Aaron Montgomery Ward, 1843—1913

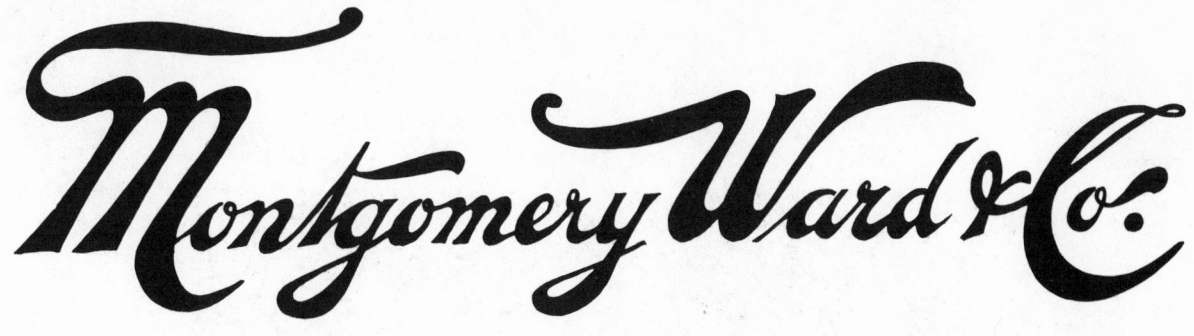

Montgomery Ward & Co.

Catalogue and Buyers' Guide

No. 57, SPRING AND SUMMER

1895

An unabridged reprint of
the original edition with a new introduction by
BORIS EMMET

DOVER PUBLICATIONS, INC.
NEW YORK

Published in Canada by General Publishing Company,
Ltd., 30 Lesmill Road, Don Mills, Toronto, Ontario.
Published in the United Kingdom by Constable and Company, Ltd., 10 Orange Street, London WC 2.

This Dover edition, first published in 1969, is an unabridged republication of the Spring and Summer Montgomery Ward & Co. Catalogue, published in 1895. This edition also contains a new introduction by Boris Emmet and a new table of contents prepared especially for this edition.

Readers are hereby informed that the prices quoted in this catalogue are no longer valid, nor are these items available from the publisher.

Standard Book Number (paperbound): 486-22377-9
Standard Book Number (clothbound): 486-22409-0
Library of Congress Catalog Card Number: 78-86339

Manufactured in the United States of America
Dover Publications, Inc.
180 Varick Street
New York, N.Y. 10014

INTRODUCTION
to the Dover Edition

Few events could have been more exciting in the typical rural home of 1895 than the arrival of the new Montgomery Ward catalogue. For the women, it meant fashions, what everyone was wearing in Chicago and New York; for the men, farm implements, tools. Children had a dazzling glimpse of the adult world, and even farm animals and pets were provided for in this "most complete store on earth" that brought as much instruction and delight to its readers then as it does to its more sophisticated browsers now.

The company which mailed copies of this catalogue was a young business giant which in its twenty-three years of operation had expanded its original capital of $2400 into annual sales of about four million dollars. It had simultaneously altered the quality of rural life, which at that time made up two-thirds of the population of America.

Prior to the founding of Ward's, most of the items needed for the rural family were purchased from local merchants who—except for occasional visits of peddlers and agents—constituted the nexus between the wants of farmers and villagers and the "manufactories." The old-time general merchandise store not only supplied its customers with dry goods and groceries, but also dealt in hardware, tools, and such medicines as Turlington's Balsam of Life and Steer's Opodildoc. In addition, the store was the rendezvous, the oasis where farmers gathered to exchange crop intelligence, berate politicians, railroads and trusts and to enjoy a friendly drink of whiskey and swap earthy jokes.

The country store was also a substitute newspaper, and passing travelers kept the merchant posted on state and national news. From the orders he filled, he knew who was sick, who was expecting a baby, who had relatives coming. Besides this, he was the business adviser to the community and usually a pillar of the church (often located in the attic over his store, sharing the space with some fraternal order). Not infrequently he was also the local postmaster, reading and writing letters for the illiterate.

The local merchant was thus a man of considerable power, but that power was based to a great extent on the farmer's prosperity, in which the merchant held a vital stake and which he had to estimate in advance in order to determine how much credit he could safely advance to any farmer. Credit was the basis of most purchases. For most of the year the farmer would draw against his expected income in buying from his local merchant; after the harvest, he would settle with the merchant and then dig in for another protracted period of buying on credit.

The merchant, in turn, found himself squeezed on both sides. His turnover was slow, his sources of supply often uncertain, and his cost of goods high. The wholesaler and the jobber added their margins before the small retail merchant could add his own markup. And since many farmers had to buy on credit, the merchant was often forced to sell the same way, which further raised the price of goods to the ultimate consumer.

This method of buying and selling on borrowed money involved huge interest charges paid by the merchants to local bankers. To the interest charges were added cost of goods, transportation, markup to cover the cost of doing business, and profit. Since the local merchant was patronized by a relatively small number of customers, he could not risk carrying in stock a full assortment of goods or novel items that were slow sellers. An inability to move such merchandise could be fatal.

Despite the often inadequate stock carried in many local stores and the high prices of goods, there was one pleasant aspect of shopping there: the customer could spend months looking over goods at intervals before making his mind up to buy. And most of his buying was on the basis of customer's needs, not mere desire. His primary purchases were of necessity the goods he needed to farm and to feed his family: plows and harness, fatback and flour, meal and molasses. His clothes were almost entirely utilitarian, designed to afford whatever warmth might be necessary and meet minimum standards of modesty and decency. Appearance and fit were allowed wide latitude. Clothes had to be durable and comfortable enough to stand up under work on the farm and in the kitchen or to present an acceptable appearance at church.

Even with these simple requirements, the farmer often became dissatisfied with many phases of local retailing. In sparsely settled parts he found himself forced to ride miles by horseback to reach the nearest store. If he was unable to leave his farm chores to go himself, he was compelled to send some member of his family or a hired hand, and the results of this indirect purchasing were not always happy.

Yet the farmer had little choice. There was no mail-order business of any real consequence until 1872 (though mail order had operated in New England on a miniscule scale as early as 1830), no rural free delivery until 1896, and no parcel post until 1913. By the late 1860's there had sprung up hundreds of small mail-order concerns such as that opened in Augusta, Maine, in 1856 by a man named E. C. Allen, who offered such "specialties" as "washing powders," engravings, chromos, "paper goods," paper plates, and napkins. But until 1872, when Wards entered the scene, there was no mail-order house which could fill all the needs of all members of the rural family from grandma to the family dog.

Aaron Montgomery Ward was a former local store manager and traveling dry-goods salesman who had worked and lived among farmers for many years. He knew their living habits, their likes and dislikes, their complaints about the high cost of goods. He knew, for instance, that farmers had recently formed the Patrons of Husbandry, known as the Grange, the basic tenet of which was cooperative purchasing "to save the farmer money by eliminating the middleman."

Ward also hoped to eliminate the middleman—and credit risks—by buying directly from manufacturers for cash and selling to farmers directly for cash. The greater the quantity he could buy, the cheaper would be the unit cost to him and to his customers. A small profit on each transaction could become a considerable sum through sufficient turnover.

In 1872 Aaron Montgomery Ward and his brother-in-law George R. Thorne combined forces. Ward supplied $1600, Thorne $800. This original capital of $2400 was the startlingly small sum that started Montgomery Ward & Co. The fledgling firm established business and warehouse quarters in Chicago on Clark and Kinzie Streets in a room 12 by 14 feet.

For promotional purposes Ward and Thorne used initially a single sheet, 8 by 12 inches, listing their offerings and information on how to order them. By 1874 this sheet had grown to an eight-page booklet. Later in the same year it reached 72 pages. The catalogue claimed that "by purchasing with us you save 40 to 100 per cent which are the profits of the middlemen." The title page proclaimed Montgomery Ward & Co. "the cheapest cash house in the country," and perhaps more important, "the Original Grange Supply House selling to Grangers, other farmers and mechanics at the lowest wholesale prices." Goods were sent by express subject to examination, the customers paying the shipping expenses and the cost of goods "only if satisfied." The merchandise lines at the time included notions, hose and gloves, hat trimmings, toilet goods, letter paper, needles, cutlery, jewelry and watches, fans and parasols, stereoscopes and albums, trunks and handbags, harness, Grange regalia, dry goods, clothing, hats and caps, boots and shoes, and simple patent medicines.

By the early 1880's almost every item in Ward's catalogue was illustrated by a woodcut. In 1884 the catalogue's 240 pages listed nearly 10,000 items. Two years later Montgomery Ward & Co. began construction in Chicago of its own building for its rapidly expanding business. The new structure which was occupied in 1887 provided 140,000 square feet of space. The catalogue now in the reader's hands stated, "We believe in blowing our own horn; no one else seems willing to do it for us." During the year 1889 alone, Ward's received one million letters and sent out 1,850,000 letters, 405,000 packages of merchandise by mail, 700,000 postal cards, and 460,000 packages of third-class mail. By the middle 1890's the catalogue numbered 540 pages, listed 24,000 items, and brought in an annual volume of business in excess of three million dollars.

The company now began to use the slogan "Our mail-order business is the largest in the United States." This was true. By 1895 its sales had reached the four-million mark, its catalogue over 600 pages; it would be several years before its rival Sears Roebuck (founded in 1886, fourteen years after Ward's) began seriously to challenge it.

The basic business policies which led to Montgomery Ward's success may be summarized as:

1. Buying and selling for cash, which eliminated interest charges in the purchase of goods and in financing customers, thereby lowering prices.
2. Unconditional guarantee of merchandise.
3. An advertising technique which radiated friendliness and care beyond consummation of sale.
4. Huge assortment of goods. At one time in 1883 the

company inventory was advertised to be $500,000, a fantastic figure in those times. The company could afford to take great risks because it had only one inventory which served all the customers in the United States. A policy of comprehensive assortments à la Ward's might have spelled bankruptcy for the small local merchant whose service geography was very limited and number of customers relatively small.

From the very beginning Montgomery Ward & Co. had on its catalogue covers "The Original Grange Supply House" or "The Wholesale Grange Supply House." Grangers initially enjoyed special privileges in their purchases from Ward's. Orders sent in by Grange officials or countersigned by Grange seal did not have to be paid upon receipt of goods; they received an automatic 10-day extension. Ward's awareness of the importance to its business of this arrangement with the Grange was reflected not only in its general catalogues, but also in all mailings sent out.

The tone of Ward's promotional literature was always friendly, based on a verbal camaraderie which sounded sincere and straightforward. The company frequently issued invitations to customers to visit its Chicago headquarters to see what a great place Ward's was. During the Columbian Exposition, it was said to have been visited by 285,000 of its customers.

No less significant was the fact that potential buyers were constantly reminded in the simplest language that goods found defective could be returned. If goods were not as represented, Ward's paid the cost of transportation both ways. This policy was probably one of Ward's most effective ways of meeting the rising and understandably bitter opposition of local retail merchants to mail-order houses.

If Ward's, and later Sears, grew to be giants, it was in spite of the opposition of the local merchants, which was persistent and virulent, increasing from year to year in almost direct proportion to the prosperity enjoyed by such houses.

This opposition took many forms. In some small towns merchants were able to exert sufficient community pressure to compel townsfolk to burn their mail-order catalogues in the public square in a grand auto-da-fé. Local storekeepers offered prizes to those bringing in the greatest number of catalogues for destruction; elsewhere a straight ten cents per book was paid to provide fuel for the bonfire. Another device was to admit free to a moving-picture theater every child who brought a mail-order catalogue for destruction. A candidate for

mayor of Warsaw, Iowa, declared he would discharge any city employee found purchasing from a mail-order company.

Contests were locally organized to encourage customers to write poetry uncomplimentary to mail order. Some ministers declared mail order "ungodly—irreligious." In all these cases the power held by the local merchant was evident. He had the strong backing of local banks, local newspapers, the public officials themselves. Even the local postmasters tried now and then to sabotage mail-order operations. The whole maze of demeaning epithets that grew up became part of the language. Montgomery Ward became "Monkey Wards," and Sears, "Shears and Sawbuck."

Nor was the opposition limited to small communities. As early as November 8, 1873, when Montgomery Ward & Co. was only one year old, the Chicago *Tribune* had said: "Grangers Beware! Don't patronize Montgomery Ward & Company—they are Dead Beats. Another attempt at swindling has come to light." Ward's prices were quoted as being conspicuously low, and those who patronized Ward's were called "gulls" and "dupes." The *Tribune* retracted these statements on December 24, but the tone had been set for many of the subsequent attacks on mail order.

From the perspective of today, one can feel that the inadequate system of retail distribution would sooner or later have cracked under its own dead weight even without the mail-order companies. It is easy enough to see, in retrospect, that better roads, motion pictures, improved communications, the automobile—in short, the whole march of technological progress—would have had, as indeed it did, a profound effect on the operating techniques of retail merchants.

If local merchants, however, and public officials were for years hostile toward Ward's, it is obvious from its booming sales that somewhere it had millions of friends. And these, of course, were the people who used the mail-order catalogue, ordered from it, found themselves illustrated in it, and even allowed it to color their view of life.

Any book tells its readers something of the age that produced it; but this 1895 Montgomery Ward catalogue, reprinted here for the first time, holds a mirror up to the culture of its times in an astonishing way. Here is the very look and feel of the world of the 1890's: what people wore, what they read, how they cooked, traveled, spent their leisure time, tried out labor-saving devices. For the social historian, this big book is an invaluable account of the trends of the last third of the nineteenth century. For the rest of us, it provides an exercise in nostalgia, seeing what kind of life our grandparents lived, or simply in understanding the recent background of our own age.

For Ward's, it was a matter of profit, not browsing pleasure. The pictures were supplied, not for our amusement, but to illustrate, where possible, every item in the book, from windmills to pen points. Prices were clearly marked and, from our point of view, pleasantly reasonable. Seventy-five cents for a man's summer jacket could certainly bring few complaints of overcharging; though we must remember that this was at a time when civil service employees earned the good wage of $21.23 a week and Congregational ministers were expected to live comfortably on $787 a year.

The illustrations are almost entirely line cuts, many of them supplied either from a stock cut house or the manufacturer. This was one of the last catalogues to use line cuts; the twentieth century brought with it the use of halftones, which were, in their primitive state, no improvement at all. Color was finally added to the catalogue of 1909.

Wherever there was an extra inch of unfilled space, the company inserted an "institutional" ad such as "A Good Workman requires Good Tools" or "Ignorance is less provoking than Dishonesty, But it costs you Just as Much." Whereas the body type is a fairly modern standard six-point size, these homilies are all set in Victorian type which looked archaic then and may have represented an attempt by the company to make the reader feel that, while modern, the organization had old traditions and was a staid, reliable outfit.

Some of the catalogue's thirty-eight departments (machinery, buggies, stoves, bicycles, sewing machines) were supplemented by additional booklets, and groceries were sold only through such a booklet and not listed in the catalogue. Elsewhere allocation of space was based largely on sales expectancy. Of its 622 pages, 378 were devoted to the ten largest departments: Guns and Sporting Goods, Hardware, Watches and Jewelry, Clothing, Books, Dry Goods, Harnesses and Saddlery, Furniture, Tinware and Cutlery, Crockery and Glassware.

According to the *Dry Goods Department* of the 1895 catalogue, the housewife of the gay 90's was not gay; she was busy! She had the opportunity to make almost every item in her family's wardrobe. She could make her own sheets, weave her own carpets, quilt her own quilts, even sew tents for family camping trips.

Where the catalogue has only four pages of suits for ladies and children, it devoted 31 well-packed pages to listings of fabrics she could buy, such as alpaca, serges, cashmere, mohairs, wool, brocades, lawns, ginghams, velvets. If she weren't sure of the quality of the fabric, samples would be sent upon request. She was encouraged to order full bolts of fabric because it "costs less to do when we don't have to unroll." If she couldn't use a full bolt of 56 yards of fancy black sateen at 11½ cents per yard, "perhaps a neighbor would be glad to take part of it." From this a beautiful waist could be made for 40 cents (a saving compared to a ready-made at 75 cents); at such a bargain who cared if her neighbor was making a sateen waist exactly like her own?

The linen section included not only fabrics but also ready-made glass-towels, doilies and table cloths. The catalogue assured the housewife that she was making a great savings buying from this department because "Linens are an article of merchandise on which the country merchants make big profits. This is why peddlers always carry linens. As merchants do not sell a great quantity of any one article, they are obliged to pay the wholesaler a big price, and for the same reason have to add large profits."

The *Trimmings and Notions Department* (p. 77) gave additional ways for the housewife to keep her hands busy: in sewing, knitting, and embroidering such items as pillow shams and tray cloths. For $1.40 she could buy a Gem Tufting and Embroidery Machine to make Turkish rugs, curtains, piano spreads or table covers—all so simple that "a ten year-old child could operate it."

Ready-made suits, such as those on page 34, were a welcome item for women who were beginning to appreciate the advantage of leisure. Shirt waists occupied an entire page because "for a small outlay of money, your old dress skirt worn with a nice laundered waist provides you with a cool, comfortable and up-to-date costume that will astonish you."

Books were a large part of life in that pre-television age, and we should not be surprised to find a 39-page *Book Department* (p. 38). Then, as now, three types of book predominated: best-sellers (*Peck's Bad Boy*), classics (Browning), and how-to-do-it books including reference works. Among the 3000 titles were such bargains as the 15-cent *How to Kill Time in Chicago*, the helpful *How to Make and Use a Telephone*, or the newest work of Mr. Kipling, *The Jungle Book*. There were discreet manuals for ladies, *The Physical Life of*

Women (the male version was called *The Transmission of Life*), cookbooks, and veterinarian manuals ("don't be cruel to your horses, read about their care"). Visiting cards, including mourning cards, testify to the day's social practices, just as a 12-page *Stationery Department* (p. 110) tells of a time when people wrote longer letters than they do now.

The American's extreme concern with cleanliness did not begin in the twentieth century, as the eight-page *Sanitary Department* (p. 102) shows. The facilities may have been primitive, but there was no end of sanitary equipment the housewife might buy. A whole page is devoted to soap because Montgomery Ward was "a large buyer of toilet soaps, hence are enabled to get unusually low prices from manufacturers." The purchaser had her choice of "Lemon Juice Complexion Soap" which was excellent for freckles and sunburn, or "Williams Medicated Jersey Cream Toilet Soap" which contained "pure rich cream from Jersey Cows" and served to heal "babies' rash, also chaps and sores . . . prevents pimples." If these didn't suit her she could choose cocoanut oil soap, transparent soap, tooth soap, and even a special soap for the family dog.

In this section the housewife could find anything from nail brushes to paint brushes. If it was hair brushes she wanted, she could buy either a plain manual one (ten cents to a dollar) or a more exotic electric hair brush ("the most powerful magnetic brush ever made; cures headache, neuralgia, rheumatism, prevents hair from falling out and aids in restoring gray hair to its natural color. In the back of this brush are embedded strongly charged magnets in contact with which are the fine, highly polished steel wires which form the brush so that when applied to the head or flesh, currents of magnetic electricity flow from the magnet through the wires"). This brush sold for $1.25 or $1.50 "for the new improved model with extra magnet in handle."

If her hair was too unmanageable even for this brush, she could do what the young lady of today does—cover it with a wig. Hair was as much an obsession then as it is today, as the large number of wigs, wiglets and falls found in the *Notions Department* (p. 122) shows.

To obtain a wig it was necessary to "send samples of hair, as hair goods cannot be returned except to be exchanged for another shade of the same quality." If the lady's hair were red, gray, golden, or "drab" she would be required to pay 25 to 50 cents extra for her hair piece. She could buy puff bangs "parted, the latest style" for $3.50, a "French hair switch" for $5.00 to $10.00, or, if she were really desperate, a full wig for $10 to $18.00. She was then ready to put on her new hat (p. 131), especially decorated for her by Montgomery Ward for 15 to 50 cents plus the cost of trimming. The entire upper half of her head would have then been furnished by this catalogue.

Nor was the male neglected by the hair goods department of the Montgomery Ward catalogue. He could order a full beard on wire for a dollar; a mustache or goatee for a dime, and side whiskers for 75 cents. If he needed a full wig, he could use the detailed measuring instructions, measure his head, and order a toupee.

All these were to some degree status symbols, but nothing more so than a pocket watch (*Watches and Jewelry Department,* p. 135) which could instantly give any young clerk the glow of a millionaire. The large department also reflects America's long concern with time and promptness—an outgrowth perhaps of its Puritan background.

The dollar watch is conspicuously absent here, and the watches listed are of the elegant and expensive type. How many orders were filled for the $112.70 solid gold case, 20-ruby jewel nickel movement "Montgomery Ward and Company Extra Railroad Timer" to be worn dangling from the vest of a $10.00 suit of clothes? For the man who could not afford something that expensive there was available for $3.65 "a watch, destined to fill a long felt want; in fact, a watch that is both good and cheap. The case is silverine and is a man's medium size . . . looks as well as silver and wears better." Ward's insisted that this seven-jewel stem-winder would "run as well as an Elgin or Waltham."

Since jewelry couldn't be made at home, it occupies a surprising 26 pages of the catalogue (compared to 12 pages for ladies' clothing), running from ear drops to scarf pins, mourning jewelry, and even a solid gold bib for baby. Plain gold wedding bands started at 95 cents though the bridegroom with serious financial worries could buy a gold-finish band for as little as 3 cents—or the farsighted one a dozen for a quarter. If the lady's finger was somewhat fat, the 95-cent staple price soared to $1.50.

The Optical Goods Department (p. 203) tells of a time when eyeglasses were fitted more casually than they are today. A test-yourself chart (for old-sight, near-sight, or astigmatism) was considered adequate for ordering any of the lenses provided.

Also in the section were such scientific instruments as Portable Electro-Medical Batteries ("magnetic instruments" for the "worst cases of paralysis, rheumatism, neuralgia and all nervous diseases"). Americans had become fascinated with the magic of electricity in the decade after Edison's incandescent lamp lit the city of New York. If electricity could light a city, it was felt, it could surely cure peoples' ills.

In a home-centered age, 14 pages in the *Games Department* (p. 224) tell of home games from parlor quoits to the game of "Electors and Presidential Puzzle"— probably a big seller with a presidential election in the offing. Another 14 pages of *Musical Instruments* (p. 238) underline the same tendency to make one's own entertainment at home with a parlor organ or concertina. There were only three pages (p. 252) devoted to *Artist's Materials,* but even that shows a greater nationwide interest than one would have suspected in this period.

What young lady of the 1890's, having studied the *Toiletries and Drugs* section (p. 255), waited patiently for her Ward's package and then hid her 20-cent box of "Tetlow's Refinement—a combination box of face powder containing lily white rouge and eyebrow pencil" or her 10-cent eyebrow pencil "for imparting dark colors to eyebrows and lashes"? While the lady of 1895 could, as we have seen, wear wigs and wiglets and curl her hair, she obviously could not do much more to her face than apply some face powder. She might use Florida Water, colognes or perfumes, but she could not color her cheeks or lips with anything red or pink.

From this section of the catalogue the housewife could keep her family in good shape with Ward's "Beef, Wine and Iron" pills, Compound Cathartic pills, or the "Great Russian Corn and Bunion Exterminator." The doctor was not just a telephone call away, so when the children got sick she would need "Cook's Neutralizing Cordial," a "pleasant anti-acid and laxative preparation" which cured "piles, habitual costiveness, diarrhoea, sour stomach, indigestion, summer complaint of children."

If horses and cattle got sick there were Condition Powders, and for the family's teeth, there was "Cook's Chlorate Dentrifice" which was "not a drug and will have no bad effect upon the enamel. By its daily use the teeth will become white and smooth . . . contains no soap, and hence will not fill the mouth with nasty soapsuds."

The major portion of the *Clothing Department* (p. 267) was given to men's and boy's clothing. The lady of the house was encouraged to "insist upon it that the men of your family dress well provided they do so without increased cost."

There were nine styles of men's suits available and four for boys, but each style could be made up in many different fabrics and this determined the price of the suit. For $28 the well-dressed men could buy a double breasted Prince Albert suit in "Superfine imported black crepe cloth, fine new goods similar to broadcloth." The suit was especially suited for "ministers, physicians, and professional men."

Montgomery Ward's specialty was the $10 suit, a "wonderful success" which "inspired us to put forth greater efforts in this line." For the man who had limited funds and probably needed his suit only occasionally, there was the $3 "round cornered sack suit" available in black- and gold-lined diagonal cotton worsted. There were suits for everyone: children's suits and suits for youths with long pants; corduroy suits, street-car conductors' suits and even Grand Army suits. If this didn't satisfy the purchaser, he could have a suit custom-tailored for as little as $15.

For the ladies and girls there were things that they might not want to make for themselves: underwear, gloves, knitwear, cloaks, shawls, and caps and bonnets. The corset department occupied almost four pages, and the torturous garments with their laces and stays were called "light, comfortable, well shaped and very durable . . . soft and pliable . . . give thorough support." They were truly the foundation of the Gibson girl.

Not only people were well-dressed by Montgomery Ward; their animals were too. In this, the golden age of the horse, it does not surprise us to find 29 pages in the *Harness and Saddlery Department* (p. 311) given to combs, fly nets, brushes and saddles (Montgomery Ward insisted that they were the place to buy harness because "Chicago is headquarters for leather, so we are able to do more than ordinarily well in such goods"). We might, however, be surprised to find here goat harnesses, or Gray Siberian Dog robes for $8.25; if one didn't like the idea of sitting under a dog robe, a robe made of goat or prairie wolf could be substituted.

The *Hardware Department* (p. 352), one of the largest, listed almost every conceivable nut, bolt, hook or screw, with three pages of door locks alone and a page of doors to put them on. With equipment included here, the farmer could butcher his animals, prune his own trees, shear his own sheep, or do his own blacksmithing, bricklaying and plumbing.

One of the great successes of Montgomery Ward was its listing of lavor-saving devices for the woman of the house, devices she could buy only from the catalogue. For $1.75 she could buy a wringer for her washday, for 75 cents a "self-heating iron." She could make ice-cream with an up-to-date ice-cream freezer or for $14.10, have the "solid ash antique finished hand carved" refrigerator holding 35 pounds of ice. This marvelous new gadget operated on the principle that "ice being placed on the false bottom becomes very cold and heavy, and falls through the opening into the provision chamber below, forcing the warm air up through the flues, where it strikes the ice, is condensed and cooled." It would even keep crackers and gingersnaps crisp and dry.

Two other departments filled out the housewife's kitchen: the *Stove Department* (p. 418), and *Tinware and Cutlery* (p. 427), carrying items from rat traps to a Magic Milk Shake Machine ($6.00).

Men found a special interest in the *Guns and Sporting Goods Department* (p. 449). The length of this, the largest department in the catalogue, with 30 of its 59 pages devoted to firearms and ammunition, would seem to indicate that America's obsession with guns is pre-Hollywood, a deeply embedded feature of the American character. People who made gun purchases must have been considered somewhat special because "guns can be sent C.O.D. only when $5.00 is sent with order. Do not return dirty and rusty guns and expect us to take them back."

Revolvers, shown on three pages, could not be sent to minors in the State of Illinois, but other states had no such regulations. A purchaser from the State of Illinois had to send Montgomery Ward a letter assuring the company that he was not a minor and that he wanted to purchase the gun for self-protection.

After the purchaser equipped himself with the proper rifle, he could choose other necessities for hunting: hunter's clothing, decoys, and muzzles and whips for his dogs. The man who didn't like hunting would find here the necessary equipment for lawn tennis, baseball, football, fishing and camping.

Shoes (p. 508) were a staple part of mail-order catalogues, and if they make us smile today, you may be sure that readers of 1895 considered them very stylish. Five pages presented ladies shoes from "Trilby's" to satin slippers, but most women probably bought the "common sense shoe" recommended for "strength and toughness." Ten pages of men's shoes included cowboy boots and even preacher's baptismal boots. Children had a single page, and parents were encouraged to buy "Child's ankle-supporting shoes" because "no child with weak ankles should be without them."

Whether one wanted a bicycle (p. 555), a buggy (p. 579), or a rolling pin (p. 574), it was all here, as was the following particularly amusing labor-saving device in the *Dairy* section: "Lamb's Adjustable Animal Power for Churns, Separators, etc." (p. 568). The "power" was a treadmill on which the farmer could place one or two dogs or a pair of sheep or goats. As the animals ran, the treadmill moved, thereby causing whatever was hooked into it to move also. "The Powers are quickly and easily attached to any kind of churn, or can be used for doing a great deal of farm labor, usually done by the man or maid or the farmer's wife. You can just as well save the wife and maid this ever tiresome task, as well as the time that is expended in churning and like work, by making your dog, goat, or sheep do all this labor as well and the labor required in many of the farm duties." A two-sheep power cost $23 and the One Dog Power was available for $15.

If the housewife didn't have a "Lamb's Adjustable Animal Power," she had to be her own source of power for her ironer, washing machine or mangle, and if she could not afford any of these fancy labor-saving machines, she could purchase a washboard in the *Woodenware Department* (p. 572) for 25 cents.

It is easy to see that the catalogue mirrored the life of the times. Simply to look at its pages is to reenter the past, recapture the excitement of that moment in 1895 (and many other years) when the Ward's catalogue was delivered to the rural homes that made up America. For this writer, however, it has an additional meaning. Having been in the retail business most of his life (though not with Ward's), he can still admire the selling technique shown throughout the catalogue. Despite an occasional exaggeration, there is a sense of honesty in the book and the sort of friendliness and care for the customer that go beyond the mere requirements of a sale.

Even now, almost one hundred years after the founding of Ward's, the ordering of merchandise via catalogue is a multi-billion-dollar business. The 1968 reports of the two colossi of the catalogue business—Sears and Ward's—indicate that more than one-fifth of their sales arrive via catalogue. Only recently J. C. Penney which for decades successfully sold only over the counter started selling also by catalogue. Despite the increase of shopping centers, automobiles, and large discount stores, the American family apparently still enjoys doing its shopping in the comfort of home.

BORIS EMMET

New York, New York
April, 1969

TABLE OF CONTENTS

No. 57.

Catalogue and Buyers' Guide

SPRING AND SUMMER 1895

MONTGOMERY WARD & Co.

111, 112, 113, 114, 115 AND 116 MICHIGAN AVENUE, CHICAGO, ILL.

Please Read Remarks and Rules Before Ordering.

No. 57.

REMARKS.

Our business was organized in 1872 to meet the wants of the Patrons of Husbandry, from whom we then received our main support. We did not, however, refuse the patronage of any person, knowing that the more goods we handled the cheaper we could sell them.

Our goods, with few exceptions, are sold in quantities to suit the purchaser at prices quoted.

We employ no agents or traveling collectors.

The prices we quote are for goods in our store. All expenses for transportation of both goods and money must be paid by the purchaser.

We cheerfully answer inquiries.

All orders sent us from previous catalogues will be filled from Catalogue No. 57 until 58 is issued. Values are subject to the fluctuations of the market, without notice to the purchaser.

NOTICE—Our Catalogues are issued early in March and September of each year. Please preserve this copy until September 1, 1895, then write us for No. 58, inclosing 15 cents for postage or expressage (we send catalogue by express when we can do so to advantage).

All claims must be made within 10 days after receipt of goods.

To conduct our business in a successful and satisfactory manner, it is necessary to have certain rules to govern our movements. We therefore, in order to prevent all misunderstanding, invite your careful attention to the following:

RULES FOR SHIPMENT OF GOODS.

Freight Shipments.

RULE 1. We will ship goods by freight to ANY ONE if money accompanies the order.

We will ship goods by freight in our own name and collect the bill through your banker, if sufficient money is sent us with the order to cover freight charges. Be sure you give us the name and location of your bank.

Our responsibility ceases when we have obtained a receipt in good order from the transportation company.

We make claims on the Transportation Companies for loss or damage of goods in transit, if reported to us, but such claims are for your benefit, not ours.

Freight must be prepaid to points which have no agent. Where there is an agent it is not necessary as there is no difference in charges. *We make no charge for cartage or cases.*

Express Shipments.

RULE 2. Goods will be sent by express, C. O. D. (collect on delivery) when, in our opinion, the articles ordered are suitable. Value, bulk, weight, class, distance, etc., will determine our acceptance or refusal of all such orders. We will not send C. O. D. for amounts under $5.00. To insure the certain shipment of goods by express C. O. D., sufficient money should at least be sent to pay all possible transportation charges. We guarantee that goods shipped by us shall be as represented and of full value, and if not satisfactory we will exchange for other goods or refund the money paid for them, at the option of the purchaser.

No goods will be sent by Express to points off a railway, unless paid for. Express and Freight rates from Chicago to any point can be obtained of the local agent or by writing to us. We use cases or boxes for express shipments only when necessary to secure safety of contents, but make no charge for them.

Goods shipped by Express C. O. D. may be examined at the Express office, in presence of agent. Please do not abuse this privilege by disarranging the goods or occupying too much of the agent's time. While we are willing that the purchaser shall examine the goods, and be satisfied that they are as ordered before paying for them, the Express companies and their representatives dislike the trouble, annoyance and

No. 57, 2nd Edition, March, 1895.

risk attending it, and the privilege is extended to you on condition that it is not abused.

We repeat that we will guarantee all packages to contain the goods ordered and of full value.

If express shipments are to be prepaid, be sure to allow money for that purpose. There is no necessity for prepayment unless you are sending goods to some friend. The charges are exactly the same at either end of the line.

Mail Shipments.

RULE 3. Postage on goods by mail is 1 cent per ounce, or fraction thereof, being 16 cents per pound. No one package must exceed 4 lbs., but any number of packages may be sent to the same address, weighing 4 lbs. or less each. Packages can be sent by registered mail for 8 cents per package extra. We would advise insuring all mail shipments, as the insurance fee is usually less than the cost of registering, and in case of loss the shipment is duplicated.

We positively require cash in advance for goods and postage. Send enough and we will return the amount overpaid, if any. The invoice or bill will generally follow the goods within two days. Sometimes, when the amount is small and the account is balanced, we do not send the bill.

Explosives, poisonous or inflammable articles are unmailable. Sharp pointed instruments and glass, such as, Needles, Knives, Pens, Lantern Slides, etc., can go in mailing cases at an extra cost of 5 cents. Liquids may be inclosed in vials, packed in wooden boxes, as provided in U. S. Postal Laws. Allow 5 cents for liquid cases. We are constantly sending large quantities of goods by mail to all parts of the country, and with very few exceptions goods reach their destination.

All goods sent by mail are at purchaser's risk unless insured. We can assume no responsibility after goods are deposited in postoffice. We advise insuring everything of value.

Insure Your Mail Packages.

We have perfected a plan of Postal Insurance and will, until further notice, insure mail packages *when so instructed* for 5 cents for each package of $5.00 or under in value, 10 cents for packages valued at from $5.00 to $10.00, and 5 cents for each additional $5.00 in value. If you want your packages insured be sure to write "Insure" on your order, and inclose the insurance fee. Prompt notification of failure to receive packages is necessary to secure adjustments.

After reading the foregoing Rules, BE SURE to say HOW you want your goods shipped, whether by Freight, EXPRESS or MAIL.

How to Order.

Commence your order similar to the sample heading on page 2, following the order of directions as there given, *and always say at the top of the order how much money you inclose;* also read our rules regarding the shipment of goods. Write your name, P.O. address, shipping point, etc., PLAINLY. It is best to make Express orders exceed $5 in value, and freight orders exceed 100 lbs. in weight. *We often refuse to ship small orders, as the cost of transportation would consume your saving.* We desire that our goods shall cost you LESS under all circumstances than you can possibly obtain them through any other source. To equalize or reduce the cost of transportation, we advise the sending of club orders. ANY ONE can get up a club. Your Freight or Express Agent can usually give you the rate per 100 lbs. from Chicago. If you have questions to ask, or wish to refer to other matters, write your communication on a separate sheet of paper, give your P. O. address, and sign your name in full. Do not ask questions on sheet used for orders, as our Corresponding and Order departments are in different parts of the building, consequently such questions may not receive attention. (See cash discounts, page 2.)

DISCOUNTS FOR CASH.

Rule 4. DISCOUNT FOR CASH.—Until further notice we will allow the following discounts, *when money accompanies the Order. AND IN NO OTHER CASE:*

On orders amounting to $ 20.00 and up to $ 50.00, 2 per ct. discount.
On orders amounting to   50.00 and up to 100.00, 3 per ct. discount.
On orders amounting to 100.00 and up to 150.00, 4 per ct. discount.
On orders amounting to 150.00 and upward, 5 per ct. discount.

On orders for groceries, amounting to $20.00 and over, we allow 2 per cent discount (except on sugar, which is *net* in all cases).

These discounts will not be allowed unless sufficient money is sent to pay the *WHOLE ORDER*, and will in no case be allowed on C. O. D. orders.

Our object is to treat it as a *Cash Sale*, and close the transaction at one entry, thus saving trouble and expense of keeping an account; therefore be sure to send enough. If you send too much we will refund the balance with the bill. If any balance is due you not convenient to refund in stamps, we will send it in the form of a Treasurer's Draft, or in some form simply and easily negotiated. We do not refund or claim balances of less than 5 cents. We particularly desire every one to make inquiries about us before sending us an order.

OUR RESPONSIBILITY.

To those unacquainted with us, our ability and willingness to perform our part of the contract, we refer you to any resident or business house of this city, and, by permission, to the First National Bank of Chicago, the largest bank in America—capital and surplus six millions of dollars.

Always inclose stamps for reply when writing TO ANY ONE for references.

We do not wish to be classed with the numerous swindlers of our city, and particularly desire every person to make inquiry about us before giving us an order. If this plan is always followed, honest men will be supported, and swindlers die out.

(Our financial standing can be ascertained of any of the commercial agencies or of any reputable bank in America.)

HOW TO SEND MONEY.

It is perfectly safe to send money in the following manner, viz.: Bank Draft, Postal Money Order, or Express Money Order, and in cash by Express, charges prepaid, because in case of miscarriage the loss will be made good.

NOTICE.—Drafts or Checks on Aberdeen, Atlanta, Atchison, Albany, Baltimore, Buffalo, Bismarck, Cincinnati. Columbus, Ohio; Cleveland, Denver, Des Moines, Duluth, Detroit, Dubuque, Fargo, Indianapolis, Kansas City, Lincoln, Neb., Louisville, Milwaukee, Minneapolis, Mitchell, S. Dak.; Omaha, Philadelphia, Pittsburg, Portland, Ore., St. Paul, St. Louis, St. Joseph, Mo., San Francisco, Sioux City, Sioux Falls, Toledo, Troy, Topeka, Washington, Yankton, will be received at par. On other towns we deduct the banker's charge for collection and exchange, which varies from 10c. to 50c., according to amount and distance.

☞ **Orders accompanied by individual checks on local banks will be delayed until checks are collected. Expense of collection will be charged.**

We will not be responsible for currency or coin sent by open mail nor for money sent in Registered Letters, although we consider this last method practically safe if they are carefully sealed. We advise the use of two envelopes—one within the other. When sending a Postoffice Money Order, disregard instructions on back and inclose it in your letter with order for goods.

When gold or silver becomes worn so as to be light weight, it is only worth what it will bring as bullion, which is about 10 per cent. less than its face value. Do not send us worn and defaced coin and expect to get its face value. Defaced 5c. coins have no value.

NOTICE.—We do not care to take postage stamps, but to accommodate our customers who live where there is no Postal Money Order office, where it is difficult to make change in currency, we will accept them for amounts under $5.00. From points where Postal Money Order and express offices are established, we will not accept stamps in larger amounts than $1.00, except at a discount of 2 to 3 per cent.

We recommend the Express Money Order system of remitting, because it is safe, simple and economical. There is no use sending money or stamps where access can be had to an Express Office.

NOTE.—Do not send Money or Stamps in a letter by open mail. Many such letters never reach their destination, and we are often blamed for it. Always when possible send money by some of the forms mentioned above.

RETURNING GOODS.

Parties desiring to return goods bought of us and sent as ordered must do so immediately on receipt of them. We are perfectly willing to make exchanges or refund the money, but if the goods are as represented by us, the return charges must be paid by the purchaser. Goods used or damaged after leaving our hands cannot be returned unless by special agreement.

Extract from U. S. Postal Laws: "All packages of merchandise sent through the mails must be so wrapped or enveloped that their contents may be readily examined by postmasters, without destroying the wrapper." Tie the packages firmly with twine, but do not seal.

NEVER SEAL packages returned by mail, or enclose written matter, as by doing so it subjects the whole to double letter postage (4 cents per ounce) and the sender thereof to a fine of $10.00, provided parties to whom it is addressed refuse to pay extra postage. When packages of merchandise are returned to us sealed, or contain written matter, we shall deduct the extra amount of postage paid by us from the value of the goods returned.

When you send goods by mail, write your name and address, AND NOTHING ELSE, ON THE OUTSIDE of the parcel, or enclose a PRINTED CARD only. Send letter of instruction by mail, but DO NOT INCLOSE IT IN PACKAGE WITH GOODS. For rates of postage, see Rule 3, page 1.

Never return goods by freight unless the weight exceeds 25 lbs , nor by express unless the weight is under 25 lbs. Before returning goods write us for instructions. When you return goods by express or freight, put your letter of instructions, if possible, inside the package. Be sure to give the invoice number of all goods returned; this will save us lots of trouble.

All claims for damages, shortage, etc., must be made within 10 days after receipt of goods.

NOTE.—We decline to be held responsible for delays, errors, etc., in adjusting accounts for goods returned to us without the name and address of the sender on the outside. Our business is much too large for us to identify anything unless plainly marked.

SPECIAL CATALOGUES.

We publish a large number of special catalogues for which see inside rear cover.

SAMPLES.

We make no charge for samples of dry goods, and for that reason we request you when writing for them, to be very explicit in stating exactly what is wanted, giving Catalogue Number when possible, if not the width, price quality, color. etc., so that we can send you just what you need, instead of a great lot of samples that are of no use to you and cost us considerable money.

HOW IT PAYS

To get up club orders. Please observe that we allow a discount for cash when money accompanies the order. The discount is rated according to amount of goods purchased. (See Rule 4.) Now, suppose you want $40 worth of goods and you can persuade your neighbors to club with you. The following will illustrate the profit.

Your order............................... $40.00
Neighbor A.... .... 17.00 his share of discount, 00c.
Neighbor B .... 9.00 his share of discount, 00c.
Neighbor C......................... 30.00 his share of discount, 60c.
Neighbor D......................... 8.00 his share of discount, 00c.
Neighbor E......................... 20.00 his share of discount, 40c.
Neighbor F......................... 6.00 his share of discount, 00c.
Neighbor G.... .... 26.00 his share of discount, 52c.

                                $156.00 $1.52

You get 5 per cent. discount on $156.00, which is $7.80, and pay out $1.52 to your neighbors, leaving you a profit of $6 28, to say nothing of what you saved by getting the goods at our prices. This would pay well for an evening's work. Your neighbors would gain, as well as yourself, in the reduced proportionate freight charges.

In making the above estimate, it is supposed no groceries are ordered, as the discount on groceries is 2 per cent. on amounts over $20.00, excepting sugar (no discount on sugar). If the above order is for $100.00 worth of dry goods and $56.00 worth of groceries (no sugar), then the discount would be 5 per cent. on $100 00 and 2 per cent. on $56.00. It pays to buy of us on any terms.

SAMPLE HEADING FOR ORDER.

We inclose 2 order blanks in each Catalogue sent you, and will furnish more on application, free. It is not absolutely necessary to have these blanks, but they are a great convenience and prevent many mistakes. If you do not happen to have any handy, try to conform to the sample heading here given, to prevent error:

MESSRS. MONTGOMERY WARD CO.,

111 to 116 Michigan Avenue, CHICAGO, ILL.

Please Send to
Name ....
Postoffice ....
County ....
State ....

How to be shipped (See rules in Catalogue, page 1)...

Inclosed please find $.................................
{ State here the amount of money sent and whether Draft, Express Money Order, Postal Order, Postal Note, Currency or Stamps.

The following articles are selected from Catalogue No.........................Grocery List No.................
(Always mention number of Catalogue or Grocery List from which order is taken)

No. of Article in Catalogue.	Quantity.	ARTICLES WANTED.	SIZES, COLORS, etc.	PRICE.	TOTAL AMOUNT

INDEX.

Ladies....

For the Spring and Summer Season of 1895, our variety of Merchandise that interests the ladies, is the most satisfactory that we have ever offered.

NOVELTIES IN DRESS GOODS AND SUITINGS
GOODS FOR SUMMER WEAR

(Look over our quotations of the above and write us for samples.)

NEW EFFECTS IN OUR DRESSMAKING DEPARTMENT—Our force of designers, fitters, and dressmakers is thoroughly competent. **Our Special Dressmaking Catalogue "E,"** postage 2 cents, will show you what we can do in this line.

LADIES' SHOES. The largest line carried by one house in the United States. Nearly 100 styles to select from. We offer them with but one profit added.

Binder Twine—Season 1895

Do not fail to write for Samples and Prices of our BINDER TWINE if you are a buyer. We have nearly 1,000 tons contracted for and will be able to quote a low figure. WRITE BEFORE JUNE FIRST, if you can, as our supply is liable to be exhausted.

Shot Guns

No one ever "swears off" on the M. W. & Co. HAMMERLESS. The habit of using one becomes firmly fixed after one application. It is recognized as the fore-runner of all low-priced Hammerless Guns, though it does not take a back seat anywhere when quality, hard wearing, and good shooting are mentioned. Why not order one with the understanding that you will return it in good condition within three days and get you money back if the gun doesn't suit you. **See Prices and Description on Page 449.**

Potato Bugs

This will be the greatest potato year on record. Potatoes are about the surest crop there is if you take care of the bugs. Our PARIS GREEN is good and pure, and we feel very sure that our price is the lowest quoted by any house in the United States. **Write us.**

DESCRIPTIVE ILLUSTRATED PRICE LIST.

SPRING AND ══ No. 57. ══ SUMMER 1895.

Montgomery Ward & Co.

111 TO 116 MICHIGAN AVENUE, - - CHICAGO, ILL.

ALL GOODS IN THIS PRICE LIST SOLD SUBJECT TO THE FLUCTUATIONS OF THE MARKET.

DRESS GOODS DEPARTMENT.

Choicest weaves and newest productions of Foreign and Domestic looms for Spring and Summer season 1895.

Note Reduced Prices.

Our purchase of dress goods for this season far exceeds in both quantity and quality any previous season's collection. All prices have been revised on the new tariff basis, and no other mercantile house has ever before been able to offer such magnificent values as will be found through our entire line. Samples are always cheerfully sent upon request. We only ask that such requests be as specific as possible. Indefinite orders necessitate the sending of large quantities of samples for which there is no need and which means considerable expense to us, both in goods used and additional postage.

A special piece price will be found quoted on many of our lines. We were induced to adopt this feature owing to the numerous inquiries which we receive from merchants, clubs and individuals, asking for special quotations on large quantities. It costs us less to do business when we do not have to unroll, measure and cut goods. What we save in cost of handling, and often more, we are willing to allow to those of our customers who buy their goods in original packages. Where piece prices have been omitted we will be glad to quote same upon request. If you cannot use a full piece perhaps a neighbor would be glad to take part of it, and in this way both can make a saving.

Under no circumstances will we allow "piece prices" where we cut goods.

Colored Alpaca, Cashmere, Henrietta, Serge, Etc.

We buy all of the following lines direct from the manufacturers at the lowest possible cost, which enables us to save to our patrons the retailers' profit.

Free wool and the present low rate *of import duties* on foreign made goods have had an effect on fabric values which permits us to quote prices lower than any heretofore ever heard of. Many of the choicest lines are manufactured exclusively for Montgomery Ward & Co., and cannot be procured elsewhere.

1. Royal Serge, 22 inches wide, in plain, solid colors. The lowest priced piece dyed dress goods ever sold. Makes a very good looking cheap dress. Colors: Cardinal, wine, brown, gray, sapphire blue, navy blue, myrtle green or black. Per yard..................................$0.05
Full piece of about 50 yards, 4¾ cents per yard.

5. Alpaca, single fold, 22 inches wide, half wool, wears well, looks well, and don't cost much. Colors: Slate, gray, tan, golden brown, medium brown, seal brown, purple, national blue, royal blue, myrtle, cardinal, garnet, wine, navy or black; also staple mixture in brown, light gray or medium gray. Per yard.....................08½
Full piece of about 50 yards, 8 cents per yard.

8. Union Cashmere, light, medium or dark slate, olive, medium blue, medium brown, seal, golden brown, cardinal, garnet, myrtle, navy or black; 22 inches wide, single fold. Per yard.... .09
Full piece of 50 yards, 8¾ cents per yard.

10. Pacific-Mohair Cashmere, 22 inches wide, single fold, in mixtures only of dark and medium shades of brown or gray, in light, medium or dark shades. These goods are always in demand among ladies of quiet tastes, who prefer them to the more decided colorings. Per yard............09¼
Full piece of about 50 yards, 9 cents per yard.

12. English or Union Cashmere, double fold, 27 inches wide. This is a staple goods, and universally worn. We can furnish all the fashionable spring and summer shades, with the exception of light or evening shades. These are not made in this quality. Colors: Wine, garnet, cardinal, navy blue, myrtle green, slate, mahogany, tan, light brown, medium brown, seal or black. Per yard................................... .12
Full piece of about 50 yards, 11½ cents per yard.
NOTE—Nos. 5, 8, 10 and 12 are not made in cream, white or evening shades.

14. Henrietta Cloth, double fold, width 36 inches. This is a novel production in cotton, made from the best stock and woven to show a fine and distinct twill, almost equal in appearance to a fine French Henrietta. We have it in a complete new range of colors, including all the fashionable shades to be worn this season. Colors are: Cream, pink, light blue, nile green, canary, purple, slate, medium blue, tan, old rose, sapphire, cardinal, wine, medium brown, dark brown, navy blue, bronze, myrtle green or black. *This black is perfectly fast color and will not crock.* Per yard....................................12½
Full piece of about 50 yards, 12 cents per yard.

18. Cashmere, double fold, 36 inches wide, all wool filling. All the fashionable colors, among which are the following: Drab, gray, dark slate, sapphire blue, navy, olive green, myrtle, cardinal, garnet, wine, tan, golden brown, medium plum, heliotrope, sage green, hussar blue, old rose, seal brown, purple, black, marine blue, light blue, pink or cream. Per yard.......... .20
Full piece of about 50 yards, 19½ cents per yard.

19. Heavy Cashmere, double-fold, 39 inches wide, all wool filling, cotton warp. Colors: Tan, gray, slate, old rose, reseda, sapphire blue, olive, cardinal, wine, golden brown, medium brown, seal, navy, myrtle or black. Also high colors: Purple, azure blue, sky blue, pink or cream. Per yard.. .24
Full piece of about 60 yards, 23 cents per yard.

20. English Cashmere, finest quality, double fold, 36 inches wide. We can furnish all seasonable shades. For colors, see No 18. Per yard....... .25
Full piece of about 50 yards, 24¼ cents per yard.

21. Cashmere, all wool, imported goods, double fold, 34 inches wide. Colors: Navy, wine, garnet, cardinal, myrtle, dark brown, golden brown, tan, beige, old rose, gobelin blue, slate, gray, heliotrope, cream or black. Per yard............24½
Full piece of about 55 yards, 24 cents per yard.

23. Cashmere Serge, reversible, strictly all wool, 45 inches wide, equal to anything retailed at 60 cents. We have all the fashionable shades, light or dark navy blue, sapphire blue, tan, golden brown, medium brown, seal brown, myrtle green, cardinal, garnet, wine, slate, gray, old rose, sage, cream or black. Experts pronounce this the cheapest and best serge ever offered. Per yard.................................. .39

24. Cashmere, all wool, Henrietta finish, 38 inches wide, double fold, former half-dollar quality. Colors: Navy, plum, medium blue, cream, light blue, pink, nile green, sage, bronze, mahogany, seal, dark brown, golden brown, medium brown, myrtle, tan, cardinal, garnet, wine, old rose, sapphire, gobelin, heliotrope, beige, olive, purple, black, gray or slate. Per yard............ .35

25. Cashmere, all wool, Henrietta finish, 45 inches wide. Colors: Navy blue, sapphire blue, plum, wine, garnet, cardinal, olive, myrtle, green, golden brown, medium brown, seal brown, tan, old rose, slate, gray, cream or black. Per yard................................... ... .45

26. Imported French Henrietta, all wool, 38 inches wide, finest quality, in the following colors: Old rose, reseda, nile, heliotrope, lavender, eminence purple, light blue, pink, cardinal, scarlet, white, cream, seal brown, medium brown, golden brown, bronze, black, olive, myrtle, navy blue, gray, tan, slate, wine, salmon, gobelin, sapphire, and all other seasonable colors. We would like to have you compare these goods with what others sell at seventy-five cents. Per yard.................................... .57

30. Schilbach's Imported Henrietta, all wool, 45 inches wide. This make of Henrietta is conceded to be the finest cloth in the world, ranking second to none. Most other houses carry other makes which affords larger profits, none of which can, however, approach the genuine Schilbach goods in weight, richness of colors or in their magnificent silky finish. We are importing large quantities of these henriettas direct from the manufactures and have decided to make them a feature of our dress goods department. Colors: Dark navy, light navy, sapphire blue, peacock, cardinal, garnet, wine, gobelin blue, mahogany, royal purple, olive, plum, golden brown, medium brown, seal brown, sage green (reseda), bronze, dark tan, light tan, myrtle, heliotrope, slate, medium gray, light gray, bright blue, majenta, eminence purple, nile, old rose, pink, lavender, light blue, cream or black. Last season's retail price, $1.25 per yard.
Our new tariff price, per yard....................$0.65

32. Imported India Cashmere, 50 inches wide, made of finest Australian wool, twilled on both sides, highest finish, and made in all the fashionable street shades, as follows: Myrtle, navy blue, seal, medium brown, slate, medium tan, light tan, sage, old rose, wine or black. The extreme width of the goods makes it economical to buy, as a few yards makes a dress.
Per yard.................. 75

Albatross.

36. Albatross Cloth, all wool, light and thin, like Nuns' veiling, only not so hard twisted wool, has a soft crepe-like appearance. Much used for party, wedding or graduating dresses. Colors: Cream, pink, light blue, nile, light gray, slate, navy, brown, tan or black. Width, 38 inches. Per yard................................$0.38

French Serges.

39. French Serge, all wool, double fold, 34 inches wide. The lowest priced foreign wool serge, ever offered. We know from comparison that ours is the best cheap serge in the market. Colors: Navy, wine, garnet, cardinal, myrtle, dark brown, golden brown, tan, old rose, gobelin blue, beige, slate, gray, heliotrope, cream or black. Per yard................................$0.25

40. French Serge, all wool, 38 inches wide, our own importations, fine twill and excellent finished cloth. We pride ourselves on the value we give. Everybody now wears serge. We have the following seasonable shades: Slate, medium gray, cardinal, garnet, wine, marine blue, navy blue, golden brown, seal brown, tan, bronze, myrtle, reseda (a new grayish green), sapphire blue, hussar blue, heliotrope, cream or black. Retailers' price, $0.60.
Our price per yard..............................37½

42. Superfine French Serge, all wool, 45 inches wide. This is very fine, beautifully finished cloth, and will give excellent wear. Serges are now used for all occasions. We can furnish all the fashionable shades as quoted in No. 40.
Usual retail price, $0.75.
Our new tariff price, per yard...................50
Serges are reversible and can be made up either side out, which is an advantage in making over a dress.

43. Extra Superfine French Serge, all wool, 45 inches wide. The best we sell. Colors: Navy, sapphire blue, cardinal, wine, gobelin blue, mahogany, royal purple, olive, golden brown, medium brown, seal, reseda, tan, myrtle, heliotrope, slate, gray, old rose, cream or black...... .75

Beige Mixtures.

45. Imported Beige Suitings, all wool, 50 inches wide. A very popular and durable cloth in serge weave; all new spring mixtures, light gray, medium gray, dark gray, light brown, dark brown, light tan, dark tan, sapphire blue, olive with brown or Gens d Arme blue with wine mixture. Per yard................................$0.55
NOTE—Five to six yards makes a stylish dress.

English Whipcord Serge.

46 English Whipcord Serge, all wool, 50 inches wide. This is one of the richest dress materials we have ever offered, and we offer it to our trade at a rare bargain. It is absolutely correct in style, and designed to meet the requirements of a dressy woman. An opportunity was presented to us to purchase the n anufacturer's entire production at considerably less than cost to make. Believing that by securing such an immense quantity of a really good cloth at an extremely low price we could thereby greatly popularize our dress goods department, we took advantage of the situation, and are consequently now in a position to offer to our friends the very best value ever offered in America. This cloth is retailed by first-class houses in Chicago at $1.50 per yard. We have the following colors: Tan, golden brown, medium brown, dark brown, light gray, slate, wine, cardinal, myrtle, navy or black. Per yard—while they last............$0.75

Shower Proof Serge.

47 Shower Proof Serge, all wool, 51 inches wide. This serge is now very popular with the ladies and is constantly growing in favor wherever introduced. It is of English manufacture, very richly finished, twilled fine like the French serges and of good medium weight. The fabric is treated with a secret preparation in finishing which, while it does not fill up the cloth or alter its appearance, renders it water or shower proof, an advantage which is readily perceived and appreciated by any lady. The only colors we handle are navy blue or black. Per yard....$0.90 Width considered, this cloth costs no more than many ordinary serges of narrower widths.

BLACK GOODS.

NOTE REDUCED PRICES AND IMPROVED QUALITIES.

Black Cashmeres and Henriettas.

We are direct importers of these goods. They come from the hands of the best dyers and finishers in the world and are unsurpassed for durability and color. Always state whether jet or blue black is wanted. Union or cotton warp goods is only made in blue black, that shade being the most serviceable in these grades.

Per yard.

50 Union Cashmere, black, 22 inches wide......$0.09
51 Black Cashmere, 27 inches wide, half wool, double fold.. .12
52 Black Cashmere, double-fold, 32 inches wide, all wool filling.. .17
54 Black, Double Fold Cashmere, 36 inches wide, cotton warp, all wool filling........................ .20
56 Henrietta, Black Union, 36 inches wide........ .25
57 Cashmere, black, 39 inches wide, cotton warp, wool filling, heavy................................ .25
58 Black Cashmere, all wool, 34 inches wide...... .24½
60 Henrietta, black, all wool, 38 inches wide, double fold.. .35
62 Henrietta, black, all wool, 38 inches wide, double fold.. .40
64 Henrietta, black, all wool, 38 inches wide...... .50
66 Henrietta, black, all wool, 38 inches wide...... .55
68 Henrietta, black, all wool, 38 inches wide...... .65
70 Henrietta, black, all wool, 38 inches wide...... .70
72 Henrietta, black, all wool, 38 inches wide...... .75
73 Henrietta, all wool, blue black or jet black, 45 inches wide.. .48
74 Henrietta, all wool, 46 inches wide, blue black or jet black.. .55
76 Henrietta, blue or jet black, all wool, 46 inches wide.. .70
78 Henrietta, fine and heavy, double-warp, Drap d'Ete finish, blue or jet black, 46 inches wide..1.00

Ecroyd's Silk Warp Henriettas.

Per yard.

80 Black Henrietta, Silk Warp, 39 inches wide, double fold..$0.85
82 Black Henrietta, Silk Warp, finer quality, 39 inches wide, double fold........................ .95
84 Black Henrietta, Silk Warp, 39 inches wide, double fold.. 1.00
86 Black Henrietta, Silk Warp, 46 inches wide, double fold, finer quality........................ 1.10
87 Black Henrietta, Silk Warp, 39 inches wide, double fold, superfine quality.................. 1.25

Priestley's "Eudora."

A new Silk Warp Black Goods, similar to silk warp henrietta, but having a new improved finish, the special feature of which is that it will not catch dust.

Per yard.

88 Black Silk Warp Eudora, 40 inches wide......$1.20
89 Black Silk Warp Eudora, 40 inches wide....... 1.35

Novelty Black Goods.

New, Plain and Fancy Weaves.

91 Black Diagonal Suiting, 22 inches wide, half wool. Good black and excellent wearing goods.$0.12
92 Black Armure or Crepe Cloth, width 36 inches, wool filling. A good wearing, firm goods, with raised pattern to resemble English crepe Much used for mourning wear. Per yard......... .15
93 Black All Wool Brocaded Goods, satin finish, handsome jacquard designs, our own importation. Very stylish this season, width 36 inches. Per yard.. .35
94 Black Mohair Brocaded Goods, all wool, 38 inches wide, figures, of which we have a beautiful variety, are woven in brilliant Turkish mohair in the wool fabric and form a contrast which almost equals silk in appearance. Designs are all new and of medium size. Per yard. .65

Dress Goods—Continued.

95 Black Persian Cashmere, all wool 38 inches wide. This is a very beautiful and dressy cloth of medium weight, having a soft, smooth finish with a luster equal to satin. Per yard........... .65
96 Important Black Striped Electoral, narrow or medium stripes in self color. New patterns; very neat and stylish. Width 40 inches. Per yard.. .80
98 Black Bengaline, all wool. A new fabric, finely corded, similar to English rep, reversible; both sides alike Width 38 inches. Per Yard.. .79

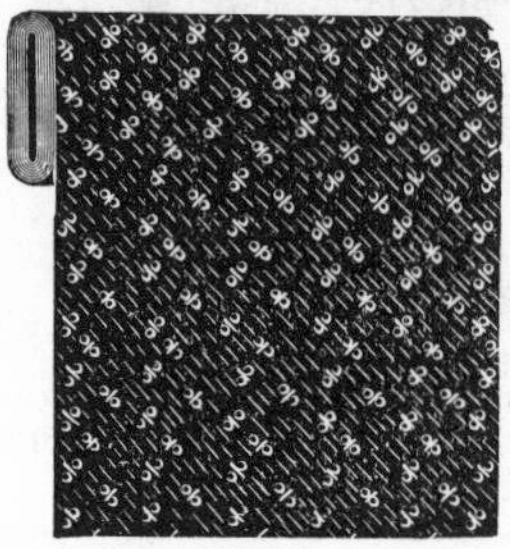

99 New Black Mohair Brocades. Width 38 inches. These styles are entirely new. The grounds are of all wool crepe weaves, or twills, through which are woven a great variety of small, tasteful designs in brilliant black mohair, giving the whole fabric a highly lustrous appearance, equal to silk. Per yard........$0.75

Per yard.

100 Black Crepon, a well-known black fabric, 38 inches wide, similar to Momie or Armure, firm but soft..$0.85
102 Black Sebastopol Fine French Dress Goods, double fold, 38 inches wide, new finish. These goods are twilled like cashmere, but have fine depressed lines running lengthwise of the cloth, giving it the appearance of a narrow, flat cord.. .74
110 All Wool Black Whipcord Suiting. A strong, good wearing cloth, a trifle heavier than henrietta; is smooth finished and shows fine raised satin finished cords running diagonally through cloth; a very popular seller. Width, 40 inches. Per yard.. .60
112 Black Drap D'Alma. A thoroughly staple and handsome dress fabric, smooth finished, similar to henrietta, only the twills are double, i. e., woven in pairs instead of singly. This cloth is especially liked for its rich draping qualities. Width, 38 inches. Per yard......... .75
114 Black Crepe Cloth, all wool, finest quality, 39 inches wide. Especially desirable for ladies in mourning. Per yard........................... .75

Black French Crepons.

The craze of the season.

115 Imported French Crepon, black, all wool, 40 inches wide, a rough, crinkly material, light in weight, and extremely stylish. Per yard..$0.65
119 Black Silk Warp Crepon, 48 inches wide, imported by M. W. & Co. direct from Paris. This we consider the handsomest black fabric shown this season. Very light weight, and of extremely fine texture. Per yard................. 1.25

Black Nuns' Veiling or Batiste.

124 Black Nuns' Veiling, half-wool, 22 inches wide..$0.16
125 Black Nuns' Veiling, all wool, 36 inches wide, double-fold.. .45
126 Black Nuns' Veiling, all wool, double-fold, 38 inches wide.. .50
127 Black Nuns' Veiling, all wool, double-fold, 42 inches wide.. .65

Black Silk Warp Sublime.

130 Black Silk Warp Sublime or Gloria Cloth Width, 48 inches. A fabric woven with a fine silk warp, and having a highly lustrous surface. Softer and more durable than pure silk, and of equal sheen or lustre. This cloth is now very much used for dresses, blouse waists and underskirts. It is strong, wears well and is economical on account of the width, as it takes fewer yards and cuts to better advantage than narrow goods. Per yard..$0.69

Black Bordered Nuns' Veiling.

For Mourning Veils and Bonnets.

135 Black Nuns' Veiling, 42 inches wide, half wool, has side band border 3 inches deep. Per yard..$0.70
136 Black Silk Warp Nuns' Veiling, 42 inches wide, 3 inch side band border. Per yard.. 1.00
138 Black Silk Warp Nuns' Veiling, extra fine, 42 inches wide, 3 inch side band border. Per yard.. 1.25

Lustrous Black Mohairs.

Dress Mohairs, perfectly dyed goods, black as jet.

Per yard.

140 Black Alpaca, 24 inches wide..............$0.19
142 Black Alpaca, 25 inches wide............... .23
144 Black Alpaca, 27 inches wide............... .30
146 Black Mohair Brilliantines, 38 inches....... .32
148 Black Mohair Brilliantines, 38 inches....... .50
150 Black Mohair Brilliantines, 38 inches....... .55
152 Black Mohair Brilliantines, 38 inches....... .60
154 Black Mohair Brilliantines, 46 inches....... .70
156 Black Mohair Brilliantines, 46 inches....... .90

Compare Our Prices with Others

Black French Serges.

For general wear there is no cloth better or more popular with the ladies than Serges. They are not so smooth or closely constructed as Henrietta, but are made of a more wiry wool, are reversible, and at present extremely stylish.

Per yard.

160 All Wool Black Serge, 36 inches wide.......$0.30
162 All Wool Black Serge, 38 inches wide....... .38
163 All Wool Black Serge, 45 inches wide....... .40
164 All Wool Black Serge, 46 inches wide....... .50
166 All Wool Black Serge, 46 inches wide....... .75
168 All Wool Black Serge, 48 inches wide....... .95

Nuns' Serge.

170 Nuns' Serge, All Wool. Jet black, 39 inches wide. This serge is very fashionable. It is of coarse weave, made of hard twisted and wiry wool, and will stand any amount of wear. Per yard..$0.45

Fancy Dress Goods.

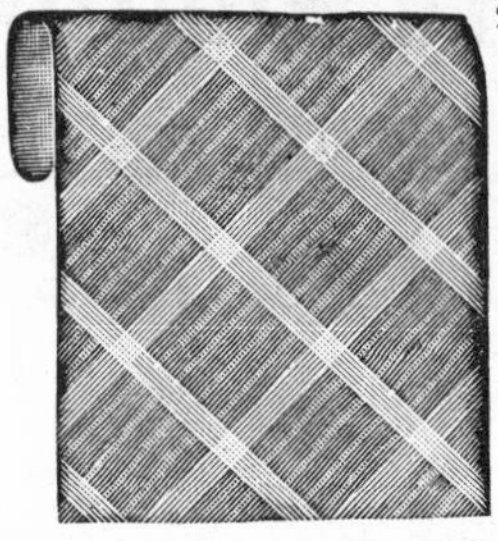

200 Cotton Twill Crown Plaids, 23 inches wide, imitation of Scotch wool designs; Highland colorings. Combinations of dark blue and green; navy and red; navy and brown; brown and white; navy and gold; wine and blue; red and blue, brown and tan; purple and green, or black and blue. Per yard........$0.04¾ Full piece of about 50 yards, 4½ cents per yard.

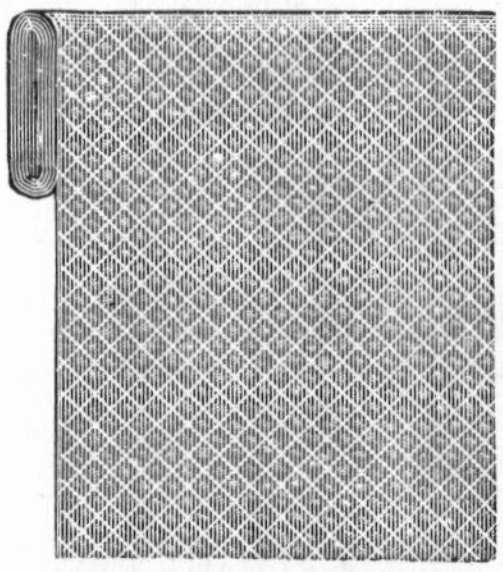

202 English Tweed Checked Suitings. A twilled cotton fabric, very sightly and durable. Colors: Dark, black grounds with small fancy checks of heliotrope and gold; brown with black or black with green. Width, 31 inches. We purchased 500 pieces of this cloth at a ridiculous price, and offer them while they last at. Per yard.............$0.08 For full piece of about 50 yards, 7¼ cents per yard.

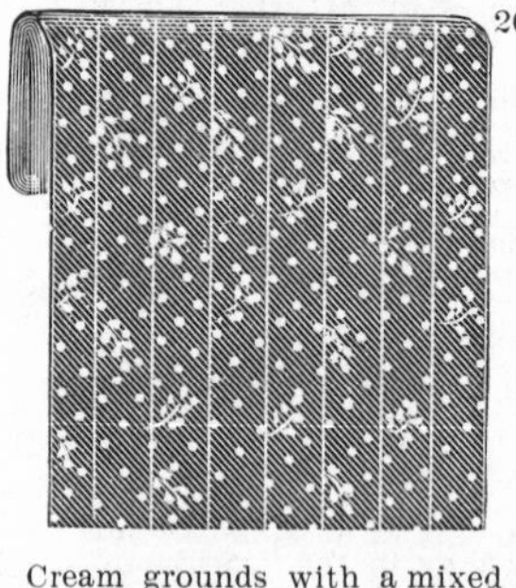

203 Pacific Satin Surah, 29 inches wide. A new cotton fabric of a surah twill weave, light and dark colors printed in neat, tasteful designs. Dark grounds are black, wine, navy or sapphire blue with fine dotted stripes and tiny dots of white over which is scattered a small floral figure in pretty colors. Fast black grounds with a variety of small neat figures in white. Cream grounds with a mixed chene design closely covering ground work, copied from silk pattern; color combinations in the figures are heliotrope, black and dull green; pink and black; light blue, tan and wine; light blue and black; pink and wine; light blue, wine and majenta. All of these colorings are on cream grounds. Made to sell for 12½ cents. Our price, per yard..$0.08 For full piece of about 50 yards, 7½ cents per yard.

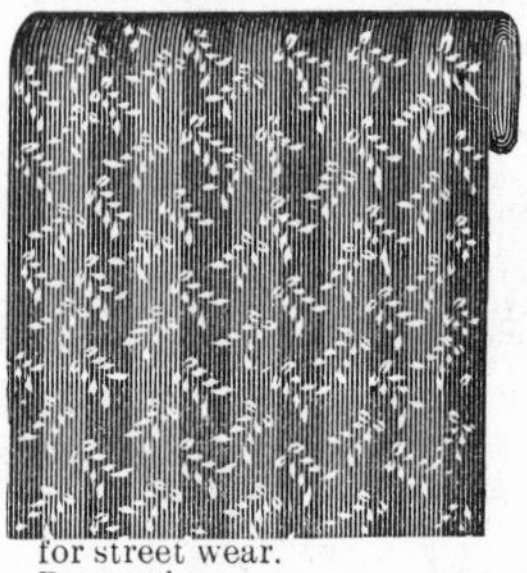

204 Inverness Flannels, 30 inches wide, fleeced back, twilled on right side like cashmere, and printed in Persian striped designs or small fancy spots; the latter are on black, seal, or wine grounds. Persian effects are in combinations of navy and cardinal, or wine and old rose. A very pretty and comfortable cloth for tea gowns, wrappers or for street wear. Per yard..$0.10 Full piece of about 50 yards, 9½ cents per yard.

GROCERY LIST ISSUED MONTHLY

Free Upon Request.

Dress Goods—Continued.

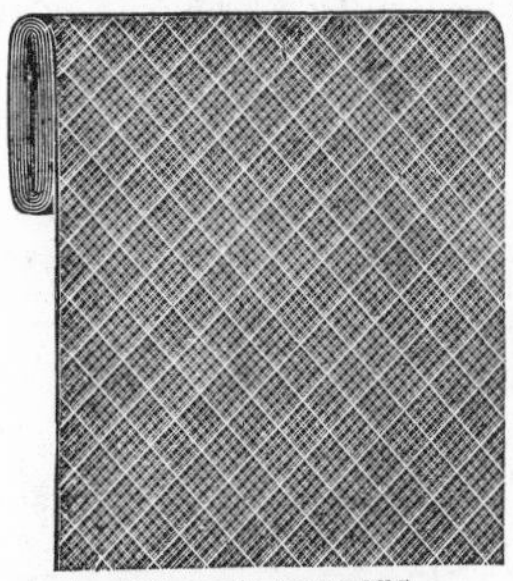

206 Scotia Suitings, 28 inches wide; a twilled cotton dress goods, medium weight, double fold. Patterns are small checks and 1 inch plaids copied from fine English suitings. Predominating colors are brown with lines of blue, or medium blue ground with lines of red and black; a cloth that will wear well and look well.
Per yard........$0.09
Full piece of about 50 yards, 8¾ cents per yard.

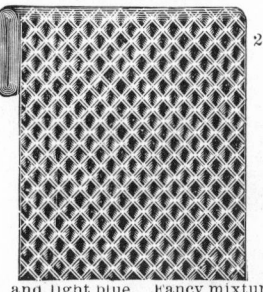

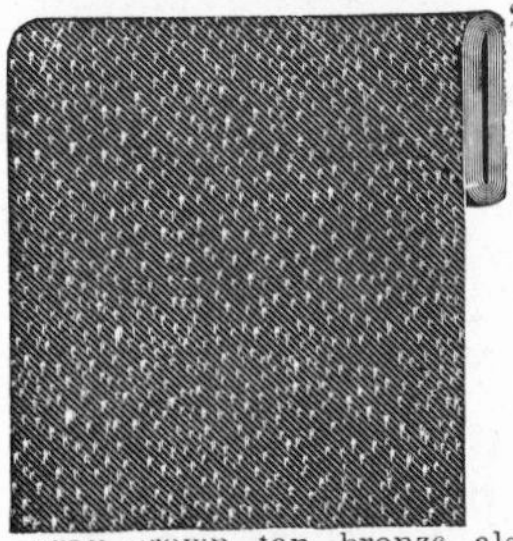

208 Claremont Suiting, double-fold, 32 inches wide; new spring colorings. This is one of the best made low priced suitings that we ever received. We considered them of such extraordinary good value that we purchased all that the mill had. The styles are in tweed effects. Pin checks, fine stripes and bourette mixtures in light, medium or dark gray, brown, tan, bronze, also new combinations of pinkish tan and garnet, or heliotrope and brown.
Per yard....................$0.12½
Full piece of about 50 yards, 11¾ cents per yard. The above goods are all owned and the sale controlled exclusively by M. W. & Co., and we know that for style and quality nothing in the regular market at near the price approaches them.

210 Fairmount Checked Suiting, 28 inches wide, double fold. This is one of the prettiest low priced dress goods we ever opened. Checks and colorings are exact copies of imported goods worth $1.00 per yard. Colors combined are: Pea green, light brown and white; light brown tan and white; navy, light brown and white; navy and light blue. Fancy mixture of green, gold, red and white, or myrtle, red, gold and white.
Per yard....................$0.12½
Full piece of about 45 yards, 12 cents per yard.

211 Fine Checked Suitings, 28-inches wide, double fold. New and attractive styles for genteel wear; from their appearance you could never guess their cost, they look to be worth several times the price quoted. Colors are: Tan and white; slate and white; green and white; blue, wine and white; wine, black and white.
Per yard....................$0.12
Full piece of about 50 yards, 11¾ cents.

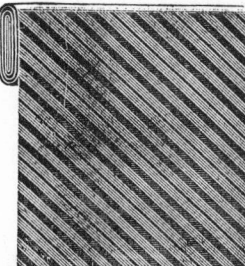

216 Worsted Diagonal, 22 inches wide, very popular for bias back waists, etc.; fine line of colors, good wearing goods. Medium or dark gray, navy blue, myrtle, golden brown, medium brown seal, cardinal, garnet, wine, sapphire, beige, tan or black.
Per yard........$0.12
For full piece of about 52 yards, 11 cents per yard.

218 Brocaded Alpaca, 22 inches wide, half wool. Colors: Golden brown, dark brown, beige, tan, old rose, myrtle, slate, light gray, seal, olive, cardinal, garnet, wine, navy, sapphire or black.
Per yard............$0.12
Price, full piece of about 54 yards, 11¼ cents per yard.

Our Next Catalogue, No. 58, will be issued *Sept. 1, 1895.*

Dress Goods—Continued.

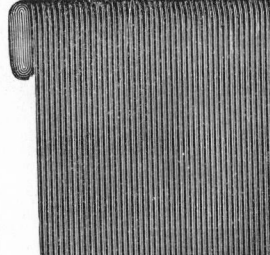

224 Striped Wash Poplin for dresses and skirts, in neat, narrow, medium or wide stripes of black and gray. This is a thoroughly staple fabric, fast colors, does not show dirt and wears like iron. Width, 28 inches.
Per yard....$0.10
Price per yard, full piece of about 50 yards, 9½ cents per yard.

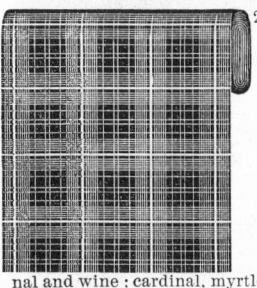

225 Endurance Dress Plaids, double fold, 27 inches wide. Very pretty for children. The cloth is a cashmere twill, well made and nicely finished. The plaids are of medium size and are formed by cross lines of several contrasting shades prettily blended. The combinations are as follows: Scarlet navy and gold; navy, cardinal and white; myrtle, cardinal and wine; cardinal, myrtle and navy; mahogany, navy and white; navy, green and white; navy, cardinal and gold.
Per yard....................$0.12½
For full piece of about 50 yards, 11¾ cents per yard.

226 Bourette Suitings, double fold, 27 inches wide. This is a well-made cloth for the price, and will give good service. The ground or body colors are: Wine, black, myrtle green, brown or navy checked or plaided and and speckled over with small bright knotted or bourette threads; also made in small and medium shepherd checks in black and white.
Per yard....................$0.13
Price for full piece of about 50 yards, 12¼ cents per yard.

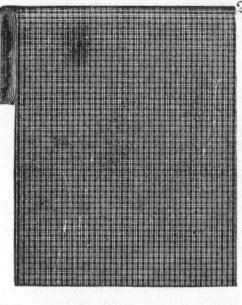

227 Bradford Checked Suitings, double fold, 28 inches wide. These goods were copied from and closely resemble the newest styles in high priced English all wool suitings. The checks are very small and are in the following color combinations: Brown, red and olive; brown and blue, brown and black; brown and slate; brown and green; blue and gold.
Per yard..........$0.12
Full piece of about 50 yards, 11¼c. per yard.

228 Diagonal Melange Suitings, 33 inches wide, cotton warp, wool filling. A very desirable line of quiet mixtures for spring wear. This cloth is especially desirable for traveling or shopping dresses, as it does not catch or show dust. Mixtures are in green, tan, brown, gray, or blue effects. Per yard..........................$0.18
Full piece of about 50 yards, 17 cents per yard.

229 Fancy Mixed Diagonals, half wool, 36 inches wide. This is a good looking and serviceable material and will make a very pretty dress. They were made to retail at not less than 30 cents. We bought them at a bargain and will offer them as such while they last. Colors: Red brown, medium brown, olive, slate, wine, or green. Per yard.............................$0.18
Full piece of about 50 yards, 17¼ cents per yard.

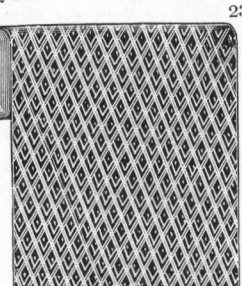

230 Manchester Fancy Worsted Brocades, 33 inches wide, double fold, cotton warp, worsted filling and small neat designs woven in bright, silky mohair. This is a staple fabric and always in demand. Colors are: Slate, golden brown, medium brown, seal, garnet, wine, cardinal, myrtle, navy or black. (Usual price, 25 cents). Our price, per yard.......$0.15
Full piece of about 50 yards, 14½ cents per yard.

Dress Goods—Continued.

231 Chameleon Fancy Brocades, two color effects in small diamond pattern, similar to 230. Pattern is woven of bright worsted in contrasting shade to ground color. Width is 33 inches, double fold. Colors are: Brown with blue; cardinal with blue; wine with bronze; light brown with myrtle; myrtle with wine; brown with black; brown with olive; blue with wine.
Per yard....................$0.15
Full piece of about 50 yards, 14½ cents per yard.

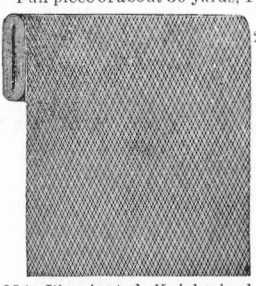

232 Double Fold Fancy Brocaded Suiting. Width, 33 inches. We have the following solid colors, in which are woven small patterns in bright silky mohair, in self color; brown, navy, tan, gray, cardinal, myrtle or black. Per yard, $0.19. For full piece of about 50 yards, 18 cents per yard.

234 Illuminated Knickerbocker Suitings, part wool, 32 inches wide, double fold. Very stylish. The filling in the cloth is interwoven with tiny knotted thread of contrasting colors, which produces a fine speckled effect. The colors combined are: Seal brown and gold; dark gray and white; dark green and emerald; navy and bright blue; wine and red; slate and white.
Price per yard..................................$0.16
For full piece of about 50 yards, 15 cents per yard.

242 Fine Diagonal Whipcord Suiting, half wool, 32 inches wide, double fold. A strong, good wearing cloth and made in a stylish range of colors. Prominent shades are navy blue, wine, myrtle green, golden brown, tan, medium or seal brown, slate, cardinal or black.
Per yard..$0.18
For full piece of about 50 yards, 17¼ cents per yard.

248 New Brocatelle Suitings, width 34 inches, double fold, half wool. Small brocaded figure on solid grounds in contrasting colors, producing an illuminated or iridescent effect. Combinations are of gray and black; black and gold; brown and brown or gray and brown.
Per yard........$0.22
For full piece of about 50 yards, 21 cents per yard.

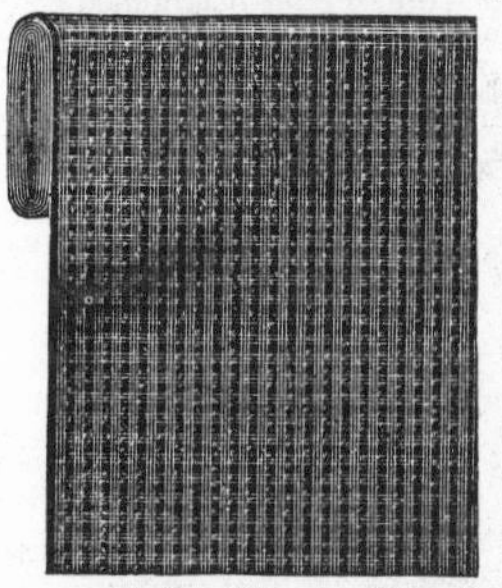

256 New Bourette Suitings, double fold, 32 inches wide, part wool. This is a very handsome and stylish material, soft finish, and looks like all wool. The styles are exact copies of the latest imported novelties. The colored bourette threads form the following mixtures: Brown and blue; brown and olive; brown and tan; brown and gray; brown and green or brown and wine.
Per yard..........$0.22
Full piece of about 50 yards, 21 cents per yard.

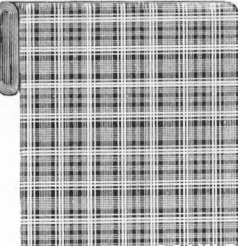

257 Worsted Scotch Plaids, cotton warp, worsted filling, double fold, 32 inches wide. These goods are made by the Arlington mills and for intrinsic value are the best plaids on the market. They are absolutely fast colors, will wash and stand any amount of hard wear. These bright effects are much in demand now for fancy dress waists and children's dresses. Plaids are all small or medium broken effects in scarlet with green, blue and gold.
Per yard..............................$0.25
Full piece of about 50 yards, 24¼ cents per yard.

Our BOOK Department
Has become Very Popular.

EXAMINE THE QUOTATIONS.

Dress Goods—Continued.

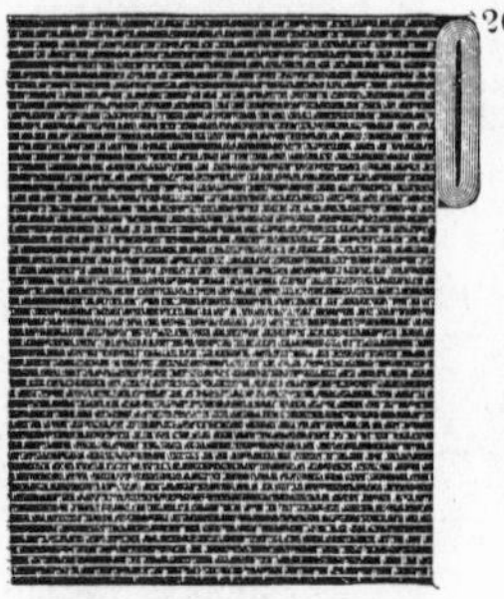

260 Bon Ton Mixtures. A new line of fashionable suitings, 33 inches wide, double fold, new spring colorings. The cloth is beautifully woven and the styles are all genteel and quiet in colorings. The warp is cotton while the filling is a mixture of silk and wool; the silk showing in small speckled mixture on medium grounds with fine hairline stripe. Colors are: Gray, heliotrope with green, tan, blue, brown or a new light shade of green.
Per yard............$0.25
Full piece of about 50 yards, 23½ cents per yard.

268 Pointelle Suiting, double fold. 32 inches wide, all wool filling. It is smooth finished, woven on the diagonal order with fine bright colored threads, forming small illuminated spots on background; very genteel. Colors are: Tan, slate, plum, cardinal, golden brown, seal brown, navy blue, myrtle or black; illuminating threads are red and gold. Per yard............ .23
Full piece of about 50 yards, 22 cents per yard.

270 Paris Pin Check Suitings, 32 inches wide, double fold. This is a fine plain weave, very neat and stylish. half wool. The tiny checks are formed of two or more contrasting colors. We have the following effects: Brown, black and gray; olive and gold; brown and navy; black and red; navy, wine and brown, or green and brown. We think this is one of the prettiest low-priced fabrics shown this season.
Per yard.. .25
Full piece of about 50 yards, 24 cents per yard.

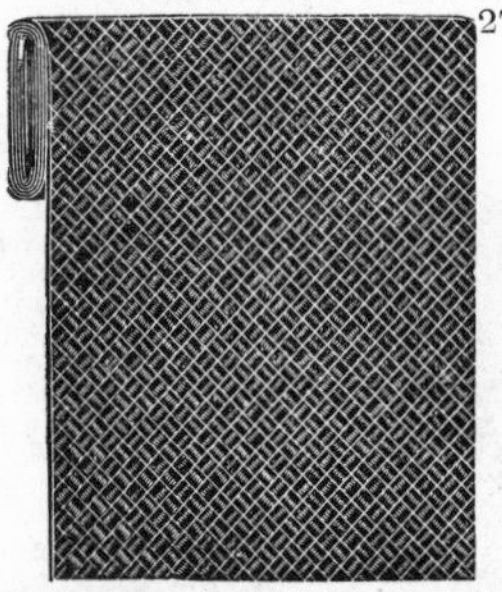

272 New Matelasse Suiting, 36 inches wide, all wool filling, cotton warp. This is an exact copy of an expensive imported novelty, and unless closely examined could not be told from goods costing one dollar per yard. Two or more colors are combined in weaving each style. We have the following combinations: Wine and brown; navy and gold; navy, red and green; black and gold; black, green and tan.
Per yard............$0.30
Full piece of about 50 yards, 29 cents per yard.

274 Arlington Fancy Diagonals, 36 inches wide, half wool, double fold. This is one of the richest domestic dress fabrics shown this season. The predominating colors are: Myrtle green, navy, wine, cardinal, seal, golden brown, sapphire blue, or tan, each color being brightened by fine interwoven bright threads of contrasting colors. Per yard..............................$0.35
Full piece of about 50 yards, 34 cents per yard.

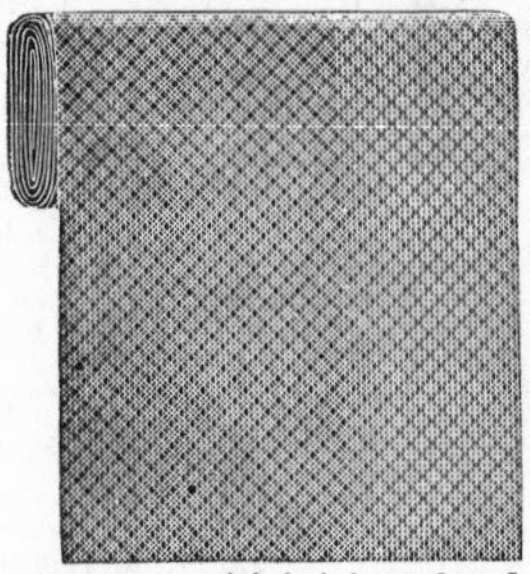

275 Illuminated Novelty Suiting, 36 inches wide, not all wool but the cotton warp is so skillfully interwoven that it requires a close examination to detect it. In style and appearance this cloth is equal to anything in the market at 75 cents. Colors are: Tan, reseda green, slate, wine, golden brown, medium brown, seal, navy or myrtle. These ground colors are interwoven with bright colored threads forming small designs. Must be seen to be appreciated.
Per yard..$0.40

276 Trafalgar Double and Twist Suitings, 36 inches wide, three-fourths wool, double fold. This is an unusually substantial weave and will make a very serviceable and rich-looking dress. Looks equal to an imported cloth. In appearance it resembles pepper and salt mixture, excepting that the mixtures are combinations of various fashionable colors produced by weaving doubled and twisted colored threads. We show the following styles: Brown, blue and orange; blue and red; olive and blue; cadet blue and black; wine and blue, or black and orange.
Per yard..$0.35

WE GUARANTEE EVERYTHING TO BE AS REPRESENTED.

Our Guarantee has always been found good.

Dress Goods—Continued.

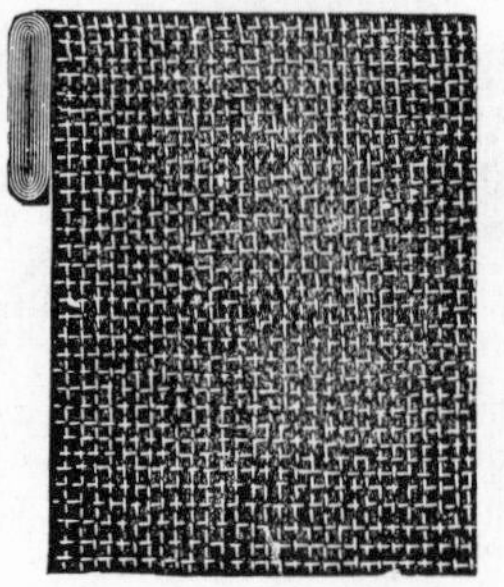

278 Silk and wool Novelty Suiting, 36 inches wide, double fold. A rich, soft wool material, in new color combinations for spring and summer. We have the following styles. The first named color is the wool or body shade, into which is closely woven the contrasting color in silk bourettes: Olive green and gold; tan and gold; light gray and blue; dark brown and blue; light brown and gold. All light effects.
Per yard,........$0.39

Covert Cloths.

For wide all wool Covert Cloth see No. 3236.

Covert cloths are among the most fashionable of the new dress fabrics, and are in great demand for stylish street wear. They come in mixture effects of various colors, the mixtures being formed by different colored yarns which are doubled and twisted before weaving. They do not show dust or wear, and are therefore very economical.

281 Covert Suitings, 32 inches wide, double-fold, part wool. Predominating colors are: Tan, brown, wine, blue, gray, blue and gold or gray mixture. Per yard..............................$0.20
Full piece of about 50 yards, 19¼ cents per yard.

282 Covert Suitings, 36 inches wide, half wool. Color combinations are: Tan and gray; brown and gold; brown and gray; blue and brown; gray. Per yard.................................. .39
Full piece of about 50 yards, 37½ cents per yard.

Brocaded Brilliantines.

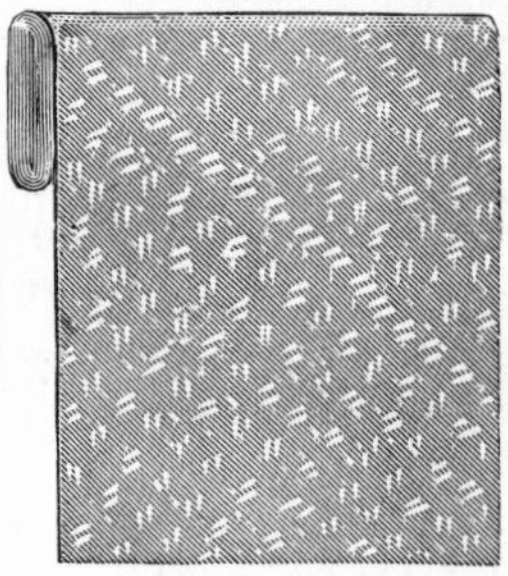

284 Brocaded Mohair Brilliantines, rich and lustrous as silk, small, neat designs in self color. Width 38 inches. Shades are: Light gray, slate, light green, wine, tan, golden brown, medium brown, seal, navy, myrtle or black. This line we expect will be one of the greatest sellers of the season.
Per yard........$0.45
Full price of about 50 yards, 42½ cts. per yard.

New All Wool Fancies.

Our own importations. The prettiest effects we ever brought out, and the cost no more than asked in most places for cotton mixed goods.

Fancy Vigoureux Suiting.

286 All Wool Vigoureux Suiting, in narrow hairline stripes. A fine blending of harmonizing colors; quiet and genteel. no loud or positive effects. We have light grayish blue interwoven with wine and olive; brown and cream; tan and cream; wine, olive and ecru; olive and cream.
Width, 37 inches. Per yard...................$0.37½

287 All Wool Novelty Vigoureux Suiting, entirely new design; weight and finish especially adapted for spring and summer wear. Color combinations are: French gray and ecru; cream, olive and old rose; cream and tan; seal brown and white; turquoise blue, white and garnet; olive cream and brown; electric blue and white; gray and white. Width. 37 inches. These goods should be seen in the piece, Per yard........... .48

288 Pin Check Vigoureux Suiting, all wool, 38 inches wide, double fold. A very neat and stylish fabric for general wear; new importation for spring 1895. Colors are: Grayish blue, tan, light gray, dark gray, brown or green.
Per yard.. .49

Colored All Wool Brocades.

JACQUARD DESIGNS.

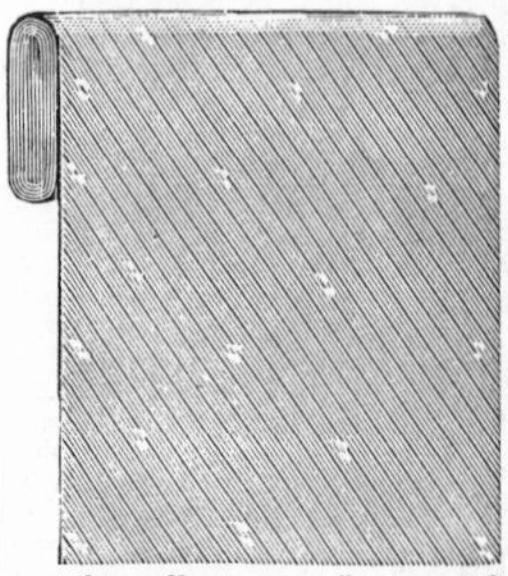

289 Jacquard Brocaded Suiting, all wool, 35 inches wide, double fold, piece-dyed fancy weaves will be very popular this season. These goods are made in Saxony, Germany, expressly for Montgomery Ward & Co., and in this line we believe we have the lowest priced all wool novelty ever put on the market. The cloth is satin finished, with fine diagonal lines and small woven figures. Colors: Navy, cardinal, wine, tan, gray, old rose, sapphire blue, heliotrope, golden brown, medium brown, seal, myrtle, olive or black. Per yard...............$0.35
For full piece of about 55 yards, 33½ cents per yard.

Dress Goods—Continued.

290 Wool Checked Suitings, spring colorings. A very handsome and stylish line of small even checks. The cloth is all wool, medium weight, and we safely recommend it for satisfactory service. Colors are: Tan and gray, blue and tan, light green and mauve, brown and gray, brown and blue, brown and gray, navy and slate. Width, 36 inches.
Per yard..$0.48

292 Hekla Suiting, all wool, 38 inches wide, double-fold, latest importations. We are especially proud of this line as it is one the neatest effects brought out this season. It is a fine mixture, having through it almost invisible hair line stripes so close together as to form part of the mixture. Colors are combined as follows: Beige, cardinal and olive; gray cardinal and olive; tan cardinal and olive; tan, olive and black, or black and cardinal.
Per yard.. .60

French Crepon.

Every lady this season wants a crepon dress. Must have it if she has any desire to be in style. This fabric is especially adapted to the prevailing style of dress—large sleeves and wide skirts.

295 French Crepon, all wool, 41 inches wide. Colors: Beige, reseda, bluet—the new shade of blue, old rose, gray, wine, medium brown, golden brown, tan, navy, cardinal, cream, lilac, nile, light blue, heliotrope, magenta or jacqueminot, black.
Per yard..$0.65

Colored or Black Silk Warp Sublime.

298 Silk and Wool Sublime, 38 inches wide, double fold. Warp is of finest spun silk, filling of wool. These goods are so woven that the silk is thrown to the surface, producing a luster equal to all silk, yet much more durable. It is the richest plain fabric in the market and has become very popular with fine trade. Colors are: Ecru, light tan, dark tan, golden brown, silver gray, light blue, navy, cardinal, cream or black.
Per yard..$0.90

Whipcord Suitings.

They come in all staple and leading shades. The cloth resembles serge, but is firmer and smoother, not so woolly, and does not catch dust, etc. This cloth has always been very successful with us. We strongly recommend it for wear and elegance.

304 Imported All Wool Whipcord Suiting, medium weight, very fine and rich in finish, adapted to all kinds of wear. We import these goods in large quantities and buy only from the best makers in France. We show the following fashionable shades this season: Gray, cardinal, garnet, wine, golden brown, seal brown, tan, gobelin blue, purple, reseda green or black. Width, 40 inches. Per yard....................$0.55

306 Extra Heavy Whipcord Suiting, all wool, 38 inches wide. The weight and beauty of this cloth must be seen to be appreciated. It drapes beautifully, and the cords being raised prominently gives it a very rich and uncommon appearance; for service it cannot be equaled. Colors are: Myrtle green, light navy blue, dark navy blue or black. Usually sold at 85 cents.
Per yard.. .60

Dress Flannels and Tricots.

312 All Wool Newton Sackings, a low-priced but nicely finished dress flannel, one that will be found thoroughly satisfactory in wearing qualities. We have them in a complete range of colors, as follows: Tan, seal brown, medium brown, slate, golden brown, gray, cardinal, light navy, wine, garnet, myrtle, sapphire, blue gray mixture, navy, black, light, medium or dark gray mixture or brown mixture. Width, 28 inches.
Per yard.. .22
Full piece about 35 yards, 21 cents per yard.

316 All Wool Tricot or Bengaline, 36 inches wide. Makes a nice durable dress for general wear. Colors are: Navy blue, slate, tan, myrtle, olive, plum, cardinal, wine, medium brown, seal or black. Per yard........................ .33
Price of full piece of about 50 yards, 32 cents per yard.

318 All Wool Flannel Suiting, cloth finished, double fold, 40 inches wide. A thoroughly staple dress goods, of which we sell great quantities; good weight and pressed finish; all seasonable colors in plain and mixtures. Plain colors are: Navy blue, marine blue, sapphire blue, myrtle green, sage green, olive, tan, golden brown, medium brown, seal brown, cardinal, wine, slate or black. Mixtures in dark, medium or light gray; dark, medium or light brown. Fancy mixtures in dark blue, green or brown.
Per yard.. .37½
Price of full piece of about 40 yards, 36½ cents per yard.

A MILLION PEOPLE

Found our methods worth trying last year.

Worsted Storm Serges.

For quotations on extra wide serges see Nos. 3220-3222.

Storm Serges have taken a prominent place among the leading staple dress materials. No other fabric has yet been introduced that will equal these goods for appearance and wearing qualities. No lady's wardrobe is complete without a Storm Serge dress. They are also extensively used for skirts, to be worn with fancy silk or wash waists.

320 Storm Serge, 36 inches wide, all worsted filling, cotton warp. A splendid-looking and durable cloth. Colors: Navy blue or black. Per yard..$0.24
Full piece of about 50 yards, 22½ cents per yard.

323 Storm Serge, 36 inches wide. All pure worsted warp and filling. (Note.—Real Storm Serges are made only from worsted, which is a longer fiber, more wiry and more expensive than the softer and shorter fibre wools. In this quality we can furnish black or navy blue. Per yard.. .35
Full piece of about 50 yards, 33⅓ cents per yard.

325 Storm Serge, 38 inches wide. All pure worsted. A handsome cloth and one that we recommend for wear. Colors: Black or navy blue. Per yard.. .49
Full piece of about 50 yards, 47½ cents per yard.

Novelty Storm Serge.

A Bargain.

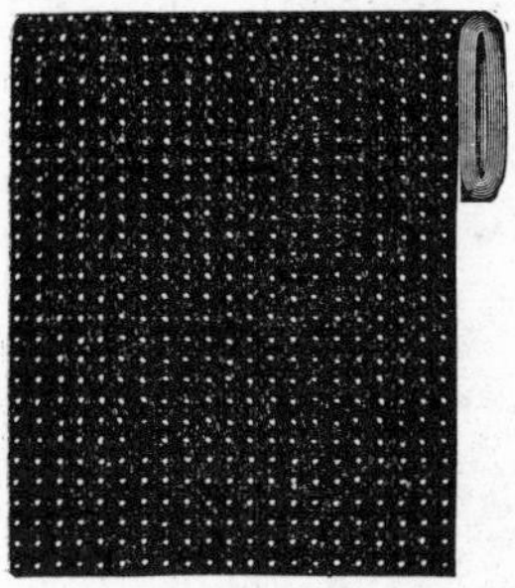

327 Fancy Storm Serge Suiting. All pure worsted, 36 inches wide, double fold, black, the only color, through which is woven fine white threads, producing a tiny pin point effect; a remarkably pretty and stylish cloth for street costumes. We have but limited quantity and can get no more. Actual value, 55 cents. Price until sold, $0.37½.
Full piece of about 50 yards, 36 cents per yard.

Heavy Wool Serges.

329 All Wool Cheviot Serge, similar in construction to Storm Serge, but without the harsh feeling which distinguishes the latter. This is one of our best selling serges and one that has always given great satisfaction: for the price it is one of the best values ever offered. Colors are: Tan, golden brown, medium brown, cardinal, light navy, dark navy or black; width, 36 inches. Per yard.. .35
Full piece of about 50 yards, 34½ cents per yard.

Gray and Black Brocaded Fancies

334 Gray Brocaded Dress Goods. All wool, 38 inches wide, handsome Jacquard designs in fine tracing effects of black on gray grounds. The cloth is of medium weight, a satin finished face and is very desirable for ladies of quiet tastes or mature years who do not care for colors, yet want a change from black. Also used for second mourning. Per yard..$0.50

Moreen Skirting.

NOTE REDUCED PRICE.

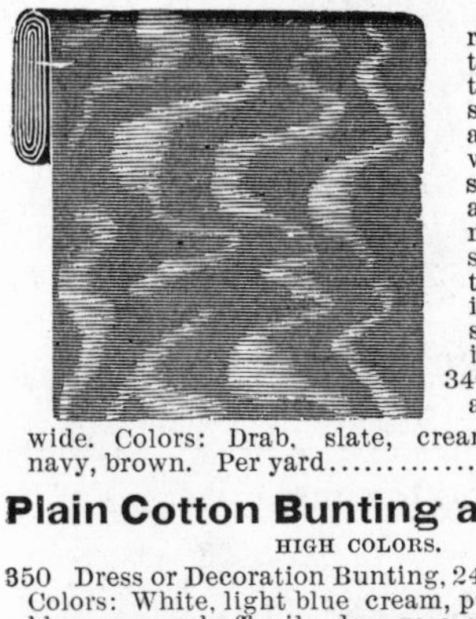

Moreen Skirting resembles an extremely heavy watered gros grained silk. It is especially adapted for wear with the prevailing styles in dress skirts as its stiffness makes the skirt stand out or flare at the bottom, which is the effect now sought for by fashionable women.

340 Moreen Skirting all wool, 25 inches wide. Colors: Drab, slate, cream, black, garnet, navy, brown. Per yard..$0.40

Plain Cotton Bunting and Crepes.

HIGH COLORS.

350 Dress or Decoration Bunting, 24 inches wide. Colors: White, light blue cream, pink, medium blue, canary, buff, nile, deep rose, pink, yellow, lilac, pea green, apple green, cardinal, navy or gold. The red, white and blue is much used for decoration A better one we think than you can get elsewhere. Per yard..$0.04
Price for full piece of about 65 yards, 3¾ cents per yard.

Dress Goods—Continued.

352 Plain Colored Bunting, 36 inches wide, double fold. A strong, well made cloth, very pretty and much used for fancy dresses, dainty quilts, curtains and draperies. Colors: Pink, light blue, nile green, apple green, deep rose, yellow, cardinal, cream or white. Per yard..... .06
Full piece of about 55 yards, 5½ cents per yard.

354 Pekin Crepe or Momie Cloth, 29 inches wide, used for fancy party dresses, draperies, etc.; plain colors only, comes in the following shades: Cream, light blue, pink, lavender, nile, yellow, cardinal or black. Per yard.. .09
Full piece of about 50 yards, 8½ cents per yard.

356 Fine Bulgarian Crepe, 28 inches wide, a soft rich draping, crinkling cloth, resembling the Oriental or Turkish cotton crepes. Pretty for party dresses or summer wear, also for fancy work. Shades are: Cream, white, canary, yellow, pink, light blue, lilac, nile, red, orange, tan or black. Per yard.. .12
Full piece of about 45 yards, 11¼ cents per yard.

357 Serpentine Crepe, 28 inches wide. This is one of the most popular of the crepe weaves and looks the same as the high priced wool crepes now so much used for fashionable wear. We can furnish all colors quoted in 356. Per yard.. .14
Full piece of about 50 yards, 13¼ cents per yard.

359 Art Novelty Crepon. The loveliest, daintiest cotton crepe you ever saw; width 28 inches. Made in all of the light colors: Cream, pink, light blue, canary, lilac, orange, white, ecru, nile, cardinal or black. Per yard.. .20
Full piece of about 45 yards, 18½ cents per yard.

Challies, Lawns and Cotton Novelties.

PRINTED AND PLAIN.

Newest Styles for Spring and Summer 1895.

Plain Black Lawns.

365 Plain Fast Black Jaconet Lawn, width 30 inches. This is a good firm cloth, well finished and not rotted in the dye. Jet black. Per yard..$0.06
Full piece about 40 yards, 5¾ cents per yard.

366 Fast Black Plain Fine Organdie Lawn, width 30 inches. A clear, brilliant black. Cloth is perfectly finished, fine and sheer....... .08½
Full piece of about 40 yards, 8 cents per yard.

Challies.

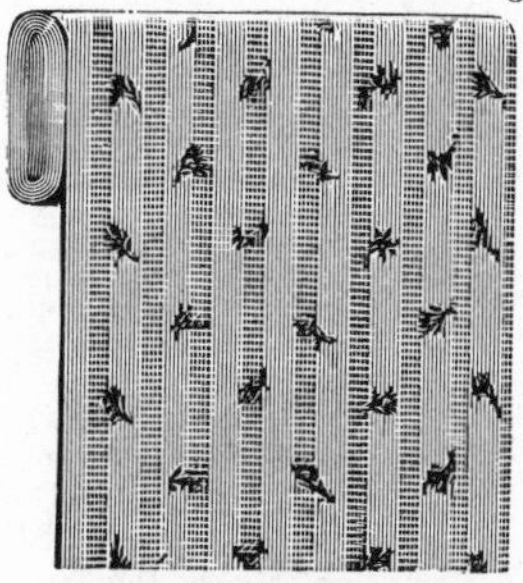

368 Figured Cotton Challies, 23 inches wide. New small floral and dash effects in heliotrope, pink, nile or light blue, on cream white grounds. Quarter inch fancy stripes in pink, light blue, nile, tan or heliotrope on cream white ground, over which is also printed small tasteful floral patterns. This is beyond a question the best cheap challie ever sold.
Per yard.......$0.03½
Full piece of about 50 yards, 3⅜ cents per yd.

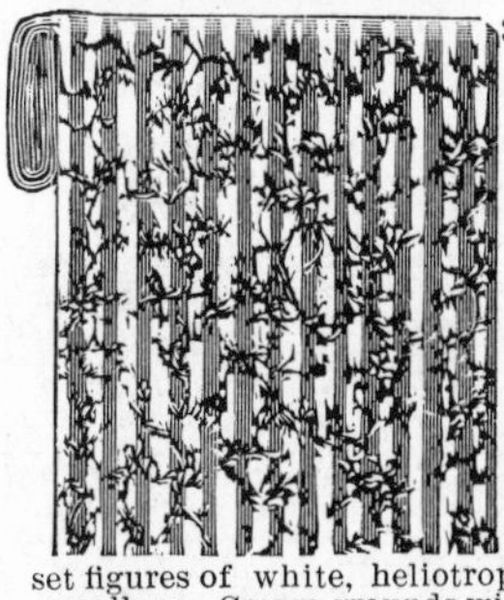

369 Best Figured Cotton Challies, 23 inches wide. All the finest and newest goods. Venetian muslins or Pacifics. Cream grounds with small floral designs in heliotrope, light blue, garnet or gold, combined with dashes, leaves and flowered stripes; or cream grounds in heliotrope, tan, pink, blue or nile green. Shadings of other bright colors; black grounds with small set figures of white, heliotrope, pink, turquoise blue or yellow. Cream grounds with fine Stripes and tiny Dresden floral designs in pink, heliotrope or blue with contrasting shades. Per yard $0.04½
Full pieces of about 50 yards, 4¼ cents per yard.

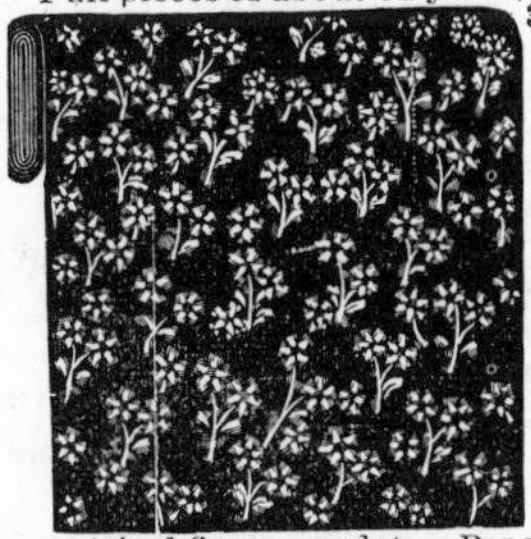

375 Pacific Half Wool Figured Challie or Nuns' Veiling, width 22 inches. Almost equal in appearance and feeling to the imported all wool challies. The ground colors are: Cream, black or navy blue, over which are exquisitely printed designs, small or medium sized, showing beautiful flowers, either set or combined with vine tracings, also set geometrical figures or dots. Per yard..............$0.16
Full piece of about 50 yards, 15½ cents per yard.

376 Plain Pacific Half Wool Challie or Nuns' Veiling, 22 inches wide. Black, cardinal, navy, olive, gray, pink, light blue, cream or tan only. Compare our prices with others.. .15
Price for full piece of about 50 yards, 14½ cents per yard.

Dress Goods—Continued.

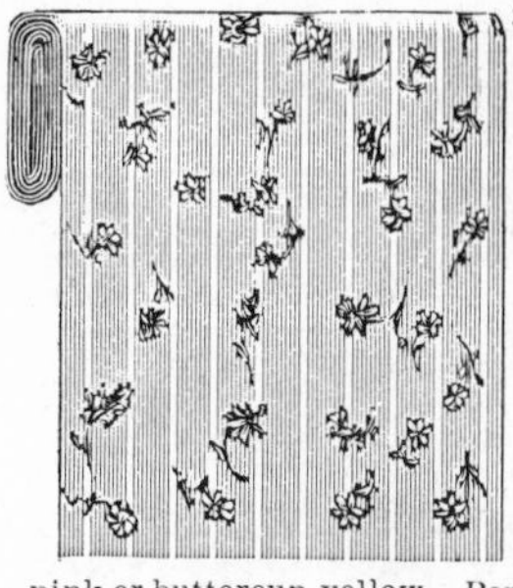

378 Silk Striped Imported French Challie, 27 inches wide all wool filling, fine cotton warp, looks and handles like the finest all wool goods. This is one of the prettiest challies yet produced. The grounds are all cream with narrow silk stripes 1 in. apart running through. Over all is printed small dainty floral designs in gray, heliotrope, garnet, blue, mahogany, brown with blue, pink or buttercup yellow. Per yard. $0.25
Full piece of about 50 yards, 23½ cents per yard.

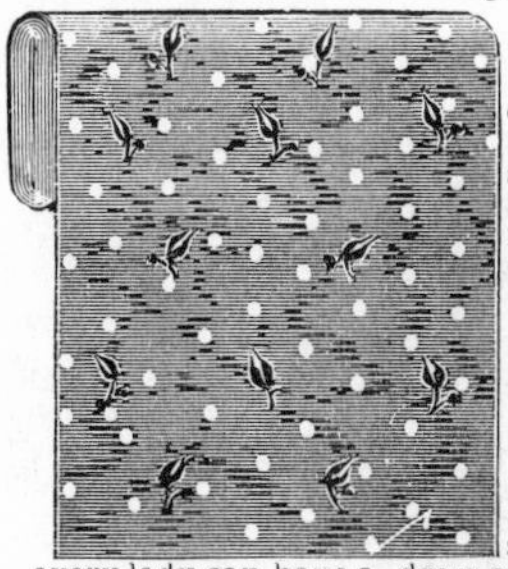

385 Finest Imported French Challies, all wool, 30 inches wide. The quality and designs of these goods are so exquisitely beautiful that a printed description can only convey the most meager conception of their beauty. In former seasons the high price which these goods commanded made it possible for only the finest trade to use them. The new tariff has made the cost of this season's importations so low that now nearly every lady can have a dress or house gown of these serviceable yet dainty creations of French weavers at a very moderate cost. Some of the color combinations are: Wine, heliotrope and olive; lavender and heliotrope; cream, gold and olive; cream, gold and heliotrope; cardinal and black; dark brown, tan and blue; black, gray and heliotrope; French gray, white and lilac; pink, olive and deep rose. Stripes in white, nile and pink combination, tan and heliotrope, black, white and heliotrope, or navy, white and heliotrope.
Per yard..$0.39
Last season's price for same qualities, 60 cents per yard.

Swivel Silks.

386 Swivel Silks, 27 inches wide. This line of summer goods is very popular and is one of the prettiest fabrics ever made. It is on the zephyr gingham order but is woven with a silk warp which is brought out on the surface, forming neat and showy designs such as small, even and broken blocks, squares, lace pattern stripes, dashes, etc. Colors are: light heliotrope, pink, ecru, light blue, nile, corn yellow, lemon, blue, gray or cream.
Per yard..$0.37½

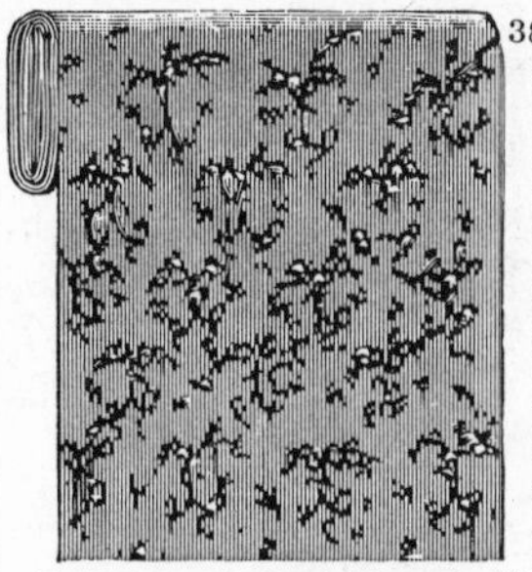

388 Crepoline, a new cotton summer dress fabric, 28 inches wide. It is a fine crepe or momie weave, firm texture, looks like wool albatross, printed in floral designs, artistic vine tracings, etc. Light grounds are: Cream, light blue, ecru or lavender, printed in pretty contrasting colors. Dark grounds are: Seal, navy, olive, wine or black.
Per yard..............$0.08
Full piece of about 50 yards, 7½ cents. Regular price of above goods 12½ cents.

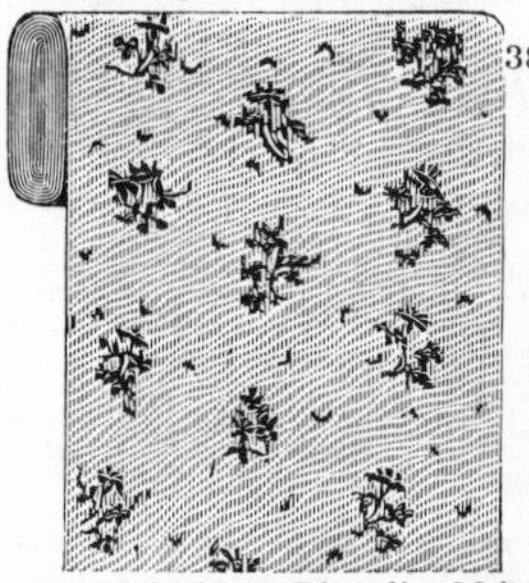

389 Figured Crepe Picardie, 26 inches wide. A new crinkled cotton goods made by same process as Gauffre silk, light tinted grounds printed over with neat floral design. Colors are: Light blue, pink, cream, lilac, salmon or deep rose.
Per yard.......$0.07½
Full piece of about 50 yards, 6¾ cents per yard.

390 Plain Crepe Picardie, 26 inches wide. Same goods as above, but plain solid colors; very showy and pretty for party dresses or fancy waists. Colors: Lilac, pink, light blue, nile, black, cream, cardinal, yellow, white, navy, deep rose, tan or wine. $0.07
Full piece of about 50 yards, 6½ cents.

EVERY WOMAN SHOULD HAVE A SEWING MACHINE,

Dress Goods—Continued.

391 Royal Epingeline. A handsome printed cotton dress fabric, with the appearance and draping qualities of wool goods. The filling is woven with double threads, forming fine horizontal cord or rib. Grounds are cream, with large floral designs in beautiful artistic shadings. This fabric is especially pretty for house gowns. We have but one case of 50 pieces, which we secured at about one-half actual value. Color combinations in flowers are: blue with old rose and olive; old rose with grey and olive; old rose with heliotrope and olive; heliotrope with gold and olive; violet with pink and olive. Per yard, while they last..........................$0.10½
Full price of about 50 yards, 10 cents per yard.

392 Fancy Cotton Duck Suiting. 28 inches wide. These goods are very stylish and durable and are in great demand for Summer out-door dresses and Eton suits. We have a pretty range of light stripes sprinkled over with tiny dots of same color as stripe on white grounds. Colors: Light blue, pink, gray, tan or heliotrope; also indigo blue grounds with small white polka dot or hair line stripes. Per yard..................$0.08½
Full price of about 50 yards, 8 cents per yard.

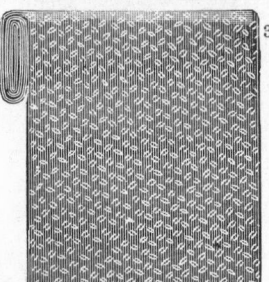

393 Flutter Duck Suiting, fine double cable cloth, very stylish and pretty. The best duck in the market. Grounds in white, tan, porcelain blue, navy blue (pure indigo dye). Small figures, dots and stripes in white, blue, black or red.
Per yard......$0.12½
Full price of about 50 yards, 11¾ cents per yard.

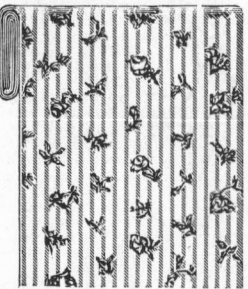

394 Cashmere Sublime, 28 inches wide. A special job, but 1 case to sell. This is a very neat and pretty wash fabric, woven with a twill same as cashmere. Styles are narrow even stripes on cream ground in pink, light blue, tan, heliotrope, over which are printed small rose and bud design, in pretty, contrasting shades.
Per yard........$0.09
Full piece of about 50 yards, 8½ cents per yard.

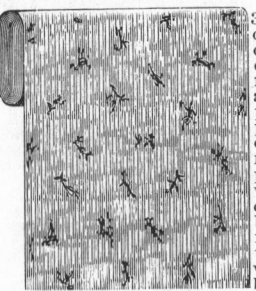

395 Shantong Pongee, India silk finish. 30 inches wide. This is one of the best selling summer fabrics, and makes a delightfully cool and pretty dress. It is a plain weave, very fine, on the muslin order, but not so sheer or transparent as mull or lawn; will wash perfectly. In dark grounds we have black, with small wild flower design in heliotrope and gold; navy, with gold and rose color; brown, with gold and heliotrope. Light styles have a tiny rosebud figure on fancy grounds, representing printed yarn effects. Colors: Light blue, pink, tan, heliotrope or gray. We secured these goods at considerable less than value. Retail price is 14 cents. Our price, per yard....$0.10
Full piece of about 50 yards, 9½ cents per yard.

Dress Goods—Continued.

396 Fayal Crepe, 28 inches wide. This is one of the best bargains of the season. We thought so well of this fabric that we bought the manufacturer's entire stock. It is a crinkly crepe weave, soft and graceful in draping qualities and of fashion's most approved patterns. The designs are small and true to nature in their artistic beauty of color blendings. On cream grounds the combinations are: Heliotrope and olive; heliotrope, blue and olive; garnet gold and olive; pink, gold and olive; blue, pink and olive. Light blue ground with gold and olive; lilac ground with heliotrope, gold and olive; pink ground with mahogany, light blue and olive. Retail value of this fabric, 15 cents per yard. We shall use these as a leader at, per yard...$0.10
Full piece of about 28 yards, 9¾ cents per yard.

397 Taffeta Moire, 27 inches wide, a new production in cotton goods; comes in black grounds finished so as to look just like Moire Antique silk. Designs are handsome floral effects in pink, blue, gold or heliotrope in combination with other harmonizing tints.
Per yard......$0.16
Full piece of about 50 yards, 15 cents per yard.

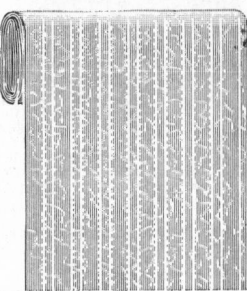

398 Marie-Antoinette Lace Stripe Mull. A new thin cotton goods with a hard finish. Particularly adapted to the present style of immense sleeves and wide skirts. This is one of the extremely chic and rechere productions of the season and must be seen to be appreciated. The grounds are plain or covered with quaint scrolls, dots, flowers in indistinct chene effects through which are run lace cord stripes, which add much to their beauty and strengthen the fabric. Colors are: Nile green, pink, light blue, cream or corn yellow. Per yard.......................$0.16
Full piece of about 45 yards 15¼ cents per yard.

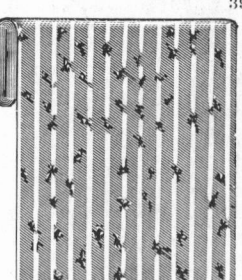

399 Imported French Plisse. The daintiest, prettiest wash fabric you ever saw. It is a fine and sheer zephyr weave in delicate tints through which at intervals of every half inch is woven a narrow crinkled or puckered stripe of white; over all is printed a tiny leaf design in black. Ground colors are: Light heliotrope, light blue, a light dull green, pink, corn yellow, or black with white figure. Per yard....................................$0.30

Plain Sateens.

400 Garner's Fine Sateen, plain colors; width 31 inches. We have all of the following colors now: Cream, light blue, pink, cardinal, lilac, navy, wine, gray, myrtle, golden brown, old gold, old rose, medium brown, marine blue, seal brown, mahogany. Price, per yard..............$0.10
For full piece about 50 yards, 9½ cents per yard.

402 Garner's Extra Fine Sateen, plain solid colors; width 31 inches. We can furnish all colors as quoted in No. 400. Per yard.......... .16
For full piece of about 50 yards, 15 cents per yard.

Figured Sateens.

A SPECIAL JOB.

404 Dresden Figured Sateens, 31 inches wide; sold everywhere at 12½ cents. We purchased a large quantity at less than value and intend to use them as a leader for our wash goods department. Grounds are black, seal brown or navy, on which is printed various floral and small set designs, dashes, etc., in blue, pink, heliotrope, red and gold combinations.
Price, while they last, per yard.... ......$0.07¾
Full piece of about 50 yards, 7½ cents per yard.

405 Pacific Fine Sateens, 31 inches wide. Ground colors are: Brown, gobelin blue, old rose, navy or light gray. Grounds are closely covered with a leaf design, soft tones of same color, or contrasting shade with a scattering of small, bright flowers.
Per yard..$0.10
For full piece of about 50 yards, 9¼ cents per yard.

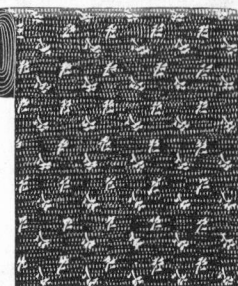

406 Fine Henrietta Sateens, 31 inches wide, black grounds only. Designs are small floral patterns, with dotted or plain backgrounds; all tasteful and pretty styles copied from china silks. The colors in figures are: Pink and olive, light blue and olive, gold and olive heliotrope and olive, leaf green and olive, or heliotrope and gray.
Per yard........$0.12
Full piece of about 50 yards, 11 cents per yard.

407 Satin Milo Checks, 26 inches wide. A new sateen in small shepherd check. Very stylish for dresses and waists, looks just like silk. Checks are in the following color combinations: Pink and gray, tan and drab, purple and green, heliotrope and olive, blue and brown, navy and white, or black and white.
Per yard........$0.15
Full piece of about 50 yards, 14¼ cents per yard.

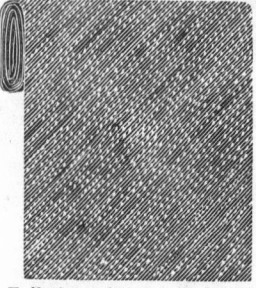

408 London Fancy Sateens, 30 inches wide. Printed in a new silk design, a diagonal effect produced by irregular broken dashes, almost completely covering background. Grounds are all black, and are in the following combination: Black and white, black and green, black and blue, black and heliotrope, or black and gray.
Per yard........$0.16
Full piece of about 50 yards, 15 cents per yard.

Dress Goods—Continued.

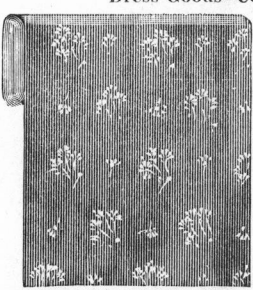

409 Extra Fine Paris Sateens, 31 inches wide, superb henrietta finish. New artistic designs in small Dresden china effects. They are all so pretty that it would be difficult to select the prettiest. Grounds are all black and tiny flowers and buds are in following combinations: Heliotrope, green and gold; pink, green and white; heliotrope, green and white; blue, gold and white; gold, green and white. Per yard ...$0.17
Full piece of about 50 yards, 16 cents per yard.

410 Alsace Imported Sateens, 31 inches wide. These sateens are absolutely fast colors, have a magnificent henrietta finish and represent the highest art in printing. The grounds are fast black over which is a sprinkling of tiny pin dots in contrasting color and graceful floral designs of medium size, in beautiful colorings. We have the following styles: Brown dots with heliotrope and green flower; gray dots with pink and green flower; gold dots with dahlia and green flower; green dots with gray and gold flower; pink dots with blue and olive flower; gold dots with mahogany and blue flower. Per yard.....................$0.19
Full piece of about 50 yards, 18 cents per yard.

411 Imported Printed Brocades, 28 inches wide. This is a new sateen in fast black, with a woven brocade stripe and slanting dash pattern which looks like silk. It is absolutely fast color and will make a durable, stylish and elegant dress. Printed designs are arranged over the brocaded surface and are in the following colors: Heliotrope, tan and olive; light brown, blue and olive; slate and light gray; olive, gray and gold. Per yard.....................$0.28
Full piece of about 50 yards, 27 cents per yard.

412 Finest Imported French Sateens, 30 inches wide. Nothing handsomer made in sateens than these goods. The cloth is made from the finest Egyptian cotton and is woven to show a woven moire or watered background which looks like silk and is an effect which domestic manufacturers have been unable to reproduce. The grounds are black, with artistic clusters of pin spots in heliotrope, blue, green, cerise, gold, brown or gray; also navy ground with white. These goods are designed for the finest trade and cannot fail to be appreciated. Per yard.....................$0.34

Fast Black Sateens.

Our Fast Black Sateens will stand soap and water, perspiration, exposure to the sun and air, salts of lemon and every kind of acid that will not destroy the fiber of the cloth without fading, leaving the goods as strong as any other black, and with a surface that will not crock.

	Width in inches.	Per yard.
413 Fast Black Sateen.................	28	$0.08
Price of full piece of about 50 yards, 7½ cents per yard.		
414 Fast Black Sateen, fine quality. A special value.......................	31	.09
Price for full price of about 50 yards, 8½ cents per yard.		
416 Fast Black Sateen.................	34	.14
Price for full piece of about 58 yards, 13½ cents per yard.		
418 Super Sateens, fine double fold..	36	.18
Price for full piece of about 43 yards, 17 cents per yard.		
420 Extra Super Sateens, double fold.	36	.27
Price for full piece of about 41 yards, 25 cents per yard.		

Henrietta Fast Black Sateens.

These goods, while cotton, are so woven, dyed and finished as to be an exact imitation of black henrietta or cashmere, and the color is guaranteed. Heretofore sateens have always been made with a hard, close shining surface, which proclaimed their cheapness and made them unyielding, hot and close.
In these goods all objections have been removed, while their good features have been retained as to wearing qualities, dye, etc.

Per yard.
422 Black Cashmere Sateen, width 29 inches....$0.12
Price for full piece of about 53 yards, 11¼ cents per yard.
424 Black Henrietta Sateens, width 32 inches.... .16
Price of full piece of about 48 yards, 15½ cents per yard.
426 Black Henrietta Sateens, width 32 inches... .23
Price for full piece of about 43 yards, 22 cents per yard.
428 Black Henrietta Sateens, width 32 inches... .26
Price for full piece of about 44 yards, 25 cents per yard.

Fancy Fast Black Sateens.

BLACK AND WHITE.

Per yard.
430 Surah Sateen, fast black, 30 inches wide, with single hair lines of white an inch apart, white polka dot or small figures. The cheapest figured fast black sateen ever sold. Price......$0.12
Price for full piece of about 56 yards, 11½ cents per yard.

Fast Black Brocades.

433 Fast Black Brocaded Sateens with colored figures, width 30 inches. This is a new line that bids fair to be a great seller. It is a rich and permanent black with small woven brocaded designs printed over at close intervals with triangular clusters of small dots in white, heliotrope, cardinal, pink or gold. The dressiest cloth ever made for the price.
Per yard.........$0.18
Full piece of about 50 yards, 17¼c. per yard.
435 Fast Black Brocaded Sateens, plain solid black, width 30 inches. We show a handsome line of patterns in this cloth and consider it excellent value.
Per yard.....................$0.19
Full piece of about 50 yards, 18 cents per yard.

436 Imported Satin Brocaded Sateen, width 30 inches. Finest cloth made. Woven under a new process from finest Egyptian cotton. New patterns in floral and scroll effects. The richest black sateen you ever saw.
Per yard.........$0.25
Full piece of about 55 yards, 24 cents per yard.

Linen Dress Silks.

New Importation for Spring 1895.

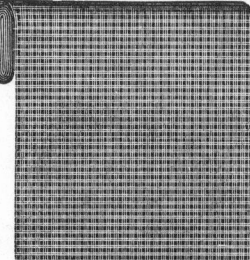

440 A linen dress fabric, 24 inches wide, woven in checks, stripes and plaids, in exact imitation of the latest style summer silks. The colors are perfectly fast, and will not change while the fabric remains. The cloth is very fine, not too heavy, can be washed and will "do up" perfectly. They are finished exactly like silk and cannot be told from it, except by close inspection, while they will last several times as long. Checks are even or broken, and come in the following color combinations: Black and white; navy blue and gold; navy and white; black and gold; gray and black; navy and cream; navy and red; medium blue and gold; blue and ecru; garnet and white; wine, gold and white; light blue and white; light blue and gray. Plaids are combinations of brown, cardinal and cream bronze, navy and gold; golden brown, gray and white; light blue, white and gold. Stripes are: Blue and white hair line; brown, white and gold; black with white hair line; black and white medium or broken stripe; brown and white; navy and red or medium blue and white hair line; Chambray mixtures in steel or blue with narrow white stripes. Price per yard..................$0.28

Dress Goods—Continued.

442 Brocaded Linen Dress Silks, 24 inches wide, entirely new. The designs are small and neat and have all the brilliant lustre of a silk, yet having the great firmness and wearing qualities of linen. A perfect wash fabric for dresses or fancy waists. Many of these styles cannot be duplicated outside of our stock, as they are manufactured for and imported only by Montgomery Ward & Co. Colors are: Gray, tan, pink, light blue, navy, brown, olive, beige or wine.
Per yard........................$0.38

Dress Linen.

These goods are made in the "natural" flax color only, and are not dyed in shades. Used for dresses or traveling dusters.

Per yard.
444 Dress Linen, width, 32 inches................$0.20
Price for full piece of about 46 yards, 19 cents per yard.
446 Dress Linen, width, 32 inches................ .25
Price for full piece of about 43 yards, 23 cents per yard.
448 Dress Linen, width, 34 inches................ .30
Price for full piece of about 44 yards, 28 cents per yard.

Real Manchester Chambray.

The most popular wash fabric made.

Note our price! Is it right?
These goods are so well known that little need be said regarding them. Every lady knows how well they take starch, how perfectly they "do up."
Ours we have finished perfectly soft and free from dressing.
The plain colors match the fancies and are often used in making combination costumes. We contract for immense quantities of these goods annually, being one of the largest purchasers in America. Therefore are able to offer them to our customers at the lowest possible price. *Send for samples.*

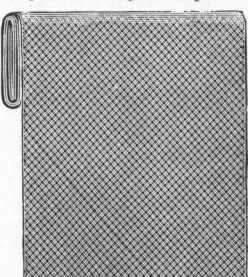

PRICE BY THE PIECE.
We will make a price of 9½c. a yard on any No. of chambray if you buy at one time a full piece of any one style and color of about 45 yards.
462 Dice Checked Linen Finished Chambray; width 24 inches. Colors: Navy, heliotrope, brown, deep pink or steel combined with white. Very neat and dainty.
Per yard.....................$0.10

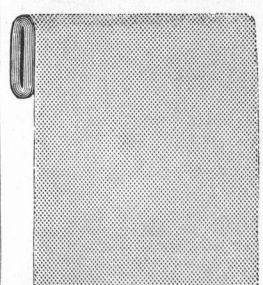

466 Polka Dot Chambray, linen finish, 24 in., a fine small pin dot in darker shade of self color. Colors: Navy, steel gray, brown, deep pink or heliotrope.
Per yard.........$0.10
466 Plain Chambrays in the following colors: Steel, brown, light blue, navy, light pink, deep pink or heliotrope. Width 24 in.
Per yard.........$0.10

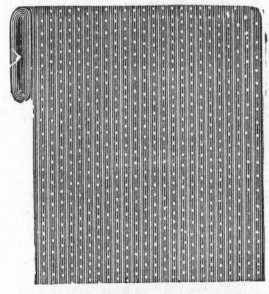

467 Brocaded Striped Linen Finished Chambray, 24 inches wide, perfect washing colors, soft finish. Brocade figure is in deeper tone of ground color, through which is run narrow hair line stripes of white. Colors: Deep pink, heliotrope, navy, brown or steel.
Per yard.........$0.10

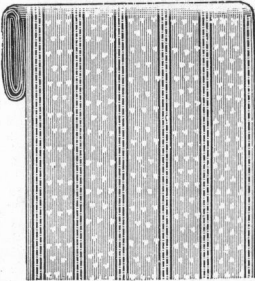

470 Brocaded Wide Striped Linen Finished Chambray, 24 inches wide. Small neat brocaded design in ground color with fine double stripes of white, one inch apart. Colors: Heliotrope, navy, brown, deep pink or steel.
Per yard.........$0.10

Dress Goods—Continued.

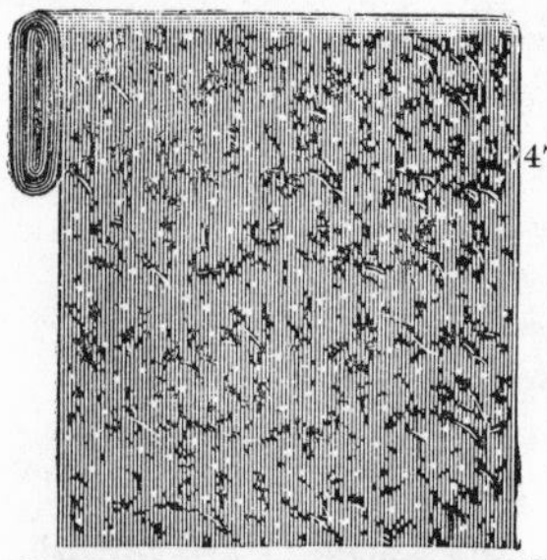

471 Brocaded Linen Finished Chambray, 24 inches wide, vine pattern, a neat running design. Colors: Steel, brown, deep pink, heliotrope or navy. Per yard........$0.10

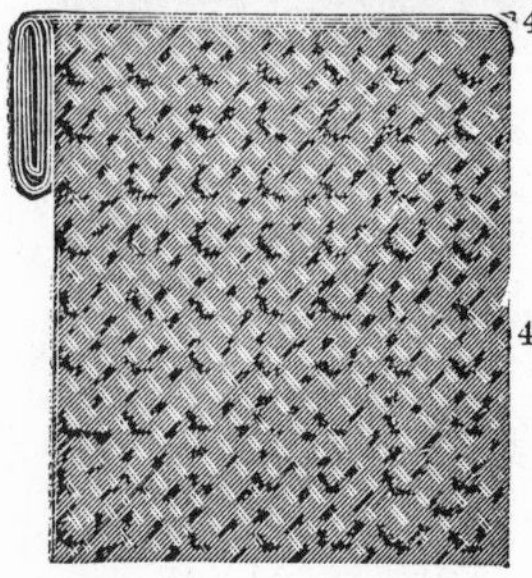

473 Swivel Brocaded Linen Finished Chambray, 24 inches wide. A small dash or swivel pattern of solid color, a deeper shade than ground tone. Colors: Steel, deep pink, heliotrope, navy or brown. Per yard.........$0.10

474 New Brocaded Linen Finished Chambray. Colors: Navy, brown, steel, deep pink or heliotrope. Per yard........$0.10

Ginghams.

The remarkably low prices at which we offer leading standard makes of Ginghams marks them as unquestionably the most economical cotton dress material that can be bought, the color in Ginghams being produced by colored yarns (dyed before weaving). Their superiority over piece dyed and printed good for hard wear is easily apparent. Buying these goods in large quantities from manufacturers we have been enabled to secure extraordinary values, among which are the well-known *Amoskeag Staple Apron Ginghams, best quality*, usually sold at from 8 to 9 cents per yard. Our price is 5 cents. Nearly every housekeeper knows these goods. See what you can buy them for elsewhere.

Apron Styles.

500 Old Virginia Staple Apron Check Ginghams, 27 inches wide, small and medium even checks, in blue and white, brown and white, or green and white. Per yard..............................$0.03¾
No less for any quantities.

502 Manchester Staple Apron Ginghams, good and strong, small, medium or large even or broken checks, in blue, brown, green or black with white. Full pieces contain about 50 yards. Same price for any quantity. Per yard........ .04¾

506 Amoskeag Best Standard Apron Ginghams. These goods are so well known that little need be said regarding them. They are acknowledged to be the most evenly woven, clearly colored and heaviest ginghams that can be bought. We have checks in the various sizes; pin head, small, medium and large (about ¼ inch square), also small broken check. The colors are: Blue and white, brown and white, green and white, pink and white, or black and white. Usually retailed at 8 cents. Per yard........................$0.05
No less for any quantity.

508 Turkey Red and White Apron Checks, blocks or plaids in Lancaster and Amoskeag goods, fast colors. No stripes. State whether you want small, medium or large checks or plaids; width 27 inches. Per yard.............................. .07¾
Price for full piece of about 44 yards, 7½ cents per yard.

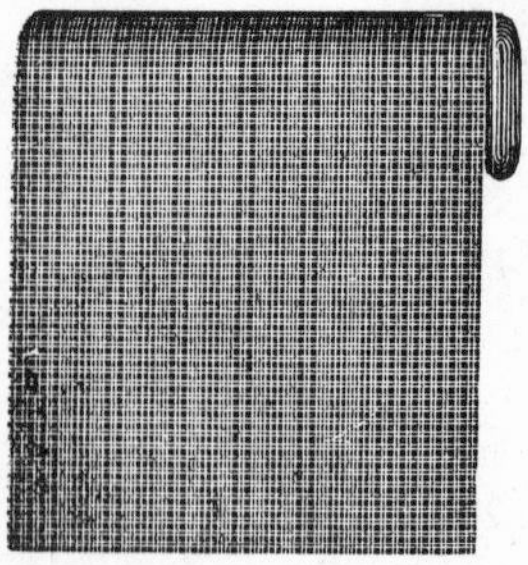

514 Bordered or Side Band Apron or Skirting Gingham; fine and strong, fast colors, best quality, 33 inches wide with 5 inch borders woven in different style checks from body of goods; the width makes the length of skirt or apron; for the latter it requires 1¼ to 1½ yards. Goods are made in small or medium checks only of blue and white or brown and white
Per yard..$0.09
Price for full piece of about 50 yards, 8½ cents per yard.

GENTLEMEN—

Send for our Dressmaking Catalogue, and show the Ladies how they can put on more style and save something.

Fancy Check Ginghams.

520 Fancy Ginghams for children's dresses and aprons, small checks and plaids in medium or dark fast colors, good wearing quality. Checks are even or broken styles, with combinations of three or more colors, in narrow lines or shaded effects, browns, tans, blues, etc.; width, 27 inches. Per yard..................................$0.06
Full piece of about 50 yards, 5⅞ cents per yard.

522 Best Fancy Ginghams, similar style to No. 520, only finer quality. Best standard goods. Predominating colors are: Brown, navy blue, tan, slate or wine, mixed with red or other colors in fine thread lines. Per yard...................... .07
Full piece about 50 yards, 6¾ cents per yard.

Dress Ginghams.

PLAIDS AND STRIPES.

525 Velasco Dress Ginghams, 27 inches wide. This is our cheapest number and a really good thing for the price. The styles are plaids or stripes and the predominating colors light or dark as follows: Navy, brown, pink, light blue or wine. Per yard.......................................$0.04½
No cheaper for any quantity; full piece contains about 50 yards.

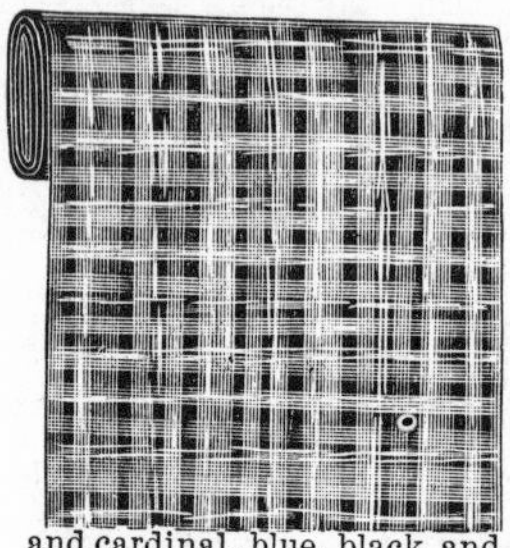

526 Mentone Dress Gingham, 27 inches wide. This gingham has got to be an old standby with us; we try to beat it each season, but without success, the cloth is good and the styles are far ahead of anything else near the price; this seasons colorings are as follows: Medium size plaids in navy and red; navy and gold; blue, cardinal and white; gray and cardinal, blue, black and white; brown, gold and blue; brown, gold and red; and bright Scotch effects in cardinal, gold and green, or cardinal, blue and white; the stripes are in blue and brown, tan and blue; black and white ground with tan and cardinal stripes; dark steel ground, with black and tan stripes or black ground with narrow and medium white stripes.
Per yard........ ...$0.05
For full piece of about 50 yards, per yard, 4¾ cents.

528 Aberdeen Dress Gingham, 27 inches wide. This cloth resembles a seersucker having a smooth linen finish; it is of very good weight, closely woven and will undoubtedly wear well; the styles are rather small plaids, and narrow stripes, in the following colors: Plaids, navy and white, wine and white; light blue and white; black and white, pink, blue and white; tan, black and white; or blue, pink and white; the stripes have blue mixed or brown mixed grounds with either pink and white, or light blue and white narrow lines; if you want a cheap gingham for good service, this is the one.
Per yard..$0.06
For full piece of about 50 yards, price per yard 5¾ cents.

529 Normandie or West Brook Ginghams, 27 inches wide; cloth good. We know of nothing equal to it at the price. Styles unlimited; plaids and stripes in every conceivable combination of color. These are some of them: Plaids, in heliotrope, gold and white; tan, gold and white; pink, gold and white; sapphire, gold and white, or brown gold and white; navy and cardinal; cardinal and green; navy and white, or brown and white; speckled grounds with gold bars; brown and white with snowflake effect; tan and red; pretty gray combinations; electric blue and gold, or black and white. Stripes are in medium blue, with fine gold or red lines; also medium size stripes in blue, wine, gold or brown on speckled groundwork, and black and white narrow or medium stripes.
Per yard...$0.07
Price for full piece of about 45 yards, 6¾ cents per yard.

Genoa Crape.

530 Genoa Crape is really a Novelty. Gingham crapes are the correct thing this season. The novelty, however, is not its only recommendation; it is good all-around cloth, is strong and finished quite soft, and the weaving very pretty. The style effect is a fancy stripe, about one-quarter of an inch wide, with a space of about half an inch between. The stripe is of crape or puckered weave and in white, while the space between forms the groundwork and is woven in tiny checks in the following colors: White, light brown, light blue, pink, dark brown, heliotrope or navy. The price, too, is one of its strong points and is the lowest ever quoted on these goods. Per yard, only...........................$0.07
For full piece of about 36 yards, 6¾ cents per yard.

531 Fine Seersucker Ginghams, made from hard twisted cotton and smooth finished. Quiet staple styles for common wear. Fast colors, made to withstand frequent washing. We have medium and small checks formed by small white cross bars on ground of brown, navy or black mixture. Stripes in the same colors. Plain colors, brown, blue or gray. Width, 27 inches. Per yard..........................$0.07½
Full piece of about 50 yards, 7⅛ cents per yard.

Dress Goods—Continued.

532 Amoskeag Seersucker, 27 inches wide, in stripes only. The wearing qualities of this cloth are too well known to need any comment, it is made especially for wear and frequent washing, one coloring is dark blue mixed ground with fine single hair line stripe in white, also double stripes or wider effects made of three or five lines running close together. The other colorings which are more dressy are grounds of pink, heliotrope, dark blue mixed or dark brown mixed with ½ inch stripes made up of narrow lines of pretty light colors. You can always depend on Amoskeag goods. Per yard.................................. .08
For full piece of about 45 yards, 7½ cents per yard.

533 Renfrew Gingham, 27 inches wide. The best weight and styles of standard dress gingham; the special features of this line are neat styles and dark and medium colorings. There are checks in gold and wine; brown and gold; gray and black, or brown, black and white; plaids in dark mixtures, brown, gold and black; brown and pink; tan and red; green, gold and white; blue and gold; tan and green; blue, white and cardinal; or black and white. Stripes are in tan and red; gray and gold; gold and black speckled; pink and black, gray and black brown and black; tan and green; sapphire and tan; or black and white. Per yard........................... .08½
For full piece of about 44 yards, 8¼ cents per yard.

535 Criterion Gingham, 27 inches wide. This is a fine zephyr cloth at a low price. We have bought it especially for children, though as the styles run small this season, it is just as suitable for ladies' wear, where something light and pretty is wanted. There is only one style, a tiny broken check; the colorings are these: Heliotrope and white; navy and white, or light blue and white. We have sold this gingham at 12½ cents other years; it is a much nicer thing than the price indicates. Per yard..................... .09
Price for full piece of about 42 yards, 8½ cents per yard.

Greylock Pointille.

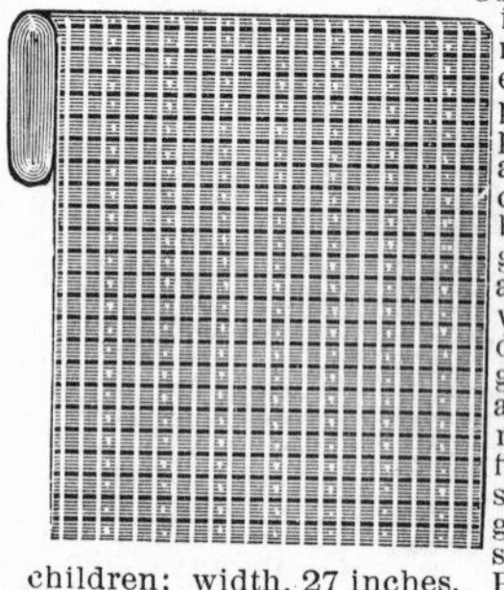

538 Greylock Pointille is a gingham cloth of a new fancy weave, a novelty of the season, but pretty enough to be reproduced many times again. There are five colors: Tan, pink, light blue, brown or navy; on grounds of these colors are fine cross bars of white and navy, and a darker shade of the ground work; the other, a stripe, is formed by means of a little woven figure in every third space crossing the goods; being a neat design is very suitable for children; width, 27 inches. Per yard...........$0.10
For full piece of about 50 yards, 9½ cents per yard.

544 Toile du Nord Gingham is perhaps the best known of all others. It is weighty, smooth and evenly finished, and especially adapted to withstand the hard usages of the laundry; consequently we need only quote this season's styles. Plain colors are in pink, light blue, dark blue mixed, gray, gobelin, brown mixed, navy or seal brown, dark staple checks or stripes in navy, black, brown, or steel and white; even small checks in pink and white, blue and white, black and white, or brown and white; white grounds with small or medium bars of pink, blue, navy, heliotrope, brown or black, light blue or pink; grounds with small bars of white, fancy checks of blue and tan, pink and grey, navy and tan, or light fancy mixed colors; plaids in grey and heliotrope, tan and pink, navy and white, brown and white, or black and white; narrow even stripes in pink and white or blue and white, and wider stripes in pink, tan, gray, light blue, navy, brown, or black and white. Width 27 inches.
Per yard $0.10
For full piece of about 44 yards, 9¼ cents

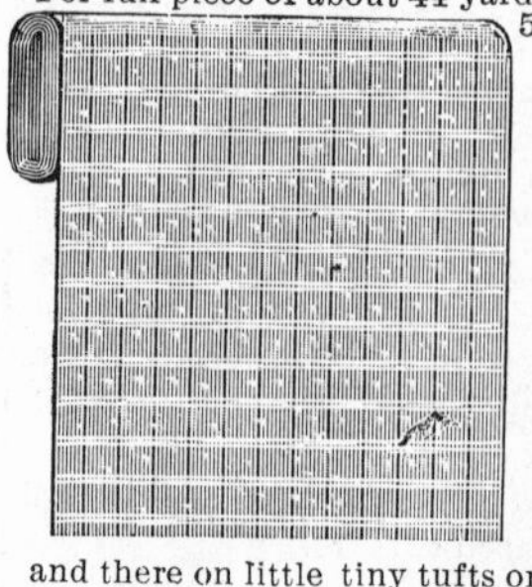

546 Knickerbocker Gingham, 27 inches wide. This effect was produced in dark colors last fall. The work was fully appreciated, so it has reappeared in dainty spring colorings now; the styles are bars, stripes or broken checks in light work, and the knickerbocker effect is produced by weaving scattered threads of bright color through the cloth, which appear here and there on little tiny tufts or knots; there are some bourette effects on a plain ground. The color effects are always tasty, and predominate as follows: Grey, tan, light blue, pink or brown.
Per yard..$0.10
Full piece of about 42 yards, 9¼ cents.

Anything FOR Anybody.

Dress Goods—Continued.

549 Fine Scotch Zephyr Gingham, 27 inches wide. The color effects of these goods seem to increase in beauty each succeeding year. This season they are prettier than ever, and look almost too dainty to wear and soil, although they wash perfectly. The styles are small even checks in tan and white; heliotrope and white; blue and white; pink and white; brown and white, or black and white, also bars of the same colors on white grounds; fancy light checks or plaids on white grounds are these combinations: Heliotrope and tan; pink and blue; and some with pink or blue grounds; black and white broken checks, and very pretty tan grounds with fine stripes of cardinal, navy, brown or white. Per yard....$0.12½
Price for full piece of about 40 yards, 12 cents per yard.

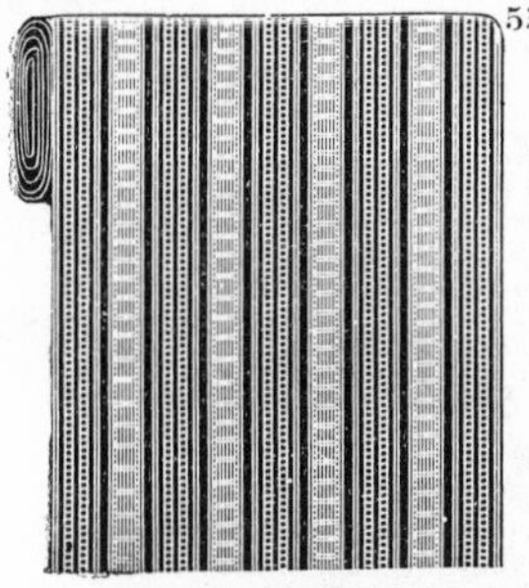

551 Armadale Lace Striped Zephyr, 27 inches wide. The showiest and prettiest gingham ever offered at a low price. Our former purchases of this gingham were sold at 15 cents per yard, which was then considered cheap and it was the biggest seller we ever had. Our present stock has been bought at about one-half cost to manufacture and we took all in sight. It is a bargain that we feel sure will be appreciated and serve as a splendid advertisement for our gingham department. The ground colors are of plain chambray weave broken with stripes of white into which are introduced small squares of open lace work; the stripes are outlined with raised cord interwoven which adds strength and beauty to the cloth. Colors fast. They are in the following combinations. Light blue and white; light gray and white; brown and white; navy and white; pink and white; tan and white; old rose and white, or black; heliotrope and white.
Per yard, while they last..........................$0.10
Full piece of about 48 yards, 9¼ cents per yard.

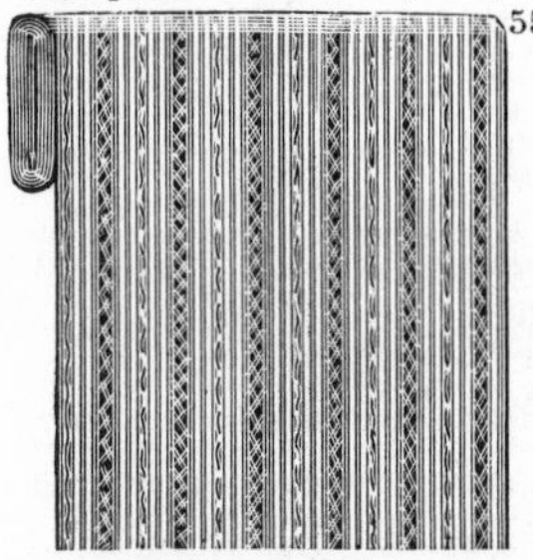

554 Merlin Lace Stripe Novelty Gingham, 28 inches wide. This is an exact copy of one of the finest French novelties of this season. The cut will give an idea of style, but the fineness of work and beauty of color can only be known by seeing. The colors are, light blue, tan, pink and heliotrope; one style has narrow white lace work and fine stripe of brown; another has a fine cord stripe in black and white; white ground work with narrow raised stripes of pink, tan or light blue is a very dainty effect.
Per yard..$0.20

560 Fancy French Ginghams, 32 inches wide. This is the finest work of the season, made expressly for high class retail trade. The styles and colorings are exquisite, such as French art alone could produce; we quote some of the prettiest styles, Pink ground with checks of raised threads of cream, and a small maltese cross of light mixed colors between; the same style with nile and white, cream, tan and brown, ecru and mixed colors, white heliotrope and light green; small tweedy checks in pure white grounds with narrow cross bars of pink, light blue, tan, brown, black, nile or heliotrope; small staple or shepherd checks. Children's styles in pink, light blue, navy, brown or black with white narrow fancy woven stripes in all of the above color combinations. We will be glad to submit samples of these goods for we believe that to see is to buy. Their beauty is irresistible. Per yard.......................... .24
Full piece of about 40 yards, 22½ cents per yard.

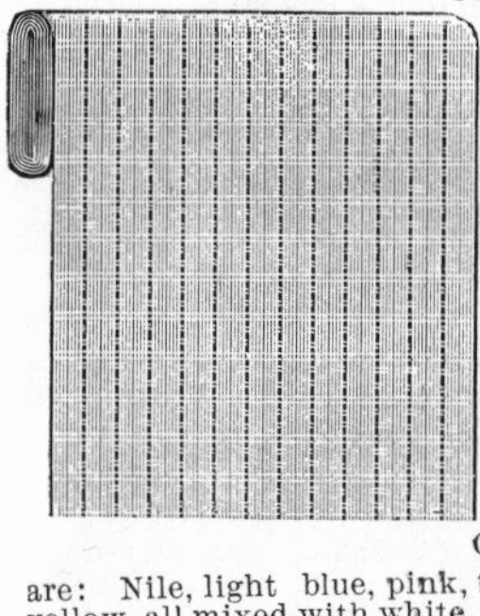

562 Japonette, 26 inches wide. This is a novelty weave in zephyr cloth. It was introduced last season and proved so successful that it was made again for this season. The styles are all new and a vast improvement over those of last year. They come in stripe and crossbar plaid effects, also checks. The patterns are formed by prominent raised cords of various plain or mixed colors to form harmonious contrasts with ground tints. Colors predominating are: Nile, light blue, pink, tan, navy heliotrope or yellow, all mixed with white and forming the daintiest combinations imagineable.
Per yard.......................................$0.25
Full piece of about 40 yards, 23½ cents per yard.

SILK DEPARTMENT.

NOTE.—It is well to remember that we cannot always match samples selected perfectly, and often in such cases use our best judgement in filling orders. Original lines from which quotations are made become sold out and cannot be duplicated in every feature, shade or pattern, and sometimes texture may vary slightly from original, but we always aim to give an equal value, better if possible. It is clearly to our interest to do so. This applies to all kinds of dry goods.

Samples

of all silks and satins will be sent upon request, but in such small pieces as to be useless for fancy or crazy-patch-work. We send very small pieces and only to intending purchasers. Order by number and give price. We shall be pleased to furnish samples of any silk you may want not found quoted here. For our guidance, give color, name, width and about the price you expect to pay.

Black Silk.

NOTICE OUR REDUCED PRICES.

Nearly every lady aims to have at least one black silk dress, yet few realize how much depends upon the character of the house they buy from. Few lines offer better opportunities to unscrupulous dealers for making immense profits than do black dress silks. While width is often an important factor in regulating prices we have given most particular attention in selecting our lines to securing only those silks which combined the greatest weight with the richest color and the softest or most pliable finish. Our stock contains all the fashionable weaves and our revised quotations should make this department especially attractive to buyers.

Black Bengaline or Crystal Silk.

A heavily corded black silk.

		Width in inches.	Per yard.
600	Black Bengaline Silk..............	18	$0.45
601	Black Bengaline Silk..............	19	.90
602	Black Bengaline Silk..............	20	1.00
603	Black Bengaline Silk..............	21	1.25
604	Black Bengaline Silk..............	21	1.50

Black Radzimir.

		Width in inches.	Per yard.
608	Black Radzimir Silk, a popular weave, good weight, soft finish, will not break or crack. This silk has a smooth, even surface, but is so woven as to look like corded goods	20	$0.90

Black Gros Grain Silk.

650 Black Silk, gros grain, 18 inches............$0.65
Price full piece of about 75 yards, five per cent less than yard price on all silk.

652	Black Silk, gros grain, 19 inches..........	.85
654	Black Silk, gros grain, 23 inches..........	.95
656	Black Silk, gros grain, 24 inches..........	1.10
658	Black Silk, gros grain, 24 inches..........	1.35
660	Black Silk, gros grain, 22 inches..........	1.50
662	Black Silk, gros grain, 22 inches..........	1.75

All black and colored silk is cut straight.

Black Armure Silk.

664 20 inches wide, very small seeded design....$0.90

Black Peau d'Soie.

Peau d'Soie Silk is a plain weave, heavy in weight, but very soft and pliable in finish and absolutely unbreakable.

665	Black Peau d'Soie Silk, 20 inches wide......	$1.00
666	Black Peau d'Soie Silk, 21 inches wide......	1.20
667	Black Peau d'Soie Silk, 21 inches wide......	1.40

Black Faille Francaise Silk.

This Silk is much softer than gros grain and shows a heavier cord. It does not break or cut readily and is a very popular seller.

670	Black Faille Francaise Silk.	Width, 19 in..	$0.60
672	Black Faille Francaise Silk.	Width, 20 in..	.85
674	Black Faille Francaise Silk.	Width, 24 in..	.95
676	Black Faille Francaise Silk.	Width, 21 in..	1.17
678	Black Faille Francaise Silk.	Width, 21½ in	1.45
680	Black Faille Francaise Silk.	Width, 21¾ in	1.65
682	Black Faille Francaise Silk.	Width, 22 in..	1.85

Black Satin Duchesse.

Black Satin Duchesse is now very fashionable and is one of the most durable silks made.

		Per yard.
684	Black Satin Duchesse, 20 inches wide.......	$0.95
685	Black Satin Duchesse, 20 inches wide.......	1.10
686	Black Satin Duchesse, 20 inches wide.......	1.25

Black Satin Rhadame Silk.

		Width in inches.	Per yard.
690	Black Satin Rhadame............	18	$0.59
692	Black Satin Rhadame............	19	.70
694	Black Satin Rhadame............	20	.85
696	Black Satin Rhadame............	24	1.00
698	Black Satin Rhadame............	24	1.30

Black Surah Silk.

		Width in inches.	Per yard.
710	Black Surah Silk, double warp..	19	$0.50
712	Black Surah Silk, double warp..	22	.70
714	Black Surah Silk, double warp..	23	.90
716	Black Surah Silk, double warp..	23	1.00

Black Moire or Watered Silk.

		Width in inches.	Per yard.
718	Black Moire Silk..................	21	$0.98
720	Black Moire Silk..................	21	1.10
722	Black Moire Silk..................	21	1.35
724	Black Moire Silk..................	22	1.60

Black Moire Antique Silk.

Moire Silks are used extensively for trimmings and also dresses this season.

		Per yard.
725	Black Moire Antique, 21 inches wide........	$1.45
726	Black Moire Antique, 21 inches wide........	1.70
727	Black Moire Antique, 21 inches wide........	2.25

Black Brocaded Silk.

Small, medium and large designs, very rich and always in demand. Per yard.

728	18 inches wide..................................	$0.75
730	22 inches wide..................................	1.00
731	22 inches wide..................................	1.25
732	22 inches wide..................................	1.50
733	22 inches wide..................................	1.75
735	Black Brocaded Taffeta Silk, 19 inches wide, small neat designs..................................	.89

Black Brocaded Gros Grain Silk.

738 Black Gros Grain Silk, 21 inches wide, brocaded in neat small designs. This is a very heavy and durable silk and quite new: makes handsome dresses or waists. Per yard...........$0.85

Colored Brocaded Silk.

740 Brocaded Silks. Very handsome for waists, trimmings or combinations. They all come in two toned effects and are in the following colors, first named shade being the ground, second color the figure: Black and white, black and blue, black and gold, black and green, black and cardinal, black and heliotrope, navy and old gold, golden brown and dark brown.
Width, 19 inches. Per yard.......... ....$0.85

Colored Moire or Watered Silk.

748 We can furnish all seasonable shades in this line, including the different shades of brown, blue, green or red. Colored Moire Silk, 19 inches wide.......................................$0.75

Colored Moire Antique.

Shades for Spring and Summer, 1895.

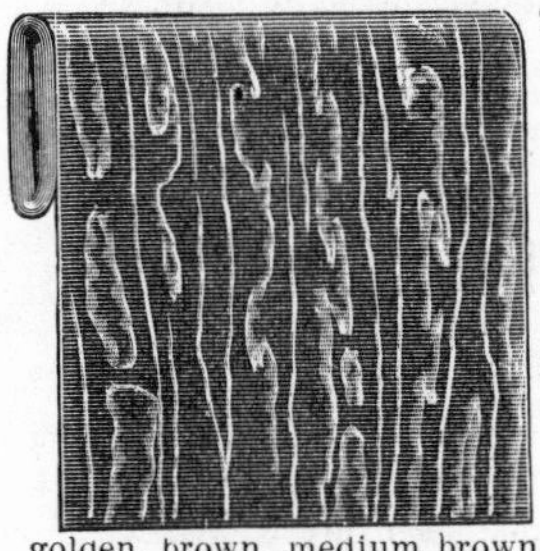

750 A new line of colored Moire Antique Silk for dresses and trimmings. Very rich and stylish. Equal in appearance to $1.50 goods. Colors are: Cerise or majenta, bluet, light blue, pink, cream, deep lavender, gobelin blue, gray, old rose, tan, olive, heliotrope, cardinal, wine, garnet, myrtle, royal blue, royal purple, navy blue, golden, brown, medium brown, seal brown or black. Width, 19 inches. Per yard.............. ....$0.49

Changeable Satins.

754 Excelsior Changeable Satins, 23 inches wide. Warp is of one color, filling of another, producing a changeable effect. The showiest and best cheap silk made for fancy dress waists or costumes. Colors are: Navy with red; mahogany with black; golden brown with gobelin, golden brown with dark blue; cardinal with green; gray with black; golden brown. Per yard............$0.35

Colored Crystal Bengaline Silks.

A heavily corded silk, soft and pliable; will not slip, cut or crack. Very fashionable.

770 Colored Bengaline Crystal Silk, width 18 inches; a very sightly line at a low price. All leading street and evening shades. Colors: Golden brown, medium or seal brown, navy, garnet, gray, medium blue, old rose, olive. lilac, royal purple, heliotrope, blue, myrtle green, wine, cardinal, tan, black, pink, nile, cream or light blue. Per yard..........................$0.40

774 Armure Crystal Silks, 18 inches wide, a heavy crystal weave over which is a small seeded Armure pattern. A new production. All colors as above. Per yard .50

778 Colored Bengaline High Class Silk, width 20 inches. Colors: White, cream, slate, gray, tan, gobelin, wine, old rose, navy, myrtle, golden brown, medium brown. Per yard....... 1.00

779 Colored Bengaline Crystal Silk, heavy cord, width 20 inches. A special bargain that cannot be duplicated. Only colors are: Myrtle. navy, golden brown, medium brown, heliotrope, old rose, light gray or light green. Per yard........ 75

Colored Dress Silks.

Per yard.

Please notice what we say about silk samples under department heading, page 11.

790 Plain Colored Gros Grain Silk, 18 inches wide, fine and soft. Colors: Green, prune, heliotrope, maroon, ecru, reseda, gray, drab, terra cotta, beige, fawn, mode, serpent, tan, slate, old rose, mahogany, claret, cardinal, bronze, myrtle, garnet, wine, olive, plum navy, peacock, sapphire, gobelin, national or cadet blue...$0.74

Plain or Changeable Taffeta Silks.

796 Plain Taffeta Silk, 19 inches wide, similar to gros grain, but of finer weave and higher luster. We have all seasonable colors. Per yard........$0.85

797 Changeable Taffeta Silk, 19 inches wide. Color combinations are: Old rose with olive; cardinal with navy; myrtle with red; navy with black; green with brown; blue with brown; blue with orange; blue with gold; black with brown; red with black; blue with ecru; gold with heliotrope. Per yard.. .80

Changeable Surahs.

Changeable effects continue to be a prominent feature of the silk business. They are used for all purposes—dresses, waists, linings or trimmings.

800 Changeable Surah, warp of one color, filling of another, produces the changeable effect. We can furnish harmonious combinations for almost any color. A few of the combinations are: Heliotrope with gray; olive with old rose; heliotrope with myrtle; brown with myrtle; black with brown; sapphire and black; cardinal and gray; gray and black, or olive and cardinal. Width, 18 inches. Per yard....................$0.50

Black and White Striped Taffeta Silk.

802 Black and White Striped Taffeta Silk, 18 inches wide. Stripes are neat, small effects in white hair lines, arranged evenly or irregularly on black grounds. Per yard......................$0.50

Brocaded Taffeta Silks.

Changeable Effects.

804 Brocaded Taffeta Silk, 19 inches wide, a beautiful line of small changeable designs suitable for waists, trimmings, or dresses. The predominating or ground colors are: Golden brown, myrtle green, dark brown, navy blue, garnet or gobelin blue, into which are woven bits of bright colors. Per yard $0.65

806 Brocaded Novelty Taffeta, two and three color tone combinations similar to above, but heavier and richer. We show a beautiful range of patterns. The principal styles are stripes in pink and light green; cerise or majenta and light green; light blue and tan; navy and gray; black and cardinal; steel and pink; corn yellow and black; cardinal and sapphire blue; gobelin blue and brown; navy and cardinal or black and gray; scattered over the stripes are small brilliant figures which show in strong relief. Per yard.. .75

Changeable Novelty Silk.

808 Changeable Armure Novelty Silks, 19 inches wide, small fancy design. Combinations of olive and old rose: myrtle, navy or black with cardinal; myrtle with gold; magenta with olive; brown with tan or gold. Per yard.................. .50

Colored Surah Silks.

Please notice what we say about silk samples under department head, page 11.

810 Colored Surah Silks, 18 inches wide, colors same as 813...................................$0.29

813 Colored Double Warp Surah Silks, 19 inches wide, extra values for trimming or dresses. Comes in the following colors: Green (all shades), heliotrope, maroon, salmon, ecru, reseda, gray, drab, beige, fawn, serpent, tan, slate, cream, old rose, mahogany, claret, cardinal, peacock, navy, gobelin, azure, cadet, sky, royal or national blue, white, pink, bronze, garnet, lilac, orange, shrimp, wine, olive, plum, nile, lemon, rose, and all the new shades as fast as they appear. Per yard.............................. .50

Plaid Silks.

815 Plaid Surah Silks, 24 inches wide. Plaids are now extremely stylish for waists and trimmings. We have some very rich effects in bright color combinations. The plaids show handsomely in the piece, but samples cannot show them accurately. Pretty effects on navy, scarlet and white; navy, brown and ecru, or garnet, white and blue. Per yard..............$0.90

A New Silk for Waists.

820 Black Brocaded Taffeta, 19 inches wide, has small and beautiful designs of brilliant black over which is embroidered a small star flower design in colors. The design is about the size of a half dime and about three inches apart. This pattern is confined to M. W. & Co. for Chicago and cannot be obtained elsewhere. Colors are: Black with cardinal, light blue, old rose, lilac, gold, green, cerise, bluet or white. Per yard...$0.85

Checked Japanese Taffeta Silk.

824 Japanese Taffeta Silk, in small shepherd check for waists or dresses, 21 inches wide. These checks are in great demand for summer dresses and waists. Jap. Taffeta is a new production and differs from the Swiss or French goods inasmuch as it is firmer and is soft finish, whereas the other goods are crisp and harsh. Color combinations are: Pink and black; gray and blue; blue and white, tan; blue and red; blue and gold; blue and red or black and white. Per yard...$0.47

Gauffre or Crinkled Silk Pongee.

828 Gauffre Silk Pongee, 21 inches wide. This is a new and very popular silk for fancy dress waists, neckwear or hat trimmings. It is a thin pongee, crinkled in a large and showy crepe pattern. This one is the latest production, and comes in a crinkly or puckered stripe effect. Stripes about ½ inch wide. All the dainty fancy shades: Maize or corn yellow, cream, pink, light blue, nile green, old rose, lilac, cardinal, ecru, navy, pearl white, gobelin, blue, cerise or black. Per yard.............................. ....$0.35

Printed Plisse Silks.

830 Printed Plisse Silk, 20 inches wide. This is the newest idea in gauffre or crinkled silks, and is the daintiest, loveliest fabric you ever saw for the price. Nothing could be prettier for waists or combinations. It is a small, crinkly stripe pattern in white grounds over which is printed beautiful little floral designs in heliotrope, garnet, bluet, golden brown, cardinal or cerise. Per yard...$0.55

Wide Chiffon.

835 Silk Chiffon, 48 inches wide. A thin, gauze-like material that is very handsome, and is now much used for dress waists and costumes for evening wear; also for neckwear and millinery trimmings. Colors are: Cardinal, cream, yellow lavender, cerise, bluet or black. Per yard.. $0.65

Colored Faille Francaise Silk.

840 Colored Faille Francaise Silk, 19 inches wide, good weight, nicely corded, and lustrous finish. Is soft and pliable and will not cut or crack; can furnish colors as in 842; also other fashionable shades. Per yard......................$0.89

Colored Satin Rhadame.

860 Colored Satin Rhadame. Width 19 inches. All the new and fashionable colors. Silks of this class will be extensively used this season for trimmings and dresses. Colors: Seal, medium or golden brown, myrtle, reseda, navy, sapphire blue, peacock blue, wine, cardinal, slate, tan or purple. Per yard..$1.00

Colored Satin Duchesse.

862 Colored Satin Duchesse, 20 inches wide, all the fashionable shades. Per yard.............. 1.19

Black Satins for Trimmings or Dresses.

		Per yard.
870	Black Satin, 19 inches	$0.50
872	Black Satin, 22 inches	.75
874	Black Satin, 24 inches	1.00

Colored Satins.

878 Colored Satins. Ivory, cream, sky, rose, nile, lilac, lavender, salmon, yellow, serpent, reseda, scarlet, cardinal, garnet, wine, claret, navy, marine olive, bronze, sapphire, gendarme, old rose, beige, mahogany, prune, heliotrope, myrtle, or brown. Satins are made in such a multitude of shades that we can usually furnish any shade or match any sample. Width, 18 inches...$0.25

880 Colored Satin, all colors as above.............. .45

882 Colored Satin, we can furnish colors above quoted. Width, 18 inches............................ .60

For quilted satins, see index.

Oil Silks for Hat Sweat Bands and Arm Shields or Medicinal Purposes.

Per yard.

888 Oil Silk, 25 inches wide......................$0.85
Price for full piece of about 5 yards, 80 cents per yard.

Kai Ki Wash Silks.

Fast colors, especially designed for summer waists and dresses. Nothing so delightfully cool as these silks.

890 Kai Ki Wash Silks, best qualities, 21 inches wide. New importations for 1895. This season's stock includes the largest and handsomest collection of styles that has ever been shown in these goods. We have narrow, even and broken stripes in the following colors: Gray and white; brown and white; navy and white; pink and white; red and white; light blue and white; wine and white; tan, pink and gold; heliotrope, pink and gold; green, light blue and gold; gray, pink and light blue; dove, pink and white; lavender, gray and white; pink, light blue and gray. Also small, even checks in rose and olive; garnet and white; black and white; navy and white; cardinal and black, or navy and white. Per yard...$0.39

A Novelty.

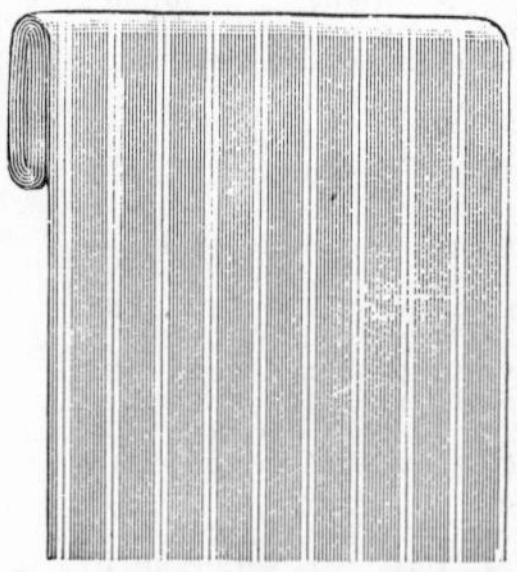

892 Cable Cord Kai Ki Silk, 21 inches wide. The prettiest wash silk made. Grounds are in plain tints with narrow stripes formed by fine raised cords of white silk. Makes an extremely strong silk and a decided novelty. Colors: Light blue and white; rose pink and white; brown and white; cardinal and white; navy and white, or black and white. Per yard.........$0.50

Shantung or Pongee Silk.

894 Pongee Silk in natural color, not dyed in shades, but made only in a pure flax tint, 19 to 20 inches wide, used for traveling dresses, negligee wear, fancy work, etc...............$0.25
For full piece of about 18 yards, per piece....... 4.25

895 Natural Color Pongee Silk, 26 inches wide, good quality. Per yard.............................. .35
For full piece of about 15 yards.................. 4.75

Printed Shantung Silk.

898 Printed Shantung or Natural Pongee Silk, 19 inches wide. This is something entirely new, never shown in this country before, but the idea is so good that a large demand for the goods is already assured. They are sold only by the piece. Original lengths are put up in China, 19 to 19½ yards in a piece, just enough for a dress. Owing to the fact that we do not open or cut these pieces, we cannot furnish samples. The ground color is ecru—the natural Pongee tint, on which is printed a small floral design in pink with olive green leaves; heliotrope with olive; blue with brown leaves. A vine pattern comes in dark blue, brown or olive. Price, per piece....................................$6.25

Plain China Silks.

NOTE REDUCED PRICES

900 Plain China Silk, 19 inches wide, solid colors only, for drapery, party dresses, fancy work, mantels, scarfs, decorative art work and trimming lightweight fabrics. Black, white cream, light blue, nile, lavender, pink, rose and shrimp, old rose, mahogany, canary, yellow, orange, sapphire, gendarme, garnet, cardinal, gobelin, navy, marine, gray, reseda, bronze, golden, dark or medium brown. Per yard $0.22

902 Plain Japanese Habutai Silk 20 inches wide; our own importation, fine and firm, woven, dyed and finished in Japan. The best low priced silk sold by anybody. Colors: Light blue, pink, yellow, orange, gray, dove, ecru, lilac, heliotrope, nile, old rose, cardinal, wine, navy, golden brown, dark brown, sapphire blue, cream or black. Per yard.. .35

904 Plain Japanese Habutai Silk, 23 inches wide, woven in Japan, dyed and finished in Lyons, France. This silk is much softer and finer woven than China silks and equally strong. The weaving, which is done on hand looms, is perfect and entirely free from the coarse threads or knots usually found in Canton China silks. The colors are absolutely fast and sun-proof, and the silk can be washed like linen without injury to color or finish. Importing, as we do, vast quantities of this silk each season, we are enabled to sell it at a price which would be impossible were we to buy from American stocks. Colors are: Tan, copper, light blue, pink, shrimp or salmon, cream, white, nile, light olive, dark olive, buff or maize, yellow, orange, lilac, reseda or sage green, cardinal, mahogany, gobelin blue, sapphire blue, navy blue, myrtle, old rose, wine, golden brown, gray, slate, seal brown or black. Per yard.. .48

Plain Black Japanese Dress Silks.

911 Imported Black Habutai Silk, 24 inches wide. Per yard.......................................$0.45

913 Imported Black Habutai Silk, 27 inches wide. Per yard.. .50

914 Imported Black Habutai Silk, fine quality, 27 inches wide. Per yard............................ .70

916 Imported Black Habutai Silk, finer quality than above. We highly recommend this grade for service. Per yard................................ .80

Plain Black "Shower Proof" Silks.

918 Plain Black Japanese Silk, treated with a new process which renders it rain or waterproof. In appearance it does not differ from the regular lines of Japanese silks. Width, 23 inches. Per yard $0.60

919 Plain Black "Shower Proof" Silk. Width, 27 inches. Per yard.. .75

Cream Habutai Silks.

920 Plain Habutai Silk in natural (cream) color only; width, 20 inches. This is a very soft, light weight of silk of Japanese make. It is exceedingly strong in construction and sold in great quantities for party dresses, fancy work and underwear. It is especially desirable for the latter purpose, as it washes like cotton. Per yard...$0.35

922 Plain Natural Habutai Silk, cream color only; width, 27 inches. Per yard.................. .50

Figured China Silks.

We are to-day one of the largest American importers of these goods and are therefore able to offer our customers the choicest and newest designs. Many of them made exclusively for us. We undoubtedly offer the best values obtainable in summer silks.

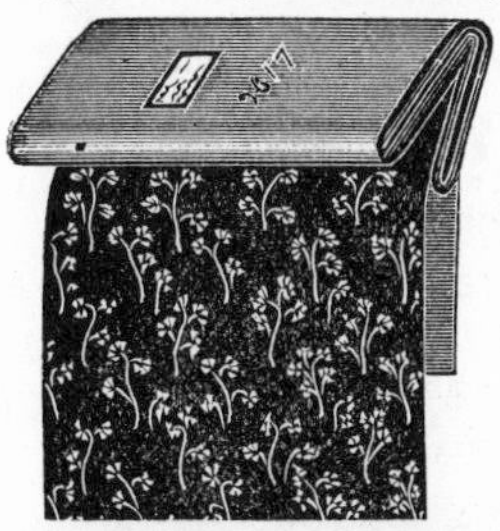

930 Figured China Silk, 18 inches wide. A choice collection of small floral designs in white on grounds of dark and medium colors. Navy, brown, myrtle, black, wine, cardinal, tan, golden brown, slate.
Per yard......$0.22½

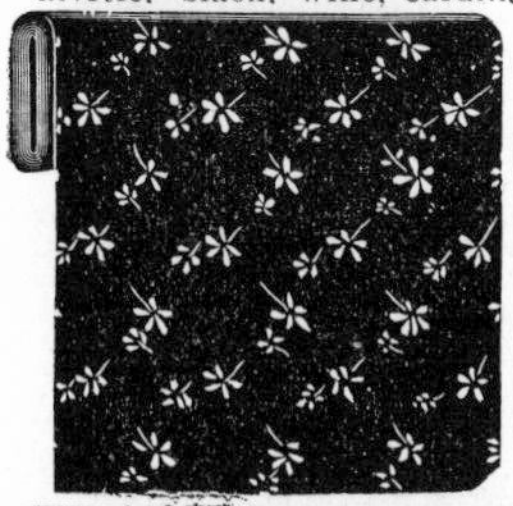

932 Imported China Silk, 21 inches wide. Small floral patterns on colored grounds in all the season's fashionable colors: Navy, myrtle, dark brown, golden brown, wine cardinal, gray, slate, tan, old rose, cream, black. This is a special value.
Per yard.... $0.30

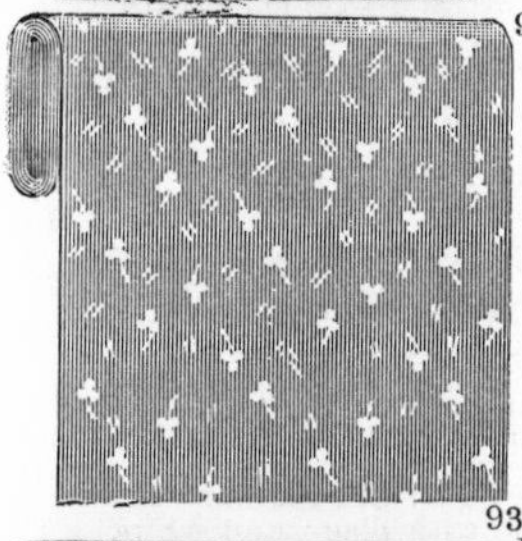

934 Pongee Faconne; width 21 inches. This is a plain Habutai silk, light and soft in texture, with tiny brocaded figures woven in self colors. A very handsome and durable novelty for dresses and silk waists. Colors are, golden brown, cream, light blue, pink, lavender, olive, nile, old rose, cardinal, navy or black.
Per yard....... $0.50

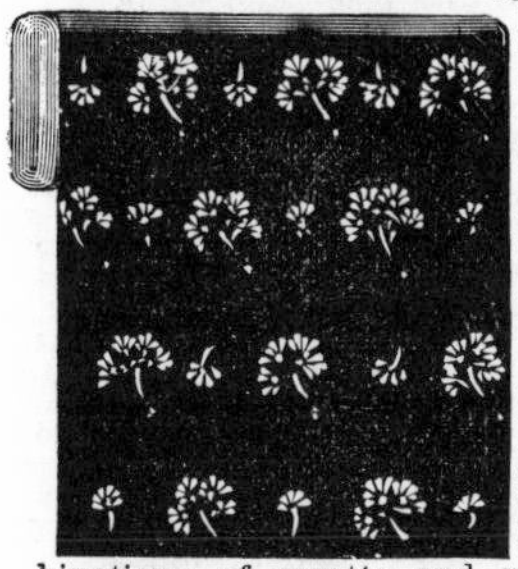

936 Printed Japanese Habutai Silks, 23 inches wide. Importations for season of 1895. These silks are perfectly fast colors. Dyed and printed in Lyons by the most improved process. There are no better silks shown in America. The designs for this season are medium floral clusters in a new shaded effect and a hair line stripe with tiny pin dots between, over which is an irregular scattering of larger dots. In the latter style we have combinations of myrtle and pink; black and green; wine and white; brown and white; navy and white; navy and gold; black and white; black and blue; black and pink; black and heliotrope; black and majenta or cerise; black and gold. Floral designs are in black and pink; black and apple green; black and turquoise; blue, black and white; navy and white; navy and gold; brown and white; wine and white; myrtle and pink or black and purple.

These silks are all woven on hand looms and are absolutely free from coarse threads, specks or imperfections. Per yard..................................$0.60

Drapery Silks.

Per yard.

950 Drapery Silks, 32 inches wide, in solid colors. It is suitable for drapery, linings, trimmings, fancy work, decorations, etc. Colors: Pink, orange, yellow, nile, apple green, old rose, tan, sapphire, gobelin, cream and mahogany only..$0.48

952 Drapery Silk, etc., as above, figured in large designs. Suitable for throws, sash curtains, mantel drapes, etc.................................... .58

For cotton goods in imitation of the above, see Nos. 1886-1888.

Japanese Gold Stamped Crepe Drapery.

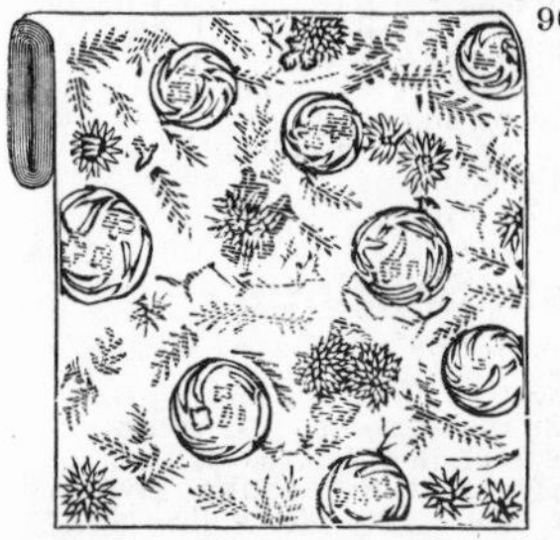

960 Japanese Cotton Drapery Crepe, gold stamped, 27 inches wide. Very handsome, durable and economical for window draperies, mantels, headrests, sofa pillows, and various other decorative purposes, designs are floral scrolls in gold combined with pretty colors on grounds of the following shades: Yellow, corn or maize, white, nile green, old gold, olive, light blue, medium blue, old rose, dark old rose. This cloth is also largely sold for fancy costumes. Per yard..............$0.20
For full piece of 25 yards, 18½ cents per yard.

Rare Bargains in Brocades.

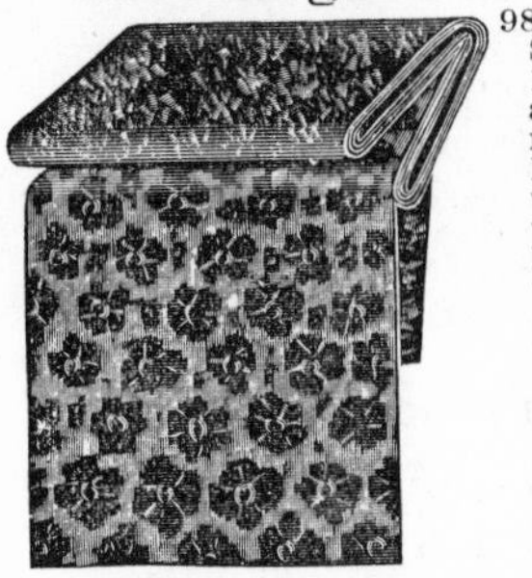

980 Black Brocaded Silk Velvets; width 19 inches, medium and small designs, rich in color and style. Many velvets will be worn this season for wraps and trimmings, hence this lot which we purchased at much under their value should attract unusual attention from close buyers. The price at which we offer them until sold is less than ¼ their actual value.
Per yard.......$0.25

VELVETS AND VELVETEENS.

Royal Silk Finish Velveteens, Black.

Per yard.

982 Black Velveteen, 17½ inches wide..........$0.22
Price for full piece of about 36 yards, 5 per cent. less than cut piece price on all velveteens.

984 Black Royal Velveteen, 18 inches wide...... .35

986 Black Royal Silk Finish Velveteen, 22 inches wide...... .... .50

988 Black Royal Silk Finish Velveteen, 22 inches wide. .... .60

990 Black Royal Silk Finish Velveteen, heavy, 22 inches wide........................ .75

Black Velutina.

A heavy, lustrous velveteen, made by an improved process, and the nearest approach to a Lyons all silk velvet in appearance that has ever been produced.

992 Black Velutina, 24 inches wide.. ....$0.90

994 Black Velutina, heavy, 26 inches wide...... 1.30

Colored Velveteens, Silk Finish.

Velvets and Velveteens are to be much used for fashionable trimmings. We have all desirable shades.

1000 Silk Finish, Colored Velveteens. A good value for low price; width 18 inches; colors as follows: Cream, pink, beige, moss olive, bronze, myrtle, sky blue, azure blue, royal blue, navy, gray, dark slate, gobelin, old rose, peacock blue, gold, golden brown, Havana brown, medium or seal brown, mahogany, cardinal, garnet, wine, sapphire or purple. Per yard.................$0.23

1002 Colored Velveteen, silk finish, 20 inches wide. Can furnish all colors as in 1000. Price per yard.. .35

1004 Colored Velveteens, silk finish, 22 inches wide. For colors see 1000. Per yard........... .50

Moleskin.

1020 White Moleskin, for painting, fancy work, etc.; 26 inches wide, fine and heavy, not made in colors. Per yard..............................$1.75

Black Silk Velvets.

Exceptional Values.

NOTE.—We do not cut any black or colored velvets on the bias. All velvets, silks, etc., are cut straight only.

1024 Black Silk Velvets.

Width,	18 in.	18 in.	18 in.	18 in.	18 in.	18 in.
Per yd..	75c	$1.00	$1.25	$1.50	$1.75	$2.00

Price for full piece of about 25 yards, 5 per cent less than for a cut piece on all velvets.

Colored Silk Velvets.

We positively have the best values in velvets that can be found anywhere. Our stock is so complete we can usually match any sample or furnish any color made. Per yard.

1030 Colored Silk Velvets, Croise back, 18 inches wide, in the following colors: Cream, white, pink, light blue, cardinal, garnet, myrtle, coach green, golden brown, lilac, mahogany, old rose, reseda, heliotrope, prune or black, medium brown, seal brown, moss olive, drab, purple, navy, marine, terra cotta, sapphire, peacock blue or claret.......................................$0.75

1032 Colored Silk Croise Velvet, 18 inches wide, all colors as above................................ 1.00

1034 Colored Silk Croise Velvet, 19 inches wide, colors as in 1030.................................$1.25

Silk Plushes.

Mottled Finish.

Per yard.

1054 Mottled Silk Plush, 18 inches wide; colors as follows: Nile, lavender, old gold, serpent, reseda, scarlet, cardinal, garnet, wine, claret, navy, olive, bronze, sapphire, mahogany, prune, heliotrope, myrtle, brown, castor, copper, gobelin golden brown...$0.75

1056 Mottled Silk Plush, 18 inches wide. We have all the colors in 1054 (except evening or light shades) given above, and the new shades as fast as dyed. Per yard........................ 1.00

1058 Mottled or Marbelized Silk Plush, 24 inches wide. A job lot to close. We have the following shades only in this width and will have no more when sold: Cadet blue, reseda (a gray or sage green) gray, old rose, gobelin blue, sapphire blue, peacock blue, myrtle green, gold, mahogany, cardinal, navy, medium brown or black.
Per yard.. .65

1070 Silk Seal Plush in brown only; width 24 inches. Used for jackets, capes, etc.
Price, per yard.. 2.25

PRINT DEPARTMENT.

Leader No. 1.

1100 Best Standard Dark Prints, including all the leading brands, Garner, Gloucester, Allen, Hamilton, Pacific, etc. These are dark colorings only, always scarce at this time of year. We have secured all we could, enough we believe, to see us through. We will cut any number of yards, but do not care to sell more than 5 whole pieces at one time, so that orders at the end of the season may be filled. If you prefer any particular color order it; we have most every dark color in this line, but if not, will send something near.
Price, per yard.......................... ......$0.03½

Leader No. 2.

1102 Best Standard Light or Medium Colored Prints, similar goods to above excepting the color. Of these we have bought an immense supply, had to, to sell them at the price. We will cut any length, or sell any quantity. Our contracts for these prints extend all through the season, so all wants will be supplied. If you have any choice of color, order it; your country merchants pay 5 cents for these goods, our price to you. Per yard $0.04

Staple Styles.

1103 Fast Color Prints, in small figures, red and white, or pink and white checks or plaids, also pink or blue grounds with white polka dots or hair line stripes. Per yard.........................$0.05
Price for full piece about 50 yards, same.

1104 Full Standard Print, in dark brown and white small apron checks; very neat and will not show dirt, Per yard............................ .05
Price for full piece about 50 yards, same,

1106 Frock Prints, very small figures, in pink, buff or purple. Per yard........................ .06
Price for full piece about 50 yards, 5¾ cents.

1108 Hair Line Striped Prints, fast colors in purple and white, and pink and white. Per yard.......................... 06
Price for full piece about 50 yards, 5½ cents per yard.

1110 Oil Prints, green ground, yellow and black small figures; canary, with red and black small figure; red ground, with yellow and black figure. Per yard.... .... .06
Price for full piece about 50 yards, 5⅞ cents per yard.

1112 Washington Oil Blue Frock Prints are not so dark as indigo; they are printed in a small floral design of a little lighter shade than the ground work and are neat and pretty for children. Per yard.................................... .06
Price for full piece of about 50 yards, per yard, 5⅞ cents.

Shepherd Checks.

1118 Black and White Shepherd Checked Print. Checks run from pin checks up to those a half inch square. All fast colors and all perfectly printed. Just the thing for aprons, dresses and children's wear. Per yard......................... .06
Price for full piece of about 50 yards, 5¾ cents per yard.

Novelty Prints.

These are the best spring and summer work, and are a little nicer than ever before; the styles described are of the early shipments; the printing may differ somewhat later, but the colorings will not change all through the season.

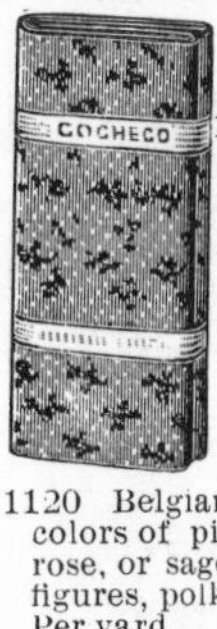

1119 Cocheco Novelty Print Dress Patterns. These are the best work of the season; nothing but good styles; put up in dress lengths of 10 yards. Try a pattern if you want a pretty one. Just new from the mills. Colors are: Grey, tan, brown, pink or light blue.
Per pattern.......................$0.50

1120 Belgian Dress Prints, in predominating colors of pink, tan, heliotrope, pea green, old rose, or sage green. The printing is in small figures, polka dots, or figured stripes.
Per yard...$0.05
Price for full piece of about 50 yards, 4⅞ cents.

1122 Diamond Chambray Prints are printed in chambray effects as the name implies; one of the most taking styles is a wavy stripe in pink and white, blue and white, navy and white, or black and white. Other styles are dots or rings on pink, blue, heliotrope or cardinal grounds.
Per yard.. .05
Price for full piece of about 50 yards, 4⅞ cents.

1124 Goblin Blue Dress Prints; only one color in this line, but it is a favorite, more popular every year. The color is neither dark nor light, the printing is in white, small figures or stripes.
Per yard..$0.05½
Price for full piece of about 50 yards, 4⅞ cents per yard.

Bicycles will soon be more common than buggies. Better have one.

Prints—Continued.

1126 Satin Finish Dress Prints; these are made in dark or medium colors, also in some of the daintest light effects. Some of the best styles are navy ground, with white polka dots, or hair line stripes; ground of crepe effect with figures in grey, gobelin, tan, pea green, pink, heliotrope or light blue; one of the dainty styles is a tiny check of delicate colorings, such as pink and grey, blue and white, etc. Per yard............. .05¾
Price for full piece of about 50 yards, 5½ cents per yard.

1128 Simpson's Dress Percales in light or medium colorings. The styles are all good and are represented by fancy checks in old rose, pea green, grey, cardinal; pink, blue, brown or black and white, hair line stripes, or polka dots on the following grounds: Nile, heliotrope, tan, blue or pink, also fancy stripes in the same colors, and an endless variety of floral designs on either white or light grounds, some of them very small, others larger.
Per yard.. .05¾
Price for full piece of about 20 yards, 5½ cents per yard.

1130 Pacific Fancy Dress Prints, in medium or dark colorings. One pretty style is a pebble design in brown, sapphire, or cardinal another is rather small flower printed in white on the following grounds: Medium blue, tan, pea green, grey or wine. Then there are tan or grey grounds speckled with bright mixed colors, and stripes in any of the colors mentioned. Per yard...... .05¾
For full piece of about 50 yards, 5½ cents per yard.

1131 Garnet Foulard Print, very neat and stylish; made in solid garnet grounds, with small foulard silk pattern of white or gold. The figures are dots, rings, flowers, floral or plain stripes.
Per yard.. .05¾
For full piece of about 50 yards, 5½ cents per yard.

1132 Navy Blue Fancy Prints, 25 inches wide. Navy blue grounds, with small and medium floral and set figures; figured stripes, stars, dots and dashes in cardinal or gold. Per yard....... .05¾
For full piece of about 50 yards, 5½ cents per yard.

Silverine Print.

1133 Silverine Print, a black and white speckled or diagonal groundwork with small, medium or large figures of gold or mixed colors, also polka dots. The general color effect is rather dark.
Per yard.. .05¾
Price for full piece of about 50 yards. Per yard, 5½ cents.

Cocheco Fast Black Novelties.

1134 Fast Black Prints, solid black grounds with colored printing. There are dots, small figures, or hair line strips in gold, also medium floral designs in mixed colors of heliotrope and gold, blue and gold, or green and gold. Per yard..... .05¾
Price for full piece of about 50 yards, per yard, 5½ cents.

Dahlia Print.

1135 Dahlia Print does not represent the many hues of the flower its name suggests; the color effect, however, is its chief attraction, it being of a rich damask red. The printing is in floral or set figures, pretty broken checks or stripes, also diagonal, or watered effects. A little black and white is introduced, which gives a pleasing relief to the dominant color; it is one of the favorites this season. Width, 25 inches. Per yard.. .06
For full piece of about 50 yards. Per yard..... .05¾

Windsor Resille.

1136 Windsor Resille, the color effects of this novelty without doubt surpass all other print work of the season. The seasonable shades are represented in the ground work, cream, ecru, heliotrope, pink; tan, grey, pea green, nile green, or black; in one floral design the ground is almost entirely covered with printing of different colors with good effect; another style, and very pretty, is delicate vine tracing. These are printed on either of the colored grounds mentioned. Width, 25 inches. Per yard...................... .07
For full piece of about 50 yards, per yard, 6¾ cents.

Turkey Red Dress Prints.

1138 Turkey Red Oil Print with either black or white printing. The styles are small or medium figures, polka dots, bars, stripes, plain or floral, or sporting patterns. Per yard................ $0.05
For full piece of about 50 yards, 4⅞c. per yard.

1140 Cardinal and Black Wool Checks or small plaids of black on cardinal grounds, fast colors; exceedingly attractive for children's dresses; printed in exact imitation of wool goods. Per yard.. .05½
Price for full piece, about 50 yards, 5¼ cents per yard.

1144 German Percale in Turkey Red. Checks, plaids or stripes of white, fast color. Extra strong cloth. Width, 30 inches. Per yard...... .08
Price for full piece, about 44 yards, 7¾ cents per yard.

1148 Extra Wide Turkey Red Fancy Prints, 31 inches wide, cloth fine and strong, fast color. Red ground with medium or large size white figures or stripes. Per yard....-.................. .11
Price for full piece, about 45 yards, 10¾ cents.

Flannel Print.

A New Production.

Popular for children's dresses or wrappere.

1150 Flannel Print, 26 inches wide. The cloth very firm and is teazled or closely napped, so as to exactly resemble the fine French figured flannels. It is only made in cardinal grounds, over which are printed small or medium black figures, vine tracings or small polka dots.
Per yard..$0.06½
Price for full piece of about 43 yards, 6¼ cents per yard.

Indigo Blue Prints.

1160 Indigo Blue Prints, solid blue grounds, figured, dotted or striped with white; width 25 inches. Per yard..............................$0.05
Price for full piece of about 50 yards, 4¾ cents per yard.

1162 Plain Indigo Blue Print Cloth, no figures; width 25 inches. Per yard..................... .05
Price for full piece of about 50 yards, 4¾ cents per yard.

1164 Blue and Gold Indigo Prints, small and medium figure or stripes of gold on indigo blue ground. Per yard................................ .06
Price for full piece of about 50 yards, 5¾ cents per yard.

1166 Dutch Blue Print, 30 inches wide, polka dots, medium or small figures or stripes in white or gold; checks in white only. Per yard........ .09
Price for full piece of about 50 yards, 8¾ cents per yard.

1167 Plain or solid Indigo Blue Print Cloth, quality as above; width, 30 inches. Per yard.. 09
Price for full piece of about 50 yards, 8¾ cents per yard.

1168 Dutch Indigo Print, 31 inches wide, white figured stripes, checks. Per yard......... 10½
Price for full piece of about 43 yards, 10¼ cents per yard.

1170 German Extra Heavy Indigo Blue Print, 33 inches wide, solid blue ground, with figures, stripes or bars of white. Per yard............... .12½
Price for full piece of about 50 yards, 12¼ cents per yard.

Extra Wide Print.

1172 Sterling Dress Print; on extra heavy cloth in dark colors only, printed in medium size figures. The colors are: Sapphire, navy, brown or black; some of the designs are balls, also flowers; the black grounds have either colored or white figures. This is a print made especially for wear. Width, 29 inches.
Per yard..$0.08
Price for full piece of about 50 yards, 7¾ cents per yard.

1174 Extra Wide Costume Print, very fine, fast colors; width, 32 inches. Designs are all new. Ground or predominating colors are: Black with gold; black with white; black with heliotrope, or mixed colored flowers; navy ground with white or gold. Designs are floral effects, stripes and set figures, medium or small.
Per yard.. .10
Full piece of about 50 yards, 9½ cents per yard.

Shirting Prints.

1180 Shirting Prints, white ground, with figures black, red, blue, brown, black and red or black and blue. Checks in blue, pink or black. Stripes in black, blue or red and cheviot effects and sporting patterns for boys' waists in combinations of black and red, or black and blue.
Per yard..$0.04
Full piece of about 50 yards, 3⅞ cents per yard.

Percales or Cambrics.

This fabric will have an immense sale the coming season, on account of the growing popularity of ladies' shirt waists. We are going to meet the demand in every particular. The following quotations contain a fine variety of this season's styles. The cloth and printing are the best work, and the prices beat all.

1181 Crown Percale, 30 inches wide, in stripes or polka dots only; the stripes are even lines of blue and white, pink and white or black and white, either hair-line or about ⅛ of an inch wide; the dots are on pink or light blue grounds.
Per yard..............................$0.06¾
For full piece of about 50 yards, per yard 6½ cents.

1182 Steel River Percale, 31 inches wide, in the following styles: Hair-line stripes or polka dots on blue or pink ground, narrow stripes on wine colored grounds, and wider dotted or fancy stripes on white, blue, or pink grounds, hair-line stripes, checks, dots or small figures on white ground; these are in black, blue or pink, also larger figures in the same colors and some in mixed colors. Per yard...................... .08
For full piece of about 42 yards, per yard 7¾ cents.

1184 Harmony Percale or Penang, 36 inches wide. This is a superior cloth and extra wide; the cloth is fine, yet heavy, and the styles printed for high class trade; the grounds are either white pink or blue. There are polka dots, stripes exclusive figures, small or medium size, on the white ground of black, pink, blue or mixed colors, and of white on pink or blue grounds; sporting patterns are on white, pink or blue grounds and include drums, bicycles, etc.
Per yard.. .12
Price for full piece of about 50 yards, 11½ cents.

Black and White Prints.

1185 Black ground with small, medium, or large figures of white: also hair-line or figured stripes; patterns are new, neat and pretty.
Per yard..$0.05
Full piece of about 50 yards, per yard. .4⅞ cents.

1186 Simpson's Black and White Prints; styles similar to above. Per yard.......................... .05
For full piece of about 50 yards, per yard 5¾ cenes.

Silver Gray Prints.

1187 Silver Gray Prints, with small, medium, or large designs, stripes or plaids. A nice print for elderly ladies, genteel and serviceable.
Per yard.. .05
For full piece of about 50 yards, per yard 4⅞ cents.

1188 Simpson's Silver Gray Print, styles similar to above. Per yard...................... .06
For full piece of about 50 yards, per yard 5⅓ cants.

Bed Quilt, Comforter or Robe Prints.

1190 Comforter Print, high colors, fancy, large patterns. Regular width. Per yard..........$0.04½
Full piece of about 50 yards, 4¼ cents per yard.

1192 Riverpoint Robe Prints, black ground with red figures, or red ground with white or gold figures. Per yard.............................. .05
Full piece of about 50 yards, 4⅞ cents per yard.

1194 Portsmouth Comforter Prints, patterns mostly large, bright colors; cloth good and firm.
Per yard.. .05¼
Full piece of about 50 yards, 5¼ cents per yard.

1196 Hamilton Twilled Drapery, also for comforters. Wears splendidly. Colors bright and clean. Per yard.......................... .06
Full piece of about 50 yards, 5¾ cents per yard.

1198 Russian Turkey Red Robe Print, black figures on red ground, medium sized designs. Per yard.. .06
Price full piece of about 50 yards, 5¾ cents per yard.. .06

1200 Pacific Comfort Print, absolutely fast colors, made in large handsome designs, bringing out beautiful color effects. Medium and dark colors predominating. Per yard........ .06
Price full piece of about 50 yards, 5¾ cents per yard.

1202 Washington Oil Prints, black ground with red figure, or red ground with black and white figure. Fast colors. Per yard.............. .07½
Price full piece of adout 50 yards, 7¼ cents per yard.

Tabby Cats.

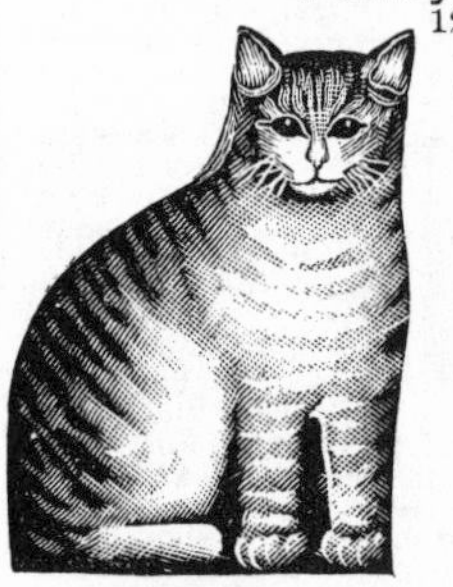

1210 Tabby Cat Prints. No home complete without a cat. Each half yard of cloth is printed in three pictures. Front, back and feet with outlined margin for cutting. These pictures are to be cut out, sewed together and stuffed with sawdust or cotton, and the result is a life size Maltese tabby, cat in sitting position. The most natural thing of the kind ever produced. Every yard contains two cats. Also have same goods with kittens, 8 to the yard.
Per yard.............$0.13½

Indestructible Dolls.

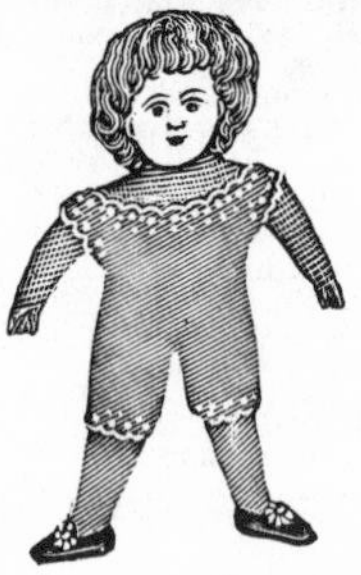

1212 A Printed Cambric, heavier and stronger than the cats. Each half yard contains 1 complete doll, front and back, printed in perfect imitation of fine bisques; same color tints. This doll will stand any amount of hardship and will please the little ones immensely. Per yard. $0.13½

Other Toy Prints.

1213 Toy Prints, similar to above in the following figures. Two to the yard. Tatters, Bow-wow, Floss, bunny, hen and chickens, rooster, owl, monkey, pickininny, bisque doll, Punch and Judy, jointed doll, Little Lord Fauntleroy.
Eight to the yard. Little Tatters, Little Bow-wow, little Jocko, baby elephant.
Twelve to the yard. Brownies.
Price, per yard $0.13½

Regents Shirtings.

For Shirts, Waists or Dresses.

1215 Regents Shirtings. A beautiful line of extra heavy Percales, 36 inches wide, fast colors and handsome styles in plain or figured stripes, dots and fancy designs. Colors: Pink, gray, tan, light blue or white grounds; splendid effects for wrappers and shirt waists. This line is extraordinary in value. A special deal with the mill. Regular price, 12½ cents. Our price per yard..............................$0.09
Full piece of about 48 yards, 8½ cents per yard.

Drapery Prints.

For Furniture Coverings or Draperies.

1218 Allen Twill Drapery Print, 25 inches wide, in large handsome designs or smaller flowers on the following colored grounds: Cream, ecru, sapphire, wine, navy, light blue or brown. Per yard $0.06
For full piece of about 50 yards, 5¾ cents per yard.

1220 Purdah Rep Drapery, 29 inches wide, similar weave to the imported English cretonne. They come in the following color grounds with large harmonizing floral designs: Gray, ecru, cream, wine, navy, black. Per yard .... .12
For full piece of about 50 yards, 11 cents per yard.

1222 Cameo Drapery, 30 inches wide, in handsome patterns and rich colorings. Cloth is good and strong, and woven in twilled effects. They will drape beautifully. Designs are medium or large, and highly artistic in shadings. Colors of ground work: Tan, black, brown, navy, wine, cream, light blue or slate. Per yard .... .12
For full piece of about 50 yards, 11 cents per yard.

Solid Colored Print.

1230 Plain colored prints in the following colors: Cardinal, orange, gray, medium brown seal brown, green, dark blue, scarlet, tan, black or medium blue; 25 inches wide. Per yard $0.05
Price for full piece of about 50 yards, 4⅞ cents per yard.

1232 Plain Oil Turkey Red Prints, 25 inches wide .... .05
Price for full piece of about 50 yards, 4⅞ cents per yard.

1234 Plain Turkey Red Oil Prints, 25 inches, better grade .... .07
Price for full piece of about 50 yards, 6¾ cents per yard.

1236 Plain Turkey Red Oil Prints, 31 inches wide .... .10
Price for full piece of about 40 yards, 9 cents per yard.

1238 Plain Turkey Red Oil Prints, 36 inches wide .... .12
Price for full piece of about 50 yards, 11¼ cents per yard.

1240 Twilled Turkey Red Oil Prints, 31 inches, plain color 15
Price for full piece of about 50 yards, 14½ cents per yard.

Oil Prints.

1242 Oil prints in orange, blue or green, 24 inches wide, plain colors only $0.06
Price for full piece of about 54 yards, 5⅞ cents per yard.

National Decoration Bunting.

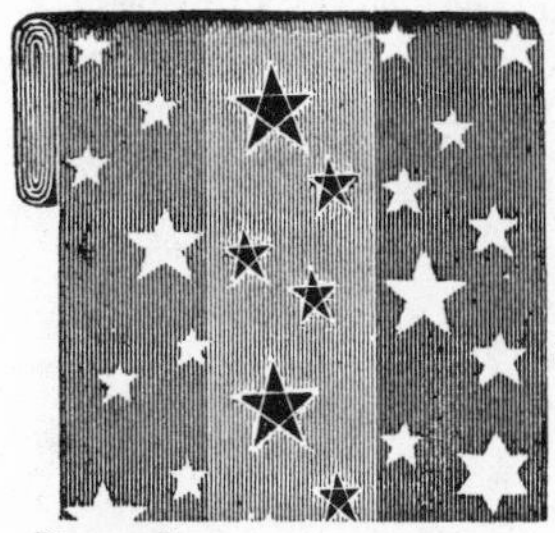

We handle large quantities of Decoration Buntings, and are particularly well prepared to supply large orders. Entertainment and Decoration committees will save money by sending to us for their supplies.

1246 Print Cloth similar to Bunting, printed in red, white and blue stripes, with stars, 21 inches wide. Per yard $0.04½
Price for full piece of about 65 yards, 4¼ cents per yard.

1248 Red, white or blue bunting, 25 inches wide. Plain solid colors, for festooning or draping. In ordering always specify the colors wanted. Per yard .... .04
Full piece, about 55 yards, 3⅞ cents per yard.

1250 Tri-color Bunting, width 25 inches striped in wide bands of red, white and blue; plain, no stars. Per yard .... .05
Full piece, about 50 yards, 4¾ cents per yard.

1252 Flag Bunting, 28 inches wide, made with 2 or 4 flags to the yard. Price, per yard .... .06
Price for full piece of about 53 yards, 5¾ cents per yard.

For solid color bunting in national and other fancy colors, see No. 350.

BABY CARRIAGES.

Our Line is Very Complete and our styles are the best.

Prices are lower this year than ever before.

Don't Neglect the Baby.

DOMESTICS.

ANY GOODS NOT QUOTED HERE WILL BE FURNISHED AT LOWEST MARKET PRICE AND SAMPLES, MARKED WITH WIDTH AND PRICE, SENT ON APPLICATION.

Large contracts which we have made with leading manufacturers this season are on a much lower and more favorable basis than ever before. This will be more readily appreciated by referring to the *extraordinarily low prices* we are now enabled to quote on well known *Standard Cottons, If low prices are an inducement, we should beyond doubt have your trade on Domestics.*

Unbleached Sheeting.

Per yard.

1305 Standard LL Unbleached Sheetings, 36 inches wide. We handle the following well-knpwn brands: Aurora, Badger, Atlantic, Harper. Full pieces average about 60 yards.
Price, per yard, any quantity $0.04
NOTE: LL Sheetings average about 4 yards to the pound.

1307 Unbleached Sheetings, 36 inches wide, strong and heavy. Buck's Head, Honest Width or Triumph brands. Full pieces average about 60 yards. Per yard, for any quantity .... .04¾
These sheeting average about 3¼ yards to the pound.

1310 Extra Heavy Unbleached Sheetings, 36 inches wide, Atlantic "A" or Indian Head brands. These sheetings average about 55 yards to the piece, and weigh 2⅞ yards to the pound. Per yard, for any quantity .... .05

The above prices are subject to fluctuations of the market, and are not guaranteed beyond the present stock.

Fine Unbleached Shirtings and Sheetings.

About 56 yards to a piece.

Per yard.

1312 Fine Brown Cotton, 36 inches wide, Tioga $0.04
1311 Fine Brown Cotton, 36 inches wide, Aurora B .... .05
1318 Fine Brown Cotton, 36 inches wide, Pepperell "R" .... .05
1320 Fine Brown Cotton, 36 inches wide, Lockwood .... .06
1322 Fine Brown Cotton, 39 inches wide, Pepperell "E" .... .06
1324 Fine Brown Cotton, 40 inches wide, Dwight Star .... .07½

Unbleached Cottons by the Full Piece.

Many of our customers would like to buy their sheeting by the bolt but cannot well use or afford to buy the quantity usually put up in one length. For the benefit of such we have had the most popular grades woven in 25 yard lengths and shall sell them by the piece only.

Unbleached Sheeting.

Prices reduced.

Per piece.

1330 Unbleached Sheeting, 36 inches wide, 25 yards. (when you buy 25 yards of cotton cloth for $1.00 do not expect too much. It is offered only to those who want to buy goods at a low price, regardless of quality. All the others we can recommend.) Alliance No. 4 .... $1.00
1331 Medium Unbleached Sheeting, 36 inches wide, 25 yards. Alliance No. 3 .... 1.20
1332 Medium Unbleached Sheeting, 36 inches wide, 25 yards. Alliance No. 2 .... 1.30
1333 Heavy Unbleached Sheeting, 36 inches wide, 25 yards. Alliance No. 1 .... 1.45

Unbleached Extra Wide Sheetings Pepperell.

The Pepperell Mills Wide Sheetings, while not woven as fine, close or hard as some others are universally used by hotels, hospitals and the U. S. government, as their experience teaches that a cloth woven hard is worn out more in washing in trying to get it clean and white than one slightly coarser.

These are fine enough for most any trade, wear splendidly, will not crack, and wash easily.

Width given is exact.

Per yard.

1340 Brown Pepperell Sheetings, fine, 45 inches wide $0.08½
Full piece of about 45 yards, 8 cents per yard.
1342 Brown Pepperell Sheetings, fine, 48 inches wide .... .09½
Full piece, about 45 yards, 9 cents per yard.
1344 Brown Pepperell Sheetings, fine, 58 inches wide .... .11½
Full piece, about 45 yards, 11 cents per yard.
1346 Brown Pepperell Sheetings, fine, 68 inches wide .... .13
Full piece, about 45 yards, 12 cents per yard.
1348 Brown Pepperell Sheetings, fine, 80 inches wide .... .15
Full piece, about 45 yards, 14 cents per yard.
1350 Brown Pepperell Sheetings, fine, 88 inches wide .... .17
Full piece, about 45 yards, 16 cents per yard.

Pequot.

While for general wearing qualities the Pepperell Sheetings are undoubtedly the most satisfactory medium-priced cottons on the market, there has been for some time a growing demand from many of our customers for a finer and heavier quality. We have therefore, after a careful comparison of leading brands, selected the Pequot Sheetings as being superior to all others for uniformity of thread, fineness of weave, weight and general combination of qualities, which are essential in first-class sheetings.

Per yard.

1370 Unbleached Pequot Sheeting (5/4), 45 inches wide $0.10½
Full piece of about 48 yards, 10 cents per yard.
1371 Unbleached Pequot Sheeting (6/4), 54 inches wide .... .12½
Full piece of about 48 yards, 12 cents per yard.
1372 Unbleached Pequot Sheeting (7/4), 58 inches wide .... .14
Full piece of about 48 yards, 13¼ cents per yard.
1373 Unbleached Pequot Sheeting (8/4), 68 inches wide .... .16
Full piece of about 48 yards, 15 cents per yard.
1374 Unbleached Pequot Sheeting (9/4), 80 inches wide .... .18
Full piece of about 48 yards, 17 cents per yard.
1375 Unbleached Pequot Sheeting (10/4), 88 inches wide .... .20
Full piece of about 48 yards, 19 cents per yard.

Cream or Half Bleached Cottons.

Not rotted in whitening, soft and fine, no dressing.

Per yard.

1380 Cream Bleached Cotton, 36 inches wide $0.07
Price for full piece of about 55 yards, 6¾ cents per yard.
1382 Cream Bleached Cotton, 36 inches wide .... .08
Price for full piece of about 56 yards, 7¾ cents per yard.
1384 Cream Bleached Cotton, 36 inches wide .... .09
Price for full piece of about 53 yards, 8¾ cents per yard.

Half Bleached Extra Wide Sheetings, Pepperell.

These goods are steadily growing in favor, they become white after a few times washing, once tried are always liked.

Pillow Case Widths.

Per yard.

1390 Pillow Case Cotton, Pepperell, half bleached, 42 inches wide $0.08½
Full piece of about 46 yards, 8 cents per yard.
1392 Pillow Case Cotton, Pepperell, half bleached, 46 inches wide .... .09½
Full piece of about 45 yards, 9 cents per yard.
1394 Pillow Case Cotton, Pepperell, half bleached, 50 inches wide .... .10½
Full piece of about 45 yards, 10 cents per yard.

Wider, for Sheets.

Per yard

1396 Half Bleached Sheeting, Pepperell, 54 inches .... .11½
Full piece of about 45 yards, 11 cents per yard.
1398 Half Bleached Sheeting, Pepperell, 63 inches .... .13
Full piece of about 45 yards, 12 cents per yard.
1400 Half Bleached Sheeting, Pepperell, 72 inches .... .15
Full piece of about 45 yards, 14 cents per yard.
1402 Half Bleached Sheeting, Pepperell, 79 inches .... .17
Full piece of about 45 yards, 16 cents per yard.
1404 Half Bleached Sheeting, Pepperell, 90 inches .... .19
Full piece of about 45 yards, 18 cents per yard.

Bleached Cottons.

About 55 yards to a piece.

Per yard.

1410 Bleached Cotton, 27 inches wide, "Just Out." brand $0.04
1412 Bleached Cotton, 1 yard wide, Ballardvale .05
1414 Bleached Cotton, 1 yard wide, Farmers' Choice .... .05½
1416 Bleached Cotton, 1 yard wide, Cabot .... .06
1418 Bleached Cotton, 1 yard wide, Lonsdale, soft finish .... .06½
1420 Bleached Cotton, Fruits of the Loom, 1 yard wide .... .07
1422 Bleached Cotton, 1 yard wide, Masonville .... .07½
1424 Bleached Cotton, 1 yard wide, Wamsutta .11
1426 Bleached Cotton, 1 yard wide, New York Mills .... .10
1428 Lonsdale Fine Cambric, 1 yard wide .... .08½
1430 Bleached Wamsutta, double warp, twilled for night robes, 36 inches wide .... .11
1432 Pride of the West, 36 inches wide, best bleached cotton manufactured .... .12

Bleached Cotton by the Full Piece.

Many of our customers would like to buy their sheetings by the bolt, but cannot well use or afford to buy the quality usually put up in one length. For the benefit of such we have had the most popular grades woven in 25 yards lengths and shall sell them by the piece only.

1433 Bleached Shirting or Sheeting, "Monitor Brand;" a rather heavy cloth of good even thread and finished "soft" for the needle, 25 yards in piece. Price, per bolt $1.75
1434 Fine Bleached Shirting or Sheeting, 36 inches wide, 25 yards in a piece, manufactured, bleached and branded especially for M. W. & Co., 'Purity Cottons." Per piece 1.95

Bleached Extra Wide Sheetings, Pepperell.

The Pepperell Mills Wide Sheetings, while not woven as fine, close or hard as some others, are universally used by hotels, hospitals and the U. S. government, as their experience teaches that a cloth woven hard is worn out more in washing in trying to get it clean and white than one slightly coarser.

These are fine enough for most any trade, wear splendidly, will not crack, and wash easily.

Pillow Case Widths.

Per yard.

1436 Pillow Case Cotton, Pepperell, bleached, 42 inches wide..$0.08½
Full piece of about 45 yards, 8 cents per yard.

1437 Pillow Case Cotton, Pepperell, bleached, 46 inches wide.. .09½
Full piece of about 45 yards, 9 cents per yard.

1438 Pillow Case Cotton, Pepperell, bleached, 50 inches wide.. .10½
For full piece of about 45 yards, 10 cents per yard

Sheeting Widths.

Per yard.

1439 Bleached Pepperell Sheetings, 54 inches .$0.11½
Full piece of about 45 yards, 11 cents per yard.

1440 Bleached Pepperell Sheetings, 63 inches... .13
Full piece of about 45 yards, 12 cents per yard.

1441 Bleached Pepperell Sheetings, 72 inches... .15
Full piece of about 45 yards, 14 cents per yard.

1442 Bleached Pepperell Sheetings. 79 inches... .17
Full piece of about 45 yards, 16 cents per yard.

1443 Bleached Pepperell Sheetings, 90 inches... .19
Full piece of about 45 yards, 18 cents per yard.

Twilled Bleached Sheeting Pepperell.

1443½ Bleached Pepperell Twilled Sheeting (9/4), 81 inches wide. Best sheeting made for wear
Per yard..$0.22½
Full piece of about 48 yards, 21¼ cents per yard.

PEQUOT.

Bleached Pequot Wide Sheetings.

While for general wearing qualities the Pepperell Sheetings are undoubtedly the most satisfactory medium priced cottons on the market, there has been for some time a growing demand from many of our customers for a finer and heavier quality. We have therefore, after a careful comparison of leading brands, selected the Pequot Sheetings, as being superior to all others for uniformity of thread, fineness of weave, weight and general combination of qualities which are essential in first-class sheetings.

Pillow Case Widths.

1444 Bleached Pequot Pillow Casing, 42 inches wide. Per yard..$0.10½
Full piece of about 48 yards, 10 cents per yard.

1445 Bleached Pequot Pillow Casing (5/4), 45 inches wide. Per yard.. .12
Full piece of about 48 yards, 11½ cents per yard.

1446 Bleached Pequot Pillow Casing, 50 inches wide.. .13
Full piece of about 48 yards, 12¼ cents per yard.

Sheeting Widths.

1447 Bleached Pequot Sheetings (6/4), 54 inches wide.. $0.14
Full piece of about 48 yards, 13¼ cents per yard.

1448 Bleached Pequot Sheetings (7/4), 63 inches wide.. .16
Full piece of about 48 yards, 15 cents per yard.

1449 Bleached Pequot Sheetings (8/4), 72 inches wide.. .18
Full piece of about 48 yards, 17 cents per yard.

1450 Bleached Pequot Sheetings (9/4), 81 inches wide.. .20
Full piece of about 48 yards, 19 cents per yard.

1451 Bleached Pequot Sheetings (10/4), 90 inches wide.. .21½
Full piece of about 48 yards, 20½ cents per yard.

Drilling.

1454 Unbleached Drilling, 29 inches. Per yard..$0.06
Price for full piece of about 40 yards, 5¾ cents per yard.

1456 Unbleached Drilling, best, 29 inches. Per yard.. .07
Price for full piece of about 30 yards, 6½ cents per yard.

Drilling is used for pockets, for lining pants, etc.

Boat Sail Drill.

1458 Twilled Sail Drill, 29 inches wide, unbleached weight between 6 and 7 ozs. to the yard. Much used. Woven strong. Per yard........$0.08
Price for full piece of about 60 yards, 7½ cents per yard.

Cheese, Butter and Dairy Cloth.

1460 Unbleached Cheese Cloth, 36 inches wide, F. R. D..$0.02
About 80 yards to a piece, 2,500 yards to the bale. Bale price, 1¾ cents per yard.

1462 Unbleached 36 inches. Nabob Royal Cheese Cloth.. .02¾
Price for full piece of about 65 yards, 2½ cents per yard. About 2,000 yards to a bale.

1463 Unbleached Cheese Cloth. East Hampton, 36 inches wide, extra good value........ .03½
Price for full piece of about 50 yards, 3¼ cents per yard.

1464 Unbleached Cheese Cloth, Persian extra, 36 inches wide, extra fine quality........ .04
Price for full piece of about 65 yards, 3¾ cents per yard.

1465 Bleached Butter Cloth, Jersey, 36 in. wide. 03½
Price for full piece of about 60 yards, 3¼ cents per yard.

1466 Bleached Dairy Cloth, 45 inches wide...... .04½
Price for full piece of about 120 yards, 4½ cents per yard.

Denims.

1480 Blue Denims, Haymaker..$0.08
Price for full piece of about 60 yards, 7½ cents per yard.

1482 Blue Denims, Uncasville.. .10
Price for full piece of about 60 yards, 9½ cents per yard.

1484 Blue Denims, Jaffray xxx.. .11
Price for full piece of about 60 yards, 10½ cents per yard.

1486 Blue Denims, York.. .12
Price for full piece of about 60 yards, 11¼ cents per yard.

1488 Blue Denims, Lawrence, 9 ounce.. .13
Price for full piece of about 60 yards, 12 cents per yard.

1490 Brown Denims, Jaffray xx.. .10
Price for full piece of about 60 yards, 9½ cents per yard.

1492 Brown Denims, Everitt.. .12
Price for full piece of about 60 yards, 11¼ cents per yard.

1494 Brown Denims, Amoskeag, 9 ounce.. .15
Price for full piece of about 60 yards, 14 cents per yard.

1496 Striped or Checked Denims, heavy weight, blue or brown.. .11½
Price for full piece of about 60 yards, 11 cents per yard.

1498 Striped Denims, York Mills, best made, brown stripe and blue stripe.. .12½
Price for full piece of about 60 yards, 11¾ cents per yard.

1499 Striped Denims, extra heavy weight, blue or brown fancy stripes, cassimere patterns. Per yard.. .15
Full piece of about 60 yards, 14 cents per yard.

New Denims.

1502 York Denims, wire twist and very durable. 8 ounces to the yard. Plain gray only color. Width, 28 inches. Per yard..$0.12½
Full piece of about 55 yards, 11¾ cents per yard.

1505 York Denims, wire twist, same as above, only heavier. Weight, 9 ounces to the yard. Plain gray only. Per yard.. .15
Full piece of about 55 yards, 14 cents per yard.

1508 York Mills, dark brown mixed, heavy twilled Denims. Width, 28 inches. Weight per yard, 7 ounces. Price.. .11
Price for full piece of about 57 yards, 10½ cents per yard.

1509 York Denims, dark brown mixed. Weight per yard, 8 ounces.. .12½
Price for full piece of about 55 yards, 11¾ cents per yard.

1510 York Denims, dark brown mixed. Weight per yard, 9 ounces. Price.. .15
Price for full piece of about 57 yards, 14 cents per yard.

Fancy Denims.

1512 York Fancy Mixture Denims, 28 inches wide. Blue and gold, blue and white, or blue and red. Per yard.. $0.15
Full piece of about 60 yards, 14 cents per yard.

Denim for Art Work.

1515 Fancy Colored Denim, 36 inches wide, the newest thing for fancy needle work; ladies embroider it for artistic curtains, sofa pillows, table covers, and other house decorations The colors are; Apple green, tan, old rose, yellow, light blue, gray, red with black, or red with white. Price, per yard.. $.25

Ducking.

Per yard.

1520 White Duck, 8 ounces; 29 inches wide... $0.08
Price for full piece of about 65 yards, 7½ cents per yard.

1522 White Duck, Stark, 8 ounces; 29 inches wide.. .10
Price for full piece of about 65 yards, 9½ cents per yard.

1524 White Duck, Stark, 10 ounces; 29 inches wide.. .12½
Price for full piece of about 65 yards, 11¾ cents per yard.

1526 White Duck, Stark, 12 ounces; 29 inches wide.. .15
Price for full piece of about 65 yards, 14 cents per yard.

1528 White Duck, 40 inches wide. Western Star, 8 ounces.. .17
Price for full piece of about 65 yards, 16 cents per yard.

1530 Brown or Drab Duck, 27 inches wide, for overalls, hunting coats or jumpers.. .10
Price for full piece of about 65 yards, 9¾ cents per yard.

1532 Brown or Drab Plain Colored Duck, for overalls, and jumpers; 29 inches wide; best quality.. .12½
Price for full piece of about 65 yards, 12 cents per yard.

By anticipating some of your wants and making your order 100 pounds, you can get it by freight at minimum cost.

Less than 100 pounds is charged as 100 pounds, so you can see where the saving comes in.

Wide Ducks.

The following widths and weights are the ones most used for harvester aprons, tents, stack covers, awnings, etc. Best quality, double and twisted threads. Plain white.

See index for above articles ready made.

Order No. 1540.

Width.	Weight per square yard about 20 oz. No. 6. Per yard.	Weight per square yard about 18 oz. No. 8. Per yard	Weight per square yard about 15 oz. No. 10. Per yard.
28 inch.	$0.22	$0.20	.17
30 inch.	.24	.22	.18
34 inch.	.26	.24	.20
36 inch.	.28	.26	.22
38 inch.	.30	.27	.23
40 inch.	.32	.29	.24
44 inch.	.35	.32	.27
48 inch.	.38	.34	.29
52 inch.	.42	.37	.31
56 inch.	.44	.40	.34
60 inch.	.47	.43	.36
66 inch.	.52	.47	.40
72 inch.	.56	.51	.43
84 inch.	.65	.59	.50
96 inch.	.85	.76	.65
120 inch.	1.05	.86	.81

Prices on other widths and weights quoted on application.

Price for full roll, about 100 yards, 5 per cent less than above prices.

Awning and Tent Fancy Duck.

NOTE: Scalloped Awning and Tent Trimming is made to order only. Prices will be quoted on application. Always state width of trimmings and style and quality of duck wanted.

1542 Fancy Tent Duck, width, 31 inches, in even or broken wide stripes, brown and white and blue and white; 8 ounces. Per yard...........$0.12½
Full piece about 50 yards, 12 cents per yard.

1543 Fancy High Colored Tent or Awning Duck, width, 31 inches. Orange, white and black in narrow, broken or wide even stripes. Per yard.. .15

1544 Awning Duck, red and white, in even narrow or wide stripes or wide broken stripes. Per yard.. .18

1545 Awning Duck, brown, black, green or blue, with white, in narrow, even or wide broken stripes. Per yard.. .15

1546 Awning Duck, brown and yellow or yellow and white, even wide stripes. Per yard........ .15
Full piece, about 50 yards, 5 per cent discount from above prices.

Fancy Ticking.

1550 Fancy Red, White and Blue Twilled Feather Ticking, width, 31 inches, colors fast, medium or wide stripes; good, firm cloth. Per yard....$0.12
Full piece of about 50 yards, 11½ cents per yard.

1552 Blue Plaid Ticking, 30½ inches wide, colors are fast, and plaids are medium or large. Per yard.. .10
Price for full piece of about 50 yards, 9½ cents per yard.

Bed Ticking.

These goods are made blue and white stripe only.

Per yard.

1556 Straw Ticking, Oakland B., 27 inches $0.05
Price for full piece of about 55 yards, 4¾ cents per yard.

1558 Straw Ticking, Swift River, 30 inches .. .06
Price for full piece of about 55 yards, 5½ cents per yard.

1560 Straw Ticking, Amoskeag H , 30 inches... .07
Price for full piece of about 55 yards, 6½ cents per yard.

1562 Ticking, Amoskeag G., 31 inches........... .08
Price for full piece of about 55 yards, 7½ cents per yard.

1564 Amoskeag D , new improved, 31 inches... .10
Price for full piece of about 55 yards, 9½ cents per yard.

1566 Feather Ticking, Amoskeag A., new improved, 31 inches.. .11
Price for full piece of about 55 yards, 10½ cents per yard.

1568 Feather Ticking, Amoskeag ACA., best plain tick made, new improved, 32 inches..... .12½
Price for full piece of about 55 yards, 11¾ cents per yard.

1570 Herring Bone Feather Ticking, 31 inches wide, blue and white stripe only, very heavy and firm.. .15
Price for full piece of about 55 yards, 14 cents per yard.

1572 Amoskeag Tick, ACA., 36 inches wide..... .18
Price for full piece of about 55 yards, 17 cents per yard.

1574 Conestoga Ticking, 60 inches wide, double fold. Blue and white narrow stripes. Tick can be made with sewing but two seams. Heavy cloth, fast colors.. .32½

We try to say what we mean and to mean what we say.

Sateen Twilled Skirting or Awning Tick.

Per yard.

Nothing made for the purpose that will give such long wear for the money.

1580 Skirting Sateen Twill, double-fold, 32 inches wide; body of goods is drab color and stripes are of cardinal or navy $0.10
Price for full piece of about 50 yards, 9¼ cents per yard.

1584 Sateen Twilled Skirting, Amoskeag, 32 inches wide, drab, striped with cardinal, white and gold or cardinal, brown and blue. Heavier and stronger than above. Thoroughly good and serviceable. Weight, 8 ounces to the yard. .15
Price for full piece of about 50 yards, 14½ cents per yard.

1586 Sateen Twilled Skirting, finest thing made, 32 inches wide, superior color combinations. They are navy ground with fine white stripes, drab ground with fine stripes of gray and brown, drab with red, gray and gold, or drab with blue and gray. Per yard .... .25
For full piece of about 50 yards, 22½ cents per yard.

Montgomery Ward & Co.'s Alliance Carpet Warp.

Our Alliance Warp is carefully made of good cotton, hard and evenly twisted, of uniform size and long reel, 4 ply, No. 8½ yarn, 90 inch reel: five pounds will make 25 yards of yard wide carpet. We do not sell less than 5 pounds of white or any one color.

Per pound.

1590 White Allance Cotton Warp (sold in 5 pound bundles only), net weight $0.15

1592 Colored Alliance Cotton Warp (sold in 5 pound bundles only), net weight .... .17
Colored Carpet Warp comes in brown, orange, red, green, black or medium blue; one color in each bundle. Special prices will be given on quantities of 300 pounds or more.

Weaving Cotton or Cotton Yarn for Hand Looms.

1594 White Weaving Cotton, single thread, numbers 8, 10 and 12. We do not sell less than 5 pounds, one bundle. Per pound $0.15

1596 Colored Weaving Cotton, No. 10, only size. Colors: Brown, red, blue, green, old gold, yellow, orange or black; sold in 5 pound bundles of one color only. Per pound .... .25

Bags and Sacks.

All our grain sacks except No. 1600, are seamless, will hold two bushels and are perfect. *No discount on grain bags.*

	Each.	Bale Price.
1600 Grain Bags, 2 bushels, good and strong	$0.12	$11.00
1604 Grain Bags, 2 bushels, American A.	.13	12.00
1606 Grain Bags, 2 bushels, Rock City	.16½	15.50
1608 Stark A Bags, 2 bushels	.17	16.00

Grain bags are put up 100 to the bale. We sell any quantity. Bags are sold subject to the fluctuation of the market. Each. Per Bale.

1610 Wool Sacks, size, 90x40 inches; weight, 3¼ pounds $0.28 $25.00
Prices herewith quoted are not guaranteed. We shall charge market value the day order is filled.
Burlaps fluctuate every day in price, 1-16 to ¼ cents.

1612 Burlap Wheat Bags, 2 bushels.
8 oz., 5c. 10 oz., 6c. 12 oz., 7c.

1614 Burlap Wheat Bags, 4 bushels.
8 oz., 7c. 10 oz., 8c. 12 oz., 9c.

Burlap Sacking.

1616 Weight per yard.

7 oz.	8 oz.	9 oz.	10 oz.	11 oz.	12 oz.
3¾c.	4c.	4¼c.	5c.	5½c.	6c.

Price for full piece of about 225 yards, ¼ cent less per yard than for cut length. Above is 40 inches wide, about 225 yards in each piece. Special prices will be furnished on large quantities of Burlap.
If you use any amount you should certainly write us.

COTTON BATTING.

Almost all dealers sell cotton batting by the roll, and while nothing may be said regarding their weight, people suppose they are getting 16 ounce rolls, as they have always been put up that way. *Almost all dealers have their batts put up to-day with but 12 ounces or ¾ of a pound to a roll,* which makes comparisons of the prices by the roll obviously unfair, unless weight is taken into consideration.

All our rolls weigh about 16 ounces—1 pound each (except No. 1630, the cheapest). We say about 16 ounces, as they are as near that uniform weight as can be put up. Some may exceed that while others may be a trifle under. The average is one pound each. Our batts are patent folded, and are not simply a wad of cotton to be repicked and put into the quilt in bunches. Each batt is nicely papered, is folded and will open up, all the same thickness, 36 inches wide and 7 feet long.

Cotton batting is put up 50 pounds to the bale, and if sold in that quantity an extra discount of 5 per cent will be allowed. Per roll.

1630 Cotton Batting, Telephone E 1 .... $0.07
1632 Cotton Batting, fair quality, M. W. & Co., D. .08
1634 Cotton Batting, good quality, M. W. & Co., B .... .10
1636 Cotton Batting, better quality, M. W. & Co., B B .... .12
1638 Cotton Batting, fine quality, M. W. & Co., A .... .13
1640 Cotton Batting, clean white, M. W. & Co., A A .... .15
1642 Snow White Cotton Batting, 16 ounce roll, used for medical purposes, baby quilts, etc.; extra long staple, no specks. Per roll .... .25

2—2nd

Cotton Wadding.

Per sheet.

1644 Cotton Wadding, slate color only, good cotton, nicely glazed; size about 32 inches by 36 inches. Per dozen sheets $0.20 $0.03

1646 Cotton Wadding, white, nicely finished, clean and white; size, about 28 inches by 39 inches. Per dozen sheets $0.25 03

SHIRTINGS.

Our shirting stock will be found fully up to our standard for completness of assortment and good value. We aim to have every good thing on the market, and at right prices always.

1660 Southern Plaid Shirtings. These goods are well known, and are sold largely in the southern states. They come in plaids and checks of brown, or blue and white, or fancy effects. Not fine quality, but made of strong cotton, and are good value for the price. Width, 22 inches. Per yard $0.04½
Full piece of about 58 yards, 4 cents per yard.

1662 Shirtings in checks, plaids or stripes, blue and white, brown and white, and blue and brown checks; good weight; 25 inches wide .... .07
Price for full piece of about 53 yards, 6½ cents per yard.

1664 Shirtings in checks or plaids, blue and white, excellent goods at moderate price; 28 inches wide .... .08
Price of full piece of about 56 yards, 7½ cents per yard.

1666 Twilled Shirting, in stripes only, blue, brown or shaded. These goods are real good and strong; 27 inches .... .08½
Price for full piece of about 54 yards, 8 cents per yard.

1668 Heavy Twilled Shirtings, small checked patterns. Medium brown, dark brown or dark blue combined with white or red, gold and other colors: 27 inches wide .... .09
Price for full piece of about 54 yards, 8½ cents per yard.

1672 Amoskeag Excelsior Shirting, in checks, plaids or stripes, blue and white, brown and white, or red, white and blue. We particularly recommend these goods; 30 inches wide .... .09
Price for full piece of about 54 yards, 8½ cents per yard.

1674 Old Fashioned Hickory Stripe, in blue and white or brown and white, reliable goods, good weight; 27 inches wide .... .09
Price for full piece of about 57 yards, 8½ cents per yard.

1675 Old Hickory Striped Shirtings strong and heavy, better than above, blue and white or brown and white .... .10
Full piece of about 50 yards, 9½ cents per yard.

1676 Clarendon Extra Heavy and Fine Shirting or jumper cloth, neat styles, fast colors. Made in checks or plaids, in blue and white only. Width, 30 inches .... .10
Price for full piece of about 61 yards, 9½ cents per yard.

1678 Shirtings, heavy wire twist, and double cable, in checks, plaids, or stripes; blue, brown or fancy colorings; 27 inches wide .... .12½
Price for full piece of about 49 yards, 12 cents per yard.

1680 Shirtings, best goods, made expressly for M. W. & Co.'s trade, in checks and plaids; small, medium or large, blue and white, red and white, or red, white and blue, also in pin checks in blue and white, and stripes in blue and white only; nothing better made; 31 inches wide ...... .15
Price for full piece of about 53 yards, 14 cents per yard.

1682 Shirting, same goods as above, but wider; 33 inches wide .... .16
Price for full piece of about 54 yards, 15 cents per yard.

Cheviot Shirtings.

1686 Beverly Chevoit Shirtings, 27 inches wide. For strength, evenness of cloth, weight and beauty of patterns we believe this shirting surpasses every other line ever sold at this price. Styles are fine thread stripes of red, gold or white, on dark navy or indigo ground; dark blue mixed ground with small wine check; brown gounds with narrow fancy stripe, or medium red and white mixed stripe on brown. Per yard $0.09
Price for full piece of about 50 yards, 8½ cents per yard.

1688 Cheviot Shirting, in small or medium checks, also stripes in blue, brown or fancy colorings, light, medium or dark: 27 inches wide. .10
Price for full piece of about 54 yards, 9½ cents per yard.

1690 Cheviot Shirting made in blue and white or blue, red and white checks; heavy weight; 27 inches wide .... .12
Price for full piece of about 50 yards, 11½ cents per yard.

1692 Cheviot Shirting, double fold, fine goods, light weight, checks in blue and white, brown and white, dark mixed pin check, stripes in blue and white, brown and white, and fancy coloring; width, 27 inches .... .12
Price for full piece of about 50 yards, 11½ cents per yard.

1694 Hercules Cheviot. A shirting of extraordinary strength and wearing qualities. It is made in plain blue mixture, also stripes of red on blue ground; width, 27 inches .... .10
Price for full piece of about 50 yards, 9½ cents per yard.

INSURED MAIL PACKAGES.
See Page 1.

A New Shirting.

1696 Fast Black "Bull-Hide" twilled shirting. Same as No. 1708, but in black ground with small figures or stripes of white. Per yard $0.11½
Full piece of about 50 yards, 10¾ cents per yard.

Napped Shirting.

1698 Amoskeag Napped Shirting, fluffy on the wrong side, similar to cotton flannel, extra warm, in stripes only, brown or fancy coloring, 27 inches wide $0.11
Price for full piece of about 50 yards, 10½ cents per yard.

1700 Amoskeag Napped Shirting, same as above, but in checks and plaids only; brown, blue, red, white and blue, and other fancy colorings, 27 inches wide .... .12
Price for full piece of about 50 yards, 11½ cents per yard.

Indigo Twilled Shirting.

1708 Indigo Twilled Shirting, blue drill ground with small white figures, stripes and checks, similar in appearance to the Indigo calico, but with a sateen finish and soft; made expressly for shirts, colors guaranteed; 28 inches wide .. $0.12½
Price for full piece of about 42 yards, 12 cents per yard.

1710 Plain Indigo Twilled Drill Shirting, 56½ inches wide, color fast, cloth woven strong and firm .... .12
Price for full piece of about 45 yards, 11½ cents per yard.

Moleskin Shirting.

Also used for Dresses.

1720 A new production, woven plain and printed on one side. The other side is fleeced or napped. Cloth is very fine and strong, good weight and is sure to be popular; styles are checks, plaids or stripes; checks are in gray or brown mixed ground with gold or white lines; stripes are slate, tan, drab or gray mixture, broken and chevron stripes; plaids are light or medium gray or brown mixture with black bars, width 28½ inches. Per yard .... .12½
Price for full piece of about 55 yards, 12 cents per yard.

LINING DEPATMENT.

Silesias, Percalines, Corset Jeans, Fancy Sateens, Crinolines, Grass Cloths, Wigans, Paddings, Canvas, Hair Cloths, Cambrics, Paper Cambrics, Farmer's Satins, Fiber Chamois, Imitation Hair Cloths, Taffeta Skirt Linings, etc.

Robe Lining see No. 4240.
Quilted Linings see No. 3500.

A noticeable fact of late has been the growing demand for better grades of linings. People are beginning to appreciate the importance of using good linings in wearing apparel of all kinds, as by so doing much is added to the fit, wearing qualities and general appearance of one's attire. Best wearing results are obtained from loosely woven effects in dress materials, by making them over strong linings, perfectly fitted to withstand the strain on seams.

We have given special attention to this department, and know that we can furnish better linings for less money than any other house in America. We buy direct from the manufacturers and handle only goods of known merit.

A New Departure.

For the convenience of many of our customers who may want to purchase dress linings, but do not care to make up the necessary list from stock quotations, we have had *Lining Sets* put up in different qualities and staple colors, each set containing an average quantity of the different linings most commonly sold for a dress. Considering the quality and quantity of materials these *Lining Sets* are much cheaper than you could buy the goods for in the usual way from retail houses.

1740 Lining Set, put up in drab, slate, brown or black. Contains 6 yards kid finished cambric skirt lining, 2 yards drilling or corset jean waist lining, 1 yard wigan skirt stiffening. Per set $0.40

1742 Lining Set, all colors as above. Contains 6 yards kid finished cambric skirt lining, 2 yards good silesia waist lining, 1 yard French elastic canvas skirt stiffening. Per set .... .55

1744 Lining Set, black only. Contains 6 yards fast black, kid finished cambric, 2 yards silesia, black one side and white on the other, 1 yard best French elastic canvas. Per set .... .85

1746 Lining Set, put up in drab, slate, brown or black. Contains 6 yards kid finished cambric skirt lining, 2 yards silk finished percaline waist lining, 1½ yard cotton hair cloth skirt stiffening. Per set .... .65

1748 Lining Set, put up in drab or brown. Contains 2 yards of fancy figured percaline waist lining, 6 yards of taffeta or rustle lining for skirt, and 1 yard of French linen canvas. Per set 1.00

Corset Jeans for Waist Linings.

1750 Biddeford Corset Jeans, drab, slate, light or dark brown, and black or white. Per yard .. $0.05
Price for full piece of about 55 yards, 4⅞ cents per yard.

1752 Naumkeag Corset Jeans, best sateen finish, light drab, slate, light or dark brown, black or white. Per yard .... .07
Price for full piece of about 48 yards, 6½ cents per yard.

Write out what you want, enclose the money, tell where to send and we do the rest. Easiest thing in the World.

Cambric or Skirt Linings.

Standard Quality.

1756 Best. Soft Kid Finished Cambric. Colors: Slate, drab, gray, light, medium or dark brown, black, tan, myrtle, navy or wine. All dark, staple shades; 27 inches wide. Per yard......$0.03½
Price for full piece of about 55 yards no less.

1757 Soft Kid Finished Cambric, 27 inches wide, high colors: Cream, white, pink, light blue, scarlet, yellow, etc. Per yard.................. .04½
Full piece of about 55 yards, 4¼ cents per yard.

1758 Fast Black Cambric, warranted perfectly fast dye; 27 inches wide...................... .06
Price for full piece of about 49 yards, 5¾ cents per yard.

1760 Soft Finished Cambric, black one side white the other; 27 inches wide...................... .07
Price for full piece of about 50 yards, 6¾ cents per yard.

1762 Paper Cambric, double fold, in black, brown, drab or slate; 36 inches wide.... .... .06
Price for full piece of about 53 yards, 5¾ cents per yard.

1764 Paper Cambric, double fold, in high colors. Red, pink, white, light blue, dark blue or green; 36 inches wide...................................... .07
Price for full piece of about 54 yards, 6¾ cents per yard.

A New Skirt Lining.

1765 Taffeta or Rustle Lining is an improved skirt lining, universally used by first-class dressmakers; it is of fine texture, light weight, watered and highly finished. It has just enough stiffness and makes a pleasing rustling sound when worn, resembling silk; is a superior skirt lining in every way. The colors are: Tan, medium brown, seal brown, light gray, medium drab, dark slate, black or white; width, 25 inches. Per yard..$0.08½
Price for full piece of about 55 yards, 8 cents per yard.

Farmers' Satin and Italian Cloth.

Per yard.

1766 Farmers' Satin, black; 27 inches wide.....$0.25
Full piece of about 50 yards, 23½ cents per yard.

1768 Farmers' Satin, black; 27 inches wide...... .50
Full piece of about 50 yards, 48 cents per yard.

1770 Farmers' Satin, black, 54 inches wide...... 1.00
Price for full piece of about 54 yards, 95 cents per yard.

1772 Farmers' Satin, black; 54 inches wide.... 1.25
Price for full piece of about 50 yards, $1 14 per yard.

1774 Farmers' Satin, black: 54 inches wide....... 1.40
Price for full piece of about 40 yards, $1.30 per yard.

1776 Farmers' Satin, 27 inches wide, fine quality. Colors: Navy blue, bottle green, old gold, wine, tan, golden brown, light blue, medium blue, dark brown and scarlet.................... .40
Full piece of about 28 yards, 37 cents per yard.

Fine Fancy Sateen Linings.

1780 Fancy Sateen Lining, 36 inches wide, made in drab or slate, with small fancy figures printed in fast colors. Per yard................$0.19
Full piece of about 50 yards, 18 cents per yard.

1782 Extra Fine Sateen Lining, 38 inches wide, black on one side tan and drab on the other, over which is printed neat designs in fast colors. This class of linings is now much used. Per yard .... .25
Full piece of about 50 yards, 24 cents per yard.

Silesias.

For waist lining and tailors' use, 36 inches wide.

1790 Fernwood Silesia, made in black and all staple shades. A very good lining, much better than usually sold at 10 cents. Per yard..........$0.08
For full piece of about 60 yards, 7¾ cents per yard.

1792 Silesia, in plain colors, good and firm...... .10
Price for full piece of about 60 yards, 9 cents per yard.

1794 Silesia, fine quality, all colors. We recommend this grade.................................. .15
Price for full piece of about 60 yards, 14 cents per yard.

1796 Fast Black Silesia, 36 inches wide.......... .16
Price for full piece of about 55 yards, 15 cents per yard.

1798 Silesia, black one side, white the other, or drab one side and black the other............ .16
Full piece of about 58 yards, 15 cents per yard.

Fancy Silesias.

1800 Silesia, fancy check, stripes or figures; medium colors.. .15
Price for full price of about 60 yards, 13½ cents per yard.

1802 Silesia, light colored stripe or fancy pattern .18
Full piece of about 60 yards, 16 cents per yard.

1804 Silesia, fancy colored, checked one side, black the other.. .20
Full piece of about 45 yards, 18 cents per yard.

Percaline.

A soft waist lining now much used. While light in weight, it is firm and does not stretch, and is preferred to any other lining by ladies who have their dresses tightly fitted; owing to its light silky texture it does not make bulky seams or enlarge the size of the dress waist.

Per yard

1806 Percaline, Moire silk finished, all colors, 36 inches wide..$0.12½
Full piece of about 55 yards, 12 cents per yard.

Figured China Percaline.

Per yard.

1808 Fancy Figured Percaline, the nicest summer waist lining, light weight, plain colored back, either in grey or tan, with pretty figures of another color; some are striped, this lining is usually retailed for about 20 cents, we have secured a bargain and make the price, per yard....$0.10
For full piece of about 40 yards, 9½ cents per yard.

Linings for Stiffenings.

For bottoms of dresses, collars and cuffs and tailors' use.

Linings of this class are in great demand owing to the present styles of wide bottom, flared or bell-shaped skirts Per yard.

1810 Wigan, black, gray, brown or white, similar to crinoline, but stiffer, with less body than canvas; 33 inches wide..................................$0.07½
Full piece of about 55 yards, 7 cents per yard.

1811 Grass Cloth, a very light weight, wiry stiffening much used for skirts and interlinings for large sleeves now so fashionable. It keeps the latter in shape without noticeably increasing the weight. Colors: Gray, brown, black or natural tan. Per yard.................................. .08
Full piece of about 30 yards, 7½ cents per yard.

1812 Padding, a stiff, glazed lining for bottom of dresses, in black, cream brown or slate; 27 inches wide.. .12
Price for full piece of about 66 yards, 11½ cents per yard.

1813 Elastic Canvas, good quality, used for skirt stiffening. Black, brown or gray; width, 25 inches. Per yard... ....$0.12
Full piece of about 50 yards, 11¼ cents per yd.

1814 Linen Canvas, French elastic, the best lining for bottoms of dresses; it retains its stiffness longer than any other lining; no dress can set well without it. Colors: White, natural linen, brown, gray or black. Medium grade. Per yard, .15
Price for full piece of about 50 yards, 13 cents per yard.

1816 Linen French Elastic Canvas, better quality than the above. Per yard.................. .20
Price for full piece of about 50 yards, 19 cents per yard.

1818 A New Crinoline, gray striped, elastic finish, 25 inches wide. Especially adapted for use in present style skirts.............................. .10
Full piece of about 50 yards, 8¾ cents per yard.

1820 Crinoline, 20 inches wide, for lining collars, cuffs, skirts, sleeves, etc., in black, brown, slate or white. Per yard........................ .08
Full piece of 12 yards, 80 cents per piece.

Linings—Continued.

1822 Crinoline, width 33 inches; black, brown, slate or white; extra heavy.......................... .12
Price for full piece of about 30 yards, 11½ cents per yard.

1824 Black Barred Crinoline, 33 inches wide.... .13
Price for full piece of about 30 yards, 12 cents per yard.

1826 Tailors' Canvas, natural color only......... .15

1827 Tailors' Canvas, natural color only, better than above... .18

1828 Imitation Hair Cloth, gray striped, width 17 inches; for skirt stiffening. This is a new light-weight stiffening, made of elastic cotton, in exact imitation in color and texture of the imported hair cloth, and costs very much less. Price, per yard... .25
Price for full piece of about 45 yards, 23½ cents per yard.

1830 Gray Hair Cloth, 16 inches wide............ .60
Price for full piece of about 65 yards, 50 cents per yard.

1832 Buckram, similar to wigan, 24 inches wide, put up in rolls, in black or white only.
Per yard.. .12
Price for full piece of about 8 yards, 85 cents.

Fibre Chamois.

1835 Fibre Chamois is a new interlining, made of the felted fibre of the spruce tree, and is intended by the manufacturers to take the place of almost every other kind of lining made. It is of light weight, a square yard of No. 10 weighing but 2⅛ ounces; is used for puffed sleeves and flare skirts, and if crushed will regain its original shape by slightly shaking. As a cloak interlining is without doubt a good thing. There are three weights—No. 10, light; No. 20, medium; No. 30, heavy. These are 64 inches (more than 1¾ yards) wide.
Our price, per yard $0.32½
For full piece of 10 yards, 30 cents per yard.

Linen Scrim.

1836 Linen Scrim for stiffening sleeves, etc., black, slate, brown, tan or cream, width 27 inch.
Per yard..$0.14
Full piece of about 45 yards, 12⅛ cents per yard.

1837 Linen Scrim, white, width 25 inches.
Per yard.. .15
Full piece of about 45 yards, 13⅛ cents per yard.

Serge Coat Lining.

1840 Mohair Serge Lining, 32 inches wide. Black or brown only. Per yard...............................$0.55

WHITE GOODS DEPARTMENT.

We make a specialty of *White Goods*. Our purchases are of such a magnitude each season, that we are enabled to offer extraordinary values in each line. Write us for samples and compare qualities with what other houses sell. We feel safe in asserting that no other house which reaches and is accessible to the consumer, can compete with the values we give in foreign and domestic white goods

Apron and Skirting Lawns.

Made with broad band, fancy openwork, satin stripes and imitation hemstitching borders on one side of goods, for bottom of skirts, aprons, etc.

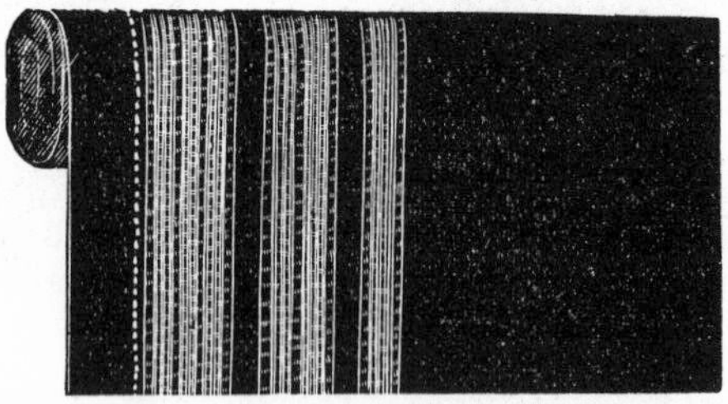

1851 White Apron or Skirting Lawn, 39 inches wide. The cloth is fairly fine, and clearly made with a wide lace border in three styles; five single rows of lace work, three double rows, or two rows of three together. They all have a wide imitation hemstitched hem at bottom.
Per yard...$0.08
Full piece about 54 yards, 7½ cents per yard.

1852 Plain White Apron or Skirting Lawn, width, 39 inches. A clean, strong cloth of even weave, has wide border composed of three double bands, five single bands or four graduated bands, lace openwork with eight-inch imitation hemstitched hem at bottom.
Per yard... .10
Full piece about 54 yards, 9 cents per yard.

1856 White Apron or Skirting Lawn, 40 inches wide, a smooth sheer lawn with broad band borders in three styles; eleven even narrow sateen stripes, twelve narrow sateen stripes divided into threes, or three rows containing six narrow stripes each. Stripes are woven to have the appearance of tucking. Per yard............ .12
Full piece about 55 yards, 11 cents per yard.

1857 White Fine Lace Checked Apron Lawn, 40 inches wide, border is formed by alternate stripes of sateen and lace work, and is in three styles; narrow even stripes; wide even stripes, or wide broken stripes. Per yard................ .12½
Full piece of about 55 yards, 12 cents per yard.

1858 Fine White Apron or Flouncing Lawn, 40 inches wide. This cloth is beautifully fine and sheer and the borders the prettiest you ever saw; they are in three styles, fine lace work separated by nine graduated bands of sateen edged with fancy cord; ten narrow sateen bands with fine lace work between and wider band of each at top and bottom; six bands composed of five tiny sateen stripes with lace check between each band and imitation hemstitched hem at bottom. Per yard .... .16
Full piece of about 55 yards, 15 cents per yard.

1859 Plain White Apron or Flouncing Lawn, 40 inches wide, with a narrow row of drawn work seven inches from the bottom, giving the appearance of a real hemstitched border. The cloth is evenly woven and the border is of double thickness. Per yard............................ .14
Full piece or about 55 yards, 13 cents per yard.

1860 Fine White Apron or Flouncing Lawn, 40 inches wide, with border composed of even or broken satin stripes, separated by several rows hemstitched open work. A very handsome lawn. Per yard......................... .... .15
Full piece of about 55 yards, 14 cents per yard.

1861 Fancy Apron or Skirting Lawn, 39 inches wide, a very fine quality of white lawn with side borders composed of several rows of heavy satin bands, printed over with a graceful and dainty trailing vine pattern in pink, light blue, heliotrope or gold. One of the prettiest styles imaginable Per yard............................ .20
Full piece of about 50 yards, 15 cents per yard.

Hemstitched Apron and Flouncing Lawns.

Per yard.

1868 Ladies' White Hemstitched Apron or Flouncing Lawn, 37 inches wide, with 5-inch hem. Good lawn, and at the price should be a rapid seller....... ....$0.18
For full piece of about 30 yards, 17 cents per yd.

Drapery or Curtain Fabrics.

1880 Figured Silkaline, 36 inches wide, large floral designs in exact imitation of drapery silks. Very pretty for inexpensive mantel drapes, curtains, sofa pillows, head rests, etc.; also used for covering fine quilts. Colors are: Nile green, olive, white, light blue, old rose, gold or orange. Per yard.... ....$0.08
Full piece of about 60 yards, 7½ cents per yard.

1886 Plain Vestibule Drapery, also called Silkaline, because of its close resemblance to silk drapery. It is 30 inches wide, solid colored and in the following shades only: Old rose, orange, lemon or reseda. Its uses: Lining for heavy winter window curtains, for book cases, covering for bureau cushions, toilet sets, lining of transoms, window curtain drapery, and its peculiar silk-like finish makes it adapted to dress purposes. Per yard... .... .12½
Full piece of about 50 yards, 11½ cents per yard.

White Goods—Continued.

1888 Figured Silk-aline Drapery; width, 30 in.; best goods, improved finish, new loop design in quiet contrasting colors on grounds of cream, light blue, gold, old blue or gobelin, salmon. Very ornamental for sofa pillows, head rests draperies, throws, or covering for fine comfortables. Per yard.......$0.14 Full piece of about 50 yards, 13 cents per yard.

Drapery Swiss.

1900 Imported White Dotted Swiss Muslin, for curtains and drapery; also used for dresses; three styles, small, medium and large lappet spots. Width, 30 inches. For sash curtains, or in place of the more expensive lace curtains; it is very pretty; also used for covering toilet sets. Per yard............$0.12½ Full piece of about 50 yards, 12 cents per yard.

1901 Imported Drapery Swiss, 30 inches wide, small or medium size dots, better quality than above. Per yard............ .15 Full piece of about 50 yards, 14 cents per yard.

1902 Dotted or Figured Curtain Muslin, 40 inches wide, small dots, medium dots, crescent pattern or cluster spot pattern. Very pretty and washes perfectly. Per yard............... .16 Full piece of about 50 yards, 15 cents per yard.

1903 Colored Figured Curtain Muslin, 40 inches wide, white grounds with a maltese cross design in red, gold or blue; a good seller. Per yard... .17 Full piece of about 50 yards, 16¼ cents per yard.

1904 White Imported Swiss Drapery, 36 inches wide, small dots, medium dots or fancy lattice figure outlined with raised cords. Per yard.... .18 Full piece of about 50 yards, 17 cents per yard.

1906 Imported Curtain Swiss, white with woven coin spots and pretty side border, tape effect, also fine corded stripe and figure with neat border, width 30 inches; will make dainty and stylish wash curtains. Price, per yard......... .15 Full piece of about 50 yards, 14¼ cents per yard.

1909 New Figured Curtain Swiss, 36 inches wide, imported. We have three new designs all of which are extremely stylish and pretty. Bowknot pattern, Empire pattern (wreath), cluster dot pattern. This is one of the most stylish window dressings that we have been able to find. Per yard................................ .20 Full piece of about 50 yards, 19 cents per yard.

1910 New Imported Drapery Swiss, all white, 36 inches wide; designs are small and are in leaded stained glass effects, being outlined with fine raised cords. Some patterns have center of lace open work. Price, per yard... .... .22 Full piece of about 50 yards, 20 cents per yard.

Plain White Curtain Organdie.

1911 Plain White Organdie, very stylish and much used now for ruffled window curtains. It washes perfectly, and is very serviceable; width is 48 inches. This fabric is also extensively used for white dresses. Price, per yard.......... .15 Full piece of about 40 yards, 14½ cents per yard.

Point d'Esprit.

1912 Point d'Esprit. A white lace net of small mesh with tiny worked spots scattered profusely over it. Much used for sash curtains, bed draperies, chamber curtains or in making toilet sets, splashers, etc. Width, 48 inches. Per yard.... .22 Full piece of about 50 yards, 20½ cents per yard.

Scarf Embroidery or Bureau Scrim

1913 Embroidery Scrim, 18 inches wide, fast edges. Can be used plain or worked with worsted, silk, linen or cotton, and with or without ribbons in or under open work at sides. Makes a very cheap, easily washed, lasting tidy or scarf. Per yard...$0.15

1914 Scarf Scrim, 18 inches wide, selvedge edges, plain center, as above, but it has more openwork at the sides. Center can be worked, left plain or threads drawn to make design wanted. Two rows openwork each side. Per yard......$0.20

1916 Cream, 18 inches wide, with coarse mesh in center, two rows of tied openwork at each side, hemstitched selvedge edge of finer scrim. Makes pretty fancy work. Per yard................... .25

1918 Cream Scrim, 18 inches wide; will wash and iron perfectly. Made in two patterns. Fine scrim in center, one row of three-inch openwork and heavy thread pattern at either side; heavy hemstitched selvedge edge, with three rows of openwork and heavy thread design in center; patterns look like hand-work; very pretty. Per yard................................... .30

1920 Deep Cream Embroidery Scrim, 19 inches wide, with hemstitched parted openwork and bands of light blue, gold or pink on both sides. Please state which color you want.............. .32

1922 Bolting Cloth Embroidery Scrim, 18 inches wide, fine as silk. Has exquisite tied openwork in center of two twilled bands separated by delicate hemstitching on both edges. The center is plain, edges fast. This is an extra rich pattern, and will make very dainty art work with the proper needle work and taste displayed..... .42

Plain Curtain Scrim.

1926 Plain Scrim, cream color; width 36 inches; makes good looking but inexpensive curtains for bed rooms, etc. Per yard...................$0.12 Full piece of about 40 yards, 11¾ cents per yard.

1928 Plain Curtain Scrim, fine quality, cream color; width 36 inches; will wear and wash well. Nice for curtains, splashes, tidies, etc. Per yard... .25 Full piece of about 40 yards, 23½ cents per yard.

Fast Black Wash Goods.

These goods are all absolutely fast black—will not crock nor grow rusty after repeated washing. Will stand all ordinary acid tests, and are not rotted in dyeing. For a light weight, cool dress nothing is more serviceable and generally satisfactory. We have a splendid line of patterns. Samples will be cheerfully sent upon request.

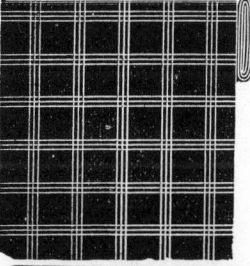

1930 Fast Black Check and Broken Plaid Lawn, 28 inches wide; three patterns, small, medium and large. Per yard.. .....$0.10 Full piece of about 50 yards, 9¼ cents per yard. These cuts do not properly represent the goods. The designs are much enlarged to plainly show patterns.

1936 Fast Black Hemstitched, checked and Plaid Lawn, 28 inches wide. Five patterns, small, medium, and large, even and fancy. Good cloth, good styles. Per yard.......$0.15 Full piece of about 50 yards, 14 cents per yard.

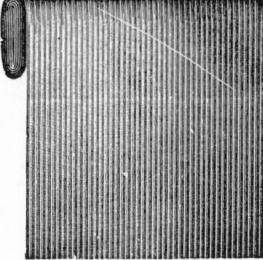

1937 Fast Black Corded Stripe Lawn, neat pattern. Width, 28 inches. Per yard.......$0.10 Full piece of about 50 yards, 9¾ cents per yard.

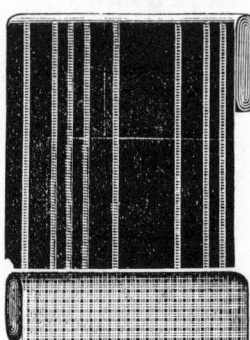

1938 Fast Black Hemstitched Lawn in five designs, narrow, medium and wide stripes. Width, 28 inches. The cloth is extra close and firm, and the hemstitching an exact imitation of that done by hand..........$0.16 Full piece of about 50 yards, 15 cents per yard.

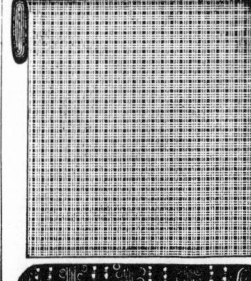

1939 Fast Black Checked Lawn, small pattern and good sellers; width, 28 inches. Per yard.......$0.12 Full piece of about 50 yards, 11¼ cents per yard.

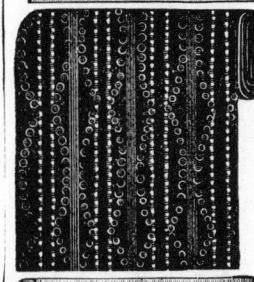

1940 Fast Black Brocaded Striped Lawn, stripes separated by a row of imitation hemstitched lace openwork, sateen stripe shows a brocaded design. Per yard.......$0.14 Full piece of about 50 yards, 13¼ cents per yard.

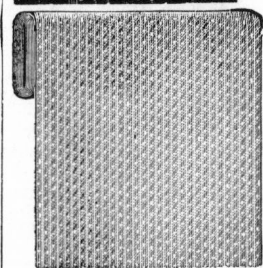

1941 Fast Black Dimity Swiss, 28 in. wide. A sheer and pretty swiss lawn in narrow corded stripes, with tiny worked spots between. Neat and serviceable. Per yard.......$0.16 Full piece of about 50 yards, 15 cents per yard.

Plain Black India Linen.

While called linen, it is not, but resembles lawn, and is made from a fine grade of Sea Island cotton, carefully and evenly spun, and taking on a soft, silky finish. Ours are bright black, fast colors; will not crock, and we know upon comparison with others will be found cheap.

1960 Plain Black India Linen, 29 inches wide..$0.10 Price for full piece of about 24 yards, 9½ cents per yard.

1964 Plain Black India Linen, 30 inches wide.... .15 Price for full piece of about 24 yards, 14 cents per yard.

1966 Plain Black India Linen, 30 inches wide.. .17 Price for full piece of about 24 yards, 16¼ cents per yard.

1968 Plain Black India Linen, 30 inches wide... .23 Price for full piece of about 24 yards, 21¼ cents per yard.

1970 Plain Black India Linen, 30 inches wide.. .33 Price for full piece of about 24 yards, 31 cents per yard.

Nainsooks.

We take especial pride in our Nainsooks; our sales are so large, our purchasing power so great, that we are enabled to offer exceptional values.

Plain White Nainsooks.

English Manufacture.

Our goods will be found upon comparison to be firmer and heavier than usually sold.

1980 Plain Nainsook, fine and sheer, 31 inches wide... ... .$0.12 Price for full piece of about 20 yards, 11 cents per yard.

1982 Plain Nainsook, fine and sheer, 31 inches wide................................ .15 Price for full piece of about 20 yards, 14 cents per yard.

1983 Plain Nainsook, fine and sheer, 36 inches wide. Per yard............................... 17 Price for full piece of about 20 yards, 16 cents per yard.

1984 Plain Nainsook, fine and sheer, 36 inches wide.................................... .20 Price for full piece of about 20 yards, 18 cents per yard.

1986 Plain Nainsook, fine and sheer, 36 inches wide.................................... .25 Price for full piece of about 20 yards, 23 cents per yard.

White Lace Striped Lawns.

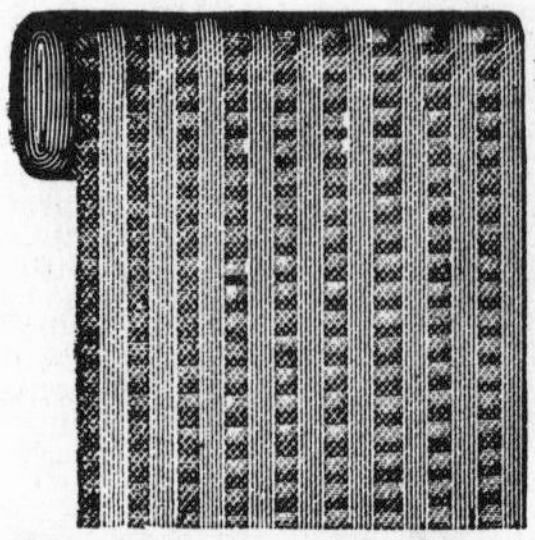

1990 White Lace Striped Lawn; width, 27 inches: fine open lace work in three widths of stripes, narrow or medium, even stripes or medium broken, Price, per yard.$0.07
For full piece, about 50 yards, 6¾ cents per yard.

1991 White Lace Striped Lawn, 25 inches wide. Three patterns: Narrow, medium or wide stripes. Per yard.................................$0.08
Full piece of about 50 yards, 7½ cents per yard.

1992 White Lace Striped Lawn, 28 inches wide. This number is a rare bargain. We bought it from an English manufacturer at very much less than value. It is fine and sheer, has satin stripes about half an inch apart through which run fine openwork stripes; about every three inches is a heavier corded lace stripe. The effect is exceedingly pretty. Actual value 18 cents. Our price, while they last. Per yard................ .10
Full piece of about 50 yards, 9¼ cents per yard.

1993 White Brocaded Stripe and Lace Openwork Lawn, very pretty; 28 inches wide. Three styles: Narrow, medium and wide stripes. Per yard.. .12
Full piece of about 50 yards, 11¼ cents per yard.

1994 White Lace Striped Lawn, 28 inches wide. This is another great bargain, bought at same time as No. 1992, but is a finer quality. The style is very similar, being a combination of satin stripes and fine drawn openwork on the sheerest of lawn. The lace work, of which there is a half-inch stripe every three inches, is the most delicate and dainty work imaginable. Retailer's price for this material is 20 cents. Ours, while it lasts. Per yard.................... .12½
For full piece of about 50 yards, 11¾ cents per yard.

1996 White Corded Lace Stripe Lawn, 26 inches wide; very strong and showy; a favorite. Three styles: Narrow, medium or wide stripes. Per yard.. .14
Full piece of about 50 yards, 13 cents per yard.

1997 White Fine Lace Striped Lawn, 28 inches wide, one of the prettiest lace effects of the season. We have these styles—narrow, medium and wide stripes. Per yard.......................... .15
Full piece of about 50 yards, 14 cents per yard.

1998 White Lace Striped Lawn with dots between the stripes. A new effect, very dainty and stylish, width 28 inches. We have three styles—narrow, medium and wide stripes.
Per yard.. .18
Full price of about 50 yards, 17 cents per yard.

Satin Striped Nainsook.

Bookfold.

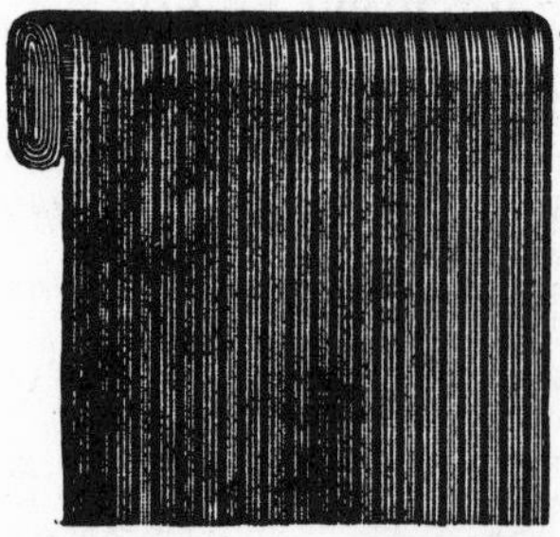

2000 White Satin; Striped Nainsook width, 25 inches; a good looking cloth at a low price. We have three styles. Hair line stripe, narrow single stripe or medium herringbone stripe. Per yard....$0.08
For full piece of about 24 yards, 7½ cents per yard.

2002 White Satin Striped Nainsook, finer than above; width, 26 inches, 3 styles—fine hair line stripe, narrow herring bone, even stripe, or medium broken or uneven herringbone stripe.
Per yard..$0.10
Full piece, about 24 yards, 9¼ cents per yard.

2003 White Satin Striped Nainsook, 27 inches wide, better quality than above. Three styles; narrow, medium or wide stripes.
Per yard.. .12
Full piece of about 50 yards, 11¼ cents.

2004 White Satin Striped Nainsook; width, 26 inches. A fine quality, one that will wear and wash well. Come in four styles; hair line stripe, fine broken stripe, narrow, even or medinm size broken herringbone stripes. Per yard.......... .15
Full piece, about 24 yards, 14 cents per yard.

2006 Extra Fine White Satin Striped Nainsook; width, 27 inches; fine, clear bleach and superior satin finish. Comes in four styles; hair line stripe, narrow single line stripe, narrow single herringbone or broken herringbone stripes.
Per yard.. .20
Full piece of about 24 yards, 18 cents per yard.

INSURE YOUR PACKAGES. Mail packages may be insured against loss by paying a fee of 5 cents for each $5.00 in value. Write "Insured Mail" on your order, enclose the money, and we will do the rest.

Checked White Nainsook.

Longfold.

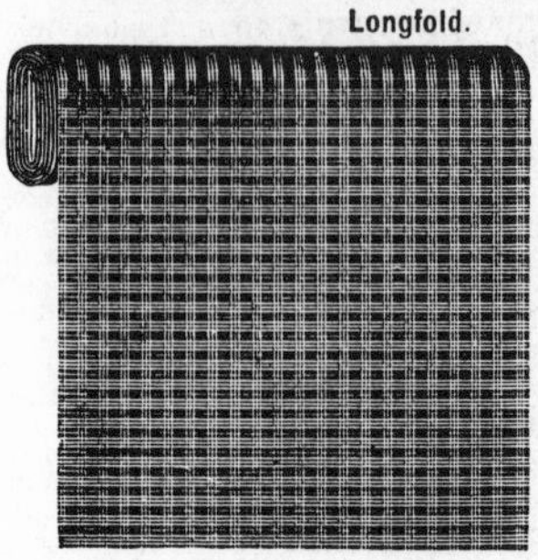

2010 Nainsook Checks, 25 inches wide, and in three patterns; small, medium and large. Did you ever buy one so low before? At the price, the cloths and patterns are surprisingly good; a leader for prices.
Per yd...$0.04½
Same price for full piece of about 50 yards.

2012 Checked Medium or Dice Pattern Nainsook, 25 inches wide; checks are small. Comparison of prices will show we are headquarters for white goods $0.06
Price for full piece of about 50 yards, 5½ cents per yard.

Bookfold.

2014 White Nainsook, Checks and Plaids; width 25 inches. Have three different styles; pin check, small dice checks, small bar checks. Per yard..$0.07
For full piece of about 24 yards, 7¼ cents per yard.

2016 White Nainsook Checks; width, 27 inches, A good quality at a popular price. Have four styles; pin check, small line check, small dice check, ¾-inch satin bar check or large dice check, Per yard.............................. .10
For full piece of about 24 yards, 9½ cents per yard.

2018 Fine Nainsook Checks and Plaids, 28 inches wide, 4 patterns; Pin check, small dice check, small single bar check, or 1-inch broken line plaid. Per yard.............................. .15
Full piece of about 24 yards, 14 cents per yard.

2020 Extra Fine Nainsook, Checks and Plaids, width, 30 inches. A handsome cloth, one that will wear and retain its fine finish after repeated washings. Comes in four patterns: Pin check, small dice check, small single satin bar check, or 2-inch broken satin line plaid. Per yard.... .20
Full piece of about 24 yards, 18 cents per yard.

White Victoria Lawns.

There goods are woven the same as India Linens, but are not so thin or sheer.

2030 White Victoria Lawn, 25 inches wide. Not cheese cloth because low-priced, but made of even threads, smoothly woven, well bleached and strong. Your merchant cannot buy it for any less. Per yard................................$0.05
Price for full piece of about 24 yards, 4¾ cents per yard.

2032 White Vicioria Lawn, 26 inches wide; has the qualities of the above number, made by the same mill, but finer. Don't judge the quality by the price; buy some or send for samples, then you will buy. Per yard.............................. .06
Price for full piece of about 50 yards, 5¼ cents per yard.

2034 White Victoria Lawn, 30 inches wide, better. .08
Price for full piece of about 24 yards, 7 cents per yard.

2036 White Victoria Lawn, 30 inches wide. A very good seller.............................. .10
Price for full piece of about 24 yards, 9½ cents per yard.

2038 White Victoria Lawn, 32 inches wide; well liked.............................. .12
Price for full piece of about 24 yards, 11 cents per yard.

2040 White Victoria Lawn, 32 inches wide; very fine weave and excellent finish. Per yard...... .15
Price for full piece of about 24 yards, 14 cents per yard.

2042 White Victoria Lawn, 32 inches wide; a highly finished, clean and sheer lawn, free from all specks or imperfections so often found in such goods. Per yard.............................. .18
Full piece of about 24 yards, 16¾ cents per yard.

White Striped Lawns.

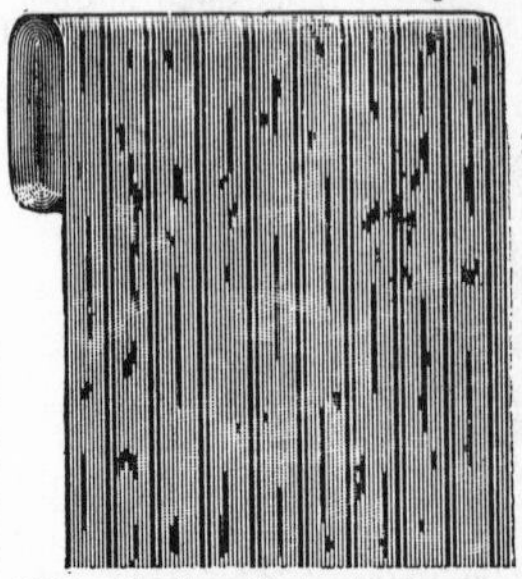

2058 White Corded Stripe Lawn, neat and serviceable, 25 inches wide; one line, two line or three line stripes.
Per yard.....$0.05½
Full piece of about 50 yards, 5¼ cents per yard.

2059 White Striped Lawn, 25 inches wide, splendid value for the price. Three patterns; narrow single line, double line, medium space between, or four line with space of plain lawn between. Per yard.............................. $0.07
Full piece of about 50 yards, 6¾ cents per yard.

2061 White Satin Stripe Lawns, 27 inches wide, three staple patterns. Narrow single, double or triple stripes. Per yard.............................. .08
Full piece of about 50 yards, 7¾ cents per yard.

Lawns—Continued.

2064 White Fancy Satin Stripe lawns, 28 inches wide; new and sightly patterns and a good wearing cloth; three styles, narrow, medium or wide stripes. Per yard.............................. .10
Full piece of about 50 yards, 9¼ cents per yard.

2065 White Satin and Corded Stripe Lawns, 27 inches wide, a strong and well made cloth; will stand frequent washings. We have three patterns: Wide, medium or narrow. Per yard..... .10
Full piece of about 50 yards, 9¼ cents per yard.

2067 White Satin Stripe and Dotted Lawn, 28 inches wide. A new and very pretty effect, different from anything before made. The cloth is substantially made and comes in three styles, narrow, medium or wide stripes.
Per yard..$0.12½
Full piece of about 50 yards, 11¾ cents per yard.

2069 White Fancy Corded Stripe Lawn, 28 inches wide. This is a decidedly novel and pretty pattern. It has a raised wavy cord following the stripes, the space between being cross-lined, forming small checks. We have three widths, single, double or triple cord stripes.
Per yard..$0.16
For full piece of about 50 yards, 15 cents per yard.

Checked and Plaid Lawns.

2070 White Checked Lawns, 25 inches wide, checks formed by slightly raised cords; three styles, small, medium or large checks.
Per yard..$0.06
Full piece of about 50 yards, 5¾ cents per yard.

2071 White Plaid Lawn, 26 inches wide, a good substantial cloth for the price. The styles: Half inch check, one inch plaid formed by double cross bars or two inch broken plaid. Per yard. .07½
Full piece of about 50 yards, 7¼ cents per yard.

2072 White Fancy Checked Lawn, 27 inches wide. Three sizes, small, medium or large. A neat and pretty style. Per yard.............................. .10
Full piece of about 50 yards, 9½ cents per yard.

2073 White Plaid Lawn, 27½ inches wide, plaid formed by an arrangement of narrow satin lines running each way, leaving a medium square of plain lawn between. Two sizes, one seven line and one eight line plaid. Per yard.. .10
Full piece of about 50 yards, 9½ cents per yard.

Lace Checked Lawn.

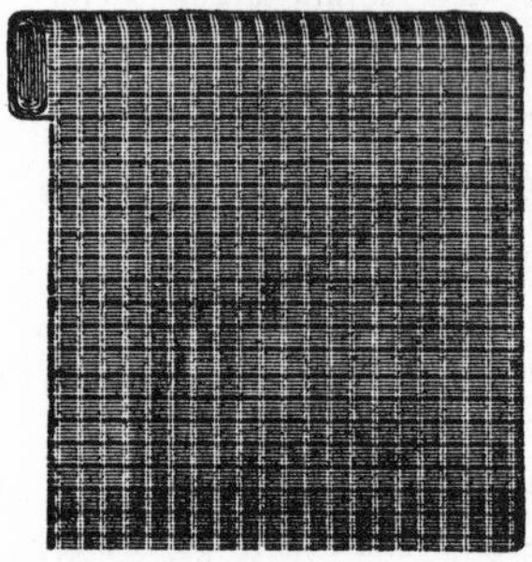

2076 White Lace Checked Lawn, 26 inches wide. Good quality, checks formed by rows of drawn openwork firmly made. We have four styles, one inch single line, one-inch double line, one and-one-half inch triple line, two inch quadruple.
Per yard...$0.12
Full piece of about 50 yards, 11¼ cents per yard.

2078 White Lace Checked Lawn, 27 inches wide. Hemstiched openwork. Similar to above but finer in quality. We have three styles, small, medium or large checks. A very pretty lawn.
Per yard..$0.15
Full piece of about 50 yards, 14 cents per yard.

2080 Fine Lace Plaids; width 28 inches. Body of goods is a fine lace weave, through which run satin bars forming plaids. Have two styles; one-inch even or square plaids and two inch broken bar plaid. Will make a delightfully cool summer dress. Per yard.............................. .20
Full piece of about 50 yards, 18 cents per yard.

White Welt or Heavy Corded Pique.

Now much used for children's wear and ladies' suits or vests.

2085 White Welt Pique, 27 inches wide, fine cord. Per yard..$0.14
Full piece of about 40 yards, 13¼ cents per yard

2086 White Welt Pique, 27 inches wide. Two styles: Fine or heavy cord. Per yard.............. .18
Full piece of about 40 yards, 17 cents per yard.

2087 White Welt Pique, 27 inches wide. Wide, heavy cord; splendid quality. Per yard.............. .25
Full piece of about 40 yards, 23½ cents per yard.

Fancy Welt Pique.

2088 White Fancy Pique, 26½ inches wide, two styles, one a narrow stripe formed with two extra heavy cords in pairs, the other with four heavy cords arranged together. Per yard $0.16
Full piece of about 40 yards, 15 cents per yard.

2089 White Fancy Pique, 28 inches wide. A very neat and handsome lace stripe design, in three styles, narrow, medium broken or wide.
Per yard.. .22
Full piece of about 40 yards, 21 cents per yard.

White Marseilles.

2090 White Marseilles, 25 inches wide; a heavy white goods similar to Pique, but made in birdseye fancy checked patterns. We have two styles, small or medium size. Per yard.......... .24
Full piece of about 40 yards, 23 cents per yard.

Pique Brilliant.

PRETTY FOR CHILDREN'S DRESSES.

2092 White Pique Brilliant, 28 inches wide. A very pretty cloth, not so heavy as welt pique. Pattern is a small brilliant woven spot. Per yard........ .15
Full piece of about 40 yards, 14 cents per yard

2093 White Pique Brilliant, 27½ inches wide, finer quality than above. Two styles, small or medium size patterns. Per yard.............. .18
Full piece of about 40 yards, 17 cents per yard.

White Cotton Canvas or Duck Suiting.

Very stylish now for Ladies' or Misses' Eton or Blazer Suits. *Also for Men's Duck Trousers or Waiters' Coats.*

2095 White Cotton Duck Suiting, 28 inches wide. Per yard....... .10
Full piece of about 50 yards, 9½ cents per yard.

2096 White Cotton Duck Suiting, 28 inches wide, better quality, double thread. Per yard....12½
Full piece of about 50 yards, 11½ cents per yard.

Plain White India Linen.

The name is a misnomer; it is not linen, but a fine grade of Sea Island cotton woven like fine sheer lawn, but smoother finished, and is much used. Kindly send for samples and compare ours with others of the same price.

Per yard.

2100 India Linen, 30 inches wide..............$0.08
Price for full piece of about 24 yards, 7½ cents per yard.

2102 India Linen, 30 inches wide.......... .10
Price for full piece of about 24 yards, 9 cents per yard.

2104 India Linen, 30 inches wide......... ......12½
Price for full piece of about 24 yards, 11½ cents per yard.

2106 India Linen, 30 inches wide................ .15
Price for full piece of about 24 yards, 14½ cents per yard.

2108 India Linen, 30 inches wide................ .20
Price for full piece of about 24 yards, 18½ cents per yard.

2110 India Linen, 30 inches wide................ .25
Price for full piece of about 24 yards, 23½ cents per yard.

2112 India Linen, 36 inches wide.... .... .30
Price for full piece of about 24 yards, 28½ cents per yard.

Ecru India Linen.

2116 Ecru or Deep Cream India Linen, 30 inches wide. Per yard..................................$0.10
Full piece of about 24 yards, 9¾ cents per yard.

2118 Ecru or Deep Cream India Linen, 30 inches wide; finer quality. Per yard................... .12
Full piece of about 24 yards, 11½ cents per yard.

Swiss Mull.

Our prices are right. Send for samples and prove it.

Per yard.

2130 Swiss Mull, 25 inches wide.................$0.09
Price for full piece of about 24 yards, 8½ cents per yard.

2132 Swiss Mull, 30 inches wide................ .11
Price for full piece of about 24 yards, 10 cents per yard,

2134 Swiss Mull, 30 inches wide................ .15
Price for full piece of about 24 yards, 14 cents per yard.

2135 Swiss Mull, 30 inches wide 20
Price for full piece of about 24 yards, 19 cents per yard.

India Dimity.

Dimities are perhaps the most popular line of fancy white goods in demand this season. Their beautiful sheer textures and fine dainty patterns are a very strong recommendation to favor.

2136 Striped Dimity, white, 28 inches wide, made in three styles—fine single cord line, three line and four line cords. Per yard..........$0.12½
For full piece of about 35 yards, 11½ cents per yard.

2138 Striped India Dimity, 32 inches wide, very thin and sheer, but strong and wears well. Much used for children's dresses. Have three styles, single, double or three line stripes, all narrow and formed by raised threads or cords woven into plain goods. Per yard.............. .17
Full piece of about 30 yards, 15½ cents per yard.

2140 Fine Checked White Dimity, 30 inches wide. Three patterns—checks formed by tiny cords woven each way forming the checks. We have the single, double or treble line.
Per yard.. .20
Full piece of about 30 yards, 19 cents per yard.

2141 Fine Striped India Dimity, 32 inches wide. Very sheer and fine. Three widths—narrow, medium or wide stripes. Stripes are formed by grouping the fine raised thread lines.
Per yard... .... .25
Full piece of about 30 yards, 23½ cents per yard.

2142 Checked India Dimity; width, 32 inches. Very sheer, but strong and durable. Made of finest India cotton. Is far prettier, and will outwear many of the heavier fabrics. Have two styles—single or double cord line checks. Very small. Per yard............................ .35
Full piece of about 30 yards, 32 cents per yard.

White Figured, Striped and Dotted Swiss.

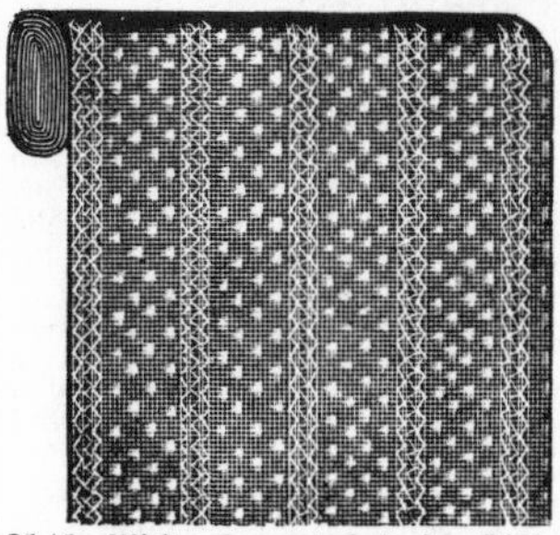

2147 White Dotted and Figured Swiss; width, 24 inches. A good thing at the price, which is very low for real Swiss. Three styles: fine or medium size dots and medium size oblong figure.
Per yard..$.08½
Price for full piece of about 30 yards, 8¼ cents per yard.

2148 White Imported Swiss. 24½ inches wide; two styles; small dot or medium figure—a Maltese cross design. Per yard...................... .10
Full piece of about 30 yards, 9¼ cents per yard.

2149 White Imported Swiss, 26 inches wide; two styles; Grecian scroll stripe or a combination of dot and medium figure. Per yard....... .12
Full piece of about 30 yards, 11½ cents per yard.

2150 White Imported Fancy Swiss, 26 inches wide; two styles, one a lace stripe with dotted space between, the other a small Maltese cross. Per yard..................................... .15
Full piece of about 30 yards, 14½ cents per yard.

2151 White Imported Dotted Swiss, 26 inches wide; four styles: small dot, medium dot, large dot, size of nickel or large dot, size of quarter dollar; a fine and serviceable swiss; one of our best sellers. Per yard......................... .16
Full piece of about 30 yards, 15½ cents per yard.

2152 White Imported Dotted Striped Swiss, 26 inches wide. This is a very popular number with us and is really very pretty. Two styles; a fancy stripe with medium dots or a fancy wavy stripe with small dots. Per yard......... .17
Full piece of about 30 yards, 16 cents per yard.

2153 White Imported Dotted Swiss, 27 inches wide; two sizes; very small or small medium dots. Per yard.................................... .20
Full piece of about 30 yards, 19 cents per yard.

2154 White Imported Dotted or Fancy Swiss, 30 inches wide, a popular number. We have two styles—pin dots or corded stripes with dotted space between; a beauty. Per yard.............$0.25
Full piece of about 30 yards, 24 cents per yard.

2156 White Imported Dotted Swiss, 30 inches wide. A fine quality with dots firmly woven. Three styles—pin dots, medium dots or large dots. Per yard .... .30
Full piece of about 30 yards, 23 cents per yard.

2157 White Imported Fancy Figured Swiss, 30 inches wide, exceedingly fine; a beautiful line, of newest patterns. We have four styles—a small figure with narrow line stripe, a small fancy sprig, a star and dot combined or medium size fancy figure. These patterns are all perfectly embroidered, and will stand any amount of washing. Per yard.................. .38
Full piece of about 30 yards, 36¼ cents per yard.

2158 White Imported Dotted Swiss, 30 inches wide. Dots are firm and beautifully worked on very fine swiss; have three sizes, pin dot, small dot or medium size dot. Per yard.............. .40
Full piece of about 30 yards, 38 cents per yard.

Fancy Colored Swisses.

2159 White Swiss with colored dots, width 26 inches. Neat and pretty for dresses or fancy household decorations; dots are small and are of the following colors: Pink, light blue, red or gold. Per yard.................................. .16
Full piece of about 30 yards, 15 cents per yard.

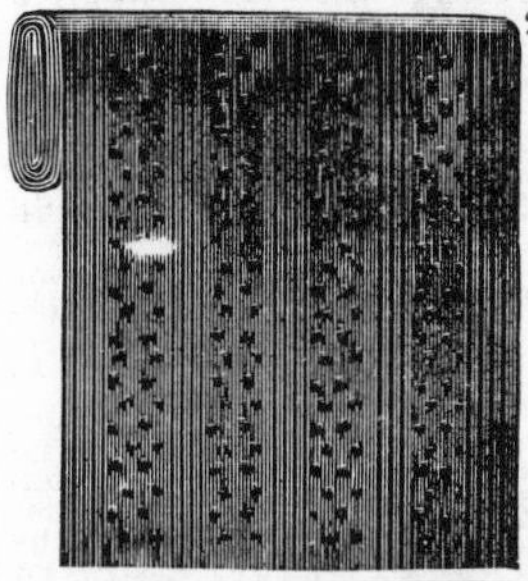

2160 Striped and Dotted Solid Colored Swiss, 26 inches wide. The prettiest swiss you ever saw for fancy party dresses; pattern is lace cord, striped with fine worked dots in spaces between the stripes; the tints are: Pink, light blue, canary yellow, cardinal or black.
Per yard $0.20
Full piece of about 30 yards, 18 cents per yard.

Fancy Printed Summer Novelties.

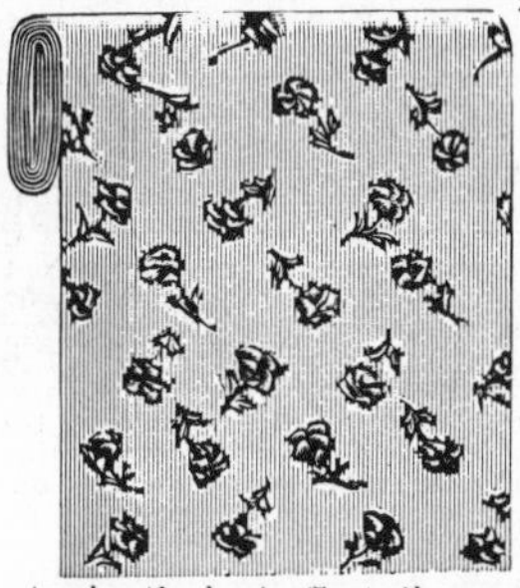

2165 Colored Printed White Lawn, 25 inches wide. This is the first and cheapest number, but unless looked at very closely might easily be taken for much higher priced goods. The design and colorings being really artistic. The printing is of single pansies with slightly bent stalk, and scattered with a careless grace over the white ground. There is just enough color in the flowers to give the best effect; they are in the following colors: Blue, red, gray and red combined; heliotrope, olive, or gold. The colors are nicely shaded, the stalks being mostly green. Per yard...... ......$0.07½
For full piece of about 50 yards, 7 cents per yard.

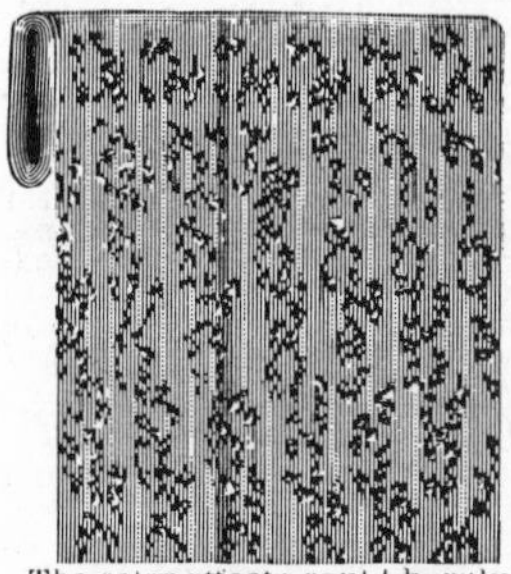

2166 Colored Printed White Lawn, 25 in. wide. This is just as pretty as the one above, though quite unlike it in detail. The lawn is not woven perfectly plain, but has an almost invisible strip of fine cords. The printing is of violets, some having long stalks, form wavy stripes about two inches apart; single violets with short stems being scattered between The color effects could hardly be better. They are: Blue with a little gold; red with green and gold; shades of grey, heliotrope and green; gold and green. Per yard.......... ....$0.08
For full piece of about 50 yards, 7¼ cents per yard.

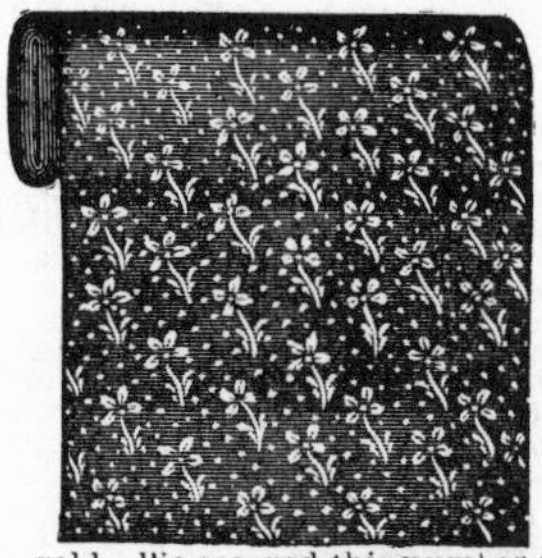

2167 Printed Dotted White Muslin, 30 inches wide, a handsome and inexpensive material for summer dresses. The cloth is fine and even, with small white dots set rather closely, and is printed all over with a medium floral design in beautifully blended colors. The general effects are of heliotrope, pink blue or gold We secured this number at a bargain by buying a large quantity and will let you share it while it lasts. Regular value 12½ cents.
Our price, per yard.......................... .08½
Full piece of about 50 yards, 8 cents per yard.

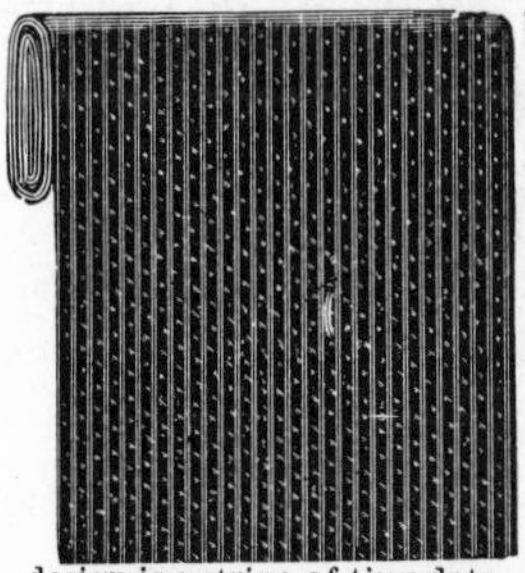

2168 Colored Lawn with printed Stripes, 27 inches wide; this is a nice, fine lawn and the style of printing, being exceedingly neat, should be a very popular number. The colors too are all good, dark as well as light; there is black and white, heliotrope and white navy and white, pink and white, or blue and white. The grounds are the color and the design white; the design is a stripe of tiny dots, and one-quarter of an inch apart; between the stripes are other dots a trifle larger and rest far enough apart to produce a very pleasing and genteel effect. The blue and pink are both pretty, full shades, the navy or black are equally good where something dark is wanted. Per yard.................. .10
For full piece of about 50 yards, 9½ cents per yard.

2169 White Corded Dimity, with Colored Dot, 28 inches wide. This is one of the staple items of fancy white goods, and appears every year as regularly as the season itself. Unless it had been an exceptionally good thing it would have died out long ago. But it has an increased sale every succeeding year. The ground is white, with fine corded lines, some evenly spaced, others in a broken effect; the dots, which are of the smallest pin-head size, are the only printing; the ground is quite thickly covered with them, but being very fine the color effect is light. Dots are of the following colors: Blue, pink, heliotrope or black. Per yard............... .10
For full piece of about 45 yards, 9½ cents per yard.

A Word to the Wise is Sufficient.

Lawns—Continued.

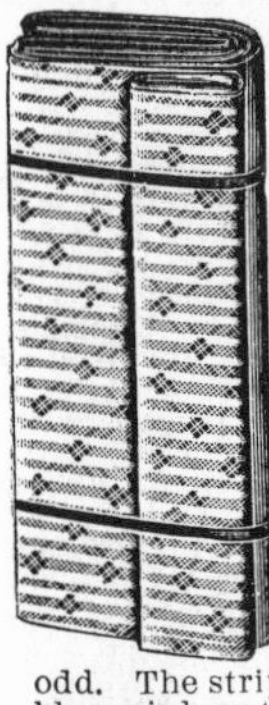

2170 Grecian Lawn, 40 inches wide; a firm and splendid washing fabric for ladies' shirt waists, dresses or wrappers. The principal feature of this work is its unique style; the color effect is rather light, the groundwork being formed by light colored stripes an eighth of an inch wide and one-half an inch apart. On a white ground over this is printed a diamond shaped figure made up of four smaller diamonds, those falling on the colored stripes being white and those on the white taking the color of the stripe. The figures are edged with a darker shade of color which gives tone to the whole design which, though it seems simple in detail, is of a superior style of work and will appeal principally to those who are seeking something odd. The stripes and figures are of gray, light blue, pink or tan. Per yard......................$0.10
Full piece of about 45 yards, 9½ cents per yard.

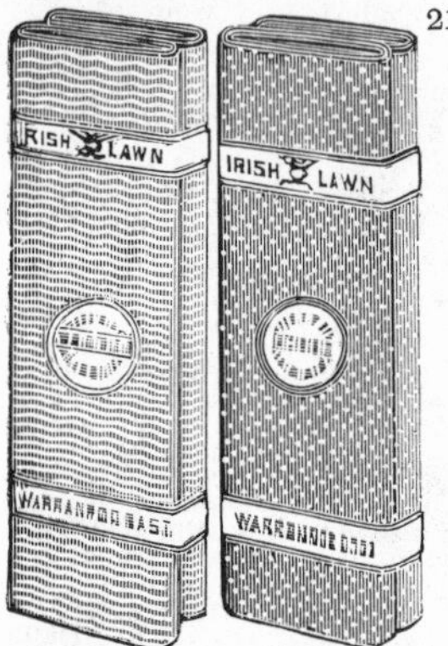

2172 Figured Irish Lawn, 39 inches wide, made by the Waukegan Mills, the most popular wash fabric of the season for Ladies' Shirt Waists, Summer dresses or wrappers; fast colors. Last year our trade was immense in these goods, and this year we intend to double it. We have secured a fine array of styles, something we fancy to suit the most fastidious; the cloth has real merit, and will wear well, will stand any amount of washing and "do up" perfectly. The black grounds with white dots, stripes, or small figures are exceedingly neat; tan grounds too are quite a feature this year, and printed with dots of brighter color is one of the prettiest styles; dots are in black, brown, red or blue; the same colors are printed in stripes. Another nobby effect is a wavy stripe of either nile, light blue, pink or black on a white ground; navy blue grounds with white dot. The following colored grounds have a stylish scroll design of white on gobelin blue, tan, pink or heliotrope. We also have the following plain solid colors: Tan, gobelin blue, pink or black. There are many inferior imitations of this fabric now on the market. The best and genuine Irish Lawns are retailed at not less than 12½ cents, usually 15 cents. Quantity makes price, so we have contracted for such an immense quantity that we will be able to continue our special price of per yard $0.10
Full piece of about 36 yards, 9¾ cents per yard.

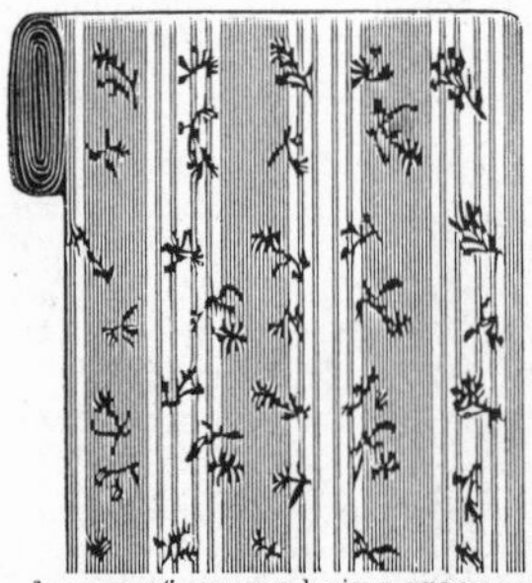

2173 Saxony Satin Striped and Printed Lawn, 27 inches wide; this is one of the light summer styles and would impress almost anyone as being very sweet and pretty; the ground is white, fine plain lawn with sateen stripes some ecru, others broken; over the groundwork is a dainty design of small colored flowers, buds, and leaves, the leaves of course being green, and the flowers printed in the following nicely shaded colors: Heliotrope, blue or pink; the general effect is light and fairy like. Per yard............. ....$0.12
Full piece of about 45 yards, 11½ cents per yard.

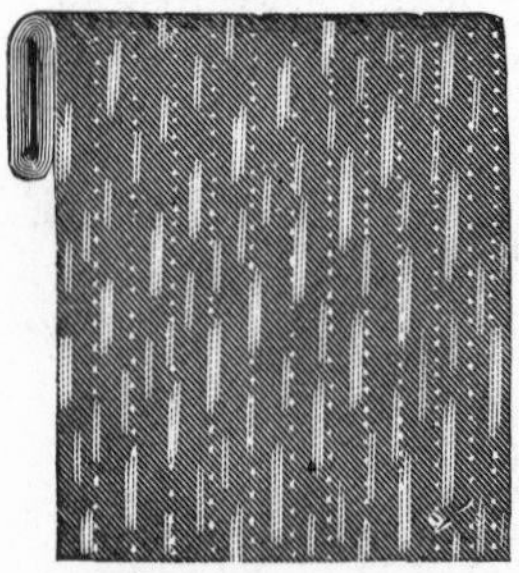

2174 Black Lawn, with colored printing, 27 inches wide. This is an unusually attractive novelty. For a dark effect it is one of the most stylish things we have ever seen. The printing is a tiny colored polka dot all over the black ground, and a broken stripe design, composed of rather longer dots and being printed to appear like illuminated dashes. They are about an inch in length, or rather longer, and run singly, double or three together. The color seems stronger in the center of the figure, and the dots smaller at the end of it. The printing is in the following colors, on black grounds only: Medium blue, old rose, heliotrope, gold or cardinal. Per yard...............................$0.12½
Full piece of about 45 yards, 11¾ cents per yard.

Lawns—Continued.

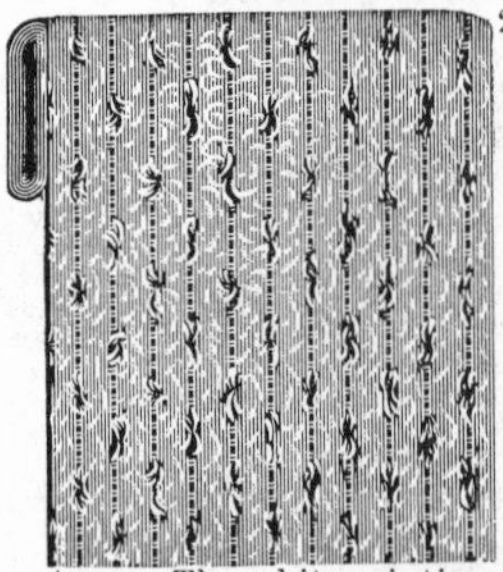

2175 Colored Lace Stripe and printed Lawn, 29 inches wide. Though the ground colors in this line are rather light, the general effects are somewhat darker than one might imagine, owing to the printing pretty well covering the ground colors. This cloth has a fine, lace stripe about an inch apart, and the printing is in black and white, on grounds of light blue, tan, pink or heliotrope. The white printing takes the form of a small crescent design or fine, close, dotted work, while the black is in a small floral or other fancy figure. The cloth is fine and the general effect novel and artistic. Per yard..................$0.12½
Full piece of about 45 yards, 11½ cents per yard.

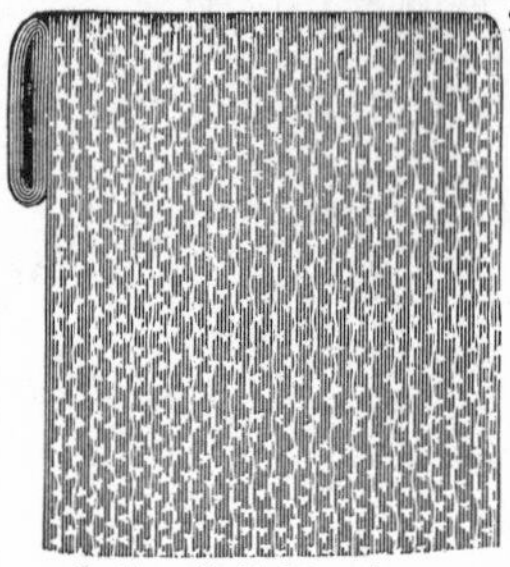

2176 Colored Figured Corded Dimity, 28 inches wide. This exquisite novelty might be considered the typical one of this season's styles. The figures are generally small this year, the colorings and work prettier than ever before; this one in particular we think a little more dainty in its general effect than anything else brought out; the corded ground work is very popular, and all soft light colors seemed to have been dyed especially for this design, which is simplicity itself. The colors are: Light blue, pink, heliotrope, nile, or black. These are the ground colors, the small floral figure is of white. For children's wear this seems perfect also for ladies where something dainty is desired. Send for samples. Per yard..........$0.12½
Full piece of about 45 yards, 11½ cents per yard.

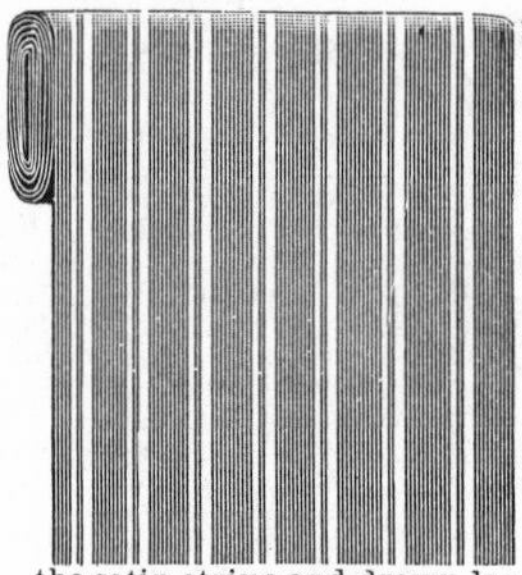

2178 Light Colored Lace and Satin Striped Lawn, 28 inches wide. This is a novelty without printing; the pretty weaving effects and delicate color tints are its features of beauty; the colors are cream, pale blue, heliotrope, or pink. The satin stripes in each color are of a slightly lighter shade than the groundwork, which gives a two-toned effect, besides the satin stripe and drawn lace work. There is a fine raised thread design. These are woven alternately, where something light and lacey is desired; there is nothing prettier. Per yard...................... $0.14
For full piece of about 45 yards, 13 cents per yard.

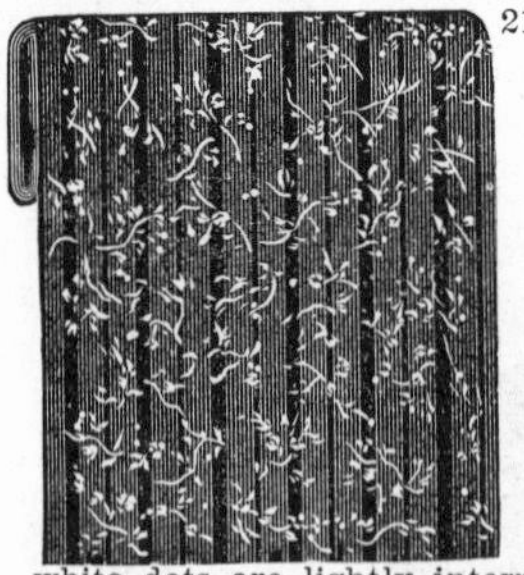

2180 Black Striped Lawn, with Colored Printing, 28 inches wide; the groundwork is fast plain black, with fancy woven brilliant stripes of same color; over this is printed a graceful design of flowers, moss rose buds, small green leaves, and tiny wild flowers in pretty bright colors; same effects are in heliotrope, green and gold; pink, green and blue, or heliotrope blue and gold; small white dots are lightly intermixed with the flower sprays, and though not prominent, add greatly to the effect. We consider it the best style of the seasons in dark lawns. It should be seen to be appreciated.
Per yard......... .. ..$0.14
Full piece of about 45 yards, 13 cents per yard.

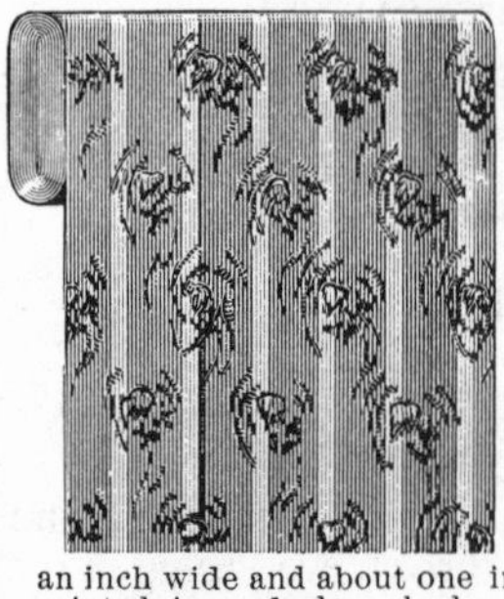

2182 Colored Figured Empress Dimity, 28 inches wide; this is one of the larger designs of this season's novelties; the dimity is in the corded weave, and the color effect of ground is striped as follows: Blue with white, pink with white, heliotrope with white, tan with white, or gray with white; the white stripes are about one-third of an inch wide and about one inch apart; over this is printed in a darker shade of the ground color a medium sized leaf and twig; these appear every few inches along the white lines with a drooping effect; intermixed with and surrounding these leaves is a design of fine dotted curves, apparently revolving round and about the leaves, but never touching them; the effect is stylish in the extreme.
Per yard...$0.16
Full piece of about 45 yards, 15 cents per yard.

Colored Silk Mull.

2190 Colored Silk Mull, 45 inches wide, in cream pink and light blue only. Per yard $0.39

Colored Mull de Paris.

For linings, hat trimmings and the many uses that a dainty, stylish woman can put it to, this is indispensable

Per yard.

2194 Mull de Paris, 24 inches wide, white.......$0.20
Price for full piece of about 24 yards, 19 cents per yard.

2196 Colored Mull de Paris, 24 inches wide, cream .... .22
Price for full piece of about 24 yards, 20 cents per yard.

2198 Colored Mull de Paris, 24 inches wide, pink or light blue.................................. .23
Price for full piece of about 24 yards, 21 cents per yard.

2200 Colored Mull de Paris, 24 inches wide, black.. .25
Price for full piece of about 24 yards, 23 cents per yard.

Silk Bolting Cloth.

Cream color only; used to paint on, or embroider for ends of scarfs, tidies, toilet sets, handkerchief cases, cravat cases, etc. Width, 40 inches.

2202 Silk Bolting Cloth, No. 3½. Per yard......$0.80
2204 Silk Bolting Cloth, No. 3½. Per yard...... 1.00

Prices on heavy Silk Bolting Cloth, all qualities, for milling purposes, furnished on application.

Tarletan.

Per yard.

2206 Colored Tarletan, 45 inches wide; green white, blue, pink, medium blue, rose or black..$0.12
Price for full piece of about 16¾ yards, 11½ cents per yard,

Decorative Fancy Art Tidies, Stand Covers, and Side-Board Linen.

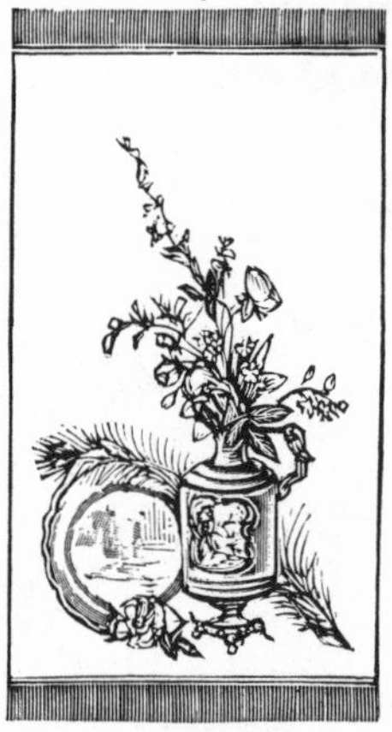

2250 Sateen Tidy, fringed ends; size, 15x30 inches. Cream colors with handsome vase and floral design in brown and light blue and other colorings; colors fast.
Each................ $0.12
Per dozen 1.35

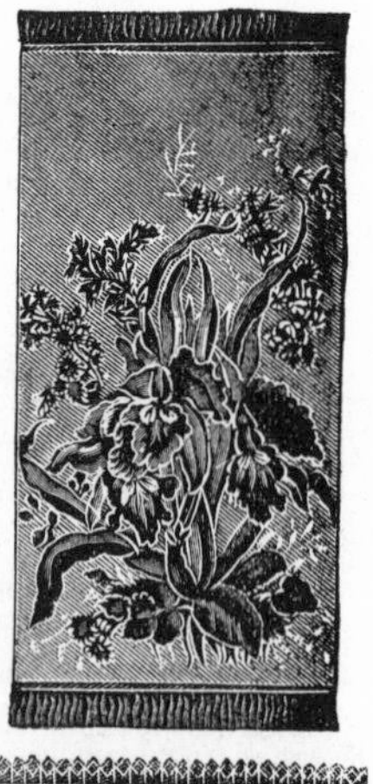

2252 Hand Painted Tidy. Size, 15x30 inches. Fast colors; fringed on both ends, sides hemmed. Flowers are tiger lily, purple lilies, etc., in natural colors, as are leaves and flowering vines. The term "hand painted" is a commercial one. They are printed in exact imitation. Backgrounds are cream, pink, blue, ecru or salmon.
Each... ....$0.12
Per dozen.............. 1.35

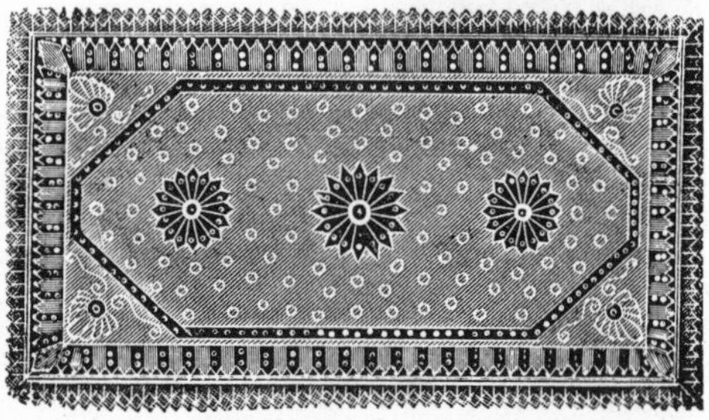

2254 All Over Lace Covered Tidy; size, 20x36 inches. Groundwork is cream, pink, olive or salmon, over which is a design to represent lace, with body of goods in different colors showing through. Edge is trimmed all around with fine 1½ inch wide lace. Colors fast. A very handsome ornament. Each..........................$0.25

Linen Covers—Continued.

2256 Tinsel Embroidered and Painted sateen scarf or Tidy. New designs and pretty as silk. Size, 14½x40 inches; fringed on both ends. Colors are; golden yellow,light blue or shrimp pink and green.
Each..............$0.22
Per dozen........ 2.45

2258 New Sateen decorative scarfs with hand-painted bolting cloth end; size, 14x42 inches. A handsome ornament at a low price; colors: Light blue, golden yellow or shrimp pink.
Each..............$0.25
Per dozen........ 2.50

2260 Tapestry Tidy; size, 20x30 inches. The center is a richly colored reproduction of painting on rare and costly tapestries. Edge is hemmed; both ends fringed; ground colors: Cream,blue, pink,ecru, or shrimp.
Each..............$0 16
Per dozen........ 1.75

2162 Fringed Cotton Stand Cover, 33x33 inches. The material is a fancy weave with hand painted design on each corner. Colors are: Light blue, orange, light green or pink. Each..$0.35
Per dozen 4.00

A New Novelty.

2263 Fancy Canvas Duck Table Covers, 41x41 inches. These covers are made of good quality white cotton duck or canvas with colored linen fringe all around to match tint of the corner design, which is outlined in tinted silk, the center being painted in same color. The tints are: Nile green, pink, light blue or gold. These covers are really very pretty.
Each $0.75

2264 Fancy Canvas Duck Stand Cover, same design and colors as above. Size, 28x28 inches.
Each .... .40
2265 Fancy Canvas Duck Mats, same design and colors as 2263. Size, 16x16 inches. Each ... .15
2266 Fancy Canvas Duck Bureau or Dresser Scarfs, same design and colors as 2263. Size, 22x48 inches. Each .... .50

Laundry Bags.

2269 Laundry Bag; size, 14x 25 inches; made from heavy figured drapery sateen, with white cotton drawing cord and tassels. A very useful and attractive article and a big seller. Colors: Old rose, tan or olive.
Each......................$0.25

Fringed Scarfing.

2270 A novelty in linen, for making tray cloths, table, sideboard or dresser scarfs, also pretty for splashers and useful in a dozen different ways. It is a white Momie linen, fringed on both sides, 17 inches wide; has a broad damask band or stripe through the center in either red, blue or gold.
Price, per yard..$0.22

Reversible Turkish Tidies, Scarfs and Throws.

These goods are made of looped threads like a Turkish towel only finished softer. The designs and color combinations are all bright and pretty. Colors show different on both sides, making them reversible.

2280 Fancy Stripe Tidy, diamond pattern, ends fringed; size, 14x33 inches. Predominating colors are light blue, gold, cardinal or green.
Each..............$0.12
Per dozen........ 1.35

2284 Scotch Thistle Tidy. size, 15x36 inches; has thistle pattern woven in colors on pretty contrasting grounds. Predominating colors: Pink, blue, red or olive.
Each..............$0.15
Per dozen........ 1.70

2288 Stork Pattern Table Scarf, 15x44 inches. A big seller; has figure of stork woven in contrasting colors, natural as life. Color are: Cardinal, ecru or wine.
Each..............$0.20
Per dozen......... 2.25

2289 Medallion Scarf; size, 17½x43 inches. Wreath of morning glory with bird in center. Ground colors are: Pink, light blue, ecru or white.
Each...........$0.22
Per dozen.......... 2.45

2290 Swan Tidy. This is a new pattern and promises to be a big seller; has picture of swan and spray of flowers woven in contrasting colors to ground or body colors, which are in olive. cardinal, magenta or peacock blue. Size, 17x45 inches.
Each.............$$0.25
Per dozen........ 2.75

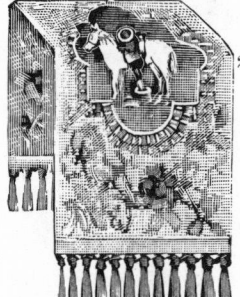

2291 Reversible Turkish Tidy Scarf in high colors. New designs showing small boy mounting the horse. Ground tints are light orange, canary yellow or pink. Size, 16x36 inches.
Each..... ....$0.25
Per dozen......... 2.70

2292 Floral Scarf; size 16x54 inches, extra long. Lily pattern in relief on contrasting grounds. Colors predominating are: Peacock blue, pink, cardinal, yellow, etc. Very rich and handsome.
Each.............$0.29
Per dozen........ 3.33

2295 New Terry Stand Cover, 37x37 inches; light grounds, white pink, light blue or ecru, with handsome center and border in gold, pink, blue, olive and other contrasting colors. Knotted fringe all around.
Each..........$0.39
Per dozen..... 4.50

Brocaded Jacquard Reversible Scarfs and Covers.

Measurement includes fringe.

We can furnish pink, buff, violet, light blue or white in any of these goods.

2300 Chair Scarf, 19x40 inches. Knotted fringe with raised design in white on body of scarf, and beautifully colored ends, as per illustration. In all colors as given above.
Each..............$0.35

2302 Mantel Scarf in all colors as 2300, 16x55 inches. Has a white center, with assorted colored designs and highly colored, figured ends. Knotted fringe.
Each...... ....$0.40

Scarfs and Covers—Continued.

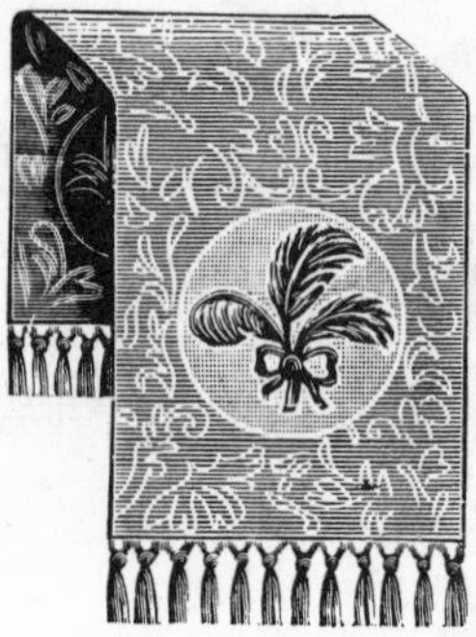

2304 Bureau Cover. A lovely thing. See colors 2300. Size 23 x 50 inches. Knotted fringe, has beautiful colored border of grapes and leaves. Each....$0.55

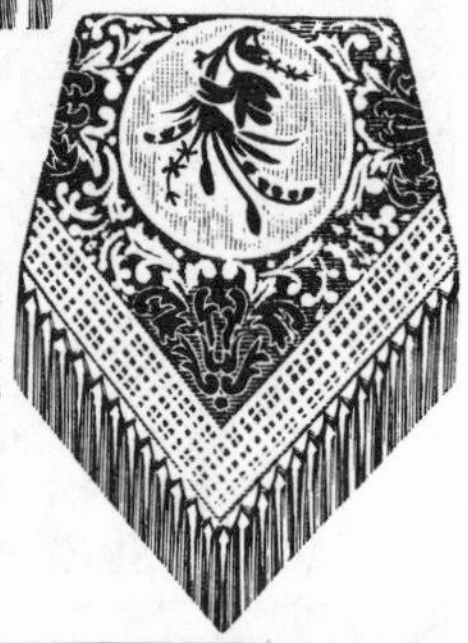

2306 Table Cover, with artistic raised design in white over the entire surface and sombre shaded colored designs in each corner and center. Size 37 inches square. Knotted fringe all around. Each..$0.47

LINEN DEPARTMENT.

Linens are an article of merchandise on which the country merchants make big profits. This is why peddlers always carry linens. As merchants do not sell a great quantity of any one article, they are obliged to pay the wholesaler a big price, and for the same reason have to add large profits. We who import direct, or buy of manufactures here, are in a position to sell to you at about the same price they pay. You can save money by buying your linens of us.

Genuine Turkish Towels.

Extra heavy—double-ply yarn—soft finish—no starch.

STRIPED.	Each.	Per doz.
2350 Striped Bath Towel, half bleached, has narrow red stripes through center and side border. Size. 12x28 inches..	$0.04	$0.45
2352 Striped Bath Towel; has three stripes in three bright colors, and narrow end border fringed. Size 16x30 inches. Half bleached....	.06	.70
2356 Striped Bath Towel, durable; centre stripes of one color, three band side side stripes of another. Fringed end border. 18x36 inches	.09	1.00

Bleached Turkish Towels.

Pure white, with neat red end border, fringed, fast edges, describes them all. Size and quality determine their cost.

2360	Size, 14 x30 inches.	Each, $0.07	Per doz.	$0.78
2362	Size, 16 x35 inches.	Each, .10	Per doz	1.10
2364	Size, 17 x38 inches.	Each, .14	Per doz.	1.50
2368	Size, 20 x42 inches.	Each, .19	Per doz.	2.20
2370	Size, 22½x46 inches.	Each, .22	Per doz.	2.50
2374	Size, 23 x45 inches.	Each, .29	Per doz.	3.25

2374 is extra fine and heavy, fancy corded border.

Unbleached Turkish Towels.

Cream color, fast edges, fringed with colored end border, soft finish double ply yarn, tells everything regarding them. We guarantee their value. Cost, of course, is determined by size and quality.

2380	Size, 15x30 inches.	Each $0.05	Per doz.	$0.55
2382	Size, 16x31 inches.	Each .07	Per doz..	.75
2384	Size, 18x39 inches.	Each .10	Per doz.	1.10
2386	Size, 23x44 inches.	Each .14	Per doz..	1.50
2388	Size, 23x50 inches.	Each 16	Per doz..	1.85
2390	Size, 22x44 inches.	Each .18	Per doz..	2.00
2392	Size, 24x46 inches.	Each .20	Per doz..	2.25
2394	Size, 26x56 inches.	Each .25	Per doz..	2.85

Hard Linen Finish, extra large and heavy.

2396 Size, 28x54 inches, Each $0.35 Per doz.. 4.00

White Turkish Toweling or Terry.

The following Terry or Turkish Toweling is for children's cloaking, roller towels, etc.

Per yard.

2398 White Turkish Toweling, 18 inches wide..$0.15
Price for full piece of about 28 yards, 13½ cents per yard.

2400 Terry, white, 26 inches wide.................. .25
Price for full piece of about 28 yards, 24 cents per yard.

2402 Terry, white, 26 inches wide................ .35
Price for full piece of about 28 yards, 33 cents per yard.

2404 Terry, white, 27 inches wide.................. .40
Price for full piece of about 30 yards, 37 cents per yard.

Brown Terry.

2410 Brown Terry, 26 inches wide. Per yd.....$0.32
Price for full piece of about 28 yards, 31 cents per yard.

Wash Rags or Dusters.

Made from Turkish Toweling for this purpose, after the style of small square Turkish towel.

2416 Wash Rags, half bleached, plain and red or blue striped, 10x10. Each......................$0.03
Per dozen.................................... .25

2418 Wash Rags, bleached, size, 10x11.
Each..................$0.04 Per doz............ .35

2420 Wash Rags, bleached, size, 12x14.
Each................$0.05. Per dozen.......... .50

Cotton and Linen Diaper.

Best quality made.

Cotton and linen diaper come in pieces of 10 yards each, manufacturers' measure. We do not sell less than a piece, or cut samples of these goods.

		Per piece.
2430	Cotton Diaper, 18 incher wide.............	$0.45
2432	Cotton Diaper, 20 inches wide.............	.55
2434	Cotton Diaper, 22 inches wide.............	.65
2436	Cotton Diaper, 24 inches wide.............	.70
2438	Cotton Diaper, 27 inches wide.............	.75
2440	Linen Diaper, 16 inches wide..............	1.25
2442	Linen Diaper, 18 inches wide..............	1.35
2444	Linen Diaper, 20 inches wide..............	1.40
2446	Linen Diaper, 22 inches wide..............	1.65
2448	Linen Diaper, 24 inches wide..............	2.00

Cotton Crash.

Per yard.

2452 Cotton Huck Crash. 15 inches wide, unbleached.......................................$0.04½
Price for full piece of about 25 yards, 4 cents per yard.

2456 Twilled Cotton Crash, 15 inches wide, unbleached... .05
Price for full piece of about 25 yards, 4¾ cents per yard

2458 Checked Cotton Glass Toweling, 16 inches wide. White with red lines, small or medium checks. Per yard................................. .05
Price for full piece of about 50 yards, 4½ cents per yard.

2462 Unbleached Honeycomb Crash, 17 inches wide.. .06
Price for full piece of 25 yards, 5¾ cents per yard.

Linen Crash or Toweling.

We beat the world on low priced Crashes,

Per yard.

2470 Brown Linen (unbleached) Crash; 16 in...$0.06
Price for full piece of about 50 yards, 5½ cents per yard.

2472 Brown Linen Plain Crash, 17 inches...... .06½
Price for full piece of about 50 yards, 6¼ cents per yard.

2474 Brown Linen Plain Crash, 19 inches...... .07½
Price for full piece of about 50 yards, 7¼ cents per yard.

2478 Bleached Linen Crash, plain, 14 inches.... .06
Price for full piece of about 50 yards, 5½ cents per yard.

2482 Bleached Linen Crash, 19 inches.......... .08
Price for full piece of about 50 yards, 7¾ cents per yard.

2486 Half Bleached Twilled Crash, 17 inches... .08½
Price for full piece of about 50 yards, 8 cents per yard.

2488 Union Crash, half bleached, heavy twilled, 17 inches... 08
Price for full piece of about 50 yards, 7½ cents per yard.

2490 Stevens' Unbleached Linen Crash, 18 inches wide .... .10
Price for full piece of about 25 yards, 9 cents per yard.

2492 Rycroft's Unbleached Linen Twilled Crash, 18 inches wide.................................. .11
Price for full piece of about 40 yards, 10 cents per yard.

2494 Bleached twilled Crash, all linen, strong, red border, 18 inches.......................... .10
Price for full piece of about 50 yards, 9¾ cents per yard.

2498 Glass Toweling, red or blue check, 16 inches wide.. .07
Price for full piece of about 50 yards, 6½ cents per yard.

2500 Glass Toweling, red or blue check, 18 inches wide.. .08
Price for full piece of about 50 yards, 7½ cents per yard.

2504 Stevens' Russia Crash, bleached, 15½ inches wide.. .10
Price for full piece of about 25 yards, 9¼ cents per yard.

2506 Stevens' Russia Crash, bleached, 17 inches wide .... .11
Price for full piece of about 25 yards, 10½ cents per yard.

2508 Plain Hotel Crash, bleached, extra heavy for hard wear, 17 inches wide.................. .12½
Price for full piece of about 40 yards, 11½ cents per yard.

2510 Bleached Huckaback Linen Crash, 15 inches wide...................................... .14
Price for full piece of about 40 yards, 13 cents per yard.

2512 Bleached Huckaback Linen Crash. 18 inches wide...................................... .17
Price for full piece of about 40 yards. 15½ cents per yard.

All Linen Sheeting and Pillow Casing.

Also much used now for art embroidery with colored linen or wash silk in making splashers, tidies, stand covers, etc.

2520 Bleached Linen Pillow Casing. width 45 inches. Per yard.....................................$0.45

2524 Bleached Linen Pillow Casing, width 54 inches. Per yard.................................... .60

2526 Bleached Linen Sheeting, width 90 inches. Per yard.. .95

Tint Bleached Embroidery Crash.

Much used nowadays for stamped work splashers, tidies, drawn work, etc. Worked with fast colored marking cotton or linen, it makes not only very pretty but thoroughly durable fancy work.

		Per yard.
2530	16 inches wide Embroidery Crash..........	$0.16
2532	18 inches wide Embroidery Crash..........	.20
2534	20 inches wide Embroidery Crash..........	.22
2536	24 inches wide Embroidery Crash..........	.24

Fancy Embroidery Crash.

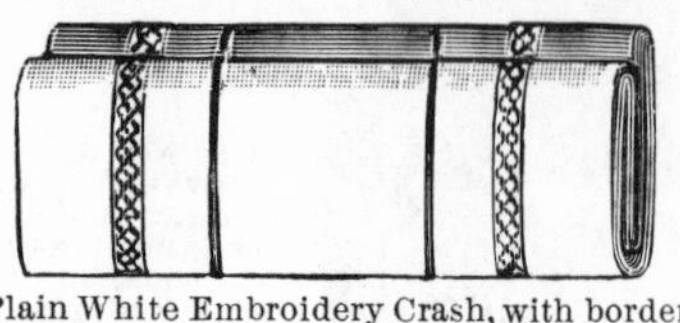

2538 Plain White Embroidery Crash, with border on both sides of drawn open work. Width, 16 inches. Per yard..................................$0.18
Full piece of about 30 yards, 17 cents per yard.

Cotton Towels.

We sell any quantity at a proportionate dozen price.

Per doz.

2542 Soft Finish Cotton Honey Comb Towel, unbleached. Size, 15x30 inches. Per dozen...$0.50

2548 Cotton Honey Comb Towel, cream, size 20x42 inches. Per dozen........................ .75

2552 Cotton Honey Comb Towel, half bleached, 21x44 inches.. 1.00

2554 Cotton Towels, Honey Comb, extra heavy, half bleached, fancy border, fringed, a bargain. Size, 20x43 inches................................. 1.25

2555 White Cotton Crepe or Oat Meal Towel: absorbent and good for wear. Size, 17x34 inches, Per dozen.................................. .84

Linen Huckaback Towels.

ALL LINEN HUCK TOWELS, with colored borders. The best wearing towels made.

Sizes given on all towels include fringe.

		Price each.	Per dozen.
2560	14x24 inches..........	7c..................	$0.70
2562	15x24 inches..........	9c..................	.95
2564	16x30 inches..........	10c.................	1.10
2566	16½x32 inches.........	12c.................	1.30
2568	20x40 inches..........	16c.................	1.80
2570	20x42 inches..........	18c.................	2.15
2572	20x41 inches..........	20c.................	2.25
2574	20x42 inches..........	28c. goodvalue......	3.00

Huckaback Hemmed and Hemstitched Towels.

There is to-day a large and growing demand for hemstitched towels. The leading city hotels and steamship companies, who are the largest consumers of linens have recognized the economy of buying hemstitched goods, and now use nothing else. Housekeepers who pride themselves on their linens are now using this class of work extensively. It does not fray out and show wear, as does most fringed goods, but always looks fresh and neat.

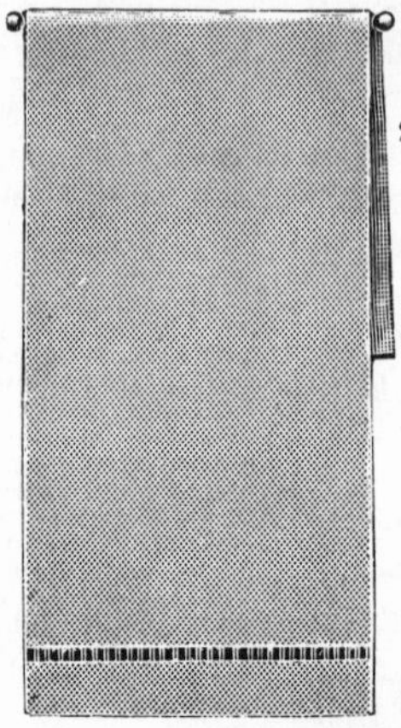

2576 White Huckaback Towel, hemmed ends. A serviceable towel at a low price. Size, 16x34 inches. Colored end borders in blue, red or salmon. Each......$0.15
Price, per dozen.... 1.65

2580 Real Hemstitched White Linen Huck Towels. Size, 18x37 inches, colored, end borders in red, blue or white.
Each................. .22
Price, per dozen.... 2.45

2582 Real Hemstitched White Linen Huck Towels. Extra heavy. Size, 20x40 inches. A splendid towel. Each.... .25
Price, per dozen.... 2.90

We issue a Special Illustrated Book Catalogue, quoting all Latest Books. It will save you money. Send 6 cents to pay postage.

Towels—Continued.

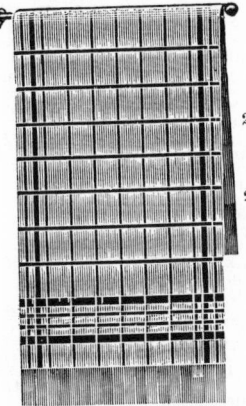

2584 White Hemstitched Momie Linen Towel, new striped pattern, size, 19x44 inches.
Each .... .22½
Per dozen 2.50

2586 White Fancy Linen Huck Towel, assorted patterns, all white, size, 22x43 inches, on ornamental and splendid wearing towel.
Each .... .32½
Per dozen 3.75

Linen Glass Towels.

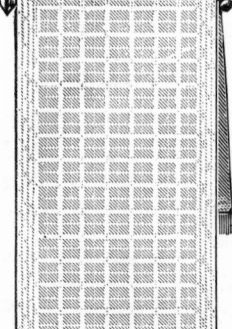

2590 Half Linen, Red Checked Glass Towels, size, 12x24 inches.
Each $0.04½
Per dozen .,..... .50

2592 Red Checked Glass Towel, better than above, size 14 x 28 inches.
Each $0.06
Per dozen .... .65

Striped Twilled Linen Towels.

2598 Linen Twilled Towels, striped with fine lines of red or blue, size 16x32. Each $0.11
Per dozen 1.13

2600 Linen Twilled Towel, striped as above, but larger, size 17x37. Each .... .14
Per dozen 1.40

All Linen Dice Pattern Towels.

2604 Linen Dice Towels, cream bleached, strong and heavy, size 21x24 inches. A bargain.
Each $0.15
Per dozen 1.75

Crepe Towel.

2606 White Crepe Towels, red border, size 17x32, inches. These towels will give good service. They have a hard, rough frictional surface, resembling crepe or momie in appearance and are strong favorites with many people. Each $0.11
Per dozen 1.20

2608 White Crepe Towels, same as above, size 17x34 inches. Each .... .12
Per dozen 1.35

Half Bleached Damask Towels.

Note reduced price.

2610 Red, Blue or Red and Blue Bordered Damask Towel, all linen, half bleached, assorted patterns in center and on ends. Size, 14x26.
Each $0.07
Per dozen .... .78

2612 Damask, Half Bleached Towel, with side color line and end border in red. Has Egyptian scroll around outside, and medallion center patterns. Cupid with cymbals, etc. Size, 16x32 inches.
Each $0.12
Per dozen 1.25

2614 Damask Towel, half bleached, with red side line and wide, red figured end border. The centers have woven pictures of croquet players and similar designs. Size, 17½x35 inches.
Each $0.14
Per dozen 1.47

2616 Large Loom Center Pattern, Red Bordered Fringed Towel. Made for wear as well as looks. Size, 18x37 in. We have various center designs like and similar to cut.
Each $0.15
Per dozen 1.70

2618 Large Towel, quality same as above with clearly woven loom pictures in center, representing various subjects from life. Size, 20x40 inches. Each ... $0.17
Per dozen 1.90

2620 Same as above in designs, weave and quality. Size, 21x44.
Each $0.20
Per dozen 2.25

2624 Extra Large Bureau Towel, half bleached, center designs, and an extra wide figured red end border. Has double line red side border. A very good, large towel for the money. Size, 22x42 inches.
Each $0.23
Per dozen 2.55

2628 Cream Bleached Broche Towel. Size, 18x36 inches; a well made all linen towel with red floral designs worked in center medallion effect; but a limited quantity of these towels to sell.
Each $0.24
Per dozen 2.75

Towels—Continued.

Bleached Damask Towel with floral medallion center patterns, red line side borders triple red end borders having woven designs in harmony with center.

2636 Size, 18x36.
Each $0.20
Per dozen 2.25

2637 Extra Large Bleached German Damask Towel, soft finish, strong and heavy, all linen. Has wide end borders in red, blue, gold or plain white; size, 25x 52 inches. The largest towel ever sold at the price. Each $0.27½
Per dozen 3.25

2640 Bleached Damask Towel, knotted fringe, red border. A very pretty and good wearing towel, size 18x38 inches. Each....$0.12
Per dozen 1.35

2641 Bleached All Linen Damask Towel; knotted fringe. Colored end borders: Red, blue, gold or plain white. This is a new importation and splendid value for a small towel. Size, 17x35 inches. Each.... $0 15
Per dozen 1.65

2642 Bleached All Linen Damask Towel. Good quality; has knotted fringe and two rows openwork on each end; between the rows is a broad fancy damask band in pink, blue, red or white. Size, 17x36 inches. This is the cheapest openwork linen towel ever sold.
Each... .... $0.17
Per dozen 1.95

2643 Bleached Knotted Fringe Damask Towel. Plain white. Pattern is not in center, but all over towel in fern leaves. roses, etc. Good designs, well bleached yarns and closely woven. Size, 20x40. Each.....$0.21
Per dozen 2.26

2644 All White, Pure Bleach satin Damask Towel, exquisite designs, knotted and plaited fringe, and two rows of fine hand tied openwork across each end. Size of towel, 20x42 inches.
Each $0.32
Per dozen 3.50

Towels—Continued.

2646 Extra Large Bleached Knotted Fringe Damask Towel. Answers nicely for bureau or dresser on account of its size and handsome design. Size, 24x50. All white. Each......$0.41
Per doz............ 4.67

2647 Bleached, All Linen Damask Towel, good quality: made for practical service, yet pretty withal: ends are hemmed and have colored or white borders through the center of which runs a row of drawn openwork. Size, 20x40 in.
Each..............$0.25
Per doz............ 2.80

2648 German Broche or Embroidered Border Towel. Reversible, extra large; size, 23x50 inches; all pure linen; German manufacture; heavy, soft and fine. Brocaded damask patterns. Borders are in wide bands; handsome designs. Colors: Gold or blue. Knotted fringe ends. We closed out importer's stock of these towels at much under their value. There will be no more of them. They cannot be duplicated out of any stock under 60 cents each. Our price while they last.
Each..............$0.40
Per doz........... 4.60

2649 All Linen Damask Towel, knotted fringe and one row of tied openwork through border. Borders are in plain white, red, blue or gold. Size of towel, 17x35 inches. A very handsome towel of exceptional value.
Each..............$0.16
Per doz........... 1.75

2652 All Linen Damask Towel, knotted fringe, two rows of openwork; figured borders in pink, red, blue, gold salmon or plain white. Size, 19x40.
Each..............$0.23
Per dozen......... 2.32

2653 All Linen Damask Towel, scattered floral design in center. Wide white or colored end border, with two rows of tied openwork; borders of red, blue or salmon; size of towel, 20x44 inches.
Each...........$0.22½
Per dozen...... 2.50

Towels—Continued.

2654 All Linen Bleached Damask Towel; style shown in cut. Knotted and plaited fringe, wide colored border with a row of double hand tied openwork, brocaded stripe damask center. Colors are: Pink, light blue, red, gold or plain white; size, 20x42 in.
Each..............$0.24
Per dozen........ 2.75

2655 Bleached Damask Towel, extra large and fine. Has wide colored damask borders with two rows of drawn openwork. All linen. Borders are red, blue or gold. This is one of the largest and showiest towels for the price ever shown. Size, 22½x49 inches. Each.....$0.27
Per dozen.......... 3.12

2656 Knotted Fringe, all linen bleached damask towel, strong and serviceable, size 22x48 inches. Has wide colored damask borders, red, blue, gold or white. Size and quality considered this is an exceptional value.
Each.........$0.27½
Per dozen..... 3.15

2658 Plain White Brocaded Damask Towel. All linen, knotted fringe, plaited heading with hand tied, drawn openwork; a beauty. Size, 20 x 42 inches.
Each..........$0.35
Per dozen....... 3.85

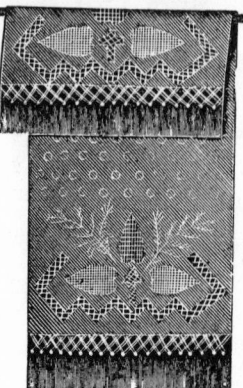

2662 Fine Damask Towel, all linen, extra large size, measures 25x47 in. Knotted fringe and wide damask borders of red, blue or plain white. A splendid towel and one of the best values we ever offered.
Each........$0.28
Per dozen... 3.25

2670 Momie Figured Damask Tied Openwork Linen Towel, size, 22x48 inches. Criscross tied fringe, both ends. Openwork cannot fray or ravel. An elegant ornament.
Each....$0.65
Per dozen.... 7.50

2670.

Towels—Continued.

2678 Fancy White Brocaded Damask Towel; size, 22x44 inches. Knotted fringe and handsome drawn openwork design on end. Makes a very handsome and durable tidy.
Each.........$0.45
Per dozen........ 5.25

Bleached Linen Napkins.

For Bleached Table Damask with napkins to match See Nos. 3040-3041-3042.

Sold in dozens or half dozens.

These goods are all pure bleached flax. Irish, Scotch and German manufacture, our own importations and selected with especial regard to wearing qualities. New and elegant patterns; sizes given are actual measurement. Price governs quality.

	Size in inches.	Per doz.
2692 Bleached Linen Napkin..	13½x14½	$0.60
2694 Bleached Linen Damask Napkin, fine qual ty.........	16½x16½	.75
2696 Bleached Linen Damask Napkin....	17 x17	.85
2698 Bleached Linen Damask Napkin, better....	17 x17	1.00
2699 Cream or Half bleached German Dice Napkins, union, made for hard common wear. Matches No. 2976 Damask....	18 x18	.69
2700 Bleached Soft Finish, Heavy German Linen Napkin, dice pattern..............	18 x18	1.10
2701 German Silver Bleach Napkins, all linen, heavy and fine, soft finish; pattern and quality matches table damask Nos. 2989-2990	18 x18	1.15
2702 German Silver Bleach Napkins, all linen, extra fine, soft finish, small polka dot pattern. Matches table covers Nos. 2914-15-16	18 x18	1.65
2703 German Silver Bleach Damask Napkin. Same quality and pattern as above. Matches table covers Nos. 2914-15-16....................	24 x24	2.90
2704 Bleached Damask Linen Dinner Napkin...............	20 x20	1.40
2706 Bleached Damask Linen Dinner Napkin........	20 x20	1.60
2708 Bleached Damask Linen Dinner Napkin, finer quality.	20 x20	1.75
2710 Bleached Satin Damask Dinner Napkin, extra fine....	20 x20	2.00
2712 Bleached Linen Damask Napkin, large size.............	21 x21	1.20
2714 Bleached Damask Napkin all linen....................	21 x21	1.50
2716 Bleached Damask Linen Dinner Napkin, fine and large	22 x22	2.00
2718 Dinner Napkin, Satin Damask, bleached, good quality....................	22 x22	2.25
2720 Satin Damask, Bleached Linen Dinner Napkin; very fine, large....................	22 x22	2.50
2722 Extra Large Bleached Satin Damask Linen Napkin, superfine quality......... ..	24 x24	3.00
2724 Bleached Double Damask Linen, extra superfine, satin finish.................	24 x24	3.50

Laces, Embroideries, Etc.

Our line this season is better than it has been. Look it up.
Page 76.

Linen Class or Fruit Doylies.

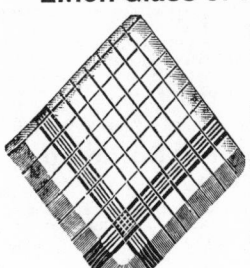

Bleached Linen Glass or Fruit Napkins, red or blue hair-line check, red border, fringed on all sides.
2730 Red or Blue Checked Doylies, 11x11 inches.
Per dozen........$0.20
2732 Red or Blue Checked Doylies, 14x15 inches.
Per dozen......$0.35
2734 Red or Blue Checked Doylies, 14x15 inches,
Per dozen.......$0.45

Colored Border Doylies.

	Size in inches.	Per doz.
2740 Bleached Linen Doylies, dice pattern, with colored band borders in red, blue or pure white fringed all round. Per dozen................	13x13	$0.40

Half Bleached Linen Doylies, Red Border.

	Size in inches.	Per doz.
2744 Linen Doylies, cardinal border, fringed on all sides....	12x12	$0.60
2746 Linen Doylies, red border fringed on all sides.............	15½x15½	.73

Pure Bleached Doylies.

	Size in inches.	Per doz.
2750 Plain Bleached Linen Doylies, border and center figured pattern...............	11½x12	$0 45
2752 Plain Bleached Linen Doylies with center pattern and border fringed......	13x13	.60
2754 Bleached Linen Doylies, plain white border, fringed	16x16	.80

Turkey Red Scotch Fruit Doylies.

For Fruit and Table Use.

	Size in ins.	Per doz.
2770 Turkey Red and White Doylies, fringed, fast colors	12x12	$0.40
2772 Turkey Red and White Fringed Doylies. neat pattern, fast color...............	15x15	.62
2774 Turkey Red and White Fringed Doylies, elegant pattern, fast colors.............	18x18	.80
2778 Turkey Red Doylies fringed. fast colors.....	20x20	1.45

Fancy Doylies.

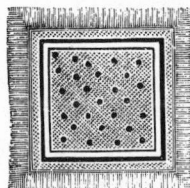

2780 Square All Linen Dentists' Doylies, also very useful and pretty for table or household decoration. We have two styles, square momie linen fringed, in white only, or satin damask in gold, pink or blue with small brocaded dots in center; fast colors, all pretty. Size, 7x7 inches. State style or color wanted.
Per dozen $0.25

For table decorations and ornaments.
2782 Square All Linen Momie Center Doylies, fringed all around; size, 7½ inches square; useful in a hundred ways. Per dozen...... .25
2784 Colored Octagonal or Eight-sided, All Linen Doylie or Mat, 7x7 inches, colored fast red, light blue, white or mahogany; has basket weave edges and fancy center, with fringe all round; as much used for ornamental mats as for table use. Per dozen............................. .50

2786 Round White Damask Doylies, 10 inches in diameter, fringed; Useful for table decorations, as stands for dishes, for cake baskets; very fine; we do not sell less than ¼ dozen.
Price, per dozen....$0.50
2788 Same as above, but square, same size.
Per dozen.........$0.50

2790 Round White Damask Doylies, fringed, 8 inches in diameter, same as 2786, but finer quality. Price, per dozen.........................$0.75
2792 Square White Damask Doylies, fringed, size, 8x8 inches, same quality as 2790. Price, per dozen............................ .75

Our capacity is 10 orders a minute.

Doylies—Continued.

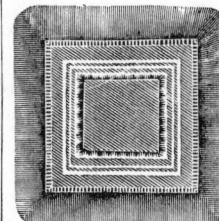

2794 White Satin Damask, Fringed. Hemstitched Doylie, 8x8 inches; we do not sell less than ¼ dozen.
Price, per doz......$1.00
2796 Same as above; size, 9½x9½ inches; colors: Light blue, pink or gold; useful as vase or lamp mats, for toilet covers, bureau ornaments, or to render beautiful a table set in white; fast colors. We do not sell less than ¼ dozen. Per doz......$1.25

2798 Fancy Colored Linen Fruit Doylie, size, 13x13 inches. fringed all around; colors are: Pink, blue, gold, natural or flax tint, also chocolate. Price, per dozen......................$0.85

Tray Cloths.

2800 All Linen Tray Cloths, fringed all around; size, 18 x25 inches; damask is fine and the pattern is pretty; they are plain white and have colored border of red, pink, gold or light blue. Colors are fast. For center of table, to put under platters, for children's use, or to cover a soiled place on an otherwise clean cloth, they are indispensable.
Each.................$0.15
2802 Tray Cloths, all linen, all white or bordered with red, gold or blue lines; fringed all around; in colors fast. Size, 22x30 inches, finer linen than above.
Each...................$0.22

2804 White All Linen Momie Tray Cloth or Tidy; 16x26 inches; has tied openwork border; fringed all around. Retailers who carry such goods usually ask fancy prices; by way of contrast we will sell them each at...........$0.22

2806 Tray Cloth; 16x33 inches; momie linen, with tied zigzag openwork its entire length and flowered damask center of pink, light blue, red, buff or lemon. A wonderful addition to any table, stand or bureau.
Each.......$0.35
2808 Same as above, any color; size, 16x52.
Each.......$0.50
2810 Same as above, any color; size, 16x66.
Each........$0.70

Dresser Scarfs.

2812 White Linen Crepe Sideboard or Dresser Scarfs, size, 16x50 in. The end shows design in hand tied openwork, beautifully executed, fringed border.
Price, each.........$0.40

2813 White Momie Linen Sideboard or Dresser Scarf; knotted fringe, with plaited heading and drawn openwork design on both ends.
Size, 16½x63 inches.
Each...............$0.60

2814 Cream Momie Linen Sideboard or Bureau Scarfs. A job. Drawn openwork border all around and star pattern of openwork on ends. Size, 16x51 inches.
Each...............$0.30
2815 Cream Momie Linen Sideboard or Bureau Scarf. Same as above. Size, 16x68 inches.
Each...............$0.45

2816 All Linen Tray Cloth or Stand Cover, flowered damask center, tied fringe all around, and two rows of openwork on all edges. Size, 25x30 inches; very pretty and cheap, white only.
Each .$0.40

2817 White Satin Damask Sideboard or Dresser Scarfs; also much used as a runner for center of dining table, laid over the table cloth. This is a special lot that we bought at about one-half actual value. There will be no more when these are sold. The damask is of fine quality, with beautifully finished drawn openwork forming a wide stripe through center into which can be inserted rows of ribbon; narrow openwork lines on sides. Size, 16x51 inches. Each.................$0.49
2818 White Satin Damask Openwork Scarf or Runner. Same as 2817. Size, 16x68 inches.
Each .... .65

2824 Momie Linen Bureau or Sideboard Scarf; size, 16x51 inches. Has fancy colored band through center. Colors: Red, blue, pink or gold. Fringed all around.
Each.....$0.25

2825 Momie Linen Bureau or Sideboard Scarf; same quality and colors as above. Size, 16x68 inches.
Each,...... .32

Lunch Cloths.

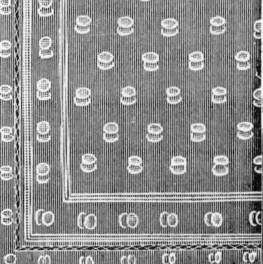

2826 Hemstitched Bleached Linen Damask Lunch Cloths, a special line; size, 30x30 inches. Neat designs and real hemstitched openwork border all around.
Each $0.60

Lunch Cloths—Continued.

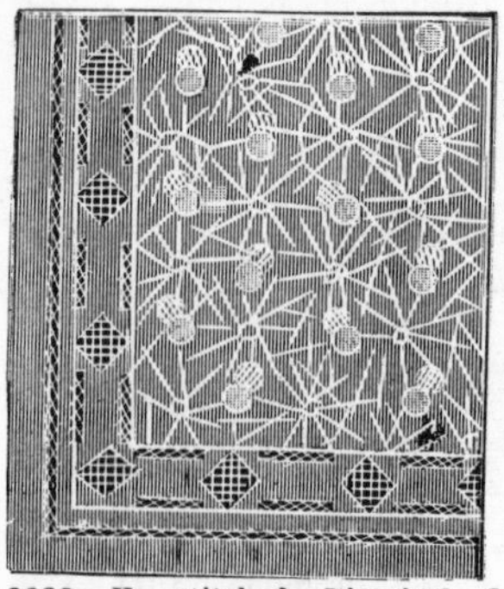

2827 Hemstitched Bleached Linen Damask Lunch Cloths. Handsome patterns, with fancy border all around of drawn openwork; real hemstitching. Our price is about 30 per cent. less than actual value; size, 31x31 inches. Each.........$1.10

2828 Hemstitched Bleached Linen Damask Lunch cloths, fancy openwork border, same as above; size, 46x46 inches. Each............... $1.90

Fancy Stand or Table Covers.

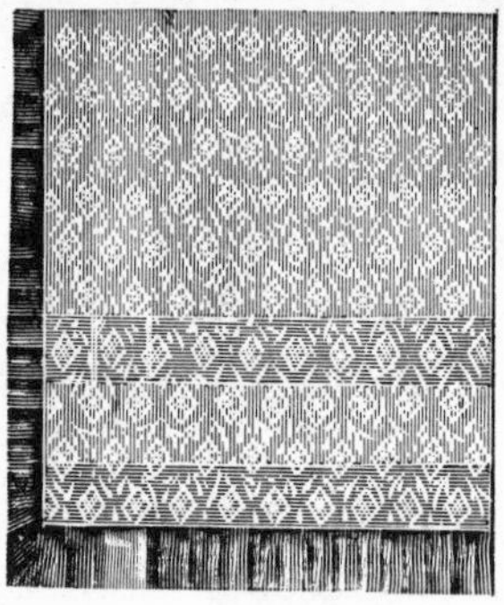

2829 Cotton Tapestry Table Covers; size, 52x58 inches; fringed all around. A soft, pretty cover, looks like raw silk. Colors: Old gold with brown and green border; bright blue, with ecru and brown border; light blue, with brown and ecru border; slate, with orange and garnet. Each.........$0.45

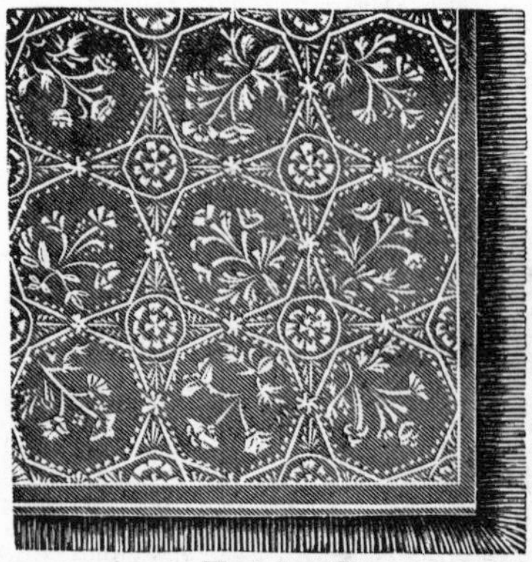

2832—Fancy Colored All Linen Table Cover, fringed all around. Size, 52x53 inches. A very pretty cloth and one that will wash perfectly. Colors are: Pink, blue, or straw color. Each $0.69

Table Covers.

Our assortment will be found complete, and the prices we know are right. Table cloths are rapidly taking the place of that sold by the yard. They cost no more, require no labor to prepare them for use, and look infinitely better, as they have end borders, which yard goods do not have. Measurements given are the actual sizes, including fringe.

Turkey Red and White Covers.

Each.

2850 Turkey Red Covers, cheapest ever offered. Fringed border on both sides, fast colors. Size 54x58 inches. actual measure..................... $0.39

2852 Table Cover, turkey red and white, fringed border on both edges; colors fast. Size, 54x70 inches.. .49

2854 Turkey Red Cover, same as above, but larger. Size, 54x90 inches....................... .65

2856 Turkey Red and White Combination Table Cloths, oil colors, fringed on all sides. Best goods made.

Size..............................	$\frac{5}{4}$	$\frac{6}{4}$	$\frac{7}{4}$
Inches..............................	32x32	45x45	54x55
Prices, each..............................	30c.	60c.	90c.
Size..............................	$\frac{8}{4}$	$\frac{10}{4}$	$\frac{12}{4}$
Inches..............................	66x70	66x88	66x100
Prices, each..............................	$1.17	$1.41	$1.95

Brown and White Table Cloth. A Leader.

Each.

2866 All Linen Table Cloths, 48x58 inches in size. Bleached threads one way, unbleached (called brown in the trade) threads the other way. Strong and serviceable.......... ... .$0.50

Loom Damask Table Cloths, Red Border.

NOTE REVISED PRICES.

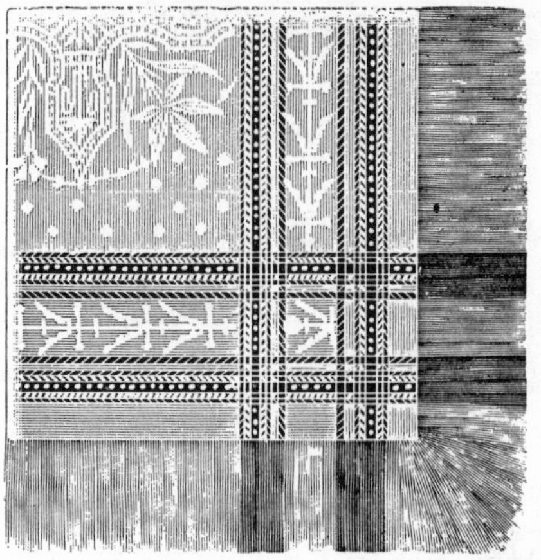

We sell vast quantities of these covers and find that they give universal satisfaction where a heavy and sightly cloth is desired for common wear. They come in a large range of patterns; borders are a deep bright red and fast color. The cloth thickens with washing.

2870 All Linen Cover; size, 50x61 inches ($\frac{8}{4}$). Each...$0.50

2871 All Linen Cover; size, 50x70 inches ($\frac{8}{10}$). Each... .65

2872 All Linen Cover; size, 50x79 inches ($\frac{8}{12}$). Each... .75

2873 All Linen Cover; size, 50x88 inches ($\frac{8}{14}$). Each... .85

2874 All Linen Cover; size, 50x97 inches ($\frac{8}{16}$). Each... .90

2875 All Linen Cover: size, 50x106 inches ($\frac{8}{18}$). Each... 1.00

2876 All Linen Cover; size, 50x115 inches ($\frac{8}{20}$). Each... 1.10

Cream Linen fringed cloths, red border, similar to above line but much finer and wider.

2880 Size, 60x68 inches ($\frac{8}{4}$). Each..............$1.00
2882 Size, 60x85 inches ($\frac{8}{10}$). Each.............. 1.35
2883 Size, 60x98 inches ($\frac{8}{12}$). Each.............. 1.65

Union Linen Red Bordered Covers.

Same styles as preceding Nos. Cheapest cloths made.

2884 Size, 50x60 inches ($\frac{8}{4}$). Each.............$0.45
2885 Size, 50x70 inches ($\frac{8}{10}$). Each.............. .55
2886 Size, 50x78 inches ($\frac{8}{12}$). Each.............. .65
2887 Size, 50x88 inches ($\frac{8}{14}$). Each.............. .70
2888 Size, 50x98 inches ($\frac{8}{16}$). Each.............. .80
2889 Size, 50x105 inches ($\frac{8}{18}$). Each.............. .90

Bleached Fringed Table Cloths.

Bleached Linen Fringed Cloths, handsome brocaded Damask center patterns with rich Damask border. Fringe all around. We believ, they are the best, low priced bleached cloths in the market. They are in three sizes as follows: Each.

2890 Size, 58x65 inches.............................. $1.00
2892 Size, 58x88 inches.............................. 1.35
2894 Size, 58x100 inches.............................. 1.65

Colored Border and White Union Table Cloths.

Dice pattern, German manufacture, fine and soft finish, borders in white, red, gold, blue or pink.

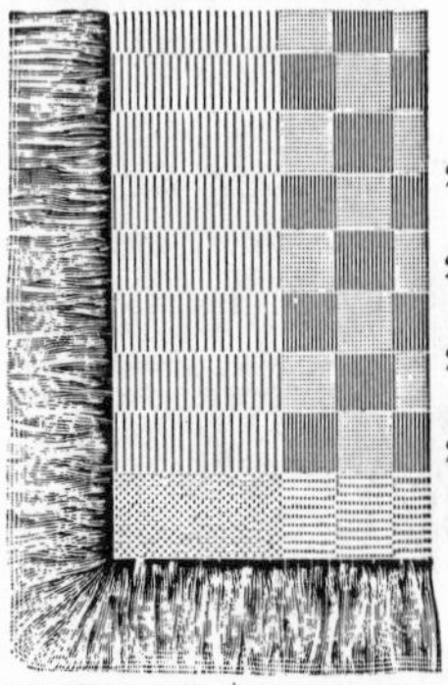

2895 Fringed Table Cloth ($\frac{8}{4}$), 52x63 inches Each.....................$0.70

2896 Fringed Table Cloth ($\frac{8}{10}$), 52x79 inches Each..................... .95

2897 Fringed Table Cloth ($\frac{8}{12}$), 52x84 inches. Each..................... 1.12

2898 Fringed Table Cloth ($\frac{8}{14}$), 52x96 inches. Each..................... 1.25

Our Underwear Department has been entirely revised.

All Linen Bleached Goods.

These goods are made in Austria, are woven from fine bleached yarns and have the soft feeling peculiar to Austrian linens. No starch used. They come in broken dice patterns and are fringed all round.

Each.

2900 Size, 61x68 inches.............................. $1.00
2902 Size, 61x83 inches.............................. 1.25
2904 Size, 61x100 inches.............................. 1.50

Bleached Colored Bordered Cloth.

Same manufacture as the plain. Same class of goods. Border is in lines, making a noticeable, but not conspicuous edging. Colors: Red, pink, buff, blue; fringe on all sides. All linen.

Each.

2908 Size, 58x66 inches..............................$1.10
2910 Size, 58x84 inches.............................. 1.35
2912 Size, 58x100 inches.............................. 1.60

Real Silver Bleached German Linen Table Cloths.

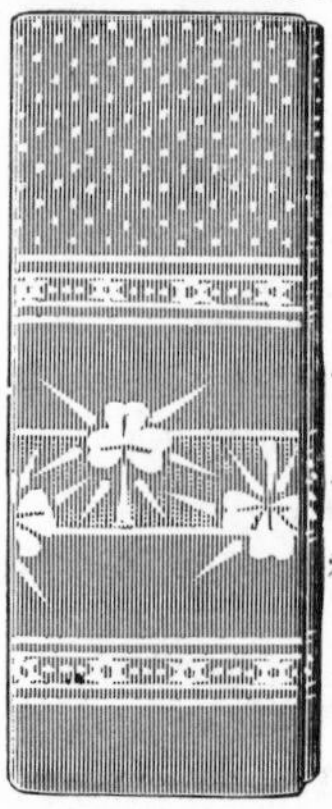

The most serviceable table cloth linen made. Soft finish, no dressing. A feature of this linen is that it grows handsomer after repeated washings. *For Napkins to match these cloths, see Nos. 2702-2703.*

2914 Silver Bleached Table Cloth, dot pattern, size, $\frac{8}{4}$x70x72 inches. Each..............................$1.90

2915 Silver Bleached Table Cloth, dot pattern, size, $\frac{8}{10}$x70x90 inches. Each..............................$2.40

2916 Silver Bleached Table Cloth, dot pattern, size, $\frac{8}{12}$x70x108 inches. Each..............................$2.95

Table Cloth and Napkin Sets.

Each Set in a Box.

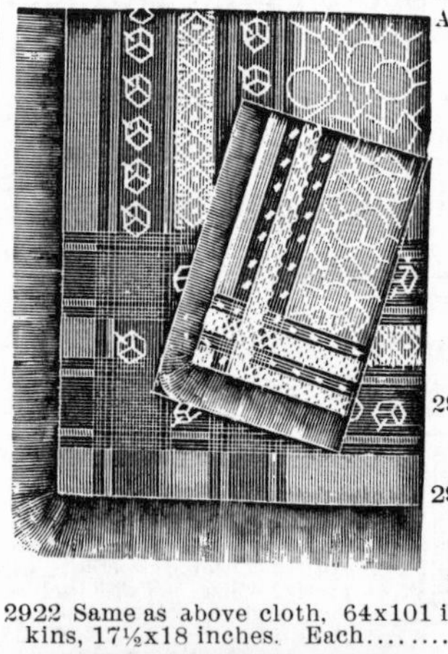

All Linen Colored Border Fringed Table Cloth, size, 65x66 inches and 12 all linen colored border fringed napkins; size, 17½x18 inches. We can furnish borders of red, blue, yellow, salmon, gold or plain white. These goods are our own importation and are very cheap.

2920 Each set comes put up in a neat box. Price, per set......$2.25

2921 Same as above cloth, 63x85 inches; napkins, 17x17. Each........$2.67

2922 Same as above cloth, 64x101 inches; napkins, 17½x18 inches. Each.................... 3.00

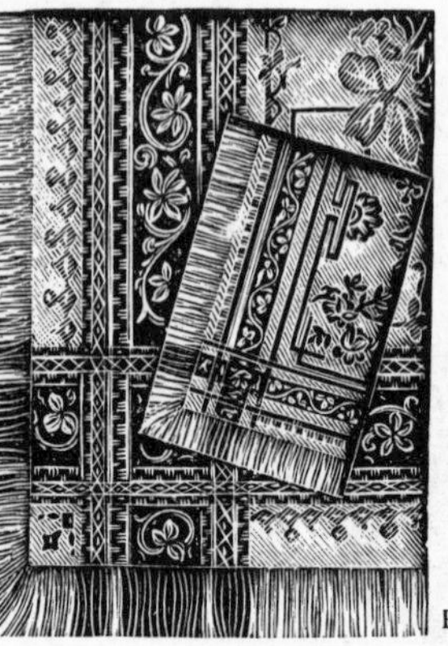

Colored Border. All Linen Table Set. Has fine damask cloth, fringe all around, with fast colored border of light blue, red, pink, gold or plain white, and 12 fringed napkins with colored borders to match cloth.

2924 Cloth, size, 62x64; napkins, 14¾x15½ inches. Price per set $2.67

2925 Cloth, size, 66x85; napkins, 14¾x15½ inches. Price per set $3.00

2926 Cloth, size, 63x99; napkins, 15x15½ inches. Price, per set, $3.50

INSURE YOUR PACKAGES.—Mail packages may be insured against loss by paying a fee of 5 cents for each $5.00 in value. Write "Insured Mail" on your order, enclose the money, and we will do the rest.

Table Sets—Continued.

All Linen, Open-work Colored Border Table Set. Damask is fine, colors are fast, and patterns are new. As cut shows, it has two rows of openwork on cloth, fringed all around, brocaded in center. Napkins have colored borders to match cloth. Colors: Red, light blue, pink, gold or plain white.

2928 Cloth, 63x84 inches, napkins 15x15½ inches. Per set..... $3.50

2929 Cloth, 75x100 inches, napkins 15x15½ inches. Per set...... $4.00

2931 All Linen Table Set, cloth and napkins fringed all around. Colors: Red, gold, light blue, pink or white. Size of cloth, 59x82 in.; napkins, 15x15 inches. Per set..... $2.10

2932 All Linen Table Set, same quality and colors as above; size of cloth, 59x98 inches; napkins, 15x15 inches. Per set...... $2.40

New Cheap Sets.
THE CHEAPEST WE EVER SOLD.

2934 Fringed Linen Table Set; consists of 1 table cloth and 1 dozen napkins. Dice pattern, bleached. Made with red border or all white cloth 50x68 in.; napkins, 12 x 12 inches. Per set...... $1.25

2935 Fringe Linen Table Set. Same as above. Cloth, 50x85 inches; napkins, 12 x 12 inches. Per set...... $1.50

2936 Fringed Linen Table Set. Same as above. Cloth, 50x100 inches; napkins, 12x12 inches. Per set..... $1.75

Turkey Red Damask.
We buy from manufacturers only. On this line we can't be beat.

Sold by the yard; patterns are squares, stripes and fancy designs with borders.   Per yard.

2940 Turkey Red and White Damask, 50 inches wide; best in America for the price............ $0.18
Full piece of about 27 yards, 16½ cents per yard.

2944 Turkey Red and White Damask, 58 inches wide .... .25
Price for full piece of about 27 yards, 24 cents per yard.

2946 Turkey Red and White Table Damask, 58 inches wide; fast colors; handsome designs. This damask is a leader with us and we believe it to be the best cloth ever sold at this price.... .33
Price for full piece of about 27 yards, 31½ cents per yard.

2947 Solid Cardinal Brocaded Damask, 58 inches wide; border of same color. Per yard........ .38
For full piece of about 30 yards, 36 cents per yard

Damask—Continued.

2948 Turkey Red and White Table Damask, 58 inches wide; fast colors; oil boiled,.... $0.40
Price for full piece of about 27 yards, 39 cents per yard.

2950 Cardinal and White Fancy Checked Damask, 58 inches wide. Very slightly goods. Colors absolutely fast. Per yard............... $0.37½
Price for full piece of about 27 yards, 36½ cents per yard.

2952 Imported Turkey Red Damask, absolutely fast color. New styles, which we think the prettiest ever shown. Grounds are all in red with white designs or mottled effects, (see illustration), over which are arranged handsome designs in solid red, forming a bold relief. Width, 58 inches. Per yard $0.56
For full piece of about 50 yards, 47½ cents per yard.

2954 Turkey Red and White Figured Damask, 58 inches wide; warranted oil colors, perfectly fast.................. $0.55
Price for full piece of about 27 yards, 53 cents per yard.

2952

Turkey Red Damask, Fancy Colored Border.

2960 Imported Turkey Red and Green Damask, 58 inches wide, with green border 8 inches wide. Oil colors, perfectly fast. Flowered or dice patterns......... ....$0.45
Price for full piece of about 27 yards, 43 cents per yard.

2962 Imported Turkey Red and Green Damask, 58 inches wide, with flowered or Grecian border 8 inches wide, of green; patterns are either block or floral and are warranted absolutely fast colors.. .50
Price for full piece of about 27 yards, 48 cents per yard.

2964 Imported Turkey Red and Green Damask, 58 inches wide, with green flowers or blocks; has an 8 inch border of red and green, with lines of black. Dice or fancy pattern. Perfectly fast colors.. .... .60
Price for full piece of about 27 yards, 57 cents per yard.

Van Dyke Fancy Colored Damask.

2966 Van Dyke Fancy Colored Damask, 58 inches wide, a new importation; very pretty and fast colors. The patterns are graceful and artistic, with harmonizing borders. Color combinations are: Cardinal and gold; blue and old gold; cardinal and blue, or two shades of old gold combined. Per yard......................$0.39

Half Bleached Union Table Linen.
PRICES REDUCED.
Half Bleached Union Linen Table Cloth, in square or dice pattern. Squares are made small, medium or large and broken dice effects. Where low-priced goods will answer, these are the best you can get. They are made in three widths. We have all patterns in all widths.   Per yard.

2970 Union Table Linen, 46 inches wide........$0.18
Price for full piece of about 43 yards, 17½ cents per yard.

2972 Union Table Linen, 50 inches wide.. .... .. .22
Price for full piece of about 43 yards, 21½ cents per yard.

2974 Union Table Linen, 54 inches wide........ .25
Price for full piece of about 43 yards, 24 cents per yard.

2976 Union Table Linen, dice or broken square pattern; German manufacture; 67 inches wide. Per yard.. .49
For full piece of about 45 yards, 47½ cents per yard.

All Linen Half Bleached Table Linen.
Patterns are even or broken squares. Cloth is all linen and well woven for hard wear and frequent washings.   Per yard.

2980 Half Bleached Dice Linen, 56 inches wide. Per yard $0.35
For full piece of about 43 yards, 33½ cents per yard.

2982 Half Bleached Dice Linen, 58 inches wide. Per yard .... .50
Price for full piece of about 43 yards, 47½ cents per yard.

Extra Heavy German Table Linen.
This cloth has no dressing in it, but is made with a wash finish. Patterns are even or broken dice or squares. It is made more especially for hotels and restaurants, where a cloth receives frequent washing and hard usage.
Per yard.

2986 Heavy German Table Linen, 54 inches wide..................................$0.40
Price for full piece of about 43 yards, 38 cents per yard.

2988 Heavy German Table Linen, 58 inches wide.. .50
Price for full piece of about 43 yards, 49 cents per yard.

German Silver Bleached Table Damask.

NOTE—For Napkins to match see No. 2701.
Cut shows border design only.

2989 German Silver Bleached Damask in small neat patterns. The best wearing linen made. Soft finish, no starch. Width, 54 inches. Per yard...... $0.45
Full piece of about 36 yards, 42½ cents per yard.

2990 German Silver Bleached Damask, 60 inches wide. Per yard........ $0.50
Full piece of about 36 yards, 48 cents per yard.

Red Bordered, Half Bleached Table Linen.
Patterns are even or broken dice. Cloth is good and will thicken slightly after washing, and also become whiter.
Per yard.

2992 Half Bleached Table Linen, red border, 55 inches wide $0.33
Full piece of about 42 yards, 32 cents per yard.

2994 Half Bleached Table Linen, red border, 58 inches wide .... .50
Full piece of about 43 yards, 48 cents per yard.

Half Bleached Linen Damask.
Differs from the above in that the patterns are not in squares, but in figures, floral designs. etc., with a woven side border.   Per yard.

3000 Half Bleached 54-inch Damask, all linen ..$0.32
3002 Half Bleached 56-inch Damask, all linen.. .40
3004 Half Bleached 58-inch Damask, all linen, better than the above....................... .50
3006 Cream Damask, very fine, all linen, 67 inches wide.................................... .60

Bleached Damask.
Bleached table linen is so much used we have taken great care to present only those we could recommend for width, finish, wear, pattern and bleach. We believe it to be to your interest to buy your linen of us. Many of the patterns are confined to us; not shown elsewhere.
Per yard.

3020 Bleached Union Damask, 54 inches wide.$0.28½
Full piece of about 25 yards, 27½ cents per yard.

3022 Bleached All Linen Damask, 54 inches wide.. .39
Full piece of about 25 yards, 37½ cents per yard.

3024 Bleached All Linen Damask, 62 inches wide.. .47
Full piece of about 25 yards, 46 cents per yard.

3026 Bleached All Linen Damask, 62 inches wide, still better.............................. .56
Full piece of about 25 yards, 55 cents per yard.

3028 Bleached All Linen Damask, 63 inches wide, still better.............................. .70
Full piece of about 25 yards, 68 cents per yard.

3030 All Linen Bleached Imported Satin Table Damask, elegant patterns, 68 inches wide. We pride ourselves on the value we give.......... .80

3032 Pure Linen White Satin Damask, 72 inches (two yards wide), beautiful patterns,........... 1.00

New special designs with napkins to match, either ⅝ or ¾ sizes.

3040 Bleached All Linen Satin Finished Damask; width, 68 inches; special designs. Per yard............$1.00

3041 Fine Bleached Damask Napkins; size, 20x20 inches; same quality and design as No. 3040 Damask. Per dozen................. $2.35

3042 Large and Fine Bleached Damask Dinner Napkins; size, 24x24 inches; same quality and pattern as above napkins and damask. We recommend the above goods where fine and perfect service is desired. Per dozen................. $3.40

Irish Bosom Linen.
For Shirt Bosoms, Collars, Cuffs, etc.   Per yard.
3060 Irish Linen 36 inches wide.................$0.28
Price for full piece of about 22 yards, 27 cents per yard.
3062 Irish Linen, 36 inches wide, better......... .35
Price for full piece of about 22 yards, 34 cents per yard.
3064 Irish Linen, 36 inches wide.............. .40
Price for full piece of about 22 yards, 38 cents per yard.
3066 Irish Linen, 36 inches wide................ .60

Butchers' Linen.

Used for re-enforcing shirt bosoms, embroidery, drawnwork, etc.

Per yard.

3068 Unbleached Butchers' Linen, 36 inches wide $0.25
Price for full piece of about 24 yards, 24 cents per yard.
3070 Unbleached Butchers' Linen, 40 inches wide ...... .27
Price for full piece of about 24 yards, 26 cents per yard.
3074 Unbleached Butchers' Linen, 40 inches wide ...... .37
Price for full piece of about 24 yards, 36 cents per yard.
3078 Bleached Butchers' Linen, 29 inches wide .25
Price for full piece of about 25 yards, 24 cents per yard.
3080 Bleached Butchers' Linen, 29 inches wide. .30
Price for full piece of about 24 yafds, 29 cents per yard.
3082 Bleached Butchers' Linen, 36 inches wide. .35
Price for full piece of about 24 yards, 33 cents per yard.
3084 Bleached Butchers' Linen, 40 inches wide, .40
Price for full piece of about 24 yards, 38 cents per yard.

Brown Linen Drilling.

Per yard.

3090 Brown or Unbleached Linen Drilling, twilled, good weight; for men's clothing, etc.; width, 26 inches $0.25

White Cotton Table Felting.

It is also called silent cloth, as when placed under the table cloth it dulls the sound of placing china on the table, makes the cloth look whiter, does not allow hot dishes to spoil the finish of the table, and is universally used when perfect table service is desired. We have it in cream white only.

Per yard.

3094 Table Felting, white only, double napped, good weight, 54 inches wide. Per yard $0.35
3096 Table Felting, double napped, thick, and soft, 54 inches wide. Alabama XX ...... .50
3098 Table Felting, 66 inches wide, extra thick, and soft, double napped, Howard ...... .65

Excelsior Quilted Table Pads, or Silence Cloths.

Pure white made of two layers of white cotton cloth with wadding between and quilted perfectly, clean and free from lint.

3100 Table Pads, quilted, size, 54x63 in. Each.. $1.50
3101 Table Pads, quilted, size, 63x72 in. Each.. 1.75
3102 Table Pads, quilted, size, 63x90 in. Each.. 2.25
3103 Table Pads, quilted, size, 68x108 in. Each. 2.95

WOOLEN DEPARTMENT.

In this department we carry a large and varied assortment of ladies' heavy weight and extra width *Dress Goods, Jacket Cloths, Cloakings, Men's and Boys' Cassimeres* and *Corduroys*. As we purchase all of these goods direct from manufacturers and in very large quantities, we can always save our customers "the middlemen's profit," and often more.

Ladies' Cloth.

New Spring shades for Capes, Dresses, Wraps, etc.
3204 Ladies' Cloth, 50 inches wide, fine Union wool mixtures. A nicely finished cloth, good weight and one that will give satisfactory wear. Colors are dark or light gray mixture, light brown, in plain or mixture, slate, heliotrope, seal brown or mahogany, black. Per yard $0.35
Full piece of about 50 yards, 32 cents per yard.
3206 Ladies' Cloth, fine, closely woven, perfect finish, absolutely all wool, 50 inches wide, for fashionable and durable dresses. We claim for this cloth that it is far superior in quality and finish to any half dollar ladies' cloth on the market. Buy a pattern and compare it with others. Colors: Slate, black, light navy, dark navy, garnet, electric blue, brown, light brown, beige, cardinal, wine, myrtle, sapphire, olive, plain gray, tan, seal brown, also mixtures in light gray, medium gray, dark gray, light or dark brown mixtures; also illuminated mixtures in brown or blue. Per yard ...... .45
Price for full piece of about 50 yards, 43 cents per yard.
3210 Extra Fine Habit Cloth, 52 inches wide, all wool, very heavy, handsomely finished, new shades. This cloth will compare favorably with any 90 cent cloth in the market. Write for samples before purchasing eleswhere. Colors: Tan, slate, light gray, seal brown, golden brown, myrtle, medium brown, sapphire blue, navy blue, wine, black; also mixtures in dark iron gray, medium gray, light gray, light or medium brown. Per yard ...... .65
Full piece of about 50 yards, 63 cents per yard.

Broadcloths.

New Shades for Spring and Summer.

NOTE:—Broadcloths will be very extensively used for ladies' capes, dresses, wraps, etc. It is a fabric that is unusually durable and elegant for out-door gowns.

Our lines have been selected with great care. They are manufactured especially for us, and we believe them to be unapproachable in values.
3212 All Wool Broadcloth, 50 inches wide, twilled back and rich glossy face; finish is in the weave, not put on with rollers and sizing; colors are: Seal brown, tan, beige, myrtle, garnet or wine, old rose, purple, sapphire blue, slate, light gray, navy blue or black. Per yard $0.75
3214 Columbia Fine Broadcloth, all wool, superb lustrous finish, 52 inches wide; 6 yards makes a handsome dress. Colors are; Seal brown, medium brown, golden brown, light tan, dark tan, bronze, wine, marine or light navy, dark navy, silver gray, medium gray, slate, old rose, purple, cardinal or black. Per yard 1.00
We claim this cloth to be equal to any sold elsewhere at $1.50.
3216 Imported Broadcloth, very fine all wool, 54 inches wide. Colors: Seal, medium or golden brown, black, fawn, tan, wine, myrtle, navy, slate, bronze, purple, white or cream. Per yard 1.80

Storm Serge.

The popularity of Storm Serge does not diminish. No other fabric yet produced combines the wearing qualities and style of this cloth. Suited, as it is, to wear on nearly all occasions, no woman's wardrobe is quite complete without a Storm Serge dress. The width of these goods also makes them economical.
3220 All Worsted Storm Serge, 50 inches wide, a good cloth, made from extra long combed wool. Colors as follows: Black, light navy, dark navy or myrtle green. Per yard $0.60
3222 English All Worsted Storm Serge, a splendid heavy cloth, fine and firm, made from hard twisted wiry wools; an original and perfect wear resisting serge. Colors are: Myrtle, navy or black; width, 50 inches. Per yard ...... .75

Silk and Wool Mixed Costume Cloth.

This cloth is especially adapted for fashionable trade. Many ladies who display quiet taste in dress selections, but do not always want plain goods, will find this fabric peculiarly suited to their wants. It is firm and well woven. Very wide, so that a few yards suffice for a dress, and will make up attractively either plain or with Velvet trimmings.
3232 Silk and Wool Mixed Suiting, 50 inches wide, in the following plain mixtures: Pepper and salt style, gray and white, brown and white, blue and white, wine and white or blue and gold. Per yard $0.68

A Hummer.

3233 Wide Wale Serge, 50 inches wide; colors navy blue or black only. Made especially for walking costumes or general out door wear. Will make splendid skirts to wear with shirt waists, or fine Eton suits. It is of medium weight, and although not all wool, has the appearance of it. The texture is firm; will wear like wire. It was made to sell at 40 cents. Circumstances placed it in our hands at our own price. We will let you share the bargain at Per yard $0.25
Full piece of about 45 yards, per yard, 24 cents.

Fancy Wool Suitings.

For tailormade street gowns.

3234 Fancy Wool Suiting, 50 inches wide, entirely new, and the handsomest wide cloth shown this season. It is made from twisted wools of contrasting colors, so as to produce a fine seeded effect. Color combinations are: Black and gold; wine and black; navy and gold; black and red; olive and gold; turquoise blue black and gold. Per yard $0.50

Covert Cloth Suiting.

The newest cloth for ladies' tailor-made costumes.
3236 Covert Cloth Suiting, all wool, 50 inches wide; a handsome cloth, strong and heavy. Covert cloth is woven from wool of two contrasting colors, which form a fine mixture effect. The back of the cloth is in contrasting color to the face, and is often used as a trimming. We have the following combinations: dark gray mixture; olive and gold; light grayish brown; light and dark brown; dark blue and gray; tan and seal.
Per yard $0.69

Heavy Woolens, Cloakings, Overcoatings, Etc.

3240 Old Homestead Cloaking, 27 inches wide; quite heavy. Plaided, striped or checked in tan and light brown or dark colors, also diagonal effects in dark colors. Needs no lining. Not made of fine wool, but will wear well $0.40
Price for full piece of about 50 yards, 36 cents per yard.

Diagonal Jacket Cloth.

A job to close;

3243 Diagonal Jacket Cloth, 50 inches wide; also used for heavy dresses; a very strong and handsome cloth; weight about 14 ounces to the yard. Only styles tan or gray mixtures. Present actual value, $1.00 per yard. Price while they last $0.47½

Sheeting in 25 yard lengths, a quantity you can afford to buy.

Cheviot Cloakings.

The most popular cloth of the day.

3244 Heavy Weight Cheviot Cloaking, 56 inches wide. The best value for the money that is offered anywhere. We have it in black or navy blue. Per yard $1.00

Diagonal Cloaking.

A special job.

3246 Diagonal Cloakings, 50 inches wide, medium heavy weight. A very strong and good looking cloth made to sell at $1.50 per yard. We secured the lot at a bargain and took all the mill had. Color Gray. Price, while they last. Per yard $0.75

Fine Cheviot Cloaking.

3249 Fine Cheviot, 54 inches wide, medium weight. A very durable and stylish cloth, not too heavy, and especially adapted for children's and misses' cloaks. Colors: Cardinal, coachman's drab. Per yard $1.39
3250 Heavy Cloaking, 54 inches wide. A rich finished, smooth faced cloth. Color: Light brown. Per yard 1.60

Tan Boucle Ulstering or Coating.

3252 Boucle Cloth; width, 56 inches: Tan color only. For fashionable jackets, ulsters or cloaks. This is a remarkably handsome cloth; good weight. It is plain, smooth weave, over the surface of which is the boucle effects, produced by curly mohair noils of same colors, woven irregularly through the cloth, and having the appearance of silk tufts. These goods are sold by fashionable retailers at $2.00 per yard. Our price, per yard $1.25

Cashmere Mixture Cloakings.

3253 Cashmere Mixture Cloakings, 54 inches wide. A heavy weight, good wearing cloth, entirely new and extremely stylish. Manufacturers of fashionable cloaks and jackets have purchased this cloth very freely, and predict for it a very large sale. Colors are: Dark brown mixture or black mixture. Per yard $1.68

Colored Beaver Cloakings.

These goods are too well known to require any introduction.
3254 Beaver Cloakings, 56 inches wide. A splendid, heavy cloth with fine fur face, smooth as satin, high finish. Colors: Brown, navy blue, myrtle green or black. Per yard $1.50

Black Beaver.

3260 Black Ashuelot Beaver, wool filling, 54 inches wide $0.95
Price for full piece of about 50 yards, 90 cents per yard.
3262 Black Wool Beaver, 54 inches wide; a good cloth 1.50
3264 Black Wool Beaver, extra face, fur back, 54 inches wide 2.25
3266 Black All Wool Beaver, 54 inches wide, best 3.50

Black Kersey.

3267 Gladstone Black Kersey, 54 inches wide; a handsomely finished cloaking of great durability. Color is a bright and permanent black. Per yard 1.75

Repellent or Waterproof.

NOTE—We sell great quantities of Repellents for serviceable "Knock-about" dresses, under skirts, men's shirts and children's suits. No better wearing cloth can be made.
3271 Dark Gray Repellent Suiting, 50 inches wide, a heavy and well made cloth; would be cheap at 35 cents. We have received a lot of about 100 pieces which we will offer while they last at: Per yard $0.25
Full piece of about 50 yards, 23¼ cents per yard.
3273 Repellent Suiting, 50 inches wide, strong and heavy. Colors: Dark blue, black or brown. We have just closed out a large eastern mill's stock of this cloth (about 300 pieces) and consider it one of the best purchases we ever made. The cloth was made to sell for 50 cents and is good value at that price. Goods forced on a dull market, nerve and ready cash explain our purchase. We offer them to our customers while they last at: Per yard ...... .29
Full piece of about 50 yards, 27½ cents per yard.
3274 Repellent or waterproof cloth, good weight, navy blue, gray mixture, brown mixture, black mixture or wine, width 54 inches. Per yard.... .50
Full piece of about 50 yards, 48 cents per yard.

Cottonades and Cotton Worsteds.

3280 Cottonades, width 27 inches, made in stripes; dark grounds with bright color lines. Per yard $0.12
Full piece, about 50 yards, 11¼ cents per yard.
3286 Hyde Park Cottonades; width, 27 inches. A well made, strong, good wearing cloth. Splendid pattern, copied from foreign worsted. Checks in black, gray and red; black, brown and red, or black, brown and blue. Narrow stripes in black and gray black and brown, or mixed black, gray and brown stripe. Per yard ...... .16
Full piece, about 50 pards, 15 cents per yard.
3288 Cottonades, best goods; stripes, checks or mixtures in black and white, blue and white or brown and white; width, 27 inches. Per yard.. $0.18
Price for full piece of about 50 yards, 17 cents per yard.

Cottonades -Continued.

3290 Cotton Worsted, in stripes only, black and blue, black and gray or black and brown; the cloth is firm and of good weight. The colors and patterns are extremely neat; the stripes are narrow and woven to resemble either a fine diagonal or herringbone effect; width, 27 inches. Per yard .... .22
Full piece of about 50 yards, 20½ cents per yard.

3292 Cotton Worsted, 27 inches wide, soft, fleeced back, splendid weight. Styles are exact copies of imported worsteds. Medium and dark narrow stripes and checks. This we believe to be the best value, considering style and quality, that has ever been offered. Per yard........... .25
Full piece of about 50 yards, 23½ cents per yard.

3294 Northwestern Diagonal; width, 27 inches, soft finish, firmly woven and heavy weight. Will stand any amount of wear; looks like all wool. Grounds are black with mixtures of red, gold, or white. Per yard .... .30

Imported Fustian.

This is also called moleskin; it is very close, heavy weight, hard twisted cotton goods, with a surface resembling cashmere; has wonderful wearing qualities and is much used where clothing has rough usage.

Per yard.

3296. Fustian, drab only; 27 inches wide......$0.75

Kentucky Jeans.

Per yard.

3300 Kentucky Jeans, 27 inches wide; in black mixed, brown mixed or medium gray; medium weight, good and strong. Price, per yard... ...$0.10
Price for full piece of about 50 yards, 9¼ cents per yard.

3302 Kentucky Jeans. Good cloth, 27 inches wide. Made in gray mixed and black or brown mixed. Per yard....... .... .12
Price for full piece of about 50 yards, 11¼ cents per yard.

3304 Kentucky Jeans These are most excellent goods at the price. We bought a great quantity and make a low price to sell them quickly. Send for samples. These are a great bargain. Colors: Medium gray, dark gray, light gray, brown, black or gold mixed. Per yard................. .16
Price for full piece of about 50 yards, 15 cents per yard.

3306 Kentucky Jeans, good weight, strong and serviceable. Cannot be beat for the price. Colors: Light, medium or dark gray; sheep's gray or brown; width, 27 inches. Per yard.... .22
Price for full piece of about 50 yards, 20½ cents per yard.

3308 Kentucky Jeans, light, medium or dark gray, sheep's gray, gold, brown or black mixed. Good sterling goods, heavy weight. Per yard.. .30
Price for full piece of about 50 yards, 28 cents per yard.

3312 Kentucky Jeans, all wool filling, light, medium or dark gray, sheep's gray, black mixed, brown or black. Per yard...... .... .40
Price for full piece, about 50 yards, 37½ cents per yard.

Imported Corduroy.

Per yard,

For clothing, carriage cushions, etc.

3320 Corduroy, for men's wear, heavy and strong; 27 inches wide; drab or brown only....$0.50
Price for full piece, about 50 yards, 48 cents per yard.

3322 Corduroy, medium weight, for men's clothing, finer than above. Colors: Drab, brown or black................................... .65
Price for for full piece, about 50 yards, 63 cents per yard.

3324 Corduroy, in myrtle or navy................ .70
Price for full piece of about 50 yards, 68 cents per yard.

3326 Fine Corded Corduroy, good goods, strong and stout. Colors: Drab, brown or black........ .85
Price for full piece of about 50 yards. 82 cents per yard.

3328 Heavy Corduroy, 27 inches wide; in black, brown, light otter, dead grass, or drab.... ... .85
Price for full piece of about 50 yards, 83 cents per yard.

3330 Heavy Corduroy in partridge mixture. Has a fine mottled effect, as seen on the breast of partridge. Brown or gray mixtures; width, 27 inches. Per yard........ .... .85
Price for full piece of about 50 yards, 82 cents per yard.

3332 Corduroy, 57 inches wide; odorless; extra heavy; navy and myrtle only.................. .90

Cloth and Cassimeres.

Two Big Bargains.

3340 Oxford Twill Cassimere, a black mixed heavy suiting; bought at auction at about half its real value. Has only one fault; will wear too long. You won't get tired of it though; it's neat style. Width, 27 inches. Per yard $0.18
Price for full piece of about 50 yards, 17 cents per yard.

3342 Zebra Cassimere, brother to the above in point of value, though the styles are quite different. These are checks or plaids, in mixtures of gray, with black and a little bright color combined. It is a good, medium weight cloth, wool one way, and is usually sold for 35 cents a yard; width, 27 inches. Per yard..................
Price for full piece of about 50 yards, 18½ cents per yard.

Cassimeres—Continued.

3344 North Adams Worsteds; width, 27 inches. Small checks in black and brown, or brown and gray; stripes in black and gray, brown mixed, and red or black and blue Soft, nice feeling goods, and will wear well. Per yard .... .23

3347 Sterling Cassimeres; width, 27 inches. Splendidly constructed goods, medium weight, styles copied from English suiting. Invisible checks in black and gray or black and brown, narrow herringbone stripes in brown and gray, bl ck, gray and red or brown gray and red; half inch striped diagonals in black or brown with gray. Also plain diagonal mixtures in dark gray or brown. Per yard...... .... .28
Full piece of about 50 yards, 26½ cents per yard.

3352 Satinet Panting and Suiting, cotton warp, check or stripes in brown and black, or gray and black mixture; fast colors, 27 inches wide...... .30

3354 Fine Cassimeres, 27 inches wide, nicely woven, good wearing goods; styles are pin checks or neat stripes in gray, brown or black mixed .32½

3356 Guernsey Cassimere; width, 27 inches, fine goods for wear, styles neat; quiet colors, small checks in gray or light brown; narrow stripe in medium brown........................... .37½

3358 Heavy Kersey, rough, all wool, plain mixtures, checks or stripes, in gray and brown mixed; 27 inches wide, ... .45

3360 Cassimere Suitings, all wool, most gray, light medium or dark, in plain checks, broken checks or stripes; also in plain gray or brown mixed. This is a favorable line of goods for boys' wear, and will also make good suits for men; 27 inches wide.................. ..... .50

3362 Fine Cassimere Suitings, all wool, a similar line of goods to that above, but heavier weight. We recommend it. These goods come from reliable mills. Styles are plain mixtures in gray or brown, fine invisible checks in gray with red or black; brown with gray or black; black with gray; 27 inches wide.................... .75

3364 Cassimere Suitings and Pantings, heavy, in gray, brown or black mixed stripes, checks and plaids, good weight for men's wear; 27 inches wide......... .... .85

3368 Plain Navy Blue Smooth Cloth for suits; 54 inches wide, all wool......................... 1.30

*** **Our next Catalogue will be sent only to those who send us 15 cents for postage.**

Navy Blue Cloth.

3376 Middlesex Dark Blue Flannel Suiting, for men's or boys' wear; width, 54 inches, weight, 14 ounces. Per yard..........................$2.25

3378 Middlesex Flannel Suiting, dark blue for men's or boys' wear; width, 54 inches; weight, 16 ounces. Per yard............................ 3.00

Astrakhans and Seal Plushes.

3390 Black Astrakhan, short curl, mingled with glossy mohair, 50 inches wide.......... ....$2.15

3392 Brown Astrakhan, better grade, 50 inches wide.. 2.50

3394 Astrakhan, black, medium curl, 50 inches wide.. 3.00

3398 Astrakhan, brown, larger curl, 50 inches wide.. 4.00

3400 Chinchilla, or black and white Astrakhan, 50 inches.. 2.75

3402 Chinchilla, or black and white Astrakhan, 50 inches; better.................................. 3.65

3406 Chinchilla, or black and white Astrakhan, 50 inches; best.................................... 5.00

3410 Silk Seal Plush, 50 inches wide.......... 7.50

3412 Silk Seal Plush, 50 inches wide; better.... 9.00

3414 Silk Seal Plush, 50 inches wide; like sealskin.. 10.50

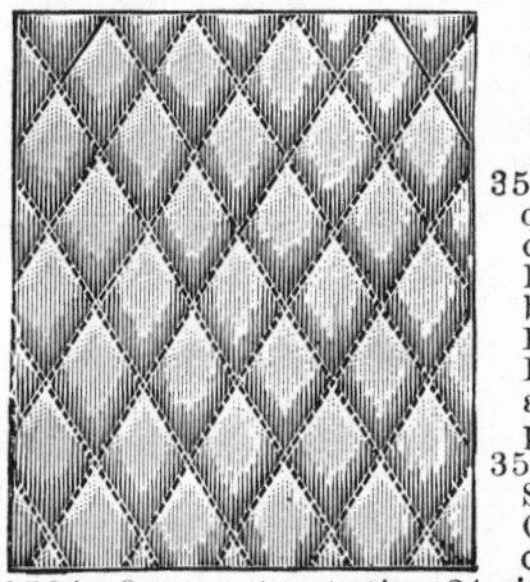

Quilted Linings.

3500 Quilted Sateen, good quality. Colors: Black, cardinal, pink, old gold, light blue, wine, or brown; 27 inches wide. Per yard...........$0.50
Price for full piece of about 42 yards, 47 cents per yard.

3502 Quilted Farmers' Satin, 27 inches wide. Colors: Black or brown only.....................$0.65

3504 Quilted Silk Satin, 24 inches wide. Colors: Seal brown, medium brown, black, cardinal, old gold, wine, navy, light blue, pink, orange, cream and white...................................$0.75

3506 Better Quality Silk Satin, 24 inches wide; same colors as in No. 3504....................... 1.00

FLANNEL DEPARTMENT.

In this department we have in stock and quoted almost every flannel made. We have described them so the different kinds can be easily recognized and values ascertained without seeing the goods or sending for samples. We, however, send samples cheerfully upon request, and should we not have quoted what you want will gladly get it for you.

Outing Flannels.

Each succeeding year brings out more styles and priettier than the preceding one. The many uses to which the outing cloths of to-day are put seem almost indescribable. No other fabric yet produced can take their place. Their peculiar downy feeling, soft and delicate color shadings and light weight seem to form a combination which establishes some particular use for the cloth in nearly every person's wardrobe. They are very largely in demand now for Men's and Boys' Shirts, Blouse Waists for Ladies and Children; dresses for outing or house wear and wrappers. They are also extensively used for night gowns in the softer weaves. Our new styles in outings are now open. *Send for samples.* We can do you good. Our stock is immense in quantity and styles. Early orders secure best selections. Choice styles become scarce as the season advances.

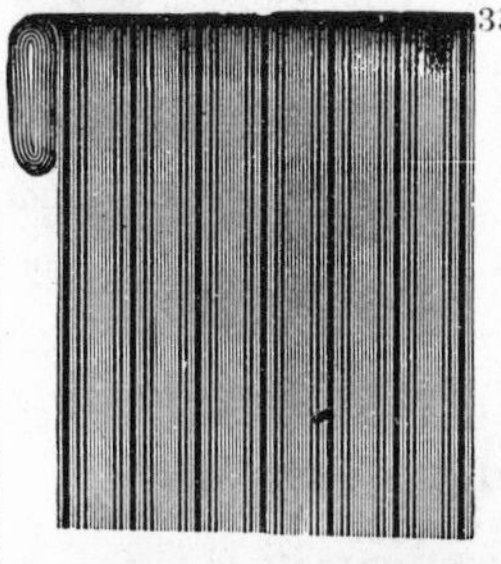

3507 Outing Flannel, 27 inches wide. A very choice line of neat and attractive styles in the following combined colors: Light blue and navy; brown and navy; light blue navy and red; navy and orange; navy and gold or brown and red. We venture to say that this is the best fancy outing cloth ever offered at so low a price.
Per yard...........$0.04¾
Full piece of about 50 yards, 4½ cents per yard.

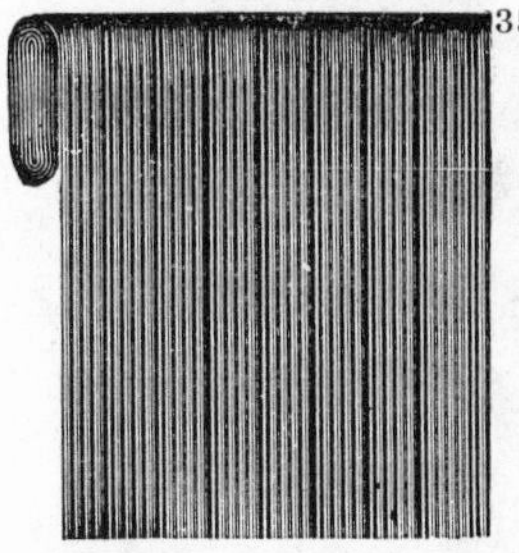

3508 Trilby Outing Flannel, 27 inches wide; soft and fleecy, very superior to anything sold before at the price. Stripes only in following predominating colors: Cream, gray, light blue, light brown or tan.
Per yard..... .....$0.06
Psice for full piece of about 50 yards, per yard 5½ cents.

Index, Pink Pages.

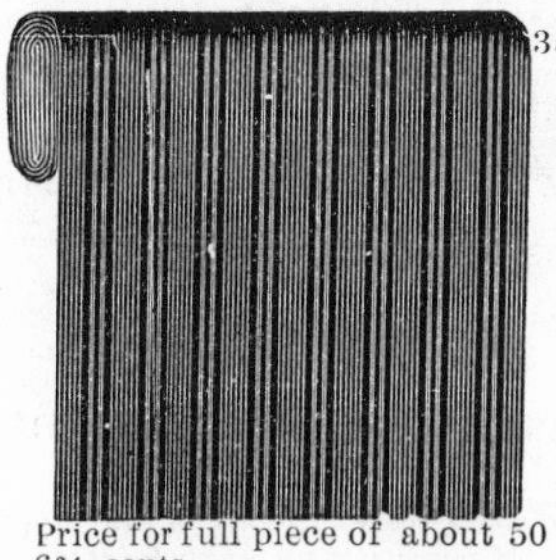

3510 Marcella Outings, a beautiful line of checks; the cloth is firm, nicely teazled, and the color combinations exquisitely. These are some of them, gold and blue; gray and pink; blue and red; gray and red; light blue and pink; tan and white; brown and blue, or two shades of gray.
Per yard......$0.07½
Price for full piece of about 50 yards, per yard 6¾ cents.

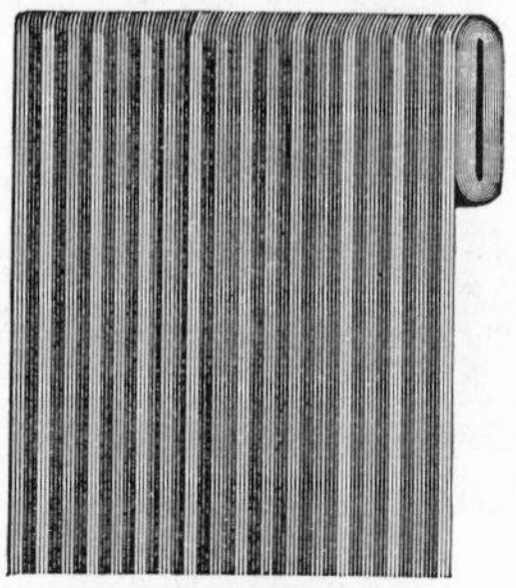

3511 Coventry Flannelettes, width 27 inches. An entirely new cloth, soft and downy to the touch. Grounds are rather dark, and are woven in a fine speckled effect after the style of new dress fabrics. Stripes are in navy and gold, wine and blue, or brown and gold. Checks in navy and gold, blue, wine and white, or blue, gold and white.
Per yard......$0.09
Full piece of about 50 yards, 8½ cents per yard.

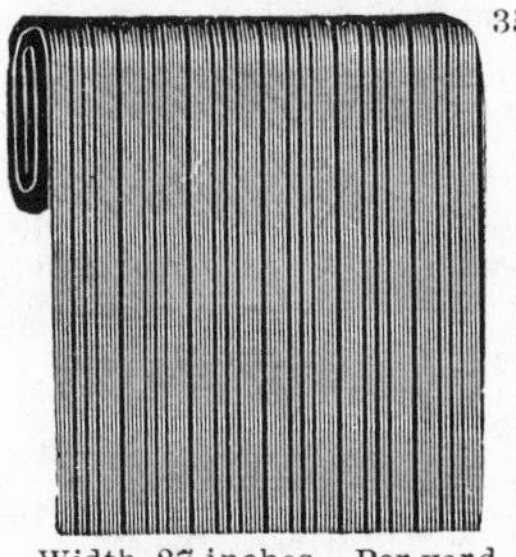

3514 Wayside Suiting. The prettiest line of narrow stripes you ever saw for the price. Styles are all new. Cloth close and fine, perfectly finished. Colors are quiet and genteel or light and dainty combinations on white grounds. Colors in stripes are: Light blue, cream and gold; pink cream and gold; lilac, cream and gold, gray, cream and pink; brown, cream and gold; gray, brown and gold.
Width, 27 inches. Per yard.... ....$0.10
Full piece of about 50 yards, 9¼ cents per yard.

Outing Flannels—Continued.

3516 Striped and Checked Outing Flannel width, 27 inches, dark and medium colors. A closely napped cloth, fine and strong, one that will wear well and always look well. In checks we can furnish the following styles: Tan and red; gray shaded; black and tan; brown and tan; gray and blue. Stripes are: blue and tan; gray and tan; wine and gray, white hair line, tan and black hair line.
Per yard .... .09½
Full piece of about 54 yards, 9 cents per yard.

3520 Plain Domett Outing Flannels, 27 inches wide. Light, medium or dark gray; blue, gray, pink or blue, tan or brown, mixed. Good looking goods, and good to wear. Per yard .... .08½
Price for full piece of about 50 yards, 8 cents per yard.

3524 English Flannelettes and Teazle Downs. The softest and loveliest cloth you ever handled. Comes in light and medium colorings. The light colorings are the daintiest effects ever produced, and rival the costly eiderdown. We also have them in plain pink, light blue or cream. The newest and prettiest style this season is the knickerbocker effect, which is produced with threads of bright colored silk, lightly scattered, and appearing in little tufts here and there. They come in the following color combinations: Light blue, with brown; pink with blue; brown with gold, or ecru with orange. Other styles are: Broken checks in pink, gray, brown, light blue or fancy mixed; even checks in blue, brown, pink or gray; hair line stripes, cream with blue, or cream with pink; and broken stripes in pink or blue. Width, 28 inches. Per yard $0.10
Price for full piece of about 50 yards, 9½ cents per yard.

3525 Southdown Flannels, 28 inches wide. A thick, heavily napped flannelette, soft as eider down. Especially adapted for house wrappers, morning gowns and underskirts. Styles are broken or irregular stripes, softly shaded, not too pronounced. Colors combined are: Gray, wine and gold; brown, wine and gold; gray, navy and gold.
Per yard ...,...... $0.12
Full piece of about 50 yards, 11 cents per yard.

3526 Heavy Wool Mixed Twilled Outing Flannel, 30 inches wide. A splendid cloth for hard wear. Forty per cent. wool. Especially good for men's shirts or ladies' underskirts. Styles are broken stripes in tan with red, wine with blue, or blue with red. Per yard .... .17
Full piece of about 50 yards, 16 cents per yard.

3528 Extra Fine Outing Flannel, part wool Filling; fine cotton warp; has the touch and feel of fine imported cloth, and costs much less. It is made in stripes only, in the following colors, on cream-white grounds: Blue, pink, tan, or tan with cardinal thread combined on cream. Width, 32 inches. We consider them extra value at $0.20
Price for full piece of about 40 yards, 19 cents per yard.

Silk Embroidered Flannels.

New Designs.   Note Reduced Price.

Embroidery is done with a smooth twisted silk, giving more service and is more showy than the flat silk usually used. The work is all done on a specially selected cream white 36-inch all wool flannel, with two-inch folded edge. Designs are all new and are handsomer and greater width embroidery than can be found elsewhere at the same prices.

It is not customary to sample embroidered flannels, as very accurate descriptions are given and expense of sampling is great. However, where selections cannot otherwise be made we will send samples upon request.
Per yard

3530 Width of embroidery 1½ inches, small neat spray designs $0.55
3532 Width of embroidery 2¾ inches, olive branch design .... .65
3534 Width of embroidery 3 inches, double crescent design, detached pattern .... .78
3536 Width of embroidery 3½ inches, snow ball and vine pattern; very pretty .... .82

3537 Width of embroidery 4½ inches, artistic design, vine and crescent. See cut No. 3537; ½ size of work.... $0.87

3538 Width of embroidery 5 inches, floral scroll design. See cut No. 3538; ½ size of work $0.90

3540 Width of embroidery 5¾ inches, elaborate design, clover leaf, blue bell, crescent and vine. See cut No. 3540; shows ½ size of work...... .... $1.05

3541 Width of embroidery 6 inches, beautiful floral scroll with center of design or flower in drawn or openwork. A novelty. See cut No. 3541; shows ½ size of work............. $1.20

Hemstitched Embroidered Flannel.
Cream White Only.

3542 Hemstitched Flannel, with small running design, vine and bud. Per yard....$0.60
3543 Hemstitched Flannel, border worked in connected block dice pattern. Crescent and spray above. See cut 2218; shows work ½ actual size. Per yard $0.69

Opera Flannel.   Per yard.

3544 Opera or Pressed Flannel, 25 inches wide, fine, soft wool, nicely finished, much used for babies, ladies' dressing sacques, fancy work, etc. Colors: Navy, royal, azure, light or gas-light blue, wine, garnet, cardinal, scarlet, cream, pink, gold, salmon, yellow, black, red, brown, light, medium or dark gray mixed. Other colors we cannot get, as they are not made.......$0.32
Price for full piece of about 20 yards, 30 cents per yard.

Basket Weave Flannel.

3545 Matelasse Suiting (Opera Flannel), basket weave, fine all wool fabric, for basques, sacques or children's wear; nothing more elegant when made; will wash. Colors: Royal blue, scarlet, seal or black. These are the only colors now made; 25 to 27 inches wide........$0.45
Price for full piece, about 26 yards, 43 cents per yard.

French Printed Flannels.
For Wrappers and Dressing Sacques.

3546 French Printed Flannels; all wool 27 inches wide; a beautiful assortment of designs, small and medium size; also stripes. Among the styles shown are navy grounds with white hair line stripes or polka dot; cream ground with light blue or pink hair line stripes; cream or light blue grounds with flower designs. Width, 27 inches.
Per yard $0.50

Twilled Opera Flannel.

3549 Twilled Pressed Flannel, 27 inches wide. This flannel will supply a long felt want for something with a little more body than the plain woven opera flannel; it is made, if anything, from a softer yarn, spun from finest Australian wool, finished equal to the French goods, and the color shades have been carefully selected; they are as follows: Cream, pink, light blue, tan, grey, cardinal, wine, brown, navy or black. Per yard...............$0.35
Price for full piece of about 36 yards, per yard, 32½ cents.

Plain Eider Down.

3550 Plain Eider Down, elastic back. Eider down is a fine fabric with an elastic back so finished that it resembles a sheep fleece closely sheared. Where beauty, combined with warmth and gossamer lightness is wanted, this is most desirable. Width, 24 inches; colors: Light blue, navy blue, pink, cream white, medium brown, cardinal, French gray, garnet, old gold, black, tan, fawn, mixtures in light or dark gray $0.30
Price for full piece of about 23 yards, 28 cents per yard.
3551 Plain Eider Down 36 inches wide; all colors as above. All wool face, heavy fleece........ .45
Price for full piece of about 22 yards, 42½ cents per yard.

Striped Eider Down.

Note—Striped and Fancy Eider Downs are used for children's cloaks, Afghans and ladies' morning house gowns.

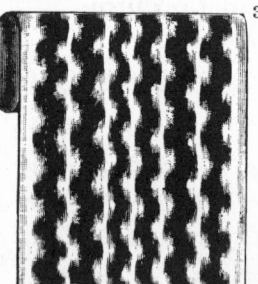

3552 Capella Cloakings, 26 inches wide. This is a very fancy striped eider down; very dainty in colorings and novel in design. The stripes are irregular or zigzag, and are mostly in dark shades on light harmonizing grounds, space between stripes is about two inches. Colors are: Brown on cream; pink on light blue; white on tan; or black on gray. Per yard........$0.38

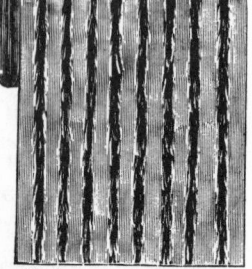

3553 Moretta Cloaking, 27 inches wide. This is one of the prettiest novelties ever produced. It is a plain eider down weave, in solid colors, with fine, long, silky mohair woven in narrow stripes of contrasting colors about two inches apart. We are especially proud of this line. Colors are: Cream ground with stripes of light blue, pink or brown; pink with brown; light blue with brown; ecru with blue or pink; tan with brown; tan with shaded wine and olive; gray with black, garnet with black; light blue with white; or pink with shaded wine and olive. Per yard........$0.49
3554 Fairy Cloakings, 26 inches wide. This is one of the finest and daintiest of the eider down novelties. The styles are in mottled and shaded stripes; irregular combinations on various tints in each style. Prominent effects are: Cream with light blue and pink; cream with pink and brown; cream with brown and tan; cream with tan and light blue; white with gray and ecru. Per yard .... .60

Lamb's Wool.

SIMILAR TO EIDER DOWN.

3562 Lamb's Wool, 26 inches wide. This goods is very largely sold now for babies' cloaks, afghans and ladies' morning gowns. It has the soft down-like feeling of eider down, but the face is of a fine, soft curly wool, instead of being plain like the latter goods. Colors are: Pink, tan, ecru, light blue, cream, cardinal, plain light gray or dark gray mixture. Per yard............$0.45

Llama Cloth.

A NOVELTY.

3563 Llama Cloth, 26 inches wide; made for children's short cloaks; trims handsomely with velvet. This is an entirely new cloth and one of the most stylish materials yet put on the market. It is similar to eider down, but heavier and having a longer and more hairy fleece. We have a mottled effect, which is a combination of gray, brown, red and blue; Other styles are garnet and gray, tan and gray, cardinal and gray, light gray, pink or blue. Per yard..............$0.50

Fancy Cotton Eider Down.

SOMETHING NEW.

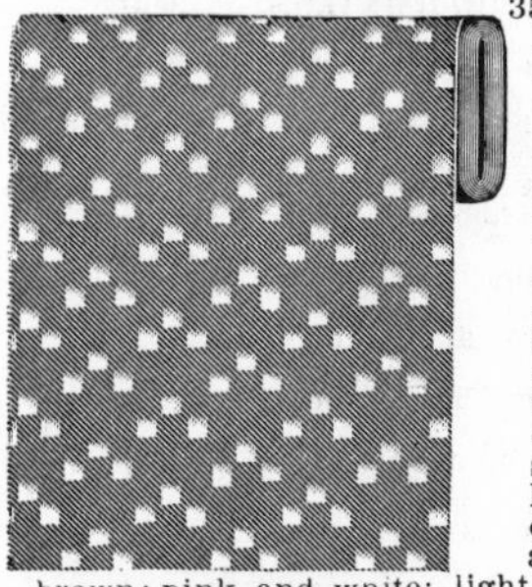

3564 Cotton Eider Down, 27 inches wide. A splendid imitation of the wool goods. Can only be distinguished after a close examination. This will undoubtedly be a big seller on account of its handsome appearance and remarkably low price. The design is a cluster of three small squares in contrasting colors on solid grounds. We have the following combinations: Brown and ecru; tan and brown; pink and white; light gray and white; ecru and white; light blue and white. Stripes in gray with pink, or brown with ecru. Per yard............$0.15
Full piece of about 20 yards, 14¼ cents per yard.

Unmade Skirt Patterns.

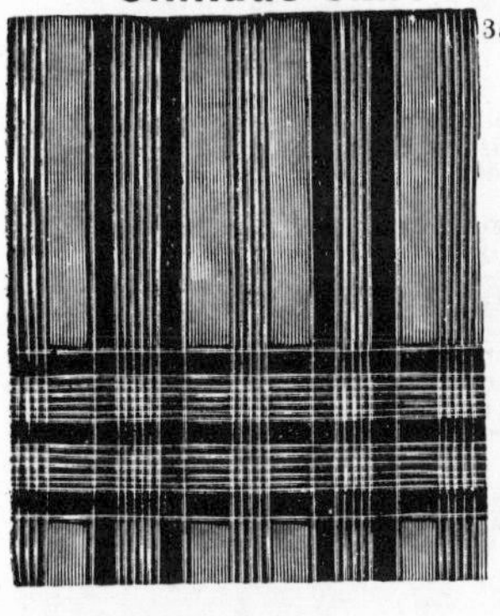

3580 Methuen Domestic Flannel Unmade Skirts. The width of goods makes length of skirt (38 inches), pattern 2¼ yards long, large enough for any lady. We sell great quantities of these skirts. Each one is put up separately and nicely folded. They are made with striped body and plaid borders in following combinations: Gray, with black and blue; blue with gray or red with gray.
Price, each..............$0.28
Price, per dozen.............3.15

3582 All Wool Skirt Patterns, the best low-price all wool skirt shown by anybody; length of skirt, 40 inches; width, 80 inches. Colors: Cardinal and black; blue and black; gray and black; black and white. All neat stripes with plaided border in same color. Each..........62½

3584 All Wool Skirt Patterns, heavier and finer than above; length of skirt, 40 inches; length of pattern, 2¼ yards; the heaviest skirt and the prettiest patterns we have ever shown at the price. Color combinations are; Blue and black; scarlet and black; gray and black; in wide stripes and plaid borders; also brown and cream; broken stripes and narrow stripes in gray and black, with cardinal bourette threads in border. Each..........85

3586 Skirt Patterns, all wool, same size as above; better goods; very fine, soft and heavy. Colors are: Black and red; black and blue; black and gray; black and white..........1.00

3588 Cashmere Wool Skirts, extra fine, all wool; same size as above; weight, 16 to 17 ounces. Solid colors: Black, navy, dark gray or brown, with fancy striped borders. Price, while they last. Each..........1.35

Flannel Skirting by the Yard.

3600 All Wool Flannel Skirtings, 38 inches wide, made in stripes, with plain or checked border, in red and black; blue and black; gray or black; or white and black; 2¼ yards make a skirt. Price, per yard..........$0.45

3602 Wool Skirting, 38 inches wide, fine pressed flannel, entirely new patterns and colors; all stripes; plain borders; a few of the colors are: Cardinal, wine, navy, tan, reseda or brown. Bright knotted threads woven in border. Per yard..........50

3604 All Wool Flannel Skirting, extra heavy, 38 inches wide; colors as in 3600. Per yard.... .65

3—2nd

Plain White Union Flannel.

A union of cotton and wool, woven plain; no cotton threads, but the cotton used is carded into the wool before it is spun. The width and the amount of wool together with the weight determines the price. The higher the price the more wool and the greater the width. The higher grades feel and look like all wool and are generally sold as such. We guarantee to give full value. Made only in cream white.

Per yard.
3630 Plain White Union Flannel, 24 inches wide..........$0.12½
3632 Plain White Union Flannel, 24 inches wide.......... .15
Price for full piece of about 34 yards, 5 per cent. less than quoted cut length price.
3634 Plain White Union Flannel, 27 inches..... .20
3638 Plain White Union Flannel, 27 inches..... .30
3640 Plain White Union Flannel, 27 inches..... .35
3642 Plain White Union Flannel, 31 inches..... .40

White, Fine Cotton Warp, Wool Filled, Plain Flannel.

Per yard.
3650 Width, 27 inches..........$0.25
Price for full piece of about 36 yards, 22½ cents per yard.
3652 Width, 26 inches.......... .34
Price for full piece of about 36 yards, 32 cents per yard.

All Wool Plain White Flannels.

Made in cream white, of fine wool, perfectly finished, free from specks and of good weight.

Per yard.
3660 Width, 27 inches..........$0.25
Price for full piece of about 41 yards, 24 cents per yard.
3668 Width, 27 inches.......... .30
3670 Width, 27 inches.......... .35
3674 Width, 32 inches.......... .40
3676 Width, 32 inches.......... .45
3678 Width, 36 inches.......... .50
3682 Width, 36 inches.......... .60

Silk Warp Flannel, Extra Fine Wool Filling, Plain White.

Per yard.
3690 Width, 32 inches..........$0.75
Price for full piece of about 27 yards, 70 cents per yard.
3692 Width, 36 inches.......... .85
Price for full piece of about 37 yards, 80 cents per yard.

White Domett or all Cotton Shaker, Plain White Flannel.

While all cotton, they are soft and woolly, being napped to imitate wool goods, and as they do not shrink, answer nicely when used for a purpose where frequent washing is needed.

Per yard.
3700 Width, 27 inches..........$0.04½
This number, while the lowest priced, is an exceptionally fine piece of goods for the money, and much superior to any bleached cotton flannel at the price.
3701 Width, 27 inches..........$0.06
3702 Width, 27 inches.......... .08
3704 Width, 27 inches.......... .10
3708 Width, 30 inches.......... .12½
3710 Width, 30 inches.......... .15

Union Domett or Wool Mixed Shaker—Plain White.

The best grades are nearly all wool. These goods are made for service.

Per yard.
3724 Width, 29 inches..........$0.20
3728 Width, 30 inches.......... .25
3730 Width, 34 inches.......... .30

White Wool Shaker Flannel, Plain.

SPLENDID GOODS FOR THE PRICE.

Per yard.
3740 Width, 34 inches..........$0.35
3742 Width, 36 inches.......... .40

Wool Filled Cotton Warp, Twilled White Flannel.

Per yard.
3750 Width, 27 inches..........$0.25
3754 Width, 28 inches.......... .35

All Wool White Twilled.

Per yard.
3760 Width, 26 inches..........$0.35
3762 Width, 28 inches.......... .40

Plain Scarlet Domett Flannel.

All cotton, finely teazled or napped on both sides; much used for skirts, underwear or children's garments.

Per yard.
3770 Plain Scarlet Domett Flannel, 27 inches wide, good color and absolutely fast..........$0.10
Price for full piece of about 50 yards, 9 cents per yard.

Our Book Department is again crowded out. Must have more room. Why? Consult Our Prices.

Plain All Red Wool Flannel.

Per yard.
3778 Width, about 20 inches..........$0.12½
3780 Width, about 24 inches.......... .15
3782 Width, about 24 inches.......... .20
3784 Width, about 27 inches.......... .25
3786 Width, about 27 inches.......... .30
3790 Width, about 32 inches.......... .35

Plain Orange All Wool Flannel.

Per yard.
3800 Width, 22 inches..........$0.16
3802 Width, about 25 inches.......... .20
3804 Width, about 27 inches.......... .25
3806 Width, about 27 inches.......... .30

Plain Blue Gray, All Wool Flannel.

Per yard.
3808 Width, about 22 inches..........$0.20
3810 Width, about 25 inches.......... 25
3814 Width, about 26 inches.......... .35

All Wool Plain Black Mixed.

Per yard.
3820 About 24 inches wide..........$0.30
3822 About 25 inches wide.......... .35

Medium Blue All Wool Flannel Plain Weave.

Per yard.
3826 Width, 26 inches..........$0.25

Fast Black, All Wool Twilled Flannel.

Per yard.
3830 Black Twilled Flannel, 28 inches wide. All wool and fast color. A strong, good wearing flannel made to meet the present demand for black shirts and under garments..........$0.30

All Wool Scarlet Twilled Flannel.

Our Scarlet Twilled Flannels are all, "Anti-Rheumatic" goods, all medicinally dyed, free from any odor, made from good wool and excellent value.

Per yard.
3838 About 25 inches wide..........$0.15
3840 About 26 inches wide.......... 20
Price for full piece of about 60 yards, 5 per cent. less than cut price.
3842 About 27 inches wide.......... .25
3844 About 27 inches wide.......... .30
3846 About 27 inches wide, weight, 6 ounces per yard.......... .35
3848 About 27 inches wide.......... 40
3850 About 27 inches wide.......... .50

California Flannels.

ALL WOOL SCARLET TWILLED.

The flannels are made of the finest selected domestic wool and perfectly woven. They are evenly dyed: fast colors, only the best dyes being used. Nothing nicer in the market.

Per yard.
3856 Width 28 inches, 5 oz. (A)..........$0.35
3858 Width, 28 inches, 6 oz. (C).......... .40
3860 Width, 28 inches, 7 oz. (E).......... .45

All Wool Navy Twilled Flannel.

These goods are genuine indigo dye. No logwood or aniline being used; are fast in color, of good weight and because sold by every merchant and well known by customers are sold at a small profit.

Per yard.
3862 Width, 24 inches..........$0.15
3864 Width, 24 inches.......... .20
3866 Width, 27 inches.......... .25
3868 Width, 27 inches.......... .30
3870 Width, 27 inches, weight 5 ounces, per yard.......... .35
3872 Width, 28 inches.......... .40
3874 Width, 28 inches.......... .50

California Flannel.

All Wool Navy Twill.

Same quality as scarlet.

Per yard.
3880 Width, 28 inches, 5 oz. (A)..........$0.35
3882 Width, 28 inches, 6 oz. (C).......... .40
3884 Width, 28 inches, 7 oz. (E).......... .45

Blue Gray Wool Twilled Flannel.

Per yard.
3890 Width, about 27 inches, wool mixed..........$0.25
3896 Width, about 27 inches, all wool.......... .30
3898 Width, about 27 inches, all wool.......... .40

Union Blue Gray Twilled Flannel.

Per yard.
3900 Width, about 27 inches..........$0.12½
3904 Width, about 27 inches.......... .18

Irish Frieze, Blue Gray Mixture.

Cotton Warp, wool mixed filling. Price governs quality.

Per yard.
3910 Width, 27 inches, weight 4½ oz..........$0.12½
3912 Width, 27 inches, weight 5 oz.......... .16
3914 Width, 27 inches, weight 6 oz.......... .18
3916 Width, 27 inches, weight 8 oz.......... .20

We handle every known make of Gun and Revolver.

Irish Frieze, Pink Mixture.

Same as 3910–16.

For Skirts or Shirting.

		Per yard
3920	Width, 27 inches, weight 4½ oz	$0.12½
3922	Width, 27 inches, weight 5 oz	.16
3924	Width, 27 inches, weight 6 oz	.18
3926	Width, 27 inches, weight 8 oz	.20

All Wool Plain Scarlet Shaker Flannel.

Especially suitable for underwear. Heavier than any other plain weave. Honest goods.

		Per yard.
3930	Width, 27 inches	$0.25
3931	Width, 27 inches	.30
3932	Width, 31 inches	.35
3934	Width, 36 inches	.40

Plain Mascoma, Colored Shaker, all Wool Filling, Cotton Warp.

		Per yard.
3940	Width, 27 inches, blue mixed	$0.30
3942	Width, 27 inches, brown mixed	.30
3944	Width, 27 inches, black mixed	.30

Twilled Mascoma Colored Shaker All Wool Filling, Cotton Warp.

		Per yard.
3950	Width, 28 inches, blue mixed	$0.35
3952	Width, 28 inches, black mixed	.35
3954	Width, 28 inches, brown mixed	.35

Mascoma All Wool Shaker Flannel.

A fine heavy weight for shirts and underwear.

		Per yard.
3958	Width, 28 inches, gray mixture	$0.37½
3959	Width, 28 inches, brown mixture	.37½

Shirting and Dress Flannel.

Per yard.

4100 Farmers' Wool Mixed Shirting Flannels, 27 inches wide, about ¼ cotton, ¾ wool. Our leader. Made in plaids and checks only. Small and medium size, even and broken. Black and red or blue and black............$0.15
Price for full piece of about 50 yards, 14 cents per yard.

4104 Longman's Union, 4 Ounce Flannel, strong and serviceable, 27 inches wide. Colors are: Red and black; red and gray or blue and black; checks are small medium plaids.............. .18
Price for full piece of about 50 yards, 17 cents per yard.

4106 All Wool, full 4 ounces to the yard, Shirt Flannel, 27 inches wide. Styles are in checks, plaids and stripes. Colors: Red and gray, red and black or blue and black; broken checks or plaids; red and black, blue and black or gray and blue; even checks; stripes in gray with fine white stripes.............. .22
Price for full piece of about 50 yards, 21 cents per yard.

4108 All Wool, 5 ounces to each yard. Shirting Flannel; width 27 inches. Made plain and in checks, even and broken plaids. Color combinations are: Black and white; gray and white; gray and cardinal; gray and blue; gray, red and blue, or plain gray. .... .25
Price for full piece of about 45 yards, 24 cents per yard.

4110 The best 27-inch, 5-Ounce Dress and Shirting Flannel made. Made plain, striped, checked and plaided. Colors: Plain gray; even checks in red and black and blue and black; broken checks in gray, wine and white; small plaid in gray and white or blue gray, gold and navy; half inch stripes in black and gray, hair line stripes in gray and white.............. .30
Price for full piece of about 55 yards, 29 cents per yard

4116 Greenland All Wool Twilled 8 Ounce Shirting, checks, plaids and stripes. Made for the northwest trade. A big seller. Checks, broken plaids or stripes in red and black, blue and black, black and white; plain colors: Gray, navy or scarlet; width, 27 inches. .... .40
Price for full piece of about 38 yards, 39 cents per yard.

New Dress Plaids.

4120 Dresden Plaid Flannels, 27 inches wide. A soft napped flannel in bright checks or small plaids copied from the imported German flannels. Very pretty for children's wear, ladies' house sacques, etc. Colors are: Red and gray; gray and white; red and slate; red and black; black and white; blue and red, or red and tan.
Per yard. $0.17
Price for full piece of about 50 yards, 16 cents per yard.

DAIRY GOODS.

We quote very low prices on churns, butter workers, milk cans and all other dairy supplies. See Index for quotations.

Northwestern Mackinaw Flannels or Blanketing.

These goods were made especially for us and are superior stock to any other line in the market. They are all wool, made from the finest combed yarns, fast colors, and 54 inches wide. They are especially adapted for outdoor wear, for shirts, jackets or women's skirts, and are extensively used in lumber camps and throughout the Northwest

SCARLET MACKINAW.

		Per yard
4200	Mackinaw flannel, scarlet, 16 ounces	$0.69
4202	Mackinaw flannel, scarlet, 20 ounces	.80
4204	Mackinaw flannel, scarlet, 24 ounces	1.05

NAVY BLUE MACKINAW.

4208	Mackinaw flannel, navy, 16 ounces	.69
4210	Mackinaw flannel, navy, 20 ounces	.80
4212	Mackinaw flannel, navy, 24 ounces	1.05

⅞ SCARLET OR NAVY TWILLED FLANNEL.

4213 Twilled All Wool Shirting Flannel; width, 54 inches, weight, 12 ounces; very strong....... .80

Wool Felt Robe Lining.

4240 All Wool Figured Felt Robe Lining, 54 inches wide. Is firm, made for wear, and is figured in small design of red and black, brown and cream, etc.............. $0.75
Price for full piece of about 50 yards, 70 cents per yard.

White Flannel Sheeting.

4250 White all wool flannel sheeting; width 79 inches. Per yard.............. $1.25

Linsey.

Linsey is much used on account of its durability for shirting, skirts or children's dresses. We have a splendid assortment of styles in small and medium checks and broken plaids; same styles as higher priced shirting flannels.

4262 Atlanta Linsey in broken checks and plaids. Black and red, blue and black, or blue, red and gray. Width, 27 inches.
Per yard.............. $0.12½
Price for full piece of about 50 yards, 11¾ cents per yard.

4264 Linsey Plaid, fine quality, styles and colors same as above. Width, 27 inches...... ...... .15
Price for full piece of about 50 yards, 14 cents per yard

A New Flannel.

4270 Alhambra Guinea Hen Shaker Flannel, 29 inches wide. Mottled effect like guinea hen's feathers. Very soft and thick napped on both sides. Colors: Brown blue or gray mixed. Per yard.............. $0
Price for full piece about of 30 yards, 11½ cents per yard.

Unbleached Cotton Flannel.

Our Cotton Flannels are the Nashua brand, which are noted for having a longer nap and firmer back than any other line made. They cost less of us than others ask for ordinary grades.

Per yard.

REVISED LIST.

4495 Unbleached Cotton Flannel, cheapest made, width, 25 inches.............. $0.04
Full piece of about 60 yards, 3¾ cents per yard.

4500 Unbleached Cotton Flannel, width, 25 inches. .... .05
Price for full piece of about 58 yards, 4⅞ cents per yard.

Cotton Flannel—Continued. Per yard.

4502 Unbleached Cotton Flannel, width, 27 inches............. .06½
Price for full piece of about 58 yards, 6¼ cents per yard.

4504 Unbleached Cotton Flannel, width, 30 inches............. .08½
Price for full piece of about 58 yards, 8⅛ cents per yard.

4506 Unbleached Cotton Flannel, width, 33 inches. Compare this with the 10 cent quality others sell.... .10
Price for full piece of about 67 yards, 9¾ cents per yard.

4508 Unbleached Cotton Flannel, heavy weight, width. 31 inches............. .12
Price for full piece of about 55 yards, 11½ cents per yard.

4512 Unbleached Cotton Flannel, width 32 inches, extra heavy twilled back, and thick napping............. .15
Price for full piece of about 55 yards, 14¼ cents per yard.

Bleached Cotton Flannel.

Per yard.

4520 Bleached Cotton Flannel, width, 24 inches............. $0.06½
Price for full piece of about 58 yards, 6¼ cents per yard.

4522 Bleached Cotton Flannel, width, 26 inches, ... .08½
Price for full piece of about 58 yards, 8¼ cents per yard.

4524 Bleached Cotton Flannel, width 26 inches .10
Price for full piece of about 57 yards, 9½ cents per yard.

4526 Bleached Cotton Flannel, width, 28 inches............. .12
Price for full piece of about 55 yards, 11¼ cents per yard.

4528 Bleached Cotton Flannel, heavy weight, width, 28½ inches............. .14
Price for full piece of about 55 yards, 13¼ cents per yard.

4530 Bleached Cotton Flannel, width, 29½ inches, extra heavy............. .15½
Price for full piece of about 54 yards, 15 cents per yard.

Colored Cotton Flannel or Drapery Plushes.

Used for Portieres, Wall Hangings, Linings, etc.

Per yard

4550 Colored Cotton Flannel, old gold, medium and navy blue, olive, wine, cardinal, scarlet, drab or brown, 25½ inches $0.09
Price for full piece of about 54 yards, 8½ cents per yard.

4554 Colored Cotton Flannels, high colors, blue, scarlet, garnet, brown, slate, drab and gold, 27 inches.............. .12½
Price for full piece of about 55 yards, 11¼ cents per yard.

4556 Heavy Cotton Plushes, 28 inches wide: plain colors, Cardinal, scarlet, wine, pink, claret, blue, drab, slate, brown, old gold........ .15
Price for full piece of about 55 yards, 13 cents per yard.

LADIES' AND CHILDREN'S SUIT DEPARTMENT.

Ready Made Wrappers and Tea Gowns; dresses made to order. Styles absolutely correct up to date.
NOTE.—We cannot furnish samples of wrappers or other ready-made garments. Samples of any garments which we quote to measure and make up in our custom department will be cheerfully sent upon request.
SPECIAL.—*We can make to order any dress shown in the Standard Fashion Catalogue or other Catalogues.* Samples of dress materials and any information desired will be furnished upon request.
Write for our Special Dressmaking Catalogue No. E., mailed free of charge.
See our Special Catalogue E for rules for measurement.
Ready-made wrappers, gowns and dresses are made in the following scale of sizes only.

Bust, 32 in. Length, 54 in.   Bust, 36 in. Length, 56 in.   Bust, 40 in. Length, 58 in.
Bust, 34 in. Length, 56 in.   Bust, 38 in. Length, 58 in.   Bust, 42 in. Length, 58 in.

Spring and Summer Styles.

Every garment quoted by us this season has been selected with great care and for style and finish cannot be surpassed by any other line of *ready made goods on the market.*

5600 Ladies' Ready Made Wrappers, made of new light prints. Waist half lined, circular yoke with ruffle, large sleeves and belt; best wrapper sold anywhere for so low a price.
Each $0.59
Per dozen 6.65

5601 Ladies' Ready Made Wrappers, made of new light prints, yoke lined, has wide circular ruffle stitched in around yoke, no exposed edges. Half belt and large sleeves, Watteau back from yoke.
Each. $0.75
Per dozen 8.50

Wrappers—Continued.

5603 Ladies' Ready Made Wrappers, made of indigo blue standard prints, neat patterns, stripes and figures, waist half lined. Circular yoke with wide ruffle, Watteau pleat from collar, large sleeves, half-belt and pocket.
Each..................$0.75
Per dozen...... ....8.75

5604 Ladies' Ready Made Wrappers, made of good cotton challies in cream grounds with neat floral designs, stripes, etc. of pretty harmonizing colors. Style, same as 5603, lined waist. Each. $0.90

5603-4

5605-6

5605 Ladies' Ready Made Wrappers, made of light chambray prints: new colorings, such as light blue, pink, heliotrope or tan; neat and pretty patterns, made with a square yoke with wide ruffles, with collar notched in back; large sleeves, Watteau pleats from yoke, half belt and pocket; waist half lined. Each $0.85
Per dozen............. 9.25

5606 Ladies' Ready Made Wrappers. Same style as 5605; made of Pembrook suiting, a twilled cotton fabric; strong and durable, also very pretty; colors are dark and printed in fine mixture effects, resembling tweed. Each....................$1.25

5607 Ladies' Ready Made Wrappers, made of standard mourning prints; black grounds, with neat, white designs; half lined waist, new, rounded yoke, with gathered front; ruffle has a gathered heading and is outlined with narrow white braid trimming, which is also on the wide notched back collar and cuffs; Watteau pleat from yoke; loose front, with detached fitted waist lining; belt and pocket, large sleeves.
Each ....$0.98.   Per dozen........$11.50

5609 Ladies' Ready Made Wrappers, made from best standard light prints, waists half lined, new yoke with two points in front and one in back, edged with full wide ruffle, wide collar with deep pointed back; Watteau pleat from yoke, large sleeves, half belt and pocket. Each....$ 1.00
Per dozen........... 11.50

5610 Ladies' Ready Made Wrappers. Same style as 5607; made of Henrietta finished plain fast black sateen, lined waist.
Each.................$1.45

5611 Ladies' Ready Made Wrappers. Same style as 5607; made of printed satin Surah; a twilled cotton goods resembling

5609

cashmere; printed in stylish combinations of colors; light grounds, black or mourning grounds, with small white figures, or wine, navy, sapphire or black, with colored designs, striped effects.
Each...................$1.50

5612 Ladies' Ready Made Wrappers, made from standard indigo or mourning prints, neat patterns, waist half lined, double pointed yoke front and back outlined with fancy wash braid, trimming of same on collars and cuffs, wide ruffle over shoulders, full puff sleeves gathered in at elbows. Wateau pleat from yoke, half belt and pocket.
Each ....$ 1.00
Per dozen.......................... 11.50

5612

Wrappers—Continued.

5614   **5615**

5614 Ladies' Ready Made Wrappers, made from best indigo blue prints, in neat patterns, half lined waist, full front and back with a gathered heading at the square yoke; very wide ruffle, extending over shoulders, large sleeves; the gathered heading at yoke, the edge of ruffle, collar and cuffs are trimmed with a narrow piping of plain scarlet; has a pocket and is held to form with a half belt. This garment will be a big seller. Each.........$1.10 Per dozen.....$12.80

5615 Ladies' Ready Made Wrappers, made of best standard prints, light and medium colors, waist half lined, circular yoke with wide ruffle all around, fancy wash braid trimming on edge of ruffle, around collar and cuffs, yoke full and gathered in front to collar, large sleeves, half belt and Wateau pleat from yoke, detached, fitted waist lining. Each...........$ 1.15
Per dozen....... .. .. 13.50

5617 Ladies' Ready Made Wrappers, made of best soft sateen finished prints, new light effects, lined waist, lining being detached and close fitting, circular yoke, with wide, full ruffle all around and trimmed with fancy wash braid; same is also on collars and cuffs; large puff sleeves gathered at elbow; Wateau pleat from yoke, fitted back and belted front.
Each.................$1.20
Per dozen 14.00

5618 Ladies' Ready Made Wrappers, made from figured crepoline in light or dark grounds. This is a handsome light weight cotton goods not so heavy as sateen. It is a momie or crepe weave, printed in handsomely colored floral or vine patterns. Made same style as 5617, without braid. Each. $1.25

5617-18

5619   **5621**

5619 Ladies' Ready Made Wrappers, made from best indigo blue prints, half lined waist; circular yoke with wide scalloped ruffle and collar of plain blue;

edges of scallops are worked with a button-hole stitch over white cord, making a substantial trimming, Wateau pleat from yoke; large sleeves, half belt holds loose front to form, fitted back. Each..........$1.25
Per dozen... ....14.25

5621 Ladies' Ready Made Wrapper, made from light percales; waist half lined, square yoke, with wide ruffle all around; both ruffles and collar are edged with narrow wash lace, large sleeves, Wateau pleat from yoke, fitted back and held to form in front with half belt. Each.........$1.25 Per dozen........ $14.25

5623 Ladies' Ready Made Wrappers, made of best standard mourning prints, very neat patterns, in figured stripes, and small patterns of white, on fast black grounds. We consider this the prettiest and best mourning wrapper offered this season. Yoke is of plain black, and is made with two points in front and one in back, around which is a wide ruffle. Outlining the yoke and around collar and cuffs is a row of fancy black and white wash braid, waist half lined, large sleeves, side pockets, fitted back and loose front, held to form with half belt, Wateau pleat from yoke.
Each...................$ 1.40
Per dozen.............16.25

5623

5625 Ladies' Ready Made Wrapper, made of fine Henrietta finished sateen, in newest designs; black grounds with figures, in neat combinations of colors, heliotrope, blue, rose, gold, etc. Waist half lined; has circular yoke, around which is a full wide ruffle collar, cuffs and ruffle trimmed in narrow baby ribbon to match shade in figure; fitted back, Wateau pleat from yoke, front loose and held to form with half belt. Each....$ 1.50
Per dozen........... 17.00

5625

5631 Ladies' Ready Made Wrappers, made of heavy percale, in newest light colorings, perfect washing. This is one of the best made and prettiest garments in the line, and will be found very serviceable. Waist is half lined, has circular yoke and double scalloped ruffle, scallops bound with cord and worked in buttonhole stitching, Wateau pleat from yoke, fitted back and loose front, held to form with half belt, side pocket and large sleeves. We strongly recommend this garment for style and wear.
Each.................$ 1.50
Per dozen...........17.25

5631

5633 Ladies' Ready Made Wrappers, made of fine cambric lawns, similar styles to percales, but the fabric is much finer and more sheer; colors, light and dainty; waist, half lined; has a wide double sailor collar, pointed in back to resemble yoke, very wide ruffle, extending from collar, and finished all round with narrow valenciennes lace, fancy wash braid around collar, new, large sleeves, gathered in at wrist, with fancy trimming, and wide flowing cuffs, double faced and trimmed in lace, fitted back, with Wateau pleat from yoke, front loose and held to form with half belt, side pocket. This wrapper is perfectly made, and is the daintest garment in our line. Each.........$ 1 75
Per dozen.......... 20.00

Wrappers—Continued.

5635 Ladies' Ready Made Wrappers. Made of English cotton warp cashmere, detached fitted waist lining, skirt unlined, shirred front and full Wateau back with shirred heading. New immense puff sleeves, tight fitted from elbow, loose front held to form with half belt; collar, cuffs and belt trimmed in narrow baby ribbon to match garment; colors are: Cardinal, wine, navy, golden brown or black. Each............$2.50

Ladies' Tea Gowns.

MADE TO MEASURE.

5651 Ladies' Tea Gowns, made of cotton warp English cashmere, in navy blue, cardinal, wine, golden brown, gray or black, full puff sleeves full loose front and back, shirred at yoke, wide ruffle over shoulders, lined throughout.....$5.00

5635

5654   5651

5654 Ladies' Tea Gowns, made of all wool reversible serge, fine twill, lined throughout, has large balloon sleeves, wide ruffle and collar trimmed with narrow silk ribbon, full Wateau pleats in back from collar. Colors: Cardinal, wine, navy blue or black, or any other seasonable colors. Each.............$6.00

5656   5658

5656 Ladies' Tea Gowns made to measure, of finest quality all wool Henrietta, colors: Cardinal, wine, golden brown, navy, light gray or any other seasonable colors. Made with Wateau back from collar, full loose front, wide cape ruffle extending to waist, full puff sleeves with ruffle at elbow lined throughout...$9.00
5658 Ladies' Tea Gowns, made to measure from finest all wool French Challie, new designs in light or dark effects, grounds in cream black, navy blue or brown. Made with standing roll collar, pointed yoke front and back with Wateau pleat from yoke, wide cape revers of plain China silk to shade of figure, cuffs of same, also facing of collar; belt of silk ribbon to match silk trimming, large double puff sleeves with ruffle at elbow, lined throughout Each........$9.00

Children's and Misses' Dresses.

Ready Made.

5681 Child's Calico Wrapper, made of light ground American prints, shirred at neck and finished with narrow ruffle, full sleeves finished with ruffle.

Ages	2 yrs.	4 yrs.	6 yrs.	8 yrs.
Price	$0.25	$0.25	$0.30	$0.35

Dresses—Continued.

5683 Child's Wash Dress, made of printed percale in light and dark effects, neat patterns, large sleeves, square yoke with ruffled heading for skirt, ruffle around neck and sleeves.

Ages	2 yrs.	4 yrs.	6 yrs.	8 yrs.
Price	$0.45	$0.45	$0.50	$0.60

5685 Childs' Wash Dress, made of strong, plain, chambray gingham, in navy blue mixture, square yoke covered with a very wide circular collar made with two points, front and back, edge trimmed in fancy wash braid, full bishop sleeves with braid trimming on cuffs.

Ages	2 yrs.	4 yrs.	6 yrs.	8 yrs.
Price	$0.50	$0.55	$0.65	$0.75

5687 Little Girls' Dresses, made of best staple gingham; small checks in navy blue, brown, or pink, with white; yoke of white all over tucking; trimming of white Hamburg edging.

Ages	2 yrs.	3 yrs.	4 yrs.	5 yrs.	Each	$0.69

5689 Child's Wash Dress, made of extra fine quality, zephyr ginghams in light dainty checks and broken plaids, circular yoke with full wide ruffle all around trimmed on edges and headed with fancy wash braid, same on collar and cuffs, full bishop sleeves.

Ages	2 yrs.	4 yrs.	6 yrs	8 yrs
Price	$0.70	$0.75	$0.80	$0.90

5690 Little Girl's Dress, made of small checked baby flannel, in pink, light blue, tan, scarlet or gray. The daintiest fabric you ever saw Round yoke, wide circular ruffle, full bishop sleeves.

Ages	1 yr.	2 yrs.	3 yrs.	4 yrs.	5 yrs.	6 yrs.
Price	$0.75	$0.95	$1.00	$1.10	$1.20	$1.30

5691 Little Girl's Dress, made of printed flannelette, in scarlet and black only. Small neat designs in black on scarlet grounds; full front with girdle, wide sash at back, full bishop sleeves; girdle, cuffs, collar and bottom of skirt trimmed in all wool black hercules braid.

Ages	2 yrs.	3 yrs.	4 yrs.	5 yrs.	6 yrs.	7 yrs.	8 yrs.	9 yrs.
Price	$1.25	$1.35	$1.45	$1.55	$1.75	$1.95	$2.15	$2.35

Age, 10 years, $2.50.

5693 Child's Wash Dress, made of light prints, in fancy wash braid, felled seams and a splendid dress for the price.

Ages	4 yrs.	6 yrs.	8 yrs.
Price	$0.50	$0.50	$0.55
Ages	10 yrs.	12 yrs.	14 yrs.
Price	$0.60	$0.65	$0.75

5694 Girls' Calico Dresses, made of light prints, wide, deep ruffle forms square yoke, wide turned collar, pointed front and back, full bishop sleeves, and felled seams throughout.

Ages	6 yrs.	8 yrs.
Prices	$0.50	$0.55
Ages	10 yrs.	12 yrs.
Prices	$0.60	$0.65
Ages	14 yrs.	

5695 Girls' Wash Dresses, made of strong blue checked ginghams, very serviceable for school wear. Full, wide ruffle over shoulders, turned collar trimmed in fancy wash braid, braid also forms heading for ruffle which outlines a pointed yoke; two rows braid on cuffs and around waist forming a belt.

Ages	6 yrs.	8 yrs.	10 yrs.	12 yrs.	14 yrs.
Prices	$0.65	$0.70	$0.75	$0.85	$0.95

5697 Girls' Wash Dresses, made of very fine light ginghams, neat broken fancy checks in pink, blue, tan, etc, very pretty and handsomely made, square yoke around which is a wide, full ruffle headed with two rows fancy wash braid; braid on collar and two rows around cuffs, felled seams throughout.

Ages	4 yrs.	6 yrs.	8 yrs.	10 yrs.	12 yrs.	14 yrs.
Prices	$0.90	$0.95	$1.00	$1.15	$1.25	$1.35

Ladies' Newport Suits.

Not made to order, stock sizes only.

See note under department heading, page 24 for scale of sizes.

5700 Ladies' Newport Suit, ready made, consists of jacket and skirt to be worn with shirt waists. Jacket is made with Tuxedo back, large leg-o'-mutton sleeves, wide revers in front, double stitched seams, inside seams bound, new organ piped skirt, very full and wide, deep turned ed hem at bottom. Made of good looking and serviceable repellent cloth, in navy blue or black.
Per suit........$4.90

5702 Ladies' Newport Suit, same style as above. Made of strong repellent cloth. Collar, cuffs and bottom of skirt trimmed with black worsted hercules braid. Colors: Black or navy blue only.
Per suit........$5.50

Ladies' Suits—Continued.

5704 Ladies' Newport Suit, same style as 5700, made of heavy all-wool storm serge, trimmed with two rows of folded satin rhadame on collar, cuffs and bottom of skirt. Colors: Black or navy blue only. A stylish and splendid wearing suit. Per suit.......................$5.95

5705 Ladies' Newport Suit, same style as 5700, made of heavy English whip cord, trimmed in narrow folds of satin. Navy blue or black only. Very serviceable and elegant. Per suit.....$7.50
5708 Ladies' Newport Suit, same style as 5700, made of fine all wool broadcloth, high finished; collar, cuffs and bottom of skirt trimmed with narrow fold of moire silk, very elegant. Colors: Black, brown, light or dark navy blue.
Per suit.....$8.50
5709 Ladies' Newport Suit, made of all wool cheviot serge in navy blue; new organ pipe skirt, double breasted jacket, double stitching around skirt and jacket, immense sleeves, made in first-class style. Per suit $8.75
5711 Ladies' Newport Suit, made of stylish tweed suiting, in light brown and white mixture. Very neat and serviceable, will not show dust or wear. Same style as 5709. Per suit...$9.00

5709

Ready Made Dress Skirts.

To be worn with shirt or blouse waists. Length 42 in. Waist, 24, 26, 28 in.

Our shirts are all cut after the latest models, are substantially and correctly made, and much cheaper than you can make them yourself. A ready made dress skirt and a few changes of shirt waists constitutes an economical and up to date outfit for any woman

5714 Ladies' Ready Made Dress Skirts black or navy blue repellent cloth, three pleats in back, 4 inch hem at bottom and 3 rows stitching. Back of skirt lined with canvas. Each. $2.75
5716 Ladies' Ready Made Dress Skirts same as cut. Four organ pipe pleats in back, made of all wool fine serge in navy blue or black, 3 in. hem at bottom with 2 rows stitching.

5714 & 5716

Back is lined with silesia which covers the stiffening used to hold pleats in shape. Each $4.00
5718 Ladies' Ready Made Skirts made of all wool cheviot serge, in navy blue or black. Three organ pipe pleats in back, 3 inch hem at bottom and three rows stitching, stiff interlining holds pleats in shape; skirt lined throughout with silesia. Each.........$4.50

Soft or Unlaundered Waists.

Sizes, 32 to 42 inches bust measure.

5801 A Job Lot of Ladies' Fine White Waists, last season's stock; regular values 90 cents to $1.50 each.
Closing price, each..$0.45
5803 Light Calico Waists, neat patterns, full front, large sleeves and belt, all sizes. Each.......$0.25
Per dozen...........2.90
5805 Indigo Blue Print Waists, neat patterns, large sleeves and belt, all sizes. Each.....$0.35
Per dozen 4.00
5806 Light Calico Waists, made with large sleeves, full front and belt, neat patterns and a well made waist for the price, all

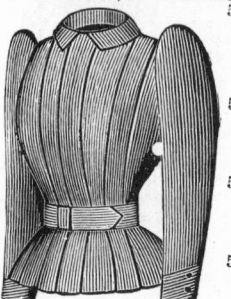

5803.

sizes. Each .....$0.37½   Per dozen $4.25

Waists—Continued.

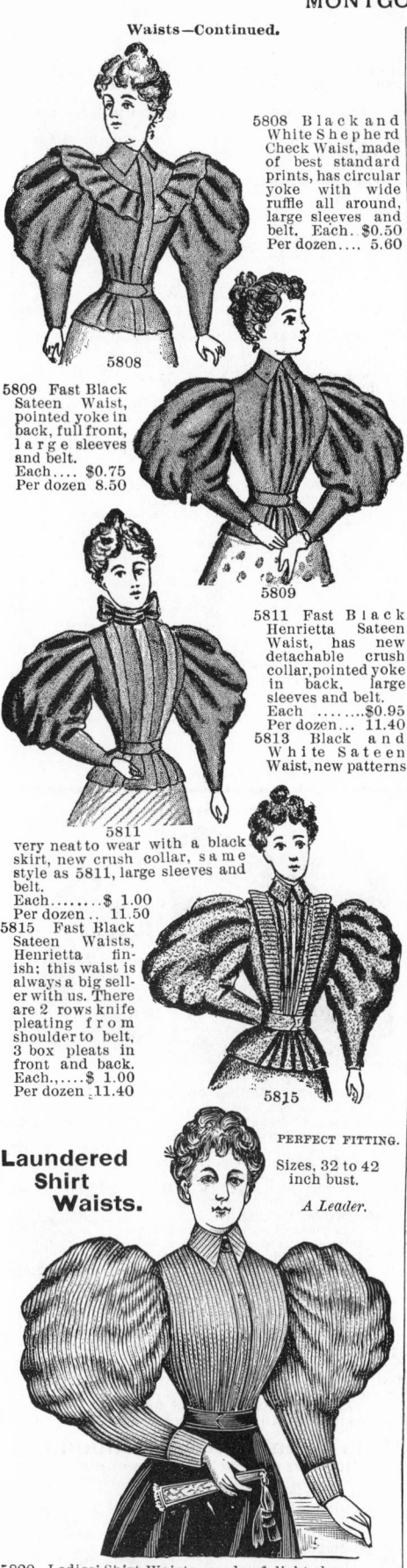

5808 Black and White Shepherd Check Waist, made of best standard prints, has circular yoke with wide ruffle all around, large sleeves and belt. Each. $0.50 Per dozen.... 5.60

5808

5809 Fast Black Sateen Waist, pointed yoke in back, full front, large sleeves and belt. Each.... $0.75 Per dozen 8.50

5809

5811 Fast Black Henrietta Sateen Waist, has new detachable crush collar, pointed yoke in back, large sleeves and belt. Each ....$0.95 Per dozen... 11.40

5813 Black and White Sateen Waist, new patterns

5811

very neat to wear with a black skirt, new crush collar, same style as 5811, large sleeves and belt. Each.......$ 1.00 Per dozen.. 11.50

5815 Fast Black Sateen Waists, Henrietta finish; this waist is always a big seller with us. There are 2 rows knife pleating from shoulder to belt, 3 box pleats in front and back. Each.,....$ 1.00 Per dozen .11.40

5815

Laundered Shirt Waists.

PERFECT FITTING.

Sizes, 32 to 42 inch bust.

A Leader.

5820 Ladies' Shirt Waists, made of light chambray prints; in pink, blue, heliotrope, gray or tan stripes or figures, also checks in pink, blue or gray, stiff laundered collar and cuffs, plain belt, all felled French seams, pointed shirt yoke in back. Each........$0.48 Per dozen... .... 5.60

5822 Ladies' Shirt Waists, made of good percale, in blue, pink or gray stripes, also in fancy figures on blue, pink or heliotrope; felled French

Waists—Continued.

seams, large sleeves, plain belt, stiff laundcollar and cuffs, pointed shirt yoke in back, full front. Each.....$0.69 Per dozen. 8.00

5824 Ladies' Shirt Waists, faultlessly made of fine percale, in a great variety of new patterns and colors; some styles as follows: Stripes in tan and white covered.

with a small black dot; indigo blue and white; light blue and white, pink and white; black and white; assorted small figures on blue, pink or heliotrope; plain solid pink, blue, white or fast black: made with large sleeves, felled French seams, perfect fitting stiff laundered collar and cuffs, re-enforced pointed shirt yoke in back, full front, belt. Each.......$0.85 Per dozen.......... .. .. 9 75

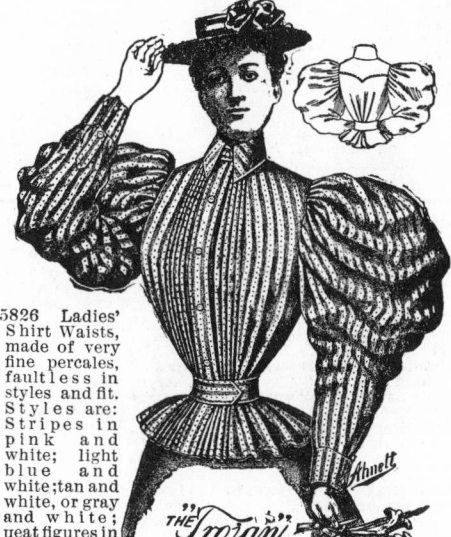

5826 Ladies' Shirt Waists, made of very fine percales, faultless in styles and fit. Styles are: Stripes in pink and white; light blue and white; tan and white, or gray and white; ueat figures in blue, pink or heliotrope; plain solid pink, blue or buff, with narrow piped edge of white on front pleat, cuffs and collars, also a line of new fancy persian patterns

"Trojan" N9 1065

in pink, nile, blue or heliotrope; immense sleeves, re-enforced pointed shirt yoke in back, full front, felled French seams, stiff laundered collar and cuffs, belt. Each........$ 1.00 Per dozen... 11.50

5828 Ladies' Shirt Waists, made of fine percales, beautiful and stylish patterns, fast colors; a perfect and faultless waist in every detail. We show the following styles: Stripes in light blue, buff, nile or golden

"The Trojan" N9 1017

Waists—Continued.

yellow (the later is quite new and very stylish), also black and white stripe; tan or buff with small navy dots or black with white polka dots. This waist has immense sleeves, all bound seams, re-enforced pointed shirt yoke in back, full front, perfectly laundered collar and cuffs, belt. Each.$1.25. Per dozen.$14.25

Misses' Shirt Waists.

Sizes, 10 years, 12 years, 14 years, 16 years.

5832 Misses' Shirt Waists, all sizes, made of fine chambray prints in neat patterns, good fast colors, stiff laundered collar and cuffs, pointed shirt yoke in back, full in front, plain belt. Colors; Pink, light blue or dark blue, felled French seams, large sleeves. Each.......$0.60 Per dozen.. 6.75

Ladies' Silk Waists.

Ready made. Stock sizes only, 32 to 42 inches bust.

5840 Ladies' Long Silk Waists, made of black double warp surah silk, large sleeves, turnover collar, full front, back made with a pointed shirt yoke, from which the silk is gathered full and held to form with plain belt, light muslin lining. Each ..$4.00

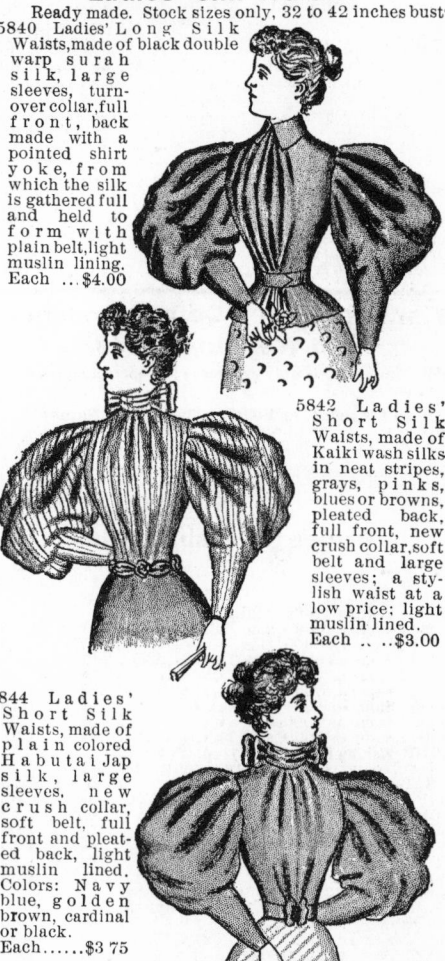

5842 Ladies' Short Silk Waists, made of Kaiki wash silks in neat stripes, grays, pinks, blues or browns, pleated back, full front, new crush collar, soft belt and large sleeves; a stylish waist at a low price; light muslin lined. Each $3.00

5844 Ladies' Short Silk Waists, made of plain colored Habutai Jap silk, large sleeves, new crush collar, soft belt, full front and pleated back, light muslin lined. Colors: Navy blue, golden brown, cardinal or black. Each.....$3 75

Ladies' and Misses' Shirt Waists.

The up-to-date woman this season will have her wardrobe *plentifully supplied with shirt waists* They are the correct thing for general wear and are by far the most becoming and sensible article of woman's attire to receive fashion's universal approval.

At a very small outlay of m ney a woman may now be possessed of several distinct changes of apparel.

Your old dress skirt worn with a neat laundered waist provides you with a cool, comfortable and up-to-date costume that will quite astonish you. *If you haven't a suitable skirt we can sell you one ready made cheaper than you can make it.*

Our new waists have been made for us by the best manufacturers of such lines in this country and are absolutely perfect in every detail. We are especially proud of our styles and values.

The correct waist for this season is made with a soft or unstarched body and stiff laundered collars and cuffs. Soft or unlaundered waists are also much worn.

BOOK DEPARTMENT.

(Books bought on special order cannot be returned.) *No books taken back or exchanged if sent as ordered.* All prices quoted are for books in our store, charges for transportation to be paid by purchaser. Those wishing to have books sent by mail will find the approximate amount required for postage in addition to cost of book appended to each quotation or else in a table under the general heading under which the book is classed.

We give below a table showing about size in inches of the different books on our list. These measurements sometimes vary, but will serve to give a general idea of the dimensions of any of our books.

16 mo..............4x6½ in. Royal 8 vo..7½x10 in. 12 mo............4½x7½ in. Quarto....8½x10½ in. 8 vo..........6½x9 in. Imp. Quarto..12x9 in.

(*In ordering books give name and number.*) Any books not found in this department we will be pleased to furnish upon application, school books included. Send 5 cents for postage for special complete Illustrated Book Catalogue.

We also issue, a complete medical and scientific book catalogue, complete rural book catalogue and complete educational (school book) catalogue. Send for them.

INDEX.

Visiting, Regret, Correspondence and Wedding Cards.

This line of cards only embraces the correct styles now in use.

Prices for printing Visiting Cards, one Name:

25 Cards	50 Cards	100 Cards	300 Cards
$0.25	$0.35	$0.50	$0.75

Wedding, Regret and Correspondence:

100 Cards	300 Cards	500 Cards
$1.50	$1.75	$2.00

Prices for Plain Cards.

	Per Pkg. of 25 Cards.	Per Box of 300 Cards.
6000 **Visiting Cards,** plain white, 4 ply, very stylish (HT), size 3¼x1¼	$0.06	$0.55
6001 Same as 6000, size 3½x1⅔ (HC)	.07	.75
6002 Same as 6000, size 3¾x1¾ (HX)	.08	.85
6003 Same as 6000, size 4x2 (HA)	.09	.95
6004 Same as 6000, size 4¼x2¼ (HM)	.10	1.05
6005 Same as 6000, size 3x2 (CB)	.11	1.15
6006 Same as 6000, size 3¼x2¼ (CE)	.12	1.25
6007 Same as 6000, size 3½x2½ (CR)	.13	1.35
6010 **Visiting Cards,** 8 ply, plain white bevel edge (HT). Very latest; size 3x1¾	.07	.75
6011 Same as 6010, size 3¼x1⅞ (CX)	.08	.85
6012 Same as 6010, size 3½x2 (CH)	.09	.95
6013 Same as 6010, size 3¾x2¼ (CA)	.10	1.05
6014 Same as 6010, size 4x2½ (CE)	.11	1.15
6015 Same as 6010, size 2x3 (CB)	.12	1.25
6016 Same as 6010, size 3¼x2¼ (CE)	.13	1.35
6020 **Visiting Cards,** 8 ply, White Cards with gold bevel edges, neat and stylish, size 3x1¾ (CT)	.08	.85
6021 Same as 6020, size 3¼x1⅞ (CX)	.09	.95
6022 Same as 6020, size 3½x2 (CA)	.10	1.05
6023 Same as 6020, size 3¾x2¼ (CA)	.11	1.15
6024 Same as 6020, size 4x2½ (CM)	.12	1.25
6025 Same as 6020, size 2x3 (CB)	.13	1.35
6026 Same as 6020, size 3¾x1 (CE)	.14	1.45
6028 **Visiting Cards,** with notched bevel border, 8 ply, a novelty, size 3x1¾ (CH)	.09	.95
6029 Same as 6028, size 3¼x1⅞ (CX)	.10	1.05
6030 Same as 6028, size 3½x2 (CH)	.11	1.15
6031 Same as 6028, size 2x3 (CB)	.12	1.25
6032 Same as 6028, size 3¼x2¼ (CE)	.13	1.35
		Per Dz. boxes.
6035 **Visiting Cards,** pure white, the very latest and best, put up in boxes of 25 cards and 25 envelopes to match, size of cards 3½x2	.25	$2.70
6036 Same as 6035, in box with envelopes, size 3½x2½	.35	3.00
	Per Pkg. of 25 Cards.	Per Box of 300 Cards.
6037 **Mourning Cards,** 25 in package, with ⅛ inch black border, size 2x3½	$0.10	$1.05
6038 Same as 6037, size 2½x3½	.11	1.15

Wedding, Correspondence and Regret Cards.

	Per Pkg. of 25 Cards.	Per Box of 100 Cards.
6040 Plain White 3 ply cards (C90), 25 in box, with envelopes to match, size 4½x3½	$0.14	$0.45
6041 Same as 6040, with gold edge, in box with envelopes (C91)	.15	.52
6042 Plain White Bevel Edge (CAH) Cards, 25 in box, with envelopes to match, size 4½x3½	.28	.96
6043 Same as 6042, with gold edge cards (CAX)	.30	1.05
6044 Ragged Edge Bevel Cards, 25 in box, with envelopes, size 4½x3½ (CAM)	.33	1.10
6045 Same as 6044, with gold edges (CAB)	.36	1.28
	Box of 100	Per 1000
6048 Large Double Cards to fold in center, size open 4½x6¾. Bevel notched edges, a beautiful wedding card (CAEH)	$0.90	$7.50
6049 Same as 6048, with fancy notched border, red and gold	1.00	8.50

Fancy Memorandums.

This line numbers 6060 to 6072; embraces entirely new goods, separate and distinct from styles heretofore sold by us. (*Not How Cheap But How Good.*)

	Each.	Per Doz.
6060 American Russia, leather lined limp covers, ruled faint, 60 leaves, size 2½x3¾ (A1.)	$0.50	$5.50
6061 Same as 6060. Indexed with cover stamped visits (AE)	.55	6.00
6062 American Russia, ruled faint, 60 leaves with pencil attached (Stamped Visits). Size 2½x3¾ (A7.)	.65	7.00
6063 Same as 6062. Stamped Cash Account, without pencil (A8.)	.55	6.00
6064 American Russia (A9.) Ruled faint, 60 leaves, stamped engagements.	.50	5.40
6065 American Russia, 60 leaves, indexed, stamped visiting list, with pencil attached. Size 3x4 (A 25.)	.70	7.75
6067 American Russia, 60 leaves, ruled dollars and cents. Size 3⅝x5. Stamped cash account (A 44.)	.75	8.25
6068 Same as 6067, stamped engagements with printed heading (A 47.)	.75	8.25
6069 Same as 6067, stamped household expenses (A 48.)	.75	8.25
6070 American Russia, 60 leaves. Size 3⅝x5⅞. Indexed and stamped addresses (A 52.)	.80	8.75
6071 Same as 6070, faint ruled, plain, 96 leaves (A 54.)	.90	9.50
6072 Genuine Seal, leather binding, leather lined. Size 2¼x4⅞. Cross Bar Ruling	.75	8.25

Memorandums.

Numbers 6074 to 6081 all open on end.

	Each.	Per doz.
6074 Red Leather Vest Pocket Memorandum, size 2½x4½ (V-C. H. B. R.) 40 leaves, green edges, quadrille ruling	$0.07	$0.75
6075 Red Leather Memorandum, 60 leaves, ruled for dollars and cents, green edges. Size 3⅝x6 (V—CH EA)	.13	1.45
6077 Same as 6075, with band and pocket extra (V—CHEB)	0.18	1.80
6078 American Russian Leather Memorandum, 50 leaves, vest pocket. Size, 2¾x4½, gilt edges. (V—CXEA). Ruled for dollars and cents	.14	1.50
6079 Same quality as 6078, with band and pocket extra. Size 3¾x6. 72 leaves. Ruled dollars and cents. (V—CXCO)	.22	2.45
6080 American Russian Leather. 72 leaves. Ruled dollars and cents. Gilt edges. Size 4¼x7 (V—CXRM½)	.25	2.70
6081 Extra Black Morocco Leather Memorandum, containing linen paper, gold edges. Size 3⅝x6. Ruled dollars and cents. (V—CHBX). 96 leaves	.28	3.10

Side Opening Memorandums.

(Numbers 6083 to 6091 Open on Side.)

	Each.	Per doz.
6083 Red Leather Memorandum. Size 2½x4½. 40 leaves, green edges, quadrille ruling. (V—CHBR)	$0.07.	$0.75
6084 Extra Red Leather Memorandum, gilt edges. 50 leaves. Size 2¾x4½. Ruled dollars and cents. Fine paper. (V—CXEH)	.14	1.50
6085 Red Leather Memorandum 60 leaves. Ruled for dollars and cents. Green edges. Size 3⅝x6. (V—CHEH)	.13	1.45
6087 Black Morocco Memorandum. 60 leaves. Ruled dollars and cents. Size 3½x5½. (B—ABH) Red edges	.20	2.25
6088 Same as 6087. Size 2¾x4½. (B—ABT)	.18	1.80

Memorandums—Continued.

6090 Extra Black Morocco Leather, containing linen paper. Size 3⅝x6. Ruled dollars and cents. (V—CHBM) 96 leaves .... Each .28, Per Doz. 3.10

6091 Same as 6079, only open on side. (V—CXRM) .... .25, 2.70

Indexed Memorandums.

(All Are Side Opening.)

Each, Per doz.

6093 American Russia Vest Pocket Memorandum. 60 leaves. Size 2¼x5⅝. (V—CT). Indexed throughout $0.14, $1.50

6094 American Russia Memorandum, indexed throughout. Size 3¾x5¾. Gold edges. Ruled dollars and cents. 70 leaves. (V—CXAT¾) .... .22, 2.45

6095 Buyers' Book, American Russia leather. 150 leaves. Ruled in quadrille. Size 4¼x6¾. Indexed throughout. (V—CXPB) .... .40, 4.50

6096 Same as 6095, excepting index in front. (V—CXPM) .... .40, 4.50

Pencil Memorandums.

Each. Per doz.

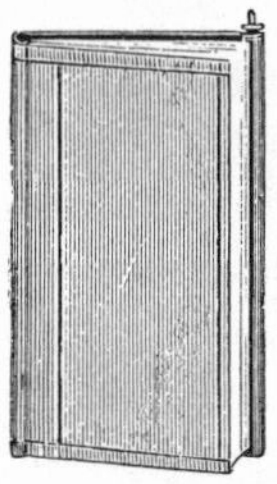

6098 American Russia Leather, vest pocket, open on side. 40 leaves, with pencil attachment. Size 2½x5½, (B — R A O) Quadrille ruling .. $0.23, $2.40

6099 Same as 6098. Size 3½x6. Ruled dollars and cents .. .30, 3.25

Removable Memorandums.

Each, Per doz.

6100 Leather Covered. Size 2½x4¼, red edges. 40 ruled leaves, open on end with movable insides. (B—OT CB) $0.15, $1.60

6102 Insides for above .... .04, .40

6103 Leather Covered. Size 3x6, same as above, 6100. (N—CRHT) .... .19, 2.10

6104 Insides for 6103 .... .06, .60

6105 American Russia. Size 3¾x6, end open, with rubber band and pocket. 60 leaves .... .25, 3.00

6106 Insides for 6105 .... .05, .50

6107 Extra Fine Russia Memorandum, with silk rubber band, leather lined, with pocket. Size 3¾x6. Cloth bound insides. 40 leaves. Gilt edge .... .35, 3.50

6108 Insides for 6107, gold edges .... .08, 85

Flap Memorandums.

Each Contains One Pocket and Pencil Holder.

Each. Per doz

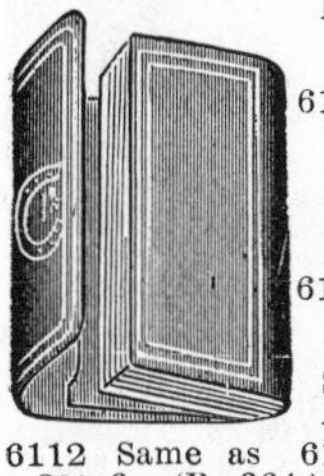

6109 Extra Sheep Leather Memo andum. 48 leaves. Ruled for dollars and cents. Size 3x5¼. (V—PTX) .. $0.12, 1.35

6110 Extra Sheep Memorandum. 50 leaves. Same as 6109. Size, 3¼x5¾. (B—AEA) .... .15, 1.65

6112 Same as 6109, except in size 3¾x6. (B—364.) .... .20, 2.20

6114 Same as 6109. Size 3½x6. 96 leaves. (V—PTA½) .... .22, 2.50

6116 Same as 6109. Size 4x6.. 96 leaves. (B—AEO) .... .25, 2.75

6117 American Morocco, gilt edges, with pencil holder and pocket. 60 leaves. Size 3¼x6. Ruled for dollars and cents. (B—AOP) .... .30, 3.25

6118 Same as 6117. Size 4x6½. Hip pocket size. (B—AOX) .... .40, 4.50

Memorandums.

Each. Per doz.

6122 Lithographed Manilla Covers. Size 2¼x5¼. Vest pocket size, 20 pages, quadrille ruling (V-BTC) $0.01, $0.10

6123 Imitation Black Morocco Leather Vest Pocket Memorandum, size 2¼x5½, 34 leaves, quadrille ruling (V-CATX) .... .03, .32

6124 Same as 6123, size 2½x4½ (V-CATC) .... .04, .40

6126 Fancy Manilla Memorandum, size 4x6¾, open on end, ruled for dollars and cents, 48 leaves (B-CXTM) .... .03, .30

6127 Same as 6126, open on side (B-CXTB) .... .03, .30

6128 Same as 6126, containing 72 leaves, open on end (B-CXTP) .... .04, .40

6129 Same as 6128, open on side (B-CXTO) .... .04, .40

6131 Pressboard Cover, containing extra good paper, size 3¾x6, end open. 40 leaves, ruled dollars and cents (V-HCH) .... .04, .40

6132 Same as 6131, side open (V-HCX) .... .04, .40

6133 Manilla Cover, cloth back, 68 leaves, open on end, size 3½x5¾ (V-CHE½) .... .03, .30

6139 Same as 6133, open on side .... .03, .30

Memorandums—Continued.

6141 Same as 6133, containing better quality of paper, 72 leaves, open on side (V-BCX) .... .05, .50

6142 Same as 6141, open on end (V-BCT) .... .05, .50

6144 Extra Large Memorandum, size 4⅛x6⅝, 96 leaves, end open (V-HXB) .06, .65

6145 Same as 6144, open on side (V-HXM) .... .06, .65

6147 Memorandum, good quality, size 4x7, manilla cover, 48 leaves, good paper (V-HCM) end open .... .07, .75

6148 Same as 6147, side open (V-HCA) .07, .75

Duck Memorandums.

Numbers 6150 to 6157 are all durably bound in duck cloth, and contain a good quality of paper. Ruled dollars and cents. Each. Per doz.

6150 Size 3¼x8¼, 72 leaves (V-CXHA) side open $0.05, $0.50

6151 Size 3¼x8¼, 48 leaves (V-CXAM) side open .... .05, .50

6152 Size 3¾x6, 72 leaves (V-CXHC) side open .... .05, .50

6153 Size 3¾x6, 72 leaves (V-CXHX) end open .... .05, .50

6154 Size 4x7, 48 leaves (V-CXAX) end open .... .05, .50

6155 Size 4x7, 48 leaves (V-CXAH) side open .... .05, .50

6156 Butcher Books, with flap pencil holder and pocket, size 3¼x5, 50 leaves (B-MAH) .... .09, 1.00

6157 Same as 6156, size 3x5¾, 40 leaves (B-MAM) .... .11, 1.20

Heavy Board Sheep Memorandums.

Numbers 6160 to 6166, open on side, durably bound in sheep, contain good white paper, ruled in dollars and cents. Each. Per doz.

6160 Size 3⅝x5⅞, 50 leaves (B-HXM) ... $0.10, $1.00

6161 Size 3⅝x5⅞, 96 leaves (B-HXE) ... .13, 1.45

6162 Size 4¼x6¾, 50 leaves (B-HMX) ... .15, 1.70

6163 Size 4¾x7⅞, 50 leaves (B-HMP½) ... .18, 2.00

6165 Lumber and Log Tally Book, ruled for 16 spaces, "Log" size, 4⅛x6¾, 72 leaves (B-CBXH) sheep binding ... .17, 1.95

6166 Same as 6165 for (Lumber) 32 spaces, sheep binding (B-CBXA) ... .17, 1.95

Grocers', Butchers' and General Store, Pass and Counter Books.

Each. Per doz.

6170 Butchers' Pass Book, manilla paper cover, size 3½x6, 18 leaves (V-ACX) $0.01, $0.10

6171 Butchers' Pass Book, manilla cover, size 3½x6, 38 leaves (B-COTH⅝) .02, .20

6172 Same as 6171, Grocers' Book (B-COTX⅝).. .02, .20

6173 Butchers' Book, same as 6170, extra good quality, size 3½x6½ ..... .03, .30

6174 Butchers' or Grocers' Counter Day Books, size 5½x11¼, manilla cover, cloth backs, good yellow manilla paper, 48 leaves (B-COMH½) .... .04, .40

6175 Same as 6174, 90 leaves (B-COMH) .... .05, .50

6176 Large Size Counter Books, duck cloth binding, size 7¾x11¾, 90 leaves, day book ruling .... .10, 1.00

Time Books.

Each. Per doz.

6180 Time Book, manilla cover, size 4¼x6¾, 24 leaves, containing wage tables. *Weekly* (V-HTX) $0.03, $0.28

6181 Same as 6180 *Monthly* (V-HTC) ... .03, .28

6182 Time Book, canvas cover, 48 leaves, size 4¼x6¾ *Weekly* (V-COP) .... .06, .65

6183 Same as 6182 *Monthly* (V-COX) ... .06, .65

6185 Time Book, heavy duck cover, green edges, containing 150 leaves, size 4¼x6¾, *Weekly* (V-COE) .... .20, 2.25

6186 Same as 6185, *Monthly* (V-COR).. .20, 2.25

6187 Time Book, full bound sheep with pencil holder, size 4½x7, 56 leaves, good paper .... .22, 2.40

6189 Time Book, flap sheep bound with pencil attachment, size 4½x7, 56 leaves (B—ECX½) *Monthly* .... .28, 3.10

6190 Time Book, heavy board sheep binding, size 4¾x7, 56 leaves (B—ECP) *Monthly* .... .18, 2 00

Notes, Drafts, Receipts.

Receipts.

Each. Per doz.

6192 Pocket Receipts, printed on good paper, size 2x7, 50 leaves, pressboard cover $0.04, $0.40

6193 Pocket Receipts, size 2½x8, board cover with stubs, 50 leaves .... .06, .55

6194 Standard Pocket Receipts, fancy printed forms, 50 in pad, size 3¼x11¼ .... .08, .85

6195 Same as 6194, 100 in pad .... .14, 1.50

6196 Rent Receipts, good paper, pocket size, 50 in pad, size 2x7 .... .04, .40

Notes and Drafts.

Each. Per doz.

6197 Pocket Note Books, printed on good paper, 50 leaves, size 2x7, pressboard covers $0.04, $0.40

6198 Standard Note Book, lithographed forms on good paper, size 3¼x11¼, 50 leaves .... .08, .85

6199 Same as 6198, 100 leaves .... .14, 1.50

6200 Pocket Draft Books, printed on good paper, 50 leaves, size 2x7, pressboard covers .... .04, .40

6201 Standard Draft Books, lithographed forms on good paper, size 3¼x11¼, 50 leaves .... .08, .85

6202 Same as 6201, 100 leaves .... .14, 1.50

Check Books.

Each. Per doz.

6204 Fine Lithographed Check Books, 100 in pad (Pay to Order), size 3¼x10¾, R. B. C. $0.15, $1.65

6205 Fine Lithographed Check Books, size 3¼x10½ (Pay to Bearer), R.B.C½ .15, 1.65

Ready Printed Statements and Bill Heads.

Please note that these statements and bill heads are not printed with name, address, etc., to order. Read quotations carefully.

Each. Per doz.

6206 Bill Heads, printed in black with blank line for buyer and seller, containing 50 and 100 bills, extra heavy white paper, 50 in pad $0.09, $0.90
100 in pad .... .15, 1.70

6208 Statement Heads, printed in black with blank line for buyer and seller, containing 50 and 100 statements, 50 in pad .... .09, .90
100 in pad .... .15, 1.70

Note Books.

6214 Regiment Note Book, containing good paper, 48 leaves, lithographed cover, faint ruled for either pen or pencil, size 5⅞x9¼. Each $0.03
Per doz .... .35

6216 See Saw Note Book, manilla printed cover, 60 leaves for pen or pencil, size 5¾x8¾. Faint ruled. Each $0.04
Per doz .... .48

6217 Stenographers' and reporters' note book, faint ruled good paper, manilla cover, 80 leaves, size 5¾x9.
Each $0.05
Per doz .... .50

Each. Per doz.

6219 Wolf Note Book, red lithographed cover, 58 leaves, faint ruled for pen or pencil, size 6x9¼ $0.05, $0.50

6220 Eagle Note, same as 6219, 80 leaves .... .06, .65

6222 Royal E. C. Note Book, heavy manilla cover, extra fine paper, faint ruled, size 5¾x8½, 72 leaves .... .07, .75

6223 Same as 6222. Pocket size .... .07, .75

6224 United States Mail Students' Note Book, manilla cover, extra fine paper, 62 leaves, size 6x9 .... .08, .85

6225 Columbian Souvenir Note Book with illustrations, red manilla cover, 100 leaves, size 4½x8½. Extra fine paper, ruled .... .10, 1.00

Composition and Exercise Books.

Numbers 6230 to 6237 are all bound in limp manilla covers, containing good paper, ruled; size each 7x8.

Each. Per doz.

6230 Playmates composition, 12 leaves .. $0.02, $0.20

6231 Bad Boy composition, 24 leaves .... .03, .30

6232 War composition, 40 leaves .... .04, .42

6233 Jolly Boys composition, 48 leaves .. .04, .42

6234 Jolly Girls composition, 80 leaves .. .07, .75

6235 Steamship composition, 60 leaves .. .05, .50

6236 Navy composition, 96 leaves .... .08, .85

6237 Agate composition, 32 leaves .... .05, .50

6240 Duck Cloth binding, 36 leaves ..... .05, .50

6241 Duck Cloth binding, 72 leaves ..... .10, 1.10

6242 Duck Cloth binding, 100 leaves .... .15, 1.60

6243 Our best bound in duck, heavy boards, Russia corners, extra good paper, 72 leaves .... .20, 2.25

Drawing Books.

6245 Drawing Books, heavy covers, super quality white drawing paper, fifteen leaves, each leaf separated by fine tissue, 6x9½ inches.
Each............$0.04
Per dozen...... .40
6246 Same as 6245, size 9½x12 inches.
Each.............$0.07 Per dozen.............$0.75

SCALE BOOKS.

Fairbank's Standard.

6247 Scale Book, size 8½x13, containing 500 weigh forms printed on good paper with stubs. Bound in heavy boards. Marble paper sides and cloth backs. Retail price.......................$1.00
Our price...........$0.48 Per dozen..........5.00

Howe Scale Books.

6248 Same quality and size as 6247, Each.....$0.48
Per dozen..$5.00

United States Standard.

6249 Same quality as 6247. Each...............$0.48
Per dozen............................,.....$5.00

Pocket Ledger.

6251 Pocket Ledger, sheep bound, no flap or pocket, 50 leaves, size 2¾x6. Each............$0.12
Per dozen...1.25

Indexes.

6253 Size 7¼x12, super white paper, flexible pressboard covers, cloth back, 2 letters to each leaf..$0.10
6254 Size 8¼x13¾, extra white paper, full duck bound, leaf to a letter............................. .48
Per dozen..5.00

Invoice Books.

Each.
6256 Invoice Books for pasting bills in, size 10x14¼, bound in marble paper, sides, leather backs and corners, P. E. P. 180 pages......$0.85
6257 Invoice Books same as 6256, size 12¾x17¾, 240 pages, P. E. T...............................1.90
6258 Demy Invoice Books, size 11½x16¼, indexed and paged, 240 pages, P. E. M............1.80

Letter Files.

6260 The "Boss" File is the very best letter file ever sold at the price. Is strongly made, has wood ends, joints stayed with cloth; also has what no other low-priced file possesses, a self-working spring in cover. Has index printed on both sides, which is held in file with patent metal tags. Price, each····........................$0.50
Per dozen...5.40
Weight 1 lb. 13 oz.
6261 The "Chicago" Letter File, wood frame, fancy paper covered, size 10½x11¾x3. Weights 30 oz. Each....................................... .25
Per dozen..2.75

Copying Presses.

6263 Plain and substantial black enamel finish with wheel, same as cut.
No. 1. Size, 9x11....$3.75
" 2. Size, 10x12.... 4.00
" 3. Size, 10x15.... 4.50
" 4. Size, 12x18.... 8.25
" 5. Size, 11x16.... 6.25
" 6. Size, 15x20....11.50
" 7. Size, 18x22....13.50
" 8. Size, 20x24....17.25

Each.
6265 Copying brushes, 3 inches wide.............$0.25
6266 Water Bowls for copying, iron tube........ .20

Letter Copying Books.

ALL TISSUE.

6267 Letter Copying Books, good quality paper, cloth sides, paged and indexed.

Pages.	Size, 9x11	Prices each.		Pages.	Size, 10x12	Prices each,
No. 1	300	$1.00		No. 4	300	$1.10
No. 2	500	1.20		No. 5	500	1.45
No. 3	1,000	1.70		No. 6	1,000	1.85

Full Duck Letter Copying Books.

6269 Containing good quality of Japanese tissue paper, durably bound in duck.

No. of pages.	Size.	Price each.	Per doz.
No. 1—	500	10x12	$0.62	$ 7.25
No. 2—	700	"	.84	9.75
No. 3—1,000	"	1 12	13.00

Bookkeeping Blanks.

6272 Extra well made line of cheap bookkeeping blanks, containing good white paper, bound in heavy board manilla covers, with side titles. Each book contains 200 pages; the line embraces Journals, Day, Cash and Ledgers. All are flat opening books.
Each........................$0.20
Per set, 4 books............ .70
Per dozen....................2.00

Blank Books.

We have adopted the "hundred" page plan for its simplicity and convenience. In ordering please state exactly what you want, whether Day Book, Journal, Record, Cash, S. E. or D. E. Ledgers or Long Day Books.
N. B.—Postage on blank books is usually more than the cost of the book, being 16c. per pound. We would advise when ordering these goods to make the order large enough for freight shipment.

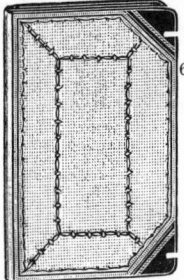

6278 Cap Folio, bound in Slate Duck, Russia corners, fine white paper, containing from 100 to 400 leaves. Ruled in Single Entry and Double Entry Ledgers, Records, Cash and Journals. The Journals in this line are used for both Day and Journals.

Size 8x12¾.

No. pages	100	150	200	250	300	400
Price each	$0.18	.27	.36	.45	.54	.72
Per dozen	1.75	3.00	3.75	4.00	6.00	8.25

6279 Cap Full Bound Flat Opening, Duck with Russia corners, gold title stamp. Extra heavy fine white paper. One of the best and cheapest books made.
N. B.—The smallest book in this line is 250 pages. Ruled in Records, Cash Journals, Ledgers and Broad Day Books.

Size 8½x13.

No. pages	250	300	350	400	450	500
Price each	$0.65	.78	.91	1.04	1.17	1.30
Per dozen	7.25	8.75	10.50	11.75	12.60	13.80

6280 Full Bound Sheep, flat opening with Russia corners, extra superfine heavy white paper, ruled in Journals, Cash, Long and Broad Day Books, Records and D. E. Ledgers, containing 250 to 800 pages.
N. B.—This line is ruled in units, making a separate line for every figure entered, which enables anyone to keep all figures a uniform size.

Size 8½x13.

No. pages	250	300	400	500	600	800
Price, each	$0.75	.90	1.20	1.50	1.80	2.40
Per dozen	8.40	9.75	13.75	16.00	19.00	25.00

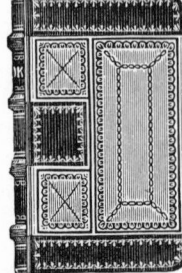

6281 M. W. & Co.'s Special Made. Full Bound Duck, with genuine Russia ends, back and bands, flat opening. Superior quality white wove paper, containing 300 to 1,000 pages. Ruled in Day Books, Journals, Cash, Records and D. E. Ledgers. All books in this line are ruled in units, making a separate line for every figure entered.

Size 9¼x14¼.

No. pages	300	400	500	600	800	1,000
Price, each	$1.20	1.60	2.00	2.40	3.20	4.00
Per dozen	12.50	16.50	20.75	25.00	33.50	42.00

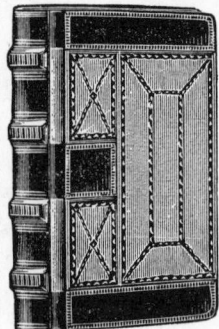

6283 *Our New Line,* full Bound Sheep, American Russia ends and bands, marble edge, flat opening, unit ruled. This line only comes in Double Entry Ledgers, Journals and Cash Books. The Double Entry Ledgers contain short accounts, and cloth index. All books in this line are ruled in unit lines. Special extra heavy paper.
Can also furnish 6 column Journals in this line, 400 pages, at $3.50 each.

Size 11½x16¼.

No. of pages	500	600	800
Price, each	$ 3.50	4.20	5.60
Per dozen	37.25	45.00	60.00

Hotel Registers.

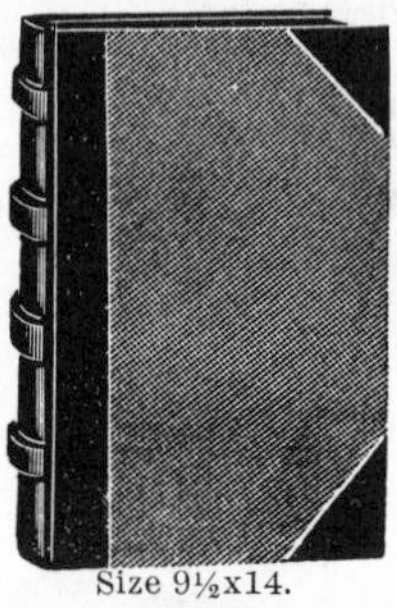

6284 Hotel Register, cloth bound, with genuine Russia backs. Printed head with name left blank to be written or stamped with rubber stamp. These are used by all the leading hotels in the country.
No. pages...250 300 400 500
Pr. each.$1.88 2.25 3.00 3.75

Miniature Blank Books.
(For personal and smaller accounts.)

6285 Bound in Duck and Agate Paper, with title stamp on cover; good white paper, ruled in Journals, Day Books, Records, Cash and S. E. and D.E. Ledgers, containing 100 pages. Our price, each.......... $0.30
Per dozen..............................3.25
Duck bound............................ .20
Per dozen..............................2.00

Size 4½x6¼.

6286 Bound in Red Leather, Stiff Cover, with gold title stamp on cover; extra fine paper, containing 200 pages. Ruled in any ruling. Our price each....$0.50
Per dozen...........................5.00

Size 4¼x7.

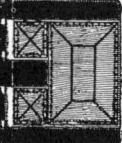

6287 Our Leader. Full Bound Sheep with Russia ends and bands, flat opening, containing 300 leaves of superior quality paper. Ruled in Journals, Cash, Day Books, Records, S. E. and D. E. Ledgers. Best book made. Our special price, each..$1.60
Per dozen.............................18.50

Size 10x8½.

Manifold Letter and Note Book.

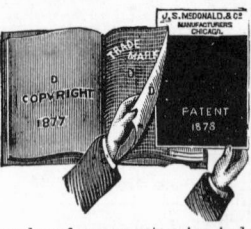

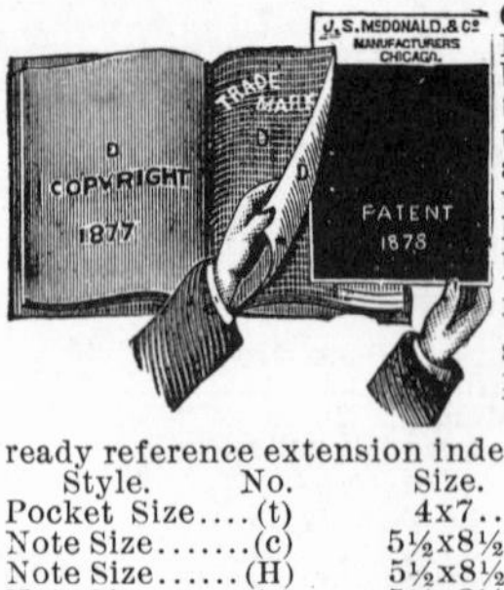

6290 Manifold Letter Books. A sheet of carbon paper is placed between two leaves, and the letter is written with a stylus or lead pencil; when finished the lower leaf is torn off and the upper remains as a copy. Each book is furnished with carbon paper and stylus with directions for using. Indexed books have patented ready reference extension index.

Style.	No.	Size.	No. Leaves.	Price.
Pocket Size	(t)	4x7	200	$0.60
Note Size	(c)	5½x8½	100	.60
Note Size	(H)	5½x8½	200	.95
Note Size	(a)	5½x8½	300	1.20
Large Note	(aX)	6 x9½	300	1.35
Large Note	(aB)	6 x9½ paged and indexed	500	2.00
Letter Size	(M)	8½x11	200	1.35
Letter Size	(B)	8½x11 paged and indexed	300	2.00
Letter size	(E)	8½x11 paged and indexed	500	2.35
Letter Size	(R)	8½x11 paged and indexed	500	2.15
Note Size	(P)	7 x10 paged and indexed	300	1.50

6291 Made of all tissue paper for those who desire to use their own note and letter heads.

Note Size	(O)	7 x10 paged and indexed	500	2.00

Atlases, Latest Editions.

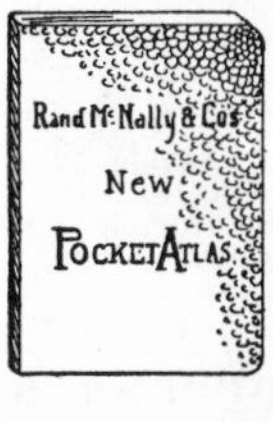

6295 New Rand, McNally & Co.'s Pocket Atlas of the World. Containing county maps of all States and Territories in the United States, and the Provinces of the Dominion of Canada, together with descriptive, statistical and historical matter pertaining to each, and indexed lists of their counties, population, etc.; also colored skeleton maps of the continents showing all countries of the world. Retail price, each......$0.25
Our price........................ .18
Per dozen........................ 1.90
Postage each, extra, 4c.

New Handy Atlas.

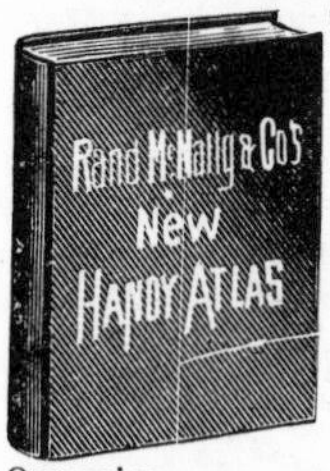

6297 This new atlas contains county maps of the United States and Dominion of Canada in colors, also descriptive, statistical and historical matter pertaining to each State or Province; indexed list of all counties with area and population; a ready reference list alphabetically arranged of all towns and villages, with population of 1890, also colored maps of all countries of the world, with diagrams, etc. Bound in limp cloth. 382 pages, size 5¾x8.
Retail price..................$1.00
Our price................$0.55 Postage.......... .10

Montgomery Ward & Co.'s New Home and Library Gazetteer and Indexed Atlas of the World, 345 pages.

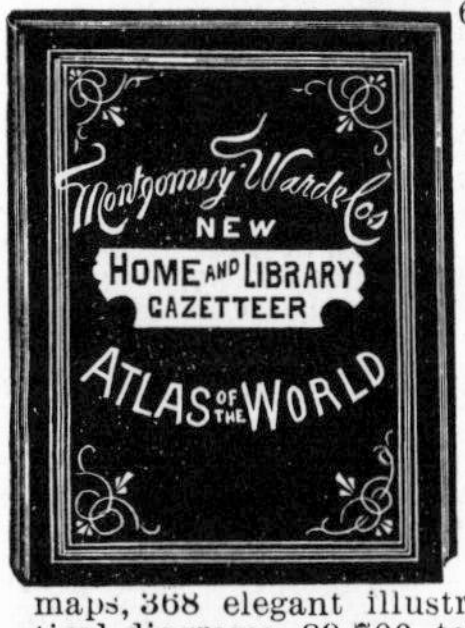

6298 Containing complete 1890 census population of every city, town and incorporated village in the United States, alphabetically arranged, and all information relative to same. Authentic. Containing the latest colored indexed maps of every State and Territory in the United States, every province of Canada, and every country in the world, together with historical, descriptive, and statistical information pertaining to each, embellished with 125 colored maps, 368 elegant illustrations, 612 colored statistical diagrams, 89,700 towns, villages and hamlets. Size, when closed, 11½x14½ inches. Complete in one volume. Atlases comparing with this would retail for not less than $5.00 to $10.00. Bound in the best English cloth, gold side stamp.
Our price..$2.25
Bound in half Morocco, gold side stamp. Our price.. 2.75
Weight, 104 ounces. Postage 55 cents extra.

School, Family and Library Globes.

A copy of the Globe Manual will accompany each globe.

The Manual gives explanation of the terms used in geography and astronomy, and the phenomena of mathematical geography, including temperature and ocean currents, and forty-five problems on the use of globes, with rules and illustrative examples; also several valuable tables.

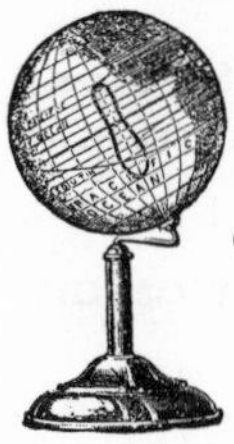

6300 Our New eight inch globe (C. T. M.) mounted on a beautiful nickel plated stand, inclined axis absolutely correct. Manufacturer's price $8.00.
Our price....... $4.00

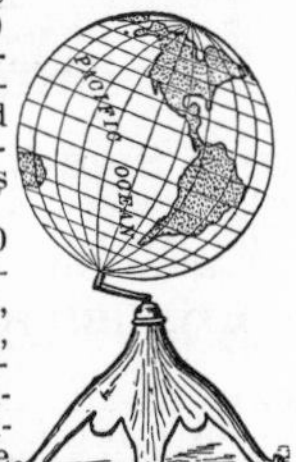

6301

6301 New Plain Terrestrial 12 inch globe, 23 inches in height, mounted on a nickel-plated stand, guaranteed correct. Manufacturer's price $15.00.
Our price........$5.00

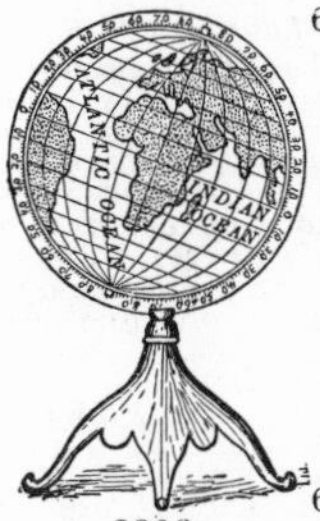

6302

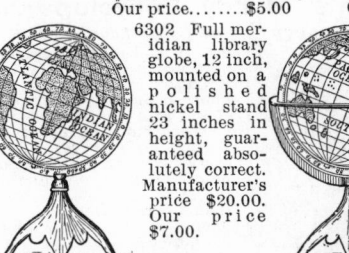

6302 Full meridian library globe, 12 inch, mounted on a polished nickel stand 23 inches in height, guaranteed absolutely correct. Manufacturer's price $20.00. Our price $7.00.

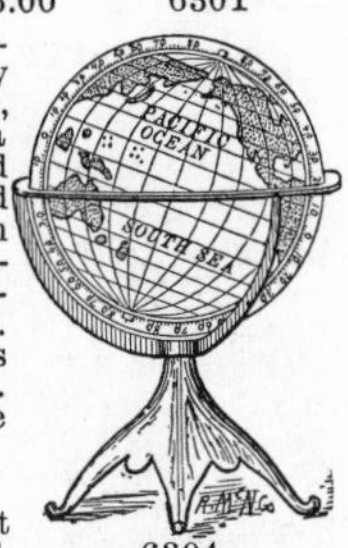

6304

6304 Our best full mounted globe, 12 inches in diameter, 23 inches in height mounted on a beautiful nickel-plated stand, guaranteed absolutely correct, manufacturer's price $25.00 Our price..........................$9.00

Maps—Continued.

6306 A large map of the world, with a special map of the United States, England and Wales, Germany, Norway and Sweden. Comprehensive diagrams of mountains and rivers, and alphabetically arranged compilation describing every country in the world, and its location indexed. The only reversible map showing Rand, McNally & Co.'s latest general map of the United States, size 66x46. Bound with tape; sticks, top and bottom, ready to hang on the wall. Our special prepaid price..............$0.90
Per dozen..10.00

6307 **State Maps.** Folded neatly into pocket size. We have maps of every State and Territory in the United States, without exception. In ordering *be sure and give name of State and Territory wanted.* Each......$0.15. Per dozen.......... 1.60
By mail, extra, each.................................. .02

POCKET MAPS OF FOREIGN COUNTRIES. Series 6310.

Afghanistan, indexed, board cover...............$0.18
Africa, 21x28 inches, with an inset map, on an enlarged scale, of the Suez Canal............... .52
Alaska, 50x28 inches............................ .70
Argentine Republic, Chile, Paraguay and Uruguay (new), 21x28 inches...................... .52
Asia, 21x14 inches.............................. .35
Australia and New Zealand, 21x14 inches, with plans of Sydney and Port Jackson............... .35
Austro-Hungarian Monarchy, 21x14 inches, with plan of Vienna................................ .35
Belgium and The Netherlands, 21x14 inches, with plan of Brussels, index to cities, towns, etc..... .35
Brazil and Guiana (new), 21x28 inches........... .52
British Columbia, 14x21 inches.................. .35
Central America (new), 28x21 inches............. .52
China, 21x14 inches............................. .35
China, Farther India, and Indian Archipelago, indexed, board cover............................ .18
Colombia and Venezuela (new), 28x21 inches.... .52
Cuba, 21x14 inches.............................. .35
Denmark, 14x11 inches, with Northern portion of the German Empire, comprising Schleswig-Holstein and Lauenburg........................ .35
Egypt and the Egyptian Soudan, paper cover..... .18
England and Wales, 21x14 inches, with index to cities, towns, etc.............................. .52
Europe, 21x14 inches............................ .35
France, 21x14 inches, with plan of Paris, index to cities, towns, etc........................... .52
Germany (new), 35x28 inches, with index to cities, towns, etc.............................. .70
Greece and the Ionian Islands, 21x14 inches..... .35
India, Indo-China, and Farther India, 21x14 inches, with plans of Calcutta and Bombay..... .35
Ireland, 21x14 inches, with index to cities, towns, etc.................................... .52
Italy, 21x14 inches............................. .35
Japan, in two sheets, 21x14 inches, each.......... .52
Mexico (new), 28x21 inches...................... .52
North America, 21x14 inches, showing the West India Islands and Central America............. .35
Oceanica, 21x14 inches.......................... .35
Palestine, 21x14 inches, with plats showing environs of Jerusalem, journeyings of Christ, and sketch showing divisions into tribes............ .35
Persia and Afghanistan, 14x11 inches............$0.35
Peru and Bolivia (new), 28x21 inches............ .52
Russia (European), 21x14 inches................. .35
Scotland, 21x14 in., with index to cities, towns, etc. .52
South America (new), 28x21 inches.............. .52
Spain and Portugal, 21x14 inches, with plans of Madrid and Lisbon............................. .35
Sweden and Norway, 21x14 inches................ .35
Switzerland, 21x14 inches....................... .35
Turkey in Asia (Asia Minor) and Transcaucasia, 21x14 inches.................................. .35
Turkey in Europe, 21x14 inches.................. .35
West Indies, 18x14 inches....................... .35
On above maps, postage, extra, 5c.

Rand, McNally & Co.'s New Large Scale Wall Maps. Series 6311.

Sent to any address, charges prepaid upon receipt of prices quoted.

STATE.	Size.	Scale to 1 inch.	* Half Mount'd	† Full Mount'd
California & Nevada	34x46	18 miles	$1.50	$2.25
Colorado	36x26	12 "	1.25	2.25
Florida	36x48	10 "	......	2.25
Illinois	35x55	8 "	1.50	2.50
Indiana	28x42	8 "	1.25	2.25
Indian Territory	34x26	12 "	......	1.50
Iowa	48x36	8 "	1.25	2.25
Kansas	56x32	8 "	1.25	2.25
Michigan	41x58	8 "	1.50	2.50
Minnesota	40x56	8 "	1.25	2.25
Mississippi	51x58	7 "	1.25	2.25
Missouri	48x40	8 "	1.25	2.25
Montana	38x25	16 "	1.00	1.75
Nebraska	61x34	8 "	1.50	2.50
New England States	41x58	10 "	......	3.00
New Mexico Ty	30x26	18 "	......	1.50
New York	34x31	10 "	......	2.25
North Dakota	50x36	8 "	1.50	2.50
Ohio	51x44	6 "	1.50	2.50
Pennsylvania	40x25	8 "	......	2.25
South Dakota	52x36	8 "	1.50	2.50
Tennessee	58x24	9 "	......	2.25
Texas	63x46	15 "	......	4.00
United States	66x46	45 "	......	4.00
Washington	60x41	8 "	1.50	2.50
West Virginia	44x38	7 "	......	2.50
Wisconsin	41x58	8 "	1.25	2.25

Globe Series of School Maps. Series No. 6312.

Prices of Wall Maps.	Size.	Price.
Western Hemisphere	41x58 inches.	$3.60
Eastern Hemisphere	41x58 "	3.60
North America	41x58 "	3.60
South America	41x52 "	3.60
United States, Canada and Mexico	41x58 "	4.50
Europe	41x52 "	3.60
Asia	41x52 "	3.60
Africa	41x52 "	3.60

The above maps forwarded to any address by mail or express upon receipt of price quoted.

How to Kill Time in Chicago.

6314 The Stranger's Guide to the World's Fair City. Where to go and how to get there, with map and illustrations of all public buildings, etc. Anyone who intends to visit the greatest city on earth should have this book.
Our special price......$0.15 Postage............$0 05

Montgomery Ward & Co.'s New Indexed Map of Chicago.

6315 Guaranteed the latest and best, printed in colors. Price..$0.04
Per dozen.. .40
Postage, each.. .02

Dictionary Holders.

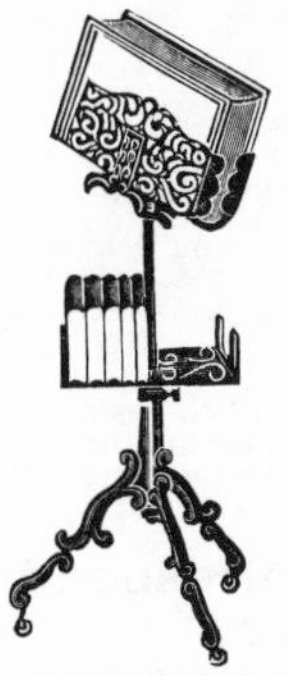

Harvard.

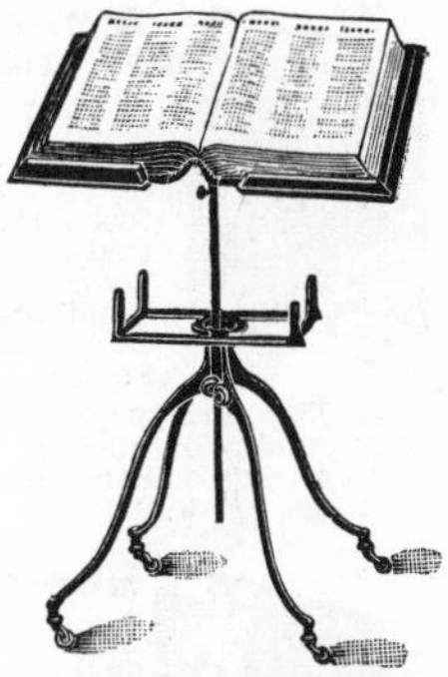

Noyes.

Noyes Holders.

Perfectly adjustable to any height or angle and is pivoted to turn any angle. Suitable for holding dictionaries, bibles, albums or large books of any kind.

6317 All iron, bronzed and nickel-plated, polished walnut case, four legs on casters. Has book rack below to hold 8 or 10 volumes—a great convenience.
Retail price, each....$4.00 Our price..........$2.60

6318 All wire, level top, no pivot or casters, light and strong. Folds up for shipment.
Retail price, each....$3.00 Our price..........$1.45

Harvard Holders.

Are durable and practicable. The sides are operated by double acting springs, the book being firmly clamped while closed and resting on a level surface when open. The adjustment to books of different sizes, and the inclination to any angle, are effected by a single screw.

6320 Complete with casters and revolving bookshelf, all nickel-plated finish.
Retail price........$8.00 Our price........$3.95

6321 Same as No. 6320, finished in black japan.
Retail price........$5.50 Our price........$2.60

6322 Same as 6321 in finish, without shelf or casters.
Retail price........$4.00 Our price........$2.05

6323 Same as 6320, finished in antique copper, suitable for office or parlor.
Retail price........$8.00 Our price........$3.80

WORKS OF REFERENCE.

American Encyclopædic Dictionary.

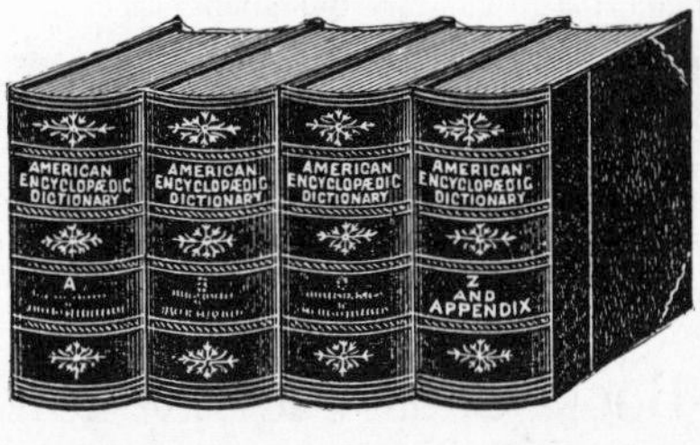

6325—An entirely new accurate, practical and inexhaustive work of reference to all the words in the English language, with a full account of their origin, meaning, pronunciation and use. Edited by Robert Hunter, A. M., F. G. S. Containing 250,000 words, or 160,000 more than the Webster International. A complete encyclopædia and dictionary combined. 2,000 illustrations.

Dictionaries—Continued.

It gives over 50,000 important cyclopædic subjects not given in any of the standard cyclopædias. It is the embodiment of many dictionaries in one, embracing Botany, Chemistry, Mineralogy, Zoology, Anatomy, Law, Medicine, Electricity, etc. It is also complete as a classical and Biblical dictionary, and is a perfect glossary of the English language. Well and durably bound, as follows:
Cloth, per set of 4 Volumes, *complete*............$6.50
½ Morocco, per set of 4 Volumes, *complete*....... 8.50
Library Sheep," " " , *complete*....... 9.50
Total weight of 4 volumes, 28 lbs. Sample pages sent upon application.

Alibone's Quotations.

6326 Complete in three volumes. A valuable work for every home, library and academy, containing POETICAL QUOTATIONS covering the entire field of British and American poet y, from Chaucer to Tennyson, with copious indexes. Both authors and subjects alphabetically arranged.
PROSE QUOTATIONS, from Socrates to Macaulay, with indices; authors, 544; subjects, 571; quotations, 8,810.
GREAT AUTHORS of all ages. Being selections from the prose works of eminent writers, from the time of Pericles to the present day. By S. Austin Alibone, LL. D. Set of three volumes, complete..$6.00
Any volume, separate.............................. 2.10
Postage, each...................................... .24

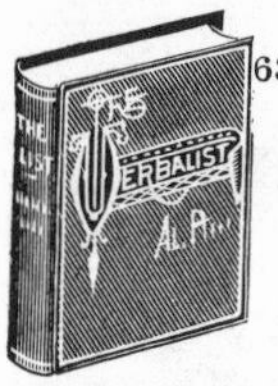

Ayres', Alfred, Works.

6327 The Orthoepist, a pronouncing manual, containing about three thousand five hundred words, including a considerable number of the names of foreign authors, artists, etc., that are often mispronounced. 18mo.
Retail price.........................$1.25
Our price.............................. .90
Postage, extra, 10c.
6329 The Verbalist, a manual devoted to brief discussions of the right and wrong use of words. 18mo. Retail price $1.25. Our price... .90
Postage, extra, 10c.

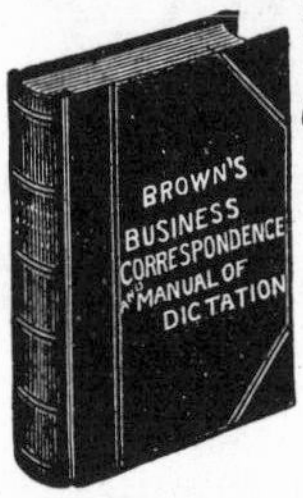

Business Correspondence.

6330 Brown's Business Correspondence and Manual of Dictation, for the use of Teachers and Students of Stenography and Typewriting, containing selected letters of actual correspondence in Banking, Insurance, Railroad and Mercantile Business; a chapter on Punctuation, Spelling and Use of Capital Letters; together with a full and complete Spelling List of 27,000 words.
Our price.......................$0.75
Postage, extra 12c.

Cruden's Complete Concordance.

6331 Complete Concordance of the Holy Bible (unabridged edition). Large 8vo., cloth........$1.00
Full leather.. 1.85
Postage, extra, 32c.

Cushing's Manual.

6332 Of Parliamentary Practice, being rules for conducting business in deliberative assemblies.
Cloth, 16 mo $0.35
Postage, extra, 4c.

Reader's Reference Library. Series 6333.

Crown 8vo., half morocco, gilt top.

	Each— Retail price.	Our price.
Chambers' Concise Gazetteer of the World	$2.50	$1.75
Brewer's Reader's Hand-book	3.50	2.45
Brewer's Dictionary of Phrase and Fable	2.50	1.75
Brewer's Dictionary of Miracles	2.50	1.75
Brewer's Historic Note-book	3.50	2.45
Edwards's Words, Facts and Phrases	2.50	1.75
Worcester's Comprehensive Dictionary	2.50	1.75
Ancient and Modern Familiar Quotations	2.50	1.75
Bombaugh's Gleaning for the Curious	3.50	2.45
Soule's Synonyms	2.75	1.93
Roget's Thesaurus	2.50	1.75
The Writer's Hand-book	2.50	1.75
Walsh's Hand-book of Literary Curiosities	3.50	2.45
Great Truths by Great Authors	2 50	1 75

Postage, each, extra 15c.

Our new Medical and Scientific Book Catalogue is now ready. Send 2 cents to pay postage.

Chambers' Encyclopædia.

Special attention given to American subjects.
The New Chambers' Encyclopædia.

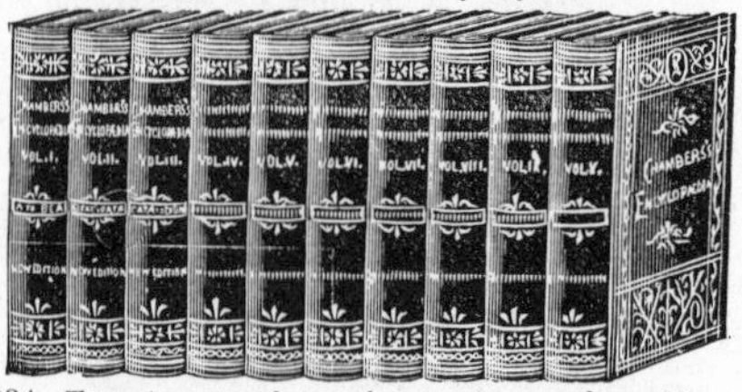

6334 Twenty years later than any encyclopædia in the market. New type, new subjects, new illustrations, new maps. A complete dictionary of art, science, history, literature, fable, mythology. biography, geography, etc. Handsomely illustrated with maps and numerous wood engravings.
Specimen pages sent on application.
Complete in Sets: Ten volumes:
Cloth...................$18.90
Sheep.................. 25.20 Half Morocco...... $27.35
Weight, 50 lbs.

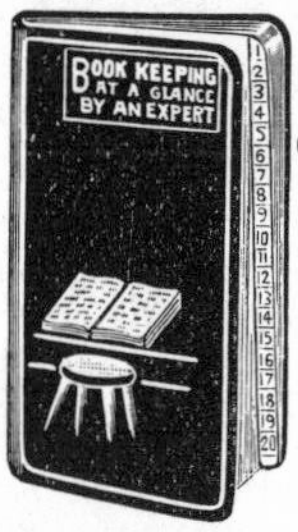

Book-keeping at a Glance.

6335 By Expert J. T. Brierly. A simple and concise method of practical book-keeping, with instructions for the proper keeping of books and accounts, and numerous explanations and forms used in a commercial business, showing an entire set of books, based upon actual transactions; how to take off a trial balance sheet, and finally close and balance accounts. 144 pages. Size 2¾x5; Russia leather.
Retail price $0.50
Our price.. .38
With patent index.................................... .50
Postage, extra, 5c.

Chambers' Encyclopædia.

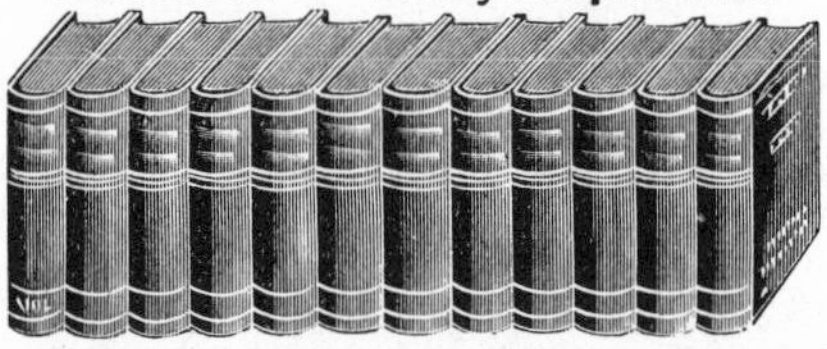

A library of universal knowledge for the people, being a complete reprint of the Edinburgh and London edition of Chambers' Encyclopædia, with very large additions upon topics of special interest to American readers, and giving American statistics of population down to and including the census of 1890, containing more than 27,000 specially prepared articles giving pointed, practical, explicit and most interesting and instructive information.
6338 Red and Gold Edition. Bound in blue cloth with stampings on side and back in red ink and gold. Retail price..$10.00. Our price..........$6.50
6339 Popular Edition. Bound in brown cloth with gold title on back. Retail price, $7.00.
Our price.. 4.50

Chambers' English Literature.

6340 4 volumes. Cloth. 12mo.
Per set 4 volumes. $3.00
Postage .... .48

Crabb's English Synonyms.

6341 Explained in alphabetical order, to which is added an index to the words. Illustrated by G. Crabb.
Retail price $1.25; our price.................. . $0.88
Postage, extra.. .12

Conklin's Handy Manual.

(New Edition 1894, containing full census of 1890.)

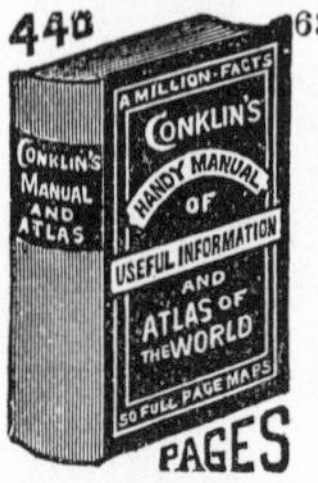

6342 Conklin's Handy Manual and Atlas of the World, by Professor Conklin, of Hamilton University. A full description of every country in the world; 440 pages of information, facts, calculations, receipts, processes, rules, business forms, legal items, etc., over 2,000 subjects of value. Conklin's Manual in limp cloth. Each......$0.15
Per dozen. 1.65
Conklin's Manual in stiff cloth, gold embossed, library style.
Each..................................$0.30
Per dozen...... .... 3.25
Extra by mail: limp.. .03
Cloth... .05
Can be furnished in German at same prices.

Coffin's Interest Tables.

6343 Interest tables at ½, 1, 2, 3, 3½, 4, 4½, 5, 6, 7, 8 and 10 per cent. per annum. By John Coffin. Best book in print on this subject.
Retail price $1.00. Our price.....................$0.75
Postage 10c. extra.

Cassell's Latin Dictionary.

6344 Latin-English and English-Latin, by J. R. Beard, D. D. Cloth. 12mo. 892 pages.
Retail price $1.50; our price.....................$1.05
Postage, extra .... .14

Drill Tactics.

LATEST EDITIONS.

6346 **Government Edition.** infantry drill regulations, approved by the President Oct. 3, 1891. These books were printed with those ordered by the war department for issue to the army.
Paper...$0.26
Leather.. .65
Postage, extra, 6c.

Duffey's Ladies' and Gentlemen's Etiquette.

6347 A complete manual of the manner and dress of American society. Retail price........$1.50
Our price.. 1.05
Postage.......... .... .12

Dick's Encyclopædia.

6348 DICK'S ENCYCLOPÆDIA OF PRACTICAL RECEIPTS AND PROCESSES, containing 6,422 practical receipts on all subjects. By Wm. B. Dick. 607 pages, royal octavo. Price, cloth.............$3.50
Bound in sheep, an ornament to any library $4.50. Extra by mail............ .... .35

Encyclopædia Britannica.

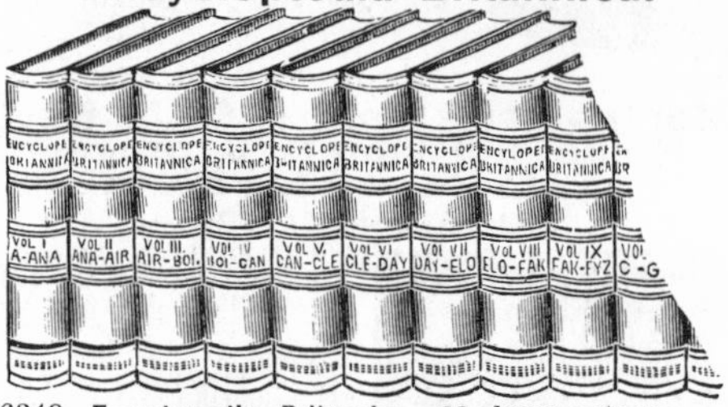

6349 **Encyclopædia Britannica. 30** large octavo volumes (Allen Reprint), 25 volumes, Encyclopædia Britannica and 5 volumes American Supplement. This new reprint edition includes all of the American copyrighted articles, and is the only word for word, page for page, volume for volume, reprint, unaltered from the original ever published. Over 1,500 contributors, 20,-500 pages, 8,000 illustrations, etc.
Single volumes, green silk cloth.................$ 1.25
Full set, 30 vols., green silk cloth............... 35.00
Single volume, ½ Russia............................ 1.45
Full set, 30 vols., ½ Russia........................ 42.00
Single volumes, ½ Russia extra.................. 1.65
Full set, 30 vols., ½ Russia extra................ 48.00
Postage on single volumes......................... .28
In ordering single volumes, always state what volume or volumes are wanted.
Set of 30 vols. weighs 125 lbs., packed in box.

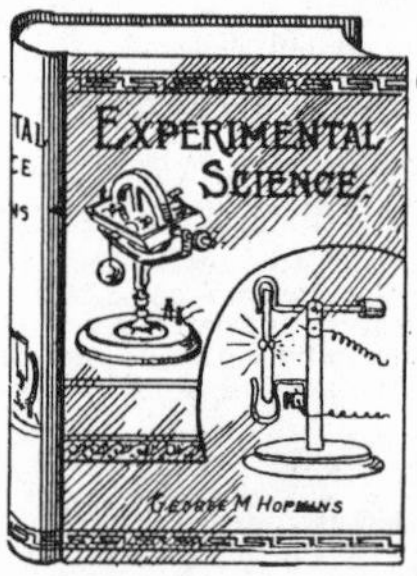

Experimemtal Science.

6350 Experimental Science by George M. Hopkins; this book is full of interest and value for teachers, students and others who desire to impart or obtain a practical knowledge of physics; 740 pages, over 680 illustrations, elegantly bound in cloth. Fourteenth edition, revised and enlarged.
Retail price............$4.00
Our price 3.00
Postage 40 cents extra.

English-Swedish and Swedish-English Dictionary.

6351 Full explanations of all words. Bound in half leather. Each.......................................$1.25
Postage, extra, 10 cents.

English and Dano-Norwegian Dictionary.

6353 New stereotype edition, revised and improved, half Russia binding. Each............$1.50
Postage, 10 cents extra.

Edison's Handy Encyclopædia.

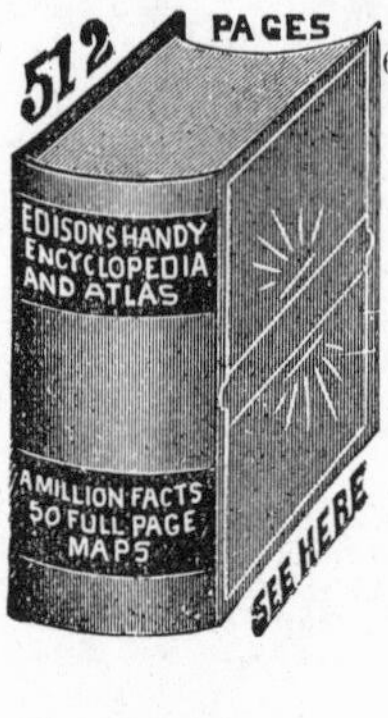

New Census Edition of 1891-92.

6354 Of general information a universal atlas, edited by Thos. F. Edison. Much in little. Five hundred and twelve pages of closely printed matter. A reference encyclopædia, contains a million facts of great value to everyone, also a compilation of practical facts on practical subjects.
Bound in limp cloth.
Each...................................$0.15
Per dozen............................. 1.65
Cloth covers, embossed titles, library style. Each......$0.30
Per dozen.............................. 3.25
Postage, each, limp....... .03
Library.................. ... .04

Encyclopædia of Quotations.

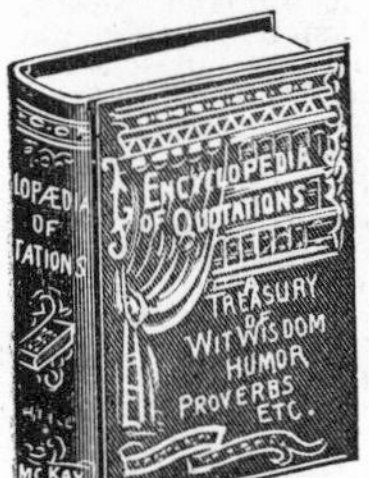

6356 A treasury of wisdom, wit and humor; odd comparisons and proverbs. Authors, 931; subjects, 1,393; quotations, 10,299. Compiled and arranged by Adam Woolever. Royal octavo, cloth, gilt,
Retail price............... $1.75
Our price 1.00
Postage, extra............ .32

Flowers.

6357 Their language, poetry, sentiment, etc. *Red-line edition.* 18mo. Cloth, beveled gilt edges. Retail price $1.25
Our price............... .88
Postage .... .10

Everybody's Guide to Music.

6358 With illustrated chapters on singing and the cultivation of the voice; full and explicit helps to the piano and organ; complete dictionary of musical terms. By Josiah Booth. pp. vi., 176. Square 16mo., cloth.
Retail price............... $0.75
Our price............... .55
Postage, extra, 4c.

Fallow's, Rt. Rev. Samuel,

6359 100,000 Synonyms and Antonyms; or Synonyms and Words of Opposite Meaning, with an appendix. 16mo, cloth. Retail price. $1.00
Our price .... .70
Postage, extra............... .12

Favorite Illustrated Dictionary.

6360 A Dictionary of the English language, from the best authorities; 32,000 words and phrases, 670 illustrations. Retail price.......... $0.25
Our price............... .12
Per dozen 1.25
Postage, 3 cents.

Good Manners.

6362 A Manual of Etiquette. *Red-line edition.* Square, 18mo. Cloth, gilt edges.
Retail price............... $1.25
Our price .... .88
Postage, extra, 10 cents.

Gaskell's Compendium of Business Forms.

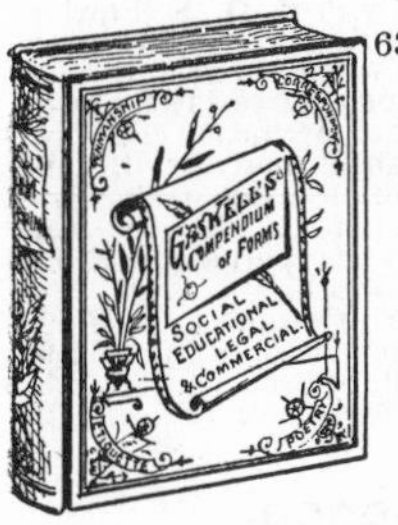

6363 Educational, social, legal and commercial, embracing self-teaching penmanship, book-keeping, laws, etiquette, agricultural, mining, receipts, etc. By G. A. Gaskell; 935 pages; cloth. This edition has been revised and enlarged by Loomis T. Palmer, making it a complete encyclopædia of reference. Also contains beautiful illustrations throughout.
Subscription price........ $6.00
Our price............... 2.80
Postage .... .48

Gaskell's Penmanship.

6364 Gaskell's Complete Compendium of Elegant Writing, comprised in a new series of twenty beautiful COPY SLIPS for self-instruction; one large plate of fancy and ornamental penwork and a book of instruction, complete in a packet. Our price, per set............... $0.25
Postage............... .04

Gaskell's Guide to Writing, Pen Flourishing, Lettering and Letter Writing.

6365 With Gems from American and European penmen, and portraits and sketches, being a complete self-teaching guide to plain and artistic work of every description possible for the use of the pen. By G. A. Gaskell. Profusely illustrated with original plates expressly for this book. Our price............... $0.60
Postage............... .12

Hill's Manual.

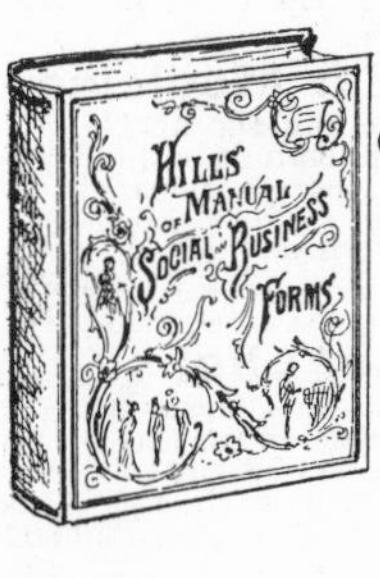

6366 Of Social and Business forms, a guide to correct writing and approved methods in speaking and acting in the various relations of life. New enlarged edition. Illustrated and corrected to date. By Thos. E. Hill, author of Morals and Manners, Hill Banking System, etc
Subscription price $6.00
Our price............... 1.95
Postage............... .45

How to Pronounce 10,000 Difficult Words.

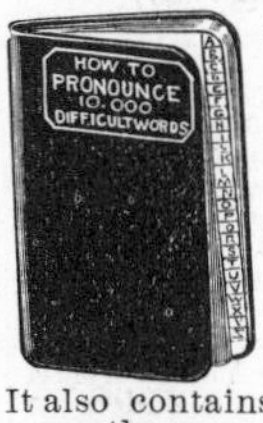

6367 An authoritative hand-book of words in common use. There are few persons whose education is so complete as to insure the correct pronunciation of all the words met with in daily reading. Czar, Boucicault, Isolate, Balmoral, Boulanger, Coup d' etat, etc., are cases in point. These words with very many others of the same kind will be found in the book. The aid offered to the reader or speaker by it is very great. It also contains an extended list of words often incorrectly pronounced.
By F. M. Payne; 128 pages, bound in Russia, indexed. Retail price 50c., our price 38c. Postage, extra, 3c.

Masson's New French-English and English-French Dictionary.

6369 Of the French language, uniform with above, giving new words recently introduced in French.
Retail price $1.00. Our price............... $0.70
Per dozen............... 8.00
Mail, 15 cents extra.

Mythology.

6370 **Manual of Mythology.** By Alex. S. Murray, For the use of schools, art students and general readers. Founded on the works of Petiscus, Preller and Welcker. With 45 plates on tinted paper, representing nearly 100 mythological subjects. Crown, 8vo. Our price............ $1.45
Postage, 16c. extra.

New Webster Vest-Pocket Dictionary.

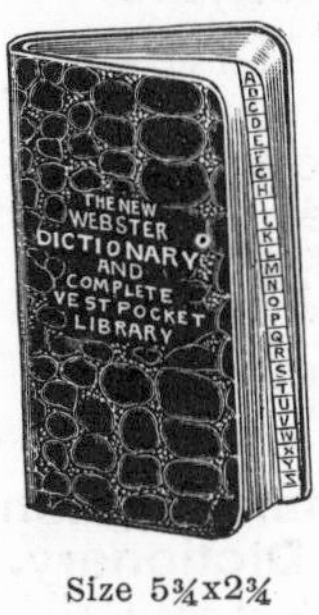

Size 5¾x2¾

6371 An entirely new and original compilation from the famous Webster's great work. Its size and general make-up are such as to render this beautiful little book for ready reference in Spelling, Meaning of Words, Correct Pronunciation, Synonyms, Irregular Verbs and Habitual Mistakes. Simple, Practical, Invaluable. It includes the Gazetteer of the World. Something new and especially useful.
Limp cloth, retail price.... $0.25
Our price .... .15
Per dozen............... 1.65
Full Morocco, indexed, retail price............... .50
Our price............... .30
Per dozen............... 3.25
Postage, each............... .04

Nuttall's Standard Dictionary of the English Language.

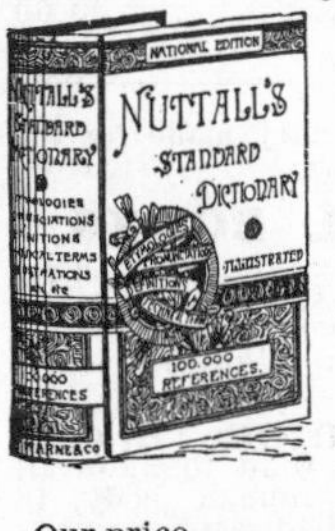

6372 Handiest Lexicon in the world. In large crown 8vo.; 832 pages.
PRINCIPAL FEATURES: New, clear type, 100,000 references containing all new words introduced into common parlance, science and literature. It is an etymological dictionary, giving derivations and meanings of all root words. It is illustrated, contains tables of pronunciation of classical, geometrical and scriptural names and for scholastic and home use is undoubtedly the handiest dictionary extant.
Cloth, retail price........... $1.50
Our price............... .75
Same, with patented index............... 1.00
Half Morocco, indexed............... 1.78
Postage, each............... .20

Law at a Glance, or Every Man His Own Counselor.

6373 Is a new epitome of the laws of the different States of our Union and those of the General Government of the United States, and will be found invaluable to those who are forced to appeal to the law, as well as the large class who wish to avoid it. The whole is alphabetically arranged so as to make reference to it easy.
Retail price............... $1.00
Our price............... .70
Postage, extra............... .12

Popular Handbooks. Series No. 6374.

	Retail price.	Our price
Cavendish on Whist	$0 50	$0.35

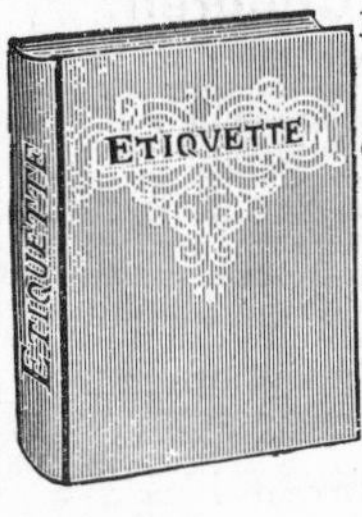

	Retail price.	Our price
Etiquette. By Agnes H. Morton, B. O. Cloth binding	.50	.35
Correspondence. By Agnes H. Morton, B. O. Cloth binding	.50	.35
Handbook of Pronunciation. By John H. Bechtel. Cloth binding	.50	.35
Punctuation. By Paul Allardyce. Cloth binding	.50	.35

Series No. 6374—Continued.

	Retail price.	Our price
The Debater's Treasury. By Wm. Pittenger. Cloth binding	.50	.35
Oratory. By Rev. Henry Ward Beecher. Cloth binding	.50	.35
Quotations. By Agnes H. Morton, B. O. Cloth binding	.50	.35
Practical Synonyms. By John H. Bechtle Cloth binding	.50	.35
The Art of Conversation. By J. P. Mahaffy. Cloth binding	.50	.35

Any of the above 9 books, postage 6c. each.

Parson's Laws of Business.

6375 For all the States and Territories of the Union and the Dominion of Canada, with forms and directions for all transactions. New revised edition, 8vo., cloth, 866 pages.
Subscription price, $3.75. Our price.......... $2.30
Sheep.............. $2.65. Postage, extra..... .30

Popular American Dictionary.

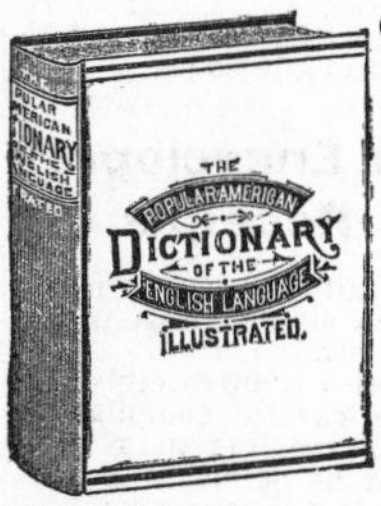

6378 Illustrated. A complete library in itself. Contains beside the dictionary proper a mass of information never before gathered within the compass of one volume. Revised from latest and best English and American authorities. 12mo., cloth, embossed sides and back.
Retail price.............. $1.00
Our price............... .30
Per dozen............... 3.25
Extra by mail............... .10

Reed's Rules.

6379 The latest recognized book of Parliamentary law for every one in any way connected with societies, clubs or organizations of any kind. By Thos. B. Reed. ex-speaker of the House of Representatives Cloth, 16mo. Retail price, $0.75. Our price.......... $0.52
Full seal leather............... .88
Postage, extra, 6c.

Roberts' Rules of Order.

6380 For Deliberative Assemblies. By Lieut. Col. H. M. Roberts, Corps of Engineers, U. S. A. 168th thousandth. Pocket size. Cloth $0.55
Postage, extra, 6c.

Ropp's Commercial Calculator.

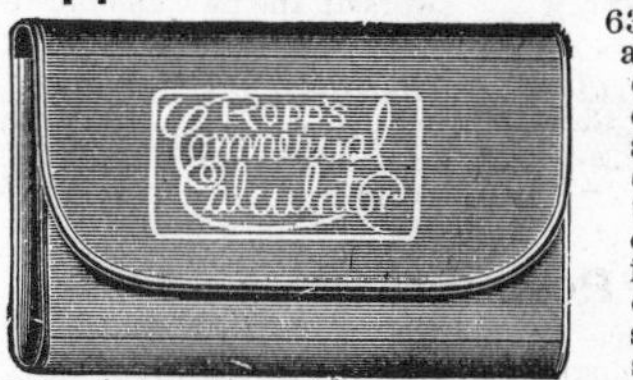

6381 Contains a new system of commercial tables, also a practical arithmetic for practical purposes, in which is embodied the shortest and simplest rules, easy, interesting tables, a new process for adding long columns, explanations to nearly all tables in both English and German. The tables of wages, interest, grain, log and lumber are worth many times the price of the work. No. C paper. Each..... $0.16
Per dozen............... 1.75
No. H. Leatherette. Each, $0.35. Per dozen... $3.50
No. A Morocco. Each..... .70. Per dozen... 7.50
No. M Kid. Each .... .90. Per dozen... 9.50
Postage, each. 6c.

Reference Books, Series 6382.

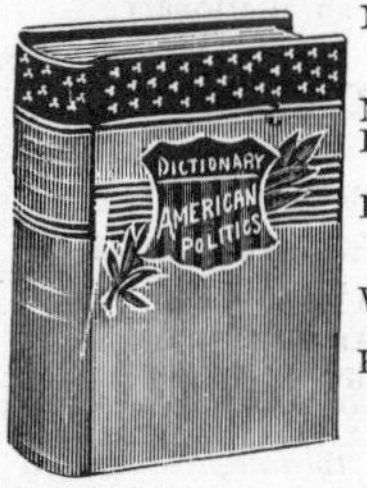

National Standard History of the United States. By Everit Brown.
National Standard Encyclopædia.
Law Without Lawyers. By Henry B. Corey.
Dictionary of American Politics. By Everit Brown and Albert Strauss.
What Everyone Should Know. By S. H. Burt.
Readers' Reference Hand-Book. By H. C. Faulkner and W. H. Van Orden.
Writers' Reference Handbook. By Jennie T. Wandle and H. C. Faulkner.
Etiquette? Health and Beauty. By Francis Stevens and Francis M. Smith.
Cyclopædia of Natural History. By Charles C. Abbott.
Why, When and Where. By Robert Thorne, M. A.
National Standard Dictionary, Illustrated; containing 40,000 words.
All are handsomely bound in cloth, 12mo.
Retail price $1.00. Our price, each............ $0.65
Postage, each............... .15

Roget's Thesaurus of English Words and Phrases.

6383 New edition, revised and enlarged by the author's son, J. L. Roget. Crown 8vo., cloth.
Retail price........ $2 00 Our price............ $1.40
Postage 16 cents extra.

Our Mail Order Methods have become generally recognized as correct.

Stamp Albums.

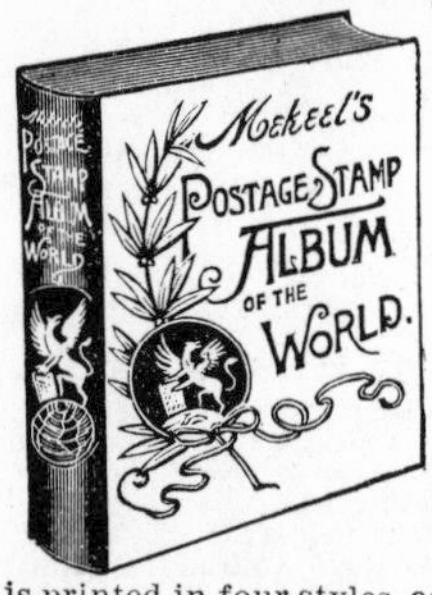

6385 **Mekeel's Postage Stamp Album of the World** is acknowledged to be the standard album. Its latest edition that has just been placed on sale is receiving the support of stamp collectors the world over.

This album contains spaces for the famous Columbian series now in use, a feature not included in any other album, and also provides for all other stamps issued to date. The illustration at the left gives a good idea of its general appearance, and the album measures 9x12 inches. It is printed in four styles, as follows:

No. 1—Half bound, cloth and boards..............$1.05
No. 2—Full cloth, black and gilt.......................1.75
No. 3—Full cloth, black and gilt, with stubs.....2.45
No. 4—Extra, full leather, stubs and gilt edges...5.25
Postage, extra...42

Scientific American Encyclopædia of Receipts.

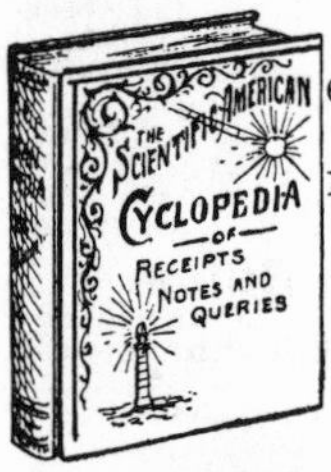

6386 Beautifully bound in cloth with gold title stamps, large print, and fully illustrated. Notes and queries, 1,200 receipts and 680 pages; a careful compilation of most useful receipts and replies published in the Scientific American for the last fifty years. 675 pages. Cloth, retail price .$5.00
Our price.............................3.65
Postage, 40 cents.

Smith's Bible Dictionary.

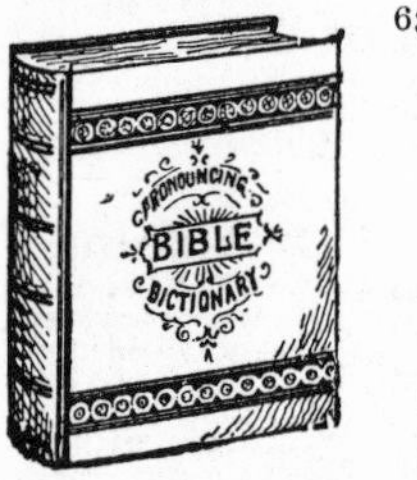

6387 Comprising antiquities, biography, geography, natural history, etc., with numerous illustrations and maps. A history of books of the Bible, also containing Cruden's complete concordance and 4,000 questions and answers on the new and old testaments. Cloth, marbled edges.
Retail price, cloth.......$2.50
Our price,....................1.05
Retail price, sheep......3.00
Our price.....................1.60
Postage, 28c extra.

Smith-Peloubet Dictionary.

6388 Dictionary of the Bible. Comprising its antiquities, biography, geography, natural history and literature. Edited by William Smith, LL.D. Revised and adapted to the present use of Sunday-school teachers and Bible students. By Rev. F. N. and M. A. Peloubet. With eight colored maps and 440 engravings on wood, 8vo.

	Retail price.	Our price
Cloth, extra	$2.00	$1.40
Full Sheep	3.00	2.10

Postage, extra, 20c.

Wessely's Spanish Dictionary.

6390 New pocket Spanish-English dictionary, 12 mo. Cloth...........$0.55 Postage, extra, 10c.

Wessely's Italian Dictionary.

6391 New pocket dictionary of the Italian and English language, 12 mo. Cloth..$0.55 Postage, 10c

Webster's International Dictionary

The New Webster.

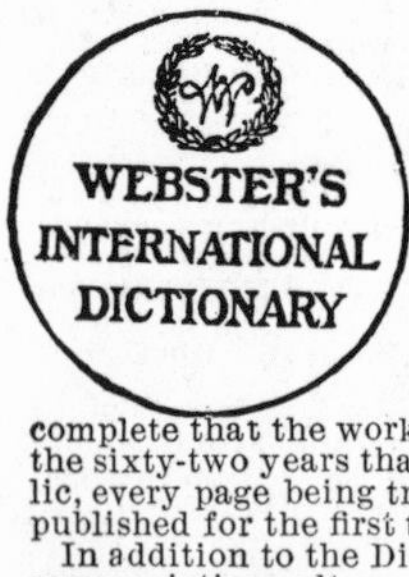

6394 The authentic Webster's Unabridged Dictionary, comprising the issues of 1864, '79 and '84, all still copyrighted, is now thoroughly revised and enlarged, under the supervision of Noah Porter, D. D., LL. D., of Yale University, and as a distinguishing title bears the name, Webster's International Dictionary. This last revision is by far the most complete that the work has ever undergone during the sixty-two years that it has been before the public, every page being treated as if the book was now published for the first time.

In addition to the Dictionary of Words, with their pronunciation, alternative spellings, etymology, and various meanings, illustrated by quotations and numerous engravings, there are several valuable appendices, comprising: A pronouncing gazetteer of the world. Vocabularies of Scripture, Greek, Latin and English proper names. A dictionary of the noted names of fiction. A brief history of the English language. A dictionary of foreign quotations, words, phrases, proverbs, etc. A biographical dictionary with 10,000 names. A classified selection of illustrations (filling 82 pages), etc., etc.

Library Sheep Binding.	Retail price	$10.00
" " "	Our price	8.50
" " "	Indexed	9.25

Postage extra, $1.08.

Reprint of Webster's Unabridged Dictionary of the English Language.

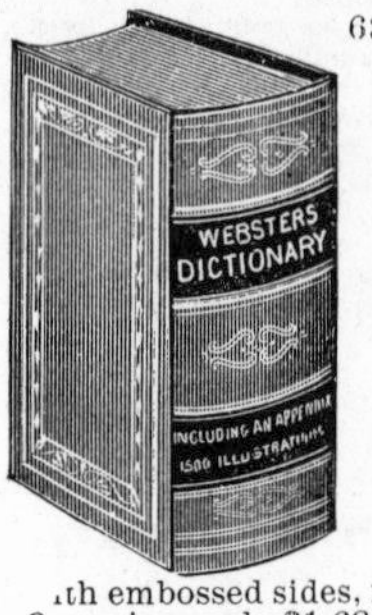

6395 Noah Webster's Dictionary of the English Language. The copyright having expired enables us to furnish the reprint. Pronunciations exhibited by the divisions of words into syllables, by accentuation or by general rules. Revised and enlarged by Chauncey A. Goodrich, professor in Yale College, to which has been added an appendix of 10,000 words and 1,500 illustrations, with pronouncing vocabularies of scripture, classical and geographical terms and a dictionary of mercantile and legal terms. Substantially bound in sheep, with embossed sides, marbled edges.
Our price, only $1.68. With patent Index......$2.25
Postage, 68 cents extra.

Webster's Every Man His Own Lawyer.

6396 A compendium of business and domestic law and equity; comprising the rights and wrongs of individuals. A handy guide in all law and business transactions and negotiations. Civil and commercial relations of everyday life. The special laws of every State and Territory in the United States, 12mo., cloth, gilt. Library.
Our price, only.................................$0.75
Postage...13

Word-Book of Synonyms.

6397 Of the English Language. By Thos. P. Peabody. The most complete in the English language. 12mo. Cloth.............................$0.30
Postage, 6 cents.

Young's Analytical Concordance to the Bible.

6398 Containing every word in alphabetical order, arranged under its Greek or Hebrew origin, with the original meaning of each, and pronunciation. With the latest information on Biblical Geography and Antiquities, etc. By Robert Young, LL. D. Quarto. Retail price, $5.00. Our price..........................$3.75
Postage, 48c. extra.

Zahner's New German-English and English-German Dictionary.

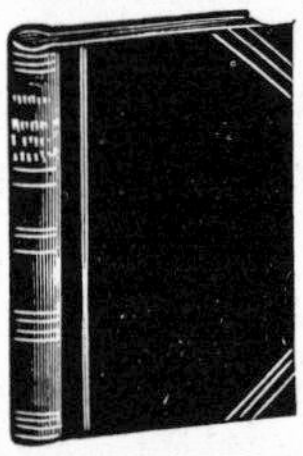

6400 A Dictionary of the English-German and German-English, arranged in separate parts. By Carl Zahner. Contains pronunciations, definitions, etc. Illustrated. 462 pages, finely bound, leather backs, gilt stamp. Large crown, 8vo.
Retail price..........................$1.00
Our price................................70
Per dozen..............................8.00
Postage, each..........................15
The best dictionary made for the price.

MEDICAL BOOKS.

We list below only a partial list of family medical books which are all standard on the subjects they treat. (Doctors and students will find it profitable to have our special medical and scientific book catalogue.) Send 2c. for postage.

Dr. Foote's Plain Home Talk.

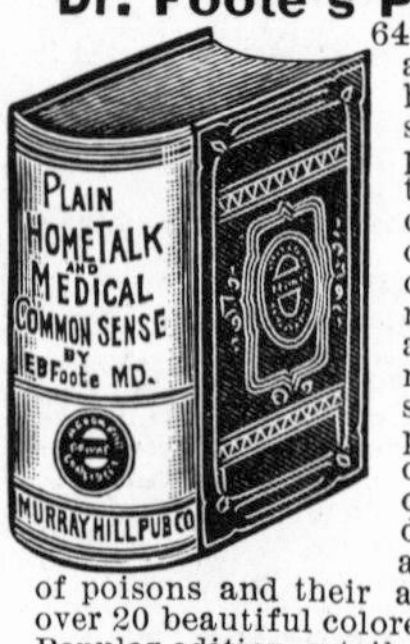

6405 If you want to know all about the human body, in health and disease, nature's secrets revealed, how life is perpetuated, health maintained, disease induced, death delayed, how to marry your own mate, and transmit wealth of health to posterity, read the most popular, comprehensive and useful book treating of medical, social and sexual science. An appendix of great practical utility made up of over 200 prescriptions or receipts for acute and chronic disorders common to adults and children, a complete table of poisons and their antidotes; illustrated by over 20 beautiful colored lithographs.
Popular edition, retail price $1.50 Our price...$0.85
Standard " " " 3.25 " " 1.35
Postage, 14 and 18 cents extra.

6406 Same printed in the German language at same prices.

The Care of Children.

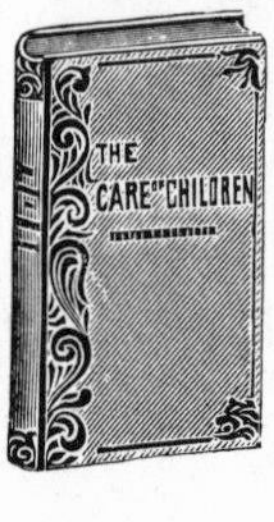

6407 By Elizabeth Robinson Scovil, superintendent of the Newport Hospital and associate editor of the Ladies' Home Journal. The book contains chapters on: Food, Clothing, Beds and Bedding, Baby's Toilet, Baths, Care of Teeth, Eyes, Ears, Hair, Nails and Feet Ailments, Physical Deformities, Diseases of Children, How to Act in Emergencies, Physical Culture, Care of Girls and the Care of Boys. 12mo. 348 pages.
Cloth. Price.............................$1.00
Our price...................................$0.70
Postage, 10 cents extra.

New Physician.

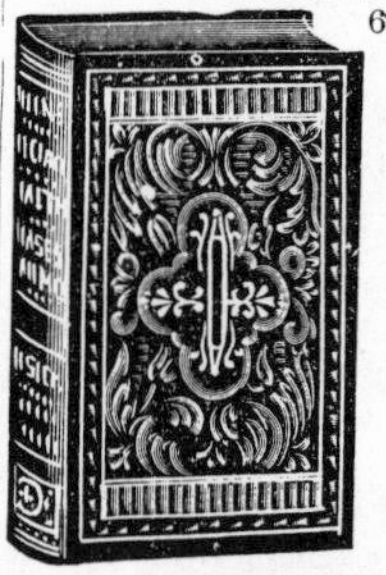

6408 Gunn & Jordan's Newest Revised Physician, being the first new domestic physician or home book of health by John C. Gunn, M. D., originally as enlarged and now issued with renewed copyright to the author, who prepared the large additions made to it during the six years from earliest publications. Johnson H. Jordan, M. D. Large octavo, 1,200 pages. Bound in leather, with marble edges.
Subscription price.........$6.00
Our price..........................4.00
Postage................................36
Can be furnished in the German language at same price.

Ladies' Medical Guide.

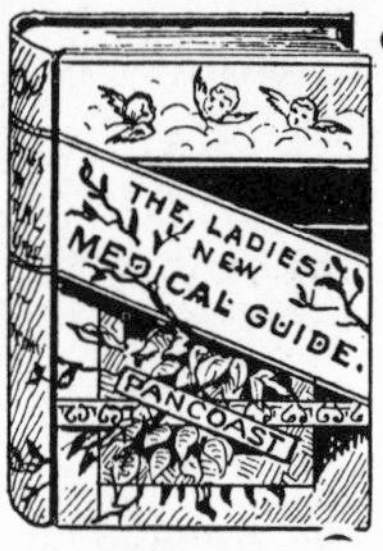

6409 By S. Pancoast, M. D., instructor, counselor and friend, explaining nature and mystery of reproductive organs in both sexes. Handsomely bound in cloth. Containing 682 pages, with working chart, showing all external parts of the human body. Also hundreds of other illustrations.
Subscription price.......$2 50
Our price......................1.60
Full Morocco.................1.90
Postage...........................19

Cowan's Science of New Life.

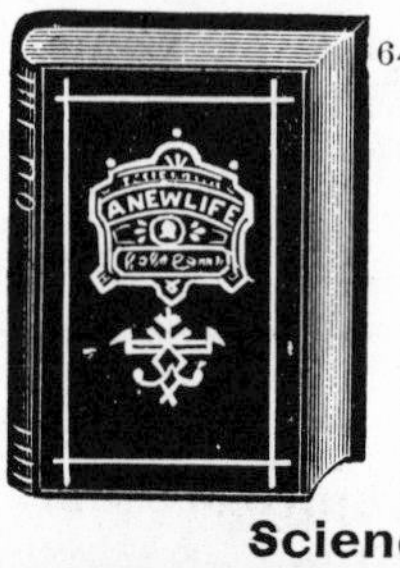

6410 By John Cowan, M. D. A book well worth possessing by every thoughtful man and woman. The "Science of a New Life" has received the highest testimonials and commendations from leading medical and religious critics; 400 pages; 100 illustrations. 8 vo. English cloth, gilt side and back stamps......................$2.05
8 vo. leather, sprinkled edges, ...2.40
½ Morocco.....................2.75
Postage, extra..................24

Science of Life.

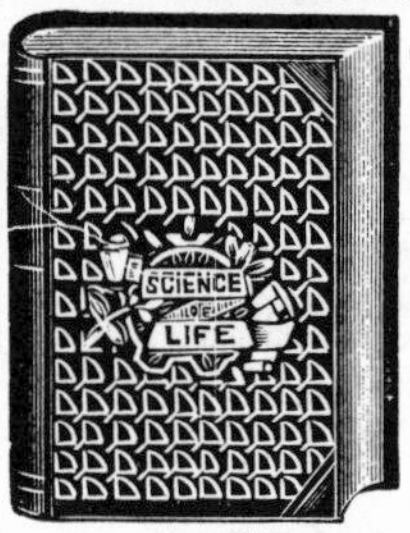

6411 By Prof O. S. Fowler; containing chapters on manhood, womanhood and their relations. Love, laws, power, selection or mutual adaption, courtship, married life and perfect children, male vigor and female health and beauty perpetuated. 1,050 pages, cloth.
Subscription price......$3.75
Our price.......................1.95
Full Morocco.................2.35
Postage..........................26

Human Science.

6412 Uniform with above by same author. Physiology, phrenology, etc.
Subscription price...$3.75
Our price...1.95
Postage, extra..26
Full Morocco..2.35

Physical Life of Woman.

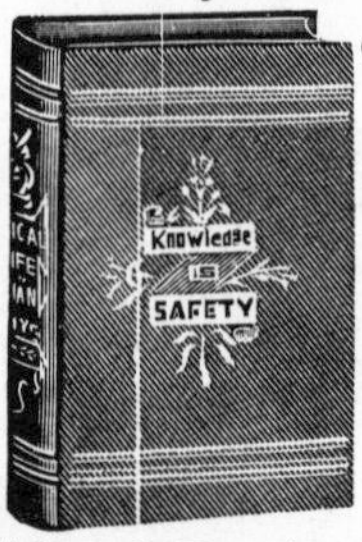

6414 By George H. Napheys, A. M., M. D. Advice to the maiden, wife and mother. A new edition, revised to the latest date, with a life of the author. This is the only work on the delicate topic of woman recommended for popular reading by the most distinguished physicians, eminent divines, prominent educators, leading medical journals, and the press generally.
Subscription price, cloth..$2.00
Our price..........................80
Postage..............................12

Hand-Book of Popular Medicine.

6415 Uniform with above, embracing the anatomy and physiology of the human body; instructions for nursing the sick; home gymnastics; the domestic treatment of ordinary diseases and accidents of children and adults. 12mo., cloth, gilt back and side.........................$0.80
Postage...12

Transmission of Life.

6416 Uniform with "Physical Life of Woman." Counsels of the nature and hygiene of the masculine functions. New edition, revised and enlarged. Large 12mo., cloth, gilt back and side...$0.80
Postage...12

What Women Should Know.

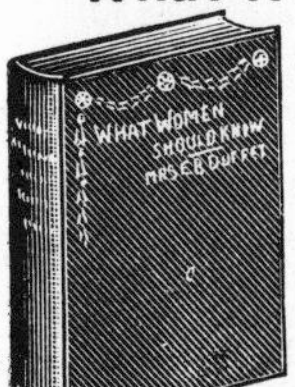

6417 What Women Should Know About Women, by Mrs. E. B. Duffy. Containing practical information for wives and mothers. 16 mo., cloth; handsomely bound.
Retail price..................$1.00
Our price.................. .52
Postage.................. .07

Stepping Stone.

6418 To Homeopathy and Health, by E. H. Rudick, M. D. (Exam.) Physician to Reading and Berkshire Homeopathic Dispensary. 12mo., cloth..........$0.75. Postage..........$0.10

Medical Dictionary.

6419 Complete pronouncing medical dictionary, embracing the terminology of medicine, kindred sciences, with their signification, etymology, etc., also Latin terms and phrases occurring in Medicine, Anatomy, Pharmacy, etc. By Joseph Thomas, M. D., LL. D.
Retail price..................$4.00
Our price.................. 2.40
Full Sheep.................. 2.80
Postage.................. .34

United States Dispensatory.

6420 Latest edition, enlarged and improved. Illustrated, 8vo., sheep binding.
Retail price..................$8.00
Our price.................. 6.10
With Dennison's patent index.................. 6.85
Postage.................. .40

Gray's Anatomy.

6421 Descriptive and surgical; a new American from the thirteenth English edition, revised by W. W. Keen, M. D., to which is added Holden's Landmarks, medical and surgical. 1,098 pages, 685 illustrations.
Cloth, retail price..................$6.00
Our price.................. 4.95
Leather, retail price.................. 7.00
Our price.................. 5.75
Postage, extra.................. .55
Above with colored plate, $1.25 extra.

Chemistry.

6422 Essentials of Chemistry. By Witthaus.
Retail price..................$1.00
Our price.................. .80
Postage.................. .08

N. B.—Net prices made on any medical work published.

Dr. Chase's Receipt Books.

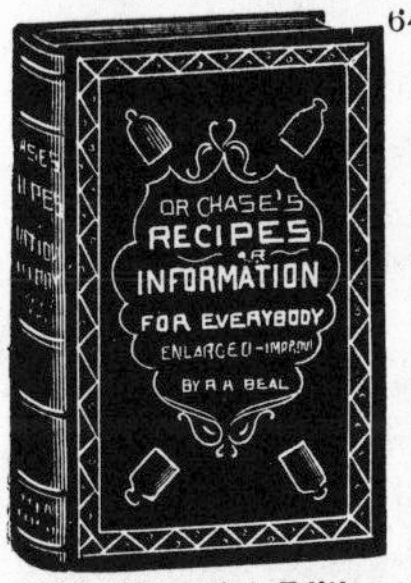

6423 Dr. Chase's Receipts or Information for Everybody is now enlarged and improved by the publisher, containing 648 pages and 2,000 receipts. The new edition gives in plain language full directions for the successful treatment of all leading diseases to which man, woman or child is heir; as well as those for horses and cattle, being the results of long experience of some of the most scientific physicians.
Subscription price..................$2.00
Our price.................. 1.05
Postage.................. .12

6424 **Memorial Edition** of Dr. Chase's Receipts. Sold by subscription for $2.75. Our price......$2.05
Postage, 22c. extra.

COOK BOOKS.

ALL ARE THE BEST PRACTICAL EDITIONS.

White House Cook Book.

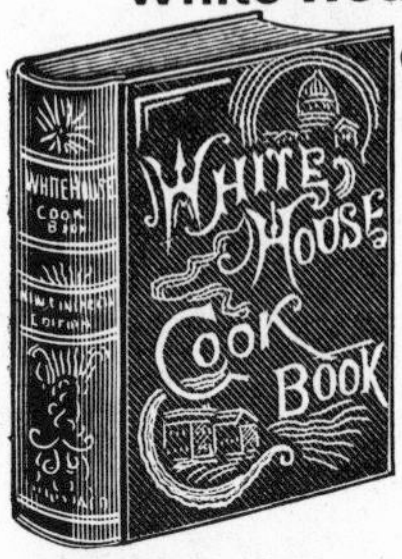

6425 The genuine edition, containing cooking, toilet and household recipes, menus dinner, giving table etiquette, care of the sick, health suggestions, etc. By Mrs. F. L. Gillette and Hugo Ziemann, steward of the White House. 569 pages, bound in oilcloth.
Subscription price..................$3.00
Our price.................. .98
Postage.................. .28
German edition same price.

Common Sense in the Household.

6426 A manual of practical housewifery. New edition by Marion Harland. Retail price.......$1.75
Our price, oilcloth binding.................. 1.22
Postage.................. .14

Buckeye Cookery.

6427 With hints on practical housekeeping; 8vo. oilcloth. Retail price..................$1.75
Our price..................$1.20. Postage.................. .14

Miss Parloa's Original Appledore Cook Book.

6428 Considered the best ever offered to American housekeepers. Bound in oilcloth.
Retail price..........$1.25. Our price..........$0.88
Postage.................. 0.10

Jessup Whitehead's Cook Books.

6429 Cooking for Profit; adapted for all who serve meals for a price. Cloth..................$2.20
American Pastry Cook.................. 1.50
Hotel Meat Cooking.................. 1.50
Family Cook Book.................. 1.25
Steward's Handbook.................. 2.25
Postage, each.................. .18

Miss Neill's Cook Book and Encyclopædia.

6430 Receipts for the use of families, etc. Every receipt has been carefully tested by experienced housekeepers. 315 pages, handsomely bound in green oilcloth..................$0.25
Postage.................. .10
Same bound in paper covers.................. .10
Postage.................. .03

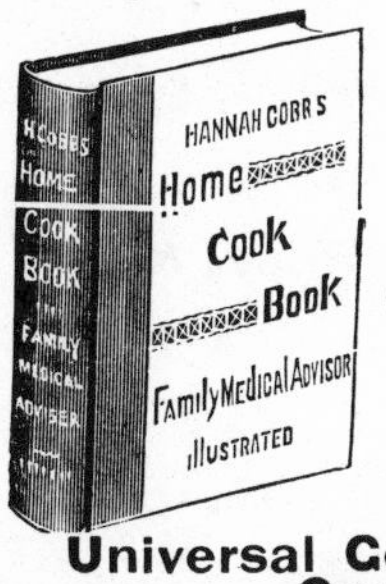

Hannah Cobb's Home Cook Book and Family Medical Adviser.

6431 A thoroughly easy, practical family cook book and medical adviser; eight full page illustrations and 100 engravings.
Oilcloth binding........$0.50
Postage, 14 cents extra.

Universal German-American Cook Book.

6432 In the German language. 12mo. cloth.....$0.35
Postage.................. .10

Boston Cook Book.

6433 What to Do and What Not to Do in Cooking. By Mrs. D. A. Lincoln, of the Boston Cooking School. 12mo., cloth, $1.40. Postage......$0.12

Practical Books on Architecture, Building and Carpentry, Painting and Decorating.

Carpentry Made Easy.

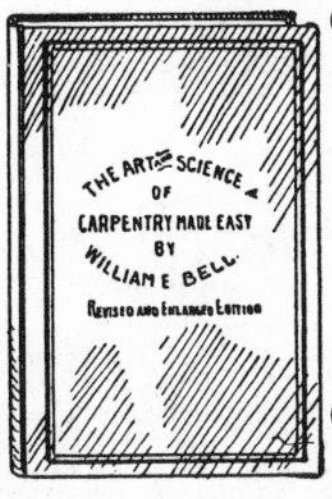

6434 By Wm. E. Bell. With instructions in building balloon frames, barns, mills, warehouses, church spires, etc. Comprising also a system of bridge building, estimates of cost and valuable tables, illustrated with 44 plates, 8vo., cloth.
Retail price..................$5.00
Our price.................. 3.50
Postage.................. .22

How to Join Moldings.

6435 The art of mitering and copying. By O. B. Maginnis Illustrated..................$0.75
Postage.................. .08

Log Cabins.

6436 How to build and furnish them By William S. Wicks. Numerous illustrations..........$1.05

Draugthman's Manual.

6437 Or How Can I Learn Architecture? Containing hints to inquirers and directions in draughtmanship. By F. T. Camp.... $0.40. Postage...$0.06

Cottages.

6438 Or Hints on Economical Building, containing twenty-four plates of medium and low price houses. By A. W. Brunner..$0.75. Postage....$0.08

Architectural Drawing.

6439 Or How to Make the Working Drawings for Buildings. Just suited for students, carpenters and builders..................$1.75
Postage.................. .12

The Hardwood Finisher.

6440 With rules and directions for finishing in natural colors, and in antique, mahogany, cherry, birch, walnut, oak, ash, redwood, sycamore, pine and all other domestic woods; also for filling, staining, polishing, dyeing, gilding and bronzing. Compiled and edited by Fred. T. Hodgson. Each......$0.75. Postage..........$0.08

Gould's Carpenters' and Builders' Assistant and Woodworkers' Guide.

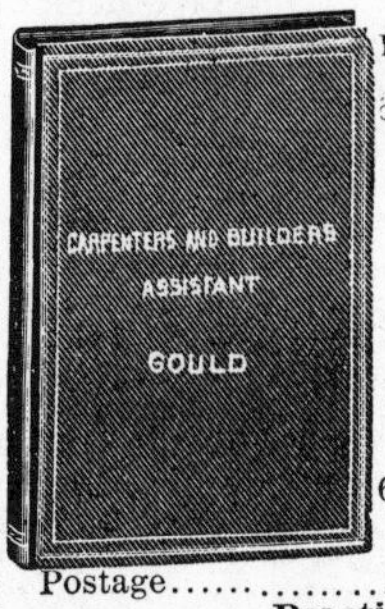

6441 This work is intended to combine all the knowledge the workman requires to construct any design in carpentry by an easy system of lines. By L. D Gould, architect and practical builder. Revised and enlarged edition, cloth, 8vo.
Retail price..................$2.50
Our price.................. 1.95
Postage.................. .12

Practical Stair Building.

6442 A complete instructor in this art. By Fred. Hodgson. 12mo, cloth..................$0.75
Postage.................. .08

Practical Carpentry.

6443 A clear and correct guide to laying out all carpenters' and joiners' work, 300 illustrations. By Fred Hodgson..................$0.75
Postage.................. .06

Steel Square, Part 1st

6444 Its uses, etc. By Fred. Hodgson. 12mo., cloth..........$0.75. Postage..........$0.08

Steel Square, Part 2d.

6445 A continuation to part first, giving new problems. By Fred Hodgson. 12mo., cloth....$0.75
Postage.................. .08

New System of Hand Railing.

6446 Or How to Cut Hand Railing for Circular and Other Stairs Square from the Plank. By Fred Hodgson. 12mo., cloth..................$0.75
Postage.................. .08

The Slide Rule and How to Use It.

6447 Rules are given for the measurement of all kinds of boards and planks. Timber in the round or square. Glazier's work, painting, brickwork, etc. Paper covers..................$0.18
Postage.................. .02

The Builders' Guide and Estimator's Price Book.

6448 Containing current prices of all building material, price of labor, etc. By Fred. T. Hodgson. 12mo..................$1.50
Postage.................. .12

Moore's Universal Assistant.

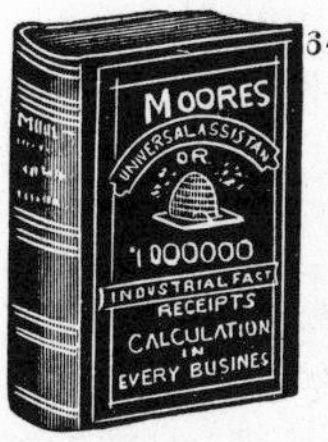

6449 A complete mechanic, containing over one million industrial facts, calculations, receipts, processes, trade secrets, rules, business forms, legal items, etc., in every occupation from the household to the manufactory. By R. Moore. Cloth, 500 illustrations.
Subscription price..................$3.00
Our price.................. 1.25
Half leather, our price....... 1.75

Hand Saws.

6450 Their Use, Care and Abuse. How to Select and how to File Them. This work is intended for woodworkers generally. Cloth, our price, only..................$0.75
Postage.................. .08

Barn Plans and Outbuildings.

6451 Two hundred and fifty illustrations. A most valuable work. Full of ideas, hints, suggestions, plans, etc., for the construction of barns and outbuildings, by practical writers. Recently published. Cloth, 12mo..................$1.10
Postage.................. .10

Homes for Home Builders.

6452 Edited and arranged by D. M. King, architect, of New York. Farm and village house plans; also plans of barns, stables, poultry houses, etc., in great variety. Cloth, 12mo....$1.10
Postage.................. .10

Reed's House Plans for Everybody.

6453 By S. B. Reed. This useful volume meets the wants of persons of moderate means, and gives a wide range of designs, from a dwelling costing $250 up to $8,000, and adapted to farm village and town residences. Profusely illustrated. Cloth, black and gold, 12mo..................$1.10
Postage.................. .10

Reed's Cottage Houses

6454 By S. B. Reed, author of "House Plans for Everybody," etc. For village and cottage homes. Together with complete plans and specifications. With over 100 illustrations. General descriptions, and detailed estimates of materials, constructions, and cost are given with each plan. Cloth, 12mo..................$0.90
Postage.................. .10

Hints and Practical Information.

6455 For cabinet makers, upholsterers and furniture men generally, together with a description of all kinds of finishings. Cloth, gilt.
Our price, only..................$0.75
Postage.................. .08

Hints for Painters, Decorators and Paper Hangers.

6456 A selection of useful rules and suggestions for house, ship and furniture painting, gilding, color mixing, etc. Paper covers, our price......$0.18
Postage.................. .02

The Complete House Builder.

6457 Containing 50 plans and specifications of houses, etc., for town and country. Our price..$0.16
Postage.................. .02

Mechanical Arts Simplified.

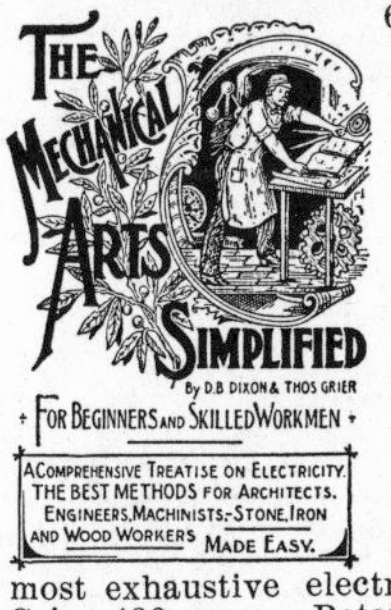

6458 A work of reference for the use of architects, architectural iron workers, builders, blacksmiths, bookkeepers, boilermakers, contractors, civil, mechanical, hydraulic, mining, stationary, marine and locomotive engineers, foremen of machine shops, fireman, master mechanics of railroads, master car builders, machine shop proprietors, machinery jobbers, machinists, pattern makers, roadmasters, and business men generally. Compiled and arranged by D. B. Dixon, and with the most exhaustive electrical department by Thos. G. Grier, 480 pages. Retail price..................$2.50
Our price.................. 1.75
Postage.................. .14

Practical Draughting,

6459 A series of practical illustrations in draughting. By Pemberton. 12mo., cloth.......$0.75
Postage.................. .08

Painters,' Varnishers' and Gilders' Companion,

6460 A most practical work on this subject. 12mo., cloth..................$1.15
Postage.................. .14

American Plumbing.

6461 By Alfred Revill. For master plumbers, architects, builders, apprentices, and householders. A compendium of practical plumbing from solder-making to high class open work. The only work on plumbing containing a complete drainage system, elevation and plan for use of architects and plumbers. Retail price. $2.00
Our price........ 1.40
Postage........ .12

How to Paint.

6462 By Gardner. Cloth, 12mo........ $0.75
Postage........ .08

Everybody's Paint Book.

6463 Full particulars for mixing and applying paints are given. It also tells about varnishes, polishing, staining, kalsomining, etc., as well as how to renovate furniture. Illustrated. Handsomely bound in extra cloth........ $0.75
Postage........ .08

The Complete Carriage and Wagon Painter.

6464 This work of nearly 200 pages gives detailed directions for painting carriages, wagons and sleighs, besides full instruction in lettering, scrolling, ornamenting, striping, varnishing, and coloring, with numerous recipes for mixing colors. It contains nearly 200 illustrations.... $0.75
Postage........ .08

Practical Paper Hanger.

6465 A handbook on wall decorations in paper and other materials, with practical instructions on hanging them. By J. S. Jennings. 8vo., cloth........ $1.65
Postage........ .12

Plaster and Plastering.

6466 A complete guide, illustrated with forty figures for ceilings; also preparation and application of plaster, stucco, cements, etc. 12mo., cloth........ $0.75
Postage........ .08

PRACTICAL BOOKS FOR ENGINEERS, FIREMEN, ELECTRICIANS, ETC.

Roper's Engineer and Firemen's Books

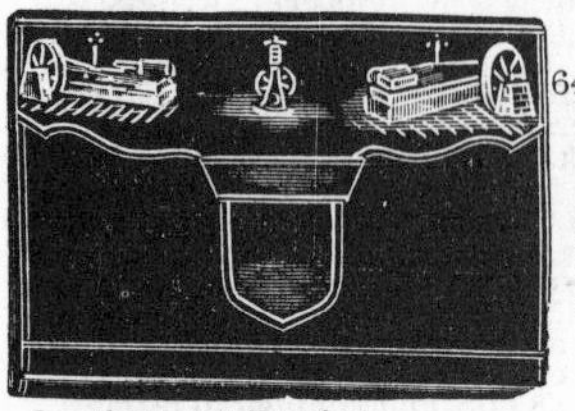

6467 **Roper's Handbook** for Stationary, Locomotive and Marine Engines, 3,000 subjects, 1,316 paragraphs, 876 questions and answers, fully illustrated.

Leather, retail price........ $3.50
Our price........ 2.50
Postage........ .10

Roper's Hand-Book of Land and Marine Engines.

6468 Containing a description and illustrations of every description of land and marine engine in use at the date of its publication, whether simple or compound, horizontal, vertical, beam, steeple, direct acting, back action, geered oscillating, trunk or rotary. Retail price........ $3.50
Our price........ 2.50
Postage........ .10

Roper's Hand-Book of Modern Steam Fire Engines.

6469 The only book of the kind ever published in this country. It contains descriptions and illustrations of all the best types of steam fire engines and fire-pumps. Retail price........ $3.50
Our price........ 2.50
Postage........ .10

Roper's Hand-Book of the Locomotive.

6470 One of the most valuable treatises ever written on the subject, as it is so plain and practical that any engineer or fireman that can read can easily understand it. Retail price.... $2.50
Our price........ 1.80
Postage........ .08

Roper's Use and Abuse of the Steam Boiler.

6471 Containing illustrations and descriptions of all classes of steam boilers in use at the present day. Plain cylinder flue, double deck, to set up, fire and manage the same.
Retail price........ $2.00
Our price........ 1.45
Postage........ .08

Roper's Catechism of High Pressure Steam Engines.

6472 Written in the form of question and answer, for the use of engineers of limited education and experience. Retail price........ $2.00
Our price........ 1.45
Postage........ .06

Roper's Questions and Answers for Engineers.

6473 Contains all the questions that an engineer will be asked when undergoing an examination for the purpose of procuring a license, with the answers to the same. Retail price........ $3.00
Our price........ 2.15
Postage........ .04

Roper's Instructions and Suggestions for Engineers and Firemen.

6474 This little book is made up of a series of suggestions and instructions, the result of recent experiments and the best modern practice in the care of steam engines and boilers.
Retail price........ $2.00
Our price........ 1.45
Postage........ .04

Roper's Care and Management of the Steam Boiler.

6475 One of the most practical works ever published on this subject, with a great amount of information of immense value to owners of steam boilers, engineers and firemen, expressed in plain, practical language. Retail price...... $2.00
Our price........ 1.45
Postage........ .06

Roper's Young Engineer's Own Book.

6476 Containing an explanation of the principal theories of the steam engine. For the use of educational instructions where students are intended to engage in mechanical pursuits, and for the private instruction of youths who show an inclination for steam engineering. By Stephen Roper. With 106 illustrations, 363 pages, 18mo., tuck, gilt edge. Retail price...... $3.00
Our price........ 2.15
Postage........ .10

Haswell's Engineers' Pocket Book.

6477 New edition, revised and enlarged. 12 mo. Pocket book style.
Retail price........ $4.00
Our price........ 3.00
Postage........ .12

Works of Joshua Rose, M. E.

Modern Steam Engines.

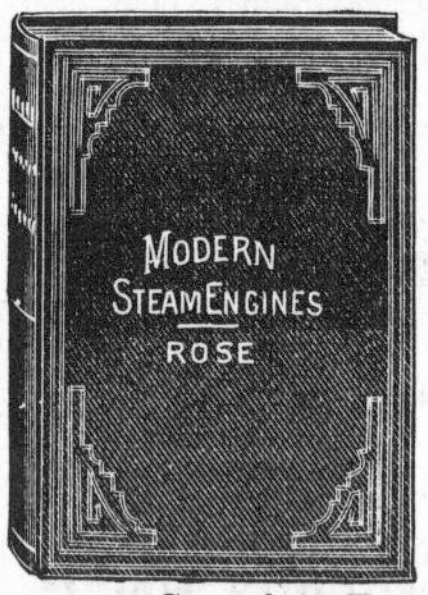

6478 An Elementary Treatise upon the Steam Engine, written in plain language, for use in the workshop, as well as in the drawing office, giving full explanations of the construction of modern steam engines; including diagrams, showing their actual operation. Illustrated New Revised Edition, 357 pages, 453 Engravings.
Retail price........ $6.00
Our price........ 4.90

Complete Practical Machinist.

6479 Embracing all subjects for machinists, 356 illustrations, 439 pages; cloth.
Retail price, $2.50. Our price........ 1.95

Steam Boilers.

6480 Just published. A practical treatise on boiler construction and examination; 73 Engravings, 258 pages, cloth.
Retail price, $2.50. Our price........ 1.95

Mechanical Drawing Self Taught.

6481 Containing instructions in the selection of drawing instruments, elementary instructions in practical mechanical drawing, simple geometry, etc. By Joshua Rose. Fully illustrated.
Retail price........ $4.00
Our price........ 3.00
Add 10 per cent. extra for postage if sent by mail on all Rose books.

Books on Blacksmithing.

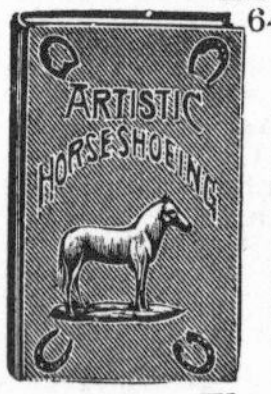

6482 Artistic Horseshoeing. A Practical and Scientific Treatise, giving Improved Methods of Shoeing, with Special Directions for Shaping Shoe to Cure Different Diseases of the Foot, and for the Correction of Faulty Action in Trotters. By George E. Rich. 62 Illustrations, 153 pages.
Retail price........ $1.00
Our price........ .75
Postage, 10 cts.

The Practical Horseshoer.

6483 This work treats of and illustrates proper shapes of shoes for different diseases of the feet, the various methods of Shoeing Vicious and Ugly Horses or Mules, and a great variety of tools suitable and useful in horseshoeing; how to shoe horses to Cure Contraction, to Prevent Interfering or Overreaching; best methods of Treating Corns—whether Cold or Hot-Fitting is—best, etc. 12mo. Cloth.
Retail price........ $1.00
Our price........ .75
Postage, 10 cts. extra.

Practical Blacksmithing.

6484 A Collection of Articles Contributed at Different Times by Skilled Workmen to the columns of "The Blacksmith and Wheelwright," and Covering nearly the Whole Range of Blacksmithing, from the Simplest Job of Work to some of the Most Complex Forgings. Compiled and edited by M. T. Richardson. Complete in four large volumes; 1,000 illustrations, 1,069 pages. Single volumes, each 75c.
Retail price, per set, $4.00. Our price, $2.80
Postage, 48 cts. extra.

Mechanics' Library.

6485 The mechanics' complete Library of modern rules, facts, processes, etc., for the Engineer, Artisan, Electrician, etc. This valuable compendium, compiled expressly for the workshop, is plain, comprehensive and devoid of complicated rules and problems. It contains diagrams and plans for machinists, pattern-makers, draughtsmen, boiler makers and tinsmiths, etc.
Cloth, retail price........ $1.00
Our price........ .70
Full leather, retail price........ 2.00
Our price........ 1.00
Postage........ .10

Stevenson's Illustrated Practical Tests.

6486 Examination and ready reference book for Stationary, Locomotive and Marine Engineers, Firemen, Electricians and Machinists to procure Steam Engineer's License. Retail price..... $1.00
Our price........ .68
Postage........ .06

Zwicker's Practical Instructor in Questions and Answers for Machinists.

6488 Firemen, Electricians and Steam Engineers. Revised edition. By Philip H. Zwicker.
Retail price........ $1.00
Our price........ .68
Postage........ .06

Standard Electrical Dictionary.

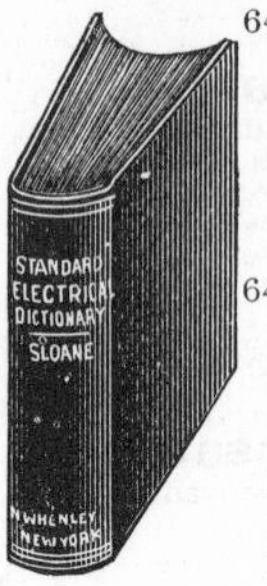

6490 Containing 624 pages, 350 illustrations, covering the subject of electricity thoroughly. Handsomely bound in cloth, gilt.
Retail price........ $3.00
Our price........ 2.00
Postage........ .16

Electricity Simplified.

6491 By T. O'Connor Sloane, A. M., E. M., Ph. D. This work is the simplest ever published on the subject of electricity. The object of "Electricity Simplified" is to make the subject as plain as possible.
Retail price........ $1.00
Our price........ .75
Postage........ .08

Dynamo Tenders' Hand-Book.

6492 By F. B. Badt. 70 Illustrations.
Retail price........ $1.00
Our price........ .75
Postage........ .06

Incandescent Wiring Hand-Book.

6493 41 Illustrations and 5 tables. By F.B. Badt.
Retail price........ $1.00
Our price........ .75
Postage........ .06

Bell Hangers' Hand-Book.

6494 By F. B. Badt. 97 illustrations. Just the book for those engaged in selling, installing or handling electric batteries, electric bells, elevator, house or hotel annunciators, burglar and fire alarms, electric gas lighting apparatus, electric heat regulating apparatus, etc., etc.
Retail price........ $1.00
Our price........ .75
Postage........ .06

Electric Toy Making.

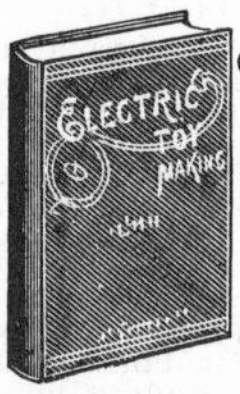

6496 Dynamo Building and Electric Motor Construction. By T. O'Connor Sloane, A. M., E. M., Ph. D. This work treats of the making at home of electrical toys, electrical apparatus, motors, dynamos and instruments. The work is especially designed for amateurs and young folks.
Retail price........ $1.00
Our price........ .75
Postage........ .08

Arithmetic of Electricity.

6497 By T. O'Connor Sloane, A. M., E. M., Ph. D. A practical treatise on electrical calculations of all kinds, reduced to a series of rules, all of the simplest forms, and involving only ordinary arithmetic. Retail price........ $1.00
Our price........ .75
Postage........ .06

A. B. C. of Electricity.

6498 By W. H. Meadowcraft, 13th edition. Cloth, limp binding. Retail price........ $0.50
Our price........ .38
Postage........ .06

Electricity for Engineers.

6499 By Chas. Desmond. Constant Current. A clear and comprehensive treatise on the principles, construction and operation of Dynamos, Motors, Lamps, Indicator and Measuring Instruments; also a full explanation of the electrical terms used in the work. Alternate Current Apparatus. Containing an explanation of the principles governing the generation of, and a description of the instruments and machinery used in connection with Alternate Electrical Current. Illustrated. Revised edition, 12mo. Cloth........ $1.90

How to Become a Successful Electrician.

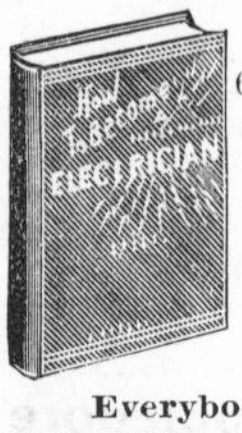

6500 By Prof. T. O'Connor Sloane. This work is designed to tell "How to Become a Successful Electrician," without the outlay usually spent in acquiring the profession. Illustrated.
Retail price........ $1.00
Our price........ .75
Postage........ .06

Everybody's Hand Book of Electricity.

6503 With glossary of electrical terms and tables for wiring. By Edward Trevert. 120 pages, 50 illustrations. Cloth. 12mo. Retail price.... $0.50
Our price........ 0.38
Postage, extra........ 0.06

Dynamos and Electric Motors.

6504 And All About Them. By Edward Trevert. Cloth, 12mo. Retail price $0.50
Our price .... .38
Postage, extra .... .06

Electricity and Its Recent Applications.

6505 By Edward Trevert. A book complete on all subjects of electricity. Retail price $2.00
Our price 1.45
Postage, extra .... .12

Electric Railway Engineering.

6506 Embracing practical hints upon power hous , dynamos, motor, and line construction. By Edward Trevert. Cloth, 12mo. Retail price $2.00
Our price 1.45
Postage, extra .... .14

How to Build Dynamo-Electric Machinery.

6507 A complete and practical work on this subject, 350 pages, numerous illustrations. By Edward Trevert. Retail price $2.50
Our price 1.80
Postage, extra .... .20

Questions and Answers About Electricity.

6509 A first book for students. Theory of electricity and magnetism. By E. T. Bubier. Cloth, 12mo. Retail price $0.50
Our price .... .38
Postage, extra .... .05

Hand-Book of Wiring Tables,

6510 For arc, incandescent lighting and motor circuits. By A. E. Watson. Retail price....$0.75
Our price .... .55
Postage extra .... .06

Cary's How to Make and Use a Telephone.

6511 A thorough and practical work on this subject. Cloth, illustrated. Retail price $1.00
Our price .... .75
Postage, extra .... .08

Electrical Instrument Making.

6513 By S. R. Bottone. A thorough and practical work on this subject. Illustrated.
Retail price........$0.50 Our price..............$0.38
Postage, extra .... .06

Electric Bells and all About Them.

6514 By S. R. Bottone. Illustrated. Cloth.
Retail price........$0.50 Our price..............$0.38
Postage, extra .... .06

Electric Motors.

6515 A complete simple work on this subject by Bottone and Beale. Illustrated.
Retail price........$0.75 Our price..............$0.60
Postage, extra .... .08

Electro Plating.

6516 By E. Trevert. A complete and simple work on electro plating. Illustrated.
Retail price........$0.50 Our price..............$0.38
Postage .... .06

Modern Practice of the Electric Telegraph.

6517 By Franklin L. Pope. This work has just been revised, enlarged and brought up to date. Fully illustrated. A practical work for learners.
Retail price........$1.50 Our price..............$1.25
Postage, extra .... .10

Practical Surveyor's Guide.

6518 By Duncan. Containing necessary information to make any person of common capacity a finished land surveyor, without the aid of a teacher. Fully illustrated. Retail price......$1.50
Our price 1.15
Postage, extra .... .12

Manual of Wood Carving.

6519 With practical instructions for learners of the art; 128 illustrations. By William Bemrose, Jr., 15th edition. Retail price..............$2.50
Our price 2.00
Postage .... .16

Sign Writing and Glass Embossing.

6520 A complete practical illustrated manual of this art. By James Callingham. 260 pages. Cloth 12mo. Retail price $1.50
Our price 1.15
Postage .... .10

Mineralogy Simplified.

6521 By Henri Erni. Easy methods of identifying minerals, including ores, by means of the blowpipe; 121 engravings, 395 pages.
Retail price $3.00
Our price 2.35
Postage .... .18

American Miller and Millwright's Assistant.

6522 By W. C. Hughes. A practical work on the subject. Retail price $1.50
Our price 1.15
Postage, 10 cents extra.

Watch Repairer's Hand-Book.

6523 Complete guide to the beginner in taking apart and putting together; also cleaning all watches. By Kemlo. Illustrated; 93 pages.
Retail price $1.25
Our price .... .90
Postage, 10 cents extra.

Assayers' Guide.

6524 Or practical directions to assayers, miners and smelters for the tests by heat and wet processes for metals, gold, silver, coal, etc. By O. M. Lieber; 133 pages, cloth. Retail price.......$1.50
Our price 1.05
Postage, 10 cents extra.

The Moulders' and Founders' Pocket Guide.

6526 A practical work on moulding and rounding in green sand, dry sand, loam and cement. By F. Overman; 44 engravings, 342 pages.
Retail price $2.00
Our price 1.60
Postage, extra .... .12

SERIES OF PHOTO PUBLICATIONS.

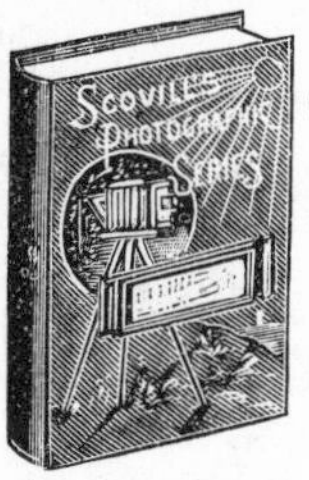

The Photographic Instructor.

6528 Edited by W. L. Lincoln Adams; consisting of the comprehensive series of practical lessons issued to the Chautauqua School of Photography, revised and enlarged, with an appendix of over thirty pages on the nature and use of the various chemicals and substances employed in photographic practice (Sco-26); 200 pages. Illuminated paper covers $0.88
Library edition 1.35

The Amateur Photograher.

6529 A complete guide for beginners. By W. F. Carleton: paper covers $0.20

The Ferrotype and How to Make It.

6530 By E. M. Estabrooke (Ant 5); cloth bound.$0.95

Modern Dry Plates.

6532 Or Emulsion Photography. By Dr. J. M. Eder, the eminent German authority on gelatine. Translated by Mr. Horace Milner and edited by Mr. H. Baden Pritchard, F. C. S. 138 pages, large, 12mo. (A-7.) Cloth ....$ .88

The Art and Practice of Silver Printing.

6533 By H. P. Robertson and Capt. Arney. Price $0.75

The Modern Practice of Retouching.

6534 As practiced by M. Piquepe and other celebrated experts. (Eighth edition.) Paper covers $0.42
Library edition. (S-7) 0.68

Hardwich's Photographic Chemistry.

6535 A manual of photographic chemistry, theoretical and practical. (Ninth edition.) Edited by J. Traill Taylor. Leatherette binding. (S-12)..$1.75

Photographic Printing Methods.

6536 By Rev. W. H. Burbank (Sco-22). A practical guide to the professional and amateur worker. A volume of more than 200 pages, substantially bound in cloth $0.88

N. B.—Any book on Photography or Lantern Publication not found in this list we will supply at a less price than the publishers.

MAGIC LANTERN PUBLICATIONS.

The Optical Lantern.

6537 Illustrated. By Andrew Pringle. Paper covers $0.80
Cloth bound (S-34) 1.35

Lantern Slides by Photographic Methods.

6538 By Andrew Pringle. (S-35) Paper covers. 63 cents. Cloth bound $1.05

Wilson's Lantern Journeys.

6539 By Edward C. Wilson. In three volumes. Gives incidents and facts in entertaining style of about 2,000 places and things. Cloth bound. Per volume $1.75

Optical Projection.

6540 A book of the lantern, being a practical guide to the working of the magic lantern and containing precise directions for making lantern pictures; cloth bound $1.80

Agricultural and Rural Books.

The following line of books are only a partial list of the many works on this subject carried in stock by us. If you are in want of others on all subjects pertaining to the farm, etc., send for our free Descriptive Rural Catalogue.

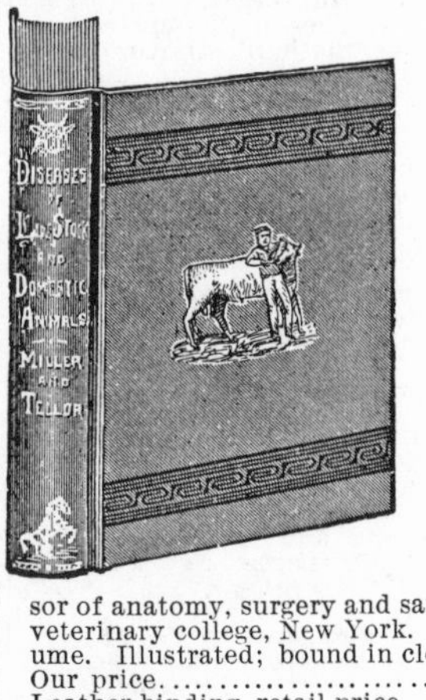

6545 **Disease of Live Stock.** By Miller, W. B. E., D. V. S., and Teller, Lloyd V. Diseases of Live Stock, or a popular guide for the treatment of all domestic animals, including horses, cattle, sheep, swine, dogs and poultry. By W. B. E. Miller, D. V. S., president of the Veterinary Association, etc., etc.; Lloyd V. Teller, M. D., and Willis P. Hazard, editors of the *Guernsey Breeders Journal*, "Breeders' Hand-book,"etc. A. Leautard, professor of anatomy, surgery and sanitary medicine to the veterinary college, New York. One large octave volume. Illustrated; bound in cloth, Retail.......$2.50
Our price 1.25
Leather binding, retail price 3.00
Our price 1.80
Postage .... .24

Agricultural Books—Continued.

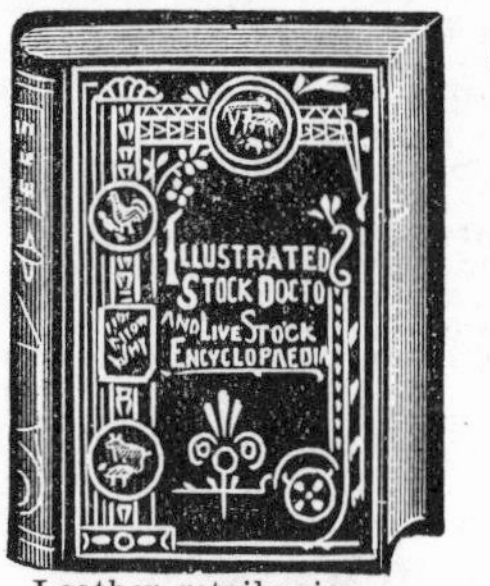

6547 **Manning's Illustrated Stock Doctor.** Horses, cattle, sheep, swine, poultry, bees and dogs. By J. Russell Manning, M. D. V. S. With all the facts concerning the various breeds and characteristics, breaking, training, sheltering, buying, selling, profitable use and general care; embracing all the diseases to which they are subject.
Cloth, retail price $3.75
Our price 2.00
Leather, retail price 4.50
Our price 2.50
Postage .... .22

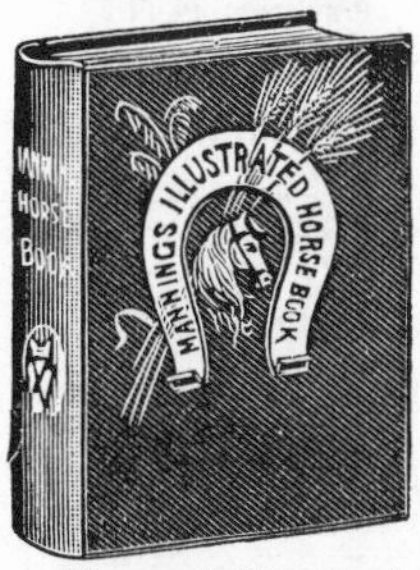

6548 **Manning's Illustrated Horse Book.** By J. R. Manning, giving, among other things, the most recent approved and humane methods for breaking, training and breeding; also the prevention and cure of disease, etc.; 515 pages, containing colored and other illustrations. Retail price..$2.50
Our price 1.25
Postage, 30c. extra.

Magner's Standard Horse and Stock Book.

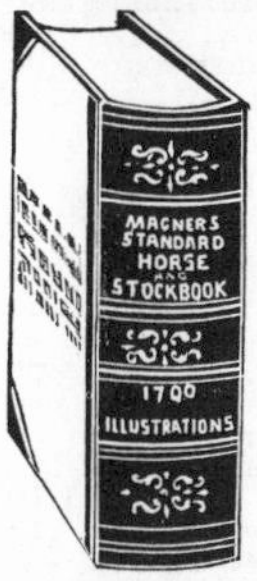

6549 A Complete Pictorial Encyclopædia of Practical Reference for horse and stock owners, all secrets of taming and educating unbroken and vicious horses, with the details of breaking up all habits to which horses are subject; their diseases, abuses, and remedies; also cattle, dogs, bees, sheep, swine, poultry, etc., 1,200 pages, 1,700 illustrations, ½ Russia binding.
Retail price $6.00
Our price 3.00
Postage, extra .... .60

Horses.

6575 **Stonehenge's Eve y Horse Owner's Cyclopædia.** Cloth, 8vo $2.75
Postage .... .22
6576 **Riley on the Mule.** Cloth, 12mo 1.10
Postage .... .10
6577 **Stonehenge on the Horse in the Stable and Field.** Cloth, 12mo 1.50
Postage .... .16
6578 **Herbert's Hints to Horsekeepers.** Cloth, 12mo.. 1.35
Postage .... .10
6579 **Armitage. Every Man His Own Horse Doctor.** Large octavo 5.65
Postage .... .52
6580 **Dadd's American Reformed Horse Book.** Cloth 8vo 1.85
Postage .... .18
6581 **Percheron Horse,** by Du Hays and Weld. Cloth, 12mo .... .38
Postage .... .06
6582 **How to Handle and Educate Vicious Horses,** by Oscar R. Gleason. Cloth, 12mo .... .38
Postage .... .06
6583 **Dadd's Modern Horse Doctor.** Cloth, 12mo.... 1.10
Postage .... .10
6585 **Youatt and Spooner on the Horse.** Cloth, 12mo. 1.10
Postage .... .10
6586 **The Saddle Horse.** Cloth, 12mo .... .75
Postage .... .08
6587 **Mayhew's Illustrated Horse Management.** Cloth, 12mo 2.25
Postage .... .22
6589 **Gleason's Veterinary Hand-Book** and System of Horse Training .... .95
Postage .... .15
6590 **History, Diseases and Treatmen of the Horse,** by Youatt. Cloth, 12mo 1.50
Postage .... .12
6591 **Animal Castration,** by A. Leautard. Cloth, 12mo 1.50
Postage .... .12
6592 **The Winter Care of Horses and Cattle,** 8vo. paper .... .30
Postage .... .03
6593 **The Bridle Bits,** by Battersby. Cloth, 12mo. .75
Postage .... .08
6596 **Every Man His Own Veterinarian,** by George S. Heatley. Cloth, 12mo 1.85
Postage .... .16
6597 **Horses Teeth,** by W. H. Clark, Dentistry, etc. 1.50
Postage .... .12

N. B.—Send for Descriptive Catalogue of above Books.

Don't be Cruel

TO YOUR HORSES. READ ABOUT THEIR CARE.

Sheep and Swine.

6602 **Stewart's Shepherd's Manual,** by Henry Stewart, cloth, 12mo $1.10
Postage .... .12

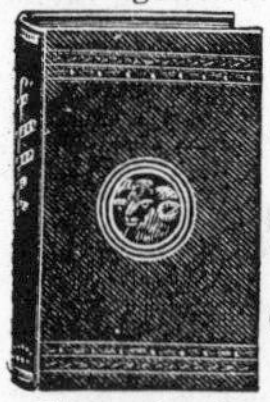

6603 **The American Merino.** For wool or for mutton. Cloth, 12mo. 1.10
Postage .... .10
6604 **A Treatise on the Diseases of Sheep,** by J. H. Steel. 8vo. Cloth 3.35
Postage .... .16
6605 **Harris, on the Pig.** Cloth, 12mo 1.10
Postage .... .10
6606 **Coburn's Swine Husbandry,** by F. D. Coburn. Cloth, 12mo 1.34
Postage .... .10
N. B.—Send for Descriptive Catalogue of above Books

Poultry and Bees.

6610 **Profits in Poultry.** Cloth, 12mo $0.75
Postage .... .10

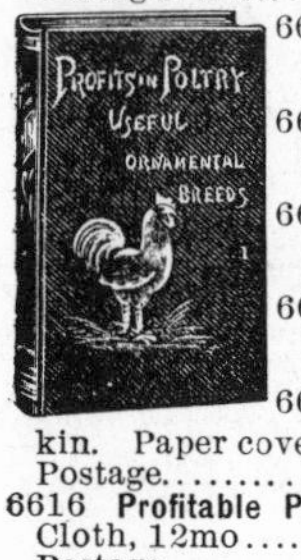

6611 **Wright's Practical Poultry Keeper.** Cloth, 12mo 1.45
Postage .... .14
6612 **Lewis' Practical Poultry Book.** 100 engravings. Cloth, 8vo 1.10
Postage .... .14
6613 **Johnson's Practical Poultry Keeping.** Paper, 12mo .... .38
Postage .... .04
6614 **Poultry Culture,** by I. K. Felch. Cloth, 12mo 1.10
Postage .... .12
6615 **Duck Culture,** by Jas. Rankin. Paper cover .... .42
Postage .... .04
6616 **Profitable Poultry Keeper,** by Stephen Beal. Cloth, 12mo 1.10
Postage .... .12
6617 **Quimby's New Bee Keeping.** Cloth, 12mo 1.10
6618 **King's Bee-Keeper's Text Book.** Cloth, 12mo. .80
Postage .... .10
6619 **Root's A. B. C. of Bee Culture.** Large octavo. .90
Postage .... .14

Cattle.

6622 **The Dairyman's Manual,** by Henry Stewart. Cloth, 12mo., $1.45. Postage $0.12
6623 **Willard's Practical Dairy Husbandry.** Cloth, 8vo 2.25
Postage .... .22

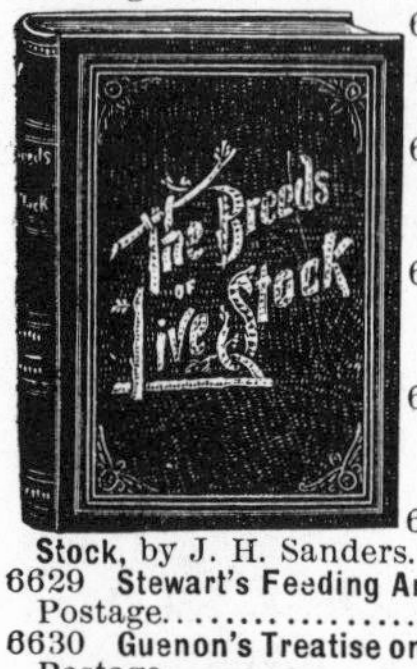

6624 **Willard's Practical Butter Book.** Cloth, 12mo .... .75
Postage .... .10
6625 **Dadd's American Cattle Doctor.** Cloth, 12mo 1.10
Postage .... .12
6626 **Cattle Breeding,** by William Warfield. Cloth, 12mo 1.50
Postage .... .12
6627 **A Manual of Cattle Feeding,** by H. P. Armsby. Cloth, 12mo 1.35
Postage .... .12
6628 **The Breeds of Live Stock,** by J. H. Sanders. Cloth $2.25. Postage. .32
6629 **Stewart's Feeding Animals.** Cloth, 12mo 1.50
Postage .... .12
6630 **Guenon's Treatise on Milch Cows,** by T. J. Hand .75
Postage .... .10

Farm and Garden.

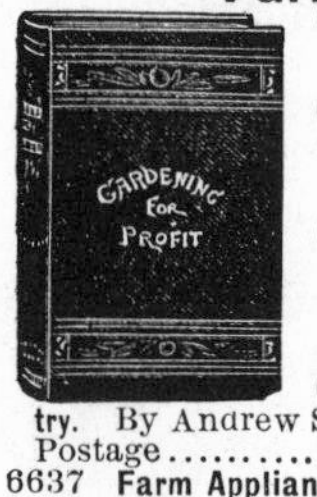

6633 **Allen's N w A erican Farm Book.** Cloth, 12mo $1.85
Postage .... .14
6634 **Henderson's Gardening for Profit.** By Peter Henderson. (New Edition.) Cloth, 12mo. 1.45
Postage .... .14
6635 **Henderson's Gardening for Pleasure.** By Peter Henderson. (New Edition.) Cloth, 12 mo 1.45
Postage .... .14
6636 **Fuller's Practical Forestry.** By Andrew S. Fuller. Cloth, 12mo 1.10
Postage .... .10
6637 **Farm Appliances.** 250 illustrations. Cloth, 12mo., $0.75. Postage .... .10
6638 **Fences, Gates and Bridges.** A valuable work. Cloth, 12mo .... .75
Postage .... .10
6639 **Farm Conveniences.** A Manual of What to do and How to do it 1.10
Postage .... .10
6640 **French's Farm Drainage.** Cloth, 12mo 1.10
Postage .... .12
6641 **The N w Onion Culture.** By. B. L. Grenier. Paper .... .38
Postage .... .04
6642 **New Potato Culture.** By E. S. Carman Paper. .38
Cloth .... .55
Postage, each .... .06
6643 **Trees and Tree Planting.** By J. S. Brisbin. Cloth, 12mo 1.10
Postage .... .10
6644 **How to Make the Garden Pay.** By Grenier 1.65
Postage .... .14
6645 **Maple Sugar and Sugar Bush.** By Prof. A. J. Cook .... .35
Postage .... .04
6646 **Harris' Talks on Manures.** Cloth, 12mo 1.30
Postage .... .12
6647 **Silos, Ensilage and Silage.** Cloth, 12mo .... .30
Postage .... .08
6648 **Kalamazoo Celery Culture.** By G. Bochove & Bro .... .38
Postage .... .04

Farm and Garden—Continued.

6650 **Flax Culture,** Paper cover .... .23
Postage .... .03
6651 **Butter and Butter Making.** By W. P. Hazard. Paper .... .20
Postage .... .03
6652 **Waring's Book of the Farm.** By Geo. E. Waring, Jr. Cloth, 12mo 1.40
Postage .... .16
6653 **Thomas' Farm Implements and Machinery.** Their Construction and Use. Cloth, 12mo 1.10
Postage .... .14
6655 **Broom Corn and Brooms** .... .38
Postage .... .04
6657 **Wheat Culture.** By Curtiss .... .38
Postage .... .04
6658 **Bennett's Farm Law.** Cloth .... .55
Postage .... .06
6659 **Tomato Culture.** Paper cover .... .23
Postage .... .05
6660 **A. B. C. of Potato Culture.** Leatherette .... .23
Postage .... .05
6661 **Tile Drainage.** Leatherette .... .23
Postage .... .05

Fruits and Flowers.

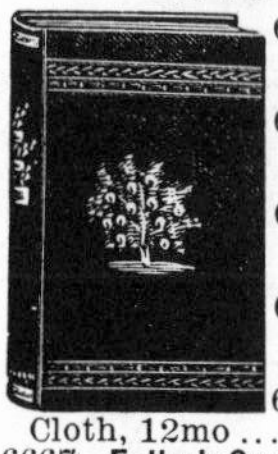

6662 **Barry's Fruit Garden.** Illustrated. Cloth. 12 mo $1.45
Postage .... .14
6663 **Fulton's Peach Culture.** Cloth, 12mo 1.10
Postage .... .10
6664 **Quinn's Pear Culture.** Cloth, 12mo .... .75
Postage .... .08
6665 **Webb's Cape Cod Cranberries.** Paper, 12mo .... .30
Postage .... .04
6666 **The Cider Maker's Hand-Book** Cloth, 12mo .... $0.75 Postage, .08
6667 **Fuller's Small Fruit Culturist** 1.10
Postage .... .10
6668 **Fuller's Grape Culturist** 1.10
Postage .... .10
6669 **Fuller's Strawberry Culturist** .... .18
Postage .... .04
6670 **White's Cranberry Culture** .... .90
Postage .... .10
6671 **Chorlton's Grape Growers' Guide.** Cloth, 12mo .55
Postage .... .08
6672 **Henderson's Practical Floriculture,** By Peter Henderson. Cloth, 12mo. $1.10. Postage .... .12
6673 **Henderson's Hand-Book of Plants** (new). Cloth, 8vo. $3.00. Postage .... .22
6674 **Horticultural Buildings.** By F. A. Hawks. The construction, etc. Cloth, 8vo. $1.10. Postage .... .16
6676 **Maple Sugar and the Sugar Bu h.** 8vo. paper .23
Postage .... .03
6678 **A B C of Strawberry Culture.** Leatherette .... .23
Postage .... .05
REMEMBER! We issue a Special Descriptive Catalogue on all books pertaining to the FARM, also a large Special BOOK Catalogue, which will be mailed upon receipt of 6 cents to pay postage. Send for them.

SPORTSMAN'S BOOKS.
Hunting and Shooting.
Shooting on Upland Marsh and Stream.

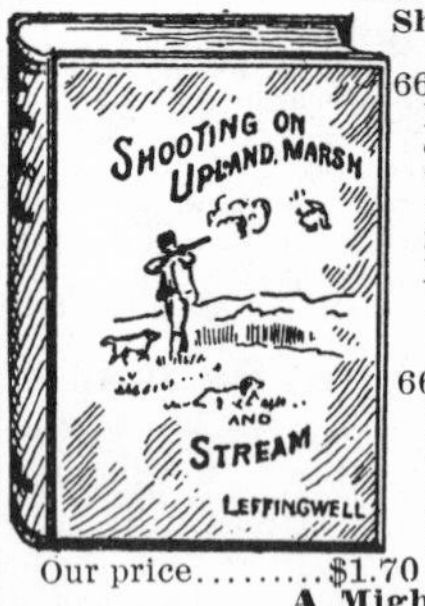

Shooting on Upland, Marsh and Stream.

6685 Edited by William Bruce Leffingwell (Horace). A most comprehensive work on game, their habits etc.; 8vo.; 473 pages, cloth. Retail price $3.50. Our price $2.40
Half morocco 3.00
Postage, extra, 28c.

Wild Fowl Shooting.

6686 Their habits, resorts, flights, and most successful methods of hunting. By Wm. Bruce Leffingwell: illustrated, 8vo.; cloth.
Retail price $2.50
Our price .... $1.70 Postage, extra .... .22

A Mighty Hunter.

6687 The Adventures of Charles L. Youngblood on the Plains and Mountains. Cloth, illustrated. Retail price $1.00. Our price $0.70
Postage 10c.

The Big Game of North America.

6688 Its habits, habitat, haunts and characteristics; how, when and where to hunt it. A book for the sportsman and naturalist. By G. O. Shields (Coquina). 80 illustrations, 600 pages, cloth. Retail price $3.50
Our price .... $2.40 Half morocco 3.00
Postage, extra, 30c.

Cruisings in the Cascades.

6690 Travel, Exploration, Amateur Photography, Hunting and Fishing, and Life Among the Cowboys. 12mo. Cloth. 300 pages.
Retail price $2.00. Our price $1.40
Half morocco 2.00

The Gun and Its Development.

6691 With Notes on Shooting. By W. W. Greener. Breechloading rifles, sporting rifles, shotguns, gunmaking, choice of guns, chokeboring, gun trials, theories and experiments. Fully illustrated. Cloth, 770 pages. New edition. Retail price $2.50. Our price $1.75
Postage, extra, 26c.

The Breechloader and How to Use It.

6692 Written for people who have neither time nor means to make the sport a life study. By W. W. Greener. 288 pages. Illustrated.
Retail price $1.00 Our price $0.75
Postage, extra, 8c.

The Art of Shooting.

6694. An Illustrated Treatise on the Art of Shooting, w th extracts from the best authorities. By Charles Lancaster. Illustrated with numerous drawings from instantaneous photographs. Retail price $3.00. Our price $2.15
Postage, extra, 14c.

Wing and Glass Ball Shooting.

6695 With the Rifle. Containing instructions for beginners in snap-shooting, and exposure of some of the popular fallacies in regard to it. By H.C. Bliss. Retail price 50c. Our price $0.38
Postage, extra, 2c.

How I Became a Crack Shot.

6696 By W. M. Farrow. Hints to beginners; 205 pages. Cloth. Price 80c Postage, 8c.

Gunsmith's Manual.

6698 A complete hand-book for the American Gunsmith, being a practical guide to all branches of the trade. With numerous engravings and diagrams and plates. Cloth. Retail price $2.00
Our price 1.40
Postage .... .14

Trajectories of Hunting Rifles.

6699 Trajectories of American Hunting Rifles. A series of tests made at the Creedmoor Range. Paper; 96 pages. Illustrated. Retail price $0.50
Our price .... .38
Postage .... .04

Field, Cover and Trap-Shooting.

6700 By Captain Adam H. Bogardus, Champion Wing Shot of the World. Embracing Hints for Skilled Marksmen; Instructions for Young Sportsmen; Haunts and Habits of Game Birds; Flight and Resorts of Waterfowl; Breeding and Breaking of Dogs. Cloth; 493 pages. Retail price $2.00
Our price 1.45

Frank Forester's Field Sports.

6701 Of the United States and British Provinces of North America. Embracing the Game of North America. By Henry William Herbert. Illustrated. Fourteenth Edition. 2 Vols., cloth, crown, 8vo.
Retail price $4.00
Our price 2.80
Postage, extra .... .38

American Big Game Hunting.

6702 The Book of the Boone and Crockett Club. Editors, Theodore Roosevelt and George Bird Grinnell. Illustrated. Cloth, 345 pages.
Retail price $2.50
Our price 1.85
Postage .... .14

The Complete Sportsman.

6704 A Manual of scientific and practical knowledge designed for the instruction and information of all votaries of the gun. By Howland Gasper. Illustrated. Cloth, 277 pages. Retail price $2.00
Our price 1.45
Postage .... .14

"The Wilderness Hunter."

6705 It is satisfactory to be able to welcome in Mr. Theodore Roosevelt's "The Wilderness Hunter," a noteworthy and valuable addition to the very brief list of good books on American big game hunting.
Retail price $3.50
Our price 2.63
Postage .... .18

Hunting Trips of a Ranchman.

6706 Sketches of Sport on the Northern Cattle Plains. By Theodore Roosevelt. Illustrated with 26 full page illustrations. Cloth, 350 pages.
Retail price $3.50
Our price 2.63
Postage, extra .... .18

Modern American Rifles.

6708 By A. C. Gould (Ralph Greenwood). Fully illustrated. Royal 8vo. The only practical book issued; over 300 pages. It describes modern American rifles; mode of manufacturing; description of appliances used by riflemen for hunting and target shooting. Retail price $2.00
Our price 1.50
Postage, extra .... .14

Game Laws in Brief.

6709 Laws of the United States and Canada relating to game and fish seasons. For the guidance of sportsmen and anglers. Paper. Retail price $0.25
Our price .... .18
Postage .... .04

Trap Shooter's Ready Reckoner.

6710 A series of tables showing at a glance the division of purses under all conditions with entries from one to fifty for individuals, club and tournaments. By J. C. Clark. Retail price $0.25
Our price .... .18
Postage .... .04

Art of Wing Shooting.

6711 A practical treatise on the use of the shotgun, illustrated by sketches and easy reading how to become a crack shot. By Wm. Bruce Leffingwell.
12 mo., cloth $0.70
Paper covers .... .35
Postage, extra, cloth $0.10; paper, $0.04.

TRAPPING AND ANGLING.

Gibson's Camp Life in the Woods.

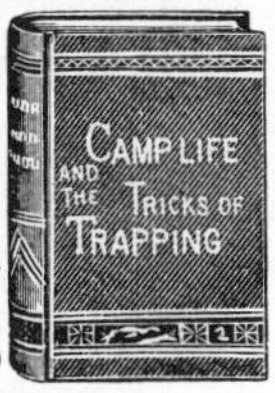

6712 Camp life in the woods, and the tricks of trappers and trap making. Containing comprehensive hints on camp shelter of all kinds, boat and canoe building, and valuable suggestions on trappers' food, etc. Valuable recipes for the curing and tanning of fur skins, etc. By W. Hamilton Gibson. 300 pages. Illustrated by the author. 16 mo. Cloth $0.75
Postage, extra .... .10

The Trappers' Guide.

6713 By S. Newhouse. A manual of instruction for capturing all kinds of fur-bearing animals and curing their skins. Illustrated. Cloth. Retail price ....$0.50. Our price $0.38
Postage .... .05

Hunter and Trapper.

6714 The best modes of hunting and trapping are fully explained, and foxes, deer, bears, etc., fall into his traps readily by following his directions. By Halsey Thrasher, an old and experienced sportsman. Cloth, 12mo.
Retail price .... $0.75. Our price $0.55
Postage .... .08

Brown's Taxidermist's Manual.

6715 A New and Improved Edition. The standard guide for the collection and preservation of specimens of birds, animals, reptiles, etc.; fully illustrated. Cloth, 12mo. Retail price. .$1.00
Our price .... .75
Postage .... .08

Batty's Practical Taxidermy and Home Decoration.

6716 By Joseph H. Batty. An entirely new and complete as well as authentic work on taxidermy—giving in detail full directions for collecting and mounting animals, birds, reptiles, fish, insects and general objects of natural history. 125 illustrations. Cloth, 12mo.
Retail price $1.50
Our price 1.10
Postage, extra .... .10

The Amateur Trapper and Trap-Maker's Guide.

6717 A complete treatise on the art of trapping, snaring and netting; containing directions for constructing the most approved traps, snares, nets and deadfalls, and the most successful baits for attracting all kinds of animals, birds, etc., with their special uses in each case; also practical receipts for preparing skins and furs for market, and for tanning them, with instructions for stuffing specimens of birds and animals in the most natural manner. Illustrated. 16mo, paper cover. $0.35
Bound in boards, cloth back .... .50

The Taxidermist's Manual.

6718 Containing complete instructions in the art of taxidermy, with directions how to prepare, mount and preserve all kinds of birds, animals and insects. By Graham Allen. Profusely illustrated.
Large 16mo $0.18

The Hunter and Angler.

6719 A handy manual of hunting, trapping and angling, with valuable hints in regard to guns, rods, game, fish and baits; including instructions for the care and medical treatment of dogs. Illustrated.
Large 16mo $0.18

BIRDS.

Key to North American Birds.

6721 Third Revised Edition. By Elliott Coues, M.A., M.D. Ph. D. It contains a concise account of every species of living and fossil bird at present known on the continent north of the boundary line between Mexico and the United States, including Greenland. Illustrated with over 500 wood engravings. 1 vol., royal octavo, vellum cloth. Retail price $7.50
Our price 6.85

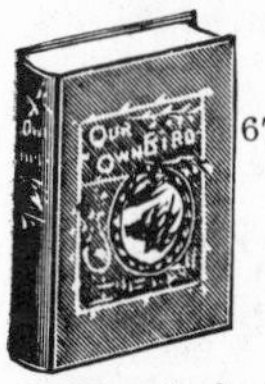

Our Own Birds.

6722 A familiar natural history of the birds of the U. S. By Wm. L. Baily; beautifully illustrated.
Retail price $1.25
Our price .... .88
Postage, extra .... .10

Murphy's American Game Bird Shooting.

6723 This work on game birds is written entirely from a sportsman's standpoint, being intended not only to describe their haunts and habits, but also the various methods employed in this country and Europe for bagging them. Cloth.
Retail price $2.50. Our price $1.85
Postage .... .14

Nest and Eggs of North American Birds.

6724 By Oliver Davie. Fourth edition. Illustrated. Cloth. 455 pages, with index.
Retail price $2.00. Our price $1.45
Postage .... .14

Hints and Points for Sportsmen.

6726 Compiled by "Seneca." This compilation comprises six hundred and odd wrinkles and suggestions for the shooter, fisherman, dog owner, yachtman, canoeist and camper.
Retail price $150. Our price $1.10
Postage .... .10

Woodcraft.

6727 By Messmuk. 140 pages on this subject.
Our price $0.75
Postage .... .10

4—3rd

FISHING.

Book of the Black Bass.

6729 Comprising its complete scientific and life history, together with a practical treatise on angling and fly-fishing, and a full description of tools, tackle and implements. By James A. Henshall, M. D. Illustrated. Cloth, 470 pages.
Retail price ....$3.00 Our price $2.25
Postage .... .14

Practical Trout Culture.

6730 By J. H. Slack, M. B. A useful and practical work, showing how the farmer may grow crops in his pond just as he does in his fields. Illustrated. Cloth, 143 pages. Price $0.70
Postage 10

Fishing With the Fly.

6732 Fifteen full page colored plates illustrating over 100 flies. New edition, 335 pages.
Our price only ....$2.10 Postage $0.14

Fly Fishing and Fly Making.

6733 By J. H. Keene, with plates of actual material for making flies. 159 pages. Cloth $1.25
Postage .... .10

American Game and Fishes.

6734 By G. O. Shields, and 19 other standard authorities on this subject. 8 vo. 580 pages.
Cloth. Retail price ...$2.50 Our price $1.75
Postage .... .22

A. B. C. of Carp Culture.

6735 A treatise on the German, or European Carp, by Root, Miller and Finley. 8vo. Paper $0.23
Postage, extra .... .04

CANOEING AND CAMPING.

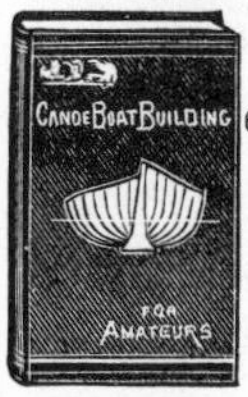

Canoe and Boat Building.

6739 A Complete Manual for Amateurs. Containing plain and comprehensive directions for the construction of Canoes, Rowing and Sailing Boats and Hunting Craft. By W. P. Stephens. Retail price $2.00. Our price $1.45
Postage, 16c.

Practical Boat Building for Amateurs.

6740 By Adrian Neison. Cloth. A practical and complete work. Cloth, 106 pages.
Retail price ....$1.00. Our price $0.80
Postage, 10c.

Canoe and Camp Cookery.

6742 A practical Cook Book for Canoeists, Corinthian Sailors and Outers. By Seneca. Cloth, 96 pages.
Retail price $1 00
Our price .... .75
Postage, 10c.

Canvas Canoes and How to Build Them.

6743 By Parker B. Field. With a plan and all dimensions. 48 pages. Retail price $0.50
Our price .... .38
Postage, 3c.

The Sailing Boat.

6744 Practical instructions for its management, together with "Nautical Vocabulary," "Weather Indications," and "Rules for Sailing Boat Matches." By C. E. Prescott. Pocket edition. Flexible cloth. 12mo.
Retail price $0.25
Our price .... .18
Postage, 4c.

The Oarsman's Manual.

6745 Containing practical instructions in rowing and sculling for amateurs and professionals. By W. Beach. Illustrated. Large 16mo $0.18
Postage, 3c.

Dick's Yachting and Sailing.

6747 Containing practical instructions in all that pertains to the construction, rigging and management of all kinds of yachts. Illustrated. 12mo. Cloth, gilt $0.50
Postage, 6c.

How to Camp Out.

6748 By Gould. Cloth, 16mo. Price $0.55
Postage, 8c.

Camping and Camp Outfits.

6749 A manual of instruction for young and old sportsmen. By G. O. Shields ("Coquina"). Contains practical points on how to dress for camping trips, what to carry, how to select camp sites. Thirty illustrations. 12mo., 200 pages; cloth. Retail price $1.25
Our price .... .88
Postage, 10c.

DOGS.

Dogs of Great Britain, America and Other Countries.

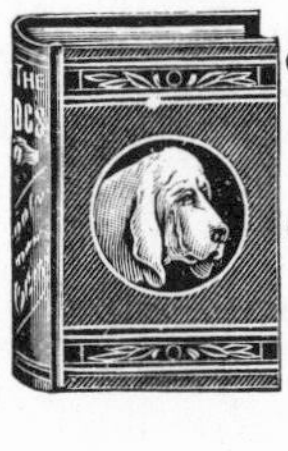

6751 Enlarged and revised. Cloth, 12mo. $1.45
Postage .... .12

Diseases of Dogs.

6752 Hugh Dalziel. The author is one of the first British authorities on dogs. 116 pages. Paper...$0.40
Postage .... .04

Training vs. Breaking.

6753 By S. T. Hammond. This is a book for dog owners, who by its directions can successfully train their hunting dogs. 163 pages. Cloth $0.88
Postage .... .08

The Spaniel and Its Breaking.

6754 By F. H. F. Mercer. Cloth. Illustrated.
Price $0.88
Postage .... .08

American Book of the Dog.

6755 The origin, development, utility, breeding, training, deseases and kennel management. By G. O. Shields. 8 vo., 700 pages. Cloth $2.45
Postage .... .26

First Lessons in Training.

6756 With points and standards of all breeds of dogs. Paper, 106 pages. Price $0.40
Postage .... .04

Scientific Education of Dogs for the Gun.

6757 By "H. H." The results of thirty-seven years' practical experience. 220 pages. Cloth $2.25
Postage .... .12

Modern Training.

6759 Handling and Kennel Management. By B. Waters. Illustrated. Cloth, 373 pages. Retail $2.00, our price $1.45. Postage, 14 c.

Altemus Library.

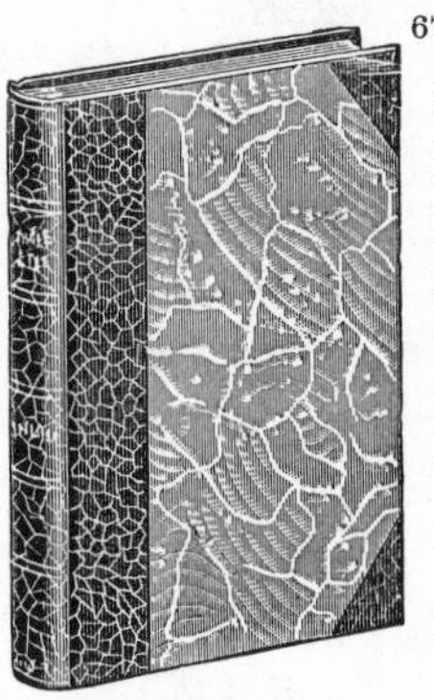

6762 Altemus Library. All beautifully bound in half crushed levant with gilt tops, handsomely printed on calendered paper, large clear type. A most beautiful holiday and gift book.
Retail price $1.50
Our price 88
6763 Presentation Cloth Edition. Each $0.48
Postage, each .... .08

Sesame and Lilies, Ruskin
Pleasures of Life, Lubbock;
Bacon's Essays.
Thoughts, Marcus Aurelius Antoinus.
Discourses, Epictetus.
Emerson's Essays, First Series.
Emerson's Essays, Second Series.
Cranford .... Mrs Gaskell
Imitation of Christ .... Thomas A'Kempis
Vicar of Wakefield .... Goldsmith.
Chesterfield's Letters ....
Idle Thoughts of an Idle Fellow .... Jerome
Tales from Shakespeare .... Charles and Mary Lamb
Natural Law in the Spiritual World .... Drummond
Addresses .... Drummond
Evolution of Man .... Drummond
My Point of View .... Selections from Drummond
The Scarlet Letter .... Hawthorne
Representative Men .... Emerson
My King and His Service .... Havergal
Reveries of a Bachelor .... Ik. Marvel
House of the Seven Gables .... Hawthorne
Dream Life .... Ik. Marvel
Rab and His Friends, Marjorie Fleming, etc .... Brown
Essays of Elia .... Lamb
Sartor Resartus .... Carlyle
Heroes and Hero Worship .... Carlyle
Ethics of the Dust .... Ruskin
A Window in Thrums .... J. M. Barrie
Mosses from an Old Manse .... Hawthorne
Twice Told Tales .... Hawthorne
Uncle Tom's Cabin .... Stowe

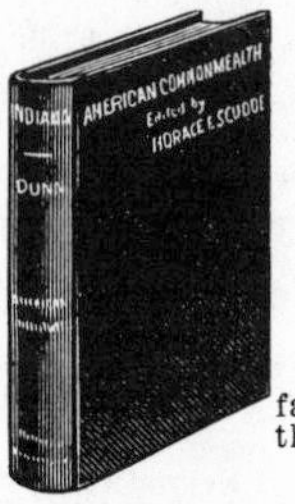

American Statesmen. Series No. 6764.

Bound Uniform in cloth, 12 mo.
Retail price, each $1.25
Our price, each .... .88
A series of biographies of men famous in the political history of the United States.

Daniel Webster.	By Henry Cabot Lodge.
Albert Gallatin.	By John Austin Stevens.
James Madison.	By Sidney Howard Gay.
John Adams.	By John T. Morse, Jr.
John Marshall.	By Allan B. Margruder.
Samuel Adams.	By J. K. Hosmer.
Thomas H. Benton.	By Theodore Roosevelt.
Henry Clay, 2 vols.	By Carl Schurz.
Patrick Henry.	By Moses Coit Tyler
Gouverneur Morris.	By Theodore Roosevelt.
Martin Van Buren.	By E. M. Shepard.
George Washington, 2 vols.	By Henry Cabot Lodge.
Benjamin Franklin.	By John T. Morse, Jr.
John Jay.	By George Pellew.
Lewis Cass.	By Andrew C. McLaughlin
John Quincy Adams.	By John T. Morse, Jr.
Alexander Hamilton.	By Henry Cabot Lodge.
John C. Calhoun.	By Dr. Von Holst,
Andrew Jackson.	By Prof. W. G. Sumner.
John Randolph.	By Henry Adams.
James Monroe.	By D. C. Gilman.
Thomas Jefferson.	By John T. Morse, Jr.
Abraham Lincoln, 2 vols.	By John T. Morse, Jr.

Postage, each $0.10

99782

American Commonwealths. Series No. 6766.

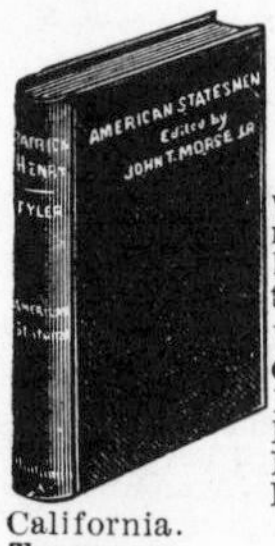

A series of Histories of the Commonwealths of the United States, with maps. Edited by Horace E. Scudder. Bound in silk cloth, gilt tops, large type, etc.

Virginia.	By John Eston Cooke.
Oregon.	By William Barrows.
Maryland.	By William H. Browne.
Kentucky.	By N. S. Shaler.
Michigan.	By T. M. Cooley.
Kansas.	By L. W. Spring.
California.	By Josiah Royce.
Tennessee.	By James Phelan.
New York.	By E. H. Roberts, Vol. 1
New York.	By E. H. Roberts, Vol. 2.
Connecticut.	By Alex. Johnson.
Missouri.	By Lucien Carr.
Indiana.	By J. P. Dunn, Jr.
Ohio.	By Rufus King.
Vermont.	By Rowland E. Robinson.
New Jersey.	By Austin Scott.
Pennsylvania.	By Wayne MacVeagh.
Illinois.	By E. G. Mason.
South Carolina.	By Edward McCrady, Jr.

Our price $0.88
Postage, extra, each .... .12

Alcott's, Louisa M., Stories. Series No. 6768.

"Miss Alcott is the benefactor of households".

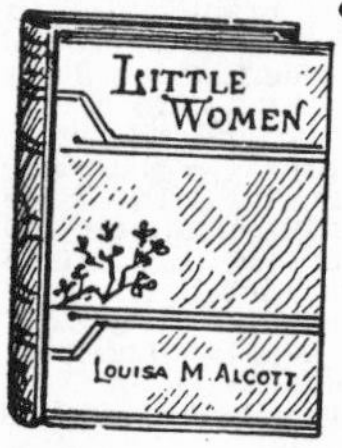

Little Men.
Little Women.
Eight Cousins
Jack and Jill.
Work.
Moods.
Life Letters and Journals.
Hospital Sketches.
Modern Mephistopheles.
Rose in Bloom.
Jo's Boys.
Old Fashioned Girl.
Under the Lilacs.

Each 12mo., cloth. Retail price, each $1.50
Our price, each .... .98
Postage .... .12

Comic Tragedies.

6769 Written by "Jo" and "Meg," and acted by the "Little Women," with a foreword by "Meg." Portraits of Jo and Meg, and a view of the house in which they lived. 16mo., cloth. Uniform with Miss Alcott's books. Retail price $1.50
Our price .... .98

Alcott's Garland Series. Series No. 6770.

A Garland for Girls.	Proverb Stories.
Silver Pitcher's	Spinning Wheel Stories.

Retail price, each $1.25
Our price, each .... .88
Postage .... .10

Aunt Jo's Scrap Bag Series. Series No. 6771.

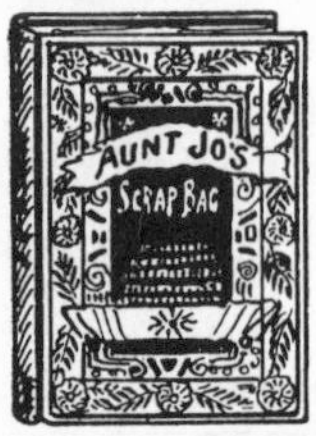

My Boys.
Cupid and Chow Chow.
My Girls.
Jimmie's Cruise in the Pinafore
An Old Fashioned Thanksgiving.
Shawl Straps.
16mo., cloth.
Retail price, each $1.00
Our price, each .... .70
Set of 6 vols 4.10
Postage, each .... .08

Arthur's, T. S., Works. Series No. 6773.

(Temperance Series.)

Durably bound in cloth, 12mo., 12 volumes, containing:

The Wedding Guest.	Our Homes.
Words of Cheer.	Grappling with the Monster.
Cast Adrift.	Mother's Rule.
Woman to the Rescue.	Friends and Neighbors.
Danger.	The True Path.
Saved as by Fire.	Three Years in a Mantrap.

Retail price, per set $6.00
Our price 3.75
Single volumes, each .... .33
Postage, each, per volume .... .10

Ten Nights in a Bar Room.

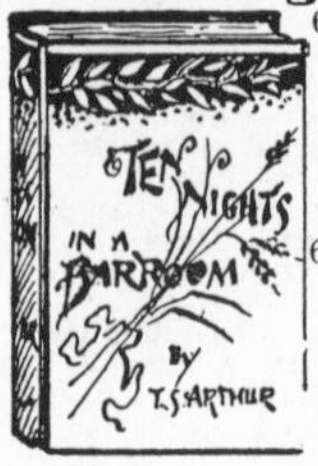

6774 Ten Nights in a Bar Room, And What I Saw There. By T. S. Arthur. A new edition in large type of this famous book, 12mo. Illustrated. Retail price $1.25
Our price reduced to .... .45
Postage .... .10

6775 **Home Stories.** 6 vols. Sold only in sets.
Sowing the Wind.
Hidden Wings.
Sunshine at Home.
Not Anything for Peace.
The Peace Makers.
After a Shadow.
Price $2.00

Abbott's, Willis J., American Wars.

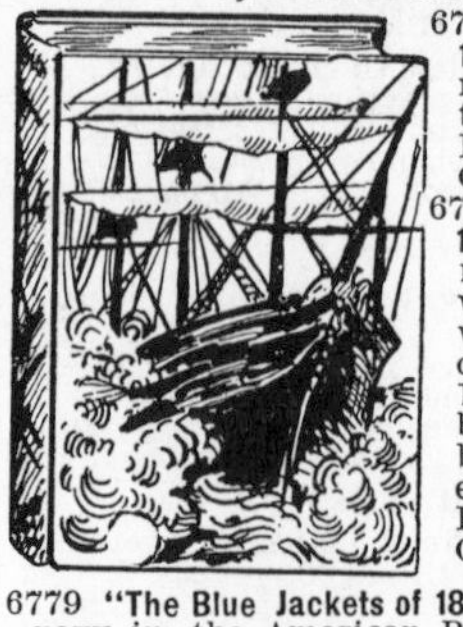

6777 **"The Blue Jackets of 1776."** A history of the navy. 32 full page illustrations. Large 4to., cloth.
Retail price $2.00
Our price, only 1.25

6778 **"The Blue Jackets of 1812."** A history of the naval battles of the second war with Great Britain, to which is prefixed an account of the French war of 1798, with 32 illustrations. by W. C. Jackson, and 50 by H. W. McVickar. A new edition, large 4to., cloth.
Retail price $2.00
Our price, only 1.25

6779 **"The Blue Jackets of 1861."** A history of the navy in the American Rebellion; with many full page pictures of great interest. A new edition, 4to., cloth.. Retail price $2.00
Our price, only 1.25

6780 **"The Battle Fields of 1861."** The initial volume of a History of the land forces of the War for the Union, with many illustrations, 4to, cloth. Retail price ..... $2.00 Our price only .. $1.25

6781 **"Battle Fields and Camp Fires."** The second volume of the History of the Land Forces in the War for the Union, fully illustrated by W. C. Jackson, 4to, cloth. Retail price $2.00
Our price, only 1.25

6782 **"Battle Field and Victory."** The third volume of the History of the land force in the War for the Union, 4to, cloth. Retail price $2.00
Our price, only 1.25
Postage on above six, each .... .25

Abbott's American Pioneers and Patriots series. Series No. 6785.

By John S. C. Abbott. A series illustrating the early history and settlement of our country.

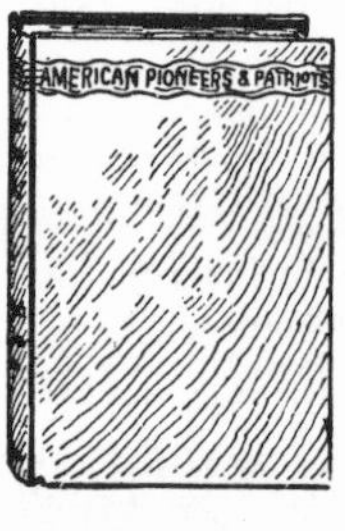

George Washington.
Kit Carson.
LaSalle.
Miles Standish.
Paul Jones.
Peter Stuyvesant.
Benjamin Franklin.
Captain Kidd.
Columbus.
Daniel Boone.
David Crockett.
De Soto.
Each in one volume, 12mo. Illustrated.
Per volume $0.75
Postage, each .... .10
Per set of 12 vols. 8.00

Alger, Horatio, Jr.'s Popular Juvenile Books for Boys.

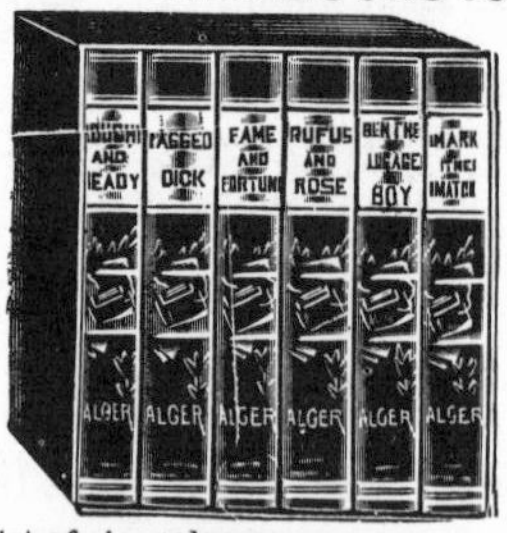

12mo., cloth. Illustrated.

6786 **Ragged Dick Series.** 12mo., cloth.
Ragged Dick.
Fame and Fortune.
Mark, the Match Boy.
Rough and Ready.
Ben, the Luggage Boy.
Rufus and Rose.

Set of six volumes $5.25
Single volumes, each .... .88

6787 **Tattered Tom Stories.** 12mo., cloth. **First Series.** Illustrated.

Tattered Tom.	Phil the Fiddler.
Paul the Peddler.	Slow and Sure.

Set of four volumes $3.50
Single volumes, each .... .88

6788 **Tattered Tom Stories.** 12mo., cloth. **Second Series.** Illustrated.

Julius.	Sam's Chance.
The Young Outlaw.	The Telegraph Boy.

Set of four volumes $3.50
Single volume, each .... .88

6789 **Campaign Series.** 12mo., cloth. Illustrated.
Frank's Campaign. Paul Prescott's Charge.
Charles Codman's Cruise.
Set of three volumes $2.50
Single volumes, each .... .88

6790 **Luck and Pluck Series.** 12mo., cloth. **First Series.** Illustrated.

Luck and Pluck	Strong and Steady.
Sink or Swim.	Strive and Succeed.

Set of four volumes $3.50
Single volumes, each .... .88

6791 **Luck and Pluck Series.** 12mo., cloth. **Second Series.** Illustrated.

Try and Trust.	Risen from the Ranks.
Bound to Rise.	Herbert Carter's Legacy.

Set of four volumes $3.50
Single volume, each .... .88

6792 **Brave and Bold Series.** 12mo., cloth. Illustrated.

Brave and bold.	Shifting for Himself.
Jack Ward	Wait and Hope.

Set of four volumes $3.50
Single volumes, each .... .88

Juvenile Books—Continued.

6793 **Pacific Series.** 12mo., cloth. Illustrated.

The Young Adventurer.	The Young Explorer.
The Young Miner.	Ben's Nugget.

Set of four volumes $3.50
Single volume, each .... .88

6794 **Atlantic Series.** 12mo., cloth. Illustrated.

Young Circus Rider	Hector's Inheritance.
Do and Dare.	Helping Himself.

Set of four volumes $3.50
Single volumes, each .... .88

6795 **Way to Success Series.** By Horatio Alger, Jr., 4 vols., 12mo., cloth.

Bob Burton.	The Store Boy.
Luke Walton.	Struggling Upward.

Set of four volumes $3.50
Single volumes, each .... .88

6796 **New World Series.** By Horatio Alger, Jr,

Digging for Gold.	Facing the World.
In a New World.	

Set of three volumes, $2.50. Single volumes, each $0.88
Postage extra, per vol .... .10

6798 **Only an Irish Boy.** By Horatio Alger, Jr. 12mo $0.88

6800 **Victor Vane.** By Horatio Alger, Jr. 12mo.. $0.88

Arabian Nights' Entertainments.

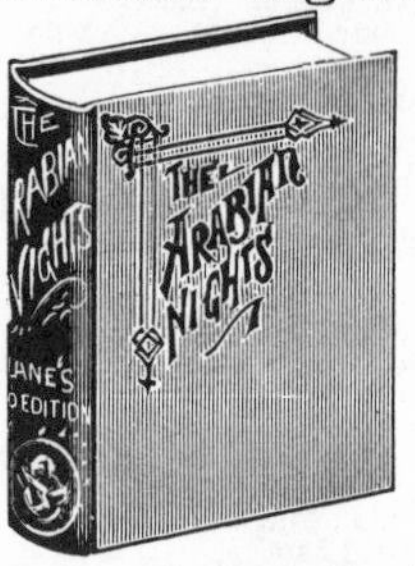

6802 Translated from the Original Arabic by Edward William Lane. Handsomely illustrated with one hundred and fifty illustrations. Revised and enlarged edition. Royal octavo. Cloth.
Retail price $2.00
Our price 1.40
Postage, 32c. extra.

Alger Series for Boys. Series 6804.

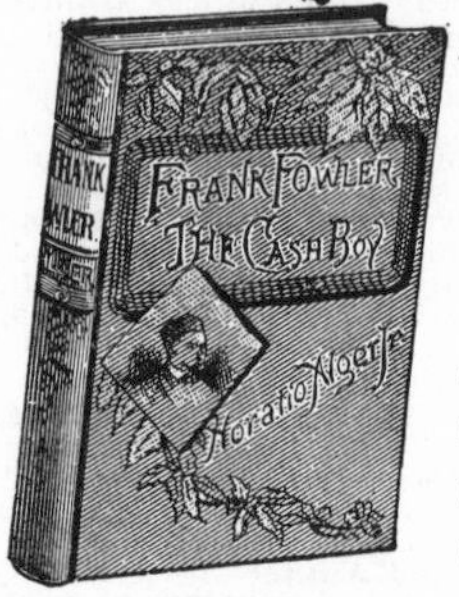

A series of spirited stories for boys, by popular writers. Each illustrated, uniform in size, bound in handsome cloth binding.
Retail price each ... $1.00
Our price, each ..... .52
Postage, each 12 cents extra.

Adrift in the Wilds. By Edward S. Ellis.
The Boy Cruisers. By St. George Rathborne.
Budd Boyd's Triumph. By William P. Chipman.
Captain Kidd's Gold. By James Franklin Fitts.
Captured by Apes. By Harry Prentice.
Captured by Zulus. By Harry Prentice.
The Castaways. By James Otis.
Dan, the Newsboy. By Horatio Alger, Jr.
The Errand Boy. By Horatio Alger, Jr.
Frank Fowler, the Cash Boy. By Horatio Alger, Jr.
Guy Harris, the Runaway. By Harry Castlemon.
The Island Treasure. By Frank H Converse.
Jaunt Through Java. By Edward S. Ellis.
Joe's Luck. By Horatio Alger, Jr.
Julian Mortimer. By Harry Castlemon
Lost in the Canon. By Alfred R. Calhoun.
Roy Gilbert's Search. By William P. Chipman.
A Runaway Brig. By James Otis.
Search for the Silver City. By James Otis.
The Slate-Picker. By Harry Prentice,
Tom Temple's Career. By Horatio Alger, Jr.
Tom Thatcher's Fortune. By Horatio Alger, Jr.
Tom, the Bootblack. By Horatio Alger, Jr.
Tom, the Ready. By Randolph Hill.
Tony, the Hero. By Horatio Alger, Jr.
The Train Boy. By Horatio Alger, Jr.
The Treasure Finders. By James Otis.
A Young Hero. By Edward S. Ellis.

Burnham, Clara Louise, Works. Series No. 6805.

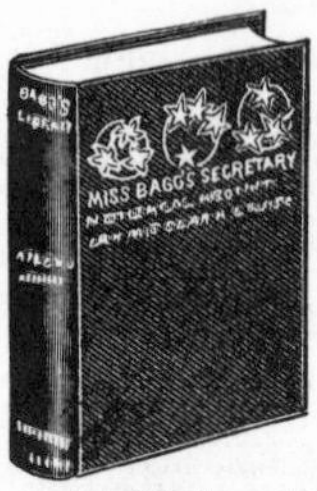

12mo, cloth.	Retail price.	Our price.
Young Maids and Old.	$1.50	$1.05
Next Door	1.25	.88
No Gentlemen	1.25	.88
A Sane Lunatic	1.25	.88
Miss Bagg's Secretary.	1.25	.88
Mistress of Beech Knoll	1.25	.88

Postage, each, 10c extra.

Buffalo Bill, From Prairie to Palace.

6807 Compiled by John M. Burke, by authority of General W. F. Cody (Buffalo Bill). Profusely illustrated. The title of this book tells something of the wide range of interest covered by its 275 pages. Illustrated, paper cover $0.35
Handsome cloth binding .... .75

Bellamy, Edward, Works,

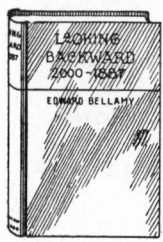

Looking Backward.

6808 By Edward Bellamy. The greatest and most interesting book out; over 500,000 sold. Handsomely bound in silk cloth, 12mo.
Retail price $1.00
Our price................ .68
Paper covers............ .33
Postage, extra, cloth, 10 cents. Paper, 4c.

Black, William, Works.

6810 Complete Works of William Black, handsomely bound in cloth, black and gold. Library edition, 12 volumes. Per set....................$5.25

Bacon's (Lord) Essays.

6811 Essays and Historical Works, complete in one volume, 12mo., cloth.........................$0.52
Postage, 10c.

Bronte, Charlotte, Works.

6812 Set contains the following: Jane Eyre Shirley, The Professor, Emma and Poems, Tenant of Wildfell Hall, Villette, Wuthering Heights and Life. Six volumes, cloth, gilt top, 12mo.............................$4.50
Six volumes, half calf........................... 9.00
Postage, extra, 70c.
6813 Popular edition of Bronte's Works. 4 volumes, cloth, 12mo............................ 1.98
Postage, 50c. extra.

Burnett, Frances Hodson, Works.

Little Lord Fauntleroy.

6815 By Frances Hodgson Burnett. A charming serial for young folks. Elegantly illustrated and bound in fine English cloth, square 8vo.
Price $1.40
Postage...................... .22
6816 **Giovana and the Other.** 8vo., cloth. Illustrated.
Retail price $1.50
Our price.................. 1.05
6817 **Sarah Crew.** What happened at Miss Minchin's. Illustrated, 8vo., cloth. Retail price....$1.00
Our price.................. .70
6818 **Little Saint Elizabeth,** and other stories, 8vo., cloth. Retail price................................$1.50
Our price.................. 1.05
Postage...................... .15
6819 **The One I know Best of All,** a memory of the mind of a child, 12mo., cloth.
Retail price...............$2.00
Our price.................. 1.40
Postage...................... .12

Browning, Robert, Poetical and Dramatic Works.

6820 New Riverside Edition. The text from the latest English edition, revised and rearranged by Mr. Browning, with portrait and index; 7 volumes; Crown, 8vo.; gilt tops; cloth.
Retail price, $11.50 Our price................$7.90
Single volumes, each........................ 1.25

Barr, Amelia, Works.
Series 6822.

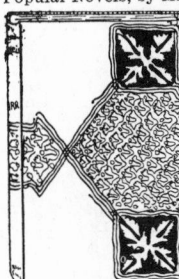

Popular Novels, by Mrs. Amelia Barr, 12mo., cloth.
The Squire of Sandal Side.
A Border Shepherdess.
Paul and Christina.
Feet of Clay.
The Household of McNeil.
Friend Olivia.
She Loved a Sailor.
Remember the Alamo.
Jan Vedder's Wife.
The Last of the Macallisters.
A Daughter of Fife.
Between Two Lovers.
The Bow of Orange Ribbon.
A Sister of Esau, new.
Master of His Fate.
Retail price $1.25
Our price, per volume, only...................... .88
Postage................... .12

Jan Vedder's Wife.

6824 New 16mo edition. Cloth...................$0.30
Postage... .08

Bow of Orange Ribbon.

6825 New 16mo. edition. Cloth................$0.30
Postage, extra.. .... .08

Bolton, Sarah K., Works.
Series 6827.

All uniform binding, large type and cloth. Illustrated. Large 12mo.

Famous Types of Womanhood.
Famous English Statesmen.
Famous English Authors of the Nineteenth Century.
Famous European Artists.
Famous American Authors.
Famous American Statesmen.
Famous Men of Science.
Girls Who Became Famous.
Poor Boys Who Became Famous.
Famous Leaders Among Men.
Famous Voyagers.
Retail price, each $1.50
Our price 1.00
Postage extra, each ...... .12

Blaine, Jas. C., Works.
Twenty Years in Congress.

6829 By James G. Blaine, 2 vols, 8vo., cloth.
Subscription price...................$7.50
Our price........................... 5.00
2 vols., 8vo. sheep, subscription price........... 9.50
Our price........................... 6.40
Postage............................ .75

Best Presentation Editions.
Series No. 6830.

All are bound in padded American seal binding, dark colors, round corners, gold edges, with handsome stamp on sides; containing good paper, print and ext. a illustrations.
Ben Hur. By Lew Wallace.
Fair God. By Lew Wallace.
Romola. By George Eliot.
Bitter Sweet. By J. G. Holland.
Scarlet Letter. By Hawthorne.
Jane Eyre. By Bronte.
Hypatia. By Kingsley.
Wide, Wide World. By Wetherell.
Marble Faun. By Hawthorne.
Uncle Tom's Cabin. By H. B. Stowe.
Ramona. By Helen H. Jackson.
Lorna Doone. By R. D. Blackmore.
Kathrina. By Holland.
Retail price, each...................................$3.00
Our price, each................................... 2.10
Postage, each, 12 cents.

Beaconsfield, Lord (Disraeli), Works of.

6833 7 vols., 12mo. cloth, sold only in sets........$6.30
  I. Coningsby and Tancred.
  II. Sibyl and Beaconsfield's Life.
  III. Vivian Grey.
  IV. Venetia and the Rise of Iskander.
  V. Endymion and Miriam Alroy.
  VI. Lothair and Contarini Fleming.
  VII. Henrietta Temple and the Young Duke.

Barrie, J. M., Famous Works.
Series 6835.

Nicely bound and printed. 12mo., cloth.

	Retail price.	Our price.
The Little Minister, illustrated	$1.25	$0.88
Two of Them, illustrated	1.25	.88
Auld Licht Idyll	1.00	.70
An Edinburgh Eleven	1.00	.70
A Tillyloss Scandal	1.00	.70
A Window in Thrums	1.00	.70
When a Man's Single	1.00	.70
Better Dead, and My Lady Nicotine	1.00	.70

Postage, each, 10c. extra.

Boswell, James.

6836 Life of Samuel Johnson, 4 volumes........$2.10

Bill Nye's History of the United States.

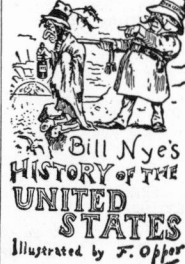

6838 A humorous story of the discovery, settlement and development of the United States, by Bill Nye. Illustrated by F. Opper. Crown 8 vo.; 150 illustrations.
Retail price................$2.00
Our price.................. 1.40
Postage, 20c. extra.

Birthday Books.

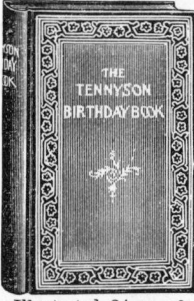

6840 **Tennyson's Birthday Book.** Edited by Emily Shakespeare, handsomely bound in cloth; fully illustrated, 32mo.
Retail price.............$1.00
Our price............. .50
6841 **Shakespeare Birthday Book.** With portrait and twelve illustrations. 24mo., cloth, 65c.; seal.
6842 **Scripture Birthday Book.** Arranged by Rev. A. C. Ryle, Bishop of Liverpool. Illustrated, 24mo. cloth.
Price...................$0.65
6843 **The Poet's Birthday Book.** With original poems for each month by Longfellow, Whittier, Will Carleton and others. Illustrated. 24mo., cloth. Price........$0.65
6844 **Little Folk's Birthday Book.** Arranged by Amanda B. Harris. Three hundred and sixty-five little poems and pictures. Square 24mo., cloth, tinted edges. Price........$0.65
6845 **Sands of Time.** A beautiful book of birthday gems from the great poets. Fine cloth, full gilt. Price........$0.50

6846 A beautiful series of new birthday books in fine bindings, each is bound in padded leather, round corners and gold edges.
  Scott, Shakespeare, Hemans, Burns, Wordsworth.
Retail price, each...... $1.25
Our price.................. .88
Postage, each, extra...... .08
6847 Same as 6846. Can be furnished in a more elaborate style of binding with perfumed covers. Each..................$1.40

Crowell's New Illustrated Library.
Series 6850.

The publishers have spared neither pains nor expense in their efforts to make this new line of standard books the finest that has ever been produced at so low a price. The paper, type, and illustrations are of the highest excellence, while the beauty of the styles of bindings adapt these volumes to a large class of buyers for home, library and gift purposes. Each set contains 2 volumes, bound in white and gold cloths with full gilt top.
Retail price, per set of 2 volumes............ $3.00
Our price, per set of 2 volumes.................. 2.10

Alhambra (The) and Sketch Book. By Washington Irving. Printed on fine paper and illustrated with 42 reproductions of photographs and original illustrations by eminent artists. Photogravure frontispiece.
Anna Karenina. By Count Lyof N. Tolstoi. Printed on on fine paper, with photogravure portrait and ten original illustrations by Paul Frenzeny.
Boswells' Life of Johnson. Edited by Mowbray Morris. Printed from new plates on fine paper, with 34 portraits. Photogravure frontispiece.
Cambridge Book of Poetry and Song. Edited by Charlotte Fiske Bates. Printed on fine paper, and illustrated with photogravure portraits of Longfellow and Whittier, and original illustrations by the best artists. This edition contains 40 fac-simile poems in autographs.
Count of Monte Cristo (The). By Alexander Dumas. Complete and accurate translation. Printed from new plates on fine paper. With 18 new illustrations by Frank T. Merrill. Photogravure frontispieces.
French Revolution (The). By Thomas Carlyle. Printed from new plates on fine paper, and illustrated with 34 portraits and reproductions of famous paintings. Photogravure frontispieces.
Ivanhoe. By Sir Walter Scott. Printed from new plates on fine paper. With 18 new illustrations by H. M. Eaton. Photogravure frontispieces.
Les Miserables. By Victor Hugo. Printed on fine paper. With 32 original illustrations by the best French artists. Photogravure frontispieces.
Lorna Doone. By R. D. Blackmore. Printed from new plates on fine paper. With 18 new illustrations by Frank T. Merrill. Photogravure frontispiece.
Romola. By George Eliot. Printed on fine paper and illustrated with 34 reproductions of Florintine photographs. Photogravure frontispieces.
Tennyson's Poetical Works. Printed on fine paper and illustrated with photogravure portraits and original illustrations by best artists.
Three Musketeers (The). By Alexander Dumas. With new introduction by his son, and 250 illustrations by Maurice Leloir. Photogravure frontispieces. Complete and accurate translation.
Tom Brown at Oxford By Thomas Hughes. Printed on fine paper, and illustrated with 34 reproductions of fine photographs of the picturesque features of Oxford, Photogravure frontispieces.
Tom Brown's School Days. By Thomas Hughes. Printed on fine paper and fully illustrated by H. W. Pierce. Photogravure frontispieces.
Postage, extra, per set 32c.

Children's Favorite Classics. Series 6852.

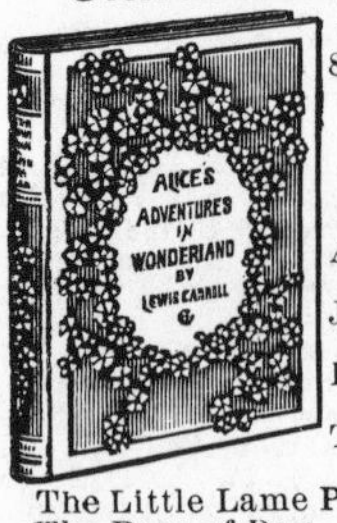

8vo Edition. Printed from new plates on fine paper, with colored borders. Fully illustrated, including colored frontispiece and vignette title. Attractively bound in white and colors.
Alice's Adventures in Wonderland. By Lewis Carroll
Jackanapes and Daddy Darwin. By Mrs. J. H. Ewing.
Lob Lie by the Fire. By Mrs. J. H. Ewing.
The Adventures of a Brownie. By Miss Mulock.
The Little Lame Prince.............By Miss Mulock.
The Peep of Day.
The Story of a Short Life........By Mrs. J. H. Ewing.
Through the Looking Glass.........By Lewis Carroll.
Per set of 8 volumes..............................$6.50
Retail price, each....$1.25 Our price, each.... .88
Postage, each, extra 12c.

Cooper, J. Fenimore, Works.

6853 Complete Works of Cooper, 16 volumes, large type, calendered paper, fully illustrated, 12mo., silk cloth, gilt tops. Retail price, $12; our price...$8.40
Half calf, gilt tops...................................16.00
6854 **Leatherstocking Tales**—5 vols. Library style. 12mo. Cloth. The Pathfinder, The Deerslayer, The Prairie, Last of the Mohicans, The Pioneers. Retail price, $3.50; our price.............. 1.75
Half calf.......... .... 5.00
6855 **Leatherstocking Tales**—Avon edition. 5 vols. 12mo. Cloth.................................. .98
6857 **Sea Tales**—5 vols. Library style. 12mo., cloth. The Pilot, The Two Admirals, The Water Witch, Wing and Wing. The Red Rover. Retail price, $3.50; our price, $1.75. Half calf 5.00
6859 **Sea Tales**—Avon edition. 5 vols. 12mo., cloth .98

Carleton, William, Works.

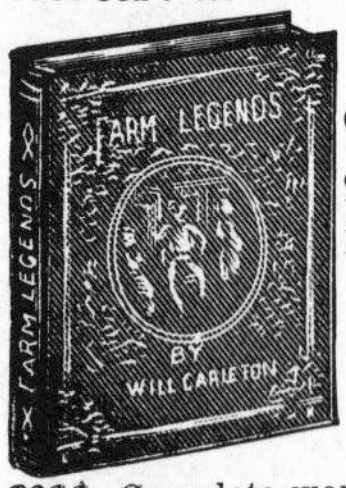

6861 Handsomely bound in silk cloth, beautifully illustrated, 8vo.
City Festivals, City Legends,
Farm Ballads, City Ballads,
Farm Festivals, Farm Legends.
Retail price each...........$2.00
Our price, each 1.40
Complete set of 6 volumes, 8.00
Postage, per vol., 16 cents extra.

Carlyle, Thomas, Works.

6862 Complete works, 10 volumes, large type, calendered paper. 12mo., cloth, gilt tops.......$7.50

Frederick The Great.

6864 New Edition by Thomas Carlyle, 12mo., cloth, gilt tops, 4 volumes...................... $3.00

Carlyle's Complete Works.

6865 New Library Edition, 10 volumes, 12mo., ornamental cloth.............................. $5.00

French Revolution.

6867 New Library Edition, 12mo., 2 volumes.. $0.75
half calf 1.98

Campaigns of the Civil War. Series 6870.

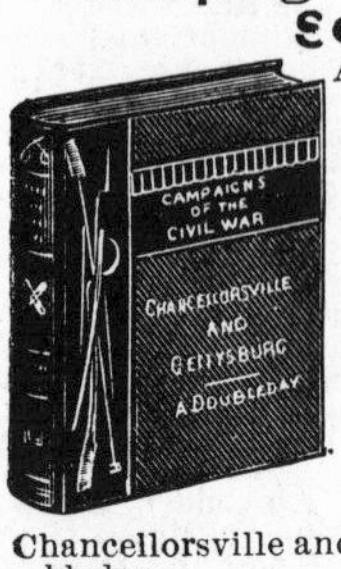

All beautifully bound in cloth and illustrated with maps and plans.
Retail price, each............$1.00
Our price........................ .70
Outbreak of the Rebellion. By G. Nicholay.
From Fort Henry to Corinth. By Hon. M. F. Force.
The Peninsula; McClellan's Campaign of 1862. By A. S. Webb.
The Army Under Pope. By John C. Ropes.
Antietam to Fredericksburg. By F. W. Palfrey.
Chancellorsville and Gettysburg. By Abner Doubleday.
Army of the Cumberland. By H. M. Cist.
The Mississippi. By F. V. Green.
Atlanta. By Hon. J. D. Cox.
March to the Sea. By Hon. J. D. Cox.
Shenandoah Valley. By Geo. A. Pond.
Virginia Campaigns of '64-5. By Andrew A. Humphreys.
Statistical Record of the Armies of the U. S. By Frederick Phisterer.
Blockade of the Cruisers. By J. R Soley.
Atlantic Coast. By Daniel Ammen.
Gulf and Inland Waters. By A. T. Mahan.
16 volumes complete, $10.25. Postage, extra..$0.10

Coffin, C. C., Works. Series 6872.

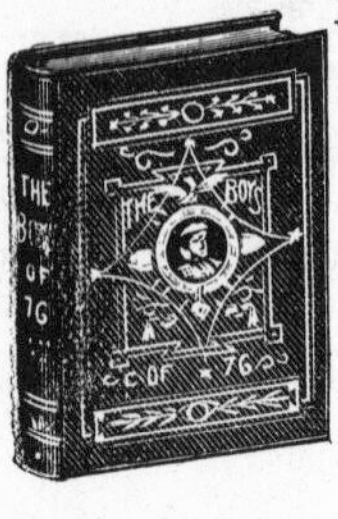

Works of C. C. Coffin. All handsomely bound in cloth, with gold title stamps.
Building Up the Nation.
The Boys of '76.
Marching to Victory.
Story of Liberty
Old Times in the Colonies.
Freedom Triumphant.
Redeeming The Republic.
Drum Beat of the Nation.
Abraham Lincoln.
Retail price, each $3.00
Our price 2.10
Per set of 9 volumes 18.50

Cumming, Gordon, Works.

6873 Wild Men and Wild Beasts, or Scenes in Camp and Jungle. 18 illustrations. 12mo., cloth. Retail price $1.50. Our price..........$1.10
Postage, 12 cents extra.

Carey, Rosa N., Girl's Books.

6874 New Edition, complete works, 10 volumes, 12mo., cloth.....................................$4.00

Crawford, F. Marion, Works. Series 6876.

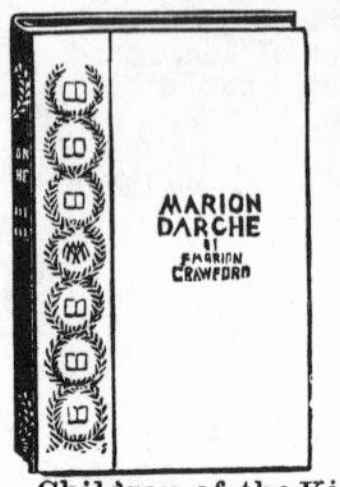

In uniform cloth binding. 12mo.
Mr. Issacs. A Tale of Modern India.
Zorrster.
Dr. Claudius. A True Story.
A Tale of a Lonely Parish.
Saracinesca.
Marzio's Crucifix.
The Three Fates.
With the Immortals.
Greifenstein.
Sant' Ilario. A Sequel to "Saracinesca."
A Cigarette Maker's Romance.
Khaled. A Tale of Arabia.
The Witch of Prague.
Children of the King. Marion Darche.
Pietro Ghisleri. To Leeward.
A Roman Singer. Paul Patoff.
An American Politician. Per vol.
Retail price..........$1.00 Our price.... .....$0.70

Katherine Lauerdale.

6877 A new book, by F. Marion Crawford, 2 vols., 12 mo., cloth.
Retail price.......................................$2.00
Our price.. 1.40

Love in Idleness.

6878 New. By F. Marion Crawford.
Retail price.......................................$2.00
Our price.. 1.40
Postage, 12 cents.

The Ralstons.

6879 Just published. By F. Marion Crawford. 2 vols., 12 mo. Retail price.......................$2.00
Our price.. 1.40
Postage, extra.. .22

Castlemon, Harry, Popular Juvenile Books for Boys.

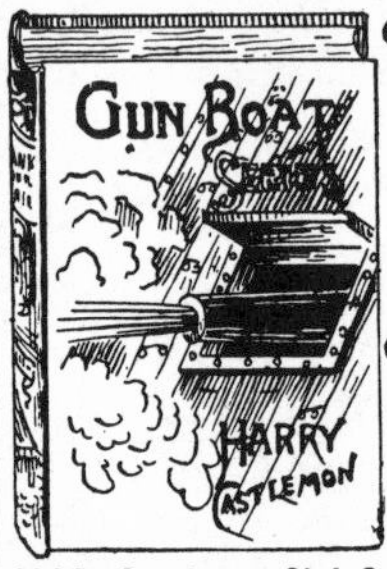

6880 **Gunboat Series.** 12 mo., cloth, illustrated.
Frank on a Gunboat.
Frank before Vicksburg.
Frank on Lower Mississippi.
Frank the Young Naturalist.
Frank in the Woods.
Frank on the Prairie.
Set of six volumes.......$5.25
Single volume, each........ .88
6881 **Rocky Mountain Series.** 12 mo., cloth, illustrated.
Frank among the Rancheros.
Frank in the Mountains.
Frank at Don Carlos' Ranche.
Set of three volumes.... $2.63
Single volume........... .88
6882 **Sportsmen Club Series.** 12 mo., cloth, illustrated.
The Sportsmen's Club in the Saddle.
The Sportsmen's Club Afloat.
The Sportsmen's Club Among Trappers.
Set of three volumes $2.63
Single volumes, each.............................. .88
6883 **Frank Nelson Series,** 12 mo., cloth, illustrated.
Showed Up. Frank in the Forecastle. The Boy Traders.
Set of three volumes...............................$2.63
Single volumes .... .88
6884 **The Boy Trapper Series.** 12 mo., cloth, illustrated.
The Buried Treasure. The Boy Trapper. The Mail Carrier.
Set of three volumes...............................$2.63
Single volume, each................................ .88
6885 **Roughing It Series.** 12 mo., cloth, illustrated.
George in Camp. George at the Wheel. George at the Fort.
Set of three volumes...............................$2.63
Single volumes, each............................... .88
6886 **Rod and Gun Series.** 12 mo., cloth, illustrated.
Don Gordon's Shooting Box. Rod and Gun Club. The Young Wild Fowlers.
Set of three volumes $2.63
Single volumes, each .... .88
6887 **Go Ahead Series.** 12 mo., cloth, illustrated.
Tom Newcombe. Go Ahead. No Moss.
Set of three volumes $2.63
Single volumes, each............................... .88
6888 **War Series.** 12 mo., cloth.
True to His Colors. Marcy the Blockade Runner. Rodney the Partisan. Marcy the Refugee. Rodney the Overseer. Sailor Jack the Trader.
6 volumes in a box.................................$5.25
Single volumes, each............................... .88
6889 **Forest and Stream Series.** 12mo., cloth, illustrated. Joe Wayring.
Snagged and Sunk. Steel Horse.
3 volumes in a box.................................$2.63
Single volumes, each .... .88

Books—Continued.

6890 **Hunter Series.** 12mo., cloth, illustrated. Oscar in Africa. Two Ways of Becoming a Hunter. Camp in the Foot Hills.
Three volumes in box $2.63
Single volumes, each................................ .88
6891 **Our Fellows, or Skirmishes with the Swamp Dragoons.** 16mo., cloth .... .88
Postage on Castlemon books, each, 10 cents.

Custer, Mrs. E. B., Works. Tenting on the Plains.

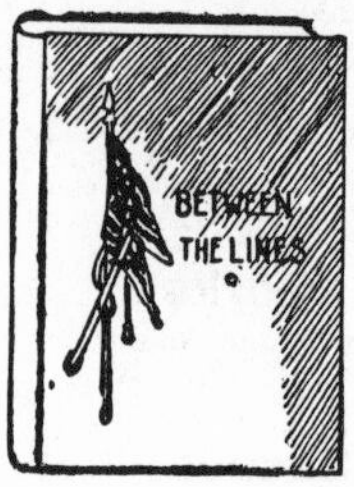

6894 By Mrs. E. B. Custer, containing the life and career of Gen. Geo. A. Custer and camp life on the plains. 702 pages. Beautifully bound in silk cloth and side stamping in colors. Subscription price, $3.50. Our price.........$2.40
Postage........................ .24
Small edition.................. .75
Postage........................ .09

Boots and Saddles.

Retail price. Our price.
6895 By Mrs. E. B. Custer, with portrait and map. 12mo., cloth $1.50 $1.05

Corelli, Marie, Works of.

6896 New beautiful presentation edition, handsomely bound in blue and green cloth, with gold embossed designs.
The Soul of Lilith; A Romance of Two Worlds; Wormwood; Vendetta, and My Wonderful Wife; Ardath; Thelma.

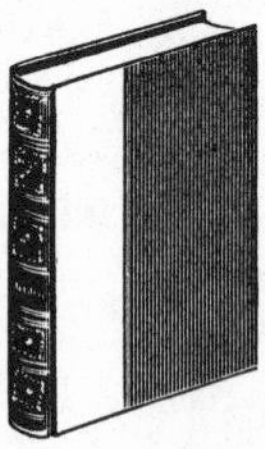

Retail price, each.......... ....$1.00
Our price........................ .70
Per set 6 volumes............... 4.10
Postage, extra, each............ .10
6897 **Corelli Works,** library edition. 6 volumes, 12mo., cloth. Complete...............................$3.00

Corelli Works, Avon Edition.

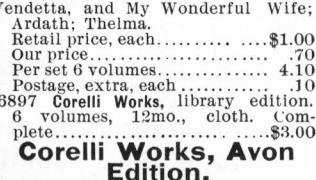

6898 4 volumes, 12mo. A Romance of Two Worlds; Thelma; Vendetta; Wormwood. Cloth, imperial half bound, full gilt back, per set...$0 72

Dumas, Alexander, Works. Series No. 6900.

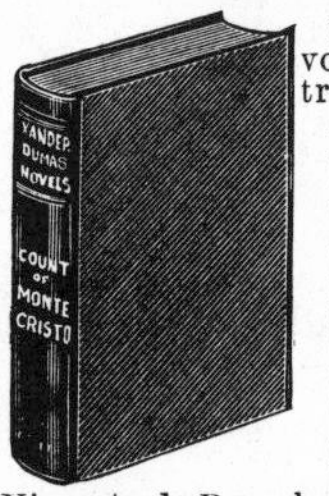

Standard Edition. 15 vols., each volume containing 6 full page illustrations. 12mo., cloth.
The Count of Monte Cristo.
Twenty Years After.
Marguerite de Valois.
Forty-five Guardsmen.
The Regent's Daughter.
Memoirs of a Physician.
Taking the Bastile.
The Queen's Necklace.
The Countess de Charney.
The Three Musketeers.
Chicot, the Jester.
The Conspirators.
Vicomte de Bragelonne. 2 vols. The Chevalier de Maison Rouge.
Per vol.:
Retail price, each, $1.25. Our price, each.....$ 0.88
Per set, cloth:
Retail price, $18.75. Our price 12.00
Half calf:
Retail price 30.00
Our price.. 20.00

Avon Edition. Series 6901.

12mo., cloth, 6 volumes. Sold only in sets.
"The D'Artagnan Romances." The Three Guardsmen.
Twenty Years After. The Vicomte de Bragelonne.
Louise de La Vallerie.
The Man in the Iron Mask. The Son of Porthos.
Cloth, Im. Hf. Bound, full gilt back. Per set.
Retail price.......................................$4.00
Our price.. 1.08
6902 Count of Monte Cristo, 2 vols., 12mo., cloth.
Retail price.. 1.50
Our price .... .75
6903 Same as 6902, cheaper cloth binding......... .48
Postage, 24 cents per set.

Doyle, A. Conan, Works of.

	Retail price.	Our price.
6905—12mo., cloth.		
The White Company, illustrated.....	$1.25	$0.88
The Doings of Raffles Haw, and A Study in Scarlet....................	1.00	.70
The Firm of Girdlestone..............	1.00	.70
Micah Clarke........................	1.00	.70
At the Sign of the Four.............	1.00	.70
My Friend, the Murderer.............	1.00	.70
Adventures of Sherlock Holmes......	1.50	1.05
Sherlock Holmes, 2d series..........	1.50	1.05
The Refugees........................	1.75	1.25
Round the Red Lamp..................	1.50	1.05

Postage, extra, each 12 cents.

Doyle's Works.

6906 Popular Edition, sold only in sets, 5 vols., cloth, gilt.
Firm of Girdlestone. Micah Clarke.
White Company, The. My Friend, the Murderer,
Sign of the Four, and A Study in Scarlet. and Doings of Raffles Haw.
Retail price, $4.50. Our price...... ....$2.50

Dickens, Charles, Works.

6909 New Library Edition, 15 volumes, beautifully illustrated, large type, calendered paper. 12mo., silk cloth, gilt tops. Retail price...15.00
Our price..8.75

Dickens' Works.

6910 New Popular Edition, 15 volumes, large type, 12mo, cloth. Retail price...............$9.00
Our price..5.00
Half calf..14.98

Dickens' Works.

6911 New Columbus Edition, 15 volumes, large type, good paper, 12mo., cloth. Retail price...$5.00
Our price..3.75

Deland, Margaret, Works.

6913 Beautifully bound in cloth, 12mo.
The Old Garden.
John Ward, Preacher.
Sidney (A Novel).
Retail price, each.........................$1.25
Our price..88
Postage, extra.....................................10

Davis, Richard Harding, Works.

6914 Each 12mo., cloth extra.

	Retail price.	Our price.
Our English Cousins	$1.25	$0.88
West From a Car Window	1.25	.88
Rulers of the Mediterranean	1.25	.88
Van Bibber, and others	1.00	.70

Postage, extra, 12 cents each.

Evans, Augusta J., Works. Series 6917.

Almost every one is familiar with this author's writings. The books are all durably bound in cloth, with gold trimmings; size 5½ x 7½; large type and good paper.

Beulah, Inez, Macaria, Retail price, each, $1.75 Our price, $1.28 St. Elmo, Vashti, Infelice. At the Mercy of Tiberius. Retail price. $2.00. Our price.........$1.35
Postage, each..............14

Ely, Prof. R. T., Works.

6918 Labor Movement in America. All 12mo., cloth binding. By Prof. Richhard T. Ely.
Retail price..................................$1.50
Our price..1.05
6919 Problems of To-Day. A Discussion of Tariff, Taxation and Monopolies. By Prof. Richard T. Ely. 12mo. Revised and enlarged edition.
Retail price..................................1.50
Our price..1.05
6920. Social Aspects of Christianity. By Prof. Richard T. Ely. Retail price................90
Our price..65
6921 Taxation in American States and Cities. 12mo.
Retail price..................................1.75
Our price..1.23
Postage, each.....................................12
6922 Socialism and Social Reform. By Prof. Ely. 12mo. Cloth.
Retail price..................................1.50
Our price..1.05
Postage, extra, 12c.

Emerson, R. W., Works.

6923 Two vols., cloth, 12 mo.
Representative Men.
Nature, Addresses and Lectures.
Retail price..................................$2.00
Our price..1.05
Postage..24

Emerson's Essays.

6924 (Ralph Waldo) Printed from new plates on fine laid paper and tastefully bound in uniform style, in two volumes.
Essays, First Series complete.
Essays, Second Series complete.
Per set of two volumes, gilt top............................$0.94
Half calf..1.95
Postage, extra.....................................28

6925 Avon Edition of Emerson's Essays, 2 volumes, cloth.
12 mo...$0.38
Postage..20

Emerson's Complete Works.

6926 Complete works of Ralph Waldo Emerson, with portraits. 12 volumes; 12mo., cloth; gilt top. Price per set..........................$14.60

Emerson's Handy Volumes.

6928 Beautiful 16mo. edition, containing Emerson's Essays, 1st and 2nd volumes and Representative Men, bound in vellum cloth, with gold stampings. 3 volumes in box to match........$0.78
Postage, extra, 22c.

Eliot, George, Works.

6930 New Library Edition. 8 volumes. Illustrated, large type. 12mo., cloth. Gilt tops (complete).
Retail price..................................$8.00
Our price..4.25

Eliot's Works.

6931 New Standard Edition. 8 volumes. Large type. Ornamental, cloth, 12mo. (complete).
Retail price..................................$5.50
Our price..3.00
Half calf..8.00

Eliot's Works.

6932 New Popular Edition. 6 volumes. 12mo.
Cloth...$1.25

Eggleston, Edward, Works. Series 6935.

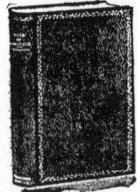

	Retail price.	Our price.
Roxy. Illustrated. 12mo	$1.50	$1.05
The Circuit Rider. Illustrated. 12mo	1.50	1.05
The End of the World. Illustrated. 12mo	1.50	1.05
The Graysons. 12mo	1.50	1.05
The Hoosier Schoolmaster. Illustrated. 12mo	1.25	.88
The Mystery of Metropolisville. Illustrated. 12mo	1.50	1.05
The Hoosier Schoolboy. Illustrated. 12mo	1.00	.70
Queer Stories for Boys and Girls. 12mo	1.00	.70
The Faith Doctor. 12mo	1.50	1.05

Postage, each, extra, 12c.

Ewing (Juliana Horatio) Works. Series 6937.

Six to Sixteen,
A Flat-Iron for a Farthing.
A Great Emergency, and Other Tales.
Mrs. Overtheway's Remembrances and Other Tales.
Jan of the Windmill.
Jacknapes and Other Tales.
We and the World.
Melchoir's Dream.
Lob-Lie-by-the-Fire.
9 vols., 12 mo. Illustrated..........................$2.50
Single volumes, each....$0.30. Postage, each...10

Ellis, Edward S., Works.

6938 Log Cabin Series. By Edward S. Ellis, 3 volumes, 12mo., cloth.
Camp Fire and Wigwam.
Footprints in the Forest.
Lost Trail.
Set of 3 Volumes, ...$2.50
Single volumes, each..........88
6939 Deerfoot Series. By Edward S. Ellis, 3 volumes, 12mo., cloth.
Hunters of the Ozark.
Camp in the Mountains.
The Lost War Trail.
In set of 3 volumes..........$2.50
Single volume, ...88
6940 Boy Pioneer Series. By Edward S. Ellis, 3 volumes, 12mo., cloth,
Ned in the Block House.   Ned in the Woods.
Ned on the River.
In sets of 3 volumes..........$2.50
Single volumes, each..........88
6941 Wildwood Series. By Edward S. Ellis. 12mo., cloth.
Through Forest and Fire. On the Trail of the Moose.
Across Texas.
Per set of 3 volumes..$2.50 Single volumes...$0.88
6942 Wyoming Series. By E. S. Ellis.
Wyoming.   Storm Mountain.
Cabin on the Clearing.
3 volumes, 12 mo., cloth..........................$2.50
Single volumes, each....................88
6944 River and Wilderness Series. By E. S. Ellis.
River Fugitives.   Wilderness Fugitives.
Lena—Wingo the Mohawk.
3 volumes, complete..............................$2.50
Single volumes, each....................88
6945 War Whoop Series. By Lieut. Jayne, (E. S. Ellis).
Lost in the Wilderness.   The Cave in the Mountain.
In the Pecos Country.
Per set of 3 volumes.............................$2.50
Single volumes, each....................88
6946 Great Cattle Trail. By Ed. Ellis. 12mo....$0.88
Postage, extra, on Ellis' books, per vol. 10c.

Ebers, George, Works.

6949 Beautiful cloth binding, printed on super-calendered paper and from new plates.
Homo Sum.   Egyptian Princess.   Uarda.
Joshua.   Bride of the Nile.   Only a Word.
The Emperor.
Sold only in sets of 7 volumes. Retail price....$8.00
Our price.........$6.00 Postage...............72
6950 George Ebers' Works. Popular Edition, 4 volumes, cloth, 12 mo......$2.48 Postage......44

Series 6951.—New Books.

This series is creating a great "hurrah" among readers. Bound in cloth, with silver stampings.
Retail price, each..............................$0.75
Our price, each.......................................52
The Devil's Playground. By John Mackie.
In the Midst of Alarms. By Robt. Barr.
Face and Mask. By ——
Postage, each 08

Elsie, Books, The Series 6952.

By Martha Finley, in 20 volumes, 12mo., cloth.

Elsie Dinsmore.
Elsie's Girlhood.
Elsie's Holiday at Roselands.
Elsie's Womanhood.
Elsie's Motherhood.
Elsie's Children.
Elsie's Widowhood.
Grandmother Elsie.
Elsie Yachting with the Raymonds.
Elsie's Vacation.
Elsie at Viameda.
Elsie's New Relations.
Elsie at Nantucket.
The Two Elsies.
Elsie's Kith and Kin.
Elsie's Friends at Woodburn.
Christmas with Grandma Elsie.
Elsie and the Raymonds.
Elsie at Ion.
Elsie at the World's Fair.
Retail price, each....$1.25   Our price, each....$0.75
Postage..10
Complete set of 20 volumes...................14.50

6953 Quarter Century Edition of the famous Elsie Dinsmore. By Martha Finley. 16mo. Bound in cloth, decorated in ink and silver. A beautiful present for girls.
Retail price.................................$0.75
Our price 35
Postage, extra.............................08

Full Watered Silk Edition. Series 6956.

Consisting of twenty-one volumes of the best works in English and American literature. Beautifully printed on fine paper, and bound in full watered silk, gold stamping, gilt edges, silk headbands, ribbon marker, rich linings. Each of the volumes contain a photogravure and a photogravure title page.
Retail price, per volume, boxed............$1.50
Our price, each............................75
Postage, extra, 10c.

Drummond, Henry.......Greatest Things in the World, and other Addresses.
Eliot, George.....................Ramola. Vol. I.
   "   "   ....Ramola. Vol. II.
   "   "   ....Mill on the Floss. Vol. I.
   "   "   ....Mill on the Floss. Vol. II.
Hawthorne, Nathaniel............Scarlet Letter.
   "   "   ......Mosses from an Old Manse.
   "   "   .....Twice Told Tales. Vol. I.
   "   "   .....Twice Told Tales. Vol. II.
Mulock, Miss..................John Halifax. Vol. I.
Mulock, Miss...............John Halifax. Vol. II.
Sewall, Anna..........................Black Beauty.
St. Pierre, Benardin de ....Paul and Virginia.
Tennyson, Lord.......................The Princess.
Warner, Susan .....Wide, Wide World. Vol. I.
Warner, Susan .....Wide, Wide World. Vol. II.
Yonge, Charlotte M..............Book of Golden Deeds.

Fireside Series for Girls. Series 6958.

A carefully selected series of books for girls, written by authors of acknowledged reputation; will win the hearts of all girl readers.
Retail price, each....$1.00
Our price, each........52
Esther. By Rosa Nouchette Carey. Illustrated.
A World of Girls: The Story of a School. By L. T. Meade. Illustrated.
The Heir of Redcliffe. By Charlotte M. Yonge. Illustrated.
The Story of a Short Life. By Juliana Horatio Ewing. Illustrated.
A Sweet Girl Graduate. By L. T. Meade. Illustrated.
Our Bessie. By Rosa Nouchette Carey. Illustrated.
Six to Sixteen: A Story for Girls. By Juliana Horatio Ewing. Illustrated.
The Dove in the Eagle's Nest. By Charlotte M. Yonge. Illustrated.
Giannetta: A Girl's Story of Herself. By Rosa Mulholland. Illustrated.
Jan of the Windmill: A Story of the Plains. By Juliana Horatio Ewing. Illustrated.

Series No. 6958—Continued.

Averil. By Rosa Nouchette Carey. Illustrated.
Alice in Wonderland and Alice through a Looking Glass. 2 vols. in one. By Lewis Carroll. Illustrated.
Merle's Crusade. By Rosa Nouchette Carey. Illustrated.
Girl Neighbors; or, The Old Fashion and the New. By Sarah Tytler. Illustrated.
Polly: A New Fashioned Girl. By L.T Meade. Illustrated.
Aunt Diana. By Rosa N. Carey. Illustrated.
At the Back of the North Wind. By Geo. McDonald.
A Chaplet of Pearls By Charlotte M. Yonge.
Days of Bruce. By Grace Aguilar.
Water Babies. By Rev. Chas. Kingsley.
Uniform cloth binding.
Retail price, each....$1.00 Our price, each....$0.52
Postage, each extra, 12 cents.

Fleming, May Agnes, Novels. Series 6960.

Guy Earlscourt's Wife.
A Wonderful Woman.
A Terrible Secret.
A Mad Marriage.
Norine's Revenge.
One Night's Mystery.
Kate Danton.
Silent and True.
Maud Percy's Secret.
The Queen of the Isle.
Edith Percival (new).
Heir of Carlton.
Carried by Storm.
Lost for a Woman.
A Wife's Tragedy.
A Changed Heart.
Pride and Passion.
Sharing Her Crime.
A Wronged Wife.
The Actress' Daughter.
The Midnight Queen.

12mo., cloth. Retail price..........$1.50
Our price, each..........$0.98. Postage .... .12

Famous African Explorers and Adventurers.

6961 2 volumes, cloth, 12mo. Per set (2 volumes). $0.75
Postage .... .24

Famous Frontiersmen, Pioneers and Scouts.

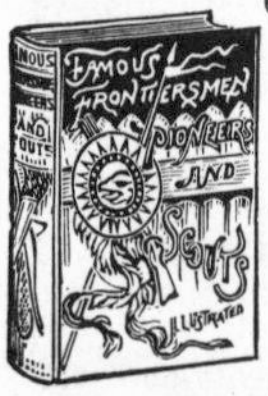

6962 A thrilling narrative of the lives of Boone, Crawford, Gitty, Finney, McCullough, Wetzel, Kenton, Clark, Brady, Crocket, Houston, Carson, California Joe, Wild Bill, Texas Jack, Buffalo Bill and Captain Jack, including Custer's last fight and Cook's recent campaign; 550 pages, illustrated. Bound in cloth, with gold stamps.
Our special price..........$0.75
Postage.......... .20

Finley Books, The. Series 6963.

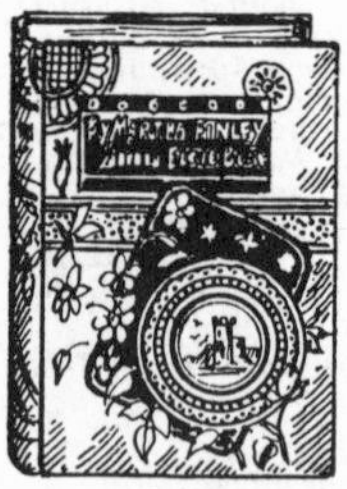

By Martha Finley, 12mo., cloth.

Old Fashioned Boy.
Wanted, a Pedigree.
The Thorn in the Nest.
Signing the Contract.
Casella.
Our Fred.

All are bound in beautiful cloth with gold emblematic title stamps, large print and calendered paper. Retail price.........$1.25
Our price.......... .75
Postage.......... .10

Fielding, Henry, Works.

6965 New Edition of Tom Jones in two Volumes, 1 mo. Cloth. Retail price, $1.50. Our price...$0.75
Postage, 24 cents extra.

Fairmount Series. Series 6968.

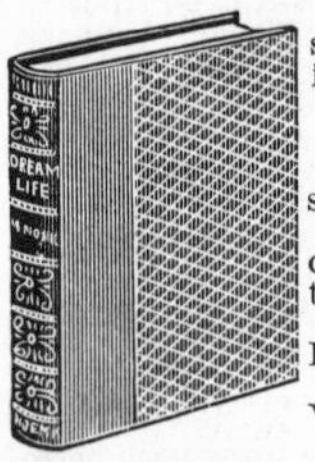

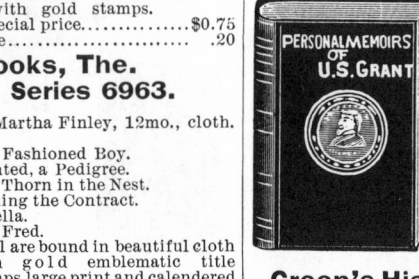

Comprising standard and fast-selling classics, beautifully bound in half Russia.
Retail price, each..........$0.75
Our price, each .... .52
Pleasures of Life, Tales from Shakespeare, Sesame and Lilies.
Bacon's Essays, Thoughts of Marcus Aurelius, Discourses of Epictetus.
Emerson's Essays 1st, Emerson's Essays 2nd, Representative Men.
Cranford, Reveries of a Bachelor, Vicar of Wakefield.
Dream of Life, Scarlet Letter, House of Seven Gables.
Sartor Resartus, Chesterfield's Letters, Heroes and Hero Worship. Postage, each..........$0.08

Golden Gleams of Thought.

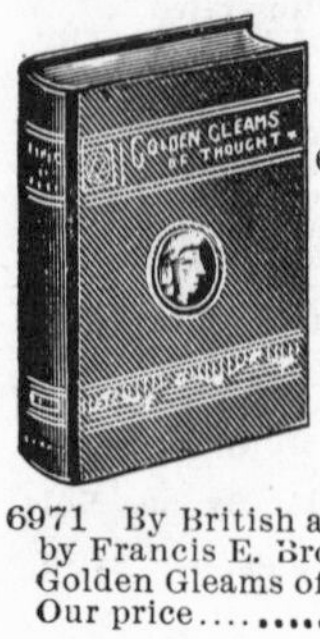

6970 Thoughts from the Words of Leading Orators, Divines, Philosophers, Statesmen and Poets. By Rev. S. P. Linn. Handsomely bound in silk cloth with gold edges. Retail price..........$1.50
Our price.......... 1.05
Postage, 14c. extra.

Golden Poems.

6971 By British and American authors, edited by Francis E. Browne Uniform binding with Golden Gleams of Thought. Retail price.......$1.50
Our price.......... 1.05

Grote's Greece.

6972 4 vols., silk cloth binding, new plates, large print, calender paper. Retail price.......$6.00
Our price.......... 3.00
Half calf binding.......... 3.98
Postage.......... .66

Goethe, J. W. Von, Works of.

6973 5 vols. Illustrated, 12mo., cloth, gilt top..$5.00
5 vols. Illustrated., 12mo., half calf, gilt top.... 7.50

I. Autobiography of Goethe.
II. Wilhelm Meister's Apprenticeship and Travels.
III. Elective Affinities, Sorrows of Werther, Travels in Italy, etc.
IV. Faust and Dramatic Works.
V. Poems of Goethe, Phigenia, Torguato Tasso, etc.

Guizot's France.

6974 8 vols., cloth (best edition). Retail price.$12.00
Our price.......... 6.25
Half calf binding.......... 7.95
Postage.......... .96

Guizot's England.

6976 4 vols. Retail price..........$6.50
Our price.......... 3.00
Half calf binding.......... 4.20
Postage.......... .55

Greenwood, Grace, Works.

6977 These works are handsomely bound and illustrated, 12mo., cloth. "Stories of My Childhood." "History of My Pets."
Retail price, each....$1.50 Our price, each.... .75
Postage, each.......... .10

Goethe's William Meister.

6978 2 volumes; cloth. 12mo.
Per set, 2 volumes..........$1.50
Postage.......... .24

Goethe's Faust and Dramatic Works.

6980 2 volumes; cloth. 12mo.
Per set, 2 volumes..........$1.50
Postage.......... .24

Grant and His Travels.

6981 2 volumes; cloth, 12mo. Per set (2 vols)....$0.75
Postage.......... .24

Grant's Memoirs. 2 Vols.

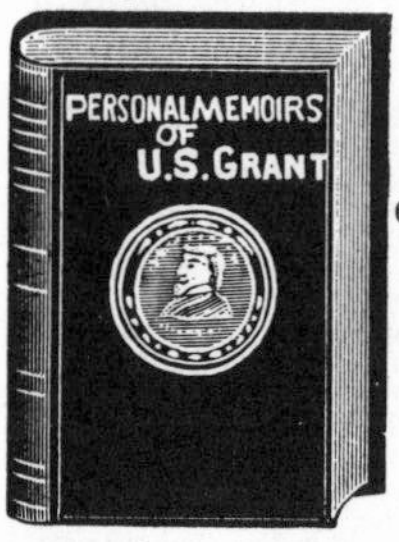

ORIGINAL EDITION.

6982 Personal Memoirs of U. S. Grant, with portraits, maps, etc., 2 volumes, 1,231 pages. Cloth and gilt.
Subscription price......$7.00
Our price.......... 3.25
Postage, 50 cents extra.
Subscription price in sheep, library binding..10.00
Our price.......... 4.50
Postage, 50c. extra.

Green's History of the English People.

Please note that we do not sell less than a full set.
6984 History of the English People. By John Richard Green. Printed from new plates, large clear type. 5 volumes, large 12mo., cloth.
Publishers' price..........$6.00
Our price.......... 2.00
Half calf, 5 vols.......... 4.95
Postage.......... .48

Short History of the English People.

6985 By John R. Green, with colored maps and tables. 12mo., cloth..........$1.05
Postage, extra.......... .10

Gibbon's Roman Empire.

6986 History of the Decline and Fall of the Roman Empire. By Edward Gibbon. With Dean Milman's notes complete. New edition, containing over 2,000 pages. 6 Volumes, 12mo., cloth $2.50
6 Volumes. 12mo., half calf.......... 6.00
6987 **Gibbon's Roman Empire.** new vellum cloth edition, gilt tops, 5 volumes, large type........ 2.15
6989 **Popular Edition.** Gibbons Roman Empire. 5 volumes, 12mo., cloth.... .. .. 1.75

Hawthorne, Nathaniel, Works.

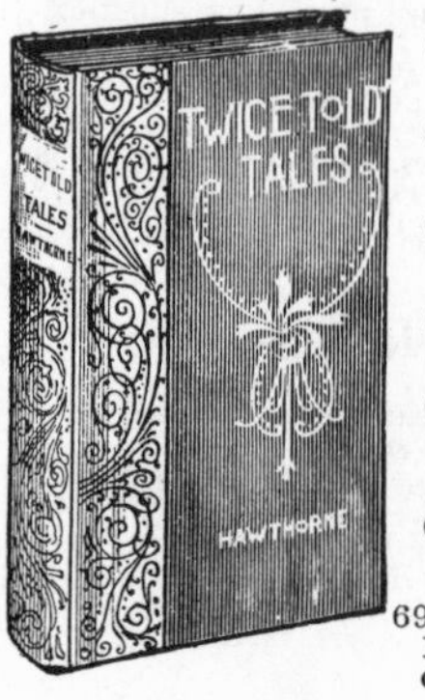

Price.
6991 **Scarlet Letter.** 16mo., cloth, red and white..........$0.22
6992 **House of the Seven Gables.** 16mo., red and white cloth.......... .22
6993 **A Wonder-book for Girls and Boys.** 16mo., red and white cloth. .22
6994 **Mosses From an Old Manse.** 16mo., red and white cloth. .22
6995 **The Snow Image, and Other Twice Told Tales.** 16mo., red and white cloth.......... .22
6996 **Twice Told Tales.** 16mo., red and white cloth.......... .22
6997 **Blithdale Romances,** 16mo., red and white cloth.......... .22

Books—Continued.

6998 **Marble Faun,** By Nathanial Hawthorne 12mo., cloth, gilt top.
Retail price..........$2.00 Our price.......... 1.45
Postage, 12 cents extra.
6999 **Hawthorne's Works.** 12mo., cloth, library style, 5 volumes. Retail price.......... 3.00
Our price, per set of 5 volumes.......... 1.75
Postage, extra.......... .65

Marble Faun.

7000 Beautiful 2 volume holiday edition of Marble Faun, by Hawthorne. Retail price......$6.00
Our price.......... 4.35
Postage, 24 cents extra.

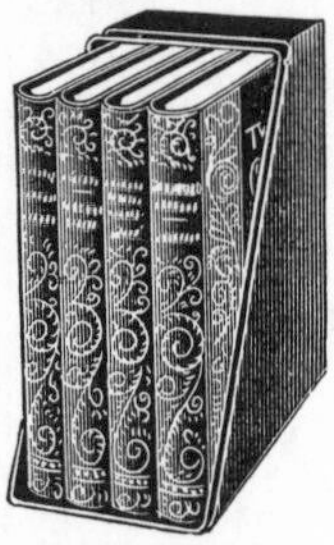

Hawthorne's Works.

7001 New Beautiful 16mo. presentation edition, containing Scarlet Letter, Twice Told Tales, Mosses from and Old Manse and House of the Seven Gables. Red and white vellum cloth with box to match.
Per set of volumes......$0.98
Postage, extra 30 cents.

Habberton, John, Works.

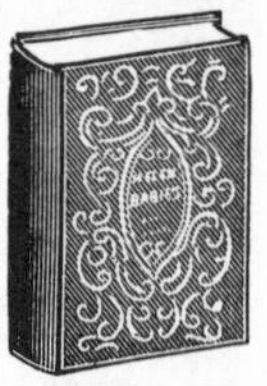

7002 **Helen's Babies,** by Jno. Habberton. Cloth, 16mo., new edition. Retail price $0.75
Our price.......... .30
Postage, extra.......... .09

Holmes' Mrs. Mary J., Novels. Series 7005.

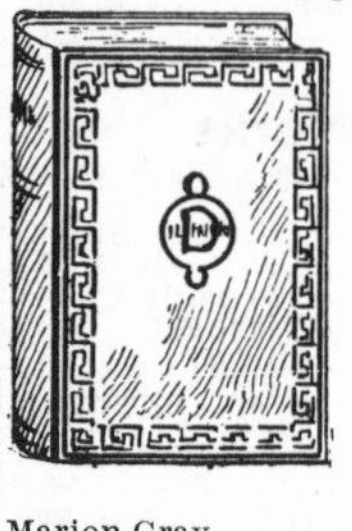

Daisy Thornton.
Chateau D'Or.
Darkness and Daylight.
Hugh Worthington.
Cameron Pride.
Rose Mather.
Ethelyn's Mistake.
Millbank.
Edna Browning.
West Lawn.
Mildred.
Forest House.
Madeline.
Marguerite (New).
Homestead on the Hillside.
Lena Rivers.
Cousin Maude.
Meadow Brook.
Dora Dean.
Gretchen (New).
Christmas Stories.
Marion Gray
Edith Lyle.
Queenie Hetherton.
Bessie's Fortune (New).
English Orphans.
Tempest and Sunshine.

Retail price, each..........$1.50
Our price, each........$0.98. Postage.......... .12

Harland, Marion, Works. Series 7006.

Alone.
Nemesis.
Ruby's Husband.
Phemie's T'mpt'n.
Helen Gardner.
Husbands and Homes
Hidden Path.
Miriam.
At Last.
The Empty Heart.
Jessamine
Moss Side.
Sunny Bank.
My Little Love.
From My Youth Up.
True as Steel.

Retail price, per volume..........$1.50
Our price " " .... .98

Holland, Dr. J. C., Complete Works. Series 7007.

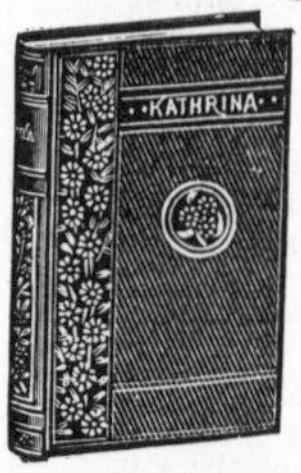

New edition with the author's latest revisions. In 16 volumes.
The Mistress of the Manse.
Puritan's Guests, and other Poems.
Titcomb's Letters to Young People.
Plain Talks on Family Subjects.
Concerning the Jones Family.
Every Day Topics (Second Series).
Seven Oaks.
Lessons in Life.
Kathrina.
Gold Foil.
Miss Gilbert's Career.
The Bay Path.
Arthur Bonnicastle.
Bitter Sweet.
Every Day Topics. (First Series.)
Nicholas Minturn.

Bound in English cloth, small 12mo. Sold in separate volumes, at..........$0.88
Or in sets of 16 volumes..........13.75
Postage, per volume, extra.......... .10

Holland's Poetical Works.

7008 **The Complete Poetical Writings** of Dr. J. G. Holland. With illustrations by C. S. Reinhart, C. C. Griswold, and Mary Hallock Foote, and a portrait by Wyatt Eaton. From new stereotype plates. 8vo., handsome cloth binding.
Retail price..........$3 50
Our price..........$2.58. Postage, 14 cents extra.

Harris' Works of Miriam Coles.

Series 7009.

Rutledge.
The Sutherlands.
A Perfect Adonis
Phœbe.
St. Phillips.
Happy-go-Lucky.
Frank Warrington.
Missy.
Rich Vandermarck.
Retail price..............$1.25
Our price............ .88
Postage, extra........... .10

Holland.

7010 A new book by Edmondo de Amics, printed from new electrotype plates. Carefully printed, illustrated with 44 photogravure illustrations and map. Two volumes, ornamental cloth, gilt tops. Retail price.......................$5.00
Our price................................... 3.50
Postage, extra............................ .28

Hale, Edward E., Works.
Series 7011.

All beautifully bound in English silk cloth, with gold title stamps.
Cloth, 16mo.
Stories of War.
Stories of Adventure.
Stories of Invention.
Stories of Sea.
Stories of Discovery.
Retail price...................$1.00
Our price.............. .70
Postage, 8c.

7012 Hale's Works Continued; all nicely bound and printed. Cloth, 12mos.:
A Man Without a Country.   His Level Best.
What Career.   In His Name.
Christmas Eve and Christ-
mas Day.
Retail price..................................$1.25
Our price, each................................. .88
Postage, each.................................. .10

Holmes, Oliver Wendell, Works.
Series 7013.

New Riverside edition, with portraits and notes.
Cloth, gilt tops.
Autocrat at the Breakfast   Mortal Antipathy.
Table.   Pages from an Old Vol-
Professor at the Breakfast   ume in Life.
Table.   Medical Essays.
Poet at the Breakfast Ta-   One Hundred Days in Eu-
ble.   rope.
Over the Tea Cups.   Guardian Angel.
Elsie Venner.
Retail price.........................$1.50
Our price........................... 1.05
Postage, extra....................... .12

Autocrat at the Breakfast Table.

7014 New popular edition by Oliver Wendell Holmes, containing also many of his favorite poems. Cloth. 12 mo. Gilt top.
Retail price.............................$1.00
Our price............................... .52
Postage, extra, 12 cents.

Howell's, Wm. D., Works.
Series No. 7016.

Venetian Life.   Suburban Sketches.
Italian Journeys.   Lady of Aroostock.
Chance Acquaintance.   The Undiscovered Coun-
A Foregone Conclusion.   try.
Indian Summer.   The Minister's Charge.
Rise of Silas Lapham.   A Fearful Responsibility
A Woman's Reason.   Dr. Breen's Practice.
Their Wedding Journey.
Each 12mo., cloth. Retail price.............. $1.50
Our price.............................. 1.05
Postage, 12 cents.

Hume's History of England.

7017 From the invasion of Julius Cæsar to the abdication of James the Second, 1688. By David Hume. Best edition, new; 5 volumes, 12mo., cloth; extra. Per set, $2.00. ½ calf, per set..$5.95

Harte, Bret, Latest Work.
Series 7018.

Handsomely bound in cloth, 12mo.
Cressy.
Heritage of Deadlow Marsh
Luck of Roaring Camp.
Tales of the Argonauts.
Ward of the Golden Gate.
Sappho of Green Springs.
First Family of Tasajera.
Mrs. Skagg's Husband.
Retail price $1.25
Our price, each.............. .88
Postage, extra................ .10

Other Harte Books.
Series 7019.

Story of a Mine.   Drift from Two Shores.
     A Law unto Herself.
Retail price, $1.00. Our price....................$0.70
Postage, extra .... .12

Howard, Blanche Willis, Works.

7021 Beautifully bound in cloth, 12mo.
One Summer.   One Year Abroad.
Aunt Serena.   A Fellow and His Wife.
Retail price, each $1.25. Our price............. $0.88

Other Howard Books.

7022 The Open Door.   Aulnay Tower.
Retail price, $1.50. Our price....................$1.05

Histories of the Old World.

7024 A series of popular histories. Each 1 vol., 8vo., with frontispiece. Cloth extra.
Italy.   Russia.
Austria.   Prussia.
     By John S. C. Abbott.
Turkey, by Edson L.   Egypt, by J. C. McCoan.
Clarke.   Germany, by Baring-
     Gould.
Retail price, each, $1.50. Our price, each......$0.90
Postage, 12 cents each. extra.

Hugo, Victor, Novels.

7027 Cloth binding. Fully illus-
trated.
Les Miserables.
Ninety Three.
Toilers of the Sea.
Notre Dame.
By Order of the King.
Hi tory of a Crime.
Retail price, each..............$1.25
Our price, each................. .75
Postage, each.................. .12
Complete set of 6 vols........ 4.40

7028 Les Miserables, By Victor Hugo; 2 vol. Cloth $0.75
Postage...................... .24
7029 Les Miserables, Fine Avon edition, 5 volumes, cloth...... .98
Postage...................... .38

Hughes, Thomas, Works.

7030 Set containing Tom Brown's Schooldays and Tom Brown at Oxford; 2 vols., cloth.
Retail price, per set........................$1.50
Our price................................. .75
7031 Two vols., half calf.................. 1.98
7032 Same as 7030, Avon edition; 12mo. Cloth, 2 vols .... .38
Postage, per set, 22c extra.

Heavenly Twins, The.

7034 By Sarah Grand. In one large 12mo. volume of nearly 700 pages. Extra cloth, laid paper.
"Mme Grand is concerned sim-
ply to make earth more habitable and life better worth living—especially for women...She does use plain lan-
guage, and a good deal of it; but everybody knows that the offenses which rouse her wrath are by no means products of her imagination."
Retail price $1.00. Our price $0.70
Postage .... .12
Paper cover................... .32
Postage .... .05

Holly, Marietta, Works.
Series 7035.

Too much cannot be said of this author's humorous writings. "Will drive the blues out of a bag of indigo." All are handsomely bound in English silk cloth, with gold title stamps, and contain numerous illustrations.

	Retail price.	Our price.
Samantha at the World's Fair	$2.50	$1.95
Samantha at the Centennial	2.50	1.45
My Opinions, and Betsy Bobbitt's	2.50	1.45
Small Edition	1.00	.70
My Wayward Pardner	2.50	1.45
Sweet Cicely	2.00	1.32
Samantha at Saratoga	1.75	.98
Small Edition	.50	.35
Samantha among the Colored Folks	1.50	1.05
Samantha Among the Brethren	2.50	1.45

N. B.—All $1.45 books mail at 26c., and 75c. and 98c. ones at 12c.

Irving, Washington, Works.

7038 The Alhambra. Beautifully illustrated with a photogravure frontispiece and 16 fine half-tone plates from special photographs. Exquisitely bound with rich Moorish decorations on side and back in gold and colors; handsomely covered and boxed.
One volume, octavo, gilt top, parti-colored cloth. Retail price $2.00. Our price............$1.40
7039 The Conquest of Granada. Uni-
form with above............$1.40
7040 The set, two volumes. Alhambra and Granada.....$2.70
Postage, each, extra, 16 cents.

7042 Irving's Works. Standard Edition, 9 volumes, large type, printed on calendered paper, illustrated, 12mo. silk cloth, gilt tops $6.00
Half calf, gilt tops............................... 9.00
7044 Popular Edition Irving's Works. 8 volumes complete, 12mo., cloth............................ 4.00
7045 Rugby Edition. Irving's works, 6 volumes, Without the Life of Washington. 12mo., cloth. 2.44
7046 Irving's Life and Voyages of Columbus. 2 vol-
umes, cloth, 12mo................................ .75
7047 Irving's Life of Washington. 2 volumes, 12mo., cloth.. .75

New Ingersoll Library.

By Robt. G. Inger-
soll.

Series 7050.

	Retail price.	Our price.
Ingersoll's Complete Lectures, 8vo., ½ calf	$5.00	$3.50
Ingersoll's Forty-four Lectures, 12mo., cloth	1.00	.70
Ingersoll's Prose Poems, 12mo., cloth	2.50	1.75
Ingersoll's Gods,12mo., cloth	1.00	.70
Ingersoll's Ghosts, 12mo., cloth	1.00	.70
Ingersoll's Moses, 12mo., cloth	1.00	.70
Ingersoll's Interviews, 12mo., cloth	1.00	.70
Ingersoll's Mistakes, 12mo., cloth	1.00	.70
Ingersoll's Wit, Wisdom and Eloquence 12mo., cloth	.75	.50
Ingersoll's Great Speeches 12mo., cloth	.75	.50

Postage, each, extra 12c., except on Complete Lectures, for which add 40c.

Ireland.

7052 Its history, scenery, people, etc., ancient abbeys, towers, castles and other romantic features; a grand descriptive and historical work with over 500 illus-
trations, 1,400 pages. Ev-
ery Irishman should have this book as well as others.
Retail price...........$3.75
Our price............ 1.75
Postage, each......... .50

Jackson, Helen, Works.
Series 7055.

"Ramona," handsomely bound in English silk cloth with gold emblematic title stamps, 12mo., cloth
Retail price..............$1.50
Our price................ 1.00
Postage, extra............ .10

	Retail price.	Our price.
Verses	$1.00	$0.70
Sonnets and Lyric	1.00	.75
A Calender of Sonnets	2.00	1.45
Complete Poems	1.50	1.05
Bits of Travel	1.25	.88
Bits of Travel at Home	1.50	1.05
Bits of Talk about Home Matters	1.00	.70
Bits of Talk in Verse and Prose, for Young People	1.00	.75
Nelly's Silver Mine	1.50	1.05
Mercy Philbrick's Choice	1.00	.75
Hetty's Strange History	1.00	.75
A Century of Dishonor	1.50	1.05
Zeph	1.25	.88
Glimpse of Three Coats	1.50	1.05

Postage, each, 10c.

Josephus' Works.

7056 3 vols., printed on fine calendered paper, from new plates. Bound in fine cloth.
Retail price.........$3.00 | Our price.........$1.75
½ calf, retail price... 5.00 | Our price......... 3.00
Postage.................................... .45

7057 "Josephus." Complete works of Flavius Josephus, the celebrated Jewish historian. Comprising the history and antiquaries of Jews, with the destruction of Jerusalem by Romans.
8vo., cloth......................$1.20
Full sheep................... 1.60
Full morocco............... 1.50
Padded binding............. 1.80
Postage..................... .36

Keightley, Thomas, Works.

7060 History of England from the earliest period to the present time. Illustrated. 2 volumes, 12mo.
Cloth...$0.70
7061 History of Greece, with maps, 2 volumes, 12mo., cloth.......... .70
7062 History of Rome, 2 volumes, 12mo., cloth.... .70
Postage, per set, 32c. extra.

Kipling's, Rudyard, Works.

7064 7 vols., 12mo., cloth, gilt top...............$6.00
7 vols., 12mo., half calf, gilt top................. 9.75
Also separately, in cloth, elegant gilt top, per volume....................................... .88

Departmental Ditties, Barrack Room Ballads, and Other Verses.
Plain Tales From the Hills.
Soldiers Three, and in Black and White.
The Phantom Rickshaw, and Wee Willie Winkle.
The Light That Failed.
The Story of The Gadsbys.
Mine Own People. Including Dinah Shadd and Other Stories.
Postage, each 10c.

The Jungle Book.

7067 A new book by Rudyard Kipling, 12 mo., cloth. Retail price.................$1.50
Our price..................................... 1.05
Postage, extra...................................... .12

King, Capt. Chas., Novels. Series 7068.

12mo. Cloth.
The Colonel's Daughter.
Between the Lines.
Marion's Fate.
Capt. Blake.
Foes in Ambush.
Campaigning with Crook.
Colonel's Xmas Dinner.
Cadet Days.
Under Fire.
Retail price, each.........$1.25
Our price, each............ .88
Postage, each................ .12

Other King Books. Series 7069.

A War-time Wooing.
Kitty's Conquest.
Laramie.
Starlight Ranch.
The Deserter from the Ranks.
Two Soldiers, etc.
Waring's Peril.
An Initial Experience.
Retail price....................................$1.00
Our price....................................... .70
Postage, each...................... .12

Kingsley, Rev. Chas., Works.

7070 8 vols., containing Alton Locke, Yeast, Hereward, Two Years Ago. Heroes and Poets, Westward Ho, Water Babies, Hypatia. Sold only in sets. Retail price, $8.00. Our price.........$4.80
Postage... .98

Knight's Half Hours with the Best Authors.

7071 With Biographical and Critical Notes, by Charles Knight. New edition; handsomely bound in cloth; gilt top; finely illustrated.
4 vols., retail price $4.00 | Our price.....$2.50
½ Russia, retail " 6.00 | Our price............. 3.25
Postage.. .42
7072 Large 8vo., 3 vol. edition, cloth........... 2.10
Postage.. .50

Knight's History of England.

7073 New Standard Edition; large type, illustrated, 9 volumes, 12 mo., cloth, gilt top.
Retail price...$9.00
Our price... 6.75

CATALOGUE No. 58

Will be issued about September 1st, 1895.
Send 15 cents for postage.

Lincoln's Stories and Speeches.

7076 Including early life stories, professional stories, White House incidents, war stories, etc. Also his speeches chronologically arranged from 1832 to his last speech in Washington, April 11, 1865, etc. Illustrated. 16mo., cloth. Retail price........................$1.00
Our price........................ .70
Postage, extra, 14 cents.

Lamb's Essays.

7078 Lamb's Essays, standard edition, 2 vols., 12mo, cloth..................................$0.85
Half calf.................................... 2.00
Postage....................................... .26

Lamb's Essays.

7079 2 vols., cloth, 12mo., in a box containing 1st and 2d essays of Elia. Retail price......... .75
Our price, per set.................... .38
Postage.................................. .22

Lamb's Works.

7080 The complete Standard Edition of Charles Lamb's works, edited, with life, etc., by Sir Thomas N. Talford, corrected and revised with portrait. The most elegant edition published; bound in uniform cloth, 3 volumes, octavo. Price reduced from $7.50
Per set, only........................ 3.00
Postage................................. .45

Lytton, Lord Bulwer, Works.

7082 The complete works of this favorite author. Very nicely printed, desirably bound. Gilt tops; illustrated. 13 vols. Retail price.. 12.00
Our price............................... 7.50
Half calf binding......................... 13.00
7083 Bulwer Lytton's Works, popular edition, 13 vols., cloth................................. 3.75

Lowell, James Russell, Works.

7084 Cloth, 12mo., 3 vols.
Among my Books, 1st series.
Among my books, 2d series.
My Study Windows.
Retail price, each..................................$2 00
Our price................................... 1.45
Per set, 3 vols........................... 4.20
Postage, each volume, extra..................... .14

Longfellow, Henry W., Works.

7085 Outre Mer. a pilgrimage beyond the sea 16mo., white and green cloth. Each...$0.22
7086 Hyperion. A romance. 16 mo., green and white cloth. Each................. .22
Postage, each................ .08

Evangeline.

7087 A tale of Arcadia, by Henry W. Longfellow, illustrated Presentation edition. Red and white cloth. Retail price, 40 cents. Our price, .22
Postage, extra..................................... .07

Lyall, Edna, Works.

7090 Complete in 7 vols., 12 mo., cloth, in a box (large type). Standard Edition.
Won by Waiting.   In the Golden Days.
Donovan.   A Hardy Norseman.
We Two   Max Hereford's Dream.
Knight Errant.   Derrick Vaughan, Novelist.
Autobiography of a Slander.
12 mo., cloth, 7 volumes..........................$3.00
Half calf..10.00
7091 Popular Edition Edna Lyall's Works.
6 volumes, cloth, gilt tops.......................$2.08
Half calf... 5.50
7092 Avon Edition Edna Lyall's works, 6 volumes, 12mo., cloth............................. 1.08

Library of Travel and Adventure. Series 7094.

Octavo volumes, richly illustrated.
Ran Away From the Dutch. From the Dutch of Perelaer. With ten full-page illustrations. Octavo, cloth.
The Wild Tribes of the Soudan. By F. L. James, with many full-page illustrations. Octavo, cloth.
Golden Days of '49. A tale of California Diggings. By Kirke Monroe. Illustrated. Octavo, cloth. Postage, each 14 cents extra.
Price, each.......................................$0.98

Lossing, Benson J. Works.

7095 New edition of Eminent Americans; 2 volumes, 12mo., cloth. Retail price.................$1.50
Our price.. .75
Postage, extra, 26 cents.

Macaulay, Thomas B., Works.

7098 Macaulay's Speeches. 2 volumes, containing the complete speeches of the noted historian. 12mo., cloth...................................$0.75
Postage, extra..................................... .24

Macaulay's History of England. Standard Edition.

7099 The History of England from the accession of James the II. Library edition. calendered paper, large type, 5 vols. Gilt tops $1.75
Same bound in ½ calf. 5.00

Popular Edition.

7100 Macaulay's History of England, popular edition. 5 vols., cloth.........$0.98
Postage, per set........ .48

Macaulay's Essays and Poems.

Critical and Miscellaneous Essays and Poems. Fine large type, new electrotype plates, printed on good paper.
7101 Three volumes. 12mo., cloth, gilt. (Publisher's price, $2.50.)
Our price.......................................$1 10
The same bound in half calf.................... 3.00
Postage.. .37

McCarthy's History of Our Own Times.

7103 The only edition with index. By Justin McCarthy. Printed from new plates on fine paper. Large clear type, with complete index; foot notes; revised and brought down to date. Retail price............$4.00
Our price.. 2.10
7104 Four volumes in two; cloth. Standard edition. Our price, per set........................$1.20
The same bound in half calf....... .... 2.10
Postage, per set................................... .28

Miller, Joaquin, Works. Series 7106.

New and revised edition of Songs of the Sierras, by Joaquin Miller. 12mo., cloth. Retail $1.50
Our price, each................ 1.05
Postage...................... .10
New and revised edition of Songs of Summer Lands, by Joaquin Miller, 12mo., cloth.
Retail price................... 1.50
Our price, each.............. 1.05
Postage........................ .10
In Classic Shades, by Joaquin Miller. 12mo., cloth...... 1.05
Postage......................... .10

Marryatt's Popular Tales. Series 7108.

Beautiful illustrated edition, handsomely bound in English silk cloth.
The King's Own.   Frank Mildway.
Masterman Ready.   Little Savage.
Peter Simple.   Olla P, drida.
Newton Forster.   Valerie.
The Mission.   Settlers in Canada.
Monsier Violet.   Pirate and Three Cutters.
The Dog Fiend.   Rattlin the Reefer.
Percival Keene.   Jacob Faithful.
Phantom Ship.   Pacha of Many Tales,
Poor Jack.   Children of the New
Japhet in Search of a   Forest.
Father.   The Privateersman.
The Poacher.   Midshipman Easy.
Retail price.........$1.00 Our price, each......$0.70
Postage, extra..................................... 10

Morley, John, Works.

7109 English Men of Letters, 2 volumes, 12mo., cloth...........$1.00 Postage, 24c. extra.

McClellan's Own Story.

7110 The War for the Union, the soldiers who fought it, etc., by Geo. B. McClellan.
Retail price.......................................$3.75
Our price.. 2.25
Postage, extra..................................... .26

Mulock, Miss, Works. Series 7114.

Library edition. Illustrated. 12mo.
My Mother and I.   A Noble Life.
Hannah.   A Hero.
Olive.   The Fairy Book.
Ogilvies.   Studies from Life.
A Brave Lady.   Sermons Out of Church.
Woman's Kingdom.   The Laurel Bush.
Mistress and Maid.   A Legacy.
Unkind Word, etc.   Young Mrs. Jardine.
Head of the Family.   His Little Mother, etc.
John Halifax.   Plain Speaking.
Agatha's Husband.   Miss Tommy.
A Life for a Life.   King Arthur.
Two Marriages.   About Money, etc.
   Christian's Mistake.
Per vol.: Retail price....$0.90 Our price $0.65
Postage, each, extra...... .10

INSURE YOUR PACKAGES. Mail packages may be insured against loss by paying a fee of 5 cents for each $5.00 in value. Write "Insured Mail" on your order, enclose the money, and we will do the rest.

Mildred Books.
Series 7115.

A companion to the Elsie books.

By Martha Finley.

Mildred Keith.
Mildred at Roselands.
Mildred's Married Life.
Mildred and Elsie,
Mildred at Home.
Mildred's Boys and Girls.
Handsomely bound in English silk cloth with gold title stamps, calendered paper and large print.
Retail price, each......$1.25
Our price, each......... .75
Postage................ .10

Mitchell, Donald G., Works.

7116 Reveries of a Bachelor. No American writer since the days of Irving uses the English language as "Ik. Marvel." Handsomely bound in cloth in colors.
Retail price................$0.50
Our price.................. .22
Postage................... .08
7117 Dream Life. By Donald G. Mitchell. Same binding as above.
Each.........................$0.22
Postage.................... .08

Mill on Liberty.

7118 On Liberty, by John Stuart Mill, should be read by every man, woman and child who has intelligence enough to know the real meaning of the word "liberty." One volume, plain type, bound in fine cloth...........................$0.52
7119 Independent Treasury System of the United States. By David Kinley, A. B., assistant and Fellow in Economics in the University of Wisconsin. 12mo. Cloth. Retail price.................... 1.50
Our price........$1.05 Postage, 12 cents extra.
7120 Repudiation of State Debts in the United States. By William A. Scott, Ph. D., Assistant Professor of Political Economy in the University of Wisconsin. 12mo. Cloth.
Retail price........$1.50 Our price.......... 1.05
Postage, 12 cents extra.

McDonald, George, Works.
Series 7121.

With illustrations on wood and steel. Being the first collected uniform edition of the author's writings; 23 vols., 12mo., cloth.

Annals of a Quiet Neighborhood.
The Seaboard Parish.
Guild Court.
Alec Forbes of Howglen.
Robert Falconer.
The Vicar's Daughter.
Paul Faber, Surgeon.
Thomas Wingfold, Curate.
Wilfred Cumbermede.
Sir Gibbie.
St. George and St. Michael.
What's Mine's Mine.

Phantastes.
The Portant.
David Elginbrod.
Adela Cathcart.
Malcolm.
The Marquis of Lossie.
Warlock o' Glenwarlock.
Mary Marston.
Weighed and Wanting.
Donal Grant.
Stephen Archer.
There and Back.

Retail price, each....$1.50 Our price $0.95
Postage, extra........ .12

Napoleon Bonaparte, Memoirs of.

7123 By Bourrienne, his private secretary; to which are added an account of the important events of the hundred days of Napoleon's surrender to the English, and of his residence and death at St. Helena. Beautifully bound and illustrated. 4 vols. Cloth. Retail price.......$5.00
Our price... 3.45
Postage, 50 cents extra.

Napoleon Bonaparte.

7125 By Jno. S. C. Abbott; illustrated maps and portraits on steel, 2 volumes, 8 vo.
Retail price.......................................$7.00
Our price.. 5.00

Oliver Optic's Standard Books.

All of the following series are handsomely bound in cloth, 12mo. and illustrated.

7126 Blue and Gray Series.
Taken by the Enemy.
A Victorious Union.
Stand by the Union.
Fighting for the Right.
On the Blockade.
Within the Enemy's Lines.
6 volumes, per set.........$5.85
Each, per volume .... .98
7127 Army and Navy Series.
Soldier Boy.
Sailor Boy.
Young Lieutenant.
Brave Old Salt.
Yankee Middy.
Fighting Joe.
6 volumes, cloth............ 5.85
Single volume, each........ .98
7128 Yacht Club Series
Little Bobtail.
Dorcas Club.
Coming Wave.
Money Makers.
Yacht Club.
Ocean Born.
6 volumes, cloth................... 5.85
Single volumes, each.............. .98

Books—Continued.

7130 Young America Abroad Series.
Dikes and Ditches.
Outward Bound.
Red Cross.
Down the Rhine.
Palace and Cottage.
Shamrock and Thistle.
6 volumes complete.............................. 5.85
Single volumes, each............................ .98
7131 Young America Abroad, 2d Series.
Cross and Crescent.
Isles of the Seas.
Northern Lands.
Sunny Shores.
Up the Baltic.
Vine and Olive.
6 volumes complete, per set...................... 5.85
Single volumes, each............................ .98
7132 All Over the World Series.
A Missing Million.
A Young Knight Errant.
A Millionaire at Sixteen.
Strange Sights Abroad.
4 volumes complete............................. 3.40
Single volumes, each........................... .87
Postage on any Optic Book, 12 cents each extra.

Paine, Thomas, Works.

7135 Age of Reason.
12mo., cloth..$0.40
Paper......, ... .16
Postage 4 and 10c.
7136 Rights of Man.
12mo., cloth $0.40
Paper covers .16
7137 Theological Works of Thos. Paine, containing Age of Reason, Examination of the Prophecies, Letters to Bishop Llandoff, etc., 12mo., cloth.
Retail price..$1.50
Our price...... .75
Postage........ .12
7138 Political Works Complete, Containing Rights of Man, Common Sense and the Crisis. Cloth, 12mo.
Retail price..$1.50
Our price...... .75
Postage........ .12

7139 Life of Thomas Paine. New edition complete. 12 mo., cloth. Retail price...... ...... .75
Our price.. .52
Postage.. .10

Pansy Books.
Series 7140.

Among the substantial reasons of the great popularity of the "Pansy Books" is their truth to nature and to life. All are handsomely bound in English silk cloth with gold embossed title stamps, and contain large bold type and calendered paper.

Aunt Hannah, Martha and John.
Chautauqua Girls at Home.
Christie's Christmas.
Crissy's Endeavor.
Divers Women.
Echoing and Re-echoing.
Eighty-Seven.
Endless Chain (An).
Ester Ried.
Modern Prophet.
Man of the House.
New Graft on the Family Tree (A).
One Commonplace Day.
Pocket Measure (The).
Profiles.
Ruth Erskine's Crosses.
Randolphs (The).
Sevenfold Trouble (A).
Sidney Martin's Christmas.
Spun from Fact.
Stephen Mitchell's Journey.
Those Boys.
Three People.
Tip Lewis and His Lamp.
Twenty Minutes Late.
Wise and Otherwise.
Wanted.
Ester Ried Yet Speaking.
Four Girls at Chautauqua.
From Different Standpoints
Hall in the Grove (The).
Her Associate Members.
Household Puzzle.
Interrupted.
John Remington, Martyr.
Judge Burnham's Daughters.
Julia Ried.
King's Daughter (The).
Little Fishers and Their Nets.
Links in Rebecca's Life.
Miss Dee Dunmore Bryant.
Mrs. Solomon Smith Looking On.
Modern Exodus (A).
Only Ten Cents.
Retail price, each............................$1.50
Our price.................................... .98
Ordering in lots of 10, at one time, 95c. each.
Postage, each, 10c. extra.

Pansy Books.
Series 7141.

Cunning Workmen.
Dr. Dean's Way.
Grandpapa's Darlings.
Miss Priscilla Hunter
Mrs. Dean's Way.
What She Said.
Bound in extra cloth, 12mo.
Retail price, each............................$1.25
Our price.................................... .85
Postage .... .09

Phelps, Elizabeth Stewart, Works,
Series 7145.

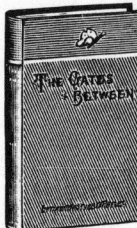

The Gates Series, 3 vols., cloth, 12 mo.
Retail price. Our price.
The Gates Ajar....$1.50 $1.05
Beyond the Gates. 1.25 .88
The Gates Between 1.25 .88
Per set of three volumes........ 4.00 2.75
Postage, each, 12c.

Gypsy Books.

7146 Gypsy Brenton. Gypsy's Cousin Joy. Gypsy's Sowing and Reaping. Gypsy's Year at the Golden Crescent.
4 vols., 16mo., cloth, each....................$0.65
Or in set, boxed......... .... 2.50

Poetical Works.
Red Line Poets.
Series 7147.

Our new line of beautiful Red Line Poets are the best bound, best paper and largest print. All are handsomely bound in cloth, with gold edges.
Retail price, each....... .. $1.25
Our price, each............. .48
In lots of 10 or more,........ .45

Arnold (Edwin).
*Aurora Leigh.
Ayrton.
Beauties of Shakespeare.
British Female Poets.
*Browning (Mrs.)
*Browning (Robt.)
*Bryant (W. C.)
Burns.
*Byron.
Calverly.
Campbell
Chaucer.
*Childe Harold.
Christian Year.
Coleridge.
Cook, E.Eliza.
Cowper.
Crabbe.
*Dante.
Dryden.
Emerson.
Eliot (Geo.)
*Familiar Quotations.
Famous Poems.
*Favorite Poems.
*Faust (Goethe).
Freeman's Poems.
*Gems, 1,001.
*Goethe's Poems.
*Golden Treasury.
*Goldsmith.
Gray (Thomas).
Greene Marlowe & Johnson.
Half Hours with Poets.
Halleck, Fitz-Greene.
Heber Bishop.
Heine.
*Hemans.
Hubert.
*Hood.
Holmes' Early Poems.
*Hugo (Victor).
*Illiad (Homer's).
Imitation of Christ.
*Ingoldsby Legends.
Irish Humorous Poems
Irish Melodies.
*Jean Ingelow.
*Keats.
Kingsley (Chas.).
*Lady of the Lake.
*Lalla Rookh.

*Lay of the Last Minstrel
*Longfellow. Early Poems.
*Lowell. Early Poems.
*Lucile.
Macaulay.
*Marmion.
*Meridth (Owen)
*Milton.
*Moore.
Motherwell.
Mulock (Miss).
*Odyssey.
Ossian.
Paradise Lost.
*Pilgrims Progress.
*Poe (Edgar A.).
Poetry of Flowers.
Poetry of Love.
Poetry of Passion.
Poetry of Sentiment.
Poets of America.
Pope.
Praed.
*Proctor.
*Red Letter Poems.
Religious Poems.
Rogers.
Rossetti (Dante G.)
*Schiller.
*Scott.
Scottish Poems.
*Shakespeare.
Shelley.
Shipton (Anna).
Smith, (Alex.).
Songs Household.
Songs Sacred.
Southey.
Spanish Ballads.
Spencer.
Surf and Wave.
Swinburne.
Tasso.
*Tennyson.
Thackeray.
Thompson
Tupper.
Virgil.
War Songs.
Wesley.
White Kirke.
*Whittier (J. G.). Early
Willis. [Poems.
*Wordsworth.

Beautiful Edition of Woodbine Poets.

7148 Any of the above Red Line Poets marked * can be furnished in beautiful padded binding with full gold edges, suitable for presentation purposes.
Retail price, each.............$1.50
Our price, each............... .95
Lots of 10 at one time....... .90
Postage, each............... .12

This Catalogue is our only salesman.

Poets' Presentation Edition.
Series 7150.

Consisting of fifteen volumes of the best p ets. Beautifully printed on fine paper and bound in parti-colored cloth. Elaborately embossed from a new design in genuine gold. Gilt tops, ribbon markers. All of the volumes contain photogravures and photogr.vure title pages.
Retail price, each.........$0.75
Our price, each............ .42
Postage, each, extra....... .08

Arnold, Sir Edwin............ ... .Light of Asia.
Aytoun, Wm. Edmunston.........Lays of the Scottish Cavaliers.
Browning, Robert. ....Selections.
Byron, Lord.......... ....Childe Harold's Pilgrimage.
Longfellow, Henry W ....Earlier Poems.
Lowell, James Russell.................Earlier Poems.
Macaulay, Lord ....Lays of Ancient Rome.
Meredith, Owen...... ....Lucile.
Moore, Thomas.......................Lalla Rookh.
Poe, Edgar Allan.......... ....Poems.
Scott, Sir Walter.....................Lady of the Lake.
Tennyson, Lord..........................Princess
Tennyson, Lord..................Idylls of the King.
Lennyson, Lord.......................In Memoriam.
Whittier, John Greenleaf...............Earlier Poems.

Westminster Edition of Poets.
Series 7155.

New Cover Design, beautifully decorated in white, gold and colors, full gilt edges. Each book in a box with printed wrappers, 12mo.
Retail price, each.... ....$1.25
Our price, each.............. .75

Browning (Mrs).   Lalla Rookh.
Browning (Robert).   Longfellow (Early Poems).
Bryant.   Lowell.
Burns.   Lucile.
Byron.   Meredith.
Eliot.   Milton.
Familiar Quotations.   Moore.
Favorite Poems.   Procter.
Golden Treasury.   Red Letter Poems.
Goldsmith.   Scott.
Hemans.   Tennyson.
Ingelow.   Whittier (Early Poems).
Lady of the Lake.
Postage, each, extra, 12 cents.

Beautiful Illustrative Octavos.
7158 Bound in flexible leather. All are superbly illustrated. Each one volume complete.
Christmas Carol. By Dickens.
Hanging of the Crane. By Longfellow.
Dream of Fair Women. By Tennyson.
Retail price, each..................................$2.00
Our price, each.................................. 1.40
Postage, each 12 cents.

The Cow Boy Poet.

7159 Ranch Verses by the Poet Ranchman (Larry Chittenden), containing 190 pages of bright, sparkling poetry, and which has received the highest indorsement from our leading critics; handsomely bound in cloth and illustrated.
Retail price..............$1.50
Our price.............. 1.05
Postage, 10c extra.

Household Edition of Poets.
Series 7160.
Complete Editions.

The volumes are of convenient size, good type and desirable for private and library use. Illustrated, 12mo., cloth binding.
Aldrich.   Emerson.
Harte (Bret)   Holmes.
Longfellow.   Lowell.
Meredith.   Taylor.
Tennyson.   Whittier.
Carey
Retail price, each........$1.50
Our price, each. 1.00

Wilcox, Ella Wheeler, Poems.

7162 Ella Wheeler Wilcox Poems; over 300,000 copies have been sold.
Poems of Passion. 12mo., cloth. Handsomely illustrated; cloth binding.
Retail price...........$1.00
Our price........... .65
Poems of Pleasure, 12mo.
Retail price......... $1.00
Our price............. .65
Maurine and other Poems.
Retail price............$1.00
Our price.............. .65
Postage, each.......... .10
3 vol. set in box....... 1.85
Any of above can be had in presentation binding, full white vellum, for $1.10 each.

Family Poets.
Series 7165.
Complete Editions.

Beautifully bound in cloth and illustrated, 8 vo.
Longfellow.
Tennyson.
Lucille.
Whittier
George Eliot.
Mrs. Browning.
Golden Treasury.
Robert Browning.
Lowell.
Holmes.
Princess.
Ingelow.
Burns.
Lalla Rookh.
Favorite Poems.
Red Letter Poems.

Retail price, each.......$2.00 Our price, each..$1.40
Postage, each, 14 cents.

Whitman, Walt, Poems by.
7167 Leaves of Grass, by Walt Whitman, in one volume; comprises all the author's poetical works down to 1892; large 8vo., gilt top, cloth.
Retail price......................................$2.50
Our price.. 1.45
Postage... .18

Poems of Passion by Ella Wheeler Wilcox.

7168 New 16 mo. edition; illustrated. A beautiful presentation edition.
Retail price......................$0.75
Our price....................... .50
Postage, extra .... .08

NEW EDITION OF THE POETS.
Embossed Leather, New Style.
Series 7170.
Complete Edition.

Our Octave Poets, padded sides, burnished yellow edges. The handsomest, most unique and desirable edition ever offered at the remarkably low price. Large royal 8vos., in the following Complete Works: Byron, Burns, Hemans, Josephus, Moore, Milton, Shakespeare, Scott.
Retail price of this edition is $3.50 per volume.
Our price, per vol. $1.80
Postage. .... .30

Encyclopædia of Poetry.

7172 Fireside Encyclopædia of Poetry, collected and arranged by Henry T. Coates. Twenty-eighth edition, enlarged and thoroughly revised, and containing portraits of prominent American poets, with fac-similes of their handwriting.
Each poem has been given complete, and great care has been taken to follow the most authentic and approved editions of the respective authors.

Here will be found the most important poems by prominent authors, besides other poems of note and popularity.

	Retail price.	Our price.
Imperial 8vo.; cloth extra; gilt side and edges	$5.00	$3.50
Half calf, gilt	7.50	5.25
Full morocco, antique; gilt edges	7.50	5.25

Olive Edition of Poets.
Series 7173.

All are handsomely bound in Genuine Embossed Persian Leather, stamped in gold, with full round gold edges, and are without a doubt the finest line ever offered by us for presentation purposes.
Moore.
Mrs. Browning.
Scott.
Bryant.
Robert Browning.
Whittier.
Byron.   Jean Ingelow.
Burns.   Lalla Rookh.
Shakespeare.   Longfellow.
Lady of the Lake.   Lucile.
Tennyson.   Lowell
Milton.
Retail price, each....$3.50. Our price each.......$1.95
Postage, each........... .14

Parkman, Francis', Works.
7174 The California and Oregon Trail, A work depicting Indian life and adventures in the Rocky mountains and prairies of the West. Cloth, gilt top. Retail price...................................$1.50
Our price........$0.75. Postage, extra...... .14

Plutarch's Lives of Illustrious Men.
Langshorne's translation. Texts and notes complete, with index. Large type, good paper, and tastefully bound.
7175 Four volumes, 12mo. Cloth, gilt, in box. .$2.20
Bound in half calf.................................$3.75
7176 Popular Edition. Three volumes, 12mo. Ornamental cloth...... . ... 1.76

Prescott, Wm. H., Works.
7178 New Popular Edition, Illustrated. 16 vols. complete. 12mo., cloth Retail price............$16.50
Our price.. 11.50
7179 Conquest of Mexico. 3 vols. 12mo., cloth. Classic Edition.. 1.05
7180 Conquest of Mexico. Popular Edition. 2 vols., 12mo., cloth.......... .... .75
7181 Conquest of Peru. Classic Edition. 2 vols., 12mo., cloth........ .... .90
7182 Conquest of Peru. Popular Edition. 2 vols., 12 mo., cloth.......................... .75
7183 Ferdinand and Isabella, Classic Edition. 3 vols., 12mo., cloth.......................... 1.05
7184 Ferdinand and Isabella. Popular Edition, 2 vols., 12mo., cloth.......................... .75
7186 Prescott's Reign of Phillip II, 3 vols., 12mo., cloth. Retail price, $3.75. Our price........... 2.60
7187 Prescott's Reign of Charles V, 3 vols., cloth. 12mo. Retail price, $3.75. Our price........... 2.60

Peck, Geo. W., Works.

7190 Peck's Bad Boy and His Pa, and Bad Boy and the Groceryman. Complete in one volume, beautifully illustrated, handsomely bound in cloth. Size 8¼x6½, 368 pages.
Retail price..............$1.50
Our price............... .88
Same in paper binding... .35
Postage, extra............ .06

7191 Peck, 12 mos.   Each Bound in cloth.
Bad Boy and his Pa.   Bad Boy and the Groceryman
Peck's Sunshine.
Peck's Boss Book. Retail price, each..........$0.50
Our price......$0.25. Postage, each, extra..... .10

"Peep-O'Day" Series.
7193 Peep-of-Day Series.
Line Upon Line.   Peep-of-Day,
Precept Upon Precept.
Three volumes in set, cloth bound, 16mo.
Price per set, only............................$0.65
(Retail price of above, $1.50.) Postage, 20 cents.

Roe, Edward P., Works.
Series 7198.

Barriers Burned Away.
What Can She Do.
Opening of a Chestnut Burr.
Near to Nature's Heart.
From Jest to Earnest.
A Knight of the XIXth Century.
A Face Illumined.
A Day of Fate.
Without a Home.
His Sombre Rivals.
A Young Girl's Wooing.
An Original Belle.
Driven Back to Eden.
Nature's Serial Story.
He Fell in Love With His Wife.
The Earth Trembled.
Miss Lou.
Taken Alive.
The Home Acre.
Success With Small Fruits.
12 mo., cloth. Retail price, $1.50
Our price............. .93
19 volumes complete.......17.00
Postage........$0.12.

Barriers Burned Away.

7199 By E. P. Roe. New presentation edition. 16mo., cloth, red and white.
Retail price..............$0.50
Our price............ .30

Opening of a Chestnut Burr.

7200 Same binding and style as "Barriers Burned Away,".. ....$0.30
Postage, each, 8 cents.

Ruskin, John, Works.

7201 Complete Works of Jno. Ruskin, handsomely bound in 13 volumes. Cloth, gilt tops. Large type, colored and other illustrations.
Retail price, per set..........................$13.00
Our price; per set.................... 8.90
Same, bound in half calf.................... 19.00
7202 Ruskin's Stones of Venice, 2 volumes; cloth, 12 mo.
Per set. 2 volumes.............................. 2.10
Postage, 26 cents.
7203 Ruskin's Modern Painters. 3 volumes; cloth, 12mo.
Per set, 3 volumes.............. 2.95
Postage, 38 cents.

Rambaud, Alfred, Works.

7205 History of Russia from the earliest times to 1877. 2 volumes, 12mo., cloth. Retail price, $1.00
Our price......... .70
Postage, 24 cents extra.

Reade, Chas., Novels.
Series 7207.

Perilous Secret.
A Woman Hater.
Love Me Little, Love Me Long.
The Cloister and the Hearth.
It is Never Too Late to Mend.
Peg Woffington, Etc.
Good Stories.
A Simpleton and the Wandering Heir.
Put Yourself in His Place.
Hard Cash.
Foul Play.
White Lies.
Griffith Gaunt.
A Terrible Temptation.
Illustrated., 12mo., cloth.

Per volume.......... $0.52 Postage..........$0.10
7209 Complete Works of Chas. Reade, in 8 large 12mo., volumes, cloth 8.25

Rawlinson, George C., Works.

	Retail price.	Our price.
7210 Seven Great Monarchies of the Ancient Eastern World. Standard. Edition, with 7 maps and 760 illustrations; 3 vols.. 12mo., cloth..........	$3.50	$2.80
Popular Edition. 3 vols., 12mo., half calf............	4.00	3.00
7211 Ancient Egypt. Students' edition, with numerous illustrations. 2 vols., 8vo	3.00	1.80
7213 Popular Edition. 2 vols.,12mo., half calf.........................	3.00	2.00
7214 Complete Works, comprising "The Ancient Monarchies," "Ancient Egypt." "Religions of the Ancient World," and "Historians' Evidence—Egypt and Babylon." Standard edition, with maps and illustrations, 7 vols.,12mo..........................	9.25	6.60

Add for postage 10 per cent. extra.

Rollin, Charles, Works.

7218 Rollin's ancient history of the Egyptians, Carthaginians, Assyrians, Babylonians. Medes and Persians, Macedonians and Grecians, 4 vols., 12mo., cloth.... $3.00 Half calf.............. 4.00
7219 Popular Edition Rollin's Ancient History. 4 vols., cloth......$1 95 Postage................ .46

Ridpath, Jno. Clark, Works.

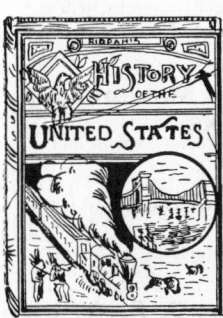

7220 History of the United States, from Aboriginal times to the present day, embracing an account of the Aborigines, the Norsemen in the new world, discoveries by Spaniards, English and French. Planting of settlements, growth of colonies, struggle of liberty, establishment of the Union, the civil war, centennial of independence, and recent annals of the Republic brought down to the year of 1891. Illustrated with charts, portraits and diagrams. Large 8vo., 782 pages. Subscription price, $4.00.
Our price ....$2.75.

7222 Large cheap edition, same contents as above Retail price.............$3.00
Our price............. 1.50 Postage, each........ .50

Riley, James Whitcomb, Works.
Series 7224.

Green Fields and Running Brooks.
Neighborly Poems.
Armazindy (New).
Sketches in Prose and occasional verses.
Afterwhiles, poems dialect and serious.
Pipes, O'Pan, five sketches and fifty poems.
Rhymes of Childhood, 101 poems.
Flying Islands of the Night.
Above, each, 12mo.,cloth, gilt top.
Retail price, each............$1.25
Our price......................$0.88
Postage, extra, each......... .10

Poems Here at Home.

7226 A new book by James Whitcomb Riley, 12mo , cloth. Retail price............$1.50
Our price..........$1.05 Postage, extra....... .10

Old Fashioned Roses.

7227 By James Whitcomb Riley, 12mo. Blue and white vellum cloth. Retail price...........$1.75
Our price........................ 1.30
Postage, extra .09

Stowe, Harriet Beecher, Works.

7229 Uncle Tom's Cabin New edition. 16 mo., handsomely bound in two colors, cloth.
Retail price.....................$0.50
Our price........................ .18
Postage........................ .07
7230 Fine 2 volume illustrated edition; a beautiful present.
Bound in silk cloth............$2.85

Other Stowe Books.
Series 7231.

Bound in English silk cloth.

Agnes of Sorrento.
The Mayflower.
Oldtown Folks.
My Wife and I.
We and Our Neighbors.
Pearl of Orr's Island.
Dred (Nina Gordon).
A Minister Wooing.
Poganuc People.
Uncle Tom's Cabin.
Retail price........$1.50 Our price............$1.05
Postage, each................ .... .12

Stretton, Hesba, Works.
Series 7232.

12mo., cloth.
Through the Needle's Eye.
In Prison and Out.
Cobwebs and Cables.
Carols.
Bede's Charity.
David Lloyd's Last Will.
Hester Morley's Promise.
Doctor's Dilemma.

Retail price..............$1.00 Our price......$0.70
Postage, each................................ .. .12

Stevens, Ann S., Works.

7234 All are well bound and printed, 12mo., cloth with gold title stamps.
Doubly False.
Gold Brick.
Mabel's Mistake.
Norston's Rest.
Palaces and Prisons.
Fashion and Famine.
The Heiress.
Mary Derwent.
The Old Homestead.
Bertha's Engagements.
Retail price..................................$0.60
Our price........................ .27
Complete set of 10 volumes................... 2.25
Postage, each, 10c. extra.

Schiller, Frederick, Works.

7235 Complete Works of Schiller. Illustrated. 4 volumes, 12 mo., cloth. Containing:
The Thirty Years' War. Historical Dramas.
Romances and Dramas. Poems and Essays.
Retail price, per set..$6.00 Our price.........$4.00
Same bound in half calf.................... 6.00

Southworth, Mrs. E. D. E. N., Works.
Series 7236.

Durably bound in cloth. 12mo.

Ishmael, or in the Depths.
Ishmael, or the Depths From.
Bridal Eve.
Bride of Llewellyn.
Curse of Clifton.
Deserted Wife.
How He Won Her.
The Lost Heiress.
Love's Labor Won.
Lost Heir of Linlithgow.
Allworth Abbey.
Discarded Daughter.
Fair Play.
Fatal Marriage.
The Fortune Seeker.
Gypsy's Prophecy.
Mystery of Dark Hollow.

Series 7239—Continued.

A Noble Lord.
Retribution.
Vivia, or the Secret Power.
Artists' Love.
Beautiful Fiend.
Bride's Fate.
Changed Brides.
Christmas Guest.
Cruel as the Grave.
Family Doom.
Fatal Secret.
India, or Pearl.
Lady of the Isle.
Maiden Widow.
Missing Bride.
The Mother-in-law.
A Noble Woman.
Phantom Wedding.
Prince of Darkness.
Soldier's Orphans.
Spectre Lover.
Three Beauties.
Tried for Her Life.
The Two Sisters.
Victor's Triumph.
Widow's Son.
Retail price, each....$0.50 Our price...........$0.27
Complete set of 43 volumes....................10.00
Postage, extra, each..................... .10

Hidden Hand.

7237 By Mrs. E. D. E. N. Southworth, Cloth, 12mo. Retail price....................$1.25
Our price .... .60
Postage, 10 cents extra.

Shakespeare's Complete Works.
Handy Complete Edition.

7239 Complete, 3 Volume Edition, illustrated, good clear type, printed on extra paper, vellum cloth, 12 mo., gilt top, leather label.
Retail price........................$4.00
Our price..................... 1.85
Postage..................... .36

New Cabinet Edition.

7240 Shakespeare's Complete Works. Large type edition. 8 vols., 16 mo., by J. Talfourd Blair, fully illustrated, bound in English cloth, red edges, in box uniform with binding.
Our price.....................$4.00
Bound in French morocco, gilt edges........ 6.75
Weight, 7 pounds.

Shakespeare's Works.

7241 New 4 volume 12mo. edition complete, large type and illustrated. Cloth, 4 vols......$1.50
Half calf, 4 vols....... 3.98

Shakespeare's Complete Works.

7243 Large 8vo. edition, large type and illustrated. Retail price, $2.75. Our price........ $1.23
Postage, extra .... .38

Shakespeare.

7244 Handy Volume Edition. Complete in 13 volumes, with glossary, green cloth, red edges, and maroon cloth, orange edges. In a cloth box.
Retail price, $7.50. Our price.................. 3.98

The Ariel Shakespeare.

STUDENTS' EDITION.
Series 7248.

It would seem difficult to find place for another edition of Shakespeare, but the Ariel edition will be found to differ in so many respects, from any other e ition that it is thought no justification is needed for its existence. The distinctive features of the edition are as follows:
Each play is in a separate volume.
The size of the volume is 3½x5 inches and about a half inch in thickness—of comfortable bulk for the pocket.
The page is clearly printed from an entirely new font of brevier type.
The text is complete and unabridged, and conforms to the latest scholarly editions.
As illustrations, the charming designs by Frank Howard (first published in 1833), five hundred in all, have been effectively reproduced, making a series of delicate outline plates.
16mo., cloth.

The Tempest.
A Midsummer Night's Dream.
The Merchant of Venice.
As You Like It.
Much Ado About Nothing.
Twelfth Night.
The Winter's Tale.
Hamlet.
Othello.
Macbeth.
King Lear.
Julius Cæsar.
Romeo and Juliet.
Anthony and Cleopatra.
Henry VI (First Part).
Henry VI (Second Part).
Henry VI (Third Part).
Troilus and Cressida.
Coriolanus.
Titus Andronicus.
Timon of Athens.
King John.
Richard II.
Henry IV (First Part)
Henry IV (Second Part)
Henry V.
Richard III.
Henry VIII.
The Two Gentlemen of Verona.
The Merry Wives of Windsor.
Measure for Measure.
The Comedy of Errors.
Love's Labor Lost.
Taming of the Shrew.
All's Well that Ends Well
Cymbeline.
Pericles.
Poems.
Sonnets.
Glossary and index of characters, etc.
Retail price, each 50c. Our price...............$0.30
Complete set of 40 volumes... ....11.00
Postage, each, extra, 5c.

Subscription Books.
Series 7250.

We desire to call your attention to our special line of finely illustrated and attractive publications which agents are selling throughout the country for from $3.00 to $5.00 each.
Our price, each....$0.98

Story of the Wild West. By Buffalo Bill.
Columbus and Columbia. A complete history of the United States. By Jno. Clark Ridpath and Jas. G. Blaine.
Footprints of the World's History. By. Jno. Clark Ridpath.
Story of Man. By J. W. Buel.
Heroes of the Dark Continent, and How Stanley Found Emin Pasha.
Life and Work of James G. Blaine.
Exile Life in Siberia. By J. W. Buel.
The Living World. A complete natural history. By. J. W. Buel.
Sea and Land. By J. W. Buel.
The World's Wonders, as seen by great tropical and Polar explorers. By J. W. Buel.
Heroes of The Plains. Wild Bill, Buffalo Bill and all famous scouts.
United States Secret Service. By Gen. Lafayette Baker.
Pictorial History of the Civil War. A full account of our late war.
Pictorial History of the U. S. By James D. McCabe.
Museum of Wonders, or Curiosities of the Whole World.
Barnum's Wild Beasts and Reptiles of the World. By P. T. Barnum.
Postage, each, extra, 32 cents.

Sue, Eugene, Works.

7255 **Wandering Jew.** Library Edition. 2 volumes, 12mo., cloth.
Retail price, $1.50. Our price..................$0.75
7256 **Wandering Jew.** Columbus Edition. 2 volumes...................................40
7258 **Mysteries of Paris.** Library Edition. 2 volumes, 12mo., cloth.....................75
7259 **Mysteries of Paris.** Columbus Edition. 2 volumes, 12mo., cloth....................40

Sheridan's Troopers on the Border.

7260 Being an account of a winter's campaign on the plains with General Sheridan. By Randolph DeB. Keim. With portrait and seven full-page illustrations. 12mo., full gilt back and side.
Retail price $1.00
Our price....................70
Postage, extra, 10c.

Sheridan, Gen. Philip H., Personal Memoirs of.

	Retail price.	Our price.
7261 With steel and wood portraits of Sheridan and his famous generals. 2 vols., 8vo. Cloth, ½ Morocco..........	$8.00	$4.00

Postage, extra 62c.

Smiles, Samuel, Works.
Series 7264

Bound in cloth, 12 mo.
Self Help.
Character.
Duty.
Thrift.
Life and Labor.
Retail price, per set $3.75
Our price 2.25
Single volumes, each.......50
Postage, each.................10

Stockton, Frank R., Works.

7265 **Stories of the Three Burglars.** 16 mo., cloth, in green and silver.
Retail price..............$0.60
Our price....................35
Postage 08
7267 **The Great War Syndicate.** 12 mo.
Price, cloth.............$0.70
Postage 10
Pomona's Travels (new). By F. R. Stockton, 12mo., illustrated...................$1.40

Stockton's Novels.

7268 Cloth. 12mo. Illustrated.
The Late Mrs. Null. | Christmas Wreck.
The Lady or the Tiger. | Rudder Grange.
Rudder Grangers Abroad. | House of Martha.
Retail price, each....$1.25 Our price, each....$0.88
Postage, extra 10

Smith, F. Hopkinson, Works.

7269 **Col. Carter of Cartersville.** By F Hopkinson Smith. Illustrated by E. W. Kemble. The author of this book has created a great sensation among critics. Bound in two colors, cloth.
Retail price................$1.25
Our price...................88
Postage, extra 08

Sidney, Margaret, Books.
Series 7270.

Margaret Sidney divides with Louisa M. Alcott and Mrs. Burnett the honors of having depicted the most charming child-life with which modern literature is acquainted. Each square 12mo., cloth.
Five Little Peppers and How They Grew.
Five Little Peppers Midway.
Five Little Peppers Grown Up.
Retail price, each.....$1.50 Our price, each....$1.00
Set of 3 volumes..............................2.90
Postage, each..................................12

Sherman's Memoirs.

7272 Memoirs of General W. T. Sherman, written by himself, to which are added chapters completing his life, and including his funeral obsequies. Prepared by W. Fletcher Johnson, Esq., and carefully reviewed by Maj. Gen. O. O. Howard, U. S. A. Illustrated; contains full page portraits of the author and other prominent generals; 2 volumes, 8vo.; 853 pages, bound in silk cloth. Subscription price.........$6.00
Our price..3.00
Postage, extra 50

Sketch Book.

7273 An entirely new 16mo. edition of the Sketch Book, by Washington Irving. Large type and handsomely bound in vellum cloth.
Retail price.......... ....$0.75
Our price.....................30
Postage, extra.................08

Scott, Sir Walter, Works.
Waverly Novels.

7277 An entirely new large type edition of Waverly Novels, red vellum cloth, leathered labels, gilt tops, 24 volumes, sold in single volumes or complete set.
Ivanhoe. | Waverly.
Guy Mannering. | Black Dwarf and Old Mortality.
The Heart of Mid-Lothian. |
The Bride of Lammermoor and a Legend of Montrose | The Monastery.
| The Abbot.
| Kenilworth.
Anne of Geirstein. | Count Robert of Paris.
Chronicles of the Canongate. | The Antiquary.
| Rob Roy.
The Fortunes of Nigel. | Peveril of the Peak.
Quentin Durward. | St. Ronan's Well.
Redgauntlet | The Talisman, and Castle Dangerous.
The Pirate. | Woodstock.
The Betrothed. |
The Fair Maid of Perth. |
Retail price per vol., $1.00; Our price per vol.$ 0.50
Complete set of 24 volumes....................11.00

Waverly Novels.

7279 Standard Edition. 12 volumes. 12mo., cloth, gilt tops..............................$6.25

Waverly Novels.

7280 Popular Edition. Library Edition. 12mo., cloth, 12 volumes...........................$ 4.50
Half calf 12.00
7281 Waverly Novels. Columbus Edition. 12 volumes, 12mo., cloth...................... 3.60

Tales of a Grandfather.

7282 Or History of Scotland. By Sir Walter Scott; 4 volumes, 12mo., cloth, gilt top.
Retail price...............................$4.00
Our price................................... 2.20

Taine's English Literature.

7283 New Standard Library Edition. 4 vols., cloth, 12mos., gilt tops........................$4.75

Tess of the D'Urbervilles.

7284 A Pure Woman, Faithfully Presented. By Thomas Hardy. Illustrated. Crown 8vo.
Retail price................................$1.50
Our price.................................. 1.05
Postage, extra 12 cents.

Twelve Decisive Battles.

7286 Of the War. A history of the Eastern and Western campaigns in relation to the actions. 520 pages. Illustrated. Cloth.................$2.25
Postage................................ ... .26

Trowbridge, J. T., Novels.
Series 7287.

A new uniform edition, all handsomely bound in silk cloth, with gold title stamps. Large, bold type, etc.
Coupon Bonds.
Cudjo's Cave.
The Drummer Boy.
Farewell's Folly.
Martin Merrivale, His (X) Mark.
Neighbor Jackwood.
Neighbor's Wives.
The Three Scouts.
Per volume...................$1.10
Postage......................12

Jack Hazard Series.
Series 7289.

By J. T. Trowbridge. Six volumes. 12mo., cloth.
Jack Hazard and His Fortunes. | Doing His Best.
Fast Friends. | Lawrence's Adventures.
The Young Surveyor.
Per set of six volumes, only....................$5.25
Per volume, separately.........................88
Postage, each..................................12

The Electrical Boy.

7290 Or The Career of Richard Greatman and George Greatthings. By Prof. John Trowbridge, of Harvard University. Illustrated. 16mo., cloth. Retail price........................$1.50
Our price................................... 1.00
Postage, 12 cents extra.

Trilby.

7290½ By George Du Maurier, author of "Peter Ibbetson." With 120 illustrations by the author, 12mo., cloth.

Henry James says: "The three Englishmen—the little, beautiful, lovable genius, the mighty man with whiskers, and the would-be-Andalusian Scot—inspire us at the very outset with a clinging comradeship. As for Trilby herself, it strikes me that few heroines of fiction have from the first announced themselves so unmistakably as fatal to the reader's peace. Her beauty is almost terrible; almost calculated to make us bashful, the bold familiarity with life with which she already stands there. It is but too plain that we are to suffer the last extremity from Trilby. We love her so much that we are vaguely uneasy for her; considerably inclined even to pray for her......It all belongs to the sociable, audible air, the irresponsible personal pitch of a style so talked and smoked, so drawn, so danced, so played, so whistled and sung, that it never occurs to us even to ask ourselves whether it is written."
Retail price..................................$1.75
Our price.................................... 1.23
Postage, extra.................................12

Ten Years a Cowboy.

7291 Ten years a Cowboy. The story, romance and adventure of life on the plains, with the varied experiences as a cowboy, stock owner, rancher, etc.: finely illustrated with many full-page illustrations. 470 pages.
Cloth.........................$0.50
Paper covers...............15
Postage, 12 and 4 cents.

Taylor's Views Afoot.

7292 Of Europe Seen with Knapsack and Staff. By Bayard J. Taylor. Well illustrated. Printed on fine laid paper, and bound tastefully in fine English cloth, gilt top, large 12mo.
Retail price................................$0.75
Our price, only...............................52
Postage......................................12

Thackeray, Wm. Makepeace, Works.

7295 **Standard Edition,** 10 volumes, 12mo., cloth, illustrated. Retail price........................$9.00
Our price................................... 6.00
Half calf...................................10.00
7296 **Popular Edition,** 10 volumes, illustrated, 12mo., cloth. Retail price 7.50
Our price................................... 4 10
7297 **Columbus Edition,** 10 volumes, 12mo., cloth.
Retail price................................. 5.00
Our price................................... 3.10

Thompson, Judge, D. P., Works.

7298 Containing Green Mountain Boys and Locke Amsden; 2 volumes, 12mo., cloth.
Retail price................................$1.50
Our price.....................................75

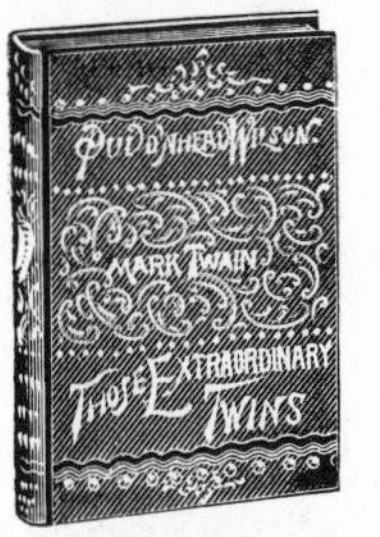

TWAIN, MARK, BOOKS. Series 7300.

All bound in fine English silk cloth, with gold title stamps, printed on supercalendered paper with large print, and containing numerous beautiful illustrations.

		Retail price.	Our price.
Pudd'nhead Wilson (new)	Cloth	$2.50	$1.80
Tom Sawyer	"	2.75	1.60
Small Edition	"	1.00	.70
Innocents Abroad	"	3.50	1.98
Tramp Abroad	"	3.50	1.98
Huckleberry Finn	"	2.75	1.60
Small Edition	"	1.00	.70
Prince and Pauper	"	3.00	1.75
Small Edition	"	1.00	.70
Connecticut Yankee	"	3.00	1.90
Library of Humor	"	3.50	1.98
Roughing It	"	3.50	1.98
Sketches	"	3.00	1.75
Small Edition	"	1.00	.70
Gilded Age	"	3.50	1.98
Stolen White Elephant	"	1.25	.88
Life on the Mississippi	"	3.50	1.98
American Claimant	"	1.50	1.05
Tom Sawyer Abroad	"	1.50	1.05
Million Dollar Bank Note	"	1.00	.70

N. B.—Postage on $1.60, $1.75 and $1.98 books, 24c; on 75c. books, 10c.

Tourgee's Popular Novels.

7301 By Judge Albion W. Tourgee. 12mo., cloth. Fully illustrated.
A Fool's Errand. Bricks Without Straw.
Hot Plowshares. A Royal Gentleman.
Figs and Thistles.
Retail price, each....$1.50. Our price, each...$1.05
Postage, each 12

Fool's Errand.

7302 New 16mo., Red and White Edition. Cloth.
Retail price.....$0.50. Our price.....$0.35
Postage, ...08

Uncle Jeremiah at the World's Fair

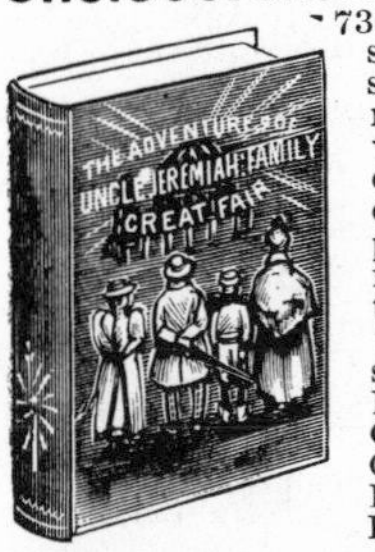

7304 By Quondam. Their Observations and Triumphs. With sixty illustrations and illuminated cover by Mayer. This is a vivid story of sight-seeing, ludicrous mishaps, exciting incidents and happy romance, as experienced by a bright county family determined to see every thing worth seeing in their visit to the World's Columbian Exposition.
Retail price, paper.....$0.25
Our price.....15
Cloth binding.....35
Postage, cloth.....10
Paper.....02

Ward, Mrs. Humphrey, Works.

7306 Marcella, a new book, 2 vols., 12mo.....$1 40
Robert Elsmere, 12mo.....52
David Grieve, 12mo.....70
Postage, extra, per vol.....12

Wright, Henrietta Christian, Works. Series 7308.

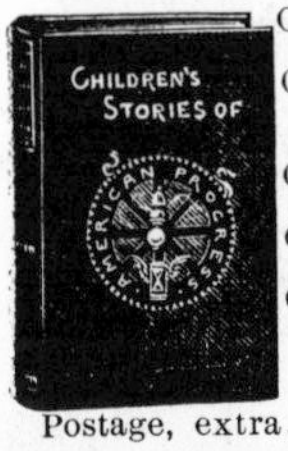

Children's Stories in English Literature. Tales from Shakespeare. 12mo.
Children's Stories in English Literature. Shakespeare to Tennyson. 12mo.
Children's Stories of the Great Scientists. Illustrated, 12mo.
Children's Stories in American History. Illustrated, 12mo.
Children's Stories of American Progress. Illustrated, 12mo.
Per set of 5 volumes.....$4.25
Single volumes.....88
Postage, extra.....10

Works by Susan Warner (Elizabeth Wetherell), and her Sister, Anna B. Warner. Series 7309.

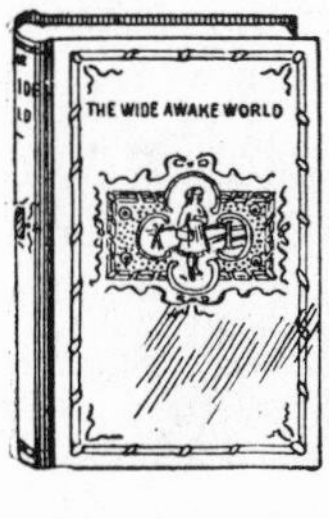

New Editions of Warner Books, finely bound and printed. Wide, Wide World; cloth, 12mo.
Retail price.....$1.00
Our price.....52
Paper cover.....15
Queechy, cloth, 12mo.
Retail Price.....1.50
Our price.....78

Other Warner Books.

7310 Each cloth, 12mo.
Dollars and Cents.
My Brother's Keeper.
Say and Seal.
Hills of the Shatemuc
Retail price, each.....$1.50
Our price.....1.05
Postage, each.....10

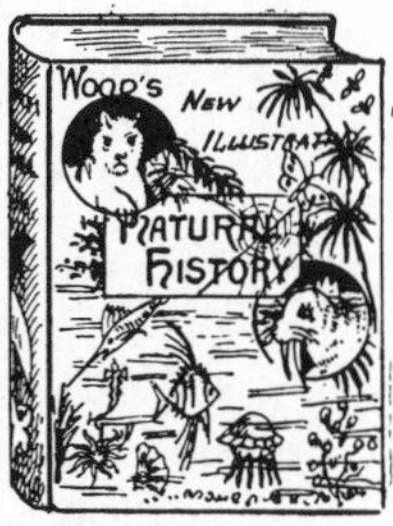

Wood's Natural History.

7311 New illustrated edition with hundreds of designs by Wolf, Zwecker, Weir, Coleman and others. Large octavo, nearly 800 pages, cloth, gilt, side and back titles.
Retail price.....$4.00
Our price.....2.75
Postage.....22

Wood's Natural History.

7312 New Edition, fully illustrated.
Retail price.....$1.25
Our price.....58
Same, board covers.....38
Postage, each.....24

Whitney, Mrs. A. D. T., Works. Series 7316.

All beautifully bound in cloth, 12mo.

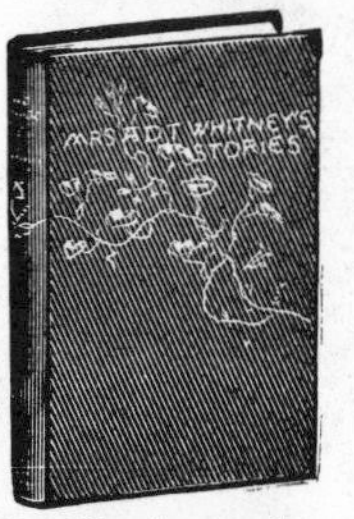

Sight and Insights, 2 vols.
Odd or Even.
Bonnyborough.
Boys at Chiquase.
Homespun Yarns.
Mother Goose.
Hitherto.
Ascutney Street.
Faith Gartney's Girlhood.
Patience Strong's Outings.
The Gayworthy's.
Leslie Goldwaites' Life.
We Girls.
Real Folks.
The Other Girls.
Golden Gossip.

Retail price, each.....$1.25
Our price, each.....88
Postage.....12

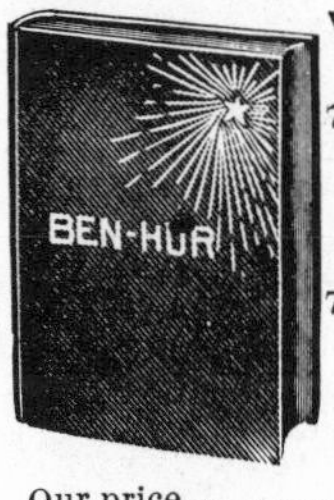

Works of Gen. Lew Wallace.

7320 **Ben Hur.** A tale of Christ. Cloth, 12mo.
Retail price.....$1.50
Our price.....90
Same, bound in half leather, gilt top.....1.45
7321 **Ben Hur,** Garfield edition, 2 volumes beautifully illustrated in photogravures, bound in fine silk, stamped in gold.
Retail price, per set.....7.00
Our price.....4.90
7322 **Fair God.** Or the last of the Tzins. 12mo., cloth. Retail price.....1.50
Our price.....92
7323 **Boyhood of Christ.** Illustrated quarto. Full leather binding. Retail price.....3.50
Our price.....2.50
7324 **Prince of India.** Or why Constantinople Fell. (Just published.) By Lew Wallace, 2 volumes, 16 mo., cloth. Retail price.....2.50
Our price.....1.75
Same, bound in half leather, 2 vols., gilt tops.. 2.80
Add 12 cents each extra per volume for postage.

Warner, Charles Dudley, Works. Series 7325.

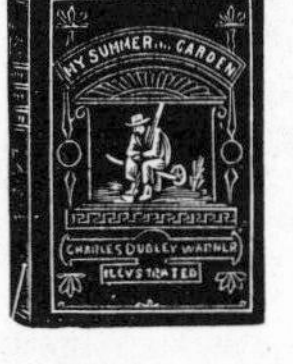

All beautifully bound in cloth with gold title stamps.
My Summer in the Garden.
Retail price.....$1.50
Our price.....1.05
Saunterings (In Europe).
Retail price.....1.25
Our price.....88
Backlog Studies. Retail price.. 1.50
Our price.....1.05
Baddeck and That Sort of Thing
Retail price.....1.00
Our price.....70
My Winter on the Nile. Retail price.....2.00
Our price.....1.40
In the Levant. Retail price.....2.00
Our price.....1.40
Roundabout Journey. Retail price.....1.50
Our price.....1.05
In the Wilderness. Retail price.....1.00
Our price.....70
On Horseback, a Tour in Virginia, Carolina and Tennessee Retail price.....1.25
Our price.....87
Studies in the Southwest. Retail price.....1.75
Our price.....1.23
Postage.....12

Wonders of Art and Archeology. Series 7328.

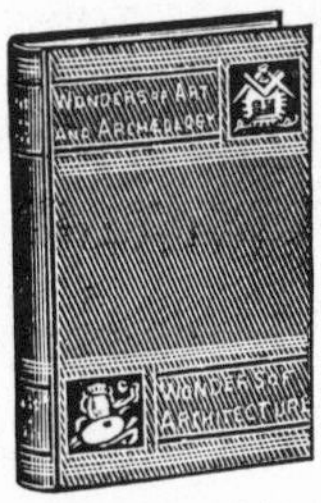

Egypt, 3,300 Years Ago, or Rameses the Great, by F. De Lanoye. With 40 illustrations.
The Wonders of Sculpture, from the French of Louis Viardot. With chapter on American Sculpture, by Clarence Cook. With 62 illustrations.
Wonders of Glass-making, its description and History from the Earliest Times to the Present, by A. Sauzay. With 63 illustrations.
Wonders of European Arts, Translated from the French of Louis Viardot. With 11 illustrations.
Pompeii and the Pompeians, by Marc Monnier. With 32 illustrations.
Wonders of Architecture, by M. Lefeere. To which is added a chapter on English Architecture, by R. Donald. With 60 illustrations.
The Wonders of Italian Art, by Louis Viardot. With 28 illustrations.
The Wonders of Engraving, by George Duplessis. With 34 illustrations. Retail price.....$1.00
Our price.....75
The set, 8 vols. in box.....5.90
Postage, extra, per vol.....10

The Wonders of Man and Nature. Series 7331.

Intelligence of Animals, with illustrated Anecdotes. From the French of Earnest Menaut. With 54 illustrations.
Mountain Adventures. Compiled from the Note Books of Distinguished Travelers, including Whymper and Tyndall. Edited, with additions, by Hon. J. P. Headley. With 41 illustrations.
Bodily Strength and Skill, by Guillaume Depping. With 70 illustrations.
Wonderful Escapes, by F. Bernard. With 26 illustrations.
Thunder and Lightning, by W. DeFonville. With 39 illustrations, nearly all full-page.
Adventures on the Great Hunting Grounds of the World, by Victor Meunler. With 22 illustrations.
Wonders of the Human Body. From the French of A. Le Pileur, Doctor of Medicine With 42 illustrations.
The Sublime in Nature, From Descriptions of Celebrated Travelers and Writers. By Ferdinand LeLanoye. With 44 illustrations. 12mo. Each. Retail price $1.00
Our price.....75
The set, 8 volumes, in box.....5.90
Postage, extra, per vol.....10

The Wonders of Science. Series 7332.

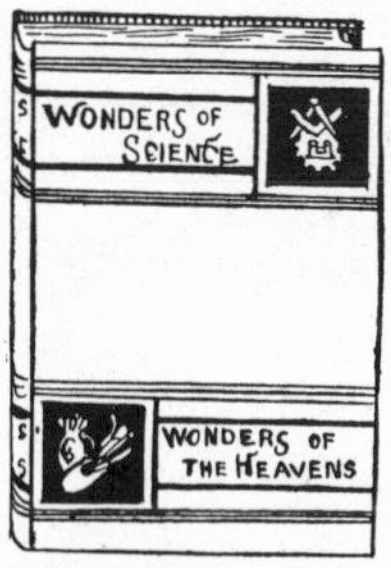

Wonders of Heat, by A. Cazin. With 93 illustrations.
Wonders of Heaven, by C. Flammarion. With 48 illustrations.
Wonders of the Optics, by F. Marion. With 71 illustrations.
The Sun, by Guillemin. With 58 illustrations.
Wonders of Acoustics, or the Phenomena of Sound, by R. Rodau. With 110 illustrations.
Wonders of Water, by G. Tissadler. Illustrated. With 64 engravings and charts.
Wonders of the Moon, A. Guillemin. With 43 illustrations.
Meteors, Areolites, Storms and Atmospheric Phenomena, by Zurcher and Margolle. With 23 illustrations.
Per set, 8 volumes in a box.....$5.90
Any volume sold separate, price, each.....75

Washington and His Generals.

7334 By Headley. 2 vols., cloth.....$1.00
Postage, 24c. extra.

Wiggins, Kate D., Works.

7335 Each 12mo., illustrated.

	Retail price.	Our price.
Birds Christmas Carol	$0.50	$0.38
Story of Patsy	.60	.45
Timothy's Quest	1.00	.70
Kindergarten	1.00	.70

Postage, each, extra, 10 cents.

World's Great Nations.

7338 Beautifully illustrated book showing characters and dress of all nations in the world. Handsomely bound in cloth and containing numerous illustrations. This is the only book in print showing and giving the most accurate history of each nationality.
Subscription price.....$5.00
Our price.....1.58
Postage, 46c. extra.

World's Fair and Midway Plaisance.

7339 Comprising 217 rare photographs of the most attractive sights, scenes and people of the exposition, bound in illuminated paper cover.
Retail price.....$0.50
Our price.....18
Cloth edition.....46
Postage, paper.....05
Postage, cloth.....08

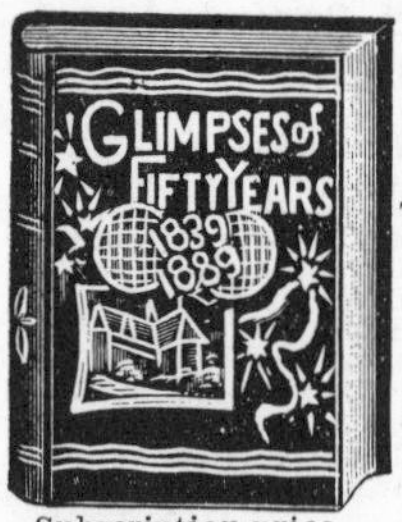

Williard, Frances, E., Works.

Glimpses of 50 Years.

7341 By Frances E. Willard. Prepared by special and unanimous request of the National Woman's Christian Temperance Union Convention of 1887, with an introduction by Hannah Whithall Smith (H. W. S.), author of "The Christian's Secret of a Happy Life." Cloth, 700 pages.

Subscription price.....$2.75 Our price.........$1.75
Postage.. .28

Yonge, Charlotte M., Works.

7346 12mo., cloth. Young Folks' Histories, 4 vols. Per set....................................$1.40
France, Rome, Germany, Greece. Postage, 48 cents extra.

Burt's Library of the World's Best Books.

Series 7350.

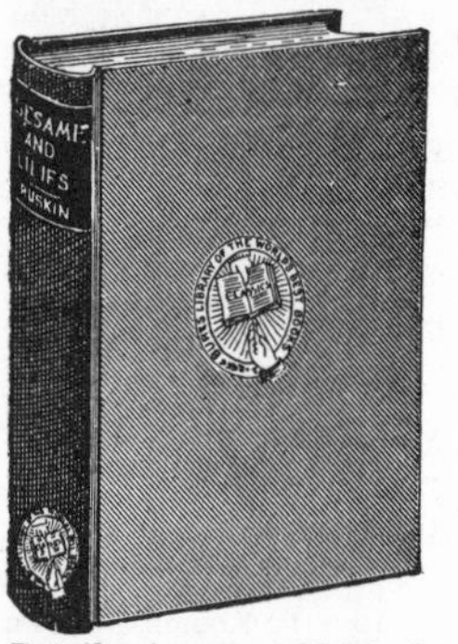

This series comprises titles selected from the standard works of the world's literature. The books are neatly and durably bound, printed on good paper, with extra margins, in large, clear type, uniform in price, size and binding. The text in every case is thoroughly reliable and unabridged, gilt tops.
Retail price,each $1.00
Our price, each.... .63
In lots of 10 at one time............. .60
Postage, 12 cts. extra.
Beautiful ½ calf binding, gilt tops.
Retail price.......$2.00 Our price, each.......$1.30
Lots of 10, each.. 1.25
Postage, each, extra, 22 cents.

Adam Bede. By Geo. Eliot.
Amiel's Journal. Translated by Mrs. Humphrey Ward.
Around the World in the Yacht Sunbeam. By Mrs. Brassey.
Bacon's Essays. By Francis Bacon.
Cloister on the Hearth. By Chas. Reade.
Confession of an Opium-Eater. By Thomas De Quincey.
Consuelo. By George Sand.
Complete Angler. By Walton & Cotton.
Corinne. By Madame De Stael.
Countess of Rudolstadt. By George Sand.
Count of Monte Cristo. Vol. 1. By Dumas.
Count of Monte Cristo, Vol. 2. By Dumas.
Crown of Wild Olive. By John Ruskin.
Daniel Deronda. By George Eliot.
Dante's Divine Comedy. Translated by Rev. H. F. Cary.
Data of Ethics. By Herbert Spencer.
David Copperfield. By Charles Dickens.
Deerslayer, The. By James Fenimore Cooper.
Descent of Man. By Charles Darwin.
Discourses of Epictetus. Translated by G. Long.
Dream Life. By Ik. Marvel.
East Lynne. By Mrs. Henry Wood.
Early Days of Christianity. By F. W. Farrar.
Egyptian Princess, An. By George Ebers.
Essays of Elia. By Charles Lamb
Emerson's Essays. By Ralph Waldo Emerson.
French Revolution. Vol. 1. By Thomas Carlyle.
French Revolution. Vol. 2.
Faust, Goethe's. Translated by Anna Swanwick.
Fifteen Decisive Battles of the World. By E. S. Creasy.
First Principles. By Herbert Spencer.
Fragments of Science. By Jno. Tyndall.
Henry Esmond. William M. Thackeray.
Heroes and Hero Worship. By Thomas Carlyle.
History of Civilization in Europe. By Guizot.
History of Pendennis. By William M. Thackeray.
History of Our Own Times, Vol. 1. By Justin McCarthy.
History of Our Own Times, Vol. 2.
Holy Roman Empire, The. By James Bryce.
House of the Seven Gables. By Nathanial Hawthorne.
Hypatia. By Charles Kingsley.
Ivanhoe. By Sir Walter Scott.
Jane Eyre. By Charlotte Bronte.
John Halifax, Gentleman. By Miss Mulock.
Kenilworth. By Sir Walter Scott.
Knickerbocker's History of New York. By Washington Irving.
Koran, The. Translated by George Sale.
Last Days of Pompeii. By Bulwer-Lytton.
Last of the Barons. By Bulwer-Lytton.
Last of the Mohicans. By James Fenimore Cooper.
Life of Christ. By Frederick W. Farrar.
Les Miserables, Vol. 1. By Victor Hugo.
Les Miserables, Vol. 2.
Light of Asia, The. By Sir Edwin Arnold.
Lorna Doone. By R. D. Blackmore.
Lucile. By Owen Meredith
Makers of Florence. By Mrs. Oliphant.
Makers of Venice. By Mrs. Oliphant.
Meditations of Marcus Aurelius. Translated by George Long.
Middlemarch. By G. Eliot.
Mill on the Floss. By George Eliot.
Moonstone, The. By Wilkie Collins.
Mosses from an Old Manse. By Nathaniel Hawthorne
Newcomes, The. By William M. Thackeray.
Nicholas Nickleby. By Charles Dickens.

Series 7350—Continued.

Old Curiosity Shop. By Charles Dickens.
Oliver Twist. By Charles Dickens.
Origin of Species. By Charles Darwin.
On the Heights. By Berthold Auerbach.
Other Worlds than Ours. By Richard A. Proctor.
Past and Present. By Thomas Carlyle.
Pathfinder, The. By Jas. Fenimore Cooper.
Picciola. By X. B. Saintine.
Pickwick Papers. By Charles Dickens.
Pilgrim's Progress. By John Bunyan.
Pioneers, The. By James Fenimore Cooper.
Prairie, The. By J. F. Cooper
Pride and Prejudice. By Jane Austin
Reign of Law. By Duke of Argyle
Reveries of a Bachelor. By Ik. Marvel.
Romola. By George Eliot.
Sartor Resartus. By Thomas Carlyle.
Scarlet Letter, The. By Nathaniel Hawthorne.
Schopenhaur's Essays. Translated by T. B. Saunders.
Self-Help. By Samuel Smiles.
Seekers After God. By F. W. Farrar.
Sesame and Lilies. By John Ruskin.
Sense and Sensibility. By Jane Austin.
Seven Lamps of Architecture. By John Ruskin.
Sketch-Book, The. By Washington Irving.
Thirty Years' War. By Frederick Schiller.
Thousand Miles Up the Nile, A. By Amelia B. Edwards.
Twice Told Tales. By Nathaniel Hawthorne.
Uarda. By George Ebers.
Uncle Tom's Cabin. By Harriet Beecher Stowe.
Undine, and Other Tales. By Le Da Motte Fouque.
Unity of Nature. By Duke of Argyle.
Vanity Fair. By William M. Thackeray.
Vicar of Wakefield. By Oliver Goldsmith.
Virginians, The. By William M. Thackeray
Westward Ho! By Charles Kingsley.
Woman in White, The. By Wilkie Collins.

Modern Library.

7352 The best works of modern authors carefully selected and edited, suitable for any library and attractive to readers of the most refined tastes, at a low price; printed in clear, readable type, on fine paper and bound in a neat, durable style; cloth; gilt top.
Retail price........$0.75
Our price............ .45
Lots of 10 at one time, 42 cents each.
Postage each, extra, 12 cents.

Micah Clarke. By A. Conan Doyle.
A Study in Scarlet. By A. Conan Doyle.
The Sign of The Four. By A. Conan Doyle.
The Firm of Girdlestone. By A. Conan Doyle.
The Captain of The Polestar and other Tales. By A. Conan Doyle.
The Second Wife. By E. Marlitt.
The Owl's Nest. By E. Marlitt.
The Princess of The Moor. By E. Marlitt.
Old Mam'selle's Secret. By E. Marlitt.
Not Like Other Girls. By Rosa Nouchette Carey.
Only The Governess. By Rosa Nouchette Carey.
A Romance of Two Worlds. By Marie Corelli
Thelma. By Marie Corelli.
Ardath. By Marie Corelli.
Vendetta. By Marie Corelli.
Wormwood. By Marie Corelli.
Eyes Like The Sea. By Maurus Jokai.
Won By Waiting. By Edna Lyall.

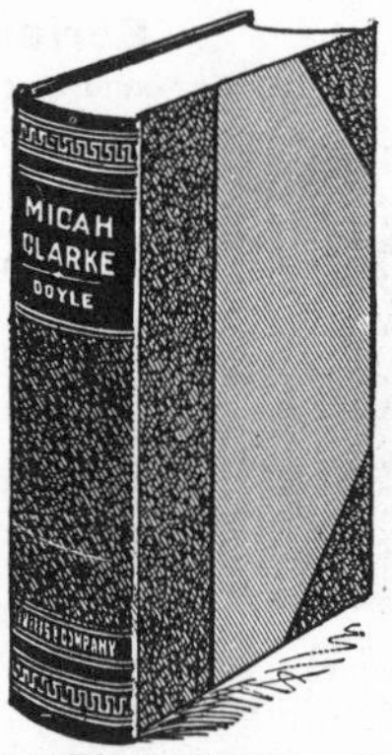

The First Violin. By Jessie Fothergill.
The Special Correspondent. By Jules Verne.
The Deemster. By Hall Caine.
The Bondman. By Hall Caine.
The Shadow of a Crime. By Hall Caine.
Lucile. By Owen Meredith.
The Chaplain's Daughter. W. Heimburg.
In the Depths. By W. Heimburg.
For Another's Fault. By W. Heimburg.
Memoirs of a Physician. By Alexandre Dumas.
Joseph Balsamo. By Alexandre Dumas.
The Queen's Necklace. By Alexandre Dumas.
A Debt of Hatred. By Georges Ohnet.
Nimrod & Co. By Georges Ohnet.
A Wedding Trip. By Emilia Pardo Bazon.

Library Editions of the New Oxford and Princeton 12 Mos.

Series 7355.

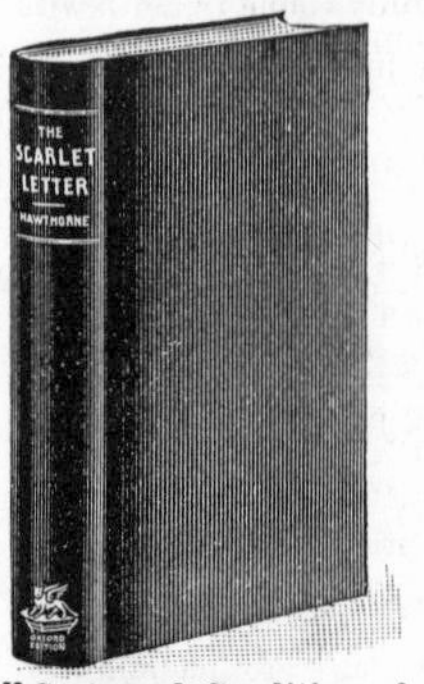

One hundred and fifty choice and favorite books by authors of world-wide repute. These editions are printed on fine paper, well bound with best cloth, headbands, and gilt top, and contain the chief works of fiction and other good standard books. Size, 5¼x7½.
Retail price, each...$0.50
Our price, each...... .25
In lots of 25 copies at one time.......... .23
Per hundred copies. .21
Postage, each, extra .10

All Sorts and Condition of Men. By Walter Besant and James Rice.
Antiquary, The. By Sir Walter Scott.
Abbot, The. By Sir Walter Scott
Adam Bede. By George Elliot.
Æsop's Fables.

Series 7355—Continued.

Airy Fairy Lilian. By "The Duchess,"
Alhambra. By Washington Irving.
Andersen's Fairy Tales. By H. C. Andersen.
Arabian Nights Entertainment.
Bacon's Essays.
Balzac's Shorter Stories. By Honore de Balzac.
Black Beauty. By Anna Sewell.
Barnaby Rudge. By Charles Dickens.
Bride of Lammermoore. By Sir Walter Scott.
Confessions of an English Opium Eater. By Thomas De Quincey.
Conscript, The. By Alexander Dumas.
Consuelo. By George Sand.
Count of Monte Cristo, The. By Alexander Dumas.
Children of the Abby. By Regina Maria Roache.
Child's History of England. By Charles Dickens.
Christmas Stories. By Charles Dickens.
Coningsby. By Lord Beaconsfield.
Crown of Wild Olive. By John Ruskin.
Daniel Deronda. By George Eliot.
Daniel Boone. By C. H. Hartliy.
David Crockett. By Himself.
Deldee, or the Iron Hand. By Florence Warden.
David Copperfield. By Charles Dickens.
Daughter of Heth, A. By William Black.
Donald Ross of Heimra. By William Black.
Dora Thorne. By Charlotte M. Braeme.
Dream Life. By Ik. Marvel.
Deerslayer. By J. Fenimore Cooper.
Dombey & Son. By Charles Dickens.
Donovan. By Edna Lyall.
Don Quixote. By Cervantes.
East Lynne. By Mrs. Henry Wood.
Edmond Dantes. By Alexander Dumas.
Emerson's Essays.
Eugene Aram. By Lord Lytton.
Essays of Elia, The. By Charles Lamb.
Far from the Madding Crowd. By Thomas Hardy.
Felix Holt. By George Eliot.
File No. 113. By Emile Gaboriau.
For Lilias. By Rosa Nouchette Carey.
Flying Dutchman. By W. Clark Russell.
Frederick the Great and His Court. By L. Muhlbach.
First Violin, The. By Jessie Fothergill.
French Revolution, The. By Thomas Carlyle
Goethe's Faust.
Gold Elsie. By E. Marlitt.
Great Expectations. By Charles Dickens.
Grimm's Fairy Tales (Illus) By Brothers Grimm.
Gulliver's Travels. By Dean Swift.
Guy Mannering. By Sir Walter Scott.
Heroes and Hero Worship. By Thomas Carlyle.
Hunchback of Notre Dame, The. By Victor Hugo.
Hardy Norseman, A. By Edna Lyall.
Harry Lorrequer By Charles Lever.
Handy Andy. By samuel Lover.
House of the Seven Gables. By Nathaniel Hawthorne.
House on the Marsh. By Florence Warden.
Hypatia. By Charles Kingsley.
Ivanhoe. By Sir Walter Scott.
In the Golden Days. By Edna Lyall.
Jane Eyre. By Charlotte Bronte.
John Halifax. By Miss Mullock.
Kenilworth. By Sir Walter Scott.
Knickerbrocker History of N. Y. By Washington Irving.
Knight Errant. By Edna Lyall.
Kit Carson. By Charles Burnett.
Last Days of Pompeii. By Lord Lytton.
Lady Audley's Secret. By Miss M. E. Braddon.
Lamplighter. The. By Maria S. Cummins.
Longfellow's Poems.
Last of the Mohicans. By J. Fenimore Cooper.
Lorna Doone. By R. D Blackmore.
Lover or Friend. By Rosa Nouchette Carey.
Louis de le Vallerie. By Alexander Dumas.
Love and Liberty. By Alexander Dumas.
Lucille. By Owen Meredith.
Martin Chuzzlewit. By Charles Dickens.
Middlemarch. By George Eliot.
Mill on the Floss. By George Eliot.
Mysterious Island, The. By Jules Verne.
Man in the Iron Mask, The. By Alex. Dumas.
Michael Strogoff. By Jules Verne.
Miseries of Paris. By Eugene Sue.
Mysteries of Paris, The. By Eugene Sue.
Natural Law in the Spiritual World. By Prof. Drummond.
Nicholas Nickleby. By Charles Dickens.
Old Curiosity Shop. By Charles Dickens.
Old Mam'selle's Secret. By E. Marlitt.
Oliver Twist. By Charles Dickens.
Our Mutual Friend. By Charles Dickens.
Pathfinder, The. By J. Fenimore Cooper
Paul and Virginia. By B. de Saint Pierre.
Pioneers, The. By J. Fenimore Cooper.
Plutarch's Lives.
Poe's Tales. By Edgar A. Poe.
Prairie, The. By J. Fenimore Cooper.
Pair of Blue Eyes, A. By Thomas Hardy.
Pickwick Papers. By Charles Dickens.
Pilgrims Progress. By John Bunyan.
Prime Minister, The. By Anthony Trollope.
Robinson Crusoe. By Daniel Defoe.
Rob Roy. By Sir Walter Scott.
Romance of a Poor Young Man. By Feuillet.
Rory O'Moore. By Samuel Lover.
Romola. By George Eliot.
Reveries of a Bachelor. By Ik. Marvel.
Rienzi. By Sir E. Bulwer-Lytton.
Romance of Two Worlds, A. By Marie Corelli.
Sartor Resartus. By Thomas Carlyle.
Son of Parthos, The. By Alexander Dumas.
Story of an African Farm, The. By Ralph Iron.
Scarlet Letter, The. By Nathaniel Hawthorne.
Scottish Chiefs. By Jane Porter.
Search for Basil Lyndhurst. By Rosa N. Cary.
Self-Help. By S. Smiles.
Sesame and Lilies. By John Ruskin.
Silence of Dean Maitland. By Maxwell Gray.
Sketch Book. By Washington Irving.
Spuire's Legacy. By Mary Cecil Hay
Swiss Family Robinson. By Montolieu and Wyss.

Series 7355—Continued.

Tale of Two Cities. By Charles Dickens.
Thaddeus of Warsaw. By Jane Porter.
Three Guardsmen, The. By Alexander Dumas.
Ties—Human and Divine. By B. L. Farjeon.
Tom Brown's School Days. By Thomas Hughes.
Tom Brown at Oxford. By Thomas Hughes.
Tour of the World in 80 days. By Jules Verne.
Twenty Years After. By Alexander Dumas.
20,000 Leagues Under the Sea. By Jules Verne.
Twice Told Tales. By Nathaniel Hawthorne.
Two Years Before the Mast. By R. H. Dana, Jr.
Uncle Tom's Cabin. By Harriet Beecher Stowe.
Vicompte, de Bragelonne, The. By Alex. Dumas.
Vanity Fair. By W. M. Thackeray.
Vicar of Wakefield. By Oliver Goldsmith.
Waverly. By Sir W. Scott.
We Two. By Edna Lyall.
Wide, Wide World, The. By Susan Warner,
Woman's Face, A. By Florence Warden.
Woman's Love Story, A. Bertha M. Clay.
White Company, The. By A. Conan Doyle,
Whittier's Poems.
Woman in White, The. By Wilkie Collins.
Won by Waiting. By Edna Lyall.

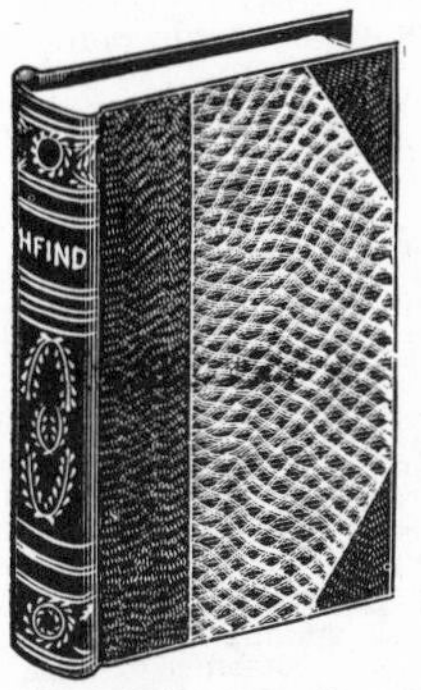

The Avon 12mos. Series 7360.

Printed in large type upon good paper, cloth. Imitation half-bound, full gilt back, head bands and fancy linings. The books in this series average 1⅛ inches in thickness, and it is by far the finest edition of 12mos. ever sold at a low price. The present list of titles embrace 234.

Retail price, each......$0.35
Our price, each.. ..... .18
Lots of twenty-five, each.......... ...... .16
Lots of one hundred, each 14
Postage, each, extra .10

Adam Bede. By George Elliot.
Æsop's Fables.
Allen Quartermain. By H. Rider Haggard.
All Sorts and Conditions of Men. By Walter Besant and James Rice.
Andersen's Fairy Tales.
Anna Karenine. By Count Lyof Tolstoi.
April's Lady. By "The Duchess."
Arabian Nights' Entertainment.
Armorel of Lyonesse. By Walter Besant.
At The World's Mercy. By Florence Warden.
Averil. By Rosa Nouchette Cary.
Babylon. By Grant Allen.
Bacon's Essays.
Balzac's Shorter Stories. By Honore de Balzac.
Bazil; or, The Crossed Path. By Wilkie Collins.
Beyond Pardon. By Charlotte M. Braeme.
Black Beauty. By Anna Sewell.
Blind Fate. By Mrs. Alexander.
Born Coquette, A. By "The Duchess."
Camille. By Alexander Dumas.
Cast Up by The Sea. By Sir Samuel W. Baker.
Children of The Abbey, The. By Regina Maria Roche.
Child's History of England, A. By Charles Dickens.
Christie Johnstone. By Charles Reade.
Claribel's Love Story. By Charlotte M. Braeme.
Confessions of an English Opium Eater. By Thomas de Quincey.
Conscript, The. By Alexander Dumas.
Consuelo. By George Sand.
Countess of Rudolstadt, The. By George Sand.
Count of Monte Cristo, The. By Alex. Dumas.
Cousin Harry. By Mrs. Grey
Crooked Path, A. By Mrs. Alexander.
Crown of Shame, A. By Florence Marryat,
Daughter of Heth, A. By William Black.
Dawn. By H R. Haggard.
Dead Secret, The. By Wilkie Collins.
Deemster, The. By H. Caine
Deerslayer, The. By J. Fenimore Cooper.
Deldee, the Ward of Warringham. By Florence Warden.
Devil's Die, The. By Grant Allen.
Diana Carew. By Mrs. Forrester.
Dick's Sweetheart. By "The Duchess."
Donald Ross of Heimra. By William Black.
Donovan. By Edna Lyall.
Dora Thorne. By Charlotte M. Braeme.
Doris' Fortune. By Florence Warden.
Dream Life. By Ik. Marvel.
Duke's Secret, The. By Charlotte M. Braeme.
East Lynne. By Mrs. Henry Wood.
Edmond Dantes. By Alexander Dumas.
Emerson's Essays, First Series.
Emerson's Essays, Second Series.
Essays of Elia, The. By Charles Lamb.
Fair Women. By Mrs. Forrester.
Family Secrets. By the Author of "Pique."
Fanchon, the Cricket. By George Sand.
Father and Daughter. By Frederika Bremer.
Fiery Ordeal, A. By Charlotte M. Braeme.
First Violin, The. By Jessie Fothergill.
Forging the Fetters. By Mrs. Alexander.
Four Sisters, The. By Frederika Bremer.
French Revolution, The. By Thomas Carlyle.
From Out the Gloom. By Charlotte M. Braeme.
Frontiersmen, The. By Gustave Aimard.
Frozen Pirate, The. By W. Clark Russel.
Goethe's Faust. By Anna Swanwick.
Golden Heart, A. By Charlotte M. Braeme.
Gulliver's Travels.
Grimm's Fairy Tales.
Guilderoy. By Ouida.
Handy Andy. By S. Lover.
Hardy Norsman, A. By Edna Lyall.
Harry Lorrequer. By Charles Lever.
Heir of Linne, The. By Robert Buchanan.
Heriot's Choice. By Rosa Nouchette Carey.
Heroes and Hero Worship. By Thomas Carlyle.
Hon. Mrs. Vereker, The. By "The Duchess."
House of the Seven Gables, The. By Nathaniel Hawthorne.
House on the Marsh, The. By Florence Warden.

Series 736 —Continued.

Hunchback of Notre Dame, The. By Victor Hugo.
I Have Lived and Loved. By Mrs. Forrester.
Indiana. By George Sand.
In the Golden Days. By Edna Lyall.
In the Heart of the Storm. By Maxwell Gray.
Ivanhoe. By Sir W. Scott.
Jane Eyre. By Charlotte Bronte.
Jealousy. By George Sand.
Jet. By Mrs. Annie Edwards.
John Halifax. By Miss Mulock.
Kenilworth. By Sir Walter Scott.
King Solomon's Mines. By H. Rider Haggard.
Kit and Kitty. By R. D. Blackmore.
Kith and Kin. By Jessie Fothergill.
Knight Errant. By Edna Lyall.
Lady Audley's Secret. By Miss M. E. Braddon.
Lady Branksmere. By "The Duchess."
Lamplighter, The. By Maria S. Cummins.
Last Days of Pompeii, The. By Sir E. Bulwer-Lytton.
Last Essays of Elia, The. By Charles Lamb.
Last of the Mohicans, The. By J. Fenimore Cooper.
Legacy of Cain, The. By Wilkie Collins.
Life's Remorse, A. By "The Duchess."
Little Irish Girl, A. By "The Duchess."
Little Rebel, A. By "The Duchess."
Longfellow's Early Poems.
Lord Lisle's Daughter. By Charlotte M. Braeme.
Lord Lynne's Choice. By Charlotte M. Braeme.
Lorna Doone. By R. D. Blackmore.
Lost Love, The. By Mrs. Oliphant.
Louise de la Vallerie. By Alexander Dumas.
Love and Liberty. By Alexander Dumas.
Lover or Friend. By Rosa Nouchette Carey.
Lucile. By Owen Meredith.
Macdermots of Ballycloran, The. By Anthony Trollope.
Madcap Violet. By William Black.
Mad Love, A. By Charlotte M. Braeme.
Man in the Iron Mask, The. By Alexander Dumas.
March in the Ranks, A. By Jessie Fothergill.
Margaret Maitland. By Mrs. Oliphant.
Marriage at Sea. By W. Clark Russell.
Married at Last. By Annie Thomas.
Married Beneath Him. By James Payne.
Marvel. By "The Duchess."
Mary St. John. By Rosa Nouchette Carey.
Master Rockafeller's Voyage. By W. Clark Russell.
Matchmaker, The. By Beatrice Reynolds.
Merle's Crusade. By Rosa Nouchette Carey.
Michael Strogoff. By Jules Verne.
Miseries of Paris, The. By Eugene Sue
Modern Circe. A. By "The Duchess."
Molly Bawn. By "The Duchess."
Mona's Choice. By Mrs. Alexander.
My Danish Sweetheart. By W. Clark Russell.
My Hero. By Mrs. Forrester.
Mysteries of Paris, The. By Eugene Sue.
Mystery of Mrs. Blencarrow, The. By Mrs. Oliphant
Nellie's Memories. By Rosa Nouchette Carey.
Not Like Other Girls. By Rosa Nouchette Carey.
Old Curiosity Shop, The. By Charles Dickens.
Old House at Sandwich, The. By Joseph Hatton.
Old Mam'selle's Secret, The. By E. Marlitt.
Oliver Twist. By Dickens.
One Life. One Love. By Miss M. E. Braddon.
Only the Governess. By Rosa Nouchette Carey.
Other Man's Wife, The. By John Strange Winter.
Our Bessie. By Rosa Nouchette Carey.
Pathfinder, The. By J. Fenimore Cooper.
Paul and Virginia. By B. de Saint Pierre.
Peg Woffington. By Charles Reade.
Phra, the Phœnician, The Wonderful Adventures of. Retold by Edwin Lester Arnold.
Pilgrim's Progress. By John Bunyan.
Pioneers, The. By J. Fenimore Cooper.
Plutarch's Lives.
Poe's Tales. By Edg. A. Poe.
Prairie, The. By J. Fenimore Cooper.
Prince of Darkness, A. By Florence Warden.
Queenie's Whim. By Rosa Nouchette Carey.
Reproach of Annesley, The. By Maxwell Gray.
Reveries of a Bachelor. By Ik. Marvel.
Rienzi. By Sir E. Bulwer-Lytton.
Robinson Crusoe. By Daniel Defoe.
Rogue's Life, A. By Wilkie Collins.
Romance of Two Worlds, A. By Marie Corelli.
Romola. By Geoege Eliot.
Rory O'Moore. By S. Lover.
Rose Douglas. By the Author of "Pique."
Ruffino. By Ouida.
Sartor Resartus. By Thomas Carlyle.
Scarlet Letter, The. By Nathaniel Hawthorne.
Scottish Chiefs, The. By Miss Jane Porter.
Sealed Packet, The. By T. Adolphus Trollope.
Search for Basil Lyndhurst, The. By Rosa Nouchette Carey.
Second Thoughts. By Rhoda Broughton.
Self Sacrifice. By Mrs. Oliphant.
Shadow of a Sin. The. By Charlotte M. Braeme.
She. By H. Rider Haggard.
Sketch Book, The. By Washington Irving.
Silence of Dean Maitland, The. By Maxwell Gray.
Son of Porthos, The. By Alexander Dumas.
St. Katharine's by the Tower. By Walter Besant.
Story of an African Farm, The. By Ralph Iron.
Story of Elizabeth, The. By Miss Thackeray.
Sunshine and Roses. By Charlotte M. Braeme.
Swiss Family Robinson.
Terrible Temptation, A. By Charles Reade.
Thaddeus of Warsaw. By Miss Jane Porter.
Thelma. By Marie Corelli.
This Wicked World. By Mrs. H. Lovett.
Thorns and Orange Blossoms. By Charlotte M. Braeme.
Three Guardsmen, The. By Alexander Dumas.
Three Men in a Boat. By Jerome K. Jerome.
Thrown on the World. By Charlotte M. Braeme.
Tom Brown at Oxford. By Thomas Hughes.
Tom Brown's Schooldays. By Thomas Hughes.
Tour of the World in Eighty Days, The. By Jules Verne.
Twenty Thousand Leagues Under the Sea. By Jules Verne.
Twenty Years After. By Alexander Dumas.
Two Kisses. By Hawley Smart.
Two Orphans, The. By R. D'Ennery.
Two Years Before the Mast. By R. H. Dana, Jr.
Uncle Max. By Rosa Nouchette Carey.
Uncle Tom's Cabin. By Harriet Beecher Stowe.
Under Currents. By "The Duchess."
Under Two Flags. By Ouida

Series 7360—Continued.

Vagrant Wife, A. By Florence Warden.
Vanity Fair. By W. M. Thackeray.
Vendetta. By Marie Corelli
Vicar of Wakefield The. By Oliver Goldsmith.
Viscomte de Bragelonne, The. By Alex. Dumas.
Vivian, the Beauty. By Mrs. Annie Edwards.
Waverly. By Sir Walter Scott.
Weaker Than a Woman. By Charlotte M. Braeme.
Wee Wifie. By Rosa Nouchette Carey.
We Two. By Edna Lyall.
What Gold Cannot Buy. By Mrs. Alexander.
When a Man's Single. By J. M. Barrie.
White Company, The. By A. Conan Doyle.
Whittier's Poems.
Wide, Wide World, The. By Elizabeth Wetherell.
Wife in Name Only. By Charlotte M. Braeme.
Willy Reilly. By William Carleton.
Witch's Head, The. By H. Rider Haggard.
Woman in White, The. By Wilkie Collins.
Woman's Face, A. By Florence Warden.
Woman's Heart, A. By Mrs. Alexander.
Woman's Thoughts About Women, A. By Miss Mulock.
Woman's War, A. By Charlotte M. Braeme.
Won by Waiting. By Edna Lyall.
Wooed and Married. By Rosa Nouchette Carey.
Wooing O't, The. By Mrs. Alexander.
Wormwood. By Marie Corelli.
Yellow Mask, The. By Wilkie Collins.

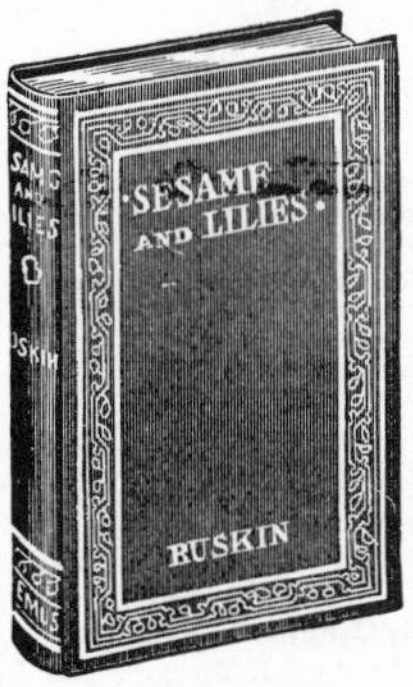

Our Beautiful Presentation Line of Dainty 16 Mos. Series 7362.

We present this season a line of cloth books, that for price, dainty and beautiful bindings cannot be excelled. All are large type, printed on good paper. Size, 4¼x6. Cloth, 16 mo.

Retail price, each......$0.40
Our price, each........ .22
In lots of 25 copies... .20
In lots of 50 copies.... .19
Postage, each. extra.... .07

Cranford. By Mrs. Gaskell.
A Window in Thrums. By James Barrie.
Rab and His Friends.
Vicar of Wakefield. By Goldsmith.
Idle Thoughts of an Idle Fellow. By Jerome K. Jerome.
Tales from Shakespeare. By Lamb.
Sesame and Lilies. By Ruskin.
Ethics of the Dust.
Pleasures of Life. By Lubbock.
Scarlet Letter. By Hawthorne.
House of the Seven Gables. By Hawthorne.
Mosses from an Old Manse. By Hawthorne.
Twice-Told Tales. By Hawthorne.
Bacon's Essays. By Bacon.
Emerson's Essays, First Series.
Emerson's Essays, Second Series.
Queen of the Air, The. By John Ruskin.
Romola. By Geo. Eliot. Vol. I
Romola. By Geo. Eliot. Vol. II.
Lady of the Lake. By Sir Walter Scott.
Lalla Rookh. By Sir Thomas Moore.
Lays of Ancient Rome. By Lord Macaulay.
Lays of the Scottish Cavaliers. By William Edmunston Aytoun.
Light of Asia. By Sir Edwin Arnold.
Longfellow's Poems.
Lowell, James Russell, Poems.
Lucile. By Owen Meredith.
Lorna Doone. Vol. I. By R. D. Blackmore.
Lorna Doone. Vol. II. By R. D. Blackmore.
Mornings in Florence. By John Ruskin.
Greatest Thing in the World, and other addresses. By Henry Drummond.
Idylls of the King. By Lord Tennyson.
In Memoriam. By Lord Tennyson.
A Book of Golden Deeds. By C. M. Yonge.
Browning (Robt.), Selections.
Representative Men. By Emerson.
Thoughts. By Marcus Aurelius.
Discourses of Epictetus.
Imitation of Christ. By A'Kempis.
Addresses. By Drummond.
Chesterfield's Letters.
Reveries of a Bachelor. By Mitchell.
Dream Life. By Mitchell.
Sartor Resartus. By Carlyle.
Heroes and Hero Worship. By Carlyle.
Uncle Tom's Cabin. By Stowe.
Story of an African Farm. By Olive Schreiner.
Whittier's Poems.
Wide, Wide World. By Susan Warner, Vol. I.
Wide, Wide World, By Susan Warner. Vol. II.
Past and Present. By Thomas Carlyle.
Princess, The. By Lord Tennyson.
Sign of the Four. By A. Conan Doyle.
A Study in Scarlet. By A. Conan Doyle.
Black Beauty. By Anna Sewall.
Childe Harold's Pilgrimage. By Lord Byron.
Coming Race, The. By Lord Lytton.
French Revolution, Vol. 1. Carlyle.
French Revolution, Vol. 2. Carlyle.
Dickens' Story Teller.
Dickens' Shorter Stories.
Dreams. Olive Shriener.
Evangeline. Longfellow.
Favorite Poems.
Frankenstein. Mrs. Shelley.
John Halifax. Vol. 1. Mrs. Mulock.
John Halifax. Vol. 2. Mrs. Mulock.
Love Letters of a Worldly Woman. Clifford.
Mill on the Floss. Vol. 1. Eliot.
Mill on the Floss. Vol. 2. Eliot.
Paul and Virginia. St. Pierre.
Poe's Poems.
Ships That Pass in the Night. Harraden.
Sketch Book. Irving.
Tennyson's Poems. Vol. 1
Tennyson's Poems. Vol. 2

Selected Paper Covered Books.

Series 7363.

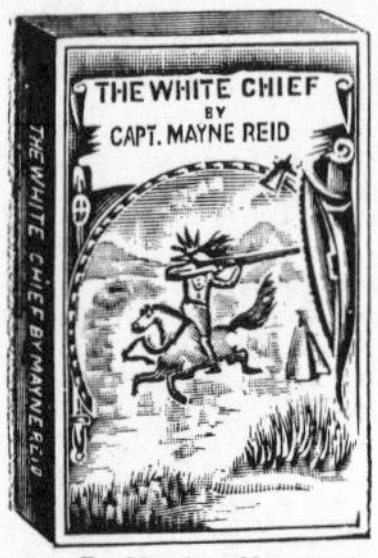

This line is devoted to strictly copyrighted novels by our foremost American writers. All are durably bound in paper covers and contain large, bold print.
Retail price, each........$0.25
Our price.................. .16
In ordering lots of 10 copies at one time, each.. .15
Postage, each, extra..... .03

By Marion Harland.
Alone.
True as Steel.
The Hidden Path.
Ruby's Husband.
Nemesis.
Sunnybank,
Moss Side.
At Last.
Miriam.
Husbands and Homes.
My Little Love.
Phenice's Temptation.

By May Agnes Fleming.
Guy Earlscourt's Wife.
A Wonderful Woman.
A Terrible Secret.
A Mad Marriage.
A Wife's Tragedy.
One Night's Mystery.
Sharing her Crime.
Silent and True.
A Wronged Wife.
Kate Danton.
Norine's Revenge.
Pride and Passion.
Heir of Charleton.
A Changed Heart.
Maud Percy's Secret
Lost for a Woman.

By Mrs. E. D. E. N. Southworth.
Ishmael, or in the depths.
Ishmael or from the depths.
Retribution.
The Deserted Wife.
Mystery of Dark Hollow.
A Noble Lord.
Lost Heir of Linlithgow.
Curse of Clifton.
Bride of Llewellyn.
The Fatal Marriage.
Allworth Abbey.
The Fortune Seeker.
The Bridal Eve.
The Lost Heiress.
Love's Labor Won.
Gipsy's Prophecy.
Vivia, or the Secret Power.
Fair Play.
How he Won Her.
The Discarded Daughter.
Changed Brides.
Bride's Fate,
Wife's Victory.
Fatal Secret.
Cruel as the Grave.
Maiden Widow.

By John Habberton.
Helen's Babies.
Mrs. Mayburn's Twins.

By Mary J. Holmes.
Ethelyn's Mistake.
Millbank.
Edith Lyle.
Tempest and Sunshine.
Lena Rivers.
The English Orphans.
Marian Gray.
Darkness and Daylight.
Cameron Pride.
Rose Mather.

By Julie P. Smith.
Kiss and Be Friends.
Widow Goldsmith's Daughter.
Chris and Otho.
Ten Old Maids.
The Widower.
The Married Belle.

By Captain Mayne Reid.
The Rifle Rangers.
The Wood Rangers.
Osceola, the Seminole.
The Headless Horseman.
The Wild Huntress.
Rangers and Regulators.
The White Gauntlet.
The White Chief.
The Hunter's Feast.
The War Trail.
The Quadroon.
The Tiger Hunter.
Lost Lenore.
The Maroon.
Wild Life.
The Scalp Hunters.

By Caroline Lee Hentz.
Linda, or the Young Pilot.
Robert Graham.
Marcus Warland, or the Long Moss Spring.
Rena, or the Snow Bird.
Eoline, or Magnolia Vale.
Planter's Northern Bride.

By Ann S. Stephens.
Fashion and Famine.
Palace and Prison.
Doubly False.
Norston's Rest.
Bertha's Engagement.
The Reigning Belle.
The Heiress.
The Gold Brick.
Mary Derwent.
Ruby Gray's Strategy.
The Old Homestead.
Mabel's Mistake.

By Geo. W. Peck.
Peck's Bad Boy and His Pa.
Peck's Bad Boy and the Groceryman.
Peck's Fun.
Peck's Sunshine.
Peck's Irish Friend.
Peck's Boss Book.

Ideal Library.

Series 7365.

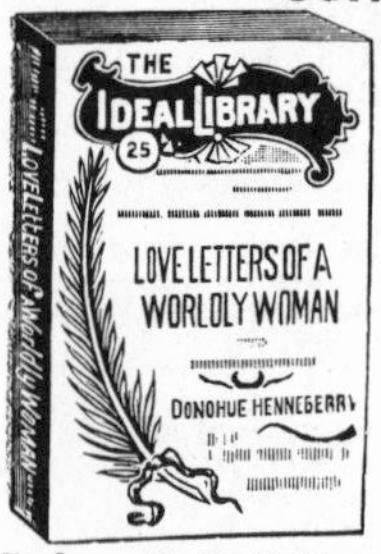

Representative works of authors of established merit only will be included in "The Ideal Library." All the numbers are printed from new, large type on a good quality of paper and bound in such a way that they open easily and flexibly, thus making their perusal a pleasure and a comfort. 12mo., paper covers. Retail price, each, 25 cents.
Our price, each..........$0.08
Per hundred, assorted, each .07
Postage, each, extra 2c.

Dodo. By E. F. Benson.
John Halifax. By Miss Mulock.
The Last of the Mohicans. By J. Fenimore Cooper.
Sketch Book. By Washington Irving.
Ships That Pass in the Night. By Beatrice Harraden.
Deerslayer. By J. Fenimore Cooper.
Oliver Twist. By Dickens.
The Evil Genius. By Wilkie Collins.
Marvel. By The Duchess.
Pathfinder. By J. Fenimore Cooper.
Pioneers. By J. Fenimore Cooper.
Conquest of Granada. By Washington Irving.
Prairie. By J. Fenimore Cooper.
Shadowed to Europe. By James Mooney.
Love Letters of a Worldly Woman. By Mrs. W. K. Clifford.
Vendetta. By Marie Corelli.
Tour of the World in 80 days. By Jules Verne.
Cruise of the Black Prince. By Lovett Cameron.
Cosmopolis. By Paul Bourget.
Strange World. By Miss M. E. Braddon.
Gulliver's Travels. By Swift.

Series 7365—Continued.

Thorns and Orange Blossoms. By Bertha M. Clay.
Lady Valworth's Diamonds. By The Duchess.
A False Start. By Hawley Smart.
Kenelm Chillingley. By Lord Lytton.
Last Days of Pompeii. By Lord Lytton.
Astoria. By Washington Irving.
Adam Bede. By George Eliot.
The Legacy of Cain. By Wilkie Collins.
A Marriage at Sea. By W. Clark Russell.
Captain Bonneville. By Washington Irving.
Romola. By George Eliot.
The Mysterious Island. By Jules Verne.
Bracebridge Hall. By Washington Irving.
Twenty Thousand Leagues Under the Sea. By Jules Verne.
A Crooked Path. By Mrs. Alexander.
The Mill on the Floss. By George Eliot.
Heart and Science. By Wilkie Collins.
Called Back. By Hugh Conway.
A Pair of Blue Eyes. By Bertha M. Clay.
The Blue Veil. By Fortune Du Boisgobey.
Puck. By Ouida.
Dark Days. By Hugh Conway.
The Lamplighter. By Maria Cummins.
Madcap Violet. By William Black.
The Missing Rubies.
Camille. By Alex. Dumas.
Love's Mystery. By Henri Greville.
Vanity Fair. By W. M. Thackeray.
The Wide, Wide World. By E. Wetherell.
Willy Rielly. By Will Carleton.
My Misadventure. By Frank Barrett.
Bound by a Spell. By Hugh Conway.
Beautiful Jim. By John S. Winter.
The Red Camelia. By Fortune Du Boisgobey.
Woman Against Woman. By Mrs. M. E. Holmes.
Black Beauty. By Anna Sewell.
On Her Wedding Morn. By Bertha M. Clay.
Sunshine and Roses. By Bertha M. Clay.
Hunted Down. Max Hilary.
Harry Lorrequer. By Charles Lever.
Natural Law in the Spiritual World. By Drummond.
Dorothy. By Henrietta Hume.
The Duke's Secret. By Bertha M. Clay.
Diana Carew. By Mrs. Forrester.
Mystery of Blencarrow. By Mrs. Oliphant.
Kenilworth. By Sir Walter Scott.
Dark Marriage Morn. By Bertha M. Clay.
Jess. By H. Rider Haggard
Cleopatra. By H. Rider Haggard.
Salmagundi. By Washington Irving.
Tales of a Traveler. Washington Irving.
Silas Marner. By George Eliot.
The New Magdalen. By Wilkie Collins.
Two Women in Black. By James Mooney.
Belinda. By Rhoda Broughton.
Coward and Coquette. By Mrs. F. Mann.
Lord Lynne's Choice. By Bertha M. Clay.
Breezie Langton. By Hawley Smart.
Ivanhoe. By Walter Scott.
Jane Eyre. By Charlotte Bronte
Claribel's Love Story. By Bertha M. Clay.
Felix Holt. By G. Eliot.
Allan Quartermain. By H. Rider Haggard.
The Alhambra. Washington Irving.
Thrown on the World. By Bertha M. Clay.
The Old Mamselle's Secret. By E. Marlitt.
The Mystery of a Hansom Cab. By Fergus W. Hume.
A Man of Samples. By Maher.
What's Bred in the Bone. By Grant Allen.
A Yellow Aster. By Iota.
As in a Looking Glass. By F. C. Phillips.
All in the Wild March Morning.
Her Desperate Victory. By Mrs. Rayne.
The Son of Clemenceau Alexander Dumas, Jr.
A Glorious Galop. By Hawley Smart.
Conquest of Spain. By Washington Irving.
Vivian, the Beauty. By Mrs. Annie Edwards.
Vicar of Wakefield. By Oliver Goldsmith.
Only One Sin. By Bertha M. Clay.
East Lynne. By Mrs. Henry Wood.
Thelma. By Marie Corelli.
King Solomon's Mines. By H. Rider Haggard.
The Hon. Mrs. Verecker. By The Duchess.
Miawa's Revenge. By H. Rider Haggard.
Mildred Trevanion. By The Duchess.
Uarda. By George Ebers.
She. By H. Rider Haggard.
A Life's Remorse. By The Duchess.
Mr. Meeson's Will. By H. Rider Haggard.
A Romance of Two Worlds. By Marie Corelli.
Ethan Brand. By Hawthorne.
Dora Thorne. By Bertha M. Clay.
Beyond Pardon. By Bertha M. Clay.
Paul and Virginia. By De St. Pierre.
Handy Andy. By Samuel Lover
Peter's Soul. By George Ohnet.
A Golden Heart. By Bertha M. Clay.
Children of the Abbey. By Regina Marie Roche.
A Mad Love. By Bertha M. Clay.
Fern Leaves. By Fanny Fern.
For Him.
The Frozen Pirate. By W. Clark Russell.
The Tents of Shem. By Grant Allen.
Wife in Name Only. By Bertha M. Clay.
One Maid's Mischief. By Geo. Manville Fenn.
My Danish Sweetheart. By W. Clark Russell.
A Woman's Face. By Florence Warden.
Eve. By S. Baring Gould.
Mystery of St. James Park By J. P. Burton.
The Dream of Love. By Zola.
The Reproach of Annesley. By Maxwell Grey.
Roland Oliver. By Justin McCarthy, M. P.
The Dark House. By Geo. Manville Fenn.
Crayon Papers. By Washington Irving.
Hunter Quartermain's Story. By H. Rider Haggard.
Jack in the Forcastle. By Martingale.
We Two. By Edna Lyall.
Donovan. By Edna Lyall.
Knight Errant. By Edna Lyall.
Louise de la Valliere. By Alexander Dumas.
Wee Wifie. By Rosa Nouchette Carey.
Edmund Dantes. By Alexander Dumas.
Dangerous Cat's Paw. By David Christie Murray.
A Dangerous Woman. By Gilbert A. Pierce.
Mary St John. By Rosa Nouchette Carey.

Series 7365—Continued.

Her Sister's Betrothed. By Bertha M. Clay.
Love's Chain Broken. By Bertha M. Clay.
Allan's Wife. By H. Rider Haggard.
Foiled by Loving. By Bertha M. Clay.
Twenty Years After. By Alexander Dumas.
In the Golden Days. By Edna Lyall.
The Son of Porthos. By Alexander Dumas.
Lover or Friend. By Rosa Nouchette Carey.
The Man with the Iron Mask. By A. Dumas.
Court Royal. By S. Baring Gould.
The First Violin. By Jessie Fothergill.
Mystery of a Turkish Bath. By Rita.
The Count of Monte Cristo. By Alexander Dumas.
Three Guardsmen. By Alexander Dumas.
To Be or Not To Be. By Mrs. Alexander.
Scenes of Clerical Life. By George Eliot.
Lady Branksmere. By The Duchess.
An Egyptian Princess. By George Ebers.
From Out the Gloom. By Bertha M. Clay.
Her Only Sin. By Bertha M. Clay.
Dick's Sweetheart. By The Duchess.
Flames. By E. Werner.
Saddle and Saber. By Hawley Smart.
A Young Girl's Love. By Bertha M. Clay.
A Woman's Error. By Bertha M. Clay.
Wilfrid Cumbermede. By Geo. Macdonald.
Won by Waiting. By Edna Lyall.
Undercurrents. By The Duchess.
The House Party. By Ouida.
Forging the Fetters. By Mrs. Alexander.
Lucile. By Owen Meredith.
Viscount de Bragelonne. By Alexander Dumas.
Woman's War. By Bertha M. Clay.
Wooed and Married. By Rosa Nouchette Carey.
Michael Strogoff. By Jules Verne.
A Hardy Norseman. By Edna Lyall.
Study in Scarlet. By A. Conan Doyle.
Sign of the Four. By A. Conan Doyle.
Idle Thoughts of An Idle Fellow. By Jerome K. Jerome.
Beyond the City. By A. Conan Doyle.
Bird of Passage. By Beatrice Harraden.
Micah Clarke. By A Conan Doyle.

Artistic Gift Books.

Magnificent examples of book making. The best literary talent and artistic skill have combined to place these among the very finest publications issued.

Shakespeare's Heroes and Heroines.

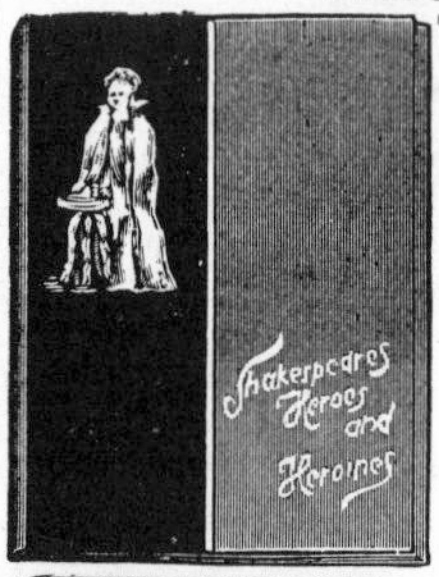

7372 Dedicated, by special permission, to Mr. Henry Irving. A series of 16 full page plates, beautifully printed after designs by Sir A. Calcot, R. A.; C. R. Leslie, R. A.; D. Maclise, R. A.; A. Redgrave, R. A.; S. Hart, R. A., etc. Interleaved with quotations from Shakespeare. Large quarto volume, bound in two-color cloth, gold titles, etc.
Retail price..........$3.50
Our price............. 2.45
Postage, extra.. ..... .22

Tennyson's Heroes and Heroines.

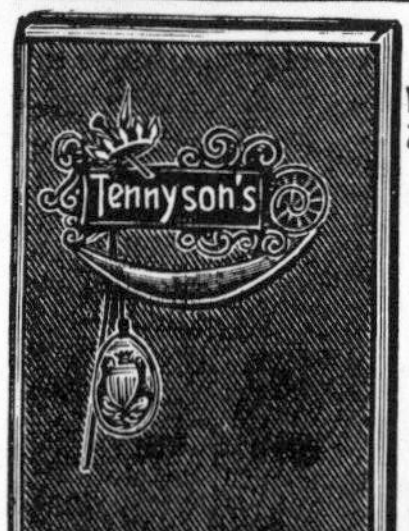

7374 Dedicated, by special permission, to Lord Tennyson. 16 colored illustrations by S. Boyers and Marcus Stone, interleaved by 104 pages of quotations from the late poet laureate's works. Illuminated by pen drawings by J. Pauline Sunter. Size, 8¾x11⅜.
Retail price............$3.50
Our price............... 2.45
Postage................. .22

Boys of the Bible.

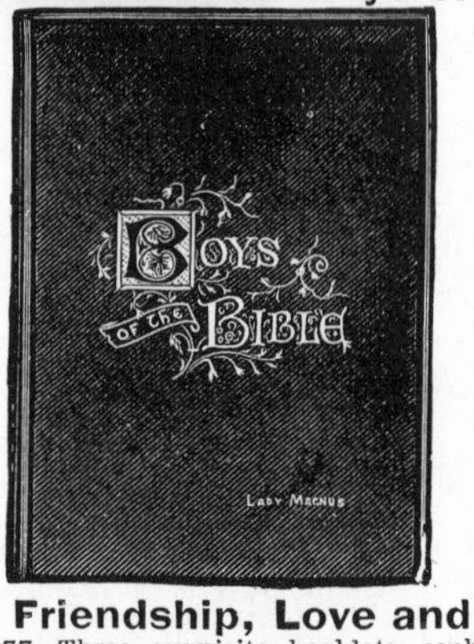

7376 Bible Stories, retold by Lady Magnus in her inimitable style; 65 pages of most artistic illustrations in color, by Henry Rylands, and in monochrome By John Lawson. Bound in cloth, gold stamping side and back, gilt top; size, 7¾x10¼. Retail price $2.00. Our price. $1.40 Postage 16c. extra.

Friendship, Love and Kisses.

7377 Three exquisite booklets, each containing selections from the poets by Volney Streamer, appropriate to its title. Artistic color illustrations, by F. Corbin, Price and others. Each book contains 80 pages, bound in parti-colored cloth, gilt top and each set in fancy box; exquisite gift for all times. Size, 4x6¼. Retail price, per set $2.50. Our price $1.75. Postage, 32c.

Arabian Nights.

7378 The best tales from the "Arabian Nights," arranged for the young by Helen Marion Burnside, and illustrated by 12 full page color plates by W. and F. Brundage. Certainly the handsomest edition of this most interesting work ever issued. Heavy board covers; illuminated. Size, 8x10. Quarto. Retail price $1.50. Our price......$1.00

7379 Same as above, bound in cloth with rich gold stamping on cover. Gold edges. Retail price $2.00. Our price.....$1.35 Postage, 26c.

Year Book of American Authors.

7380 American Literature selected and edited by Ida Scott Taylor. Containing 366 pages. Highly colored and artistic illustrations by C. Klein. Bound in white cloth, gold stamping side and back; gilt top. Size, 5x9. Retail price $1.50. Our price.......$1.00 Postage, 12c.

Black Beauty.

7381 A new and handsome illustrated edition of this famous and interesting story of a horse. Richly bound in cloth with red band and gold stampings. Retail price, $1.50 Our price, 80c. Postage, extra, 18c. This book should be read by everybody who rides, drives, or cares for horses.

World's Fair Photographs.

7382 A grand collection of art pictures of 160 full page views; size, 11x13, taken from the original photographs of all the principal buildings of the Fair and Midway Plaisance; each view is described authentic and accurate. Cloth, quarto. Retail price, $3.00. Our price...$1.30 Postage, 30c. extra

New Editions of Art and Gift Books.

The Finest Editions Ever Placed on the Market.
THE DORE BIBLE GALLERY.

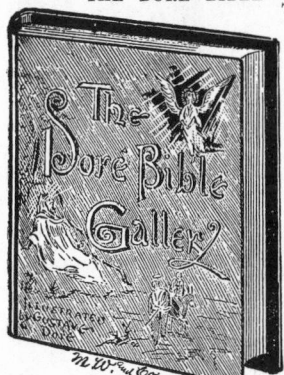

7383 A complete pictorial summary of Biblical Narrative from Genesis to Revelations, containing one hundred full-page illustrations by Gustave Dore. Arranged in chronological order and accompanied by descriptive explanations. The illustrations are unequaled. The work will be found equally acceptable to either Protestants or Catholics. Bound in cloth with full gold edges. Retail price..........$3.50 Our price..... 1.00 Bound in full morocco 2.25

7384 Cloth, same as above, in the German language. Retail price............................ 4.00 Our price.. 1.00 Postage, each............................ .38

N. B.—Our Special Book Catalogue contains many quotations on both cloth and paper novels not found in this Catalogue. Send 5c. to pay postage.

5-3d

The Life of Christ.

7385 The Life of Jesus Christ. By Canon Farrar, D. D., F. R. S., Archdeacon of Westminster. Illustrated with a large number of full-page engravings by Gustave Dore and others; also reproductions in original oil colors of famous paintings by Raphael, Rubens and other great painters. 500 pages, 9x11 inches. Bound in extra fine cloth.

Publisher's price.......$2.75 Our price..........$1.00

Dante's Inferno.

7386 Poetry and Art, with seventy-five full page illustrations by Gustave Dore. Translated from the original by Henry Francis Cary, M. A. Edited by H. C. Welsh, A. M.; a book worthy of its subject. The printing and binding are the finest. Royal quarto; size, 9⅝x12 inches. Bound in extra fine English cloth, emblematic design, full gilt, gold edges. Price..$1.05. Full morocco, gold edges.
Price...........$2.25 Postage....... .. .38

Bible Stories.

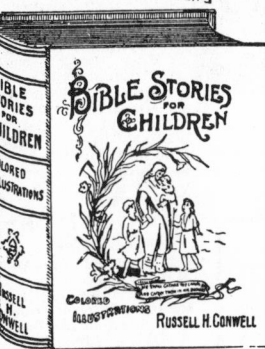

7387 By Russell H. Conwell, pastor of "The Temple," Phila. (The largest church in America.) Contains Bible stories from Genesis to Revelations, told in a simple manner, including stories of Bible heroes. Over 200 full-page illustrations and 12 colored plates. Cloth. Retail price..$3.50 Our price..... 1.25 Postage....... .30

Milton's Paradise Lost.

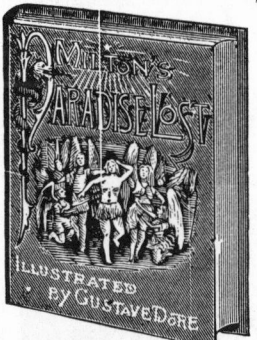

7388 A masterpiece of poetry and art, embellished with FIFTY superb full-page engravings by Gustave Dore. Edited by Henry C. Walsh, A. M. The type, printing and costly binding combined, make this the most elegant, attractive and valuable art publication of the day. Royal quarto; size, 9¾x12 inches. Bound in extra fine English cloth, emblematic design, full gilt, gold edges..$1.05 Bound in full morocco, gold edges ......$2.25 Postage.......... .38

Tennyson's Idylls of the King.

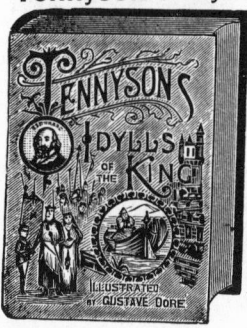

7390 New Edition. Embellished with 37 magnificent full-page engravings by Gustave Dore, the renowned French artist. Brilliant rays of fairy romance from the lights of genius. The Poet Laureate gives new interest to the old and hoary legends handed down from the days of the early bards. Imperial quarto; size, 11x14½ inches. Bound in extra fine English cloth. Emblematic design, full gilt, gold edges. Retail price.....$7.00 Our price....... 2.95
Postage, 52c.

Dante's Purgatory and Paradise.

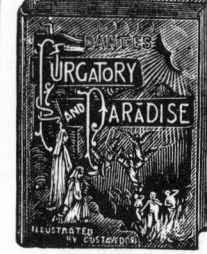

7391 Translated from the original of Dante's Alighieri and illustrated with designs of M. Gustave Dore, with critical and explanatory notes. Retail price........$2.50 Our price, cloth... 1.05 Postage............. .38 Full morocco....... 2.25

Ancient Mariner.

7392 Ancient Mariner, by Coleridge. New edition; embellished with 46 full-page engravings by the renowned artist, Gustave Dore; edited by Henry C. Walsh, A. M. No one can read the poem without being the wiser and better for it. A masterpiece of art and an ornament to any home. Large imperial quarto; size, 11x14½ inches. Bound in extra cloth, full gilt. Retail price....$6.00 Our price............. 2.05 Postage .. .. .22

Paul and Virginia.

7394 By Bernadin de Saint Pierre. This well known story fully illustrated with numerous full-page engravings, on highly calendered paper, with gold edges. Bound in fine English cloth. Emblematic designs in gold, silver and ink. Quarto size. Retail price, cloth ......$3.00 Our price.................. 1.05 Bound in full morocco.. 1.85 Postage.................. .28

Hell up to Date.

Something altogether new! The humorous hit of the age!

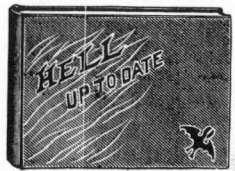

7396 The journey of R. Polasco Drant, newspaper correspondent, through the Infernal Regions, as reported by himself. Illustrated by Art Young. Dore's famous drawings illustrating Dante's "Inferno" are familiar to everybody, and it is, perhaps, for this reason that Art Young's clever book appeals so readily to all who see it. The illustrations will wring from the most critical the admission that here we have a decided addition to the wealth of American humor. The text describes an imaginary trip to the domain of Satan. Popular edition, small quarto, in extra silk cloth binding.
Retail price..........$1.00 Our price..........$0.75 Paper covers.................................... .35 Postage, extra.................................... .12

The Pilgrim's Progress.

7397 By John Bunyan. Illustrated with 100 engravings. This is highly attractive as well as very valuable. Bound in extra fine English cloth; emblematic design in gold, silver and ink. Gold edges. Retail price.....$2.50 Our price..... .70 Bound in full morocco........... 1.85 Postage.......... .28

Child's History of England.

7398 (New) A Child's History of England, by Charles Dickens, embellished with 75 engravings by the eminent historical illustrators, A. DeNeuville, Gilbert Bayard and others. Size, 9x10. Magnificently bound in fine English cloth with gold edges. Retail price........... $3.50 Our price................. 1.05 Postage.................. .36

Robinson Crusoe.

7400 Robinson Crusoe, by Daniel DeFoe. This edition has just been published regardless of expense; 120 illustrations by Walter Paget. Size, 7½x9¾.
Retail price.............$3.50
Our price.................. 1.05
Postage 36
N. B.—We guarantee this book to be the largest and best edition of Robinson Crusoe ever published.

Glimpses of the World.

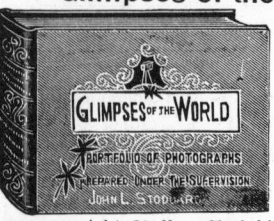

7403 Glimpses of the World, a portfolio of photographs of the marvelous works of God and man; prepared under the supervision of the distinguished traveler, John L. Stoddard. Containing 54 elaborate views of all parts of the world. Size, 12 x 14; 6.00 pages; weight, 8¼ lbs. Cloth binding, stamped in gold. Retail price....................$6.50
Our price.................................. 2.98
Half Morocco.............................. 3.50
Full Russia................................. 3.95
Postage, extra............................ .72
7404 Large Cheap Edition Stoddard Glimpses, cloth...................................... 1.25

Around the World in Eighty Minutes.

7406 Containing 106 photographs, size, 5¾x7 inches, of the most prominent views in the world, with an entertaining and instructive description of each view, by W. S. Walsh. This work is superior in mechanical execution to anything of the kind ever made, and is sold at about one-third the price asked for work of inferior quality; 224 pages.

	Retail price	Our price
Illuminated paper covers..........	$0.50	$0.38
Fine English cloth and silver.....	1.00	.70

Postage, extra, 10 cents.

Adventures of Don Quixote De La Mancha.

7407 Translated from the French of Miguel De Cervantes Saavedra, by Charles Jarvis, Esq., memoir of Cervantes and a notice of his works, 800 beautiful engravings, 100 full page plates in tint, illustrated by Gustave Dore and Tony Johannot. Beautiful cloth binding, gold edges.
Retail price.........................$4.00
Our price 2.25
Postage, extra, 34 cents.

Famous Paintings of the World.

7408 A grand collection of the most famous paintings of the world reproduced in half-tone illustrations, containing over 300 pages; size, 10 x14. Durably bound in the best English silk cloth. Retail price............................$5.00
Our price.................................. 2.65
Postage, 36 cents extra.

Napoleon From Corsica to St. Helena.

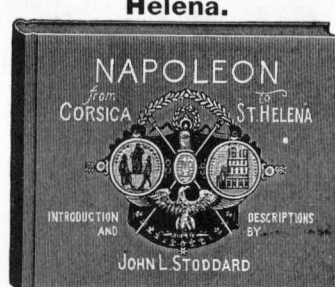

7409 331 beautiful engravings, forming a pictorial history of the "Man of Destiny." Text by the noted Napoleon scholar, John L. Stoddard. A superb volume, 11¼ x 14 inches, printed on an extra quality of enameled paper and bound in dark green cloth, with the Napoleonic coat of arms gold-embossed on cover. This work pictures every important episode in Napoleon's wonderful career, and all the important personages associated with him. The originals of the pictures reproduced have a monetary value of upward of $4,000,000, and include portraits of Napoleon by such celebrated artists as Meissonier, Delaroche, David and Gerard; battle scenes, pictures of Napoleon's marshals and generals, and of Josephine, Marie Louise and the King of Rome. Accompanying each book and included in the price is an artistic litho-

graphic reproduction in two colors of celebrated "Snuff-Box Portrait," by Paul Delaroche. This reproduction, made by the French proccess, direct from the original in the National Gallery of France, is 22 x 28 inches in size, and is usually sold by art dealers at twice the price asked for the book and picture.
Retail price of book, including portrait........$2.50
Our price of book, including portrait........... 1.75
Postage complete..............................38

Sights and Scenes of the World.

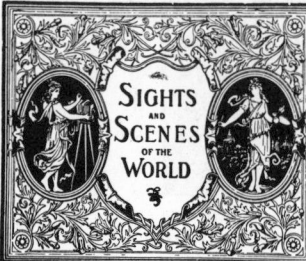

7510 The greatest public buildings, temples and churches men have reared; the gigantic ruins of past ages; the homes of celebrated people; perfect photographs of places; where notable events have taken place; the most beautiful paintings, statuary, oblisks and monuments; the wonderful things in nature of mountain, lake and desert, from the poles to the equator; in short, a grouping of the most interesting things the earth affords to look upon. Beautiful cloth binding, size, 11¼x14½, containing nearly 700 pages; 3 50 illustrations.
Retail price.... ......$6.50   Our price.........$2.60

Bible Pictures and Stories.

7411 Nearly one hundred of the most important incidents of sacred history are grouped in this attractive volume, forming a chronological panorama of the Holy Bible that is both instructive and interesting. The work cannot fail to instill into the young mind a love and desire for greater knowledge of the Holy Book itself. Although Bible pictures and stories are primarily intended for the young, it is full of interest for those more advanced in years. Elegant heavy paper, extra large type; fine English cloth binding; emblematic design in gold and ink. Size, 7x8½ inches. Retail price......................$1.25
Our price............$0.70   Postage, extra........ .18

America Illustrated.

7412 A perfect panorama of American scenery. Full of splendid illustrations. Imperial quarto. Edited by J. David Williams. The purpose of this work is to make people acquainted with superb creations of nature.
Publisher's price.. $2.00
Our price........... 1.00
Postage............ .20

Egypt Illustrated.

7413 Egypt fully illustrated with full page engravings, sketches, etc., showing all points of interest all through Egypt and the Holy Land, on heavy tinted paper with gold edges. Bound in fine English cloth, extra gilt and colors. Size, 9½x12 in. Publisher's price.. 2.50
Our price......... $1.00
Postage............ .30

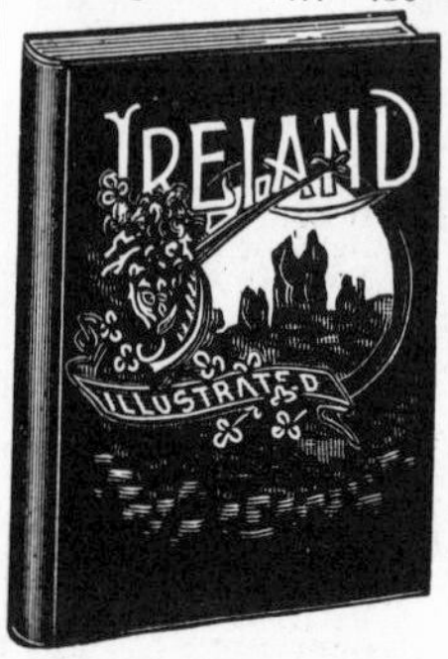

Ireland Illustrated.

7414 Edited by Richard Lovett, M.A.; fully illustrated with pen and pencil sketches, maps, engravings, etc. Any Irishman or others who wish to see the beautiful lakes of Killarney should have this book. On heavy tinted paper, with gold edge. Bound in fine English cloth, extra gilt and colored side title; boxed. Sizes, 9½x12 in.
Retail price $2.50
Our price......... 1.00
Postage......... .30

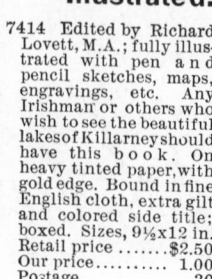

Germany Illustrated.

7416 Germany fully illustrated with numerous engravings, sketches, etc., on heavy tinted paper with gold edges. Bound in fine English cloth, title in extra guilt and colors. Size, 9½x12 in. Boxed. This book shows beautiful scenery up the Rhine, Black Forest, Northern Germany, The Tyrol, Eastern Alps, etc.
Retail price ...$2.50
Our price.......... 1.00
Postage....... .30

India Illustrated.

7417 India fully illustrated with numerous full-page engravings, sketches, etc., on heavy tinted paper with gold edges. Bound in fine English cloth. Size, 9¼ x12 inches. Revised and enlarged by Prof. Edward P. Twing, M A., member of the Royal Asiatic Society.
Retail price......$2.50
Our price, Boxed. 1.00
Postage............ .30

Europe Illustrated.

7418 Edited by F. K. Warren, R. B. S. Illustrated with numerous full-page engravings and wood engravings by the best artists. This book is the best and cheapest ever published which shows Europe as it is. Large 4to. cloth, extra gilt edges. Retail, $2.50 Boxed, each........ 1.00
Postage.... 20

England Illustrated.

7419 Printed from new plates on fine laid paper, bound in cloth. Large 8vo.; size, about 9½x12 inches. Beautifully illustrated with over 200 engravings of all places of note in England.
Retail price $3.00
Our price, only.......... 1.00
Postage............. .20

Palestine Illustrated.

7420 Large 8vo, size, about 9½x12 inches, bound in fine cloth, fully illustrated and printed on laid paper from new plates. This work shows all journeys through Palestine, its scenery, rivers, mountains, etc. The only complete work ever published.
Retail price............ $2.00
Our price, only......... 1.00
Postage .... .20

Scotland Illustrated.

7421 This beautiful illustrated book of Scotland has just been published at an enormous expense, and contains views of all principal Scotland scenery. Handsomely bound in fine English cloth with gold emblematic designs and full gold edges.
Retail price................$3.00
Our price................. 1.00
Postage .... .20

California Illustrated (New).

7422 Handsomely bound in fine English cloth with full gold edges, size, 9x12 in. Showing all points of interest in beautiful full-page engravings, large new type and super-calender paper.
Retail price..............$3.00
Our price.............. 1.00
Postage .... .20

BOOKLETS, REWARD OF MERIT CARDS, ETC.

Series 7424. New Leather Style of Gift Books.

These books are handsomely bound in full embossed leather, with gold edges, and contain beautiful poems and stories, beautifully illustrated. Retail price..............................$2.00
Our price...85

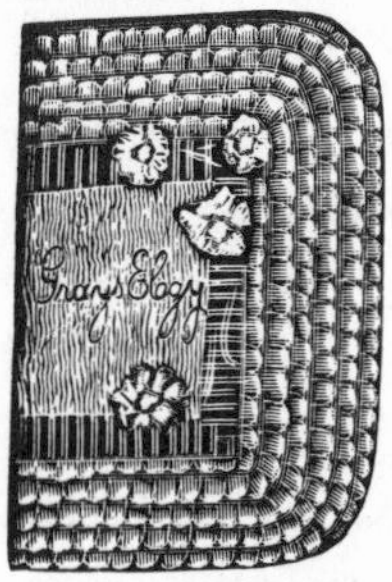

Gray's Elegy.
Low Back Car.
Shakespeare Songs.
May Queen.
Lucy Gray.
Pride of the Village.
Christmas Stories.
The Bells.
Cotter's Saturday Night.
Deserted Village.
Greenland's Icy Mountains.
Beauties of Tennyson.
Night Before Christmas.
Bingen on the Rhine.
Lady Clare.
Gems from Tennyson.
Each......................$0 85
Per dozen..................8.75
Postage.......................10

Beautiful Ivorines. Series 7426.

Bound with ivory surface of various tints and designs, gilt edges; can be washed when soiled without injury. Ret il price.............$1.50
Our price..66

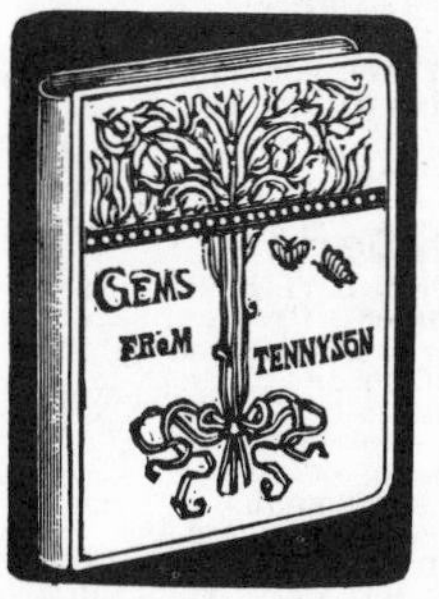

Gray's Elegy.
The Bells.
Greenland's Icy Mountains.
Beauties of Tennyson.
Night before Christmas.
Bingen on the Rhine.
Lady Clare.
Gems from Tennyson.
Come into the Garden, Maud.
My Faith looks up to Thee.
Glorious Song of Old.
Tramp, the Boys are Marching.
Swanee River.
Marching through Georgia.
Nellie Was a Lady.
His Beloved Sleep.
Massa in the Cold Ground.
My Old Kentucky Home.
Tenting on the Old Camp Ground.
Dora, by Tennyson.
Home, Sweet Home.
Rock of Ages.
Calm Night.
Our Father in Heaven.
Lord is My Shepherd.
Curfew Must Not Ring To-Night.
Ring Out, Wild Bells.
Each......................$0.66
Per dozen......................7.25
Postage..........................08

Artistic Booklets.

Refined and inexpensive substitutes for costly presents. Entirely new and original styles; dainty, artistic, rich and appropriate. Thecolor work subjects have been taken from the prominent art galleries of the world.

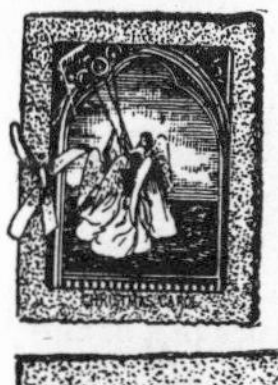

Booklets.

7427 **Incomparable Ribbon Booklets**. The very best in the market; six kinds. Size, 4½x3, containing 8 pages of verse, 25 in a box, assorted, with envelopes.
Each..........................$0.03
Per doz..............................30
Per 100............................2.00

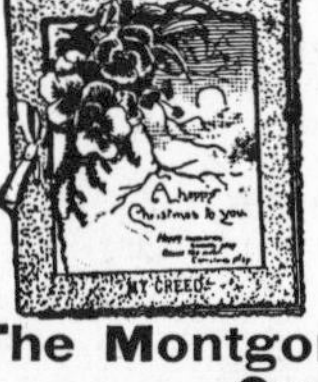

7429 **Beautiful Ribbon Booklets**. Size, 6¼x5¼. 8 pages of verse. Gold title, front mounted with beautiful cards. 12 titles assorted, 1 dozen in box, with envelopes.
Each..........................$0.08
Per doz..............................85
Per 100............................6.90

The Montgomery Ward & Co.'s Cartoon No. 1.

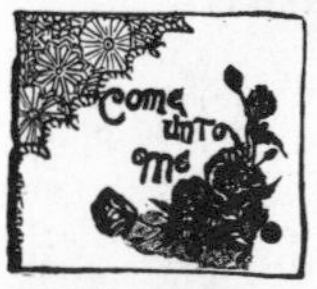

7430 One dozen assorted booklets, all shapes and sizes, painted in beautiful colors, with handsome heavy covers embossed with gold and colored titles, containing 16 pages each; would retail from 15 to 25 cents.
Our price per cartoon.......$0.76
Per dozen cartoons..........8.50

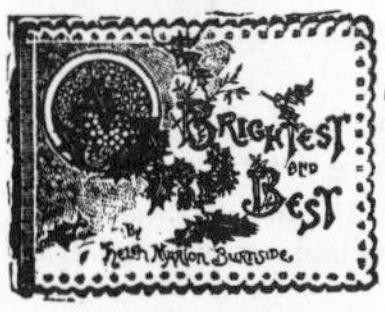

Cartoon No. 2.

7431 Same as cartoon No. 1, only larger and better quality; 12 booklets.
Price per cartoon......$ 1.25
Per dozen cartoons.... 11.50

Cartoon No. 3.

7432 Our best, containing 12 of the very choicest booklets, each containing 16 pages of verse and colored illustrations (*This is big value.*)
Our price per cartoon..............$ 1.80
Per doz. cartoons .. 20.00

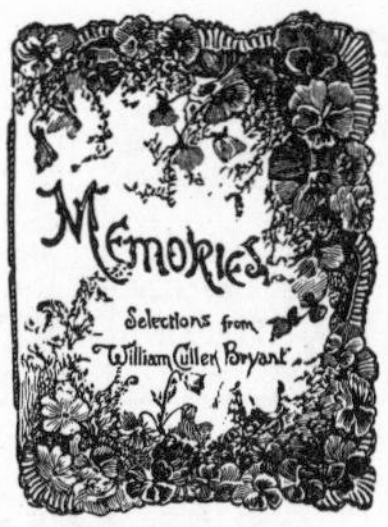

Rock of Ages Series.

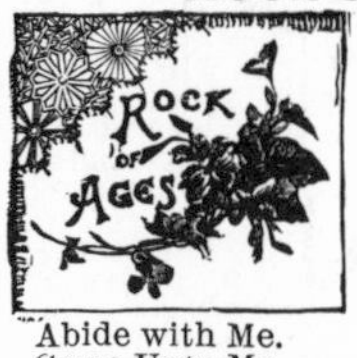

7434 Comprising exquisite shapes and styles. 16 pages of colored illustrations and verse. Average sizes, 3¼x3¾.
Angel Faces.
Lead Kindly, Light.
19th Psalm.
Rock of Ages.
Hark, My Soul.
Angel Voices.
Abide with Me.
Come Unto Me.
God Is Our Refuge.
Lord Is My Shepherd.
Retail price, each, 15c, Our price...............$0.07
Per dozen, assorted.........................75

Paths of Peace Series.

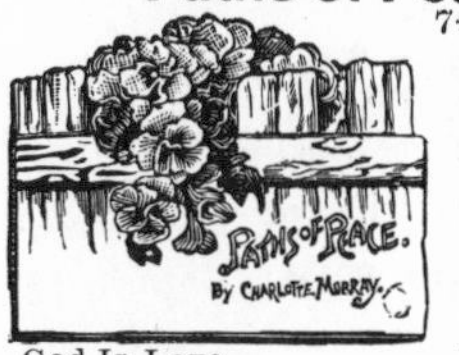

7435 Beautiful series of booklets in color with heavy embossed covers. 16 pages of verse. Average size, 4½x4.
Happy Days.
God's Sweet Will.
Kittendon.
New Year's Greetings.
With Kind Thoughts.
Paths of Peace.
God Is Love.
Watching and Waiting
Token of Remembrance.
Dolly's Darlings.
Christmas Wishes.
My Message.
In Him We Live.
Hoping and Trusting.
Bouquet of Good Wishes.
Happy Hours Attend You.
Sweet Violets.
Christmas Carol.
Sun of My Soul.
Brightest and Best.
Paths of Holiness.
Fair Fortune Favor You.
Snowdrops.
Beneath Thy Wings.
Retail price, each, 25c. Our price, each.........$0.15
Per dozen, assorted...........................1.65

Forget Me Not Series.

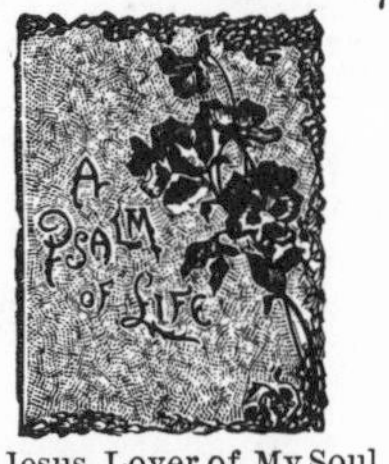

7437 A novel series of cut-out embossed booklets, each containing 16 pages of beautiful colored illustrations. Average size, 6½x3¼.
God Bless You.
Forget Me Not.
With All That's Kind and True.
Nearer, My God, to Thee.
Psalm of Life.
Home, Sweet Home.
Heavenly Helps.
Hearty Good Wishes.
The Heavenly Babe.
With All Good Wishes.
Jesus, Lover of My Soul.
Nearer to Thee.
Retail price, each, 35c. Our price, each........$0.18
Per dozen, assorted...........................1.95

The Legend Beautiful Series.

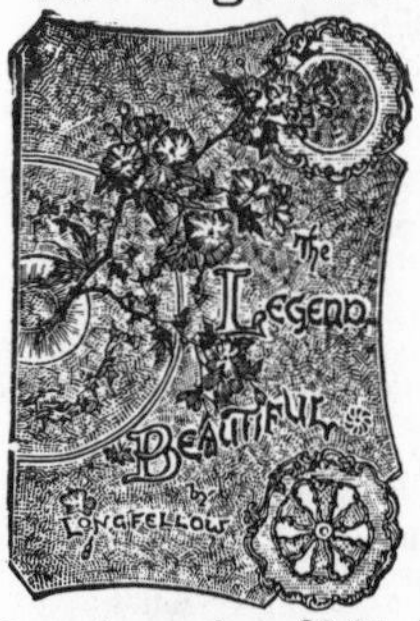

7438 A series of incomparable booklets, containing sixteen pages of the most exquisite illustrations in colors, with verse. Average size, 5½x7 each, in a box.
Cathedral Voices,
More Precious Than Rubies.
Ivy Leaves.
Bells Across the Snow.
The Legend Beautiful.
Sonnets from Shakespeare.
Living Leaves.
God Be With You.
Life and Light.
Memories.
Retail price, each..$0.50
Our price, each....$0.35 Per dozen, assorted... 3.60

Poet Series.

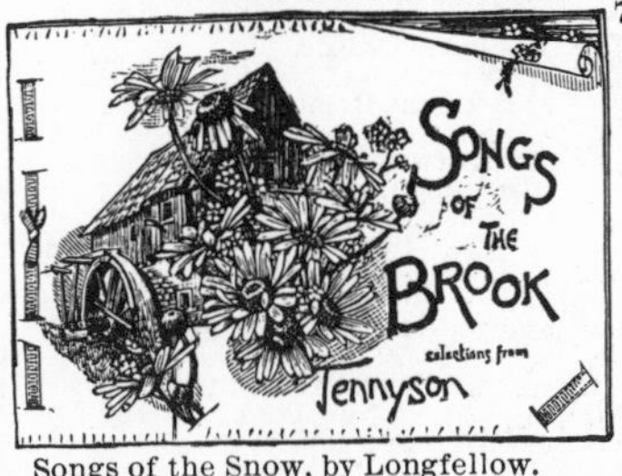

7439 A Series of Poems by Tennyson, Longfellow and Havergal, each containing 16 pages of exquisite illustrations, with beautiful embossed covers; average size, 10x7.
Songs of the Snow, by Longfellow.
Songs of the Brook, by Tennyson.
Retail price, each..............................$0.75
Our price, each.....................................52
Per dozen, assorted.............................5.75

Reward of Merit Cards.

We quote below a very complete line of reward of merit cards which have just been imported by us from one of the largest card establishments in Europe, and in buying direct we are enabled to supply our many customers at regular jobbers' prices. Cards all come 10 in a package, assorted, with or without scripture text. Weight 3 oz. per bundle.

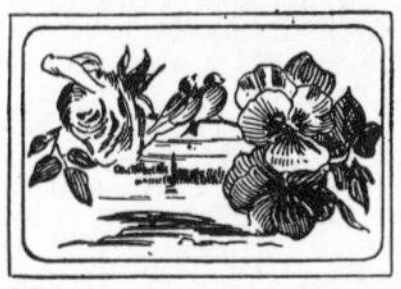

Reward Card.

7468 Beautiful design in fancy colors. Winter landscape with birds; 8 kinds. Size, 3x4¼.
Per bdle. of 10....$0.05
Per box of 100.... .40

7469 Same with Scripture text.
Per bdle. of 10..................................05
Per box of 100..................................40

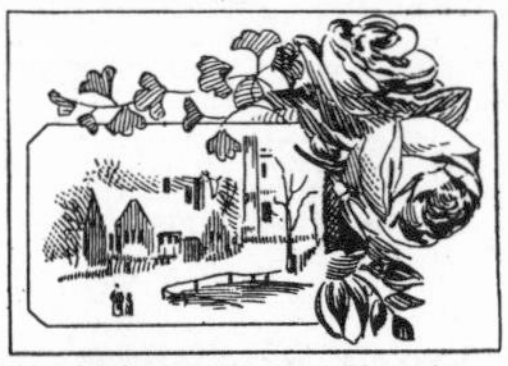

7470 Beautiful embossed card. Winter scenes, 8 kinds, all frosted. Printed in colors. Size, 3¾x5½.
Per bdle of 10.$0.07
Per box of 100. .60

7471 Scripture Text. Showing girl playing with doll. Per bdle. of 10......................$0.07
Per box of 100.......................................60

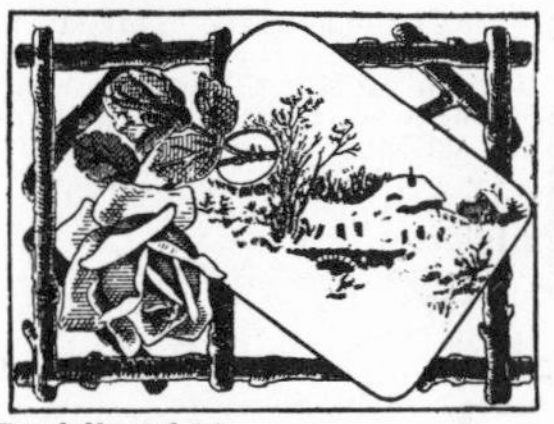

Reward Card.

7472 Beautiful embossed card, showing a winter scene by moonlight. Printed in 8 different colors; frosted, 4 kinds. Size, 4¼x6¼.
Per bdle. of 10..............................$0.10
Per box of 100......................................90

7474 Scripture Text Card. Size, 4½x5. Showing spray of flowers in colors. Per bdle. of 10......$0.10
Per box of 100......................................90

Reward Card.

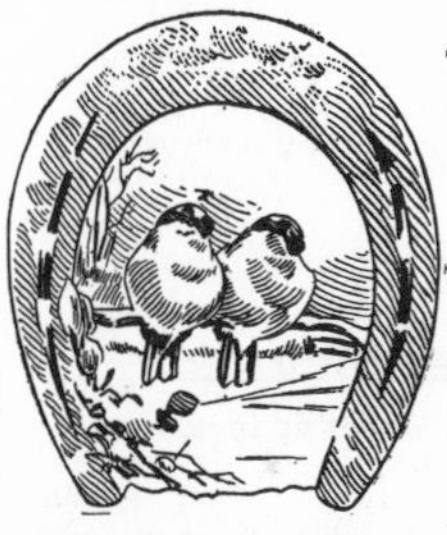

7475 Handsome Card, showing horseshoe and landscape; 4 designs, frosted, in beautiful colors. Size, 4¼x5½.
Per bdle. of 10......$0.15
Per box of 100....... 1.35

7476 Scripture Text Card, showing birds and landscape. Size, 4½x6.
Per bdle. of 10......$0.15
Per box of 100...... 1.35

7478 Beautifully highly finished card, showing landscape; in 8 colors, with fancy cut out border; frosted, 8 kinds. Size, 4x6.
Per bdle. of 10....$0.12
Per box of 100.... 1.05

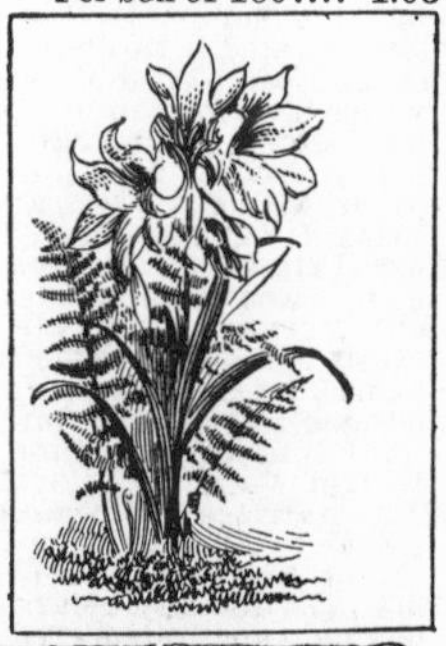

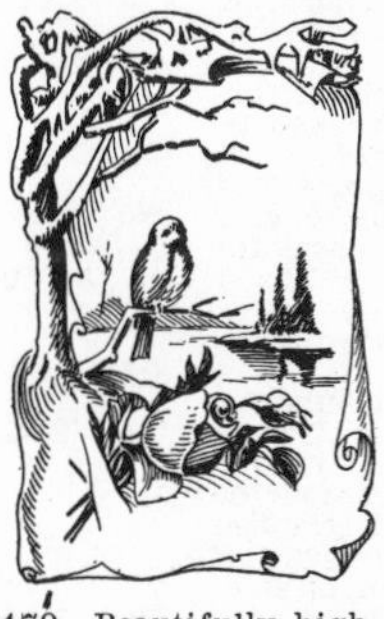

7479 Beautifully highly colored card, frosted, showing beautiful plants, etc., 4 kinds, with fancy cut out border. Size, 5x6¼.
Per pkg. of 10 cards. $0.20
Per box of 100. 1.80

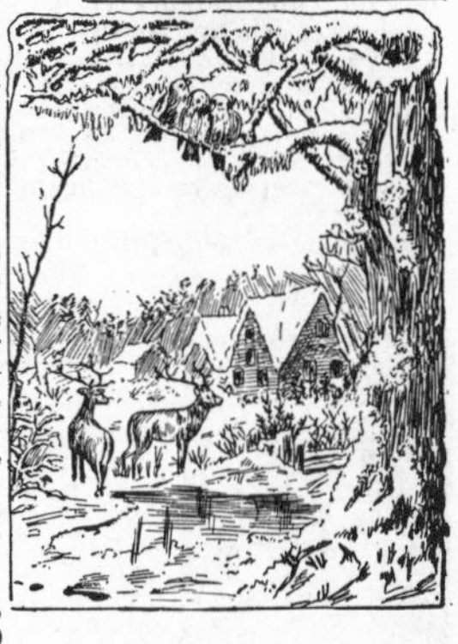

7480 Scripture Text Card, 5x6½. Showing spray of flowers in frame.
Per pkg. of 10 cards. $0.20
Per box of 100. 1.80

7481 This card we have imported for the purpose of giving our customers a large size novelty. There are 3 kinds, showing landscapes, etc., highly colored, frosted, and cut out borders. Size, 9x10.
Per pkg. of 10. cards..... $0.55
Per box of 100 5.00

Silk Corded Reward Cards.

This line embraces a series of genuine novelties, being superior to the old style fringed card. They are made of heavy cardboard, plain and embossed, highly colored designs with full silk corded edges; also cord for hanging. Each in envelope.

7483   Reward Card, showing spray of flowers; 8 different designs, 2¼x3¾. Price each.$0.03
    Price per doz............. .30
7484   Reward Card, showing beautiful landscape in winter; frosted, 12 kinds. Size, 3x4½.
    Price, each $0.05
    Price, per doz......... .50
7485   Reward Card, showing old church in winter, etc., frosted, 12 kinds, size, 4x6. Price, each .. .07
    Price, per dozen .... .75
7486   Reward Card, showing flowers, landscapes, etc., frosted, 12 kinds. Size, 4½x6¼.
    Price, each..................... .08
    Price, per dozen .... .85
7487   Reward Card, showing beautiful waterscape, bird, flowers, etc.; frosted, 12 kinds. Size, 6x8. Price, each .... .10
    Price, per doz.................. 1.00

Reward of Merit Booklets.

Our New Idea.

We have had made expressly for us a beautiful, low-priced line of Reward of Merit Booklets which can be used for both day and Sunday schools.

          Each. Doz
7491   Reward of Merit Booklet, size, 4¼x3, 8 pages, fancy cover, assorted kinds.......$0.03 $0.30
7492   Reward of Merit Booklets, size, 5¼x4¼, 8 pages, assorted kinds.......... .05   .50
7493   Reward of Merit Booklets, size, 6¼x5¼, 8 pages, assorted kinds.......... .08   .85

Scrap Book Pictures.

7495   "Giant" assortment, 50 large sheets in a box, average size, 9x8¾.
Price, per box........$1.05. Per dozen sheets $0.28
Weight, 15 ounces.
7496   The "Wonder" Scrap Picture, Average size, 13½x9½ inches. Flowers, animals and children; the finest scrap pictures ever shown. 25 sheets in a box.
Price, per box.................................. 1.25
Per dozen sheets............................ .65
Weight, per box, 20 ounces.

Marriage Certificates.

All new and beautiful designs put up in heavy pasteboard tubes ready for mailing.
       Weight, each, 4 oz.   Each. Per doz.
7497   Printed with blanks for names of parties, witnesses, pastor, date and location. Size, 10x8.........$0.03 $0.30
7498   Printed on heavy paper, lithographed at top, with places for names, location and dates. Size, 11x14........ .08   .84
7499   Printed on cardboard, lithographed at top, spaces at side, which may or may not be used for photographs; places for names, location and dates. Size, 11x14 .15   1.50
7500   Episcopal form on white heavy paper, with monogram and description, spaces for names and dates. Size, 11x14 .07   .75
7501   Printed on cardboard, blanks for names, location and dates. Size, 14x19 .25   2.50
7502   Marriage Certificate, size, 15x18, printed on heavy cardboard, space for names, dates, etc., beautiful lithographed designs at top, also large bouquet of roses, full size and natural color, on side. Weight, 7 oz...... .50   5.25
7503   Marriage Certificate, same style and size as No. 7502, with openings for two cabinet photographs. Weight, 7 oz.... .50   5.25
7504   New 1895 style Marriage Certificate, printed on fine super-calendered paper with extra fine enamel finish and beautiful illustration. Size 11x14. Each.........................$0.25
Per dozen.............................. 2.75
7505   Wedding Souvenir, consists of five sheets of parchment, bound by white silk cord and tassel; size, 5½x6½, printed in the highest style of art. Containing certificate texts, etc. Each.$0.26
Per dozen.............................. 2.90
7506   Same as 7505, printed on linen paper.
Each................................$0.20
Per dozen.............................. 2.25

Wedding Bells.

7608   **Our Wedding Bells,** consists of a book, size, 7x8¾ inches. embossed leather, having a pretty design of wedding bells. The book is complete with a marriage certificate, several pages for names of guests present at the ceremony; 21 pages of appropriate quotations. Each in neat box. Weight, 16 oz. Price, each..$0.90

Family Records.

7509   Containing Marriage Certificate, Marriage Vow, United Benediction, Births, Our Baby, etc. Beautifully printed in colors with a verse to each subject. Handsomely bound in cloth and illustrated.
Retail price..................$1.50
Our price.................... .90
Postage..................... .10

Brownie Books.

7510   By Palmer Cox. The most amusing books for the children published. All have heavy board covers, and are illustrated throughout. Each contains about 150 pages.
The Brownies at Home.
Another Brownie Book.
The Brownies; Their Book.
The Brownies Around the World (new).
Retail price, each.....$1.50   Our price..........$1.05
Postage, extra, each 24 cents.

The Knockabout Club Series. Series 7512.

A most instructive series of books for young people on history, travel and adventure. All are beautifully illustrated. By Fred. A. Ober. Illustrated cloth covers.
The Knockabout Club in North Africa.
The Knockabout Club in Spain.
The Knockabout Club in the Antilles.
The Knockabout Club in the Tropics.
The Knockabout Club in the Everglades.
The Knockabout Club on the Spanish Main.
The Knockabout Club in Search of Treasure.
The Knockabout Club in the Woods.
The Knockabout Club Alongshore.
Retail price, each......$1.50   Our price........$0.75
Per dozen, assorted................................ 8.50
Postage, extra, each 20 cents.

Grimm's Household Fairy Tales.

7514   A large quarto of 284 pages, 8½x10¼ inches, containing over one hundred illustrations in black by that clever artist. R. Andre, together with a beautiful colored frontispiece. It is bound in elegantly covered board covers.
Retail price, each........$1.50   Our price......$0.60
Postage, extra.................................. .24

Half Hours With the Bible.

7516   An epitome of the histories contained in the Old and New Testaments; 350 pages. Royal 16mo. One hundred and fifty illustrations.
Retail price.. ....$1.50   Our price.......$0.60
Postage.................................... .24

Elephant Series.

7527   New edition, new covers, and pretty books added to the assortment, making the series one of the best on our list.
Alphabet of Animals.
Alphabet of Birds.
Frog Frolics.
E. Elephant, Esq.
Monkey Tricks.
Doggie Pranks.
Apple Pie A. B. C.
Doggie's Doings.
Playful Pussy.
The Daisy Chain.

Daisy Painting Book.   Donkey Days.
Here We Are Again.   Birds and Beasts.
Our Animal Friends.   One, Two, Three.
Day in the Country.   Dicky Birds.
Mail Cart.   Baby's Letter.
   Each..............$0.10.   Per dozen, assorted, $0.95

Aunt Louisa's Big Picture Books.

7530   Comprising some of the best and most popular toy books. They are elegantly printed in oil colors, on good paper.
Alphabet of Country Scenes.
Doings of the Alphabet.
Henny Penny.
Jack and the Beanstalk.
Red Riding Hood.
Robinson Crusoe.
A Merry A B C.
Our Zoo at Home.
Childhood's Happy Days.
Our Own Sailor Dolly.
Mr. Punch and his Tricks.

Drummer Boy.   Dolly's Lovers.
Kriss Kringle.   Dorothy Dumps and the
Merry Little Maid.   Yellow Bird.
Thr ugh the Alphabet.   From a Merry Little Maid.
Scenes from Showland.   From the Realm of Story
Rip Van Winkle.   Land.
Tit, Tiny and Tittens.   Crust and Crumbs.
Three Little Kittens.   A New Book.
Three Christmas Boxes.   Jap Dollie.
Visit to the Menagerie.   Mr. T yman.
Yankee Doodle.   Pretty Poll's Painting
Reynard the Fox.   Book.
The Bible Alphabet.   Behind the Bars.
   Each.............$0.18.   Per dozen, assorted... $2.00

Round the World Series.

7531   14 pages with colored and monochrome illustrations. Four kinds assorted. Size,9½x12½.
Our Village.   The Dog that would a
The Cat's Courtship.   Soldier be.
Adventures of A B C.   Sketches at the Zoo.
Little Sunbeams.   Twelfth Night Revels.
Mixed Pickles.   Come to Our Circus.
Let Me Look.   Scenes from Showland.
Happy Faces in Many   Our Animal Kingdom.
   Places.
   Each............................$0.30
   One dozen assorted............... 3.25

Linen Books.

Numbers from 7533 to 7537 are printed on linen cloth in colors.

Little A B C Books.

7533   A showy little Alphabet Book at a very modest price. Each letter is illustrated with a common object, having beneath it a name for a spelling lesson. Each $0.04
Per dozen.............................. .35

7536   Favorite Old Nursery Stories, selected for their special excellence. Newly illustrated and enlarged. Six full-page pictures, elegantly printed in colors. Covers in colors and very handsome.

Cinderella.
Red Riding-Hood.
Babes in the Wood.
Jack and the Bean Stalk.
Puss in Boots.
The Three Bears.

Tom Thumb   Goody Two-Shoes.
A B C of Animals.   Every Baby's A B C.
Boys' and Girls' A B C   Noah's Ark A B C.
Mother Goose.
   Each.................................$0.18
   Per dozen, assorted...... .... 1.90

Cock Robin Series.

7537   Superbly illustrated, each having six full-page pictures, in oil colors, together with eight pages of reading. The covers have elegant pictures on both front and back, and are varnished.
Bo Peep, Mother Goose Melodies.
Tommy Tucker, Mother Goose Melodies.
Old King Cole, Mother Goose Melodies.
Cock Robin,   Tom Thumb.
Goody Two-Shoes.   Old Woman and Pig.
Little Pigs.   House that Jack Built.
Apple Pie.   A B C Merry Alphabet.
Child's First Book.   Jolly Animal A B C.
Child's Home A B C.
   Each.................................$0.25
   Per dozen, assorted............... 2.75

STANDARD RELIGIOUS WORKS.
Rev. J. H. Ingraham's Works.

7545   All beautifully bound in cloth, 600 pages, 12 mo.
Throne of David.
Pillar of Fire.
Prince of the House of David.
   Each $1.05
   Postage...................... .12

Endeavor Doins' Down to the Corners.

7548   By Rev. J. F. Cowan. Square 12mo. Illustrated.
A delightfully realistic account by "Brother Jonathan Hayseeds" of the Christian Endeavor work in a country village.
Retail Price..........$1.50   Our Price........$1.05

Ecce Homo.

7549   A Survey of the Life and Work of Jesus Christ. By J. R. Seeley, M. A. 16mo..........$0.70
Postage, 10 cents.

Peloubet's Notes.

7551   And questions on international Sunday-school lessons for 1895.
Retail price....................................$1.25
Our price..................... .88
Postage...................... .10

Murray, Rev. Andrew.

12mo., cloth.
                    Retail   Our
7552   price.   price.
Abide in Christ..................$1.00 $0.75
Believe in Christ................ 1.25   .90
Children for Christ, The......... 1.25   .90
Holy in Christ.................. 1.00   .75
Like Christ.................... 1.00   .75
New Life, The................. 1.00   .75
Spirit of Christ, The .... 1.25   .90
With Christ in the School of Prayer... 1.00   .75
Postage, each, 10 cents.

*** All orders are filled from the latest Catalogue. We shall, whenever possible, on orders from old Catalogues, give the nearest we have, and wish to explain that we change our quotations so as to be able to give the latest styles and better values.

Spurgeon, Rev. Chas. H., Works. Series 7553.

	Retail price.	Our price.
Feathers for Arrows, 12mo	$1.00	$0.70
Spurgeon's Gems, 12mo	1.00	.70
The Golden Alphabet, 12mo	1.00	.70
My Sermon Notes, 4 vols., in box, 12mo.	4.00	2.80
Gleanings Among the Sheaves, 18mo, gilt top	.60	.48
All of Grace. 16mo	.50	.35
According to Promise. 16mo	.50	.35
Twelve Christmas Sermons. 8vo	.50	.35
Twelve New Year Sermons. 8vo	.50	.35
Twelve Sermons on the Resurrection. 8vo	.50	.35
Twelve Striking Sermons. 8vo	.50	.35
Twelve Soul Winning Sermons. 8vo	.50	.35

Add for postage 10 per cent. extra.

World's Congress of Religions.

7554 Edited by Prof. C. M. Stevens, Ph. D., with introduction by Rev. H. W. Thomas, D. D., containing a full and correct account of the gathering of religious leaders from every country at the World's Fair. Fully illustrated.
Paper covers $0.35
Silk cloth .... .75

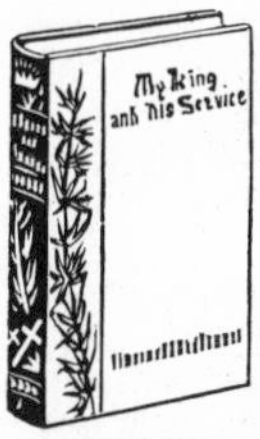

Havergal, Francis Ridley, Works.

7556 My King and His Service. New 16mo edition. Vellum cloth.
Retail price, ... $0.50
Our price .... .35

Havergal 32mos.

7557 Beautifully bound in cloth.
Retail price, each $0.25
Our price, each .... .18

Little Pillows. Kept for the Master's Use.
Morning Bells. Loyal Responses.
Morning Stars. My King.
My Bible Studies. Royal Bounty.
Royal Commandments. Royal Invitation.
Postage, each .... .03

Abiding Series.

7559 Ornamental cloth, 32mos.
Abiding. Peace.
Confiding. Rest.
Retail price, each 50c Our price, each $0.38
Per set 1.40
Postage, each, extra .... .03

Smith, Hannah W., Works.

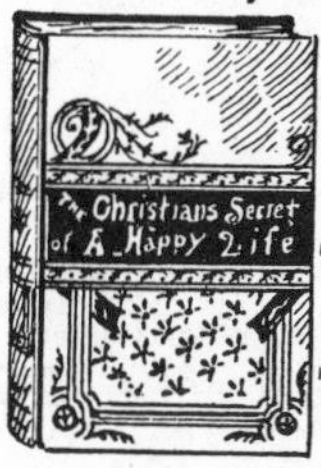

Christian Secret.

7560 **Christian's Secret of a Happy Life.** By Hannah Whitall Smith. New and enlarged edition. Cloth. 12mo. Price $0.53
Postage .... .10
7561 **The Open Secret;** or, the Bible Explaining Itself. 12mo. Cloth. Retail price, $1.00 Our price. $0.70
Postage .... .10
7562 **Every-Day Religion;** or, the Common-Sense Teaching of the Bible. By Hannah Whitall Smith. 12mo. Cloth $0.70
Postage .... .10

Between the Lights.

7563 Thoughts for the Quiet Hour. By Fanny B. Bates. 12mo. Cloth $0.88
Postage .... .12

Daily Text Book.

7565 Beautifully printed in two colors. 64mo, cloth extra, gilt edges.
Daily Bread (Our). Daily Guide (Our).
Daily Duty (Our). Daily Light (Our).
Daily Food (Our). Daily Portion (Our).
Retail price, each...$0.25 Our price $0.15
Per set of 6 volumes .... .83
Postage, extra, each 3c.

Prentiss, Elizabeth, Works.

7566 Stepping Heavenward. Cloth, 12mo. It is a story of life and faith, with the charm of naturalness and human sympathy. This makes it acceptable, as well as pure, strong and helpful. Retail price..$1.00
Our price .... .85

Aunt Jane's Hero. 12mo, cloth $0.85
Flower of the Family. 12mo, cloth .... .85
Home at Greylock. 12mo, cloth .... .85
Pemaquid. 12mo, cloth .... .85
Urbane and His Friends. 12mo, cloth .... .85
Postage, each, 10c. extra.

Beautiful Tree of Life.

7567 One of the most poetic and charming pictures in the whole Bible is that portion of scripture in Revelation above quoted, describing the Tree of Life; 512 pages, 100 illustrations. 8vo, cloth. Retail price $2.00
Our price .... .75
Postage, 22c. extra.

Royal Road.

7568 A new work by Marian Harland; 12mo, cloth $1.05
Postage, 12c. extra.

Why We Went.

7569 A new book by Jno. Habberton, author of Helen's Babies; 12mo, cloth.
Retail price .... $1.50 Our price. $1.05
Postage, extra. 12c.

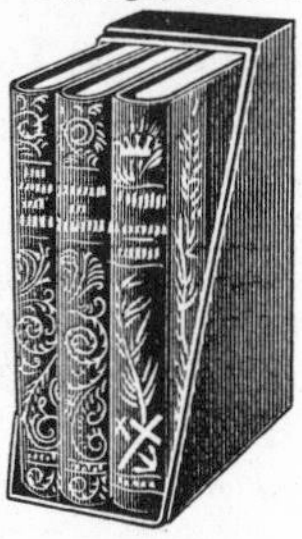

Divinity Classics.

7571 Containing Addresses, by Drummond; Imitation of Christ, by A'Kempis; and My King and His Service, by Havergal. Beautiful presentation edition, white and lavender vellum cloth in box to match. 16mo, 3 vols.
Per set of 3 volumes $0.88
Postage, extra, 26 cents.

Drummond, Henry, Works.

NEW SCIENTIFIC WORK.

7573 **The Ascent of Man.** By Henry Drummond, F. G. S. In this new work an attempt is made to tell in a plain way a few of the things which science is now seeing with regard to the "A cent of Man." Though its standpoint is evolution and its subject man, this book is far from being designed to prove that man has relations, compromising or otherwise, with lower animals. Its theme is "ascent," not "descent." 12mo, cloth. Retail price .... $2.00. Our price $1.40
Postage, extra, 16 cents.
7574 **Natural Law in the Spiritual World.** 16mo, blue cloth, silver stampings, yellow edges.
Retail price .... $0.75 Our price .... .40
Postage, 8 cents.
7575 **My Point of View.** By Prof. Henry Drummond. A beautiful presentation edition; bound in white vellum, with designs in silver, and silver top. Retail price .... .75
Our price .... .52
Postage, 8 cents.
7576 **Addresses.** By Prof. Henry Drummond. Four books bound in one volume. Half blue vellum. Each .... .22
For full white vellum, silver stamping, each... .52
Postage .... .08
7577 **Cup of Loving Serv.ce.** Presentation binding, same as above .... .75
7578 **Pax Vobiscum.** Presentation binding .... .75
7579 **What is a Christian.** A talk on books .... .27

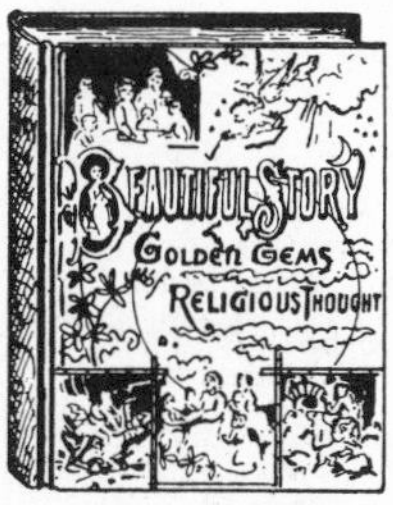

Talmage Books.

7583 **"The Beautiful Story,"** by T. DeWitt Talmage. This is the companion book to the Bible History of all sacred events recorded in the Bible. Handsomely bound in cloth with silver and gold stampings.
Subscription price $3.50
Our price 1.20
Postage .... .36

7584 **The New Beautiful Story.** By J. W. Buel and T. DeWitt Talmage, the great companion book to the Bible. 600 pages, beautifully illustrated. 8vo, cloth. Retail price $3.50. Our price $1.40
Postage, extra, 32 cents.
7585 **The Pathway of Life.** By T. DeWitt Talmage, containing 576 pages, 300 illustrations, and numerous colored plates. 8vo, cloth.
Retail price.... $3.50. Our price 1.20
Postage, extra, 30 cents.
7586 **From Manger to Throne.** By T. DeWitt Talmage. A companion book to above. Subscription price .... $3.75 Our price 1.40
Postage, 32 cents.
7589 **Night Scenes of City Life.** By T. DeWitt Talmage. Cloth, 12mo. Retail price .... .75
Our price .... .35
Postage .... .10
7591 **Traps for Men.** By T. DeWitt Talmage.
Cloth, 12mo. Retail price .... .75
Our price .... .35
Postage .... .10
7592 **Sermons in the Holy Land.** By T. DeWitt Talmage. Retail price .... .75
Our price .... .35
Postage .... .10
7593 **Crumbs Swept Up..** By T. DeWitt Talmage.
12mo, cloth .... .52
Postage .... .12
7594 **Wedding Ring.** By T. DeWitt Talmage.
12mo, cloth .... .35
Postage .... .10
7595 **Woman.** Her Power and Privileges. By T. DeWitt Talmage. 12mo, cloth .... .35
Postage .... .10
7596 **Battle for Bread.** By T. DeWitt Talmage.
12mo, cloth .... $0.35 Postage .... .10

Fishing Tackle.
We are Headquarters

History of the Conflict Between Religion and Science.

7598 By Dr. Wm. J. Draper. 12mo., cloth.
Retail price .... $1.75 Our price $1.23
Postage, extra, 12 cents.

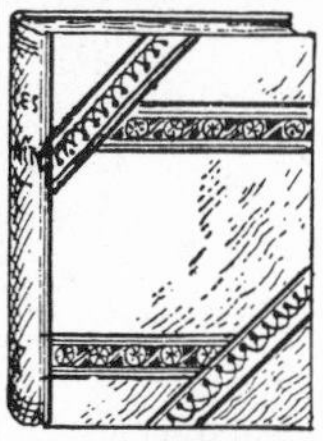

7600 **Jesus the Messiah.** An abridged edition of the Life and Times of Jesus the Messiah. By Alfred Endersheim with preface by Prof. W. Sandage, of Oxford. 8vo. Cloth bound. 659 pages. Price $1.25
Postage .... .15

Fishin' Jimmy Series

7601 Each 16mo. Blue cloth
Aunt Dorothy. By Margaret J. Preston.
Aunt Liefy. By Annie T. Slosson.
Fishin' Jimmy. By Annie T. Slosson.
Gentleman Jim. By Mrs. E. Prentiss.
Jack's Hymn. By Elizabeth Olmis.
Katie, a Daughter of the King. By Mary A. Gilmore.
The Las' Day. By Imogen Clark.
A Poppy Garden. By Emily Malbone Morgan.
Retail price .... $0.60 Our price $0.45
Postage, each, 6 cents.

Porter, Rose, Works.

7602 **Women's Thoughts for Women.** 16mo., cloth. $0.38
7603 **Men's Thoughts for Men.** 16mo., cloth ..... .38
Postage, each .... .06

Edersheim, Rev. Alfred, D. D., Ph. D.

7605 **The Bible History.** 7 vols. 12mo., cloth.
1. The World Before the Flood, and History of the Patriarchs.
2. The Exodus and Wanderings in the Wilderness.
3. Israel in Canaan under Joshua and the Judges.
4. Israel under Samuel, Saul and David, to the Birth of Solomon.
5. Israel and Judah from the Birth of Solomon to the Reign of Ahab.
6. Israel and Judah from Ahab to the Decline of the two Kingdoms.
7. Israel and Judah from the Decline of the two Kingdoms to the Assyrian and Babylonian Captivity. Containing full Scripture References and Subject Indexes to the whole series.

Each, $0.70; the set, in a neat box $4.10
7606 **Elisha the Prophet;** the Lessons of His History and Times. 12mo., cloth $0.70
7607 **Sketches of Jewish Life,** in illustration of the New Testament. 12mo., cloth .... .88
7608 **The Temple;** its Ministry and Services at the Time of Jesus Christ. 12mo., cloth .... .88
Postage, each, extra, ... .10

Lathrop, Rev. S. C.

7609 **Fifty Years and Beyond;** or, Old Age and How to Enjoy It. 35th thousand. 12 mo., cloth.... $0.70
Postage .... .10

Moody, D. L., Works.

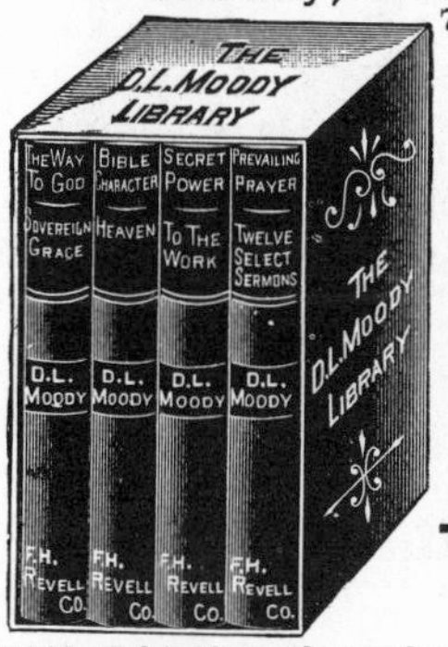

7611 The D. L. Moody Library, 4 vols., in box. 12 mo., cloth.
A new edition in new binding, containing the following eight books.
The Way to God.
Sovereign Grace.
Secret Power.
To the Work.
Bible Characters.
Heaven.
Prevailing Prayer.
Twelve Select Sermons.
Retail price $4.00
Our price 2.80
Postage, extra, 52c.

The Home Beyond, or Views of Heaven.

7612 Taken from the works of over 400 prominent thinkers and writers, by Rt. Rev. Samuel Fallows, D.D. Complete treatise on the following: Man, Life, Death, the Dying, the Death of Children, Immortality, the Resurrection, Heaven, Recognition, Angelic Ministry, Saintly Sympathy. Over 80 full-page engravings, 512 pages, royal 8vo. Retail price $2.00
Our price 1.00
Postage, extra .... .24

Daily Strength for Daily Needs.

7613 "As Thy Days so Shall Thy Strength Be." A selection for every day in the year. Selected by the editor of "Quiet Hours." Retail price.... $1.00
Our price .... .70
Postage, extra, 12 cents.
7614 **Evidences of Christianity.** By T. Watson, D.D. Comprising Jenyn's Internal Evidences, etc. 12mo., cloth $0.60
Postage .... .10
7615 **Seekers after God.** By F. W. Farrar, D. D. 12mo., cloth .... .63
7616 **Early Days of Christianity.** By F. W. Farrar, D. D. 12mo., gilt top .... .63
Postage .... .10
7617 **Geikie's Life and Works of Christ.** By Cunningham Geikie, D. D. 12mo., cloth, gilt top... .75
Postage .... .12

Books—Continued.

7618 **Koran (The)**; or, Alkoran of Mohammed. "The Bible of the East." Translated into English from the original Arabic, with notes and a preliminary discourse, by George Sale. With maps and plans, demy, 800 pp., gilt top...$1.85
Postage, 16 cents extra.

7619 **Nights Scenes in the Bible.** By Daniel March, D. D. This book shuts out the glare of day, and seeks instruction in the silent night; 544 pages.
Cloth 1.00
Postage .... .22

7620 **Kitto's Cyclopædia of Biblical Literature.** 2 vols. Cloth, 12mo. Per set, 2 volumes 2.70

7621 **D'Aubigne's History of the Reformation.** 5 vols. Cloth, 12mo. Per set, 5 volumes 3.25

7622 **Geikie's Hours with the Bibles,** 3 volumes. Cloth, 12mo. Per set of 3 volumes 2.65
Half Russia 4.25

7623 **Gold Dust.** By Charlotte M. Yonge. A collection of golden counsels for sanctification of daily life. Bound in white leatherette .... .40
Venetian seal, limp, round corners, gilt .... .60
Postage .... .08

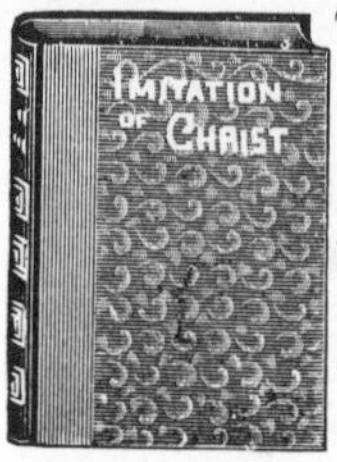

7624 **Imitation of Christ.** By Thos. A'Kempis Beautifully bound in ½ white vellum cloth, stamped in gold, $0.22. Bound in French seal, limp, gold edges, $0.56. Persian calf, red under gold edge, $0.90. Postage, each..$0.08

7625 **Christian Year.** Rivington's 18mo. edition, bound in French seal, gilt edges, $0.55. Postage, 6 cents.

7626 **Geikie's Holy Land.** By Cunningham Geikie. 2 vols. Cloth, 12mo $2.25
Postage, 26 cents extra.

Men of the Bible.

Series No. 7628
12mo. Cloth.

Abraham. By Rev. W. J. Dean.
Daniel. By H. Deane, D.D.
David. By Rev. W. J. Dean.
Elijah. By Prof. W. Milligan, D. D.
Ezra and Nehemiah. By Rev. Canon Rawlinson.
Gideon and Judges. By J. M. Lang, D. D.
Isaac and Jacob. By Rev. Canon Rawlinson.
Isaiah. By Rev. Canon Driver.
Jeremiah. By Rev. Canon Cheyne.
Jesus the Christ. By F. J. Vallings.
Joshua. By Rev. W. J. Dean.
Kings of Israel and Judah. By Rev. Canon Rawlinson.
Minor Prophets, The. By F. W. Farrar, D. D.
Moses. By Rev. Canon Rawlinson.
Samuel and Saul. By Rev. W. J. Dean.
Solomon. By F. W. Farrar, D. D.
St. Paul. By Prof. Iverach, D. D.
Retail price, each $1.00
Our Price .... $0.75 Postage, extra.... .10

Henry's Commentaries.

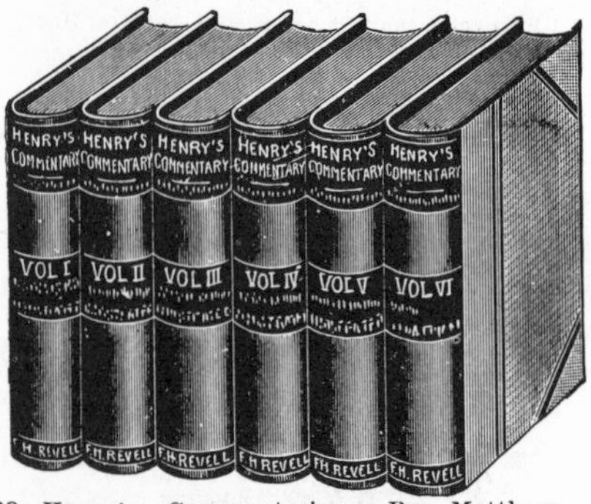

7 29 Henry's Commentaries. By Matthew Henry. A new, large type edition 6 vols. Cloth.
Retail price .... $15.00 Our price.... $10.50
Half morocco .... 18.00 Our price.... 12.60
Postage, extra, $1.40.

Jamieson Fausset and Brown's Bible Commentary.

7630 Complete in 4 volumes. Combines the best features of Matthew Henry, Adam Clarke, etc. Illustrated with maps, tables, etc. Four royal, 8vo. volumes $5.20
Postage .... .70

McIntosh, C. H., Works.

7631 Notes by C. H. M , on the Pentateuch.
Genesis, Exodus,
Leviticus, Numbers,
Deuteronomy, 2 vols., 16mo., cloth. Each.... $0.52
6 volumes in box 3.05
These books are not commentaries, in the ordinary understanding of that word; they are of a more popular style, helpful, suggestive, inspiring.

Menzies, Mrs. Stephen.

7632 **How to Mark your Bible.** With prefatory note by D. L. Moody. 8vo., paper $0.25
Cloth .... .52
"It is an excellent method for Bible students, teachers and preachers."

McNeill, Rev. John.

7633 **Sermons by the Rev. John McNeill.** Vols. I., II. and III., each containing 26 sermons. 12mo., cloth. Each .... $1.05 Postage, each.... $0.12

Paton, John G., D.D.

7634 **John G. Paton, Missionary to the New Hebrides.** An autobiography edited by his brother, with an introductory note by Rev. A. T. Pierson, D.D. New illustrated edition, 2 vols., boxed 12mo., cloth $1.60

Stalker, Prof. James, M. A., D.D.

7635 **The Life of Jesus Christ.** 12mo., cloth $0.42
Postage .... .08

Willard, Frances E.

7636 **Nineteen Beautiful Years**; or, Sketches of a Girl's Life, with preface by John G. Whittier. New and revised edition, 12mo., cloth $0.52
Postage .... .08

POCKET, TEACHERS' AND FAMILY BIBLES.

Names will be engraved on any leather Bible for 20c. per name extra.

International Pocket Bibles.

Pearl type Bibles. Without References. Six maps; thin paper. Size, 3¼x5⅝x¾ inches.

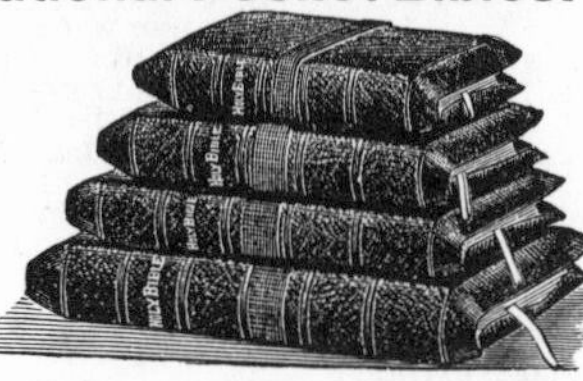

7640 **Imitation Roan,** red edges, half padded, round corners, gold side title $0.26
7641 **French Morocco,** gilt edge, flexible boards, round corners, gold title embossed designs .... .38
7642 **French Morocco,** red under gold edges, divinity circuit, round corners .... .58
7643 **Imitation Ivory,** red under gold edges, round corners. Illuminated side title with clasp. Can be used for wedding gift .... .70

Ruby Type Bibles.

Without reference; size, 3¼x5⅝x1; six maps.
7645 **Imitation Roan,** gold edges, half padded, round corners, gold side title $0.40
7646 **French Morocco,** gold edges, flexible round corners, gold side title 0.55
7647 **French Morocco,** red under gold edges, divinity circuit, round corners, gold side and back title .... .80

Emerald Type Bibles.

Without references; size, 3½x5¼; six maps.
7649 **Imitation Roan,** red edges, limp, round corners, gold titles $0.56
7650 **French Morocco,** divinity circuit, round corners, red under gold edges, leather lined 1.48

Minion Type Bibles.

Without references; size, 3¾x5¾x1¼; six maps.
7652 **Imitation Roan,** red edge, half padded, round corners, gold side titles $0.60
7653 **French Morocco,** red burnished edges, flexible boards, round corners, gold titles, floral design .... .80
7654 **French Seal,** red under gold edges, divinity circuit, round corners, leather lined 1.60

Bourgeois Type Bibles.

Without references; size, 4½x6⅝x1⅛; six maps.
7655 **Imitation Roan,** red edges, flexible boards, round corners, gold side titles $1.10
7656 **French Morocco,** divinity circuit, round corners, red under gold edges $1.95

Small Pica Type Bibles.

Without references; size, 6x8⅛x1¼; six maps.
7657 **Imitation Roan,** red burnished edges, round corners, side and back title $1.25
7658 **French Morocco,** gold edges, round corners, flexible, gold titles 1.50
7659 **French Seal,** gold edges, divinity circuit, round corners 2.25

International Students' Reference Bibles.

Containing subject index. Harmony of the Gospels, chronological tables and maps.
Bibles 7660 to 7667 are reference.

Pearl Type.

Size, 3¾x5¾.
7660 **Imitation Roan,** gold edges, boards, round corners $0.52
7661 **French Morocco,** Turkey grain, red under gold edges. Each .... .74
7662 **French Morocco,** divinity circuit, Turkey grain, red under gold edges, round corners, gilt side and back title. Each .... .85

Ruby Type Bibles.

Size, 3¾x5¾.
7663 **French Seal,** red and gold edges, limp, round corners, gold side and back titles. Each $0.85
7664 **French Seal,** divinity circuit, red under gold edges, round corners, gold side and back title. Each 1.15

Minion Type Bibles.

Size, 5¼x7½.
7665 **French Morocco,** divinity circuit, red under gold edges, round corners, leather lined. Each $2.25

Bourgeois Type Bibles.

Size, 5¼x7¾.
7666 **Imitation Roan,** gilt edges, flexible boards, round corners, gold titles. Each $1.60
7667 **French Seal,** divinity circuit, gold edges, round corners, gold side and back title 3.10

Bagster Edition, Comprehensive Teachers' Bibles.

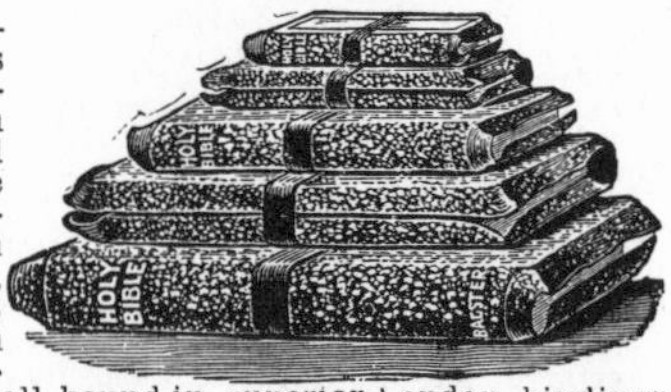

With entirely new aids and new concordance on an improved plan. There are 1,850 subjects noted in this edition, being 1,278 more than other editions contain; all bound in superior London bindings and printed on the best papers.

7668 **French Seal,** divinity circuit, round corners, pearl type, size, 6x3⅞x1¼.
Retail price $1.50
Our price 1.00
Same with Dennison's patent index 1.85
7671 **French Seal,** divinity circuit, round corners, gold edges, ruby type, size, 6½x 4¼x1¼
Retail price $2.50
Our price 1.65
7672 **French Seal,** divinity circuit, round corners, gold edges, nonpareil type, size, 7½x5x¼.
Retail price $2.75
Our price 2.00
7673 **Same** as 7672, with Dennison's patent index 2.90
7674 **Levant Morocco,** divinity circuit, leather lined, silk sewed, round corners, gold edge, minion type, size, 8½x5¼x1¼, with clasp.
Retail price $6.00
Our price 4.90
7675 **Same** as 7674, with Dennison's patent index 5.65
7677 **French Seal,** divinity circuit, bourgeois type, round corners, goldedges; size, 9¾x 5½x 1½. Retail price $6.00
Our price 4.10
7678 **Persian Levant,** divinity circuit, leather lined, silk sewed, bourgeois type, round corners, gold edges. Retail price $7.00
Our price 5.00
7679 **Levant Morocco,** divinity circuit, round corners, gold edges, leather lined, silk sewed, bourgeois type. Retail price $10.00
Our price 7.75
7680 **Same** as 7679, with Dennison's patent index 8.50

Genuine Oxford Teachers' Bibles.

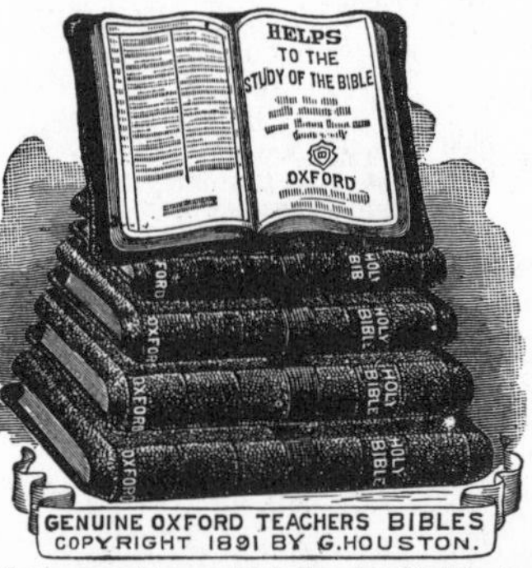

7683 **French Seal,** divinity circuit, round corners, gold edges, pearl type. Size, 4x5½. Retail price $1.50. Our price $0.95
7684 **Persian Levant,** divinity circuit, leather lined, silk sewed, round corners, red under gold edges, pearl type. Retail price $2.50. Our price $2.05
7685 **Same** as 7684, with Dennison's patent index $2.80
7686 **Same** as 7684, printed on India paper 2.90
7687 **Persian Levant,** divinity circuit, leather lined, silk sewed, round corners, red under gold edges, ruby type, size, 4¼6½.
Retail price each $3.50
Our price 2.75
7689 **Same** as 7687, printed on India paper with Dennison's patent index 4.40
7690 **Palestine Levant,** divinity circuit, leather lined, silk sewed, round corners, red under gold edges, nonpareil type, size, 4½x7.
Retail price 4.00
Our price 3.15
7691 **Same** as 7690, printed on India paper 4.75
7693 **French Seal,** divinity circuit, illustrated, round corners, gold edges, minion type, size, 5x7¾.
Retail price 3.50
Our price 1.95
7694 **Persian Levant,** divinity circuit, leather lined, silk sewed, round corners, red under gold edges, minion type, size, 5x7¾.
Retail price 5.00
Our price 3.50
7695 **Same** as 7694, with Dennison's patent index 4.25
7696 **Same** as 7694, printed on India paper 5.00
7698 **Levant Morocco,** divinity circuit, calf lined to edge, silk sewed, round corners, red under gold edges, minion type, size, 5x7½.
Retail price 6.00
Our price 4.30
7699 **Same** as 7698, with Dennison's patent index 5.05
7700 **Same** as 7698, printed on India paper, indexed 7.00

Bibles—Continued.

7701 **Persian Levant.** Divinity Circuit, leather lined, silk sewed, red under gold edge, round corners, bourgeois type, size 9⅜x6½.
Retail price..........$7.50 Our price..........$5.45
7702 **Same as 7701,** printed on India paper..... 7.00
7703 **The New Large Type Oxford Bible,** Persian Levant, leather lined, silk sewed, red under gold edges, round corners, long primer type. About the same size as small pica.
Retail price..........$8.00 Our price..........$5.00
7705 **Same as 7703** printed on India paper.......6.00

Wide Margin Bible.

7708 **Levant Morocco,** Divinity Circuit, calf lined, silk sewed, round corners, red under gold edges, minion type, with wide margin for MS. notes, size 7x9⅜x1¾
Retail price..13.00
Our price...10.00

The Holman Self-Pronouncing S. S. Teachers' Bible.

A complete library of Scriptural knowledge in small compass, adapted to all classes. Indispensable to clergymen, students, S. S. teachers and to all who would study the Word of God intelligently.

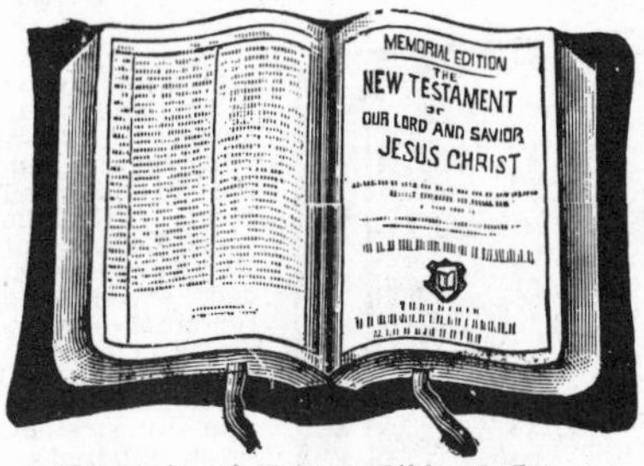

Exact size of Holman Bible, 5x7¾.

Minion Type.

7710 (A) Minion Type, Grained Cloth, red edges. Retail price..........................$2.25
Our price..1.35
7711 (B) Minion Type, French Seal, round corners, gilt edges. Retail price.................. 3.25
Our price..1.95
7712 (C) Minion Type, French Seal, divinity circuit, round corners, gilt edges. Retail price. 3.75
Our price..2.35
With Dennison's Patent Index.........................3.30
7713 (D) Minion Type, French Seal, divinity circuit, leather lined, round corners, red under gold edges. Retail price........................ 4.75
Our price..3.00
With Dennison's Patent Index.........................3.95
7714 (E) Minion Type, Persian Seal, divinity circuit, silk sewed, round corners, gold edges.
Retail price........$5.50 Our price.............. 3.50
With Dennison's Patent Index.........................4.45
7715 (F) Minion Type, Palestine Levant, divinity circuit, leather lined, silk sewed, round corners, red under gold edges. Retail price........ 6.00
Our price..3.95
With Dennison's Patent Index.........................4.90
7717 (G) Minion Type, Levant, divinity circuit, calf lined, silk sewed, round corners, red under gold edges. Retail price........................ 7.00
Our price..4.25
With Dennison's Patent Index.........................5.20
7718 (N) *India Paper* edition, best Levant, divinity circuit, calf lined, silk sewed, round corners, gold edges. Retail price.................. 9.00
Our price..6.00
With Dennison's Patent Index.........................6.95
7719 (O) *India Paper*, Seal Skin, divinity circuit, calf lined, silk sewed, round corners, red under gold edges. Retail price..................14.00
Our price..9.50
With Dennison's Patent Index........................10.45

Bourgeois Type.

SIZE 6x8.

7721 (H) Bourgeois Type, Grained Cloth, red edges. Retail price............................ 3.50
Our price..2.50
7722 (J) Bourgeois Type, French Seal, limp, round corners, gold edges. Retail price........ 4.50
Our price..3.00
7723 (K) Bourgeois Type, French Seal, divinity circuit, round corners, red under gold edges.
Retail price..........$5.00 Our price........... 3.40
With Dennison's Patent Index.........................4.35
7724 (L) Bourgeois Type, French Seal, divinity circuit, leather lined, round corners, red under gold edges. Retail price...................... 6.00
Our price..4.00
With Dennison's Patent Index.........................4.90
7725 (M) Bourgeois Type, Persian Seal, divinity circuit, leather lined, silk sewed, round corners, red under gold edges. Retail price 6.50
Our price..4.55
With Dennison's Patent Index.........................5.45
7726 (P) Bourgeois Type, Palestine Levant, divinity circuit, leather lined, silk sewed, round corners, red under gold edges. Retail price.. 7.50
Our price..5.00
With Dennison's Patent Index.........................5.95
7727 (R) Bourgeois Type, Levant Morocco, divinity circuit, calf lined, silk sewed, rounnd corners, red under gold edges. Retail price........ 8.50
Our price..5.75
With Dennison's Patent Index.........................6.65
Add 25c. each extra on all Teachers' Bibles if by mail.

"International" German Teachers' Bibles. Bourgeois. 8vo.

Recognizing the demand for a series of German Teachers' Bibles to correspond with the English lines, we have added an entirely new set of German Bible plates in bourgeois type. The page is a convenient size, and the book may be easily carried. The references are especially full. The bibles have a very complete set of helps and the best maps, prepared by men of high scholarship. These bibles have all the excellent qualities of the English bibles, in paper, printing and manufacture. This will be the only line of German Teachers' Bibles in the world.

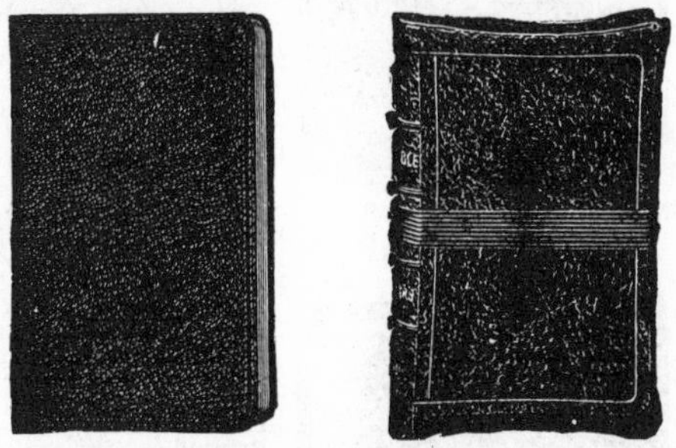

TEACHERS' EDITION, WITHOUT APOCRYPHA. THIN PAPER

Size, 5½x8½ inches.

	Retail price.	Our price.
7728 French Morocco, gilt edges, heavy boards, round corners, family record	$3.00	$1.90
7729 Algerian Morocco, red and gold edges, divinity circuit, round corners, family record, leather lined	4.00	3.00
7730 Levant, red and gold edges, divinity circuit, round corners, family record, paneled calf, lined to edge	6.00	4.10
7731 Algerian Morocco, red and gold edges, divinity circuit, round corners, family record, extra grained lining to edge	5.00	3.75

Above Bibles with Dennison's patent index, 72 notches, $1.00 extra.

American Reprint. Oxford S. S. Teachers' Bibles.

All of our editions of the Oxford Bible are printed from fac-simile plates of the University press, Oxford, England.

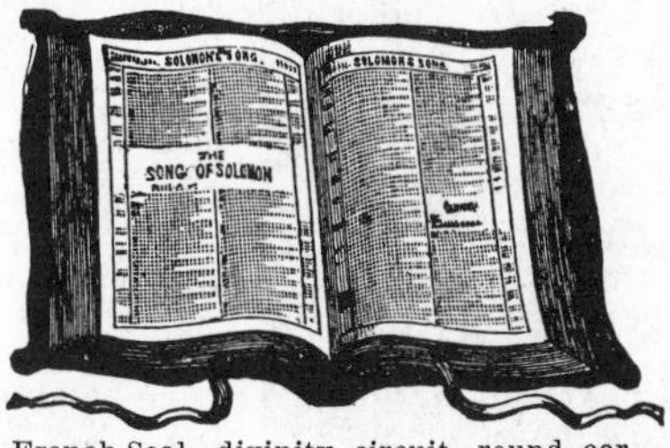

7732 French Seal, divinity circuit, round corners, gold edges, minion type, size, 5x7½.
Retail price...$3.50
Our price..1.25
Same with patent index...............................1.88
7733 Russian Seal, divinity circuit, leather lined, round corners, gold edges, minion type.
Retail price...5.50
Our price..1.80
Same with patent index...............................2.45

Prayer Books.

We take the liberty of announcing to our many customers that the new Standard Prayer Book adopted by the Convention of 1892 is now ready.

Minion Type.

Size, 2⅛x3¾.

7734 **Prayer Book,** plain cloth, white edges. Each.$0.20
7735 **Prayer Book,** Japanese seal, limp, round corners, gilt edges. Each............... .32
7736 **Prayer Book,** French seal, limp, round corners, gilt edges, with gilt cross on cover. Each................................ .48
7737 **Prayer Book,** French pebble grain, limp, round corners, red under gold edges. Each.... .62
7738 **Prayer Book,** Persian calf, limp, round corners, gilt edges, gold cross. Each.......... .58

Bourgeois Type.

Size, 3¼x7.

7739 **Prayer Book,** plain cloth, white edges. Each.$0.18
7740 **Prayer Book,** French seal, limp, round corners, gilt edges and gilt cross. Each........ .58
7741 **Prayer Book,** French pebble grain, limp, round corners, red under gold edges. Each..... .75
7742 **Prayer Book,** French rutland grain, divinity circuit, round corners, gold edge. Each........ .90

WOULD BE POOR POLICY

To misrepresent our goods knowingly, therefore do not hesitate to place confidence in our Buyer's Guide. If goods are not as represented we will cheerfully refund purchase price and pay all transportation charges.

Long Primer Prayer Books.

Size, 3½x7¾.

7743 **Prayer Book,** French, round corners, limp, gilt seal, gold edges. Each..................... .85
7744 **Prayer Book,** Syrian, Levant, limp, round corners, red under gold edges. Each.......... 1.50

Pica 12mo. Prayer Books.

Size, 4½x6⅛.

7745 **Prayer Book,** French seal, gilt edges. Each.$0.98
7746 **Prayer Book,** French duplex, limp, round corners, gilt edges. Each................... 1.20
7747 **Prayer Book,** French rutland grain, divinity circuit, round corners, gilt edges. Each........ 1.65
7748 **Prayer Book,** Persian calf, limp, round corners, gilt edges and gilt cross. Each........ 1.50

Testaments.

7749 **Testament,** ruby type; size, 2½x3¾. French seal, limp, gilt edges. Each...............$0.20
7750 **Testament,** ruby type, French seal, divinity circuit, gilt edges. Each....................... .36
7751 **Testament,** ruby type, paper enameled, flush sprinkled edges. Each, 7c. Per doz............ .70

Testaments and Psalms.

7752 **Testament,** French seal, ruby type, limp, gilt edge, size, 4x2¾. Each..................$0.28
7753 **Testament,** French seal, divinity circuit, round corners, gilt edges, size, 4x2¾.
Each.. .45
7754 **Testament,** grain cloth, size, 5⅝x7½, red edges, pica type. Each......................... .75
7755 **Testament,** French seal, limp, round corners, gilt edges, size, 5⅝x7½, pica type. Each....... 1.00
N. B.—Add 10 per cent. for postage on testaments.

Hymnals.

7756 Hymnals, 48mo, 3⅞x2⅝ inches, boards, white edges. Each...........................$0.24
7757 Hymnal, French seal, broken glass design, size, 3½x5½, red under gold edges, large type.
Each.. 1.50
7758 Hymnals, French seal, sizes, 5x7½, broken glass design, pica type, red under gold edges.
Each.. 2.05
7759 Hymnals, grain cloth, size, 5x7½, pica type, plain edges. Each.......................... .75

Prayer Books and Hymnals.

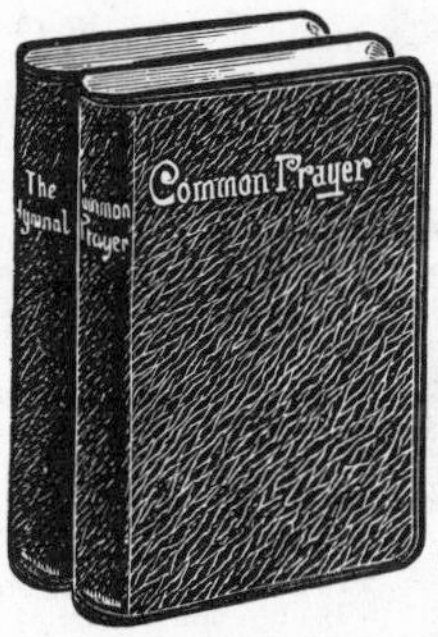

7760 Japanese Seal, limp round corners, gold edge, size, 2⅝x3⅞.
Each $0.75
7761 Prayer and Hymnal, French seal, limp, round corners, gold edges and gold cross..........$1.00
7762 Prayer and Hymnal, French pebble grain, limp, round corners, red under gold edges, gold roll $1.50
7763 Prayer and Hymnal, Syrian Levant, limp, red under gold edges, gold roll, blind ties.
Each..............$2.00
N. B.—All above Prayers and Hymnals are minion type books.

Catholic Prayer Books.

(In English.) Each.

7765 Catholic Prayer Book, 48mo., black cloth binding, white edges.............................$0.16
7766 Catholic Prayer Book, same as above. Bound in French calf, limp, round corners, gold edges.. .45
7767 Catholic Prayer Book, 32mo., bound in arabesque, with gilt center and edges............ .40
7769 Catholic Prayer Book 32mo., bound in French seal, with stamp and gilt edges, round corners.. .75
7780 Catholic Prayer Book, manual of prayer for use of the Faithful, with Epistles and Gospels, the Mass and Stations of the Cross. Bound in fine Persian, padded sides, gilt cross and title, red under gold edges; large type.
Price, each... 1.50
7781 Catholic Prayer Book, with all approved devotions for the Church and home, with Epistles and Gospels for all Sundays and Holy days of the year; bound in German calf, limp, gilt filled, gilt title and monogram on side, round corners, red under gold, solid edges, large type. Each.. 2.50
7782 Vest Pocket Catholic Prayer Book, 32mo., long, for the vest pocket; bound in fine Persian flexible leather, red under gold edges.
Each, only.. .70
7783 Combination Set, Key of Heaven and Epistles and Gospels. Bound in fine Persian, duplex, red under gold edges, 32mo., only......... 2.50
7784 Combination Set, Key of Heaven, H. C. A. H., 2 vols. in a fine French kid case with handle; books are bound in a smooth French kid, red under gold edges.............................. 3.00

N. B.—Names will be stamped in gold on leather Bibles, Prayer Books, etc., for 20 cents per name.

Catholic Prayer Books.
(In German.)

7785 Fuerer Zum Himmel, 32mo.................$0.40
7787 Fuerer Zum Himmel, 32mo., bound in embossed leather, gilt edges......................... .75
7789 Fuerer Zum Himmel, 32mo., bound in fine Russia, round corners, gilt edges, boxed........ 1.25

French Prayer Books.

7790 French Catholic Prayer Books. Bound in very handsome binding, gilt edges; our special price.. 1.50

Greek Testament.

7791 Greek Testament. With Lexicon and Supplement. By Gulielmi Greenfield. Second American Revised Edition, with Lexicon and Supplement, giving various readings adopted by the English and American revisers, 1881, and other valuable information, 24mo., cloth............. .55
Postage... .10

Family, Pulpit and Reference Bibles.

7795 Bible. Imitation Leather, full gilt side, panel design, gilt edges. Printed on fine white paper, pica type, marginal references. Contains the King James Version of the Old and New Testaments; map of Palestine in colors; life of our Lord and Savior, illustrated; numerous full page Dore and other engravings; new and beautiful marriage certificate and family record; index to Holy Bible; tables of Scripture weights, measures and coins, and alphabetical table of proper names. Size, 10½x12¾. Retail price.......................$3.00
Our price....................................... 1.25

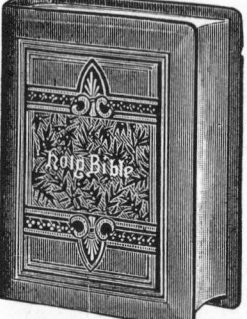

7796 Bible. Bound in American morocco, London antique gold side and back title; comb edges, cloth joints, containing same contents as Bible No. 7795 and in addition Smith's Bible Dictionary. Size, 10½ x12¾ (No. 3). Retail price...$4.25
Our price...... 1.85

7797 Quarto Family Bible, containing the Old and New Testaments, with revised version of the New Testament appended. History of the Books of the Bible, illustrated, complete Bible analysis. Concordance, Psalms in meter. Profusely illustrated with numerous full page Dore and other engravings, marriage certificates and family record in gold and colors. Bound in padded American morocco, full gilt edges, gilt side title, cloth joints (6½).
Price.............$2.90
Same with nickel clasp $3.15

7798 Bible. American morocco; new arabesque design, gold title on side and back; marbled edges. King James version Old and New Testaments, 12 full page Dore engravings, colored maps, life of our Lord, etc. Apocrypha, Concordance and Psalms, revised New Testament and family record. Contains also same as 7795.
Price, each...$2.30
Same Bible with nickel clasp..... 2.50

Bibles—Continued.

7800 Bible. French Morocco; wine color, antique raised panel sides, gold title on side and back, gold corners, gold edges. Contains also same as 7797 and in addition illuminated plate.
Extra fine Family Record.
Life of our Lord.
Scenes in the Life of Christ and Apostle Paul.
Scenes in Jerusalem, Egypt, Assyria.
Customs, arts and sciences.
Religious rites and emblems.
Wanderings of the Israelites, Idols and Idolatry of the Ancients and Scenes in Palestine, fully illustrated. Price each, $3.25. Same Bible with nickel clasp, $3.50

7801 American Calf, basket pattern, soft padded sides, round corners, gold side and back title, squares rolled with gold, gilt edges, cloth joints. Printed on fine white paper, pica type, marginal references. Contains the King James version of the Old and New Testaments, with the revised version of the New Testament appended, and in addition thereto the Apocrypha, Concordance, Psalms in meter, Smith's Bible Dictionary, with 700 illustrations, history of the religious denominations of the world, illustrated, numerous full page Dore and other engravings; steel and chromatic plates; handsome marriage certificate and family record in black and gold; chronological index; tables of scripture measures, weights and coins, and alphabetical table of proper names........$3.45
Same bible with nickel clasp.................... 3.70

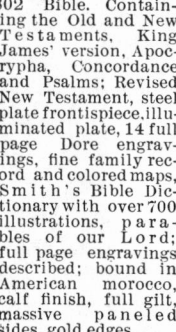

7802 Bible. Containing the Old and New Testaments, King James' version, Apocrypha, Concordance and Psalms; Revised New Testament, steel plate frontispiece, illuminated plate, 14 full page Dore engravings, fine family record and colored maps, Smith's Bible Dictionary with over 700 illustrations, parables of our Lord; full page engravings described; bound in American morocco, calf finish, full gilt, massive paneled sides, gold edges.
Price............$3.68
Same Bible with nickel clasp...............$3.88

7803 Bible. French morocco. A beautiful design, soft padded sides, round corners, squares rolled with gold side and back stamps, gilt edges. Contains King James' version of the Old and New Testaments, appended Concordance and Psalms in meter, Smith's Bible Dictionary, Bible Analysis. Family Records. Marriage Certificate. Illustrated with numerous Dore engravings.
Retail price.......$8.50
Our price........ 5.05
Same Bible with nickel clasp....... 5.45

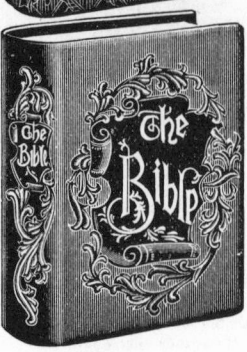

7805 Bible containing the King James version of the Old and New Testaments, with 12 full page engravings, col'd maps, life of our Lord, Apocrypha, Concordance and Psalms, revised New Testament. Bible Dictionary illustrated, 112 pages, steel plate frontispiece and fine Family Record. Bound in pebble German morocco, new scroll design, gold title and edges..$4.25
Same Bible with nickel clasp....$4.50

Bibles—Continued.

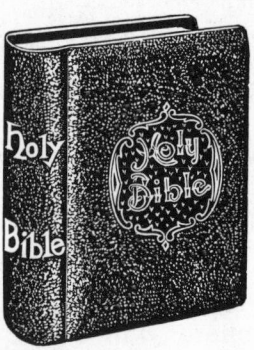

7806 Bible, containing the Old and New Testaments, Apocrypha, Concordance and Psalms, Revised New Testament printed on super calendered paper, 2 steel engravings, 24 full page Dore engravings, 2 illuminated plates, extra fine Family Record and Smith's Bible Dictionary, illustrated, 112 pages. Bible History, and Analysis, illustrated, 72 pages. Illustrated Cyclopædia, illustrated, 96 pages. Complete Instructor and Guide, illustrated, 54 pages. Parables of Our Lord, illustrated, 32 pages. Pebbled Persian morocco, new ornamental scroll design, embossed gold title and edges, squares rolled in gold, covers round cornered...$6.25
Same Bible with fine nickel clasp................ 6.65

7807 Bible, printed marginal references. Contains the King James Version of the Old and New Testaments, with the Revised Version of the New Testament appended, and in addition thereto the Apocrypha; Concordance and Psalms; Smith's Bible Dictionary, new edition, illustrated with seven hundred engravings; Bible History and Analysis, illustrated; Cyclopædia of the Bible. Marriage Certificate in black and gold.
German morocco, basket pattern, unique design, soft padded sides, round corners, squares rolled with gold, gold edges.......................................$5.25
Same Bible with clasp..........................$5.50

7809 Containing the authorized version Old Testament and parallel New Testament. Large quarto size 12½-x10½. Ours is the only edition having both versions of the New Testament in parallel columns. Numerous Bibical illustrations in black and colors; history of the Bible; marriage certificate and family record; maps, etc. All of our editions contain a new pronouncing dictionary of nearly 4,000 scriptural proper names, giving their derivation and meaning and the passage where they first occur. Bound in French morocco, padded sides, round corners, gold edges. Price, each...$2.95
Same Bible, with nickel clasp.................... 3.25

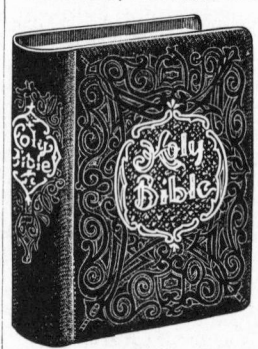

7810 Bible. This magnificent edition of the Holy Bible was made in London. The plates were cast from clear, open pica type. Contains the Old and New Testaments, Apocrypha, Concordance, Psalms in meter, revised version of the New Testament appended, Smith's Pronouncing Bible Dictionary, new edition, with seven hundred illustrations, Bible Analysis, illustrated with numerous engravings, Bible History, seventy-four pages. illustrated Cyclopædia of the Bible embracing Eastern Manners and Customs, Animals of the Bible, Plants, Flowers, and Fruits of the Bible, Wanderings of the Israelites, Idols and Idolatry of the Ancients, Jewish Worship Explained, Countries and Nations of the Bible, Palestine, Canaan or the Holy Land, City and Environs of Jerusalem, Life of our Lord and Savior Jesus Christ, Missionary Journeys of St. Paul, Prophecies of the Bible Dictionary of Names, Symbolical Language of the Scriptures, Coins of the Bible. Profusely illustrated with numerous new and original Illuminations, fine steel line engravings, colored maps, family record and marriage certificate in colors, etc. Gallery of Bible illustrations and the parables of our Lord illustrated with full-page engravings and fully described. Bound in Turkey morocco, new ornamental scroll design, Gold title and edges. Retail price $12.00. Our price..$9.00
Same Bible with heavy nickel clasp.............. 9.50

New Parallel Bibles.

The Authorized and the Revised Versions of both Old and New Testaments in Parallel Columns. Line for Line, upon each page, Large Quarto size 12½x10¼. Two Bibles in one volume.

All Bibles numbering from 7812 to 7824 are Parallel.

7812 Bible bound in imitation leather paneled gold sides, comb edges containing new pronouncing dictionary of proper names concordance to scriptures. Ten line and sixteen full line engravings marriage certificate and family records. Retail price $3 50. Our price $1.98

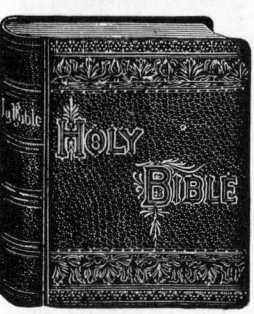

7813 Bible. Grained American morocco, padded sides, round corners, gold edges. Ten line and sixteen full-page Dore engravings. A complete concordance to the Holy Scriptures. Map of Palestine in colors. Marriage certificate and family record. The revisers' preface to Old and New Testaments, and the readings and renderings preferred by the American committee of revisers; a chronological index to the Bible, giving years when remarkable events occurred and the passages wherein they are recorded; a history of the Bible; a summary of its contents; a chapter upon Evangelists and Deacons; and many other valuable aids and helps to Bible students. $3.75
Smae with nickel clasp............................. 4.10

7814 The authorized and the revised version of both Old and New Testaments, in parallel columns, line for line, upon each page. Larger type than any other parallel Bible. Nearly 200 p ges more of Bible text. People's Family Edition (312). Two steel line and 32 full-page Dore engravings; Smith's Pronouncing Bible Dictionary (600 illustrations); a complete Concordance to Old and New Testaments; brilliantly illuminated Scripture text; map of Palestine in colors; Marriage Certificate and Family Record in black and gold; gallery of 72 Scripture illustrations; 16 portraits of founders chronological tables; the harmony of the four gospels, etc., etc. Large quarto, size, 12½x10¼. Two Bibles in one volume. American morocco, raised panel, gold title and gold edges. Each........$4.30
Same with nickel clasp............................. 4.70

7815 The authorized and the revised versions of both Old and New Testaments in parallel columns, line for line, upon each page. Large quarto size. 12½x 10½. Two Bibles in one volume. Every proper name is divided into syllables, and an accent mark is placed over the syllable upon which emphasis should rest. All of our editions contain a new pronouncing dictionary of nearly 4,000 Scriptural proper names giving their derivation and meaning and the passage where they first occur. Bound in rich French morocco padded sides, round corners, red and gold edges.
Each.................................$5.00
Same Bible with nickel clasp..................... 5.40

Always allow money for postage. If you send too much we will return it.

Bibles—Continued.

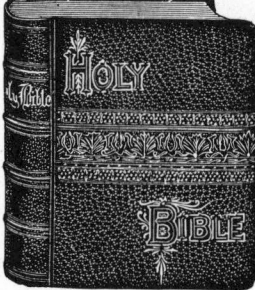

7818 The Authorized and the Revised Version of both old and New Testaments in parallel columns, line for line, upon each page. Two Bibles in one volume. Larger type than any other Parallel Bibles. Nearly 200 pages more of Bible texts Superfine family edition. Enlarged size, 12¾x10¾. 2,000 pages. Over 1,000 illustrations. In these Bibles both the text and the collateral features are printed within rules. The pages are one-half inch longer and three-eighths wider than those in any other Parallel Bible. Fine super-calendered paper is used. Containing twelve magnificently executed full page illustrations of Bible scenes from steel line plates. The subjects have been selected from the greatest masterpieces of sacred art. The Parables of our Lord, illustrated with ten full-page engravings, thirty-four full-page Dore engravings. Sixteen lithographic maps of Holy lands. Two beautiful illuminated Scripture texts. Smith's Pronouncing Bible Dictionary, (600 illustrations); a complete Concordance. Customs, Chronological Tables, Marriage Certificate and Family Record, etc. French morocco, London antique, padded sides, round corners; solid red under gold edges. NEW DESIGN. $6.50
Same with heavy nickel clasp.................... 7.00

Superfine Family Edition, Gilt Edged.

7817 Levant Morocco, London antique, super extra cushion bevel solid edges, red under gold round corners. New design. Size 12¾x 10¾. (*Best Bible made*) Containing twelve magnificently executed full-page illustrations of Bible Scenes from steel line plates. The subjects have been selected from the greatest masterpieces of sacred art. The plates have been engraved especially for us by the best artists in this country.
The Peerless Hormann Gallery or New Testament illustrations, 24 full-page monochromatic plates.
The Parables of our Lord, illustrated with ten full-page engravings. Thirty-four full-page Dore engravings.
Colored Lithograph Maps of Holy Lands.
Smith's Pronouncing Bible Dictionary (600 illustrations); a complete Concordance; four thousand questions and answers upon Old and New Testaments for use of teachers and students; History of the Books of the Bible, illustrated by forty-eight full-page engravings; gallery of ninety-six Scripture illustrations; sixteen portraits of Founders or eminent heads of Religious Denominations; the Lives of Apostles and Evangelists; Christ and His Kingdom, illustrated; forty views of Palestine from photographs; Coins and Gems, illustrated; Manners and Customs; Chronological Tables; Marriage Certificate and Family Record, etc. Retail price $24.00
Our price.................................... 13.00
Same with extra fine clasp.................... 13.75

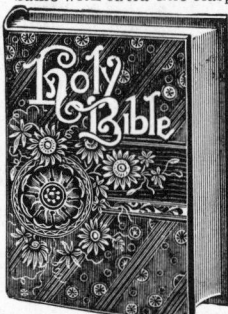

7819 Bible contains the Self-Pronouncing Text of the authorized (King James) and Revised Versions of the Old and New Testaments, arranged in parallel columns, line for line. Two colored and sixteen full-page Dore engravings, a complete concordance to the Holy Scriptures, maps of the Holy Land, and numerous biblical illustrations. Psalms of David in meter, chronological index to the Holy Bible, giving years when remarkable events occurred and passages wherein they are recorded; history of the Holy Bible a summary of its contents, and many valuable aids and helps to bible students; marriage certificate and family record. Imitation of leather arabesque, paneled, full gold sides, gilt edges.................................$1.85
Same Bible, with clasp........................... 2.10

... SAMPLES ...

We make no charge for samples, and for that reason we request you, when writing for them, to be very explicit in stating exactly what is wanted, giving Catalogue Number when possible; if not, the width, price, quality, color, etc., so that we can send you just what you need, instead of a great lot of samples that are of no use to you and cost us considerable money.

Bibles—Continued.

8720 Bible contains the authorized King James and Revised Versions, arranged in parallel columns; good, clear type; white paper; full-page engravings. Size, 10½x12½. Contains, also, the same as bible No. 7819. Bound in American morocco, arabesque, paneled, comb edges.
Retail price......$3.50
Our price........ 2.10
Same Bible with clasp.............. 2.35

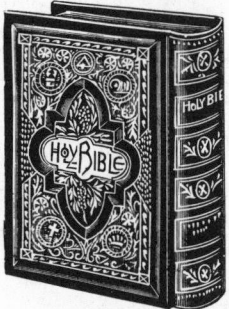

7821 Bible contains same as No. 7819, and in addition two colored and 16 full-page Dore engravings; a complete concordance to the Holy Scriptures, maps of the Holy Land and biblical illustrations, Psalms of David in meter, chronological index, history of the Bible, valuable helps to bible students; marriage certificate, etc. Handsomely bound in American morocco, raised panel, full gold edges, gold sides and back. Size, 10½x12½.
Retail price........$6.50
Our price.......... 3.90
Same Bible with clasp................... 4.15

7822 Bible, contains same as No. 7819, and in addition 2 fine steel and 24 full-page engravings. Parables of our Lord, 10 colored engravings. History of bible. Smith's Bible Dictionary, natural history, coins of bible, religious denominations of the world. Bible teachers' text book. Complete concordance. Psalms in meter. Bound in beautiful French morocco. Padded sides, new design, round corners, gold edges, squares rolled in gold. Retail price......$8.50   Our price,......$4.75
Same Bible with clasp........................... 5.00

7824 Bible. contains same as bibles No. 7819, 7821, No. 7822, and in addition six beautiful steel and 32 full-page Dore engravings, two superb chromo lithographic plates, illustrating the proverbs of Solomon, and faith, hope and charity. Parables of our Lord, illustrated bible stories for the young, with 72 illustrations. Aids and helps to bible students, etc. Bound in rich Persian morocco, padded sides, round corners, red under gold edges. Size 10½x 12½. Retail price....$9.50   Our price.........$5.75
Same bible with clasp........................... 6.20

New German Bibles.

7825 Bible. Dr. Martin Luther's Translation. Printed from entirely new electrotype plates, large, clear type on fine white paper and contains more collateral and pictorial matter than any other German Bible. Large quarto, size, 12½x10½, with Apocrypha and Concordance. Smith's Dictionary, 500 illustrations. Family edition, containing Old and New Testaments, Apocrypha, Concordance, the Parables of our Lord, illustrated with ten full-page engravings. Map of Palestine in colors, Marriage Certificate and Family Record, Life of Christ and other illustrated aids and helps to Bible students.
Price.........$3.50
7826 Bible. Same contents as No. 7825 and in addition more matter and illustration. Bound in French Morocco (514), raised panel, full gold sides and edges.
Each........$5.80 Same with nickel clasp......$6.05

Swedish Bibles.

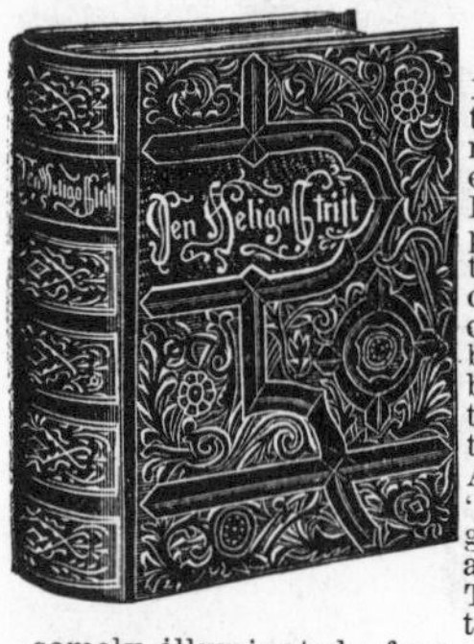

Large quarto. Size 12½ x 10½. Containing the Old and New Testaments, The Apocrypha, etc., etc. A complete Bible Dictionary. 112 pages, Over 400 illustrations. These are the finest dictionaries that have ever appeared in family bibles. Also the Parables of our Lord, illustrated; the Famous Portraits of Christ and his Apostles from Da Vinci's "Last Supper;" an elegant Marriage Certificate and Family Record; the Ten Commandments and the Lord's Prayer, handsomely illuminated; four superb chromatic plates descriptive of the Tabernacle, Jewish worship, etc., photograph cards, etc. With a complete commentary and explanatory notes, by H. M. Melin, professor of theology in the University of Lund.

7827 American morocco, arbesque paneled, comb edges $3.75
7828 American morocco, full gold sides, back and edges, containing the parables of our Lord, printed in rich colors, views from photographs of the Holy Land, many more full-page illustrations (603) 6.00
Swedish Bible, clasps extra .... .40

Catholic Bibles.

Approved Holy Catholic Bibles.

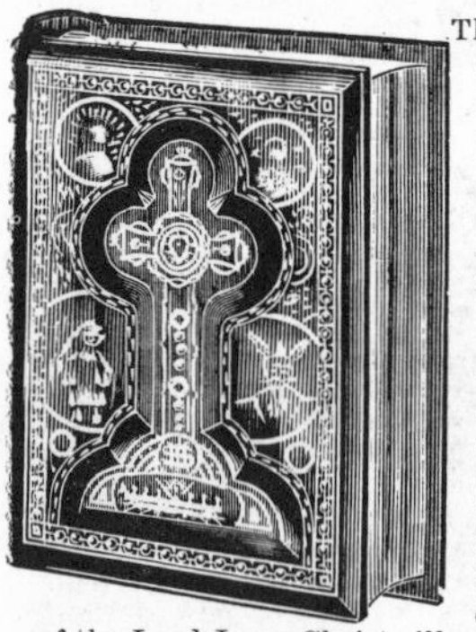

The best and cheapest edition published. Printed with the approbation of the bishops and clergy of the United States and Great Britian. Contains the entire canonical Scriptures according to the decree of the Council of Trent, translated from the Latin Vulgate. Also comprehensive history of the books of the Holy Catholic Bible, Catholic Dictionary of the Bible, profusely illustrated, full page steel and wood engravings, twelve maps of the Holy Land in colors. The parables of the Lord Jesus Christ illustrated; comprehensive helps to the study of the Holy Catholic Bible, illuminated view of the tabernacle and its furniture; Historical and Chronological Index, Statistical, Chronological and Reference Table; Marriage Certificate, Family Record and Photograph Album printed in colors. The whole embellished with hundreds of beautiful engravings.

7829 Quarto Bible, American morocco, paneled sides, marble edges (A) Each $4.65
7830 Quarto Bible, genuine morocco, paneled full gold sides and edges (C) 6.75
Catholic Bible, clasps extra .... .40

The Jennie June Series of Manuals for Ladies.

Series 7835.

The Jennie June Series of books are adapted for the instruction of ladies who desire to learn all branches of fancy work. Paper covers. Retail price $0.50
Our price .... .35

Needle Work. By Jennie June. Illustrated.
Knitting and Crocheting. By Jennie June. Illustrated.
Ladies' Fancy Work. By Jennie June. 700 illustrations.
Letters and Monograms. By Jennie June. Illustrated.
Postage, each, extra $0.06

7836 **Boy's Modern Playmate.** A book of games and sport. Cloth, 816 pages. Retail price 3.00
Our price .... $1.15 Postage .... .22
7837 **Girl's Home Companion** A book of pastime, work and play. Cloth, 716 pages 1.15
Postage .... .22

Series 7838.

Pitman's Manual of Phonography. A Complete System of Phonetic Shorthand. This Manual of Isaac Pitman's System, which is now being introduced as the Text-Book of Phonography in our educational institutions, has been revised and corrected. Convenient pocket size $0.30

Key to the Manual of Phonography. This gives, in Shorthand, all the exercises contained in the "Manual," without the aid of a teacher. Uniform in size with the "Manual." Price .... .15

The Phonographic Teacher. This is a Practical Guide to Isaac Pitman's System of Phonography. The "Teacher," with its Key, is a complete and thorough self-instructor in the art of Phonography. Convenient pocket size .... .15

Key to the Phonographic Teacher. This enables the learner to verify and correct his phonographic studies of the Exercises contained in the "Phonographic Teacher." Price .... .15

Pitman's Phonographic Reporter, or Reporter's Companion. The Reporter's Style of the Pitman System, by which fluent speakers can be reported verbatim, greatly reducing both time and labor, and insuring rapidity and accuracy .. .45

Popular Hand Books.

We have arranged these books according to the various subjects of which they treat.

RATES BY MAIL.

On all books in the following list, where we do not mention the amount required, extra, to prepay expense of mailing, it will be as follows:

All 8, 10 or 13 cent books, 2 cents; all 35 cent books, 5 cents; all 18 and 20 cent books, 4 cents.

ORDER BY NAME AND NUMBERS.

Books on Card Games, Dice, Chess, Etc.

7839 **Games of Patience, or Solitaire with Cards.** Containing sixty-four games, illustrated with about fifty explanatory full-page tableaux of games of patience. By Wm. B. Dick, quarto, 144 pages, board cover $0.50
7840 **Blackbridge's Complete Poker Player.** A practical Guide Book to the American national game. Small quarto, 173 pages, paper cover $0.35
7841 **The American Hoyle.** Containing all the games of skill and chance, as played in this country at the present time, being "an authority on all disputed points." By "Trumps." Eleventh edition, comprising Card Games, Chess, Checkers, Dominoes, Backgammon, Dice, Billiards, and all the Field Games. New and revised. 16mo., 388 pages, paper cover. $0.35
Boards .... .60
Bound in cloth 1.00
7842 **Robertson's Guide to the Game of Draughts.** This is an exhaustive work on the game of Draughts, with full instructions for learners, the standard laws of the game, the name of the games and their formation. By John Robertson.
Bound in cloth, 8vo, 320 pages $2.00
7844 **Spayth's Game of Draughts.** By Henry Spayth. This book is designed as a supplement to the author's first work, "The American Draught Player;" but is complete in itself. The score of 364 games, together with 34 novel, instructive and ingenious "critical positions." Cloth, gilt back and side, $1.00
7845 **Spayth's Draughts or Checkers for Beginners.** This treatise was written by Henry Spayth, the celebrated player, and is by far the most complete and instructive elementary work on draughts ever published. Cloth, gilt side $0.50
7847 **Handbook of Whist.** By Wm. R. Dick. Containing Poole's and Clay's Rules for playing the modern scientific games, the club rules of whist ... $0.18
7848 **Marache's Manual of Chess.** Containing preliminary rules for beginners: fifty opening of games, By N. Marache, 16mo., cloth, gilt edge $0.35
7849 **How Gamblers Win or the Secrets of Advantage Playing Exposed.** A complete and scientific expose of the manner of playing all the various advantages of cards. 16mo., paper cover $0.20
7851 **One Hundred Tricks with Cards.** By J. H. Green, the reformed gambler. 16mo., paper $0.20

Dialogue and Recitation Books, Theatricals, Speakers, Etc.

7852 **Dutch, French and Yankee Dialect.** Recitations, by Wm. B. Dick. A standard and reliable work by a well-known author. Paper covers $0.20
7853 **Brudder Bone's Book of Stump Speeches** and Burlesque Orations, Also containing Humorous Lectures, Ethiopian Dialogues, Plantation Scenes, Negro Farces and Burlesques; 188 pages, 16 mo., paper cover $0.20
7855 **Tambo's End-Man's Minstrel Gags.** A collection of Ethiopian Dialogues, Plantation Scenes, Eccentric Doings, Humorous Lectures, Laughable Interludes, End-men's Jokes, Burlesque Speeches, Witticisms, Conundrums, Yarns, Plantation Songs and Dances, etc., etc. 16 mo., 144 pages, illuminated paper cover $0.20
7856 **Howard's Recitations, Comic, Serious, and Pathetic.** Being a collection of Fresh Recitations in prose and poetry, suitable for Anniversaries, Exhibitions, Sociables and Evening Parties. 180 pages, 16mo., paper cover $0.20
7857 **Kavanaugh's New Speeches and Dialogues,** for young children. Especially adapted for School Exhibitions and Juvenile Celebrations. 16mo., paper covers $0.20
7858 **Dick's Comic and Dialect Recitations.** A capital collection of Comic Recitations, Ludicrous Dialogues, Funny Stories, Laughable Descriptive Pieces, and Imitable Parodies in Yankee, Dutch, Irish and Chinese Dialects. Paper covers $0.20
7859 **Kavanaugh's Exhibition Reciter.** For very little children. A collection of bright Recitations and short Speeches for children from three to ten years old, also a May-Day Festival for little children. In illuminated paper covers $0.20
7860 **Ogden's Skeleton Essays, or Authorship in Outline.** Consisting of condensed Treatises on popular subjects, with references to sources of information, and direction how to enlarge them into Essays, or expand them into Lectures. Paper covers, $0.35. Bound in boards $0.60
7861 **Barber's American Handbook of Ready-made Speeches.** Containing 150 original examples of humorous and serious speeches. Paper cover. $0.35
Bound in boards, cloth back .... .50
7862 **Ogden's Model Speeches,** for school occasions. Original Addresses and Orations on everything pertaining to school life, including Practical Hints on Extempore Speaking. Paper covers $0.35
7863 **Graham's School Dialogues,** for young people. Containing New and Original Dramatic Dialogues intended for anniversaries and exhibitions. Paper covers $0.20
7864 **McBride's All Kinds of Dialogues.** A collection of Original, Humorous and Dramatic Dialogues, introducing Yankee, French, Irish, Dutch and other characters. By H. Elliott McBride. 16mo., illuminated paper cover $0.20
7865 **Wilson's Book of Recitations and Dialogues,** with instructions in Elocution and Declamation. Containing a choice selection of poetical and prose recitations. 186 pages, 16mo., paper cover $0.20

Hand Books—Continued.

7866 **Martine's Droll Dialogues and Laughable** Recitations. By Arthur Martine, author of the "Martine Letter-Writer," etc. A collection of humorous Dialogues, Comic Recitations and Ludicrous Farces, adapted for School Celebrations and Home Amusements. 182 pages, large 16mo., paper cover $0.20
7867 **McBride's New Dialogues.** Especially designed for School and Literary Amateur Entertainments; containing entirely new and original dialogues, introducing Irish, Yankee and other eccentric characters. By H. McBride. 16 mo., 173 pages, illuminated paper cover $0.20
7868 **Dick's Comic Dialogues.** A collection of easy, effective and dramatic dialogues, bright, witty and full of droll "Situations," specially adapted for performance by young people. 16mo., paper covers. Price $0.20
7870 **Dick's Parlor Exhibitions.** Containing a varied collection of elegant Amusements, equally adapted to the parlor and the hall, entirely within the range of Amateurs. By Wm. B. Dick. 16mo., 160 pages, illustrated cover $0.20
7871 **Frost's Books of Tableaux** and shadow pantomimes. Containing a choice collection of Tableaux of Living Pictures, with directions for arranging the stage. 180 pages, 16mo., paper cover $0.20
7872 **McBride's Choice Dialogues.** Containing original and characteristic dialogues for school exhibitions and other amateur juvenile entertainments. By H. Elliott McBride. Illuminated paper cover .. $0.20
Bound in boards, cloth back .... .35
7873 **Dick's Ethiopian Scenes,** variety sketches, and stump speeches. Containing end-men's jokes, negro interludes and farces, fresh dialogues, for interlocutor and banjo, new stump speeches, jokes, quips and gags. 178 pages. Paper covers. Price $0.20
7874 **Child's Own Speaker.** By E. C. and L. J. Rook. A collection of Recitations, Motion Songs, Concert Pieces, Dialogues and Tableaux. For children of six years. Paper binding $0.10
Boards .... .18
7875 **Little People's Speaker.** By Mrs. J. W. Shoemaker. A superior collection of Recitations and Readings, mostly in verse. For children of nine years. Paper binding $0 10
Boards .... .18
7876 **Young People's Speaker.** By E. C. and L. J. Rook. Comprises Recitations for the different Holidays, Temperance Pieces, Patriotic Speeches, etc. For children of twelve years. Paper binding $0.10
Boards .... .18
7877 **Young Folks' Recitations.** By Mrs. J. W. Shoemaker. An excellent collection of recitations adapted to the various needs of young people's entertainments. For children of fifteen years. Paper binding $0.10
Boards .... .18
7880 **Little People's Dialogues.** By Clara J. Denton. All new and original. Everything bright and fresh. For children of ten years $0.18
Paper binding $0.18
Boards .... .30
7881 **Young Folks' Dialogues.** By Charles C. Shoemaker, Everything specially written for this volume. For children of fifteen years.
Paper binding $0.18
Boards .... .30
7883 **Humorous Dialogues and Dramas.** By Charles C. Shoemaker. All the dialogues are bright and taking and sure to prove most successful in their presentation.
Paper binding $0.20
Cloth .... .35
7885 **Holiday Selections.** For readings and recitations. By Sara S. Rice. The selections are especially adapted to Christmas, New Year's, St. Valentine's Day, Washington's Birthday, Easter, Arbor Day, Decoration Day, Fourth of July and Thanksgiving.
Paper binding $0.20
Cloth .... .35
7887 **Sunday-School Selections.** For readings and recitations. By John Bechtel. An excellent collection, suited to church socials, Sunday-school concerts, teachers' gatherings, Christian Endeavor Societies, Young Men's Christian Associations, anniversary occasions, etc.
Paper binding $0.20
Cloth .... .35
7888 **Temperance Selections.** For readings and recitations. By John H. Bechtel. This collection comprises speeches and essays from the most eminent clergymen, speakers and writers of the century.
Paper binding $0.20
Cloth .... .35

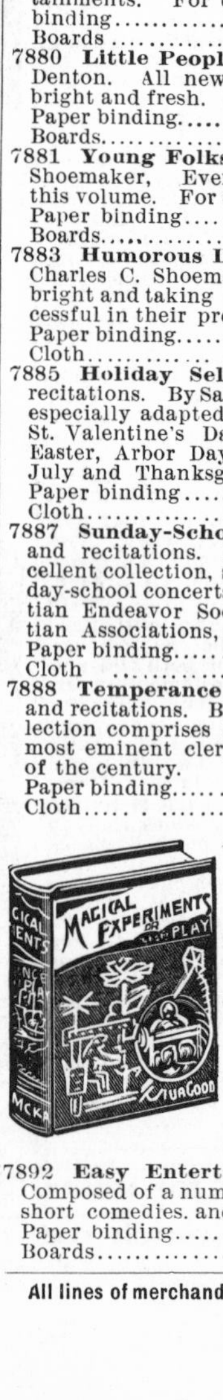

7890 **Magic.** Illustrated and explained; a book for young and old. By Arthur Good. A series of 200 amusing, popular, scientific experiments meant for the recreation of old and young. 165 fine illustrations. Square 12mo., gilt back and side ... $0.88
7891 **Young Folks' Entertainments.** By E. C. and L. J. Rook. Contains motion songs, concert pieces, pantomimes, tambourine and fan drills, tableaux, etc.
Paper binding $0.18
Boards .... .30

7892 **Easy Entertainments for Young People.** Composed of a number of original and simple plays, short comedies, and other attractive entertainments.
Paper binding $0.18
Boards .... .30

All lines of merchandise very generally reduced in price.

Receipt and Practical Hand-Books. etc.

7893 Guide to Success; or, How to do Business. Affording excellent advice in regard to the choice of a persuit in the different branches of business and the necessary qualifications for each. Paper, 16mo..$0.18

7894 Chilton's One Thousand Secrets and Wrinkles. A book for hints and helps for everyday emergencies. Containing 1,000 useful hints and receipts. 236 pages, paper covers. Price............$0.20

7895 Draper's Six Hundred Ways to Make Money. A reliable compendium of valuable receipts for making articles in constant demand, of ready sale. 144 pages, paper cover. Price........................$0.20

7896 The American Boy's Manual of Practical Mechanics. A complete hand-book for the instruction and guidance of youthful amateurs in turning in wood, metal, etc.; the construction of model steam engines and steamboats: boat and canoe building; telegraphy and the batteries employed; electrotyping; dioramas; sand; glass-blowing, and gilding on glass; magic lanterns and calcium lights; aquaria; telescopes, balloons and fireworks and other useful and ornamental appliances. Fully illustrated, 169 pages, 8vo., paper covers........................$0.35

7897 The Painter's Hand-Book. A thorough guide to all that pertains to internal and external plain and tasteful house painting, with valuable receipts, hints and information to amateurs and experts.......$0.18

7898 Dick's Home Made Candies, or How to Make Candy in the Kitchen. Containing complete directions for making all the newest and most delicious cream confections, with boiled syrup...........$0.18

7899 Arts of Beauty, or Secrets of a Lady's Toilet. With hints to gentlemen on the arts of fascination. By Madame Lola Montez, Countess of Landsfeldt. 16mo., paper cover......................$0.18

7901 Dunn's Fencing Instructor. A complete manual of the art of fencing, giving a plain description of the lines of engagement, position, salute and assault, and attacks and parries illustrated. Large 16mo., paper cover........................$0.18

7902 The Young Gymnast. Containing thorough instructions for the gymnasium, with exercises with the leaping pole, horizontal and parallel bars, trapeze, dumb-bells and Indian clubs; including directions for training, and for the treatment of accidental injuries. Illustrated. Large 16mo...........$0.18

7903 The Amateur Printer, or Type-Setting at Home. It teaches how to set type in the stick, transfer the matter to the galley and make it up in forms; how to take and correct proofs; any amateur can become a good printer by applying the information it contains. Paper covers....................$0.18

7904 Brigg's Practical Tanner. A most practical work on this subject. Explained so everyone can tan and prepare hides in a simple and practical manner........................$0.18

7905 Day's Book-Keeping Without a Master. Containing the Rudiments of Book-Keeping in single and double entry........................$0.35

7906 The Young Reporter or How to Write Shorthand. A complete Phonographic Teacher. By the aid of this work any person of the most ordinary intelligence may learn to write Shorthand and report speeches and sermons in a short time. Large 16mo, bound in boards, with cloth back. Price.......$0.35

7907 How to Write a Composition. Many hours are often wasted trying to write a plain composition. This book affords a perfect skeleton of 117 different subjects. Paper cover........................$0.20

7908 Live and Learn. A guide for all who wish to speak and write correctly. Containing examples of one thousand mistakes of daily occurrence in speaking, writing and pronunciation. Large 16mo., 206 pages, paper cover........................$0.20

7909 French Self Taught, by Franz Thimm. A new system for universal self tuition; with complete English pronunciation of every word. Price....$0.18

7910 German Self Taught, by Franz Thimm. Uniform with "French Self-Taught"............$0.18

7911 Spanish Self Taught, by Franz Thimm. Uniform with "French Self-Taught." Price.......$0.18

7912 Italian Self Taught, by Franz Thimm. Uniform with "French Self-Taught"...............$0.18

7913 How to Become a Public Speaker. By William Pittenger. This work shows in a simple and concise way how any person of ordinary perseverance and average intelligence may become a ready and effective public speaker. Paper binding..$0.20
Cloth...35

7914 Ventriloquism Self-Taught. A thoroughly reliable guide to the art of voice-throwing and vocal mimicry by an entirely novel system, with graduated exercises, including full instructions for imitating various musical instruments, wood-sawing, birds, bees, etc.; how to work ventriloquial puppets, and useful hints on entertaining. By Robert Ganthony.
....$0.18

Books of Amusement.

7915 Book of Riddles and 500 Home Amusements. Brimful of new things, and a really valuable book; 60 engravings, 16mo., paper cover.......$0.20

7916 Dick's One Hundred Amusements for Evening parties, picnics and society gatherings, Explained by 65 engravings. Paper covers....$0.20

7917 Dick's Original Album Verses and Acrostics. Containing original Verses for Autograph Albums; to accompany bouquets; for Birthday Aniversaries; for Wooden, Tin, Crystal Silver and Golden Weddings; being appended to each. Paper covers..........$0.35

7918 Parlor Tricks with Cards. Containing explanations of all the deceptions with playing cards ever invented; the whole illustrated and made easy, with 70 engravings. Large 16mo., paper cover........$0.20

7919 The Book of 500 Curious Puzzles. Contains all kinds of entertaining paradoxes. Illustrated with numerous engravings. Paper cover..........$0.20

Books—Continued.

7920 The Fireside Magician or the Art of Natural Magic Made Easy—Being a familiar and scientific explanation of Ledgerdemain, Physical Amusement, Recreative Chemistry, Diversion with Cards and all the minor mysteries of mechanical magic, with explanatory engravings. Compiled from original sources. By Paul Preston. 132 pages. 16mo., paper cover.$0.20

7921 How to Amuse an Evening Party. A complete collection of Comic Diversions, Scientific Recreations, and Evening Amusements. Profusely illustrated with nearly 200 fine wood cuts. Large 16mo., paper cover.
....$0.20

7922 Howard's Book of Conundrums and Riddles. Containing over 1,200 of the best Conundrums Riddles, Enigmas, Ingenious Catches and Amusing Sells ever invented. 16mo., paper cover.......$0.20

7923 The Parlor Magician or One Hundred Tricks for the drawing-room. Illustrated and clearly explained, with 121 engravings. Paper cover....$0.20

7924 Hermann's Hand-Book of Magic. Large 16mo., paper cover........................$0.20

Masonic Books.

7927 Duncan's Masonic Ritual and Monitor, or Guide to the Three Symbolic Degrees of the Ancient York Rite, Entered Apprentice, Fellow Craft and Master Mason. And to the degrees of Mark Master, Past Master, Most Excellent Master and the Royal Arch, by Malcom C. Duncan. Explained and interpreted by copious notes and numerous engravings. Leather tucks (pocketbook style) with gilt edge.........$2.00
Cloth.......................................1.50

7928 Richardson's Monitor of Freemasonry. A complete guide to the various ceremonies and routine in Freemasons' Lodges, Chapters, Encampments, Hierarchites, etc., the most reliable book on the subject extant. 16mo., cloth, gilt.....................$0.80
Leather Tucks (pocketbook style), gilt edge.......1.25
Extra by mail...................................06

7929 Lander's Revised Work of Odd-Fellowship. Containing all the lectures complete, with regulations for opening, conducting and closing a lodge; together with forms of initiation, charges of various officers, etc. Complete work in the different degrees, with the amendments and alterations adopted by the Sovereign Grand Lodge, at the session held in Toronto, Canada, September, 1880. 16mo., paper cover...........$0.18
Per doz.......................................1.80

7930 Morgan's Freemasonry Exposed and Explained Paper cover, octavo.................$0.18

7931 Lester's "Look to the East." Containing the Webb Work of the Entered Apprentice, Fellow Craft, and Master Mason's Degrees, with their Opening and Closing Ceremonies, Lectures, etc. Ritually and Monitorially complete. Edited by Ralph P. Lester. This is a complete Pocket Manual of the First Three Degrees of Masonry. Bound in cloth..........$1.30
Bound in Leather Tucks (pocketbook style), gilt edges.......................................1.75

7932 Allyn's Ritual of Freemasonry. Containing a complete key to the following degrees: Entered Apprentice, Fellow Craft, Master Mason, Mark Master, Past Master, Excellent Master, Royal Arch, Royal Master, Select Master, Ark and Dove, Super-Excellent Master, Knights of Constantinople, Secret Monitor, Heroine of Jericho, Knights or Three Kings, Mediterranean Pass, Knights of the Red Cross, Knights Templar, Knights of Malta, Knights of the Christian Mark and Guards of the Conclave, Knights of the Holy Sepulchre, Holy and Thrice Illustrious Order of the Cross, Secret Master, Perfect Master, Intimate Secretary, Provost and Judge, Intendant of the Buildings, or Master in Israel, Elected Knights of Nine, Elected Grand Master Sublime Knights Elected, Grand Master Architect, Knights of the Ninth Arch, Grand Elect, Perfect and Sublime Mason. Including the Key to the Royal Arch, Cipher, and to the Phi Beta Kappa, Orange, and Odd Fellows' Societies. By Avery Allyn, K. R. C. K. T. K.M., etc. Illustrated with thirty copperplate engravings. 12mo., cloth..$3.25

7933 Hyrum. The House of Wisdom or Solomon's House. Being the secret Ritual of a Learned Society, devoted to the cultivation and advancement of Experimental and Occult Philosophy and the Sciences. By A. Tylor. Illustrated with Diagrams. A correct narrative, in accordance with the very latest changes made by authority, of the progress of a neophyte through the House of Solomon. The story is told in symbolic cipher for the guidance of the initiated in mysteries which are not revealed to the profane. Bound in leather, pocketbook style............$2.00

7934 Robert's Ritual of the Knights of Pythias. The Revised Ritual for Subordinate Lodges adopted by the Supreme Lodge, August 29, 1892. Edited by Douglas Roberts. Illustrated by Diagrams of the Castle Hall. It includes the Opening and Closing Ceremonies; Official Visits; and the Initiation into the Ranks of Page, Esquire, and Knights, fully explained. Paper covers.........................$0.35
Bound in cloth...........................70

Letter Writers and Etiquette.

7935 Dick's Common Sense Letter Writer. Containing 360 Sensible, Social and Business Letters, with appropriate answers on all possible subjects, etc. By William B. Dick. 16mo., bound in boards, cloth back...$0.35

7936 Dick's Commercial Letter Writer and Book of Business Forms. Containing entirely original Models of Letters on business subjects, with appropriate replies; also several specimens of Continuous Correspondence, exhibiting by a series of letters the progress and completion of Mercantile Transactions. By William B. Dick. 200 pages, 16mo., bound in boards.......................................$0.35

7937 Worcester's Letter Writer and Book of Business forms for ladies and gentlemen. Containing accurate directions for conducting correspondence, with 276 specimen letters adapted to every age and situation in life. 216 pages. Bound in boards......$0.35

Books—Continued.

7938 North's Book of Love Letters. With directions how to write and when to use them, and 120 specimen letters, suitable for lovers of any age and conditio , and under all circumstances. By Ingoldsby North. 16mo. bound in boards........................$0.35

7939 Chesterfield's Letter Writer and Complete Book of Etiquette. 16mo., bound in boards.... $0.35

7940 Martine's Hand-Book of Etiquette. A most valuable book. 16mo., bound in boards........$0.35

7941 How to Behave in Society. A hand-book of etiquette for ladies and gentlemen, with rules for correct deportment, correspondence and forms of invitations, etc.. with valuable hints in regard to engagements, weddings, balls and other occasions..$0.18

Ready Reckoners.

7942 Dick's Log and Lumber Measure. A complete set of tables, with full instructions for their use, showing at a glance the cubical contents of logs, and Doyle's tables of the feet of inch boards they contain. All the tables are new, reliable and proved correct. Bound in boards.........................$0.20

**7943 Brisbane's Golden Ready Reckoner—Or lightning calculator, a valuable assistant to farmers, traders and housekeepers, in buying and selling all kinds of commodities. 18mo., bound in boards, with cloth back. Price........................$0.20

7944 Scribner's Lumber and Log Book. For ship and boat builders, lumber merchants, sawmill men, farmers and mechanics. Being a correct measurement of all kinds and sizes of lumber. Being the most complete book of the kind ever published. Price....$0.20
Postage..02

Boxing, Etc.

7945 Ned Donnelly's Art of Boxing. A thorough manual of sparring and self-defense, illustrated with forty engravings, showing the various blows, stops and guards. By Ned Donnelly. Advice to those who desire to perfect themselves in the manly art. 121 pages. Price........................$0.18

7946 The Laws of Athletics. How to preserve and improve the health, strength and beauty, and to correct personal defects caused by the want of physical exercise; how to train for walking, running, rowing, etc. By William Wood, professor of gymnastics,18mo., paper cover........................$0.18

7947 Dick's Art of Wrestling. A hand-book of thorough instruction in wrestling, fully illustrated by well designed engravings, exhibiting all the aggressive and defensive positions necessary for success. Paper covers. Price........................$0.18

7948 Dick's Dumb-Bell and Indian-Club Exercises. Containing practical and progressive instruction in the use of dumb-bells and Indian clubs, illustrated, and very plainly explained. Paper cover. $0.18

Music and Dancing.

7949 Dick's Quadrille Call Book and Ball Room Prompter. Containing clear directions how to call out the figures of every dance, with the quantity of music necessary for each figure, and explanation of all figures and steps which occur in plain and fancy quadrilles, besides seventy pages of dance music for the piano. Paper cover, $0.35 Bound in boards, $0.50

7950 Frank Converse's Complete Banjo Instructor, without a master. Containing a choice collection of banjo solos, hornpipes, reels, jigs, walk-arounds, songs and banjo stories, progressively arranged and explained. Boards, cloth back............$0.35

Fortune Tellers and Dream Books.

7951 Day's Fortune Telling Cards. Solution of uncertain and intricate questions, relative to love, luck, lotteries, matrimony, business matters, journeys and future events generally. Is inclosed in a case on which are printed directions for using the cards......$0.20

7952 The Gipsy Witches' Dream Book and Fortune Teller. Containing a complete alphabetical list of the dreams, with their significations, also the art of foretelling future events by cards, dice, dominoes, tea and coffee grounds, etc., and a full list of lucky days, weeks, months, etc....................$0.18

7953 Madame Le Normand's Fortune Teller. An entertaining book. Said to have been written by Madame Le Normand, the celebrated French fortune teller. Bound in boards........................$0.28

7954 Mother Shipton's Oriental Dream Book. Being a reliable interpretation of dreams, visions, apparitions, etc., together with a history of remarkable dreams proven true as interpreted. Collected and arranged from the most celebrated masters. Paper covers........................$0.20

7955 The Egyptian Dream Book and Fortune Teller. Containing an alphabetical list of dreams, with their signification and their lucky numbers, to which is added a treatise on chiromancy, and concluding with a chapter on phrenology. Illustrated with explanatory diagrams. Bound in board cover..$0.28

7956 Madame Le Marchand's Fortune Teller and Dreamer's Dictionary. Containing a complete dictionary of dreams, alphabetically arranged. Bound in board covers........................$0.28

7958 Napoleon's Dream Book and Book of Fate. Giving the methods of fortune-telling by Napoleon's celebrated Oraculum, by tea leaves, by dreams, with answers to various questions. Paper...........$0.18

Love and Courtship.

7959 The Language of Flowers. A complete dictionary of the Language of Flowers, and the sentiments which they express. 16mo., paper............$0.10

7960 The Art and Etiquette of Love. A manual of Love, Courtship and Matrimony. Containing sensible advice in relation to all the circumstances incident to the tender passion from the commencement of courtship until after marriage. Large 16mo., 176 pages, paper cover........................$0.20

7961 How to Win and How to Woo. 16mo....$0.08

7962 The Lovers' Guide to Courtship and Marriage. A dissertation of Love and Lovers, with wise suggestions for successful courtship. Large 16mo $0.18

Books on Wines and Liquors.

7963 **How to Mix all Kinds of Fancy Drinks.** A complete Bartender's Guide. Containing directions for mixing all the beverages used in the United States, in endless variety. 16mo., 1 vol., illuminated paper cover....$0.35
16mo., 1 vol., cloth.... .50

7964 **The Bordeaux Wine and Liquor Dealers' Guide.** A Treatise on the Manufacture, Rectifying and Reduction of Liquors, without the use of poisonous or deleterious ingredients, and on the preparation of Wines, Cordials, etc., directions for brewing Ale, Porter, etc., and compounding Wines, Bitters and Punches, and Coloring and Beading for Liquors. 12mo., cloth....$1.75

7965 **Fleischman's Art of Blending and Compounding Liquors and Wines.** Showing how the favorite brands of Whiskies, Brandies and other Liquors and Wines are prepared by Rectifiers, etc., preparing the finest qualities of Liquors, Cordials, Bitters, etc., and everything in it is NEW, RELIABLE AND THOROUGH. 12mo., cloth. Our price....$1.50

7966 **The French Wine and Liquor Manufacturer.** A practical Guide and Receipt Book for the Liquor Merchant on the Manufacture and Imitation of Brandy, Rum, Gin and Whisky, with Rules for the Manufacture and Management of all kinds of Wines, by Mixing, Boiling and Fermentation. To which is added Descriptive Articles on Alcohol, Distillation, Maceration, and the use of the Hydrometer; with Tables, Comparative Scale, and Rules for Purchasing, Reducing and Raising the Strength of Alcohol, etc. Illustrated with descriptive diagrams and engravings. By John Rack. Bound in cloth. Price....$2.25

7967 **Monzert's Practical Distiller.** A complete and thorough Treatise on the art of Distilling and Rectifying Alcohol, Liquors, Essences, etc., by the latest and most improved methods, combined in one pro ess. It explains the principles of Alcoholometry, with correct tables of comparative percentages by weight and by volume. Degrees of Proof and corresponding Specific Gravity. By Leonard Monzert. Bound in cloth, 12mo....$2.25

7968 **The Manufacture of Liquors, Wines and Cordials without the Aid of Distillation.** This work also includes the best receipts for the manufacture of Effervescing Beverages and Syrups, Vinegar and Bitters. It also tells how to make Cider without apples, to convert Cider into all kinds of Wines, to make strong Vinegar in 24 hours, to distinguish Imported from Domestic Liquors, to make fine Colorings for Wines and Liquors, to make Neutral Spirits, to rectify Whisky, to make Old Barrels look new, to make New Barrels look old, to detect Poisonous Liquors, to become a successful Liquor Merchant, to be an Expert Bartender, to make wholesome Liquors and Wines at very low cost and large profits, and a good deal more useful information for the trade. By Pierre Lacour. 12mo., cloth, price....$1.75

Humorous Books.

7969 **Jolly Joker, or Laugh All Round.** An immense collection of the Funniest Jokes, profusely illustrated. 12mo., 144 pages, illustrated cover....$0.18
Postage.... .04

7970 **Mrs. Partington's Carpet-Bag of Fun.** Containing the Queer Sayings of Mrs. Partington, and the funny sayings of her remarkable son Isaac. Illustrated ornamental paper cover....$0.20

7971 **Very, Very Funny.** Containing the cream of the funny things from Puck, Detroit Free Press, Peck's Sun, Texas Siftings, Arkansas Traveler, etc., etc. Profusely illustrated; the best book for the money ever offered; each, 8c. Per dozen....$0.85
Postage.... .02

7972 **Sut Lovingood.** Yarns spun by a "Natural Born Durn'd Fool." By George W. Harris. Illustrated with eight fine full-page engravings. 12mo., cloth, beveled edge....$1.00
Postage.... .15

7973 **Uncle Josh's Trunk Full of Fun.** Containing the richest Collection of Comical Stories, Cruel Sells, etc. Illustrated with nearly 200 Funny Engravings. Paper....$0.10

7974 **Ned Turner's Circus Joke Book.** A collection of the best Jokes, Bon Mots, Repartees, Gems of Wit and Funny Sayings and Doings of Ned Turner. 18mo....$0.08

7975 **Ned Turner's Clown Joke Book.** Containing the best Jokes and Gems of Wit, composed and delivered by the favorite Equestrian Clown and Ethiopian Comedian, Ned Turner, 18mo....$0.08

7976 **Talks.** By George Thatcher, the celebrated minstrel. It contains all of Mr. Thatcher's monologues, stump speeches, songs, poems, parodies, jokes, etc. Paper binding....$0.18

Treasury of Humor.

7977 Composed of Good Humor, Choice Dialect, and Choice Humor, three of the most popular books of their kind ever published
Cloth, beautifully bound....$1.05
Postage, extra, 12 cents.

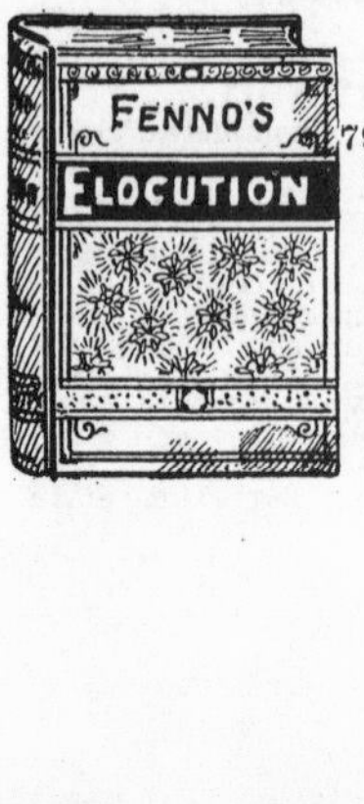

Fenno's Elocution

7978 The Science and Art of Elocution, or How to Read and Speak. Embracing a comprehensive and systematic series of exercises for gesture, calisthenics and the cultivation of the voice; with a collection of nearly 150 literary gems for reading and speaking.
Retail price....$1.50
Our price.... 1.00
Postage.... .12

Practical Elocution.

7980 By J. W. Shoemaker, A. M. This work is the outgrowth of actual class-room experience, and is a practical common-sense treatment of the whole subject. It is the best and most popular text book extant. Cloth binding.
Retail price....$1.25
Our price.... .88
Postage, extra, 12c.

Spalding's Library of Athletic Sports.

Baseball Guide for 1895 will be ready April 1st.

Series 7985.

Spalding's Official Baseball Guide for 1895. The standard authority on baseball, and only complete baseball guide published....$0.08
Per dozen.... .90
Postage.... .02

Base Ball.

By Walter Camp. Specially adapted for Colleges and Preparatory Schools. Price.... .08

Hand Ball Guide.

By Maurice W. Deshong. Regulation court and its construction, rules of the game and sketches of famous experts. Price.... .08

Foot Ball Guide for 1895.

Revised by Walter Camp; New Rules and Referee's Book. Authorized and adopted by the American Intercollegiate Association for the season of 1894-95. Price.... .08

Lawn Tennis.

By O. S. Campbell, champion player of America. Valuable for experts as well as beginners. Price....$0.08

Croquet.

Revised and corrected by the National Association, containing latest rules. Price.... .08

Bowling.

By A. E. Vogell. Containing instructions how to bowl, score, handicap, and rules for playing the various games. Price.... .08

Curling, Hockey and Polo.

By James S. Mitchell. Containing rules and regulations, with diagram of field of play. Price .08

Spalding's Manly Sports—Indian Club Swinging and Manual of Boxing. Illustrated. Each.... .20
Per dozen.... 2.00
Postage.... .04

Spalding's Official Sporting Rules. Contains the latest rules governing all sports up to date, and very complete. Retail price....$0.50
Our price.... .38
Postage.... .06

Athlete's Guide.

Articles on training, by H. S. Cornish, and rules for the government of athletic games. Price....$0.08

Indian Clubs and Dumb Bells.

By J. H. Dougherty, amateur champion of America. It contains 49 illustrations, and gives full instructions in the use of clubs and bells. Price....$0.08

Skating.

By Geo. D. Phillips. History of skating from its earliest appearance to the present day. Price....$0.08

Life and Battles of James J. Corbett.

The book embraces all the notable incidents in Champion Corbett's unique career. Price....$0.08

Prose and Poetry for Young People.

7986 Composed of Child's Own Speaker, Little People's Speaker, Young People's Speaker, and Young Folk's Recitations. Suitable as a prize or gift book for children and youths from six to fifteen years of age.
Cloth binding....$0.75
Postage, extra, 10 cents.

Shoemaker's Best Selections.

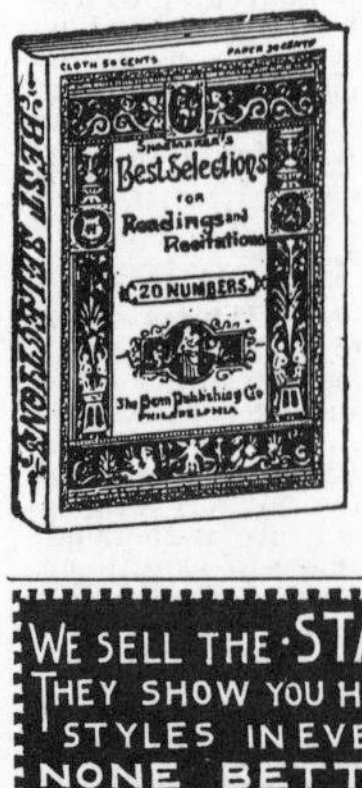

7987 For Readings and Recitations. Formerly "The Elocutionist's Annual" Each number is compiled by a different elocutionist of prominence. It is beyond doubt the best series of speakers published. Number 22 just out.
Paper binding, each...$0.20
Cloth binding, each... .35
Numbers 1 to 22 now ready.

Dick's Recitations and Readings.

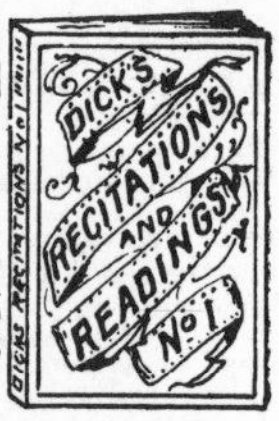

7988 **Dick's Recitations and Readings.** Numbers one to twenty-one are fully compiled with humorous, pathetic, eloquent, patriotic and sentimental pieces. Retail price....$0.30
Our price.... .18

Fenno's Favorites.

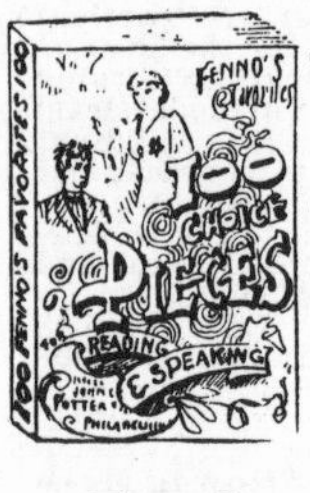

7989 **Fenno's Favorite** for reading and speaking with marked gestures, analyzed selections, explanatory notes, etc., by Frank Fenno, A. M., graduate of National School of Oratory. Ten numbers now ready. Each number contains over 100 choice selections.
Retail price....$0.30
Our price.... .20
Postage.... .04
Always give number wanted.

The Grammar of Palmistry.

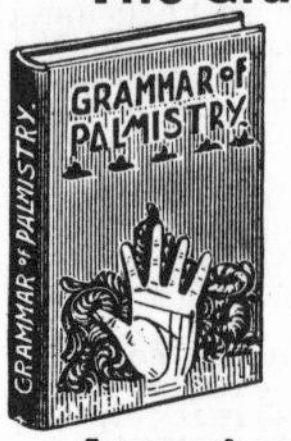

7990 By Katharine St. Hill, with eighteen illustrations. Reading character correctly by the lines of the hand and its conformation is one of the most amusing as well as interesting pastimes. Palmistry, as this art is called, is gaining new votaries every day.
16 mo., cloth....$0.52
Postage.... .08

American Amateur Dramas. Series 7995.

A collection of new copyrighted plays suitable for amateur performance, especially adapted for Lodges, Clubs, Sunday Schools, Public Schools, etc. Each, per copy, 12 cents. *except where otherwise noted.* Per dozen, $1.30. Postage, 1 cent each. The figures in columns at the right denote the number of characters. M., male; F., Female.

ONE ACT FARCES AND COMEDIETTAS.	M.	F.
An Irish Engagement (lively and laughable)	4	2
A Peculiar Position (funny and bright)	5	3
Popping the Question (always brings down the house)	2	4
Which is Which? (bright and graceful)	3	3
Lend me Five Shillings (provokes continuous mirth)	5	2
How to Tame Your Mother-in-Law (extravagantly comical)	4	2
Mulcahy's Cat (Irish low life in New York)	2	1
All in der Family (comic Dutch sketch)	4	2
Funnibone's Fix (irresistibly ludicrous)	6	2
A Cup of Tea (a spirited piece that acts exceedingly well)	3	1
"To Let, Furnished" (contains a good dude character)	3	1
The Obstinate Family (popular and very entertaining)	3	3
More Blunders Than One (comical Irish farce)	4	3
The Stage-Struck Yankee (funny straight through)	4	2
The Vermont Wool Dealer (suits every body)	5	3
The Women's Club (snappy and funny)	4	8
Twenty and Forty (contains a frisky old maid)	4	6
Betsy Baker (creates explosive laughter)	2	2
Freezing a Mother-in-Law (a screaming farce)	3	2
At Sixes and Sevens (a gay piece; sure of making a hit)	3	4
Change Partners (comic and vivacious)	2	3
A Dark Night's Business (full of uproarious Irish fun)	3	1
A Purty Shure Cure (temperance and comic)	2	1
My Neighbor's Wife (sprightly and ludicrous)	3	3
Who Got the Pig? (an Irish jury case)	3	1
Turn Him Out (wildly farcial)	3	2
Pipes and Perdition (a mother-in-law comedy)	2	2
Dot Mad Tog (Dutch and Irish courtship)	2	2
His First Brief (breezy and funny)	3	2
Dot Quied Lotchings (Dutch boarding-house sketch)	5	1
My Precious Betsey (indescribably funny)	4	4
The Ould Man's Coat Tails (Irish farce)	3	1
DRAMA AND COMEDIES.		
Imogene, or The Witch's Secret; 4 acts; strong and realistic drama; 2¼ hours	8	4
Crawford's Claim ("Nugget Nell"): 4 acts; good rattling drama; 2¼ hours	9	3
Tried and True (drama of city life); 3 acts; 2¼ hours	8	3
"Strife!" (the great labor play); 3 acts; 2¼ hours	9	4

Series 7995—Continued.

	M.	F.
Under a Cloud (breezy comedy-drama): 2 acts; 1½ hours	5	2
Saved from the Wreck (maritime serio-comic drama); 3 acts; 2 hours	8	3
Between two Fires (military drama); 3 acts; 2 hours	8	3
By Force of Impulse, or "Off to the War" (military drama); 5 acts) 2½ hours	9	3
The Woven Web (a flawless war drama); 4 acts; 2½ hours	7	3
Uncle Tom's Cabin (new copyright version); drama; 5 acts; 2¼ hours	7	5
Charity; 4 acts (a play of great merit); 2¼ hours	8	3
The Daughter of the Stars; drama; 2 acts; 1¾ hours	4	3
My Awful Dad (always makes a brilliant hit); comedy; 3 acts; 2 hours	6	6
Engaged (a mirthful society comedy); 3 acts; 2¼ hours	5	5
The Wanderer's Return ("Enoch Arden"); drama; 4 acts; 2½ hours	6	4
The Cricket on the Hearth (Dickens); drama; 3 acts, 2 hours	6	6
Single Life (uproariously funny); 3 acts; 2 hours	5	5
Married Life (side-splitting all through) comedy; 3 acts; 2 hours	5	5
Our Boys (the most succe sful play ever written); comedy; 3 acts; 2 hours	6	4
Miriam's Crime (good serio-comic drama); 3 acts; 2 hours	5	2
Meg's Diversion (pathos and humor); drama; 2 acts; 1¾ hours	5	3
A Scrap of Paper (full of healthy fun); comedy; 3 acts; 2 hours	6	6
Woodcock's Little Game (comical mother-in-law play); 2 acts; 1 hour	4	4
Partners for Life (a good "society" play); comedy; 3 acts; 2 hours	7	4
Lady Audley's Secret (dramatized from Miss Braddon's novel); 2 acts; 1¼ hours	4	3

Series 7995—Continued.

	M.	F.
Not So Bad after All, or "Is Marriage a Failure?"; comedy; 3 acts; 2 hours	6	5
Timothy Delano's Courtship (Yankee comedy); 2 acts; 1 hour	2	3
Sweethearts (humor and pathos); comedy; 2 acts; 1 hour	2	2
Uncle Jack (funny, with a good moral); comedy; 1 act; 1¼ hours	3	4

PLAYS FOR MALE CHARACTERS.

The Lost Heir; drama; 3 acts (excellent plot of unflagging interest)	10
"Medica;" roaring farce; 1 act (sure to please)	7
Wanted, a Confidential Clerk; farce; 1 act (comical and spirited)	6
Old Cronies; farce; 1 act (full of rollicking fun)	2
The Bachelor's Bedroom, or Two in the Morning; farce; 1 act	2
April Fools; farce; 1 act (brisk, bright and comic)	3
The Darkey Wood Dealer; farce; 1 act (a sure success)	3
Mischievous Bob; comic drama; 1 act	6
The Wrong Bottle; temperance sketch; 1 act	2
Well Fixed for a Rainy Day; temperance drama; 1 act	5
The Harvest Storm; drama; 1 act (unflagging in interest)	10
Furnished Apartments; farce; 1 act (very laughable)	5
The Widow's Proposals; farce; 1 act ("Widow Bedott")	3

PLAYS FOR FEMALE CHARACTEES.

Who's to Inherit? comedy; 1 act (brisk and humorous)	9
Mrs. Willis' Will; comedy; 1 act (neat and funny)	5
My Aunt's Heiress; comedy; 1 act ("Cinderella" plot)	11

Series 7995—Continued.

	M.	F.
"The Sweet Family;" burlesque; 1 act (will make a mummy laugh)		8
A Lesson in Elegance, or The Glass of Fashion; society comedy; 1 act		4
Murder Will Out; farce; 1 act (very laughable)		6
A Slight Mistake; comedy with a good moral; 1 act		5

TEMPERANCE PLAYS.

	M.	F.
Two Drams of Brandy; 1 act	2	2
Under the Curse; 1 act	3	2
Broken Promises; 5 acts (always makes a deep impression)	6	3
Ten Nights in a Bar-Room; 5 acts (new copyright version)	7	4
The Stolen Child; 2 acts	6	3

Series 7796.

Price 18 cents each. Per dozen, $2.00.
Postage, 1 cent each.

	M.	F.
Breaking his Bonds; comedy-drama; 4 acts	6	3
The Jail Bird; comedy-drama; 5 acts	6	3
Golden Gulch; border drama; 3 acts	11	3
The Man from Maine; comedy-drama; 5 acts	9	3
Shaun Aroon; stirring Irish drama; 3 acts	7	3
The Deacon; comedy-drama; 5 acts (simply immense)	6	6
The Japanese Wedding; costume pantomime	3	10
An Old Plantation Night (musical entertainment)	4	4

The Gypsies' Festival (juvenile cantata). Numerous characters.

The Court of King Christmas (juvenile cantata). Numerous characters.

King Winter's Carnival (children's operetta). Ten speaking parts and chorus.

Helmer's Actors' Make-up Book (indispensible to every actor).

Townsend's "Amateur Theatricals" (the very best guide book published).

LACE DEPARTMENT

American or Pillow Case Lace.

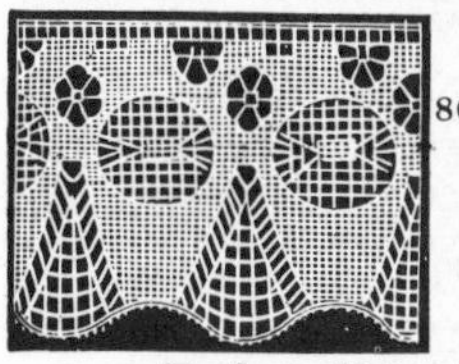

8000 Heavy white cotton wash lace.
Width, 1⅝ in., 2⅝ in., 3⅛ in., 4 in., 5½ in.
Per piece of 12 yards, 22c., 32c., 40c., 50c., 65c.

Point d' Ireland Lace.

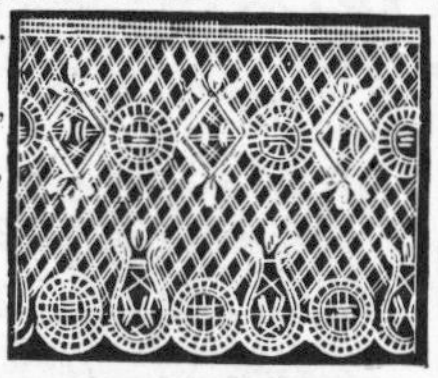

8003 Point d' Ireland Lace Cream Color.
Width, 1⅞ in., 4 in., 6¼ in., 8½ in., 11¾ in.
Per yard, 4c., 7c., 11c., 15c., 20c.

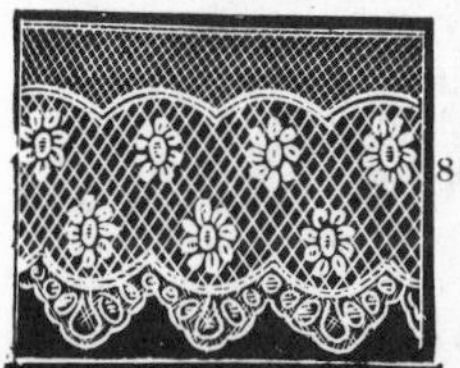

8005 Point d' Ireland Lace, net top, cream color.
Width, 4¼ in., 5½ in., 7 in., 9½ in.
Per yard, 10c., 12c., 14c., 18c.

Oriental Laces.

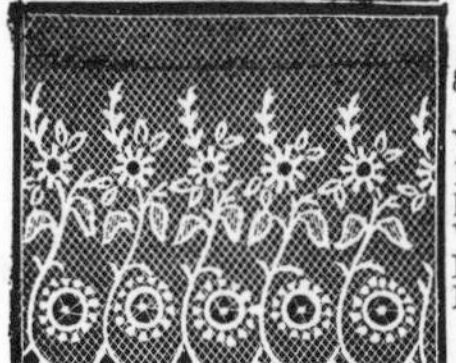

8007 Ivory Color Oriental Laces.

Width of work	2 in.	3¼ in.
Full width	2⅞ in.	4⅝ in.
Per yard	$0.07	$0.11
Width of work	4 in.	5½ in.
Full width	6½ in.	9¼ in.
Per yard	$0.14	$0.18

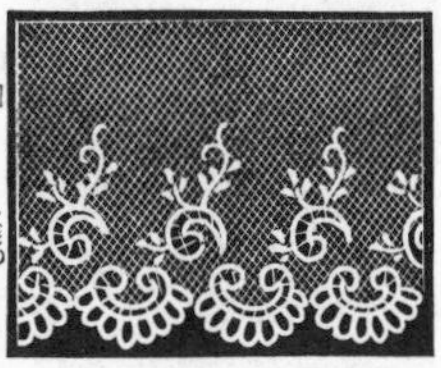

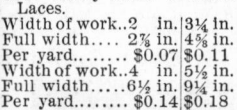

8009 Cream Color Oriental Laces, with loop edge.

	Inches.	
Full width	5¼	11
Width of work	2⅝	6½
Per yard	$0.15	$0.25

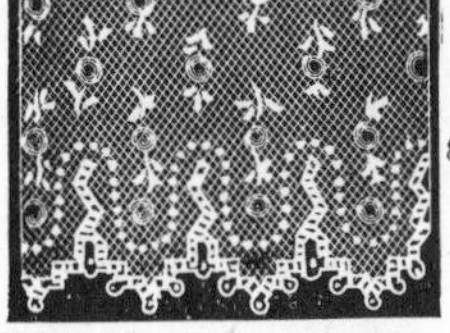

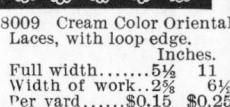

8014 Cream Color Oriental Laces, extra applique work on fine net.

Full width	6¼ in.	8 in.	11 in.
Width of work	2⅞ in.	4¾ in.	6½ in.
Per yard	$0.20	$0.30	$0.40

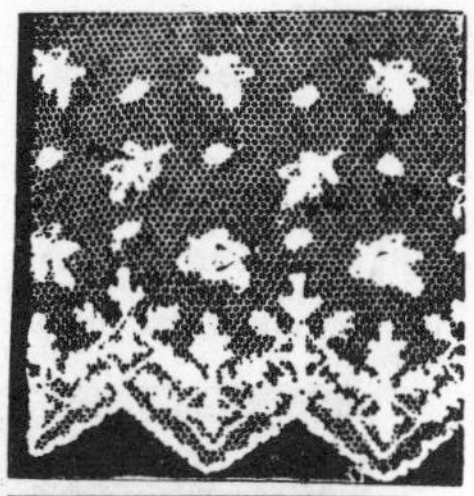

8016 Oriental Ivory Lace.
Width, 1¾ in.
Per yard $0.08
Per 12 yards ...... .85

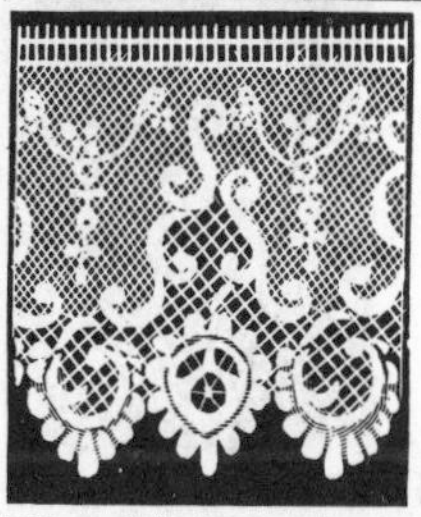

8018 Irish Point Heavy Cotton Cream Lace, for dress and cape trimming, Vandyke scallop.

Width	4 in.	5 in.	6½ in.
Per yard	$0.15	$0.20	$0.29
Width	7¾ in.	9¾ in.	
Per yard	$0.34	$0.40	

Plat Valenciennes Lace Edgings and Inserting.

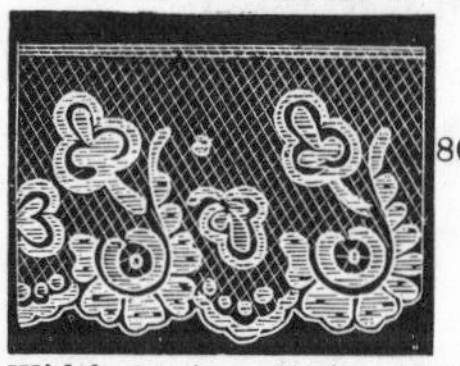

8020 Plat Valenciennes Lace Edgings, new pattern. See cut.

Width	1½ in.	2⅛ in.	2½ in.	3⅜ in.	4⅜ in.	4¾ in.
Per yd.	$0.05	$0.06	$0.09	$0.10	$0.12	$0.14
Per 12 yards	.54	.65	.95	1.00	1.30	1.50

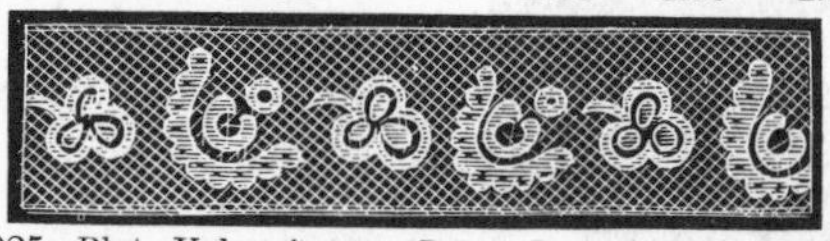

8025 Plat Valenciennes Lace Insertion to match edges No. 8020—1¼ in. wide.
Per yard .... $0.05 Per 12 yards $0.55

French Valenciennes Lace Edgings and Insertions, White.

(12 yards in piece. We do not cut pieces.)

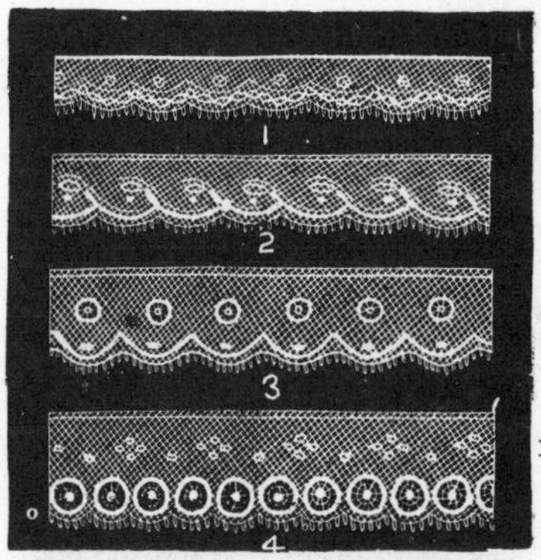

8030 ⅜ in. wide, 25c. per piece.
½ in. wide. 30c. per piece.
¾ in. wide 39c. per piece.
1 in. wide, 50c. per piece.

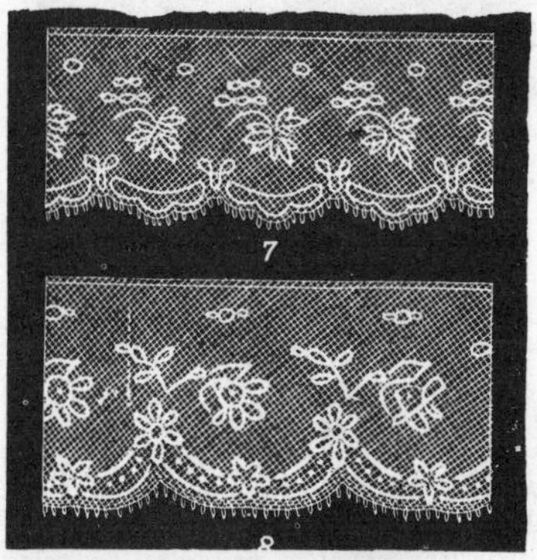

8031 1¼ in. wide, 70c. per piece.
1½ inches wide, 95c. per piece.
1¾ inches wide, $1.20 per piece.

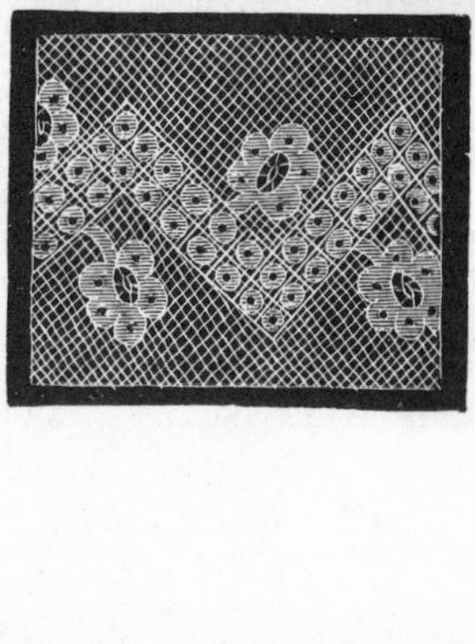

8032—
No. 9 Inserting, ½ inch wide, 40c. per piece.
No. 10 Inserting, ¾ inch wide, 45c. per piece.
No. 11 Inserting, 1 inch wide, 50c. per piece.

Lace—Continued.

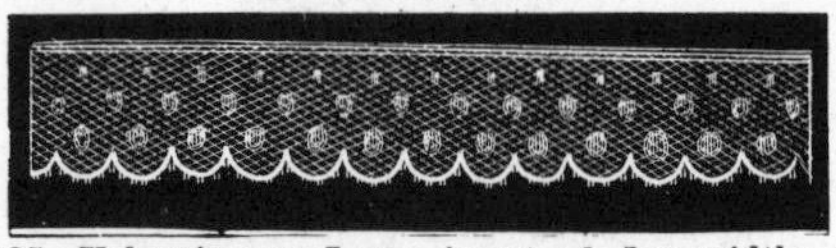

8035 Valenciennes Laces, in set of five widths to match, new. See cut.

Width	½ in.	⅝ in.	¾ in.	1 in.	1¼ in.
Per piece of 12 yds	$0.25	$0.33	$0.40	$0.45	$0.55

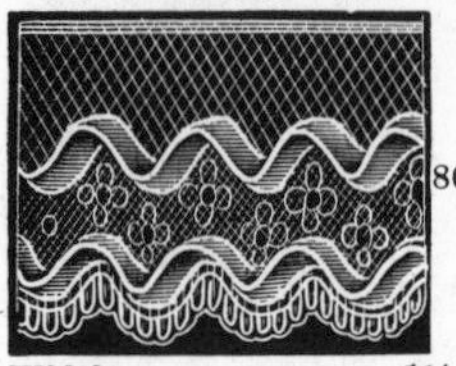

8038 Point de Paris Ivory Lace, nice quality.

Width	1½ in.	2½ in.	3⅜ in.	4⅜ in.
Per yard	$0.09	$0.14	$0.16	$0.20

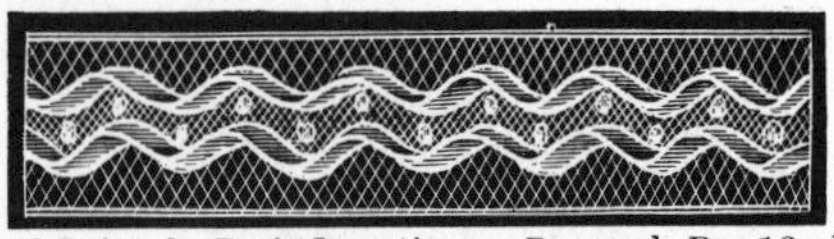

8040 Point de Paris Insertion to match 8038 edges. Width, 1¾ inches...... Per yard. $0.10 Per 12 yds. $1.00

White Linen Torchon Lace.

(We quote until sold.)

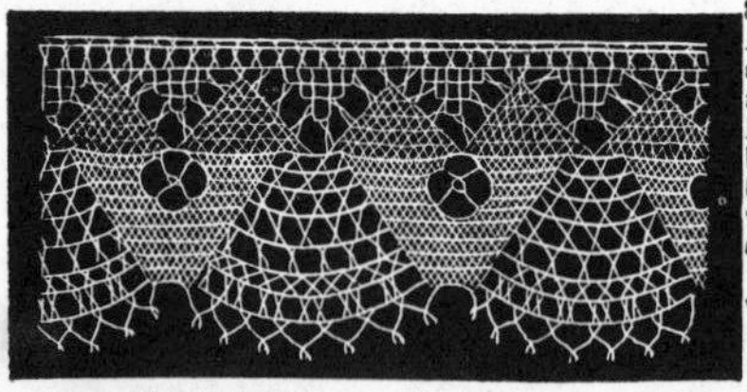

8065 All linen Torchon Lace, heavy thread; a splendid lace for wash goods, underwear, and curtains.

No.	Width.	Per yard.	Per 12 yards.
17	3⅜ in.	$0.09	$1.00
21	4¼ in.	.10	1.10

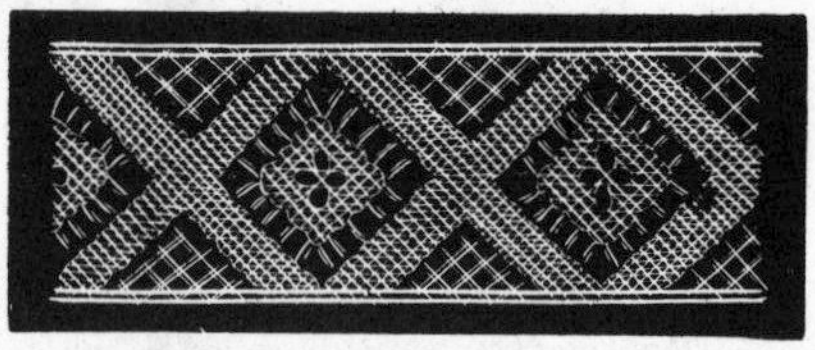

8066 All Linen Torchon Inserting to match above edge.

No.	Width.	Per yard.	Per 12 yards.
10	1⅜ in.	$0.05	$0.50
11	1⅝ in.	.06	.55
17	3¼ in.	.09	0.95

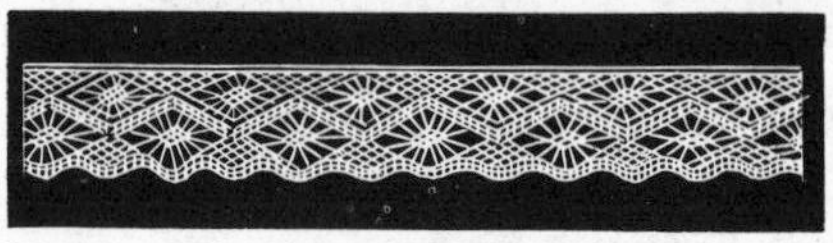

8070 Linen Torchon Lace, nice quality.

Width.	Per yard.	Per 12 yds.
⅜ in.	$0.02	$0.22
½ in.	.03	.33
¾ in.	.04	.43
1 in.	.06	.65
1½ in.	.08	.85

Real Hand-Made Torchon Laces, All Linen.

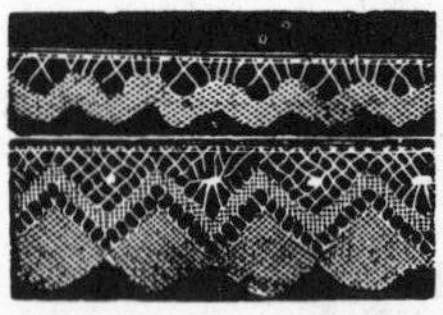

8080 Torchon Linen Edge, ⅝ to ¾ inch, heavy.
Per yard........$0.06
Per 12 yards.... .65

8082 Torchon Linen Edge, 1 inch, heavy.
Per yard........$0.07
Per 12 yards.... .75

8083 Torchon Linen Edge, 1¼in,, heavy. Per yard........$0.09
Per 12 yards........1.00

8085 Torchon Linen Edge, 1¼ inch, finer. Per yard........ .11
Per 12 yards........1.20

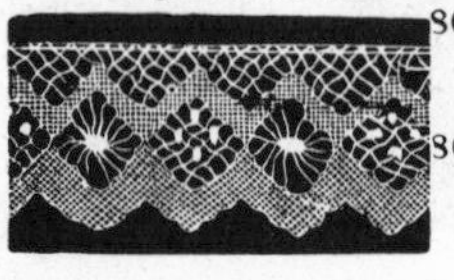

8087 Torchon Linen Edge, 2¼ inches, heavy
Per yard..............$0.11
Per 12 yards.............1.20

8089 Torchon Linen Edge, 2 inches, finer.
Per yard..............$0.14
Per 12 yards.... ..... 1.40

Lace—Continued.

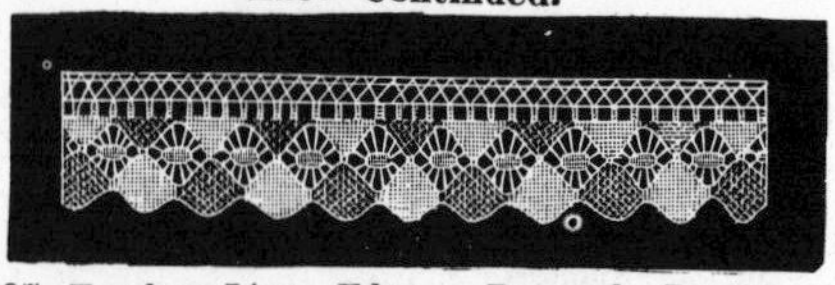

	Per yard.	Per 12 yds.
8097 Torchon Linen Edge, ⅞ inch, very fine	$0.18	$1.95
8098 Torchon Linen Edge, 1⅛ inch, extra fine	.20	2.15
8100 Torchon Linen Edge, 1½ inch, extra fine	.25	2.75

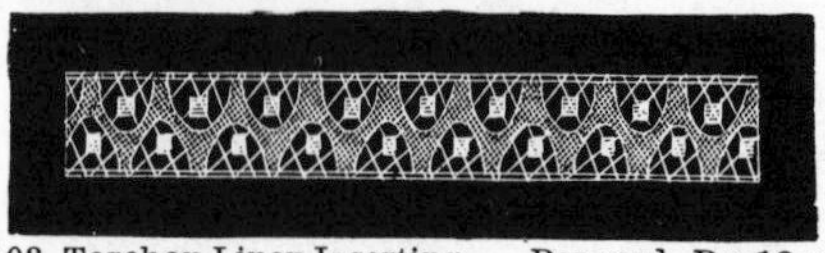

	Per yard.	Per 12 yds.
8103 Torchon Linen Inserting, heavy thread to match heavy edges. 1 inch wide	$0.07	$0.75
8105 Torchon Linen Inserting, heavy, to match above heavy edges, 1½ inch	.11	1.20
8110 Torchon Linen Inserting, fine, 1 inch to match 8097, 8098 and 8100	.17	1.85

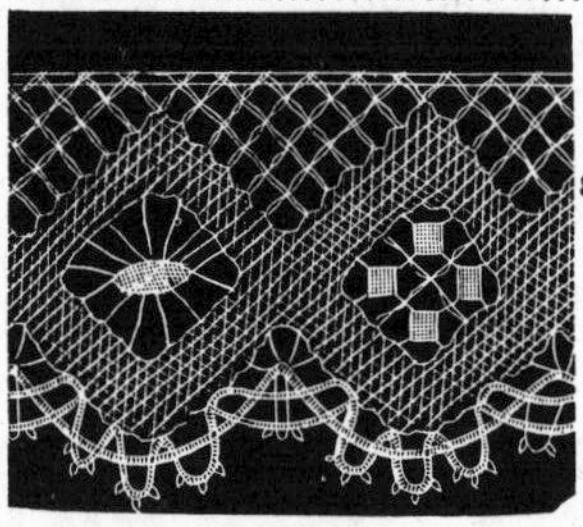

8115 Torchon Linen Edge, heavy thread. See cut. 3½ to 4 inches.
Per yard.....$0.16
Per 12 yards...1.75

Silk Lace Chiffon.

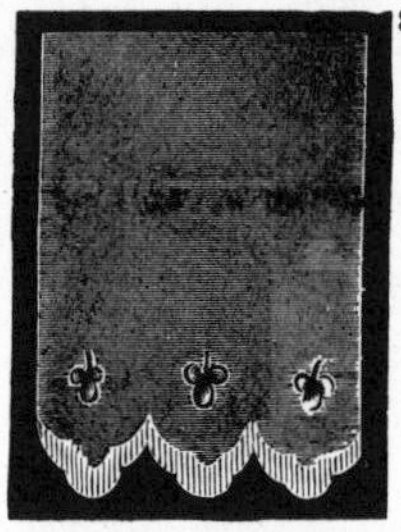

8122 All Silk Lace Chiffon (4 inches), silk embroidered edge, and one row silk embroidery above the edge. Note the colors: Black, white, cream, beige, brown, cardinal, sky blue, nile green, gray, lavender or heliotrope, navy blue and maize or corn. Per yard..............$0.20

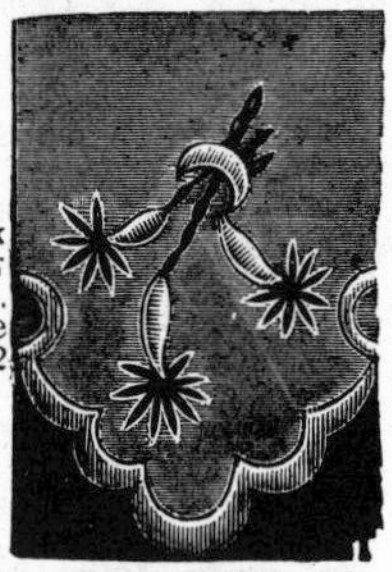

8125 Silk Chiffon, with silk embroidered edge and heavy embroidery in all colors. Width, 3¾ to 4½ inches. See cut. Per yard..........$0.32

Silk Lace Edgings.

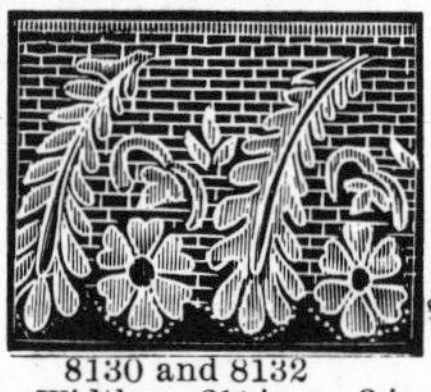

8130 and 8132

8130 Black Silk Spanish Guipure Lace.

Width,	2¼ in.	3 in.	3½ in	4½ in.	6 in.
Per yard,	$0.08	$0.10	$0.12	$0.15	$0.20

8132 Cream Silk Spanish Guipure Lace; same pattern as black No. 8130.

Width,	2¼ in.	3 in.	3½ in.	4½ in.	6 in.
Per yard.	$0.08	$0.10	$0.12	$0.15	$0.20

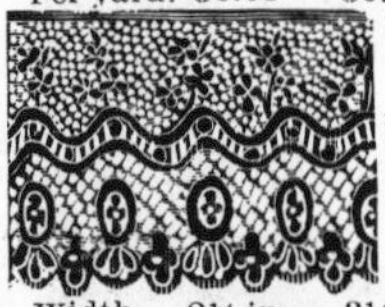

8134 Black Silk Chantilly Lace.

Width,	2⅛ in.	3¼ in.	3¾ in.	4½ in.	5½ in.
Per yard,	$0.09	$0.11	$0.14	$0.17	$0.20

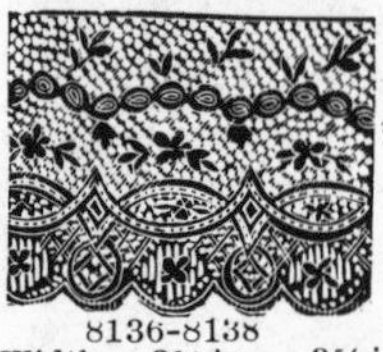

8136-8138

8136 Black Silk Chantilly Lace, new pattern. See cut.

Width,	3⅛ in.	3⅝ in.	4¾ in.	6¼ in.	7⅜ in.
Per yd.	$0.12	$0.18	$0.21	$0.32	$0.36

8138 Cream Silk Chantilly Lace, same as No. 8136 black.

Width,	3⅛ in.	3⅝ in.	4¾ in.	6¼ in.	7⅜ in.
Per yd.	$0.12	$0.18	$0.21	$0.32	$0.36

Silk Laces.

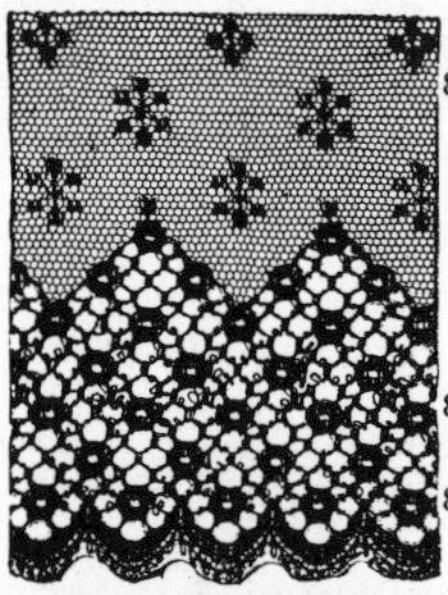

8143 Black Guipure Chantilly Lace.
Width. 3⅛ Per Yard. $0.17

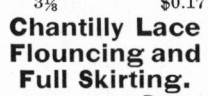

Chantilly Lace Flouncing and Full Skirting.

	Per yard.
8147 Black Silk Chantilly Lace Flouncing, 40 to 43 ins. wide	$1.00
8149 Black Silk Chantilly Lace Flouncing, 40 to 43 inches	$1.40

Fine Fedora Lace.

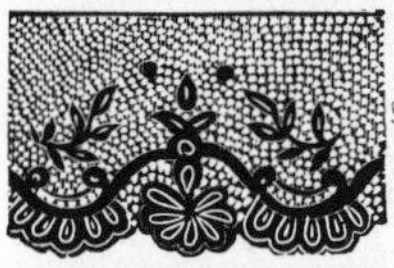

8153 Fine Black Silk Fedora Lace.

Width,	3½ in.	4⅞ in.	5¾ in.
Per yd.	$0.30	$0.40	$0.50

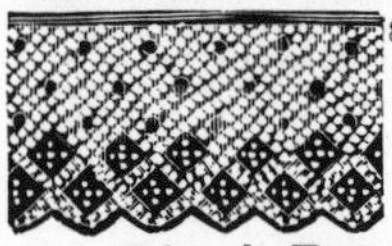

8155 Cheap Black Silk Lace, heavy thread.

Width—	3½ in.	5¼ in.	7 in.	9¼ in.
Per yard—	$0.12	$0.16	$0.22	$0.28

Black Bourdonne Laces.

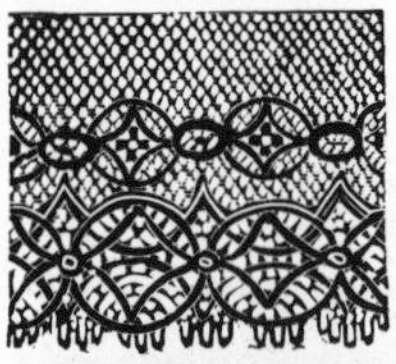

8160 Black Silk Bourdonne Lace, with net top. See cut.

Width	3¼ in.	5¾ in.
Per yard	$0.19	$0.30
Width	7 in.	9¼ in.
Per yard	$0.33	$0.49

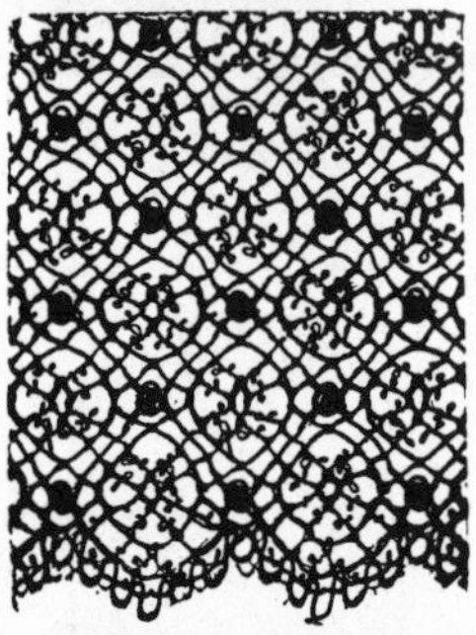

8162 Black Silk Bourdonne Lace, all over pattern, See cut.

Width..	3¼ in.	5¼in.
Per yard,	$0.25	$0.35
Width..	6½ in.	8½ in.
Per yard,	$0.45	$0.55
Width		10¼ in.
Per yard		$0.65

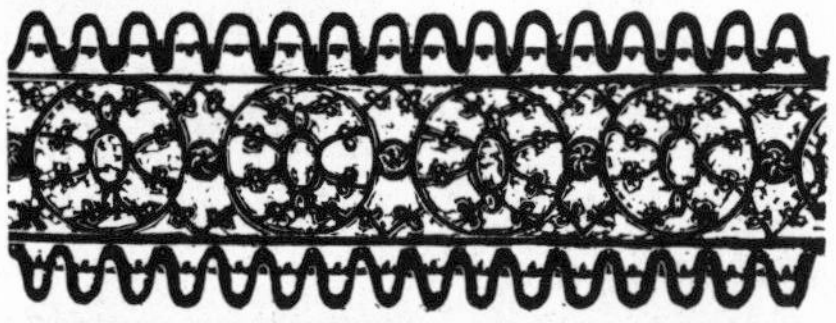

8164 Black Silk Bourdonne Lace Insertion to match edgings, Width 1½ in. Per yard........$0.12

Black Lace Drapery Nets.

(45 inches wide.)

8170 Plain Black Russian or La Tosca silk drapery net, for overdresses. Per yard..........$1.00

8172 Plain Black Brussels Net, heavy thread, all silk, for over dresses. Per yard........... 1.00

All Over Spanish Guipure Lace.

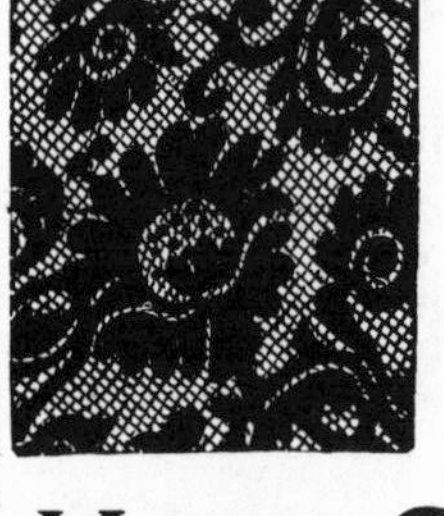

8185 Black Silk Spanish Guipure Lace, 14 inches wide. Per yard......$0.75
27 inches wide.
Per yard............ 1.50

MEN'S CLOTHING.

Quotations entirely changed.
Latest styles and fabrics.
Prices can't be beat.

Black Silk Scarfs.

Special line black silk Spanish lace scarfs, all with purled edges, at about one-half their real value. We quote until sold as they cannot be duplicated.

Each
8188 Black Silk Lace Scarfs, 7½x56 inches.....$0.40
8190 Black Silk Lace Scarfs, 7½x58 inches...... .50
8192 Black Silk Lace Scarfs, 9½x70 inches...... .60
8196 Black Silk Lace Scarfs, extra quality,8x56 inches.. .70
8200 Black Silk Lace Scarfs, extra quality and size, 10½x76 inches........................... .80
8202 Black Silk Lace Scarfs, extra quality and size, 12x74 inches.......................... 1.00

Silk Lace Scarfs.

8206 Cream Spanish All Silk Lace Scarfs. Until sold....................................$1.25

Silk Lace Fichus.

Special value in black; see quotations below.

8210 Black Silk Spanish Guipure Lace Fichus, purled edges all around; length 53 inches by 12 inches at center. Each........................$0.50

Fancy Net Veilings.

8250 Chenille Spot, all silk veiling, 14 in. wide. Per yard......................$0.09
Cream and black only.

Per yard.
8253 All Silk Veiling, with large chenille spots, 14 in. wide. Colors: Black, cream, navy and brown....................................$0.13
8254 Fine Point d' Esprit Silk Net Veiling, with fine dot effect, 14 inches wide. Colors: Black, cream, navy and brown.................... .17
8258 Black Silk Tuxedo Net Veiling, 13 inches wide.. .09
8260 Black Silk Net Veiling with fine jet beads, width 14 inches................................ .16
8262 Silk Net Veiling with small chenille spot, width 27 inches. Colors: Black and cream only .22
8264 Sewing Silk Veiling, both fast edges, 13 inches wide, all silk. Colors: Seal brown, medium brown, golden brown, tan, navy blue, drab, slate, myrtle green, white, cream, black; also white with black edge...................... .20
8266 Teutonic Silk Veiling, 12 inches wide, with four stripes above scalloped embroidered edge. Colors: Cardinal, wine, terra cotta,myrtle green. Until sold.................................... .10

Barege Wool Veilings.

In Colors, Black, Brown, Gray, Green and Blue.
Per yard.
8280 Barege Wool Veilng, single fold, fast edges, good quality.....................................$0.18
8282 Barege Veiling, medium quality,double fold .20
8284 Barege Veiling, best and finest, double fold .25

Brussels Nets or Wash Blondes.

Per yard.
8286 Wash Blonde, cream, 26 in...............$0.15
8288 Blonde Net, spot figure,white or cream,27in. .15
8291 Spot Blonde Net, white or cream, finer, 27 in. wide................................... .22
8293 Darned or Embroidered Net, 72 in., white only..................................... .30
8295 White Darned or Embroidered Net, 72 in... .42

White Silk Illusion.

Per yard.
8305 White Illusion, 1 yard wide.............$0.32
8307 White Silk Illusion for bridal veils, etc., 72 in. wide.................................. .75

Black Silk Brussels Nets.

WE QUOTE UNTIL SOLD.
Plain and Figured.   Per yard.
8310 Black Silk Net, fine quality, medium, neat figure, 27 in. wide.........................$0.50
8312 Black Silk Net, plain, 27 in. wide.......... .45
8314 Black Silk Net, plain, 27 in. wide.......... .60

Black English Crepe.

8320--   For Veiling and Trimming.
Width.........27 in.   28 in.   36 in.   41 in.
Per yard.......$0.95 $1.20 $2.00 $3.00

Ladies' Silk Ties.

8340 Japanese (washable) Silk Ties, 5x35 in., drawn hemstitch. Each............$0.20
8342 Japanese (washable) Silk Ties, 6x39 in., drawn hemstitch. Each............$0.25
NOTE.--Colors in above: Pink, light blue, navy, cardinal. nile green, yellow, cream and black.

8344 Ladies' or Children's Surah Silk Bows; solid colors: Black, cream, nile green, pink, blue, orange,brown,tan,navy, cardinal and heliotrope, all with elastic ribbon for putting on readily. Each............$0.25
Per Dozen..................... 2.70

White Embroidered Ties.

8350 White Hemstitch Lawn Ties, embroidered ends. (Size 4¼x44 inch.)
Each....................$0.10
Per dozen............. 1.00
8352 White Hemstitch Lawn Ties, embroidered ends, larger. Each..........$0.12
Per dozen............. 1.25
8354 White Lawn Ties, scalloped embroidered ends, 4¾ x44 inch. Each......$0.16
8356 White Lawn Ties, scalloped embroidered ends, 6x 44 inch. Each...... $0.18
Per dozen.............$1.95

New Collars.

8365 Cream Lace Collars, 6 inches wide (3550)
Each $0.25

8367 Cream Lace Collars, scallop pattern, width 7¾ inches. (3582).
Each...............$0.33

8369 Cream Heavy Lace Collars, width 7 inches. (3585.) Each.....$0.37

8371 Cream Applique Lace Collars, width 9 in. (3393.) Each.....$0.65

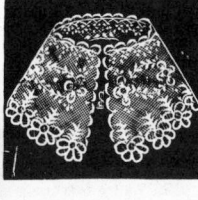

8373 Cream Vandyke Point Lace Collars, extra heavy, width 7 in. (3559.) Each....$0.75

8375 Irish Point Applique Collars, width 5½ inches. (3117).
Each.......... .....$0.20

8377 Finer Irish Point Collars, width 4½ inches (3345). Each. ...$0.35

8378 Guipure Open Work Sailor Collars. (3226).
Each...............$0.20

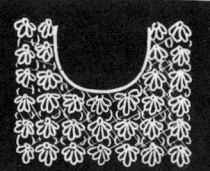

8379 Point de gene Heavy Lace Collars, sailor style (3330). Each.$0.29

New Neckwear.

SEE FOOT NOTE FOR COLORS.

8380 Ladies' Stock Collars, rosette front, fancy wave silk, plain colors (731).
Each................$0.40

8382 Ladies' Stock Collars, rosette front, plain Japanese silk. Each....................$0.50
8384 Ladies' Stock Collars, rosette front, crepe de chien silk. Each............................. .50

8388 Ladies' Stock Collars, fancy wave silk, butterfly front (729).
Each................$0.47

8394 Ottoman Corded Silk Stock Collars, butterfly front (733). Each............................$0 65

8400 Jabot Ladies' Neckwear, cream oriental lace, satin ribbon bow and satin neck band with lace over same (744).
Each................$0.65

8402 Ladies' Cape Lace Neckwear with three rows narrow satin ribbon, 10 inches wide at back, 8 inches wide at front (759).
Each..................$0.65

8404 Ladies' Japanese Silk Chemisette with four plaits up and down front and three in collar, assorted colors (735).
Each.................$0.69

8406 Ladies' Japanese Silk Waist Front with cascade and belt; butterfly collar, assorted colors (752).
Each..................$0.97

8408 Combination Cape Silk and Lace Neckwear, extra large and very dressy (713).
Each.................,...$1.25

NOTE.--All the collars above in the following colors: Old rose, new nile, pink, sky blue, maize, cardinal, lavender, black, cream, cerise and bluet.

A Bargain.

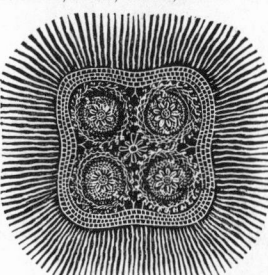

8414 Hand Crocheted Tidies. Size, 18x18 to outside of fringe. Size inside of fringe, 11 x 11. These tidies are worth 50c. at retail, but our price will be .20 cents each until sold, or $2.25 per dozen.

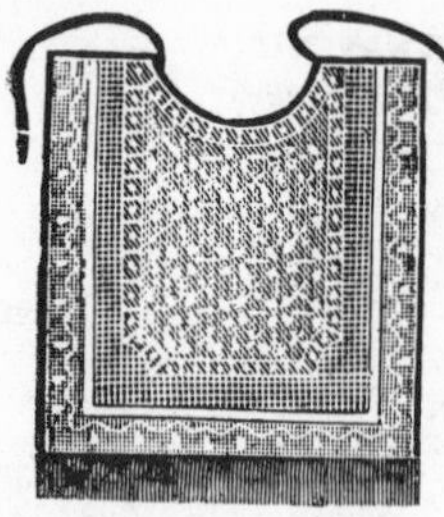

Children's Feeders.

8416 Cotton Feeders, fancy printed designs, fast colors. Size 10x12.
Each........$0.05
Per doz........ .50

8418 Fine Cloth Feeders, fancy colored designs, large size.
Each........$0.10
Per dozen........ 1.10

Baby Bibs.

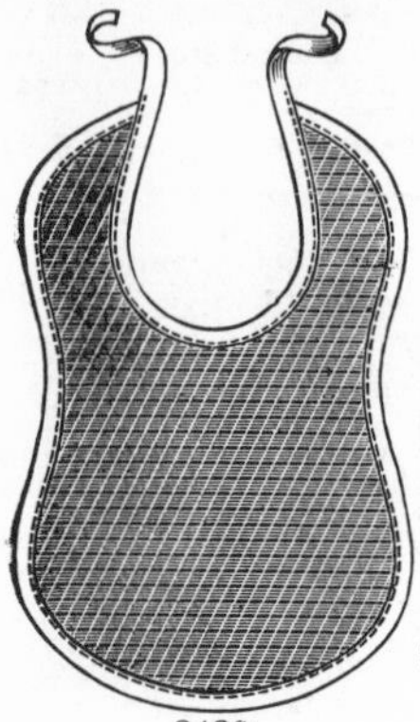

8420

8420 Honey Comb Bibs with bound edge.
Each........$0.04
Per doz........ .37

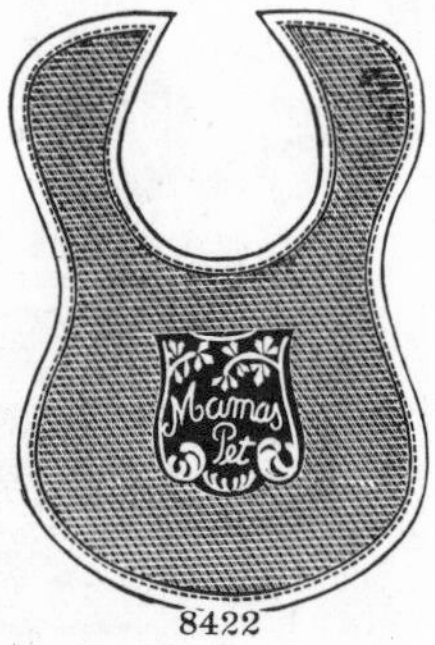

8422

8422 Honey Comb Bibs, bound edge and colored medallion. Each....$0.06
Per doz........ .60

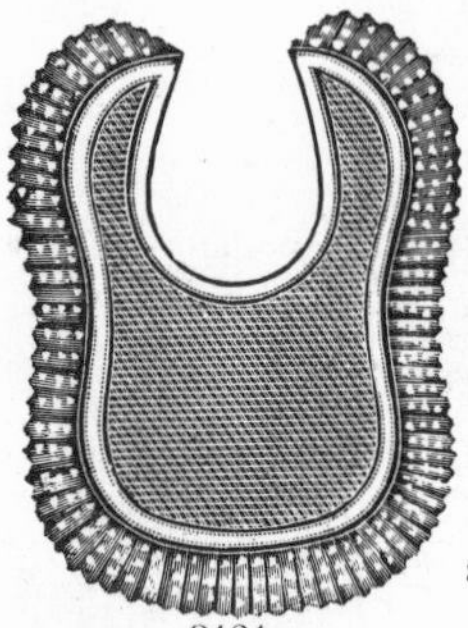

8424

8424 Honey Comb Bibs taped, and wash lace edge.
Each........$0.06
Per doz........ .60

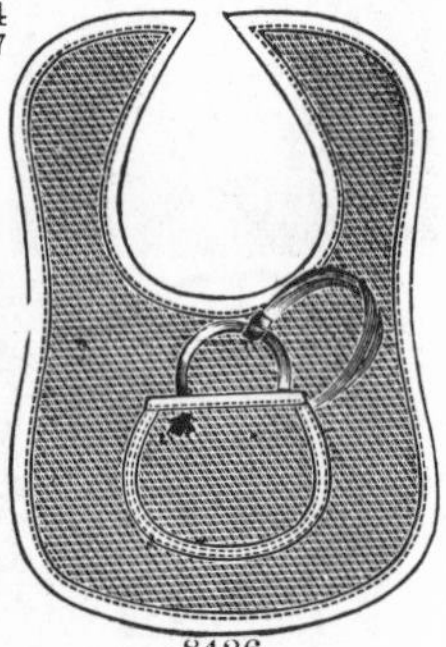

8426

8426 Honey Comb Bibs; bound edge, with bound pocket and bone ring.
Each........$0.07
Per doz........ .75

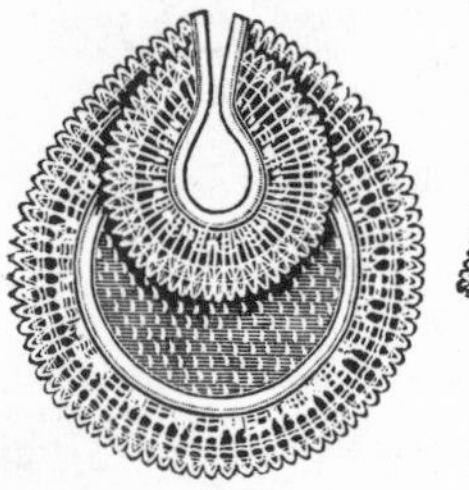

8428

8428 New Round Pattern Bibs; figured pique-fleeced on back, lace edge.
Each........$0.09
Per doz........ .95

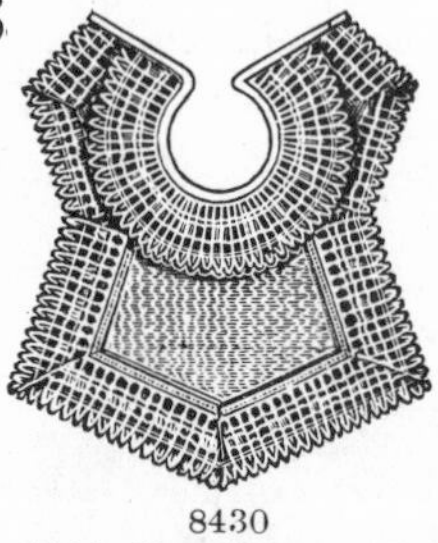

8430

8430 New Pattern Bibs; fancy cloth fleeced back, lace edge.
Each........$0.09
Per doz........ .95

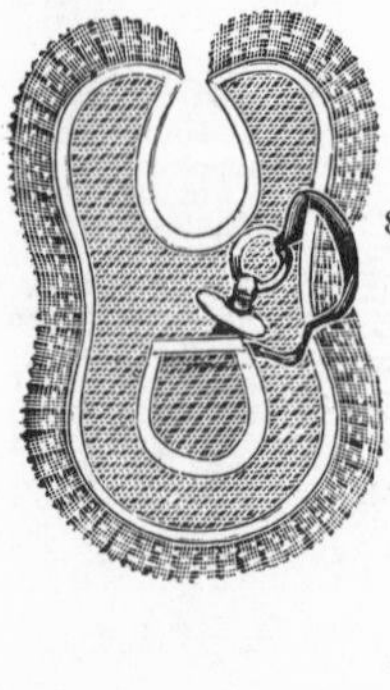

8431 Solid Comfort Baby Bib, with black rubber nipple lace edge and honey comb cloth.
Each........$0.10
Per doz........ 1.10

Bibs—Continued.

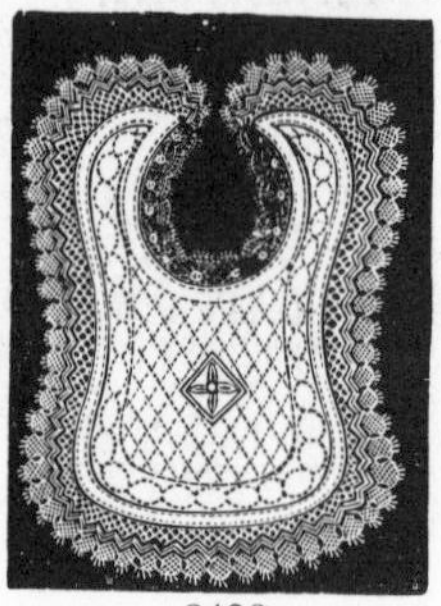

8432

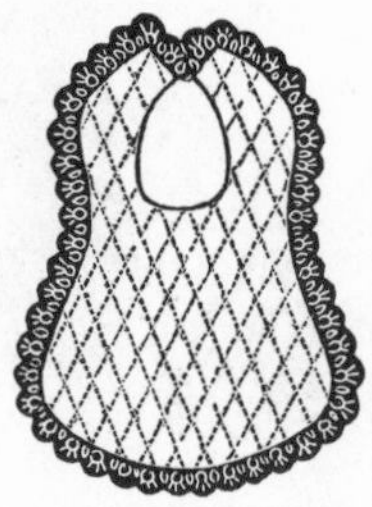

8434

8432 Quilted Bibs with wash lace edge.
Each........$0.10
Per doz........ 1.05

8434 Fine Imported Bibs; hand made; quilted and padded; wash lace edge. Each........ .18
Per doz........ 1.95

Finishing or Trimming Braids.

These braids are 6 yards to the piece and standard quality.

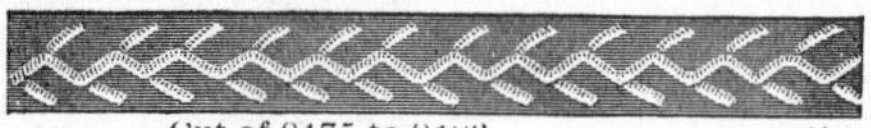

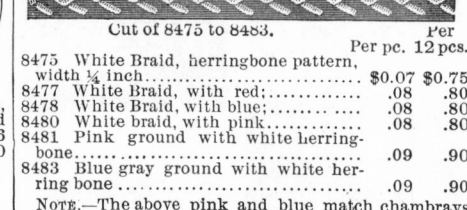

Cut of 8475 to 8483.

		Per pc.	Per 12 pcs.
8475	White Braid, herringbone pattern, width ¼ inch........	$0.07	$0.75
8477	White Braid, with red;........	.08	.80
8478	White Braid, with blue;........	.08	.80
8480	White braid, with pink........	.08	.80
8481	Pink ground with white herring-bone........	.09	.90
8483	Blue gray ground with white herring bone........	.09	.90

NOTE.—The above pink and blue match chambrays or ginghams.

8485 White braid........$0.07 $0.70

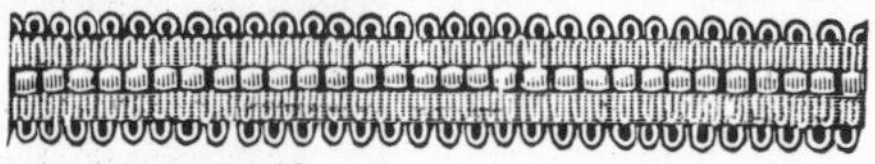

8487 White braid........$0.06 $0.60

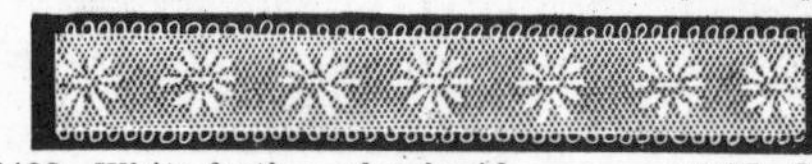

8489 White feather edge braid. $0.07 $0.70

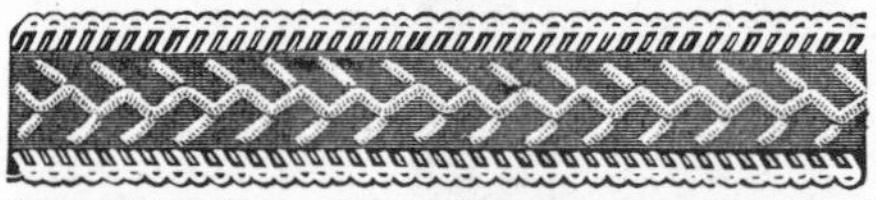

8491 White loop edge braid........$0.10 $1.05

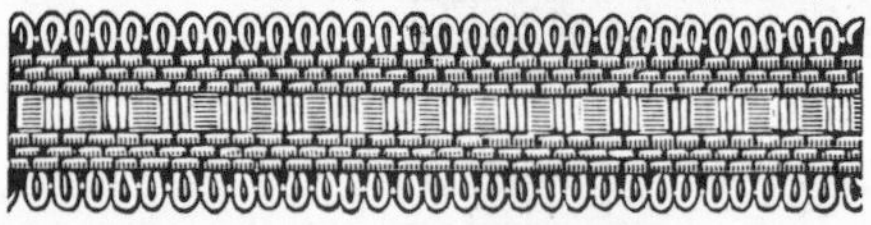

8493 White fancy feather edge braid. ⅜ inch wide........$0.09 $0.90

8495 White braid.. $0.08 $0.80

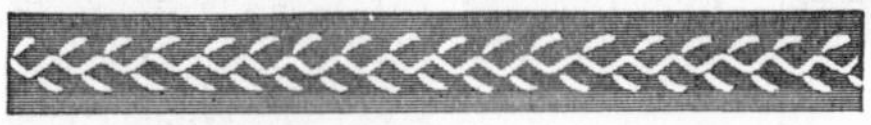

8497 Extra fine white herringbone braid........$0.11 $1.20

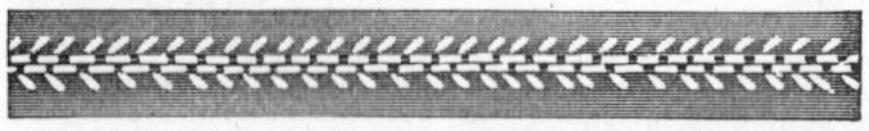

8499 Extra fine white braid........$0.12 $1.30

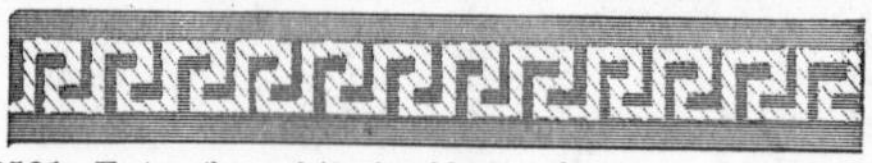

8501 Extra fine white braid, Grecian pattern........$0.14 $1.45

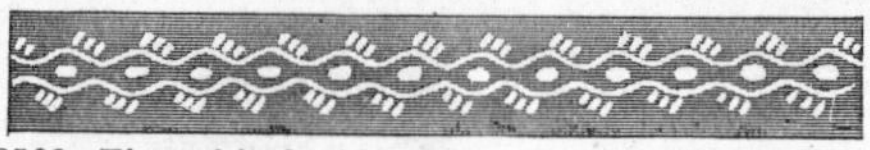

8503 Fine white braid... $0.10 $1.05

8505 White braid........$0.09 $0.90

EMBROIDERY DEPARTMENT.

We quote width of embroidery or work, the cloth being about double this width.

Colored Embroideries.

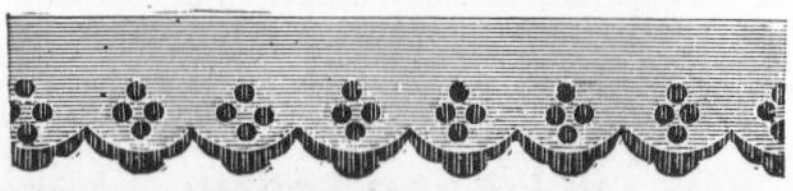

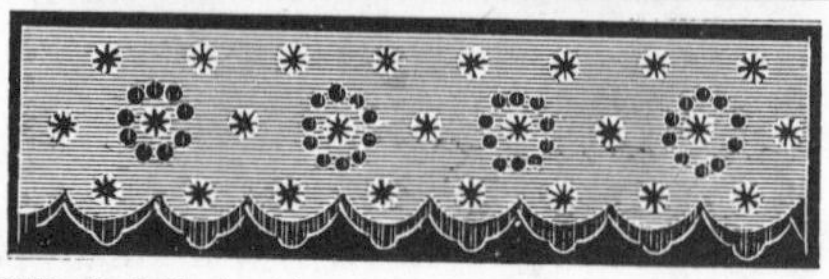

8550 Red Embroidery on white cloth.

Width....	⅜ in.	½ in.	¾ in.	1 in.	1⅜ in.
Per yard..	$0.03	.04½	.06	.07	.09

8555 Blue Embroidery on white cloth.

Width....	⅜ in.	½ in.	¾ in.	1 in.	1⅜ in.
Per yard..	$0.03	.04½	.06	.07	.09

8560 White Embroidery on red cloth.

Width....	½ in.	¾ in.	1 in.	1¼ in.	2 in.
Per yard.	$0.03½	.05	.06	.07	.09

8565 White Embroidery on navy blue cloth.

Width....	½ in.	¾ in.	1 in.	1¼ in.	2 in.
Per yard.	$0.03¼	.05	.06	.07	.09

White Cambric Embroidered Edgings.

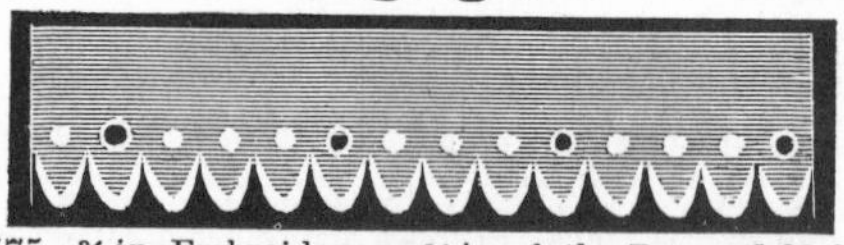

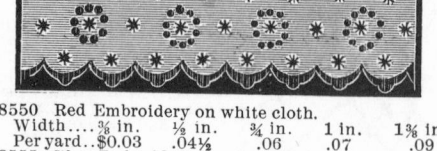

8575 ⅜ in. Embroidery on ¾ in. cloth. Per yard.$0.02
8577 ½ in. Embroidery on 1 in. cloth. " .03

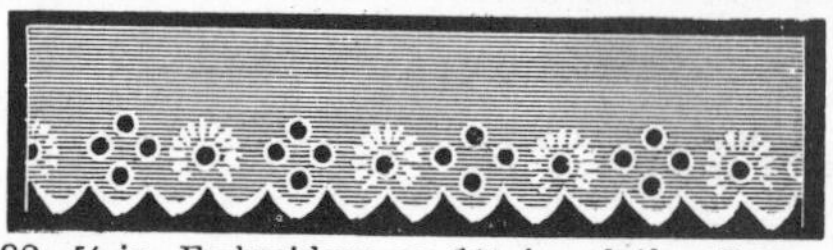

8580 ⅝ in. Embroidery on 1⅛ in. cloth. Per yard........$0.03½

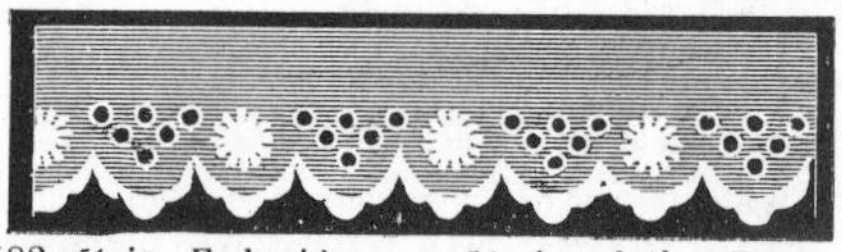

8582 ⅝ in. Embroidery on 1⅛ in. cloth. Per yard........$0.04

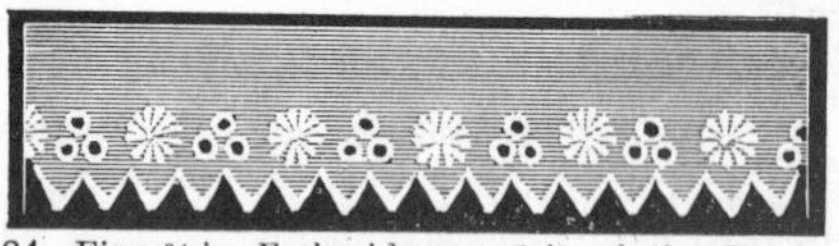

8584 Fine ⅜ in. Embroidery on 1 in. cloth. Per yard........$0.05

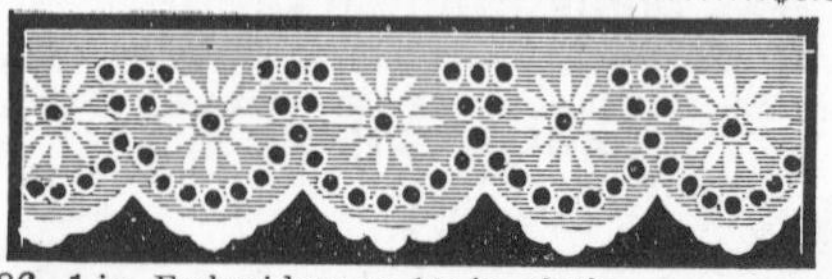

8586 1 in. Embroidery on 1¾ in. cloth. Per yard........$0.06

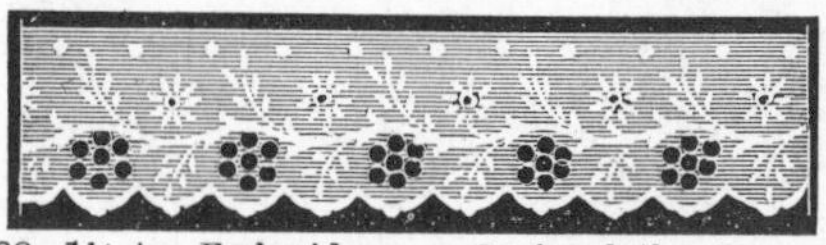

8588 1⅛ in. Embroidery on 2⅜ in. cloth. Per yard........$0.07

8590 1⅛ in. Embroidery on 2¾ in. cloth. Per yard........$0.08

Embroideries—Continued.

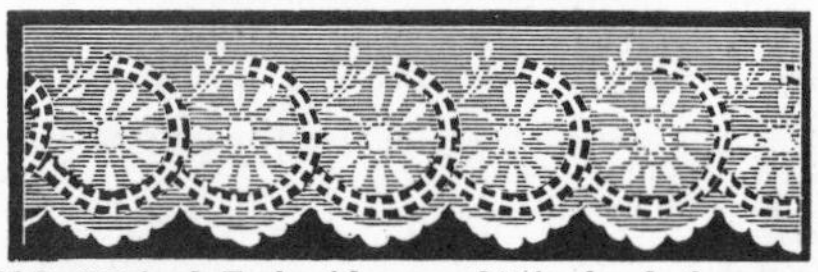

8592 1⅝ inch Embroidery on 2⅞ inch cloth. Per yard..$0.09½

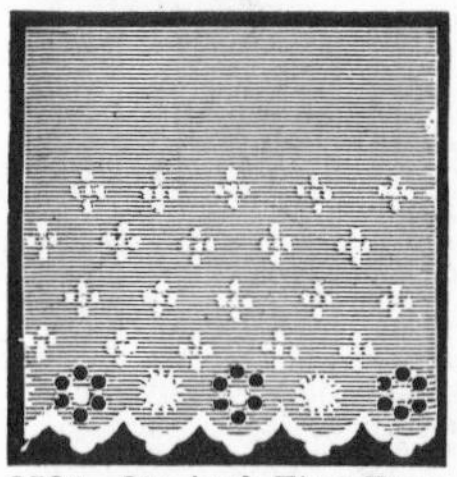

8594 2¼ inch Fine Embroidery on 4⅝ inch cloth. Per yard...$0.11

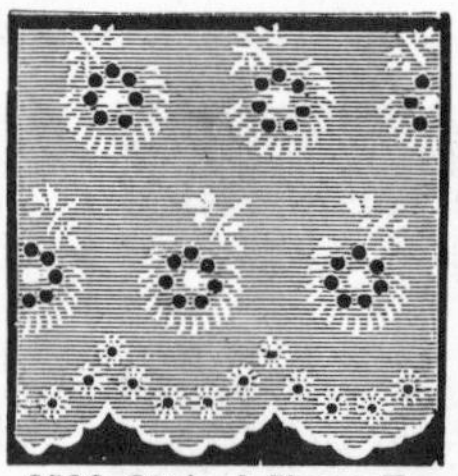

8596 2¾ inch Showy Embroidery on 5¼ inch cloth. Per yard..$0.12

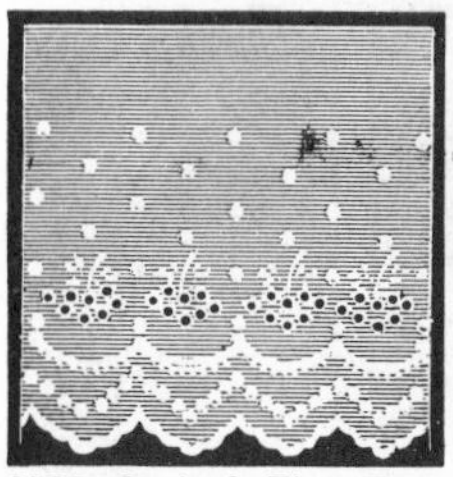

8598 3¼ inch Fine Embroidery on 7 inch cloth. Per yard...........$0.15

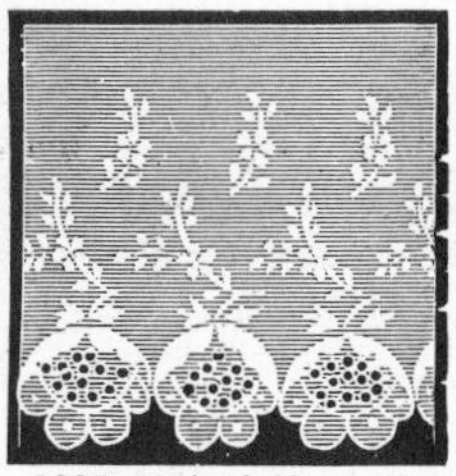

8605 4⅛ inch Showy Embroidery on 8¼ inch cloth. Per yard..$0.18

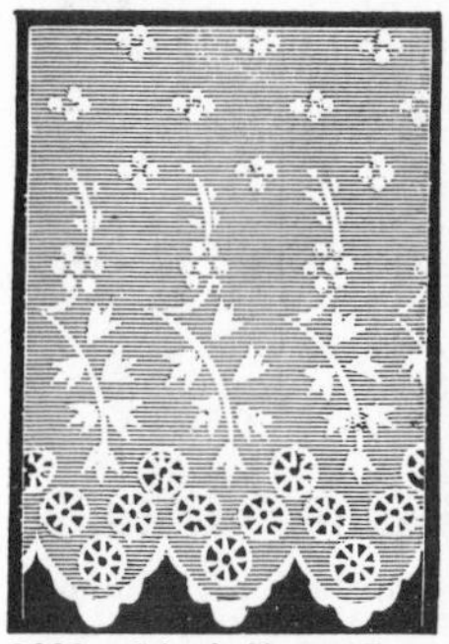

8608 7 inch Showy Embroidery on 14 inch cloth. Per yard ..$0.24

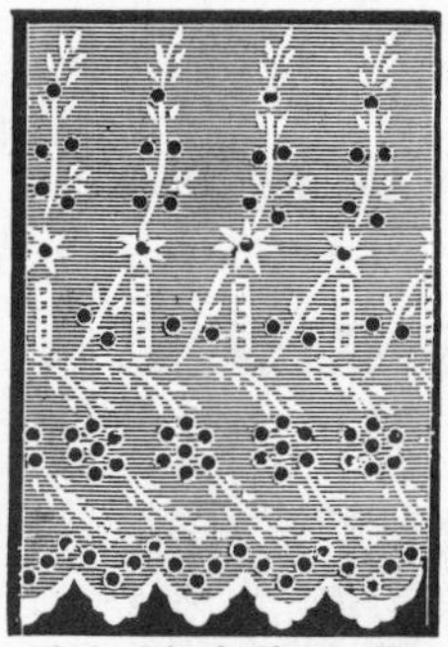

8612 8 inch Showy Embroidery on 16½ inch cloth. Per yard. .$0.27

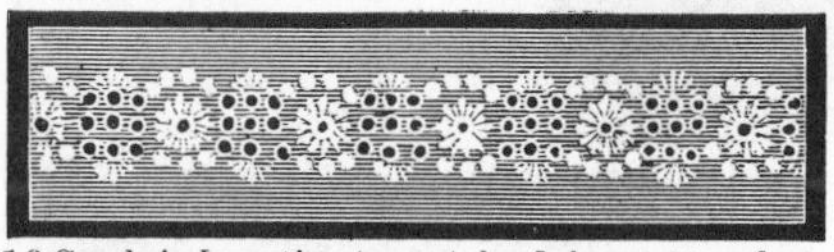

8616 Cambric Insertion to match edgings, ¾ inch Embroidery on 1½ inch cloth.................. .$0.05

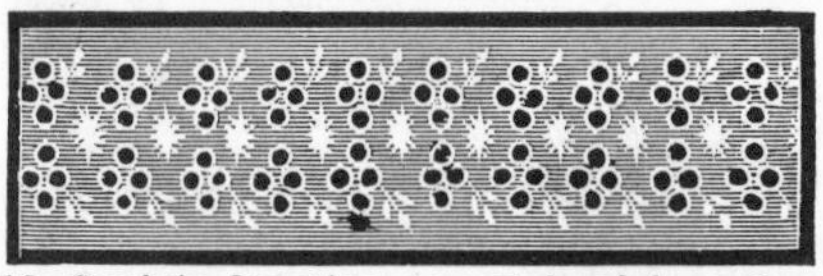

8618 Cambric Insertion to match edgings, 1 inch Embroidery on 1⅞ inch cloth..............$0.07

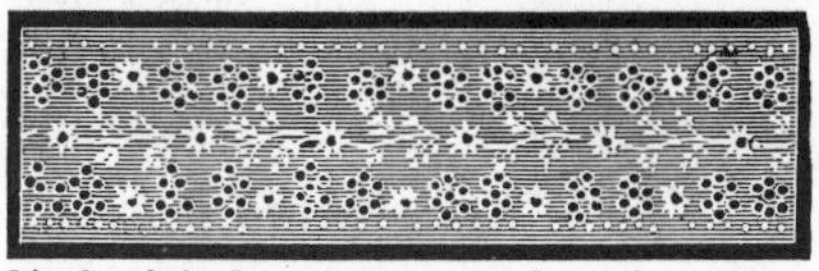

8621 Cambric Insertion to match edgings, 1⅝ inch Embroidery on 3 inch cloth..... ....$0.11

LADIES' SILK WEB BELTS

With Sterling Silver Buckles, will be fashionable again this Spring. We illustrate the newest of Belts and other Summer Jewelry

6--2nd

Irish Point Cambric Embroideries.

OPEN WORK EDGINGS ON WIDE CLOTH.

8625 Link Pattern Edging, 1⅛ inch embroidery on 3⅜ inch cloth. Per yard..............$0.07

8630 Link Pattern Edging, 1⅛ inch, finer, on 2⅞ inch cloth. Per yard.............$0.09

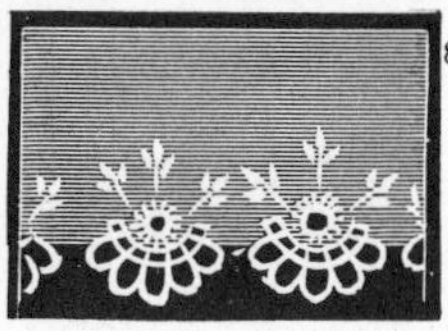

8635 Open Work Edging, 1 inch embroidery on 3¾ inch cloth. Per yard...............$0.10

8640 Irish Point 2 inch embroidery on 3⅞ inch cloth. Per yard..............$0.11

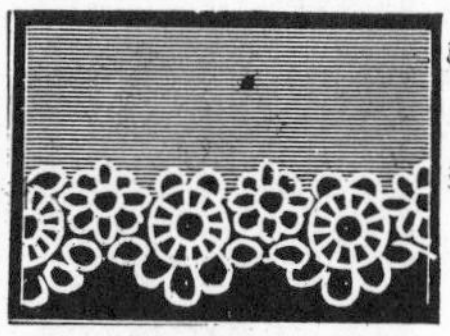

8645 Irish Point Edging, 1 inch embroidery on 4 inch cloth. Per yard..............$0.12

8650 Irish Point Edging, 1⅛ inch embroidery on 4½ inch cloth Per yard..............$0.14

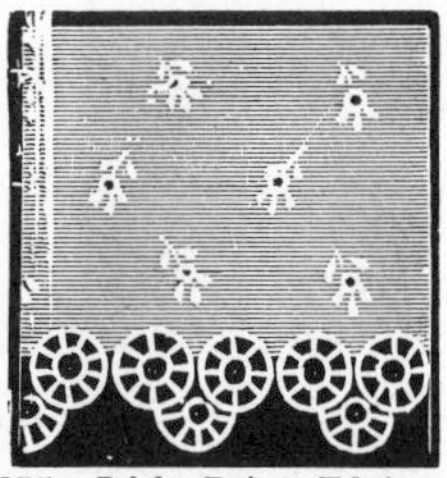

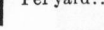

8655 Irish Point Edging, with 3½ inch embroidery on 7 inch cloth. Per yard..............$0.16

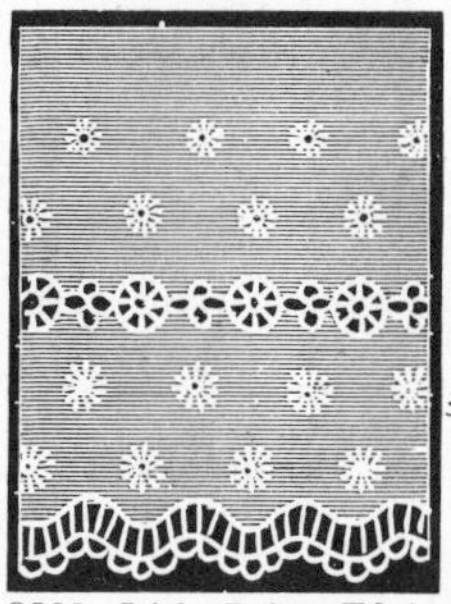

8660 Irish Point Edging, with band insertion above, 4¾ inch embroidery on 10 in cloth. Per yd., $0.20

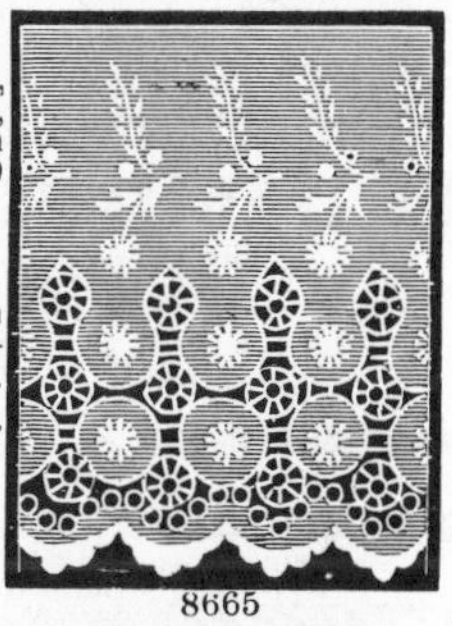

8665

8665 Cambric Edging, with Irish point open work embroidery, 6 inches wide, on 12 inch cloth. Per yard.............$0.27

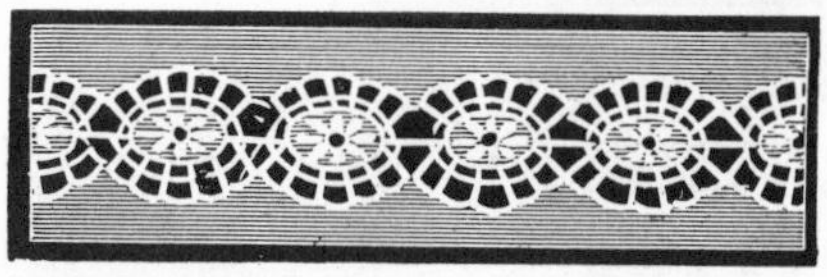

8670 Link Pattern Irish Point Insertion to match edgings, ⅝ inch work on 1¼ inch cloth. Per yard..$0.04

8675 Irish Point Insertion to match edgings, 1 inch Embroidery on 2 inch cloth. Per yard..........$0.08

8680 Irish Point Insertion to match edgings, 1 inch embroidery on 2 inch cloth. Per yard.... .....$0.12

Cambric Revere Embroideries.

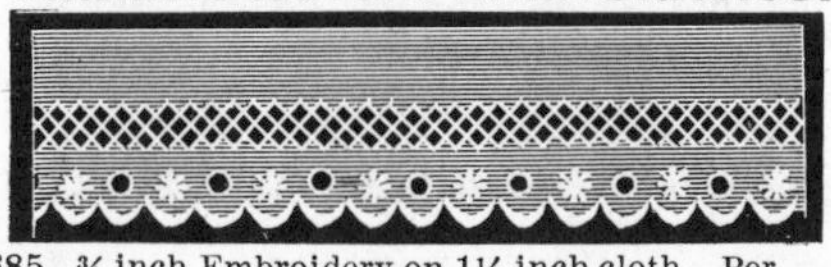

8685 ¾ inch Embroidery on 1½ inch cloth. Per yard..$0.03½

8690 ⅞ inch Embroidery on 1¼ inch cloth. Per yard..$0.05

Embroideries—Continued.

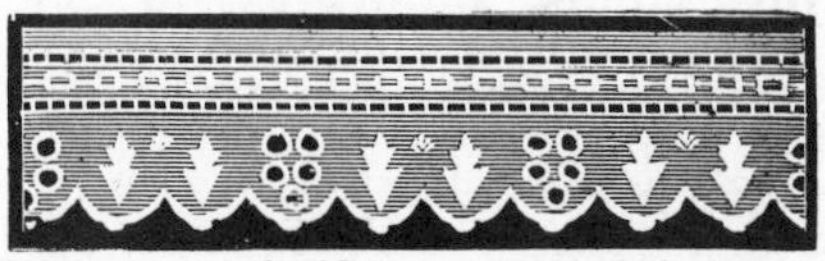

8695 1⅜ inch Embroidery on 2⅛ inch cloth. Per yard..$0.06

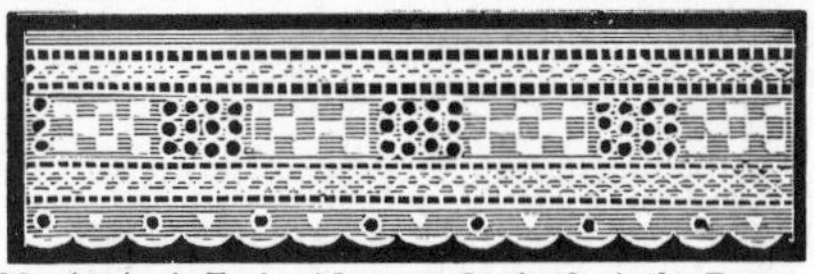

8700 1⅝ inch Embroidery on 2⅜ inch cloth. Per yard..$0.09

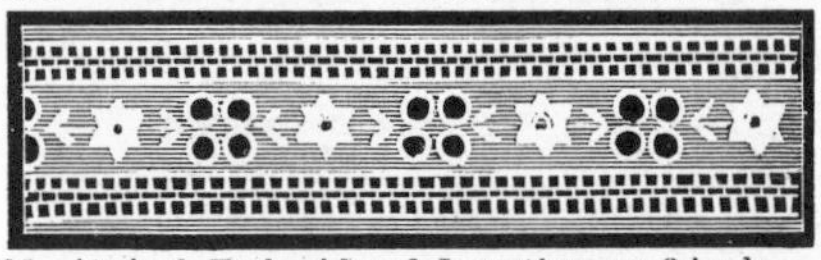

8705 1¼ inch Embroidered Insertion on 2 inch cloth to match above edgings. Per yard........$0.05

Fine Nainsook Embroideries.

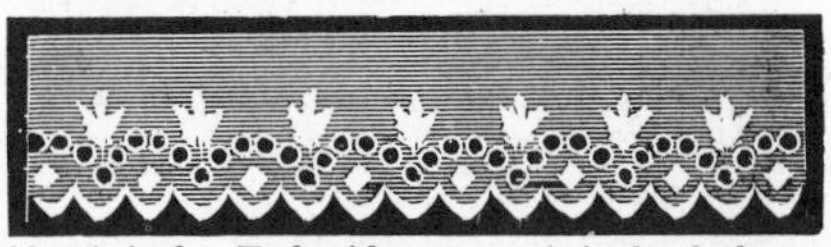

8710 ½ inch' Embroidery on 1 inch cloth. Per yard..............................$0.05

8715 ⅞ inch Embroidery on 1⅝ inch cloth. Per yard..$0.08

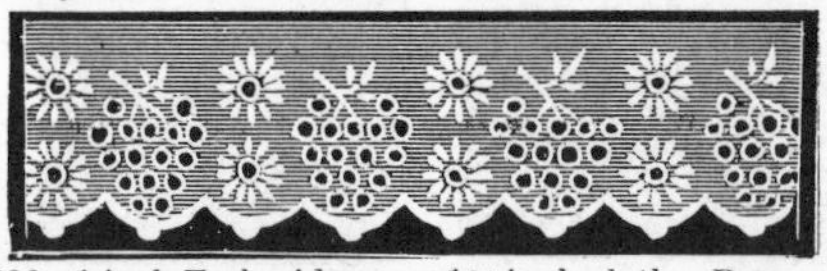

8720 1 inch Embroidery on 1¾ inch cloth. Per yard..$0.09

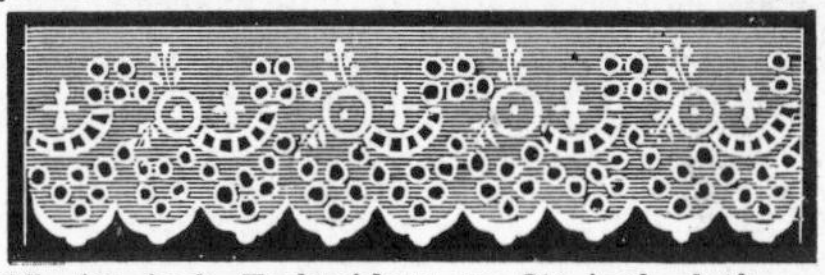

8725 1⅜ inch Embroidery on 2¼ inch cloth. Per yard.... ....$0.10

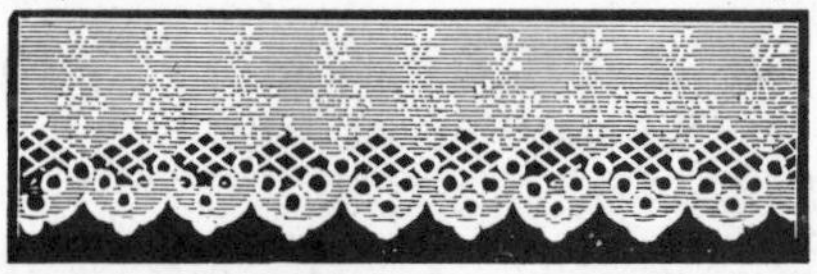

8730 1¼ inch Embroidery on 2⅝ inch cloth. Per yard............$0.12

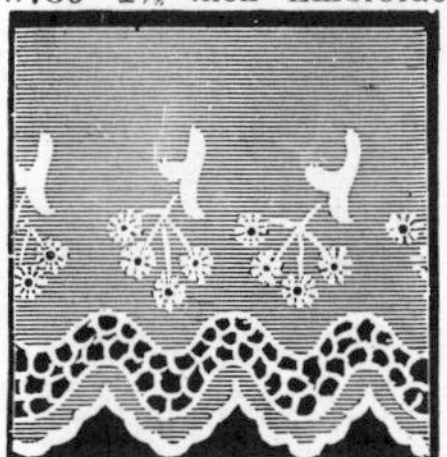

8733

8733 Nainsook Edging, Irish point effect. 2⅛ inch Embroidery on 3¾ inch cloth. Per yard............$0.14

8735 Fine Open Work Edge with all over dots above edge, making embroidery 3⅜ inches wide on 8¼ inch cloth. This is very dainty. Per yard............$0.19

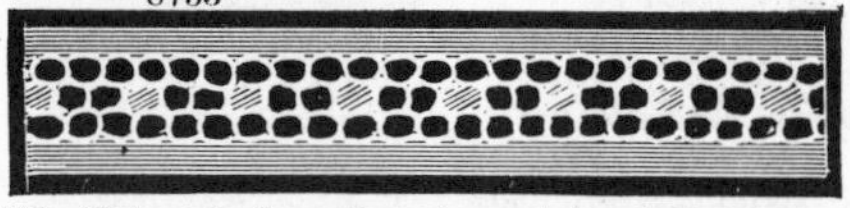

8740 Nainsook Insertion to match edges. ⅜ inch embroidery on 1 inch cloth. Per yard.... $0.07

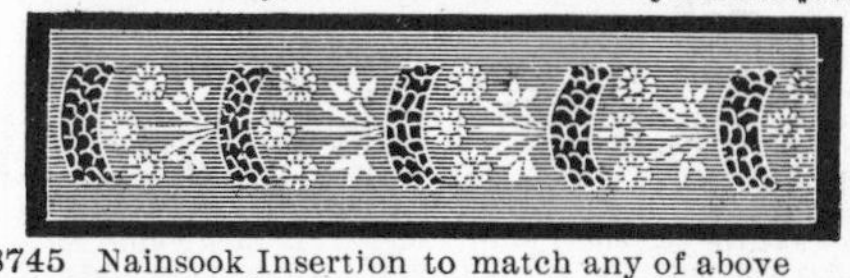

8745 Nainsook Insertion to match any of above six patterns of edgings. ¾ inch embroidery on 1¾ inch cloth. Per yard.....................$0.10

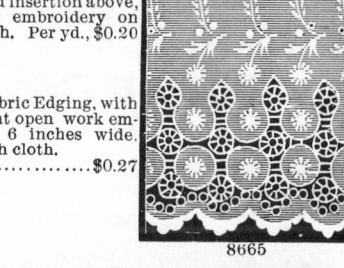

White Suisse Embroidered Edgings and Insertions

Swiss edgings are similar in styles to cuts of Cambric and Nainsook Edgings.

Per yard.

8750 Suisse Edgings, ⅜inch embroidery on ¾ to 1 inch cloth.................................$0.03
8752 Suisse Edging, 1 inch embroidery on 2 inch cloth...................................... .05
8754 Suisse Edging, 1¼ inch embroidery on 2¼ inch cloth.................................. .06
8758 Suisse Edging, finer, 1 inch embroidery on 2¼ inch cloth.............................. .08
8760 Suisse Edging, 2 inch embroidery, on 4 inch cloth.................................... .10
8762 Suisse Edging, 3¼ inch embroidery on 6¾ inch cloth.................................. .14
8764 Suisse Edging, showy pattern, 4 inch embroidery on 8½ inch cloth................... .19

Dotted Suisse Edgings.

Per yard.

8771 Dotted Suisse Edging, link edge, all over embroidery. Width, 3¾ inch.................$0.13½
8773 Dotted Suisse Edging, double loop edge, all over embroidery. 4⅛ inches wide....... .16
8775 Fine Dotted Suisse Edging, with open work Irish point edge, all over embroidery, 5⅝ inches wide................................... .20

Suisse Insertions.

WILL MATCH SUISSE EDGINGS.

Per yard.

8780 Suisse Two-Row Link Insertion, ⅜ inch embroidery on ⅞ inch cloth...................$0.04
8782 Suisse Insertion, ¾-inch embroidery on 1¾ inch cloth.................................. .06
8784 Suisse Insertion, 1⅛-inch embroidery on 2¼-inch cloth................................ .07
8786 Suisse Insertion, 1⅜ inch embroidery 2¾ inch cloth................................... .10

White Cambric and Suisse All Over Embroidery.

All our Cambric and Suisse Embroidery for yokes, sleeves and children's garments 2½ to 23 inches wide. Price governs work and quality.

8804 Cambric All Over Embroidery. Per yard..$0.35
8807 Cambric All Over Embroidery. Per yard. .50
8810 Cambric All Over Embroidery. Per yard. .75
8815 Cambric All Over Embroidery. Per yard. 1.00
8820 Suisse All Over Embroidery, 23 inches wide.. .30
8824 Suisse All Over Embroidery, 23 inches wide.. .50
8826 Suisse All Over Embroidery, 23 inches wide.. .75
8830 Suisse All Over Embroidery, 23 inches wide.. 1.00

Suisse Flouncings.

27 and 45 inches wide, manufacturers' measure. These goods come in 4½ yard patterns.

 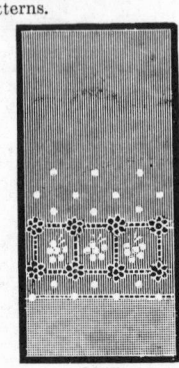

8840   8845

8840 White Suisse Flouncings, 27 inches wide, with 3-inch hemstitch, with Irish point open work and embroidery 6 inches wide above hemstitch. Per yard....................................$0.40
Per pattern.. 1.58
8845 White Suisse Flouncing, 27 inches wide, with 3½ inch hemstitch, and fine band embroidery above hemstitch 3½ inches wide.
Per yard.. .49
Per pattern.. 2.10
8851 White Suisse Flouncing, 27 inches wide, fine scalloped edge and 7 inch embroidery.
Per yard.. .43
Per pattern.. 1.80

Flouncings—Continued.

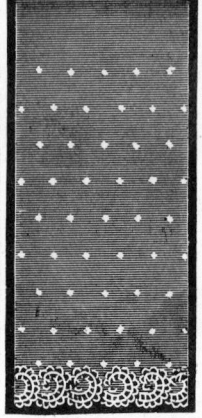

8855 White Suisse Flouncing, 27 inches wide, with scalloped edge and 10 inch embroidery; fine work.
Per yard.................$0.55
Per pattern............. 2.15

8858 White Suisse Flouncing, 42 inches wide, with wide hemstitch, and 20 inch embroidery above hemstitch.
Per yard.................$0.43
Assorted patterns, similar to cut. Per pattern. 1.80
(4½ yards in pattern.)

8865 White Suisse Flouncing, 42 inches wide, with wide hemstitch, and 20 inch embroidery above hemstitch.
Per yard.................$0.55
Per pattern............. 2.15

TRIMMING DEPARTMENT.

Tinsel Cords.

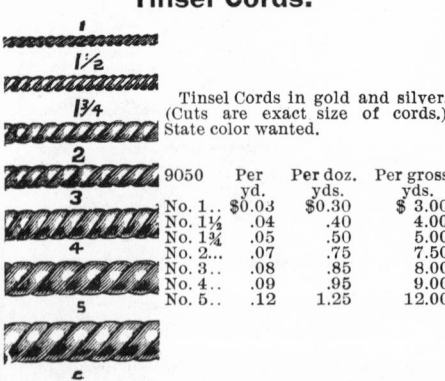

Tinsel Cords in gold and silver. (Cuts are exact size of cords.) State color wanted.

9050	Per yd.	Per doz. yds.	Per gross yds.
No. 1..	$0.03	$0.30	$3.00
No. 1½..	.04	.40	4.00
No. 1¾..	.05	.50	5.00
No. 2..	.07	.75	7.50
No. 3..	.08	.85	8.00
No. 4..	.09	.95	9.00
No. 5..	.12	1.25	12.00

Silk Lacing and Trimming Cord.

9052 Silk Cord Laces, black and colored, with keyed ends.

Length	1 yd.	1½ yds.	2 yds.	2½ yds.	3 yds.
Each	$0.05	$0.06	$0.08	$0.10	$0.12
Per dozen	.50	.60	.85	1.08	1.30

                      Per yd.   Per doz.
9055 Silk Lacing Cord, black and all colors...$0.03 $0.25
Per piece of 36 yards, 67 cents.
9060 Silk Gimp Cord, same style as shown in cuts of 9050, size of No. 3, black and colors...................... .05   .50

9080 Cable Cord, silk, black and all colors. See cut for style and size. Per yard.............$0.08
Per dozen.. .85

Silk Tassels.

9100 Silk Tassels, in black and all colors, 3 inches. Each.........................$0.05
Per dozen................................... .55

9100

Gold and Silver Soutache Braid.

1½ These cuts are the exact size of braid.
9130 Solid Gold Color Soutache Braid.

No.	1½	2
Per yard,	3c	4c
Pr. dz. yds.	30c	40c

9132 Solid Silver Color Soutache Braid.

No.	1½	2
Per yard,	4c.	5c.
Per dz. yds.	40c.	50c.

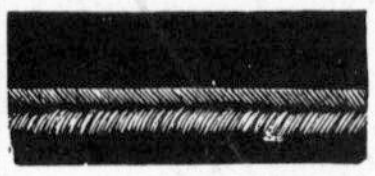

2

Flat Gold and Silver Braid.

9134 Tinsel Braid, solid gold color.

No.	Width.	Per yard.	Per dozen.
2	1-8 in.	$0.02	$0.16
3	3-16 in.	.02	.20
5	1-4 in.	.04	.40
10	7-16 in.	.07	.75
14	3-4 in.	.10	1.00

9136 Solid silver color, tinsel braid.

No.	Width.	Per yard.	Per dozen.
4	1-4 in.	$0.04	$0.40
6	5-16 in.	.05	.50
10	1-2 in.	.08	.85

Trimming Braids.

1¼

9138 Black Mohair Soutache Braid. See cuts, which are exact size.

1¾

No.	Per yard.	Per 12 yards.
1¼	$0.02	$0.16
1¾	.02	.20

Hercules Braid.

9140 Mohair Hercules Braid, in solid black and cream color.

No.	Width.	Per yard.	Per 12 yds.
2	⅛ in.	$0.01	$0.08
4	5-16 in.	.01½	.16
6	½ in.	.02	.22
10	1 in.	.03½	.38
12	1¼ in.	.04	.44
16	1½ in.	.06	.55

9143 Mohair Hercules Braid, in plain solid colors, brown, navy, cardinal, gray and myrtle green.

No.	Width.	Per yard.	Per doz. yds.
4	5-16 in.	$0.02	$0.20
6	½ in.	.03	.28
8	1 in.	.04	.36
12	1¼ in.	.05	.48

9148 Mohair Trimming Braid, with fancy silk edge, black only.

No.	Width.	Per yd.	Per 12 yds
4	⅜ in.	$0.04	$0.44
6	⅝ in.	.05	.55
8	⅞ in.	.06	.60
12	1⅛ in.	.08	.85
16	1⅝ in.	.10	1.05

Sultana Braid.

9150 Patented Fancy Braid, width 3-16 inch, center silk and edge Mifin metal (gold thread). This braid is the most popular edging for trimming dresses as well as all fancy work. It turns well and has the advantage to be sewed on easily by machine on account of its center. There is also an advantage that after sewing on this braid, the effect is not spoiled, and that it lays firm and smooth on the object it is attached to. Colors: Black, cardinal, navy blue, slate, dark brown, myrtle green. Per yard......$0.07
Per dozen yards.................................... .75
Per gross.. 8.50

Braids—Continued.

9151 Silk Trimming Braid, $\frac{3}{16}$-inch wide, in black, cream, cardinal, dark and navy blue, tan, grey and brown (412-3). Per yard.....................$0.04
Per dozen yards...........................$0.40

9153 Fine Mohair Wave trimming braid, black only. See cut.

No.	Width.	Per yard.	Per 12 yds.
4	$\frac{3}{8}$ in.	$0.04	$0.45
6	$\frac{1}{2}$ in.	.06	.65
8	11-16 in.	.08	.85
10	$\frac{7}{8}$ in.	.10	.95

Fine Silk Braid.

9154—Black Silk Trimming Braid, corded pattern, with fancy edge. See cut.

No.	Width.	Per yard.	Per 12 yds.
4	$\frac{1}{4}$ in.	$0.04	$0.44
6	$\frac{3}{8}$ in.	.06	.65
10	$\frac{5}{8}$ in.	.10	.95
12	$\frac{3}{4}$ in.	.12	1.25
16	1 in.	.14	1.55
20	$1\frac{3}{8}$ in.	.18	2.00

Tinsel Trimmings.

9155 Tinsel edge in plain gold, silver and steel.
Also gold and silver combination, $\frac{1}{2}$ inch wide.
Per yard......$0.13. Per 12 yards.............$1.40

Dress Trimmings, Passementeries, Gimps, Etc.

9158 Silk Gimp, in black, cream and colors, width $\frac{5}{8}$ in. (9229F). Per yard.................$0.08
Per doz..85

Silk Moss Trimmings.

We quote until sold. Make first and second choice of colors.

9186 Silk Moss Trimming in all staple shades, also plain white, cream and black; width $1\frac{1}{8}$ inch. Per yard...$0.25
Per dozen.. 2.75

9187 Silk Moss Trimming, $1\frac{3}{4}$ to 2 ins. wide. Black and colors, until sold....................$0.25 $2.75

9189 Black Silk Band Trimming, $\frac{5}{8}$ inch wide. Per yard...........$0.07
Per 12 yards........ .76

9195 Black Silk Gimp, $\frac{5}{8}$ inch wide. Per yard...$0.08
Per 12 yards.......................... 85

Colored Silk Trimming.

9201 New Point Silk and Satin Cord Trimming, width $\frac{1}{2}$ inch, in black, cream and colors. Per yard..$0.10
Per 12 yards........................... .. .. 1.00

9203 New Point Silk and Satin Cord Trimming, width $1\frac{3}{8}$ inch, in black, cream and colors. Per yard..$0.25
Per 12 yards.................................... 2.75

Vandyke Silk Trimmings.

9207 Vandyke Trimming in black silk and satin cord, with fine open work, $2\frac{1}{2}$x5 inches deep. Each...$0.10
Per yard of 14 ornaments $1.00

9207.

9210   9208

9208 Black Vandyke Trimming, silk and satin cord, with open work, size 2 in. wide, 4 in. deep.
Each $0.10
Per yard of 18 ornaments.................... 1.60
9210 Same as 9208, $2\frac{1}{2}$ inches wide, $6\frac{1}{4}$ in. deep.
Each .... .12
Per yard of 16 ornaments.................... 1.65

Dress and Cloak Ornaments.

9212 Bl'k Silk Cord Loop 5 inches long with olive. Each.. .$0.10
Per doz. .$1.00

9214 Black Silk Cord Loops, 5 inches long; see cut(1039). Each..........$0.18
Per dozen..... 1.75

9216 Black Silk Cord Loop; see cut. Each...$0.20
Per doz. 2.00

9218 Black Mohair loops for men's overcoats, 11 inches long. Each..........................$0.25

Black Bead Trimmings.

9220 Black Bead Trimming, $\frac{1}{2}$ inch wide
Per yard..$0.07
Per 12 yards................................. .75

9221 Black Bead Gimp, with cut squares $\frac{1}{4}$ inch wide. See cut. Per yard $0.07
Per dozen yards.............................. .75

Bead Trimming—Continued.

9222 Black Bead Edge, $\frac{3}{8}$ inch wide. Per yard..$0.08
Per 12 yards.. .85

9231 Black Bead Edge, fan pattern; width, 9-16 inch. Per yard................................$0 12
Per 12 yards.. 1.25

9233 Black Band Bead Trimming, $\frac{3}{4}$ inch wide.
Per yard............$0.14. Per 12 yards.......$1.50

9235 Fine Black Cut Bead Edge, hand made, $\frac{1}{2}$ inch wide. Per yard, $0.15. Per 12 yards.....$1.60

9237 Black Bead Pendant Trimming, width $\frac{3}{4}$ inch. Per yard......$0.16. Per 12 yards......$1.70

9247 Black Bead and Spangle Trimming, width $\frac{3}{4}$ inch. Per yard......$0.15. Per 12 yards.....$1.6)

9251 Black Bead and Spangle Trimming, fine cut beads, width $\frac{3}{8}$ inch. Per yard.............$0.21
Per 12 yards 2.15

9253 Black Bead and Spangle Band Trimming, with one row spangles, to match 9255 two rows, $\frac{1}{2}$ inch wide. Per yard, $0.16. Per 12 yards.. $1.70

9255 Black Bead and Spangle Band Trimming, with two rows spangles, to match 9253, width $\frac{7}{8}$ inch. Per yard $0.32

9256—Black Italian bead, Trimming serpentine pattern, width 2in.
Per yard.........$0.35. Per 12 yards.........$3.75

9257 Black Bead Trimming, fine cut beads, with cut nail heads, leaf pattern, $2\frac{1}{4}$ inches wide. See cut. Per yard.................................$0.75
9258 Black Italian Cut Bead Trimming, leaf pattern, $2\frac{1}{4}$ inches wide, similar to cut 9257. Per yard.........$0.43. Per dozen............. 4.75

Steel Bead Trimming.

9284 Steel Color, Bullion Trimming, ¾ inch wide. Will trim nicely on any color of dress goods Per yard.................................$0.50
Per 12 yards.. 5.50

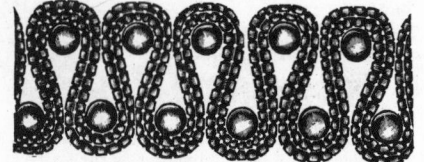

9287 Fine Crystal Bead and Pearl Trimming. Width 1 inch. Per yard.......................$0.65

9310 Iridescent Cut Bead Ornaments, in colors to match set 9440. Bronze, green, olive, slate, dark blue, steel, gold, medium and seal brown and wine only. See cut.
Each............................$0.05
Per yd. of 18 to 21 ornaments, .75

Colored Bead Ornaments.

9315 Iridescent Cut Bead Ornaments, in slate, medium and seal brown, bronze and steel only; 3x5; until sold.
Each...........................$0.08
Per yard of 12 ornaments.., .90

9310

9318 Iridescent Cut Bead Ornaments, in colors: Dark blue, slate, gobelin, golden and seal brown only. Size 3x8¼; 12 ornaments to yard. To match set 9440.
Each........$0.10
Per yard.... 1.00

9322 Fine Cut Steel Bead Ornaments, in bright steel or silver colors only. Size 2x4½ inches.
Each........$0.10

9315
Per yard of 18 ornaments......$1.65

9318

9326 Fine Cut Steel Bead Ornaments, in bright steel or silver color only. Size 2⅝x5 inches.
Each...................$0.15
9332 Fine Cut Steel Bead Ornaments, in gold and black combination only.
Each..................$0.10

9322-26   9332

Fine Trimmings at Low Prices to Close

9338   9342   9344
9338 Fine Cut Bead Ornaments, in steel and black combination only. 2¾x6 inches. Each..$0.10
Per yard of 13 ornaments...................... 1.00
9342 Fine Cut Bead Ornaments, in gold and black combination only. 2½x6¾ inches. Each. .10
Per yard of 14 ornaments...................... 1.00
9344 Fine Cut Bead Ornaments, in gold and black combination only. 4x8 inches. Each. ... .12
Per yard of 10 ornaments...................... 1.00

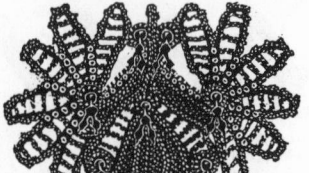

9348
9348 Fine Cut Iridescent Beaded Ornaments, very rich; for headdress, shoulder epaulette, panel, etc. Size 5x7½ inches, in colors: Brown, navy, olive and amber.
Each.....................................$0.25

Black Beaded Ornaments.

Just one-third price to close.
9356 Black Italian Cut Bead Ornaments, long and stylish; 2 inches wide by 8 inches long. Each,............................$0.06
9358 Same as 9356; 2 inches wide by 10 inches long. Each....................$0.07
9362 Same as 9356 and 9358; 2 inches wide by 13 inches long. Each.........$0.08   9356-58-62

Black Bead Ornaments.

(ONE-HALF PRICE TO CLOSE.)

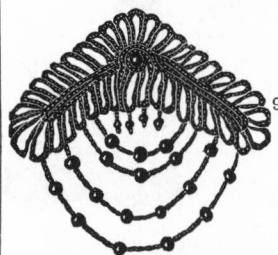

9386 Black Bead Epaulette. See cut.
Each...........$0.10
Per doz........ 1.00

9386

9388 Black Bead Epaulette.
Each $0.15

9388

9404 Black Epaulette combination of Italian cut bead and silk cord.
Each ..$0.13

9404

New Bead Garnitures.

9432 Black Jet Bead Garniture. To be worn as shown on figure or at back as well as front. Each..............$1.10

9434 Black Garniture, jet beads and spangles, with 5 crossbars.
Each............ ..$1.50

9436 Black Garniture. Cut beads, large and small.
Each $1.40

9438 Black Garniture. Fine cut beads. Cut shows front and back view.
Each.....................................$2.30

Black and Colored Bead Sets.

Note the reduction in prices. We quote only until sold
9440 Colored Bead Sets, 5 pieces, in bronze and wine only. Per set....... ....$0.60
Postage... .13
9445 Black Italian Cut Bead Sets, with large oblong beads, making a very rich set; 5 pieces.
Per set....................................$1.69

BUTTON DEPARTMENT.

Jet Dress Buttons.

	Per Doz.	Per Gross.
9800 Black Ball Cut Jet Dress Buttons.......	$0.04	$0.40
9805 Black Ball Cut Jet Dress Buttons, larger	.05	.50

9800   9805
9808 Black Cut Jet Ball Dress Buttons, one size larger than 9805..................... .06   .65

9827   9829   9831
Cuts are exact size of Buttons.

	Per Doz.	Per Gross
9827 Fine Jet Buttons, polished, smooth edges	$0.05	$0.50
9829 Fine Jet Buttons, polished, smooth edges..............	.05	.50
9831 Fine Jet Buttons, polished, smooth rim edge..............	.05	.50

9833   9836   9838
Cuts are exact size of Buttons.

	Per Doz.	Per Gross.
9833 Fine Jet Buttons, dull polished, smooth rim edges.......	$0.05	$0.50
9836 Fine Jet Buttons, polished points in crescent.............	.05	.50
9838 Fine Dull Jet Buttons, polished points...................	.05	.50

Fancy Metal Dress Buttons.

9880 Metal Dress Buttons in all colorings. No black.
Per doz..........$0.05
Per gross......... .50
9883 New Metal Dress Buttons in assorted tints and black.
Per doz.........$0.08
9880   Per gross......... .75   9883

9889 New Metal Dress Buttons in assorted tints and black.
Per dozen...........$0.08
Per gross .... .75

9889
9895 New Bright Steel Dress Buttons, with cut steel points; a high grade button similar to No. 9900. Per dozen $0.25
Per gross................................ 2.50

9900 New Metal Dress Buttons, in assorted tints, with four cut steel points; a high grade button.
Per dozen........................$0.25
Per gross....................... 2.50

9930 Fine French Dress Buttons, with 5 cut steel points. in new shadings. No black.
Per doz.........$0.25
Per gross........... 2.75
9930   9935
9935 Fine Metal Dress Buttons, in all the new shades, and black. Per doz...................$0.22
Per gross................................. 2.25

Black and Colored Crochet Buttons.

10000   Black and Colored Ball Crochet Buttons with metal shank, 16 line; see cut.
Per dozen .....$0.15.   Per gross.....$1.65

16L

Silk Dress Buttons.

10035 Silk Tailor Buttons, black and colors, 22 line. Per dozen..$0.08.   Per gross........$0.75

Button Molds.

10045   Button Molds, small to large.
Per gross, 10 cents to................$0.50

Colored Vest, Coat and Cloak Buttons.

(We sell any quantity.)

10047 Black Lasting Button, iron back.

Line	22	30	38
12 dozen for	$0.35	0.50	0.65

10049 Black Lasting Button, silk back.

Line	22	30	38
12 d zen for	$0.75	1.00	2.00

	Per doz.	Per gross.
10051 Black Worsted Diagonal Buttons, stripe, 24 line; see cut of 10247	$0.08	$0.75
10053 Black Worsted Diagonal Buttons, stripe, 30 line; see cut of 10247	.10	1.00
10056 Black Worsted Diagonal Buttons, 38 line, 1 inch	.14	1.40

Fancy Brass Buttons.

10070 Fancy Brass Buttons for ladies' or boys' clothing; see cuts for styles.

Lines	18	20	22
Per dozen	$0.08	$0.09	$0.10
Per gross	.80	.90	1.00

Brass Buttons-Fire Gilt.

	22	25	30
10105 Brass Buttons, oval topped, navy style.			
Line	22	25	30
Per dozen	$0.10	$0.12	$0.14
Per gross	1.05	1.30	1.50

Vest.   Coat.   Overcoat.

10107 Grand Army Republic Buttons, gold plated, oval topped.

	Per doz.	Per gross.
Vest	$0.18	$1.75
Coat	.22	2.35
Overcoat	.25	2.65

Vest.   Coat.   Overcoat.

10109 Officers' Gold-plated Buttons.

	Per doz.	Per gross.
Vest	$0.18	$1.75
Coat	.23	2.50
Overcoat	.26	2.65

Fancy Pearl Dress Buttons.

Job Prices For Fine Goods.

10140-43   **10131**   **10133**

Per doz.

10131   Smoked Pearl Dress Buttons, in figure and stripe. Size ⅝ in. See cut.................$0.13
10133   Combination Metal with pearl centers and steel points, dress buttons. Colors: Navy blue, myrtle green and wine. Size ⅝ in.; nice goods.
See cut..16
10140   White Pearl Dress Buttons, with eight (8) steel points. A fine high grade button.
Size ⅝ in. See cut.......................................25
10143 Cream or Oriental Pearl Dress Buttons, with eight steel points. Size ⅝ in. Very nice goods.
See cut...25

Imitation Pearl Buttons.

10145 Polished Horn, imitation smoked pearl buttons, flat.

Size line	20	22	24
Per dozen	$0.04	.04	.04
Per gross	.45	.45	.45

10148   Polished Horn, imitation white pearl button, flat

Size line	20	22	24
Per dozen	$0.04	.06	.06
Per gross	.45	.60	.60

Pearl Dress Buttons.

10151 White Pearl Dress Buttons, flat; two holes.

Line	18	22	24	26	28	30
Per doz.	$0.08	.09	.10	.12	.12	.12
Per gross	.79	.95	1 05	1.25	1.25	1.25

10153 Smoked Pearl Dress Buttons.

Line	18	22	24	26	28	30
Per doz.	$0.05	.07	.09	.11	.15	.15
Per gross	.50	.75	.90	1.10	1.65	1.65

10159 Superfine Clear White Pearl Buttons, flat; two holes; nice quality.

Size line	18	20	22	24	26	28
Per doz.	$0.10	.12	.15	.16	.18	.20
Per gross	1.10	1.20	1.40	1.60	1.85	2.20

10167 Super White Full Ball Pearl Button, with holes to sew through. Size line 18.
Per doz.....................................$0.25
Per gross...................................2.70

10169 Super White Full Ball Pearl Buttons, self shank. Size line 18.
Per doz.....$0.30 Per gross...........3.20

Pearl Shirt Buttons.

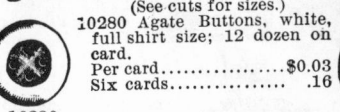

These illustrations are 12 lines. The Buttons we quote are 16 lines, two sizes larger than above cuts.
10175 White Pearl Shirt Buttons, 16 line, four patterns. Per doz......$0.09 Per gross.......$0.95
10179 "Duplex" Pearl Shirt Buttons, assorted patterns, on cards. 16 line. See cuts. Per doz..$0.12
Per gross..1.35

White Pearl Buttons for Cloaks, Jackets, Dresses, etc.

10190 White Pearl Buttons, 4 holes.

Size line	24	36	45	55	60
Per dozen	$0.20	.50	.75	.90	1.25

Button Scale.

Showing sizes of Buttons from 8 to 50 line.

8 10 12 14 16 18 20 22 24 26 28 30 32 34 36 40 50

Bone or Vegetable Ivory Buttons.

10221 Full Ball Bone Buttons, self shank, in white, cream, black and colors. Nice for wash goods. Per dozen.$0.05
Per gross...........50

10225 Plain Vegetable Ivory Buttons, in colors, white, rose, drab, slate, tan, light blue, ecru, mode, cardinal, red, brown, purple, wine, light brown, navy, myrtle and black; 22 line, plain with self shank and stud back.
Per dozen........$0.05
Per gross...........50

10228 Fancy Oval Vegetable Ivory Buttons, fine finish, 7 cuttings; assorted colors.
Per doz..............$0.05
Per gross............50

Vest, Coat, Cloak, Ulster and Overcoat Buttons.

First quality for men's and boys' wear, also ladies' jackets, ulsters, cloaks and all outside garments.
10230 Plain Black Horn Buttons, 4 holes. 24 line, vest size. Per doz..................$0.05
Per Gross.......................................50
10235 Fancy Black Horn Buttons, checkerboard pattern, smooth rim edge. 24 line, vest size.
Per doz.....................................$0.05
Per gross.......................................50

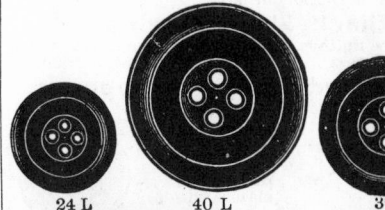

24 L   40 L   30 L

10240 Rubber Buttons, flat, in black only.
See cuts 24 L, 30 L.

	Per doz.	
Per doz.	$0.08	$0.10
Per gross	.80	1.00

40 L

Per dozen............$0.16
Per gross............1.65

46 L   **46 L**

Per dozen............$0.18
Per gross............1.85

10247 Rubber Buttons, flat, self shank, fancy, stripe pattern; in black only.

Per doz.	$0.10	$0.12
Per gross	1.05	1.25

24 L   **30 L**

Agate Buttons, White and Colored.

(See cuts for sizes.)

10280 Agate Buttons, white, full shirt size; 12 dozen on card.
Per card.................$0.03
Six cards.................16

10280   **10282**

	Per gross.	Per doz.
10282 Agate Buttons, white, large	$0.07	$0.42

10285 Agate Buttons, white, large.

Per gross	$0.09
Per 72 doz	.48

10288 Agate Buttons, white, large.

Per gross	$0.10
Per 72 doz	.50

10288   **10285**

	Per gross. 72 doz.	Per.
10291 Agate Buttons, white, largest or full underclothing size	$0.11	$0.60
10293 Agate Buttons, white, colored edge, shirt size (No. 1½)	.14	.75
10295 Agate Buttons, colored edge, shirt size (No. 20)	.25	1.35
10297 Agate Buttons, white, colored edge, extra large size	.35	1.80

10291

Nos. 10293, 10295 and 10297 come with brown, black, green, pink, red or blue edges. Please mention color wanted.

White Fancy Pearl Agates.

(See cuts for style and size.)

10300 Pearl Agate Buttons.
Per gross...$0.08
10302 Pearl Agate Buttons.
Per 12 dozen...................$0.14
10304 Pearl Agate Buttons.
Per gross..............................$0.20
10305 Pearl Agate Buttons.
Per gross...............................$0.25

10304   **10302**   **10300**   **10305**

Pant Buttons.

	Per gross.	Per great gross.
10320 Black Metal Buttons, small or fly size	$0.05	$0.55
10324 Black Metal Buttons, suspender size	.06	.65
10328 Black Solid Metal Susp..nder Buttons	.09	.85
10330 Brass Fly Buttons, best quality	.08	.80
10332 Brass Suspender Buttons, best quality	.09	.85

Pant buttons are put up in one gross boxes. We do not sell less than one box.

Black Shoe Buttons.

10335 Shoe Buttons, black, 16 line, common size. Per great gross..........$0.50. Per gross......$0.05

Button and Drawers Supporter.

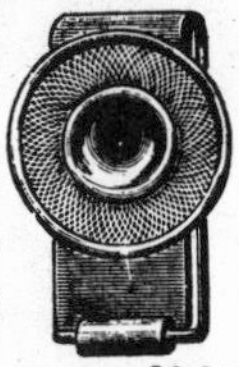

10342 Chapman's Button and Drawer Supporter; can replace a button at a moment's notice; nicely nickel plated, convenient and substantial. Each..........$0.04
Per dozen..........$0.40 Per gross..........4.30

10343 Padlock Buttons can be used for pants, coats, vests, drawers, overalls, jumpers and children's clothing. Can be put on instantly, will not pull off, can be removed at pleasure. Put up one dozen buttons in box (black), 8 (suspender and 4 fly) with locks and needle. Per box..........$0.07
Per dozen..........$0.75. Per gross........7.00

Something New.

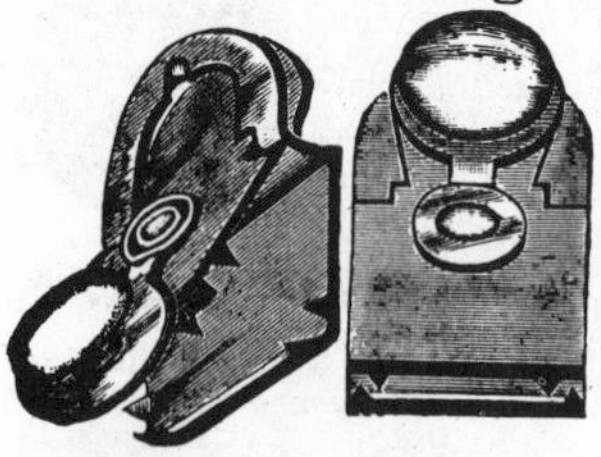

10344 Adjustable Nickel Plated Bachelor Button; for use as a pants button, scarf holder, drawer and hose supporter. Very simple and easy to use.
Each.......$0.04
Per dozen... .40
Per gross....4.00

Open.   Closed.

10345 Turn Lock Button; can be instantly attached or removed, no needle required. Colors: Black, gilt and silver. Snap an extra one on pants band, always ready to replace a missing button. Per 1 dozen box..........$0.07
Per doz. boxes..........$0.70

Fig 2

Hand Snap Buttons.

By the use of these buttons the traveling man, the farmer, the laborer, the mechanic, the growing boy and his father, of any profession, can instantly replace his missing buttons.

	Per box.	Per dozen boxes.	Per gross boxes.
10346 Black, Gold or Silvered Metal Snap Fly Buttons, one dozen in box	$0.06	$0.65	$6.75
10350 Black, Gold or Silvered Metal Snap Suspender Buttons, one dozen in box	.07	.70	7.75

Pants and Vests Buckles.

	Each.	Per dozen
10400 Duplex Pants Buckles, self-adjusting, 4 strands. for vests and pants	$0.09	$0.85
10402 Duplex Patent Buckles, 6 springs	.10	.95
10404 Pants Buckles, common silvered or black. Per gross		.18

Excelsior Button Fastener.

A very economical and substantial article. Buttons can be attached in a moment. Full directions accompany each box.
The Excelsior Button Fastener can be used to fasten buttons on shoes, clothing, gloves, rubber coats, etc.

10410 Excelsior Button Fastener, per gross.....$0.12
Per great gross..........1.25

10417 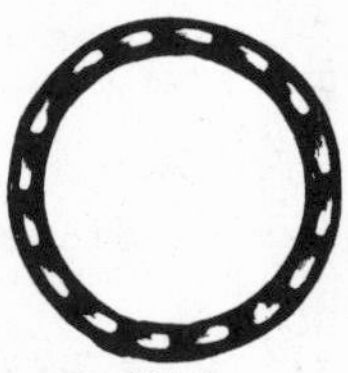   10419

10417 Polished Flat Steel Split Key Rings, one dozen assorted sizes on card. Each..........$0.03
Per doz..........$0.25 Per gross..........2.25
10419 Polished Hammered Steel Split Key Rings, extra quality, one dozen assorted sizes on card.
Each....$0.04. Per doz...$0.35 Per gross...3.25

10421 Polished Steel Key Chains, 18 inches long, Assorted styles in dozen. Each..........$0.07
Per doz..........$0.65 Per gross..........6.50
10423 Polished Steel Key Chains, with split key rings: 18 inches long. Assorted styles in dozen.
Each..........08
Per doz..........$0.80 Per gross..........8.50
10425 Polished Steel Key Chains, extra quality, finely polished, 18 inches long. Assorted styles in doz. Each..........15
Per doz..........1.50
Per gross..........16.00

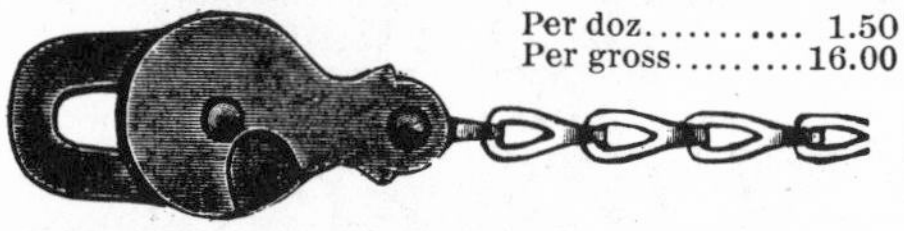

10427 Aluminum Key Chain, with patent key ring holder, length 20 inches; weighs one-fifth of an ounce. Each..........$0.15
Per doz..........$1.50 Per gross..........16.00

10429 Superior Steel Tweezers, with ear spoon, nickel plated, 2⅜ inches long. Each..........$0.07
Per doz..........$0.65 Per gross..........6.50

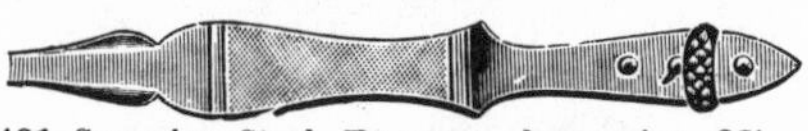

10431 Superior Steel Tweezers, large size, 2⅜ inches long. Each..........$0.07
Per doz..........$0.65 Per gross..........6.50

10433 Superior Steel Tweezers, double, large at one end and small at the other, 3⅛ inches long.
Each..........$0.07
Per doz..........$0.65 Per gross..........6.50
NOTE—The above three styles of tweezers assorted on card of one dozen.

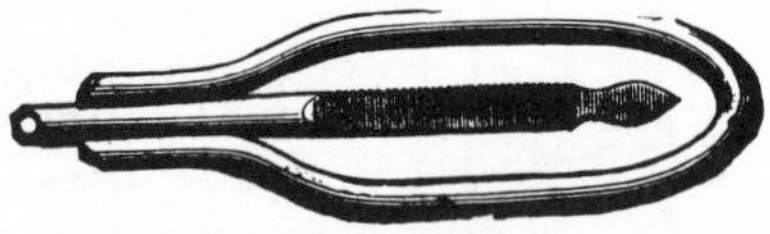

10434 Finger Nail Cleaner, Trimmer and File combined, folding style for pocket; made from polished steel. Each....$0.15. Per doz........$1.50

Button Hooks.

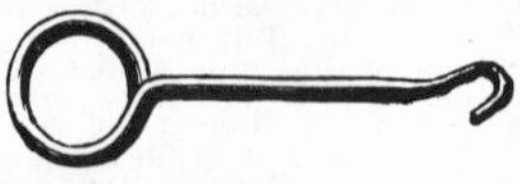

10435 Wire Button Hooks, 3½ inches long.
Per dozen..........$0.02
Per gross..........20

10437 Wood Handle Button Hooks, 3½ inches long.
Per dozen..........$0.04
Per gross..........42

Tracing Wheels.

NO. 10 TRACING WHEEL.

10439 Tracing Wheels, hardwood handles, wheel blued steel, teeth sharp and perfect. Each.....$0.05
Per dozen..........45
Per gross..........4.50

NO. 15 TRACING WHEEL.

10441 Tracing Wheels. Same as 10439, but with finger rest. Each..........$0.06
Per dozen..........65
Per gross..........6.50

Tracing Wheels—Continued.

NO. 20 TRACING WHEEL.

10443 Double Adjustable Tracing Wheels, teeth sharp and perfect. All metal parts nickle plated, antique oak handles. Each..........$0.10
Per dozen..........95
Per gross..........10.50

NO.35

10447 Reversible Tracing Wheels. When not in use wheel is enclosed in nickle handle; can be carried in pocket, a perfect high grade wheel.
Each..........$0.10
Per dozen..........95
Per gross..........10.50

Crochet Needles or Hooks.

10462 Nickel Plated Steel Crochet Hooks, assorted fine, medium and coarse. Each..........$0.03
Per dozen..........30

10478 Star Crochet Set, two bone and two steel crochet hooks in white wood box. Each..........05
Per dozen..........45

PINS.

Adamantine Pins.

(In packages of one dozen papers.)

10490 Size	2	3	4
Per package	14c	12c	11c
10491 Size	2	3	4
Per package	25c	22c	20c

10492 Book pins, 6 rows of 40 pins each, 240 pins, one row of black. All ne plus ultra high grade brass pins. Three sizes in book.
Per paper..........$0.05
Per doz..........48

10495 The Favorite Velvet Pin Cushion contains a full paper of the best steel pins. No. 3.
Each..........$0.04
Per dozen..........40

THE FAVORITE

10506 Black Pins, per box of 50..........$0.03
10508 Black Toilet Pins, in box, solid heads.
Per box..........04
Per dozen..........42

10510 Fancy Chromo Pins. Card contains 25 jet head block pins and 25 small fancy head block pins.
Per card..........$0.04
Per dozen..........40
Per gross..........4.25

10512 Cube of Black and White Pins, with black, white and assorted fancy heads.
Each..........$0.05
Per dozen..........50
Per gross..........5.50

10515 Brass Box of Black Pins, with bright set heads.
Each..........$0.04
Per dozen..........42
Per gross.....4.40

We issue a Special Medical and Scientific Book Catalogue. Send 2 cents to pay postage.

Sensible Safety and Blanket Pins.

The cheapest, most practical and best made double sided shield safety pins on the market.

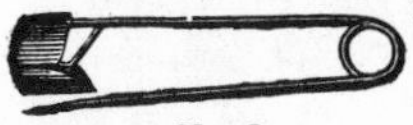

No. 2

10520 Silver-plated sensible Safety Pins. No. 2.
Per dozen..............$0.02
Per gross.............. .22

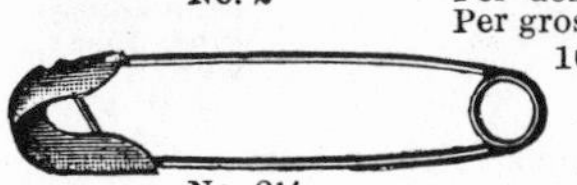

No. 2½

10522 Silver-plated Sensible Safety Pins. No. 2½
Per dozen ..$0.02½
Per gross.... .28

No. 3.

10524 Same as 10520-10522.
Per dozen......$0.03. Per gross............$0.31

10525 Large Safety Sensible Blanket Pin, 4 in. long. The heaviest, best finished and most practical blanket pin made; nickel-plated, put up ½ dozen on card, ½ gross in box. Each........$0.04
Per dozen......$0.40. Per gross.............$4.00

Hat and Shawl Pins.

10541 Hat Pins, steel, with black heads, 6 inches long. Per dozen......$0.04. Per gross.........$0.35
10542 White head 5 inch Hat Pins, blued steel. Each.................. $0.01. Six for........... .04
Per dozen.......... .06
10544 Black Jet, Cut Head Hat Pins, 5 inch blued. Each.... .... $0.01. Six for............ .04
Per dozen.......... .06
10545 Shawl or Belt Pins, black, large heads. Per dozen............ $0.03. Per gross..........$0.26
10547 Shawl Pins, fancy heads, steel chains, Per pair .... .08
Per dozen.......... .75

Hair Pins.

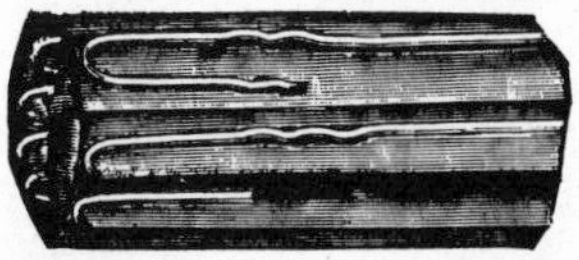

10555 Hairpins, crimped or straight, 5 pins to paper, 8 papers to roll, 10 rolls to bundle. Per roll .$0.02
Per package of 10 rolls. $0.13

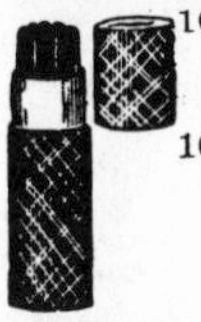

10557 Invisible Hairpins, about 50 in a box. Per box...... ..$0.03 Per doz. boxes. .30

10560 Hairpins, wood cabinet contains 50 hairpins; per box, 4 cts.; per dozen boxes, 40c. until sold.

10562 New Countess Hairpin in wood cabinet, 60 assorted pins.
Per box...... ....$0.04
Per dozen .... .40

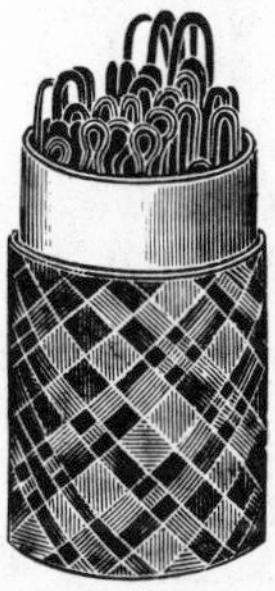

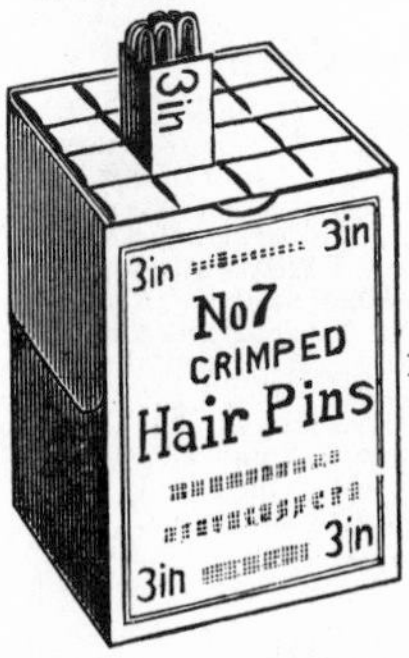
3in
3in
3in
No7
CRIMPED
Hair Pins
3in
3in

10565 Package Hairpins, 16 small boxes containing 20 hairpins each, or 320 in package.
Per package............$0.14
Per dozen...... .... 1.50

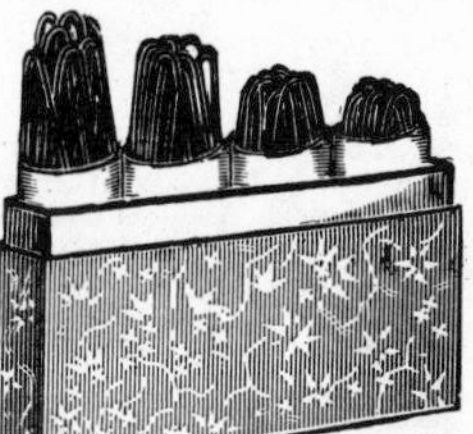

10568 New Cabinet, fine black wire Hair Pins, in 4 sizes, crimped and straight. 100 pins, pr bx. $0.06
Per dozen...... .60

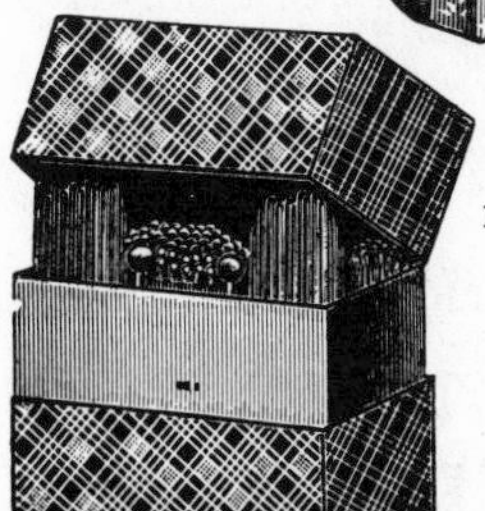

10569 Unique Cabinet. A combination put up in convenient and attractive form, 100 assorted hairpins, 100 toilet pins, 30 black pins and 4 jet shawl or belt pins. Each............$0.09
Per dozen.......... .95

Rubber Hairpins.

10580 Rubber Hairpins, crimped, put up in boxes of one dozen.
Per box..........$0.10
Per dozen..... 1.00
10582 Rubber Hairpins, straight, in boxes of one dozen. Per box..... .10
Per dozen boxes.......... 1.00

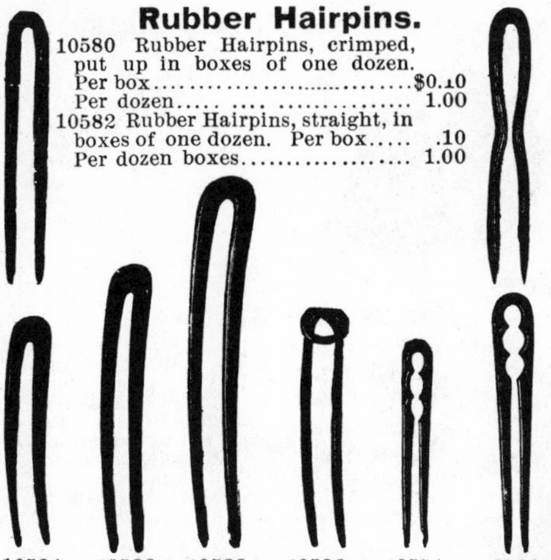

10584. 10586. 10588. 10592. 10594. 10596.

10584 Polished Rubber Hair Pins, 3¼ in. Each.$0.03
Per doz.......... .28
10586 Polished Rubber Hair Pins, 4¼ in. Each. .04
Per doz.......... .35
10588 Polished Rubber Hair Pins, 5 in. Each... .05
Per doz.......... .45
10592 Polished Twist Top Rubber Hair Pins, 3¼ in. Each.......... .04
Per doz.......... .38
10594 Fancy Rubber Hair or Braid Pin, 3 in. Each.......... .04
Per doz.......... .38
10596 Fancy Rubber Hair or Braid Pin, 3¾ in. Each.......... .05
Per doz.......... .50

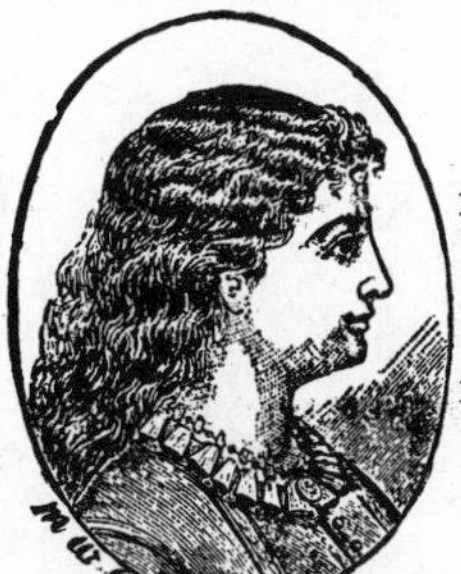

Hair Crimper

10600 Common Sense Hair Crimpers made of lead with woven covers, 12 in package. 2 in. 3 in.
Per pkg. 3c. 4c.
Per doz. pkg.30c. 40c.
10602 Duplex Hair Crimpers, nickel plate.
Per pair....... ......$0.02
Per dozen pairs.... . .20

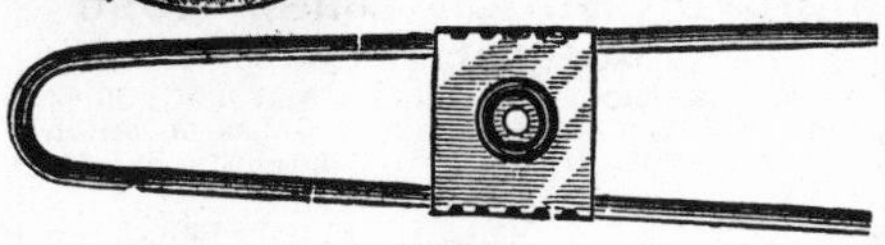

10602

Thimbles.

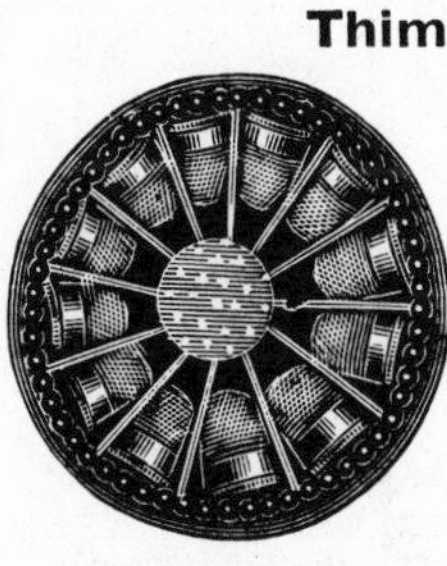

10622 Silver Plated thimbles, in round box, glass tops, closed ends; put up one dozen in a box, assorted sizes.
Per gross...........$1.30
Per box .... .12
10624 Sterling Plated Thimbles, one dozen closed tops, in box, assorted sizes.
Per gross $3.25
Per dozen .... .35
Each............ .04

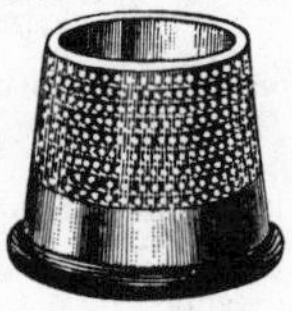

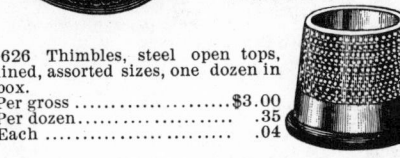

10626 Thimbles, steel open tops, lined, assorted sizes, one dozen in box.
Per gross $3.00
Per dozen.................. .35
Each .... .04

10630 Steel Thimbles, electro-silver lined, closed tops. Each.......... .03
Per box of 3 doz.......... .75
Per gross.......... 2.60
10632 Rubber Thimbles, closed, assorted sizes. Each.......... .10
Per doz.......... 1.08

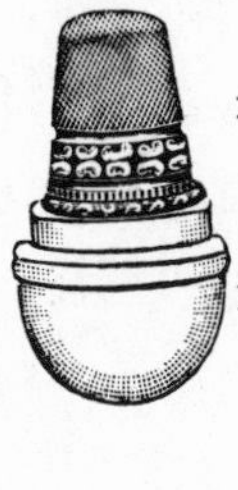

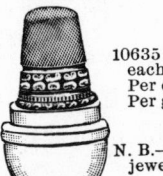

10635 Aluminum Thimbles, one each in wood box. Each........$0.05
Per doz.......... .45
Per gross.......... 4.50

N. B.—For silver and gold thimbles see jewelry department.

Cuff Holders.

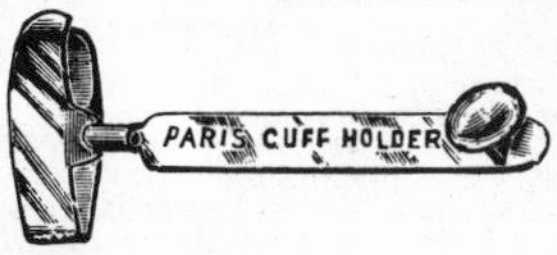
PARIS CUFF HOLDER

10660 The Paris Cuff Holder, with lever button, very practical. Per pair $0.10
Per dozen..... 1.00
Per gross......10.50

PAT. FEB. 5 1889
WIZARD

10665 The Wizard Cuff Holders improved, nickel plated.
Per pair......$ 0.12
Per doz 1.20
Per gross.... 12.00

Necktie Holders.

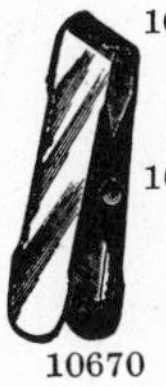

10670 The Standard Tie Holder, nickel plated, small and neat. Each, 3 cts., 2 for 5 cts.
Per doz............$0.18
10671 The Excelsior Men's Drawer Supporters, very simple, hooking to pants band, nickel plated.
Per pair...........$0.05
10670 Per 12 pairs .... .50

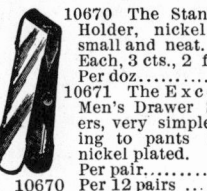

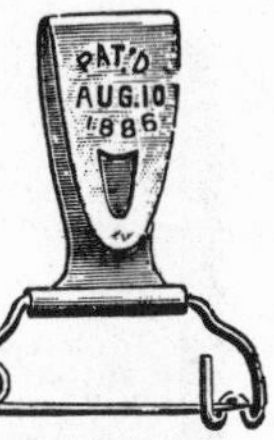
PAT'D
AUG.10
1886

10671

Patent Coat Collar Spring.

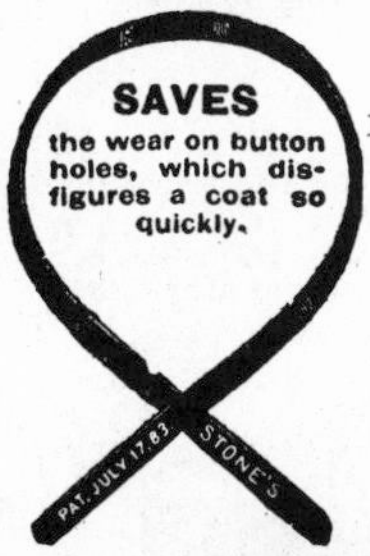
SAVES
the wear on button holes, which disfigures a coat so quickly.

10678 Patent Adjustable Coat Collar Spring. The spring is made from best oil-tempered steel, formed to fit the coat under the collar. By its use the coat collar and lapels always retain their shape.
Each $0.08
Per dozen.. .... .75
Per gross.................. 7.50
Postage.................. .04

Tape Measures.

	Each.	Per doz.
10680 Imitation Linen Tape Measure. 60 inches long	$0.02	$0.08
10683 Tape Measures, ½ inch wide, 60 inches long, figured on both sides	.04	.30
10686 Tailor's Tape Measures, double stitched, 60 inches long, figured on both sides	.08	.75

Needles.

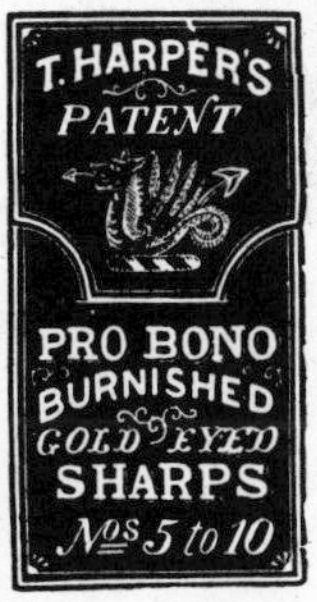
T. HARPER'S
PATENT
PRO BONO
BURNISHED
GOLD EYED
SHARPS
Nos 5 to 10

10733 Harper's Best Needles, in patent wrappers, cloth stuck, oval eyes, sharps, the finest quality that can be manufactured, except the gold-eyed; solid sizes 1, 2, 3, 4, 5, 6, 7, 8, 9, 10, and assorted 1 to 5, 3 to 9, 4 to 8, and 5 to 10, 40 papers for $1.25; 10 papers for 38c., or 1 paper for 4c.
10735 Harper's Best Gold-Eyed Needles, in patent wrappers, cloth stuck, sharps. The very finest quality that can be manufactured; solid numbers 1, 2, 3, 4, 5, 6, 7, 8, 9 and 10, and assorted sizes same as in 10733; 40 papers for $1.50; 10 for 45 cents; 1 for 5 cents. Give numbers wanted.

Lightning Needles.

Sewing Made Easy. A New Idea.

The Lightning Needle.

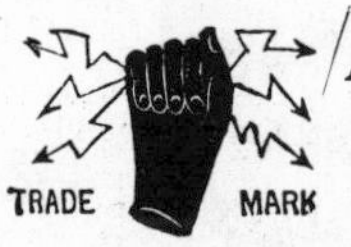
TRADE
MARK

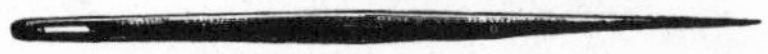

Being tapered from the center to the eye forces itself through the fabric without effort. Try it and you will like it.

10740 The Lightning Hand Sewing Needles, one push sufficient to pass the entire needle through the fabric. The eyes of the 8, 9, 10 are as large as those found in 5, 6 and 7 of other makes, enabling the user to do better and finer sewing, permitting a coarser thread to be used in a fine needle. We quote in Sharps (long) only. Sizes 1, 2, 3, 4, 5, 6, 7, 8, 9, 10, 11, 12, 5 to 10, 4 to 8, 3 to 9, 1 to 6. Per paper..........$0.04
Per 10 papers.......... .35
Per 40 papers (1,000 needles).......... 1.25

We import all our Musical Instruments directly from Germany.

Henry Milward & Sons Calyx-Eyed Needles.

Kratz's Patent
No. 5221-84.

This needle is made to meet a want patent to every one, namely, a needle that will thread without the annoying process of passing the end of the cotton through the eye. The cotton is slipped through a slit above the eye, as shown by the accompanying sketch. Invaluable for failing sight.

10744 Milward's Calyx-Eyed Needles; 10 needles in a paper, 100 papers to the thousand. Solid sizes. Nos. 3, 4, 5, 6, 7, 8 and 9. Assorted sizes, 3 to 9, 4 to 8, 5 to 9; in sharps only.
Per paper.....................$0.07
10 papers..........$0.60   1,000 needles..   5.00

10746 Glover's Needles, solid sizes, Nos. 1,2,3,4,5,6,7,8. Per paper... .08
Per 10 papers........................ .75
Per 40 papers or 1,000 needles..... 2.75
10750 Steel Knitting Needles, best quality, in package of 3 dozen, Nos. 12 to 20, No. 12 being very coarse.
Per set of five needles.............. .04
10751 Steel Knitting Needles, in sets of five, in wooden case. See cut. Per set.................................. .04
Per dozen............................ .40
10753 Double Long Cotton Darning Needles, 5 in paper, assorted 1 to 5. Per paper...................... .02
Per 3 papers.......................... .05
Per 12 papers......................... .16
10754 Large Wool Darning Needles 5 in paper, 14 to 18.
Per paper.......................... .02
Per 3 papers.......................... .05
Per 12 papers......................... .16
10755 Darning Needles, per box of 10 papers, come solid numbers in a paper and

are assorted as follows: 1, 14; 2, 15; 3, 16;   2, 18;   2, 17; No. 14 being the coarsest and No. 18 finest; per **box** of 10 papers, 250 needles, assorted as above, 33c; per paper, not assorted, 4c.

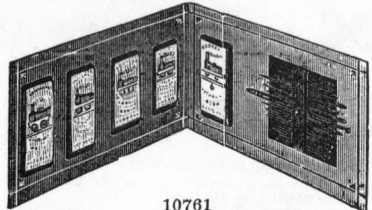

10761

10761 The Excelsior Needle Case contains five **papers** good English needles (sharps and 15 assorted single needles, tape darners, etc.), cambric stuck. Retail price 25c. Our price, each..$0.08
Per dozen...............$0.60   Per gross....... 4.75

10763 Imperial Toilet Case, large 3 fold. Size, closed 4½ x 7 inches Contains 100 fine

cloth stuck sewing needles (4 papers) besides an **assortment** of 40 varieties of all other large needles, bonnet, hat, shawl, and 96 white pins, **a** total of 238 useful articles   Each..........$0.18
Per dozen...............$1.50   Per gross.........16.50

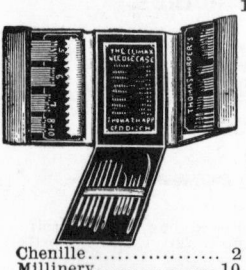

10774 Our Climax Needle Case, size, closed 2¾ x 4 inches, in fancy assorted leatherette case.
Contains—
Sewing needles.......80
Darning needles......10
Glove needles........ 5
Packing needles...... 1
Carpet sharps........ 3
Double long.......... 2
Yarn................. 2
Betweens (tailor)....25
Crewel............... 5
Tapestry............. 2
Surgeon.............. 1
Bodkin 2

Chenille............. 2
Millinery............10

Total 150 best Harper's Gold-eyed Needles. Quantity and quality considered, this is the cheapest needle case in market.
Each................$0.50
Per dozen............ 5.50

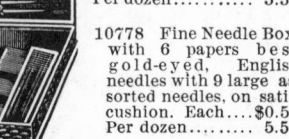

10778 Fine Needle Box, with 6 papers best gold-eyed, English needles with 9 large assorted needles, on satin cushion. Each....$0.50
Per dozen......... 5.50

Emery Bags.

10780 Emery Bag for polishing needles.
Each...............$0.09
Per doz............. .95

Wire Sleeve Supporters, Arm Bands and Garters.

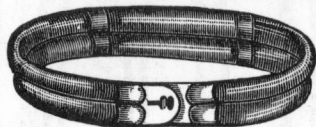

10836 Patent Duplex Ventilated Men's Arm Bands or Ladies' Garters, fine nickeled steel wire, one pair in box
Each $0.10. Per dozen..........$0.95
Postage .... .04

Hose Supporters.

10855 Men's Elastic Web Garters, plain web; see cut; per pair...........$0.10
Per dozen........................... .95
10860 Men's Silk Garters, fine, one pair in box (see cut). Black, white and assorted colors. Per pair $0.25
Per dozen. 2.70

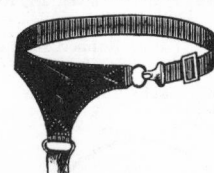

10864 Men's Silk and Satin Paris Garter, in colors and black. One pair in a box. Very fine.
Per pair..........$0.35
Per dozen........ 3.75

10864

10870 Ladies' Silk Garters, extra fine, with satin bows, in black, white and assorted colors; one pair in box.
Per pair...$0.45
Per dozen. 4.50

10870

Improved Button Clasp Hose Supporters.

The button fastener is the simplest and best. Never cuts the stocking, never slips or lets go, has no stitching. Our supporters are made of lisle elastic in black and white.

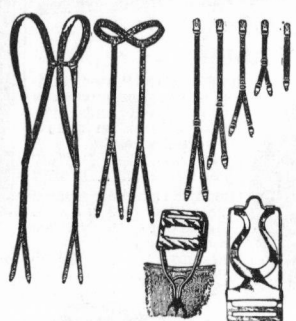

10900 Babies' Single Strap Supporter.
Per pair...$0.07
Per dozen... .70
10902 Babies' Double Strap Supporters.
Per pair... $0.09
Per dozen.. .90
10904 Misses' Two Strap Supporters.
Per pair... $0.10
Per dozen.. 1.00
10906 Young Ladies' Two Strap Supporters.
Per pair... $0.12
Per dozen.. 1.15

	Per pair.	Per doz
10908 Ladies' Two Strap Hose Supporters...................	$0.13	$1.25
10910 Ladies' Belts with hose supporters...........	.18	1.95
10913 Ladies' Shoulder Braces with hose supporters..........	.23	2.40
10915 Misses' Shoulder Braces with hose supporters..........	.18	1.95
10917 Children's Shoulder Braces with hose supporters.........	.17	1.75

10931 Ladies' Black or White Sateen Combination Belt, with hose supporters and points for safety belt; size 24 to 34 in. (see cut.) Each.................$0.25
Per dozen........................ 2.65

10932 Ladies' Suspenders for supporting skirt.
Per pair......................$0.10
Per dozen..................... 1.00

Supporters—Continued.

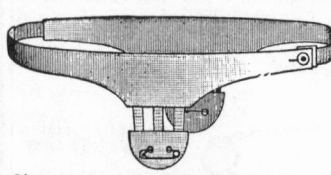

10935 Ladies' Faultless Serviette Supporter, made of soft sateen with a rubber band across hips. Meets with universal approval.

Sizes are every inch from 22 to 36; ask for one inch larger than your exact waist measure.
Each............................$0.25
Per dozen....................... 2.75
10936 The Faultless Serviette or Absorbent Health Napkin; economical, comfortable, healthful. Recommended by physicians and fast superseding birdseye linen, more absorbent, antiseptic, no washing, burned after using, invaluable while traveling, cheaper than laundering. medium size. Sold by the package of 1 doz. only. Per dozen.................$0.50
Extra by mail........................ .12

Daisy Hose Supporters.

10937 Child's Shoulder Hose Supporters, in black, white and drab, with improved button clasp. No. 1, age 1 to 3; No. 2, age 3 to 5. Try them and you will like them.
Per pair.......................$0.16
Per dozen....................... 1.65

10937—Nos. 1 and 2.

(IMPROVED CLASP.)

10938 Shoulder Hose Supporters in black, white and drab. No. 3, age 5 to 7: No. 4, age 7 to 9.
Per pair $0.18
Per dozen 1.80
10940 Shoulder Hose Supporters, in black, white and drab. No. 5, age 9 to 11; No. 6, misses.
Per pair $0.23
Per dozen 2.50
10942 Shoulder Hose Supporters, in black, white and drab. No. 7, ladies' size.
Per pair $0.25
Per dozen 2.65

10938-40-42)

Daisy Child's Waists.

10944 Child's Waist, Hose and Skirt Supporter combined. Quite new and a great success. Made of corset jean with elastic straps; has two rows of buttons, one for panties, the other for skirts. Easily laundered. Made in four sizes; colors: Black, white and drab. No. 1, 1 to 2 years, length, 9½ inches. No. 1 only has a diaper attachment.
No. 2, 2 to 5 years, length 11½ in.
No. 3, 5 to 8 years, length 12½ in.
No. 4, 8 to 11 years, length 14 in.
In ordering give size and color.
Each $0.40
Per dozen.................... 4.30

10946 Cupid Snap Waist for Children, Combination Hose Supporter, Waist and Shoulder Brace; no buttons, no button holes, no buckles. Everything goes on with a snap; can be removed or *put on* in a second's time.
Each.......................$0.50
Postage...................... .05
NOTE. If for girl send exact size of petticoat around the waist; for boy, size of kilts or pants around waist.

(Black only.)

Peerless Abdominal Supporter.

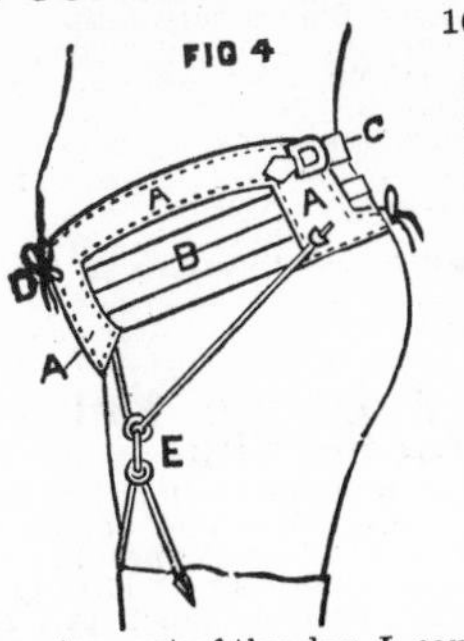

10948 If the most important inventions of any age have been those which afforded the greatest relief to human suffering, then the Peerless Elastic Abdominal Supporter must be classed with the best of them. "It is a perfect blessing," writes one lady Another says: "For three months I have been unable to take sufficient exercise to keep up my bodily health, but with the aid of this supporter I can walk as well as I ever could." Another says: "Instead of being compelled to lie down the greater part of the day I can go up and down stairs with the agility of a school girl." As a supporter before and a swathe after confinement it is unequaled. Its extreme lightness, openness and elasticity allow perfect freedom of movements, and it covers so little surface that it is not heating, while it gives perfect support.

Ladies whose household duties require them to stand or walk a great deal, causing much fatigue and exhaustion, should not be without one. It has been thoroughly tested by leading physicians who have given it their cordial indorsement. It is worn over the under flannels. In taking the measure for it, get the number of inches around the largest part of the abdomen, just below the hip bones. When properly adjusted it is glove-fitting. Satisfaction guaranteed or money refunded. Postage 10c. extra.

Sizes from 26 to 48 inches. Price each.........$2.50

Size 43 will fit a person measuring 45 inches around.

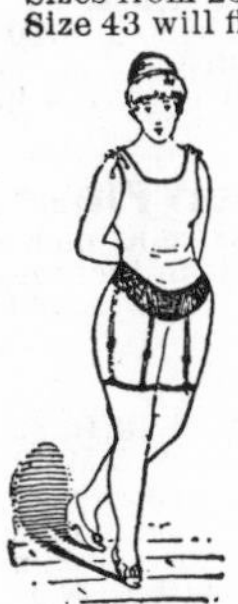

10950 Madame Schack's Dress Reform Abdominal and Hose Supporter; where shapeliness, comfort and health are desired it is indispensible—recommended to reduce corpulency and to all who suffer from weakness of their sex. Size, 28 to 44. Measure tightly around the fleshy part of the hips, *deducting two inches* to get the size wanted. Postage 10c. extra.
Each......$2.00

Non-Elastic Webbing.

10958 White Non-Elastic	½ in.	⅝ in.	¾ in.	1 in.
Per yard	$0.02	$0.02	$0.02	$0.02½
Per piece, 12 yards	.15	.17	.20	.25
10961 Black Non-Elastic. Width	½ in.	⅝ in.	¾ in.	1 in.
Per yard	$0.02	$0.02	$0.02½	$0.03
Per 12 yards	.18	.20	.25	.28

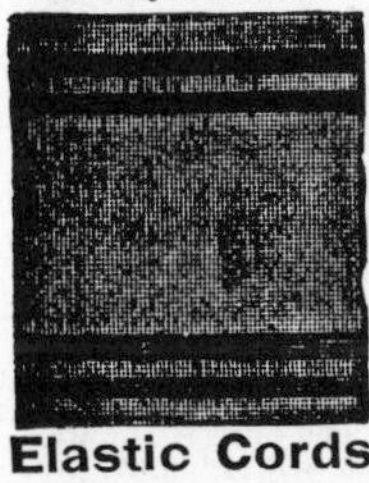

Heavy Elastic Truss Webs.

10962 Heavy Elastic, for trusses, artificial limbs, etc.

Width.	Per yard.
¾ inch	$0.12
1 inch	.14
1½ inch	.25
2 inch	.30

NOTE. If 25 yard pieces are wanted we will make special price.

Elastic Cords and Garter Webs.

Per piece.
10965 Elastic Cord, black lustre, small.........$0.14
10967 Elastic Cord, black lustre, medium...... .17
10969 Elastic Cord, black lustre, large.......... .20

Elastic Cords come in pieces of 24 yards each, manufacturer's measure. We do not sell less than a piece.

PLAIN BLACK ELASTIC BRAID.

10972 Per piece of 12 yards.. ⅜in. 30c. ½in. 40c. ⅝in. 45c. ¾in. 45c.

PLAIN WHITE ELASTIC BRAID.
Per piece of 12 yards.

10976........ ⅜in. 35c. ½in. 40c. ⅝in. 45c. ¾in 45c.

Fancy Garter Webs.

10978 Fancy Plaid and Stripe Garter Elastic, bright colors. Width ¾ inch. Per yard.........$0.04
Per piece 12 yards............ .35
10980 Fancy Plaid and Stripe Garter Elastic, bright colors, heavy, ⅞ inch wide. Per yard.... .05
Per piece, 12 yards............ .50

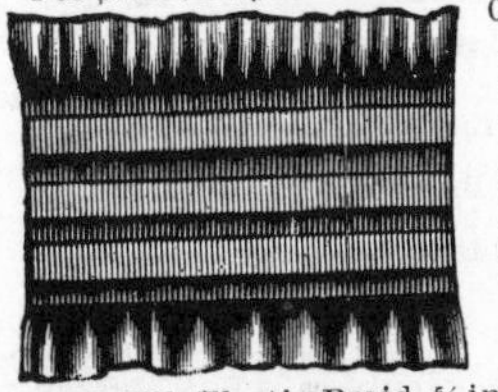

10985 Fancy Elastic striped garter web, with frill edge, 1 inch wide, blue with white stripe, blue with red stripe, gold with black stripe, cardinal with white stripe, black with white stripe, Per yard....$0.07
Per piece, 10 yds.. .60

10986 Silk Elastic Braid, ⅝ inch wide, pure quality, plain colors, black, white, scarlet, cardinal, pink, light and medium blue, old gold and orange. Per yard............$0.16
10989 Silk Elastic Braid, ⅞ inch wide, same quality and color as 10986. Per yard.......... .23

STAR BRAID OR BINDING.

Worsted Black Skirt or Coat Braid.

11000	No. 61	No. 69	No. 85	No. 89
	½ in.	⅝ in.	¾ in.	⅞ in.
Per piece of 24 yds.	48c.	60c.	70c.	80c.

11002 Star Skirt Braid, all colors. Per roll 4c; per dozen rolls, 45c.

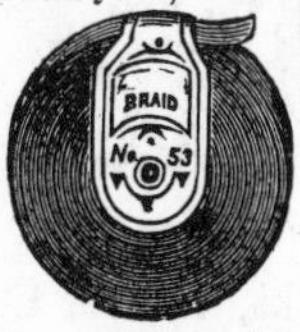

11004 Alpaca Trimming Braid, in black, white and colors. No. 29 ¼ inch wide, per piece of 24 yards, manufacturer's measure, 15c. We do not cut.

Bias Velvet Dress Facing.

11007 Blue Label Velveteen Skirt Binding, 1¼ in. wide, 3 yards long. Assorted staple shades.
Each..........$0.08
Per doz.......... .85
11008 Velveteen Dress Binding, 4 yard pieces, two inches wide, black only. Per piece.........$0.14

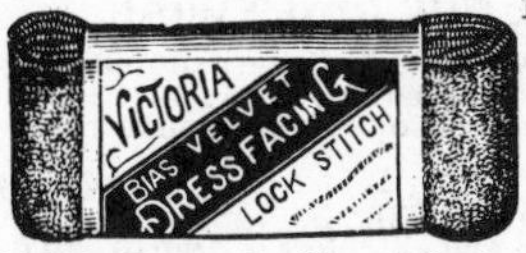

11009 Empress Velveteen, Extra quality Dress Binding, 1¼ in. wide, 4 yards long, all colors.
Per piece.......$0.15
Per dozen...... 1.65

11012 Extra Quality Velveteen Dress Binding, 4 yard pieces, two inches wide, black only.
Per piece.......... .25

Black Silk Coat Binding.

(Fine quality.)

Put up in pieces of 24 yards each, manufacturer's measure. We do not sample them nor sell less than one piece.

11015 Nos.	14	16	18	20	22
Width	7/16 in.	½ in.	9/16 in.	10/16 in.	11/16 in.
Per piece	$1.10	$1.20	$1.30	$1.60	$1.88

Colored Silk Binding.

11018 Silk Braid, ½ in. wide, for binding or trimming, all colors, 22 yards in piece.
Per yard, $0.08. Per piece..........$1.40

Cotton Tape, Black and White.

(3 yards.)

11025 Nos.	6	8	10	12	14
Width	⅜	½	9/16	10/16	¾
Per dozen	15c	18c	20c	23c	25c

Extra Super White Cotton Tape.

11027 About 4 yards in roll

Width	¼	⅜	½	⅝	¾	⅞	1 in
Per doz	30c.	35c.	40c.	50c.	60c.	70c.	80c.
Each	3c.	3½c.	4c.	5c.	6c.	7c.	8c.

Hook and Eye Tape.

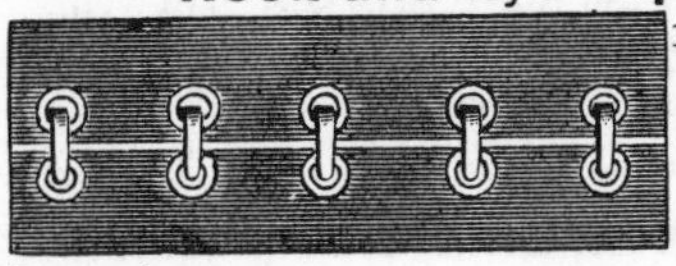

11042 Hook and Eye Tape, ready to be sewed on garment; black, white and drab.
Per yard..........$0.06
Per piece 12 yards.......... .65

Hooks and Eyes.

	No. 2.	No. 3	No. 4
11049 Extra Adamantine. Per gross	4c.		8c.
11051 Extra Silvered	8c.		
11053 Extra Japanned		5c.	6c.

SHRIMPTON'S

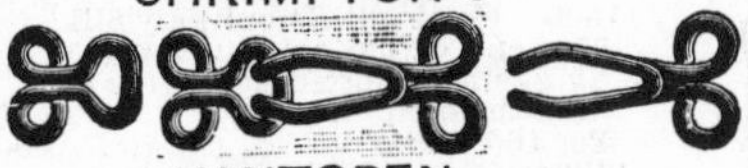

KANTOPEN.

11058—Kant-open Hooks and Eyes. Nos. 3 and 4.
Black or silvered, 2 dozen on card.
Per card..........$0.05
Per gross.......... .25
Per great gross.......... 2.75

The DeLong Patent Hook and Eye.

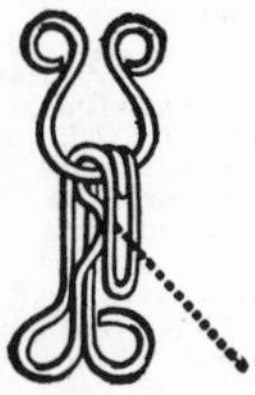

See that Hump?

11059 DeLong Patent Hook and Eye; fine white silvered.	No. 3.	No. 4.
Per cord of 2 dozen	$0.10	$0.10
Per gross	0.55	0.55
Per great gross	6.00	6.00

11061 DeLong Patent Hook and Eye Black.	No. 3.	No. 4.
Per card of 2 dozen	$0.10	$0.10
Per gross	0.55	0.55
Per great gross	6.00	6.00

Shoe Laces.

	Per doz.	Per gross.
11066 Round Glace Braid, ¾ yard.	$0.03	$0.33
11070 Round Glace Braid, 1 yard.	.04	.40
11072 Round Glace Braid, 1¼ yd.	.05	.45
11073 Round Glace Braid, 1½ yd.	.05½	.55

Corset Laces.

11090 Cotton Round. Length	2 yds.	2½ yds.	3 yds.
Per doz	$0.07	$0.09	$0.10
Per gross	.75	.90	1.10

	Per doz.	Per gross.
11092 Cotton White Elastic Corset Laces, heavy, No. 20, 2 yard laces	$0.25	$2.75
11094 Cotton White Elastic Corset Laces, No. 30, heavy, 2½ yard lace	.30	3.25

The Magic Dress Stays.

Cheap but good.

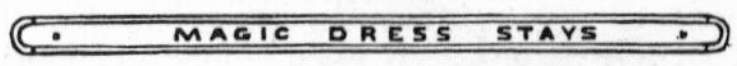

11108 Magic Cloth Covered Dress Stays, fine steel, with smooth tipped ends. Colors: White and black. Lengths, 7, 8, 9, 10 in. Per doz..$0.05
Per gross.......... .48
11109 Magic Dress Stay, sets of 9 stays, in white and black. Per set.......... .04
Per dozen.......... .40

The Very Dress Stays.

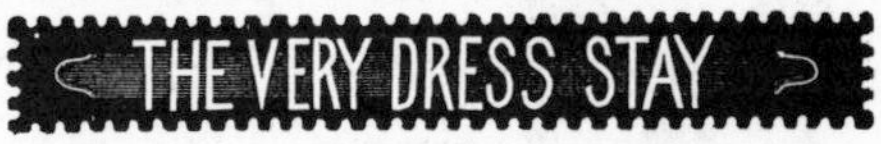

11110 Made of superior steel, enameled so it will not rust; smooth metal tips, covered with good ateen, in drab, gold, black, white, pink, blue, and red. Lengths, 6, 7, 8, 9 and 10 inches.
Per dozen.......... 0.10
Per gross.......... .95
11112 The Very Dress Stay, sets consisting of 9 stays, assorted as follows: 4/7, 2/8, 2/9, 1/10, in black, white, drab and gray. Per set.......... .09
Per dozen.......... 1.00
Per box of 25 sets.......... 1.80

Sterling Dress Stays.

11115 Made of superior quality of clock spring steel, smooth metal tips on ends, reinforced at each end by a linen tip to prevent wearing through at the ends (the weakest part), covered with a superior quality of sateen, both front and back, stitched at each side of steel to prevent coming out. Warranted waterproof. In lengths from 6 to 12 inches. Colors: Drab, gold, black, mottled slate, white, pink, light blue, red, dove. Per dozen..........$0.18
Per gross.......... 1.70
11118 The Sterling Dress Stay, sets consisting of 9 stays, assorted as follows: 4/7, 2/8, 2/9, 1/10; in black, white, drab and gray. Per set.......... .14
Per dozen sets.......... 1.50

Superior Dress Bone.

MANUFACTURED FROM FRENCH HORN.

Has the natural elasticity of whalebone, while it is capable of much finer finish.

11145 Width	5-16 in.	5-16 in.
Length	8 in.	10 in.
Per dozen	8c.	10c.
Per gross	$0.85	$1.10

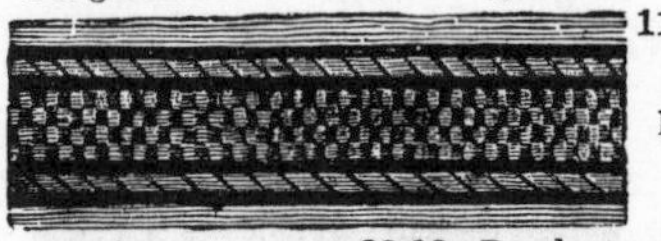

11147 Bone Casing, cotton, 9 yard piece, in black, white and drab.
Per piece..........$0.08 Per dozen pieces....$0.85

Corset Clasps and Steels.

11157 Corset Clasps, Jean covered, double steel, 5 hooks, in drab or white. Per pair..........$0.07
Per dozen.......... .65

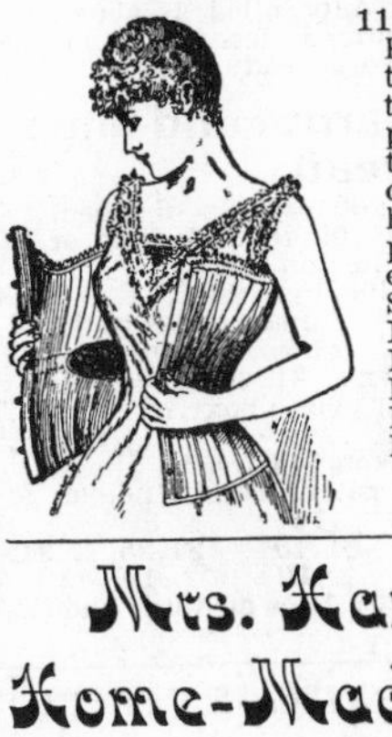

11158 The Pearl Corset Shield. Prevents corsets breaking at the waist and hips. If attached to new corset, will prevent breaking, and give three times the service. It can be used after corset sides have become broken, and will protect the body from the ends of broken stays.
Sizes No. 1 for 18-23 corset.
No. 2 for 23-28 corset.
No. 3 for 28-36 corset.
Per pair..........$0.23
Per dozen pairs.......... 2.50
Per gross pairs..........24.00

Ladies' Dress Shields.

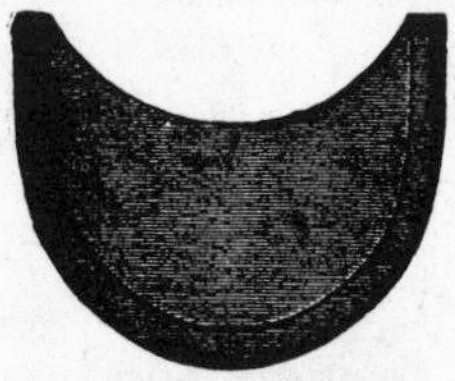

11160 Our Own Stockinet Dress Shields. A good shield for low price.

Size	2, med.	3, large.
Per pair	$0.07	$0.09
Per doz.	.75	.90

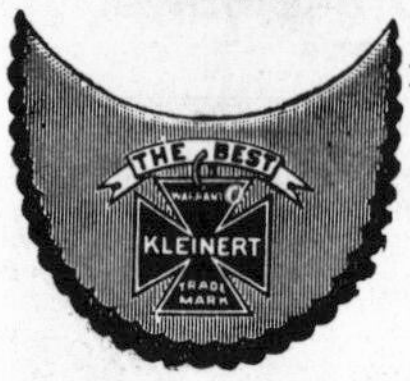

11163 Seamless Stockinet Dress Shield. Extra fine, soft as kid, pliable and elastic. They retain their shape and can be washed.

Size.	2, med.	3, large.
Per pair	$0.14	$0.16
Per doz.	1.45	1.75

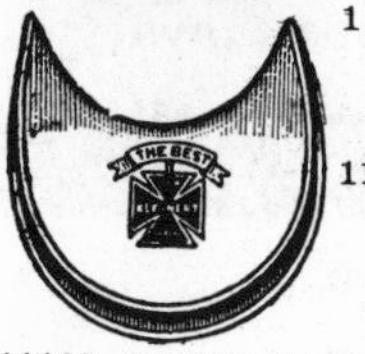

11164 Queen Pure Gum Dress Shields.

Size.	2, med.	3, large.
Per pair	$0.12	$0.14
Per doz.	1.20	1.40

11166 O. K. Pure Gum Dress Shields. Nainsook-covered, fully warranted.

Size.	2, med.	3, large.
Per pair	14c	16c
Per doz.	$1.40	$1.75

11168 Best Feather Weight Dress Shields.

Size	2, med.	3, large.
Per pair	$0.14	$0.16
Per doz	1.45	1.75

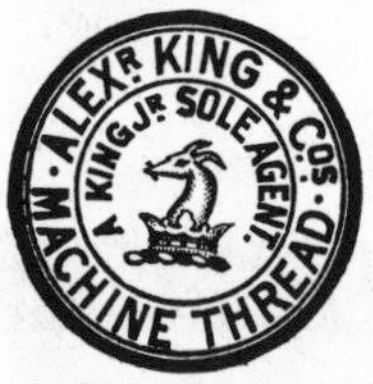

11180 Alex. King & Co.'s 200 yards soft finish machine thread, white and black, all numbers. Per spool 2c. Per dozen, 20 cents.

11182 Alex. King & Co.'s 400 yards soft finish white and black. All numbers. This thread is not glazed, so there is no limit to its uses in the household; will do hand or machine sewing like any six cord thread. Per spool 4c. Per dozen......$0.40

11184 Alex. King & Co.'s 500 yds. glace thread in white and black. All numbers; the best 500 yds. in the market, and the most economical for all kinds of hand or machine sewing; warranted full measure. Per spool 4c. Per dozen.........$0.45

The N. E. W. Spool Cotton.

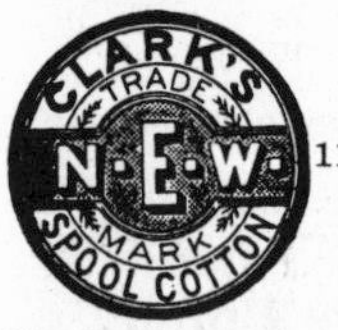

We strongly recommend it.

11194 The William Clark Company's N. E. W. Spool Cotton, the best 6 cord machine thread; try it and be convinced. Black, white and colors. Nos. 8 to 60.
Per spool..$0.04 Per doz...$0.45

If ordered in 10 doz. lots and upwards we will discount 6 per cent for cash.

Clark's O. N. T. Spool Cotton.

11196 Geo. A. Clark & Bros. Best Six Cord O. N. T. Spool Cotton. 200 yards, black, white and colored. Per spool ....$0.04 Per dozen...$0.45

Clark's O. N. T. Cabinets.

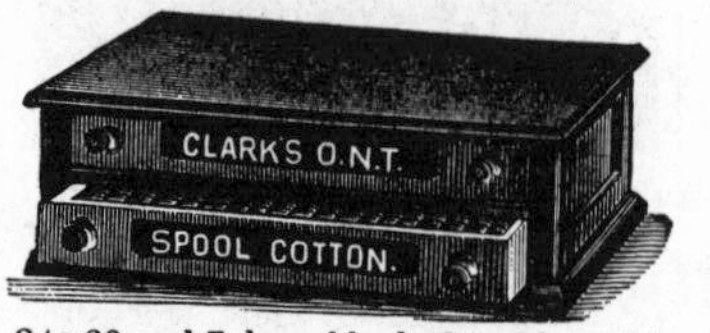

11198—Clark's O. N. T. Spool Cabinet, 2 drawers, holding 25 dozen spools thread, 18 doz. spools white Nos. 8 to 60 and 7 doz. black, 8 to 60, making a nice assortment. Sold only filled as above, at 45 cents per dozen for the thread, less 6 per cent cash. No charge for cabinets boxed ready to ship.

Spool Linen, Carpet and Shoe Thread.

11219 Barbour's 3 Cord, 200 Yard Spool Linen. None better. Nos. 25 to 100 in dark blue or black, whitish brown, white and drabs.
Per spool..............$0.08 Per dozen..........$0.86

11222 Our Special Carpet Thread comes in the following colors: Black, brown, green, red, drabs, slates, whity browns; 40 skeins and 16 ounces to the pound. Per pound box............ .70
Per ¼ pound.................................. .20

11226 Barbour's Shoemakers' Thread, linen, half bleached, in 2 ounce balls, 8 balls to pound,

Nos.	9	10	3	12
Price per pound..	$1.00	$1.10	$1.35	$1.50
Price per ball....	.14	.16	.18	.20

NOTE.—No. 9 is coarse, No. 10 is medium and No. 3 and No. 12 are finer.

A word to the wise is generally sufficient to get the adviser into trouble.

Corticelli Sewing Silk.

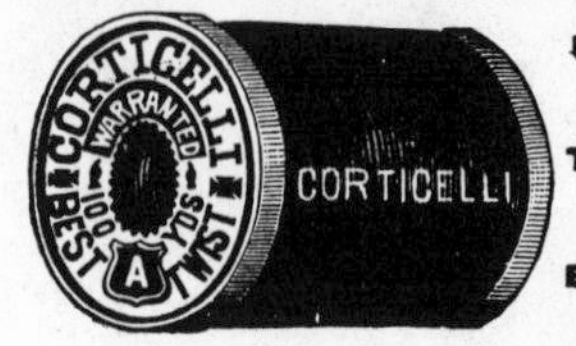

LADIES, TRY IT!

The Best Sewing Silk Made.

Every Spool Warranted.

Full Length, Smooth and Strong.

Ask for CORTICELLI Silks, Twists, Etc.

Try it. Compare it with any other quality in the market and you will find it absolutely the best. Every spool warranted full length, strong and smooth, as they are made from the finest quality raw material. Full assortment of colors always on hand. For sale by all leading jobbers and retailers all over the United States.

Sewing Silk and Twist.

Corticelli silk is warranted full size and full length. Black spool silks are marked OO, O, A, B, C and D. No. OO being the finest. Colored spool silks come in letter "A" only.

	Per doz.	Per spool.
11260 Corticelli Sewing Silk, 50 yard spools, black, white and all colors.....	$0.40	$0.03½
11262 Corticelli Sewing Silk, 100 yard spools, black, white and all colors.....	.80	.07
11264 Clark's Pure Dye Sewing Silk, 100 yard spools, good quality, black only....	.60	.06
11267 Corticelli Button Hole Twist, 10 yard spools, black, white and all colors. Put up 25 spools in box for 30 cents; per hundred spools, $1.20..........	.18	.01½
11271 Corticelli Machine Twist, black, white and all colors, 1 oz. spools, 12 spools to pound, sizes OOO, OO, O, A, B, C, D, E, EE, F, FF..............	6.50	.55

Corticelli Embroidery Silk on Spool.

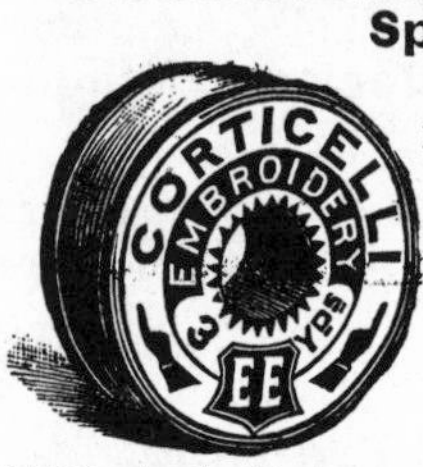

11279 Corticelli Embroidery Silk on Spools, 3 yards, size EE, in all colors.
Per spool $0.00¾
Per dozen........... .08
Per 100............. .60
Postage 5 cents per dozen.

11280 Corticelli Wash Spool Embroidery Silk (10 yds), for feather stitching, fringe, tassels, and for every kind of fancy work. This is the best size, EE, 12 spools in box, solid colors.
Per spool..$0.04
Per dozen.. .40

Skein Embroidery Silk.

11293 Florence Wash Embroidery Silk, in plain colors, 16 skeins in half ounce packages, assorted to order. Per skein.....................$0.02
Per ½ oz... .25
Per 1 oz... .50

11295 Colored Waste Embroidery Silk, all colors, odds and ends. Nice for fancy work and for our new Gem Embroidery—machine
Per 1 ounce package.............................. .37

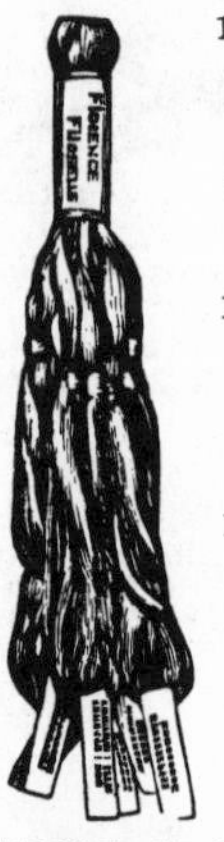

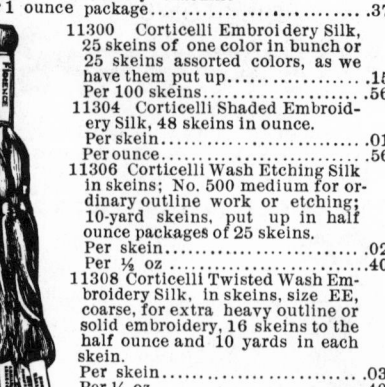

11300 Corticelli Embroidery Silk, 25 skeins of one color in bunch or 25 skeins assorted colors, as we have them put up.................. .15
Per 100 skeins....................... .56

11304 Corticelli Shaded Embroidery Silk, 48 skeins in ounce.
Per skein.............................. .01½
Per ounce.............................. .56

11306 Corticelli Wash Etching Silk in skeins; No. 500 medium for ordinary outline work or etching; 10-yard skeins, put up in half ounce packages of 25 skeins.
Per skein.............................. .02
Per ½ oz............................... .40

11308 Corticelli Twisted Wash Embroidery Silk, in skeins, size EE, coarse, for extra heavy outline or solid embroidery, 16 skeins to the half ounce and 10 yards in each skein.
Per skein.............................. .03
Per ½ oz............................... .40
Per oz................................. .75

11309 Corticelli Wash Embroidery Silk, whip cord (three cord). 25 yards on each ball. Per ball, .07
Per doz.. .80

NOTE.—11306 is expressly for outline embroidery and needle work on various kinds of material which requires washing; 11308 is for art needle work of every description on material which requires washing. Each skein of these silks is double knotted, making it impossible to tangle the thread. The shade number is also attached to each skein for the convenience of dealers and customers.

Skein Embroidery Silk—Continued.

11310 Corticelli Wash Rope Embroidery Silk, fast dye, size G, very coarse, ½ oz. of 16 skeins, in package, 3½ yards in skein. Per skein......$0.03
Per ½ oz...............$0.40. Per oz............ .75

11311 Corticelli Wash Filo Silk, black, white and colors. Per skein.................................$0.03
Per 16 skeins.. .45
Per 32 skeins.. .85

11313 Corticelli Roman Floss—16 skeins in ½ oz. bunch. Per skein................................ .03
Per 16 skeins.. .45
Per 32 skeins.. .85

Corticelli and Florence Knitting and Crochet Silk.

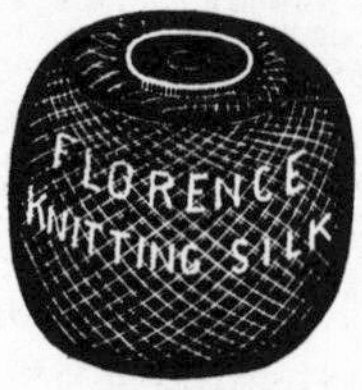

11318

11318 Florence Knitting Silk; black, white and colors, put up, 8 balls of 4 ounces in a box. No. 300 is coarse and in greatest demand. Each ball contains ½ oz. of silk, measuring 150 yards. No. 500 is fine; each ball contains ½ oz. of silk, measuring 250 yards. This silk is for knitting mittens, stockings and other articles which require washing.
Per ½ oz. ball.............$0.24
Per box, 4 oz., 8 balls.....1.75
Per lb., 32 balls........... 6.80

No. 500 in Florence Knitting and Crochet Silk can be had in black, white, cream and cream white only.

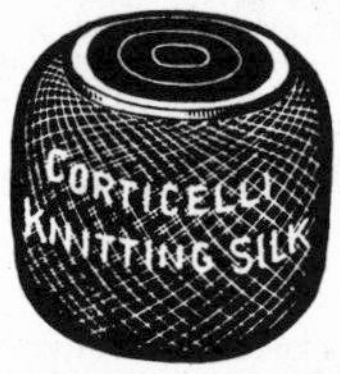

11320 Corticelli Knitting and Crochet Silk, high luster, for knitting, crocheting, embroidering; sold only in size 300, put up same as 11318, in colors, also black, white and cream.
Per ½ oz. ball............$0.30
Per box of 8 balls.......... 2.40
Per lb., 32 balls............ 9.60

White Linen Floss.

11338 Linen Floss, assorted sizes, or solid numbers as below, Nos. aa3, aa6, aA, aa, AA, in packages.
Per package of 12 skeins..............................$0.30
Per box of 4 dozen skeins.............................. 1.10

11342 Linen Floss, solid numbers.

No.	1	2	3	4	5	6
Per dozen skeins	$0 32	$0.35	$0 38	$0.40	$0.42	$0.46
Per box 4doz.sk'ns.	1.15	1.25	1.35	1.45	1.52	1.75

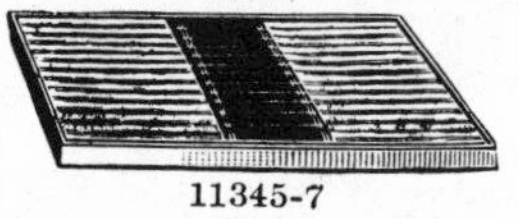

11345-7

11345 Scotch Colored Linen Floss, in luster, finish for embroidery and outline work; comes in skeins of 65 yards in assorted solid colors, and black and white No. 8.
Per gross of 12 dozen skeins.............................$5.50
Per ¼ gross, solid color in box......................... 1.50
Per dozen skeins... .55
Per skein.. .05

11347 Real Scotch Colored Linen Floss, same as 11345, but coarser (No. 4), 45 yards to skein.
Per gross..$5.50
Per ¼ gross.. 1.50
Per dozen.. .55
Per skein.. .05

Colored Twines For Ladies' Fancy Work.

11358 Superior Macrame Cord or Seine Twines; in all colors. Soft laid. No. 12 put up in balls, 4 balls to the lb., 2 pounds in a box. (Manufacturer's weight, 12 oz. to lb.) Per ball.........$0.08
8 balls.. .55

11359 Macrame Cord, unbleached only in numbers 6 fine, 9 and 12 medium and 16 and 20 coarse. Per ball, $0.06. Per 8 balls.................$0.44

11360 Oriental Cotton Crochet Cord for ladies' fancy work. About one-third size of No. 12 seine or Macrame cord, size of druggists small wrapping twine, fine cord; hard twist, in all colors, and white, cream and unbleached. Put up in 2 lb. boxes, 8 balls to lb.
Price, 1 ball, 5 cents; 8 balls.......................... .35
16 balls... .65

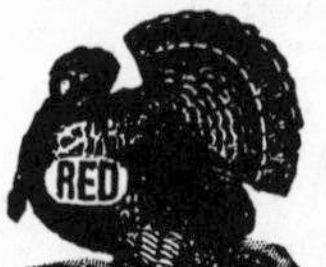

"H B" Embroidery COTTON.

TRADE MARK. ON SPOOLS.

WILL NOT CROCK OR WASH OUT.

H. B. Embroidery Cotton on spools, plain solid colors, turkey red, black and white, 3 colors only; Nos. 8, 10, 12, 14, 16, 18, 20, 22, 24.

	Per ball.	Per doz.
11424 Turkey Red H. B. Embroidery Cotton..............	$0.02	$0.20
11427 Solid Black H. B. Embroidery Cotton..............	.02	.20
11429 Plain White H. B. Embroidery Cotton..............	.02	.20

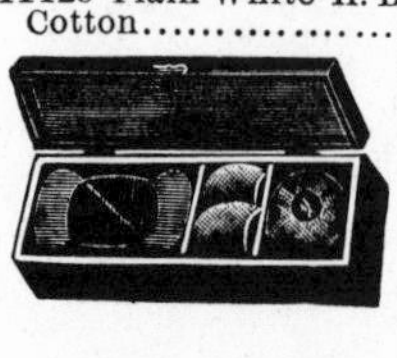

11431 Wood box with one 200 yard ball white crochet cotton, 4 balls H. B. turkey red embroidery cotton, and 6 cards fast black tiger darning cotton. Per box..$0.25
Per dozen............... 2.50

Embroidery Cotton.

11434 Embroidery Cotton, white, best C. B. French. Nos. 6 to 16. Per dozen skeins $0.20
11438 Embroidery Cotton, red only, best C. B. French. Nos. 6 to 24. Per dozen skeins .... .20

Clark's Crochet Cotton on 200 Yard Balls.

11444 Clark's Crochet Cotton, on 200 yard balls, white only; large balls, Nos. 5, 10, 15, 20, 25, 30, 40, 50, 60, 70, 80. Per ball $0.05
Per box, 10 balls .... .44
11446 Clark's Crochet Cotton, on 200 yard balls. Nos. 30, 40, 50, 60 in solid colors. Cream, ecru, pinks, salmon, mahogany, moss greens, navy, fast red, fast black, blues, yellow, orange, heliotrope, nile green, lilac, olive green, lavender, peacock, old gold, rose, old rose. Per ball.. $0.05
Per 10 balls .... .44
11447 Clark's Crochet Cotton, on 200 yard balls. Shaded colors; Nos. 30 and 50 only, white and blues; white and pinks; white and yellows; white and lilacs; white and nile green; white and moss green; white, blue and pink; white, yellow and pink; white, green and pink; white, blue and yellow; white and cream; white and salmon; white and ecrus; shaded yellows; shaded creams; red white and blue; olive green; peacocks; lilacs; old golds; old rose; heliotropes; moss greens; pinks; blues; ecru. Per ball $0.05
Per 10 balls .... .44

Note.—The above colored and shaded crochet cottons are new and novel. Send for sample skein of any color or combination named above, or for sample wheel showing work.

11456 Real Scotch Mending Linen, for darning silk, lisle thread, balbriggan or cotton hosiery. It meets a long-felt want, and is indispensable to every lady's work basket; 13 yards on card; in all staple shades and *fast black*.
Per card $0.02½
Per dozen .... .25
Per gross 2.70

11460 Woven Initial Letters, 50 in box, for marking household linen, etc.; any letter.
Per box $0.07
Per dozen .... .75

Cotton and Worsted Darning Yarn.

11470 Dorcas Darning Cotton, 30 yards on card, in all plain colors and mixed blue and white, brown and white, red and white, and black and white. Per dozen.. $0.07
Per gross .... .75
11473 Tiger Darning Cotton, *fast black*; per card $0.01
Per dozen .... .10
Per gross 1.15

11475 Dorcas Darning Worsted in all plain colors and black and white; per card $0.02
Per dozen .... .20

Knitting Cotton.

11480 White Dorcas Knitting Cotton, full weight, superfine four (4) thread, put up 8 balls to pound, 2 lbs. in box. Order any quantity; Nos. 6 to 24.
Per ball $0.05
Per pound .... .35
11482 Dorcas Knitting Cotton, navy blue; same description as above (11480); Nos. 8 to 16.
Per pound $0.40
11484 Dorcas Knitting Cotton, blue and white mixed; Nos. 8 to 16,
Per pound $0.40

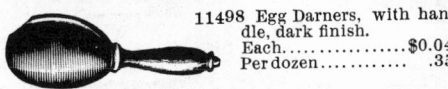

11498 Egg Darners, with handle, dark finish.
Each $0.04
Per dozen .... .35

Everything we sell you is worth the money.

We will not handle trash.

COLLARS AND CUFFS.

Boys' Collars.

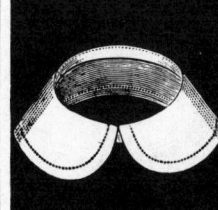

11530 Boys' Plain White Fine Linen Collars; see cut; size, 12 to 13½.
Each $0.12
Per dozen............ 1.30
11532 Boys' Colored Percale Collars, assorted.
Each $0.05
Per dozen.. .... .55

Ladies' Collars and Cuffs.
(Be sure and give size wanted when ordering.)

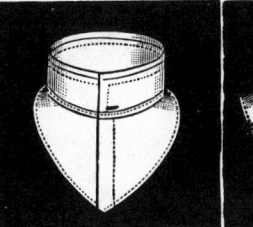

11535   11537

	Each.	Per Doz.
11535 Ladies' Medium Width Linen Collars, with cape; sizes,12½ to 15.	$0.11	$1.20
11537 Ladies' Roll Point Linen Collars, with cape; sizes, 12 to 15.....	.13	1.45

11539 Ladies' Linen White Wing Collars, with cape; sizes, 12½ to 15.
Each $0.11
Per dozen........... 1.20

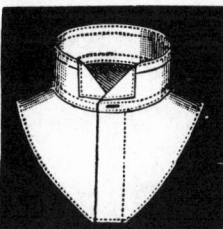

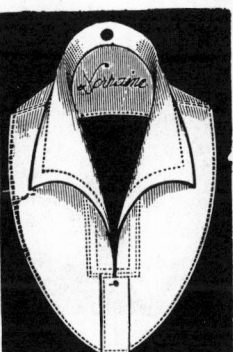

11541 Ladies' White or Colored Loraine Roll Collars, made in one size only which will fit any neck. Each $0.25
Per dozen.......... 2.75

11543 Ladies' Plain White Linen Cuffs; sizes, 7, 7½, 8, 8½. Per pair....$0.11
Per dozen............ 1.20

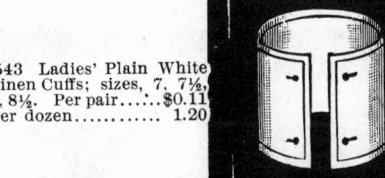

11545 Ladies' Roll Back Linen Cuffs; sizes, 7, 7½, 8, 8½. Per pair...$0.25

Ladies' Colored Cuffs.
11548 Ladies' Pique Washable Cuffs, red and blue stripe. Per doz. pair, $0.50. Per pair $0.05

Ladies' Chemisettes.

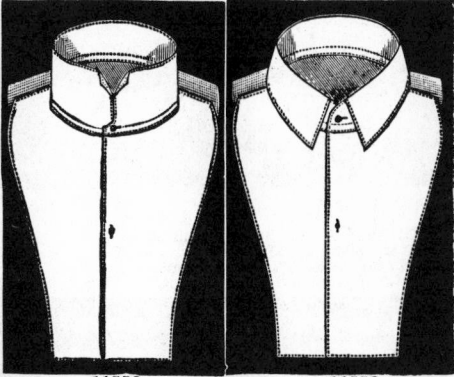

11550   11552
11550 Ladies' White Linen Chemisettes, with turndown collar, sizes, 12½ to 15, Each...... ....$0.25
11552 Ladies' White Linen Chemisettes, see cut, sizes, 12½ to 15. Each....................$0.25

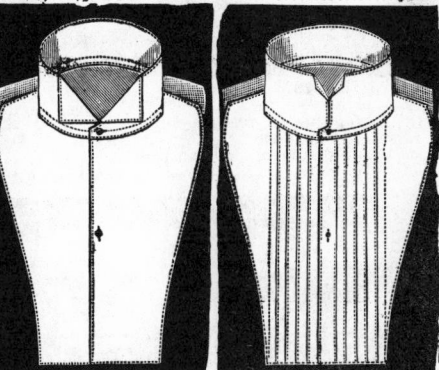

11554   11556   Each.
11554 Ladies' Plain White Chemisette, with wing collar. Sizes, 12½ to 15.... ....$0.25
11556 Ladies' Tucked Chemisette, standing collar, small points. Sizes, 12½ to 15.............. .25

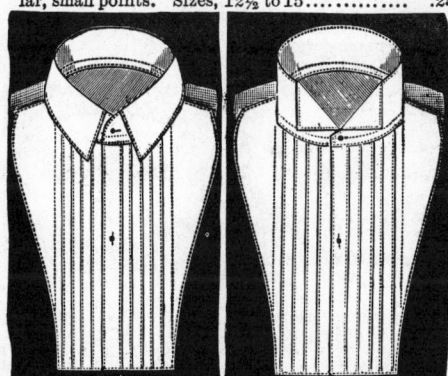

11558.   11560.   Each.
11558 Ladies' White Tucked Chemisette, lay down collar. Sizes, 12½ to 15............$0.25
11560 Ladies' White Tucked Chemisette, plain wing. Sizes, 12½ to 15.... .25

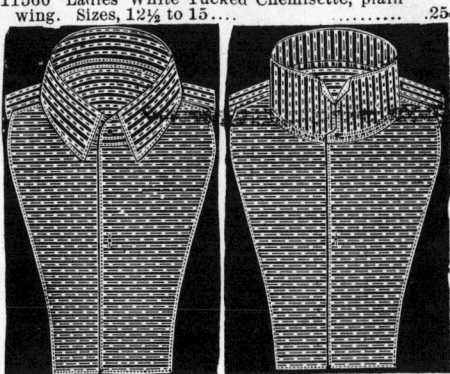

11562   11565
11562 Ladies' Colored Chemisette, assorted, red, blue and black. Sizes, 12½ to 15. ...$0.25
11565 Ladies' Colored Chemisette, assorted, red, blue and black. Sizes, 12½ to 15. Each.. .25
11567 Ladies' Cuffs, to match above fancy chemisettes. Sizes, 7½ to 8. Per pair .... .25

Men's Collars and Cuffs.

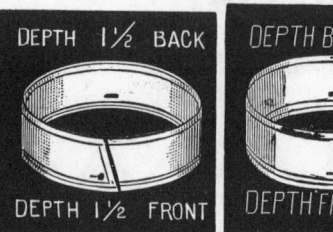

11575 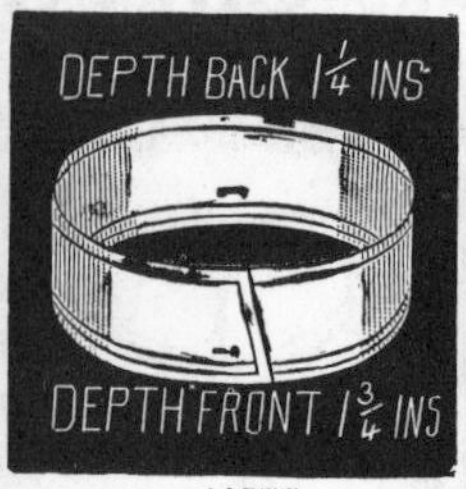   11577

	Each.	Per Doz.
11575 Men's Cresco Plain Standing Collars; sizes, 14 to 18	$0.10	$1.10
11577 Men's Renfrew Plain Standing Collars; sizes, 14 to 18	.10	1.10

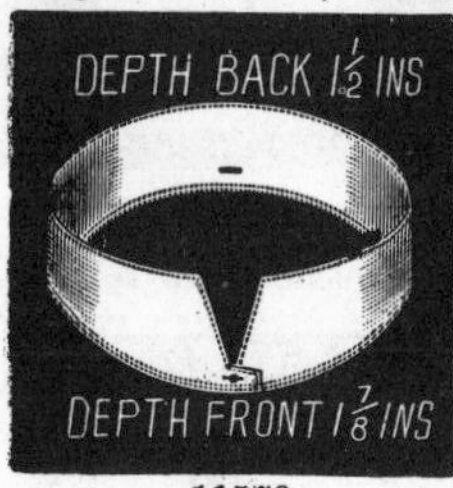

11579 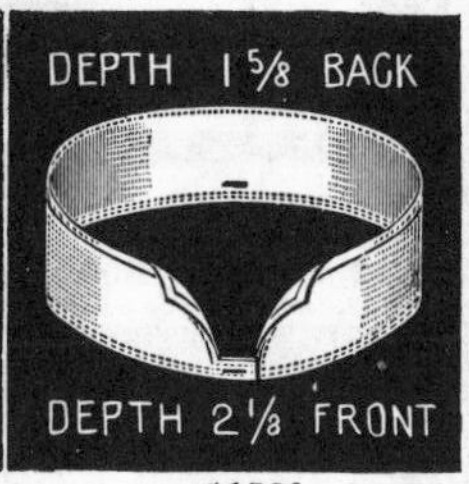   11581

	Each.	Per Doz.
11579 Men's Rutland V Front Collars; sizes, 14 to 18	$0.10	$1.10
11581 Men's Belmont Collars; sizes, 14 to 18	.10	1.10

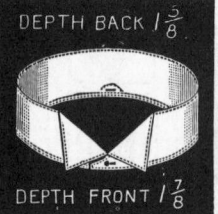 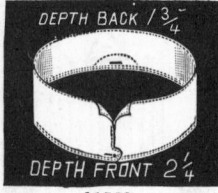

11583 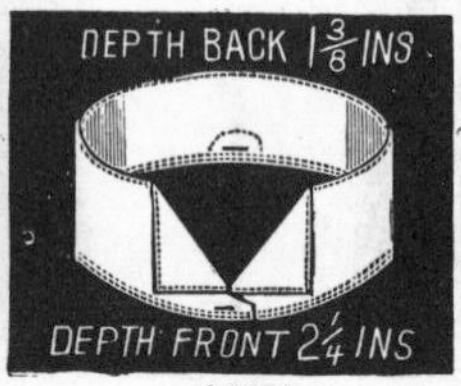   11585

	Each.	Per Doz.
11583 Boy's and Men's Irving Collars; sizes, 12½ to 18	$0.10	$1.10
11585 Men's Calumet Collars; sizes, 14 to 17½	.10	1.10

11587   11589

	Each.	Per Doz.
11587 Men's Manala Wing Collars; sizes, 14 to 18½	$0 10	$1.10
11589 Men's Willard Collars; sizes, 14 to 17½	$0.10	$1.10

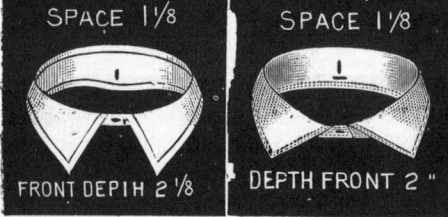

11591   11593

	Each.	Per Doz.
11591 Men's Kendall Lay Down Collars; sizes, 14 to 18	$0.10	$1.10
11593 Men's Shannon Lay Down Collars; sizes, 14 to 19½	10	1.10

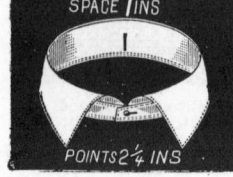

11595 Men's English Roll Collars; sizes, 14 to 18.
Each $0.10
Per dozen 1.10

Men's Linen Collars.
4-ply extra quality.

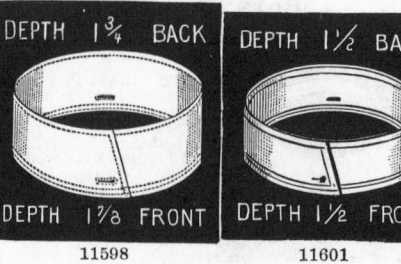

11598   11601

	Each.	Per doz.
11598 Men's Alaska Linen 4-ply Standing Collars, 14 to 18	$0.13	$1.35
11601 Men's Puritan 4-ply Linen Collars, 14 to 18	.13	1.35

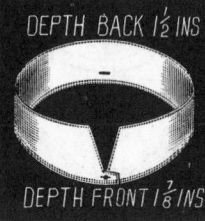 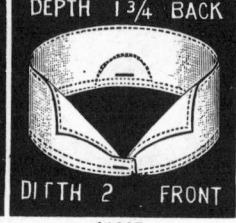

11603   11605

	Each.	Per doz.
11603 Men's Americus 4-ply Linen Collars, 14 to 18	$0.13	$1.35
11605 Men's Frontenac 4-ply Linen Collars, 14 to 18	.13	1.35

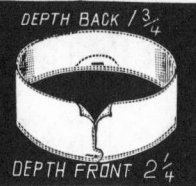

11607 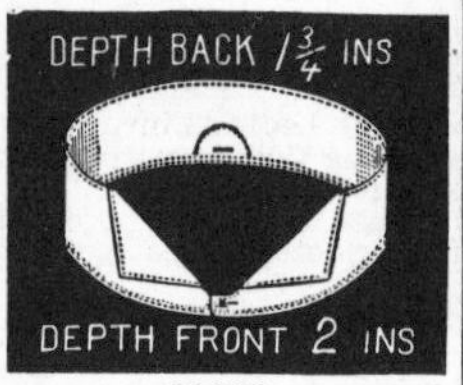   11609

	Each.	Per doz.
11607 Men's Otisco 4-ply Linen Collars, 14 to 18	$0.13	$1.35
11609 Men's Hector 4-ply Linen Collars, 14 to 18	.13	1.35

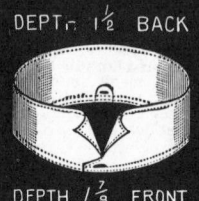

11612 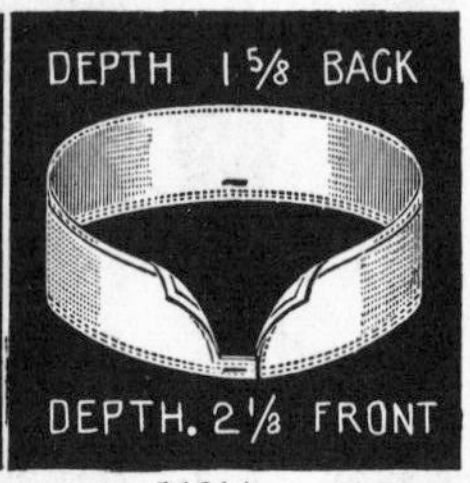   11614

	Each.	Per doz.
11612 Men's Magnet 4-ply Linen Collars, 14 to 18	$0.13	$1.35
11614 Men's Volante 4-ply Linen Collars, 14 to 18	.13	1.35

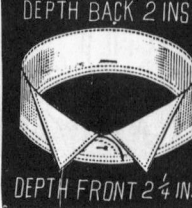 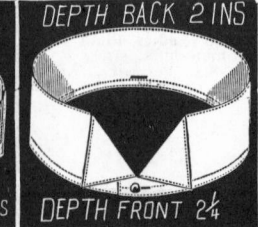

11617   11619

	Each.	Per doz.
11617 Men's Admiral 4-ply Linen Collars, 14 to 18	.13	1.35
11619 Men's Victory 4-ply Linen Collars, 14 to 17½	.13	1.35

If any of your friends want one of our catalogues you will do us a favor by asking him (or her) to send to us for one, enclosing 15 cents in stamps to pay postage or expressage.

Our assortment of Men's Furnishing Goods is up to date.

Men's Collars—Continued.

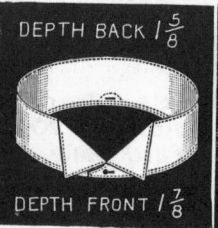 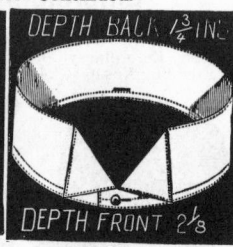

11622   11625

	Each	Per doz.
11622 Men's Manola 4-ply Linen Collars, 14 to 19	.13	1.35
11625 Men's York 4-ply Linen Collars, 14 to 17½	.13	1.35

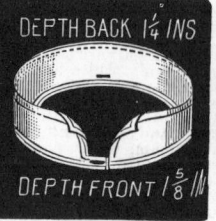 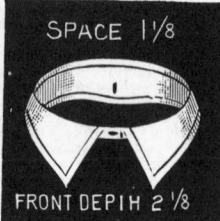

11627   11630

	Each	Per doz.
11627 Men's Claymore 4-ply Linen Collars, 14 to 18½	.13	1.35
11630 Men's Maitland 4-ply Linen Collars, 14 to 19½	.13	1.35

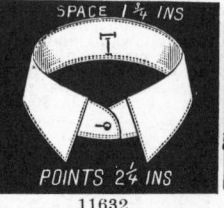

11632 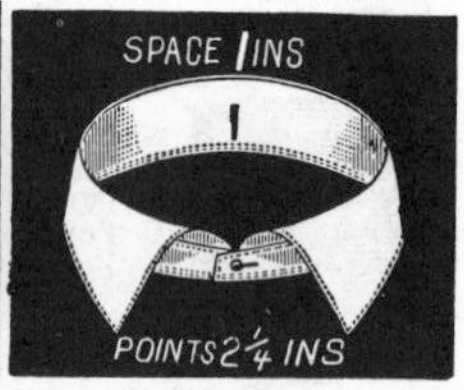   11634

	Each.	Per doz.
11632 Men's St. Leger 4-ply Linen Collars, 14 to 18	.13	1.35
11634 Men's Roll Tadousac 4-ply Linen Collars, 14 to 18	.13	1.35

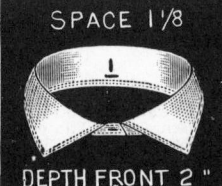

11636 Men's Jerome 4-ply Linen Collars, 14 to 19½
Each $0.13
Per doz 1.35

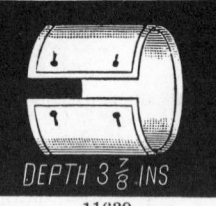 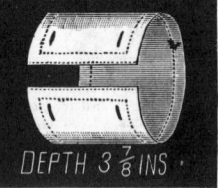

11639   11641

	Per pair.	Per doz.
11639 Men's Plain Linen 4-ply Cuffs, sizes, 10 to 11½ inch	$0.15	$1.65
11641 Men's Plain Linen 4-ply Cuffs, sizes, 10 to 11½	.18	1.95

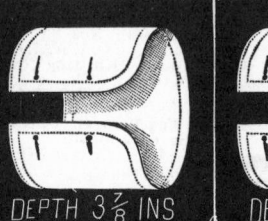 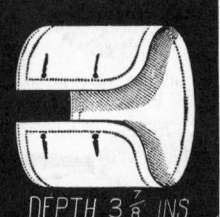

11643.   11646.

	Per pair.	Per doz.
11643 Men's Linen Cuffs, 4-ply, sizes, 10 to 11½	.18	1.95
11646 Men's Astor, Welt Edge, Extra Heavy Linen Cuffs. Sizes, 10 to 11½	.25	2.70

Cuffs—Continued.

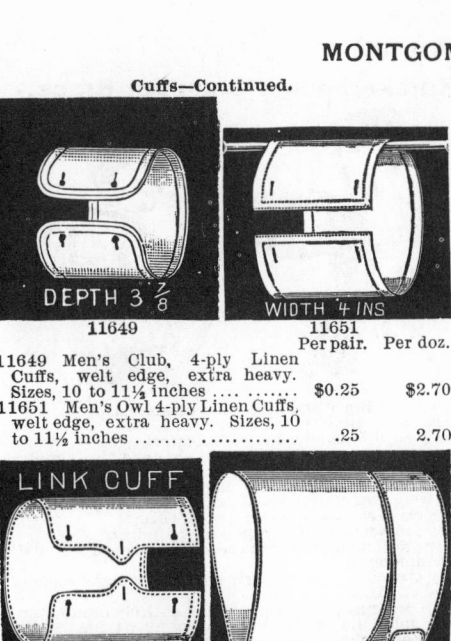

11649 **11651**
Per pair. Per doz.

11649 Men's Club, 4-ply Linen Cuffs, welt edge, extra heavy. Sizes, 10 to 11½ inches $0.25 $2.70
11651 Men's Owl 4-ply Linen Cuffs, welt edge, extra heavy. Sizes, 10 to 11½ inches .... .25 2.70

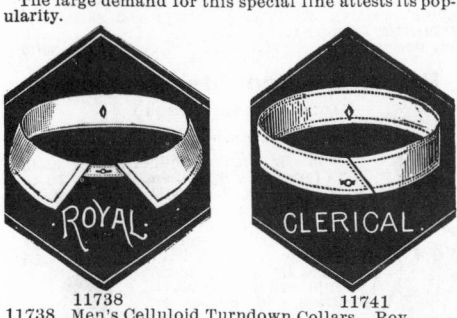

11653 **11655**
Per pair. Per doz.

11653 Men's Saladin Reversible Link Cuffs, 4-ply linen. Sizes, 10 to 11½ inches $0.25 $2.75
11655 Men's New Link Cuffs, 4-ply linen. Sizes, 9½ to 11½ inches .... .25 2.75

Celluloid Waterproof Bosoms Collars and Cuffs.

Note new prices.

To those desiring the **finest quality** of waterproof goods, we specially recommend the "Celluloid." These goods are made of the very best material, and have an **interlining of linen,** being the **only** waterproof collars and cuffs so made. Stronger and more durable than any other goods in the market.

The large demand for this special line attests its popularity.

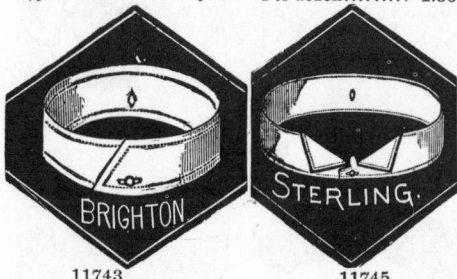

11738 **11741**

11738 Men's Celluloid Turndown Collars, Royal. Sizes, 12 to 18½, front, 1⅞ in. Each $0.15
Per dozen 1.50
11741 Men's Celluloid Plain Standing Collars, Clerical. Sizes, 12 to 19½, front, 1½ in., back, 1⅝ in. Each .... $0.15. Per dozen 1.50

11743 Men's Celluloid Collars, Brighton. Sizes, 13 to 18, front, 1¾ in., back, 1⅝ in. See cut. Each $0.15
Per dozen 1.50

11745 Men's Celluloid Standing Wing Collars, Sterling. Sizes, 12 to 18, front, 2 in., back, 1¾ in. Each .. $0.15
Per dozen 1.50
11754 Men's Peerless Celluloid Cuffs, plain, square; sizes, 10 to 11½, width 3½ inches. Per dozen 3.00
11756 Men's Eureka Celluloid Cuffs, plain, round. Sizes, 10 to 11½.
Per pair $0.30
Per dozen 3.00

11754

Celluloid Shirt Fronts.
Will Button on Neck Band of any Shirt.

11763 **11761**

11761 Celluloid Shirt Fronts; see cut. Size, 6½ inches wide, 7 inches long. Each $0.35
Per dozen 3.75
11763 Celluloid Shirt Fronts, large, 6⅜x12 inches. Each ..... $0.60 Per dozen 6.00

Sleeve Protectors.

Per pair. Per doz.

11810 Men's Good Print Oversleeves, patent rubber top $0.10 $1.00
11816 Oversleeves, standard prints, small neat checks, plain black and indigo blue dots, rubber or snap. .14 1.40

SUSPENDERS.

Postage 3 to 5c. per pair extra.   Per pair. Per doz.
11920 Boys' Suspenders, leather ends... $0.05 $0.50
11922 Boys' Braid End Suspenders....... .10 1.10
11924 Youth's Suspenders, braid ends, finer. .15 1.50
11926 Youth's Fine Suspenders, silk ends, push buckles.................... .20 2.10

Men's Heavy Suspenders.

11930 Men's Suspenders, 40 inches, cushion back web, buckeye tape ends, wire buckles.
Per pair $0.15
Per dozen 1.60

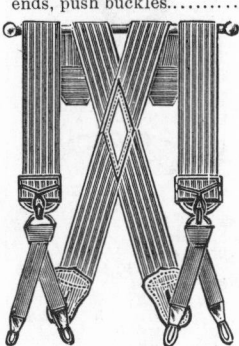

11930

11960 Men's Extra Heavy 40 inch Suspenders, cushion back web, cross (X) back, heavy wire buckles, cowhide leather ends.
Per pair $0.25
Per dozen 2.75

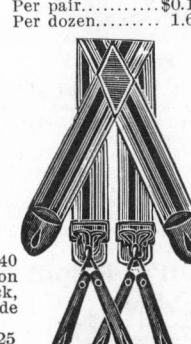

11960

11962 Our one-piece back suspenders, heavy web, solid nickel buckles, lined and stitched cowhide leather ends extra, lengths.
Per pair $0.35
Per dozen 3.75

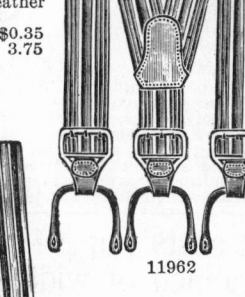

11962

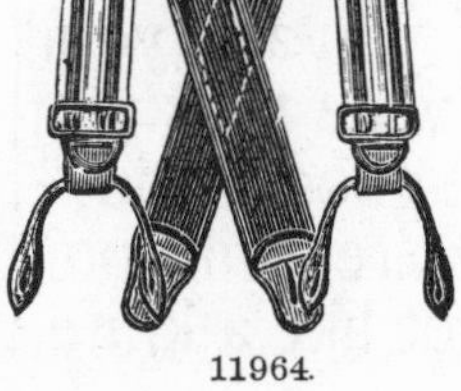

11964 Miners', Farmers' and Mechanics' *Monarch* Suspenders, extra heavy cushion back web, extra length, solid 1 piece, leather ends, warranted. See cut
Per pair $0.45
Per dozen 4.85

11964

Suspenders—Continued.

11966 Our Heavy Cushion Back Farmers' Suspenders, extra length, with best cowhide leather ends, solid nickel buckles, one-piece back. See cut.
Per pair $0.45
Per dozen 5.00

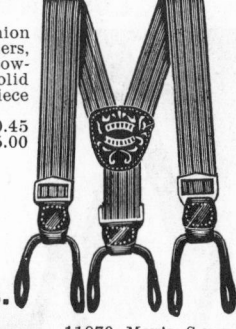

Men's Dress Suspenders.

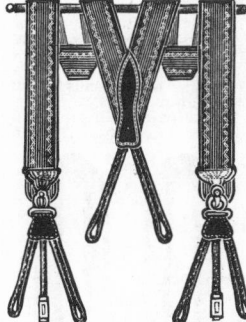

11970 Men's Suspenders; fancy web and drawer straps.
Per pair $0.10
Per dozen 1.10
11972 Men's Suspenders; fancy web or white, with drawer straps.
Per pair $0.15
Per dozen.... 1.65
11975 Men's Suspenders; fancy web or white, with drawer straps.
Per pair $0.20
Per dozen.... 2.10
11978 Men's Suspenders; fancy web or white, with drawer straps.
Per pair $0.25
Per dozen 2.65

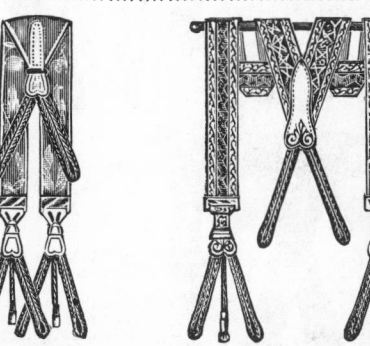

11990 **12006**

11990 Men's Fine Elastic Web Suspenders, silk braid ends and drawer straps and best cast-off push buckles. Each $0.30
Per dozen 3.25
12006 Men's Fine Dress Suspenders, silk braid ends and drawer straps, best cast-off buckles.
Per pair $0.40
Per dozen............................ 4.25

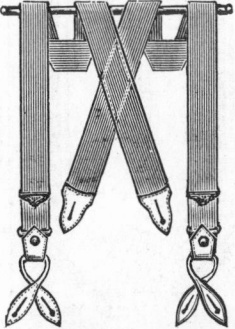

12008 Men's Fine Elastic Suspenders; extra quality, with slides and cast off buttons, colored leather ends to match elastic.
Per pair $0.50
Per dozen......... 5.40

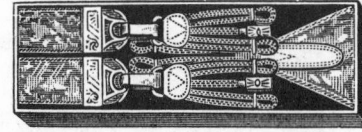

12012 Men's Silk Embroidered Fancy Dress Suspenders, assorted colors, one pair in a box, with silk braid ends and drawerstraps. See cut. Per pair $0.50
Per dozen.............................. 5.40

DON'T FORGET
Our 13 Special Catalogues, covering a wide range of Merchandise.

SPECIAL STYLES OF SUSPENDERS.

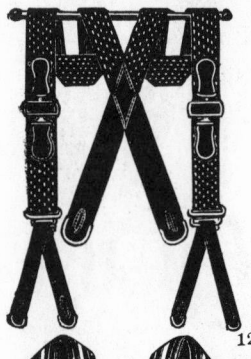

Guyot Suspenders.

12015 Non-Elastic Guyot Suspenders, narrow web, tape ends; no rubber in web, except from backpiece down.
Per pair..........$0.25
Per doz.......... 2.70

12017 Elastic Suspenders, two-piece embossed leather back with porous web between; wire buckles; braid ends and drawer straps.
Per pair...........$0.25
Per dozen... ....2.75

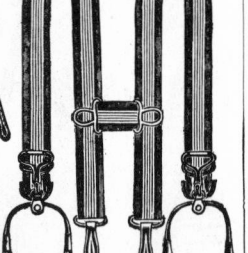

12017

12019 Elastic Suspenders with straight across movable back piece, round cord ends running over boxwood pulleys.
Per pair...........$0.30
Per doz.......... 3.52

12019

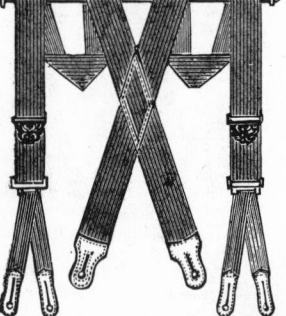

12021 Men's Fine Suspenders, with gilt slides and adjustable ends.
Per pair....$0.40
Per doz..... 4.25

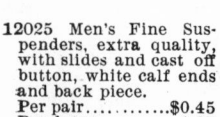

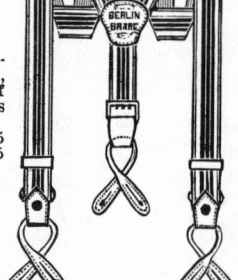

12025 Men's Fine Suspenders, extra quality, with slides and cast off button, white calf ends and back piece.
Per pair............$0.45
Per dozen..........4.85

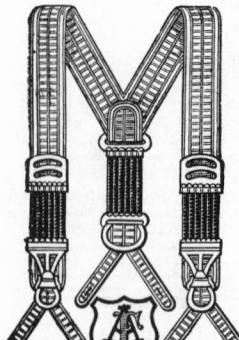

Armstrong Suspenders.

12027 Armstrong Suspenders, plain and fancy, non-elastic web, with duplex patent spiral buckles. See cut.
Per pair.........$0.40
Per doz...... 4.50
12029 Armstrong Suspenders, same as description as No.12027 but better.
Per pair.........$0.50
Per dozen....... 5.50

Pan American Suspenders.

12031 Men's Fine Suspenders. Imitation lace back piece, with silk worked buttonholes, bound ends, silk braid ends and drawer straps; white glove calf backpiece; one pair in box. See cut.
Per pair..........$0.75 Per dozen..............$8.00

Fine Satin Suspenders.

12033 Men's Plain Satin Suspenders, gilt slides, elastic cord ends. Solid colors and black, white or cream. Per pair......$0.50 Per dozen......5.40
12035 Men's Plain Satin Suspenders, satin lined, silk elastic ends. A fine dress suspender; one pair in box, solid colors and black,white or cream
Per pair............................$0.75
Per dozen............................8.10
12037 Men's Fine Satin Embroidered Suspenders; satin lined, silk elastic ends, one pair in box, choice goods,assorted colors, and black or white.
Per pair............................$1.00
Per dozen............................11.00
12039 Men's Fine Satin Embroidered Suspenders in black, white and colors as above, with satin lining and silk elastic ends. These are choice, high grade goods; one pair in box. They will make an elegant present for a gentleman.
Per pair............................$1.35
Per dozen............................ 15.00

12037-39

Montgomery Ward & Co.'s Shoulder Braces.

Front 12041   Back 12043
Per pr. Per doz.

12041 Men's Shoulder Braces and Suspenders combined in one, made of good web, nickel buckles, braid ends, calf trimmings.........................$0.45 $4.85
12043 Men's Shoulder Braces and Suspenders combined, same as above with roller end............................   .45   4.85
12045 Men's shoulder braces, extra quality, silk finish, elastic web, silk laid braided ends and drawer straps. See cut 12041........ 75   8.00

Pratt's Patent Shoulder Braces.

12047
12047 Pratt's Patent Combination Men's Shoulder Braces and Suspenders, assorted sizes, No. 3 being small, No. 4, med., and No.'s 5 and 6 large.......
12049 Pratt's Patent Combination Ladies' Shoulder Braces and Suspenders in assorted sizes, small, med. and large...

	12049 Per pr, Per doz.
$0.75	$8.10
.75	8.10

It costs but $4.00 for each extra inch of width of tire on your wagon.   If you and your neighbors used wide tires you would soon have good roads — no ruts. Narrow tires will spoil any road; they cut like a knife.

Knickerbocker Shoulder Brace.

A Shoulder Brace and Suspender combined.
No harness—simple—unlike all others.
Easily adjusted and worn with comfort.
A gentle or powerful brace is obtained by simply loosening or tightening the buckles.
A perfect skirt supporter for ladies.
The weight of clothes rests mainly upon the shoulders.
Physicians everywhere recommend them.
They promote free respiration of the lungs.
They prevent children from becoming stooped or round shouldered.
They are made to fit properly all sizes of men, women, and children.
In ordering give chest measure entirely around the body under the arms; adults sizes, 32, 34, 36, 38, 40, etc. Youth's sizes (for boys and girls). 24, 26, 28 and 30 inches.
12052 Men's Knickerbocker Shoulder Braces, non elastic web, colored and white. (No. 3.)
Per pair............................$0.60
Per dozen............................6.00
12054 Men's Knickerbocker Shoulder Braces, figured patterns, fine web, colored and white. (No. 2.) Per pair........................ 85
Per dozen............................9.00
12056 Men's Knickerbocker Shoulder Braces, silk faced web, fine, colored and white. Per pair............................1.25
Per dozen............................12.00
12058 Boy's Knickerbocker Shoulder Braces, non-elastic web, colored or white. Per pair.... .60
Per dozen............................6.00
12059 Ladies' Knickerbocker Shoulder Braces. non-elastic web, white only. Improved skirt supporter. Per pair 60
Per dozen............................6.00
12061 Girl's Knickerbocker Shoulder Braces, non elastic web, white only. Improved skirt supporter. Per pair................................60
Per dozen............................6.00

Dr. Gray's Shoulder Braces.

(LADIES' BACK SUPPORTING.)

Full Directions Accompanying Each Brace.

12065 Dr. Gray's Shoulder Braces made in four sizes: extra small waist 16 to 20, small waist 18 to 23, medium waist 24 to 27, large waist 28 to 33.
Medium and large, each. $1.50
Extra small and small, each...... 1.25
Postage... .... .15
2075 Dr. Gray's Back Supporting Shoulder Brace and Suspender for men and boys, high grade goods which possess real merit.

Made in three sizes. Boys' will fit a boy 4 ft. 8 in. to 5 ft. 2 in. tall; 26 to 29 in. waist measure. Price $1.75. Young men's will fit a young man 5 ft. 2 in. to 5 ft. 8 in. tall; 27 to 32 in. waist measure. Price $2.00. Men's will fit a man 5 ft. 8 in. to 6 ft. 2 in. tall; 28 to 34 in. waist measure. Price....$2.25
Postage................................20

Men s and Boys' Silk and Lawn Bows.

12152 Black Silk Shield Bows, for men's and boys' wear.
Each.......5, 10 and 15c.
Per dozen.....50c., $1.00 and $1.50.

12157 Fancy Silk and Satin Shield Bows, for men and boys, assorted colors.
Each.............8c and 12c.
Per dozen...$0.75 and $1.25
Each. Per doz.
12161 White Lawn Shield Bows, small for turndown collars................$0.05 $0.50
12164 White Lawn Shield Bows, finer, with embroidered ends, for turndown collars.............. .... .10   1.00

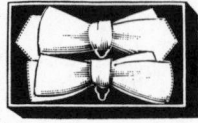

12168 White Lawn Shield Bows, pointed and square ends, two in box.
Each............................$0.15
Per box of two.......... .25
Per dozen.............. 1.40

Neckwear—Continued.

12172 Colored Lawn Shield Bows, two styles; new. (See cut.)
Each.....................$0.13
Per dozen..............1.40

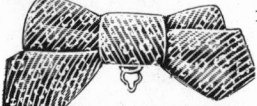

12174 Silk and Satin Fancy Shield Bows, assorted colors and plain black and white.
Each...................$0.20
Per dozen.........2.10

Band Bows, Plain and Embroidered.

12175 Plain White Lawn Bows, with band, two styles, pointed and square ends, small.
Each.......................$0.05
Per dozen..........50
Each. Per doz.

12177 Plain White Lawn Bows, with band, two styles, square and pointed ends, silk stitched, medium size.......$0.08 $0.85

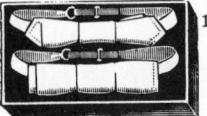

12178 Plain White Lawn Band Bows, two styles.
Each.....................$0.10
Per dozen..............1.00

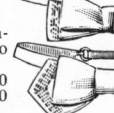

12181 White Lawn Silk Embroidered Band Bows, two styles.
Each $0.10
Per dozen 1.00

12183 White Lawn Silk Embroidered Band Bows, two styles, in box.
Each $0.18
Per box of two..........32
Per dozen..............1.75

12185 White Lawn Silk Embroidered Band Bows, two styles, in box.
Each $0.20
Per box of two........36
Per dozen.............2.00

12187 White Lawn Silk Embroidered Band Bows, two styles, in box.
Each...................$0.20
Per box of two........36
Per dozen.............2.00

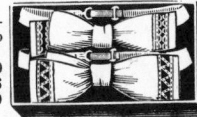

12189 Plain White Lawn Band Bows, two styles, in box.
Each $0.20
Per box of two........36
Per dozen 2.00

Silk, Satin and Lawn Bows.

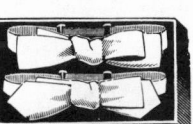

12213 Plain Satin and Gros Grain Silk Band Bows, satin lined in black or white.
Each.............$0.20
Per doz 2.15

12216 Plain Satin and Gros Grain Silk Band Bows, larger size, black or white. Each........$0.25
Per dozen................2.65

12219 Plain Black, Extra Quality Satin and Gros Grain Silk Stock Bows worn by men and ladies.
Each.........$0.40

12221 Silk and Satin Band Bows, assorted colors and black and white.
Each..............$0.25
Per dozen.........2.50

12221

12223 The New Pull Band Bows can be adjusted to suit. In fine assorted silk and satin fancies, also plain black and white.
Each $0.25
Per dozen.. 2.75

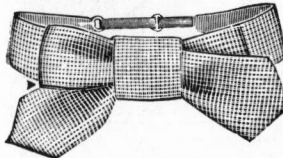

Neckwear—Continued.

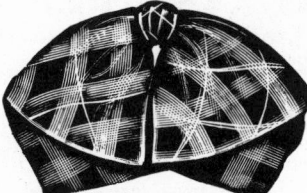

12228 Large Butterfly Silk Bows, with elastic bands; nice for boys.
Each......$0.25
Per dozen, 2.65

Men's Folded String Ties.

This cut represents the ties as they appear when tied on the neck.

12280 Men's Black Folded Gros Grain Silk Ties.
Width ....¾ in.   1 in.
Each..................... $0.15 $0.25
Per dozen................ 1.65   2.70
12283 Light Cotton Print String Tie. Per dozen.............................$0.10
12284 Light Cheviot Printed, Folded String Ties, 1⅛ inch wide. Can be laundered. Each........ .04
Per dozen......................... .45
12286 Light Folded Tubular String Ties, assorted neat styles, 1¼ inch wide. Can be laundered. Each ... ... .13
Per dozen......................... 1.45
12287 Plain White Folded Lawn Ties. Per dozen................................... .10
12289 Plain White Folded Lawn Ties, silk stitched, pointed ends. Per dozen............... .20

Windsor Ties.

	Each.	Per doz.
12301 Windsor Scarfs, fine sateen, black ground, with white stripes or polka dots.............................	.07	.72
12303 Windsor Scarfs, fine sateen, navy blue ground, in stripes and figures	.07	.72
12311 Windsor Scarfs, fine surah silk, assorted.............................	.25	2.70
12313 Windsor Scarfs, suarh silks, solid colors and black, white and cream...	.25	2.70
12315 Fine All Silk Windsor Scarfs, assorted fancies....................	.35	3.75
12320 Extra Fine All Silk Windsor Scarfs, fancy assorted..............	.45	4.30

New Line Japanese Silk Windsors.

FOR LADIES AND GENTLEMEN.

	Each.	Per doz.
12322 Japanese Silk Windsors, fancy light and dark. Size, 4½x34 inches.	.15	1.50
12324 Japanese Silk Windsors, fancy light and dark. Size, 5x36 inches..	.18	1.85
12326 Japanese Silk Windsors, fancy light and dark. Size, 5½x38 inches.	.25	2.70

New Crystal Weave Summer Neckwear.

Cna be laundered.

NOTE—These crystal weaves come in solid or fancy stripe, light, medium and navy blue, pink, cream. black.

12328 Club String Ties, crystal weave, in plain shades and contrasting stripes.
Each.....................................$0.18
Per dozen............................... 1.85

12331 Band Bows, crystal weave, square and pointed ends.
Each........$0.20
Per dozen.... 2.10

Neckwaer—Continued.

12333 Four-in-Hand, Crystal Weave Ties; natty.
Each................ ..$0.25
Per dozen............... 2.56

Summer Neckwear.

12340 Pique Fancy Teck Scarfs, in light, medium and dark shades and plain white. Each........$0.05
Per dozen.......................55
12342 Pique Fancy Teck Scarfs, in light shades. Each...............$0.10   14340-42-44
Per dozen................................ 1.10
12344 White Only, Embossed Teck Scarfs. See cut. Each...............................$0.10
Per dozen. 1.10
12346 Fine Lawn Flowing End Tecks, assorted light and medium shades.
Each.................$0.20
Per dozen.......... 2.10

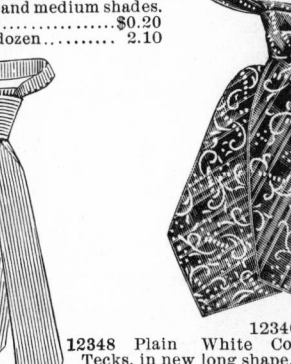

12346

12348 Plain White Corded Pique Tecks, in new long shape. See cut.
Each $0.20
Per dozen....................... 2.10

Four-in-Hand Ties.

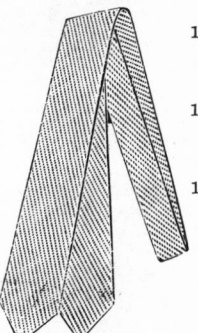

12348

12350 Pique Four-in-Hand Ties, light and medium, assorted and plain white.
Each....................$0.05
Per dozen...............55
12352 New Narrow Four-in-Hand Ties, zephyrs, light and medium; can be laundered.
Each..................$0.15
Per dozen............. 1.50
12354 Plain White Corded Pique Four-in-Hand Ties, square ends; can be laundered. Each....$0.18
Per dozen.............. 1.89

12352

12356 Plain White Corded Pique Scarfs, new graduated shapes; pointed ends; washable. Each....$0.25
Per dozen........... 2.65

12356

12358 White Corded Pique Four-in-Hand Ties, embroidered with silk in contrasting colors.
Each......................$0.20
Per dozen................... 2.10

All orders receive the same attention as if you were at our counters.

Four-in-Hand Silk Ties.

Prices govern quality.
12382 Silk and Satin Four-in-Hand Ties.
Each.................... $0.20
Per dozen 2.15
12384 Silk Four-in-Hand Ties, nice assortment. Each.......... .25
Per dozen 2.50
12388 Silk and Satin Four-in-Hand Ties, satin-lined, fine assortment; also plain black and white.
Each .... .40
Per dozen.... .... 4.25
12392 Silk and Satin Four-in-Hand Ties, graduated and even, all colors, plain shades and black and white.
Each .... .50
Per dozen............. 5.50
12394 New Narrow Plain Black Four-in-Hand Ties, in watered moire, plain gros grain and plain satin. Each.................................. .50
12395 New Narrow Four-in-Hand Ties, in light, medium and dark silk and satin. Each........ $0.50
Per dozen 5.40

Men's Silk and Satin Neckwear. Teck Scarfs.

12425 Silk and Satin Scarfs, finely assorted. Each..$0.20 Per doz..$2.15
12427 Silk and Satin Scarfs, all colors and black. Each..$0.25 Per dozen..$2.65

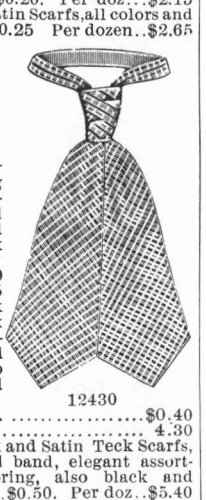

12425-27

12430 Windsorette Flowing Teck Scarf, assorted and black and white; in silk and satin. Each.... $0.30 Per doz. 3.25
12432 Fine Silk and Satin Teck Scarfs, assorted, light and dark, also black and white.
Each $0.40
Per dozen.................. 4.30
12434 Fine Silk and Satin Teck Scarfs, finer, with full band, elegant assortment of coloring, also black and white. Each..$0.50. Per doz..$5.40
12436 New Combination Scarfs, combined in plain and fancies; silk and satin. Each.................. $0.40
Per dozen.................. 4.30

12430

12432-34

12438 De Joinville Teck Scarfs, choice fancy colorings.
Each..$0.50 Per dozen. 5.40

12436

12438

12440 New Double Apron Teck Scarfs, in choice colorings, also black and white. Each.....$0.43
Per dozen.............. 4.75

Puff Scarfs.

12486 Puff Scarfs, fine assorted silks, satin lined, assorted colors and black.
Each.. $0.40

12440   12486

HANDKERCHIEF DEPARTMENT.

Boys' Handkerchiefs.

12495 Boys' White Handkerchiefs, narrow hemstitched, with colored woven border. Each.....$0.09
Per dozen.. .90

Men's Handkerchiefs.

We sell any quantity. Prices govern quality.
12498 Men's Turkey Red Printed Handkerchiefs, good quality.

Size, in inches	16x17	19x20	23x24	28x28
Per dozen	38c.	48c.	60c.	80c.

NOTE.—The above Turkey Red Handkerchiefs are sold by manufacturers and dealers as 18, 21, 24 and 28 inches square, but they are not, so we give actual size rather than mislead in quotations.
12501 Men's White Cotton Brocade Hemmed Handkerchiefs, 18x19; Per dozen $0.45

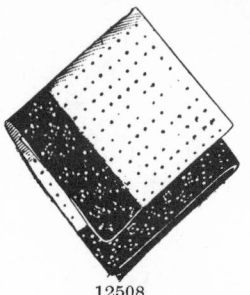

12504 Cotton Brocade Handkerchiefs, white and cream center with red band borders.
Per doz...........$0.45
12505 Men's Indigo Blue Handkerchiefs, hemmed,
Per dozen.........$0.75
12508 Men's Duplex Reversible Handkerchiefs, fine wash twills, white and cream centers, blue borders. Each..$0.09
Per dozen....... .90

12508

Men's Handkerchiefs.

Colored Printed Borders.

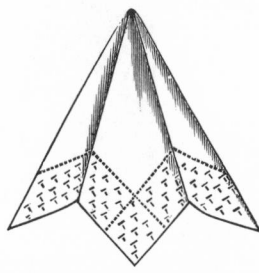

12518 Men's White Hemmed Printed Colored Border Handkerchiefs.
Each..........$0.05
Per dozen....... .55
12520 Men's White Cotton Hemmed Handkerchiefs, with printed colored border.
Each $0.06
Per doz ...... .65

12524 Men's White Hemstitched Handkerchiefs, ½ inch printed assorted borders. Each.........$0.08
Per dozen.. .85
12526 Men's White Hemstitched Handkerchiefs, fancy printed wide borders. Each............... .10
Per dozen.. 1.05
12530 Men's Hemstitched Fine White All Linen Handkerchiefs, printed colored border.
Each.................$0.25 Per dozen....... 2.75

Men's Initial Handkerchiefs.

12533 Men's White Initial Handkerchiefs, 1 inch hemstich.
Each.............$0.25
Per dozen....... 2.70

Men's Plain White Handkerchiefs.

And Hemstitched Handkerchiefs, Cotton and Linen.

	Each.	Per doz.
12534 Men's Hemmed Plain White Cotton Handkerchief	$0.04	$0.40
12536 Men's Hemmed Handkerchiefs, plain white cotton, linen finish	.07	.75
12538 Men's Hemmed Handkerchiefs, plain white cotton, fine and large	.09	.95
12542 Men's Hemstitched Handkerchiefs, plain white cotton, fine and large	.09	.95

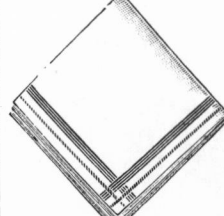

12546 Men's Fine White Hemstitched Handkerchief, 1¾ inch hem.
Each.................$0.12
Per doz....... 1.30

	Each.	Per doz.
12548 Men's Plain White All Linen Hemmed Handkerchiefs	$0.14	$1.50
12550 Men's Plain White All Linen Hemmed Handkerchiefs	.20	2.10
12556 Men's Plain White All Linen Hemmed Handkerchiefs	.25	2.85
12567 Men's Plain White All Linen Hemstitched Handkerchiefs	.25	2.70
12571 Men's Plain White All Linen Hemstitched Handkerchiefs	.35	3.75

New Japonette Handkerchiefs.

	Each.	Per doz.
12581 Fine Imitation Silk Handkerchiefs, hemstitched, cream color only; a soft wash handkerchief	$0.15	$1.65

Ladies' Plain White Handkerchiefs Hemmed and Stitched.

	Each.	Per doz.
12600 Ladies' Plain White All Linen Hemmed Handkerchiefs	$0.05	$0.60
12603 Ladies' Plain White Cotton Hemstitched Handkerchiefs	.05	.55
12605 Ladies' Fine White Hemstitched Handkerchiefs, soft finish	.10	1.00
12607 Ladies' Linen Hemstitched Handkerchiefs, plain white, ½-inch hem	.10	1.10
12608 Ladies' Plain White All Linen Hemstitched Handkerchiefs	.13	1.45
12610 Ladies' All Linen, Narrow and Revere Handkerchiefs	.13	1.45
12613 Ladies' Plain White All Linen Hemstitched Handkerchiefs	.18	1.95
12615 Ladies' Plain White All Linen Hemstitched Handkerchiefs	.25	2.65

Handkerchiefs, White with Colored Printed Borders.

12620 Ladies' or Children's Handkerchiefs, white with colored printed border.
Per doz........$0.30
12626 Ladies' Hemmed Printed Border Handkerchiefs.
Per doz........$0.35
12628 Ladies' Hemstitched Printed Border Handkerchiefs.
Per doz........$0.50

12638 Ladies' Hemstitched Printed Bordered Handkerchiefs.
Each..................$0.07
Per doz................ .75
12644 Ladies' Wide Hemstitched Fine Printed Border, Mull Handkerchiefs.
Each..................$0.10
Per dozen.............. 1.10

12645 Children's Handkerchiefs, white with assorted fancy pictures.
Each...............$0.03
Per doz............. .30

Just Out. The Brownie Handkerchief.

12646 Brownie H'dkfs. for the children; printed in fast colors on the finest lawn, in six designs, two of each, but like designs are different in color so that no two in a dozen are alike. Each set of six hdkfs. has 37 of the principal figures of the Brownie Band. Per dozen.............................. ....60c.

Handkerchiefs—Continued.

12648 White Hemstitch Handkerchief, with printed colored border and silk embroidered flower in one corner. See cut.
Each.........$0.08
Per doz.......85

12660 Ladies' Scalloped Edge, Fancy Colored Print Border Handkerchiefs.
Each.........$0.07
Per dozen...........75

Black Border Handkerchiefs.

12663 Ladies' Black Print Borders Scalloped Edge Handkerchiefs.
Each.............$0.07
Per dozen...........75

12666 Ladies' Hemstitched Handkerchiefs, white with assorted black borders. Each.............$0.12
Per dozen...........1.30

Ladies' Embroidered Handkerchiefs

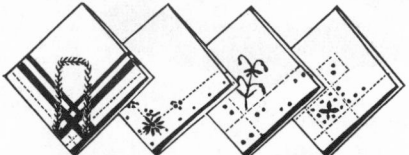

12669 Ladies' White and Colored, Hemstitched Handkerchiefs, Embroidered in 4 corners, assorted patterns. Each.............$0.07
Per dozen...........75
12675 Ladies' White Embroidered Handkerchiefs, hemstitch. 7 patterns. Each...................12
Per dozen...................1.30

12696 Ladies' White Embroidered Handkerchiefs, with fast scalloped edges, embroidered in white. Very neat and showy and special value; assorted patterns
Each..........$0.10
Per dozen......1.10

White Embroidered Handkerchiefs.

SPECIAL VALUES

12708 White Scalloped Edge Embroidered Handkerchiefs. 10 patterns.
Each..........$0.15
Per dozen.....1.65
12710 White All Linen Handkerchiefs, Scalloped and Embroidered, 6 patterns.
Each..........$0.25
Per dozen....2.70

Handkerchiefs—Continued.

12712 White Mull Handkerchiefs, with delicate tinted border and French Val. lace edge.
Each.............$0.15
Per dozen..........1.65

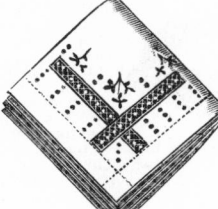

12716 Ladies' Fine White Hemstitched Handkerchief, embroidered in four corners and with French Val. lace inserting.
Each.............$0.25
Per dozen..........2.70

Ladies' Initial Handkerchiefs.

12718 Ladies' White Initial Handkerchiefs, half inch hemstitch.
Each.............$0.10
Per dozen..........1.10
12722 Ladies' White Initial Handkerchief, all linen, one inch hemstitch.
Each.............$0.25
Per dozen.........2.70

Silk Embroidered Handkerchiefs.

Assorted Patterns.

12735 Embroidered Japanese Silk Handkerchiefs in plain, white and colored tints.
Each...........$0.10
Per dozen.....1.10

12737 Embroidered Japanese Revere Silk Handkerchiefs, in plain white and colored tints.
Each...........$0.14
Per dozen.........1.50

12739 Embroidered Japanese Silk Handkerchiefs, in plain white and colored tints.
Each.........$0.20
Per dozen.....2.15

12740 Embroidered Japanese Silk Handkerchiefs, with and without revere, in plain white and colored tints.
Each.............$0.25
Per dozen.........2.70

Ladies' Initial Handkerchiefs.

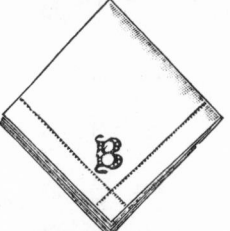

12751 Japanese White Silk Handkerchiefs, size, 14x14 inches with hemstitch and silk embroidered initial.
Each.............$0.25
Per dozen..........2.70

Men's Initial Handkerchiefs.

12755 White Japanese Initial Silk Handkerchief, 19 inches with 1½ inch hemstitch.
Each.........$0.43
Per doz.......4.75

12759 Initial Handkerchiefs, fine white Japanese silk, 1½ inch hemstitch, 22 inches square.
Each.........$0.68
Per dozen.......7.65
NOTE—Initial handkerchiefs come in all letters except I, O, Q, U, V, X, Y, and Z.

Japanese Silk Handkerchiefs.
(For Ladies, Men and Children.)

12761 Japanese Silk Handkerchiefs, plain white. 1½ inch hemstich.

Size	20 in	22 in
Each	$0.40	$0.45
Per dozen	4.00	4.75

12763 Japanese Silk Handkerchiefs, plain white twilled, fine quality, 1½ inch hemstitch.

Size	20 in.	22 in.	24 in.
Each	$0.55	$0.65	$0.75
Per dozen	6.00	7.00	8.10

12765 Japanese Silk Handkerchiefs, plain white, fine, extra quality, 1 inch hemstitch.

Size	20 in.	22 in.	24 in.
Each	$0.65	$0.75	$0.85
Per dozen	7.00	8.10	9.25

12770 Japanese Silk Handkerchiefs, plain black, 20 inch with 1½ inch hemstitch. Each.........$0.50
Per dozen.....................5.50

Brocade Silk Handkerchiefs.

12785 Brocade Silk Hdkfs. in assorted colors. Each.$0.20
Per dozen.....2.15
12788 Brocade Silk Handkerchiefs, assorted colors with contrasting stripes for border
Each.........$0.30
Per dozen...3.25

12790 Brocade Silk Handkerchiefs, 2-toned effects and solid colors.
Each......$0.40
Per dozen..4.25
12792 Brocade Silk Handkerchiefs, 2-toned effects and solid colors, extra quality.
Each.............$0.65   Per dozen...........$7.00

USE THE WM. CLARK CO.'S "N-E-W" SIX CORD SPOOL COTTON.

Mufflers.

MUFFLERS, ALL GRADES, FOR LADIES, MEN AND CHILDREN

	Each.	Per dozen.
12795 Cream Cotton Mufflers, with contrasting printed dots	$0.13	$1.40
12798 Duplex Indigo Blue Mufflers, 33 in. square, fast colors	.20	2.15
12803 Colored Mufflers, wool effects, in plaids and stripes, in dark combination colors	.25	2.70
12805 Mufflers, wool effects in plaids, medium colors	.32	3.60
12813 Assorted Dark Mufflers, silk mixed, and black and white, and gray and white mixed	.45	4.90

Silk Mufflers.

12835 All Silk Brocade Mufflers in solid cream, black, steel mixed and assorted colors.
Each $0.87
Per dozen 9.35
12840 All Silk Brocade Mufflers in solid black and cream.
Each .... $ 1.15
Per dozen 12.00
12848 All Silk Brocade Mufflers in solid cream and black, fine quality.
Each $1.50
Per dozen 16.20
12852 All Silk Brocade Mufflers in solid cream or black only, fine quality.
Each $2.00
Per dozen 22.00

LADIES' BELTS.

Always Mention Waist Measure When Ordering Belts.

13002 Black Velvet Belt, cloth lined, two inches wide; fancy oxidized buckle. Each $0.15
Per dozen 1.50
Postage, 8 cents.

13004 Fancy Embossed Calf "Melba" Belt, with lower edge notched to fit over skirt band; 2 inches wide; fancy embossed metal buckle; tan, in sizes 24 to 32 inches; black, in sizes 24 to 38 inches.
Each $0.25
Postage, 8 cents.

13006 Fancy Embossed Calf "Melba" Belt, lower edge notched to fit over skirt band; 2½ inches wide; two prong buckle; tan, in sizes 24 to 32 inches; black, in sizes 24 to 38 inches. Each. $0.35
Postage, 10 cents.

13008 Fancy Perforated Calf "Melba" Belt, lower edge notched to fit over skirt-band; 2½ inches wide; two prong buckle. Sizes, 24 to 30 inches in tan or black. Each $0.35
Postage, 10 cents.

13010 Seal Grained Calf "Melba" Belt, with lower edge notched to fit over skirt band; 2½ inches; wide; fancy silvered metal buckle, black only, in sizes 24 to 38 inches. Each $0.45
Postage, 10 cents.

Ladies' Belts—Continued.

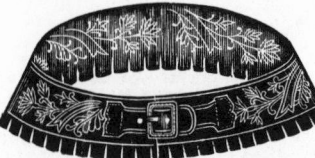

13012 Fine Fancy Embossed Calf "Melba" Belt, with lower edge notched to fit over skirt band; 3½ inches wide; shield strap and buckle, tan or black, in sizes 24 to 32 inches. Each $0.50
Postage, 10 cents.

13014 Fine Calf "Calve" Belt, shaped to fit over skirt band; front studded with cut steel point ornaments; edges pinked and perforated, square buckles, tan, in sizes 24 to 32 inches, black, 24 to 38 inches.
Each $0.55
Postage, 10 cents.

13016 Seal Grained Calf "Calve" Belt, shaped to fit over skirt band, fancy silvered metal ornament on front, square buckles, black only. in sizes 24 to 38 inches. Each $0.55
Postage, 10 cents.

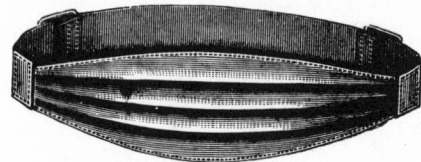

13018   13020 and   13026

13018 Fine Calf Sash Belt with two square nickeled buckles; tan only, 24 to 30 *inches*. Weight packed, 8 ounces. Each $0.45
13020 Seal Grain Calf Sash Belt with two square buckles; black only: *24 to 30 inches.* Weight, packed, 8 ounces. Each .... .45

Men's Leather Belts.

13026 Men's Fine Calf Sash Belt, tan only; two rings and square buckle. Lengths up to 42 inches. *Mention waist measure* when ordering. Weight, packed, 10 ounces. Each $0.60

13028 Boy's or Men's Solid Calf Ring Belt, 2 inches wide; tan only, in sizes 26 to 42 inches.
Mention waist measure when ordering. Each.... $0.25
Postage, 10 cents.

13030 Men's Fine Grained Calf Ring Belt, with leather covered buckle and rings; two inches wide tan only, in sizes 32 to 42 inches. *Mention waist measure* when ordering. Each $0.55
Postage, 10 cents.

13032 Men's Fine Calf Ring Belt, with leather covered two-prong buckle and rings; 2½ inches wide; tan only, in sizes 32 to 42 inches. *Mention waist measure* when ordering. Each $0.60
Postage, 10 cents.

Ladies' Web Belts.

A NEW AND ATTRACTIVE LINE.

13039 and 13041

13039 Ladies' Silk Web Belt, 2 inches wide; fancy embossed silvered metal buckle. Cardinal, cream, navy blue, in sizes 24 to 32 inches; black, 24 to 40 inches. Each $0.25
Postage, 3 cents.

13041 Ladies' Silk Web Belt, 2½ inches wide; fancy embossed silvered metal buckle. Cardinal, cream, navy blue, in sizes 24 to 32 inches; black, 24 to 40 inches. Each $0.35
Postage, 4 cents.

13043 and 13045

13043 Ladies' Fine Ottoman Silk Belt, 2 inches wide with handsome silvered buckle. Cardinal, cream, navy blue, black, in sizes 24 to 32 inches.
Each $0.40
Postage, 4 cents.

13045 Ladies' Fine Ottoman Silk Web Belt 2½ inches wide, with handsome silvered buckle. Cardinal, cream, navy blue, black, in sizes 24 to 32 inches. Each $0.45
Mention waist measure to avoid delay in filling order.

13047— Ladies' Fine Silk Web Belt, 2½ inches wide, handsome silvered buckle. Cardinal, cream, navy blue, black, in sizes 24 to 32 inches.
Each $0.50
Postage, 4 cents.

13049 Ladies' Fine All Silk Web Belt, 2½ inches wide, with fine handsome buckle; black only, in sizes 24 to 32 inches. Each $0.65
Postage, 4 cents.

13051 Belt and 13057 Buckle.

13051 Ladies' Fine Silk Web Belt, 2 inches wide, with extra fine platinum-bronze buckle, which is *guaranteed not to tarnish or discolor*, and is more durable than sterling silver; black only, in sizes 24 to 32 inches. Each $0.95
Postage, 5 cents.

Materials for Ladies' Belts.

13057 Extra Fine Platinum-Bronze Belt Buckle, guaranteed not to tarnish or discolor, and more durable than sterling silver, highly embossed and finished. See 13051 illustration.
Each $0.75
Postage, 4 cents.

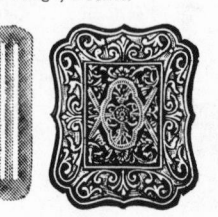

13059 Extra Fine Platinum-Bronze Belt Buckle, superior to sterling silver for strength and durability: guaranteed not to tarnish or discolor; highly embossed and finished.
Each. ... $0.85

Belt Materials—Continued.

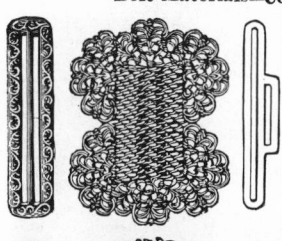

13061 Fine Silvered Belt Buckle, very handsomely embossed and finished. Each........$0.35

13063 Fine Silvered Belt Buckle, with satin finished etched center. Each......$0.30

13065 Ladies' Belt Buckle, gilt silvered finish, handsomely embossed pattern. Each......$0.25

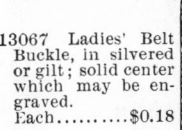

13067 Ladies' Belt Buckle, in silvered or gilt; solid center which may be engraved. Each.........$0.18

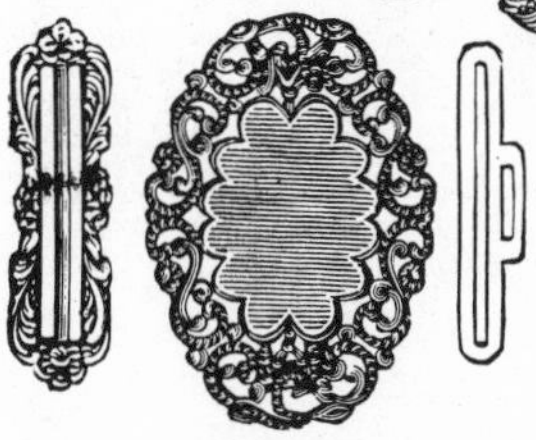

13069 Ladies' Fancy Belt Buckle, gilt or silvered finish. Each..........$0.12

13071 Ladies' Fancy Belt Buckle, silvered or gilt finish. Each.........$0.08

13077 Ladies' Fancy Belt Pins, in gilt, silvered or black finish; assorted styles. Each.........$0.05

13079 Ladies' Fancy Belt Pins, in gilt or silvered finish; assorted styles. Each.........$0.08

13081 Ladies' Heavy Silvered Finish Belt Pins, satin finish, plain or fancy. Each.........$0.12

13083 Ladies' Sterling Silver Belt Pins, satin or bright finish, plain or fancy. Each.........$0.35

"Holdfast" Belt Attachment.

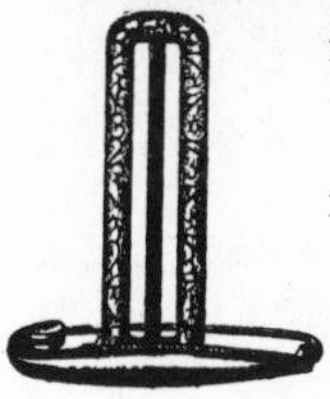

13085 "Holdfast" Belt Attachment, combining slide and belt pin, fancy embossed, silvered finish, for 2-inch webbing. Each.........$0.08

13087 "Holdfast" Belt Attachment, for 2½-inch webbing, otherwise same as 13085. Each.........$0.10

Webbings for Ladies' Belts.

Important to remember: that beltings cut according to your order *cannot be returned.*

Always allow one quarter yard in addition to waist measure when ordering belting, as that much is necessary for hemming and taking up on the slide.

13089 "Infanta" Novelty Belting, a fancy webbing interwoven with gilt tinsel thread, 2 inches wide; in cream, cardinal, navy blue, black. Allow quarter yard in addition to waist measure, when ordering. Per yard.........$0.15

13091 Fine Silk Web Belting, 2 inches wide, colors: Cardinal, cream,navy blue, black; allow quarter yard in addition to waist measure when ordering. Per yard.........$0.20

13093 Fine Silk Web Belting, 2½ inches wide; colors: cardinal, cream, navy blue, black, allow quarter yard in addition to waist measure when ordering. Per yard.........25

13095 Extra Fine All Silk Web Belting, 2 inches wide; colors: Cardinal,cream, navy blue, black; allow quarter yard in addition to waist measure when ordering. Per yard.........0.25

13097 Extra Fine All Silk Web Belting, 2½ inches wide; colors: Cardinal,cream, navy blue, black; allow one quarter yard in addition to waist measure when ordering. Per yard.........0.35

Ladies' Shopping Bags.

NOTICE.—We are out of all bags not quoted in this catalogue, and cannot obtain them, as they are no longer manufactured, and we will be obliged to substitute from our present stock on all orders for bags selected from former catalogues.

13099 Ladies' Shopping Bag, of seal grained cloth leatherette, with large outside pocket trimmed with leather and three oxidized ornaments; sateen top with drawing strings; two leather handles; size, 9¾x9¾. Weight, packed, 17 ounces. Each.........$0.43

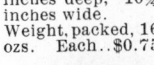

13103 Ladies' Shopping Bag, of seal grain cloth leatherette, bound all around with silk gimp cord, one large and 2 small outside pockets with oxidized catches; sateen top with drawing strings; 2 leather handles; 10¼ inches deep, 10¼ inches wide. Weight, packed, 16 ozs. Each..$0.75

13105 Ladies' Shopping Bag, of seal grain leather, with rounded bottom and ends, two leather handles; sateen top with drawing strings; size, 10 x 10 x 2¾. A handsome and roomy bag. Weight, packed, 18 ounces. Each.........$1 00

13108 Ladies' Shopping Bag of seal grain leather with rounded bottom and ends, large gusseted outside pocket with oxidized catch; two leather handles; sateen top with drawing strings. Size, 10 x10x2¾. A stylish, handsome and roomy bag. Weight, packed, 20 ozs. Each..$1.25

OUTING FLANNELS

GROW PRETTIER EACH SEASON.

Our New Stock Excels Them All.

SEND FOR SAMPLES.

Shopping Bags—Continued.

13116 Shopping Bags, extra fine calf,Suede finish, pinked edges, silk stitched all around; size, 8¼x11½ inches, with silk gimp drawing cords. Color: Mouse (or drab). Handsome and very durable. Weight, 5 ounces. Each.........$0.93

13117 Shopping Bags, extra fine calf, Suede finish; size,9½x12½ inches. Colors: Mouse (or drab), purple, brown; otherwise same as 13116. Weight, 6 ounces. Each.........$1.40

13118 Shopping Bags, extra fine calf, Suede finish, pinked edges, silk stitched all around; size, 8¼x11½ inches, silk gimp drawing cords; No. 5C, mouse color, with fine stripe, imitating corduroy. Very handsome, stylish and durable. Weight, 5 ounces. $1.45

13116-17-18

Ladies' Chatelaine Bags.

13122 Misses' Chatelaine Bag, of black lizard grained leather with oxidized frame, with ball catch, nickeled chains and belt hook; size, 4x4. Weight, packed, 5 ounces. Each.........$0.25

13124 Ladies' Chatelaine Bag of seal grained leather; size, 5½x5; black japanned riveted frame with nickeled spring catch, leather straps and belt hook. Weight, packed, 10 ounces. Each.........$0.50

13125 Ladies' Chatelaine Bag of lizard grained leather, cloth lined; size, 5½x5½; black riveted frame with patented nickeled catch, leather covered belthook and straps. Weight, packed, 11 ounces. Each.........$0.65

13127 Ladies' Chatelaine Bag of seal grained leather with outside pocket, black riveted frame with patented nickeled catch; size, 5¾x5¼; inside pocket, leather lined, leather covered belt-hook with swinging ring, leather straps. Weight, packed, 9 ounces. Each.........$0.80

13128 Ladies' Cleopatra Bag of seal grained leather with flap and oxidized catch; gusseted all around; size,5½x5¾; leather covered belt hook, leather straps; inside pocket; cloth lined. Weight, packed, 10 ounces. Until sold, each..$1.00

13129 Ladies' Chateline Bag of fine Vienna calf leather, with leather covered riveted frame, nickeled spring catch; size, 5½x5½; leather lined; inside pocket; leather covered belthook with swinging ring; leather straps. Weight, packed, 11 ounces. Each.........$1.50

Ladies' Pocket Books.

NOTICE.—Our pocket books are selected from the best makes in the country, and we are prepared to offer the latest and best styles and qualities in the market at very reasonable prices.

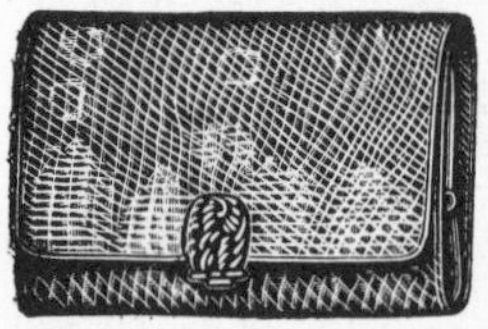

13132 Light American Lizard Grained Leather with silvered catch, leather-faced flap, cloth lined, coin pocket with snap frame, and four regular pockets. Size, 2¾x4. Weight, packed, 4 ounces. Each..$0.25

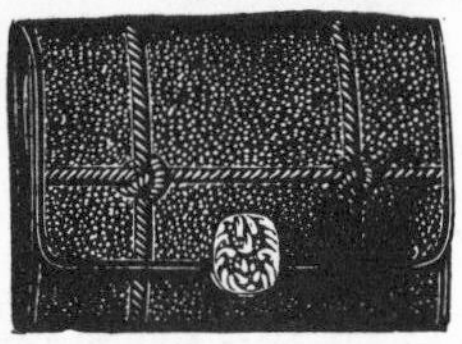

13134 Embossed Morocco Grain Leather with silvered catch and two ornaments on flap, leather faced, coin pocket with snap frame and four regular pockets. Size, 2½x4 inches. Weight, packed, 4 ounces. Each....$0.25

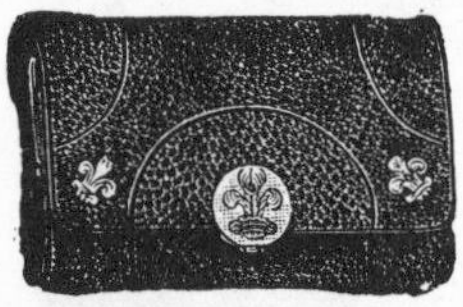

13143 Seal Grain Leather, embossed, silvered catch and two ornaments on flap, leather faced and lined, four regular pockets and coin pocket with nickeled snap frame. Size, 2⅝ x 4½ inches. Each..............$0.50

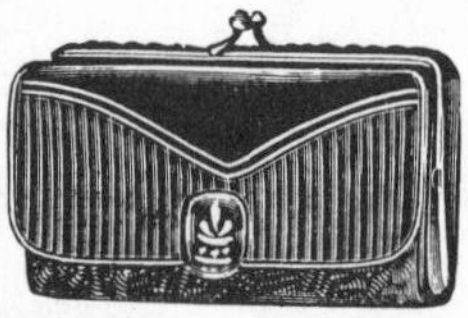

13145 Seal Grain Leather with fancy embossed fine calf flap; oxidized catch, outside card pocket and coin pocket with fancy nickeled frame, two regular pockets under flap; size, 2¾x 4½ inches. Each...........$0.50

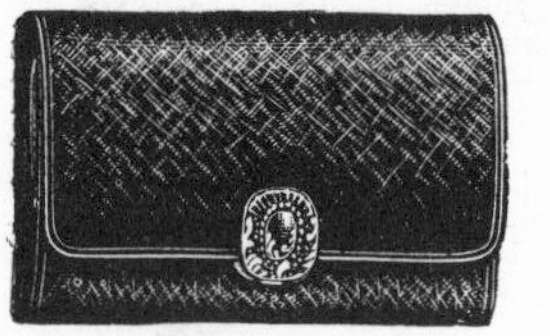

13149 Colored Grained Calf Leather, with silvered catch; leather faced and lined, four regular pockets and coin pocket with nickeled snap frame; size, 2¾ x4½ inches. Each...........$0.65 Postage .... .05

Ladies' Combination Pocket Books.

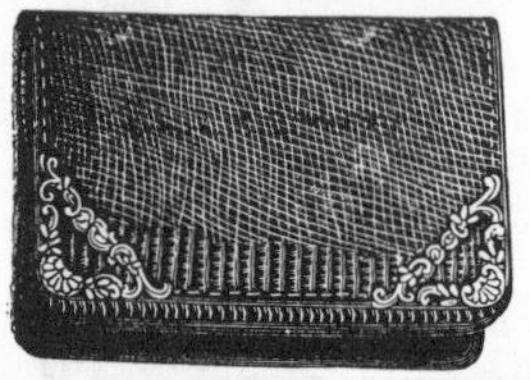

13152 Light American Lizard Grained Leather, silver metal corners, card pocket in flap, coin-pocket with snap-frame, and three regular pockets. 2¾ x4⅛ inches. Weight, packed, 3 ounces. Each..........$0.25

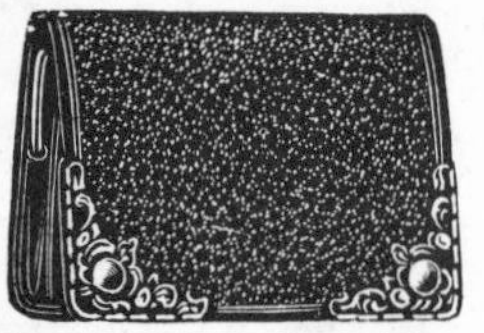

13155 Seal Grained Leather, with silvered metal corners, leather-faced card pocket in flap, coin pocket with snap frame and three regular pockets. Size, 2¾x4⅛ inches. Weight, packed, 3 ounces. Each $0.25

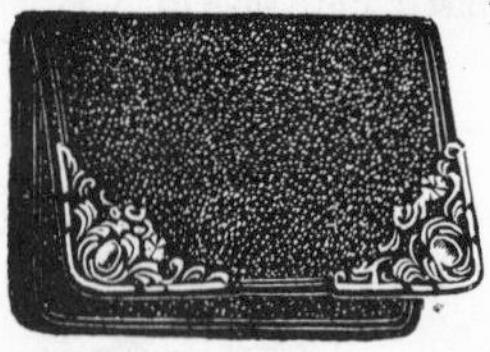

13157 Seal Grain Leather, with large oxidized corners, gusseted pocket with flap and tuck, and regular card pocket, coin pocket with snap frame, and two regular pockets. Size, 3x4½ inches. Weight, 4 packed, ounces. Each...$0.50

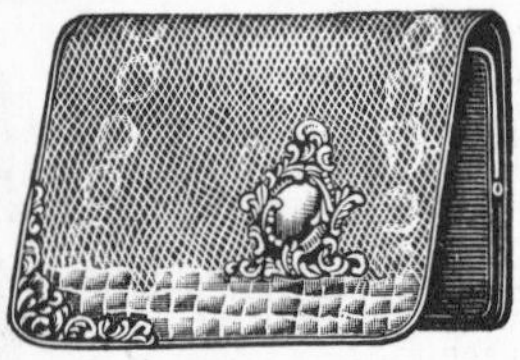

13159 Light American Lizard Grained Leather with large gilt corner and fancy ornaments on flap, leather faced and lined, one regular card pocket and one gusseted, with flap and tuck; coin pocket with snap frame, and two regular pockets. 3⅛x4½ inches. Weight, packed, 4 ounces. Each.....................................$0.50

Pocket Books—Continued.

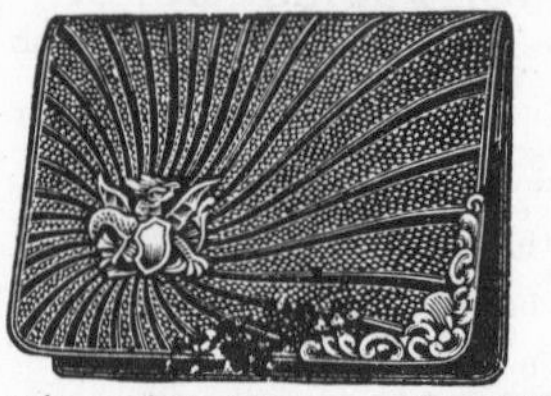

13161 Fancy Embossed Morocco Grain Leather, with large oxidized corner and fancy ornaments on flap, leather faced and lined, one regular card pocket and one gusseted, with flap and tuck; coin pocket with snap frame and two regular pockets. 3⅛x4½ inches. Weight, packed, 4 ounces. Each...$0.50

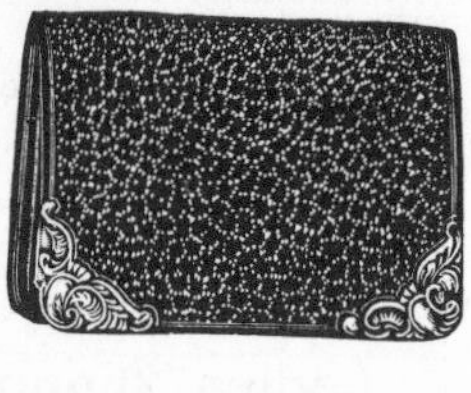

13163 Real Seal Leather, with sterling silver corner ornaments; leather faced and lined; regular card pocket and one gusseted, with flap and tuck; coin pocket with fine snap frame and two regular pockets; 3⅛x4½ inches. Weight, packed, 4 ounces. Each.............$0.85

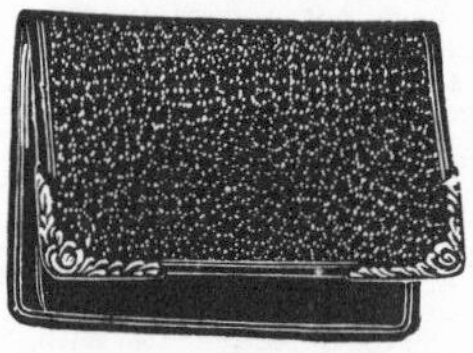

13166 Fine Genuine Seal Leather, with genuine sterling silver corners; leather faced; card pocket with flap and one regular card pocket; coin pocket with nickeled snap frame and two regular pockets. Size, 3x4½ inches. Weight, packed, 4 oz. Each $1.10

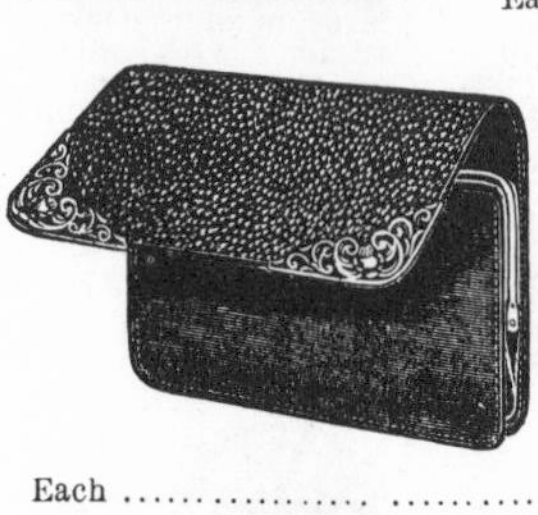

13168 Extra Fine Colored Vienna Calf Leather, with genuine sterling silver corners; faced with smooth calf; card pocket with flap and one regular card pocket; coin pocket with nickeled snap frame and two regular pockets; size, 3x 4½ inches. Weight, packed, 4 oz. Each $1.30

Card Cases.

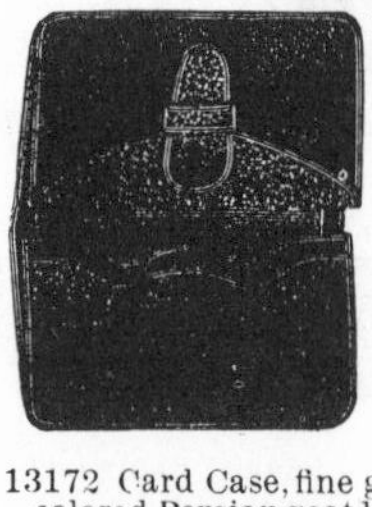

13170 Card Case of seal grain leather, faced with same; size, 2¾x4½ inches; two regular and two gusseted pockets. Weight, packed, 3 ounces. Each.............. ....$0.47

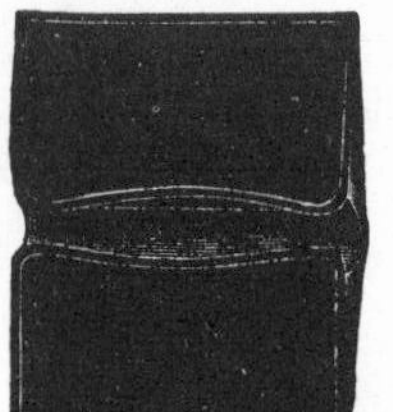

13172 Card Case, fine grained colored Persian goat leather, faced with same; size, 2¾x 4½ inches; two gusseted pockets. Weight, packed, 3 oz. Each $0.55

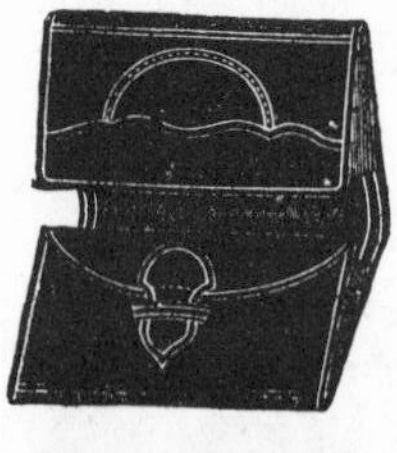

13174 Card Case of pebbled grain leather; vest pocket size, 2⅝x4½; leather faced and lined; one regular and two gusseted pockets, and three stamp pockets. Weight, packed, 3 ounces. Each....................$0.50

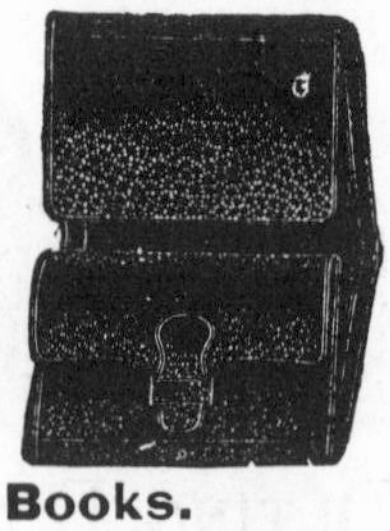

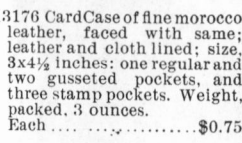

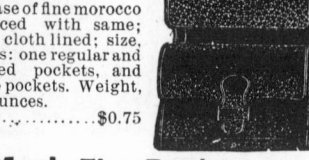

13176 Card Case of fine morocco leather, faced with same; leather and cloth lined; size, 3x4½ inches; one regular and two gusseted pockets, and three stamp pockets. Weight, packed, 3 ounces. Each.... ....$0.75

Men's Flap Books.

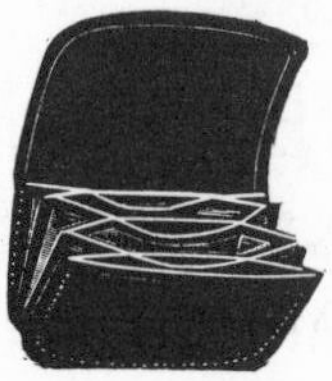

13181 Men's Flap Book of fine, smooth calf, bound and stitched all around, leather faced; four regular and three small, all leather pockets. Size, 2⅝x4½. Weight, packed, 4 ounces. Each..............................$0.50

Pocket Books—Continued.

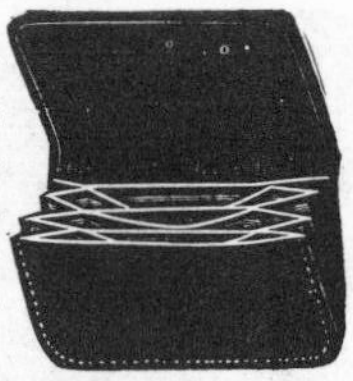

13183 Men's Flap Book of Real Russia Leather, bound and stitched all around; leather faced flap; four regular and three smaller all leather pockets. Size, 2⅝x4¼ inches. A very handsome and durable book. Weight, packed, 4 ounces. Each.............................$0.60

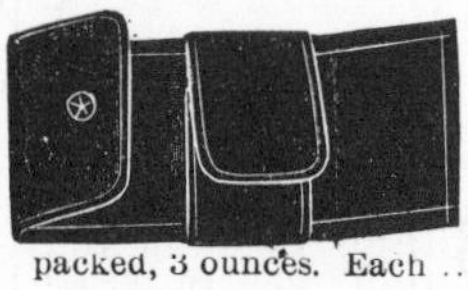

13186 Men's Bill Holder or Boodle Book, of morocco grained leather, faced and lined with leather; two flaps for holding bills. Size, closed, 2⅞x3½ inches; button lock on flap. Weight; packed, 3 ounces. Each $0.40

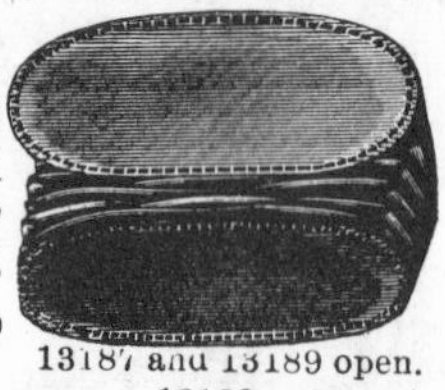

13187 and 13189 open.

13187 Men's Patent Box Flap Book of seal grained leather, with outside card pocket: five regular and four smaller cloth pockets, bound and stitched; size, 2⅝x4 inches. Weight, packed, 3 ounces. Each..................$0.40

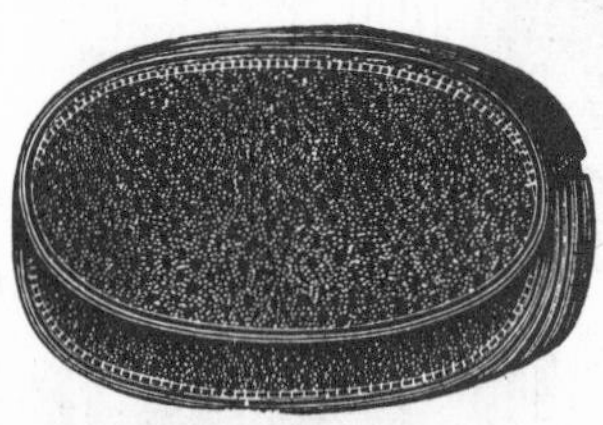

13187 and 13189 closed.

13189 Men's Patent Box Flap of seal grained leather with outside card pocket; five regular and four smaller sateen pockets, bound and stitched; size, 2⅞x4½ inches. Weight, packed, 4 ounces. Each... .$0.55

Men's Strap Books.

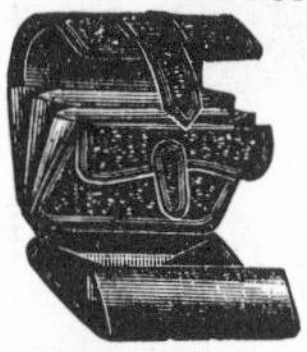

13190-13192

13190 Colored Morocco Leather size, 2⅝x4½ inches; leather faced; three small and four regular *all leather* pockets, bound and stitched, and bill fold. Weight, packed, 4 ounces. Each............ $0.55

13192 Extra Fine Calf, size, 2⅝x4⅝ inches, leather faced; four regular and three smaller *all leather* pockets, bound and stitched, bellows style; card pocket and bill fold with flap and tuck strap. Each..................................$0.95 Postage.. .04

Men's Sheep and Calf Books.

Natural Colors.

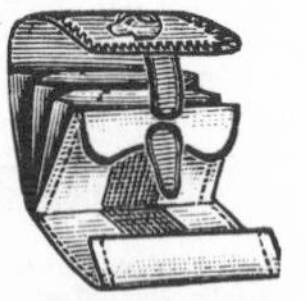

13207 Sheep (calf finish) stamped, size, 2¾x4¾, stitched all around; leather faced flap, cloth lined, 4 pockets and bill fold. Weight, packed, 3 ounces. Each................................$0.17

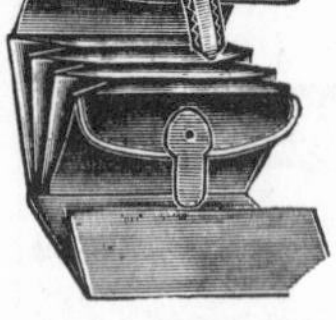

13208 Heavy Sheep, calf finish, size, 2¾x4¾, stitched all around; leather faced, cloth lined; *coin pocket* and four regular pockets and bill fold. Weight, packed, 4 ounces. Each..............$0.25

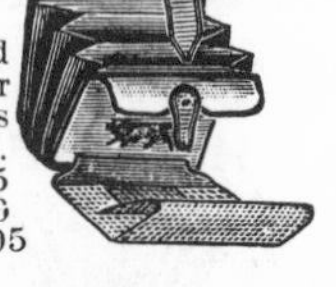

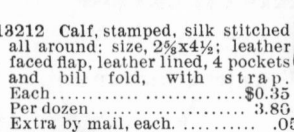

13212 Calf, stamped, silk stitched all around; size, 2⅝x4½; leather faced flap, leather lined, 4 pockets and bill fold, with strap. Each........... ....$0.35 Per dozen..................... 3.80 Extra by mail, each. .... .05

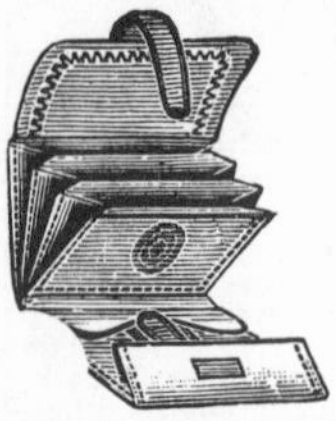

13218 Size, 2⅝x4½, calf (all leather), stamped, silk stitched, 3 small and 4 regular bellows pockets, drop bill fold, with flap and tuck strap. Each .... $0.50 Postage......................... .04

Have your Mail Packages Insured.
See Page 1.

Pocket Books—Continued.

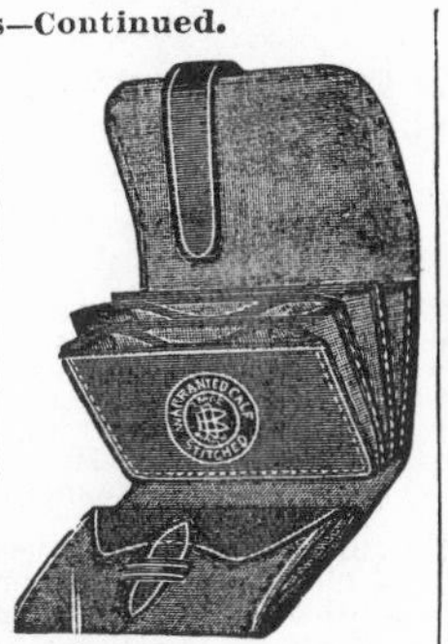

13222 Extra Fine Eng'ish Finish Calf (all leathe), securely stitched; faced with white kid; 3 small and 4 regular white lambskin bellows pockets, bound and stitched and drop bill fold with flap and strap. Size, 2¾x4¾ inches. Weight, packed, 4 ounces. Each.......$0.75

Hip-Pocket Books.

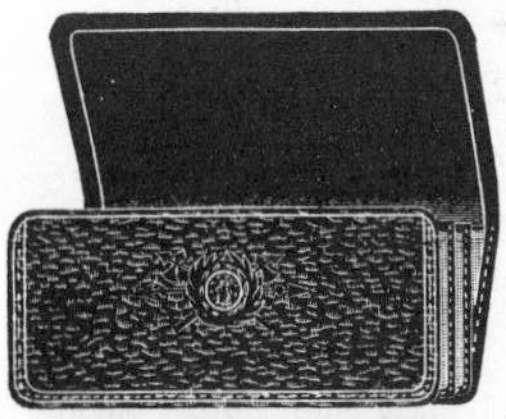

13242 Hip-Pocket Book of seal grained leather with button lock; size, 3 x 6½ inches; canvas faced; four regular and three smaller canvas pockets, bound and stitched, bellows style; weight, packed, 4 ounces. Each...........$0.25

Bill Books.

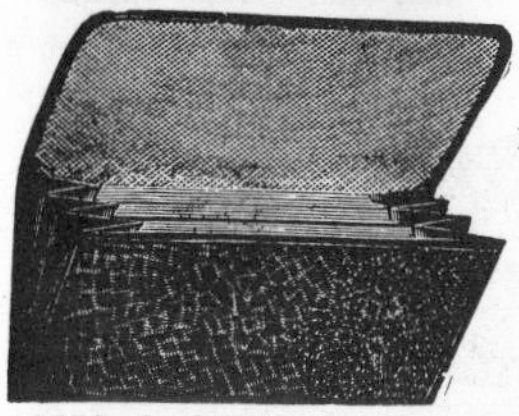

13250 Seal Grain Leather Bill Book, size 3½x8 inches; cloth faced and lined, four pockets.
Each $0.17
Postage .... .05

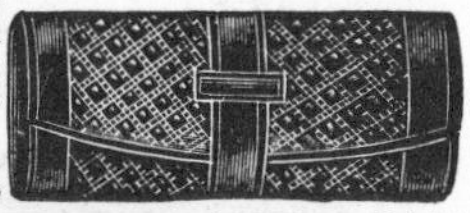

13253 Seal Grain Leather with plain corners and tuck strap; size, 3⅜x8; inches cloth faced and lined. four pockets. Weight, packed, 5 ounces. Each $0.25

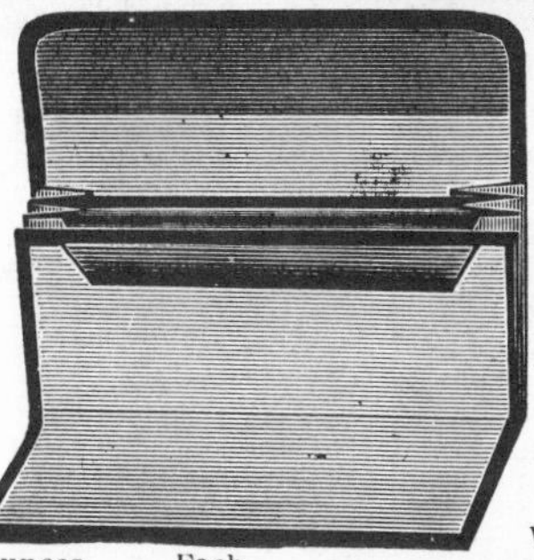

13258 Bill Book of American Russia leather, denominational style, with cardboard leaves for separating one, two, five, ten, twenty and fifty-dollar bills; one regular gusseted pocket and one ticket pocket; cloth and canvas faced; size, 3¾x8 inches. Weight, packed, 6 ounces. Each $0.45

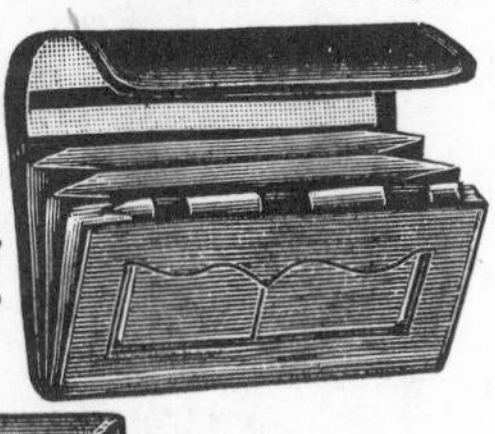

13262 Colored grained leather, size, 3⅝x8 in.; canvas faced, cloth lined; four regular pockets and two stamp pockets; lead pencil and memorandum book,
Each..............$0.40
Postage........... .05

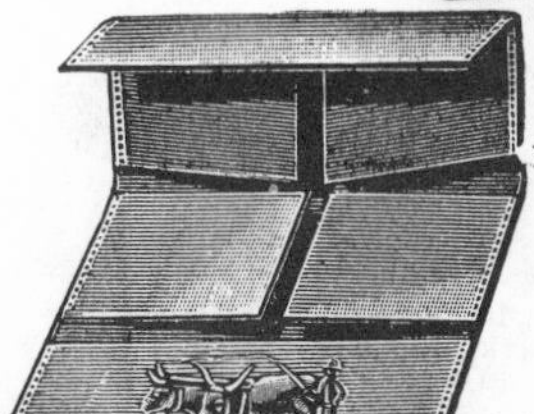

13265 English Finish Sheep, three fold style, *all leather*, size, 4x8 inches; two bill folds in center; two pockets.
Each...........$0.50
Postage .... .04

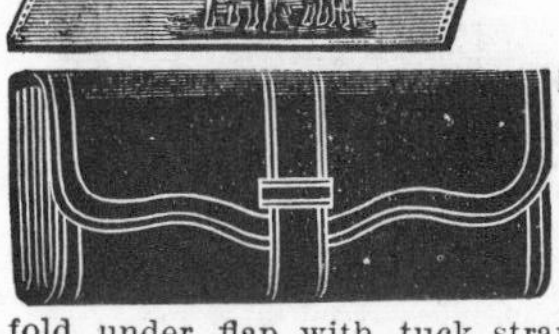

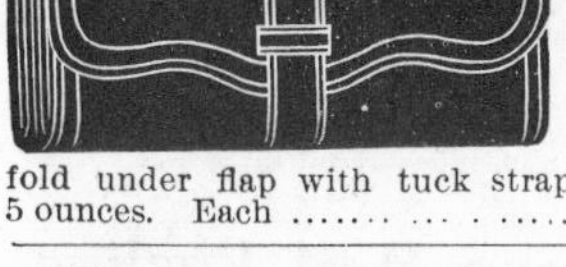

13266 Bill Book of colored grain leather with strap, size, 3⅝x8 inches, leather faced, cloth lined, three regular pockets, bill holder and "Secret" bill fold under flap with tuck strap. Weight, packed. 5 ounces. Each $0.60

Note our prices on Guns, Ammunition, etc.

Pocket Books—Continued.

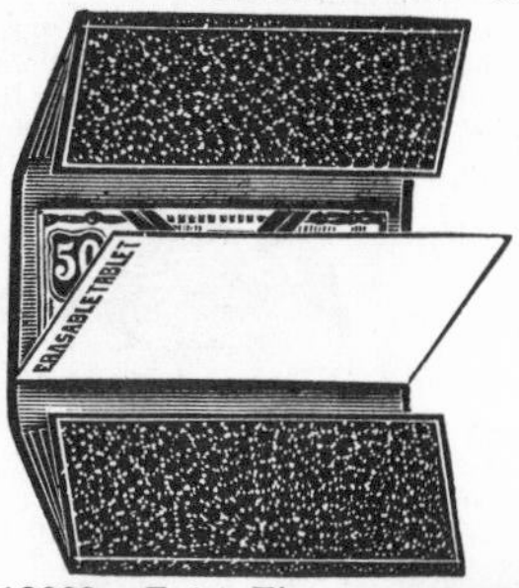

13268 Bill Book of long grained American Russia leather faced with same, cloth lined, size, 3¾x8 inches, two regular gusseted pockets, "Witch" bill holders and erasable memorandum tablet for lead pencil, in center. Weight, packed, 5 ounces.
Each............$0.50

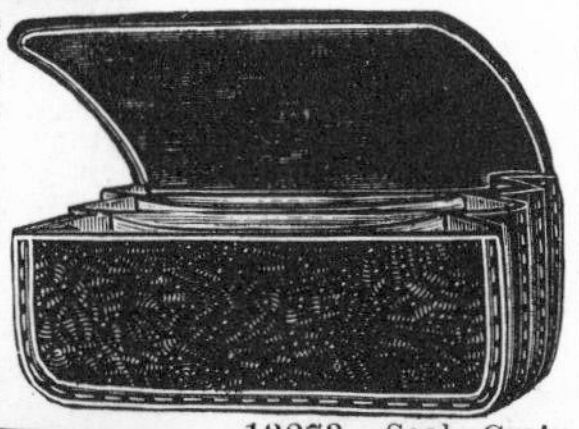

13269 Extra Fine English finish sheep, all leather bound and stitched all around; size, 3¾x8¼ in., three regular and two smaller pockets, bellows style, very light, flexible and durable.
Each $0.60
Postage...... .04

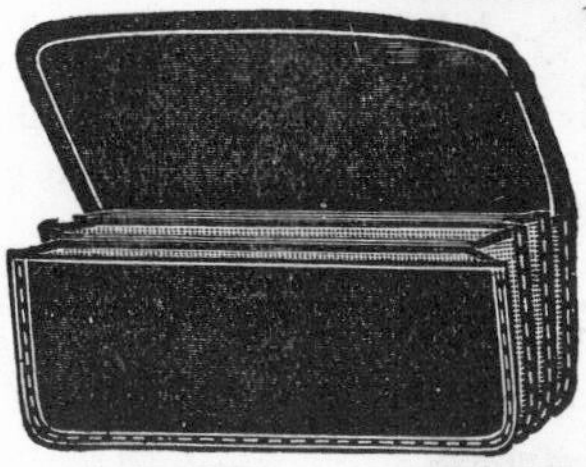

13273 Seal Grain Leather Bill Book; large, size, 4x9 in.; all leather, bound and securely stitched; three regular and two smaller pockets, bellows style.
Each........$0.75
Postage..... .05

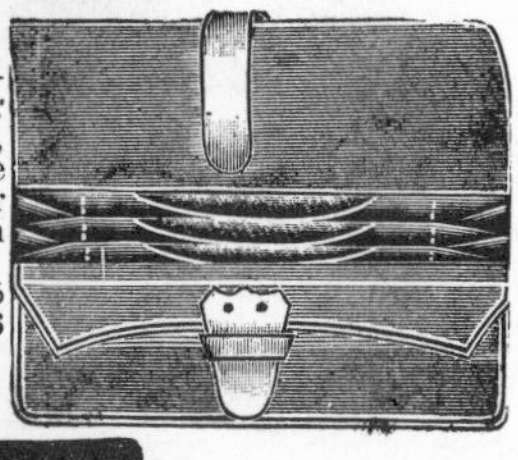

13278 Solid Calf, natural color, *all leather;* securely stitched; size, 3¾x8⅝; inches three small and four regular pockets; bill-fold with flap and tuck strap.
Each $0.95
Postage .... .06

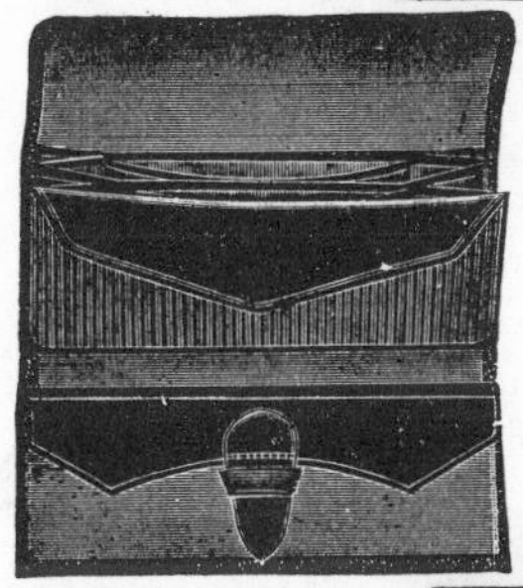

13284 Fine Calf Bill Book, size, 3½x8 inches; leather faced; three regular and two smaller canvas pockets, bound and stitched; ticket and two stamp pockets; drop bill fold with flap and tuck strap.
Each $1.15
Postage...... .05

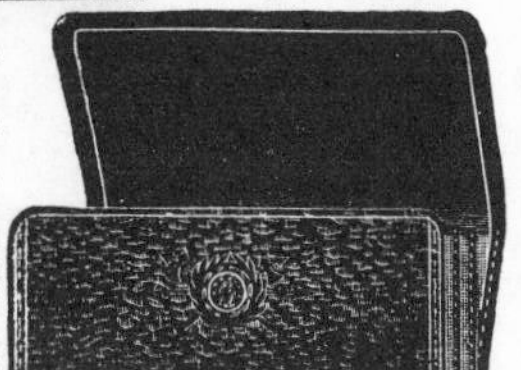

13287 Fine Persian Grain Leather Bill Book, size, 3¾ x8½ inches; leather faced; three regular and two smaller (all leather) pockets, bound and stitched, bellows style; card, ticket and two stamp pockets.
Each........... $1.25
Postage........... .05

Extra Large Bill Books.

FOR POLICIES. DEEDS. DOCUMENTS, ETC.

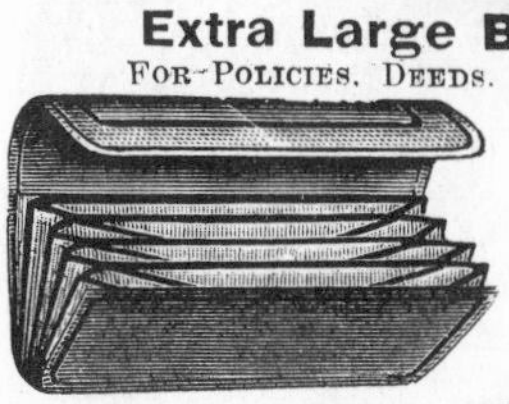

13293 American Russia Leather Bill Book, size, 4⅜x10¼ inches: canvas faced; five regular and four smaller canvas pockets, bound and stitched, bellows style.
Each.............$0.70
Postage........... .06

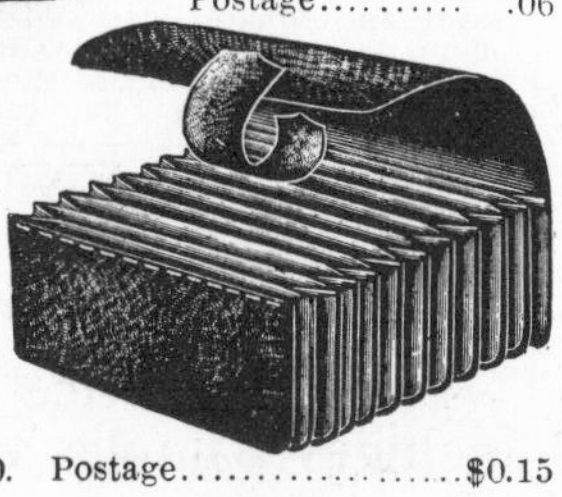

13297 Extra Large Bill Book with strap, *Bankers' Case Style*, made of long grained American Russia leather; size, 5⅝x10½ inches, faced with leather; 12 small and 13 regular canvas pockets, bound and stitched, bellows style.
Each..........$1.40. Postage....................$0.15

Pocket Books—Continued.

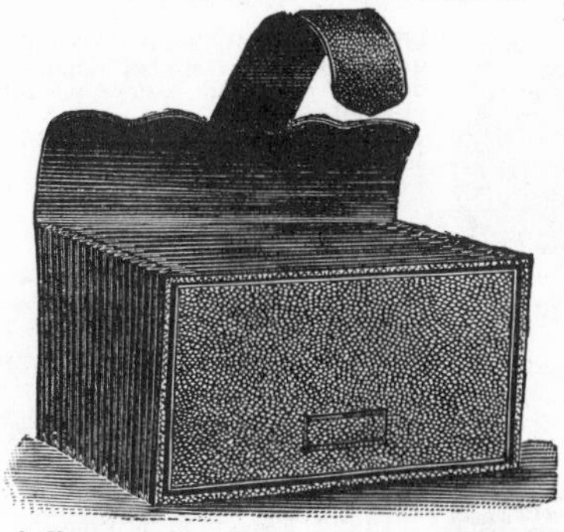

13300—Bankers' Case of seal grained leather; 13 pockets (metal stayed) two letters and one month to each pocket and one pocket for sundries; size closed, 9½x 5½x2 in., bellows style, cloth gussets. Weight packed, 27 ounces.
Our special price, each.......... ....$1.65

Purses.

In measuring purses we first give depth of purse and then width across the frame.

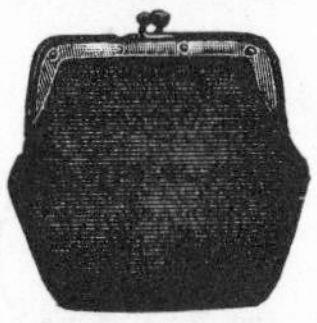

13302 Vest Pocket Purse of fine brown kid, with nickeled riveted frame, ball catch; size, 1¾x1¾ inches. Weighs, 2 ounces.
Each.............. ....$0.04
Per dozen................. .42
Per gross................... 4.50

13304 Buckskin Flat Purse, nickeled riveted frame, ball catch; size, 2½x2¼ inches. Weight, 2 ounces.
Each........... . ...$0.04

13306 Fine Kid Flat Purse with nickeled riveted *over lapping frame* which prevents small coin from slipping out; chamois lined; size, 2¾x3 inches.
Each $0.10
Postage.............. .02

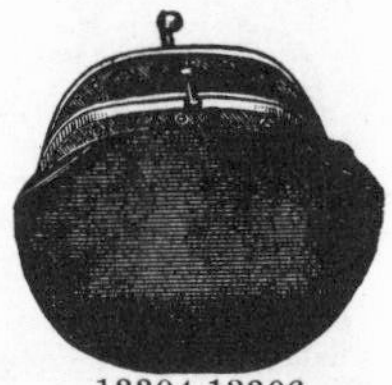

13304-13306

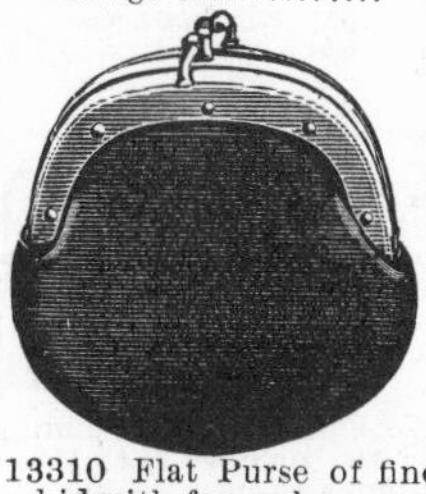

13308 Fine Kid Flat Purse with nickeled riveted frame, with partition; three-ball catch, chamois lined, two pockets; size, 3x2⅞ Each...........$0.15
Per dozen............. 1.60
Postage................. .03

13310 Flat Purse of fine brown kid with fancy hammered nickeled solid frame; ball catch; size, 2¾x2⅛ in.; lined with white kid; inside pocket with frame. Weight packed, 3 ounces.
Each $0.18
Per dozen............ . .. 1.90

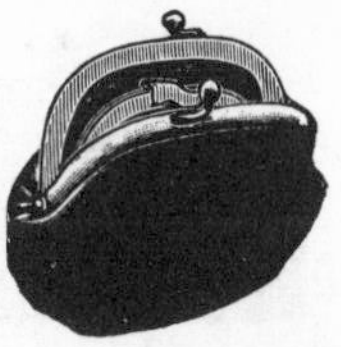

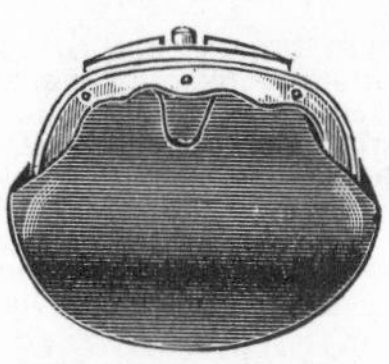

13315 Flat Purse of fine brown kid, nickeled riveted frame with center partition; size, 3x3 inches; chamois lined; two pockets. Weight, packed, 3 ounces.
Each $0.20
Per dozen............. 2.10

13317 Bag Shape Purse of fine brown kid with side gussets and welt; nickeled riveted frame with partition; size, 2¾x3 inches; chamois lined; two pockets. Weight, packed, 3 ounces. Each........$0.22
Per dozen............. 2.40

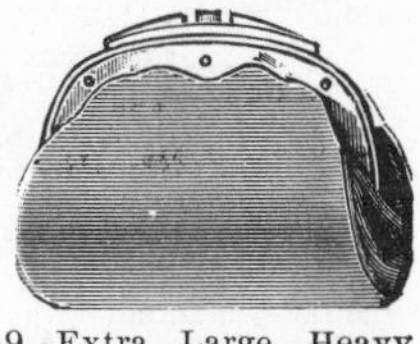

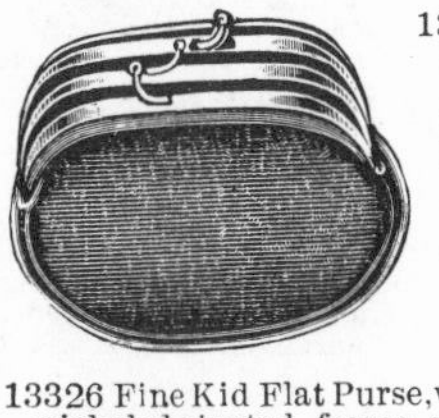

13319 Extra Large Heavy Black Kid Purse, chamois lined, three pockets, 3¾x4 inches; nickeled riveted frame, ball catch; weight, packed, 5 ounces.
Each.......................$0.19

13326 Fine Kid Flat Purse, with nickeled riveted frame, with overlapping partitions which prevent small coins from dropping out; two pockets; chamois lined; size, 2⅝x3 inches.
Each $0.20
Per dozen............... 2.10
Postage................., .03

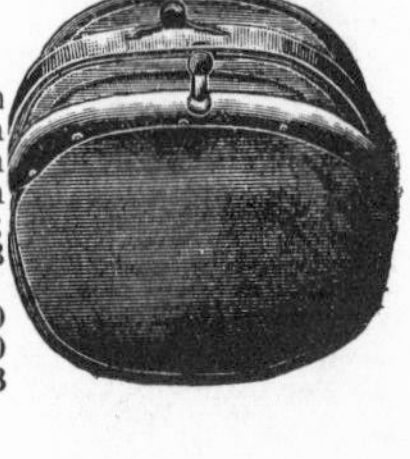

Purses—Continued.

13329 Size, 3x3¼, Heavy Ooze Kid gusseted; riveted nickel frame, with double partition; three pockets, chamois lined.
Each...........................$0.32
Per dozen.....................3.25
Postage.........................04

13332 Flat Purse of Buckskin, size, 3x3 inches; nickeled riveted frame with partition; chamois lined; two pockets. Weight, packed, 3 ounces.
Each................$0.20
Per dozen............2.10

13337 Extra Large Fine Buck Purse, bag shape, with side gussets; nickel riveted frame, with ball catch; three pockets; chamois lined; size 3¼x4 inches. Weight, 5 ounces.
Each..................$0.23
Per dozen.............2.50

13339 Bag Shape Purse of fine oozed calf leather, Plymouth buck finish, with side gussets and welts; size, 2¾x 3 inches; fine nickeled riveted frame with partition; lined with white kid; inside pocket with frame and three regular pockets. Weight, packed, 3 ounces.
Each................................$0 30
Per dozen....................... 3.00

13341 Fine Calf Purse, bag shape, with side gussets and welt, size, 2½x3¼ inches; finely polished nickeled riveted frame, ball catch; kid lined; inside pocket with frame, and two regular pockets. Weight, packed, 3 ounces.
Each..............$0.40

13345 Fancy Mottled Celluloid Purse, bag shape, leather gussets; nickeled frame; size 2x3 inches; white kid lined; inside pocket with frame and two regular pockets. Weight, packed, 3 ounces. Each.............$0.20
Per dozen....... .... 2.00

13347 Fáncy Mottled Celluloid Purse, oblong bag shape, leather gussets; size, 2¼x3½ inches; polished nickeled frame with gilt partition; lined with colored chamois; two pockets. Weight, packed, 4 ounces.
Each.....................$0.28
Per dozen...............3.00

11349 Fancy Mottled Celluloid Purse, oblong bag shape, leather gussets and welt; size, 2½x4¼ inches; polished fancy nickeled frame, white kid lined; inside pocket with frame and two regular pockets. Weight, packed, 4 ounces.
Each.......... ....$0.32
Per dozen....................3.25

13351 Imported Kid Purse for Pocket Knife; nickeled frame with ball catch; assorted sizes. Weight packed, 2 ounce. Each..................$0,08
Per dozen.........................80

Draw String Pouches.

13359 Oozed Leather Coin or Tobacco Pouch, with draw strings; 4x3½ inches. Weight, packed, 2 ounces Each.........$0.05
Per dozen....................50

13359 and 13361

13361 Oozed Leather Coin or Tobacco Pouch, with draw strings; 5x4 inches. Weight, packed, 3 ounces. Each.................$0.08
Per dozen.................................75

Pouches—Continued.

13363 German or Brewers' Pouch. This is the best pouch manufactured for tobacco or coin; has inside pocket for gold, made from solid piece of leather.
Each......$0.13
Per dozen.. 1.40
Postage .... .03

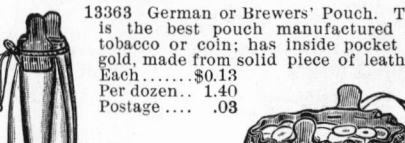

Closed.   13363 and 13365   Open.

13365 German or Brewers' Pouch, *extra large size;* two inside pockets. Weight, packed, 4 ounces. Each..................................$0.19
Per dozen.....................................2.00

13367 Fine Genuine Buckskin Pouch, made from six pieces, light and dark alternating, securely stitched with silk, buckskin top with colored macrame drawing strings: 5½ inches deep, 5 inches wide, suitable for coin or smoking tobacco.
Each..........................$0.22
Per dozen....................2.40

13367

Tobacco Pouches.

13369 "Velvet" Rubber Tobacco Pouch, self-closing, tan color. Diameter, 3⅜ in. Keeps tobacco moist and clean.
Each.............................$0.21
Per dozen........... .. 2.20
Postage.......................02

BRUSHES.
Wire Metallic Hair Brushes.

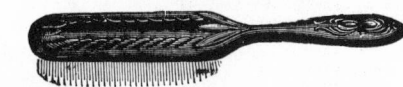

13381 Metallic Brush, 7 rows oblong, small size, Florence hard rubber back. Weight, packed (each). 5 ounces. Each...... ....$0.10
Per dozen.......................................1.10

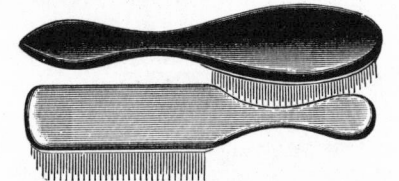

13383 Metallic Hair Brushes, medium size, oval and square, black enameled and light wood; half dozen in' box. Weight, packed (each), 6 ounces. Each.... ....$0.15
Per box, half dozen.............................75

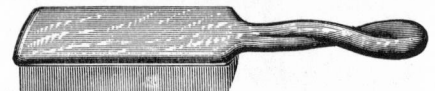

13385 Metallic Hair Brushes, large, assorted, black enameled and light wood twist handles; half dozen in box. Weight, packed (each), 7 ounces. Each.................. ....$0.25
Per box, half dozen 1.25

13387 Metallic Hair Brushes, large size; assorted oval and square, black enameled backs, with floral decorations; half dozen in box. Weight, packed (each), 7 ounces. Each $0.35
Per box, half dozen.... ....1.80

Hair Brushes—Continued.

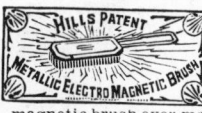

13395 ELECTRIC BRUSHES. HILL'S PATENT METALLIC ELECTRO-MAGNETIC BRUSH. RUBBER BACK.
The manufacturer makes the following statement:
It is the most powerful magnetic brush ever made; cures headache, neuralgia, rheumatism, prevents hair from falling out and aids in restoring gray hair to its natural color. In the back of this brush are embedded strongly-charged magnets, in contact with which are the fine, highly polished steel wires which form the brush so that when applied to the head or flesh, currents of magnetic electricity flow from the magnet through the wires.
Price.............................$1.25
Brush weighs 10 ounces.
13398 The New and Improved Hill's Electric Brush, has extra magnet in handle.
Price $1.50
Brush weighs 10 ounces.

Hair Brushes.

13400 Infants' White Goat Hair Brushes, fine and soft. Each.....$0.25
Per dozen............................2.60
Weight, packed, 5 ounces.

13404 Hair Brush, oval, large size, cherry back, gray center with outside row of white bristles. Weight, packed, 7 ounces. Each..............$0.20
Per doz...2.15

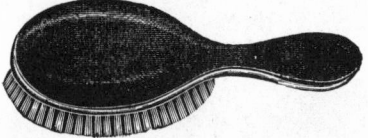

13408 Hair Brush, oval, medium size, polished Walnut back, all white bristles, 11 row. Weight, packed, 6 ounces. Each........................$0.25
Per doz..2.75

13411 Hair Brush, square, medium size, polished olivewood back, all pure white bristles, 9 row. Weight, packed, 6 ounces. Each, $0.35. Per doz.$3.75

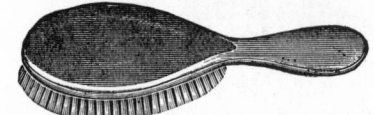

13414 Hair Brush, oval, large size, veneered back, long unbleached Russia bristles, 11 row. Weight, packed, 7 ounces. Each..............$0.40
Per doz...4.25

13418 Hair Brush, oval, large size, polished redwood back, curved handle, long white penetrating bristles, 13 row. Weight, packed, 7 ounces.
Each..............$0.50. Per doz.............$5.25

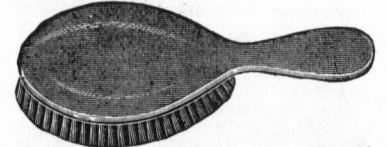

13422 Barbers' Hair Brush, oval, large size, polished redwood back, gray Russia penetrating bristles, 15 row. Weight, packed, 8 ounces. Each.....................$0.50. Per doz.........$5.25

13426 Barbers' Hair Brush, oval, large size, finely polished dark redwood back, long gray Russia penetrating bristles, stiff, 11 row. Weight, packed, 8 ounces. Each................$0.68
Per doz.......... ....7.25

Ideal Hair Brushes.

13430–32

"Ideal" Hair Brushes, genuine Siberian bristles, black with a single bristle substituted for tufts, and set in an elastic air cushioned base. Will penetrate any growth of hair without effort. Does not injure the hair or scalp, and will remove dandruff without irritating the scalp. Clean, light and durable.
13430 Hair Brushes, cherry wood back, black Siberian bristles, medium size (C). Each.......$0.65
Brush weighs 6 ounces. Per dozen............ 7.00
13432 Hair Brushes, cherry wood back, black Siberian bristles, large size (H). Each.......... .75
Brush weighs 7 ounces. Per dozen 8.10

Celluloid Hair Brushes.

13436 Celluloid Hair Brush, 12 rows white bristles, size, 8⅜ x 2⅜. Weight, packed, 5 ounces. Our special price, each.......$0.50

13438 Celluloid Hair Brush, fancy backs, 12 rows white bristles, size, 8⅜x2⅜. Weight, packed, 6 ounces.
Each...............$0.60 Per dozen... .... 6.50

Florence Hair Brushes.

Hare Rubber Backs.

13440 Black, All Bristle Hair Brush, with black figured back; a good brush. Weight, packed, 7 ounces.
Each..............$0.23 Per dozen.............$2.50

13442 Hair Brush, Florence hard rubber backs, fine white Russia bristles.
Each...............$0.35 Per dozen.............$3.75
Brush weighs 6 ounces.

13444 Black, All Bristle Hair Brush, hard rubber back. See cut. Each, $0.45. Per dozen.......$4.75
Brush weighs 8 ounces.

13446 Hair Brushes, Florence hard rubber backs, fine white Russia bristles.
Assorted designs, similar to cut.
Each...............$0.55 Per dozen.......... $6.00
Brush weighs 8 ounces.

13450 Florence Hair Brush extra fine white Russian Okatka bristles, 15 row, carved back and handle, 9¼ in. long. Each brush in a box. Weight packed, 9 ounces.
Each $1.00

13453 Cosmeon Hair Brush with pebbled aluminum back and long white Russia penetrating bristles, medium size; very handsome. Weight, packed, 7 ounces.
Each.........................$1.00

"COSMEON" HAIR BRUSH
ENTIRE SURFACE UNCHANGEABLE
PURE ALUMINUM

Flesh and Bath Brushes.

13490 Long Curved Flesh Brush, *for dry use* (not for water); alternate rows of black and white bristles; light satinwood back. Weight, packed, 10 ounces. Each.........................$0.50
Per dozen. 5.25
Leiner's Patent Combined Bath and Flesh Brushes, guaranteed for wet or dry use. Superior friction brushes made from select bristles woven into twisted wire; very durable and popular.

13493 Leiner's Bath and Flesh Brush, metallic back, curved handle, which may be detached and reversed; web strap on back for use without handle. Weight, packed, 10 ounces.
Each..................$0.48. Per doz............$5.32

13497 Leiner's Bath and Flesh Brush, long and curved, with three rows of superior bristles. Weight, packed, 12 ounces. Each $0.80
Per dozen.. 9.25

Perfection Corn File.

13498— The greatest thing on the market for a speedy and painless removal of corns. A practical, perfect remedy. Can be operated by any child. No danger of blood poisoning or lock-jaw. Made of genuine African Salamander skin, and truly antiseptic.
Price, each.........$0.20 Per dozen..........$1.75
Per gross.......................................21.00
Give it a trial.

Tooth Brushes.

HINTS IN REGARD TO USE AND CARE OF TOOTH BRUSHES.
Never lay a wet brush away, but put it upright in an open dish.
A new brush should be soaked in cool water about twenty minutes before using the first time.
If some of the bristles begin to work up in use, do not draw them out, but trim them off, and your brush will last longer.
Bristles will be injured if brushes are put away wet and left for several days to dry. For the same reason the backs split and the brushes become offensive in smell, and discolored.
Tooth Brushes are not expensive. It is wiser to throw an old brush away than be annoyed in trying to make it last a while longer.
Tooth brushes should be selected according to requirements of the individual. A soft brush used with much pressure would break down the bristles, while a stiffer brush would stand the work.

Note.—For Tooth Soap and Powder, see Index.

13500-02 13510 13514 13512 13506
13500 Tooth Brushes, good, cheap brush.
Each.................$0.06 Per dozen $0.65
Weight per dozen, 12 ounces.
13502 Tooth Brushes, good.
Each.................$0.10 Per dozen 1.00
Weight, per dozen, 14 ounces.
13504 Tooth Brushes, fine quality.
Each.................$0.15 Per dozen.......... 1.50
Weight, per dozen, 15 ounces.
13506 Tooth Brushes, superior quality.
Each.................$0.18 Per dozen.......... 1.95
Weight, per dozen, 17 ounces.
13510 Tooth Brushes, standard M. W. & Co., warranted, extra fine.
Each .. ..$0.25 Per dozen.......... 2.60

Tooth Brushes—Continued.

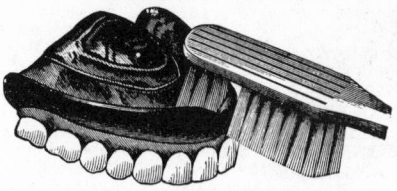

13512
13512 Tooth Brushes, Florence dental plate, extra quality, for cleaning artificial teeth.
Each.................$0.29. Per dozen.......$3.10
Weight, per dozen, 16 ounces.
13514 The "Prophylactic" Tooth Brush: a perfect cleanser of the teeth; is constructed upon principles of dental science. the bristles being in separate and distinctly pointed tufts, that they may be forced *between the teeth* as well as to cleanse the surface. Directions for use are given with each brush.
Each.................$0.29 Per dozen............ 3.10
Weight, per dozen, 16 ounces

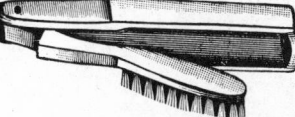

13516 Folding Pocket Tooth Brush, all bristle brush.
Each....$0.25
Per doz .2.60

Nail and Hand Brushes.

13530   Each. Per doz.
13520 Hand Brushes, 4 row, imported fiber, hardwood back, 4 inches in length; also useful in house cleaning, kitchen work, etc $0.04 $0.40
Weight, per dozen, 20 ounces.
13524 Nail Brushes, 6 row, all white bristles, bone back............................ .15 1.50
Weight, per dozen, 14 ounces.
13526 Nail Brushes, 8 row, all white bristles.. .20 2.00
13530 Nail Brushes, 8 row. all white bristles, with wings. See cut........... .25 2.60
Weight, per dozen, 22 ounces.

Shaving or Lather Brushes.

For shaving soap see Index.

                                Each Per doz.
13542 Plunger Shaving Brushes, good quality bristles. Weight, packed, 3 ounces.................................$0.10 $1.00
13544 Shaving Brush, large, all light French bristles, firmly secured in the binding; durable enameled handle. Weight, packed, 3 ounces. Retail price, 25 cents. Our price.................... .15 1.50
13546 Shaving Brush, good quality, all bristles. Weight, packed, 3 ounces...... .25 2.50

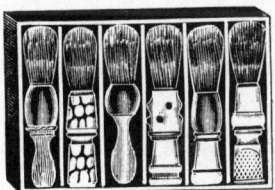

13551 Shaving Brush, medium size, fine quality of pure badger bristles, oval end; assortment of handles in box of half dozen. Weight (per box), packed, 20 ounces. Each.$0 40
Per box of six brushes.........$2.10

13534 "Imperial" Lather Brush, large size; fine white bristles 2½ inches long, square cut; firmly set in black hard rubber handle a perfect and satisfactory brush. Weight, packed, 3 ounces.
Each.........................$0.50
Per dozen........................ 5.35

Barbers' Dusters.

13558 Barbers' Dusters, all white horse hair: full length 9 inches; weighs 4 ounces.
Each.......................................$0.45
Per dozen...................................... 4.80

Cloth Brushes.

13562 Cloth Brush, black center, with outside row of black and white bristles, redwood back. Weight, packed, 8 ozs.

Each.................$0.25 Per dozen..........$2.50

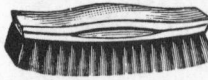

13564 Cloth Brushes, all white bristles, white satin-wood back. A fine brush. Weight, packed, 8 ounces. Each.... ....$0.50
Per dozen...... ..... 5.40

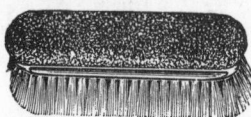

13567 Hat or Cloth Brush, white horse-hair, 6 rows, plush back; small size, 5½ inches long. Weight, packed, 5 oz.
Each $0.25
Per dozen....... 2.50

Shoe Polishers.

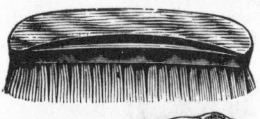

13575 Shoe Polisher or Cloth Brush of all black bristles, with polished hardwood back. Weight, packed, 8 ounces.
Each...........$0.20
Per dozen...... 2 10
13579 Sunshine polisher, solid mass of fine elastic bristles, 1½ inches long, same as in set 13625. 
Each $0.60
Per dozen...... 6.85
Brush weighs 11 ozs.

13579-13625

Blacking Daubers.

13583 Blacking Dauber, stencil brush style, made of pure black bristles, with metal ferrule, light hardwood handle. Weight, packed, 4 ounces. Each ....$0.10 Per dozen..... ...$1.00

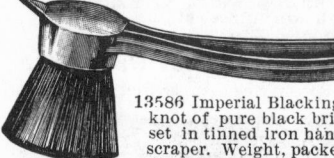

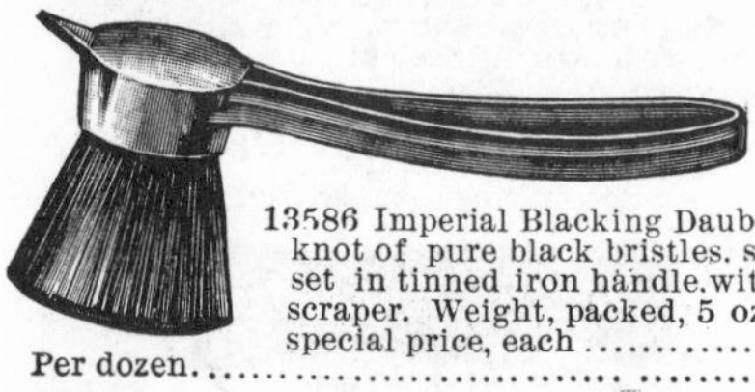

13586 Imperial Blacking Dauber, solid knot of pure black bristles. securely set in tinned iron handle. with mud-scraper. Weight, packed, 5 ozs. Our special price, each $0.10
Per dozen.................................. 1.00

13589 Our T. M. C. Dauber. solid knot, extra stiff bristle, improved scraper, tilted polished, nickel handle. Weight, packed, 5 ounces. Each.......................$0.15
Per dozen.. .... 1.65

13593 Best Shoe Blacking in a perfect box. No soiled fingers, no tight covers, no wasted blacking. See cut. Small sizes per box...$0.05
Per dozen .... .50
Box weighs 4 oz.

Blacking Brushes.

13600 Blacking Brush, mixed bristle; a good brush.
Each $0.15
Per dozen........... 1.50
Brush weighs 8 ounces.
13604 Blacking Brush, all bristle, a good one. Weight, packed, 11 ounces.
Each....................$0.25 Per dozen.......$2.50
13608 Blacking Brush, all bristle, large, full and heavy.
Each.............$0.50
Per dozen 5.40
Brush weighs 14 ozs.

Blacking Sets.

 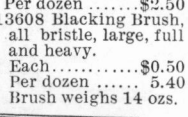

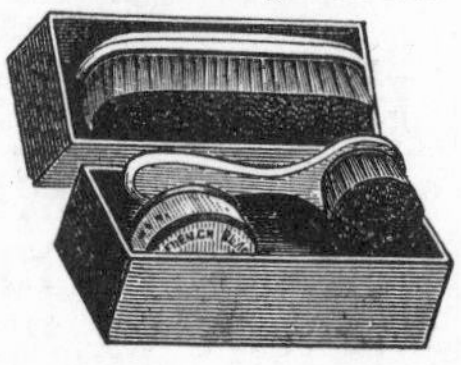

13610 Blacking Set, in neat box; polisher, dauber and box of blacking.
Each $0.25
Per dozen........ 2.65
Set weighs 11 ounces.

Blacking Sets—Continued.

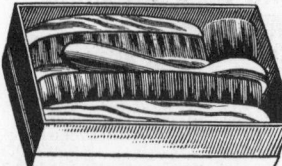

13614 Blacking Set in box; has bristle polisher, mud brush and dauber.
Each......$0.45
Per dozen. 4.80
Postage.... .14

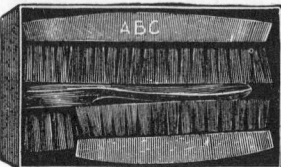

13618 Shoe Blacking Set, containing polisher, mud brush and dauber of good quality, with polished antique oak solid backs. Weight, packed, 16 ounces;
Each $0.50
Per dozen.. 5.40

13625 "Sunshine" Shoe Blacking Set, contains the perfect "Sunshine" polisher (No. 13579), dauber and box of blacking in stamped cloth case and is intended for consumers of good goods. Weight, packed, 20 ozs. Our special price, each $0.85

Dust or Counter Brushes.

13626 Counter Brush, all bristles. gray center, black outside.
Each $0.25
Per dozen... 2.65
13626-8
13628 Dust Brushes. American bristles, plain handles. Each, 45c. Per dozen..............$4.90
Dust brushes weigh 9 ounces each.

Turkey Feather Dusters.

		Each.	Per doz.
13630	10 inches.....	$0.22	$2.25
13632	12 inches.....	.30	3.00
13634	14 inches.....	.36	3.80
13636	15 inches.....	.40	4.30
13638	16 inches.....	.45	4.80

Weight, 9 to 12 ounces.

Feather Dusters.

13640 Body Feather Duster, 8-inch handle and 6-inch feathers.
Each $0.10
Per dozen...................... 1.00
Weight, 6 ounces.
13642 Body Dusters, full and soft, 10-inch handle and 7-inch feathers.
Each..........$0.15
Per dozen 1.65
Weight, 8 ounces.

The woven down duster, flat. not round, has no equal; double faced soft, downy wiper that gathers up the dust and when filled with dust can be taken from the room and beaten out in a moment.

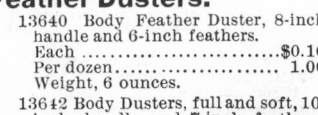

13640 and 13642   13646-48
13646 (No. 1) Duster, 8-inch handle, all dark down, 7x9 inch, double faced brush.
Each...$0.75
Per dozen.. 7.50
Weight, 6 ounces.
13648 (No. 2) 16-inch handle, duster 8x11, all dark downs, same as No. 1. Weight, 8 ounces.
Each.................................... .90
Per dozen..................................... 8.75

Paint Brushes.

Hints in regard to care and use of paint brushes.

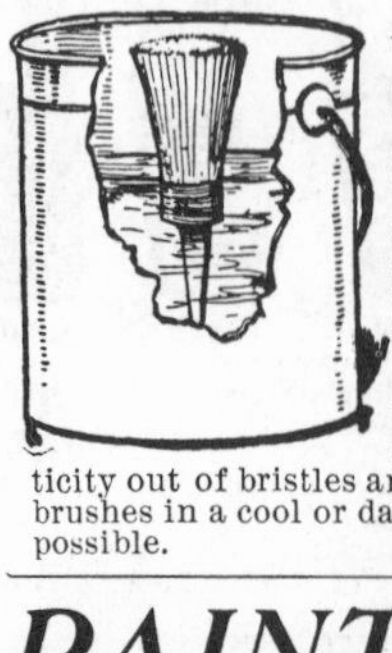

Swelling a new brush is a very important item in the future usefulness of that tool. A new paint or varnish brush *should not be put in water with bristles down*, for water soaked bristles will always work flabby, and fine bristles nearly always twist. Put your brush in water *with handle down* (as shown in illustration), letting water come just to the point where bristles emerge from binding. This will swell the handle without soaking elasticity out of bristles and making them flabby. Keep brushes in a cool or damp spot, as near the floor as possible.

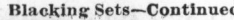

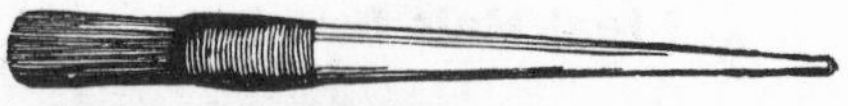

13685 French Sash Tools, all white bristles, short ferrule, wire bound, a fair jobbing brush. Length of bristles 1½ to 2 inches.

Manufacturers' number ..	2	4	6	8
Price. each..............	$0.03	$0.04	$0.06	$0.08
Per dozen.....•••	.30	.45	.60	.85
Weight, each..............	3 oz.	3 oz.	4 oz.	4 oz.

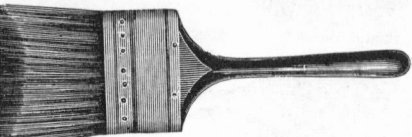

13689 Extra Gloss Oval Paint or Varnish Brush, warranted all pure white bristles, wire bound; cement set; *must not be put in Alcohol Shellac;* will work well in paint or varnish.

Size numbers..	6	4	2	3-O	6-O
Price, each....$0.10	.10	$0.16	$0.23	$0.40	$0.67
Per dozen.....	1.10	1.75	2.45	4.40	7.50
Weight, each..	4 oz.	4 oz.	4 oz.	5 oz.	8 oz.

13692 English Chiseled Flat Varnish Brush, light French bristles, cement set; *must not be put in Alcohol Shellac;* black wood handle.

Size	1 in.	1½ in.	2 in.	2½ in.	3 in.
Price, each....$0.08	.08	$0.12	$0.16	$0.23	$0.28
Per dozen.......	.80	1.20	1.65	2.35	2.95
Weight, each......	2 oz.	3 oz.	3 oz.	4 oz.	4 oz.

13694 and 13697.

13694 Extra Chiseled Flat Bristle Flowing Varnish Brush, superior Chinese (black) bristles, double thick cement set; *must not be put in Alcohol Shellec;* brass bound; unequaled for fine work, elasticity and durability.

Weight, each....	3 oz.	4 oz.	4 oz.	5 oz.	5 oz.
Width......	1 in.	1½ in.	2 in.	2½ in.	3 in.
Price, each......	$0.12	$0.15	$0.23	$0.34	$0.40

Per set of five, one of each size.................. 1.10

13697 Extra Chiseled Flat Bristle Flowing Varnish Brush; glue set, for use in Alcohol Shellac, (*must not be put in water*); otherwise same as 13694.

Weight, each.....	3 oz.	4 oz.	4 oz.	5 oz.	5 oz.
Width, each......	1 in.	1½ in.	2 in.	2½ in.	3 in.
Price.............	$0.12	$0.15	$0.23	$0.34	$0.40

Per set of five, one of each size..................$1.10

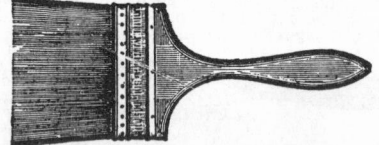

13698 Ajax Wall Paint Brush, all light bristles, metal bound; handy brush for common use, floor and barn painting, pasting, etc.

		Each.	Per dozen.	Weight, each.
No.	0--2½ in. wide.	$0.14	$1.40	4 oz.
No.	1--3 in. wide.	.18	1.85	5 oz.
No.	2--3½ in. wide.	.24	2.50	6 oz.
No.	3--4 in. wide.	.31	3.25	7 oz.
No.	4--4½ in. wide.	.40	4.10	8 oz.

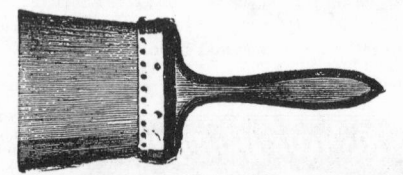

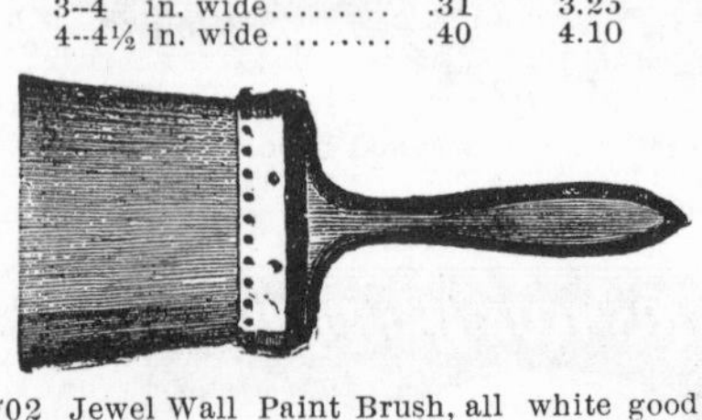

13702 Jewel Wall Paint Brush, all white good Russia bristles, brass bound; an excellent painters' brush.

		Each.	Per doz.	Weight. each
No. 1	3 inches wide.	$0.30	$3.25	6 ounces.
No. 2	3¼ inches wide.	.40	4.25	8 ounces.
No. 3	4 inches wide.	.50	5.40	9 ounces.
No. 4	4½ inches wide.	.65	7.00	11 ounces.

Paint Brushes—Continued.

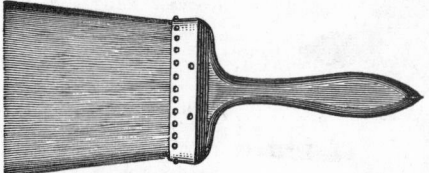

13704 O. K. Super Wall Paint Brush. best white Russia bristles, *extra long and heavy*, brass bound; excellent working brush for painters' use.

	Each.	Weight each.
No. 12 3½ inches wide	$0.65	10 ounces.
No. 13 4 inches wide	.85	11 ounces.

13708 Victor Stucco Wall Paint Brush, good all white Russia bristles, long stock, leather bound, full and elastic; splendid working brush for practical purposes.

	Each.	Per doz.	Weight, each.
No. 30 3½ inches wide	$1.00	$10.50	9 ounces.
No. 35 4 inches wide	1.25	13.35	11 ounces.

Whitewash Brushes.

Keep your brushes in a cool place, and soak them well before using. Never put whitewash brushes in newly slaked lime, as it will rot the bristles.

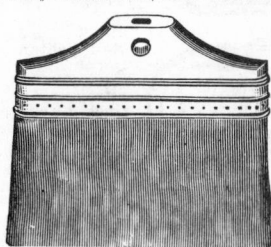

13712 "B" Whitewash Head, white mixed middle with outside row of white French bristles, metal bound; good brush for rough outside work.

	Each.	Per doz.	Weight, each.
No 0 6 inches wide	$0.20	$2.00	7 ounces.
No. 2 7 inches wide	.28	3.00	9 ounces.
No. 4 8 inches wide	.33	3.60	11 ounces.
No. 7 9 inches wide	.50	5.25	14 ounces.

13714 A. W. Druid Whitewash Head, all white pure bristles, metallic bound.

	Each.	Per doz.	Weight, each.
No. 1 6 inches wide	$0.30	$3.20	8 ounces.
No. 3 7 inches wide	.40	4.20	10 ounces.
No. 5 8 inches wide	.53	5.65	12 ounces.
No. 7 9 inches wide	.70	7.50	14 ounces.

13716 Queen Whitewash Head, long all white bristles, metal bound; good brush for general purposes.

	Each.	Per doz.	Weigh each.
No. 1 7 inches wide	$0.60	$6.40	10 ounces.
No. 2 7½ inches wide	.65	7.00	12 ounces.
No. 3 8 inches wide	.80	8.50	14 ounces.
No. 4 8½ inches wide	.85	9.00	16 ounces.

13718 Acme Whitewash Head, all white bristles, extra long, brass bound; a satisfactory and good working brush.

	Each.	Weight, each.
No. 15 7½ inches wide	$0.85	13 ounces.
No. 25 8 inches wide	1.05	15 ounces.
No. 35 8½ inches wide	1.30	17 ounces.

Paints! Paints!
Paints! Paints!

Be sure and write for our color card of Paints.

If you are thinking of painting a house, our book "Hints on the Selection of Colors" will be sent free upon application.

Calcimine Brushes.

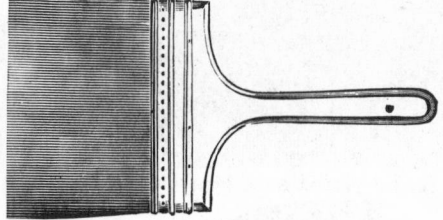

13724

13722 Atlantic Calcimine Brush, all white bristles, metallic bound. Good brush for family use.

	Each.	Weight, Each.
No. 6 6 inches wide	$0.75	14 ounces.
No. 7 7 inches wide	.95	17 ounces.
No. 8 8 inches wide	1.25	20 ounces.

13724 Extra Standard Calcimine Brush, good, long yellow Russia bristles, brass bound. An excellent brush for practical use.

	Each.	Weight, Each.
No. 17 7 inches wide	$2.00	20 ounces.
No. 18 8 inches wide	2 65	24 ounces.

13728 Painters' Duster, long, gray stock, mixed quality, large size Good cheap brush. Each...$0.45

13731 Paper Hangers' Smoothing Brush, two rows stiff, yellow Russia bristles, wire drawn, ten inches wide. Weight, packed, 8 ounces. Each...$0.75

13734 Paper Hangers' Patented Smoothing Brush and Roller Combined. No. 20, 10 inches wide, two rows bristles, roller on one end of handle. Each...1.20

13736 Paper Hangers' Paste Brush, 7 inches wide, all white bristles, metal bound. Each...1.25

Graining Combs.

13738 American Leather Graining Combs, 20 inches. Weight, packed, 4 ounces. Per set....45

13739 Taylor's English Steel Graining Combs, in tin compartment case. Weight packed. 15 ounces. Per set...1.25

COMBS.

13745 Pure Aluminum Dressing Comb, coarse and fine, 7½ inches long, 1⅛ inches wide, highly polished, very light, strong and durable. Each...$0.75

13749 and 13751.

13749 Paragon Metallic Dressing Comb, nickel plated, coarse and fine, 1 inch wide, 5½ inches long. Weight, per dozen, 14 ounces. Each...$0.05 Per dozen...$0.50

13751 Paragon Metallic Dressing Comb. 1 inch wide, 6½ inches long. Weight, packed, 16 ounces. Each...$0.06 Per dozen...$0.65

Raw Horn Dressing Combs With Metallic Backs.

13755 Nickel Plated Back Dressing Combs, raw horn, 7 inches. See cut. Each...$0.12 Per dozen...1.25 Weight, per dozen, 15 ounces.

13760 Nickel Plated Back Hotel Comb, raw horn, all coarse. See cut. Each...$0.12 Per dozen...1.25 Weight, per dozen, 15 ounces.

Raw Horn Barber Combs.

13762 Polished Horn Barber Combs. All coarse, 7 inch, ½ inch teeth. Each...$0.10 Per dozen...90 Weight, per dozen, 7 ounces.

13764 Polished Horn Combs, coarse and fine. See cut. Each...$0.10 Per dozen...90

Celluloid Combs.

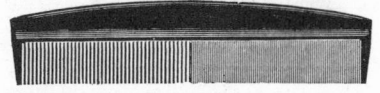

13768 Celluloid Dressing Comb, 7 inch; 1 inch teeth, in blue, red, pink and white. Each...$0.09 Per dozen...90 Weight, per dozen, 9 ounces.

Rubber Dressing Combs.

13778 Hard Rubber Dressing Comb, 1½ inches wide, heavy curved back.

Length	7 in.	8 in.
Each	$0.06	$0.08
Per dozen	.65	.75
Weight, per dozen	10 oz.	12 oz.

13781 Atlantic India Rubber Dressing Combs, 8 inches. See cut. Weight, per dozen, 16 ounces. Each...$0.10 Per dozen...$0.90

13783 Atlantic India Rubber Dressing Combs, 8 inches See cut. Weight, per dozen, 16 ounces. Each...$0.12 Per dozen...1.10

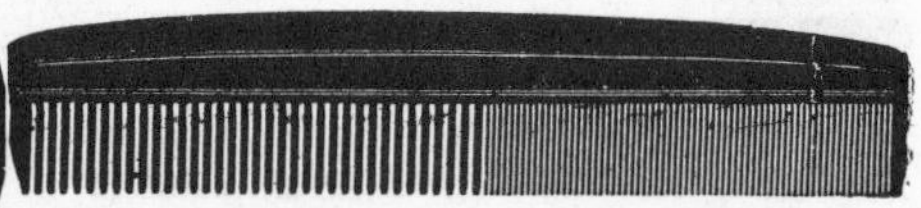

13785 Hard Rubber Dressing Comb. 1¾ inches wide, heavy curved quill back; length, 8 inches. Weight, per dozen, 16 ounces. Each...$0.12 Per dozen...1.25

13787 Hard Rubber Dressing Comb, 1⅞ inches wide, wide fancy back; length, 8 inches. Weight, per dozen, 16 ounces. Each...$0.12 Per dozen...1.30

13789 Goodyear Extra Heavy Rubber Dressing Combs, 8 inches. Weight, per dozen, 16 ounces. Each...$0.20 Per dozen...2.10

13790 Fine High Grade Dressing Combs, grailed teeth. Weight, per dozen, 17 ounces. Each...$0.25 Per dozen...2.70

13798 Dressing Combs, rubber, toilet. Each...$0.35 Per dozen...3.75 Weight, per dozen, 26 ounces.

Combs—Continued.

13805 Slant Barber Combs, fine quality rubber, unbreakable; length, 7½ inches. Weight, per dozen, 8 ounces. Each.......... ....$0.13
Per dozen.. 1.20

Rubber Pocket Combs.

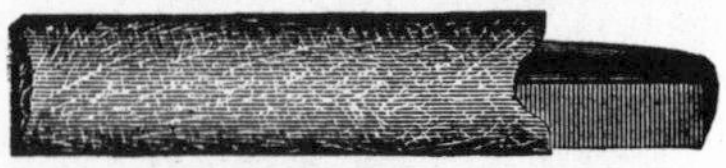

13807 Hard Rubber Pocket Comb, ¾ inch wide, curved back, coarse and fine, length, 4 inches; in leatherette slide case. Weight, per dozen, 5 ounces. Each...............................$0.05
Per dozen................................ .... .50

13809 Hard Rubber Pocket Comb, of superior quality and finish, length, 4½ inches; in sliding case. Weight, per dozen, 6 ounces.
Each $0.10
Per dozen... .... .95

Unbreakable Combs.

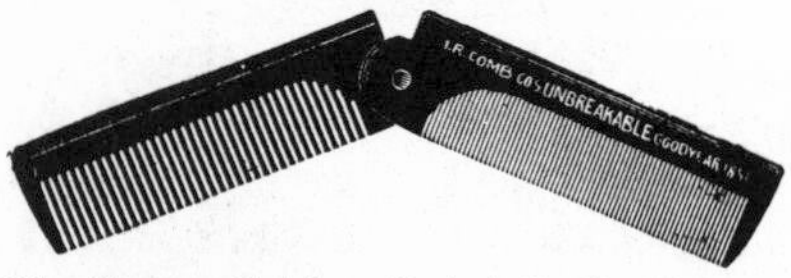

13812 Siamese Folding Pocket Comb of unbreakable hard rubber, coarse and fine; length, closed, 3⅛ inches. Weight, per dozen, 6 ounces. Each...... ....$0.12 Per dozen...........$1.15

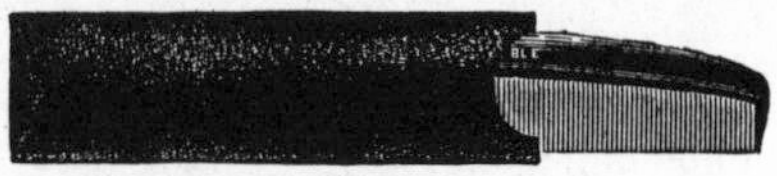

13815 Unbreakable Rubber Pocket Comb, curved back, coarse and fine, 4½ inches; in leatherette slide; neat pocket comb for hair or mustache. Weight, per dozen, 5 ounces. Each............$0.12
Per dozen... 1.10

13821 Samson Unbreakable Rubber Dressing Comb, coarse and fine; 8 inches long, 1½ inches wide. Weight, per dozen, 16 ounces. Each....$0.16
Per dozen... 1.65

13825 Unbreakable Rubber Dressing Comb, all coa se, 1½ inches wide, length 8 inches. Weight, per dozen, 16 ounces. Each............$0.16
Per dozen... 1.65

The above lines of unbreakable combs are especially recommended for service and cheapness.

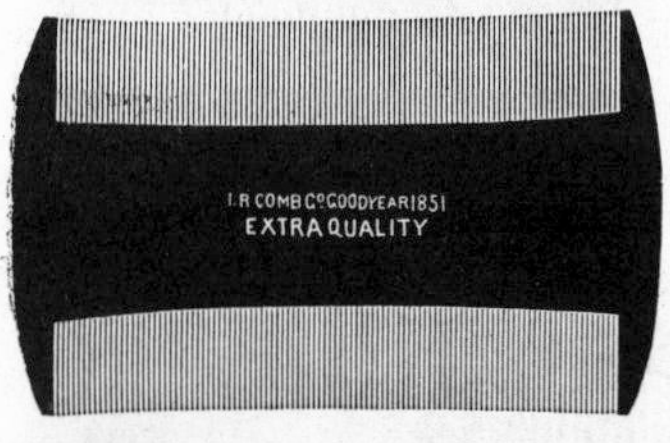

13826 Superior Quality. Fine Tooth India Rubber Combs
Each....$0.08
Per doz. .85

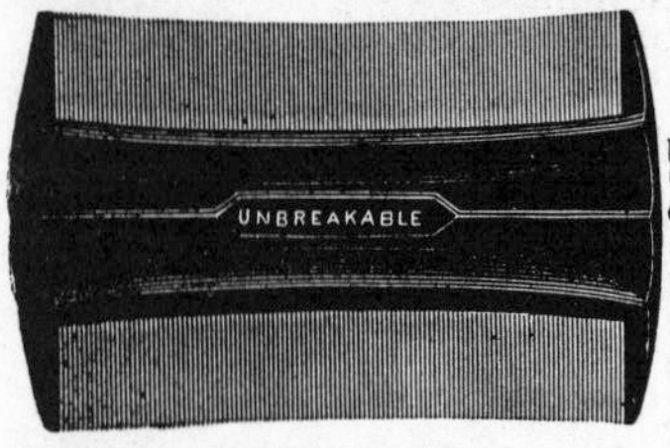

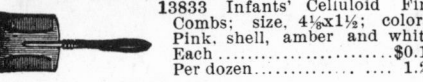

13830 Unbreakable Fine Tooth Rubber Combs, Fine; see cut.
Each... $0.10
Per doz. 1.10

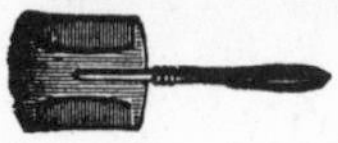

13833 Infants' Celluloid Fine Combs; size, 4⅛x1½; colors: Pink, shell, amber and white.
Each $0.12
Per dozen.............. .... 1.25

Combs—Continued.

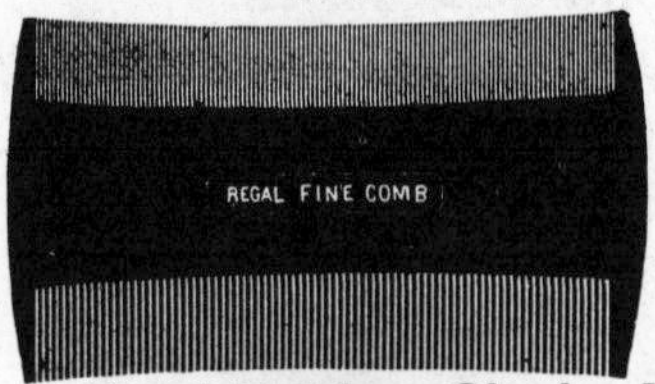

13836 Fine Rubber Combs, one side fine, the other coarse; see cut.
Each...$0.08
Per doz. .85
Weight, per dozen, 6 ounces.

Hard Rubber Circle Combs.

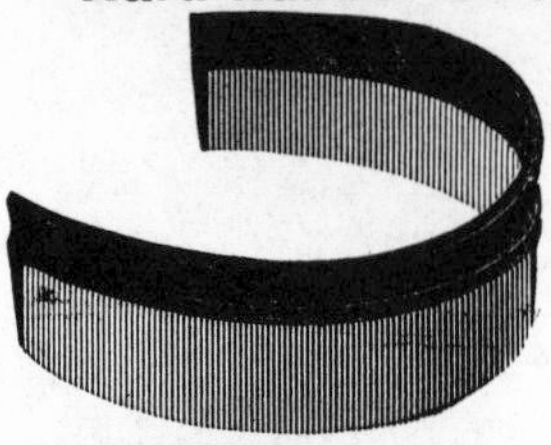

13846 Unbreakable Rubber Circle or Round Comb, ribbed top. Weight, per dozen, 9 ounces.
Each.........$0.08
Per dozen..... .80

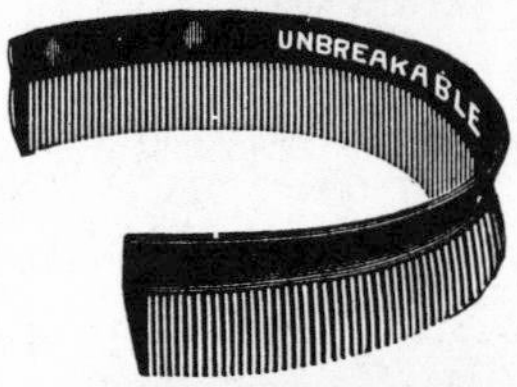

13849 Unbreakable Round Combs, rubber; weight, per doz, 9 ounces.
Each $0.12
Per doz.......... 1.20

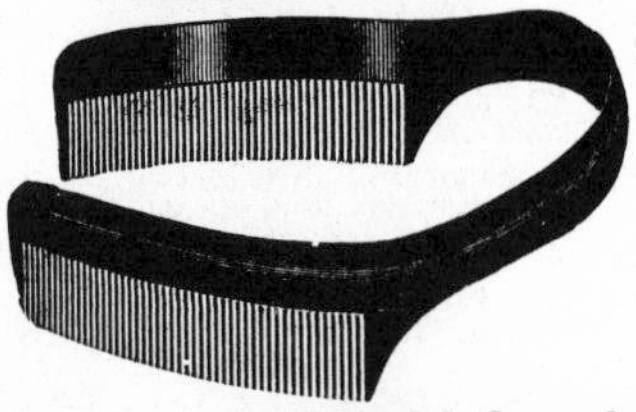

13852 Hard Rubber Combination Side and Round Comb, curved back. Weight, per dozen, 9 ounces.
Each.... $0.10
Per doz.. 1.00

Celluloid Combs.

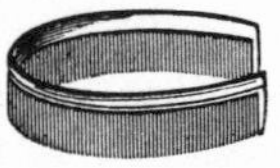

13854 Circle or Round Combs, celluloid, in colors blue, red, shell and white; plain tops.
Each $0.06
Per dozen...................... .65

Goodyear's Hard Rubber Syringes.

(Postage 3 to 5 cents each.)

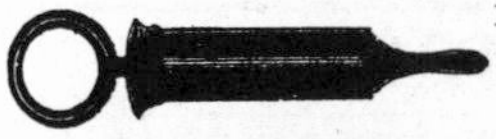

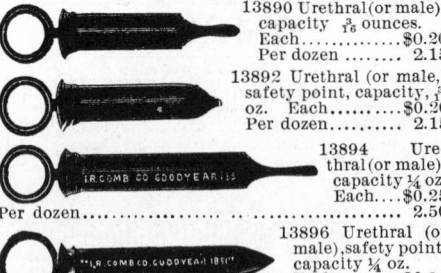

13890 Urethral (or male), capacity $\frac{3}{16}$ ounces.
Each..............$0.20
Per dozen 2.15

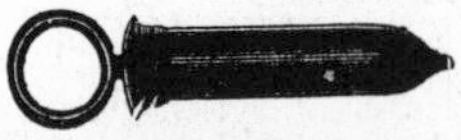

13892 Urethral (or male,) safety point, capacity, $\frac{3}{16}$ oz. Each..........$0.20
Per dozen.......... 2.15

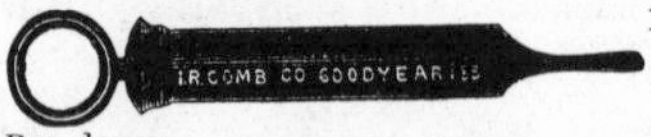

13894 Urethral (or male), capacity ¼ oz.
Each....$0.25
Per dozen.............. .... 2.50

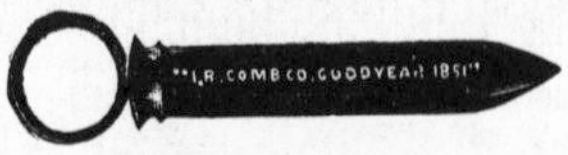

13896 Urethral (or male), safety point, capacity ¼ oz.
Each $0.30
Per dozen.... 3.00

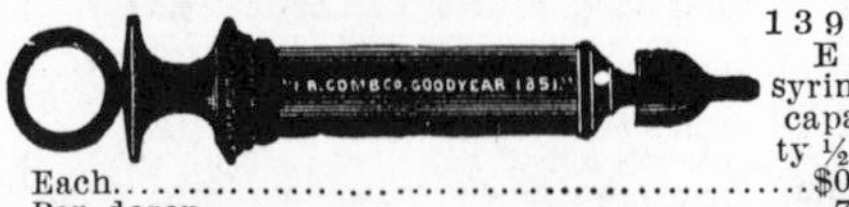

13901 Ear syringe, capacity ½ oz.
Each..$0.70
Per dozen... 7.00

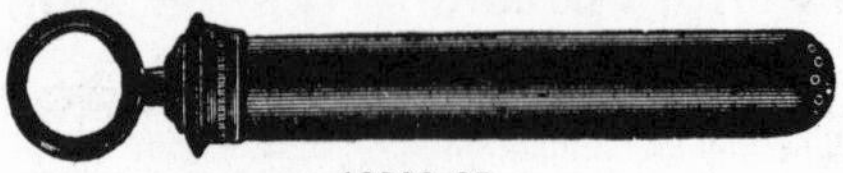

13903-05

13903 Vaginal Syringe, capacity 1 oz.
Each...$0.45
Per dozen........ .... 4.50
13905 Vaginal Syringe, capacity 2 oz. Each...... .60
Per dozen.. 6.00

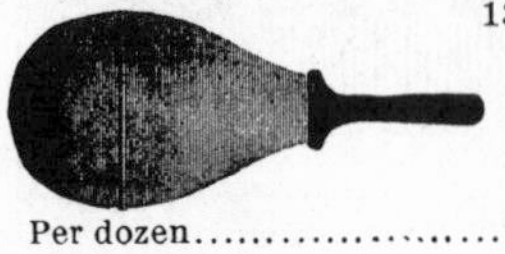

13907 Goodyear Infant Syringe, capacity 1 ounce, soft rubber bulb with hard rubber infant's rectal pipe. Weight, packed, 4 oz.
Each...............$0.20
Per dozen.. 2.15

Syringes—Continued.

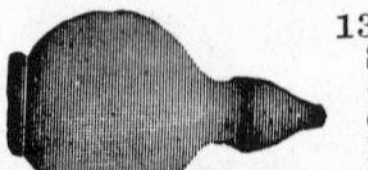

13908 Goodyear Nasal and Ear Syringe, all soft rubber; capacity, ¾-ounce. Weight, packed, 3 ounces.
Each........................$0.20
Per dozen 2.00

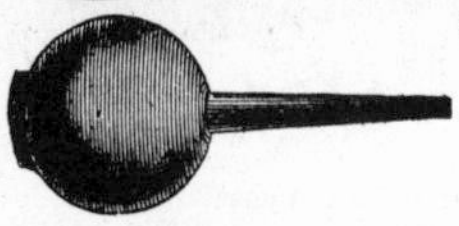

13909 Eye, Ear, Ulcer and Abcess Syringe, capacity 1 ounce; injection tube is made of very soft and flexible rubber, and will not injure or pain the inflamed part. Weight, packed, 3 ounces. Each...........................$0.20
Per dozen 2.00

Challenge Bulb Syringes.

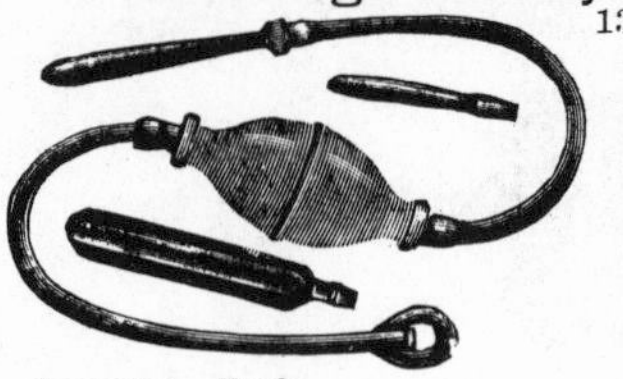

13910 Our Challenge Bulb Syringe, 3 hard rubber pipes, infant rectal, and large vaginal irrigator, made from fine Para stock, and we challenge comparison for actual value. Weight, packed, 8 ounces. Each $0.50
Per dozen 5.40

Goodyear Bulb Syringes.

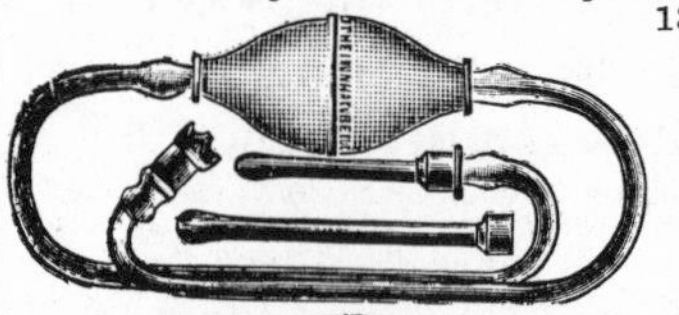

13928 Enterprise Crown Syringe, with two metal pipes. A good, cheap Springe.
Each....$0.40
Per doz. 4.00
Postage, .09

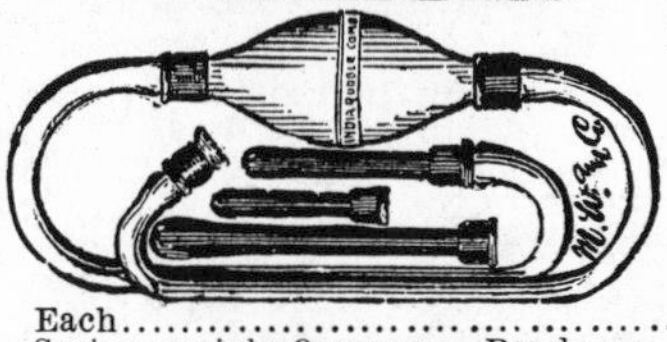

13933 The Metropolitan Crown Syringe, hard rubber fittings, three hard rubber pipes, in neat box; see cut.
Each...$0.65
Syringe weighs 9 ounces. Per dozen............ 6.75

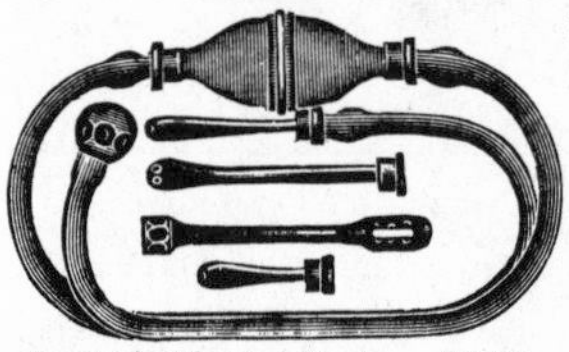

13935 Goodyear Crown Syringe, constructed of the best quality of dark soft rubber, with hard rubber infant, rectal and vaginal pipes and improved vaginal irrigator; in wood box. Weight, packed, 12 oz. Each....$1.00. Per dozen....$10.25

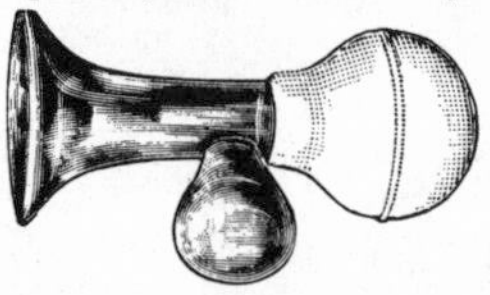

13940 "English" Breast Pump, one in box. Weight, packed, 8 oz.
Each..............$0.22
Per dozen.......... 2.25

Continuous Flow Syringes.

All intermittent syringes inject more or less air, which is invariably drawn back into the tube while the bulb is expanding and re-filling, and is often painful and dangerous. These syringes have a steady and continuous flow, which can be gentle or strong at the easy control of the user. High medical authorities indorse them as being safe, easy to operate and perfect in cleanliness, durability and efficiency. *First-class goods, made of the finest Para rubber* and **Warranted reliable in every respect.**

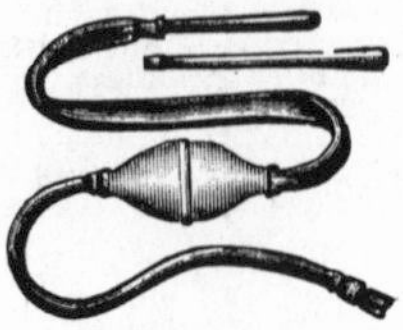

13944 "Omega" No. 4 Syringe (continuous flow), hard rubber vaginal and rectal pipes; no screw threads; valves secured from loss; pipes attached by inserting in soft rubber socket. Packed in octagon box. Weight, packed, 9 ounces.
Each.....................$0.75

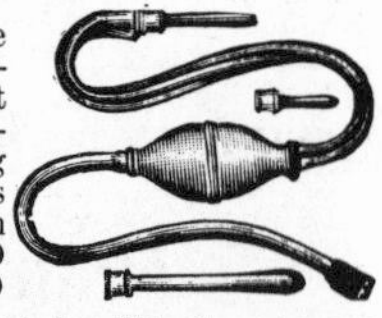

13946 "Omega" No. 3 Syringe (continuous flow), hard rubber vaginal, rectal and infant pipes; noiseless sinker. Improved method of coupling bulb and tubing, that secures valves from loss. Packed in oval box. Weight, packed, 9 ounces. Each..........$1.00

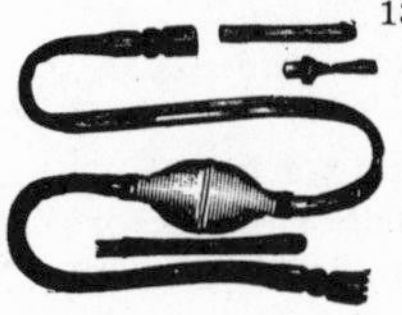

13948 "Alpha E" Syringe, (continuous flow), has no screw threads or washers, therefore cannot leak; injecting tubes being attached by an improved soft rubber joint socket; hard rubber infant, rectal and vaginal pipes; in cloth case. Weight, packed, 12 ounces. Each........$1.50

Syringes—Continued.

13950 "Alpha D" Syringe (continuous flow), fitted without extra large valve chambers; hard rubber infant, rectal, vaginal and nasal pipes, and improved *Vaginal Irrigating Spray;* noiseless and noncorrosive sinker end; packed in neat cloth case. Weight, packed.13 ounces
Each $1.75

Female Syringe.

13952 *"Tyrian" Female Syringe,* for cleansing the vaginal passages of all discharges; especially adapted *for injections of hot water;* the liquid being driven from the syringe when bulb is compressed and drawn back into it on relaxing the pressure, thus giving an opportunity to thoroughly wash the diseased parts. Capacity eight ounces. Made of one piece of *Soft Rubber,* with removable hard rubber shield. Having no valves or connections cannot get out of order. Weight, packed, 13 ounces.   Each.............. $1.25

The Ladies' Syringe.

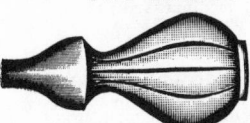

13954 Ladies' Syringe is the only PERFECT vaginal syringe in the world. Constructed upon the principle of *Injection* and *Suction* (a plan generally admitted by the medical profession as the only correct and efficient one); it cleanses the passages of all discharges to *perfection;* is very easily cleaned. During the injections not a drop of fluid need be spilled on clothing, etc. Consists simply of one piece of fine soft rubber. Full instructions for use with each syringe. Weight, packed, 17 ounces. Each.................... $2.50

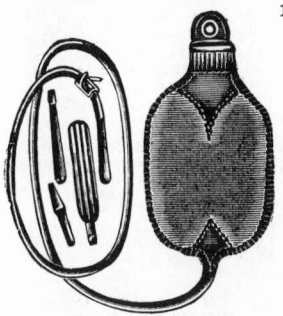

13956 "Perfection" Fountain Syringes, made from *pure rubber,* with hard rubber connections, hard rubber vaginal, rectal and infant pipes, and vaginal irrigator, about six feet pure rubber tubing, with shut off.

	Price each.
2 Quarts	$0.90
3 Quarts	1.00
4 Quarts	1.10

	Per dozen.
2 Quarts	$9.50
3 Quarts	10.50
4 Quarts	11.65

Combination Water Bottle and Fountain Syringe.

First class goods, made from **Pure Rubber** *of high grade:* perfect in durability and all other respects, and guaranteed to give satisfaction.

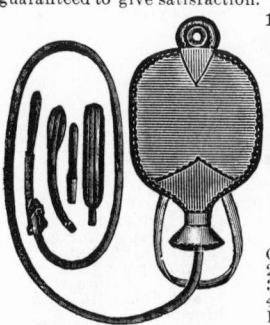

13959 "Perfection" Combination Water Bottle and Fountain Syringe, fitted with hard rubber connection, infant, rectal, bent vaginal and nasal pipes, and vaginal irrigator; six feet pure rubber tubing, with shut-off attachment. Packed in strong black cloth box.

Capacity.	Price, each.
2 Quarts	$1.50
3 Quarts	1.60
4 Quarts	1.70

Postage, 23 to 30c. ea.

Capacity.	Per dozen.
2 Quarts	$15.00
3 Quarts	15.75
4 Quarts	16 50

Challenge Hot Water Bottles.

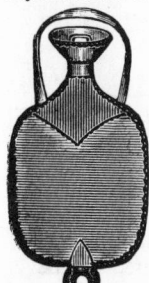

13960 Challenge Hot Water Bottles, pure rubber, high grade goods. Note our prices.

Capacity.	Price each.	Per doz.
2 Quarts	$0.75	$7.50
3 Quarts	.80	7.75
4 Quarts	.85	8.13

Postage, 18 to 25 cents.

Goodyear Crown Water Bottles.

(Hard Rubber Stopper.)

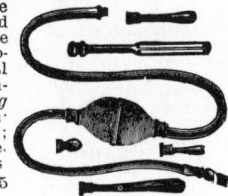

13963 Goodyear Crown Water Bottles, hard rubber stopper. These are pure rubber and warranted. Fountain Syringe Attachments quoted below will fit these water bottles.

Capacity.	Price. each.	Per doz.
2 Quarts	$1.10	$10.75
3 Quarts	1.20	11.75
4 Quarts	1.30	12.50

NOTE.—See Fountain Syringe Attachments No. 13967 which fit water bottles No. 13963.

Fountain Syringe Attachment.

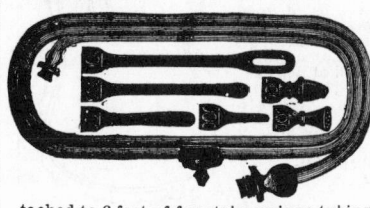

13967—Fountain Syringe Attachment for above water bottles No. 13963 has hard rubber connection attached to 6 feet of fountain syringe tubing, a shut-off and full set of pipes (hard rubber); cannot spill in any position, either hanging or on shelf or mantel.
Per set................................... $ 0.95
Per dozen.................................... 10.80

Rubber Tubing for Syringes.

13975 White Rubber Tubing for Bulb Syringe.
Per foot $0.04
13978 Corrugated White Rubber Tubing for Fountain Syringe. Per foot.................... .04

Seamless Rubber Nipples.

REGULAR STYLE.

		Each.	Per doz.
13980	White Rubber	$0.02	$0.20
13982	Black Rubber	.02½	.25
13984	Maroon Rubber (4)	.03	.30

13980-82-84

Davidson's "Safety" Nipples, celebrated for purity and durability.

		Each.	Per doz.
13986	Safety Nipples, White	$0.03	$0.30
13987	Safety Nipples, Black	.04	.40
13989	Safety Nipples, Maroon	.04	.40

13986-87-89

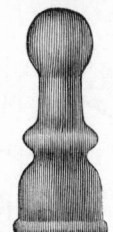

Davidson's "Health" Nipples, made from finest quality Para rubber; can be attached to any bottle where common nipple is used; is constructed so that infant can obtain a strong hold, and renders nursing easy.

		Each.	Per doz.
13992	"Health" Nipples, White	$0.04	$0.40
13993	"Health" Nipples, Black	.04	.45
13994	"Health" Nipples, Maroon	.04	.45

13992-93-94

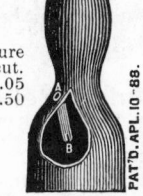

13996 Mizpah Valve Nipples, from pure gum, black only, with valve. See cut.
Each.... .... $0.05
Per dozen .... .50

PAT'D. APL. 10-88.

13996

Soft Nipple Shield.

14005 Soft Nipple Shield in black, white and maroon.
Each................... $0.05
Per dozen............. .50

Finger Cots.

14010 Rubber Finger Cots. Each....... $0.04
Per dozen.................................... .35
Per gross..................................... 3.50
Postage, 5 cents per dozen.

Teething Rings and Pads.

14012 White Rubber Teething Rings for babies.
Each $0.05
Per dozen............ ...... .50
14015 English Teething Pads, dark pure gum rubber; the infants' delight. Each........... $0.08
Per dozen............. .75

Nursing Bottles.

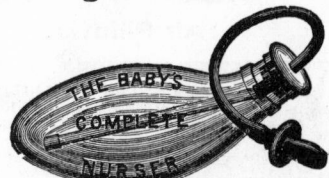

14025 Medallion Nursing Bottle, with white rubber fittings.
Each..$0.10
Per dz.   .95
Weight, packed, 12 ounces.

14028 Nursing Bottles, M. W. & Co., No.1, fitted complete with best maroon or black rubber fittings, and 2 brushes in box. Each............. $0.20
Per dozen...................................... 2.10
Nurser weighs 12 ounces.

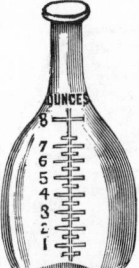

14033 Nursing Flask with rubber nipple, graduated, capacity 8 ounces; made from flint glass.
Each $0.10
Per dozen.................... .95

Nursing Bottle Fittings, Etc.

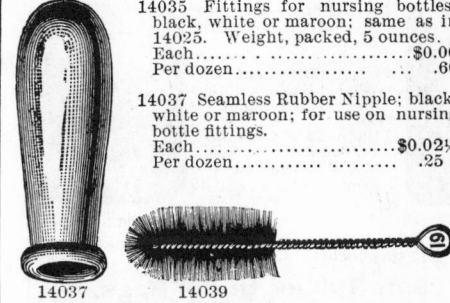

14035 Fittings for nursing bottles; black, white or maroon; same as in 14025. Weight, packed, 5 ounces.
Each........ .... $0.06
Per dozen................. ... .60

14037 Seamless Rubber Nipple; black, white or maroon; for use on nursing bottle fittings.
Each........................ $0.02½
Per dozen................. .25

14037   14039

14039 Bottle Brush, for cleaning nursing bottles.
Each $0.02
Per dozen................................. .20
14042 Tube Brush on finely plated twisted wire, for cleaning nursing bottle tubes. Each...... .01
Per dozen....................................... .07

Rubber Tubing.

14043 Pure Gum Black Rubber Tubing, for nursing bottle fittings. Per foot.................... $0.04
14044 Maroon Rubber Tubing, for nursing bottle fittings. Per foot..................... $0.04

Plant Sprinkler.

14046 Plant Sprinkler, for spraying plants and flowers without injuring them, or soaking the earth, and without soiling everything else near them. May also be used for sprinkling clothing in the laundry, spraying carpets and clothing to prevent moths, spraying disinfectants in the sick room, etc. Preferable in every way to the tin dipper or watering pot. Medium size; capacity 6 ounces; weight, packed, 8 ounces.
Our special price, each........................ $0.55

We can't correct errors if you won't give us a chance.

Invalid Rings.

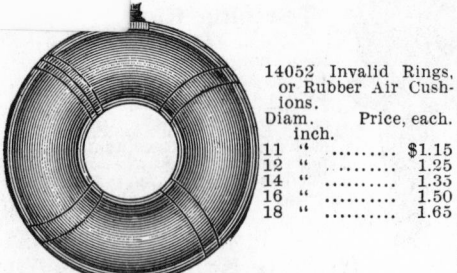

14052 Invalid Rings, or Rubber Air Cushions.

Diam. inch.	Price, each.
11 "	$1.15
12 "	1.25
14 "	1.35
16 "	1.50
18 "	1.65

Air Pillows.

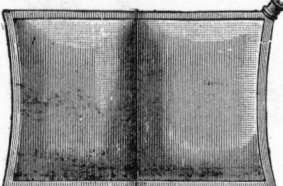

14054 Rubber Air Pillows, sateen covered.

Size.	Each.
9x13 in	$1.25
10x16 in	1.50
12x18 in	2.00
14x23 in	2.25

Bed Pans.

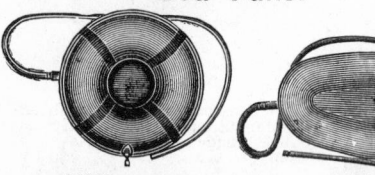

14056 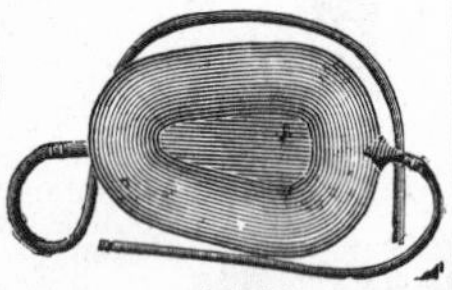   14058

14056 Round Bed Pan, with outlet tube; slate colored soft rubber. Each..................$2.00
14058 Oval Bed Pan, with outlet tube; slate colored soft rubber. Each..................... 2.75

Ice Bags.

For use in case of sunstroke, high fevers, etc.

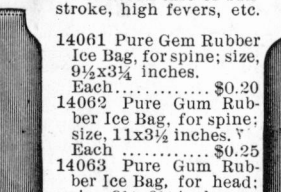
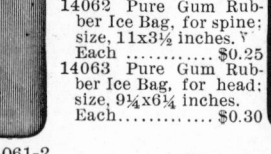

14061 Pure Gem Rubber Ice Bag, for spine; size, 9½x3¼ inches.
Each............ $0.20
14062 Pure Gum Rubber Ice Bag, for spine; size, 11x3½ inches.
Each............ $0.25
14063 Pure Gum Rubber Ice Bag, for head; size, 9¼x6¼ inches.
Each............ $0.30

14061-2   14063-14064

14064 Pure Gum Rubber Ice Bag, for head; size, 11x6½ inches. Each.....................$0.35

Soft Rubber Urinal Bags.

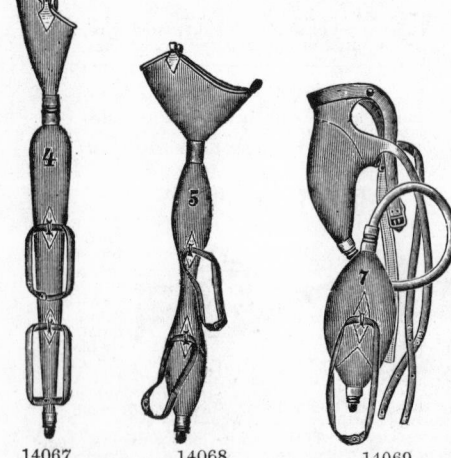

14067   14068   14069

14067 Soft Rubber Urinal Bag, French pattern: day and night use for male. Each.............$0 95
14068 Soft Rubber Urinal Bag, French pattern; day and night use for female. Each........... .95
14069 Soft Rubber Urinal Bag, improved French pattern: day and night use for male. Each.... 2.00

Have your Mail Packages insured. See page 1.

Nursery Rubber Sheeting.

IN WHITE ONLY.

14071 Width	27 in.	36 in.	45 in.	54 in.
Price, per yard	40c.	60c.	75c.	$0.95
Weight, per yard	15 oz.	18 oz.	22 oz.	28 oz.

Diapers.

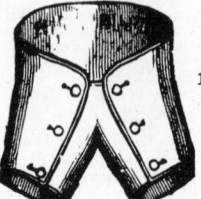

14073 Rubber Diaper Drawers. Come in 3 sizes –small medium and large.
Each...................$0.25
Per dozen............... 2.75
Diaper weighs 6 ounces.

Rubber Bibs.

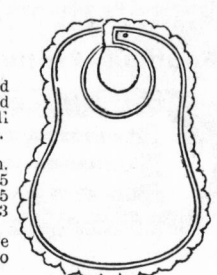

14075 Rubber Bibs of good quality rubber cloth, pinked edges and braided all around with colored braid. Buttons at back of neck. Length.10 in. 11 in. 12 in.
Each...................$0.15
Per dozen............... 1.75
Postage on rubber bibs, 3 cents.
NOTE.—Rubber bibs are measured from chin to lower end.

Waterproof Bibs and Aprons.

14080 Waterproof Bibs of enameled cloth, bound with tape with neck ties. Size, 9x12 inches. Weight, packed, 3 ounces.
Each...................$0.04
Per dozen............... .35

14080

14084 Child's Waterproof Bib, enameled oil, cloth, bound with tape. pocket and tape ties. Weight, packed, 4 ozs.
Each.............$0.10
Per dozen........ .95

14086 Child's Waterproof Apron with loops for arms; enameled oil-cloth bound with tape. Weight, packed, 5 ounces.
Each........ ......$0.10
Per doz.......... .95

14084

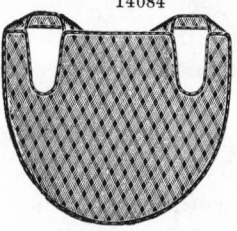

14086

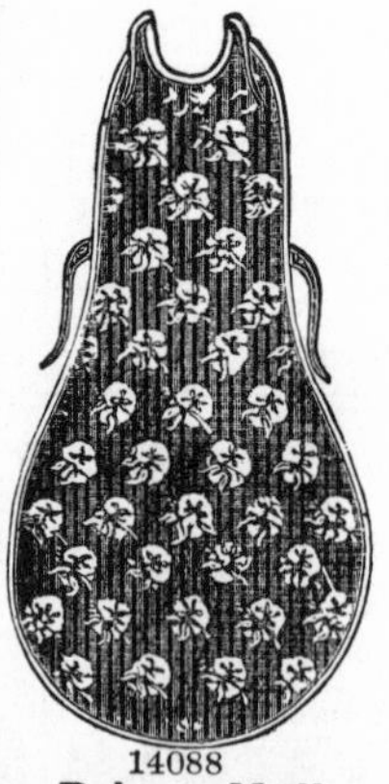

14088 Ladies' Waterproof Bib Apron, enameled oil-cloth, bound all around with tape; ties for neck and waist. Weight, packed, 8 ounces.
Each.................$0.20
Per doz................ 2.15

14088

Prime Yellow Chamois Skin.

We call your attention to our large line or *First Quality* chamois skins, and to a few of their many useful qualities.

Small sizes suitable for ladies' face toilet purposes, for applying powder, etc.; for making chest protectors, undervests and underwear; for lining clothing in cold climates, and for lining watch and pistol pockets they are equal to buckskin; for cleaning and polishing jewelry, silverware, cutlery, guns, revolvers, glassware, mirrors, windows, painted woodwork, buggies and any smooth surface, they are unequaled, as they do not scratch, and leave no lint. Can be used wet or dry. If dry and stiff, after having been used wet, a few rubs between the hands will make them soft.

The size given is the average size in a dozen.

14100—	No.	1	3	5	7
Size—inches		6x5	9½x8½	12x10	17x15
Each		6c.	10c.	28c.	40c.
Per dozen		60c.	$1.00	$2.80	$4.25

14100	No.	10	11	14
Size—inches		20x19	24x22	30x28
Each		55c.	65c.	95c.
Per dozen		$5.75	$7.00	$9.95

Sponges.

14105 Yellow Toilet Sponges, fine texture, bleached, small size; for use with shaving mug, etc. Each........................$0.04
Per dozen............................... .38
Per case (100 pieces)..................... 2.80
14107 Yellow Toilet Sponges, fine texture, bleached; medium size; for general toilet use
Each........................$0.10
Per dozen............................... .95
Per case (100 pieces)..................... 7.00
14109 Florida Toilet Sponge, bleached, medium in texture, for general toilet purposes.

	Each	Per doz	Pr. case 100 pcs.
No. H, small	$0.05	$0.48	$3.50
No. F, medium	.10	.95	7.00
No. E, medium large	.15	1.45	10.50

14116 Pure Sheep's Wool Sponges, free from sand; unbleached, natural color, very durable. For household, carriage and general cleaning and for bath.
No. 10, medium, about 8 in pound.
Each........................ .30
Per pound..................... 2.30

14118 Extra Fine Pure "Sheep's Wool" Bath Sponges, free from sand, choice grade of fine, soft sponges for bathing purposes, also suitable for cleaning highly polished surface, glass, etc.
Each.
No. 16, medium small, 15 to 20 in pound................$0.20

Toilet or Watercloset Paper.

14120 "Capital" Toilet Paper, No. 1 quality; 1,000 (4½x6½ in.) sheets in package, with improved wire loop. Weight, packed, 12 ounces.
Per package........................$0.08
Per dozen packages.................... .80
Per case (100 packages)............... 6.25
14121 Plain (not perforated) Roll Toilet Paper, 4½ inches wide; weight, packed, 8 ounces.
Per roll.............................. .04
Per dozen rolls...................... .40
Per case (100 rolls) 3.00

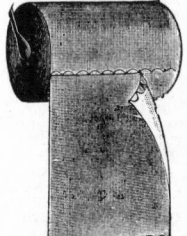

14122 Perforated Roll Toilet Paper, fair quality; Jumbo roll 4¾ inches wide. Weight, packed, 12 ounces
Per roll................$0.06
Per dozen rolls......... .60
Per case (100 rolls)..... 4.50
14123 Perforated Roll Toilet Paper, No. 1 quality; guaranteed to contain 1,000 sheets; 5 inches wide. Weight, packed, 12 ounces.
Per roll................$0.10
Per dozen rolls........ 1.00
Per case (100 roll)....... 7.50

14122

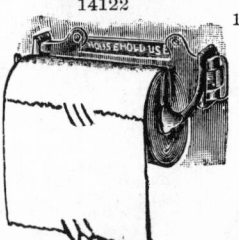

14124 "Honest Count" Divided Roll Toilet Paper, made from *first quality pure tissue;* WARRANTED TO CONTAIN 1,000 square sheets to each roll. Weight, packed, 13 ounces. Per roll...$0.12
Per dozen rolls..... 1.28
Per case (100 rolls).10.00

14124 Roll in 14127 Fixture.

14125 Springfield Oval Toilet Paper, for use in No. 14126 Fixture; weight, packed, 8 ounces. Fixture will be sent free with case of paper.
Per Roll.........$0.08
Per dozen rolls... .90
Per case(100 rolls)7.25

14125 roll in 14126 Fixture.

CHICAGO

. . . IS NOW THE . . .

Commercial Center of America

and is recognized as the Largest and Closest Market for Manufactured Goods in America.

Fixtures for Toilet Papers.

14126 Springfield Toilet Paper Fixture, for families, hotels, factories, public buildings, etc.: for Springfield Oval Roll Paper, No. 14125; locks paper on the fixture and delivers only one sheet at a time. Convenient, Economical, Durable, Noiseless. Japanned finish. Weight, packed, 3 lbs.
Each $0.38
Per dozen 4.00

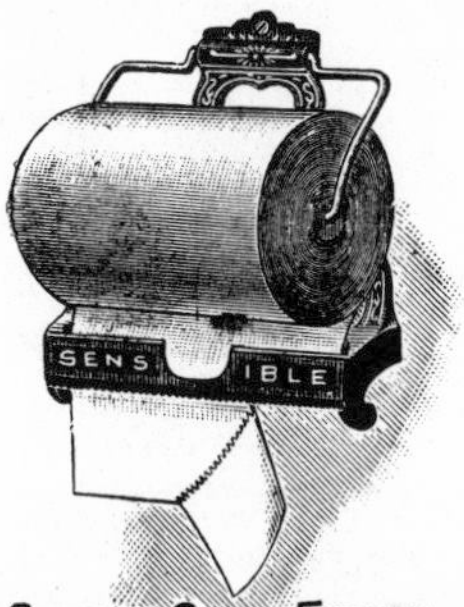

SENSIBLE CLOSET FIXTURE.

14127 "Household", Toilet Paper Fixture, bronze finish; has automatic tension; is complete and cannot get out of order. FOR 14124 PAPER.
Each $0.12
Weighs 12 ounces.

14128 "Sensible" Fixture *for roll toilet papers*, bronze finish; two parts only—roll holder and gauge with cut-off edge. The best fixture in the market. Weight, packed, 12 ounces.
Each $0.12
Per dozen 1.10

Paper Napkins.

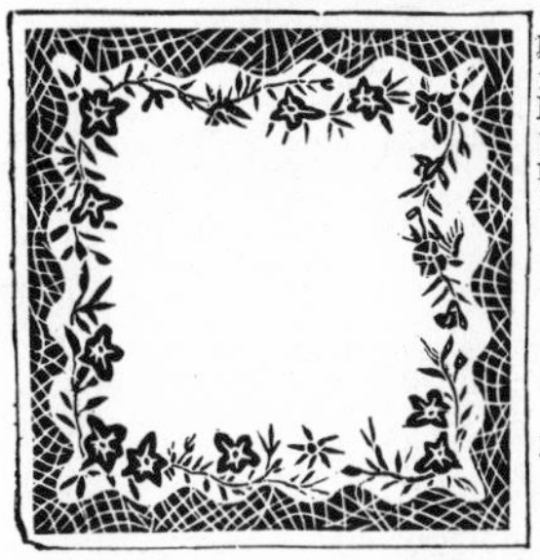

Suitable for use in home decoration and for tourists, travelers, lawn parties, lunches, picnics, fairs, restaurants, etc.

14130 American Tissue Napkins, Japanese designs in assorted colors, size, about 15x15, superior quality.
Per 100 ...... $0.25
Per 1,000 ...... 2.00

14132 Japanese Paper Napkins, creped; fancy designs in bright colors, medium large size, 100 weigh 15 ounces.
Per 100 .... $0.50 Per 1,000 .... $4.50

Toothpicks.

14135 Hard Wood Toothpicks, double pointed, 2,300 in a box, for hotels, restaurants, etc.
Per box $0.03
Per dozen boxes .... .30
Per case (100 boxes) 2.25

14138 "World's Fair," "Velvet Finish" Wood Toothpicks, compressed, rounded, polished and double pointed. *The best wood pick made.* For family use. Per box .... .05
Per dozen boxes .... .60
Per cartoon, 25 boxes 1.20

14140 Quill Toothpicks, about 15 picks in bunch.
Per bunch .... .03
Per package, 40 bunches .... .95

TOILET SOAPS.

We are large buyers of toilet soaps, hence are enabled to get unusually low prices from manufacturers. We carry a large and well assorted stock and our toilet soap trade is one of the largest in the West.

Improved American White Castile.

14151 Improved American Castile Toilet Soap, 100 per cent. pure: our own brand. Guaranteed to produce the cleanest and most purifying lather. We do not sell less than a box of this soap. Order a box, and if it does not suit you, notify us, and we will see that it costs you nothing. Parties ordering other goods can have a sample BAR put in their order free of charge. This is our leader in toilet soaps. Cut in 4 ounce square cakes, 16 cakes in a box (about 4 pounds in box).
Price, per box $0 50
In lots of 6 boxes or more, 45c. per box.

Cocoanut Oil Toilet Soaps.

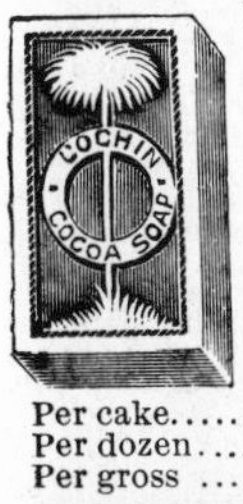

14153 Pure Cocoanut Oil Soap. This soap gives the same results when used in very hard water that an ordinary soap would have in soft water. Made expressly for Dakota, Utah, Arizona trade, or wherever there is a trace of alkali in the water. Cocoanut Oil Soap can, of course, be used in soft as well as hard water. It makes a wonderful suds, possesses a decided cocoanut odor, and some persons will use no other. Cakes, ⅞x1⅞x3 inches; 1 dozen cakes in a box.
Per cake $0.03
Per dozen .... .30
Per gross 3.00

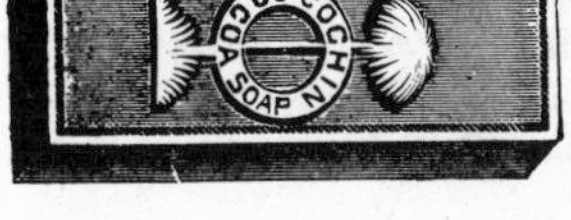

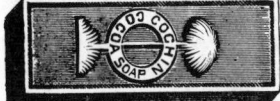

14154 Pure Cocoanut Oil Soap, in 8-ounce bars, size, 5⅜x9½ inches
Per bar. $0.08
Per box (20 bars). $1.30

Milled Toilet Soaps.

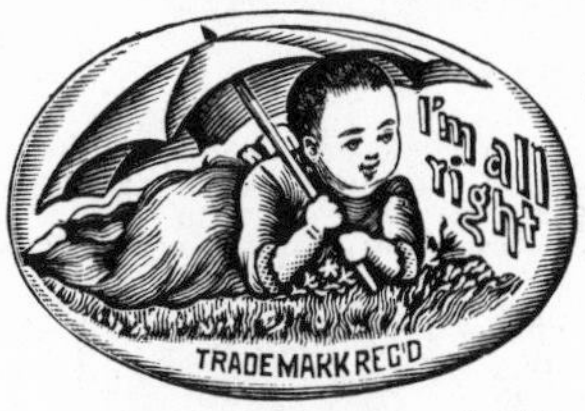

14162 "I'm All Right" Milled Toilet Soap, large oval cakes, pink and white, 12 in box.
Per cake $0.04
Per dozen ... .40

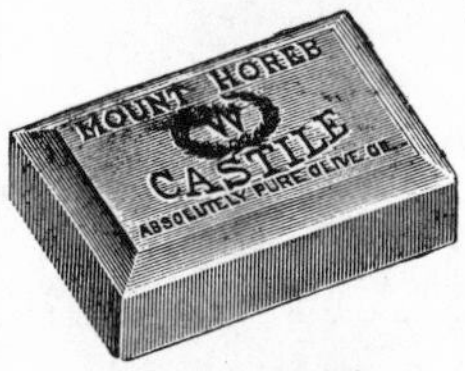

14165 "Mount Horeb" Castile, a pure, natural color olive oil soap made of the finest selected oil imported for this purpose, unexcelled for delicacy and cleansing, softening qualities; superior to much of the imported Castile soap.
Per cake $0.05
Per bx., 1 doz. cakes. .45

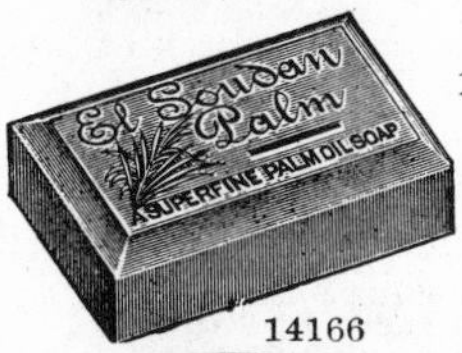

14166

14166 "*El Soudan*" *Palm*, a superfine toilet soap, made from the finest selected African palm oil, imported expressly for this purpose.
Per cake $0 05
Per dozen cakes ..... .45

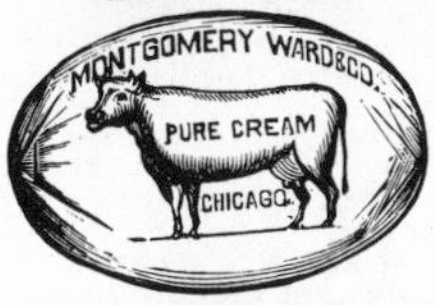

14169 Montgomery Ward & Co.'s "Pure Cream" Toilet Soap, a fine milled delicately perfumed toilet soap, medium oval cakes, 3 cakes (each wrapped) in box. Per cake $0.04
Per box (3 cakes) .... .11
Per dozen .... .40

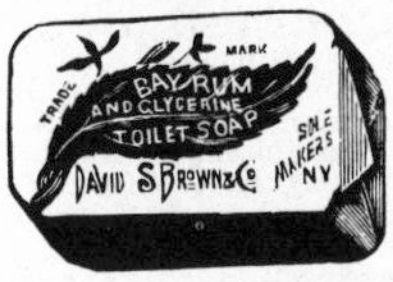

14180 "Fine Milled Bay Rum and Glycerine" Toilet Soap, wrapped, 3 cakes in box (see cut).
Each $0.08
Per dozen .... .84
Postage .... .05

Transparent Soaps.

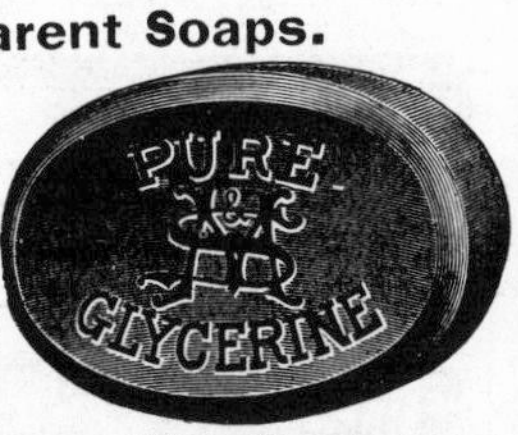

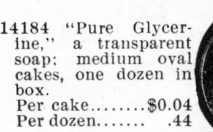

14184 "Pure Glycerine," a transparent soap; medium oval cakes, one dozen in box.
Per cake $0.04
Per dozen .... .44

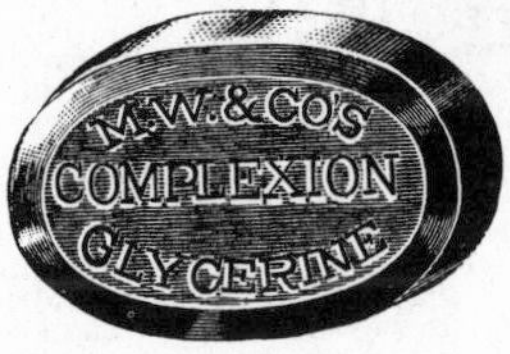

14188 Montgomery Ward & Co.'s (our own brand) Complexion Glycerine Soap. A fine transparent soap guaranteed to be perfectly pure and sweet; unexcelled for the toilet and bath; makes a copious lather, is very emollient and produces a smooth skin. Fully equal to imported soaps at one-half the price. Per cake $0.10
Per box (3 cakes) ...... $0.25 Per dozen .... .95
Postage 05

Pear's English Soaps.

14193 Pear's Unscented Transparent Soap. Per cake $0.09
14195 Pear's Transparent Glycerine Soap, scented. Per cake .... .14

Boquet Soaps.

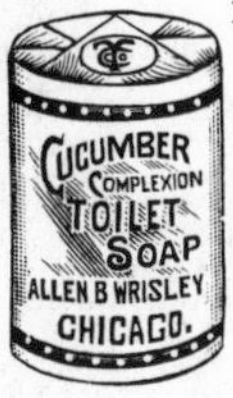

14202 "Cucumber" Complexion Toilet Soap, delicately perfumed, fragrant and refreshing; combines the healthful cleansing of pure soap, with the grateful emollient qualities of cucumber juice; medium oval cakes, each wrapped; 3 cakes in box.
Per cake $0.09
Per box, three cakes .... .25
Per dozen .... .95

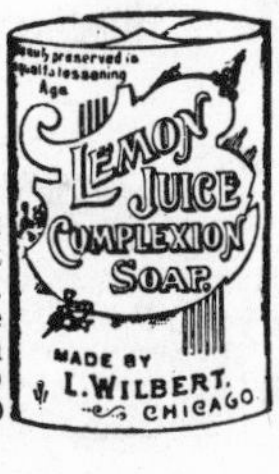

14205 "Lemon Juice" Complexion Soap, a nicely perfumed milled toilet soap; *excellent for freckles, sunburn, tan, etc. Very popular.* Each cake in handsome wrapper, 3 cakes in box. Per cake $0.09
Per dozen cakes 1.00

Toilet Soaps—Continued.

14208 Twentieth Century Toilet Soaps, fine milled and perfumed, Glycerine, Honey and Oatmeal; nicely wrapped, 3 cakes in box.
Per cake $0.08
Per box .... .22
Per dozen .... .80

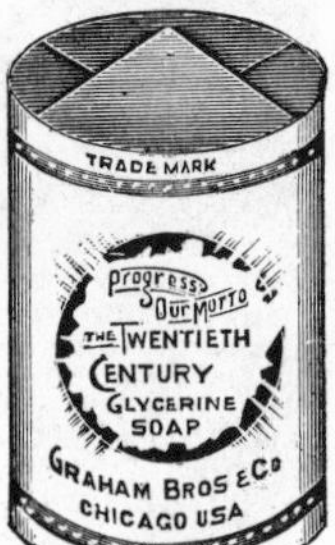

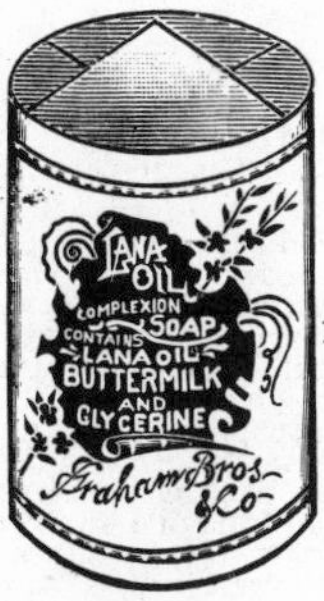

14210 Lana Oil Complexion Soap, contains Lana Oil, Buttermilk and Glycerine, for preserving the skin and leaving it soft and pliable; each cake wrapped, 3 cakes in box. Per cake $0.09
Per box, three cakes .... .25
Per dozen .... .95

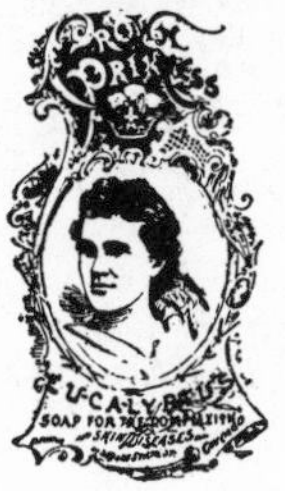

14212 Crown Princess Eu-ca-lyp-tus Soap, *for the complexion*, from pure vegetable oils, contains no perfume except Oil of Eu-ca-lyp-tus which is the principal ingredient; it whitens the skin and leaves it fresh and youthful in appearance; for scalp, hair, skin diseases, pimples, blackheads, brown spots, freckles, sunburn and tan it has no equal. Regular price, 25 cents. Our special price, per cake ... $0.10
Per box, 3 cakes .... .25
Per dozen .... .90

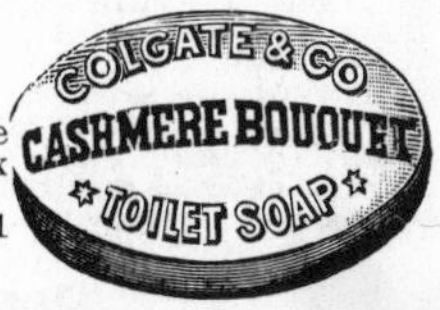

14213 Colgate's Cashmere Bouquet Soap, genuine; six cakes in box.
Per cake $0.21

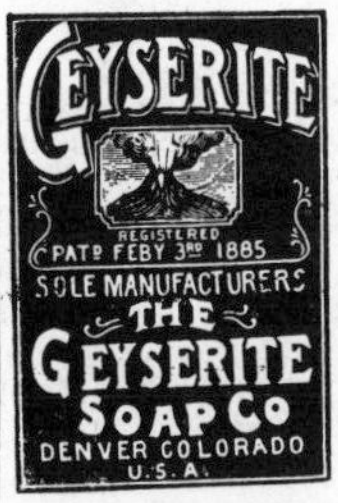

Medicated Soaps.

14215 Geyserite, nature's own medicinal soap; a product of Geyser action, holding in solution potash, soda, lime, iron, magnesia and sulphur, which, chemically combined with a pure vegetable oil compound, forms a pure, cleansing and healing toilet soap; heals cuts, burns, bruises, eczema and eruptions of the skin: try Geyserite for the complexion. Per cake $0.04
Per dozen .... .42
Hotel box (100 cakes) 3.00

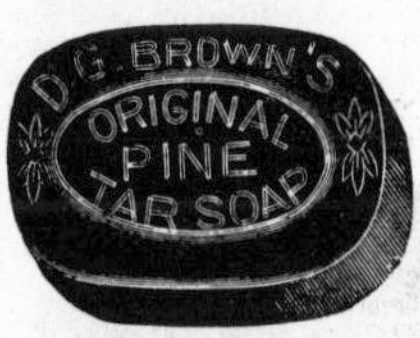

14216 *Brown's "Pine Tar,"* a superior, pure, *non-irritating* and effective soap, which can be used in hard, or soft water, contains the natural healing of *pure Vegetable Oils*, makes the skin soft, elastic and healthy; prevents chapped hands; cures Tetter and Salt Rheum; removes dandruff. *Retail Price 10 cents per cake.* Our special price, per cake $0.05
Per box (one dozen cakes) .... .48

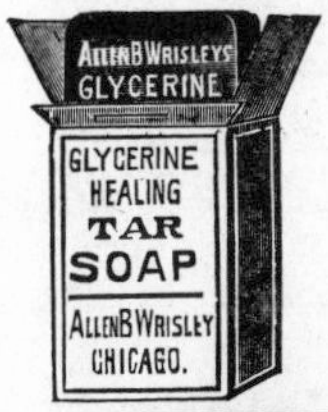

14217 "Glycerine Healing Tar" Soap, an absolutely pure soap, combining curative properties of glycerine and tar; can be used in hard water and will keep hands soft and smooth. Made especially for farmers, mechanics and people doing rough work. Large eight ounce cake in box.
Per cake $0.07
Per dozen cakes .... .75
Postage .... .10

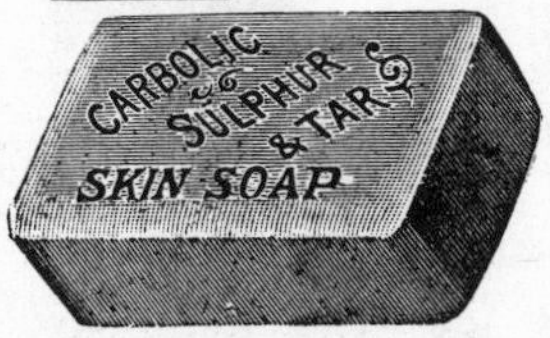

14219 Carbolic Sulphur and Tar Soap for the complexion and diseases of the skin.
Per cake $0.08
Per dozen ..... .80

14221 Carbolic Acid Soap, for man and beast. Excellent for the skin under all conditions, but especially beneficial when used for washing bruises, burns, cuts, old sores, itchings, etc. Each cake wrapped, six cakes in box.
Per cake $0.08
Per dozen cakes .... .80

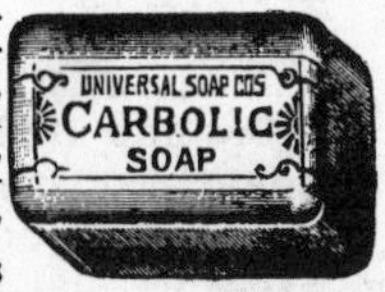

Toilet Soaps—Continued.

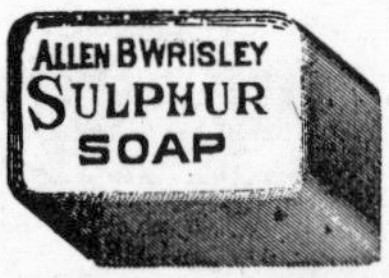

14223 Wrisley's "Sulphur Bath" Soap, for beautifying the complexion; a remedy for skin diseases. It affords the benefits of the sulphur bath to every household; 3 cakes in box.
Per cake $0.08
Per dozen cakes .... .80

14227 Packer's Tar Soap. Perfectly pure. Excellent for toilet, bath and nursery use. A natural balm for skin diseases. A delightful cleanser of hair and scalp. Usual price, 25 cents per cake. Our price, per cake. $0.18 Per dozen cakes $2.05

14229 Genuine Cuticura Medicated Toilet Soap. Per cake, 14 cents. Drug store price 25 cents per cake.

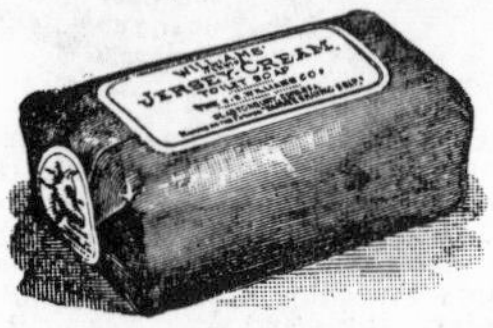

14235 Williams' Medicated Jersey Cream Toilet Soap; contains *pure, rich cream from Jersey Cows* combined with other curative properties recommended in treatment of skin diseases; softening, soothing, healing, cooling, refreshing and invigorating; for toilet, bath and nursery purposes: heals babies' rash, also chaps and sores; cools sunburn, feverish irritations, etc.; prevents acute and chronic eczema, pimples, etc. Per cake $0.20
Per box (3 cakes) .... $0 57 Per dozen cakes 2.10

STIEFEL'S MEDICACTED SOAPS.

Known as the Standard Medicated Soaps of the World.

3 cakes in a box.	Per cake.	Per box.	Per doz.
14245 "Borax," a remedy for chronic skin diseases, chilblain, itch, freckles, liver spots and eruptions. A beautifier of the complexion	$0.17	$0.48	$1.75
14247 "Carbolic Acid Glycerine," a protection against contagious diseases, wash in surgical operations, healing remedy in supurating skin disease. Excellent for tetter and similar skin diseases and a safeguard against vermine and insect stings	.17	.48	1.75
14249 "Freckle," a pleasant and most effective remedy for freckles, tan, liver spots and other unseemly eruptions of the skin.	.17	.48	1.75

Dog Soap.

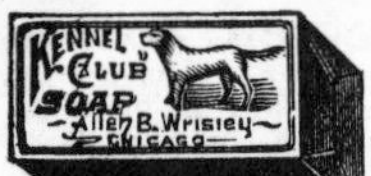

14254 "Kennel Club" Dog Soap; will kill fleas and other insects and give relief in skin diseases.
Per cake $0.08
Per dozen cakes .... .75

SHAVING SOAP.

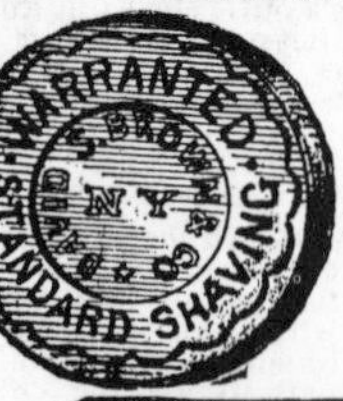

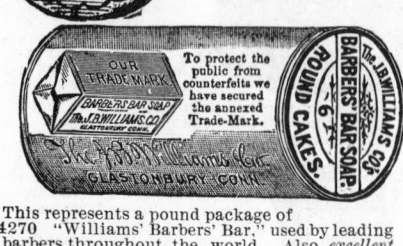

14261 Standard Shaving Soap a good, pure, white soap; six round cakes to pound package. Per cake $0.04
Per dozen .... .40

14264 Genuine Cuticura Shaving Soap, medicated; square cup cakes; makes an excellent lather. Per cake, $0.12½

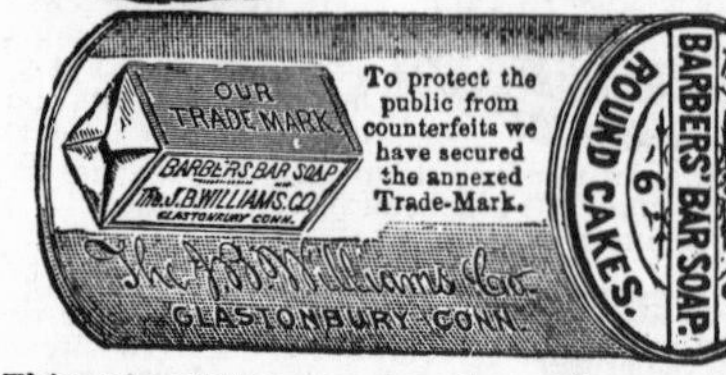

This represents a pound package of
14270 "Williams' Barbers' Bar," used by leading barbers throughout the world. Also *excellent for bath, toilet and nursery purposes*, keeping the skin always soft and smooth. Six round cakes to package.
Box of 10 pounds (60 cakes) $2.70
Per cake .... .06
Per dozen cakes .... .60

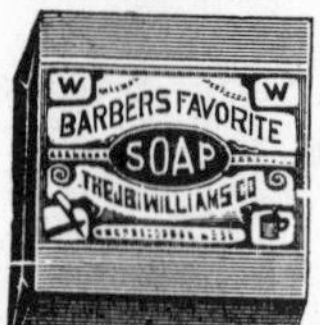

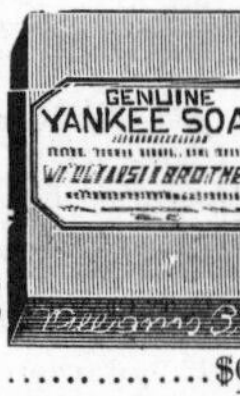

14275 "Barbers' Favorite," a very popular shaving soap. Per cake $0.08 Per dozen .75

14280 "Genuine Yankee," the most famous shaving soap in the market.
Per cake $0.09
Per dozen cakes 1.00

See our DRUG LIST for a complete line of Toilet Articles, also elsewhere in this catalogue. (See Index on pink pages.)

Shaving Soaps—Continued.

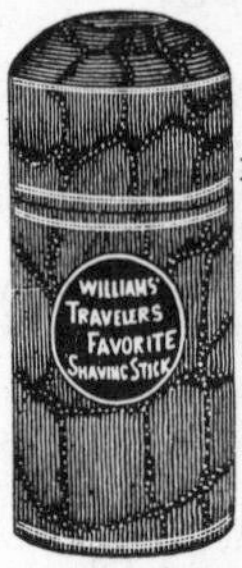

14284 "Williams' Travelers' Favorite" Shaving Stick. A pure, white soap, exquisitely perfumed with finest Attar of Roses; in leatherette covered metal box.
Per stick $0.19
Per dozen sticks 1.90
Postage .... .06

Tooth Soap.

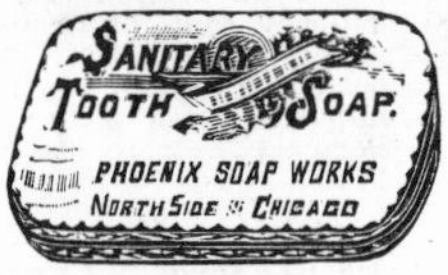

14289 "Sanitary," the Perfect Tooth Soap, for cleaning, beautying and preserving the teeth, hardening the gums and keeping the breath sweet; warranted not injurious; in metallic box. Retail price, 25 cents.
Our price, per box .. $0.12 Per dozen boxes ... $1.25

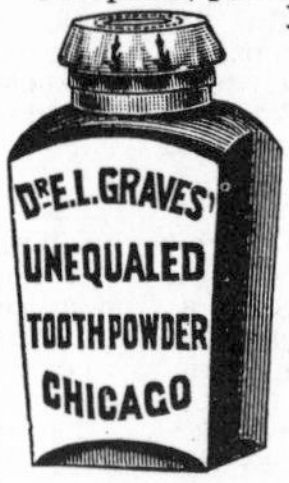

14292 Dr. Graves' Unequaled Tooth Powder, pure, pleasant, harmless; cleans, brightens, beautifies and saves the teeth; cures soft and bleeding gums, makes fillings last. Highly recommended by dentists. Drug store price 25 cents. Weight, packed, 10 ounces.
Our special price, 2 oz. bottle, $0.18
Per dozen 1.85

14294 Dr. Graves' Unequaled Tooth Powder, 4 ounce wide mouth bottle. Drug store price 50 cents. Weight, packed, 12 ounces.
Our special price ...... $0.35 Per dozen $3 75

Pomatum and Cosmetiques.

(To be used same as cosmetic.)

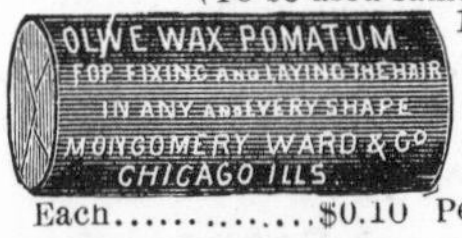

14296 Olive Wax Pomatum. for fixing and laying the hair, whiskers or mustaches. Highly perfumed; each stick wrapped in tinfoil.
Each .... $0.10 Per dozen $0.70

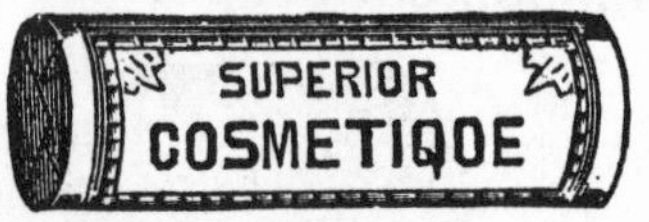

14301 Superior Cosmetique, black, pink or white; each stick wrapped in foil. Retail price, 10c. Our special price—
Per stick .... $0.05 Per dozen sticks $0.45

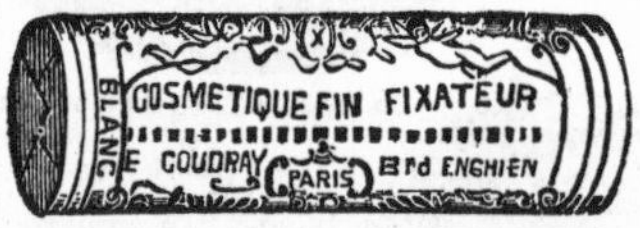

14303 French Cosmetique, round stick, wrapped in foil, black, pink or white. Retail price, 10c. Our special price—
Per stick .... $0.05 Per dozen sticks $0.45

Shampoo Paste.

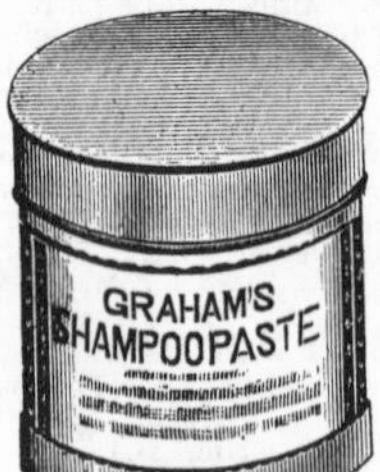

14306 Graham's Shampoo Paste. Removes dandruff, leaves the hair soft and keeps scalp in healthy condition. Produces the finest foam, is the most economical shampoo and is unexcelled as a cleanser
Per box $0.18
Per dozen 1.75
Box weighs 8 ounces.

Clothes and Glove Cleaner.

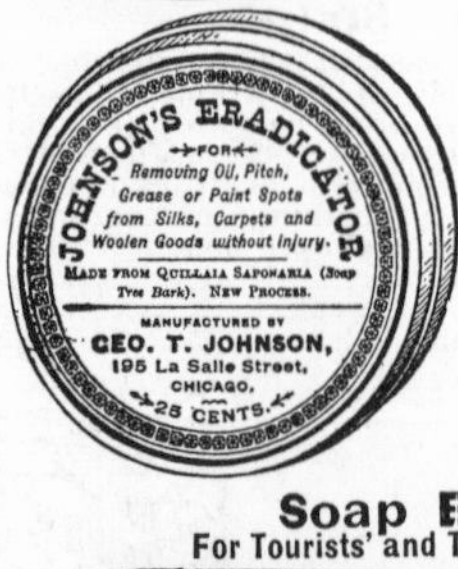

14310 "Johnson's Eradicator," made from "Quillaia" bark from the South American Soap Tree; for removing stains, oil, pitch, grease, dirt and paint spots from silks, woolen goods, carpets, etc..without injury. Excellent for cleaning kid gloves, leaving them soft, dry and pliable. Retail price 25c per box.
Our special price, per box $0.12
Postage .... .04

Soap Boxes.

For Tourists' and Travelerers' Use.

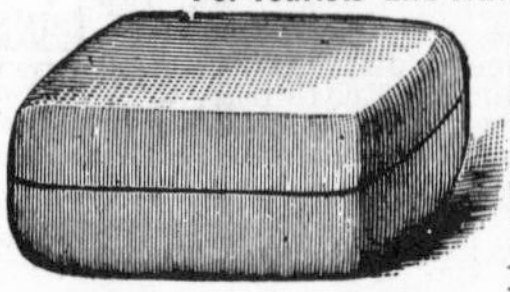

14313 Celluloid Soap Box, white, size. 3½x2¾ x1⅝ inches; loose cover, handsome and very durable. Weight, packed, 5 ounces.
Our special price, Each $0.25

STATIONERY DEPARTMENT.

Envelopes.

No. Description.	Prices. 250	500	1,000
14401 Envelopes, manilla, No. 3, Drug, 2$\frac{5}{16}$x3⅝ in., 1,000 in box. Weight, per box, 46 ounces	......	......	$0.38
14403 Envelopes, manilla coin, open end, No. 3, 2½x4¼ in., 500 in box. Weight, per box. 30 ounces	......	$0.28	.48
14405 Envelopes, manilla, No. 5, 3x5½ in., No. 440, XXX stock. (500 in box). Weight, per box, 46 ounces	......	.30	.53
14407 Envelopes, manilla, No. 6, 3⅝x6 in., No. 440, XXX stock, (500 in box). Weight per box, 52 ounces	......	.35	.60
14409 Envelopes, manilla, No. 6¾, size, 3$\frac{9}{16}$x6½ in., No. 440, XXX stock (500 in box). Weight, per box, 61 ounces	......	.40	.70
14414 Envelopes, white, No. 5, 3x5½ in., No. 350, XX stock. Weight, per box of 250, 32 ounces.	$0.25	.42	.75
14416 Envelopes, white, No. 6, 3⅝x6 in., No. 350, XX stock. Weight, per box of 250, 35 ounces.	.28	.47	.85
14422 Envelopes, white, No. 5, 3x5½ in., No. 250, XX super stock. Weight, per box of 250, 32 ounces.	.28	.47	.85
14424 Envelopes, white, No. 6, 3⅝x6 in., No. 250, XX super stock. Weight, per box of 250, 36 ounces	.30	.55	1.00
14430 Envelopes, Duplex; white outside, blue inside, *writing cannot show through;* No. 5, 3x5½ in., high cut, No. 850, XX super stock. Weight, per box of 250, 32 ounces.	.35	.65	1.15
14434 Envelopes, Duplex; white outside, blue inside, *writing cannot show through;* No. 6½, 3½x6¼ in., high cut, No. 850, XX super stock. Weight, per box of 250, 40 ounces.	.40	.75	1.40
14438 Envelopes, cream wove commercial high cut, No. 5, 3x5½ in., No. 160, XXX super extra stock. Weight, per box of 250, 37 ounces. Per 100, ... 22c	.38	.70	1.35
14442 Envelopes, cream wove, commercial high cut, No. 6, 3⅝x6 in., No. 160, XXX super extra stock. Weight, per box of 250, 41 ounces Per 100 .... 25c.	.45	.85	1.50
14456 Envelopes, cream wove, baronial high cut, No. 4, 3¾x4⅝ in., No. 160, XXX super extra stock. Weight, per box of 250, 36 ounces. Per 100 .... 23c	.45	.82	1.40
14463 Envelopes, cream wove, baronial high cut, No. 5, 4¼x5¼ in., No. 160, XXX super extra stock. Weight, per box of 250, 43 ounces. Per 100 .... 25c.	.45	.85	1.50
14468 Envelopes, Silk Fiber, four tints in box, No. 6, size, 3⅝x6 in., XX super extra stock (500 in box). Weight, per box, 56 ounces	......	.85	1.60
14471 Envelopes, linen, cream, high cut, No. 6, 3⅝x6 in. Old Hampden Bond. Very light in weight and *suitable for use in foreign correspondence.* Weight, per box of 250 24 ounces. Per 100, ... 25 c	.50	.90	1.75
14475 Envelopes, white wove official No. 9, 3⅞x8⅞ in., No. 150 XX super extra stock. Weight, per box of 250, 56 ounces. Per 100, 35c.	.65	1.25	2.35
14478 Envelopes, manilla, official No. 10, 4⅛x9½ in., No. 450, XXXX stock. Weight per box of 500, 7½ lbs. Per 100 .... 25c.	.45	.85	1.45

Writing Papers—Ruled and Folded.

Postage on paper and envelopes is usually more than cost of goods—16c. per pound. N. B.—A ream of paper contains 480 sheets; ¼ ream contains 120 sheets.

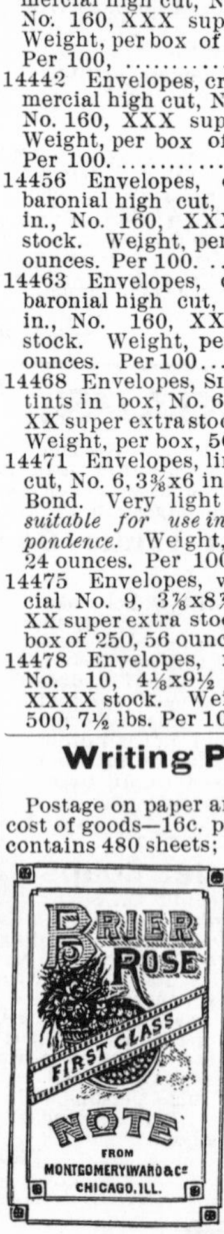

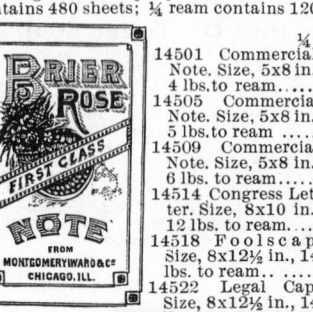

	Per ¼ Ream.	Per Ream.
14501 Commercial Note. Size, 5x8 in., 4 lbs. to ream	$0.12	$0.40
14505 Commercial Note. Size, 5x8 in., 5 lbs. to ream	.14	.50
14509 Commercial Note. Size, 5x8 in., 6 lbs. to ream	.17	.60
14514 Congress Letter. Size, 8x10 in., 12 lbs. to ream	.33	1.20
14518 Foolscap, Size, 8x12½ in., 14 lbs. to ream	.39	1.40
14522 Legal Cap. Size, 8x12½ in., 14 lbs. to ream	.39	1.40

"The party who shakes the tree doesn't always get the most apples."

Superfine Writing Papers—Ruled and Folded

Our "Superfine" papers will be found to be just what is needed by those who require *good paper* for business and general correspondence.

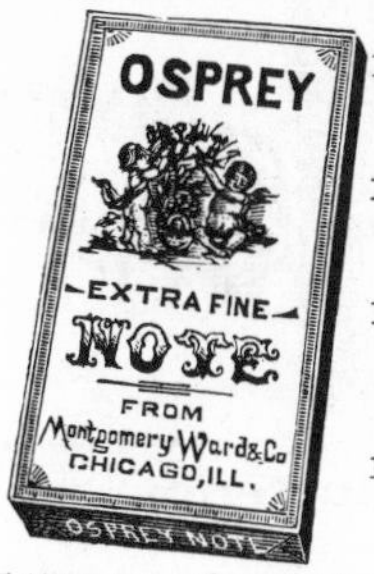

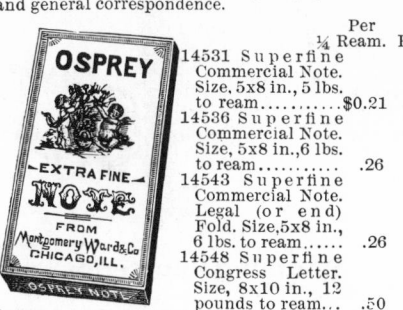

	Per ¼ Ream.	Per Ream.
14531 Superfine Commercial Note. Size, 5x8 in., 5 lbs. to ream	$0.21	$0.75
14536 Superfine Commercial Note. Size, 5x8 in., 6 lbs. to ream	.26	.90
14543 Superfine Commercial Note. Legal (or end) Fold. Size, 5x8 in., 6 lbs. to ream	.26	.90
14548 Superfine Congress Letter. Size, 8x10 in., 12 pounds to ream	.50	1.80
14552 Superfine Foolscap. Size, 8x12½ in., 14 lbs. to ream	.60	2.10
14558 Superfine Legal Cap. Size, 8x12½ in., 14 lbs. to ream	.60	2.10

Single Sheet Papers.

"Superfine" White Wove Single Sheet Writing Papers, *ruled one side only*, for business purposes. Put up in packages of 500 sheets, and we do not sell less than package.

	Per Package.
14560 Superfine 6-lb. Note Heads; size, 5½x8½ inches; half ream (500 sheets) in package	$0.42
14561 Superfine 7-lb. Royal Packet Note Heads; size, 6x9½ inches; half ream (500 sheets) in package	.50
14562 Superfine 12-lb. Folio Letter Heads; size, 8½x11 inches; half ream (500 sheets) in package	.84
14563 Superfine 6-lb. Statement Heads. No. 6; size, 5½x8½ inches; half ream (500 sheets) in package	.45
14564 Superfine 14-lb. Bill Heads, No. 6; size, 8½ x4¾ inches; half ream (500 sheets) in package	.35
14565 Superfine 14-lb Bill Heads, No. 4; size, 8½ x7 inches; half ream (500 sheets) in package	.52
14566 Superfine 14-lb Bill Heads, No. 3; size, 8½ x9¼ inches; half ream (500 sheets) in package	.70
14567 Superfine 14-lb Bill Heads, No. 2; size, 8½ x14 inches; half ream (500 sheets) in package	1.05

Fine Note Papers

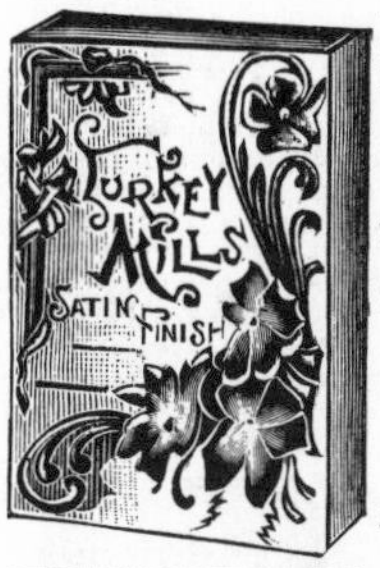

14582 Pound Package of Turkey Mills, Satin Finish Cream Wove Ruled Octavo Note Paper. Weight, packed, 18 ounces. Per package (one pound)....$0.20

Note–14456 Envelopes are suitable for use with 14582 paper.

14584 Mayflower Linen Commercial Note Paper, a coarse cream laid, smooth finish, ruled paper, size, 5x8 inches; quarter ream (120) in box; weight, packed, 26 oz. Per box, $0.30
Per ream.................. 1.05

14586 Mayflower Linen Commercial Note, *unruled*, otherwise same as 14584. Per box, $0.30. Per ream, $1.05.

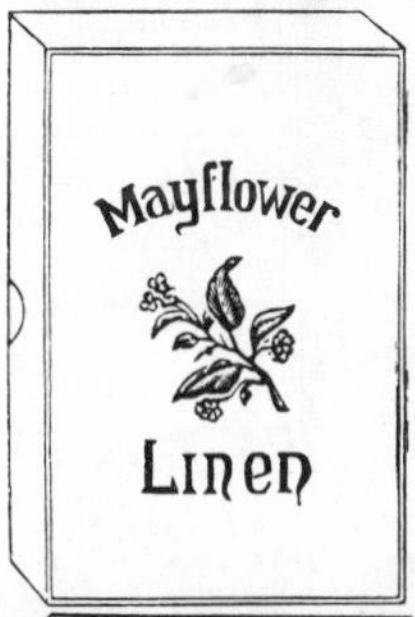

14588 Envelopes, Mayflower Linen. No. 5 Baronial (or square) to match 14584 and 14586 papers; one-eighth thousand (125) in box; weight, packed, 25 ounces. Per box.....$0.30
Per 1,000 .... 2.10

Fine Correspondence Note Papers

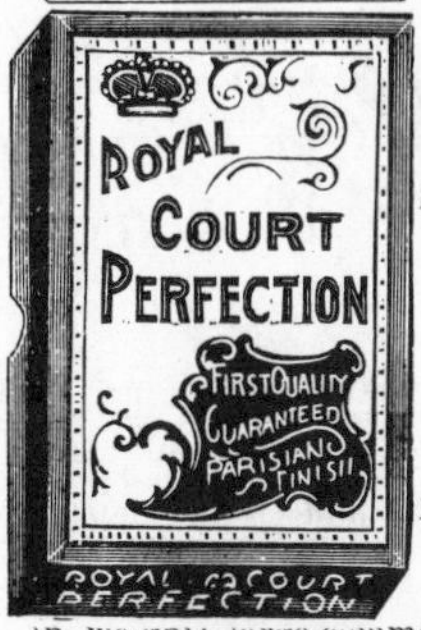

14590 Royal Court Perfection Note Paper, for fine correspondence; guaranteed *first quality*, water marked, high finish cream wove octavo note, ruled; quarter ream (120 sheets) in box; weight, packed, 26 ounces. Our special price:
Per box.............. $0.45
Per ream.............. 1.60

14592 Envelopes, Royal Court Perfection. guaranteed *first quality* cream wove baronial (or square) octavo size, to match 14590 paper; one-eighth thousand (125) in box; weight, packed, 20 ounces. Our special price per box. $0.45
Per 1,000.................. 3.00

14594 "Overland Mail," *for foreign correspondence*; an extra thin, smooth finish, waterlined paper, very light in weight; large commercial note; size, 5½x8½ in.; quarter ream (120 sheets) in package; weight, packed, 12 ounces. Our special price, per package......$0.38

14596 "Overland Mail," waterlined, *for foreign correspondence*; large letter size, 8¼x10¼in.; quarter ream (120 sheets) in package; weight, packed, 22 ounces.
Our special price, per package.................. .75

Note Paper—Continued.

14598 "Overland Mail" Envelopes, No. 6; size, 3⅝x5⅞; for use with 14594 and 14596 papers.
Per 100.................................. 35

Desk or Scratch Pads.

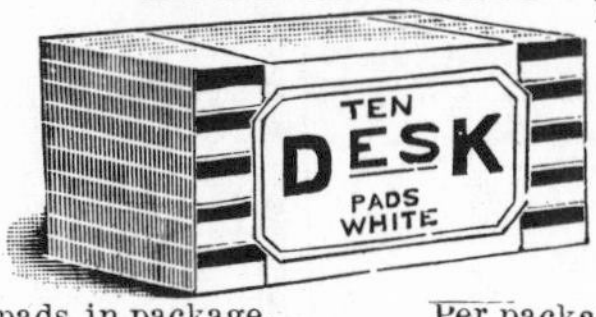

Desk or Scratch Pads, made from white laid, smooth finish paper for pen or pencil; 72 leaves, bound on end with detachable cloth binding. Put up 10 pads in package.

Number	Size.	Each.	Per package of ten.	Per 100.	Weight. per pkg.
14600	3 x4¾	$0.01½	$0.12½	$1.00	17 oz.
14604	3½x6	.02	.16	1.35	26 oz.
14609	4½x7	.02½	.22½	2.00	36 oz.
14613	5x8	.03½	.30	2.60	47 oz.

Pencil Tablets.

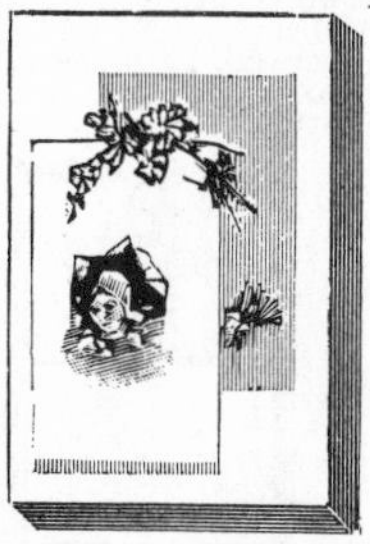

14617 "Penny" Talbets, for pencil use; handsome cover, lithographed in colors, juvenile designs; 64 pages white paper, ruled; size, 4x6 inches. Weight, packed (per dozen), 20 ounces. Each...........$0.01
Per dozen .... .09
Per gross.................. 1.00

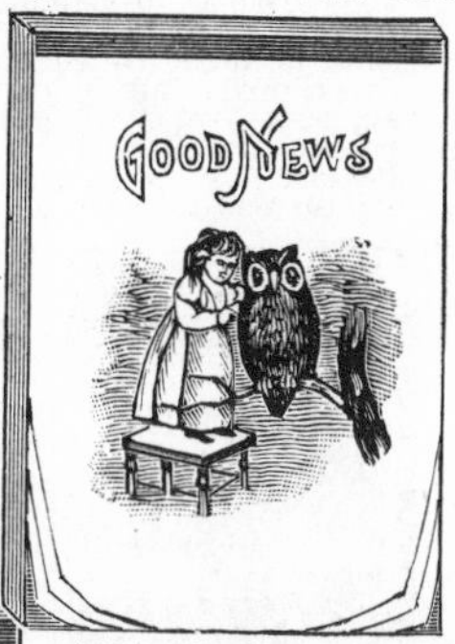

14621 "Good News" Pencil Tablet, cover printed in colors; 200 pages white paper, ruled, *permanently bound and perforated*. Size, 6x9 inches. Weight, packed, 8 ozs.
Each $0.03
Per dozen........ .32
Per 100............ 2.50

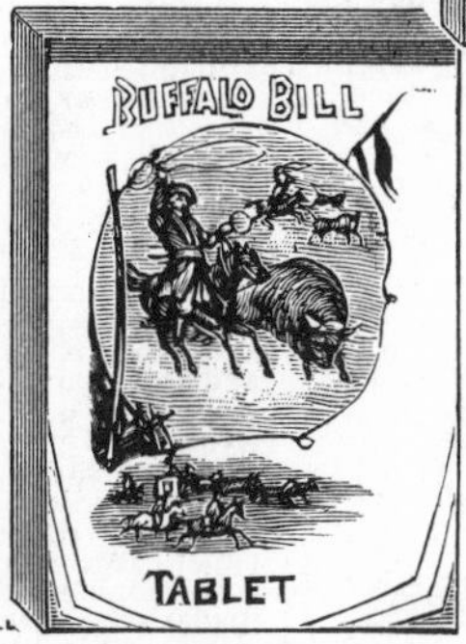

14624 "Buffalo Bill" Pencil Tablets, cover printed in colors; 480 pages white paper; ruled; *permanently bound and perforated*. Size, 6x9 inches. Weight, packed, 18 ounces.
Each $0.06
Per dozen......... .67
Per 100........... 5.25

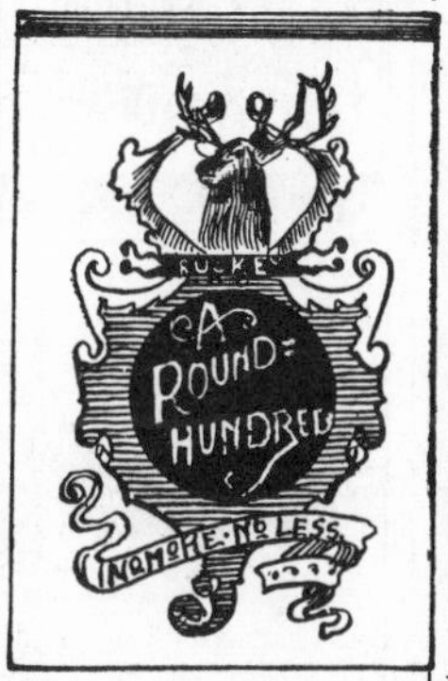

14627 "Round Hundred" Tablet, for pen or pencil use, cardboard cover, printed in two colors; size, 5x8, 100 leaves good manilla paper, ruled. Weight, packed, 7 ounces. Each.....$0.03
Per dozen.......... .32
Per 100............ 2.50

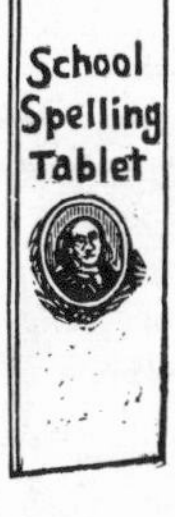

14630 School Spelling Tablet, size, 2¾x 8¾ inches; printed cardboard cover; 160 pages cream paper, practice ruling. Weight, packed, 5 oz. Each.............. $0.03
Per dozen.......................... .32
Per 100.......................... 2.50

Writing Tablets.

NOTICE.-Writing tablets are rapidly superseding the ordinary note and letter papers for general correspondence, as they are much more convenient.

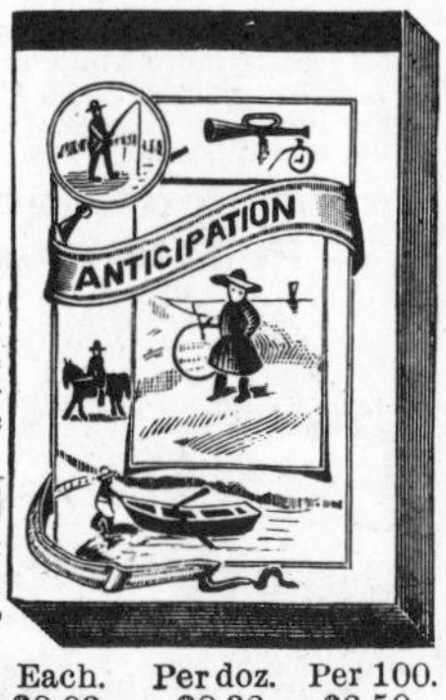

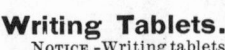

"Anticipation" Writing Tablets, tinted cardboard cover; printed in colors cream wove, ruled writing paper. Weight (each), packed, 6 ounces.

	Pages.	Each.	Per doz.	Per 100.
14635 Com'l Note	110	$0.03	$0.32	$2.50
14637 Packet Note.	80	.03	.32	2.50
14639 Letter	48	.03	.32	2.50

Writing Tablets—Continued.

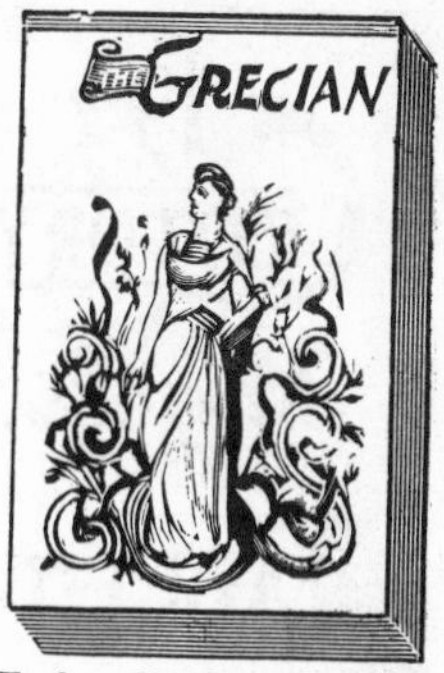

"Grecian" Writing Tablets, tinted glazed board cover embossed and lithographed in colors and gold, with blotter attached; fine, white smooth finish ruled writing paper.
Weight, packed, 10 ounces.

	Pages.	Each.	Per doz.	Per 100.
14642 Com'l Note	160	$0.06	$0.65	$5.00
14645 Packet Note	110	.06	.65	5.00
14648 Letter	70	.06	.65	5.00

"Favorite" Writing Tablets, for penmanship practice work in schools.

14652 Smooth finish white paper with two-line ruling; 80 pages; size, 8x6 inches. Weight, packed, 6 ounces each. Retail price, 10 cents each.
Our special price, each..$0.06 Per dozen.......$0.65
Per 100.................................. 5.00

14655 Smooth finish white paper with four-line ruling, otherwise same as 14652.
Our price, each $0.06
Per dozen.................................... .65
Per 100.. 5.00

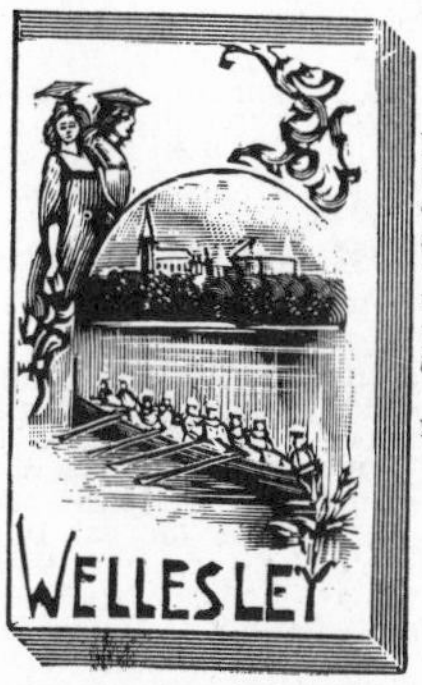

"Wellesley" Writing Tablets, pebbled board cover, handsomely lithographed in colors and gold, with blotter attached; *superfine quality* of white wove smooth finish ruled writing paper. Weight, packed, 12 ounces each. *Retail price 15 cents each.*

NOTICE OUR SPECIAL PRICES.

A large value line.

	Pages.	Each.	Per doz.	Per 100
14672 Com'l Note	200	$0.09	$0.96	$7.50
14676 Packet Note	130	.09	.96	7.50
14679 Letter	90	.09	.96	7.50

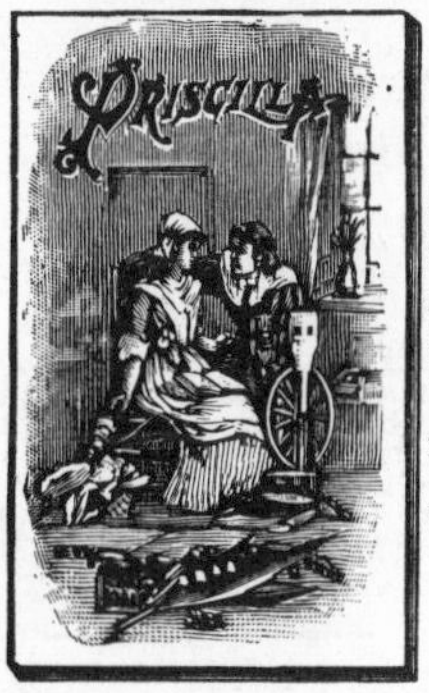

"Priscilla" Writing Tablets, glazed board covers, lithographed in colors and gold, with blotter attached. *Fine grade cream laid, antique finish linen paper, ruled.* Large value line. Regular price 15c. each.

NOTICE OUR SPECIAL PRICES.

Weight, packed, 8oz. each.

	Size.	Each.	Per doz.
14683 Commercial Note	5 x 8	$0.09	$0.95
14686 Packet Note	5½x 9	.09	.95
14689 Letter	8 x10	.09	95

"Prince of India" Writing Tablets; tinted glazed board cover, handsomely lithographed in colors and gold, with blotter attached; sixty leaves, superfine plate finish, cream wove ruled writing paper. Retail prices, 20, 25 and 30 cents each.

NOTICE OUR SPECIAL PRICES.

	Size.	Each.	Per doz.	Weight each.
14692	5x8	$0.11	$1.15	9oz.
14696	5¾x9	.14	1.45	11oz.
14699	8x10	.18	1.95	17oz.

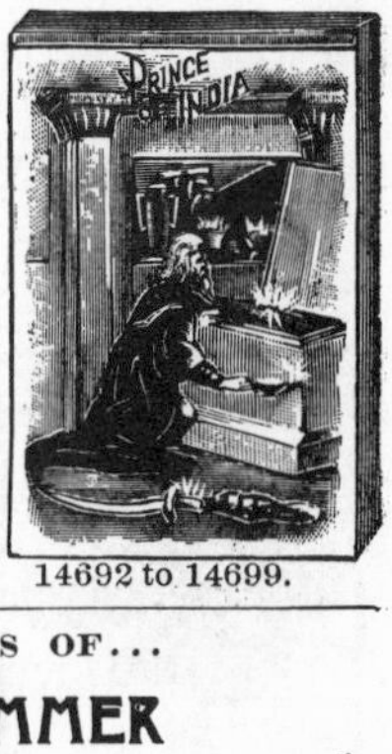

14692 to 14699.

...OUR LINES OF...
SPRING AND SUMMER
DRESS GOODS
ARE FINE.

Writing Tablets—Continued.

"19th Century' Writing Tablets; handsome board cover embossed in imitation of seal leather and printed in gold, with blotter attached. *Extra Superfine quality of fine cream laid smooth finish writing paper, ruled.* Retail prices 30, 40 and 50 cents each.

NOTICE OUR SPECIAL PRICES.

We recommend this line to those who desire high grade goods.

14713 to 14731

Size.	Each.	Per doz.	Wt. each.
14713 Com'l Note. 5½x8½	$0.17	$1.80	12 oz.
14715 Packet Note 6 x9½	.22	2.40	14 oz.
14717 Letter...... 8¼x10¾	.30	3.20	22 oz.

"19th Century" Writing Tablets. *Eighty sheets extra fine, high plate finish, white Parchment paper, ruled,* very light in weight, suitable for foreign and for lengthy correspondence.

Size.	Each.	Per doz.	Wt. each.
14720 Com'l Note..5½x8½	$0.17	$1.80	9 oz.
14722 Packet Note.6 x9½	.22	2.40	10 oz.
14724 Letter........8¼x10¾	.30	3.20	14 oz.

"19th Century" Writing Tablets, *unruled;* otherwise same as 14720 to 14724.

Size.	Each.	Per doz.	Wt. each.
14727 Com'l Note..5½x8½	$0.17	$1.80	9 oz.
14729 Packet Note.6 x9½	.22	2.40	10 oz.
14731 Letter........8¼x10¾	.30	3.20	14 oz.

Book-keeping Blanks.

For Practice Work in Schools and Colleges.

14735   Book-keeping Blanks, good quality white paper, blank book finish, thirty-six pages to book; colored press-board covers, printed; size 8½x14 inches; ruled as follows; Journal, Double Entry Ledger, Day Book, Record, Cash Book, Single Entry Ledger, Sales Book, Trial Balance. Weight each, 7 ounces. *Always mention kind of ruling wanted.*
Each $0.08
Per dozen.................... .75

PAPETERIES.
Paper and Envelopes in Boxes.

All boxes contain 24 sheets of paper and envelopes to match, unless otherwise described.

14752 Fine Cream Laid, smooth octavo note paper with square envelopes to match,in tinted box. Weight, packed, 8 ounces.
Per box... ....$0.07
Per doz. boxes.......... .72

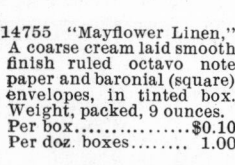

14755 "Mayflower Linen," A coarse cream laid smooth finish ruled octavo note paper and baronial (square) envelopes, in tinted box. Weight, packed, 9 ounces.
Per box................$0.10
Per doz. boxes........ 1.00

14761 "Century Linen," fine white wove, medium finish, ruled octavo note paper and baronial (square) envelopes; in tinted box with printed title. Weight, packed, 9 ounces.
Per box..........$0.15
Per dozen boxes.. 1.52

Fapeteries—Continued.

14766 Superfine Heavy Cream Wove plate finish ruled octavo note paper and baronial envelopes to match, in tinted box. Weight, packed, 10 ounces.
Per box.................$0.17
Per doz. boxes.......... 1.75

14769 Fine Wove smooth finish tinted ruled octavo note paper and baronial envelopes to match, 6 boxes (six different tints of paper) in carton. Weight, per box, packed, 10 ounces.
Per box................$0.18
Per carton (6 boxes).. .95

14773 "Silk Fibre" Papeterie, wedding size (5x7) note paper and envelopes to match, made from the genuine silk fibre' smooth finish tinted writing paper, four tints in carton of six boxes. Weight, per box, packed, 10 ounces.
Per box $0.18
Per carton (6 boxes)..... .95

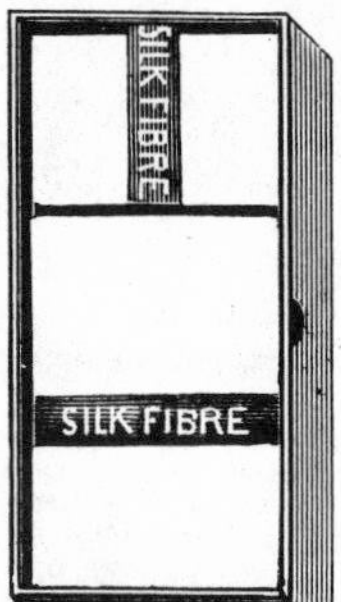

14786 "Overland Mail' Commercial note paper and Baronial (square) envelopes; an extra thin, light weight,smooth finish waterlined, pure linen paper *for use in foreign correspondence;* in plain box with printed title.
Weight, packed, 6 ounces.
Per box.........$0..00   Per dozen boxes........$2.20

14793 "French Quadrille" octavo note paper and baronial envelopes, thin, light weight, smooth finish, waterlined (both ways),pure linen paper for fine correspondence, in plain box with title printed. Weight, packed, 7 ounces.
Per box.........$0.21
Per doz. bxs........ 2.20

14797 Extra superfine plate finish, heavy cream wove, ruled octavo note paper (tied with ribbon) baronial envelopes and neat blotter, in tinted box with title printed in bronze. Weight, packed, 12 ounces,
Per box.... ....$0.21
Per dozen boxes... 2.16

14799 Whiting's Longfellow Linen (azure tinted), laid, water-marked, octavo note paper and baronial envelopes to match. In plain box, cover printed in color and gold. Weight, packed, 10 ounces.
Per box................$0.24
Per dozen boxes 2.50

Ragged Edged Papeteries.

14806 "Royal Linen;" extra fine, cream ruled, *ragged edge,* octavo note paper and baronial (square) envelopes; in tinted box with printed title. Weight, pack'd,10 ounces.
Per box.....$0.20
Per doz bxs. 2.00

Cold Edged Papeteries.

14808 Superfine wove tinted ruled octavo note paper with pure gold edge round corners, two tints in box, baronial envelopes to match, in tinted box. Weight, packed, 10 ounces.
Per box.................$0.20
Per dozen.............. 2.00

Mourning Papeteries.

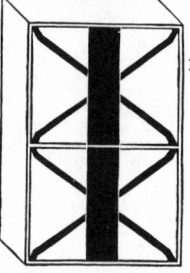

14810 Superfine cream wove, smooth finish, ruled octavo note paper with narrow mourning border, and baronial envelopes to match. Weight, packed, 9 ounces.
Per box..................$0.25
Per dozen boxes......... 2.50

Decorated Papeteries.

14811 Cream wove, ruled, octavo paper with floral decorations in colors and assorted designs, baronial (square) envelopes, in tinted box. Weight, packed, 9 ounces.
Per box.........$0.12
Per doz bxs.... 1.25

14816 Cream wove, ruled, smooth finish octavo note paper with days of the week in colors printed in upper left hand corner of sheet, seven designs in box, baronial envelopes to match. Weight, packed, 10 ounces.
Per box................$0.14
Per dozen boxes....... 1.50

14820 First-class cream wove, ruled, octavo note paper, with quotations from Longfellow, Whittier, Shakespeare or Tennyson, in upper left hand corner of sheet, four designs in box, baronial envelopes Weight, packed, 10 ounces.
Per box..................$0.16
Per dozen boxes... ,... 1.60

14822 Superfine cream wove, ruled octavo paper with *large handsome floral decorations in colors and assorted designs;* baronial (square) envelopes; in tinted box. Weight, packed, 10 ounces.
Per box.......$0.20
Per doz bxs.... 2.05

14825 Superfine cream wove, ruled octavo note paper with embossed floral design in upper and lower left hand corners of sheet; baronial envelopes, with embossed floral design in upper left hand corner, and fancy cut flap. Weight, packed. 11 ounces.
Per box..........$0.23
Per doz........... 2.35

Juvenile Papeteries.
For Misses' and Children's Correspondence.

14827.   14828.

14827 Cream Wove, ruled Juvenile (3¼x4¼ inches), note paper and envelopes to match; in colored chromo-top box. Weight, packed, 5 ounces. Per box....................$0.07
Per dozen boxes............................ .72
14828 Superfine cream wove, ruled juvenile (4x5½ inches) note paper, *with embossed decorations* in colors and assorted designs, with envelopes to match, in tinted box. Weight, packed, 7 ounces. Per box.................$0.12
Per dozen boxes............................ 1.20

14837 Misses' Silk Plush Work Box, size 5x4x2¾; furnished with bone tape-needle, bodkin and crochet hook; cream wove juvenile note paper and envelopes to match. Weight, packed, 13 oz.
Each $0.40

Papeteries in Fancy Boxes.

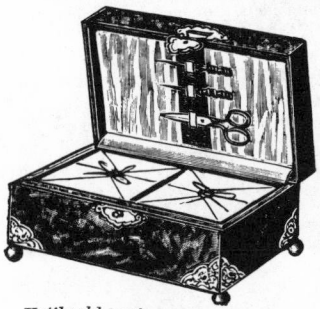

14855 SilkPlush Work Box with silvered center and corner ornaments and catch; size, 8x5½x2¾, cover lined with puffed satin and furnished with bodkin, crochet-hook and scissors; cream wove ruled octavo note paper and baronial envelopes. Weight, packed 20 oz.
Until sold, each.......$0.82

14857 Celluloid Handkerchief Box with silvered corner ornaments, catch and hinges; size, 5¾ x5¾x3; cover and box lined with satin; 12 cream correspondence cards and envelopes to match. Weight, packed, 20 oz.
Until sold.
Each. $0.85

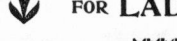

Kai Ki Wash Silks

▼ FOR LADIES' WAISTS.

The PRETTIEST LINE EVER LANDED

. . . IS NOW SHOWN IN OUR . . .

SILK DEPARTMENT

A Request will bring you Samples.

YOU WRITE THE ORDER,

Enclose the money and we do the rest. Easiest thing in the world.

8—2nd

Celluloid Boxes—Continued.

14859 Celluloid Glove Box, with silvered corner ornaments, catch and hinges; size, 10¾x3¾x3, cover and box lined with satin; 24 cream correspondence cards and envelopes to match. Weight, packed, 22 ounces.
Until sold, each................................ ...$0.85

14861 Silk Plush Work Box, with silvered handle and corner ornaments, catch and hinges; size, 8x5⅜x3; cover lined, with puffed satin and plush and furnished with bodkin, crochet-hook, glove-hook and scissors, cream wove, ruled octavo note paper and baronial envelopes. Weight, packed, 24 ounces. *Until* sold, each...............$1.05

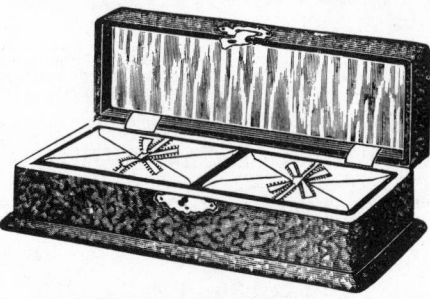

14864 Silk Plush Glove Box with three silvered ornaments, catch and hinges; size,13x4x3; cover lined with puffed satin; cream correspondence cards and envelopes to match. Weight, packed, 26 ounces. *Until sold*, each.............$1.00

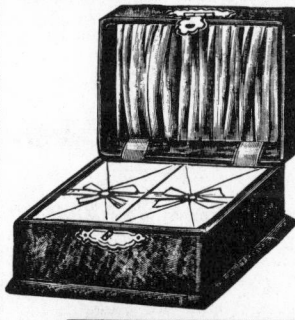

14868 Silk Plush Handkerchief Box with three silvered ornaments, catch and hinges; size, 8¼x 6¼x3; cover lined with puffed satin; cream wove ruled octavo note paper and baronial envelopes. Weight, packed, 26 ounces.
Each.......$1.00

14370 Fine Silk Plush Glove Box, with embossed celluloid ornament on cover; etched oxidized corner ornaments and fancy catch, nickeled hinges, 11¾x4x3 inches; cover lined with puffed satin; cream correspondence cards and envelopes to match. Weight, packed, 25 ounces.
Each.................................$1.20

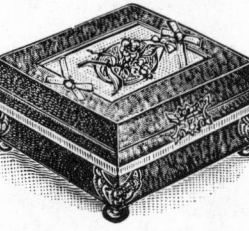

14872 Fine Silk Plush Handkerchief Box, with embossed celluloid ornament on cover; etched oxidized corner ornaments and fancy catch, nickeled hinges; 6½x6½x3 inches, cover-lined with puffed satin; cream wove ruled note paper and envelopes to match. Weight, packed, 23 ounces.
Each $1.20

Plush Boxes—Continued.

14876 Colored Leather Jewel Box with silvered hinges, hasp, padlock and key; beveled extension top and base; size, 7¾x5½x4 inches, removable tray with four compartments; cover, tray, and box lined with puffed satin; cream note paper and envelopes to match. Weight, packed, 33 ounces.
Each.............$1.65

14884 Fancy Shape Box, embossed celluloid with colored floral design on cover, silvered catch, hinges, corner ornaments and ball feet; cover lined with fine puffed satin; cream wove ruled note paper and envelopes (ribbon tied) to match. Weight, packed, 26 ounces.
Until Sold, each.............$1.50

Blotting Papers.

14925 "Star" Blotting Paper, put up 12 in package 4x9½ inches, assorted colors in package. Weight, 4 ounces. Per package...............$0.04
Per dozen packages............ .40
14927 "Climax" Heavy Standard Blotting Paper, 12 sheets, 4x9½ inches, assorted colors in package. Weighs 5 oz. Per package........... .06
Per dozen packages............ .60
14929 "Climax" heavy colored blotting paper, 19x24 inches; blue, buff, cherry. Per sheet..... .05
Per dozen......... 45

Desk Blotting Pads.
Without Blotting Paper.

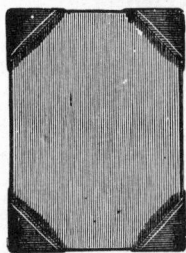

14931 Desk Blotting Pad, size, 19¼x24¼, made of heavy binders' board, covered with blue paper, red roan leather corners, morocco paper back; for holding full sized (19x24) sheets of blotting paper. Weight packed, 32 ounces.
Each (without blotting paper).............$0.30
Per dozen.......... 2.75

Colored Shelf Paper.

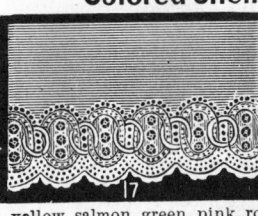

4933 Shelf Paper, pinked in fancy designs, each sheet 8½ inches wide, 33 inches long. Various patterns. Twenty-four sheets in quire, 6 quires in gross. We do not sell less than one quire of a color. Colors: Red, lilac, yellow, salmon, green, pink, rose, brown, blue, white. Quire weighs 6 ounces. Per quire...............$0.03
Per gross..................... .12

Lace Shelf Paper.

14935 Lace Shelf Paper, made from a high grade, smooth finish, heavy book paper, pinked and embossed; in pieces 12 inches wide and ten yards long; four colors: white, blue, pink, yellow. Weight (per piece) packed, 7 ounces. Per piece....$0.06
Per box, 12 pieces....................... .63

Paper Festooning.

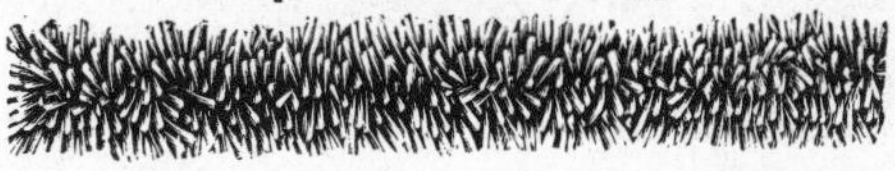

14937 Moss Paper Festooning, for decorating halls, arches, stands, stores, etc, made of tissue paper on strong hemp twine; well made and very durable; 10 yards in roll, red, white and blue combined; also solid colors--white, red, blue, pink, green, yellow, lilac. Roll weighs 8 ounces. *Sold by the roll only.* Per roll (10 yds)...$0.30
Per dozen rolls............................ 3.20
See Index for Japanese Lanterns.

Automatic Shading Pens.

For engrossing, fancy lettering, show card writing, etc.

15001 Nos.   0   1   2   3   4   5
Widths.   1-16 in.   ⅛ in.   3-16 in.   ¼ in.   ⅜ in.   ½ in.
Each, 15c; Per dozen, $1.65.
15002 No. 6, ⅝ inch wide. Each....................$0.20
15003 No. 8, ⅞ inch wide. Each....................20

Ink for Automatic Shading Pens.

15004 Shading Pen Ink, prepared especially for use with automatic shading pens; in wide-mouth, round flint glass, 1½ ounce bottles. Colors: red, violet, blue, green, crimson, black, yellow, brown. Per bottle.......................$0.10
Per dozen bottles.............................. 1.10

"Montgomery Ward & Co.'s Steel Pens."

Illustrations show exact size of pens.
"Montgomery Ward & Co.'s (our own brand) Steel Pens are high grade first-class pens, and *warranted perfect in every particular;* fully equal to any steel pens in market which sell for $1.00 per gross. GIVE THEM A TRIAL.

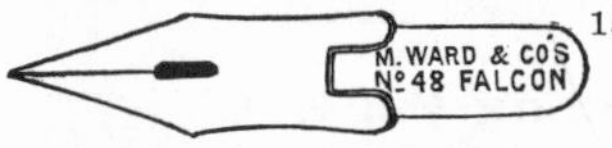

15008 "M. W. & Co.s" Falcon. (No. 48), gray finish, med. point and perfect action. The most popular style in market for general business use. **Per gross**......$0.60
Per dozen.................................... .07

15011 "M.W. & Co.'s" College (No. 1604), gray finish, fine point and double elastic action. The favorite style for professional penmen and instructors in penmanship.
Per gross....$0.60 Per ¼ gross.... $0.17

Esterbrook's Steel Pens.

15023 "Bank" (No. 14), bronze finish; medium point; an excellent and popular pen for business use. 
Per dozen........$0.07 Per gross.............$0.48

15026 "Falcon" (No.048), bronze finish, medium point. The most popular pen in use for general business purposes. 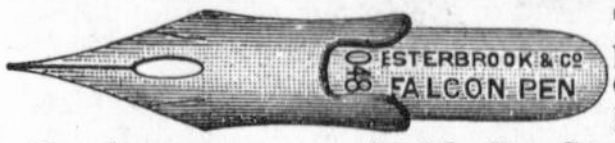
Per dozen........ $0.06 Per Gross $0.48

15029 "Extra Fine Elastic" (No. 128), gray finish. The favorite pen for college and professional penmen Per dozen........ ...$0.06
Per gross...................................... .52

15035 "Short Nib Engrossing," or Stub (No 161, F) bronze finish, medium fine stub. Very popular. Per dozen.......$0.08
Per gross.................................... .60

15037 "Ladies' Falcon" (No.182), bronze finish. Fine and easy action.
Per dozen...........06
Per gross.............44

15039 "School" (444), bronze finish, medium fine. Largely used in the public schools.
Per dozen.............06 
Per gross.............40

15045 "Mammoth Falcon" (No. 340, B), bronze finish; easy action. For general correspondence and for bank, shipping and entry clerks' use. Twelve pens and a holder to suit on card.
Per card............$0.24 Postage......... $0.03

Esterbrook's Celebrated Steel Pens in metallic boxes, containing one doz. pens each. Postage one cent per box; eight cents per dozen.

15046 School and Fine Pens, selected assortment of styles. Per box.............$0.06
Per dozen boxes...............................60
15048 Superior Business Pens, selected assortment of styles. Per box 06
Per dozen boxes...............................60
15050 Assorted Stub or engrossing Pens, specially selected for use by lawyers and professional men. Per box...............06
Per dozen boxes.............................60

Spencerian Steel Pens.

15053 "College" (No. 1), point fine, elastic and action perfect, largely used by the best penmen in the country. 
Per gross....................................$0.80
Per ¼ gross...................................25
15060 "School" (No. 5), point fine, medium in flexibility.
Per gross.........$0.80
Per ¼ gross...................................25 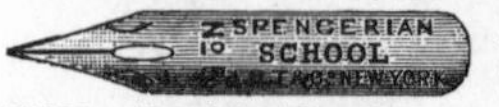
15062 "Bank" (No. 9), point long and flexible; great favorite with accountants, tellers, etc. 
Per gross....................................$0.80
Per ¼ gross...................................25

Gillott's Steel Pens.

15071 "Principality Pen" (No. 1), extra fine point, and will make heavy down-stroke. Excellent in flourishing and ornamental pen work. Per dozen.............$0.10
Per gross...................................90 
15075 "Ladies' Pen" (No. 170), extra fine point. Designed especially for ladies' use. Per doz.$0.08
Per gross...................................65 
15079 "Victoria" (No. 303) The original extra fine pen and most widely used.
Per dozen......$0.10
Per gross........ .90 
15081 "Public Pen" (No. 404), with bead, fine point. Very popular for fine writing and school use.
Per dozen......$0.06
Per gross....................................49
15083 "Magnum Quill" Pen (No. 601 E. F.), extra fine point; for fine and ordinary writing; very popular for general use. 
Per gross....................................$0.83
Per ¼ gross...................................25
15084 "Double Elastic" (No. 604 E. F.), extra fine point. The original double elastic pen, a favorite with professors of penmanship and teachers in business colleges. Per gross...$0.60
Per ¼ gross...................................20

Job Lot Steel Pens.

15086 Job Lot Steel pens, assorted styles; one gross in box, *Sold by the gross only.*
Per gross..........................$0.25
Postage.........05
15090 "Colorado" (No. 2), golden finish; a flexible and non-corrosive yellow metal pen. Sold by the gross only.
Per gross.........$0.24

Fountain Pen.

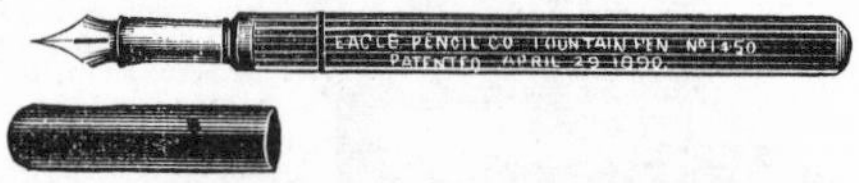

15103 Eagle Fountain Pen, a metallic case with cap, contains glass vial filled with ink to which is attached the feeder holding a non-corrosive (golden) pen. The most complete, useful, convenient fountain pen in use. Each...........$0.08
Per dozen....................................85
15105 Glass Vials, filled with ink for use with 15103 fountain pen. Per dozen...............25
15107 "Eagle Pen" (golden), non-corrosive, for use in 15103 Fountain pen.
Per dozen......$0.07
Per gross.............60 
15109 Eagle Fountain Pen; assortment contains one fountain pen No. 15103, three extra vials, No. 15105, and one dozen extra pens, No. 15107, in neat compartment box. A complete, popular and useful outfit. Weight, packed, 5 ounces. Per box.............$0.20
Per dozen boxes.............................. 2.00

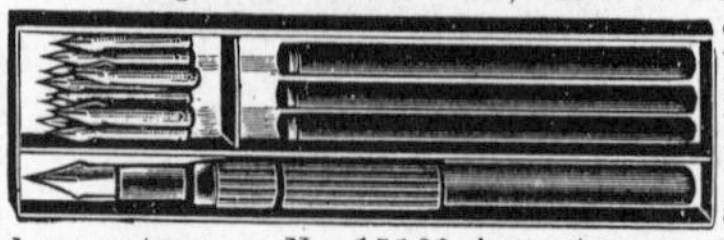

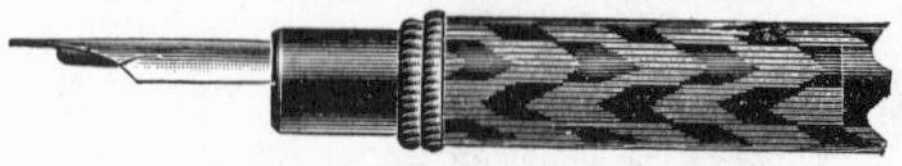

15112 The Student Fountain Pen; a reliable fountain pen, made of hard rubber, with chased barrel, fitted with gilt pen; any straight steel pen may be used if desired; directions for using and filler accompany each pen. Weight packed 4 ounces. Retails at 50 cents.
Our price, each.......................$0.35
Per dozen.................................... 3.50

For High Grade Fountain Pens see Jewelry Department.

15114 Fountain Pen Filler, straight point glass with seamless rubber bulb. Each.............$0.04
Per dozen.......................... .35

Glass Writing Pens.

PAT. SEP 90.

15117 Glass Writing Pen; fluted and twisted glass pen point in nickeled barrel with black enameled holder. Each....................$0.09
Per dozen....................................95

Ruling Pen.

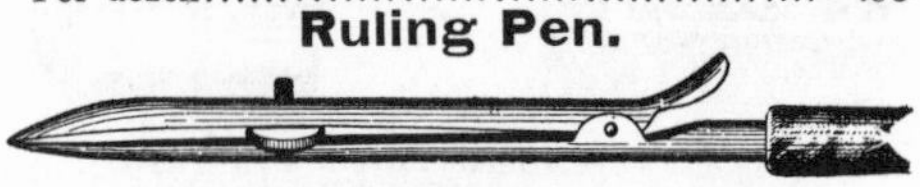

15119 Spencerian Ruling or Bow Pen, glass finish wood handle, imitating mottled rubber; nickel plated double blade with flat spring at joint to keep points together; slight pressure on finger-plate causes blades to spread so that filler or spoon-shaped blade may be inserted in ink-stand and enough ink taken and retained when closed upon smaller blade to rule 36 lines six inches long, with one dip in ink. The best ruling pen made for book-keepers' use and general purposes.
Weight, packed, 2 ounces. Each.............$0.20
Per dozen.................................... 2.00

Penholders.

Postage on penholders 4c. to 6c. per dozen.

15125 Straight Penholders, fluted cedar handles, with binding tips, for school use. Per dozen...$0.03
Per gross....................................32

15127, 15132
15127 Swell Penholders, polished cedar handles, with steel tips, medium size. Each.............$0.02
Per dozen.........$0.15 Per gross........... 1.40
15132 Swell Penholders, enameled handles with nickeled tips; large size. Each...........03
Per dozen.........$0.25 Per gross........... 2.60

15134 Or-tho-dac-tyl-ic Penholder (*without pen*) with finger-rests which assist the hand to assume the proper position in writing; recommended by instructors in penmanship.
Each (without pen)......................$0.04
Per dozen 40
Per gross.................................... 3.60

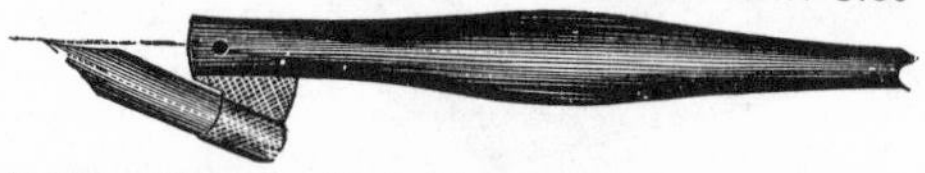

15135 Oblique Penholder, polished swell handle, with brass tip (*without pen*); large size. Largely used by card-writers and experts in penmanship. Each..............................$0.04
Per dozen....................................40

15137 The "Bank" Penholder, combined wood and cork, long taper polished cedar handles, cork tips and metal grip for pen. The "touch" of cork is very agreeable and easy, and does not tire fingers. Each.....................$0.06
Per dozen....................................65

15140 Faber's Aluminum Penholder, fluted aluminum tip with black taper handle. Steel pen in each holder. Our special price, each.....$0.07
Per dozen.................................. 0.75

15143 Pure Aluminum Penholder, fancy spiral taper handle. Each.........................$0.20
Per dozen.................................. 2.00

15153 Rubber Penholder, long, with flange (21) black or mottled. Each.........................$0.11

15156 Rubber Penholder, short, reversible, black, or mottled. Each.........................$0.18

15158 Rubber Penholder, pocket reversible, large size, for Nos 5, 6, or 7 gold pens; black or mottled. Each.........................$0.23
Per dozen.................................. 2.40

Styluses.

FOR WRITING ON MANIFOLD PAPER.

15162 Stylus, steel point, nickel mounted, black japanned swell taper handle. Each............$0.08
Per doz. .... .85

15165 and 15168.

15165 Stylus, porcelain point, nickel mounted black japanned swell taper handle. Each....$0.08
Per doz... .85
15168 Stylus, real agate point, gold mounted, black japanned swell taper handle. Each......$0.30
Per doz... 3.00

Dixon's American Graphite Pencils.

Per doz. Per gross.

15200 Round, plain cedar, 7 inches long......................$0.03 $0.30
Weight per dozen, 3 oz.

DIXON'S ARTISAN No 268

15204 and 15208

15204 Round, polished cedar, with inserted rubber eraser (see cut)..........$0.07 $0.75
Weight, per dozen, 4 ounces.
15208 Round, black or red polished, with inserted rubber eraser (see cut).. .08 .85
Weight, per dozen, 4 ounces.

TIP-TOP 315

15212 Dixon's "Tip Top," round, maroon finish, gilt stamp, No. 2 lead, short nickel tip and rubber eraser. Weight per dozen, 4 ounces..................$0.14 $1.40

ROVER No 317

15216 Dixon's "Rover," tablet or ladies' size, round, maroon finish, gilt stamp, No. 2 lead, short nickeled tip and rubber eraser. Weight per dozen 4 oz... .$0.14 $1.40

MONTGOMERY WARD & CO CLIMAX

15220 "Montgomery Ward & Co. Climax." Round, maroon finish, gilt stamp, Nos. 2 and 3 grades; with nickeled tip and rubber eraser.............$0 20 $2.00
Weight per dozen, 4 oz.

DIXON'S CABINET

15224 Dixon's "Cabinet." round, satin finish, gold stamp, Nos. 2 and 3 leads of high grade, fitted with nickeled tips carrying an erasive rubber of superior quality $0.30 $3.00
Weight, per dozen, 5 oz.

DIXON'S SECRETARY

15228 Dixon's "Secretary," round, satin finish, tablet size (3-16 in. diameter) gilt stamp. Nos. 2 and 3 leads of high grade, nickeled tip with rubber eraser $0.30 $3.00
Weight per dozen, 5 oz.

DIXON'S HighSchool SM

15232 Dixon's "High School," round shape, satin finish; leads of fine quality and carefully graded in seven degrees of hardness: (S)—Soft. (SM)—Soft medium. (MB) Medium black. (M)—Medium hard. (MH)—Medium hard. (H)—Hard. (VH)—Very hard. Peculiarly suited to school use.............$0.30 $3.25
Weight per dozen, 5 oz.

DIXON'S SECRETARY No3

15236 Dixon's "Secretary," hexagon shape, tablet size (diameter, ¼ inch), Nos. 2 and 3 leads, nickeled tip with rubber eraser. Weight per doz.. 5 oz .$0.35 $3.50

DIXON'S AMBASSADOR No2

15240 Dixon's "Ambassador" Pencil, tapering in shape, handsomely finished; Nos. 2 and 3 leads of high grade; inserted rubber eraser of best quality; very popular..................$0.40 $4.50
Weight per dozen, 5 oz.

DIXON'S AMERICAN GRAPHITE SM

15244 Dixon's "Fine Polygrade" Pencils, round shape, gold stamp, satin finish, smooth, tough leads in 7 grades of hardness: (S)—Soft. (SM)—Soft medium. (MB)—Medium black. (M)—Medium. (MH)—Medium hard. (H)—Hard. (VH)—Very hard.........$0.42 $4.50
Weight, per dozen, 5 oz.

Pencils—Continued.

DIXON'S TRI-LATERAL

15248 Dixon's "Tri-Lateral" Pencil, triangular shape fits the fingers, does not tire hand from continuous use, nor roll when laid on a slanting desk; handsomely finished; Nos. 2 and 3 leads of high grade; nickeled tip with rubber eraser...................$0.40 $4.40
Weight per dozen, 5 oz.

DIXON'S AMERICAN GRAPHITE SM-No2 116

15252 Dixon's "Fine Polygrade" Pencils, hexagon shape, gold stamp, satin finish. Smooth, tough leads in 7 grades of hardness. (S)—Soft. (SM)—Soft medium. (MB)—Medium black. (M)—medium. (MH)—Medium hard. (H)—Hard. (VH) Very hard.............$0.55 $6.00
Weight, per dozen, 5 oz.

PROGRAMME

15259 "Programme" Pencils, round, enameled in colors, with gilt tip and ring. Suitable for use in lady's memorandum book............................$0.20 $2.00

CARPENTER

15262 Carpenters' Pencil, oval polished. cedar, 7 inches long...................$0.18 $1.75
Weight per dozen, 5 oz.
15265 Carpenters' Pencil, oval polished cedar, 9 inches long................. .20 2.00
Weight per dozen, 7 oz.
15268 Dixon's ' Framers' " Carpenter's Pencil, octagon shape, maroon finish; (H)—Hard, tough leads, chisel point, 7 inches long......................... .30 3.20
Weight, per dozen, 6 ounces.

Colored Crayon Pencils.

819-DIXON'S-BLUE

Each. Per doz.
15274 Crayon Pencils, blue lead, round, polished cedar, 7 inches long $0.03 $0.32
Weight per dozen, 5 oz.
15278 Crayon Pencils, red lead, round, polished cedar, 7 inches long......... .03 .32
15282 Crayon Pencils, green lead, round, polished cedar, 7 inches long......... .03 .32
Weight per doz, 5 oz.

DIXON'S BEST BLUE 350

15286 "Dixon's Best" Blue Crayon Pencil, round shape, gold stamp, highly finished, 7 inches long.............. .07 .75
Weight, per dozen, 6 oz.

DIXON'S OPERATORS' PENCIL No300

15290 Dixon's "Operator" Pencil; satin finish; extra soft and thick, rich black lead; for free-hand drawing, etc. .42 4.50
Weight, packed, 6 oz.

15295 Dixon's Colored Crayon Pencils in sets, for map drawing in schools: 4 inches long: one each of light blue, brown, green, yellow, dark blue, red, in chromo box. Weight, packed, 3 oz.
Per box......................$0.07
Per dozen boxes...................... .70

15299 "Dixon's Best" Colored Crayon Pencils in sets, *for drawing class, artists' and teachers' use:* round gold stamp, highly finished; length, 7 in. Smooth, tough, easy marking leads in vivid colors; six colors in box: Black, brown, red, blue, yellow, green, in slide box. Per box.............. $0.40
Postage...................... .04

Copying Crayon Pencils.

15302 "Eagle" Ink Crayon, (Purple) No. 1, (very soft), extra copying. A substitute for ink. Letters written with this grade can be copied by slightly dampening the copying paper.
Each................$0.08 Per doz........$0.85
15304 "Eagle" Ink Crayon (Purple) No. 2 (medium soft), copying. For general use. Each.... .08
Per dozen............... .85
15306 "Eagle" Ink Crayon, (Purple) No. 3 (medium hard), copying. For order books and memorandums and for office use. Will not blur by pages rubbing together. Each............... .08
Per dozen............... .85
15308 "Eagle" Ink Crayon, (Purple) No. 4, very hard and smooth; non-erasive; more durable and will hold a point longer than any other pencil of equal smoothness. Each....$0.08 Per dozen.... .85
Postage, 4 cents per dozen.
15310 "Sun" Copying Crayon, Purple. Each....$0.04
Per dozen............... .35
15311 "Sun" Copying Crayon, Blue. Each...... .04
Per dozen............... .35
15312 "Sun" Copying Crayon, Red. Each........ .04
Per dozen............... .35

Automatic Pencils and Leads.

Each. Per doz.

15314 "Eagle" Automatic Pencil (*Stop Gauge*), with copying ink lead, which writes black and copies green; length 5 inches. For extra leads see No. 15316...............................$0.08 $0.85
15316 Copying Ink Leads (write black and copy green) for use in Automatic Pencil No. 15314, 3 leads in metallic box. Per box. .08 .75
15318 Automatic Pencils, with purple copying lead (stop gauge), length 5 inches................................. .18 2.00
Weight, per dozen, 7 ounces.
15322 Purple Copying Ink leads, for use in No. 15318 pencil; three leads in flat box; per box.............. .15 1.60

Propel and Repel Pencils.

15325 "Wire Nail" Propel and Repel Pencil. A novel pencil imitating a wire nail. Bright nickel finish, black lead, length 4 inches.
Each................$0.08 Per dozen..........$0.85
15329 Black Leads for 15325 pencils: six leads in box. Per box. .... .08

Slide Pencils.

15330 The Business Pocket Pencil, chased rubber barrel with gilt tips; screwed tip holds lead, which will slide into barrel when closed; length closed 3¾ inches. Each....................$0.20
Per dozen 2.00
15331 Black Leads for 15330 Business Pencil; 4 leads in box. Per box. .06

15332 "Magic" Vest Pocket Sliding Pencil; nickel plated sliding holder fitted with round cedar lead pencil; length closed 3 inches. A handy device for using up short pieces of lead pencils. Each.................$0.04 Per dozen...... .40

Lumber Pencils.

DIXON'S No 361 JAPANNED HEXAGON LUMBER PENCIL

15335 to 15343

15335 Dixon's "Regular" Black Lumber Pencil, hexagon shape; japanned finish; ½ inch in diameter, 4¾ inches long. Weight, per dozen, 18 ounces.
Each........... .$0.05 Per dozen.........$0.45
Per gross.............. 5.00
15337 Dixon's "Extra Soft" Black Lumber Pencil, for green lumber, hexagon shape, paper covered; otherwise same as 15335.
Each................$0.05 Per dozen........... .45
Per gross.............. 5.00
15340 Dixon's Red Lumber Pencil, hexagon shape; paper covered; otherwise ame as 15335.
Each................$0.08 Per dozen........... .80
Per gross.............. 9.00
15343 Dixon's Blue Lumber Pencil, hexagon shape; paper covered; otherwise same as 15335.
Each................$0.08 Per dozen........... .80
Per gross.............. 9.00

Acme Indelible Marking Pencils.

ACME PENCIL

15345 Acme Indelible Marking Pencil. Length, 4 inches; one dozen in box, in black, blue, red or assorted colors; will not rub or wash off. Indispensable to farmers and shippers of produce for marking goods.
Each................$0.03 Per dozen...........$0.25
Weight, per dozen, 7 ounces.

Slate Pencils.

15347 **Pure Aluminum** Slate Pencil for Stone Slates, no sharpening required, will not wear out, always ready for use; quickly erased with damp sponge or cloth; will not injure the slate surface; a pure aluminum pencil point attached to enameled swell taper handle. Each......$0.04
Per dozen............................. .40

DIXON'S SLATE 845

15348 Best Natural Slate, encased in cedar wood like lead pencils. Length, 7' inches. Weight, per dozen, 4 ounces. Per doz.........$0.07
Per gross...................... .75

There is nothing we want to do more than to correct errors. ~:~ ~:~

Slate Pencils—Continued.

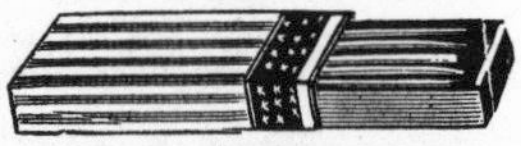

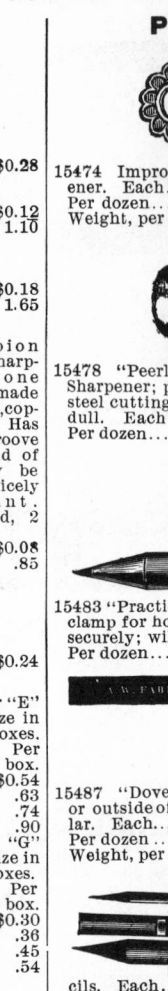

15349 Best German Slate Pencils, union; pointed, in sliding pasteboard box containing 12 pencils. A convenient box for scholars. Per box, $0.03. Per dozen boxes $0.28
Weight, per box, 5 ounces.

15352 Best German Slate Pencils, gray, pointed; length, 5½ inches; 100 in box. Per box $0.12
Per 1,000 (10 boxes) 1.10
Weight, per box, 26 ounces.

15355 American Soapstone Slate Pencils, 5½ inches long, pointed, 100 in box. Weight per box, packed, 32 ounces. Per box $0.18
Per 1,000 (10 boxes) 1.65

Slate Pencil Sharpener.

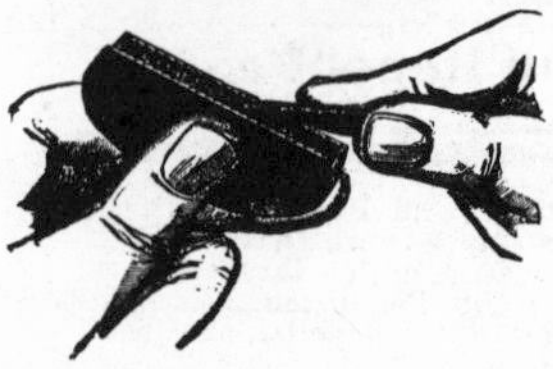

15356 Champion Slate Pencil Sharpener (for stone slate pencils), made of chilled iron, coppered finish. Has corrugated groove in which end of pencil may be reduced to a nicely tapered point. Weight, packed, 2 ounces.
Each ....$0.01 Per doz $0.08
Per gross .... .85

Tailors' Chalk.

15358 "Gilt Edge" Tailors' Chalk, for *Dressmakers', Tailors' and Cutters' use*; superior quality, 72 pieces white, red and blue assorted, in neat wooden box. Weight, packed, 42 ounces.
Per box $0.24

Shipping Tags.

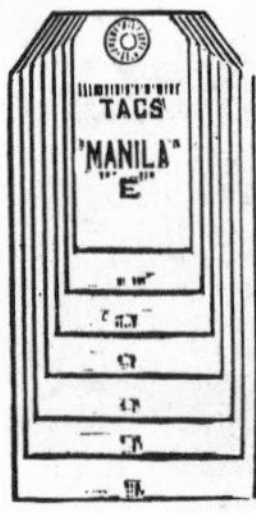

15363 Shipping Tags, manilla or "E" standard quality, 100 of one size in box; we do not break or assort boxes.

		Weight, per box.	Per box.
No. 3E,	3¾x1⅞ inches	3¼ lbs.	$0.54
No. 4E,	4¼x2⅛ inches	4 lbs.	.63
No. 5E,	4¾x2⅜ inches	5¼ lbs.	.74
No. 6E,	5¼x2⅝ inches	6½ lbs.	.90

15365 Shipping Tags, manilla "G" or cheap quality, 1,000 of one size in box, we do not break or assort boxes.

		Weight, per box.	Per box.
No. 3G,	3¾x1⅞ inches	2¾ lbs.	$0.30
No 4G,	4¼x2⅛ inches	3½ lbs.	.36
No 5G,	4¾x2⅜ inches	4¼ lbs.	.45
No. 6G,	5¼x2⅝ inches	7½ lbs.	.54

15367 Tourists' Tags, one dozen manilla tags with strings attached, in envelope, for tourists' or family use. Weight, packed, 3 ounces. Per envelope $0.08
Per box (12 envelopes) .... .80

Paper Knives.

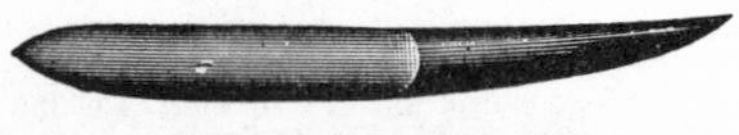

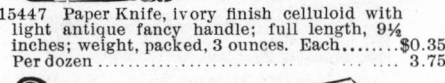

15445 Paper Knife, ivory finish celluloid with handle imitating walrus tooth; full length, 7½ inches; weight, packed, 3 ounces. Each......$0.20
Per dozen 2.00

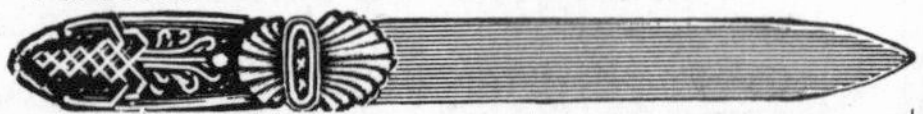

15447 Paper Knife, ivory finish celluloid with light antique fancy handle; full length, 9⅛ inches; weight, packed, 3 ounces. Each........$0.35
Per dozen 3.75

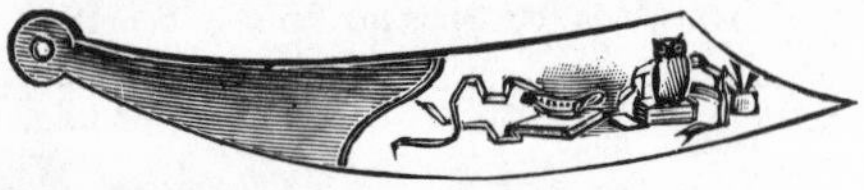

15449 Paper Knife, ivory finish celluloid scimiter shape, with fancy embossed design on blade; full length, 8½ inches; weight, packed, 3 ounces; 3 designs in dozen. Each.............$0.45
Per dozen (assorted designs) 4.75

Steel Ink Eraser.

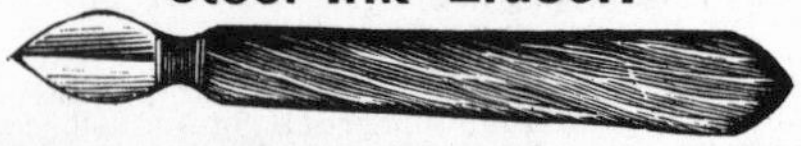

15457 Steel Ink Eraser with spear point; cocoa wood handle, length, 5 inches. Each..........$0.25

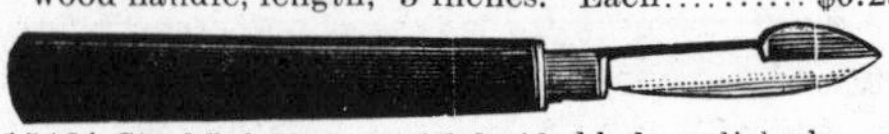

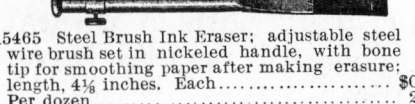

15461 Steel Ink Eraser with knife blade, polished ebony handle; length, 6 inches.
Each $0.40

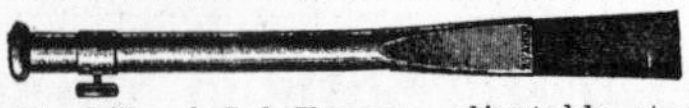

15465 Steel Brush Ink Eraser; adjustable steel wire brush set in nickeled handle, with bone tip for smoothing paper after making erasure; length, 4⅛ inches. Each $0.20
Per dozen 2.00

Pencil Sharpeners.

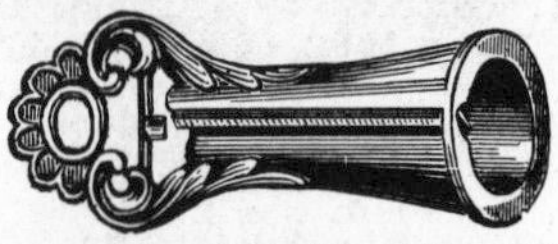

15474 Improved Long Bevel Lead Pencil Sharpener. Each $0.06
Per dozen .... .60
Weight, per dozen, 6 ounces.

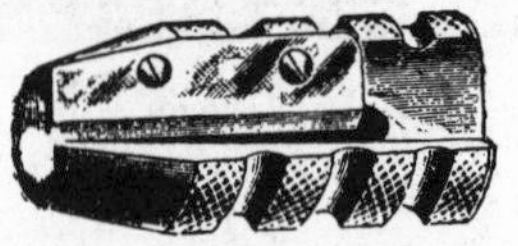

15478 "Peerless" Long Bevel Lead Pencil Sharpener; polished solid brass barrel with fine steel cutting blade, which may be ground when dull. Each $0.15
Per dozen 1.50

Pencil Holders.

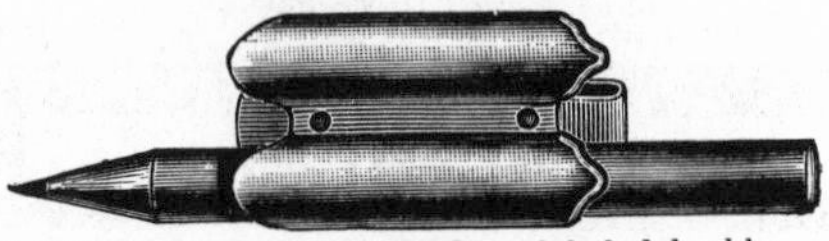

15483 "Practical" Pencil Holder, nickeled double clamp for holding two pencils; holds pencils securely; will not work off. Each. $0.05
Per dozen .... .45

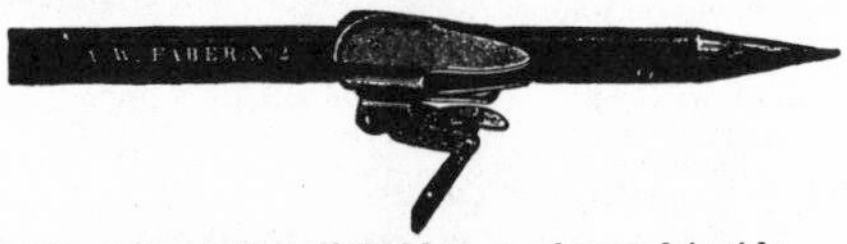

15487 "Dove" Pencil Holder, can be used inside or outside of pocket; nickeled finish; very popular. Each $0.08
Per dozen .... .85
Weight, per dozen, 5 ounces.

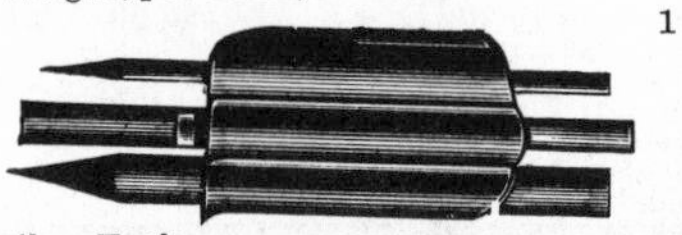

15491—"Triplicate" Pencil Holder, nickeled finish; for three pencils. Each $0.08
Per dozen .... .85

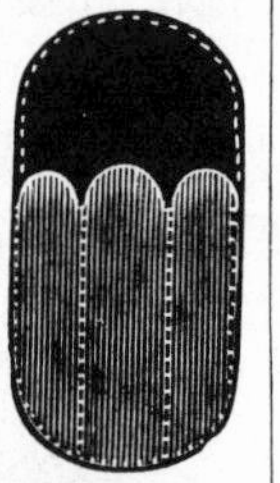

15495 Stylographic" Safety Pocket, will hold three fountain pens or lead pencils; imitation black Russia leather.
Each $0.10
Per dozen 1.00
Postage .... .02

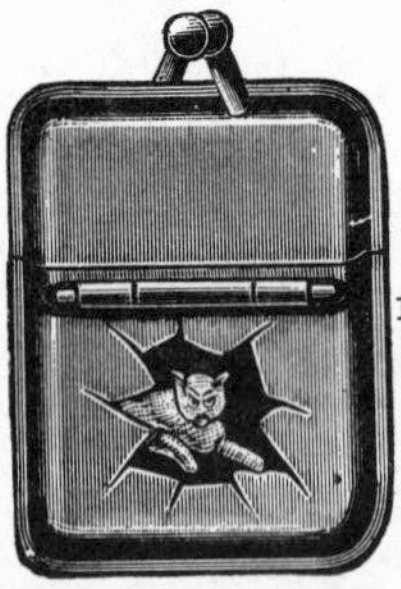

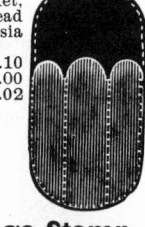

Postage Stamp Boxes.

15504 "Champion" Fancy Metallic Postage Stamp Box, ball catch, nickeled, gilt, silvered or oxidized finish. Size, 1⅝x1¼ inches.
Each $0.08
Per dozen .... .85

Paper Fasteners.

Do your own binding. Use the "Commercial" and "Victor" Paper Fasteners for binding manuscripts, pamphlets, documents, records, legal or any other papers for preservation and reference.

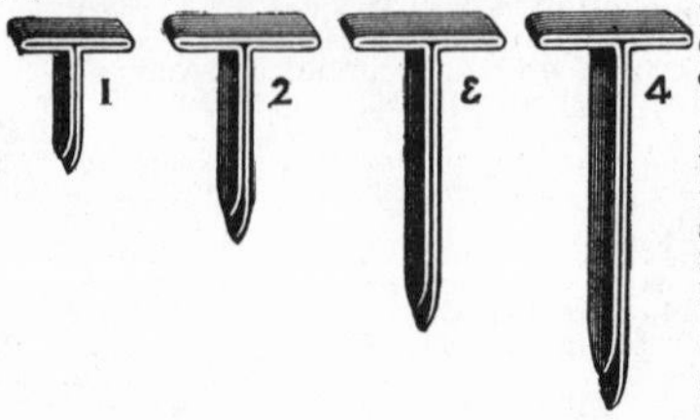

15507 Commercial Paper Fasteners, made from best quality brass and will not break in bending Flat heads 100 of one size in brass box.

No.	Length.	Per 100	Per Carton, 1000	Wt. per 100
1	¼ inch.	$0.10	$0.80	2 oz.
2	½ inch.	.12	1.00	3 oz.
3	¾ inch.	.14	1.20	3 oz
4	1 inch.	.17	1.40	3 oz

Catalogue No. 58 will be ready Sept. 1, 1895.

Paper Fasteners—Continued

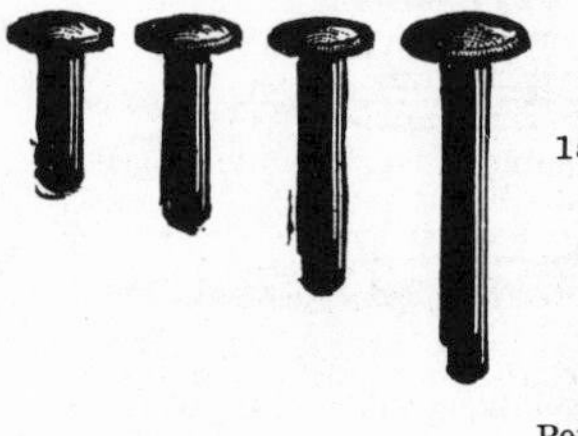

15512 Commercial Round Head Paper Fasteners; 100 of one size in brass box.

No.	Length.	Per 100	Per Carton, 1000	Wt. per 100
1	¼ inch.	$0.12	$1.00	2 oz.
2	½ inch.	.14	1.20	3 oz.
3	¾ inch.	.19	1.60	3 oz.
4	1 inch.	.24	2.00	4 oz.

Victor Staple Driver.

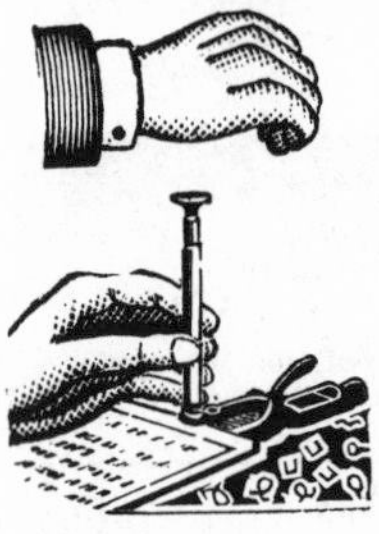

15515 Victor Staple Driver, for binding books, papers, pamphlets, etc., putting down cloth or matting, putting up curtains, shades on rollers, and driving small steel staples for a hundred purposes. Requires no skill to use it, staple is placed in holder, driven to place and driver returns to place ready for use. Packed in neat wood box containing driver, clincher and 400 assorted staples.
Each $0.40
Per dozen 4.25
Postage .... .12

15518 Staples for "Victor Driver, 3-16, ¼, ⅜ or ½ inch. 500 of one size in box. Do not break or assort boxes. Per box .... .10
Weight, per box, 3 ounces.

Victor Letter Balance.

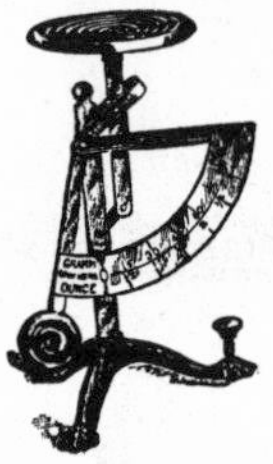

15524 Victor Letter Balance, will accurately weigh from one-half to three ounces; nickel plated platform, brass frame work, japanned iron base with thumb-screw to regulate any unevenness of surface on which balance is placed. Weight, packed, 5 ounces.
Our price, each $0.20

Rubber Erasers.

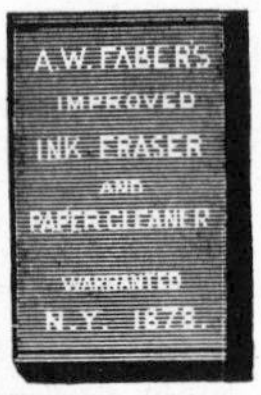

15530 Faber's Improved Ink Eraser and Paper Cleaner.
Each $0.04
Per doz .... .40
Weight, per doz., 5 oz.

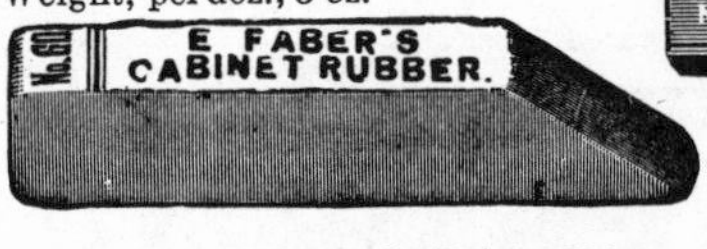

15532 Cabinet Bevel Point Oblong Rubber Eraser, velvet finish; superior quality; small size; weight, per dozen, 4 ounces. Each.......$0.01
Per doz..........$0.09 Per pound (120 pcs.) .80

15533 Cabinet Eraser; medium size; weight, per dozen, 6 ounces. Each .... .03
Per dozen......$0.30 Per pound (40 pieces).. .80

15535 Cabinet Eraser; large size; weight per dozen, 12 ounces. Each .... .05
Per dozen.......$0.50 Per pound (20 pieces).. .80

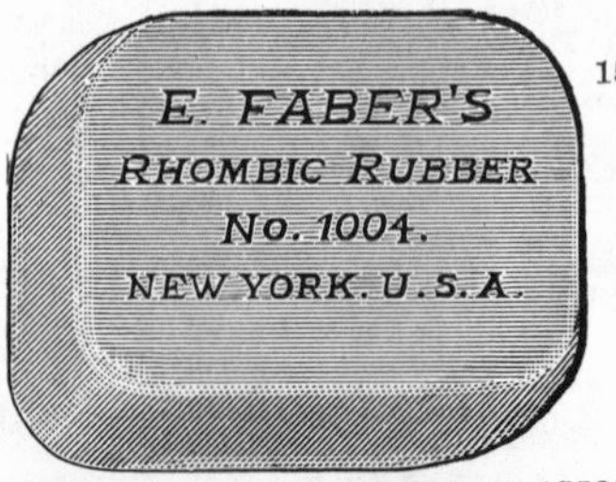

15537 Rhombic Rubber Eraser, with four sharply beveled edges which will erase typewriter, ink or pencil marks.
Each $0.04
Per doz.. .42

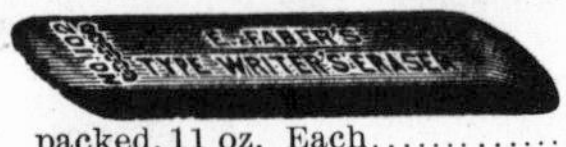

15538 Faber's "Typewriter's" Eraser, large size Weight, per doz., packed, 11 oz. Each .... .08
Per dozen .... .80

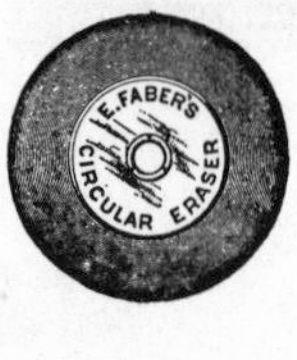

15540 Faber's Circular Eraser, made of a new compound, mounted on nickel plated disks, and will readily erase both ink and pencil marks.
Each $0.04
Per dozen .... .40

Erasers—Continued.

15542 Combined Ink and Pencil Eraser; beveled erasive rubbers, with composition centers. Each......$0.08 Per dozen ... .75

Pure Rubber Bands.

15547 Cabinet of assorted pure rubber bands *for home and office use.* Assortment of sizes up to one-half inch wide and 2½ inches in length. Weight, packed, 4 ounces. Per box......$0.25

15557 THREAD BANDS. One gross in a box. We do not sell less than a box.

Nos.	8	10	12	14
Length	⅞ in.	1¼ in.	1⅝ in.	2 in.
Per box	8c.	10c.	12c.	14c.
Per dozen boxes	85·.	$1.00	$1.20	$1.40
Weight, per doz. boxes.	11 oz.	11 oz.	14 oz.	14 oz.

15564 Rubber Bands, one-quarter inch wide.

Number.	Length.	Per doz.	Per gross.
000¼	3 in.	$0.07	$0.70
0000¼	3½ in.	.09	.80

15568 Rubber Bands, one-half inch wide.

Number.	Length.	Per doz.	Per gross.
00½	2½ in.	$0.11	$1.05
000½	3 in.	.12	1.15
0000½	3½ in	.14	1.25

15572 Rubber Bands, three-quarters inch wide.

Number.	Length.	Per doz.	Per gross.
000¾	3 in.	$0.15	$1.50
0000¾	3½ in.	.18	1.75

We do not sell less than one dozen of a size, Nos. 15564 to 15572 Bands.

15574 Heavy Rubber Bands, ⅝ inch wide.

Number.	Length.	Each.	Per doz.
105	5 in.	$0.05	$0.45
107	7 in.	.06	.60
109	9 in.	.07	.75

Our new Trade Mark LEUGER, H.H. COLLINS IMPROVED EUREKA INK ERADICATOR 27 UNION SQUARE N.Y. Adopted Jan. 1, 1894. REMOVING AN INK BLOT

15578 Improved Eureka Ink Eradicator, removes ink from paper and clothing without injury, also removes fruit, coffee, tobacco and wine stains from linen, lace and household goods without injury; directions for using accompany each box. Weight packed, 13 ounces. Per box. $0.20 Per dozen boxes....................................... 2.00

Ink.

For complete quotations of Ink, see Grocery List.

15580 Thomas' Stylographic Ink, black; absolutely non-corrosive; for use in fountain pens. 4 oz. bottles; per bottle, $0.12 Dozen bottles..$1.25 Bottle weighs 17 ounces.

15582 Sanford's Fountain Filler Blue Black Ink, for use in stylographic and fountain pens; writes blue and changes to black; 4 ounce flint glass bottle with filler; a cap screws into sleeve on neck of bottle, which holds bulb and filler in place and seals bottle. Weight, packed, 15 ounces. Per bottle........................$0.17

15584 Sanford's Gloss Black Ink, for ornamental penmanship, card writing, engrossing, e c.; dries jet black with a smooth, glossy surface like varnish; in 1½ ounce round bottle. Weight, packed, 10 ounces. Per bottle..................$0.07 Per dozen bottles......... .70

Indelible Ink.

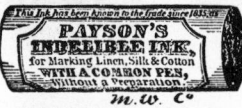

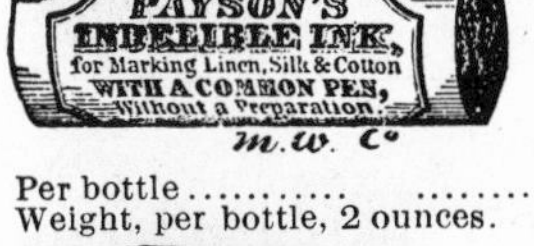

PAYSON'S INDELIBLE INK, for Marking Linen, Silk & Cotton WITH A COMMON PEN, Without a Preparation m.w.Cº

15586 Payson's Indelible Ink, for marking linen, silk, and cotton with a common pen; no preparation is required. Per bottle .... $0.20 Weight, per bottle, 2 ounces.

15588 Sanford's Indelible Ink, writes dark, changes to deep black and is permanent; put up in practical bottle, with stretcher for holding fabric while marking, and pen and penholder in decorated tin box. Weight, packed, 4 ounces.. $0.20

Indelible Ink—Continued.

Nº 1007 EAGLE INDELIBLE LINEN MARKER

15590 Eagle Indelible Linen Marker; will mark linen and cotton fabric without injuring the goods, and as soon as marks are made they appear jet black and remain thoroughly indelible; no heating or ironing necessary. Dampen the cloth slightly, rub the mordant over it several times and then use the pointed marker with slight pressure. Weight, packed, 2 ounces.

Each $0.08
Per dozen .... .85

Mucilage.

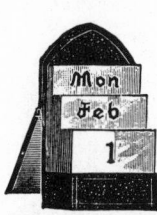

IMPERIAL MUCILAGE CHICAGO INK CO CHICAGO

15592 "Imperial" Sponge Top Mucilage Bottle, filled with a strong, clear mucilage; has a direct feed and will not clog. Good value at the price. Weight, packed, 12 ounces.
Per bottle.............................$0.13
Per dozen bottles.............. 1.20

Sealing Wax

SANFORD'S SEALING WAX

15595 Sanford's No. 2 Red Express Sealing Wax; 4 four-ounce sticks to pound, or 8 two-ounce sticks to pound. Per (4 oz.) stick...............$0.12
Per (2 oz.) stick................... .06
Per pound (either size)......... .35

15597 Sanford's Green Express Sealing Wax; 4 or 8 sticks to the pound box. Per (4 oz.) stick... .12
Per (2 oz.) stick..................... .06
Per pound (either size)......... .35

15598 Superfine London Black Letter Sealing Wax. Per (1 oz.) stick........................ .05
Per (2 oz.) stick .... .10
Per pound (either size) .... .70

Initial Seals.

B

15599 Initial Seal for Sealing Wax; length, 2½ inches, black enameled handle, nickeled metal die with rustic initial letter. Our special price, each..............$0.10
Per dozen 1.00

15600 Initial Seal for use with Sealing Wax; length, 3 inches, black enameled handle, nickeled metal die with Old English initial letter. Our price, each....................................$0.17
Per dozen 1.85

Perpetual Calendar.

Mon Feb 1   January SUN MON TUES WED THUR FRI SAT

Perpetual Calendars, good for any year; suitable for holiday and birthday gifts.

15603 and 15609   **15606**

15603 Perpetual Calendar, grain leather case with fancy cloth back and rest, heavy cardboard slips with name and number of days and name of months, 4 inches high, 2 inches wide. Weight, packed, 4 ounces. Our special price, each.......$0 50

15606 Perpetual Calendar, finely polished, Persian grained leather case with English silk cloth back and rest, heavy cardboard slips with names of months and days, and numbers of days in colors protected by transparent celluloid slides, 4¾ inches high, 2½ inches wide. Weight, packed, 4 ounces. Our special price, each....... .65

15609 Perpetual Calendar, colored tripe leather case with English silk cloth back and rest; ivory finish celluloid slips with names of months and days, and numbers of days in bold figures, 4 inches high, 2 inches wide. Weight, packed, 5 ounces. Our special price, each..... .65

Inkstands.

15612 Flint Glass, with metal screw cap, for use in writing desks.
Each..........................$0.07
Per dozen.......................... .75
Weight, 3 ounces.

15621 Practical or Common Sense Inkstand. No evaporation, no spilling of ink. Same style as safety inks and, but without cork in bottom.
Weight, packed, 18 ounces.
Each........................$0.12
Per dozen 1.20

Inkstands—Continued.

15623 *"Sterling"* Automatic inkstand, saves 75 per cent. in ink, or more than its cost, in six months; seals ink from atmosphere and prevents evaporation; will not overflow, delivers ink to the pen in perfect liquid form, has no plugs to be adjusted and no detachable parts to be mislaid or lost. Weight, packed, 20 ounces. Our special price, each.$0 40

15624 Extra Soft Rubber Valves for Sterling Inkstand. Each...... ....$0.10

15629 Inkstand. Double, enameled finish, 4½ inches high, with two revolving "Star" bottles, heavy flint glass. Weight, packed, 28 ounces.
Each....................$0.35
Per dozen.......... 3.75

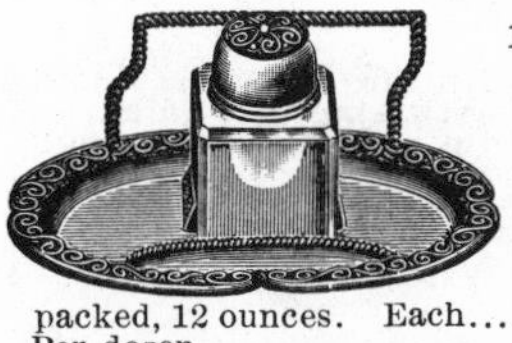

15631 Inkstand, fancy embossed silvered metal base with tray for pens and twisted wire pen rack, crystal glass ink well with cap of silvered metal; 2½ inches high; base, 5x3¾ inches. Weight, packed, 12 ounces. Each....................$0.20
Per dozen.......................... 2.10

15635 Inkstand, rolled steel base, pen-rack and hinged cover, nickel plated and highly polished, with pressed crystal glass ink bottle; 2¾ inches high, 3¾ in. base. Weight packed, 15 ounces. Each..........$0.45

15639 Inkstand, maroon finish, iron base and pen-rack, with rope pattern crystal glass sponge, cup and two ink-wells, with fancy iron caps; 3¼ inches high; base, 9¾x4¼ inches. Weight, packed, 4½ pounds. Too heavy to go by mail. Each..$0.50

Pocket Inkstands.

FOR TRAVELERS' AND TOURISTS' USE.

15646 Lignum Vitæ Wood Inkstand with screw top, 2 inches high, 1¼ inches in diameter; leakage impossible, polished. Weight, 3 ounces. Each..........$0.12
Per dozen........................ 1.25

15650 Inkstand covered with fine grade of leather, double spring covers, silvered finish inside; 1¾ inches in diameter. Weight, packed, 3 ounces. Our special price, each...$0.30

Paper Clips.

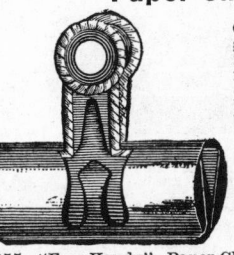

"Ever-Handy" Paper Clips, for holding together notes, receipts, invoices, letters and memoranda of every description, made from best spring steel and brass, double strength.

15653 "Ever Handy" Paper Clip, small size, with jaws 1½ inches wide. Each..............$0.04
Per dozen........ .40

15655 "Ever-Handy" Paper Clip, medium size, with jaws 2½ inches wide. Each..............$0.06
Per dozen.. .60

Board Clips.

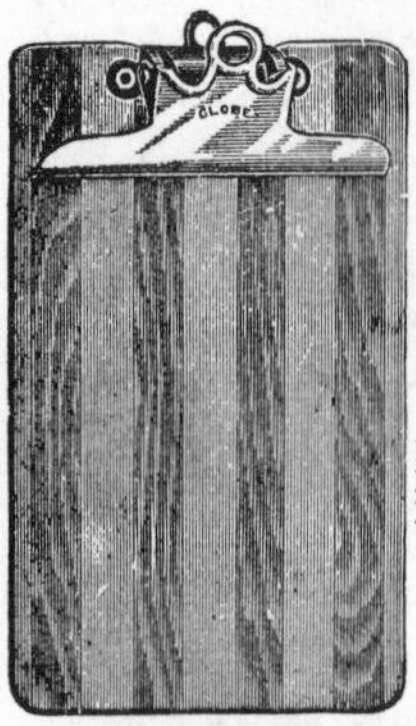

Striped Wood Board, Nickeled Clip, with brass wire spring, improved metal shoulder for papers to square against, and metal eye to hang up by. The best made and finished board clip on the market.

	Each.	Per doz.
15657 Note Size	$0.28	$3.05
15658 Letter Size	.31	3.35
15659 Cap Size	.34	3.65

Paper Files.

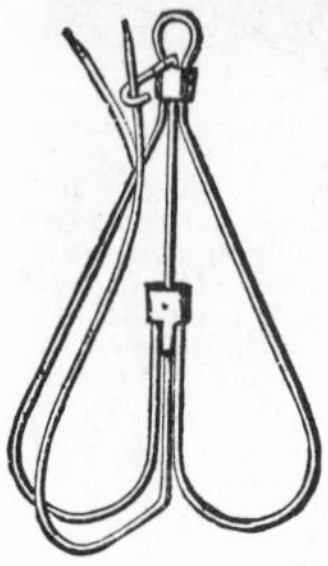

15665 Hanging Paper File, tinned wire back and hook with protected point. Weight, packed, 9 ounces.
Each $0.04
Per dozen .... .40

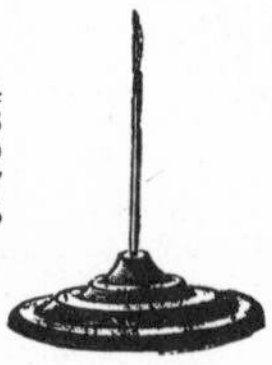

15667 Jumbo Standing Paper File, 4 inch lacquered iron base, wire 8 inches long. Weight, packed, 9 ounces. Each $0.07
Per dozen .... .75

PEN RACKS.

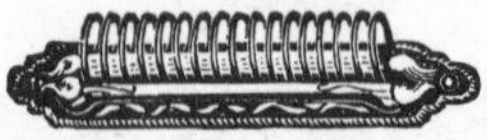

15672 Keep's Patent Perfection Spiral Pen Rack, each coil permanently but loosely held by loops in base thus preventing springs from being weakened or displaced by use; size, 6¼x1¼x1⅛ inches. Weight, packed, 3 ounces. Each $0.08
Per dozen .... .80

Wooden Rulers.

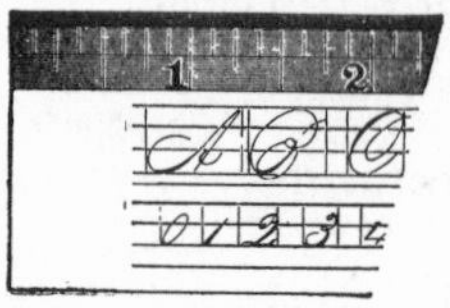

15685 Spencerian Script Ruler, a heavy maple ruler 1⅜ inches wide, 15 inches long, divided into eighths of inches; copies of penmanship printed on both sides of ruler. Suitable for school or office use. Weight, per dozen, packed, 2 pounds.
Each.. .... $0.04
Per dozen .... .40

15687 Spencerian Script Ruler, with inlaid brass edge; length 15 inches; otherwise same as 15685. Weight, packed, (per dozen), 2½ pounds.
Each $0.08
Per dozen .... .85

Scholars' Companions.

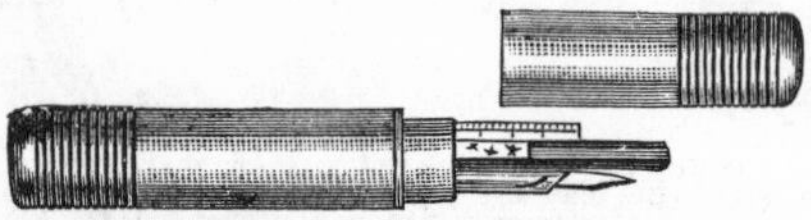

15700 Whitewood Box Scholars' Companion; furnished with lead pencil, pen, penholder, slate pencil and six inch wood ruler. Weighs, 3 oz.
Each $0.03
Per dozen .... .30

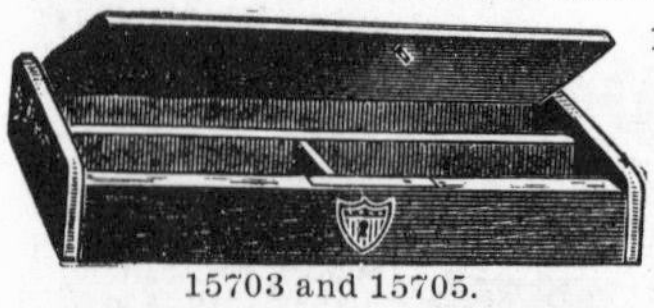

15703 and 15705.

15703 "Magic Hingeless" Scholars' Companion, highly polished basswood box with three compartments and lock and key. 8¼x2⅜x1⅛ inches. Weight, packed, 6 ounces. Each $0.05
Per dozen .... .45

15705 "Magic Hingeless" Scholars' Companion, furnished with rubber eraser, lead pencil, slate pencil, penholder and pen; otherwise same as 15703. Weight, packed, 7 ounces.
Each .... .08
Per dozen .... .75

Scholars' Companions—Continued.

15707 "Magic Hingeless" Scholars' Companion, highly polished hardwood body *with inlaid butternut top;* three compartments for fittings; lock and key. 8¼x2⅜x1⅛ inches. Weight, packed, 6 ounces.
Each $0.08
Per dozen .... .75

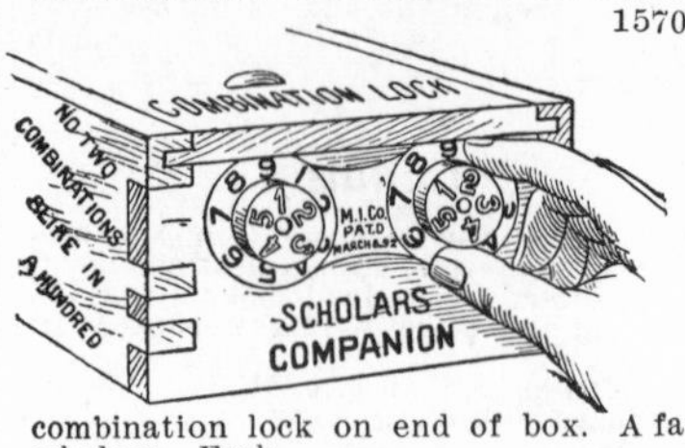

15709 "Combination Lock" Scholars' Companion, hardwood box, with three compartments; sliding cover fastened by combination lock on end of box. A favorite with scholars. Each $0.08
Per dozen .... .75
Postage .... .06

Chalk Crayons.

15715 White Chalk Crayons, round; one gross in box. Weight, 2½ pounds.
Per box $0.05
Per dozen boxes .... .54

15717 Colored Chalk Crayons, round; one gross *assorted colors* in box. Weight, 2½ pounds.
Per box (one gross) .... .30
Per dozen boxes 3.25

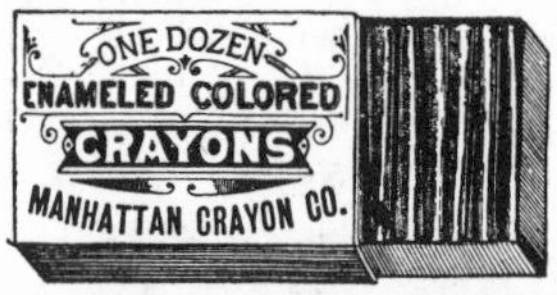

15719 Enameled Colored Chalk Crayons, 12 pieces, assorted colors in slide box. Weight, packed, 5 ounces.
Per box $0.04
Per doz boxes .... .40

15721 "ALPHA DUSTLESS CRAYON" makes a firm clean mark; will not soil hands or clothing, nor scratch or glaze the board; it is DUSTLESS and will not injure the throats of teachers and pupils. It is durable and will last six times as long as common chalk crayons. Weight, per box, 4 lbs. Per box (one gross) .... .55
Per dozen boxes 6.00
We do not sell less than a box of Chalk Crayons.

Blackboard Erasers.

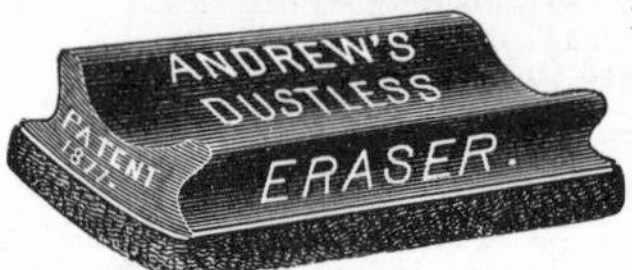

15726 Andrews' Dustless Blackboard Eraser, made of *wool felt*, so woven that the rubbing is done by the ends of the fiber; it gathers and holds the dust, cleans the board thoroughly, is easily cleaned, and very durable. Weight, packed, 4 ounces.
Each $0.08
Per dozen .... .80
Per gross 8.00

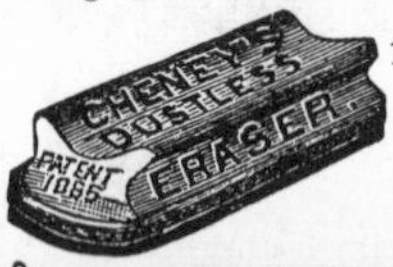

15729 Cheney's Dustless Eraser, colored felt, firmly secured to block, a substantial eraser. Weight, packed, 3 ounces. Each $0.04
Per dozen .... .40

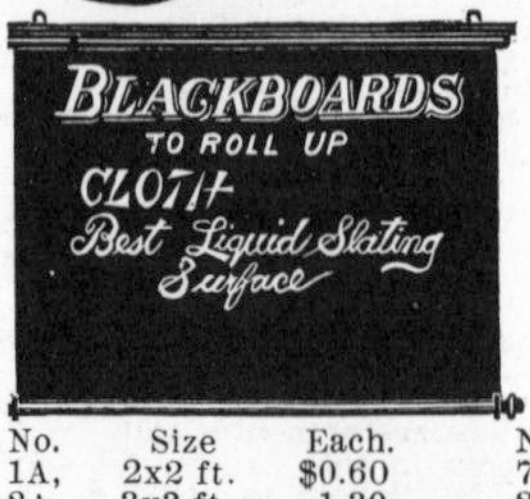

Portable Blackboards.

15735 Portable Blackboard of cloth with best black liquid slating surface on both sides, mounted on rollers with hook and rings complete for hanging.

No.	Size	Each.	No.	Size.	Each.
1A,	2x2 ft.	$0.60	7A,	4x4 ft.	$2.25
2A,	3x3 ft.	1.30	8A,	4x5 ft.	2.75
3A,	3x4 ft.	1.75	9A,	4x6 ft.	3.25
4A,	3x5 ft.	2.25	10A,	4x7 ft.	3.85
5A,	3x6 ft.	2.75			

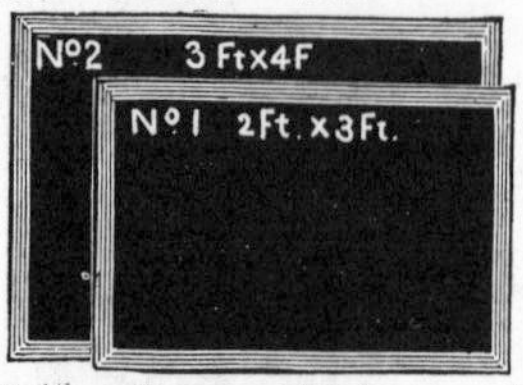

15737 Portable Blackboard of hyloplate, slated both sides; with ash frame; for use on wall, easel or table.

No.	Size.	Each.	No.	Size.	Each.
1B,	2x3 ft.	$3.00	4B,	3½x5	$6.40
2B,	3x4 ft.	4.15	5B,	4 x6	8.25
3B,	3x4½ ft.	5.25			

Slated Paper and Cloth.

For Blackboards; excellent for any flat surface.

15738— Per yard.
No. 26. Paper, 3 feet wide, slated one side, black $0.52
No. 25. Paper, 4 feet wide, slated one side, black .... .66

15739—
No. 24. Cloth, 3 feet wide, slated one side, black .... .60
No. 23. Cloth, 4 feet wide, slated one side, black .... .73
No. 22. Cloth, 3 feet wide, slated two sides, black .... .73
No. 21. Cloth, 4 feet wide, slated two sides, black .... .88

Liquid Slating for Blackboads.

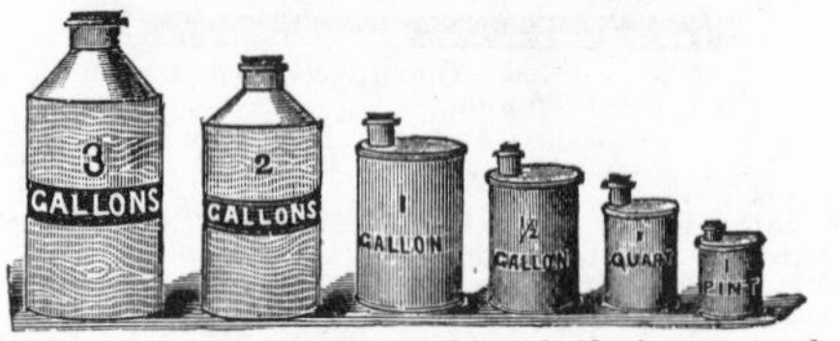

15741 Best Alcohol Black Liquid Slating; may be applied to hard finish plaster, paper, boards, or to old blackboards of any kind; does not become greasy; is not easily scratched; does not crack, blister or glaze when applied to suitable surface according to directions which accompany each can; dries in a few minutes, hardens in a day. A gallon will cover about 250 square feet, 3 coats. Put up in tin cans. Cannot be sent by mail.
Per pint .... $0.60   Per half-gallon ... $2.00
Per quart .... 1.10   Per gallon 4.00

15742 Flat Brush for applying liquid slating; 3 inches wide. Each $0.75

School Bags.

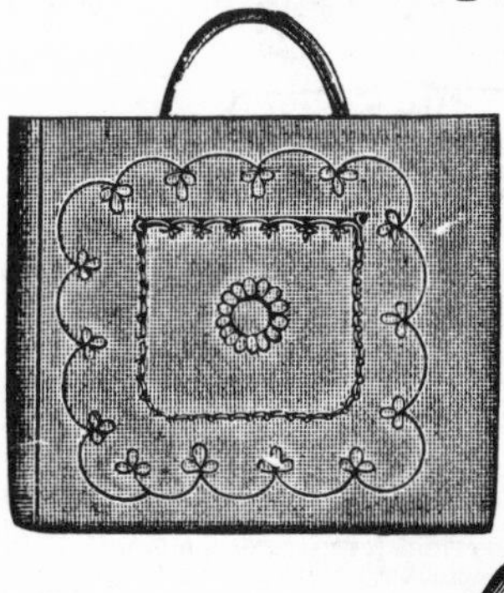

15743 School Bags, Burlap embroidered with colored braid; with pocket; 11½x14 inches. Weight, packed, 5 ounces
Each $0.08
Per dozen. .80

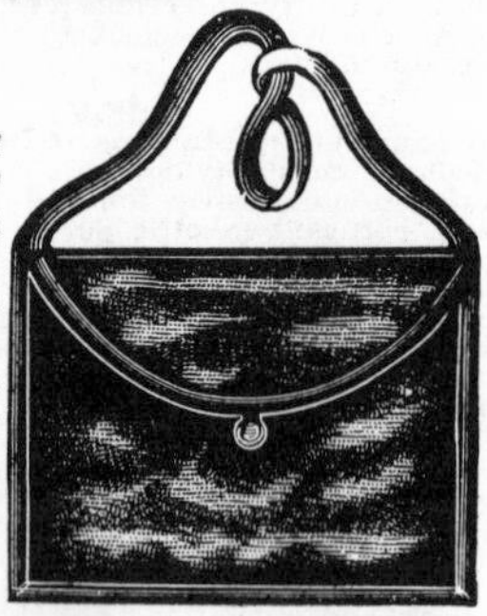

15745 Waterproof School Bags; made of enameled cloth, with flap and leather shoulder strap. Weight, packed, 5 ounces.

	Each.	Per Doz
14 inches...	8c	$0.85
16 inches...	10c	1.05

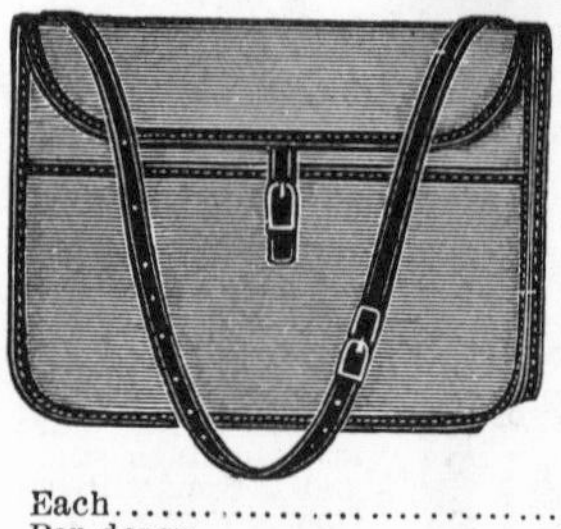

15749 School Bag, brown duck bound and stitched all around, large pocket 6 inches deep across front of bag; flap fastens with buckle and strap; grain leather shoulder strap with buckle; size, 9½x14 with 2¼ inch gusset, making a very roomy bag. Weight, packed 6 ounces.
Each $0.18
Per dozen 1.90

School Bags—Continued.

15751 School Bag. A new, strong, fancy bag, made of heavy colored cotton cord, lined with colored cambric. Very durable. 9¾x13½ inches. Each....$0.18
Per dozen........ 1.90

15753 Fancy *School* Bag, made of colored cotton cord of various shades, lined with colored cambric and finished with heavy cord drawing strings; 13½x17 inches.
Each............$0.20
Per dozen........ 2.00

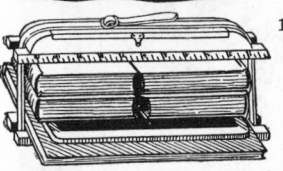

15755 The Scholars' Combination Carryall; combining book-clamp, 12-inch ruler and scholars' companion; hardwood, nicely finished, with stout leather straps and buckle. Weight, packed, 9 ounces. Each....................$0.20
Per dozen...................... 2.00

Slate Sponges.

15758 Sponges for cleaning school slates; fairsize, medium in texture, bleached and cleaned.
Per dozen...........$0.08
Per gross............. .80

School Slates With Wood Frames.

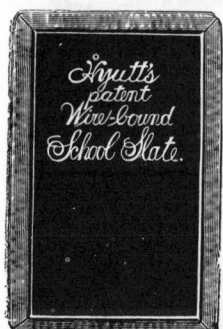

"Hyatt" Patent Wire Bound School Slates combine strength, lightness, durability and uniformity of finish of surface; being wire-bound *they cannot come apart*, and machine-smoothed they present an absolutely even writing surface, free from ridges.

Size.	Each.	Per doz.	Weight, each
15760 6x9..........$0.04		$0.42	18 oz.
7x11.......... .05		.48	22 oz.
8x12.......... .06		.60	25 oz.
6x9, 12 dozen in case, per case.....$4.75			
7x11, 10 dozen in case, per case......... 4.50			
8x12, 8 dozen in case, per case......... 4.50			

"Hyatt" Noiseless Slates.

Strength, lightness and durability combined. Best quality slate with perfectly finished even writing surface, free from ridges. Frame is *wire bound* (cannot come apart) and covered with fine bright red (fast color) wool felt, securely fastened.
15762 "Hyatt" Noiseless Slate, single.

Size.........Each.	Per doz.	Weight, each.
6x9...........$0.08	$0.80	18 oz.
7x11.......... .10	1.00	23 oz.
8x12.......... .12	1.20	26 oz.
6x9, 12 dozen in case, per case................. ..$9.00		
7x11, 10 dozen in case, per case............... 9.00		
8x12, 8 dozen in case, per case 9.00		

15764 "Hyatt" Noiseless Slate, double, hinged with strong webbing, firmly riveted to frames.

Size.	Each.	Per doz.	Weight, each.
7x11...........$0.20		$2.00	40 oz.
8x12.......... .24		2.40	46 oz.
7x11, 5 dozen in case, per case...................$9.00			
8x12, 4 dozen in case, per case................... 9.00			

Slates.—Continued.

15768 Hyatt "Peerless" Noiseless Slate with non-erasable *colored lines* on one side, produced by patent process which leaves slate surface perfectly smooth and even; felt covered wire bound frame: size, 6x9 inches. Weight, packed, 18 ounces.
Each...........$0.12
Per dozen........ 1.25
Per case of 12 dozen...........14.25

Silicate Book Slates.

Superior quality, strongly made, bound in fine black cloth covers Superior slate surface *for the slate pencil*. For school or office use.

	Size.	Ea.	Per dz.
15772 6 surfaces,	5x8½	$0.25	$2.70
6 "	6x9	.35	3.80

Silicate Book Slates, neatly and strongly bound in fine cloth, with superior IVORINE SURFACE *for the lead pencil;* for the pocket.

		Size.	Each.	Per doz.
15775	6 surfaces,	3x5	$0.15	$1.60
	10 "	3¼x5½	.25	2.70

15772-15775

Writing Desks.

15823 Butternut Desks (*for juveniles*), varnished; top beveled, paneled, and has black and gilt center ornament, beveled extension base, flannel lined, furnished with screw top inkstand; size, 11x7½x2½. Weight, 28 ounces. Each........$0.40

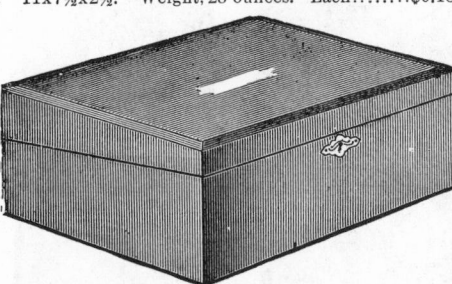

15836 Oak Desk, nice varnish finish, bevel edge, polished brass name and key plates, inside folds banded and lined with velvet; furnished with inkstand; size, 12x8x3½. Weighs 55 ounces.
Each................ ....$1.40

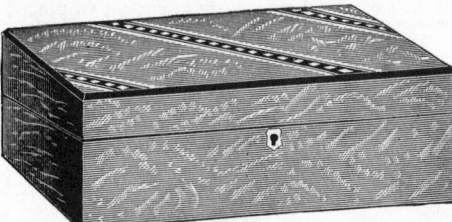

15837 Veneered Oak Desk, bevel edge, gilt and black band ornament, brass name plate. Fitted with walnut reeded folds and lined with colored flannel; furnished with inkstand. Size 12¾x9x4¼. Weighs 53 ounces. Each.........$1.50

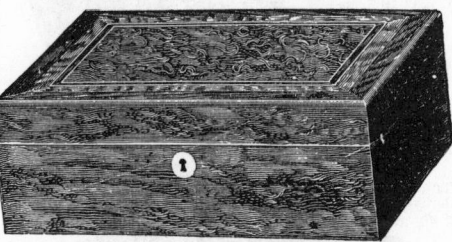

15842 Inlaid Desk, nicely polished, bevel edge, polished brass name plate; inside folds reeded and lined with colored velvet: furnished with inkstand. Size, 13x9x4½. Weighs 64 ounces.
Each..................................$2.75

Portfolios.

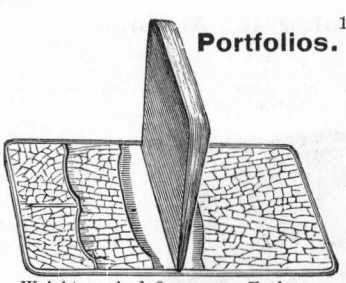

15850 Tinted Canvas Portfolio, bound with leather and stitched all around; two large and two smaller pockets for stationery; large sheets of blotting paper in center; size, closed, 8¼x11¼ inches.
Weight, packed, 9 ounces. Each.............$0.50

Ladies' Writing Companion.

15859 Writing Companion of fancy embossed cloth leatherette; size, 7½x12½ inches; oxidized metal cap inkstand; compartment for stamps and pens; large gusseted pocket and two smaller pockets for stationery; enameled nickeled tip penholder. Weight, packed, 24 ounces.
Each..............$0.80

Work Boxes.

15875 Oak Work Box, filled and varnished, bevel edge, ornamented with gilt bands, stationary mirror inside of cover, fitted with removable walnut tray containing three compartments and pin-cushion. Size, 12x8x3½. Weighs, 42 oz....$0.90

Bicycles

This year's sales expected to be the largest on record.

Our Hawthorne at $65.00 and White Star at $45.00 are both high grade.

You can't begin to do so well at the price.

Photograph Albums.

NOTE.—COMPLAINTS ARE OFTEN MADE THAT *"openings are too small for pictures."* Album openings are of standard size. Photograph mounts should be trimmed to suit the size of album opening. Care should be taken in inserting and removing pictures.

16007 Moire Plush Album with large nickeled word "Album" and extension clasp; tinted interior with openings for 20 cabinets and 16 cards; size, 8½x10½ in. Weight, packed, 60 oz. Each......$0.75

16019 Silk Plush Album with large handsome floral ornament of nicely colored embossed celluloid; silvered extension clasp, light interior with floral decorations in color and gold; openings for 26 cabinets and 16 cards; size,8¾x11 in. Weight, packed, 5 pounds. Too heavy to go by mail. Each....$2.00

16022 Silk Plush Album with full celluloid front cover, handsomely embossed word "Album" and floral ornaments in colors; silvered extension clasp, light interior with decorations in gold, openings for 26 cabinets and 16 cards; size, 8¾x10½. Weight, packed, 5½ pounds. Too heavy to go by mail. Each....$2.25

16071 Seal Grain Leather Longfellow Album with floral embossing on front cover; gilt extension clasp; light tinted interior with openings for 60 cabinets; size, 7¾x16 inches. Too heavy to go by mail. Weight, packed, 6 lbs. Each....................$2.50

Albums—Continued.

16073 Moire Plush Longfellow Album with nickeled word "Album" and extension clasp; tinted interior with openings for 48 cabinets; size, 7x16 inches. Weight, packed, 4½ lbs. Too heavy to go by mail. Each.............$1.35

16080 Silk Plush Longfellow Album, with celluloid front cover ornamented with embossed word "Album" and flowers in colors; silvered extension clasp; tinted interior with floral decorations in gold; openings for 60 cabinets; size,7½x16inches. Weight, packed, 6¼ lbs. Too heavy to go by mail. Each $3.00

16089 Silk Plush Upright Album, with celluloid word "Album," silvered extension clasp; drawer in base for odd pictures; light interior with floral decorations in gold; openings for 60 cabinets; 12¼ inches high. 10½ inch base. Weight, packed, 6½ lbs. Too heavy to go by mail. Each. $2.75

16075 Silk Plush Longfellow Album, with large handsome word "Album" in colored celluloid; silvered extension clasp; tinted interior with floral decorations in gold; openings for 60 cabinets; size, 7½x16 inches. Weight, packed, 6¼lbs. Too heavy to go by mail. Each.....$2.25

16085 Fine Silk Plush Longfellow Album with full celluloid front cover, ornamented with embossed word "Cabinets" and handsome floral designs in colors; silvered extension clasp; light interior with handsomely lithographed floral decorations; openings for 64 cabinets; size, 7½x16 inches. Weight, packed, 6¾ lbs. Too heavy to go by mail. Each.............$4.00

Albums—Continued.

16090 Silk Plush Upright Album, with plate glass trefoil mirror, silvered catch and ornaments; adjustable swivel back; tinted interior with decorations in color and gold; openings for 60 cabinets and 15 cards; 11½ inches high, 14 inch base. Weight, packed, 7 lbs. Too heavy to go by mail. Each......................$3.50

16099 Fine Fancy Embossed Celluloid Upright Album, top and front ornamented with colored flowers, drawer in base for odd pictures; light interior with lithographed floral decorations, openings for 64 cabinets; 12 inches high. Weight, packed, 9 lbs. Too heavy to go by mail. Each........ ....$6.00

Pocket Photograph Cases.

16100 Pocket Photograph Case of fine seal grained calf leather (very durable), with openings for two cabinet pictures; size, closed, 5x7 inches. Weight, packed, 3 ounces. Each....................................$0.60

16102 Pocket Photograph Case, with openings for four cabinet pictures; otherwise same as No. 16100. Weight, packed, 5 ounces. Each....................................$1.20

Scrap Books.

See Index for quotations on scrap book pictures. We have a very fine assortment.

Scrap Book, full cloth covers, with stamped corners and back; word "Album" embossed in gold; 36 pages, heavy white paper, colored edges, patent back.

Number.	Size.	Each.	Per doz.	Weight, each
16113	10¼x12¾	$0.30	$3.00	22 ounces.
16117	11¼x14	.35	3.50	27 ounces.

Scrap Books—Continued.

16118 Scrap Book, heavy covers bound in cloth, stamped in silver and black, patent back. Size, 12⅜x15 inches; 60 pages, extra heavy white paper, with colored edges. Each, 64 cents. Weight, packed, 45 ounces.

No Mucilage or Brush Required.

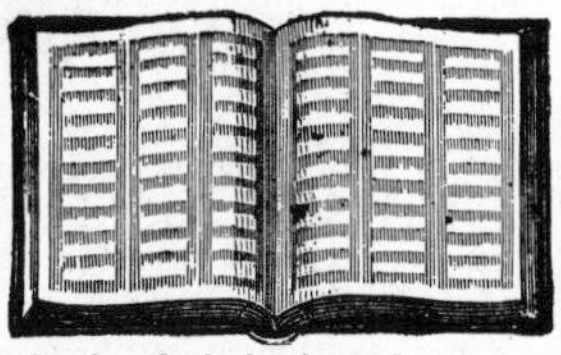

The convenience of the ready-gummed page and the simplicity of the arrangement for pasting is such that those who once use this scrap book never return to the old style.

Mark Twain's Scrap Book, cloth back and corners, marble paper sides; a very serviceable and reliable book.

16121 Size, 6⅜x9⅜ inches, 64 pages, 2 gummed columns to page. Each........................$0.38
Extra by mail, each.....$0.13 Per dozen....... 4.10

16123 Size 8½ x 11 inches, 64 pages, 3 gummed columns to page.
Each.................$0.55
Per dozen 6.00
Extra by mail, each. .20

16127 Mark Twain's Scrap Book, bound in full cloth, with fan and butterfly design stamped in three colors, making a very neat and tasty book. Size, 10½ x12 inches, 64 pages, 3 gummed columns to page.
Each $1.15
Postage .... .30

Autograph Albums.

Autograph Album, fine silk plush, with silver word "Album," about 60 pages tinted paper of good quality, with gold edges.

No.	Size.	Each.	Per doz.	Weight, each.
16150	3¾x6	$0.37	$3.85	7 ounces.
16153	4¼x7	.43	4.60	10 ounces.
16155	5 x8	.53	5.60	11 ounces.

Ladies' Book Sets.

16165 Ladies' Book Set, three books in sliding case, CASH, NOTES and VISITS. Flexible leatherette cover, gilt titles; about thirty leaves, quadrille ruled. Size, in case, 4½x2⅛x⅝.
Per set...................... .05
Per dozen sets .... .40
Postage........................ .04

Dominoes.

16205 Dominoes, natural wood embossed, with red dots; ⅞x1⅝; set of 28 pieces, in cardboard box. Weighs 7 ounces. Per set........$0.08
Per dozen sets........... .80

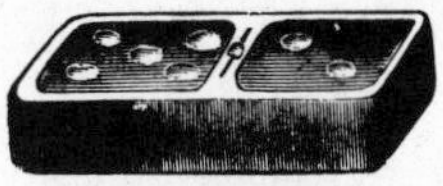

16207 "Crown" Dominoes, black, round corners, white dots; 28 pieces in cardboard box.
Per set.............$0.20
Per dozen sets.......2.10

16210 "Black" Dominoes, embossed, with white enamel dots; ⅞ x1¾; set of 28 pieces in heavy cardboard box. Weighs 11 ounces.
Per set..................$0.35 Per doz. sets.....$3.25

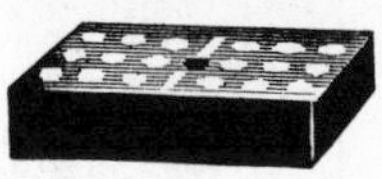

16212 "Double Nine" Black Dominoes, embossed, with white enamel dots; ⅞x1¾; set of 55 pieces in wood frame box, *More persons can play and the game has greater possibilities.* Weighs 23 ounces. Per set..................$0.75

Dominoes—Continued.

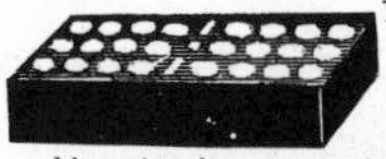

16216 "Double Twelve" Black Dominoes, embossed, with enameled dots; ⅞x1¾; set of 91 pieces in wood frame box. VERY INTRICATE AND NOVEL, *making domino games doubly interesting.* Weighs 36 ounces. Per set.....................$1.25

Checker Men.

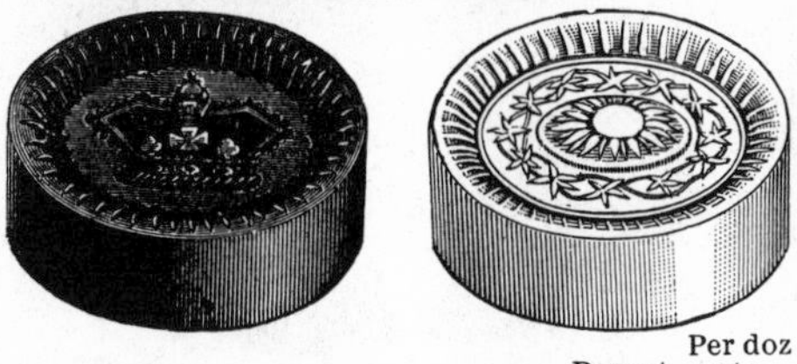

Per set. Per doz. sets.

16225 Checkers, hardwood, natural and black, 1 inch in diameter, 24 pieces in set; set weighs 5 ounces...........$0.04 $0.35
16227 Checkers, star hardwood, white and black, 1⅛ inches in diameter, 30 pieces in set; set weighs 7 ounces.... .06   60
16229 Checkers, polished, interlocking natural and black; 1⅛ inches in diameter, 30 pieces in set; set weighs 7 oz.. .12   1 25

Chess or Checker Boards.

16246 Folding Chess or Checker Board, bound in black cloth, embossed in gilt; backgammon back, 1¼ inch red and black squares; size, open, 14x 14 Weight, packed, 15 oz. Each $0.50
Per dozen....................... 5.25

Backgammon Boards

16258 Backgammon Board, walnut frame, brass hinged, imitation leather top with gilt border, red and black squares; size, open, 15x15½; furnished with dice, 2 dice-cups and set (30 pieces) wood checkers. Weight, packed, 35 ounces.
Each............. ....$1.00

Chess Men.

16264 French Wood Chess Men, black and white, in white wood boxes. Per set.. $0.45
Postage.. .10

16268 Fine Boxwood Chess Men, *Staunton Pattern,* black and white polished: in dove-tailed polished hardwood box with sliding cover. Weight, packed, 18 ounces.
Per set...................................$1.00

Dice.

No. 1.    No.7

16271 Bone Dice No.3..
No. 1. ⁵⁄₁₆ inch. Per dozen........................$0.06
Postage................... .02
No. 3. ⅜ inch. Per dozen....................... .11
Postage................... .03
No. 7. ⁷⁄₁₆ inch. Per dozen....................... .20
Postage .... .05

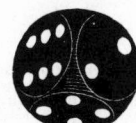   

No. D 1.   No. D 2.

16275 Black Diamond Dice, made of black composition with white enameled sunken dots, rounded corners.
No. D 1, ½ inch. Per dozen......................$0.15
Weight, packed, 3 ounces.
No. D 2, ⅝ inch. Per dozen..................... .30
Weight, packed, 4 ounces.

Dice—Continued.

16276 "Celluloid" Poker Dice, representing ace, king, queen, jack, ten and nine spots; ivory finish celluloid. PERFECT GOODS. Set of five pieces in box. Weight, packed, 4 ounces.
Per set.................$0.65

Dice Cups.

16279 Heavy Solid Sole Leather Dice Cup. Natural color, securely stitched, medium size.
Each..............................$0.18
Per dozen........................ 1.85
Postage.......................... .04

Cribbage Boards.

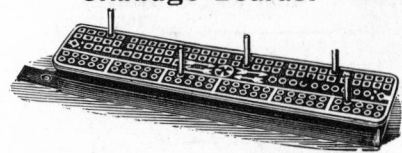

16291 Le Count's Cribbage Board, polished, nickeled metal plate with drilled holes; stained whitewood base with compartment containing six cribbage pins. Size, 2¼x9¾ inches. Weight, packed, 17 ounces. Our special price, each....$0.40

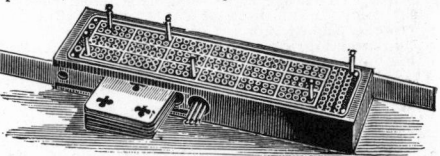

16295 Le Count's Patent Cribbage Board, polished, nickeled metal plate with three double rows drilled holes, to score for three or six players; base of polished black walnut with compartments for two packs of cards and one containing nine steel cribbage pins. Size, 2⅜x10½ inches. Weight, packed, 20 ounces.
Our special price, each........................$0.80

Poker Chips.

16341 Composition Poker Chips, ivory finish, warranted not to chip or warp, 1¼ inches in diameter, 100 in box assorted as follows: 50 white, 25 red, 25 blue. Weight, packed, 25 oz.
Per box of 100. .... $0 30
Per 1000...... 2.75
16345 Composition Poker Chips, ivory finish, first quality, warranted not to chip or warp; 1½ inches in diameter; 100 in box, assorted as follows: 50 white, 25 red, 25 blue. Weight, packed, 28 ounces. Per box of 100.............$0.35
Per 1000...... 3 00

16351 Decorated Poker Chips, for playing "Penny Ante," 100 in box, assorted as follows: 50 white of numeral 1, 25 red of numeral 5, 25 blue of numeral 10. Size, 1½ inches. Weight, per box (100), 28 ounces.
Per bx of 100.$1.25
Per 1000 .... 10.70

16355 "Lily" Design Poker Chips, 1½ inches in diameter; 100 chips in box, assorted as follows: 50 white, 25 blue, 25 red. Can supply in no other assortment of colors unless ordered in lots of 1000 or more; will then be assorted as desired. Weight (per box) packed, 28 ounces.
Per box of 100.$1.20
Per 1000. .. ..10.75

16358 "Bull's Head" Design Poker Chips, 1½ inches in diameter; 100 chips in box, assorted as follows: 50 white, 25 blue, 25 red. Cannot supply in any other assortment of colors unless ordered in lots of 1000 or more; may then be assorted as desired. Weight (per box), packed, 28 ounces.
Per box of 100.$1.20
Per 1000......10.75

Poker Sets.

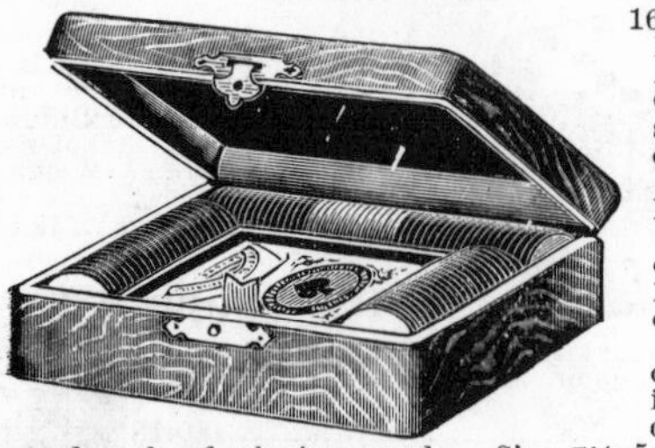

16367—Polished Antique Oak Box, silvered catch and hinges, lined with flannel. contains 100 poker chips in assorted colors, 1¼ inches in diameter, and pack of playing cards. Size, 7½x5x2. Weight, packed, 34 ounces.
Our special price, each.......................... $1.10

Game Counters.

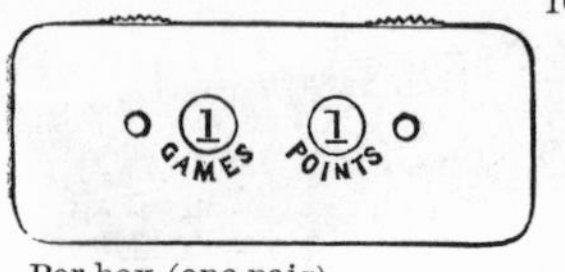

16371 Game Counters of ivory finish celluloid, 3x1$\frac{1}{16}$ inches, two wheels, one for games and one for points, one pair in pebbled paper sliding box. Our special price.
Per box (one pair)................................ $0.25
Per dozen.. 2.70

Playing Card Boxes.

16378 Playing Card Box, made from English sole leather, telescope style, securely stitched, russet color, for one pack of cards. Size, 4x3x1. Weight, packed, 3 oz.
Our special price, each.......................... $0.25
Per dozen.. 2.70

Duplicate Whist Sets at Popular Prices.

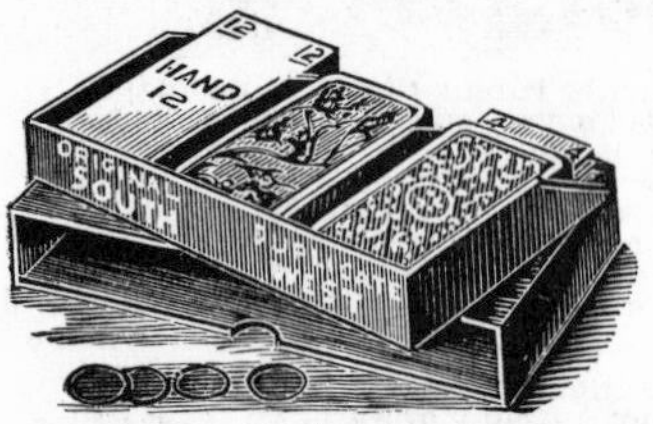

16390 "Tokalon" Duplicate Whist Set; consists of four slide boxes, suitably marked for each player, each box having three divisions, and each division will hold three hands, or a complete pack of cards; dividers of a separate color for each player; score-cards and directions for playing in each set. Size 8½x5x4¼. Weight, packed, 24 ounces. Our special price, per set........ $0.40
Extra score cards for 16390, 100 in package.
Per package.. .40

Whist Sets—Continued.

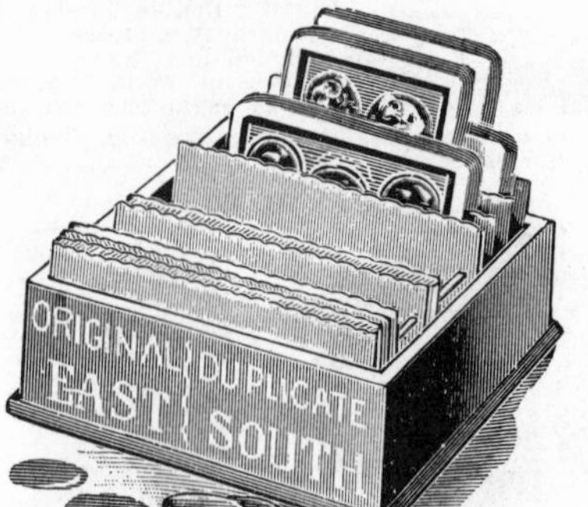

16393 "Tokalon" Duplicate Whist Set, complete for 12 hands; four Russia red leatherette boxes (as shown in illustration), each fitted with movable card-board dividers, score-cards, counters and directions for playing in box; size, 11¼x5¾x4¼ inches. Weight, packed, 38 ounces. Our special price, per set. . $0.80
16396 "Tokalon" Duplicate Whist Set, complete for 12 hands; four colored English silk cloth boxes (as shown in illustration) in large pebbled black cloth box, with telescope cover stamped in gold; furnished same as 16393. Weight, packed, 44 ounces. Our special price, per set.. 1.60
Extra score cards for 16393 and 16396, 100 in package. Per package.............................. .80

Playing Cards.

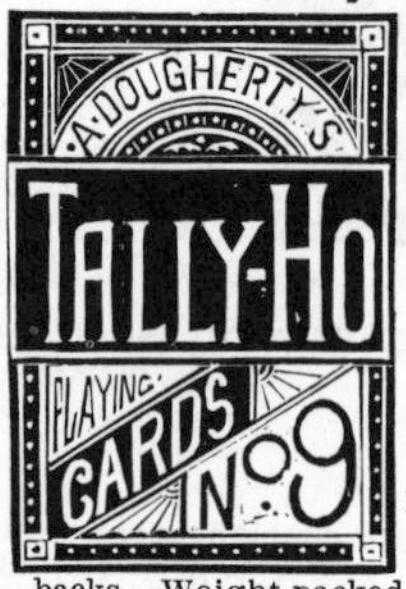

Our line of playing cards is of the best standard quality, and they will commend themselves by the following distinguishable features: Excellence of stock, artistic and accurate printing, superior slip, finish and cutting; designs of faces and backs from sketches by prominent artists. Incomparable jokers, all original designs, artistic and handsome decoration of pack boxes and wrappers.

16440 Steamboat No. 0, round cornered, double indexed; star, plaid, wave and calico backs. Weight packed, 4 ounces. Per pack.... $0.08
Per dozen packs.. .85
Per gross packs.. 9.60
16445 "Occidental" No. 09, assortment of fancy backs, enameled. Weight packed, 4 oz. Per pack, $0.13
Per dozen packs.... $1.40 Per gross packs.... $16.00

Playing Cards—Continued.

16450 "Tally-Ho" No. 9, round cornered, double index, enameled; large variety of handsomely designed backs in different tints and colors; the best enambled card at the price in market. Weight, packed, 4 ounces. Per pack........... $0.17
Per dozen packs.. 1.85
Per gross packs.. 21.00
16455 "Club" No. 50, *second quality*, made from linen stock, enameled finish. Weight, packed, 4 ounces. Per pack.. .20
Per dozen packs.. 2.00
Per gross packs.. 23.00
16461 'Climax" No. 14, enambled, round cornered "*linen cards*," double indexed, beautifully designed backs in tints and colors. Weight packed, 4 ounces. Per pack.. .30
Per dozen packs.. 3.35
Per dozen gross packs.. 38.50
16465 "Barcelona" No. 49, "Spanish Monte Cards;" 48 cards in pack; assortment of backs and colors. Weight, packed, 3 ounces.
Per pack.. .30
Per dozen packs.. 3.35
Per gross packs.. 38.50
16470 "Tournament Whist" No. 63, size, 2¼x3½ inches, highly enameled; handsome backs; made expressly for "Whist" "Bezique," "Solitaire," "Pinochle," and all full-handed games. Weight, packed, 4 ounces. Per pack.......... .30
Per dozen packs.. 3.35
Per gross packs.. 38.50
16490 "Oriental" No. 91 X, dark tinted backs, beautifully designed and printed in gold, with gold edges. A dainty and exquisite card for use in social gatherings. Weight, packed, 4 ounces. Per pack.. .35
Per dozen packs.. 4.00
16496 "Indicators" No. 50, made of best linen stock; assortment of handsomely designed backs in tints and colors. *The best playing cards made.* Recommended for club use. Weight, packed, 4 ounces. Per pack.. .55
Per dozen packs.. 6.00

LAST year we sold more goods than ever before, which shows that people know where to save when they have to.

Why not save all you can all the time.

STAMPED AND FANCY GOODS DEPARTMENT.

Stamped Linen Squares.

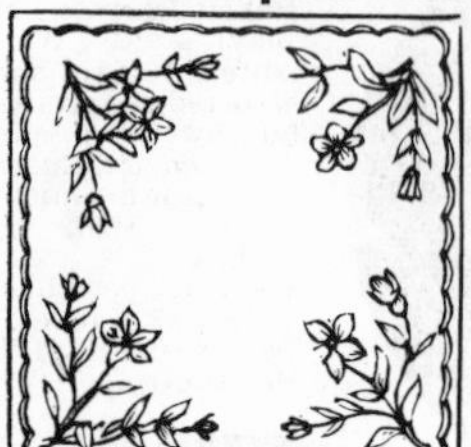

16500 Raw Edge Linen, stamped with floral centers to be worked with filo silk; scalloped edges square and round to be buttonholed with wash embroidery silk.
Size....5 in., 7, 9, 12.
Each.$0.03, .04, .06, .09.
Size..15 in., 18, 20, 24.
Each.$0.12, .18, .30, .35.

Honiton Laces.

			Per yard.	Per Doz.
16505	Honiton Lace.	(437)	$0.13	$1.45
16507	Honiton Lace.	(792)	.11	1.20
16509	Honiton Lace.	(790)	.08	.85
16511	Honiton Lace.	(463)	.13	1.45
16513	Honiton Lace.	(410)	.11	1.20
16515	Honiton Lace.	(417)	.11	1.20
16517	Honiton Lace.	(320)	.08	.85

Through an error the illustrations of Honiton Laces were left out. See page 134 for illustrations.

Honiton Designs.

16519 Fine Quality Linen Squares, stamped in artistic Honiton designs. Honiton lace to be basted on the design, then embroidered with wash embroidery silk, the upper row in the long and short button-hole stitch, the outer edge in the scallop as designed. When complete, cut out the linen underneath the medallion; these patterns are suitable for above laces, and produce a very effective piece of embroidery.

Size, inches.	5	7	9	12	15	18	21	24
Each	5c.	7c	9c.	12c.	20c.	28c.	50c.	75c.

Photo Frames.

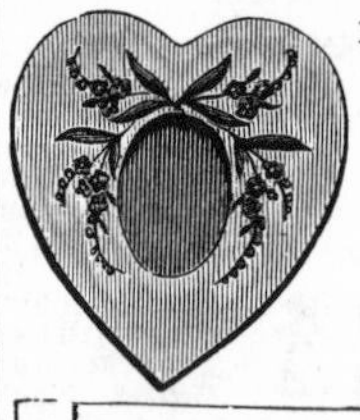

16521 One of the latest novelties in embroidery; cardboard mountings, to be covered with the linen which is stamped ready for embroidery. After the linen is embroidered, cut it out along the dotted lines, span it over the front piece and glue, then fasten the back to the front with the little screws sent with frame; comes in three shapes; heart, octagon and oblong; size, 9x11 inches.
Each.......... $0.38

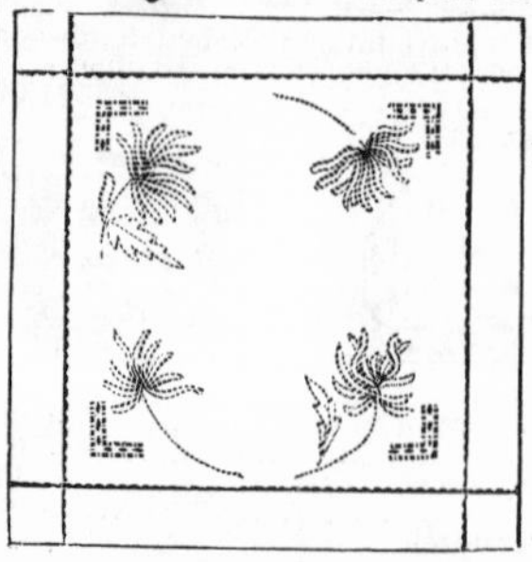

16523 Hemstitched Linen Squares, fine quality with openwork corners; stamped with choicest designs for outlining and Kensington embroidery.
Sizes.12 in. 18 in.
Each. 25c. 40c.
Sizes.24 in. 30 in.
Each. 60c. 75c.

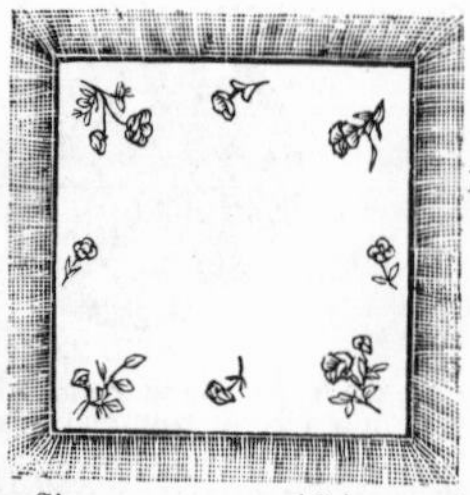

16525 White Cotton Duck Squares, stamped in new designs; 1½ inch fringe headed with colored cross stitching.

Size	12 in.	18 in.	24 in.	30 in.
Each	10c.	18c.	25c.	40c.

16527 Tray Cloth, same style as 16525; 18x27 inches.
Each.. $0.20

Table Covers.

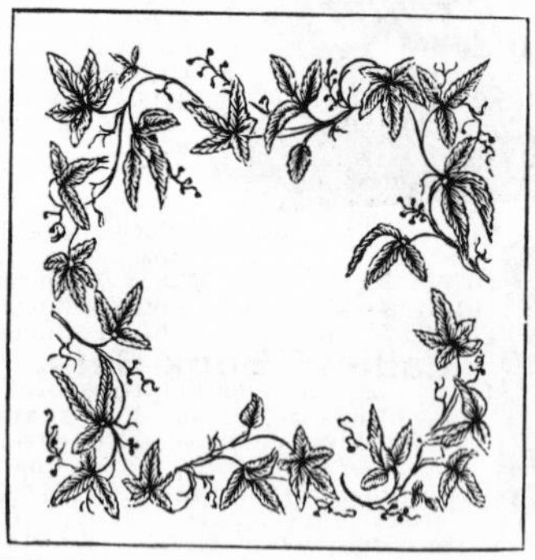

16535 White Cotton Drill Table Covers, one yard square, stamped in colors, to be outlined or embroidered with different colors of linen embroidery thread. (See 16547.)
Each... $0.25

16537 Table Cover, white bedford cord, tinted as above, 36 inches Each.. .45
16539 Table Cover, tinted denim, one yard square, stamped in scroll and floral designs to be worked in linen embroidery thread; the plain scroll lines outlined with Japanese gold thread, which is sewed on like a braid. Colors: Light blue, yellow, medium green and red.
Each.. .50

Sofa Cushion Covers.

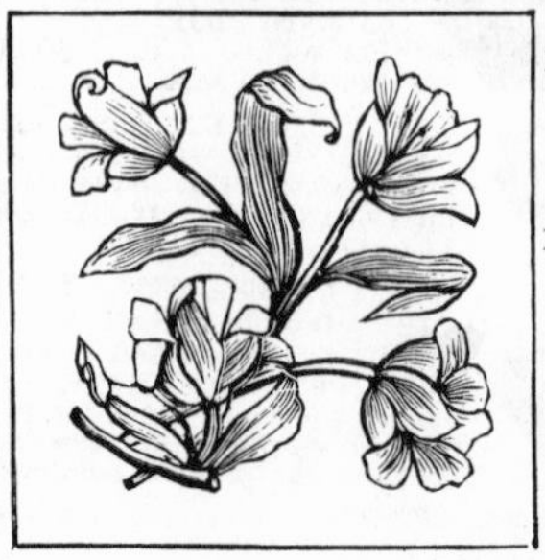

16541 Cushion Cover white cotton drill, tinted in floral and scroll designs; 24x24 inches.
Each.......... $0.20
16543 Cushion Cover, tinted denim, 24x24 inches; floral and scroll designs to be worked like above denim covers. Colors: Light blue, yellow, green and red. Each.... $0.35

Doylies.

16545 White Cotton Drill Doylies, stamped in colors, to be worked as above. Size, 9x9 inches. Each$0.06
12x12 inches. Each.................... .12

Embroidery Thread.

16547 Linen Embroidery Thread, in colors for working above covers, etc. Per skein..........$0.03
Per dozen skeins........................... .30
When this thread is ordered for working above articles, we select suitable shades to match colors of stamping. It takes from twelve o fifteen skeins for working table cover and six to ten for cushion covers.

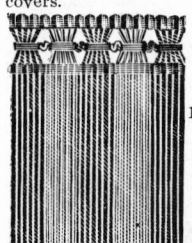

Linen Fringe.

16551 Linen Fringe for finishing edge of table covers. Comes in plain white also in white with green, white with yellow and white with brown.
Per yard...................$0.08

Stamped Tray Cloths.
Assorted Designs.

16553 Stamped Tray Cloths, white cotton duck, 18x27 in. Each......$0.10
16555 Stamped and Fringed Tray Cloths, all linen, 19x25 in. Each......$0.18
16557 Stamped and Fringed Tray Cloths, all linen momie, 19x27 inches. Each......$0.30
16559 Stamped Tray Cloths, white linen, fine quality, 19x27 in. Each...$0.35
16561 Stamped and Fringed Tray Cloths, all linen momie, 19x29 inches. Each.............$0.40
16563 Stamped and Fringed Tray Cloths, open work, all linen momie, 20x30 inches. Each.... .45
16565 Hemstitched Tray Cloths, fine quality linen with drawnwork edges and corners, stamped in assorted new designs. See cut 16502 for illustration, 18x27 inches. Each .... .55

Stamped Splashers.

16575 Stamped Splashers, white cotton duck; size, 18x28 inches. Each.......................$0.10
16577 Stamped Splashers, plain linen, fringed; size, 19x32 inches. Each....................... .18
16579 Stamped Splashers, plain linen, with row of openwork; fringed; size, 19x32 inches. Each... .25
16581 Stamped Splashers, all linen momie, scalloped with knotted fringe; size, 19x32 inches. Each... .32
16583 Stamped Splashers, all linen momie, openwork in center and corners; fringed; size, 17x31 inches. Each............................. .38
16585 Stamped Splashers, all linen momie, openwork all around; fringed; size, 19x32 inches. Each... .40

WALL PAPER

Is remarkably cheap. You should keep your rooms well papered; it is so bright and cheerful.

Stamped Fringed Linen Scarfs.

16590 Stamped and Fringed Scarfs, plain linen.
Size.	Each.
16x54 in.	$0.25
16x72 in.	.35

16592 Stamped and Fringed Scarfs, plain linen, with row of open work on both ends.
Size.	Each.
16x54 in.	$0.32
16x72 in.	.40

16594 Stamped Linen Momie Scarfs, scalloped ends with knot.ed fringe.
Size.	Each.
16x54 in.	$0.35
16x72 in.	.45

16596 Stamped Linen Momie Scarfs, openwork center and sides, knotted fringe.
Size, 16x54 inches. Each... ....$0.45
Size, 16x72 inches. Each..................... .58

Stamping Outfits.

We have the perforated stamping patterns in the latest designs, also liquids for stamping. We design monograms and special patterns to order. We have (3) three stamping outfits, the finest in the market. See quotations following.
In each of these outfits can be found designs suitable for any kind of embroidery. There are no two patterns alike in these three outfits.
16629 Stamping Outfit No. 4 contains 22 patterns and one complete alphabet, with box of powder. Each..................................$0.45
Postage....................................... .12
16633 Stamping Outfit No. 1 contains 75 patterns and one complete alphabet and one box of powder. Each................................ .85
Postage....................................... .15
16643 Stamping Outfit No. 2 contains 40 patterns and one complete alphabet but larger designs and letters than No. 16633, and one box of powder. Each................................ .85
Postage....................................... .15
16658 Liquid for stamping black.
2 ounce bottle, each........................... .12
5 ounce bottle, each........................... .25
Cannot go by mail.
16661 Stamping Powder, white and blue.
Per box....................................... .12

Stamping Patterns.

16668 We furnish special patterns to order, but as the variety is great we cannot describe them. Prices range from 5 to 75 cents each. Give a full and clear description of your wants and we will send you good value for your money, and allow three to five days to complete them
In ordering, give style of pattern, STYLE you prefer, and PURPOSE of its use.

Tissue Paper Flower Outfits.

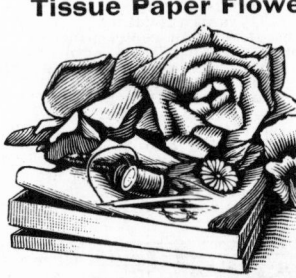

16673 Our 25c. package in patent envelope, containing 12 half sheets assorted tissues, wire tubing for stems and leaves, culots, sprays and instruction book. Each..... $0.25
Postage... .08

16673—76
16676 Our Beginners' Outfit contains 12 sheets assorted fine tissue paper, 2 dozen wires for stems, 1 dozen each cut spray, culots, daisy petals, ½ dozen daisy centers, 1 piece tubing for stems, ½ dozen leaves, circular showing designs and explanations for making doll dresses, etc., and book of instruction. Each............$0.35
Postage. .... .11
16685 Our Complete Outfit of tissue paper for making paper flowers, decorative articles, tissue paper dolls, etc., contains 36 sheets (15x20) assorted fine tissue, 1 piece tubing each, small, large and moss rose, 1 dozen each culots, sprays and natural moss, 1 spool hair and cotton covered wire, 1 dozen wire stems, 1 dozen leaves, ½ dozen each poppy centers, poppy buds, rose centers, daisy centers, 1 dozen daisy petals, 1 pair pincers, 4 dolls' heads, 4 pairs legs, 4 body forms, 4 dress forms and circular showing designs and giving explanations for making dresses, and book of instruction. Each........ 1.00
Postage....................................... .20

Imported Tissue Paper.

For making paper flowers, fancy articles, and producing pretty effects in decorating.

16691—	Per sheet.	Per quire.
White............................	$0.01	$0.15
Light Greens......................	.01	.20
Medium Greens...................	.02	.25
Olive and Leaf Greens............	.02	.25
Light Pinks.......................	.01	.20
Medium Pinks....................	.02	.25
Bright Pinks.....................	.03	.40
Bright Rose......................	.05	.80
Bright and Deep Reds............	.05	.80
Light Yellows....................	.01	.20
Medium Yellow..................	.02	.25
Medium Orange..................	.02	.25
Deep Orange.....................	.03	.40
Light Blues......................	.01	.20
Medium and Dark Blues..........	.02	.25
Light and Medium Lilac..........	.02	.25
Purples..........................	.03	.35
Browns..........................	.02	.30
Black............................	.02	.30

16695 Crepe Tissue Paper, suited to the following and many other uses: For making lamp and candle shades, screens, fans, tablecloths, napkins, flower pot covers, fancy decorations for special occasions where striking effects are desired. Rolls 20 inches wide and about 10 feet in length, in the following colors: Virgin white, light and dark amber, pale and dark coral, apple, grass, peacock, sea, nile and moss greens, canary, gold, terra cotta, heliotrope, ruby, orange, light and dark pink, jet black, violet, purple, apricot, light and nut brown, light, royal and dark blue, yellow, green. Weight, packed, 9 ounces.
Per roll........ ....$0.28

Fine Pillow Shams.

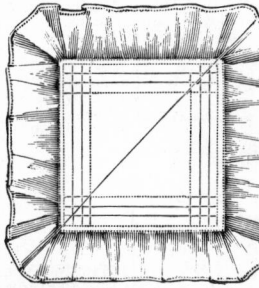

16699 Fine Lawn Pillow Shams, 3 tucks and deep ruffle. Per pair..$1.00

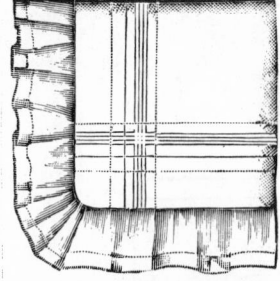

16701 Fine Lawn Pillow Shams, with 3 narrow and 2 wide tucks, wide hem and deep ruffle.
Per pair........$1.25

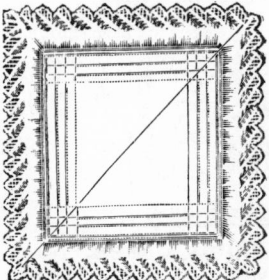

16703 Fine Lawn Pillow Shams, with 3 tucks and Suisse embroidery ruffle.
Per pair...... $1.68

16705 Fine Mull Pillow Shams, with wide hem and ruffle of Suisse embroidery.
Per pair...... $1.88

Stamped Muslin Pillow Shams.

Per pair. Per doz. pair.

16707 Stamped Muslin Pillow Sham, not hemmed. Assorted patterns, 28x25 ....$0.20 $2.00

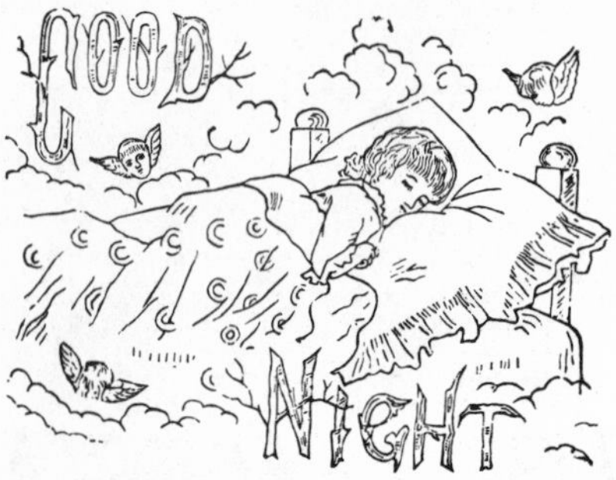

16710 Hemstitched Stamped Muslin Pillow Shams, assorted patterns. Per pair...$0.35 and .50

Embroidered Pillow Shams.

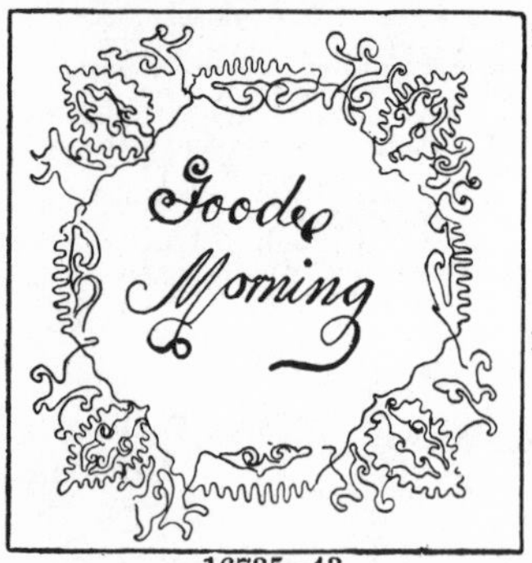

16735—43

16735 White Muslin Pillow Shams, 30x30. Embroidered in fast dyered, with Good Night on one and Good Morning on the other. Per pair, $0.38

16743 White Muslin Pillow Shams, 30x30. Embroidered in white, with Good Night on one and Good Morning on the other. Per pair, $0.35

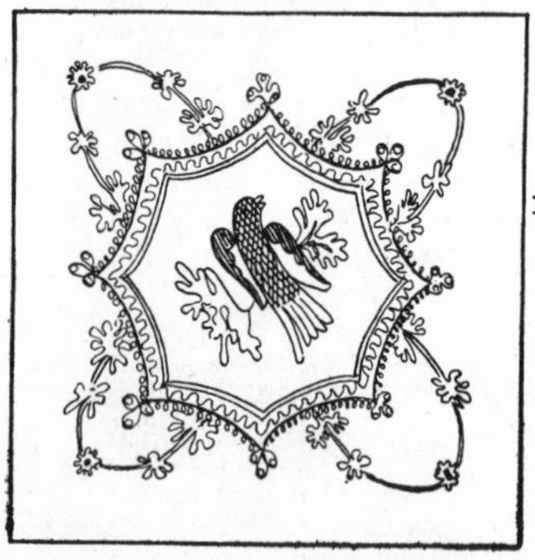

16748 White Muslin Pillow Shams, 30x30. Embroidered in fast dye red. Per pair, $0.43

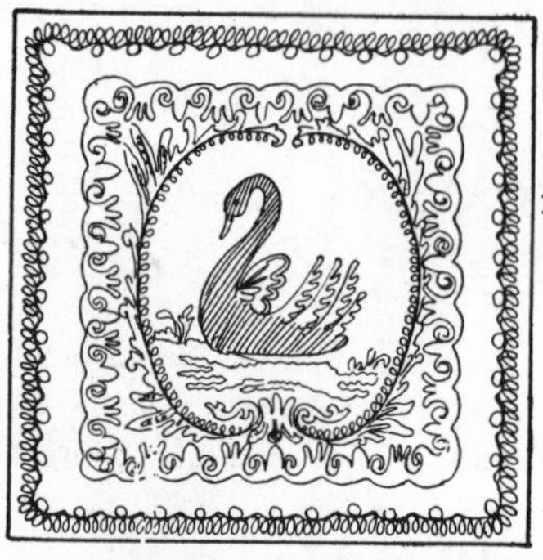

16752 White Muslin Pillow Shams, 30x30. Embroidered in fast dye red. Per pair, $0.60

Muslin Pillow Cases.

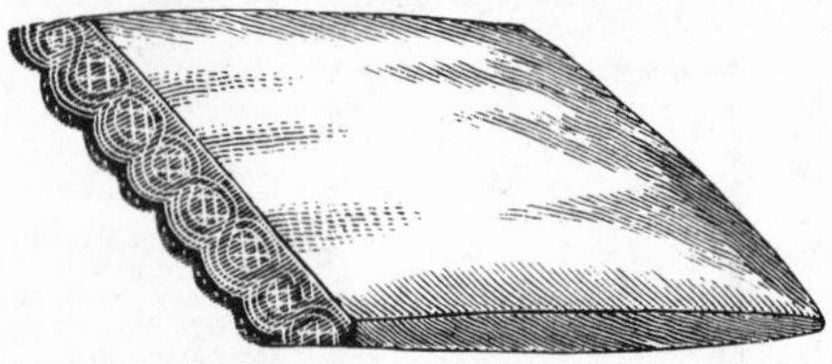

16763 Bleached, Hemmed Pillow Cases, with American lace. Size, 22x35. Per pair..........$0.40
Per dozen pairs.................................... 4.35

Plain Muslin Pillow Cases.

16768 Bleached, Hemmed Pillow Cases, same as above, 16763, without lace. Per pair...$0.30
Per dozen pairs.................................... 3.40

Pepperell Bleached Bed Sheets.

16774 Bed Sheets, 2½ yards long by 2 yards wide, made from good bleached sheeting, hemmed. Each $0.50
Per one dozen sheets............................ 5.75

16788 Bleached Muslin Sheets, 2½ yards long by 2¼ yards wide. Each............................ .60
Per one dozen sheets............................ 6.75

Ottoman Burlap Patterns.

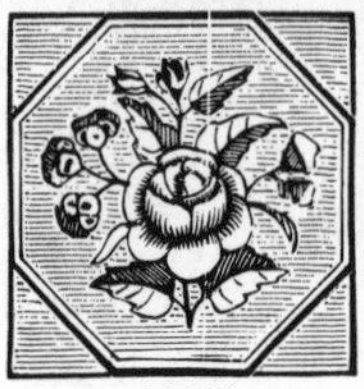

16808

16795 Ottoman, Dog's head in center, handsome border, size, 20x20 inches. Each............ .....$0.12

16801 Ottoman, Cat's Head in center, octagon border in two colors. Size 20x20 inches. Each.....................$0.12

16805 Ottoman, Branch of Roses in center, oval border. Size, 14x20 inches. Each.....................$0.10

16808 Ottoman, Floral Center of Roses, Pansies, and Bell Flowers, octagon border. Size 20x20 inches. See cut. Each.........................$0._2

Burlap Rug Patterns.

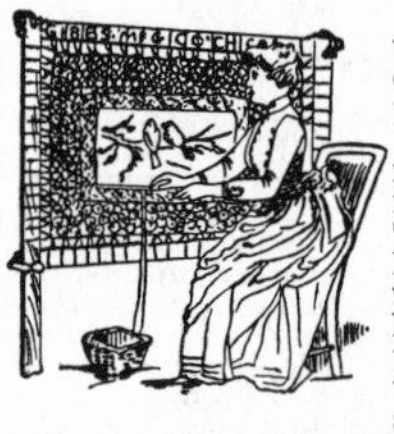

Turkish and Assorted Patterns. We show two patterns only, but quote 15 patterns, as per quotations below.

The above cut represents the manner of placing our patterns in the frames for working. Take 4 slats similar to bed slats. Place them as shown in cut; then fasten corners together, leaving the inside large enough to hold the pattern and about two inches between pattern and frame, so as to stretch the pattern. Then, after hemming the pattern, sew it into frame as shown in the cut, stretching tightly and square. Then proceed to work the pattern by following the lines with the various colors designated.

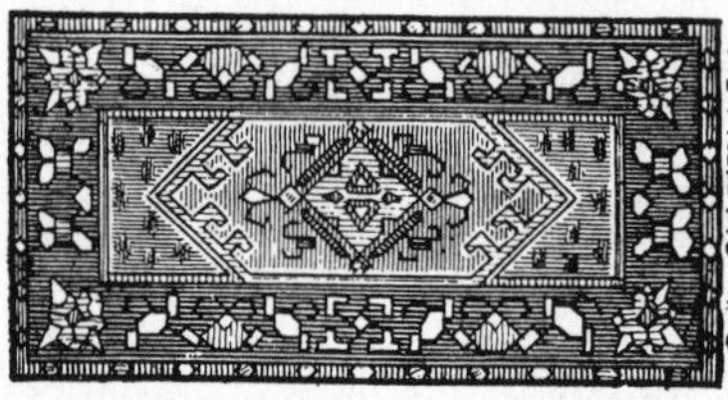

16815 Turkish Design. Size, 16 in. by 1 yard; price, 23 cents. Similar to cut (136).

16820 Bouquet of Roses in center, surrounded by scroll in old gold and brown; geometric border, with roses in corners. Size, ½x1 yd. (40). Price.................................... $0 23

16823 Spaniel Dog lying on center panel; spray of roses at each end, scroll border. This pattern is an unusual favorite. Size, ½x1 yard (19). Price .23

16825 Lilies, Rosebuds and Pansies in center surrounded by scroll of old gold and brown combined with Mosaic border. Size, ⅝x1⅛ yards (43). Price.............................. .27

16827 Oval Panel, with fine Stag's Head in center, Grecian border. Size, ⅝x1⅛ yards (80). Price .28

16831 Life Size Cat lying on a carpet; unique rustic border in three colors, an easy and popular pattern. Size, ⅝x1⅛ yards (24). Price....... .28

16838 Large cluster of roses in center panel; combination border, with handsome scrolls. Size, ¾x1¼ yards (96). Price................ .35

16840 Spaniel Dog lying on Mosaic carpet, surrounded with a unique oval, with twined ash leaves, scroll in corners of plain border. Size, ¾x1¼ yards (36). Price.................. .35

16841 Turkish Design, similar to 16815. Size, ¾x1¼ yards (150). Price........................ .37

16843 Stag by the Lake; heavy rich border of scroll work; beautiful landscape in center. Size, ¾x1½ yards (22). Price.............................. .42

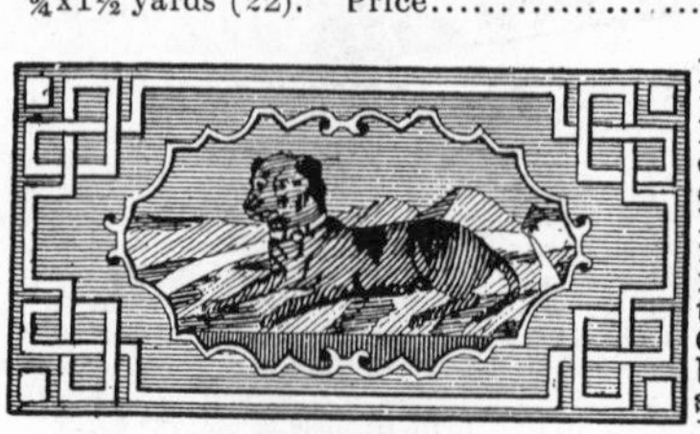

16844

16844—Large, intelligent-looking dog lying on a lawn, lake and mountain in the distance. Grecian border. Size ¾ x 1½ yards (91.)
Price $0.42

16849 Cat and Three Playful Kittens, with handsome scroll border. Size ¾x1½ yards (39). Price .42

16855 Bouquet of Morning Glories, Lilies, etc., in center; Grecian border. Size ¾x1½ yards (90). Price................................. .42

16868 Large Lion lying in the foreground with another in distance. Landscape with luxurious tropical plants. Size ⅞x1¾ yards (7). Price... .50

16877 Turkish Design. Size ⅞x1¾ yards (170). Price.. .60

Material Used in Working the Patterns.

Every household has its supply of odds and ends, rags and ravelings, which can be woven into articles of beauty and utility. Rags worked into the proper patterns with the improved rag machine produce very rich and handsome rugs and ottomans, having a tapestry effect which gives no suggestion of the cheapness of the material.

Some prefer to work colored yarn with their rags, others use fancy yarns altogether. In the latter case it may be estimated that it will require from one-quarter to one-half pound of yarn to every square foot of canvas worked, according as you want the article, light or heavier. One-half pound of good yarn to the square foot will make a rug nearly three-quarters of an inch thick

Colored Rug Yarn.

Order No. 16881.

Yarn especially manufactured for this purpose and kept in stock by us can be supplied in any quantity.

The average amount of yarn required to fill our patterns is shown in the following list; but for the weight of each separate color we refer you to our yarn list which we will send when asked for.

	Pounds.
No. 136	1⅝
" 19, 40	2
" 24, 43, 80	2¾
" 36, 96, 150	3½
" 39, 90, 91	4½
" 22	4¾
" 7, 170	5½
Ottomans, 6, 7, 8	⅞
Ottomans, 2	¾

The above ingrain carpet yarn, assorted colors, 4 skeins to pound. Per skein.......................$0.20
Per pound.. .75

The Gem Tufting and Embroidery Machine.

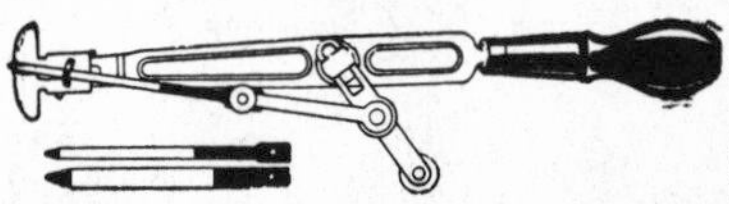

16888 Has four needles. Will work rags, yarn, zephyr and silk. A machine for $1.40 that makes Turkish Rugs, Ottomans, Curtains, Stair Carpets, Hoods, Mittens, Slippers, Quilts, Piano Spreads or Table Covers, which have all the gorgeous appearance of the genuine Turkish or Persian design. So simple that a ten year old child can operate it. With this machine you can beautify your homes and teach your children to be industrious. Special instructions with each machine. Postage 7 cents. Each..$1.40

Canvas.

16890 Java Canvas, white, 18 in. Per yard.....$0.20
16892 Penelope Canvas, 27 in. Per yard..... .. .25

Ladies' Gingham Aprons.

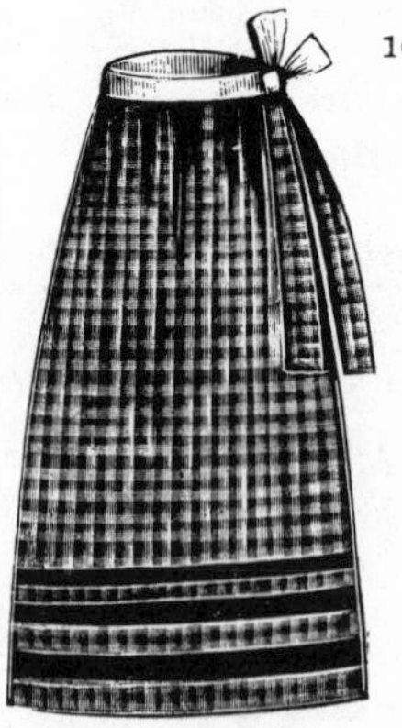

16895 Ladies' Good Gingham Aprons, assorted checks, in brown, green and blue, 38 inches long, 45 inches wide. See cut. Each.........$0.25
Per dozen.............. 2.75

Ladies' White Aprons.

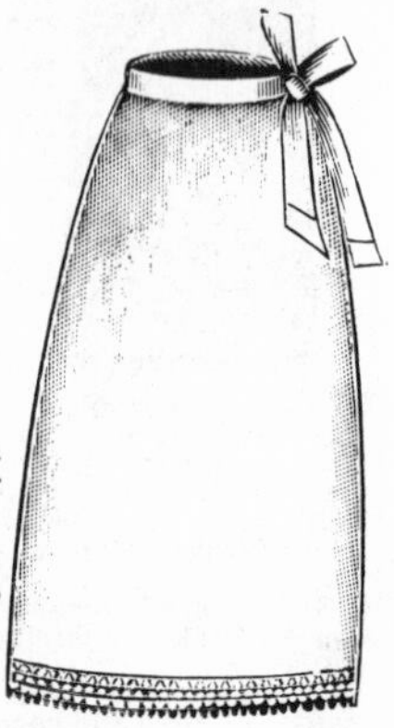

16900 Ladies' White Muslin Aprons, good quality, trimmed with lace and strings. See cut (1625).
Each.............. ..$0.15
Per dozen.............. 1.65

Aluminum Cooking Utensils

Are Fast Displacing Tin and Iron – so Light and Clean.

Aprons—Continued.

16903 Ladies' White Muslin Aprons, with four inch hem, three 1½-inch tucks and strings. See cut.
Each $0.25
Per dozen........... 2.70

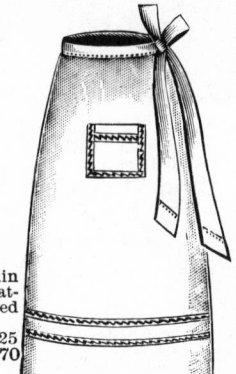

16906 Ladies' White Muslin Aprons, with pocket; neatly trimmed with colored finishing braid. See cut.
Each................$0.25
Per dozen........... 2.70

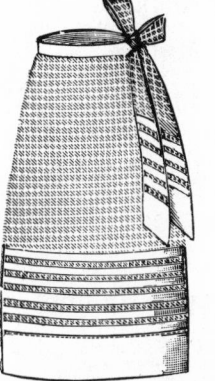

16909   16912

16909 Ladies' Check Nainsook Aprons, with satin finish muslin stripes, 2½ inch wide hem and strings. See cut.
Each............$0.30 Per dozen $3.25
16912 Ladies' White Muslin Aprons, with one wide tuck, three small ones, 2½ inch hem and strings. See cut.
Each..............$0.30 Per dozen............ 3.25

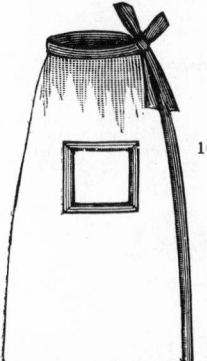

16916 Ladies' White Muslin Aprons, with two pockets and strings, neatly trimmed with band of colored chambray. See cut.
Each....................$0.35
Per dozen..... ....3.90

16920 Ladies' White Muslin Aprons, good quality, wide strings, 5¼ inch wide hem, 3¼ inch band of Suisse inserting with fancy edge. See cut (1714)
Each..... ....$0.40
Per dozen............... 4.50

Aprons—Continued.

16922 Ladies' White Muslin Aprons, fine quality, with 6-inch deep hem headed with band of Suisse insertion and four tucks, strings; (4662) see cut. Each.$0.50

16922

Stamped Aprons.

Our stamping is permanent, is done with liquid, and will not mar or rub off.

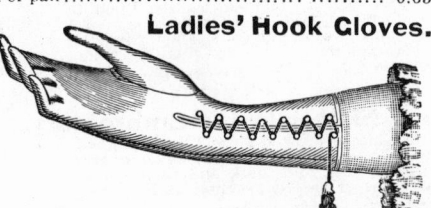

16930

16930 White Muslin Apron, hemmed and stamped in assorted designs.
Each...............................$0.22
Per dozen 2.35

GLOVE DEPARTMENT.

We do not warrant kid gloves. Carelessness in fitting will ruin any glove. To insure satisfaction the glove must be put on with great care the first time, remembering that the more you pull the tighter the glove will become. Put the fingers in first, smooth by rubbing from the tips of the fingers (never push between the fingers), then rub the thumb on and push the glove up. Never take hold of the top of the glove. By observing the above, gloves will fit better and wear longer.

N. B.—In ordering gloves, especially kid, be sure always to give color and size wanted. To determine your size measure closely around the hand across the knuckles. If sizes of kid gloves are sent as ordered and have been tried on, *they will not be exchanged.*

Ladies' Button Gloves.

7019 Norma Ladies' Kid Gloves, with 4 large pearl buttons. Colors: Brown, tan, mode, slate, red, navy blue, white and black. Sizes, 5½ to 8.
Per pair $1.00

17021 La Reine Kid Gloves, with 4 large pearl buttons, which match color of glove and embroidery Colors: Brown, tan, mode, slate, red, navy blue, white and black. Sizes, 5½ to 7½. Per pair.. $1.25
17023 Franconia, real French kid gloves, with four large pearl buttons and embroidery to match color of glove. Colors: Black, brown, tan, mode, slate, red and navy blue. Sizes, 5½ to 7½. Per pair.... 1.50
17026 Lothair, Ladies 4-button Kid Gloves, white only. Sizes, 5¾ to 8. Per pair.................. 1.00
17028 LaTosca, Ladies' 4-button Kid Gloves, quoted only until sold in the following sizes and colors: Tan color, sizes, 7½, 7¾ and 8. Brown, sizes, 7¾ and 8, Grey, 7½, 7¾ and 8. Per pair................................... 0.65

Ladies' Hook Gloves.

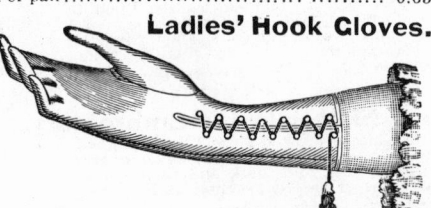

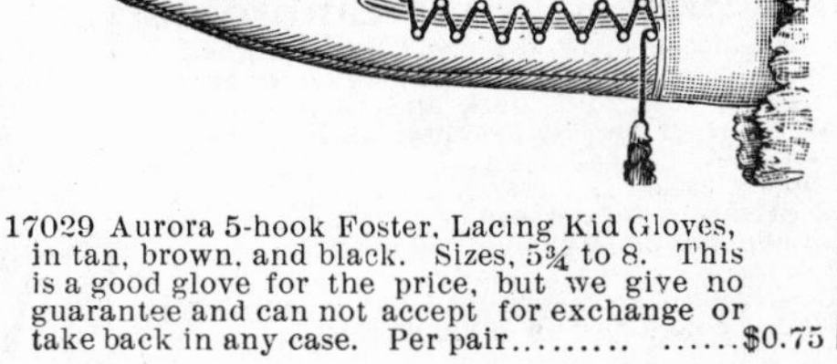

17029 Aurora 5-hook Foster, Lacing Kid Gloves, in tan, brown, and black. Sizes, 5¾ to 8. This is a good glove for the price, but we give no guarantee and can not accept for exchange or take back in any case. Per pair........ ......$0.75

Gloves—Continued.

17030 Duchess Kid Gloves, 5-hook, Foster lacing, with embroidery to match color of glove. Colors: Black, brown, tan, mode and slate. The best $1.00 glove in the market. Our price .... .95
17034 Duchess Kid Gloves, 7-hook Foster lacing; embroidery to match color of glove. Colors: Black, brown, tan, mode and slate. Per pair 1.10
17036 Lothair Kid Gloves, 5-hook, Foster lacing. Colors: Brown, tan, mode, slate, red, navy blue, white and black. Sizes, 5¾ to 8 Per pair 1.10
17038 La Reine Kid Gloves, 5-hook, Foster lacing; embroidery to match color of glove. Colors: Black, brown, tan, mode, slate, blue, red and green. Per pair................................. 1.35

Ladies' Undressed Kid Gloves.

17052 Ariadne Kid Gloves, 5-hook, Foster lacing Suede, embroidery to match color of glove. Colors: Black, brown, tan, mode and slate. Per pair.......................................$1.10
17056 Richmond Kid Gloves; 5-hook, Foster lacing, Suede; embroidery to match color of glove. Colors: Black, brown, tan and slate. Per pair.. 1.25

Undressed Mousquetaire Kid Gloves.

17070 Ariadne 8-button Length Suede Mousquetaire, with 3 buttons at wrist, and embroidery to match glove. Colors: Black, brown, tan, mode, slate, white, cardinal, pink, lemon, navy blue and dark green. Sizes, 5½ to 7½. Per pair..... ....$1.35

17072 Seville, 12-button length Suede Mousquetaire. Colors: Black, tan, mode, cardinal, pink, lemon, light blue, lilac and white. Sizes, 5½ to 6¾. Per pair................................$2.60
17076 Seville, 16-button length Suede Mousquetaires. Colors: Black, white, lemon, cardinal, light blue and pink. Sizes, 5½ to 6¾. Per pair.. 3.10
17078 Seville, 20-button length Suede Mousquetaire. Colors: Black, tan, lilac, white, lemon, cardinal, light blue and pink. Sizes, 5½ to 6¾. Per pair.................................... 3.60
17080 Bellaire, 12-button length Suede Mousquetaire; white only. Sizes, 5½ to 6¾. Per pair 1.75
17082 Bellaire, 16-button length Suede Mousquetaire; white only. Sizes, 5½ to 6¾. Per pair 2.25

Biarritz Gloves.

17095-99

17095 Biarritz, 6-button length closed wrist Mousquetaire, partly white stitching and partly embroidery to match color of glove. Colors: Black, brown, tan, slate, red, navy blue, white and pearl; sizes, 5¾ to 7½. Per pair...........$0.95
17099 Chamois, 6-button length Mousquetaire. Colors: White and yellow; sizes, 5½ to 7½. Per pair.... ... ... .87

Ladies' Gauntlet Gloves.

17104 Ladies' Gauntlet Undressed Mocha; good weight, nice for driving. Colors: Tan, brown and black. Per pair..$1.10
17108 Ladies' Gauntlet Dressed Kid Gloves, one button. See cut. Colors: Brown, tan and reddish tans; sizes 6 to 7¾. Per pair.....ι.......$1.25
17110 Ladies' Mocha gauntlet, 2 button gloves. Black only; sizes, 5¾ to 8. Per pair..... ......$1.50

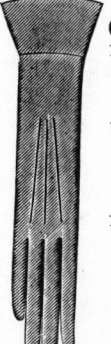

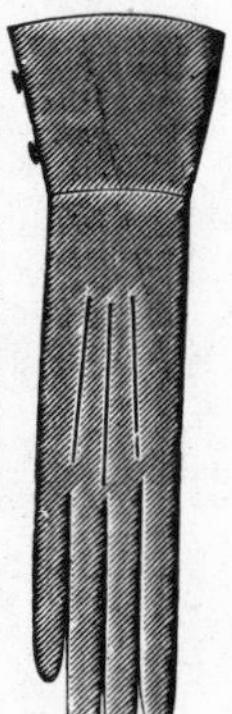

Men's Kid Gloves.

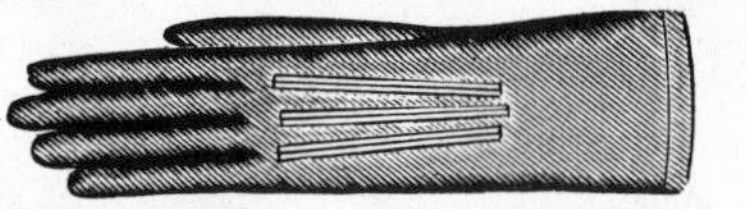

17108   17110

17148 Men's Kid Gloves, stitched backs. Colors: Tan, brown, red and white; sizes, 7¼ to 10. Per pair....... ....$1.00
17151 Men's Fine Dress Kid Gloves, Pique back. Colors: Tan, brown, red and white; sizes, 7½ to 10 Per pair............................... 1.35

Ladies' Jersey Gloves.

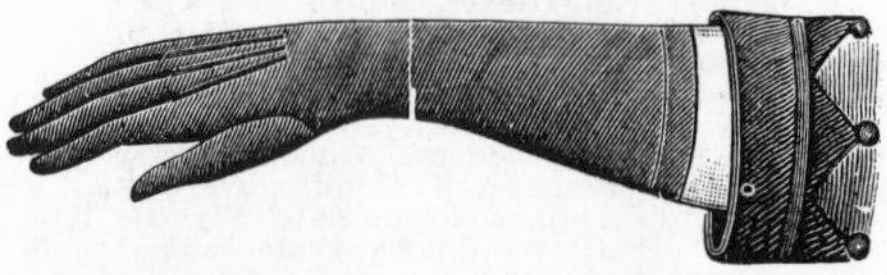

Per pair. Per doz.
17155 Ladies' Fast Black Gloves, pointed backs, length 12 inches....... ...$0.15 $1.65
17157 Ladies' Jersey Gloves, silk embroidered backs. Colors: Slates, tans, browns............ .15 1.65

Ladies' Taffeta Gloves.

Per pair. Per doz
17161 Ladies' Fast Black Taffeta Silk Gloves..........$0.25 $2.70
17163 Ladies' Fast Black Taffeta Silk Gloves, kid point. Per pair............ .30 3.25
17165 Ladies' Fast Black Taffeta Silk Gloves, kid point.......... .43 4.50
17168 Ladies' Fast Black Taffeta Silk Gloves, fine quality.......... .50 5.40

Ladies' Gauntlet Gloves.

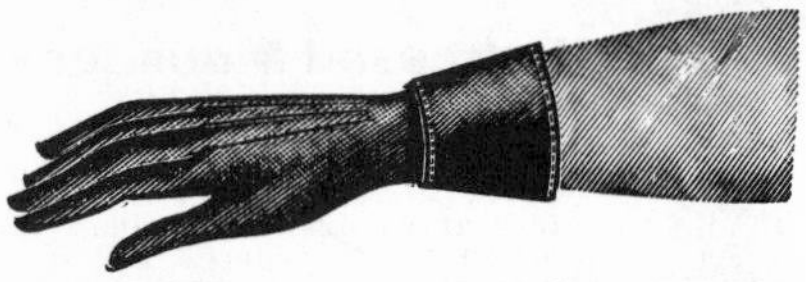

Per pair. Per doz
17174 Ladies' Gauntlet Gloves, Berlin lisle, tan shades..........$0.25 $2.70

Ladies' Pure Silk Gloves.

Per pair. Per doz.
17185 Ladies' Pure Silk Black Gloves, fine silk pointed backs..........$0.50 $5.40
17186 Ladies' Pure Silk Cream Color Gloves, silk pointed backs.......... .50

Kayser Patent Finger Tipped Gloves, have a guarantee ticket in each pair, that entitles the customer to a new pair *Free*, if the tips wear out before the gloves.

17188 Kayser Pure Silk Gloves; these are 3-ply at finger ends and are guaranteed not to wear out at finger ends first; sizes 6½ to 8½. Black only. Per pair..........$0.65
17189 Kayser Pure Silk Gloves. These are 3 ply at finger ends, and are guaranteed not to wear out at finger ends first. Sizes, 6 to 8½. Per pair.......... .85

Misses' Gloves.

Per pair, Per doz.
17200 Misses' Fast Black Berlin Gloves.......... $0.12 $1.35
17202 Misses' Berlin Gloves, in tan, brown and gray.... .12 1.35

Ladies' and Misses' Silk Mitts.

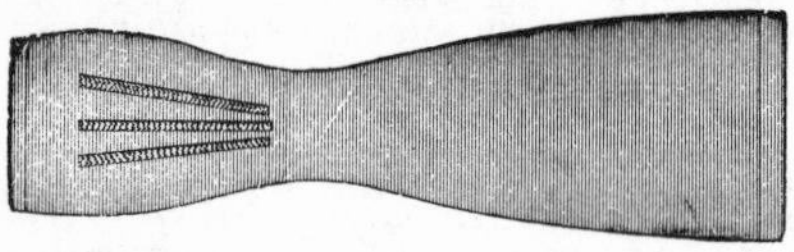

Per pair. Per doz.
17204 Misses' Black Silk Jersey Mitts, pointed backs.......... $0.20 $2.15
17208 Misses' Black Silk Jersey Mitts, pointed backs.......... .25 2.70
17210 Misses' Silk Mitts, in cream, tan, brown, cardinal, pink and light blue.......... .25
17211 Ladies' Black Silk Jersey Mitts, silk pointed backs 20 2.10
17217 Ladies' Black Silk Jersey Mitts, silk pointed backs.......... .25 2.70
17223 Ladies' Colored Silk Mitts, in cream, pink, sky blue, cardinal, navy blue, dark brown, tan and gray.......... .25 2.70
17226 Ladies' Black Silk Jersey Mitts, fine, with silk pointed backs and inserted thumb.......... 35 3.60
17228 Ladies' Black Silk Mitts, fine silk pointed backs, glove thumb .40
17230 Ladies' Cream Color Silk Mitts, same as above No. 17228.... .40
17232 Ladies' Black Silk Mitts, extra quality, silk pointed backs, glove thumb.......... .50
17234 Ladies' Cream Color Silk Mitts, same as above No. 17232.... .50
17236 Ladies' Extra Quality Black Silk Mitts, fine silk pointed backs and glove thumb.......... .60
17238 Special Extra Quality Black Silk Mitts, silk pointed backs and glove thumb.......... .68
17242 Ladies' Silk Mitts for evening or party wear; length 18 inches. Colors: Cream, blue and pink...... .65

Ladies' Extra Size Silk Mitts.

Per pair. Per doz.
17243 Ladies Black Silk Jersey Mitts, silk pointed backs, large size $0.25 $2.70
17250 Ladies' Black Silk Jersey Mitts, silk pointed backs, extra size 35 3.75
17254 Ladies' Black Silk Jersey Mitts, pointed backs, extra quality and size.......... .50 5.40

Men's Gloves.

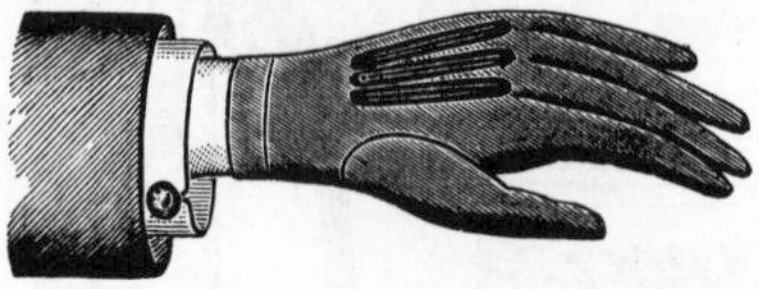

Per pair. Per doz.
17259 Men's White Berlin Gloves, plain Jersey.......... $0.15 $1.65
17263 Men's Fine Silk Taffeta Gloves, in brown, tan and slate colors.......... .50

Ornaments for Fancy Work.

Silk and chenille or plush tufts in fancy colors for fancy work. Cuts are from ⅛ to ¾ size of goods. No blacks except in No. 17351 tufts.

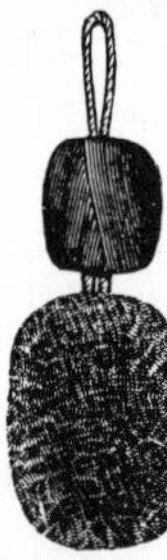

17353

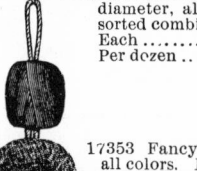

17351 Silk Ball Tufts, ⅝ inch in diameter, all colors and assorted combinations. Each..........$0.01 Per dozen.......... .10

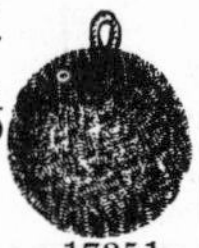

17351

17353 Fancy Silk Pompons, 2¼ inch long, all colors. Each..........$0.04 Per dozen.......... .43

17359 Tassel for fancy work in the new shades; length, 4 inches. Each..........$0.04 Per dozen.......... .40

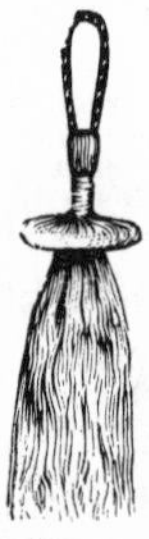

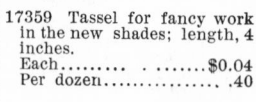

17359

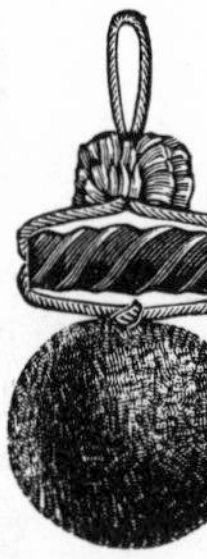

17363

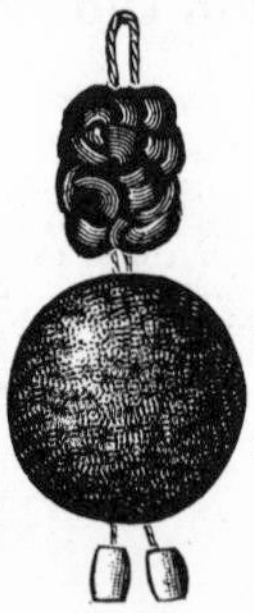

17367

17363 Fancy Silk Pompons, 2 inches long. Each..........$0.04 Per dozen.......... .43
17367 Fancy Silk Pompons, with two drops; length, 2½ inches. Each..........$0.04 Per dozen.......... .43

Fancy Cords.

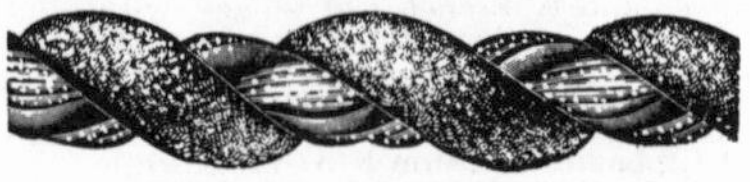

17375—77.

17375 Madrid Fancy cord, silk chenille and tinsel; for fancy work; all colors and black, white and cream. Per yard..........$0.06 Per dozen yards.......... .60
17377 Fine Berlin Combination Silk Chenille and Gold Tinsel Cord. Very handsome for all kinds of fancy work and as a fancy trimming cord for costumes, etc. See cut. Black and colors. Per yard.......... .08 Per dozen.......... .85

Fancy Materials for Embroidery.

17380 Kismet or Frosted Tinsel Thread. 12 balls in box, in plain colors: Gold, silver, canary, blue, pink, steel, gold, dark and light copper, light blue, green, red, fansy blue, yellow, copper, etc. Per ball..........$0.02 Per dozen balls.......... .20
17382 Arrasene for embroidery in all colors, put up in bunches of 12 skeins. Per bunch.......... .15 Per dozen.......... 1.50
17386 Ribbosene or Braidene for embroidery, white and colors, put up in bunches of 12 skeins. Per bunch.......... .20

Embroidery Material—Continued.

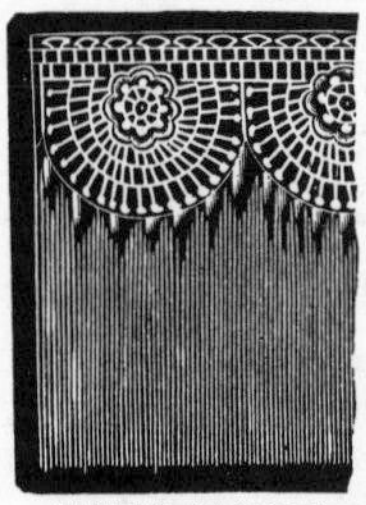

SAMPLE OF WORK.

17388 Twilled Lace Thread for crocheting, knitting and all kinds of fancy work; it is unequaled by any crochet thread in the market. We have it in all numbers from 20 to 100 in both white and ecru. The twill is a new feature, giving a much better appearance to the work than the common three and six cord threads now in use. A trial will satisfy you as to the superiority over all others. No. 20, 30, 40, 50, 60, 70, all 200 yards, on each spool; we can supply samples. If you are interested send for them. Per spool..........$0.05 Per box (10 spools).......... .45

Gold Threads for Embroidery.

17390 Imitation Gold Thread, 12 yards in a bunch. Per bunch..........$0.15
17392 Frosted Gold Thread, 12 yards in a bunch. Per bunch.......... .15
17394 Crochet Gold Thread. Per ball.......... .11
17396 Washable Gold Thread, sizes 7, 8, 9. Per skein.......... .05
17398 Washable Gold Cord. Per skein.......... .05
17399 Japanese Gold Thread, fine. Per skein.... .11
17400 Japanese Gold Thread, medium. Per skein .15
17401 Japanese Gold Thread, coarse. Per skein. .20

Spangles.

17402 Gold or Silver Spangles. Sizes, ¼ to ⅜ in. Per ounce..........$0.14

Embroidery Hoops.

17406 Embroidery Hoops, 4, 5, and 6 inches in diameter. Per pair..........$0.05
7 to 12 inches. Per pair.......... .06

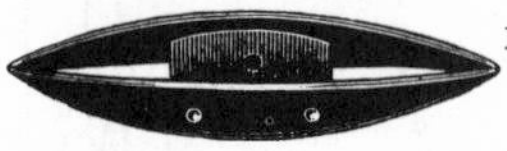

17408 Rubber Tatting Shuttles, finely polished. Each ...$0.15 Per dozen........ 1.50

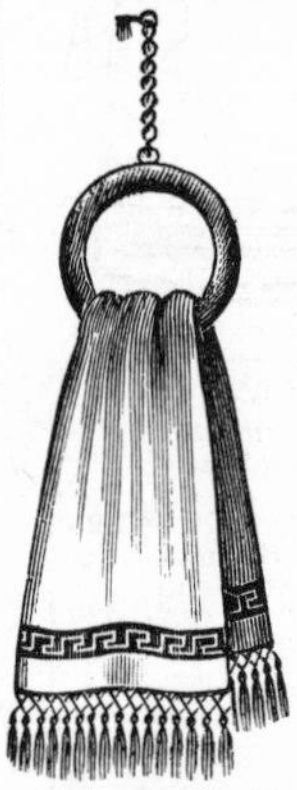

Fancy Towel Holders.

17410 Towel Rings in ebony, rosewood, mahogany and antique oak. Large, each......$0.10 Per dozen.......... 1.00
17412 Towel Ring. Consists of polished hardwood ring with brass chain and hook. Price, without towel. Each, large,..........$0.12 Per dozen.......... 1.20

Pin Cushion Novelties.

Until sold.

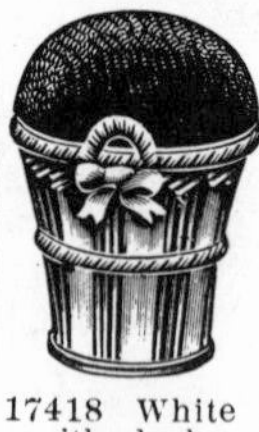

17416 White Metal Basket with push cushion; see cut: Each.......$0.10 Postage.......... .05

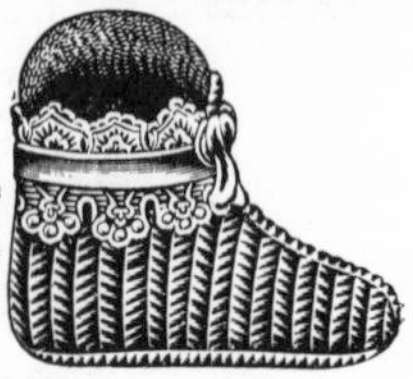

17418 White Metal Bootee with plush cushion; see cut. Each..........$0.10 Postage.......... .04

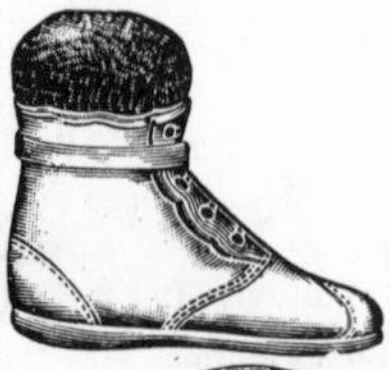

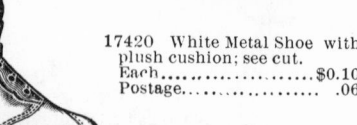

17420 White Metal Shoe with plush cushion; see cut. Each..........$0.10 Postage.......... .06

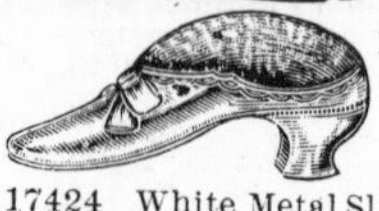

17422 White Metal Slipper with plush cushion, length, 5½ inch; see cut. Each......$0.15 Postage.......... .08
17424 White Metal Slipper with plush cushion, length, 4 inch; see cut. Each..........$0.10 Postage.......... .05

WRITE US on any Business Topic.

Folding Silk Fans.

17435 Silk Fans, with dainty floral and gold decorations; colors: pink, white, cream, Nilegreen, light blue and light yellow. Each........$0.45

17437 Black Silk Fans, with new floral and gold decorations. Each .... .45

17439 Black Silk Fans, decorated in gold and spangles, with floral designs; polished wood sticks, decorated in either gold or silver: 13 inch. Each...................................... .68

17441 Silk Fans, with artistic floral and silver designs; fancy sticks, decorated in silver; colors: pink, light blue and white. See cut; 13 inch. Each................................... .98

17443 Large Black Satin Face Fans, China silk backs, fancy polished wood sticks; 13 inch. Each... .60

17445 Black Sateen Fans, black polished wood sticks. Each.................................. .20

17447 White Imitation Linen Fans, floral decorations, natural wood sticks. Each............ .15

Feather Fans.

17449 New Feather Fans, both sides alike; colors: pink, light blue and white. 14 in. See cut. Each.........$0.50

THE "TELESCOPE" PAT'D FAN

17454 Telescope Cloth Fans, leatherette covered tubes; tan, red and black. Each..........$0.15

17466 Telescope Fans inclosed in an imitation cigar. Each........... $0.15 Per dozen 1.50

"TELESCOPE" FANCY SHAPE.

PATENTED.

17468 New Telescope White Cloth Fans, decorated; four new fancy shapes. Each...........................$0.25

"FATINITZA" FANCY SHAPE.

PATENTED.

17470 New Fatinitza Cloth Fans in tan, red and black, decorated; four new fancy shapes. Each......... ....$0.15

THE "FATINITZA" PAT'D FAN

17472 Fatinitza Fan; fine cloth with leather handle; black only. Each..............$0 20

17474 Daisy Fans, plain white cambric, with daisy bouquet. See cut open and closed. Each..............$0.25

Fans—Continued.

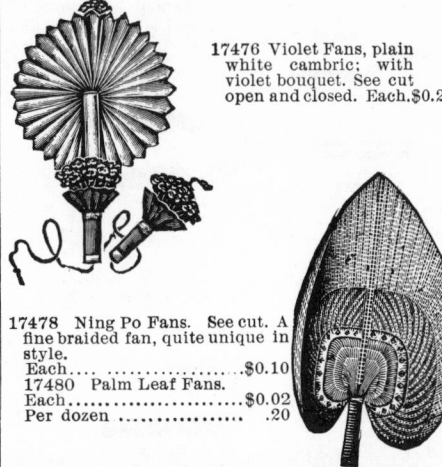

17476 Violet Fans, plain white cambric; with violet bouquet. See cut open and closed. Each.$0.23

17478 Ning Po Fans. See cut. A fine braided fan, quite unique in style. Each $0.10
17480 Palm Leaf Fans. Each ....$0.02 Per dozen .... .20

HAIR GOODS.

When ordering, send samples of hair, as hair goods cannot be returned except to be exchanged for another shade of the same quality.

Drab, red, gray and golden shades in switches, waves, bangs, etc., will be charged 25 to 50 per cent. extra.

N. B.—Be sure you understand what you are ordering before sending for hair goods, as they can not be returned. In ordering send sample of shade wanted, free from oil, folded up in a paper, pinned to your order and marked "Sample," to avoid any mistake.

17520 Puff Bang. Parted. the latest style, designed for the best trade. Made on ventilated foundation, with hair lace part. See cut. Each $3.50

La Toska Bang

17530 La Toska Bang. Ladies who do not require large, heavy front will find this a little gem; light and fluffy, ventilated foundation. Each, until sold $1.25

Feather Bang.

17536 Feather Bang, of fine natural curly hair. See cut. Each.................$2.50

17575 Princess Bang, made of natural curly hair on weft; a popular bang, being light and easily attached, Each......$0.50

Emma Wave.

17581 Emma Wave, invisible hair lace foundation, natural curly hair, 3 inch part, 12 inch from side to side. Each, until sold.. ....$3.00

17618 Kid Hair Curlers, neat and nice for curling the hair; 12 in package.

Length	3½ in.	4 in.	4½ in.
Per package	$0.06	$0.08	$0.10

Human Hair Switches.

17634 Short Stem Hair Switches in all ordinary and medium shades; extra shades will cost from 25 to 50 per cent. extra.

Weigh About.	Length About.	Price, each
2 ounces	20 inches	$0.65
2 ounces	20 inches	.90
2 ounces	22 inches	1.25
3 ounces	22 inches	1.50
3 ounces	24 inches	2.25
3½ ounces	26 inches	3.25

NOTE.—The above 65c. switch has long stem.

French hair switches can be made to order from $5.00 to $10.00 each.

17642 Gray Hair Switches, fine quality, short stem. Be sure to send sample of hair.

Weight.	Length.	Each.
2 ounces	18 inches	$1.75
2¼ ounces	22 inches	3.00
3 ounces	23 inches	4.00
3 ounces	25 inches	6.00

NOTE.—The above prices are for medium shades of gray. Where extra white is ordered it will cost ½ or 50 per cent. more.

17634-42

Hair Nets.

	Each.	Per doz.
17644 Invisible Hair Nets of double hair, for front only	$0.05	$0.55
17668 Hair Nets, silk, all colors and gray, for back hair	.08	.85
17686 Hair Nets, all colors, for back hair	.10	1.00
17691 Hair Nets, Gerster, coarse, hand made, for back hair	.15	1 50

Ladies' Wigs.

17699 These wigs are all ventilated on a delicate open mesh foundation. They are perfect in fit, having a graceful and natural appearance not found in wigs of other manufacture. Each.

Short hair, cotton foundation	$10.00
Short hair, silk foundation	12.00
Hair, 18 inches long	15.00
Hair, 24 inches long	18.00

This is only for ordinary shades; light and half gray are worth 25 per cent. more; if very gray, 50 per cent more.

Full Beards.

17709 On wire	$1.00
17713 Ventilated	2.00

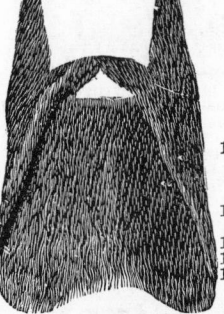

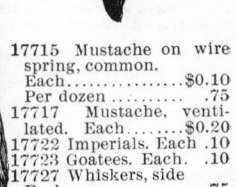

17715 Mustache on wire spring, common. Each.........$0.10 Per dozen .... .75
17717 Mustache, ventilated. Each.......$0.20
17722 Imperials. Each .10
17723 Goatees. Each. .10
17727 Whiskers, side Each................ .75

The above come in dark and medium shades only.

Men's Wigs.

Directions for measuring the head for a wig, to insure a good fit. Mention number of inches.

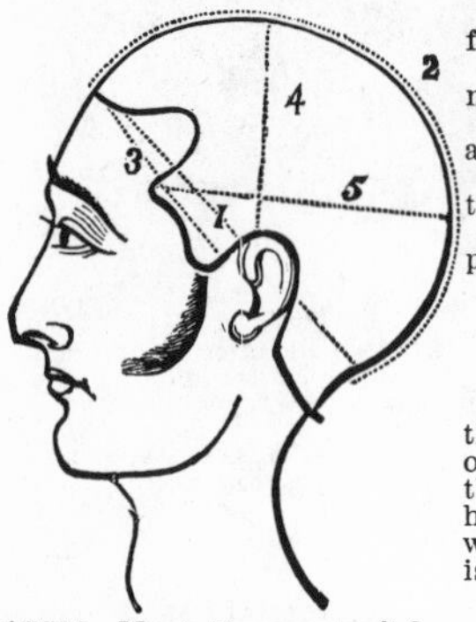

No. 1. The circumference of the head.
No. 2. Forehead to nape of the neck.
No. 3. Ear to ear, across the forehead.
No. 4. Ear to ear, over the top.
No. 5. Temple to temple, around the back.

TO MEASURE FOR A TOUPEE.

Cut a piece of paper the exact size and shape of the bald spot; also the measure around the head, and mention which side the parting is on.

Each

17730 Men's Toupee, weft foundation.........$ 5.50
17733 Men's Toupee Wigs, ventilated foundation.. 10.00
17735 Toupee Paste, for keeping the same in place. Per stick.................................50
17737 Men's Full Wigs for street wear, weft seam, with crown cotton foundation.......... 8.00
17739 Men's Wigs, silk foundation, vegetable net seam.. 12.00
17755 Men's Wigs, silk foundation, gauze net seam.. 15.00
17758 Men's Wigs, silk foundation, hair lace ....$18.00 to 21.00
Extra shades will be charged according to color.
17764 Minstrel Wigs. Each....................$0.75
NOTE.—In addition to above list of men's wigs, we can furnish all kinds of wigs for either ladies or men, for stage, masquerade or character purposes.
17768 Grease Paints, 8 colors in a box, for make-up purposes. Per box....................$1.00

WHAT would you think of a city man if he let the paint peel off his house?
What do you suppose the city man thinks of you under the same circumstances?

Curling and Crimping Irons.

Postage, 12c.
NOTE.—Curling irons or combs cannot be returned after once heating.

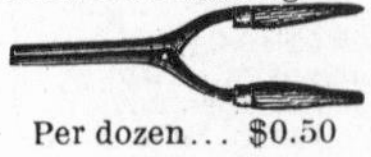

17794 Small Duke Hair or Mustache Curling Iron, polished steel, nickel plated, six inches long. Each......$0.05
Per dozen... $0.50
Postage.................. .02

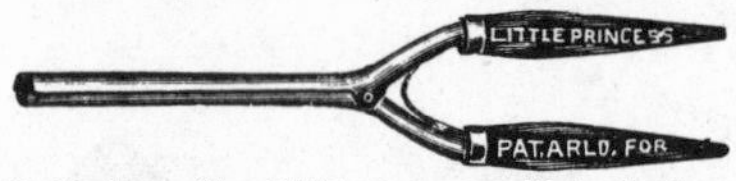

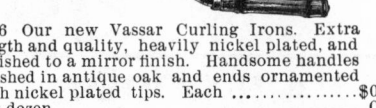

17796 Medium Size Little Princess Hair Curler. 7¼ inches, fine nickeled steel, wood handles, best spring. See cut. Each..........$0.06
Per dozen .... .65
Postage .... .05
17798 Full Size Princess Curling Irons, in fine nickeled steel, wood handles, best springs. See cut. (1.) Each.......... .07
Per dozen .... .75
Postage .... .06

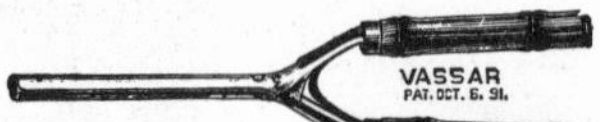

17806 Our new Vassar Curling Irons. Extra length and quality, heavily nickel plated, and polished to a mirror finish. Handsome handles finished in antique oak and ends ornamented with nickel plated tips. Each $0.10
Per dozen 0.95

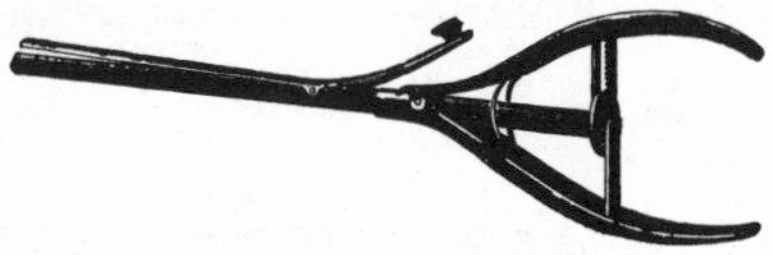

17813 The Automatic Hair Curling Iron. Press the handle and the rod curls your hair. It's done in a minute.
Each $0.30
Postage .... .06

Waving Irons.

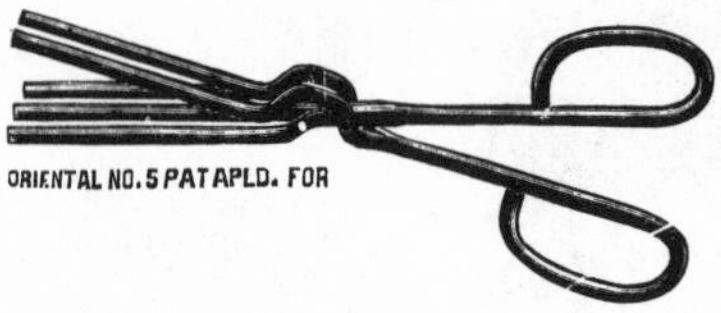

17815 Oriental No. 5. Made of polished steel and handsomely nickel plated. Each, 20c.

Peerless Lamp Chimney Stove.

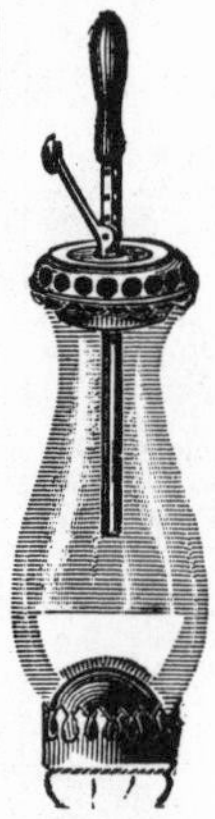

17818 Peerless Lamp Chimney Stove, invaluable for convenience and economy; so compact that it can be carried in the pocket. To heat curling iron use as shown on this cut. To heat cup of water remove loose top and all the heat of the lamp will come in direct contact with bottom of cup. Made of brass, nickel plated; put up one in box.
Each $0.15
Per dozen 1.50

Curling Iron Heater.

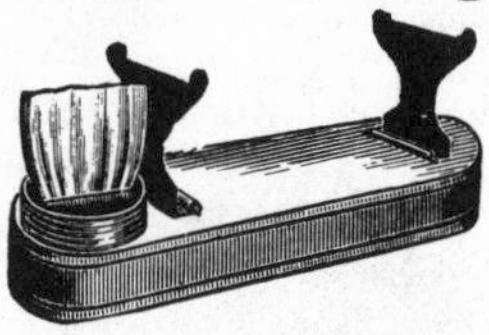

17820 This Curling Iron Heater is very convenient; nickel plated, can be entirely closed so a person can carry in pocket.
Each..............$0.16
Per dozen......... 1.60

Beads.

We do not sell less quantities than quoted.
17844 Cut Steel Beads. Per bunch..............$0.10
17846 Cut Gold Beads. Per bunch.............. .15
17850 Seed Beads. White, crystal, green, blue and black; weight, 3 ounces. Per bunch....... .10
Yellow, red and pink. Per bunch.............. .15
17853 Basket Beads in bunches of 12 strings, 40 beads on a string. Colors: Crystal and black.
Per bunch.............. .03
Per doz n bunches.............. .30
17855 Basket Beads, same quantity as above. Colors: White, pink, blue, silver, gold, coral, lemon, green, ruby. Per bunch.............. .05
Per dozen bunches.............. .48

White and Colored Crepe for Trimming Ladies' and Children's Straw Hats, Etc.

17857 Crepe in black, white, cream, pink, navy, cardinal, green, tan, brown, gray, and yellow. Width, 16 inches.
Per yard $0.15

RIBBON DEPARTMENT.

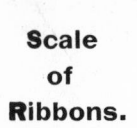

Scale of Ribbons.

No.	In. Wide.
40	3 1-2
22	2 5-8
16	2 3-8
12	2
9	1 5-8
7	1 1-4
5	1
4	3-4
3	5-8
2	7-16
1 1-2	1-4

NOTE.—The above ribbon scale shows width of each number. All ribbons are put up 10 yards to piece.

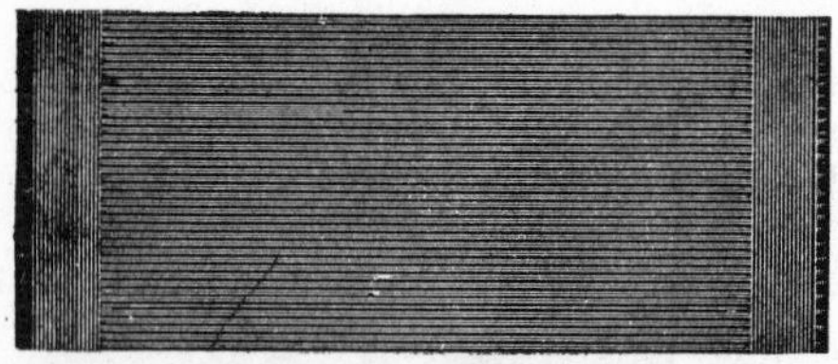

17900 All Silk Gros Grain Ribbons, satin edges or plain satin gros grain, good quality for low-priced ribbon, assorted staple shades and plain black.

Numbers	2	5	7	9	12	16	22	30
Per yard	$0.03½	.05	.06	.08	.10	.12	.14	.16
Per pc. 10 yds.	.32	.45	.55	.70	.85	1.00	1.15	1.40

Nos. 22 and 30 in black only.

Satin and Gros Grain Ribbons.

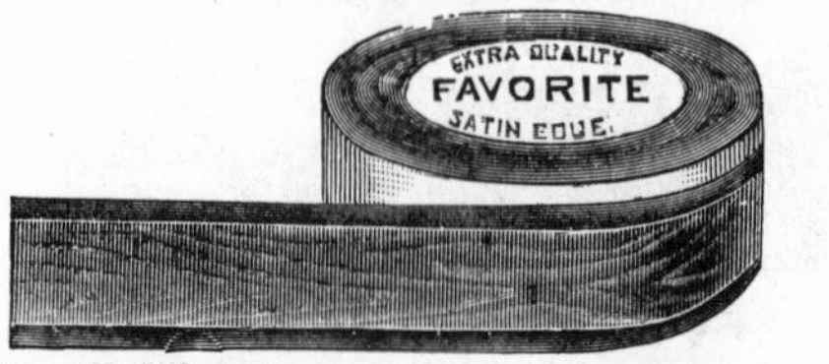

17905 All Silk Gros Grain Ribbons, heavy and finer quality, satin edges, assorted shades and plain black.

Numbers	2	3	5	7	9	12	16	22	30
Per yard,	$0.05	.6	.9	.11	.13	16	.20	.23	.28
Piece 10 yds	.45	.55	.75	.95	1.10	1.45	1.75	2.05	2.50

No 30 in black only.

We Sell More SHOOTING IRONS than Any Other House in America. Prices are Right.

Ribbons—Continued.

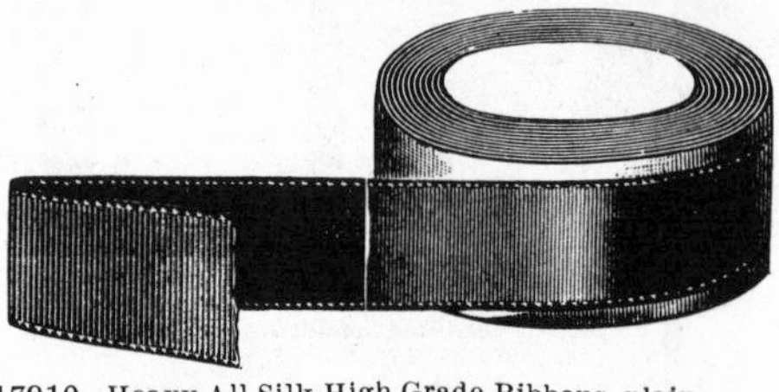

17910 Heavy All Silk High Grade Ribbons, plain satin one side, gros grain the other, fast woven edges, in solid black and colors.

Numbers....	2	3	5	7	9	12	16	22	30	40
Width, in...	7/16	⅝	1⅛	1 5/16	1⅝	2	2⅜	2⅞	3¼	3⅝
Per yard.	$0.05	.06	.09	.11	.13	.16	.20	.25	.28	.33
Pr pc. 10 yd	.43	.55	.70	.90	1.10	1.40	1.75	2.15	2.50	3.05

Nos. 30 and 40 black only.

17912 Plain Black Faille or Gros Grain Ribbon, nice quality, all silk, heavy

Numbers.....	5	7	9	12	16	22	30
Per yard.....	$0.09	.11	.13	.18	.21	.25	.28
Per piece.....	.80	.95	1.15	1.60	1.75	2.10	2.40

17915 Heavy Black Double Face Satin Ribbon, extra quality, all silk.

Numbers.....	5	7	9	12	16	22	40
Per yard.....	$0.10	.12	.16	.20	.23	.28	.35
Per piece.....	.85	1.05	1.45	1.75	2.00	2.45	3.10

Moire Watered Ribbons.

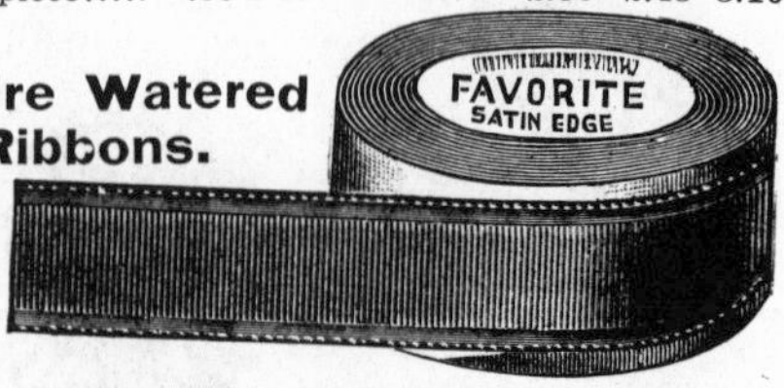

17920 All Silk Gros Grain Moire Watered Fine Ribbons, satin edges, black and colors.

Numbers......	2	5	7	9	12	16
Price, per yard.	$0.06	.09	.11	.13	.16	.20
Per piece 10 yds.	.50	.75	1.00	1.20	1.45	1.80

Binding Ribbon.

17930 Taffeta or Binding Ribbon, in black, white, brown, cardinal, scarlet, cherry, orange, pink and green. Per piece..............................$0.13

Baby Ribbon.

17932 All Silk Picot Edge Baby Ribbons, ¼ inch wide. Colors: White, cream, blues, pinks, old rose, cardinals, greens, yellow, orange, lilac, brown, navy, black. Per piece $0.14

Sash Ribbon.

17935 Sash Ribbon, extra quality, moire watered, 8½ inches wide; black only. Per yard.......$0.75

Fancy Ribbons.

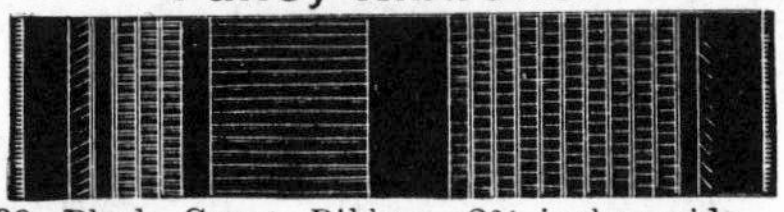

17939 Black Gauze Ribbon, 2¾ inches wide. Per yard $0.15
Per piece 1.25

17941 Black and Steel Combination Silk Ribbon, 2¾ inches wide. Per yard .... .19
Per piece 1.75

17943 Silk Ribbon, satin one side, gros grain the other; colors: Black, cream, light yellow, light blue, pink, nile green, navy blue, three browns, sage, olive and emerald green, rose and scarlet; width, 3¼ inches. Per yard .... .22
Per piece 1.95

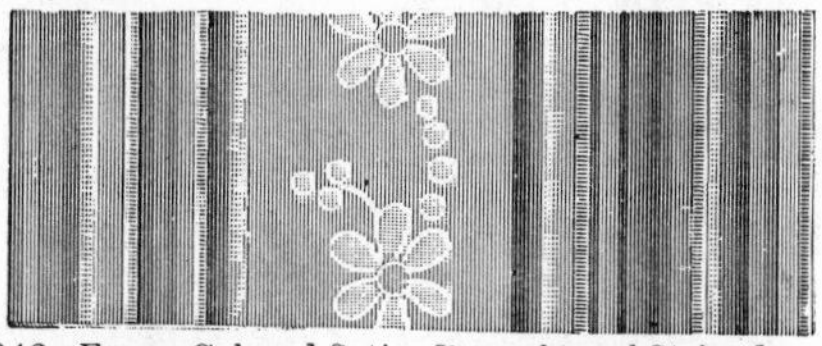

17946 Fancy Colored Satin Brocade and Striped Ribbons; colors: Cream, maize, rose, light blue, lilac, apple green, new blue, cherry, ecru and brown; a very handsome combination ribbon; width, 2⅞ inches. Per yard $0.28
Per piece 2.50

17948 Heavy All Silk Cord Edge Taffeta Ribbons; colors: Cream, light blue, rose, olive green, cherry, leghorn, turquoise, scarlet, navy blue, tan, brown and black; a new trimming ribbon; width, 3½ inches. Per yard .... .32
Per piece 2.95

17949 Fine All Silk Ribbon, 3⅜ inches wide, black only. See cut. Per yard $0.32

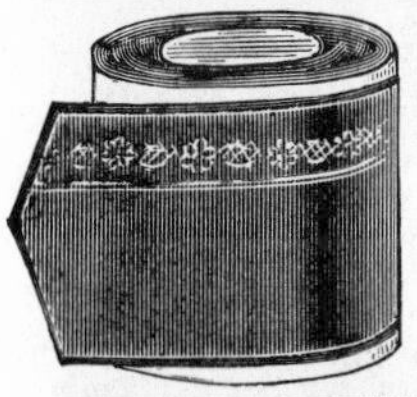

7950 Black Silk Gros Grain Ribbon, woven imitation lace border in contrasting colors: Black with white edge. We quote only until sold. Per yard.........$0.27
Per piece, 10 yards..... 2.45

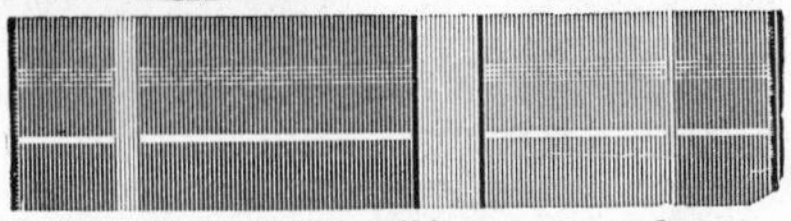

17952 Fancy Plaid Silk Ribbons, assorted combination of colors; width, 3⅛ inches. Per yard.$0.30
Per piece 2.75

Lining Sets.

****
****

A popular and original feature of our LINING DEPARTMENT. They save you time and money.

9—2nd

Ribbons—Continued.

17954 Fancy Brocaded Fine Satin Ribbon, black only; width, 3 inches. Per yard $0.32
Per piece 2.75

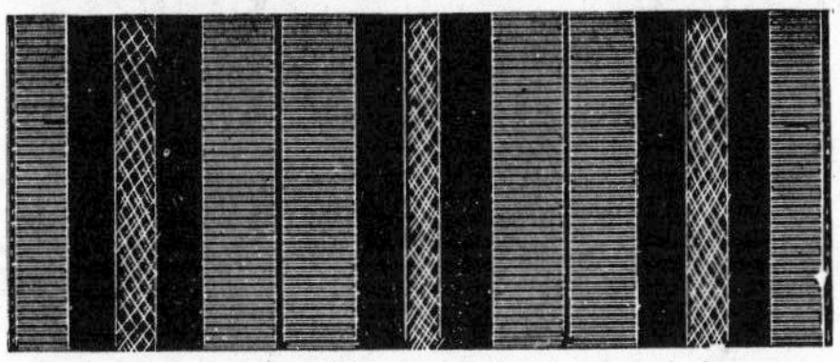

17956 Fine Black Ribbon, with openwork lace stripes; nice quality; width, 3⅜ inches. Per yard $0.43
Per piece 3.90

Duchesse Velvet Ribbons, Black Only.

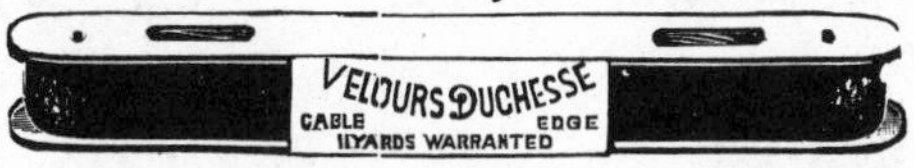

17960 The New Duchesse Black Velvet Ribbons, just introduced into the American market; surpasses all other. It is specially adapted for dress trimmings. Cannot be injured brushing, as it has a silk cable edge, and will replace the satin velvet ribbons at a much less price.

Number	1¾	2¼	3¼	4	5½	6½	8	11
Width	⅜in.	7/16in.	9/16in.	¾in.	1in.	1¼in.	1½in.	2in
Per yd.	$0.05	.06	.08	.09	.12	.15	.18	.25
Pr pc 11 yd.	.45	.50	.70	.90	1.10	1.50	1.75	2.35

17962 Black Velvet Ribbons, fast edges, fair quality.

Number	1½	2½	3½	5	6½	8	10	12
Width	5/16in.	7/16in	11/16in.	1in.	1¼in,	1½in.	1¾in.	2in
Per yd.	$0.03	.05	.06	.08	.11	.14	.17	.20
Pr pc 10 yd.	.25	.40	.55	.75	1.00	1.25	1.45	1.70

Colored Velvet Ribbons.

17964 Colored Velvet Ribbons in a variety of shades, until sold. When we have not the shade wanted, none will be sent.

Nos.	2	4	5	7	9	12
Per piece	$0.75	$1.00	$1.25	$1.75	$2.00	$2.50
Per yard	.08	.10	.14	.18	.22	.26

Satin Back Black Velvet Ribbon.

17966 Satin Back Black Velvet Ribbons, fast woven edges, nice quality for ties, hat or dress trimming.

Numbers	4	5	7	9	12	16
Width	¾in.	15/16in.	1⅛in.	1½in.	1¾in.	2¼in.
Per yard	$0.12	$0.15	$0.18	$0.23	$0.30	$0.36
Per pc. 10 yd.	1.05	1.35	1.70	2.10	2.80	3.15

Remnants.

17968 Remnants of silk ribbons from ½ to 2½ inches wide, assorted colors; lengths, ½ to 1½ yards. Put up in 10 yard packages. Per package, $0.75 to $1.00.

Black Ostrich Tips.

Good Value.

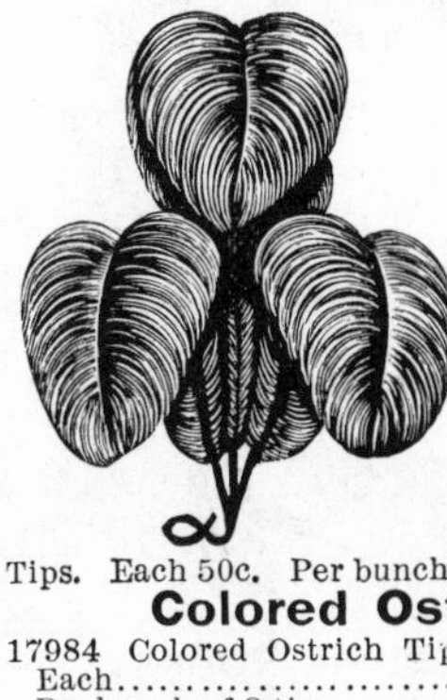

17970 Black Ostrich Tips. Each 10c. Per bunch of 3 tips $0.25

17972 Black Ostrich Tips. Each 14c. Per bunch of 3 tips..$0.35

17973 Black Ostrich Tips. Each 16c. Per bunch of 3 tips..$0.45

17976 Black Ostrich Tips. Each 20c. Per bunch of 3 tips..$0.55

17978 Black Ostrich Tips, fine. Each 30c. Per bunch of 3 tips..$0.75

17980 Black Ostrich Tips. Each 35c. Per bunch of 3 tips..$1.00

17982 Black Ostrich Tips. Each 50c. Per bunch of 3 tips $1.40

Colored Ostrich Tips.

17984 Colored Ostrich Tips. Assorted colors. Each $0.14
Per bunch of 3 tips .... .35

17986 Colored Ostrich Tips. Assorted colors. Each .... .18
Per bunch of 3 tips .... .50

17990 Colored Ostrich Tips. Assorted colors. Each .... .22
Per bunch of 3 tips .... .60

17993 Colored Ostrich Tips. Assorted colors. Each .... .30
Per bunch of 3 tips .... .85

17995 Colored Ostrich Tips. Assorted colors. Each .... .50
Per bunch of 3 tips 1.50

Princess Ostrich Tips.

New Style—See cut.

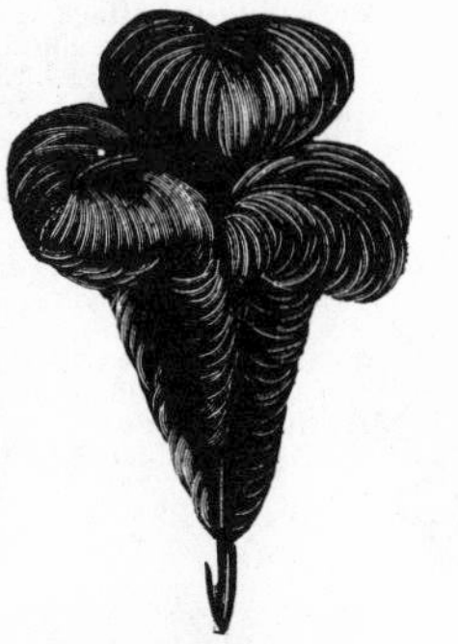

Princess.

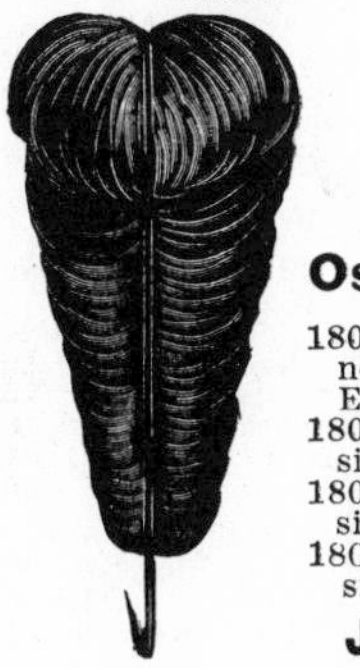

17997 Black Princess Ostrich Tips. Per bunch of three $0.35

18001 Black Princess Ostrich Tips. Per bunch of three $0.43

18003 Black Princess Ostrich Tips. Per bunch of three $0.50

18005 Black Princess Ostrich Tips. Per bunch of three $0.75

18007 Black Princess Ostrich Tips; extra fine. Per bunch of three............$0.90

Ostrich Half Plumes.

18009 Colored Half Plumes. All the new and staple shades. Each $0.45

18011 Black Ostrich Half Plumes, single. Each $0.25

18013 Black Ostrich Half Plumes, single. Each................$0.42

18015 Black Ostrich Half Plumes. single. Each..55c., 68c. and 85c.

Jetted Ostrich Tips.

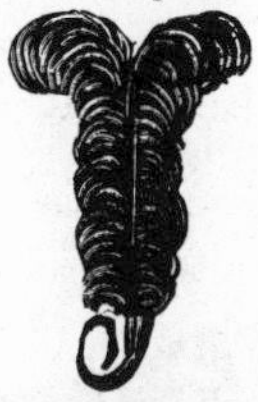

18019 Black Ostrich Tips, Prince of Wales, jetted. Per bunch of two............$0.45

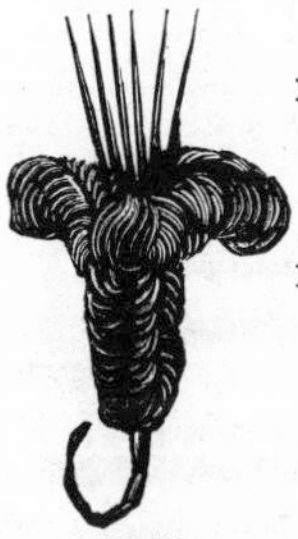

18021

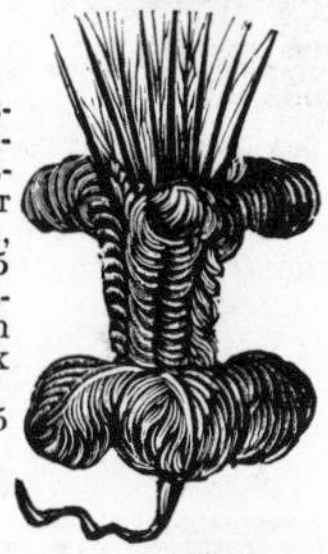

18023

18021 Black Ostrich Tips, Princess, with Aigrettes, jetted. Per bunch of three, ...$0.55

18023 Black Ostrich Tips, with Aigrettes and six (6) jetted tips. Per bunch..$0.75

New Buckles.

The popular ornaments for stock collars, dresses, hats, etc.

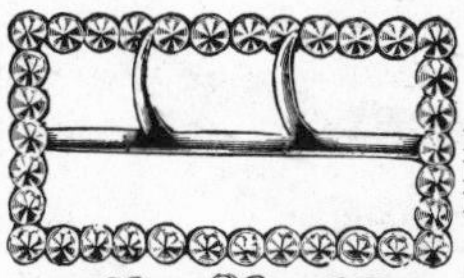

18035 Cut Steel Buckles, riveted.

Size.	Each.
1 inch, one prong.	$0.08
1¼ inch, two prong..	.10
1½ inch, two prong..	.12
1¾ inch, two prong..	.14
2 inch, three prong..	.16

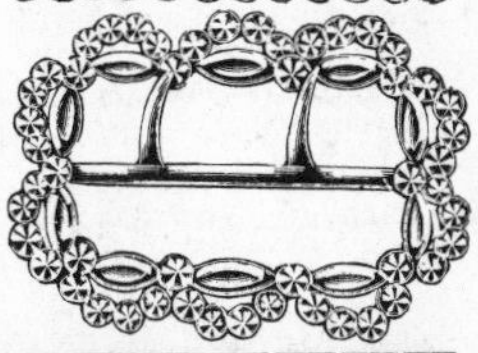

18037 Cut Steel Buckles, fine quality, riveted.

Size.	Each.
1 inch, two prong...	$0.18
1½ inch, two prong.	.23
2 inch, three prong..	.27

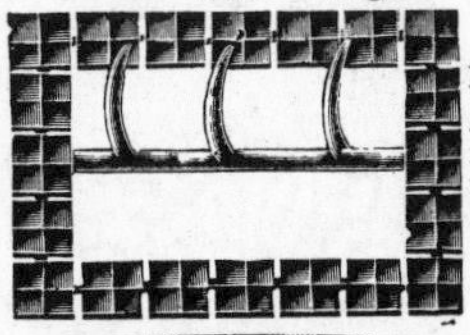

18039 Jet Buckles.

Size.	Each.
1 inch, two prong....	$0.07
1¼ inch, two prong..	.08
1½ inch, two prong..	.12
1¾ inch, three prong	.14

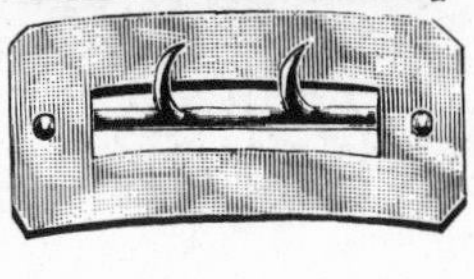

18041 White Pearl Buckles, two prong.

Size.	Each.
1 inch.........	$0.18
1½ inch.........	.23
2 inch.........	.27

Ornaments—Continued.

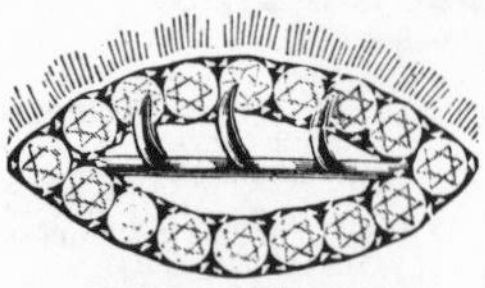

18043   Rhinestone Buckles, gilt mountings.
Size.   Each.
¾ in., one prong, $0.13
1¼ in., two prong,   .16
1½ in., two prong,   .19

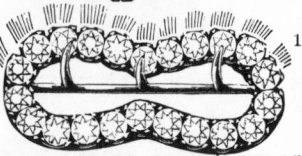

18045   Rinestone Buckles, gilt mountings, like cut.
1¾ in. Each, $0.27

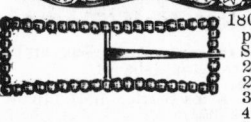

18047   Rhinestone Buckles, gilt mountings, like cut; 2¼ inch
Each.....$0.29

18049   Gilt Buckles, rope pattern, style of cut.

Size.	Each.
2 inches	$0.12
2½ inches	.15
3⅛ inches	.18
4 inches	.21
5 inches	.25

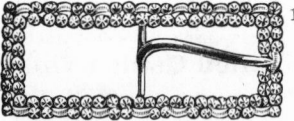

18051   Cut Steel Buckles, riveted.

Size.	Each.
2½ inches..	$0.21
3¼ inches..	.26
3¾ inches..	.32

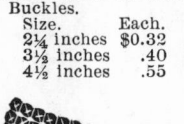

18054   Steel Riveted Buckles.

Size.	Each.
2¼ inches	$0.32
3½ inches	.40
4½ inches	.55

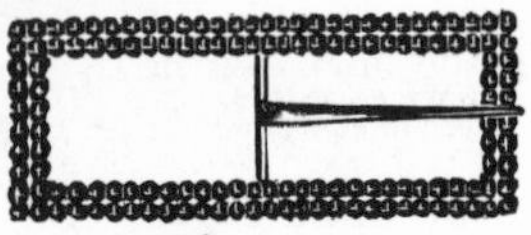

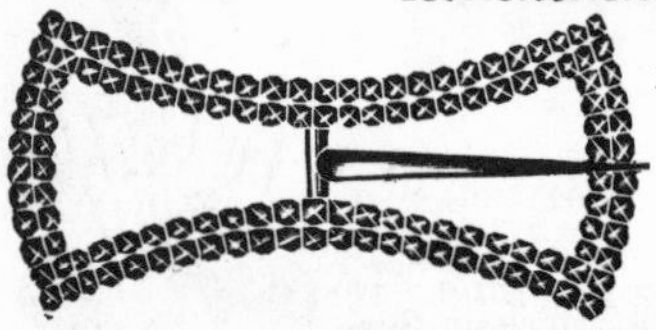

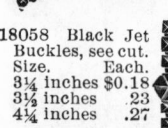

18056   Steel Riveted Buckles.

Size.	Each.
3¼ in..	$0.40
4 in..	.45
5 in..	.50

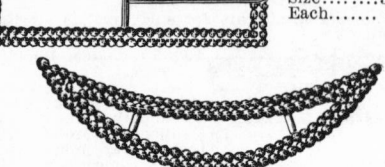

18058   Black Jet Buckles, see cut.

Size.	Each.
3¼ inches	$0.18
3½ inches	.23
4¼ inches	.27

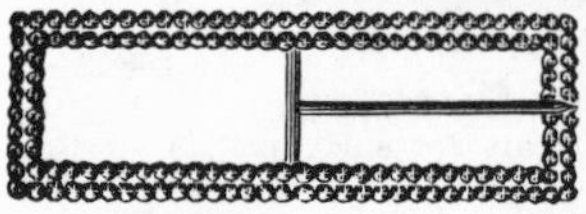

18060   Black Jet Riveted Buckle.
Size........3¾ in.
Each....... $0.40

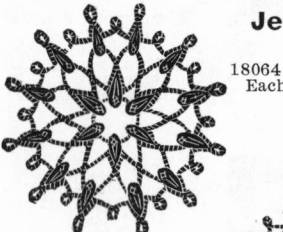

18062   Steel Slides, riveted. Size, 4¼ in.   Each, $0.45

Jet Crowns.

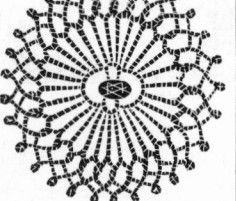

18064   Black Jet Crowns. Each.......15c. 20c. 25c.

18066   Black Jet Crowns. 5 inch.
Each..............$0.30

Ornaments—Continued.

18068   Black Jet Crowns. 5 inches.
Each......45c. and 75c.

Ornaments.

 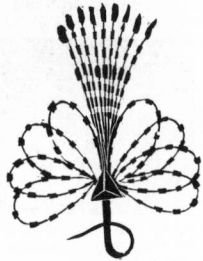

18070   18072
18070   Jetted Ornaments (see cut), 12 piquets.
Each.................................... $0.20
18072   Jetted Ornaments; size, 5½x5½ inches.
See cut. Each................................... .25

18074   Fancy Top Jet Pins, assorted styles. Each.................... $0.10

Roses.

Our line of flowers for this season, contains a new and varied assortment of designs and colors; many of the patterns being our own importation, giving the customer good quality and choice colors at popular prices.

18095   Half Blown Rose and Bud, leaves and rubber stems; colors: Red, jack, yellow cream, tea and pink.
Each.....................$0.10
18097   Full Blown Rose, grasses, leaves and piquets, same colors as 18095. . $0.10
Per bunch of three sprays ....$.025
18099   Spray of Two Full Blown Roses with leaves, grasses and piquets; colors: Red, pink, cream, yellow, rose and tea..
.........................$0.14
Per bunch of three sprays....
.........................$0.35

18095

18101   Full Blown Rose, two buds fine leaves and rubber stems; colors: Cream, yellow, tea, rose, pink, scarlet ..$0.15
18103   Wild Rose Spray; three natural roses, fine leaves and rubber stems; colors: Cream, yellow, coral, rose, light blue, tea, pink, and scarlet....$.160
18104   Wild Rose Spray: 6 roses, all satin petals, rubber stems; colors: Pink, yellow, rose, new blue and red.
Each.....................$0.16

18103

Velvet Roses.

18106   Three Velvet Roses; fine quality, shaded centers: colors: Rose, coral, new blue, heliotrope, tea, yellow and green (3377).
Each.....................$0.20
18108   Three Roses; pure silk and velvet, rubber stems; colors: Pink, rose, new blue, coral, heliotrope, apricot, red, yellow and shaded green (3480).
Each. $0.25

18108

Roses—Continued

18110   Six Pure Silk and Velvet Roses, rubber stems; colors: Pink, tea, rose magenta, blue, yellow, apricot; gold and combinations of lilac with pink, and yellow with green. (3445).
Each.........................$0.40
8112   Three Roses and Three Buds; all of fine pure silk velvet, with rubber stems; colors: Pink, red, rose, new blue, yellow, green, green shaded, and combinations of pink and green (3458). Each.....$0.50
18115   Three Crush Roses and Three Buds, all of finest quality pure silk velvet in rich shades; colors: Pink, tea, yellow, rose bluet, red, magenta, green, green shaded and combination of pink and green (3454)..$0.68
18117   Two Beautiful Half Blown Roses, two buds of finest quality silk velvet, muslin and silk, rubber stems; colors: Rose, tea, red and yellow (3196)..................$0.75

18110

Sprays.

18119   Spray of China Asters with leaves and grasses; colors: Pink, heliotrope, red, yellow, rose and cream (2006)...................$0.15
Per bunch of three sprays $0.39
18121   Wild Rose, velvet petals with cluster of lilies of the valley, grasses and leaves; colors: Tea, cream, red, pink and rose (115)...........$0.16
Per bunch of three sprays $0.42
18123   Assorted Sprays, a great variety of patterns and colors. Value, 25c and 30c; to close. Each..$0.15 and$0.20

18119

18125   Bunch of Velvet Forget me-nots, with leaves and grasses; colors: Light blue, cream, pink, coral, yellow and rose, (49). Each.......$0.17
18127   Bunch of Apple Blossoms, full blossoms with natural buds, fine quality; colors: Pink, cream, yellow, coral, light blue, heliotrope and rose.
Each $0.16
18129   Bunch of Lilies-of-the-Valley, white only, with green leaves. Each $0.18

18125

18131   Spray of Geraniums with natural buds and leaves; colors: Pink, rose, red, white, cream and apricot. (83)
Each $0.22
18133   Bunch of Velvet Geraniums, nine blossoms; buds and rubber stems; colors: Scarlet, pink, rose, coral and yellow (618). Each $0.25
18135   Bunch of Silk Velvet Geraniums, fifteen blossoms, with buds and rubber stems; colors: Scarlet, pink, rose, coral and yellow (628).
Each $0.45

18135

18137   Bunch of silk Velvet Pansies: four blossoms, with buds, leaves and rubber stems; natural shades (87). Each.....................$0.25
18139   Bunch of three Silk Velvet Pansies and Buds; natural shades (11015). Each.....................$0.40
18141   Bunch of six Silk Velvet and Satin Pansies; buds and rubber stems; natural shades (4359). Each $0.52

18141

Sprays—Continued.

18143 Spray of Fine Lilacs, with natural and two large velvet begonia leaves. Colors: Lilac, white, yellow and coral (208). Each.........................$0.35

18145 Large Bunch of Lilacs: four sprays. Colors: White, light and dark lilac (7454). Per bunch................$0.42
Per single spray.......... .13

18147 Bunch of Sweet Peas and Buds, with rubber stems; assorted natural shades in a bunch (11168). Each...........$0.28

18149 Spray of five Large Half Blown Buds, leaves and rubber stems; colors: Pink, yellow, cream, tea, jack and red, like cut (7396). Each......................$0.30

18151 Spray of six Buttercups and Buds all satin petals, yellow centers; colors: Pink, rose, yellow, cream, new blue, brown and black, (7438). Each...$0.30

18153 Bunch of fine Velvet Verbenas, with leaves; dainty colorings in white, cream, yellow, light blue, bluet, pink, rose and scarlet (72). Each $0.30

18149

18155 Bunch of twelve fine Velvet Primroses, moss stems, green piquets tipped in colors to match flowers, which come in white, yellow, pink, rose, red, heliotrope and new blue. See Cut (15160). Each............$0.35

18157 Bunch of Heather, fine velvet blossoms, moss stems and piquets similar to above and in the same colors (433). Each............$0.40

18155

18159 Bunch of twelve Wheatheads. Colors: White, yellow, coral, rose, apricot and Nile (11462). Each......................... .40

18161 Spray of five Velvet Cornflowers, with moss stems, velvet leaves. Colors: Light blue, lavender, light and dark shades of bluet or new blue (402). Each.................................. .45

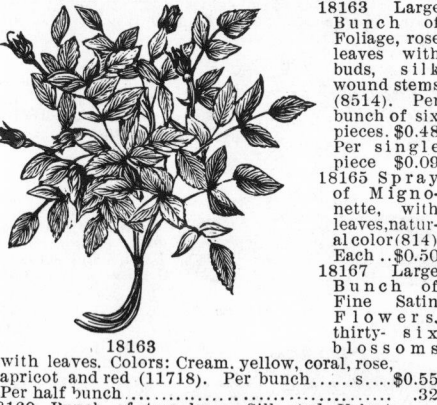

18163 Large Bunch of Foliage, rose leaves with buds, silk wound stems (8514). Per bunch of six pieces. $0.48
Per single piece $0.09

18165 Spray of Mignonette, with leaves, natural color (814). Each ..$0.50

18167 Large Bunch of Fine Satin Flowers, thirty-six blossoms with leaves. Colors: Cream, yellow, coral, rose, apricot and red (11718). Per bunch......s...$0.55
Per half bunch... .32

18163

18169 Bunch of two large Silk and Velvet Poppies, with buds and rubber stems. Colors: Red, jack, yellow, pink and new blue (530). Each... .55

18171 Bunch of twelve Half Blown Buds, fine quality, rubber stems. Colors: Pink, tea, yellow, jack and cream (7489). Each.................. .60

Rose Sprays.

18173 Assorted Rose Sprays, in nice line of colors, all good value. Former price 40 and 50 cents. To close. Each... ....$0.35

18175 Long Spray of six Velvet and Muslin Roses, buds, ivy leaves and rubber stems. Colors: Pink, rose, yellow, cream, magenta and new blue (2059 Each)......$0.45

18177 Long Spray of two Large Double Muslin Roses, fine quality, with seven buds, leaves and rubber stems. Colors: Dark red, pink, white, yellow and tea (2045). Each $0.55

Sprays—Continued.

18179. Long Spray, two full blown roses, three buds, velvet, silk and muslin petals. fine quality leaves, and rubber stems. Colors: Yellow, pink, jack, light yellow and new blue. See cut (2008) Each $0.60

18181 Long Spray, two large half blown roses, four buds, fine quality muslin, long rubber stems and leaves, similar style to above cut. Colors: Deep red, jack, yellow, pink and tea (2027). Each.... $0.60

18183 Long Spray, six full blown roses, on wound silk and rubber stems, clustered with

18179

ivy leaves. Colors: Pink, tea, jack and red (246). Each.................................. .70

18185 Long Spray, two large muslin and velvet poppies and buds on long moss stems, arranged with forget-me-nots and fine leaves. Colors: red, yellow, tea, pink and rose (2021) Each.... .60

18187 Spray of natural green velvet and muslin Ivy Leaves with berries, rich shadings, long rubber stems. Each....''''......... .... 1.10

Wreaths.
New dainty styles for children's hats.

18190 Bluebell Wreaths; colors: White, cream, yellow, rose, light blue, heliotrope and red (41041) Each...................$.0.23

18192 Wreath of 42 Daisies, fine: colors: White, cream, yellow, rose and pink (41087). Each $0.28

18194 Long, full Wreath of Primroses; white, cream, yellow, rose, light blue, heliotrope and red (41061). Each..................$0.28

18196 Wreath of fine wild Roses, fine muslin natural centers, same colors as above (41114). Each.........$0.30

18198 Wreath of fine Wild Roses, fine muslin natural centers, same colors as above (41109). Each-..$.045

41190

18200 Wreath of eleven fine quality Rosebuds, arranged with bunches of lilacs, fine leaves and rubber stems. Colors: Pink, tea yellow and cream. Each.........................$0.50

Small Flowers, Materials, Etc.

18202 Violets. natural shades, in bunches of three dozen. Per bunch...................$0.06

18204 Frosted Violets, natural shades. Per dozen.........$0.12

18206 Frosted Violets, white only. Per dozen....................$0.12

18208 Muslin Violets, natural shades. Per dozen.........$0.18

18210 Large Velvet Violets, natural shades. Per dozen. ..$0.18

18212 Satin Violets, fine quality, natural shades. Per dozen. $0.18

18214 Velvet Buttercups. Colors: Red, rose, green, pink and new blue. Per dozen............$0.16

18216 Forget-Me-Nots, velvet. Colors: Red, pink, light blue, new blue, cream and yellow. Per dozen.................................... .10

18218 Forget-Me-Nots. velvet. on four-inch moss stems: ten blossoms on a stem, Colors: Light blue, rose, coral, yellow and red. Per dozen stems .... .18

18220 Hyacinths, 3 blossoms on a stem. Colors: White, lavender, blue, pink, yellow, cream and magenta. Per dozen stems .... .16

18222 Rosebuds; pink, yellow, tea and red. Each...................$0.04 Per dozen......... .37

18224 Clover Blossoms, with extra long stems. Colors: Red, rose and yellow. Per bunch of 3 dozen, until sold................................... .20

18226 Daisies; white, pink, yellow and blue, with brown and yellow centers. Per dozen ...... .25

Black Flowers.

18228 Black Spray Wild Roses satin leaves and jet piquets (394). Per spray.....................$0.20
Per bunch of 3 sprays......................... .48

18230 Black Satin Violets. Per bunch of 3 doz. .25

18234 Spray of Black Satin Wild Roses, jetted centers and jetted leaves (5810). Per spray.... .28

18236 Bunch of Three Black Satin Roses, with black, gold or white centers (3464). Per bunch... .28

18239 Bunch of Black and White Flowers, satin leaves, jet piquets (5820). Per spray.... .35

18240 Spray of Black Satin Buds, leaves and jet piquets (309). Per spray......... .48

Black Flowers—Continued.

18242 Spray of Black Satin Flowers and Leaves, piquets and rubber stems (324). Per spray. .55

18244 Bunch of Chrysanthemums, fine silk, three flowers and buds (6434). Per spray...... .62

18246 Spray of Lillies, fine black silk, satin leaves, chenille piquets, rubber stems (387). Per spray .... .70

Orange Blossoms.

18278 Orange Blossoms, Bridal Sets, fine quality wax blossoms with buds and green leaves; each set contains wreath and bouquet. Each......$1.50, $2.00 and $3.00

18280 Orange Blossom Sprays, fine wax blossoms with buds and leaves. Each......50, 75c. and 1.00

18285 Orange Blossom Bouquets, same as above.
Small. Each...................................... .15

18290 Confirmation Wreaths, white. Each....... .20

18295 Confirmation Bouquets, white. Per spray. .08
Per bunch of 2 sprays......................... .15

MILLINERY DEPARTMENT.

We again invite the attention of our customers to this department. We can furnish any style of of trimmed or untrimmed Hats in any desired quality or cost; see illustrations and quotations following. We also carry in stock a full line of Ribbons, Fancy Flowers, Wreaths, Sprays, Ostrich Tips, Plumes, Birds. Jetted Ornaments, Aigrettes, etc., etc. A reasonable charge will be made for trimming, from 15c. to 50c. These prices are for the work only. Any made Hat or Bonnet made or trimmed to order cannot be returned or exchanged.

Misses' Straw Hats.

18352— Misses' or Children's Canton Fancy Edged Trimmed Hats, assorted styles. Colors, white ecru, brown, navy blue and cardinal. Each.............. .. $0.35

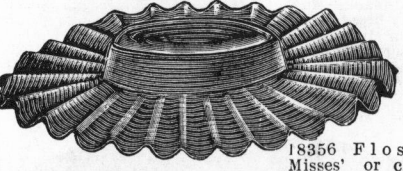

18356 Flossie. Misses' or children's Fine Canton Hats, colors and white. Each...$0.23
Fancy Lace Braid, colors and white. Each..... .40

18362— Chrysanthemum. Misses' or children's Union Milan and fancy braid, fancy edge. Black and colors. Each......................................$0.35
Canton Braid, with fancy edge; colors, no black .... .38
Fancy Rustic and hair braid, colors only........ .75

18368 Gypsy Same description as Chrysanthemum. Misses' or children's, Union Milan and fancy braid, fancy edge, black and colors.........................$0.35
Canton Braid with fancy edge, colored only, no black... .38
Fancy Rustic and hair braid, colors only.......... .75

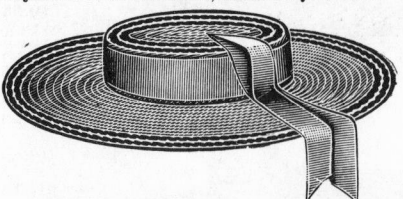

18374 Pinafore. Trimmed sailor, ribbon band, Canton braid, black, brown, ecru and navy. ... $0.22
Union Milan, grosgrain, ribbon band, black and colors... .60

Ladies' and Misses Sailors.

18378 Seersucker Sailor, in blue and white stripe, cardinal and white, black and white, cashmere band and under brim................$0.35

18384—Dartmouth Sailor Fine Canton, untrimmed in black, white and colors. Each.$0.25

Union Milan, untrimmed, black and colors. Each. .40
China Milan, trimmed with gros grain band, black and colors. Each....................50
Union Milan, trimmed with gros grain band, and colors. Each.......................68
Fine Milan, trimmed with gros grain band, black and colors. Each.................. 1.45

18388 Corwin, Sailor, untrimmed, Union Milan, black and colors. Each...$0.55

Fine Rustic Braid, black and colors.. .... .60
Fine Milan, black and colors................ 1.45

Leghorn Flats.

18394 Leghorn Flats, black only.
Each.... $0.50, $0.75, $0.90, $1.10, $1.40 and $1.75
18398 Leghorn Flats, white only.
Each...$0.25, $0.50, $0.75, $0.90, $1.10, $1.40 and $1.75.
18404 Child's White Leghorn Flats. Each......$0.35

Flats, For Ladies, Misses or Children.

18408 Canton, plain braid; brown, navy, ecru and black. Each....................$0.25
Fancy braid; black and colors....................35
Union Milan and hair, with wide, fancy braid, insertion; black and colors.....................60
Black Chips..................90
Colored Chips.......... 1.20

18412 Idlewild High Crown Flats, India Leghorn black only........................$0.50
Fancy Lace Braid, black and colors............68

Untrimmed Hats.

18416 Triumph, Hair Braid. fancy edge, black only. Each......$0.40

Hair Braid, Milan edge, black only..............$0.65
Hair Braid, fancy edge, black only..............68
Lace Braid, fancy edge, black and colors.......75
Black Chip....................90
Colored Chip.................... 1.20

18420 Osborne-Union Milan and hair, fancy edges, black and colors. Each. $0.35
Fancy Straw Crown, with Union Milan rim; fancy edge, black and colors.$0.50
Union Milan and hair, wide fancy braid insertion, black and colors...........................60
Neopolitan, with fancy bernina, chip edges, black only.................... .90

18424 Criterion. Same description and prices as 18420. Osborne.

18428 Helvetia Union Milan, and hair with fancy edge, black and colors. Each.... $0.35

Lace Hair, Union Milan insertion and edge, black only. Each................................ .60
Union Milan, black and colors.................. .55

18432 Monterey. Same description and prices as 18428. Helvetia.

18436 Arlington. Same description and prices as 18428 Helvetia

18440 Canterbury. Same description and price as 18428 Helvetia.

18444 Rainsford. Fancy straw crown, with Union Milan rim and fancy edge; black and colors. Each........................$0.50
Lace hair, union milan insertion and edge, black only. Each .... .90
Neopolitan, fancy bernina chip edge, black only. Each........................ .. .. .90

18448 Matinee, China Milan lace insertion, black and colors......................................$0.40 Each.
Fancy Braid, black and colors....................60
Black Chip....................75
Black Chip, fine quality........................ 1.10
Colored Chip........................... 1.40

18452 Woodford. Hair braid, with fancy braid insertion, black only. Each..$0.40

Hair Braid, Milan edge, black only.............60
Fancy Chip and lace mixed, black and colors.... .90

18456 Ideal. Lace braid. Milan edge, black and colors. Each..$0.37
Hair Braid, Milan edge, black only. Each .$0.60
Lace Braid, chip edge and insertion, black and colors. Each...... $0.95

18460—Elaine, Lacebr'd, Milan edge, blk. and colors. Ea.$0.37
Union Milan, black only. Each 40
Union Milan, finer, black only. Each 62
Hair Braid, fancy edge, black only. Each.........68

18464 Randolph Canton braid, black only. Each..$0.22
Milan Braid, black only. Each..$0.50
Hair Braid, Milan edge and insertion, black only.........$0.60

18468 Avenell, Hair Braid, with fancy insertion, black only. Each....$0.40
Hair Braid, Milan edge, black only. Each.................$0.60
Fancy Braid, black and colors. Each.............68

18470 Hermione. Union Milan, black only. Each.$0.40
Hair Braid, fancy insertion, black only Each.....................$0.40
Lace Braid, Milan edges, black and colors. Each$0.37
Hair Braid, Milan insertion black only. Each.. .60

18474—Minuette. Hair braid, with fancy insertion, black only. Each$0.40

Fancy Braid, black and colors.......................43
Lace and Chip, mixed, black and colors.........65

18478 Avon. Open fancy straw, black and colors. Each..............$0.42
Hair Braid, with insertion $0.60
Italian Straw crown, Milan, with lace insertion, rim, black and colors.................$0.68

18482 Cassette. Union Milan and hair, fancy edge, black only. Each..$0.35

Fancy Straw Crown, Union Milan rim, fancy edge, black and colors. Each....................50
Union Milan, black and colors. Each...........55
Black Chip... 50

18486 Lilian. Union Milan and hair, fancy edge, black and colors. Each........$0.35
Fancy Straw Crown, Union Milan rim and fancy edge, black and colors. Each.....$0.50
Union Milan, black and colors....................55
Hair, fancy lace hair edge, black only........ .. .60
Black Chip.......................90

18490 Kent. Same description and prices as 18486 Lilian...

18494 Windsor. Union Milan and hair, fancy edge, black and colors. Each.........$0.35

Union Milan, black and colors....................55
Black Chip.......................90

18498 Essex. Same description and prices as 18494 Windsor.

18502 Bijou. Union Milan, black and colors.................$0.55
Hair Braid, fancy straw edge, black only.................$0.60
All Lace braid, black only.. .90
Fancy Bernina Chip, black and colors.................$0.95

18506 Beatrice. Union Milan, black only. $0.50
Union Milan, finer, black only .68
Black Hair Braid, chip edge.. .68
Hair Braid, fancy edge, black only 60

Frames.

	Each.
18508 Wire Frames, toques and bonnets........	$0.18
Hats........	.25
18510 Buckram Frames, toques and bonnets....	.09
Hats........	.12

Fez Caps.

18718 Children's Fez Caps, in navy and cardinal.
Each.................$0.25
18720 Fez Caps, large size, navy and cardinal.
Each.................$0.35

Trimmed Hats.

18724 Corrine. Fine black silk lace hat, with jet ed e, crown and band; trimmed with wide fancy silk ribbon, rhinestone buckle, large spray of fine velvet and muslin flowers and velvet forget-me-nots. Each.................................$5.00

18726 Arlington. Open braid hat, fancy edge trimmed with wide silk ribbon, lace and two bunches of small flowers with foliage. Colors: Brown, ecru and black. Each. ..,.......$1.30

18728 Wanda. Open braid, fancy edge, trimmed with wide satin and gros grain ribbon, lace, fancy pin and fine velvet flowers with foliage. Colors: Brown, ecru and black. Each...................$1.75

18730 Canterbury. Misses' hats of fancy braid, trimmed with large bow of wide all silk plaid ribbon, large gilt buckle, two bunches of silk and velvet flowers. Colors: Brown, navy, ecru and black. Each.............. ....$2.15

Trimmed Hats—Continued.

18735 Mignon. Fancy lace braid, satin wire under brim, trimmed with wide satin and gros grain ribbon, fine steel buckle, two bunches of velvet flowers. Colors: Navy, brown, ecru and black, Each...... ....$2.25

18740 Orleans Turban. Fine hair braid, trimmed with folds of velvet, two bunches of black satin violets, rosette of wide satin ribbon and bunch of silk and velvet flowers. This braid comes only in black, but we trim in colored flowers.
Each.......... ....$2.45

18746 Lucllle. Fancy braid faced with gold tricotine, satin wire edge; trimmed with large bow of wide all silk ribbon, two fancy pins, large bunch of roses with buds and foliage Colors: Navy, brown and ecru with ribbon to match, or in black with colored ribbon. Please state what color ribbon is desired when ordering. Each.......... . . ..$2.65

18748 Avery. Fancy straw braid, trimmed with velvet folds, steele buckle. Wide all silk ribbon, two bunches of fine velvet flowers, Colors: Brown, ecru and black. Each $2.75

Trimmed Hats—Continued.

18750 Season. Fancy braid, lace edge, satin wire under brim; trimmed with large bow of wide all silk ribbon, rhinestone buckle, large bunch of roses with buds and leaves. Colors: Navy, brown, ecru and black. Each....... ....$2.85

18754 Cassette. Fancy braid, trimmed with velvet fold, large bow and rosettes of wide, all silk ribbon, jet or steel buckle and two bunches of small flowers. Colors: Brown, ecru and black. Each $3.10

18765 Lillian Young lady's hat; fine leghorn trimmed with wide, all silk ribbon, two small steel buckles and two bunches of fine silk and velvet roses. White or black leghorn with colored ribbon. State color of ribbon preferred. Each............ .... .:..............._........$3.40

18771 Venice Bonnet. Fine, fancy braid, velvet facing; trimmed with velvet, wide silk lace, two jet pins, bunch of small velvet flowers. jetted aigrette, velvet ribbon, bows and ties. Black only. Each......$3.75

Trimmed Hats –Continued.

18775 **Triumph.** Lace braid, fancy edge, faced with gold tricotine, two rows satin wire, trimmed with three bands of velvet around crown, wide fancy, all silk ribbon, rhinestone buckle, wide lace, bunch of fine silk and velvet flowers, with foliage; colors: Brown, ecru and black. Each..$3.65

Trimmed Hats—Continued.

18785 **Rainsford.** Fine lace braid, high crown fancy edge; trimmed with wide velvet fold, velvet bands around crown, large bows of wide, all silk ribbon, two fine jet pins. Violets, fine velvet flowers with buds; black only. Each.......$4.25

Trimmed Hats—Continued.

18791 **Puzzle.** Child's Hat, rustic braid, trimmed with all silk ribbon, cream lace and small flowers. Colors: Navy, brown, ecru and white, Each..$1.15

Ready-Made Wrappers.

New styles—are superior in every way to former lines.

Excellent values are shown in this department.

Honiton Lace Illustrations.

See quotations on page 122.

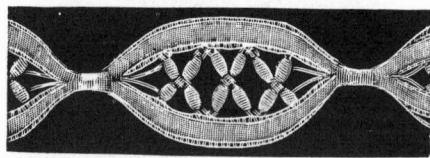

16505

16507

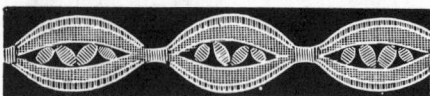

16509

16511

16513

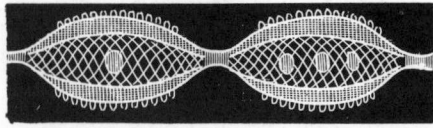

16515

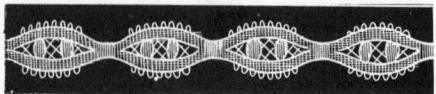

16517

WHAT ONE GETS

Is measured to a great extent by what one goes after. Go after the right thing in the right way and you are fairly sure of right results.

There is such a thing as going after the right thing the wrong way, or the wrong thing the right way. Be careful not to fall into these too common errors.

The way to make a saving in purchasing your necessities of life is to write us for freight rates from Chicago to your town, figure up our prices as per quotations in our various catalogues, compare the *total* with the *total* cost of the same goods if purchased from your local dealers. This is the right way, and we feel sure of getting our share of your trade if you will do as we suggest.

Judicious buying means money in the savings bank.

CHICAGO.

WATCH DEPARTMENT.

Men's 18 Size Solid 14-K Gold Stem Wind Watches, with Elgin, Hampden or Waltham Movements. Prices of Elgin Watches and Solid Gold Cases.

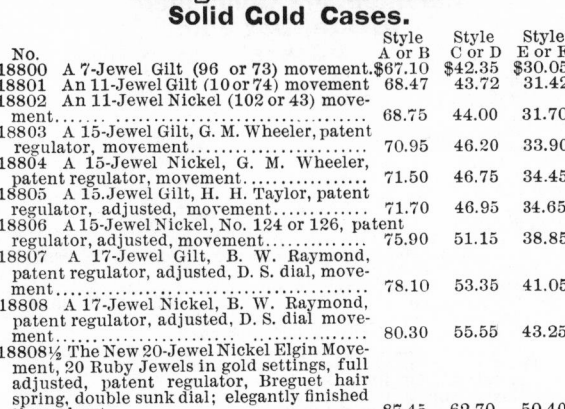

No.		Style A or B	Style C or D	Style E or F
18800	A 7-Jewel Gilt (96 or 73) movement.	$67.10	$42.35	$30.05
18801	An 11-Jewel Gilt (10 or 74) movement	68.47	43.72	31.42
18802	An 11-Jewel Nickel (102 or 43) movement.	68.75	44.00	31.70
18803	A 15-Jewel Gilt, G. M. Wheeler, patent regulator, movement.	70.95	46.20	33.90
18804	A 15-Jewel Nickel, G. M. Wheeler, patent regulator, movement.	71.50	46.75	34.45
18805	A 15-Jewel Gilt, H. H. Taylor, patent regulator, adjusted, movement.	71.70	46.95	34.65
18806	A 15-Jewel Nickel, No. 124 or 126, patent regulator, adjusted, movement.	75.90	51.15	38.85
18807	A 17-Jewel Gilt, B. W. Raymond, patent regulator, adjusted, D. S. dial, movement.	78.10	53.35	41.05
18808	A 17-Jewel Nickel, B. W. Raymond, patent regulator, adjusted, D. S. dial movement.	80.30	55.55	43.25
18808½	The New 20-Jewel Nickel Elgin Movement, 20 Ruby Jewels in gold settings, full adjusted, patent regulator, Breguet hair spring, double sunk dial; elegantly finished throughout.	87.45	62.70	50.40

Style A, Raised Ornaments, Large Diamond in Center. Weight, 55 pwt. 14-K Solid Gold. Case without movement, $62.70.

Style B, 14-K Solid Gold Box Joint Case. Weight, 58 pwt. Raised Ornaments, large Diamond in Horse's Eye. Case without movement, $62.70.

Prices of Waltham Watches with Solid Gold Cases.

No.		Style A or B	Style C or D	Style E or F
18809	A 7-Jewel Gilt (1) movement.	$67.05	$42.30	$30.00
18810	An 11-Jewel Gilt (3) movement.	68.45	43.70	31.40
18811	An 11-Jewel Nickel (3) movement.	68.70	43.95	31.65
18812	A 15-Jewel Gilt P. S. Bartlett, patent regulator, movement.	70.90	46.15	33.85
18813	A 15-Jewel Nickel P. S. Bartlett, patent regulator, movement.	71.45	46.70	34.40
18814	A 15-Jewel Gilt P. S. Bartlett, patent regulator, adjusted, D. S. dial, movement.	73.10	48.35	36.05
18815	A 15-Jewel Nickel, P. S. Bartlett, patent regulator, adjusted, D. S. dial, movement.	73.65	48.90	36.60
18816	A 17-Jewel Gilt (25) patent regulator, adjusted, D. S. dial, movement.	75.85	51.10	38.80
18817	A 17-Jewel Gilt, Appleton-Tracy, patent regulator, adjusted, D. S. dial, movement.	78.05	53.30	41.00
18818	A 17-Jewel Nickel, 35 or Appleton Tracy, patent regulator, adjusted, D. S. dial, movement.	80.25	55.50	43.20
18819	A 17-Jewel Crescent St. Nickel, patent regulator, adjusted, D. S. dial, movement.	84.70	59.95	47.65
18819½	The New 17-Jewel Waltham Vanguard, Gold Settings, gold, patent regulator, full adjusted, double sunk dial. Highest grade 18 size Waltham movement ever made.	95.70	70.95	58.65

Prices of Complete Hampden Watches in Solid Gold Cases.

No		Style A or B	Style C or D	Style E or F
18820	A 7-Jewel gilt movement.	$67.00	$42.25	$29.95
18821	An 11-Jewel gilt movement.	68.40	43.65	31.35
18822	An 11-Jewel nickel movement.	68.65	43.90	31.60
18823	A 16-Jewel, nickel, No. 44 or 64 "Dueber" movement, patent regulator.	71.40	46.65	34.35
18824	A 17-Ruby Jewel, nickel, No. 43 or 63 "J. C. Dueber," movement, adjusted patent regulator, D. S. Dial.	75.80	51.05	38.75
18825	A 17-Ruby Jewel, nickel, No. 47 or 67 "J. C. Dueber Special" movement, adjusted patent regulator, D. S. Dial.	77.60	52.85	41.55
18826	A 17-Ruby Jewel, nickel, Dueber "New Railway" movement, fully adjusted, gold patent regulator, D. S. Dial.	87.60	62.85	51.50
18827	A 17-Ruby Jewel, nickel, Dueber, "Special Railway" movement, fully adjusted, gold patent regulator, D. S. Dial.	97.40	72.85	61.50

Prices of Montgomery Ward & Co's Special Guarantee Watches in Solid Gold Cases.

No.		Style A or B	Style C or D	Style E or F
18828	A 16-Ruby Jewel, nickel movement, named "Montgomery Ward & Co., Extra 16 Jeweled."	$77.70	$52.95	$40.65
18829	A 20-Ruby Jewel, nickel movement named "Montgomery Ward & Co., Extra Railroad Timer."	112.70	87.95	75.65

The Montgomery Ward & Co. Special Guarantee Movements are made especially for us and are the best value for the money in the market. Each movement of this brand is accompanied by Our Special Guarantee Certificate.

For Men's 16 Size Solid Gold Watches, see page 144.

Style A.

Style B.

Style C. 50 pwt. Solid 14-K Gold Case...$37.95

Style D.   50 pwt., 14-K Solid Gold Case. $37.95.

Style E.   Solid 14-K Gold Case.........$25.65

Style F.   Solid 14-K Gold Case·........$25.65

The celebrated H. H. Taylor Elgin Watch Movement has been discontinued by the Elgin Company. We bought a large lot cheap, and we are now furnishing this full jeweled adjusted movement at only a slight advance over the price of unadjusted movement. See quotation 18805.

Style M. Case only. Htg., $17.05. O. F., $15.40

Style N. Case only. Htg., $17.05.   O. F., $1540

Men's 18 Size, 14 K. Gold Filled, Stem Wind, Watches. Guaranteed for 20 Years.

Prices of Complete Elgin Watches in Either of these Boss, 20-Year Guarantee, 14K Gold Filled, 18 Size, Box Joint Cases.

No.		Hunting case.	Open Face case.
18850	A 7-Jewel Gilt (96 or 73) move't...	$21.45	$19.80
18851	An 11-Jewel Gilt (10 or 74) move't.	22.83	21.18
18852	An 11-Jewel Nickel (102 or 43) movement................	23.10	21.45
18853	A 15-Jewel Gilt G. M. Wheeler, Patent Regulator, movement	25.30	23.65
18854	A 15-Jewel Nickel G. M. Wheeler, Patent Regulator, movement	25.85	24.20
18855	15-Jewel Gilt H. H. Taylor. Patent Regulator, Adjusted, movement......	26.05	24.40
18856	A 15-Jewel Nickel, 126 or 124, Patent Regulator, Adjusted, movement...	30.25	28.60
18857	A 17-Jewel Gilt B. W. Raymond, Patent Regulator, Adjusted, double sunk dial, movement................	32.45	30.80
18858	A 17-Jewel Nickel B. W. Raymond, Patent Regulator, Adjusted, double sunk dial, movement................	34.65	33.00
18858½	The new 20-Jewel Nickel Elgin movement, 20 Ruby Jewels in gold settings, full adjusted, patent regulator, Breguet hair spring, double sunk dial, elegantly finished throughout......	40.45	39.35

Prices of Complete Waltham Watches in either of these Boss, 20 Year Guarantee, 14K Gold Filled 18 size, box Joint Cases.

No.		Hunting case.	Open Face case.
18859	A 7-Jewel Gilt (1) movement.......	$20.35	$19.25
18860	An 11-Jewel Gilt (3) movement.....	21.73	20.63
18861	An 11-Jewel Nickel (3) movementt-	22.00	20.90
18862	A 15-Jewel Gilt, P. S. Bartlett, pa... ent regulator, movement.............	24.20	23.10
18863	A 15-Jewel Nickel, P. S. Bartlett, patent regulator, movement............	24.75	23.65
18864	A 15-Jewel Gilt P. S. Bartlett, patent regulator, adjusted, double sunk dial, movement................	26.40	25.30
18865	A 15-Jewel Nickel P. S. Bartlett, patent regulator, adjusted, double sunk dial, movement................	26.95	25.85
18866	17-Jewel Gilt, No. 25, patent regulator, adjusted, double sunk dial, movement................	29.15	28.05
18867	A 17-Jewel Gilt Appleton-Tracy, patent regulator, adjusted, double sunk dial. movement...............	31.35	30.25
18868	A 17-Jewel Nickel Appleton-Tracy or 35, patent regulator, adjusted, double sunk dial, movement.............	33.55	32.45
18869	A 17-Jewel Nickel Crescent St., patent regulator, adjusted, double sunk dial, movement................	37.95	36.85
18870	The Vanguard. New Waltham movement, 17 jewels, in gold settings, gold patent regulator, full adjusted, elaborately finished. Highest grade 18 size Waltham movement ever made......	48.95	47.85

Prices of Complete Hampden Watches in either of these Dueber 14K Gold Filled 20-Year Guarantee Cases.

No.		Hunting case.	Open face. case.
18871	A 7-Jewel Gilt "Exp. Bal." Movement	$19.80	$18.70
18872	An 11-Jewel Gilt "Exp. Bal." Movement	21.17	20.07
18873	An 11-Jewel Nickel "Exp. Bal." Movement	21.45	20.35
18874	A 16-Jewel, nickel, No. 44 or 64, "Dueber" movement, patent regulator.	24.20	23.10
18875	A 17-Ruby Jewel, nickel, No. 43 or 63, "J. C. Dueber" movement, adjusted, patent regulator, D. S. Dial.............	28.60	27.50
18876	A 17-Ruby Jewel, nickel, No. 47 or 67, "J. C. Dueber Special" movement, adjusted, patent regulator, D. S. Dial................	30.30	29.20
18877	A 17-Ruby Jewel, nickel, Dueber "New Railway" movement, fully adjusted, gold patent regulator, D. S. Dial	40.30	39.20
18878	A 17-Ruby Jewel, nickel, Dueber "Special Railway" movement, fully adjusted, gold patent regulator, D. S. Dial.	50.30	49.20

Prices of Montgomery Ward & Co.'s Special guarantee watches in these Dueber 14K Filled 20-Year Guarantee Cases.

No.		Hunting case.	Open face case.
18879	A 16-Ruby Jewel, nickel movement, named Montgomery Ward & Co,, Extra 16-Jewel."................	$30.40	$29.30
18880	A 20-Ruby Jewel, nickel movement, named "Montgomery Ward & Co., Extra Railroad Timer."...............	65 40	64.30

Style O Case only. Htg.,$15.95. O. F., $14.85

Style P.   Caseonly. Htg.,$15.95. O. F., $14.85

Style T. Case only. Htg ,$15.40. O. F., $14.30

Style U. Case only. Htg ,$15.40. O F., $14.30

Notice the reduction we make in price of H. H. Taylor Adjusted Elgin movements.   No more to be had when this lot is sold.   See quotation 18855.

Men's 16 Size 14K Gold Filled, Stem Wind Watches. Guaranteed 20 Years.

Style A1. Case only. Htg., $13.20. O. F., $12.10

Style B1. Case only. Htg., $13.20. O. F., $12.10

Style C1. Case only. Htg., $13.20. O. F., $12.10

Style D1. Case only. Htg., $13.20. O. F., $12.10

Style E1. Case only. Htg., $13.20. O. F., $12.10

Style F1. Case only. Htg., $13.20. O. F., $12.10

Style G1. Case only. Htg., $13.20. O. F., $12.10

Prices of Complete Elgin or Hampden Watches in any 16 size, 20 year guarantee, 14K filled case, on this page.
Elgin Watches.

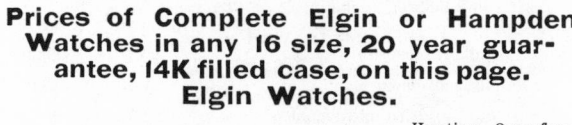

	Hunting case.	Open face case.
18881 A 7-Jewel, gilt mov't, No. 114 or 104.....	$17.60	$16.50
18882 An 11-Jewel, gilt mov't, No. 92 or 105 ..	18.92	17.82
18883 An 11-Jewel, nickel mov't, No. 127 or 128	19.45	18 35
18884 A 15-Jewel, gilt mov't, No. 2 or 106......	20.90	19.80
18885 A 15-Jewel, gilt adjusted mov't, No. 3 or 107	23.60	22.50
18886 A 15-Jewel, nickel adjusted mov't, No. 4 or 108	25.85	24.75
18887 A 15-Jewel, nickel full adjusted mov't, No. 86	32.45	31.35

Hampden Watches.

	Hunting case.	Open face case.
18888 An 11-Jewel, gilt, movement, No. 110...	$18.90	$17.80
18889 A 13-Jewel, nickel movement, No. 109...	21.95	20.85
18890 A 17-Jewel, nickel movement, patent regulator, No 108	23.65	22.55
18891 A 17-Jewel, nickel, movement, patent regulator, adjusted, No. 107 .... :..	25.80	24.70
18892 A 17-Jewel, nickel, adjusted movement, patent regulator, No. 106	29.15	28.05
18893 A 17-Jewel, nickel, full adjusted movement, patent regulator, No. 105	40.15	39.05
18894 A 17-Jewel, nickel, full adjusted movement, patent regulator, No. 104	51.15	50 05
18894½ A 16-Jewel, nickel, patent regulator, Montgomery Ward & Co. movement	22.50	21.40

Style H1. Case only. Htg., $13.20. O. F., $12.10

For Men's 12-Size Filled and 16-Size Gold Cases. See page 144.

Men's 18 Size Dueber & Boss 14-K Gold Filled Stem Wind Watches. 20-Year Guarantee. Fitted with Elgin, Waltham, Hampden or M. W. & Co.'s Movements Complete.

The prices given below are for watch movements mentioned, fitted in any of the 14-K filled, 20 year guarantee cases illustrated on **this page and page 139.** All the cases on **page 138 and 139** are same price. Take your choice.

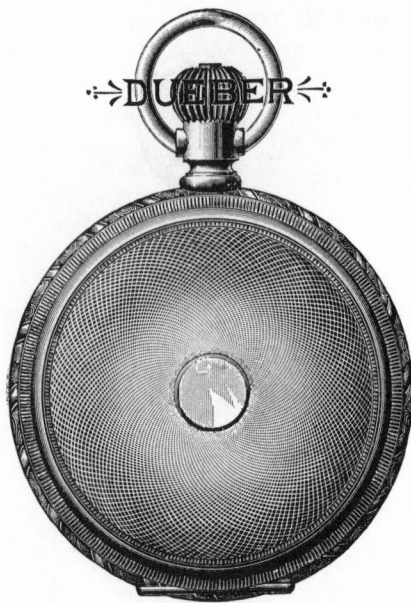

Style J1. Case only. Htg., $12.10; O. F., $11.00.

Style K1. Case only. Htg., $12.10; O. F., $11.00

Complete Hampden Watches.

No.		Hunting case	Open face case.
18895	7-Jewel, Gilt, expansion balance	$16.50	$15.40
18896	11-Jewel, Gilt, expansion balance	17.87	16.77
18897	11-Jewel, Nickel, expansion balance	18.15	17.05
18898	A 16-Jewel, Nickel, No. 44 or 64, "Dueber" movement, patent regulator	20.90	19.80
18899	A 15-Jewel Gilt, No. 49 or 69 "Dueber" movement, patent regulator adjusted	22.55	21.45
18900	A 17-Ruby Jewel, Nickel, No. 43 or 63, "J. C. Dueber" movement, adjusted, patent regulator, D. S. Dial	25.30	24.20
18901	A 17-Ruby Jewel, Nickel, No. 47 or 67, "J. C. Dueber Special" movement, adjusted, patent regulator, D. S. dial	27.00	25.90
18902	A 17-Ruby Jewel, Nickel, Dueber, "New Railway" movement, fully adjusted, gold patent regulator, D. S. dial	37.00	35.90
18903	17-Ruby Jewel, Nickel, Dueber "Special Railway" movement, fully adjusted, gold, patent regulator, D. S. dial	47.00	45.90

Complete Waltham Watches.

No.		Hunting	Open face
18904	A 7-Jewel, Gilt, (1) movement	$16.55	$15.45
18905	An 11-Jewel Gilt (3) movement	17.90	16.80
18906	An 11-Jewel Nickel (3) movement	18.20	17.10
18907	A 15-Jewel, Gilt, P. S. Bartlett patent regulator movement	20.35	19.25
18908	A 15-Jewel, Nickel, P. S. Bartlett patent regulator movement	20.95	19.85
18909	A 15-Jewel, Gilt, P. S. Bartlett patent regulator, adjusted, double sunk dial, movement	22.60	21.50
18910	A 15-Jewel, Nickel, P. S, Bartlett, patent regulator, adjusted, double sunk dial, movement	23.10	22.00
18911	A 17-Jewel, Gilt, No. 25, patent regulator, adjusted, double sunk dial, movement	25.35	24.25
18912	A 17-Jewel, Gilt, Appleton & Tracy patent regulator, adjusted, double sunk dial, movement	27.80	26.40
18913	A 17-Jewel, Nickel, Appleton & Tracy, or 35, patent regulator, adjusted, double sunk dial, movement	29.70	28.60
18914	A 17-Jewel, Nickel, Crescent St., patent regulator, adjusted, double sunk dial, movement	34.10	33.00
18914½	**The Vanguard.** A New Waltham Movement, 17 Jewels in gold settings, gold patent regulator, adjusted, double sunk dial, elaborately finished	45.10	44.00

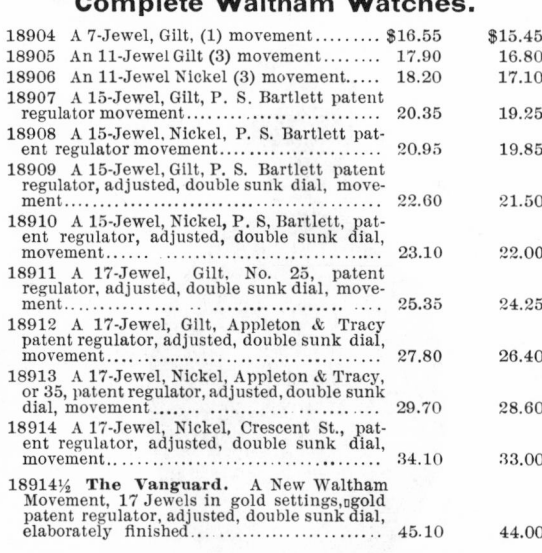
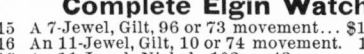

Style L1. Case only. Htg., $12.10; O. F., $11.00.

Style M1. Case only. Htg., $12.10; O. F., $11.00

Complete Elgin Watches.

No.		Hunting	Open face
18915	A 7-Jewel, Gilt, 96 or 73 movement	$16.60	$15.50
18916	An 11-Jewel, Gilt, 10 or 74 movement.	17.95	16.85
18917	An 11-Jewel, Nickel, 102 or 43 movement	18.25	17.15
18918	A 15-Jewel, Gilt, G. M. Wheeler, patent regulator movement	20.40	19.30
18919	A 15-Jewel Nickel G.M. Wheeler, patent regulator, movement	21.00	19.90
18920	A 15-Jewel, Gilt, H. H. Taylor Patent Regulator, adjusted, movement	21.15	20.05
18921	A 15-Jewel, Nickel 126 or 124, patent regulator, adjusted, movement	23.10	22.00
18922	A 17-Jewel, Gilt, B. W. Raymond, patent regulator, adjusted, double sunk dial, movement	27.55	26.45
18923	A 17-Jewel, Nickel, B. W. Raymond, patent regulator, adjusted, double sunk dial, movement	29.75	28.65
18923½	The New 20-Jewel, Nickel, Elgin Movement, 20-ruby jewels in gold settings; full adjusted, patent regulator, Breguet hair spring, double sunk dial; elegantly finished throughout	36.57	35.47

Montgomery Ward & Co.'s Special Guarantee Watches.

No.		Hunting	Open face
18924	A 16-Ruby Jewel, Nickel, movement named "Montgomery Ward & Co. Extra 16 Jeweled"	$27.10	$26.00
18925	A 20-Ruby Jewel, Nickel, movement named "Montgomery Ward & Co. Extra Railroad Timer"	52.10	51.00

Our Special Guarantee Movements are made up for us and are absolutely the best watches in the world for the price. Each movement contains our Special Guarantee Certificate.

Style N1. Case only. Htg., $12.10: O. F., $11 00.

Style O1. Case only. Htg., $12.10; O. F., $11.00

The Celebrated H. H. Taylor Watch has been discontinued by the Elgin Watch Co. We bought the last lot cheap, and while they last, we will sell these full-jeweled, adjusted watches at only a slight advance on the unadjusted grades. See quotation No. 18920.

Men's 18 Size 14K Filled, Stem Wind Watches.   Guaranteed 20 Years.
For Prices with Elgin, Waltham or Hampden Movements See Page 138.

Style P1. Case only. Htg., $12.10; Open Face, $11.00.

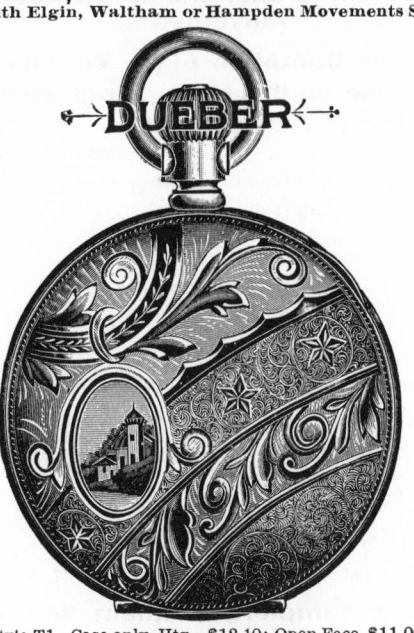

Style T1. Case only. Htg., $12.10; Open Face, $11.00.

Style U1. Case only. Htg., $12.10; Open Face, $11.00

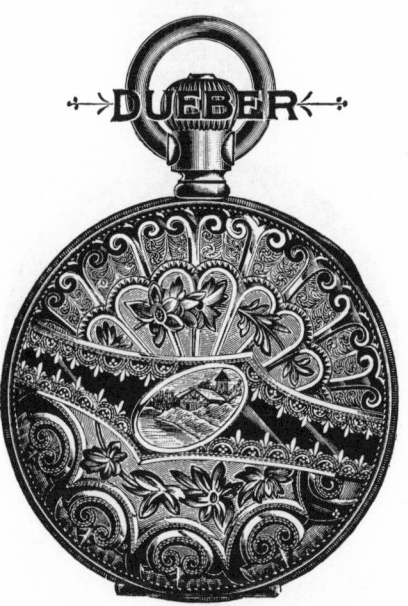

Style A2. Case only. Htg., $12.10; Open Face, $11.00.

Style B2. Case only. Htg., $12.10; Open Face, $11.00.

Style C2. Case only. Htg., $12.16; Open Face, $11.00

Style D2. Case only. Htg., $12.10; Open Face, $11.00.

Style E2. Case only, Htg., $12.10; Open Face, $11.00.

Style F2. Case only Htg., $12.10; Open Face, $11.00

Men's 18 Size 10K Filled, Stem Wind Watches. Guaranteed 15 Years, with Elgin, Waltham and Hampden Movements.

Style G2. Case only. Htg. $8.25; O. F. $7.15.

Style J2. Case only. Htg. $8.25; O. F. $7.15.

Style L2. Case only. Htg. $8.25; O. F. $7.15.

Prices of Complete Elgin Watches in any case on this page. Gold Filled. 15 Year guarantee.

No.	Hunting case.	Open face case.
18926 A 7-Jewel Gilt (96 or 73) Movement......	$12.65	$11.55
18927 An 11-Jewel Gilt (10 or 74) Movement....	14.02	12.92
18928 An 11-Jewel Nickel (102 or 43) Movement..............................	14.30	13.20
18929 A 15-Jewel Gilt G. M. Wheeler Movement, patent regulator..............................	16.50	15.40
18930 A 15-Jewel Nickel G. M. Wheeler Movement, patent regulator....................	17.05	15.95
18931 A 15-Jewel Gilt H. H. Taylor Adjusted Movement, patent regulator....................	17.25	16.15
18932 A 15-Jewel Nickel No. (124 or 126) Adjusted Movement, patent regulator.............	18.25	18.15
18933 A 17-Jewel Gilt B. W. Raymond Adjusted Movement, patent regulator, D. S. D............	23.65	22.55
18934 A 17-Jewel Nickel B. W. Raymond Adjusted Movement, patent regulator, D. S. D....	25.85	24.75
18934½ The New 20-Jewel Nickel Elgin Movement. 20 ruby jewels in gold settings, full adjusted, patent regulator, Breguet hair spring, double sunk dial, elegantly finished throughout	32.75	31.65

Price of Complete Waltham Watches in any case on this page. 15 year guarantee 10K Gold Filled.

No.	Hunting case.	Open face case.
18935 A 7-Jewel Gilt No. 1 Movement..........	$12.60	$11.50
18936 An 11-Jewel Gilt No. 3 Movement.......	14.10	13.00
18937 An 11-Jewel Nickel No. 3 Movement.....	14.25	13.15
18938 A 15-Jewel Gilt P. S. Bartlett Movement, patent regulator.......	16.45	15.35
18939 A 15-Jewel Nickel P. S. Bartlett Movement, patent regulator...................	17.00	15.90
18940 A 15-Jewel Gilt P. S. Bartlett Adjusted Movement, patent regulator, D. S. Dial........	18.70	17.60
18941 A 15-Jewel Nickel P. S. Bartlett Adjusted Movement, patent regulator, D. S. Dial........	19.20	18.10
18942 A 17-Jewel Gilt No. 25 Adjusted Movement, patent regulator......................	21.40	20.30
18943 A 17-Jewel Gilt Appleton-Tracy Adjusted Movement, patent regulator, D. S. Dial........	23.60	22.50
18944 A 17-Jewel Nickel Appleton-Tracy Adjusted Movement, patent regulator, D. S. Dial.	25.80	24.70
18945 A 17-Jewel Nickel Crescent St. Adjusted Movement, patent regulator, D. S. Dial........	30.25	29.15
18946 The Vanguard New Waltham Movement, 17 jewels, gold settings, gold patent regulator, full adjusted, elegantly finished................	42.35	41.25

Prices of Complete Hampden Watches in any case on this page, 10K Gold Filled. Warranted 15 Years.

No.	Hunting case.	Open face case.
18947 A 7-Jewel, gilt, exp. bal. mov't...........	$12.55	$11.45
18948 An 11-Jewel, gilt, exp. bal. mov't.........	13.95	12.85
18949 An 11-Jewel, nickel, exp. bal. mov't......	14.20	13.10
18950 A 16-Jewel, nickel, No. 44 or 64 "Deuber" mov't, patent regulator...........	16.95	15.85
18951 A 17-Ruby Jewel, nickel, No. 43 or 63, "J. C. Dueber," adjusted patent regulator, D. S. Dial, mov't....................	21.35	20.25
18952 A 17-Ruby Jewel, nickel, No. 47 or 67, "J. C. Dueber" special movement, adjusted, patent regulator, D. S. Dial...............	23.15	22.05
18953 A 17-Ruby Jewel, nickel, "Dueber New Railway" movement fully adjusted, gold patent regulator, D. S. Dial......................	33.15	32.05
18954 A 17-Ruby Jewel, nickel, "Dueber Special Railway" movement, fully adjusted, gold patent regulator, D. S. Dial......................	43.15	42.05

Prices of Montgomery Ward & Co. Special Guarantee Watches in any gold filled case on this page.

No.	Hunting case.	Open face case.
18955 A 16-Ruby Jewel, nickel movement, named "Montgomery Ward & Co., extra 16 jeweled."........................	$27.65	$26.00
18956 A 20-Ruby Jeweled, nickel movement, named "Montgomery Ward & Co., extra railroad timer."..................................	62.65	61.00

Sty H2. Case only. Htg. $8.25; O. F. $7.15

Style K2. Case only. Htg. $8.25; O. F. $7.15

Style M2. Case only. Htg. $8.25; O. F. $7 15

The Elgin Watch Co. have discontinued making the celebrated H. H. Taylor watch. We have purchased the last lot, and while they last we will sell these full jeweled adjusted movements at only a slight advance over the unadjusted grade. See quotation No. 18931.

Dust Proof Screw Bezel and Back Stem Wind Watches.

These Dust Proof Cases are the strongest and most durable cases made. The Monarch Cases, styles N2, P2 and U2, are 14k gold filled, warranted 21 years. Montauk Cases, styles O2, T2 and A3, are 10k filled, warranted 15 years.

Prices of Complete Elgin Watches in Dust Proof Screw Bezel Filled Cases.

	14K Styles. N 2 P 2 U 2	10K Styles. O 2 T 2 A 3
18957 A 7-Jewel Gilt (96 or 73) movement...	$13 20	$ 9.35
18958 An 11-Jewel Gilt (10 or 74) movement.	14.57	10.72
18959 An 11-Jewel Nickel (102 or 43) movement	14.85	11.00
18960 A 15-Jewel Gilt G. M. Wheeler, Movement, patent regulator.....................	17.05	13.20
18961 A 15-Jewel Nickel G. M. Wheeler Movement, patent regulator...............	17.60	13.75
18962 A 15-Jewel Gilt H. H. Taylor Adjusted Movement, patent regulator.............	17.80	13.95
18963 A 15-Jewel Nickel No. 124 Adjusted Movement, patent regulator.............	22.00	18.15
18964 A 17-Jewel Gilt B. W. Raymond Adjusted Movement, patent regulator, D.S.D.	24.20	20.35
18965 A 17-Jewel Nickel B. W. Raymond Adjusted Movement, patent regulator, D. S. D.	26.40	22.55
18965½. The New 20-Jewel, Nickel Elgin Movement, 20 Jewels in gold settings, full adjusted, Breguet hairspring, patent regulator, double sunk dial, elegantly finished throughout	33.30	29.45

Prices of Complete Waltham Watches in Dust Proof Screw Bezel Filled Cases.

	14K Styles. N 2 P 2 U 2	10K Styles. O 2 T 2 A 3
18966 A 7-Jewel Gilt No. 1 Movement..	$13.15	$9.30
18967 An 11-Jewel Gilt No. 3 Movement	14.55	10.70
18968 An 11-Jewel Nickel No. 3 Movement...	14.80	10.95
18969 A 15-Jewel Gilt P. S. Bartlett Movement, patent regulator....................	17.00	13.15
18970 A 15-Jewel Nickel P. S. Bartlett Movement, patent regulator....................	17.55	13.70
18971 A 15-Jewel Gilt P. S. Bartlett Adjusted Movement, patent regulator, D.S. Dial....	19.25	15.40
18972 A 15-Jewel Nickel P. S. Bartlett Adjusted Mov't., patent reg., D. S. Dial......	19.75	15.90
18973 A 17-Jewel Gilt No. 25 Adjusted Movement, patent regulator................	21.95	18.10
18974 A 17-Jewel Gilt Appleton-Tracy Adj. Mov't., patent regulator, D. S. Dial.........	24.15	20.30
18975 A 17-Jewel Nickel Appleton-Tracy Adj. Mov't., patent regulator, D. S. Dial......	26.35	22.50
18976 A 17-Jewel Crescent St., Adj. Mov't., patent regulator, D. S. Dial................	30.80	26.95
18977 The Vanguard New Waltham Mov't., 17 Jewels in gold settings, gold patent regulator, full adjusted, elaborately finished.....	41.80	37.95

Prices of Complete Hampden Watches in Dust Proof Screw Bezel Filled Cases.

	14K Styles. N 2 P 2 U 2	10K Styles. O 2 T 2 A 3
18978 A 7-Jewel Gilt Exp. Bal. Mov't.........	$13.10	$9.25
18979 An 11-Jewel, Gilt Exp. Bal. Mov't......	14.55	10.65
18980 An 11-Jewel, Nickel Exp. Bal. Mov't..	14.75	10 90
18981 A 16-Jewel, Nickel, No. 44 or 64 "Dueber" movement, patent regulator..........	17.50	13.65
18982 A 17-Ruby Jewel, nickel, No. 43 or 63 "J. C Dueber" movement, adjusted patent regulator, D. S. Dial........	21.90	18.05
18983 A 17-Ruby Jewel, nickel, No 47 or 67 "J. C. Dueber" Specia movement, adjusted, patent regulator, D. S. Dial........	23.70	19.85
18984 A 17-Ruby Jewel, nickel, "Dueber New Railway" movement, fully adjusted, gold patent regulator, D.S. Dial................	33.70	29.85
18985 A 17-Ruby Jewel, nickel, "Dueber Special Railway" movement, fully adjusted, gold patent regulator, D. S. Dial...........	43.70	39.85

Prices of Complete Montgomery Ward & Co.'s Special Guarantee Watches in Screw Bezel Cases.

	14K Styles. N 2 P 2 U 2	10K Styles. O 2 T 2 A 3
18986 A 16-Ruby Jewel, nickel movement named "Montgomery Ward & Co. Extra 16-Jeweled."....	$23.80	$19.95
18987 A 20 Ruby Jewel, nickel, movement named "Montgomery Ward & Co. Extra Railroad Timer.".	58.80	54.95

Style N2. Case only. 14k filled $8.80

Style P2. Case only. 14k filled $8 80

Style U2. Case only. 14k filled $8.80

Style O2. Case only. 10k filled $4.95

Style T2. Case only. 10k filled $4.95

Style A3. Case only. 10k filled $4.95

Notice our Reduced prices on the Celebrated H. H. Taylor Watch No. 18962. The Elgin Co. have discontinued this grade and we bought the last lot cheap. While they last you can buy these full-jeweled adjusted watches at a slight advance on the unadjusted grades. See No. 18962.

SPECIAL BARGAINS IN MEN'S STEM WIND WATCHES.

Every watch on this page is quoted at a specially low price. They are leaders with us and only the large quantity we sell enables us to quote such low prices.

$3.65   **$3.65**

18988 Solid Silver Hunting Case, beautifully engraved, fitted with 11-jewel nickel movement, micrometer expansion balance, stem wind and set, highly finished and accurately regulated, making the most elegant gentleman's watch ever sold for such a low price. In addition to watch we include a full length coin silver chain, No. 19402, and a handsome roll plate charm. We engrave initials on the watch when so ordered without extra cnarge.
Price, complete.. ....$8.50

18989 Here's a Watch, destined to fill a long felt want; in fact, a watch that is both good and cheap. The case is silverine and is a man,s medium size. It looks as well as silver and wears better. The movement is a 7-jewel nickel stem wind and set, with expansion balance, and is finely finished throughout. As to time keeping quality, we have this watch made for us, with the stipulation that, every movement must be subjected to a trial before leaving the factory, and that it must run as well as an Elgin or Waltham 7-jewel movement. We confidently recommend it as the best low-priced watch in the world. Price.......................$3.65

18990 Solid Silver 5 oz. Hunting Case, large 18 size stem,wind and set, fitted with 11-jewel, Waltham, Elgin or Hampden movement, expansion balance, stem wind and set, perfectly regulated and warranted to keep accurate time; also a solid silver double strand chain included. See cut above.
Price of watch and chain, complete .. .$15.75

A Howard for   Watch $27.50.

18991 An 18 size, American movement, jeweled in the escapement, expansion balance, stem wind and set, of A1 time keeping quality, fully warranted, cased in a silverine open face case, making a splendid watch for the price.
.............................$4.10
8991A A similar movement in hunting style, silverine case...................$4.80

18992 Elegant Boss 14k Filled Hunting Case, with solid gold bow, crown and joints; warranted for 20 years; fitted with genuine Howard Full Jewel Patent Regulator, stem wind and set movement, fully guaranteed. This quotation is a special one which will be withdrawn as soon as the limited supply of these watches is disposed of. Price only $27.50
With engraved case 29.50

18993 The Celebrated H. H. Taylor, Elgin movement, 15-jewel, patent regulator, adjusted to heat and cold, stem wind and pendant set, fitted in dust proof screw bezel and back, gold filled case, guaranteed 15 years. engraved like illustration; special price for this lot of watches while they last $12.95
Same movement in solid silver, 3 oz. screw bezel and back case...........................$12.00
Same movement in 14k filled screw bezel, case guaranteed 20 years................................$17.80

Notice our special offer on the celebrated H. H. Taylor watches quoted on pages 135 to 141,

18 Size Stem Wind, Solid Silver, Silveroid and Silver Filled Watches.
Waltham Screw, Bezel and Solid Back Cases.

Styles 4X and 3X have gold ring around stem and gold reflectors inside bezel.

Price of case only.

Style 4X. 4 oz., solid silver screw bezel plain............$9.35
   "   3X. 3 "   "   "   "   " 8.25
   "   2X. 3 " filled "   "   " 3.30
   "   1X. 3 " nickel "   "   " 1.10

Extra for gold inlaid backs on any of above cases except style 1X, $1.10. Designs; Horse. Locomotive and Stag. Style IX not made gold inlaid.

Fahys Screw Bezel and Back Cases.

Style 4W. 4 oz., solid silver screw B. & B. plain.........$5.77
Style 3W. 3 oz.,   "   "   "   " 4.67
Style 2W. 3 oz., filled "   "   " 3.30
Style 1W. 3 oz., ore   "   "   " 1.10
Style W. 3 oz., "   "   " engraved......... 1.35

Extra for gold inlaid backs on any of above cases except 1W and W, $1.10. 1W and W are not made with gold inlaid backs.

Style 4W. Gold Inlaid.....................$6 87

Style 4X, Gold Inlaid $10.45

For prices of these cases with movements, see below.

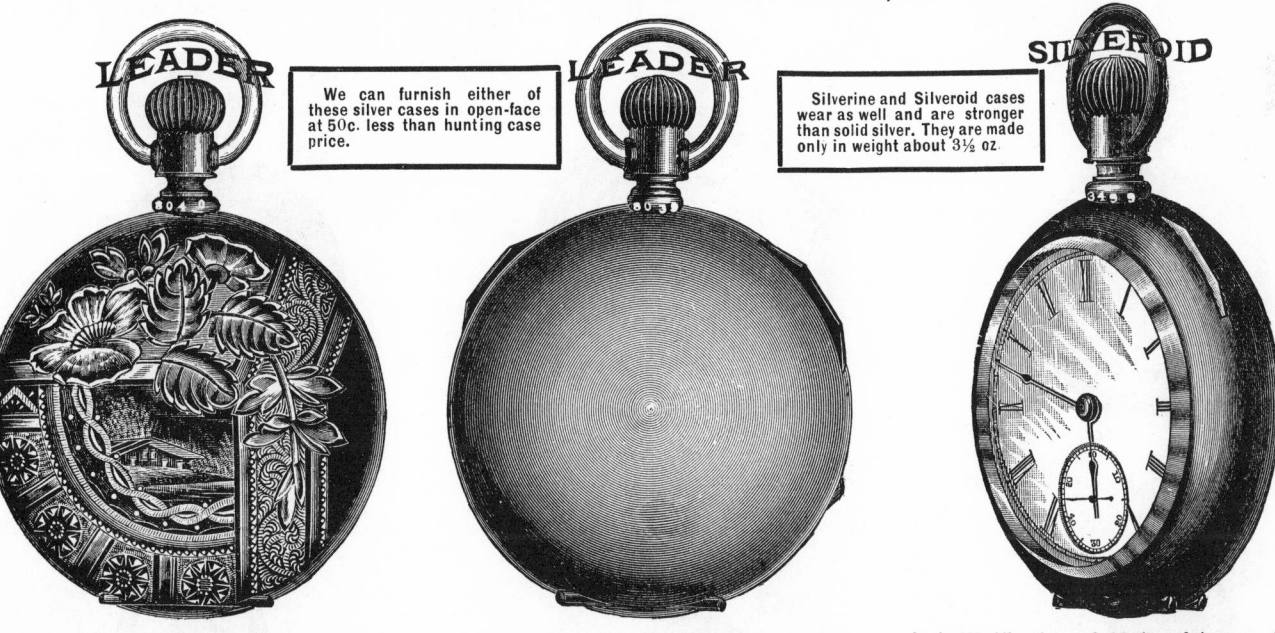

We can furnish either of these silver cases in open-face at 50c. less than hunting case price.

Silverine and Silveroid cases wear as well and are stronger than solid silver. They are made only in weight about 3½ oz.

Style 4S. Silver 4 oz., Htg. Case only ....$7.42.
Style 3S. "   3 "   "   "   .... 6.05.

Style 4R. Silver 4oz., Htg. Case only .....$6.87.
  " 3R   "   3 "   "   "   ..... 5 50.

Style 3V. Silverine o. f 18 size, plain case alone.$0.85
  " 2V.   "   "   18 " Eng. Stag " " 1.35
  " 1V.   "   Htg. 18 " plain " " 1.50

We can furnish open-face silverine cases, style of No. 18993, page 142, for 25c more than price of plain case.

Prices of Elgin, Waltham and Hampden Watches Complete.	Style 3V	Style 1X or 1W	Style W or 2V	Style 1V	Style 2X or 2W	Style 3W	Styze 3R	Style 4W	Style 3S	Style 4R	Style 4S	Style 3X	Style 4X
18993½ 7-Jewel, nickel, Trenton or Standard....................	$ 4.10	$ 4.40	$ 4.75	$ 4.80	$ 6.60	$ 8.00	$ 8.80	$ 9.07	$ 9.35	$10.17	$10.72	$11.55	$12.65
18994 7-Jewel, gilt, Elgin, Waltham or Hampden................	5.22	5.50	5.75	5.90	7.70	9.07	9.90	10.17	10 45	11.27	11.82	12 65	13.75
18995 11 " " " "	6.62	6.87	7.12	7.27	9.08	10,44	11.27	11.54	11.82	12.64	13.19	14.02	15.12
18996 15 " " G. M. Wheeler, Elgin or No. 15 Waltham gilt...................................	9.10	9.35	9.60	9.75	11.55	12,92	13.75	14.02	14.30	15.12	15.67	16.50	17.60
18997 15-Jewel, nickel, G. M. Wheeler, Elgin, No. 15 nickel Waltham, or No. —64 Hampden..........................	9.65	9.90	10.15	10.30	12.10	13.47	14.30	14.57	14.85	15.67	16.22	17 05	18.15
18997½ 15-Jewel, gilt adjusted, H. H. Taylor, Elgin..........	9.85	10.10	10.35	10.50	12.30	13.67	14.50	14.77	15.05	15.87	16.42	17.25	18.35
18998 15-Jewel, gilt, adj. P. S. Bartlett, Waltham or No. 49 Hampden....................................	11.30	11.55	11.80	11.95	13.75	15.12	15.95	16.22	16.50	17.32	17.87	18.70	19.80
18999 15-Jewel, nickel adj. 124 Elgin or P. S. Bartlett, Waltham.........................	11.85	12.10	12.35	12.50	14.30	15.67	16.50	16.77	17.05	17.87	18.42	19.25	20.35
19000 17-Jewel, gilt, adj. No. 25 Waltham or 17 jewel Hampden, J. C. Dueber nickel	14.05	14.30	14.55	14.70	16.50	17.87	18.70	18.97	19.25	20.07	20.62	21.45	22.55
19001 17-Jewel, gilt, B. W. Raymond, Elgin or Appleton, Tracy & Co., Waltham 17-jewel....................	16.25	16.50	16.75	16.90	18.70	20.06	20.90	21.17	21.45	22.27	22.82	23.65	24.75
19002 17-Jewel, nickel, B. W. Raymond, Elgin or Appleton, Tracy & Co., Waltham....................	18.45	18.70	18.95	19.10	20.90	22.26	23.10	23.37	23.65	24.47	25.02	25.85	26.95
19003 17-Jewel, nickel, Crescent Street Waltham............	22.85	23.10	23.35	23.50	25.30	26.66	27.50	27.77	28.05	28.87	29.42	30.25	31.35
19004 17-Jewel, nickel, New Railway Hampden......	25.75	26.10	26.35	26.50	28.30	29.67	30.50	30.77	31.05	31.87	32.42	33.25	34.35
19005 17-Jewel, nickel, Vanguard, Waltham................	33.85	34.10	34.35	34.50	36.30	37.66	38.50	38.77	39 05	39.87	40.42	41.25	42.35
19006 17-Jewel, nickel, Special Railway Hampden............	35.75	36.10	36.35	36.50	38.30	39.67	40.50	40.77	41.05	41.87	42.42	43.25	44.25

The Elgin Watch Co. have discontinued the celebrated H. H. Taylor Watch. We bought the last lot cheap, and while they last we will sell this full jeweled adjusted watch at a slight advance over the unadjusted grade. See No. 18997 1-2.

SPECIAL BARGAINS IN WATCHES.

19007 Our "Lady Grange" Bargain. An elegant 14k solid gold case, fitted with our 16 Ruby jewel nickel expansion bal. Breguet hairspring, adjusted movement, the "Lady Grange." This movement is accompanied by our special guarantee certificate and is warranted when properly regulated to run perfectly. The outfit includes a beautiful solid gold Victoria chain, and a handsome oak case, silver trimmed, with lock and key,
Price only.................$27.00

19008 Another Special Offer. Ladies O Size, gold filled case. Warranted five years. Beautifully engraved and fitted with Elgin or Waltham, 7 jewel movement, stem wind and set. Price....$8.80
19009½ Same as above but case guaranteed 15 years...................$11.00

19009 A New Special Bargain in Ladies' Watches. Dueber 14k filled case, guaranteed 20 years; elegant star and vermicelli engraving, exactly like illustration, fitted with a 13-jewel nickel U. S. Waltham movement, stem wind and set. A beautiful roll plate chain and elegant oak case, silver trimmed, with lock and key. Price only.......................$16.00

19010 Ladies' or Misses' Chatelaine Watch 0 size, 14k gold filled, open face, engraved case, guaranteed for 20 years. Fitted with Elgin or Waltham movement. Stem wind and set. Price...........................$10.00

19011 Boys' Nickel Watch. This is a first-class article, guaranteed to keep good time. Movement is stem wind and set.
Price with nickel case.......................$3.00
Price, with solid silver case..................4.50

19012 Solid Silver Open Face Chatelaine Watch, ladies' or misses' size, beautifully engraved case, with nickel cylinder movement, stem wind and set, gold hands and second hand, plain or fancy dial. Price........................$7.00
19013 Same movement without second hand, fitted in plain, nickel, open face case............4.25

The postage on a watch is 12 cents. See page 1 for Insurance Mail.

We charge for engraving initials 2½c per letter for script, 5½c for Old English

19014 Men's 16 Size 14k Solid Gold Hunting Case, fitted with 11-jewel Elgin, Waltham or Hampden movement.
Price each............................$31.00
19014½ Same with full jewel movement.
Price each............................$33.50

19015 A new size in watches—12 size. Just the thing for gentlemen who want a small size watch, or ladies who prefer a size larger than regular. This 14k filled 20-year guarantee hunting case, plain or engraved, with 11-jewel Elgin, Waltham or Hampden movement, stem wind and set. Price.............$16.75
Fitted with 15-Jewel Movement..... ....21.75

19016 Men's 16 Size, 14k Heavy Solid Gold Case, full engraved, fitted with full jewel Waltham, Elgin or Hampden movement, hunting style, stem wind and set..........................$43.25

LADIES' 6 SIZE 14K SOLID GOLD STEM WIND WATCHES.
For Prices With Elgin, Waltham or Hampden Movements See Table Below.

Style B3. 2 Diamonds, 3 Rubies, any name, furnished in one week's time. Case only, $27.30

Style C3. Raised ornaments, 1 Diamond. Case only, $28.00.

Style D3. Fancy engraved, 1 Diamond Case only, $25.00.

Style E3. Plain polished, 1 Diamond. Case only, $24 00.

Style F3, Heavy Raised Ornaments. Case only, $24.00.

Style G3. Fancy Engraved. Case only, $20.00.

Style H3. Fancy Engraved. Case only, $22.50.

Style J3. Fancy Engraved. Case only, $20.00.

Style K3. Fancy Engraved. Case only, $22.50.

Style L3. Fancy Engraved. Case only, $19.00

Style M3. Fancy Engraved. Case only, $19 00.

Style N3. Fancy Engraved Case only, $19.00.

Catalogue No.	Prices of Complete Watches.	Style B3	Style C3	Style D3	Styles E3 & F3	Styles H3 & K3	Styles J3 & G3	Styles L3 M3 N3
19027 A	7-Jewel Gilt Exp. Bal. Elgin, Waltham or Hampden Mov't............	$32.25	$33.02	$29.95	$28.95	$27.45	$24.95	$23.95
19028 An 11	" " " " " " " "	33.63	34 40	32.10	31.10	29.60	27.10	26.10
19029 An 11	" Nickel " " " " "	34 18	34.95	31.88	30.88	29.38	26.88	25 88
19030 An 11	" " " " " " " Jewels in Settings	35.00	35 77	32.70	31.70	30.20	27.70	26.70
19032 A 15	" " " " " " " " "	38.30	39.07	36.00	35.00	33.50	31.00	30.00
19033 A 16	" " " " " " " " "	39.30	40 07	37.00	35.96	34.45	31.95	30.95
19034 A 17	" " " " " " " " "	49.30	50.07	47.00	46.00	44.50	42.00	41.00
19035 A 15	" " " " " Montgomery Ward & Co.'s Mov't with Special Guarantee Certificate.............	35.30	36.00	33.00	32.00	30.50	28.00	27.00
19036 A	16-Jewel Nickel Chronometer Bal., Montgomery Ward & Co. Mov't, with Special Guarantee Certificate........................	42 30	43.00	40.00	39.00	37.50	34.95	33.95

Montgomery Ward & Co. Movements are made to run. They are the best value we can offer. We send a written guarantee with each movement, and every purchaser is insured satisfaction.
We charge for engraving initials 2½ cents per letter for script style; 5 cents for Old English.

10—2nd

LADIES' 6 SIZE SOLID 14K GOLD STEM WIND WATCHES.
For Prices with Elgin, Waltham or Hampden Movements, See Table Below.

Style O3.   Fancy Engraved.
Case only, $18.50.

Style P3.   Fancy Engraved.
Case only, $18.50.

Style T3.   Raised Ornaments.
Case only, $16.00.

Style U3.   Fancy Engraved.
Case only, $18.50.

Style A4.   Fancy Engraved.
Case only, $15.00.

Style B4.   Fancy Engraved.
Case only, $14.50.

Style C4.   Fancy Engraved.
Case only, $14.50.

Style D4.   Fancy Engraved.
Case only, $14.50.

Style E4.   Fancy Engraved.
Case only, $13.00.

Style F4.   Fancy Engraved.
Case only, $13.00.

Style G4.   Fancy Engraved.
Case only, $12.50.

Style H4.   Fancy Engraved.
Case only, $12.00.

Prices of Complete Watches.

Catalogue Number.	Style. H 4	Style. G 4	Styles. E 4 F 4	Styles. D 4 C 4 B 4	Style. A 4	Style. T 3	Styles. U 3 P 3 O 3
19037 A 7-Jewel, Gilt, Expansion Balance, Elgin, Waltham or Hampden Movement..............	$16.95	$17.45	$17.95	$19.45	$19.95	$20.95	$23.45
19038 An 11-Jewel, Gilt, Expansion Balance, Elgin or Waltham Movement	18.32	18.82	19.32	20.82	21.32	22.32	24.82
19039 An 11-Jewel, Nickel, Expansion Balance, Elgin or Waltham Movement....................	18.87	19.37	19.87	21.37	21.87	22.87	25.37
19040 An 11-Jewel, Nickel in Settings, Expansion Balance, Waltham or Hampden Movement....	19.70	20.20	20.70	22.20	22.70	23.70	26.20
19042 A 15-Jewel, Nickel in Settings, Expansion Balance, Elgin, Waltham or Hampden Movement	23.00	23.50	24.00	25.50	26.00	27.00	29.50
19043 A 16-Jewel, Nickel in Settings, Expansion Balance, Hampden Movement...	24.10	24.60	25.10	26.60	27.10	28.10	30.60
19044 A 17-Jewel, Nickel in Settings, Expansion Balance, Elgin, Waltham or Hampden Movement	34.00	34.50	35.00	36.50	37.00	38.00	40.50
19045 A 15-Jewel, Nickel in Settings, Expansion Balance, Montgomery Ward & Co. Movement with Special Guarantee Certificate....................	20.00	20.45	20.90	22.45	22.95	23.95	26.45
19046 A 16-Jewel, Nickel Chronometer Balance, Montgomery Ward & Co. Movement, with Special Guarantee Certificate....................	27.05	27.55	28.05	29.55	30.05	31.05	33.55

We Charge for Engraving 2½ Cents per Letter for Script Style, 5 Cents for Old English.

LADIES' O SIZE SOLID 14K GOLD STEM WIND WATCHES.
For Prices with Elgin or Waltham Movements, See Table Below.

Style J4. Raised Ornaments. 1 Diamond. Case only, $23.50.

Style K4. Raised Ornaments. 1 Diamond. Case only, $23.50.

Style L4. Raised, Ornaments. 1 Diamond. Case only, $23.50.

Style M4. 2 Rubies, 1 Diamond. Case only, $23.50.

Style N4. Raised Ornaments. Case only, $19.25.

Style O4. 3 Emeralds, 1 Diamond. Case only, $19.25.

Style P4. Raised Ornaments. Case only, $19.00,

Style T4. Fancy Eng., 1 Diamond. Case only, $19.00.

Style U4. Fancy Engraved. Case only, $16.00.

Style A5. Fancy Engraved. Case only, $16.00.

Style B5. Fancy Engraved. Case only, $16.00.

Style C5. Fancy Engraved. Case only, $15.00.

Style D5. Fancy Engraved. $15.00.

Style E5. Fancy Engraved. Case only, $15.00.

Style F5. Fancy Engraved. Case only, $11.50.

Style G5. Fancy Engraved. Case only, $11.50.

Style H5. Fancy Engraved. Case only, $11.00.

Style J5. Case only. Engine Turned, $11.00.

Catalogue No.	**Prices of Complete Watches.**	Styles J5 H5	Styles G5 F5	Styles E5 D5 C5	Styles B5 A5 U4	Styles T4 P4	Styles O4 N4	Styles M4 L4 K4 J4
19047	A 7-Jewel, Gilt, Expansion Balance, Elgin or Waltham Movement........	$15.95	$16.45	$19.90	$20.90	$23.90	$24.15	$28.40
19048	An 11-Jewel, Gilt, Expansion Balance, Elgin or Waltham Movement	17.32	17.82	21.31	22.31	25.31	25.56	29.81
19049	An 11-Jewel, Nickel, Expansion Balance, Elgin or Waltham Movement.	17.87	18.37	21.86	22.86	25.86	26.11	30.36
19051	A 15-Jewel, Nickel, Expansion Balance, Elgin or Waltham Movement...	22.00	22.50	26.05	27.05	30.05	30.30	34.55
19052	A 17-Jewel, Nickel, Expansion Balance, Elgin or Waltham Movement...	33.00	33.50	37.05	38.05	41.05	41.30	45.55

We guarantee all Watch Movements for one year. We don't mean by this that they are intended to last only a year, but we give purchasers this length of time to thoroughly **test** their watches, and if they fail to perform satisfactorily they can be returned to us and exchanged or repaired free of charge.

LADIES' 6 SIZE 14K GOLD FILLED STEM WIND WATCHES, GUARANTEED 20 YEARS.

For Prices with Elgin, Waltham or Hampden Movements, See Table Below.

Style K5. Raised Gold Ornaments, 1 diamond. Case only, $11.55.

Style L5. Raised Gold Ornaments, 1 diamond. Case only, $11.55.

Style M5. Fancy Engraved, 1-Diamond. Case only, $11.00.

Style N5. Fancy Engraved, 1-Diamond. Case only, $11.00.

Style O5. Fancy Engraved Case only, $9.90.

Style P5. Fancy Engraved. Case only, $9.90.

Style T5. Fancy Engraved. Case only, $8.80.

Style U5. Fancy Engraved Case only, $8.80.

Style A6. Fancy Engraved. Case only, $8.80.

Style B6. Fancy Engraved. Case only, $8.90.

Style C6. Fancy Engraved. Case only, $8.90.

Style D6. Fancy Engraved. Case only, $8.90.

Catalogue Number.	**Prices of Complete Watches.**	Styles. D 6 C 6 B 6	Styles. A 6 U 5 T 5	Styles. P 5 O 5	Styles. N 5 M 5	Styles. L 5 K 5
19053	A 7-Jewel, Gilt Expansion Balance Elgin, Waltham or Hampden Movement	$13.85	$13.75	$14.85	$15.95	$16.50
19054	An 11-Jewel, Gilt Expansion Balance Elgin or Waltham Movement	15.22	15.12	16.22	17.32	18.87
19055	An 11-Jewel, Nickel Expansion Balance Elgin or Waltham Movement	15.77	15.67	16.77	17.87	19.42
19056	An 11-Jewel, Nickel in Settings, Expansion Balance Elgin, Waltham or Hampden Movement	16.60	16.50	17.60	18.70	20.25
19058	A 15-Jewel, Nickel in Settings, Expansion Balance Elgin, Waltham or Hampden Movement	19.90	19.80	20.95	22.05	23.60
19059	A 16-Jewel, Nickel in Settings, Expansion Balance Hampden Movement	20.90	20.80	21.90	23.00	24.55
19060	A 17-Jewel, Nickel in Settings, Expansion Balance Elgin, Waltham or Hampden Movement	30.90	30.80	31.90	33.00	34.55
19061	A 15-Jewel, Nickel in Settings, Expansion Balance Montgomery Ward & Co. Movement, with special guarantee certificate	16.90	16.80	17.90	19.00	20.55
19062	A 16-Jewel, Nickel Chronometer Balance Montgomery Ward & Co. Movement, special guarantee certificate	23.90	23.80	24.90	26.00	27.55

We charge for engraving 2 1-2 cents per letter for script style, 5 cents for Old English.

LADIES' 6 SIZE 14K GOLD FILLED, 20-YEAR GUARANTEE STEM WIND WATCHES.
For Prices with Elgin, Waltham or Hampden Movements, See Table Below.

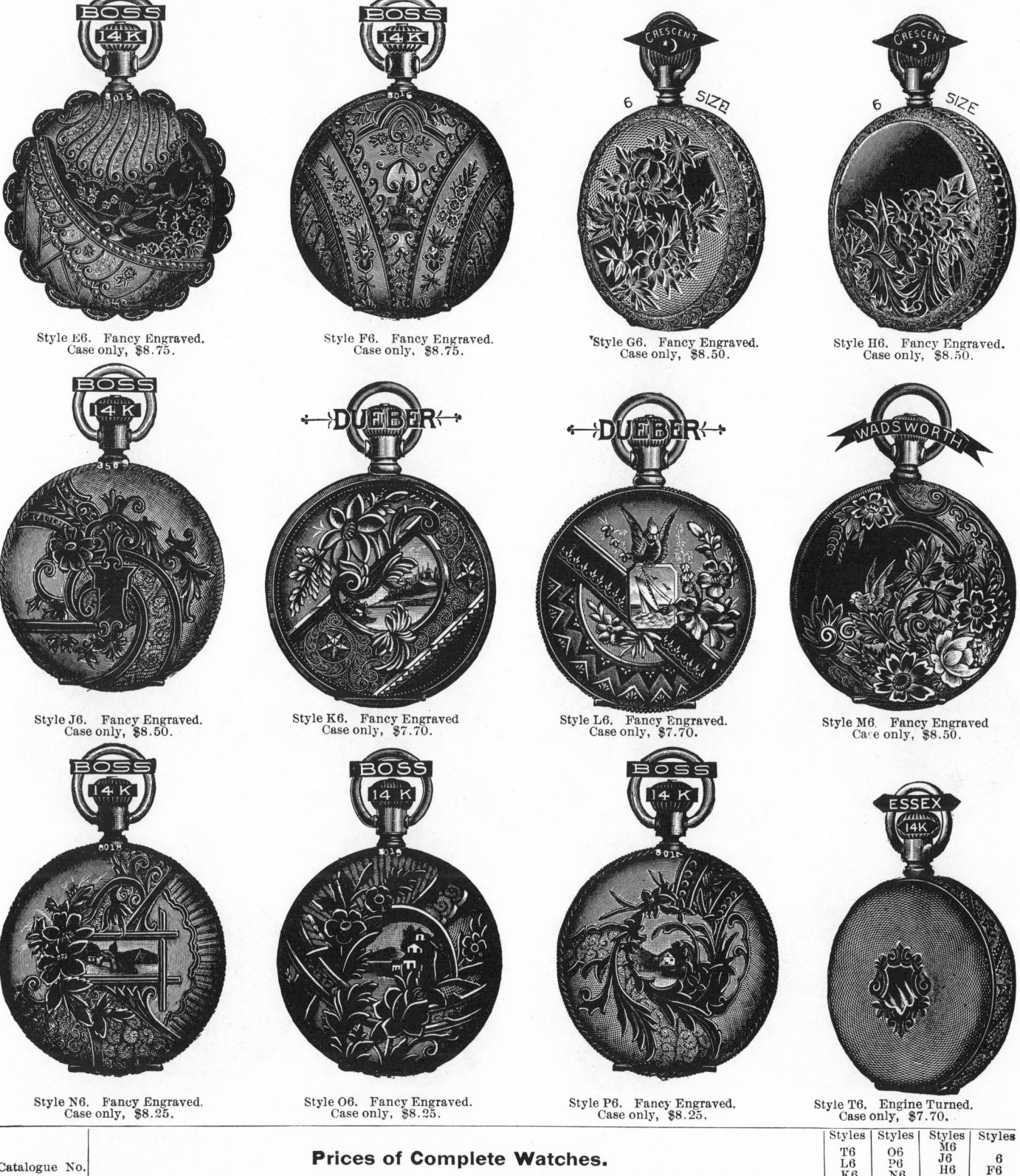

Style E6. Fancy Engraved.
Case only, $8.75.

Style F6. Fancy Engraved.
Case only, $8.75.

'Style G6. Fancy Engraved.
Case only, $8.50.

Style H6. Fancy Engraved.
Case only, $8.50.

Style J6. Fancy Engraved.
Case only, $8.50.

Style K6. Fancy Engraved
Case only, $7.70.

Style L6. Fancy Engraved.
Case only, $7.70.

Style M6. Fancy Engraved
Case only, $8.50.

Style N6. Fancy Engraved.
Case only, $8.25.

Style O6. Fancy Engraved.
Case only, $8.25.

Style P6. Fancy Engraved.
Case only, $8.25.

Style T6. Engine Turned.
Case only, $7.70.

Catalogue No.	Prices of Complete Watches.	Styles T6 L6 K6	Styles O6 P6 N6	Styles M6 J6 H6 G6	Styles 6 F6
19070	A 7-Jewel, Gilt, Expansion Balance, Elgin, Waltham or Hampden Movement...	$12.65	$13.25	$13.52	$13.78
19071	An 11-Jewel, Gilt, Expansion Balance, Elgin or Waltham Movement..	14.02	14.62	14.89	15.16
19072	An 11-Jewel, Nickel, Expansion Balance, Elgin or Waltham Movement..	14.57	15.17	15.44	15.71
19073	An 11-Jewel, Nickel in Settings, Expansion Balance, Waltham or Hampden Movement.	15.40	16.00	16.27	16.54
19075	A 15-Jewel, Nickel in Settings, Expansion Balance, Elgin, Waltham or Hampden Movement.	18.70	19.30	19.57	19.84
19076	A 16-Jewel, Nickel in Settings, Expansion Balance, Hampden Movement.....................................	19.70	20.30	20.57	20.84
19077	A 17-Jewel, Nickel in Settings, Expansion Balance, Elgin, Waltham or Hampden Movement............................	29.70	30.30	30.57	30.84
19078	A 15-Jewel, Nickel in Settings, Expansion Balance, Montgomery Ward & Co. Movement. with Special Guarantee Certificate	15.70	16.30	16.57	16.84
19079	A 1 -Jewel, Nickel, Chronometer Balance, Montgomery Ward & Co. Movement, with Special Guarantee Certificate......	22.70	23.30	23.57	23.85

Montgomery Ward & Co., Movements are the most accurate time-keeping watches made for the money. We send a guarantee certificate with each one.
We do watch repairing of all kinds at the lowest prices consistent with good work; send for our watch repair price list

LADIES' O SIZE 14K GOLD FILLED, 20-YEAR GUARANTEE, STEM WIND WATCHES.

For Prices with Elgin or Waltham Movement, See Table Below.

Style U6. Case Only, $9.90.

Style A7. Case Only, $9.90.

Style B7. Case Only, $8.25.

Style C7. Case Only, $9.35.

Style D7. Case Only, $9.35.

Style E7. Case Only, $8.25.

Style F7. Case Only, $8.25.

Style G7. Case Only, $9.35.

Style H7. Case Only, $8.80.

Style J7. Case Only, $8.80.

Style K7. Case Only, $8.80.

Style L7. Case Only, $8.80.

Style M7. Case Only, $7.15.

Style N7. Case Only, $7.70.

Style O7. Case Only, $7.70.

Style P7. Case Only, $7.70.

Style T7. Case Only, $7.70

Style U7. Case Only, $7.15.

CATALOGUE. NUMBER	Prices of Complete Watches.	Styles U7 M7	Styles P7 T7 O7 N7	Styles F7 E7 B7	Styles J7 K7 H7 L7	Styles D7 C7 G7	Styles. A7 U6
19080 A	7-Jewel Gilt Expansion Balance, Elgin or Waltham Movement...	$12.10	$12.65	$13.21	$13.76	$14 25	$14.80
19081 An	11-Jewel Gilt Expansion Balance, Elgin or Waltham Movement...	13.47	14.00	14.54	15.11	15.66	15.20
19082 An	11-Jewel Nickel Expansion Balance, Elgin or Waltham Movement.	14.02	14.58	15.13	15.68	16.24	16.79
19083 An	11-Jewel, Nickel in Settings Expansion Balance, Waltham Movement...	14.85	15.40	15.97	16.52	17.14	17.68
19085 A	15-Jewel, Nickel in Settings, Expansion Balance, Elgin or Waltham Movement ...	18.15	18.72	19.23	19.78	20.23	20.80
19087 A	17-Jewel, Nickel in Settings, Expansion Balance, Elgin or Waltham Movement...	29.15	29.69	30.23	30.79	31.21	31.78

Postage on a watch is 8c. See page 1 for Mail Insurance. We charge for engraving names or initials 2½c. per letter for script; 5c. for Old English.

We have a complete and elaborate Watch Repair Department, employing the best class of labor and doing first-class work at low prices.
Send for our repair price list.

Watchmakers' Tools, Materials and Supplies.

We illustrate below a line of Watchmakers' and Jewelers' tools. Lack of space will allow us to illustrate but a few of the most useful and desirable, and even these illustrations we have had to reduce to the smallest possible space. However, we will furnish goods of standard make and size and of the very best quality. Price we guarantee as low as any and in some instances below the market. If articles desired are not illustrated or quoted, allow market price and give accurate description of same and we will furnish. When ordering material, always send samples if possible, if not, fully describe size and make of watch or clock for which parts are intended. When placing orders for small articles in this line, where price is unknown, you will save both time and trouble by making a remittance of sufficient funds to cover all possible charges. We always refund any balance there may be in your favor.

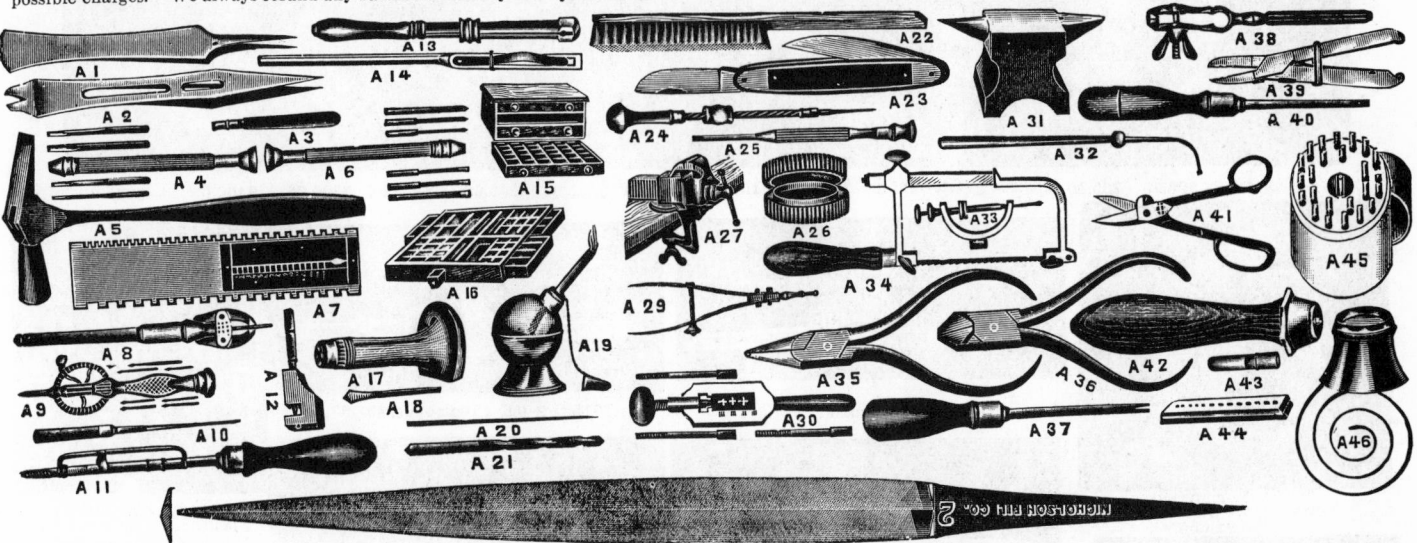

No. A. 75. This cut shows average length of watchmakers' files.

Our New Lathe for Watchmakers' Use.

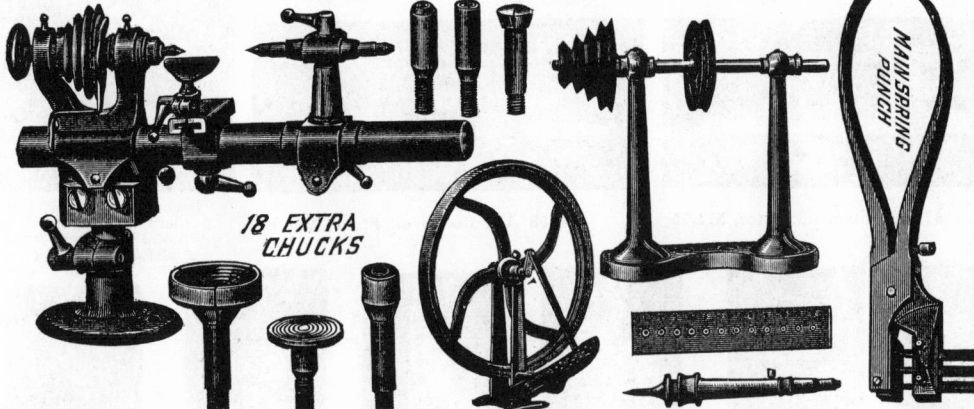

18 EXTRA CHUCKS

Jeweling Tool.

Our New Improved Lathe.
With Index Pointer and Latch.

This Lathe is by far the best made for the price in the market. It is nickel-plated with hardened spindles and bearings; the bed is made of steel, giving it a fine, high polish, free from all imperfections. We warrant them to be perfect in every part; the cone is made of steel with three steps, with **INDEX POINTER** and latch at *cone, as shown in cut*, with rubber knob on the end; the tailstock is provided with hard taper center, hardened and ground; the bed can be raised to suit the operator and can be removed with ease.

Length of bed, 10 inches. Bed to center, 1½ inches.

Lathe complete, with 18 extra chucks. Price. $22.00
Counter Shaft extra......3.00
Foot Wheel " 3.50
No. A 160 Improved Mainspring Punch... 1.25
No. A 175 Complete Jeweling Tool (see cut) 1.50
Silver Plating Liquid, a good thing. See quotations A 146, this page.

Watch and Clock material cannot be exchanged. Always send sample of parts wanted. Outer end of mainspring, with one inch of spring, will always bring the right kind.

Silver and Gold Solution for Plating without a Battery. See Nos. A 146 and 147.

No 73.	O. No. A. 75.	R. No. A 71.	M. No. A 7	S.

No. A 95.—Each 20c.
Cuts F O. R M. and S. show width and shape, length as above.

No.			No.		
A 50	Alcohol Cups....................each	$0.35	A 71	Files, small, round and square....each	$0.12
A 31	Anvil (jewelers')...............each	.75	A 73	Files, flat, regular..............each	.35
A 53	Blow Pipes, common brass.........each	.25	A 75	Files, rounding and entering......each	.35
A 32	Blow Pipes, nickel plated, with ball...each	.50	A 77	Files, screw head................each	.25
A 23	Bench Knife (jewelers'), with case		A 7	Gauge Mainspring.................each	1.00
	opener..........................each	.50	A 79	Gauge, Degree, nickel-plated, with rule, each	1.00
A 55	Buffs, Chamois, or Felt, round or flat. each	.20	A 5	Hammers, according to size....each .40 to	.75
A 22	Brushes, best bristle, watch or clock, each	.30	A 81	Hammers' Handles, ebony.........each	.25
A 59	Burnishers, jewel and other....each .25 to	.75	A 83	Hands, Watch, per pair, 10c.; per doz. pair	.50
A 10	Broaches, Stub's best quality, assorted		A 84	Hands, 2d. each, per pair, 10c: per doz. pair	.50
	sizes from No. 75 to 40......per dozen	1.00	A 85	Hands, Clock, per pair, 5c.; per doz. pair	.42
A 3	Broach Handle....................each	.10	A 17	Handles, adjustable, for graver or small	
A 20	Broaches, Swiss joint.........per dozen	.25		files..........................each	.15
A 16	Cabinet, for small material.......each	1.50	A 42	Handles, adjustable, for medium files each	.25
A 15	Cabinet, for large material........each	4.50	A 87	Jeweling Tools, Swiss, in box......each	1.50
A 20	Calipers, Pinion, plain...........each	.25	A 89	Jewelers' Cement, per bottle........each	.25
A 61	Calipers, regular brass...........each	.30	A 91	Jewel Pin Setter.................each	.88
A 63	Calipers, nickel plated, with bar and		A 43	Jewel Bottle....................each	.03
	screw..........................each	.65	A 93	Keys, Watch, common..........per dozen	.25
A 40	Clock Screwdriver................each	.28	A 95	Keys, Watch, wind any watch (see cut) each	.20
A 37	Clock wire bender................each	.20	A 97	Keys, Watch, for bench use........each	.50
A 65	Counter Sinks, per set of three.....	1.00	A 99	Keys, Clock, Iron or brass........each	.10
A 67	Counter Sinks, per set of six......	2.00	A 19	Lamps, Alcohol, patented, large......each	1.75
A 6	Counter Sinks, adjustable handle, per		A101	Lamps, Alcohol, faceted glass......each	.88
	set.............................	.75	A103	Mainsprings, Watch, each 25c....per doz	1.75
A 26	Cups, Oil, for watch or clock......each	.20	A105	Mainsprings, Clock, 1 day........each	.15
A 18	Drills, common ....per dozen	.36	A107	Mainsprings, Clock, 8 day........each	.45
A 21	Drills, Morse, Twist, assorted....per dozen	1.25	A100	Oil, Watch or Clock, per bottle......each	.20
A 33	Drills, Stock, common............each	.50	A111	Oiler, Watch....................each	.15
A 09	Drill Bow, to use with above .. ....each	.20	A113	Oil Stone, best Arkansas, in box......each	1.00
A 24	Drill Stock, patent spiral........each	.65	A 13	Pin Slide, common medium........each	.35
A 9	Drill Stock, patent guard........each	1.00	A 38	Pin Vise, hollow handle..........each	.75
A 46	Eyeglass, Watchmakers' common...each	.30	A 8	Pin Vise, nickel plated, patented....each	1.25
A 46	Eyeglass, Watchmakers', with coil		A146	Plating Solution, silver, per bottle........	1.00
	spring..........................each	.50	A147	Plating Solution, gold, per bottle........	2.50

No.		
A 12	Punch, mainspring, English..........each	$0.75
A117	Punch, mainspring, Swiss (3 punches),	
	each............................	125.
A 45	Punches, set of 24, with hollow stake,	
	in hardwood box, per set............	1.25
A 35	Plyers, round, square or snipe bill....each	.65
A 36	Plyers, Stub's best side cutting......each	1.00
A119	Plyers, cutting, regular Swiss.... ....each	.65
A 41	Shears and Wire Cutters..............each	1.25
A 11	Screw Holder and Driver combined...each	.75
A 25	Screwdriver, Watch................each	.25
A 4	Screwdriver, Watch, adjustable, 4	
	sizes, per set....................	.60
A 14	Second Hand Holder, nickel plated...each	.40
A 44	Stake, Riveting, hard steel........each	.25
A 34	Saw Frame, Swiss, extra quality,	
	nickel plated....................	1.10
A121	Saws for above ....per doz.	.15
A123	Saw Frames, Stubs'................each	1.75
A125	Saw Blades, Stubs'................each	.25
A127	Soldering, copper................each	.20
A129	Soldering fluid, per bottle........each	.25
A131	Solder, Silver........per package	1.00
	gold........per package	2.00
A 30	Screw Stock and Dies, per set..........	2.00
A 1	Tweezers, fine medium or heavy.....each	.35
A 2	Tweezers and hand raiser..........each	.45
A 39	Tongs, 2 hole, hand..............each	.40
A 27	Vise, jewelers', 1½ in. jaw........each	1.75
A133	Vise, amateur....................each	.40
A137	Watch Glasses, hunting style, each, fitted	.10
A139	Watch Glasses, per ½ dozen of one No....	.15
A141	Watch Glasses, assorted, per gross....	2.50
A143	Watch Glasses, thick, open face, fitted, each	.20
A155	Watch Glasses, thick open face, per doz....	.40

DIAMOND DEPARTMENT.

We illustrate on this and the following pages the newest and most desirable styles of Diamond Jewelry. Our Diamonds are guaranteed to be perfect, pure white stones. Prices are the lowest, consistent with good quality, and we willingly refund money on any article which fails to come up to expectation, if it is returned at once.

APPROXIMATE SIZES OF STONES.

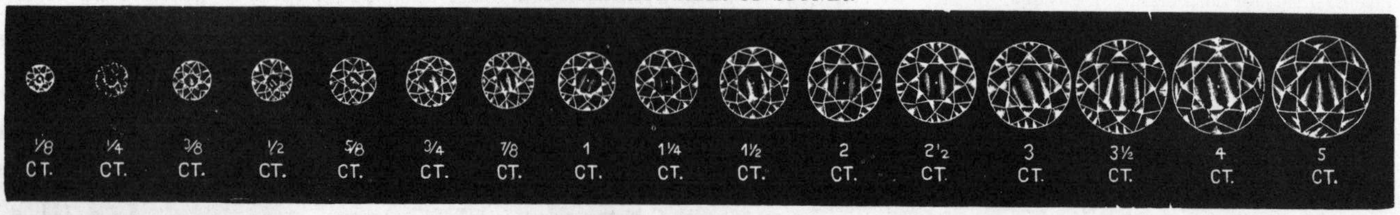
1/8 CT.
1/4 CT.
3/8 CT.
1/2 CT.
5/8 CT.
3/4 CT.
7/8 CT.
1 CT.
1 1/4 CT.
1 1/2 CT.
2 CT.
2 1/2 CT.
3 CT.
3 1/2 CT.
4 CT.
5 CT.

$7.00 $15.00 $23.75 $35.50 $52.60 $71.50 $92.00 $118.00 $156.00 $190.00 $235.00 $290.00 $350.00 $390.00 $450.00 $675.00

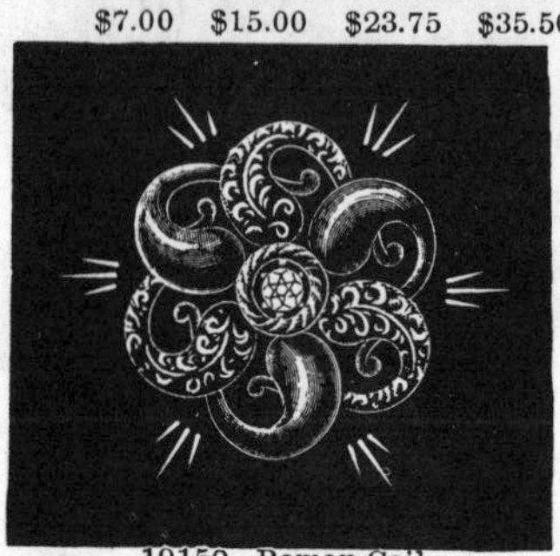

19150 Roman Coil Brooch, 1/8k Diamond center, $13.50.

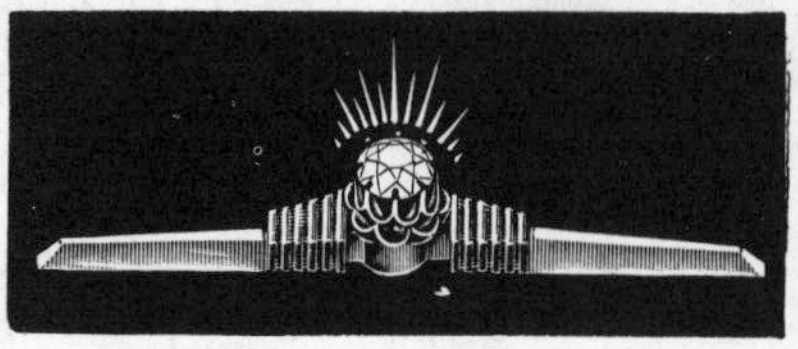

19151 3/8K Diamond, $27.00.

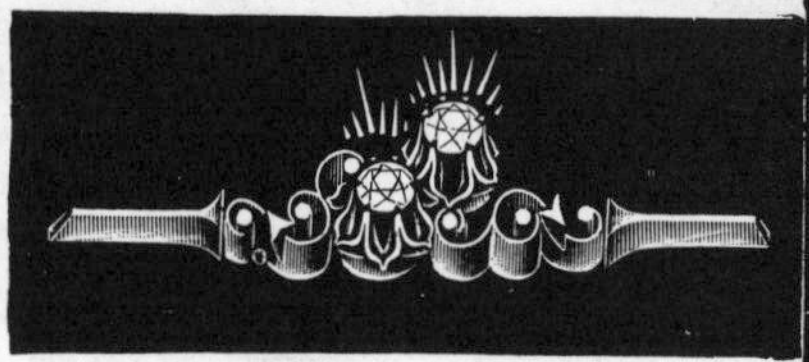

19152 2 1/4K Diamonds, $37.50.

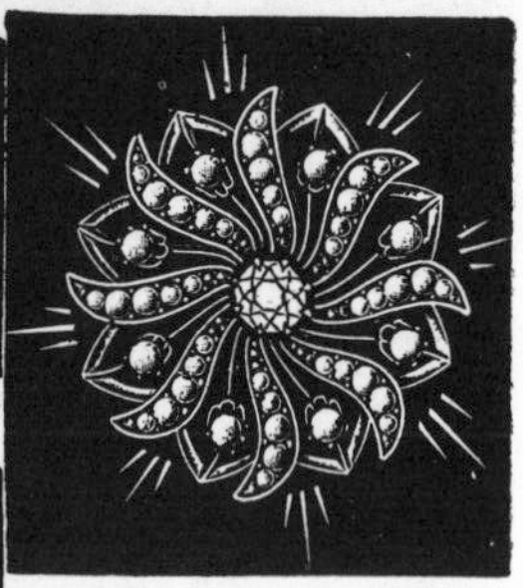

19153 Elegant Pearl and Diamond Brooch or Necklace Pendant; can be worn either way. $48.00.

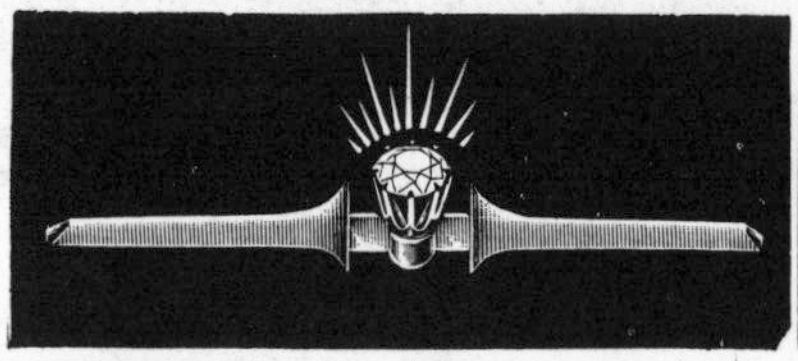

19154 1/4K Diamond. Price, $18.75.

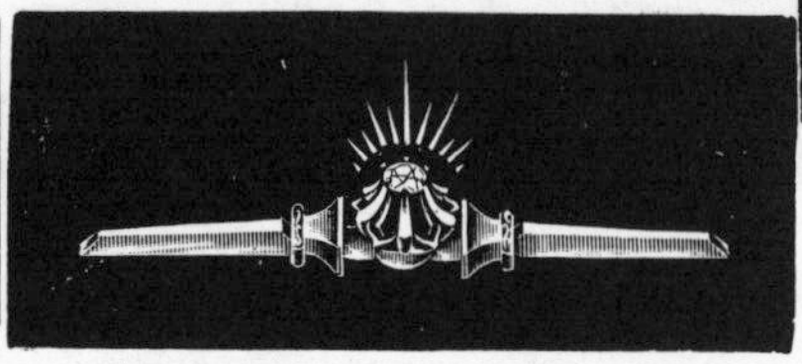

19155 3/16K Diamond. Price, $13.75

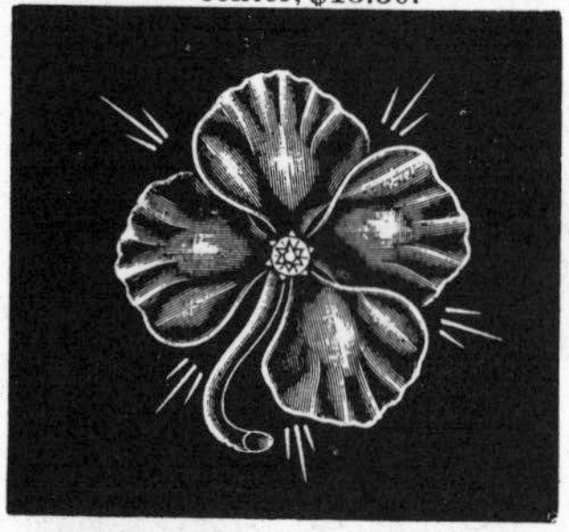

19156 Roman Leaf Brooch, Diamond center. Price, $11.50

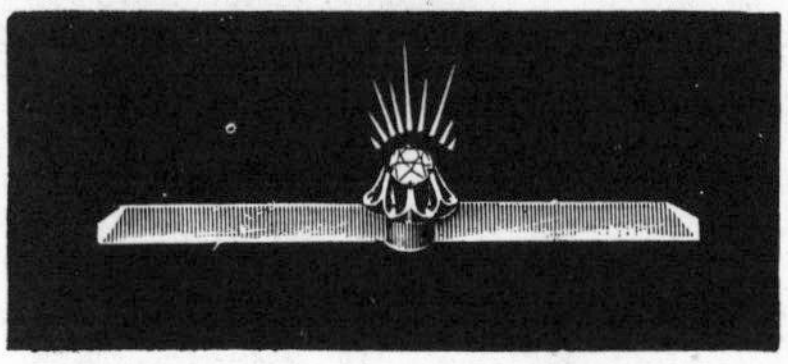

19157 1/8K Diamond. Price, $11.75

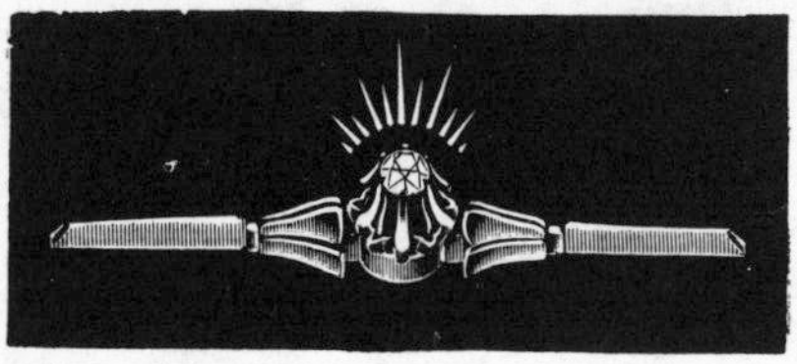

19158 1/8K Diamond. Price, $10.50

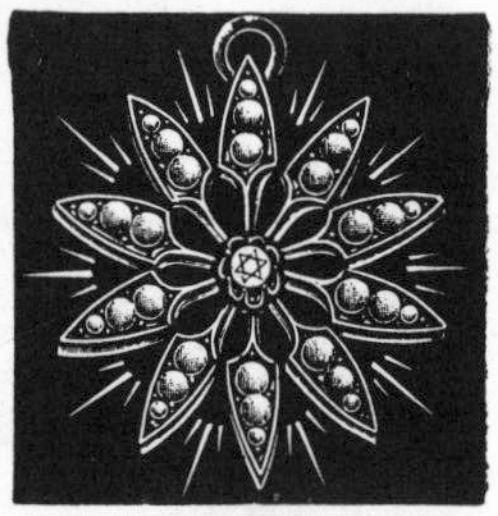

19159 Brooch or Pendant, Pearls and Diamond in center. Price $31.50

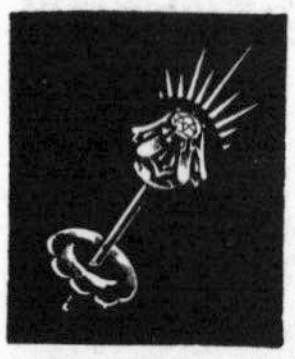

19160 1/8K. Price, per pair, $12.00

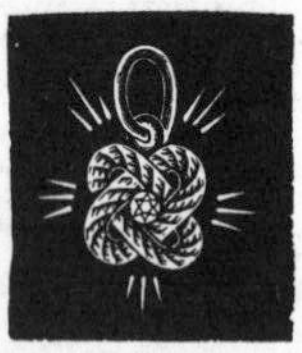

19161 Diamond center. Price, per pair, $9.00

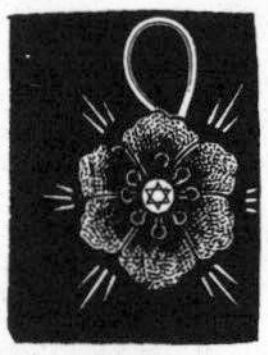

19162 Diamond center. Price, pair, $10.25

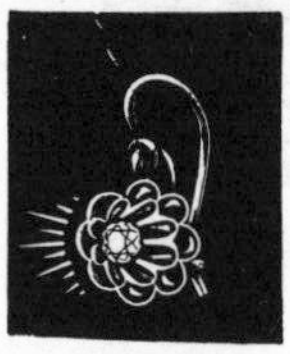

19163 1/8K Price, per pair, $10.50

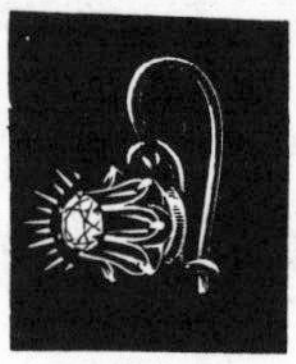

19164 1/4K Price, per pair, $17.50

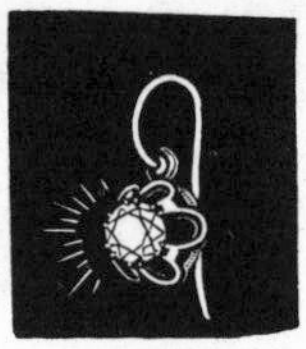

19165 1/2K Price, per pair, $35.00

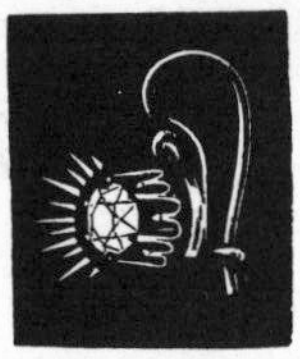

19166 3/4K Price, per pair, $44.00

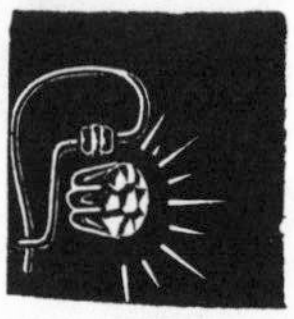

19167 1K, Price, per pair, $69.00

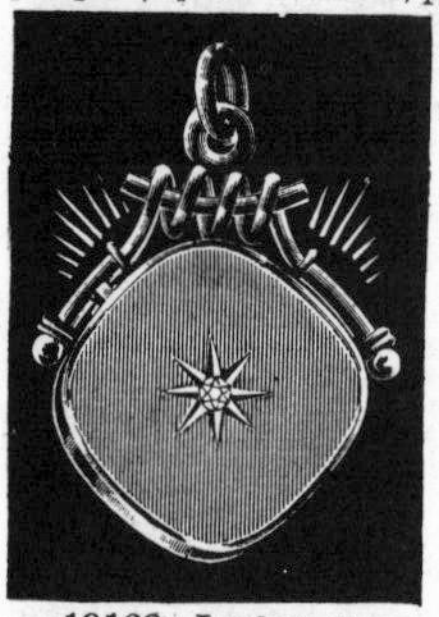

19169 Locket, 2 pictures, Diamond. Price, $10.75.

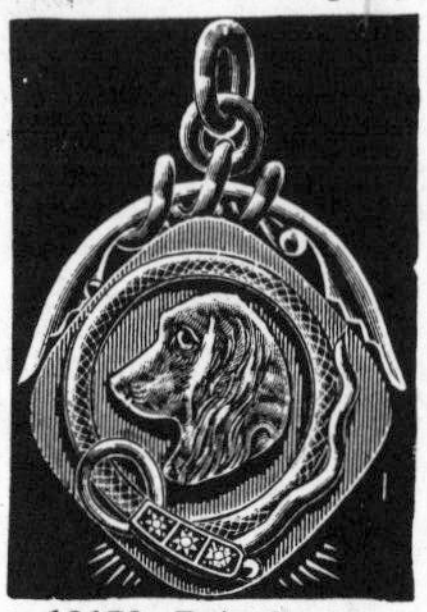

19170 Raised gold head and whip, 3 Diamonds. Price, $14.74

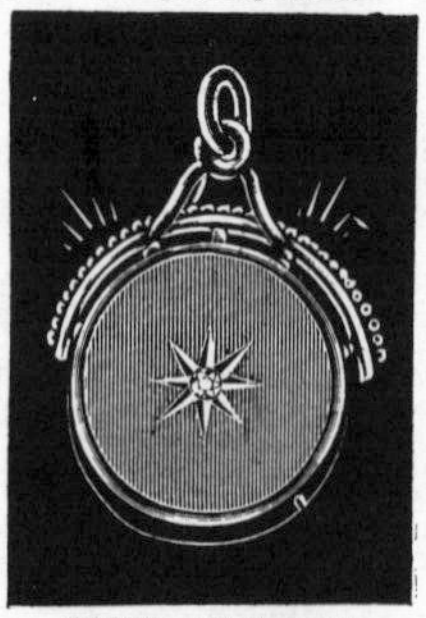

19171 Plain satin finish, 1 Diamond. Price, $9.25

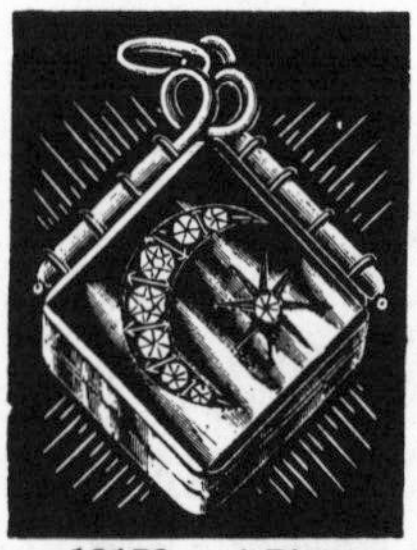

19172 1 Picture Locket, 8 Diamonds. Price, $15.00

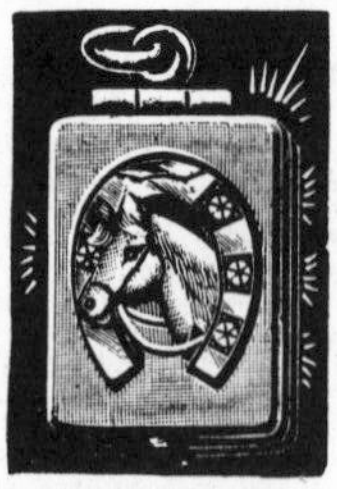

19173 Raised Horse shoe and horse head, set with 4 real diamonds, 2 pictures. Price, $10.50

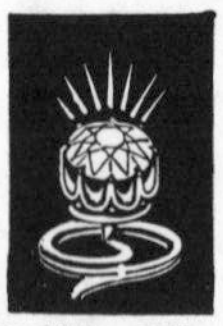

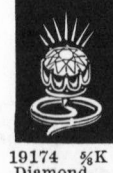

19174 5/8K Diamond. Price, $40.00

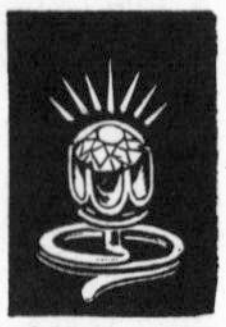

19175 1/4K Diamond. Price, $16.00

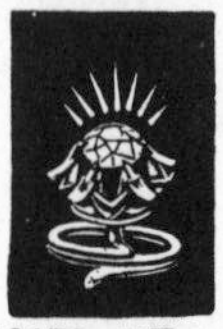

19176 1/4K Diamond. Price, $16.50

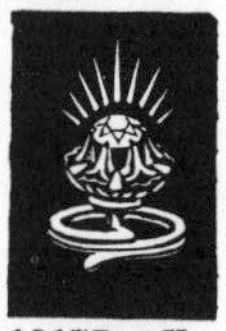

19177 1/16K Diamond. Price, $6.75

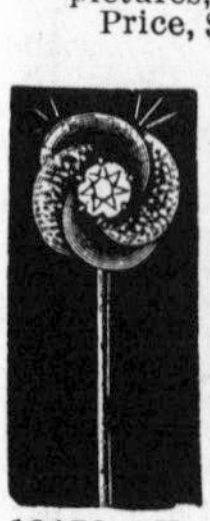

19178 3/16K Diamond complete, $12.50.

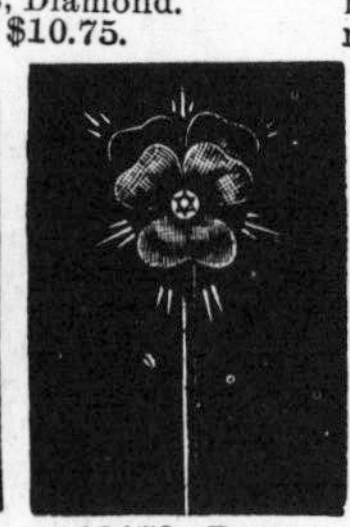

19179 Roman Gold Pansy, Diamond center, scarf pin, $5.50

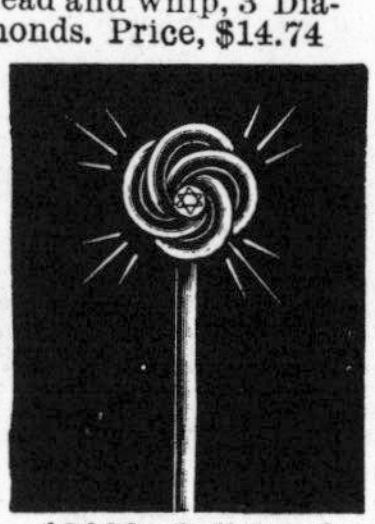

19180 Coil Scarf Pin, Diamond center. Price, $5.00.

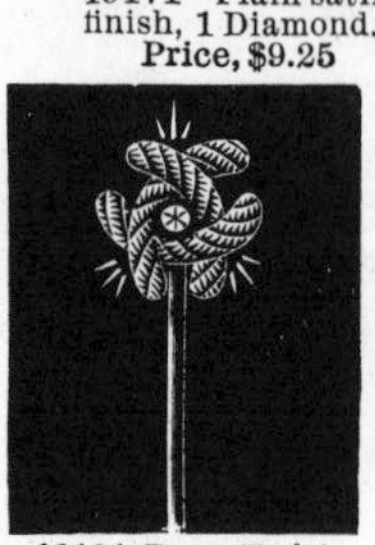

19181 Rope Twist Scarf Pin, Diamond center. Price, $5.75

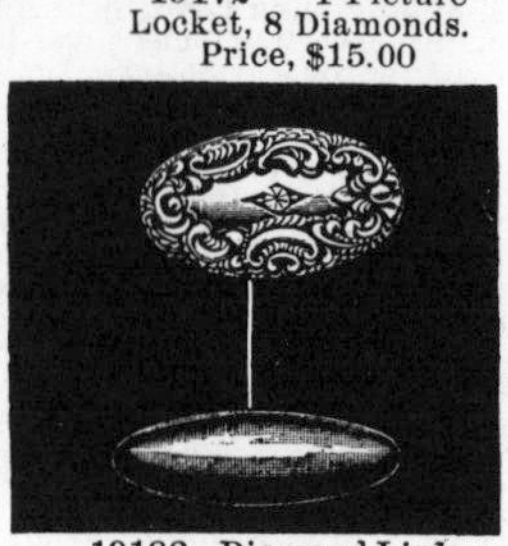

19182 Diamond Link Cuff Buttons. Price, per pair, $12.50.

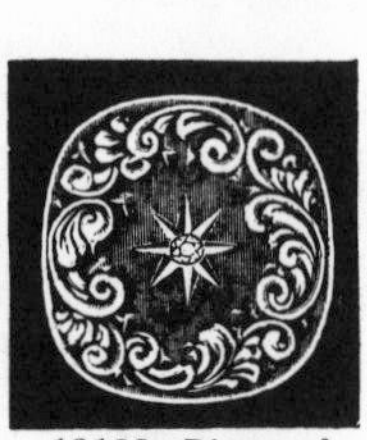

19183 Diamond Cuff Buttons. Price, per pair, $9.00

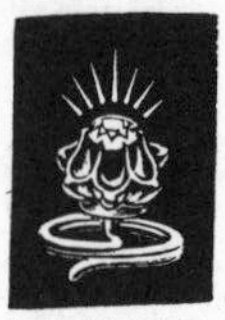

19184 1/8K Diamond. Price, $9.25

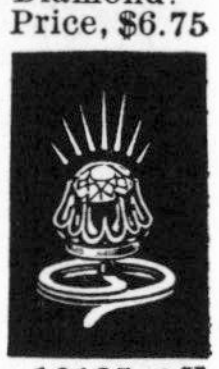

19185 3/16K Diamond Price, $12.00

SOLID GOLD RINGS, GENUINE DIAMOND SETS.

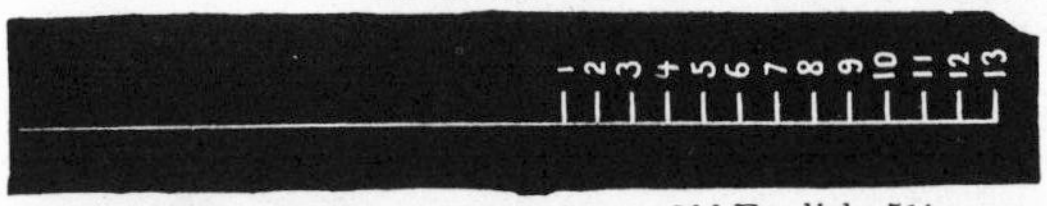

Always send size when ordering rings. Send us a 2 cent stamp and we will send you a ring gauge to measure your finger. If you have not time for this, measure finger as per instructions below.

This cut represents gauge for a size of rings. Measure your finger with a narrow piece of paper, not wider than ⅛ inch, place the paper upon the gauge so that the end touches the edge of the cut on the left. The figure at the other end of the paper gives the size of the ring wanted.

Engraving, per letter, Script, 2½c.; Old English, 5½c.

We ask you when inspecting this page to bear in mind that the Diamonds are all carefully selected with the view of giving you the very best possible value for your money. The mountings are all guaranteed 14K solid gold. Any diamond ring which does not prove satisfactory upon inspection can be returned to us for exchange, or we will refund money.

19190 1K Diamond. Tiffany Setting. Price, $119.00

19191 1K Diamond Flat Setting. Price, $118.00

19192 ½K Diamond. Tiffany Setting. Price, $37.00.

19193 ⅜K Diamond, chased and polished setting. Price, $25.50.

19194 $\frac{5}{16}$K Diamond, chased, Roman setting. Price, $21.50.

19195 ¼K Diamond. chased setting. Price, $17.25.

19196 ⅜K Diamond, chased setting. Price, $27.00.

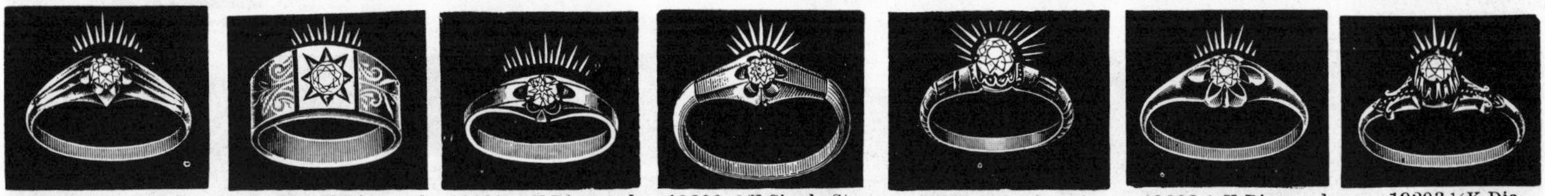

19197 ¼K Diamond polished setting. Price, $17.50.

19198 ¼K Diamond, engraved setting. Price, $19.25.

19199 $\frac{3}{16}$K Diamond. Price, $15.00.

19200 $\frac{3}{16}$K Single Stone Diamond, English setting, half round shank. Price, $15.00.

19201 ½K, Chased Mounting. Price, $38.00.

19202 ¼K Diamond. Price, $17.25.

19203 ¼K Diamond, high setting. Price, 18.10

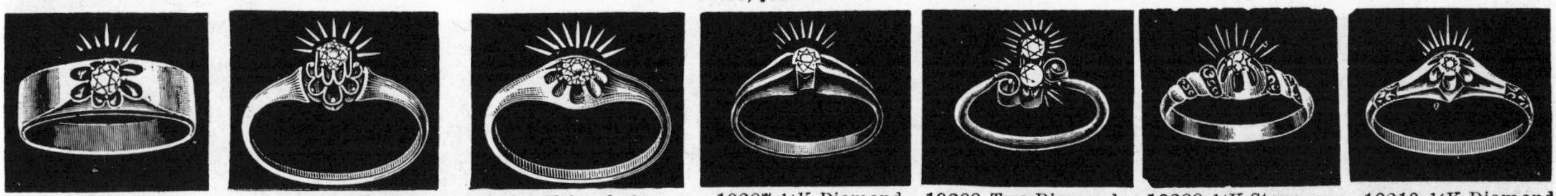

19204 ⅛K Diamond, heavy mounting. Price, $12.25.

19205 ⅛K Single Stone Diamond Ring, crown setting. Price, $11.25.

19206 ⅛K Single Stone Diamond Ring. Price, $11.25.

19207 ⅛K Diamond. Price, $9.50.

19208 Two Diamonds. Price, $10.00.

19209 ⅛K Stone, engraved setting. Price, $10.50.

19210 ⅛K Diamond chased setting. Price, $10.50.

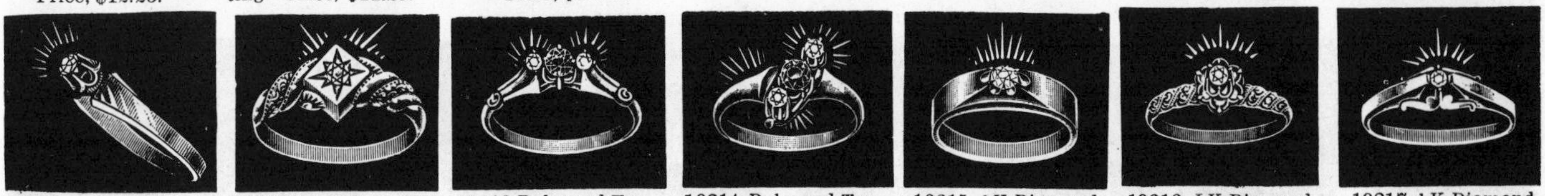

19211 ⅛K Fine, Genuine Diamond. Price, $9.00.

19212 $\frac{1}{16}$K Diamond in fancy chased setting. Price, $7.75.

19213 Ruby and Two Diamonds. Price, $11.25.

19214 Ruby and Two Diamonds. Price, $11.20.

19215 $\frac{1}{16}$K Diamond, flat, polished setting. Price, $7.50.

19216 $\frac{1}{16}$K Diamond. Price, $7.00.

19217 $\frac{1}{16}$K Diamond Price, $6.75.

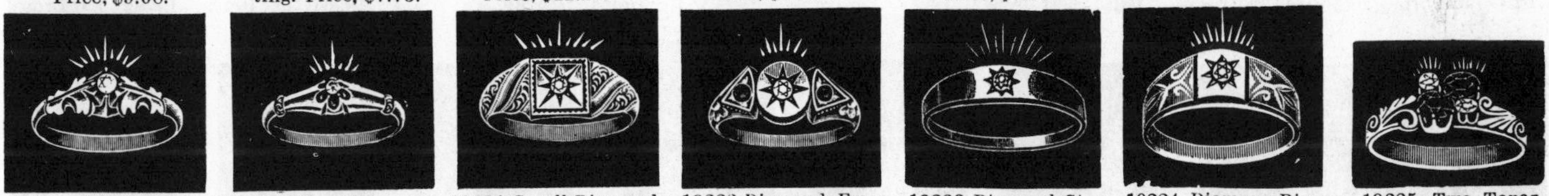

19218 $\frac{1}{16}$K Diamond. Price, $6.50.

19220 Misses' Diamond Ring; sizes, 3 to 6. Price, $3.75.

19221 Small Diamond, engraved mounting. Price, $2.80.

19222 Diamond, Emerald and Ruby, Roman colored mounting. Price, $7.00.

19223 Diamond Star Setting. Price, $4.25.

19224 Diamong Ring, chased setting. Price, $3.00.

19225 Two Topaz, Two Diamonds, Price, $5.00.

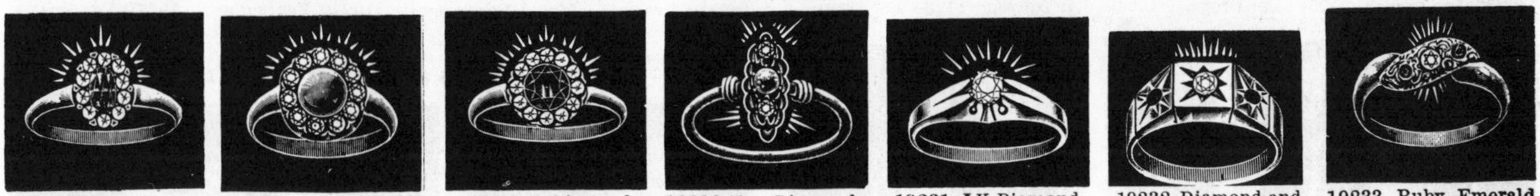

19226 Ruby and Ten Diamonds. Price, $8.75.

19227 Opal and Eleven Diamonds. Price, $18.50.

19228 Sapphire and Twelve Diamonds. Price, $13.00.
19229 Same, with Ruby and Diamonds. Price, $13.50.

19230 Two Diamonds and Opal Center, round wire setting. Price, $12.00.

19231 $\frac{3}{16}$K Diamond, plain mounting. Price, $15.50.

19232 Diamond and Ruby Ring, polished setting. Price, $9.00.

19233 Ruby, Emerald and Diamond Snake Ring Price, $10.75.

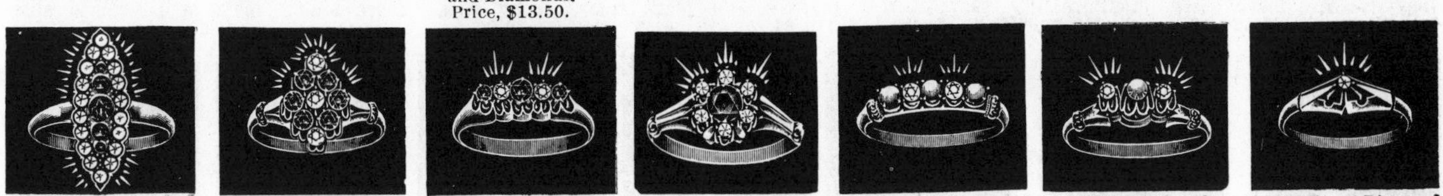

19234 Five Emeralds and Eighteen Diamonds. Price, $15.50.
19235 Same, with Opals and Diamonds. Price, $16.50.

19236 Six Rubies and Two Diamonds. Price, $6.75.

19237 Three Emeralds and Diamonds. Price, $10.25.

19238 Ruby and Six Diamonds. Price, $7.75,

19239 Three Pearls and Two Diamonds. Price, $12.00

19240 Pearl and Two Diamonds. Price, $8.00.

19241 Misses' Diamond Ring; sizes, 2 to 6. Price, $3.50.

Send a 2 cent stamp for one of our patent ring gauges, with which you can measure your finger exactly and thus avoid the risk of getting the the wrong size ring.

CEYLON BRILLIANTS.

Cut from Rock Crystal. The finest imitation diamond in the world. Mounted in solid gold diamond mountings. These stones are imported by us, and each card is stamped with our registered trade mark. They have nearly the brilliancy of diamonds at a fraction of the cost.

Directions for their care: As soon as the stone commences to lose its brilliancy it should be washed thoroughly in clear water, to which a few drops of Ammonia have been added, using soap and a jeweler's brush (see A22, page 151); rinse in clear water, and dry in boxwood sawdust. (For sale by us at 10c. per package.)

If these directions are followed, the stones will be as brilliant as ever. If unsatisfactory results are obtained, they may be returned to us for cleaning free of any expense except transportation charges.

19244 Star and Crescent Brooch. 14 Stones, $7.50   19245 Lace Pin, seven Stones, $4.50.   19246 Crescent Brooch, 13 Stones, $6.25   19247 Solitaire Star, Worn as Brooch or Pendant, $6.50.

19248 Solitaire Lace Pin, $4.00   19249 Brooch, two Stones, $5.00.   19250 Solitaire Lace Pin, $3.25.

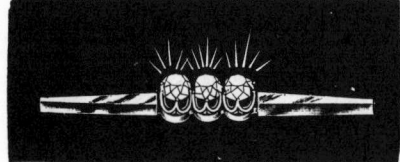
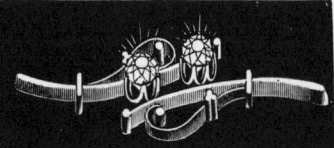

19251 Three Stone Lace Pin, $4.25.   19252 Two Stone Lace Pin, $5.00.   19253 Solitaire Lace Pin, $4.15.

19254 Solitaire Star. Can be worn as Brooch or Pendant, $6.25.

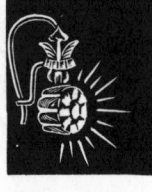

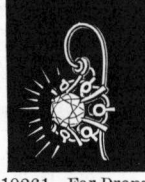

19255 Ear Drops, $3.50.   19256 Ear Drops, $4.75.   19257 Ear Drops, $3.25.   19258 Ear Drops, $3.00.   19259 Ear Drops. $3.75.   19260 Ear Drops, $4.00.   19261 Ear Drops, $3.80.   19262 Ear Drops, $5.00.

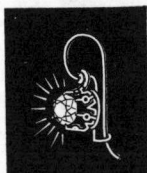

19263 Ear Drops, $3.10.   19264 Ear Drops, $2.75.   19265 Ear Drops, $2.90.   19263 Ear Drop $2.80.   19267 Ear Drops. $3.50.   19268 Ear Screws, $2.95.   19269 Ear Screws, $3.95.   19270 Ear Screws, $3.75.

Mountings are all Solid Gold.

19271 Scarf Pin, $2.00.   19272 Scarf Pin, $2.10.   19273 Scarf Pin, $1.75.   19274 Scarf Pin, $1.90.   19275 Scarf Pin, $1.25.   19276 Stud, $1.75.   19277 Stud, $2.00.   19278 Stud, $1.00.   19279 Stud, $1.50.   19280 Stud, $1.80.

19281 Ring, $7.00.   19282 Ring, $5.00.   19283 Ring, $5.50.   19284 Three Stone Ring, $7.50.   19285 Ring, $3.50.   19286 Ring, $2.25.   19287 Ring, $4.25.

All Mountings on this Page are Solid Gold. Stones are exact size of Illustrations.

Send a 2 cent stamp for one of our patent ring gauges to measure the finger, and avoid mistakes in ordering wrong sizes.

MEN'S SOLID GOLD VEST CHAINS. Length, 12 inches.
In 10K and 14K Quality.

Note.—These goods are sold by weight, price being for 10k., 76c per pwt. and 14k., 90c per pwt.
Goods will be furnished exactly as represented and at prices quoted; if other weights or patterns are required 10 days should be allowed in which to make same
We will make to order any pattern or weight at proportionate cost.

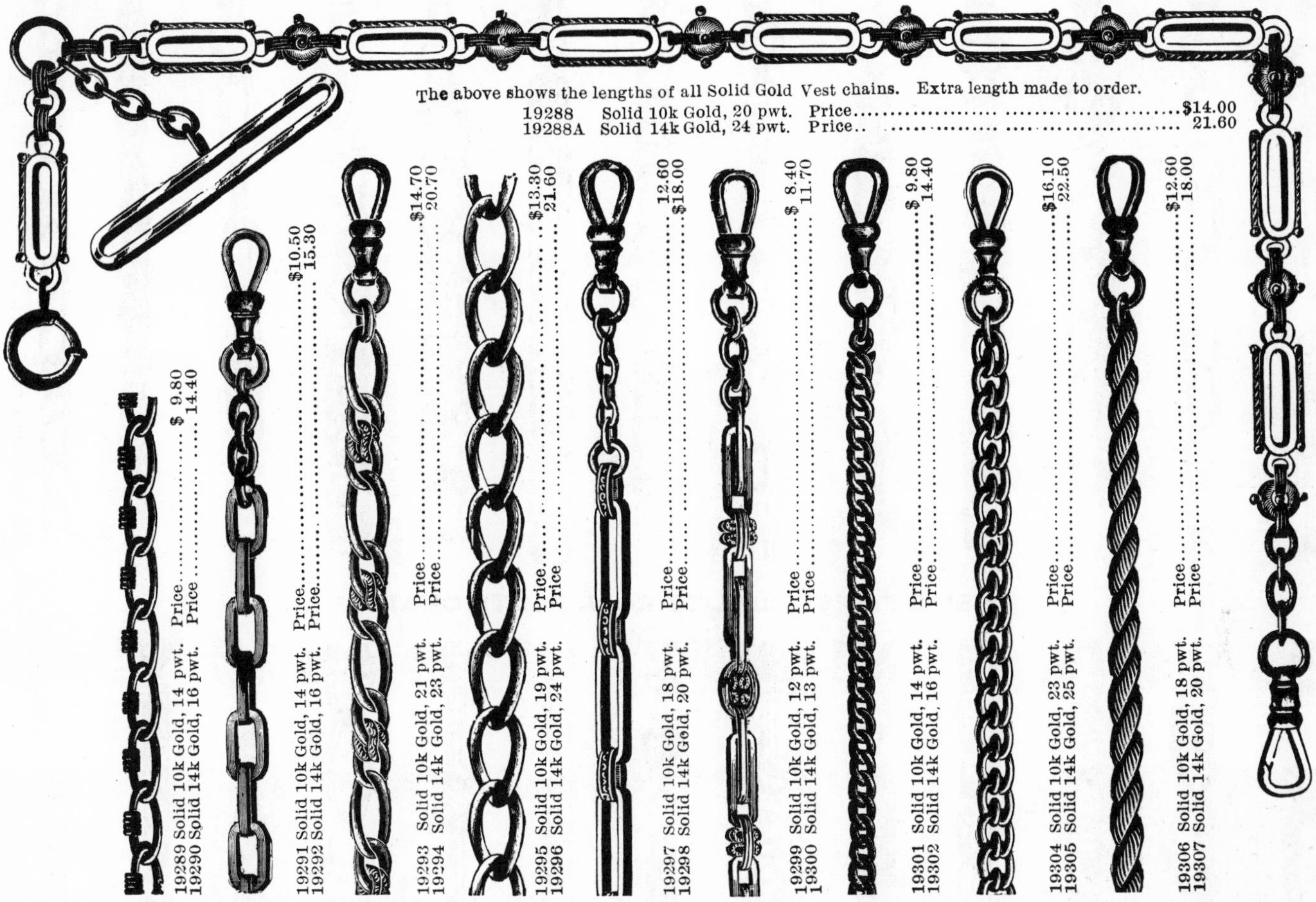

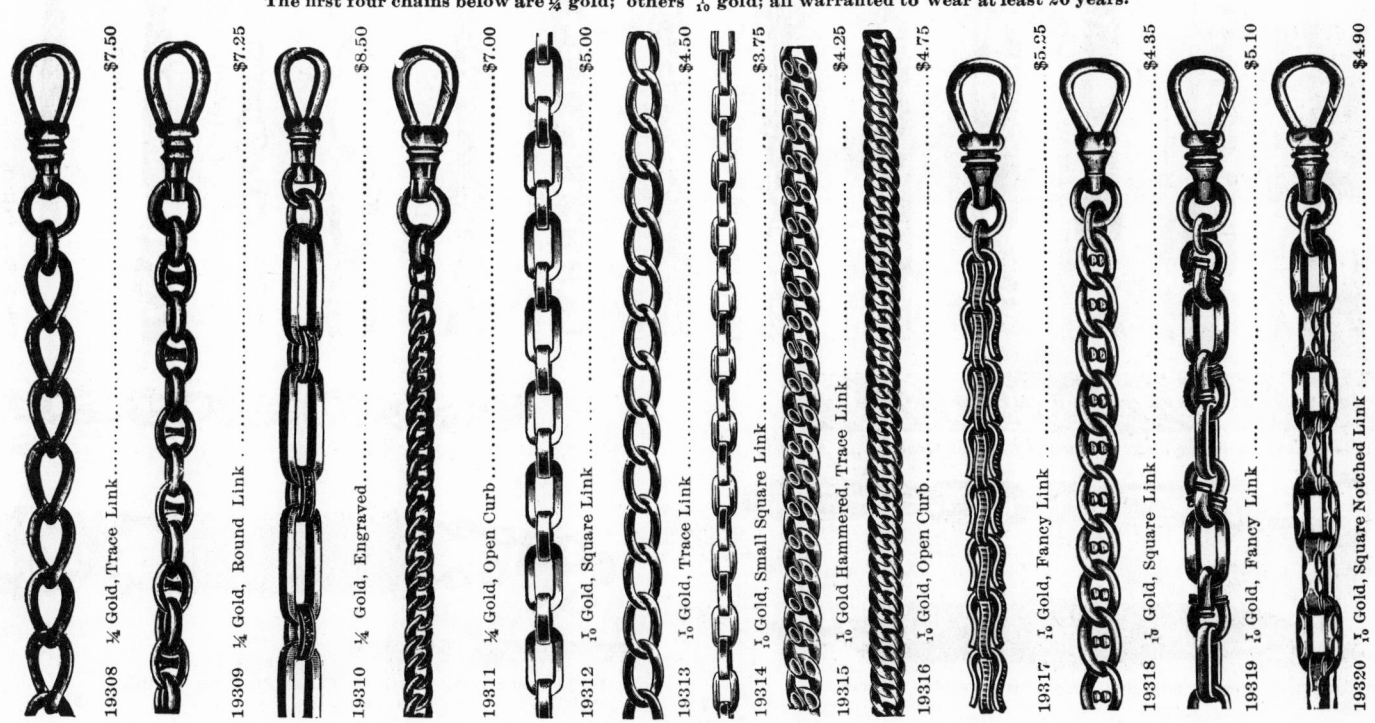

The above shows the lengths of all Solid Gold Vest chains. Extra length made to order.

19288 Solid 10k Gold, 20 pwt. Price........ $14.00
19288A Solid 14k Gold, 24 pwt. Price........ 21.60

19289 Solid 10k Gold, 14 pwt. Price........ $ 9.80
19290 Solid 14k Gold, 16 pwt. Price........ 14.40

19291 Solid 10k Gold, 14 pwt. Price........ $10.50
19292 Solid 14k Gold, 16 pwt. Price........ 15.30

19293 Solid 10k Gold, 21 pwt. Price........ $14.70
19294 Solid 14k Gold, 23 pwt. Price........ 20.70

19295 Solid 10k Gold, 19 pwt. Price........ $13.30
19296 Solid 14k Gold, 24 pwt. Price........ 21.60

19297 Solid 10k Gold, 18 pwt. Price........ 12.60
19298 Solid 14k Gold, 20 pwt. Price........ $18.00

19299 Solid 10k Gold, 12 pwt. Price........ $ 8.40
19300 Solid 14k Gold, 13 pwt. Price........ 11.70

19301 Solid 10k Gold, 14 pwt. Price........ $ 9.80
19302 Solid 14k Gold, 16 pwt. Price........ 14.40

19304 Solid 10k Gold, 23 pwt. Price........ $16.10
19305 Solid 14k Gold, 25 pwt. Price........ 22.50

19306 Solid 10k Gold, 18 pwt. Price........ $12.60
19307 Solid 14k Gold, 20 pwt. Price........ 18.00

Seamless Gold Filled Vest Chains, with Gold Soldered Links.

The first four chains below are ¼ gold; others $\frac{1}{10}$ gold; all warranted to wear at least 20 years.

19308 ¼ Gold, Trace Link........ $7.50
19309 ¼ Gold, Round Link........ $7.25
19310 ¼ Gold, Engraved........ $8.50
19311 ¼ Gold, Open Curb........ $7.00
19312 $\frac{1}{10}$ Gold, Square Link........ $5.00
19313 $\frac{1}{10}$ Gold, Trace Link........ $4.50
19314 $\frac{1}{10}$ Gold, Small Square Link........ $3.75
19315 $\frac{1}{10}$ Gold Hammered, Trace Link........ $4.25
19316 $\frac{1}{10}$ Gold, Open Curb........ $4.75
19317 $\frac{1}{10}$ Gold, Fancy Link........ $5.25
19318 $\frac{1}{10}$ Gold, Square Link........ $4.35
19319 $\frac{1}{10}$ Gold, Fancy Link........ $5.10
19320 $\frac{1}{10}$ Gold, Square Notched Link........ $4.90

All Chains on this page are full length, 12 inches. Any chain on this page can be sent by mail for 2 cents. See page 1 for Mail Insurance.

MEN'S GOLD FILLED VEST CHAINS.   Warranted to Give Perfect Satisfaction.

MEN'S FINEST QUALITY ROLL PLATE CHAINS.

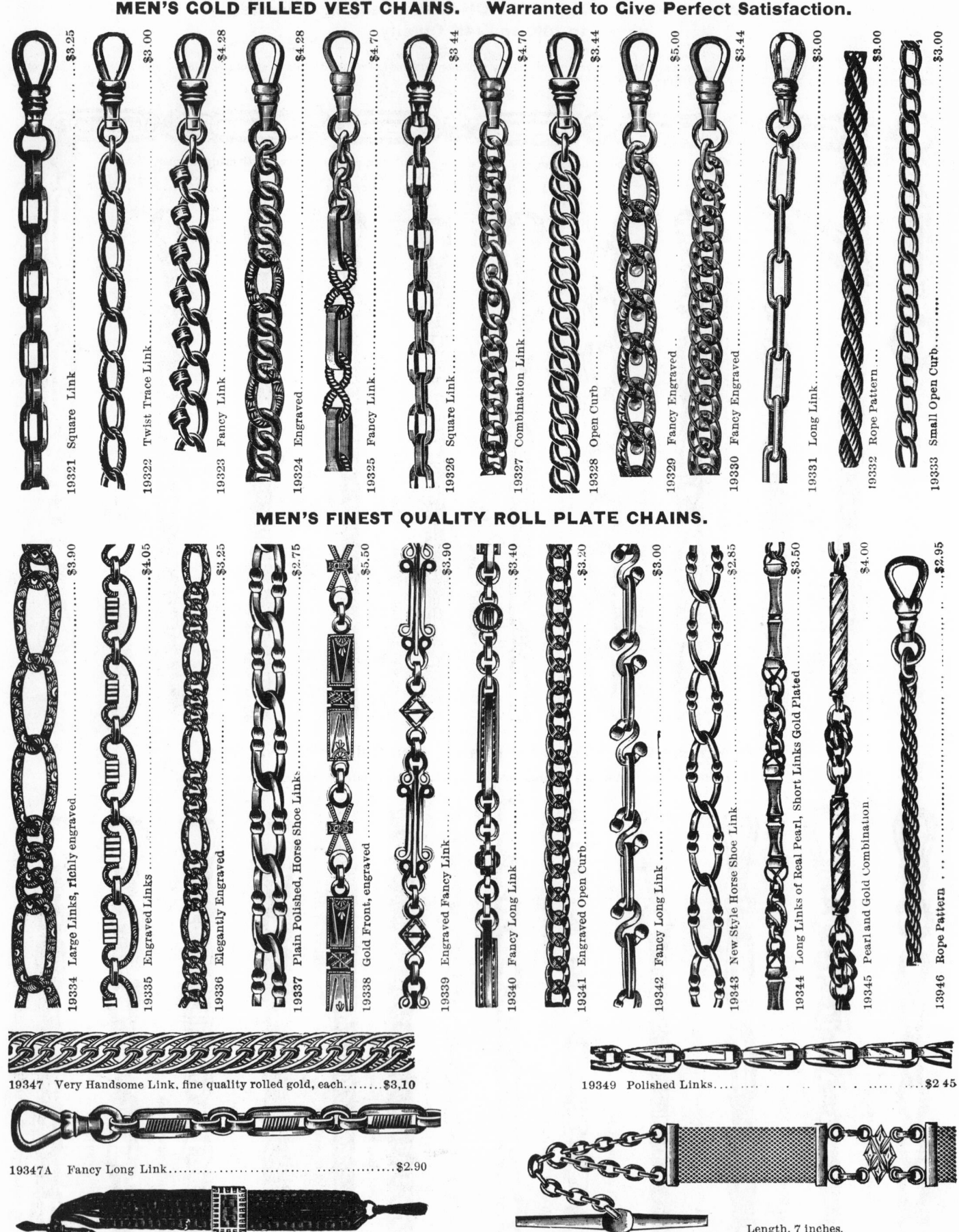

19334 Large Links, richly engraved $3.90
19335 Engraved Links $4.05
19336 Elegantly Engraved $3.25
19337 Plain Polished, Horse Shoe Links $2.75
19338 Gold Front, engraved $5.50
19339 Engraved Fancy Link $3.90
19340 Fancy Long Link $3.40
19341 Engraved Open Curb $3.20
19342 Fancy Long Link $3.00
19343 New Style Horse Shoe Link $2.85
19344 Long Links of Real Pearl, Short Links Gold Plated $3.50
19345 Pearl and Gold Combination $4.00
13946 Rope Pattern $2.95

19321 Square Link $3.25
19322 Twist Trace Link $3.00
19323 Fancy Link $4.28
19324 Engraved $4.28
19325 Fancy Link $4.70
19326 Square Link $3.44
19327 Combination Link $4.70
19328 Open Curb $3.44
19329 Fancy Engraved $5.00
19330 Fancy Engraved $3.44
19331 Long Link $3.00
19332 Rope Pattern $3.00
19333 Small Open Curb $3.00

19347   Very Handsome Link, fine quality rolled gold, each $3.10

19347A   Fancy Long Link $2.90

19348   Best Quality Silk Braid Vest, Plated Slide, 7 inches
long.   Each $0 35

19349   Polished Links $2 45

Length, 7 inches.
19350   Aluminum, with Pearl Center Piece, very stylish.
Each $1 75

All Chains on this page except Nos. 19348 and 19350 are full length, 12 inches.

MEN'S ROLL PLATE VEST CHAINS—FULL REGULAR LENGTH.

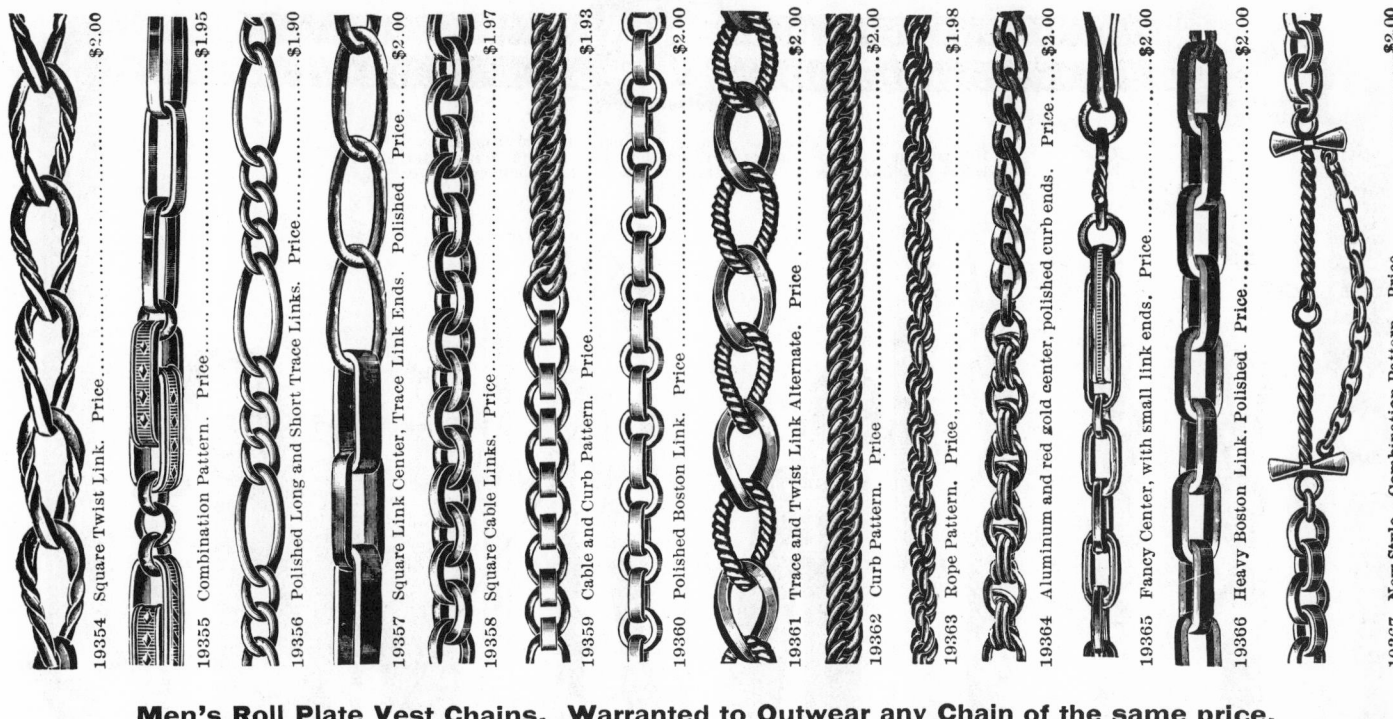

19354 Square Twist Link. Price....$2.00
19355 Combination Pattern. Price....$1.95
19356 Polished Long and Short Trace Links. Price....$1.90
19357 Square Link Center, Trace Link Ends. Polished. Price....$2.00
19358 Square Cable Links. Price....$1.97
19359 Cable and Curb Pattern. Price....$1.93
19360 Polished Boston Link. Price....$2.00
19361 Trace and Twist Link Alternate. Price....$2.00
19362 Curb Pattern. Price....$2.00
19363 Rope Pattern. Price....$1.98
19364 Aluminum and red gold center, polished curb ends. Price....$2.00
19365 Fancy Center, with small link ends. Price....$2.00
19366 Heavy Boston Link. Polished. Price....$2.00
19367 New Style. Combination Pattern. Price....$2.00

Men's Roll Plate Vest Chains. Warranted to Outwear any Chain of the same price.

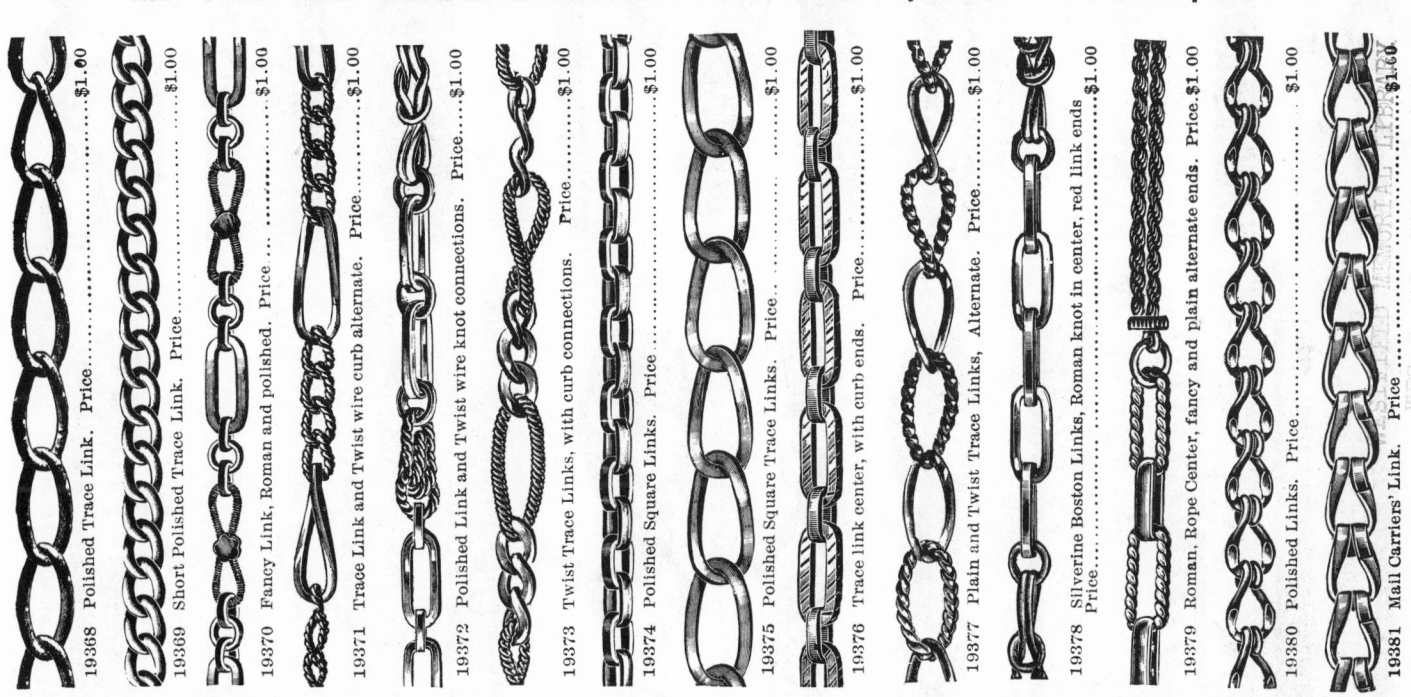

19368 Polished Trace Link. Price....$1.00
19369 Short Polished Trace Link. Price....$1.00
19370 Fancy Link, Roman and polished. Price....$1.00
19371 Trace Link and Twist wire curb alternate. Price....$1.00
19372 Polished Link and Twist wire knot connections. Price....$1.00
19373 Twist Trace Links, with curb connections. Price....$1.00
19374 Polished Square Links. Price....$1.00
19375 Polished Square Trace Links. Price....$1.00
19376 Trace link center, with curb ends. Price....$1.00
19377 Plain and Twist Trace Links, Alternate. Price....$1.00
19378 Silverine Boston Links, Roman knot in center, red link ends. Price....$1.00
19379 Roman, Rope Center, fancy and plain alternate ends. Price....$1.00
19380 Polished Links. Price....$1.00
19381 Mail Carriers' Link. Price....$1.00

Aluminum Vest Chains.
Light as wood. Strong as steel. Never tarnish.

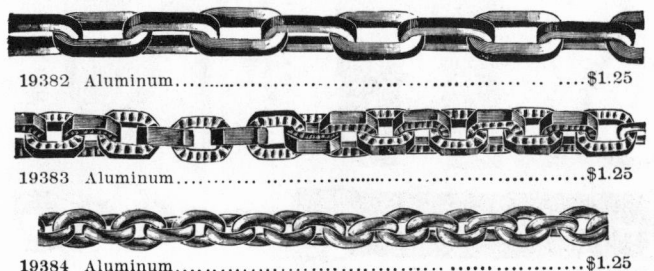

19382 Aluminum....$1.25

19383 Aluminum....$1.25

19384 Aluminum....$1.25

Pony, or Boys' Size Roll Plate Chains.
8½ inches long with drop piece for charm

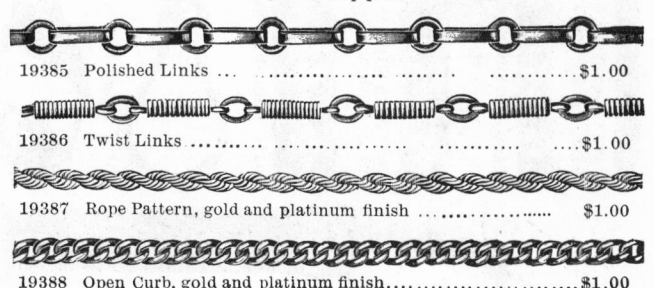

19385 Polished Links $1.00

19386 Twist Links $1.00

19387 Rope Pattern, gold and platinum finish $1.00

19388 Open Curb, gold and platinum finish.....................$1.00

All chains on this page are full length, 12 inches, except the Boys' chains.

MEN'S ROLLED PLATE AND SILVER VEST CHAINS.

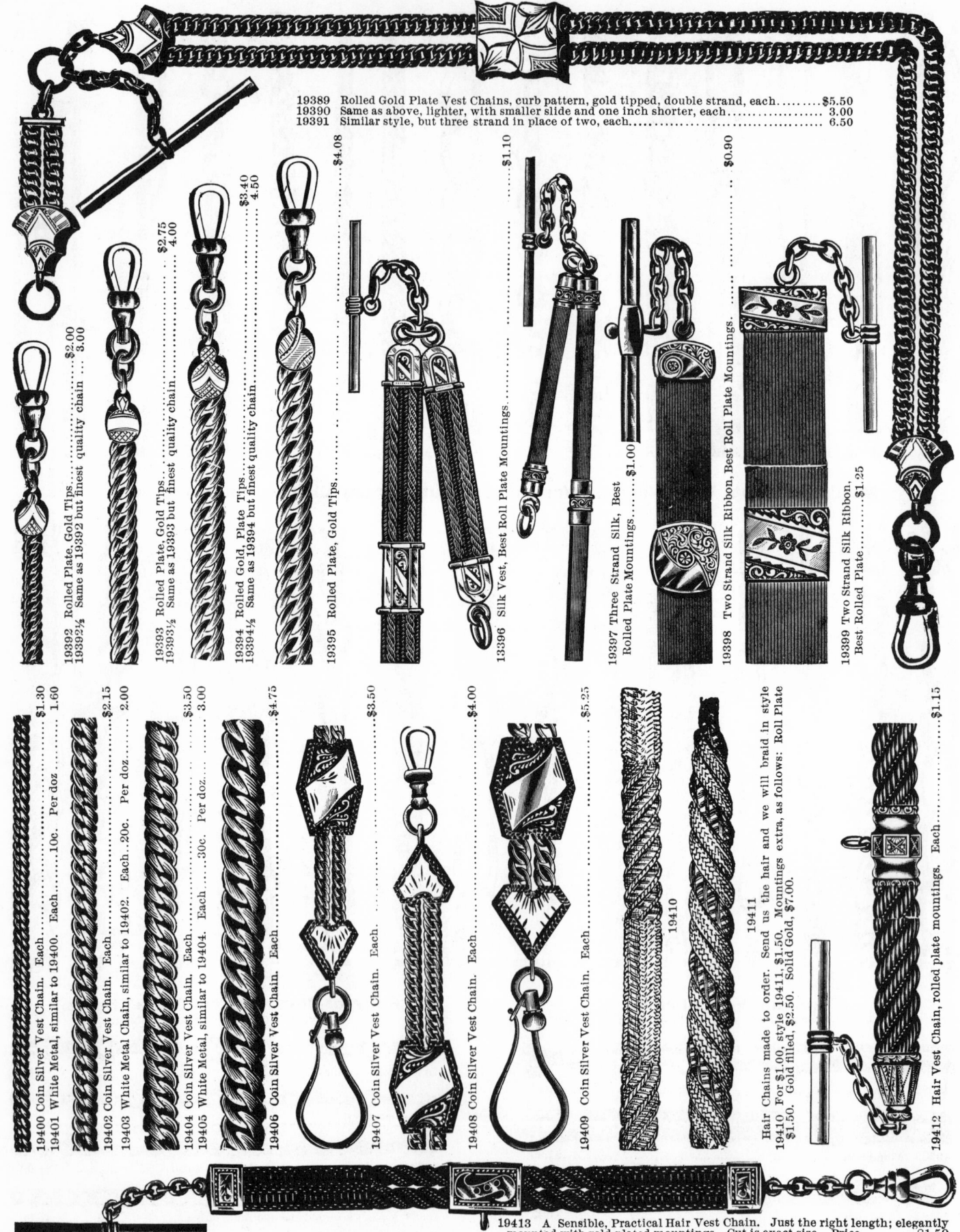

19389 Rolled Gold Plate Vest Chains, curb pattern, gold tipped, double strand, each.........$5.50
19390 Same as above, lighter, with smaller slide and one inch shorter, each.................. 3.00
19391 Similar style, but three strand in place of two, each................................. 6.50

$4.08

$3.40
4.50

$2.75
4.00

$2.00
3.00

$1.10

$0.90

19392 Rolled Plate, Gold Tips............$2.00
19392½ Same as 19392 but finest quality chain ... 3.00

19393 Rolled Plate, Gold Tips.. $2.75
19393½ Same as 19393 but finest quality chain. 4.00

19394 Rolled Gold, Plate Tips........ $3.40
19394½ Same as 19394 but finest quality chain...... 4.50

19395 Rolled Plate, Gold Tips............$4.08

13396 Silk Vest, Best Roll Plate Mountings............$1.10

19397 Three Strand Silk, Best Rolled Plate Mountings........$1.00

19398 Two Strand Silk Ribbon, Best Roll Plate Mountings............$0.90

19399 Two Strand Silk Ribbon, Best Rolled Plate........$1.25

$1.30
1.60

$2.15
2.00

$3.50
3.00

$4.75

$3.50

$4.00

$5.25

$1.15

19400 Coin Silver Vest Chain. Each............$1.30
19401 White Metal, similar to 19400. Per doz.......... 1.60

19402 Coin Silver Vest Chain. Each............$2.15
19403 White Metal Chain, similar to 19402. Per doz....... 2.00

19404 Coin Silver Vest Chain. Each............$3.50
19405 White Metal, similar to 19404. Per doz........ 3.00

19406 Coin Silver Vest Chain. Each............$4.75

19407 Coin Silver Vest Chain. Each...........$3.50

19408 Coin Silver Vest Chain. Each............$4.00

19409 Coin Silver Vest Chain. Each............$5.25

19410

19411

Hair Chains made to order. Send us the hair and we will braid in style 19410. For $1.00, style 19411, $1.50. Mountings extra, as follows: Roll Plate $1.50. Gold filled, $2.50. Solid Gold, $7.00.

19412 Hair Vest Chain, rolled plate mountings. Each............$1.15

19413 A Sensible, Practical Hair Vest Chain. Just the right length; elegantly mounted with gold plated mountings. Cut is exact size, Price...........$1.50

All chains on this page, except No. 19413, are full regular length.

Ladies' Roll Plate and Solid Gold Guard Chains, Nos. 19414 to 19424 are 50 inches Long.

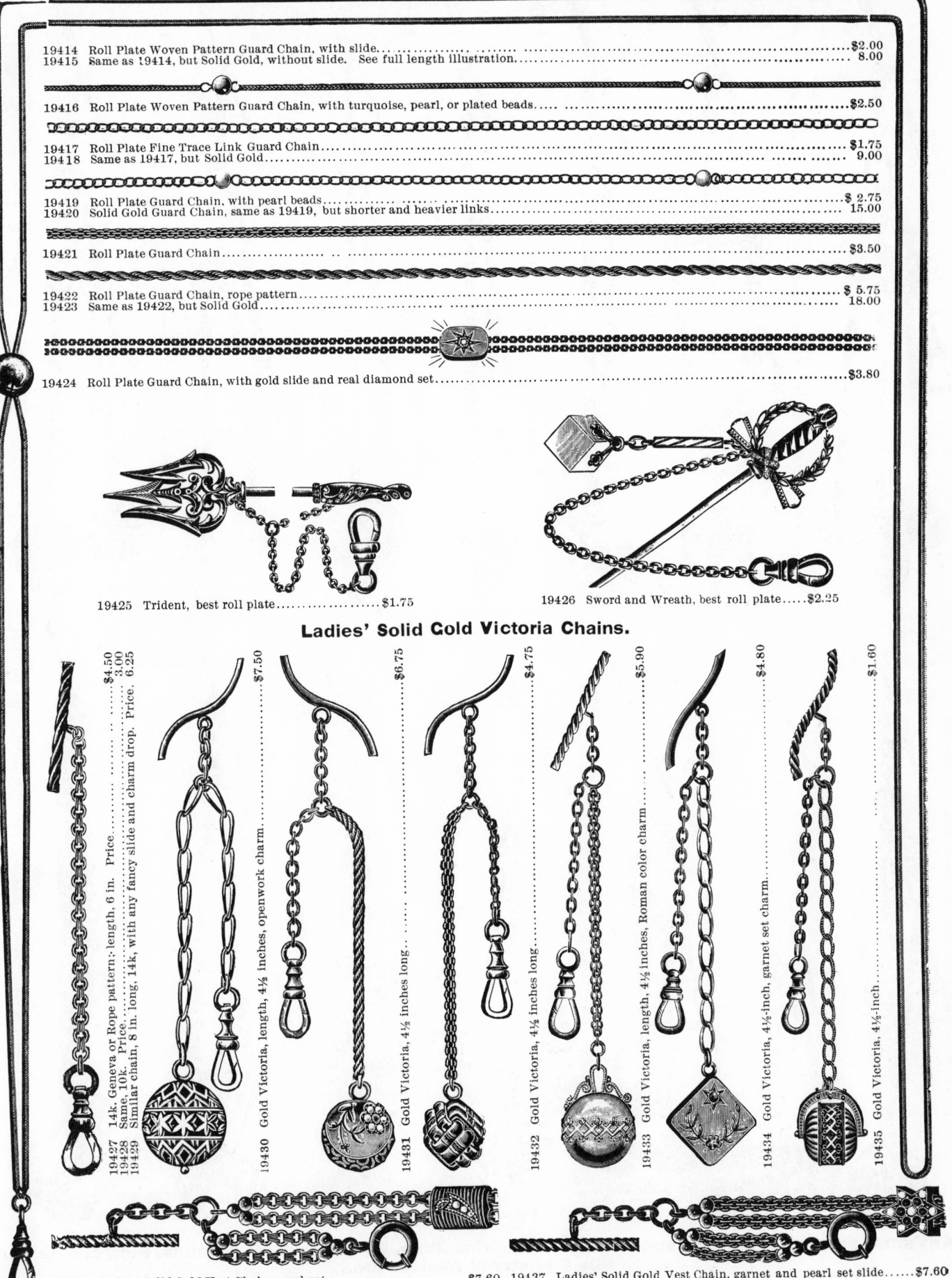

19414   Roll Plate Woven Pattern Guard Chain, with slide..$2.00
19415   Same as 19414, but Solid Gold, without slide.   See full length illustration......................8.00

19416   Roll Plate Woven Pattern Guard Chain, with turquoise, pearl, or plated beads.....................$2.50

19417   Roll Plate Fine Trace Link Guard Chain...$1.75
19418   Same as 19417, but Solid Gold..9.00

19419   Roll Plate Guard Chain, with pearl beads..$ 2.75
19420   Solid Gold Guard Chain, same as 19419, but shorter and heavier links............................15.00

19421   Roll Plate Guard Chain..$3.50

19422   Roll Plate Guard Chain, rope pattern...$ 5.75
19423   Same as 19422, but Solid Gold...18.00

19424   Roll Plate Guard Chain, with gold slide and real diamond set......................................$3.80

19425   Trident, best roll plate.....................$1.75

19426   Sword and Wreath, best roll plate.....$2.25

Ladies' Solid Gold Victoria Chains.

19427   14k. Geneva or Rope pattern, length, 6 in.   Price........$4.50
19428   Same, 10k. Price........3.00
19429   Similar chain, 8 in. long, 14k, with any fancy slide and charm drop. Price. 6.25

19430   Gold Victoria, length, 4½ inches, openwork charm.......$7.50

19431   Gold Victoria, 4½ inches long.......$6.75

19432   Gold Victoria, 4½ inches long.......$4.75

19433   Gold Victoria, length, 4½ inches, Roman color charm.......$5.90

19434   Gold Victoria, 4½-inch, garnet set charm.......$4.80

19435   Gold Victoria, 4½-inch.......$1.60

19436   Ladies' Solid Gold Vest Chain, pearl set. $7.60

19437   Ladies' Solid Gold Vest Chain, garnet and pearl set slide......$7.60

Ladies' Best Quality Roll Plate Victoria Chains.

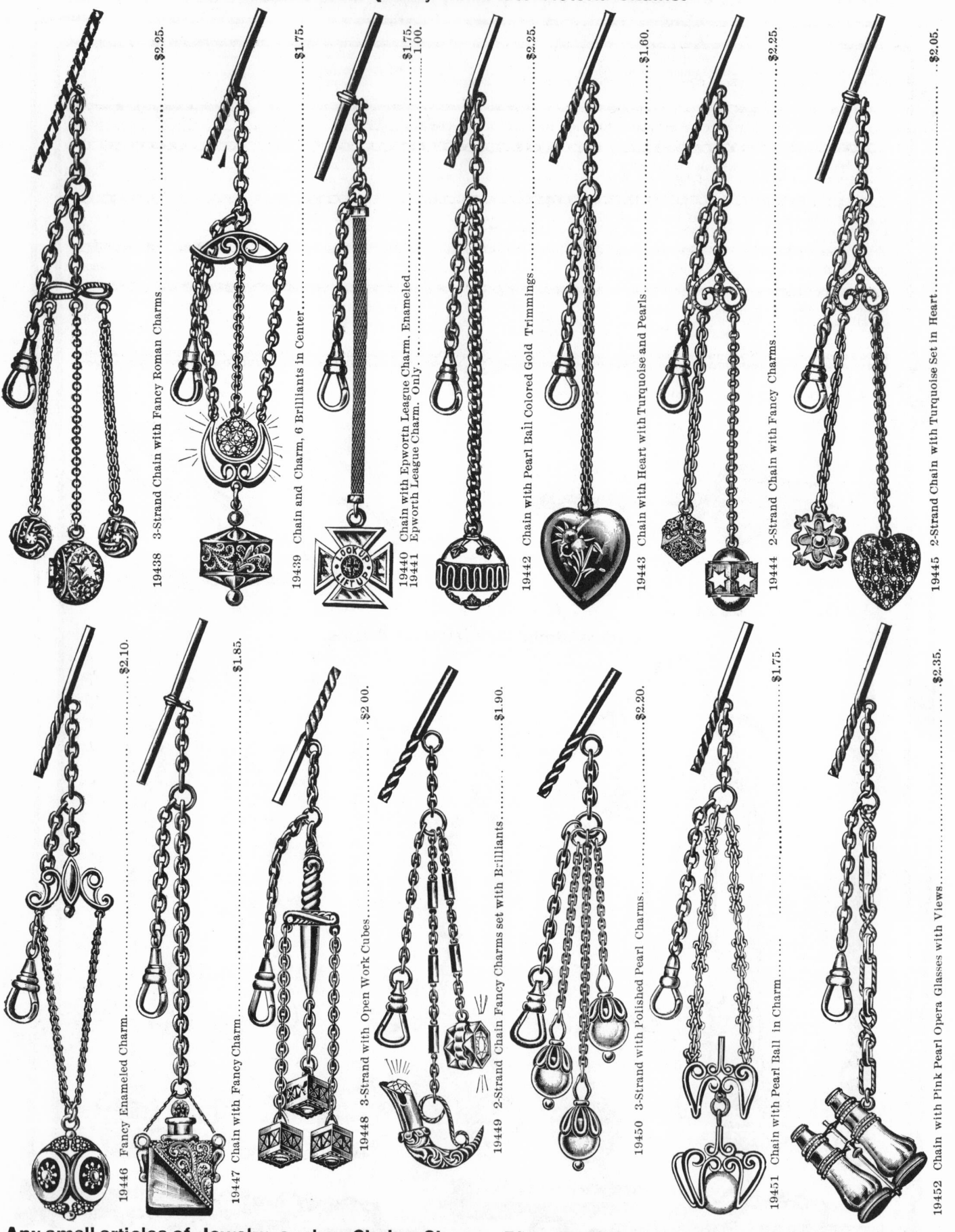

19438   3-Strand Chain with Fancy Roman Charms..........$2.25.

19439   Chain and Charm, 6 Brilliants in Center..........$1.75.

19440   Chain with Epworth League Charm. Enameled..........$1.75.
19441   Epworth League Charm. Only..........1.00.

19442   Chain with Pearl Ball Colored Gold Trimmings..........$2.25.

19443   Chain with Heart with Turquoise and Pearls..........$1.60.

19444   2-Strand Chain with Fancy Charms..........$2.25.

19445   2-Strand Chain with Turquoise Set in Heart..........$2.05.

19446   Fancy Enameled Charm..........$2.10.

19447   Chain with Fancy Charm..........$1.85.

19448   3-Strand with Open Work Cubes..........$2 00.

19449   2-Strand Chain Fancy Charms set with Brilliants..........$1.90.

19450   3-Strand with Polished Pearl Charms..........$2.20.

19451   Chain with Pearl Ball in Charm..........$1.75.

19452   Chain with Pink Pearl Opera Glasses with Views..........$2.35.

Any small articles of Jewelry, such as Chains, Charms, Pins, Ear Drops, Cuff Buttons, Etc., can be sent by Registered Mail for 10c.

LADIES' BEST QUALITY ROLL PLATE VICTORIA CHAINS.

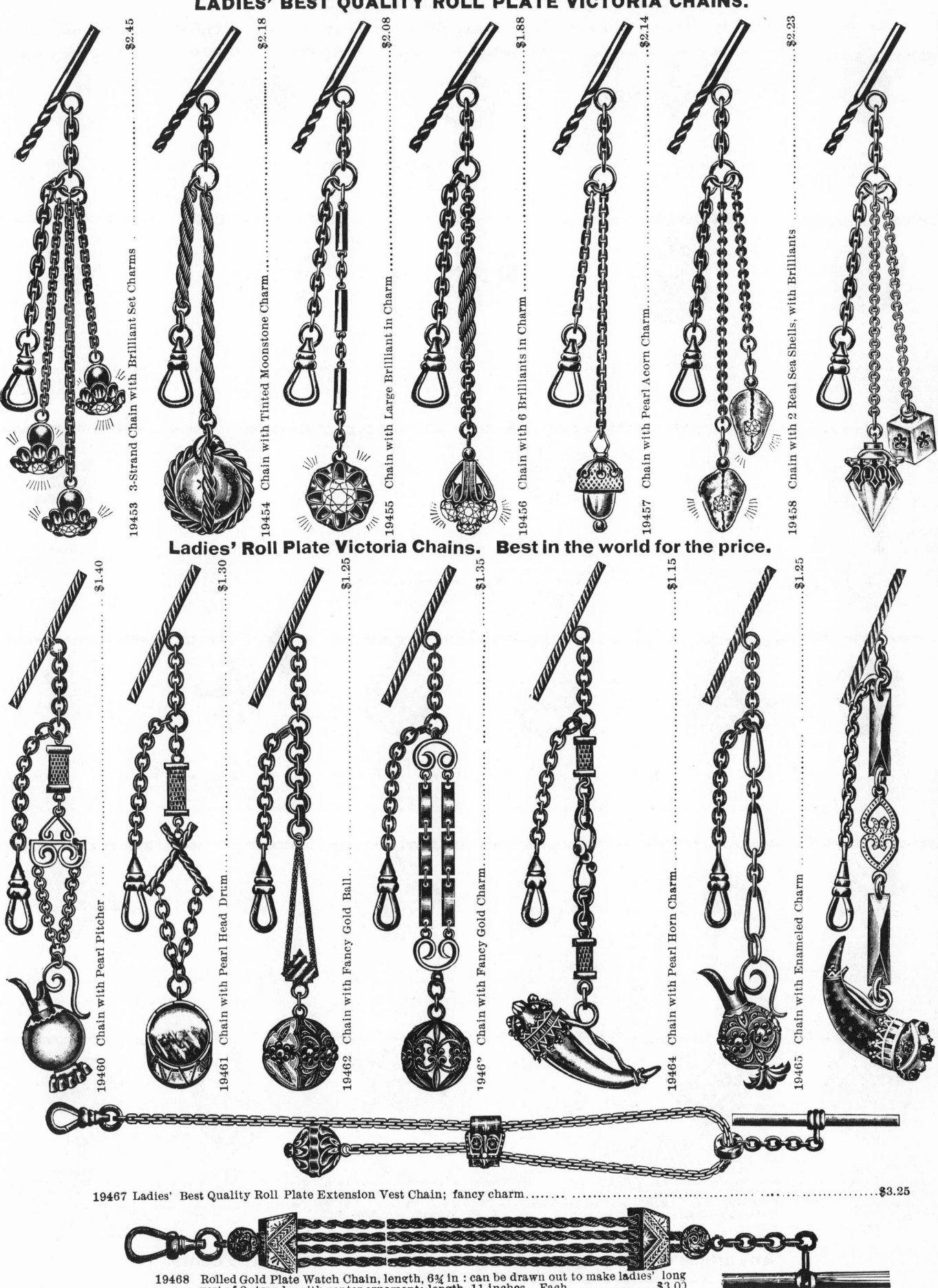

$2.45   19453   3-Strand Chain with Brilliant Set Charms

$2.18   19454   Chain with Tinted Moonstone Charm

$2.08   19455   Chain with Large Brilliant in Charm

$1.88   19456   Chain with 6 Brilliants in Charm

$2.14   19457   Chain with Pearl Acorn Charm

$2.23   19458   Chain with 2 Real Sea Shells, with Brilliants

$2.28   19459   Chain with Polished Pearl Charms

Ladies' Roll Plate Victoria Chains.   Best in the world for the price.

$1.40   19460   Chain with Pearl Pitcher

$1.30   19461   Chain with Pearl Head Drum

$1.25   19462   Chain with Fancy Gold Ball

$1.35   1946?   Chain with Fancy Gold Charm

$1.15   19464   Chain with Pearl Horn Charm

$1.25   19465   Chain with Enameled Charm

$1.15   19466   Chain with Pearl Horn Charm, with Pearl Links

19467 Ladies' Best Quality Roll Plate Extension Vest Chain; fancy charm...... $3.25

19468 Rolled Gold Plate Watch Chain, length, 6¾ in : can be drawn out to make ladies' long vest of 2 strands, with center ornament: length, 11 inches. Each $3.00

SOLID GOLD NECKLACES AND PENDANTS.

These Chains are from 12 to 13 inches in length; if wanted longer than regular size, extra price must be allowed, and extra time in which to make.

19470
Solid Gold, Turquoise Settings.
Price, complete, $4.40.
Pendant, separate, $1.00.

19471
Solid Gold, Turquoise, Pearl
and Garnet Sets.
Price, $2.75.

19472
Solid Gold, Turquoise and Pearls
Price, complete, $3.50.
Pendant, separate, $2.00.

19473
Solid Gold, Enameled Flower,
with Real Diamond.
Complete, $5.50.
Pendant, only, $3.00.

19474
Solid Gold, Pearl Settings.
Price, complete. $4.20
Pendant, separate, $2.60.

19475
Extra Heavy Gold Link with
Diamond Set Pendant.
Complete, $7.50. Pendant,
only, $3.50.

19476
Fine Gold Necklace with Real
Diamond Set Pendant. Price.
$8.05. Same with Topaz in
place of Diamond. Price $6.00

19477
Fine Gold Necklace,
Pendant Set with Pearl and
Ruby, $5.00. Pendant,
only, $2.75.

19478
Star Pendant Set with
Opal in Center and Pearls around.
Complete, $7.50, Pendant
only, $5.00.

19479
Fine Chain with Small
Roman Color Heart Charm,
Pearl Set, complete, $2.75.
Pendant, only, $1.00.

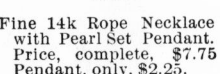

19480
Fine 14k Rope Necklace
with Pearl Set Pendant.
Price, complete, $7.75
Pendant, only, $2.25.

19481
Fine 10k Chain with
Stone Set Pendant,
$3.00.

19482
Fine Light 10k Chain with
Stone Set Pendant. Price,
complete, $5.10. Pend-
ant only, $2.10.

19483
Medium Size 10k Chain,
with Flower Pendant set
with Real Diamond.
Price, complete, $4.00

19484
Cable Link 10k Chain,
with Roman Color Heart
Pendant; sapphire and
pearl sets. Price,
complete, $4.50.

19485
Fine Woven Gold Chain
with Enameled and Pearl
Set Pendant. Price, com-
plete, $4.89. Pendant
separate, $2.75.

19486
Fine 10k Gold Chain, with
real Diamond Set Locket.
Price, complete..$6.75
Lockets, separate. 4.00

19487
Fine long link Chain, Pearl
Set Pendant.
Price, complete..$4.80
Pendant, separate 2.75

19488
Fine link gold Chain, with
real Pearl Set Pendant.
Price. complete..$6.70
Pendant, separate 3.25

19489
Heavy Rope Chain, with
real set Pearl Pendant.
Price, complete..$6.75
Pendant, separate 2.50

19490
Fine Gold Chain, with
Pearl, Stone Set Pendant.
Price, complete..$4.19
Pendant, separate 2.12

19491
Fine Gold Chain with Pearl
and Fancy Stone Set Pendant
Price, complete..$6.78
Pendant, separate 3.50

19492
Fine Woven Gold Chain, with
pearl and F--re OpalSet Pend-
ant.
Price, complete........$8.00
Pendant. separate. 5.00

19493
10k Gold Chain, with
Heart and Clover Leaf
Pendant, 3 sapphires in
center pearls around
edge. Price complete, $5.75

19494
Fine Gold Chain, Enam-
eled and Pearl Set Pendant.
Price, complete. $4.30
Pendant, separate.... 2.30

19495
Fine Gold Chain, Enam-
eled and Pearl Set Pend-
ant.
Price, complete......$5.00
Pendant, separate ... 2.95

19496
Fine 10k Gold Chain, with
Sun Burst Pendant, sap-
phire set.
Price, complete......$3.75

19497.
Fine Strong Chain, with
Enameled, Pearl Set Pen-
dant.
Price, complete.... $6.75
Pendant, separate.. 3.25

19498
Solid 10k.,Gold Chain,Fancy
Pearl and Stone Set Pendant.
Price, complete.......$7.00
Pendant, separate..... 3.25

19499
Fine Woven Gold Chain,
Pearl ,Stone Set Pendant.
Price, complete......$7.50
Pendant, separate... 3.75

19500
10k Gold Chain,with Wreath
Pendant, green gold leaves,
and five pearl sets.
Price, complete.......$5.50

19502
Fine Woven Gold Chain,
Pearl and Opal Set Pen-
dant. Price $7.00
Pendant, separate.. 4.25

19503
Fine Gold Chain, with Pearl
Set Pendant.............$4.75
Pendant only.... ...... 2.75

19504
Fine 10k Chain, with
Roman Color Heart
Charm, pearl set in cen-
ter and fine brilliants
around edge.
Price complete....$5.00

Any article on this page can be sent by registered mail for 10 cents.

Our charge for engraving initials is 2 1-2 cents per letter for Script, 5 cents for Old English.

BEST ROLLED PLATED NECKLACES AND BACELETS.

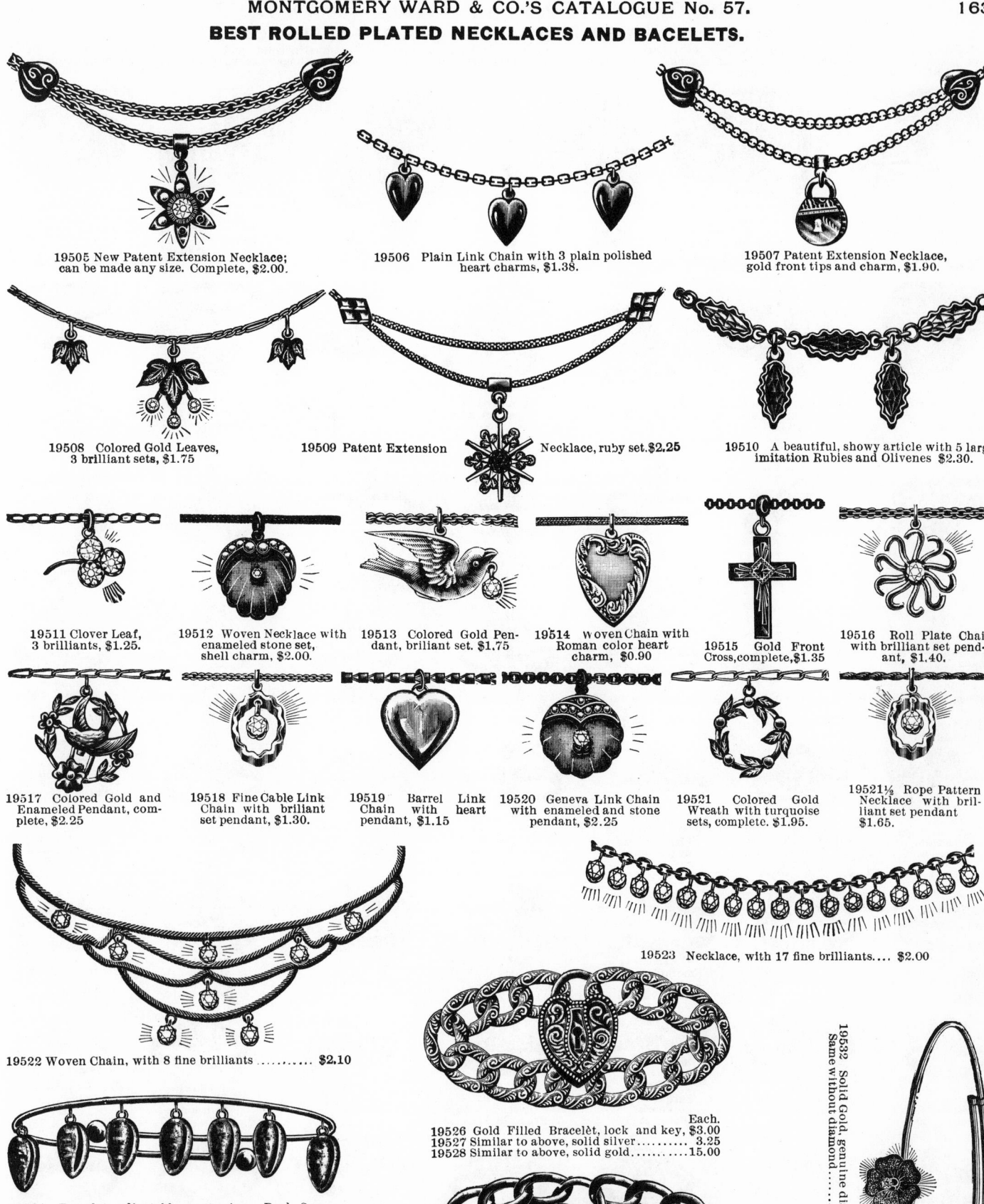

19505 New Patent Extension Necklace; can be made any size. Complete, $2.00.

19506 Plain Link Chain with 3 plain polished heart charms, $1.38.

19507 Patent Extension Necklace, gold front tips and charm, $1.90.

19508 Colored Gold Leaves, 3 brilliant sets, $1.75

19509 Patent Extension   Necklace, ruby set. $2.25

19510 A beautiful, showy article with 5 large imitation Rubies and Olivenes $2.30.

19511 Clover Leaf, 3 brilliants, $1.25.

19512 Woven Necklace with enameled stone set, shell charm, $2.00.

19513 Colored Gold Pendant, briliant set. $1.75

19514 Woven Chain with Roman color heart charm, $0.90

19515 Gold Front Cross, complete, $1.35

19516 Roll Plate Chain with brilliant set pendant, $1.40.

19517 Colored Gold and Enameled Pendant, complete, $2.25

19518 Fine Cable Link Chain with brilliant set pendant, $1.30.

19519 Barrel Link Chain with heart pendant, $1.15

19520 Geneva Link Chain with enameled and stone pendant, $2.25

19521 Colored Gold Wreath with turquoise sets, complete. $1.95.

19521½ Rope Pattern Necklace with brilliant set pendant $1.65.

19522 Woven Chain, with 8 fine brilliants $2.10

19523 Necklace, with 17 fine brilliants.... $2.00

19524 Bracelet, adjustable as to size. Real Sea Shell Bangles. Price................................$0.50

19525 Rolled Plate, Garnet and Brilliant Bracelet. Each...$1.30

19526 Gold Filled Bracelèt, lock and key, $3.00
19527 Similar to above, solid silver.......... 3.25
19528 Similar to above, solid gold...........15.00

19529 Gold Filled Bracelet, lock and key....$2.75
19530 Similar to above, solid silver......... 2.90
19531 Similar to above, solid gold...........13.50

19532 Solid Gold, genuine diamond. Each......$7.25
Same without diamond........ 4.50

LADIES' AND MEN'S RINGS, BEST QUALITY SOLID GOLD.

We illustrate below the largest and finest line of set rings we have ever shown. All the mountings are best quality solid gold. Nos. 19533 to 19540 are gent's rings, sizes 6 to 12. Nos. 19541 to 19591 are ladies' rings. Sizes, 5¼ to 8¼; extra large sizes, cost extra. Always send finger size when ordering. See instructions at top of page 153, or send 2c. stamp for finger gauge.

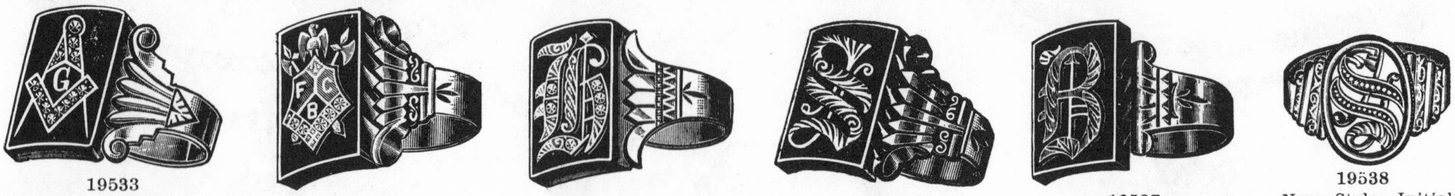

19533 Masonic, or Odd Fellows Ring, heavy shank, 12 Diamonds, $14.00. 19534½ Same as above with any initial, $14.00

19534 K. of P., Odd Fellows, or Masonic Ring, Raised Emblem, 6 Diamonds, $7.50

19535 Initial Ring, Raised initial, 6 Diamonds, any letter, $7.80

19536 Initial Ring, Raised initial, no Diamonds, any letter, $5.00

19537 Initial Ring, same style as 19536, but not quite so heavy, $3.00

19538 New Style Initial Band Ring, all made from 1 piece of gold. Price, $3.25. With 6 diamonds, $6.50

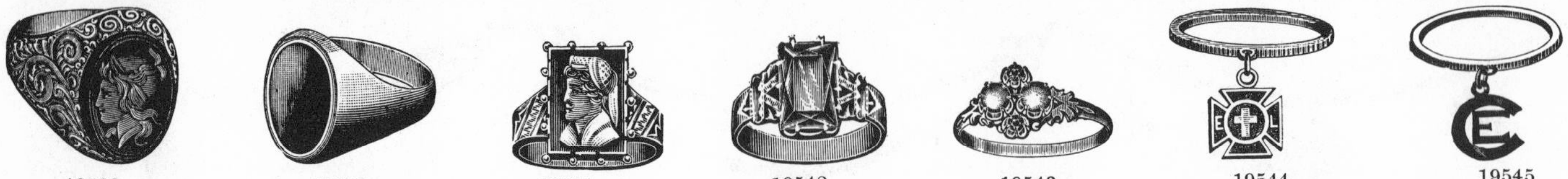

19539 Men's Tiger Eye Set, Carved Shank, $5.75

19540 Men's Real Carbuncle, Plain Durable Shank, $6.00

19541 Pink and White Cameo, Boys' or Ladies' Ring, $1.75

19542 Amethyst or, Topaz Set, $1.60

19543 Opals and Rubys, $5.50

19544 Epworth League Bangle Ring, $0.95. Same in solid silver, $0.30

19545 Christian Endeavor Bangle Ring, $0.90. Same in solid silver, $0.30

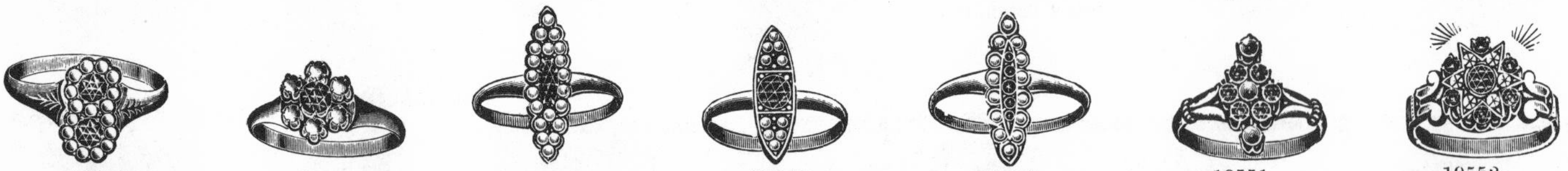

19546 Ruby and Emerald Centers and Pearls around edge, $4.85

19547 Ruby Center and 6 Pearls. Price, $3.85

19548 Marquise Style, Emeralds and Pearls. Price, $4.50

19549 Marquise Style, Ruby and Pearls. Price, $3.50

19550 Marquise Style, Olivene and Pearls. Price, $4.00

19551 6 Garnets and 3 Moonstones. Price, $4.55

19552 6 Diamond Star and 7 Emeralds. Price, $9.00

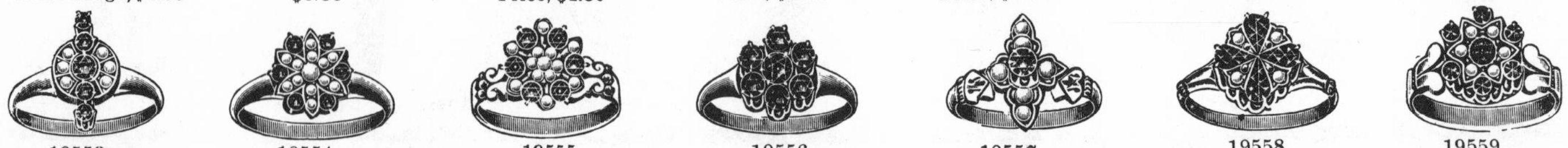

19553 Rubies, Emeralds and Pearls. Price, $4.30

19554 Rubies, Emeralds and Pearls. Price, $5.25

19555 Rubies, Emeralds and Pearls. Price, $5.50

19556 Olivene Center and 6 Pink Topaz. Price, $3.75

19557 Ruby Center and 6 Pearls. Price, $4.75

19558 4 Rubies, 4 Pearls. Price, $5.00

19559 Amethyst and Pearls. Price, $6.00

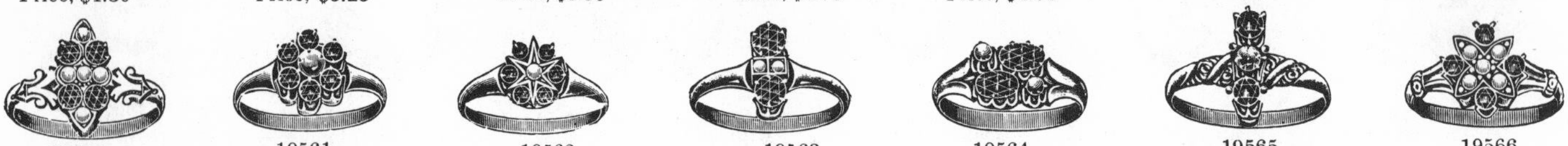

19560 Olivenes, Topaz and Pearls. Price, $4.35

19561 Moonstone Center and 6 Pink Topaz. Price, $3.70

19562 Pearl Center and 6 Pink Topaz. Price, $3.65

19563 2 Rubies and 2 Pearls. Price, $2.25

19564 2 Rubies and 2 Moonstones. Price, $3.25

19565 1 Opal and 2 Rubies. Price, $3.85

19566 4 Sapphires and 4 Pearls. Price, $4.10

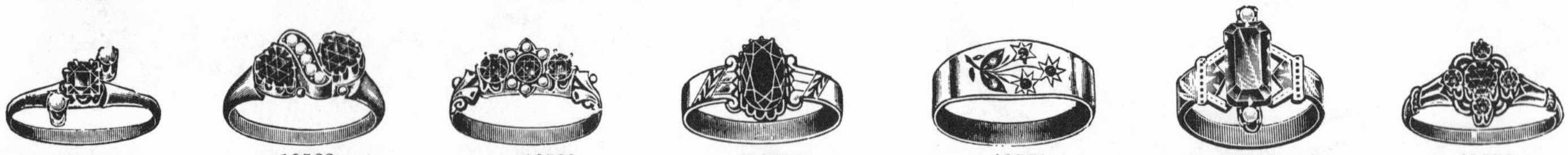

19567 Emerald and Pearls. Price, $2.50

19568 2 Heart-Shape Rubies, 5 Pearls. Price, $3.00

19569 Emerald, Rubies and Pearls. Price, $3.90

19570 Emerald or Garnet. Price, $1.50

19571 Flat Band, Assorted Sets. Price, $2.00

19572 Garnet and Pearls. Price, $2.17

19573 Olivene Center, 4 Pink Topaz. Price, $3.95

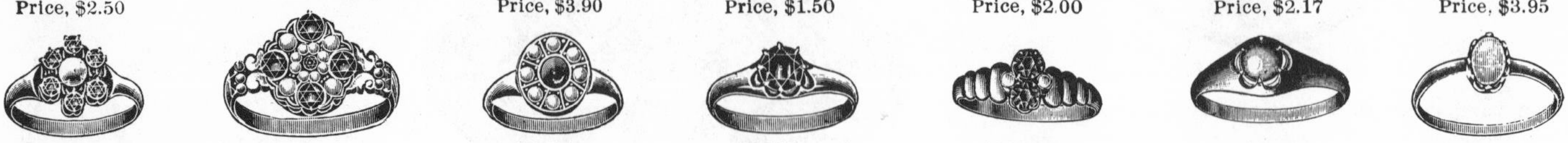

19573½ Moonstone and 6 Olivenes. Price, $3.25

19574 Pearls, Emeralds and Rubies. Price, $5.00

19574½ Turquoise and Pearls. Price, $2.60

19575 Diamond Cut Olivene. Price, $3.00

19575½ Rubies and Pearls. Price, $1.90

19576 Fine Large Turquoise. Price, $2.40

19577 Fine Opal Set. Price, $4.25

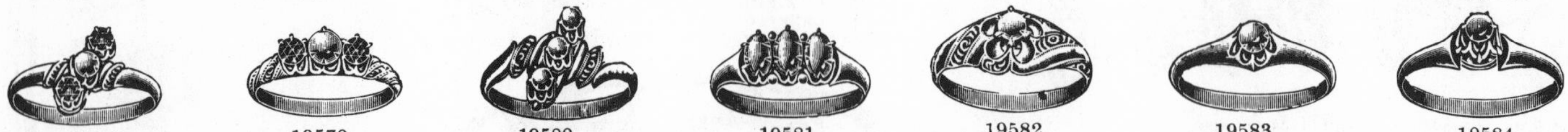

19578 Opal, Ruby and Emerald. Price, $3.75

19579 Opal and 2 Rubies. Price, $3.60

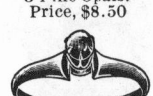

19580 3 Fine Opals. Price, $8.50

19581 3 Large Opals. Price, $7.00

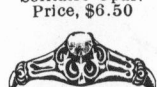

19582 Solitaire Opal. Price, $6.50

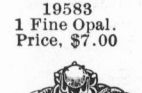

19583 1 Fine Opal. Price, $7.00

19584 Solitaire Opal. Price, $4.00

19585 Diamond Cut Amethyst. Price, $3.40

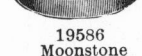

19586 Moonstone. Price, $4.40

19587 Moonstone. Price, $2.10

19588 5 Pearls. Price, $8.25

19589 Single Pearl. Price, $7.25

19590 Single Small Pearl. Price, $4.10

19591 Single Small Pearl. Price, $3 80

Send a two cent stamp for one of our patent ring gauges, with which you can measure the finger exactly and avoid mistakes in ordering.

BEST QUALITY SOLID GOLD BAND RINGS.

The price of these rings is governed entirely by the weight; the higher the price the heavier the ring. Some of the cuts make one ring look heavier than others at the same price, but the actual weight is in proportion to the price.

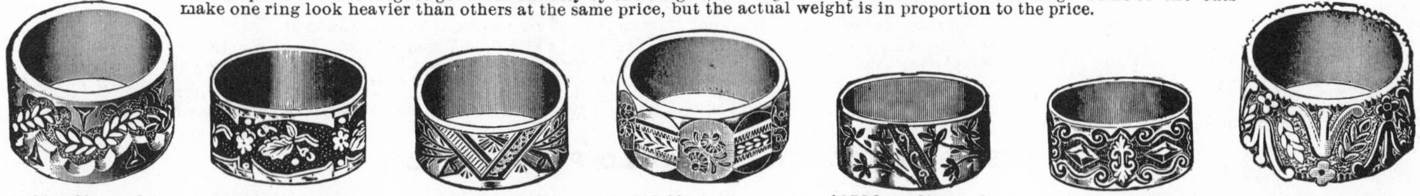

19592 Sizes, 6½ to 11 Price.....$3.60
19593 Sizes. 6½ to 10½. Price...$2.50
19594 Sizes, 6½ to 11. Price......$3.50
19595 Sizes, 6¼ to 11. Price..............$2.43
19596 Sizes, 6½ to 11. Price.......$2.60
19597 Sizes, 6½ to 11. Price.$3.00
19598 Sizes, 6¼ to 11 Price...........$3.20

19599 Sizes, 6½ to 11. Price......$2.75
19600 Sizes, 6½ to 11. Price...$2.60
19601 Sizes, 6½ to 10½. Price..$2.10
19602 Sizes, 6¼ to 11. Price...$2.80
19603 Sizes, 6 to 10. Price...$1.88
19604 Sizes, 6½ to 11. Price. ...$2.00
19605 Heavy Oval. Sizes, 6 to 11½..$3.00 In Sterling silver, .85

19606 Sizes, 6 to 10½. Price...$1 90
19607 Sizes, 6½ to 11. Price.. $2.45
19608 Sizes, 6½ to 11. Price.$1.95
19609 Sizes, 6¼ to 11. Price $2.05
19610 Sizes, 6½ to 11 Price.. $2.30
19611 Sizes, 6½ to 11. Price.. $1.90
19612 Sizes, 6¼ to 11. Price.. $1.84

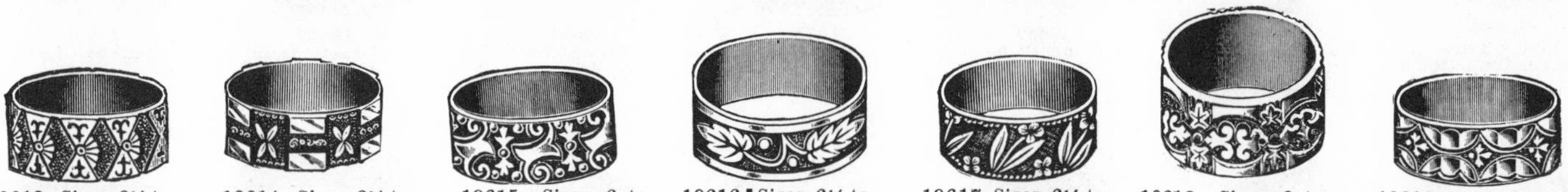

19613 Sizes, 6¼ to 11. Price....$2.20
19614 Sizes, 6¼ to 11. Price....$2.15
19615 Sizes, 6 to 10½. Price..$1.65
19616 Sizes, 6½ to 11. Price...$1.97
19617 Sizes, 6¼ to 11. Price...$1.84
19618 Sizes, 6 to 10. Price....$1.40
19619 Sizes, 6 to 10. Price....$1.35

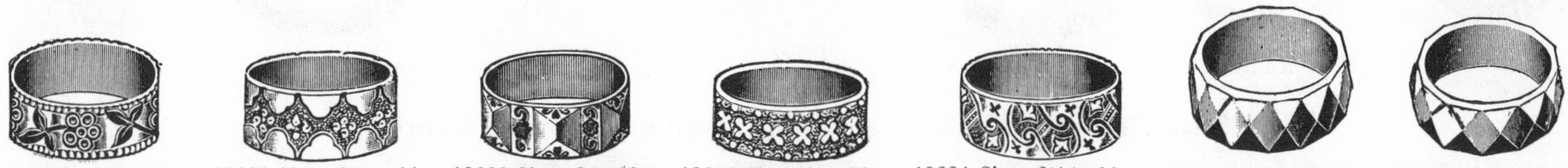

19620 Sizes, 6 to 10½. Price....$1.78
19621 Sizes, 6½ to 11. Price....$2 15
19622 Sizes, 6 to 10. Price....$1.30
19623 Sizes, 6 to 10. Price....$1.72
19624 Sizes, 6¼ to 11. Price...$1.94
19625 Sizes, 5¼ to 9. Price....$1.05
19626 Sizes, 3 to 6½. Price..65c.

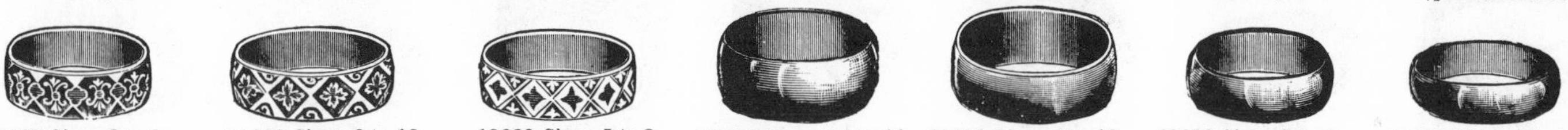

19627 Sizes, 3 to 8. Price....85c.
19628 Sizes, 6 to 10 Price....$1.25
19629 Sizes, 5 to 8. Price .. 88c.
19630 Sizes, 6½ to 11. Price....$2.25
19631 Sizes, 6 to 10. Price....$1.50
19632 Sizes, 5 to 8. Price....95c.
19633 Sizes, 2 to 5. Price....67c.

Misses' Rings, Size 4 to 7 only.

19634 2 Emeralds, 2 Pearls. Price, $2.00
19635 Turquoise and Pearls. Price, $2.00
19636 2 Rubies and 1 Pearl. Price, $1.85
19637 Amethyst Set. Price, $1.00.
19638 Single Ruby. Price, $1.50
19639 Ruby and Pearls. Price, $1.25
19640 Emerald and Pearls. Price, $1.78

Children's Rings, Size 0 to 5 Unless Otherwise Quoted.

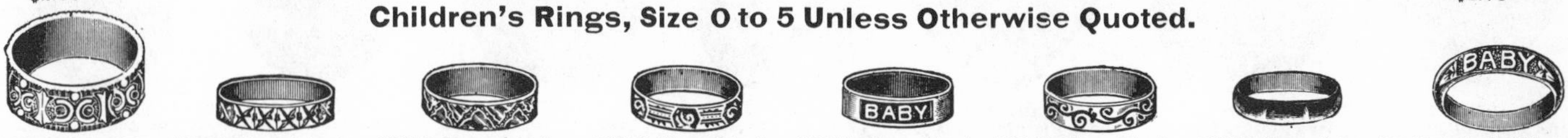

19643 Sizes, 3 to 6½. Price..68c.
19644 Sizes, 0 to 4. Price 54c
19645 Sizes, 1 to 5. Price....58c.
19646 Sizes, 1 to 5, Price....55c.
19647 Sizes, 0 to 4. Price....60c.
19648 Sizes, 0 to 5. Price....65c.
19649 Sizes, 0 to 3. Price.50c.
19649½ Gold Filled Baby Ring. Sizes 0 to 6. Price, $0.25

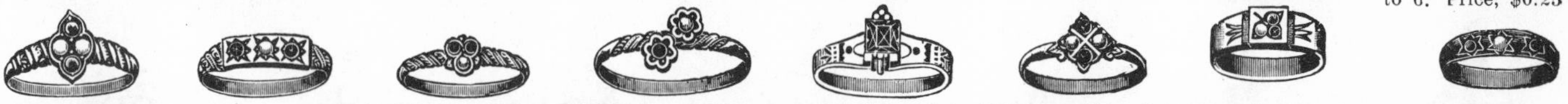

19650 Garnets and Pearls. Price,90c.
19651 Garnets and Pearl. Price,$1.05
19652 Garnets and Pearl. Price,95c.
19653 Turquoise and Pearl. Price,$1.10
19654 Garnet Set. Price..$1.00
19655 Garnets and Pearls. Price.$1.25
19656 Garnet, Pearl & Turquoise.Price$1.05
19657 Turquoise and Pearls. Price.$1.30

A Plain Solid 18K Gold Ring is the Proper Thing for a Wedding Ring.

Multiply the No. of pwt. by the cost per pwt which will give the cost of ring complete.

Flat. Flat. Flat. Oval. Oval Oval. Oval

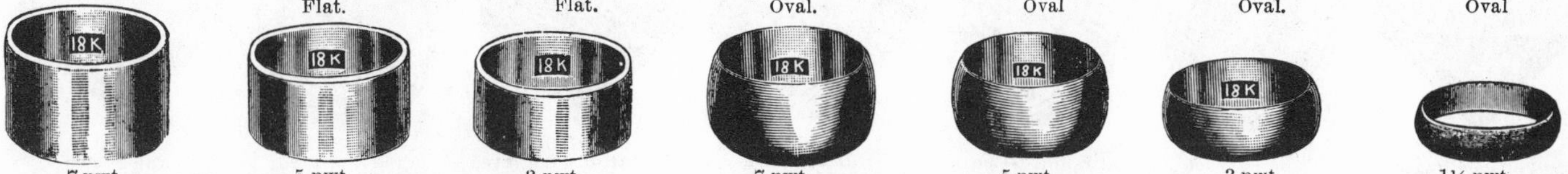

7 pwt. 5 pwt. 3 pwt. 7 pwt. 5 pwt. 3 pwt. 1¼ pwt.

19658 Flat 18k Solid Gold Bands, per pennyweight	$1.00	19662 Plain Oval 18k Rings, per pennyweight	$1.00
19659 Flat 16k Solid Gold Bands, per pennyweight	.90	19663 Plain Oval 16k Rings, per pennyweight	.90
19660 Flat 14k Solid Gold Bands, per pennyweight	.80	19664 Plain Oval 14k Rings, per pennyweight	.80
19661 Flat 10k Solid Gold Bands, per pennyweight	.60	19665 Pl in Oval 10k Rings, per pennyweight	.60

NOTE.—Plain Rings as above are not furnished lighter than 3 pwt., except at advance upon pennyweight price of 30c. per pwt.

SEND A TWO CENT STAMP FOR ONE OF OUR PATENT RING GAUGES WITH WHICH YOU CAN MEASURE YOUR FINGER CORRECTLY AND AVOID MISTAKES WHEN ORDERING.

Plain 18k Gold Filled Rings.—See Illustrations at bottom of page 165.

Similar in appearance to Nos. 19658 and 19662; wear for years like solid gold.
We do not engrave filled rings, as the engraving cannot be removed and ring exchanged if it fails to fit.

19666 Plain 18k Gold Filled, Oval, size of 7 pennyweight, each..............$2.00	19672 Extra Quality Flat Gold Filled, size of 3 pennyweight............... $1.85
19667 Plain 18k Gold Filled, Oval, size of 5 pennyweight, each............. 1.55	19673 Extra Quality Plain Oval Gold Filled, size of 7 pennyweight.... .... 2.62
19668 Plain 18k Gold Filled, Oval, size of 3 pennyweight, each............. 1.25	19674 Extra Quality Plain Oval Gold Filled, size of 5 pennyweight............. 2.00
19669 Plain 18k Gold Filled, Oval, size of 2 pennyweight, each.... .... .75	19675 Extra Quality Plain Oval Gold Filled, size of 3 pennyweight............. 1.62
19670 Extra Quality Flat Gold Filled, size of 7 pennyweight............. ... 3.00	19676 Extra Quality Plain Oval Gold Filled. Child's size of 1¼ penny-
19671 Extra Quality Flat Gold Filled, size of 5 pennyweight 2.25	weight .... .75

BEST QUALITY ROLLED GOLD PLATE RINGS.

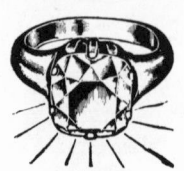      

19679 Large Imitation Diamond. $0.75   19680 Tiger Eye Cameo Set. $0.68   19681 Bloodstone Set. Glove Ring. $0.65   19682 Gent's Black Cameo $0.70   19683 Gold Stone Set. $0.75   19684 Tiger Eye Stone, fancy setting. $0.48   19686 Carbuncle Garnet. $0.80

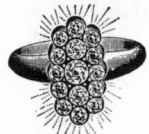  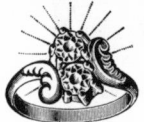  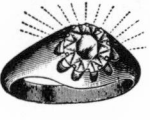  

19687 Cluster Imitation Diamonds and Rubies. $0.85   19688 Gold Stone Set, encrusted with Brilliants. $0.55   19689 Imitation Diamond and Ruby. $0.60   19690 Three White Stone Brilliants. $0.75   19691 Fine Solitaire Brilliant. $0.78   19692 Faceted Setting, on Brilliant. $0.75   19693 Fine Solitaire Brilliant. $0.50

19694 Misses' Brilliant Set. $0.40   19695 Three Brilliants. $0.42   19696 Emerald and Brilliants. $1.00   19697 Ruby and Brill $0.65   19698 4 Imitation Diamonds. $0.62   19699 Good Finish, plain wedding style, each 3c; per doz. 25c.   19700 Misses' Friendship Ring. $0.25

COIN SILVER RINGS. Good Style and Finish. Always Send Size.

    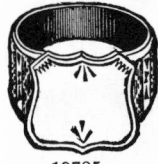  

19701 Coin Silver. Double Hearts. $0.18   19702 Gold Hands $0.55   19703 Silver Shield Top $0.30   19704 Silver Shield Top. $0.65   19705 Silver Gold Top $0.85   19706 Plain Silver. $0.40   19707 Sterling Silver. Stone Set Eyes. $1.34

SOLID GOLD LOCKETS AND CHARMS.—Prices, Each.

19708 Fine Roman Pendant, Diamond Set. $10.50. 19709 Same without Diamond. $6.50   19710 Two Picture Locket, Raised Colored Gold Ornamentation. $6.00   19711 Two Pictures, Raised Ornamentation. $6.25   19712 Two Pictures, Raised Colored Ornamentation. Very Handsome. $6.50   19713 Two Pictures, Raised Rococo Edge, Real Diamond. $7.75   19714 Two Pictures, Handsome Engraving, Real Diamond. $6.04   19715 Two Pictures, Rococo Edge, Real. Diamond. $6.25

19716 Fine Polished Engraved Locket for Two Pictures, ₁⁵k Diamond in Center. $7.50   19717 Fine Polished Engraved Locket for Two Pictures, ₁⁵k Diamond in Center. $7.25   19718 Satin Finish Chased Locket for Two Pictures, ₁⁵k Diamond in Center. $7.00   19719 Raised Gold Flowers, K. of P. Emblem. Two Pictures. $7.25. Can furnish Masonic or Odd Fellows at same price.   19720 Beautifully Engraved Locket for Two Pictures. $4.25   19721 Fine Engraved Front Locket, for Two Pictures. $4.00   19722 Satin Finish Chased Locket, for Two Pictures. $4.50

All of these Lockets have plain back where initial or any emblem can be engraved. We charge for script engraving 2½ cents per letter. Old English 5 cents per lette

SOLID GOLD LOCKETS AND CHARMS.

Many of the lower priced lockets and charms quoted below, although known as solid gold and sold as such by all jewelers, have the backs strengthened inside with silver solder. We guarantee all to wear as well as any goods made at the price.

19724
Heart Locket. Diamond set. $10.50
19725 Same without Diamond. $7.00

19726
Extra quality Diamond set $7.50

19727
Gold Locket Engraved. 2 pictures $3.50

19728
Bright Engraved Locket. 2 pictures. $2.95

19729
Satin Chased Locket. 2 pictures $3.00

19730
Hand Engraved Charm. $3.00

19731
Odd Fellows' Locket. Enameled in colors. 2 pictures. $4.40. K. of P. or Masonic, same price.

19732
Raised Gold Birds and Flowers. 2 pictures. $3.55

19733
Roman Chased Locket. 2 pictures. $3.45

19734
Bright Engraved Locket. 2 pictures. $1.95

19735
Bright Engraved Locket. 2 pictures $1.90

19736
Bright Engraved Locket. 2 pictures. $2.23

19737
Satin Finish Locket. Diamond set. $3.09
9738 Same without Diamond. $2.00

19739
Satin Finish Locket. Diamond set. $3.05
19740 Same without Diamond. $2.05

19741
Engraved Locket. 2 pictures. Diamond set. $4.80

19742
Gold Star Pendant. Pearl sets. $1.88

19743
Fancy Gold Pendant. Sapphire and Pearls. $2.45

19744
Gold Pendant Pearl set. $1.75

19745
Roman Charm. Ruby, Pearl and Sapphire. $2.15

19746
Roman Heart Charm. Pearl sets. $2.26

19747
oman Chased Charm, Pearl set. $1.75

19748
Roman Heart Charm. Pearl set. $1.25

19749
Roman Heart Charm. Diamond set. $3.00

19750
Engraved Heart Locket. 2 pictures. $3.35

Best Rolled Plate Lockets and Charms.

19751
Aluminum. Heavily Gold Plated; light and durable. Garnet eyes. $1.25

19752
Aluminum. Heavy Gold Plated. Garnet eyes $1.15

19753
Aluminum. Heavy Gold Plated Garnet eyes. $1.30

19754
Gold Filled Locket. 2 pictures. $1.55

19755
Chased and Engraved Locket. 1 picture, 75c.

19756
Filled Locket. 2 pictures Brilliant set. $1.27

19757
Filled Locket. 2 pictures. $1.37

19758
Gold Filled Locket. 2 pictures. $1.67

19759
Chased Locket. 1 picture $0.78

19760
Stone Set. 1 picture. $1.15

19761
Fine Intaglio. Sea Charm. $0.68

19762
HorseShoe Charm $1.54

19763
Fine Roman Locket. 6 Brilliants. 1 picture. $1.42

19764
Raised Wreath. 1 picture. $0.84

19765
Satin Finish. 1 picture. $0.73

19766
Filled Locket 2 pictures $1.00

19767
Engraved. 1 picture. $0 79

19768
A Perfect Practical Compass. Warranted. $1.20

19769
Crystal Charm. $0.92

BEST QUALITY ROLLED PLATE LOCKETS AND CHARMS.

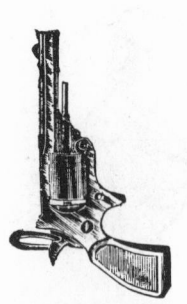
19770
Rolled Plate Pearl
Handle Revolver.
Each, 40c.

19771
Fancy Stone Set Locket.
Each, $1.20

19772
Fine Rolled Plate Charm.
Each, 59c.

19773
Rolled Plate Locket.
Each, 63c.

19774
Fancy 4 Color Stone.
Each, 95c.

19775
Fancy Stone Set 1
Picture Locket.
Each, 85c.

19776
Gold Side Fancy Stone
Set, 1 Picture Locket.
Each, $1.18

19777
Fancy Edge Stone
Set, 2 Pictures, 75c.

19778
Real Crystal Ball Charm.
Each, $1.03

19779
Compass Charm.
Each, $1.25

19780
Raised Gold Dogs, 1
Picture, $1.56

19781
Crystal Ball.
Each, 64c.

19782
Rolled Plate, Gold Sides.
Each, $1.30

19783
Fancy Stone Set
Locket. Each, 80c.

19784
Fancy Rolled Plate,
Stone Eyes. Each, 55c.

19785
Fancy Gold Plate,
2 Picture Locket.
Each, 65c.

19786
Rolled Plate Opera
Glasses, World's Fair
Views. Each, 65c.

19787
Fancy Center, Plain
Edge. Each, 50c.

19788
Black and Gold
Stone Charm.
Each, 97c.

19789
Fancy Gold Side 2
Picture Locket.
Each, 64c.

19790
Fancy 3 Color Stone.
Each, 95c.

19791
Raised Colored Gold 1
Picture Locket, 90c.

19792
Rolled Plate Stone Set,
1 Picture. Each, 80c.

19793
Roman Stone Set,
1 picture. Each, 78c

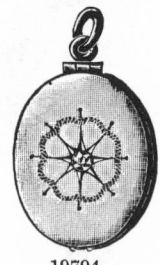
19794
1 Picture Chased Stone
Set Locket. Each, 81c.

19795
Pearl Horn Charm.
Each, 68c.

19796
4 Colors, Barrel Charm
Each, 95c.

19797
Rolled Plate Locket,
2 pictures, Each, 60c.

19798
Extra Quality.
Each, $1.35

19799
Each, 67c.

19800
Stone Set Locket.
Each, 88c

19801
Fine Roman Locket, 6
Brilliants, 1 Picture.
Each, $1.49

19802
Love Locket, 1 Picture,
Brilliant Set.
Each, 91c.

19803
Stone Set Locket.
Each, 88c.

19804
Fancy Colored Gold
1 Picture Locket.
Each, 60c.

19805
Plow, Two Colors. Each, $1.25

19806
Roman Color, Garnet Eyes.
Each, $1.00

19807
Book Locket, 2 Pictures.
Each, 98c.

19808
Roman Heart Locket,
1 Picture. Each, 63c.

19809
Roman Finish, Garnet
Eyes. Each, 50c.

19810
Stone Base.
Each, $1.25

ROLL PLATE WATCH CHARMS.

19815
Odd Fellow. Each, 32c.

19816
Raised Emblem,
Stone Back.
Each, 35c

19817
Colored Head.
Each, 32c.

19818
Fancy Colors.
Each, 32c.

19819
Brilliant Set.
Each, 32c.

19820
Engraved Front.
Each, 32c.

19821
Brilliant Set.
Each, 32c.

19822
Each, 32c.

19823
Colored Landscape.
Each, 32c.

19824
Colored Landscape
Each, 32c.

19825
Stone Base.
Each, 32c.

19826
Colored Head.
Each, 32c.

19827
Each, 32c.

19828
White Enamel Shoe.
Each, 32c.

19829 Pearl Center
With Brilliant.
Each, 32c

19830
Each, 32c.

19831
Each, 32c

19832
Brilliant Set
Each, 32c.

19833
Red Set.
Each, 32c.

19834
Each, 32c.

19835 Stone Set.
Each, 37c.

19836
Colored
Hour Glass
Each, 65c.

19837
Pearl Shoe.
Each, 74c.

19838
Anchor Compass
Each, 32c.

19839
Compass Charm.
Each, 35c.

19840
Rolled Plate, Stone Set.
Each, 33c.

19841
Silver and Pearl.
Each, 33c.

19842 Wheel Compass.
Each, 40c.

19843
Watch Compass
Each, 38c.

19844
Stone Side
Charm. Each, 28c.

19845
Fancy Stone Side
Charm. Each, 28

19846
Fancy Compass
Each, 36c.

19847
Crystal Ball.
Wound with
Twisted Wire
Each, 52.

World's Fair
Views.

19848 Telescope,
eight different
views of princi-
pal World's Fair
buildings. Price,
each........$0.10

19849
Rolled Plate Stone Set
Charm. Each, 25c.

19850
Buggy. Each, 34c.

19851
Stone Set
Charm. Each, 32

19852
Raised Flowers.
Each, 39c.

Any
Letter.

19852½
Silver, 10c.
Plate, 11c.

19853
Engraved.
Each, 36c.

19854
Brilliant Set.
Each, 39.

19855
Pearl Head Tam-
bourine. Each, 68c.

19856
Pearl Horse Head.
Each, 67c.

BEST QUALITY ROLL PLATE AND GOLD FILLED CUFF BUTTONS.--Prices per Pair.

ALL OUR CUFF BUTTONS, EXCEPT LINK BUTTONS, HAVE PATENT LEVER BACKS.

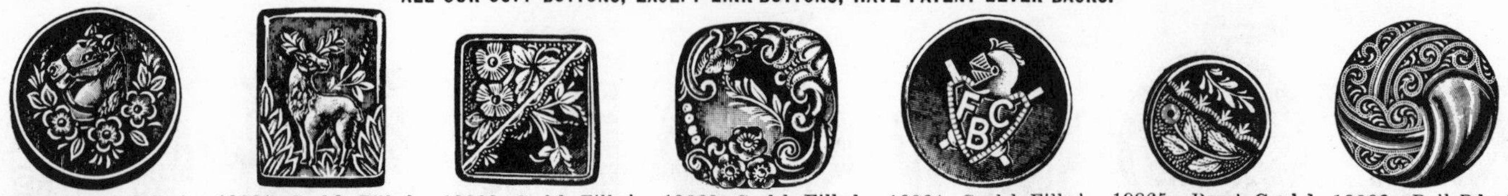

19860 Gold Filled, raised, gold ornaments.......... $2.00

19861 Gold Filled, raised, gold stag. Price.......... $1.90

19862 Gold Filled, colored, gold flowers. Price..........$1.85

19863 Gold Filled, colored, gold flowers. Price..........$1.75

19864 Gold Filled. raised gold, K. of P. emblem........$1.65 Same in Masonic or Odd Fellows...$1.65

19865 Boys' Gold Filled, colored gold flowers $1.25

19866 Roll Plate. polished........$0.85

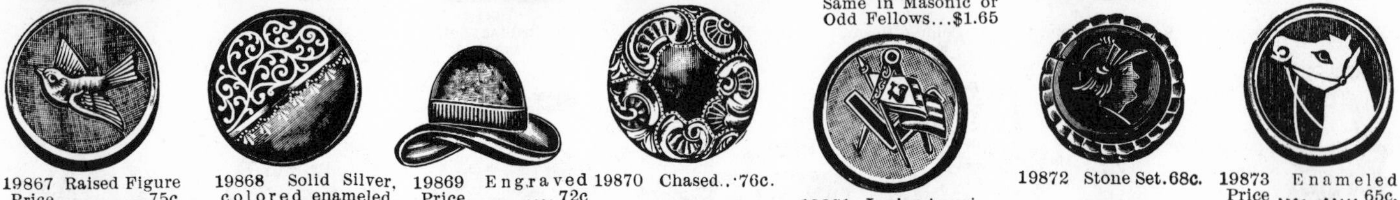

19867 Raised Figure Price ....75c.

19868 Solid Silver, colored enameled. Price... .... 70c.

19869 Engraved Price.. . .... 72c

19870 Chased..·76c.

19871 Junior American Mechanics... 67c. Furnish any emblem.

19872 Stone Set.68c.

19873 Enameled Price.... ...... 65c.

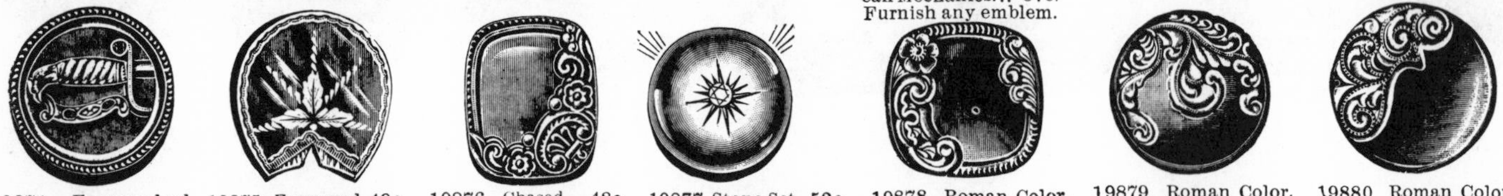

19874 Enameled Sword ....50c.

19875 Engraved.49c.

19876 Chased...48c

19877 Stone Set..52c.

19878 Roman Color. Price........... 47c

19879 Roman Color. Price........... 51c.

19880 Roman Color. Price............ 46c.

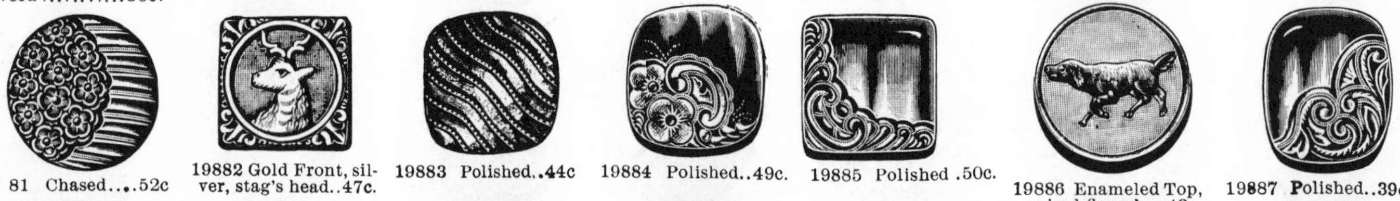

19 81 Chased....52c

19882 Gold Front, silver, stag's head..47c.

19883 Polished..44c

19884 Polished..49c.

19885 Polished .50c.

19886 Enameled Top, raised figure....43c.

19887 Polished..39c.

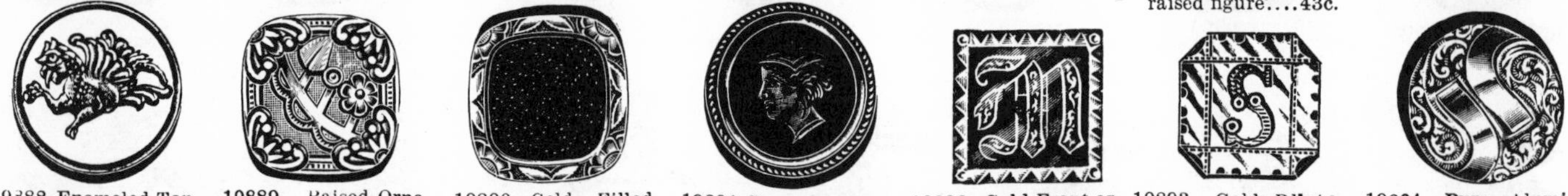

19888 Enameled Top, raised figure.....35c

19889 Raised Ornaments............38c.

19890 Gold Filled, gold stone set, 85c.

19891 Stone Set..41c.

19892 Gold Front or Onyx, any initial. Price $1.00

19893 Gold Plate (give letter wanted). Price...... ......35c.

19894 Pure Aluminum. Price $0.10

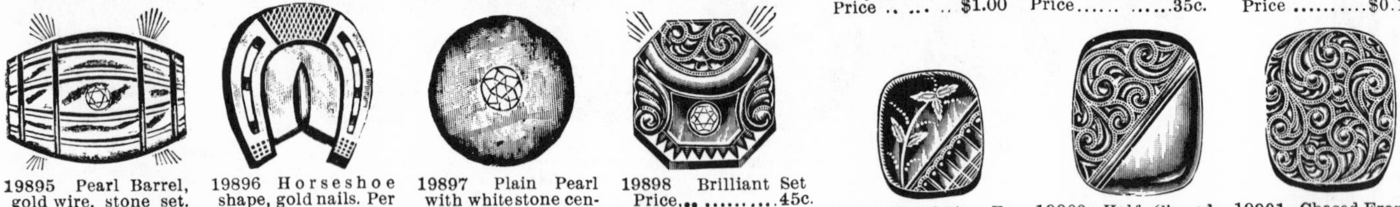

19895 Pearl Barrel, gold wire, stone set. Price $0.42

19896 Horseshoe shape, gold nails. Per pair. ....75c.

19897 Plain Pearl with whitestone center. Price.......$0.30
19897½ Without Stone, 20c

19898 Brilliant Set Price,.. ....45c.

19899 Boys' Size, Engraved. Price...42c.

19900 Half Chased, Price...... .....25c

19901 Chased Front Price...........23c

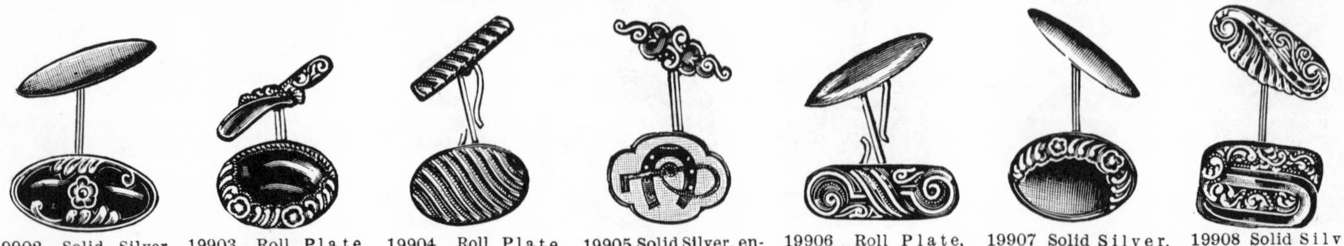

19902 Solid Silver, enameled........68c,

19903 Roll Plate, link buttons....65c.

19904 Roll Plate, link buttons.... 50c,

19905 Solid Silver, enameled..........45c.

19906 Roll Plate, polished........46c.

19907 Solid Silver, Price............42c.

19908 Solid Silver, Price............39c.

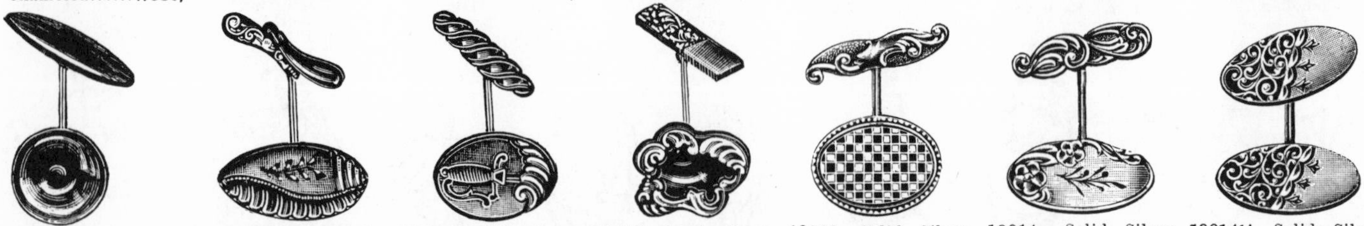

19909 Roll Plate, polished.........83c.

19910 Gold Filled, engraved link buttons........... $1.10

19911 Solid Silver enameled link buttons..............80c.

19912 Solid Silver, enameled Sword. Price..............85c.

19913 Solid Silver enameled........90c

19914 Solid Silver enameled.........95c.

19914½ Solid Silver enameled...... $1.25

SOLID GOLD CUFF BUTTONS.

All our cuff buttons except link buttons have patent lever backs.

19915 Roman Color, plain and engraved. Price, $4.00

19916 Chased Roman Coil. Price, $3.50

19917 Engraved, Satin Finish. Price, $3.90

19917A Plain and Chased. Price $3.60

19918 Fine Strong Button, handsomely chased. Price, $3.50

19919 Gold Inital; any letter. Price, $3.00

19920 Thick, Flat Heavy Buttons, hand engraved. Price, $4.50

19921 Gold Emblem I. O. O. F. Masonic or K P same price. Price, $3.00

19922 Gold Raised Emblem, Masonic, Odd Fellows or K. P. Per pair, $5.00

19923 Head and Wreath of colored gold raised upon heavy gold buttons. Per pair, $5.00

19924 Medium size, new design fancy chasing. Per pair, $3.00

19925 Polished Raised Edge. Per pair, $2.85

19926 Bright Polish, hand chased. Per pair, $2.00

19927 Plain Satin, ladies' or boys'. Per pair, $2.25

19928 Roman Chased Diamond center Per pair, $5.50

19929 Plain Roman, Diamond center Per pair, $4.75

19930 Chased, Diamond center. Per pair, $5.00

19931 Chased Edge. Per pair, $2.75

19932 Gold Chameleons. Per pair, $4.25

19933 Chased. Per pair, $3.50

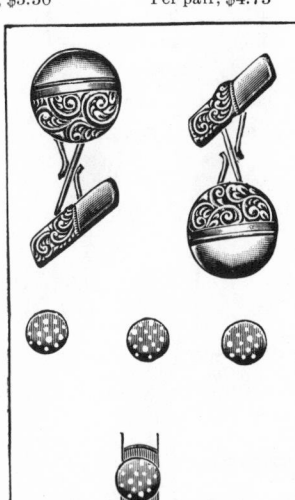

19935 Ladies' roll plate combination set, collar, dress and cuff buttons. Per set, 65c
19935A Same silver plated. Per set, $0.30

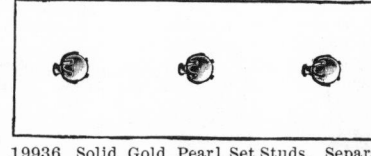

19936 Solid Gold, Pearl Set Studs. Separable backs. Per set, $2.50. Each, 85c.

19937 Solid Gold Top Polished Studs. Separable backs. Per set, $1.25.

19938 Solid Gold Top, Pearl Set Studs. Separable backs. Per set, $2.25

19939 Ladies' Solid Silver Combination Set, collar, dress and cuff buttons. Per set, 78c

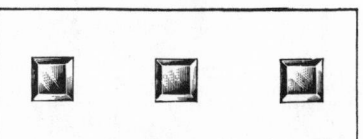

19940 Solid Gold Top, Polished Studs. Separable backs. Per set, $1.40

19941 Solid Gold Brilliant 90c

19942 Solid Gold, Brilliant 85c

19943 Solid Gold, Brilliant 80c

19944 Solid Gold Top Separable Studs. Per set, $1.35
19945 Same, but roll plate.   "   .25
19946   "   "   white or blackstone   "   .25

19947 Roll Plate, Brilliant. 25c.

19948 Roll Plate, Brilliant. 30c.

19949 Ruby Doublet. 32c.

19950 Pearl set. 30c.

19951 Pearl set. 20c.

19952 Real Moonstone, solid gold, 75c.

19953 Pearl Set, solid gold. $1.00

19954 Fine Pearl Set, solid gold. $2.00

For finest imitation Diamond Studs, see Ceylon Brilliants, Page 154.

FINE SOLID GOLD SCARF AND STICK PINS.
Worn by Ladies and Gentlemen.

 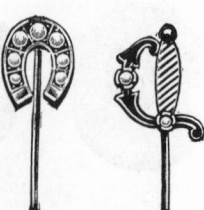      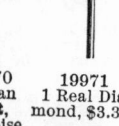

19960 Enameled Sword, $2.63 | 19961 Pearl Set Horseshoe, $2.00. | 19962 Enameled Handle, 2 Pearls, $1.35 | 19963 Ruby and Pearl Sets, $1.25 | 19964 Engraved Handle, 1 Pearl, $1.25 | 19965 Pearl Set, $2.50 | 19966 Pearl Set Crown, $3.50 | 19967 Pearls and Turquoise $2.00 | 19968 Real Diamond and Pearl, $3.50 | 19969 Crescent Star, Turquoise, and Pearls, $1.60 | 19970 Roman Heart, Turquoise, 9 Pearls, $2.30 | 19971 1 Real Diamond, $3.35

 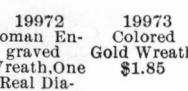      

19972 Roman Engraved Wreath, One Real Diamond, $3.75 | 19973 Colored Gold Wreath, $1.85 | 19974 Emerald and Pearl Wreath, $1.50 | 19975 Enameled Leaves, Whole Pearls, $2.00 | 19976 Roman Battle Ax, Pearls and Turquoise Sets, $2.40 | 19977 Engraved Battle Ax, Turquoise Set, $0.88 | 19978 Bright Gold Two Pearls, $1.90 | 19979 Ruby, Emerald and Sapphire, $0.90 | 19980 Flying Wings, Ruby and Pearls, $2.95 | 19981 Three Moon Stones, $1.05 | 19982 Sheaf and Sickle, $1.00 | 19983 Dumb Bell, Two Pearls, $1.50

 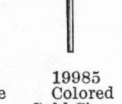    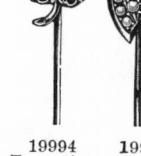

19984 Alligator, One Emerald Set, $1.00 | 19985 Colored Gold Chameleon, $1.50 | 19986 Colored Green Gold, $1.50 | 19987 Epworth League, Solid Gold,$1.00 Solid Silver, .35 | 19988 Green Colored Gold, $2.00 | 19989 Colored Gold, $1.75 | 19990 Green Gold, One Pearl, $2.50 | 19991 Colored Gold, One Brilliant, $1.25 | 19992 Roman Coil, Ruby Set, $0.95 | 19993 Bright Gold, One Diamond, $3.75 | 19994 Turquoise and Pearls, $2.00 | 19995 Battle Ax, Pearl Set, $1.85

19996 Chip Diamond in Pansy, $1.25 | 19997 Garnet Set, Flower, $0.59 | 19998 Gold Hand, Pearl Set, $1.25 | 19999 Roman Leaf, One Diamond, $2.75 | 20000 Roman Coil, One Diamond, $3.00 | 20001 Three Fine Brilliants, $1.00. | 20002 Bright Gold, One Imitation Diamond, $1.25 | 20003 Large Imitation Pearl, $0.85 | 20004 Pearl Set, $0.75 | 20005 One Fine Brilliant, $0.92 | 20006 Pearl Set, Flower, $0.98 | 20007 Thistle, Colored Gold, $1.50

BEST QUALITY ROLL PLATE SCARF OR STICK PINS.

  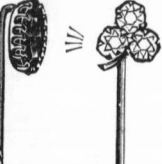     

20008 Pearl Ball, $0.38 | 20009 Single Brilliant, $0.25 | 20010 Ruby Set, $0.26 | 20011 Single Topaz, $0.42 | 20012 Three Brilliants, $0.40 | 2001 Bright Finish, Seven Brilliants, $0.50 | 20014 Single Ruby, $0.32 | 20015 Imitation Pearl, $0.30 | 20016 Colored Leaf, One Brilliant, $0.29 | 20017 Engraved Front, $0.36 | 20018 Colored Leaf, One Brilliant, $0.27 | 20019 Solid Silver, Pearl Top,$0.35

20020 Plated Horseshoe and Real Sea Shell, $0.50 | 20021 Stone Set, $0.29 | 20022 Pearl Wreath, $0.29 | 20023 Serpent, Emerald and Rubies, $0.40 | 20024 Real Sea Shell, Pearl Center, $0.34 | 20025 One Brilliant, $0.23 | 20026 Aluminum Owl, $0.53 | 20027 Single Brilliant $0.25 | 20028 Pearl with Plated Letter, any Initial. $0.15 | 20029 Odd Fellows, $0.26 | 20030 Masonic, $0.25 | 20031 K. of P., $0.23

BEST QUALITY ROLL PLATE SCARF AND STICK PINS.

These little pins are very popular with ladies as well as gentlemen.   They are worn by ladies in the same manner as an ordinary brooch pin.

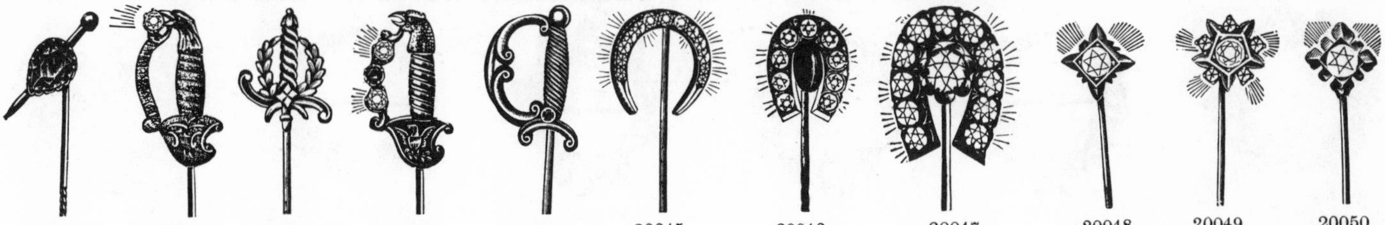

| 20040 Amethyst. $0.33 | 20041 Stone Set Sword. $0.28 | 20042 Wreath and Sword. $0.22 | 20043 Ruby and 2 Brilliant Sets. $0.34 | 20044 Enameled, 1 Brilliant. $0.30 | 20045 Gold Front, 12 Brilliants. $0.87 | 20046 Cat's Eye and Brilliants. $1.00 | 20047 12 Fine Brilliants. $1.50 | 20048 Gold Front, 1 Brilliant. $0.50 | 20049 Brilliant and Sapphires. $0.68 | 20050 Gold Front 1 Brilliant. $0.55 |

| 20051 Stone Set, 1 Brilliant $0.63 | 20052 Pearl Set. $0.85 | 20053 Stone Set. $0.50 | 20054 Garnet Set Fly, $0.78 | 20055 Stone Set. $0.48 | 20056 Gold Front. $0.30 | 20057 4 Rubies and 1 Brilliant. $0.57 | 20058 Horseshoe with 9 Brilliants. $1.50 | 20059 Brilliant and 4 Rubies. $0.63 | 20060 Colored Gold, $0.90 | 20061 / 20062 Stones set in Handles. $0.18 / $0.18 |

| 20063 4 Amethysts and 1 Brilliant. $0.73 | 20064 Garnet Set. $0.23 | 20065 Garnet Set. $0.23 | 20066 Gold Front, Pearl Set. $0.70 | 20067 Colored Gold. $0.32 | 20068 Gold Front 5 Brilliants, $0.60 | 20069 Real Coral. $0.55 | 20070 Coronet. $0.42 | 20071 Gold Front, 12 Brilliants. $0.90 | 20072 Gold Front, 12 Brilliants. $0.50 | 20073 Stone Set. $0.42 | 20074 Oxidized Silver. $0.55 |

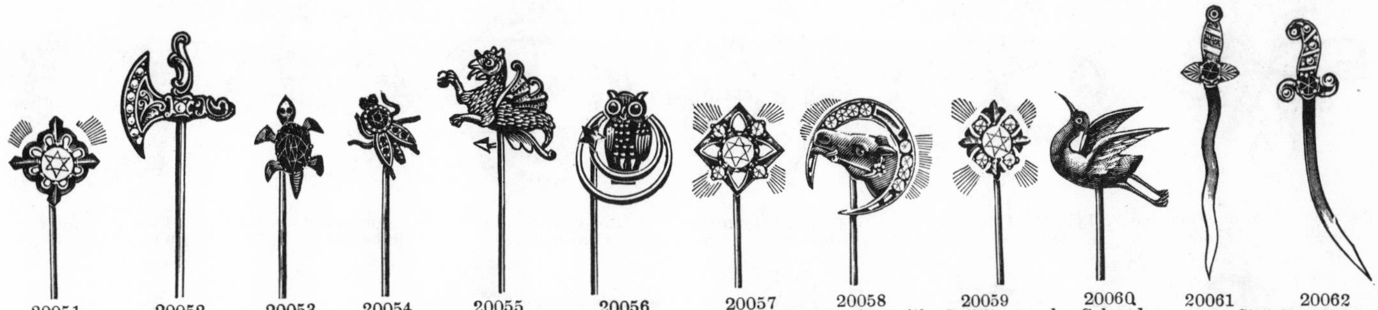

STERLING SILVER AND SILVER PLATED SCARF OR STICK PINS.

| 20075 Silver Head. $0.20 | 20076 Silver Head. $0.22 | 20077 Agate Head. $0.18 | 20078 Christian Endeavor. $0.14 | 20079 Silver Leaf. $0.20 | 20080 Silver Bird. $0.18 | 20081 Silver Battle Ax, new $0.25 | 20082 Silver Leaf. $0.15 | 20083 Silver Plume. $0.19 | 20084 Silver Butterfly. $0.24 | 20085 Silver Butterfly. $0.23 | 20086 Silver Battle Ax, $0.15 |

COLLAR BUTTONS GOLD AND GOLD PLATED.—Prices, Each.

Nos. 20087 to 20093 are solderless, one piece buttons.

| 20087 Stationary Top, solid gold. $1.25. 20088 Same in gold filled. $0.30 | 20089 Stationary Top, gold filled, $0.29. 20090 Same in solid gold. $1.10 | 20091 Stationary Top, gold filled, $0.25. 20092 Same in solid gold. $1.05 | 20093 Stationary Top, gold filled, $0.20. 20094 Same in solid gold. $1.00 | 20095 Lever Top, Roll plate. $0.25 | 20096 Lever Top, Roll plate. $0.15 20097 Same in solid gold. $1.00 | 20098 Lever Top, Roll plate, $0.10 20099 Same in solid gold, $0.85 | 20100 Back Lever roll plate. $0.20 20101 Same in solid gold $1.25 |

| 20102 Separable Stone Set $0.15 | 20103 Separable Gold Front. $0.35. 20103½ Same Solid Gold. $1.25 | 20104 Separable, Stone Set. $0.15 | 20105 Stone Set, plate 22c. Gold. $1.25 | 20106 Ladies' Brilliant Set, $0.25. 20107 Gold Diamond Set, $3.50 20107A Same in Rolled Plate 15c | 20108 Roll Plate Tie Holder. $0.15 | 20109 Pearl, $0.10 Per doz. $1.09. 20110 Bone, $0.01 Per doz. $0.10 | 20111 Pearl back, Shoe front. $0.13 Aluminum. $0.10 |

SOLID GOLD BROOCH AND LACE PINS.

We offer a larger line of solid gold goods than ever before. Prices have been reduced in many instances so that a solid gold article can be purchased for little more than plate. We call especial attention to our elegant line of Wreath Pins, the most fashionable patterns now worn.

20120
Colored Gold Leaves,
3 Diamonds. $6.50.

20121
Roman Gold Wreath,
Diamond Set. $3.75.

20122
Roman Gold Wreath,
1 Turquoise Set. $3.55.

20123
Roman Gold Wreath,
10 Whole Pearls. $4.75.

20124
Roman Gold Wreath,
Fine Opal Set. $4.50.

20125
Crescent Diamond
Center. $4.50.

20126
Polished Mounting, Fine
Amethyst Sets. $3.00.

20127
Polished, Fine Garnet
Center. $3.25

20128
Polished Mounting,
Brilliant Set. $2.25.

20129
Roman Gold, Pearl
Center. $4.25.

20130
Polished Mounting,
Ruby Center. $2.75.

20131
Enameled Leaves,
4 Whole Pearls. $3.65.

20132 Diamond Mounting, 2 Fine
Brilliants. $3.10.

20133 Engraved Gold Swallows,
Pearl Sets. $4.75.

20134 Roman Gold Leaves,
2 Pearl Sets. $2.85.

20135 Polished Gold Mounting,
2 Ruby Doublets. $2.10.

20136 Polished Mounting, Real
Moonstone Set. $2.00.

20137 Heavy Gold Mounting, Fine
Whole Pearl Set. $5.00.

20138 Polished Gold Mounting,
Brilliant Set. $1.90.

20139 Polished Gold Mounting,
3 Brilliant Sets. $2.65.

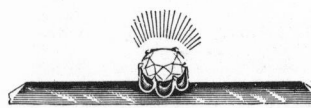
20140 Polished Gold Mounting, Large
Brilliant Set. $1.75.

20141 Heavy Gold Mounting, 3 Fine
Whole Pearl Sets. $4.25.

20142 Polished Gold Mounting,
3 Brilliant Sets. $2.10.

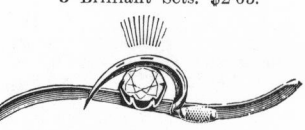
20143 Polished Gold Mounting,
1 Brilliant Set. $2.20.

20144 Polished Gold Battle Ax, Removable
Scabbard Handle. $4.00.

20145 Polished Gold, Real Amethyst
Set $2.35.

20146 Bright Gold Sword Pin, Real
Pearl Sets, Removable Scabbard. $4.75.

20147 Solid, Heavy and Handsome
Diamond Set. $2.75.

20148 Roman Gold Leaves, 3
Whole Pearl Sets. $2.85.

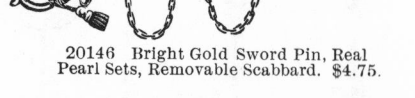

20149 Solid and Fine; any name
engraved. Each, $1.50.

20150 Solid Gold. $1.25.

20151 Solid Bright Gold, Chased. Very
neat. Each, $2.00.

20152 Extra Heavy Solid Gold, Chased and
Enameled. Each, $3.25.

20153 Misses' or Child's Solid Gold
Lace Pin, chased and stone
set. Each, $1.12.
20154 Similar, with real diamond. Each, $2.50.

20155 Solid Gold, assorted styles, chasing
extra heavy. Each, $3.75.

20156 Solid Gold, Roman Color, set with
real pearl. Each, $1.88

20157 Heavy Gold Mounting, Fine Brilliant
Set. Each, $2.90

20158 Solid Gold, set with rubies and
pearls. Each, $3.00.

20159 Solid Gold and Chased and Stone
Set. Each, $1.40.
20160 Same with real diamond. $3.50.

BEST QUALITY ROLL PLATE LACE PINS.

WE CALL ESPECIAL ATTENTION TO OUR LINE OF WREATH, SWORD AND BATTLE AX PINS, THE LATEST NOVELTIES.

20165 Horseshoe and Whip, Brilliant Sets. Price, $1.15.

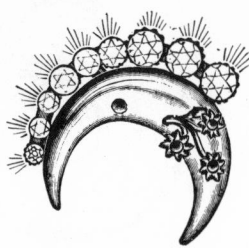

20166 Pearl Crescent, Brilliant Sets. Price, 94c.

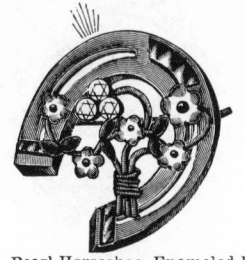

20167 Pearl Horseshoe, Enameled Flowers and 3 Brilliants in clover leaf. Price, 63c.

20168 Enameled Leaves, Brilliant Sets. Price, 85c.

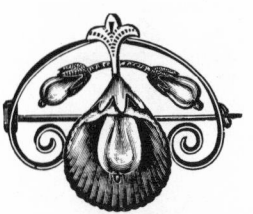

20169 Real Sea Shell and Pearl Flowers. Price, 92c.

20170 Real Sea Shells, Rolled Plate Trimmings. Price, 88c.

20171 Pearl Flowers, Colored Gold Leaves and One Brilliant Price, 79c.

20172 Roman Color Wreath, Enameled Leaves and Brilliant Sets. Price, 74c.

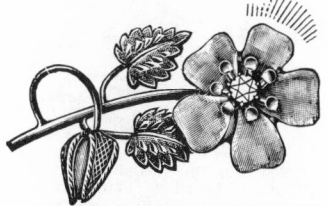

20173 Beautiful Pink Pearl in Bud and Flower, colored leaves. Price, 94c.

20174 White Pearl, Roll Plate Mounting. Price, 75c.

20175 Gold Front, Fine Brilliant Sets. Price. $1.25.

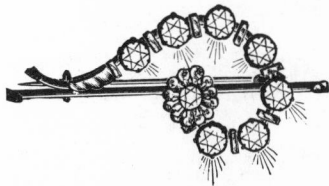

20176 Gold Front, Fine Brilliant Sets. Price, $1.08.

20177 Pearl Ball Brilliant Sets. Price, 71c.

20178 Pearl Balls, Roll Plate Mounting. Price, 76c.

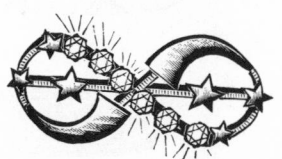

20179 Fine Gold Front with 6 Extra Quality Brilliants. Price, $1.15.

20180 Real Sea Shell with Colored Gold Ship and Polished Oar. Price 86c.

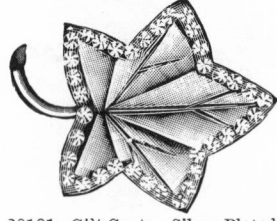

20181 Gilt Center, Silver Plated Edge. Price, 20c.

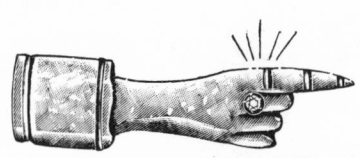

20182 Pearl Hand, Brilliant in Ring Price, 29c.

20183 Pear Shaped Amethyst with Colored Leaves and Chased Gold Wire. Price, 52c.

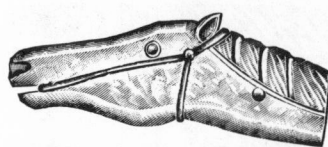

20184 Pearl Head, Roll Plate Bridle. Price, 32c.

20185 Real Sea Shell, Pearl Balls and Roll Plate Trimmings. Price, 77c.

20186 Polished Sword with 7 Brilliants in Handle. Price, 86c.

20187 Enameled Handle with Brilliant Pendant. Price, 50c.

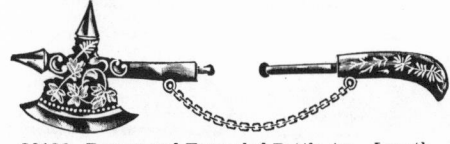

20188 Roman and Enameled Battle Ax. Length, 3½ inches. Price, 65c.

20189 Roman Color Handle, Polished Blade and Scabbard. Price, 50c.
20190 Same, but Solid Silver. Price, 55c.

20191 Pearl Battle Ax, with Gold Plate Trimmings. Price, 79c.

BEST ROLL PLATE GOLD FRONT LACE PINS AND BABY PINS.

20192 Fine Gold Front with Chain and Acorn Pendant. Price, $1.05.

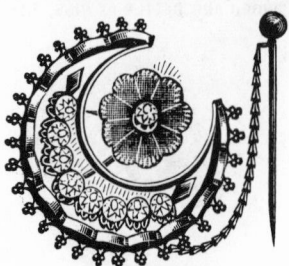

20193 **Extra** Quality Gold Front, Polished and Set with Stones. Price, each, $1.25

20194 Handsome **Pearl** Crescent, mounted in Rolled Gold, with 3 Brilliants. Price, 93c.

20195 Roman and Bright Coil with fine Brilliant. Price, $1.35.

20196 Fancy Gold Front. Price, $1.15.

20197 Gold Front, 1 Brilliant. Price, $1.14.

20198 Gold Front Star, 1 Brilliant. Price, $1.16.

20199 Engraved Colored Gold Leaves with 3 fine Brilliants. Price, $1.25.

20200 Engraved Roman Leaf, with fine Brilliant. Price, $1.08.

20201 Polished Gold Front, 1 fine Brilliant. Price, $1.15.

20202 Polished Gold Front, 1 Brilliant. Price, $1.28.

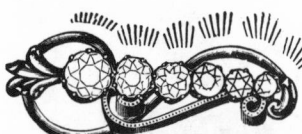

20203 Six Fine Brilliants, Extra Rolled Gold Setting. Price, 82c.

20204 Engraved Gold Front. Price, 65c.

20205 Engraved Gold Front. Price, 60c.

20206 Polished and Engraved Gold Front Price, 72c

20207 Engraved Gold Front. Price, 79c.

20208 Engraved Gold Front. Price, 53c

20209 Pearl with Gold Filled Bands. Price, 30c.

20210 Engraved Gold Front. Price, 64c.

20211 Engraved Gold Front. Price, 52c.

20212 Gold Front Scimitar. Price, 66c.

20213 Chased Gold Front Battle Ax with Scabbard Handle. Price, 85c.

20214 Polished Gold Front, Turquoise and Garnet Sets. Price, 52c.

20215 Roman Color with Turquoise and Pearl Sets. Price, 89c.

Roll Plate and Gold Front Baby Pins.

20216 Engraved Front, gold plate on sterling silver. Per pair, 60c.

20217 Gold Plate on Sterling Silver. Per pair, 70c.

20218 Gold Front, Raised Letters. Per pair, 48c.

20219 Engraved Front, gold plate on sterling silver. Per pair, 65c.

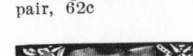

20220 Gold plate on sterling silver. Per pair, 62c

20221 Solid Sterling Silver, Blue Enameled. Per pair, 57c.

20222 Gold Plate on Sterling Silver. Per pair, 58c.

20223 Gold Front, Stone Set. Per pair, 50c.

22024 Engraved Gold Front. Per pair, 54c.

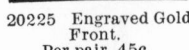

20225 Engraved Gold Front. Per pair, 45c,

22226 Gold Plate, Stone Set, Per pair, 32c.

29227½ Gold Front. Per pair, 40c.

20228 Bright, Polished. Per pair, 35c.

20229 Hard Blue Enamel, Gold Plate. Per pair, 25c.

20230 Gold Plated Enameled Letters, Baby Per pair, 36c.

ROLL PLATE AND STERLING SILVER LACE PINS.—Price, Each.

20231   Silver Plated "Brownie" Pin the latest novelty, enameled in colors. 35c.

20232   Silver Leaf Enameled, 1 Brilliant. Price, 27c.
20233   Same in gold plate, 26c.
20234

Silver Plated and Enameled "Brownie" Pin, new and pretty, 30c.

'20234½   New "Brownie" Pin, Silver Plated and Enameled in Colors, 33c.

20235   Pearl Handle, Colored Enameled Leaves, 1 Brilliant. 3¾ inches long.   Price, 84c.

20236   Pearl Set. Price, 39c.

20237   Brilliant Set. Price, 33c.

20238   Brilliant Set. Price, 38c.

20239   Garnet Sets. Price, 51c.

20240   Solid Silver Battle Axe. Price, 65c.

20241   Turquoise Set. Price, 31c.

20242   Garnet and Brilliant Sets, Price, 38c.

20243   Garnet Set.   Price, 18c.

20244   Garnet Set.   Price, 18c.

20245   Garnet Set.   Price, 18c.

20246   Garnet Set.   Price, 18c.

20247   Colored Leaves, Cream-Tinted Moonstone Center.   Price, 54c.

20248   Cameo Set Price, 36c.

20249   Moonstone Set. Price, 40c.

20250   Garnet Set. Price, 42c.

20251   Gold Front Lace Pin, any name engraved (give name wanted). Price, complete, 50.

20252   Name Pins, gold plate. Give name wanted.
Price. each..$0.25

Ada,	Edith,	Ida,	Lizzie,	Nettie.
Alice,	Emma,	Irene,	Mary,	Nellie.
Annie,	Effie,	Jessie,	Mattie,	Nancy,
Agnes,	Ethel,	Jennie,	Mamie,	Ollie,
Belle,	Flora,	Julia,	Maggie,	Olive,
Bertha,	Fannie,	Josie,	Minnie,	Ruth,
Blanche,	Florence,	Kate,	Mabel,	Rose,
Cora,	Grace,	Katie,	May,	Rebecca
Clara,	Gertie,	Lucy,	Martha,	Susie,
Carrie,	Helen,	Lillie,	Margie,	Stella,
Dora,	Hannah,	Louise,	Maude,	Sarah,
Ella,	Hattie,	Lottie,	Nora,	Winnie.

No names furnished except those quoted in above list.

Coral and Gold.
20253   Misses' Set, Drawn Gold Wire. set with coral. Per set, $1.00. Pin or drops separate. Each, 50c.

20254   Sterling Silver, bright and beautiful. Price, 50c.

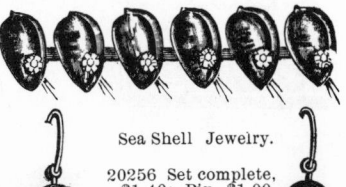

Sea Shell Jewelry.

20256 Set complete, $1.40; Pin, $1.00. Drops, 40c.

20257   Solid Sterling Silver Chameleon Pin. Has four joints in body, and when worn, moves in a life-like manner. A great novelty. Price, $1.50.

20255   Ladies' Set, Pin and Drops, Coral and Gold Wire. Complete, $1.80. Pin or drops separate. Each, 90c.

Postage on any article on this page, 2c.

HAT PINS. Price, Each.

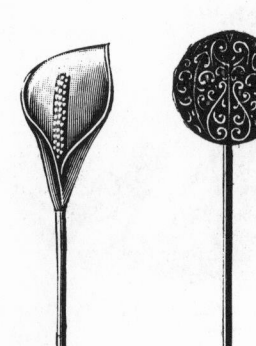    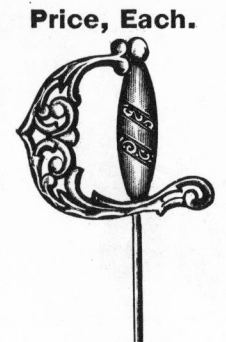   

| 20258 Silver Plated Hat Pin. Price, 15c. | 20259 Sterling Silver Hat Pin. Price, 60c. | 20260 Sterling Silver Hat Pin. Price, 30c. | 20261 Sterling Silver Enameled Hat Pin. Price, 50c. | 20262 Sterling Silver Hat Pin. Price, 80c. | 20263 Best Gold Plate Hat Pin. Price, $1.00. | 20264 Sterling Silver Hat Pin. Price, 40c. | 20265 Tinted Moonstone Hat Pin. Price, 25c. |

Best Quality Roll Plate Stick Pins. Price, Each.

 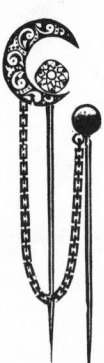 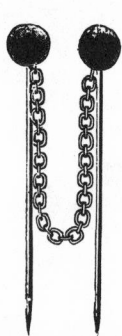 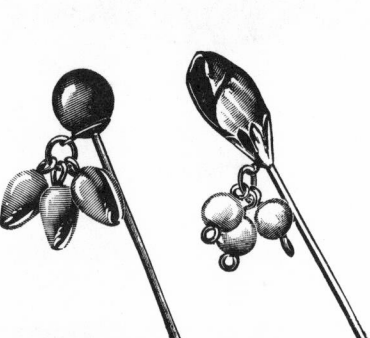 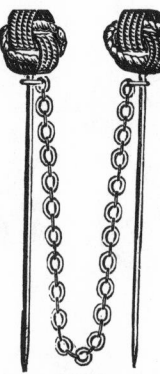 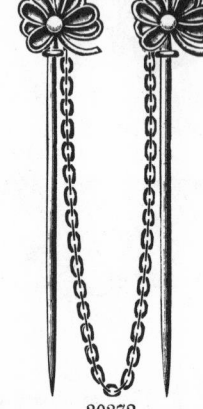

20266 Fine Quality Rolled Gold Sword Pins, per pair, 70c.

20267 Fine Quality Plate Stone Set, per pair, 50c.

20268 Plain Rolled Gold Balls, per pair, 18c.

20269 Tinted Moonstone Ball and 3 real Sea Shells, 25c.

20270 Real Sea shell Top and 3 Moonstone Balls, 35c.

20271 Twist Knot, per pair, 50c.

20272 Black Enameled Pearl Set Flowers, solid gold, $3.50.

Gold Front and Solid Gold Pins and Button Sets.

 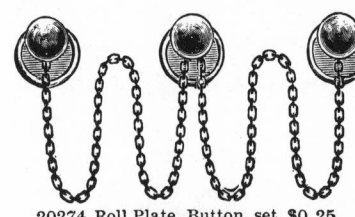  

20273 Child's Gold Front Pin, Set engraved, per set, 75c.

20274 Roll Plate Button, set, $0.25
20275 Solid Gold Top " " 1.00
20276 Solid Gold " " 1.75

20277 Child's Gold Front Pin Set. Per set, 65c.

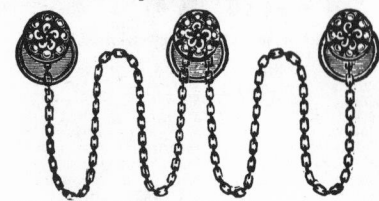 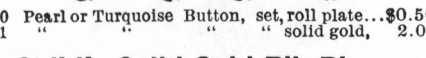

20278 Roll Plate Button, set, ... $0.75
20279 Enameled Solid Gold Button, set 2.25

20280 Pearl or Turquoise Button, set, roll plate... $0.50
20281 " " " " solid gold, 2.00

20282 Roman Gold, Pearl Set, solid Gold Button Set, $3.00.

Child's Solid Gold Bib Pins.

20283 Roman Gold, chased edge per pair, $2.75.

20284 Bright Gold, blue enameled, per pair, $3.00.

20285 Bright Gold, enameled, per pair, $2.75.

20286 Engraved, per pair, $2.50.

20287 Engraved, per pair, $2.60.

 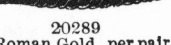  

20288 Engraved, per pair, $1.88.

20289 Roman Gold, per pair, $1.80.

20290 Engraved, per pair $2 30.

20291 Engraved, per pair, $2.00.

20292 Roman Gold, Turquoise set, per pair, $1.60.

 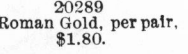    

20293 Plain Center. Per pair, $1.80.

20294 Plain Polished. Per pair, $150.

20295 Solid Gold, chased, round edge. Per pair, $1.40.

20296 Plain Solid Gold; can engrave any name. Price, each, $1.00.

20297 Fine Gold, hand engraved. Each, 95c.

Any of the above Baby Pins sold singly at one-half the pair price.

LADIES' AND MISSES' SOLID GOLD EAR DROPS.--Price Per Pair.
Note the very low prices on Solid gold Jewelry this year.

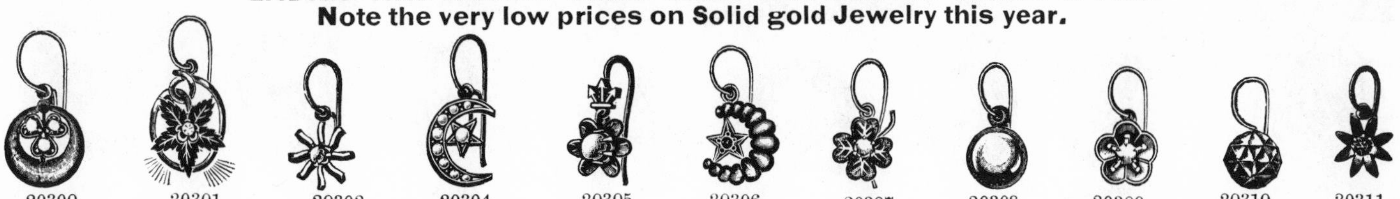

20300 Roman Gold, Pearl Sets, $1.60. — 20301 Roman Gold, Diamond Set, $5.00. — 20302 Bright Gold, Pearl Set, $2.00. — 20304 Star and Crescent, Pearl Set, $3.00. — 20305 Large Pearl, Set $2.00. — 20306 Roman Gold, Turquoise Set $2.25. — 20307 Pearl Set, Flower, $1.75 — 20308 Polished, Ball, $1.25 — 20309 Pearl Set, Flower, $1.90. — 20310 Polished, Faceted Ball, $1.00. — 20311 Ruby Set, Flower. $1.60.

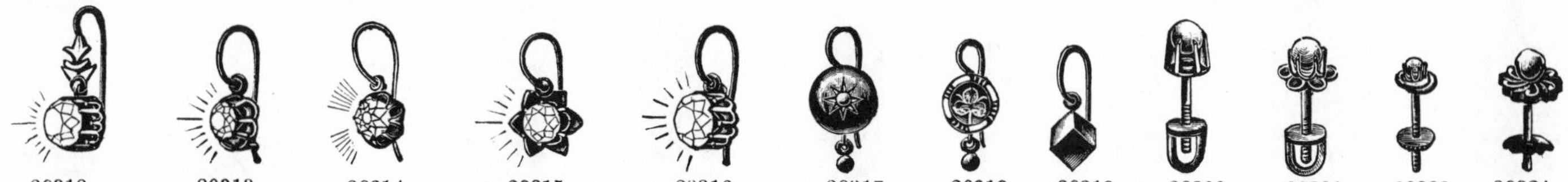

20312 Brilliant Set, $1.25. — 20313 Brilliant Set, $1.40. — 20314 Brilliant Set, $1.10 — 20315 Brilliant Set, $1.30. — 20316 Brilliant Set, $1.50. — 20317 Pearl Set, $1.15. — 20318 Engraved, $1.00. — 20319 Polished Cube, $1.00. — 20320 Pearl Set Screw Back, $1.80. — 20321 Moonstone Set, $1.65. — 20322 Pearl Set, $1.35. — 20324 Fine Pearl Set, $3.00

Roll Plate Ear Drops.

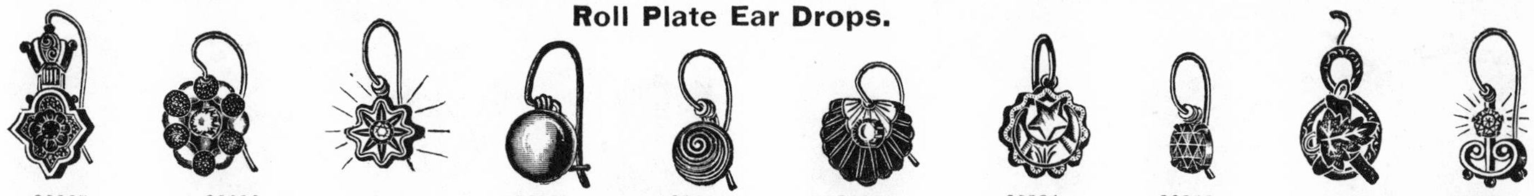

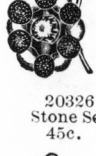

20325 Garnet Set 55c. — 20326 Stone Set, 45c. — 20327 Brilliant Set, 80c. — 20328 Polished Ball, Gold Wire, 60c. — 20329 Real Sea Shell, 40c. — 20330 Pearl Set 34c. — 20331 Gold Front, Gold Wire, 75c. — 20332 Amethyst Sets, 58c. — 20333 Coral Wire Drops, 95c. — 20334 Brilliant Sets, 57c.

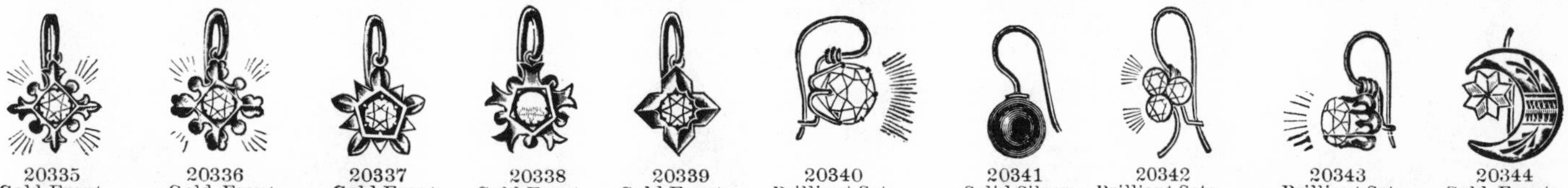

20335 Gold Front, Gold Wires, Brilliant Set, 90c. — 20336 Gold Front, Gold Wires, Brilliant Set, 88c. — 20337 Gold Front, Gold Wires, Emerald Set, 92c. — 20338 Gold Front, Gold Wires, Moonstone Set, 86c. — 20339 Gold Front, Gold Wires, Ruby Set, 84c. — 20340 Brilliant Set, Gold Wires, 70c. — 20341 Solid Silver Ball, 40c. — 20342 Brilliant Sets, 61c. — 20343 Brilliant Set, 25c. — 20344 Gold Front, Gold Wire, 62c

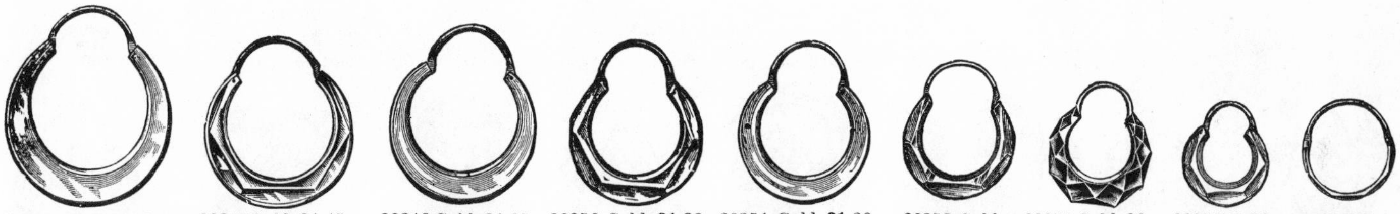

20345 18k Gold $1.50; 20346 Plate, 63c. — 20347 Gold, $1.45. — 20348 Gold, $1.25; 20349 Plate, 50c. — 20350 Gold, $1 38. — 20351 Gold, $1.20; 20352 Plate, 40c. — 20353 Gold, $1 00 — 20354 Gold, 98c.; 20355 Plate, 33c. — 20356 Gold, 75c. — 20357 Gold, 70c.; 20358 Plate, 30c

Real Onyx and Jet Mourning Jewelry.

20359 Onyx Gold Mounted, $9.50.
20360 Same, Roll Plate Mounted, $1.50

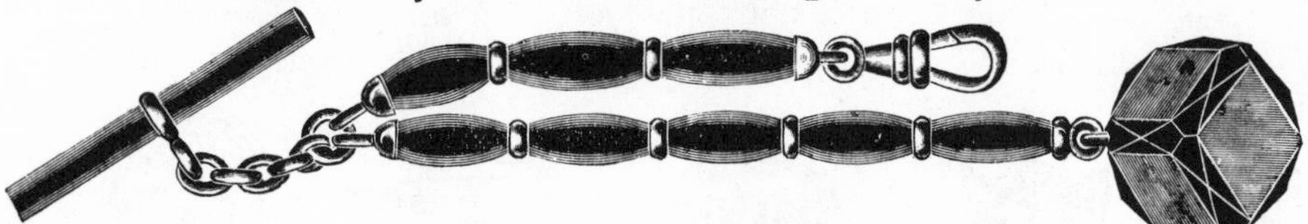

20361 Jet Victoria Chain, Roll Plate Trimmings, $1.00.

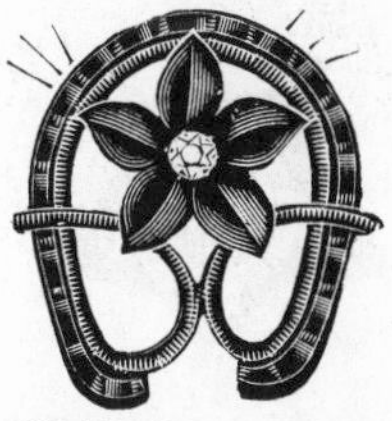

20363 Black Brooch Pin, with Brilliant Set. 30c.

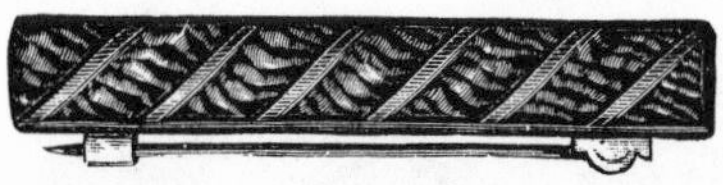

20362 Black Jet Bar Pin, 25c.

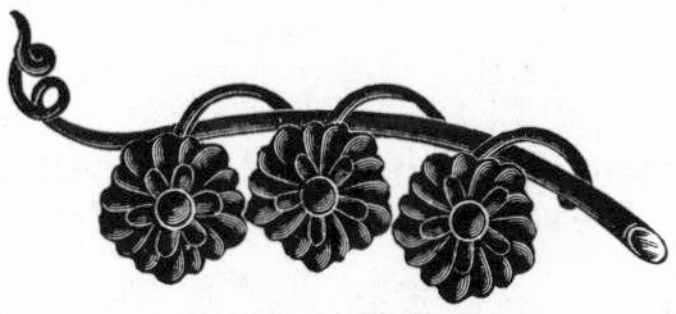

20364 Roll Plate Mounted, 85c.

20365 Onyx Pearl Set, Solid Gold, $8.00
20366 Same, Roll Plate, 75c.

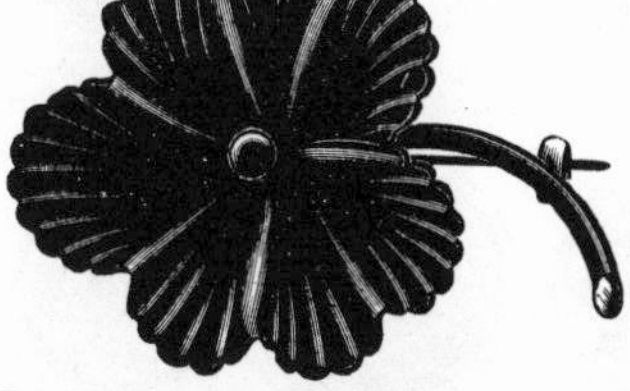

20367 Onyx Gold Mounted, $6.00.
20368 Same, Roll Plate, 80c.

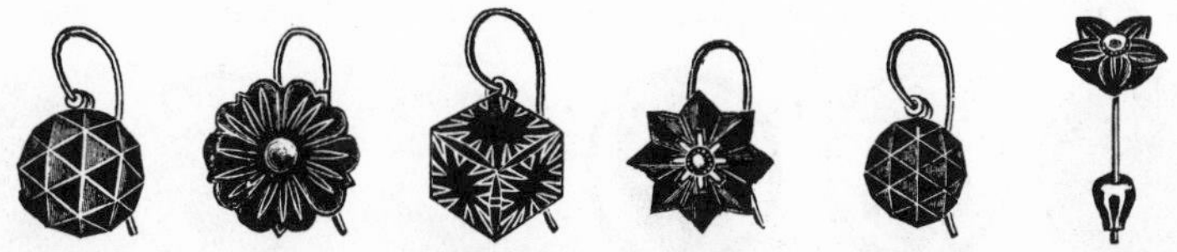

20369 Solid Gold Wires, $1.25. — 20370 Roll Plate Wires, 50c. — 20371 Roll Plate Wires, 55c. — 20372 Roll Plate, Pearl Set, 70c. — 20373 Solid Gold, 89c. — 20374 Solid Gold, Pearl Set, $1.50.

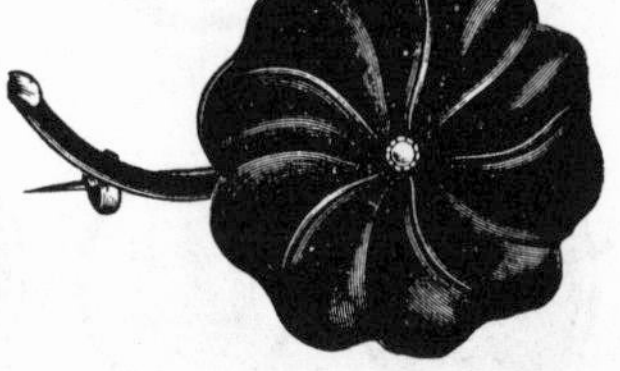

20375 Pearl Set Onyx, Solid Gold, $6.50.
20376 Same, in Roll Plate, 90c.

SOLID GOLD AND ROLL PLATE EMBLEM PINS AND BUTTONS.
Enameled in Appropriate Colors.

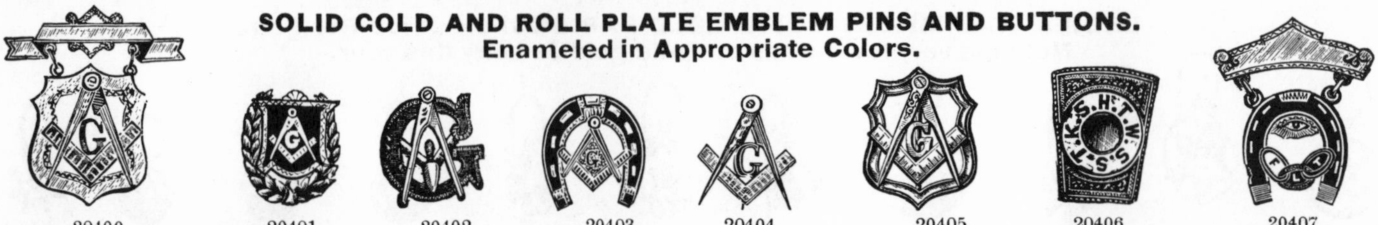

20400 Masonic. Roll Plate, $0.70. Solid Gold, 1.25.

20401 Masonic. Roll Plate, $0 55. Solid Gold, 1.02

20402 Masonic. Roll Plate, $0.45. Solid Gold, .78.

20403 Masonic. Roll Plate, $0.45. Solid Gold, .80.

20404 Masonic. Roll Plate, $0.25. Solid Gold, .50.

20405 Masonic. Roll Plate, $0.45. Solid Gold, .63.

20406 Masonic. Roll Plate, $0.50. Solid Gold, .71.

20407 Odd Fellows. Roll Plate, $0.70. Solid Gold, $1.21.

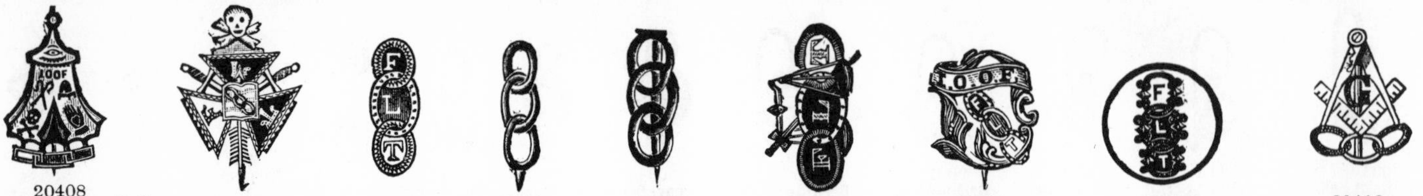

20408 Odd Fellows. Roll Plate, $0.40. Solid Gold, .90.

20409 Odd Fellows. Roll Plate, $0.50. Solid Gold, .95.

20410 Roll Plate, $0.38. Solid Gold. .53.

20411 Roll Plate, $0.50. Solid Gold, .88.

20412 Roll Plate, $0.60. Solid Gold, 1.13.

20413 Odd Fellows. Roll Plate, $0.40. Solid Gold, .67.

20414 Odd Fellows. Solid Gold, $0.70.

20415 Odd Fellows. Roll Plate, $0.45. Solid Gold, .90.

20416 I. O. O. F. and Masonic. Roll Plate, $0.25 Solid Gold, .52

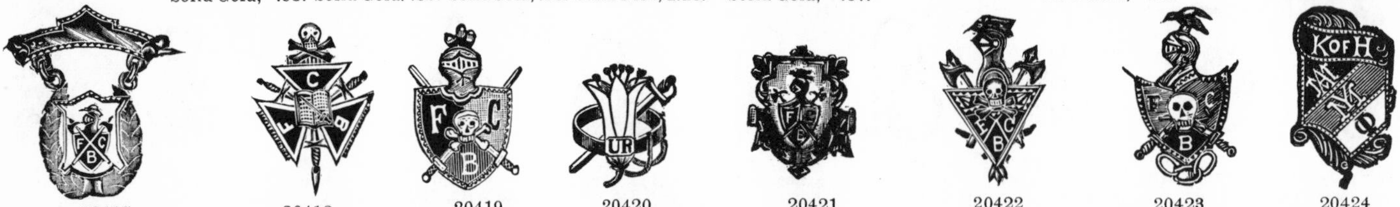

20417 K. of P. Roll Plate, $0.75. Solid Gold, 1.30.

20418 K. of P. Roll Plate, $0.75. Solid Gold,$1.25.

20419 K. of P. Roll Plate. $0.45. Solid Gold, .80.

20420 U. R. K. of P. Roll Plate, $0.50. Solid Gold, .94.

20421 K. of P. Roll Plate, $0.50. Solid Gold, .91.

20422 K. of P. Roll Plate, $0.45. Solid Gold, .85.

20423 I. O. O. F. and K. of P. Solid Gold, .95.

20424 Knights of Honor. Roll Plate, $0.55 Solid Gold, .93

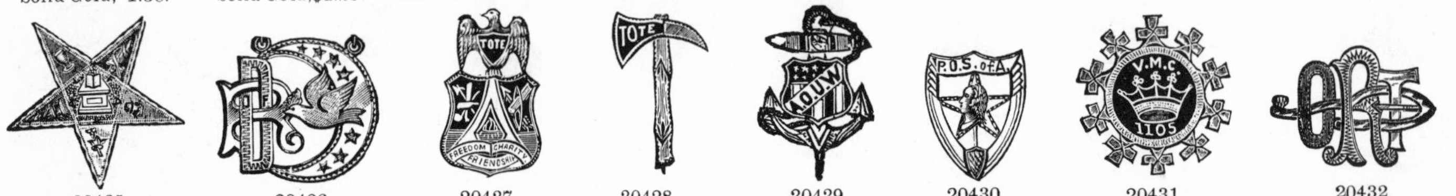

20425 Eastern Star. Roll Plate, $0.65 Solid Gold, 1.24.

20426 D. of Reb. Roll Plate, $0 60. Solid Gold, 1.14.

20427 Red Men's. Roll Plate, $0.55. Solid Gold, .92.

20428 Red Men's. Roll Plate, $0.45. Solid Gold, .80.

20429 A. O. U. W. Roll Plate, $0.40. Solid Gold, .65.

20430 P. O. S. of A. Roll Plate, $0.35. Solid Gold, .62.

20431 Royal Arc. Roll Plate, $.60. Solid Gold, 1.00.

20432 Telegraphers'. Roll Plate, $0.50. Solid Gold, .96.

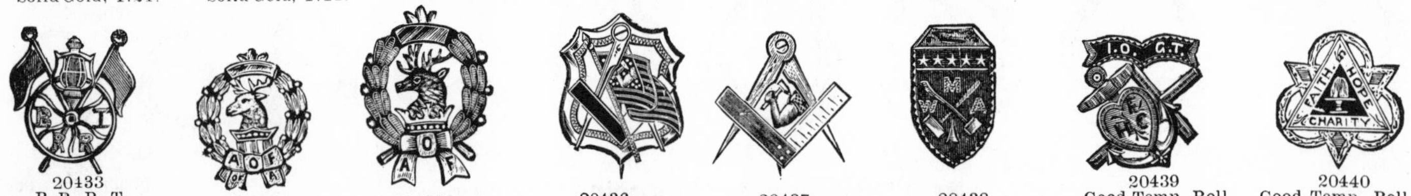

20433 B. R. R. T. Solid Gold, $0 95

20434 A. O. F. of A. Roll Plate, $0 50. Solid Gold, 1.25.

20435 A. O. F. Roll Plate, $0.65. Solid Gold, 1.50

20436 Jr. O. A. M. Roll Plate, $0.50. Solid Gold, 1.00

20437 Sr. O. A. M. Roll Plate, $0.60. Solid Gold, .40

20438 Mod. Woodm'n. Roll Plate, $0.50. Solid Gold, .86.

20439 Good Temp. Roll Plate, $0.60. Solid Gold, .86

20440 Good Temp. Roll Plate, $0.55 Solid Gold, .81.

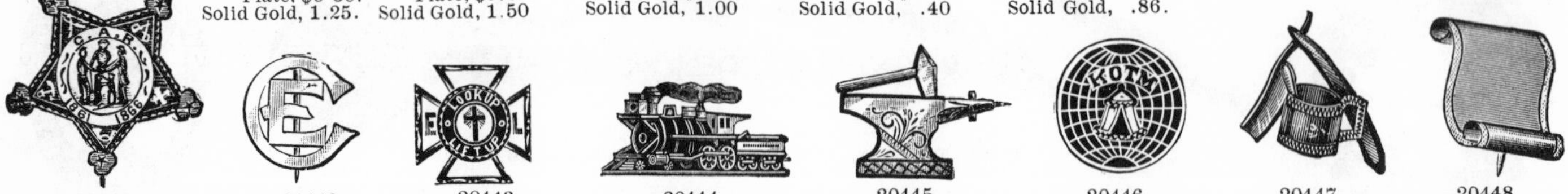

20441 G. A. R. Roll Plate, $0.60. Solid Gold, 1.08.

20442 Christian Endeavor. Gold, $0.95. Silver, .50.

20443 Ep. League. Roll Plate, $0.40. Solid Gold, .70.

20444 Locomotive. Solid Gold, $0.79.

20445 Blacksmiths' Pin. Solid Gold, $0.62.

20446 K. O. T. M. Roll Plate, $0.45. Solid Gold, .85.

20447 Barbers'. Solid Gold, $0.57.

20448 Any Engraving. Solid Gold, $1.06.

Lapel Buttons, Enameled in Appropriate Colors, Screw Backs.

Price, Solid Gold, Each, 87 Cents. Roll Plate, Each, 38 Cents.

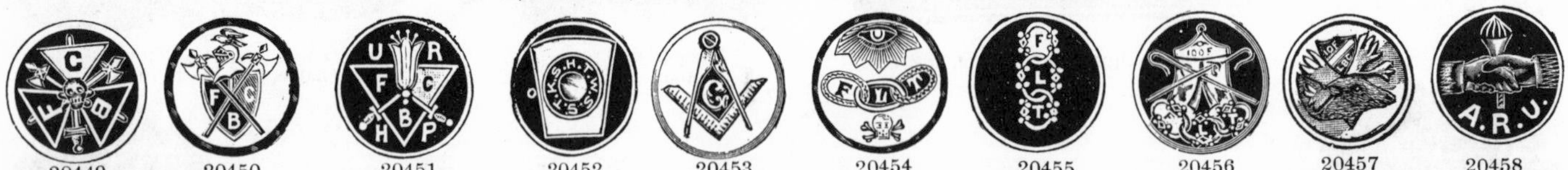

20449 K. of P

20450 K. of P.

20451 K. of P

20452 Masonic.

20453 Masonic.

20454 Odd Fellows.

20455 Odd Fellows.

20456 Odd Fellows.

20457 Ind. Foresters.

20458 Am. R. R. Union.

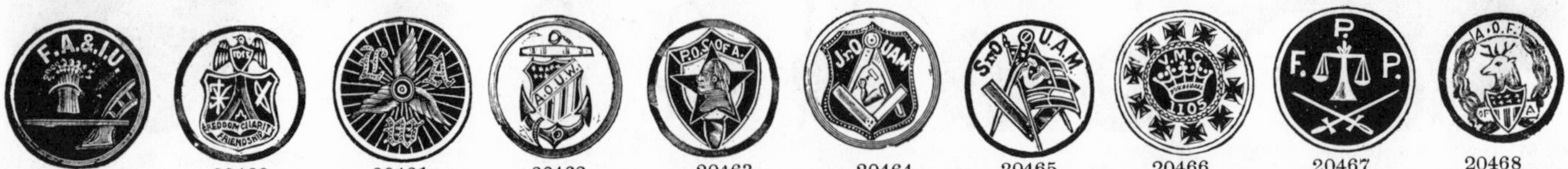

20459 Farmers' Alliance.

20460 Red Men

20461 Wheelmen.

20462 A. O. U. W.

20463 P. O. S. of A.

20464 Jr. O. U. A. M.

20465 Sr. O. U. A. M.

20466 Royal Arcanum.

20467 A. P. A.

20468 A. O. F.

SOLID GOLD AND ROLL PLATE EMBLEM CHARMS—Enameled in Appropriate Colors.

20469 Odd Fellows.
Solid Gold, $3.50
Roll Plate, 1.10

20470 Odd Fellows.
Solid Gold, $3.00
Roll Plate, 1.00

20471 Masonic.
Roll Plate, $1.00
Solid Gold, 3.25

20472 Masonic.
Roll Plate, 75c.
Solid Gold, $2.25

20473 Odd Fellows.
Roll Plate, $0.95
Solid Gold, 2.00

20474 Foresters.
Roll Plate, $1.00
Solid Gold, 3.50

20475 A. O. U. W.
Roll Plate, $0.90
Solid Gold, 3.75

20476 Masonic.
Roll plate, $1.15
Solid Gold, 3.50

20477 K. of P.
Roll Plate, $0.90
Solid Gold, 2.00

20478 K. of P.
Roll Plate $1.20,
Solid Gold, 3.50

20479 Grand Army Charm
roll plate, enameled
in colors, $1.00

20480 Woodmen.
Roll Plate, $1.05
Solid Gold, $4.00

20481 Sr. O.U.A.M.
Roll Plate, $1.25
Solid Gold, 5.00

20482 I. O. F.
Roll Plate, $1.00
Solid Gold, 4.25

20483 Odd Fellows,
locket, 2 pictures,
raised emblem.
Solid Gold only, $7.75

20484 Masonic
Locket, 2 pictures,
solid gold only,
raised emblem $6.50.
K. P. or Odd Fellow
same price.

20485 Masonic.
Roll Plate, 75c.
Solid Gold, $3.00

20486 P. O. S. of A.
Roll Plate, $1.10
Solid Gold, 5.00

20487 Jr. O. U. A M.
Roll Plate, $1.15
Solid Gold, 5.70

20488 K. of P.
Roll Plate,
$1.50

20489 Roll Plate,
Pearl Center, Masonic
or Odd Fellows.
$1.25

20490 Jr. Am.
Mechanics.
Roll Plate, 75c.

20491 Epworth
League. Roll
Plate, 80c.

20492 Roll Plate,
any emblem,
assorted shapes.
55c.

20493 K. of P,
Roll Plate, $1.75
Solid Gold, 8.00

20494 Royal Arcanum
Roll Plate, $1.35
Solid Gold, 5.00

20495 Masonic Key-
stone. Roll Plate
Top, 85c.
Solid Gold Top, $1.50

20496 Masonic
Keystone. Solid
Gold, $4.50
Roll Plate, $1.25.

20497 Knights Templar.
Solid Gold $18.00
Roll Plate, 4.00

20498 Masonic and
Odd Fellows.
Roll Plate, $1.25
Solid Gold, $4.00

20499 K. of P.
Roll Plate, $1.25
Solid Gold, 7.00

20500 K. of P.
Roll Plate. $1.75
Solid Gold, 9.50

20501 K. of P.
Roll Plate, $3.75
Solid Gold, 16.00

20502 Odd Fellows.
Roll Plate, $1.75
Solid Gold, 9.00

20503 Any Emblem.
Roll Plate on Pearl
Cross, $1.50

SHELL HAIR PINS WITH SOLID GOLD, SILVER AND PLATED TOPS.

Prices, Each.

20510
Shell Pin. Sterling Silver
Raised Ornaments. Cut
full size. $0.90

20511
Shell Pin. Sterling Silver
Raised Ornament. Cut
one-half size. $1.75

20512
Fine Filigree Work,
Sterling Silver Top. Cut
one-half size. $2.35

20513
Shell Prongs. Silver Plated
Top. Cut one-half size.
$0.55

20514
Shell Pin. Sterling Silver
Raised Ornament. Cut
one-half size. $1.50

20516
Shell Prong. Sterling Silver Top
Very showy.
Cut full size. $0.95

20517
Shell Pin. Solid Gold
Raised Ornament.
Cut one-half size. $3.75

20518
Shell Pin. Solid Gold
Raised Ornament.
Cut one-half size. $4.00

20519
Shell Pin. Silver Plated
Raised Ornament.
Cut one-half size. $0.64

20520
Shell Pin. Sterling Silver
Raised Ornament.
Cut one-half size. $1.45

20521
Shell Pin. Sterling Silver
Top. Cut one-half size.
$2.50

20522
Shell Pin. Sterling Silver
Raised Ornament.
Cut full size. $0.75

20523
Shell Pin. Sterling Silver
Raised Ornament.
Cut one-half size. $1.25

20524
Shell Prong. Gold Plate
Head. Very handsome.
Cut one-half size. $1.50

20525
Shell Battle Ax, with
sterling silver raised
ornamentation.
Price, $1.00

20526
Shell Pin. Sterling Silver
Raised Wreath. Cut
one-half size. $1.35

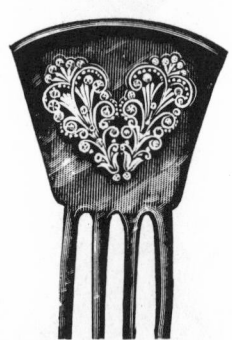

20527
Silver Plated Raised
Ornament. Cut
one-half size. $0.60

20528
Shell Prongs. Silver Plated
Top. Cut one-half
size. $0.50

20529
Shell Prongs. Gold
Plated Top. Cut one-
half size. $0.48

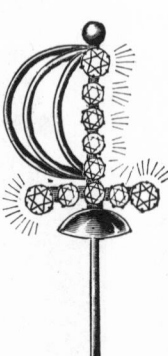

20530
Rolled Plate.
Set with Brilliants
Price, $0.48

20531
Roman Color Top with polished
points of good rolled gold
Length, 5½ inches. $0.25

20532
Shell, with raised solid
silver ornaments
Price, 90c.

20533
Shell Side Comb, with sterling silver scroll top, length,
2 inches. Per pair, 70c.

IMITATION TORTOISE SHELL HAIR ORNAMENTS.--Prices, Each.

We recommend for durability the ornaments described as Celluloid. They are very light and will bend double without breaking.

20534 Imitation Shell; width, 2¾ inches; length, 5¾ inches. Price, 55c.

20535 Celluloid Imitation Shell; width, 2¾ inches; length, 4½ inches. Price, 38c.

20536 Celluloid Imitation Shell; width, 2¾ inches; length, 4¾ inches Price, 39c.

20537 Choice Pattern Imitation Shell Pin; length, 5 inches. Price, 20c.

20538 Black Imitation Jet; width, 2½ inches; length, 4¾ inches; Price, 23c.

    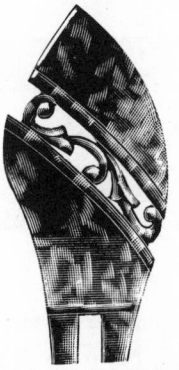  

20539 Celluloid Imitation Shell; width, 1¾ inches; length, 6 inches. Price, 40c.

20540 Celluloid Imitation Shell; width, 1¾ inches; length, 6¾ inches, Price, 45c.

20541 Celluloid Imitation Shell; width, 2 inches; length, 6½ inches. Price, 38c.

20542 Celluloid Imitation Shell; width, 1¾ inches; length, 8 inches. Price, 26c.

20543 Celluloid Imitation Shell; width, 1¾ inches; length, 6 inches. Price, 27c.

20544 Celluloid Imitation Shell; width, 1½ inches; length, 6½ in. Price, 25c.

20545 Celluloid Imitation Shell; width, 1½ inches; length, 5¼ in. Price, 33c.

   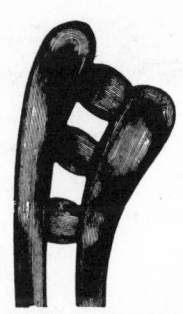 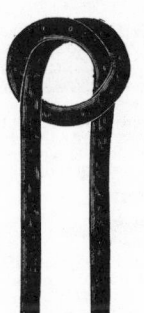 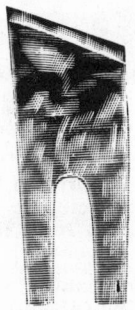 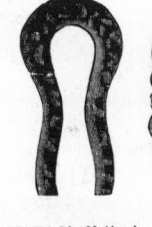 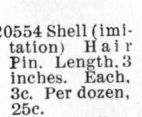 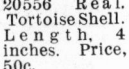

20546 Assorted Imitation Shell; amber or black; similar to cut; length, 5½ inches; width, 1½ inches. Special price on this lot, 19c

20547 Fancy Top Shell Side Combs. Per pair, 50c.
20548 Imitation. Per pair, 20c.

20549 Real Shell Side Combs. Per pair, 48c.
20550 Imitation. Per pair, 10c.

20551 Smooth Plain Top, good and strong. Length, 5 inches. Each, 9c; per dozen. $1.00.

20552 Strong Heavy Twist Pin. Length, 5 inches. Each, 25c.

20553 Imitation Shell; width, 1¼ inches; length, 5 in. Price, 10c.

20554 Shell (imitation) Hair Pin. Length, 3 inches. Each, 3c. Per dozen, 25c.
20555 Similar, smaller and lighter. Price, 1c.

20556 Real Tortoise Shell. Length, 4 inches. Price, 50c.

Real Tortoise Shell Hair Ornaments.

20557 Real Tortoise Shell Pin. Price, 90c.

20558 Real Shell; width, 1⅝ inches; length, 6 inches. Price, $1.20.

20559 Real Shell; width, 2 inches; length, 5¼ inches. Price, $1.60.
20560 Same as above, but plain edge. Price, $1.00.

20561 Real Shell; width, 2 inches; length, 5¼ inches. Price, $1.25.

20562 Real Tortoise Shell; regular length, 6 inches. Price, $1.50.

20563 Real Shell Back Combs; plain and rich. Dimensions, 3x3½. Price, $1.60.
20564 Same as above, but imitation shell Price, 25c.

FOUNTAIN PENS.

NOTE—Fountain Pens are rapidly superseding all other styles and kinds for practical use. The best value will be found in **Montgomery Ward & Co.'s Special** "The Best," manufactured especially for us. GIVE THEM A TRIAL. *They are fully guaranteed*, and we refund money if they fail to give satisfaction.

20565 Our Perfect Fountain Holder, fitted with No. 2 14K Gold Pen...$1.10
20566 Same style, but larger holder fitted with No. 4 14K Gold Pen 2.75

20567 Hexagon Brown Rubber Perfect Holder, with No. 2 14K Gold Pen...1.50

20568 Twist, Perfect Fountain Holder, with No. 2 14K Gold Pen...1.60

20569 Ladies' Gold Mounted Perfect Holder, with No. 2 14K Gold Pen...1.90

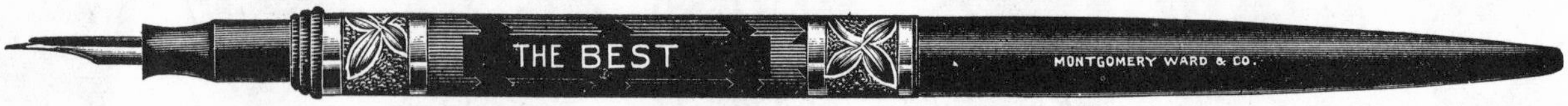

20570 Gentlemen's Gold Mounted Perfect Holder, with No. 2 14K Gold Pen 2.00
20570A Same as No. 20570, but larger holder with No. 5 pen..3.50

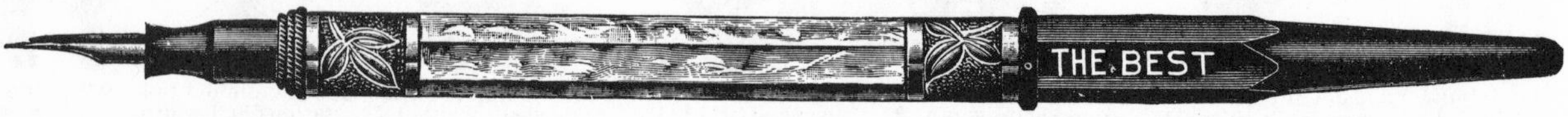

20571 Gentlemen's Pearl Holder, fitted with No. 216K Gold Pen..5.00

20572 The Scribbler Fountain Pen. We offer to our patrons under this title a fountain pen which will equal in quality, beauty and durability any fountain pen **ever** manufactured at a low price. The cut gives a very faint idea of its appearance. The barrel is made of purest Para Rubber, with best rubber cap. Pen is perfect in shape, not **flattened out**, and is made of solid gold, guaranteed to assay **not less than** 14K. Price, 65 cents. If not as represented above in every particular, your money will be promptly refunded. Cost of mailing is only 2 cents.

The P. S. Fountain Pen.
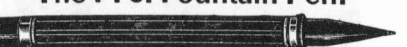

20573 The P. S. Fountain Pen, best hard rubber holder, fitted with Gillott's fine point, or Esterbrook stub pen. This article is reliable, in fact the only one that we know of made to hold steel pens. Price each............$0.35

NOTE—We make a specialty of repairing fountain pens and replacing missing parts.

Independent Stylographic Pen.

20574 The Celebrated Independent Stylographic Pen, made of best quality hard rubber, Platinum point and needle, alloyed with iridium, not affected by any kind of ink. Will not leak or blot and is always ready for use. Each.$0.75

Send pen to us with 75 cents, and we will repair and refund balance of money with pen. This method saves time and correspondence.

GOLD AND SILVER MOUNTED PENS AND PENCILS.
ILLUSTRATIONS ARE TWO-THIRDS SIZE.

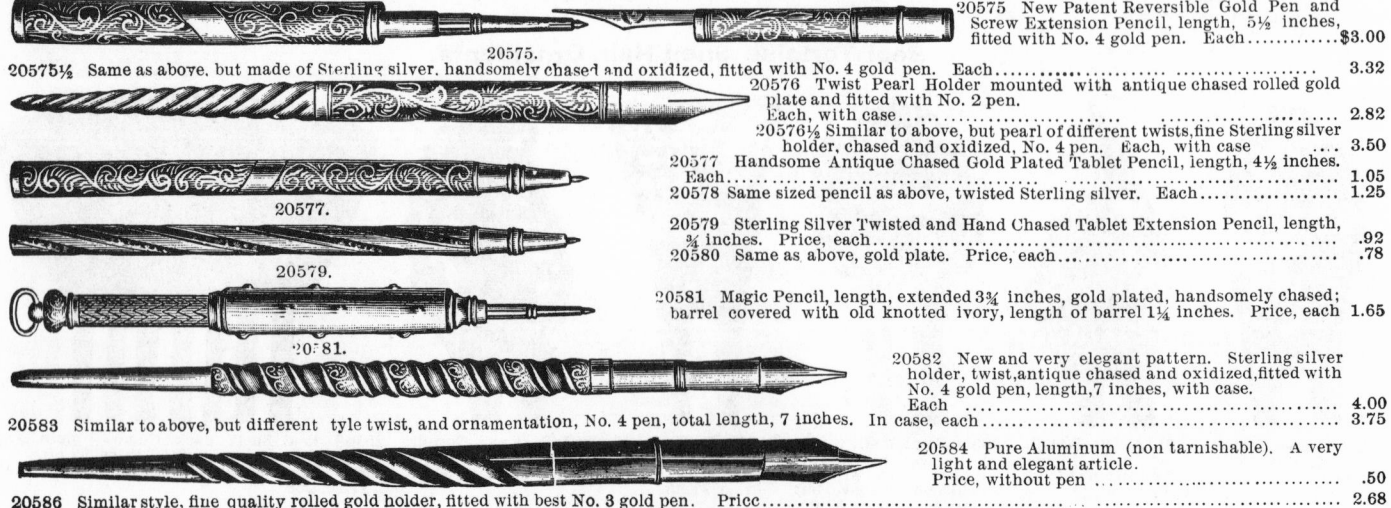

20575.

20575 New Patent Reversible Gold Pen and Screw Extension Pencil, length, 5½ inches, fitted with No. 4 gold pen. Each............$3.00

20575½ Same as above, but made of Sterling silver, handsomely chased and oxidized, fitted with No. 4 gold pen. Each.................................3.32

20576 Twist Pearl Holder mounted with antique chased rolled gold plate and fitted with No. 2 pen. Each, with case.........................2.82

20576½ Similar to above, but pearl of different twists, fine Sterling silver holder, chased and oxidized, No. 4 pen. Each, with case 3.50

20577 Handsome Antique Chased Gold Plated Tablet Pencil, length, 4½ inches. Each...1.05

20577.

20578 Same sized pencil as above, twisted Sterling silver. Each...................1.25

20579 Sterling Silver Twisted and Hand Chased Tablet Extension Pencil, length, ¾ inches. Price, each...92

20579.

20580 Same as above, gold plate. Price, each...78

20581 Magic Pencil, length, extended 3¾ inches, gold plated, handsomely chased; barrel covered with old knotted ivory, length of barrel 1¼ inches. Price, each 1.65

20581.

20582 New and very elegant pattern. Sterling silver holder, twist, antique chased and oxidized, fitted with No. 4 gold pen, length, 7 inches, with case. Each...4.00

20583 Similar to above, but different style twist, and ornamentation, No. 4 pen, total length, 7 inches. In case, each......................................3.75

20584 Pure Aluminum (non tarnishable). A very light and elegant article. Price, without pen 50

20586 Similar style, fine quality rolled gold holder, fitted with best No. 3 gold pen. Price...2.68

Plush Cases for Pens, 75c. Each.

GOLD PENS, HOLDERS, PENCILS, ETC.

In this line of goods we are able to give unusually good value at prices quoted, as we have large quantities of these goods made especially to our order; the pens are of 14k gold, and known as diamond pointed; the mountings are best 14k plate, and will wear a lifetime. Nos. 20587 to 20594 are all cased in neat satin lined boxes at prices quoted. Postage on cased goods, 4 to 6c. extra.

20587 Fine Pearl Holder, best rolled plate mountings, 14k Pen, No. 1 or 2. Fitted into satin-lined case as shown by No. 20600. Price, each, $1.65.

20588 No. 3, 14k Pen. Best rolled plate mountings, fine pearl holder. Fitted in case similar to No. 20600. Price, each, $1.90.

20589 No. 4, 14k Pen. Fine Pearl Holder, best rolled plate mountings. Fitted in case similar to No. 20600. Price, each, $2.15.

20590 No. 5, 14k Pen. Fine Pearl Holder, best rolled plate mountings. Fitted in case similar to No. 20600. Price, each, $2.50.

20591 No. 4 Pen. Fine Pearl Holder, solid sterling silver mountings, handsomely chased. Fitted in case similar to 20600. Price, each, $2.25.
20592 Same as above, with No. 5 pen. Price. each, $2.45.

20593 No. 5 Pen. Ebony Desk Holder, rolled plate mountings. Fitted with leather covered satin lined box. Price, each, $1.48

20594 No. 4 Pen. Ebony Desk Holder, rolled plate mountings. Fitted in leather covered satin lined box. Price, each, $1.25.

20595 No. 4 Pen. Black Enameled Holder. rolled plate mountings, screw pencil in end. Price, each, $1.75.

20596 No. 4 Pen. Rolled Plate Telescope Holder. closes to vest pocket size. Price, each, $1.45.
20597 No. 5 Pen, otherwise same as above. Price, each, $1.75.

20598 No. 5 Pen. Fine Chased Rolled Plate Holder; combination screw pencil. Price, each, $1.75.

20599 Men's Propelling and Repelling Pencil; gold trimmed; takes full size and length of lead. A business pencil. Each, $0.35,

20600 Antique Chased Gold Plate Holder; handle of knotted ivory, fitted with No. 2 gold pen, and furnished with morocco, satin lined case; total length, 7 inches. Each.................$1.90
20601 Similar to above, old knotted ivory holder, mounted in sterling silver, handsome antique chasing, fitted with No. 4 gold pen, morocco case. Each..................... 2.00

20602 Assorted Colors, Twist Pearl Holder, mounted in fine rolled gold plate, and fitted with No. 3 gold pen. Length of above, 7 inches. Price in morocco case, each........................$1.90

We charge for engraving on articles of Jewelry, Watches, etc., 2½ cents per letter for script style; 5 cents for Old English style.
We can furnish Plush Cases for Pens at 75 cents each.

Gold Pens repointed and repaired. Send pen and 42c; this will cover expense if pen can be repaired at all.

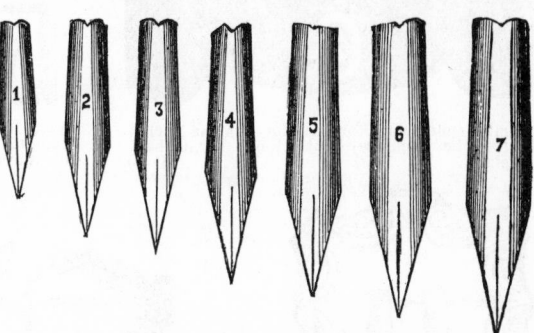

GOLD PENS. (CUTS FULL SIZE.)

PRICES, EACH.

Nos.	1	2	3	4	5	6	7
20604 14k.........	$0.65	$0.75	$0.82	$1.05	$1.18	$1.55	$1.85
20605 10k....			.50	.60	.80	.90	

10k pens not made smaller than No. 3.

Cut full size.

20606 Magic Screw Pencil, sterling silver mountings, elegantly chased and oxidized, stone set. Come in assorted patterns. Price, each... . ...$1.38

20607 Rolled Plate Magic Pencil, elegantly chased   Price, $0.83

20608 Sterling Silver, chased and oxidized. Stone in head of snake. Each................... ....$2.68

20609 Sterling Silver, gold mounted, assorted designs. Price, each...$1.00

20610 Rolled Plate Magic Pencil, ebony mounting. Price, each......$0.50

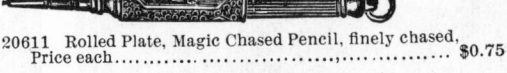

20611 Rolled Plate, Magic Chased Pencil, finely chased, Price each... $0.75

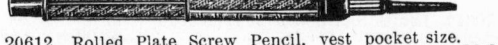

20612 Rolled Plate Screw Pencil, vest pocket size. Price, each...$0.30

Cut one-half size.

20613 Rolled Plate Tooth Pick, with solid gold pick. Price, each...$0.25
20613A No. 20613 Toothpick in leather case........... 0.35

For Fountain and Stylographic Pens see preceding page.

Sterling Silver and Plated Belt Pins; Czarina Neck Buckles, Belts, Garters, Etc.

20625 Sterling Silver Belt Pin....$0.50

20626 Sterling Silver Belt Pin....$0.40
20627 Same in Silver Plate....... .20.

20628 Roll Gold Plate Belt Pin...........$0.75.

20629 Gold Plate, Roman Color Czarina Buckle for the neck, without ribbon. Cut half size.................. - $1.25

20630 Roll Gold Plate Buckle, for neck or dress ornament,$0.50

20631 Sterling Silver Veil Clasp; very useful........$0.60

20632 Sterling Silver Buckle, for neck or dress ornament.................$0.65

20633 Sterling Silver Buckle, for neck or dress ornament...............$0.60

20634 Sterling Silver Czarina Neck Buckle. Cut full size, $0.60

20635 Rolled Gold Plate Czarina Neck Buckle. Cut full size.... $0.45

20636 Rolled Gold Plate Czarina Neck Buckle. Cut full size, $0.55

20637 Sterling Silver Umbrella Clasp........$0.35

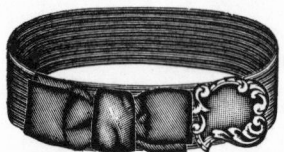

20638 Silk Elastic Garter, with solid silver clasps. Per pair........$3.25

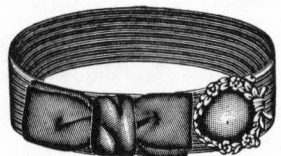

20639 Silk Elastic Garter, with solid silver clasps. Per pair........$3.00

20640 Silk Elastic Garters, with solid silver clasps. Per pair $2.00
20641 Silk Elastic Garters, similar to No. 20640, but with plated clasps. Per pair..........................$0.85

20642 Silk Elastic Garters, with solid silver adjustable clasps. Per Pair............................$1.75

20643 Ladies' Sterling Silver Trimmed Belt; finest silk web, assorted colors.....................$2.50

20644 Ladies' Sterling Silver Trimmed Belt, finest silk web, assorted colors....................$2.00

20645 Ladies' Sterling Silver Trimmed Belt, best silk web assorted colors....................$1.90
20646 Same as No. 20645,but silver plated buckle. 1.10

20647 Ladies' Sterling Silver Trimmed Belt, finest silk web, assorted colors.....................$3.00

20648 Ladies' Sterling Silver Trimmed Belt, finest silk web, assorted colors.....................$2.75

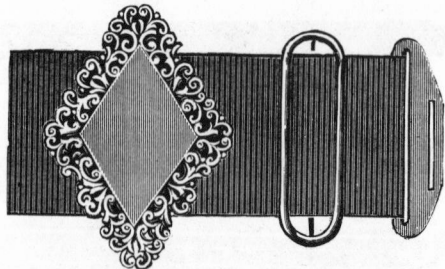

20649 Ladies' Silver Plated Trimmed Belt, good quality web, assorted colors................$0.85

20650
Cabinet Frame. Silver Plated and Enameled in Colors. 6 inches high. $0.80

20651
Card Size Photo Frame. Silver Plated and Enameled in Colors. 4½ inches high.$0.80

20652
Sterling Key Chain, 17 inch, $2.25

20653
Silver Plated Pin Tray. $0.35

20654
Silver Plated Jewelry Tray. $0.40

We engrave 2 or 3 letter monograms on belts Nos. 20647-20648, or 20649 for 25 cents.

GOLD HEAD CANES, THIMBLES, NOVELTIES AND ALUMINUM WARE.

Cuts are ½ Size.
20700 An Extra Quality 14k Gold Filled Cane Head, the top plate solid gold, handsomely chased and warranted for 20 yrs. Stick is ¾ inch ebony. Price, $13.50

20701 Superior Quality Gold Head Cane, latest pattern and finest quality of chasings; a cane that will last a lifetime; ⅞ inch ebony stick.
Price $20.00

(Always send size.)

20702 A Fifteen Year Guaranteed Gold Filled Head, handsomely chased; 1 inch ebony stick.
Price............$10.00

NOTE.—We furnish Gold Headed Canes, any size from ⅜ in. to 1¼ in. at proportionate prices; satisfactory value guaranteed.

This cut is exact size; other cuts are reduced. 20703 Gold Plated Head (cut is exact size) handsomely chased; ½ in. ebony stick. Price..........$2.50

SILVER THIMBLES.

20704 Aluminum, Very light, 10c.
20705 Silver, 25c,

20706 Silver, better quality, 33c.

20707 Silver Chased, fancy patterns. 45c.

20708 Silver, extra quality, ornamental band, 55c.

GOLD FILLED THIMBLES.

20709 Silver gold band, assorted chasings, $1.00.

20710 14k Solid Gold, each $4.00. 20710½ 10k Solid Gold, each, $3.12.

20711 Plain Gold filled, each, 82c. 20711½ Same, solid gold, $2.90.

20712 Fancy Octagon, gold filled assorted chasing, each, $1.40.

20746 Gold Plated and Enameled Handle Paper Cutter. Length, 5½ inches. $1.00

20747 Silver Plated and Enameled Handle Paper Cutter. Length, 6 inches. $0.50

20748 Sterling Silver Handle, Pearl Blade Bookmark. $1.25

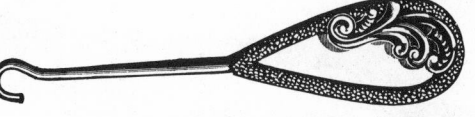

20749 Sterling Silver Glove Buttoner. $0.60

20750 Sterling Silver Handle, Pearl Blade Bookmark and Paper Cutter. $1.30

20751 Fine Steel Cutting Blades. mounted with sterling silver handles These are choice articles for holiday gifts. $2.90

20752 Pearl Bookmark and Paper Cutter $0.50

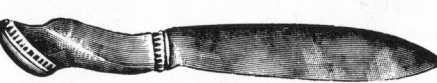

20753 Pearl Paper Cutter, 5 inches long. $0.80

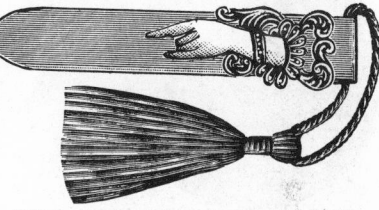

20754 Sterling Silver Bookmark. $0.55

PURE ALUMINUM WARE.

Tea Ball.

Sugar Bowl.

Sugar Shaker.

Syrup Pitcher

Cup.

T. P. Holder

Bon Bon.

20755 Pure Aluminum, Tea Ball, total length, 7 in. Ball 1½ in. dia. Each, $0.50.

20756 Pure Aluminum Sugar Bowl Satin and Polished Finish. Height, 5 inches. Each, $2.00

20757 Pure Aluminum, Chased and Polished. Height, 4½ inches. Each, $1.25

20758 Pure Aluminum Syrup Pitcher, Bright Polished. Height, 6 inches. Each, $1.75

20759 Child's Cup, Satin and Polished Finish. Height 3 inches. $0.75

20760 Pure Aluminum Match or Tooth Pick Holder. Silver Finish; height 2¼ inches. $0.50

20761 Pure Aluminum Fancy Edge, Twist Wire Handle; dimensions, 4x5 inches. Each, $0.85

Candlestick.
Nut Tray.
Mustard Cup.
Salt and Pepper.
Candle Stick.
Funnel.

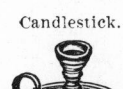      

20765 Pure Aluminum Candlestick; dimensions, 2½ x 4 inches. Each, $0.65

20766 Pure Aluminum Nut or Bon-Bon Tray; diameter, 4 inches. Each, $0.55

20768 Aluminum Cover and Spoon; cup and base is glass. Each, $0.75

20769 Fine Finish, like silver; height, 4 in. Salt or Pepper. Each, $0.65

20771 Pure Aluminum, handsome as silver. Height, 6 inches. Each, $0.75 Height, 8 inches. 1.45

20772 Pure Aluminum; mirror polish. Each. 3 inch............$0.50 4 inch........... .68 5 inch, with strainer, .75

20774 Aluminum. Each, $0.10

These goods never require cleaning or polishing as do similar goods made of other metals.

SOLID STERLING SILVER FLAT WARE.   Guaranteed $\frac{925}{1000}$ Fine.

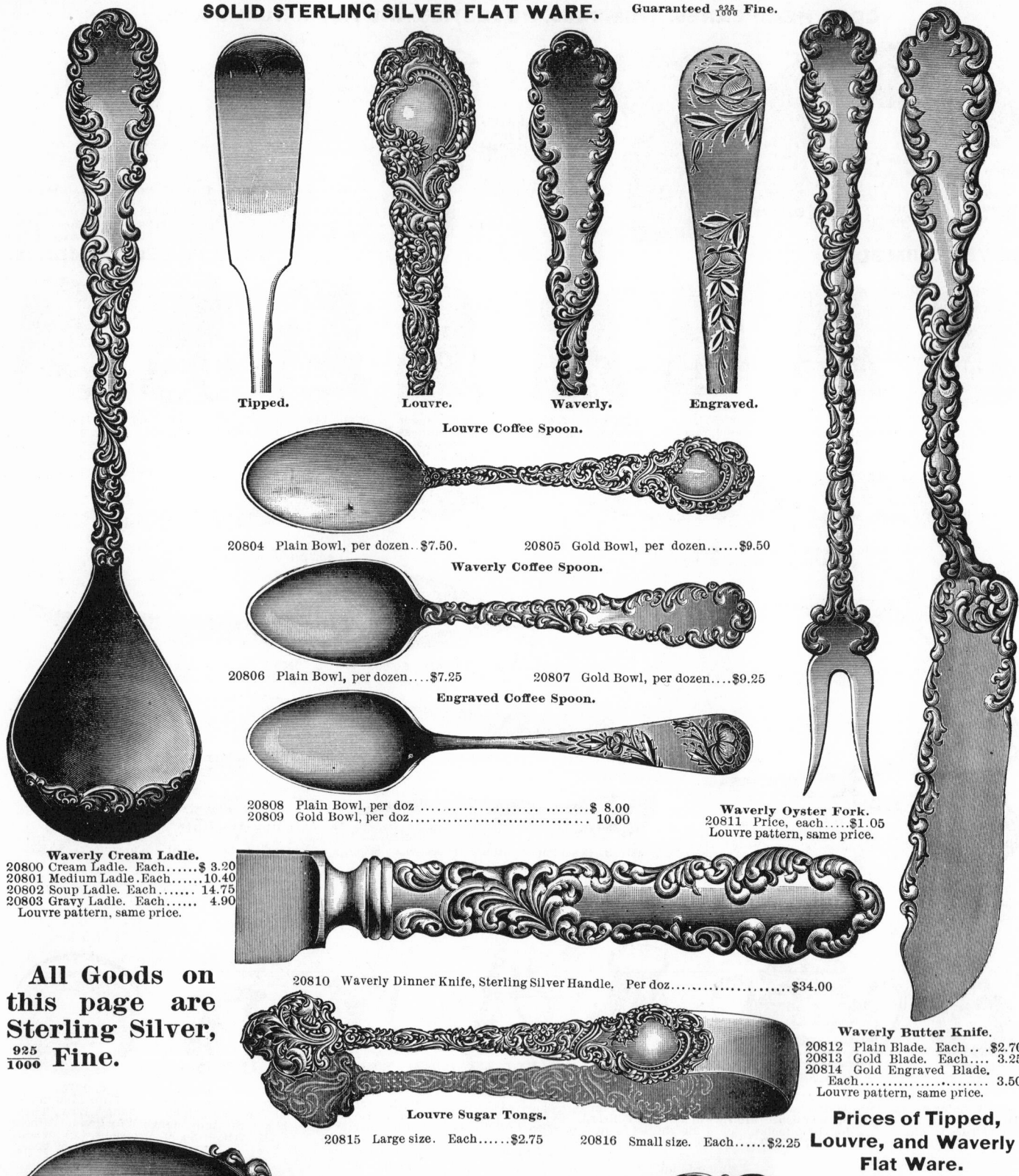

Tipped.   **Louvre.**   **Waverly.**   **Engraved.**

Louvre Coffee Spoon.

20804   Plain Bowl, per dozen..$7.50.   20805   Gold Bowl, per dozen......$9.50

Waverly Coffee Spoon.

20806   Plain Bowl, per dozen....$7.25   20807   Gold Bowl, per dozen....$9.25

Engraved Coffee Spoon.

20808   Plain Bowl, per doz ....$ 8.00
20809   Gold Bowl, per doz................................ 10.00

Waverly Oyster Fork.
20811   Price, each.....$1.05
Louvre pattern, same price.

Waverly Cream Ladle.
20800 Cream Ladle. Each.....$ 3.20
20801 Medium Ladle.Each......10.40
20802 Soup Ladle. Each.......14.75
20803 Gravy Ladle. Each...... 4.90
Louvre pattern, same price.

All Goods on this page are Sterling Silver, $\frac{925}{1000}$ Fine.

20810   Waverly Dinner Knife, Sterling Silver Handle.   Per doz......................$34.00

Waverly Butter Knife.
20812   Plain Blade. Each ...$2.70
20813   Gold Blade. Each.... 3.25
20814   Gold Engraved Blade.
     Each......................... 3.50
Louvre pattern, same price.

Louvre Sugar Tongs.

20815   Large size. Each......$2.75   20816   Small size. Each......$2.25

Prices of Tipped, Louvre, and Waverly Flat Ware.

Tea Spoons, 6 oz....Per doz.	$ 6.60
Tea Spoons, 8 oz....Per doz.	8.80
Table Spoons, 18 oz. Per doz.	19.80
Medium Forks, 18 oz. Per doz.	19.80
Dessert Spoons, 14 oz. Per doz	15.40
Dessert Forks, 14 oz. Per doz.	15.40
Sugar Shells. Each.........	1.70
Butter Knives. Each........	2.70

Waverly Sugar Shell.
20817   Plain Bowl ....Each. $1.70
20818   Gold Lined Bowl .... Each. 2.00
20819   Gold Lined Engraved Bowl.. ...Each. 2.25
Louvre pattern, same price.

For price of engraved pattern add to price of Waverly, $1.50 per doz. for Tea Spoons; $2.25 per doz. for Dessert Spoons and Forks; $2.50 per doz. for Table Spoon and Forks; 25c. each for Butter Knives and Sugar Spoons. See Our Prices for Engraving Names and Initials at Bottom of Next Page.

THE CELEBRATED ROGER BROS. "1847" FLAT WARE.

Sold by jewelers the world over as the best plated ware made. Compare our prices with your jeweler's, and notice how much you can save by ordering from us.

20900	Solid Crucible Steel Knives, plain or frosted, 9 inches long, hand burnished, triple plate Per dozen $3.40
20901	Forks to match. Per dozen.. 3.40
20902	DessertKnives to match, 7¼ inches long. Per dozen...................................... 3.20
20903	Dessert Forks to match 3.20
20904	Three piece Carving Set to match 3.50

20905	Table Knives, arabesque handles, like or similar to cut, bright finish. triple plate. Per dozen $4.25		20911	Quadruple Plate on Nickel Silver, hollow handle, arabesque, bright finish knives. Per dozen........$6.00
20906	Forks to match. Per dozen 4.30		20912	Forks to match. Per dozen 6.00
20907	Three-piece Carving Set to match.................... 4.50		20913	Three-piece Carving Set to match................. 6.00
20908	Fruit Knives to match, per set (6)..................... 1.75			
20910	Nut Picks to match, per set (6)..................... 1.50			

Patterns.	Tea Spoons.		Table Spoons.		Dessert Spoons.		Medium Forks		Dessert Forks.	
	Extra plate. Per doz.	Triple plate. Per doz.	Extra Plate. Per doz.	Triple plate. Per doz.	Extra Plate. Per doz.	Triple plate. Per doz.	Extra plate. Per doz.	Triple plate. Per doz.	Extra plate. Per doz.	Triple plate. Per doz.
20914 Tipped ...	$2.48	$3.98	$4.95	$7.86	$4.37	$6.71	$4.97	$7.89	$4.40	$6.73
20915 Shell,.....	2.76	4.20	5.44	8.40	4.95	7.26	5.42	8.41	4.90	7.31
20916 Portland.	2.79	4.23	5.47	8.43	4.98	7.31	5.44	8.44	4.92	7.34
20917 Savoy.....	2.81	4.26	5.48	8.44	5.01	7.36	5.47	8.48	4.94	7.37
20918 Columbia.	2.82	4.27	5.51	8.47	5.02	7.37	5 49	8.40	4.95	7.36

Tipped.   Savoy.   Shell.   Portland.   Columbia.

We illustrate below a few fancy pieces of the famous "Rogers Bros." "1847" Brand. We can furnish either of these articles in any of the four fancy pattern shown above.

Patterns.	Butter Knives.	Sugar Shells.	Pickle Forks.	Coffee Spoons.	Mustard Spoons.
	Extra or Standard Plate.	Extra or Standard Plate.	Extra or Standard Plate.	Extra or Standard Plate.	Extra or Standard Plate.
20919 Tipped........	$0.48 each	$0.40 each	$0.32 each	Not made.	$0.22 each
20920 Shell..........	.50 each	.44 each	Not made.	$3.75 doz.	.33 each
20921 Portland.....	.51 each	.45 each	$0.46 each	3.77 doz.	.35 each
20922 Columbia.....	.52 each	.47 each	Not made.	3.79 doz.	36 each
20923 Savoy	.53 each	.49 each	Not made.	3.80 doz.	.38 each

Fancy Pieces.	Standard Plate.	Each.
20924	Pie Knife, any fancy pattern.............	$2.08
20925	Cake Knife, any fancy pattern.........	2.05
20926	Cream Ladles, any fancy pattern........	.85
20927	Gravy Ladle, any fancy pattern..........	1.25
20928	Berry Spoons, any fancy pattern........	1.35
20929	Sugar Tongs, any fancy pattern.........	1.00
20930	Salt Spoons, any fancy pattern..........	.21
20931	Soup Ladles, any fancy pattern.........	2.51
20931½	Oyster Forks.any fancy pattern. Per doz	4.10

SEE OUR RATES FOR ENGRAVING, AT BOTTOM OF THIS PAGE.

Butter Knife. Cut ¾ size.

20932 Columbia Butter Knife, triple plate. Each.......................... ....$0.75

Sugar Spoon, ¾ size

Coffee Spoon. Cuts full size.

20933 Primrose Coffee Spoons, extra plate. Per dozen..........................$3.75
20934 Primrose Coffee Spoons, triple plate. Per dozen.......................... 4.75

20937 Columbia Sugar Shell, triple plate. Each.............. ...$0.65

Cut full size.

20935 Savoy Coffee Spoons, extra plate. Per dozen...........................$3.80
20936 Savoy Coffee Spoons, triple plate. Per dozen.............................. 4.70

20938 Portland Salt Spoon, extra plate. Each....... ....$0.31

Cut full size.

We charge for engraving table flat ware, spoons, forks, etc,, 1 1-2 c, per letter for script engraving on lots of six or more pieces. On all other work our charge is 2 1-2 c. per letter for script style, 5 c, for Old English.

20939 Embossed Small Sugar Tongs, made in embossed pattern only. Each $0.75
20940 Sugar Tongs, larger size, any fancy pattern. Each......... 1.00

We sell any quantity of our table ware from one piece upward at dozen rates.

MONTGOMERY WARD & CO.'S GUARANTEED FLAT WARE.

These goods are made for us especially by one of the largest factories of America. They are stamped with our name and the makers are under forfeit to keep the quality up to our standard, which is the very best it is possible to produce. By making contracts for large quantities of these goods we are enabled to place them with our customers at prices much lower than any of the standard brands of plated ware. Each original package of forks, spoons, etc., contains our "Guarantee Certificate," which authorizes the purchaser to return any ware bearing our name in case it should not prove as represented in every particular, and we will refund money or replace the goods.

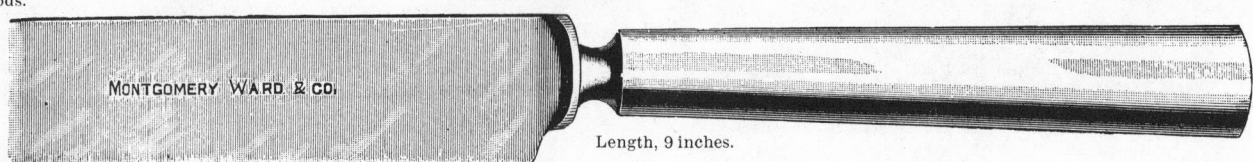

Length, 9 inches.

20950   Montgomery Ward & Co.'s Extra Crucible Steel Knife, extra quality triple plate. Hand burnished, polished or satin finished handles, making positively the best knife offered at the price. Per dozen...$2.95

20951   Forks to match. Made of Solid Nickel Silver and extra heavy plated. Per dozen.. 2.95

NOTE.—These goods are put up in a handsome box bearing our name and trade-mark; also a guarantee that they will give perfect satisfaction or money will be refunded. If you want the best for your money, order them.

PATTERNS.	Tea Spoons. Per Doz.		Table Spoons. Per Doz.		Dessert Sp'ns Per Doz.		Med'm Forks Per Doz.		Dess'rt Forks Per Doz.	
	Extra plate.	Triple plate.	Extra plate.	Triple plate.	Extra plate.	Triple plate.	Extra plate.	Triple plate.	Extra plate.	Triple plate.
20952 Tipped..	$1.95	$2.98	$3.70	$5.90	$3.25	$4.94	$3.68	$5.85	$3.20	$4.98
20953 Windsor	1.97	3.00	3.75	6.05	3.30	5.00	3.74	5.94	3.28	5.05
20954 Chicago	2.00	3.04	3.85	6.20	3.45	5.25	3.80	6.00	3.35	5.10
20955 Cardinal	2.04	3.10	3.95	6.35	3.50	5.35	3.90	6.10	3.55	5.20
20956 Majestic	2.08	3.20	4.10	6.40	3.54	5.40	4.00	6.25	3.58	5.30
20957 Shell....	2.10	3.25	4.25	6.50	3.60	5.50	4.12	6.30	3.65	5.45

PATTERNS.	Butt'r Knives Each.		Sugar Shells. Each.		Pickle Forks. Each.		Coffee Sp'ns. Per Doz.	M'st'rd Sp'ns. Each.	
	Extra plate.	Triple plate.	Extra plate.	Triple plate.	Extra plate.	Triple plate.	Gilt Bowls, extra per set, $1.00. Not made.	Extra plate. Not made.	Triple plate.
20958 Tipped..	$0.38	$0.55	$0.25	$0.39	$0.26	$0.41	$3.65	$0.19	$0.37
20959 Windsor	.40	.60	.28	.43	29	.44	3.67	.20	.47
20960 Chicago.	.45	.65	.35	.54	.32	.49	3.67	.21	.47
20961 Cardinal	.50	.68	.42	.60	.47	.55	3.69	.21	.49
20962 Majestic	.52	.70	.45	.62	.50	.65	3.68	.22	.49
20963 Shell	.55	.72	.48	.65	.63	.60	3.70	.25	.52

Tipped.   Windsor.   Cardinal   Shell.   Chicago.   Majestic.

20964   Shell Coffee Spoons. Per dozen...$3.70

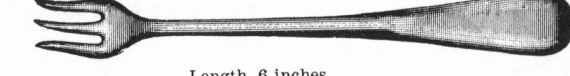

20965   Majestic Coffee Spoons. Per dozen...$3.68

50966   Chicago Butter Knife. Each...$0.45

Length, 6 inches.

20967   Oyster Forks, Windsor pattern. (This pattern matches well with any set.) See cut. Standard plate. Each.............$0.33 Per doz.....$3.00

20968   Oyster Forks, hand engraved, solid silver finish, heavy Standard plate. Each.........................$0.70 Per doz........................... 7.70

Bargains in Forks and Spoons.

We have a lot of Rogers and M. W. & Co. best triple plate goods, fancy patterns,from old catalogue,to close out as follows:

		Triple Plate.	Extra Plate.
20970	Rogers or M. W. & Co. Fancy Dessert Spoons, per doz.	$4.00	$3.00
20971	Rogers or M. W. & Co. Fancy Table Forks.........	4.00	3.00
20972	Rogers or M. W. & Co. Fancy Dessert Forks........	3.75	2.30
20973	Rogers or M. W. & Co. Fancy Dessert Spoons.......	3.75	2.30

Used for Ice Cream Soda. Length, 5 inches.

20974   Bar Spoon, warranted; see cut; long French twist handle, Standard plate. Per doz...........................$3.77

20975   Fluted Julep Strainers, warranted, Standard plate. Each.. .60

20976   Assorted Fancy Pattern Pickle Forks. Each.............$0.20

20977   Chicago Gravy Ladle. Each.........................$0.90

OUR CELEBRATED PANAMA SILVER TABLEWARE AT REDUCED PRICES.

The immense quantity which we used last year, of these popular goods, together with the lowered price of metals, has enabled us to offer our Panama Silver Ware this year at greatly reduced prices. Quality will remain exactly as heretofore.

Panama Silver is the metal of the century. It is solid and not plated, and will not tarnish when exposed to the atmosphere.

Forks, spoons, butter knives and sugar shells now made of the new metal are superior to silver plated goods in point of non-tarnishing, and are equal to sterling silver for durability.

We guarantee them to wear longer than any other metal goods made. As there is no plate to wear off, any silver powder, polish, chalk or electroine can be used to clean them.

They are put up in neat packages, each one bearing our brand and trade mark, which we consider a sufficient guarantee as to their quality.

They are made only in Windsor patterns, as shown in illustration marked "Windsor," on this page.

See our rates for engraving spoons, forks, etc., at bottom of previous page.

New Price List of Panama Silver.

		Per doz.
20978	Teaspoons, Windsor pattern..................................	$1.10
20979	Dessert Spoons, Windsor pattern..........................	1.90
20980	Tablespoons, Windsor pattern.............................	2.20
20981	Medium Forks, Windsor pattern............................	2.20
		Each.
20982	Sugar Shells, Windsor pattern.............................	$0.21
20983	Butter Knives, Windsor pattern............................	.21

Purchasers of these goods, not finding them perfectly satisfactory, may return them in exchange for other goods, or we will refund the purchase price.

We have discontinued the sale of Panama Silver Knives, as we find the blades do not retain the temper. We recommend our No. 20950 knives, to match Panama Silver forks and spoons in appearance and durability.

SILVER PLATED FANCY PIECES.
Made by the Most Reliable Manufacturers.

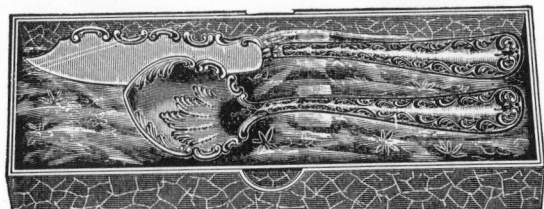

21000 Majestic Sugar Spoon and Butter Knife, in satin
    lined box...$1.30
    Any fancy pattern same price.

21001 Shell Pie Knife, in satin lined box..................$2.10
    Any fancy pattern pie knife same price.

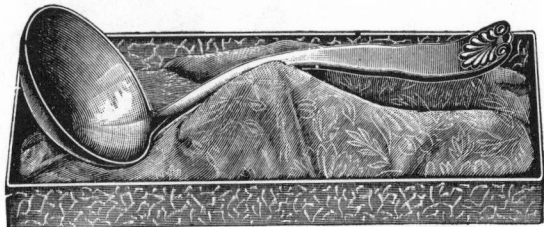

21002 Shell Cream Ladle, in satin lined box $1.00
    Any fancy pattern cream ladle same price.

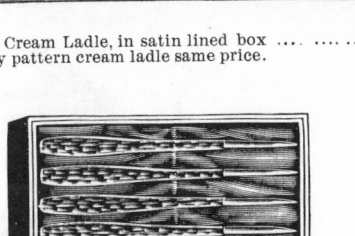

21003 Set of 6 Fancy Nut Picks, in satin lined case.
    Per set $0.75

21004 Nut Cracker, in satin lined box. Each..............$0.50

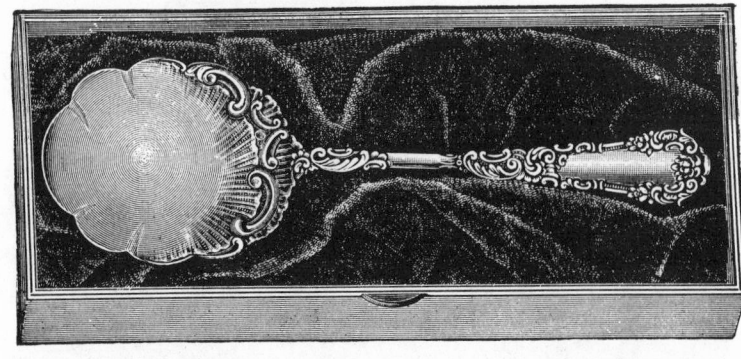

21008 Yale Berry Spoon, in plush lined case...............................$1.25

21009

21009 Majestic Child's Set of 3 pieces; knife,
    fork and spoon.   Heavy A 1 plate on best
    white metal.   Each set in satin lined case.
    Per set...$1.25
    Savoy, Portland or Shell (1847) Child's Sets.
    same price.

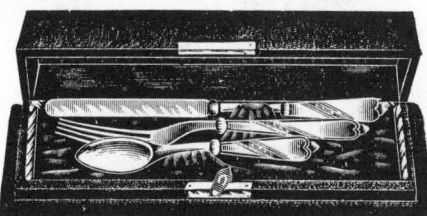

21010 Three pieces, Chicago Pattern; in fine
    silk plush case, A 1 goods. Per set.........$2.25
21011 Child's Sterling Silver Fork and Spoon,
    with Pearl Handle Knife, all in plush case.
    Per set............. .... 7.50

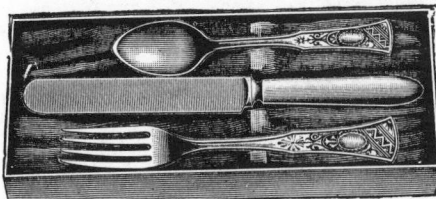

21012 Fancy Fork and Spoon, plain steel knife,
    in satin lined box..............................$0.65
21013 Child's Set, 3 pieces in box............... .25

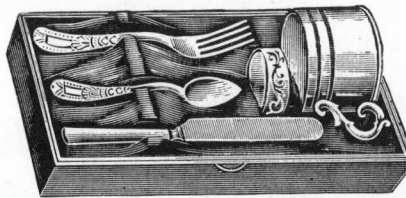

21014 Child's Silver Plate Knife, Fork, Spoon,
    Gold Lined Cup and Napkin Ring in satin lined
    case $1.25

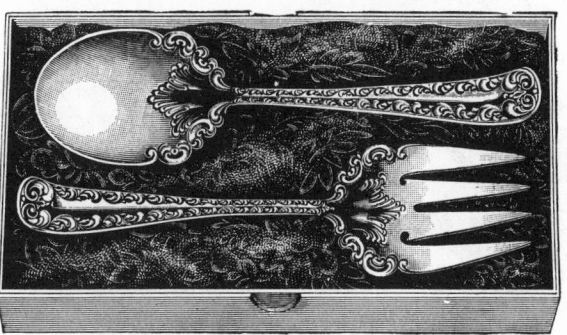

21005 Majestic Salad Fork and Spoon, in satin lined box ...$2.95

21006 Nut Cracker and 6 Picks in case
    Heavy Silver Plate.....................$1.75

"Standard" Silver Plated Ware.

This ware is known as fine White Metal, silver plated, and is fair ware at
the low price quoted.

21015 1 package (6) Tea Spoons; per package ....$0.25. Postage..........$0.06
21016 1 package (3) Table Spoons; per package .. .25. Postage.......... .06
21017 1 package (3) Medium Forks; per package   .25. Postage.......... .06

**FIRST QUALITY QUADRUPLE SILVER PLATED WARE—
QUALITY GUARANTEED.**

21120   Quadruple Plate Tea Set, 6 pieces, including waiter, $35.45; without waiter, 5-piece set, $25.45.
21121   Coffee, 9½ inches, $6.60   21122—**Tea**, 7½ inches, $5.75.   21123—Sugar, 6½ inches, $4.55.   21124—Cream, 4½ inches, $4.30   21125—Spoon. 4½ inches, $4.20
Coffee holds 3½ pints; Pitcher and Spoon Holder are gold-lined.

21130   Tea, $5.50.   21131   Spoon Holder, $4.00.   21132   Sugar, $4.25.   21133   Cream, $4.10.   21134   Coffee, $6.25.
Coffee holds 3½ pints; 8 inches high. Other pieces in proportion.   Cream and Spoon gold-lined.

21135   Tea, $4.00   21136   Cream. $2.75.   21137   Sugar, $3.00.   21138   Spoon Holder, $2.70.   21139   Coffee, $4.50.
Coffee, 3½ pints capacity, 8½ inches.   Spoon Holder and Cream Pitcher gold-lined.

21140   Coffee, $4.00.   21141   Spoon Holder, $2.00.   21142   Sugar, $2.50.   21143   Cream, $2.00.   21144   Tea, $3.50.

21145   E l e g a n t   Embossed
Crumb Tray and Scraper, $3.00.
21146   Cream, $3.85.
21147   Spoon to match, $3.90
Coffee, 8½ inches, 3½ pints.   Cream and Spoon gold-lined.
21148   Sugar, $3.80.
21149   Coffee, $5.75
21150   Tea to match, $5.25.
Syrup Pitchers and Butter Dishes to match above shown on pages 189 and 190.
We charge for engraving 2 1-2c per letter for script style, 5c for Old English.

BEST QUALITY QUADRUPLE SILVER PLATED WARE. QUALITY GUARANTEED.

21151 Crystal Glass Berry
Dish, $3.00.
Height, 11 inches.

21152 Beautifully Decorat-
ed Ruby Glass Berry
Dish, $4.75.
Height, 11 inches.

21153 Fancy Rose Glass Berry
Dish, $4.00.
Height, 10½ inches.

21154 Imitation Cut
Glass Berry Dish,
$2.60.
Height, 8½ inches.

21155 Fancy Rose Glass Berry Dish.
$4.90. Height, 11 inches.

21156 Large Fancy Glass Berry
Dish, $5.25. Height, 10 inches.

21157 Crystal Glass Berry Dish,
with Spoon, $4.40. Height, 10 in.

21158 Crystal Glass Berry Dish.
$4.50. Height, 7 inches.

21159 Crystal Glass Berry Dish,
$2.90 Height, 8½ inches.

21160 5-Bottle Caster,
Chased Border, $5.50.

21161 6-Bottle Caster,
Chased Border, $4.25.

21162 5-Bottle Caster,
Chased Border, $4.00.

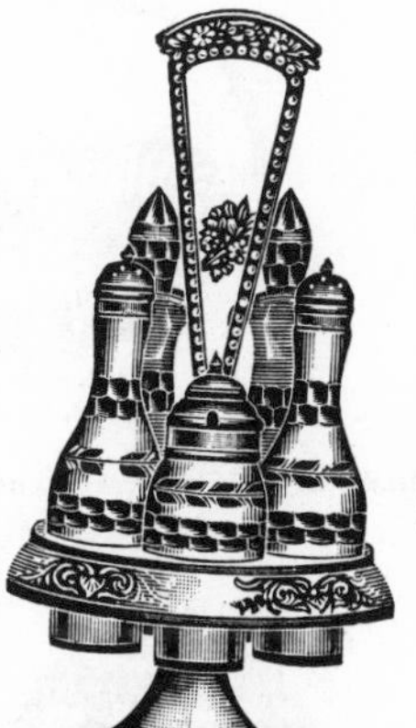

21163 5 Bottle Caster,
Chased Border, $3.25.

21164 5-Bottle Satin ngraved
Caster, $4.50.

21165 Tilting Water Set, Satin Engraved Goblet and Slop, gold lined, $12.25. Height, 21 inches.

21166 Tilting Water Set, Handsomely Engraved Goblet, gold
lined, $19.75.

21167 3-Piece Water Set. Complete..........$11.75
21168 Pitcher only. Height, 7½ inches. Price. 6.40
21169 12-inch Tray.................. 3.25
21170 Goblet. Height, 5 inches.... .... 2.10

21171 4-Piece Satin Engraved and Embossed Water Set..$13.50
21172 Pitcher... .... 4.50
21173 Goblet, gold lined............................... 2.25
21174 Slop, gold lined................................. 2.25
21175 Waiter................................... 4.50

Thorn's Silver Polish, Liquid Form, 15c. per Bottle. Powder, 10c. per Box.

13—2nd

BEST QUALITY QUADRUPLE SILVER PLATED WARE. QUALITY GUARANTEED.
Cake Baskets, Etc.

21179 Rich Heavy Border, Embossed Handle. Dimensions, 9x9. Price, $6.50.

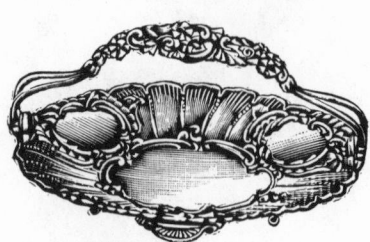

21180 Fancy Edge and Handles, Dia-9 inches. Price, $4.00.

21181 Chased Rococo Border. Price, $3.50.

21182 Embossed, Center Fancy edge. Height, 9 inches. Price, $3.00

21183 Rich Repousse Border, Low, Heavy Base. Height, 10 inches. Price, $3.25.

21184 Chased Inside and Border. Price, $3.40.

21185 Pink Opaque Glass, Nicely Decorated Pickle Jar. Height, 7 inches. Price, $3.75.

21186 Crystal Glass Pickle Caster. Price, $1.80.

21187 Ruby Decorated Glass. Price, $2.35.

21188 Fancy Glass Pickle Caster in Silver Plated frame. Price, $2.50

21189 Embossed Bon Bon. Price, $3.25.

21190 Embossed Gold Lined Bon Bon. Price, $1.95.

21191 Satin Finish Bon Bon. Price, $2.80.

21192 Gold Lined Bon Bon Tray. Price, $2.00.

21193 Elegantly Decorated Ruby Glass Pickle Caster. Height, 10 in. Price, $3.50,

Thorn's Silver Polish, Liquid Form, 15 cents per bottle. Powder, 10 cents per box.

21194 Butter Dish. Height, 9 in. Price, $4.00.

21195 Butter Dish. Height, 6½ in. Price, $3.50.

21196 Butter Dish, Satin Finish, Embossed Wreath. Price, $3.25.

21197 Butter Dish, Satin Chased. Price, $2.75.

21198 Butter Dish, Glass Base Plated Cover. Price, $1.25.

21199 Caster. 2 Vinegar, Pepper, Salt and Mustard. Price, $3.00.

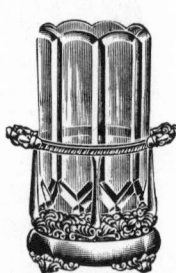

21200 Celery Dish, Crystal Glass. Price, $2.25.

21201 Celery Glass, Silver Plated Frame. Height, 10 in. Price, $1.40.

21202 Bread Tray. Price, $3.00.

21203 Decorated Ruby Glass Sugar and Cream, Quadruple Plated Frame. Price, $4.50.

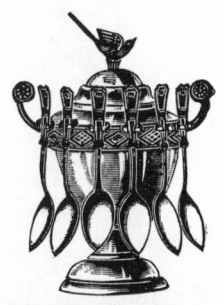

21204 Combination Sugar Bowl and Spoon Holder, without spoons. Height, 8 in. Price, $2.50.

We charge for engraving 2½ cents per letter for script style, 5 cents for Old English.

Best Quality Quadruple Silver Plated Ware.   Quality Guaranteed.

21210   Three-piece Dessert Set, fancy chased, $10.50
21211 Cream, gold lined, $3.45.   21212   Sugar, $3.55.   21213 Spoon gold, lined $3.50.

21214   Satin Bright Cut Dessert Set, cream and spoon goldlined. $9.00.
21215   Cream, $3.00.   21216   Sugar, $2.90.   21217   Spoon Holder, $3.00.

CHURCH SERVICE OR COMMUNION SET.
Best Quality Plate, Plain Polished.

21218 Plain Polished Syrup, $2.90.

21219 Satin Engraved Syrup, $3.00.

21220 Satin Engraved Syrup and Plate, $3.75.

21221 Satin Engraved Syrup and Plate, $3.25.

21224 Dessert Set, Sugar and Cream, embossed, gold lined, $3.90.   Height, 2½ inches.

21222   Fancy Chased Card Receiver, $4.00.

21223 Satin Engraved Card Receiver $3.25. Length, 7¾ in.

21225   Card Stand, embossed $2.00. Diameter, 6 inches.

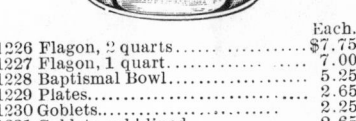

	Each.
21226 Flagon, 2 quarts	$7.75
21227 Flagon, 1 quart	7.00
21228 Baptismal Bowl	5.25
21229 Plates	2.65
21230 Goblets	2.25
21231 Goblets, gold lined	2.65

Electric Call-Bell.

21232   Fruit or Nut Bowl, raised decorations, gold lined, Height, 8 inches, $6.75.

21233   Porcelain Lined Baking Dish for vegetables, puddings, etc.   The porcelain lining is removable and will stand the heat, $4.25

21235 Large Size Pocket Flask with collapsion cup, cover screw top, $3.00

21236 Bell, electric. Price, $1.25.

21237 Call Bell, quadruple silver plate. Height, 4½ inches, Each.... ....$1.00

21238 Call Bell, silver plated bronze base. Height about 6 inches.   Assorted styles, similar to cut. Each.$0.75

21240   Elegant Satin Engraved Gold Lined Shaving Mug and Brush, removable compartment, $5.50
21240½. Brush only, $2.15.

21241 Satin engraved Shaving Mug and brush, gold lined $3.00
21241½. Brush only, $1.25.

21242   Screw top, Satin Engraved Pocket Flask, $2.00

21243   Fancy Chased Hairpin Box. $1.25.

21244   Satin Chased Smoking Set, 4 pieces, $5.00.

21245 Pin Tray, chased border, 3x2¼ inches, $1.50.

21246   Gold Lined Tooth Pick Holder, Height, 2 in. $1.55.

21247 Chased Pick Holder. Height, 2 in. $1.40.

21248 Chased Pick Holder. Height, 2¼ in. $1.50.

21249   Engraved Match Holder. Height, 2 in. $1.00.

21250 Fancy Pick Holder. Height, 2 in. $1.25.

BEST QUALITY QUADRUPLE PLATED NAPKIN RINGS. QUALITY GUARANTEED.

21260
Price, 20c.

21261
Price, 36c.

21262
Price, 38c.

21263
Solid Silver. Price, $1.50.

21264
Price, 70c.

21265
Price, 85c

21266
Price, 68c.

21267
Price, 85c.

21268
Price, 83c.

21269
Price, $1.05.

21270
Price, 88c.

21271
Price, 75c.

21272
Price, 70c.

21273
Price, 50c.

21274
Price, 69c.

21275
Height, 2½ in. Price, $1.25.

21276
Price, $1.65.

CHILDREN'S CUPS.

All Best Quality.

21277 Chased and Gold Lined.
Price, $2.40.

21278 Chased and Gold Lined.
Price. $2.10.

21279 Chased and Gold Lined.
Price, $1.40.

21280 Embossed.
Price, $1.75

21281 Chased and Gold Lined
Price, $1.93.

21282
Price. $1.85.

21283
Chased Gold Lined Cup.
Price, $1.75.

21284 Chased and Gold Lined.
Price, $1.25.

21285 Aluminum Collapsion Cup;
height, open, 2½ in.; closed, ⅞ in.;
weight, 1 oz. Will never tarnish.
Price, 75c.

21286 Collapsion Cup; height,
open, 2½ in.; closed, 1 in.
Price, $1.00

21287. Tea Cup.
Bright Cut, Gold Lined
Price, $2.75.

21288 New design Cup and Saucer,
Elegantly Chased; height, 3 in. Price,
$3.00. With mustache guard, $3.50.

21289 Coffee Cup. Mustache Guard.
Bright Cut, Gold Lined.
Price, $3.15.

21290 Embossed Gold Lined Cup
and Saucer.
Price, $2.50.

We Charge for engraving 2 1-2 cents per letter for Script Style, 5 cents for Old English.

EXTRA PLATE SILVERWARE.

Under this heading we quote a line of goods not up to the regular Quadruple Plate Goods, but a line that is well made, one that with reasonable care will last for many years. The styles are all of the latest and most desirable. For prizes, or for occasional use they are unsurpassed.

Caster

21291   Extra Plate Caster, 5 bottles; height, 15 inches. A beauty at the price; looks as well as a $6.00 caster. Each.................$0.90

Caster

21292   Extra Plate 5 Bottle Caster; height, 15 in. Heavier base and better bottles than No. 21291. Each.................$1.50

Caster

21293   Elegant Extra Plate 5 Bottle Caster. Height, 17 in. Beautiful bottles, with call bell in handle. Each.................$2.75

Water Set

21294   Extra Plate Water Set; chased cup, gold lined. Height, 19 in. Set complete.......$7.50

Pickle Caster

21295   Extra Plate Pickle Caster, tongs attached. Height, 11½ inches. Each.....................$1.00

Syrup

21296   Triple Plate with Extended Base, Height, 5½ inches.   Price. ...$1.25

Sugar

21297   Combination Sugar Bowl and Spoonholder for 12 spoons. Height, 6½ inches. Price, without spoons, $1.38

Berry

21298   Large Fruit Stand Glass Dish; extra plate frame and base. Height, 8 inches. Each....$1.25

Berry

21299   Large Glass Fruit Dish, metal frame, extra plate, Height, 6½ inches. Each.....................$1.50

Cake

21300 Beautiful Cake Basket. Height, 10 inches. Each.....................$1 50

Butter

21302   Extra Plate Butter Dish; chased. Height, 7¼ inches. Each $1.25

TRIPLE PLATE 4-PIECE TEA SET.
Satin Finish, Elegantly Chased.

Teapot

21304 Height, 9 inches. Price.. .... $2.75

Sugar Bowl

21306 Height, 6 inches. Price $1.85

Spoon Holder

21308 Height, 4 inches. Price. $1.65

Creamer

21310 Height, 3½ inches. Price $1.62

Sugar

21312   Fancy Colored Glass Sugar Bowl in silver plated frame with sugar shell attached. Price, $1.35

Butter

21314   Extra Butter Dish; Height, 6 inches; chased. Price............ $1.35

A TRIPLE PLATE 6-PIECE TEA SET FOR $6.50.

21316   Triple Plate 4-Piece Tea Set, Sugar Bowl not shown, complete, $7.00
Each piece separate $1.75.

21325 Coffee. Height, 7 inches Price $1.25.

21326 Butter Height, 6 inches. Price $1.25.

21327 Sugar. Height, 5 inches. Price $1.00.

21328 Spoon Holder. Height, 4½ inches. Price $1.00.

21329 Cream Pitcher. Height, 4½ inches. Price $1.00

21330 Syrup. Height, 5 inches. Price $1.00.

CLOCK DEPARTMENT.

We warrant every Clock we sell to keep good time.

Bee Time Nickel Clocks.

22999 Cut ¾ size. One day time. Ansonia make; dial is 2 inches in diameter, with bevel cut glass; the smallest clock made that keeps good time.
Price............$0.85
Postage, extra..... .09

22999

Bee Alarm.

23000 Same size as No. 22999, but with alarm; the smallest alarm clock made in the country; warranted to give satisfaction; dial 2 inches.
Price............$1.25
Postage, extra . .12

23000

23001

Progressor.

Please note price—compare with your retail jeweler. A better alarm clock for the money cannot be produced.
23001 Dial is 4 inches.
Price............$0.57
23002 The celebrated Waterbury Sunrise Alarm. Similar in appearance to 23001 but finer and more accurate timekeeper. Price.$0.78
23003 Same clock, as 23001, with calendar attachment,
Price............$0.80
Postage, extra, on Nos. 23001, 23002 and 23003, 22c.

Sure-Call Alarm.

23004 The best alarm clock made. Will not fail to wake you up. Rings for over a minute. Dial is 2 in., height 4½ in. Nickel or gilt finish; fine movement; cut steel pinions; double roller escapement.
Price............$1.50
Postage............. .24

23004

Electric Alarm.

23005 Double telephone bells. Rings for three minutes. Fine adjusted movement, cut steel pinions, double roller escapement. A very accurate timepiece. Height 5½ inches; dial, 2 inches. Nickel or gilt finish.
Price............$3.00
Postage........ .30

23005

Boudoir.

23006 A beautiful little porcelain clock, suitable for bed-room or sitting-room; decorated porcelain case, one day Waterbury movement; height, 7 inches.
Price............$2.30

23006

23007

Cupid's Dart.

23007 A handsome ornament as well as a good timekeeper, finished in silver or bronze, with fancy dial. Height, 6 inches, Ansonia movement, dial, 2 inches.

Price........ $3.20
Postage, extra .26

Frolic No. 2.

23008 Another handsome little clock in Silver or Bronze finish; 2-inch fancy dial; Ansonia movement. Warranted a good timepiece. Height, 7½ inches.
Price.........$3.00

23008

Magic.

23009 This is one of the prettiest and most graceful little clocks ever made. It comes in Silver or Bronze finish; has 2-inch fancy dial. Ansonia movement. A good timepiece and a beautiful ornament. Height, 9¼ inches.

Price..........$3.25

23009

Croquette.

23010 Another style of Ansonia fancy Silver and Bronze finish clock. A good timekeeper; 2-inch fancy dial. Height, 8¼ inches.
Price.......................... $3.25

23010

New Short Wind Waterbury.

Front.

Back.

23011 A Perfect Stem Wind Watch, good movement, made by the Waterbury Clock Co. Stem wind and set, porcelain dial, fancy embossed case; dial, 1¾ in.; same diameter as an ordinary men's size watch. Can be hung up or carried in the pocket; warranted to keep time. Price......................$1.35
Postage, 5c.
23011½ Same as above, but winds from back.
Price......................$1.25

Cupid Wreath.

23012 A beautiful little clock. Silver finish; 2-inch dial, an accurate timepiece, with cut steel pinions. Height, 5 inches.

Price............$2.00

23012

Tourist.

Glass Sides, Nickel and Gilt finish; 2½-inch dial. Good, accurate timepiece and a reliable and ornamental alarm clock.

23013 One-day alarm.
Price..........$1.85
23014 One-day strike.
Price..........$2.00
Height, 7 inches.

23013

Windsor.

23015 A new and handsome novelty alarm clock. Elegant decorated porcelain, with fancy silver dial. As ornamental as it is useful.

Price............$3.75
Height, 8¼ inches.

23015

Dayton.

23016 Antique oak case. Height 23 in., Ansonia movement, 6-in. dial, hour and half-hour strike on wire bell.
Price............$3.00
23017 Same with gong bell.
Price............$3.30
Alarm, extra...... .40
Weight, boxed, 17 lbs.

CLOCK DEPARTMENT—Continued.

Oakland.

23018 Black walnut case. Height, 23 in., carved top, s i d e s and base, A very handsome and desirable clock, fully w a r r a n t e d. Eight-day, half hour strike on wire bell, Waterbury movement. .... $3.90.
Eight-day, half-hour gong strike $4.30
Alarm, 40c. extra

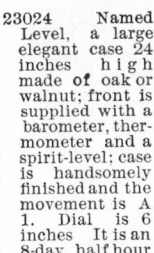

23018

Level.

23024 Named Level, a large elegant case 24 inches h i g h made of oak or walnut; front is supplied with a barometer, thermometer and a spirit-level; case is handsomely finished and the movement is A 1. Dial is 6 inches It is an 8-day, half strike on wire bell.
Price $3.75
23024 A S a m e with gong strike
Price $4.15
Alarm, 40 c extra
Weight, boxed, about 35 lbs.

23024

Napier.

23030 Antique oak furniture is now the style. Here you have a clock that will match; height, 23½ in., with a barometer and thermometer attached. making it quite the thing. Price, 8-day wire bell, $4.75
23031 Same w i t h gong bell.
Price $5.25
Alarm, 40c. extra.
Weight, boxed, 28 pounds.

23030

No. Forty-Four.

A calendar clock with alarm.
23019 An elegant carved w a l n u t clock; 8-day strike with alarm and calendar. Movement is of fine construction. Calendar is perpetual, showing day of week, month, day of month. Guaranteed accurate and reliable; case is 24 inches high; dials, on each, 6 inches.
Price $5.25
Without alarm, 40c less.
Weight boxed, 30 bs.

23019

Albany.

23025 Black walnut case. Height, 24 in. Carved t o p and base. A very l a r g e, p l a i n b u t h a n d s o m e clock, with an extra d e e p-sounding bell. The dial being 8 in. diameter, can be readily seen in any sized room. A very desirable clock for dining or general room, 8-day, half-hour strike on cathedral gong. $4.80
Alarm, additional, 40c.

23025

President.

23032 Plain, rich looking case of either oak or walnut, fluted columns; height, 21⅝ in.; dial, 6 in.; 8-day strike, wire bell.
Price, each... ...$3.25
23033 Same, with gong or cathedral bell.
Price.............$3.75
Alarm, extra, 40c.
Weight, boxed, 28 lbs

23032

No. Forty.

23020 An 8-day, oak cased, perpetual calendar clock, Height, 24 in., dials are each 6 in. A handsome and reliable article.
Strikes hours on wire bell. Calendar is perpetual
Price........$6.40
Weight, boxed, 30 lbs.
Not made with alarm.

23020

Buffalo.

23026— Large, showy, elegantly and substantially made; gives time of day and day of month, accurate and reliable; case black walnut, richly ornamented; height, 26⅞ in.; dial, 8 in.; 8-day, h a l f hour, wire bell strike, with calendar.
Price....$3.70
23027 S a m e, gong bell $4.10
Weight, 30 lbs. N o t m a d e with alarm.

23026

Corona.

23034 Black w a l n u t case; one-day time and wire bell strike; height, 17½ inches; 5-inch dial.
Price.............$2.25
Alarm, extra...... .40
Weight, boxed, 20 lbs.
Allow for box, 10 cents.

23034

Monarch.

23035 This is indeed a "Monarch," both in name and appearance. Made of fine black walnut, with bronze ornaments and French sash on dial. Has drawer in base of clock. Height, 25 inches; dial, 6 in.; 8-day half-hour strike on wire bell.
Price.............$6.15
23036 · Same, with gong bell.
Price.............$6.35
Alarm, extra.. .40
Weight, boxed, 22 lbs.

23035

Gibson.

23021 Handsome O a k Cased clock, barometer a n d thermometer attached; 8-day, wire bell strike. Height, 24 in., dial 6 in.
Price..............$3.38
23022 Same, with gong strike.
Price..............$3.88
Alarm, 40 cents extra.
Weight, 25 pounds.

23021

Berkeley.

23028 A Pretty Ansonia Black walnut clock; height 23 inches, 6 in. dial. Half-hour strike on wire bell.
Price........$3.10
23029 Same, with gong bell.
Price.......$3.35
Alarm, extra, 40c
Weight, b o x e d, 17½ lbs.

CLOCK DEPARTMENT—Continued.

Dakota.

23037 An elegantly polished oak cabinet clock, suitable for parlor or dining-room: 8-day; half-hour strike: cathedral gong, 5-inch gilt dial. Height, 15 inches.
Price..$4.00

23037

23038

Occidental.

A large, showy clock, walnut or oak gilt trimmed, gilt figures; mirror sides. New Haven 8-day movement.
23038 8-Day Strike $5.75
23039 8-Day Gong Strike $6.00
Alarm, extra.... .40
Height, 24 inches.

Cato.

23040 Polished oak, same finish and movement as No. 23037.
Price...$4.10

23040

Montana.

23041 Here is the biggest bargain ever offered, in 8-day clocks; compare the price of this with others and then send us your order. Clock is 22 inches high, made in oak or walnut: strike on wire bell
Price $2.00
Alarm, extra... .30

Seth Thomas Clocks.

Bangor.

23042 A Seth Thomas clock. Handsome black walnut case; height 21 in.; dial 6 in.; 8-day, spring, wire bell strike; like all Thomas clocks, is a good timekeeper.
Price...........$4.10
Alarm, extra.. .40
Weight, boxed, 25 lbs

23042

23043

Tampa.

23043 Another of the famous Seth Thomas clocks. Elegant black walnut case; height, 22 in., dial, 6 in., 8-day spring strike on cathedral bell.
Price.......$5.75
Alarm 40 cents additional.
Weight, boxed, 28 lbs.

New York.

23044 The cheapest Seth Thomas clock ever offered. Best Seth Thomas black walnut 8-day movement, half hour strike; made only with alarm and wire bell. Height, 22 in.
Price..........$3.85
Weight, boxed, 27 lbs.

Study No. 3.

23045 Study No. 3. An elegant polished oak hanging clock, 8-day, Waterbury weight movement: very accurate timepiece; glass sides; 8-inch silver dial; gong strike.
Price..............$8.75
Height, 22¼ inches.

23044

Augutsa.

23046 An 8-day weight striking clock. Oak case, cabinet finish. A beautiful ornament and a perfect timepiece. Length of case, 50¾ in. Dial is silver with black figures. 10 in. in diameter, brass weights and chains.
Price...............$16.75
Weight, boxed, 60 lbs.
Not made with alarm.

23046

Carlton.

A Black walnut regulator at the price of an ordinary mantel clock. Warranted perfect. Height 42 in.. dial 8 in.
23047 Eight-day time.......$5.65
23047½ Eight-day, half-hour, slow strike on gong........ .....$6.80
Not made with alarm.
Weight, boxed for shipment, 35 lbs.

23047

Study No. 4.

23048 Polished oak hanging clock, very handsome: 8-day Waterbury weight movement; very accurate timepiece; glass sides; 8-inch silver dial, gong strike.
Price.............$12.50
Height, 35¼ inches.

23048

Drop Octagon.

Especially adapted for use in school houses or churches; a polished veneered mahogany or rosewood finish, spring regulator.
23049 8-day; 8-inch dial $2.85
23050 8-day; 10-inch dial $4.00
23051 8-day; 12-inch calendar strike..........$5.00

23051

NOTE.—This quotation is upon the clock made by the Waterbury Clock Co. For Seth Thomas make add $1.00 to above prices, except No. 23049; not made by Seth Thomas Co.

CLOCK DEPARTMENT—Continued.
Fine Mantle Clocks.

"Lisle."

23053   Enameled iron case with gilt trimmings (will not tarnish). Height, 11 inches; 8-day, half-hour strike on cathedral gong bell, visible escapement. Price.............................$9.30
Same, with plain dial.... .... 7.25
Weight, boxed, 24 lbs.

Catalena.

23054   A new and graceful design in enameled iron with gilt trimmings; plain white or fancy gilt dial, 8-day, half hour strike, cathedral gong; movement made by the Waterbury Clock Co. Price, with American gilt or white dial, with visible escapement.........$8.00
Weight, boxed, 32 lbs.

Porcelain B.

23055   Fine porcelain clock, decorated with gold with three colored panels. You cannot imagine the beauty of this clock by looking at the cut; it must be seen to be appreciated. These clocks have formerly been so high priced that we could not use them, but we have made a deal with the makers so that we can offer them to you at a very reasonable price. You should have one of them for your parlor. Price.....................$15.30
Weight, boxed, 28½ lbs.

"Boston Extra."

23056   A very neat, handsome enameled iron case clock with Ansonia works. Height, 11 inches, 8-day, half-hour strike on gong bell, visible escapement. Price....$10.00
Plain dial, price.. 8.75
Weight, boxed, 34 lbs.

Berlin.

23057   Clock is enameled iron case, with gold figures, 8-day Ansonia movement, half-hour strike on cathedral gong bell, with visible escapement. Price............... ....$7.60
Plain dial, white or gold, price 5.75
Weight, boxed, 25 lbs.

Rosalind.

23058   One of the handsomest enameled iron case clocks made; is 12¼ inches high, with rich bronze trimmings and gold scroll work; 8-day, half-hour strike on cathedral gong bell, with visible escapement, like cut. Price...........................$12.60
With plain dial................................ .. 10.50
Weight, boxed, 32 lbs.

Amiens.

23059   Clock is Ansonia make, with enameled iron case set with gilt trimmings; 8-day, half-hour strike on cathedral gong bell; height, 10¼ in.
Plain dial, white or gold................... $ 8.85
Porcelain dial, visible escapement........ 10.50

La France.

23060   8-Day enameled iron Ansonia movement, with bronze urn, cathedral gong half-hour strike. Bronze trimmings with visible escapement ..$9.00
23061   Without visible escapement........$7.75

"Alford."

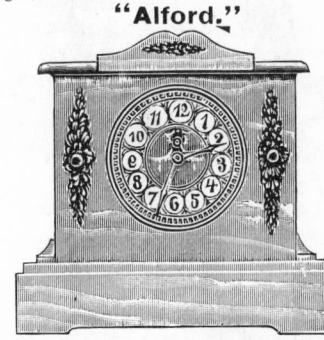

23062   Beautiful onyx, of the best quality, an 8-day Ansonia movement, with porcelain or gilt dial. Price..$14.50
Weight, boxed, 40 lbs.

Petite.

23063   Marbleized iron case, superior 8-day movement, fancy dial, half-hour strike on gong bell. Height, 9¾ inches, weight, boxed, 25 lbs.
Price...$5.50

Neptune.

23064   8-Day, half-hour gong strike, movement. Dial 5 inches, height, 11⅜ inches, length, 10 inches. American white dial, Roman or Arabic figures............ ....$7.00
Porcelain dial, Roman or Arabic figures....... 7.60
American gilt dial, Arabic figures....... 7.10
Visible escapement additional................ .70

"Ecuador."

23065   This richly enameled iron boudoir clock, 8-day gong, hour strike. Height, 9 inches, width, 10 inches, dial, 4½ inches. Gross w'ght, boxed, 30 lbs.
Price. $5.75

CLOCK DEPARTMENT—Continued.
Fine Mantel Clocks.

Our Seth Thomas Leader.

23066 Seth Thomas marbleized mantel clock. Case is elegantly enameled in exact imitation of Mexican onyx; warranted not to crack or peel; gilt ornaments and fancy gilt dial; movement is best Seth Thomas make; 8 day, half-hour strike; cathedral gong; 16½ inches wide, 12 inches high. Weight boxed, 11 lbs.
Price....................................$5.75

"Brennus."

23067 Very handsome mantel clock, finished in bronze. Height, 15 inches. New Haven movement; 8-day; half-hour strike on cathedral gong bell.
Price..........................$15.75
Weight, boxed, 53 pounds.

"Magnolia."

23068 Original design, highly artistic, marbleized wood case with gilt ornaments. Supplied with high class 8-day Star movement, half-hour strike and deep-toned gong. Dial, 5½ inches; height, 13 inches; length, 16½ inches.
American white dial, Roman or Arabic figures.... $6.95
American gilt dial, Arabic figures..... .... 6.90
Porcelain or bronzed dial.............................. 7.50
Gross weight, boxed, 24 lbs.

Seth Thomas.

23069 A handsome, marbleized wood mantel clock, with the celebrated Seth Thomas movement: 8-day, half-hour strike, cathedral gong: 5-inch dial. White or gilt. Height, 11 inches; width of base, 16½ inches. Price................ .... $6.75

Seth Thomas.

23070 An elegant marbleized wood, Seth Thomas 8-day, half-hour strike, cathedral gong clock; height, 12 inches; base, 15 inches; dial, 5 inches.
Price........................ ....$8.00

Washington.

23071 Enameled iron, 8-day, half-hour strike, cathedral gong, New Haven movement; gilt trimmings; height, 10½ inches
Price.................. . ...$7.75

23072 Clock Ornament; bronze: 4 inches high, Price, $1.25.

23073 Elegant Bronze Figure for clock ornament. Height, 6 inches. Price reduced to $1.10. Weight, 16 ounces.

$64,800 in Silver in the original of this figure.

Buffalo Bill.
A Clock Ornament.

23074 Handsome Bronze Horse, surmounted by a typical western rider. Splendid piece of work. Height, 10 inches. Weight, 5 lbs.
Price.........$1.35

23075 Height, 13 inches. Price, each, $1.00.

23076 Warrior. Height, 10½ inches. Each, $3.25. Per pair, $6.00.

23077 Exact reproduction of the famous Montana Silver Statue of Justice exhibited at the World's Fair. This is the only reproduction in the market and is a most valuable souvenir of the fair. The figure, globe and eagle are heavily silver plated; base is gold plated.
Height, 12 inches. Price.................$2.95
Height, 20 inches. Price.... .... 6.00

23078 Height, 14 inches. Price, each, $1.50.

23079 Pitcher. Height, 21 inches. Price each $2.90.

OPTICAL GOODS DEPARTMENT.

In this department we include optical goods of all kinds, surveyors', mathematical, meteorological and scientific instruments, drawing instruments and material. We are in a position to furnish nearly everything made in goods of the classes mentioned, whether listed or not. Send us your order and we will make the price right. Write for list of glass eyes for birds and animals.

We have arranged with a leading oculist of this city whereby all orders involving the least question as to the possibility of a perpect fit, will be submitted to him.

Parties ordering spectacles or eyeglasses will please observe the following directions which are required to insure proper glasses:

1st. State if glasses have been used and for what purpose, reading or for more distant objects.

2d. If glasses have not been previously used, state whether vision is defective for near objects, for distant objects, or for both near and distant objects, and if gasses wanted are for reading or walking purposes.

3d. State what the distance is (inches) from the center of one pupil to the center of the other. Measure with a rule or tape across the nose. Is the bridge of the nose prominent or flat?

4th. Give age. 5th. State if glasses wanted are for reading or distant objects.

Type For Testing the Sight.

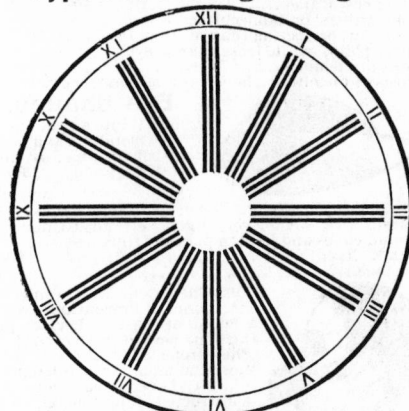

For Old Sight.

Let the customer, while holding the page in a good light at 12 to 14 inches distant from the eye, state the finest print that can be read at that distance. The number over the paragraph will be about the number of convex glasses for reading and sewing.

For Near Sight.

Let the customer state the farthest distance from the eyes at which paragraph No. 24 can be *distinctly* seen. The number of inches so obtained between the card and the eyes will correspond approximately with the number of concave lenses required.

Astigmatism.

If some of the arms in the above figure appear more distinct than others, the presence of astigmatism is indicated. The defect can only be corrected by cylindrical lenses, carefully ground to the oculist's order, or by personal fitting.

No. 48.

The smallest size letters on this card should be read easily at fifteen inches from the eye. If you cannot do so you should wear spectacles. It does not pay to buy cheap spectacles.

No. 36.

They distort the rays of light, disturb the angles of vision, cause pain and discomfort and injure the

No. 30.

eyesight. When it is necessary to hold work or reading matter farther than fifteen

No. 26.

inches from the eyes in order to see distinctly, it is a sure sign of failing vision,

No. 24.

and much annoyance, discomfort and pain will be prevented by

No. 18.

having a pair of glasses fitted.

No. 16,

Buy no other kind.

No. 14.

Crystalline are

No. 10.

the best

Spectacles.

NOTE:—All spectacles costing 50 cents or more are furnished with neat leather case without charge.

Spectacles or Eyeglasses, when sent by mail, allow 5 cents extra for postage.

All spectacles and eyeglasses listed are fitted in focal numbers from 5 to 72; special focal numbers, and prescription lenses fitted to order.

We can fit new lenses to old spectacles or eyeglass frames at a cost of from 25 to 50 cents, according to work to be done.

Straight Temple Spectacles.

Single Temple.

	Per pair.	Per doz.
23500 Steel Frame Spectacles, single temples, plano convex lenses, all numbers	$0.10	$1.00
23501 Steel Frame Spectacles, single temples, two screws in joint, well finished, all numbers, plano convex lenses	.25	2.50
23502 Steel Spectacles, single temples, periscopic lenses, good finish	.50	5.20
23503 Spectacles, highly tempered steel; single temples, extra finish, first quality periscopic convex lenses	.75	7.65
23504 Single Temple, solid nickel frame, finest quality, periscopic convex lenses	.75	7.65
23505 Alumnico Frames (resembling silver). *Will not rust.* Fitted with finest crystal, periscopic convex, or concave lenses	1.10	11.00
23506 Coin Silver Spectacles, good weight and fitted with first quality lenses	1.40	15.00
23507 Steel Spectacles, blue tempered, fitted with finest periscopic Brazilian pebble lenses; retail price, $2.50. Our price	1.75	18.00

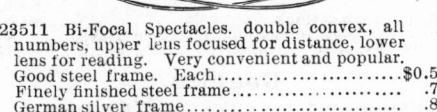

23510 Gold Filled, straight temple, round eye wire spectacles of exceptional value.

For those who are partial to gold spectacles, but cannot afford to wear them, they are especially recommended. Finely finished, with periscopic convex lenses, all focal numbers.

Price, each $1.25

23511 Bi-Focal Spectacles, double convex, all numbers, upper lens focused for distance, lower lens for reading. Very convenient and popular.

Good steel frame. Each	$0.50
Finely finished steel frame	.75
German silver frame	.85
Coin silver frame, genuine	1.50
Gold filled frame, with cemented lenses	1.95

Sliding or Extension Temple Spectacles.

Sliding or extension Temples, when closed, have the advantage of taking up less room than the ordinary style. They are often preferred by elderly people.

23512 Sliding Extension Temples, finest periscopic lense, coin silver mountings $2.25

23513 Same as No. 23512, mounted in solid gold frame, 10 karat.

Retail price ....$12.00 Our price........ 8.50

Riding or Hook-Bow Spectacles.

Riding or hook bows are usually recommended for glasses that are worn for distance or for a continued length of time.

23514 Alumnico Metal Spectacles, resembling silver, well finished hook temples, concave or convex lenses. Each $1.25

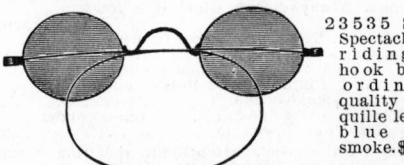

23515 Bronzed Steel Spectacles, with riding or hook temple bows reaching behind ears, with double or periscopic convex lenses. Each $0.75

Riding or Hook Bows

23516 Bronzed Steel Spectacles, same as above, but fitted with concave or near sighted lenses. Each $0.75

23517 Steel Spectacles, with riding or hook bows, fine finish, light weight, nickel plated, convex lenses. Each 1.25

23518 Same as above, fitted with concave or near sighted lenses. Each 1.25

23519 Steel Spectacles, riding bow or hook temples, fine finish with grooved periscopic concave lenses, first quality making the frame almost invisible, for near sighted people 1.85

Spectacles—Continued.

23520 Frameless Spectacles, hook temples, bronzed steel mounted, with periscopic convex lenses, first quality ..... .80

23521 Same as 23520, fitted with concave or near sighted lenses. Each ..... .85

23522 Gold Filled Spectacles, hook bows, fitted with either periscopic concave or convex lenses. Each 1 35

Solid Gold Spectacles, Straight Temples.

Set with Finest Quality Periscopic Lenses, Per Pair.

23523 Gold Spectacles, round eye wire, flat temples, 8 karat, good medium weight $3.70

23524 Same as 23523, 10 karat 4.00

23525 Same as 23523, 14 karat 4.90

Frames furnished in flat finish at same price, if preferred.

Solid Gold Spectacles, Riding or Hook Bow Temples.

Set with Finest Quality Periscopic Lenses. Per

23526 Solid Gold Spectacles, round eye wire, pair. hook temples, good medium weight, 8 karat $3.80

23527 Same as 23526, 10 karat 4.20

23528 Same as 23526, 14 karat 5.00

Nos. 23523 to 23528, inclusive, light weight, 25 cents less; heavy weight 25 to 50 cents per pair additional.

23529 Solid Gold Spectacles, hook bows. This is one of the most popular styles, 14 karat.

Retail price $7.00. Our price $5.25

23530 Solid Gold Frameless or Skeleton Spectacles, hook bows, made in 14 karat only.

Retail price $6.00. Our price 4.75

Half-eye or pulpit pattern spectacles, also side light spectacles, tinted, furnished at low prices.

Colored Lens Spectacles.

Without Focus.

23532—Coquille Spectacles for, weak eyes, shell shaped, smoke or blue lenses, straight temples, steel frame, ordinary quality. Price $0.20

23533 Coquille Spectacles, blue or smoke lenses, better quality and finish, first quality lenses, straight temples ..... .35

23534 Coquille Spectacles, blue or smoke lenses, straight temples, extra fine finish, ground and polished Coquille lenses 1.25

23535 Steel Spectacles, riding or hook bows, ordinary quality Coquille lenses blue or smoke. $0.25

23536 Steel Spectacles, riding or hook bows good quality, Coquille lenses, blue or smoke $0.50

23537 Steel Spectacles, riding or hook bows, extra finish, with fine quality ground Coquille blue or smoke lenses 1.25

23538 Steel Spectacles, riding or hook bows, fitted with *flat lenses*, smoked or blue in light, medium or dark shades, nickel plaited frame 1.20

When ordering *colored* spectacles, always mention shade of lenses desired.

Eyeglasses.

All eyeglasses costing over 50 cents are furnished with a neat leather case and silk cord without charge. Each.

23539 Hard rubber frame, plano convex lenses, good value $0.10

23541 Vulcanized rubber frame, good quality, periscopic lenses, steel spring nose piece ..... .25

23542 Hard rubber frame, first quality, periscopic lenses, convex or concave, adjustable spring nose guard ..... .50

23543 Zylonite (or celluloid) frames; very light weight, highest quality, convex or concave periscopic lenses, with adjustable spring nose piece (see cut of 23546), a fine glass 1.00

23545 Steel frame, fine finish; periscopic convex lenses ..... .55

If you need Spectacles or Eyeglasses, your order is safe with us. We can fit you if anyone can.

Eye Glasses—Continued.

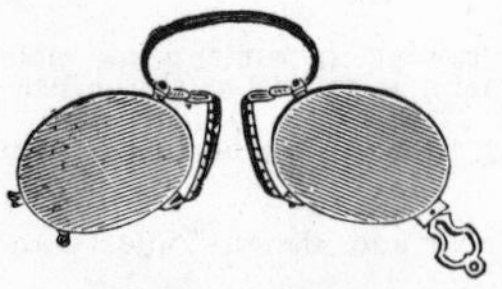

23546 Steel frame, good finish periscopic lenses, with patent adjustable spring nose guard, a very comfortable glass; all numbers............. .90

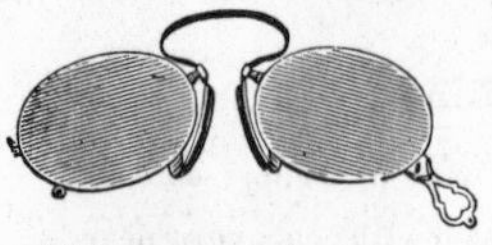

23547 Steel frames grooved periscopic concave lenses, first quality, semi-invisible frames, a beautiful and deservedly popular glass for near-sightedness.. 1.00

23548 Steel frames, fine finish, double or periscopic convex Brazilian pebble lenses. Nothing better.. 1.75

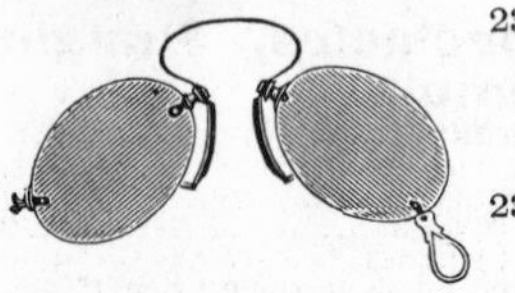

23549 Frameless Eyeglasses, double or periscopic convex or concave lenses, good quality.......... .50

23550 Frameless Eyeglasses, same as 23549, extrafine finish, fitted with patent adjustable nose guard.................... .75

23551 Alumnico Frame (resembling silver), periscopic lenses, good quality...................... 1.10

23552 Gold Filled Eyeglasses, seamless gold filled frame with adjustable spring, solid or offset guards. Recommended for those who cannot afford solid gold. Fitted with cork nose pieces, making a light, comfortable, well appearing and popular glass. Has first quality periscopic lenses. 1.25

Gold Eyeglasses.

Assay and Workmanship Guaranteed.

23553 Solid gold frame, first quality periscopic lenses, regular weight, round eye wire.

	8 karat.	10 karat.	14 karat.
Price, each........	$3.00	$3.50	$4.50

Each.

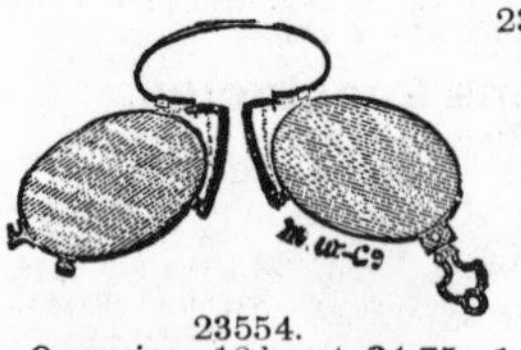

23554 Solid Gold Frame, with first quality periscopic lenses, medium weight, round eye wire, with self-adjusting springnose pieces (see cut); a very desirable glass. Retails at $7.00 and $9.00.

23554.

Our price—10 karat, $4.75; 14 karat............ $6.50

23555 Frameless Gold Eyeglasses with periscopic lenses, first quality (see cut of 23549.) Retails at $7.00. Our price, 10 karat............ 4.25

Cork guards to nose pieces of any eyeglasses to which they can be fitted, 15c. extra.

Colored Lens Eyeglasses.

Nos. 23556 to 23559 are made with either Coquille or flat lenses. Always specify which style you want.

Each.

23556 Rubber Eyeglasses, rubber frames, Coquille or flat lenses, smoke or blue $0.25

23557 Same as 23556, with first quality lenses.. .50

23558 Steel Frames, finest finish, Coquille or flat lenses, smoke or blue.............................. .50

23559 Same, extra fine finish, with finest ground Coquille or flat lenses............................ 1.25

NOTE—We give special attention to repairing spectacles and eyeglasses, and guarantee first-class work at a reasonable cost.

Spectacle and Eyeglass Cases.

Spectacle and eyeglass cases, when sent by mail, allow 2c. extra for postage. Each. Per doz.

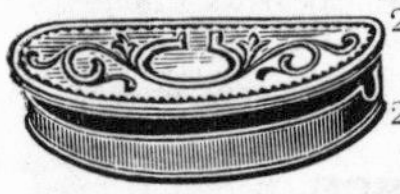

	Each.	Per doz.
23561 Eyeglass Case, nickel, velvet lined........	$0.20	$2.00
23562 Spectacle Case, 6 in. hammered, open end, nickel plated..........	.20	2.00
23563 Spectacle Case, fine planished or japanned tin, side opening with patent snap catch, length, 6⅛ inches........	.15	1.50
23563½ Riding Bow Spectacle Case, 5 inch, side opening, planished tin......	.14	1.40
23564 Spectacle Case, tin, patent open end; length, 6¼ inches........	.12	.10
23565 Spectacle Cases, tin, side opening; length, 7 inches........	.10	1.00
23566 Spectacle Cases, leather, open end, common	.05	.50
23567 Spectacle Cases, fine leather, open or closed end	.09	0.95

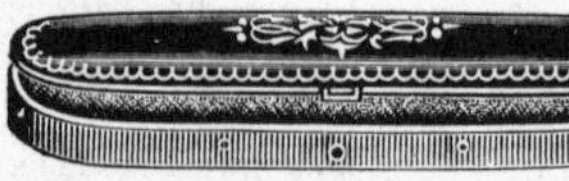

23568 Spectacle Cases, papier mache, inlaid design, closed or open end, or side opening with spring catch, made 6¾ inches for straight temple, and 4¾ for riding bow specs...... .... Each. 0.25 Per doz $2 10

Eye Glass Cases—Continued.

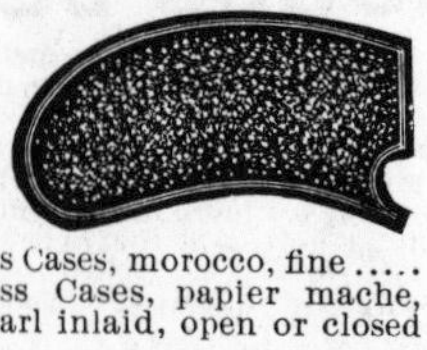

	Each.	Per doz.
23570 Eyeglass Cases, morocco, fine.....	.07	.70
23571 Eyeglass Cases, papier mache, metal or pearl inlaid, open or closed end..........................	.25	2.25

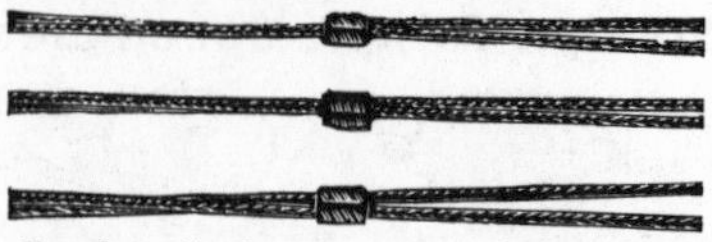

	Each.	Per doz.
23573 Eyeglass Cords, pure silk, light weight, with bead slide.................	$ .05	$ .50
23574 Eyeglass Cords, pure silk, fast dye, medium weight, with silk covered slide....................	.08	.75
23575 Eyeglass Cords, pure silk, fast dye, extra heavy weight, with silk covered slide....................	.10	1.00

Eyeglass Chains and Hooks.

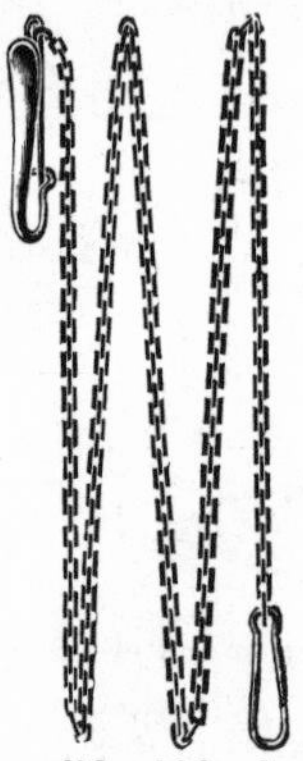

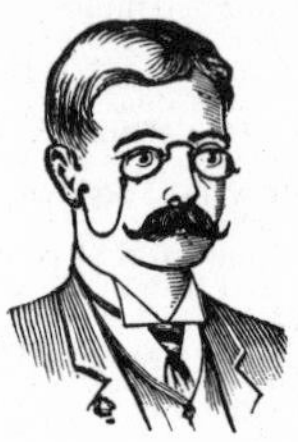

23576

22576 New Model Eyeglass Chain and Hook, rolled gold.
Each.............. $0.70
Solid gold......... 2.00

23577 Eyeglass Chain, solid gold hook and holder. Each.............. $2.25

23578 Same, 1-10 rolled gold.......................... 1.00

23579 Gold Eyeglass Chain, with snap holder and hair pin. Each.. 2.75

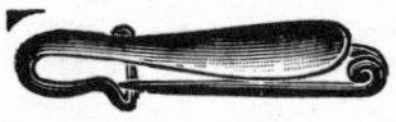

Each.

23580 Eyeglass Hook, solid gold $0.90

23581 Eyeglass Hooks, gold plated, engraved.... .35

23582 Eyeglass, japanned steel.......................... .07

Goggles.

When ordering goggles, state color of lenses desired.

Each. Per doz.

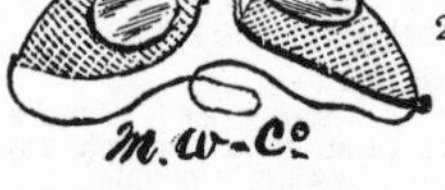

23583 Goggles, wire gauze, blue, smoke, green or white lenses, each in tin box................................ $0.08 $0.75
Postage, 2 cents per pair.

23584 Goggles or Eye protectors, good finish, velvet bound edges, in leather case, blue, smoke or white lenses...... .35 3.50
Postage, 2 cents per pair.

23585 Railroad or Driving Spectacles, blue or smoke lenses, velvet bound, straight temple bows .... .75 7.50
Postage, 5 cents per pair.

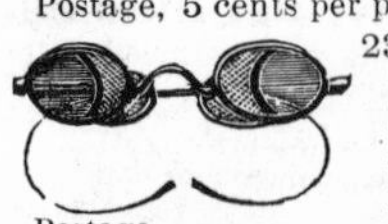

23586 Driving Spectacles, well finished, steel frame, hook temples, fine clear or *smoke* lenses, folding wire gauze protecting shields.
Each.......................... $1.25
Postage......................... .05

Mica Eye Protector.

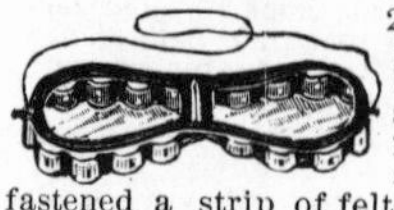

23589 Wholly protects the eye from the entrance of foreign bodies. It consists of a light metal rim. Each section of the rim holds a sheet of mica around which is securely fastened a strip of felt, perforated so that perfect ventilation is secured. A silk elastic cord is attached to each, encircling the head of the wearer and holding the protector in place. Made in clear, smoke, or blue. Price.. $0.30
Postage.. .05

When ordering goods to be shipped by mail, have them insured. See page 1.

Shooting and Millers' Spectacles.

All shooting spectacles furnished with neat case free of charge.

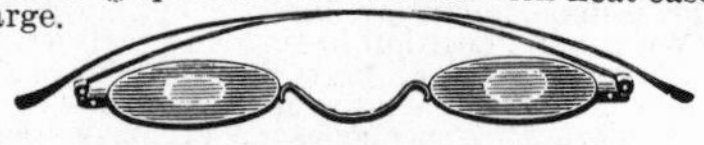

Shooting Spectacles.	Each.	Per doz.
23590 Shooting Spectacles improve the vision wonderfully when viewing a field or landscape, and prevent the eye becoming affected by strong light. Amber colored shooting lenses.......	$0.25	$2.50
23591 Shooting Spectacles, with fine quality of amber lenses and riding or hook bow frame	.50	5.50
23592 Millers' or Stonecutters' Spectacles, for protecting the eyes from injury; plain, white lenses, large eyes, turn pin temples.........................	.20	2.00

Postage on either shooting or millers' spectacles, 5c.

Eye Shades.

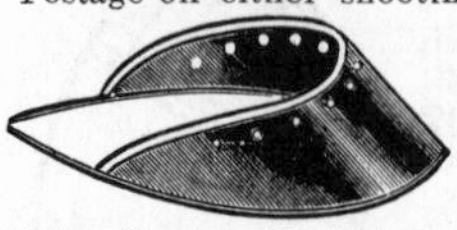

23594 White's Eye Shade, with metal rim and leather bound edge, as illustrated. Each...... $0.12
Postage .... .03

23595 Feather Weight Green Celluloid Transparent Eye Shade, very light, self adjusting, bound edges and held in place by ribbon elastic band. Each.............................. $0.18
Postage,.......... .... .02

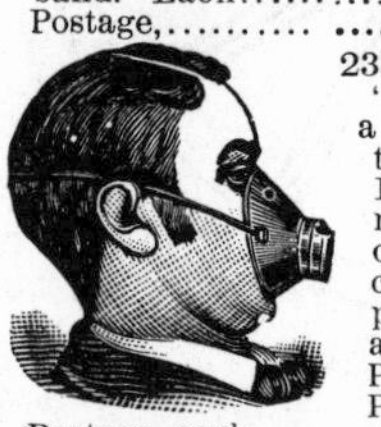

23596 The Patent Dust Protector. "An ounce of Prevention is worth a Pound of Cure." Perfect protection, perfect ventilation. Dust protector for protecting the nose and mouth from inhalations of dust of every character. It is constructed of light metal, nickel plated, is handsomely finished, and will last several years.
Price, each.................. $0.90
Price, per dozen............ 8.50
Postage, each........................... .05

Ear Trumpets and Tubes.

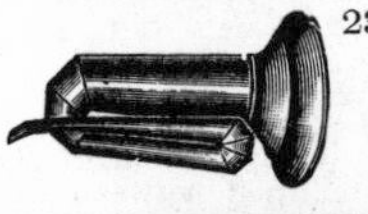

23597 Bugle-Shape Ear Trumpet, japanned metal, made in three sizes, small, medium or large.
Each.................................... $2.25

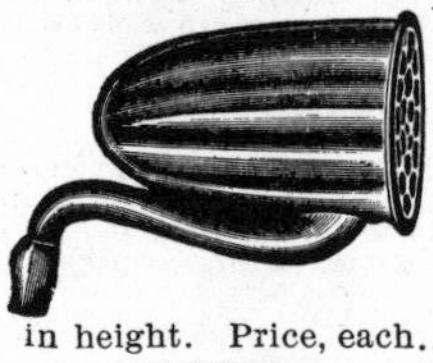

23598 London Hearing Horns, designed for those who are moderately deaf, as they can easily be carried in the pocket and concealed in the hand when in use. Finished in black oxidized and in sizes from 2½ to 4 inches in height. Price, each......................... 2.50

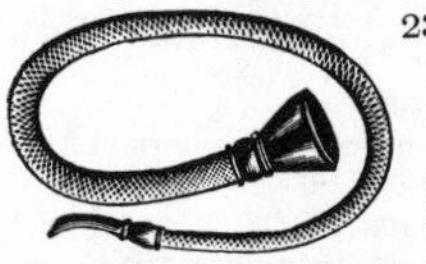

23599 Conversation Tubes, rubber ends, flexible mohair, conical shape tube, 3 feet in length; this tube suits the most obstinate cases of deafness.
Price, each............ 2.75

Field or Marine Glasses.

All have fine achromatic lens; the expression, 24 line or 26-line, gives the diameter of the largest lens in the glass, there being 11 lines to the inch.

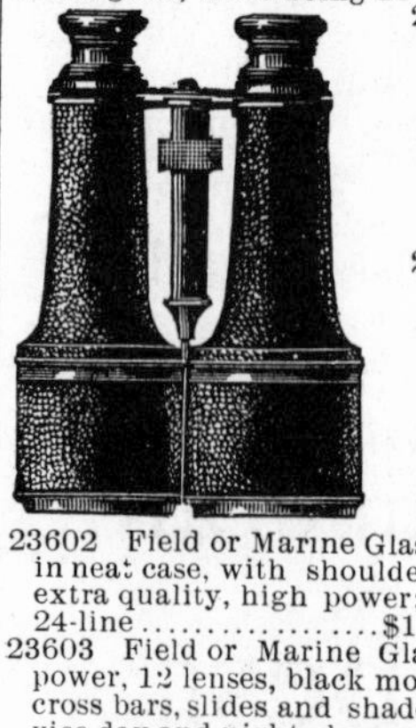

23600 Field or Marine Glasses, extension hood, in neat case with shoulder strap. A good, strong glass for ordinary work.
24-line.............. $8.25
26-line................ 9.00
Weight, 2¼ lbs.

23601 Field or Marine Glasses, extension hood, in neat case, with shoulder strap. This glass is a little more powerful than the preceding.
24-line.............. 10.24
26-line.............. 10.85
Weight, 2¾ lbs.

23602 Field or Marine Glasses, extension hood, in neat case, with shoulder strap, finest finish, extra quality, high power; weight, 2½ pounds.
24-line.................. $13.50 26-line......... 15.25

23603 Field or Marine Glasses, highest known power, 12 lenses, black morocco body, japanned cross bars, slides and shades, U. S. Signal Service day and night glasses. 26-line, 2½ pounds $24.00

23604 Tourists' Field Glasses, with short body and long draw tubes, morocco covered, 19-line objectives, achromatic; length, when closed, about 4 inches; when extended, about 5½ inches. Price, including case and strap......... 8.75
Weight, complete, 1 pound 4 ounces.

23605 Stockman's Ranch or U. S. Cavalry Field Glass. 22-line, large eye pieces, patented spring adjustment, so that tubes may be drawn out or closed instantly without altering adjustment to sight. Measures 5 inches closed and 7½ inches extended, finely finished, perfect optical construction. Put up in sole leather case, with straps for carrying. Weight, complete, 2½ lbs.
Price.. 23.00

Opera Glasses.

All have fine achromatic lenses.

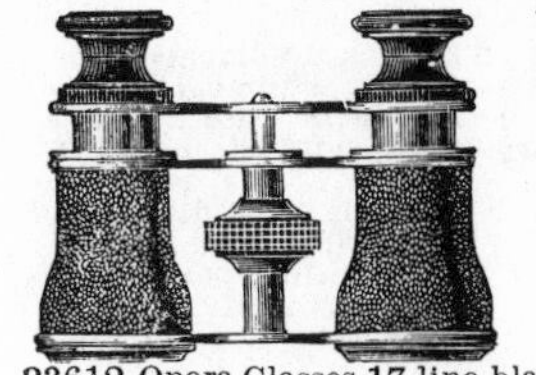

23610 Opera Glasses, 15 line, black leather, covered and enameled frame, morocco case. Each............ $2.75

23611 Opera Glasses, 15-line, black leather covered and enameled frame, morocco case. Each........ $4.12

23612 Opera Glasses, 17-line, black leather covered and enameled frame, morocco case. Each.. $5.22

23613 Opera Glasses, 15-line, black morocco covered and enameled frame. The best plain, reliable glass obtainable; in neat leather case. Each.................. $5.50

23614 Opera Glasses, 17-line, black morocco covered and enameled frame, in neat leather case. This glass is the same quality as 23613, but is full size larger. Each.................. 6.25

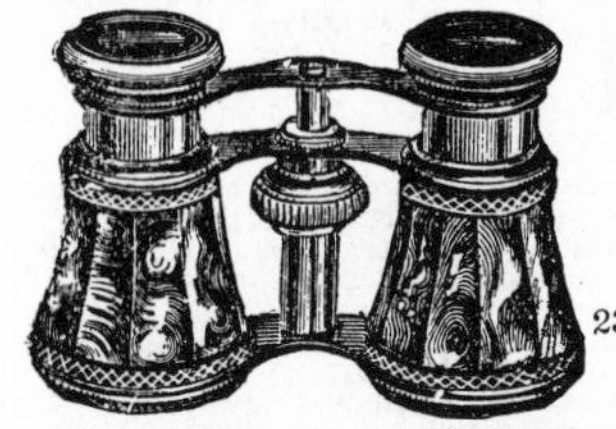

23615 Lamier fancy Pearl Opera Glass, 13-line objective, pearl tops and full nickeled draw tubes and cross bars; good power and exceptional value; has no superior at the price. Wgt., 6 oz.. $5.00

23616 White Pearl Opera Glasses, gilt cross bars and slides, in morocco case; 15-line, very fine achromatic lens. Each.. $10.00

23617 Oriental Pearl (light or dark) Opera Glasses, gilt cross bars and slides; in morocco case; 15-line, very finest achromatic lens, each.. 12.00

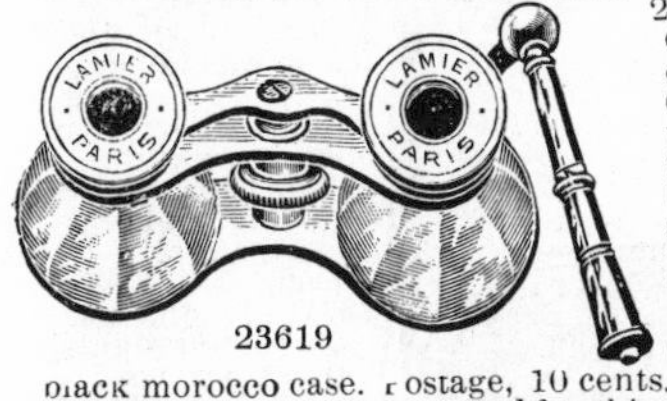

23619

23618 Genuine Colmont Smoked Pearl Opera Glasses, 15 line, with high pearl tops, aluminum bars and tubes, special high power lenses. This glass weighs but 5 ounces; in black morocco case. Postage, 10 cents. Price. $20.00

Opera Glasses weigh, wrapped for shipment, 10 ounces each.

23619 Oriental Pearl Opera Glass, with handle nickel mounted. A superior glass, popular with the ladies, new and elegant in design, perfect in optical construction and of exceptional value. Weight, 9 ounces. Price, each.................. $12.75

Spy Glasses and Telescopes.

All have fine achromatic lenses. Each.

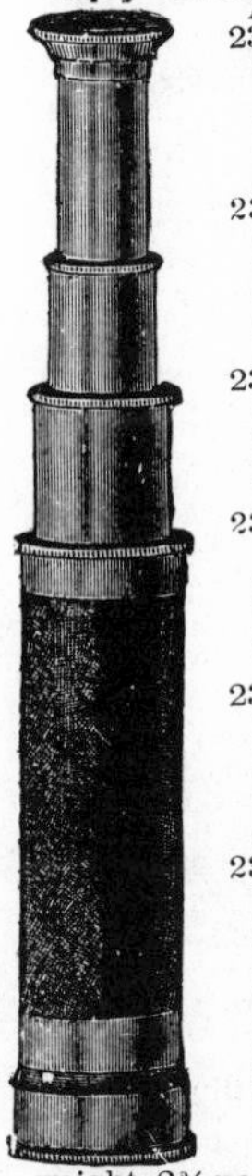

23620 Spy Glass; size, when closed, 4¾ inches long, when open, 13¾ inches long; 10-line, leather covered, 4 sections; power, 10 diameters.................. $1.85
Postage.................. .10

23621 Spy Glass; size, when closed, 6 inches long; when open, 16½ inches long; 14-line, leather covered, 4 sections; power, 15 diameters.................. 2.80
Postage.................. .15

23622 Spy Glass; size, when closed, 8 inches long; when open, 22 inches long; 16-line, 4 sections; power, 20 diameters.................. 4.25
Postage.................. .25

23623 Spy Glass; size, when closed, 10 inches long, when open, 30 inches long; 19-line, 4 sections and extension hood, leather covered; power, 25 diameters 6.10
Weight, 35 ounces.

23624 Spy Glass; size, when closed, 10½ inches long; when open, 36 inches long; 22-line, 5 sections, black morocco body, burnished brass tubes, a superior finished glass, weight 3 pounds.................. 9.50

23625 Spy Glass, superior lenses, unequaled for definition; 5 sections, burnished brass draws, body of elegant polished mahogany wood, brass trimmings, sun glass to eye piece. It affords excellent views of the sun, moon, satellites, etc., in addition to its terrestrial powers; 22-line, power, 30 diameters; 11 to 36 inches (extreme range 12 to 16 miles); weight, 2¾ pounds. Price.................. $14.25

23626 Spy Glass, superior quality lenses, 5 sections and sunshade or hood, burnished brass draw tubes, stitched morocco covered body with loops for sling straps. Adjustable sun glass to eye piece and provided with an additional section for astronomical observations, affording excellent views of the sun, moon, satellites, etc., in addition to its terrestrial powers; length, when closed 11 inches, when extended, 36 inches; 22-line, weight, 3¼ lbs.................. 16.00

23627 Spy Glass, same general description as above; 27-line objectives, brass mountings, morocco covered, extension hood sun glass to eye piece, with extra 6-inch celestial tube; length, when closed, 13 inches; when extended, 48 inches; weight, complete, 4¾ pounds..... 25.00

Telescopes—Continued.

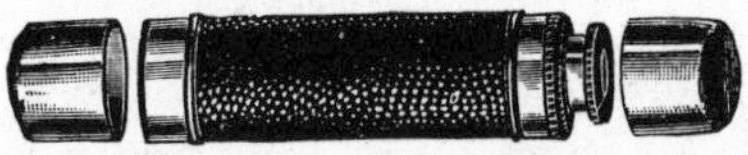

23628 New Achromatic Pocket Telescope; size, when closed, 5⅛ inches, when open, 14¾ inches, 10-line, black morocco covered body, full nickel plate draw tubes, round polished nickel caps for both ends; power, 10 diameters. Price.........$3.25 Postage............$0.10

23629 Same as above, but 12-line; length, when closed, 5 inches; when open, 16 inches; power, 15 diameter. Price..$3.75 Postage............ .12

23630 Same as 23628 but 14-line; length, when closed, 6¾ inches; when open, 17½ inches; power, 20 diameters. Price................ $4.50
Postage.................. .15

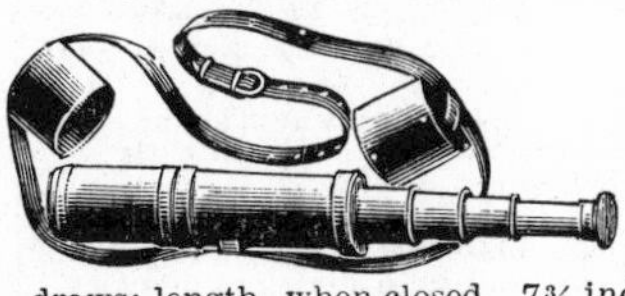

23631 Tourists' Spy Glasses, brass body oxidized, morocco covered, with sunshade and leather caps and straps; has 4 draws; length, when closed, 7¾ inches; when extended, 29 inches; 19-line; weight, 1¾ pounds.................. $15.00

23632 The Rifle Range Telescope, like cut, and as described above, but larger and more powerful; length, when closed, 11 inches; when extended, 36 inches; power, 33 diameters; has 4 draws; warranted to show in a clear atmosphere a bullet mark at 1,000 yards; 22-line; weight, 3 pounds.................. 21.00

23635 Astronomical Telescope, brass body, 38 inches long, 3-inch diameter achromatic objective. Separate 17-inch eye piece for terrestrial observation; power, 50 diameters, and 8-inch celestial eye piece, power 125 diameters. Rack and pinion for adjustment of focus, vertical and horizontal movement, mounted upon a short enameled iron folding tripod. Packs complete into a strong wood case with handle. Price, each.................. 52.00

23636 The above, with the addition of a full size, strong, hard wood tripod.................. 64.00

Microscopes.

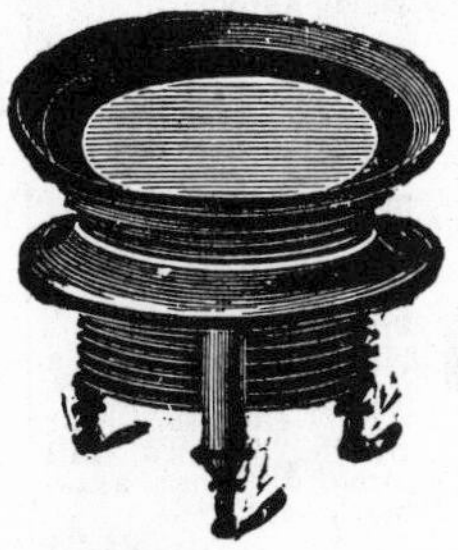

23640 Tripod Microscope; especially adapted to close examination of ores, fabrics, leaves, grasses, etc. The focus is adjustable to fit any eye. Brass frame and legs, double lens.
Each.................. $0.39
Per dozen.................. 3.90
Postage.................. .05

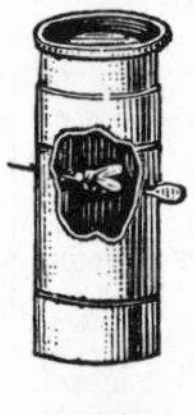

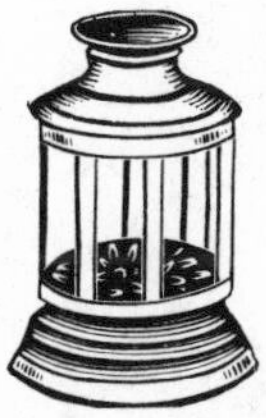

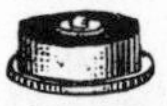

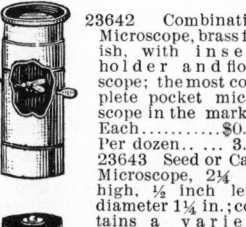

23642 Combination Microscope, brass finish, with insect holder and flora-scope; the most complete pocket microscope in the market.
Each........... $0.35
Per dozen........ 3.25

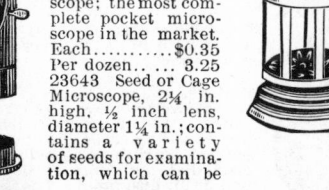

23643 Seed or Cage Microscope, 2¼ in. high, ½ inch lens, diameter 1¼ in.; contains a variety of seeds for examination, which can be exchanged as desired Each...$0.15
Per dozen.................. 1.25
Postage.................. .05

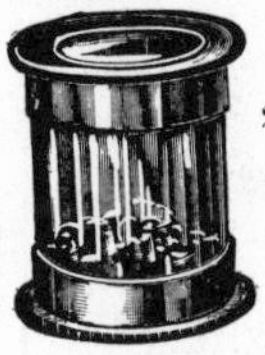

23644 Seed Microscope, good lens nickel plated mounting, size, 1⅝ inch high, 1½ inch diameter. This instrument is used to examine variation of seeds and is also adapted for examination of bugs or insects alive, which is a feature presented by none but high price instruments.
Price, each.................. $0.25
Per dozen.................. 2.50
Postage each.................. .05

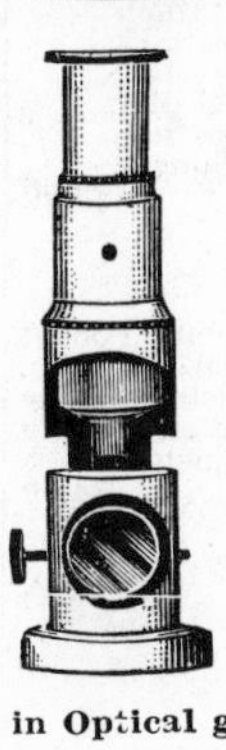

23646 Scholars' Microscope, designed for use of young persons who wish something beyond the powers yielded by a simple microscope. The lenses are accurately ground, and the entire instrument substantially made with a vertical brass body 7 inches high, mirror beneath stage for illumination of transparent objects, one eyepiece, one objective, giving a power of 40 diameters, 1,600 area, neatly packed in French polished case, with two glass slips. 1 prepared object, 1 pair brass forceps.
Each.................. $2.25
Postage.................. .25

Microscopes—Continued.

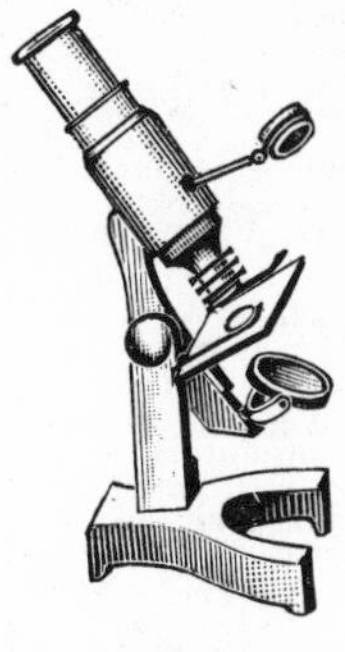

23647 Students' Compound Microscope, stands 6 inches high when inclined as in cut, 10 in. when drawn out; has bronzed base, with hinge, allowing instrument to be used at any convenient angle; body of finely polished brass, large and firm stage, with brass springs for holding object. Beneath stage is mirror with universal motion for illuminating transparent objects. We furnish each instrument with the following accessories: 2 crown glass objectives, affording magnifying powers of every range, from 30 to 75 diameters (500 to 7,500 areas), 2 plain glass slips, 1 prepared object in a neat box. Each.................. $4.00
Weight, 1½ pounds.

23648

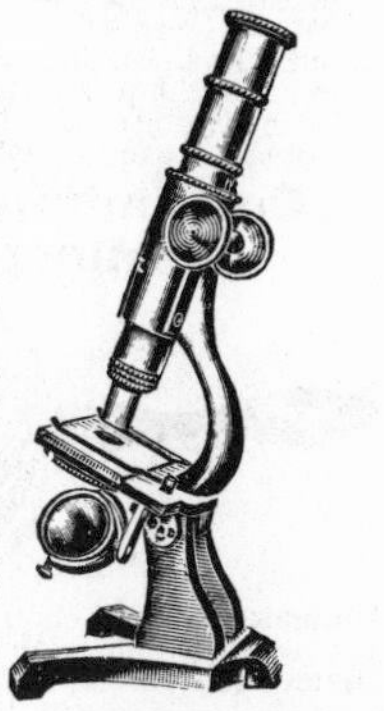

23648 Students' Compound Microscope, same as 23647, but has triple objective, separable, giving three powers, from 30 to 125 diameters of from 500 to 10,000 areas, and condensing lens for illuminating opaque objects, Each............ $6.00
Weight, 1¾ pounds.

23649 American Model, extra large microscope, with reflecting racks and jointed frame; has square stage with revolving diaphragm, and has double rack and pinion adjustments. Height, 12 in.; has japanned base, brass achromatic tubes; power, about 200 diameters.
Price.................. $15.00
Weight, 5 pounds.

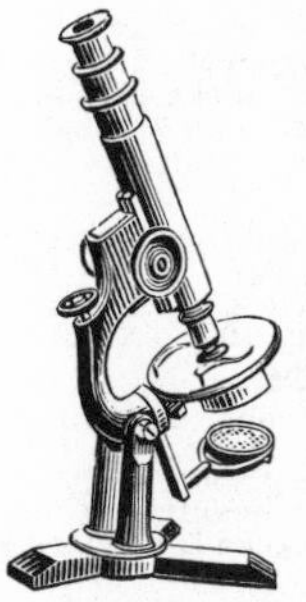

23650 Model Microscope with one eyepiece, two objectives—¾ inches and 1-5 inches; magnifying power 70 and 295 diameters, and may be fitted to range from 50 to 1,440 diameter, with extra eyepieces and objectives, if required. Is fitted with perfect rack and pinion, for coarse adjustment, and micrometer screw for delicate adjustment; brass circular stage and sub-stage ring and dome diaphragm; plain and concave mirror on adjustable bar for transparent or opaque objects, and provided with society screw. The instrument packs into an upright polished case with drawer for accessories and receptacles for eyepieces and objectives, lock and key and handle for carrying. Weight, complete, about 11½ pounds; size of case, 7x9x13 inches. Price, for each outfit.......... $45.00

Magnifying Glasses.

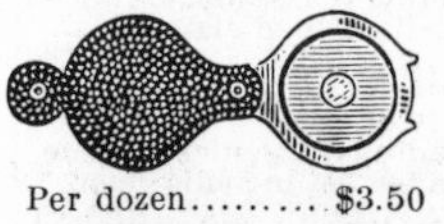

23654 Magnifying Glasses, single lens, ⅝ inch diameter with diaphragm, rubber case. This is a very powerful glass for its size. Each.......... $0.35
Per dozen.......... $3.50 Postage.......... .03

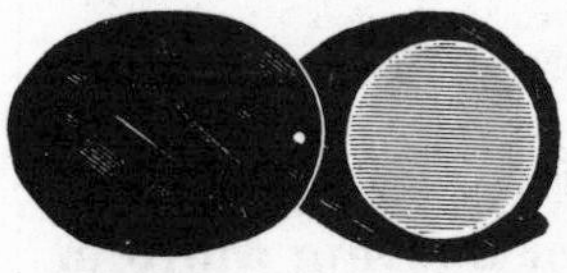

23655 Magnifying Glass, single lens, ¾ inch diameter, rubber case.
Each....... $0.25
Per dozen.. 2.50
Postage..... .02

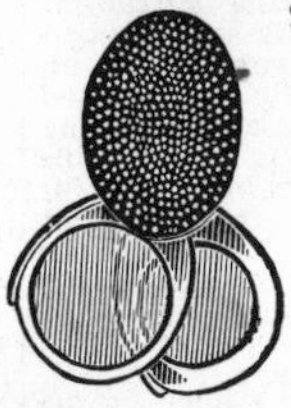

23656 Magnifying Glass, single lens, 1¼ inch diameter, oxidized case. Each.................. $0.50
Per dozen.................. 5.00
Postage.................. .02

23657 Magnifying Glass, single lens, 2 inch diameter, rubber case. Is also a fine sun glass.
Each.................. $1.00
Per dozen.................. 11.00
Postage.................. .05

	Each.	Per doz
23658 Magnifying Glass, double lens, ¾ inch diameter, rubber case........ Postage, 5 cents.	$0.40	$4.00
23659 Magnifying Glass, double lens, 1¼ inch diameter oxidized case...... Postage, 5 cents.	.70	7.25
23660 Magnifying Glass, double lens, 1 inch diameter, rubber case......... Postage, 5 cents.	.60	6.25
23661 Magnifying Glass, double lens, 1¼ inch diameter, rubber case........ Postage, 5 cents.	.80	9.00
23662 Magnifying Glass, double lens, 1¾ inch diameter, rubber case, also a fine sun glass. This is a very powerful glass.................. Postage, 5 cents.	1.25	13,50

Our very large trade in Optical goods is due solely to the merit of the goods we handle.

Magnifying Glasses—Continued.

23663 Prospector's Magnifier and Sun Glass, double lens, 1⅝ inches and 1 inch diameter; rubber case. A glass of high magnifying power. Each.... 2.00
Postage, 5 cents.

23664 Magnifying Glass, folding, 3 lenses, 5, ¾ and ⅞ inch rubber case. .75 8.00
Postage, 5 cents.

23665 Pocket Magnifier, German silver case and rim. Diameter, 1¼ inch... 1 lens. .50 2 lens. .70
Postage, 5 cents.

23666 Watchmakers' Lens, mounted in hard rubber, 2 to 4 inch focus..... .30
Postage, 5 cents.

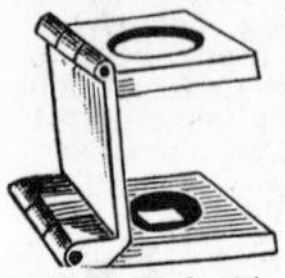

23667 Pick Glasses or Linen Testers Very convenient for use as a pocket magnifier, giving good power and folding into the smallest possible space. Finish, nickeled, with achromatic lenses. Each............$0.60
Per dozen........................ 6.50
Postage, 5 cents.

23668 Pick Glasses or Linen Testers, same as preceding, but not so powerful nor as highly finished; brass. Each..........................$0.25
Postage, 5 c ents. Per dozen.................... 2.50

Coddington's Magnifiers or Miners' Glasses.

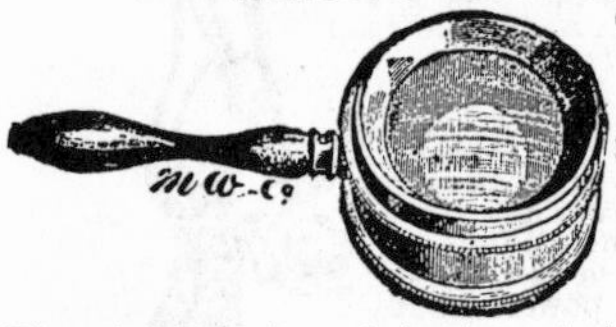

Our miners glasses are the most powerful obtainable.

23675 Coddington Magnifier or Miner's Glass, brass frame with handle.

Diameter, ⅝ inch, each (postage, 4c.) $1.00
Diameter, 1 inch, each (postage, 6c.)............. 1.25
Diameter, 1⅜ inch, each (postage, 8c.)............ 1.50

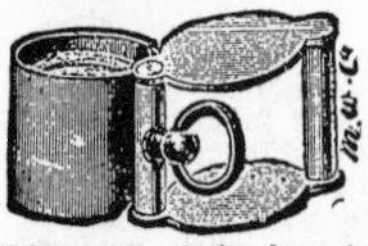

23676 Coddington Magnifier or Miner's Glass, nickeled case, folding cover, with ring, superior lenses.

Diameter, ¾ inch, price, each (postage 4c)........$1.25
Diameter, 1 inch, price. each (postage 6c)........ 1.50
Diameter, 1¼ inch, price, each (postage 8c)....... 1.75
Diameter, 1⅝ inch, price, each (postage 10c)...... 2.10

Reading Glasses

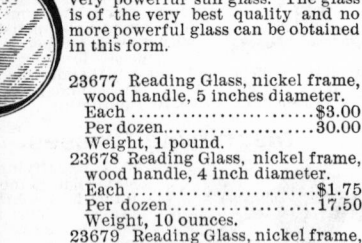

These glasses are used to magnify letters in reading, and are also a very powerful sun glass. The glass is of the very best quality and no more powerful glass can be obtained in this form.

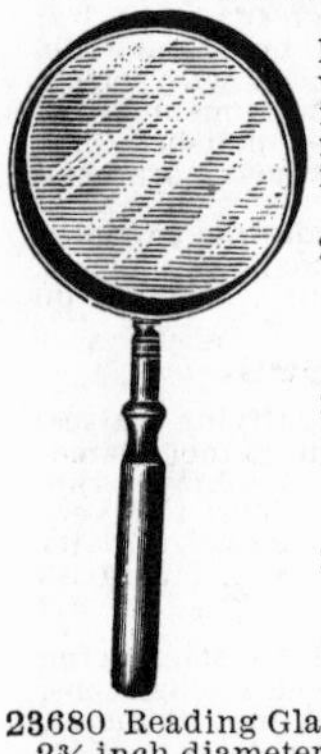

23677 Reading Glass, nickel frame, wood handle, 5 inches diameter.
Each.........................$3.00
Per dozen....................30.00
Weight, 1 pound.

23678 Reading Glass, nickel frame, wood handle, 4 inch diameter.
Each.........................$1.75
Per dozen....................17.50
Weight, 10 ounces.

23679 Reading Glass, nickel frame, wood handle, 3½ inch diameter.
Each.........................$1.12
Per dozen....................11.25
Weight, 8 ounces.

23680 Reading Glass, nickel frame, wood handle, 2¾ inch diameter. Each..$0.84 Per dozen..... 9.00
Weight, 6 ounces.

23681 Reading Glass. nickel frame, wood handle, 2¼ inch diameter. Each..$0.55 Per dozen.... 6.00
Weight, 4 ounces.

Magnifying or Shaving Mirrors.

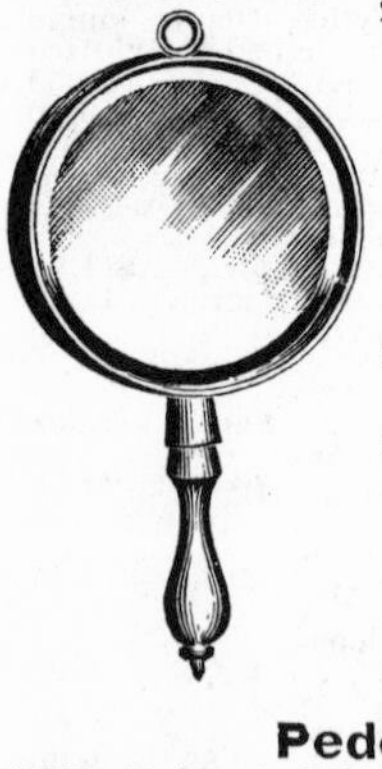

23682 Magnifying Mirrors or Toilet Hand Glasses, having a plain or ordinary mirror on one side, while the reversed side contains a magnifying mirror, making a valuable and convenient hand glass for shaving and general toilet use; ebonized frames, diameter, 4 inches. Each....$1.00
Weight, 8 ounces.

23683 Same as above, but 5 inches in diameter.
Weight, 12 oz. Each....$1.30

23684 Similar to above, but better quality, and fitted with an adjustable metal handle, so that the mirror may stand without holding or be hung up as desired; nothing better of this kind made; diameter, 6 inches. Each.........$2.50
Weight, 20 ounces

Pedometers.

23685 Pedometers, for showing distance walked when carried in the pocket, in nickel plated watch case dial, indicating 12 miles, and reading to quarters of miles. Postage 10c. Each...$4.30

23686 Pedometer, for measuring distances walked, watch pattern, nickel case, registering to 100 miles. Postage, 10c. Each.................... 4.75

Compasses.

The postage on compasses is 5c., except where quoted otherwise.

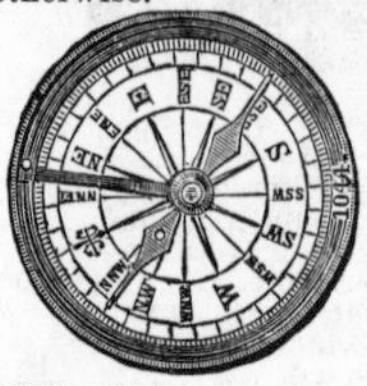

23690 Pocket Compass, watch shape, open face, paper dial, brass case with ring.

	Each.	per doz.
Diam., 1 inch	$0.15	$1.60
Diam., 1½ in.....	.20	2.00
Diam., 2 in.......	.25	2.50

23691 Brass Compass with cap cover, paper dial.
Diameter, 1½ in,, each 25c. Per dozen.... .....$2.40
Diameter, 1¾ in., each, 30c. Per doz............ 2.75

23692 Pocket Compass, open face, brass case with ring, silvered metal dial, diameter, 1¾ inches.
Each... .40
Per dozen...................................... 4.00

23694 Pocket Compass, open face, watch shape, brass, with handle, silvered metal dial and with stop; diameter, 1¾ inches. Each.... .... .60
Per dozen...................................... 6.50

23696 Pocket Compass, brass, heavy milled edge cover, silvered metal dial with divisions, jeweled, cap to needle and with sliding stop.
Diameter, 1¾ inches. Each.............. .75
Diameter, 2 inches. Each.................. 1.00
Diameter, 2¼ inches. Each................. 1.25
Postage.. .10

23697 Pocket Compass, brass metal dial, hinge cover, jeweled cap to needle, slide stop, full circle division, diameter 1¾ inches. Each........$ 1.04
Per dozen...................................... 10.25
Diameter, 2 inches. Each...................... 1.50
Per dozen...................................... 15.00
Postage.. .10

23698 Pocket Compass, nickel plated, finely engraved metal dial, slip cover, automatic stop, jeweled English bar needle, full circle division.

Diameter	2½ in.	3 in.
Each	$2.50	$3.00
Postage		.15

23700 Pocket Compass, brass, diameter, 3¼ in., English bar needle, dial marked for double degrees and raised circle division to level of needle, extra heavy convex crystal, automatic stop, slip cover. Each........................ 3.75
Postage.. .15

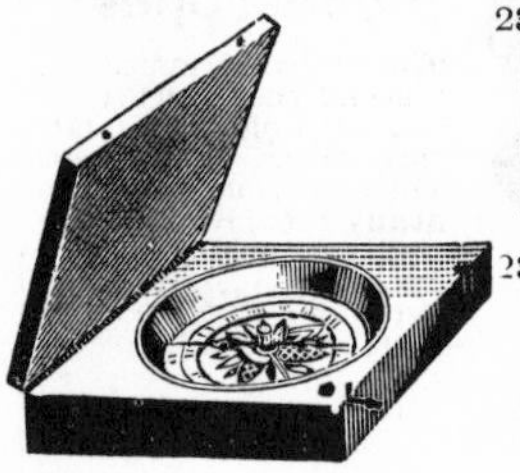

23701 Wood Case Compass, square shape, diameter 2¾ in. metal dial, automatic stop, agate cap.
Each............$0.75
Per dozen.......... 7.50
Postage 10 cents.

23702 Wood Case Compass, same size. English bar needle, jeweled, full circle division, automatic stop.
Each...........$ 1.25
Per dozen...................................... 12.00
Postage.. .10

23703 Wood Case Compass, same description as 23702, but with raised dial. Each. 1.75
Per dozen...................................... 17.50
Postage.. .10

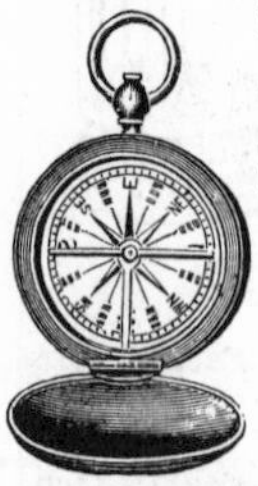

23704 Wood Case Compass, same as above, with the addition of a cyclometer attachment.
Each...................................... $2.25
Postage.................................... .10

23705 Pocket Compass, silvered metal, watch shape, 2 inches diameter, hinged spring cover, automatic stop, jeweled, English bar needle, silver metal dial, with full divisions, and practically dust proof.
Price, each........................$3.50

23706 Military Compass, bronze, 2 inches diameter, hinged cover, jeweled, English bar needle, handsomely marked metal dial, automatic stop, full divisions, with degrees marked from 0 to 90. A durable and beautiful instrument. Weight, 4⅛ ounces. Price...............$5.00

23707 A Woodman's Reliable Compass, 2¾ inch diameter, made for rough service, double thick oxidized case, hinged cover, automatic stop, jeweled, English bar needle, silvered metal dial, full divisions, degrees marked from 0 to 360, heavy beveled covered glass, weight, 9½ ounces.
Price, each.....................................$4.90

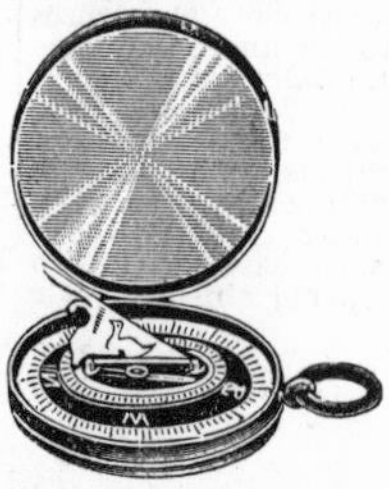

23707½ Sun Dial Pocket Compass, Jeweled needle, full circle divisions, slide stop, nickel plated folding case, 2 inch diameter.
Price, each.......... ....$4.00

Boat Compasses.

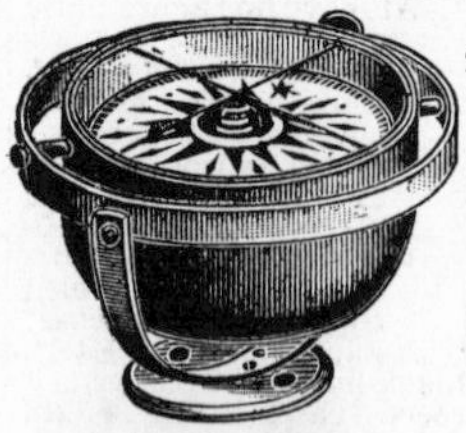

23708 Boat Compass skeleton, brass gimbal mounting, with base having screw holes, designed to fasten in any position. Floating card dial with agate cap, 1¾ inch diameter. A little beauty.
Each..............$3.50
Postage............ .08

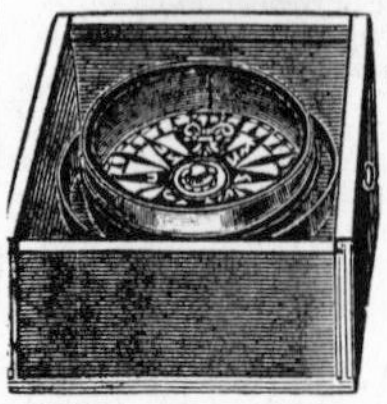

23709 These Boat Compasses have brass bowls and gimbal rings, and are mounted in strong oak box and sliding cover. The cards are jeweled and mounted on hardened pivots. The bowls are heavily weighted to assure steadiness.

6 inch box..........3½ inch card.........Each $4.50
8 inch box.............5 inch card........Each 6.00
10 inch box............7 inch card........Each 8.00

23710 Boat Compasses, same construction as No. 23709, but mounted in dove-tailed mahogany box with sliding cover.
4 inch box...........4¼ inch card..........Each 4.00
6 inch box...........3½ inch card..........Each 5.00

23711 Yacht Compass, with Singer's jeweled floating card dial, brass bowl casing on gimbals in burnished brass slip cover case.
8¼ inch box..........2½ inch card.........Each 5.50

Folding Sight Compasses.

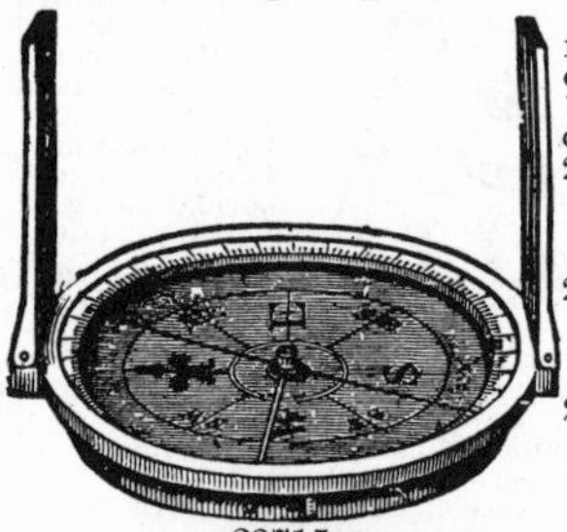

23715

Very serviceable for retracing lines once surveyed. Weight, about ten ounces each.

23715 2 in. needle, folding sights in leather case.
Each $4.25

23716 2¼ in. needle, folding sights, in leather case.
Each.......$5.75

23717 2½ in. needle, folding sights in leather case. Each..$6.00

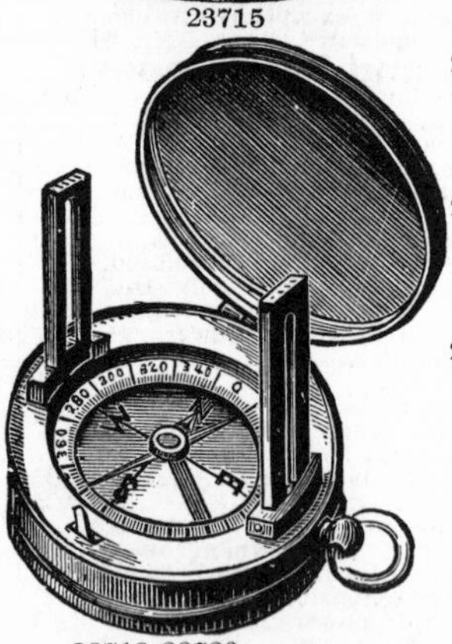

23718-23720

23718 2 inch diameter bar needle hinge cover, nickel plated. folding sights.
Each......$4.30

23719 2⅝ inches diameter, bar needle, hinge cover nickel plated, folding sights.
Each.........$5.00

23720 2¾ inch diameter bar needle, hinge cover nickel plated, folding sights.
Each........$6.20

Prices on larger size or more expensive compasses furnished upon request. Give description of compass wanted if you can.

Clinometer Compass.

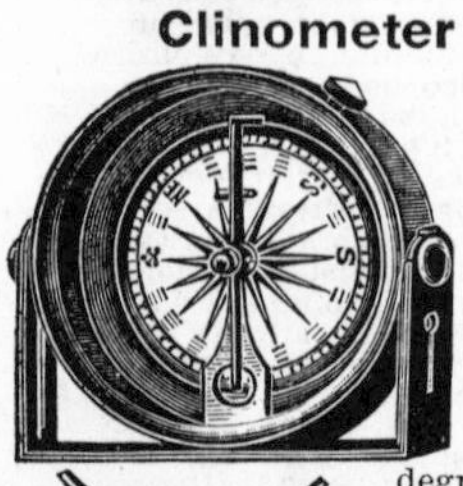

23721 Combined Sight Compass and Clinometer. bronze case, slip cover, silvered dial, graduated to one degree, edge bar needle, with agate center and automatic stop. Pivoted sights, which are turned down to form a base when used as clinometer; can be used for levels or inclinations, in inches, per yard or in degrees. 3 inch diameter.
Each, in morocco case....$8.50
Postage.... 15

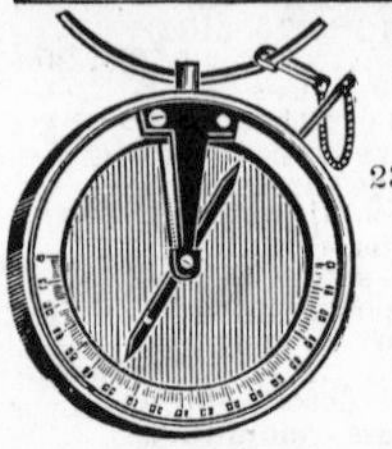

23722 Dip Needle Compass, for prospecting for minerals; a well made and accurate miners dipping needle compass. Brass rim and nickel plated dial. Each instrument in morocco case. Price, each........$9.75

NO CHARGE FOR BOXING OR CARTAGE

SURVEYORS' COMPASSES.
Folding Sights.

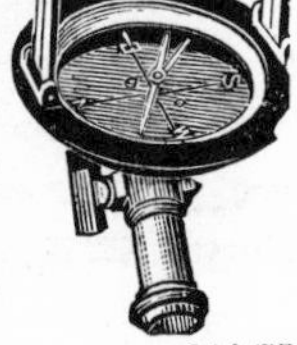

23723 2½ inch needle, folding sights, ball socket, Jacob staff mountings.... .... $6.96
Weight, 1 pound.
23724 2¾ inch needle, folding sights, ball socket, Jacob staff mountings.................$8.00
Weight, 1¼ pounds.
23725 3½ inch needle, folding sights, ball sockets, Jacob staff mountings...................$9.00
Weight, 1½ pounds.
23726 3⅛ inch needle, folding sights, ball socket, with two levels, Jacob staff mountings. Each.............$11.75
Weight, 2½ pounds.
23727 4⅛ inch needle, folding sight, ball socket, with two levels, Jacob staff mountings.
Weight, 2¼ pounds.
Each...................... $13.25

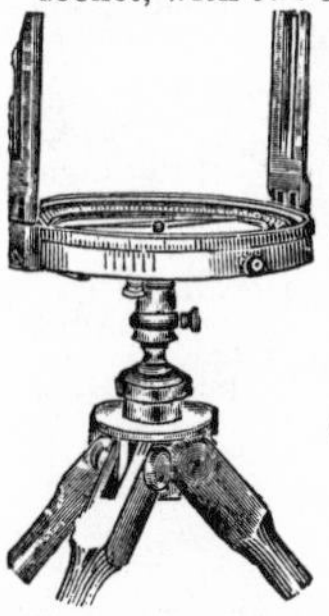

23728 Tripod, with Jacob staff top for compasses. Each..$2.40
23729 Jacob staff with metal shoes. Each............. $0.90
Weight, 2¼ pounds.
23730 Vernier Compass, 3½ inch needle, folding sights, two levels, with tripod. Each.........$19.00
Without tripod 15.00
Weight, complete, 7 pounds.
Weight, without tripod, 2½ lbs.
23731 Vernier Compass, 4½ inch needle, folding sights, two levels, with tripod. Each........$21.00
Without tripod 17.00
Weight, complete, 7½ lbs.
Weight, without tripod, 3 lbs.

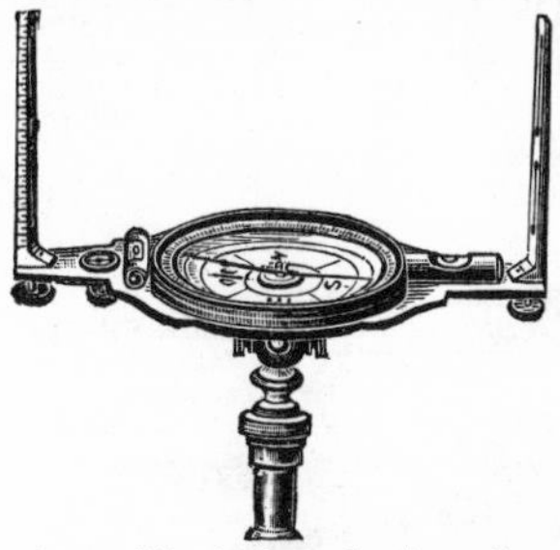

23732 High Grade Vernier Compass, 5 inch needle with Vernier inside compass circle, two straight levels, Jacob staff mountings, brass cover, outkeeper, vernier under the glass for adding or subtracting the magnetic variations of the needle, sights graduated for taking angle of elevation and depression; in mahogany box with lock and strap for carrying. Without tripod, price, $35.00 With tripod, price $40.00

The Vernier Transit or Transit Compass.

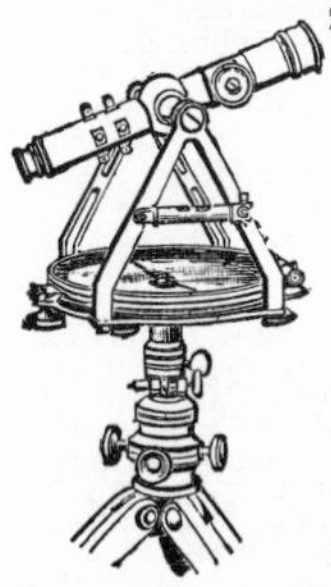

23734 This instrument will be found very convenient for country surveyors who want to do good land surveying and not invest so much money for a regular transit. It is provided with a very substantial leveling arrangement, has 2 straight levels, and in place of the sights it has a strong telescope, 8 inches long, with cross-hairs complete, like the telescope of a transit. Ths needle is 5½ inches long, with variation plate inside the circle. The instrument is not heavier than an ordinary compass; weight, without tripod, 8 lbs., and can easily be carried by passing the arm through between telescope axis and plate. It also has a clamp and tangent screw to center. It is packed in a nice mahogany box containing magnifying glass, adjusting pin and shade. Price, with light tripod..$75.00

Levels and Transit.

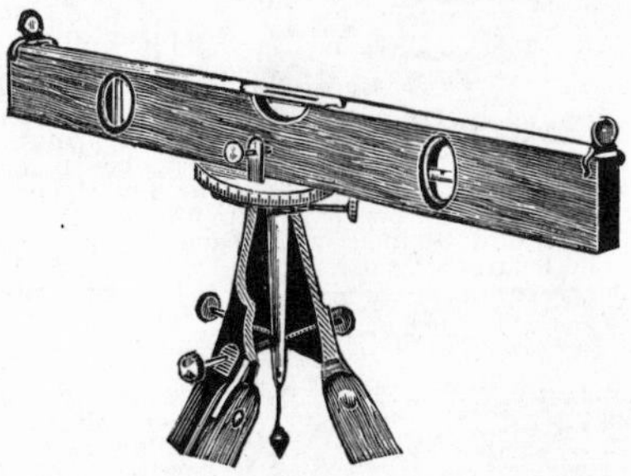

23735 Merrell's Leveling Instrument. This apparatus is designed for the use of builders, carpenters, masons, sewermen, graders, etc. The parts comprising the complete instrument consists of 1 tripod stand, 1 transit, 1 pointer, 1 target, two leveling sights, and all necessary screws, etc., and does not include level, tripod legs or tangent staff; as the first item you probably have, and the last two are easily made. Our price for the instrument, parts and attachments is...$9.00

Levels—Continued.

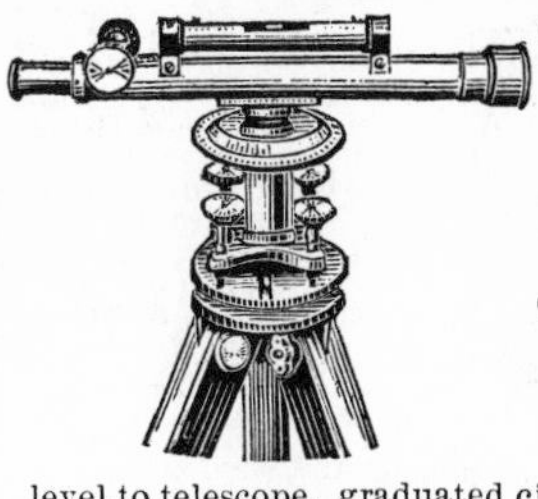

23736 Farmers' and Builders' Drainage and Leveling Instrument, complete with wooden tripod and metal base, for use on walls of buildings in course of erection.
Telescope 11 inches long with rack and pinion adjustment, two-mile range, best achromatic objectives with cross hairs level to telescope, graduated circle with clamp and leveling screws. Price, with carrying case..$35.00
Weight, complete. 3½ pounds.

NOTE.—The addition of a compass, mounted on telescope under the level, furnished, if desired, without extra charge.

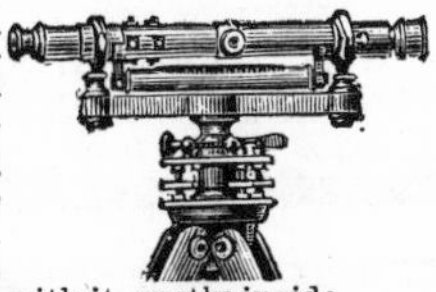

23737 New Improved Leveling Instrument. The principal features of this level are its compactness and lightness. It has a long, stout center of phosphor bronze, and the rings of telescope are of the hardest bell metal. The cross bar is cast hollow, carrying with it, partly inside, the clamp and tangent screw, so they always keep the same relative position to telescope on the right hand side of observer. If desired we provide the inside of wyes with agate bearings at an additional cost of $10.00, as this protects the wyes against wear from the turning of telescope, the cause of frequent adjustment; it is quite an important improvement. The telescope has an adjustable arrangement to keep cross wires in an exact horizontal position, consisting of a projecting pin on the collars. When this pin is brought in contact with this adjustable screw the wire is horizontal. This permits the collars to lay in the wyes without the least strain, and the telescope can be revolved without opening the clasps. Weight of instrument, with 18 inch telescope, 9¼ lbs.
Price of 18 in., Y level, each..................$110.00

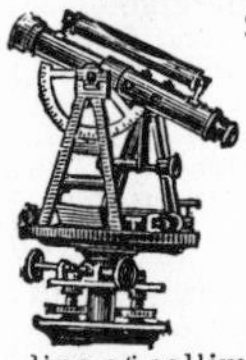

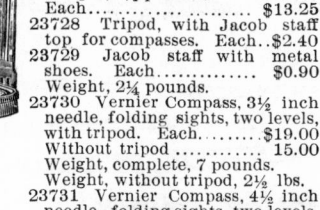

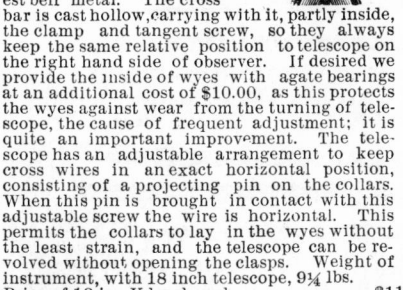

23738 Engineers' Transit, Horizontal Circle, with double Verniers, read to minutes or 30" or 20" if desired, graduations silvered, improved Spring Tangent Screws, shifting center to set instruments exactly over a given point, improved telescope 11 inches long, magnifying 25 times, exactly balanced and reversing on both ends, eye-piece provided with improved screw arrangements to focus cross wires, the line of collimation correct on all distances, long compound centers of phosphor bronze, improved tripod. Weight, 13½ lbs., packed in box containing plumb-bob, screwdriver, magnifier and adjusting pins and shade. Price.........$165.00
23739 Same as above, but with level and clamp to telescope.......................................180.00
23740 Same as No. 23739 but with full circle or arc of 3½ inch radius, the arc being fastened with a clamp to the telescope axis, so that instrument can be used as plain transit.
Price.. 200.00

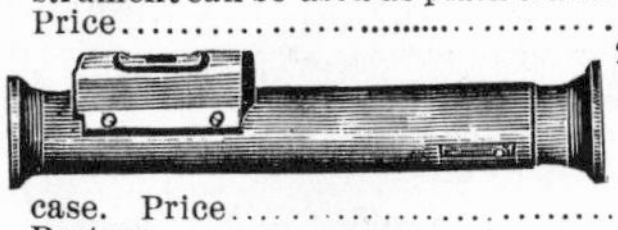

23741 Locke's Hand Level, 5 inches long, nickel plated, in neat leather case. Price.....................................$6.00
Postage........ .... .10

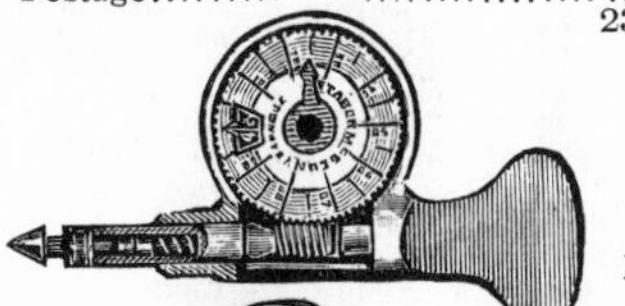

23742 Speed Indicator. The Tabor Revolution Counter, with stop motion. A good, simple speed indicator. Each........$0.90
Postage.... .05

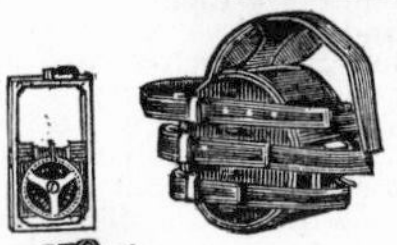

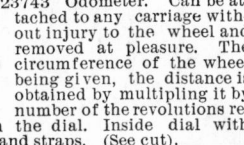

23743 Odometer. Can be attached to any carriage without injury to the wheel and removed at pleasure. The circumference of the wheel being given, the distance is obtained by multipling it by number of the revolutions recorded upon the dial. Inside dial with leather case and straps. (See cut).
Price..$12.75

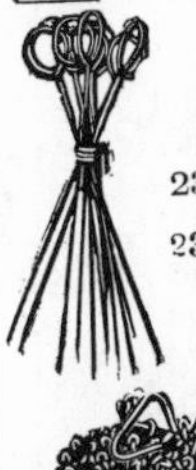

23744 Best Steel Arrows or marking pins, 15-inch, 11 in set. Price, per set.$1.05
23745 Iron Arrows or marking pins, 11 in set, 15-inch... .60

Measuring Chains.
Of Steel and Iron.

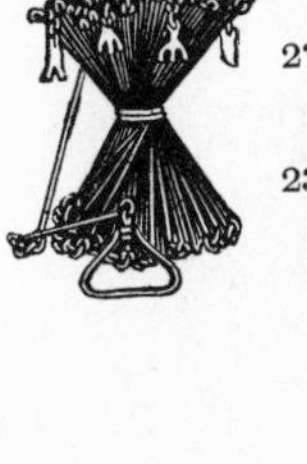

23746 Steel, best grade, brazed links and rings; brass handles.

Feet,	33	50	66	100
Each,	$4.65	$5.70	$8.75	$9.80

23748 Steel, Oval Rings, not brazed, brass handles.

Feet,	33	50	66	100
Each,	$3.15	$4.10	$5.75	$6.90

23750 Iron, Oval Rings, brass handles.

Feet,	33	50	66	100
Each,	$2.20	$3.10	$3.75	$4.80

Improved Tape Chains.

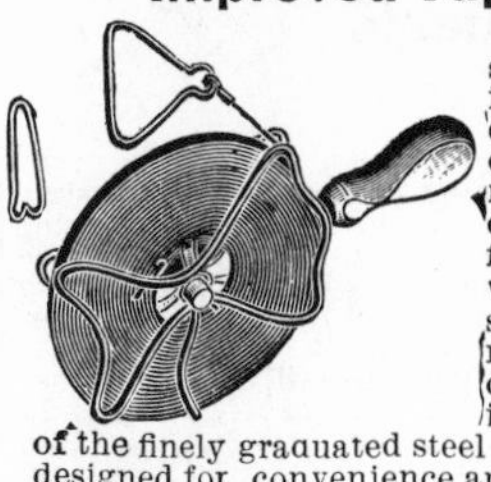

These tapes are made of superior steel, about ¼ inch wide, graduated every foot by a brass rivet, end feet in 10ths and the number of feet are stamped on brass plates every five feet. They are provided with a handy, substantial reel and a pair of round, detachable handles. These tapes are not intended to take the place of the finely graduated steel tapes, but are especially designed for convenience and durability to replace the heavy chains in all land surveying, railroad and canal work and town plotting. For country, field and town work, these tapes have given excellent satisfaction. They can be dragged through wood and, brush, etc., and if they are nickel-plated, they do not rust and do not require any oiling or cleaning after being used.

23751 50 feet long, graduated every foot, end feet in 10ths, nickel-plated. Each..................$4.50
23752 50 feet long, graduated every foot, end feet in 10ths, plain. Each........................... 3.60
23753 66 feet long, graduated every link, nickel-plated. Each...................................... 5.40
23754 66 feet long, graduated every link, plain. Each.. 4.50
23755 100 feet long, graduated every foot, end feet in 10ths, nickel-plated. Each.............. 5.85
23756 100 feet long, graduated every foot, end feet in 10ths, plain. Each........................ 4.50

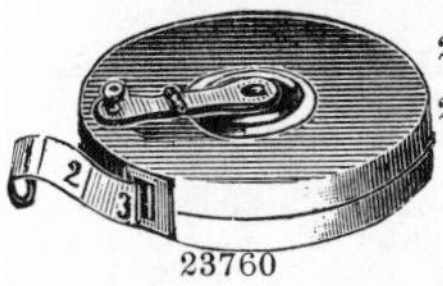

23760

23758 Timber Scribes, medium.................$0.75
23759 Timber Scribes, large, extra heavy, with steel gouging blade.......$1.00

Surveyors' and Engineers' Measuring Tapes.

23760 Metallic Measuring Tapes, enameled waterproof linen, wire warp; in leather cases; folding handle; marked feet and 12ths; links on back.

25 ft.	33 ft.	50 ft.	66 ft.	75 ft.	100 ft.
$1.75	$2.00	$2.50	$2.75	$3.00	$4.00

23761 Metallic Tapes, same description, but divided 1-10 foot, for engineers' use.

25 ft.	33 ft.	50 ft.	66 ft.	75 ft.	100 ft.
$1.75	$2.00	$2.50	$2.75	$3.00	$4.00

23762 Steel Tapes, in leather case, folding flush handle; nickel trimmings; marked feet and inches; links on back.

25 ft.	33 ft.	50 ft.	66 ft.	75 ft.	100 ft.
$3.75	$4.50	$6.00	$7.75	$9.00	$11.00

23763 Steel Tapes, same description, but divided in tenths of foot instead of inches; for engineers' use.

25 ft.	33 ft.	50 ft.	66 ft.	75 ft.	100 ft.
$3.75	$4.50	$6.00	$7.75	$9.00	$11.00

Steel and Linen Pocket Tapes.

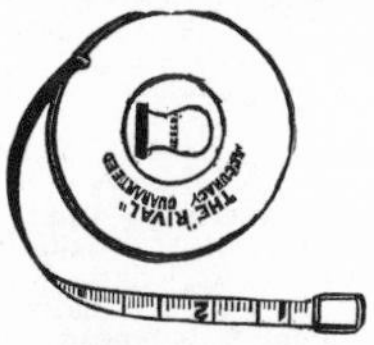

23764 Steel Pocket Tapes, very light, flush handle, divided 1-12 foot, 25 feet long. Weight, 6 ounces.
Each..................$3.00
23765 Same description as above, 50 feet long. Weight, 9 oz.
Each $3.65

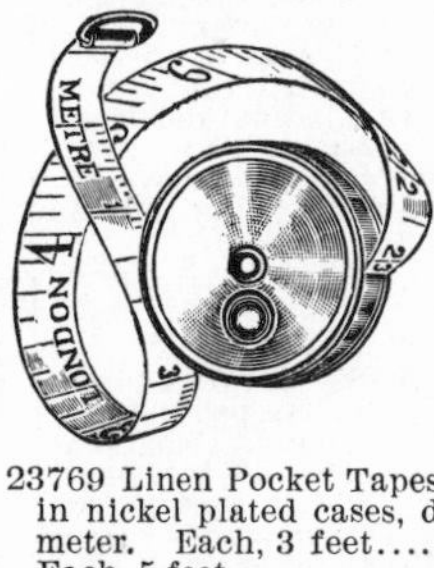

23766 Steel Pocket Tapes, with spring and stop in German silver cases, divided 1-16 inch.

3 ft.	6 ft.	9 ft.	12 ft.
$0.95	$1.25	$1.75	$2.25

23767 Divided in 1-16 inch and meter.

3 ft.	6 ft.	9 ft.	12 ft.
$1.35	$2.10	$2.70	$3.40

23768 Divided in 1-16 inch on one side and in 1-10 inch on the other side. Length, 6 ft. Each..$1.50

23769 Linen Pocket Tapes, with spring and stop, in nickel plated cases, divided into inches and meter. Each, 3 feet..........................$0.40
Each, 5 feet.. .50
23770 Best Water-Proof Linen Spring Pocket Tapes, in German silver cases, with stop, divided inches and meter. Each, 3 feet.............. .60
Each, 6 feet.. .85
23771 Spring Tape Measures, in nickel cases, at half price until sold........................... .10
Other tapes and graduation furnished on short notice.

...INQUIRIES...

CONCERNING SURVEYORS' DRAWING, MATHEMATICAL AND SCIENTIFIC INSTRUMENTS CHEERFULLY ANSWERED.

Mathematical and Drawing Instruments.

23775 Pencil Compass, adapted to every variety of drawing where accurate instruments are required. Especially valuable for school uses. Simply adjusted. The leg is strengthened by a brace and moving sleeve as shown in cut. Make any size circle from ½ in. to 8 in. in diameter. Price, each, including good quality nickel rubber tipped pencil...........................$0.25
Per dozen...........................1.50
Postage.................................02
Special price in large quantities.

Polygraph.

23777 Draws and designs, giving correct curves and degrees. 10,000 mathematical figures can easily be produced. The greatest drawing assistant ever invented. Put up in neat box, with full explanations, directions for use and specimens of drawings.
Nickel plated, each.....$0.25
Per dozen................2.50
Postage 05

Drawing Instruments in Cases.

Nickel Plated Drawing Instruments, with improved pen and pencil points, in pocket cases with round corners and bar locks.

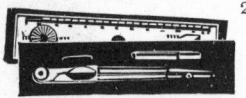

23778 School Divider, nickel plated, 5 in. long, with pencil point adjustment, metal box of leads, in sliding, velvet-lined case. Weight, 2 ounces.
Per set..........$0 25 Per doz. sets...........$2.50

23780 Set with 4¾ inch dividers, with pen and pencil points, rule and leads.
Per set........$0.45
Weight, 4 ounces.

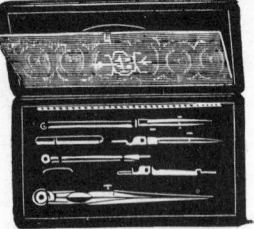

23781 Set with 4¾ inch dividers, with pen and pencil points, lengthening bar and ruling pen, rule and leads and metal protractor.
Per set......$0.75
Weight, 6 ounces.

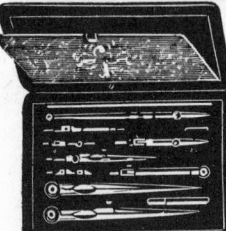

23782 Set with 4¾ inch dividers, with pen and pencil point, lengthening bar, 4¼ inch plain dividers, 3 inch needle point divider with pen and pencil points and improved ruling pen, rule, leads and metal protractor.
Weight, 8 ounces.
Per set $1.35

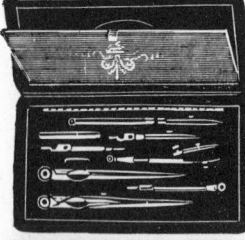

23783 Set with 4¾ inch dividers, pen and pencil points, lengthening bar, 4¼ inch plain dividers, spring bow pen, improved ruling pen, rule, leads and metal protractor.
Weight, 8 ounces.
Per set.........$1.60

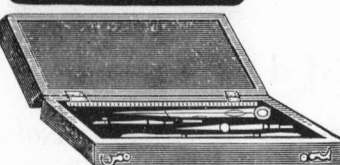

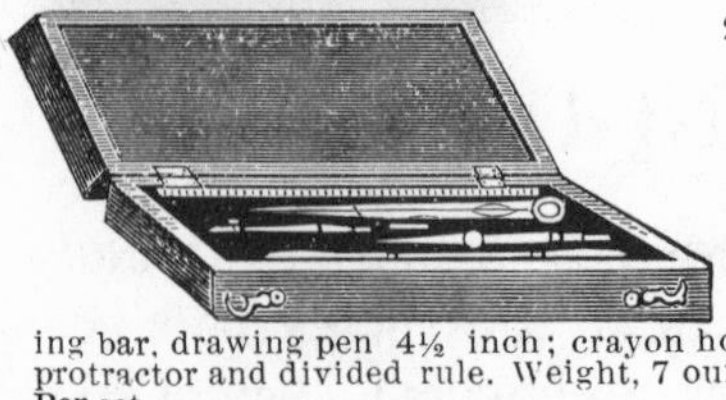

23785 Mahogany Box, containing 4½ inch brass compasses, with pens, pencil point and lengthening bar, drawing pen 4½ inch; crayon holder, horn protractor and divided rule. Weight, 7 ounces.
Per set...............................$0.75

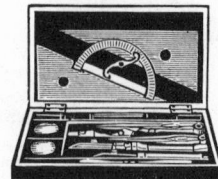

23787 Mahogany Case, brass instruments, 4½ inch compasses with pen, pencil point and lengthening bar, 4½ inch plain dividers, 4½ inch drawing pen, 7 inch scale, 3½ inch protractor, crayon holder, 3 triangles, colors, brushes, etc., very low at the price we ask. Weight, 15 ounces Per set......$1.75
23789 Rosewood Case, with lock and key, brass instruments set in tray, 6½ in. compasses, with pen and pencil points and lengthening bar, 4½ in. plain dividers, 4 in. compass with pen and pencil points, ruling pen, brass and horn protractors, divided rule. Weight, 1¼ pounds.
Per set $3.25

Swiss Drawing Instruments.

Of German silver, steel points and high finish

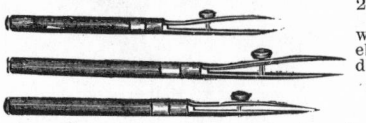

23791 Ruling Pen, with spring ebony handle, 4½ in.. .....$0.85
23792 Ruling Pen, with spring, ebony handle, 5 inches...........................$0.90
23793 Ruling Pen, with spring, ebony handle, 5½ inches.................................1.00

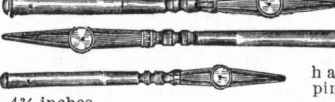

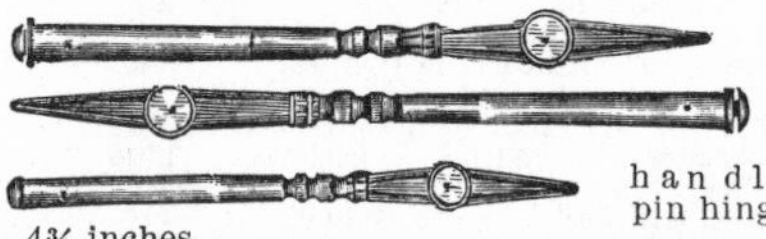

23794 Ruling Pen—ivory handle, with pin hinge joint. 4¾ inches.......................$1.25
23795 Ruling Pen, ivory handle, with pin hinge joint, 5½ inches......................1.50
23796 Ruling Pen, ivory handle, with pin hinge joint, 6½ inches........................1.75

23797 Curved Pen improved.
By loosening the screw at the end of handle, the bar running through hollow center acts as a pivot for the pen, which will follow any curve readily without blotting the edges of the curve ruler.
If the upper screw is fastened, it can be used as a drawing pen, and is useful for ruling into corners and for fine work. Each................................$1.75

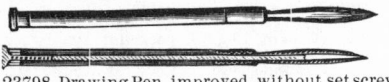

23798 Drawing Pen. improved, without set screw.
The pen opens and closes by turning a thumbscrew at the upper end of handle, making the screw through the blades unnecessary and a displacement of the nibs sideways impossible. As there is no obstruction to the sight in working this pen is perfect for work. Each................................$1.55

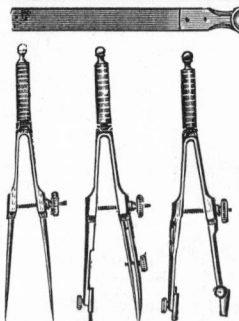

23799 Swedish Detail Ruling Pens, for long lines, 5 inches....$1.25
23800 Swedish Detail Ruling Pens, for long lines, 7 inches... 1.50
23801 Steel Spring Bow Dividers, 3½ inch metal handle.....$1.90
23802 Steel Spring Bow Pencil, 3½ inch metal handle.........$2.00
23803 Steel Spring Bow Pen, 3½ inch metal handle..........$2.00
23804 Set of Bows, composed of Nos. 23801-2 and 3 in case $6.25

23805 Dotting Instrument, with 6 wheels in case....................$3.65
NOTE.--By throwing back the spring the wheels of different patterns are inserted.

ALTENEDER PATTERN.

All pencil points arranged to hold Faber's leads.

23806 Plain Dividers. 4½ in. pivot joint. Price... $1.75.
23806½ Plain Dividers, 6 inch pivot joint......$2.25

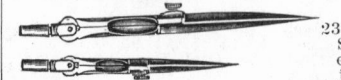

23807 Hair Spring Dividers, 4½ inch pivot joint.... $2.50
23808 Hair Spring Dividers, 6 inch pivot, joint, $3.00

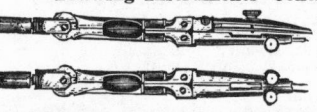

23809 Compasses, 4½ inch fixed needle and pencil points, pivot joint. Price...$3.75
23810 Compasses, 4½ in., with pen, pencil and needle points, pivot joint......3.75
23811 Compasses, 4¼ in. with pen, pencil and needle points, hair spring 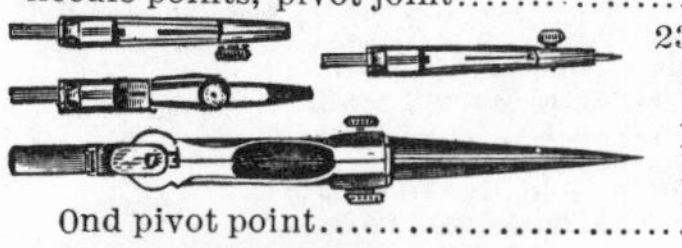

Ond pivot point.......................$5.75

23812 Compasses, 6 in. fixed needle point hair spring and pencil, pen points, lengthening bar and pivot joint $7.50
23816 Compasses, 6 in. pencil, pen and needle points, lengthening bar, pivot joint ..$7.25

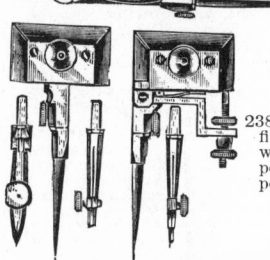

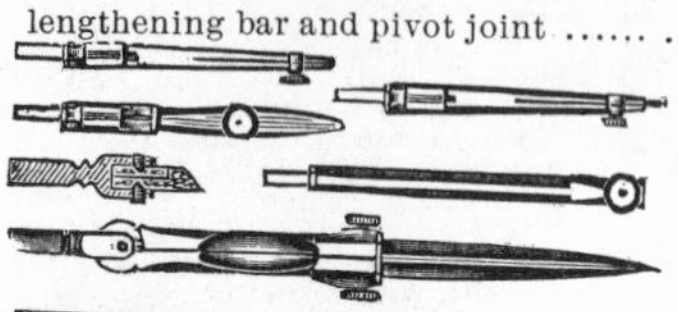

23817 Beam Compass, to fit on any straight edge, with two steel points, pencil, pen and needle points............$8.00

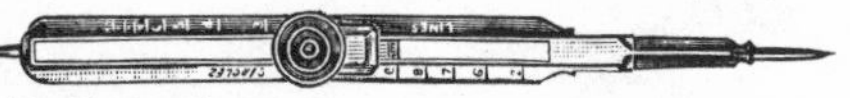

23818 Proportional Dividers, 7½ inch, for lines and circles, in case....................$8.00

23819 Proportional Dividers, 7¾ inch, with rack adjustment for lines, circles, plains and solids, in case $11.00

Pivot Joint—Swiss Instruments, in Cases.

23820 Set of pivot joint instruments containing 4 inch ruling pen, with joint and ivory handle, plain divider 4½ inch, pivot joint compasses 4½ inches, with pen, pencil and needle points; box of leads. Complete in pocket morocco case. Each $9.00

23822 Set of pivot joint instruments, in pocket morocco case, containing compass, pivot compass, pivot joint, 6 inch, with fixed needle point and pen and pencil points, lengthening bar, ruling pen 4½ inch, with spring ruling pen 5½ inch, fine joint, steel spring bow pen 5½ inch, fine joint, steel spring bow pen 3½ inch, metal handle, plain divider, 6 inch pivot joint, box leads....................$15.00

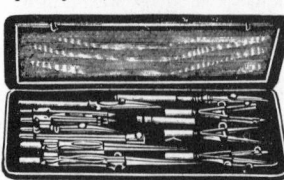

23823 Set pivot joint instruments in pocket morocco case. Containing 12 pieces plain divider, 6 inch, pivot joint steel spring bow divider, 3½ inch metal steel spring bow pencil, 3½ inch metal handle, steel spring bow pen 3½ inch, metal handle, ruling pen, 4½ inch, with spring ebony handle, ruling pen 5½ inch, fine joint, compasses pivot joint 6 inch with pencil, pen, needle points and lengthening bar, box of leads.......$19.00

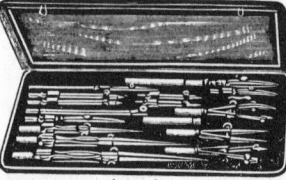

23824 Set of pivot joint instruments in pocket morocco case. Containing sixteen pieces, as follows: Compasses, pivot joint, 6 in., with pencil, pen, needle point and lengthening bar, compasses, pivot joint. 4½ inch, with pencil, pen and needle point, hair spring divider, pivot joint, 6 inch steel spring bow divider, 3½ inch metal handle, steel spring bow pencil, 3½ inch metal handle, steel spring bow pen. 3½ inch metal handle, ruling pen, 4½ inch, with spring and ebony handle, ruling pen 5½ inch, with fine joint. Box leads...........$26.00

Extra Fine German Instruments.

Made of superior German silver and Steel.
All pencil points are arranged to hold Faber's leads.

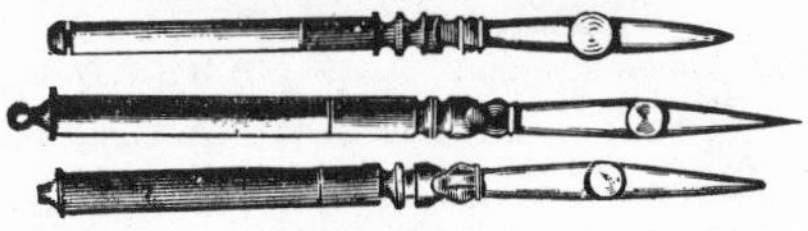

23825 Drawing Pen, no joint, 4¾ inch, black handle $0.18
23826 Drawing Pen, no joint, 5 inch, white handle .... .25
23827 Drawing Pen, 4 inch, not jointed, ivory handle .... .35
23828 Drawing Pen. 5 inch, ordinary joint, ivory handle .... .50
23831 Drawing Pen, 4½ inch, fine joint and needle point, ivory handle .... .75
23833 Drawing Pen, 5½ inch, fine joint and needle point, ivory handle .... .85

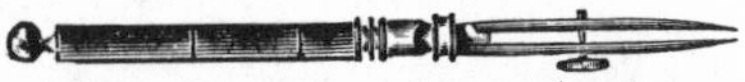

23836 Drawing Pen, 5½ inch, with German silver blades for colored inks, fine joint, needle point, ivory handle .... .85

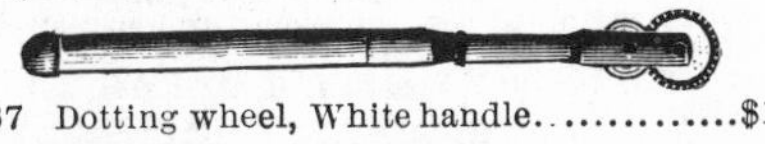

23837 Dotting wheel, White handle $1.00

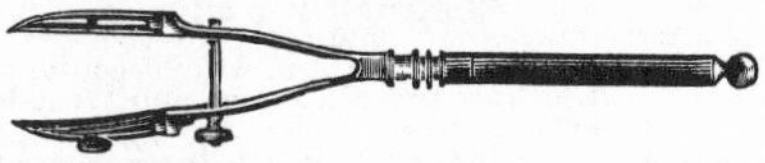

23838 Railroad Pen, 5½ inches, two pens with joint, ivory handle $2.25

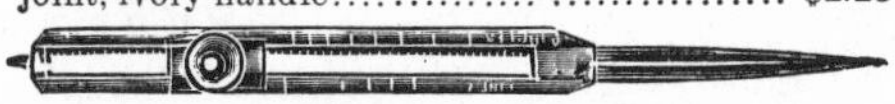

23839 Proportional Divider, German silver, 6¼ inches, in case. Each $2.25
23840 Proportional Dividers, brass, 6¼ inches, in case. Each 1.75
23841 Proportional Dividers, German silver, 7 inches, with rack movement for lines and circles, in case. Each 3.75

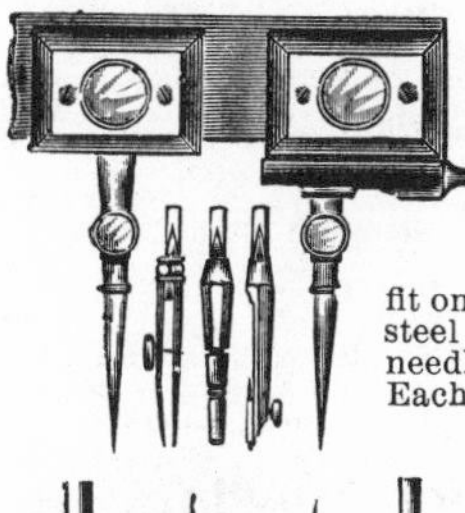

23842 Beam Compass, to fit on any straight edge, with two needle points, pen and pencil points, in leather case. Each $4.75
23843 Beam Compass to fit on any straight edge, with 2 steel points, pencil, pen and needle points. Each, in case $6.50

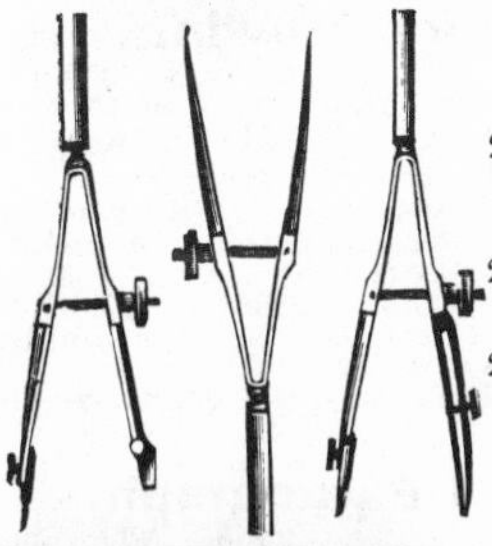

23844 Steel Spring Bow Dividers, 3½ in., round points, metal handle $1.10
23845 Steel Spring Bow Pencil, 3½ in. needle, metal handle $1.25
23846 Steel Spring Bow Pen 3½ in. needle points, metal handle $1.25

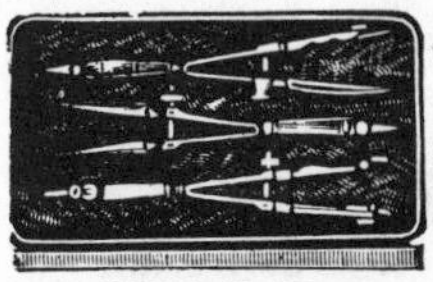

23847 Leather Case, containing set of bows, as illustrated, white handles. $4.25
23848 Leather Case, containing set of bows; metal handles $3.75

23844-45-46

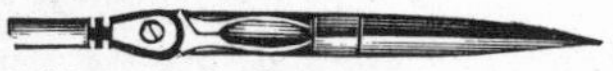

23849 Dividers, 3½ inches, with handles $1.00

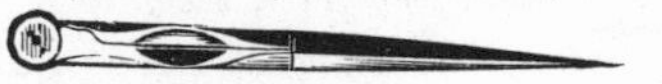

23850 Plain Dividers, 5 inch $0.75
23851 Plain Dividers, 6 inch .... .85

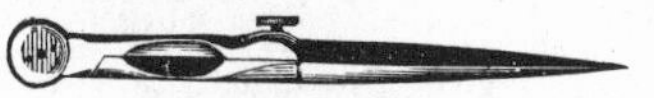

23852 Hair Spring Dividers, 5 inch $1.35
23853 Hair Spring Dividers, 6 inch 1.75

EXAMINE OUR . . . .

Lace Quotations.

. . . . We have Increased the Line.

14—2nd

Drawing Instruments—Continued.

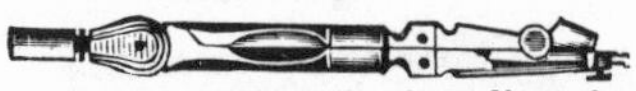

23854 Compasses, 3½ inch, fixed needle and pencil points, with handle $1.90

23855 Compasses, 3½ inch, fixed needle and pen points, with handle $1.90

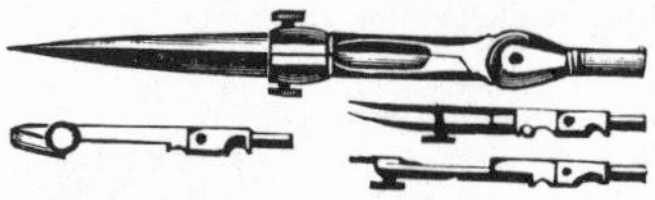

23856 Compasses, 3½ inch, with handle, pen, pencil and fixed needle point $2.60

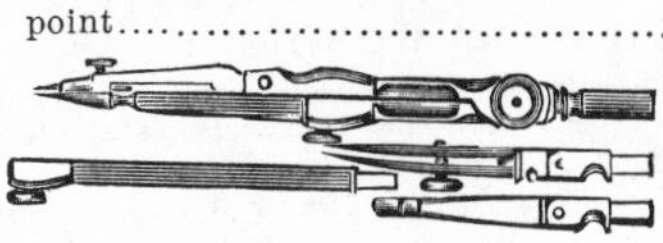

23857 Compass, 4½ in., with handle, pen, pencil, lengthening bar, divider and fixed needle points $3.50

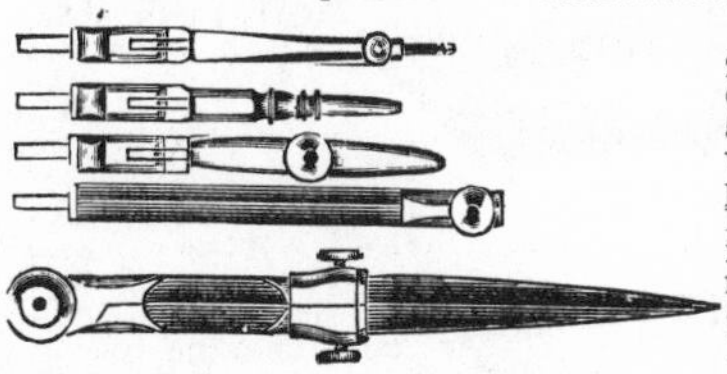

23859—Compass, 5½ inch, with pen, pencil, lengthening bar, needle and divider points. Each $3.00

Extra Fine German Instruments.

IN POCKET MOROCCO CASE.

Maroon colored velvet lining. Best quality German silver. All pencil points are arranged to hold Faber's leads.

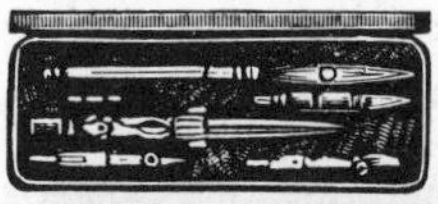

23865 Contents: 3½ inch compass, with handle, pen pencil and needle points, 4 inch ruling pen, lead case and key. Each $3.75

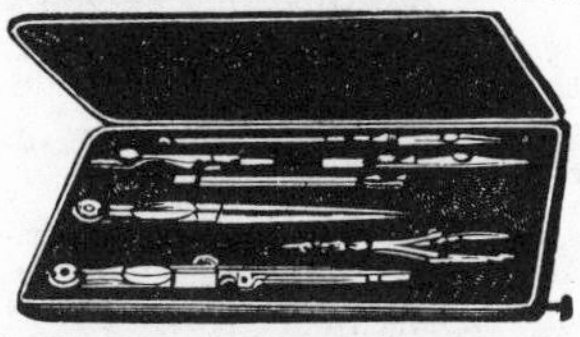

23866 Contents: 5 inch compasses with fixed needle point, pen, pencil, and lengthening bar, 5 in. dividers, steel spring bow, pen, drawing pen with hinge and pin, lead case and key $5.75

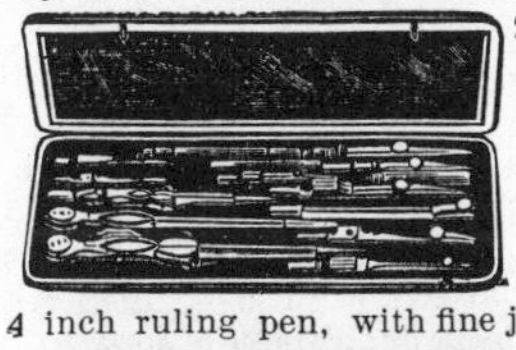

23867 Contents: 5½ in. compasses, with pen, pencil, needle points, and lengthening bar, 5 in. plain divider, 3½ in. compasses, with pen, pencil and needle points, 5½ inch ruling pen, with hinge and 4 inch ruling pen, with fine joint. Each $7.75

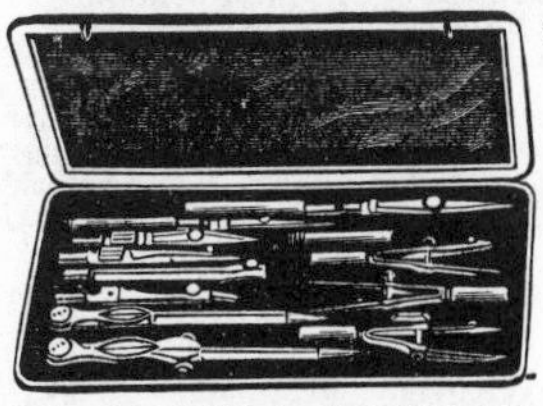

23868 Contents: 5½ inch compasses with pen, pencil, needle points and lengthening bar, 5 inch plain dividers, 3½ inch steel spring bow dividers, metal handle, 3½ inch steel spring bow pencil, metal handle, 3½ inch steel spring bow pen, metal handles; 5½ inch ruling pen, with hinge and pin, 4 inch ruling pen, with joint, box with leads and key. Each $9.00

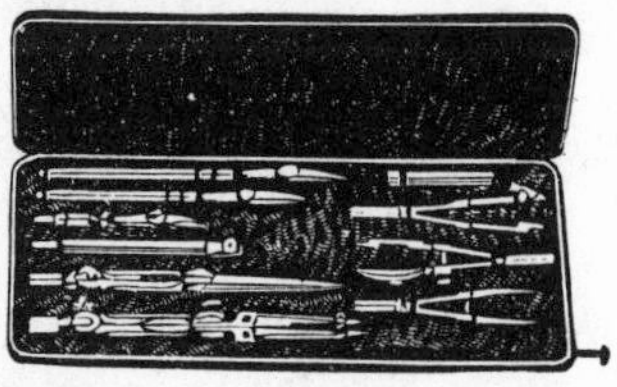

23869 Set of German Pivot Joint Instruments; Alteneder pattern; in pocket morocco case with velvet lining. Contents: Dividers, 6 inch fixed needle. joint pen pencil, lengthening bar, 5 inch hair spring dividers, 3½ inch steel spring bow spacers, 2 round points, metal handle, 3½ inch steel spring bow pencil, needle point, metal handle, 3½ inch steel spring bow pencil, needle point, metal handle. 4½ inch drawing pen, ebony handle, lead case and adjusting key. Each $10.00

HAWTHORNE AND WHITE STAR Bicycles have no peer. Send for Special Bicycle Catalogue if interested.

Drawing Instruments—Continued.

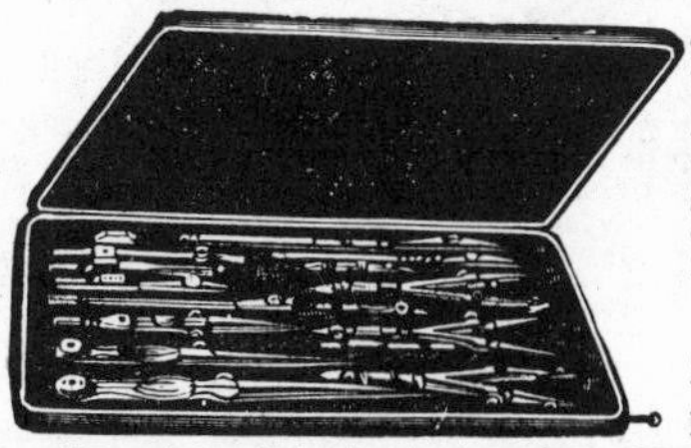

23870 Contents: 5½ in. compasses with pencil, needle points and lengthening bar, 5 inch plain dividers, 3½ inch bow compass, with pen, pencil and needle points, 3 inch steel spring pen, 3 inch spring bow pencil, 3 inch spring bow dividers, 5½ inch ruling pen with hinge and pin, 4 inch ruling pen, lead case and key. Each $12.00

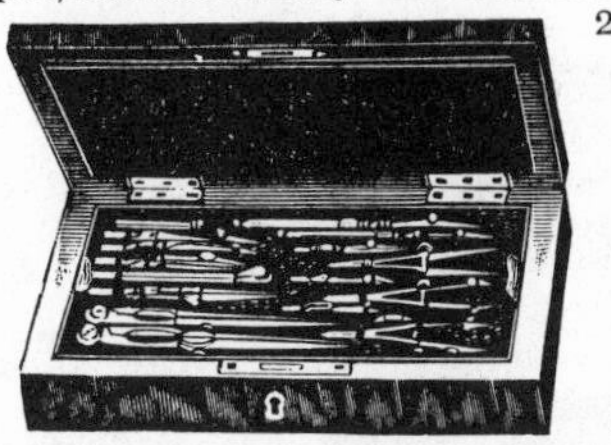

23871 Polished Walnut Case with tray, lock and key. Contents: 5½ inch compasses, with pen, pencil, needle points and lengthening bars, 5 inch dividers, 3½ inch bow compasses, with pen, pencil and needle points, 3 inch steel spring bow pen, 3 inch spring bow pencil, 3 inch spring bow dividers, 5½ inch ruling pen with hinge and pin, 4 inch ruling pen, lead case and key. Each $15.00

Protractors.

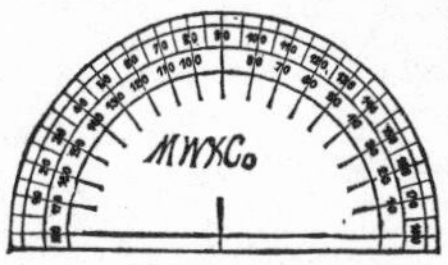

Each.
23880 Brass Protractors, whole degrees; diameter, 3½ in. $0.10
23881 Horn Protractors, whole degrees, 4 inch .... .15
23882 Brass Protractors, half circle, whole degrees, 4 inch diameter .... .25
23883 Horn Protractors, half-circle, half degrees 5 inches diameter .... .25
23884 German Silver Protractors, half-circle, half degrees, 5 inch diameter .... .75
23885 Railroad Curve Protractors, horn, diameter 8 inches; half degrees, with 23 circular curves from half to 8 degrees, a radius of 400 feet to the inch 1.50
Larger and more expensive protractors furnished when ordered.

Paper Protractors.

Each.
23900 Large Bristol Board, 14-inch, full circle, ¼ degree $0.35
23901 Large Drawing Paper, 14-inch, full circle, ¼ degree .... .30
23902 Large Fine Tracing Paper, 14-inch, full circle, ¼ degree .... .25
23903 Boxwood Protractor, 6 inches long, 1¾ inches wide, scales of ¼, ½, ¾, to 1 to the foot; scale of cords; diagonal scales .... .35
NOTE. Ivory Protractors, extra quality, from $1.00 to $4.00 each

Rules and Scales.

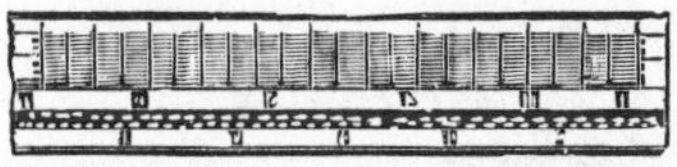

23904 Plotting Scales, boxwood, 6 inches $0.10
23905 Plotting Scales, ivory, 6 inches .... .75

Machine Divided Scales.

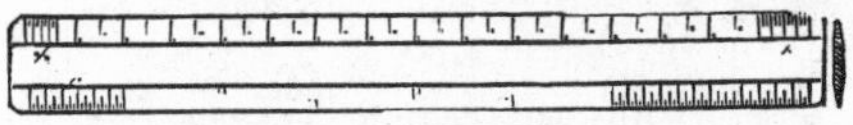

U. S. STANDARD.

23906 Best Quality Flat Boxwood Scales, beveled and divided on both sides; divided ⅛, ¼, ½, 1 inch, and on reverse side, ⅜, ¾, 1½, 3 inch, to foot. Each.
24 inches long $2.60
18 inches long 2.00
12 inches long 1.20
6 inches long .... .75

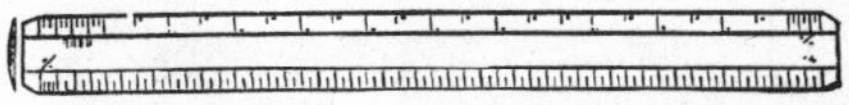

23908 Best Quality Flat Boxwood Scales, divided ⅛, ¼, ½, 1 inch, to foot.
24 inches long $1.75
18 inches long 1.30
12 inches long .... .75
6 inches long .... .50

Triangular Architects' Scales.

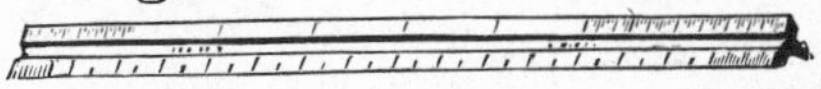

			Each.
23910—	Inch.	div. ¼, ⅛, ½, 1, ⅜, ¾, 1½	
Triangular,	6 Boxwood ...	3, 3/16, 3/32, 1/16 in. to the ft.	$0.80
"	12 Boxwood ...	"	1.50
"	12 Metalic	"	3.00
"	12 *Ivorine* edges	"	3.00
"	18 Boxwood	"	2.50
"	24	"	4.00

Triangular Engineers' Chain Scales.

						Each.
23911—	Inch.	div.10,20,30,40,50				
Triangular	6 Boxwood......	60 parts to the in.				$0.80
"	12 Boxwood......	"	"	"		1.50
"	12 Metalic........	"	"	"		3.00
"	12 *Ivorine* edges..	"	"	"		3.00
"	18 Boxwood......	"	"	"		2.50
"	24	"	"	"		4.00

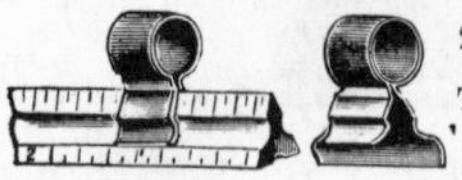

23912 Triangular Scale Guard or Holder This appliance is made of plated metal. It can be attached to any part of the scale, and overcomes the necessity of searching for the scale when in use.
Each...$0.25

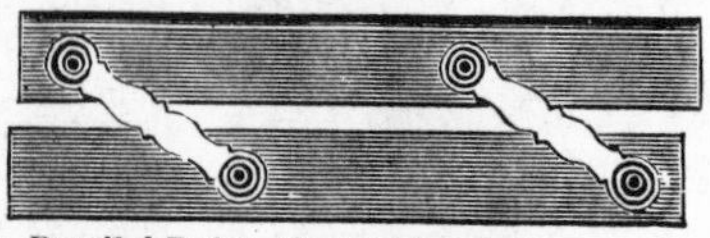

23913 Parallel Rules, ebony, brass bars.

Length..............	6	9	12	18	24
Price, each........	$0.18	$0.35	$0.40	$0.65	$1.50

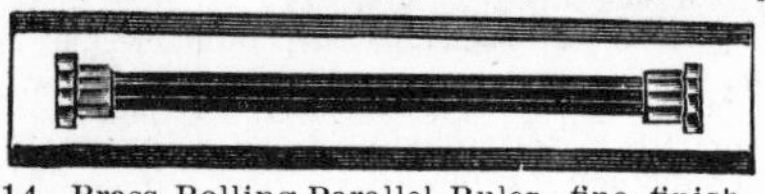

23914 Brass Rolling Parallel Ruler, fine finish,
18 inches...$10.00
15 inches... 8.75
12 inches... 6 75
23915 Ebony Rolling Parallel Ruler, 18 inches... 4.50
15 inches... 3.75
12 inches... 3.00
23916 German Silver Rolling Paralell Ruler.
18-inches...14.00
15-inches...11.50
12-inches... 9.50

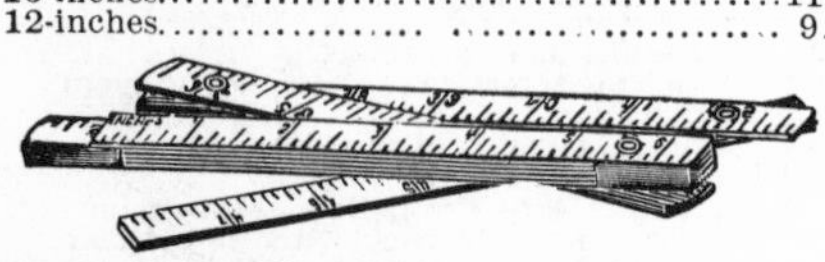

Engineers' Skeleton Pocket Rule, flexible and light, will not shrink, very accurate, has self-acting springs, which keep the rule in a straight position.
23918 Skeleton Rule, self-acting springs, 2 feet, 4 folds, 1-16 inches, on both sides..............$0.25
23919 Skeleton Rule, self-acting springs, 4 feet, 8 fold, 1-16 inches on one side, meters on other .50
23920 Skeleton Rule, self-acting springs, 4 feet, 8 folds, 1-16 inches on both sides .... .50
23921 Faber's 12-inch Boxwood Rule, divided into 1-16 inches, ⅜ inch wide. Each........ .10
23922 Faber's, Boxwood Rule, divided into 1-16 inches; width 1½ inches, brass edge.

Length.......	12	15	18	24 inches.
Each.........	40c.	50c.	60c.	75c.

23923 Faber's Maple Rule, divided into 1-8, 1-16, double inlaid brass edge, rubber plugs to prevent slipping.

Length..............	12	15	18 inches.
Each..	25c.	30c.	35c.

See Index for quotations on school and office rules.

Triangles.

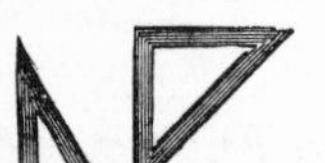

All triangles measured this way

30°x60° 45°

23925 Cherry Triangles, framed, mortised joints 30°x60°

Size	7	9	11	14 in.
Each...	18c	20c	25c	35c.

23926 Cherry Triangles, framed, mortised joints, 45°.

Size	5	7	9	11 in-
Each	18c.	20c.	25c.	35c.

23927 Transparent, "Ambro" Triangles, open center, 30°x60°.

Size...:	5	7	8	12	16 inch.
Each..............	35c.	50c.	60c.	$1.00	$2.40

23928 Transparent "Ambro" Triangles, open center, 45°.

Size..........	4	6	10	14	18 inch.
Each.............	30c.	60c.	$1.15	$2 40	$4.00.

Straight Edges.

23930 Cherry, one edge beveled—

Size.	18	24	30	36	42 inch.
Each......................	20c.	25c.	30c.	40c.	50c.

23931 Mahogany, Ebony Lined.

Size..........................	24	30	36	42	48 inch.
One edge beveled. Each..	$0.55	70	1.00	1.25	1.60

23932 Steel Straight Edges, nickel plated, one edge beveled, the other square

Size................	15	18	24	30	36 inch.
Each......	$1.75	$2.00	$3.00	$4.00	$5.00
Size...............	42	48	60	72 inch.	
Each	$6.50	$8.00	$11.00	$15.00	

When ordering goods to be shipped by mail, have them insured. See page 1.

T Squares.

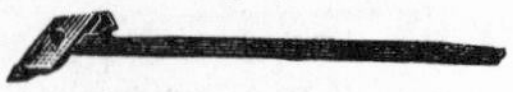

23935 Cherry Blade and Fixed head.

Size......	15	18	24	36	48 inch
Each..............	25c	30c	40c	60c	90c

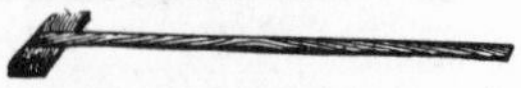

23936 Cherry Blade and Movable Head.

Size......	15	18	24	36	48 inch.
Each.........	50c.	70c.	90c.	$1.00	1.50

23937 Mahogany, Ebony Lined, *Fixed* Head.

Size,	24	30	36	42	48	54	60 inch
Each.	$1.20	$1.50	$1.75	$2.00	2.50	$3.25	$4.00

Drawing Boards.

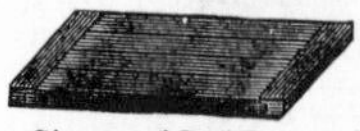

23940 Pinewood, with two drawing surfaces and side ledges.

Size	12x17	15x21	20x25	23x31 in.
Each	65c.	95c.	$1.25	$1.50

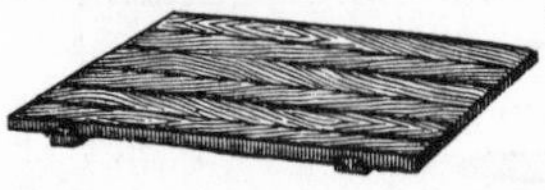

23941 Pinewood, with hardwood ledges dove tailed into the board to allow contraction and expansion.

Size.........	20x24	23x31	31x42
Each................................	$1.60	$2.25	$3.50

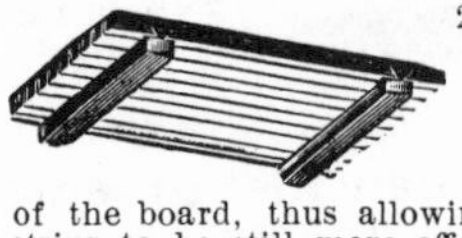

23942 Pinewood, with hardwood ledges, dovetailed into the board to allow contraction and expansion, and groove sunk in ⅜ the thickness of the board, thus allowing the narrow wooden strips to be still more effectually controlled by the hardwood ledges.

Size	31x42	36x55	42x60 inches.
Each	$4.00	$6.25	$7.25

Larger drawing boards of any size and style made to order.

Folding Stands.

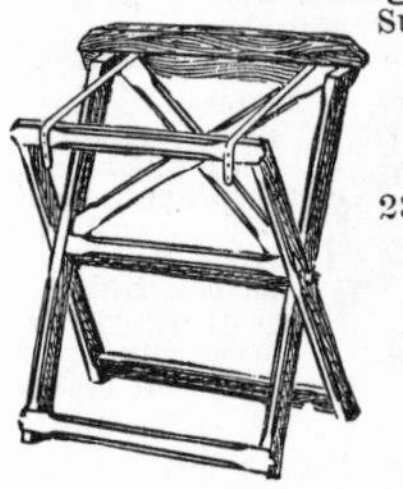

Substantially made and nicely finished with adjustable leather straps to set to convenient height and hinged top board to set the drawing board slanting.
23943 Folding Stand of hardwood, each, $7.00.
Further quotations on T squares, straight edges, triangles, irregular curves and drawing boards furnished on application.

Thumb Tacks.

23946 German Silver, swedged and round heads, ⅜ inch diameter, per dozen........................$0.20
Round heads, ½ inch diameter, per dozen......... .25
23947 Brass, swedged head, same as preceding.
Round heads, $\frac{5}{16}$ inch dameter, per dozen .... .12
Round head, ½ inch diameter, per dozen.......... .18
23948 "Bayonet" Tacks made of one piece of steel, a portion of the head forming the point ⅜ inches diameter. Price, per box of 100, including a tack lifter.. .50
Same, $\frac{7}{16}$ inch diameter, per box.................... .75
NOTE—We are prepared to quote prices on any quality and size of drawing and detail paper, tracing cloth, tracing paper, "Blue Process" paper, cross section and profile paper.

Chinese or India Ink.

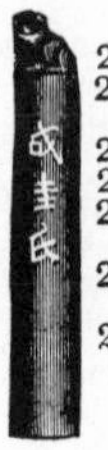

23950 Black, oval polished, 2¼ inch........$0.10
23951 Lion Head Black, oval polished, 3 inch.. .25
23953 Square black, super, 2⅞ inch ..... .40
23954 Square, black, super. super, 3⅝ inch .90
23955 Square Blue, Chinese Inks, about 2¾ inch................................. .50
23956 Square, Red, Chinese Inks, about 2¼ inch.................... .... .50
23957 Square, Yellow, Chinese Inks, about 2¾ inch.. .50

Liquid Drawing Inks.

23958 Higgin's Waterproof Black Ink, per bottle..$0.20

Slate Ink Slabs.

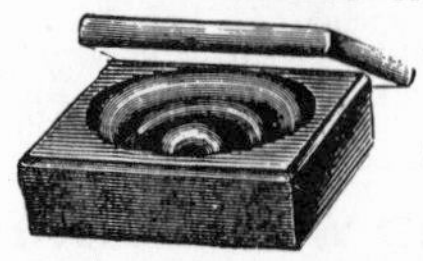

23960 3½ in. square, with heavy glass cover.
Each.....................$0.45
23961 5 inch square with heavy glass cover.
Each.............. .65

For quotations of ordinary office supplies, pencils, etc., see index.

A. W. Faber's Lead Pencils.

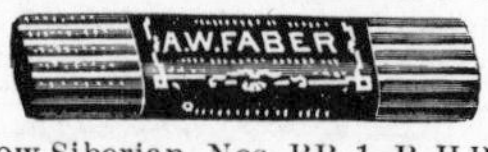

23962 Yellow Siberian, Nos. BB-1, B, H B-2, F-3 H, HH-4, 3 H, 4 H, 5 H, 6 H. Per dozen..........$1.20
Nos. 1, 2, 3 and 4 form a collection especially suited for ordinary use.
23963 Red Hexagon, Nos. 1, 2, 3, 4, 5.............$0.75

23964 Artists' Pencil, with Siberian lead, double pointed. Each..$0.35
23965 Artists' Pencil, with Siberian lead, single pointed. Each.............................. .25

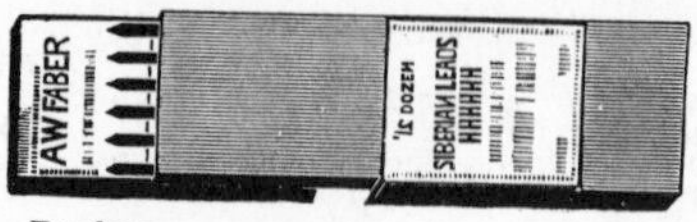

23966 Siberian Leads, 6 in box, No. 2 B to 6 H.
Per box...$0.65
23967 Regular Leads, 6 in box, No. 1 to 5.
Per box.. .35
Leads in boxes are not assorted.

L. & C. Hardtmuth's Lead Pencils.

Leads, Colored Pencils and Chalk.

L. & C. Hardtmuth are the oldest and largest pencil manufacturers in the world.
23970 "Koh-i-Noor," Nos. B, H B, F, H, 2 H, 3 H, 4 H, 5 H, 6 H. Per doz...............................$1.25
Every dozen done up separately in a box.
By a new process of manufacture the graphite assumes a highly compressed form, which secures for it remarkable lasting qualities, the pencil point remaining sharp for a surprisingly long time. For the draftsman and others, where the preservation of a fine point is of importance, the Koh-i-Noor pencils and leads will be found invaluable.
23971 Hardtmuth's Red Hexagon, Nos. B, H B, F, H, 2 H, 3 H, 4 H. Per doz............................$0.75
23972 Artists' Pencil, with Koh-i-Noor lead, double pointed Each.............. .35
23973 Artists' Pencil, with Koh-i-Noor lead, single pointed. Each........................ .25
23974 Koh-i-Noor Leads, 6 in box; Nos. H B, 4 H, 6 H. Per box........................ .65
23975 L. & C. Hardtmuth's Wax Crayons, in wood; No. 90 Yellow; No. 52 Orange Chrome; No. 57 Raw Sienna; No. 60 Vandyke Brown; No. 63 Sepia; No. 67 Sap Green; No. 71 Light Green; No. 75 Cobalt Blue; No. 78 Dark Blue; No. 80 Violet Carmine; No. 85 Vermillion; No. 87 Rose Madder. Per doz............................ 1.20
23976 L. & C. Hardtmuth's Red Pencils. Per doz. .75
23977 L. & C. Hardtmuth's Blue Pencils.
Per dozen... .75
23978 L. & C. Hardtmuth's Red and Blue Combination Pencils. Per doz...................... .75
23980 L. & C. Hardtmuth's Round Lumber Crayons, Black. Per doz.................. .60
23981 L. & C. Hardtmuth's Round Lumber Crayons, Blue Per doz.................... .60
23982 L. & C. Hardtmuth's Round Lumber Crayons, Red. Per doz........................ .75

Steel Pens for Drawing.

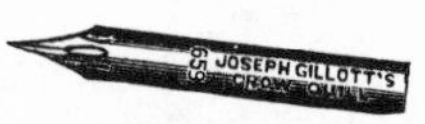

23983 Gillott's Crow Quills, on cards with holder. Per card of 1 doz..................$0.60

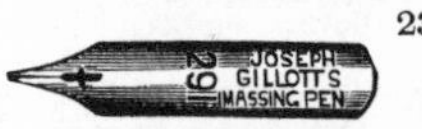

23984 Gillott's Mapping Pens, on cards, with holder. Per card of 1 doz......$0.60

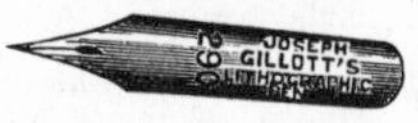

23985 Gillott's Lithographic Pens, on cards, with holder.
Per card of 1 doz.....$0.60

The Improved Pantograph.

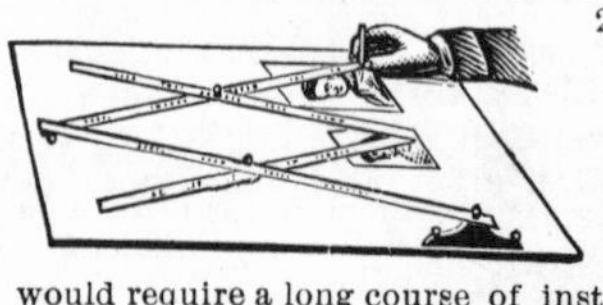

23986 The Improved Pantograph is a simple mechanical apparatus made of hardwood, enabling any person to do at once that which would require a long course of instruction and practice to accomplish in the usual way. Photographs may be made in drawing to life size. Music, engravings, maps, ornamental designs, fancy letters, monograms and patterns may be enlarged to any required size by the use of this convenient instrument. Price, each..............$0.20
Per dozen.. 2.00
23987 Improved Pantograph, higher grade, brass mounted, movable point, an elbow joint pencil holder, divisions in figures. Price, each. .85
23988 Hardwood Pantograph, with brass wheel and elbow, joint pencil holder, movable point, polished black figures, arms 17 inches long with 49 holes, numbered. Put up in a neat box.
Each.. 1.60
23989 Conte's Genuine French Pantograph, for enlarging, reducing or copying any design.
Whatever difficulties may be presented by a complicated design, the Conte Pantograph can reproduce it in a very few minutes; on account of its simplicity and its utility it has been adopted by many engineers of all countries.
Made of finely polished hardwood, with nickel plated screws and trimmings. Divided into millimetres
Each, with full directions...........................$2.00

Carbon Paper.

23990 Black Transfer Carbon Impression Paper, for drawing or painting, for outlining work of every description on any surface desired. Nos. 23990 to 23992 papers are prepared on one side only, and are not intended for manifold use.

Size, 10x15. Per sheet	$0.05
Per dozen	.50
Per quire	.90
23991 Size, 20x30. Per sheet	.15
Per dozen	1.20
Per quire	2.30

23992 Transfer Carbon Impression Papers, in colors, red, blue, green, yellow, brown and white. Size, 11x18.

Per sheet	.09
Per dozen	.85
Per quire	1.60

23993 Transfer Carbon Impression Paper, prepared on *both* sides for manifold use. Made in *black* only. Sizes, 20x30.

Per sheet	.20
Per dozen	2.00
Per quire	3.50

Drawing Paper in Sheets.

WHATMAN'S HAND-MADE.

The Whatman paper differs in surface as follows, viz.:

C. P. signifies "COLD PRESSED," and has a slightly grained surface; used for general drawings and finely finished water color drawings.

H. P. signifies "HOT PRESSED," and has a smooth surface; mostly used for very fine drawings and pen-and-ink sketches.

R. signifies "ROUGH," and has a coarsely grained surface; used for very bold drawing and water color work (Torchon paper).

In ordering please specify which surface is desired, C. P., H. P. or R.

We furnish all sizes of Whatman's papers, but we list only the following ones, because they are most profitable to buy, as they are made of heavier paper, and cost no more in proportion to size than the smaller sheets; we cut the sheets up if desired, thus furnishing small sheets of heavier paper.

24000 Whatman's with H. P. or C. P. surface, select quality.

	Per quire.
Imperial, 22x30 inches	$2.75
Double Elephant, 27x40 inches	5.00

24001 Whatman's with R. surface, selected best quality (Torchon paper).

	Per quire.
Imperial, 22x30 inches	$3.15
Double Elephant, 27x40 inches	5.40

24002 Whatman's extra heavy, with surface as below, selected quality.

	Quire.	Sheet.
Imperial, 22x30, H. P., C. P. or R.	$ 7.25	$0.35
Double Elephant, 27x40, C., P. or R.	10.75	.50

24003 "Napoleon Cold Pressed" Drawing Paper. Smooth surface. For water color and pen-and-ink work.
Double Elephant, 27x40. Per quire $4.50

24004 "Lincoln" Drawing Paper. Slightly grained surface. Principally used for architectural drawings.
Double Elephant, 27x40. Per quire 3.00

24005 "Lessing" Drawing Paper Smooth surface for line work in ink or pencil, very tough. Much used for mechanical and civil engineers' drawings and surveyors' maps.
Double Elephant, 27x40. Per quire 3.00

DRAWING PAPER IN SHEETS.

24006 Standard Drawing Paper especially adapted for colleges and schools.

		Per quire
Cap	14x17 inches	$0.25
Demy	15x20 inches	.40
Medium	17x22 inches	.55
Royal	19x24 inches	.75
Imperial	22x30 inches	1.00
Double Elephant	27x40 inches	2.00

24007 "Cream" Drawing Paper. For description see No. 24009.
Double Elephant, 27x40 in. Per quire 2.00

24008 Patent Office Bristol Board, plain, 10x15 inches. Per dozen ..... .50

24009 "Ivory White" Bristol Board. For pen-and-ink drawings.

	Per Sheet
20x30 inches	$0.25
30x40 inches	.40

Drawing Paper in Rolls.

24010 "Orion" Detail Paper, cold pressed, is expressly made for drafting purposes, of selected stock, with slightly grained surface. It stands erasing to fair extent, and will take India ink and pencil well.

	Per roll of 100 yards. Med.	Thick.	Per roll of 10 yards. Med.	Thick.
36 in. wide	$4.00	$4.50	$0.50	$0.60
42 in. wide	4.50	5.50	.60	.70
48 in. wide	5.25	6.75	.70	.80
54 in. wide	6.00	8.00	.80	1.00

24011 "Teuton" Detail Drawing Paper, white, extremely tough, will not break in folding, with best erasing quality and suitable for pencil, ink and color work. Only done up in rolls of 25, 50 and 100 yards length; 36 or 62 inches wide.

	Per 100 yds.	Per 50 yds.	Per 25 yds.
36 in. wide	$ 9.00	$ 4.75	$ 2.50
62 in. wide	13.50	7.00	3.75

24012 Cream Drawing Paper. Is the finest paper in the market for preliminary and general drawing and sketching. It will stand erasing perfectly, and will take ink, pencil and water color well. Unlike other papers of similar kind, it will not break in folding. Its cream tint is agreeable to the eye, and will admit of much handling without soiling.

	Per 100 yds.	Per 25 yds.	Per yd.
21 in. wide	$ 6.00	$1.75	$0.08
36 in. wide	10.50	3.00	.15
42 in. wide	14.25	4.00	.20
62 in. wide	17.50	5.00	.25

Drawing Paper—Continued.

24013 "Silver Gray" Drawing Paper. Its pleasing tint sets drawings off to advantage. Has excellent erasing quality, and is of superior stock. In rolls of about 35-40 lbs., 25c per lb.

	Per 100 yds.	50 yds.	25 yds.	Per yd.
27 in. wide	$ 8.00	$ 4.25	$ 2.25	$ 0.10
36 in. wide	10.50	5.50	3.00	.15
62 in. wide	17.50	9.25	5.00	25

24014 "Standard" Drawing Paper. Is a strong white paper, excellent erasing properties, with slightly grained surface, suitable for work in ink, pencil and color.

	Per 50 yds.	Per 25 yds.	Per yd.
27 in. wide	$ 5.60	$3.00	$0.15
36 in. wide	7.20	4.00	.20
42 in. wide	8.75	4.75	.24
62 in. wide	14.25	7.40	.35

24015 "Super Super Egg Shell" Drawing Paper. It is made of the best paper stock. Owing to its peculiar surface, drawings made upon it show up most effectively. Unsurpassed for perspective drawing and water color work.

	Per 25 yds.	Per 10 yds.	Per yd.
36 in. wide	$ 6.75	$2.85	$0.33
42 in. wide	7.50	3.25	.36
58 in. wide	9.75	4.20	.47

24016 Super Super Cold Pressed Drawing Paper. Is made of the same stock as the preceding and differs from it only in the surface, which is cold pressed or medium smooth.

	Per 25 yards.	Per 10 yds.	Per yd.
36 in. wide	$ 6.75	$2.85	$0.32
42 in. wide	7.50	3.25	.36
58 in. wide	9.75	4.20	.47

Mounted Roll Drawing Papers.

For maps and other valuable drawings made to last, that should not tear or break by much hadling or folding, the following papers mounted on muslin will be best adapted.

24020 "Standard" Mounted. The same paper as described under 24014.

	10 yds.	Yard.
36 in. wide	$ 6.50	$0.80
42 in. wide	7.30	.90
56 in. wide	10.25	1.20

24021 "Super Super Eggshell," Mounted. The same paper as described under 24015.

	10 yds.	Yard.
36 in. wide	$ 7.85	$1.00
42 in. wide	8.85	1.10
58 in. wide	11.75	1.40

24022 "Super Super Cold Pressed," Mounted. The same paper as described under 24016.

	10 yds.	Yard.
36 in. wide	$ 7.85	$1.00
42 in. wide	8.85	1.10
58 in. wide	11.75	1.40

Tracing Cloth and Tracing Paper.

24023 "Imperial" Tracing Cloth, one side glazed, the other dull.

	Per roll of 24 yards.	Per yard.
30 in. wide	$ 6 90	$0.35
36 in. wide	7.60	40
42 in. wide	10.50	.50

24025 Tracing Parchment, a strong, transparent "German" paper for pencil or ink.

Size, 20x30. Per sheet	$0.05
Per quire	.85
Size, 30x40. Per sheet	.10
Per quire	1.80

24026 "Vegetable" Tracing Paper.

	Per quire.
Cap. 13x17 inch	$0.90
Royal, 19x25 inch	2.00
Imperial, 22x28 inch	2.50

24027 "Orion" Detail Tracing Paper for pencil.
40 in. wide, per roll of 100 yards 2.50
48 in. wide, per roll of 100 yards 3.25

24028 "Advance" Tracing Paper, medium thick.
42 in. wide. Per roll of 20 yds. 1.50

24030 "Natural" Tracing Paper. Unglazed. The best for detail or full size tracings.

	Per roll of 44 yds.	22 yds.
54 in. wide	$5.00	$2.50

24031 "Natural" Tracing and Sketching Paper.
62 in. wide, per roll of 50 yds $3.50

24032 "Parchment" Tracing Paper. Thin, most suitable for tracing from blue prints.
42 in. wide. Per roll of 20 yards $2.00

24033 "Parchment" Tracing Paper, very fine, medium thick.
37 in. wide. Per roll of 20 yards 3.25

Blue Print Paper.

PREPARED READY FOR USE.

Are freshly made when ordered, and will not spoil in several months if properly kept. See metal tubes, No. 24039. The Hyperion Parchment Blue Print Papers are the toughest in the market. They will keep the best and make the finest prints.

24035 "Hyperion Satin," medium thick.

Width	27 in.	30 in.	36 in	42 in.
Prepared, per roll of 10 yds	$1.15	$1.25	$1.40	$1.60
Prepared, per roll of 50 yds	4.00	4.25	4.90	5.25

24036 "Hyperion Parchment," medium thick.

Width	24 in.	30 in.	36 in.	42 in.
Prepared, per roll of 10 yds	$1.30	$1.50	$1.60	$1.80
Prepared, per roll of 50 yds	4.50	5.25	6.00	6.75

24037 "Hyperion Cloth."
Prepared, per roll of 10 yds., 36 in. wide 3.75
Prepared, per roll of 10 yds., 42 in. wide 4.75

Blue Print Paper—Continued.

24038 "White Hyperion Erasing Fluid" for making alterations and additions on blue print.
Per bottle $0.25

24039 Air Tight Metal Tubes for keeping cut rolls of prepared blue print paper dark and dry, and also well adapted for the safe keeping of valuable plans and tracings.
38 in. long, 4 in. diam., holding 50 to 100 yds ... 1.50
42 in. long, 4 in. diam. holding 50 to 100 yds .. 2.00

24040 Blue Print Frames made of hardwood, with brass mountings, cushions and thick frames.

	Polished plate glass.	Frame only.
20x24 in.	$9.75	$6.00
24x30 in.	12.00	8.00
28x36 in.	16.25	10.00
30x42 in.	21.60	12.40
36x50 in.	40.00	19.75

Profile Papers.

24041 "Perfect" Profile Paper, plate A. Printed in orange or green, 22 in. wide, in rolls of 50 yards. Per yard $0.30
When ordering please state color.

24042 "Perfect" Profile Paper, plate B. Printed in orange or green, 22 in. wide, in rolls of 50 yds. Per yd $0.30

Stereoscopes.

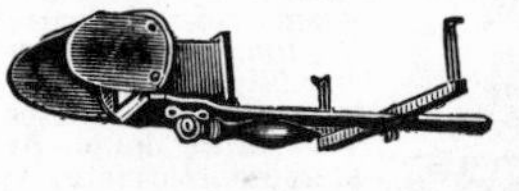

4045 Stereoscope, oiled mahogany with polished hood and good glasses, folding handle.
Each $0.25
Per dozen $2 75

24046 Stereoscope, oiled cherry, with polished cherry hood; folding handle, glasses warranted to focus. Each $0.40
Per doz 4.00

	Each.	Per doz.
24047 Stereoscopes, frame of black walnut, oil finish, hood of rosewood, polished. Extra quality lens, folding handle	$0.75	$7.50
24048 Stereoscopes, frame and hood polished gray satinwood, polished nickel trimmings, folding handle finely polished, 1½ inch lenses	1.25	
24049 Stereoscopes, frame and hood, of polished tulip wood, polished nickel trimmings, folding handle finely polished, 1½ inch lenses	1.25	

24050 Stereoscope, plush covered, satin lined hood, high grade lenses, collapsing frame of rosewood and nickel, folding nickel handle.
Each $2.00

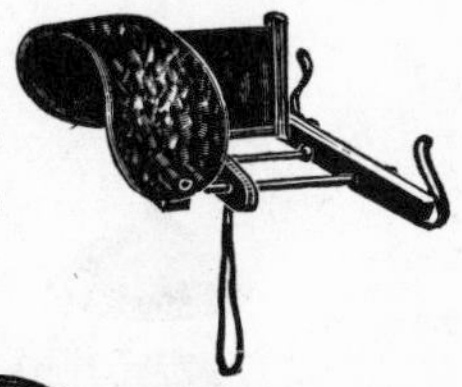

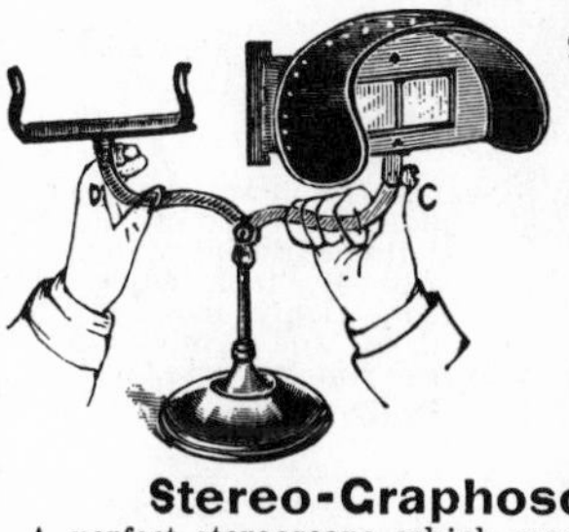

24051 Folding Stereoscope with stand, plush covered hood, satin lined. The folding frame is of rosewood and nickel, high grade lenses, and instrument folds into very compact form. Highly polished nickel stand
Each $3.25

Stereo-Graphoscopes.

A perfect stereoscope, which may be changed to a graphoscope, for looking at photographs and single pictures by reversing the lenses.
Weight, 14 to 18 ounces. each.

Fig. 1.

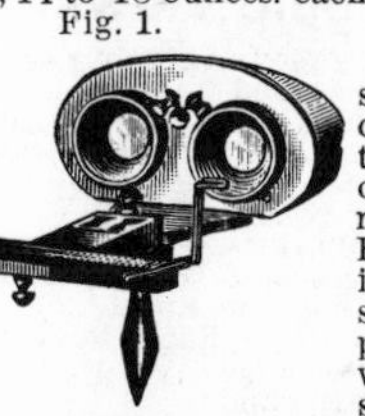

When the lenses are set so the small knobs on the eye pieces touch the knob in the center of holder, the instrument is stereoptic, as in Fig. 1; when using this instrument as a stereoscope, always place the picture between the wires and adjust the sliding picture holder to get the proper focus.

Fig. 2.

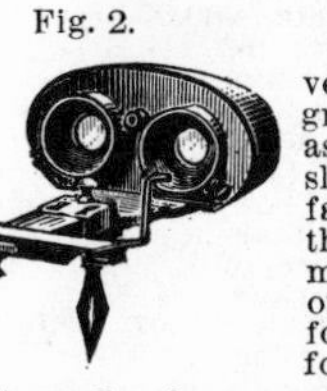

When the lenses are reversed as in Fig. 2, it is graphoscopic. When using as a graphoscope, shut the sliding picture holder up as far as it will go; then hold the picture in the hand and move to the right or left, up or down, to get the proper focus. Clean the lense before using.

	Each.	Per doz.
24052 Stereo-Graphoscopes, oiled cherry, with polished cherry hood, screw handle	$0.50	$5.40
24053 Stereo-Graphoscopes. oiled cherry, with polished cherry hood, large lenses in polished frames, folding handles	.85	9.00

Stereo-Graphoscopes—Continued.

24054 Stereo-Graphoscope, made of varnished sycamore, with polished walnut stand, nickel eyelets and 4-inch lens. Upper lens for viewing photographs, engravings or any single view; lower lens for looking at stereoscopic or double views. Extreme height, 15 in.; length of sliding adjustment, bar, for focus, 10 in.; weight, 1½ pounds.
Price, each............$2.50

24055 Stereo-Graphoscope, polished mahogany, same size as above, but with nickel, weighted stand and eyelets, 4-inch lens. Weight, 3 pounds.
Price, each........$3.50

24056 Stereo-Graphoscope made of polished oak, with nickel trimmings folding box form; size when closed, 8x10x3½ inches. Has sliding form adjustment, fine stereoscopic lenses for viewing double or stereoscoptic pictures, and 4½ in. graphoscope lens for viewing photographs or other single pictures. Weight, 4½ lbs.
Each....... $7.75

24057 Stereo-Graphoscope with patent collapsing focusing frame. Stereoscope hood is of seal leather, satin lined, frame and stand of highly polished nickel. On opposite end of frame from stereoscope is placed a 4½ inch nickel mounted graphoscopic lens, which can be removed when desired. This is a very beautiful instrument and is extremely ornamental as well as useful. Weight, 5½ lbs. Price...$8.25

24058 Graphoscope. Very highly finished in nickel, sliding telescope movement with 4½ inch adjustable lens, richly mounted in nickel and revolving on a heavy nickel base. Weight, 2¼ lbs. Price.... . $4.00

Stereoscopic Views.

NOTE.—All Stereoscopic Views, are our assortment. We can not fill orders for special subjects.
Postage on views, 6 cents to 9 cents per dozen.
Special prices will be made for large quantities of stereoscopic views or stereoscopes. State quantities wanted when writing for prices
For Stereoscopic View Baskets, see index.
Medium Quality Stereoscopic Views, mounted on light weight, tinted card board mounts.

	Each.	Per dz.	Per 100
24060 Stereoscopic Views, large assortment of American and Foreign Landscapes. Plain.	$0.05	$0.40	$3.00
24061 Stereoscopic Views of Yellowstone Park and Western Sporting Scenes. Plain.	.05	.45	3.50
24062 Stereoscopic Views, a fine assortment of Chicago Park and Boulevard Scenes. Plain.	.05	.50	4.00
24063 Stereoscopic Views, Scandinavian Scenery. Pictures of interesting places in Norway, Sweden and Denmark. Plain..	.07	.60	4.00
24064 Stereoscopic Views. English Group Series. Interesting and amusing subjects. Plain..	.07	.65	5.00
24065 Stereoscopic Views, Group Series. Pictures of children, comic scenes, etc, *handsomely colored*	.07	70	5.00
24066 Stereoscopic Views, handsomely colored, American and Foreign Landscapes............	.07	.75	5.00

Stereoscopic Views—Continued.

Artistic Series, first quality Stereoscopic Views, mounted on extra heavy cardboard. Mounts of large size.

	Each.	Pr dz.	Pr 100
24070 Stereoscopic Views, a fine assortment of American landscapes, principal cities, Mackinaw Island, etc.........	$0.08	$0.75	$5.00
24071 Stereoscopic Views, from original negatives of exciting sporting scenes. Duck shooting, deer hunting, canoeing and camping. Plain..............	.09	.95	7.60
24072 Stereoscopic Views, Pictures of places of interest in Chicago. A fine assortment of park and boulevard scenes. Plain.....................	.10	1.00	7.75
24073 Stereoscopic Views, a superior line of views of the Dells of the Wisconsin River and Niagara Falls, from original negatives. Plain...................	.10	1.00	7.75
24074 Stereoscopic Views, a fine assortment of views of Florida and Alaskan landscapes Plain.................	.10	1.00	7.75
24075 Stereoscopic Views of the ruins of the Johnstown, Pa. and Conemaugh Valley disaster. The greatest casualty in American history. Plain............	.10	1.00	7.75
24076 Stereoscopic Views, Yellowstone National Park and scenes along the Hudson. New Series, finely finished. Plain...	.10	1.00	7.75
24077 Stereoscopic Views, very choice series of American landscapes, finely finished and handsomely colored................	.10	1.00	7.75
24078 Stereoscopic Views, finest artistic series published; choice landscapes, mounted on best card board mounts and artistically colored........	.15	1.50	10.00
24079 Stereoscopic Views, a choice assortment of the best subjects of the "White City," World's Fair Stereoscopic Views that are well mounted and first quality finish...................	.10	1.00	7.75
24080 Stereoscopic Views of seven subjects—Caravals "Columbus Fleet," Spain's Exhibit to World's Fair; artistic; size, 4½x7 inches...................	.15	Per set....	.90

Graphoscopic Views.

24081 World's Fair Photographic Views of *special value.* We offer an assortment of 42 subjects, 8x 10, mounted, first class photographs of exceptional fine subjects, both interior and exterior views of the World's Columbian Exposition. These photographs are worth three times what we ask for them. We will also include what we have left of 20 cent views, also cabinet size. "Cold Storage" fire and "Ferris wheel" photographs. Price, assorted, per dozen.............$1.00

24081½ World's Fair Photographs, 18x22, mounted. Six subjects. Fine selection for framing or hanging up as they are. We offer these large pictures at less than half their value. Our price, each, $0.40. Per set................$2.00

24081¾ Chicago Views, about seventy-five subjects, all first-class work; new interesting photographs of Chicago Parks, Boulevards, Public Buildings, Street Scenes, Stock Yards, Pullman Views and Reproduction of Works of Art and Statuary from the Art Institute. Size of photos, 6x8 inches. Each, unmounted for album, No.
2456.................................$0.35
Per dozen.............................. 3.60
Each, mounted on 10x12 card mounts.......... .40
Per dozen.............................. 4.20

Card and Cabinet Photographs.

All photographs are our own selections. We do not fill orders for specific subjects.
24082 Cabinet size Photographs of actresses, good finish, assorted. Each............................$0.05
Per dozen..... .... .50
24083 Cabinet size Photographs, comic subjects, very amusing. Each........................... .06
Per dozen........................... .60
24084 Cabinet size Photographs, taken from life, of prominent actresses of the vaudeville stage, in full costume, extra finish and mounted on super-calendered cards. Each.................... .15
Per dozen........................... 1.50
24085 Cabinet size Photographs of Celebrities of the theatrical world. These photos are gems of art in every respect and equal the productions of the leading photographers of the country. A large and choice selection of subjects. Each $0.25
Per dozen............................... 2.50
Postage on cabinet photographs, 7 cents per dozen.
24086 Card Photographs, large assortment of actresses. Per dozen........................... .15
Per 100.. 1.00
Postage 3 cents per dozen.

Aneroid Barometers.
(For Farmers, Horticulturists, etc.)

Directions for reading accompany each barometer. Barometers must be carefully handled and adjusted; they are delicate instruments and should not be handled by anyone who does not know how to use them.

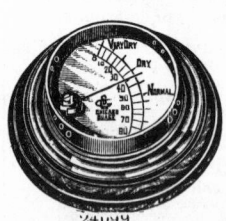

24087 Aneroid Barometer, nickel plated case, open face, card dial, diameter 2¾ inches, weight, 7 oz. Each....................$1.75
24088 Aneroid Barometer, nickel plated case, open face, card dial; diameter, 4 inches; weight, 10 oz. Each....................$3.25
24089 Universal Aneroid Barometer, closed porcelain dial, accurate and reliable, bronze finished case, 5 inch dial, weight, 1 lb. Each..................$6.00
24090 Aneroid Barometer, polished brass case, 5½ inch diameter, silvered metal dial with aperture in center exposing working parts of instrument, Fahrenheit thermometer and beveled edge plate glass cover. A beautiful and accurate instrument in velvet-lined case; weight, 2 lbs. Price..........$12.00
24091 Holosteric Aneroid Barometer, same general description as above, but 8 inches in diameter, and supplied with two thermometers, Fahrenheit and Centigrade, weight in velvet lined case, 4½ lbs. Price......$18.00
24092 "Standard" Aneroid Barometer, carved wood frame, 31 in. long, porcelain dial, 8 inches in diameter, opal plate glass thermometer, beveled edge, 10 in. long, weight, 10 lbs. Price.....$20.00

24092

24093 Mercurial Barometer and Thermometer. Extra heavy tube mounted in polished oak frames. Scales are black oxidized metal and divisions are in white lines and figures. Length, about 40 inches. Price.........................$5.00

Pocket Aneroid and Altitude Barometers.

24094 Pocket Aneroid Barometer, compensated for temperature and reading to 16,000 feet for altitude. This may be used for measuring height as well as foretelling the weather. Nickel, watch size, 1⅞ in. diameter, metal dial, open face, put up in plush-lined morocco case. Weight, 4½ ounces.
Each.................................$9.50
24095 Pocket Aneroid Barometer, compensated for temperature and reading to 16,000 feet altitude. Brass open face, metal dial, covered with heavy beveled glass; size, 1⅞ in.; put in neat morocco case, silk lined. Each........ 14.00
Weight, 4 ounces.
24096 Pocket Aneroid Barometer, compensated, same general description as preceding; special finish, extra size, 2½ in. diameter, with beveled altitude scale, reading to 16,000 feet. Weight, 7 ounces.
Each.. ....$17.00

Moisture Gauge.

24098 Moisture Gauge or Hygrometer for determining the humidity of the atmosphere or percentage of moisture in the air. Used out of doors or in the house. and in incubators. Moisture gauge, with metal back.
Each.................$0.90
Postage.............. .05
24099 Moisture Gauge mounted on wooden base. Each......... 1.25
Postage............. .10

24099

24100 German Hygrometer, brass case, card dial. This instrument is guaranteed accurate. measure, 2¼ in. diameter, weight, 4 ounces, suitable to use in connection with our Incubator Thermometer.
Price, each...........$1.75
24101 German Hygrometer, nickel case card dial, 3¼ inch diameter and mounted on 6 inch wood base, making handsome instrument. Weight, 8 ounces.
Price, each..........$2.25

24100

THE PROOF OF THE PUDDING is in the asking for more.

The Fact That Our Customers Trade with Us Year After Year
Speaks for Itself.

There is Economy in the "Mail Order Business."

Thermometers.

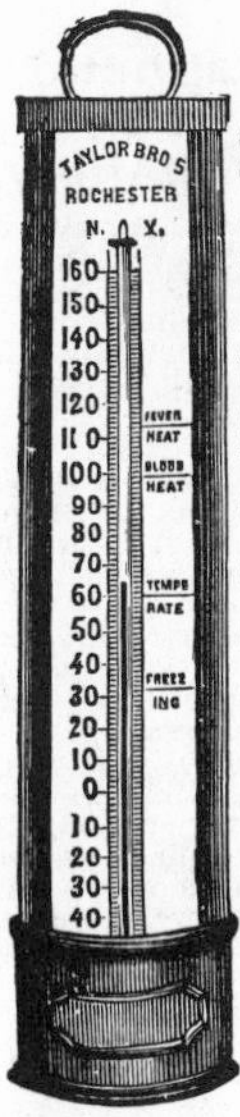

NOTE.—Thermometers *should not* be shipped by mail. We *cannot* be responsible for breakage.

Thermometers, japanned tin case, tested tubes of standard size and reliable for ordinary use. Packed half dozen in wood box. The 8-inch and 10-inch are mercury instruments with range from about 20 below zero to about 120 above. The 12-inch are spirit with scale reading down to 30 to 50 below zero.

24105 Length, 8 inches. Each...$0.25
    Per dozen.........................2.50
24106 Length, 10 inches. Each....35
    Per dozen.........................3.50
24107 Length, 12 inches. Each....45
    Per dozen.........................4.50
24108 Thermometers, Standard, with *seasoned tubes*, tested and graduated with *special* care as to accuracy. Scale tubes and case extra heavy, mounted with bright metal clasps. No better or more accurate thermometers can be made. Signal service flag stamped on face of each as a guarantee of correctness. Length, 10 inches.
    Each.......................$0.90
24109 Length, 12 inches.
    Each..............................1.15
24110 Length, 14 inches.
    Each..............................1.50

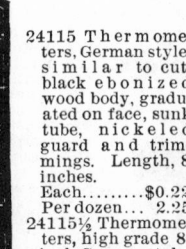

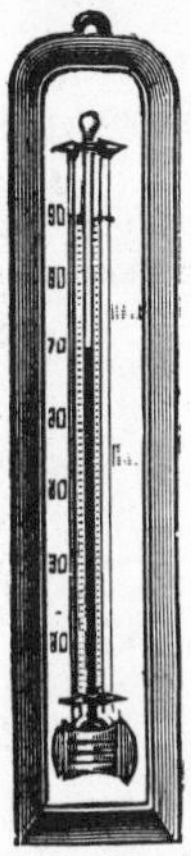

24111 Standard House Thermometer, with 8-inch metal scale. mounted on solid oak back and graduated in large figures and degrees, reading from 30 to 90 above zero. Magnifying tube filled with red fluid making a most desirable and accurate instrument specially adapted for indoor use.
    Price.........................$1.10

24112 Thermometer, same design as above, except has 8-inch metal scale graduated from 20 degrees below to 120 degrees above zero; standard mercury, white back tube, and is practice for either indoor or outdoor use.
    Price...................... $0.85

24113 Same style as above, with 10 inch scale, graduated from 30 below to 120 degrees above zero.
    Price, each.....................$1.20

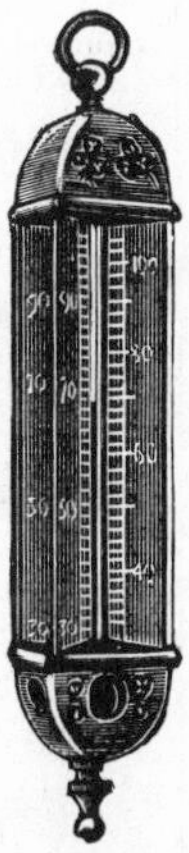

24114 Radial Scale Thermometer, designed to be suspended by an accompanying chain and snap; can be read at a distance from every side of the room. Handsome oxidized metal frame and scale graduated in large figures and degrees, reading from 30 to 100 degrees above zero. Bulb is filled with red fluid and protected on all sides.
Price.............................$1.25

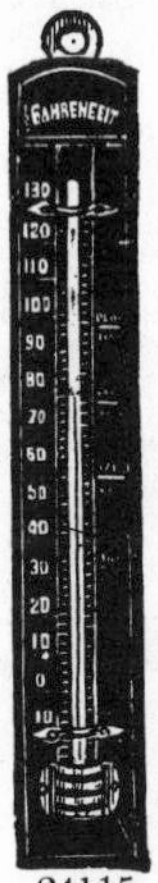

24115 Thermometers, German style, similar to cut, black ebonized wood body, graduated on face, sunk tube, nickeled guard and trimmings. Length, 8 inches.
    Each..........$0.22
    Per dozen... 2.25
24115½ Thermometers, high grade 8-inch, German style, oval top, boxwood finish, magnifying mercury, filled sunken tube, graduation plain in double degrees. Reliable for either indoor or out of door use.
    Price, each..$0.44
24116 Window Thermometers, 10 inch cylinder glass with porcelain scale, nickel arms, accurate, convenient and good value.
    Each.................$0.90
24117 Window Thermometer, heavy plate glass figured, annealed, polished beveled edges with brass supports to hold thermometer several inches from the wall or sash. A superb and accurate instrument; 10 inches.
Price, each.............$1.50

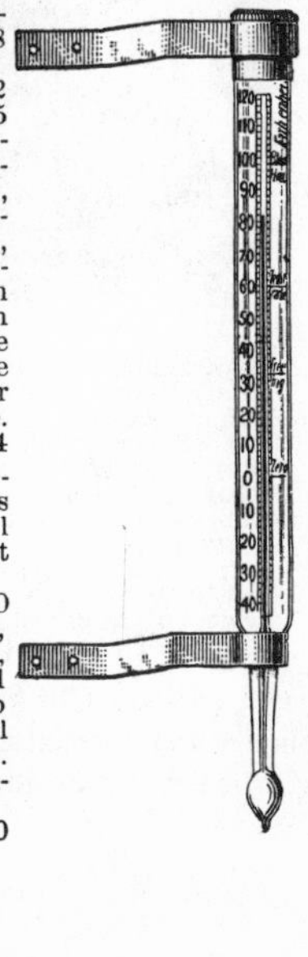

Thermometers—Continued.

24118 Metal Frame Vestibule Thermometers, filigree pattern, neat finish. Entire length, 11 inches. Graduated 8-inch metal scale with brass guard over bulb.
    Price.... $0.75
24119 Standard Metal Frame Thermometer, filigree design, neat finish. A handsome mantle ornament. Has heavy beveled edge 8-inch metal scale with etched graduation and burnished brass guard over bulb.

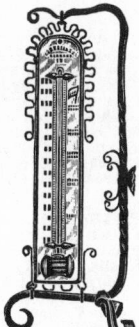

24119

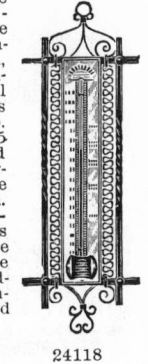

24118

Entire length, 11½ in. Price.............$1.50

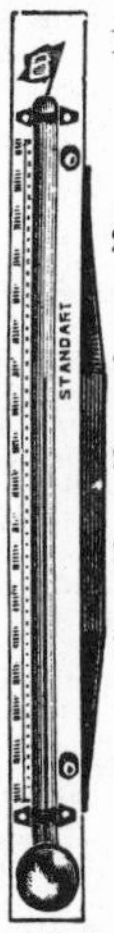

Registering Thermometers.

24120 U. S. Signal Service Standard Thermometers, 12 inches long, with brass insulating strap to fasten in position. Degrees etched on metal seal. Each.....................$2.50
24121 Same size and style as above, but minimum self-registering thermometer.
    Each $3.50
24122 Same size and style as 24092, but maximum self-acting thermometer
    Each $3.50
24123 Minimum Thermometer, very accurate, registers to 50 degrees below zero.
    Each $1.60
24124 Minimum Thermometer, 10 in. boxwood, self-registering, accurate and good value, scale reading from 40 below to 120 above zero. Each........................$0.85

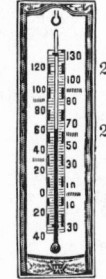

Distance Thermometers.

Unequaled for convenience, accuracy and fine appearance. The term Distance Thermometer is applied for the reason that by using large, distinct figures printed in black, gold or silver and alternating them either side of the scale, the temperature can be read at a glance at a distance of from 12 to 30 feet.

24125 Distance Thermometer, enameled metal, black figures, japan case. Size, 2x9 inches.
    Price.....................$0.22
24126 Distance Thermometer, black enameled plate, white figures, mounted on bevel edged back of highly polished wood. Size, 2½x9 inches.
    Price....................$0.65

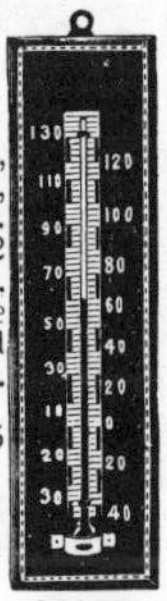

24125   22126

Chemical and Clinical Thermometers.

24130 Solid Glass Chemical Thermometers, graduations etched on tube or porcelain scale up to 300 degrees and 600 degrees. Each.............$2.00
24131 Clinical Thermometers, self-registering, 4 inches, in neat hard rubber case, straight pattern, with bulb. Very accurate. Each.......... 1.00
24132 Clinical Thermometers, self-registering, 4 inch, in black enameled case with gilt band, safety chain and clasp. Cannot be lost out of pocket. A clinical certificate for accuracy accompanies each thermometer. Each............ 2.00

Pocket Thermometers.

24133 Pocket Thermometer, accurate and convenient, mounted in imitation cigar.
    Price, each........ $0.25
    Per dozen............ 2.70
Brewers', Confectioners,' Evaporating, Chemical Incubating and Angle Thermometers furnished at lowest prices.

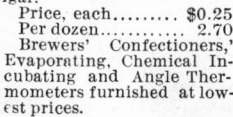

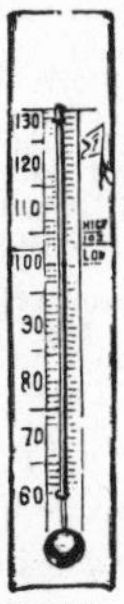

Incubating Thermometers.

24134 Incubating Thermometer, with graduated metal scale, 6 inches. Very sensitive and accurate. Each.$0.50
    Per dozen...................... 5.00
NOTE.—See quotation of No. 24089-92. Moisture Gauges.
NOTE—4½-inch Incubator Thermometer furnished in same style and price as the 6-inch.

24134

Dairy Thermometers.

24135 Churn Thermometers, with flanged scale tested at 62° for churning, and graduated from 30 to 90 degrees.
    Each.................$0.15
    Per dozen.......... 1.50
24136 Dairy Thermometers, with flange (see cut). For general dairy use; 8-inch.
    Each.................$0.15
    Per dozen.......... 1.50
    10-inch, each..... .20
    Per dozen.......... 2.25
24137 All Glass Thermometers for dairy use, also suitable for bath and weather purposes.
    Each.................$0.25
    Per dozen.......... 2.00
24138 All Glass Standard Floating Dairy Thermometer, a new and superior instrument; 9 inches long, with swell tube, so that thermometer floats upright.
    Price, each........$0.50
    Price, per dozen 5.00....

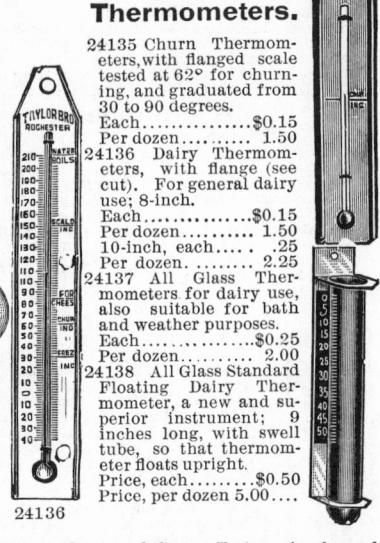

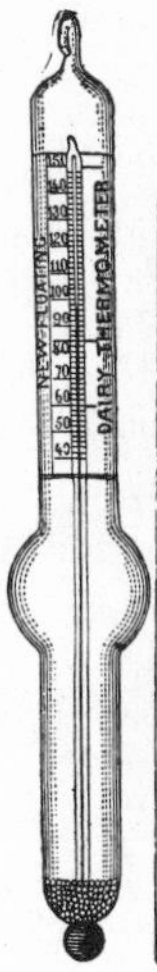

24138. 24136

24139 Brown's Improved Cream Tester, simple and practical. Each $0.25
    Per dozen.. 2.75
24140 The "Acme" All Glass Milk Tester. Hick's patent.
    Price...$0.50
Instructions for using No. 24140, Hick's Acme Milk Tester: Dip the instrument in the vessel of milk. When nearly full place the forefinger on the top to prevent the milk escaping, lift it out of the vessel and hold it up to the light. If the milk is pure the blue bead will gradually rise to the surface. If it contains water the bead will slowly sink.
NOTE—Thermometers should not be shipped by mail; we cannot be responsible for breakage.

Storm Glass and Thermometers.

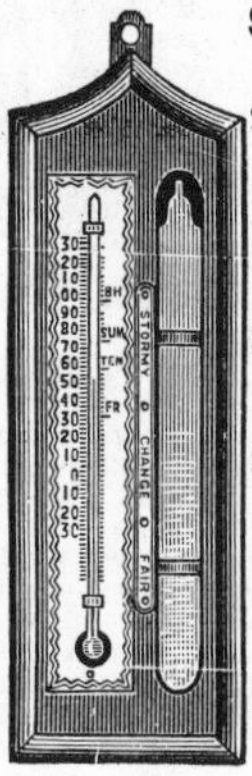

24142 Storm Glass Thermometer and Barometer combined; walnut case. Size, 3¼x9 inches. See cut. The most popular instrument of the kind ever introduced.
    Each.............................$0.20
    Per dozen........................ 2.00
24143 Polished Copper Case, Storm Glass and Thermometer, mounted with copper trimmings. Size,9x2¼ inches.
    Price, each.....................$0.50
24144 Carved Antique Oak Storm Glass, 6½-inch metal scale thermometer, and 6-inch etched bottle. Size, 10x4½ inches.
    Price, each.....................$0.90

Bath and Hot-Bed Thermometer.

24145 Bath Thermometer in square wooden frame 12 inches long. with round handle, enclosed glass cylinder thermometer 8 inches long. with Dr. Forbes' specifications of proper temperature, Price. each......$0.48
24146 Hot-Bed Thermometer; a hard wood, round 15-inch frame with handle, box wood scale, red spirit, fitted with sharp-pointed hollow brass ferrule to penetrate the soil. Indispensable to the florist or gardener.
    Price, each.........................$1.80
24147 Confectioners' Thermometer, heavy copper case, 12 inches long, accurate scale reading up to 350 or 400 degrees. Each $1.75
24148 Evaporating Thermometers, for fruit evaporating, ovens, dry kilns, etc., 10-inch flanged scale, extra heavy reading to 300 degrees and over. Each................$1.65

Lactometer.

24150 For testing the quality of milk. Of great value to dairymen and farmers determining the relative value of cows by testing their milk; showing the effects produced by changes in the animal's food—different articles of diet produce milk of different density. Fill a jar with milk, allowing it to cool to the temperature of 60 degrees, immerse the lactometer and notice marks opposite surface of milk. The marks signify as follows:
P—Pure milk.
¾—3 parts milk and one part water.
½—2 parts milk and 2 parts water.
¼—1 part milk and 3 parts water.
W—All water.
Any immediate value can be determined by the decimal scale on the opposite side, zero being water and 100 pure milk.
    Each.............$0.35. Per dozen............$3.75

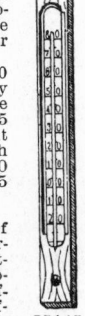

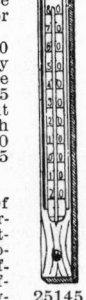

25145

Urinometers.

24151 Urinometers for determining the specific gravity of the urine; is an indicator of the condition of the same, as related to the general health. A circular accompanies each instrument, giving full instructions as to how it should be used. Urinometer, complete with jar, inclosed in round wood box. Each $0.35

Hydrometers.

24153 Can Furnish hydrometers for any of the following purposes (give name and number when ordering).

1. Acid.	9. Spirit plain.
2. Alkali.	10. Bark (for tanners).
3. Sugar and Syrup.	11. Liquids heavier than water.
4. Vinegar.	12. Liquids lighter than water.
5. Salt, 0 to 50.	13. Sacchrometers.
6. Salinometer, 0 to 100.	14 Ammonia.
7. Cider.	15. Coal Oil.
8. Shellac.	

Price of any of the above, 50c.

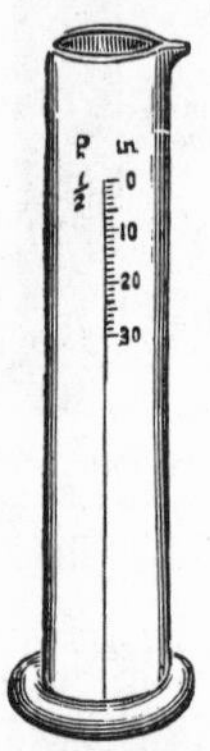

24156

24155 Hydrometer Jars, with foot and pouring spout, plain.
Height, 10 inches; diameter, 1½ inches, each $0.40
Per dozen 4.25
Height, 12 inches; diameter, 2 inches, each .... .50
Per dozen 5.00
Height, 15 inches; diameter, 2 inches, each .... .60
Per dozen 6.00
Weight, 6 to 8 ounces.

24156 Hydrometer Jars, with foot and pouring spout; engraved, degrees marked from zero to 30.
Height, 10 inches. diameter, 1½ inches, each .... .60
Per dozen 6.25
Height, 12 inches, diameter, 2 inches, each .... .75
Per dozen 7.50
Height, 15 inches, diameter, 2 inches, each .... .85
Per dozen 8.50
Weight, from 6 to 8 ounces.

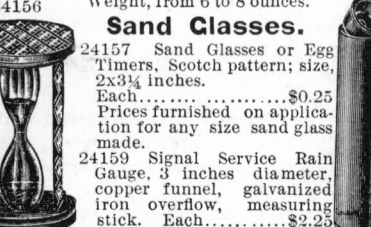

Sand Glasses.

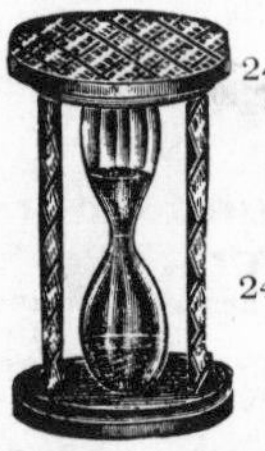

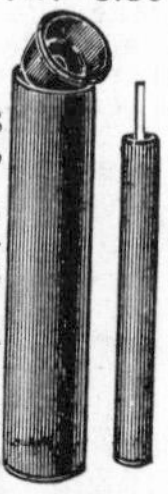

24157 Sand Glasses or Egg Timers, Scotch pattern; size, 2x3¼ inches.
Each $0.25
Prices furnished on application for any size sand glass made.

24159 Signal Service Rain Gauge, 3 inches diameter, copper funnel, galvanized iron overflow, measuring stick. Each $2.25

ELECTRICAL GOODS.

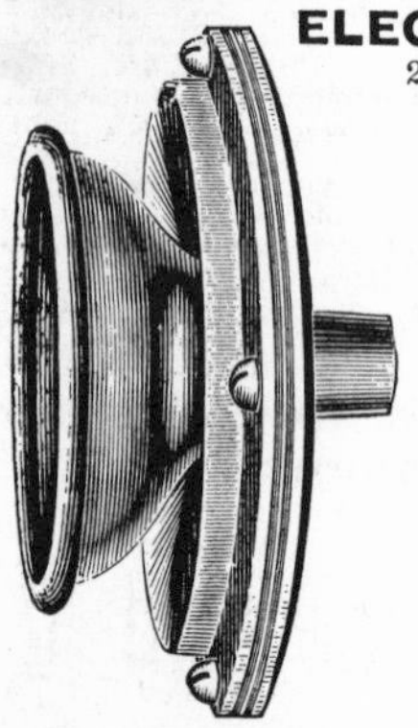

24170 The Elgin Accoustic Telephone, made wholly of metal, nickel plated, self-supporting, not even a screw to hold it in place. The telephone will work on a line ½ mile long, and is the neatest, most durable and best working mechanical telephone on the market. Telephones, per pair (2), with 200 feet wire, wire for hangers and directions for putting the phone in working order complete.
Weight, 3½ lbs $5.00

24171 Copper Wire, No. 18, for Elgin Phone, per pound (125 feet) $0.31

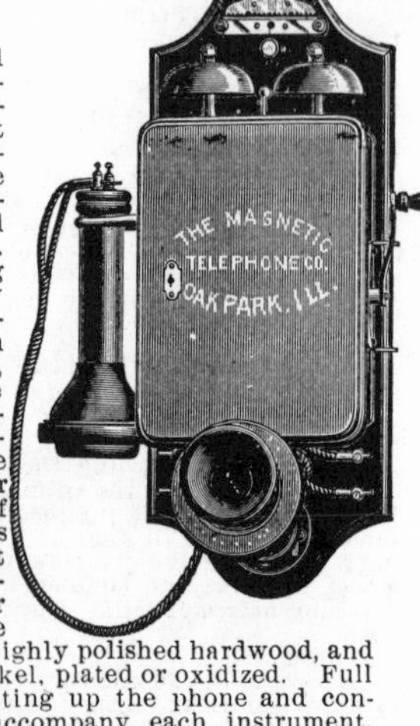

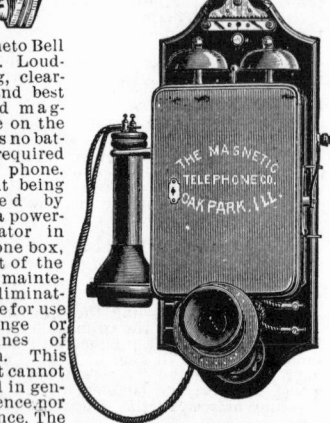

24172 Magneto Bell Telephone. Loudest talking, clearest tone and best constructed magneto phone on the market. As no batteries are required with this phone. the current being generated by means of a powerful generator in the telephone box, a large part of the expense of maintenance is eliminated. Suitable for use for exchange or private lines of any length. This instrument cannot be excelled in general excellence nor in appearance. The boxes being of highly polished hardwood, and metal parts of nickel, plated or oxidized. Full directions for putting up the phone and constructing lines accompany each instrument. Prices quoted below are for phone complete and do not include any materials for line construction. Weight, each phone, 15 lbs. Price, per phone $18.00
Price, per pair, complete for two stations 35.00
For quotations of wire, insulators, etc., see No. 24218.

Portable Electro-Medical Batteries.

These magnetic instruments are of undoubted value as the instruments through whose agency physicians effected almost miraculous cures. Our most learned doctors and physicians acknowledge their efficiency in even the worst cases of paralysis, rheumatism, neuralgia, and in fact, all nervous diseases. These machines may be used by all invalids with perfect safety. When doctors fail to effect a cure with drugs and medicines, and electricity is resorted to in the last stage of disease, even then, under such immense disadvantages, electricity often cures.

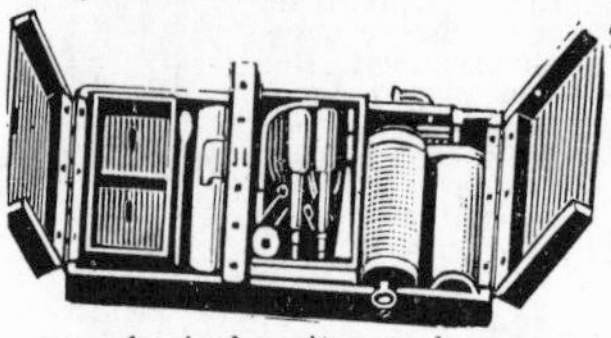

24175 Gaiffe's Battery, three currents, with silk covered conducting cords, two insulated handles, one metallic brush, one olive shaped exciter, one spherical exciter and one vial of bisulphate of mercury. In polished mahogany case, 7½x4x1¼ in. Complete, with full directions. Weight, 1¼ lbs. $7.75

24176 Gaiffe's Battery, with same size coil as in preceding, producing two currents instead of three. Mounted in single cover mahogany case, 6½x4x1¼ inches, containing two insulated handles and one vial bisulphate of mercury.
Weight, 1 pound. Each $6.25

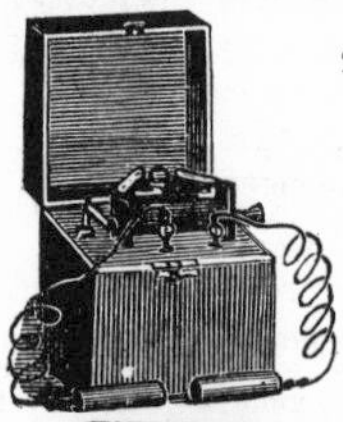

24177 The Crown Family Battery. The merits of this battery will be easily appreciated as possessing neatness of design and simplicity of operating. A pleasant and uniform electric current, both mild and powerful. Three different and distinct currents are produced—the primary, secondary, and both combined in intensity. Mounted in polished cherry case with nickel handles. Size, 6x5¼x5¼ inches, with full directions for using. Highly recommended. Weight, 2¼ lbs.
Price, complete $3.50

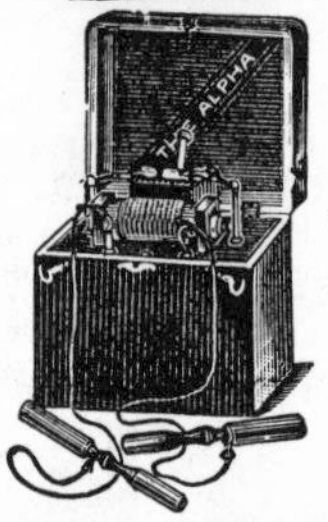

24178 Alpha Faradic Family Medical Battery, constructed upon improved scientific principles and designed for private or professional use. Full description of apparatus, directions for operating and directions for making solution furnished with each instrument. Weight, 3½ lbs.
Each $5.00

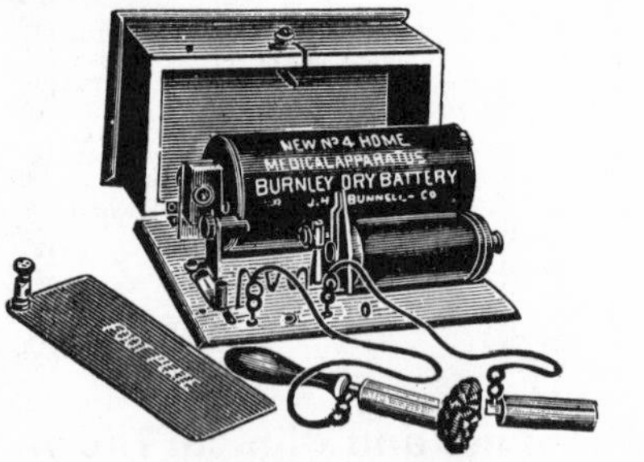

24179 The New Home Electro-Medical Apparatus, with dry battery. This battery is the most convenient and reliable of any hundreds of forms ever introduced. It is reliable, because with its dry battery so much less care is necessary to avoid getting it out of order than is required with any other known form. The entire absence of acids, liquors or salts will be appreciated by any one who has ever had occasion to use a medical battery. The appliance furnished with the apparatus consists of foot-plate, sponge, cords and handles (electrodes). The electrode having a wooden handle is used as a sponge-holder when required. The size of the apparatus is 3¼x5x8¼ inches. Weight, 4 pounds.
Price, complete ..... $7.00 Extra battery, per cell $0.75
Extra Sponge Holder .50 Extra Handles, pair .. .75
Extra Metallic Hair Brush, electrode 1.25
Extra Cords, 4 feet, per pair .... .50

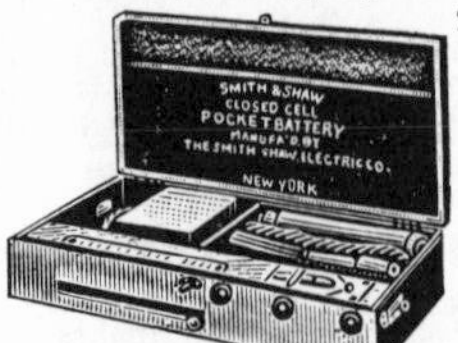

24180 The Genuine Smith & Shaw Portable Pocket Battery. Powerful current. The most practicable and thorough pocket battery made. Cells cannot spill contents.
Price, with two cells (weight 1¾ lb) ... $8.50
Price, with three cells (weight, 2 lbs $10.00

Magnetic Electro Battery.

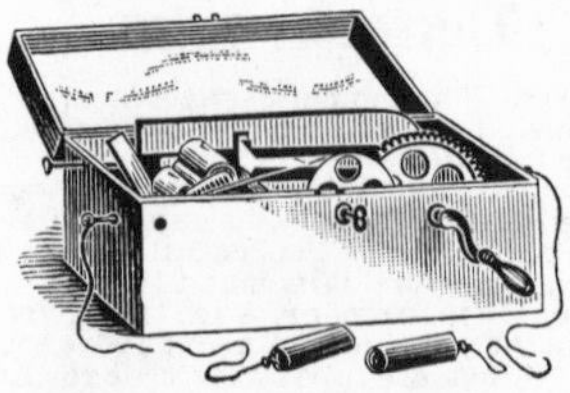

24182 Davis & Kidder's Genuine Magneto-Electric Machines.
Price, each. $7.25
Weigh, 6¾ lbs.

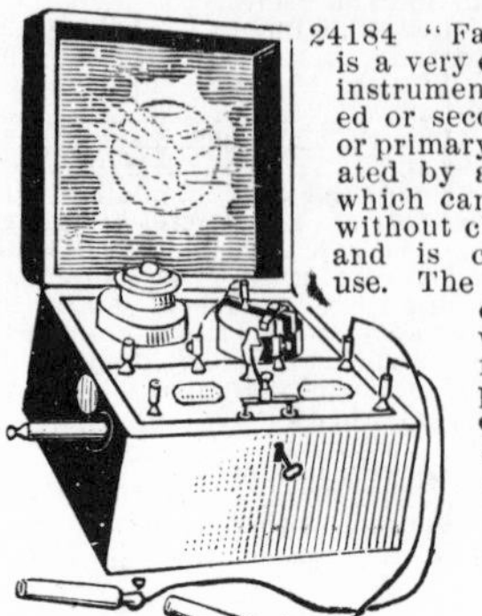

24184 "Family" Battery. This is a very effective and portable instrument, produces the induced or secondary, and the direct or primary current, and is operated by an open battery which can be used for months without changing the solution and is constantly ready for use. The power may be increased by gradually withdrawing the tube from the helix. In polished black walnut case with cords and handles; weight, 8 lbs.
Each $10.00

Medical Battery Parts.

Order No. 24185 and be sure to specify what Battery the parts are for.	**Each.**
Zincs for the Crown Family Battery	$0.20
Carbons for same	.25
Glass Jars for same	.25
Tops complete for same, zinc and carbon attached.	.65
Zincs for the Alpha Battery	.25
Carbons for same	.25
Glass Jars for same	.25
Zinc for Family Battery. Per pair	.50
Postage on pair zincs	.18
Platinas for same	1.00
Clamps for same	.25
Cords for same. Per pair	.50
Glass Jars for same	.25
Metal Springs for Magnetic Battery	.10
Cord belt for same	.05
Bisulphate Mercury for use with batteries Nos. 24175, 24176 and 24180 per ounce	.10
Price, per ½ lb. bottle	.75
Price, per 1 lb. bottle	1.25
Bichromate Potassium for use with batteries, Nos. 24177 and 24178. Per lb	.35

Medical Induction Coil, Without Battery.

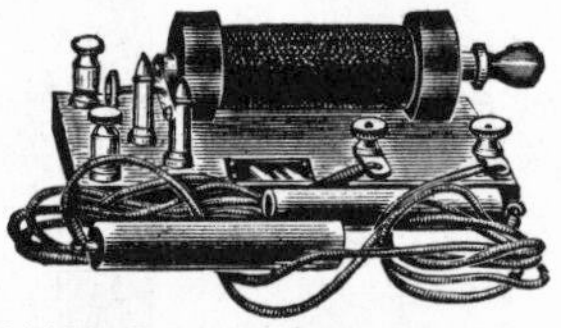

24186 Induction Coil, mounted on neat wooden stand with pair of hand electrodes and sponge holder of best quality. Can be operated with any acid battery. Price, without battery $3.50

24187 Same as above, complete with dry battery cell, ready for use. Weight, 3½ pounds. 4.00

Electric Motors.

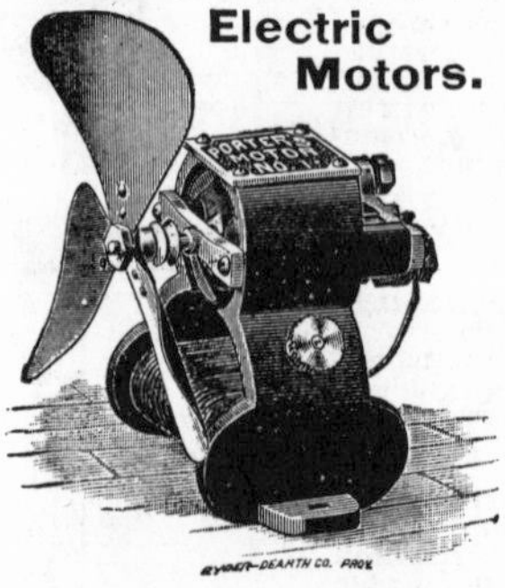

The Porter Electric Motor, a practical machine for a little money. An entirely novel principle underlies the construction both electrically and mechanically, insuring simplicity, low cost, reduced size, diminished weight, higher speed and wonderful economy in power required to operate them.

24190 The No. 1. Motor, although a very small one in size, is highly efficient. With one cell of acid battery it will operate a small dental lathe, a fan, a revolving window stand, an egg beater, a music-box, etc. It is no toy. Its electrical efficiency is about $\frac{1}{32}$ horse power, or from 35 to 40 watts on a continuous run. No better motor can be furnished to meet the wishes of young students engaged in the study of experimental physics. Its efficiency will surprise the user. Weight, 1¾ pounds. Price, each $2.90

24191 The No. 2 Motor, same construction as above, but larger size, weighing 3 pounds and capacity of $\frac{1}{16}$ horse power. Price 4.75

WE CARRY IN STOCK a full line of DRUGS, CHEMICALS, PHARMACEUTICAL PREPARATIONS, Etc., Etc., and can fill orders promptly and correctly. An experienced druggist is in charge, and he will compound prescriptions when so ordered. Send for our Drug List. Mailed free.

Electric Motors—Continued.

24192 The Porter Electric Motor No. 3. Size, 5½ in. long x 4½ in. high x 4¼ in. wide. The No. 3 Motor will suffice to run a sewing machine nicely; a cooling and ventilating fan; a lathe, buffer or grinding machine, such as are used in jewelers' and dentists' work, etc. It requires about 20 amperes of current under pressure of 6 to 10 volts. At normal speed of 2,200 revolutions per minute using four cells of battery it will yield an efficiency of about 1/12 horse power; four cells will answer to operate any household sewing machine. For its size and power, this motor (No. 3) is equal to any domestic electric motor sold to-day, and costs from one-third to one-half less money. Weighs 6 pounds.
Price each.. 9.00

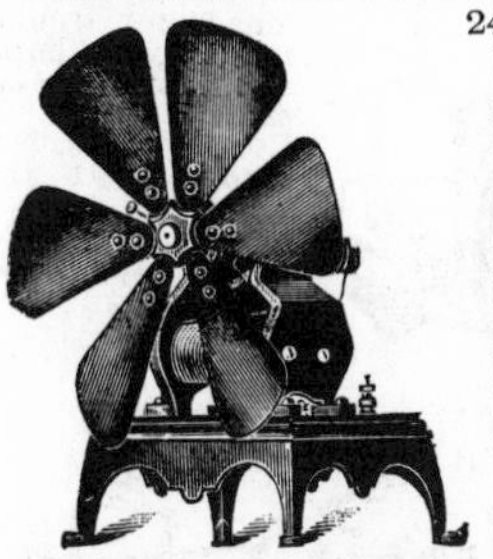

24193 The Porter Electric Motor No. 3, with stands, same size, description and capacity as the No. 24192, but provided with iron stand so that motor is sufficiently elevated to allow the use of a 10 in. 6 blade ventilating fan. Both the No. 24192 and No. 24193 are furnished with switch for instantly starting and stopping the machine.
Total weight, 7½ lbs.
Price..............$11.00

Battery Outfit for No. 3 Porter Motor.

24194 For operating sewing machine or doing other work requiring same power as sewing machine.

4 cells, 6x8, Battery,	@	$2.00	$8.00
2 lbs. Battery Powder (4 chg.)	@	50	1 00
			$9.00

NOTE—When doing work requiring less power than a sewing machine, or when using the No. 1 or No. 2 Motors, use a less number of cells of battery than four. We will furnish one or more cells at above prices. When purchasing battery outfit for the No. 1 or No. 2 Motors, order a one point switch at 25 cents, as these sizes are not provided with switch.

Fans for Motors.

Order No. 24195

4 Inch	3 Blades.	Each, $0.25
5 "	3 "	" .35
6 "	4 "	" .40
8 "	4 "	" .75
10 "	6 "	" 1.25

Switches.

Order No. 24197.
Round, hardwood base,

1 Point.	2 Point.	3 Point.
25 cents.	30 cents.	35 cents.

Telegraph Apparatus.

High Grade Telegraph Instruments.

NOTE—Instruments wound to but 5 ohms are designed for local lines, practice use, etc. Those wound to 20 ohms resistance are practical working instruments for all short lines up to 10 or 15 miles in length.

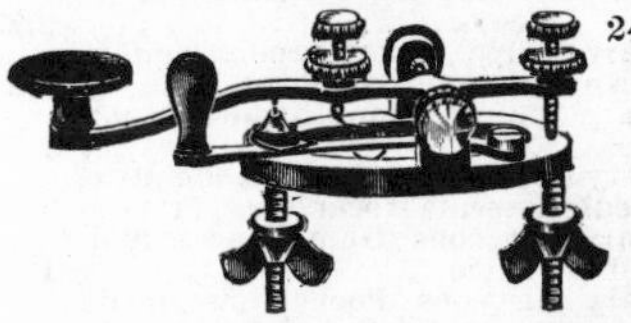

24200 Steel Lever Solid Trunnion Leg Key. This key in more durable and in every respect better than any other for rapid and perfect Morse sending.
The lever is only one-half the weight of the ordinary brass lever, as generally made. The entire lever and trunnions together being made of fine wrought steel, the common defect of loose trunnions is avoided, the strength of a heavy brass lever is obtained with much less weight of metal, and by the perfect bearing which the solid trunnion gives, together with the use of the hardened platina points, sticking is absolutely prevented. The size and proportions are such as to make it the most perfect operating key possible to obtain, either for the hand of the skilled and rapid expert or the beginner. Price, each, $1.50. Postage............$0.10
24201 Steel Lever, Solid Trunnion Desk Key. Exactly the same in construction as No. 24200, except that it is made without legs. A beautiful and perfect instrument for use on fine desks, or wherever a legless key is preferable.
Price, each........$2.00 Postage.............. .10
24202 The Giant Sounder is now recognized throughout America as the best standard of excellence in sounders. It gives a loud, clear sound with just half the amount of local battery required for other forms of sounders. Wound with fine wire to 20 ohms resistance for main line use (without relay), on lines up to 15 miles in length. Each, $2.50. Postage.... .... .20
24203 Giant Sounder, same as above, but wound to 5 ohms resistance. Each, $2.00. Postage... .20

Telegraph Apparatus—Continued.

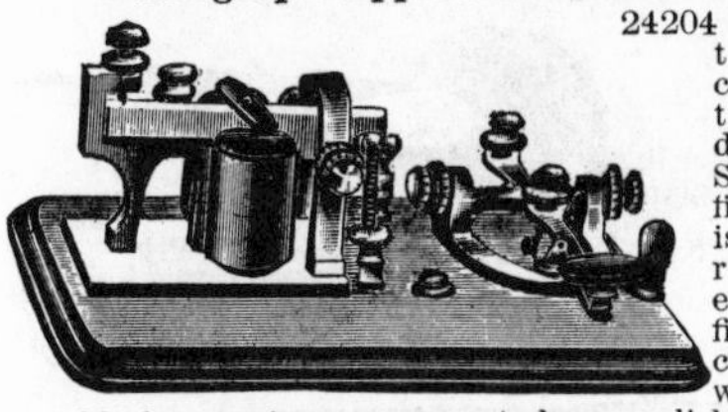

24204 Combination Set consists of the Standard Giant Sounder, finely finished with rubber-covered coils, fine silk-covered wire wound to 20 ohms resistance, mounted on polished mahogany base, with a steel lever key. The handsomest and most perfect set of short line instruments ever produced. Each........$4.00 Postage.........$0.35
24205 Same as 24204, but wound to 5 ohms.
Each................$3.50 Postage............ .35

Learners' Telegraph Instruments.

THE AJAX LEARNERS' SET.

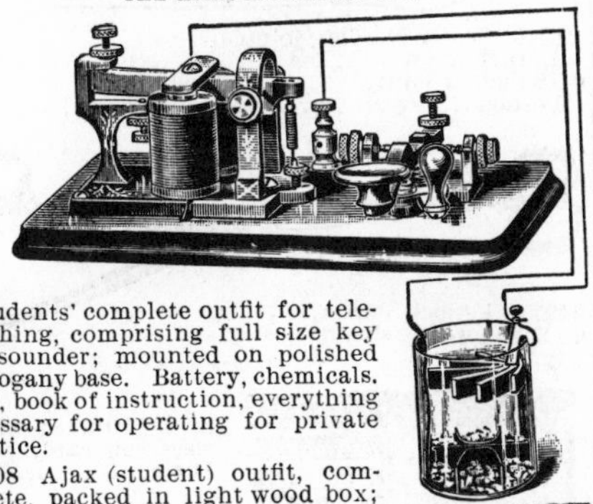

Students' complete outfit for telegraphing, comprising full size key and sounder; mounted on polished mahogany base. Battery, chemicals, wire, book of instruction, everything necessary for operating for private practice.
24208 Ajax (student) outfit, complete, packed in light wood box; weight, 10½ lbs........................$3.50
24209 Instruments only, mounted on base; weight, 2 pounds........................ 2.80
24210 Instrument only (3), mounted on base; sounder wound for long distance. This instrument should be used on lines of half a mile or more, as it will give better results. Weight, 2 pounds........................ 3.50
24213 Battery Cells, extra, complete; weight, 5 pounds; 5x7 size........................ .65
24214 Battery Jars, 1¾ pounds.............. .25
24215 Zinc, complete; weight, 1¾ pounds....... .30
24216 Copper; weight, 5 ounces.............. .20
24217 Blue Vitriol. Per pound.............. .09

Estimate for Half Mile Private Line.

24218 Two No. 24208 instruments, wound with fine wire, at $3.50	$7.00
½ mile No. 12 B B Galvanized Iron Wire, 85 pounds, at 9c	7.65
14 Pony Glass Insulators, at 5c	.70
15 Oak Brackets, at 3c	.45
5 Cells Gravity Battery, at 65c	3.25
2 pounds Office Wire, at 40c	.80
2 pounds Blue Vitriol, at 9c	1.08
	$20.93

The above estimate is for a practical working line, not a toy.

Quotations given on main line relays, combination sets, sounders, keys, etc., upon application. We can furnish anything used in telegraphy at a discount from usual prices. Electrical supplies of any kind quoted upon request.

Electric Door Bells and Appliances.

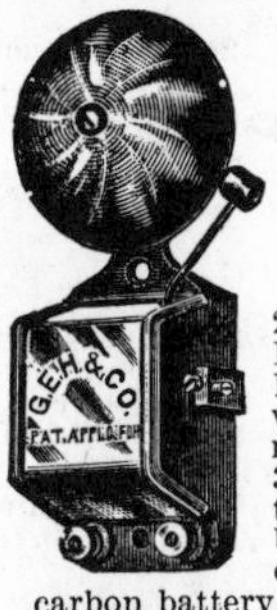

24225 Our "Standard" Three Inch Electric Bell. The design of bell is new and novel; has perfect adjustment. Price, each..............$0.75
Postage.............................. .15
24226 Bell Outfit, consisting of our 3-inch bell, 1 cell, Carbon battery, 1 bronze push botton, 1 lb. (150 ft.) wire, sal ammonaic and package staples and tape Price $2.50

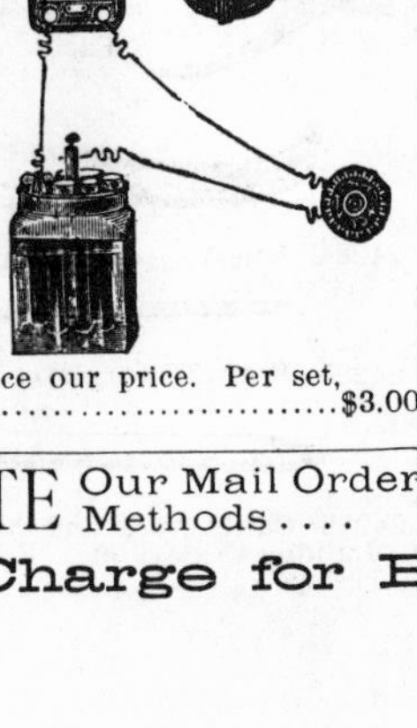

24227—Electric Bell Sets, with walnut push, 3-in. electric gong bell, one diamond carbon battery, 100 feet of insulated wire, screws, staples and tape. Packed in wooden box. Weight, 6¼ pounds.
Per set..............$2.75
24228 Electric Bell Set; same as No. 24227, except has fancy bronze push and 3-inch black walnut box bell. Notice our price. Per set, complete............................$3.00
Weight, 7½ pounds.

Batteries.

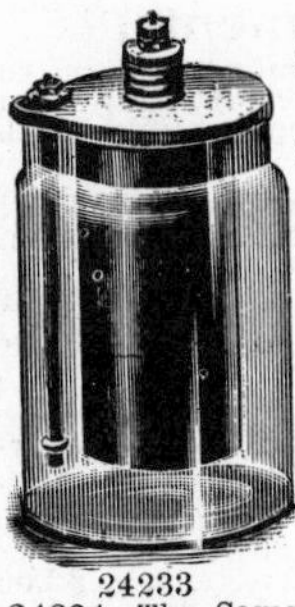

24233

24230 M. W. & Co. Carbon Battery, complete; weight, 3½ pounds.
Each..............................$0.50
24231 Leclanche Disque Batteries, complete with box of sal ammoniac; weight, 4 lbs. Each.....$0.75
24232 The Imperial Dry Battery; height, 6½ inches; diameter, 2½ inches; ready for use; does not freeze or evaporate. The most compact, practical battery for general use made; weight, 2¼ lbs.
Each..............................$0.90
24233 The Hayden, a most powerful and enduring open circuit battery; weight, 2½ lbs. Price......$1.00
Push buttons, sal ammoniac, wire, etc.
24234 The Samson No. 2; the best battery for gas engine work. Price..................$1.10
24235 Push Buttons, wood. Each.......... .15
24236 Push Buttons, fancy bronze.............. .50
24237 Push Buttons, floor.............. .40
24238 Sal Ammoniac, in paper boxes. Per box (6 ounces).............. .10
In bulk, per pound.............. .20
24239 Annunciator Wire, for use with eleceric bells. Per pound (150 feet).............. .25

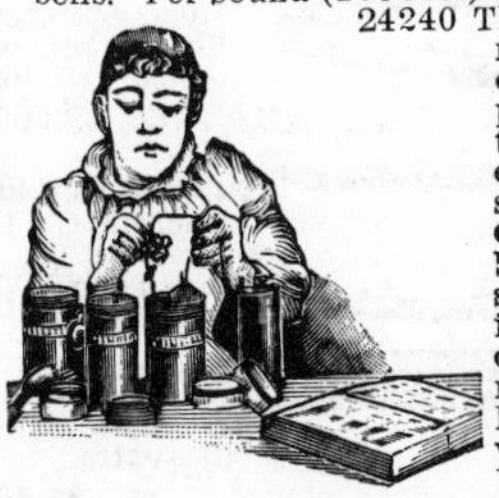

24240 The Amateur Plating Outfit. The best low-priced outfit on the market for plating small articles, teaspoons, etc. Plates equally well with gold, silver, nickel or copper. Outfit consists of 2 dry batteries, 2 glass tanks, solutions, salts, book of instructions, and all other necessities for making a complete outfit. Packed in strong oak box with hinge cover. Weight, 9½ pounds.
Price..................................$5.00
NOTE.—If you are interested in larger plating outfits send to us for complete catalogue of outfits and material.

Electric Insoles.

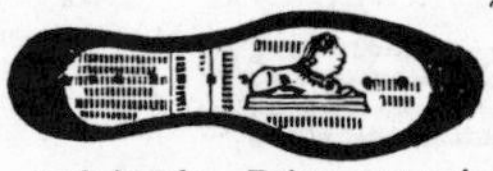

24242 Electric Insoles. Sure foot warmers. Recommended by many. State size of shoe worn. Has zinc and copper battery in each insole. Price, per pair..................$0.75
Postage.............................. .04

Electric Battery Plasters.

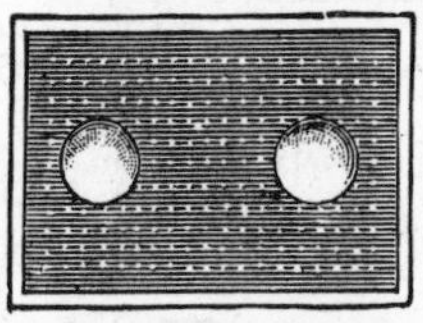

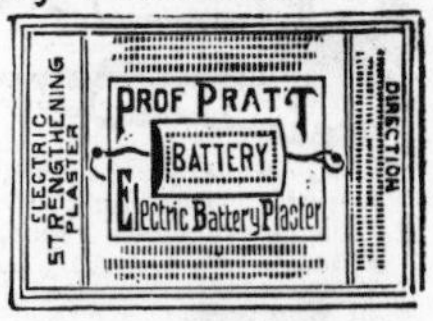

24243 The Lion Electric Battery Plaster has 2 silver disks on face of plaster, connected with a perfect copper and zinc battery on back, which guarantees a current of electricity. This current is diffused throughout the whole system. The battery can be charged with vinegar and used a number of times. Cures all aches and pains instantly. Each..................$0.45
Send for circular of Electric Belts and Specialties

The Remedial Heater or Pocket Stove.

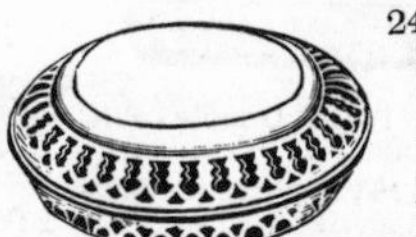

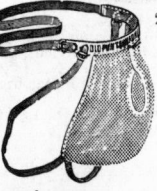

24244 Designed for the treatment of ear or toothache, colic, diseases of women and children where the application of external heat is necessary. It can be carried in the overcoat pocket, and used as a finger warmer. It is made of metal, nickel plated, and measures 3½x1 inch. There is nothing about it to get out of order and no possible danger of fire escaping from the heat chamber. Heat is produced by the burning of a small tablet of a slowly combustible substance, principally made up of carbon. One of these will burn with an even heat for about two hours and continuous heat may be obtained by replacing the consumed carbon by another.
Price, complete, packed in neat wood box, with one dozen carbons..............................$0.85
Postage $0.15 Extra carbons, per doz......... .10

Surgical Instruments.

NOTE—We are prepared to furnish prices of Human Dental Forceps, Surgical Appliances of all kinds. Deformity Apparatus, Elastic Stockings, Supports, etc.

O-P-C Suspensory.

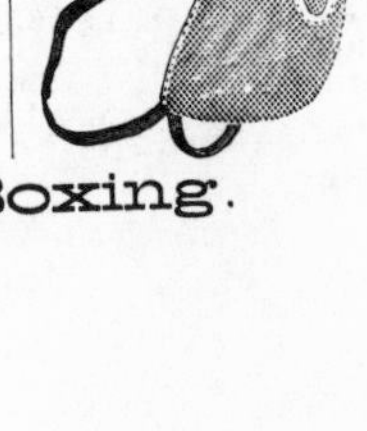

24245 Automatically adjustable and never fails to fit and give satisfaction. For comfort, security, durability and elegance the best in the world. Order by number. Give size, large, medium or small.
No. 2, lisle..............................$0.75
No. 3, silk.............................. 1.25
No. 4, all silk.............................. 1.75
No. 5, all silk, fancy colors. 2.25

Veterinary Instruments.

In veterinary goods we illustrate only a few instruments that are commonly used by everyone owning a horse, but we are in a position to supply anything made in this line, and will quote prices upon application.

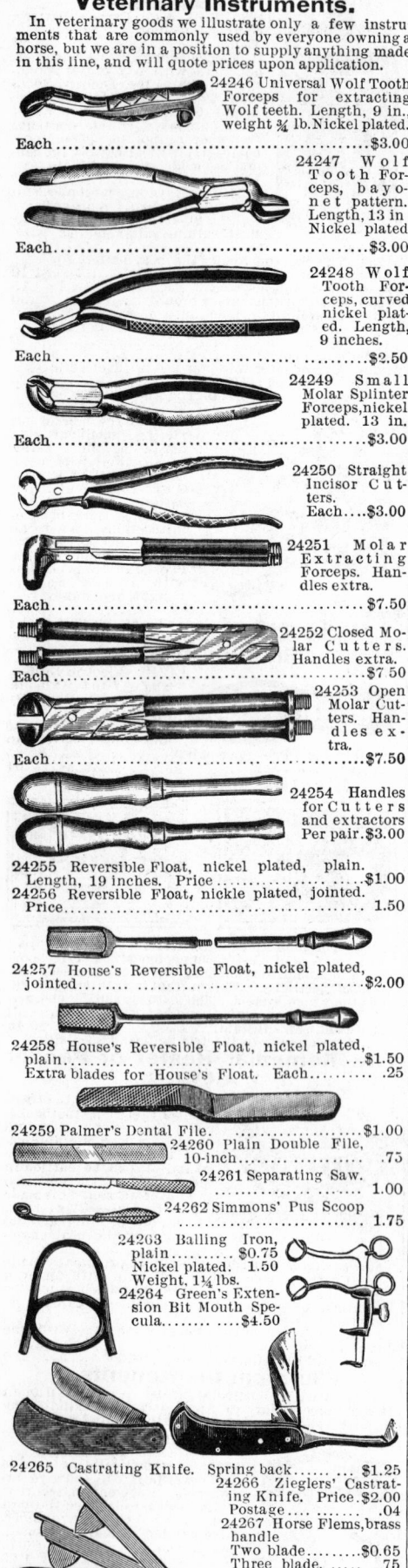

24246 Universal Wolf Tooth Forceps for extracting Wolf teeth. Length, 9 in., weight ¾ lb. Nickel plated.
Each $3.00

24247 Wolf Tooth Forceps, bayonet pattern. Length, 13 in. Nickel plated
Each $3.00

24248 Wolf Tooth Forceps, curved nickel plated. Length, 9 inches.
Each $2.50

24249 Small Molar Splinter Forceps, nickel plated. 13 in.
Each $3.00

24250 Straight Incisor Cutters. Each $3.00

24251 Molar Extracting Forceps. Handles extra.
Each $7.50

24252 Closed Molar Cutters. Handles extra.
Each $7.50

24253 Open Molar Cutters. Handles extra.
Each $7.50

24254 Handles for Cutters and extractors Per pair.$3.00

24255 Reversible Float, nickel plated, plain. Length, 19 inches. Price $1.00
24256 Reversible Float, nickle plated, jointed. Price 1.50

24257 House's Reversible Float, nickel plated, jointed $2.00

24258 House's Reversible Float, nickel plated, plain $1.50
Extra blades for House's Float. Each 25

24259 Palmer's Dental File. $1.00
24260 Plain Double File, 10-inch 75
24261 Separating Saw. 1.00
24262 Simmons' Pus Scoop 1.75

24263 Balling Iron, plain $0.75
Nickel plated. 1.50
Weight, 1¼ lbs.
24264 Green's Extension Bit Mouth Specula $4.50

24265 Castrating Knife. Spring back $1.25
24266 Zieglers' Castrating Knife. Price. $2.00
Postage 04
24267 Horse Flems, brass handle
Two blade $0.65
Three blade. ..... .75
Postage 50

Veterinary Instruments—Continued.

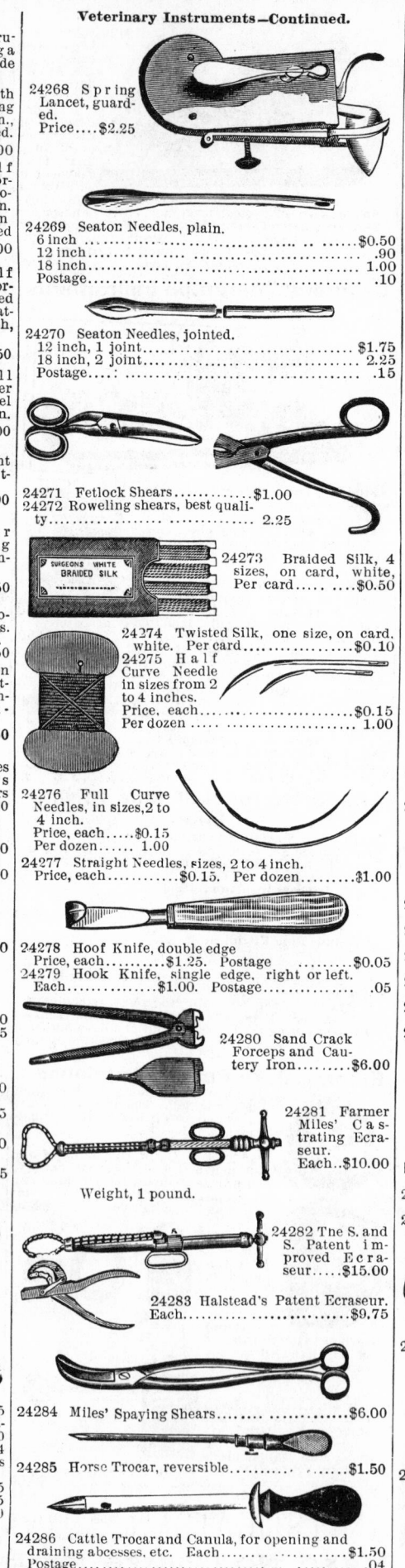

24268 Spring Lancet, guarded. Price....$2.25

24269 Seaton Needles, plain.
6 inch $0.50
12 inch 90
18 inch 1.00
Postage 10

24270 Seaton Needles, jointed.
12 inch, 1 joint $1.75
18 inch, 2 joint 2.25
Postage 15

24271 Fetlock Shears $1.00
24272 Roweling shears, best quality 2.25

24273 Braided Silk, 4 sizes, on card, white, Per card $0.50

24274 Twisted Silk, one size, on card. white. Per card $0.10
24275 Half Curve Needle in sizes from 2 to 4 inches. Price, each $0.15
Per dozen 1.00

24276 Full Curve Needles, in sizes, 2 to 4 inch. Price, each $0.15
Per dozen 1.00
24277 Straight Needles, sizes, 2 to 4 inch. Price, each ....$0.15. Per dozen $1.00

24278 Hoof Knife, double edge Price, each ....$1.25. Postage $0.05
24279 Hook Knife, single edge, right or left. Each ....$1.00. Postage 05

24280 Sand Crack Forceps and Cautery Iron $6.00

24281 Farmer Miles' Castrating Ecraseur. Each ..$10.00

Weight, 1 pound.

24282 The S. and S. Patent improved Ecraseur $15.00

24283 Halstead's Patent Ecraseur. Each $9.75

24284 Miles' Spaying Shears $6.00

24285 Horse Trocar, reversible $1.50

24286 Cattle Trocar and Canula, for opening and draining abcesses, etc. Each $1.50
Postage 04

Veterinary Instruments—Continued.

24287 Pig Extracting Forceps. Each $3.50
24288 Drenching Horn for administering medicine to horses; japanned.
Each $0.85
Weight, 1½ pounds.

24289 Burton's Drenching Bit. No longer any trouble to give your horse medicine. One man can do it. Used by horsemen throughout the country,
Price $2.75
Weight 1¼ pounds.

24290 Mouth Speculum. S. & S. patent, easy of operation; it holds the mouth open so that an examination of the teeth can be made with the greatest ease. Nickel plated.
Price $9.50
Weight, 4 pounds.

24291 Veterinary Thermometer. 6-inch, sensitive self-registering, in pocket case. Price $1.50
24292 Horse Catheter, best quality $2.00
24293 Horse Catheter same as above, second quality. Price $1.75

24294 Metal Mare Catheter. $1.50
24295 Metal Mare Catheter, jointed $2.00

24296 Injection Syringes, metal 16 ounces.
Weight, 1½ pounds. Price $1.00
24 ounces, weight, 2½ pounds. Price 2.00
36 ounces, weight, 3¾ pounds. Price 2.50
24297 Veterinary Balling Gun, nickel plated, 15 inch length. Price 2.25
24298 Veterinary Scalpel, ebony handle, right or left. Specify which is wanted. Price 1.25
24299 Veterinary Scalpel, ebony handle, double edge. Price 1.50
24300 Veterinary Hypodermic Syringe, complete, with three needles, needle trocar, etc., Price.. 3.50
24301 Veterinary Surgeons' Gum Lancet, folding, black handle. Price 1.50
24302 Veterinary Surgeons' Pocket Case, made of best morocco, and containing an assortment of twelve instruments. Price 20.00

24303 Syringes for administering medicine to horses and other animals. Quittor Hard Rubber, two pipes. Price, each ..$1.50

24304 Syringes, same as preceding, but of metal, nickel plated, Quittor, two pipes. Price, each...$2.50
24305 Veterinary Hard Rubber Horse Syringes, capacity, 24 ounces. Each $3.75

24306 Dehorning Saw, plain finish $1.50

24307 Gouging Forceps, nickel plated $3.50

24308 Whisson's Improved Pig Forceps: has points of excellence which make it a most practical instrument, and may be used upon either small or large sows with equal satisfaction. The instrument is made of malleable iron, tinned to prevent rusting. Will not tear the sow or otherwise injure the animal in operation, Price $1.00

Coin, Silver Milking Tubes, Etc.

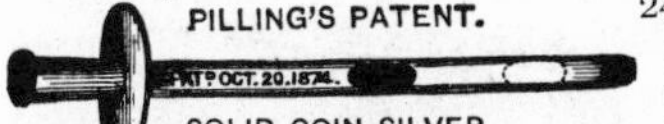

24310 Coin Silver Milking Tubes, for sore and obstructed teats, and hard milking cows; made of pure coin silver and can be used with absolute safety, set of 4 tubes, 1¾ inches long, in neat box, with full directions for use....$1.60
Single tubes, each.... .43

Special length	2¼ in.	2¾ in.	3¼ in.	3¾ in.
Each	55c	70c.	80c.	95c.

Postage, 2 cents.

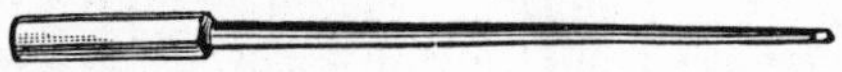

24311 Grooved Director, or instrument for opening cows' teats, with full directions for using.
Each....$0.60
Per dozen.... 6.00
Postage.... 0.02

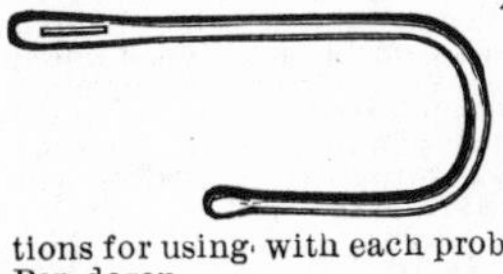

24312 Lead Probes for treatment of stricture and obstructed teats; also for enlarging the opening in cows' teats; made in three sizes, small, medium and large; full directions for using with each probe. Each....$0.20
Per dozen.... 2.00
24313 Cow Teat Slitter, best implement steel, nickeled sheath, 5 inch length. Each.... 1.25

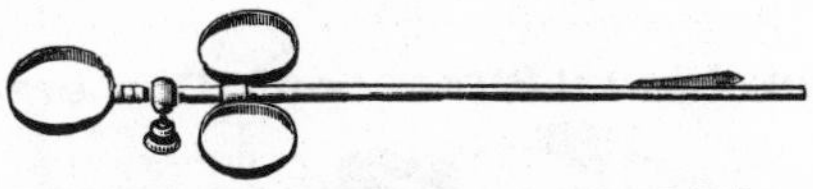

24314 Stricture Cutter, for cows' teats, 7 inch length, made of best implement steel. Each....$2.60

Poultry Instruments.

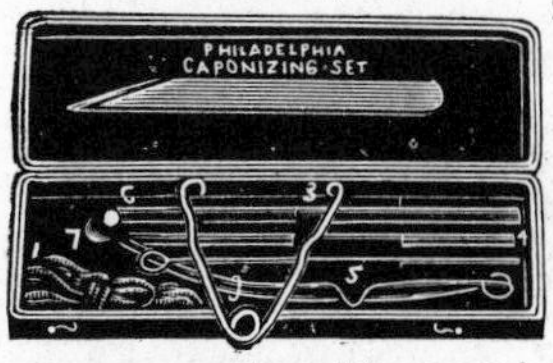

24315 It is well understood that poultrymen can double their profits by caponizing their chicks. The operation is very simple, the instructions being so explicit that any one, after a careful reading, will be able to perform the operation with proper instruments.

The demand for capons far exceeds the supply, even at an advanced price.

The Philadelphia Caponizing Set contains the best instruments on the market; and at the price at which they are offered no one who keeps chickens can afford to neglect the opportunity of increasing their profits.

Price, per set, in velvet lined case (see cut), with book, "Complete Guide for Caponizing"....$2.50
Postage.... .10

French Poultry Killing Knife.

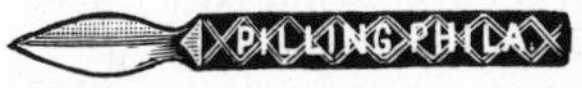

24316 Every poultry raiser should have one. They are made of finely tempered instrument steel, with nickeled handle; will last a lifetime.
Each.... $0.40. Postage....$0.05

We are prepared to furnish nearly everything in Veterinary Instruments. We handle only the BEST.

The Philadelphia Poultry Market.

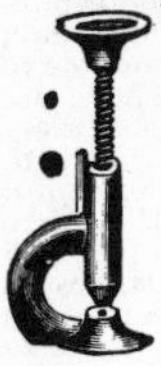

24317 Do you keep a record of chickens? The different breeds, hatches, etc., should be kept. There is no better or quicker way than by this marker, as over 200 different marks can be made by punching we between toes, for instance between first and second toes of right foot can mean Wyandotte or Plymouth Rock; between second and third toes, White Leghorn or Lanshan, so that hundreds of private marks can be made, not only to keep records, but by your private marks you can secure yourself from the chicken thief. They are well made with steel spring and cutter, nicely nickel plated.
Price....$0,18. Postage....$0.05

Gape Worm Extractor.

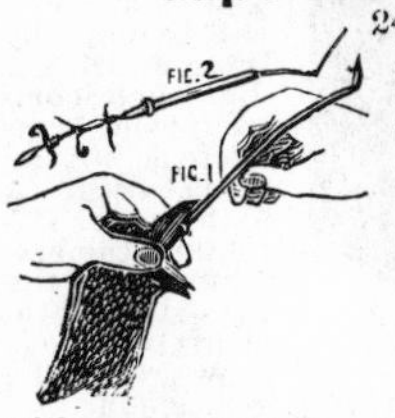

24318 The disease commonly known as Gapes is caused by a small worm in the windpipe of fowls. When the chick seems to gasp frequently it is a sure indication of Gapes, and it should receive attention at once. The only sure cure is to remove the worms by mechanical means. You will save time and money by having on hand a Gape Worm Extractor. The extractor quickly removes, without injury to the chick, the worms and matter from the windpipe, and effects an instant cure. The instrument is made of brass and will last a lifetime. The cut shows the manner of using the instrument. One chick saved pays price of instrument. Price....$0.30
Postage.... .03

Ladies! **Don't fail to note our varied new line of Embroideries and Suisse Flouncings. Styles and prices will surely interest you.**

PHOTOGRAPHIC GOODS DEPARTMENT.

NOTE.—We do not sell Cameras or outfits on trial, nor can they be returned after having been used. The goods quoted by us are the same old by *all* photographic stock houses, and are staple articles of merchandise.

Failure to produce a good negative is in nearly every case due to the want of carefulness or lack of skill on the part of the operator. While anyone can now learn to take a good photograph at a small outlay of time and money, yet the first few efforts must not be expected to equal the work of one proficient in the art. Do not expect to set up in photography as a means of support with one of our *low priced* outfits. Taking photographs for your own amusement, for the home circle or for your friends, and finishing portraits for a discriminating public are entirely different subjects.

Portrait work requires a high grade lens and camera, while excellent pictures of landscapes can be made with cameras, fitted with a single view lens; of course the picture is much better in detail when a rectilinear lens is used. If you desire any make of camera or lens not found listed in this catalogue, write us for prices, giving name of camera and manufacturer's name. We will cheerfully answer all questions of this nature, and will mail special catalogues of photographic apparatus to those desiring same.

Hand Cameras.

Since the introduction of the Hand Camera, picture making has been so simplified that the possibilities of photography are brought within the reach of all. The Amateur Photographer is now found among persons in nearly every walk of life. The business man finds photography a valuable assistant as well as a pleasant recreation, while for the tourist and pleasure seeker it has many charms. Surely there is no more pleasant souvenir of vacation rambles than photographs, taken by yourself, of the various scenes and incidents connected with your outing. Many recollections are thus preserved, and the history of the pleasant holiday is brought to mind by a glance at the finished picture long afterward.

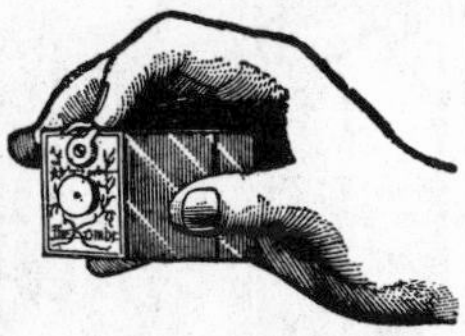

24350 THE KOMBI. A small, thoroughly practical, pocket camera; made of metal, bronze finished, measures 2x1⅝ inches, and weighs, when loaded for twenty-five exposures, about four ounces. It takes films and makes a picture 1⅛x1⅛ inches square, or a circle picture 1⅛ inches in diameter. With the camera is combined a magnifying graphoscope, for viewing the photographs when developed and printed upon a strip of translucent material.
Price, in cloth-covered case....$3.50
1 Roll Film, for 25 exposures.... .20
1 Box of 5 Rolls of Film (for 25 exposures each) 1.00
Complete Developing and Printing Outfit.... 3.00
Magazine containing extra loading.... 1.50
Rubber Loading Sleeve.... .60
No. 2 Staff Tripod with plate.... 2.00

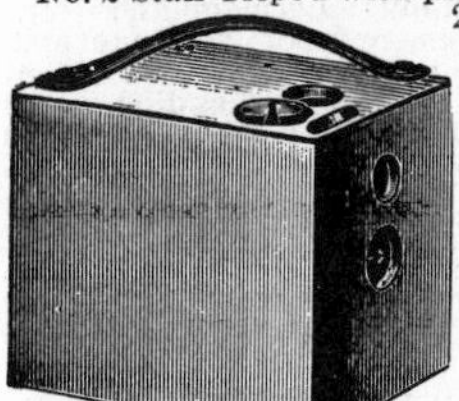

24351 THE BULL'S EYE (Daylight) CAMERA. Provided with a roll of film that may be placed in position or removed without the necessity of a dark room. The Film Cartridge is provided at either end with a length of opaque cloth to protect it from the light when being placed in position or removed from the camera in daylight, thus making a *Daylight Camera.* The cartridge is easily adjusted and removed and may be sent by mail to be developed and printed to any photo-goods dealer or photographer if you should not wish to finish the picture yourself. The camera is made in best possible manner and has an achromatic lens, of universal focus, set to take pictures at any distance over 8 feet away. No focusing required, simply aim the camera, push the spring (which is always set) and turn the key. When twelve exposures have been made, which uses up the roll of film; the cartridge is removed and a fresh one inserted.

Hand Cameras—Continued.

The Bull's Eye takes a picture either square or circle, 3½ inches in diameter. Size, 5¾x4¾x4½ inches. Weight, about two pounds.
Price, with wood case covered with grain leather $7.50
Price includes 1 film cartridge and book of instructions.
Extra cartridges, for 12 pictures. Each....$0.55
24352 THE BULL'S EYE CAMERA for 4x5 pictures, uses light proof film cartridges for 12 exposures, and is a larger and more complete investment than 24351. Size, 5½x6½x8¼. Weight, 2½ lbs., covered with grain leather. Price, each....$14.00
Extra cartridges, for 12 pictures, each.... .90

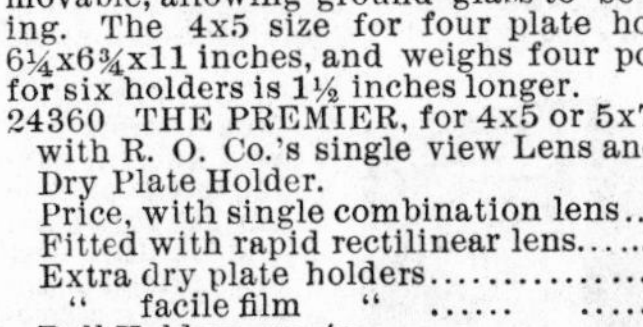

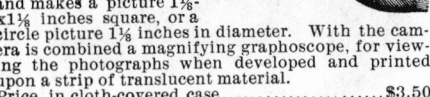

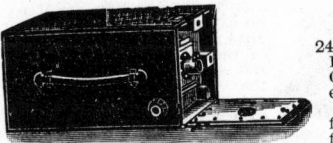

24353 THE PREMIER CAMERA, for either glass plates, cut films or roll films. A high grade "all around" instrument. They are fitted with the new silent shutter, and either single view or double combination lenses of the well known R. O. Co.'s make. Boxes are well made, covered with grain leather, and are made to carry either four or six double plate holders. Each camera is provided with two view finders and two tripod plates, so that either vertical or horizontal pictures can be made. The back panel is removable, allowing ground glass to be seen for focusing. The 4x5 size for four plate holders measures 6¼x6¾x11 inches, and weighs four pounds. The box for six holders is 1½ inches longer.

24360 THE PREMIER, for 4x5 or 5x7 pictures, fitted with R. O. Co.'s single view Lens and *one* Perfection Dry Plate Holder.

	4x5	5x7
Price, with single combination lens...	$13.50	$18.00
Fitted with rapid rectilinear lens....	18.90	27.00
Extra dry plate holders....	.90	1.12
" facile film "	1.13	1.35
Roll Holders, *empty*....	7.25	9.00

24354 THE PREMIER No. 2 is the regular Premier with the addition of swing back and rising and falling front. In other respects the description of the regular Premier applies to the No. 2. The swing back and rising and falling front are used principally when using the camera on a tripod, and are of especial advantage when taking architectural subjects and tall buildings. A hand camera with these improvements possesses all the advantages of a regular tripod camera.

	Size 4x5	Size 5x7
No. 2 Premier with single view lens and 1 plate holder....	$16.20	$21.60
No. 2 Premier with rapid rectilinear lens and 1 plate holder....	21.50	30.50

We make no charge for cases or cartage.

Hand Cameras—Continued.

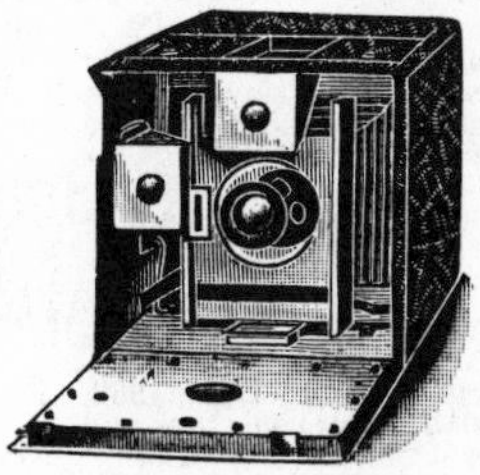

24355 THE ROCHESTER, a high-grade hand camera for making 4x5 pictures, using glass plates. Fitted with Gundlach Rapid Retigraphic Lens and one plate holder.
Price....$25.00
Rochester plate holders, 4x5. Each.... .90

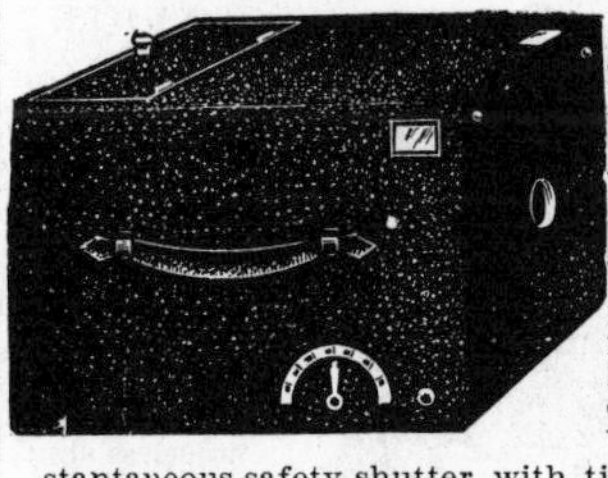

24356 THE NIGHT HAWK CAMERA, the best *cheap* 4x5 camera ever placed before the public; uses *glass plates.* The Night Hawk can be focused either with ground glass or focusing dial, and is fitted with a rapid achromatic lens for instantaneous and general work; also an instantaneous safety shutter, with time exposure stop. These cameras are made of the best material, and the workmanship and finish first-class. Can be had either polished antique oak, or in morocco leather covering. Price includes one plate holder and full instructions.
Price, antique oak....$4.80
Price, morocco covered.... 6.75
Extra plate holders, 4x5, each.... .90

TO one who is not afraid of a little labor, no more pleasant hobby can be followed up than

=Photography.=

Folding Hand Cameras.

Folding cameras are favorites with the amateur photographer, as by the style of their construction much greater compactness is secured than it is possible to obtain with the regular style boxes. They are extremely simple to open, ready for use. Merely lower the front of camera, which forms a bed, and draw the front with lens forward until the pinion engages in the rack, and the final adjustment is made with the apparatus placed at the front for that purpose.

The appearance of these folding cameras are especially handsome, as the entire front and bed are made of polished mahogany or cherry, which contrasts perfectly with the black leather covering.

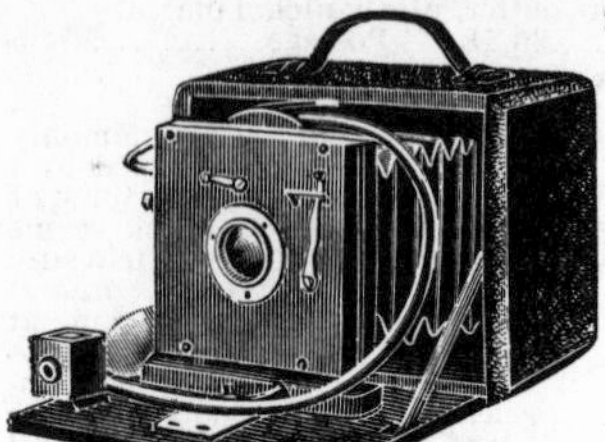

24357 THE BO PEEP FOLDING CAMERA. The "Bo-Peep" will be found by those desiring a light and compact hand camera to be just the thing, being a high grade. 4x5 folding camera, fitted with all the latest improvements to date, at a low price. The size of the Bo-Peep is 7¼x5½x4¾ inches, and it weighs but 2¾ pounds; has a rising and falling front board, swing back, and is fitted with a new time and instantaneous shutter with bulb attachment and patent anastigmat lense. Price includes one plate holder.

Price, 4x5	$13.75
Price, 5x7	22.50
Extra, 4x5, double plate holders, each	.90
" 5x7, " " " "	1.12

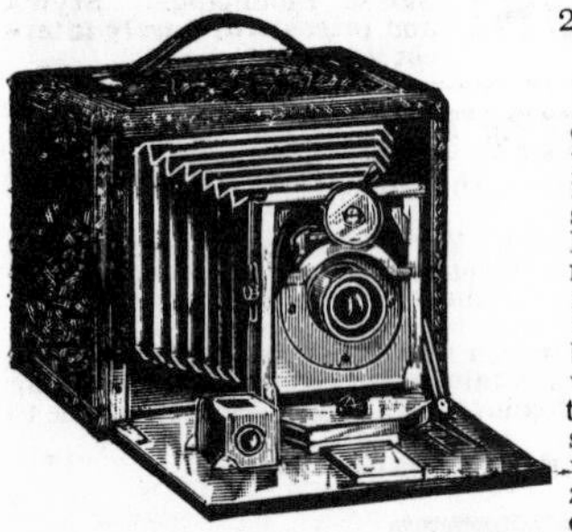

24358 THE FOLDING PREMO CAMERA is a most complete and practical little instrument, possessing all the latest improvements. Has rising and falling front, swing back, reversible view finder and two tripod plates, so that either vertical or horizontal pictures can be taken. The shutter is of special construction, and the lens is a rapid rectilinear of great power, made specially for this camera. A roll holder can be used in this style Premo when desired.

	4x5	5x7	6½x8½
With one dry plate holder. Prices	$27.00	$34.00	$45.00
Extra plate holders	1.13	1.35	1.60
Film holders	1.28	1.45	1.70
Roll holders	7.25	9.00	14.60

24359 THE FOLDING PREMO CAMERA—Style "B." Almost identical with No. 24362, except that it is fitted with *single view* lens and roll holder cannot be used in it.

	4x5	5x7
Premo B, with one plate-holder. Prices	$18.00	$24.25

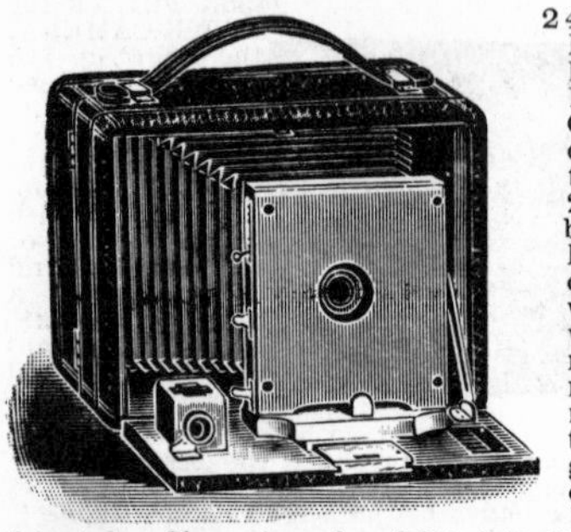

24360 THE FOLDING PREMO CAMERA-Style "D" Cheaper in construction than Nos. 24358, 24359 but a thoroughly practical camera. Fitted with single view lens with rigid diaphrams, and new noiseless shutter. Either glass plates or cut films can be used in this style. Size, when closed 5½x5 ⅝x6¼ inches; weighs 2 pounds and holds three plate holders.

Price, 4x5 .... $10.75

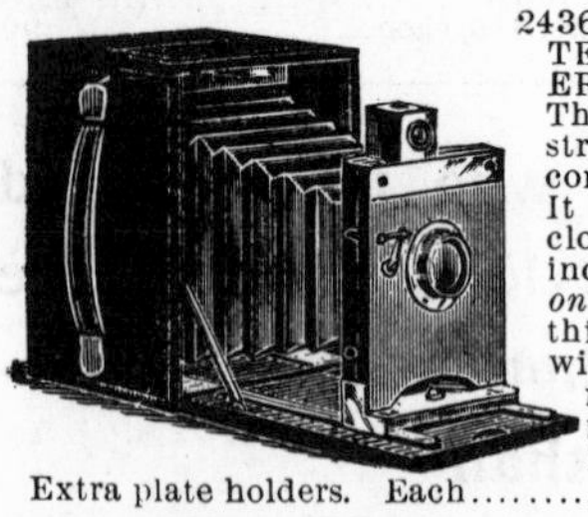

24361 THE ROCHESTER FOLDING CAMERA for 4x5 pictures. This is one of the strongest and most compact of its kind. It measures, when closed, but 4¾x5½x7 inches. *Glass plates only* can be used in this camera. Fitted with high grade symmetrical lens, with rotating diaphrams

Price $22.50

Extra plate holders. Each $0.90

24362 THE ROCHESTER FOLDING CAMERA, fitted with rapid symmetrical lens, and silent shutter for time and instantaneous exposures.

Price with one plate holder $35.00

Extra plate holders, 5x7. Each 1.13

Magazine Hand Cameras.

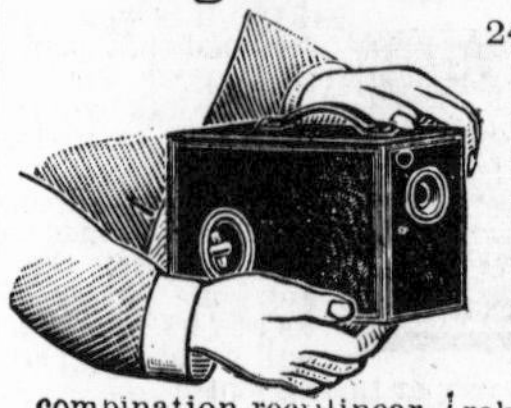

24363 THE TROKONET CAMERA, Style "C." For cut films or glass plates. For 4x5 pictures. Capacity, 30 cut-sheet films or 12 glass plate without reloading. Size, 6¼x7¼x11¼ inches. Weight, when loaded, 4¾ pounds. This Trokonet is provided with a Gundlach double combination rectilinear Trokonet lens, two finders, instantaneous and time shutter, with adjustable speed, focusing rack and pinion with scale for focusing, counter for exposures, and two sockets for tripod screws. The C Trokonet is handsomely finished and covered with morocco leather. Price of C Trokonet, loaded with 30 cut sheet films $31.50

24364 THE TROKONET, Style D. For films or glass plates. The D Trokonet is exactly the same as the C Trokonet, excepting that it has a single, instead of a double, combination lens. This lens is equal to any high grade single combination lens. Price of D Trokonet, loaded, with 25 cut-sheet films $18.75

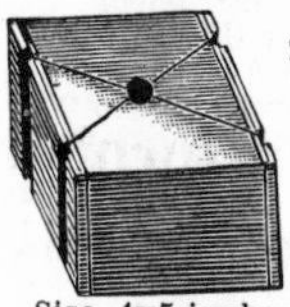

24365 THE TROKONET FILMS makes the Trokonet system possible. The film is sold in packages as here illustrated. Every film is attached to a paper septum, and as the latter costs nothing may be thrown in the waste basket after the films have been developed.

Size, 4x5 inches, in packages of 30 .... $2.25

24366 Septums for Glass Dry Plates or Films; Size, 4x5 inches, 1 dozen in a package .... .60

Full directions in each package how to use Glass Dry Plates in Trokonets

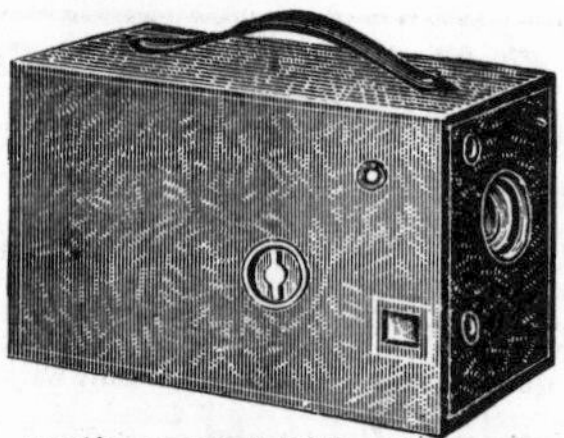

24367 THE SUNART MAGAZINE CAMERA, for 4x5 pictures. Uses cut-sheet films, capacity 24 films without reloading. The Sunart is the latest and best magazine camera placed on the market. It is 5⅝ inches wide, 6¾ inches high and 10⅛ inches long, neatly covered with seal grain morocco, with convenient handle for carrying. Has two finders covering same field as the lens. The lens is a Bausch & Lomb rapid rectilinear with rotating stops, and covers a 4x5 film to the extreme edge with full opening. The shutter is of an improved construction that *permits being reset without exposing the film, for either time or instantaneous exposure.* The working parts are so simple, a child can operate them. Price $45.00

24368 SUNART FILMS, loaded in carrier, per package of 24 .... $1.50

SUNART FILMS, loaded in carriers, per package of 12 .... .80

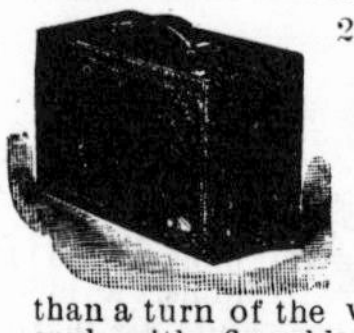

24369 THE HEATHERINGTON MAGAZINE CAMERA No. 1, 4x5 size, for glass plates or cut films; is a box of the ordinary hand camera size, strongly and carefully made, that will carry six glass plates or cut films always ready for exposure without opening the box and with no other movement than a turn of the wrist. Size, 6x6½x9 inches, covered with fine black seal grain leather, fitted with rotary shutter that can be set for either time or instantaneous exposure, and fine achromatic lens.

Price $20.00

View Cameras.

View cameras are not suitable for making Ferrotype (tin type) pictures. This line of photographic work requires camera and lenses of special construction. Prices of Ferro-type outfits will be quoted upon application.

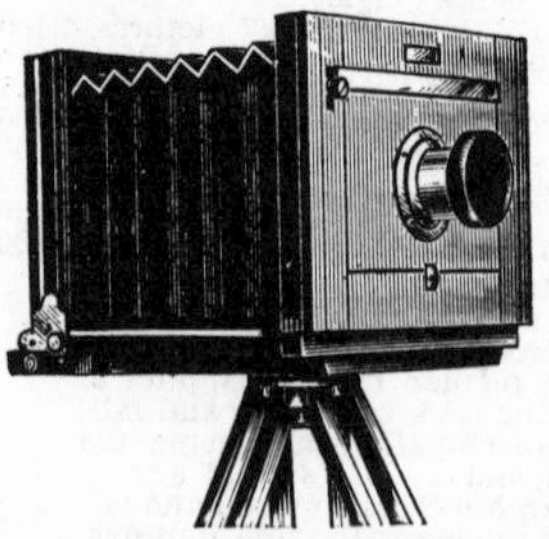

24370 The New Model Camera is well known, having been on the market for years, and is the best low priced camera manufactured. Made of selected cherry, with nickel trimmings, has folding bed, sliding front, and is reversible. With each camera is furnished one R. O. Co.'s single view lens, standard folding tripod, one perfection plate holder, and carrying case with handle, *except size 8x10 where neither tripod nor lens are included in price*

For pictures.	No swing.	Single swing.
3¼x4¼	$7.88	$8.75
4x5	7.90	8.80
4¼x6½	8.70	9.63
5x7	9.65	10.50
5x8	9.70	10.55
6½x8½	11.38	13.23
8x10	11.40	13.25

The New Model Improved.

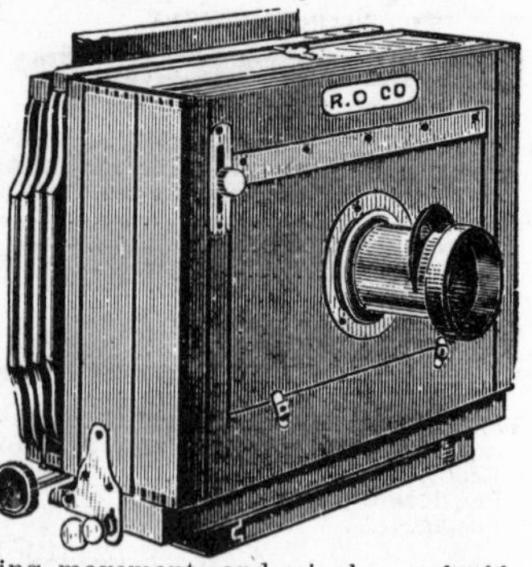

24371 This camera is made after the general style of the preceding but better finished. It has the reputation of being the most popular camera in America, made of mahogany, with nickel trimming, has sliding front folding bed and is reversible, has rack and pinion focusing movement and single or double swing back. With each camera is included one of R. O. Co's, single view lens, Carlton sliding tripod, one perfection plate holder and carrying case, except size 8x10, where price includes neither lens nor tripod.

For picture.	Single swing.	Double swing.
3¼x4¼	$11.37	$13.12
4 x5	12.25	14.00
4¼x6½	14.10	15.75
5 x7	17.50	18.80
5 x8	8.55	18.85
6½x8½	19.25	21.00
8 x10	13.15	14.87

New Model Steroscopic Cameras.

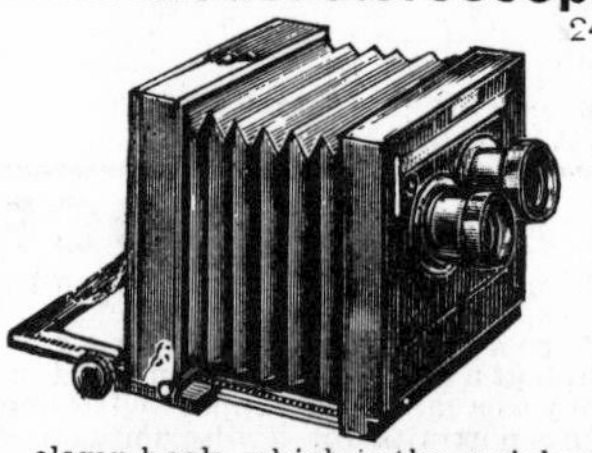

24372 New Model Stereoscopic Camera is patterned closely after the New Model Improved, having rack and pinion for focusing, sliding front, folding bed, and is reversible by means of an adjustable reversing clamp. The folding bed is held rigid by a clamp hook, which is the quickest, easiest and best device yet produced for the purpose. The partition and front board are removable so that the camera may be used, if desired, for other than stereoscopic pictures, by the addition of a lens of sufficient size to cover the full plate. Each camera is inclosed in a neat canvas case, with room for two extra Perfection Holders. Price for 5x8, including pair of No. 1 R. O. Co.'s View lenses, matched, Carlton sliding tripod and one Perfection holder $19.25

Use No. 24409 Perfection Plate Holder in New Model, New Model Improved and New Model Stereoscopic Camera.

The Normandie Reversible Back Camera.

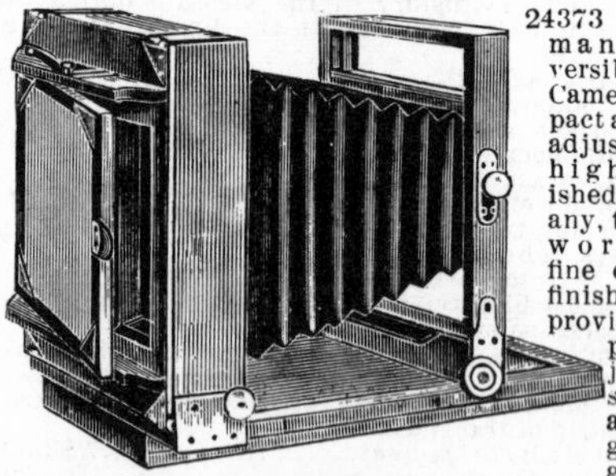

24373 The Normandie Reversible Back Camera, compact and easily adjustable, of highly polished mahogany, the metal work being fine draw file finish. It is provided with patent adjustable, spring-actuated ground glass always in position and never in the way. The front portion of the bed is provided with hinges, so as to drop or to fold under the camera when in use with wide angle lenses of short focus. It is made rigid by use of patent clamp hooks, and is provided with double rack and pinion movement and front focus. The back of this camera is completely reversible, and the slides can be drawn from bottom as well as from top or either side. The Normandie is fitted with the Zephyr double dry plate holder up to 8x10 inclusive; above that size with the Eclipse holder. Where extra holders are required, either the Eclipse or Zephyr may be ordered. Price includes one double plate holder and telescopic brass-bound carrying case, but no lens or tripod.

Size.	Single swing.	Double swing.	Zephy. plate holders, to 8x10.	Eclipse holders.
4 x 5	$13.12	$14.87	$1.08	
4 x 6½	15.75	17.50	1.13	$1.13
5 x 7	15.80	17.55	1.15	1.15
5 x 8	17.60	19.25	1.25	1.25
6½x 8½	19.30	21.87	1.45	1.45
8 x10	21.90	24.50	1.65	1.65
10 x12	30.62	34.12	......	5.40
11 x14	39.38	42.88	......	6.30
14 x17	56.87	60.37	..	9.00

The Carlton Camera.

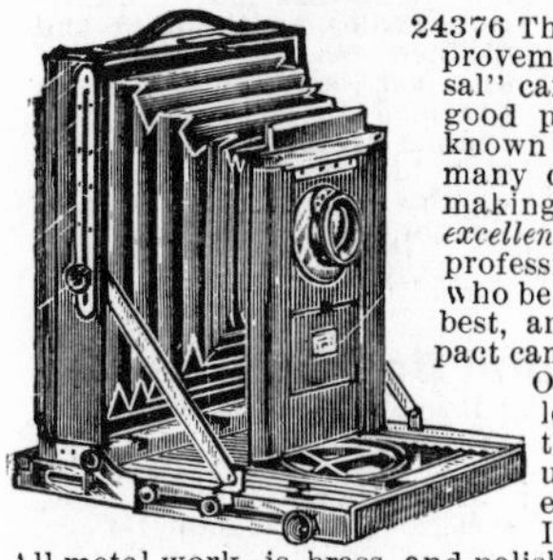

24376 The "Carlton" is an improvement on the "Universal" camera, having all the good points of that well-known box, and in addition many qualities of its own, making it the camera *par excellence* to the amateur or professional photographer who believes in having the best, and is the most compact camera in the market. Owing to the extra length of the bellows, the camera can be used for copying and enlarging, if desired. It has reversible back. All metal work is brass and polished lacquered. The camera box is made of select mahogany, highly polished. The bed carries its own tripod top, adapted to our No. 24451 Combination Tripod. The top is of metal, neatly fitted in the bed, and revolves easily and smoothly, permitting the operator to adjust camera in any direction. A small milled head screw fastens it firmly in position. The Carlton cameras, in sizes to 8x10 inclusive, are furnished with either a long or short canvas case. The former carries the camera and three holders only; the latter will hold the camera, six holders, combination tripod, and in sizes to 6½x8½ inclusive, there is a compartment for lenses. In ordering, specify style of case desired

		Price.
Size of view......4 x5	Double swing......	$30.62
" " 4¼x6½	" "	31.50
" " 5 x7	" "	35.00
" " 5 x8	" "	36.75
" " 6½x8½	" "	39.37
" " 8 x10	" "	43.75

Horseman's No. 2 "Eclipse" Outfit.

POLISHED CHERRY CAMERA, WITH TRIPOD AND COMPLETE CHEMICAL OUTFIT.

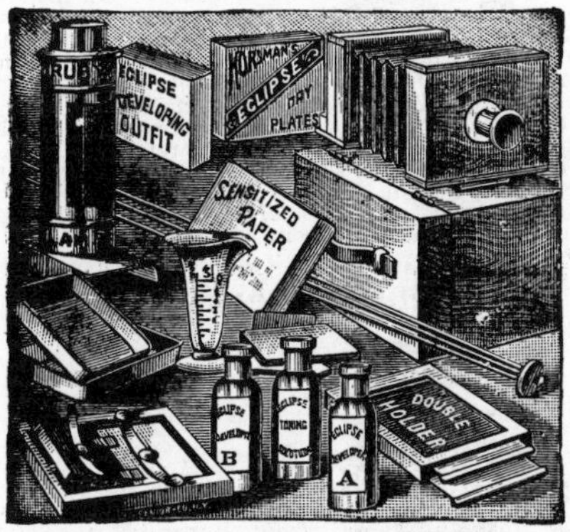

24380 The No. 2 "Eclipse" is gotten up to fill a popular demand. It consists of a hardwood camera, for plate size 3¼x4¼ inches, with leatherette bellows, brass mounted lens, hinged ground glass, double plate holder, tripod and carrying case; weight of above 2 lbs. The chemical outfit for developing and printing which goes with the above contains: Ruby lamp, ½ dozen dry plates, 2 japanned iron trays, 2 bottles developer; 1 box hyposulphite soda, 12 sheets sensitized paper, 1 printing frame, 1 bottle toning solution, 1 dozen bevel edged card mounts. Weight, complete, 10 pounds. Price for complete outfit............$4.50

Horseman's No. 3 "Eclipse" Outfit.

24381 The No. 3 Eclipse Camera makes a full size cabinet photograph or view; size, 4¼x6½ inches. This outfit consists of polished hardwood camera with folding bed and double plate holder, brass mounted lens, with set of stocks, folding tripod, carrying case, printing frame and complete chemical outfit.
Price, for complete outfit...........................$9.00
Weight, complete, 15 pounds.

SUNDRIES FOR HORSEMAN'S ECLIPSE OUTFITS.

Plate Holders, 3¼x4¼, for No. 2. Each.........$0.45
Plate Holders, 4¼x6½, for No, 3. Each.......... .90
"A" and "B" Eclipse Developer, per bottle...... .10
Eclipse Toning Solution........................... .10
We do not handle the Ripley Dry Plates. See quotations of dry plates of standard brands.

OUR

Custom Tailoring Department

Offers excellent opportunities to those who des re Good Clothes at Low Prices. See page 273.

View Finder.

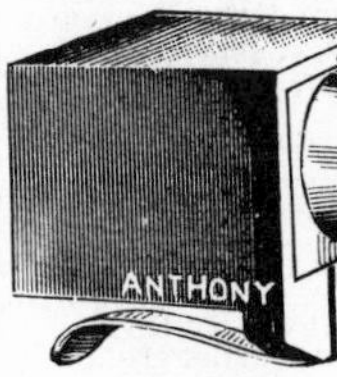

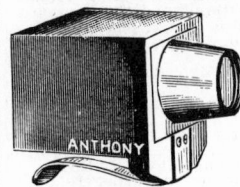

24382

24382 The View Finder is in reality a miniature camera, and is attached to top of a view camera in taking instantaneous pictures of moving objects. The same view is seen on the small screen as is reflected in the camera, and by observing the screen of the finder the exact moment for the exposure can be told; it can be attached to any camera. Price $1.35

Lenses.

A lens can always be used to take pictures smaller than the plate which it is designed to cover. For instance a 5x8 lens can be used to make 4x5 pictures but nothing larger than 5x8. Upon request special prices will be quoted upon Dallmeyer, Darlot, Gray or Clark lenses; in fact upon almost any tube upon the market.

M. W. & Co.'s "Crystal" Single Lens.

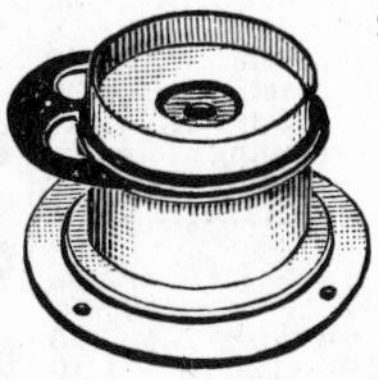

M. W. & Co.'s "Crystal."

24385 M. W. Co.'s Crystal Achromatic Single View Lenses with revolving diaphragm for landscapes; undoubtedly the best Single Achromatic Lens in the market, being much superior to any which usually accompany amateur outfits. They are so constructed as to give pictures of moderate angle with great sharpness and brilliancy.

Size of Plate.	Focus.	Price, complete.
4 x5	6 inch.	$3.85
5 x7	8 inch.	4.50
5 x8	9 inch.	5.00
6½x8½	11½ inch.	6.00
8 x10	12½ inch.	7.25
10 x12	14 inch.	8.50

R. O. & Co.'s Single View Lens.

24386 For Illustration of R. O. Single View Lens, see cut of New Model Improved Camera, No. 24371. For landscape work the single view lens is most used. It gives good results and will even make good interior and portraits. Brass with *revolving diaphragm.*

Size of Plate.	Length of Focus.	No.	Price.
4 x5	6 inch	1	$2.70
4¼x6½	8 inch	1½	3.15
5 x8	10 inch	2	3.60
6½x8½	11 inch	3	4.50
8 x10	13 inch	4	6.30

Pair No. 1 Lenses matched for Stereoscopic work, mounted on front board.......................$5.50

M. W. Co.'s Rapid Rectilinear Lens.

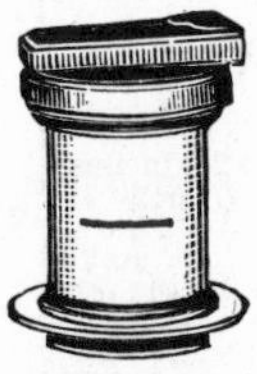

M. W. & Co.'s "Meniscus."

24387 M.W. & Co.'s Rapid Rectilinear *"Meniscus" Double* Achromatic, with set of Waterhouse stops, for portraits, groups, landscapes or instantaneous work. These lenses are not as rapid as our *Extra Rapid Rectilinear "Special"* Lenses, but to those to whom the price of the latter would be an obstacle we can only say that they will meet a long-felt want, as they possess many valuable properties peculiar to themselves.

Visible diam. of Lenses.	Size of Plates.	Back Focus.	Equiv. Focus.	Angle.	Price, complete.
1 inch.	4x5	5½ in.	$2\frac{1}{16}$ in.	75°	$ 8.00
1⅛ inch.	5x7	7½ in.	8¼ in.	75°	9.00
1¼ inch.	5x8	8¼ in.	9⅛ in.	75°	10.00
1⅝ inch.	6½x8½	11⅜ in.	12¾ in.	75°	15.00
2 inch.	8x10	$14\frac{9}{16}$ in.	16¼ in.	75°	20.00
$2\frac{5}{16}$ inch.	10x12	16 in.	18¼ in.	75°	25.00

IMMENSE -:- NUMBERS.

The things we quote in our HARDWARE DEPARTMENT are more numerous than you may think. Try counting them. All standard goods, too. We don't sell anything else.

M. W. & Co.'s Extra Rapid Recitilinear Lens.

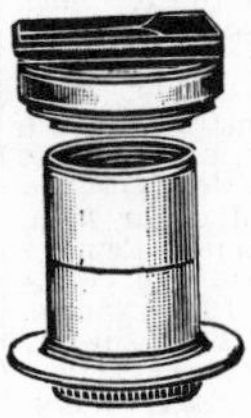

M. W. & Co.'s "Special."

24389 M.W.& Co.'s Extra Rapid Rectilinear, Apalantic Double Achromatic ("Special"). Removable hood; with set of Waterhouse diaphragms, for portraits, groups, landscapes, or instantaneous objects; highest finish and finest quality; each lens guaranteed. Stops cut and working to the standard sizes, with full aperture. These lenses cover plates to the edge and quality is equal to either of the three popular English lenses, Dallmeyer, Ross and Beck, which are much more expensive.

Visible diam. of Lenses.	Size of Plate.	Back Focus	Equiv. Focus.	Price, complete.	Price wth Iris diaphragm.
1 inch.	4x5	4⅞ in.	5½ in.	$13.50	$16.50
1¼ inch.	5x7	7½ in.	8⅛ in.	18.00	21.00
$1\frac{7}{16}$ inch.	5x8	8¼ in.	8¾ in.	20.00	28.00
1⅝ inch.	6½x8½	10¼ in.	11 in.	26.50	30.00
$2\frac{1}{32}$ inch.	8x10	12¾ in.	13⅞ in.	31.00	34.50
$2\frac{1}{16}$ inch.	10x12	14 in.	16⅛ in.	40.00	48.00
$2\frac{9}{16}$ inch.	12x16	17¾ in.	$19\frac{3}{16}$ in.	48.00	60.00
3⅛ inch.	16x20	23¼ in.	25½ in.	65.00	78.00

M. W. & Co.'s Symmetrical Wide Angular Rectilinear Lens.

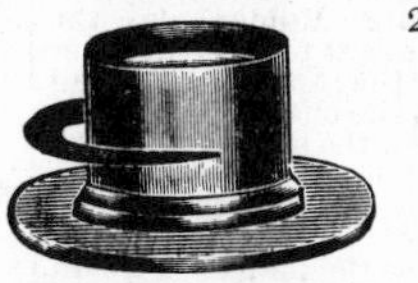

M.W. & Co."'Wide Angle" double Achromatic.

24394 M. W. & Co.'s Symmetrical "Wide Angle." Double Achromatic (Special). For work requiring great width of angle, and extra rectilinear results, such as interiors, architectural or street views, over an angle of 90 or 100 degrees, and have a remarkable depth of focus compared with other wide angle lenses. They are the most rapid wide angle lenses made. They are distinguished by the comparatively large stops with which they give sharp images, a result which is largely due to the great perfection of their polish. Revolving diaphragm. Removable hood.

Diam. of Lenses.	Size of Plate.	Equivalent Focus.	Price, complete.
$\frac{9}{16}$ inch.	4 x5	4 inch.	$12.50
⅝ inch.	5 x8	5 inch.	14.50
$\frac{11}{16}$ inch.	6½x8½	6 inch.	17.00
$\frac{13}{16}$ inch.	8 x10	7 inch.	22.00

Drop Shutters.

Special prices quoted on Hadden, Bauch & Lomb, Thornton, Packard & Low shutters upon application.

The Universal Drop Shuttere·

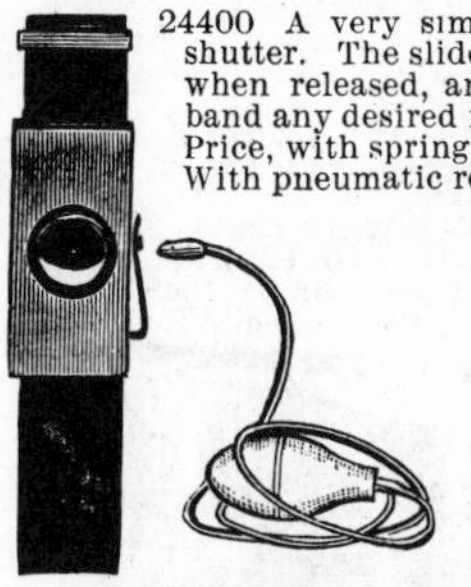

24400 A very simple yet effective form of shutter. The slide falls of its own weight when released, and by the use of rubber band any desired rapidity may be obtained.
Price, with spring release.............$0.90
With pneumatic release, bulb and tube 1.40

"Marvel Shutter.

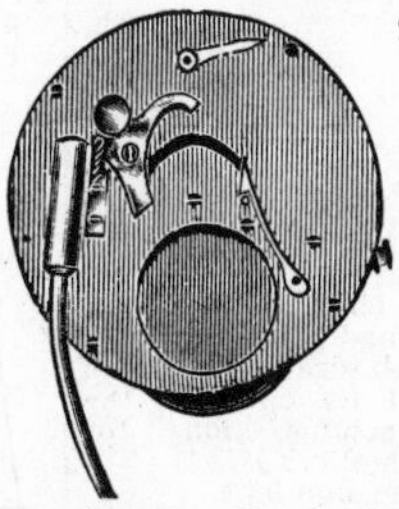

24407 Is made to fit on the front end of the lens tube, and is constructed on the simplest principles and has the following distinct advantages over any other upon the market. It is the easiest and quickest changed from time to instantaneous.

It is less liable to get out of order than any other.

It is steel bronzed over brass, with parts nickeled—therefore the handsomest in appearance.

There is absolutely no rebound, as the disk locks itself after making the exposure.

It is adjusted to the lens by a velvet-lined flance which is tightened by a screw—therefore avoiding all injury to the tube or making it necessary to cut same.

In ordering it is only necessary to measure the lens' hood with a strip of paper and forward same to us.

Size........4x5	5x8	Larger size.
Prices....$5.50	$5.50	$6.25.

New French Shutter.

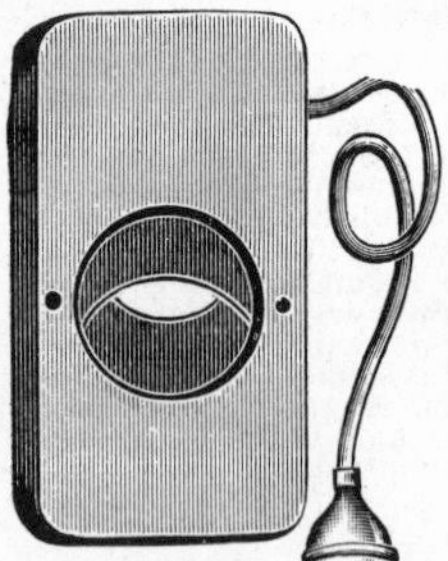

24408 A light, handsome two-wing shutter for both time and instantaneous exposures at a moderate price, handsomely nickeled. The instrument is a tube shutter, and to place same in position unscrew nickel-plated collar from back of frame. Remove the lens hood, slip collar over barrel of lens, and replace hood; fasten shutter and lens together by screwing collar in place. When ordering give diameter of both hood and barrel of lens upon which shutter is intended to be used.

Size.	Price
1¼ inch opening	$4.00
1⅝ inch opening	4.50
2⅛ inch opening	5.00

Perfcet Dry Plate Holder.

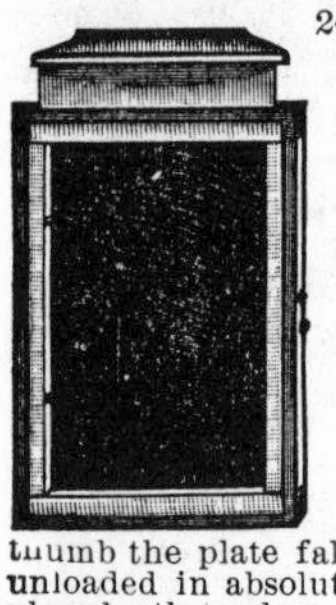

24409 The New Model, New Model Improved and New Model Stereoscopic Cameras are the *only* cameras quoted in this catalogue that these holders will fit. We can furnish almost *any* kind of plate holders at less than list price. Where ordering, *be sure to state what camera the holder it is intended to be used in.* The Perfection Double Plate Holder is the simplest and best plate holder ever placed on the market. To load this holder, the end of the plate is rested against the spring-bar at the end of the holder; then by simply pressing the spring bar with the thumb the plate falls into place. Can be loaded and unloaded in absolute darkness, as the plate is held in place by the ends only; the full width of the plate is exposed and but 1-16 inch is cut off from each end.

Size	Each	Size.	Each.
3¼x4¼	$0.90	5 x 8	$1.25
4 x5	.90	6½x 8½	1.45
4½x6½	1.12	8 x10	1.70
5 x7	1.15		

Inside Kits.

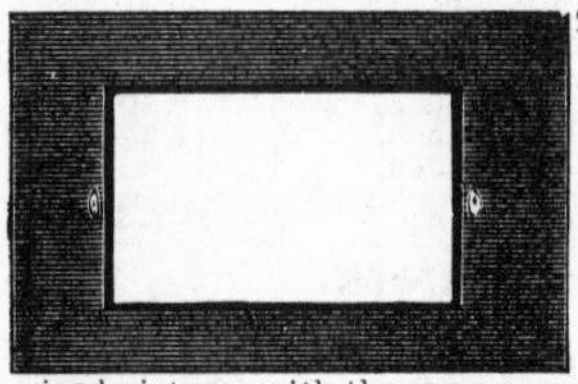

24410 Consists of thin wooden frames, made to fit in the Perfection Plate Holder with openings for smaller plate, with spring for holding plate in place. Enables anyone having a camera to take smaller sized pictures with the same apparatus.

☞ *When ordering, please mention size of plate holder as well as size of plate kits are for.*

Size.		Each.
4 x5	to hold 3¼x4¼ plates	$0.20
4¼x6½	to hold 3¼x4¼ plates	.20
5 x7	to hold 3¼x4¼ or 4x5 plates	.25
5 x8	to hold 3¼x4¼, 4x5 or 4¼x6½ plates	.25
6½x8½	to hold 4x5, 4¼x6½, 5x7 or 5x8 plates	.30
8 x 10	to hold 5x7, 5x8 or 6½x8½ plates	.35
10x12	to hold 5x7, 5x8, 6½x 8½ or 8x10 plates	.45
11x14	to hold 5x8, or 6½x8½, 8x10 or 10x12 plates	.55

Inside kits are made to hold any ONE of the sizes mentioned above, but are not adjustable to all the sizes listed.

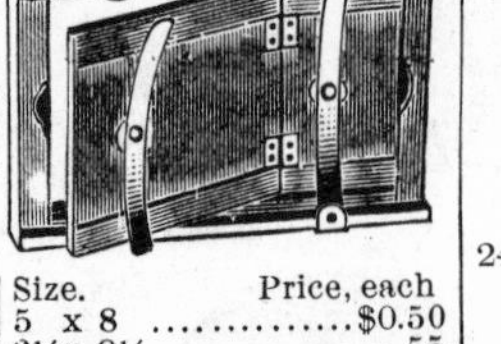

24412 The Favorite Printing Frame, especially desirable for amateurs, on account of its lightness, at the same time being equal in strength and durability to the ordinary flat printing frame.

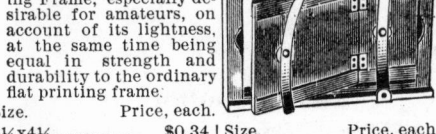

Size.	Price, each.	Size.	Price, each
3¼x4¼	$0.34	5 x 8	$0.50
4 x5	.36	6½x 8½	.55
4¼x6½	.40	8 x10	.67
5 x 7	45		

Tripods.

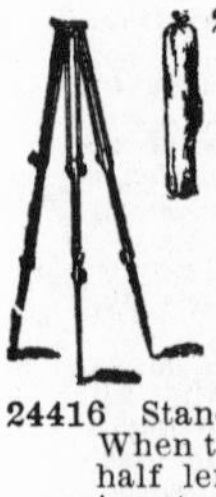

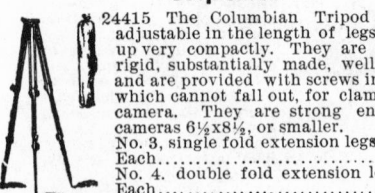

24415 The Columbian Tripod is made adjustable in the length of legs and fold up very compactly. They are perfectly rigid, substantially made, well finished and are provided with screws in the top, which cannot fall out, for clamping the camera. They are strong enough for cameras 6½x8½, or smaller.

No. 3, single fold extension legs. Each $1.75
No. 4. double fold extension legs. Each 2.25

24416 Standard Folding Trpiod, with iron head. When tripod head is removed, the legs will fold to half length. The screw remains always in the iron top ready for use and not liable to loss. It is light, strong and rigid.
Price, for cameras from 4x5 to 6½x8½ $1.80

Tripods—Continued.

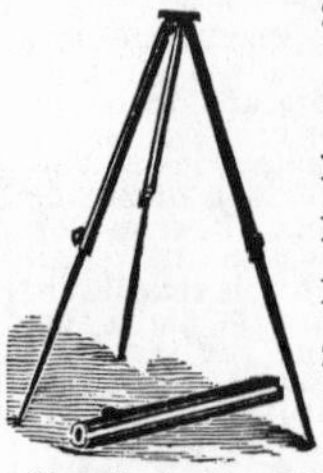

24417 Carlton's Sliding Tripod, light, strong and rigid; easy to adjust in rough places, quickly taken down, very compact

	Each.
No. 1, for 4x5 and 4¼x6½ camera	$2.25
No. 2, for 5x8 and 6½x8½ camera	2.70
No. 3, for 8x10 and 10x12 camera	3.15

24418 Combination Sliding and Folding Tripod. Length, when closed, only 22 inches; a beauty. No. 1, for cameras 3¼x4¼ to 4¼x6½ 2.75
No. 2, for cameras 5x8 and 6½x8½ 3.15
No. 3, for cameras 8x10 and 11x14 3.60

Developing Trays.

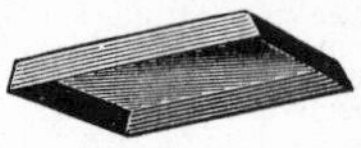

24420 Japanned Tin Developing Trays, made with two small ridges in bottom to prevent plates from adhering.

4x5, each	$0.20	6½x 8½, each	$0.30
5x8, each	.25	8 x10, each	.40
		10 x12, each	.50

24421 Developing Trays, vulcanized rubber.

4x5, each	$0.25	6½x 8½, each	$0.70
5x8, each	.55	8 x10, each	1.00
		10 x12, each	1.50

24422 Amber Glass Trays, for developing. Heavy, shallow, for plates.
4½x6½ size $0.25 | 5x8 size $0.35

24423 Papier Mache Trays.

	Each.		Each.
1 size, 3¼x4¼	$0.25	4 size, 7 x 9	$0.70
2 size, 4¼x5½	.30	5 size, 8¼x10¼	.95
3 size, 5¼x8¼	.50	6 size, 10¼x12¼	1.40

Quotations given up to size 28x34, when desired.

Funnels.

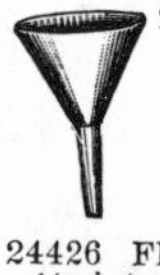

24425 Glass Funnels, for filtering, etc.

½ pint, each	$0.15
1 pint, each	.20
1 quart, each	.25
2 quarts, each	.35

24426 Fluted Glass Funnels, for filtering.

½ pint, each	$0 15
1 pint	.20

24427 Hard Rubber Funnels, not easily broken.

¼ pint, each	.40
½ pint, each	.45
1 pint, each	.50
1 quart, each	.60

Graduated Glasses.

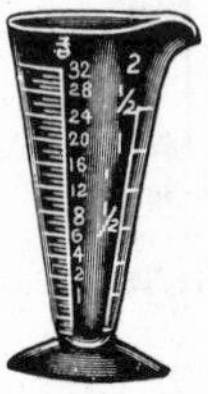

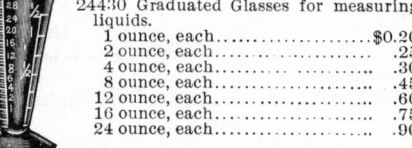

24430 Graduated Glasses for measuring liquids.

1 ounce, each	$0.20
2 ounce, each	.25
4 ounce, each	.30
8 ounce, each	.45
12 ounce, each	.60
16 ounce, each	.75
24 ounce, each	.90

Glass Mortars and Pestles.

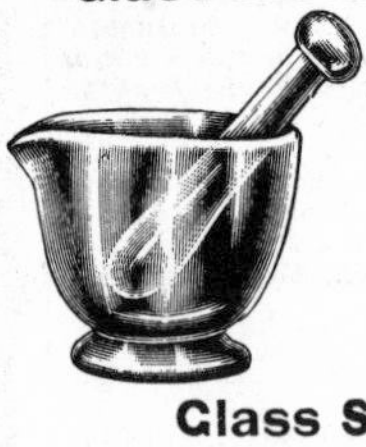

24432 1 ounce, 2½x2¼ inches. Each $0.15
2 ounce, 3x2¾ inches. Each $0.20
4 ounces, 4x3 inches. Each $0.25
8 ounce, 4¼x3½ inches. Each $0.35

Glass Spirit Lamps.

With ground glass cap.

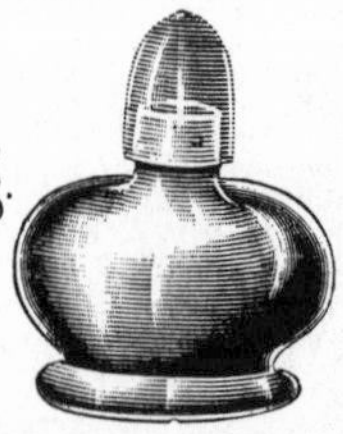

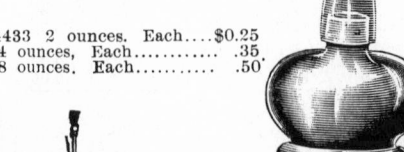

24433 2 ounces. Each $0.25
4 ounces, Each .35
8 ounces. Each .50

Scales and Weights

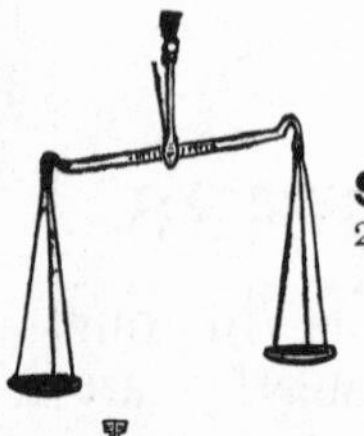

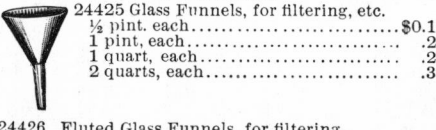

24455 Hand Scales, with weights, 5 in. beam, 2¼ inch pans, neatly put up in lined folding box.
Price $0.50
Postage .10

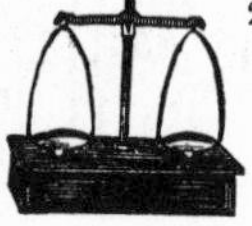

24456 Prescription Scales, with pillar and beam on polished walnut or cherry box, with drawer, 6 inch beam, 2½ inch pans, and includes full set weights.
Price $3.50
Weight, 1½ pounds.

Scales and Weights—Continued.

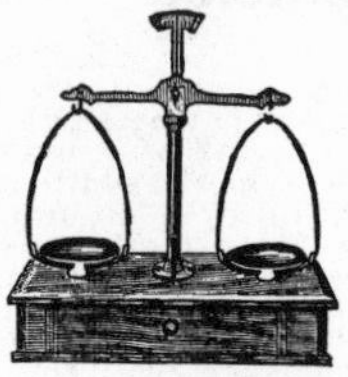

24457 The Lakeside Prescription Scales, with pillar and 8 inch beam, on finished ashwood box, with drawer. Finished in lacquered brass, and has nickel plated pans, 2¾ inch diameter. Full set weights $4.25
Weight, 1¾ pounds.

Camel's Hair and Bristle Brushes.

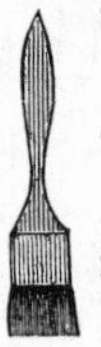

24459 Camel's Hair Brushes, for dusting off plates before using.

Width	1 in.	1½in.	2 in.	2½in.	3 in.
Each	25c.	30c.	50c.	60c.	80c.

24460 Bristle Brushes, for pasting, mounting and varnishing.

Width	1 in.	1½in.	2 in.	2½ in.	3 in.
Each	10c.	15c.	20c.	25c.	30c.

24461 Marking Brush, plain handle, white bristle. Each $0.05
Per dozen .50

24462 Marking Brush, camel's hair, plain handle. Each .07
Per dozen .75

24463 Bristle, Art Marking Brush, colored handle, a very superior brush. Each .10
Per dozen 1.00

Perfection Magazine Flash Lamp.

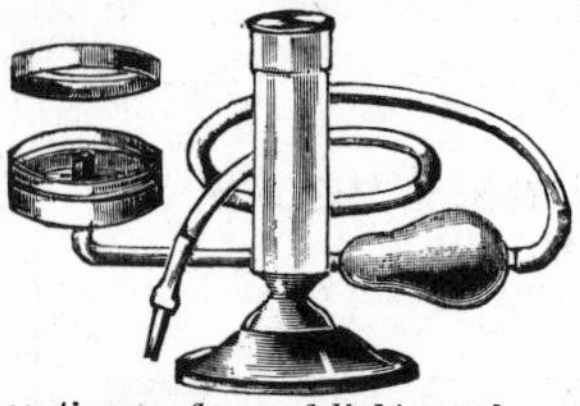

24465 The Perfection is considered the best magazine lamp yet produced for the use of pure magnesium.

The magazine, when loaded to its full capacity, contains powder sufficient for twenty flashes An instantaneous flash or a *continuous flame of light* may be produced, the length of exposure depending upon the will of the operator. The circular wick produces a large volume of flame, entirely consuming the full discharge of powder.

A mouth-piece and rubber tubing are supplied with each lamp; a bulb may be attached if preferred.

The extreme simplicity of the Perfection Lamp, the ease of manipulation, and the excellent results produced, will recommend it to all desiring a safe and thoroughly practical instrument at a low price.

Price, complete $1.80

Ruby Lanterns.

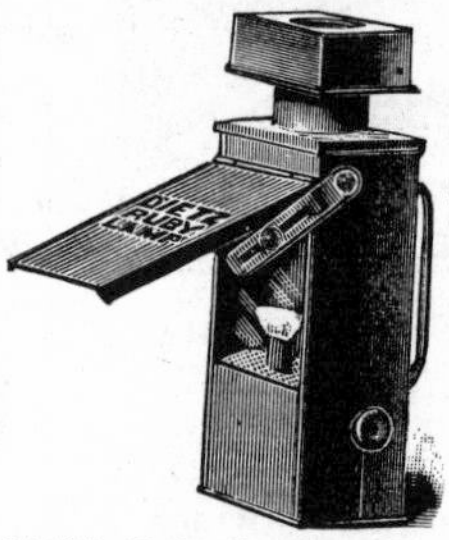

24466 Ruby (Dark-Room.) Lamp, pocket form, very portable, with ruby glass front. Burns oil. Each $0.50

24467 Ruby Lamp, same style as above, but with larger illuminating surface; made of polished brass; a first-class high-grade lamp. Price $0.85

24468 The Universal Lamp. This is a very superior lamp, one of the best on the market for the price. The combustion is perfect; it gives a steady flame, and is free from smoke and smell. Each .90

24470 Carlton Dark Room Lantern has three illuminating surfaces and reflector. A comfortable and well ventilated kerosene lantern. Price, each 1.80

24471 Tisdall's Ruby Candle Light. No dirt, oil or smell of any kind. The best light for the amateur; not easily broken, and can be carried in the pocket .90

Burnishers.

We can save you money on any burnisher made. Write for prices before purchasing elsewhere.

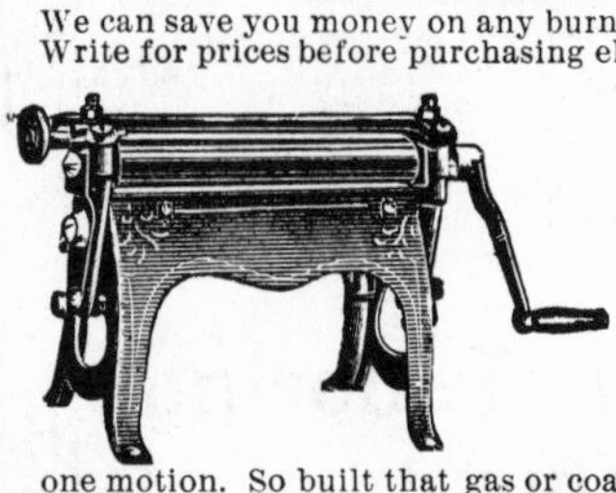

24475 Entrekin's New Victor Burnisher with patented movable burnishing tool and one wheel adjustment for giving a uniform pressure and perfect accuracy of adjustment, with one motion. So built that gas or coal oil lamp can be used for heating; 8-inch roll $9.00

24476 Entrekin's Accurate Rotary Burnisher. This machine has the one wheel adjustment, the lock nut and set screw and swing fire pan. It may be heated with oil or gas. Specify which is wanted.
Price, 10-inch roll $18.00

Burnishers—Continued.

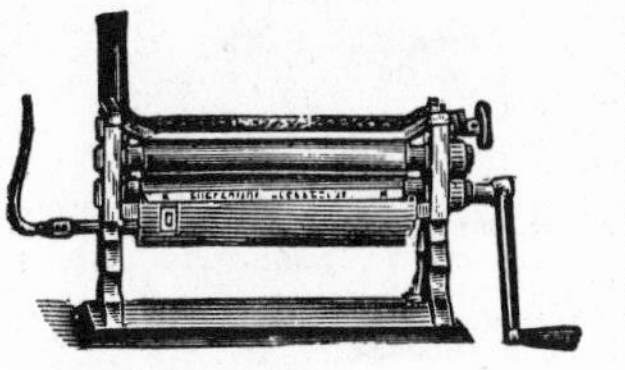

477 Smith's Amateur Columbian Polisher. Full nickel plate finish and a beauty for practical amateur work, Fitted with gas or gasoline heaters. Specify which is wanted.

Price, 8-inch roll $14.00
Weight 22 pounds.
10-inch roll, each 20.00
15-inch roll, each 27.00

24478 The Globe Enameler. Patented by Jas. H. Smith, the most perfect burnisher on the market. Spa.e cannot be spared to ennumerate the many points of excellence of this machine, but a detailed description will be mailed to any one requesting same. For gas or gasoline; state which is wanted.

Price, 10-inch roll $27.00
" 15 " " 36.00
" 20 " " 45.00
" 25 " " 54.00

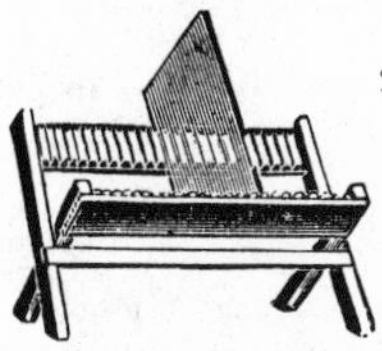

24479 A cheap and convenien accessory for the dark room, preventing the negative from scratching while drying; holds 24 negatives.
Price, each, for plates up to 6½x8½ $0.40

Class Forms.

For trimming photographic prints before mountings.

24480 Stereoscopic, arched top $0.25
3¼x3¼, square corners .... .20
4x5 .... .35
4¼x6½ .... .50
5x8 .... .50
6½x8½ .... .75

Ground Class.

SELECTED CLEAR CRYSTAL PLATE.

Order No. 24481.

Size.	Each.	Size.	Each.
4x5	$0.15	6½x8½	$0.40
4¼x6½	.20	8x10	.50
5x8	.30	10x12	.60

Ruby or Orange Class.

FOR DARK ROOMS.

Order No. 24482.

Size.	Per light.	Size.	Per light.
6½x8½	$0.20	11x14	$0.60
8x10	.35	12x20	.75
10x12	.50		

Always state whether you want ruby or orange color.

Retouching Pencils.

See 23962. Smith's Metalic Points. Each $0.23

Mailing Envelopes.

24484 Envelopes for mailing individual photographs. Mail your letter and photograph well protected in the same sealed package for 4c., and thus be assured of both reaching their destination in good order.
Price, per package of 25 envelopes $0.35
Price, per box of 250 envelopes 2.50
Postage on package of envelopes .... .25

Negative Preserves.

Weight of box of envelopes, 16 pounds.

24485 Invaluable for preserving negatives from dust, scratches, etc. Consists of stout paper envelopes open at one end, with thumb hole and printed lines for name, number and remarks referring to the negative. Fifty in a package.

	Per pkg.		Per pkg.
3¼x3¼	$0.15	5x8	$0.30
4x5 or 4¼x5½	.20	6½x8½	.32
4¼x6½	.25	8x10	.40
5x7	.28	10x12	.70

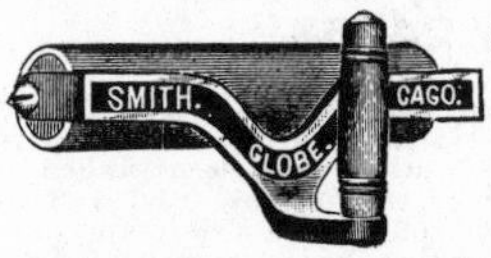

24486 Smith's Patent; the best mounter and squeegee on the market. See illustration. Light wood roller, covered with soft rubber.

Price, 6-inch ....$0.90 Price, 8-inch $1.15
Price, 10-inch 1.45

24487 Same as above, except that rollers are very heavy, made of iron.
Price, 6-inch ....$1.35 Price, 8-inch $1.60
Price, 12-inch 1.80

If We Make a Mistake... We Want to Correct It.

Don't fail to tell us about any that may occur.

Photographic Paste, Varnishes, Miscellaneous Sundries, Etc.

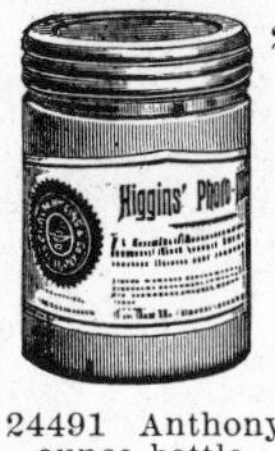

24490 Higgins' Photo Mounter: is an always ready adheser, which will not spill, spatter nor drop off the brush. Never hardens, separates or becomes gritty; does not cockle, strike through, or change the tone; never moulds sours or deteriorates in any way; a unique adhesive scientifically made to meet the special requirements of photographic mounting.
Price, per small jar $0.23
Price, per pint jar .... .45

24491 Anthony's Flint Varnish, for negatives, 6 ounce bottle .... .40
24492 Anthony's Diamond Varnish, for positives or tin types, 6 ounce bottle .... .40
24493 Anthony's Retouching Varnish; per bottle .... .50
24495 Plate Lifters, prevents soiling the fingers .10
24496 Alpha Rubber Finger Tips (in sets of 3). Per set .... .15
24498 Gossamer Focusing Cloth, best quality ... .75
24500 Hydrometers for photographers' solutions, single degree .... .50
24502 Negative Washing Boxes, adaptable from 4x5 to 8x10, best quality 3.35
24503 Anthony's Adjustable Developing Fork for plates 4x5 to 8x10, each .... .85
For plates 3¼x4¼ to 5x8 .... .60
24505 Copelin's Opaque, per bottle .... .36
24506 Lockwood's Photo Clips 05
24507 Litmus Paper, blue or red, sensitive, cut slips, put up in bottle. Price .... .14
24508 Photographer's Note Book, compact and simple, for recording exposures, neatly bound; size, 3x4½ inches. Price, including pencil ...... .25
24510 Absorbent Filtering Cotton (Lawton's), extra fine quality, ½ pound package .... .40
¼ pound package .... .25
24512 Robinson's Straight Trimmers, for trimming photographs .... .20
24514 Robinson's Revolving Photograph Trimmers .... .25
24515 C. S. Glace Polish, to apply to photographs before burnishing, ready for use. Per box .20

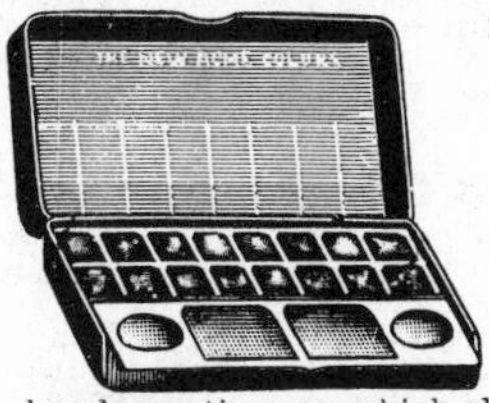

24519 The New Columbian Transparent Water Colors for coloring photoportraits or views, lantern slides, transparencies, engravings, etc., on any kind of paper. These are not liquid colors, but are moist and put up in cups, the complete sets being contained in handsome tin case, which also contains palettes and directions for use. They are easy to apply; very effective and more durable to light than any liquid colors, and as they are sold in a condensed form greater strength can be secured than with the diluted liquid colors. They are also more economical, as they neither spill, freeze nor precipitate.
Each box now contains 18 colors of all desirable shades.
No difficulty in burnishing prints after color.
Price, per box, including 245 page cloth bound book of instructions to water coloring $2.25

24520 PHOTINTO, the magic liquid colors for tinting photos, art folios, magazine pictures, etc. No experience in art necessary to learn coloring with photinto, as full directions how to do it accompanies each box, and these can be learned in ten minutes. Price, per box of six bottles, assorted colors, with directions. $0.50
Cannot be sent by mail.

Photographic Papers. Dry Plates, Etc.

24521 Filtering Paper, best gray, round, 13 in. diameter. Per pack of 10 sheets $0.10
Per pack of 100 sheets .... .75
24522 Blotting Paper white, extra heavy, for drying photographic prints, 19x24 inches.
Per sheet .... .10
Per dozen .... .75
24523 Yellow Post Paper, for dark room illumination; large size. Per sheet .... .04
Per dozen sheets .... .40
24524 Carbutt's Ruby Paper, for dark room illumination, 20x25. Per sheet .... .25

WE quote on page 186 a large assortment of Spring and Summer Novelties in

Ladies' Jewelry,

Including
BELT BUCKLES,
CZARINA NECK BUCKLES,
BELT PINS
VEIL CLASPS, ETC.

"Kloro" Aristotype Printing Paper.

24525 The best Gelatine Printing Out Paper on the market, and at prices far below those at which other papers are sold. We want this paper to be in the hands of every Photographer, amateur and professional in the country. Every *professional*, not acquainted with the merits of Kloro, who will send us his printed card and letter, head and two 2 cent stamps for postage, with a request that we give him a sample of Kloro, will be supplied with a trial package of the paper, cabinet size, free of charge. It is a reliable paper and will print with brilliant high lights, giving silky half-tones and rich transparent shadows. Can be used with combined or separate toning baths, and suitable for strong or soft negatives. Kloro Paper neither cracks, curls nor blisters. A finished Kloro print is durable and not easily scratched and marred. A perfect substitute for albumen paper

PRICES OF KLORO PAPER.		Doz.	Gross.
2¼x3⅝	Carte de Visite	$0.15	$0.75
3x4	Mantello	.15	1.00
3½x3½	Trokonet No. 1	.20	1 20
2¾x5⅝	Swiss Panel	.20	1.20
3¼x4¼		20	1.20
*3⅞x5½	Cabinet	.25	1.35
3⅞x5⅞		.25	1.35
4x5		.25	1.50
4x6		.25	1.50
4¼x6½		.30	2.00
5x7		.35	2.65
5x8		.40	3.00
5½x7½	Paris Panel	.45	3.40
6x8		.50	3.75
6½x8½		.55	4.10
7x9		.65	5.25
7½x9½		.70	5.75
8x10		.75	6.00
10x12		1.10	9.00
11x14		1.25	11.25
14x17		1.85	18.00
16x20		2.50	24.00
18x22	½ doz. $1.75	3.00	30.00
20x24	½ doz. 2.00	3.50	33.00

SECONDS.—A limited quantity of Standard Cabinet size and 4x5 trimmed Seconds at $1.00 per gross.

*STANDARD CABINET SIZE.—This size will be furnished on all orders for "Cabinets" when no special size is mentioned. Orders for all sizes under 5x7 in less than gross lots will be charged at dozen prices. 5x7 and up to 18x22 in dozens. ½ gross and gross lots only. In half-gross an additional charge of 25 cents to ⅛ of gross price will be charged for packing. For prices on toning and fixing solution see 24566.

PROOFS.—Kloro Paper, proofs, per gross cabinets, 60 cents.

Albumen Paper.

24529 *Ready Sensitized Albumen Paper. Put up in light proof packages of 2 dozen sheets.

Size.	Per pkg.	Size.	Per pkg.
3¼x4¼	$0.25	5x8	$0.72
4x5	.38	6½x8½	.95
4¼x6½	.47	8x10	1.40
5x7	.65	18x22 per doz. sheets.	2.85

Ferro-Prussiate or Blue Paper.

24530 Royal Ferro-Prussiate or Blue paper, for making blue and white pictures, very easy to manipulate, requires no toning. Prints can be made very rapidly. No chemicals required in the use of this paper. It is merely printed for about ten minutes in the sunlight, and then washed thoroughly in clean water. This paper is manufactured expressly for our trade, and is unsurpassed for brilliancy of color and finish. Will retain its sensitiveness longer than any other paper on the market. Full and complete directions for working accompanies each package. Put up in light tight packages of 24 sheets.

Size	Per pkge.	Size	Per pkge.
3¼x4¼	$0.16	5 x8	$0.40
4 x5	.20	6½x8²	.50
4¼x6²	.30	8 x10	.65
5 x7	.36		

Dry Plates.

24535 Direction for using plates accompany every package. We sell nearly all the popular brands, quotations below being for seeds 26X, Cramer's Crown, etc. The sensitometer numbers indicate the degree of rapidity, the higher the number the more rapid the plate. When ordering *always give size, brand and sensitometer number wanted.*

Size.	Per doz.	Size.	Per doz.
3¼x4¼	$0.40	6½x8½	$1.50
4 x5	.60	8 x10	2.15
4¼x6½	.80	10 x12	3.40
5 x7	1.00	11 x14	4.50
5 x8	1.13		

The New Eagle Dry Plates.

24536 Under this number we offer one of the very best plates on the market at prices which should be a consideration to every photographer, whether amateur or professional. The sensitometer No. 50X cannot be beaten for speed, quality, brilliancy or cleanliness. The No. 40XXX should be used for all landscape work where time exposures are given. The Orthochromatic are equal in rapidity to the No. 50 and especially valuable to those desiring to obtain true "color values." The "non-halation" are for interior work where the photographer is compelled to make an exposure against the light. They will stand an exposure of thirty minutes of a window through which the sun is shining, without showing any halation effect. Prices as given below are for broken lots. Special low prices will be quoted on case lots and on Process and Eagle equatorial plates specially made for use in hot climates. Be sure to state whether 50X or 40XXX are wanted.

Dry Plates—Continued.

Doz. in case.	Size.	Price per doz. Orthochromatic.	Price per doz. Nos. 50x-40xxx
40	2½x2½		$ 0.19
40	2½x4		.22
39	3¼x4¼	$ 0.41	.34
24	4 x5	.59	.49
24	4¼x5½	.68	.56
28	4¼x6½	.81	.68
22	4¾x6½	.90	.75
22	5 x7	.99	.82
22	5 x8	1.13	.94
12	6½x8½	1.49	1.24
12	7 x10	1.98	1.65
12	8 x10	2.16	1.80
3	10 x12	3.42	3.05
3	11 x14	4.50	3.75
2	14 x17	8.10	6.75
1	16 x20	11.25	9.38
1	17 x20	11.70	9.75
1	18 x22	13.95	12 62
1	20 x24	16.65	13.88

—24537

Doz. in case.	Size.	Price per doz. Regular or Orthochromate Stripping.	Price per doz. Imperial Non Halation.
39	3¼x4¼		$ 0.50
24	4 x5		.72
24	4¼x5½		.81
28	4¼x6½		.99
22	4¾x6½		1.08
22	5 x7	$ 1.31	1.26
22	5 x8	1.49	1.40
12	6½x8½	1.98	1.89
12	7 x10	2.66	2.43
12	8 x10	2.88	2.70
3	10 x12	4.95	4.28
3	11 x14	5.99	5.63
2	14 x17	10.80	10 00
1	16 x20	14.99	14.18
1	17 x20	15.57	14.63
1	18 x22	18.0C	17.33
1	20 x24	22.05	21.15

24538 Lantern Slide Platcs. Size, 3¼x4 inches, made on thin crystal glass.
Per dozen $0.50

24539 Non-Sensitized Ferrotype Plates, for collodion work or for squeegeeing aristotype prints. size, 10x14 inches. Each $0.10
Per dozen .... .75

Card Mounts.

Card mounts are cards upon which to paste the finished print. As the appearance of the finished photographs depends in no small degree upon the manner in which it is mounted, a good picture is worthy a good mount. Our mounts are put up in packages of twenty-five, and we do not break packages. Note great reduction in prices from former quotations.

24540 Plain white card board mounts, fair quality.

Size.	Per pkg.	Per 100.	Size.	Per pkg.	Per 100.
6½x8½	$0.20	$0.55	10x12	$0.35	$1.05
8 x10	.25	.70	11x14	.40	1.31

24541 Extra heavy, white card board mounts.

Size.	Per pkg.	Per 100.	Size.	Per pkg.	Per 100.
3¼x4¼	$0.10	$0.35	6½x8½	$0.40	$1.50
4 x5	.15	.40	8 x10	.55	2.00
4¼x6½	.20	.65	10x12	.85	3.00
5 x8	.30	.95	11x14	1.00	3.75

24542 Unenameled, good quality, round corners, assorted tints.

Size.	Per Pkg.	Per 100.	Size.	Per Pkg.	Per 100.
3¼x4¼	$0.10	$0.35	5¼x8½	$0.25	$0.80
4¼x5¼	.15	.45	6½x8½	.30	1.00
5 x7	.20	.55	7 x9	.35	1 25
5 x8	.22	.65	8 x10	.40	1.45

24543 Gold Bevel Edge, good quality and heavy weight, light amber and white.

Size.	Per pkg.	Per 100.	Size.	Per pkg.	Per 100.
3½x4½	$0.30	$0.90	5x8	$0.60	$2.10
4¼x5¼	.35	1.10	6½x8½	.70	2.65
4¼x6½	40	1.25	8x10	1.00	3.90
5x7	.55	1.90	10x12	2.00	7.13

24544 Bottle Green, gold bevel edges, gray back

Size.	Per pkg.	Per 100	Size.	Per pkg.	Per 100.
4¼x5¼	$0.40	$1.45	6½x8½	$1.00	$3.60
4¼x6½	.50	1.60	8x10	1.40	5.50
5x8	.70	2.50			

No. 24545 same as No. 24544 except that color is *maroon* instead of bottle green.

24546 Extra heavy, best quality mounts, with wide gold bevel edge. None better. Primrose color.

Size.	Per Pkg.	Per 100.	Size.	Per Pkg.	Per 100.
4 x5	$0.85	$3.25	6½x8½	$1.50	$5.25
4½x6½	.90	3.25	8 x10	2.00	7.50
5 x8	1.35	5.00			

24547 Extra heavy, best quality mounts, extra wide, gold bevel edge, in bottle green. An elegant card for the finest work.

Size.	Per Pkg.	Per 100.	Size.	Per Pkg.	Per 100.
4 x5	$0.95	$3.63	6½x8½	$1.60	$6.00
4¼x6½	1.00	3.63	8 x10	2.25	8.75
5 x8	1.40	5.50			

Cabinet Mounts.

	Per Pkg.	Per. 100
24548 Plain edge, round corners, cabinet mounts; rose and primrose	$0.15	$0.40
24549 Gold, bevel edge, round corners, cabinet mounts; white and primrose	.20	.70
24550 Gold, serrated edge, unenameled, cabinet mounts; rose and primrose	.25	.85
24551 Gold, bevel edge, cabinet mounts, *black* only	.40	1.45

Miscellaneous Mounts — Caterson's Ferrotype Holders, Etc.

	Per Pkg.	Per 100.
24552 Carte de Visite Mounts; size. 2½x4¼ inches; enameled back, plain face, in white, primrose, rose and pearl.	$0.10	$0.30
24553 Carre Mounts; size, 3x3 inches; gold, bevel edge, for mounting square or circle pictures 3x3 inches or less in diameter; rose and primrose	.20	65
24554 Mantello Mounts, white, enameled face, plain back, crenate edge cards 4¼x6 inches, for mounting 3x4 prints. A new and handsome mount	.35	1.20
24555 Caterson's Ferrotype Cases, assorted tints, red borders, oval opening, card size	.12	.35
24556 Caterson's Ferrotype Cases, assorted tints, cabinet size, arch top or oval openings	.30	1.00

Stereoscopic Mounts.

	Per Pkg.	Per 100
24558 Unenameled both sides, dark buff and primrose colors; size, 3½x7 in.	$0.15	$0.45
24559 Enameled face, plain back, in light buff, gray and tea colors. Size, 4x7	.25	.75

Morehouse Photograph Album.

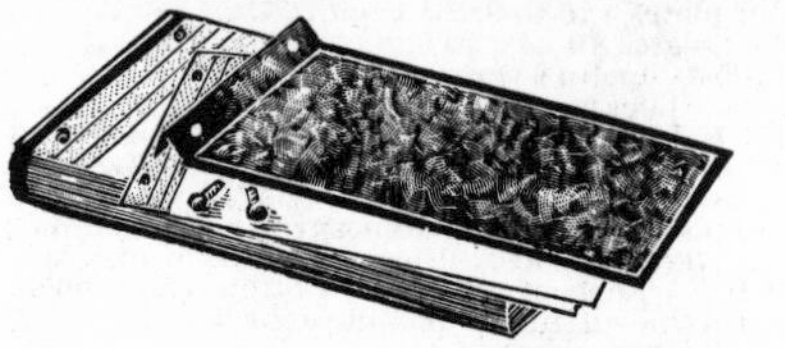

For Mounted or Unmounted Photographs.

It has an adjustable extension, thus allowing from twenty to forty pages to be put in without injuring the appearance of the book. It opens perfectly flat, allowing the leaves to fall evenly when opened at any page, and is so constructed that one or more leaves can be taken out without disturbing the balance. Made in the most desirable bindings.

For Mounted Photographs.

24560 These books are furnished with twenty-five gummed stubs, to which the already mounted photograph can be attached.

Size,	Style "A" Full Cloth	Style "B" Seal Back and Corners.	Extra gummed stubs or hinges. Per Pkg of 25.
6x7	$0.95	$1.65	$0.35
7x10	1.18	1.90	.45
10x12	1.42	2.13	.55
11x14	1.66	2.37	.65

For Unmounted Photographs.

24561 Each book is furnished with twenty-five No. 1 Mounts, with perforated stubs attached, rendering it necessary only to mount and finish photograph before putting it into book.

Size,	Style E. Bound in half leather and half cloth, embossed.	Style F. Seal grain back and corners, embossed and rolled in gold leaf.	Extra Perforated leaves. Per doz.
6x7	$1.38	$1.88	$0.35
8x10	1.85	2.38	.50
10x12	2.40	3.08	.75
11x14	2.85	3.75	1.00
14x17	3.80	4.75	1.50

Photographic Chemicals.

Remember all chemicals are bought and sold by avoirdupois weight, which is 437½ grains to the ounce, and 16 ounces to the pound, while at the same time they are mixed by apothecary's weight—480 grains to the ounce, and 12 ounces to the pound; hence, if you should get but 437½ grains of any chemical for an ounce, do not think it short weight. We do not sell chemicals in less quantities than quoted below, neither do we break packages.

Order No. 24565.

Acid, acetic, No. 8, 1-lb. bottle	$0.18
Acid, citric, 1 oz. bottle	.15
Acid, muriatic, 2 oz. bottle	.18
Acid, nitric, 1 oz. bottle	.15
Acid, nitric, ½ oz. bottle	.10
Acid, oxalic, 2 oz. bottle	.15
Acid, pyrogallic (H. & F.) 1 oz. can	.35
Acid, pyrogallic (Anthony's) 1 oz. bottle	.38
Acid, pyrogallic (Schering's) 1 oz. can	.45
Acid, pyrogallic (Mallinkrodt's) 1 oz. can	.43
Acid, salicylic, 1 oz. package	.25
Acid, salicylic, ½ oz. package	.15
Acid, sulphuric C. P., 1 oz. bottle	.15
Alcohol, ½ pint bottles, 98 per cent deodorized	.25
Alum, pulverized, 1 pound package	.18
Alum, chrome, ½ lb. bottles	.20
Ammonia, liquid conc, U. S. P. 1 lb. bottle	.32
Ammonia, bromide, 1 oz. bottle	.12
Ammonia, bichromate, bottle included, per lb.	3.00
Ammonia, carbonate, bottle incl.ded, per lb.	.60
Ammonia, chloride, 1 oz. bottle	.12
Ammonia, sulpho cyanide, 1 oz. bottle	.23

Order No. 24565—Continued.

Chloroform, 1 oz. bottle	.15
Ether, sulphuric concentrated, 1 lb. bottle	.85
Eikonogen, crystals, 1 oz. bottle	.40
Glycerine, 2 oz. bottle	.15
Glycerine, 1 oz. bottle	.08
Gold, chlor.de (liquid) 15 gr. bottle	.75
Gold, chloride (dry), Anthony's 15 gr. bottle	.35
Gold, chloride (dry), H. & F., 15 gr. bottle	.50
Hydrochinon, in tins (H. & F.,) per ounce	.45
Iodine, resub. 1 oz. bottle	.38
Iodine, tincture, 1 oz. bottle	.20
Iron, protosulphate, 1 lb. package	.08
Iron, protosulphate, 1 lb. bottle	.25
Lead, nitrate, 1 oz. bottle	.15
Lead acetate, 1 oz. bottle	.25
Lime, chloride, ¼ oz. bottle	12
Lime, chloride, in bottles, per lb	.25
Mercury, bi-chloride, 1 oz. bottle	.15
Mercury, bi-sulphate, per oz	.15
Mercury, bi-sulphate, ½ lb. bottle	.75
Mercury, bi-sulphate, 1 lb. bottle	1.25
Magnesium, pure, per oz	.40
Potass, meta-by-sulph, per oz	.35
Potassium, bromide, 2 oz. bottle	.15
Pottassium, bromide, 1 oz. bottle	.10
Pottassium, carbonate, 1 lb. bottle	.27
Pottassium, carbonate, ½ lb. bottle	.20
Pottassium, cyanide, 2 oz. bottle	.14
Pottassium, cyanide ¼ lb. bottle	.25
Pottassium, cyanide, 1 lb. bottle	.65
Pottassium, ferri-cyanide, (red prussiate), per lb	.85
Pottassium, ferro-cyanide, (yellow prussiate) per lb	.60
Pottassium, iodide, 1 oz. bottle	.35
Pottassium, neutral oxalate, 1 lb. pack	.30
Silver, nitrate, 1 oz. bottle, per oz	.65
Silver, nitrate, 8 oz. bottle, per bottle	4.00
Silver, bath solution, 40 grains strong, 1 pint bottle	1.75
Silver, bath solution, 40 grains strong, 1 quart bottle	3.25
Soda, acetate, 2 oz. bottle	.15
Soda, bi-carbonate, 1 lb. package	.12
Soda, carbonate (Sal.), 1 lb. package, granular	.10
Soda, carb. (Sal.), crystals, 1 lb. bottle	.20
Soda, citrate, 1 oz. bottle	.18
Soda, hyposulphate, per lb	.05
Soda, phosphate, ½ lb, bottle	.30
Soda, sulphite, granular, ½ lb. bottle	.30
Soda, sulphite, crystals, 1 lb. bottle	.25
Soda, tungstate, 1 oz. bottle	.15
Soda, acid sulphite, 1 lb. bottle	.38

Ready-Mixed Developers, Toning Solutions, Intensifiers, Etc. Order No. 24566.

	Each.
"Eikonogen" Developer in one solution, one of the best 8 oz. bottles	$0.30
Eikonogen Developer in one solution, one of the best. 16 oz. bottles	.54
Hydrochinon Developer in one solution. 8 oz. bottles	.27
Carbutt's Eiko-cum hydro developer, combining the good qualities of both Eikonogen and Hydrochinon, two 8 oz. bottles in pkg. Per pkg	.53
Carbutt's Pyro and Soda-Potash developer, concentrated. Two 8 oz. bottles in pkg. Per pkg	.55
Stanley's concentrated, an old favorite. Two large bottles in pkg. Per pkg	.46
M. W. & Co.'s ready prepared intensifier. Two 2 oz. in pkg with full directions. Per pkg	.65
French Azotate, a superior article for toning, 4 oz. bottle. Per bottle	.25
French Azotate, 10 oz. bottle. Per bottle	.50
M. W. & Co.'s Toning solution for albumen paper. Per 12 oz. bottle	1.00
M. W. & Co.'s Toning Solution. Per 4 oz. bottle.	.40
Kloro Concentrated Combined Toning and Fixing Solutio , ready for use. Prepared specially for Kloro paper but works equally well with nearly all gelatine papers. Per 12 oz. bottles	.45
Per gallon	2.70
Kloro *Dry* Combined Toning and fixing ingredients *without chloride of gold.* Price, per box sufficient for 1 gross cabinets	.23
Per box sufficient for 5 gross cabinets	.90
Hale's Toning powders. Per ¼ lb. box	.25
Hale s Toning powders. Per ½ lb. box	.45
Hale s Toning powders. Per 1 lb. box	.60

Developing Outfits. Order 24568.

(For producing the negative.)

The chemicals and articles which should accompany any of our cameras, and with which the negative is made, consists of the following articles, arranged in sizes according to the size of the camera used. Two japan-tin developing trays, one dozen dry plates, one 4-ounce graduated glass, one package concentrated developer, one pound hypo-soda, one pocket ruby lantern, one copy Amateur Photographer,

Arranged for 3¼x4¼ camera, price, complete	$2.18
Arranged for 4x5 camera, price, complete	2.35
Arranged for 4¼x6½ camera, price, complete	2.65
Arranged for 5x7 camera, price, complete	2.85
Arranged for 5x8 camera, price, comp'ete	3.00
Arranged for 6½x8½ camera, price, complete	3 45
Arranged for 8x10 camera, price, complete	4.35

These outfits are all that are needed to produce a perfect negative. Some additions can be made for convenience sake by those who can afford it.

Printing Oufits.
Order 24569.

(For printing, toning and finishing the picture.)
Consists of the following articles: One printing frame, one dozen aristotype paper, one 12-oz. bottle aristotype toning and fixing solution, one pack (25) good card mounts, one jar photo mounter.

Printing and Toning Outfits for 3¼x4¼ camera, price, complete.................................. $1.40
Printing and Toning Outfit for 4x5 camera, price, complete.................................. 1.47
Printing and Toning Outfit for 4¼x6½ camera, price, complete.................................. 1.53
Printing and Toning Outfit for 5x7 camera, price, complete.................................. 1.73
Printing and Toning Outfit for 5x8 camera, price, complete.................................. 1.83
Printing and Toning Outfit for 6½x8½ camera, price, complete.................................. 2.13
Printing and Toning Outfit for 8x10 camera, price, complete.................................. 2.65

We do not furnish developing and printing outfits with any of our cameras, except the Horseman's Eclipse. To price of other cameras add price of developing outfit, also price of printing outfit, and you will have the total cost of an outfit with which you can produce pictures. Additional supplies, as extras and conveniences, can be purchased at any time.

TYPEWRITERS.

24575 A perfect typewriting machine for less than $1.00. It does practical work and is so simple a child can operate it. With ordinary care it cannot get out of order. Is light and portable, weighing only 1 pound complete. Writes with practice 10 to 20 words a minute, Our price, each........................ $0 80
Postage .... .20

The American.

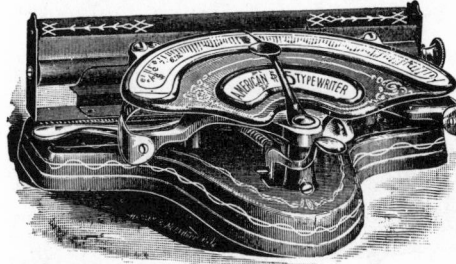

24576 The American Typewriter is complete, simple, durable and rapid. A serviceable machine at a price far below other makes, for same value. Weight, less than five pounds, as put up in sliding cover wood box. Iron base and metal parts. Writes 71 characters, capitals, small letters, figures and marks. Work always before you. An instrument for private or commercial use. Price, each........................ $5.70

Merritt.

24577 One of the best low-priced machines on the market. It writes 78 characters, and does work equal to any $100 machine made. It is a double case machine, having interchangeable METAL type, from which it prints direct; no ribbon being used. It is portable, durable, has perfect alignment, and is very cheap. The writing is done by pressing the handle into the niche indicated. Price, complete, with case..$11.00

OUR INTERESTS ARE MUTUAL!

We could not expect your orders if we did not treat you right, and without your orders we cannot live.

Odell Typewriter.

24578 This typewriter prints directly from metal type, no ribbon being used, and gives a much cleaner impression than can possibly be obtained from an ink ribbon. The Odell machine has perfect alignment and is a very good typewriter for manifold; the double case machine writes 78 characters, representing capitals, small letters, all of the punctuation marks, together with percentage marks and fractional figures. Weight, 7½ pounds.
Price, Double Case Machine............... $13.00
The Odell Typewriter lists at $20.00; our price of $13.00 gives you a discount of more than ⅓ off. We make this special offer to increase the sale and give our customers the benefit of the low price obtained by our purchasing in large quantities.

Edison Mimeograph.

24579 The Edison Mimeograph Typewriter. A practical working machine, that does perfect mimeograph work. It has steel type, keeps good alignment, prints from a ribbon, is a heavy manifolder, and is strong and durable, at same time being light and portable. Writes 78 characters, caps and small letters..... $22.00

Typewriter Supplies.

24 90 Typewriter Oil, per bottle................. $0.15
24591 Type Cleaning Brushes, each............. .20
24592 Typewriter Ink, red, purple and green, 1 oz. bottle. Each............................ .25
24595 Typewriter Ribbons for Caligraph, Remington, Smith-Premier, etc., machines, in purple, blue and green copy and black record. Each, .60
24596 Typewriter Carbon Paper for manifold work, in sizes, 8x10½; 8x12; 8x13 inches; and in colors: Purple, blue and black.
Price, per box of 100 sheets.....................2.50
24597 Typewriter Paper, "State Bond" (No. 10), superfine; medium weight.   Price, per ream (500 sheets).
Legal size, 8x13 inches................. $1.70
Ruled with marginal lines 1.80
Letter size, 8x10½ inches............ 1.50

PRINTING PRESSES, TYPE, ETC.

24614 Baltimorean Hand Inking Press, No. 5. Will print a form 1¾x3⅛ in. Weight of press and outfit, 7 pounds. Price, including press complete, one font type, package of cards, ink and furniture................................ $1.75

24615 Baltimorean Self Inker No. 9. Will print a card 2½x3¼ in. This size is especially adapted for printing small jobs, such as cards, envelopes, etc. It carries one roller, has grippers, and it is in every way a complete self-inking press.

Price of press and outfit of No. 217 type, 50 blank cards, ink and furniture................ $3.75
Weight of press and outfit, 15 pounds.
24616 Baltimorean Self-inker, No. 10. Will print a form 2½x4 in. Weight of press and outfit, 19 lbs. Price of press with one roller and outfit of 1 font of No. 217 type, 50 blank cards, ink and furniture............................ 6.00
24617 The Baltimorean Self-inker, No. 11. Will print a form 2½x4 in. Weight of press and outfit, 20 lbs. This press is extra finished, with 2 rollers and outfit of 1 font, each Nos. 200 and 217 type, 50 blank cards, ink and furniture..... 7.75
24618 The Baltimorean Self-inker, No. 12. Is larger than the two preceding presses. Will print a form 4½x6½ in., has 2 rollers and outfit of 4 fonts of type, Nos. 202, 208, 217 and 219, composing stick, planer, furniture, leads and ink. Price, complete.....................18.50
Weight of press and outfit, 80 pounds.

Type.

Our type is put up in wood cases with division for each letter, and sliding cover. Quads, spaces and figures go with every font. Weight, per font, 1¾ lbs. This type is of standard make and is full size.

No. 200   5 A   50 cts.
NEAT LETTER FOR NAMES AND OTHER USES. 123456789.

No. 202   2 A 5 a   70 cts.
J. F. W. DORMAN, Baltimore, Maryland, 1234

No. 203   2 A 5 a   70 cts.
Standard Letter for Circulars, Invitations, etc. 2

No. 204   5 A   50 cts.
LETTER-WRITER PRINT. 123

No. 208   5 A $0 50
ATTORNEY AND COUNSELLOR AT LAW 93

No. 213   2 A 5 a $1 10
Susan B. Anthony. 2

No. 214   2 A 5 a $ 95
Annual Reception. 124

No. 217   2 A 5 a $ 90
Pauline B Richards   25

No. 219   4 A $ 75
A SUCCESSFUL MAN

No. 224   3 A $1 00
CARD LETTER

The above simply shows the style of type included in each font, also the number of letters in same, taking "a" as a basis, the other letters all being in proportion.

Rollers and Chases.
Price, each.
24619 Rollers for Hand Inking Presses.......... $0.20
Rollers, with core, for self-inker No 9........... .30
Rollers, with core, for self-inker, Nos. 10-11.... .36
Chases, with screws, for No. 5 Press........... .18
Chases, with screws, for Nos. 9, 10, 11 .... .23
Chases, for No. 12 Press...................... .40

Printing Ink, Sizing and Varnish.
24620 2 ounce cans, black.................... $0.10
2 ounce cans, blue, purple or green .... .20
2 ounce cans, red or yellow................... .20
2 ounce cans, Printers' Varnish................ .20
2 ounce cans, Printers' Varnish................ .15
2 ounce cans, Gold Sizing..................... .20
1 ounce Gold Bronze.......................... .20
1 ounce Silver Bronze........................ .20
Gold Size is to be used in place of ink. Sprinkle the bronze over the printing done, to produce gold letters. By using Silver Bronze, silver letters are produced. Special list of type mailed on application.

Rubber Type Outfits.

FAMILY PRINTING OUTFIT, 3A FONT.

24621 For marking linens, books, papers, etc., and printing cards. The cheapest rubber type outfit ever offered. Can be changed quickly to any other name or wording. Useful in household or business. Consists of three printers' alphabets of type, one line type holder, bottle of indelible ink, pad and tweezers in neat paper box.
Each. ....20c.   Postage........... $0.04

Success Rubber Type Outfit, 2A, 3a.

24622 Contains five printers' alphabets (2A. 3a) of type, two sets of figures, bottle of indelible ink, one line holder and ink pad, tweezers, spaces, quads, etc., put up in neat folding cover box. Each $0.40
Postage....................................... .05

Linen Markers Rubber Type Outfit, 2A, 3a.

24623 Consists of five printers' alphabets, large and small letters of old English type, three sets figures, punctuation marks, dollar sign, type for fancy work, pad and one line holder. This outfit is for special use as a linen marker.
Price.. $0.50
Postage...................................... .10

CARD PRINTERS RUBBER TYPE OUTFIT, 2A, 3A

24625 Contains five printers' alphabets (2A3a) of light face type, specially adapted for card printing stamping envelopes, etc. In addition to letter's the outfit is provided with four sets of figures, large and small, punctuation marks, dollar and percentage signs, brackets for fancy work, pad and line holder. A very desirable outfit.
Price..$0.60
Postage.. .10

SUPERIOR RUBBER TYPE OUTFIT, 5A. 6A.

24626 It consists of eleven printers' alphabets (5A6a) of type, four sets of figures, 2 large and 2 small, punctuation marks, dollar and percentage signs, stars and brackets for fancy work, tweezers, Improved self inking pad and type holder for setting up four lines of matter. In additon to the eleven alphabets or letters the outfit contains the following sign words and sentences: "&," "and," "For Sale By," "From," "Return in ten days to." This is a *business* outfit and is the best value ever offered. Price....$2.00
Postage... .15

Pads and Inks.

24628 Stamp Ink, in red, black or violet. Per bottle..$0.15
24629 Carter's Jet Black Indelible Stamping Ink, specially prepared for use with rubber or metal stamps, and with stencils for marking cotton, linen and all textile fabrics. Full directions for use accompany each bottle. Price, per oz. bottle .10
24630 The Improved Inexhaustable Felt Stamp Pad for use with rubber type outfits, handstamps etc. Size, 4½x2¾ in. Not affected by heat, cold or pounding; always ready for use, and contains enough ink for several months' service. Put up either red, purple, blue, green or black. Weight, 5 ounces. Price.. .20
When ordering always give color of ink desired.

24632 The Victor Dater, consists of a metal holder provided with revolving rubber type and figures so arranged that by its use it is an easy matter to stamp the date on all bills and letters. In addition to the names of the months and the figures corresponding to the days of the month and the years from "1893" to "1903," the Dater contains the following words; "Rec'd," "Ans'd," "Paid." Packed in paper box with fountain pad. Price..... ....$0.35
Postage... .08

24633 The Pearl Check Protector; the cheapest protector in the market. Substantially and neatly made of iron, nickel trimmed. Answers all ordinary purposes. Weight, 1½ pounds.
Price......... ....$0.90

Chicago Check Perforator.

24634 Used and indorsed by clearing houses and stands at the head of all similar devices in point of workmanship, ease of operation and durability. It is operated with one hand and will perforate the top, center or bottom as desired; every machine warranted. Weight, complete as packed in wooden box, about 8½ pounds.
Price, each...$12 00

24635 The Acme Check Perforator, rapid and durable, awarded highest medals and diploma at World's Fair, 1893. The only single lever machine having a separate punch and dies for each figure.
Price $15.00

Columbian Brownie Stamps.

These stamps consist of a series of humorous characters, and are designed as a source of amusement for children. Each set contains some ludicrous figures and will be a great delight to the little folks.

24636 Set No. 1 comprises 2 large, 3 medium and 5 small Brownies. Self-inking pad and tablet, in paper box.
Price..................................$0.20
Postage .... .08

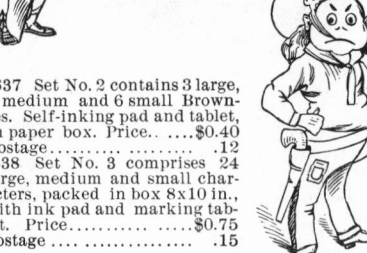

24637 Set No. 2 contains 3 large, 5 medium and 6 small Brownies. Self-inking pad and tablet, in paper box. Price.. ....$0.40
Postage.......... .... .12
24638 Set No. 3 comprises 24 large, medium and small characters, packed in box 8x10 in., with ink pad and marking tablet. Price.......... .....$0.75
Postage .... .15

Tool Chests.

24640 Boys' Tool Chest. Size of chest, 9½ inches long, 4½ inches wide, 2½ inches deep, with side cover; contains 10 assorted tools, including hand saw. This is a box for small children. Weight, 1 lb. Price, each........................$0.25
24641 Boys' Tool Chest, 11 inches long; 5½ wide, 3½ inches deep, well made; with end till; contains 10 assorted tools for boys' use. Weight, 2½ lbs. Price, complete...................... .50
24642 Boys' Too. Chest, 13¼ inches long, 6¾ inches wide, 5 inches deep, well made, with movable till and partitions, containing 10 assorted tools, better quality for boys' use. Weight, 3¾ lbs. Price, complete........................ .75
24643 Boys' Tool Chest, 15½ inches long, 8¼ inches wide, 5¾ inches deep. Extra quality, made of chestnut wood with walnut mouldings, and all nicely varnished; has movable till with partitions, containing 18 assorted tools. Weight, 4¾ lbs. Price, complete................ 1.25

24644 Youths' Tool Chest 15½ inches long, 8½ inches wide, 5¾ inches deep, made of chestnut and walnut woods, nicely varnished, heavy base and bands, with large till and compartments and bronze lifting handles and chest lock; contains 22 assorted tools as follows: 1 cast steel firmer gouge with handle, 1 cast steel screwdriver, 1 two-foot boxwood rule, 1 mallet, 1 pair compasses, 1 oil can, 1 cast steel nail punch, 1 cast steel firmer chisel with handle, 1 hand-screw, 2 cast steel nail gimlets, 1 smoothing plane, 1 cast steel regulator, 1 oil stone, 1 carpenter's mitre box, 1 trying square, 1 beechwood marking gauge, 1 cast steel saw file and handle, 1 cast steel panel saw, 1 nail hammer, 2 cast steel brad awls, handles assorted. This chest is fitted with Henry Disston & Son's or Harvey W. Pierce Co's celebrated hand and panel saw. Weight, 12 pounds. Price complete......$5.00
24645 Youths' Tool Chest made of selected chestnut and walnut woods, nicely varnished, heavy base and bands with large till and partitions, japanned lifting handles and chest locks. Size, 1 foot 9 inches long, 11¼ inches wide, 7½ inches deep. Contains 47 superior quality assorted tools. Weight,   pounds. Price........$8.00
24646 Youths' Tool Chest. Not illustrated. Size of Chest, 1 foot, 10¼ inches long, 11½ inches wide, 9¼ inches deep. Made of superior quality of black walnut and chestnut wood, nicely dovetailed, beautifully finished in oil and varnish, with heavy base and bands, folding handles, brass and bronze trimmings, and large till with partitions and chest lock; containing 70 superior quality assorted tools.
Weight, 30 pounds. Price...................$14.00

Buck Saws

24647 The Boys' Perfect Junior Buck Saw and Buck. Blades 15 in. long, made of best cast-steel. Frames and buck painted and varnished. A good, substantial article for practical use. Packed, one set complete, knocked down in a paper box. Weight 2¼ lbs.
Price.............. ....$0.50
24648 Boys' Perfect Buck-Saw and Buck. Same as preceding but larger and stronger made, with blade of saw 22 in. long. Packed in pasteboard box. Weight 6 pound.
Price......... ....$0.75

Iron Banks and Safes.

24650 The Ideal Iron Safe, made of cast iron, handsomely nickel plated. A good bank for the price. Size 3½ in. high, 3½ in. wide, 2¼ in. deep; weight, 10 ounces.
Price.......................$0.10

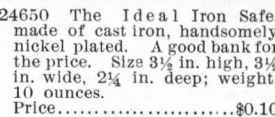

24652 The Administration Bank, with combination lock. An exact model of the World's Fair Administration Building. Made of iron, strongly constructed and nickel plated. Will receive nickels, dimes, or quarters.
Weight, 1 lb.
Price..............$0.25

24654 Security Safe, an attractive bank of novel construction with secret hinges. The combination lock is simple but effective, is handsomely nickeled; size 6x4¼x2¾ inches. Packed, one in a box.
Price $0.65

24655 Keyless Savings Bank, made of sheet steel handsomely lithographed in gold on back, blue or white enamel. Slot with interlacing springs to prevent removal of money. Register on bottom for recording deposits. Size 5½ inch high, 3⅜ inch wide, 3½ inch deep. Weight, 15 ounces. A light and thoroughly durable two combination keyless lock bank that will give satisfaction.
Price each.....................$0.85
Postage 15c.

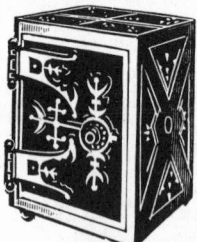

24656 The Boudoir Combination Lock Safe, with two divisions and drawers, handsomely lined with plush and satin; a practical article for every household for the safe keeping of valuables, such as money, jewels, etc., etc. It is strongly made and handsomely ornamented and embossed. Dimensions, 6x6 x8¼ inches, and weighs 13½ lbs. Comes packed in a strong wooden box, making a total weight of 16 lbs.
Price, each.............$5.00

24663 Iron Organ bank (CPO), elegantly finished, large chime of bells, dancing figures revolve when the handle is turned, the monkey deposits the coin in the vault and politely raises his hat: size, 8½ in. high, 5⅛ in. wide and 3¾ in. deep. Weight, 3¾ lbs. Each ....$0.85 This bank is too heavy to go by mail.

Our Book Department is again crowded out. Must have more room. Why? Consult Our Prices.

Safes—Continued.

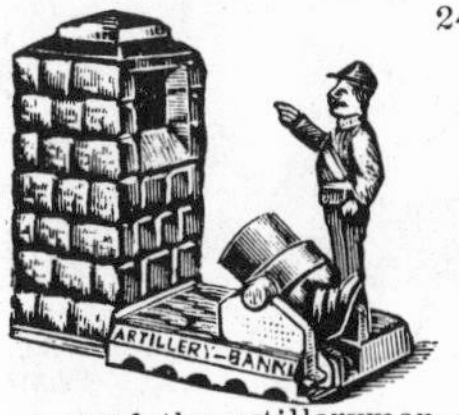

24668 The Artillery Bank, made wholly of iron, highly finished and bronzed throughout. Cannon (or mortar) is brass plated; tower and artilleryman, Japanese bronze. Place the coin in the mortar, push back the hammer and press the thumbpiece and the coin is fired into the fort or tower. Paper caps can be used if desired. The arm of the artilleryman moves up and down. Size, 6 inches high, 8 inches long. Each bank packed in wooden box. Weight, 4 pounds. Price.........$1.00

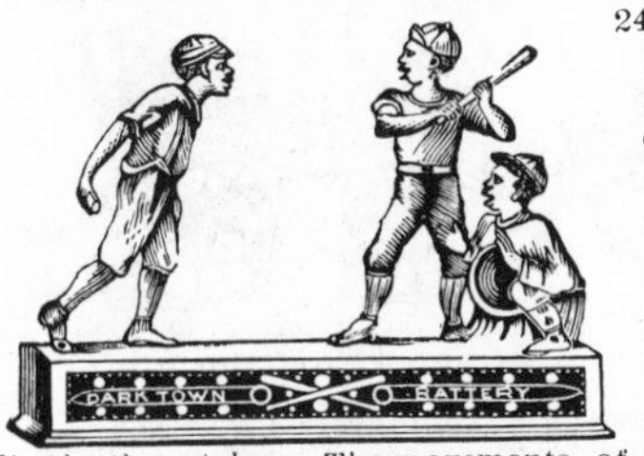

24670 The Base Ball Bank. Place a coin in the hand of the pitcher, press the lever and the coin is swiftly pitched. The batter strikes and misses, and the coin is caught and safely deposited by the catcher. The movements of all the figures are very life-like. Handsomely finished in bright colors. Length, 10 inches height, 7¼ inches; width 2¼ inches. Packed one in wooden box. Weight, 4½ lbs. Price $0.90

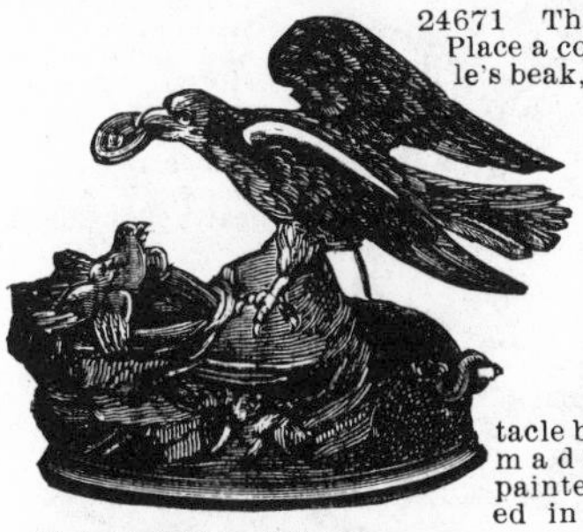

24671 The Eagle Bank. Place a coin in the Eagle's beak, press the lever, and the eagles will rise from the nest crying for food. As the eagle bends forward to feed them, the coin falls into the nest and disappears into the receptacle below. Strongly made, handsomely painted. Eagles painted in natural colors. Weight, 4 lbs. Price.......................$0.95

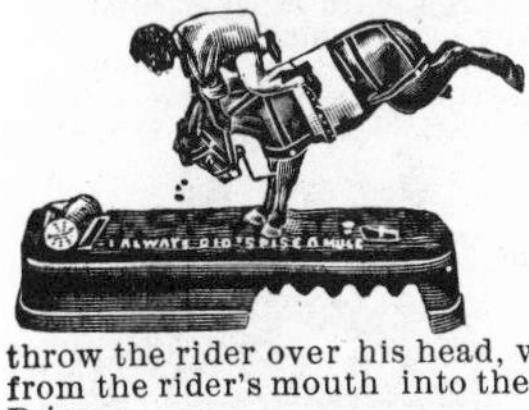

24672 The Kicking Mule Bank. Length 10½ in. Height, 8 in., width, 3 in.; made of iron and nicely finished. The mule and rider being brought into position, a slight touch on a knob at the base causes the mule to kick and throw the rider over his head, when the coin is thrown from the rider's mouth into the receptacle below. Price $0.88

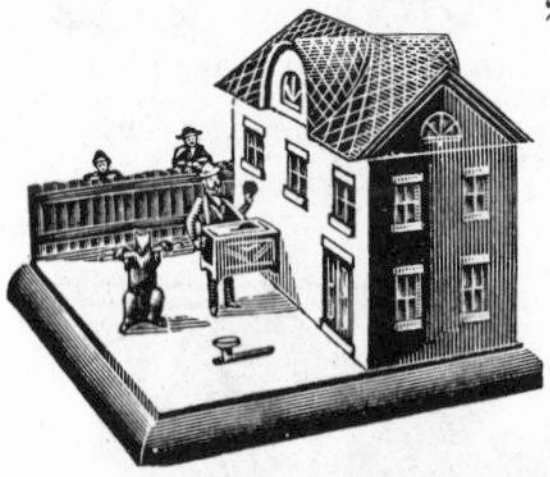

24673 The Dancing Bear Bank, with clock-work mechanism and chimes. Size 6⅞ in. long, 4¾ in. wide, 5½ in. high. This bank represents the front of a country house with an Italian organ-grinder and a bear on the lawn. After winding up the mechanism, place a coin in the slot and push the knob in front of him. He will then deposit the coin and play the organ while the bear performs his part. Handsomely painted. Packed one in a wooden box.. $0.98

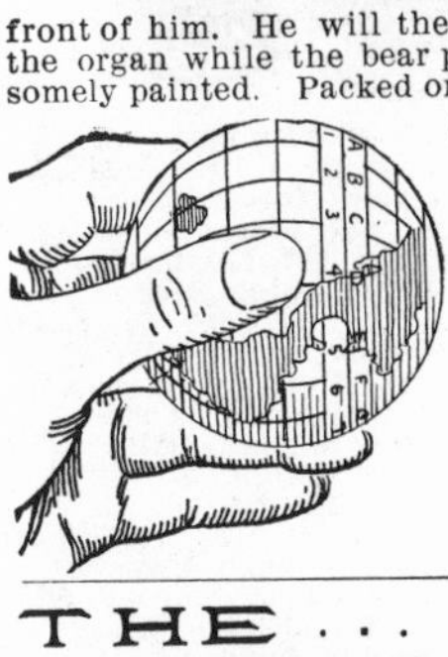

24674 The Columbian Souvenir Pocket Bank, made of nickel, globe shape, 3 inches in diameter, with map of the world engraved upon it. It is opened on the same principle that the Columbus Egg is made to stand on end. Unless the trick is known it is utterly impossible to open it. The best trick bank in the market. Weight, 3 ounces...$0.30

THE...

CONSTANT INCREASE

In the number of orders received by us is pretty good evidence that our prices are right.

15—3d

Registering Banks.

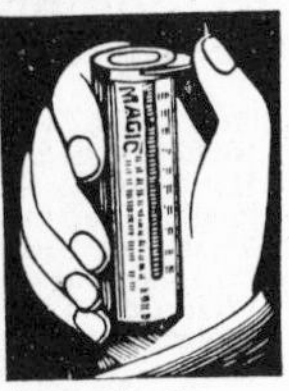

24676 The Little Gem Dime Pocket Savings Bank, locks itself and registers the amount deposited; opens automatically when $5.00 in dimes have been deposited without the use of force; is handsomely nickel plated and can be carried in the pocket without inconvenience
Each.........................$0.10
Per dozen.................... 1.00
Postage...................... .05

24677 The Magic Dime Pocket Savings Bank. Same general construction as above, but made of heavier metal. Holds $5.00 in dimes.
Price, each.............................. $0.20
Per dozen................................ 2.00

Marbles.

24713 Glass figured— Each Per doz.
5 weight per dozen 1 lb.............$0.04 $0 35
7 weight per dozen 2½ lbs........... .05 .50
9 weight per dozen 4 lbs............ .06 .65
11 weight per dozen 7 lbs........... .15 1.75

No. 24714 Large Size, glass threaded marbles for the babies. Each..................................$0.05
Per dozen .... .50

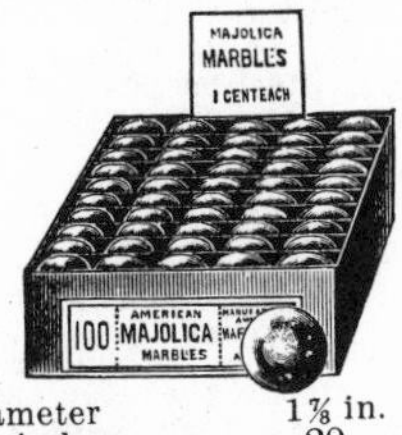

24715 American Majolica Marbles, made in new and fancy colors, and packed each size in a pasteboard box; weight, about 4½ lbs. The only novelty in the marble line that has been introduced for years. Sold only as quoted; we do not break original packages.

Diameter	1⅞ in.	1½ in.	1 in
No. in box	20	50	100
Diameter	⅞ in.	¾ in.	⅝ in.
No. in box	200	300	400

Price per box of any size, 70c.
In ordering be sure to mention size desired.

24716 Assortment of about 100 marbles, all sizes and kinds. Per bag.......................... $0.20
24717 Ballot Marbles, assorted, black and white. Per 100...................................... .35
24718 Cornelian (blood) Agates. Small, each....8 cts. Med...12 cts. Large...20 cts.

Tops.

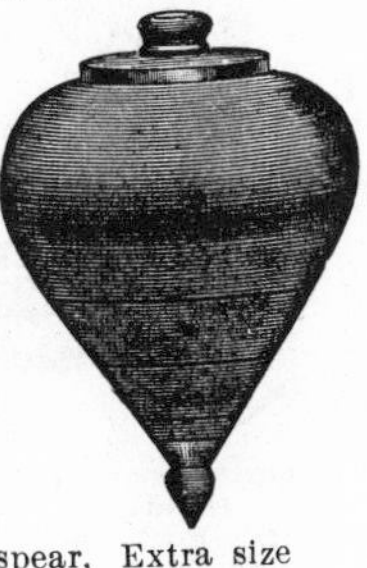

24719 Stained Wood Peg Tops, assorted colors and in four sizes. Price per doz. $0.25
24720 Hardwood Tops, extra quality, peg all the way through; brass button rivet on top. Selected hardwood, malleable iron pegs with hardened points. Per dozen...............$0.35
24721 Boxwood Tops, hardened point pegs, in assorted colors and four sizes. Per dozen.................$0.45
24722 Boxwood Tops, with spear, Extra size and weight; octagon shaped spear, just the thing to split your opponet's top wide open. No. 4 size. Per dozen..............................$0.70
24723 Lignum Vitae Tops, made of hardest known wood. Assorted sizes. Per dozen.......... .80

Toy Iron Trains.

24730 Passenger Train, small size, nickel-plated engine, tender and one coach, length of train, 11½ inches. Packed one in a box. Price..................................$0.25
24731 Passenger Train, same as above except larger; nickel plated. Length of train, 19¾ inches. Price.................................. .50
24732 Ideal Passenger Train consisting of locomotive, tender and one passenger coach of large size. Made of iron, handsomely nickeled, jointed connecting rods on drive wheels; all wheels revolve. Length of train, 30 in. Packed one in a box. See cut. Price.................. 1.00

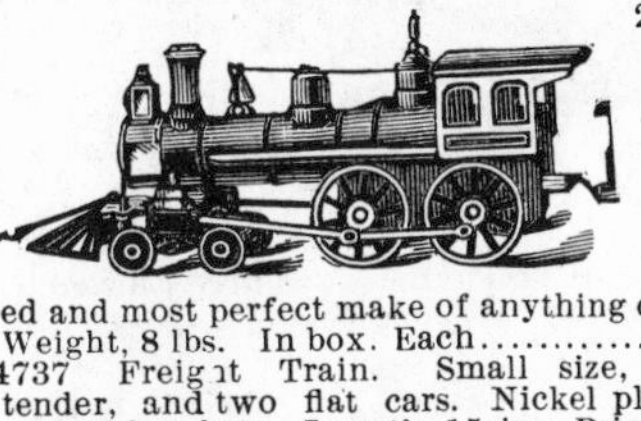

24734 Large size engine and tender, no cars; pull with a string This engine and tender are the finest finished and most perfect make of anything on the market. Weight, 8 lbs. In box. Each..............$1.50
24737 Freight Train. Small size, engine, tender, and two flat cars. Nickel plated and packed in a box. Length, 15 in. Price..... .23
24738 Freight Train, same as above but larger. Length, 25¾ in. long. Price............ .48
24739 Freight Train consisting of large size locomotive, tender and two flat cars of large size, all nickel plated. Drive wheels on engine are connected with jointed connecting rod, and all wheels revolve. Length of train, 35¼ in. Packed in a box. Price...................... .95

Toys—Continued.

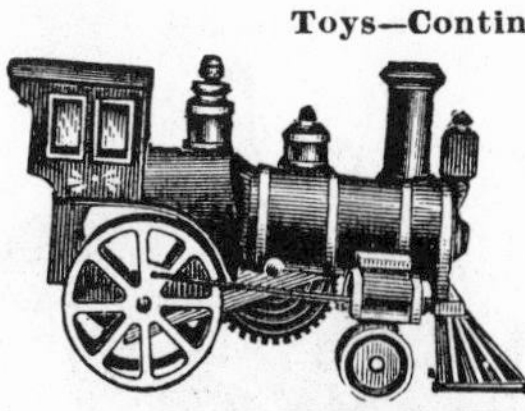

24740 Mechanical Iron Locomotive, new model and finish, guaranteed to work perfectly. Packed one in a box with tender. Length, 10 in. Weight, 2¾ lbs. Price....$1.00

Steam Toys.

Upright Engines.

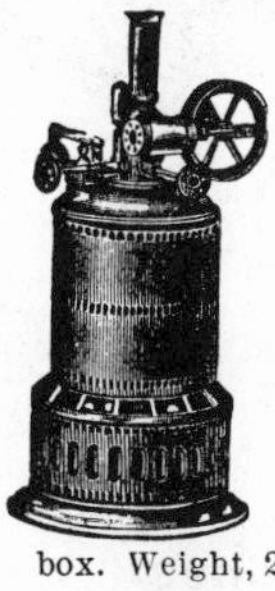

24745 The "Hero" Improved Steam Engine, the cheapest perfect running steam engine made. Postage, 8c. Price, each..................$0.20
24746 The Weeden Upright Steam Engine, American manufacture, with whistle, weighted safety valve, brass boiler, smoke stack, exhaust, starts and stops by throttle. This engine is well known all over the country. Price........$0.75. Weight, 1¾ lbs.
24747 The Weeden Upright Engine, No. 5½. Very similar in appearance to No. 24748; has water gauge and rotary governor. Height from base to top, 9½ in., height, of boiler, 3 in., diameter of boiler, 2¾ in. Each engine placed in wooden box. Weight, 2½ pounds, Price.....................$1.25

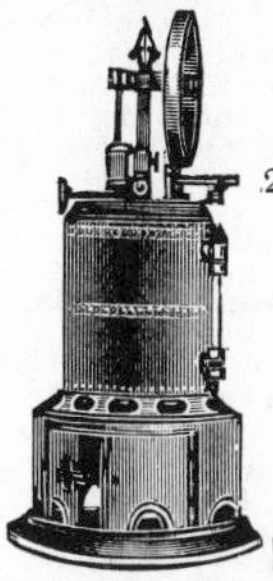

24748 Weeden Upright Engine, No. 6. This is a large and attractive upright engine. It is substantially made, and is in every respect strong and durable, and presents a fine appearance when in operation. Has brass boiler, rotary governor, water gauge, etc. Price.............................$2.50
Weight, 3½ pounds.

Horizontal Engines.

24750 The "Ajax." Each engine carefully packed in a wood box, complete with lamp, etc. A sensible, practical, instructive toy. Warranted to work perfectly. Absolutely safe. Brass boiler, with copper band, iron stand, etc. Price. each....$0.75
Extra, by mail.. .16

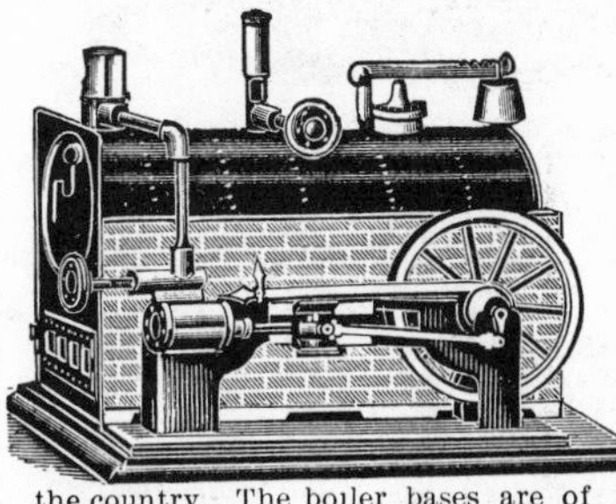

24752 The Weeden Horizontal Engine; this engine is new in style and is the type most commonly found in all manufacturing establishments throu'out the country. The boiler bases are of Russia iron, finished in black, gold and red. The other parts are brass and cast metal. Size of base, 4½x5¾ inches; length of boiler, 4¾ inches; diameter, 1⅝ inches; fly wheel, 1⅞ inches. Packed in wooden box it weighs 24 ounces, Price.......................................$1.50

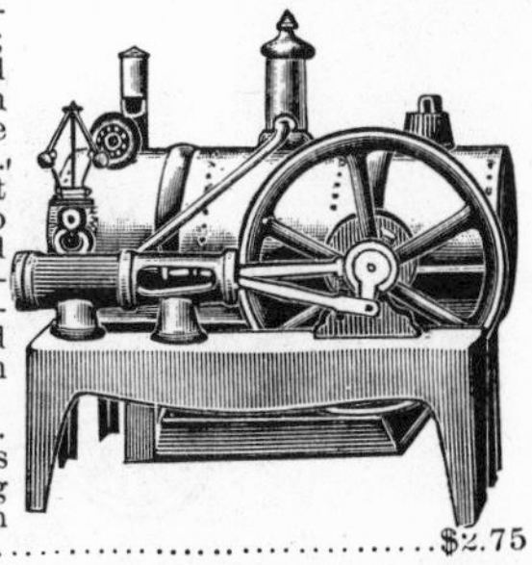

24753 New Horizontal Weeden Engine; has large polished brass boiler with steam dome, whistle and safety valve. The frame is cast malleable iron, to which the boiler and engine are firmly attached. The cylinder, steam chest and slide rest are cast in one piece and can not get out of order. The whole engine is in every way a strong and durable steam toy. Price, each..............................$2.75

"DO AS YOU WOULD BE DONE BY."

This is a rule which we try to live up to, and upon which we have built our business.

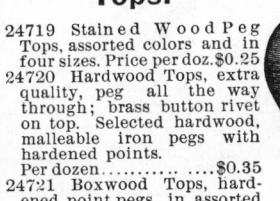

Horizontal Engines--Continued.

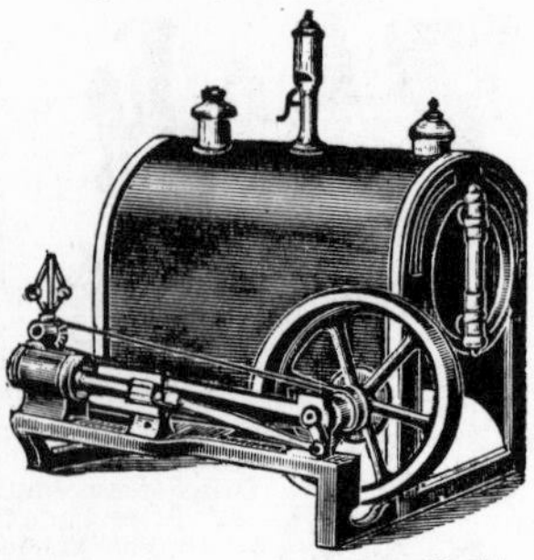

24755 Large Horizontal No. 10; this is the largest and strongest engine we handle. It has a large brass boiler enveloped with a sheet iron jacket to prevent loss of heat. The boiler trimmings are safety valve, whistle, steam dome and water gauge. The boiler frame and engine bed are made of malleable iron, well riveted and pinned together. The cylinder, steam chest and cross head slide rest are made in one piece of solid brass. The piston and rod, the crank and connecting rod, the eccentric and valve rod and slide valve are all made of brass. The balance wheel is made of malleable iron with a polished face. All parts of the engine are securely put together, well finished, and *very durable*. Each engine is carefully tested before packing. Full directions for operating engine will be found in each box, with price list of duplicate parts. Weight, 8½ pounds, Price.....$8.00

Beam and Mill Engines.

24757 The Weeden Beam Engine. This engine is modeled after and has all the essential features of a "Cornish Pumping Engine." The boiler is mounted in imitation of brick setting, including iron stays and working furnace door for management of fires. The top of Boiler is provided with Manhole, Gallows, Frame with Walking Beam, and Filler with Safety Valve. Instead of an oscillating cylinder, it has a device for the introduction of steam into a stationary vertical cylinder, consisting of Rocking Valve with Valve Rod, worked by an eccentric on the main shaft, the inlet of steam to the steam chest being controlled by a screw throttle valve. Size, 6½ in. base, 3½ in. wide, 5½ in. high. Price............$1.75

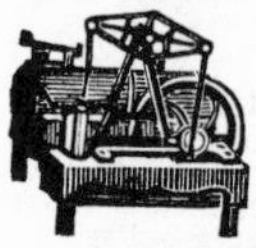

24758 The Walking Beam Engine, 7 in. long, 7 in. high, 4 in. fly wheel, 4½ in. walking beam, heavy riveted brass boiler, with safety valve. Put up, one in a neat paper box complete. Price............ ....$4.50 Weight, 4 pounds.

Steam Trains.

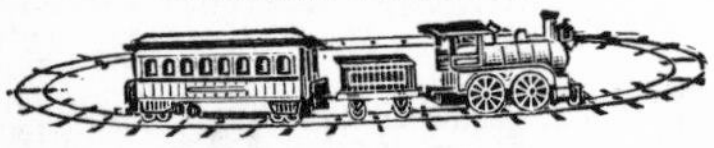

24761 Weeden Steam Locomotive, Tender and Passenger Car, with jointed track on wooden sleepers. Diameter of track, 3½ feet, locomotive, 8 inches long; car and tender in proportion. Put up in wooden box. Weight, 4 lbs. Price, for train complete $3.50

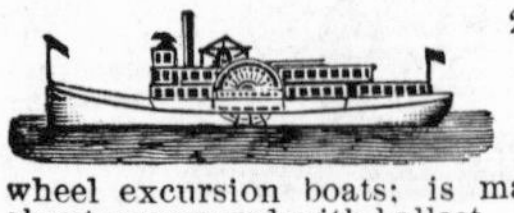

24762 The Weeden New Sidewheel Steamboat. The steamer is new, and is modeled after the modern sidewheel excursion boats; is made of tin and weighs about one pound with ballast. Will steam in a tub or tank of water or on a still water pond. Dimensions: 12 inches long, 3½ inch beam, 5 in. high. Price, complete, packed in a wooden box, $2.00; total weight, 2lbs.

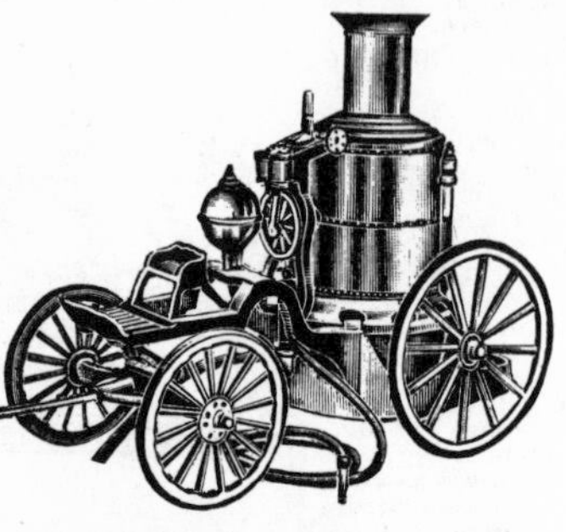

24763 New Steam Fire Engine; has all the essential parts of a modern fire engine. The boiler is polished brass attached firmly to frame and has safety valve, whistle and water gauge. It has two cylinders, pump and hose attachments; is firmly put together, and all its parts are strong and durable. Every engine is thoroughly tested before leaving the factory and fully warranted. Full directions for running the engine inclosed in each box, with price of dulicate parts. Price, eac h............................ $5.50

Our claim that this Catalogue opens the large markets to you is no idle boast. Where else can you find so much? As a genuine guide to prices it has no equal.

Attachments for Steam Engines.

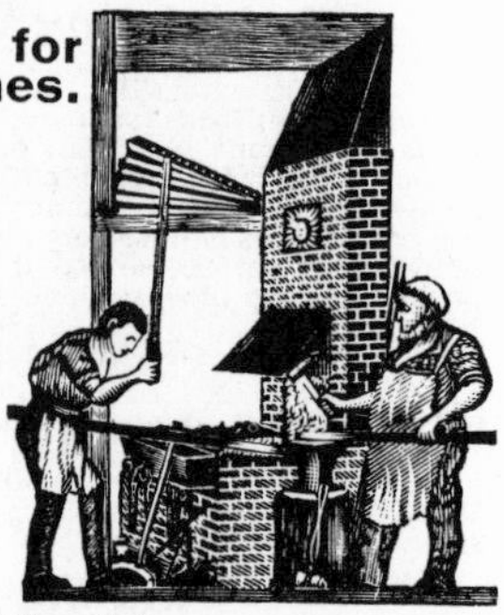

24765 The Village Blacksmith Steam Engine Attachment. Very novel and interesting. Pleases old and young alike. Weight, 1½ lbs. Each..........$0.40

Toy Machinery.

Can be operated by any of our toy steam engines.

24768	Circular Saw and Table	$0.45
24769	Turning Lathe	.55
24770	Grindstone (wood wheel)	.35
24771	Cone Pulley to connect with lathe	.20
24772	Hangers for shafting	.10
24773	Pulleys, ⅛ to 2½ in. diameter	.03

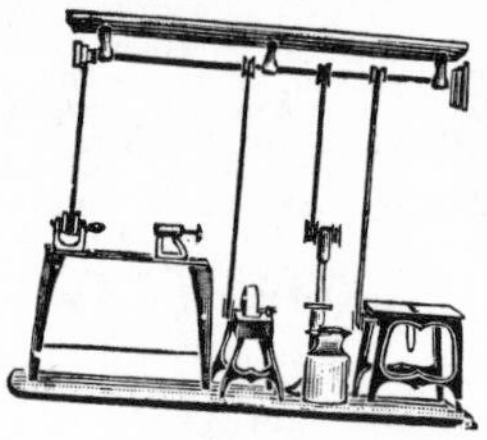

24775 The Model Toy Machine Shop, of five pieces; consists of circular saw and table, turning lathe, anvil, press drill and grind, stone mounted on wooden base, with pulleys and overhead shafting. Length, 11 inches. Weight, complete, packed in pasteboard box, 2 lbs. Price, per set. ..$0.95

Patent Hot Air Toys.

24776 Hot Air Attachments, single and double figures, made with the patented air wheel. Each, complete..$0.20

Indestructible Malleable Iron Toys.

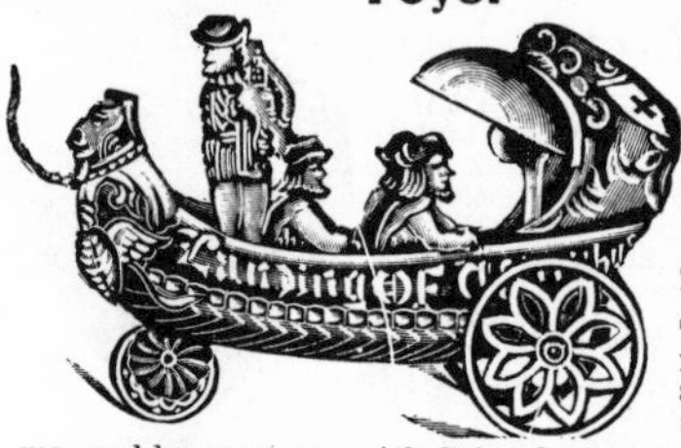

24780—Columbus Bell Toy. As the toy is drawn, each revolution of the wheels causes the bell to ring. The design represents an ancient state barge manned by oarsmen, with Columbus standing in the bow. Handsomely painted in bronze and fancy colors. Each one packed in a wood box. Length, 7½ in. Height, 5¼ in. Width, 3½ inches. Price..$0.50

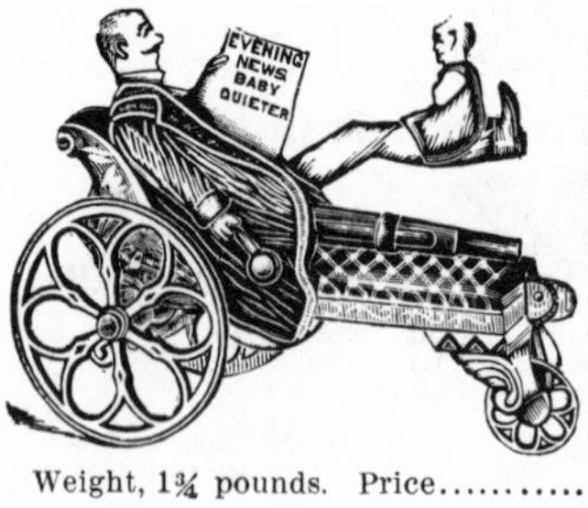

24781 The Baby Quieter Wheel Toy; as it is drawn, each revolution of the wheel rings the bell and jumps the baby. A very amusing toy; finished in fancy colors. Length, 7¼ in. Height, 6 in. Width, 3¾ in. Weight, 1¾ pounds. Price.........................$0.40

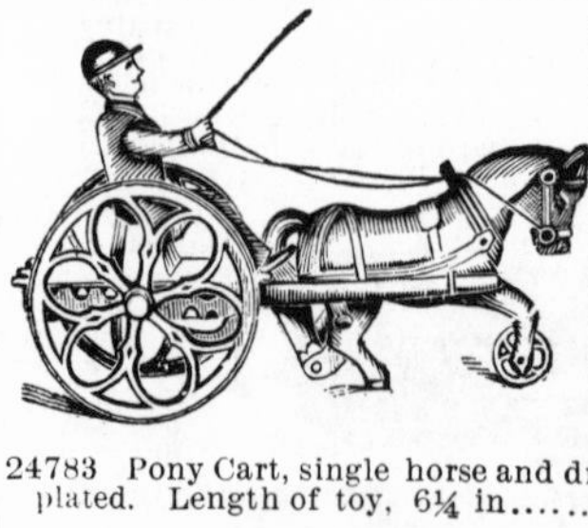

24782 The Pony Wheel Toy, made of malleable iron, handsomely finished in bright colors. Each revolution of the wheel causes the driver to strike the pony with the whip. Length, 9 in. Height, 5¼ in. Weight, 1½ lbs. Price......$0.45

24783 Pony Cart, single horse and driver, nickel plated. Length of toy, 6¼ in.................$0.25

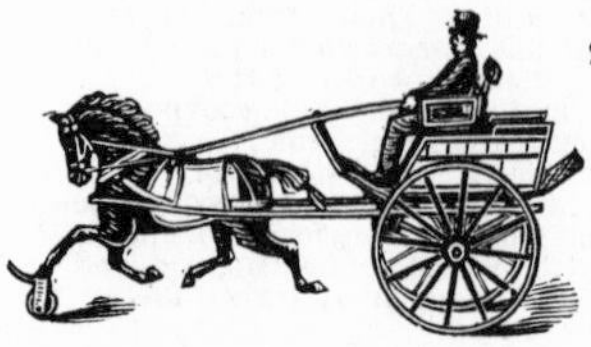

24784 Road Cart A perfect model, made of iron and nickel plated. Single horse and driver. Length of toy, 10¼ in. Price...... $0.50

Toys—Continued.

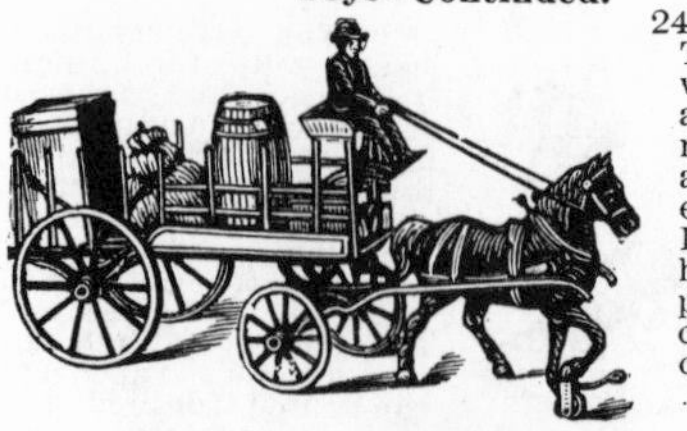

24787 Single Truck (1) with driver and load of merchandise, as represented in cut. Length, 13 in. handsomely painted in colors. Each, complete, ...$0.80

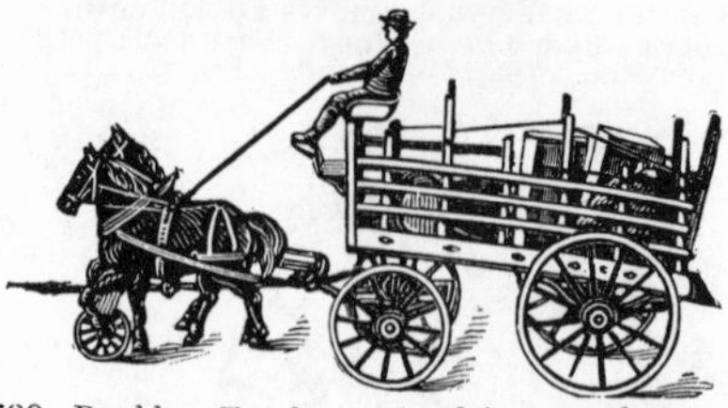

24789 Double Truck, with driver and two horses. Load consists of two boxes, two barrels and one sack of merchandise. Horses painted black, harness and running gear of truck painted a bright red, black striped. Packed one in a box; complete. Each.......................$1.75

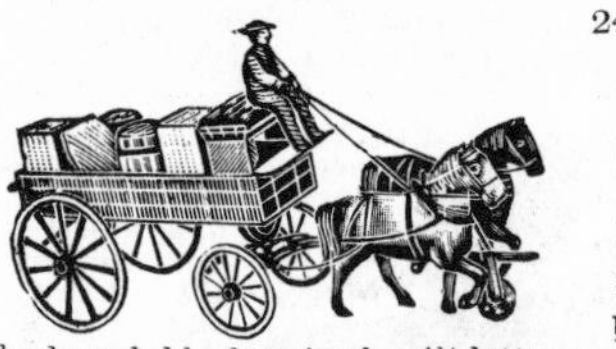

24790 Express Wagon with driver and two horses. Load consists of two boxes, and one sack. Horses painted cream color, harness black, hames red, collar black, wagon body red, black striped, gilt letters; gear yellow, black striped. Packed one in a box, complete. Each. $2.00

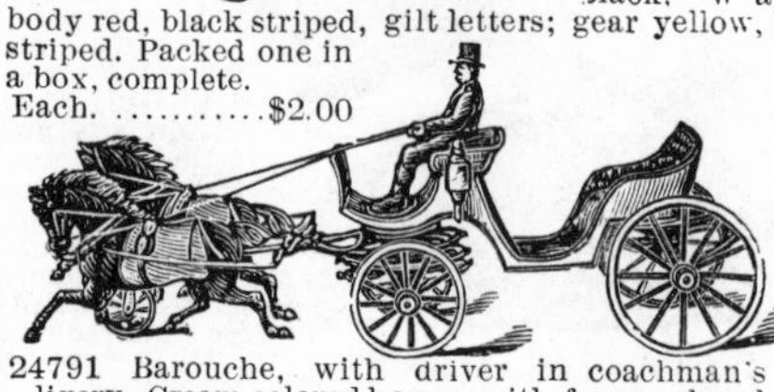

24791 Barouche, with driver in coachman's livery. Cream colored horses, with fancy colored hip blankets, running gear, maroon, gold striped; body black. Both horses trotting when toy is in motion. A particularly handsome article. Packed one in a box. Each.............$1.85

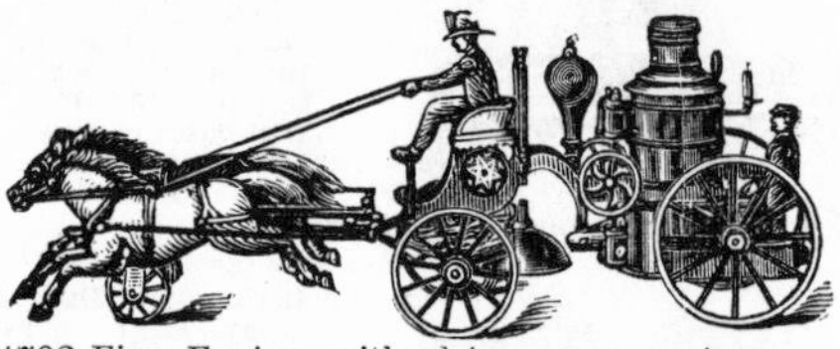

24792 Fire Engine, with driver and engineer in full regulation uniform. When in motion the horses gallop and the gong rings. A complete miniature fire engine, with nickel plated boiler and valves, Length, 18 inches; packed one in a box. Each...............................$2.00

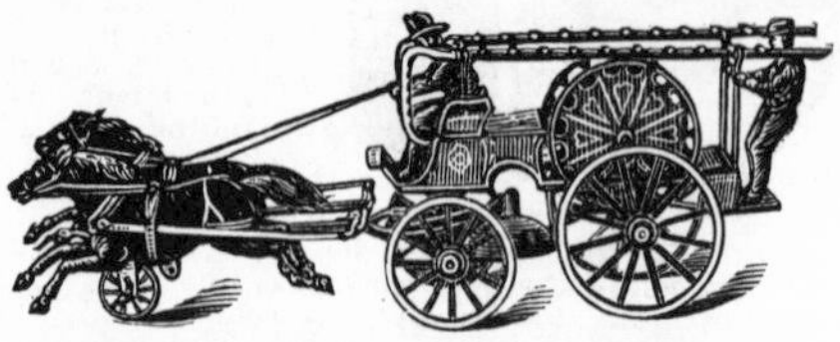

24793 Hose cart (S), with driver and fireman in full uniform, with two Pompier Corps ladders, as shown in cut. Cream colored horses with red running gear to cart and alarm gong, which rings while in motion. Whole finely painted in bright colors. A companion piece to 24792. Length, 18 in. Each.....................$2.00

24794 Hook and Ladder Truck, with driver and steersman in full uniform. Four red extension ladders, which can be united, making a ladder 51 inches in length. Two axles, gaily painted. Length, 24 inches. Too large to illustrate correctly. Must be seen to be appreciated. Each, complete.................................... 2.00

24795 The above three numbers make a complete miniature fire department. Price, per set..5.50

24796 Engine House, made of malleable iron and wood, handsomely painted in fancy colors, length, 26¼ inches; width, 10 inches; height, 18 inches. Has swinging doors, with bell at top Price, each.. 3.25

24797 The "Brave Boy" Fireman's Complete Outfit, consisting of helmet, trumpet and axe. Helmet is made of papier mache and painted black with gilt stripes and is ornamented with a gilt badge fastened to the front. Trumpet is of papier mache and axe of wood. Handsomely painted in bright colors; it is an outfit that will please any boy. Cannot be sent by mail. Price... 2.50

Toys—Continued.

24798 Artillery, made of indestructible iron and steel, in a good, substantial manner, as per cut. Horses mismated in color, gun carriage and limber dark green, red stripes. Gun dead black, brass mounted. Men in uniform. Total length of toy, 34 inches. Price. $4.00

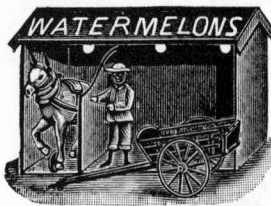

24800 Donkey Cart and stable; a new, complete, well made and finished house toy, amusing for either boys or girls. Price, each...$1.75

Mechanical Novelties.

24801 Mechanical Walking Horse, made of iron and painted. Size 8½x7 inches. After winding up the concealed spring, place the horse on the floor or any smooth surface, and it will start off at a brisk walk, as natural as life, Weight, packed in pasteboard box, 2 lbs. Each......................$2.00

24803 Mechanical Monkey; looks as much like a real monkey as it is possible to make it appear. Wind it up and it will vigorously ring a bell. Dressed in bright costumes. Packed one in a box. Price..........................$2.50

24805 Mechanical Performing Acrobats, representing two gymnasts in various feats of turning on a horizontal bar. A neat and novel toy, interesting to all. Size 8x6x6. Packed one in a heavy pasteboard box. Price ....$2.75 Weight, 3 pounds.

24806 Mechanical Jumping Dog with rider, covered with natural skin, white in color; it looks just like a real dog. Wind it up and it hops along in a most comical manner. Weight, 6 ounces. Price.......................................$0.95

Natural Skin Animals.

24809 Natural Skin Lamb, mounted on wooden base with wheels; to be drawn with a string. Price, each, ...$0.25

24810 Natural Skin Lamb, musical attachment and with rider in fancy colored costume. Mounted on wooden base, with wheels. Price.. 1.25

24812 Natural Skin Lambs, with musical attachment, mounted on wooden base, with wheels, 13x5 inches. Length of lamb, 12 inches, height to top of head, 9½ inches. They bleat as natural as life by pressing on the nose. Price.......... 1.75

24813 Natural Skin Cow, with voice, mounted on wooden base with wheels, 10x4½ inches. By pressing on the nose the cow will low as natural as life. Price, each.$0.95

We guarantee everything we sell to be just what we say it it. Neither more nor less.

Toys—Continued.

24814 Toy elephant on platform with wheels, with swinging head and fancy colored blanket. Size of platform, 8x3½ in. Length of figure, 8 in. Height, 5 in. Price $0.30

24815 Large Size Toy Elephant, with swinging head and fancy trimmed blanket; length of toy, 12 in.; height, 8½ in. Mounted on rollers concealed in each foot. Each.................... .90

24816 Natural Skin Donkey, mounted on wooden base with wheels. Press on his nose and he will bray as earnestly as though alive. Size, 6½x10 in. weight. 12 oz. Price $0.85

24819 Natural Skin Horse and Cart, as shown in cut. Length of toy, 11 inches. Price....$0.75

24820 Natural Skin Horse and Truck. See illustration of No. 24789 for style of wagon. A fine large toy 20 inches in length. Price..........$1.00

Animals Mounted on Platforms

24822 Pressed Paper Horses, patent German process, very light and handsome, small size. Each............$0.10

24823 Same description, large size. Each....... .20
24824 Same Horse as No. 24822, but harnessed to cart. Body of cart is natural wood oiled, wheels of pressed paper. Each.............. .35
24825 Saddle Horse, made of composition. with handle. Size of horse, 10 inches high, 8 inches long. Price................. .50
24826 Saddle Horse, same as No. 24825, but 12 inches high, 10 inches long and large in proportion. Price................. .96
24827 Assorted Animals, small size, on platforms. Assortment consists of tigers, elephants, wildcats, lions, bears and dogs. State kind preferred, and they will be sent if in stock. If not, substitution will be made. Each................. .25

Plush Animals.

24830 New Plush Dogs, small size, well made. Price.$0.25
24831 Our New Plush Pug Dog; nice size, and well made. Each... ....$0.50 Per dozen............. 5.40

Toy Stoves.

24835 The Pastime Toy Heating Stove. A beautiful model of the modern base burner. Has transparent red windows; base, top and urn are nickel plated; place a candle in candlestick on inside of stove, and it diffuses a warm, brilliant glow; one joint of pipe with each stove. Size of base 5¾ inches; total height, 12½ in; weight, 6 pounds. Price...........$0.90

24836 Toy Range, nickel-plated with polished edges and ornamentation. Useful and instructive toys. Size about 4x5x5 inches; packed one in a box with several utensils. Price.................$0.50

24837 Same as above but larger and with more utensils. Price.................... 1.00
24838 Large size Toy Range; a perfect working stove, nickel plated and highly ornamented. Beautiful, useful and instructive. Price includes half dozen of the most needed utensils. Size about 6 inches wide, 11 inches high, 11½ inches long. Price.................. 2.00

Child's Sad Irons.

24840 Nickel plated Toy Sad Iron, half pound size, with stand. Each............... $0.15

24841 Nickel plated Toy Sad Iron, one pound size, with stand Each..$0 20
24842 Same as No. 24841, but two pound size. A useful toy. Each..$0.24

24843

24843 Acme Toy Sad Iron with solid handle, nickel plated, with stand; small size. Each................$0.10
24844 Mrs. Pott's Toy Sad Iron, with detachable nickel plated and with handle; medium size. Each $0.25
24845 Mrs. Pott's Toy or Polishing Iron, nickel plated, with detachable walnut handle, about two pound size, large enough to be useful. Price

24844-5.
with stand, each...................................$0.35

Toy Scales.

24846 Size, without scoop, 4½ inches long, 1¾ inches high, 2 inches wide; scoop, 3¼x2 inches. Nicely painted and bronzed, and has three coppered weights. Weight, ½ pound.
Price, each...$0.10
Per dozen... 1.00
24847 Toy Scales, 4¾ inches long. 3 inches high, 2¼ inches wide, with a set of weights accompanying each scale. Nicely finished; one in box. Weight, 1¼ pounds. Each..................... .20

Chime Toys.

24850 White Metal Revolving bell chime. Gives a very pleasant musical sound Small, each...........$0.10 Weight, 3 oz. Per doz.. 1.00
24851 Same description as above, but larger size. Weight, 4 oz. Each....$0.25 Per dozen 2.20

24852 White Metal Revolving bell chime, with horse attached. Weight, 5 oz. Each......$0.22 Per doz.....2.50

The "Sea-Saw" Chimes.

24855 To be drawn with a string. As the wheels revolve, the figures at either end of the "teeter" rise and fall alternately, at same time vigorously ring a chime bell placed between them. Packed in a box. Price.........................$0.50
24856 The Young America Chime. A large, brightly painted iron chime, with large bell and flag. As toy is drawn the bell revolves and rings. Each .... .75

24858 The Roller Chime is a handsome lithographed revolving drum with metal handles; as the drum revolves on being drawn over the floor, it produces a succession of musical sounds. Weight, 1½ pounds. Each......-......$0.25

OUR MAIL ORDER
METHODS.... MEET MANY .. WANTS.

Magnetic and Electrical Toys.

24860 The Boston Motor and Battery Outfit. A new invention A motor and battery combined. It is right in line with the advancement of the age and enables young people to keep up with the times in the studies of the problems of electricity. Its construction is complete and of the best materials, with all the parts of a large motor, including armature, commutator, magnets, brushes, and a pulley for transmitting power. It is especially adapted for running small mechanical figures, toy machinery, etc., and with a good charge of compound will run a four-inch fan. Packed with full directions in wooden box. Weight, 2 pounds.
Price of outfit $1.00
Price, including fan 1.25

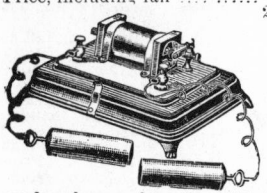

24862 The Novelty Medical Coil and Battery complete. This battery is especially designed for amusement purposes, but when required will serve the purposes of the best medical coils. It is provided with small hand regulator, and currents thus produced range from the mildest to those that are quite enough for the strongest man. The outfit consists of medical coil and battery, one pair conducting cords, pair nickel plated handles and one dozen extra battery pads. Packed in wooden box. It weighs 2½ pounds. Price......................$2.25

Magnets.

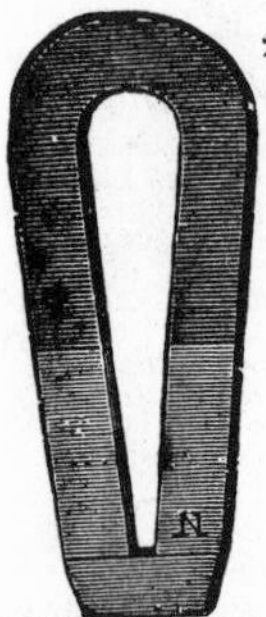

24865 Horseshoe Magnets, superior quality.

Length.	Each.	Per doz.
2 inches. Postage, each, 2c.	$0.06	$0.60
2½ inches. Postage, each, 2c.	.10	.95
3 inches. Postage, each, 3c.	.15	1.50
4 inches. Weight, each, 5 oz.	.20	2.10
6 inches. Weight, each, ¾ lb.	.45	5.00
8 inches. Weight, each, 1¼ lbs.	.85	9.25
10 inches. Weight, each, 3¾ lbs.	1.50	16.00
12 inches. Weight, each, 4½ lbs.	2.00	20.00

24866. Magnetic Loadstone,
Price in pieces of less than one pound.............10
Price per pound............................1.00

Gray Rubber Toys.

24870 Rubber Mouse, black or white, with whistle. Each........................$0.18

24873 Rubber Snakes, natural color and shape; you can have more fun with them than with a basket of monkeys. Large size, each..........$0.40
Small size, each.............................25

24874 Rubber Sheep, with whistle. Each........$0.20
24875 Rubber Goat, with whistle. Each.............$0.20

24876 Rubber Dogs, assorted kinds, poodle, mastiff, pointer, etc., Each..........$0.20

Pure White Rubber Toys.

We wish to call special attention to this line of toys. All are made of best pure white rubber, and each toy is a perfect model of the animal it represents.

24885 White Rubber Spitz Dog, with whistle: Each......$0.30
Size, 4½x7 inches

24886 White Rubber Pug Dog, with whistle.
Each................$0.30
Size, 4½x7 inches.

24887 White Rubber Newfoundland Dog, with whistle. Each...$0.30
Size, 4½x7 inches.

Toys—Continued.

24889 Rubber Sheep, Cows, Donkey and Goats, assorted large size, with whistle. Not illustrated. Each.......$0.30
24890 White Rubber Cat, with whistle. Each $0.30
Size, 4½x7 inches.

24890

RATTLER.

24895 Globe Bell Tin Rattle, wooden handle,
Each.....................................$0.05
Per dozen..................................50
24896 Globe Iron Rattles, sleigh bell pattern, japanned wood handles. Each..............06
Per dozen..................................65
24897 Same, better quality. Each...........09
Per dozen..................................85
24898 Bone Rattle, with teething ring and 4 metal bells. Each.........................20
24899 Chime Rattle, 4 chime bells on leather band, enameled handle. Each...............10
24900 Rattle and Teething Ring, one bell on enameled handle, rubber ring. Each...........12

Willow and Rattan Baby Rattles.

24901 Willow Rattles, natural color, with colored trimmings, straight handle. Each........... $0.07
Postage....................................02

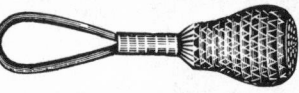

24902 Fancy Rattle, high varnished, hard finished willow and rattan woven; has bent rattan loop handle: handsome, light and durable. Price, each.......................$0.15
Postage....................................02

Rubber Rattles.

24904 Musical Rattle, with teething ring.
Each........................$0.10
Per dozen....................1.00
Rattle weighs 3 ounces.
24905 Musical Rubber Rattle, with teething ring handle; length, 6 in.; weight, 4 oz.
Each..........................$0.15
Per dozen....................1.50

24905   24904

Rubber Balls.
Hollow Balls.

24910—				
Size	10	20	30	40
Diameter and inches	1⅝	1⅞	2¼	2½
Each	$0.04	$0.06	$0.08	$0.10
Per dozen	.44	.65	.87	1.08
Weight	2 oz.	3 oz.	3 oz.	4 oz.

Solid Balls.

24911				
Size	10	20	30	40
Diameter and inches	1¼	1⅞	2¼	2½
Each	$0.05	$0.07	$0.10	$0.14
Per dozen	.50	.75	1.10	1.60
Weight	3 oz.	4 oz.	4 oz.	4 oz.

Light Inflated Balls.
The children's favorite.

24912				
Diameter and inches	1¾	2½	2¾	3
Each	$0.07	$0.10	$0.15	$0.20
Per dozen	.77	1.08	1.60	2.15
Postage, each	.02	.03	.03	.04

Stuffed Kid Balls.

24913 Kid House Balls, stuffed with cotton batting and covered with kid, making a desirable house ball for the little people. Large size.
Each.....................................$0.20
Postage....................................04
24914 Celluloid Balls, assorted colors, small size.
Each......................................$0.10
24915 Celluloid Balls, assorted colors, large size.
Each......................................$0.18

MISCELLANEOUS TOYS AND NOVELTIES.

24917 Toy Police Lanterns, 1½ in. bull's-eye, burns candle, changeable light. You should see the boys play policeman with this lantern. Throws strong light. Each.......................$0.10
Per dozen................................1.00
Postage, each..............................05

Toy Dinner Bells.

24918 Call Bell, 2¼ inch, japanned iron base, iron hammer, silvered bell, brass push or tongue. The neatest toy bell made. Each...........$0.15
Per dozen................................1.50
Postage, each..............................08
24919 Tea Bells with japanned handle. Each...05
Per dozen...................................50
24920 Rubber Balloons with trumpet ends. To be inflated by blowing into them. A good loud one. Each..........................$0.04
Per dozen...................................40

Jumping Ropes.

24921 Jute Rope, ¼ inch; length 6½ in: stained handle. Each..........................$0.04
Per dozen...................................40
Postage....................................02
24922 Jute Rope, ¼ inch; length 7 feet, japanned handles. Each......................06
Per dozen...................................60
Postage....................................03
24923 Jute Rope, ¼ inch; length 8 feet, japanned or polished handles Each...........08
Per dozen...................................80
Postage....................................03

Jack Stones.

24924 Nicely coppered. good sizes. Per doz.....$0.04
Per gross...................................30
Weight, per dozen, 2 ounces.

The Roaming Toys.

24925 Another of the world's surprises in popular toys. Made of metal and colored in gold, green and blue; led by a string. Lead it about ten feet by the string, when it will go ten feet by itself and lead you. Lots of fun for children. Weight,
5 ounces. Price, each....................$0.09
Per dozen, assorted........................75

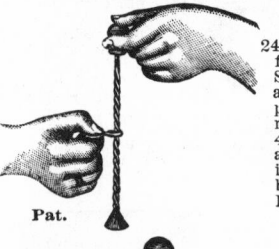

24933 The "Wonderful" Agate Spinner Simple mechanical action in this toy produces surprising results. Spinner No. 4, threaded glass agate, and directions in neat pasteboard box. Each....$0.10
Postage.........02

Pat.

24934 The Air Wheel is one of the greatest toys on earth. The aerial problem solved. Flies high through the air by a simple mechanical movement. It is an amusing and exciting toy. Old and young enjoy it. Put up complete with rod and flyers.
Price.,...................$0.10
Postage....................02

24937 Pewter Fire Department and Cavalry Outfits. These are small pewter metal apparatus, horses and men. Each set put up in pasteboard box. State which set is wanted, if you have a preference, or order both.
Price, each set..........................$0.10
Postage....................................02

Calliope Whistle.

24938 Made of wood, finished in bright colors. All of the notes can be sounded by pulling out the stopper. A good whistle, plenty of fun for boys and girls. Each...................$0.05
Per doz.....................................40
Postage....................................02

Climbing Monkey.

24939 The greatest novelty of the age. Climbs the string, moving arms and legs, and representing life in all its movements. Simple and durable. Nothing to get out of order Packed one in a box. Price............$0.25
Postage....................................07

Conjurers' Tricks and Magical Apparatus.

24940 A box of Magical Wonders. This box of clever tricks will furnish much amusement for the little folks. It contains a variety of amusing tricks, with book of instructions. Price.....$0.50

24941 Same general description as above, but containing a greater number of tricks. Sure to please. Price...................... 1.00

24942 Large size box of Magical Apparatus, containing apparatus for performing a large number of mystifying tricks, with book of instructions....................................... 1.50

Toy Reins.

24946 Toy Reins. Made of good weight and red and blue webbing with 1½ web yoke and chime bells.
Per pair...........$0.10
Postage........... .03

24947 Toy Reins, made of fine red and white 1-inch webbing, crossed leather yoke and five chime bells. Per pair............. .20
Postage................ .04

24948, Toy Rein made of extra heavy red webbing with fancy colored yoke, four brass chime bells on yoke piece. This is an especially good set. Length, 54 inches. Price per set.... .35
Postage............... .08

24949 Toy Reins. Extra heavy red and white webbing, fancy leather yoke and four large nickel chime bells. Price............. .50
Postage............... .10

24950 Toy Reins. Extra heavy red, white and blue webbing, 1 inch snap yoke; yoke and neck piece of white and tan leather. A very handsome set; 7 nickel chime bells. Weight 12 oz. Price........ .65

24951 Toy Reins, made of maroon colored leather, fancy stitched. Separate yoke piece made of black enameled leather, trimmed with fancy colored leather and stitching. Has three large silvered metal chime bells, and rings for attaching reins. Two silvered metal bells and snaps on reins. This set can be used for driving a dog or goat, as the reins can be fastened to a bit or collar by means of the snap attachments. Length, 42 inches. Put up one set in pasteboard box. Weight, 12 oz. Price per set....... .85

24952 Toy Reins, made of red, white and blue webbing, with large, fancy colored leather yoke; trimmed with 14 silvered metal chime bells. Reins attached to metal rings on yoke. A handsome, showy set for a boy of any age. Length, 48 inches. Price per set................... 1.25
Postage............................ .08

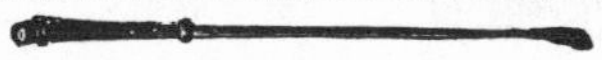

24954 Boys' whip, with loop, fancy. Each....... .05
24955 Boys' whip, 25 inches, wood stock, 22 inches, leather lash. Each....................... .08
Per dozen................... .85
24956 With whistle in handle, braided lash, as per cut. Each....................... .10
Per dozen...................... 1.00

24957 A splendid one, good length, with braided leather lash, fancy colored braided stock, whistle in end of handle. Each....................$0.15
Per dozen...................... 1.50

Dog Whips.

24958 Ten inch handle with whistle, 28 inch braided leather lash, with whip and cracker; a good article. Each........................$0.25
Per dozen...................... 2.50

Toy Watches.

24961 Toy Watch, for girls, open face, Swiss style, fancy gilt chain.
Each.................$0.08
Per dozen............. .90

24963 Toy Watch, figured hunting case, hour and minute hand, stem winder, steel vest chain. Each.............$0.10 Per dozen...... 1.00
24964 Toy Watch with bell. Wind watch up and bell will strike. Each......................... .15
Per dozen...................... 1.60
24965 Toy Watch, automatic tick movement, stem winding, hands move separately A good one. Each........................... .20
24967 Grandfather's Clock. A good imitation of the old timepiece. No doll house complete without one. Each................... .25
Postage, on toy watches.................. .03

Noah's Arks.

This toy has been a seller ever since the flood, and probably will be as long as the world stands.
24970 Noah's Ark, filled with neatly painted animals, flat ark. Each $0.10
Per dozen........... 1.00
Weight, ½ pounds.

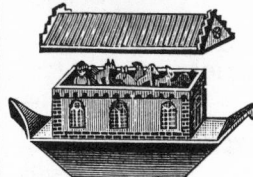

24972 Noah's Ark; boat shape, fancy; weight, 10 oz., 50c.
24973 Noah's Ark; same style as 24972, but larger and better. Each...........$0.75
Weight, 1¼ pounds.

Surprise Boxes.
(Jack in the Box.)

Surprise Boxes ranging from small to large sizes, containing figures of various forms which spring out of the box at will.
24975 Surprise Box. Each......$0.10
Per dozen.. .... 1.00
24976 Surprise Box. Each....... .25
Per dozen...... . ... 2.50

WOODEN TOYS

War Ship "Columbia."

24978 A perfect reproduction of this powerful and fast war ship, a model of strength and beauty, and the largest and most complete toy cruiser ever made. A feature is the smoke, giving the cruiser the appearance of being under full steam, and moving at a high rate of speed. It is finely lithographed, thoroughly made, and rigged with two masts; has four smoke stacks, eight ventilators, wire railing, cord, six boats, cannons, etc., and has a crew of twelve officers and sailors. All parts pack inside of boat. Full directions for setting up accompany each boat. Length, from stem to stern, 36 inches; 24 inches on top of mast. Price................................... $0.90

24980 Military Parade, has a force of 28 handsome soldiers arranged in 5 companies, commander and 2 aids, and carries 6 flags; all mounted on wheels. No cannon. Can be made to march obliquely when desired. Height of soldiers. 5½ inches. Comes packed in nice box 20 inches long, 10 in. wide, with attractive label. Price......... . ... $0.50

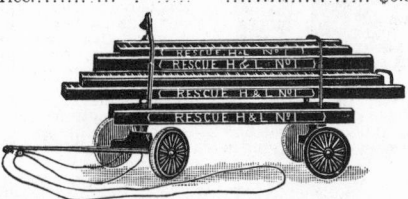

24983 Rescue Hook and Ladder Truck Co. 1; made wholly of wood. Has four handsomely painted ladders, which are so made that they can be joined together, forming one long ladder. An interesting toy for any boy. Price..........$0.50

Buffalo Bill.

24985 This is a new departure in wooden [toys] and is decidedly novel in every respect. It il[lus]trates vividly how Buffalo Bill and his sc[outs] overcame a party of ambuscaded Indians. [Every]thing out. Price......................

24986 Cinderella Coach with Blocks. A fine representation of an elegant coach with driver and footmen, drawn by a pair of horses, all lithographed in light colors

and highly ornamented. The coach contains set of blocks illustrating the story of Cinderella and the Glass Slipper. Length of coach, 10 inches; height. 11¼ inches. Packed in box. Price.. ... .$0.90

24987 Express Wagon. A new and attractive wagon, neatly ornamented and colored, very strongly made, has two wings and is easily set up. All parts pack inside the body, making a small package. Size, 13 inches long, 7 inches high. Price........$0.20

Wooden Soldiers.

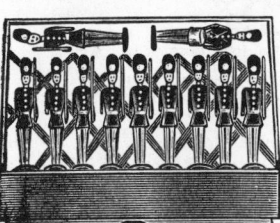

24988 Wooden Soldiers, movable, each made to stand alone. In box.
Per set......$0.20
Per doz... 2.10
24989 Wooden Soldiers, large size.
Per set.....$0.40

24993 A handsome and pleasing novelty, bright and attractive, representing a dog playing with a ball. By drawing the toy the dog jumps up and down every revolution of the Wheel, which is between his paws. Size, 15½ in. long and 9 in. high. Each...$0.23

Toy Guns and Pistols.

Toy Guns cannot be sent by mail on account of length and liability of breakage.

24994 School Drill Gun. The frequent demand for a large size boy's gun for drilling purposes in school or otherwise has induced us to introduce this gun. It is made of hardwood, well finished, and has the percussion lock to fire off paper caps; it is in size large enough for boys from 12 to 16 years of age. Stock 42 in. long. with bayonet. Each...................................$1.00
24995 Toy Gun, with bayonet and strap, measures 41 inches in length without bayonet; shoots paper cap and stick. Weight, 1¼ lbs. Each.... .90
24996 The "Harmless" Gun. Price........ .85
24998 The Swift and Sure Gun. Price.......... .25

BOOKS

Fast becoming a Store in itself, so large is the department.

Insure Your Mail Packages.

See Page 1.

Vacuum Tipped Arrows, Pistols and Rifles.

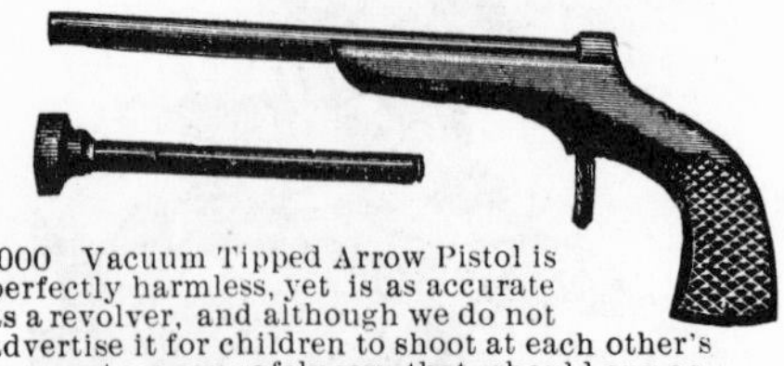

25000 Vacuum Tipped Arrow Pistol is perfectly harmless, yet is as accurate as a revolver, and although we do not advertise it for children to shoot at each other's eyes, yet we can safely say that should any accident happen it would not harm the most delicate child. It has no equal for parlor amusement or outdoor sport. Made of bronze, with polished barrel; including target. Price........ $0.50
25001 Same as above in full nickel, with target.. .75
25002 Vacuum Tipped Arrow Rifles, regulation pattern, wood stock and 16 in. bronze barrel. Price includes one arrow. Each..... .95
25003 Same as 25002, but with nickel-plated barrel. Price.... 1.40
25005 Extra arrows, each.... .15
25006 The Echo Toy Pistol. A harmless, novel and ingenious toy. No caps to endanger the eyes of the little ones, but a loud report to please the boys. It will throw a pea or bean 40 feet with remarkable accuracy. Weight, 4 ounces. Price, each.... 10
25007 The King Pop Gun. Just out, made on same principle as the well known King Air Rifle. By means of compressed air a cork is fired from the gun with a loud report. Perfectly harmless. Weight, 6 ounces. Price, each.... .25

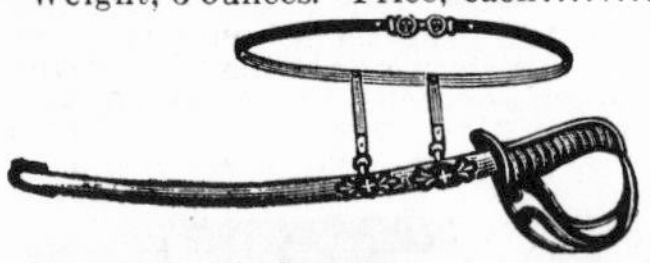

25008 Toy Swords with strap, belt and guarded handle in sheath; length, 25 in.; weight, ½ pound. Each.... $0.25

Toy Iron Cannon.

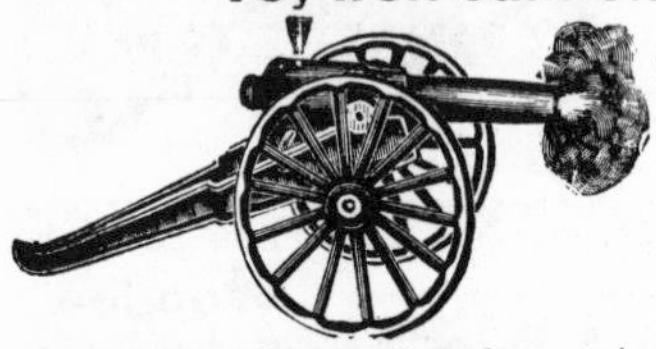

25010 Toy Iron Cannon mounted on wheels, carriage painted red, cannon black; new design. length of barrel, 3½ in.; bore, ¼ in.; weight, ¾ lbs. Price.... $0.20
25012 Iron Cannon; same description, but larger; length of barrel 5 in., bore, 5/16 inch, weight, 1¾ lbs. Price.... 38
25014 Iron Cannon, 7 in. barrel, ½ in. bore; weight, 3¾ lbs. Price.... .85
25016 Iron Cannon, 9 in. barrel, ⅝ in. bore, 7¼ lbs. weight. Price.... 1.35
25018 Jumbo Iron Cannon, 10 in. barrel, ¾ in. bore, weight, 12¼ lbs. Price.. 1.90

Brass Cannon.

25019 U. S. Regulation Pattern, solid brass, highly polished, very handsome, strong, and gives loud report, handsomely mounted on malleable iron carriage. Small size; length of barrel 4 in.; weight, 1 lb. Price.... $0.45
25020 Brass Cannon, same description, but with 5 in. barrel and ⅜ in. bore; weight, 1¾ lbs. Price.... .90
25022 Large Brass Cannon, about same description as No. 25014, but made of brass. Price..... 1.85

Wooden Cannon,

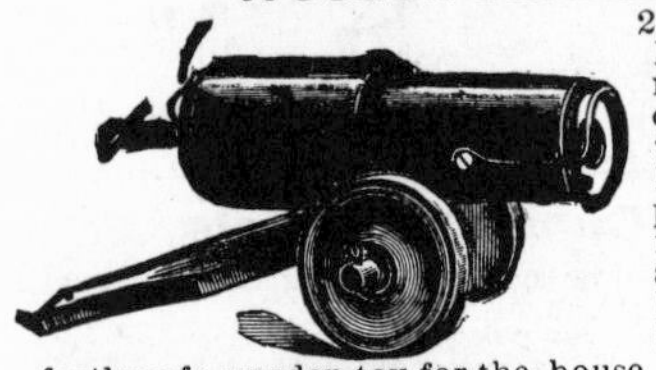

25023 Columbus Krupp Cannon, mounted in gun carriage; a large toy, weighing less than two pounds; a ten-inch gun makes a loud report but can do no harm. A perfectly safe wooden toy for the house. We can recommend it for every family where there is a small boy. Price, each.... $0.40

Toy Drums.

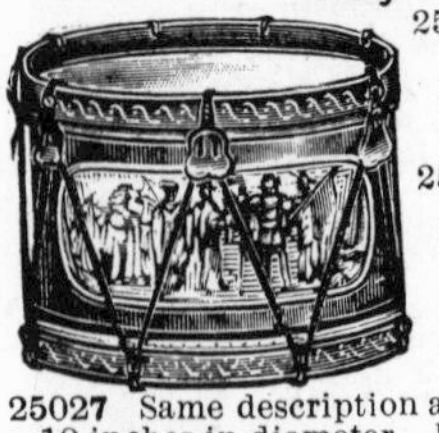

25025 Toy Drum, good quality, hammered brass body, corded with sticks, 7 inches in diameter.... $0.25
Per dozen.... 2.75
25026 Toy Drums, good quality, brass body, ornamented with lithographed picture in bright colors, corded 8 inches in diameter.
Price.... $0.50
Per dozen.... 5.40
25027 Same description as above, but larger size, 10 inches in diameter. Price .... .75
Per dozen.... 7.75
25028 Toy Drum, flat, imitation mahogany body, calfskin head, corded, enameled sticks, 10 in. diameter. Price.... 1.00
25029 Same as above, with 12 inch head. Price.. 1.50
25030 Same as above, with 14 inch head. Price.. 2.00

Toys—Continued.

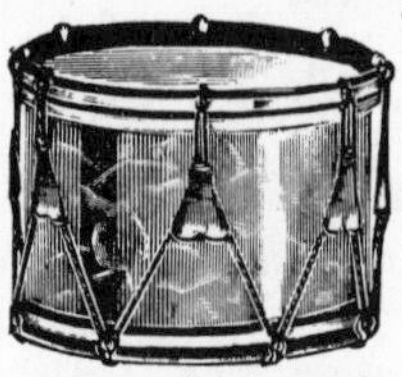

25031 Regulation Pattern, High Drum, fine 12 in. calf skin head, fancy wood body, corded, with shoulder sling and enameled sticks.
Price.... $2.25
25032 Same, with 14 inch head.
Price.... $2.50

Toy Trumpets, Bugles, Trombones, Cornets, Etc.

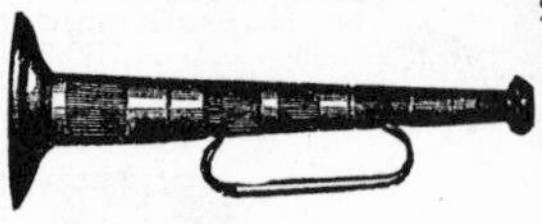

25033 Tin Toy Trumpets, nicely striped and painted, about 9 inches long. Weight, 1 ounce
Each.... $0.05
Per dozen..... .50
25035 Horn Toy Bugles about 6 inches long. Weight, 1 ounce. Each, $0.05. Per dozen...... .50
25036 Horn Bugles, 8 inches long, with mouth-piece. Each.... .12
25037 Toy Horn Bugles, with horn mouth-piece; length, about 10 inches; extra quality. Weight, 3 ounces. Each.... .20
Per dozen.... 2.25
25038 Huntsman's Bugle, double note, nickel-plated, large size. Each.... .30

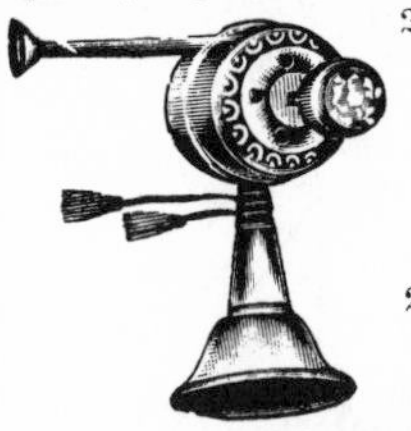

25039 French Musical Horns, silver finish. By working the lever on the under part of the instrument, and blowing steadily, the horn will play a complete tune. Has cord and tassel, as shown in cut.
Each.... $0.25
25040 French Musical Horns, same general description as No. 25039, but much larger and made of better material.
Each.... $0.40

Toy Magic Lanterns.

No other toy has been the source of so much wonderment and delight to children as the magic lantern. The line quoted below are high grade toys, and one of them will be the means of providing many hours of entertainment to the little folks.

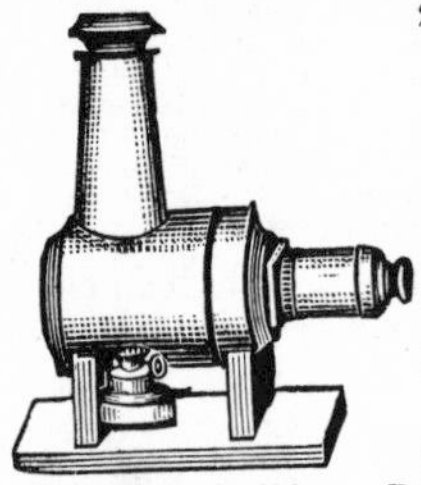

25045 Toy Magic Lantern, neatly ornamented metal body, provided with good condensing and objective lenses, and kerosene lamp, packed in neat box, with 1 dozen slides. Uses 1⅜ inch slides, and magnifies picture to 2½ or 3 feet in diameter.
Price.... $0.85
25046 Same description, but uses 1½ inch slides.
Price.... $1.15
25047 Same description, but uses 1¾ inch slides. Price.... $1.40
25048 Same description, but uses 2-inch slides. Price.... 1.85
25049 Same description, but uses 2⅜-inch slides. Price.... 2.20
25050 Same description, but uses 2¾-inch slides. Price.... 2.65
25051 Same description, but uses 3⅛-inch slides. Price.... 3.25

The "Gloria" Magic Lanterns.

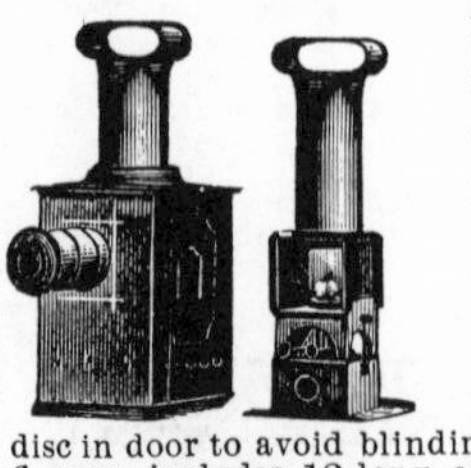

For Parlor and Amateur Entertainments. These magic lanterns combine economy and superior brilliant effects over the ordinary juvenile magic lanterns, having a duplex lamp so constructed as to avoid the necessity of using glass chimneys; metal lacquered body, nickel plated chimney and fronts, 1 crown glass condenser, 2 superior crown glass lenses in tubes, dark glass disc in door to avoid blinding vision when regulating flames; includes 12 long covered slides having from four to six subjects on each slide, Chromotrope, 1 comic movable slide, 1 welcome slide, 1 good-night slide. Complete, in neat carrying case with handle. Made in three sizes.
25053 Gloria Lantern, with 2-inch slides, showing 2-foot picture. Price.... $5.00
25054 Same, 2⅜-inch slide, showing 3-foot picture. Price.... 6.75
25055 Same, 2¾-inch slide, showing 3¾-foot picture. Price.... 8.00

We can fit you out from head to foot. Likewise your family. Even your horses.

The Polyopticon or Wonder Camera.

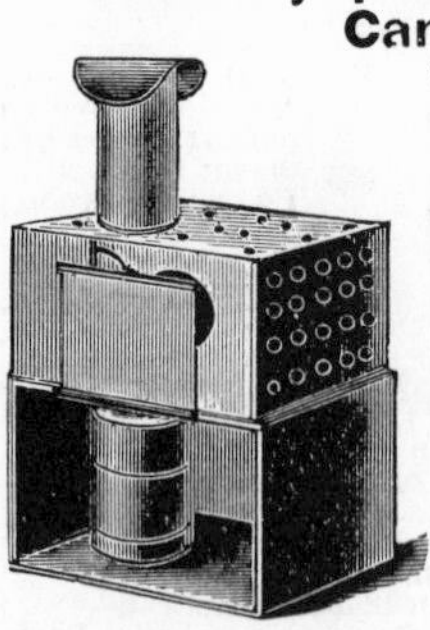

25057 Produces views on screen or wall from cuts from newspapers, magazines, portraits, comic chromo cards, photographs, flowers, comic cuts, etc., in all their colors, enlarged about 400 areas; over a hundred different pictures are given with each Polyopticon, covering almost every conceivable object; with reflector lamp and burner chimney, lens and door, with 3-inch picture window. Weight, 3½ lbs.
Price complete.... $4.40

Toy Magic Lantern Slides.

NOTE.—We cannot fill orders for any SPECIAL SUBJECTS in toy lantern slides. These slides come to us from the manufacturers put up 1 dozen in a box, and in three to five assortments only.

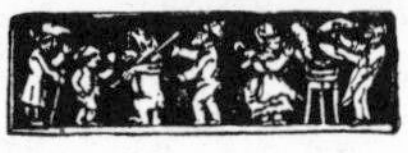

25060 Plain Slides highly colored, for amateurs; nursery tales, Mother Goose Fables, American and German scenery, World's Fair, etc.

Width	Per doz	Weight, per doz.
1⅛ in.	$0.35	7 oz.
1⅜ in.	.45	8 oz.
1½ in.	.50	10 oz.
1¾ in.	.60	15 oz.
2 in.	.90	1¼ lbs.
2⅜ in.	1.00	1½ lbs.
2¾ in.	1.50	2½ lbs.
3⅛ in.	1.75	3 lbs

25065 Movable Slides, comic colored, for amateurs.

Width	Each	Per doz	Weight, per doz.
1½ in.	10c.	$1.00	1¼ lbs.
1¾ in.	14c.	1.50	1½ lbs.
2⅜ in.	20c.	1.75	2 lbs.
3⅛ in.	25c.	2.50	3¾ lbs.
4 in.	35c.	4.00	4½ lbs.

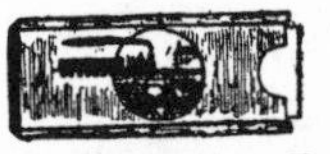

25067 Movable Slides, colored landscapes.

Width	Each	Per doz	Weight, per doz.
1¾ in.	20c.	$1.80	1 lb.
2⅜ in.	25c.	2.80	1½ lbs.
3⅛ in.	50c.	5.50	2 lbs.
4 in.	75c.	7.20	4½ lbs.

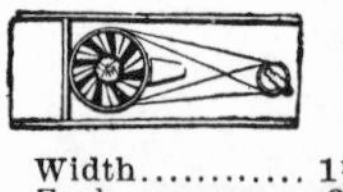

25070 Geometrical Chromotrope Slides; consist of two vari-colored wheels, revolving in opposite directions by means of a crank and belt, producing a brilliant effect

Width	1½ in.	2⅜ in.	3⅛ in.	4 in.
Each	35c.	50c.	75c.	$1.00
Postage	5c.	5c.	5c.	7c.

Magic Lanterns and Sciopticons.

For Sunday Schools, Societies, Army Posts, Home and Public Entertainments.

We carry a full stock of high grade magic lanterns, sciopticons, slides, screens and accessories, at all times. Special list of these goods sent by mail, free, upon application. We do a large business in this line, and our prices are unusually low for first quality goods.

No. 10. Improved Duplex Magic Lantern.... $ 9.50
No. 100, C. A. C. E. Magic Lantern.... 20.00
No. 300. Triplex Sciopticon.... 28.00
No 350. Headlight Sciopticon.... 36.00
No. 400. New York Model Sciopticon.... 47.00
And many others.

If you are at all interested in the subject of magic lanterns or views, do not neglect to send for our special list of magic lanterns and slides No. G. Free on application.

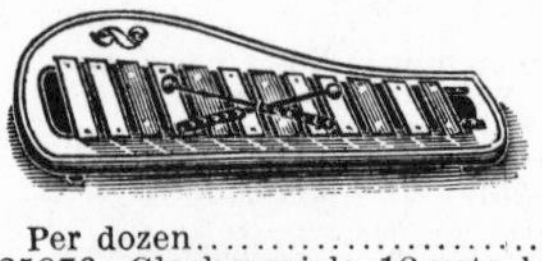

25075 Glockenspiele, or improved Metallophone, eight notes bronze keys, hardwood frame in neat paper box.
Each.... $0.25
Per dozen.... 2.70
25076 Glockenspiele, 12 note, bronze keys. Size 7x16 inches. Each.... .50
Per dozen.... 5.40
25077 Glockenspiele, 18 note, bronze keys. Size, 2x8x23¼ inches. Each.... .90
Per dozen.... 8.00

Toy Harps.

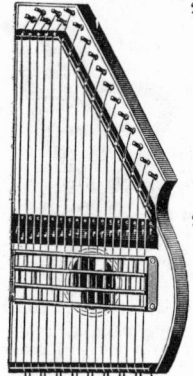

25080 The Phonoharp is not merely a toy, but a musical instrument with 15 strings and having three bars, by the use of which chords are produced to harmonize with sounds obtained by picking the strings as on a common zithern. Five sheets of music with each instrument, which can readily be played by a child. Price................$1.50

25081 The Phonoharp. This musical novelty consists of a 17 string zithern, on the face of which is fastened a nickel plated three bar shield, which protects certain strings from contact with the finger pick or thumb piece; chords are produced by drawing, pick or thumb piece, in the right hand, across the shields, while the other hand remains free to be used as a damper or to play with as performer may desire. Instrument is made of best materials, only the best piano wire being used, and is handsomely finished in a thoroughly workman-like manner. Price................$2.50

25082 Phonoharp, same general description as 25081, but larger and better, with nickel plated parts, 25 strings and 6 bars. Each............$4.00

Toy Zithern.

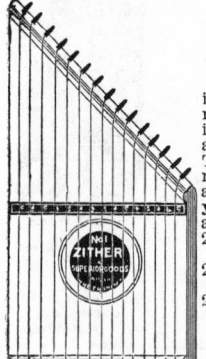

An attractive toy musical instrument, on which the cords may be learned with ease; both instructive and interesting to all. Made plain and harp shape. These goods are handsomely made and finished, and are appreciated and enjoyed by young people of all ages, as they are all tuned to concert pitch.

25084 Plain Shape, 10 strings. Each......................$0.40
25085 Plain Shape, 15 strings. Each......................$0.60
25086 Harp Shape, 22 strings. Each $0.90

Toy Violins.

25092 Toy Violin, 16 inches long, one in a box, with a bow. Each.........................$0.25
Per dozen................................ 2.75
25093 Toy Violins, 18 inches long, one in a box, with bow. Each........................ .50
Per dozen................................ 5.00
25094 Toy Violins, 20 inches long, packed in a box with folding cover and handle for carrying, with bow. Price, each............. .90

Toy Pianos.

(Cannot be sent by mail.)

25095 Square Toy Piano, as shown in cut, with high legs and open front, single cover. Size, 10x7½x8½. Rosewood. Stained and decorated front. One octave. Weight, 2½ pounds. Price..........$0.40
25096 Square Toy Piano, varnished wood case, open front with folding music rack and 15 keys. Size, 6½x10¼x9. Weight, 5 pounds. Price $0.90

25097 Square Toy Pianos, with high, turned legs and full-hinged cover to close. Size, 19½ x 10½ x 9½. Weight, 6 lbs. Price...........$1.50

Toy Pianos—Continued.

25100 Upright Toy Piano; case handsomely finished, ornamented legs and chandeliers, 15 keys. Packed one in a pasteboard box. Weight, 7¾ pounds. Price................$2.25

25101 Upright Toy Pianos; same general description as above, but larger size and with 18 keys. Size, 18x17½x10 in. Weight, 11 lbs. Price.....$3.50

25102 Upright Toy Piano; extra quality, three octaves, tuned to a perfect concert pitch. Finely carved legs. 23x24x11. Ornamented and has two gilded chandeliers. Weight, 11 pounds. Price....$5.00 Each packed in wooden case.

Blocks.

Gilt Edge Building Blocks, made of thoroughly seasoned hardwood, finely finished. The variety and quality of blocks are sufficient to build a large number of pleasing designs.

25105 No. 1 size...$0.20
25106 No. 2 size... .45
25107 No. 3 size... 1.00

25116 The Educational Toy and Building Blocks; an amusing and instructive toy, taxing the skill, ingenuity and inventive genius of the young. An Alphabet Puzzle with which it is possible to form correctly all the letters of the alphabet at once; in solid or prismatic colors, in size and shape as shown in accompanying diagrams. Specially adapted for kindergarten schools. Weight, 3¼ pounds. Price......$0.90
25119 Picture Blocks, put up in fancy folding box, containing 12 cubes, making six puzzle pictures. Sample picture with each box; very fine for children; extra quality for the price. Weight, 1 pound.
Per box..............$0.22 Per dozen..........$2.10
25120 Same as above, but larger size. Per box.... .40
25121 Westcott's Army and Navy Blocks. These picture blocks are covered with highly colored lithographs of the navies of the world. Packed in fancy colored box, illuminated cover.
Price, per box.............................$0.35
25122 Combination Picture and Alphabet Blocks, containing 20 large natural cube pictures, alphabet and puzzle blocks, 4 combination pictures packed in wood frame box, with illuminated cover. Weight, 2 pounds.
Per box..............$0.50 Per dozen........$5.50
25123 War Ship Picture Blocks, consisting of 24 large size cubes, with which can be made pictures of 6 of the famous vessels of the White Navy. Pictures are 7¾x20½ inches. Packed in neat box, with pattern pictures. Price................... .90
25124 Capital Picture Blocks, same description as above, but pictures are those of six prominent buildings at the National Capital. Price........ .90

Telescopic Picture Blocks, consisting of hollow cube blocks, covered with fancy lithographed designs. These blocks pack one into another, thus affording endless amusement for the little ones.
25127 Per set of 12 blocks..... ...$0.95

25147 Alphabet Blocks, 20 large fine cubes, with illustrations, figures and alphabet. The colors are bright and attractive, and workmanship the best. Per box......................... .75

China Toy Tea Sets.

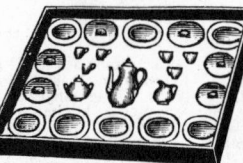

52155

25155 Set consists of cups, saucers, tea pot, sugar bowl and cream; small size; packed in paper box. Price....$0.10
25156 Same description as above but larger. Price....$0.25
25157 Set consists of decorated plates, cups, saucers, tea pot, creamer, sugar bowl; good sized dishes. Price.........................$0.50
25158 Same description, but larger. Price....... .75
25159 Same, but larger size and assortment. Price........................... 1.00
25163 White Stone China Tea Set of 24 pieces, as follows: 6 plates, 6 cups, 6 saucers, 1 sugar bowl and cover, 1 tea pot and cover, 1 creamer, 1 slop bowl. This set is large enough for a miss from 8 to 14 years of age. (Not safe to send by mail.) Weighs 8½ lbs. Per set..................$1.25 The pieces in this set are larger than usually sold in toy sets; the cups stand 2 inches high, and the plates measure 4½ inches across.

25164—Fancy Decorated Tea Set, same size and assortment as above; elegant patterns. Packed in wooden box, weight 8½ lbs. Price.$1.75

Decorated China Toy Toilet Sets.

25172 Extra Size Wash or Toilet Set, gilt lined and brilliantly decorated; a handsome set. Packed in strong box; weight, 3 lbs. Per set........$0.65
Per dozen sets 7.00

Britannia Tea Sets.

25175—Britannia Tea Sets, silver finish, consisting of tea pot sugar bowls, sugar tongs, creamer, four plates and cups, Put up in neat pasteboard box; weight, 5 ounces........................ $0.09
25176 Britannia Tea Set, silver finish, consisting of tea pot, sugar bowl, creamer, six plates, six cups, six spoons and sugar spoons. Embossed decorations; weight, 10 ounces. Price.. .22
25177 Britannia Tea Set, silver finish, consisting of tea pot, sugar bowl, creamer, six plates, six cups and six spoons. A very handsome set; weight, 1¼ pounds.....................- .45
25178 Britannia Tea Set, silver finish, consisting of tea pot, sugar bowl, creamer, spoon holder, six plates, six cups, six spoons and fancy filigree work sugar tongs. The entire set is handsomely decorated in bas-relief design, making a large showy set; weight, 3¾ pounds. Price... .85

Superior Quality Toy Tin Kitchen Sets.

25180 Tin Kitchen Set, small size; consisting of about fifteen pieces tin kitchen utensils. See illustration. Weight, 6 ounces. Price.....$0.10
25181 Tin Kitchen Set, medium size; consisting of 25 or more pieces, tin and wooden utensils. Weight, 12 ounces. Price.................... .20
25182 Tin Kitchen Set, large size, containing 30 pieces. Weight, 1¼ pounds. Price........... .40
25183 Tin Kitchen Set, Large size. Has 42 or more utensils of good size; some of the pans in Nos. 25181 and 25182 are large enough for baking small loaves, cakes, etc. Weight, 1¾ lbs. Price... .65

Superior Quality Embossed Tin Kitchens.

Painted in bright colors and very attractive to the little folks.

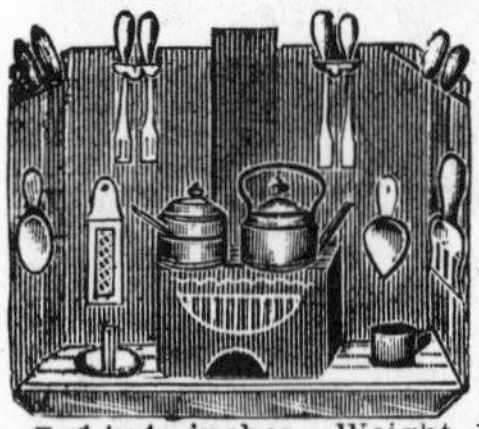

25185 Embossed Tin Kitchen, small size; contains 1-hole range and ten pieces kitchen tinware. Size, 6½ in. high, 11 in. long, 2¼ in. deep. Postage $0.15
Price.. .... .25

25186 Embossed Tin Kitchen, medium size. Has in addition a two-hole range, a water cooler and 12 utensils. Size, 7x14x4 inches. Weight, 1¾ lbs. Price.......$0.45

25187 Embossed Tin Kitchen. One of the largest and best. Two-hole range with warming oven above, water cooler and twenty pieces tin and wooden kitchen utensils of large size. Size, 8½ x19x5 inches. Weight, 2¾ lbs. Price .... .75

All of the above kitchen and kitchen sets are packed in neat boxes.

Children's Table Sets.

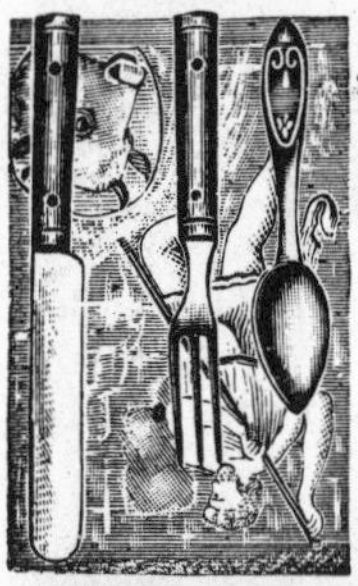

25190 Children's Memento Sets; knife fork and spoon, on card.
Per set. $0.10
Per dozen sets............ 1.00
Postage. .... .04

25191 Child's Set of three pieces, consisting of knife, fork and spoon, mounted on fancy picture card. 4½x7 inches. This set has cocobola handles, riveted with bolster and cap; blades made of good quality of steel, Per set $0.25

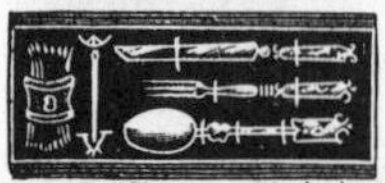

25192 Toy "Britannia" Sets, consisting of knife, fork, spoon, napkin ring and knife rest in neat box, containing 3 sets.
Per set. $0.30

25193 Box containing knife, fork, spoon and napkin ring of doll size. Price.... ...... 0.05

25194 Same, but larger size and provided in addition to above with knife rest. Price.......... .10

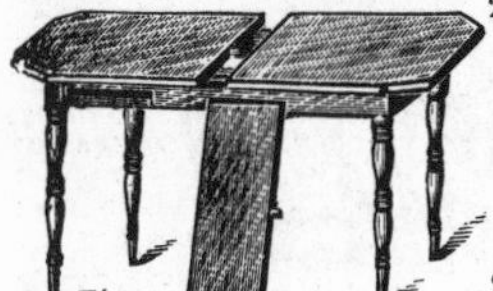

25197 Folding Table, similar to cut. Legs fold under, making it convenient to handle. Nicely made and a new thing in a toy table; size, 21 x 13 x 14½ inches.
Price, each.......$0.50

25198 Folding Table, larger than preceding, well made and useful; size, 14x24x15½ inches.
Price, each................ .... .75

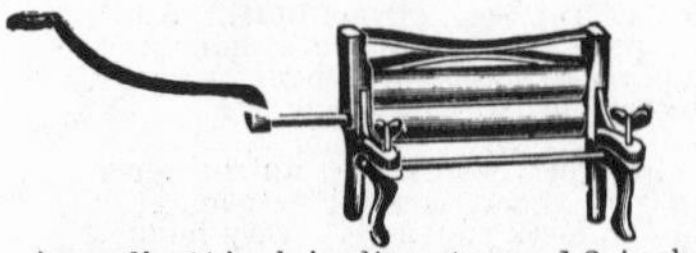

25200 The "Triumph" Toy Wringer; frame made wholly of cast metal, smooth finished, white rubber rolls, ½ inch in diameter and 3 inches long. Can be fastened to side of tub by means of thumb screws. A perfect model of the regular Triumph wringer. Weight, 1 lb. Price, each..$0.40

Unique Wash Sets.

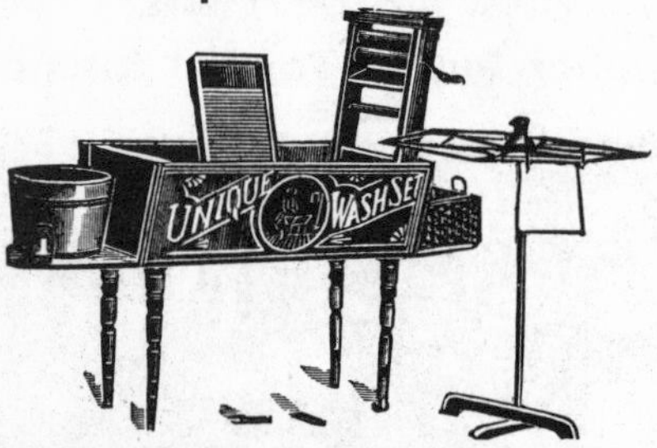

25203 Entirely new and original in design, consisting of latest style Laundry Tub, Wringer, Washboard, Pail, Basket, and double line Clothes Reel with Clothes Pins. All parts pack inside of tub. Compact, attractive and strongly made. Size, 27in. long, 13 in. high, 9 in. wide. Reel, 16 in. high. Price.... $0.90

25204 Similar in design to above. Consists of new style Laundry Tub, Wringer, Washboard, Basket, Clothes Reel and Pins. All parts pack inside of tub. Size, 18 in. long, 7 in. wide, 9½ in. high. Reel, 11 in. high. Price............ .50

25205 Toy Washing Machine. A complete practical toy for washing dolls' clothes. Modeled after pattern of a large washer. Is 6½ inches wide, 12¼ inches long, stands 7½ inches high, and is nicely painted in bright colors.
Price, each .... .95

Doll Bedsteads.

The Silver Queen Dolls' Wire Bedstead with mattress and pillows. A most perfect dolls' bed; made in three sizes

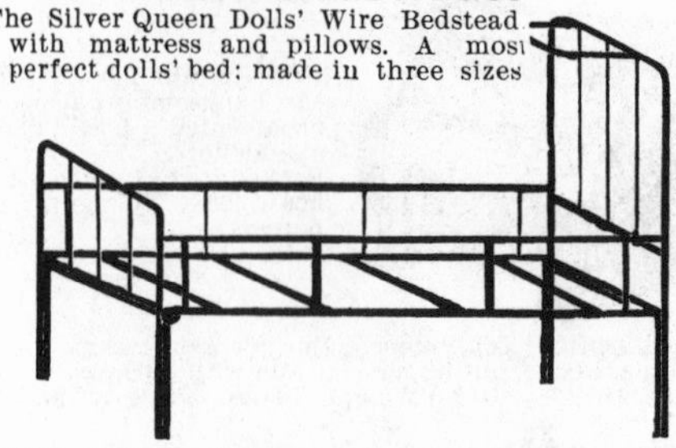

25207 18 inch. Price.. ....$0.75
25208 24 inch. Price............ .... 1.00
25209 30 inch. Price........................ 1.25

Dolls' Cane Bedstead. Strong wood frame, wrapped in fancy patterns with split cane. Has turned wood head and foot posts, and ordinary slat mattress. Made in two sizes.

25210 Small size, 10x 6 x 11 in. Each.......................$0.70

25211 Large size, 12x10x12 inch headboard. Each $0.90

These beds cannot be sent by mail.

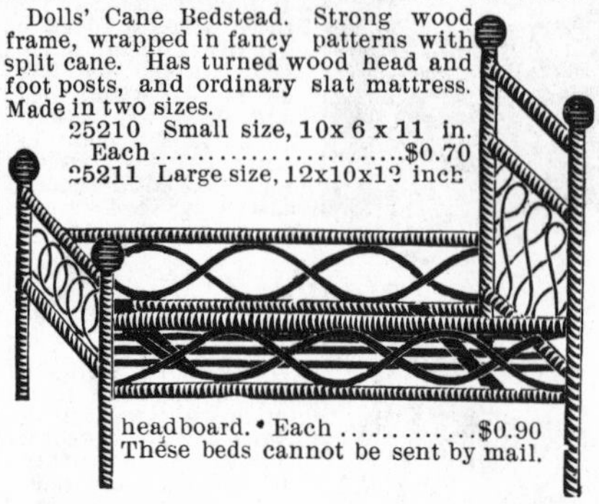

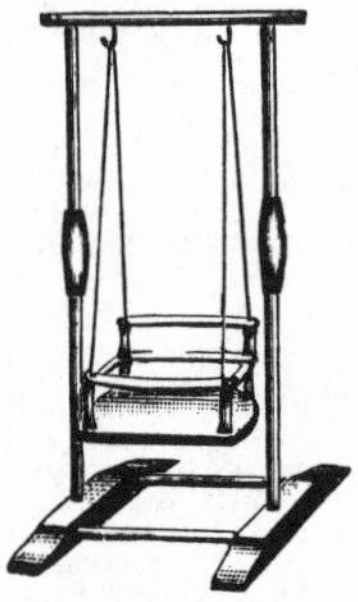

Doll Swings.

25212 Dolls' Swing; stands 20 inches high. Measures 12x12 inches at the base; the seat of the swing 7 inches across; knocks down flat. Each swing wrapped and tied in packages, 2x5x13.
Price, each...............$0.15

25213 A Doll's Swing, not illustrated. Different construction from the one quoted above, but a good swing.
Price $0.20

Doll Hammocks.

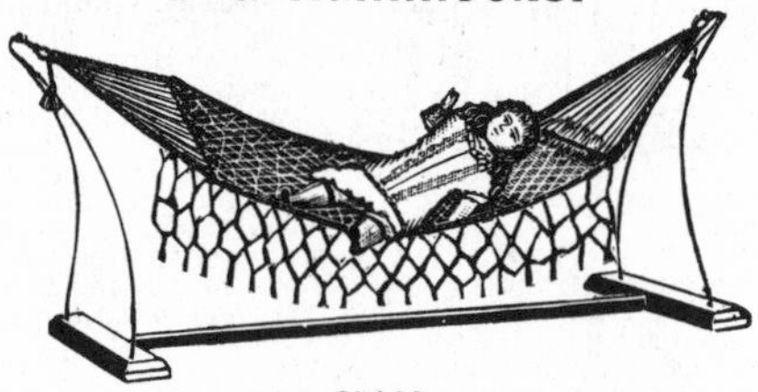

25162

25214 Toy Doll Hammocks. Made of fancy colored seine twine, hand woven, strong and durable. Metal rings in each end for suspending hammock. Length, 40 inches. Each..... $0.15
Postage 02
Stands for same, 2 ft., 6 in. long. Each........ .25

25215 Toy Doll Hammocks. Fancy colors, with spreaders. Length, 50 inches, Designed to be used with a rack stand as illustrated.
Price of hammock........ .25
Stands for same, each.... .25

25216 Toy Doll Hammocks. Fancy colors with pillow and spreaders Corded edge of extra heavy braided twine, with variegated tassels. A very superior article. Price, each .... .50

25217 Stands for same, each..................... .25

Doll Cradles.

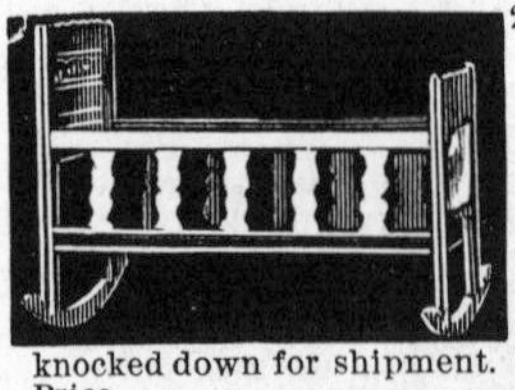

25219 Doll's Cradle made of chestnut wood, with foot and head board paneled and painted in handsome design. Will hold a 20-inch doll. Extreme length, 22 inches; height, 16 inches; width, 11 inches. Packed knocked down for shipment. Weight, 3 lbs.
Price.......................... $0.75

25220 Doll's Cradle, same style finish and wood as above, but designed to accommodate a 16-inch doll. Extreme length, 18 inches; width, 9 inches; height, 12 inches; weight, 2 pounds.
Price.... .45

25221 Doll's Cradle, same general construction, but smaller, extreme length being 15 inches; height, 8 inches; width, 7 inches; weight, 1 pounds. Price .... .25

Doll Furniture.

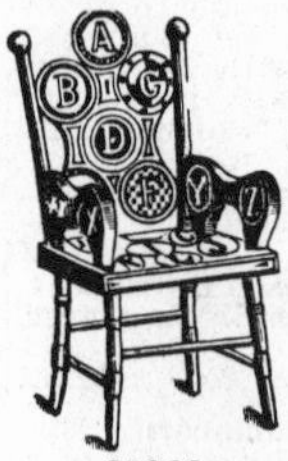

25222

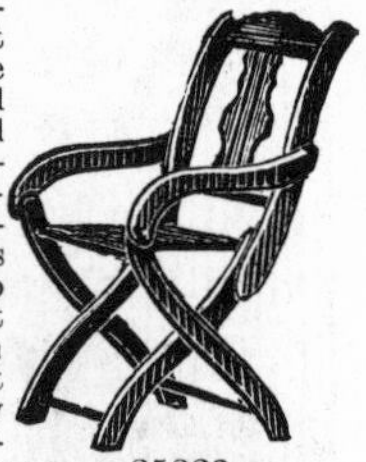

25223

25222 Alphabet Chair, made of hard wood and covered with handsomely illuminated letters. This chair is so made that it can be taken apart and set up in a few moments, affording amusement and instruction to any child. Height to top of back of chair, 11 inches; to seat, 5 inches; width, 5 inches. Weight, packed, knocked down, ½ pound. Price $0.19

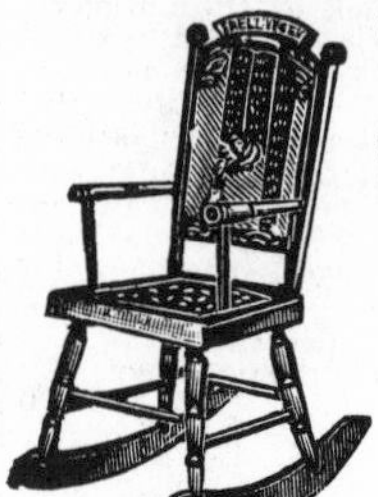

25223 Doll's Folding Chair, made of hardwood, with fancy cloth seat; height, 11½ inches.
Price. $0.20

25224 Doll's Spelling Rocker. A new feature for chairs. A large selection of words for children to learn to spell, together with a pleasing design in bright colors. Height, 14 inches. Price............$0.22

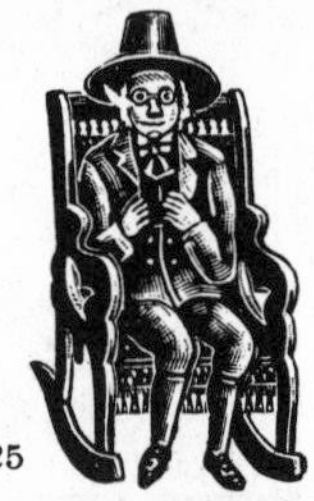

25225 Grandpa Rocker. An original and pleasing feature in rockers, consisting of handsomely designed chair represented as being occupied by grandpa, and having a very lifelike appearance. Size, 13 inches high, 6 inches wide.
Price...... . ... $0.25

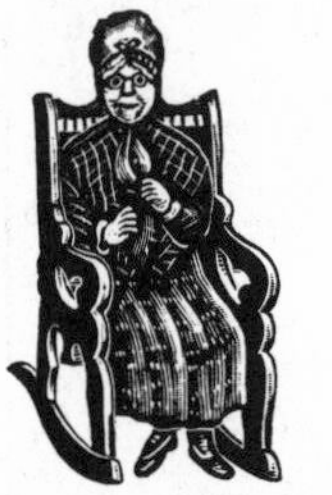

25225¼ Same, but chair is occupied by grandma.
Price.........................$0.25

25226 Doll's High Chair. Made of hardwood, smooth finish and handsomely ornamented to represent cane work. Each packed in neat pasteboard box. Height, 8 inches.
Price..........................$0.24

25227 Doll's High Chair, same construction and size as above, but has lap board with wooden dishes attached.
Price.......................$0.28

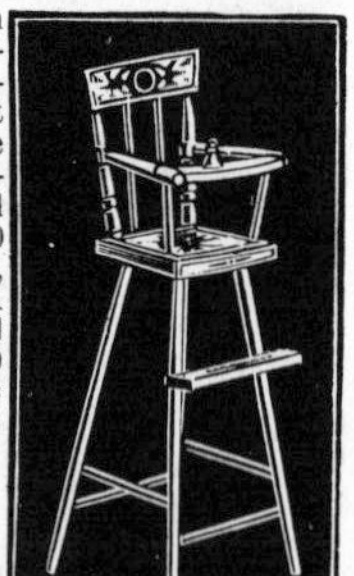

25228 Doll's Alphabet High Chair. One of the latest patterns and an exceedingly handsome chair. On the back, seat and step are lithographed the full alphabet, figures and pictures. Height, 22 in. Packed in neat box. Price $0.30

25229 Folding Alphabet Table, lithographed in bright colors. circular in shape. Ornamented with letters of the alphabet, 10 inches in diameter, 8½ inches high. Price $0.25

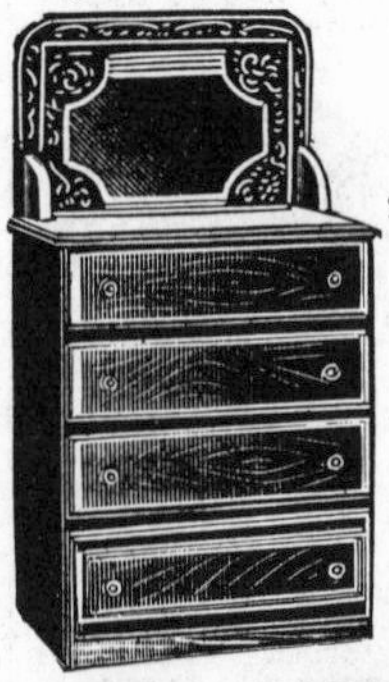

25234 Imperial Chiffonnier, a very fine and handsome piece of furniture. The drawer fronts and extension top are lithographed in perfect imitation of rich burl panels and carved work. Has 4 drawers with polished metal knob fronts. It is strongly made and finely finished, and is exceedingly attractive. Size, 9 inches long, 18 inches high.
Price $0.95

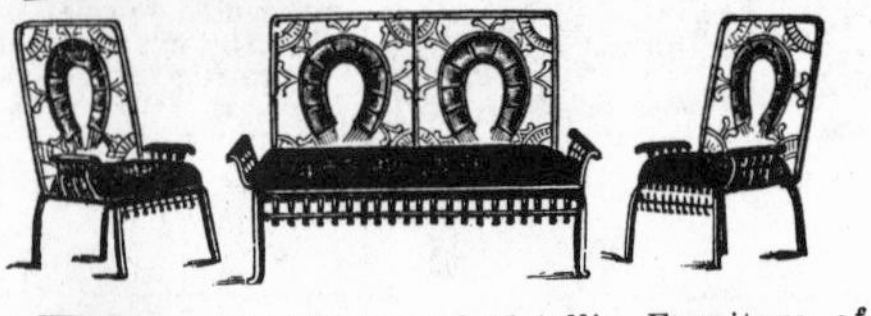

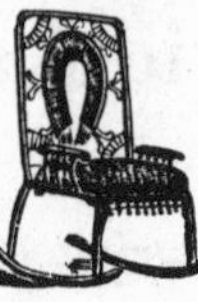

25235 Set of Metallic Furniture of artistic design, filigree patterns, consisting of four pieces: settee, rocker and two chairs, handsomely upholstered in velvet. Size of settee, 5 in. long, 4 in. high; chairs, 2 in long; rocker, 2¼ in. wide, 3½ in. high.
Price....... ....$0.35
Postage......................... .10

CHILD'S FURNITURE.

Order No. 25238.

A description and the illustration of crib does not do justice to this line of goods. The pieces are imitation enamel, corrugated, finished in white and gold, and are large enough to be of practical value.

Beds.

18 inch. Price, each	$1.00
21 inch. Price, each	1.25
24 inch. Price, each	1.50

Cribs.

18 inch, Price, each	1.25
21 inch. Price, each	1.50
24 inch. Price, each	1.88
Child's Rocker. Price, each	1.50
Child's Chair. Price, each	1.35
Child's Settee. Price, each	2.50
Dolls' Chair. Price, each	.38
Child's Chair. Price, each	.75
Child's Table. Price, each	1.13
Child's Table. Price, each	.75

Black Boards.

25240 One of the finest and most complete blackboards made. A well arranged combination of easel and desk, having a movable sawed extension, with designs for drawing on either side. The board is made of new material of best quality, smooth and warranted not to check. The desk is provided with an extra large drawer with ornamented front. The board drops forward to form the desk, showing additional designs for drawing. It is made in a substantial manner and folds very closely for shipping. Height, 48 in. Size of board, 16x19 in.
Price ... $1.00

25241 A perfect Blackboard and Easel; no cut. Has fluted standards. Complete alphabet on the frame of the board. A movable extension having designs for drawing on both sides. The back support can be easily removed so as to make a very thin package: height, 41 inches. Size of board, 18½x12½ inches.
Price ... $0.45

DOLLS.

Jointed Dolls, Bisque Heads, with Chemise.

25249 Jointed Dolls, bisque heads, flowing hair, teeth, and long plaited chemise. Length, 15½ inches.
Price ... $0.50
25250 Jointed Dolls, with bisque heads, flowing hair, teeth and long chemise. Length, 19 inches.
Price ... .90
25251 Jointed Dolls, extra large and fine, with flowing hair, teeth and long chemise, bisque heads. Length, 25 inches.
Price ... 1.90

Kid Body Dolls, Not Dressed, Jointed.

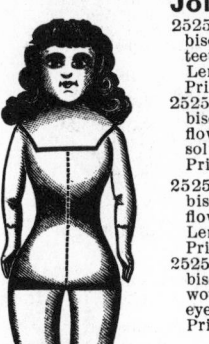

25252 Kid Body Dolls with bisque heads, flowing hair, teeth and solid eyes. Length, 12 inches.
Price ... $0.25
25253 Kid Body Dolls with bisque heads, woven wig, flowing hair, teeth and solid eyes. Length 15 in.
Price ... .50
25254 Kid Body Dolls, bisque heads, woven wig, flowing hair, and teeth. Length, 17 inches.
Price ... .75
25255 Kid Body Dolls, with bisque heads, woven wig, teeth and solid eyes. Length, 21 inches.
Price ... 1.25

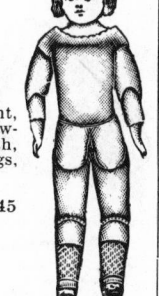

25257 Kid Body Doll, patent hip joint, jointed arms, fine bisque head, flowing hair on full woven wig, teeth, closing eyes, open work stockings, and shoes.
Length, 23 inches,
Price ... $2.45

Dressed Dolls, Patent Indestructible Heads.

25267 Indestructible Head Dressed Doll, cloth body, hair stuffed, painted hair, cloth shoes. Length, 17 inches.
Price ... $0.40
25268 Indestructible Head Dressed Doll. Same as above. 20 inches long. Price ... $0.60
25269 Indestructible Head Dressed Doll, largest size, 24 in. long. Price ... $0.80

Dressed Dolls, Cloth Bodies, with Kid Joints.

25275 Dressed Dolls, with kid joints, bisque heads and arms, teeth and flowing hair. Dressed in handsome costume; length, 13 inches.
Price ... $0.50
25276 Dressed Dolls, cloth body, kid joints, bisque heads and arms, flowing hair, teeth, shoes, stockings. Dressed in costume of handsome design and good material; length, 14¼ inches.
Price ... $0.85
25277 Dressed Dolls, cloth body, kid joints, bisque head and arms, flowing hair, teeth, solid eyes, shoes and stockings; dress is of the best *materials*, in fashionable colors and well made; length, 17 inches. Price ... $1.00
25278 Dressed Dolls, cloth body, kid joints, bisque heads, flowing hair, teeth, *solid eyes*, shoes and stockings, dressed in an elaborate costume of satin, with large turned-up hat, length, 20 inches.
Price ... 2.00

Dressed Baby Dolls, Jointed.

25280 Full Jointed Dolls, finest bisque head, flowing hair, solid eyes; long baby dress of woolen stuff and silk, neatly trimmed. See cut. Price ... $1.00
25281 Same description but larger size, and more elaborate dress. Price ... $1.45

25282 Superior quality, superfine dolls: jointed, with bisque heads, flowing hair, teeth, shoes and stockings. Dressed in "Baby" costume of nun's veiling, with cap to match. Length, 12 inches.
Each ... $0.65
25283 Same description as above, but larger. Each ... $0.90
25284 Large size "Baby" doll. Length, 16 inches. Price ... $1.50

Jointed Dolls, Dressed.

25285 Finest bisque heads, solid eyes, flowing hair, teeth, shoes and stockings. Superior quality dolls. Dress made of cotton stuff, trimmed, silk bonnet. Price ... $0.50
25287 Same description; dress of muslin and lace, bonnet trimmed with ribbon. Price ... 1.00
25288 Same description, dress and bonnet of changeable silk trimmed with ribbons. Price ... 1.15
25289 Same description: dress, finest muslin, woven through with ribbons. Full silk bonnet with silk strings and balls. Price ... 1.25
25290 Same description: dress of fine woolen goods, trimmed with silk ribbons or embroidered. Some hair lace hats, some bonnets. Price ... 2.00
25291 Same description; dress, fine cashmere trimmed with silk and lace. Full silk bonnet, lace trimmed. Price ... 2.25
25292 Same description; dress, full winter costume of fine woolen goods, trimmed with plush and ribbons. Bonnet to match. Price ... 3.50

Columbus Dressed Dolls.

The costumes are works of art, made of the finest silk velvet and satin, in contrasting colors. Each Cavalier wears at his side a tiny sword. The broad cap is surmounted with an ostrich plume, while the inscription, "1493 C. Columbus, 1893" is emblazoned upon its front.
25293 Columbus Doll, jointed, bisque head, flowing hair, teeth, solid eyes. Length, 15 inches.
Price ... $1.80
25294 Columbus Doll, same description as above. Length, 18 inches. Price ... $2.50

25295 Columbus Doll, large size. Length, 21 inches. Price ... $3.25

Indestructible Wool Dolls.

25296 Worsted, dressed Girl Dolls, assorted, similar to cut. 10 inches long. Price $0.20

25297 Worsted dressed dolls, 12½ inches long. Price $0.35

25298 Worsted Dolls Dressed to represent a clown. In full costume, cap and bells. Length, 12½ inches. Price $0.50

55299 Worsted Dolls, large size, with fine knitted wool dresses. Length, 15 inches. Price $0.85

25300 Rubber Doll, musical, with knitted worsted hat and dress. Length, 7½ inches. Price.... ....$0.25

25303 Rubber Jointed Boy Doll, musical. Will turn his head from side to side and raise his hands at will. Dressed in school costume. Length, 7 inches. Price... ...... .25

Clapping Figures.

25305 Various styles and costumes, bisque heads. We formerly catalogued these figures at from 25 to 75 cts. each, but to dispose of stock we offer them at the uniform price of each.... .... $0.25

25306 Indestructible Soldiers, dressed in oilcloth suits in combination colors Length, 10½ inches. Each .... $0.10 Per doz 1.00

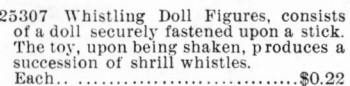

25307 Whistling Doll Figures, consists of a doll securely fastened upon a stick. The toy, upon being shaken, produces a succession of shrill whistles. Each.. .... $0.22

25308 Same as above, except that figure is that of a rabbit, covered with natural skin. Price............................ $0.20

25309 The Musical Doll Figure is a doll head fastened upon a circular music box, secured to a stick handle. Upon being revolved, beautiful music is produced. Price.......................... $0.40

25310 The Bird Musical Figure is the same style as above, but the figure is that of a bird, represented as standing over its nest. The music box is under the nest. See cut. Price.............. $0.45

Paper Dolls.

25311 Our Pets Dressing Series. A new idea in paper dolls consists of finely lithographed dolls 9¾ inches long, on heavy cardboard, cut out with easel back. Each doll has three dresses of different colors and styles with hats to match, packed in neat box. The costumes all modern styles; six different designs. Price, each .... $0.20 Postage .... .04

25312 Our Pets Paper Dolls, reduced size, same de cription as above but smaller. Price, each .... $0.12 Postage .... .03

25313 Princess and Princesses Paper Dolls, same size and description as No. 25311, but each doll is provided with four regal costumes. Price, each .... $0.23 Postage .... .04

25314 Paper Dolls, made of heavy cardboard, printed in colors, showing both front and back, furnished with four complete costumes with bonnets to match, all fashionable styles. Three designs each in separate envelopes, 4x7 inches. Price each .... $0.05 Per dozen assorted, 3 kinds.... .50 Same, size 6x10 inches, each.. .10 Per dozen, assorted, 3 kinds............ $1.00 Postage on paper dolls, each .... .02

25313

Paper Doll House.

25315 Doll houses made of extra heavy card, board, printed in bright colors. Can easily be put together by any child. Comes knocked down, and packs into small space for shipping. Each $0.35

25316 Paper Toy Furniture for children to cut out. Three styles—*Parlor, Dining-room,* and *Bed-room.* Each sheet contains a full set of beautiful new style furniture, lithographed in eleven colors, printed on fine cardboard, and elegantly embossed. Sheets are 15x17 inches. Any child can cut them out. When cut they have only to be bent, no fitting or mucilaging of parts together. When ordering specify what style is wanted. Price p r set .... .10 Per set of 3 (Parlor, Dining-Room, Bed-Room).. .25

Doll Heads.

NOTE.—The measurements on China and Bisque Doll Heads are from shoulder to shoulder and from front to back.

25317 China Heads, painted hair and eyes.

No.		Size		Price	
No.	2	Size	3x2	Price	10 cents.
"	4	"	3½x2¼	"	15 "
"	6	"	4x2½	"	20 "
"	8	"	4½x3	"	25 "
"	10	"	5x3½	"	35 "

25318 Bisque Doll Heads; none better. Woven wig, flowing hair, teeth, and solid eyes.

No	Size	Price
5	3¾x2	$0.60
7	4½x2½	.80
9	5½x3	1.00
11	6¼x3½	1.25

25319 Bisque Doll Heads, same kind as No. 25318 but with closing eyes.

No.	Size	Price
4	3¼x1¾	$0.50
6	4¼x2¼	.65
8	4¾x2¾	.85
10	6x3	1.10

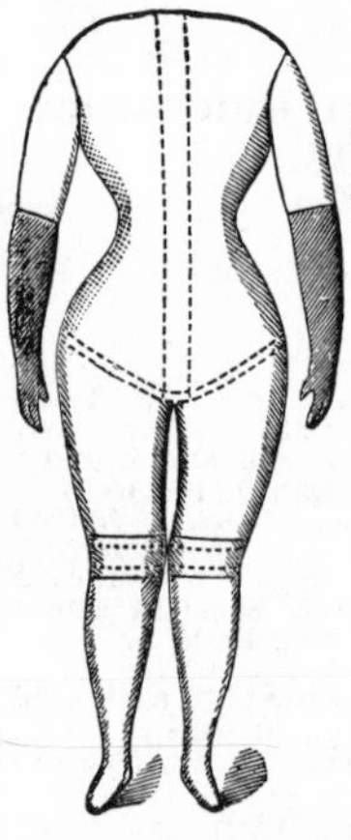

Muslin Doll Bodies.

(NO HEAD.)

25320 Doll Bodies (no head); made of white muslin, with seat, white kid arms, and removable corsets.

Length.	Each.	Per doz.
10½ inches...	$0.15	$1.60
13 inches...	.20	2.15
17 inches..	.30	3.00
19 inches...	.40	4.00

25322 Adjustable Doll Stand, made of polished steel, nickel plated; any child can easily apply it and the doll will be held firmly. This article has become a necessary part of a doll outfit. Enables the child to have doll parties, receptions, promenades, etc., and have each doll supported in any position desired.

Size and prices as follows:		Each	Doz.
No. 1	For Dolls, 3½ to 6 inches long.....	$0.10	$0.85
No. 2	For Dolls, 6½ to 11 inches long	.20	1.70
No. 3S	For Dolls, 12 to 20 inches long......	.35	3.80
No. 3	For Dolls, 16 to 24 inches long......	.50	4.25
No. 4	For Dolls, 24 to 36 inches long......	1.25	12.75

Doll Sundries.

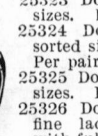

25323 Doll Shoes, assorted sizes. Per pair $0.10

25324 Doll Stockings, assorted sizes. Per pair. $0.10

25325 Doll Corsets, assorted sizes. Per pair $0.10

25326 Doll Caps, made of fine lace or embroidery, with full lace ruches. Assorted styles and sizes. Each.................. $0.20

25326 25327¼

25327 Doll Hats, made of Mull or Cambric, on wire frame. Strings to match, assorted sizes and colors. Each $0.30

25327¼ Dolls' Silk Embroidered caps, lace trimmed, ribbon strings, assorted styles and sizes. Each.... ....$0.50

25327½ Dolls' Silk Caps, plush and lace trimmed, assorted sizes and colors. Each.......... $0.40

25327¾ Dolls' Plush Caps, lace trimmed and Plush, Tam O'-Shanter shape with ornament.

25329 Each $0.35

-Doll Sundries—Continued.

25328 Doll "Tam O' Shanter" Cap and Hood, made of fine zephyr. Assorted colors. Each .... .20

25329 Doll Shetland Floss Sacques, made in combinations of two colors. Each .... .25

25330 Doll Shetland Floss Sacques, finer quality than above, trimmed with silk embroidery Each .... .40

25331 Dolls' Superfine Saxony Sacques, (15) double knit of fine Saxony wool. Handsomely embroider ed with triple row of silk floss, and finished with a row of narrow satin ribbon Each. .60

25332 Doll's Cloak, made of fine white flannel, silk embroidered. Wide collar and mutton leg sleeves, assorted sizes. Price. .... .50

25333 Doll's Cloak, made of fine Bedford cord. Trimmed with double row of silk embroidery, satin ribbons, divided collar and mutton leg sleeves. The handsomest doll's cloak on the market. Each .... .75

25334 Dolls' Saxony Bootees crocheted of fine Saxony wool, in combinations of two colors. Per pair.... .15

25335 Dolls' Bootees same style as above, but tops embroidered with silk floss, and supplied with silk ties and tassels. Per pair .... .20

GAMES.

In this department we catalogue what we confidently believe to be the best assortment of amusements for the home circle that can be found anywhere.

Folding Board Games.

Note our line of 85c games. Every game in this list, from No. 25340 to 25351 retails at $1.00 and $1.25 each. Our price, *85c each.*

25340 The new and exciting game Columbia. Is bound in durable dark green paper (imitation morocco), 22 inches, square folds in center, with fancy label, printed in best gold bronze, mounted on heavy cloth board; best quality. The game is lithographed, in colors—red, blue, gold, brown, gray, black, white and yellow; containing the portraits of all the presidents, large size, in life colors, giving the date of their birth, death and inauguration, and term of years. On the four corners are historical pictures in brilliant colors—the landing of Columbus; signing the Declaration of Independence; surrender of Cornwallis, and surrender of General Lee, with their dates. A box containing 30 disks—15 red ones and 15 blue ones; also rules for playing, with an explanation of the historical and geographical features of the game. Price each.............. .... $0.85

25341 The Presidential Election Game. The game is both simple and practical. It is elegant in appearance, it gives information concerning the electoral vote, and is played in such a manner as to combine instruction with lots of fun. Weight, 2 lbs. Price $0.85

25342 The Electoral College Game. The game played by either two or four persons, and during its progress shows the methods used in electing a President of the United States. The game is played upon a beautifully lithographed board, containing the portrait of all the presidents, the date and place of meeting of the different National Conventions, the Electoral Vote of all the States, and many more statistics of national interest. Size of board, 18x18 inches. Weight, 3½ lbs. Price........................ ...... .85

25343 The Military Game. Toy soldiers in connection with a game; every wide-awake boy will want it: handsomely lithographed box containing two armies with their commanders-in-chiefs and other officers, and toy pistols for artillery, Pistols make loud reports and discharge projectiles. Full directions for playing game in two ways, packed in box. Weight, 3½ lb. Price .85

25344 The Games at the Old Homestead Combined; consists of a backgammon board 12½x14½, checker and chess board 12½x14½, enameled finished, and the grand race game, size, 27x14-½ inches, the whole folding into a book 14½-x6¼x½ in., and packing into a fancy pasteboard box, with lithographed cover. Size, 17x9½x2 inches, containing a set of stained wood chessmen, set of checkers, two plain wood dice boxes, two dice and six colored cardboard racehorses and riders mounted on wooden stands, with directions for playing the various games. Weight, complete, 2¾ lbs. Each $0.85

The Yale-Harvard Games.
A High Class Game for Thoughtful Players.

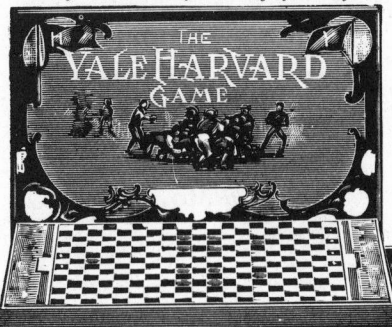

25345 A new game of skill of rare merit for two players. The basis of the game is foot-ball, the idea of each side being to carry the ball into the opposite goal. The pieces used are numbered, and can be moved as many spaces as their numbers indicate. New style of drawer game board. Price.....................................$0.85

The Limited Mail and Express Games.

25346 The new, popular board game, elegantly produced and played upon a map of the United States with miniature railroad trains, etc. The trains carry cotton from the South, tobacco from Virginia, corn from Iowa, live-stock from Texas, etc., as well as mail matter from all parts of the country. It is extremely amusing. Played on new style drawer game board (14x21 inches)..$0.85

The Soldier Boy Games.

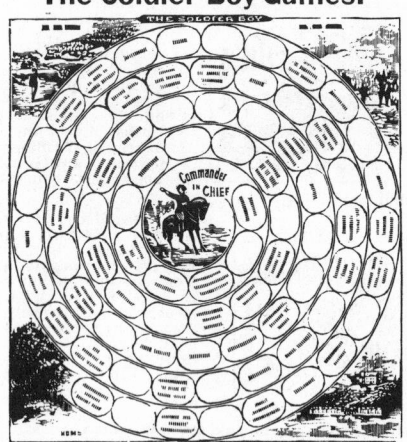

25347 A very large, showy, folding board, almost two feet square. Especially captivating for boys. With the game come four metal soldiers and spinning indicator for playing. The game relates the stirring story of the battlefield, and illustrates the promotion gained by ability, bravery and ambition. The winner of the game is the player who first attains the position of "Commander-in-Chief." Price..................$0.85

The Game of "Hopity."

25348 This is a game of skill, which can be played by two, three or four persons of any age. The particular feature of the game is the popular jumping move, pieces being allowed to jump over friend and foe alike to reach the opposite side of the board. The game is handsomely issued on a board seventeen inches square. Price.................$0.85

Games—Continued

25349 Innocence Abroad represents the journey of a party of people who travel by various routes toward the same destination, and who meet with various experiences and occurrences. A handsomely lithographed, folding board 19x19 inches, shows roads running through a very picturesque country, past farms, forests, mountains and across rivers whose course can be traced from their source to the ocean. Packed, complete, with directions in pasteboard box, 19½x10x1½ inches. Weight, 2½ pounds. Price $0.85

The Game of Travel.

25350 A handsome and instructive game, representing a journey through Europe. Metal steamships and railroad trains of different colors are used for pieces. The game is played with route tickets. The idea of the game is to make a tour to Europe as far as Constantinople, then returning to America. Played on new style patent game-board, with drawer for pieces (14x21 inches). Price.........................$0.85

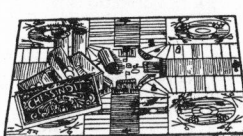

25351 Chessindia is founded upon an ancient legend wherein four rulers combine with their armies to besiege a fortress containing an immense treasure. There were four approaches to this citadel, and the one who first planted his standard upon its walls was to have the largest share of the wealth it contained. The game has been designed to represent, with its King and Knights, the march of the four armies in their attack upon the fortress. It has been called "the best of all home games," and it will interest all ages. The game is mounted upon a substantial board 18 inches square. The design of which carries out the spirit of the story. There are four sets of implements, with which two distinct games can be played, contained in a separate box. Weight, 1½ lbs. Price.........$0.85

The Game of Electors and Presidential Puzzle.

25353 Popular edition of a good game, played on handsome lithographed board with colored implements. New and exciting. Packed in box with directions for playing both games.....$0.25

25356 Solitaire; consists of a board 8x8, on one side of which is a lithograph of the well-known game of solitaire, and on the reverse a checker board; 33 cards accompany each game, all of which comes in a neat box and weighs 12 oz. Price...................................$0.25

25357 Knuckle Billiards. A peculiar new game and a very interesting one. It is simple and makes a great deal of fun. Packed, complete, in neat box with directions. Weight 10 oz. Price...$0.40

25358 The Grand Race Game, consists of a substantially cloth bound, folding board, 26x14 in. in size; printed in colors to represent a race track, including fences, etc. Has six colored cardboard horses and riders, mounted on wooden stands, two wooden dice cups and two dice. Full directions for playing accompany each game. Weight, complete, 1½ lbs. Price.......$0.45
25359 Extra fine edition, price....................60

Games—Continued.

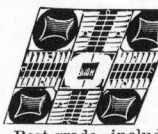

25360 Royal Game of Parchesi complete. This is an entertaining game for the family circle. It can be played by either two, three or four persons, besides greatly interesting the lookers on. Full instructions accompany each. Best grade, including a book muslin bound folding board, embossed and stamped in gold, with box containing 8 dice, 4 dice cups and 16 counters. A nicely gotten up set. Wgt., 1¾ lbs. Complete....$1.35

25361 Across the Continent is the most elaborate board game ever issued. The large folding board upon which the game is played is a bird's eye view of the United States, showing the principal cities, railway lines, etc. It is an instructive and handsome picture. In course of the game players make a trip across the Continent and back, follow the routes stated on their tickets, and pay traveling expenses. Railway tickets, toy money, fine celluloid pieces, enameled cups, and full directions with each game. It has utensils for six players, but any number can play. It is an exciting and educational amusement. Size of board, 21x42 inches. Weight, 6 pounds. Price...................$2.75
25362 Around the Circle Game, a new and attractive board game for two or more up to six players. Extremely interesting; finished in high colors, with implements and instructions packed in an attractive box. Price...................................$0.96
25363 "Jaclu," a new, interesting and instructive method of playing two games. Figures and letters. Either two or four persons may play, and as mathematics enter largely into the game it is a most entertaining one for thoughtful players. The game is played upon a handsomely finished hardwood board, 8x18 inches in size. Price, each.............$0.50

Miscellaneous Games.

25365 Disco, the Great Carom Game. The object of the game is to deposit the disk in the opponent's pocket. Each such score counts one, and a total of nine wins the game. The cues are 8 inches long, made of hardwood, and are to be held in the hand like a pencil. The disk is of steel, hollow in the center and tired with rubber. The board is of hardwood. The combinations by which the pockets may be gained are innumerable. Sure to become as popular as crokinole. Size of board, 16x28 inches $2.25

25366 Crokinole, a new and intensely interesting game for everybody, with no objectionable features. There is no game where the element of chance is smaller, as the winning of the game depends wholly upon the skill of the player. The engraving shows the board placed in position on a table, also the position of the hand in the act of playing. Size, octagon shape, 32 in. across. Made of polished ash. Each...................$3.25
25367 Made of cherry or oak, covered with fine quality of flannel $4.50
25368 Parlor Tennis. This new and fascinating game is arranged for parlor or lawn use and is played with 12 light rubber balls. Can be played individually or by sides. Weight, 3 lbs. Packed, each game complete, in pasteboard box. Price..........$1.75

25369 Parlor Quoits. Another popular and interesting game for either parlor or lawn; consists of two turned posts, firmly set in nicely finished brass, 8 inches in diameter, and four quoits five inches in diameter, made of wood, and firmly wound with heavy, fancy colored webbing. Packed in neat box with fine lithographed label on cover. Price...................................$0.90
25373 Bean Bag Game. A game of skill; is always popular. Consists of board, 9x12 inches, elevated at the end by two turned standards to give it the proper angle. Has three openings, and furnished with five wooden disks. Directions on cover of box in which the game is packed. Price...................$0

Games—Continued.

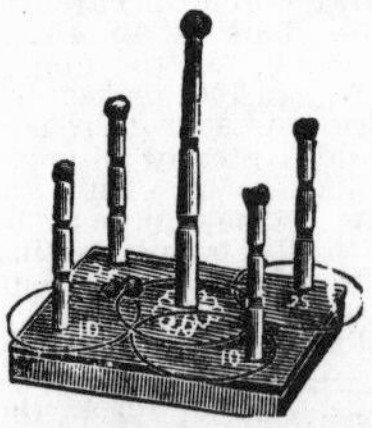

25378 Pitch-a-ring, consists of a highly polished chestnut wood box and 5 posts nicely painted and varnished. The 8 rings are plated rattan in fancy colors. A most novel and interesting game. Weight, complete, 3 lbs. Price...$0.95

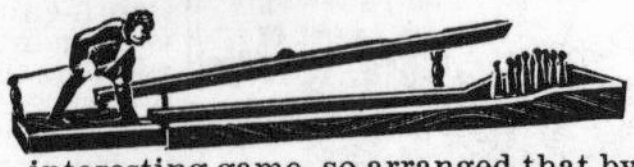

25382 The Automatic Bowling Alley. Another new and interesting game, so arranged that by pressing a knob at the end of the board the man's arm is drawn back and held by a spring; then the marble is allowed to roll down the track and strike a wire coil, releasing the arm which rolls the marble at the ten pins in a very life-like manner. Size of board, 6½x36 inches. Height of man, 6½. Packed in box. Price..................$0.75 Weight, 4½ pounds.

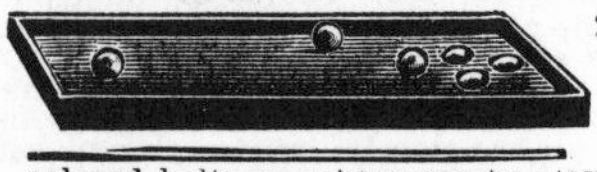

25383 Parlor Pool. A miniature pool table, 7¾x29 in., with hardwood cue and three colored balls, on which can be played a number of interesting games. Price..........................$0.85

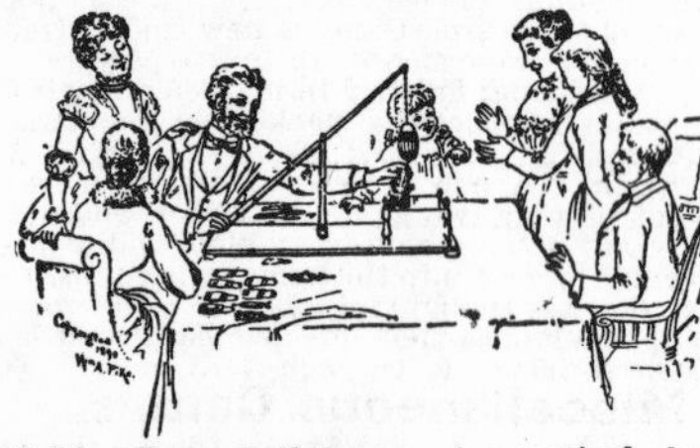

25388 Ding Dong Bell Game. A practical elucidation of the nursery rhyme Ding, Dong Bell. Can be played by any number up to twenty. Packed each game in a pasteboard box; weight, 3¾ lbs. Finely finished oak. Price...........$0.95
Same, hardwood, stained and varnished (2). Price .... .74
25389 Same, hardwood, smooth finish (1)........ .58

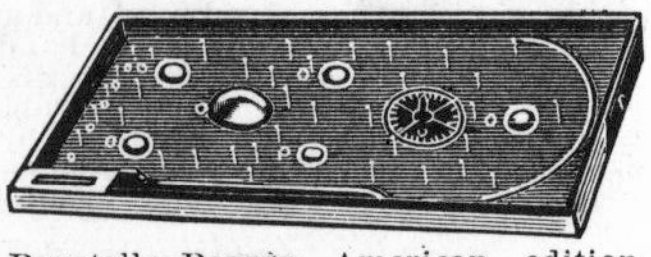

25391 Bagatelle Boards, American edition, 18 in. length; made in best possible manner, with spring cue, indicator, bell and pins. Price $0.45
25392 Bagatelle Boards, American edition, covered with oilcloth, has spring cue, brass indicator, chime bell and pins; length, 24 in.; weight, 1¾ lbs. Price $0.85

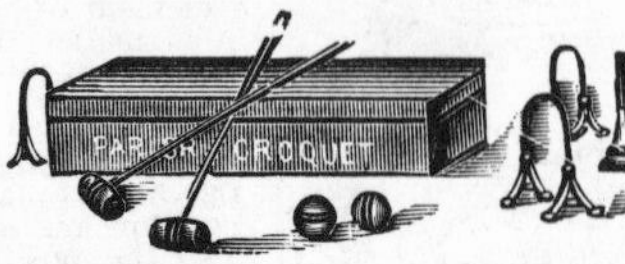

25395 Table Croquet, complete as above, but larger, with 8 balls and mallets, elegantly striped. Per set.............................. 0.80 Weight, 2¾ lbs.
25396 Parlor Croquet, suitable for playing on the floor, finely varnished and painted. Price per set, complete..............$0.85 Weight, 6 lbs

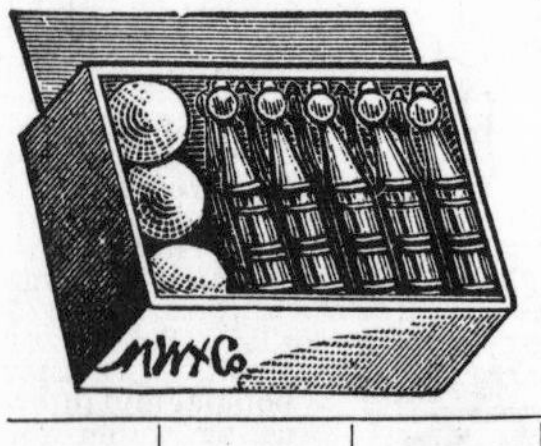

Hardwood Ten Pins.

Polished and striped complete with balls, In strong wood boxes. Well made and finished.

No.	Size.	Weight.	Per set.	Per doz.
25397	7 in.	2½ lbs.	25c.	$2.50
25398	9 in.	4 lbs.	40c.	4.00
25396	12 in.	10 lbs.	70c.	7.25

'Tis the Business of our Freight Clerk to quote rates on anything to any place.
Ask him what you want to know.

Games—Continued.

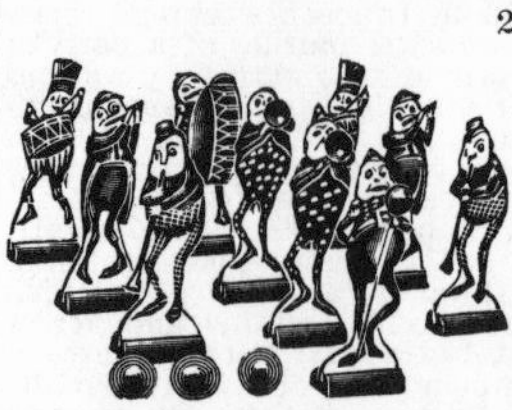

25400 Brownie Band Ten Pins. The latest style of Brownie ten pins, consisting of ten musicians with instruments, showing comical expressions and occupying laughable attitudes, each standing 8 inches high, together with 3 polished balls. Packed in a handsome labeled box. Price.............. $0.45

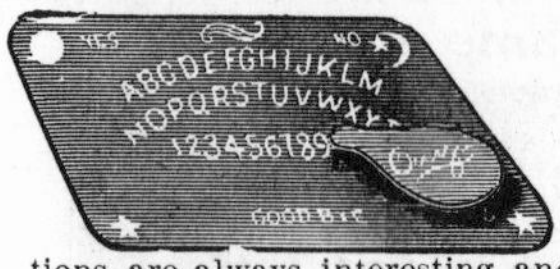

25401 Ouija, or Egyptian Luck Board. The Ouija is without a doubt a most interesting, remarkable and mysterious production. Its operations are always interesting and sometimes invaluable, answering as it does questions concerning the past, present and future. Directions for operating the Ouija accompany each board. Packed each one in a pasteboard box.
Each. $1.00
Cannot be sent by mail.

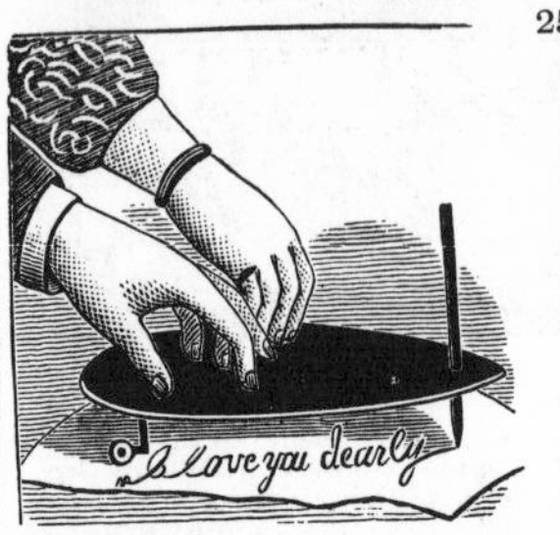

25403 The scientific Planchette Board, made on the same principle as the old and popular planchette boards of 1860. Style (No. 2), fine polished boards, cherry finish, nickel plated casters, with swivel joint, boxwood wheels, lead tip pencil with rubber. Put up in paper box with full directions and full account of its workings. Each..................................$0.95
Postage.. .10
25404 Planchette No. 3, hardwood board, varnished, brass casters, maple wheels and pencil. Put up in neat paper box with full directions,
Each... .50
Postage.. .10

Miscellaneous Parlor Games, Small.

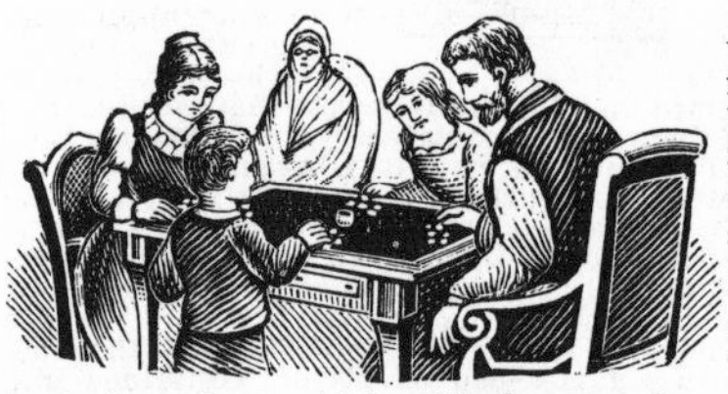

Tiddledy Winks may be played by any number of people on any small table with a thick cloth on. Each player is provided with four to six counters of the same color, and one larger one, the use of the larger one being to press to the edge of the smaller one and in that way cause it to jump into the cup, which is in the center of the table. The player who first gets all his counters into the cup wins the game.
25410 Popular edition, for four players..........$0.20
Postage.. .05
25411 Popular edition, for six players............ .40
Postage.. .08
25412 Hop Scotch Tiddledy Winks, a novel method of playing this popular game. Full directions with each game.
Price.. 45
25413 Tiddledy Winks Ten Pins, a new and entertaining combination of Tiddledy Winks and Ten Pins.
Price per set.. .50
25414 Tiddledy Winks Tennis, a good combination of Tennis and Tiddledy Winks.
Price.. .85
25415 Game Box, consisting of jumping rope, shuttlecock, cup and two balls. Finely finished in white and gold enamel. A fine present for a girl. Weight, 1 pound. Each.................... .75
25416 The Cuckoo Game. The latest society craze; consists of six handsomely printed cards 4½x4½ inches, divided 1 to 9 fancy colored squares, 54 colored counters, one wooden dice box and one cube enameled in colors corresponding with the squares on the cards. Put up in fancy lithographed covered paper box. Size, 6½x5x1¾; weight, 8 oz. Price.................... .20
25417 Cuckoo Game, with 10 cards, 2 dice cups and colored cubes, and 90 counters complete in box size, 12x5¼x1¾, weight 14 oz. Price ..... .35
25418 Cuckoo Game, with 16 cards, 4 fancy colored cups, 4 colored cubes, and 144 colored counters packed in separate box, all packed in a varnished wood box with sliding cover, size 13x5¾x2¼: weight 1¾ lbs. Price.............. .60
Full and complete directions for playing accompany each game.

Don't Forget Our Numerous SPECIAL CATALOGUES

Jack Straws.

25420 This is an old-fashioned game, but its popularity increases yearly.
Price per box with directions.......................$0.08
Per doz.. .80
By mail, extra.. .02
25421 Jack Straws, consisting of carved wooden implements, such as rakes, hoes, forks, poles, hooks, etc., put up in a neat box. The latest forms and the most difficult game; all made of carved wood. Per box.............................. .10
Per doz.. 1.00
By mail, extra.. .02

Lotto.

This famous German game has become very popular in America. It is very easily learned, and may be played by the youngest children and grown up people. Directions in each box.
25425 In paper box, 3¾x6; 6 cards; good small set. Each...$0.08
Per dozen.. .75
25426 Wood box, 4½x7½; 24 cards; numbers in bag, inside box with glasses and counters.
Each...........$0.20 Per dozen.............. 2.00
25427 Wood box, 5½x9; 18 large cards; numbers in bag, inside box wiih glasses and counters.
Each... 0.40
Per dozen.. 4.00

Card Games.

Ten Cent Series,

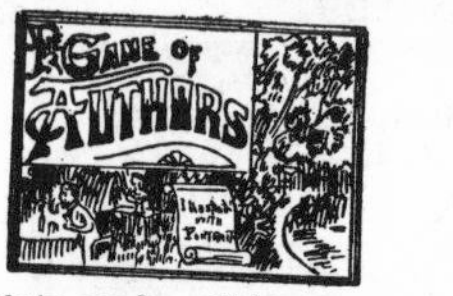

25428 Authors. This interesting little game, giving titles and works of the best authors contains classified and lettered books, and is interesting to old and young alike. Directison in each box.
Plain cards. Price $0.10
25429 Hidden Authors, different from above in manner of playing. Price.......................... .10
25430 Old Maid, a new edition of this popular game. Price.. 10
25431 Snap, an old game in a new dress; everything in the game has to do with the word snap. Price... .10
25432 Anagrams, the game of letters under a new name. Letters in plenty for playing both games. New and attractive. Price........................ .10
25433 Peter Coddle; our 10c. edition of this popular card game is complete, and equal in every respect to the usual 25c. series. Price.... .10

Card Games.

Nineteen Cent Series.

Every game in this series retails at 25 and 30 cents. Our price 19c. Postage from 4c to 10c.

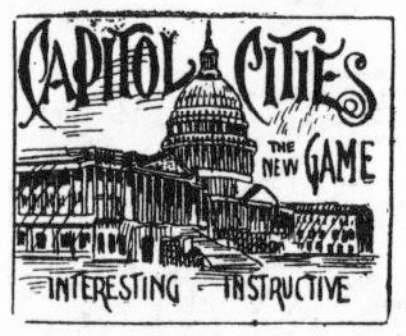

25434 Capitol Cities. A new Card Game very similar to the popular "Authors." Books are made up in the same manner as in authors, but the names of the United States are used, instead of the names of writers and their books. The game is interesting and instructive. Price.......................$0.19

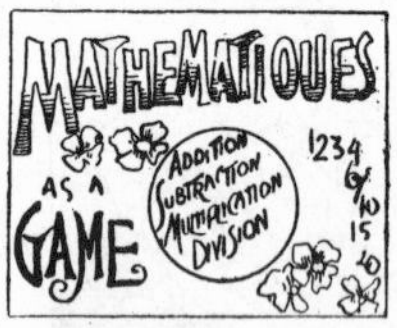

25435 Mathematiques Another of the Educational Series. Games are won on the lines of addition, subtraction, multiplication and division. An instructive and intensely fascinating game. Packed in neat box with full directions. Price...........$0.19
25436 Authors popular edition vignetted.
Price.. .19
25437 Proverbs. The old standard game revised, consisting of 100 cards containing the best proverbs, with directions for playing game seven different ways. Price.............................. .19
25438 Letters. An entertaining and popular game. Greatly improved and containing nearly 300 letters and directions for playing both Letters and Anagrams. Price....................... .19
25439 Roses. Containing 36 cards on which are printed roses, nine each of red, yellow, pink and blue. The object of the game is to avoid taking any of the blue roses, Price.............. .19
25442 **Peter Coddle.** This humorous game consists of about 200 cards, containing amusing sentences, together with a 16-page book describing in a spicy manner the adventures of Peter Coddle in New York. Parts of the story are omitted and blanks left to be supplied by the cards. One of the most amusing and comical games published. Directions in each box. Price.......... .19
25443 **Timothy Tuttle,** a new reading game giving an account of a visit to the World's Fair by a young man from the Tuttle family. Timothy tells what he saw and what he thinks of the many curious things he found in the great Exposition. Price.. .19
25444 **Fortune Telling Card Game.** It would be unwise to rely on the predictions contained in it, but young people will find it very entertaining. price.. .19
25445 **Mother Goose Old Maid.** Best quality, full assorted, superior finish cards. Price.............. .19

Card Games—Continued.

25448 **Wang** combines in its methods originality, simplicity and novelty. It is put up in very attractive form, containing 72 cards, divided into two sets, each of a different color, and one hundred metal counters called shekels. The game will never become old, as the variations are unlimited. Price.................. $0.19

Card Games.
40 Cent. Series.

The games in this series are those that usually sell at 50 cts., 60 cts., and 75 cts.

Our price. each.....................$0.40
Postage, from 6 to 12 cents.

25450 **The Wild Flower Game.** A beautiful game, consisting of more than 60 cards, lithographed with pictures of wild flowers. The game follows a course in botany, and is recommended to students.
Price.......................$0.40

25452 **Logomachy, or War of Words.** The new premium games. One of the best new parlor card games published. Full directions accompany each game; put up in handsome box, 6x8½x1 inch. Each............................$0.40

25453 **Negomi.** A new game containing forty beautifully lithographed cards and implements for counters, packed in neat box with full directions for playing. Price................ .40

25455 **American History,** an educational game, consists of sixty enameled cards on which are printed questions relating to the various headings, these questions being selected for their general interest and importance. Price........ .40

25456 **Combination Game Box,** consisting of complete Fish-pond, Checkerboard and set of checkers, set of dominoes and five dial counters, handsomely labeled.
Price.,$0.40

25457 **American Cities.** A beautiful and instructive game. Fifty-two cards printed in many colors, giving views of fifty-two different cities. Each card bears the population of the city, and a small amount of descriptive matter. In good sized boxes, 7x9 inches, with handsome label. Price...........................$0.40

25458 **The Bible Game,** arranged in form of questions from the Old and New Testaments. Prepared with the greatest care. It is the best game upon the subject so far issued. Price.......... .40

25459 **Authors,** finest edition published, in neat cloth covered box with sliding cover.
Price.................................. .40

Puzzles.
Mystic Square.

TAKE THE FIVE SMALL SQUARES, (TEN PIECES) AND WITH THEM FORM ONE PERFECT SQUARE.

25463 Follow the directions on the engraving and you will be entertained for an entire evening. Each..$0.14 Per dozen..$1.25 Postage..$0.02

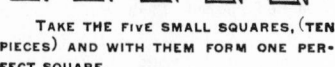

25468 **The Mystoscope.** The Wonder of How Columbus Discovered America. Directions with each.
Each.....................$0.22 Postage...........$0.05

25470 **The "Wonder" Puzzle.** The object is to place 18 pieces of 81 squares, so as to form a square, with the colors running alternately. It can be done in several different ways. If at first you don't succeed, try, try again.
Price, each.........$0.10
Postage............ .02

Puzzles—Continued.

25472 **The Ferris Wheel Puzzle** consists of a neatly made box with a glass top. Inside is a perfect miniature Ferris Wheel revolved by a button underneath. The puzzle is to place a passenger (ball) into each vacant car. Can you do it?
Price each..........$0.20
Price, per doz....... 2.10
Postage, 5c.

25474 **Three Blind Mice.** See how they run. In the center of the 7x7 inch pasteboard box is a representation of an ordinary three-spring mouse trap. Catch all three mice in this trap in the puzzle or trick; and it is a teaser.
Price, each....................$0.19
Price, per dozen.................... 2.00
Postage, 4c.

25476 **Columbus Egg.** The trick with this egg is to make it lie flat on its side. *It can be done.* A most amusing toy, or it can be used as a novel paper weight.
Price, each.............$0.09
Per dozen............. .75

25478 **Columbus Egg Puzzle.** One of the cutest and most ingenious little tricks ever devised; made of brass, handsomely nickeled, showing the bust of the great navigator (stamped in the head of each egg). Put up one in a box, with full directions how to make the egg stand on end.
Price, each..........................$0.18
Per doz............................... 2.00
Postage on either of above eggs, 2 cents each.

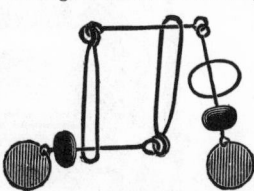

25479 **Wire Puzzle.** A collection of eight puzzles that are every one good, and from simple to complicated designs. This set with instructions for working is the most complete and in every way the best collection of wire puzzles ever offered.

Our price for the set............................$0.30

Cut Up Puzzles.

25480 **Cut-Up Jumbo Puzzles,** consisting of a large colored picture of the celebrated elephant "Jumbo," 12x15 inches, mounted on heavy board and cut up into irregular pieces, put up in a handsome box. Each box contains a complete picture, showing how pieces look when put together.
Each.........................$0.15
Per dozen.......................... 1.50
Postage.......................... .05

25481 **Blown-Up Steamboat Puzzle,** same as 25480, only the picture is that of a steamboat.
Each............................. .16
Per dozen.......................... 1.60
Postage.......................... .05

25482 **Bird Slips,** or puzzle picture game for the little folks, put up in fancy colored box.
Each............................. .18
Postage.......................... .05

25484 **A Sectional Picture Toy** of the American Fire Department, lithographed in brilliant colors on heavy cardboard and cut up, making one of the most entertaining sectional puzzle games in the market, forming when put together a complete fire department of five pieces. Packed in wood box, with lithographic label. Weight, 20 oz. Price................................ .50

25485 **Dissected Map of the United States.** This map is engraved in outline, with only the more prominent features and localities, thereby presenting to the child no more than can be easily remembered. On the back are illustrations of the prominent industries, products and animals of the country, thus combining with the map an interesting dissected picture, the whole forming a complete object lesson of the geography and natural history of the United States. Size, when put together, 22x15. Packed in pasteboard box. Weight, 1½ lbs. Price...................... .45

25486 **Dissected Map of the United States,** same size as preceding, but mounted on wood and dissected in entire states, allowing a practical comparison of the different states. Packed in wooden box. Weight, 1½ lbs. Price............ .75

If You Won't Write Us

Our twenty correspondents will lose their jobs. Their business is to write letters on business topics.

Occupations.

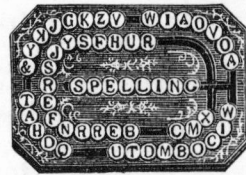

25494 **Spelling Boards.** These boards are 13½ in. long by 9 in. wide, and have 56 lettered hardwood blocks, neatly made and highly ornamented. Instructive and amusing; letters cannot come out or be placed in position upside down. Weight, 1¾ pounds. Price, each.$0.75

25496 **Picture sewing.** This game or occupation consists of a box containing a collection of cards, having traced on them outlines of various objects, which are to be sewed in colored threads. Just the thing for little girls. Box contains cards of colored threads, a perforating needle, pad, pictures, etc. Sure to Please. Price............................ $0.25

25499 **Drawing Teacher.** A neat box containing 20 different designs; perforated on heavy paper with full instructions. Each.............$0.25
Postage................ .... .06

KIND WORDS.

ORGANS AND PIANOS.
We Ship on Trial to Any Part of the United States. Read Our Offer.
ORGANS.

Our Windsor Organs are made in one of the largest and best equipped factories in this country, and we guarantee them to be equal in every way to the very best. Thousands have been sold, and with one or two exceptions every instrument has given perfect satisfaction. The actions are perfect. The cases are made of solid black walnut or oak, finely finished, and handsome in design. Our prices are lower than offered by any other house in the world for instruments of equal value. The reason why we can afford to make such low prices is because we do a strictly cash business and employ no agents. We deal directly with the consumers, and they get the benefit of the agent's profits. We warrant our Organs and Pianos for five years; also allow every purchaser the privilege of giving them a thorough trial, so there is no chance whatever for deception. This is our offer:

How We Ship Organs and Pianos on Trial.

We will ship any Windsor Organ or Piano on trial to any railroad shipping point in the United States, subject to the following conditions: Upon receipt of order we will ship the instrument to our own address, send a sight draft with bill of lading attached, to your banker's. When the shipment arrives at destination the purchaser will be required to deposit with the bank the price of the instrument, but with the understanding that the money is to be held fifteen (15) days. During this time the instrument may be given a thorough trial at your home, freight charges *one way* to be paid by purchaser. If you find that it is not in every way satisfactory you can return it to station agent at any time before the expiration of time specified and by obtaining bill of lading showing that the instrument has been returned to us in good order, and presenting same at bank, the entire amount deposited will be refunded.

We advise all purchasers, however, to send in full amount of money with order. By so doing you not only avoid all unnecessary trouble, but get the benefit of our cash discounts, (pianos excepted) which otherwise we do not allow (see rule 4, page 2); besides, when cash accompanies order we allow a trial of 30 days, and, if not satisfactory, may be returned at our expense and money will be refunded.

Description of the Windsor Organs.

We use but one style of works, having adopted the standard "ten stop double coupler" actions. They have two full sets of reeds with double riveted tongues, the celebrated Wilcox divided coupler (the best in the world) operated by two stops, heavy mouse-proof bellows, two swells, "knee" and "grand organ." They have ten stops, viz: Diapason, melodia, dulcet, echo, principal forte, celeste, cremona, piano bass coupler and treble coupler. The tone is smooth, clear and powerful and cannot be excelled at any price. This organ will last just as long and produce equally as good music as any $200 organ; in fact our manufacturers state that they cannot make us anything better as far as works are concerned. We shall handle the Windsor Organ in nine styles, as shown and described below. Every instrument guaranteed exactly as represented or may be returned at our expense. We box them and put on board of cars free of charge.

Solid Black Walnut Case, entirely new and modern in design, hand rubbed and finished in oil. Symmetrically proportioned top, with elaborately carved turnings, large French Plate bevel edged mirror in center, adjustable music desk, with pocket underneath, fancy carved brackets and scroll work throughout. Knee swell and grand organ, pedals covered with Brussels carpet. Five octaves compass, divided as follows; two octaves diapason, three melodia, three octaves celeste, two octaves principal; height, 6 feet 9 inches; length, 4 feet 3½ inches, depth, 2 feet. This is one of the most elaborate and finely finished cases ever put on the market.

25500 Windsor Organ, 5 octaves (Style 1) as described above, including stool and instruction book; boxed for shipping. Each...$60.00

25500 Style 1. Price, $60.00.

This case (style 6) is entirely new in design, handsome in appearance and though moderate in price, is one of our best styles. They are made of solid black walnut; height 81 inches, length 48 inches, depth 23, finished in oil, hand rubbed, extension top, scroll work of fancy design, elaborately carved panels at top and sides; large plate glass mirror in center panel; adjustable music rack. Lamp stands, castors, nickel plated pedal frames, best Brussels carpet on pedals. The keyboard is five octaves; compass two full set reeds, divided as follows: Two octaves diapason, three melodia, two principal, three celeste.

25504 Windsor Organ (style 6), as described above, including stool and instruction book, boxed for shipping.
Each..............$45.00
Weight boxed about 400 lbs.

25504½ Windsor Organ, same style as 25504, MADE OF OAK, including stool and instruction book, boxed for shipping.
Each..............$47.00

The Windsor Organ, Style 6.

25505 Windsor Organ, same style case as 25504 Walnut woodwork, WITH SIX OCTAVES, including *Stool and Instruction Book*, boxed. Each.........$55.00 Weight, boxed, about 450 lbs.

25505½ Windsor Organ, same style as 25504 Oak woodwork, with six octaves, including Stool and Instruction Book, boxed. Each................$57.00 Weight, boxed, about 450 lbs.

Solid black Walnut, hand-rubbed, finest oil finish, extended curtain top, elaborately carved, richly ornamented scroll and pressed work, highly polished, Lower part of center panel is of red silk plush, upper part contains a French bevel plate mirror and adjustable music rack, beaded front and end panels, lamp stands, handles, two swells, "knee" and "full organ," keyboard five octaves compass divided as follows; Two octaves diapason, three octaves melodia, two octaves principal, three octaves celeste reeds. Height, 6½ feet; depth, 2 feet; length, 4 feet. Pedals covered with Brussels carpet, brass heel plates. This is an entirely new case, solid in construction, elegant in design and finish; in fact nothing is wanting to make it perfect in every respect.

25501 Windsor Organ, Style 2, as described above, including instructor and stool (No.26038) boxed for shipping........$56.00 Weight, boxed, about 400 pounds.

25502 Windsor Organ, Style 3 same style and finish as 25501, with 6 octaves. Weight, boxed, about 450 pounds. Price, including stool and instruction book. Each................$63.00

The Windsor Organ.   Styles 2 and 3.
5 octaves, $56.00; 6 octaves, $63 00;

Description of Style 7.

Solid black walnut case; hand rubbed, oil finished, height 4 feet 8 inches, length 3 feet 9 inches, depth 21 inches; Gothic end tops, lamp stands, handles, two swells, knee and full organ, pedals covered with Brussels carpet with brass heel plates, keyboard, five octaves compass divided as follows: Two octaves diapason, three octaves melodia, two octaves principal, three octaves celeste. This case is intended more particularly for church and school purposes, the back being finished so that it can be turned toward an audience. It will prove a very acceptable and low priced case for any and all uses.

25506 Windsor Organ; style 7, as described above, including instruction book and stool (26038), boxed for shipping.
Each................$37.00 Weight, boxed, about 300 pounds.

The Windsor Organ. Chapel, Style 7.

We sell hundreds upon hundreds of Organs and scarcely ever receive a complaint.

Organs Continued.

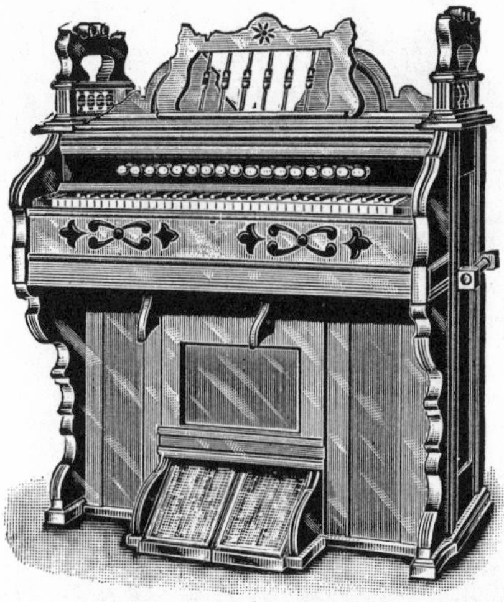

Windsor Organ, Grand Chapel Style 9 and 9½.

Description of our New Grand Chapel Organ, Style No. 9.

We have recently made some changes in our Grand Chapel Organ in the way of improvements. The style of case is about the same, but have enlarged the capacity of the bellows, also have made some changes in the action. This instrument contains 19 octaves of reeds (or in all 228 reeds) divided as follows: 2 octaves diapason, 3 octaves melodia, 3 octaves celeste, 2 octaves principal, 3 octaves flute, 3 octaves cello, 2 octaves perfection, and one octave sub bass also vox humana. It has 17 steps with porcelain knobs as follows: Diapson, echo, principal, piano, forte, cremona, celeste, dulcet, melodia, vox humana, fortisimo, flute cello, perfection, uub bass, treble coupler and bass coupler.

The case is made of either oak or black walnut, hand rubbed finish, neat and handsome in design, finished back and front, panel ends, finely carved top and cheeks, low top, height 50 inches, length 50 inches, depth 24 inches. Pedals are covered with Brussels carpet, and held down with brass plates.

25506½ Windsor Grand Chapel Organ, Style 9, as described above, including stool and instruction book. Walnut woodwork. Each ...$57.00

25506¾ Windsor Grand Chapel Organ (Style 9½), as described above, with stool and instruction book. Oak woodwork. Each ... 58.00

Weight boxed about 400 lbs.

Piano Scarfs.

(UPRIGHTS).

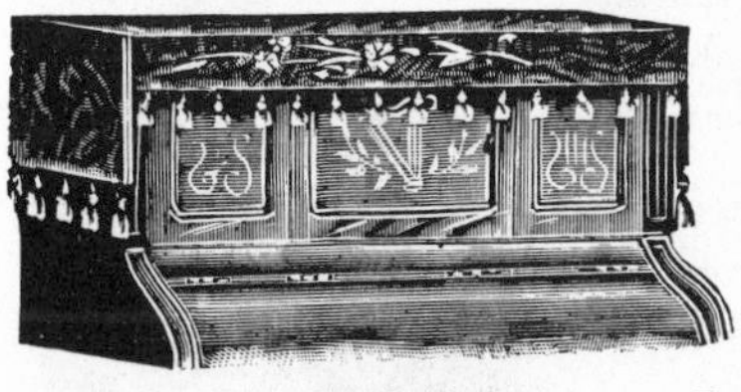

25513-14

25510 Piano Scarf with plain felt top and embroidered silk plush front and tassels, assorted colors. Each...$2.00

25512 Piano Scarf, all silk plush, good quality, plain front, trimmed with tassels, assorted colors. Each ... 3.50

25513 Piano Scarf, finest American silk plush, hand embroidered front, silk tassels, assorted colors. Each ... 4.25

25514 Piano Scarf, made of best English silk plush, hand embroidered front, trimmed with silk tassels, assorted colors. Each ... 4.75

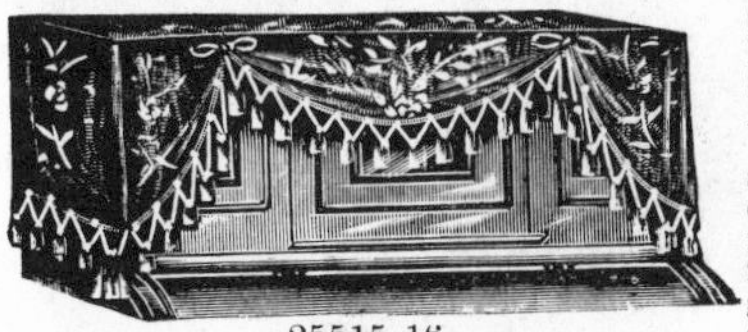

25515-16

25515 Piano Scarf, American Velours, assorted colors, made of 27-inch goods, double draped, fringed front and ends, draw cords, very pretty and durable. Each ... $4.25

25516 Piano Scarf of the finest imported velours, made of 32-inch goods, double draped, with draw cords, trimmed with fine quality knotted silk fringe, assorted colors. One of the most beautiful scarfs ever shown. Each ... 4.75

Weight of Piano Scarfs, about 3½ pounds.

Square Piano Scarfs.

25517 Piano Covers, square, made of best felt, scalloped edge, silk embroidered, 2x2½ yards, colors: Wine, olive or peacock blue; weight, 2½ pounds. Each ... $4.50

25518 Piano Covers, 2x2¾ yards square, made of best felt, scalloped edge, elegant silk embroidered; colors: Wine, olive or peacock blue; weight, 2¾ pounds. Each ... 6.00

Pianos.— Weight, boxed, 900 lbs.

Our WINDSOR pianos are comparatively new in the market, but during the past year we have done a very successful business in this line. Our sales have been large and with hardly an exception (it is impossible to please all) every instrument has given the best of satisfaction. We are daily in receipt of testimonials, praising their merits in the highest terms and it is evident that the people are beginning to realize that it is to their interests to *buy pianos at first hands* instead of paying enormous profits to middlemen. We intend to keep the Windsor up to the highest degree of excellence, and any new improvements in actions, etc., are at once adopted, as we aim to produce a piano with all modern improvements at our established prices, rather than continue on old styles at reduced prices. We therefore recommend our *Windsor Pianos*, not only for faultless mechanism, but purity and brilliancy of tone, superior workmanship, artistic design and finish of cases. In every instrument we use the double repeating actions constructed on the latest improved system, the touch is prompt and elastic and they have a remarkably pure and evenly balanced scale; full iron frame bronzed and polished; we have recently added the new "third pedal." The cases are of all the latest styles of wood, finely finished, highly polished and with finely carved trusses and panels, adjustable music rack and continuous nickel plated hinge on top and fall board; in fact great care is given to every detail with the one object in view of producing a first-class upright piano.

EVERY PIANO IS WARRANTED FOR FIVE YEARS, bears our trade mark "Windsor," also our firm name, which is positive evidence that our confidence in them is unlimited. Satisfaction is guaranteed in every case as you will see by referring to our offer on preceding page in regard to sending them out on trial.

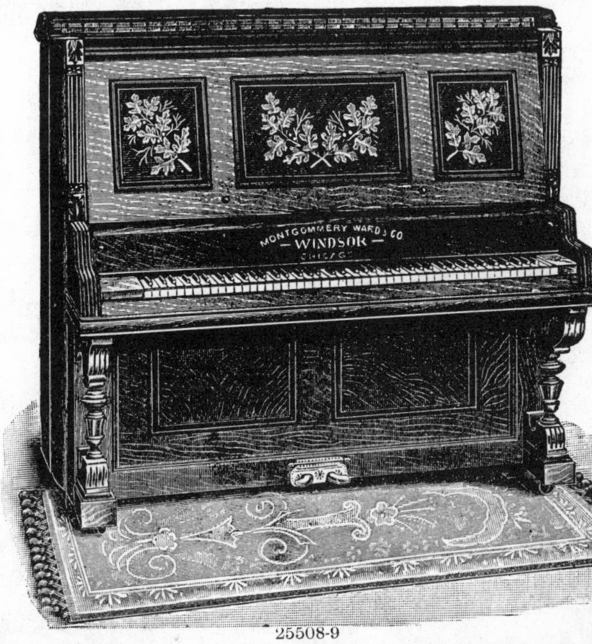

25508-9

25507 Windsor Piano (style A), as described above, 7⅓ octave, ivory keys, overstrung scale; three strings in unison (excepting wound bass strings), elastic double repeating action, with nickeled hammer, rest rail and brackets; height 53 in.; length 62 in.; depth 28¾ in. The case on this style is made of "built up" hardwood with highly polished surface and finished in imitation of Rosewood, Ebony or Mahogany. Price, including plush stool and scarf, $170.00 net (no discount).

25508 Windsor Piano (style B), same style as 25509 (see cut), with full swing front music desk, full size full iron frame, 7⅓ octave, ivory keys (overstrung scale), elastic double repeating action with nickel plated hammer rest rail and brackets; THREE PEDALS; height, 56 inches; length, 62 inches; depth, 28½ inches. This case is double mahogany veneered, highly polished and finished either in natural color, or in imitation of Rosewood or Ebony and is indeed a very handsome piano. Price, including plush stool and scarf each $195,00, net (no discount).

25509 Windsor Piano (style C), as described see cut, with full swing front music desk, full size 7⅓ octave, ivory keys, full iron frame, overstrung scale, elastic double repeating action, with nickel plated hammer rest rail and brackets; THREE PEDALS; height, 56 inches; length, 62 inches; depth, 28½ inches. This case is double veneered, highly polished and can furnish either the genuine figured American walnut, oak or San Domingo Mahogany. This piano will rank, equal, in every respect, to the very best grades. Price, including plush stool and scarf, $210.00 net (no discount.)

NOTE.—We wish it understood that our Windsor Pianos are not to be classed with the inferior instruments with which the country is being flooded, as we would not under any circumstances allow our name to be associated with any article that we could not thoroughly recommend. We have a special catalogue of our pianos and organs. Mailed free. We do not claim that they are equal to a "Steinway," which cannot be purchased at less than six hundred dollars each, but we do claim they are equal in every way to the medium grades that are sold by agents at from $350.00 to $400.00.

MUSICAL GOODS DEPARTMENT.

The new tariff law of last year has made a slight reduction in cost of imported instruments and fittings, and our prices will be found correspondingly lower.

ACCORDIONS.

Cannot be sent by mail.

We buy all our accordions direct from European manufacturers, select the style with a view to durability, quality of material, tone and workmanship, rather than to highly ornamented cases, although each instrument is highly finished. We also request a careful inspection of our prices, which we know to be lower than offered by any other dealer in the country for instruments of the same value.

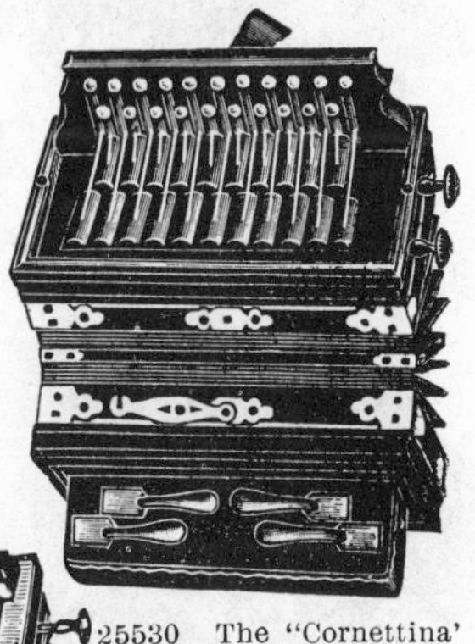

25526 Accordion, 21 long, nickel keys, 4 sets reeds, stops, 4 basses, double leather-bound bellows, ebonized case with nickel moldings. Size, 11¼x6½x6½; weight, boxed 18 pounds. Price, each .$7.75

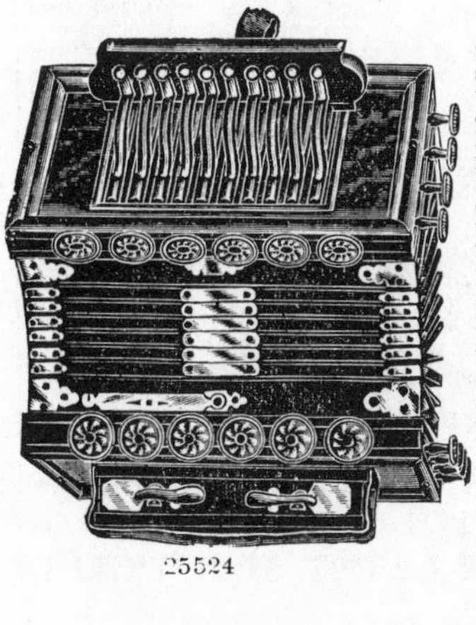

25524

25524 Professional Accordion, light wood case with mahogany moldings. Length, 13⅞, width 7⅛, depth, 9⅛ inches, 4 sets reeds, 8 stops. 10 long nickel keys, 2 basses, 6 double bellows, leather bound with nickel corners, one row fancy trumpets. Weight, boxed. 20 pounds. Each $7.90

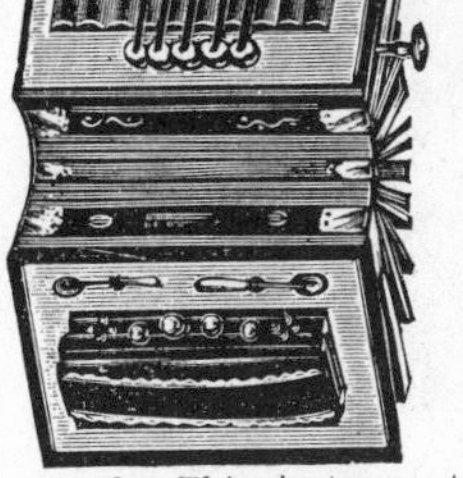

25530 The "Cornettina" Accordion is the latest novelty in this line and is bound to become a popular instrument. It consists of an ordinary accordion, full size, well made; has 2 sets reeds, 2 stops, 10 keys, 2 basses, double bellows. Directly under the regular row of keys are five extra keys, the reeds of which are tuned in imitation of the cornet or bugle, and military signals, bugle call, tec., can be perfectly executed. This instrument also has three other attachments, by which you can imitate either the cuckoo, nightingale or cock crowing. The Cornettina, with the different combinations, is capable of producing the most pleasing musical effects.

Weight, boxed, 10 pounds. Price ... $5.70

Accordions—Continued.

25532 Miniature Professional Accordion. Mahogany case; size, 10¾ x5½x7½; 3 sets of reeds,10 long nickel keys, 6 stops, 2 basses, 3 double bellows,nickel corners, 2 rows mirror trumpets, excellent tone; weight, boxed, 10 pounds.
Price, each....$5.25

25534 Accordion Ebonized Case; size, 10x5½x5¾; 2 sets reeds, 2 stops, 10 nickel keys, double bellows, open action. Weight, boxed, 7 pounds.
Price, each......$2.00

Kalbe's Imperial Accordion.

We now carry in stock an extensive line of the celebrated "Kalbe" accordions, and as we import them direct from Berlin we can afford to place them on the market at very reasonable prices. This brand of instruments has been on the market for a number of years and is without doubt the best in the world.

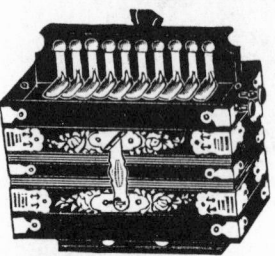

25535 Kalbe's Miniature Accordion; size, 10⅛ x5½; highly polished ebonized case, hand-painted decorations, double bellows, open action, sunken key board, 2 sets reeds, 2 stops, 10 patent nickel keys, nickel trimmings; weight, boxed, 7 pounds.
Price, each ..$3.25

25536 The Imperial Patent TWELVE KEYED Accordion. Size, 10½ x 5¼. Polished black case, double leather-bound bellows, patent nickel clasp, 2 sets broad reeds, 2 stops, 2 basses and 12 nickel keys. The extra keys are so arranged as to obviate the necessity of two rows of keys, and, being adapted for the execution of the most difficult music, are

25536

suitable for professional players; besides, are easily mastered by beginners. Weight, boxed, 8 pounds.
Price, each $3.90

25537 The Kalbe Imperial Piccolo Accordion; height, 9 in.; width, 6¼ in.; depth, 4½ in. Ten nickel keys, 2 basses, open action, double bellows, 2 sets broad reeds, one stop, leather bound bellows frame, nickel trimmings, in neat case with handle and hooks, manufactured expressly for us. Weight, boxed, 7 lbs.
Each......$4.25

25537

Accordions—Continued.

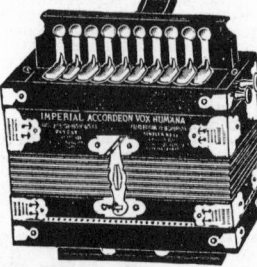

25538

25538 Kalbe's Imperial Accordion with "Vox Humana" or tremolo attachment; handsome mahogany case, highly polished. Size, 10½x5½, 2 sets extra board steelbronze reeds, 10 patent nickel keys,2 stops,open action,double bellows, nickel trimmings. Wgt., boxed 10 lbs.
Price, each,$4.75

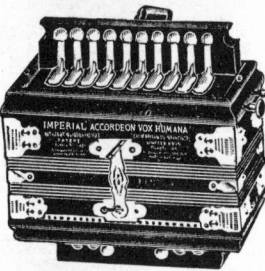

25539

25539 Kalbe's Miniature Accordion. Ebonized case, beaded moldings, bellows has 9 foids, each fold bound with nickel, 10 patent keys, 2 sets reeds, 2 stops, tremolo attachment. Weight, boxed, about 10 lbs.
Price, each, $4.90

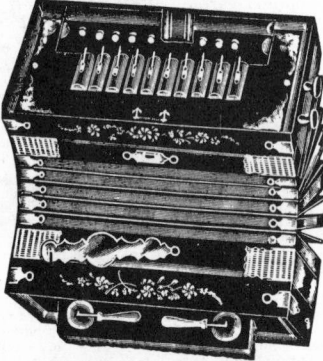

25541 Professional Imperial Accordion Size,12½x6¼, ebonized case, fine hand painted moldings, gilt ornaments, 5 double bellows, 2 sets broad steel bronze reeds, 2 stops, 10 nickel keys, nickel trimmings. Wgt., boxed, 10 lbs.
Price, each $5.75

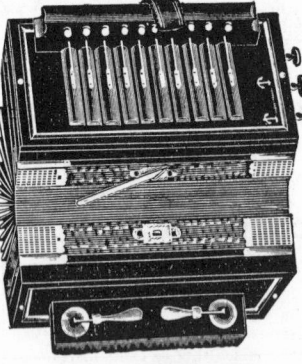

25543 Large Imperial Accordion. Size, 12x16¾, 3 sets broad steel bronze reeds, 3 stops, 10 long nickel keys, heavy nickel lined moldings. large bellows, 11 folds, each bound with nickel, making a very attractive and substantial instrument. Weight, boxed, 15 lbs.
Price, each $8.00

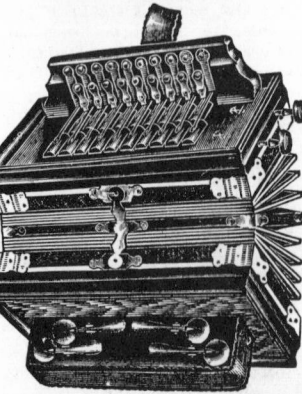

25548 Kalbe Accordion ebonized case; size, 12½ x7, 19 long nickel keys, 4 sets broad reeds, two stops, open action, double bellows, leather straps, nickel trimmings.Weight, boxed, 12 lbs.
Price....$9.00

Accordions—Continued.

25550 New Kalbe Accordion, ebonized moldings and panels, Size, 12x7x6,leatherette covered bellows, open action, 21 nickel keys, 2 stops, double bellows, 4 sets reeds, 6 basses.
Price, each ....$10.50 Weight, boxed, 15 pounds.

Flute Accordions.

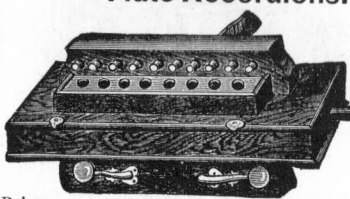

25561 FluteAccordions (no instructor) 10 keys 2 basses, metal mouthpieces.
Price..................................$0.75
Weight, 21 ounces.

25563 The Clariophon or newFlute Accordion. Length, 15 inches.

25563

diameter, 2 inches, made of wood, imitation mahogany, 10 keys, 2 basses, well made. Weight, 20 ounces. Price, each $1.10

Concertinas.

Cannot be sent by mail

(German make.)

25566 Concertinas Mahogany, full size, 20 keys, bone buttons, nickel sound rings, good tone. Weight, boxed, 6 pounds.
Price, each....$2.15

25568 Concertina, rosewood case, English pattern, morocco bound bellows,20 keys, steel reeds and loud clear tone, finely finished. Weight, boxed, 6 pounds.
Price, each......$4 25

25570 Concertinas; fine rosewcod case with elaborate German silver inlayings, leather bound bellows, 20 keys, broad reeds, heavy tone,finely finished. Wt. boxed, 8 lbs.
Price, each...$5 65

English Concertinas.

25576 Anglo-German pattern,made of mahogany, 20 keys, leather bound bellows, 5 folds, in wood case. Each .$9.40 Weight, boxed, 6 pounds.
25578 Anglo-German pattern, mahogany, steel reeds, 20 keys, leather bound bellows, 5 folds, in wood case.
Each............$11.25
Weight. boxed.7 pounds

STANDARD IS THE WORD TO BE USED IN CONNECTION WITH OUR MUSICAL GOODS. WE DO NOT SELL TRASH.

HARMONICAS. Our "Windsor."

25585 Our Improved WINDSOR Harmonicas are made expressly for us by one of the first makers of Enrope, under our own name and brand, and after giving them a thorough trial, we feel justified in pronouncing them the *best* Richters ever put on the market. They have ten single holes, 20 reeds, extra heavy nickel plated reed plates, extension ends, nickel covers. Especial attention has been given to tuning and we guarantee every one to be *absolutely perfect.* Each is stamped with firm name. Each..$0.20 Per dozen..... 2.15 Weight, each, 3 oz.

25585½ Set of four of our celebrated WINDSOR Harmonicas. No. 25585 in neat cloth covered pocket case (see cut). We send assorted keys unless otherwise instructed. Per set...$0.95

25586 The "Golden Lark" RICHTER Harmonicas, 10 single holes, 20 reeds, nickel plated reed plates, gold gilt, covers, satin finished, perfectly tuned, Each in satin lined plush case. Weight, 4 ounces. Price, each...$0.38 Per dozen...$4.05

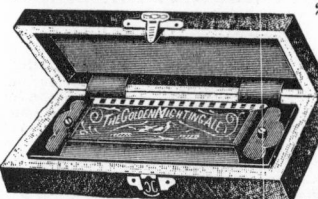

25588 The "Golden Lark" CONCERT Harmonicas. 10 double holes, 40 reeds, nickel plated reed plates, extension ends, gold gilt covers, satin finish, tuned in octaves and absolutely perfect. Each, in satin lined plush case. Price, each...$0.70 Per dozen...7.55 Weight, 5 ounces.

25592 Richter Harmonicas, fine quality 10 single holes 20 reeds brass reed plates, celluloid covers; correctly tuned. Each...$0.26 Per dozen...2.80

25593 Concert Harmonica, 10 double holes, 40 reeds, brass reed plates, celluloid covers, absolutely perfect in tone. Each...$0.45 Per dozen...4.86 The seamless celluloid shell into which the harmonica slides, acts as a resonator as well as cover for the instrument, and avoids putting the lips in contact with the brass plates.

Genuine Hohners.

Our prices on this famous line of Harmonicas are lower for a single instrument than your local dealer CAN BUY THEM in gross lots.

25596 Hohner, 10 single holes on one edge, brass reed plates, nickel covers. Each...$$0.12 Weight, 3 oz.

25597 10 double holes on one edge double reeds. nickel plated covers. Each...$0.29. Weight, 5 ounces.

25598 10 double holes on each edge, double reeds, nickel covers. Each...$0.85 Weight, 7 ounces.

16—3d

Carl Essbach's.

25600 Carl Essbach's Richter Harmonica, good quality, 10 single holes. 20 reeds, brass reed plates, nickel cover. Each...$0.10 Per dozen...1.00 Weight, 3 ounces.

25601 Carl Essbach's New French Harp, extra fine quality, pure tone, perfectly tuned; ten single holes, 20 German silver reeds, brass reed plates nickeled, nickel covers, extension ends. Each...$0.13 Per dozen...1.40 Weight, 3 ounces.

25604 Essbach's Miniature Concert Harmonica. 10 double holes, 40 reeds, brass reed plate, nickel covers. This harmonica "fills a long felt want," it being a full "concert," but of small size, therefore the tones are easily produced, besides it can be covered with the hands, same as the Richters. Each...$0.32 Per dozen...3.45 Weight, 4 oz.

Koch.

We now carry in stock the celebrated Andreas Koch Harmonicas, and can recommend them for either professionals or amateurs. They are perfectly tuned and easy to blow.

25605— Koch Richter, 10 single holes, 20 reeds, brass plates, extension ends, nickel covers, all keys. Each...$0 13 Per dozen...1.40 Weight, 3 ounces.

25506

25606 Koch Double Richter, 10 single holes on each edge, 40 reeds, brass plates, nickel covers, extension ends, assorted keys. Price, each...$0.28 Per dozen...3.00 Weight, 6 ounces.

55607

25607 Koch Professional Richter, Organtone, 16 double holes, 32 reeds tuned in octaves, brass plates, nickel covers, excellent tone; every player should have one. Price, each...$0.32 Per dozen...3.45 Weight, 5 ounces.

25609

25609 Koch Concert Harmonicas, 10 double Holes 40 reeds, brass plates, nickel covers, extension ends, every one a gem. Price, each...$0.38 Per dozen...4.05 Weight, 6 ounces.

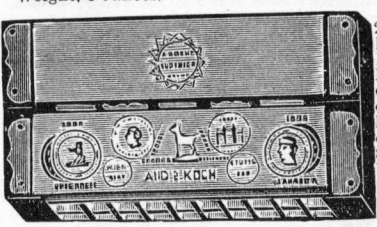

25610

25610 Koch Double Harmonica, 10 double holes on each edge 80 reeds, brass plates, nickel covers. Price, each...$0.75

Ludwig's.

25611 The Genuine Gebr, Ludwig Harmonica, Richter, pattern, 10 single holes, brass reed plates, nickeled single hole, nickel covers, extension ends, assorted keys. Weight, 3 ounces. Each...$0.10 Per dozen...1.00

Miscellaneous Makes.

25617 "Jim Dandy" Richter Harmonica, 10 single holes, brass plates, 20 reeds, nickel covers; best harmonica in the market for the money. Each...$0.05. Per dozen...$0.50 Weight, 3 ounces.

25618 Original "Emmet" Richter, good quality, 10 single holes, 20 reeds, nickel covers, bone mouthpiece, extension ends, assorted keys. Each.$0.12 Weight, 3 ounces   Per dozen...1.80

25619 Meinel's Concert Richter, 10 double holes, 20 reeds, full concert size, brass plates, extension ends, loud tone. Each..$0.18 Per dozen...$1.95 Weight, 4 ounces.

25622 The Philharmonic Concert Harmonica, excellent quality, rich tone, 10 double holes on each edge, 80 reeds, brass plates one side is tuned in octave, the other side in duet; perfectly tuned. Each...$0.70 Weight, 6 ounces.

25623 One set of four "Thie," Harmonicas in pocket case. Each has 10 single holes on one edge, brass reed plates, German silver covers, each in different key. Per set...$0.60 Weight, 12 ounces.

25624 The Philharmonic Duet Set of Harmonicas, concert size, each has 10 double holes. 40 reeds, nickel covers, one is tuned in octave, one in duet, perfectly tuned both in same key, produces excellent music when played together. Price, per set...$0.75 Weight, 7 ounces.

Bell Harmonicas.

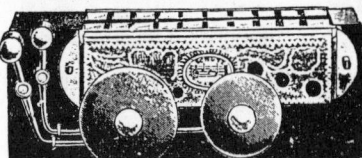

25626— Bell Harmonicas, Richter, German silver, 10 holes, 1 bell...$0 30 Weight. 4 ounces.

Harmonicas—Continued.

25628 Bell Harmonica, Richter, German silver, 10 holes, 2 bells.. $0.50
Weight, 5 ounces.
25629 Bell Harmonica, Concert, German silver, 10 holes, double, 1 bell...... . ... $0.60
Weight, 6 ounces.
25631 Bell Harmonica, Concert, German silver, 10 holes, double, 2 bells........ .... $0.80
Weight, 7 ounces.

HARMONICA POCKET CASES.

25632 Pocket Case for Richter Harmonicas, made of kid, nickel plated frame at top, with clasp.
Each................... $0.10
25633 Pocket Case for Concert Harmonica, same style as 25632.
Price, each.................. $0.15

Harmonica Holders.

25635 Excelsior Harmonica Holders (see cut) are constructed on an entirely new principle, and are giving excellent satisfaction. They consist of a wood breastplate, to which are attached heavy spring wire shoulder pieces. Harmonica of any size is held firmly in proper position for playing by two springs, thus leaving the hands free to play accompaniment on any other instrument. They are quickly and easily adjusted. Price, each $0.50. Weight, 8 ounces.
25636 Harmonica Holder, consists of heavy metal tube, painted and varnished, with opening at top for either Richter or Concert harmonicas; also opening at one end, and is used to regulate the tone and produce "tremolo" vibrations.
Each....$0.10 Per dozen...$1.00 Weight, 6 ounces.

Violin Cases.

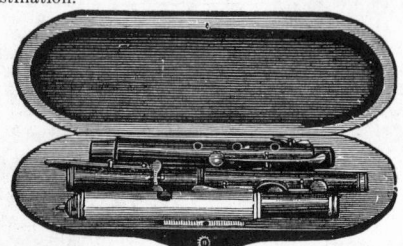

25641

25640 Wood, black, half lined with flannel, remainder with paper. Each.................... $1.00
Weight, boxed, 8 pounds.
25641 Wood, black, with lock, half lined with flannel, remainder with paper. Each........... 1.25
Weight, boxed, 8 pounds.
25641½ Brown Canvas, leather bound edges, lined with flannel, good model, opening at end. Each 1.35
25642 Wood, black, with lock and clasps, lined throughout with felt or flannel. Each 2.00
Weight, boxed, 8 pounds.
25643 Papier Mache, French, violin shape, lined with baize, lock, handle and clasps. Each.... 2.50
Weight, boxed, 10 pounds.
25645 Genuine Leather covered, black, finely finished, lined throughout with velvet, leather handles, nickel clasps. Each 4.50
Weight, boxed, 8 pounds.

Flutes.

(Instruction book free with each flute.)
No music dealer will warrant flutes, clarionets, piccolos or fifes not to check or crack. This often happens by change of temperature. Great care should be exercised in use of such instruments, not to suddenly expose to heat when they have been in cold air. They are always examined and leave in perfect shape. We will not be responsible for them after they arrive at destination.

25657

25650 D, 1 key, with tuning slide, German silver trimmed, in paper case............................ $1.65
Weight, 12 ounces.
25651 D, 4 keyed, Grenadillo, German silver rings and slide, in paper case........................... 2.80
Weight, 13 ounces.
25652 D, 6 keyed, Grenadillo, German silver rings and slide, cork joints, paper case 3.75
Weight, 14 ounces.
25654 D, 8 keyed, Grenadillo, German silver rings and slide, cork joints, in leather case........... 6.50
Weight, 26 ounces.
25655 D, made of Grenadillo with 10 German silver keys and trimmings, slide cork joints, each in fine morocco case. Price.............. 9.40
Weight, 26 ounces
25657 D, 10 keyed, Grenadillo, ivory head, with slide, in fine case, like illustration..... .... 16.70
Weight, 25 ounces.

Piccolos.

Each in Paper Case.
(Instruction Book, 45c.)
Weight, 6 to 8 ounces.

25662   Each.

25660 E flat or D, 1 key, cocoa, German silver tipped $0.55
25661 E flat or D, 1 key, cocoa, German silver tipped and tuning slide................... .90
25662 E flat or D, 4 keys, cocoa, German silver tipped and tuning slide.... .... 1.85
25663 E flat or D, 6 keys, cocoa, German silver tipped and tuning slide 2.35

25665 E flat or D, 6 keys, Grenadillo, ivory head, tuning slide, cork joints, German silver tipped.. $4.70

Flageolets.

EACH IN PASTEBOARD BOX.

25671

25667 Flageolet, Key of D, made of Grenadillo wood, German silver trimmed, one key. Each.. $1.65
25668 Flageolet, Key of Bb, Grenadillo wood, German silver trimmed, one key. Each......... 2.00
Weight, 10 ounces.
25669 Flageolet, Key of D, Grenadillo wood, 4 keys, German silver trimmings. Each......... 2.35
Weight, 10 ounces.
25671 Flageolets, Key of D, Grenadillo wood, German silver trimmings, 6 keys. Each......... 2.60
Weight, 10 ounces.

25675 Nightingale Flageolets (see cut), made of brass, nickel plated, finely finished, correctly tuned, made in following keys: Bb, C, D, Eb, F and G. Price, each, any key...............$0.25
Weight, 6 ounces.

Piccolo Flageolets.

This combination consists of a Piccolo with an extra Flageolet head and can be used as either instrument.

25678 Piccolo Flageolet, key of D, made of boxwood, German silver trimmed, 1 key.
Price, each..$1.90
25679 Piccolo Flageolet. key of D, made of Grenadillo wood, German silver trimmed, 6 keys
Each 2.80
Weight, 12 ounces.

Flute and Piccolo Cases.

25681-85.
25681 Flute Case, morocco covered, velvet lined, for 4 or 6 keyed flute. Each...................$1.85
Weight, 16 ounces.
25683 Flute Case. morocco covered, velvet lined, for 8 to 10 key flute. Each................ 2.35
Weight, 16 ounces.
25685 Piccolo Cases. morocco covered, velvet lined, for Eb or D Piccolo. Each.............. 1.30
Weight, 10 ounces.

Fifes.

(Instruction Book, 12c.)
Fifes are made in key of Bb and C only.

25687 Fifes made of Maple, brass tipped. Each...$0.20
Weight, 6 ounces.
25688 Fifes made of Cocoa, German silver tipped. Each 40
Weight, 6 ounces.
25689 Fifes made of Ebony, German silver ferrules. Each.................................. .60
Weight, 8 ounces.
25690 Fifes (Crosby) made of Ebony or Cocoa, long model U. S. Regulation pattern, long German silver ferrules. Each............ .85
Weight, 8 ounces.

25691 Fifes made of brass, nickel plated, raised holes. Weight, 10 ounces. Each...........$1.25

Flute, Fifes and Piccolo Mouthpieces.

25693-95

25693 Mouthpieces for Flute, composition, with adjustable screws $0.20
25694 Mouthpieces for Fife.............$0.12
25695 Mouthpieces for Piccolo..............$0.12
Weight, 2 ounces.

Clarionets.

Clarionets are made in the following keys only: A, Bb, C, D, and Eb. We give an instruction book free with instrument. Always mention what key is desired.
25705 Clarionet made of Grenadillo wood, black, with 13 German silver keys, German silver trimmings, any key.
Price, each.......... $11.00
Weight, 20 ounces.
25707 Clarionet, Grenadillo wood, black, Albert system, with 13 German silver keys, 2 patent rings, German silver trimmings; in any key. Price, each.... $12.50
Weight, 22 ounces.
25709 Clarionet, Grenadillo, black, Albert system, with 15 German silver keys (extra Bb and C sharp), two rings, German silver trimmings, any key.
Price, each.......... $15.00
Weight, 23 ounces.
25710 Clarionet, Albert system, made by Buffet, Crampon & Co., Paris; Grenadillo wood, 15 German silver keys, 2 rings with trill keys; each has 2 mouthpieces.
Price................. $28.00

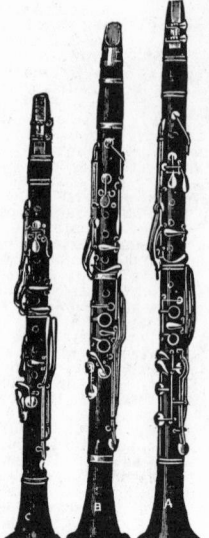

25705 25707 25709
Weight, each, 1 ounce.

Clarionet Reeds.

Give key of clarionet for which reed is wanted.
25711 "Martin" Brand, good quality, any key.
Each, $0.05. Per dozen $0.50
25712 "Le Fin" Brand, superfine quality, any key.
Each, $0.10. Per dozen.......................... 1.00
25713 "Artists" Brand, the best brand in the market, made expressly for soloists. Each... ...... .15
Per doz... 1.60

Clarionet Reed Trimmers.

25713½ Flach's Patent Clarionet Reed Trimmer and Regulator (see cut) is a new invention, and clarionet players will see at once that it is not only useful, but economical. By its use the annoyance of broken and imperfect reeds is avoided; besides, a reed can be made to last a long time. They are made entirely of metal, fitted with knife of best quality; also has fine steel file on back; can be carried in vest pocket. Price, in neat case, each..$1.75
Weight, 3 ounces.

Clarionet Reed Case.

25714 Clarionet Pocket Reed Case. leather covered, holds six reeds. Each...................$1.00
Weight. 5 ounces.

Clarionet Cases.

25716

25715 Leather Case, lined with handle strap. Give key of clarionet.
Each............... $2.00
Weight, 9 ounces.
25716 Clarionet Case (see cut), leather covered, lined with flannel, handle, hooks and lock; for set of three clarionets.
Each............... $3.50
Weight, 4 pounds.

Clarionet Music Racks.

Always state key of instrument for which rack is wanted.
25718 German Silver, with adjustable ring.
Each $1.00
Weight, 4 ounces.

25718

Clarionet Mouthpieces.

Weight, 4 ounces. Give key of Clarionet.
    Each.
25720 Cocoa or Ebony, without reed holder, any key... $0.42
25721 Cocoa or Ebony, with German Silver reed holder, any key.................................... .65

Clarionet Mouthpiece Caps.

Weight, each, 3 ounces.

25726 Clarionet Mouthpiece Cap or Protector, made of cocoa. Each $0.35

25727 Clarionet Mouthpiece Cap, nickel plated. Each .... .45

Give key of clarionet.

Music Boxes.

Cannot send through the mail, neither will we send them C. O. D. subject to examination, as they are delicately constructed, and we cannot afford to take the responsibility of having inexperienced parties handle them.

We now import our entire line of music boxes, buying of the leading manufacturers of Switzerland, and a careful inspection of description and prices given below will convince the most skeptical that we are headquarters for this line of goods.

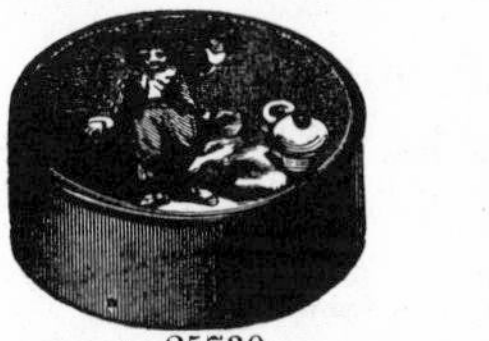

25730.

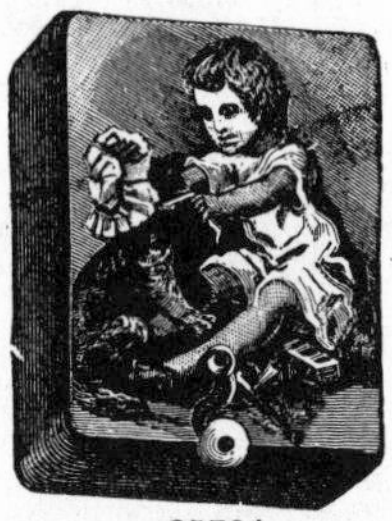

25731.

25730 Round Nickel Case, 2¾ inches in diameter, decorated top and bottom, 18 notes, one air, operated by turning small crank on top. Weight, 10 ounces.
Price, each $0.45

25731 Square Wood Case, size, 4x3½ inches, decorated top, 18 teeth, operated with crank, plays two airs. Weight, 16 ounces.
Price, each $0.75

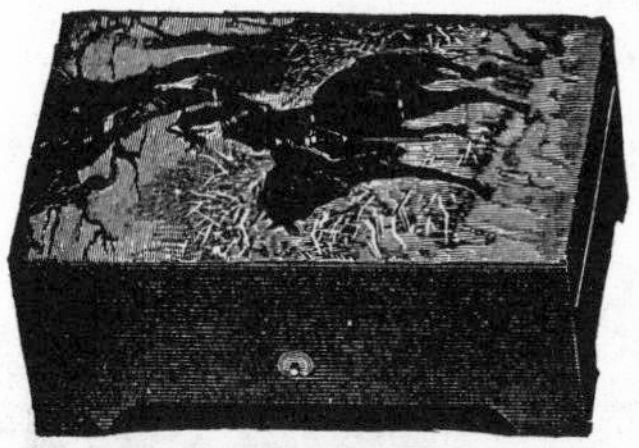

25732 Highly Polished Mahogany Case; size, 4¾x3½x2⅜, inteior glass cover to protect works, covers decorated with pretty chromos; self-acting cylinder, 2½ inches long with mainspring, winds like a watch, with attached key, has 36 notes, plays 2 airs. Weight, 16 ounces.
Each $2.65

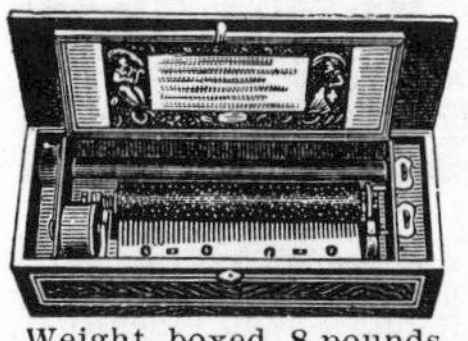

25736 Imitation Rosewood case, highly polished; size, 12x6½x4½; covers richly decoroted, bevel edges and white lines inlaid in top, also on front of box; interior glass cover; spring lever movement, starting and "change" levers, 3⅜ in. cylinder, plays 6 airs.
Weight, boxed, 8 pounds.
Price $8.10

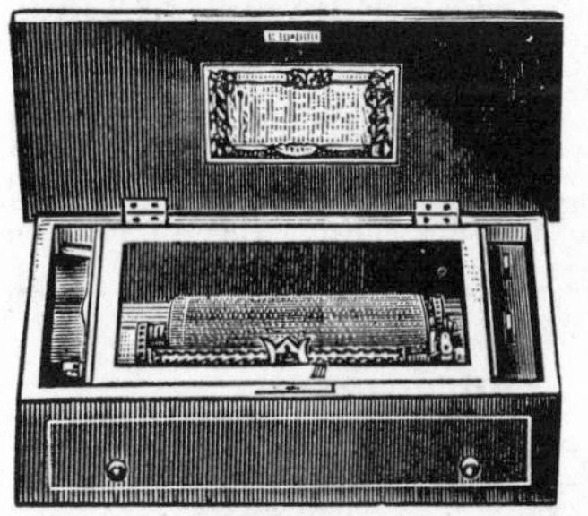

25740 Imitation Rosewood Case, size, 18x8½x5½ in., 7½ in. cylinder, cylinder tune indicator, zither attachment, Plays 10 airs. Weight, boxed, 25 lbs.
Each..$16.80

25741 Imitation Rosewood, same style as 25740, size, 20½x9x5¾, with 9¼ inch cylinder tune indicator, zither attachment; plays 12 airs. Weight, boxed, 30 lbs. Each $25.00

25742 Imitation Rosewood, same style as 25740, 23½x9½x9, 13 inch cylinder, plays 10 airs, has zither attachment, speed regulator, tune indicator; a very fine instrument. Each 30.00

...PRICES...

Speak for themselves. Compare ours with others and see how WELL ours can talk; not how loud.

The Capital Music Box.

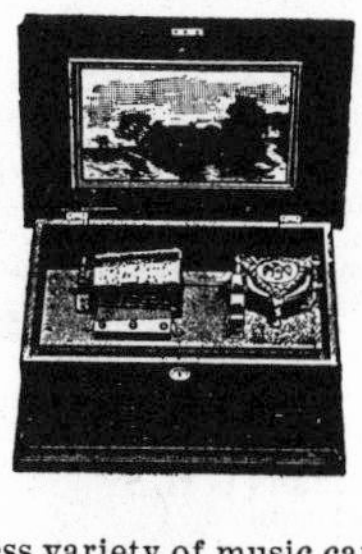

The Musical Box shown in cut is a new invention of American manufacture and is constructed upon a new system which admits of an unlimited number of tunes being obtainable at a reasonable cost for each; this feature alone insures its popularity. The construction is substantial, and cases are finished in oak or mahogany and highly polished. It has an improved and extra large spring movement which permits it to run much longer than the ordinary style. The tune cylinders are made of metal, each plays one piece, and an endless variety of music can be furnished. Zither attachment can be applied at an additional cost of $1.00.

25743 Capital Musical Box as described above, sizes 14½x11½x7, 44 notes in comb.
Price, including one tune, each $18.25
Extra tunes, each 0.30
Weight, boxed, about 25 lbs.

25744 Capital Musical Box as described above, size, 21x14x8½, 58 notes in comb. Price, including one tune. Each 35.00
Extra tunes. Each 0.40
Weight, boxed, about 50 lbs.
List of tune cylinders furnished upon application.

Mandolins.

Weight, boxed, 8 pounds.

This instrument is becoming very popular, our sales having more than doubled during the last year. We would state for the benefit of those desirous of learning to play the mandolin, that they are "tuned" same as the violin, and fingering is the same, so that one who can play a violin may easily learn to manage the mandolin. Instruction book free with each instrument.

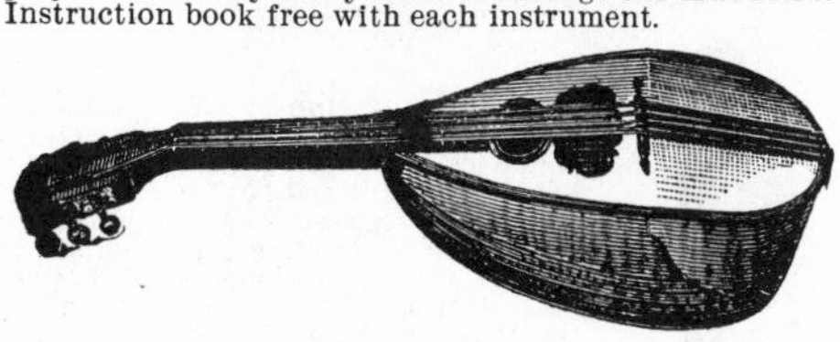

Each

25745 Mandolin, American, full size, maple and oak ribs. Highly polished, plain front, rosewood finger board, brass patent head, correct scale, finely finished, warranted for one year not to split or warp. *The best mandolin ever put on the market for the money.* Price $5.50

25746 Our Conservatory Mandolin, full size, American made, mahogany and maple ribs, rosewood band, all French polished, orange front, ebony finger board, position dots, inlaid striking piece, rosewood tipped, fully warranted. Nickel plated, patent head. Price 9.00

25747 Our Professional Concert Mandolin, American manufacture, rosewood and mahogany ribs, white inlaid edges, rosewood bound inlaid soundhole, ebony or rosewood finger board, position dots, full French polished, Italian patent head, warranted not to split or warp 13.00

25748 The Joseph Bohmann American Mandolin, full concert size, 19 maple ribs, highly polished, rosewood finger board, pearl position dots, patent tail piece, inlaying around sound hole, patent head, scale guaranteed absolutely perfect. Warranted one year. Each 15.00

Mandolin Pick.

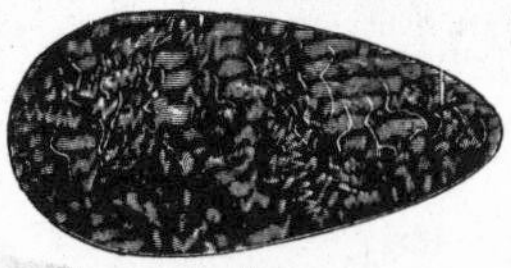

25749 Mandolin Picks, made of celluloid, imitation tortoise shell, oval pattern, *very best quality.*
Each $0.04
Per dozen .... .40

Mandolin Cases.

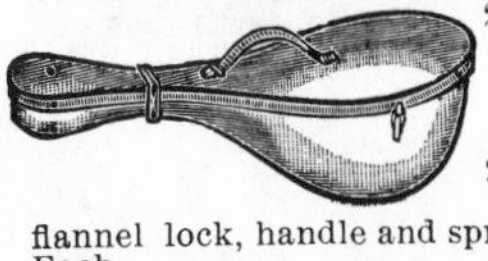

25750 Mandolin Case, made of brown canvas, leather bound, flannel lined, strap fastenings.
Each $1.00

25751 Mandolin Case, wood, black, lined with flannel lock, handle and spring clasps.
Each $2.25

25752 Mandolin Case leather, covered, russet or black color, hand sewed, flannel lined, fine quality. Each 5.50

25754 Mandolin Bags, made of green cloth.
Each .... .75

25755 Mandolin Bags, canvas, fleece lined, patent fasteners. Each .... .90

25756 Mandolin Bags, made of silk plush, extra fine quality. Each 4.50

LOOK UP

Our Agricultural Implement quotations before buying elsewhere. We can save you something.

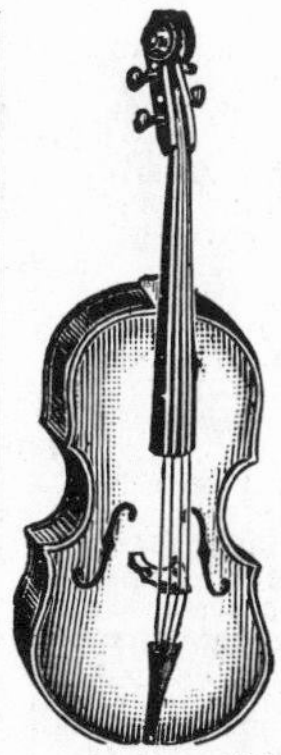

Violoncellos.

Instruction book and bow free with each Violoncello. Each one in case ready for shipping. Weight, boxed, 43 pounds.

25763 Violoncello, German make, reddish brown color, fair quality, *peg head.* Each $8.00

25764 Violoncello, better quality, dark red, good model, with *patent head.* Each $9.40

25766 Violoncello, light red color, polished, fine model, good tone, inlaid edges, brass plates, patent heads.
Each $11.75

25769 Stradivarius model, dark brown color, inlaid edges, patent head, fine quality, excellent tone.
Each $17.00

Violoncello Patent Head.

Weight, per set, 11 ounces.

25775 Iron plates and screws, maple pegs with pearl dot inlaid in head $1.65

25776 Brass plates, iron screws, maple pegs with pearl dot inlaid in head 1.80

Double Bass Viols—Patent Heads.

Instruction book and bow free with each. Weight, boxed, about 125 pounds.

25779 Double Bass, half size, dark red, shaded and polished, 3 strings, good quality. Each .. $18.40

25780 Double Bass, same size and style as No. 25779, with 4 strings. Each 19.75

25781 Double Bass, three-quarter size, 3 strings, dark red, shaded and polished, good quality. Each 20.75

25782 Double Bass, same size and style as No. 25781, with 4 strings. Each 22.50

25783 Double Bass, half size, 3 strings, dark red, polished, inlaid edges, fine quality. Each 28.20

25784 Double Bass, three-quarter size, 4 strings, dark red, polished, inlaid edges, fine quality.
Each 32.75

25785 Double Bass, three-quarter size, 4 strings, dark red, polished, inlaid edges, swelled back, extra fine quality. Each 42.30

Double Bass Bows.

25787 Maple, red painted, light wood frog.
Each $1.25
Weight, 10 ounces.

25788 Red wood, natural color, ebony frog, good quality. Each 2.35
Weight, 12 ounces.

25789 Pernambuco wood, natural color, ebony frog, German silver lined, inlaid eye (professional model). Each 4.50
Weight, 12 ounces.

Double Bass Bridges.

25795 Maple, plain scroll, good quality, for half size bass. Weight, 3 ounces. Each $0.40

25796 Maple, plain scroll, good quality, for three-quarter size bass. Weight, 4 oz. Each .... .50

Guitars.

Instruction book free with each guitar.

We handle American made Guitars exclusively, and select the instruments carefully, with the view of selling only those that we can thoroughly recommend. Guitars that are "hawked" about the country at ridiculously low prices are made simply to sell cheap, without any care being given to their musical properties. We guarantee every Guitar in our stock to be absolutely perfect in scale and to have a smooth, musical tone. They are made in the largest factories in this country, the workmanship is the very best, and we warrant each instrument regardless of price (for one year), not to crack or warp. We recommend gut and silk wound strings under all circumstances. If steel strings are to be used, however, we suggest that a tail-piece be put on the instrument, otherwise the sounding board is liable to "spring" at the bridge and in time injure the guitar.

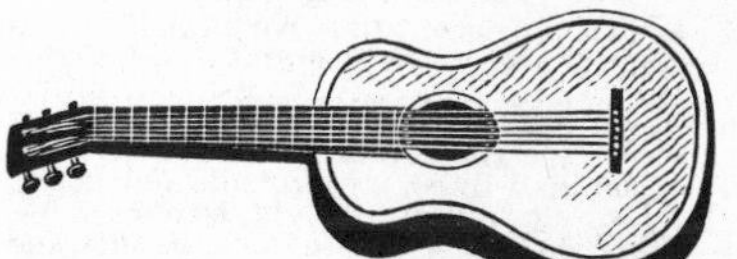

25800 OUR LEADER, American made Guitar, standard size, back and sides made of maple and handsomely finished in imitation of either rosewood, mahogany or oak, all highly polished, yellow top, imitation ebony finger board, position dots; patent head, raised frets, *warranted for one year.* Weight, boxed, about 15 lbs.
Price $3.75

25801 OUR KENWOOD, American made, standard size, back and sides made of "quarter-sawed" oak, highly polished, finely finished cedar sounding board, cedar neck, raised frets, patent head, excellent tone and warranted not to split or warp. Weight, boxed, 15 lbs.
Price, each 6.00

25803 OUR COLUMBIAN, STANDARD American made guitar, standard size, solid MAHOGANY back and sides, edges inlaid with white celluloid, highly polished rosewood finger board, correctly fretted, cedar neck, patent heads, manufactured expressly for us and warranted not to split or warp. Weight, boxed, about 15 lbs.
Price, each 9.00

Guitars—Continued.

25804 Our Columbian "CONCERT" American Guitar, same style and description as No 25803. Concert size, rich tone. Weight, boxed, about 18 lbs. Price, each 11.00

25804½ Our Columbian GRAND CONCERT American Guitar, same style as 25803. GRAND CONCERT size. A superb instrument. Weight, boxed, about 20 lbs. Price, each 13.00

25805 Our "WINDSOR" American made, Conservatory Guitar, solid rosewood back and sides, yellow cedar top, cedar neck, ebony finger board, inlaid stripe in back, standard size, finely polished, and *fully warranted in every respect*. Weight, boxed, 15 lbs. Each 12.00

25806 Our WINDSOR CONCERT Guitar, American made, same description as 25805, only they are the large or concert size, each is absolutely perfect in every respect, and warranted not to split or warp. Weight, boxed, 15 lbs. Price, each. ..14.00

NOTE.—The "Windsor" Guitars are manufactured expressly for us in one of the very best factories in the country, and we can safely say they are *the best* instruments ever offered for the money. The name Montgomery Ward & Co.'s "Windsor" is burned on inside of each.

25807 WASHBURN American Guitar, solid rosewood body, mahogany or cedar neck, patent head, ebony finger board, warranted not to split or warp, standard size. Weight, boxed, 15 lbs. Each $22.00

25808 WASHBURN American Guitar, of solid rosewood body, mahogany or cedar neck, ebony finger board, inlaid, warranted not to warp or split. Concert size. Weight, boxed, 15 lbs. Each..26.00

Capo D' Astros.

NOTE.—The Capo D'Astro is used to clamp on guitar finger board at first fret to facilitate playing in flat keys.

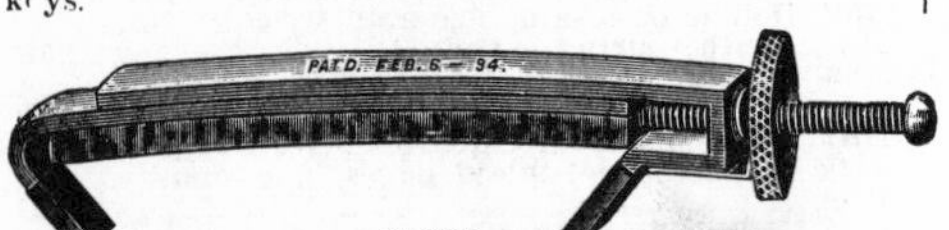

25809

25809 Capo D'Astro, nickel plated, cork lined, with adjusting screw, fit any guitar. Each.....$0.20 Weight, 3 ounces.

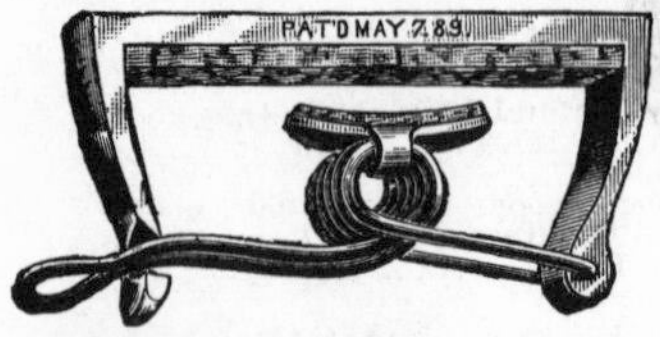

25809½ The Patent "Lightning" Capo D'Astro metal frame, nickel plated, cork lined cap, heavy spring quickly adjusted. Weight, 3 ounces. Each $0.30

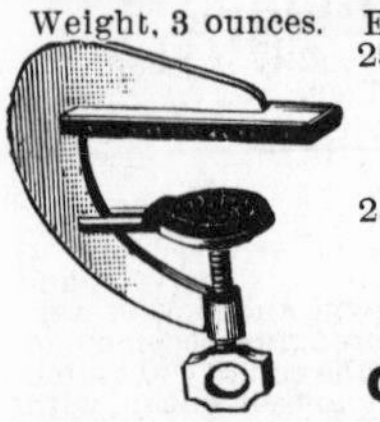

25810 Capo D'Astros, brass with cork lined string cap and adjusting screw, like cut. Weight, 3 ounces. Each $0.40

25811 Capo D'Astros, same as above, nickel plated. Weight, 3 ounces. Each $0.50

Guitar Tail Pieces.

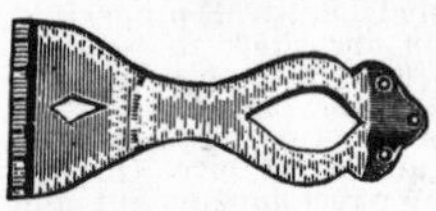

25813 Guitar Tail Pieces made of *Celluloid.* Each $0.50

25814 Guitar Tail Pieces, made of brass, nickelplated (see cut). Weight, 5 oz. Each $0.75

NOTE.—If steel strings are to be used on a guitar it is essential to the tone and durability of the instrument that they should be attached to a tail piece.

Guitar Cases.

Each.

25815 Brown canvas, leather bound, with opening in end for standard size guitar. Weight, 5½ lbs $1.50

25816 Brown canvas, same as above, for concert size guitar. Weight, 5½ lbs 1.75

25817 Wood, half lined, with handle and hooks, for standard size guitar. Weight, boxed, 18 lbs. 1.90

25818 Wood, half lined, with lock, handle and hooks, for standard size guitar. Weight, boxed, 18 lbs 2.00

25819 Wood, full lined, with lock, handle and spring clasp, for concert size guitar. Weight, boxed, 20 lbs 2.85

25822 Leather, russet color, hand sewed, finely embossed, full lined, opening in end for standard size guitars. Weight, boxed. 20 lbs 5.25

25823 Leather, russet color, same style as No. 25822, for concert size guitars 5.75

Guitar Bags.

25824 Green Felt, for either standard or concert size guitars. Weight, 9 oz 1.00
Give size of guitar.

Guitar and Banjo Frets.

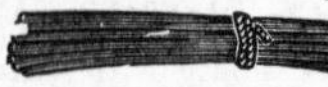

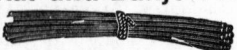

25826 Guitar or Banjo Frets, brass, per set of 18. $0.20

25827 Guitar or Banjo Frets, German silver, per set of 18 .... .30

Weight, per set, 3 oz. NOTE.—We do not break sets.

Banjos.

(Weight of banjos, boxed, 18 lbs.)
Instruction book free with banjo.

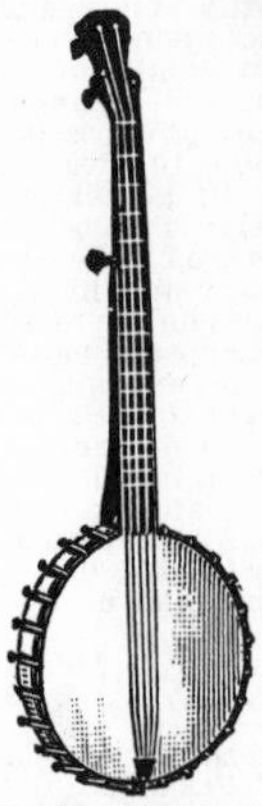

25828 Maple Shell, 10 inch, imitation cherry, sheepskin head, four brass brackets, marked frets. Each $1.75

5829 Nickel Shell, 10 inches in diameter, wood lined, imitation cherry neck, marked frets, calfskin head, 7 brass brackets. Each $2.75

25831 Nickel Shell, 11 inches in diameter, wood lined, highly polished birch neck, imitation ebony finger board, raised frets, inlaid position dots, celluloid pegs, 21 nickel brackets, calfskin head. Each $4.50

25832 Nickel Shell, 11 inches in diameter, wood lined grooved hoop, 24 nickel brackets. French polished birch neck, imitation ebony finger board, inlaid position dots, wired edge, celluloid pegs, patent tail piece, calfskin head. Each $5.50

25834 German silver Shell, 11 inches in diameter, wood lined, both edges wired, grooved hoop, 24 nickel brackets, French polished birch neck, ebony veneered finger board, fancy inlaid position dots, handsome scroll, elaborately inlaid with pearl, patent pegs No. 26212, an extra fine instrument. Each 9.00

25837 Professional Banjo, Steward model, 12 inches in diameter, nickel plated German silver shell, both edges wired, wood lined, finely polished birch neck, extra heavy strainer hoop, ebony finger board, raised frets, 29 nickel brackets, neck ornamented with pearl, calfskin head Each 13.00

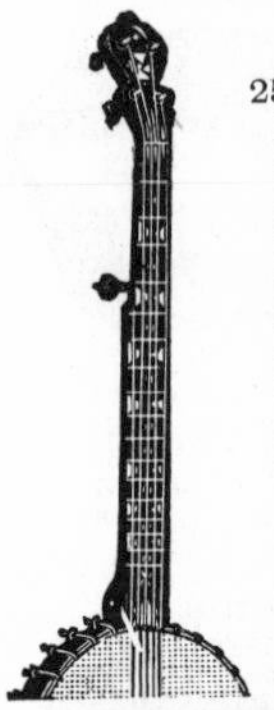

25841 Our Windsor Professional Banjo, 11 inches in diameter, polished German silver shell, 30 nickel brackets, wood lined, both edges wired, grooved corrugated hoop, patent tail piece, raised frets, French polished walnut neck, full ebony finger board extending over head piece, elaborately inlaid with pearl, back of head piece covered with ebony, German silver name plate, patent pegs, calfskin head; this banjo is a new model made expressly for us, and is one of the most beautiful as well as perfect instruments ever put on the market. Banjos of no better quality are sold daily at double our price. Each $18.00

Banjo Thimbles.

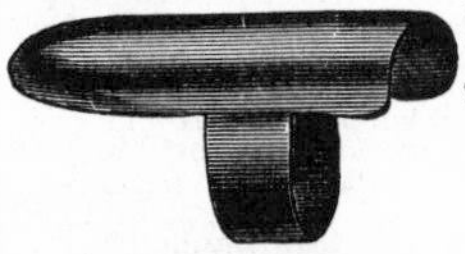

25846 Banjo Thimbles of German silver. Price, each 5c, per dozen, 50c. Weight, each, 1 ounce.

Banjo Cases.

25847 Pasteboard, marbled; weight, boxed, 12 pounds. Each $0.45

25849 Wood, black, varnished, flannel lined, with lock, handle and hooks, for 11 inch banjo; weight, boxed, 17 lbs 2.00

25851 Brown Canvas, leather bound, with opening in end for 9, 11 or 12 inch banjo; weight, 6 lbs 1.75

25852 Banjo Case, made of solid leather, flannel lined, hand sewed, fine quality, with opening at end for 11 inch banjo; weight, 7 lbs. Each 4.50

Banjo Bags.

25854 Green Felt, for 9, 10 or 11 inch banjo; weight, 7 ounces $0.90

25855 Gossamer Rubber, for 9, 10 or 11 inch banjo; weight, 9 ounces 1.35

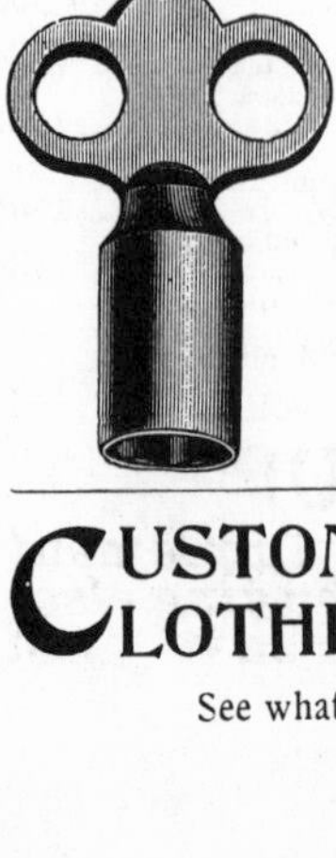

25857 Banjo Wrenches for Brackets, etc., brass. Each. 10c.

25858 Banjo Wrenches, nickel plated. Weight, 2 ounces. Each $0.20

Zithers.

(Weight, boxed, 12 lbs.)

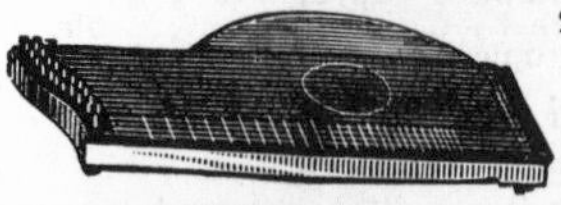

25860-61

25860 Imitation rosewood, full strung, plain head, neatly inlaid, good quality and finish, in paper box $3.75

25861 Rosewood, full strung, neatly inlaid, plain head, finely finished, in paper box $6.50

25863 Rosewood, polished, inlaid sound holes and edges, with patent head, in pasteboard case. Each 10.00

Zither Rings.

25865 German Silver, plain, each .... .03

25866 Horn, plain, each .... .05

Zither Strings.

25868 Steel and brass for finger board. Each....$0.05

25869 Accompaniment and bass, wound on steel wire. Each .... .07

25870 Full set, wound on steel wire, weight, per set, 6 ounces 1.75

NOTE.—When ordering strings for zither be sure and give number and letter of string wanted.

Zither Cases.

(Weight, boxed, 10 lbs.)

25873 Wood, black varnished, flannel lined, with lock, handle and hooks. Each $2.00

25874 Wood, black varnished, velvet lined, with lock, handle and spring clasp 6.50

Zither Tuning Pins.

25875 Steel blued, per dozen.. .... $0.20

25876 Nickel plated, per dozen .... .30

Weight, per dozen, 4 ounces.

Columbia Zither.

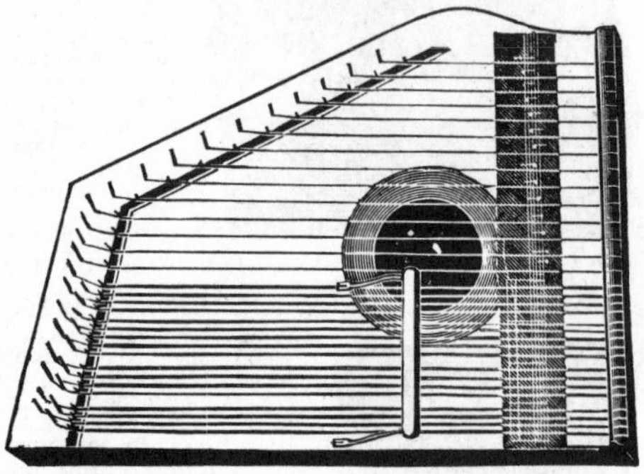

25878 Columbia Zither, is a new musical instrument similar in style and has the same quality of tone as the ordinary Zither, but by a peculiar system of tuning and, as it requires no fingering, it is in other words a *simplified Zither*. The bass strings are arranged in groups of four, which produce the necessary chords (played with left hand), and the air is played with right hand on the seventeen treble strings. Directly underneath the strings is a white celluloid scale, giving the letter of each string; also a section of the staff showing the position of different notes. It has in all 34 strings, and is easily learned. Full instructions accompany each; also a collection of good music arranged by letters and figures, so you can play without any knowledge of reading music. They are made in imitation of rosewood, finely finished Size, 17¼x14 inches. Price, including wrench and picks. Each .... $4.50 Weight, boxed, 10 lbs.

Dulcimers.

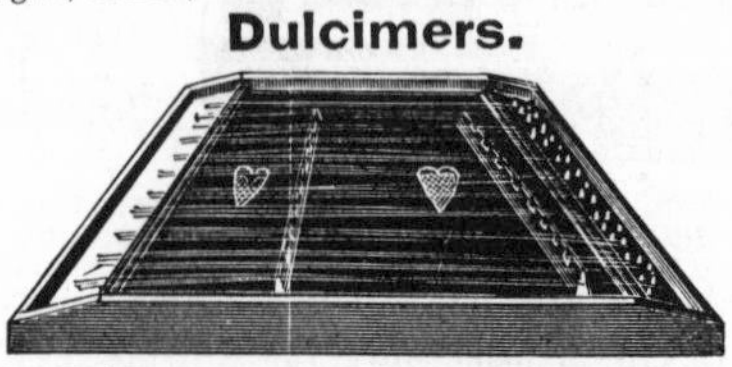

25879 Dulcimers, American made, imitation rosewood, neatly decorated body, finely finished, chromatic, can be perfectly tuned in all keys; in short, it is the most complete and carefully made instrument of the kind produced. Price, each $16.00

25880 Dulcimer Beaters, flexible handles, felt covered heads. Per pair .... .35 Weight, 4 ounces.

Dulcimer or Zither Wire.

25881 English steel, best quality, in ¼ pound coils, per lb $1.20

25882 Brass, best quality, on ½ lb. spool, per lb.. 1.00

25884 English steel on spools, 2 yards each, per dozen spools .... .45 Weight, per dozen spools, 5 ounces.

25885 Brass on spools, 2 yards each, per dozen spools .... .40 Weight, per dozen spools, 5 ounces.

Dulcimer Tuning Pins.

25887 Steel blued, with square or oblong heads. Per dozen $0.12
Weight, per dozen, 6 ounces.

Amateur Violin Outfit.

Each one with Instructor free.

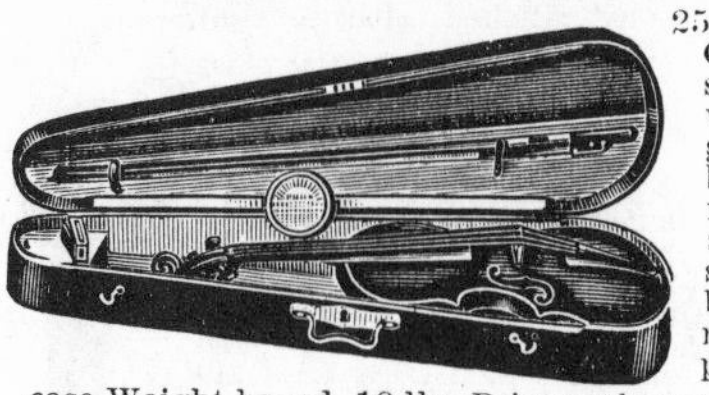

25891 Violin Outfit consisting of violin of good quality bow, box of resin, set of strings, instruction book, all in marbled pasteboard case. Weight, boxed, 10 lbs. Price, each, complete. $2.00

25892 Violin Outfit, consisting of full-sized violin, good model, bow, box of resin, set of strings, instruction book, in pasteboard case. Price, complete 2.80

25893 Violin Outfit, with better violin, bow and wood case, with handle and hooks, also strings, etc. Weight, boxed, 20 pounds. Price, each..... 4.25

25894 Violin Outfit with finely polished violin. good model and tone, bow, strings, etc., in wood case, with lock, handle and hooks. Price, complete.................................. 5.40

25895 Violin Outfit, with violin of extra fine quality, handsome model, ebony trimmings, well made, polished, smooth tone, each in full lined wood case, with patent spring clasps and lock, bow, extra set strings, etc. Weight, boxed, 20 lbs. Price, each, complete.... 9.40

Violins Alone.

(Weight, boxed, 10 pounds.)

We import our entire line of violins, comprising a large collection, and instead of putting on fabulous prices, which is the case with music dealers generally, we sell all grades on reasonable margins. We have recently added the famous "Lowendall" line, and are now in a position to supply every want from the beginner to the artist. We guarantee satisfaction in every case, and any violin purchased from us may, if unsatisfactory, be returned after a trial of five days and money will be refunded, providing the transportation charges are paid by the purchaser. Instruction book, bow and paper case free with each violin.

25900 Italian, dark red color, good model and finish. Each.......................................$3.75

25901 Light red, shaded edges, polished, excellent model, well made. Each..................... 4.45

25902 Fancy Violin, dark brown color, handsomely inlaid with pearl, fine model, highly polished. Each..................................... 4.70

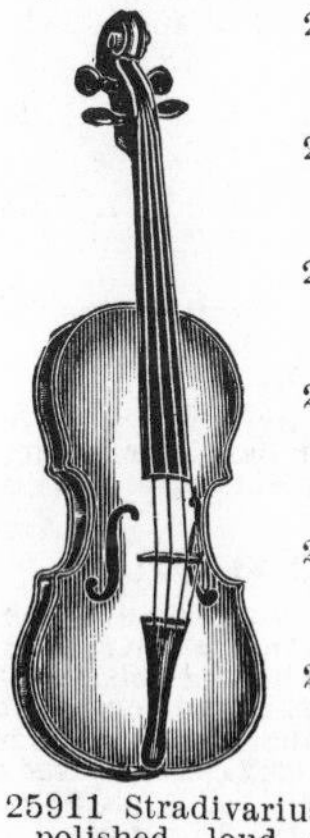

25905 Stainer Model, swelled back and top, red shaded, highly polished ebony trimmings, good tone. Each.............................$5.65

25906 Stradivarius Model, fine imitation of old amber varnish, loud, heavy tone, full ebony trimmed. Each..................................$6.50

25907 Stradivarius Model, dark red, shaded, highly polished, birdseye maple back, full ebony trimmed, good tone. Each............$7.50

25908 Fancy Violin, dark brown, polished, elaborately inlaid back with pearl and colored wood; cord rim around edges, inlaid tail piece. Each $7.75

25909 Maggini Model, fine quality, red shaded, double purfling around edges, dull finish, ebony trimmings. Each $8.45

25910 Stradivarius Model, finely carved scroll, highly polished, ebony trimmings, excellent tone. Each $9.90

25911 Stradivarius Model, light red color, highly polished, loud, clear tone, ebony trimmings. Each...11.75

25912 Stradivarius Model, American style, light red color, amber varnish, ebony trimmings. This is a new instrument and possesses a fine tone. Each 14.10

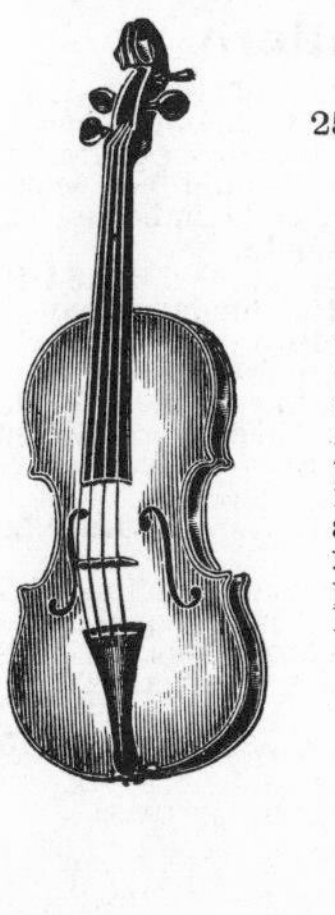

25914 Our Artist's Violin, made by Henry Eichheimer, Berlin. This is a new line of violins and on account of their exceptionally fine qualities are bound to become famous. They are of the popular rich red color, oil varnish, and polished, beautiful model (rather favoring Stradivarius), small neck, fine scroll, polished ebony trimmings and possess a tone which in *volume* and *purity* is seldom equaled in a new instrument. We guarantee *perfect* satisfaction and will refund money in any case if not perfectly satisfactory. Each...........................$23.50

Lowendall Violins.

This famous line of violins is so well and favorably known that it hardly seems necessary to make any comments. They are manufactured by the celebrated L. Lowendall, of Berlin, who is considered to be one of the best violin makers in Europe. Every instrument produced is from carefully selected materials and is intended for use by artists, which is a guarantee that they are absolutely perfect. We handle *three best* grades, import them ourselves, and sell them at prices within reach of all who wish a really first-class violin. We allow a trial of five days after receipt and if not satisfactory can be returned at our expense and we will refund money. Good bow and wood case with each free.

25917 LOWENDALL'S CONSERVATORY Violin; dark red color, fine model, full ebony trimmings, finely finished, excellent tone. Each......... $18.80

25918 LOWENDALL'S IMPERIAL violin; light red, amber oil varnish, perfect model, full ebony trimmings, rich tone, polished. A superb instrument for orchestra leader. Each........ 37.60

25919 LOWENDALL'S ARTIST'S Violin; light red color, polished, amber oil varnish, finely finished, ebony trimmings. A perfect violin in every respect. As its name implies, is *intended for the soloist*. Each 47.00

N. B.—When testing a violin be sure to tune it to "concert pitch." This can be done by using a tuning pipe or fork. You will then get full strength and volume of the tone. Violins are often condemned simply because they are tuned too low.

Boys' Violins.

(Weight, boxed, 8 pounds.)

Instruction Book and Bow free. No case.

We can furnish Boys' Violins in either half or three-quarter sizes at same price. Each.

25922 Good model, light red shaded, imitation ebony finger board..................................$2.00

25923 Dark brown color, perfect model, well made, imitation ebony trimmings................ 3.75

25924 Conservatory, fine model, amber color flamed back, ebony trimmings, good tone........ 5.60

Violas or Tenor Violins.

Prices quoted include bow and instruction book. Each

25925 Viola, light reddish color, inlaid edges, good model and finish..............................$4.70

25926 Viola, medium brown color, good model, well finished, fancy tail piece.................... 6.50

25927 Viola, Guarnerius or Stradivarius model, reddish brown color, polished, finely finished, full ebony trimmings 13.85

Violin Bows.

(Weight, packed, 10 ounces.) Each.

25931 Maple, red painted ebony, frog, bone slide and button.....................................$0.38

25932 Maple, imitation snakewood, ebony frog, pearl slide, German silver button .... .55

25933 Redwood, ebony frog, pearl inlaid dot, pearl slide, German silver button................. .85

25934 Brazil wood, ebony frog, pearl slide and eye, full German silver lined, German silver button 1.10

25936 "Remenyi," Brazil wood, dark color, ebony frog, double pearl eye, pearl slide, German silver lining and button.................................. 1.65

25937 Pernambuco wood, *extra wide*, ebony frog, pearl inlaid eye, pearl slide, German silver lining and button.. 1.85

25938 Genuine snakewood, carved ivory frog. German silver lined, fine hair..................... 2.35

25940 "Imperial" genuine Pernambuco wood, fine ebony frog, silver heart in side, full lined, extra quality hair.. 3.30

25942 "Tourte" model for artist, genuine Pernambuco wood, octagon, ebony frog, full German silver lined, finely finished, heavy hair.............. 4.20

Violin Bow Frogs with Screws.

25945 Ebony with German silver button and slide $0.22

25947 Ebony, pearl eye inlaid in slides, full German silver lined, German silver button, pearl slide.. .38

Ocarinas.

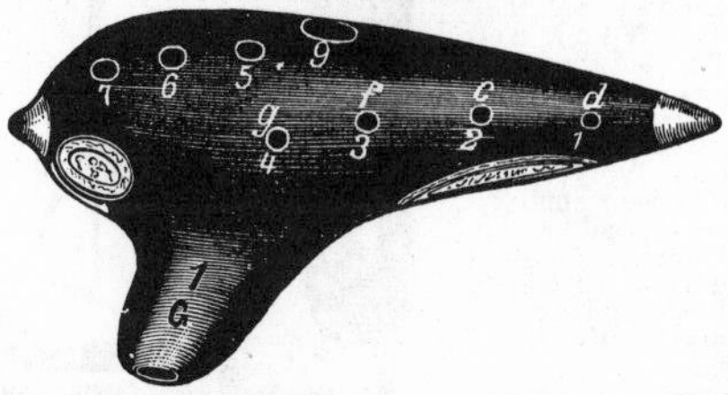

	Each.		Each.
25951 Key of C, Sop.	$0.18	25961 Key of Ab, Alto	$0.50
25952 Key of Bb, Sop.	.20	25962 Key of G, Alto.	.60
25953 Key of G, Sop.	.22	25963 Key of F, Alto.	.60
25954 Key of F, Sop.	.27	25964 Key of E, Alto.	.75
25955 Key of E, Sop.	.32	25965 Key of Eb, Alto.	.85
25956 Key of Eb, Alto	.32	25966 Key of D, Bass.	1.25
25957 Key of D, Alto	.32	25967 Key of C, Bass.	1.45
25958 Key of C, Alto.	.36	25968 Key of B, Bass.	1.55
25959 Key of Bb, Alto.	.40	25969 Key of A, Bass.	1.80
25960 Key of A, Alto.	.45	25970 Key of G, Bass.	2.15

NOTE.—When ordering quartet or sextet sets, be sure to have all the same key.

Weight of Ocarinas, sopranos, 4 oz.; altos, 14 oz.; bass, 26 oz.; contra-bass, 40 oz.

NEXT CATALOGUE No. 58 READY SEPTEMBER 1ST.

Kazoos.

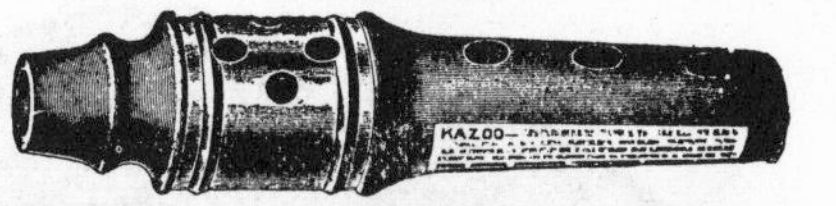

25975 Kazoos, the great musical wonder, plays any tune and anyone can play it; imitates fowls, animals, bagpipes, etc. Very popular with singing clubs and affords a great variety of amusement for one or a crowd. Directions with each. Price, each....................................$0.08
Per dozen .... .85
Postage, 2c each.

Parlor Bells.

25980 Twelve lettered blue steel bars fastened on finely gilded wood frame, key of C, perfectly tuned to concert pitch. Produces a fine effect when played with piano, organ or guitar, or as solo instrument. Price, in pasteboard box, including two beaters.....................................$1.35
Weight, 51 ounces.

Orchestra Bells.

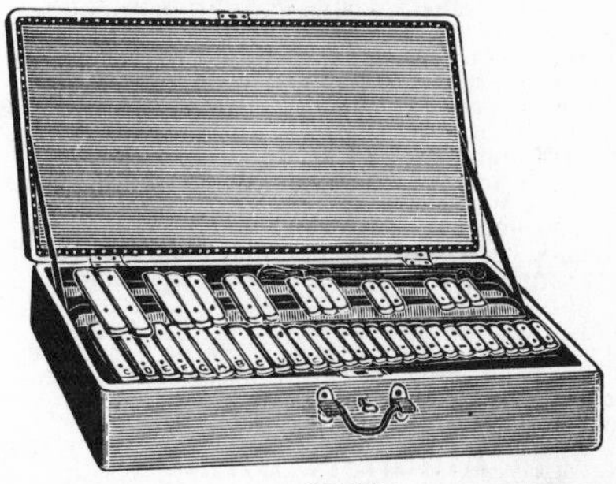

25982

These instruments are of extra fine quality and are intended for *professionals* and may be used in orchestra or for solo purposes with excellent effect. They are made with heavy polished plates of best quality steel and tuned to perfect concert pitch; mounted in strongly made, highly finished walnut case with lock and handle for carrying.

25982 Orchestra Bells, 2 octaves, chromatic scale, 25 notes. Price, complete..................$6.50
Weight, boxed, 20 pounds.

25983 Orchestra Bells, 3 octaves, chromatic scale, 37 notes. Price, complete.................. 9.50
Weight, boxed, 25 pounds.

Musical Sleigh Bells.

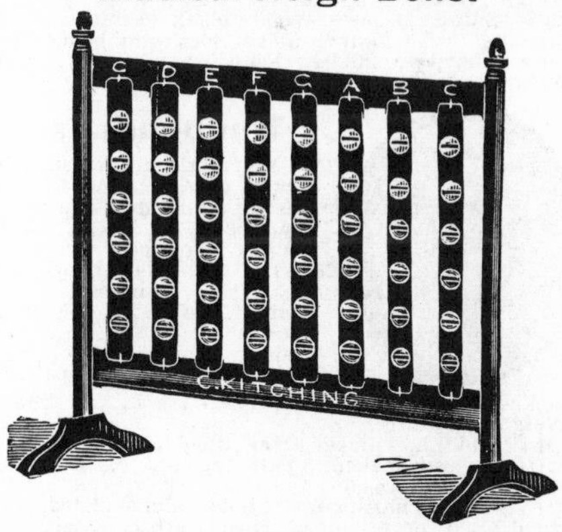

25984

25984 Musical Sleigh Bells. The above cut represents the latest in musical novelties and we believe it will prove a good seller. It consists of eight straps with six sleigh bells tuned in unison on each strap. The different sets are tuned as follows: c, d, e, f, g, a, b, c, and are attached to neatly finished wood frame; size, about 24x30 inches. Over each strap its proper letter is stamped. We thus have one full octave tuned in Bb, and all styles of music can be played with the most pleasing effect and with very little practice. They are "knocked down" and packed in pasteboard box; easily put together. Weight, 40 ounces. Per set $6.25

The Autoharp.

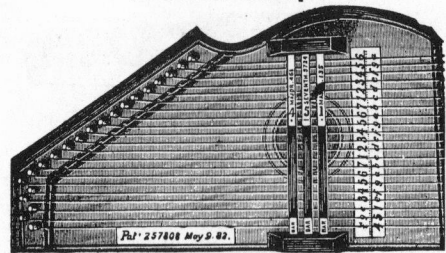

25985

(A Practical and Ingenious Musical Novelty.)

25985 Consists of a zither with an attachment for producing the chords used in accompanying music for singing or solo playing. The attachment consists of three or more bars, which are placed across the string in the center of the instrument, and are made with dampers, which deaden all the strings not used in the chord. It will therefore be seen that it is only necessary to draw the ring over every string on the instrument in order to produce a perfect chord when either of the bars are lowered. It has 18 treble strings and three bass strings, making 21 in all. Six pieces of music, a ring and full instructions are furnished with each instrument. Price, each.$2.75
Weight, 53 ounces.

25988 Autoharp No. 2¾, has 23 strings, 5 bars, producing 5 chords. Each........................ 3.60
Weight, 62 ounces.

25989 Autoharp No. 3, has 28 strings, 4 bars with shifters, producing 9 chords. Each.............. 8.60
Weight, 6 pounds.

25990 Autoharp No. 5, "Concert," top and sides rosewood veneered, edges inlaid, highly polished, has 28 strings, 5 bars with shifters, producing 13 chords. Each.... ......13.50
Weight, 6¼ pounds.

25992 Autoharp No. 6, same style as No. 5, has 32 strings, 6 bars with shifters, producing 16 chords. Each........................18.50
Weight, 8½ pounds.

Autoharp Strings.

We do not sell less than full set

25995   Full set for No. 25985............$0.40
25997   Full set for No. 25988........... .... .50
25998   Full set for No. 25989-90................ .60
25999   Full set for No. 25992............... ..... .65

Autoharp Picks.

26005   Horn, good quality. Each.............. $0.06
26006   Celluloid, good quality. Each .... .10

Autoharp Cases.

26008   Autoharp Cases, wood, black varnished, half lined with flannel, handle, hooks and lock for Nos. 25985 to 25990 inclusive. Each...$1.40
Weight, boxed, 8 pounds.

26009   Autoharp Cases, Wood, black varnished, full lined with flannel, nickel lock and hooks for autoharp No. 25992. Each.................. 2.00
Weight, boxed, 10 pounds.

Tambourines.

26010   8-inch, plain maple rim, tacked sheepskin head, suitable for drills, etc. Each.$0.35
Per dozen 3.75
Weight, 12 ounces.

26011   10-inch, plain maple rim, tacked sheepskin head.
Each...................... $0 40
Per dozen 4.30
Weight, 15 ounces.

26013   10-inch, fancy painted tacked calfskin head............................$0.70
Weight, 16 ounces.

26014   10-inch, nickel rim, lined with wood, calfskin head, tacked. 3 pair jingles............. .90
Weight, 16 ounces.

26015   10-inch, narrow metal hoop, nickel plated, wood lined, professional, tacked calfskin head, 6 set jingles. Each........................... 1.75
Weight, 24 ounces.

26017   Tambourine, Salvation Army, 11-inch maple hoop, calfskin head, 19 sets brass jingles, band fastenings.................................. 1 50
Weight, 24 ounces.

26018   Tambourine, Salvation Army, 11-inch, nickel hoop, wood lined, 19 sets of brass jingles, metal band fastenings................. • 2.00
Weight, 24 ounces.

We Make Errors

So does everyone. Our wish is to be given the opportunity to make good any mistakes which we may make. Be sure to tell us if anything goes wrong.

Bones.

Per set.
26025   Bones, rosewood, large, set of four........$0.20
Weight, 6 ounces.
26026   Bones, rosewood, small, set of four...... .15
Weight, 5 ounces.
26027   Bones, ebony, large, set of four .... .35
Weight, 7 ounces.
26028   Bones, ebony, small, set of four .... .25
Weight, 6 ounces.
26029   Bones, walnut, patent clappers, set of two .10
Weight, 3 ounces.

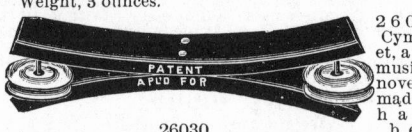

26030, Cymbalet, a new musical novelty made of hard bent wood, with two brass jingles at each end loosely attached to a steel rod, gives the same effect as the tambourine and is much easier to handle. Each.....$0.05
Per dozen .... .50
Weight, 4 ounces.

Triangles.

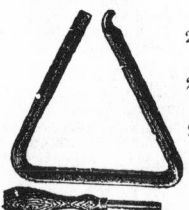

26033   6-inch, polished steel, with hammer. Each....$0.35
Weight, 9 ounces.
26034   7-inch, polished steel, with hammer. Each....$0.50
Weight, 12 ounces.
26035   8-inch, polished steel, with hammer. Weight, 15 oz.
Each................. $0.75

Piano Stools.

26038   Imitation Rosewood hardwood pedestal, iron feet, hair cloth, red or green reps. Retail price, $2.50 to $3.00. Our price............. ..$1 25
Weight, boxed, 25 lbs.

26040   Same, with plush seat, maroon or crimson.
Retail price $6.00
Our price............. 2.75
Weight, boxed, 25 lbs.

26042   Imitation Rosewood, framed, oblong seat, 13x16½ inches, handsome wood pedestal, maroon or crimson silk plush, plain or embossed. Retail price.... ....$7.20
Our price 3.50
Weight, boxed, 30 lbs.

26038

Violin Tail Pieces and Music Stands.

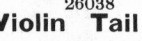

26050 Tail pieces, imitation ebony, plain, Each $0.05
26051 Tail Pieces, ebony, plain, Each $0.10
26052   Tail pieces, inlaid, similar to cut. Each....$0.28
26053   Violin Tail Pieces, made of Celluloid, finely carved, imitation ivory, or tortoise shell; very popular, Each..... $0.50
26054   Tail Pieces, very fine ebony, inlaid, similar to cut $0.70
Weight of tail pieces, 2 ounces.
26056   The "Ideal" Folding Music Stands, made of STEEL, japanned, light and convenient for carrying. Each.....$0.60 Per dozen.... ...$6.50
26058   "Ideal" Music Stands, same as above, nickel plated. Each..$1.25 Per dozen........ 13.50
Weight, 43 ounces.

26054   26056-58

Music Stand Cases.

26059   Music Stand Case, made of heavy leather, sole leather ends, hand sewed. Each. $0.90
Weight, 18 ounces.

Violin End Pins.

Weight, 1 ounce.
               Each.
26065   End Pins, maple, No. 1.......$0.03
26066   End Pins, ebony, No. 3......... .05
26067   Violin End Pins, made of ebony, polished, with "A" tuning pipe in end.................. .12

Violin Pegs.

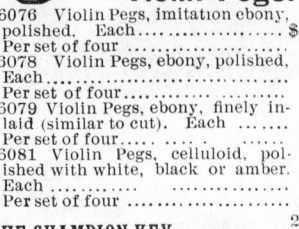

26076   Violin Pegs, imitation ebony, polished. Each.................. $0.04
Per set of four .... .12
26078   Violin Pegs, ebony, polished, Each.................... .06
Per set of four.............. .20
26079   Violin Pegs, ebony, finely inlaid (similar to cut). Each..... .20
Per set of four............. .75
26081   Violin Pegs, celluloid, polished with white, black or amber.
Each .... .08
Per set of four .... .25

THE CHAMPION KEY

Patented May 8th, 1888.

26082   The Champion Patent Violin Pegs, made of metal, nickel plated, with polished celluloid thumb piece; the best peg made; will not slip.

Each............. $0.25   Per set of four...... $0.80

Jew's Harp.

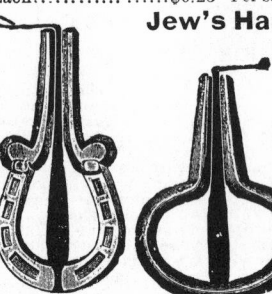

26083   English Harp, club pattern. Each.... $0.10
Weight, 2 oz.

26083   26085 to 26089
26085   Jew's Harp, common style, good quality.
Each...$0.05
Weight, 2, ounces.
26086   Jew's Harp, white metal frame, best quality, medium size.
Each .... .12
Weight, 2 ounces.
26087   Jew's Harp, large size.
Each .... .20
Weight, 3 ounces.
26088   Jew's Harp, extra large size.
Each .... .25
Weight, 3 ounces.
26089   Jew's Harp, Jumbo, lacquered.
Each .... .40
Weight, 4 ounces.

Drums.

We quote below two of the latest improved styles of snare drums. The "Prussian" pattern has squareheaded metal rods for holding the hoops in place. The "Regulation" pattern has cords and hooks.

Prussian Pattern Snare Drum.

26095   Brass Shell, 16 inches in diameter, 6 inches high, 8 rods, white metal plated hooks and trimmings, 8 rawhide snares, 2 calfskin heads. Each..............$5.00
Weight, 16 pounds.

26096   Nickel plated Shell, 16 inches in diamter, 6 inches high, 8 rods, white metal plated hooks and trimmings, 8 raw hide snares, 2 calfskin heads.
Weight, 16 lbs. Price, each.............. ....$6.00

29065-96

Regulation Pattern.

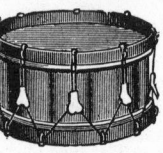

26097   Rosewood Shell (Army pattern), 16 inches in diameter, 12 inches high, best Italian hemp cord, improved snare strainer, 2 calfskin heads, tinned cord hooks.
Each............. ....$4.40
Weight, 16 pounds, boxed.

26099   Birdseye Maple Shell, 16 inches in diameter, 9½ inches high, fine varnish finish, best Italian hemp cord, tinned snare strainers, 2 calfskin heads.
Each $5.50
Weight, 14 pounds.

26101
26101   Bird'seye Maple Shell, 16 inches in diameter, 6 inches high, fine varnish finish, best quality Italian hemp cord, tinned cord hooks, 12 braces, 8 snares, new pattern snare strainers, 2 calfskin heads.
Each 5.75
Weight, 13 pounds.

Youth's Snare Drums.

26103 Brass Shell, regulation pattern, 14 inches in diameter, 7 inches high, red hoops, 6 snare with strainer, 1 calfskin and 1 sheepskin head. 2 sticks. Each...........................$3.00
Weight, 10 lbs.

26104 Brass Shell, Prussian pattern, 14 inches in diameter, 4½ inches high, 6 rods, red hoops, 6 snares with snare strainers, 1 calfskin and 1 sheepskin head, 2 sticks. Each......   3.50
Weight, 11 pounds.

Bass Drums.

26106 Regulation Pattern, bird's-eye maple shell, 24 inches in diameter, 12 inches high, 13 braces, best quality Italian hemp cord, improved cord hooks, 1 calfskin and 1 sheepskin head, 1 stick. Each.................................$10.50
Weight, 50 lbs.

26107 Regulation Pattern bird's-eye maple shell, 30 inches in diameter, 12 inches high, 14 braces best quality Italian hemp cord, improved cord hooks. 2 calfskin heads, 1 stick. Each. 13.50
Weight, 55 pounds.

Cymbals.
(TURKISH.)

26110 Composition Metal, 8 inch, with leather handles. Weight, 35 ounces.....................$4.50
26111 Composition Metal, 9 inch, with leather handles. Weight, 45 ounces.....................   5.25
26112 Composition Metal, 10 inch, with leather handles. Weight, 50 ounces.....................   6.25
(GERMAN.)
26114 Brass, 12 inch, leather handles............   2.50
Weight, 45 ounces.
26115 Brass, 13 inch, leather handles............   3.25
Weight, 50 ounces.

Calfskin Head for Drums, Banjos and Tambourines.

No.		Each
26120	12 inch Head for 10 inch shell............	$0.22
26121	13 inch Head for 11 inch shell............	.30
26122	14 inch Head for 11½ inch shell...........	.35
26123	15 inch head for 12 inch shell............	.40
26124	16 inch head for 13 inch shell............	.50
26125	17 inch Head for 14 inch shell............	.60
26126	18 inch Head for 15 inch shell............	.70
26127	19 inch Head for 16 inch shell............	.80
26128	20 inch Head for 17 inch shell............	.90
26129	22 inch Head for 19 inch shell............	1.00
26130	28 inch Head for 24 inch Bass Drum.......	1.50
26131	30 inch Head for 26 inch Bass Drum.......	1.80
26132	32 inch Head for 28 inch Bass Drum.....	2.00
26133	34 inch Head for 30 inch Bass Drum.....	2.25
26134	36 inch Head for 32 inch Bass Drum.....	2.75
26135	38 inch Head for 34 inch Bass Drum.....	3.00
26136	40 inch Head for 36 inch Bass Drum.....	3.50
26137	42 inch Head for 38 inch Bass Drum.....	4.00

Weight of calfskin drum heads: 10 to 15 inches, 4 ounces; 15 to 20 inches, 5 ounces; 20 to 28 inches, 9 ounces; 30 to 36 inches 12 ounces; 38 to 40 inches, 16 ounces.

Snare Drum Sticks.
Per pair.

26140 Rosewood, polished, weight 6 ounces.....$0.25
26142 Ebony, polished, weight 8 ounces..........   .50
26143 Ebony, with nickel plated ferrules, highly polished, weight 9 ounces......................   1.00
26145 Snakewood, highly polished, weight 9 oz..   1.20
26146 Snakewood, with nickel plated ferrules, highly polished, weight 9 ounces...............   2.00

Bass Drum Sticks.

26148 Hickory Handle; with chamois skin head. Each...$0.40
Weight, 10 ounces.

Snare Drum Slings.

26150 Red Webbing, small, for boy's drum, with snap. Each.....................................$0.25
Weight, 3 ounces.
26151 White or Striped Webbing, improved pattern, best quality with snap. Each.............   .40
Weight, 3 ounces.

Bass Drum Slings.

26152 White or Striped Webbing, improved pattern, best quality, with snap. Each...........$0.60
Weight, 4 ounces.
26153 Leather, fine quality Each................   .80
Weight, 6 ounces.

Any musical instrument made furnished at lowest rates. Also parts of all kinds of musical instruments furnished if desired.

Music Folios.
For Holding Sheet Music.

26156 Music Folio, imitation leather, spring back, handsomely embossed gilt roses on front (See cut). Each................$0.60
Weight, 26 ounces.

Music Folios—Continued.

26158 Music Folio, cloth sides, fine quality, spring back, imitation water color panel on front, surrounded with embossed gilt flowers.
Price, each.........$1.00
Weight, 26 ounces.

26158

Music Wrappers.

26160 Solid Leather Music Rolls, similar in style to No. 26161; finely finished, hand stitched in either russet, lemon or orange color.
Each...................$0.75
Weight, 9 ounces.
26161 Music Roll, made of the finest embossed leather; colors, black russet or orange.
Each...................$1.00
Weight, 8 ounces.

26161   26162

26162 Music Wrapper, made of celluloid, imitation ivory, finely embossed, lined with silk, leather strap. Each...........................$1.15
Weight, 12 ounces.

Tuning Forks.
Weight, 2 ounces.

26165 Philharmonic A............................$0.09
26166 Philharmonic C............................   .09
26167 Tuning Forks, heavy blued steel, finely finished, warranted the new American pitch; each in case. Key of A. Price, each.........   .32
26169 Tuning Fork, same quality as 26167, Key of C. Each...   .32

Tuning Pipes.

26172 Set of two, A and C, combined weight, 2 oz..$0.12
26173 E, A, D and G, combined, for tuning violin or mandolin (like cut)... $0.30
Weight, 3 ounces.
26175 Set of 5, B, G, E. A and E combined, for tuning banjo. Weight, 3 ounces.......$0.40
26176 Set of 6, E, G, B, D, A. and E combined, for tuning guitar. Weight 3 ounces.................$0.50

26173

NOTE.—New beginners on violin, mandolin, banjo or guitar will find above sets very convenient for tuning instruments. They are made of German silver, and tuned to a standard concert pitch.

Batons.

For the use of singing teachers, band masters. etc.

26180 Baton made of rosewood, polished, tapering; length, 16 inches...........................$0.25
26181 Baton made of ebony, tapering, French polished; length, 16 inches........................   .40
26182 Baton made of ebony, highly polished, inlaid ivory handle (see cut), length, 16 inches. Each...   4.00

Metronomes.

This instrument consists of a short pendulum with sliding weight; is operated by clockwork, and is fixed to measure or to beat "time" in music. They are very useful for beginners in learning to read music.
26183 Metronome, made of mahogany, Maelzel system, best French make, without bell.
Each...$2.50
26184 Metronome, same as No. 26183, with bell.
Each...........................$3.50

26186 Ruling Pens, with five lines for drawing staff; weight, 1 ounce.........................$0.10
26187 Steel Pens, with three points, for writing music; weight, per dozen, 1 ounce...............   .20

Banjo Pegs.
Weight, per set, 3 ounces.

26201 Imitation Ebony, hollow shape, polished, with pearl dot in hand.
Each.........................$0.03
26202 Side Peg to match No. 26201.
Each......................   .03
26204 Ebony, hollow shaped, polished, with pearl dot in hand. Each......   .06
26205 Side Peg to match No. 26204, Each......................   .06
26207 Celluloid, white or imitation amber, hollow shape, polished.
Each......................   .08
26208 Side Peg to match No. 26207. Each......................   .08
26209 Greek Cross, polished (see cut). Each....   .12
26210 Side Peg to match No. 26209. Each   .12

Champion Patent Banjo Pegs.

26212 Made of metal, nickel plated with polished celluloid thumb pieces, turns easily, but will not slip.
Each...................$0.25
Per set of 5.........   1.00

THE CHAMPION KEY
Pat'd May 8th, 1888

Banjo Brackets   Side Peg.
Per dozen.
Weight, per dozen, 9 ounces.

26215 Spread Eagle Pattern, brass, with bolt and nut. $0.60
26216 "Leaf" Pattern, brass, with bolt and nut......................................   .70
26217 Leaf pattern, nickel plated, with bolt and nut...................   1.00
26218 Globe Pattern, brass turned and polished, with bolt and new pattern safety nut (see cut)......................   .90
26219 Globe Pattern, nickel plated, turned and polished, with bolt and new pattern safety nut...............   1.25

26218

Banjo Tail Pieces.

26221 Ebony, common, good model and finish.
Each.........................$0.08
Weight, 1 ounce.
26223 Nickel plated, new model, strings have double purchase.
Each.........................$0.25
Weight, 3 ounces.
26224 Imitation Ivory, carved. Weight, 1 ounce.
Each.........................$0.35
26226 Wood's Patent Adjustable Banjo Tail Piece, made of a peculiar metal, highly polished, strings are easily and quickly attached, besides it will not break them. Price, each, including bolt....$0.40
Weight, 2 ounces.

26226

Banjo Bridges.

26228 Banjo Bridges, common. Each..........$0.03
26229 Banjo Bridges, better, made of ebony.....   .05
Weight, 1 oz.

Violoncello Bridges.

26232 Maple, good quality, with 2 scrolls.
Each.........................$0.18
26233 Maple, fine quality, with 3 scrolls.
Each...........................   .27
Weight each, 3 oz.

Violoncello Tail Pieces.

26236 Maple, imitation ebony finish, pearl dot inlaid on top. Each.............................$0.28
26237 Ebony, plain, best model and finish.
Each...........................   .70
Weight, each, 4 oz.

Violoncello Bows.

26240 Redwood, plain ebony frog, bone button, good quality. Each.........................$0.70
Weight, 8 oz.
26241 Redwood, ebony frog, pearl eye, German silver button. Each 1.00
Weight, 10 oz.
26242 Brazil Wood, ebony frog, double pearl eye, full German silver lined, pearl slide, German silver button. Each.......................   1.65
Weight, 10 oz.
26244 Pernambuco Wood, ebony frog, double pearl eye, full German silver lined, German silver button. Each 2.35
Weight, 10 oz.

Violoncello Bows Frog With Screws.

26247 Ebony, pearl dot inlaid in sides, pearl slide, bone button. Each....................$0.25
26248 Ebony, pearl dot inlaid in sides, German silver lined, pearl slide, German silver button. Each...   .45
Weight, 2 oz.

Bow Hair.

26255 Violin Bow Hair, white, good quality.
Per bunch.............................$0.15
26255½ Violin Bow Hair, white, finest quality.
For artists' use. Per bunch............ .20
26256 Violoncello Bow Hair, best quality, white.
Per bunch........................ .20
26257 Double Bass Bow Hair, best quality, black.
Per bunch........... .25
26258 Double Bass Bow Hair, best quality, white.
Per bunch......... .... .30
Weight, per bunch, 1 oz.

Resin.

26261 Resin in pasteboard box. Weight, 2 oz.
Per box.............................$0.03
26262 Resin, better quality, on metal spools;
weight, 3 oz. Per box.... 07
26263 Double Bass Resin, good quality, in oblong
pasteboard boxes. Per box................ .10
26264 Double Bass Resin, Koehler's Improved,
in round boxes. Per box................. .30

Violin Chin Rest.

26265 Violin Chin
Rests; ebony, dou-
ble acting screw
fastenings; good
quality.
Each.........$0.30
Weight, 6 ounces.

26266 Violin Chin
Rests, ebony; with
two nickel plated
double acting
screw fastenings
(see cut).
Each.........$0.50
Weight, 5 ounces.

26266
26267 Violin Chin Rest and Shoulder Rest combined (Becker's patent), made of celluloid and
nickel. This is a new and useful invention, as
it holds the violin in proper position for playing. Weight, 6 ounces. Each................. $1.15

Violin Finger Boards.

26268 Violin Finger Boards; ebony, polished;
weight, 6 ounces. Each...................... 0.25
26269 Violin Finger Boards; ebony, artists' model, superfine quality, French polished, for fine
violins. Each........ .... $0.50
Weight, 8 ounces.

Violin Nuts and Saddles.

26270 Violin Nut, ebony, for upper end of finger
board. Each...........................$0.04
26271 Violin Saddles, ebony, for supporting tail
piece string. Each............................. .04

Violin Bridges.

26272 Violin Bridges, good. Each.............$0.04
26273 Violin Bridges, better. Each.............. .10
Weight, 1 ounce.

Violin Mutes.

26275 Violin Mute; new model,
made of metal with patent
spring. Each............$0.08
Weight, 1 ounce.

26276 Violin Mute, made of German silver, see cut.
Each....................$0.15

26277 German Silver, with
tuning pipe A, and string
gauge....................$0.30
Weight, each, 1 ounce.

Violin Patent Heads.

26279 Violin Patent Head, brass,
engraved on sides, bone buttons.
Per set.................$0.35
26280 Violin Patent Head, nickel
plated, engraved on sides, good
quality.
Per set $0.50
Weight, each, 4 ounces.

Violin Neck.

26281 Violin Necks, maple, unfinished, carved
scroll. Each...........................$0.20
26282 Violin Necks, maple, unfinished, fine
quality, finely carved scroll. Each.............. 0.70
26283 Violin Necks, curly maple, unfinished,
best quality, finely carved scroll. Each......... 1.15
Weight, 8 oounce.

Piano Tuning Hammers.

26284
26284 Piano Tuning Hammers. Steel with extension Rosewood handle, three heads; square,
oblong and star. Price, each, complete.........$1.75
Weight, 20 ounces.

Strings.

We wish to caution our trade in buying strings
against being misled by "fancy names and high prices"
quoted by other dealers. We buy all our gut strings
(steel and wound strings are made in this country)
direct from the best European manufacturers, select
only *first quality* and are selling them at "rock bottom"
prices. A trial order will convince you that this statement is correct.
Violin and banjo strings weigh 2 oz. per set, guitar
and violoncello strings, 4 oz. per set.

Violin Strings, Cut.

		Each.	Per doz.
26285	E, best quality German, trans- parent polished, 4 lengths	$0.12	$1.25
26286	E, best quality, transparent rough finish, 4 lengths	.12	1.25
26287	A, best quality, 2½ lengths, pol- ished	.12	1.25
26288	D, best quality, 2½ length, pol- ished	.15	1.60
26289	G, fine quality gut covered with silvered wire, 1 length	.08	.85
26290	Full set of 4	.40	

Violin Strings, Cut, "Campanilla" Brand.

The Campanilla Violin Strings are of extra fine
quality, made from the finest Russian gut and are
recommended particularly for the Artist's use. *There
are none better made.*

		Each.	Per doz.
26291	E, Campanilla extra quality, 4 lengths, polished	$0 16	$1.70
26292	A, Campanilla, 2½ lengths	.16	1.70
26293	D, Campanilla, 2½ lengths	.20	2.15
26294	G, Campanilla, 1 length	.10	1.00
26295	Full Set of 4 Campanilla, 55c.		

Steel Violin Strings.

	Silver plated.	Each.	Per doz.
26298	E, 1 length, best quality	$0.02	$0.20
26299	A, 1 length, best quality	.02	.20
26300	D, 1 length, best quality, cov- ered, silver plated	.06	.65
26301	G, 1 length, best quality, cov- ered, silver plated	.06	.65
26302	Full set, 10c.		
26303	Silk Violin Strings, E, 4 lengths, very fine quality French.	.12	1.25

Banjo Strings, Cut.

		Each.	Per doz.
26305	B or 1st and E or 5th	$0.08	$0.85
26306	G or 2nd	.10	1.00
26307	E or 3d	.10	1.00
26308	A or 4th bass	.08	.85
26309	Full set of 5, best quality, 35 cents.		

Steel Banjo Strings.

		Each.	Per doz.
26312	B or 1st, and E or 5th	$0.02	$0.20
26313	G or 2d	.02	.20
26314	E or 3d	.02	.20
26315	A or 4th	.07	·65
26316	Full set of 5, per set, 12c.		

Guitar Strings.

		Each.	Per doz.
26318	E or 1st, best quality gut	$0.12	$1.25
26319	B or 2d, best quality gut	.12	1.25
26320	G or 3d, best quality gut	.15	1.60
26321	D or 4th, silvered wire on silk	.10	1.00
26322	A or 5th, silvered wire on silk	.10	1.00
26323	E or 6th, silvered wire on silk	.10	1.00
26324	Full set of 6, 60c.		

Steel Guitar Strings.

		Each.	Per doz.
26326	E or 1st silvered steel, best quality	$0.02	$0.20
26327	B or 2d, silvered steel, best quality	.02	.20
26328	G or 3d, compound silvered wire wound on steel and silk	.10	1.00
26329	D or 4th compound	.10	1.00
26330	A or 5th, compound	.10	1.00
26331	E or 6th, compound	.10	1.00
26332	Full set of 6, steel, 38c.		

Mandolin Strings.

		Each.
26334	First String, steel wire, silver plated	$0.04
26335	Second String, steel wire, silver plated	.04
26336	Third String, steel wound with silver wire	.08
26337	Fourth String, steel, wound with silver wire	.08
26338	Full set of 8	.40

Violoncello Strings.

		Each.
26340	A, best Italian	$0.15
26341	D, best Italian	.20
26342	G, best wired gut	.15
26343	C, best wired gut	.20
26344	Full set of 4 strings Per set	.65

Double Bass Strings.

		Each.
26347	G or 1st, genuine Italian, fine quality. Each	$0.60
26348	D or 2d, genuine Italian, fine quality Each	.75
26349	A or 3d, genuine Italian, fine quality Each	.90
26350	A or 3d, wound silvered wire on gut. Each	1.00
26351	E or 4th, wound, silvered wire on gut. Each	1.10
26352	Per set of 3	2.00
26353	Per set of 4	3.00

NOTE.—When ordering sets of double bass strings
state whether you want "A" string plain or wound.

String Gauges.

26354 String Gauges (Albert's)
made of brass, highly polished.
Each...................$0.25
26354½ String Gauge, same as
26354 Nickel plated.
Each...................$0 35
Weight, 1 ounce.

C. F. ALBERT
STRING GAUGE
IN 5THS
PAT. MARCH 2
1886
A G
4 3 2 1

Guitar Finger Boards.

26355 Guitar Finger Boards, ebony, plain, without frets. Each........................$0.60
26356 Guitar Finger Boards, ebony, with frets.
Each................................. 1.00
Weight, 16 ounces.

Guitar Bridges.

		Each.
26358	Ebony, plain, good model and finish	$0.20
26359	Ebony, polished, with pearl inlaid ends	.60
26360	Celluloid, imitation amber	.90

Weight, 4 ounces.

Guitar Pegs.

THE CHAMPION KEY.

Patented May 8th, 1888.

26361 The Cham-
pion Patent
Guitar Pegs (for
peg-head gui-
tars only), made
of metal, nickel
plated, cellu-
loid thumb
piece; *will not
slip.* Each.............................$0.25
Per set of 6 .... 1.25
Weight, each, 1 ounce.

Guitar Patent Heads.

26362—
Brass,
Per set,
70c.
26363—
Nickel
Plated.
Per set,
$0.90.

26362-3   Weight, 6 oz

Guitar Bridge Pins.

(Weight, per set of 5, 1 oz.)

26365 Ebony, polished, with pearl dot in end.
Each...............................$0.02
Per set of 6.................................. .10
26366 Celluloid, imitation ivory, amber or tor-
toise shell. Each.............................. .03
Per set of 6.................................. .15
26367 Ivory, polished, pearl dot in head. Each. .06
Per set of 6.................................. .30

Music Paper.

		Per quire.
26375	10 Staves, superfine royal, 10x15	$0.30
26376	12 Staves, superfine royal, 10x15	.30
26377	14 Staves, superfine royal, 10x15	.30
26378	16 Staves, superfine royal, 10x15	.30

Weight, per quire, 21 ounces.

Blank Music Books.

26382 6 Staves, 40 pages, cloth back, marbled paper covers, oblong; size, 7½x9½ in. Each....$0.15
Weight, 7 oz.
26384 8 Staves, 64 pages, same size and style as No. 26382. Each. .20
Weight, 10 oz.
26385 12 Staves, 84 pages, same size and style as No. 26382. Each. .30
Weight, 14 oz.
26386 10 Staves, 52 pages, cloth back and sides, full gilt; size, 7½x9½ in. Each. .40
Weight, 12 oz.
26387 12 Staves, 80 pages, leather back and corners, cloth sides; size, 9x11½ in. Each. .60
Weight, 22 oz.
26388 14 Staves, 80 pages, leather back and corners, cloth sides; size, 10⅛x13¾ in. Each. .75

Roller Organ.

The Roller Organs are new and very popular mechanical musical instruments, and our prices are so low that our sales are very large. The music is produced from reeds (regular organ size), 20 in number, which are perfectly tuned and covered with steel valves. The latter are operated by the music roller which is supplied with pins similar to those on an ordinary music box. The roller is made to revolve with gearing, which also drives the bellows. All the working parts are made of solid metal, easily accessible, and on the whole are well made and durable. They have a tone of good volume. Any child can play them, and we can furnish all styles of music.

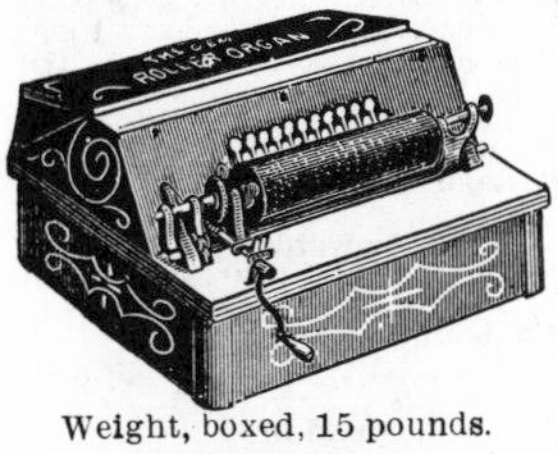

26400 The Gem Roller Organ, as described above, imitation black walnut case, length, 16 inches, width, 14 inches, height, 9 inches. Price, complete, including three rollers..$4.50
Weight, boxed, 15 pounds.

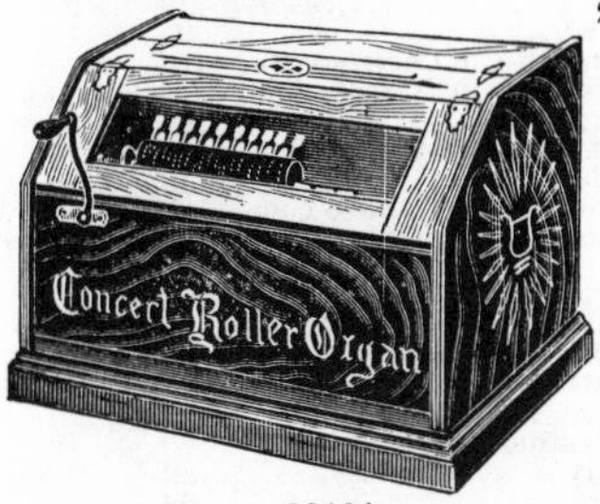

26401

26401 The Concert Roller Organ, larger in size, hence greater volume of tone, handsome black walnut case, glass top, finely finished. Length, 19 inches, width, 16 inches, height, 14 inches. Price, complete, including five rollers....$9.00
Weight, boxed, 30 pounds.

We can furnish extra rollers for above at 23c. each; per dozen, $2.50. Extra by mail, each 7cts. Each roller plays one tune. Music list furnished on application.

Band Instruments.

It is now time for bands to prepare for the political campaign of 1896. It will be "red hot," and there will be a great demand for music. The new tariff law makes quite a reduction in cost of brass instruments, besides we are getting lower prices from manufacturers on account of placing large advance orders, and a comparison of our present prices with former quotations will show that we have given our customers full benefit.

The German Piston Valve Instruments are made expressly for us by a reliable manufacturer in Germany, and we can recommend them as being equal to any German Piston line on the market.

Our Light Action French Piston Valve Instruments, made by Jules De Vere & Co., Paris, are becoming very popular; our sales have doubled during the past year and so far as we know every instrument has given perfect satisfaction.

On orders of 5 or more band instruments we will be pleased to quote special prices on application.

German Piston Valves.

Water key, music rack and German silver mouthpiece with each instrument.

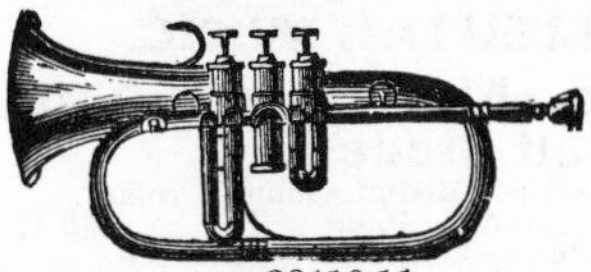

26410-11

26410 Eb Cornet, brass. Each......$5.10
26411 Eb Cornet, nickel plated. Each......$6.10
Weight, boxed, 6 pounds.
26412 Bb Cornet, brass, same style as No. 26410.$5.75
26413 Bb Cornet, nickel plated 6.70
Weight, 7 pounds.

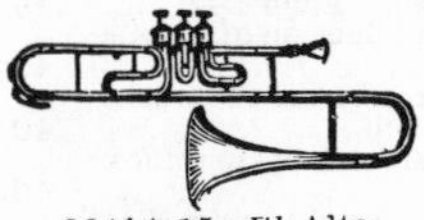

26414-15—Eb Alto.

26414 Eb Alto Valve Trombone, brass..........$7.20
26415 Eb Alto Valve Trombone, nickel plated. Each..........$9.30
Weight, boxed, 8 pounds.
26416-Bb Tenor Valve Trombone, same style as 26414, brass........ $ 9.30
26417 Bb Tenor Valve Trombone, same style as 26414, nickel plated........11.85
Weight, boxed, 9 pounds.

Piston Valves—Continued.

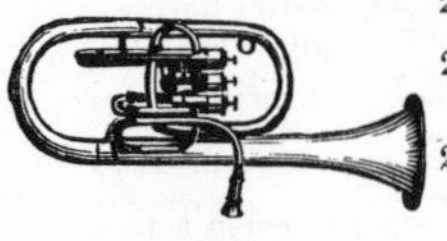

26420-21

26420 Eb Alto. Bell up, brass..........$7.20
26421 Eb Alto, Bell up, nickel plated........$9.20
Weight, boxed, 8 pounds.
26422 Bb Tenor, Bell up, Same style as 26420. Brass..........$9.30
26423 Bb Tenor, Bell up, same style as 26420, nickel plated..........11.85
Weight, boxed, 9 pounds.
26424 Bb Baritone Bell up, same style as 26420, brass..........$10.95
26425 Bb Baritone, Bell up, same style as 26420, nickel plated..........$13.75
Weight, boxed, 10 pounds.
26426 Bb Bass, Bell up, same style as 26420, brass..........$11.90
26427 Bb Bass, Bell up, same style as 26420, nickel plated..........$14.95
Weight, boxed, 15 pounds.

Eb Basses.

26428 Eb Bass, Bell up, brass..........$16.50
26429 Eb Bass, Bell up, nickel plated.......... 20.55
Weight, boxed, 18 pounds.

Improved French Piston Instruments.

With genuine light action valves, manufactured by Jules DeVere & Co., Paris. Water key, music rack and German silver mouthpiece with each instrument.

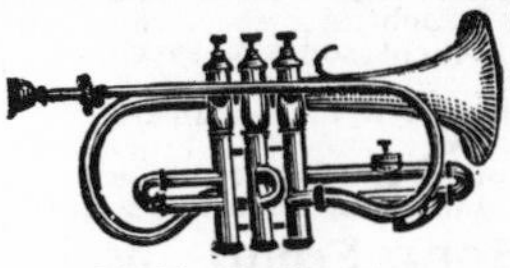

26431. Eb Cornet.

26431 Eb Cornet, brass, Each..........$6.50
26432 Eb Cornet, nickel plated........$7.50
Weight, boxed, 6 pounds.

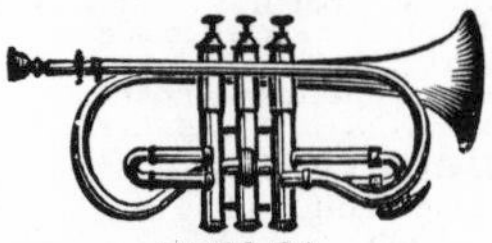

26433-34

26433 Bb Cornet, brass, Each..........$6.70
26434 Bb Cornet, nickel plated. Each..........$7.70
Weight, boxed, 7 lbs.

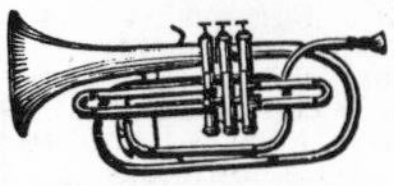

26435 Eb Solo Alto, bell front, brass. Each..........$10.70
26436 Eb Solo Alto, bell front, nickel plated. Each..........$12.75

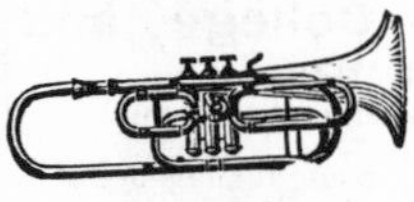

26437-38

26437 Eb Alto, Valve Trombone, bell front. Each..........$10.70
26438 Eb Alto Trombone, bell front, nickel plated. Each..........$12.75
Weight, boxed, 9 pounds.

Each.
26439 Bb Tenor Valve Trombone, same style as No. 26437. Brass..........$12.70
26440 Bb Tenor Valve Trombone, same style as No. 26437. Nickel plated..........15.20
Weight, boxed, 10 pounds.
26441 Bb Baritone Valve Trombone, same style as No. 26437. Brass..........12.75
26442 Bb Baritone Valve Trombone, same style as 26437. Nickel plated..........16.70
Weight, boxed, 11 pounds.

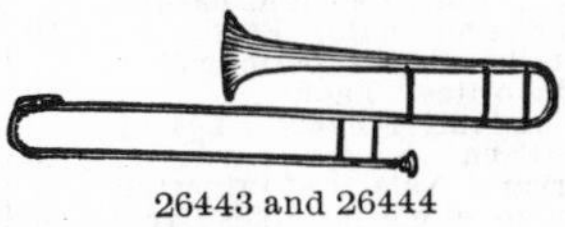

26443 and 26444

26443 Bb Tenor Slide Trombone, Brass.......$8.05
26444 Bb Tenor Slide Trombone. Weight, boxed, 8 pounds.
Nickel plated..........$10.55

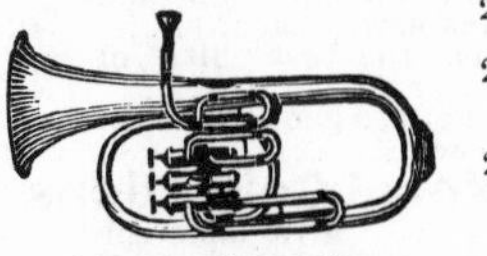

26445 and 26446

26445 Eb Alto. Bell up. Brass..........$10.70
26446 Eb Alto, bell up. Nickel plated...$12.75
Weight, boxed, 8 lbs.
26447 Bb Tenor, bell up. Same style as No. 26445. Brass..$12.70

Each.
26448 Bb Tenor, bell up, same style as No. 26445. Nickel plated..........$15.20
Weight, boxed, 10 pounds.
26449 Bb Baritone, bell up, same style as No. 26445. Brass.......... 12.75
26450 Bb Baritone, bell up, same style as No. 26445. Nickel plated..........16.70
Weight, boxed, 11 pounds.
26451 Bb Bass, bell up, same style as No. 26445. Brass..........16.25
26452 Bb Bass, bell up, same style as No. 26445. Nickel plated..........19.25
Weight, boxed, 16 pounds.

Eb Basses.

26453 Eb Bass, bell up. Brass..........$23.25
26454 Eb Bass, bell up. Nickel plated.......... 27.30
Weight, boxed, 25 pounds.

Solo Bb Cornets.

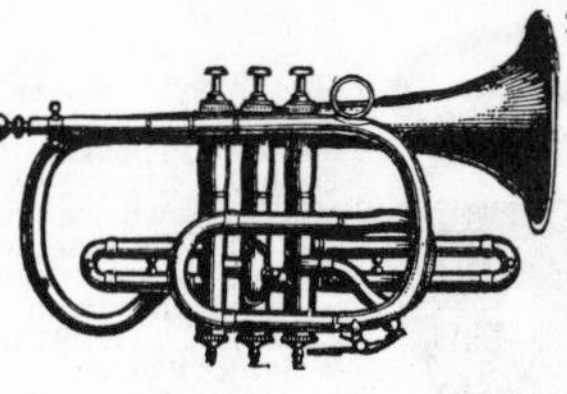

26455 Bb Cornet, Brass, long model German silver, light action, French piston valves, water key, German silver mouthpiece. "A" set piece, a superb instrument.
Price..........$8.50
Weight, boxed, 7 pounds.
26456 Bb Cornet. Same as above. Nickel plated..........$10.25
26458 Bb Cornet, light action, improved model, French manufacture, extra quality richly mounted with figured metal. German silver pistons and mouthpiece, with double water keys and "A" set piece. Brass..........$18.00
Weight, boxed, 8 pounds.
26460 Bb Cornet, same style as No. 26458. Nickel plated. Each..........$20.00
26462 Bb Cornet, same style as No. 26458. Silver plated. Each..........$26.00

Solo "C" Cornets.

26463 "C" Cornets, brass, improved model, French manufacture, light action, German silver piston valves, with water key, extra Bb crook. Each..$8.50
26464 "C" Cornet, same style as No. 26463. Nickel plated. Each.......... 10.25

Note.—We guarantee our band instruments to be in perfect condition, as each one is thoroughly examined by an experienced workman before being shipped. They also have the name of Montgomery Ward & Co. stamped in the metal.

Cornet Mutes.

26465 Cornet Mutes, nickel plated, used to place in the bell of the instrument to soften the tone for practising, or to produce the "Echo." Each.$1.25
Weight, 12 ounces.

Band Instrument Mouthpieces.

26466 German silver for Eb or Bb Cornets. Each..........$0.40
Weight, 2 ounces.
26467 German silver for altos and tenors. Each.......... .65
Weight, 2 ounces.
26468 German silver for Bb baritones, or Eb basses. Each.......... 1.00
Weight, 3 ounces.
26469 "Professional" silver plated and burnished "Higham" or "Austin" models, for Eb or Bb cornets. Each.......... .70
Weight, 2 ounces.
26471 "Professional," same as No. 26469, for altos or tenors. Weight, 3 ounces. Each..... 1.00
26472 Professional, same as No. 26469, for baritone. Weight, 3 ounces. Each.......... 1.40
26474 Professional, same as No. 26469, for Bb or Eb bass. Each.......... 1.65
Weight, 5 ounces.

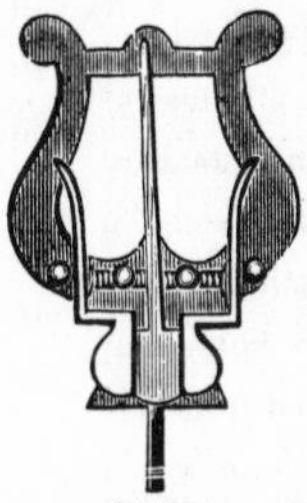

26475

Band Instrument Music Racks.

26475 Music Rack, improved pattern, 3 prongs for band instrument, brass. Each.........$0.50
26476 Music Rack, same as number 26475, nickel plated. Each..........$0.75
26477 Music Racks for slide Trombones, brass, 75 cents each; nickel plated, each $1.00.
Weight, boxed, 6 lbs.

Bugles.

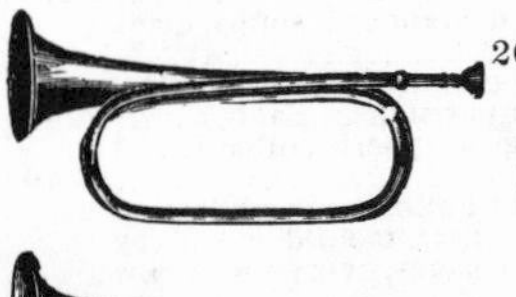

26478 Cavalry Bugles, key of F, brass. Each..........$2.00
Nickel plated. Each..........$2.75

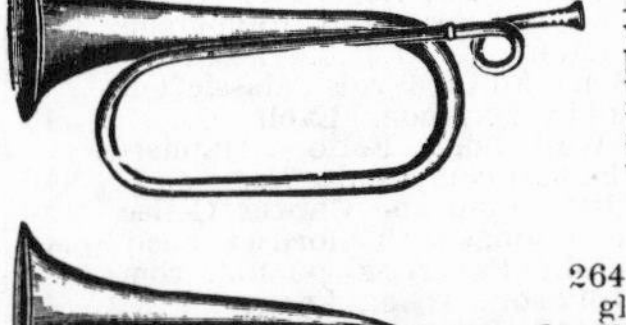

26480 Infantry Bugles, key of C, with Bb crook, brass. Each.......$2.65
Nickel plated. Each.......$3.65

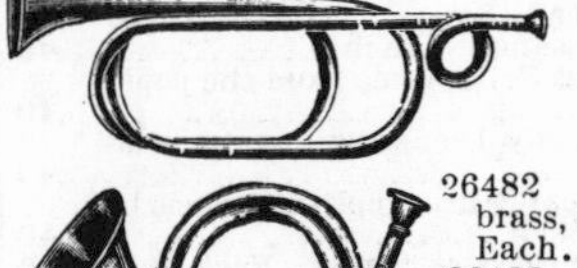

26481 Artillery Bugles, key of G, brass. Each.........$2.85
Nickel plated. Each.........$3.80

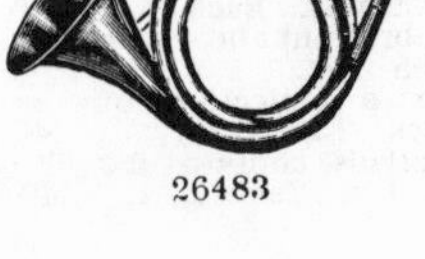

26483

26482 Hunting Horns brass, one turn. Each..........$0.90
26483 Hunting Horns, brass, three turns. Each.......... $1.30

Cornet Cases.

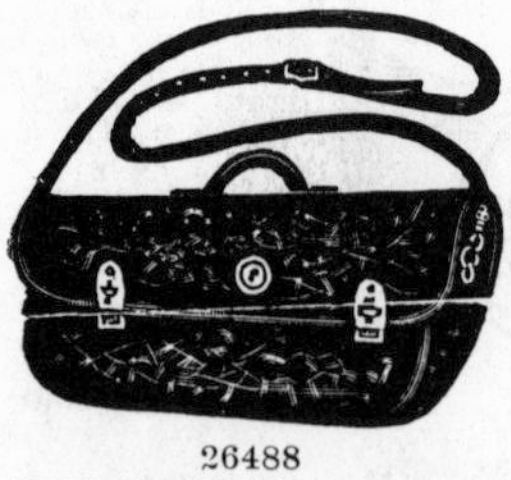

26488

26484 Wood, black varnished, lined; lock, handle and hooks. Each............$1.25

26486 Brown canvas satchel form, leather bound, flannel lined, with shoulder strap. Each............$1.00 Weight, 22 ounces.

26488 Pebbled Leather, black satchel form, flannel lined, nickel plated trimmings, with shoulder strap (see cut).......................$1.50 Weight, 25 ounces.

26489 Leather, russet color, satchel form, flannel lined, nickel plated trimmings, with shoulder strap. Weight, 25 ounces....................... 1.50

Vocal and Instrumental Musical Collections.

The most popular musical collections on the market to-day are what are known as "50 cent Folios" and as the demand is almost entirely for this style many of the best copyrights are published in this form. These books are full sheet music size printed from excellent plates on good paper with neat and attractive covers and AT OUR PRICE you can get a collection of from twenty to sixty pieces of good music at the cost of a single piece at retail. We quote below a complete list of the best publications up to date, and as the music ranges from the easiest to the most difficult grades every taste can be supplied. As our space is limited we can give only a brief description of each, but every number will be found a "gem" of its kind and sure to please. If you order these books by mail, allow 12 cents each, extra for postage.

Vocal Music.

26495 American Ballad Collection, 54 modern ballads. Each.............$0.40

26496 American Song and Chorus Collection, 68 popular copyright songs. Each.............. .40

26497 Artists' Song Folio, a selection of classic concert songs. Each............ .40

26498 Choice Baritone, and Bass Songs, an excellent collection for low voices. Each........ .40

26499 Choice English Songs, by modern composers. Each.............. .40

26501 Empress of Song, a good collection of songs of the day. Each........ .40

26502 Excelsior, baritone and bass folio, late songs by well-known composers. Each.......... .40

26503 Excelsior Song Folio, popular songs and ballads. Each.............. .40

26504 Excelsior Vocal Folio; a collection of standard songs. Each.............. .40

26505 Famous Songs, a superior collection by famous writers. Each.............. .40

26506 Floral Offering, a superior collection of concert and parlor music. Each.............. .40

26507 Folio of Standard Songs, 144 pages of vocal favorites. Each.............. .40

26508 Galaxy of Song, a compilation of standard popular songs. Each.............. .40

26509 German Songs, a late collection of standard songs by the best authors. Each.............. .40

26510 Ideal Folio, 2 vols., collection of songs in the popular style. Each.............. .40

26511 Ideal Gems of English Song, choice English songs and ballads. Each.............. .40

26512 International Song Folio, a volume of popular songs. Each.............. .40

26513 Italian Song Classics, selected from popular modern writers. Each.............. .40

26514 Musical Chatterbox, 2 volumes, new and popular songs and pieces for piano or organ for young folks. Each.............. .40

26515 Magnet, new and standard songs, duets and quartettes. Each.............. .40

26516 Millard's Songs contains many of Harrison Millard's best compositions. Each.............. .40

26517 Monarch of Song, a superb collection of popular music. Each.............. .40

26517½ The "Maywood" Folio, a new collection of popular songs and instrumental music by George Schleiforth, 111 pages, every piece new and good. Price.............. .40

26518 National Classic Song Folio, high-grade, standard songs. Each.............. .40

26519 National Song Folio, 4 vols., classic and popular songs of every grade. Each.............. .40

26520 National Waltz-Song Folio, standard waltz-songs, by the best composers. Each.............. .40

26521 Ne Plus Ultra Song and Chorus Collection, 49 well selected songs with choruses. Each. .40

26522 New and Old Favorites, popular compositions in the folk song style. Each.............. .40

26523 Old Homestead Songs. "The dear old songs our mothers' sang." Each.............. .40

26524 Operatic Song Folio, gems from the popular operas. Each.............. .40

26525 Palace Folio, royal songs by popular composers. Each.............. .40

26526 Pearls of Vocal Music, polished gems by popular writers. Each.............. .40

26527 Popular Song Classics, 2 vols. Each.............. .40

26528 Prima Donna Album, brilliant and classic music for a high voice. Each.............. .40

26529 Royal Vocal Folio, a collection of standard medium grade songs. Each.............. .40

26530 Royal Collection of Ballads, contains the latest and best ballads of the day. Each........ .40

Vocal Music—Continued.

26531 Royal Collection of Songs with Choruses, popular copyrights by famous American composers. Each.............. .40

26532 Royal Collection of Songs, standard songs by eminent hands. Each.............. .40

26533 Selected Songs, the Cream of the American and English ballads. Each.............. .40

26534 Singer's Portfolio, 2 vols., selected songs, new and very good. Each.............. .40

26535 Song Bouquet, new and popular vocal music. Each.............. .40

26537 Song Casket (Whitney's), selected popular vocal gems. Each.............. .40

26538 Song Diamonds, a collection of charming songs and ballads. Each.............. .40

26539 Song Folio, 4 vols., the best vocal music by American and foreign composers. Each.... .40

26540 Song Offering, choice songs, ballads and duets. Each.............. .40

26541 Songs of Ireland, melodious echoes from the Green Isle. Each.............. .40

26542 Songs of Scotland (Hitchcock's), gems of Caledonia in song and ballad. Each.............. .40

26543 Songs of Scotland (W. S. & Co.), 78 beautiful songs, popular with all. Each.............. .40

26545 Song Souvenir, a collection of popular vocal gems. Each.............. .40

26546 Song Treasures, charming songs and ballads in the popular vein. Each.............. .40

26548 Standard Song Album, world-famous songs by the most renowned composers. Each........ .40

26549 Standard Vocal Album, a magnificent collection of popular songs, ballads and duets. Each .40

26551 Superb Songs, the best creations of master song writers. Each.............. .40

26552 Superior Song Collection, choice and new vocal compositions. Each.............. .40

26553 Vocal Casket, excellent songs by excellent writers. Each.............. .40

26555 Vocal Folio, 2 vols., new and standard vocal favorites. Each.............. .40

26556 World's Exposition Vocal Repertoire, a collection worthy the Columbiad Each........ .40

Sacred Song Folio.

26558 Album of Sacred Music, popular solos and quartets for church and home. Each.............. .40

26559 Excelsior Sacred Folio, new sacred music by the best authors. Each.............. .40

26560 Folio of Sacred Songs, contains standard music for all voices. Each.............. .40

Vocal Duet Folios.

26562 Brainard's Vocal Duet Folio, a fine collection of popular duets. Each.............. .40

26563 Excelsior Vocal Duet Folio, selected gems from the best composers. Each.............. .40

26564 Standard Vocal Duets, choice and melodious numbers by popular writers. Each........ .40

26565 Thirty-two Vocal Duets, a collection of popular duets by the best authors. Each........ .40

26566 Vocal Duet Folio, 2 vols., well-known compositions, popular in the best sense. Each...... .40

Comic, Minstrel, College and Topical Songs.

26568 Album of Comic Songs, a collection of popular comic songs. Each.............. .40

26569 Bouquet of Comic Songs, made famous by dialect artists at home and abroad. Each....... .40

26571 Comical, Topical and Motto Songs, contains a large variety of the best songs of the day. .40

26572 Comic Casket, collection of late comic songs. Each.............. .40

26573 College Songs (octavo form), 200,000 copies sold. Best book of its kind ever issued. Each .40

26575 Comic Songs, Old and New, including some good sentimental songs with choruses. Each... .40

26576 Famous Comic Songs of England and America, popular on the stage and in the parlor. Each .40

26578 Harvest of Minstrel Songs, standard "burnt cork" favorites. Each.............. .40

26579 Minstrel Folio, 2 vols., footlight flashes, witty, sentimental and serio-comic. Each...... .40

26581 National Minstrel Folio, a superior collection of new and old favorites. Each.............. .40

26582 New Album Comique, famous songs by popular composers. Each.............. .40

26583 Songs for Harvard, Yale and Princeton Students, and everyone else who likes lively music. Each.............. .40

26585 Songs of the Past and Present, comic and sentimental songs, old and new. Each........ .40

26586 Songs of the Period, the best "hits" of recent times. Each.............. .40

26587 They're After Me, Folio, a good album of favorite comic songs. Each.............. .40

Miscellaneous Vocal Collections.

26589 Grand Army War Songs. A valuable collection of war and camp songs, to which is added a selection of memorial songs and hymns for Decoration Day, etc.; choruses all arranged for male voices, organ or piano accompaniment; 100 pages, heavy paper covers. Price..........$0.45 Extra by mail.............. .05

26590 *The Treasury of Song.* A mammoth collection of the very best vocal gems, both sacred and secular, selected from the works of the best composers. Every piece a favorite. A book of 550 pages; size, 10x7, handsomely bound in cloth. The largest collection ever put on the market. Regular price, $2.50. Our price...... 1.25 Extra by mail.............. .24

26592 Minstrel Songs, old and new, book of 214 pages, board covers, containing a collection of over 100 of the famous minstrel and plantation songs, including the most popular of the celebrated Foster melodies; arranged with piano or organ accompaniment.............. 1.25 Extra by mail.............. .18

Vocal Collections—Continued.

26593 Male Quartette and Chorus Book by J. Herbert. A new collection of music for male voices designed for use in glee club, concert, college or home; contains 108 pieces Board covers; Price, $0.55. Extra by mail.......... 0.08

26594 **The Jolly Songster,** a new collection of over 160 pages, comic and popular songs with music. Paper covers, each.............. .15 Postage.............. .05

26596 The Celebrated Dockstader Songster, containing 50 minstrel and variety songs, with words and music. Price, $0.08, Postage........ .02

26598 **The Old and New Home German Songster,** an an excellent collection of popular songs in German with music, 200 pages, paper covers. Each .15 Postage.............. .5

We can supply you with nearly anything in music whether quoted or not.

Gospel Hymns.

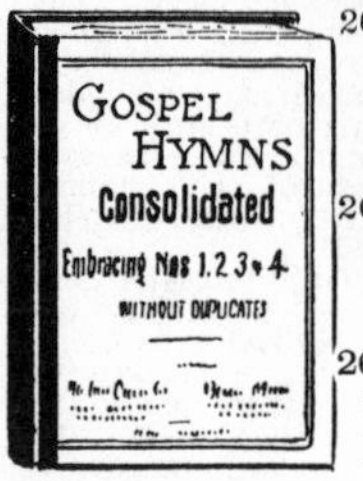

26600 Consolidated, Nos. 1, 2, 3, 4. Large type words and music 400 pages.
Each..............$0.75
Per dozen.............. 7.72
Postage.............. 10

26601 Same as 26600, bound in ½ leather, red edges, words and music. Each..............$ 1.50
Per doz.............. 15.40
Postage, each.............. .10

26602 Words only. Nos. 1, 2, 3, 4. Each..............$0.20
Per dozen.............. 2.15
Postage.............. .04

	Each.	Per doz.
26603 Gospel Hymns, No. 5, with words and music. Board covers..............	$0.30	$3.10
Postage..............	.06	
26604 Same as No. 26603, bound in limp cloth, very handsome..............	.50	5.40
Postage..............	.06	
26605 Gospel Hymns, No 6, bound in boards..............	.30	3.10
Postage..............	.06	
26606 Gospel Hymns No. 6, *Christian Endeavor* Edition, bound in boards. Each	.35	3.60
Postage..............	.06	
26607 Same as No. 26606, bound in limp cloth, very handsome..............	.50	5.40
26608 Gospel Hymns Nos. 5 and 6 combined words and music, large type, board covers..............	.60	7.00
Postage, each..............	.08	
26608½ Gospel Hymns, Nos. 5 and 6 combined words and music, small type, board covers..............	.45	5.00
Postage..............	.05	
26609 Gospel Hymns, same as No. 26608 words only..............	.22	2,30
Postage..............	.04	
26611 **Just Out, Gospel Hymn, Nos. 1 to 6** complete with words and music in one volume. Having combined these six numbers and eliminated all duplicates, we are enabled to offer this popular series of gospel hymns (739 hymns and tunes) in one volume at a reasonable figure. This edition is handsomely bound in maroon colored cloth. Price..............	1.00	11.00
Postage..............	.20	
26611¼ Gospel Hymns, 1 to 6 complete, words only, flexible cloth covers.......	.20	2.25
Postage..............	.03	

Cornet Edition.

26612 Melodies of the Gospel Hymns, Nos. 1, 2, 3, 4, consolidated. Arranged for the cornet by Hayslip, for use in Sabbath schools, Gospel meetings, etc. A piano or organ played from the regular edition will agree perfectly with the cornet played from this. Price, paper covers...$1.00 Extra by mail.............. .08

26613 Gospel Hymns, No. 5, arranged for the cornet, containing the melodies and altos of all the members. Price, paper covers.............. .80 Postage, 5c. extra.

26614 Gospel Hymns, No. 6 arranged for the cornet, paper covers. Each.............. .80 Postage, 5c. extra,

INSTRUMENTAL MUSIC.

Piano Folios,—Medium and Difficult Grades.

26620 American Artists' Edition Album, 2 vols., music of the higher grades. Each..............$0.40

26622 American Piano Collection, 50 pieces of choice piano music. Each.............. .40

26623 Chicago Collection of Standard Piano Music. Each.............. .40

26624 Columbian Collection of Piano Music, popular and high grade music. Each.............. .40

26625 Famous Favorites, a collection of classic piano music. Each.............. .40

26626 Folio of Marches, selected from the works of celebrated composers. Each.............. .40

26627 Golden Hours, an album of marches, waltzes, etc. Each.............. .40

26628 Kinkel's Folio, 2 vols., bright and sparkling music of easy and medium grades. Each.. .40

26630 Liszt's Best Compositions. Each.............. .40

26631 Operatic Folio, 2 vols., gems from the latest operas. Each.............. .40

26632 Paderewski's Concert Album. Each...... .40

Reed Organ Folios.

26635 Excelsior Organ Folio, an album of popular music. Each .40

26636 Folio Gems, popular and standard music. Each .40

26637 Folio Leaves, an excellent collection of medium grade music. Each .40

26637½ Gems of Strauss, containing 100 pieces by this great composer. Each .40

26638 Golden Folio, music of easy and medium grades. Each .40

26639 Hitchcock's New Organ Book, a folio of popular pieces in light style. Each .40

26640 National Organ Folio, a sellection of standard pieces for organ. Each .40

26641 Organ Pearls, easy and medium grade music. Each .40

26643 Parlor and Cabinet Organ Selections, vocal and instrumental music. Each .40

26645 Parlor Bouquet, medium grade music for piano or organ. Each .40

26646 Parlor Organ Folio, music of the medium and higher grades. Each .40

26647 Reed Organ Companion (Brainard's), easy pieces for organ, suitable for beginners. Each .40

26648 Reed Organ at Home, a new collection of popular music. Each .40

26649 Reed Organ Folio, music by favorite composers. Each .40

26650 Silver Folio, easy and medium style music. Each .40

26651 Superb Solos, an excellent collection of moderately difficult music, arranged for piano or organ Each .40

Duet Folios.

26653 Excelsior Four-hand Folio, popular and new duets. Each $0.40

26655 Four-hand Folio, an album of popular duets. Each .40

26656 Four-hand Folio of Popular Dance Music. Each .40

26657 National Four-hand Folio, productions of standard authors. Each .40

26658 Par Excellence Four-hand Selections, high grade duets. Each .40

26659 Pianoforte Duet Selections, a selection of medium grade pieces. Each .40

26660 Two Musical Friends' Four-hand Folio, choice music of medium difficulty. Each .40

DANCE FOLIOS.

These folios are made up of new and standard waltzes, galops, polkas, schottisches, etc., and the titles usually describe the contents of each colection. Postage, $9,12

26664 American Dance Music Collection. Each, .40
26665 Bouquet of Waltzes. Each .40
26666 Dance Casket. Each .40
26667 Dance Folio, 6 vols. Each .40
29668 Excelsior Dance Collection. Each .40
26669 Famous Dance Music. Each .40
26670 Favorite Waltzes, by Waldteufel and others. Each .40
26671 Monarch Waltz Collection. Each .40
26672 National Dance Album. Each .40
26673 National Waltz Folio. Each .40
26675 Parisian Dance Folio. Each .40
26676 Parlor Dance Folio. Each .40
26677 Queen of the Waltz Folio. Each .40
26678 Royal Collection of Dance Music. Each, .40
26679 Seaside Dance Folio, 2 vols. Each .40
26681 Standard Dance Album. Each .40
26682 Strauss' Concert Album. Each .40
26683 Strauss' Dance Collection. Each .40
26684 Strauss' Dance Folio. Each .40
26685 Strauss' Famous Collection of Waltzes. Each .40
26686 Superior Dance Collection. Each .40
26687 Waldteufel's Dance Folio, 2 vols Each, .40
26688 Waltz Album. Each .40
26689 Winner's Dance Folio, Piano or Organ. Each .40

ORCHESTRA MUSIC.

26695 The New Mammoth Collection for Violin. This book contains over 350 pieces of the latest and best music arranged for first violin, including waltzes, polkas, schottisches, galops, marches, quadrilles plain and fancy, overtures, opera selections, etc.. etc. We can also furnish all other orchestra parts to every piece at reasonable prices. This is just the book for orchestra leaders to select from. Size, 10x7, paper covers. Price, each $0.45
Postage, extra .20

26696 The Cornet Players' Pastime, a work similar to 26695, containing 1,000 cornet solos, embracing all styles of standard and popular music, all arranged, paper covers. Price. each .45
Postage, extra .20

26697 Favorite Dance Album, first series, arranged for orchestra of nine instruments, viz.: 1st and 2nd violin, cornet, clarionet, flute, viola, trombone, bass and piano; contains 11 pieces of assorted dance music, each piece new and good.
Price, each book (except piano) .25
Piano book .35
Extra by mail, each .03

26698 Favorite Dance Album, second series, arranged for same instruments as No. 26697, contains 11 pieces choice dance music.
Price, each book (except piano) .25
Piano book .35
Extra by mail, each .03

26699 Beginners' Orchestra Journal, No. 1, by A. S. Bowman. Contains 25 easy and popular pieces of dance music arranged for orchestra of 8 instruments, viz.: 1st and 2nd violin, cornet, clarionet, flute, trombone (either clef), bass and piano, each part separate.
Price, each book (except piano) .25
Piano book $0.50 Extra by mail .03

Orchestra Music—Continued.

26700 Beginners' Orchestra Journal, No. 2, by A. S. Bowman; 25 pieces dance music arranged for orchestra, same as No. 1, but contains a more difficult grade of music.
Price, each book (except piano) .25
Piano book $0.50 Extra by mail .03

26701 Popular Duets for violin and piano, No. 1. This is a new collection of the very latest music, including "Loves' Dreamland" Waltzes, Mendelssohn's "Wedding March," "Hornpipe Polka,' etc., 84 pieces, 122 pages. Full sheet, music size, paper covers. Every piece a gem.
Price, each .40
Postage, extra .10

26701½ Popular Duets. No. 1 same as No. 26701 arrarged for cornet and piano. Each .40
Postage .10

26702 Popular Duets for Violin and Piano, No. 2, contains a collection of still later music. Full sheet music size, 120 pages. These are the best collections ever put on the market in book form.
Price, each .40
Postage, extra .10

26703 Student's Recreation. A magnificent col lection of violin solos, with or without piano accompaniment. This work contains 12 well known popular airs, with variations arranged progressively from the 1st to the 7th positions. When necessary the fingering as well as the bowing is marked.
Price, violin part alone, paper covers .45
Extra by mail .05

26703½ Student's Recreation. Violin and piano, in one volume, paper covers .90
Extra by mail .12

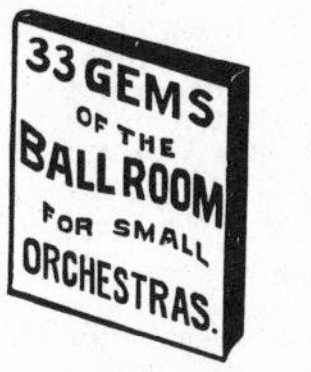

26704 Gems of the Ball Room, No 1, by McCosh and others. A collection of 33 pieces of choice dance music, all kinds, arranged for orchestra of 8 instruments, viz.: 1st and 2d violin, cornet, clarionet, flute, trombone (double clefs), bass and piano, each part separate.
Price, each book (excepting piano) $0.50
Price, each book, in lots of 5 or more (excepting piano) .45
Price piano book, each 1.00

26705 Gems of the Ball Room, No. 2. A collection of the latest dance music, arranged for orchestra of 8 instruments, same as Gems No. 1. Contains 33 pieces, including the new military schottische "Berlin," "York,' etc.
Price, each book (excepting piano) .50
Price, each book, in lots of 5 or more (excepting piano) $0.45. Price, piano books, each 1.00

26706 Gems of the Ball Room No. 3, arranged for same instruments as Nos. 1 and 2, and contains 33 pieces of new dance music, also some of the old "Contra" dances.
Price, each book (excepting piano) .50
Price, each book, in lots of 5 .45
Price piano books, each 1.00

26707 Gems of the Ball Room, No. 4, arranged for same instruments as the other numbers, contains 32 pieces of the latest and best dance music. Price, each book (excepting piano) .50
Price, each book (excepting piano) in lots of 5 .45
Price piano book 1.00

26708 Gems of the Ball Room, No. 5; this is the latest edition of these very popular orchestral collections, and contains 32 pieces of the best new dance music. Arranged for same instruments as Nos. 1 and 2.
Price, each book (excepting piano) .50
Price, each book (excepting piano) in lots of 5 .45
Price piano books 1.00
Extra by mail, each 2 cents.

There are no duplicates in Gems of the Ball Room, and every orchestra leader should have the complete set.

26709 Beauties of the Ball Room No. 1 by W. T. Kohler. This is a new collection of the very best dance music and the grade is one and two degrees more difficult than Gems of the Ball Room. 27 popular numbers, arranged for the following instruments: 1st. violin, 2nd. violin, cornet, clarionet, flute, viola, trombone, bass, piano, alto horn, and tuba.
Price, each book (excepting piano) .50
Price, each book (excepting piano) in lots of 5 .45
Price, piano book 1.00

26709½ Beauties of the Ball Room No. 2, 28 pieces. same instrumentation as No. 26709.
Price, each book (except piano) .50
Price, each book, (excepting piano), in lots of 5 .45
Piano books, each $1. Postage, each .03

26710 Echoes from the Ball Room. This collection contains everything in music essential to dancing. It includes the latest dances, also the old standards, 31 pieces, arranged for 1st and 2d violin, cornet, clarionet, bass, flute, viola, trombone and piano.
Price, each book (excepting piano) .50
Price, each book, in lots of 5 .45
Price piano books 1.00

26711 Musician's Omnibus. A book containing 1,500 pieces, arranged for violin, consisting of waltzes, polkas, schottisches, galops, quadrilles, jig and clog dances, etc. Publisher's price 2.00
Our price 1.50

26712 Ryan's 1,050 Reels and Jigs, a very popular collection of lively music arranged for Violin. Price, each $1.50 Extra by mail 0.12

26713 Opera Duets for Violin and Piano. Contains 30 standard and popular operas arranged for violin and piano. Violin part does not run above first position; best collection published. Price. violin and piano complete, one volume, board covers $1.00 Postage .14

Brass Band Music.

26715 The Combination Band Book, arranged by McCosh, just published, and is already becoming very popular, as it contains 16 pieces of choice music for every occasion. "Marches," "Quicksteps," "Waltzes," "Polkas," "Overtures," etc., etc. Just the book for young bands. Arranged for full band of twenty pieces.
Price, single book, each $0.25 Set of 6, each $0.20

26716 National Band Journal No. 1. Contains 8 pieces of music, including our national airs, together with the best of our grand old war songs, arranged for full band.
Price, all parts, complete .90
Postage 04

26717 The Ever Ready Band Books. A new collection of choice "Quicksteps," "Marches," "Waltzes," etc., by McCosh, Fox, Ruby and other composers, arranged for full brass band.
Price, single books, each .25
Set of 6 or more, each .20
Postage .04

26719 Sacred Band Journal, contains 10 familiar hymns arranged for full band. This journal is invaluable for Sunday playing, Sunday school picnics, concerts, etc. Price, all parts complete. .90

Guitar and Banjo Music.

26721 Hamilton's Banjo Folio. A splendid collection of beautiful banjo music, suitable for amateur or artist. Contains collections for solos and duets. Full sheet music size.
Each $0.40
Postage .10

26722 "Banjoists' Budget," a grand collection of 50 jigs, hornpipes, reels, clog dances, walk-arounds, etc, etc.. arranged and correctly fingered for the banjo, by A. Bauer. Best collection of banjo music published. Paper covers.
Price .45
Extra by mail .05

26724 Hitchcock's Superb Banjo Collection, 266 choice selections for banjo. Each $0.40
Extra by mail .12

26725 The Royal Guitar Folio, 1 superior collection of the latest and best guitar music, both vocal and instrumental. Arranged in good style by the best professionals, paper covers.
Each .40
Extra by mail .10

26727 The Guitarist (*Vocal*). We confidently claim for this collection of guitar music a place at the head of all similar productions. It is not an instruction book, but a collection of the latest and best music with accompaniments for guitar. Full sheet music size bound in cloth.
Price 1.10
Extra by mail .11

26729 The Guitarist (*Instrumental*). A collection of new and standard waltzes, polkas, marches, etc., arranged for the guitar in the most artistic manner. Bound in cloth. Price 1.10
Extra by mail .11

26731 Instrumental Guitar Folio. Contains standard pieces. Easy and moderately difficult.
Each .40
Extra by mail .12

Mandolin Folios.

26735 Benjamin's Amateur Collection for Mandolin and Guitar, with piano accompaniment. Contains 13 easy and popular pieces. Each $0.30
Postage .04

26736 Excelsior Mandolin and Guitar Folio, containing late and popular selections in easy style. Each .40
Postage .10

26737 Excelsior Mandolin and Piano Folio, 27 popular pieces. Each .40
Postage .10

26738 Society Dance Journal, a fine collection of dance music for mandolin and piano. Each .40
Postage .12

Miscellaneous.

26745 The True Musical Directory, an invaluable book containing all the musical terms, their definitions, etc., now in common use $0.20
Postage .03

26747 The True Piano Tuner, containing concise instruction for tuning and regulating pianos. This useful little book will be welcomed by all amateurs who wish to know more about the structure and care of instruments. Price .25
Postage .03

26749 Organ Voicing and Tuning, a thoroughly practical work on organ tuning, voicing and repairing. This book is illustrated and a careful study of it will obviate the necessity of sending for a tuner every time your organ gets out of order. Each .25
Postage .03

26751 Rudiments of Music, a concise and thoroughly practical course of instruction on the art of singing by note; prepared by J. R. Murray. Teachers, classes and individuals will find in the above inexpensive work everything necessary to a complete understanding of the art of reading and singing by note. Each .10
Postage .02

26752 Palmer's Theory of Music, a practical guide to the study of thorough bass, harmony and composition, and for acquiring a knowledge of the science of music in a short time with or without the aid of a teacher. Each .90
Postage .05

We make NO CHARGE for Boxing.

Miscellaneous—Continued.

26753 The Normal Music Hand Book, by Geo. F. Root. This work contains statements of elementary principles, short lectures, full method of teaching singing classes, elementary harmony and composition. Also a defining and pronouncing index of musical terms. Price, complete (5 books in one). Each 2.60
Postage .... .10

26754 Root's New Course in Voice Culture and Singing, by Frederic W. Root. This is a graded course, adapted to guide the young voice correct the faults of mature singers and develop the voice systematically. State whether it is wanted for male or female voice. Price 1.40
Extra by mail .... .10

Instruction Books for Musical Instruments.

PIANO.

26765 Lebert & Stark, Piano School, Parts 1, 2 and 3, board covers; retail price, per volume....$2.00
Our price, per volume 1.25
Postage .... .14

26766 Karl Merz's Piano Method, complete.
Publisher's price $3.00
Our price, ... 2.00
Postage .... .24

26768 Richardson's New Method for Pianos; revised edition; publisher's price 3.00
Our price 2.10
Postage .... .28

26769 Root's New Musical Curriculum, complete and revised. Publisher's price, ... 3.00
Our price 2.10
Postage .... .28

26771 Gordon's New School for Piano, complete.
Retail price 3.00
Our price 2.25
Postage .... .28

ORGAN.

26772 Whitney's Improved Easy Method for the Parlor Organ. New and enlarged edition. This is a new and attractive system by which the pupil may rapidly learn to play the organ. Besides a thorough course in music, this book contains a choice collection of vocal and instrumental pieces, progressively arranged, so that a careful study of each in their order will enable the student to correctly perform all the different styles of music. Publisher's price 1.50
Extra by mail .... .13
Our price .... .60

26774 White's Method of Reed Organ.
Publisher's price 2.50
Extra by mail .... .15
Our price .... .80

26775 Karl Merz's Modern Method for Reed Organ. Publisher's price 2.50
Extra by mail .... .18
Our price 1.25

26776 Getze's Method for Reed Organ. Publisher's price 2.50
Extra by mail .... .16
Our price 1.00

26777 The Model Organ Method, by Dr. Geo. F. Root. A book of graded instructions and exercises for reed organ, together with pieces, voluntaries, interludes and vocal selections.
Price, board covers 1.90
Postage .... .15

26777½ Clark's New Method for Reed Organ Complete. Price, board cover 2.00
Postage .... .25

VIOLIN.

26778 Maza's Complete Violin School. Publisher's price $2.00
Extra by mail .... .07
Our price .... .75

26779 Benjamin's Illustrated Violin Method. This is the latast publication in the way of a violin instructor, and is the best work for the beginner ever put on the market. It contains the complete elementary course, as profusely illustrated, also contains a collection of popular music, 79 pages sheet music size. Each .... .50
Extra by mail .... .05

26780 Wichtl's Young Violinist. Publisher's price 2.25
Extra by mail .... .10
Our price .... .80

26781 Henning's Practical School for Violin, complete with English and German text. Publisher's price 1.50
Our price 1.00
Extra by mail .... .14

26782 Howe's Original Violin School, new and enlarged edition. Contains complete rules and exercises together with a collection of over 450 pieces of every variety. Hundreds of old familiar airs never before published for violin. Extra large type and fine paper. Extra by mail.... .04
Each .... .40

26783 Howe's "Diamond" School for the Violin, contains complete instructions, full directions for bowing and 558 pieces of dance music.
Extra by mail .... .04
Each .... .45

BANJO.

26786½ Wessenberg's Thorough Banjo. A new and standard method for banjo, containing a complete elementary course besides a fine collection of solo and duet music, board covers.
Price, each .... .90
Extra by mail .... .10

26787½ Instruction Book of Chords for Banjo, showing position of fingers in all keys. Publisher's price .... .50
Our price .... .25
Postage .... .01

GUITAR.

26788½ Carcassi's Guitar Method, complete....$1.00
Extra by mail .... .12

26789½ Diagram School for the Guitar, by J. T. Rutledge. This is the latest and without doubt the most complete method for the guitar that has ever been offered to the public. It contains a thorough course of instruction, is profusely illustrated with diagrams of the finger boards, showing all the positions, etc., besides a fine collection of music, bound in boards. Publisher's price 2.50
Extra by mail .... .16
Our price 2.10

26790½ Instruction Book of Chords for Guitar, in all keys. Price .... .25
Postage .... .01

CORNET.

26791½ Arban's World Renowned Method for the Cornet, four books in one. This edition contains a complete method of instruction; Arban's 14 solos with variations, 60 beautiful duets for 2 cornets and the art of phrasing, consisting of 100 operatic, classic and popular melodies. Every cornetist should have one.
Price, in paper binding 1.00
Extra by mail .... .10

26792½ Arban's World Renowned Cornet Method, in cloth binding, gilt letters. Each 1.60
Extra by mail .... .16

MISCELLANEOUS.

26793½ Benjamin's Illustrated Method for the Mandolin, containing complete course in the rudiments of music, is fully illustrated and contains a choice collection of music.
Price .... .50
Extra by mail .... .05

26794½ Howe's Army and Navy Fife Instructor; containing complete course of instructions, also calls, signals and the complete camp and garrison duties as practiced in the United States Army and Navy, besides the National Airs and a large collection of marches, quicksteps, waltzes, etc., etc. Price, each, paper cover...... .40
Extra by mail .... .04

26795½ Pepper's Universal Dancing Master, Prompter's Call Book and Violinists' Guide. This work is intended as a complete instructor in the art of dancing and prompting; it contains an elaborate description of the steps and figures used in the round, square and fancy dances, including the very latest, such as the "York." "Berlin," "Lœmo," "German," etc., etc.; also an appropriate collection of music easily arranged for the violin and plainly marked for prompter's calls. Over 200 pages, board covers. Every violinist should have one of these books. Extra by mail .... .14
Price, each .... .80

26796½ Winner's Self Instructors, condensed and revised for Accordion, Organ, Violin, Guitar, Banjo, Flute, Fife and Cornet. Retail price, .25
Postage, extra .... .02
Our price .... .12

26797½ Winner's Primary School for Accordion, Organ, Violin, Guitar, Banjo, Flute, Fife, Violoncello, Clarionet and Cornet. Not condensed; unabridged. (Specify for which instrument book is wanted.) Extra by mail .... .03
Per volume .... .18

26798½ Ryan's True Instruction Books for musical instruments as follows: Accordion, Banjo, Bugle, Cornet, Concertina, Clarionet, Drum, Flageolet, Fife, Flute, Guitar, Violin, Violoncello, Double Bass, Mandolin, Harmonica, Ocarica, Zither, Eb Alto, Trombone.
Retail price .... .50
Postage, extra .... .03
Our price, each .... .25

26799½ Pepper's New Self Instructor for the Piccolo. Contains complete instructions for this popular instrument. Extra by mail .... .04
Each .... .45

26800 **Langey's Celebrated Tutors**, Coleman's Edition for the following instruments: Violin, Viola, Violoncello, Double Bass, Cornet, Clarionet, Piccolo, Flute, Oboe, Bassoon, Eb Cornet, Bb Cornet, Eb Alto, Bb Tenor (valve), Bb Tenor, Slide Trombone, Bb Baritone, Eb Bass, Drums, Fife, Zither, Mandolin, Guitar and Banjo.
Price, each, paper cover .... .75
Postage .... .07

∴ WE MUST BLOW OUR OWN HORN...

OR THE SAME,

It Will Not Be Blowed.

Artists' Materials.

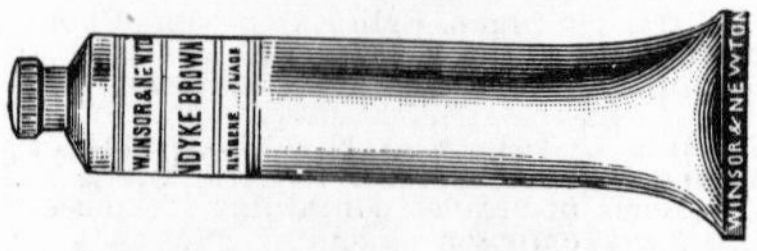

Artists Tube Oil Colors of the very best American manufacture, put up in single and double patent collapsible tubes nearly twice the regular size.

Weight of tubes as follows: Single, two ounces; double, 4 ounces; Windsor & Newton's, 3 ounces.

COMMON COLORS.

Am Vermillion (unfading	Lamp Black)
Antwerp Blue	Magenta
Asphaltum	Mauve
Bitumen	Meglip
Blue Black	Mummy
Bone Brown	Naples Yellow, light
Brown Pink	Naples Yellow, deep
Brown Ochre	Neutral Tint
Burnt Roman Ochre	New Blue
Burnt Sienna	Nottingham White
Burnt Umber	Oxford Ochre
Caledonian Brown	Olive Lake
Cappa Brown	Orpiment
Carmine Lake	Payne's Gray
Cremnitz White	Permanent Blue
Chrome, Green, Light	Purple Lake
Chrome, Green, Medium	Prussian Blue
Chrome, Green, Deep	Raw Sienna
Chrome, Yellow, Lemon,	Raw Umber
Chrome, Yellow, Medium	Roman Ochre
Chrome, Yellow, Deep	Sap Green
Chrome, Yellow, Orange	Scarlet Lake
Crimson Lake	Silver White
Chinese Blue	Sugar of Lead
Cologne Earth	Terre Verte
Cool Roman Ochre	Transparent Golden Ochre
Emerald Green	Vandyke Brown
Flake White	Venetian Red
Gamboge	Verdigris
Ivory Black	Verona Brown
Indian Lake	Yellow Lake
Indian Red	Yellow Ochre
Indigo	Zinnobar Green, Light
Italian Pink	Zinnobar Green, medium
Jaune Brilliant	Zinnobar Green, deep
King's Yellow	Zinc White
Light Red	

26801 American manufacture, single tubes. Each $0.05
26802 American manufacture, double tubes. Each .... .08
26803 Winsor & Newton's Oil Colors, in above shades, one size only. Each .... .08

SPECIAL COLORS.

Brown Madder	Citron Yellow
Cerulean Blue	English Vermilion
Chinese Vermilion	Sepia
Geranium Lake	

26805 American manufacture, single tubes. Each $0.14
26806 American manufacture, double tubes. Each .... .18
26808 Winsor & Newton's Oil Colors, in above shades, one size only. Each .... .18

Carmine No. 2	Oxide of Chromium
Cobalt Green	Oxide of Chromium, transparent
French Veronese Green	Pink Madder
Madder Lake	Rose Madder
Malachire Green	Strontian Yellow
Mineral Gray	Virdian
Orange Vermilion	Lemon Yellow
Cobalt Blue	Lemon Yellow, pale
Extract of Vermilion	Scarlet Vermilion
French Ultramarine Blue	
Indian Yellow	

26809 American manufacture, single tubes. Each $0.18
26810 American manufacture, double tubes. Each .... .23
26811 Winsor & Newton's Oil Colors, in above shades, one size only. Each .... .27

CadmiumYellow, pale Carmine, French Cadmium Yellow, Medium Purple Madder, Cadmium Yellow, Orange, Violet, Carmine, Aureolin, Burnt Carmine, Madder Carmine.

26813 American manufacture, single tubes. Each .... .23
26814 American manufacture, double tubes. Each .... .36
26815 Winsor & Newton's Oil Colors, in above shades, one size only. Each .... .45

QUADRUPLE TUBES.

Cremnitz White	Flake White
Sliver White	

26823 American manufacture. Price .... .20
26824 Price, Winsor & Newton's. Each .... .30

OUR GROCERY PRICE LIST

Contains everything kept in an ordinary grocery store, and many other things besides. All goods guaranteed as represented or money refunded.

Published Monthly. **Mailed Free.**

Winsor & Newton's Water Colors.

Moist in whole and half pans, and dry in whole and half cakes.
Weight of Water Colors, 1 ounce each.

COMMON COLORS.

Antwerp Blue	Light Red
Bistre	Mauve
Blue Black	Naples Yellow
Brown Ochre	Neutral Tint
Brown Pink	New Blue
Burnt S.enna	Olive Green
Burnt Umber	Orange Chrome
Chinese White	Payne's Gray
Chrome Yellow	Prussian Blue
Cologne Earth	Prussian Green
Deep Chrome	Raw Sienna
Emerald Green	Raw Umber
Gamboge	Roman Ochre
Hooker s Green, No. 1	Sap Green
Hooker's Green, No. 2	Terre Verte
Indigo	Vandyke Brown
Indian Red	Venetian Red
Italian Pink	Vermilion
Ivory Black	Yellow Lake
Lamp Black	Yellow Ochre

26826 Whole Pans or Cakes. Each............$0.25
26827 Half Pans or Cakes. Each............... .13

SPECIAL COLORS.

Brown Madder	Purple Lake
Cerulean Blue	Roman Sepia
Crimson Lake	Rubens Madder
Leitch's Blue (or Cyanine Blue)	Scarlet Lake
Mars Yellow	Scarlet Vermilion
Neutral Orange	Sepia
	Warm Sepia

26828 Whole Pans and Cakes. Each............$0.54
26829 Half Pans and Cakes. Each............. .27

Cobalt Blue	Violet Carmine
Indian Yellow	Veridian (or Veronese Green)
Lemon Yellow	
Orange Vermilion	Pale Cadmium Yellow
Cadmium Yellow	Cadmium Orange
Orange Vermilion	French Blue (or French Ultramarine)

26830 Whole Pans and Cakes. Each............$0.63
26831 Half Pans and Cakes. Each............. .31

Aureolin	Burnt Carmine
Carmine	Field's Orange Vermilion
Pink Madder	Rose Madder (or Madder Lake)
Gallstone	

26832 Whole Pans and Cakes. Each............ $1.00
26833 Half Pans and Cakes. Each............. .50

Madder Carmine	Smalt
Purple Madder	Ultramarine Ash.

26834 Whole Pans and Cakes. Each............ 1.30
26835 Half Pans or Cakes. Each............. .65

American Water Colors.

In Japanned Tin Boxes. Each
26841 The Royal Pocket Box, 6 colors in cakes; weight, 8 ounces....................$0.18
26842 The Imperial Pocket Box, 10 colors in cakes; weight, 9 ounces.. :............... .32
26844 The Rembrant Pocket Box, 12 pans, moist colors; weight, 11 ounces.............. .40
26845 The Murillo Pocket Box, 16 pans, moist colors, 2 tubes; weight, 12 ounces.............. .75

Artists' Prepared Canvas.

FIRST QUALITY—SMOOTH
26848 Artists' Prepared Canvas, 30 inches wide.
Price, per yard....................$0.65
Per roll of 6 yards................... 3.50
26849 Artists' Canvas, 36 inches wide; per yard. .70
Per roll of 6 yards................... 4.00
Weight, per yard, about 16 ounces.
For prices on Bolting Cloth see index.

Artists' Prepared Canvas on Stretchers.

No.	Size.	Smooth.	Size	Smooth.
		Each.		Each.
26860....	8x10	$0.30	18x30	$0.90
26861....	9x15	.40	22x36	1.35
26862....	1.x20	.55	28x48	2.20
26863....	12x24	.68	36x50	2.85
26865....	16x28	1.00	40x54	3.25

Intermediate sizes furnished at proportionate rates.
Weight on artists' canvas on stretchers; 8x10 to 9x15, 12 ounces; 10x20 to 16x24, 20 ounces; 48x30 to 22x36, 30 ounces; 28x43 to 40x54, 42 ounces.

Academy Boards.

26870— Smooth or Rough.

Size.	Weight.	Each.	Size.	Weight.	Each.
6x 9 in	10 oz.	$0.05	18x24 in	32 oz.	$0.25
9x12 in	12 oz.	.06	20x25 in	50 oz.	.35
12x18 in	18 oz.	.10	22x27 in	60 oz.	.40

Palettes.

Made of mahogany or walnut, either oval or square shape.

No.	Size.	Weight.	Price, oiled.	Price, polished.
26881	9 inch	3 oz	$0.15	$0.40
26882	10 inch	3 oz	.18	.40
26883	12 inch	4 oz	.25	.50
26884	14 inch	5 oz	.30	.75
26885	15 inch	6 oz	.35	.80

Palette Cups.

23886 Palette Cup, single, made of tin, without cover. Each...................$0.05
26887 Palette Cup, single, made of tin with cover. .10

Palette Knives.

With cocoa or ebony handle. Each.
26888 Size, 3 inch, weight 3 oz...................$0.20
26889 Size, 3½ inch, weight 3 oz................ .20
26891 Size, 4 inch, weight 4 oz............. ... .25
26892 Size, 5 inch, weight 5 oz................ .30

Oils and Varnishes.

In 2 ounce bottles. Weight, per bottle, 6 ounces.
Per bottle.
26901 Linseed Oil, purified.....................$0.13
26902 Pale Drying Oil........................... .15
26903 Strong Drying Oil........................ .15
26904 French Nut Oil .... .15
26905 French Poppy Oil .... .15
26906 Spirits Turpentine, rectified............. .14
26907 Genuine Mastic Varnish .... .40
26908 Picture Mastic Varnish .... .30
26909 Genuine Picture Copal Varnish.......... .20
26910 White Demar Varnish................... .18
26912 Oil Amber Varnish, for violins, 1 ounce bottles .... .35
26913 Spirit Amber Varnish, for violins .... .23
26914 White Lac Varnish .... .18
26915 French Retouching Varnish, for oil or water color paintings .... .25

French Siccatifs.

Weight, per bottle, 6 ounces.
26918 Siccatif de Courtrai, per bottle...........$0.23
26919 Siccatif de Harlem, per bottle............. .45

Mahl Sticks.

26925 Whitewood, 30 to 40 inches $0.18
26926 Black Walnut............................. .25
26927 Whitewood, with 4 joints, brass ferrules, varnished .... .50
Weight, 8 ounces.

Sketch Blocks.

Whatman's Solid Sketch Blocks, with rough and extra rough surface.

Each.
26932 Sketch Block; size, 5x7; weight, 7 oz.....$0.40
26934 Sketch Block; size, 7x10; weight, 8 oz.... .68
26935 Sketch Block; size, 9x12; weight, 9 oz.... 1.00
26936 Sketch Block; size, 10x14; weight, 10 oz. 1.35

Sensible Sketch Books.

Made of improved drawing paper of fine texture, particularly adapted for pencil work; will also take water color if carefully used. The paper is of a slight cream tint, and the covers of heavy cardboard, canvas covered, making a strong and durable book.

No.	Size.	Weight.	Each.
26939	5½x8	6 ounces.	$0.30
26941	6 x9	7 ounces.	.35
26943	9 x11	9 ounces.	.75
26944	10 x14	12 ounces.	.90

Impression Paper.

26945 Impression Paper, black, blue, red, green or white; size, 10x12; weight, per dozen, 5 oz.
Per sheet.................................$0.09

Sketching Easels.

26946 Patent Folding Sketching Easels, 5 feet in height, made of whitewood, with shelf and pins. Can be adjusted to hold the smallest placque or large canvas; folds in center, is light and convenient for carrying; weight, 42 ounces.
Price, each .... .75

Japanned Tin Boxes for Oil Painting Materials (empty).

Arranged to hold tube colors, palette, oil and brushes.
26947 Japanned Box, size. 11x6x1½, each..... $1.00
26948 Japanned Box, size, 13x6x2, each....... 1.35
26948 Japanned Box, size, 13x9x3, with inside lid to keep colors in place.
Each................. .... 1.50

Hard French Pastel Crayons.

26955 Box containing 12 sticks, assorted colors; weight, 4 ounces, per box....................$0.18
26956 Box containing 18 sticks, assorted colors; weight, 5 ounces, per box.................. .28
26957 Box containing 24 sticks, assorted colors; weight, 6 ounces, per box.................. .35
26958 Conte's Square Black Crayon, hard, medium and soft; weight, per dozen, 3 ounces.
Each.... .... .02
Per dozen............................... .17
26860 Crayon Holders, brass, 4-inch, each...... .09
26961 5-inch, each .... .11
26962 6-inch, each .... .13
Weight, 1 ounce.

Extra Soft French Pastel Crayons.

(Cannot be sent by mail.)

26962½ Box containing 64 crayons, assorted colors.
Each........... $2.00
26963 Box containing 126 crayons, assorted colors.
Each.........$3.75
26963½ Box (see cut) two trays, two rows, containing 160 crayons assorted colors, Each..$5.40
26964 Extra Soft Pastel Crayon, separate shades, packed in wood boxes, 1 dozen crayons of each shade in a box. No. 1 being the deepest shade.
Weight, 5 ounces. Price per box............ .45

Crayon Sauce.

26965 Conte's Crayon Sauce, put up in full packages. Price, per package $0.06
Per dozen............................... .65
Weight, 6 ounces.

Chamois Stumps.

26970 Nos.1,2 and3..$0.09 | 26973 No. 7.....$0.16
26971 Nos. 4 and 5.. .11 | 26974 No. 8 ..... .18
26972 No. 6.......... .13
Weight, each, 1 ounce.

Tortillons, Small Paper Stumps.

26980 Tortillon Stumps, 12 in package, white or gray. Per package....................$0.05

Fixatif.

For fixing crayon, charcoal or pencil drawings.
26985 2 ounce bottles, weight, six ounces.
Per bottles.............................$0.14

Amateur Crayon Outfit.

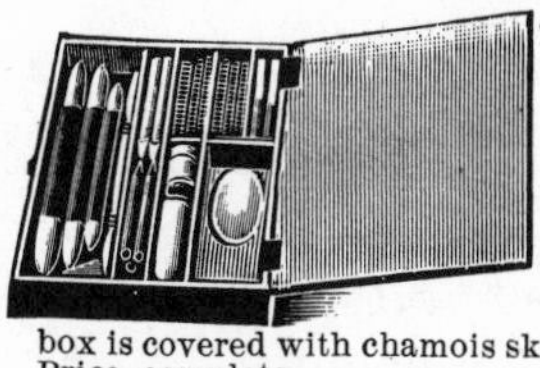

26987 Palette Crayon Box. Size, 6¾x5⅛, contains one dozen Conte black crayons, ½ dozen colored crayons, package crayon sauce, 12 tortillion stumps, 2 paper and 1 chamois stump. The lid of box is covered with chamois skin for stumping.
Price, complete....................$1.00
Weight, 12 ounces.

Tinted Crayon Paper.

26988 French Royal Crayon Paper, size, 19x24; weight, per sheet, 1 ounce. Per sheet..........$0.09
Per quire.................................... 1.20
26989 English Imperial Crayon Paper; size, 22x30; weight, per sheet, 1½ ounces. Per sheet.... .13
Per quire.................................... 2.70
26990 English Double Elephant Crayon Paper; 27x30; weight, per sheet, 12 ounces.
Per sheet................................ .22
Per quire................................ 4.05
26992 Charcoal Papers, good quality, white or tinted; size, 19x24; weight, per sheet, 1 ounce.
Per sheet................................ .05
Per quire................................ .90

Superior Bristle Artists' Brushes.

27001 Made of imported French Bristles, polished handles, round and flat.

No. 1 to 12 series.

No.		No.	
1	$0.05	7	$0.07
2	.05	8	.08
3	.06	9	.08
4	.06	10	.08
5	.07	11	.09
6	.07	12	.09

Weight, each, 3 oz.

Extra Large Bristle Brushes.

27002 Flat.

	Each.		Each.
½ inch	$0.07	1⅛ inch	$0.14
⅝ inch	.09	1¼ inch	.16
¾ inch	.10	1⅜ inch	.20
⅞ inch	.11	1½ inch	.23
1 inch	.12	1¾ inch	.26

Weight, each, 4 ounces.
"Bright's" Bristle and Landseer Bristle Brushes at same price as above.

Red Sable Brushes for Oil Colors.

27005 Round and flat, polished handles.

No.	Each.	No.	Each.
1	$0.07	7	$0.14
2	.08	8	.16
3	.09	9	.18
4	.10	10	.20
5	.11	11	.23
6	.12	12	.27

Assorted, 1 to 6, per dozen..................... 1.00
Assorted, 1 to 12, per dozen................... 1.55
Weight, each, 3 ounces.

Red Sable "Bright's" Brushes.

27007

No.	Each.	No.	Each.
1	$0.09	6	$0.20
2	.10	7	.25
3	.12	8	.30
4	.15	9	.35
5	.18		

Weight, each, 3 ounces.

French Round Badger Blenders.

27015 Polished handles.

No.	Each.	No.	Each.
1	$0.18	7	$0.60
2	.23	8	.68
3	.30	9	.78
4	.38	10	.90
5	.45	11	1.00
6	.52	12	1.10

Weight, each, 3 ounces.

Use Corticelli Sewing and Embroidery Silks.

Red Water Color Sables.

27017   Black polished handles, plated ferrules.

	Each.		Each.
No. 0 red	$0.09	No. 7 red	$0.41
1 red	.10	8 red	.50
2 red	.14	9 red	.63
3 red	.17	10 red	.81
4 red	.18	11 red	.95
5 red	.27	12 red	1.22
6 red	.32		

Weight, each, 3 ounces.

French Round Camel's Hair Lac Brushes.

27020   In tin, polished handles, large.

	Each.		Each.
No. 1	$0.09	No. 4	$0.15
2	.11	5	16
3	.13	6	18

Weight, each, 3 ounces.

Flat Camel's Hair Lac Brushes.

27025   In tin, polished handles, large.

	Each.		Each.
⅜ inch	$0.09	¾ inch	$0.15
½ inch	.09	⅞ inch	.18
⅝ inch	.13	1 inch	.23

Weight, each, 4 ounces.

Camel's Hair Brushes.

27027   Tin ferrules, polished, handles round.

	Each.		Each
No. 1	$0.05	No. 7	$0.11
2	.06	8	12
3	.07	9	.13
4	.08	10	.14
5	.09	11	.15
6	.10	12	.16

Weight, each, 3 ounces.

27035   Minature Camel's Hair Pencils, in quills; sizes from 1 to 8. Each $0.05
Per dozen, assorted .... .45
Weight, per dozen, 2 ounces.

27038   Camel's Hair Striping Brushes in quills, for carriage painting, etc. Sizes from No. 1 to No. 8. Each .... $0.05. Per dozen ..... .50

Papier Mache Plaques.

For Oil and Water Color Painting.

ROUND	EACH.						
	6 in.	7 in.	8½ in.	10 in.	12 in.	14 in.	16 in.
27050 Plain White	$0.13	18	23	27	35	45	.54
27051 Black Polished	$0.27	32	35	45	63	75	1.00

Weight, each, 6 ounces.

Porcelain Plaques.

Round, frosted surface.
It is not safe to ship porcelain plaques by mail.

27061   5 inch, weight, 4 ounces. Each $0.23
27063   7 inch, weight, 5 ounces. Each .... .38
37065   10 inch, weight, 8 ounces. Each .... .70
27067   12 inch, weight, 12 ounces. Each .... .90
27070   15 inch, weight, 16 ounces. Each 1.85

Intermediate sizes at proportionate rates.

Celluloid in Sheets.

27075   Celluloid, used for painting and novelties of all kinds; easily cut with scissors. We can furnish the following colors: White, pale blue, pink and nile green.
Sheets, size, 20x25 in. Each, $0.60. Postage..$0.08
27076   Celluloid, same as 27075 in sheets; size, 20x50 in. Each ..... $1.10. Postage .... .15
27077   Celluloid, transparent, size, 20x25.
Per sheet....$0.70   Per sheet, size, 20x50....$1.30
27078   Celluloid, translucent (imitation frosted),
Size, 20x25. Per sheet $0.70
Size 20x50. Per sheet $1.30

Amateurs' Oil Painting Outfit.

27082   Consists of sketching box, whitewood, highly polished size, 9x6, containing one tube each, chrome yellow, chrome green, burnt sienna, silver white, ivory black, yellow ochre, Naples yellow, emerald green, vandyke brown, light red permanent blue, crimson lake English vermilion; one bottle each pale drying oil, turpentine, one mahogany palette, one palette cup, one knife, one No, 1 blender, 2 flat bristle brushes, 1 sable brush, 1 small academy board and two studies. Price, complete.......$1.80
Weight, 30 ounces.

Oil Painting Outfit Complete.

27083   Oil Painting Outfit, consisting of extra fine japanned tin box, size,13x9x3 with bevel top; contains 25 tubes of oil colors, assorted, 6 bristle brushes, 4 red sable brushes, 2 Bright's bristle brushes, 1 Badger blender No. 4, 1 bottle each pale drying and poppy oil, and spirits of turpentine, steel palette knife, mahogany palette, 3 sticks charcoal and holder. Price, complete.....$6.00
Weight, boxed, 8 pounds.

Books on Oil Painting.

(Extra by mail, 4 cents.)

27086   Use of Colors. Valuable treatise on the properties of different pigments and their suitableness to use of artists and students.........$0.25
27089   Marine and Landscape Painting in Oil. Practical guide; fully illustrated.......................... .40
27092   How to Draw and Paint. The whole art of drawing and painting; containing concise instructions in outline, light and shade, perspective sketching from nature, etc.: 100 illustrations. Boards, cloth back.......................... .40
27106   Painter's Manual. A practical guide to house and sign painting, graining, varnishing, lettering, etc.; including a treatise on how to mix paints. Price, each.......................... .40
27108   Amateur Art, or Painting without a Teacher. This book teaches landscape and flower painting in oil and water colors, cameo oil painting, china painting, transfering photographs and prints to glass. coloring photos to oil and water colors, painting on velvet, silk plush, satin, wood and glass, Kensington painting, crayon portraiture, charcoal drawing, lustre painting, etc., etc.; also contains a carefully prepared table for mixing colors. Price........ 1.00
Postage........ .... .10

Lustre Paint Bronzes.

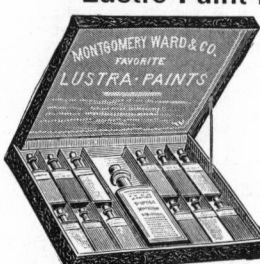

For painting on plush, velvet, silk, satin and for ornamental gilding and decorative purposes.
27125   One dozen bottles of bronze, assorted colors; also one bottle medium for mixing with the bronze. Assortment of colors in each box.

1 bottle Pale Gold.	1 Fire.
1 Rich Gold.	1 Sparkling Silver.
1 Green Gold.	1 Orange.
1 Silver.	1 Carmine.
1 Blue.	1 Lemon.
1 Green.	1 Copper.
1 Bottle Medium.	

Put up in fancy boxes, with full directions for using. Per box.............................$1.10
Weight, 24 ounces.
27130   Lustre Paints, any colors mentioned above. Per bottle............................. .10
Per 12 bottles.- 1.00
Weight, 2 ounces.
27132   Medium, for mixing with bronze. Per bottle..................................... .10
Per 12 bottles............................ 1.10
Weight, 6 ounces.
27135   "Our Favorite" Sparkling Spangles or Bronze Flitters, for decorative purposes. We can furnish the following colors: Gold, silver, copper, diamond (dust), straw yellow, orange, fire red, carmine, crimson, red, blue, violet, grass green, dark green, pink, light blue, dark blue, maroon, steel and mixed.
Price, per ounce vial, $0.15 Per dozen. $1.50
Weight, 2 oz.

Japanese Ready Mixed Paints and Enamels.

27145   Japanese Ready Mixed Paints for all kinds of artistic and decorative painting and gilding. Can be used on any article, but is intended more particularly for regilding furniture, frames and other household ornaments. We can furnish it in the following colors: Gold, silver, fire, crimson, green, blue, orange, lemon and maroon. Each bottle is packed in neat wood box, 3½x1½ in., with brush and directions for using.
Price, per box....................$0.20
Per dozen. 2.15
Weight, 5 ounces.

27146   Goldine (unmixed) the best substitute for gold leaf on the market. Used for decorating and gilding furniture frames, etc. The package contains one ounce bronze gold, one bottle mixing liquid, one brush and porcelain cup.
Price, complete $0.25
Per dozen. 2.70
Weight per package, 12 ounces.

27147   Star Enamels, ready for instant use. They are easily applied with a flat brush and produce a brilliant and lasting surface like ivory, and are washable as porcelain; can be used for painting vases, jars, chairs, tables, old furniture, baskets, bicycles, etc.; in fact, is useful for decorating anything and everything; when dry it becomes hard and durable. It is put up in cans; size, 3⅛x2⅛, and we can furnish the following shades: Pure white, ivory white, light blue, pink, green, yellow, red and black. Price, each..$0.18 Per dozen..1.95

Celluloid Novelties, Frames, Etc.

Celluloid is now being extensively used in the manufacture of fancy goods, frames, etc., as it is comparatively inexpensive, is made in all colors, and the most beautifully effects are produceed by ribbon and hand painted decorations.

Novelties.

27210   Cornucopia, made of translucent celluloid; hand-painted; cord to hang. Size, 3x8 inches. Weighs, 3 ounces. Each.. .$0.20

27212   Fancy Cornucopia, octagon shape, made of celluloid, handsomely decorated with hand-painted flowers. Size, 4½x8 in. Weight, 4 ounces. Each... $0.50

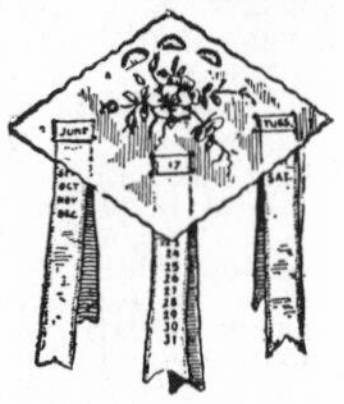

27214   Perpetual Calendar, diamond shape, made of translucent celluloid, hand-painted, three ribbons, giving month, day of week and day of month. Size, 7½x5½ inches. Weight, 4 ounces. Each... ....$0.40

27216   Perpetual Calendar, made of celluloid and white metal, imitation silver. Size, 6¾x4¾ inches. Hand-painted decorations; silk ribbons, with dates, etc. Weight, 7 ounces. Each......................$0.65

27217   Photograph Case. Size, 8x6½x 2½. Made of celluloid, silk lined, metal trimmings, holds 25 cabinets. Weight, 8 oz. Each...$1.00

27218   Jewel Box, fancy shape made of translucent celluloid, lined with silk, hand-painted. Size, 4x5 inches. Each $0.40
Weight, 12 ounces.

27220   Jewel Box of fancy shape, made of celluloid. Size, 6x6x2½. Lined with silk, metal ornament on top, metal feet, hand-decorated. Each.........$1.10

27222   Handkerchief Box; size, 6x6x3, made of semi-transparent celluloid, hand-painted decorations, extension base, corners trimmed with silver, lined with satin and perfumed.
Price, each $1.00
Weight, 8 ounces.

Novelties—Continued.

27224 Handkerchief Box, made of translucent celluloid, silk-lined, scalloped edges, trimmed with ribbon, hand-painted decorations. Each ....$1.10 Weight, 7 oz.

27228 Handkerchief Box, fancy shape, made of translucent celluloid, trimmed with metal ornaments, silk-lined, handsomely hand-painted cover, Size, 6x 6x3½. Weight, 15 ounces. Each......$1.75

27229 Glove Box, to match 27228. Size, 12x5x3½. Same style. Weight, 24 ounces. Each.........$2.10

Celluloid Cabinet Frames.

27301 Cabinet Photo Frame, made of polished celluloid, fancy shape, scroll opening. Size, 6x 7¾. easel back. Price ea $0.10 Per doz. $1.00 Weight, 4 oz.

27301

27303 Cabinet Photo Frame, size, 8½x6½, made of celluloid, scalloped edges, fancy opening, tied with silk tassels, assorted colors. Price, each ....$0 25 Weight, 6 oz.   Per doz 2.70

27305 Cabinet Frame, same style as No. 27303, double, for two cabinets. Each..... .... .50 Weight, 10 oz.   Per doz 5.40

27307 Cabinet Photo Frame, size, 8½x6½, made of transparent celluloid with silver ornaments on corner, scroll opening, tied back with silk tassels. Price, each...........$0.40 Weight, 6 oz. Per doz. 4.35

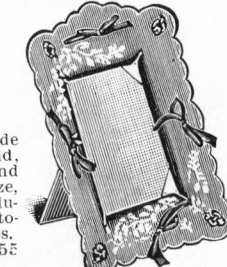

27308 Cabinet Frames made of translucent celluloid, hand painted, metal and ribbon trimmings. Size, 8½x5¼, transparent celluloid protector for photograph. Weight, 8 ounces. Each $0.55

27308

27310 Double Cabinet frame same style as 27308, with openings for two photographs. Weight, 12 ounces. Each....$1.10

27310

27312 Cabinet Frames, fancy shape, made of polished celluloid, bound with fancy white metal. Size, 10x8½ Weight, 10 ounces. Each........... $0.75

27312

27314 Cabinet Frame, size, 10x8½, fancy shape, made of translucent celluloid, metal trimmed with silver, metal ornaments. Weight, 10 ounces. Each....$0.90

Picture Frames—Continued.

Picture Frames, large sizes. We quote below a few of the most popular styles of Picture Frames, and our prices will be found exceedingly low. We carry in stock only "regular" sizes as described and we suggest to purchasers that if you do not find the *exact* size wanted in our list *cut your picture to fit a regular size if possible.* Our reason for making the suggestion is that a frame made "to order" costs nearly double a regular size of about same dimensions, besides it delays shipment at least one week. We do not send out samples of mouldings.

27320 Picture Frames, shell gilt, 3-inch moulding, pretty patterns fitted with glass.

Size	Each.	Per Doz.
8x10	$0.25	$2.70
10x12	.35	3.75
11x14	.38	4.00
14x17	.40	4.30
16x20	.45	4.85

27322 Picture Frames, 3½-inch shell moulding of receding pattern, handsome design, finished in composition of white and gilt, lacquered, each fitted with glass.

Size.	Each.	Per doz.
8x10	$0.37	$4.00
10x12	.40	4.30
11x14	.45	4.85
14x17	.50	5.40
16x20	.55	6.00

27324 Picture Frame of novel design, 3½-inch moulding, handsomely embossed face, finished white and gilt with pink tinted border. ¾-inch gilt lining reinforced with ¾-inch imitation ivory strip, very pretty frame fitted with glass.

Size.	Each.	Per doz.
8x10	$0.50	$5.40
10x12	.55	6.00
11x14	.60	6.45
14x17	.65	7.00
16x20	.70	7.50

27326 Picture Frame, 5-inch moulding, raised center, 3-inch figured and burnished gilt on inside, 2-inch steel moulding on outside, forming a large and showy frame, fitted with glass.

Size.	Each.	Per doz.
8x10	$0.55	$6.00
10x12	.60	6.45
11x14	.65	7.00
14x17	.70	7.50
16x20	.75	8.10

27328 Picture Frames of 3¼-in. beaded and polished oak, with 1-inch ornamented strip on outside, a neat and desirable frame, all fitted with glass.

Size.	Each.	Per doz.
8x10	$0.45	$4.85
10x12	.50	5.40
11x14	.55	6 00
14x17	.60	6.45
16x20	.65	7.00

27340 Picture Frame, 4-inch oak with fancy raised centre, ornamented with strip of imitation French walnut, all highly polished, suitable for fine pictures, fitted with glass.

Size.	Each.	Per doz.
8x10	$0.60	$6.45
10x12	.65	7.00
11x14	.70	7.50
14x17	.75	8.10
16x20	.80	8.65

Easels.

27437 Easels for photographs (without picture), made of twisted wire. Each.....$0.05 Per dozen. .50 Weight, 3 oz.

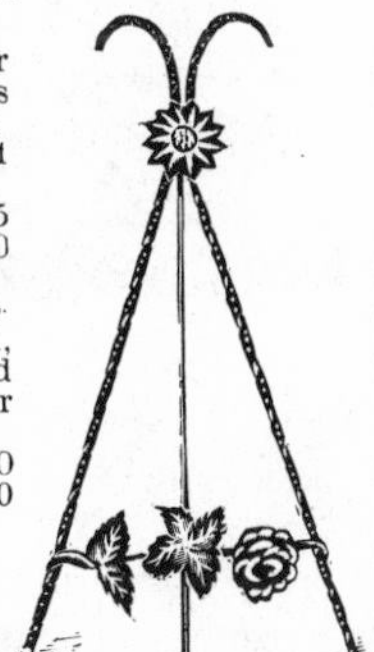

27440 Photograph Easel, made of twisted wire with silver decorations (see cut). Each...... ....$0.10 Per dozen .... 1.00 Weight, 5 ounces.

Ladies' Toilet Cases.

Manufacturers of fancy toilet and jewel cases, work boxes, etc., etc., have discarded nearly all plush, and now use celluloid almost exclusively. The reason is the latter material is more durable; is easily cleaned with water, and is susceptible to the finest embossing. In fact, it is equal in appearance to the most artistic carving. We handle the best grade, with turned corners and finest linings.

27601 Toilet Case; size, 9¾x4, made of silk plush, lined with satin. Contains bevel mirror, brush and comb. Each...................$1.00 Per dozen..............10.80 Weight, 25 ounces.

Toilet Cases—Continued.

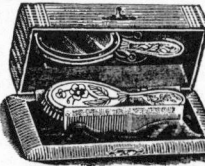

27602 Toilet Case; size, 9½x4½; made of celluloid, handsomely embossed, extension base, fine satin lining; contains white bevel mirror, brush and comb. Each...$1.50 Weight, 35 ounces.

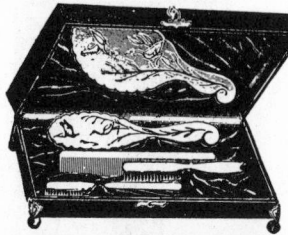

27606 Toilet Case; 10½x5½; made of silk plush lined with satin; contains white fittings, bevel mirror, comb, hair, tooth and nail brushes, assorted colors. Price, each $1.75 Weight, 26 oz.

27612 Combination Toilet and Manicure Case. Size, 11½x7. Made of celluloid sides, with handsomely embossed leaves and flowers, ribbed ends, extension base, spray of beautiful flowers embossed on center panel on top, fine satin lining; contains 10 pieces large fancy Florence fittings in white (bevel mirror). Weight, 49 ounces. Each $3.50

27618 Combination Toilet, Manicure and Odor Case. Size, closed, 11x7½ x6½. Made of fine silk plush, top and front of celluloid, with embossed scroll and floral design around edge. Cupid surrounded by wreath in center; lined throughout with satin; contains 10 pieces fancy white fittings and two odor bottles. A handsome case. Weight, packed, about 8 pounds. Each $4.50

27626 Combination Toilet and Manicure Case; size, 11 x13x4¼, finely carved celluloid base, silk plush ends, celluloid panel, 5½ inches wide over centre, on which is embossed three large sprays of colored flowers and leaves; finest satin lining, contains complete set of 12 white Florence toilet and manicure fittings, also glove stretcher. Weight, boxed, about 10 lbs. Each, $6.25

27630 Large Combination Toilet and Manicure Case; size, 15 x 13 x 4¼, made of celluloid, ivory finish, fine imitation carved ends, with two bands of colored raised flowers, two large sprays of colored flowers and leaves on top of center panel; lined with finest satin; contains handsome set of 17 pieces (including shoe horn and glove stretcher) of the finest Florence fittings, fancy pattern, raised colored flower design on back of brush and mirror. One of the best and most beautiful designs in a toilet case ever put on the market. Each............ $9.00 Weight, about 13 pounds.

Ladies' Toilet Sets in Plain Boxes.

Those who desire a toilet set of extra fine quality, and do not wish to pay for an elaborate case, will be able to make a selection from styles quoted below.

27640 Toilet Set, Florence, white; consisting of bevel mirror, length, 9½ inches, good brush, with embossed roses on back and comb, in neat pasteboard box. Per set....... $1.00 Weight, 23 ounces.

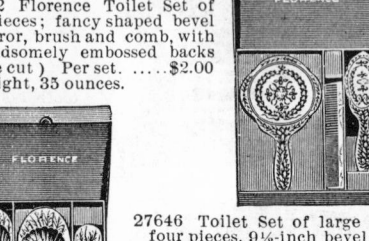

27642 Florence Toilet Set of 3 pieces; fancy shaped bevel mirror, brush and comb, with handsomely embossed backs (see cut) Per set. .....$2.00 Weight, 35 ounces.

27646 Toilet Set of large size, four pieces, 9½-inch bevel mirror, hair brush, cloth brush and comb, fancy shell pattern backs, in neat box. Per set......$2.25 Weight, 36 ounces.

27648 Toilet Set, large size fancy pattern, handsomely embossed, tinted backs, curved handles, large bevel mirror, extra fine brush with long, heavy bristles and comb. Per set.................$2.50 Weight, 36 ounces.

27650 Toilet Set of extra large size; length of mirror, 11¾ inches size of glass. 4½x 6½; large brush, with 15 rows heavy bristles; windmill design, embossed backs. Per set.................$2.85 Weight, 42 ounces.

27654 Toilet Sets in white with fancy embossed backs, consisting of five pieces, viz. bevel mirror, hair brush, cloth brush, hat brush and comb, large size, excellent quality. Per set...........$4 15 Weight, 50 ounces.

Infants' Cases.

27695 Infant's Case of Silk-Plush. sateen lined, containing powder box, brush, comb and ring of ivory, brush with fancy back, pretty box, size of case, 5x6. Weight, 16 ounces.
Each ....$ 1.00
Per dozen.................10.80

27696

27696 Infant's Case, made of fine silk plush, lined with satin; size, 6x5x3½, contains powder box, brush, comb and ring. Weight, 20 oz. Price, each....$1.35
Per dozen..........................14.50

By buying all your goods at one place you save time, trouble and money. The larger your order the less will be freight charges, as applied to each article.

Jewel Cases.

27700 Ladies' Silk Plush Jewel Case, satin lined, with two compartments, good quality, assorted colors, nickel clasp; size, 5½x4½.
Each......................$0.50
Per dozen............. 5.40
Weight, 10 ounces.

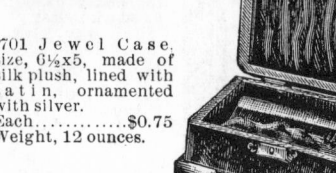

27701 Jewel Case, size, 6½x5, made of silk plush, lined with satin, ornamented with silver.
Each.............$0.75
Weight, 12 ounces.

27703 Jewel Case, size, 7 x 5 x 3 ¼, made of celluloid, ribbed ends, fancy embossing on sides; the word "Jewels" embossed in centre panel on top; satin lining, movable tray, lock and key. Each.$1.00 Weight, 22 ounces

27704 Watch Box of handsome polished oak; size, 4x4¼, metal ornaments, mirror back, lined with fine satin. Price, each, ...$1.00 Weight, 14 ounces.

Manicure Sets.

27720 Manicure Set, size, 6x3¾, made of silk plush, lined with satin; contains scissors, knife, powder box and nail polisher. Each.........$0.75 Weight, 12 ounces.

27722 Manicure Set, size, 7½x5, made of silk plush satin lined; contains 6 pieces manicure fittings. Price, each..$1.00 Weight, 12 ounces.

27727 Manicure Case, fancy shape, size, 11x8, made of the finest plush and satin; finely embossed top, contains, celluloid fittings, gold plated tips and ornaments; knife, scraper, polisher, tweezers, scissors, button hook, two powder boxes. Price, each..$3.50 Weight, 46 ounces.

27728 Jewel Case, covered with imitation seal leather gold plated trimmings, lined with the finest satin, beaded mirror on inside of cover; size, 8¾x6½; contains 8 large celluloid fittings, same as number 27727. Price, each....$4.25 Weight, 40 ounces.

Work Boxes.

27730 Work Box made of plush, satin lined, silver ornament on top; size, 5x6½. Contains 4 pieces fittings. Each.$0.50 Weight, 10 ounces.

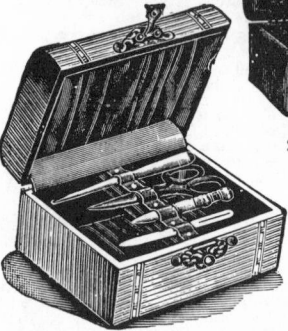

27731 Work Box; size, 4¾x3¼, made of celluloid, embossed satin lining, contains four work fittings. Each........$0.60 Weight, 8 ounces.

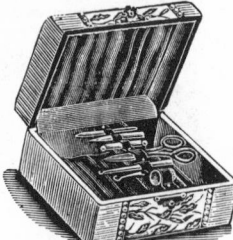

27733 Work Box; size, 8x5¾x3¼ made of celluloid, ribbed end, embossed front, handsome raised spray of colored flowers on top. Each...............$1.00

27738 Work Box; size, 9¼x5x4; made of silk plush, fancy shape large celluloid panel on top; handsomely embossed with colored flowers and leaves, satin lining, bevel mirror on inside of cover, contains 7 pieces white work fittings. Each.......$1.90 Weight, 27 ounces.

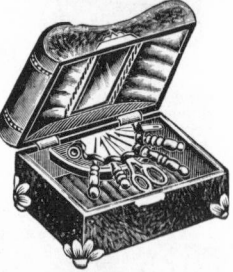

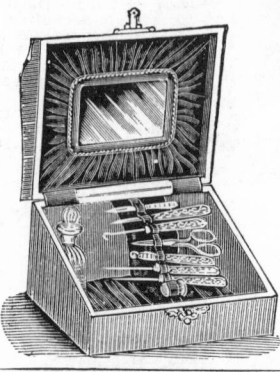

27744 Work Box, fancy shape; size, 8x6½x5, made of celluloid, ribbed sides and front, embossed top, satin lined, bevel mirror inside of cover, contains seven carved bone fittings, good scissors and odor bottle. Each...$3.00 Weight, 42 ounces.

We Are Like the Snow.

We Cover the Ground.

No House on Earth offers as many different articles as we do.

Toilet Mirrors.

27760 Plate Glass Mirror, bevel edge, with easel back, either for hand or used with back for shelf. The edges of plush in assorted colors; size, 4x6 inches, Price, each......$0.25 Per dozen.......... 2.75 Weight, 8 ounces.

27762 Tourists' Patent Mirror, 5½ in. diameter, silk plush back and sides, nickel sides, nickel and plush standard. This mirror can be adjusted to any angle, also fold together to avoid breaking. Price, each......$0.75 Per dozen........ 8.10 Weight, 15 ounces.

Hand Mirrors.

27774— Florence Hand Mirror, entirely new shape, handsomely decorated back. French plate glass size, 5x9½ inches; color black Weight, 11 ounces. Each $0.75 Per dozen 8.10

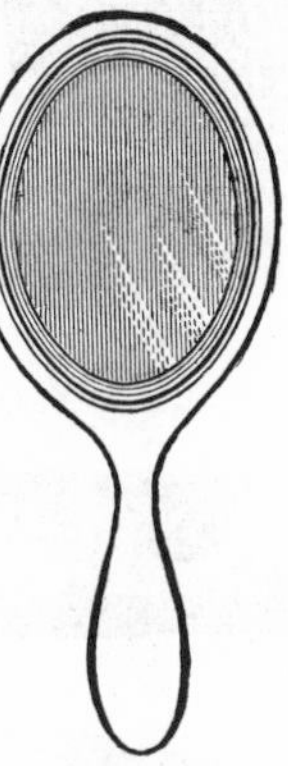

27774   27779

27779 Oval Hand Mirror, rubber back, bevel plate glass; length, 9 inches; colors black or brown; weight, 7 ounces. Each.......................$0.25

Pocket Mirrors.

27792 Pocket or Hand Mirror, size, 4¼x3, fancy nickel sides; easel back. Each..................... ....$0.10 Per dozen................. 1.00 Weight, 5 ounces.

27794 Round Mirror, 3 inches in diameter with nickel frame and folding handle. Each.$0.05 Per dozen..................... .50 27795 Round Mirror, same as 27794, 5 inches in diameter. Each.....................$0.10 Per dozen................. 1.00 27801 Round Zinc Folding Mirror, No. 1, 2½ inches in diameter. Weight, 5 ounces....$0.03 Per dozen..................... .33 27802 Same, 3 inches in diameter. 3 ounces. Each......$0.04 Per dozen................. .43 Weight, 6 ounces.

Open.

27794-802

Triplicate Mirrors.

27806 Triplicate Mirror (386) with three heavy bevel plates, size, 6x6, with fancy nickel plated frames, nickel ornament, flowered front. Price.......,$2.00 Weight, 35 oz. 27807 Triplicate Mirrors, same description as 27806, with plates; size, 8x8. Each........$3.75

27806

Write About Freight Rates.

Whisk Broom Holders.

27811 Whisk Broom Holder, with torchon back, celluloid front, hand painted. Size, 6½x6½. Each......... .$0.30 Weight, 10 oz. 27815 Whisk Broom; size, 4x6½, made of translucent celluliod, hand painted decorations, ribbons to hang; fitted with broom. Each...........$0.50 Weight, 12 oz.

27811

27815

27818 Whisk Broom Holder, size, 13x5 in. Shape of snow shoe, with heavy cord lacings, broom socket made of plush and celluloid, with handsome decorated fan embossed on front, fitted with good broom. Each..............$0.65 Weight, 15 ounces. 27819 Whisk Broom Holder. Shape of toboggan. Size,10x3½ in. Made of wood trimmed with satin ribbon. Broom socket made of celluloid, silk plush and satin, metal band, fitted with good broom. Each..............$0.85

27818   27819

Ladies' and Men's Toilet and Traveling Cases.

We quote nearly all of Men's Traveling and Shaving-Cases without razor, as every gentleman either possesses a good razor or wishes to make his own selections. When razors are desired please make selections from our regular line quoted in this catalogue, adding cost to regular price of case.

27827 Men's Toilet Set, in leather case, russet color; size 8¼x2¼, containing hair, tooth and nail brushes, comb and whisk broom. Weight, 8 oz. Price.............................$0.70 Per dozen.............. 8.15

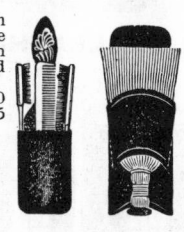

27828 Traveling Case, made of embossed leather; size, 8x2¼-x2, with neat bevel mirror, inlaid, contains solid back brush, comb, tooth and nail brushes. Weight, 10 ounces. Price, each..............$1.00

27830 Traveling case, made of embossed leather, rubber lined; size, closed, 8 x 4 x 2¾, contains solid back brush, bevel mirror, size, 3x6, comb, soap box, scissors, tooth and nail brushes and button hook. Price.......................$2.00 Weight, 22 ounces.

27830

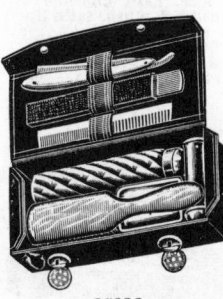

27832 Men's Traveling Case, made of sole leather; nickel clasps. Size, closed, 9x3¾x2¾; contains Torrey razor, strop, comb, solid back hair brush, nickel lather brush and soap box, tooth and nail brushes in glass bottle. Each..............$2.75 Weight, 24 ounces.

27832

Traveling Cases—Continued.

57834

27834— Ladies Traveling Case. made of fine embossed leather, size, closed 8x4x2 leather lined contains solid back hair brush, comb, nickel soapbox, perfume bottle, scissors, tooth and nail brushes, knife, nail scraper, file and button hook. Price...$3.00 Weight, 20 ounces.

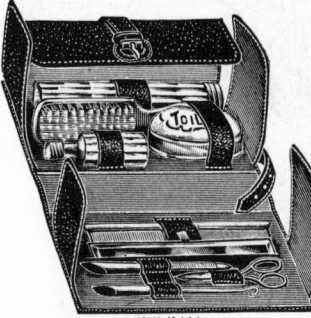

27834½ Traveling Case, made of heavy seal grain leather, size 8¾x5x2¼ fine leather lining. Contains solid back hair brush, comb, nickel soap box, tooth and nail brushes, perfume bottle, scissors, nail file, and bevel mirror.

27834½   Price, each ....$4.00 Weight, 30 ounces.

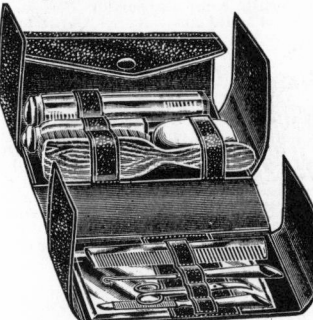

27836½ Ladies' Traveling Case made of genuine seal leather, finely finished, leather lining. size, 8½x4¼x 2¼. Contains hair brush. comb, celluloid soap box, cut glass perfume bottle, tooth and nail brushes in glass case, fine scissors, nail file, button hook and bevel mirror. Price, each........$5.50 Weight, 34 ounces.

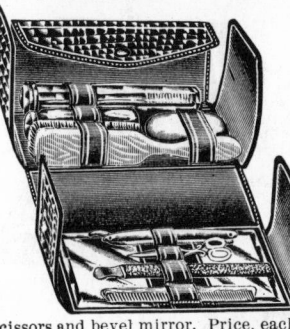

27837½ Mens' Traveling Case, of extra fine quality made of genuine alligator leather, lined with leather; size, closed, 8 ¼ x 4 x 2 ¼. Contains hair biush, comb, lather brush, tooth, and nail brushes in glass cases, celluloid soap box, Torrey razor, strop, scissors and bevel mirror. Price, each, complete..$6.00

Shaving Cases.

Nearly every gentleman possesses a razor, or at least wishes to make his own selection. For this reason we quote our Shaving Cases without razors. If you wish to order razor, please make selections from our line quoted in this catalogue and add cost to price of case.

27839 Shaving Case; size, 7x5; made of silk plush, satin lined, silver ornament on top; contains partition, mug and lather brush. Price, each........$1.25 Weight, 28 ounces.

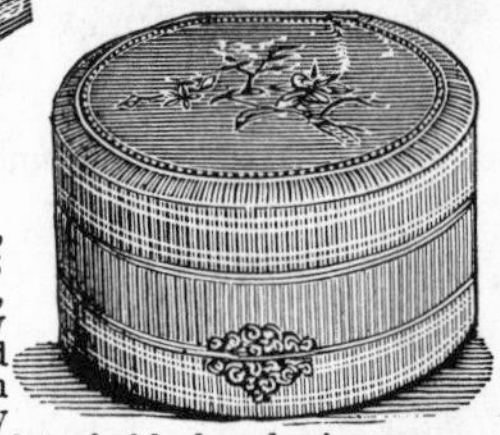

27840 Shaving Case, round pattern; size,7x4; made of celluloid, ivory finish, fancy ribbed sides, embossed panel on top, satin lined; contains fancy mug, lather brush and detachable bevel mirror. Each..$1.85 Weight, 26 ounces.

Shaving Cases—Continued.

27843 Shaving Case, fancy shape: made of silk plush, satin lined, silver ornaments on top; contains fancy mug, brush and adjustable plate mirror; size of case, 9x6¼x5½. Price, each, $3.00 Weight, 43 oz.

No razor furnished with this case.

27845 Shaving Case; size, 12x6½x4¼; made of celluloid imitation, carved sides, bevel edge, cover top finely embossed with spray of flowers, lined with satin; contains bevel mirror, fancy mug, lather brush, comb and scissors. Weight, 50 ounces. Each.... ....$3.15

27847 Shaving Case, fancy shape; size, 10x7, scalloped edges, open gilt trimming around outside, heavy embossed top, all made of silk plush lined with satin; contains detachable plush covered mirror, fancy mug, comb, lather brush and scissors. Each..............$4.50 Weight, 59 ounces.

Smoking Sets.

These cases are made in a substantial manner of good material, in artistic designs, and are "just the thing" for holiday and other presents. An ornament to any smoker's room.

27850 Smoking Set; size, 6x3¾; made of silk plush, lined with satin; contains imitation meerschaum pipe and cigar holder. Weight, 16 ounces. Each $0.70

27853 Smoking Set, made of celluloid. Size, 4x6. Metal ornament on top; satin lining, mirror on inside of cover; contains pipe, cigar holder, cigar cutter and nickel match box. Weight, 12 ounces. Each $1.00

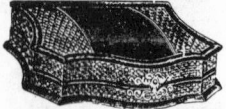

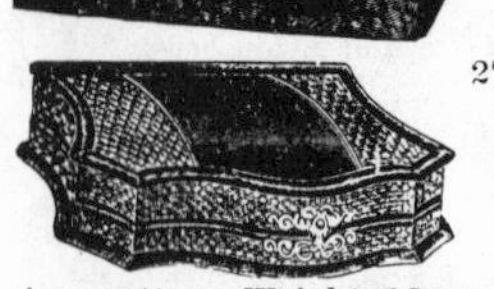

27854 Smoking Set; size, 8x6. Fancy shape, made of celluloid, finely embossed, plush edges, satin lined; contains pipe, cigar holder, cigarette holder, match-box and cigar cutter. Weight, 18 ounces. Each $2.00

Collar and Cuff Boxes.

27858 Combination Collar and Cuff Box, made of silk plush, horseshoe shape, lined with paper. Each.$0.50 Weight, 10 ounces.

Collar and Cuff Boxes—Continued.

27859 Combination Collar and Cuff Box, round pattern. Size, 6x7 inches. Made of celluloid, fancy carved sides, words "Collars and Cuffs" embossed on top, fine satin lining, tube in center for cuffs. Weight, 26 ounces. Each...............$1.00

27862 Combination Collar and Cuff Box, fancy shape, size, 9 x 7½ x 5¾, made of fine silk plush, lined with satin, silver ornaments. Price, each.. $1.50 Weight, 39 ounces.

27863 Combination Collar and Cuff Box. Size, 9¼x5¾x 5½. Made of celluloid, ivory finish, beaded ends, fancy cover, with spray of embossed colored flowers, finest satin lining, two compartments. Weight, 35 ounces. Each..........$1.90

SOLE LEATHER COLLAR AND CUFF BOXES.

Sole Leather Collar and Cuff Boxes, extra heavy sole leather top and bottom. Collar boxes 4½ inches in diameter, 3½ inches high; cuff boxes 4½ inches in diameter, 5 inches high; in red russet or orange colored leather, at prices as follows:

27865   **27865** Collar and Cuff Boxes, without handle. Per set of 2............$0.90
27866 Combination Set, collar one end, cuffs the other. Each.................................... .90
27868 Collar and Cuff Boxes, with plush sides, without handle. Per set of two. 1.50

27869 Combination Set, plush sides. Each................................$1.50
27870 Collar and Cuff Boxes, with adjustable handle. Per set of two.$1.25
27871 Collar and Cuff Boxes, with adjustable handle, plush sides. Per set of two.....................$1.75
Extra by mail, per set............. .15
27872 Combination Collar and Cuff Box and Toilet Case, made of sole leather; size, 8x4½; cuffs in one end, collars the other, toilet set in center, consisting of solid back hair brush, comb, tooth and nail brushes. Price, each......................$1.75

Handkerchief and Glove Boxes.

27874½ Glove and Handkerchief Set; size, 12x4 and 6½x6½; made of silk plush, satin lined, oval corners, raised top, glove box fitted with stretchers. Per set of two............$1.75 Weight, 36 ounces.

27875 Glove and Handkerchief Set of fancy shape, made of the best silk plush, fine satin lining, size, 12x5, 7x7½; glove box fitted with stretcher. Price, per set of two......$2.00 Weight, 40 ounces.

Handkerchief Boxes—Continued.

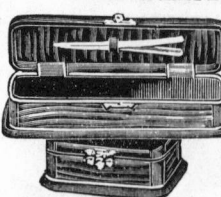

27876 Glove and Handkerchief Set, made of fine silk plush, embossed top, round corner, extension base, satin lining; fitted with glove stretcher; size of glove box, 12x4x4; size of handkerchief box, 7x 7x4. Price, each..$2.50 Weight, 45 ounces.

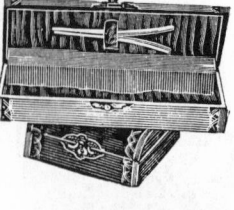

27877 Glove and Handkerchief Set, made of polished celluloid, trunk shaped, trimmed with silver metal bands, fancy center ornament, satin lining; size handkerchief box, 6⅜x6⅜x 2¾; glove box, 12½x 3¾; fitted with stretcher. Price, each...$3.25 Weight, 41 ounces.

27878 Glove and Handkerchief Set, covered with imitation seal leather, gold plated ornaments, metal feet, lined with finest satin, fitted with glove stretcher. Price, per set of two..$4.25 Weight, 48 ounces.

27878

Necktie Cases.

27879 Necktie Case; size, 14½x4. Made of silk plush, the word "neckties" in metal on top, nickel clasps, inside of cover, lined with satin. Weight, 14 ounces. Each...$0.75

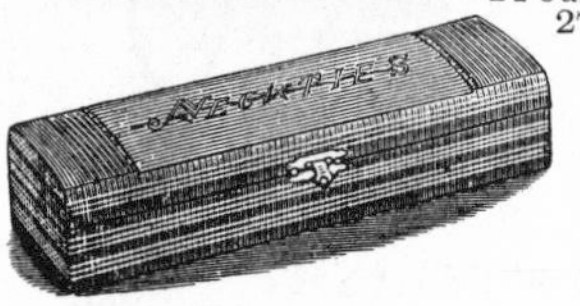

27880 Necktie Case; size, 12½x3¾x2¾, made of celluloid; fancy embossed sides and ends, the word "Necktie" embossed on top, full satin lining. Each..........$1.00 Weight, 21 ounces.

Photograph Cases.

27881 Photograph Case made of silk plush lined with satin; size, 7½x5, will hold 50 cabinets; assorted colors. Price, each....$1.00 Weight, 14 ounces.

27882 Photograph Case, size, 7½x, 5½, made either of fine silk plush or polished birds-eye maple, fancy ornament on top, metal feet and lined with finest satin. Price, each. ....$1.40 Weight, 25 ounces.

27883 Upright Photograph Case, fancy shape; size, 11x8½, ornamented celluloid front, celluloid door, handsomely embossed with colored flowers; also has the word "Photographs" across front; fine satin lining, holds 50 cabinets. Each............ ...$1.60 Weight, 20 ounces.

27884 Photograph Case, size, 9¾x7½, made of fine silk plush, ornamented with silver (see cut), lined with fine satin; will hold 100 cabinet photographs. Price ....$2.00 Weight, 25 ounces.

Photograph Cases.

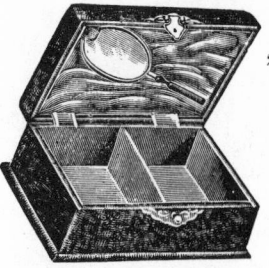

27885 Photograph Case, size, 9½x7¼, made of fine silk plush, fancy ornament on top, extension base lined with finest satin. Each box contains fine magnifying glass with 3 inch lens. Price, each....$2.50 Weight, 30 ounces.

Slipper Cases.

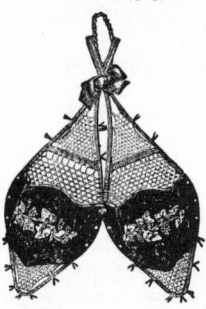

27898 Slipper Case, consisting of two snow shoes, with wood frames joined together; size, 11x16: cord lacings,slipper pockets made of silk plush with silvered metal ornaments on fronts. Each...........$1.00 Weight, 16 ounces.

DRUGGISTS' SUNDRIES, TOILET PREPARATIONS, FACE POWDERS, PERFUMES, ETC.

Face Powder.

Postage on face powder, per box...............$0.05

27902 Tetlow's Celebrated Swans' Down Face Powder, guaranteed to contain no poisonous substance; full size, white or flesh. Per box..................$0.10 Per dozen..............1.00 27907 Tetlow's "Refinement," a combination box of face powder containing lily white Rouge and Eye Brow Pencil. Per box..................$0.20 Per dozen..............2.15

27916 Pozzoni's Dove Complexion Powder, a delicate, invisible, perfumed toilet powder, and warranted perfectly harmless; either white or brunette; put up in round boxes 3 in. in diameter. Per box..................$0.20 Per dozen boxes 2.15

27917 Pozzoni's Celebrated Medicated Face Powder; put up in round wood boxes, either white or pink. Per box......................40 Per dozen boxes.................4.30

Eye Brow Pencils.

27924 Eye-Brow Pencils for imparting dark colors to the eye-brows and lashes; put up in nickel plated case; length, 2⅝ in. Each................$0.10 Per dozen...................1.00 Weight, 2 ounces.

Infant Powders, Puffs, Etc.

27925 Infant Powder, best quality. Per pkge.....$0.10 Per dozen packages............................1.00 27926 Toilet Powder Puffs, for toilet and infants' use, satin top, bone handles. Each................20

Puff Boxes.

27928 Puff Boxes, made of papier mache. Size, 3x3½. handsome Chinese decorations. Each.......$0.20 Weight, 4 ounces.

27930 Puff Boxes, similar in style to No. 27928, made of celluloid; colors, either white, pink or blue. Each.....................$0.40 Weight, 5 ounces.

Lotus Cream.

27931 Chiles' Lotus Cream is a new and effective preparation for the skin, made from the cactus plant, contains no oil or grease and is guaranteed absolutely harmless. It cures chapped hands, sore lips and all inflammation and irritation of the skin, will also remove pimples, tan and sunburn. Put up in 2½ oz bottles; weight, 10 oz. Price, per bottle......................$0.15 Per dozen 1.60

Toilet Preparations—Continued.

27933

27933 Knights Parisian Cream, a new and delicate toilet preparation which we consider superior to glycerine or camphor ice as it is not greasy or sticky and makes the skin soft and velvety; highly perfumed. Price, 2 oz. bottles.......$0.15 Per dozen..........................1.60 Weight, 12 ounces. 27934 Knight Parisian Cream, 4 oz. bottles. Each......................25 Per dozen..........................2,70 Weight, 16 ounces.

Cook's Chlorate Dentifrice.

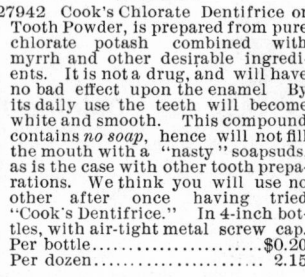

27942 Cook's Chlorate Dentifrice or Tooth Powder, is prepared from pure chlorate potash combined with myrrh and other desirable ingredients. It is not a drug, and will have no bad effect upon the enamel By its daily use the teeth will become white and smooth. This compound contains *no soap*, hence will not fill the mouth with a "nasty" soapsuds, as is the case with other tooth preparations. We think you will use no other after once having tried "Cook's Dentifrice." In 4-inch bottles, with air-tight metal screw cap. Per bottle......................$0.20 Per dozen.....................2.15

27944 *Sozodont*, per bottle.......................70 27946 *Calder's Saponaceous Dentine.* Per bottle ....20 27948 *Crosswell's Tooth Powder.* Per bottle 20

Florida Water.

28030 Florida Water is either used as a perfume for handkerchiefs or as a lotion in bathing face, arms and hands. It can be used with water for latter purposes, imparting a cool and pleasant feeling to the skin, and making it soft and clear. The ingredients are pure and simple, united with perfumes from flowers. It is of full strength and warranted excellent in all respects. Manufactured expressly for us, Our own brand, and every bottle warranted.

	Weight.	Each.	Per doz.
No. 1, 2-oz. bottle	9 oz.	$0.15	$1.40
No. 2, 4-oz. bottle	13 oz.	.25	2.70
No. 3, 8-oz. bottle	17 oz.	.45	4.86

Florida Water is packed in boxes of one doz.

Colognes and Perfumes.

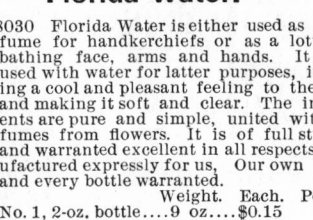

28033 Extra quality German Cologne. 1-oz. bottle........$0.14 Weight, 6 ounces. 4-oz. bottle............30 Weight, 12 ounces. 8-oz. bottle...........60 Weight, 25 ounces.

1 oz. 4 oz. 8 oz. 3½ in. 6 in. 7½ in. high.

Hoyt's German Cologne.

28035 Hoyt's Genuine German Cologne, 10 cent size. Price, per bottle.............$0.09 Per dozen.....................1.00 Weight, 6 ounces. 28036 Hoyt's German Cologne, 25 cent size. Price, per bottle... ....$0.20 Per dozen.....................2.25 Weight, 10 ounces. 28037 Hoyt's German Cologne, 50 cent size. Price, per bottle.............$0.40 Per dozen.....................4.30 Weight, 20 ounces.

Montgomery Ward & Co.'s Extracts.

Perfumes are sold throughout the country, almost exclusively by retail druggists, and like everything else in their line at enormous profits. Not only this but they seldom carry the best grades. We buy our entire line of perfumes in bulk from the best manufacturers in this country, handle *only the choicest pomade* extracts, and put them up ourselves in ordinary bottles. We are thus enabled to give our customers the very finest perfumes made at very low prices. We carry in stock the complete line of staple flower odors. Make your selection from list given below.

White Rose,   Rose Geranium,
Jockey Club,   Musk (true Tonquin),
White Lilac,

New Mown Hay.

Blue Lilies,   White Heliotrope,
Lily of the Valley,   Wood Violet,
Frangipanni,   Violet,
Persian Lilac,   Colgate's Cashmere
Crab Apple Blossom,   Bouquet,
Shandon Bells.   Japonita.

Put up in quantities to suit purchaser at prices as follows:

		Mailing weight.	Each.
28041	1 ounce bottle	11 oz.	$0.35
28042	2 ounce bottle	14 oz.	.55
28043	4 ounce bottle	16 oz.	1.00

No charge for bottles.

We guarantee the above exactly as represented. We carry the extracts in stock in bulk and bottle them ourselves. Parties desiring to buy perfumery and not bottles, will do well to order the above, as we believe in putting all the value inside of the bottles. Purchase money refunded to parties not satisfied with Montgomery Ward & Co.'s perfumes, at prices charged, upon return of same.

Perfume Novelties.

28053

28053 Handsome Perfume Vase, made in imitation of cut glass; height, 7 in. Contains 1 oz. perfume; a pretty ornament for bracket or dresser. Each......................$0.20 Per dozen.....................2.15 Weight, 12 ounces.

28055 Fancy Bisque Vase, size, 4x2, white, decorated with ribbon, with colored bisque rose and leaves on front, filled with perfume. Each......................$0.20 Per dozen ....2.15 Weight, 12 ounces.

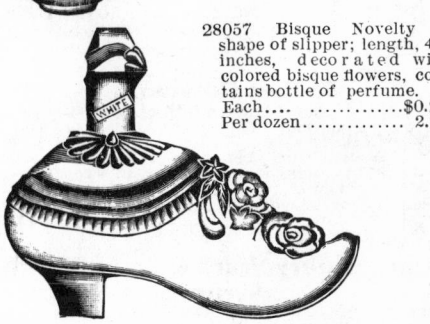

28057 Bisque Novelty in shape of slipper; length, 4½ inches, decorated with colored bisque flowers, contains bottle of perfume. Each.... ....$0.25 Per dozen.............2.70

Atomizers.

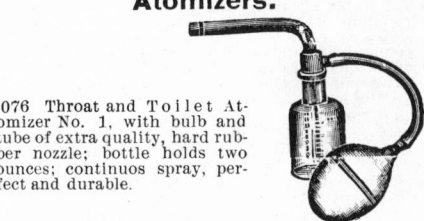

28076 Throat and Toilet Atomizer No. 1, with bulb and tube of extra quality, hard rubber nozzle; bottle holds two ounces; continuos spray, perfect and durable.

28076

Each ....$0.40 Weight, 8 ounces.

We try always to say what we mean, and to mean what we say.

Atomizers—Continued.

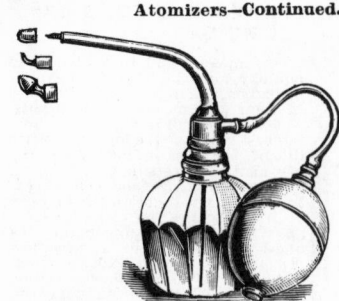

28077 Throat and Nasal Atomizer of fine quality, large bulb, continuous spray, three hard rubber screw tips; long straight tube for throat or general applications downward; tube for larynx; also Nasal tip. Each...$0.75

28078— Atomizer for spraying Oils, Vaseline, etc. Each... ...$0.70 Weight, 18 oz.

Hair Oil and Brilliantine.

28085 Bay Rum Hair Oil, an excellent dressing, made from the very best oils and bay rum, put up in 4 ounces, fancy bottles. Per bottle......$0.18 Per dozen.....$1.95 Weight, 16 ounces.

28087 White Rose Hair Oil, extra fine quality, scented with white rose, 4 ounce fancy bottles. Per bottle.............$0.20 Per dozen...........................2.15 Weight, 16 ounces.

Brilliantine.

28090 A preparation for the moustache, giving a glossy appearance; is also used for the hair; perfectly harmless, 1 ounce bottles, weight, 4 ounces. Price.............$0.20 Per dozen..............................2.15

Perfumery and oils can be sent by mail.

Bandoline, Sea Foam, Etc.

28092 Bandoline. A preparation for the hair (not a dressing) to be applied after combing to keep it in place. Put up in 1½ oz. bottles. Each.............................$0.10 Per dozen..........................1.00 Extra by mail.......................07

28095 Shampoo Powder or "Seafoam," for cleansing the scalp, put up in bottles. Each bottle contains enough powder to make one quart of the mixture. Full directions with each bottle. Price, per bottle...................$0.25 Per dozen.............................2.70 Weight, 5 ounces.

Sachet Powders.

28110 Sachet Powder in 1 oz. glass jars, four odors, viz.: White rose, heliotrope, Jockey Club and violet. Each.................$0.20 Weight, 6 oz. Per dozen................2.15

28114 Sachet Powder, packet of smaller size, containing about ¼ oz. of powder in assorted colors. Each.............................$0.10 Per dozen..............................1.08 Weight, 2 ounces.

Montgomery Ward & Co.'s Cough Syrup.

D5600 This is an old and well known preparation for relieving and curing all forms of colds. Useful in bronchial, throat and lung diseases. The formula is published on every bottle and you know just what you are taking. Your physician will tell you that this is one of the best combinations of the pharmacopœia for coughs and colds. Try a bottle and be convinced. Price, per bottle.............................$0.30 Per dozen.............................3.00

D5601 Montgomery Ward & Co.'s Beef, Wine and Iron. Each fluid ounce contains the nutritive portion of two ounces of lean beef, 4 grains of citrate of iron, dissolved in pure sherry wine. Price, per pint bottle............$0.35 Price, per dozen pints.....................3.50

NO TIME TO SPARE...
. . . WHEN DRUGS ARE WANTED.

Send for our Drug Catalogue and learn something about prices.

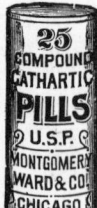

Compound Cathartic Pills.

D5602 Montgomery Ward & Co.'s Compound Cathartic Pills, sugar coated, 25 pills in neat wooden box. Compound after U. S. Pharmaceutical recipe. Per box...............................$0.11 Per dozen boxes..........................75 Weight, 2 oz.

Vegetable Liver Pills.

D5604 Montgomery Ward & Co.'s Vegetable Liver Pills, sugar coated, formula printed on outside of wrapper; put up 25 in a box. Per box................................$0.12 Per dozen boxes..........................75

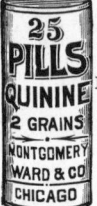

Quinine Pills.

D5608 Montgomery Ward & Co.'s Sulphate Quinine Pills, 2 grains, gelatine coated, made of absolutely pure quinine. Per bottle, 100 pills.................$0.24 Per dozen bottles.........................2.40 Weight, 3 oz.

Insect Powder.

D5610 Montgomery Ward & Co.'s Insect Powder, warranted to be of the very best quality. "Sure death" to insects. Put up in 1 lb. packages. Price, each...........................$0.35 Per dozen............................4.00

Borax.

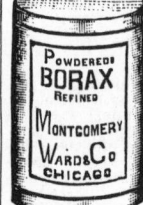

D5614 Borax, refined, powdered, put up in our own factory, and guaranteed perfect. Makes a handy and cleanly package for household use. 1 lb. package, each...........$0.17 Per dozen.....................1.80

Epsom Salts.

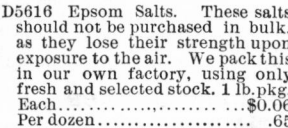

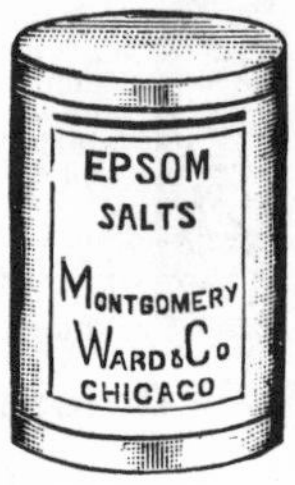

D5616 Epsom Salts. These salts should not be purchased in bulk, as they lose their strength upon exposure to the air. We pack this in our own factory, using only fresh and selected stock. 1 lb. pkg. Each...........................$0.06 Per dozen.......................65

Rochelle Salts.

D5618 Montgomery Ward & Co.'s Rochelle Salts of the very best quality, put up strictly for medical purposes. Not at all disagreeable to the taste. ½-lb. pkg., each.......................$0.30 Per dozen...........................3.25 1-lb pkg., each...........................50 Per dozen............................5.00

Sulphur.

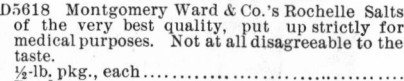

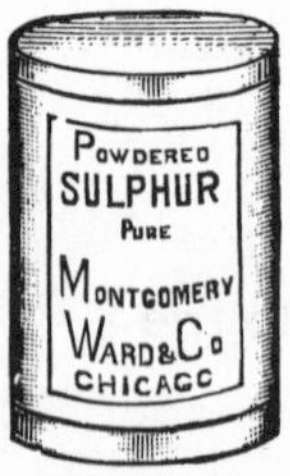

D5620 Sulphur, powdered, refined; packed in our own factory, from the brightest and cleanest stock we can buy. 1 lb. package. Each ....$0.07 Per dozen.....................80

Ammonia.

D5622 Ammonia, household, extra quality, pint bottles. Put up expressly for Montgomery Ward & Co. Per bottle.............................$0.12 Per dozen...........................1.25 Weight, 24 oz.

Spirits of Camphor.

D5624 Montgomery Ward & Co.'s Spirits of Camphor, put up in 4 oz. bottles, and guaranteed to be chemically pure. Each.....................$0.25 Per dozen...........................2.50 Weight, 10 oz.

Glycerine.

D5628 Montgomery Ward & Co.'s Glycerine, warranted absolutely pure.

	Each.	Per doz.
2 oz. bottles....	$0.10	$1.00
4 oz. bottles....	.15	1.50

Paregoric.

D5630 Montgomery Ward & Co.'s Paregoric, carefully compounded.

2 oz. bottles....	$0.15	$1.50
4 oz. bottles....	.25	2.50

Weight, 5 and 8 oz.

Peppermint.

D5632 Montgomery Ward & Co.'s Tincture of Peppermint, best quality

	Each.	Per doz.
2 oz. bottles..........	$0.15	$1.50
4 oz. bottles..........	.25	2.50

Court Plaster.

	Per Envelope.	Per doz.
D5634 Court Plaster, about 2x3 in. on silk; black, white or pink; 1 sheet in envelope......................	$0.04	$0.30
D5636 Court Plaster, about 1¼x2½ in., 3 sheets in envelope, assorted 3 colors, on muslin..................	.03	.25

Spirits Nitre.

D5638 Montgomery Ward & Co.'s Sweet Spirits Nitre, U. S. P. Absolutely pure.

	Each.	Per doz.
2 oz. bottles....	$0.15	$1.50
4 oz. bottles....	.25	2.50

Tincture of Arnica.

D5644 Tincture of Arnica, standard quality, U. S. P., made expressly for us, and quality and strength guaranteed.

4 oz. bottles (¼ pints)...............	$0.20	$2.10
8 oz. bottles (½ pints)...............	.35	3.50

Extract Hamamelis.

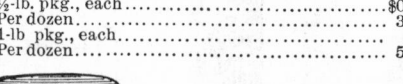

D5646 Extract of Hamamelis (or Witch Hazel). Guaranteed exactly same as Pond's Extract. Everywhere recognized as a universal all healing remedy. Undoubtedly the most valuable medicine to have in every house. Nothing equals it for sore throat, hemorrhage, sprains, bruises, wounds, sore eyes, stiff joints, in fact, is useful in nearly every accident that one can meet with. Bottled expressly for us and warranted pure. ½ pint bottle ($0.50 size). Each...$0.15 Per dozen.............................1.50 Weight, 12 oz.

1 pint bottle ($1.00 size), each....................25 Per dozen...........................2.50 Weight, 24 oz. 1 quart bottle ($1.50 size), each....................40 Per dozen.............................4.00 Weight, 45 oz.

Cook's Witch Hazel Toilet Lotion.

D5648 An elegant preparation for chapped hands, face and lips; one of the finest lotions to use, after shaving, in the market; our employes use it in preference to any other. Per bottle, 4 oz. size.................$0.18 Per dozen bottles.......................2.00

Cook's Bay Rum.

Distilled expressly for Montgomery Ward & Co. by Dr. John G. Cook, and is equal to the finest Imported. D5654 Bay Rum, quart bottle. Each...........$1.00 Per dozen.............................10.50 D5656 Bay Rum, pint bottle. Each....................60 Per dozen.............................6.00 Weight, packed, 30 ounces. D5658 Bay Rum, ½ pint bottles. Each....................35 Per dozen.............................3.50 Weight, packed, per bottle, 16 ounces. D5660 Bay Rum, ¼ pint bottle....................19 Per dozen.............................2.00 Weight, packed, 12 ounces.

Petroleum Pomade (Perfumed).

Guaranteed exactly similar to cosmoline or vaseline, and at a much lower price. D5666 Purified Petroleum Pomade or Vaseline, scented, for chapped or rough skin, blotches, pimples, sores, lip salve for toilet purposes. Nothing equals it as a hair dressing in place of the old style hair oil. Put up expressly for us, and purity guaranteed; 4 oz. bottles. Per bottle.............$0.15 Per dozen.............1.50 Extra, by mail.........21

Petroleum (Like Cosmoline).

D5668 This is a preparation made from purified petroleum oil, is similar to cosmoline and vaseline, and is the best remedy known for healing cuts, bruises, burns, etc. Plain, not perfumed.

	Each.	Per doz.
2 oz............................	$0.06	$0.50
4 oz............................	.10	1.00
1 lb. cans......................	.25	2.50

D5670 Carbolized Petroleum; same as No. D5668 with the addition of carbolic acid; 2-ounce bottles. Each.............................15 Per dozen..............................1.50

Ink Powder.

D5672 Ink Powder, put up in vials containing powder sufficient for one pint best quality of ink; colors: Green, red, black or violet. Each.............................$0.12 Per dozen..............................1.25 Per gross.............................13.50 Weight, 1 ounce each.

Cook's Cough Cure.

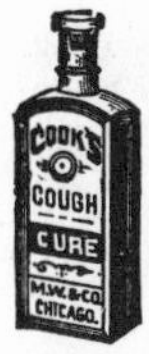

D5676 Low price, yet as efficacious as any made from an old fashioned recipe. Put up expressly for M. W. & Co. Per bottle....$0.20
Per dozen....2.00
Weight, 3 oz.
D5678 Cook's large size, ½ pint cough cure. Per bottle....75
Per dozen bottles....7.50

Flake Tar Camphor.

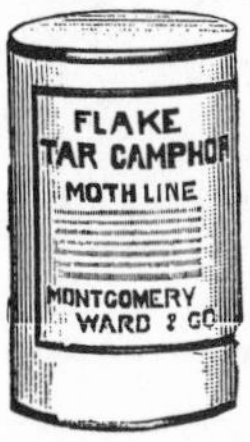

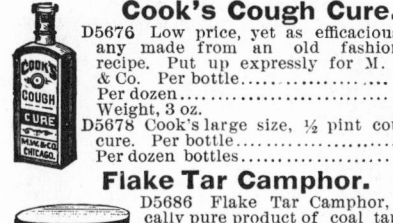

D5686 Flake Tar Camphor, a chemically pure product of coal tar for the preservation of furs, clothing, leather, etc., etc., from moths. It is free from oil or alkali and will not injure the most delicate fabrics. Put up in 1 lb. packages.
Price, per pkg....$0.25
Per dozen....2.25
Weight, 18 oz.

Cook's Eye Water.

	Each.	Per doz.
D5688 A remedy of 25 years' standing. Absolutely harmless to the yonngest infant. For weakness or inflammation of the eyes it has no equal. Moisten the eyes and drop a little inside three or four times a day. In 2 oz. bottles....	$0.15	$1.40
In 4 oz. size, with eye cup and dropper, complete in neat box....	.35	3.25

Catarrh Snuff.

D5690 Dr. Cook's Celebrated Catarrh Snuff, for nasal catarrh, hay fever, cold in the head, etc. This is a recently discovered compound; is indorsed by all the leading practitioners of this country, does not stain and affords immediate relief without causing irritation or sneezing. Put up in handy screw top bottles. Each....$0.17
Per dozen....1.90

Seidlitz Powders.

D5696 Seidlitz Powders, pure, good strength; in tin boxes, 10 powders in a box. Per box....$0.20
Per dozen....2.00
Weight, 8 oz.

Condition Powders.

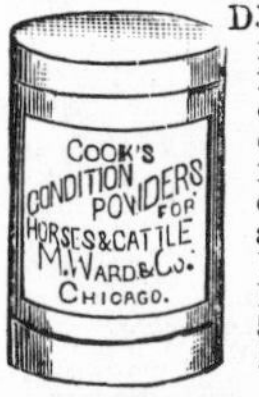

D5698 Dr. Cook's Condition Powders, for horses and cattle. Everyone owning stock has felt the need of something of this character. This is made after one of the best known formulas in existence, and will prove to be a thoroughly reliable remedy. We offer it at a popular price. 1 lb. pkg. (25c. size).
Each....$0.18
Per dozen....2.00
50c. pkg., each....35
Per dozen....3.75

Cook's Neutralizing Cordial.

D5700 Put up in 4 oz. bottles. This medicine is a pleasant, anti-(acid) and laxative preparation; very useful in piles, habitual costiveness, diarrhœa, sour stomach, indigestion, summer complaint of children, etc., etc. Per bottle....$0.28
Per dozen bottles....2.75
Weight, 12 oz.

Cook's Hair Tonic.

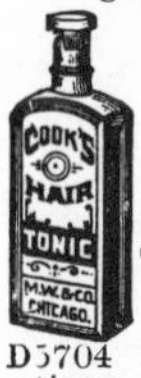

D5702 Cook's Hair Tonic for promoting the growth of hair, removing dandruff and cleansing the scalp.
Per bottle....$0.20
Per dozen....2.00

The Great Russian Corn and Bunion Exterminator.

D5704 The manufacturers claim that if directions, which accompany each bottle, are followed, a cure is certain, and as we have investigated this assertion we are satisfied that no person suffering from corns and bunions should fail to give the Russian Exterminator a trial. It requires from two to four vials to effect a cure in a bad case.
Two bottles....$0.35
Four bottles....64
Per dozen bottles....1.68
Postage, 5 cents on two bottles.

Insect Powder Guns.

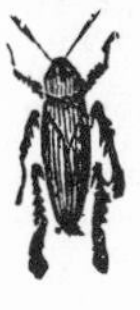

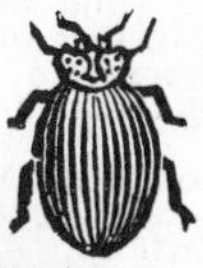

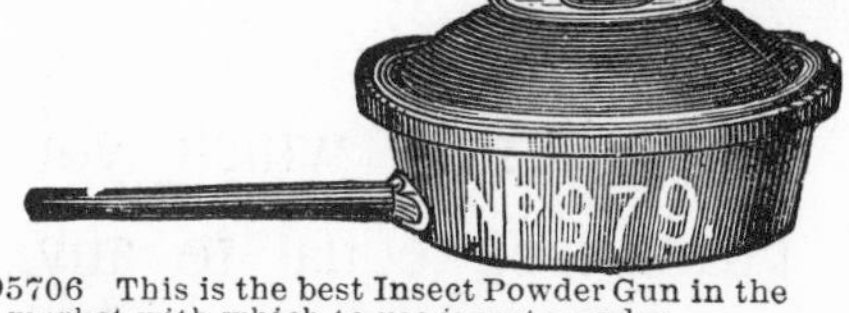

D5706 This is the best Insect Powder Gun in the market with which to use insect powder.
Each....$0.06 Per dozen....$0.50
Extra, by mail, each, about....05

Insect Powder Guns—Continued.

D5708 "Jumbo" Insect Powder Guns, same general style as D5706, made to meet a demand for as large a gun as can be held in the hand, 4 inches in diameter, holds ¼ pound of powder, bottom and spout screws off, large opening for filling. Each....$0.18
Per dozen....2.00
D5710 Dr. Cook's Insect Powder, strictly pure and guaranteed equal to anything in the market. Per package....10
Per dozen....1.10
Extra by mail, about....06

Handy Pocket Goods.

(In metal screw top air-tight glass vials).
Postage on handy pocket goods, 3 cents.

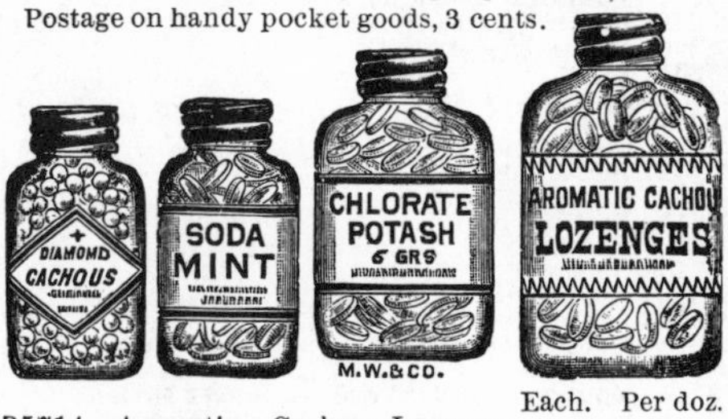

	Each.	Per doz.
D5714 Aromatic Cachou Lozenges for perfuming the breath; makes a very delicious confection; in 1 oz. vials. See cut....	$0.08	$0.85
D5716 Cachous, Diamond, for perfuming the breath; in 4 oz. vials; vest pocket size....	.08	.85
D5718 Chlorate Potash Tablets, five grains each; for sore throat, hoarseness, etc. In ½-oz vials....	.08	.85
D5720 Licorice Pellets, druggists' pure. 1 oz. vials, same as 2240....	.08	85
D5722 Soda Mint Tablets, for sour stomach, colic, flatulency, etc., ¼oz. vials, pocket style....	.08	.85
D5724 Cook's Bronchial Troches, exactly similar to Brown's cough troches, in ¼ oz. vials, as above....	.08	.85
D5726 Murate Ammonia Tablets, 3 grains each, in 1 oz. vials, as above...	.08	.85
D5728 Borax Tablets, 5 grains each, in 1 oz. vials, as above....	.08	.85
D5730 Cook's Paregoric Tablets; each tablet represents 15 drops paragoric. Dose, 1 to 4, according to age; 50 tablets in each vial....	08	.85

Montgomery Ward & Co.'s New Improved Singer Model Sewing Machine, With High Arm.

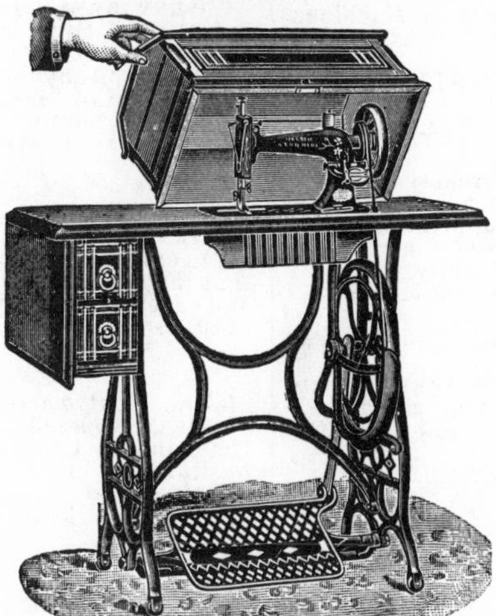

Price, $13.50.

28150 The above cut shows an exact representation of our new improved Singer Model Sewing Machine, *with high arm.* We handle one style only, No. 3, walnut drop leaf, box cover, and two drawers. Price, crated for shipment. Each....$13.50

DISTANCE

COUNTS FOR NOTHING EXCEPT TIME

AND THAT YOU CAN WELL AFFORD BY THE SAVING EFFECTED.

Description of Singer Model Sewing Machine.

The New Improved Singer Model Sewing Machine is easily managed, has a high arm, uses a self threading shuttle, automatic bobbin winder, a straight self-setting needle, makes a double thread lock stitch. It will hem, fell, bind, braid, seam, quilt, tuck, ruffle, hemstitch, or gather, and is adapted to every variety of family sewing.

The materials used in its construction are steel and iron of the best quality. Every wearing point is thoroughly hardened and smoothly finished. Case, table and drawers are finished in black walnut in the most complete and substantial manner. Every machine is warranted perfect, and if any part fails from imperfection, it will be supplied free of cost, upon return of the defective piece. The warranty does not apply to needles or shuttles, or the breakage by careless handling.

The following outfit accompanies each machine without extra charge: One dozen needles, assorted sizes, 6 bobbins, 1 gauge and screw, 1 extra check spring, 1 tucker, 1 ruffler, 1 set four widths of hemmers, 1 hemmer (used also for felling), 1 wrench, 1 screw driver, 1 oil can, 1 instruction book.

There will always be a demand for a low-priced sewing machine; for this reason we shall continue the Singer Model. We wish it understood, however, that we advise every purchaser to order our regular improved High Arm Sewing Machine, quoted on pages 263-5, as they are in *every way superior* to the Singer Model, and the difference in price is comparatively small.

Sewing Machine Needles and Attachments.

We can furnish duplicate parts for nearly every sewing machine now in use. In ordering sewing machine goods be sure and give name of machine, and *always* send sample of parts wanted, if possible. Weight of sewing machine needles; per dozen, 2 ounces.

28151 Machine Needles, Singer, the short one with plain shank used for Montgomery Ward & Co.'s old style Singer Model, Singer N. F. (new and old), also Home (old) and Blees.
Per dozen....$0.12
28153 Machine Needles, Singer, medium; the long, straight and plain shank needle.
Per dozen....12
28155 Machine Needles. Oscillating Singer for the machine having round shuttle, either flat or round shank. (Be sure and state which kind or send sample.)
Per dozen....18
28156 Machine Needles, Singer, latest improved vibrating shuttle, having flat shank.
Per doz....20
28158 Machine Needles, Montgomery Ward & Co.'s High Arm. There are three kinds. (Always send sample.)....$0.20

No. 11.
No. 12.
No' 13.

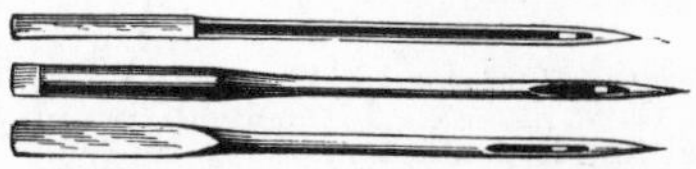

Above cuts show the different styles of our High Arm needles-

28159 Machine Needles for Montgomery Ward & Co.'s new Singer Model, No. 28150.
Per doz....$0.20
28160 Machine Needles (round shank), American (plain), Davis (old), Domestic (plain), Grover & Baker (curved or straight), Household, Home Shuttle, E. Howe, Remington (plain), St. John, Weed, Wilson, Wheeler & Wilson (curved or straight), and Wilson Oscillating: White, three kinds (round shank, flat and automatic). If not certain of the kind send a sample....18
28162 Machine Needles (flat shank), American self-setting, Crown, New Davis, Dauntless, Diamond, Ætna Improved, Florence, Howe, G. Hartford, New Howe, New Stewart, Remington, (flat shank) Royal St. John, Domestic (flat shank), Dom stic with shoulders shank, Eldredge Victor, Whitney, Wilson, Jennie June, Leader, White (flat shank), Whitehill, Springfield.
Send sample in every case....20
28164 Machine Needles, Wilcox & Gibbs....30
28166 Goodrich Tuckers. Always give name of machine for which they are wanted. Each....35
28168 One set, 4 widths of hemmers, ⅛ to 1 in. in width, with good dress binder, all nickel plated and easily managed....15
28175 Rufflers for Singer Machine....50
28176 Johnson Rufflers for other machines (be sure and give name. Each....75

SAFE DELIVERY GUARANTEED.

Sewing Machines ...AND... Baby Carriages.

SEE QUOTATIONS.

Parts for Old Style Low Arm Singer.

Postage on small parts, each, 1 cent.

28180	1 Check Spring for Singer Machine	$0.03
	Per dozen, weight, 1 ounce	.20
28181	1 Spooler Rubber for Singer Machine	.03
	Per dozen, weight, 1 ounce	.25
28182	1 Bobbin for Singer Machine	.03
	Per dozen, weight, 1 ounce	.20
28183	1 Thumbscrew for Singer Machine	.08
	Weight, 1 ounce.	
28184	Sewing Machine Belts, round, each	.10
28185	Sewing Machine Belts, flat, each	.25
	Weight, 5 ounces.	
28186	1 Set Gears	.20
	Postage	.06
28187	1 Presser Foot	.15
28188	1 Shuttle Carrier	.20
28189	1 Feed	.15
28190	1 Spooler or Bobbin Winder	.25
28191	1 Check Lever	.05
28192	1 Needle Clamp	.10
28193	1 Feed Spring	.05
29194	1 Throat Plate	.15
28195	1 Needle Bar, complete	.60
	Postage	.06
28200	Screw Drivers. Each	.05
28201	Oil Cans. Each	.08
28202	Glasses for Wheeler & Wilson	.08
28203	Bobbins for Wheeler & Wilson	.08
28204	Instruction Books for all standard grade sewing machines. Each	.15
	Give name of machine.	

Sewing Machine Shuttles.

There have been so many changes made in the running parts of different machines within the last few years that now nearly every machine in the market uses from one to three different styles of shuttles, and some few as many as five. It is absolutely necessary to send the old shuttles for a sample when a new shuttle is required. We give below the prices of a few of the most popular shuttles.

		Each.
28220	American, old style	$0.75
28221	American, No 7	.75
28222	Blees	.60
28223	Blade	1.25
28224	Crown, old style	.75
28225	Crown, cylinder	1.25
28227	Dauntless Outfit	1.25
28228	Davis, 3 styles	.80
28230	Domestic, 4 styles	.75
28231	Estey	.80
28232	Eldredge, 4 styles	.75
28234	Florenc , 2 styles	1.25
28236	Grover and Baker	1.25
28238	Howe, old	.65
28239	Howe, "B" and "G"	1.25
28241	Hartford	1.25
28242	Household	.75
28243	Helpmate	.75
28245	Jennie June	.75
28246	Leader, substitu e	1.25
28248	Montgomery Ward & Co.'s Singer Model, low arm	.32
28249	Montgomery Ward & Co.'s Singer Model, high arm	.75
28250	Montgomery Ward & Co.'s high arm, old style	.65

Shuttles—Continued.

28251	Montgomery Ward & Co.'s New Improved, Each high arm	$0.75
28253	New Home	.70
28253½	Queen	.80
28254	Remington, No. 1	.40
28255	Remington, No. 3	1.00
28256	Remington, No. 5	1.25
28257	Royal St. John, 2 styles	1.00
28258	St. John	1.00
28259	Springfield	.75
28261	Singer, N. F. and medium	.32
28262	Singer, V. S. high arm	1.00
28263	Singer, Oscillating	1.15
28265	Union	1.00
28266	Victor, old style	80
28267	Victor, latest	1.00
28268	Weed, old style	.65
28269	Weed, cylinder	1.25
28270	White, 2 styles	.75
28271	Whitehill	1.25
28272	Wilson, old style	.60
28273	Wilson, Oscillating	1.25

NOTE.—We will be pleased to quote prices on shuttles not named in this list.

Weight, 5 ounces.

See Index for Sewing Machine Oil.

28292	Magic Needle Threader to be used with any machine; a very useful and convenient article. Full directions with every threader.	
	Each	$0.05
	Per dozen	.50
	Per gross	5.00
	Extra by mail	.01

WE HAVE MADE MANY FRIENDS

Some of them have been kind enough to tell us what they think. We like to get such letters, and always try to deserve them.

We Submit a few:

SOUTH AUBURN, NEB., February 4, 1895.
Messrs. Montgomery Ward & Co., Chicago, Ill.,
GENTLEMEN:—I received one of your Cabinet Sewing Machines and find it perfect in every respect. It will compete favorably with any of the Sewing Machines on the market.
Respectfully yours,   MRS. W. H. STITZEL.

SELMA, IOWA, February 2, 1895.
Messrs. Montgomery Ward & Co., Chicago, Ill.,
GENTLEMEN:—The Sewing Machine which we purchased of you October 25, 1894, has given entire satisfaction. It is very light running and makes a beautiful stitch. In construction and appearance it is equal to Machines sold here at from $35.00 to $40.00. I cheerfully recommend this machine.
Yours respectfully,
MRS. CHARLES CRAMLET.

LOHRVILLE, IOWA, January 30th, 1895.
Messrs. Montgomery Ward & Co., Chicago, Ill.,
GENTLEMEN:—I wish to say, in regard to the MONTGOMERY WARD & Co. High Arm Machine I purchased of you some time ago, that I consider it superior to all others in stitching and light running quality, besides being an ornament to any room.
Yours respectfully,   MISS MYRTLE CAMPBELL.

HOMER CITY, PA., January 29, 1895.
Messrs. Montgomery Ward & Co., Chicago, Ill.,
GENTLEMEN:—We received the Machine purchased October 3, 1894, and are very well pleased with same. We find it just as represented. It is light running, does fine work and is perfect in every respect.
Yours respectfully,   MRS. R. W. MILLER.

NEOSHO RAPIDS, February 10, 1895.
Messrs. Montgomery Ward & Co., Chicago, Ill.,
GENTLEMEN:—I received my Machine in good condition, and my wife is well pleased with same. It does good work, and runs very lightly. I would not trade it for a $45.00 Machine my neighbor bought this winter. Yours truly,   KENNETH McDONALD.

MONONA, IOWA, January 31, 1895.
Messrs. Montgomery Ward & Co., Chicago, Ill.,
GENTLEMEN:—I wish to say, in regard to the MONTGOMERY WARD & COMPANY High Arm Sewing Machine, which I purchased some time ago, that I consider it superior to any Machine made. It is very light running; and anyone in need of a Sewing Machine will save money by buying one of these. A Machine worth from $50.00 to $60.00 sold for $19.50, and guaranteed for five years, I consider a great bargain.
Yours truly,   HENRY LICHT.

JONES VALLEY, TENN., January 29, 1895.
Messrs. Montgomery Ward & Co., Chicago, Ill.,
GENTLEMEN:—The Sewing Machine you shipped me October 30, 1894, gives entire satisfaction. My wife thinks it very light running, and that the stitch is as good as the best. We think the finish is very fine, and consider it equal in every respect to a Machine an agent asked me $40.00 for. Yours truly,   J. F. FUNK.

PARSONS, W. VA., January 29, 1895.
Messrs. Montgomery Ward & Co., Chicago, Ill.,
DEAR SIRS:—The Sewing Machine purchased by me of you some time since is a first-class piece of machinery in every respect. We hesitated to buy it on account of its cheapness, but find it equally as satisfactory as a high priced Machine of which we have had two.
Yours truly,   MRS. W. B. MAXWELL.

BELFIELD, N. D., January 30, 1895.
Messrs. Montgomery Ward & Co., Chicago, Ill.,
GENTLEMEN:—I purchased one of your MONTGOMERY WARD & COMPANY No. 5 High Arm Sewing Machines last October, and wish to say that I find it a perfect Machine in every particular. It makes a fine lock stitch, alike on both sides; and find it the easiest running machine I have ever used. I consider it equal to any $60.00 Machine now on the market.
I would also like to recommend MONTGOMERY WARD & COMPANY to those who have never bought goods from them, as a reliable house.
Yours respectfully,   MRS. W. E. KING.

DON'T WASTE YOUR MONEY by paying $35.00 for an article which you can get for $20.00. Especially an article which is guaranteed equal to any, with a guarantee as good as ours.

Our Improved High Arm in the New Drop Head Case.

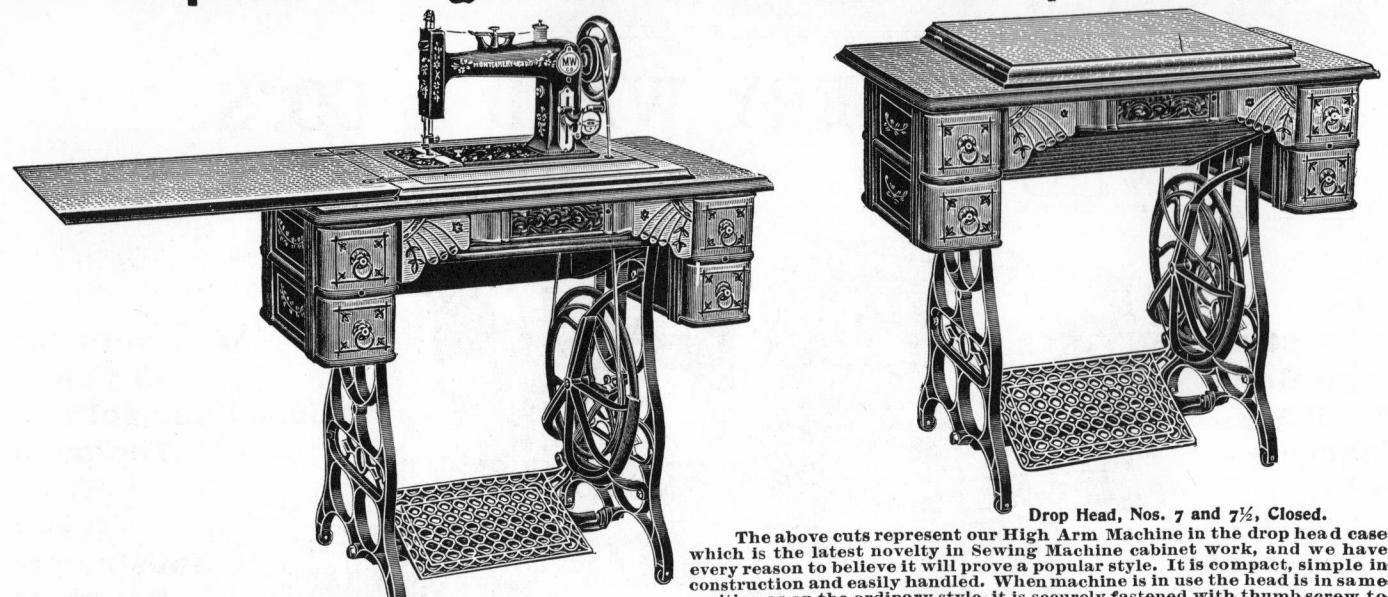

Drop Head, Nos. 7 and 7½, Closed.

The above cuts represent our High Arm Machine in the drop head case which is the latest novelty in Sewing Machine cabinet work, and we have every reason to believe it will prove a popular style. It is compact, simple in construction and easily handled. When machine is in use the head is in same position as on the ordinary style, it is securely fastened with thumb screw to drop board, and the latter is firmly supported from under side. When through using it requires only one motion of the hand to drop the head down forming a handsome table with highly polished top. The woodwork is either

Drop Head, Nos. 7 and 7½, Open.
through the table, completely out of sight. The top or leaf then folds over oak or walnut, polished and finely finished. The machine head and attachments are same as used on our other styles.

No. 7   High Arm Drop Head, Sewing Machine, 5 Drawers (see cut) Walnut Woodwork.   Each...$22.00
No. 7½ High Arm Drop Head, Sewing Machine, 5 Drawers (see cut) Oak Woodwork.   Each.. 22.20

DESCRIPTION OF OUR IMPROVED HIGH ARM SEWING MACHINES.

IN CONSTRUCTION it is similar to the Domestic with **double eccentric** for operating Shuttle and Feed Levers, **perfect in adjustment,** and if properly handled cannot get out of time. It has few bearings and **no cog wheels,** consequently it is one of the **lightest running machines made.** It is easily cleaned or oiled and on account of its simplicity is not difficult to operate.

THE HEAD is large and substantially built though neat and symmetrical in appearance. It is double jappaned, **handsomely ornamented** in colors and has large space under the arm affording ample room for handling bulky goods. The head swings on **patent hinges,** is held down with thumb screw, and bed plate is let in even with top of table.

THE BEARINGS, or parts subject to wear, **are made of fine steel,** case hardened, **adjustable,** accurately **fitted,** and can be run at a high rate of speed without injury. The levers and fly-wheel are nickel plated.

THE FEED. This important feature is the **very best;** it is a double four motion, drop feed, **perfect and positive in its action** as it has no springs, thus insuring a **uniform stitch.**

THE SHUTTLE is of the finest steel, cylindrical in form with opening at end, is **self threading, perfectly fitted,** uses a large bobbin and in action vibrates in a circular course. The shuttle spring is adjustable so that lower tension is under perfect control. The **shuttle carrier is lined with steel** to **prevent unneccessary noise** in running.

THE UPPER TENSION is on top of arm, is **easily adjusted** by means of thumb screw, is also supplied with **patent tension liberator** for releasing the work at end of seam without touching the thread.

THE STITCH is a double thread lock stitch, either long or short, the length being regulated by thumb screw on upright portion of the arm.

THE NEEDLE is straight and self-setting.

THE AUTOMATIC BOBBIN WINDER is a perfect mechanical device. The thread is evenly distributed on bobbin, thus obviating the annoyance of breaking under thread on account of carelessly wound bobbins. It is not necessary to remove work for winding bobbins. The fly wheel is released by turning thumb screw on outside and runs alone while machine stands still.

THE CABINET WORK is of the **latest design** as we use the **oval covers, skeleton drawer frames** and **full length** center drawer with **velvet lined compartments** for the attachments. The woodwork is either **oak** or **walnut,** highly polished and finished throughout in the best possible manner.

THE STAND is of pleasing design, made of the best material, finely japanned and very substantial.

THE ATTACHMENTS. We use the **best set** of sewing machine attachments ever put on the market. They are made of heavy **cold rolled steel,** highly polished and nickel plated. Every piece is guaranteed absolutely perfect, and being of steel, cannot get out of order. Each Montgomery Ward & Co. High Arm Sewing Machine will be supplied **free of charge,** with complete set of new steel attachments as follows: 1 ruffler and gatherer, 1 tucker, 1 braider, 1 binder, 1 quilter, 4 hemmers (⅛ to 1 inch); also the following accessories—1 thread cutter, 12 needles, 6 bobbins, 1 gauge and screw, 1 wrench, 2 screw drivers, 1 oil can, 1 instruction book. We make no charge for crating machines or cartage. N. B. Instruction books for our sewing machines are printed in English only.

Our High Arm Drop Cabinet Sewing Machine.

Price, $28.00.

Agents Charge $65.00,

For a machine of this style,

Our Price is $28.00.

Can you afford to make them this liberal donation, or will

YOU BUY FROM MANUFACTURERS AND SAVE THE DIFFERENCE?

High Arm Drop Cabinet, Open.   **High Arm Drop Cabinet, Closed.**

No. 8 Drop Cabinets. The above cuts represent our popular High Arm Machines in the new Automatic Drop Cabinet Case. They are supplied with the improved "drop," are easily handled and will last a lifetime. The head is raised and lowered automatically, it being only necessary to open and close the top. The case is finished in either walnut or oak, highly polished top, polished panels in back and sides, beaded and carved panel doors in front, and when closed forms a handsome and ornamental piece of furniture which may be used as a writing desk or table. There is one drawer on inside, also pockets in top of doors for the attachment, etc. Price, each $28.00. Weight, boxed, about 200 lbs.

READ THIS!!

To show our confidence in our sewing machines we make the following offer: We will ship one machine by express on 20 days' trial, to any express office on a railroad within 500 miles of Chicago, under the following conditions: When a machine arrives at the express office the person ordering it deposits with the express agent the price of the machine together with transportation charges and the return charges on the money. The express agent is instructed on each C. O. D. bill to hold the money 20 days. If by the expiration of 20 days the machine is not returned to him, the express agent sends us the money, but if returned, he pays back every cent of the money deposited to the person who deposits it, and sends us the machine at our expense both ways. If you want the machine shipped on these terms, please be particular to say so in your order.

Please note that we do not ship machines by express upon these terms to any point more than 500 miles from Chicago, as the charges would be too high, and it would be much better to ship by freight.

☞ *Machines ordered by freight and paid for may be returned if unsatisfactory, after 30 days's trial, at our expense both ways, and money will be refunded.*

We also ship our sewing machines on trial by freight, under the same conditions as organs and pianos.
For full particulars we refer you to page 238.

WE GUARANTEE SAFE DELIVERY

To any railroad point in the United States. If any parts are broken or damaged when machine arrives at destination we **hereby agree to furnish perfect duplicates free of charge** and prepay cost of transportation.

There are machines in the market similar in style to ours that are sold at lower prices, others that are delivered free of charge, but they are correspondingly inferior in quality.

We **will not** cheapen the materials or **sacrifice the slightest detail** in **workmanship**, as we aim to keep the standard of our machine **up to the highest degree of excellence.** Every machine is **thoroughly inspected**, put through the **most rigid tests** by **expert machinists** and are guaranteed **absolutely perfect** before leaving the factory. We are willing and anxious to trust our High Arm Machine on its merits alone in competition with the genuine Singers, New Home, Domestic, White, Standard, Wheeler & Wilson, Davis, or any style made. Weights are given with quotations and our freight department will cheerfully quote rates to any station upon application.

A comparison of prices will show the amount of **money you save in buying from us.**

We issue a Special Catalogue of our Sewing Machines with large cuts of every style and full descriptions; also list of testimonials received from a few of the purchasers who are using them. Mailed free to any address upon application.

CLOTHING DEPARTMENT.
SPRING AND SUMMER STYLES 1895.

Style 1.

Style 2.

Style 3.

Style 4.

Style 5. Front.

Style 5 Back.

Style 7.

Style 8.

Style 10.

Zouave.

Reefer Suit.

Kilt Suit.

Boys' Combination.

Ready To Wear Clothing.

Our Clothing Department, one of the leading departments of our house, has grown to such proportion through giving our customers exceptionally good values in the past, that we are now placed in a position practically beyond all competition this spring and summer. We will offer special inducements to all our patrons, as well as those who are skeptical about buying away from home, by sending samples of some of our special drives to convince you of the merits of our clothing, we would gladly send samples of all our clothing, but manufacturers are constantly changing their styles, and in many cases we could not match the particular pattern you would want, but we never send an inferior *quality*. Our line was never so complete, especially in medium grades and prices, which is our stronghold and is demanded by the masses. A trial order almost invariably makes a permanent customer in our Mammoth Clothing Department. We call particular attention to our $3.00 Pants, $10.00 Suits and $10.00 Overcoats.

NOTE. Remember if goods are not as represented you may return them to us and we will cheerfully refund your money.

Rules For Self Measurement.

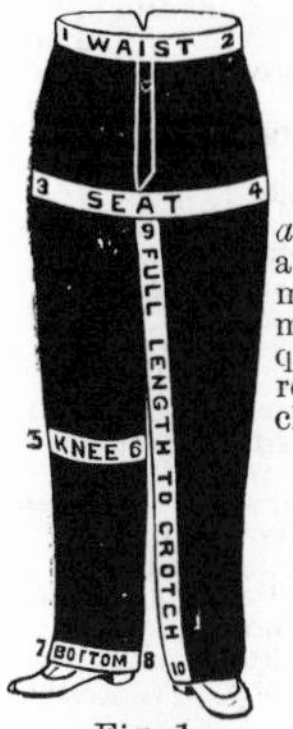

Chest, Waist and Inseam, are the only measurements required for ready made clothing.

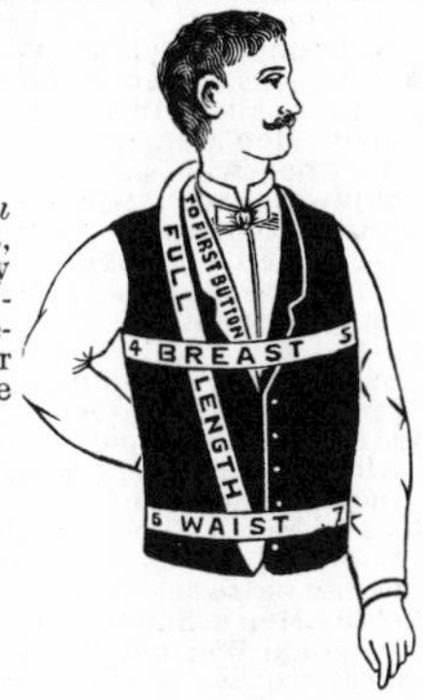

Fig 1. Fig. 2.

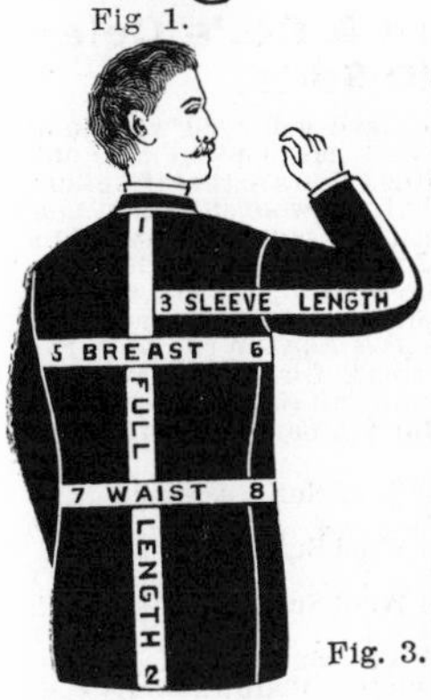

Fig. 3.

FOR COAT. Adjust tape over the breast close under the arms See Nos. 4 and 5, Fig. 2. Draw tape snugly around breast and over back. State the number of inches around chest. Give entire length of coat from 1 to 2, Fig. 3. Measure sleeve from center of back at 3 to wrist. Give number of inches around entire waist at 6 and 7, Fig. 2. For frock coat. Give length from Fig. 1 to waist line and entire length from Fig. 1 to 2.

FOR VEST. Give breast and waist measure same as for coat. Give full length and length to first button, measuring from back of neck as per illustration, Fig. 2.

FOR PANTS. State number of inches around entire waist at Fig. 1 and 2. State number of inches around hips at Fig. 3 and 4. Measure in seam from 9 to 10. State number of inches around knee at Fig 5 and 6 and around bottom at Fig. 7 and 8.

N. B. Never take coat or vest breast measure over the coat. Always take it *over the vest*, under the coat.

N. B.—The illustrated figures on page 266 show cut and shape of clothing, as follows.

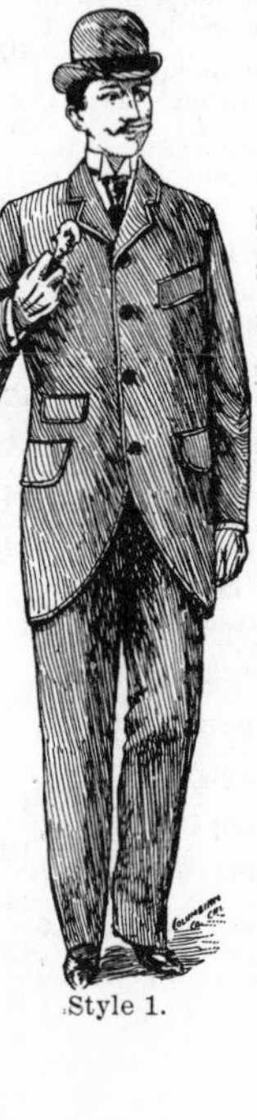

Style 1.

Style No. 1 represents Single Breasted Sack Suit.
Style No. 2 represents Single Breasted Square Cut Suit.
Style No. 3 represents Double Breasted Sack Suit.
Style No. 5 represents Three Button Cutaway, Walking or Dress Suit.
Style No. 7 represents Double Breasted Prince Albert Dress Coat.
Style No. 8 represents Full Dress Evening Suit.
Style No. 10 represents Single Breasted Fly Front Sack Overcoat.
Style No. 26 represents Children's Knee Pants Suits, corded.
Style No. 25 represents Children's Knee Pants Suits, single breasted coat.
Style No. 28 represents Children's Knee Pants Suits, with double breasted coat.
Style No. 30 represents Boys' Long Pants Suits, single breasted.
Style No. 31 represents Boys' Long Pants Suits, double breasted.

Style 1.

Men's Round Cornered Sack Suits.

30014 Men's Black and Old Gold Mixed Diagonal Cotton Worsted Suits; good value. Style 1. Per suit $3.00

30016 Men's Black and Gray Satinet Cassimere Suits; neat, small check. Style 1. Per suit 3.50

30018 Men's Round Cornered Sack Suits; fancy plaid cotton worsted, dark colors. Style 1. Per suit 4.00

30020 Men's Black and Brown, small check, satinet cassimere suits, round cornered sack. Style 1. Per suit $4.00

30022 Men's Suits, round cornered sack, black and gray, diagonal tweed; a neat pattern and extra good value. Style 1. Per suit 4.25

30024 Men's Round Cornered Sack Style Suit, black background, with small blue pin check. Domestic Worsted goods. Style 1. Per suit 4.25

30026 Men's Oxford Gray Mixed Diagonal Weave Cheviot Suits; neat and durable. Style 1. Per suit 4.50

30028 Men's Sack Suits. Dark brown and gray mixed diagonal cassimere twist, durable; will stand hard service. Style 1. Per suit..... 5.00

30030 Men's Sack Suits. Brown mixed, broken plaid cassimere. Style 1. Standard goods. Per suit 5.00

30032 Men's Sack Suits. Black and blue mixed, worsted suiting; dark colors Style 1. Per suit 5.00

Cheviot Suits.

30034 Men's Sack Suits. Dark brown and gray mixed cheviot, soft finish. Style 1. Per suit.. $5.50

30036 Men's Sack Suits. Dark blue, gray mixed cheviot, soft finish. Style 1. Very neat. Per suit 5.50

30038 Men's Sack Suits. Black cheviot, interwoven with red and blue threads; a popular pattern. Style 1. Per suit 5.75

30040 Men's Sack Suits All wool suiting; neat gray mixed pattern, medium light color. Extra value. Style 1. Per suit 6.00

30042 Men's Sack Suits. All wool plain black cheviot; made for service. Style 1. Per suit $6.00

30044 Men's Sack Suits. All wool, medium brown and gray, small fancy check patterns. Style 1. Per suit 6.50

30046 Men's Sack Suits, all wool, black and gray mixed broken check. Style 1. Per suit 6.75

30048 Men's Sack Suits. Black and gray mixed, wool hair line. Style 1. Per suit 6.75

30050 Men's Sack Suits. All wool, black and gray, small pin check pattern. Style 1. Per suit..... 7.00

30052 Men's Sack Suits. Medium and dark brown mixed wool, interwoven with gray threads. Style 1. Per suit 7.25

30054 Men's Sack Suits. Dark bluish gray, mixed wool cheviot. Very dressy. Style 1. Per suit $7.25

30056 Men's Sack Suits. All wool cheviot, black or blue. Style 1. Diagonal pattern. Per suit 7.25

30058 Men's Sack Suits. All wool, very fine diagonal pattern. Unfinished worsted, soft and fine. Very desirable suits for spring and summer. Style 1. Black or blue. Per suit........ 7.50

30060 Men's Sack Suits. Black and blue fancy plaid worsted, with invisible red threads. Style 1. Per suit 8.00

30062 Men's Sack Suits. Fancy weave, small check, black and blue mixed worsted. Very dark. Style 1. Per suit 8.00

30064 Men's Sack Suits. Brown and gray mixed, all wool cheviot. Medium colors. Style 1. Per suit 8.00

30066 Men's Round Cornered Sack Suits. All wool, very neat, brown and gray check. Good workmanship and trimmings. Style 1. Per suit 8.00

30068 Men's Round Cornered Sack Suits. Medium gray mixed invisible plaids, interwoven with faint red threads. All wool cassimere A good all round business suit. Style 1. Per suit 8.00

30070 Men's Round Cornered Sack Suits. All wool cassimere. Black background with very neat gray mixture. A serviceable and well-made suit throughout. Style 1. Per suit 8.00

30072 Men's Round Cornered Sack Suits. All wool, imported diagonal clay worsted. Dark iron gray mixture, very fine weave. Handsome, durable and neat. "Don't miss it." Style 1. Per suit 8.00

30074 Men's Round Cornered Sack Suits. All wool cassimere; very neat, modest hairline stripes of black and gray. Style 1. Per suit 8.00

30076 Men's Round Cornered Sack Suits. All wool cassimere, black and gray, pin check. A desireable pattern. Style 1. Per suit 8.25

30078 Men's Round Cornered Sack Suits. Black and gray, all wool, hairline cassimere. Style 1. Per suit 8.25

30080 Men's Imported Worsted Suits. All wool, black background with small blue pin check. Style 1. Per suit 8.50

30082 Men's Imported Worsted Suits. All wool, light bluish gray with faint sprinkling of brown, having almost the same appearance as plain gray. Very dressy. Style 1. Per suit 8.50

30084 Men's Fine Worsted Suits. Fancy weave, check pattern, dark gray color. Style I. Per suit 8.50

30086 Men's Sack Suits. All wool cassimere, small brown and light gray check mixture. Style 1. Per suit 8.75

Suits—Continued.

30088 Men's Sack Suits, all wool cassimere, black and gray, pin check pattern; excellent value. Style 1. Per suit 8.75

30090 Men's All Wool Cassimere Suits. Medium shade of gray with black mixture; well made and trimmed. Standard quality. Style 1. Per suit 8.75

30092 Men's All Wool Cassimere Sack Suits. Dark bluish gray, diagonal pattern. Imported goods. Style 1. Per suit 8.75

30094 Men's All Wool Cheviot Suits. Diagonal pattern, Plain navy blue or black. Style 1. Per suit 8.75

30096 Men's All Wool Suits. Black and gray pepper and salt mixture; very neat and substantial. Style 1. Per suit 9.50

30098 Men's All Wool Suits. Black intermingled with gray; diagonal cheviot. Extra quality trimmings. Strong and serviceable. Style 1. Per suit 9.50

30100 Men's All Wool Unfinished Worsted Suits. Navy blue or black. Fine weave, diagonal pattern, cheviot effect. Extra good value. Style 1. Per suit 9.50

30102 Men's Extra Quality Imported Clay Worsted Suits. Strictly all wool, steel gray color, fine diagonal weave, superior quality trimmings. Style 1. Per suit 9.50

30104 Men's Extra Quality Imported Clay Worsted Suits. Diagonal pattern, fine weave, strictly all wool, brown and steel gray mixed. Style 1. Per suit 9.50

30106 Men's All Wool Cassimere Sack Suits. Medium brown mixed pattern; a neat and durable business suit. Style 1. Per suit 9.50

30108 Men's All Wool Fancy Cheviot. Medium light colored English plaid. Very stylish. Style 1. Per suit 9.50

30110 Men's Fancy Worsted Suits. Black ground with broken hair line stripe of bluish gray. Style 1. Per suit 10.00

30112 Men's Fancy Cassimere Suits. All wool, black diagonal with silver silk threads. Style 1. Per suit 10.50

30114 Men's All Wool Melton Suits. Brown mixed medium shade; an ironclad suit for wear. Style 1. Per suit 10.50

30116 Men's All Wool Imported Suits. Unfinished worsted, cheviot effect, plain black or navy blue diagonal pattern; fine weave. Style 1. Per suit 10.50

30118 Men's All Wool Imported Suits. Dark and black mixed clay worsted, fine wale diagonal, Extra quality. Style 1. Per suit 10.50

30120 Men's New 3 Button Cutaway Sack Suits. Superior quality, all wool black and gray small, neat mixture; cassimere goods. Style 1. Per suit 10.75

30122 Men's Extra Quality All Wool Cassimere Suits. Very small gray pepper and salt mixture. Style 1. Per suit 10.75

30124 Men's Fine Worsted Suits. Fancy pattern, small black and blue check with an occasional red thread. Style 1. Per suit........ 11.00

30126 Men's Fine Quality Light Brown Mixed Melton Suits. All wool. Style 1. Per suit 12.00

30128 Men's Fine Quality Sack Suits. All wool cassimere. Dark iron gray, solid and durable. Style 1 Per suit 12.00

30130 Men's Imported Worsted Suits. Fine diagonal weave. Black, with blue spider web silk thread. Style 1. Per suit 13.00

30132 Men's New 3-Button Cutaway Sack Suits. All wool imported cassimere; very dark pattern, black, with small gray threads. Style 1. Per suit 13.50

30134 Men's Imported Worsted Suits. All wool. Black with fine thread of steel blue. Pin head effect. Style 1. Per suit 13.50

30136 Men's Imported Cambridge Worsted Suits. Dark blue medium wide wale diagonal pattern Style 1. Per suit 15.00

30138 Men's Imported Worsted Suits, extra long sack coats. Fancy dark blue and black mixed weave. Very small check pattern. Style 1. Per suit 15.00

30140 Men's Extra Fine Imported Clay Worsted Suits. Very dark iron gray, intermingled with invisible blue threads. Strictly all wool and first class in every respect. Style 1. Per suit.. 16.00

N. B.—All clothing quoted as *all wool*, we guarantee to be strictly so. Our all wool suits this season are better and cheaper than ever before. We earnestly solicit a trial of these goods.

Style 2.

Men's Single Breasted Sack. Square Cut Suits.

30142 Men's Dark Mixed Satinet Cassimere Suits. Small check; a good, substantial suit. Style 2. Per suit $4.00

30144 Men's Fancy Plaid Cassimere Suits. Medium gray, dark red and black mixed. Style 2. Per suit 4.50

30146 Men's Dark Blue Gray Mixed Cheviot Suits. Soft finish; very desirable. Style 2. Per suit 5.50

30148 Men's All Wool Suits. Neat, black and gray suiting, medium light color. Style 2. Special value. Per suit 6.00

30150 Men's Suits; special stock. Black and gray mixed, wool cassimere. Hairline pattern. Style 2. Per suit 6.75

30152 Men's All Wool Suits, small black and gray. pin check suiting. Neat and substantial. Style 2. Per suit 7.00

30154 Men's Fancy Wool Suits. Very small gray and black dots, on very dark brown background. Style 2. Per suit 7.50

Men's Suits—Continued.

30156 Men's All Wool Unfinished Worsted Suits. Soft diagonal cheviot effect. Plain black or navy blue. Style 2. Per suit.............. $7.50

30158 Men's All Wool Black Cheviot Suits. Perfectly plain. Style 2. Per suit.................. 8.00

30160 Men's Fancy Worsted Suits. Black and blue; very dark small square figures Style 2. Per suit.................. 8.00

30162 Men's All Wool Cheviot Suits. Blue black, with neat steel mixture. Style 2. Per suit...... 8.00

30164 Men's Suits. All wool, mocha brown with light gray mixture, soft wool finish. Style 2. Per suit.................. $° 00

30166 Men's All Wool Suits. Light gray and black mixed. A good substantial suit for millers, and other men requiring light, or medium light clothing. Style 2. Per suit.............. 9.00

30168 Men's Imported Worsted Suits. Very neat black and blue pin head check. Extra selected stock. Style 2. Per suit.............. 9.50

30170 Men's All Wool Imported Suits. Soft finish cassimere, plain fine weave diagonal pattern, wood brown. Style 2. Per suit.............. 9.50

30172 Men's All Wool English Cheviot Suits. Dark steel blue and iron gray mixed, modest mixture, dressy and neat. Style 2. Per suit... 9.50

30174 Men's Extra Fine Imported Worsted Suits. Black with silk spider web threads of red and blue. Style 2. Diagonal pattern, fine weave. Per suit.............. 10.50

30176 Men's Extra Fine All Wool Suits. Imported English cassimere; very small pin checks of brown and silver gray. Style 2. Per suit.............. $12.00

30178 Men's Superior All Wool Melton Suits. Medium dark brown mixed. Standard goods for iron clad service. Style 2. Per suit.............. 13.00

30180 Men's Imported Worsted Suits. Iron gray fancy weave; well made and trimmed throughout. Style 2. Per suit.............. 13.00

Style 3.

Double Breasted Square Cut Sack Suits.

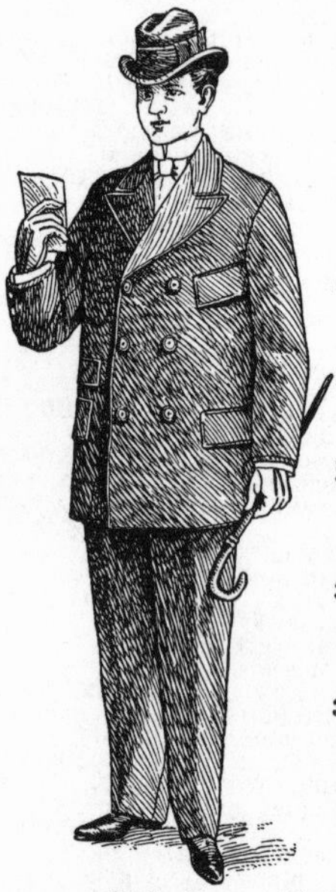

30182 Men's Black Diagonal Wool Cheviot Suits. Style 3. Per suit....$7.00

30184 Men's All Wool Cheviot Suits; diagonal pattern. Black or blue. Style 3. Per suit....$8.00

30186 Men's Melton Suits. Very darkest shade of gray. All wool. Style 3. Per suit.......$9.00

30188 Men's Fine All Wool Suits. Gray mixed, medium shade, soft finish. Style 3, Per suit......$9.50

30190 Men's Fine Imported Clay Worsted Suits. Gun powder gray. Plain and dressy. Style 3. Per suit.............$12.00

30200 Men's Fine Imported Cheviot Suits. All wool, diagonal pattern. Blue or black. Style 3. Per suit.............$12.50

30202 Men's Extra Quality Melton Suits. Cinnamon brown; all wool. All right in every respect. Style 3. Per suit..$15.00

Style 3. **Style 5.**

Three Button Cutaway Frock Suits.

30204 Men's Woll Cassimere Suits. Small check pattern, black and steel gray mixed, solid, good wearing goods. Style 5. Per suit..............$7.50

30206 Men's Fine Wool Cassimere Suits. Medium and light gray; blended plain effect, Style 5. Per suit.............. 8.75

30208 Men's Fine Wool "Tricot Long" Suits; Iron gray color. Firm and serviceable goods. Style 5. Per suit.............. 9.75

30210 Men's All Wool Suits. Plain black cheviot soft finish. Good value. Style 5. Per suit.... 10.00

30212 Men's Imported Fancy Worsted Suits. Blue black interwoven with fine blue silk threads. Style 5. Per suit.............. 12.00

30214 Men's Fine All Wool Cassimere Suits. Minute nonpareil check pattern. Bluish gray color, Extra good value. Style 5. Per suit..... 13.00

30216 Men's Fine Smooth Finished Worsted Suits. All wool, imported goods; black, interwoven with spider web gold and silver silk threads. Modest and neat effect. Style 5. Per suit.............. 13.50

30218 Men's Extra Quality English Worsted Suits. All wool, black and blue threads, woven so as to appear nearly plain black. Coat and vest bound with narrow silk braid. Style 5. Per suit.............. 14.00

30220 Men's Extra Quality English Worsted Suits. All wool, black and bluish gray mixed, very fine nonpareil or needle point check. One of the neatest suits ever made. Style 5. Per suit.............. 15.50

Men's Suits—Continued.

30222 Men's Extra Quality Imported Suits. All wool diagonal worsted. Gun powder gray; superior trimmings throughout. Style 5. Per suit.............. $16.00

30224 Men's Extra Quality Imported Suits. Dark blue crepe cloth, something new; similar to broadcloth, but softer and finer. Plain and handsome. Style 5. Per suit.............. 17.00

30226 Men's Extra Fine Imported Suits. The new crepe cloth, same as above in plain black. Style 5. Per suit.............. 17.00

30228 Men's Finest Quality Crepe Cloth Suits. Extra imported stock; dark blue. Style 5. Perfectly plain edge. Per suit.............. 24.00

30230 Men's Finest Quality Crepe Cloth Suits; same as above in plain black. Style 5. Suit.... 24.00

Old Men's Frock Suits.

30232 Men's Frock Suits. All wool cassimere; black and gray small stripes, black predominating. Large lapel pockets on skirt, 4 button front. Good, substantial suits. Style 4. Price, per suit.............. 10.00

30234 Old Men's Frock Suits. Black and gray mixed wool cassimere, gray predominating. Same style as above. Style 4. Price, per suit... 10.00

30236 Old Men's Frock Suits. Fine black and gray hairline pattern. All wool extra selected stock. Large lapel, skirt pockets. Superior trimmings. Style 4. Price, per suit.............. 12.50

Style 8.

Men's Full Dress Suits.

30238 Men's Full Dress Suits. Imported, black broadcloth. Style 8. Per suit.............. $33.00

30240 Men's Full Dress Suits. Extra fine imported broadcloth. Style 8. Per suit.......... 38.00

Style 7.

Double Breasted Prince Albert Suits.

30242 Men's All Wool Fine Diagonal Clay Worsted Suits. Black; fine weave, stitched edges. Style 7. Per Suit.............. $16.50

30244 Men's Superfine English Clay Worsted Suits. Fine wale black diagonal. Style 7, Stitched edges, Per suit.............. 19.00

30246 Men's Superfine Imported Black Crepe Cloth Suits. Fine new goods similar to broadcloth. Plain edges. An excellent suit for ministers, physicians and professional men. Style 7. Suit. 28.00

30248 Men's Double Breasted Prince Albert Suits, same goods as above in dark blue. Suit. 28.00

OUR SPECIALTIES.

Black and Blue Worsted Suits.

A black suit of clothes is always in style.

Never before have we been able to offer our customers good worsted clothing at the extremely low prices we quote this season. Our line is complete and the surpassing fineness of the garments listed below, will please as well as greatly surprise all purchasers.

N. B. Worsted Suits weigh from 4 to 5 pounds according to size and quality. Sizes run from 34 to 42 inch chest measure for coats and vests and from 30 to 40 inch waist and 30 to 35 inch inseam for pants. Half sizes are not made in ready made clothing.

30250 Men's Black Diagonal Worsted Suits; round cornered sack style, stitched edges. Style 1. Per suit.............. $5.00

30252 Men's Black Diagonal Worsted Suits; single breasted square cut style, stitched edges. Style 2. Per suit.............. 5.50

30254 Men's Genuine *All Wool* Black Clay Worsted Suits; fine diagonal weave; well made and trimmed throughout. Style 1. Per Suit... 7.45

30256 Men's Genuine *All Wool* Black Diagonal Clay Worsted Suits, same as above in style 2. Per suit.............. 7.45

30258 Men's *All Wool* Imported Black Diagonal Clay Worsted Suits, fine wale. Style 3. Double breasted sack style. Per suit.............. 7.90

30260 Men's *All Wool* Imported Black Diagonal Clay Worsted Suits; 3 button cutaway. Style 5. Per suit.............. 7.90

30262 Men's Imported Clay Worsted Suits. Black Diagonal, all wool. Style 1. Per suit.......... 8.75

30264 Men's Imported Clay Worsted Suits. Black Diagonal, all wool. Style 2. Per suit.......... 8.75

30266 Men's Imported Black Clay Worsted Suits. All wool, fine diagonal pattern. Style 5. Suit... 8.75

30268 Men's Imported Clay Worsted Suits. All wool navy blue diagonal weave. Style 5. Per suit, 8.75

30270 Men's Imported Clay Worsted Suits. All wool navy blue diagonal weave, double breasted sacks. Style 3. Per suit.............. 8.75

30272 Men's Imported Diagonal Clay Worsted Suits. All wool, black or dark blue. Style 1. Per Suit.............. 10.00

30274 Men's Imported All Wool Clay Worsted Suits. Black diagonal, medium weight. Style 2. Per suit.............. 10.00

30276 Men's Imported All Wool Clay Worsted Suits. Black diagonal; medium weight. Style 5. Per suit.............. 10.00

30278 Men's Imported All Wool Clay Worsted Suits. Black diagonal pattern. Style 1. Per suit. 11.00

30280 Men's Imported All Wool Clay Worsted Suits. Black diagonal pattern. Style 2. Per suit. 11.00

30282 Men's Imported Worsted Suits. Guaranteed high grade; very fine new pattern, small basket weave. Black or blue. Style 1. Per suit 12.00

30284 Men's Suits; same as above in style 3. Blue or black. Per suit.............. 12.00

30286 Men's Suits; same as above in style 2. Blue or black. Per suit.............. 12.00

30288 Men's Fine Imported Clay Worsted Suits, Black diagonal pattern, narrow black braid on coat and vest. Style 1. Per suit.............. 12.50

Men's Suits—Continued.

30290 Men's Fine Imported Black Diagonal Clay Worsted Suits. Narrow black braid on coat and vest. Style 5. Per suit.............. $12.50

30292 Men's Extra Quality Imported Black Diagonal Worsted Suits, stitched edges. Style 1. All wool. Per suit.............. 13.50

30294 Men's Extra Quality Imported Suits. All wool black diagonal worsted, double breasted, sack style. Fine weave. Style 3. Per suit..... 13.50

30296 Men's Extra Quality Imported Suits. Dark blue diagonal, fine wale. All Wool, Style 1. Per suit.............. 13.50

30298 Men's Suits; same style goods and color as above in style 3. Per suit.............. 13.50

30300 Men's Black Diagonal English Worsted Suits, all wool. Coat and vest bound with narrow braid. Style 1. Per suit.............. 14.00

30302 Men's Black Diagonal English Worsted Suits. Coat and vest bound with narrow braid. All wool goods. Style 5. Per suit.............. 15.00

30304 Men's English Worsted Suits. All wool, blue black, small seed pattern, stitched edges. Style 1 only. Per suit.............. 15.00

30306 Men's Fancy Imported Worsted Suits. Blue or black, small basket weave. Coat and vest bound. Style 1. Per suit.............. 15.50

30308 Men's Fancy Imported Worsted Suits. Same as above in style 2. Per suit.............. 15.50

30310 Men's Imported Cambridge Worsted Suits. All wool, wide wale diagonal pattern; 3 button cutaway sack style; similar to style 1. Seal brown color only. Per suit.............. 15.50

30312 Men's Imported Black Worsted Suits. Wide wale diagonal pattern. Style 5. Medium long. Per suit.............. 16.00

30314 Men's All Wool Imported Black Worsted Suits. Fine wale diagonal pattern. Double breasted Prince Albert. Style 7. Per suit 15.50

30316 Men's Imported Black Worsted Prince Albert Suits; same goods as above, with silk facing on lapels of coat. Style 7. Per suit.... 17.00

30318 Men's Superior Quality All Wool Suits; imported black diagonal clay worsted; fine value; extra selected stock. Style 1. Per suit. 17.50

30320 Men's Superior Quality All Wool Black Diagonal Worsted Suits; long three-button cutaway frocks. Style 5. Per suit.............. 18.00

Montgomery Ward & Co.'s Celebrated $10 Suits.

The wonderful success we have achieved with our celebrated $10 suits in the past has inspired us to put forth greater efforts in this line. We are therefore this season quoting a line of strictly all wool suits that not only boldly defy all competition, but far surpass in quality, fit and workmanship any ready-made suits ever before offered for a like sum. They are, in fact, far superior to many suits heretofore sold for a much higher price. *We sample the full line.* Write to us for samples at once. They will speak for themselves and convince you that our prices are "all right." Our stock is enormous, and all orders for regular sizes will have our immediate attention.

30322 Men's Celebrated All Wool Suits, assorted patterns. Style 1. Per suit.............. $10.00

30324 Men's Celebrated All Wool Suits, assorted patterns. Style 2. Per suit.............. 10.00

30326 Men's Celebrated All Wool Suits, assorted patterns. Style 5. Per suit.............. 10.00

30328 Men's Celebrated All Wool Suits. "Tricot Long," new style of tricot cloth. Plain colors: Medium gray, dark gray and light, brownish gray. Style 1. *Send for sample.* Per suit.... 10.00

30330 Men's All Wool Suits. "Tricot Long," same as above in style 2. Per suit.............. 10.00

30332 Men's Celebrated All Wool Suits, "Tricot Long," same as above in style 5. *Send for samples.* Per suit.............. 10.00

30334 Men's Celebrated All Wool Suits, made of imported black diagonal clay worsted. Style 1. *Send for sample.* Per suit.............. 10.00

30336 Men's Celebrated All Wool Suits, Imported black diagonal clay worsted. Style 2. *Send for Sample.* Per suit.............. 10.00

30338 Men's Celebrated All Wool Suits, imported black diagonal clay worsted. Style 5. *Send for sample.* Per suit.............. 10.00

Corduroy Suits.

Sizes 35 to 42, chest measure.

30340 Brown Corduroy, plaid cassimere lining, large game pockets on inside. Style 1.......... $12.00

30342 Drab Corduroy, plaid cassimere lining, large game pockets on inside. Styel 1........ 12.00

30344 Drab Corduroy, plaid cassimere lining, large game pockets on inside. Style 3.......... 12.75

30346 Drab Corduroy, fine cord, cassimere lining, large game pockets on inside. Style 1..... 14.00

30348 Drab Corduroy, fine cord, plaid cassimere lining. Style 3.............. 14.50

Blue Flannel Suits.

N. B.—We do not sample any ready-made clothing, except when stated. Sizes, 34 to 42.

30350 Blue Flannel Suits, light weight, all wool. Style 1.............. $9.00

30352 Blue Flannel Suits, light weight, all wool. Style 2.............. 9.00

30354 Blue Flannel Suits, light weight, all wool. Style 3.............. 10.00

30356 Indigo Blue Regulation Pilot Cloth, heavy weight. Style 2.............. 12.00

30358 Indigo Blue Regulation Pilot Cloth, heavy weight. Style 3.............. 12.75

30360 All Wool, Heavy Weight Navy Blue Regulation cloth Style 1.............. 15.00

30362 Dark Navy Blue Bullock Cloth, beaver finish. Style 1.............. 10.00

Grand Army Suits.

30364 Regulation G. A. R. Blue Flannel, fast colors; G. A. R. brass buttons. Style 2..........9.50
Sizes. 35 to 42.

Street Car Conductors' Suits.

30366 Conductors' Suits, medium weight, made of all wool navy blue flannel, fast color. Single breasted, square cut sack style. Black or brass buttons as desired. Eyelet buttonholes. The pockets are made of extra heavy canvas. The side pockets and ticket pockets of coat are bound with black leather. Good, strong and serviceable garments. Style 2. Price, per full suit..................................$11.00

30368 Conductors' Suits, extra quality, all wool navy blue Middlesex cloth, medium weight, coat pockets and hip pocket of pants bound with leather and made of heavy canvas. Built for wear. Double breasted, square cut sack. Style3. Brass or plain black bone buttons. Eyelet buttonholes. Price, per full suit.........17.50

Montgomery Ward & Co.'s "Celebrated" All Wool $3.00 Pants are World Beaters.

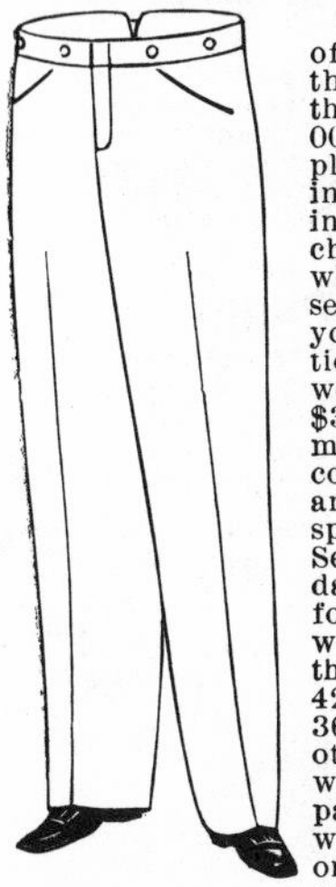

They are the most popular line of pants in the United States for the money. Those who have had them once will tell you so. 85,000 pairs sold without a just complaint. Their wonderful value induces an easy sale, and their intrinsic merits make each purchaser a regular customer. Those who have not seen them should send for samples, "it will pay you." They are without exception the best high grade "all wool" pants manufactured for $3.00. One of the largest and best manufacturers of woolens in this country supplies us with the cloth, and we will be able to furnish our spring and summer weights until September 1st, 1895. After that date we can furnish new patterns for fall and winter. Upon request we will send samples as long as they last. The sizes run from 30 to 42 inch waist measure, and 29 to 36 inch inside leg seam; sizes other than these made to order will cost from $4.00 to $5.00 per pair, according to size, providing we have the material at time of ordering. We cannot furnish coats or vests to match these pants.

N. B.—We do not send samples of any ready-made pants except our $3.00 line. When ordering pants always give waist measure first.

This lot comprises the following styles; all brand new goods and finer quality than we have ever before sold for $3.00 per pair.

30370 Men's Celebrated All Wool Cassimere Pants. Fine black and gray hairline stripe. *Send for sample.* Per pair..................$3.00
30372 Men's Celebrated All Wool Cassimere Pants, steel blue any gray hairline stripe. Per pair.................................... 3.00
30374 Men's Celebrated All Wool Cassimere Pants, medium brown and gray mixed hairline stripes. Per pair.......................... 3.00
30376 Men's Celebrated All Wool Cassimere Pants, gray mixed fancy stripe, medium color. Per pair.................................... 3.00
30378 Men's Celebrated All Wool Cassimere Pants, medium and light brown mixed stripes; very neat. Per pair.......................... 3.00
30380 Men's Celebrated Cassimere Pants; medium shade of gray with neat black stripes. Per pair.................................... 3.00
30382 Men's Celebrated All Wool Pants: made of fine quality black diagonal imported worsted. Per pair.................................... 3.00
30384 Men's Celebrated All Wool pants: made of guaranteed indigo blue flannel. Per pair... 3.00

Men's Pantaloons.

The quotations under this heading are for pants only—all men's sizes. Smallest waist, 30 inches; largest 40 inches.

All pants longer than 36 inches inside seam will have to be made to order, and will cost 50 cents to $1.00 extra, acording to the waist measure.

Before ordering pants, read instructions for measurement and remarks under the same. Be sure to make your figures plain and correct.

Summer pants weigh about 1½ pounds, winter about 2½, varying according to size and quality.

N. B.—We do not sample any pants under this heading.

30386 Men's Cottonade Pants; fancy stripe. Per pair..................................$0.75
30388 Men's Cottondale Pants; better goods. Per pair.................................... 1.00
30390 Men's Black Diagonal Cotton Worsted Pants. Per pair........................... 1 40
30392 Black and Gold Mixed Diagonal Cotton Worsted Pants............................ 1.35
30394 Dark Mixed Striped Satinet Cassimere Pants.. 1.85
30396 Gray Mixed Striped Wool Cassimere...... 2.00
30398 Men's Wool Cassimere Pants; dark mixed, fancy stripe, neat pattern; extra good value. Per pair.................................... 2.00

Men's Pantaloons—Continued.

30400 Men's Extra Quality Wool Cassimere Pants, gray and black mixed, fancy stripe. Per pair.................................... 2.25
30402 Men's Extra Quality Wool Cassimere Pants, black ground, with neat gray stripe. Per pair.................................... 2.25
30404 Men's Worsted Pants, steel blue with neat stripe. Per pair.......................... 2.50
30406 Men's Fancy Striped Wool Cassimere Pants, light and medium gray mixed. Per Pair 2.50
30408 Men's Fancy Striped Wool Cassimere Pants, light and medium brown mixed. Per pair.................................... 2.50
30410 Men's Fancy Striped All Wool Cassimere Pants, steel blue, with neat black stripe. Per pair.................................... 2.75
30412 Men's All Wool Black and Gray Hair Line Cassimere Pants, spring weight. Per pair $2.75
30414 Men's All Wool Light and Medium Brown Mixed Striped Cassimere Pants. Spring weight Per pair.................................... 2.75
30416 Men's All Wool Spring Weight Cassimere Pants; very neat brown and gray check. Per pair.................................... 3.25
30418 Men's Extra Fine All Wool Cassimere Pants, spring weight, bluish gray with fine black hairline stripe. Per pair..................... 3.50
30420 Men's Extra Fine All Wool Cassimere Pants; same as above in light gray with brown hairline stripe. The neatest pattern ever made in cassimere pants. Per pair................ 3.50
30422 Men's Extra Fine All Wool Cassimere Pants; seal brown with steel colored hairline stripes. Per pair.......................... 4.00
30424 Men's Extra Fine All Wool Cassimere Pants. Very fine black and gray pin check. Per pair.................................... 4.50
30426 Men's Imported Worsted Pants, small neat stripes of black and steel color. Per pair.................................... 4.50
30428 Men's Fine Black Worsted Pants, small corded stripe. Per pair....................... 4.00
30430 Young Men's Light Colored Pants, fine English worsted, with neat stripes of brown, cream and gray. Very handsome and dressy. Per pair.................................... 4.50
30432 Men's English Worsted Pants, fancy stripes, steel gray and black, extra quality. Per pair.................................... 5.00
30434 Men's Extra Quality English Worsted Pants blue black, narrow, fancy cord pattern. Per pair.................................... 5.50

Corduroy Pants.

30436 Brown Corduroy Pants......................$2.85
30438 Drab Corduroy Pants........................ 2.85

Black Pantaloons.

Sizes 30 to 40 inch waist measure: 30 to 35 inside seam measure.

We do not sample any pants under this heading.

30444 Black Diagonal Worsted,.....................$2.00
30446 Black Diagonal Imported Clay Worsted... 2.75
30448 Black Diagonal Worsted, corkscrew weave 4.50
30450 Black Diagonal Imported Worsted........ 5.00
30452 Black Diagonal Imported Worsted........ 5.25
30454 Black Doeskin Pants, all wool............ 6.00
30456 Black Worsted Corded...................... 5.50
30458 Blach Diagonal Clay Worsted.............. 3.00
30460 Black Diagonal Imported Clay Worsted.. 4.00

Pantaloons.—Extra Size.

Waist measures of pants, 40 to 48 inches.

Before ordering pants and vest, extra size, read instructions for measurement and remarks under same. Be sure and make your figures plain and correct.

We do not sample any goods under this heading.

30462 All Wool Black and Gray stripe Cassimere..$4.00
30464 All Wool Blue Flannel Cloth............... 4.00
30866 Fancy Stripe Gray Cassimere.............. 4.50
30468 Black Diagonal Imported Worsted....... 6.00

Overalls and Jumpers.

Light overalls weigh about 16. medium 25 and heavy 28 ounces. Jumpers weigh 20 ounces.

The quotations under this heading are all men's sizes. Smallest waist 30: largest 42: longer than 36 inch inside seam will cost 25 cents per pair extra, made to order When ordering overalls or pants always give waist measure first.

Per pair.

30470 Men's Blue Denim Overalls..................$0.50
30472 Men's Brown Denim Overalls................ .50
30474 Men's Blue Denim Overalls.................. .60
30476 Men's Brown 8-oz. Duck Overalls.......... .60
30478 Painters' White Duck Overalls. Good value; *white only.* Per pair..................... .35
30480 Painters' and Paper Hangers' White Duck Overalls, with aprons; *white only.* Per pair..... .45
30482 Painters' White Duck Waists or Jumpers; *white only.* Each............................. .35
30484 Men's Unbleached or White Duck Overalls, heavy weight............................ .60
30486 Ward's Celebrated Pantaloon Overalls, made of fancy blue or brown denim........... .80
30488 Men's 9-ounce Blue Denim Pantaloon Overalls, 3 pockets, reinforced fly............ .80
30490 Men's Brown 10-ounce Duck Pantaloon Overalls.. .80
30492 Men's Brown 10-ounce Duck Cavalry Cowboy's Overalls, reinforced on inside to bottom of pants.. 1.00
30494 Men's Blue Denim Jumpers, Amoskeag... .60
30496 Men's Unbleached or White Duck Jumpers, heavy weight............................ .60
30498 Men's Brown 8-ounce Duck Jumpers...... .60

Overalls and Jumpers—Continued.

30500 Men's Blue Full 9-ounce Denim Jumpers. .80
30502 Men's Blue Denim Apron Overalls........ .68
30504 Men's Blue and White Check Engineers' Jackets.. .42
30506 Men's Blue and White Checked Engineers' Jackets.. .35

Jean Pants.

The quotations under the heading are for PANTS only—all men's sizes. Smallest waist, 30 inches; largest, 40 inches

All pants longer than 36 inches, inside seam, will have to be made to order, and will cost from 50c. to $1.00 extra, according to waist measure.

Before ordering pants read instructions for measurement and remarks under the same. Be sure to make your figures plain and correct.

Summer pants weigh about 1½ pounds, winter, about 2½, varying according to size and quality.

KENTUCKY JEAN PANTALOONS. Each.

30508 Kentucky Jean Pants, dark gray mixed..$1.00
30510 Kentucky Jean Pants, Oxford mixed, spring bottom, B. J. style....................... 1.25
30512 Kentucky Jean Pants, Oxford mixed..... 1.50
30514 Kentucky Jean Pants, dark Oxford mixed 2.00

Coats and Vests.

The quotations under this heading are for coats and vests together. All men's sizes, 34 to 42.

Before ordering coats and vests, read instructions for measurements and remarks under the same. Be sure to make figures plain and correct.

Weight on coats and vest, 2¾ to 3¼ lbs., according to size, style and quality.

We do not sample coats and vests.

Price for coat and vest. Each.

30516 Black Diagonal Worsted, old gold mixed, all cotton. Style 1..............................$2.50
30518 Fancy Mixed Satinet Cassimeres, dark colors. Style 1................................. 3.50
30520 Men's Medium Brown Mixed Satinet Cassimere Coats and Vests. Style 1............ 3.50
30522 Men's Medium Gray Mixed Satinet Cassimere Coats and Vests. Style 1................ 3.50
30524 Men's All Wool Black Diagonal Clay Worsted Coats and Vests. Style 1............. 6.00
30526 Men's All Wool Black Diagonal Clay Worsted Coats and Vests. Style 2............. 6.00
30528 Men's All Wool Black Diagonal Clay orsted Coats and Vests. Style 5.............. 6.50
30530 All Wool Navy Blue Cloth, medium weight coat and vest. Style 1.................. 6.50
30532 All Wool Navy Blue Cloth, medium weight coat and vest. Style 2.................. 6.50
30534 All Wool Navy Blue Cloth, medium weight coat and vest. Style 3.................. 7.50
30536 All Wool Navy Blue Cloth, medium weight coat and vest, extra sizes, 43 to 48. Style 1.. 8.00
30538 Drab Corduroy, cassimere lining, two very large pockets on inside of coat. Style 1... 9.00
30540 Brown Corduroy, cassimere lining, two very large pockets on inside of coat. Style 1...$9.00
30542 Black Corduroy, colored flannel lining, fine cord. Style 1................................11.00
30544 Drab Corduroy, colored flannel lining fine cord. Style 1................................11.00
30546 Old Men's Frock Coats and Vests, made of black and gray wool hairline cassimere, lapel pockets. Style 4................................ 6.50
30548 Men's Imported Black Diagonal Clay Worsted Coats and Vests, all wool. Style 1..... 7.00
30550 All Wool Cassimere Coats and Vests, neat brown or gray mixtures. Style 1............. 7.25
30552 Men's Imported All Wool Black Diagonal Clay Worsted Coats and Vests. Style 2. Each.. 7.25
30554 Men's Imported All Wool Black Diagonal Clay Worsted Coats and Vests. Style 5. Each.. 7.50
30556 Men's Extra Fine Imported Worsted Coats and Vests; navy blue diagonal, all wool, fine wale. Style 1. Each............................ 11.50
30558 Men's Coats and Vests, same as above, in black. Style 1. Each.......................... 11.50
30560 Men's Fine All Wool Black Diagonal Worsted Coats and Vests, imported goods. Style 1. Each.. 9.00
30562 Men's Fine All Wool Imported Worsted Coats and Vests, black diagonal. Style 2. Each 9.00
30564 Men's Imported Black Diagonal Clay Worsted Coats and Vests. Style 5. Each...... 9.50
30566 Men's Fine Black Diagonal Worsted Coats and Vests, bound with narrow black silk braid. Style 1. Each.. 13.00
30568 Men's Fine Imported Black Clay Worsted Coats and Vests. Diagonal pattern. Style 5. Trimmed with narrow, black silk braid. Each.14.00
30570 Men's Long 3-Button Cutaway Frock Coats and Vests, made of imported black diagonal Clay Worsted. Very stylish Style 5....12.00
30572 Men's Long 3-Button Cutaway Frock Coats and Vests, made of imported black diagonal, very fine wale Style 5......................16.00
30574 Men's Prince Albert Coats and Vests, made of imported all wool black diagonal clay worsted, stitched edges. Style 7..................12.50
30576 Men's Prince Albert Coats and Vests, made of extra quality all wool black diagonal worsted, stitched edges. Style 7 ....15.50

NOTE. For higher priced clothing, we refer you to our custom tailoring department, where we make clothing to order in any size and style desired. *Send for samples and Catalogue R.*

LADIES—Insist upon it that the men of your family dress well, provided they can do so without increased cost. Send for Catalogue R, showing samples of cloth and prices of suits made to measure.

Men's Vests.

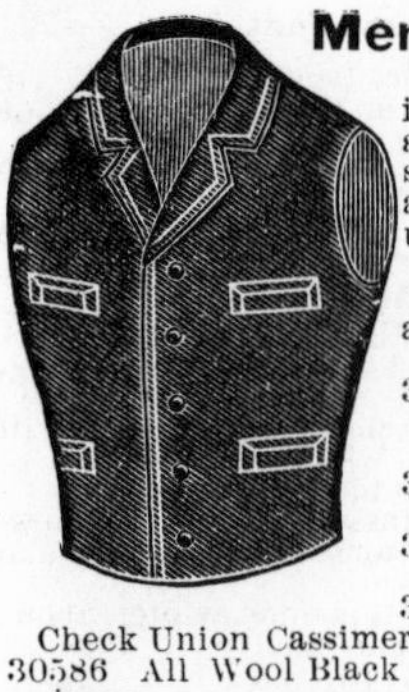

Before ordering vests, read instructions for measurement and remarks under same. Be sure to make your figures plain and correct. Size, chest measure, 34 to 42.

SINGLE VESTS ONLY.

Single vests, 10 to 15 ounces, according to size and quality.

N.B.—We do not sample vests.

30578 Black Diagonal Cotton Worsted, old gold mixed. Each $0.85
30580 Black and Grey Small Check Cassimere $1.00
30582 Black and Gray, Hairline Satinet Cassimere $1.50
30584 Black and Gray Small Check Union Cassimere $1.50
30586 All Wool Black and Gray Hailine Cassimere 2.00
30588 All Wool Blue Flannel, medium weight.. 1.75
30590 Men's All Wool Diagonal Clay Worsted Vests. Each 1.25
30592 Men's All Wool Black Diagonal Imported Clay Worsted Vests. Each 1.50
30594 Men's All Wool Black Diagonal Imported Clay Worsted Vests, fine wale. Each.... 1.75
30596 Black Diagonal Imported Clay Worsted.. 2.25
30598 Black Diagonal Imported Clay Worsted.. 2.50

Pantaloons and Vests.

The quotations under this heading are for PANTS and VESTS together. All men's sizes, chest measure from 35 to 42.

N. B.—We do not sample pants and vests. Pants and vests.

30600 All Wool Black and Gray Hairline Cassimere 4.50
30602 All Blue Flannel Cloth 5.00
30604 Black Diagonal Worsted 4.50
30606 Black Diagonal Imported Worsted 6.50
30608 Black Doeskin Pants and Black Broadcloth Vest 9.00

Coats.

The quotations under this heading are for coats only. Sizes, 35 to 42.

Before ordering coat, read instructions for measurements and remarks under same. Be sure to make your figures plain and correct.

Coats weigh from 1¾ to 2¼ pounds, according to size, style and quality.

N. B.—**We do not sample coats.** Each.

30610 Black Diagonal Cotton Worsted, old gold mixed. Style 1 .... $2.00
30612 All Wool Indigo Blue Flannel Coats. Style 1 .... 5.00
30614 Black Diagonal Imported Worsted Coats. Style 7 .... 13.00
30616 Black Broadcloth Coats. Style 7 .... 14.50

Leather Clothing.

Leather Clothing, commonly called Dongola Goat, is made of oil-tanned and dressed Rocky Mountain sheepskin. It is very soft and pliable, and is strictly waterproof and windproof. Sizes in leather clothing are 36, 38, 40, 42 and 44. No odd sizes. Weight of leather coats 3¼ to 4 pounds. Vests, 1 to 2 pounds.

30618 Black Leather Coats, double breasted, patent snap fastener buttons, plaid cassimere lining. Each $3.75
30620 Brown 10 ounce Waterproof Duck, lined with russet leather, double breasted, patent snap button 4.00
30622 Black Leather Coats, double breasted, patent snap buttons, plaid lining 4.50
30624 Black Leather Coats, double breasted, patent snap buttons, gray blanket lining 4.50
30626 Black Leather Coats, No. 1 stock, red flannel lined, double breasted, patent snap buttons. 5.00
30628 Black Leather Coats, drab corduroy lining, double breasted, patent snap buttons 5.00
30630 Black Leather Coats, Kentucky jeans lining, double breasted, patent snap buttons.... 5.00
30632 Russet Leather Coat, red flannel lining, double breasted, patent snap buttons 6.00
30634 Black Leather Coats, plaid Mackinaw lining, double breasted, patent snap buttons.... 5.75
30636 Black Leather Coats, reversible, drab corduroy, double breasted, patent snap buttons. 6.25
30638 Black Leather Coats, chamois lining, double breasted, patent buttons 6.50
30640 Brown Duck, lined with sheep pelt, corduroy collar, storm fly front, patent snap buttons. 6.50
30642 Russet Leather Coats, reversible, drab corduroy lining, double breasted, patent snap buttons.. 8.25
30644 Black Leather Coats, reversible, green corduroy, double breasted, patent snap buttons 8.50
30646 Tan Brown Genuine Ooze Calfskin Coat, reversible, soft and as pliable as cloth 11.00
30648 Black Leather Vests, red flannel lined. Each 2.50
30650 Black Leather Vests, drab corduroy lined. Each 3.00
30652 Russet Leather Vests, red flannel lined, double breasted 3.25
30654 Black Leather Vests, chamois lined 3.50
30656 Tan Brown Genuine Ooze Calfskin Vests, reversible 5.50
30658 Black Leather Pants. Per pair 4.50
30660 Black Leather Apron Pants, lined. Per pair 5.25
30662 Tan Brown Genuine Ooze Calfskin Pants. 11.00

Leather Pants are made in the following sizes only: 32, 34, 36, 38, 40 and 42 waist, and 30, 31, 32, 33 and 34 inside seam measure.

30664 Black Leather Overcoat, red and black plaid Mackinaw blanket lining. Each 9.50

Lined Duck Suits, Ulsters and Coats.

Men's sizes in duck goods are 34, 36, 38, 40, 42 and 44. No odd sizes. Duck clothing weighs as follows: Suit, 6½ and 7½ pounds; ulsters, 5 to 6½ pounds; single coats, 2 to 9 pounds.

30666 Brown Duck Coats, drab cotton flannel lined. Each $1.25
30668 Brown Duck Coats, dark gray mixed blanket lined. Each 1.50
30670 Brown Duck Coats, red cotton flannel lined, corduroy collar, Each 1.50
30672 Brown Duck Coats, lined with red Mackinaw blanketing, corduroy collar. Each 2.00
30674 Black Duck Coats, waterproof, gray blanket lined, corduroy collar. Each 2.50
30676 Men's Brown Duck Ulsters, 10 ounce goods, gray blanket lining 4.50
30678 Men's Brown Duck Ulsters, 10 ounce goods, red or blue Mackinaw lining 6.50
30680 Brown Duck Pants, gray blanket lined. Size, 32 to 42 waist, 30 to 34 leg measure. Per pair 1.50
30682 Brown Duck Pants, gray blanket lined, 32 to 42 waist, 30 to 34 leg measure. Per pair, 1.75
30684 Brown Duck Vests, gray blanket lined. Each .... .90
30686 Brown Duck Vests, gray blanket lined. Each 1.15
30688 Men's Gray Duck Suits, 10 ounce goods, gray blanket lined; full suit 5.00
30690 Men's Duck Suits, 10 ounce goods, red blanket lined 6.50
30692 Men's Duck Suits, 10 ounce goods, better lining, red blanket lined 7.35
30694 Men's Brown Duck Suits, 10 ounce goods, lined with heavy plaid Mackinaw flannel 8.50

Waiters' and Cooks' Outfits.

Each.

30696 Cooks' Jackets, single breasted, white drill, detachable buttons $1.00
30698 Cooks' Jackets, double breasted, white drill, detachable buttons 1.25
30700 Waiters' White Drill Jackets or Coats, with pockets 1.00
30702 Waiters' Black Sateen Jackets or Coats, with pockets .... .80
30704 Waiters' Black Alpaca Jackets or Coats, lined, with pockets 1.50
30706 Cooks' Bib Apron, heavy white cotton.... .30
30708 Waiters' Heavy White Cotton Apron .... .25
30710 Cook's Heavy White Muslin Caps .... .12

Barbers' and Dentists' Coats.

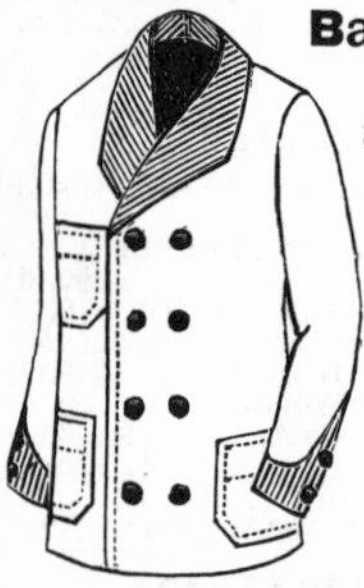

30712

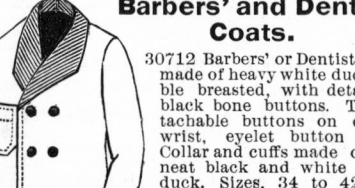

30712 Barbers' or Dentists' Coat; made of heavy white duck, double breasted, with detachable black bone buttons. Two detachable buttons on cuff at wrist, eyelet button holes. Collar and cuffs made of very neat black and white striped duck. Sizes, 34 to 42 inch breast measure. Each.... $1.50

Hot Weather Clothing.

Single Coats.

30714 Men's Summer Sack Coats; made of washable drill, light gray and drab mixed color, with fine black stripes. Sizes, 34 to 42. Each .... .75
30716 Men's Sack Coats; made of fine black and white hairline striped sateen, patch pockets. Sizes, 34 to 42. Each 1.00
30718 Men's Sack Coats; made of dark steel mixed Mohair, patch pockets. Size, 34 to 42. Each 1.15
30720 Men's Sack Coats; made of blue and white striped washable cotton cheviot; very neat. Sizes, 34 to 42. Each 1.00
30722 Men's Sack Coats; made of black cotton cassimere weave. Sizes, 34 to 42. Each 1.00
30724 Men's Black Alpaca Sack Coats. Sizes, 34 to 42. Each 1.25
30726 Men's Black Alpaca Sack Coats. Sizes, 34 to 42. Each 1.75
30728 Men's Black Alpaca Sack Coats. Sizes, 34 to 42. Each 2.50
30730 Men's Gray Mixed Brilliantine Mohair Sack Coats; superior quality, 34 to 42. Each... 1.85
30732 Men's Black Brilliantine Sack Coats. Sizes, 34 to 42. Each 3.00
30734 Men's Black Alpaca Ministerial Coats. Sizes, 34 to 42. Each 2.50
30736 Men's Extra Size Black Alpaca Ministerial Coats. Sizes, 43 to 48. Each $2.75
30738 Men's Black Drap D'Ete Ministerial Coats. Sizes, 34 to 42. Each 7.50
30740 Men's Black Cheviot Sack Coats, patch pockets. Sizes, 34 to 42. Each 2.25
30742 Men's Navy Blue Cheviot Sack Coats, patch pockets. Sizes, 34 to 42. Each 2.25
30744 Men's All Wool Sack Coats, very fine black and gray pin check; patch Pockets. Sizes, 34 to 42. Each 3.00

Alpaca Vests.

30746 Men's Black Alpaca Vests. Sizes, 34 to 42. Each $1.25
30748 Men's Black Alpaca Vests Sizes, 34 to 42. Each 1.75

Coats and Vests.

30750 Men's Sack Coats and Vests, made of light gray and drab mixed drill, with fine black stripe. Sizes, 34 to 42. Each 1.15
30752 Men's Sack Coats and Vests, made of brown mixed mohair. Sizes, 34 to 42. Each.. 2.50
30754 Men's Fine Sack Coats and Vests, made of neat gray striped mohair, patch pockets, pearl buttons. Sizes, 34 to 42. Each 3.00
30756 Men's Black Wool Cheviot Sack Coats and Vests, patch pockets. Sizes, 34 to 42. Each $3.25
30758 Men's Fine Dark Gray Diagonal Wool Cheviot Sack Coats and Vests, patch pockets. Sizes, 34 to 42. Each 3.50
30760 Men's Fine All Wool Diagonal Serge Sack Coats and Vests, patch pockets. Sizes, 34 to 42, black or navy blue. Each 4.75
30762 Men's Extra Fine All Wool Imported Serge Coats and Vests, sack style; very fine diagonal wales. Sizes, 34 to 42, black or blue. Each 6.00
30764 Men's Black Drap D'Ete Ministerial Coats and Vests, all sizes from 34 to 48 inch breast measure. Each 7.50

Linen Dusters.

30766 Men's Linen Dusters. Each $1.75

Kentucky Hemp Suits.

Sizes, 34 to 42

30768 Genuine Kentucky Hemp Suits, sack style. Something entirely new in summer clothing. Natural linen color, made of real Kentucky hemp: heavy and strong, cool and neat, patch pockets, pearl buttons, washable goods. First class in every respect Price for full suit, coat, vest and pants $4.75

White Duck Pants.

Sizes 30 to 42 Waist and 30 to 38 inch Inseam.

30770 Men's White Duck Pants, with straps for belt. These pants are made in extra length inseam and are usually worn rolled up at bottoms. Particular care should therefore be given in stating inseam measurement. Always state exact length of inseam desired. Price per pair. $0.95
30772 Men's Better Quality White Duck Washable Pants. Same style as above. Per pair 1.35
30774 Men's Washable Duck Pants, same style as above; made of white duck, with neat black and blue fine stripes, Per pair 1.50

Fancy Vests.

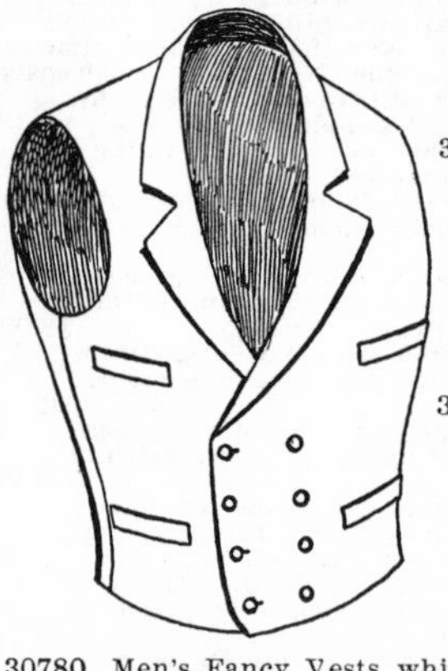

30776 Men's Fancy White Duck Vests, with neat figures of black, blue or brown. Single breasted, sizes, 34 to 42 only. Mention predominating color or color of figure desired. Each $0.80
30778 Fancy Vests, same as above in double breasted style. Each 1.00
30780 Men's Fancy Vests, white or drab duck, with small, neat figures of black, double breasted. Style, 34 to 42. Each 1.10
30782 Men's Fancy Vests, white duck, with small black figures, very neat, double breasted style. 34 to 42 chest measure. Each 1.50

Men's Spring and Fall Overcoats.

Sizes, 34 to 42 only.

30784 Light or Medium Brown and Gray Mixed Melton Overcoats. Style 10. Each $11.00
30786 Black Diagonal Clay Worsted Overcoats. Style 10. Each 12.00
30788 Dark Gray Mixed Diagonal Clay Worsted Overcoats. Style 10. Each 13.50
30790 Black or Navy Blue Wool Thibet Overcoats. Style 10. Each 14.00
30792 Gray Mixed Diagonal Cassimere Overcoats. Style 10. Each 7.50
30794 Light Brown and Gray Mixed Cassimere Overcoats. Style 10. Each 10.00

NOTICE.—A complete line of Fall and Winter ready made clothing of all kinds will be quoted in our large fall catalogue, which will be issued in September.

If you want a Buggy, Road Cart or Spring Wagon, don't, for your own sake, fail to study our prices.

Children's Suits.

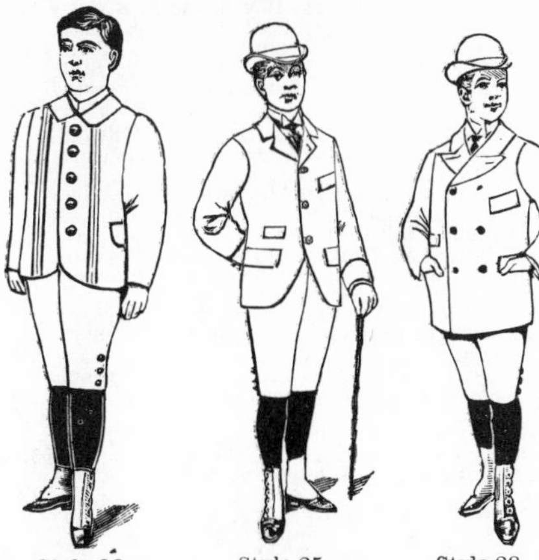

Style 26. Style 25. Style 28.

Coat and Knee Pants Suits, two pieces.

Children's Suits are made in sizes from 4 to 14 years.

N. B.—We do not sample any ready-made clothing except where so stated in quotation.

30796 Black and Gray Mixed Kentucky Jeans Suits, sack style. Each....$0.75
30798 Dark Mixed Fancy Cotton Worsted Suits, sack style. Each.... .75
30800 Dark Fancy Striped Cotton Worsted Suits, sack style. Each.... .85
30802 Fancy Striped Gray and Black Mixed Sack Suits. Each.... 1.00
30804 Plain Black Diagonal Cotton Worsted Sack Suits. Each.... 1.10
30806 Fancy Mixed Windsor Cassimere Sack Suits, medium dark colors. Each.... 1.20
30808 Black and Gray Mixed Small Check Cassimere Suits, double-breasted sack. Style 28. Very serviceable. Each.... 1.35
30810 Navy Blue Twilled Union Cassimere Suits, single breasted square cut, sack style, corded front, 4 to 14 years. Style 26.... 1.65
30812 Dark Gray Hairline Windsor Cassimere Suits, double breasted sack, style 28, 4 to 14 years.... 1.75
30814 Steel Gray and Black Mixed Twilled Wool Cassimere Suits, style 28, 4 to 14 years.... 1.90
30816 Plain Black Cheviot Double Breasted Sack Suits, 4 to 14 years. Style 28.... 2.00
30818 Medium Brown or Gray Mixed Suits, hard twisted diagonal cassimere, style 28, 4 to 14 years; mention color. Each.... 2.00
30820 Fancy Plaid Suits, style 28, wool cassimere, navy blue background, made for service, 4 to 14 years.... 2.10
30822 Dark Gray Diagonal Wool Cheviot Suits, soft finish, very neat and substantial, pants have double knees, style 28, 4 to 14 years. Each.... 2.25
30824 Fancy Wool Cassimere Suits, black, gray and steel blue mixtures, very neat patterns, double knee pants, style 28. Each.... 2.25
30826 Plain Dark Bluish Gray Wool Cheviot Suits, soft finish, style 28, 4 to 14 years. Each.. 2.25
30828 Medium and Dark Gray Fancy Mixed Wool Cassimere Suits, double knee pants, style 28, 4 to 14 years. Each.... 2.25
30830 Black or Navy Blue Soft Wool Cheviot Suits. Pants have double knees. Style 28. 4 to 14 years. Mention color wanted. Each.... 2.35
30832 Black or Navy Blue Worsted Corkscrew Sack Suits, single breasted, pleated front. Style 26. Mention color wanted. Each.... 2.40
30834 Fancy Gray Mixed Plaid Wool Cassimere Suits, silk sewed, double knees, extension band; will not rip. Style 28. Each.... 2.50
30836 Medium Brown Mixed Soft Wool Cheviot Suits, double knees. Style 28; 4 to 14 years. Each.... 2.50
30838 Gray and Black Fancy Mixed Wool Cassimere Suits; double knees, silk sewed; will not rip. An excellent suit for the money. Style 28. 2.65
30840 Drab or Brown Corduroy Suits. The most serviceable suits made. Style 28. Good weight. 3.00
30842 Brown and Gray Pin Check Wool Cassimere; double seat and knees in pants; will not rip. Style 28. Each.... 3.00
30844 Small Neat Gray Checked Cassimere Suits; fine all wool goods. Made up first-class. Style 28; 5 to 15 years. Each.... 3.25
30846 All Wool Cassimere Suits, black and gray fancy check, with neat threads of red and blue, double knees. Style 28, 5 to 14 years. Each. 3.25
30848 All Wool Plain Black Cheviot Suits, double knees. Style 28, 4 to 14 years. Each.... 3.50
30850 All Wool Cassimere Suits, light, brown and gray mixed with neat red plaid. Style 28. 5 to 15 years. Each.... 3.75
30852 All Wool Medium Dark Brown Mixed Cassimere Suits. Style, 28, 4 to 14 years. Each. 3.75
30854 Dark Fancy Worsted Suits, black with very dark red and blue plaid. Sizes, 5 to 15 years. Style 28. Each.... 4.00
30856 Imported Clay Worsted Suits, plain black or dark blue, fine wale, diagonal pattern; very dressy. Style 28. Each.... 4.00
30858 Monitor Suits. For boys who are rough on clothes; made of all wool black and gray hairline cassimere, corded front and back. Style 26. Will not rip. 4 to 14 years. Each.... 4.00
30860 All Wool Navy Blue Imported Clay Worsted Suits. Style 28, 4 to 14 years. Each.... 4.50

Children's Suits—Continued.

30862 Fine Navy Blue Tricot Cloth Suits. Style 28, 4 to 15 years Each.... 4.50
30864 All Wool Cassimere Suits. Style 28, 5 to 15 years. Medium brown: fast color. Each ... 4.50
30866 All Wool Black Diagonal Cheviot Suits. Style 28, 5 to 15 years. Each.... 4.50
30868 All Wool Medium Light Gray Checked Cassimere Suits. Very neat pattern. Style 28, 4.50
30870 Fine English Diagonal Worsted Suits, gun powder gray. Style 28. Very neat and dressy. 4 to 14 years. Each.... 4.75
30872 All Wool Fancy Brown and Gray Small Checked Cassimere Suits. Superior quality. Style 28, 5 to 15 years. Each.... 4.75
30874 Fine All Wool Imported Diagonal Clay Worsted Suits. Style 28. Two colors: Light grayish brown and dark bluish gray; very neat. Size, 6 to 15 years. Each.... 5.00
30876 Light Brown Mixed Melton Suits. Style 28. Fine imported goods. Sizes, 6 to 15 years. 5.25
30878 Fine All Wool Navy Blue Tricot Cloth Suits. Style 28. Sizes, 5 to 15 years. Each.... 6.00

N. B.—All the above suits consist of 2 pieces; jacket or coat and knee pants.

Our Windsor Combination Suits.

Four pieces, coat, 2 pair knee pants and yacht cap to match.

NOTE.—Always mention size of cap desired. *Caps run in size from 6¼ to 6⅞ only.*

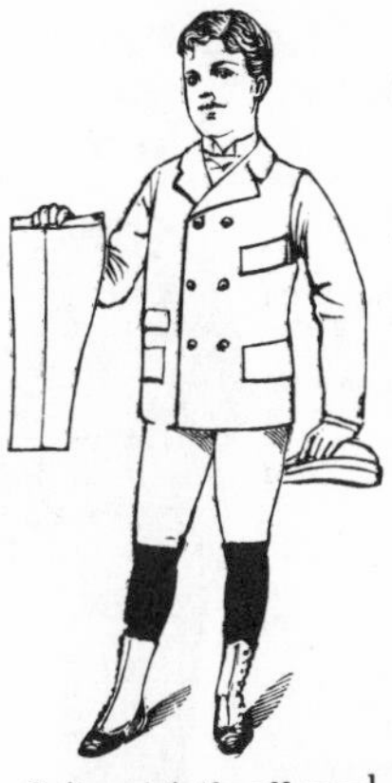

30880 Windsor Combination Suits; fancy gray mixed hard twist cassimere. Style 28, 4 pieces, coat, 2 pair pants and cap. Each....$2.25
30882 Windsor Combination Suits; small check brown, gray and black wool cassimere. Style 28. Coat, 2 pair pants and cap, 4 to 14 years. Each....$2.50
30884 Medium Brown Mixed Diagonal Cassimere, Windsor combination suits. Style 28. Coat, 2 pair pants and caps, 4 to 14 years. Each....$3.00
30886 Windsor Combination Suits; made of all wool black or navy blue diagonal cheviot; coat, 2 pair pants and cap. Style 28, 5 to 15 years per outfit. Each.$3.50
30888 Windsor Combination Suits; strictly all wool, black and gray mixed cassimere, check pattern. Coat, 2 pair pants and cap. Style 28. *How can you beat it?* Each..$3.75
30890 Windsor Combination Suits; strictly all wool cassimere, neat, brown mixed diagonal pattern. Style 28. 2 pair pants, 1 coat and a cap. 5 to 15 years. Each.... 4.00
30892 Windsor Combination Suits; same as above, in fancy gray plaid. Style 28. Each.... 4.00
30894 Windsor Combination Suits; strictly all wool, soft finished worsted. Diagonal pattern, plain black or navy blue. Coat, 2 pair pants and cap. Style 28. 4 to 15 years. Each.... 4.75
30896 Windsor Combination Suits; strictly all wool cassimere, fancy brown mixed plaid. Coat, 2 pair pants and cap. Style 28. Mention size of cap desired. Each.... 5.00
30898 Windsor Combination Suits, same as above, in fancy gray mixed plaid. Style 28. Each.... 5.00

Children's 3-Piece Suits.

Coat, Vest and Pants, 12 to 16 years only.

30900 All Wool Navy Blue Cheviot Suits, single breasted, sack style. 12 to 16 years only. Style 25. Each....$4 50
30902 All Wool Black and Gray Checked Cassimere Suits. Coat, vest and pants. Style 25. 12 to 16 years only. Each.... 5.75
30904 Navy Blue Tricot Suits, coat, vest and pants. Style 28. 12 to 16 years only. Each...$6.00
30906 All Wool Imported Diagonal Clay Worsted Suits, coat, vest and pants. Style 25; gun-powder gray; size, 12 to 16 years. Each....$6.50
30908 All Wool Black Diagonal Soft Finished Worsted Suits: same style as above; three pieces. Style 25. 10 to 15 years. Each. $6.50

Children's Reefer Suits.

We Have All the New and Nobby Styles. Sizes, 3 to 8 Years Only.

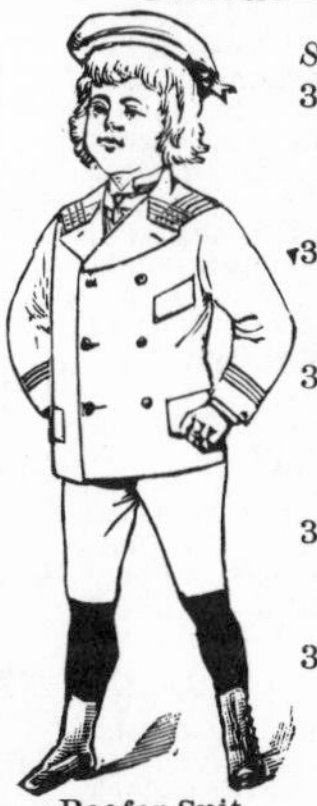

Reefer Suit.

30910 Children's Reefer Suits, jacket and knee pants; brown and gray mixed diagonal cassimere; large plain collar. Each....$1.90
30912 Reefer Suits made of dark gray diagonal cassimere; 3 to 10 years; same style as above. Each.... 2.00
30914 Reefer Suits, gray and white cassimere, mixed with black; very pretty pattern. Braided collar and cuffs. 3 to 8 years. Each.... 2.75
30916 Reefer Suits, same style as above in dark gray melton cassimere. 3 to 8 years. Each.... 2.75
30918 Reefer Suits, fancy brown and tan mixed cassimere; hercules braid trimming on collar and cuffs. 3 to 8 years. Each.... 3.00

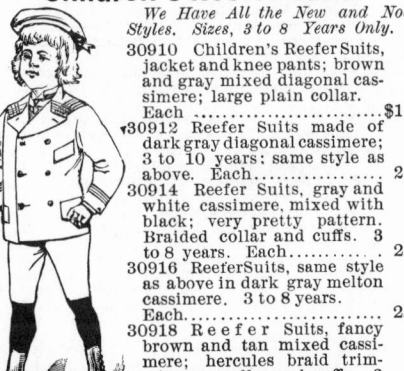

Reefer Suits—Continued.

30920 Reefer Suits, light gray wool cassimere invisible plaid; fancy braided collar and cuffs. 3 to 8 years. Each.... 3.25
30922 Reefer Suits, dark navy blue diagonal twilled cassimere, large collar and cuffs, embroidered in fancy designs, with black silk, narrow braid 3 to 8 years. Each.... 3.50
30924 Reefer Suits, "The Brownie" medium colored fancy checked wool cassimere. Large plain collar, imitation vest front, trimmed with black braid. Very popular style. 3 to 8 years. Each.... 3.50
30926 Reefer Suits, "The Brownie;" same style as above. Made of fine brown mixed plaid cassimere. 3 to 8 years. Each.... 4.00
30928 Fancy Reefer Suits, made of medium light brown wool cassimere; large collar, pockets and cuffs trimmed with 4 rows of narrow braid. Hip pocket in pants, satin knee bows and buckles. 3 to 8 years. Each.... 4.00
30930 Fancy Reefer Suits, all wool cassimere, very neat gray and brown pin check, large collar, pockets and cuffs trimmed with 3 rows of narrow brown braid, brass anchor buttons. 3 to 8 years. Each.... 4.50
30932 Fancy Reefer Suits, all wool cassimere; neat brown and cream colored broken checks, large collar, pockets and cuffs trimmed with fancy brown braid. 3 to 8 years. Each.... 4.50
30934 Fancy Reefer Suits, made of all wool black diagonal cheviot, fancy anchor brass buttons, collar, pockets and cuffs trimmed with fancy black silk braid. 3 to 8 years. Silk ribbon and fancy buckles at knees of pants; very stylish. Each.... 4.75
30936 Fancy Reefer Suits, made of fine all wool navy blue cheviot, fancy brass anchor buttons on front and cuffs, collar, pockets and cuffs trimmed with ¾-inch black mohair braid. 3 to 8 years. Fast color, square top Tam O'Shanter cap to match, included. Each.... 5.00
30938 Fancy Reefer Suits, made of extra fine all wool Scotch cheviot, seal brown and black intermingled, large sailor collar, pockets and cuffs, trimmed with fancy black braid, brass anchor buttons on front and cuffs, also at knee of pants, ½-inch black braid down side of pants. 3 to 8 years. Each.... 6.00

Juvenile Suits.

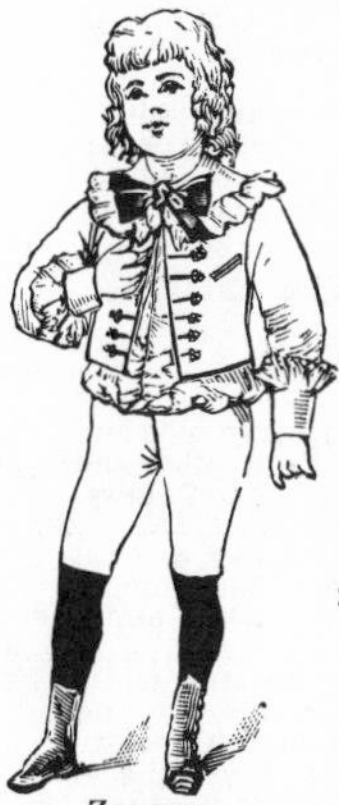

Zouave.

30940 Zouave Suits, navy blue twilled flannel, plain collar, black bead buttons on front, cuffs and knees of pants. 3 to 7 years. Each....$2.00
30942 Zouave Suits, navy blue flannel, fancy braided front and cuffs. 3 to 7 years. Each....$2.25
30944 Zouave Suits, black and gray diagonal wool cassimere, fancy braided front and cuffs, buckles and ribbon bow at knees of pants. 3 to 7 years. Each....$2.25

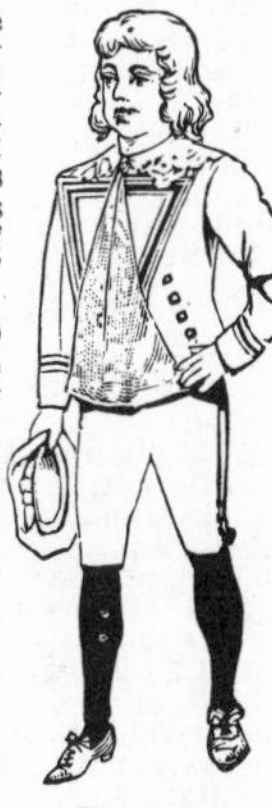

Zouave.

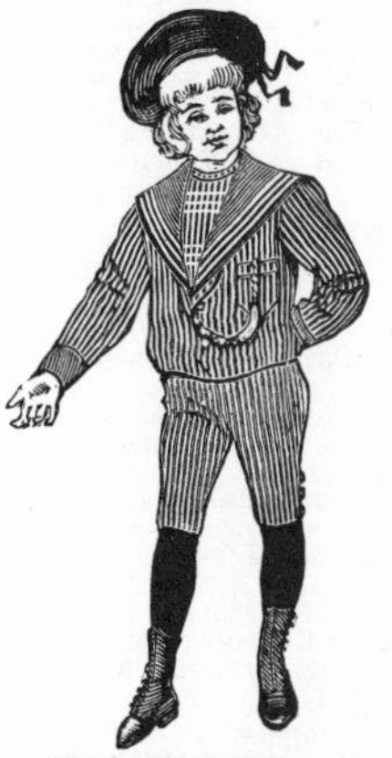

Washable Sailor.

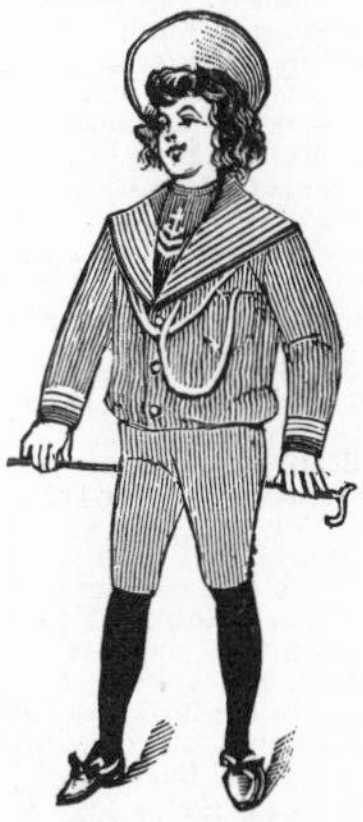

Washable Sailor

30946 Zouave Suits, fine navy blue flannel, front trimmed with neat black braid and small black buttons, buttons to match on cuffs. 3 to 7 years. Each....$2.50
30948 Zouave Suits, dark green corduroy, small button trimmings on front and cuffs, knees trimmed with silk ribbon, buckle and small button; an excellent suit. 3 to 7 years. Each.... 2.75

PAINT==Consult Us.

Juvenile Suits—Continued.

30950 Zouave Suits, fine black diagonal wool chevoit, handsome and neat, fancy narrow black silk braid trimming on front and cuffs; bow and buckle at knees. 3 to 7 years. Each..$3.00

30952 Zouave Suits, all wool navy blue twilled cloth, V-shaped braided front, fancy braided cuffs, buckle and buttons at knee. 3 to 7 years. Each 3.35

30954 Zouave Suits, fine wool cassimere, neat broken checks of brown, gray and blue; pockets, cuffs, front and entire outer edge of jacket trimmed with 2 rows of narrow brown braid; 2 rows of small buttons on each side of front and buttons to match on cuffs; pants trimmed with narrow braid and buckle, 3 to 7 years. Each 3.50

30956 Zouave Suits, light gray mixed fine wool cassimere, entire jacket bound with narrow tan-colored braid, cuffs and pockets to match, breast trimmed with 15 rows of fine tan braid in triangular shape, small tan-ornamented buttons on lower corners and cuffs; pants trimmed to match, with braid and buckles; very handsome and sure to please. 3 to 7 years. Each... 3.85

30958 Zouave Suits, blue black velvet, neatly trimmed with black silk braid and buttons; buckle and braid on pants: very dressy. 3 to 7 years. Each 4,00

30960 Zouave Suits, fine navy blue tricot cloth. Jacket richly embroidered down front and on back of skirt, with fancy narrow black silk braid. Pants bound at knee with silk ribbon and buttons. 3 to 7 years. Each $4.50

30962 Zouave Suits, fine imported black diagonal clay worsted. Large collar and front very tastefully embroidered with 3 rows of fancy, narrow, black silk braid. Cuffs trimmed to match A handsome and dressy suit for best wear. 3 to 7 years. Each 5.00

30964 Zouave Suits, fine black velvet, fancy black silk braid binding around entire jacket, collars and cuffs. Additional black silk braided designs on front and cuffs. Ribbon and buckle on pants. 3 to 7 years. Each 5.50

Blouse Sailor Suits.

Blouse and Knee Pants. 3 to 7 years.

30966 Blouse Suits, navy blue union flannel. Sailor collar, with embroidered anchors in corners. 3 to 7 years. Each..........$1.00

30968 Blouse Suits, navy blue twilled flannel. Large sailor collar, trimmed with 2 rows of black braid. Cuffs braided to match. 3 to 7 years. Each.......... 1.85

30970 Blouse Suits, dark navy blue twisted flannels; good weight. Heavy braided sailor collar, with fancy braided corners, embroidered silk star on breast, V shape front. 3 to 7 years. Each.......... 3.50

Washable Blouse Suits.

Just the thing for hot weather, always cool and neat. 3 to 7 years. Blouse jacket and knee pants. *Give them a trial.*

30972 Blouse Sailor Suit, made of navy blue and white striped cotton cheviot, sailor collar and cuffs trimmed with white braid. 3 to 7 years. Per suit..........$0.75

30974 Blouse Sailor Suit, made of tan colored duck with neat white stripe, solid tan colored cuffs and large collar trimmed with white braid. 3 to 7 years. Per suit.......... .98

30976 Blouse Sailor Suits, navy blue and white striped cotton cheviot, with solid collar and cuffs of navy blue duck, trimmed with white braid. V shaped front, with inner breast piece. 3 to 7 years. Per suit.......... 1.35

30978 Blouse Sailor Suits, heavy brown and white stripe duck; same style as above with anchor embroidered on breast piece. 3 to 7 years. Each.......... 1.75

30980 Blouse Sailor Suits, extra quality tan colored duck; fancy cuffs trimmed with pear buttons, V-shaped breast piece, with star embroidered in red; large sailor collar trimmed with seven rows of narrow red braid. 3 to 7 years. Per suit.......... 2.25

Children's Jersey Suits.

30982 All Wool Navy Blue Jersey Suits, silk ribbon bow at neck. 3 to 7 years. Each..........$2.35

30984 All Wool Navy Blue Jersey Cloth Suits, fancy braided large sailor collar. 3 to 8 years. Per suit.......... 2.65

30986 All Wool Jersey Suits, same as above; braided collar front and cuffs. 3 to 8 years. Per suit.......... 3.50

30988 All Wool Navy Blue Jersey Suits, fancy silk embroidered sailor collar and cuffs; extra inserted breast piece, embroidered with three stars. 3 to 7 years. Per suit.......... 3.75

30990 All Wool Navy Blue Jersey Suits, richly embroidered sailor collar, cuffs and inserted breast piece; double-breasted style. 3 to 8 years. Per suit.......... 4.25

NOTE—The above suits all consist of blouse, coat and knee pants. They are extra value and will give good service.

Medical and Scientific BOOKS.

We have a Special Catalogue of these works. Send 2 cents for postage. We have only standard works in this line.

Children's Kilt Suits.

These suits consist of Blouse or Jacket and Kilt Skirts. Sizes, 2 to 4 years only.

30992 Navy Blue Flannel Blouse Kilt Suits, plain button front blouse, pleated skirt trimmed with two rows of buttons. Embroidered silk anchors on corners of collar. 2 to 4 years. Per suit..........$1.50

30994 Navy Blue Twilled Flannel Blouse Kilt Suits, sailor collar and and cuffs, trimmed with black silk embroidery; embroidered anchor on breast; skirt same style as above. 2 to 4 years only. Per suit.......... 2.50

30996 All Wool Light Brown Diagonal Mixed Cassimere Kilt Suits, fancy jacket trimmed with tan colored silk braid and buttons; skirt same as above. 2 to 4 years. Per suit.......... 3.50

30998 Brown Mixed Cassimere Kilt Suits, short jacket handsomely embroidered down front and on cuffs with fancy silk braid; skirt same as above. 2 to 4 years. Per suit.......... 4.00

31000 Fine All Wool Navy Blue Flannel Kilt Suits, blouse coat, V front and large sailor collar and cuffs, richly embroidered with black braid in fancy designs. Pleated skirt embroidered on front to match blouse. 2 to 4 years. Per suit.......... 4.25

Boys' and Youths' Long Pants Suits.

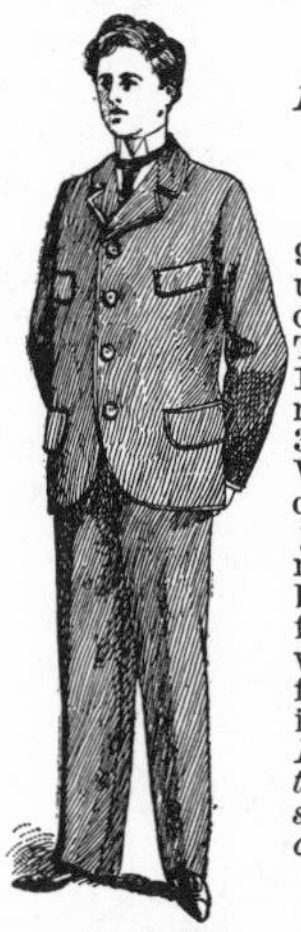

Full Suits, Coat, Vest and Pants.

Suits quoted from 9 to 13 years, measure from 25 to 29 chest measure. Those quoted from 14 to 18 years measure from 30 to 34 chest measure. Where sizes are quoted up to 19 years, the chest measure is 35 in. Pants sizes run from 26 to 32 in. waist measure and from 26 to 32 in. inseam measure. *Larger sizes than these will have to be selected from men's clothing.*

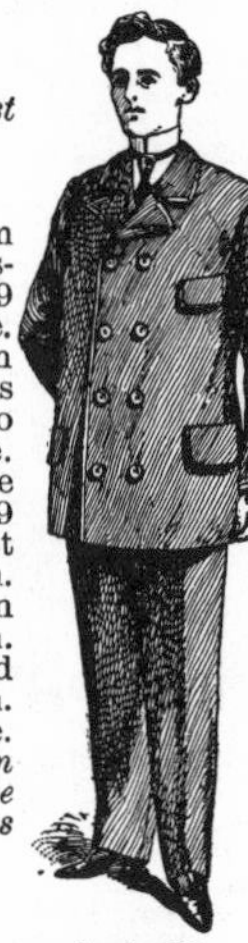

Style 30. Style 31.

31002 Youths' Black and Blue Gray Mixed Satinet Cassimere Suits. Style 30. 9 to 18 years. Each..........$2.50

31004 Black Diagonal Cotton Worsted Suits. Youths' sizes. 14 to 18 years. Style 30. Each.......... 2.75

31006 Youths' Suits, black and gray striped cotton worsted. Style 30. Neat pattern, 9 to 18 years only. Each.......... 3.00

31008 Youths' and Boys' Suits, black diagonal cotton worsted, old gold mixed. Style 30. 9 to 18 years only. Each.......... 3.00

31010 Boys' and Youths Suits; black and gray check pattern, cotton worsted. Style 30. 9 to 18 years. Each.......... 3.25

31012 Boys' and Youths' Suits, fine black and gray striped Windsor cassimere. Style 2. Single breasted, square cut. 9 to 18 years. Each.......... 3.50

31014 Youths' suits, 11 to 18 years. Dark gray mixed Windsor Cassimere. Style 30. Each..... 3.50

31016 Boys' and Youths' Suits. 9 to 18 years. Style, 2. Dark gray pin check satinet cassimere. Each.......... 3.75

31018 Boys' and Youths' Suits, 10 to t8 years Style 31 Small black and blue check Windsor cassimere. Each.......... 4.00

31020 Boys' and Youths' Cassimere Suits; small fancy check of brown and gray. Style 30. 10 to 18 years. Each.......... 4.00

31022 Boys' and Youths' Suits. Neat, fancy mixed small check gray satinet cassimere. 9 to 18 years. Style 30. Each.......... 4.25

31024 Boys' and Youths' Suits, black and gray neat striped cassimere. Style 30. 9 to 18 years. Each.......... 4.25

31026 Youths' Suits, 10 to 18 years. Black, with small blue check. Fine satinet cassimere goods; extra value. Style 2. Each.......... 4.25

31028 Boys' and Youths' Suits, 9 to 18 years. Dark gray mixed diagonal cheviot. Style 30. Each..........4.50

31030 Boys' and Youths' Suits, black diagonal corkscrew worsted. Style 30. 9 to 18 years. Each.......... 4.65

31032 Boys' and Youths' Suits. Single breasted, square cut style. Brown mixed, invisible plaid wool cassimere. Style 2. 9 to 18 years. Each. 4.75

31034 Youths' Suits. 11 to 18 years. Style 30. Dark gray diagonal, hard twisted wool cassimere. Each.......... 5.00

31036 Youths' Suits, 12 to 18 years, Style 31. Fine, dark gray, soft wool cheviot, double breasted. Each.......... 5.00

31038 Boys' and Youths' Suits. Fine, black, wool cheviot. Style 2. 10 to 18 years. Each.. 5.00

Boys' Long Pants—Continued.

31040 Youths' Suits, 13 to 19 years only. Strictly all wool, medium, gray mixed cassimere. Small, neat figure. Style 30. Each.......... 5.25

31042 Youths' Suits, 13 to 18 years only. Style 31. Fine, black wool cheviot, double breasted coat. Each.......... 5.50

31044 Youths' Suits, 12 to 18 years. All wool, gray mixed cassimere, neat, broken check pattern. Style 10. Each.......... 5.50

31046 Youths' Suits, 13 to 19 years. Style 2 Steel gray, wool cassimere. Fancy plaid pattern, with invisible red mixture. Each.......... 5.75

31048 Boys' and Youths' Suits, 10 to 19 years. Style 30. All wool navy blue or black diagonal cheviot; mention color desired. Each.......... 5.75

31050 Boys' and Youths' Suits, 9 to 18 years. All wool light gray pin check cassimere. Style 2. Each.......... 6.00

31052 Boys' and Youths' Suits, 9 to 18 years. All wool dark gray pin check cassimere. Style 30. Each.......... 6.00

31054 Boys' and Youths' Suits, 10 to 19 years. Style 2. Genuine indigo blue flannel. Each...$6.00

31056 Boys' and Youths' Suits, same as above in style 30. Each.......... 6.00

31058 Boys' and Youths' Suits, 12 to 19 years. Style 30. Made of imported all wool black diagonal clay worsted. Each.......... 6.25

31060 Boys' and Youths' Suits. Fancy imported worsted black, with neat blue plaid. Style 2. 10 to 19 years. Each.......... 6.50

31062 Youths' Suits, 14 to 19 years. All wool light gray pin check cassimere. Style 30. Each.......... 6.50

31064 Boys' and Youths' Suits, 12 to 19 years. All wool navy blue or black diagonal cheviot. Style 30. Each.......... 7.50

31066 Boys' and Youths' Suits. Style 2. 10 to 19 years. Made of medium brown, worsted finish cassimere, very neat and durable. Each.......$7.50

31068 Boys' and Youths' Suits, same as above in dark gray. Style 30. Each.......... 7.50

31070 Boys' and Youths' Suits. Style 30. 11 to 19 years. Imported black clay worsted, all wool, diagonal pattern. Each.......... 8.00

31072 Youths' Suits, fine imported worsted, diagonal pattern, navy blue. Style 30. 14 to 19 years only. Each.......... 8.00

31074 Boys' and Youths' Suits, fine imported diagonal clay worsted, gunpowder gray. Style 30. All wool. 10 to 18 years, Each.......... 8.00

31076 Youths' Suits. Style 2. 12 to 19 years. Black or blue diagonal clay worsted. Each.... 9.00

31078 Youths' Suits, fine all wool black cheviot with very slight mixture of gray, Style 30. 14 to 19 years. Each.......... 9.50

31080 Youths' All Wool Cassimere Suits, black with gray pin dots. Style 30. 14 to 19 years. Each.......... 9.50

31082 Youths' All Wool Dark Brown Scotch Cheviot Suits, invisible red mixture. Style 30. 14 to 19 years..........10.00

31084 Youths' Fine Suits, cadet blue imported worsted, with nonpareil fine black check: very pretty. Style 30. 14 to 19 years only. Each. 10.00

31086 Youths' Fine Imported Cassimere Suits, black and gray pepper and salt mixture. Style 30. 14 to 19 years. Each..........10.00

31088 Youths' Fine Suits, wide wale diagonal worsted, all wool. Style 30. 14 to 19 years. Colors: Black, blue or seal brown. Each.......10.50

Children's Knee Pants.

Weight on Knee Pants, 4 to 14 ounce, according to quality and size. Per pair.

31090 Kentucky Jeans, Oxford mixed..........$0 18
31092 Fancy Stripe Heavy Cottonade.......... .23
31094 Black Diagonal Cotton Worsted.......... .25
31096 Fancy Stripe Cotton Worsted.......... .27
31098 Fancy Stripe Cotton Worsted, better quality.......... .31
31100 Black and Gray Striped Satinet Cassimere .38
31102 Black and Gray Check Satinet Cassimere .38
31104 Gray Mixed Plaid Cheviot.......... .40
31106 Black and Gray Striped Cotton Worsted.. .45
31108 Black and Gray Diagonal Cassimere, new elastic band.......... .50
31110 Brown and Gray Mixed Plaid Cassimere.. .50
31112 Brown Mixed Double and Twist Cassimere, double knees, extension band will not rip .70
31114 Gray and Black Double and Twist Cassimere, double knees.......... .70
31116 Brown Corduroy.......... .70
31118 Drab Corduroy.......... .70
31120 Dark Gray Cheviots, double knees.......... .75
31122 All Wool Brown Mixed Cassimere, double knees.......... .85
31124 All Wool Gray Mixed Cassimere, double knees.......... .85
31126 All Wool Navy Blue Cassimere, double knees.......... .85
31128 All Wool Black and Gray Stripe Cassimere, double knees.......... .85
31130 All Wool Brown and Gray Stripe Cassimere, double knees.......... .85
31132 All Wool Blue Flannel, double knees.......... .90
31134 Brown Corduroy, heavy.......... .90
31136 Drab Corduroy, heavy.......... .90
31138 All Wool Navy Blue Jersey Cloth.......... .95
31140 All Wool Gray Pin Check, double knees, 1.00
31142 All Wool Black Diagonal Clay Worsted, 1.00
31144 All Wool Navy Blue Jersey Cloth.......... 1.25
31146 All Wool Light Brown Checked Cassimere, double seat and knees, extension band... 1.25
31148 All Wool Black Diagonal Cheviot, double seat and knees.......... 1.25
31150 All Wool Navy Blue Tricot Cloth.......... 1.35

Boys' Long Pants.

Scale of sizes in boys' pants.

Waist	27	27	28	28	29	29	29	29	30	31	31
Inside seam	26	27	27	28	29	28	29	30	30	30	31

Weight of pants under this heading 1¼ to 1½ lbs., according to size and quality.

N. B. We do not sample Boys' Pants. Per pair.

31152 Striped Cottonade, dark colors....$0.80
31154 Dark Striped Satinet Cassimere.... 1.15

Long Pants—Continued.

31156 Medium Gray Striped Cassimere.... 1.25
31158 Medium Gray Striped Union Cassimere.... 1.35
31160 Drab Corduroy.... 1.75
31162 Brown Corduroy.... 1.75
31164 Black and Very Dark Blue Striped Wool Cassimere.... 2.00
31166 Fine Black and Gray Wool Striped Cassimere.... 2.25
31168 Black and Light Gray All Wool Striped Cassimere.... 2.75
31170 Steel Gray and Black Striped Worsted.... 3.00
31172 Steel Blue with neat black stripe.... 3.50

CUSTOM TAILORING DEPARTMENT.

Workmanship First-Class. Satisfaction Guaranteed. Send for Samples—Free.

The marked success we have had during the past season in this department leads us to believe that our patrons desire to have a share of their clothing made to order. In order to meet their wishes in every respect, for the Spring and Summer season of 1895, we have greatly increased our facilities in this branch.

We quote below a few prices of our most popular Suitings, Trouserings and Overcoatings, and shall be pleased to send you *free of charge*, samples for your inspection, with full instructions for taking measure. We can make and furnish you anything in the men's tailoring line.

Our Leader: Business Men's Suit.

31225 Business Men's Suit. Made of brown or gray mixed all wool cassimere small check, or Plain black or blue cheviot. Made in Styles 1, 2, 3, and 5 only. Price per suit....$12.00

31231 Our always popular English Clay Worsted Suiting, in black or blue, made to order in Styles 1, 2, 3 or 5....$15.00
With Binding.... 17.00
Clerical Suit. Style 9.... 17.50
Prince Albert, silk faced.... 17.50
Prince Albert, silk faced and bound.... 20.00
Pants of same goods.... 4.00

31233 Fine Imported Clay Worsted Suits, to order, in styles 1, 2, 3 or 5.... 18.00
With Binding.... 20.00
Prince Albert Suits.... 21.00
With Binding.... 23.00
Clerical Suits.... 23.00
Pants.... 5.50

31235 Special Importation Clay Worsted Black or Blue Suits, to order, in styles 1, 2, 3 or 5.... 23.00
With Binding.... 25.00
Clerical Suits.... 27.00
Prince Albert Suits.... 26.00
With Binding.... 28.00
Pants.... 6.50

31237 Black All Wool Thibet Suits, to order, in styles 1, 2, 3 or 5.... 15.00
With Binding.... 17.50
Clerical Suits.... 19.00
Prince Albert Suits.... 18.00
With Binding.... 20.00
Pants.... 4.00

Have your Mail Packages insured. **See page 1.**

31246 Imported French Thibet Suits, to order in Styles 1, 2, 3 or 5.... 20.00
With Binding.... 22.00
Clerical Suits.... 24.00
Prince Albert Suits.... 23.00
With Binding.... 25.00
Pants.... 5.50

31248 Gray Tricot, long suiting suit, to order in styles 1, 2, 3 or 5....$18.00
With Binding.... 20.00
Prince Albert Suits.... 21.00
With Binding.... 23 00
Pants.... 5.00

31250 Cassimere suiting suits, to order, in styles 1, 2, 3 or 5.... 18. 0
With Binding.... 20.00
Prince Albert Suits.... 21.00
With Binding.... 23 00
Pants.... 5.50

31252 English Gray Mixed Clay Worsted Suits, to order, in styles 1, 2, 3 or 5.... 18.00
With Binding.... 20.00
Prince Albert Suits.... 21.50
With Binding.... 23.50
Pants.... 6.00

31255 Black or Blue Bird's-Eye Worsted Suits, to order, in styles 1, 2, 3 or 5.... 18.00
With Binding.... 20.00
Prince Albert Suits.... 21.00
With Binding.... 23.00
Clerical Suits.... 22.00
Pants.... 5.50

31256 Black or Blue Tricot Suits, to order, in styles 1, 2, 3 or 5.... 20.00
With Binding.... 22.00
Prince Albert Suits.... 23.00
With Binding.... 25.00
Clerical Suits.... 24.00
Pants.... 5.50

31257 Fancy Mixed Cheviot Suits, to order, in styles 1, 2, 3 or 5.... 15.00
Pants.... 4.00

31258 Fancy Diagonal Cheviot Suits, in styles 1, 2, 3 or 5.... 15.00
Pants.... 4.00

31259 Gray Mixed Cheviot Suits, to order, in styles 1, 2, 3 or 5.... 15.00

31261 Black and Gray Mixed Cheviot Suits, to order, in styles 1, 2, 3 or 5....$15.00
Pants.... 4.00

31263 Partridge Mixed Corduroy Suits in styles 1, 2, 3 or 5.... 17.00
Pants.... 4.50

31264 Brown, Black or Drab Corduroy Suits, to order, in styles 1, 2, 3 or 5.... 17.00
Pants.... 4.50

31265 Drab, Black or Brown Corduroy Suits, fine cord, to order, in styles 1, 2, 3 or 5.... 17.00
Pants.... 4.50

Trousers to Order.

31266 Fancy Black Stripe Trousering, per pair..$5.50
31267 Black Ribbed Imported Worsted Panting. 5.50
31268 Fancy Stripe Trousers.... 5.00
31270 Fancy Stripe Trousers.... 5.00
31272 Cassimere Stripe Trousers.... 4.50
31274 Striped Trousers.... 4.50

Spring Overcoats.

31283 Men's Imported Clay Worsted Overcoats. Colors: Oxford, gray, brown mixture, drab mixture, and black, lined with serge and satin sleeve lining.... 23.00

31285 Men's Light Weight Imported Brown Melton Overcoats....$20.00

Send for Catalogue "E." Ladies' Dresses to Order.

HAT DEPARTMENT.

ALL THE NEW AND STANDARD STYLES.

Particular care and attention will be devoted to all orders for hats and caps. Our facilities for packing hats are now such that they can be shipped with other goods, however heavy or bulky, with perfect safety.

N. B.—**Sizes 7⅝, 7¾, 7⅞** and **8** are extra large sizes and not usually found in ready-made stocks. Customers requiring any of these sizes can obtain prices for having same made to order upon application. In making inquiries be sure to state style, size and color wanted. It requires from five to seven weeks to have extra size hats and from five to ten days for special or extra size caps made to order.

How to Measure for a Hat.

Head size.	Inches around head.	Head size.	Inches around ead.	Head size.	Inches around head.
5⅞	18¾	6⅝	21	7⅜	23⅜
6	19	6¾	21¼	7½	23¾
6⅛	19⅜	6⅞	21⅝	7⅝	24
6¼	19¾	7	22¼	7¾	24½
6⅜	20½	7⅛	22½	7⅞	25
6½	20¾	7¼	23	8	25¼

Men's sizes run from 6¾ to 7½.

Boys' sizes from 6⅛ to 7 only; children's sizes. 6¼ to 6¾ only. If ordered out of regular sizes, will be charged at prices of those in which they are manufactured.

Do not make a mistake, If no measure is at hand use a string for measuring, and send it with your order, but pin it fast to order.

Planter Hats.

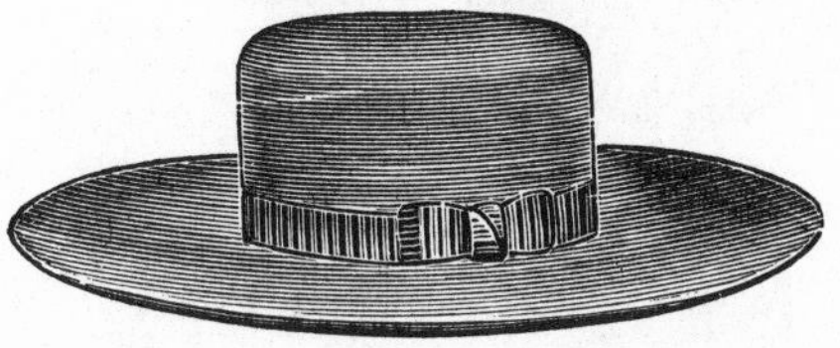

Planter.

Weight of Planter hats, 4 to 6 ounces. Sizes, 6¾ to 7⅜.

Each.

31510 Men's Saxony Wool Hats, "Planter," black or drab....$0.75
31512 Men's Saxony Wool Hats, "Planter," black or drab.... 1.00
31514 Men's Cassimere Fur Hats, "Planter," black, drab or slate.... 2.00

Average weight of all soft wool and fur hats, 4 to 6 ounces. Size, 6¾ to 7⅜.

18—2d

Cow Boys' Hats.

Cow Boys' Hats are designated by the following colors: Belly nutria is light, side nutria is medium light, and calfskin is medium dark.

Largest line of Cow Boy Hats in America—unsurpassed for style, finish and durability. Correct sizes. Popular prices. Always reliable.

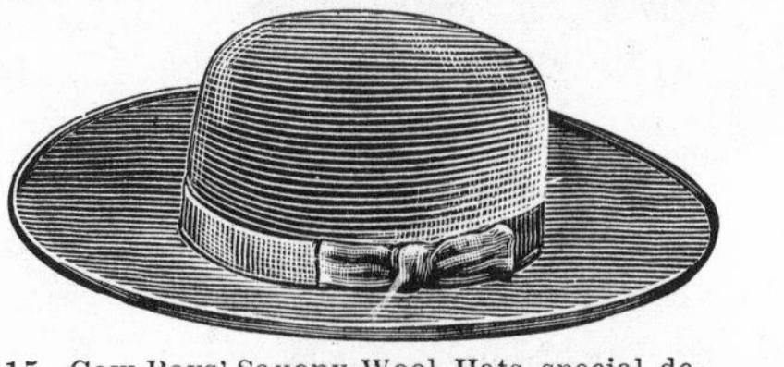

31515 Cow Boys' Saxony Wool Hats, special design, convex brim, extra reinforced edge, silk ribbon band; crown, 4¼ in.; brim, 3½ in.; weight, 6 oz.; colors, belly nutria or light calfskin; sizes, 6¾ to 7⅜. Each....$ 1.00
Per dozen.... 10.80

31517 Cow Boys' Fine Saxony Wool Hats, same style as the Broncho, 1 in. leather band and leather binding; crown, 4½ in.; brim, 4 in.; calfskin color; weight, 6 oz.; sizes, 6¾ to 7½. Each....$ 1.00 Per dozen.... 10.80

Fine Fur Cow Boy Hats.

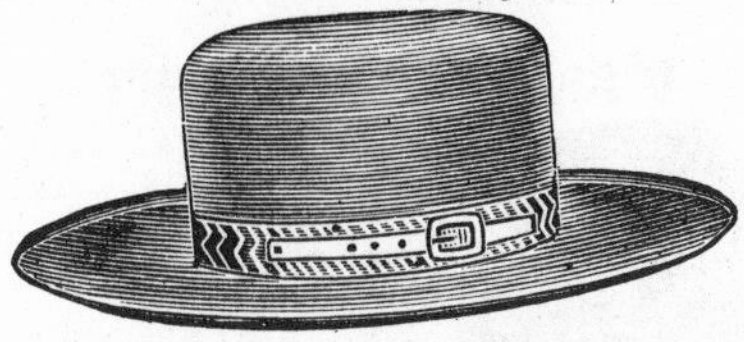

"The Broncho," 31521.

31521 Cow Boy's Sombrero Hat, calfskin color, bound with calf, 1-inch leather band; crown, 4¼ in.; brim, 3¾ in.; weight, 6 oz.; sizes, 6¾ to 7½. Each....$ 2.50 Per dozen.... 27.00

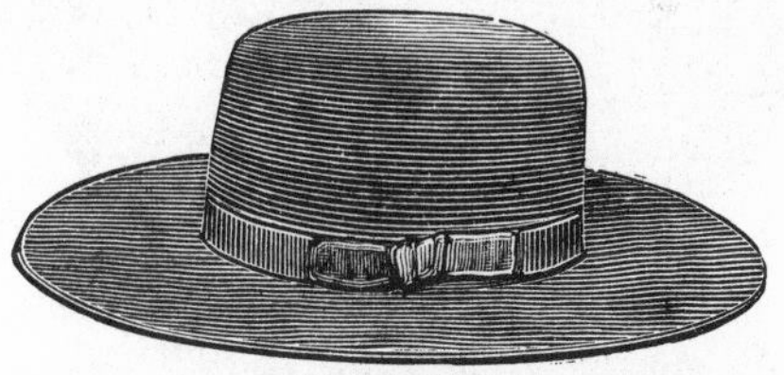

"The Scout."

31522 Cow Boys' Favorite Sombrero Hat, belly nutria color; crown, 4 in.; brim, 4 in.; raw edge; flat, stiff knife-blade brim, 1 in. silk ribbon band, silk elastic cord and eyelets; weight, 6 oz. Each....$ 3.00
Per dozen.... 32.40

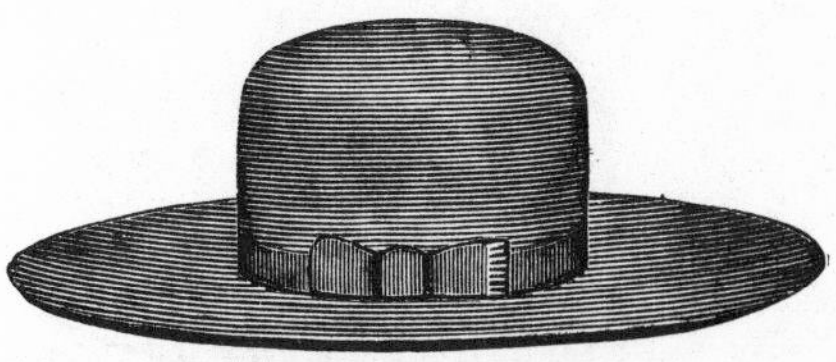

"The Montana," 31524.

31524 Cow Boys' Sombrero Hats; color: Belly nutria; silk band and binding; crown, 4½; brim, 4½ inches; weight, 7 ounces; sizes, 6¾ to 7⅜. Each....$ 3.50
Per dozen.... 37.80

It Would Be Poor Policy

To misrepresent our goods knowingly, therefore do not hesitate to place confidence in our Buyers' Guide. If goods are not as represented we will cheerfully refund purchase price and pay all transportation charges.

Hats—Continued.

"The Never Flop," 31525.

31525 Cow Boys' Sombrero Hats, 'The Never-Flop:" colors: Side nutria, silk band, no binding; crown, 4½, brim, 4 inches, weight, 8 oz., sizes, 6¾ to 7½.
Each..$ 3.50
Per dozen...37.50

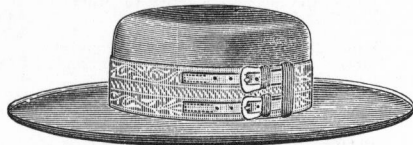

"The Mountaineer," 31527.

31527 Cow Boys' Sombrero Hats, calfskin color leather bound, 2-inch leather embossed band; crown, 4½, brim, 4 inches, weight, 10 ounces, sizes, 6¾ to 7½.
Each..$ 3.50
Per dozen...37.50
31529 Cow Boys' Sombrero Hats, color: Belly nutria, J. B. Stetson's "Boss of the Plains," silk band and binding; crown, 4½, brim, 4 inche , weight, 6 ounces, sizes 6¾ to 7⅜.
Each..$ 5.00
Per dozen...54.00

"The Texas Steer," 31531.

31531 Cow Boys' Sombrero Hats, color: Side nutria, 1⅜ embossed leather band, with four silver stars, flange brim, no binding; crown 4½, brim 5 inches, weight, 8 ounces, sizes 6¾ to 7⅜.
Each..$ 5 00
Per dozen...54.00

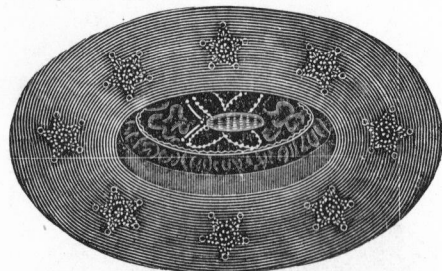

"Chief Moses," 31533.

31533 Cow Boys' Sombrero Hats, "Chief Moses," color: Belly nutria, silver band, no binding, four silver stars on crown, eight on brim, satin lined with illuminated butterfly on inside, most attractive cow boy hat for the money manufactured; 4½ inch crown, 4½ inch brim, weight, 10 ounces, sizes 6¾ to 7⅜.
Each..$ 5.00
Per dozen...54.00

"Ranch King'" 31534.

31534 Cow Boys' Sombrero Hats, "Ranch King," Mexican style. Color: Belly nutria, silver tinsel cord band, no binding, soft crown, stiff brim, crown, 6½ inches, brim, 5 inches, weight, 8 oz., size, 6¾ to 7⅜.
Each................$6.00 Per dozen.........64.80

CATALOGUE No 58
FOR FALL AND WINTER, 1895 AND 1896 . . . .
WILL BE READY SEPT. 1ST, 1895.

Hats—Continued.

31535.

31535 Cow Boys' Fancy Sombrero Hats made of of extra fine quality light brown fur felt and trimmed with gilt braid and bangles, like illustration. Price, to close them out, each..........3.00

"Pride of the West." 31537.

31537 Montgomery Ward & Co.'s Old Reliable "Pride of the West" Cow Boys' Sombrero Hat. Belly nutria color. Trimmed with silver stars on crown and under brim. Extra heavy braided roll band of silver woven cloth. Extra fine satin lining and improved sweat-band. Sizes, 6¾, 6⅞, 7, 7⅛, 7¼, 7⅜, 7½; weight, 12 oz.; 4 inch crown; 5 inch brim.
Each................$8.00 Per dozen.........86.40

Leather Hat Bands.

31538 Extra Quality Embossed Leather Hat Bands, 2 inches wide; two buckles. Weight, 4 ounces. Tan color. Each......................$0.50
Per dozen..5.40
31540 Embossed Tan Colored Leather Hat Bands, 1 inch wide. Weight, 2 ounces. Each..........20
Per doz...2.16

Men's Crushers.

Weight of Men's Crushers, 3 ounces. When sent specially by mail, allow 8 cents additional for postage.

31542 Men's Wool Crusher Hat; colors, mocha brown and black.
Each.....$0.45
Per doz.. 4.85

31542 to 31549	Each.	Per doz.
31544 Men's Fur Crusher Hat; color, mocha brown.....................	$0.70	$7.50
31546 Men's Fur Crusher Hat; color, navy blue.......................	.70	7.50
31548 Men's Fur Crusher Hat; color, navy blue or brown	.95	10.36
31549 Men's Fur Crusher Hat; color, black............................	.95	10.36

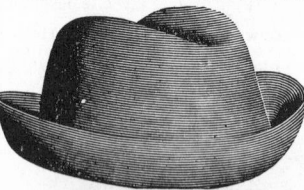

31550 Men's Black Fur Crushers, full shape crown and brim.
Each.$1.35
Per doz.—
$15.00

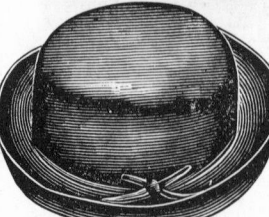

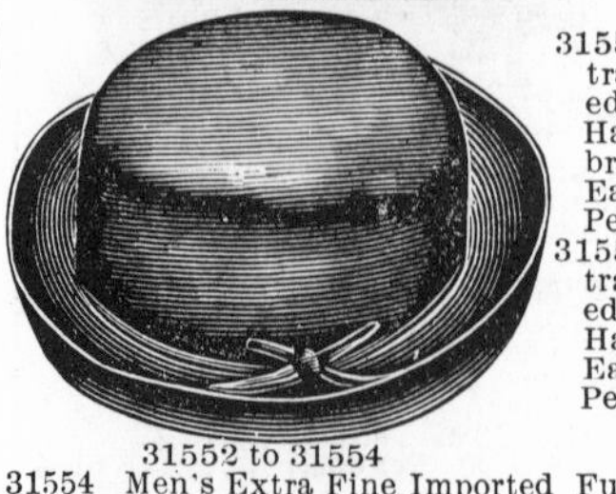

31552 Men's Extra Fine Imported Fur Crusher Hats; color, mocha brown.
Each $1.60
Per dozen...17.28
31553 Men's Extra Fine Imported Fur Crusher Hats; color, black.
Each....... $1.60
Per dozen...17.28

31552 to 31554
31554 Men's Extra Fine Imported Fur Crusher Hats: color, tan brown. Each...............$1.60
Per dozen......................................17.28

Men's Stiff Fur Hats.

31555 Men's New Spring Style Black Stiff Fur Hats, medium shape. Weight, 5 oz.
Each....................$1.35

Hats—Continued.

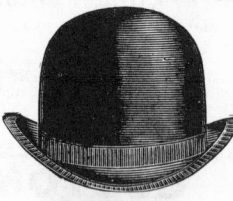

31556 Men's Black Stiff Felt Hats, new spring shape, medium crown and brim. Weight , 5 ounces. Each....$1.75

31558 Men's Latest Style Mocha Brown Stiff Fur Hats, medium crown and brim, silk ribbon band and binding. Very nobby for young men.
Each...............$2.00

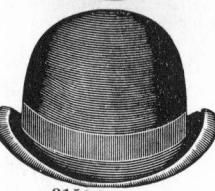

31559 Men's Latest Style Black Stiff Fur Hats similar to above. Very dressy. Each...............$2.00

31559-61
31561 Men's Black Stiff Hats, same style as above better quality. Each........................$2.75

31563 Men's New Spring Style Stiff Hats, extra quality fur felt. Full shape, black only. 6¾ to 7½. Weight, 6 ounces. Each..............$3.00

31564 Men's Extra Size Stiff Hats For men requiring extra large sizes, fine quality fur felt, black only. Weight, 6 ounces. Sizes, 7½, 7⅝, and 7¾. No small sizes. Each..............$3.00

Fedora Hats.

Note the New Styles and Prices.

For ease, comfort and style the soft Fedora hats lead all others. They are by far the most popular hats in the world to-day. We have never before been able to offer them at the extremely low prices we are quoting this season.

31565 Men's Fedora Hats, soft fur, wide silk band and binding, popular shape, satin lining. Weight, 3 ounces. Colors, black or brown.
Each.............$0.75
Per dozen...... 8.10

31565

31566 Men's Fedora Hats, fur felt, wide silk band and binding. Colors: Blue black, mocha borwn and slate. Sizes, 6¾ to 7½.
Each.............$ 1.00
Per dozen........ 10.80

31566

31567 Young Men's New Spring Style Soft Fur Fedora Hats Five different colors, viz: Black, dark blue, golden brown, light chocolate and slate. Medium shape, silk band and binding; sizes, 6¾ to to 7½.
Each.............$ 1.25
Per dozen,....... 13.50

31567

Write Us Upon Any Business
=:= =:= Topic. =:= =:=

Hats—Continued.

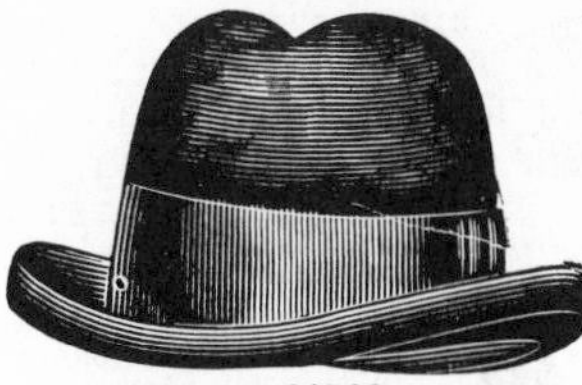

31568

31568 Men's Fedora Hats, soft fur felt, wide silk band and binding, standard shape. Colors: Black, Mocha brown, chocolate and slate. Sizes, 6¾ to 7½. Each.......$2.00

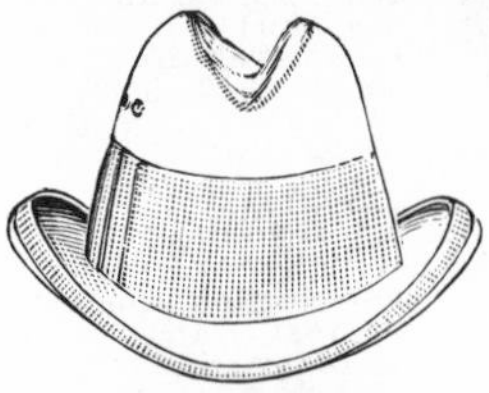

31569 Men's Fine Fur Fedora Hats, New colors for sping and summer. Wide heavy corded silk band and binding, popular shape. Colors: Pearl, dark fawn, mocha, golden brown and black. Sizes, 6¾ to 7½. Weight, 4 ounces. Each....$2.25 Per dozen........24.30

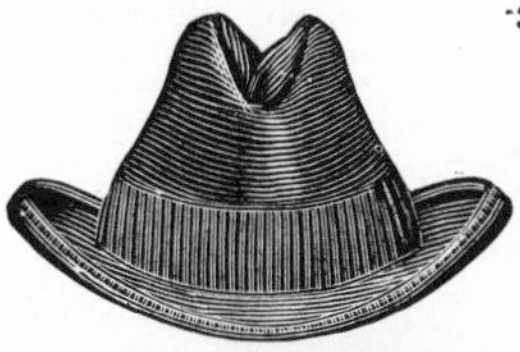

31571 Men's Fine Fur Fedora Hats. Heavy silk corded binding and wide silk ribbon band to match. 3 inch brim. Two colors: Black and mouse; Sizes, 6¾ to 7½. Weight, 4 ounces. Each...........$ 2.25 Per dozen..........24.30

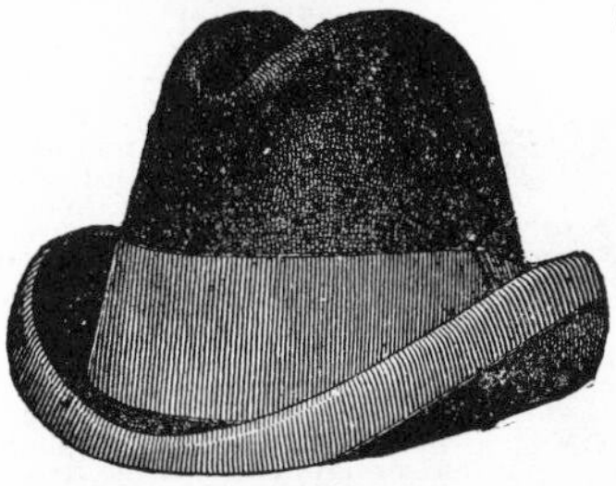

31572-75

31572 Men's Soft Fur Fedora Hats. Full shape, wide silk band and binding. Colors: Black, dark brown, gray, tan and mocha. Sizes, 6¾ to 7½. Weight, 4 oz. Each...$1.50

31575 Men's Fine Fedora Hats; superior quality fur felt. Wide, silk ribbon band and binding. Popular shape. Colors: Black, golden brown, mocha, pearl, drab and slate. Sizes, 6¾ to 7½. Each..$2.50

Men's Soft Fur Hats.

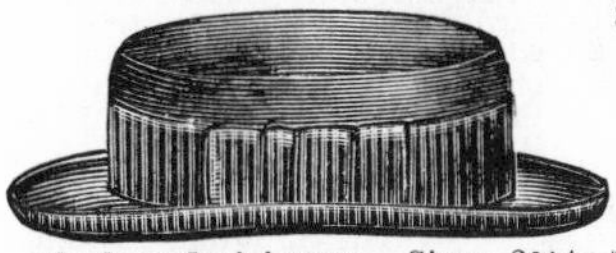

31576 *The New Pasha Hat.* Fine fur felt, selected stock. Heavy and wide silk corded ribbon band and binding. Colors: Black or dark brown. Sizes, 6¾ to 7½, 4 inch crown, 2 inch brim. Each..............................$1.85

31578 The New Pasha Hat, similar to above, but with raw edge and narrow silk ribbon band. Black or brown. 6¾ to 7½. Each....... ....1 50

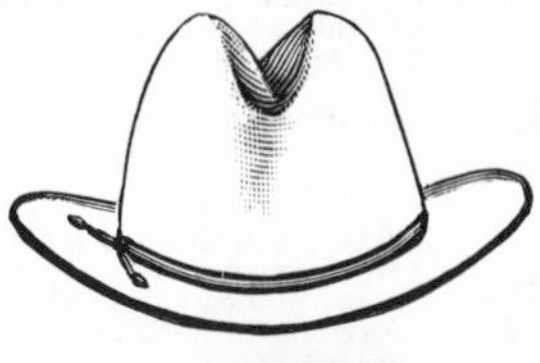

31579 *Our Special:* Men's soft fur hats, medium shape, like illustration; silk cord band; medium gray colors. Sizes, 6¾ to 7½. Each..........$1.50

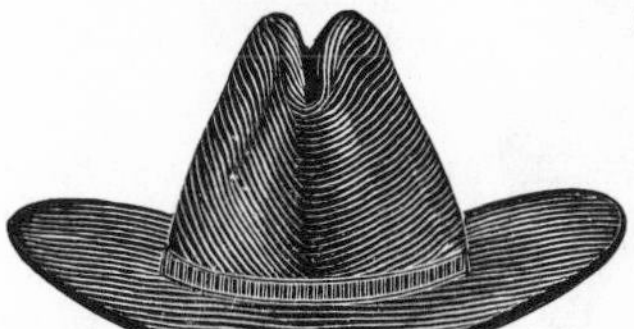

31580 *The Bush Brigadier:* Men's soft black fur hat, 4 inch brim, 6½ inch crown, small black silk ribbon band. Sizes, 6¾ to 7½; weight, 5 oz. Each....$3.00

The quotations in this catalogue, with a few exceptions, are for goods in our store.

Fifty per cent. of our orders are shipped within one day.

Hats—Continued.

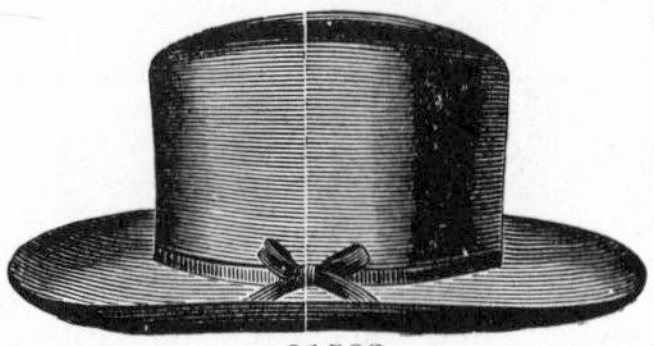

31583

31583 *The Brigadier:* Men's full shape soft black fur hats, 3 inch brim, 6¼ inch crown: high grade stock. Sizes, 6¾ to 7¾; weight, 5 oz. Each....$2.75

31584 Men's Black Fur Hats, "The Brigadier." Each.. 1.50 Per dozen.. 16.20

31585 Men's Soft Fur Hats; color: Belly nutria. or light gray. Sizes, 6¾ to 7½. The Brigadier. Each.. 2.75 Per dozen..30.00

31586 Men's Soft Fur Hats, J. B. Stetson's, The Brigadier, black only. Each..................... 4.00 Per dozen..48.00

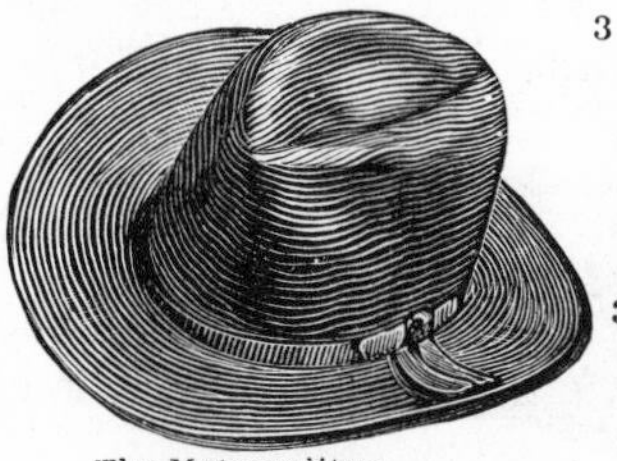

The Metropolitan.

31587 Men's Soft Fur Hats, "The Brigadier." Blue black, 6 in. crown 3½ in. brim, silk cord band; sizes 6¾ to 7½. Each......$ 2.00 Per doz.....21.60

31588 Men's Soft Fur Hats, "The Metropolitan." Black, 6 in. crown 3¼ in. brim. Narrow silk ribbon band. Sizes, 6¾ to 7½. Each................$ 2.25 Per dozen.. 24.30

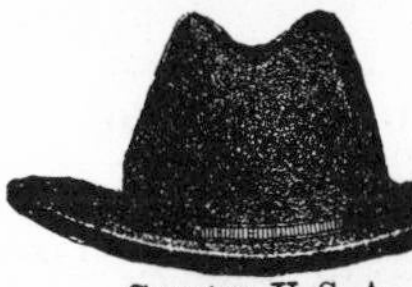

Cavalry, U. S. A.

31589 Men's Soft Fur Hats, regulation U. S. A. Cavalry, as worn by the U. S. regulars. Color: Drab or side nutria. Sizes, 6¾ to 7½. Each...........$ 1.50 Per dozen....... 16.20

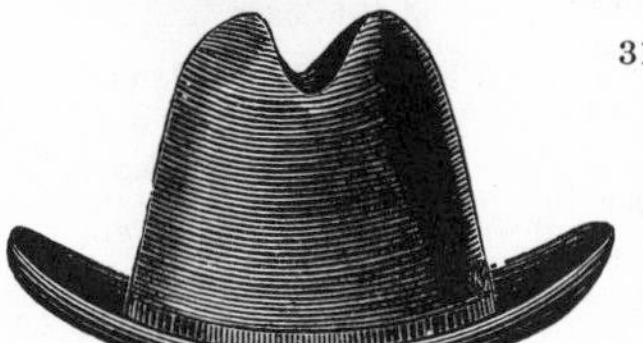

31591 Men's Soft Fur Hats, dark stone color, cord band, medium shape crown and brim, raw edge. Each....$ 1.00 Per doz.. 10.80

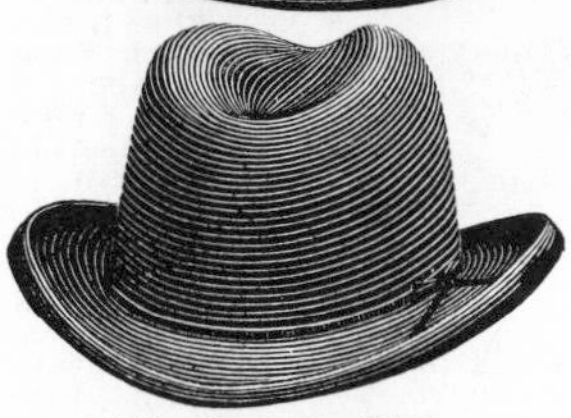

"The Commercial."

1593 Men's Soft Fur Hats, "The Commercial." Black, cord band, raw edge. Each.......$ 1.37 Per dozen.. 14.80

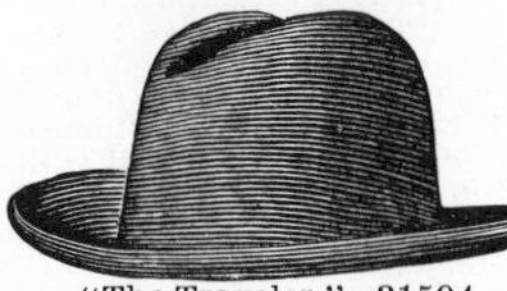

"The Traveler," 31594

31594 Men's Soft Fur Hats. "The Traveler." Black or drab; cord band. Each 6¾ to 7¾ $2 25 Per doz..... 24.90

31595 Men's Soft Fur Hats. J. B. Stetson's "The Traveler," in black. only. Each..................................$ 4.00 Per dozen.. 48.00

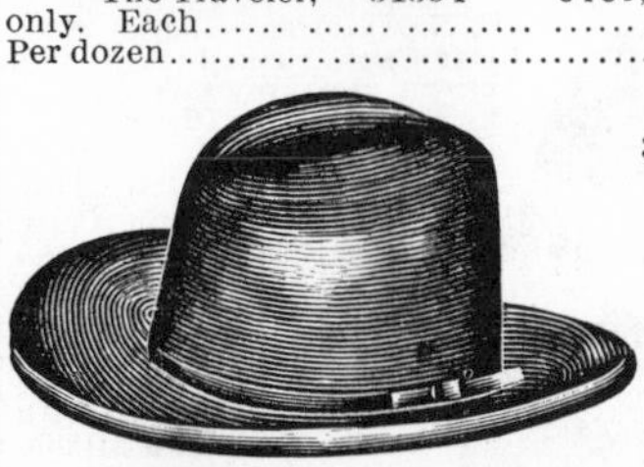

31596 Men's Soft Fur Hats. "The Governor." Dark brown or light slate, full shape. Each..$ 2.25 Per doz 24.30

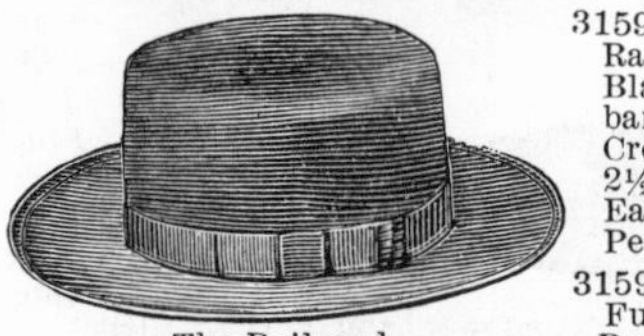

The Railroad.

31597 Mens Soft Railroad Fur Hats. Black or slate, silk band and binding. Crown, 4 in., brim 2¼ inch. Each.....$ 2.00 Per dozen.. 21.60

31598 Men's Soft Fur Hats. "The Boss Railroad Hat." XXXX quality, selected stock. Crown, 4 in., brim, 2½ in., silk band and binding, satin lined, extra quality sweat band. Colors: Black, dark brown and belly nutria. Each...................................$ 2.75 Per dozen.. 29.70

Hats—Continued.

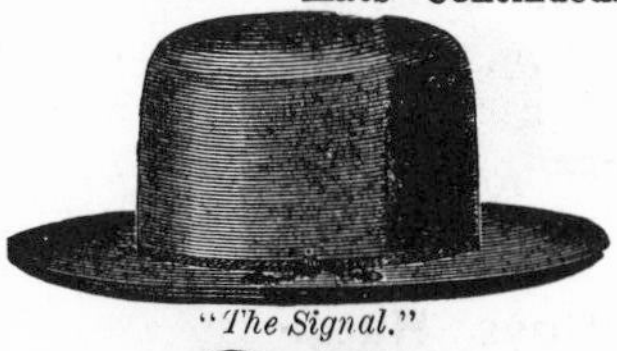

"The Signal."

31599 Men's Soft Fur Hats, "The Signal." Cord band, black or dark blue. Each.....$ 2.00 Per dozen.21.60

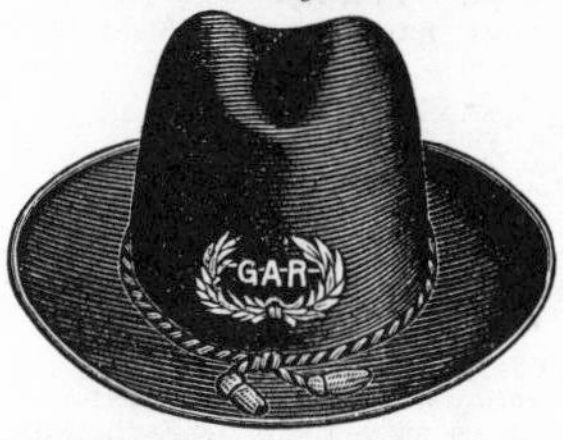

31600 Men's Wool Hats, regulation G. A. R. size, 6¾ to 7⅜. Each........$0.75 Per dozen....8.10

31601 Men's Black Fur Hats, regulation G. A. R., size 6¾ to 7⅜. Each....... $1.25 Per dozen.. 13.50

31602 Mens' G. A. R. Hats, soft black fur, superior quality, 6¾ to 7½. Each.......................$2.00

Mens's Extra Size Hats.

NOTE. Men having large heads and requiring extra size hats, such as size 7½, 7⅝ and 7¾, will find all sizes up to 7¾ quoted under Nos. 31564, 31583 and 31594 in black only. Other men's hats are not made larger than size 7½.

Men's Hats.

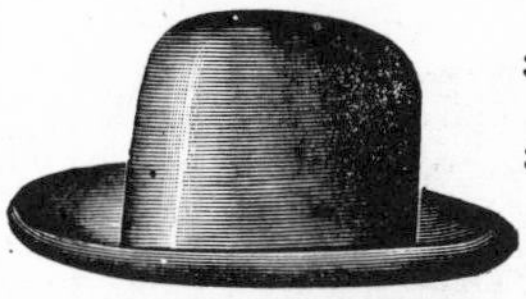

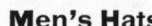

31604 Men's sWool Hats, black, 6¾ to 7⅜. Each......$0.50

31606 Men's Wool Hats, black, 6¾ to 7⅜. Each...... 0.75

Young Men's Hats.

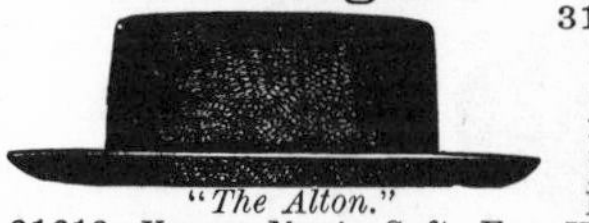

"The Alton."

31612 Men's or Young Men's soft Fur Hats, "The Alton." Cord band, raw edge, black. Each.........$ 2.00 Per dozen. ...21.60

31613 Young Men's Soft Fur Hats, "The Alton." Fawn or slate color, cord band, raw edge. Each.......................................$ 2.00 Per dozen 21.60

31615 Young Men's Soft Fur Hats, "The Alton." Black cord band, raw edge. Each...... 1.25 Per dozen.. 13.50

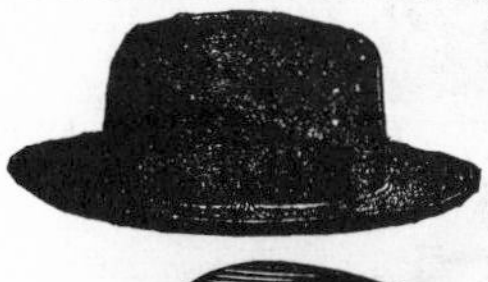

31617 Men's Soft Fur Hats, black, cord band, raw edge, crown, 4¼ inches, brim, 2⅝ inches. Each............$ 1.50 Per dozen....... 16.20

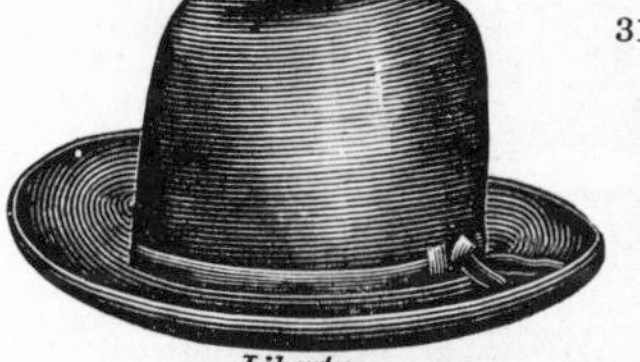

Liberty

31619 Men's Dark Blue Soft Fur Hats, "The Liberty." Raw edge, narrow silk band. Each.......$1.25 Per doz.. 13.50

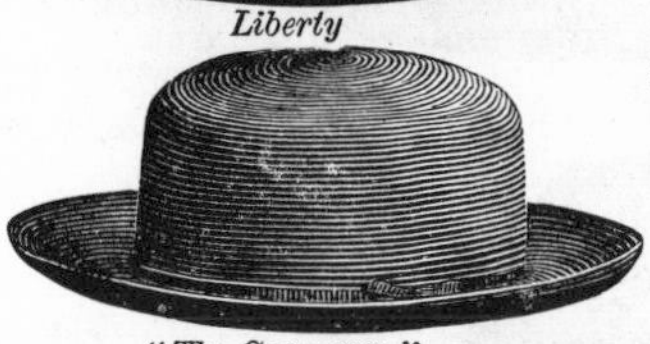

"The Gramercy."

31620 Men's Soft Black or Brown Hats, "The Gramercy." Suitable for young and middle aged men, superior quality. Each .... $2.25 Per dozen............ $24.30

Silk Hats.

N. B. We always ship the very latest style in silk hats unless otherwise ordered.

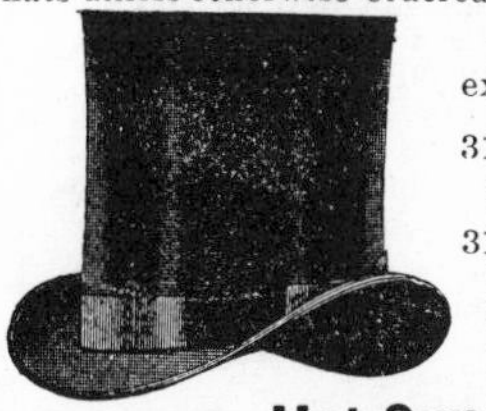

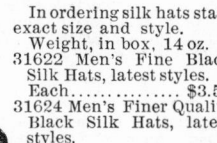

In ordering silk hats state exact size and style. Weight, in box, 14 oz.

31622 Men's Fine Black Silk Hats, latest styles. Each...............$3.50

31624 Men's Finer Quality Black Silk Hats, latest styles. Each... . ...$5.00

Hat Sundries.

31625 Leather Boxes for silk hats; tan colored, buffing leather, regular nickel lock, fancy lining; very handy in traveling. Price, each......$5.00

31628 Men's Silk Hat Brush, fine bristle edge, with silk plush padded back. Each.............. .50

31629 Black Silk Hat Cords with swivel and bar to attach to buttonhole of coat; used for all kinds of hats. Each.............................. .05

31630 G. A. R. Wreath and Cord. Per set.... : .25

Ear Muffs.

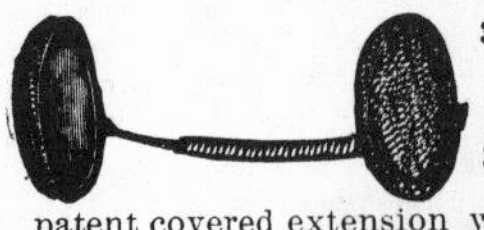

31631 Black Velvet Ear Muffs, lined.
Each...............$0.10
Per dozen............1.10
31632 Black Velvet Alaska Ear Muffs with patent covered extension wire. Each..........$0.20
Per dozen.............................2.15

Boys' Hats.

Average weight of boys' hats, 4 ounces. Sizes, 6½ to 7 only.

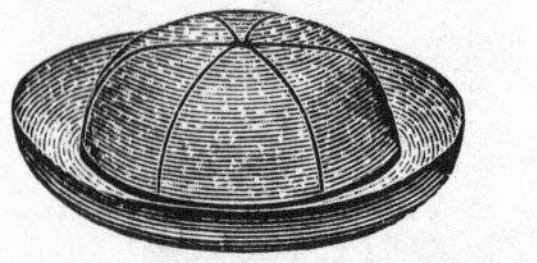

31633 Boys' Plaid Cloth Turban Hats, medium and dark colors. Fancy plaid and mixed patterns. Weight, 2 ounces, sizes, 6½ to 7. Each..$0.25
Per dozen..............................2.70

31634 Boys' Wool Hats, square crown turban, raw edge, small silk band. Colors, black, blue or brown. Weight, 3 oz.
Each..............$0.35
Per dozen.........3.78

31635 Boys Wool Hats, satin bound, satin band. Colors, blue or black. Weight, 4 oz.
Each...$0.45
Per doz. 4.85

31641 Boys' Saxony Wool Hats, round crown, crusher shape, raw edge, with band. Colors, blue black or light brown. Weight, 3 oz.
Each..............$0.50
Per dozen..........5.50

"*Boys' Derby.*"

31642 Boys' Black Stiff Fur Derby Hats, silk band and binding, satin lined. Sizes, 6½ to 7.
Each $1.00
31644 Boys' Black Stiff Fur Derby Hats, silk band and binding, satin lined. Sizes 6½ to 7. Each..$1.50

31645 Boys' Black or Brown Fur Hats, "The Fedora," 6½ to 7. Weight, 4 oz.
Each........$ 1.25
Per dozen....13.50

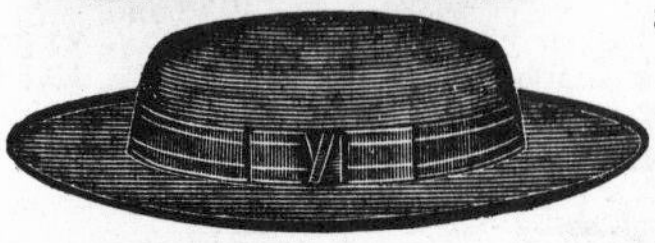

31646 Boys' Planter Hats, silk band and bound, wide brim. Colors, black or drab. Weight, 4 oz.
Each...$0.70
Per doz. 7.55

31647 Boys' Fine Fur Crushers, satin lined. Colors, blue or brown. Weight, 4 oz.
Each..........$ 0.95
Per dozen........10.26

Men's Caps.

The following caps, 31648 to 31660, are light weight caps, largely used for office, shop, railroad and general indoor wear. Average weight is about 1 ounce.
31648 Black Silkaline Skull Caps, lined. Sizes, 6¾ to 7⅝.
Good value. Each...........................$0.25
Per dozen.............................2.70

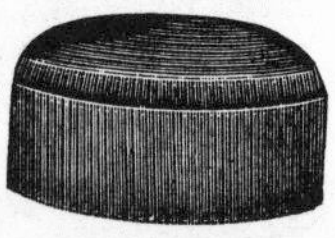

31649 Men's Silk Polo or Office Skull Caps: also used for traveling. Price governs quality.
Each.........................$0.50
Per dozen.........................5.40

31650 Men's Black Silk Caps, with visor to protect the eyes.
Each...........$ 0.50
Per dozen........ 5.40

Caps—Continued.

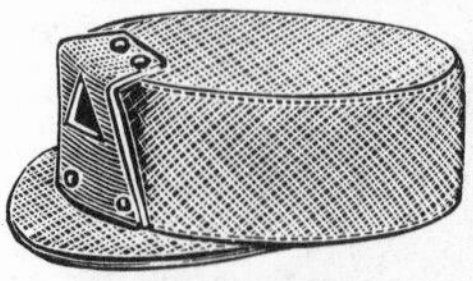

Miners' Cap.

31652 Miners' Caps. Brown duck or canvas, lined, extra heavy, stiff leather guard and socket for lamp. Each...$0.18
Per dozen......... 1.95

31653-31654

31653 Men's Cotton Shop Caps, with visor, good quality, black or cream.
Each.......................$0.10
Per doz..................1.08
31654 Men's Black Silkaline Caps, with visor, lined. Sizes, 6¾ to 7⅝. Each......... .25
Per dozen...............2.70
31655 Men's Black Silkaline Caps, lined, full shaped top, same style as 31874. Sizes, 6¾ to 7⅝
Each.......................................$0.40
Per dozen..................................4.32
31657 Men's Black Silk Caps, with visor, same shape as 31874, satin lined. Sizes, 6¾ to 7⅝.
Each....................................... .75
Per dozen..................................8.10

Engineer's Cap.

31658 Men's Black Silkaline Engineers' Caps, extra wide visor to protect the eyes. Sizes, 6¾ to 7⅝.
Each........$0.40
Per dozen...... 4.32
31660 Men's Black Silk Engineers' Caps, satin lined, extra wide visor to protect the eyes.
Each.......................................$0.70
Per dozen..................................7.50

Children's Summer Caps.

Sizes, 6¼ to 6¾.

Yacht Cap.

31662 Children's Navy Blue Flannel Yacht Caps. Sizes, 6¼ to 6¾.
Each...............$0.15
Per dozen..........1.69
31665 Children's Navy Blue or Red Flannel Yacht Caps, with cord in front. Each..........$0.20
Per dozen..................................2.15
31669 Children's Yacht Caps. Plain flannel cloth trimmed with 1-inch black hercules braid around band; cord in front. Colors: Tan, cardinal and navy blue. Sizes, 6½ to 6¾.
Each....................................... .25
Per dozen..................................2.70

31670 Children's Navy Blue Broadcloth Yacht Caps, double gilt cord in front; embroidered ornament in front of crown.
Each $0.40
Per dozen... 4.32
3167ı Children's Navy Blue Yacht Caps, made of extra quality broadcloth. Trimmed in front with heavy double gilt cords and around lower band with ½-inch gilt hercules braid. Sizes, 6¼ to 6¾. Each....$0.65
Per dozen..................................7.00

31674 Children's Fancy Caps "The Ensign," made of navy blue broadcloth, heavy double gilt cord over cr wn, trimmed around band with ½-inch gilt braid, embroidered ornament in front; sizes, 6¼ to 6¾.
Price, each.................................$0.50
Per dozen..................................5.40

"The Eton."

31675 Children's Fancy Summer Caps, "The Eton," fine brown and gray mixed cassimere; sizes, 6¼ to 6¾.
Each...................$0.45
Per dozen..............4.86
31681 Children's Eton Caps, same as above in plain navy blue. Each........$0.45
Per dozen..................................4.85

"The Brownie."

31682 Children's Fancy Summer Caps, "The Brownie," blue, gray, pin check cassimere, with cord and whistle attachment; sizes, 6¼ to 6¾.
Each..............$0.45
Per dozen..........4.86

31683 Children's Fine Broadcloth Yacht Caps, navy blue, satin lined, heavy double gilt cords in front; heavy 1-inch wide gilt band, anchor pattern, around entire lower band of cap. Rich and dressy; sizes, 6¼ to 7. Each............$0.85
Per dozen..................................9.18
31684 Children's Fine Yacht Caps, same as above with silver trimming. Each................ .85
Per dozen..................................9.18

Caps—Continued.

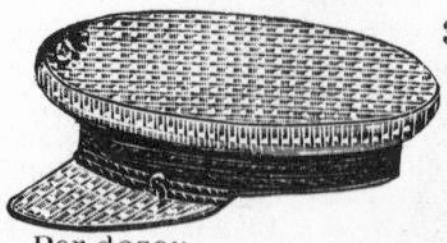

31688 Children's Summer Caps, new Russian admiral style, full top, light cream color, with small neat brown mixture; cassimere cloth. Hercules braid band.
Each...................$0.50
Per dozen..................................5.40

31695 Children's Fancy Summer Caps, made of plain colored fine flannel in the following combinations of colors: Gray and navy, cardinal and navy, and seal and tan brown, feather ornaments. Sizes, 6½ to 6¼.
Each...................$0.45
Per dozen..................................4.85

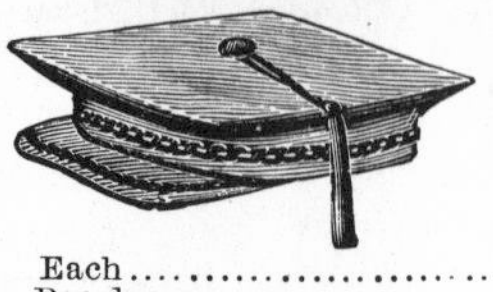

1696 Children's Fancy Summer Caps, "The Wellesly." Made of fine all wool cloth, square top, with button and silk cord in center, silk embroidered visor. Colors: Tan, seal, navy and cardinal.
Each.......................................$0.45
Per dozen..................................4.85

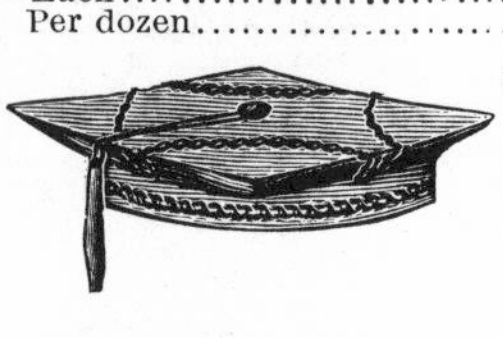

31699 Children's School Caps, Vassar style, made in all wool cloth, tastefully trimmed with combination gimp cord. Colors; Gray, tan, navy blue, cardinal and seal brown. Sizes, 6¼ to 6¾.
Each.......................................$0.45
Per dozen..................................4.85

31701 Children's Fancy Cashmere Caps, puff top, edged with silk cord, silk ornament on side. Colors: Tan, wine or navy. Sizes, 6¼ to 6¾. Each....$0.50
Per dozen..........5.40

31708 Children's Fancy Caps, "The Idlewild," made of plain red, or navy blue flannel, trimmed with neat fancy silk cord around band; sizes, 6¼ to 6¾.
Price, each................$0.45
Per dozen..................4.06

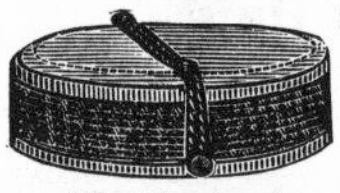

The Corporal.

31712 Children's Fancy Caps, "The Corporal," made of plain cardinal red flannel, trimmed with wide hercules braid and black silk cord; sizes, 6¼ to 6¾0
Price, each..........$0.40
Per dozen..................4.32

The Dorothy.

31716 Childrens' and Misses' Caps, "The Dorothy," made of fine navy blue wool ladies cloth. The three corners tastefully caught up at the centre of crown with loop of fancy gimp braid; very neat, sizes, 6¼ to 6⅞.
Fach................$0.50
Per dozen............5.40

The Gloriana.

31717 Children's and Misses' Caps, "The Gloriana," made of navy blue serge cloth, with feather at side.
Each $0.25
Per dozen 2.70

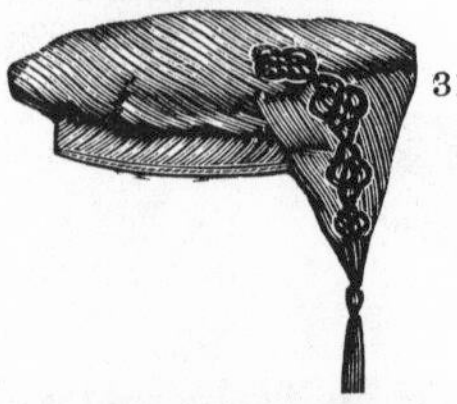

31720 Children's Caps, "New Arabian," made of red and olive diagonal changeable silk. Sizes, 6¼ to 6¾. Silk cord ornaments.
Each...................$0.50
Per dozen..............5.40

31722 Children's and Misses' Sailor Hats, made of navy blue broadcloth, 1-in h gold braid band. Sizes, 6¼ to 7.
Each.............$0 50
Per dozen..................................5.40
31724 Children's and Misses' Sailor Hats, made of fine quality, navy blue broadcloth. Imported gold ribbon band, 1 inch wide. Sizes, 6¼ to 7.
Fach....................................... .75
Per dozen..................................8.10

Caps—Continued.

31725 Children's and Misses' Sailor Hats. Extra fine navy blue broadcloth, edged around crown with neat silk cord. 1-inch imported gold ribbon around band, anchor design; satin lined. Sizes, 6¼ to 7. Each...........$ 0.95
Per dozen...........10.25

31726 Children's and Misses, Sailor Hats, same as above; with silver trimming. Each........$ 0.95
Per dozen..........10.25

31738 Children's and Misses' Caps, "The Oxford," made of fine navy blue broadcloth, black silk button and cord on top. 1-inch imported gold ribbon band, satin lined; sizes, 6¼ to 7. Each................$ 0.85
Per dozen.......... 9.18

Boys' Caps.

Sizes, 6¾ to 7.

31739 Boy's New Summer Outing Caps, wide front piece, black and white check cassimere. Very popular shape. Sizes, 6½ to 7, weight, 2 ounces. Each.............$0.45
Per dozen.......... 4.85

31741 Boys' Outing Caps, same style as above, very fine mixture of tan and gray. Also plain blue wool cassimere, Sizes, 6½ to 7. Weight, 2 ounces. Each..................45
Per dozen.......... 4.85

31742 Boys' Outing Caps, same style as above. Dark gray or navy blue, soft wool flannel. These caps are fitted with the new transparent visors; made of dark green celluloid, soft and flexible. The best protector ever invented for the eyes. We earnestly recommend them to our patrons. Sizes, 6½ to 7. Each.................$0.50
Per dozen.......... 5.40

31748 Boys' Yacht Caps, fancy mixed cassimere; dark colors. 6½ to 7. Each......... ....$0.25
Per dozen....... 2.70

Yacht Caps.

31749 Boys' Yacht Caps, dark and medium gray, mixed wool cassimer; 1 inch black hercules braid on band and visor. 6½ to 7. Each..............$0.37
Per dozen 4.00

31751 Boys' Yacht Caps. same style as above in navy blue. Each.... 37
Per dozen.......... 4.00

31753 Boys' Navy Blue Broadcloth Caps, black hercules braid trimming. Sizes, 6½ to 7. Each..................40
Per dozen.......... 4.32

31756 Boys' Yacht Caps, black and white shepherds plaid cassimere, black hercules braid trimming; sizes, 6½ to 7. Each..................45
Per dozen.......... 4.86

31758 Boys' Yacht Caps, navy blue broadcloth, satin lined, narrow patent leather strap in front, solid black curved leather visor. Each.........50
Per dozen.......... 5.40

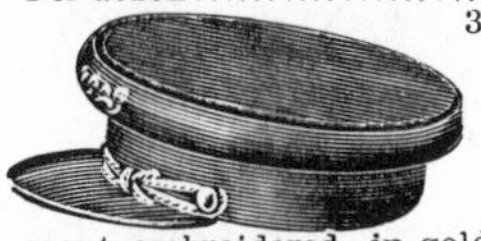

31761 "The Commodore." Boys' Extra Fine Quality Navy Blue Broadcloth Yacht Caps, satin lined, heavy braided double gold cords and buttons to match. Beautiful ornament embroidered in gold, silver and scarlet tinsel wire on front of cap. Handsomest yacht cap in the market; sizes, 6½ to 7. Each $0 75
Per dozen.......... 8.10

31762 Boys' Yacht Caps, plain navy blue broadcloth, handsome 1-inch wide silver or gold ribbon band and double silver cord in front; 6½ to 7. Each..................75
Per dozen.......... 8.10

31765 Boys' Yacht Caps, made of fine black corded silk, heavy satin lining, double silk cord in front; sizes, 6½ to 7. Each................75
Per dozen.......... 8.10

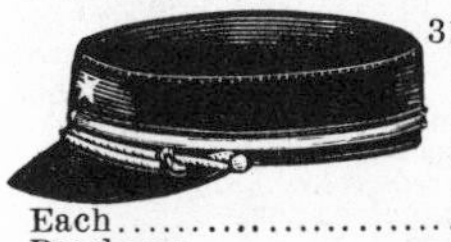

31767 Boys' Summer Caps, "The Yale," navy blue broadcloth, heavy gilt cord and braid trimmings, embroidered gilt star in front. Sizes, 6½ to 7. Each.....................$0.50
Per dozen.......... 5.40

Ladies' Caps.

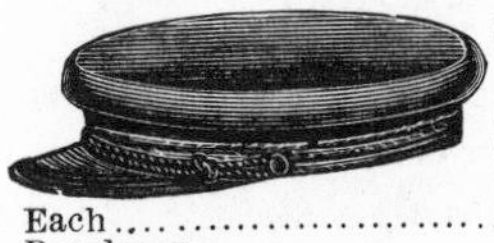

31771 Ladies' Yacht Cap "The Lucile," plain flannel with hercules braid and cord trimming; Navy, cardinal, tan and white. Sizes, 6½ to 7¼. Each..................$0.37
Per dozen.......... 4.00

Caps—Continued.

31776 Ladies' Yacht Caps, plain navy blue or white broadcloth, trimmed with hercules braid and cord. Sizes, 6½ to 7¼. Each............$0.50
Per dozen.......... 5.40

31777 Ladies' Yacht Caps, made of fine black corded silk, satin lining. Double silk cord in front. Very dressy. Sizes, 6½ to 7¼. Each:. ..75
Per dozen.......... 8.10

Men's Summer Caps.

Sizes, 6¾ to 7½.

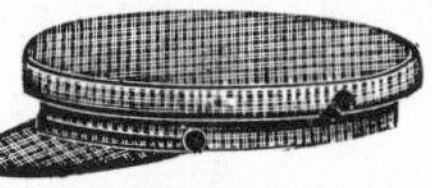

31782 Men's Yacht Caps, medium and dark mixed cassimere cloth, assorted patterns. Sizes, 6¾ to 7½. Each............$0.25
Per dozen.... ..2.70

31783 Men's Yacht Caps, navy blue wool kersey cloth, black hercules braid band, with cord in front. Each...................35
Per dozen 3.80

31785 Men's Yacht Caps, black and white shepherds plaid cassimere cloth, with black hercules braid trimming. Sizes 6¾ to 7½. Each.... .45
Per dozen.......... 4.86

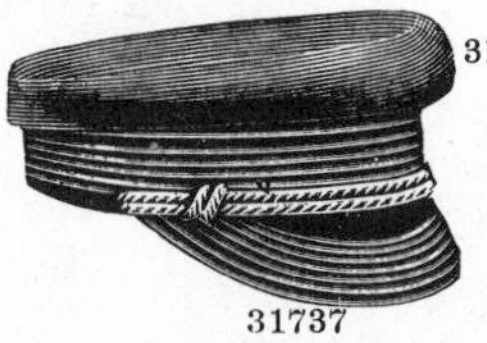

31787 Men's Yacht Caps, made of navy blue broadcloth, with black Hercules braid trimming on band and visor. Sizes, 6¾ to 7½. Each....$0.50
Per dozen.......... 5.45

31789 Men's Yacht Caps, plain black corded silk, with cord band in front. Sizes 6¾ to 7½. Each 60
Per dozen 6.45

31790 Men's Yacht Caps, extra quality, fine black silk, fine wale, heavy satin lining, double silk cord band in front, handsome and neat. Sizes, 6¾ to 7½. Each.....................$0.85
Per dozen.......... 9.18

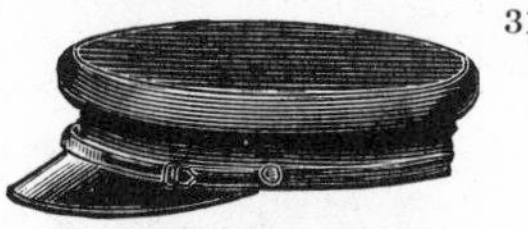

31792 Men's New Yacht Caps. "The Skipper," made of navy blue broadcloth, satin lined, solid black leather visor curved to protect the eyes. Sizes 6¾ to 7½. Each.....................$0.65
Per dozen 7.00

31794 *Men's New Outing Caps,* made of black and white shepherds plaid cassimere, extra wide visor to protect the eyes. Sizes 6¾ to 7½. Each..... .....$0.45
Per dozen........ 4.86

31796 Men's New Outing Caps, tan mixed cassimere, very neat. Extra wide visor. Sizes 6¾ to 7½. Each........$0.45 Per dozen.........$4.86

31797 Men's New Outing Caps, same shape as above; made of navy blue broadcloth. Extra wide visor made of dark green transparent celluloid. The best protector for the eyes ever invented. Sizes, 6¾ to 7½ Each.................$0.50 Per dozen.........$5.40

31799 Men's Black Silk Caps, same style as above, satin lined. A fine cap for bookkeepers and clerks, as well as for outdoor summer wear. Sizes, 6¾ to 7½. Each................$0.75 Per dozen...........$8.10

31801 Men's Black Silk Outing Caps, with extra wide silk visor. Extra fine quality. Heavy satin lining, same as above. Each................$0.85 Per dozen............$9.18

Men's Straw Hats.

N. B.—We quote but a few staple styles in straw hats, as they do not usually make a profitable shipment unless ordered with other goods. The following lines we will have in stock until July 15. After that date we cannot guarantee to supply them. Place your orders early and we will give them immediate attention. Men's sizes run from 6¾ to 7½ only. Boys' sizes from 6½ to 7 only. We cannot furnish any other sizes in straw goods.

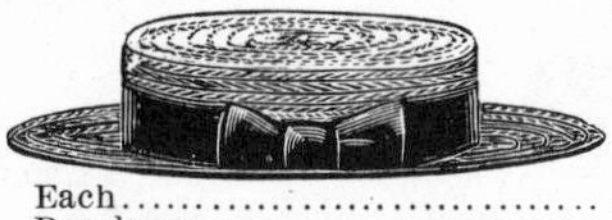

31803 Men's Straw Hats, natural straw color, with black band, medium crown and brim. Each......................$0.25
Per dozen 2.70

31807 Men's Natural Color Straw Hats, medium shape, double braided brim, 2-inch black ribbon band. Sizes, 6¾ to 7½. Each 45
Per dozen.......... 4.86

31820 Men's Mackinaw Straw Hats, similar style to above. Sizes, 6¾ to 7½. Each 50
Per dozen.......... 5.40

Hats—Continued.

31822 Men's Straw Hats, similar to superior quality, double braided, very 6¾ to 7½. Each .....
Per dozen 7.90

31824 Young Men's Featherweight Hats, made of natural color, rush straw, 2 inch black ribbon band, medium brim and crown. Sizes, 6¾ to 7⅜. Each 75
Per dozen 8.10

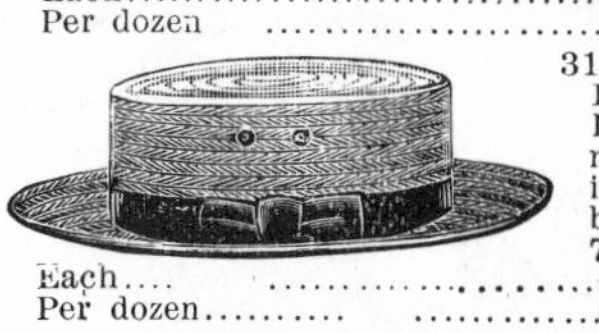

31826 Men's Plain Braided Straw Hats, high crown, medium brim 1 inch black ribbon band. Sizes, 6¾ to 7½. Each $0.50
Per dozen.......... 5.40

Boys' Straw Hats.

31828 Boys' Plain Straw Hats, black ribbon band. Sizes, 6½ to 7. Each $0.20
Per dozen..... 2.16

31830 Boys' Plain Straw Hats, curved brim, cord band. Sizes, 6½ to 7. Each...................28
Per dozen.......... 2.85

31832 Boys' Straw Hats, same style as above, made of black and white braided straw. Sizes 6½ to 7. Each..................$0.28
Per dozen.......... 2.85

31834 Boys' Staw Hats, natural color, straight brim, medium crown, black ribbon band, 6½ to 7. Each..................$0.45
Per doz..........4.85

Helmets.

31836 "The Stanley," Men's Helmet Hats, straw body covered with silesia; Dead grass color, sash band to match, complete ventilator around sweat band, weight, 2 ounces. Coolest hat in the world. Sizes 6¾ to 7⅜ only. Each.......... $0.50
Per dozen 5.40

31840 Men's Helmet Hats, similar style to above, with extra wide 3½ inch brim, nearly straight, tan color. Sizes 6¾ to 7⅜. Each.................$0.75
Per dozen.......... 8.10

Boys' Winter Caps.

Sizes 6½ to 7.

31842 Boys' Navy Blue All Wool Tricot Cloth Caps, pull-down black astrakhan band, satin lined, silk embroidered top. Each..................$0.75
Per dozen. 8.10

31844 Boys' Double Knit Wool Caps, derby ribbed, seamless, pull-down band, gray mixed or blue black. Each.................$0.25
Per dozen..........2.70

31846 Boys' Chinchilla Mask Caps, felt lined; protects face, ears and neck when drawn down; also can be worn as plain turban. Each.....................$0.40
Per dozen.......... 4.32

31848 Boys' Blue Black Beaver Mask Caps. Same style as above. Each...............$0.60
Per dozen...........6.48

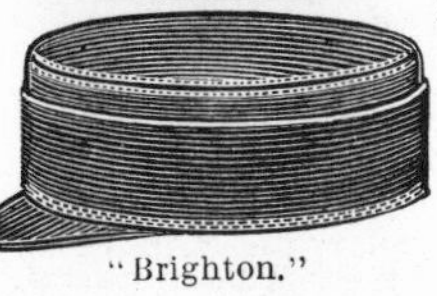

31850 Boys' Brighton Caps, dark navy blue cloth, with pull-down band; lined. Each...................$0.40
Per dozen.........4.32

"Brighton."

31851 Boys' Winsdor Caps, dark broken plaids and fancy mixtures, lined. Each.. ....$0.30
Per dozen.......... 3.24

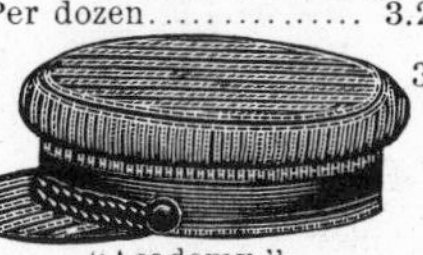

Windsor.

31852 Boys' Academy Caps, medium dark fancy plaid cassimeres, pull down band; lined. Each.................$0.50
Per dozen. 5.40

"Academy."

Caps—Continued.

31854 Boys' Black Silk Plush Turbans, pieced; silk lined, pull down band.
Each.................$0 50
Per dozen.........5.40

31855 Boys' Black Silk Plush Turbans; square crown, pull down band; lined.

31855

Each.................................$0.65
Per dozen........................7.00

31856 Boys' Black Silk Plush Winter Yachting Caps, with pull down band; neat ornament in front; lined.
Each................$0.75
Per dozen........8.10

Men's Cold Weather Caps.

Sizes, 6¾ to 7½.

31857 Men's Genuine Gray Mixed Scotch Caps, lined, full shape.
Each.............$0.30
Per dozen.......3.24

31858 Men's Genuine Scotch Caps; dark navy blue, lined; full shape.
Each.............$0.30
Per dozen........3.24

31860 Men's Chinchilla Mask Caps, felt lined, protects face, ears and neck when drawn down; also can be worn as plain turban.
Each.................$0.50
Per dozen...... ....5.40

31861 Men's Brighton Caps, assorted, dark and medium plaids, mixed cassimeres, linea. Pull down band.
Each...............$0.25
Per dozen..........2.70

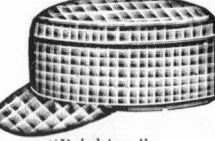
"Brighton."

31862 Men's Brighton Caps, dark navy blue cassimere, lined, pull down band.
Each...............................$0.45
Per dozen............................4.86

31863 Men's Genuine Scotch Windsor Caps, dark navy blue, lined. Each...$0 45
Per dozen........................4.86

31864 Men's Windsor Caps, extra heavy, smooth finish, blue black beaver, satin lined. Each..... ....$1.00
Per dozen........................8.10

31865 Men's Storm King Caps, made of chinchilla felt, lined, large sliding band.
Each............$0.50
Per dozen......5 40

"Storm King."

Men's Silk Plush Caps.

31867 Men's Black Silk Plush Windsor Caps, six-piece top, double roll band, satin lined.
Each............$0.75
Per dozen...........8.10

We Do No Business in Chicago.

The Mail Order Trade and Retail Trade
Cannot be successfully Combined.

OUR SPECIALTIES.
Metal Hat Badges.

The following metal badges are made of fine quality German silver, handsomely nickel plated. The prices quoted are for badges made to order, and in each case full amount of cash must accompany the order. It will require from 3 to 4 days to fill order. Badges made to order cannot be returned or exchanged unless the error is clearly ours.

BAGGAGEMAN

Each $0.65

MADERA
BAGGAGE & EXPRESS

31868 Plain Nickel Plated Badge, size, ¾x3 in. Baggageman, Porter, Drayman, City Hotel or any name not exceeding 14 letters. Weight, 1 ounce.
Per dozen.........$7.00

31869 Nickel Plated Badge, with fancy oval top; size, 3 inches long, 1 inch wide at center. Suitable for two words, such as "City Expressman" "C M. & St. P. R. R. Conductor," "City News Agent," "C. & A. Baggageman." and similar words not exceeding 20 letters. Weight, 1 ounce.
Each.............$0.85   Per dozen.........$9.18

31870 Nickel Plated Badge, with fancy oval top, 1½ inches wide at center, 4 inches long. Suitable for such words as "Omnibus Coates House," "Porter Southern Hotel," etc.
Each.......$1.35   Per dozen............$14.58

31871 Firemen's Regulation Navy Blue Cloth Caps, lined, extra heavy black leather visor. Sizes, 6¾ to 7½.
Each............$ 1.00
Per dozen...... 10.80

Fireman's Cap.

31872 Firemen's Regulation Caps, same as above, in better quality, with wire frame. Each.......... 1.50
Per dozen.................................. 16.20

31873 Baggagemen's Regulation Navy Blue Cloth Caps, with heavy curved leather visor. Sizes, 6¾ to 7½.
Each ....$ 1.25
Per dozen 13.50

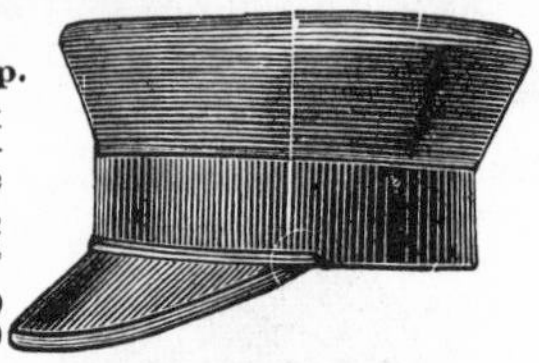

Baggageman's Cap.

31874 Men's Black Gross grain silk Conductor's Caps, same shape as illustration, wire frame. Sizes 6¾ to 7½.
Each..........$ 1.50
Par dozen.... 16.20

31875 Men's Navy Blue Cloth Conductors' Caps, without wire frame; stiff top. Sizes 6¾ to 7½.
Each............$1.00   Per dozen............$10.80

31876 Men's Blue Cloth Conductors' Caps, with patent wire cloth frame; will always keep its shape. Without badge
Each........ ...$1.50
Per dozen.....16.20

Frame Covered.

Uncovered.

Ribbon Badges

31878 Black Silk Gros Grain Ribbon Badges, printed in gold letters. We carry in stock the following: TICKET AGENT, MESSENGER, CONDUCTOR, BRAKEMAN, PORTER, NEWS AGENT, STATION AGENT, STEWARD, CAPTAIN, AGENT, DRAYMAN, HACKMAN, BELLMAN, CITY HOTEL, OMNIBUS TRANSFER and CITY EXPRESSMAN. Each.........$0.25
Printed badges with other lettering than above will have to be made to order, require five days to make, and cost 75 cents each.

31879 "News Agent," embroidered in gold wire block letters...............................$1.00

31880 "Brakeman," embroidered in gold wire block letters..... .... 1.00

CONDUCTOR

31882 "Conductor," embroidered in gold wire block letters, with double band of gold.
Each...................$1.50

Embroidered badges with over nine letters will cost 10c. for each additional letter.

THIS CATALOGUE

Enables you to buy to as much advantage as though present at our counters.

INITIALS

31883—Gilt or Silvered initials, attached pins on each letter for fastening. Cut represents ½ the size of letters. Each..$0.04
Per dozen.................................40

Military Caps.

31884 Men's Military Caps, same style as illustration, made of fine quality navy blue broadcloth, ½ inch black patent leather band in front, heavy solid black leather visor, leather sweat band. Sizes, 6¾ to 7½. Each...... .....$0.75
Per dozen...........................8.10

31886 Men's Military Caps, same as above in confederate gray. Each........................ 0.75
Per dozen...........................8.10

31888 Boys' Soldier Caps, same shape as above, with heavy double gilt cord and buttons, navy blue, sizes 6½ to 7⅛. Each......................50
Per dozen...........................5.40

31890 Boys' Soldier Caps, same as above, in cadet gray. Sizes 6½ to 7⅛. Each....................50
Per dozen...........................5.40

31892 Boys' Extra Quality Navy Blue Military Caps, heavy black leather visor, cross guns ornament in front, crown of cap trimmed with narrow gilt braid, heavy double gilt cord and buttons, gilt braid around lower band, very handsome. Sizes 6¾ to 7⅛.
Each................................ 0.75
Per dozen...........................8.10

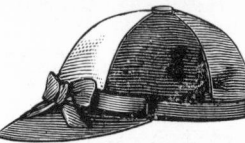

31894 Boys' University Caps, made of good quality navy blue flannel, lined; trimmed with double gilt cord and buttons; leather visor. Sizes, 6½ to 7⅛; weight, 2 oz. Flat top, navy style. Each......$0.35
Per dozen.............................3.80

31898 Jockey Caps, made of heavy satin, regulation race track style, combination colors, red and blue, red and black, red and yellow, red and green, red and white, blue and gold, red white and blue and plain colors. Sizes 6½ to 7½. Each....$1.00
Per dozen.............................10.80

SHIRTS.
Men's Negligee Shirts.

WORKING, BOATING, TENNIS, CYCLISTS', TOURISTS' FIREMEN'S AND BLUE FLANNEL SHIRTS.
Weight of men's overshirts average as follows: Light summer weight, 7 to 10 ounces; medium weights, 10 to 15 ounces; heavy weights, 18 to 25 ounces. Sizes, 14½ to 17 only. Always give neck measure.
N. B.—We do not sample overshirts,

Men's Checks and Plaid Over-shirts.

32200 Men's Overshirts; light ground cotton cheviot, broken checks. No pockets; similar to style A. Each........$0.35 Per dozen.......e..$3.78

32202 Men s Overshirts plaid domette flannel, light colors, handkerchief pocket, yoke back. Similar to style A. Each................ .45
Per dozen............................4.86

32204 Men's Overseirts, light ground sateen twill, fancy broken checks, pearl buttons, yoke back, handkerchief pocket. Similar to style A. Each. .45
Per dozen............................4.86

32206 Men's Overshirts, light ground broken check Oxford cheviot, removable studs, yoke back, handkerchief pocket. Similar to style A. Each........................$0.50 Per dozen.... 5.40

32208 Men's Overshirts, light ground sateen finish, fancy checks, removable studs, yoke back, handkerchief pocket. Similar to style B. Each..............................65
Per dozen............................7.02

32510 Men's Overshirts, made of Madrass cloth, small checks, removable studs, yoke back, handkerchief pocket. Colors: Light blue or pink ground. Similar to Style B. Each..............70
Per dozen............................7.56

32212 Men's Overshirts, made of soft finish Scotch cheviot; broken checks, assorted light colors, pearl buttons, gathered yoke, handkerchief pocket. Similar to style C. Each........ .80
Per dozen............................8.64

32214 Men's Overshirts, made of Madrass cloth, light ground, medium checks, assorted colors, removable gilt top studs, gathered yoke back, handkerchief pocket. Similar to Style B.
Each................................ 1.00
Per dozen............................10.80

32216 Men's Overshirts, made of fine zephyr cloth, light ground, small checks, silk stripes, French yoke back, removable studs, handkerchief pocket. Similar to Style B. Each....... 1.15
Per dozen.................................12.42

NEGLIGEE OVERSHIRTS.

Spring and Summer Styles, 1895.

Style A.   Style B.   Style C.   Style D.   Style E   Style F.

Style G.   Style H.   Style I.   Style J.   Style K.   Style L.

Style M.   Style N.   Style O.   Style P.   Style Q.

Style R.   Style S.   Style T.   Style U   Style V.   Style W.

Shirts—Continued.

32218 Men's Overshirts, light ground Madras cloth, medium small checks, assorted colors, gathered yoke, pearl buttons. Set in watch and handkerchief pockets. Similar to style E. Each .... 1.35 Per dozen 14.58

32220 Men's Overshirts, made of fine wool cashmere, silk stripes, light ground. Small checks, gathered yoke, pearl buttons, set in watch and handkerchief pockets. Similar to style E. Each .... 1.75 Per dozen 18.90

Men's Striped Overshirts.

32222 Men's Overshirts, striped domette flannel, Medium light colors, no pockets. Similar to style F. Each $0.25
Per dozen 2.70

32224 Men's Overshirts, light ground, fancy striped cheviot, yoke back, handkerchief pocket. Similar to style F. Each 0.30
Per dozen 3.24

32226 Men's Overshirts, made of sateen, light ground narrow stripes, yoke back, handkerchief pocket, similar to style H. Each $0.35
Per dozen 3.78

32228 Men's Overshirts, made of cotton cheviot, light blue ground, with white stripes, removable studs, yoke back hankerchief pocket. Similar to style F. Each .... $0.45 Per dozen 4.86

32230 Men's Overshirts, made of domette flannel, light ground fancy stripes, yoke back handkerchief pocket. Similar to style G. Each .... .45
Per dozen 4.86

32232 Men's Overshirts, sateen twill colors, ecru ground, neat stripes, yoke back, pearl buttons, handkerchief pocket. Similar to style G. Each .... $0.50 Per dozen 5.40

32234 Men's Overshirts, made of Oxford cheviot, light ground, with neat fancy stripes, yoke back, pearl buttons, handkerchief pocket. Similar to style H. Each $0.60
Per dozen 6.48

32236 Men's Overshirts, made of sateen twill, ecru ground, fine hairline stripes, removable nickel-top studs, yoke back, handkerchief pocket, Similar to style G. Each .... .65
Per dozen 7.02

32238 Men's Overshirts, twilled buckskin cloth, light ecru ground, fancy stripes, yoke back, pearl buttons, handkerchief pocket. Similar to style H. Each .... .70
Per dozen 7.56

32240 Men's Overshirts, fancy striped, wool mixed twilled cassimere, good weight, medium and dark colors, handkerchief pocket. Similar to style H. Each .... .75
Per dozen 8.10

32242 Men's Overshirts, made of light ground Madrass cloth with light colored fancy stripes, yoke back, pearl buttons, handkerchief pockets. Similar to style I.
Price each .... $0.85 Price per dozen 9.18

32244 Men's Overshirts, made of fine zephyr cloth, neat stripes, gathered yoke, pearl buttons, set in watch and handkerchief pockets. Colors: Light blue, pink or heliotrope ground. Similar to style E.
Price each .... $0.95 Per dozen 10.26

32246 Men's Overshirts, imitation of French flannel, light ground, with silk stripes, yoke back, pearl buttons, handkerchief pocket. Similar to style I.
Price each .... $1.10 Per dozen 11.88

32248 Men's Overshirts, made of extra fine English Madrass cloth, silk effect. Colors: Light blue ground, with neat silk stripes, gathered yoke, pearl buttons, handkerchief pocket. With non-shrinkable neck band. Similar to style I. Each .... $1.45 Per dozen 15.66

32250 Men's Overshirts, made of French botany Flannel. Colors: Light ground, neat fancy silk stripes, gathered yokes, pearl buttons, set in watch and handkerchief pockets. Non-shrinkable neck band. Similar to style E. Each ... $ 1.75
Per dozen 18.90

32252 Men's Overshirts, made of extra fine all wool, Cashmere. Colors: Light ground, narrow silk stripes, gathered yoke, pearl buttons. Watch and handkercheif pockets. Similar to style G. Each .... $ 2.00
Per dozen 21.60

Men's Plain Front Overshirts.

32254 Men's Overshirts, plain dark gray mixed Melton cloth, without pocket, small black horn buttons, similar to style K. Price each $0.45
Price per dozen 4.86

32256 Men's Overshirts, extra fine sateen, yoke back, pearl buttons, handkerchief pocket. Colors: Light, medium and dark shades of ecru: similar to style K. Price each .... .75
Price per dozen 8.10

32258 Men's Overshirts, plain weave of silk, beautiful shade of golden ecru, double pointed yoke back, gold plated studs, watch and handkerchief pockets. Similar to style K. Until sold price each 2.50
Price per dozen 27.00

Men's Pleated Front Overshirts.

32260 Men's Overshirts, cotton cheviot, light blue ground, narrow stripes, and pleated front. Similar to style L. Each $0.45
Per dozen 4.86

32262 Men's Overshirts; medium colored striped Domette flannel, pearl buttons, pleated front. Similar to style L. Each .... .50
Per dozen 5.40

32264 Men's Overshirts, fine sateen twill, light ground, neat stripes, removable studs, pleated front. Similar to style N. Each .... .65
Per dozen 7.02

Embroidered Front Overshirts.

32266 Men's Overshirts, cotton cheviot, medium ground, silk embroidered. Scroll down front pleat, collar and pocket. Similar to style M. Each .... $0.40 Per dozen $4.32

32268 Men's Overshirts, sateen twill, Colors: Light ecru ground, neat stripes. Removable studs, handkerchief pocket, silk embroidery down front pleat and on collar. Similar to style O. Each .... .60
Per dozen 6.48

32270 Men's Overshirts, good weight, striped cotton buckskin twilled cloth, with two rows of handsome silk embroidered scroll down front. Set in shield front bosom, removable studs. Colors: Light, dark or medium tan. Similar to style V. Each .... .65
Per dozen 7.02

32272 Men's Overshirts, fine, tan brown chambray. Set in bosom, yoke back, removable studs, two rows of elegant silk embroidery down bosom. Similar to style V. Each .... .70
Per dozen 7.56

32274 Men's Overshirts, cashmere twill cheviot, light ground, neat stripes, yoke back, removable studs, silk scroll down front pleat, collar and pocket. Similar to style M. Each $0.75
Per dozen 8.10

32276 Men's Overshirts, fine sateen, light fawn ground, fancy mottled stripes, yoke back, pearl buttons, handkerchief pocket, two rows of handsome silk embroidery down front pleat and on collar. Similar to style Q. Each $0.85
Per dozen 9.18

Men's Novelty Front Overshirts.

32278 Men's Overshirts, light ground, striped cotton cheviot novelty, set in bosom, with bias stripes, removable studs. Similar to style S. Each .... $0.40 Per dozen 4.32

32280 Men's Overshirts, fancy weave striped cotton chevoit, light ground, front pleat, collar and pocket, trimmed with fancy cord piping. Similar to style T. Each .... .45
Per dozen 4.86

32282 Men's Overshirts, diagonal weave cotton cheviot, medium light ground, narrow stripes, handkerchief pocket, with necktie design embroidered on front pleat, which dispenses with a detachable necktie. Similar to style U. Each .... .45
Per dozen 4.86

32284 Men's Overshirts, sateen twill, light ecru ground, fancy stripes, yoke back, handkerchief pocket; with necktie design. Similar to above, see style U. Each .... .50
Per dozen 5.40

32286 Men's Overshirts, made of fancy cotton cheviot, medium color ground, set in bosom, removable studs, silk embroidered scroll down front of bosom and on collar. Similar to style P.
Price each .... .50
Price per dozen 5.40

Black Sateen Overshirts.

32288 Men's Overshirts, plain black sateen yoke back, handkerchief pocket. Similar to style K. Each .... .45
Per dozen 4.86

32290 Men's Overshirts, black sateen with white hairline stripes, yoke back, pearl buttons, handkerchief pocket. Similar to style G. Each ...... .50
Per dozen 5.40

32292 Men's Overshirts, plain black sateen with white silk scroll embroidery down front pleat and on collar, removable studs, handkerchief pocket. Similar to style R. Each .... .55
Per dozen 5.94

32294 Men's Overshirts, plain black sateen, yoke back, pearl buttons, handkerchief pocket. Similar to style K. Each. $0.65 Per dozen 7.02

32296 Men's Overshirts, black twilled sateen, with neat white stripes yoke back, removable studs, handkerchief pocket. Similar to style J. Each .... $0.70 Per dozen 7.56

32298 Men's Overshirts, plain black sateen, fine twill, full yoke back, pearl buttons, watch and handkerchief pockets. Similar to style K. Each .... $0.90 Per dozen 9.72

Men's Working Shirts.

32300 Men's Overshirts, heavy indigo blue cheviot; small and medium sized checks straight yoke back, handkerchief pocket. Similar to style E. Each .... $0.40 Per dozen $4.32

32302 Men's Overshirts, heavy indigo blue cheviot, narrow white stripes, straight yoke back, handkerchief pocket. Similar to style G. Each. 0.45
Per dozen 4.86

32304 Men's Overshirts, plain Indigo blue, heavy buckskin twilled cheviot, without pocket. Similar to style K. Each 0.50
Per dozen 5.40

Men's Blue Overshirts.

(Prices govern quality.)

32306 Men's Blue Union Flanne. Overshirts, double breasted. Each .... $ 0.95

32308 Men's All Wool Blue Flannel Overshirts, double breasted. Each 1.25

32310 Men's All Wool Blue Flannel, double breasted, large pearl buttons. Each 1.50

32312 Men's All Wool Blue California Flannel, double breasted, large pearl buttons. Each 2.00
Per dozen 21.60

32314 Men's All Wool Blue California Flannel, double breasted, large pearl buttons. Each 2.75

32316 Special value in Men's All Wool Blue Flannel Overshirts, single breasted, pearl buttons. Until sold, each 2.30

Boys' Overshirts.

Sizes, 12½ to 14½.

32318 Boys' Overshirts, striped cotton cheviot, medium light ground. Each $0.25
Per dozen 2.70

32320 Boys' Overshirt, sateen twill, ecru ground, small checks, yoke back, pearl buttons, handkerchief pocket. Each 0.40
Per dozen 4.32

32322 Boys' Overshirts, medium colored striped domette flannel, handkerchief pocket. Each .... .40
Per dozen 4.32

32324 Boys' Overshirts, plain black sateen, yoke back, handkerchief pocket. Each .... .45
Per dozen 4.86

32326 Boys' Overshirts, cream ground sateen, assorted figures, yoke back, pearl buttons, handkerchief pocket. Each .... .65
Per dozen 7.02

32328 Boys' Overshirts, heavy twilled cotton buckskin cloth, with nap on inside, yoke back, pearl buttons, dark colors, pleated front. Each. .70
Per dozen 7.56

Boys' Shirt Waists.

Weight of cotton waists, 4 to 5 ounces; blue flannel waists, 6 to 8 ounces.

Sizes, 4 to 13.

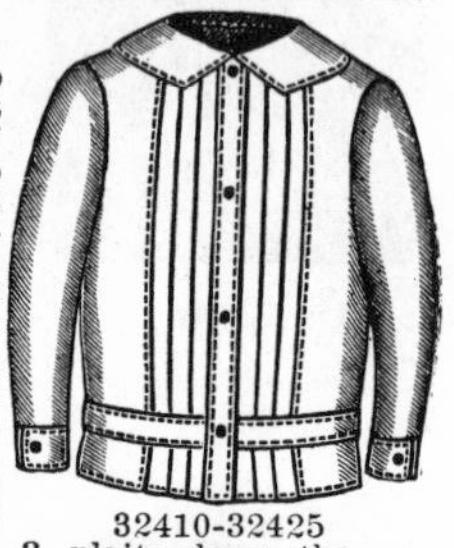

32410-32425

32410 Boys' Figured Calico Shirt Waists, plain front and back. Each $0.17
Per dozen 1.85

32412 Boys' Shirt Waists, 3 plaits down the front, assorted designs. Each $0.22
Per dozen 2.38

32413 Boys' Shirt Waists, indigo blue, assorted white figures and designs, three plaits down front. Each $0.25
Per dozen 2.70

32414 Boys' Shirt Waists, 3 plaits down the front and 2 down the back, new designs in assorted colors. Each ...... $0.30 Per dozen $3.25

32415 Boys' Shirt Waists, medium colors, neat plaid cheviot, three plaits down front. Each .... $0.30 Per dozen 3.30

32417 Boys' Shirt Waists, medium stripe, domett flannel, three plaits down front. Each ..... .30
Per dozen 3.25

32419 Boys' Shirt Waists, plaited front and back, crepe momie cloth, neat broken checks. Each .. .50
Per dozen 5.40

32421 Boys' Shirt Waists, extra fine and heavy penang cambric, 3 plaits down front and back. Each .... $0.50 Per dozen 5.40

32422 Boys' Heavy Union Flannel Shirt Waists, with pocket. Colors: Navy blue, wine, medium brown or drab. Each .... .60

32423 Boys' Shirt Waists, made from plain black sateen, plaited front and back. Each .... .50
Per dozen 5.40

32424 Boys' Laundried Shirt Waists, extra fine and heavy penang cambric; 3 plaits down front and back. Each ...... $0.75 Per dozen 8.10

33425 All Wool Fine Flannel Shirt Waists, plaited front and back, pearl buttons, medium colors. Each 1.00

32426 Boys' Shirt Waists, made from black sateen with neat white stripes, lace and button front combined, plaited front and back, Each $0.60
Per dozen 6.50

32428 Shirt Waists, made from fancy striped domett flannel, imitation French flannel, lace and button front combined. Each $0.35
Per dozen 3.78

32430 Boys' Heavy Mixed Melton Flannel Shirt Waists, with pocket, lace and button front combined; dark colors. Each .. $0.40 Per dozen .. $4.32

32431 Boys' Navy Blue All Wool Twilled Flannel Shirt Waists, with pocket, lace and button front combined. Each ...... $0.75 Per dozen $8.10

32432 Boys' All Wool Twilled Fannel Shirt Waists, pleated front and back, lace and button front combined. Colors: Wine, brown or drab. Each .... $1.00 Per dozen $10.80

32434 to 32440

32434 Boys' Shirt Waists, striped cotton cheviot, light ground, double ruffle down front, sailor collar with 1 inch ruffle. Each $0.30
Per dozen 3.24

32436 Boys' Shirt Waists, light ground striped chambray, double ruffle down rront, sailor collar, turned over cuffs with ruffle. Each $0.45
Per dozen $4.86

32438 Boys' Shirt Waists, indigo blue, fancy figured penang; double ruffle down front, sailor collar, turned over cuffs with ruffle, pleated front and back. Each. $0.55
Per dozen 5.94

32440 Boys' Shirt Waists, medium heavy stripe, cotton cheviot, double ruffle down front, sailor collar with ruffle, pleated front and back. Each .... $0.60 Per dozen 6.48

Boys' Blouse Waists.

Sizes, 4 to 13 years.

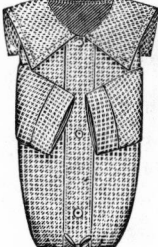

32442 Boys' Blouse Waists, fancy light ground cotton cheviot, sailor collar. Each........$0.30
Per dozen 3.24

32442

32444 Boys' Blouse Waists, plain black sateen, sailor collar. Each.....$0.35   Per dozen.... 3.78

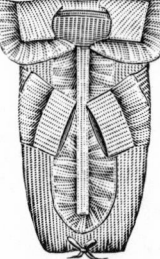

32446 Boys' Blouse Waists, light ground striped Chambray, double ruffle down front, sailor collar and turned over cuffs, with ruffle. Each..$0.40
Per dozen................. 4.32
32448 Boys' Blouse Waists, plain black sateen, double ruffle down front, sailor collar, with ruffle. Each.......$0.45
Per dozen................. 4.86

32446

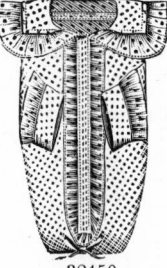

32450 Boys' Blouse Waists, soft finished percale, light ground, with combination of stripes and figures; double ruffle down front, sailor collar turned over cuffs, with ruffle. Each.....................$0.50
Per dozen................. 5.40

32450

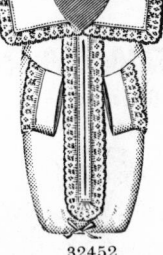

32452 Boys' Blouse Waists, fine white lawn, double row or colored narrow embroidery down front, sailor collar and turned over cuffs, trimmed with same. Colors: Navy blue or red embroidery. Each..$0.70
Per dozen................. 7.56

32452

Men's White Shirts.

32460 Men's White Shirts. "Our Leader," unlaundered, full lengths and widths, re-enforced front and back, linen bosom. Each............$0.35
3 for.......... 1.00
32462 Men's White Shirts. unlaundered, double re-enforced front and back, linen bosom. Each. .45
Per dozen 4 90
32464 Men's White Shirts, unlaundered, double re-enforced front and back, continuous facing on cuffs and back, made of New York mills muslin. Each.......................... .65
Per dozen................................... 7.00
32466 Men's White Shirts, unlaundered, double re-enforced front and back, continuous facing on cuffs and back. bosom lined with butchers' linen. One of the best shirts made. Each..... .95
Per dozen......................... 10 25
32468 Men's White Shirts, laundered, re-enforced front and back. Each.................... .75
Per dozen......................... 8.10
32470 Men's White Shirts, laundered, re-enforced front and back, made of New York mills cotton. Each.......................... .95
Per dozen......................... 10.25
32472 Men's White Shirts, laundered, re-enforced front and back, continuous facing on back and cuff, butchers' linen back on bosom. One of the best made. Each......... 1.25
Per dozen......................... 13.50

Men's Short Bosom Shirts.

32475 Men's White Laundered Shirts, the new short bosom 10 inches long, most comfortable bosom made, as it never wrinkles. Each.......$0.90
Per dozen......................... 9.72
32477 Men's White Laundered Shirts, double re-enforced front, 10 inch bosom. Each........ 1.20
Per doz........................... 13.00

Men's White and Fancy Dress Shirts.

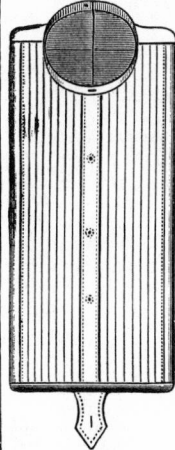

32479 Men's White Shirts laundered open front. Each ..$1.00
Per doz10.80
32481 Men's White Shirts, full dress, plaited front, made of Wamsutta muslin, re-enforced front. Each $1.25
Per doz13.50
32483 Men's White Dress Shirts, full linen bosom, open front and back, single front plait, handsomely embroidered in white
Each......................... 1.00
Per dozen....................10.80

32481

32483

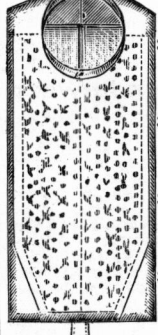

32485 Men's White Dress Shirts, full dress bosom, made from figured pique, open front and back, single front plait. Each.... 1.25
Per dozen....................13.50
32487 Men's White Laundered Shirts, open back, neat fancy colored striped bosom and attached cuffs. Each............-....$1.00
Per dozen....................10.80
32489 Men's White Laundered Shirts, open back, small polka dots on bosom and attached cuffs.
Each.........................$1.00
Per dozen....................10.80
32496 Men's Colored Laundered Shirts, open front and back, attached cuffs, neat pin stripes; plain white collars are worn but not given with these shirts. Each..$1.50

32485

32499 Men's Colored Laundered Shirts, open front and back, cuffs attached, medium colors. neat stripes; white collars are worn but not given with these shirts. Each.................. 1.50

Men's Fancy Colored Shirts.

32502 Men's Percale Shirts, medium narrow stripes, soft body, laundered collar and cuffs, attached, removable studs. Colors: pink or blue.
Each.................................$0.60
Per dozen......................... 6.48

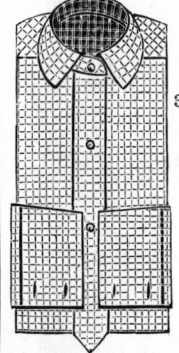

32504 Men's Percale Shirts white, ground small checks, soft body, laundered collars and cuffs attached, removable studs. Colors: Red, black, or blue.
Each.........................$ 0.95
Per dozen....................10.26

32504

32506 Men's Percale Shirts, blue, and white pin striped soft body, laundered collar and cuffs attached, removable studs. Each............ ...$ 1.00
Per dozen....................10.80
32508 Men's French Percale Shirts, broken checks and stripes, soft body, laundered collar and cuffs, pointed yoke back, Colors: Light dark, or medium tan. Each.................... 1.50
Per dozen.................... 16.20

Men's Fancy Laundered Percale Shirts.

32510 Men's Fancy Laundered Percale Shirts. Alternate medium and narrow stripes, attached collars and cuffs. Colors: Heliotrope, light blue or steel gray. Each..................$0.75
Per dozen......................... 8.10
32513 Men's Fancy Laundered Percale Shirts, white ground with small checks, one standing and one turned down collar, detached cuffs. Colors: Blue, red or black. Each.............. 1.00
Per dozen....................10.80

Shirts—Continued.

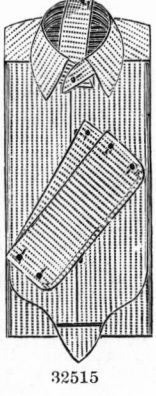

32515 Men's Fancy Laundered Percale Shirts, white ground with neat fancy stripes, one standing and one turned down collar, detached cuffs. Colors: Blue, red, or heliotrope. Each......$ 1.00
Per dozen....................10.80

32515

32517 Men's Fancy Laundered Percale Shirts, white ground, small broken check, one standing and one turned down collar, detached cuffs. Colors: Black or blue. Each..............$ 1.25
Per dozen................. 13.50

32517

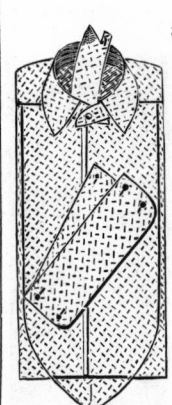

32519 Men's Fancy Laundered Percale Shirts, white ground with small figure, one standing and one turned-down collar, detached cuffs. Colors: Blue or black. Each..............$ 1.25
Per dozen................. 13.50
32521 Men's Fancy Laundered Percale Shirts, open front and back, one standing and one turned-down collar, detached cuffs, medium, narrow or hairline blue and white stripes.
Each.....................$ 1.35
Per dozen................. 14.58
32523 Men's Fancy Laundered Percale Shirts, open front and back, white ground with small black figure or dot, one standing and one turned-down collar, detached cuffs. Each ......$ 1.35
Per dozen................. 14.58
32525 Mens Fancy Laundered Percale Shirts, open front and back, narrow fancy stripes, one standing and one turned-down
32519 collar, detached reversible cuffs. Colors: Blue, chocolate or steel gray. Each..................$ 1.50
Per dozen................. 16.20
32527 Men's Fancy Laundered Percale Shirts. Open front and back. White ground, small check, one standing and one turned down collar, detached reversible cuffs. Colors: Blue or black. Each................ ....$ 1.50
Per dozen................16.20

Boys' White Shirts.

32529 Boys' White Shirts, unlaundered, re-inforced front, linen bosoms, sizes, 12 to 14.
Each.... ....$ .45
Per dozen..................... 4.86
32530 Boys' White Shirts, laundered, re-inforced front, linen bosoms, sizes, 12 to 14.
Each.......................... .65
Per dozen..................... 7.02

Boys' Fancy Percale Shirts.

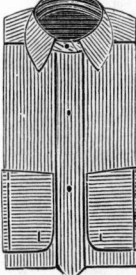

32531 Boys' Fancy Percale Shirts. Soft body, white ground with hairline stripes, attached, laundered collar and cuffs, removable studs. Colors: White, blue or black.
Each...........................$0.70
Per dozen 7.56

32532 Boys' Fancy Laundered Percale Shirts. White ground, narrow broken stripes; one standing and one turned down collar, detached cuffs. Colors: Black, blue or red.
Each...........................$ .95
Per dozen.....................10.26

Men's Night Shirts.

Weight of Night Shirts 12 ounces.

32534 Men's Fancy Trimmed Night Shirts, assorted, colored, embroidered.
Each $0.45
Per dozen 4.86
32536 Men's Plain White Night Shirts, made from fine muslin.
Each $0.60
Per dozen 6.48
32538 Men's Fancy Night Shirts, front trimmed with fancy embroidery; collar, cuffs and pocket stitched with silk.
Each $0.65
Per dozen 7.02
32540 Men's Fancy Night Shirts, made of fine quality muslin, wide silk embroidery down front; collar, cuffs and pocket stitched with silk.
Each $0.75
Per dozen 8.10

32542 Men's Fancy Night Shirts, made of fine quality muslin, handsome German design, silk embroidery down front, silk stitching on collar, pocket and cuffs. Each .... $ .90
Per dozen 9.72
32544 Men's Fancy Night Shirts, made of best quality muslin, beautiful scroll design of silk embroidery down front, pointed yoke, collar, pocket and cuffs stitched with silk. Each 1.00
Per dozen 10.80

Ladies' Summer Underwear.

Ladies' underwear weighs from 3 to 6 ounces according to size. Sizes, 3, 4, 5. No. 3 is small. Always mention size.

32550 Ladies' Jersey Ribbed Summer Vests, low neck and short sleeves. Each $0.06
Per dozen ...... .65
32552 Ladies' Ecru Jersey Ribbed Summer Vests, low neck and short sleeves, neck and armholes trimmed with cotton shell trimming Each $0.09
Per dozen 1.00

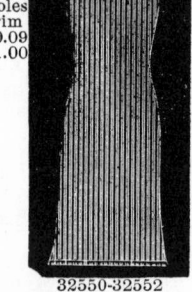

32550-32552

32554 Ladies' Ecru Jersey Ribbed Summer Vests, low V Shaped neck, short sleeves, white tape drawn through neck and armholes.
Each $0.14
Per dozen 1.51

32554

32556 Ladies' Ecru Jersey Ribbed Summer Vests, low square neck, combed Egyptian cotton, armholes and neck trimmed with narrow silk braid, bow of same.
Each $0.20
Per dozen 2.28

32556

32558 Ladies' Ecru Jersey Ribbed Summer Vests, short sleeves, handsome novelty front of fancy netted open work of Egyptian cotton; neck and armholes trimmed with narrow silk braid and bow of same.
Each $0.25
Per dozen 2.70

32558

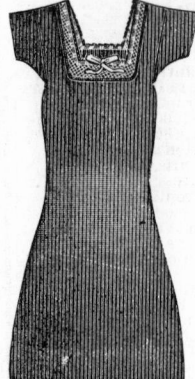

32560

32560 Ladies' Ecru Jersey Ribbed Summer Vests, low square neck, 1¼ sleeves, herringbone trimming around neck and armholes.
Each $0.25
Per dozen 2.70

32562 Ladies' Ecru Jersey Ribbed Summer Vests, high neck and long sleeves, silk cat stitching on neck. Each $0.45
Per dozen 4.90
32564 Ladies' White Gauze Summer Vests, high neck and short sleeves Each .... .25
Per dozen 2.70
32566 Ladies' White Gauze Summer Vests, high neck and long sleeves, silk trimmed neck.
Each .... .40
Per dozen 4.32

Children's Summer Underwear.

32568 Children's Jersey Ribbed Vests, low neck and short sleeves.

Ages	1 yr.	2 yr.	3 yr.	4 yr.	5 yr.
Sizes	12 in.	14 in.	16 in.	18 in.	20 in.
Price	4c.	5c.	6c.	7c.	8c.
Per doz.	$0.44	$0.54	$0.64	$0.74	$0.84
Ages		6 yr.	7 yr.	8 yr.	9 yr.
Sizes		22 in.	24 in.	26 in.	28 in.
Price		9c.	10c.	11c.	12c.
Per doz.		$0.94	$1.04	$1.14	$1.24

32570 Children's Jersey Ribbed Lisle Thread Vests, low neck and short sleeves, silk shell trimmed neck and armholes.

Ages	1 yr.	2 yr.	3 yr.	4 yr.	5 yr.
Sizes	12 in.	14 in.	16 in.	18 in.	20 in.
Price	8c.	9c.	10c.	11c.	12c.
Per doz.	$0.86	$0.96	$1.06	$1.16	$1.26
Ages		6 yr.	7 yr.	8 yr.	9 yr.
Sizes		22 in.	24 in.	26 in.	28 in.
Price		13c.	14c.	15c.	16c.
Per doz.		$1.36	$1.46	$1.56	$1.66

32572 Children's White Gauze Undervests, high neck and long sleeves.

Sizes	16 in.	18 in.	20 in.	22 in.	24 in.
Price	12c.	13c.	14c.	15c.	16c.
Per doz.	$1.30	$1.40	$1.50	$1.60	$1.70
Sizes	26 in.	28 in.	30 in.	32 in.	34 in.
Price	17c.	18c.	19c.	20c.	21c.
Per doz.	$1.80	$1.90	$2.00	$2.10	$2.20

32574 Ladies' Ecru Jersey Ribbed Sleeveless Summer Combination Suits knee lengths.
Per suit $0.45
Per dozen 4.90
32575 Ladies' Ecru Jersey Ribbed Sleeveless Summer Combination Suits, ankle lengths.
Each .... .50
Per dozen 5.40

Men's Summer Underwear.

Weight, 4 to 6 ounces.
According to Size. Always Mention Size Wanted.

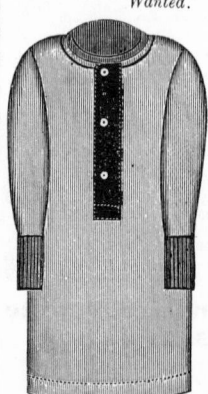

32574-32575

32578 Men's Gauze Undershirts, French ribbed neck.
Each $0.25
Per dozen 2.70

32580 Men's Gauze Drawers to match above.
Each $0.25
Per dozen 2.70
32582 Men's Gauze Undershirts, natural mixed color; fancy French ribbed neck. Each .... .30
Per dozen 3.24

32584 Men's Gauze Drawers, to match above.
Each .... $$.30
Per dozen 3.24
32586 Men's Summer Weight Balbriggan Undershirts, French ribbed neck. Each .... .35
Per dozen 3.78
32588 Men's Summer Weight Balbriggan Drawers, to match above. Each .... .35
Per dozen 3.78
32590 Men's Summer Weight Tan Brown Balbriggan Undershirts, satin front, silk stitching around neck. Each .... .45
Per dozen 4.86
32592 Men's Summer Weight Tan Brown Balbriggan Drawers, to match above. Each ...... .45
Per dozen 4.86
32594 Men's Summer Weight Light Blue Balbriggan Undershirts, French ribbed neck.
Each .... .45
Per dozen 4.86
32596 Men's Summer Weight light Blue Balbriggan Drawers, to match above. Each 0.45
Per dozen 4.86
32598 Men's Summer Weight, Genuine French Balbriggan Undershirts, fine gauze. Each ..... .50
Per dozen 5.40
32600 Men's Summer Weight, Genuine French Balbriggan Drawers to match above. Each ..... .50
Per dozen 5.40
32602 Men's Medium Weight, Natural Wool Color Undershirts. Each ...... $0.45 Per dozen 4.85
32604 Men's Medium Weight, Natural Wool Color Drawers to match above. Each .... .45
Per dozen 4.85
32606 Men's Medium Weight, Natural Wool Undershirts. Each ..... $0.70 Per dozen 7.56
32608 Men's Medium Weight, Natural Wool Drawers, to match above. Each .... .70
Per dozen 7.56
32610 Men's Unbleached Drilling Drawers, patent knit anklets Each .... .40
Per dozen 4.32
32612 Men's Bleached Jean or Drill Drawers, patent knit anklets. Each .... .45
Per dozen 4.86

Boys' Summer Underwear.

Sizes 2½ to 34.

ALWAYS MENTION SIZE.

32616 Boys' Gauze Balbriggan Color Undershirts, French ribbed neck. Each .... .25
Per dozen 2.70
32618 Boys' Gauze Balbriggan Color Drawers, to match above. Each .... .25
Per dozen 2.70
32620 Boys' Gauze Natural Mixed Undershirts, French ribbed neck .... .25
Per dozen 2.70
32622 Boys' Gauze Natural Mixed Drawers, to match above. Each .... .25
Per dozen 2.70

WINTER UNDERWEAR.

Infants' Wool Shirts.

Average weight of infants' shirts, 2 ozs

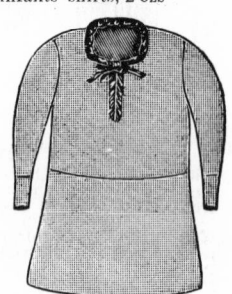

32768-32769   32770.

32768 Infants' Wrapper Vests, cream white, fine derby ribbed, ⅓ wool.

Length	10	12	14	16	18	20	inch
Sizes	1	2	3	4	5	6	
Price, each	20c	25c	30c	35c	40c	45c	

32769 Infants' Saxony Wool, Fine Derby Ribbed Knit Vests.

Length	10	12	14	16	18	20	inch.
Sizes	1	2	3	4	5	6	
Price, each	33c	37c	41c	45c	50c	55c	

32770 Infants White Saxony Wool Knit Vests or Shirts.

Length	10	12	14	16	18	20	inch
Size	1	2	3	4	5	6	
Price, each	25c	30c	35c	40c	45c	50c	
Per doz	$2.70	$3.24	$3.78	$4.32	$4.86	$5.40	

We Are Prepared...

To Meet Almost
✦ Any Want in
MEN'S UNDERWEAR.

Average Scale of Sizes in Children's Underwear

Vests. Sizes.	For age.	Pantalets. Sizes.	For age.
16 in.	1 year and under.	16 in.	1 to 1½ years.
18 in.	1 to 1½ years.	18 in.	1½ to 2 years.
20 in.	1½ to 2 years.	20 in.	2 to 4 years.
22 in.	2 to 4 years.	22 in.	4 to 6 years.
24 in.	4 to 6 years.	24 in.	6 to 8 years.
26 in.	6 to 8 years.	26 in.	8 to 10 years.
28 in.	8 to 10 years.	28 in.	10 to 12 years.
30 in.	10 to 12 years,	30 in.	12 to 13 years.
32 in.	12 to 13 years.	32 in.	13 to 14 years.
34 in.	13 to 14 years.	34 in.	13 to 14 years.

Children's Underwear.

Weight of children's underwear, 4 to 10 ounces, according to size.

32771 Children's Gray Mixed Merino Undershirts.
Sizes, 16 18 20 22 24 26 28 30 32 34 in.
Price, 6c 9c 12c 15c 18c 21c 24c 27c 30c 33c

32772 Children's Gray Mixed Merino Pantalets.
Sizes, 16 18 20 22 24 26 28 30 32 34 in.
Price, 6c 9c 12c 15c 18c 21c 24c 27c 30c 33c

32773 Children's White Merino Undershirts.
Sizes, 16 18 20 22 24 26 28 30 32 34 in.
Price, 9c 12c 15c 18c 21c 24c 27c 30c 33c 36c

32774 Children's White Merino Pantalets.
Sizes, 16 18 20 22 24 26 28 30 32 34 in.
Price, 9c 12c 15c 18c 21c 24c 27c 30c 33c 36c

32775 Children's Light Gray Mixed Merino Undershirts.
Sizes, 16 18 20 22 24 26 28 30 32 34 in.
Price. 11c 14c 17c 20c 23c 26c 29c 32c 35c 38c

32776 Children's Light Gray Mixed Merino Pantalets.
Sizes, 16 18 20 22 24 26 28 30 32 34 in.
Price, per pair—
11c 14c 17c 20c 23c 26c 29c 32c 35c 38c

32778 Children's All Wool Scarlet Undershirts.
Sizes, 16 18 20 22 24 26 28 30 32 34 in.
Price, 15c 21c 27c 33c 39c 45c 51c 57c 63c 69c

32779 Children's All Wool Scarlet Pantalets.
Sizes, 16 18 20 22 24 26 28 30 32 34 in.
Price, per pair—
15c 21c 27c 33c 39c 45c 51c 57c 63c 69c

32780 Children's Two-thirds Wool Undershirt, light gray mixed colors.
Sizes, 16 18 20 22 24 26 28 30 32 34 in.
Price, 18c 24c 30c 36c 42c 48c 54c 60c 66c 72c

32781 Children's Two-thirds Wool Pantalets, light gray mixed colors.
Sizes, 16 18 20 22 24 26 28 30 32 34 in.
Price, per pair—
18c 24c 30c. 36c 42c 48c 54c 60c 66c 72c

32782 Children's Extra Fine Natural Wool Vests, light gray color.
Sizes, 16 18 20 22 24 26 28 30 32 34 in.
Price, 35c 41c 47c 53c 59c 65c 71c 77c 83c 89c

32783 Children's Extra Fine Natural Wool Pantalets to match above.
Sizes, 16 18 20 22 24 26 28 30 32 34 in.
Price, per pair—
35c 41c 47c 53c 59c 65c 71c 77c 83c 89c

32784 Children's Knit Undershirts, fine grade, sanitary brown, mixed cotton, with heavy white fleece on inside.
Sizes, 16 18 20 22 24 26 28 30 32 34 in.
Price, 25c 28c 31c 34c 37c 40c 43c 46c 49c 52c

32785 Children's Knit Drawers, to match above.
Sizes....18 20 22 24 26 28 30 32 34 in.
Price, per pair—
28c 31c 34c 37c 40c 43c 46c 49c 52c

32788 Boys' Scotch Mixed Undershirts, sizes, 24 to 34. Each.........$0.40 Per dozen..........$4.32

32789 Boys' Scotch Mixed Drawers, sizes 24 to 34. Per pair.........$0.40 Per dozen..........$4.32

Ladies' Jersey Ribbed Vests and Pants.

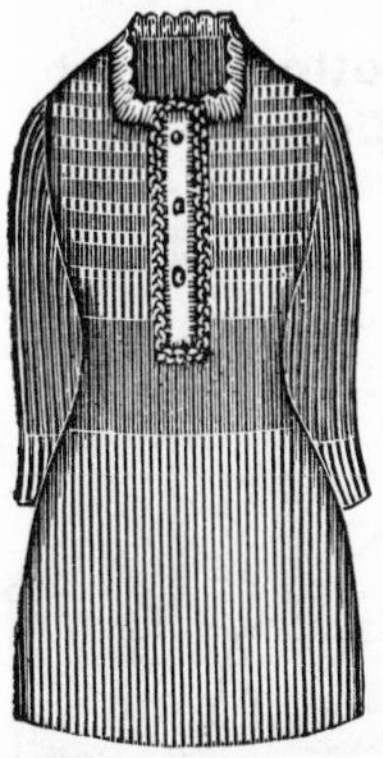

32790 Ladies' Cream Colored Jersey Knit Ribbed Vests.
Each....................$0.20
Per dozen.............. 2.16
No drawers to match above.

32792 Ladies' Jersey Knit Ribbed Vests, heavy Egyptian cotton, natural wool color,
Each....................$0.25
Per dozen............... 2.70

32793 Ladies' Drawers or Pants to match above.
Per pair..................$0.25
Per dozen.............. 2.70

32794 Ladies' Jersey Knit Ribbed Vests, heavy weight Egyptian cotton, natural wool color. Each.......$0.35
Per dozen 3.78

32795 Ladies' Jersey Knit Ribbed Drawers or Pants to match above. Each....$0.35
Per dozen............ 3.78

32796 Ladies' Jersey Knit Ribbed Ecru Vests, double combed Egyptian cotton, fancy front, silk ribbon neck. Each. ..$0.40

32797 Ladies' Jersey Knit Ribbed Drawers to match above. Each.......... .40

32798 Ladies' Jersey Knit Ribbed Vests, one-third wool, silver gray color. Each............. .50
Per dozen........... 5.40

32799 Ladies' Drawers or Pants to match above.
Each......... .50
Per dozen. 5.40

32800 Ladies' Natural Wool Color Jersey Knit Ribbed Vests, one-half worsted. Each........ .70
Per dozen.......... 7.56

32801 Ladies' Drawers or Pants to match above.
Each .70
Per dozen.......... 7.56

Ladies' Underwear—Continued.

32802 Ladies' Natural Wool Jersey Knit Ribbed Vests, all wool. Each......................... 1.00
Per dozen.............................. 10.80

32803 Ladies' Drawers or Pants to match above.
Each.................................... 1.00
Per dozen............................... 10.80

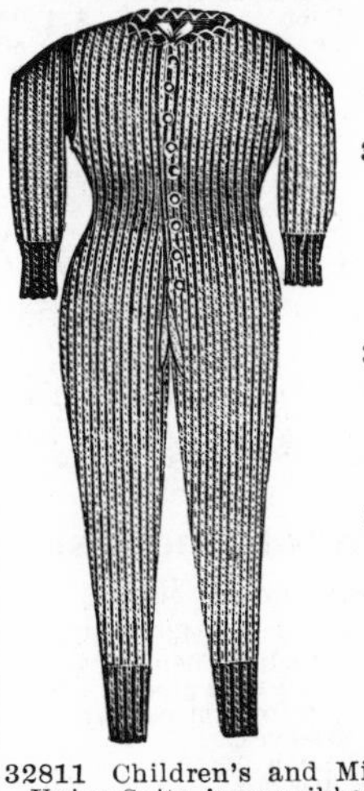

32808 Ladies' Combination or Union Suits, jersey ribbed, heavy weight cotton; natural wool color; small, medium and large.
Per suit.............$0.50
Per dozen suits...... 5.40

32809 Ladies' Combination or Union Suits, jersey ribbed, natural wool color, one-half worsted.
Per suit.............$1.00
Per dozen suits......10.80

32810 Ladies' Combination or Union Suits. Jersey ribbed, all wool, natural wool color; sizes, 2, 3, and 4. Per suit...... $ .10

32811 Children's and Misses' Combination or Union Suits, jersey ribbed, natural wool color.

Ages..................	5 and 6.	7 and 8.	9 and 10.
Sizes..................	1	2	3
Per suit..............	$0.60	$0.75	$0.90
Ages..................	11 and 12	13 and 14	
Sizes..................	4	5	
Per suit..............	$1.05	$1 20	

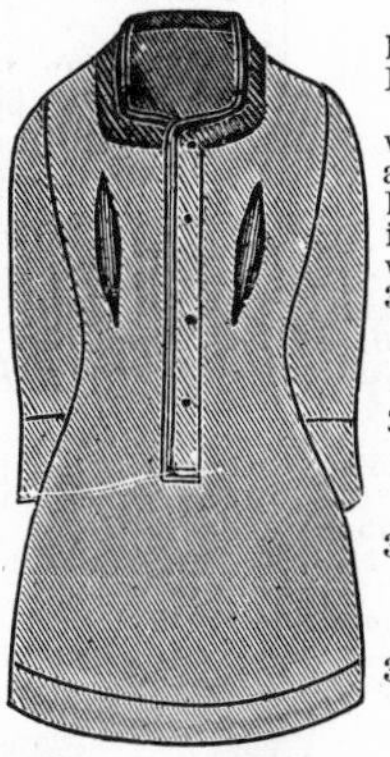

White Merino, scarlet camel's hair and natural wool vests. Price governs quality.

Weight of all ladies' underwear, 10 to 13 oz, per garment, according to size and quality. Ladies' sizes run from 28 to 40 ins. Always mention size wanted.

32812 Ladies' White Merino Vests or Wrappers, French neck. Each............$0.40
Per dozen............... 4.50

32813 Ladies' White Merino Drawers or Pants.
Each...................$0.40
Per dozen.............. 4.50

32814 Ladies' White Merino Vests or Wrappers, French neck, Each...........$0.50
Per dozen............... 5.40

32815 Ladies' White Merino Drawers or Pants. Each$.0.50
Per dozen.............. 5.40

Ladies' Natural Wool Underwear.

Always mention size wanted.

	Each.	Per doz.
32816 Ladies' Light Gray Mixed Merino Vests or Wrappers, natural wool color..................................	$0.45	$4.86
32817 Ladies' Light Gray Mixed Merino Drawers or Pants, natural wool color..	.45	4.86
32818 Ladies' Light Gray Mixed, or Natural Wool Color, Merino Vests or Wrappers..	.70	7.56
32819 Ladies' Drawers or Pants, to match above..	.70	7.56
32820 Ladies' Natural Wool Wrappers or Vests..................................	1.00	10.80
32821 Ladies' Natural Wool Drawers or Pants....................................	1.00	10.80

Ladies' Scarlet Underwear.

Always mention size wanted.

Sizes, 28 to 40 inches.	Each.	Per doz.
32822 Ladies' Scarlet Wrappers or Vests, all wool..................................	$0.75	$8.10
32823 Ladies' Scarlet Drawers or Pants, all wool..................................	.75	8.10
32824 Ladies' Scarlet Wrappers or Vests, all wool..................................	1.00	10.80
32825 Ladies' Scarlet Drawers or Pants, all wool..................................	1.00	10.80

Ladies' Camel's Hair Underwear.

Size, 28 to 38 inches.	Each.	Per doz.
32826 Ladies' Camel's Hair Mixture Wrappers or Vests........................	$1.00	$10.80
32827 Ladies' Camel's Hair Mixture Drawers or Pants..............	1.00	10.80

(Camel's Hair Mixture is very light brown.)

N. B.—Ladies' Black Wool Underwear we do not quote this season, as it does not give good satisfaction.

When ordering goods, please be sure to give name of article wanted as well as catalogue number and price.

Men's Undershirts and Drawers.

(Weight of Men's Underwear averages from 13 to 18 ounces, according to size and quality.) Men's sizes run from 34 to 44 inches in shirts, and 30 to 42 inches in drawers. *Always mention size wanted.*

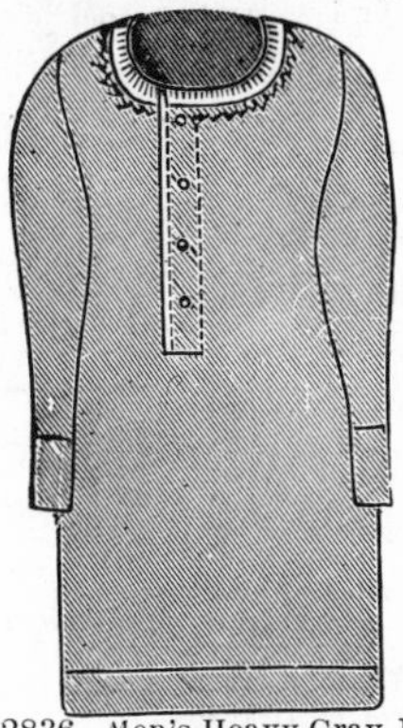

32832 Men's Heavy Scotch Gray Mixed Undershirts.
Each............. $0.40
Per dozen......... 4.32

32833 Men's Drawers, to match above.
Per pair............$0.40
Per dozen.......... 4.32

32834 Men's Plain White Merino Underhirts.
Each...............$0.40
Per dozen.......... 4.32

32835 Men's Plain White Merino Drawers.
Each...............$0.40
Per dozen.......... 4.32

	Each.	Per doz.
32836 Men's Heavy Gray Ribbed Undershirts..........................	$0.45	$4.86
32837 Men's Heavy Gray Ribbed Drawers.	.45	4.86
32838 Men's Fancy Striped Merino Undershirts..........................	.50	5.40
32839 Men's Fancy Striped Merino Drawers..........................	.50	5.40
32840 Men's Natural Wool Color Undershirts, with white fleece on inside; heavy weight..........................	.50	5.40
32841 Men's Drawers, to match above....	.50	5.5C
32844 Men's Natural Wool Undershirts, heavy weight, ribbed, for the northwest.	.65	7.00
32845 Men's Drawers, to match above...	.65	7.00
32846 Men's Light Brown or Camel's Hair Mixture Undershirts, ribbed cuff bottom..........................	.65	7.00
32847 Men's Light Brown or Camel's Hair Mixture Drawers..................	.65	7.00
32848 Men's Plain White Merino Undershirts..........................	.70	7.56
32849 Men's Plain White Merino Drawers	.70	7.56
32850 Men's Natural Wool Undershirts, ribbed cuff bottom, 65 per cent. wool...	.75	8.10
32851 Men's Natural Wool (65 per cent. wool) Drawers..........................	.75	8.10
32852 Men's Natural Wool Color Undershirts, with heavy white fleece on inside	.75	8.10
32853 Men's Drawers, to match above....	.75	8.10
32856 Men's Brown Mixed Blizzard Undershirt, best garment ever made for the northwestern and cold climates or lumber districts..........................	.90	9.72
32857 Men's Drawers, to match above...	.90	9.72
32858 Men's Fine All Wool Camel's Hair. Undershirts, drab mixed..........	1.00	10.80
32859 Men's Fine All Wool Camel's Hair Drawers, drab mixed..................	1.00	10.80
32862 Men's Natural Wool Undershirts, 90 per cent. wool, rib cuff bottom, heavy and fine, splendid value	1.00	10.80
32863 Men's Drawers, to match above...	1.00	10.80
32864 Men's Plain White Merino Undershirts..........................	1.00	10.80
32865 Men's Plain White Merino Drawers	1.00	10.80
32866 Men's Natural Wool Color Undershirts, with heavy white wool fleece on inside..........................	1.00	10.80
32867 Men's Natural Wool Color Drawers, with heavy white wool fleece on inside..........................	1.00	10.80
32872 Men's All Wool Natural Wool Color Undershirts, rib cuff bottom, heavy, fine and fluffy..................	1.25	13.50
32873 Men's Drawers, to match above...	1.25	13.50
32874 Men's Camel's Hair Color Undershirts, with extra heavy wool fleece on inside. Very warm..............	1.50	16.20
32875 Men's Camel's Hair Color Drawers, with extra heavy wool fleece on inside. Very warm..................	1.50	16.20

Men's Scarlet Undershirts and Drawers.

	Each.	Per doz.
32876 Men's All Wool Scarlet Knit Undershirts..........................	$0.75	$8.10
32877 Men's. All Wool Scarlet Knit Drawers..........................	.75	8.10
32878 Men's Undershirts, scarlet and white mixed, heavy, two threads red wool, one thread white cotton.........	.75	8.10
32879 Men's Drawers, to match above..	.75	8.10
32880 Men's All Wool Scarlet Knit Undershirts, heavy and fine. Medicated...	1.50	16.20
32881 Men's All Wool Scarlet Knit Drawers, heavy and fine. Medicated..	1.50	16.20

Men's Fine Heavy Underwear.

	Each.	Per doz.
32882 Men's Extra Heavy Natural Wool Undershirts, with fleece on inside, ribbed cuff bottom..................	$2.00	$21.60
32883 Men's Extra Heavy Natural Wool Drawers, to match above..............	2.00	21.60
32884 Men's Extra Heavy All Wool Ribbed Undershirts, light tan color, silk trimmed..........................	2.00	21.60
32885 Men's Extra Heavy All Wool Ribbed Drawers, to match above........	2.00	21.60

Men's Full Fashioned and Full Regular Made Undershirts and Drawers.

32886   Men's Undershirts, medium weight, silk mixed; made from very fine Australian wool Each, to close......................................$2.00

32887   Men's Drawers, to match above............ Each, to close.................................... 2.00

Men's Cotton Flannel Undershirts and Drawers.

Always Mention Size Wanted.

	Each.	Per doz.
32891 Men's Bleached Cotton Flannel Undershirts............................	$0.75	$8.10
32893 Men's Bleached Cotton Flannel Drawers.................................	.75	8.10
32895 Men's Unbleached Cotton Flannel Undershirts............................	.50	5.40
32897 Men's Unbleached Cotton Flannel Drawers.................................	.50	5.40
32899 Men's Unbleached Cotton Flannel Undershirts............................	.75	8.10
32900 Men's Unbleached Cotton Flannel Drawers.................................	.75	8.10

Ladies' Muslin Underwear.

Ladies' White Cotton Drawers.

Weight of Ladies' Drawers, 5 to 8 Ounces.

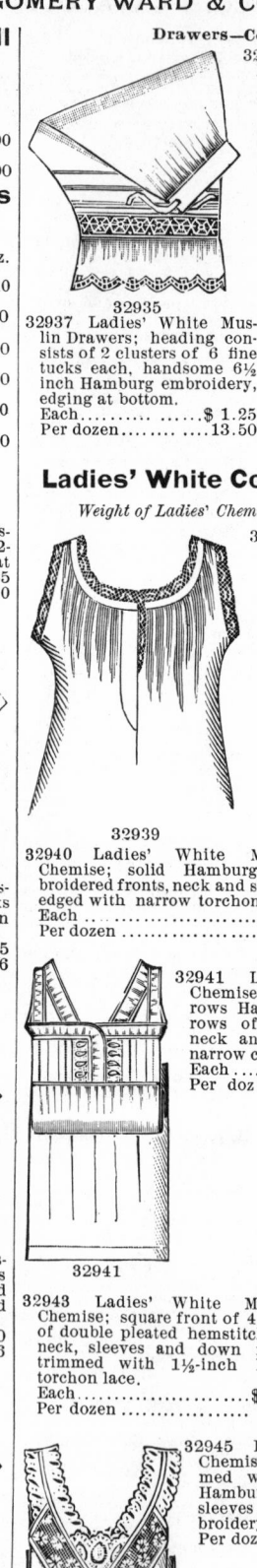

32917   Ladies' White Muslin Drawers, 3 tucks and 2-inch cambric ruffle at bottom. Each......$0.25 Per dozen........... 2.70

32917

32921   Ladies' White Muslin Drawers, cluster of 3 fine tucks, trimmed with 1½-inch Hamburg edging. Each.........$0.35 Per dozen........... 3.78

32921

32923   Ladies' White Muslin Drawers, 4 fine tucks and 2¼ inch linen torchon lace at bottom. Each.................$0.45 Per dozen........... 4.86

32923

32926   Ladies' White Muslin Drawers, 3 clusters of 3 fine tucks each, and 3½-inch Hamburg edging at bottom. Each.....$0.55 Per dozen........... 5.94

32926

32928   Ladies' White Muslin Drawers; two clusters of 2 fine tucks each and 3-inch fine, hemstitched embroidery at bottom. Each.............$0.70 Per dozen........... 7.56

32928

32930   Ladies' White Muslin Drawers; two clusters of 4 fine tucks each, bottom trimmed with handsome 6 inch Hamburg embroidered edging. Each.................$0.85 Per dozen........... 9.18

32930

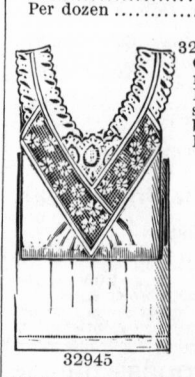

32933   Ladies' Lawn Drawers; heading of 1-inch fine valenciennes lace, inserting between 6 fine tucks, 3-inch valenciennes lace edging at bottom. Each..............$ 0.95 Per dozen..........10.27

32933

Drawers—Continued.

32935   Ladies' White Muslin Drawers; heading of 1-inch fine Hamburg insertion and 3 clusters of fine tucks, bottom trimmed with 3 inch Hamburg embroidered ruffle. Each................$ 1.00 Per dozen.....   ......10.80

32935

32937   Ladies' White Muslin Drawers; heading consists of 2 clusters of 6 fine tucks each, handsome 6½ inch Hamburg embroidery, edging at bottom. Each......... ......$ 1.25 Per dozen........ ....13.50

32937

Ladies' White Cotton Chemise.

Weight of Ladies' Chemise is 7 to 10 ounces.

32939   Ladies' White Muslin Chemise, trimmed with crochet edging on front, neck band and sleeves. Each......   . ...$0.25 Per doz............ 2.70

32939

32940   Ladies' White Muslin Chemise; solid Hamburg embroidered fronts, neck and sleeves edged with narrow torchon lace. Each ....$0.35 Per dozen 3.78

32940

32941   Ladies' White Muslin Chemise; front trimmed with 2 rows Hamburg insertion and 4 rows of 1¼-inch hemstitching, neck and sleeves trimmed with narrow cambric ruffle. Each .... $0.45 Per dozen................... 4.86

32941

32943   Ladies' White Muslin Chemise; square front of 4 rows of double pleated hemstitching, neck, sleeves and down front trimmed with 1½-inch linen torchon lace. Each........................$0.65 Per dozen 7.02

3_943

32945   Ladies' White Muslin Chemise, V shaped front, trimmed with handsome 1½-inch Hamburg insertion. Neck and sleeves edged with narrow embroidery. Each.............$0.85 Per dozen................... 9 18

32945

32947   Ladies' White Cambric Chemise; solid front of fine Valenciennes lace, with narrow tucks and herringbone trimming, and 1½ inch valenciennes lace on neck and sleeves. Each...... .... $0 95 Per dozen................. 10.26

32947

Chemise—Continued.

32950   Ladies' White Cambric Chemise, front formed by handsome solid embroidery insertion, and eight fine tucks, neck and sleeves trimmed with narrow Hamburg edging. Each..$ 1.20 Per dozen................. 12.96

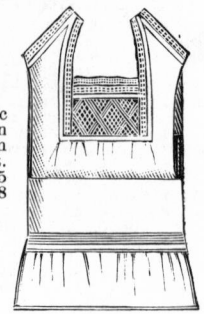

32950

Ladies' Cambric Skirt Chemise.

Weight, 6 to 8 Ounces.

32953   Ladies' White Cambric Skirt Chemise, solid torchon yoke, edged with torchon lace, tucked and ruffled skirt. Each.................$0.85 Per dozen........ ..... 9.18

32953

32955   Ladies' White Cambric Skirt Chemise, solid Hamburg yoke, edged with Hamburg, edge, skirt trimmed with Hamburg edge 1½ inches wide. Each.... ...   .$ 1.10 Per dozen.................11.88

32955

32957   Ladies' White Cambric Skirt Chemise, linen torchon yoke, front trimmed with narrow ribbon, edged with torchon lace; two clusters of three tucks each and ruffle on skirt. Each....................$ 1.25 Per dozen. 13.50

32957

32959   Ladies' White Cambric Chemise, V-shaped front formed by two ruffles of handsome three-inch Hamburg embroidery, laced with narrow feather-edge silk ribbon; neck and sleeves trimmed, with embroidery. Each.......................$ 1.30 Per dozen........... 14.04

32959

Ladies' White Cotton Night Dresses or Gowns.

Weight of Ladies' Gowns is about 10 to 16 ounces.

32961   Ladies' White Muslin Night Dress or Gowns, neck, sleeves and front, trimmed with narrow Hamburg edging, rolling collar and turned over cuffs. Each.........$0.45 Per dozen............ 4.86

33961

32963   Ladies' White Muslin Night Dress or Gown, Mother Hubbard back, V shaped front of 2½-inch Hamburg embroidery, raised shoulders, narrow Hamburg edging on neck and sleeves. Each..$0.60 Per dozen.............................. 6.40

32963

Night Dresses—Continued.

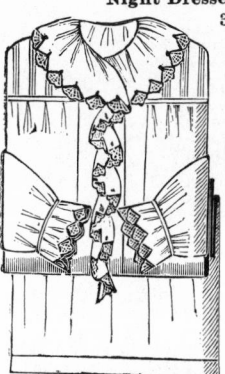

32965 Ladies' Muslin Night Dress or Gown, Mother Hubbard style, with Jarbot front of embroidered ruffle, rolling collar edged with narrow embroidery, raised shoulders, ½-inch Hamburg edging on sleeves. Each. $0.70 Per doz. $7.56

32967 Ladies' White Muslin Night Dress or Gown' Mother Hubbard style, solid tucked circular front, trimmed with 2-inch cambric ruffle and herringbone stitching, raised shoulders, cambric ruffle on neck and sleeves. Each. $0.75 Per doz. $8.10

32969 Ladies' White Muslin Night Dress or gown, Mother Hubbard back, front trimmed with 2 rows of linen torchon insertion and 4 clusters of 6 fine tucks each, neck and sleeves trimmed with narrow torchon, lace, raised shoulders. Each.... $0.90 Per dozen............ 9.72

32971 Ladies' White Muslin Night Dress or Gown, Mother Hubbard back, raised shoulders, 2 rows of 2½-inch fine Hamburg insertion, 4 rows of 6 fine tucks each handsome 1½-inch embroidery on neck, down front and sleeves, with herringbone stitching. Each......... $0.95 Per dozen............10.26

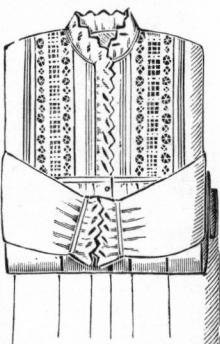

32973 Ladies' Muslin Night Dress or Gown, Mother Hubbard style, square front yoke of 2 rows of Hamburg insertion and 4 alternate rows of fine tucks, and 2-inch Hamburg ruffle, raised shoulders, neck and sleeves trimmed with embroidery, 4 fine tucks on cuff. Each..... $1.00 Per dozen............10.80

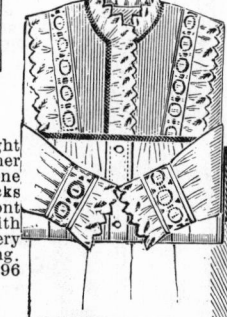

32975 Ladies' Muslin Night Dress or Gown, Mother Hubbard style, Keystone shaped front of fine tucks and insertion, neck front and sleeves trimmed with fine Hamburg embroidery and herringbone stitching. Each.. $1.20 Doz. $12.96

Night Dresses—Continued.

32977 Ladies' Muslin Night Dress or Gown, Mother Hubbard style, pleated back, raised shoulders, yoke of alternate rows of fine tuc ing, embroidered Jarbot ruffle down front, circular turned down embroidered collar. Hamburg ruffle on sleeves. Each................. $1.25 Per dozen............13.50

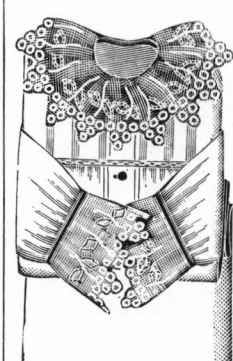

32981 Ladies' Muslin Night Dress or Gown; Mother Hubbard style, raised shoulders, yoke of 6 alternate rows of fine tucks and herringbone trimming, handsome embroidered ruffle collar and 5 inch edging on sleeves. Each............ $1.40 Per dozen..........15.12

32984 Ladies' Cambric Night Dress or Gown, Mother Hubbard back, raised shoulders, circular shaped yoke, trimmed fine with valenciennes lace edging and insertion, alternate rows of fine tucks, neck and sleeves, trimmed with valenciennes lace. Each... $1.45 Per dozen 15.66

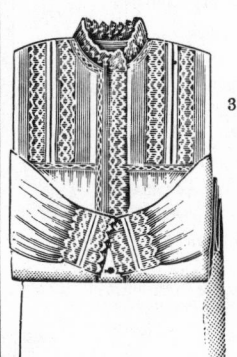

32987 Ladies' Muslin Night Dress or Grown, Mother Hubbard style, raised shoulders, yoke formed of 4 clusters of 10 fine tucks each and alternate rows of fine Hamburg edging and 2 rows of hemstitching, 1½ inch Hamburg embroidery on neck, down front and sleeves. Each................. $1.50 Per dozen 16.20

32889 Ladies' Cambric Night Dress or Gown, Mother Hubbard style, pleated back, raised shoulders, V shaped neck, solid front yoke of linen torchon lace, 4 alternate rows of herringbone trimming, sleeves and neck trimmed with same. Each. $1.75 Doz. $18.90

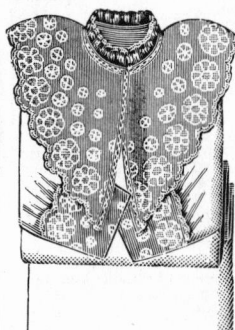

32993 Ladies' Muslin Night Dress or Gown, Morher Hubbard style, handsome pointed embroidered collar extending over shoulders, dainty turned over embroidered cuffs, neck trimmed with narrow Hamburg edge and herringbone; raised shoulders. Each...... $1.95 Per dozen 21.06

Ladies' Skirts—Continued.

Ladies' White Cotton Skirts.

Weight of ladies' skirts is 8 to 16 ounces.

32995 Ladies' White Muslin Skirts: heading of 3 tucks, with 5½-inch cambric ruffle at bottom. Each............$0.50 Per dozen...... 5 40

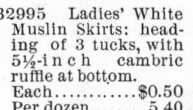

32997 Ladies' White Muslin Skirts; heading of 4 fine tucks, with 3½-inch torchon lace at bottom. Each.............$0.65 Per dozen......... 7.02

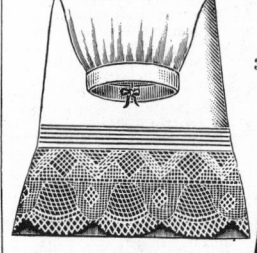

32999 Ladies' White Muslin Skirts; 4 fine tucks for heading, bottom trimmed with 5¼-inch Hamburg edging. Each......$0.75 Per dozen........ 8.10

33001 Ladies' White Muslin Skirts; heading of 4 fine tucks, with 10-inch fine Hamburg embroidery at bottom. Each............. $0.95 Per dozen.........10.26

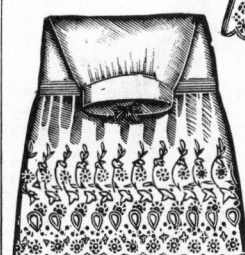
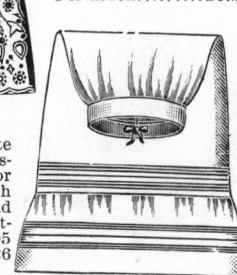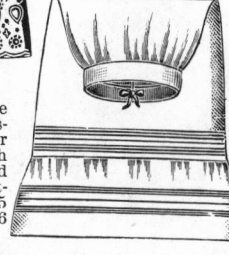

33003 Ladies' White Muslin Skirts; two clusters of 4 tucks each for heading, with 7½-inch fine cambric ruffle and alternate tucks at bottom. Each........$0.95 Per dozen.........10.26

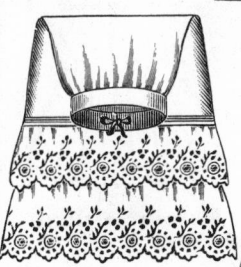
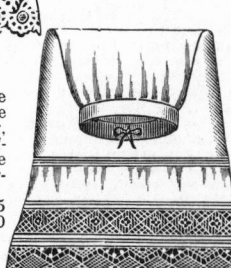

33007 Ladies' White Muslin Skirts, heading of 3 fine tucks, 2 rows of 3½-inch each Hamburg embroidered edging at bottom. Each........... $1.00 Per dozen...... 10.80

33009 Ladies' White Muslin Skirts, three fine tucks for heading, 4-inch fine cambric ruffle and two alternate rows of wide linen torchon lace at bottom. Each .... $1.25 Per dozen........ 13.50

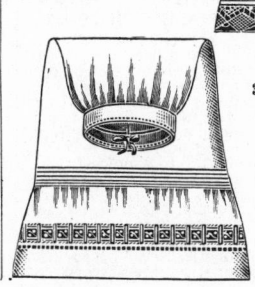

33012 Ladies' White Muslin Skirts, heading of 4 narrow tucks and 11-inch embroidered hemstitched flounce at bottom. Each... ....$1.45 Per dozen....... 15.66

Ladies' Skirts—Continued.

33014 Ladies' White Muslin Skirts, 6-inch cambric ruffle, with 3 fine tucks and 7-inch fine Valenciennes lace edging at bottom, with cambric dust ruffle.
Each........... $ 1.65
Per dozen....... 17.82

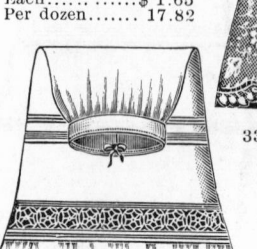

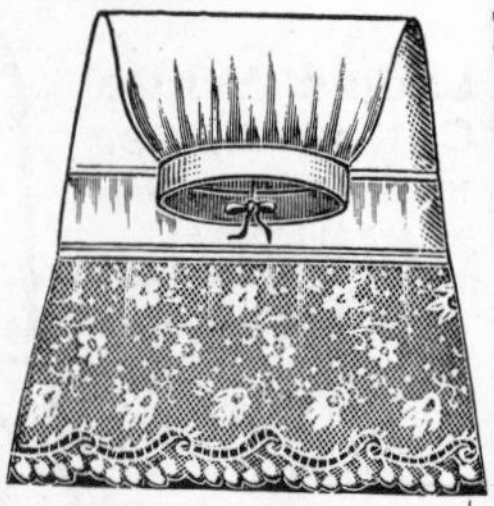

33017 Ladies' White Muslin Skirts, heading of two clusters of 4 fine tucks each, with handsome 13-inch embroidered cambric flounce, with alternate rows of tucks and Hamburg edging at bottom.
Each.......... $ 1.75
Per dozen...... 18.90

Ladies' Corset Covers.

Prices govern quality of muslin.
33018 Ladies' White Muslin Corset Covers, made plain. Each.......$0.16
Per dozen........ 1.73

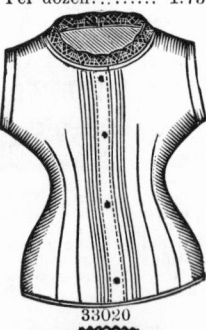

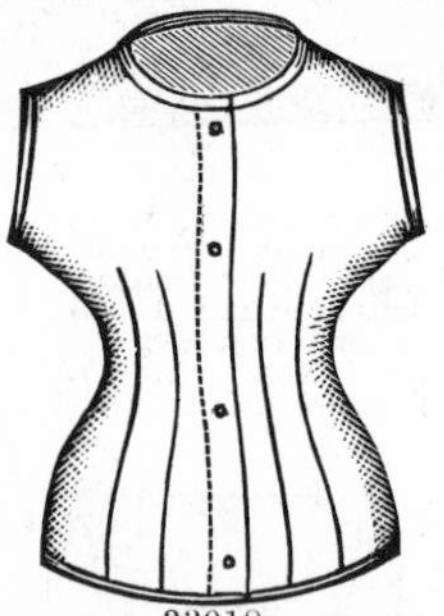

33020 Ladies' White Muslin Corset Cover, neck trimmed with trochon lace and six fine tucks down the front.
Each........ $0.23
Per dozen.......... 2.49

33022 Ladies' White Cambric Corset Covers, V shaped front trimmed with Hamburg edge.
Each................$0.33
Per dozen.......... 3.57

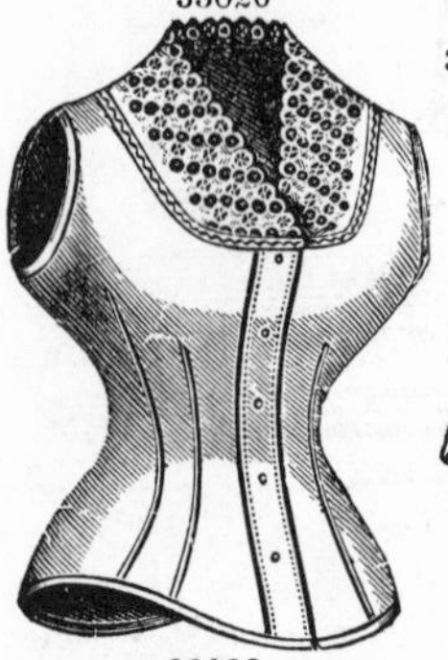

33024 Ladies' White Cambric Corset Covers; low neck, solid Hamburg yoke, edged with herringbone stitching. Each.....$0.50
Per dozen.......... 5.40

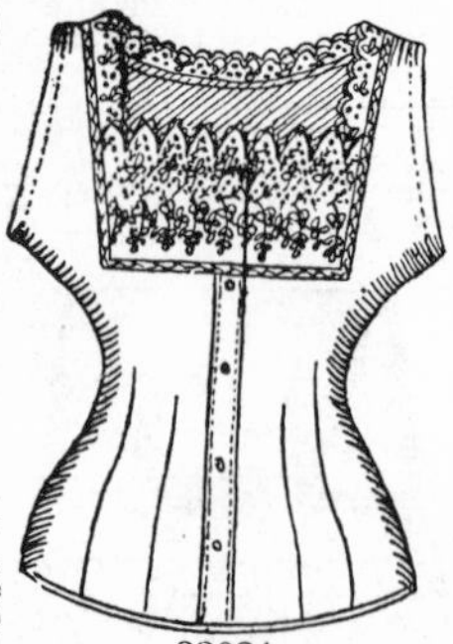

Ladies' White Muslin Bridal Trousseaux.

33026 Ladies' White Muslin Bridal Trosseau, solid Hamburg embroidery yoke on gown and chemise, 3½-inch Hamburg embroidery and 14 fine tucks forming a heading on drawers, all to match; set of 3 pieces, put up in box; weight with box, 40 ounces.
Per set $4.00
33028 Ladies' White Muslin Bridal Trosseau, gown and chemise trimmed with 4 rows of valenciennes insertion with alternate clusters of fine tucking, neck and sleeves of valenciennes lace edge; drawers, 1 row of insertion and lace edge to match, and 2 clusters of tucks; set consisting of 3 pieces put up in box. Per set..................$6.00

Children's and Misses' Muslin Underwear.

33030 Children's and Misses' Night Dress, 2 clusters of five fine tucks down front; ¾-inch ruffle and wide hem around neck. Sleeves to correspond with neck and front. Six sizes only.
Weight, 6 to 9 ounces.

Size No.		Each
1, for Miss 3 years	......	$0.37
2, for Miss 4 to 5 years,		.47
3, for Miss 6 to 7 years,		.57
4, for Miss 8 to 9 years,		.67
5, for Miss 10 to 11 years		.77
6, for Miss 12 to 13 years		.87

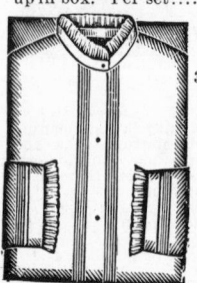

Muslin Underwear—Continued.

33032 Children's and Misses' Chemise, ¾-inch ruffle around sleeves, made of serviceable cotton. Six sizes only.
Weight, 3 to 7 ounces.

Size No. 1, for Miss 3 years, each..................	$0.22
Size No. 2. for Miss 4 to 5 years, each.............	.27
Size No. 3, for Miss 6 to 7 years, each.............	.32
Size No. 4, for Miss 8 to 9 years, each.............	.37
Size No. 5, for Miss 10 to 11 years, each..........	.42
Size No. 6, for Miss 12 to 13 years, each	.49

33038 Children's and Misses' Drawers, 1-inch hem and cluster of five fine tucks, made of serviceable cotton. Six sizes only.
Weight, 3 to 5 ounces.

Size No. 1, for Miss 3 years, each..................	$0.22
Size No. 2, for Miss 4 to 5 years, each.............	.27
Size No. 3, for Miss 6 to 7 years, each.............	.32
Size No. 4, for Miss 8 to 9 years, each.............	.37
Size No. 5, for Miss 10 to 11 years, each..........	.42
Size No. 6, for Miss 12 to 13 years, each..........	.49

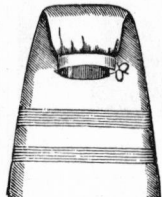

33041 Children's and Misses' Skirt 2-inch hem and two clusters of five fine tucks, with 1¼ inch space between. Six sizes only.
Weight, 3 to 7 ounces.

Size No. 1, for Miss 3 years, each....	$0.22
Size No. 2, for Miss 4 to 5 years, each..............	.27
Size No. 3, for Miss 6 to 7 years, each..............	.32
Size No. 4, for Miss 8 to 9 years, each..............	.37
Size No. 5, for Miss 10 to 11 years each..........	.42
Size No. 6, for Miss 12 to 13 years, each	.47

Infants' Robes.

Infants' robes average 6 ounces in weight.
33066 Infants' Long White Cambric Robes, 2-inch embroidery on yoke; neck and sleeves trimmed with narrow Hamburg, 3 pleats front and back, hem at bottom.
Each........................$0.45
Per dozen................... 4.86

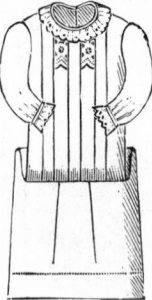

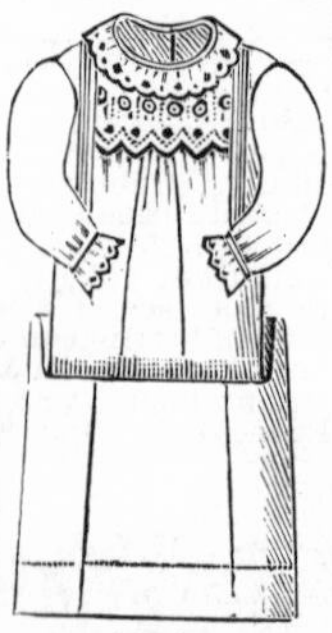

33068 Infants' Long White Cambric Robes, solid embroidered yoke, 5 fine tucks on each side, 3 pleats, back; neck and sleeves trimmed with 1-inch embroidery, herringbone trimming around sleeves; puffed shoulders, hem at bottom. Each.............$0 60
Per dozen................... 6.48

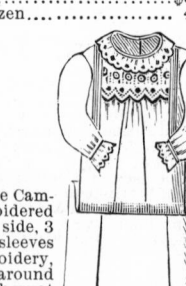

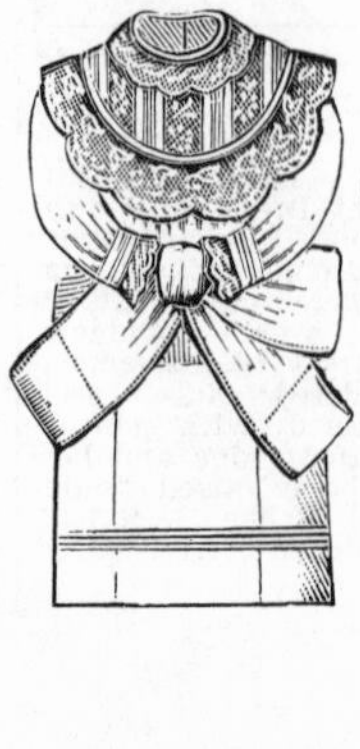

33070 Infants' Long Fine White Cambric Robes, circular yoke of fine valenciennes lace, and 3 rows of 1-inch lace to match; 2 clusters of 5 fine tucks, neck and sleeves trimmed with narrow Val. lace, 4 fine tucks on cuffs, 3 pleats in back, puff shoulders, 3 fine tucks and hem at bottom. Each.........$0.75
Per dozen................. 8.10

Infants' Robes—Continued.

33072 Infants' Long White Cambric Robes, solid embroidered yoke front and back, handsome 1½-inch Hamburg around yoke, circular shape, neck trimmed with narrow Hamburg, dainty embroidered turned over cuffs to match, puffed shoulders, 4 fine tucks and deep hem at bottom.
Each..................$0.85
Per dozen.......... 9.18

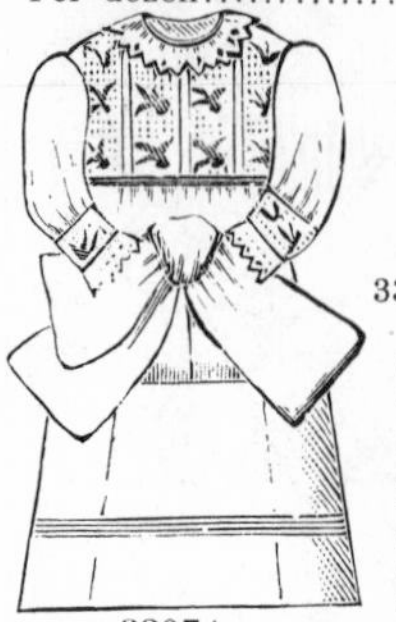

33074 Infants' Fine White Long Cambric Robes; square yoke of 4 rows 1½-inch fine Hamburg embroidery front and back, with 3 fine tucks and herringbone stitching each side, neck and sleeves edged with narrow embroidery to match, 1-inch Hamburg around cuffs, puffed shoulders, 5 fine tucks and deep hem at bottom.
Each, $1.00 Per doz...$10.80

33076 Infants' Very Fine Long White Cambric Robes, 30 fine tucks front and back of yoke, handsome embroidered ruffle extending over shoulders, embroidered turned over cuffs to match, neck trimmed with narrow Val. lace and herringbone stitching, 2-inch embroidery on streamers, puffed shoulders, deep hem at bottom.
Each ..$1.50 Per doz..$16.20

33077 Infants' Very Fine Long White Cambric Robes, 3 rows of Hamburg embroidery and 4 clusters of 5 tucks each down entire front, 3 pleats in back, narrow embroidery on neck and sleeves, cuffs trimmed with 1-inch inserting. 4 inch embroidered flounce, with 3 fine tucks at bottom.
Each..$1.75 Per dozen.$18.90

33078 Infants' Extra Fine Long White Cambric Robes, entire front trimmed with 3 rows of handsome 3-inch Hamburg embroidery and 2 clusters of 3 fine tucks each, 1 inch embroidery each side of inserting, neck and sleeves edged with Hamburg, 2¼-inch inserting on cuffs, puffed shoulders, 3-inch embroidered ruffle at bottom.
Each...$2.00 Per doz..$21.60

33079 Infants' Long White Robes, made of extra fine nainsook, elaborately trimmed with a V shaped fine embroidered ruffle over shoulders, extending front and back, beautifully turned over embroidered cuffs to match, fine Val. and herringbone stitching on neck, embroidered edge streamers, 8 fine tucks and 4-inch embroidered flounce at bottom.
Each ....$ 2.40
Per dozen.............. 25.92

Children's Short Cambric Dresses.

Sizes run from 1 to 3 year.

Children's dresses average 4 ounces in weight.
33080 Child's White Cambric Dress, three plaits down front, flounce on neck and sleeves, hemmed at bottom of skirt. No 1, 1 year; No. 2, 2 years; No. 3, 3 years.
Each................... $0.40

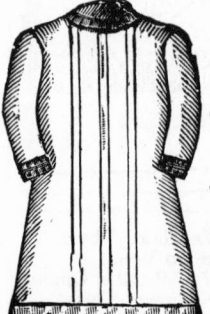

Childrens' Dresses—Continued.

33081 Child's White Cambric Dress, yoke trimmed with 4 clusters of 4 tucks each and 3 rows of narrow hemstitching, herringbone trimming with 3 pleats in back, neck and sleeves edged with narrow embroidery, puffed shoulders, hem at button. No. 1, 1 year; No. 2, 2 years; No 3, 3 years. Each...$0.60

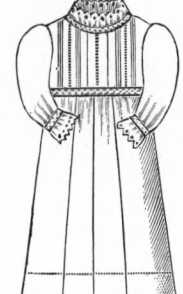

33081

33082 Child's White Cambric Dress, solid Hamburg yoke, hemmed at bottom. No. 1, 1 year; No. 2, 2 years; No. 3, 3 years. Each...........$0.60

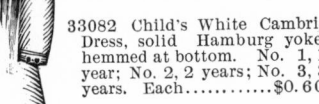

33082

33084 Child's White Cambric Dress, tucked yoke, Hamburg trimming on neck and sleeves, tucked and hemmed at bottom, No. 1, 1 year; No. 2, 2 years; No. 3, 3 years. Each.................$0.75

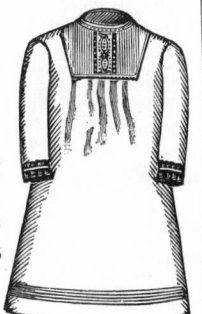

33084

33085 Child's White Cambric Dress, double circular shaped embroidered ruffled yoke, 6 pleats in back narrow embroidery edging on neck and sleeves, tucked cuffs, puffed shoulders, deep hem at bottom. No. 1. 1 year; No. 2, 2 years; No. 3, 3 years. Each.........$0.85

33085

33086 Child's White Cambric Dress, elegantly trimmed with Hamburg, on neck, sleeves and down front. Hamburg ruffle 6 inches deep at bottom. No. 1, 1 year; No. 2, 2 years; No. 3, 3. years. Each..............$1.15

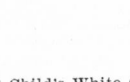

33086

Infants' Cambric and Flannel Skirts.

Children's skirts average six ounces in weight.

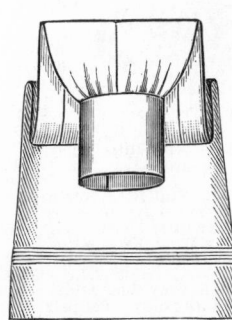

33087 Infants' Long White Cambric Skirts, white short bodice, four fine tucks and deep hem at bottom. Each...........$0.50 Per dozen....... 5.40

Infants' Skirts—Continued.

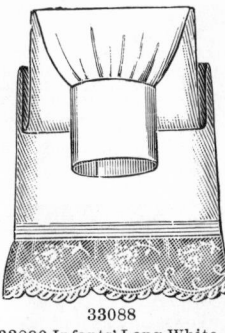

33088

33088 Infants' Long White Cambric Skirts, with short bodice, four fine tucks and three inch valenciennes lace at bottom Each.........$0.75 Per dozen....... 8.10

33090 Infants' Long White Cambric Skirts, with short bodice; handsome 1¾-inch Hamburg inserting, hemstitched around bottom, with deep hem. Each.........$ 0.95 Per dozen.........10.26

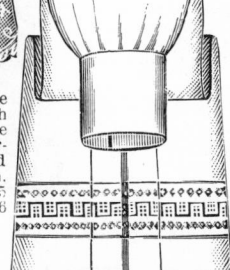

33090

33092 Infants' Long White Cambric Skirts, with short bodice; 1-inch fine valenciennes lace inserting between two clusters of 3 tucks each, and 3-inch valenciennes lace edging at bottom. Each.........$ 1.20 Per dozen.......12.96

33092

33094 Infants' Long White Cambric Skirts, with short bodice, bottom trimmed with elaborate 1-inch Hamburg embroidery inserting, between two clusters of 3 fine tucks each, and 2 inch embroidery. Each.........$ 1.25 Per dozen......13.50

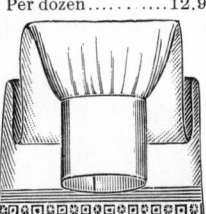

33094

Flannel Skirt.

33095 Infant's All Wool Long Flannel Skirt, scalloped and embroidered with silk at bottom one inch deep...$ 1.25 Per dozen.........13.50

33097 Infants' All Wool Long Flannel Skirts scalloped and embroidered with silk at bottom 2½ inches deep..$ 1.50 Per dozen.........16.20 Cut represents style only, not pattern of embroidery.

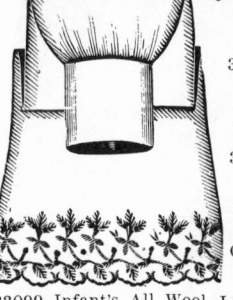

33099 Infant's All Wool Long Flannel Skirt, scalloped and embroidered with silk at bottom inches deep. Each......$1.75. Per dozen.....$21.60

Infants' Embroidered Flannel Shawls or Blankets.

33100 Infant's Cream White All Wool Flannel Shawl or Blanket; silk stitched scalloped edges and silk embroidered on corner; size, 24x24 inches. Each...................$0.70 Per dozen.................7.50

33101 Inafnt's cream White All Wool Flannel Shawl or Blanket; silk stitched, scalloped edges and silk embroidered designs on 2 corners. Size, 28x28 inches. Each..................$1.00 Per dozen.................10.80

33103 Infant's Cream White All Wool Flannel Shawl or Blanket, hemmed edge, with ½-inch satin ribbon all around, large silk embroidered floral design on 1 corner. Each..................$ 1.15 Per dozen................12.42

Flannel Shawl.

33108 Infant's Cream White All Wool Flannel Shawl or Blanket; silk stitched, scalloped edge, silk embroidered floral designs on 2 corners; colors of design, white or light blue. Size, 33x33 inches. Each..................$ 2.00 Per dozen.................21.60

Infants' Outfits.

33111 Cambric Robe, Hamburg inserting and edging down front and on sleeves...............$1.06
1 White Flannel Blanket, scalloped in silk, embroidered silk flower on corner....................70
1 Cambric Night Slip...............35
1 Cambric Day Slip...............75
1 Cambric Skirt, with waist...............82
1 Cambric Shirt, lace trimmed...............22
2 Saxony Wool Shirts, 30...............60
2 Pair Wool Bootees, 15...............30
1 Flannel Band, hemstitched, herringbone silk stitched...............20
1 Flannel Pinning Skirt, or Barrie Coat, 33 inches long...............60
1 Long Flannel Skirt, 32 inches long...............1.10

13 pieces, price per outfit...............$6.70
The above articles are sold separately if desired. Weight, 33 ounces.

33115 1 Cambric Robe, elegantly trimmed with tucking and inserting from neck to bottom......$1.75
1 Flannel Blanket, scalloped in silk, embroidered silk flower on corner...............1.25
1 Cambric Night Slip...............47
1 Cambric Day Slip...............92
1 Cambric Skirt, with waist...............87
1 Cambric Shirt, lace trimmed...............31
2 Saxony Wool Shirts, 30...............60
2 Pair Wool Bootees, 20...............40
1 Bib...............06
1 Flannel Band, hemstitched, herringbone silk stitched...............20
1 Flannel Pinning Skirt, or Barrie Coat, herringbone silk stitched...............75
1 Long Flannel Skirt, herringbone silk hemstitched...............1.25

14 pieces, price per outfit...............$8.83
The above articles are sold separately if desired. Weight, 40 ounces.

33117 Fine Muslin Robe, handsomely trimmed with inserting and fine tucking all over front. Hamburg edge around bottom...............$2.62
1 Flannel Blanket, scalloped in silk, very large silk embroidered flower on corner...............1.75
1 Cambric Night Slip...............47
1 Cambric Day Slip, trimmed down front with inserting, Hamburg flounce...............1.80
1 White Skirt, with waist, Hamburg flounce......1.12
1 Cambric Shirt, lace trimmed...............53
2 Saxony Wool Shirts, 30...............60
2 Pair Wool Bootees, 23...............46
2 Bibs, laced trimmed, 11...............22
1 Short Dress, embroidery, fine tucked yoke, skirt falling from yoke...............2.25
1 Flannel Band, herringbone silk, hemstitched..20
1 Flannel Pinning Skirt, or Barrie Coat, herringbone silk...............75
1 Long Flannel Skirt, with 3 clusters of 3 tucks each...............1.50

16 pieces, price per outfit...............$14.27
The above articles are sold separately if desired. Weight, 46 ounces.

Ladies' Summer Skirts.

Weight, 9 to 10 ozs.

33120 Ladies' Skirts, plain gray wash poplin, with 3-inch ruffle of same. Each........$0.30 Per dozen.... 3.24

33120

33122 Ladies' Skirts, blue and white striped wash poplin, with 4½-inch bias ruffle of same. Each.........$0.35 Per dozen.... 3.78

33122

33124 Ladies' Skirts, blue gray wash poplin, with white stripes, 1 inch bias heading of same, with 4 inch box pleating at bottom. Each........$0.50 Per dozen.... 5.40

33124

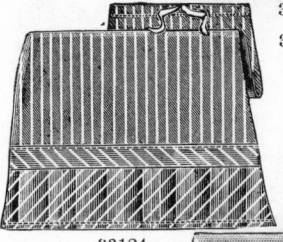

33126 Ladies' Skirts plain gray wash poplin, 3½-inch double ruffle of same, piped heading, ruffles edged with black scrolled stitching. Each....$0.70 Per dozen.... 7.56

33126

Ladies' Skirts—Continued.

33128 Ladies' Skirts, blue gray mixed with poplin, 6½-inch ruffle of same; 3 rows narrow white braid and 2 rows of rick rack around bottom of ruffle.
Each.........$0.75
Per dozen..... 8.10

33130 Ladies' Skirts steel mixed chambray 7½-inch handsome embroidered flounce, with 1½-inch plain heading and dust ruffle. Each....$0.85
Per dozen...... 9.18

33132 Ladies' Skirts, made of blue and white striped zephyr poplin, with 7-inch ruffle, 3 rows of narrow feather edge braid on ruffle, bias heading of same; also dust ruffles.
Each..........$1.00
Per dozen......10.80

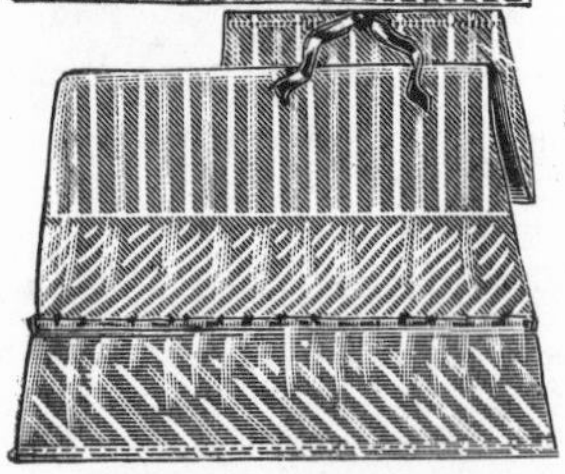

33134 Ladies' Skirts, umbrella style, made of blue and white striped zephyr poplin, with 11 inch bias flounce, and 6-inch dust ruffle.
Each..........$1.25
Per dozen.....13.50

Ladies' Black Sateen Skirts.

33136 Ladies' Plain Fast Black Sateen Skirts, with 4½-inch ruffle. Each......................$0.50
Per dozen... 5.40

33138 Ladies' Fast Black Sateen Skirts, with 3½-inch double ruffle at bottom; also dust ruffle.
Each..........$ .75
Per dozen...... 8.10

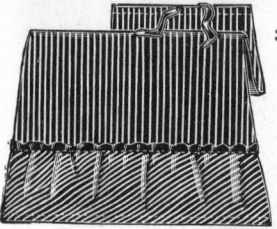

33140 Ladies' Fast Black Sateen Skirts, with narrow white stripes, 7-inch bias flounce of same, and dust ruffle.
Each..........$ .85
Per dozen..... 9.18

33142 Ladies' Fast Black Sateen Skirt, with 6 inch deep knife pleating; 2½-inch plain heading; also dust ruffle.
Each..........$ .85
Per dozen.... 9.18

33144 Ladies' Fast Black Sateen Skirts, double 1½-inch ruffle, trimmed with 2-inch black Yak lace; dust ruffle.
Each........$ 1.00
Per dozen.....10.80

Ladies' Skirts—Continued.

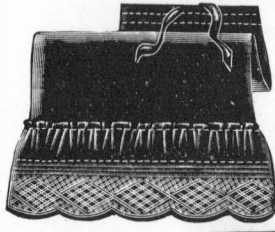

33146 Ladies' Fast Black Sateen Skirts, 5-inch ruffle with 4 fine tucks, trimmed with handsome, 3 inch black lace, wide dust ruffle.
Each .. ...$ 1.25
Per 13.50

33148 Ladies' Fast Black Sateen Skirts, plain 1½-inch heading of same, with 7½-inch ruffle, embroidered in colors; wide dust ruffle at bottom.
Each........$ 1.25
Per dozen.....13.50

33150 Ladies' Fast Black Sateen Skirts, umbrella style, with 8-inch moreen flounce, and 3 inch raised box pleating. Each...... ....$2.00
Per dozen................................21.60

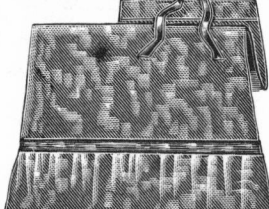

33152 Ladies' Steel Gray Moreen Skirts, 1-inch heading of same, with 5-inch moreen ruffle at bottom.
Each.... .... $2.10
Per dozen.... 22.68

Ladies' Winter Skirts.

Weight from 12 to 24 ounces.

33154 Ladies' Dark Gray Mixed Melton Skirts, 1¼ inch piped heading and 2-inch ruffle.
Each $0.60
Per dozen.. 6.48

33156 Ladies' Dark Gray Mixed Melton Skirts, black sateen heading, embroidered, 3¼-in. ruffle at bottom.
Each......$0.75
Per dozen. 8.10

33158 Ladies' Dark Gray Mixed Melton Skirts, very large, 1-in. heading, 3¾-in. ruffle.
Each.......$0.85
Per dozen.. 9.18

33160 Ladies' Gray Mixed Melton Skirts, two rows of black velvet with silk embroidered designs and 3½-in. ruffle at bottom.
Each........$ 1.00
Per dozen...10.80

33163 Ladies' Oxford Mixed Melton Skirts, 5¼-in. ruffle, elegantly embroidered with silk floss.
Each....$ 1.25
Per doz....13.50

Ladies' Skirts—Continued.

33165 Ladies' Black Sateen Skirts, lined with striped domette flannel and 14-in. heavy quilting at bottom.
Each.......... ...$0.85
Per dozen.............9.18

33167 Ladies' Fast Black Sateen Skirts, lined with striped domette flannel; 15 inch heavy quilting at bottom. Each....$1.00
Per doz...........10.80

33169 Ladies' Fast Black Sateen Skirts, lined with domette flannel, 14 inch heavy quilting, bound at bottom with velvet.
Each.................... 1.25

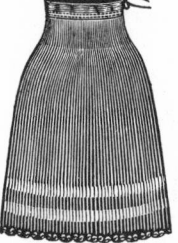

33165

Per doz....................13.50

33171 Ladies' Fast Black Sateen Skirts, lined with fast black cotton, knife pleats 4 inches deep, Each...............................1.35
Per doz...........................14.58

33173 Ladies' Fast Black Sateen Skirts, lined with fast black cotton, 6 inch ruffle, scalloped and embroidered in silk. Each...............1.50
Per doz...........................16.20

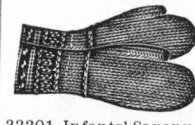

33175 Ladies' Knit Skirts, 30 inches long; made of Egyptian cotton. Colors, sanitary, mixed, only, until sold.
Each.... ....$0.35

33177 Ladies' Improved Knit All Wool Skirts, crochet stitch. Will not shrink, ravel or sag when worn. French yoke band. Length, 38 inches; weight, 16 ounces. Colors: Black, navy blue or sanitary brown, mixed.
Each........ ....$ 1.50
Per dozen............. 16.20

33175

33179 Children's and Misses' Improved Knit All Wool Skirts, crochet stitched. Will not shrink, ravel or sag. Colors: Cardinal, navy blue or sanitary brown, mixed.
Size, 18-inch. Each..........................$ 0.60
Per dozen............................... 6.48
Size, 22-inch. Each............................. .90
Per dozen............................... 9.72
Size, 26-inch. Each............................ 1.20
Per dozen............................12.96

GLOVES AND MITTS.
Infants' Misses' and Ladies' Mitts, Wool, Worsted and Silk.

Weight of children's and ladies' mitts, 1 to 3 ounces; men's 4 to 7 ounces.

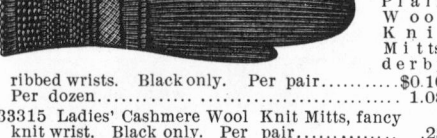

33300 Infants' Cashmere Wool Mitts, fancy silk stitched wrists. Colors: Cardinal, light blue, black or white.
Per pair....... ....$0.23
Per dozen............. 2.50

33301 Infants' Saxony Wool Mitts, fancy wrists. Colors: Cardinal, light blue, black or white.
Per pair.........$0.10 Per dozen........ 1.08

33304 Infants' Saxony Wool Mitts, silk woven in on outside. Colors: Black or white. Per pair... .35
Per dozen................................. 3.78

33306 Children's Plain Wool Mitts; color, black only.
Size 3, per pair................................. .09
Per dozen..................................... .90
Size 4, per pair................................. .10
Per dozen..................................... 1.08
Size 5, per pair................................. .11
Per dozen..................................... 1.18

33308 Children's and Misses' Cashmere Wool Mitts. Black only. Sizes 3, 4 and 5.
Per Pair.........$0.12 Per dozen............. 1.30

33310 Misses' and Children's Double Knit Wool Mitts. Made of fine Saxony wool. Black only.
Per pair.........$0.25 Per dozen............. 2.70

33312 Misses' and Children's Double Knit Wool Mitts, fancy back, made of fine Saxony yarn. Black only. Assorted sizes. Per pair...... 30
Per dozen.............................. ..... 3.24

33314 Ladies' Plain Wool Knit Mitts. derby ribbed wrists. Black only. Per pair..........$0.10
Per dozen... 1.08

33315 Ladies' Cashmere Wool Knit Mitts, fancy knit wrist. Black only. Per pair............. .25
Per dozen... 2.70

33317 Ladies' Cashmere Wool Knit Mitts, plain and fancy wrist; colors: Wine, navy blue, or seal brown. Until sold. Per pair............. .15

33319 Ladies' Fine Saxony Wool Knit Mitts, fancy openwork back. Black only. Per pair... .28
Per dozen... 3.02

33320 Ladies' Double Knit Saxony Wool Mitts, with derby ribbed wrist. Black only. Per pair .25
Per dozen....... .... 2.70

Mitts –Continued.

33323 Ladies' Fine Saxony Mitts, double knit, with neat satin bow on back. Black only.
Per pair................$0 38 Per dozen........ 4.10
33324 Ladies' Double Knit Mitts, made of fine coral Saxony yarn, fancy openwork back. Black only. Per pair.........................40
Per dozen.................................. 4.32
33325 Ladies' Double Knit Mitts, made of fine Saxony yarn, fancy open work back. Colors: Wine, seal brown or navy blue. Until sold. Per pair...................................25
33326 Ladies' Double Knit Mitts, made of fine Saxony yarn, fancy openwork stitch on back and cuff. Black only. Per pair.................50
Per dozen.................................. 5.40
33328 Ladies' Double Knit Mitts, very fine Saxony on outside, with Angora wool lining; very warm. Black only. Per pair..................60
Per dozen.................................. 6.48
33329 Ladies' Plain Silk Mitts, derby ribbed wrists. Black only. Per pair, $0.45. Per dozen.$4.86
33330 Ladies' Plain Silk Mitts, derby ribbed wrists. Colors: Wine, seal brown or navy blue. Until sold. Per pair....................35
33331 Ladies' Spun Silk Mitts, knit double, silk on outside and cashmere wool on inside. Black only. Per pair..........$0.60. Per dozen. 6.48
33332 Ladies' Spun Silk Mitts, knit double, silk on outside and cashmere wool on inside. Colors: Wine, seal brown or navy blue. Until sold, per pair...................................50
33333 Ladies' Silk Mitts, knit double, cashmere wool lined, fancy openwork stitch on back. Black only. Per pair......$1.00. Per dozen...10.80

33334 Ladies' Silk Mitts, knit double, cashmere wool lined, fancy openwork stitch on back. Colors: Wine, seal brown or navy blue. Until sold, per pair.......................$0.75
33335 Ladies' Double Silk Mitts, fancy openwork stitch on back and wrist, with neat silk cord and bell ornament on back. Black only. Per pair...........$1.50 Per dozen............16.20
33336 Ladies' Double Silk Mitts, finest grade, fancy openwork stitch on back and wrist, with neat satin bow on back. Black only. Per pair...........$2.00 Per dozen......... 21.60
33337 Ladies' Double Silk Mitts, fancy openwork stitch on back and wrist, with neat satin bow on back to match. Colors: Wine, navy blue or seal brown. Until sold, per pair....... 1.00
N. B.—Ladies' Silk Mitts make a very acceptable and useful present.
Numbers 33325, 33330, 33334 and 33337 are special bargains. The prices are below manufacturers' cost. Give first and second choice of colors.

Boys' Mitts.

33341 Boys' All Wool Heather Mixed Double Knit Mitts, for rough wear. Per pair...........$0.18
Per dozen.................................. 1.95
33342 Boys' Double Knit All Wool Mitts, wine, seal brown, navy blue or black. Per pair.......18
Per dozen.................................. 1.95
33344 Boys' Double Knit Wool Mitts, large size, colors as above. Per pair $0.20. Per dozen..... 2.16
33346 Youths' Double Knit Wool Mitts, same colors as above. Per pair....................22
Per dozen.................................. 2.38
33348 Boys' and Youths' Fulled Mackinaw Mitts, heavy weight. Per pair....$0.15. Per pair... 1.62
33349 Boys' Scotch Wool Gloves, assorted styles and sizes. Per pair......$0.25 Per dozen...... 2.75

Men's Knit Wool Mitts.

33350 Men's Double Knit Wool Mitts; colors: Black only. Per pair....$0.25 Per dozen....... 2.70
33351 Men's Double Knit Saxony Wool Mitts: black only. Per pair....$0.40 Per dozen..... 4.32
33353 Men's Double Knit Silk Mitts, lined with fine wool; black only. Per pair................... 1.25
Per dozen..................................13.50

Men's Mittens.

Weight of Men's Mitts and gloves, 4 to 9 ounces per pair

33361 Men's fulled Mackinaw Mitts, grained leather palms Per pair.$0.35
Per doz... 3.78

33361-33362
33362 Men's Fulled Mackinaw Mitts, genuine oil tanned calf palm and welted seams.
Per pair.........$0.45 Per dozen............. $4.77

We have a finely equipped Freight and Express Bureau, and will be glad to quote Freight and Express Rates to any point upon application.
19–2d

Mitts—Continued.

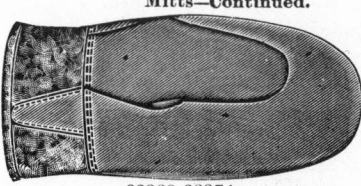

33368-33375.
33368- Men's extra heavy Esquimaux Mitts, camels' hair and wool mixed, plush lined, back and palm covered with genuine oil tanned calf, welted seams, warmest mitt made. 73
Per dozen.................................. 8.10
33374 Men's Extra Heavy Knit Wool Mitts, tufted fleece lining, back and palm covered with genuine oil tanned calf, welted seams. Per pair....85
Per dozen.................................. 9.18
33375 Men's Extra Heavy Esquimaux Mitts, camel's hair and wool mixed, fleece wool lined, back and palm covered with Plymouth buckskin, welted seams. Per pair........$ 1.00
Per dozen..................................10.80

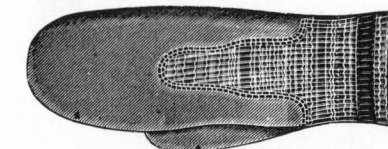

33382 to 33392.
33382 Men's Oil Tanned Grained Leather Mitts, fleece wool lined, close fitting knit wool wrist.
Per pair.............$0.40 Per dozen...........$4.32
83384 Men's Oil Tanned Genuine Calf Mitts, fleece wool lined, close fitting knit wool wrist.
Per pair.............$0.60 Per dozen........... 6.48
33386 Men's Oil Tanned Genuine Calf Mitts, fleece wool lined, close fitting knit wool wrists.
Per pair.............$0.75 Per dozen........... 8.10
33390 Men's Plymouth Buckskin Mitts, fleece wool lined, close fitting knit wool wrist, welted seams. Per pair............................. 0.85
Per dozen.................................. 9.18
33392 Men's Genuine Plymouth Buckskin Mitts, fleece wool lined, close fitting knit wool wrist.
Per pair ....$1.25 Per dozen...........13.50

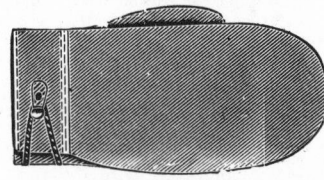

33394 to 33401½.
33394 Men's Oil Tanned Leather Mitts, string fastener, for choppers and lumbermen, unlined, welted seams. Per pair $0.40
Per dozen.................................. 4.32
33395 Men's Indian Tan Genuine Calfskin Mitts, unlined, string fastener, welted seams. Per pair...70
Per dozen.................................. 7.56
33397 Men's Plymouth Buckskin Mitts, welted seams, string fastener for choppers and lumbermen, unlined. Per pair.......................75
Per dozen.................................. 8.10
33399 Men's Asbestol Cordovan Horsehide Mitts, string fastener, welted seams, sewed with wax thread. This leather is tanned by a new process which makes it proof against heat, steam, boiling or cold water and is water proof, soft and pliable as a piece of cloth. Per pair...........80
Per dozen.................................. 9.00
33400 Men's Plymouth Buckskin Mitts, fleece lined, string fastener, welted seams. Per pair.. 1.00
Per dozen..................................10.80
33401½ Men's Reindeer Skin Mitts, fleece lined, string fastener, russet brown color, welted seams. Per pair.......$1.15 Per dozen.........12.42

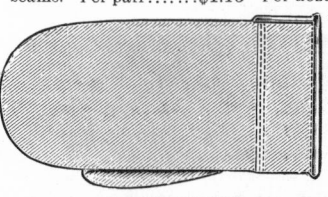

33403 Men's Genuine Oil Tanned Saranac Buckskin Chopper Mitts, unlined, welted seams. Per pair $0.85
Per dozen 9.18

33403-33406.
33406 Men's Genuine Saranac Buckskin Mitts. oil tan, fleece wool lined. Per pair.............$ 1.25
Per dozen..................................13.50

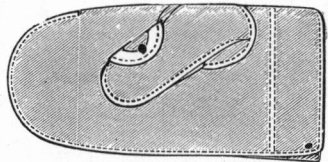

33408 Men's Extra Heavy Split Calfskin Mitts, unlined riveted thumbs for heavy, rough work. Per pr..$0.45
Per doz.. 4.86

33408 to 33414
33410 Men's Plymouth Buckskin Mitts, extra heavy, riveted thumbs. Per pair...............$ 1.00
Per dozen..................................10.80

Mitts—Continued.

33412 Men's Genuine Adirondack Jack Buck Mitts, extra heavy weight, double copper riveted thumbs. No. 2 stock. Per pair................. 1.00
Per dozen..................................10.80
33414 Men's Genuine Adirondack Jack Buck Mitts, extra heavy weight, double copper riveted thumbs. No. 1 stock. Per pair................. 1.25
Per doz..13.50

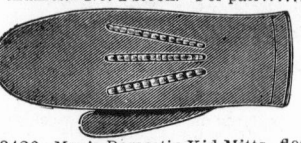

23418 Men's Domestic Kid Mitts, fleeced lined, shirred elastic wrist. Per pr....$0.50
Per doz... 5.40

33420 Men's Domestic Kid Mitts. fleeced lined, shirred elastic wrist. Per pair..$0.85 Per doz. 9.18
33422 Men's Extra Fine Domestic Kid Mitts, fleeced lined, shirred elastic wrist. Per pair... 1.25
Per dozen..................................13.50

23425 Men's One Finger Sheepskin Leather Gauntlet Mitts, unlined. Per pair.$0.35
Fer doz.. 3.78

33425-33428
33427 Men's One Finger Grained Leather Gauntlet Mitts, unlined. Per pair.....................$0.50
Per dozen.................................. 5.40
33428 Men's One Finger Gauntlet Mitts, genuine oil tanned calfskin, unlined. Per pair.......... .75
Per dozen.................................. 8.10

Men's Gloves.

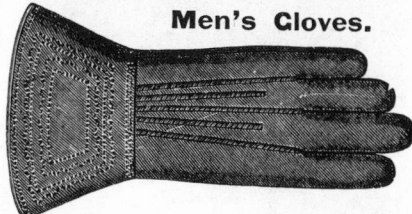

33429 Men's Gauntlet Gloves. lined. imitation Plymouth buckskin. Per pair $0.50
Fer dozen.................................. 5.40
33430 Men's Asbestol Cordovan Horsehide, Gauntlet Gloves, unlined, welted seams, sewed with wax thread, warranted water proof and not affected by heat, steam, boiling or cold water. Per pair........$1.15 Per dozen........12.00

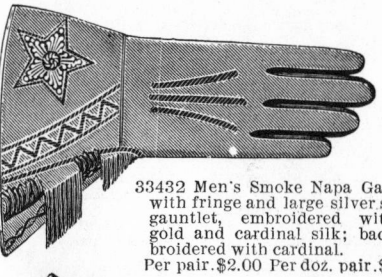

33432 Men's Smoke Napa Gauntlet with fringe and large silver star on gauntlet, embroidered with old gold and cardinal silk; back embroidered with cardinal.
Per pair.$2.00 Per doz. pair.$21.60

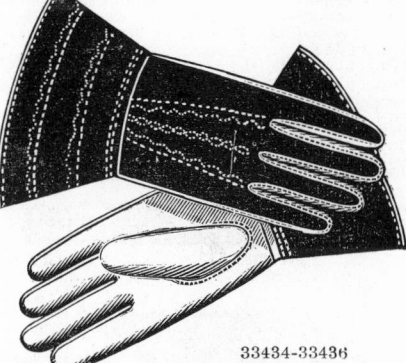

33434-33436
33434 Men's Gauntlet Gloves, Jersey cloth back and cuff. felt lined. dogskin palm. Per pair....$0.85
Per dozen.................................. 9.18
33436 Men's Gauntlet Gloves, Jersey cloth back and cuff, felt lined, napa tan buckskin palm. Per pair.............$0.95 Per dozen...........10.26

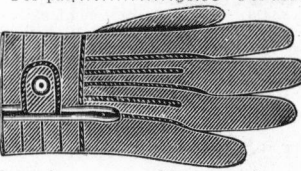

33438 Men's Genuine Oil Tanned Calfskin Gloves, welted seams, extra long wrists, one button, patent snap fastener unlined.
Per pair.........$0.85 Per dozen.............$9.18

Men's Gloves—Continued.

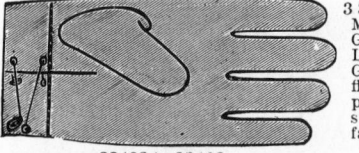

33439 Men's Grained Leather Gloves, fleece wool lined, close fitting knit wool wrist. Per pair....$0.45
Per dozen................................... 4.86
33441 Horsehide Gloves, suitable for men with small hands, or for young men, oil tanned, wool lined, close fitting knit wool wrist. Per pair.... .80
Per dozen..................................... 8.64
33443 Men's Genuine Leather Sealskin Gloves, oil tanned, fleece lined, close fitting knit wool wrist. Per pair..................................... .75
Per dozen..................................... 8.10
33445 Men's Oil Tanned Calfskin Gloves, fleece wool lined, close fitting knit wool wrist. Per pair .65
Per dozen..................................... 7.02
33446 Men's Oil Tanned Horsehide Gloves, fleece wool lined, close fitting knit wool wrist. Per pair .85
Per dozen..................................... 9.18
33447 Men's Reindeer Skin Gloves, fleece wool lined, close fitting knit wool wrist, russet brown color. Per pair................................ 1.00
Per dozen..................................10.80
33450 Men's Genuine Plymouth Buck Gloves, wool lined, close fitting knit wool wrist. Per pair 1.25
Per dozen.................................. 13.50

33454 Men's Genuine Plymouth Buck Gloves, fleece wool lined, elastic wrist, No. 1 stock.
Per pair...$1.50
Per dozen......................................16.20

33457 Men's Leather Gloves, oil tanned, welted seams, patent back snap fastener, unlined.
Per pair...$0.50
Per dozen..................................... 5.40
33458 Youths' Leather Gloves, oil tanned, welted seams, unlined, back snap fastener. Per pair ... .50
Per dozen..................................... 5.40
33463 Men's Genuine Oil Tanned Calfskin Gloves, welted seams, patent back, snap fastener. Unlined. Per pair............................. .75
Per dozen..................................... 8.10
33466 Men's Genuine Oil Tanned Saranac Buckskin Gloves, unlined, patent back snap fastener. Per pair 1.15 Per dozen.......................12.40
33468½ Men's Reindeer Skin Gloves, patent back snap fastener, unlined, russet brown color.
Per pair..........$0.85   Per dozen........ $9.18
33471 Men's Asbestol Cordovan Horsehide Gloves, patent back snap fastener, welted seams, unlined, sewed with wax thread, warranted water proof and not affected by heat, steam, or boiling water.
Per pair........ $1.00   Per dozen $10.80

33478 Men's Reindeer Skin, fleece wool lined, one button, welted seams, russet brown color.

33478
Per pair............$1.25   Per dozen.........$13.50

33480 Men's Genuine Plymouth Buckskin Gloves, fleece wool lined, welted seams, patent back string fastener

33480
Per pair............$1.50   Per dozen..........$16 20

𝔄LL OUR GOODS are sold in any quantity to suit the purchaser, except when stated differently in catalogue.

Men's Gloves—Continued.

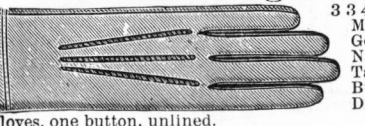

33483 Men's Grained Leather Gloves, fleece lined, patent string fastener.

33483 to 33492
Per pair. ....$0.50   Per dozen...........$5.40
33485 Men's Genuine Oil Tanned Calfskin Gloves, welted seams, patent string fastener, unlined.
Per pair............$0.75   Per dozen......... 8.10
33487 Men's Genuine Oil Dressed Calfskin Gloves, out-seam sewed, very soft on the hands, patent string fastener, unlined.
Per pair............$0.75   Per dozen 8.10
33490 Men's Indian Tan Calfskin Gloves, welted seams, patent string fasteners, unlined.
Per pair............$0.75   Per dozen 8.10
33492 Horsehide Gloves, oil tanned, suitable for men with small hands or for young men, patent string fasteners, unlined.
Per pair............$0.70   Per dozen 7.56
33492½ Men's Genuine Oil Tanned Calfskin Gloves, fleeced lined, welted seams, patent string fasteners. Per pair, $0.85   Per dozen........ 9.18

33494 Men's Gloves made from caribou stock, with double palm of oil tanned calfskin.

33494-33495
welted seams, patent string fasteners, unlined, used by gripmen and motormen or for any kind of work where hand usage comes on the palm, unlined.
Per pair.........$0.75   Per dozen $8.10
33495 Men's Gloves, same as above, with heavy fleece lining.
Per pair.........$0.85   Per dozen 9.18
33496 Men's Leather Gloves, string fastener, welted seams, with double palm of asbestol cordovan horsehide, for grip or motormen, unlined. Per pair....$1.00   Per dozen...... ....10.80

Men's Fine Driving Gloves.

33499 Men's Genuine Napa Tanned Buck Driving Gloves, one button, unlined.
Per pair.........$1.25   Per dozen...........$13.50
33500 Men's Genuine Castor Buck Driving or Walking Gloves, medium weight, two buttons.
Per pair...........$1.25.   Per doz.............13.50

Men's Dogskin Gloves.
Weight 2 ounces.

33502 Men's Unlined Dogskin Gloves, fancy backs, dark colors, no blacks.

33502-33505
Per pair............$0.60.   Per dozen.........$6.50
33503 Men's Domestic Dogskin Gloves, dark and medium colors, no blacks. Per pair............ .75
Per dozen..................................... 8.10
33504 Men's Dogskin Gloves, two buttons, dark and medium colors, no blacks. Per pair...... .. 1.00
Per dozen..................................10.80
33505 Men's Goat Driving Gloves, unlined, out-seam make, one button. Per pair.............. 1.00
Per dozen 10.80

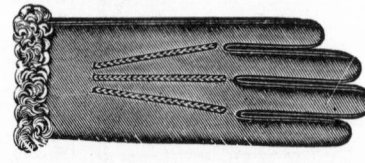

33509 Men's Domestic Kid Gloves, large sizes, lined, fur top. Per pair. ..$0.75. Per dozen...$8.10
33510 Men's Domestic Kid Gloves, wool lined, elastic wrist, fur top. Per pair................. 1.00
Per dozen..................................10.80

33512 Men's Domestic Kid Gloves one button fleece lined.
Per pair. ....$1.25 Per dozen, ...$13.50

33512-33515.
33514 Men's Dressed Mocha Kid Gloves, two button, fleece lined. Per pair..$1.50. Per dozen..$16.20
33515 Men's Domestic Kid Gloves, fleece wool, sanitary lining, outside seam, one button.
Per pair............$1.50.   Per dozen. 16.20

Husking Gloves.

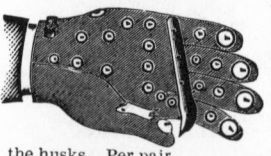

33517 Men's Husking Gloves, made from oil tanned calfskin protected with rivets where all wear comes; patent claw and husking pin attached to thumb and forefinger for tearing off the husks. Per pair......................$1.00
Per dozen 10.80
33518 Men's Husking Gloves, same as 33517, with the husker on the left hand. Per pair 1.00
Per dozen 10.80
33532 Men's Sheepskin Gauntlet Driving Mitts, the natural pelt on outside, oil tanned calf palm and thumb, fleece lined. Per pair............... .75
Per dozen..................................... 8.10

Boys' Heavy Mitts and Gloves.

33538 Boys' Grained Leather Mitts, fleece wool lining, close fitting knit wool wrist (for style of mitt see cut 33382).
Per pair........$0.35 Per dozen............$3.78
33540 Boys' Fulled Mackinaw Mitts, genuine oil tanned calf palm and thumb (for style of mitt see cut 33376).
Per Pair........$0.38 Per dozen............ 4.10
33542 Boys' Fulled Mackinaw Mitts, covered with Plymouth buckskin (for style of mitt see cut 33382). Per pair............................. .45
Per dozen..................................... 4.86
33544 Boys' Grained Leather Gloves, fleece wool lined, close fitting, knit wool wrist (for style of glove see cut 33439).
Per pair........$0.40 Per dozen.......... 4.32
33546 Boys' Plymouth Buckskin Gloves, fleece wool lined, close fitting, knit wool wrist (for style of glove see cut 33439).
Per pair........$0.60 Per dozen............ 6 48

Men's Scotch Gloves.

33548 Men's Seamless Scotch Gloves, fulled large sizes, gray and brown mixed.
Per pair..$0.25
Per doz... 2.70
33549 Men's Seamless Scotch Wool Gloves, fancy mottled, medium sizes. Per pair.................$0.35
Per dozen 3.78
33550 Men's Seamless Scotch Wool Gloves, extra heavy fancy knit backs and palms.
Per pair.........$0 45   Per dozen............ 4.86
33551 Men's Seamless Scotch Gloves, made of worsted yarn, fancy knit, plain fingers and wrist.
Per pair...........$0.50   Per dozen............ 5.40
33552 Men's Seamless Scotch Gloves, made of fine worsted yarn, fancy knit palm and back.
Per pair...........$0.60   Per dozen............ 6.48

Wristlets.
Average weight, 2 ounces.

33554 Ladies' and Men's Wristlets or Pulse Warmers, double knit ribbed worsted, black only. Per pair.$0.10
Per dozen 1.08
33555 Ladies' and Men's Wristlets or Pulse Warmers, double knit Saxony wool, black only. Per pair.....$0.12
Per doz)n 1.30
33556 Ladies' and Men's Wristlets or Pulse Warmers, double knit fine ribbed imported Saxony yarn, black only. Per pair... .20
Per dozen 2.16
33557 Ladies' and Men's Wristlets or Pulse Warmers, double knit fine ribbed imported Saxony yarn, fancy mottled. Per pair...... .25
Per dozen 2.70
33558 Ladies' and Men's Wristlets or Pulse warmers, double knit black silk Per pair...... .35
Per dozen 3.78
33559 Ladies' and Men's Wristlets or Pulse Warmers, finest rib black silk double knit.
Per pair ....$0.50   Per dozen............ 5.40

KNIT GOODS.
Ladies' and Misses' Headwear.

33751 Ladies' or Misses' Fascinators, hand made, shell stitch, made of Shetland floss: colors: Black, white, light blue or pink.
Each $0.20
Per dozen.. 2.16
33753 Ladies' or Misses' Fascinators, hand made, shell stitch, made of Shetland floss, colors: Black, white, light blue or pink.
Each $0.35
Per doz..... 3.78

33751 to 33755
33755 Ladies' or Misses' Fascinators, hand made, shell stitch, small neat pattern, made of fine Shetland floss, same colors as above. Each.$0.50
Per dozen.......................... .... 5.40

Fascinators—Continued.

33757 Ladies' or Misses' Fascinators, hand made, double knit of Shetland floss, beaded all over with bugle beads, tufted top; colors, Black, white, light blue or pink. Each......$0.50
Per dozen............ 5.40

33759 Ladies' or Misses' Fascinators, hand made, double knit of fine Shetland floss, wave tuft edges with silk floss, covered with silk floss; colors: Light blue or pink. Each......$0.70
Per dozen 7.56

33757-33759.

33761 Ladies' or Misses Fascinators, hand made, shell stitch, made of Shetland floss, edged all around with bugle beads, large tufted top, trimmed with beads. Colors: Black, white, light blue or pink. Each $0.70
Per dozen............. 7.56

33761

33763 Ladies' or Misses' Fascinators, hand made of Spanish floss, beaded all over with bugle beads. Colors: Black, white, light blue or pink. Each............$0.75
Per dozen....... 8.10

33763.

33767 Ladies' or Misses' Tab Hoods, hand made, of Shetland floss, covered with silk floss, tufted top, edged with silk. Colors: Black or white.
Each................. .80
Per dozen........... 8.64

33769 Ladies' or Misses' Tab Hoods, hand made, of Shetland floss, completely covered with waves of floss; top, back and front trimmed with satin ribbon to match. Colors: Black, white or pink. Each.....$ 1.00
Per dozen...........10.80

33771 Ladies' or Misses' Tab Hoods, hand made, of Spanish floss, beaded all over with bugle beads, tufted top; colors, black, white, wine, light blue or pink. Each........$ 1.00
Per dozen...........10.80

33771

Hoods—Continued.

33773 Ladies' Tab Hoods, large full sizes, hand made, of Shetland floss, edged with bugle beads, tufted top trimmed with beads. Colors: Black or white.
Each........... ......$0.80
Per dozen............. 8.64

33775 Ladies' or Misses' Tab Hoods, hand made, of fine imported Saxony yarn, covered with silk floss, edged with bugle beads, tufted top, trimmed with beads. Colors: Black or white.
Each. ....$ 1.25
Per dozen............13.50

33773-75

33779 Ladies' Tab Hood Fascinator, hand made, of Shetland yarn and Berlin wool, covered with silk floss, trimmed with swan's down, ribbon bow on top. Colors: Black, white, pink or wine.
Each ....$ 1.75
Per dozen...........18.90

33779

33781

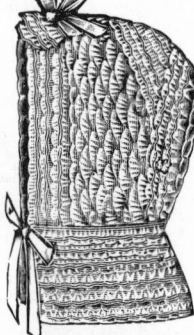

33783

33781 Ladies' Hand Made Hoods, double knit of Shetland floss, ruche top. Colors: Black, white or seal brown. Each........... ....$0.50
Per dozen.................................. 5.40

33783 Misses' Hoods, made of worsted floss, 3-inch cape. Colors: Black, white or cardinal.
Each 0.40
Per dozen................................... 4.32

33785

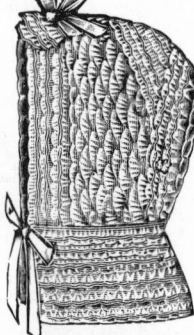

33787

33785 Ladies' or Misses' Hoods, double knit, hand made, of Shetland floss, ruche front and top, 3-inch cape. Colors: Black or white.
Each...$0.75
Per dozen................................... 8.10

33787 Ladies' Hand-Made Hoods, fine Shetland yarn, lined with teaseled yarn, three rows of shell work on front, back and top and six rows on a 6-inch cape, all edged with silk, satin ribbon, bows on top and back. Colors: Black or white.
Each ....$1.00   Per dozen...........10.80

Hoods—Continued.

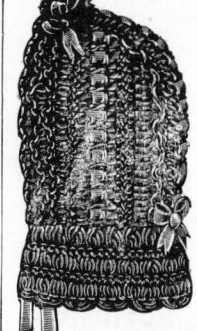

33789 Ladies' Hand Made Hoods, made of imported Saxony yarn, lined with Germantown yarn, heavy satin ribbon on sides and back, large satin bows on top and back front, sides and back edged with silk. Colors: Black, white, seal brown or wine.
Each.....................$ 1.75
Per dozen...............18.90

Infants' Knit Sacques.

33793 Infants' Knit Sacques, made of Shetland floss Colors: Plain white or light blue; also white trimmed with light blue, cardinal or pink.
Each....$0.25
Fer doz. 2.70

33795 Infants' Knit Sacques, made of Shetland floss, trimmed all around with ribbon to match, same colors as above. Each............. ....$0.50
Per dozen................................... 5.40

Men's and Boys' Knit Jackets.

Weight of boys' jackets average 1 pound, men's jackets, 1¼ to 1¾ pounds.

33800 Boys' Knit Cardigan Jackets, fancy front, for ages 6 to 10.
Each.................$0.75
Per dozen......... 8.10

33802 Boys' Knit Cardigan Jackets, fancy front, for ages 6 to 10.
Each................$1.00
Per dozen.........10.80

33804 Men's Knit Cardigan Jackets, full size; black only.
Each.................$0.75
Per dozen......... 8 10

33806 Men's Knit Cardigan Jackets, full size; black only.
Each.................$1.00
Per dozen.........10.80

33808 Men's Knit Wool Cardigan Jackets, full size; black or brown.
Each.............$1.25   Per dozen..............$13.50

33810 Men's Knit Worsted Cardigan Jackets, large size; colors, black or brown.
Each........$1.50   Per dozen..........16.20

33812 Men's Knit Worsted Cardigan Jackets, extra large sizes; colors, black or brown.
Each...........$1.75   Per dozen..........18.90

33814 Men's Knit Wool Cardigan Jackets, full sizes, double breasted; colors, black or brown.
Each.................$2.00   Per dozen.........21.60

33816 Men's Knit Worsted Cardigan Jackets, full sizes; colors, black or brown   Each............. 2.50
Per dozen...............................27.00

33818 Men's Knit Worsted Cardigan Jackets, full sizes; colors, navy blue or wine. Each......... 2.50
Per dozen...............................27.00

33820 Men's Knit Worsted Cardigan Jackets, large full sizes, double breasted; colors, black or brown. Each.............$2.75   Per dozen.....30.00

33822 Men's Knit Worsted Cardigan Jackets, extra fine, full sizes; colors, black or brown.
Each....................$3.00   Per dozen.....32.40

33824 Men's Jersey Jacket, fleeced back, heavy weight, very dressy, double breasted; black.
Each, until sold........................... 2.75

33826 Men's Jersey Knit Jackets for office wear; very neat, comfortable and dressy, fleeced back, single breasted. Colors, tan or fawn.
Each, until old............................ 3.00

Colored and White Saxony, Shetland and Knitting Worsteds.

33840 Knitting Yarns, western made, long wool, solid colors, cardinal, scarlet, seal brown, navy blue, medium blue or black. Per pound........$0.65
In packages of 5 lbs., solid colors............... 3.00

33842 Knitting Yarns, same as above, in sheep's gray or black mixed. Per pound............... .65
In packages of 5 lbs., solid colors............... 3.00

33843 Knitting Yarns, best Ohio wool, selected stock. Colors: Navy, cardinal, golden brown, black or purple. Per pound 1.00
In packages of 5 lbs., solid colors 4 50

33844 Spanish Knitting Worsted. Colors: Black, white, seal brown or navy blue. Per pound..... 1.05

Yarns—Continued.

33846 Superfine German Worsted Knitting Yarns, 4 skeins to the pound, come in the following solid colors: Medium blue, navy blue, blue, light blue, royal blue, medium brown, seal brown, gold brown, medium shade pink, scarlet cardinal, claret, wine, slate, drab, sheep's gray or black mixed. Per pound.................. 1.00
When sold in packages of 5 lbs., one color...... 4.50
Black or white. Per pound.................... .90

33847 German Worsted Knitting Yarns, 4 skeins to the lb., same colors as 33846. Per pound.. .80
Black or white. Per pound................. .70

33848 Saxony Wool, best imported. Colors: Scarlet, garnet, cardinal, claret, wine, pink, baby blue or light blue, medium blue, navy blue, seal brown, gold brown; 16 ounces to box. Per pound 1.35
Black or white. Per pound.......... 1.25

33849 Fairy Floss or Crinkled Yarn, for fancy knitting, black or white only. Per pound..... 1.00

See Our Bicycle Quotations.

Yarns—Continued.

33850 Shetland Wool, best imported. Colors: Scarlet, garnet, cardinal, claret, pink, wine, baby blue or light blue, medium blue, navy blue, seal brown, gold brown; 8 skeins to pound, 12 ounces to package, sold as 1 pound. Per package. 1.20
Black or white. Per pound 1.10
All yarns sold at manufacturer's weight.

Germantown Yarn.

33852 Germantown Yarn, plain white or plain black. Per pound.........................$1.25

33854 Germantown Yarn in the following plain shades: Seal brown, scarlet, pink, green, cardinal, wine, light blue, medium blue, navy blue, yellow, green, salmon, ashes of roses, slate, drab or purple. Per pound................................. 1.35
Germantown yarn comes put up in 10 and 12 skeins to the pound, manufacturer's weight. We do not sell less than one skein of any shade or color.

33857 Imported Ice Wool, cream white,
Per ball.....$0.02   Per box of 8 balls.......... .13

Yarns—Continued.

33859 Imported Ice Wool, black, per ball .... .02
Per box of 8 balls............................... .13

33860 Best Quality Imported Angora Wool, put up in one-quarter-pound boxes, 16 balls to the box. Colors: Brown, gray, black or white. Per ball .... $0.15   Per box 2.25

33868 Imported Berlin Zephyr Worsted or 4-ply colors: Scarlet, pink, cardinal, garnet, wine, baby blue, medium blue, dark blue, navy blue, light, medium and dark green, tan, brown, drab, olive, orange, canary, purple, black or white; 40 laps to the pound, manufacturer's weight. Per pound............................... 1.75
Per lap................................. .05

Wool Yarn.

	Per lb.
33870 Wool Yarn, white, scoured, No. C.	$0.60
33872 Wool Yarn, white shaker, No. EE.	.80
33874 Wool Yarn, blue mixed, No. A.	.60
33876 Wool Yarn, blue mixed, scoured, long wool No. 1	.80
33878 Wool Yarn, blue mixed, best Ohio wool, long staple selected stock. Per pound	1.00

CLOAK DEPARTMENT.

All Garments guaranteed exactly as represented. Ladies' garments are made in sizes 32, 34, 36, 38, 40 and 42 only.

In our Cloak Department, which has been greatly enlarged to better supply the wants of our customers on short notice, will be found the leading styles and newest materials in Children's, Misses' and Ladies' Jackets, Reefers, Capes, in all the new effects. We know our customers want full value for their money, so we have advanced another step in the right direction by giving you a higher grade of material at prices lower than ever before, and a more complete line to select from.

☞ Be sure to send bust and waist measure for cloak. (Measure over bust close under arms.) All cloaks larger than 42 inches will have to be made to order, and cost extra in proportion to size and style desired. If you require extra sized garment, send us a full description of garment wanted, being sure to state bust, length and waist measures. We will then forward measurement blank and quote exact price for having garment made to order. *N. B. We do not sample cloaks.*

Special Notice.

Fall and Winter Cloaks.

A special catalogue of fall and winter cloaks and wraps will be issued by us in October. This book will be replete with quotations and illustrations of the very latest designs in ladies', misses' and children's cold weather garments. It will be mailed to any address upon application. The immense amount of business we are doing in our cloak department, and the continual demand made upon us for garments other than those listed in our general catalogue, wherein our space is limited, leads us to issue this special catalogue; that we may better serve our many patrons and meet their wants more satisfactorily. *Remember:* The special catalogue will not be ready until about the 15th of October and will contain all the very latest styles.

LADIES' WRAPS.

For 1895, All The New Spring and Summer Styles.

Sizes, 32 to 42 inch bust measure.

33900 Ladies' Spring Capes, 21 inches long, made of good quality ladies' cloth, plaited ruffle collar, triple cape; Colors; Navy blue, tan and black. Each..$1.25

33902 Ladies' Spring Capes, 26 inches long, double cape made of wool, ladies' cloth. Handsome plaited collar trimmed with fancy braid; Colors: Tan, navy or black. Each......$1.75

33904 Ladies' Capes, 26 inches long, triple cape, with handsome, ruffled collar, made of all wool ladies' cloth Colors: Black, navy, tan and Havana brown. Each.$2.25

33906 Ladies' Spring Capes, 21 inches long; made of all wool ladies' cloth, 9-inch cream colored lace capecollar, 2-inch satin ribbon ruffle around neck and ribbon bow in front to match. Colors: Navy, Havana, tan and black. Each.......... $2.35

33908 Ladies' Spring Capes, 26 inches long; made of fine all wool cloth; edged all around with ½-inch black fancy openwork braid, braided design to match on front corners. Colors: Black, navy blue, and cardinal red. Large black silk ribbon bow tie at neck. Each.$2.75

33910 Ladies' Spring Capes, 21 inches long; made of fine quality ladies cloth, cape collar trimmed with 4-inch black lace, silk ribbon bow and ruffled neck. Colors: Navy, Havana, brown, tan and black Full sweep. Each.$2.75

33912 Ladies' Spring Capes, 23 inches long, made of light wool cloth, turndown brown velvet collar, entire cape edged with ½-inch brown braid and narrow cord braid; velvet design on front corners, light tan color only, full sweep. Each $3.00

33914 Ladies' Double Spring Capes, 21 inches long, made of all wool ladies' cloth, 4-inch black lace collar, upper cape trimmed with 2 rows of satin ribbon ½ inch wide and 4-inch black lace; full sweep. Colors: Havana, navy, tan and black. Each $3.00

33916 Ladies' Spring Capes, 24 inches long. Upper cape and collar trimmed with contrasting applique work. Made of all wool ladies' cloth. Colors: Black, tan, navy and cardinal. Each....$3.25

33918 Ladies' Spring Capes, 22 inches long, made of all wool ladies' cloth, 8 inch Parisian lace collar, with Parisian lace ornamental work across shoulders and back; satin bow tie of 2 inch ribbon. Colors: Tan, havana, navy and black. Each..........$3.35

33920 Ladies' Spring Capes, 26 inches long. All wool ladies' cloth, hemstiched, double cape, braided in fancy design, scalloped edge, ruffled collar edged with cream lace; full sweep. Colors: Navy black, tan and cardinal. Each.........$3.50

Capes—Continued.

Capes—Continued.

Capes—Continued.

33922 Ladies'Spring Capes. 25 inches long All Wool ladiescloth with large turn down collar and extra circular cape, fashionably trimmed with black applique work. Color; Black, tan, navy and cardinal. Each, $3.50

33924 Ladies' Spring Capes, 30 inches long, made of plain black light weight kersey cloth, 8-inch black lace ruffle collar and 1 row of narrow jet around neck. Particularly desirable for old ladies. Each $3.75

33926 Ladies' Spring Capes; 25in.long,made of fine All wool cloth. Sailor collar with 2-inch black silk ribbon tie, 10-inch oriental black lace across shoulders and back. Entire cape and collar edged with ¼-inch black gimp. Colors: Cardinal, navy, and black. Each $4.00

33928 Ladies'Spring Capes, 21 inches long, hemstitched edge, large black ribbon bow ties, turn down collar trimmed with fancy black braid, 5 large braided ornaments extending over shoulders and back. Colors: Tan, Havana, navy.and black, full sweep. Each........ $4.00

33930 Ladies'Spring Capes, 22 inches long, made of imported black diagonal clay worsted, double ruffle collar of black lace ornamented with black jet; 2-inch black satin ribbon streamers in back, ribbon bow tie at neck, 3-inch lace and narrow row of jet around bottom, full sweep. Each........ $4.50

33932 Ladies' Spring Capes, 27 inches long, black diagonal clay worsted, 8-inch lace ruffle collar, large ribbon bow in front and back, full sweep. Each $4.50

33934 Ladies'Spring Capes, 22 inches long, made of imported broadcloth, pleated ruffle collar of 1¾-inch ribbon, trimmed with black lace; black ribbon bow tie, shoulders and back trimmed with black braided scroll design producing a rich and handsome effect. Colors: Cardinal, red, navy blue, tan and black. Each.. ....$5.00

33936 Ladies' Spring Capes, 22 inches long, made of ladies' broadcloth; collar made of fancy bows of satin ribbon; upper cape perforated in fancy designs. Colors: Black, tan, navy, cardinal; full sweep. Each...$5.00

33938 Ladies' Spring Capes, 21 inches long, turndown collar; collar and skirt beautifully embroidered in two contrasting colors of silk braid. Full sweep. Colors: Tan, Havana, blue and black. Each........ $5.50

33940 Ladies' Spring Capes, 20 inches long, made of fine imported broadcloth. Turn down collar. Collar and bottom of skirt trimmed with narrow, fancy braid. 1½ inch fancy openwork lace two inches above bottom of skirt, fancy braided ornaments around shoulders and back. Colors: Navy, tan and black; full sweep, Each...... $5.50

33942 Ladies'Spring Capes, 32 inches long, made of imported black clay worsted, with 11-inch shoulder cape trimmed with jet and 8-inch ruffled collar. Satin ribbon bow in back and around neck. Each......... $6.00

33944 Ladies' Spring Capes, 22 inches long,double cape. B'lk broadcloth. Latest design, standing collar, with bow on side, 4 openwork designs in upper cape and two in lower cape with lace background. Colors: Black, red and navy blue. Each...$6.00

33946 Ladies' Spring Capes, 21 inches long, made of imported broadcloth, turn down collar, with applique corners, beautiful black lace and applique open work trimming around skirt; colors:Tan and brown. Each........ $6.00

33948 Ladies' Spring Capes, 21 inches long, made of fine all wool cloth, ruffle collar, trimmed with ruffled silk ribbon, cape and upper cape trimmed in latest fashi n with handsome silk embroidery; full sweep; colors: Black, tan, navy, cardinal. Each $6.50

33950 Ladies' Spring Capes, 19 inches long, made of fancy cord black ottoman silk. Four inch turn down collar of same material, overlapping 8 inch black lace collar. Shirt, collar, and lace collar all edged with jet, Moire silk ribbon tie. Each... $6.50

33952 Ladies' Spring Capes, 25 inches long, made of imported broad cloth, inlaid turn down velvet collar, double cape. Both capes, collar and skirt trimmed with six rows of neat silk stitching; full sweep. Colors: Tan, black, navy and red. Each.......................... $7.00

33954 Ladies' Capes, 24 inches long, made of royal blue broadcloth, large turn down collar; skirt and collar tastefully trimmed with black applique work. Extra full sweep; blue only. Each...$7.75

33956 Ladies' Spring Capes, 22 inches long, made of broadcloth, new standing bow collar, made of heavy satin; entire cape edged with narrow silk gimp. Body of cape trimmed in fancy lace openwork,French design. Colors: Black, cadet blue, tan and navy;full sweep. Each...... $8.25

Capes—Continued.

33958 Ladies' spring Capes, 25 inches long, made of imported broadcloth, double cape inlaid velvet collar; both capes trimmed with beautiful new design applique work of contrasting colors. Colors: Navy, cardinal, black and tan; full sweep. Each........$8.50

33960 Ladies' Capes, 22 inches long, made of fine imported broadcloth; collar made of 4 rows of heavy satin ribbon, long ribbon bow tie in front. Embroidered all over in contrasting silk braid, latest designs. Colors: Tan, navy and black. Each....$9.00

33962 Ladies' Spring Capes 23 inches long, imported broadcloth, new silk lined standing ruffle collar, collar and cape trimmed in contrasting colors with beautiful applique work. Colors: Tan, navy, black; full sweep. Each..$9.50

33964 Ladies' Spring Capes, 24 inches long, made of imported broadcloth. Double cape, upper cape, satin-lined, with large, new style lapels and turn down collar, trimmed with applique work. Very handsome and stylish. Colors: Tan, navy, black and cardinal. Each....................................... $10.00

33966 Ladies' Spring Capes, 21 inches long made of imported broadcloth. Turn down collar. These capes have trimming of black lace around bottom, braided in latest designs of silk feather edge embroidery. Narrow silk guimp around collar and down front. Colors: Bottle green, navy blue, tan and black; full sweep. Each......$10.25

33968 Ladies' Spring Capes, 22 inches long, made of black silk velvet. Bottom trimmed with 4½ inch black lace with 1-inch jet heading, high standing collar of plaited lace with 1-inch jet heading, high standing collar of plaited lace and jet ornaments. Very rich. Each......$11.00

Capes—Continued.

33970 Ladies' Spring Capes, 22 inches long, made of imported broadcloth, tan color, with cardinal red silk lining; ruffle collar, silk lined, to match lining of cape. Perforated designs, showing lining and producing handsome effect. Gilt chain ornamental fasteners. Tan color only; full sweep. Each.$10.50

33971 Ladies' Spring Capes, 22 inches long, made of fine imported kersey; collar of standing black lace, ribbon tie in front, 3-inch black lace trimming and one row of lace insertion around lower part of cape. Black only. Extra full sweep. Each....$11.50

33972 Ladies' Fine Black Ottoman Silk Capes, 21 inches long. New standing collar of same material. Double lace collar, made of one row of black lace 6 inches wide and overlapped with upper collar of cream colored lace. Satin bow and lace tie. Very handsome. Each.......$12.00

33974 Ladies' Spring Capes, 23 inches long, made of imported black kersey, perforated in beautiful designs and trimmed with black silk embroidery, high standing collar trimmed with black lace and jet. Black only. Full sweep. Each.....$13.00

33976 Ladies' Fine Black Ottoman Silk Capes, 24 inches long, trimmed with 5-inch black lace, with beading of jet heads, silk embroidered designs over shoulders and back, ruffled standing collar, black satin ribbon tie. Full sweep. Each....$14.00

33978 Ladies' Spring Capes, 26 inches long, made entirely of black satin and lace, black lace groundwork, covered with alternate rows of 3-inch satin and 5-inch black lace, trimmed with narrow jet, heavy satin ruffle collar, silk lined and trimmed with jet, large ribbon tie. Each....$15.00

Ladies' Jackets.

Sizes, 32 to 42 inches, Bust Measure.

NOTE.—We show but a few lines of Jackets, as capes will be much more fashionable and in greater demand.

33979 Ladies' Spring Jackets, 24 inches long, made of cheviot goods, double breasted, full sleeves, large pointed lapels. Colors: Black, blue or brown. Each.....$3.00

33980 Ladies' Spring Jackets, 25 inches long, light tan and gray mixed twilled cloth, inlaid velvet collar, double breasted, full sleeves, lapel pockets. Each....$3.50

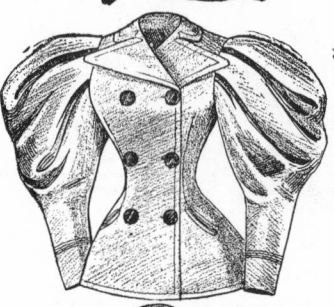

33982 Ladies' Spring Jackets, 26 inches long, tan brown soft finish diagonal cheviot, double breasted, large horn buttons, balloon sleeves, plaited back. Each..$4.25

33983 Ladies' Black Imported Clay Worsted Spring Jackets, 26 inches long, large pompadour sleeves, plaited back, curved pockets. Sizes, 32 to 42. Each......$5.00

33984 Ladies' Spring Jackets, 25 inches long, double breasted, curved pockets. Made of twilled wool cloth, large balloon sleeves. Colors: Black and navy blue. Sizes, 32 to 42. Collar and lapels, trimmed with 3 rows of narrow black braid. Each......$6.00

Children's and Misses' Jackets.

Sizes, 5 to 12 Years Only.

33985 *Children's and Misses' Jackets*, made of neat twilled wool mixed cloth, double breasted, large pompadour sleeves. Colors: Blue mixed and brown mixed. Sizes, 5 to 12 years only. Each.....$1.85

Jackets—Continued

33986 Children's and Misses' Jackets, made of navy blue twilled cloth, turn down collar and cuffs trimmed with white braid, double breasted, nickel plated buttons. Sizes, 5 to 12 years only. Each.....$2.35

33987 Children's Fancy Spring Jackets, made of all wool cloth, collar and sleeves embroidered with black silk, double breasted, brass buttons, anchor pattern, full pompadour sleeves, very stylish: Cardinal red color only. 5 to 12 years. Each.... $3.00

33989 Children's and Misses' Jackets, made of brown, mixed wool cloth, double breasted, plain brass buttons, pompadour sleeves, full large fancy turn, down collar, trimmed with brown mohair and gilt braid. Sizes, 5 to 12 years. Each...$3.25

33996 Children's and Misses' Spring Jackets, double breasted, fancy buttons, star shaped turn down collar, collar and cuffs trimmed with 2 rows each of black and white narrow braid; cardinal red color only. Very stylish. Each.... $3.50

Infants' Cloaks.

New goods, latest designs, lowest prices.

N. B.—The average weight of infants' long cashmere cloaks is 16 ounces each. Short cashmere walking jackets, 12 oz. When ordered separately by mail or special prepaid express, allow one cent per ounce extra for charges.

34341 Infants' Long Union Cashmere Cloaks, pleated collar; 9-inch cape, and bottom of cloak embroidered with silk to match. Length of cloak, 36 inches; Colors: Tan or cream.
Each . . . . $ 1.00
Per dozen............10.80
34343 Infants' Fine Union Cashmere Cloaks, 36 inches long, sateen lining, 8-inch cape and bottom of cloak embroidered with silk and ribbon to match. Mother Hubbard waist, full sleeves; colors: Tan and cream. Each...............................$1.65
Per dozen......................17 82

Infants' Cloaks—Continued.

34345 Infants' Long Cassimere Cloaks, latest style, lace and silk embroidered collar, cream colored satin ribbon streamers in back. Mother Hubbard waist, full sleeves. Cream or tan colors.
Each....................$2.75

34345

34347 Infants' Long Wool Cashmere Cloaks, new 18-inch long double cape and skirt, trimmed with heavy silk embroidery, Mother Hubbard waist, full sleeves. Tan or cream color.
Each..................$3.50

34347

34349 Infants' Long Cloaks, made of tan or cream crystal Bengaline silk. Collar, sleeve capes and cuffs richly embroidered in silk to match. Mother Hubbard waist, full sleeves. Each.........$4.00

Walking Jackets.

FOR CHILDREN FROM 1 TO 3 YEARS.

34349

34351 Infants' Mother Hubbard Cashmere Walking Jacket or Short Cloak, 7-inch cape and bottom of cloak embroidered in silk to match. Silesia lining, padded with wadding. Full sleeves, length 22, 24, 26 and 28 inches. Colors: Cream, white or tan.
Each.................$1.25
34353 Infants' Fine Cashmere Walking Jackets, with cape, Mother Hubbard waist, full sleeves, sateen lining, padded with wadding, richly embroidered on skirt and cape with silk. Length, 22, 24, 26 and 28 inches. Colors: Cream, white or tan. Weight, 12 ounces. Each...........$2.25
34355 Infant's Fine Cashmere Walking Jackets, scolloped cape, turn down collar, very full sleeves, all beautifully embroidered in white silk and narrow ribbons. 2 to 4 years; cream or tan.
Each...................$3.50

Walking Jacket.

34355

34357 Infant's Walking Jackets or Cloaks, for spring and summer, made of fine crystal or Bengaline silk, latest style, large collar, very full sleeves, collar and cuffs trimmed with fancy silk embroidery, large lace cape collar, 2 to 4 years, cream or tan.$5.50

34357

CHILDREN'S REEFER JACKETS.
New and Nobby Styles for Spring Wear.

2 to 4 years.

34359 Reefer Jackets, made of navy blue twilled flannel, double breasted, fancy brass buttons, sailor collars. 2 to 4 years. Full sleeves.
Each $1.10
4361 Reefer Jackets, made of fine navy blue, tan, brown or red twilled flannel. Full pleated sleeves, sailor collar, large fancy brass buttons, double breasted. 2 to 4 years. State color desired.
Each..............·.. $1.50

34363   **34367**

34363 Reefer Jackets, double breasted made of fine all wool ladies' cloth, large fancy silver buttons, sailor collar. Front, collar and cuffs trimmed with fancy white silk embroidery. Colors: Navy blue, royal blue, cardinal, tan, and brown. 2 to 4 years. Full sleeves.
Each..................................$2.00

34367 Reefer Jackets, double breasted, made of fine all wool twilled flannel; full sleeves, fine white pearl buttons, large sailor collar, and cuffs trimmed with three rows of narrow silk braid, 2 to 4 years, colors: Cardinal, navy, tan or brown
Each..............$2.35
34369 Reefer Jackets, fine all wool French flannel; double breasted, large fancy metal buttons, full sleeves, large latest design collar, wide
34369
lapels, collar and cuffs handsomely trimmed with fancy black braid. "A Little Beauty." Colors: Cardinal red, navy blue and tan, 2 to 5 years. Each.....................................$2.50

Washable Reefers.

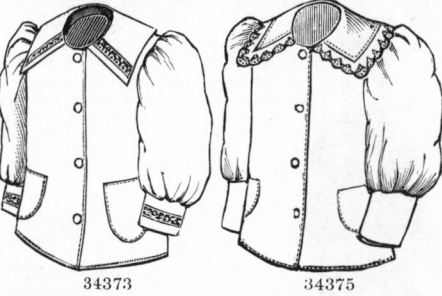

34373   **34375**

34373 Reefer Jackets, made of fine white duck; full sleeves, pearl buttons, large sailor collar and cuffs, trimmed with insertion, 2 to 4 years. Each.................................$1.15
34375 Reefer Jackets, made of fine white, corded pique. Very large sleeves, pearl buttons; large sailor collar, trimmed with white lawn, edged with scalloped Hamburg. Something new and very popular. 2 to 5 years. Each.... .... 1.85

Eider-Down Cloaks.

The following garments do not have fur trimming unless so stated in the quotation. Average weight is 16 ounces each.

34377 Infants' Eider-down Cloaks, Mother Hubbard waist, large full sleeves with cuffs, fleece lining; roll collar, small neat pin head check pattern, black and gray or tan and gray.
Lengths 22, 24, 26 and 28 inches. Each.........$0.90
Per dozen. 9.72

34379 Eider-down Cloaks, Mother Hubbard waist, pointed collar, large full sleeves, with cuffs made plain without trimming. A very neat and serviceable garment, fine fleece lining. Colors: Cream. light blue, pink, tan, cardinal, 1 to 4 years. Lengths 22, 24, 26 and 28 inches.
Each....................$1.50
Complete with muff and hood to match. Per set.......$2.50

34383 Fancy Eider-down

34370-34378 Cloaks, Mother Hubbard waist, large full sleeves with cuffs, fancy pointed collar and cuffs trimmed with 6-inch white Angora fur. These garments are made in fancy broken stripe mixture of tans, browns, grays and ecrus; we can furnish background colors in tan, light blue, pink or cream with beautiful contrasting stripes. Lengths, 22, 24, 26 and 28 inches. Weight 20 ounces, 1 to 4 years. Each....................$2.25
Complete with muff and hood to match. Per set . . 3.75

Ladies' Gossamer and Mackintosh Coats.

In taking measures for Ladies' Gossamers, measure from collar down the back to length desired; sizes, 54 to 62 inches long. No odd sizes. Weight of gossamers, put up in small box, 1½ to 2½ pounds, according to size and quality.

34385 Ladies' Best Quality Plain Silver Gray Gossamer Circular, with hood attached.
Each $1.10
34387 Ladies' Silver Gray Narrow Stripe Circular, with hood attached.
Each $1.25

34387

34389 Ladies' Silver Gray Stripe Common Sense Gossamer, with large cape and hood attached.
Each $1.75

N. B.—Single texture means a printed or woven fabric on outside, with heavy rubber coating on inside. Double texture means a printed or woven fabric on both sides with gum rubber between.

34391 Ladies' Single Texture Lady Chumley Mackintosh, with 25-inch cape attached; gray or brown stripes.
Each $2.00

34393 Ladies' Single Texture Inverness Mackintosh, with 26-inch cape attached; black or navy blue narrow wale diagonal.
Each $2.40

34395 Ladies' Single Texture Inverness Mackintosh, with large military cape, black or navy blue, corkscrew pattern. Each.$3.00

Ladies' Mackintosh.

34397 Ladies' Single Texture Inverness Mackintosh, with 26-inch cape attached. Navy blue or black cashmere twill. Each.................... 4.25
34399 Ladies' Single Texture Inverness Mackintosh, with large military cape. Steel gray, narrow wale diagonal. Each............. 5.25
34403 Ladies' Double Texture Inverness Mackintosh, with 26-inch cape attached, light plaid lining. Black or navy blue cashmere. Each... 4.50
34405 Ladies' Double Texture Mackintosh, with large military cape attached, plaid twilled lining. Navy blue or black, all wool tricot.
Each 6.00

Mackintosh Coats—Continued.

Double Cape Mackintosh.

34407 Ladies' Single Texture Mackintosh, with detachable double cape, 17 and 27 inches long; navy blue diagonal with narrow stripe.
Each.........$3.50
34409 Ladies' Double Texture Mackintosh with detachable double cape, 16 and 30 inches long; black or navy blue cashmere, fancy lining.
Each..........$6.25
34411 Ladies' Single Texture Mackintosh, with detachable double cape, 16 and 27 inches long, lined with handsome Scotch plad silk finish serge. Navy blue or black. all wool tricot.
Each. ...$9.25

34413 Ladies' Single Texture Mackintosh, with detachable triple cape, 26 inches. Black or navy blue cashmere. Each....$3.50
34415 Ladies' Single Texture Mackintosh, with detachable triple cape. Navy blue or black diagonal, narrow wale. Each $4.25
34417 Ladies' Double Texture Mackintosh, with detachable triple cape, fancy woven lining. Black or navy blue cashmere. Each.... $6.50

Misses' Gossamer and Mackintosh Coats.

Tripple Cape Mackintosh

34419 Misses' Best Quality Silver Gray Gossamer Circular, with hood attached. Sizes, 34 to 50 inches long. Each $1.00
34421 Misses' Single Texture Mackintosh, with 22-inch attached cape. Brown and black broken check. Sizes, 36 to 52 inches long. Each...... 2.25
34423 Misses' Single Texture Mackintosh, with 19-inch attached cape. Navy blue cashmere serge. Sizes, 36 to 52 inches long. Each...... 3.50
34425 Misses' Double Texture Mackintosh, with 20-inch attached cape. Navy blue cashmere, fancy plaid lining. Sizes, 36 to 52 inches long.. 4.75
34427 Misses' Double Texture Mackintosh, with detachable double cape. Navy blue, fine cashmere, with light plaid woven lining. Sizes, 34 to 50 inches long. Each........................ 5.00

Men's Mackintosh Coats.

Sizes, 34, 36, 38, 40, 42, 44, 46, 48. Chest measure to be taken over the coat it is to be worn over.
34429 Men's Double Texture Mackintosh Coat, with detachable cape, black diagonal, with fancy plaid lining. Each....................$3.75
34433 Men's Double Texture Macikntosh Coat, with detachable cape, patent ventilated arm holes, small gray checks and stripes, plaid lining. Each...........$3.75
34435 Men's Double Texture Mackintosh Coat, with detachable cape, narrow wale, dark navy blue diagonal, fancy plaid lining......$4.25
34437 Men's Double Texture Mackintosh Coat, same as above, in black.........$4.25
34439 Men's Double Texture Mackintosh Coat, with detachable cape, black cashmere, with fancy plaid lining. Each....................$5.95
34441 Men's Double Texture Mackintosh Coat, same as above, in dark navy blue. Each........ 5.95
34443 Men's Double Texture Mackintosh Coat, with detachable cape, all wool, dark navy blue, tricot, black cashmere twill lining. Each...... 8.00
34445 Men's Double Texture Mackintosh Coat, same as above in black. Each.......... 8.00
34447 Men's Double Texture Mackintosh Coat, with detachable cape, all wool dark navy blue serge, with fancy plaid woven lining, patent ventilated shoulders. Each...................11.50
34449 Men's Double Texture Mackintosh Coat, with detachhble cape, all wool black cheviot, fancy plaid woven lining. Each.............13.00

Men's Mackintosh Box Coats.

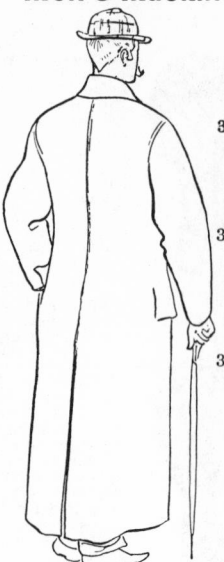

34451 Men's Double Texture Mackintosh Box Coats, double breasted, all wool black tricot, ventilated arm pits, fancy plaid lining, silk velvet collar.
Each.... . ...$7.50
34452 Men's Double Texture Mackintosh Box Coats, double ,breastedlight brown pin check cassimere, ventilated arm pits, fancy plaid woven lining, silk velvet collar, a very nobby coat. Each............$11.50
34453 Men's Double Texture Mackintosh Box Coat, double breasted, dark navy, blue or black, all wool serge, silk velvet collar, plaid lining, ventilated arm pits. Each.........$11.75

Box Coat.

Medium and Heavy Weight Rubber Clothing.

N. B.—We do not sample rubber or mackintosh coats, except where so stated.

34454 Men's Medium Weight Fine Black Rubber Coats, fancy plaid back; 50 inches long, double breasted..$2.15
34456 Men's Medium Weight Coats, wine color, velvet collar, fancy plaid back, double breasted........$2.50
34458 Men's Medium Heavy Black Rubber Coats, fancy plaid back, double breasted. $2.75
34460 Men's Medium Weight Black Rubber Coats, fancy plaid back, double breasted. $3.00
34462 Men's Medium Heavy Black Rubber Coats, fancy plaid back, double breasted. $3.25
34464 Men's Medium Weight Black Rubber Coats, patent ventilate epaulet shoulders, fancy plaid back, double breasted................$3.50

34466 Men's Heavy Black Rubber Coats, fancy striped twilled back, double breasted....$3.50
34468 Men's Medium Heavy Black Rubber Coats, double back, fancy sateen back, double breasted, velvet collar....................... 3.60
34470 Men's Heavy Weight Black Rubber Coats, double back, buff colored, twilled drill back, double breasted...................... 3.75
34472 Men's Medium Weight Black Rubber Coats, extra long double back, fancy striped back, double breasted...................... 4.00
34474 Firemen's Regulation Rubber Coats, double coated, extra wide fly front, with snaps and rings, straps and buckles on sleeves and neck...................... 4.00
34476 Policemen's Regulation Rubber Coats, fancy plaid back, double back, patent ventilated shoulders, patent ball and socket buttons, straps on sleeves, pocket for billy and shield for star 5.00

Men's Heavy Rubber Clothing.

Weight of rubber clothing, 3½ to 5½ pounds according to size and quality.
Sizes on men's clothing are as follows:

Size,	3	4	5	6	7
Chest	36	38	40	42	44

We do not guarantee our rubber clothing, but sell only the best made.
34477 Rubber Coats, on heavy sheeting, black luster finish, officers' length...............$1.60
34479 Rubber Coats, on heavy sheeting, dull finish, officers' length...................... 2.00
34481 Rubber Coats, on heavy sheeting, dull finish, mountaineers' length, extra long...... 2.75
34483 Rubber Coats, on heavy drill, dull finish, officers' length...................... 2.25
34487 Rubber Coats, on heavy drill, dull finish, mountaineers' length, extra long, can be buttoned around legs and made a riding coat if desired...................... 3.00

WE ARE LEADERS....
* But are willing to follow good leads. Anything to improve.

Boys' Rubber and Mackintosh Coats.

34489 Boys' Rubber Coats, on heavy sheeting, black, luster finish. Sizes, 24 to 34 chest measure.... $1.50

34491 Boys' Rubber Coats, on heavy sheeting, black, dull finish. Sizes, 24 to 34 chest measure, 1.85

34493 Boys' Double Texture Mackintosh Coat, with detachable cape, dark navy blue cashmere with f ncy plaid lining. Sizes, 26 to 36 chest measure. Each.... 3.25

34495 Boys' Double Texture Mackintosh Coats, with detachable cape. Narrow wale black diagonal, with fancy plaid lining. Sizes, 26 to 36 chest maasure. Each.... 3.75

Men's Rubber Leggings, Hats and Blankets. Each,

34496 Rubber Camp Blankets, on heavy sheeting, with ball and socket fastener. Size, 45x72 inches. Weight, 3½ pounds.... $1.25

34498 Rubber U. S. A. Poncho Blankets, on heavy sheeting. Size, 45x72 inches. Weight, 3 pounds 1.35

Per pair.

34500 Rubber Leggings, long, black luster.... $0.78

34502 Rubber Leggings, long, black, dull finish. .90

34503 Rubber Leggings, on drill, long, black luster finish 88

34504 Rubber Leggings, on drilling, long, black dull finish.... 1.00

Postage on rubber leggings, 18 to 20 c. per pair.

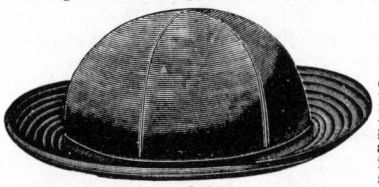

34506— Men's Round Crown Rubber Hats. For gunning and fishing, they are indispensible.

34506

as they are a great protection from rain, wind and snow. They are light and flexible, and can be carried in the trousers' pocket. Each $0.25

Each.

34508 Rubber Caps, with capes, black luster.... $0.50

34509 Ladies' Gossamer Rubber Sleeves, 16 inches long Per pair.... .35

34510 Gossamer Hat Covers, for stiff hats.... .20

Rubber Gloves and Mittens.

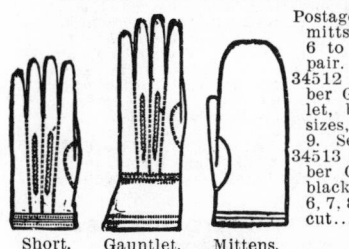

Postage on Rubber mitts and gloves, 6 to 9 cents per pair.

34512 Ladies' Rubber Gloves, gauntlet, black or tan, sizes, 6, 7, 8 and 9. See cut. $1.20

34513 Ladies' Rubber Gloves, short, black or tan, sizes, 6, 7, 8 and 9, See cut.... $1.00

Short. Gauntlet. Mittens.

34514 Men's Rubber Gloves, heavy, short; sizes, 10 to 15. See cut. Black or tan.... 1.15

34516 Men's Rubber Gloves, gauntlet, black or tan; sizes, 10 to 15. See cut.... 1.50

34518 Men's Extra Heavy Rubber Mittens. See cut.... 1.15

34520 Men's Wool Lined Rubber Mittens; black 1.35

34522 Ladies' White Rubber Aprons, with bib, medium size.... .85

34524 Ladies' White Rubber Aprons, with bib, large size.... 1.10

34526 Pure Gum or Rubber Tissue, used by tailors for bottom of pants, ladies' arm shields, rents or tares in ladies' dress fabrics can be mended without sewing, by placing a small piece of tissue under the cloth and press with a hot iron. Used for all kinds of invisible patching; 36 inches wide, about 7½ yards to the pound. Per pound.... $2.25. Per yard.... .33

34527 Gossamer Rubber Cloth, black only, 36 inches wide. Per yard.... .35

34528 Double Texture Mackintosh Cloth, all wool, black Tricot with fancy plaid lining; 36 inches wide, for making coats, cloaks and Mackintoshes. Per yard.... 1.25

Extra Quality, Yellow Oil Clothing, double made.

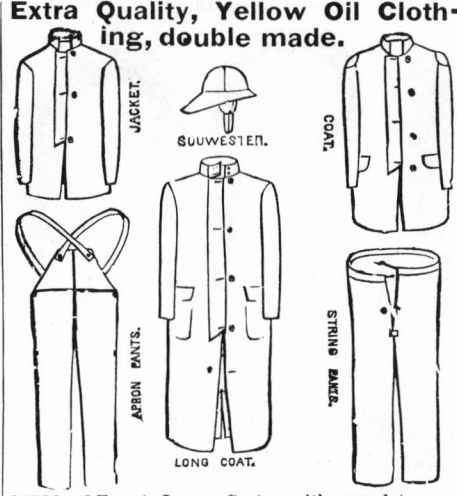

JACKET.   SOUWESTER.   COAT.

APRON PANTS.   STRING PANTS.

LONG COAT.

34530 Officers' Long Coats, with epaulets, patched and elastic inside sleeves; weight, 5 lbs.... $2.00

34531 Frock or Half Coats, with epaulets, patched and elastic inside sleeves; weight, 3¾ lbs.... 1.40

34532 Jackets, short and plain, weight, 3 lbs.... 1.00

34533 String Pants; weight, 2½ lbs.... .90

34534 Apron Pants; weight, 2½ lbs.... 1.00

34535 Squam Sou'wester, yellow; weight, 7 oz.. .25

34536 Cape Ann Sou' wester; weight, 8oz.... .50

Extra Quality, Black Oil Clothing.

34537 Officers' Long Coats, with epaulets, patched and elastic inside sleeves; weight, 3¾ lbs.. $2.10

34538 Jackets, short and plain; weight, 3 lbs.... 1.10

34539 String Pants; weight, 2½ lbs.... 1.00

34540 Apron Pants; weight, 2¾ lbs.... 1.10

34541 Squam Sou'wester, black; weight, 7 oz... .30

34542 Cape Ann Sou'wester, black; weight, 8 oz. .60

34543 Waterproof Dressing, or prepared oil. A superior dressing for oiled clothing; keeps the goods soft and waterproof. Put up in pint cans, black. Per pint.... .30

34544 Yellow Oil Dressing. Per pint.... 30

34545 Pommel Slicker, stockman's long coat, riding or walking; weight, 6¼ lbs. Yellow duck brand.... 2.40

34546 Black Pommel Slicker, same as above.... 2.50

Ladies' Black Parasols.

34547 Ladies' Parasol, 20 inches, black satin ebony handle. Each.... $1.00

34548 Ladies' Parasol, 20 inches, black with narrow and wide combination stripes, ebony crook handle. Each.... 1.50

34549 Ladies' Parasol, 20 inches, black surrah silk, ebony crook handle. Each.... 2.00

34550 Ladies' Parasols, 20 inches, black surrah silk with 4-inch ruffle, ebony crook handle. Each.... 2.50

34551 Ladies' Parasols, 20 inches, black corded silk, with narrow satin stripes, ebony crook handles. Each.... 3.50

Price governs quality on all black silk parasols.

Ladies' White and Fancy Parasols.

34552 Ladies' Parasol, 20 inches, dimity lawn, ecru or b ue, small scattering dots, lace stripe. Twisted quail handle. Each.... $0.90

34553 Ladies' Parasol, 20 inches, midsummer sateen finish. Blue clouded figures, white ribs, white enameled, carved, straight or ball shape handle. Each.... 1.00

34554 Ladies' Parasol, 20 inches, heavy white duck. White ribs, white closed loop, enamel handles, cord and tassel. Each.... 1.25

34555 Ladies' Parasol, 20 inches, white China silk, medium wide and narrow satin stripes on top and bottom; plain center, white enamel ribs, closed loop handle, cord and tassel. Each.... 1.50

34556 Ladies' Parasol, 20 inches, white satin, with 5-inch single ruffle, white enameled ribs, satin puff on top. white crook handle. Each.... 2.00

34557 Ladies' Parasol, 20 inches, cream and white watered, Moire silk, imitation crape pattern, white ribs, silk puff to match, silk cord and tassel, white crook handle. Each.... 3.00

Children's Parasols.

34558 Children's Cambric Parasols, 12 inch. Colors: Cardinal pink, or blue. Each.... $0.25

34559 Children's Fancy Sateen finish Parasols, 14-inch, with small fancy checks. Each.... .50

34560 Children's Parasols, scolloped edge satin, 12 inch. Colors: cardinal or blue. Each.... .75

UMBRELLA DEPARTMENT.

NEW GOODS, LATEST DESIGNS.

LADIES' AND GENTLEMEN'S UMBRELLAS.

Weight of umbrellas, 1 to 1¾ lbs. The illustrations of umbrella handles below do not always represent the exact pattern of those quoted, but simply give an outline style of handles. Weight on Gingham Umbrellas, 1½ to 1¾ lbs., silk umbrellas 1 to 1¼ lbs.

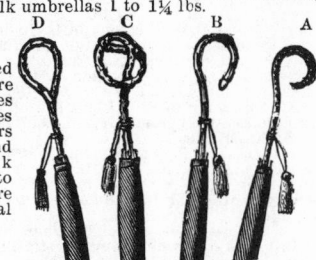

D   C   B   A

Umbrellas marked 26 inch measure 25inch; 28 inches measure 27 inch All manufacturers of umbrellas and parasols mark them from 1 to 1½ inches more than the actual measure.

34570 Ladies' Good Quality Black Sateen Umbrellas, fancy metal handles. Style F. 8-rib, solid frames. Size. 26 inches. Each.... $0.65

34572 Ladies' Black Cotton Gloria Umbrellas, natural oak loop handles. 8-rib paragon frames. Size, 26 inches. Each.... 0.85

34574 Ladies' Fine Black cotton Gloria Umbrellas, natural wood closed loop handles. Style D. 8-rib paragon frames. Size, 26 inches. Each.. 0.90

34576 Ladies' Black English Gloria Umbrellas. Acacia or oak loops. 8-rib paragon frames. Size, 26 inches. Each.... 1.00

34578 Ladies' Best Black Cotton Gloria Umbrellas, horn black handles, with silver band. Style F. 8-rib paragon frame. Size, 26 inches. Each.... $1.15

34580 Ladies' Black Twilled Silk Gloria Umbrellas, black ebony handle. Style D. 8-rib paragon frames. Size, 26 inches. Each.... 1.25

34582 Ladies' Black Silk Gloria Umbrellas, one piece Acacia wood, crook handles. Style A, with tassel. 8-rib paragon frame. Size, 26 inches.... 1.35

34584 Ladies' Black Silk Gloria Umbrellas, twisted or closed loop, Congo handles. Styles C or D, with tassel. 8-rib paragon frame. Size, 26 inches. Each.... 1.50

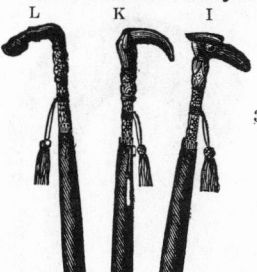

H   G   F   E

34586 Ladies' Black Silk Gloria Umbrellas, solid black rubber loop handles. Style D. with tassel; 8 rib paragon frame. Size, 26 inches. Each $1.50

34588 Ladies' Black English Silk Gloria Tight Rolling Umbrellas, imported open or closed wood loop handles, steel rod. Case and tassel. 8-rib paragon frame. Size, 26 in. ches. Each $1.75

34590 Ladies' Black Silk Gloria Umbrellas. fancy Dresden hook handle. Style F, with narrow gold band. Steel rod and tassel. 8-rib paragon frame. Size, 26 inches. Each.... 2.00

34592 Ladies' Extra Quality Union Black Twilled Silk Gloria Umbrellas, engraved gold hook handles. Style F. Steel rod, case and tassels, 8-rib paragon frame. Size, 26 inches. Each.... 2.40

34594 Ladies' Black Union Twilled Silk Uubrellas, handsome torter shell hook handles, with go d band. Style B. Steel rod, case and tassels. 8-rib, paragon frame. Size 26 inches. Each.... 2.50

34596 Ladies' Fine Quality Black Union Twilled Silk Umbrellas, imported congo twisted and closed loop wood handles. Styles C or D. Steel rod, case and tassels. 8-rib paragon frame. Size, 26 inches. Each.... 3.00

34598 Ladies' Black Union Taffeta Silk Umbrellas, fine quality, beautiful white pearl hook handles with gold band. Style F. Case and tassels. 8-rib paragon frame. Size, 26 inches. Each 3.75

Gentlemen's Umbrellas. New and Carefully Selected Stock.

L   K   I

34600 Men's Black Gingham Umbrellas, 7-rib solid frame, crook or straight wood han les.

Sizes	28-inch.	30-inch.	32-inch.
Each	$.50	$0.60	$0.70

Umbrellas—Continued.

34602 Men's Black Scotch Gingham Umbrellas, carved wood, crooked or straight handles, 8-rib solid frame.

Sizes	28-inch.	30-inch.	32-inch.
Each	$0.65	$0.75	$0.85

34604 Men's Black Scotch Gingham Umbrellas, same as above with 10 ribs.

Sizes	28-inch.	30-inch.	32-inch.
Each	$0.75	$0.85	$1.00

34606 Men's Fine Black Scotch Gingham Umbrellas, natural wood, crook or straight handles, 8-rib paragon frame.

Sizes	28-inch.	30-inch.	32-inch.
Each	$1.00	$1.10	$1.25

34608 Men's Black Cotton Gloria Umbrellas, acacia wood, hook handles, style G, trimmed with silver band, 8-rib paragon frame.

Sizes	28-inch.	30-inch.	32 inch.
Each	$1.00.	$1.15.	$1.25

34610 Men's Extra Fine Black Scotch Gingham, Umbrella 8-rib paragon frame, bamboo crook or straight handles.

Sizes	28-inch.	30-inch.	32 inch.
Each	$1.10.	$1.25.	$1 35.

34612 Men's Fast Black Guaranteed Sateen, metal crook handles, style K, 8-rib solid frame. Size, 28 inches. Each .... .85

34614 Men's Black Scotch Gingham Umbrellas, 16-rib solid frame, crook or straight wooden handles. Size, 28 inches. Each .... .95

34616 Men's Black Cotton Gloria Umbrellas, natural wood, crook or straight handles 8-rib paragon frame. Size, 28 inches. Each 1.00

34618 Men's Fine Black Cotton Twilled Gloria Umbrellas, 8-rib paragon frame, imported Acacia wood, crook handles. Style G. Size, 28 inches. Each 1.50

34620 Men's English Black Taffeta Silk, tight roller umbrellas; imported Prince of Wales or opera, wood, crook handles, steel rod, case and tassels; 8-rib paragon frame. Size, 28 inches. Each 1.95

34622 Men's Black Cotton Gloria Umbrellas, silver trimmed, natural wood handles, 8-rib solid frame.

Sizes	28-inch.	30-inch.
Each	$0.85	$1.00

34624 Men's Black, English Gloria Umbrellas, olive and Acacia wood, crook and straight handles, 8-rib paragon frame.

Sizes	28-inch,	30-inch.
Each	$1.25	$1.35

34626 Men's Fine Black Twilled Union Silk Umbrellas, 8-rib paragon frame. Natural wood, crook and straight handles, styles, H or K, with silk tassel.

Sizes	26	28	30 inches.
Each	$1.35	$1.55	$1.75

34628 Men's Fine Black Silk Gloria Umbrellas, Weichsel wood, crook or straight handles. Style H or G, with tassel. 8-rib paragon frame.

Sizes	26-inch.	28-inch
Each	$1.75	$2.00

34630 Men's Fine Black Silk Gloria Umbrellas, 8-rib paragon frame, imitation buck horn handle. Style M, with narrow silver band, case and tassel.

Sizes	26-inch	28-inch.
Each	$2.40	$2.60

34632 Men's Fine Quality Black Silk Gloria Umbrellas, steel rod natural wood, hook and straight handles styles H or K; leather case and tassel; 8-rib paragon frame.

Sizes	26-inch.	28-inch.
Each	$2.50	$2.75

34634 Men's Black Twilled Union Silk Umbrellas, handsome Tortoise shell handle, opera-hook. Styles I or K, with gold band, case and tassel; 8-rib paragon frame steel rod.

Sizes	26-inch.	28-inch.
Each	$3.35	$3.65

34636 Men's Fine Black Taffeta Umbrellas, steel rod. imported Congo or Wreichsel wood, Prince of Wales crook handles. Leather case and tassel: 8 rib paragon frame.

Sizes.	26-inch.	28-inch.
Each	$3.75	$4.00

34638 Men's Fine Black Taffeta Silk Umbrellas, 7-rib paragon frame; steel rod, fine imported Congo or Wreichsel, Prince of Wales hook handles. Styles G or M. Leather case. Can be used for cane and umbrella combined, 1½-inch steel ferrule at bottom of case.

Sizes	26-inch.	27-inch.	28-inch.
Each	$4.50	$4.75	$5.00

Canes and Walking Sticks.

NOTICE.—We catalogue but a few lines of canes, but can supply our customers with any kind of cane desired, provided same is in the market, at lowest possible price. Styles and designs of walking sticks are constantly changing, new novelties being added and old ones discontinued. We therefore quote but a few staple styles. If you wish anything special in this line write to us and we will cheerfully quote prices.

34643 Natural Hickory Crook Canes, selected stock, shellac finish. Small, light stick.
Price each...... $0.25
Per doz......... 2.70

34645 Natural Hickory Crook Canes, same as above. Medium size.
Each.............. $0.30
Per doz.......... 3.25

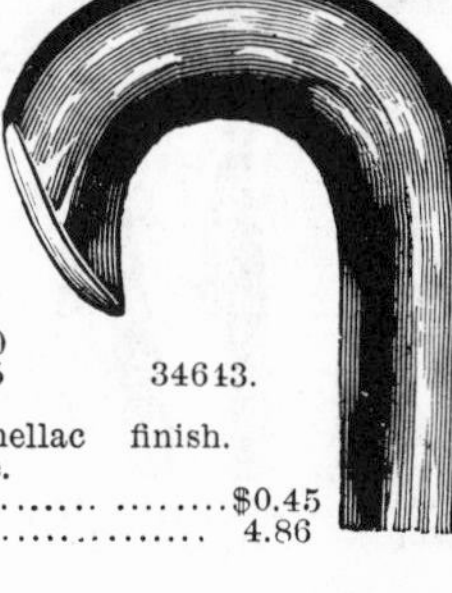

34643.

34646 Large size Hickory Crook Canes, shellac finish. Strong and serviceable.
Each $0.45
Per dozen 4.86

Canes—Continued.

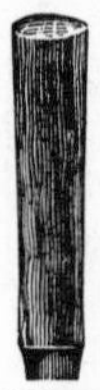

36647

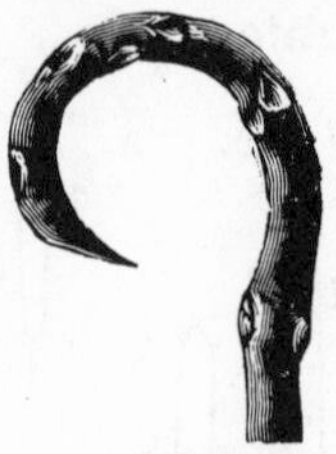

34648

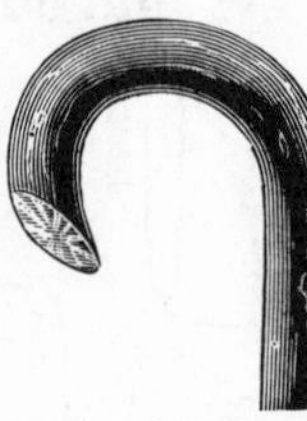

34653

34647 Straight Hickory Canes, medium size. finely finished and varnished. Each $0.10
Per dozen 1.00

34648 Congo Crook Canes. natural color, nickel plated, steel tip ferrule; large or medium szie. Very popular. Each .... .75

34651 Weischel Wood Crook Canes, natural color, nickel plated steel tipped ferrule, medium size. Each .... .80

34653 Weichsel Wood Canes, crook handle, nickel ferrule, steel tipped, plain solid sterling silver ornament on top of crook, medium size, natural color. Each 1.35

34655 Congo Canes, natural color. rough knotty finish; trimmed around cane, below, crook handle, with a one-inch band of solid sterling silver. Medium and large sizes. Each 1.00

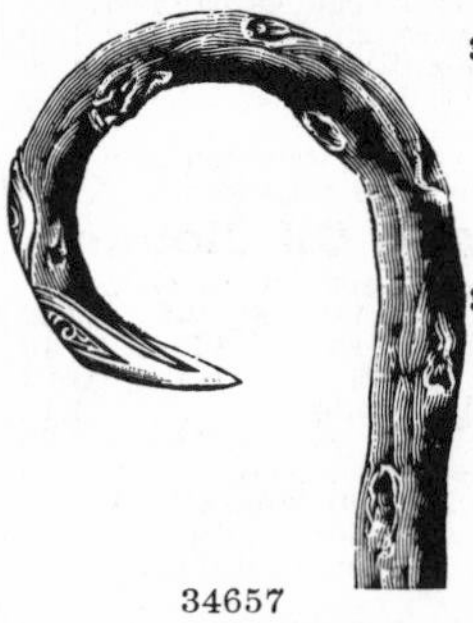

34657

34657 Natural Congo Crook Canes, nickel ferrules, steel tipped, very handsomely engraved, silver plated ornament on tip of crook, medium or large size.
Each $1.25

34659 Natural Congo Crook Canes, same style as above with plain solid sterling ornament covering end of crook, very neat and fashionable. Heavy or medium size.
Each $1.50

Canes in Dozen Lots.

The following canes we sell in dozen lots only, unless otherwise noted in quotation, as they are cheap canes, and do not make a profitable shipment when sent singly.

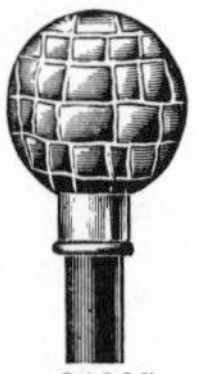

34667

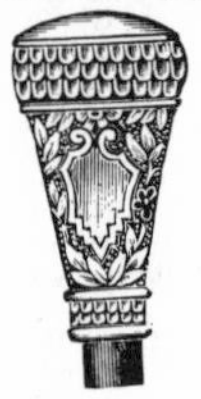

34667

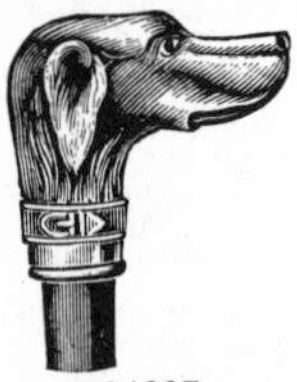

34667

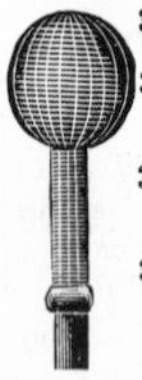

34668

34661 Natural Bamboo Picnic Canes, small size Per dozen $0.23

34663 Natural Bamboo Canes, with novelty tops, assorted if desired. Per dozen $0.35

34665 Natural Bamboo Canes, with vegetable ivory heads. Animal designs. Per dozen $0.85

34667 Rattan Canes, assorted designs, fancy metal tops, animals, balls, etc. Per dozen $1.00

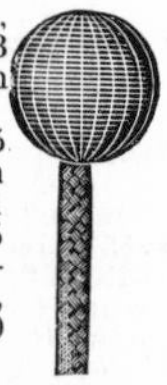

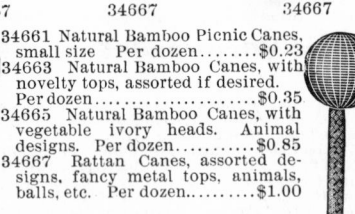

34669

34668 Loaded Canes. Extra heavy spun cloth covered heads. Strong and durable. Sold singly or by the dozen. Each .... .25
Per dozen 2.70

34669 Loaded Canes, spun cloth covered heads and steel rods. Each .... .15
Per dozen 1.58

34670 Loaded Canes. Rattan sticks, spun cloth covered heads .... .13
Per dozen 1.25

34672 Cane Racks, made of heavy seine twine, Size, 5x5 feet Each .... .75

34675 Wooden Cane Rings, for cane racks. Size, 1⅛, 1¼, 1½ and 1¾ inches inside measurement. Per 100 .... .75

Cane and Umbrella Straps.

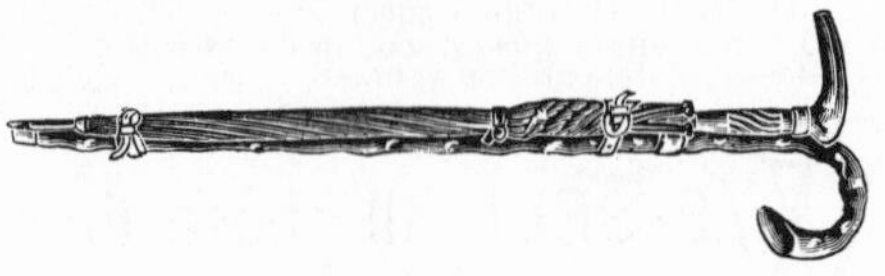

34678

34678 Natural Color, Fine Finish Leather Straps. Used for strapping unbrella and cane together. Very useful in traveling. Per pair $0.23

SHAWL DEPARTMENT.

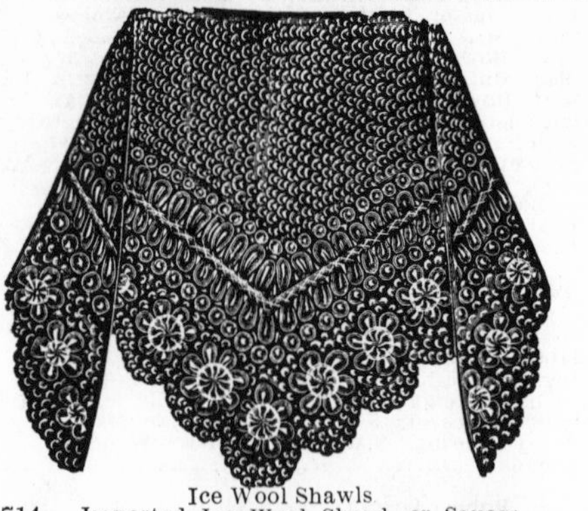

Ice Wool Shawls

34714 Imported Ice Wool Shawl or Square, very heavy border eight inches deep of rings and a beautiful design, new stitch; size, 38x38. Colors: Black or white. Each $2.00

34716 Imported Ice Wool Shawl or Squares, very heavy and fine, 10 inch, extra heavy border in new elegant designs; size, 42x42. Colors: Black or white. Each 3.00

Knit Wool Squares or Shawls.

34718 Imported French Wool Squares or Shawls, made of imported Shetland wool yarn. Size, 30x30 inches. Black or white only. Each .. $0.45

34720 Imported French Wool Squares or Shawls, made of fine Shetland wool yarn; sixe, 35x35 inches. Black or white only. Each .... .90

34722 Imported French Honeycomb Zephyr. Floss Knit Wool Squares; size, 46x46 inches. Colors: Pink or light blue; very fine tints. Each $1.25

Cashmere Shawls.

The weight of cashmere shawls varies from 9 to 22 ounces, according to quality.

34730 Cashmere Shawls, all wool twilled, wool fringe, 58x58 inches; colors: Black or cream. Each $1.20

34732 Cashmere Shawls, all wool twilled, wool fringe, 60x60 inches; colors: Black or cream. 1.50

34734 Cashmere Shawls, quality F11 twill. 60x 60 inches, all wool fringe, 3½ inches, two knot; colors: cardinal, medium blue, black or white. 2.00

34736 Cashmere Shawls, finer quality, F14 twill, 62x62 inches, 4 knot, 3½ inches wide, colors: Cardinal, wine, light blue, black or white...... 2.50

34738 Cashmere Shawls, all wool, twilled, silk embroidered, with silk fringe 5 inches deep; sizes, 60x60 inches; color, medium blue. Each, until sold 3.25

34740 Cashmere Shawls, fine quality. No. 836, 61x65 inches; 10 inch silk fringe, 5 knot, finely embroidered; colors: Light blue, tan, chocolate. Until sold 5.00

Black Cashmere Shawls.

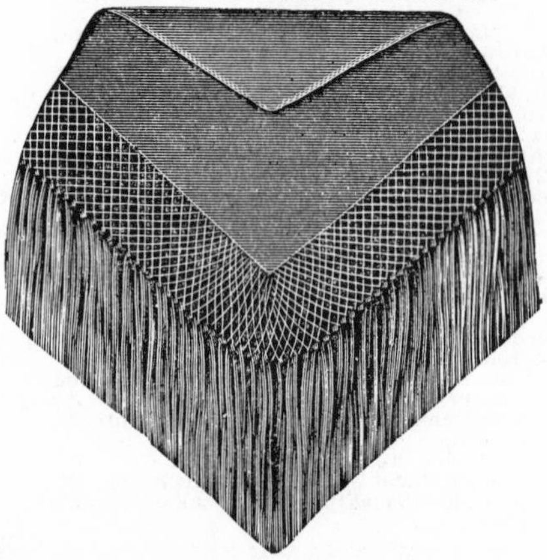

Measurements of all shawls under this heading do not include the silk fringe.

34742 Black Cashmere Shawls, all wool, with 5 knot silk fringe 5 inches deep, alike on all sides size 56x56 inches. Each $2.25

34744 Black Cashmere Shawls, all wool, with 5 knot silk fringe, 7 inches deep, alike on all sides, size, 57x57 inches. Each 3.00

34746 Black Cashmere Shawls, all wool, with 5 knot silk fringe 7 inches deep, alike on all sides, size 62x62 inches. Each 3.75

34748 Black Cashmere Shawls, all wool, with 5 knot silk fringe 8 inches deep, alike on all sides, size, 66x66 inches. Each 5.00

34750 Black Cashmere Shawls, all wool, with 7 knot silk fringe 8 inches deep, alike on all sides. size, 62x62 inches. Each 5.50

34752 Black Cashmere Shawls, all wool, with 7 knot silk fringe 8 inches deep, alike on all sides, size, 62x62 inches. Each 6.00

Shawls—Continued.

34754 Black Delaine Shawls, all wool with 7 inch crepe border. Size, 70x70 inches. Each..$6.00
34756 Black Cashmere Shawls, wool fringe, 67x 135 inches. Each.... 4.00
34758 Black Cashmere Shawls, wool fringe, 67x 135 inches. Each.... 4.75
34760 Black Cashmere Shawls, wool fringe, 72x 144 inches. Each.... 6.50
34762 Black Cashmere Shawls, wool fringe, 72x 144 inches. Each.... 8.50
34764 Black Cashmere Shawls, wool fringe, 72x 144 inches. Each.........$10.00. $12.00 and $15.00

Broche and Paisley Shawls.

34768 Shawls, ladies' French broche, fine......$ 9.00
35769 Shawls, ladies' French broche, fine...... 12.00
34771 Shawls, ladies' Paisley, with black center, only.... 11.00
34772 Shawls, ladies' Paisley, with black center.... 14.00
34773 Shawls, ladies' Paisley, with black center....$15.00 to 29.00
34774 Ladies' Double Paisley and Broche Shawls from....$10.00 to 40.00
(Price governs quality.)

Shoulder Shawls.

Also used for misses and children. Each.

34776 Shawl, misses' and children's mixed plaids. Medium and bright colors. Size, 34x34. Each.$0.40
34778 Shawls, misses' or children's mixed plaids and checks, medium and bright colors. Size, 36x36. Each.... .70
34780 Shawls, misses' or children's, mixed plaids and checks, dark, medium and bright colors. Size, 40x40. Each.... .90

Ladies' Single Wool Shawls.

34782 Shawls, ladies', all wool, Western manufacture, square, 67½x67½, gray or brown plaids; also mournings and blacks....$2.25
34784 Shawls, ladies', all wool, fine and heavy, square, 72x72, gray or brown plaids, high colors; also mourning or plain blacks.... 3.00

Ladies' Double Wool Shawls.

Each.

34786 Shawls, ladies', all wool, brown or gray double, 63x126....$3.00
34788 Shawls, ladies', all wool, gray, double, 63x126.... 3.75
34790 Shawls, ladies', all wool, browns, double, 63x126.... 3.75
34792 Shawls, ladies', all wool, Western manuufacture, gray or brown mixed, and plaids, double, 67½x135.... 4.75
34794 Shawls, ladies', all wool, Western manufacture, mourning and plain blacks, double, 67½x135.... 4.75
34796 Shawls, ladies', all wool, heavy and fine, high colored plaids, double, 72x144.... 5.75
34798 Shawls, ladies', all wool, heavy and fine, grays and browns, plain centers or plaids, also mourning or plain black, double, 72x144....... 6.25

Beaver and Velvet Shawls.

NOTICE—Beaver and Velvet Shawls vary in size from 66x66 inches in the cheaper grades to 72x72 inches in the finer grades. The average weight is from 2 to 4 lbs.

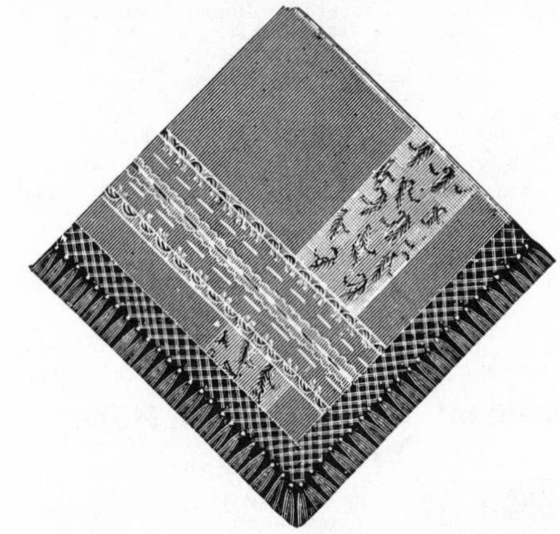

Beaver Shawl.

34802 Beaver Shawls, one knot fringe, figured border, reversible; gray or brown; weight, 3¼ lbs. Each....$1.75
34804 Beaver Shawls, one knot fringe, reversible; neat border; brown or gray; weight, 2¼ pounds. Each....$2.75
34806 Beaver Shawls, one knot fringe, reversible; figured design on border, medium colors, brown or gray; weight, 2 lbs. Each.....$ 3.25
34808 Beaver Shawls, one knot fringe, fancy figured border, reversible; brown or gray; weight, 2¾ lbs. Each.... 3.75
34810 Velvet Shawls, one knot fringe, flower borders, reversible; medium and dark colors, brown or gray; weight, 2⅛ lbs. Each.... 4.75
34814 Velvet Shawls, reversible, one-knot fringe, new fancy design borders, tan, brown, gray or mourning. Weight, 3⅜ lbs. Price, each....$6.25
34816 Plain Black Beaver Shawls, very heavy. Weight, 3¾ lbs. Price, each.... 5.25
34820 Reversible Velvet Shawls, fine quality, one knot fringe, plain mixtures gray or brown. Weight, 2¾ lbs. Price, each.... 7.25

Shawls—Continued.

34822 Very Fine Imported Velvet Shawls, reversible, floral design borders, three knot fringe, brown, tan or gray. Weight, 2¾ lbs. Price,$7.75
34824 Imported Velvet Shawls, extra quality, reversible floral design borders, three knot fringe, brown, tan or gray. Weight, 2½ lbs. Price, each.... 9.00
34828 Beaver Velvet Shawls, superior quality, reversible, floral design borders, double-knot fringe, brown, gray or tan. Weight, 3¼ lbs. Price, each....10.50
34830 Imported Beaver Shawls, extra selected stock, reversible, new, very neat design borders, three knot fringe, brown, gray, tan, fawns or mourning. Weight, 3 lbs. Price, each....11.00
34840 Imported Beaver Shawls, extra selected stock, reversible, flowered border designs, three-knot fringe, brown, tan, fawn, gray or mourning. Weight, 3 lbs. Price, each....12.00

BLANKET DEPARTMENT.

White Bed Blankets.

10-4 11-4 represents the length of the blanket, not the width, manufacturer's measurement.

Per pair.

34860 White Cotton Bed Blankets, 10-4; weight, 2 lbs....$0.65
34863 Twilled White Bed Blankets, cotton fleece, 10-4; weight, 3¾ lbs.... .95
34864 Twilled White Bed Blankets, cotton fleece, 11-4; weight, 4¼ lbs.... 1.15
34867 White Bed Blankets, all wool, colored borders, 10-4; weight, 4 lbs.... 2.75
34868 White Bed Blankets, all wool, colored borders, 11-4; weight, 5 lbs.... 3.50
34872 Hamilton White Bed Blankets, fancy striped colored borders, 10-4; weight, 4½ lbs.. 3.00
34875 All Wool "Mercer" White Bed Blankets, assorted colored borders, 10-4; weight, 4 lbs.... 3.75
34876 All Wool "Mercer" White Bed Blankets, assorted colored borders, 11-4; weight, 5 lbs.. 4.50
34880 All Wool "Longmont" White Bed Blankets, fine selected stock, fine colored borders, 11-4; weight, 5½ lbs.... 6.00
34884 All Wool "Yosemite" White Bed Blankets, very fine and fluffy, very fine borders, 11-4; weight, 5½ lbs.... 6.50
34888 All Wool "Morrave" White Bed Blankets, extra fine and heavy, elegant colored borders, 11-4; size, 72x80; weight, 5½ lbs.... 7.00
34892 All Wool "Mervale" White Bed Blankets, fancy colored borders, 10-4; size, 64x78; weight, 4½ lbs.... 4.00
34893 All Wool "Mervale" White Bed Blankets, fancy colored borders, 11-4; size, 72x80; weight, 5½ lbs.... 5.00

N. B.—Sizes given on above blankets are for one only; pair is just double the size.

Scarlet Bed or Camp Blankets.

34901 Scarlet Blankets, all wool.

Weight,	4 lbs.	5 lbs.	6 lbs.
Sizes,	56x72	64x76	66x82
Per pair	$3.00	$3.75	$4.50

N. B.—Sizes given on previous blankets are for one blanket only; pair is just double the size.

34906 Silver Gray Bed Blankets, "Arcadian," fine wool filling, colored cotton warp, 10-4; size, 62x76. Per pair....$2.50
34907 Silver Gray Bed Blankets, "Arcadian," fine wool filling, colored cotton warp, 11-4; size, 78x82, Per pair.... 3.25
34910 Atwood Gray Cotton Blankets. 10-4. Weight, 2¼ lbs. Per pair.... .60
34914 Silver Gray Blankets, cotton and wool mixed, for bed or camp.

Weight...4 lbs.		5 lbs.	6 lbs.	8 lbs.
Sizes......48x70		56x76	64x80	74x86
Per pair...$1.30	until sold,	1.50	1.95	2.90

All Wool Colored Blankets.

34922 Seneca All Wool Gray Bed Blankets, 10-4; weight, 4½ lbs. Per pair....$ 3.75
34923 Seneca All Wool Gray Bed Blankets; 11-4; weight, 5½ lbs. Per pair.... 4.75
34926 "Sonora" All Wool Bed Blankets, fine and heavy, light brownish gray color; 10-4; size, 64 x78; weight, 5 lbs. Per pair.... 6.00
34927 "Sonora" All Wool Bed Blankets, fine and heavy, light brownish gray color; 11-4; size, 72x80; weight, 6 lbs. Per pair.... 7.00

Bed Quilts or Quilted Comfortables.

Sizes given are as cut. Comfortables when made up vary a little each way.

Bed quilts are too heavy to send by mail. See Rule 3 on Page 1.

34940 Bed Quilts, covered with common print, robe pattern, red lined. Size, 48x70; weight, 5 lbs. Each.........$0.50 Per dozen $5.40
34941 Bed Quilts, covered with common robe print, red lined; size, 54x70; weight, 5½ lbs. Each..............$0.60 Per dozen.... 6.48
34942 Bed Quilts, covered with robe print on both sides; size, 60x72; weight, 6¼lbs Each..............$0.75 Per dozen.... 8.10
34943 Bed Quilts, covered with furniture print, red lined; size, 66x73; weight, 6½ lbs. Each..............$0.85 Per dozen.... 9.18
34944 Bed Quilts, covered with furniture print, red lined; size, 68x73; weight, 6¾ lbs. Each ....$0.95 Per dozen....10.26
34945 Bed Quilts, covered with figured sateen, red lined; size, 68x73; weight, 6¾ lbs. Each..............$1.15 Per dozen....11.42

Bed Quilts—Continued.

34946 Bed Quilts, covered with twilled furniture print, red lined; size, 70x75; weight, 7½ lbs. Each..........$1.25 Per dozen $13.50
34947 Bed Quilts, covered with figured sateen, red lined; size, 68x73; filled with cotton; weight, 7¼ lbs. Each.... 1.35
Per dozen....14.58
34948 Bed Quilts, twilled sateen, red lined, carded cotton filling, fancy quilted; size, 72x78; weight, 7 lbs. Each.... 1.50
Per dozen....16.20
34949 Bed Quilts, twilled sateen, bordered, red lined, carded cotton filling; weight, 7 lbs. Each. 2.00
Per dozen....21.60
34950 Bed Quilts, figured sateen, bordered, red lined, extra carded cotton filling; size, 74x78; weight, 7¼ lbs. Each.... 2.25
Per dozen....24.30
34951 Bed Quilts, imported chintz, center pattern, extra carded cotton filling; size, 80x80; weight, 7¼ lbs. Each.... 2.75
Per dozen....29.70
34952 Bed Quilts, covered with figured sateen on both sides, filled with pure swan's down; soft, light, warm and healthy; 69x75. Each.... 3.75
Per dozen....40.50

Toilet Quilts.

Each.

34975 Honeycomb Quilts, white, 1½ lbs.... ....$0.65
34976 Honeycomb Quilts, white, Diamond brand, 2½ lbs.... .90
34977 Bates' Celebrated Maltelasse Quilt, imitation Marseilles; weight, 3¼ lbs.... 1.10
34980 Mitcheline Quilt, white center with pink border; reverse side, pink center with white border; size, 80x90.... 1.50
34982 Mitcheline Quilt, white center with beautiful flower designs; borders, canary, blue, pink, salmon, Nile green, ecru or buff; all reversible; size, 80x90.... 2.50

Marseilles Toilet Quilts.

Each.

34986 Marseilles Quilts, white, 3 lbs....$1.50
34988 Marseilles Quilts, white, 3½ lbs.... 2.00
34990 Marseilles Quilts, white, 4½ lbs.... 2.50
34992 Marseilles Quilts, white, 4¾ lbs.... 3.00
34994 Marseilles Quilts, white, 5 lbs.... 3.75
34996 Marseilles Quilts, white, 5 lbs.... 4.25

Marseilles Quilts are all imported and of good value for the money. Price governs quality in all cases.

HOSIERY DEPARTMENT

NOTE—Always give the inch size, never the shoe size, for hosiery. If you wear a No. 4 shoe don't order a No. 4 hose, but 9 inch hose, etc.

Scale of Sizes.

No 1	Ladies' Shoe takes about 8 inch hose.
No. 2	Ladies' Shoe takes about 8½ in. hose.
No. 3 and 4	Ladies' Shoe takes about 9 in. hose.
No. 5 and 6	Ladies' Shoe takes about 9½ inch hose.
No. 7	Ladies' Shoe takes about 10 inch hose.

Very small and very large sizes must be ordered from the better qualities, as the low priced domestic hose are put up only in medium sizes.

We sell half dozens at dozen rate in hosiery. All hosiery is quoted per dozen pairs, or per pair.

Average weight of ladies' cotton hose, 28 to 32 oz. to the dozen, or 2½ oz. to a pair.

Ladies' Solid Colored Cotton Hose, Patent Seams.

All hose quoted fast black are absolutely stainless or money refunded. All hose described as out size have extra wide tops.

36000 Ladies' Fine Cotton Hose, fast black. Per pair....$0.05
Per dozen.... .55
36001 Ladies' Fine Cotton Hose, fast black, slate or tan. Per pair.... .08
Per dozen.... 0.85
36002 Ladies' Heavy Cotton Hose plain fast black. Per pair.... .09
Per dozen.... 1.00

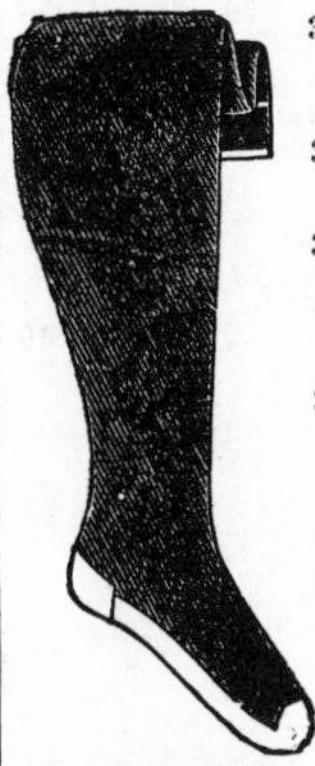

36003 Ladies' Extra Fine Cotton Hose, fast black or tan.
Per pair....$0.10
Per dozen.... 1.10
36004 Ladies' Extra Heavy Cotton Hose, fast black. Per pair....$0.10
Per dozen.... 1.10
36005 Ladies' Super fine Hose, made of fine combed Egyptian cotton, fast black or tan.
Per pair....$0.11
Per dozen.... 1.25
36006 Ladies' Superfine Cotton Hose, extra length, double soles, double heels and toes, fast black, white soles. (In 5 doz. lots, $1.00 net, per doz.) Per pair....$0.10
Per dozen....$1.10
36007 Extra Superfine Cotton Hose, extra length, double soles, double heels and toes, fast black. (In 5 doz. lots, $1.12½ net per dozen.)
Per pair....$0.11
Per dozen.... 1.25
36008 Ladies' Super Stout Heavy Ribbed Cotton Hose, double soles, double heels and toes, fast black. Per pair.... .13
Per dozen.... 1.40

Ladies' Hose--Continued.

36009 Ladies' Fine Cotton Hose, ribbed, fast black or tan. Per pair...$0.11
Per dozen.. 1.20
36010 Ladies' Extra Heavy Ribbed Cotton Hose, double heels and toes, fast black.
Per pair...$0.12
Per dozen . 1.35

36009   36010

36012 Ladies' Heavy Ribbed Cotton Hose, fast black. Per pair................................. 0.10
Per dozen.................................... 1.10

Ladies' Super Stout Seamless Cotton Hose.

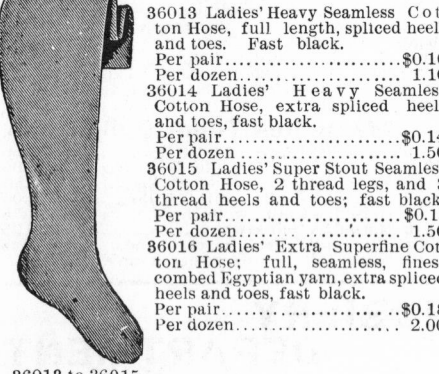

36013 Ladies' Heavy Seamless Cotton Hose, full length, spliced heels and toes. Fast black.
Per pair........................$0.10
Per dozen..................... 1.10
36014 Ladies' Heavy Seamless Cotton Hose, extra spliced heels and toes, fast black.
Per pair........................$0.14
Per dozen..................... 1.50
36015 Ladies' Super Stout Seamless Cotton Hose, 2 thread legs, and 3 thread heels and toes; fast black.
Per pair........................$0.15
Per dozen..................... 1.50
36016 Ladies' Extra Superfine Cotton Hose; full, seamless, finest combed Egyptian yarn, extra spliced heels and toes, fast black.
Per pair........................$0.18
Per dozen..................... 2.00

36013 to 36015

36017 Ladies' Super Stout Cotton Hose, double thread, full regular made, double heels and toes. fast black; a very durable. seamless stocking. (In 5 doz. lots 1.30 per dozen. Per pair........ .14
Per dozen.......................... 1.50

Ladies' Solid Colored Cotton Hose, Regular Made, Imported.

36018 Ladies' Superfine Cotton Hose, full regular made, fast black, spliced heels and toes.
Per pair........................$0.17
Per dozen..................... 1.85
36019 Ladies' Super Stout Cotton Hose, full regular made, double soles, high spliced heels and toes, extra length, fast black.
Per pair........................$0.20
Per dozen..................... 2.25
36020 Ladies' Super Stout Full Fashioned 2 Thread Imported Cotton Hose, extra high *double* heels *double* soles and *double* toes, fast black.
Per pair........................$0.25
Per dozen..................... 2.85
36021 Ladies' Superfine Cotton Hose, made of real Maco 2-thread yarn, double heels and toes, fast black or tan, full regular made.
Per pair..$0.25 Per dozen..$2.85

36018-26

36022 Ladies' Superfine Cotton Hose. made of real Maco 2-thread yarn, extra velvet finish, *double soles*, extra *high double heels* and *toes*, colors, fast black or tan. Per pair..............$0.30
Per dozen..................... 3.25
36023 Ladies' Extra Super Stout 3 Thread Cotton Hose, 6-thread heels and toes, full regular made, fast black; very durable.
Per pair....................................$0.30
Per dozen.......................... 3.25
36024 Ladies' Extra Fine 2-Thread Cotton Hose, made of real Maco yarn, fine velvety finish, extra length, double heels and toes, fast black or tan. Per pair..................................... .33
Per dozen..................... 3.60
36025 Ladies' Super Fine Cotton Hose, made of fine double thread Maco yarn, extra length, high spliced heels, double soles and toes, fast black. Per pair........................ .33
Per dozen..................... 3.60
36026 Ladies' Extra Velvet Fnish Cotton Hose, made of 3-thread combed Maco yarn, *double high spliced heels* and *toes, double soles*, extra length, full fashioned, full regular made. Colors: Fast black or tan. Per pair............ .35
Per dozen..................... 3.85

Ladies' Hose—Continued.

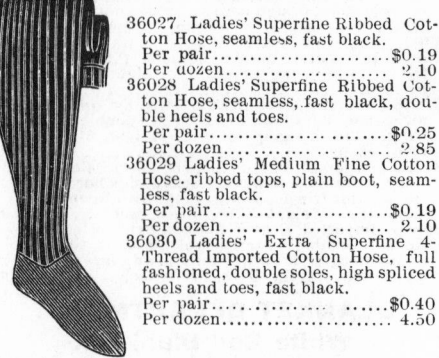

36027 Ladies' Superfine Ribbed Cotton Hose, seamless, fast black.
Per pair........................$0.19
Per dozen.................. 2.10
36028 Ladies' Superfine Ribbed Cotton Hose, seamless, fast black, double heels and toes.
Per pair........................$0.25
Per dozen.................. 2.85
36029 Ladies' Medium Fine Cotton Hose. ribbed tops, plain boot, seamless, fast black.
Per pair........................$0.19
Per dozen.................. 2.10
36030 Ladies' Extra Superfine 4-Thread Imported Cotton Hose, full fashioned, double soles, high spliced heels and toes, fast black.
Per pair........................$0.40
Per dozen.................. 4.50

36031 Our Ladies' Indestructible Cotton Hose, made of extra fine yarn, ingrain, double soles, double heels and toes. A new pair given in change for every pair that proves unsatisfactory in color or wear. Indestructible black, only.
Per pair.................................... .50
Per dozen.................................. 5.50

Ladies' Out Size Cotton Hose.

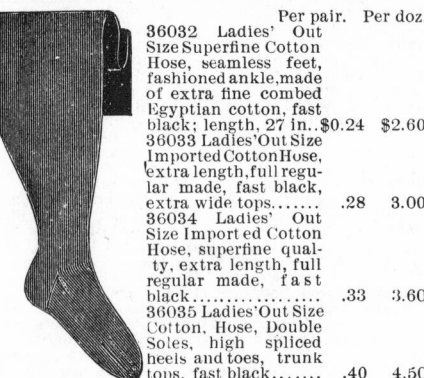

	Per pair.	Per doz.
36032 Ladies' Out Size Superfine Cotton Hose, seamless feet, fashioned ankle, made of extra fine combed Egyptian cotton, fast black; length, 27 in..	$0.24	$2.60
36033 Ladies' Out Size Imported Cotton Hose, extra length, full regular made, fast black, extra wide tops......	.28	3.00
36034 Ladies' Out Size Imported Cotton Hose, superfine quality, extra length, full regular made, fast black......	.33	3.60
36035 Ladies' Out Size Cotton, Hose, Double Soles, high spliced heels and toes, trunk tops, fast black......	.40	4.50

Ladies' Opera Hose.

36036 Ladies' Opera Hose, seamless, fast black, 32 to 34 inches long. Per pair.................$0.25
Per dozen.................... 2.85
36037 Ladies' Opera Hose, extra length, fast black, 34 in., full regular made. Per pair....... .35
Per dozen.................... 3.85
36038 Ladies' Superfine Opera Length Hose, double spliced heels and toes, fast black, or tan.
Per pair........................... .45
Per dozen.................... 5.00
36039 Ladies' Opera Length Hose, extra fine lisle thread, full regular made, fast colors. Pink, black, flesh, cardinal, sky or lavender.
Per pair....... 1.00
Per dozen....... 11.00

Ladies' Domestic Lisle Thread Hose.

36041 Ladies' Lisle Finished Hose, patented seams, fashioned ankles, tans, russets, or fast black. Per pair......................$0.12
Per dozen.................... 1.35
36042 Ladies' Superfine Lisle Finished Cotton Hose, plain, seamless, fast black. Per pair.... . .18
Per dozen.................... 2.00
36043 Ladies' Extra Superfine 2-thread Lisle Finished Hose. Made of finest combed Egyptian cotton, plain black, seamless. Per pair......... .22
Per dozen..... 2.40

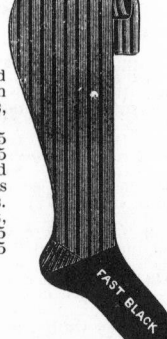

36044 Ladies' Fancy Ribbed Lisle Thread Hose, extra high spliced heels, French toes, seamless, fast black.
Per pair...................$0.25
Per dozen.............. 2.85
36046 Ladies' French Ribbed Lisle Thread Hose, seamless extra spliced heels and toes. Colors stainless, tan, russet, cardinal. Per pair.......$0.25
Per dozen.............. 2.85

Ladies' Superfine Imported Lisle Thread Hose.

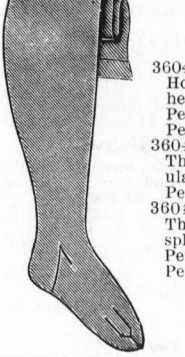

36047 Ladies' Fine Lisle Thread Hose, full regular made, spliced heels and toes, fast black.
Per pair........................$0.25
Per dozen.................. 2.85
36048 Ladies' Superfine Lisle Thread Hose, fast black, full regular made. Per pair........$0.35
Per dozen.................. 3.85
36049 Ladies' Extra Superfine Lisle Thread Hose, double soles, high spliced heels and toes, fast black.
Per pair......................$0.40
Per dozen.................. 4.50

36050 Ladies' Extra Quality Brilliant Lisle Thread Hose, 4 thread throughout and 6-thread heels and toes, fast black. Per pair............$0.50
Per dozen.................. 5.50
33051 Ladies' Extra Heavy Imported Lisle Thread Hose, double soles, high spliced heels and toes, fast black. per pair...................$0.65
Per dozen 7.00
36052 Ladies' Fine Lisle Thread Hose, assorted colors, tans, pink, cream, light blue. Per pair $0.50
Per dozen..................... 5.50

Ladies' Silk and Plaited Hosiery.

36053 Ladies' Fine Ingrain Silk Plaited Hose, full regular made, fast black, double heel and toe. Per pair......................$0.65
Per dozen.................. 6.70
36054 Ladies' Extra Silky Finished Lisle Hose, full fashioned, double heels and toes, extra lengths. fast black, cardinal, pink, sky, cream, tan. lavender. Per pair.................. 1.00
Per dozen..................11.00
36055 Ladies' Extra Fine All Silk Hose, fast black, extra high spliced heels, French toes, full regular made. Per pair.................. 1.25
Per dozen..................14.00
36056 Ladies' Stout Spun Silk Hose full regular made, fast black only. Per pair.................. 1.65
Per dozen..................18.25
36057 Ladies' Extra Quality Fine Silk Hose, Paris fashioned, fast black only.
Per pair..................................... 2.25
Per dozen 24.00

Ladies' Fleece Lined Cotton Hose.

NOTE—Fleece lined hose are for ladies who will not wear wool, but for whom the ordinary cotton hose are too light for winter wear. Out sizes are extra in the legs.
36061 Ladies' Heavy Fleeced Cotton Hose, full regular made, fast black. Per pair............$0.25
Per dozen.................. 2.85
36062 Ladies' Extra Fine Fleeced Egyptian Cotton Hose, full regular made, double heels and toes, fast black. Per pair...................... .45
Per dozen.................. 5.00
36063 Ladies' Out Size Fleece Lined Cotton Hose, extra wide tops, double heels and toes, fast black, full regular made.
Per pair..................................... .25
Per dozen.................. 2.85
36065 Ladies' Extra Out Size Fleece Lined Cotton Hose, extra heavy, double heels and toes; fast black, full regular made. Per pair............... .35
Per dozen 3.85

Ladies' Black Cotton Hose, White Feet.

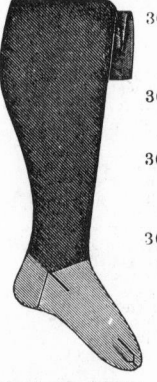

36066 Ladies' Black Cotton Hose full regular made, fast black, with unbleached or sanitary feet.
Per pair.......................$0.25
Per dozen..................... 2.85
36067 Ladies' Superfine Cotton Hose, full regular made. unbleached feet, fast black tops. Per pair.$0.30
Per dozen..................... 3.25
36068 Ladies' Extra Superfine Cotton Hose, fast black, unbleached feet.
Per pair..... ....$0.35
Per dozen..................... 3.85
36069 Ladies' Extra Fine Lisle Thread Sanitary Hose, fast black, with pure soft unbleached maco feet, high spliced heels, double soles. A very comfortable summer stocking.
Per pair $0.44
Per dozen 4.80

Unbleached Soles.
36066 to 9.

Ladies' French Mixed Cotton Hose

36070 Ladies' French Mixed Cotton Hose, Oxford and Cambridge gray. Per pair..................$0.05
Per dozen................................. .59

36071 Ladies' French Mixed Cotton Hose, Oxford and Cambridge gray, extra heavy, extra wide, ribbed tops. Per pair........................ .09
Per dozen................................. .99

36072 Ladies' Super Stout Cotton Hose, full seamless heels, color Oxford, or Cambridge gray. Per pair................................ .09
Per dozen................................. .99

36074 Ladies' Heavy 2-Thread Cotton Hose, extra length, full seamless heels; colors, tan, drab or slate. Per pair........................ .09
Per dozen................................. .99

Ladies' French and Fancy Mixed Seamless Cotton Hose, Knitted.

36075 Ladies' Heavy Seamless Cotton Hose, German knitted, double heels and toes, in brown or blue mixed with white; weight, per doz., 40 ounces. Per pair........$0.08
Per dozen pairs.................. .85

36076 Ladies' or Men's Extra Heavy German Knitted Seamless Cotton Hose, brown or blue mixed (in 5 dozen lots, $1.10 per dozen).
Per pair.....................$0.11
Per dozen.................... 1.25

36077 Ladies' or Men's Extra Heavy Rockford Hand Finished Seamless Cotton Hose, warranted made of 2-threads yarn and 4-ply heels and toes, extra length. Colors, brown mixed or blue mixed (in 5 dozen lots, $1.35 per dozen).
Per pair.....................$0.13
Per dozen.................... 1.40
Weight, per dozen, 48 ounces.

36079 Ladies' Extra Heavy Seamless Cotton Hose, double thread, extra spliced heels and toes; fast black only. Per pair........$0.14

36075 to 36079
Per dozen.................... 1.50
Weight per dozen, 48 ounces.

Ladies' Unbleached Balbriggan Hose.

Weight, per dozen, 28 to 32 ounces.
36085 Ladies' Unbleached Balbriggan Hose, patent seams. Per pair......$0.07 Per dozen.......$0.72
36087 Ladies' Unbleached Balbriggan Hose, extra wide tops, patent seams. Per pair........... .11
Per dozen.................... 1.20
36088 Ladies' Unbleached Balbriggan Hose, made of extra fine Maco yarn, patent seams.
Per pair........$0.14 Per dozen.... 1.50

36090 Ladies' Unbleached Balbriggan Hose, seamless. Per pair......$0.14
Per dozen.................... 1.50
36092 Ladies' Unbleached Balbriggan Hose, full regular made.
Per pair.....................$0.19
Per dozen.................... 2.00
36093 Ladies' Hose, unbleached balbriggan, full regular made, imported. Per pair.................$0.25
Per dozen.................... 2.85
36096 Ladies' Superfine Balbriggan Hose, unbleached, full regular made, imported. Per pair.................$0.30
Per dozen.................... 3.25
36097 Ladies' Unbleached Balbriggan Hose, full regular made, extra wide.
Per pair.....................$0.35
Per dozen.................... 3.80

Ladies' White Cotton Hose.

36090-7
Weight, per dozen, 20 to 32 ounces.
	Per pair.	Per doz.
36106 Ladies' Cotton Hose, white......	$0.10	$1.10
36107 Ladies' Cotton Hose, white.......	.14	1.50
36108 Ladies' White Cotton Hose, full regular made.......	.25	2.85

Ladies' Striped Cotton Hose.

Weight, per doz., 20 to 26 ounces.

36110 Ladies' Cotton Striped Hose.
Per pair....$0.05
Per dozen... .59
36113 Ladies' Fancy Balbriggan Hose, stripes of cardinal and white, black and white.
Per pair....$0.08
Per dozen... .85
36114 Ladies' Fancy Cotton Hose, fancy stripes.
Per pair....$0.09
Per dozen. 1.00
36117 Ladies' Cotton Hose, extra length, in black and white, red and white, or blue and white stripes.

36119   36110 to 36118
Per pair.......................$0.10
Per dozen...................... 1.10

Ladies' Hose—Continued.

36118 Ladies' Super Stout 2-Ply Cotton Hose, full seamless heels, extra length. Colors, purple, or brick red and white, clouded.
Per pair............................ .11
Per dozen........................ 1.25
36119 Ladies' Super Stout Cotton Hose, 2-thread, drop stitch, seamless heels. Colors, two shades of tan and slate.
Per pair............................ .09
Per dozen........................ 1.00
36120 Ladies' Fancy Striped Balbriggan Hose, regular made, seamless, double heels and toes, unbleached ground with stripes of cardinal, navy or black.
Per pair............................$0.15
Per dozen........................ 1.60

Ladies' Solid and Party Colored Cotton Hose, Specials.

36121 Ladies' Super Fine Cotton Hose, Richelieu rib, fast black or tan, solid colors.
Per pair......$0.11
Per dozen.... 1.20
36122 Ladies' Fancy Cotton Hose, fast black boot, high colored tops,
Per pair.......$0.14
Per dozen.... 1.50
36123 Ladies' Superfine Imported Cotton Hose, extra length, spliced heels and toes, plain fast black boot, assorted colored tops.
Per pair..$0.25
Per doz... 2.85
36124 Ladies' Fine Lisle Thread Hose, plain black boot high, colored tops, fast colors.

36121-22   36123 24
Per pair............$0.45   Per dozen.....$5.00

36125 Ladies' Lisle Thread Hose, Richelieu ribbed, black boot, high colored tops, similar to cut.
Per pair.........................$0.35
Per dozen...................... 3.85
36126 Ladies' Heavy Lisle Thread Hose, Richelieu or military ribbed, black boot, light colored tops.
Per pair.........................$0.50
Per dozen...................... 5.50

36125-26

36127 Ladies' Extra Fine Lisle Thread Hose, Richelieu ribbed, black boot, fancy striped tops.
Per pair.........................$0.50
Per dozen...................... 5.50

36128 Ladies' Extra Quality Lisle Thread Hose, plain or drop stitched, fancy vandyke ankles, black boot, high colored tops.
Per pair......................$ 1.00
Per dozen......................11.00

36128

Ladies' Merino Hose.

NOTE—Merino hose are wool and cotton blended.
36131 Ladies' Extra Heavy Merino Hose, seamless, black. Per pair.........................$0.19
Per dozen...................... 2.00
36132 Ladies' Heavy Merino Hose, seamless, double heels and toes, black only. Per pair.... 0.20
Per dozen...................... 2.25
36133 Ladies' Heavy Merino Hose, plain, seamless, double heels and toes, dark gray. Per pair.$0.20
Per dozen...................... 2.25

Ladies' Medium Weight All Wool Seamless Hose.

Average weight per dozen, 42 oz.
Average weight per pair, 3½ ounces.
36135 Medium Weight All Wool Hose, double heels and toes, black only. Per pair............$0.20
Per dozen...................... 2.25
36136 Ladies' Medium Weight All Wool Hose, extra length, ribbed welted tops, double heels and toes, black only. Per pair............ .21
Per dozen...................... 2.30
36137 Ladies' Medium Weight Plain All Wool Hose, seamless, double heels and toes. Colors: Oxford mixed, blue mixed. Per pair........... .24
Per dozen...................... 2.75
36138 Ladies' All Wool Ribbed Hose, seamless, double heels and toes, medium weight, black.
Per pair............................ 0.25
Per dozen...................... 2.85
36140 Ladies' Extra Out Size All Wool Hose, medium weight, double heels and toes, seamless, black, extra length, plain legs, ribbed welt tops.
Per pair............................ 0.37
Per dozen...................... 4.00
36143 Ladies' Worsted Hose, seamless, double heels and toes, gray only. Per pair............ .40
Per dozen...................... 4.50

Ladies' Heavy Knitted Seamless Wool Hose.

36144 Ladies' Extra Heavy Wool Mixed Seamless Hose, double heels and toes. Black only.
Per pair.....................$0.18 Per dozen....$2.00

Ladies' Cashmere Hose.

Average weight per dozen, 42 ounces.
Average weight per pair, 3½ ounces.
36154 Ladies' Super Stout Plain Cashmere Hose, all wool, seamless, double heels and toes, extra length, black only. Per pair.....................$0.35
Per dozen...................... 3.85
36156 Ladies' Heavy All Wool Cashmere Hose, double heels and toes, seamless, shaped legs, black only. Per pair.................... .25
Per dozen...................... 2.75

36158 Ladies' Super Stout All Wool Hose, full seamless fashioned ankles, double heels and toes, extra length; black or tan.
Per pair.....................$0.39
Per dozen.................... 4.25
36159 Ladies' Super Stout Cashmere Hose, extra quality, full regular made, London length, full fashioned feet, double heels and toes. Fast black.
Per pair..................... .45
Per dozen.................... 5.0

36162 Ladies' Heavy 2 Thread Out Size, Plain Cashmere Hose, extra wide tops, seamless, double heels and toes, black only.
Per pair.....................$0.50
Per dozen.................... 5.50
36167 Ladies' Extra Quality Genuine English Cashmere Hose, black, natural gray, high double heel and toe.
Per pair.....................$0.75
Per dozen.................... 8.00
36168 Ladies' Fine English Cashmere Hose, full regular made, extra length, fashioned feet, double heels and toes, black only.
Per pair.....................$0.35
Per dozen.................... 3.85

36162 O. S.

Misses' and Children's Solid Colored Hose.

Average weight, per dozen, 20 to 30 ounces.
Average weight, per pair, 2 ounces.

SCALE OF SIZES.
To avoid mistakes always give the INCH SIZE for hose.
Never give size of shoe.
1 Infants' Shoe takes....................	4-inch hose.
2 and 3 Infants' Shoe takes.............	4½-inch hose.
4 Infants' Shoe takes...................	5-inch hose.
5 Infants' Shoe takes...................	5½-inch hose.
6 and 7 Children's Shoe takes..........	6-inch hose.
8 Children's Shoe takes................	6½-inch hose.
9 and 10 Children's Shoe takes.........	7-inch hose.
11 Misses' Shoe takes..................	7½-inch hose.
12 Misses' Shoe takes..................	8-inch hose.
13, 1 and 2 Misses' Shoe takes.........	8-8½-inch hose.

36170 Infants' Plain Cotton Hose; full length fine gauge, absolutely fast black.
Sizes................	.4 and 4½ in.	5 and 5½ in.
Per pair..............	$0.05	$0.06
Per dozen.............	.59	.65

Use the William Clark Co.'s N-E-W Six Cord Spool Cotton.

Children's Hose—Continued.

36171 Misses' or Boys' Super Stout Ribbed Cotton Hose, fast black.

Sizes,	5 and 6 in.	7 and 7½ in.
Per pair	$0.07	$0.08
Per dozen	.75	.85
Sizes	8 and 8½ in.	9 and 9½ in.
Per pair	$0.09	$0.10
Per dozen	.95	1.10

36172 Children's Heavy Ribbed Cotton Hose, fast black only.

Sizes	5 and 5½ in.	6 and 6½ in.
Per pair	$0.07	$0.08
Per dozen	.75	.87

36173 Misses' Solid Colored Cotton Hose, plain fast black, extra length, fine gauge, patent seams.

Sizes	6 and 6½ in.	7 and 7½ in.	8 and 8½ in.
Per pair	$0.07	$0.07½	$0.08
Per dozen	.70	.75	.85

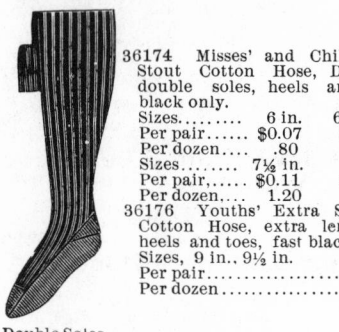

36174 Misses' and Children's Super Stout Cotton Hose, Derby ribbed, double soles, heels and toes, fast black only.

Sizes	6 in.	6½ in.	7 in.
Per pair	$0.07	$0.08	$0.10
Per dozen	.80	.90	1.05
Sizes	7½ in.	8 in.	8½ in.
Per pair	$0.11	$0.12	$0.13
Per dozen	1.20	1.35	1.45

36176 Youths' Extra Stout Ribbed Cotton Hose, extra length, double heels and toes, fast black.

Sizes, 9 in. 9½ in.	
Per pair	$0.12½
Per dozen	1.35

Double Soles.
36174-76

Misses' and Children's Seamless Cotton Hose.

36180 Super Stout Ribbed Cotton Hose, seamless, fast black, reinforced heels and toes.

Sizes	6 in.	6½ in.	7 in.	7½ in.	8 in.	8½ in.
Per pair	$0.08	$0.09	$0.10	$0.11	$0.12	$0.13
Per dozen	.85	.94	1.07	1.20	1.33	1.47

36182 Super Stout Ribbed Cotton Hose, seamless, reinforced heels and toes; black, warranted fast.

Sizes	6 in.	6½ in.	7 in.	7½ in.	8 in.	8½ in.
Per pair	$0.09	$0.10	$0.11	$0.12	$0.13	$0.14
Per dozen	.95	1.07	1.20	1.35	1.49	1.60

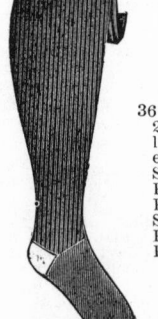

36183 Misses' or Boys' Super Stout 2-Thread Ribbed Cotton Hose, seamless, reinforced heels and toes, extra length.

Sizes	6 in.	6½ in.	7 in.
Per pair	$0.10	$0.11	$0.12
Per dozen	1.00	1.10	1.20
Sizes	7½ in.	8 in.	8½ in.
Per pair	$0.13	$0.14	$0.15
Per dozen	1.35	1.50	1.65

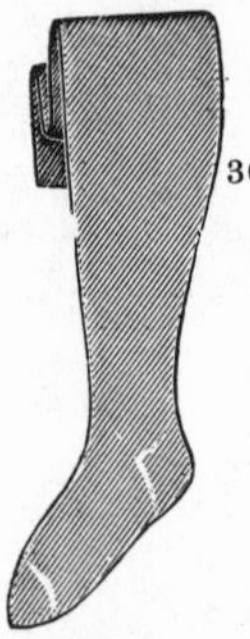

36184 Misses' and Children's Fine Plain Imported Cotton Hose full regular made, extra length, black only.

Sizes	5 in.	5½ in.	6 in.	6½ in.
Per pair	$0.14	$0.15	$0.17	$0.18
Per dozen	1.50	1.60	1.75	1.90
Sizes	7 in.	7½ in.	8 in.	8½ in.
Per pair	$0.19	$0.20	$0.22	$0.23
Per dozen	2.05	2.20	2.35	2.45

36184-5
36185 Misses' Plain Seamless Cotton Hose, double heels and toes, extra length.

Sizes	6 in.	6½ in.	7 in.	7½ in.	8 in.	8½ in.
Per pair	$0.08	$0.09	$0.10	$0.12	$0.13	$0.14
Per dozen	.90	1.00	1.15	1.25	1.40	1.50

Misses' and Boys' French Mixed Cotton Hose.

36186 Misses' and Children's Heavy Ribbed Cotton Hose, patent seams, brown mixed.

Sizes	7 to 7 in.	8 to 8½ in.
Per pair	$0.07	$0.08
Per dozen	.75	.85

36187 Misses' Super Stout Ribbed Cotton Hose, Oxford or Cambridge gray, or black and white mixed. Sizes, 7½ to 8½. Per pair $0.09
Per dozen .95

Misses' and Boys' Super Stout Seamless Cotton Hose.

36190 Misses' or Boys' Super Stout Seamless Ribbed Cotton Hose, Rockford style, double heels and toes. Oxford mixed, black and white mixed.

Sizes	6 in.	6½ in.	7½ in.	7½ in.
Per pair	$0.08	$0.09	$0.10	$0.11
Per dozen	.85	.95	1.07	1.20
Sizes	8 in.	8½ in.	9 in.	9½ in.
Per pair	$0.12	$0.13	$0.14	$0.15
Per dozen	1.33	1.45	1 55	1.65

36191 Misses' and Children's Super Stout Plain Seamless Cotton Hose, dark gray mixture; a good serviceable school stocking.

Sizes	6½ in.	7½ in.
Per pair	$0.07½	$0.08½
Per dozen	.80	.90
Sizes	8½ in.	
Per pair	$0.09½	
Per dozen	1.00	

Misses' or Boys' Seamless Heavy French Ribbed Fast Colored Cotton Hose.

NOTE.—All hosiery quoted as fast black is absolutely stainless. Money refunded if not as represented.

36193 Boys' Extra Heavy Knickerbocker Hose extra length, seamless, double heels and toes, fast black.

Sizes	7 in.	7½ in.	8 in.	8½ in.
Per pair	$0.13	$0.14	$0.15	$0.17
Per dozen	1.45	1.60	1.70	1.80
Sizes	9 in.	9½ in.	10 in.	
Per pair	$0.18	$0.19	$0.21	
Per dozen	1.95	2.05	2.20	

36194 Misses' or Boys' Super Stout Ribbed Cotton Hose, extra length, double heels and toes, double knees, seamless; fast black.

Sizes	6 in.	6½ in.	7 in.	7½ in.	8 in.	8½ in.
Per pair	$0.13	$0.14	$0.15	$0.16	$0.18	$0.19
Per dozen	1.40	1.54	1.67	1.80	1.94	2.05

36196 Misses' and Boys' Super Stout Fine Gauge Ribbed Cotton Hose, genuine 2-thread, double heels and toes, extra length; absolutely fast black or russet tans.

Sizes	6 in.	6½ in.	7 in.
Per pair	$0.15	$0.16	$0.18
Per dozen	1.60	1.75	1.90
Sizes	7½ in.	8 in.	8½ in.
Per pair	$0.19	$0.20	$0.21
Per dozen	2.05	2.20	2.35

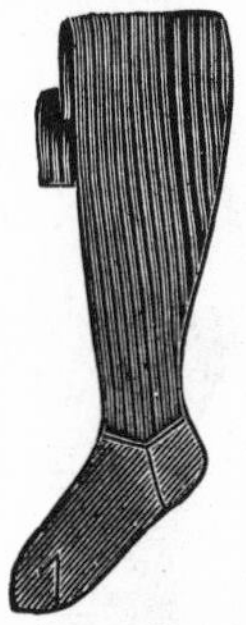

36197 Boys' Extra Super Stout Derby Ribbed 3-Thread Cotton Hose, extra length, double heels and toes, solid ingrain; color, fast black; for cycling, outdoor sport, etc.

Sizes	6 in.	6½ in.	7 in.	7½ in.
Per pair	$0.15	$0.17	$0.18	$0.19
Per doz.	1.60	1.75	1.90	2.05
Sizes	8 in.	8½ in.	9 in.	9½ in.
Per pair	$0.20	$0.21	$0.23	$0.24
Per doz.	2.20	2.35	2.50	2.60

36199 Boys' Extra Heavy Ribbed 4-Thread Knickerbocker or Cycling Cotton Hose, extra length, double spliced heels and toes; fast black. Very durable; double knees.

Sizes	7 in.	7½ in.	8 in.	8½ in.
Per pr.	$0.19	$0.20	$0.21	$0.23
Per dz.	2.05	2.20	2.35	2.50
Sizes	9 in.	9½ in.	10 in.	
Per pair	$0.24	$0.25	$0.26	
Per dozen	2.60	2.75	2 90	

36200 Misses' Extra Heavy Lisle Spun Cotton Hose, extra fine quality, ribbed, extra spliced heels and toes, fast black

Sizes	6 in.	6½ in.	7 in.
Per pair	$0.21	$0.22	$0.24
Per dozen	2.35	2.47	2.60
Sizes	7½ in.	8 in.	8½ in.
Per pair	$0.25	$0.26	$0.27
Per dozen	2.75	2.90	3.00

36201 Boys' Lisle Finished Ribbed Cotton Hose, superior quality, fast black, seamless, double heels and toes.

Sizes	7 in.	7½ in.	8in.	8½ in.	9in.	9½ in.	10in.
Per doz.	$2.40	2.55	2.70	2.80	2.95	3.10	3.25

36203 Misses' and Children's Extra Superfine French Cotton Hose, full regular made, imported, made of Egyptian cotton; fast black.

Sizes	6 in.	6½ in.	7 in.	7½ in.	8 in.	8½ in.	9 in.
Per pair	0.21	0.22	0.24	0.25	0.26	0.27	0.29
Per doz.	$2.35	2.47	2.60	2.75	2.90	3.00	3.15

Men's Ribbed Cotton Hose.

36207 Men's Heavy Ribbed Cotton Hose, seamless, fast black. Sizes, 10 to 11 in. Per pair $0.25
Per dozen 2.85

36208 Men's Extra Heavy Ribbed Cotton Hose, seamless, fast black. Sizes, 10 to 11 in. Per pair .35
Per dozen 3.85

Misses' and Children's Lisle Thread Hose.

36211 Misses' and Children's Extra Fine Egyptian Lisle Thread Hose, fine ribbed, seamless, double heels and toes, extra length; fast black or tan.

Sizes	6 in.	6½ in.	7 in.	7½ in.	8 in.	8½ in.
Per pr.	$0.18	$0.19	$0.20	$0.21	$0.22	$0.24
Per doz	1.95	2.07	2.20	2.35	2.47	2.60

36212 Misses' and Children's Extra Superfine Egyptian Lisle Thread Hose, French ribbed legs, seamless feet, double heels and toes; fast black.

Size	5 in.	5½ in.	6 in.	6½ in.
Per pair	.20	.21	.22	.24
Per doz.	$2.20	$2.35	$2.50	$2.60
Size	7 in.	7½ in.	8 in.	8½ in.
Per pair	$0.25	$0.26	$0.27	$0.28
Per doz.	2.75	2.90	3.00	3.15

Misses' and Boys' Merino Hose.

36219 Boys' Extra Heavy Ribbed Merino Hose, good, solid, durable, seamless, double heels and toes; black only.

Sizes.	Per pair	Per dozen.
7 in.	$0.21	$2.27
7½	.22	2.40
8	.23	2.55
8½	.24	2.67
9	.25	2.80
9½	.27	3.00

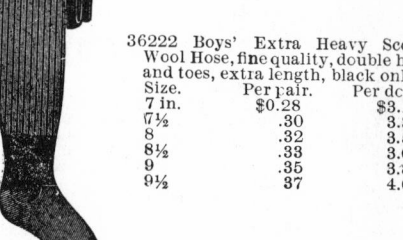

36222 Boys' Extra Heavy Scotch Wool Hose, fine quality, double heels and toes, extra length, black only.

Size.	Per pair.	Per dozen.
7 in.	$0.28	$3.15
7½	.30	3.30
8	.32	3.50
8½	.33	3.65
9	.35	3.80
9½	37	4.00

36223 Misses' or Boys' Extra Heavy all Pure Worsted Hose, warm and durable, warranted 4-thread, extra length, double heels and toes; black only.

Sizes.	Per pair.	Per dozen.
6 in	$0.35	$3.87
6½	.38	4.25
7	.40	4.55
7½	.43	4.70
8	.45	4.95
8½	.47	5.20
9	.50	5.50
9½	.55	5.75

36225 Boys' Extra Heavy Norway Stockings, all pure wool, best and warmest for zero weather; sizes, 9 and 9½ in., ribbed legs; length, 23 inches. Colors, black, gray or scarlet.

Per pair $0.40
Per dozen 4.50

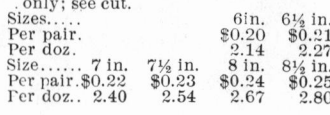

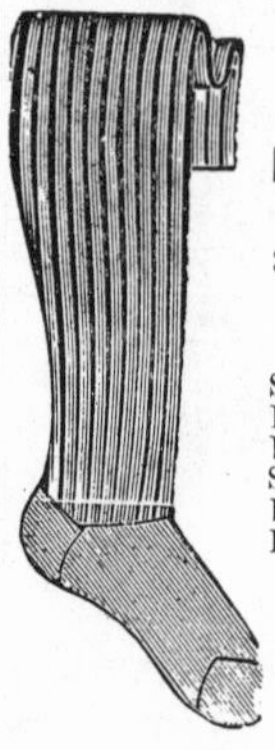

Misses' Solid Colored Cashmere Hose.

36226 Misses' Solid Colored Ribbed All Wool Hose, full fashioned seamless feet, double heels and toes, black only; see cut.

Sizes	6in.	6½ in.
Per pair	$0.20	$0.21
Per doz.	2.14	2.27
Size	7 in.	7½ in.	8 in.	8½ in.
Per pair	$0.22	$0.23	$0.24	$0.25
Per doz.	2.40	2.54	2.67	2.80

Misses' Hose—Continued.

36231 Misses' or Boys' Heavy All Wool Seamless Hose, cashmere finish, ribbed, extra length, double heels and toes, in black only.

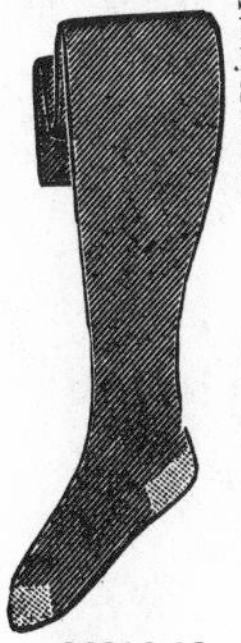

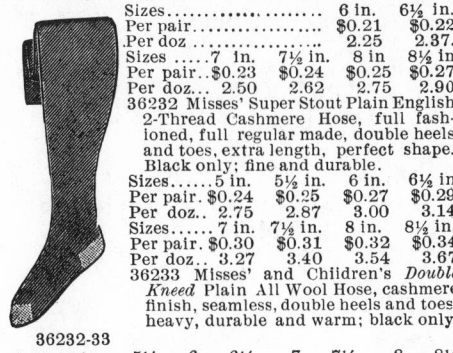

Sizes	6 in.	6½ in.
Per pair	$0.21	$0.22
Per doz	2.25	2.37

Sizes	7 in.	7½ in.	8 in	8½ in
Per pair	$0.23	$0.24	$0.25	$0.27
Per doz	2.50	2.62	2.75	2.90

36232 Misses' Super Stout Plain English 2-Thread Cashmere Hose, full fashioned, full regular made, double heels and toes, extra length, perfect shape. Black only; fine and durable.

Sizes	5 in.	5½ in.	6 in.	6½ in
Per pair	$0.24	$0.25	$0.27	$0.29
Per doz.	2.75	2.87	3.00	3.14
Sizes	7 in.	7½ in.	8 in.	8½ in.
Per pair	$0.30	$0.31	$0.32	$0.34
Per doz.	3.27	3.40	3.54	3.67

36233 Misses' and Children's *Double Kneed* Plain All Wool Hose, cashmere finish, seamless, double heels and toes, heavy, durable and warm; black only.

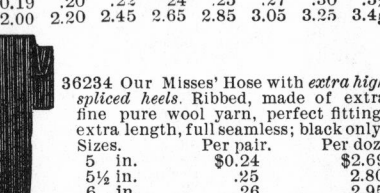

36232-33

Sizes	5 in.	5½	6	6½	7	7½	8	8½
Per pr.	$0.19	.20	.22	24	.25	.27	.30	.32
Per doz.	2.00	2.20	2.45	2.65	2.85	3.05	3.25	3.45

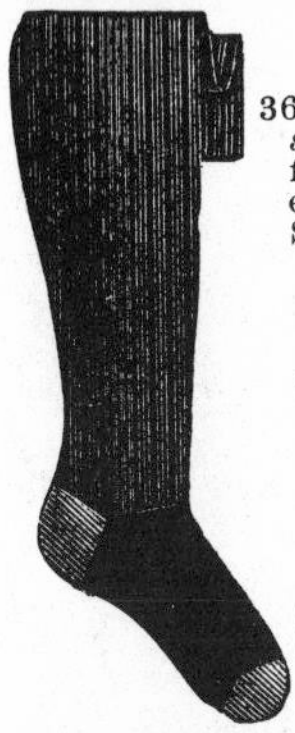

36234 Our Misses' Hose with *extra high spliced heels*. Ribbed, made of extra fine pure wool yarn, perfect fitting, extra length, full seamless; black only.

Sizes.	Per pair.	Per doz.
5 in.	$0.24	$2.69
5½ in.	.25	2.80
6 in.	.26	2.95
6½ in.	.28	3.07
7 in.	.30	3.25
7½ in.	.32	3.40
8 in.	.33	3.60
8½ in.	.35	3.75

36235 Misses' and Children's Imported Cashmere Hose, superfine quality, black, full regular made, extra length.

Sizes	5 in.	5½	6	6½	7	7½	8	8½
Per pr.	$0.34	.37	.39	.41	.44	.47	.50	55
Per dz.	3.75	4.00	4.30	4.55	4.80	5.15	5.50	5.90

Children's Drawer Leggings.

36238 Extra Saxony Drawer Leggings, in black only, for misses and children.

	Ages, 2 to 5 yrs.		Ages, 5 to 8 yrs.			Ages, 8 to 12 yrs.	
Sizes—	16 in. 18	20	22	24	26	28	30
Per pair—	$0.50 .60	70	.80	.90	1.00	1.10	1.20
Per dozen—	$5.50 6 70	7.70	8 70	9.70	10.70	11.70	12.70

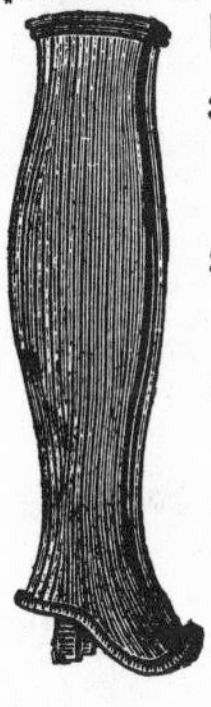

Fine All Wool Leggings.

BLACK ONLY.

36239 Ladies' Extra Heavy Wool Leggings.

Sizes	28 in.	30 in.	32 in.
Per pair	$0.39.	.42	.45
Per dozen	4.35	4.67	5.00

36240 Fine Worsted Leggings, Children's.

Sizes	16 in.	18 in.	20 in.
Per pair	$0.25	.30	.35
Per dozen	2.85	3.35	3.65

36241 Extra Fine Pure Saxony Leggings. Misses' and young ladies'

Sizes	24 in.	26 in.	28 in.
Per pair	$0.50	$0.55	$0.60
Per dozen	5.50	6.00	6.50
Ladies' sizes		30 in.	32 in.
Per pair		$0.65	$0.70
Per dozen		7.00	7.60

All Wool Stockinet or Stockings Made Easy.

36242 Heavy All Wool Ribbed Stockinet. Colors: Black or cardinal. With this material the economical housekeeper can make her entire outfit of children's stockings, mitts and wristlets at a very small cost. Stockinet is put up in rolls weighing from 3½ to 4 pounds, and measures about 9 yards to each pound. Price for full rolls, per pound $0.90
Price for less than full roll, per pound 1.00

Stocking Saving Knee Protectors.

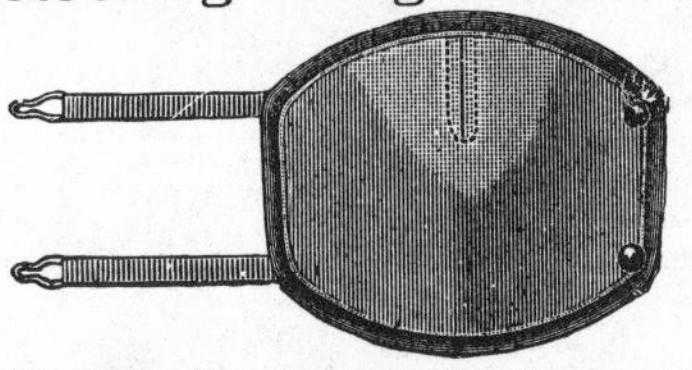

Weight, 2 ounces to a pair. Nos. 2, 3 and 4; ages 1 to 10.

36243 The New Improved Stocking Saving Knee Protector is made of extra heavy Jersey cloth. It fits closely to the knee. Per dozen $2.00
Per pair .... .20
36244 Stocking Saving Knee Protectors, made of leather. Per pair ... $0.20 Per dozen 2.00

Children's Heavy Wool Knit Hose.

36245 Misses' and Children's Extra Heavy Wool Mixed Seamless Hose, double heels and toes. Black.

Sizes	6½ in.	7½ in.	8½ in.
Per pair	$0.13	$0.15	$0.17
Per dozen	1.35	1.60	1.85

Infants' Seamless Cotton Hose.

36249 Infants' Fine Seamless Cotton Hose, plain, fast black. Sizes, 4½ to 5½. Per pair $0.09
Per dozen 1.00
36250 Infants' Fine Seamless Ribbed Cotton Hose. Sizes, 4½ to 5½. Fast black or tan.
Per Pair .... .09
Per dozen 1.00
36251 Infants' Extra Fine Seamless Ribbed Cotton Hose, extra length, black or tan. Per pair .15
Per dozen 1.60
36252 Infants' Seamless Ribbed Cotton Hose, superfine quality, fast black or tan. Sizes, 4 to 5½. Per pair .... .11
Per dozen 1.25

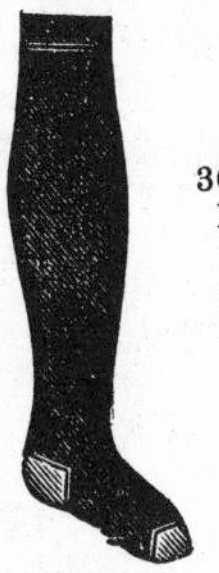

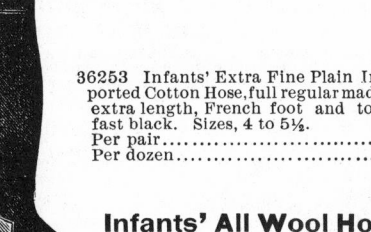

36253 Infants' Extra Fine Plain Imported Cotton Hose, full regular made, extra length, French foot and toe; fast black. Sizes, 4 to 5½.
Per pair $0.15
Per dozen 1.65

Infants' All Wool Hose.

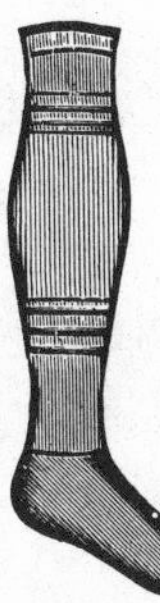

36254 Infants' All Wool Ribbed Hose red only. Sizes, 4 to 5 inches.
Per dozen $0.59
Per pair .... .05
36255 Infants' Fine Wool Hose, solid colors, fashioned seamless feet, navy, cardinal, seal. Sizes, 4 to 5½ inches.
Per pair $0.10
Per dozen 1.10
36256 Infants' Extra Fine All Worsted Hose. Seamless; black only. Sizes, 4 inches to 5½ inches. Per pair $0.15
Per dozen 1.65
36257 Infants' Superfine Saxony Wool Ribbed Hose, seamless, in black, Sizes, 4 to 5½ inches. Per pair $0.19
Per dozen 2.00

36258 Infants' Plain Worsted Hose, black, with colored silk heels and toes, seamless. Sizes, 4 to 5½. Per pair .... .20
Per dozen 2.25
36259 Infants' Extra Fine Ribbed Saxony Hose, extra length, black, with colored silk heels and toes or cream white. Sizes, 4 to 5½. Per pair .... .25
Per dozen 2.85
36260 Infants' Ribbed Extra Heavy Saxony Hose, 2 ply, in black only, Sizes, 4½ to 5½. Per pair .. .19
Per dozen 2.00
36261 Infants' Ribbed Extra Fine Saxony Hose, full regular made, seamless, black only. Sizes, 4 to 5¼. Per pair .... .25
Per dozen 2.85
36262 Infants' ¾ Socks, fine Saxony wool, plain black with colored silk heels and toes, plain legs, ribbed tops. Sizes, 4 to 5¼. Per pair .... .15
Per dozen 1.60

Infants' Wool Bootees.

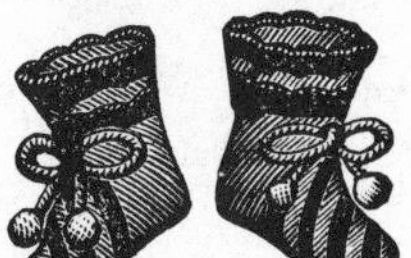

Colors, assorted; weight, 1 ounce per pair.
36263 Infants' Wool Bootees, fancy knitted.
Per pair $0.10
Per dozen 1.00

36264 Infants' Wool Bootees, heavier and larger.
Per pair $0.15
Per dozen 1.65
36265 Infants' Wool Bootees, finer quality, fancy crocheted. Per pair .... .20
Per dozen 2.25
36266 Infants' Fancy Knitted Bootees, still finer quality. Per pair .... .25
Per dozen 2.80

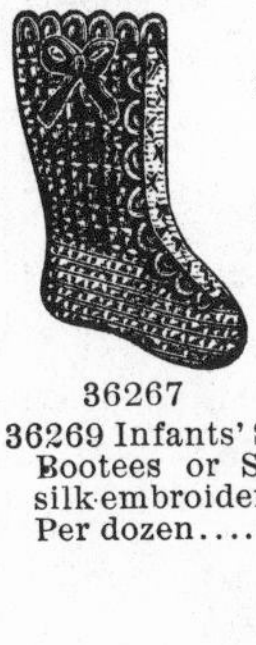

36267

36267 Infants' Hand Crocheted Wool Bootees, fine quality, silk stitched.
Per pair $0.30
Per dozen 3.25
36268 Infants' Fancy Hand Crocheted Wool Bootees, extra fancy top, extra fine quality. Per pair $0.35
Per dozen 3.80

36269 Infants' Superfine Crocheted Saxony Wool Bootees or Socks, very neat and close made, silk embroidered in pink, blue or cream. Per pair, $0.25
Per dozen 2.85

Men's Unbleached Cotton Half Hose.

All sizes above 11 in. are 25 to 50c. per dozen extra.
All hosiery is quoted per dozen pairs.
Do not order extra large sizes unless so quoted.
Always give size in inches.
Average weight, per dozen, 26 to 32 ounces.

SCALE OF SIZES.

No. 5	Men's shoes take	9-inch sock.
No. 6	Men's shoes take	9½-inch sock.
Nos. 7 and 8	Men's shoes take	10-inch sock.
No. 9	Men's shoes take	10½-inch sock.
No. 10	Men's shoes take	11-inch sock.

36270 Men's Unbleached Cotton Half Hose, open top.
Per pair $0.02
Per dozen .... .20

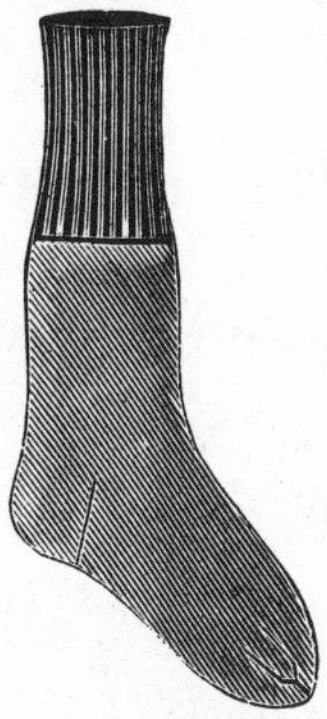

Style 36273-87

36272 Men's Imitation British Half Hose, unbleached, finished seams.
Per pair $0.05
Per dozen pairs .... .59
36273 Men's British Half Hose, unbleached, finished seams, superfine quality. (In 5 dozen lots, per dozen, 70c.)
Per pair $0.07
Per dozen pairs .... .75
36274 Men's Super Stout British Half Hose, unbleached. (In 5 dozen lots, per dozen, 80c.)
Per pair $0.08
Per dozen pairs .... .85
36275 Men's Medium Weight Seamless Half Hose, unbleached, extra spliced heel and toe, ribbed top.
Per pair $0 10
Per dozen pairs 1.10

	Per pair.	Per doz.
36277 Men's Super Stout British Half Hose, unbleached, double heels and toes, fashioned. (In 5 dozen lots, per dozen, $0.95)	$0.09	$1.00
36278 Men's Extra Heavy Seamless 3-Ply Cotton Socks, unbleached, 4-ply heels and toes, ribbed tops. (5 dozen lots, $1.12½ per dozen)	.11	1.25
36279 Super Stout British Half Hose, seamless, unbleached, double heels and toes. (In 5 dozen lots, per dozen, $1.35)	.14	1.50
36280 Men's Superfine Unbleached British Cotton Half Hose, double heels and toes, English ribbed tops. (In 5 dozen lots, $1.35 per dozen)	.14	1.50
36285 Men's Unbleached British Half Hose, super stout, seamless, imported	.19	2.00
36286 Men's Cotton Unbleached British Half Hose, super stout, seamless, imported	.20	2.25
36287 Men's Cotton Unbleached British Half Hose, superfine, extra length, seamless, imported	.25	2.80

Men's Balbriggan Half Hose.

Average weight, per dozen, 26 to 35 ounces

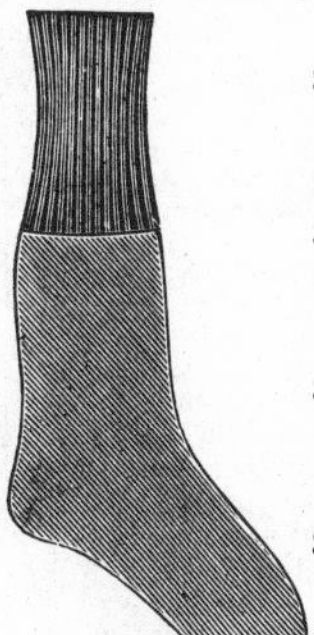

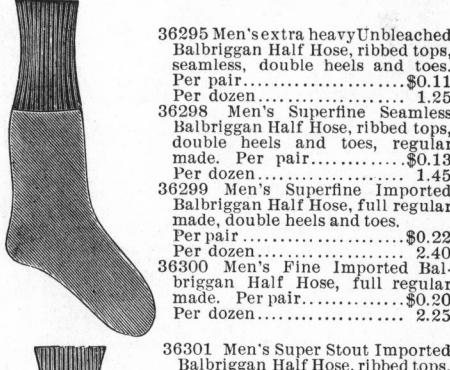

36295 Men's extra heavy Unbleached Balbriggan Half Hose, ribbed tops, seamless, double heels and toes.
Per pair $0.11
Per dozen 1.25
36298 Men's Superfine Seamless Balbriggan Half Hose, ribbed tops, double heels and toes, regular made. Per pair $0.13
Per dozen 1.45
36299 Men's Superfine Imported Balbriggan Half Hose, full regular made, double heels and toes.
Per pair $0.22
Per dozen 2.40
36300 Men's Fine Imported Balbriggan Half Hose, full regular made. Per pair $0.20
Per dozen 2.25

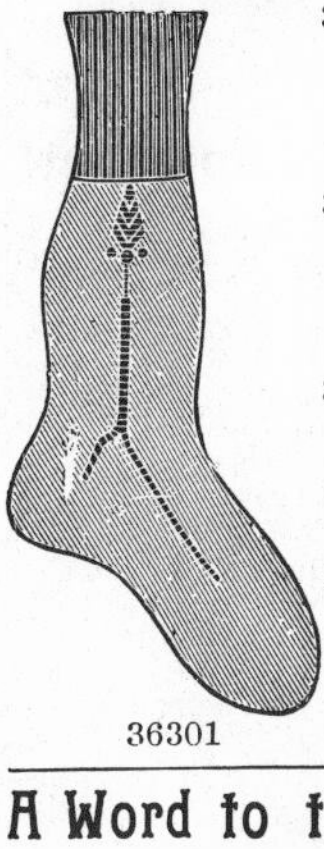

36301

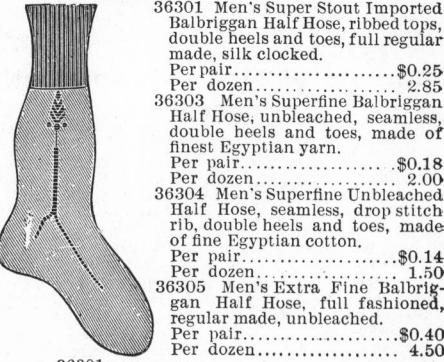

36301 Men's Super Stout Imported Balbriggan Half Hose, ribbed tops, double heels and toes, full regular made, silk clocked.
Per pair $0.25
Per dozen 2.85
36303 Men's Superfine Balbriggan Half Hose, unbleached, seamless, double heels and toes, made of finest Egyptian yarn.
Per pair $0.18
Per dozen 2.00
36304 Men's Superfine Unbleached Half Hose, seamless, drop stitch rib, double heels and toes, made of fine Egyptian cotton.
Per pair $0.14
Per dozen 1.50
36305 Men's Extra Fine Balbriggan Half Hose, full fashioned, regular made, unbleached.
Per pair $0.40
Per dozen 4.50

A Word to the Wise is Sufficient.

Men's Shaw-Knit Cotton Socks.

Average weight, per dozen, 32 oz. All Shaw-knit socks have gusseted heels and full regular seamless feet.

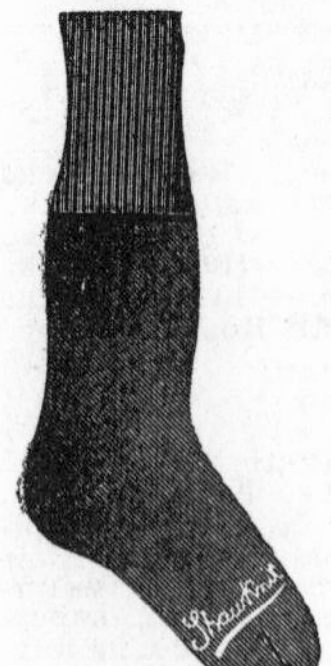

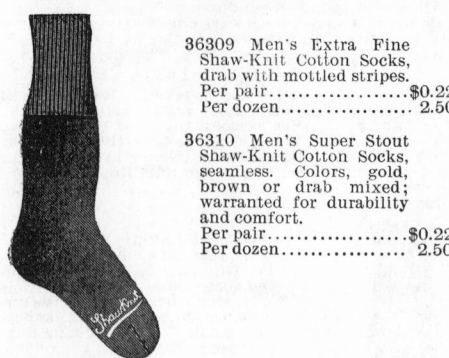

36309 Men's Extra Fine Shaw-Knit Cotton Socks, drab with mottled stripes.
Per pair....................$0.22
Per dozen.................. 2.50

36310 Men's Super Stout Shaw-Knit Cotton Socks, seamless. Colors, gold, brown or drab mixed; warranted for durability and comfort.
Per pair....................$0.22
Per dozen.................. 2.50

Men's 3-Ply Seamless Knit Cotton Socks.

Every pair guaranteed.

36311 Men's Super Stout Seamless Cotton Socks, genuine 3-thread, extra spliced heels and toes. Colors: Blue, slate or fast black.
Per pair....................$0.14
Per dozen.................. 1.50

36312 Men's Extra Heavy Seamless Knit Cotton Socks, 3-ply yarn and 4-ply heels and toes; very durable and comfortable on the foot. Colors: Solid tans and modes. Per pair.................. .14
Per dozen.................. 1.50

36313 Men's Extra Fine Perfect Fitting Seamless Cotton Socks, gusseted, made of extra fine pure Egyptian yarn. Color, sanitary gray only.
Per pair.................. .13
Per dozen.................. 1.45

36314 Men's Extra Superfine Seamless Cotton Half Hose, perfect fitting, gusseted, double heels and toes, fine Maco yarn. Colors: Absolutely fast black, slate or tans. Per pair........ .14
Per dozen.................. 1.50

Men's Celebrated Rockford Seamless Half Hose.

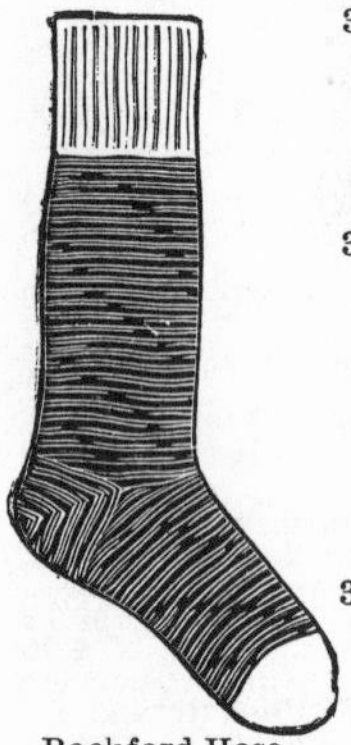

Rockford Hose.

36320 Men's Blue or Brown Mixed Rockford Seamless Half Hose, cotton, light weight, 4-ply heels and toes. Lot 101. (In 5 dozen lots, 55½c. net, per doz.) Weight, per doz., 28 oz. Per pair....$0.05
Per dozen, net.............. .59

36322 "The Sterling" Rockford Fancy Mixed Seamless Cotton Socks, medium weight, 4-ply heels and toes. Colors: Black and white, Spanish brown and white, gold and white, assorted in each doz. (In 5 doz. lots, 65c. per doz.) Lot No. 301; weight, 32 oz.
Per pair....................$0.07
Per dozen.................. .70

36324 "The Standard" Blue or Brown Mixed Seamless Rockford Cotton Half Hose, heavy weight, 4-ply heels and toes. (In 5 doz. lots, 80c. per doz.) Weight, 40 oz. Per pair....................$0.08
Per dozen.................. .87

36327 Men's Ribbed Top Rockford Socks, extra heavy, seamless, 4-ply heels and toes, blue or brown mixed (style 901). (In 5 dozen lots 95c. per dozen.) Per pair....$0.10 Per dozen........ 1.10

36328 Men's Super Stout Seamless Cotton Half Hose, made of genuine 3-ply yarn and 4-ply heels and toes. Gold and brown mixed, ribbed tops.
Per pair........$0.11 Per dozen.............. 1.20

39329 Men's Extra Stout 3-Thread Cotton Half Hose. 4-thread heels and toes, made of a fine quality of soft yarn, ribbed tops, seamless feet, unsurpassed for durability. Colors, two shades drab and Oxford gray. Per pair.................. .15
Per dozen.................. 1.60

Odd Lots of Men's Cotton Half Hose.

Average weight, 26 to 33 ounces per dozen.

36335 Men's Fancy Mixed or Striped Cotton Half Hose. (In 5 doz. lots, 42½ cents per dozen.) Per pair.................. $0.04
Per dozen.................. .45

36336 Men's Fancy Mixed Superfine Cotton Half Hose, gold, brown or drab mixed Per pair.... .05
Per dozen.................. .59

36337 Men's Fancy Mixed Cotton Half Hose, ribbed tops, assorted styles. (In 5 dozen lots, 62½ cents per dozen.) Per pair.................. .06
Per dozen.................. .65

36338 Men's Fancy Mixed Cotton Half Hose, ribbed tops, fine gauge. Full seamless heel.
Per pair.................. .08
Per dozen.................. .85
(In 5 dozen lots, 79 cents per dozen.)

Men's Heavy Seamless Ribbed Top Cotton Socks.

	Per pair.	Per doz.
36339 Men's Extra Heavy Cotton Socks, full seamless ribbed tops. Color: Pink, blue or gold mixed..........	.08	.85
36340 Men's Heavy Blue or Brown Mixed Cotton Half Hose, seamless. (In 5 dozen lots, 79 cents per dozen)........	.08	.85
36341 Men's Extra Heavy Seamless Half Hose, double heels and toes, Spanish brown mixed or blue mixed, large sizes, ribbed tops. (In 5 dozen lots, $1.05 per dozen)........	10	1.10
36342 Men's Extra Heavy Seamless Cotton Socks, double heels and toes, rib tops, extra large sizes. Colors: Blue or brown mixed. (In 5 dozen lots, $1.10 per dozen.)........	.11	1.25
36343 Men's Medium Weight Seamless Cotton Socks, extra large, brown, gold or drab mixed; sizes, 11 to 12½ only. (In 5 dozen lots, $1.00 per dozen)........	.10	1.10

Men's Fine Fancy Mixed Seamless Socks.

N. B.—These are just as comfortable, and will outwear imported half hose at double their prices.

36344 Men's Cotton Half Hose, seamless; colors: Gold, brown and drab mixed. Per pair.........$0.07
Per dozen.................. .79

36345 Men's Super Stout Double Thread Seamless Cotton Half Hose, 4-ply heels and toes, gold brown or drab mixed. Will wear well.
Per pair.................. .09
Per dozen.................. 1.00

36346 Men's Super Stout Seamless Cotton Socks, made of genuine 3-ply yarn and 4-ply heels and toes. Very durable and comfortable on the feet.
Per pair.................. .10
Per dozen.................. 1.10

36347 Men's Extra Super Stout Seamless Cotton Socks, made of extra 3-ply yarn and 4-ply heels and toes. Perfectly indestructible. Gold mixed, or Spanish brown mixed. Per pair...... .11
Per dozen.................. 1.25

36348 Men's Cotton Half Hose, extra super stout, seamless, ribbed tops, double heels and toes, fast ingrain. Colors: Slate, tan, mode, russet.
Per pair........ $0.12 Per dozen........... 1.35

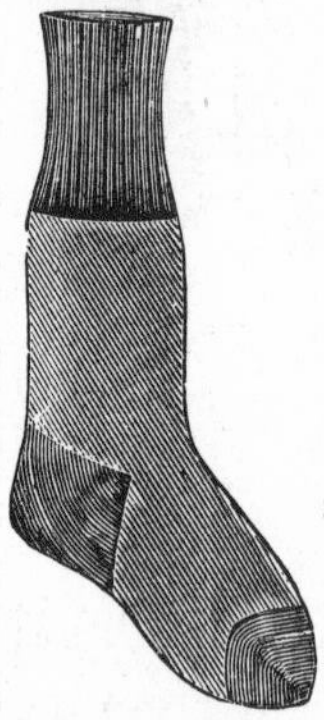

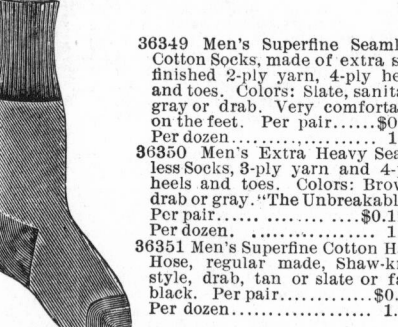

36349 Men's Superfine Seamless Cotton Socks, made of extra soft finished 2-ply yarn, 4-ply heels and toes. Colors: Slate, sanitary gray or drab. Very comfortable on the feet. Per pair......$0.11
Per dozen.................. 1.25

36350 Men's Extra Heavy Seamless Socks, 3-ply yarn and 4-ply heels and toes. Colors: Brown, drab or gray. "The Unbreakable."
Per pair..................$0.12½
Per dozen.................. 1.39

36351 Men's Superfine Cotton Half Hose, regular made, Shaw-knit style, drab, tan or slate or fast black. Per pair.............$0.14
Per dozen.................. 1.50

36352 Men's Ex-Superfine Cotton Half Hose, regular made and gusseted heels and toes. Colors: Slate, tans and drabs. Per pair..................$ .18
Per dozen.................. 2.00

Men's Colored Plain Cotton Half Hose.

Weight, about 32 ounces to a dozen.
(Black, guaranteed fast and stainless, or money refunded.)

36353 Men's Plain Seamless Half Hose, full regular made, fast black, tan or modes. Per pair...$0.10
Per dozen.................. 1.10

36354 Men's Superfine Cotton Half Hose, imported, full regular made, double heels and toes; absolutely fast black, modes or tans. (In 5 dozen lots, $1.50 per dozen.) Per pair........ .15
Per dozen.................. 1.65

36355 Men's Superfine Seamless Cotton Half Hose, full regular made. Colors: Modes or tans. Per pair.................. .12
Per dozen.................. 1.35

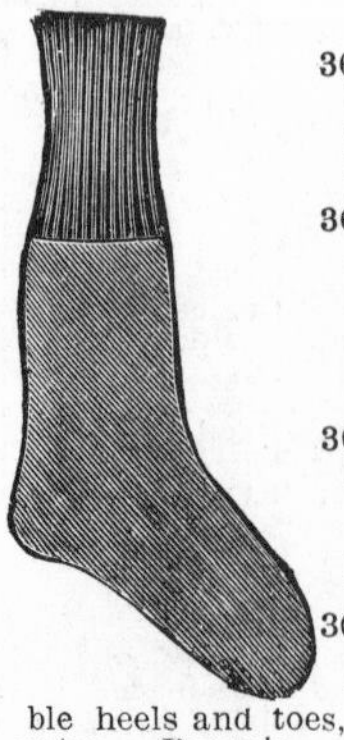

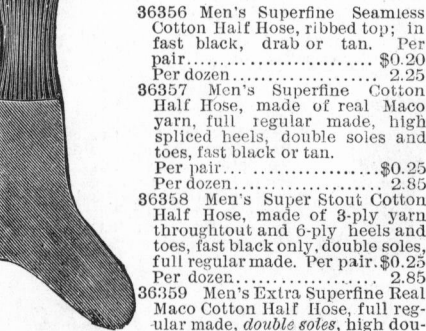

36356 Men's Superfine Seamless Cotton Half Hose, ribbed top; in fast black, drab or tan. Per pair.................. $0.20
Per dozen.................. 2.25

36357 Men's Superfine Cotton Half Hose, made of real Maco yarn, full regular made, high spliced heels, double soles and toes, fast black or tan.
Per pair...................$0.25
Per dozen.................. 2.85

36358 Men's Super Stout Cotton Half Hose, made of 3-ply yarn throughtout and 6-ply heels and toes, fast black only, double soles, full regular made. Per pair.$0.25
Per dozen.................. 2.85

36359 Men's Extra Superfine Real Maco Cotton Half Hose, full regular made, *double soles*, high double heels and toes, velvet finish. Colors, fast black or tan. Per pair....$0.28 Per dozen............$3.00

Men's Half Hose—Continued.

36360 Men's Extra Superfine Fast Black English Cotton Half Hose, full regular double soles, double heels and toes. Per pair.. .30
Per dozen.................. 3.25

36361 Men's Extra Fine Half Hose, made of real Maco yarn, light weight in tan, drab or fast black. Per pair.................. .25
Per dozen.................. 2.85

36362 M. W. & Co.'s *Guarantee* Socks. Made of extra fine lisle spun ingrain yarn. Return any pair that does not give satisfaction in *wear* or *color*, and we will give you a new pair in exchange. Indestructible black only.
Per pair.................. 0.33
Per dozen.................. 3.60

Men's Domestic Lisle Thread Half Hose.

36364 Men's Superfine 2-Thread Lisle Finished Half Hose, seamless. 4-ply heels and toes, very durable. Colors: Fast black, tan or slate.
Per pair....................$0.15
Per dozen.................. 1.66

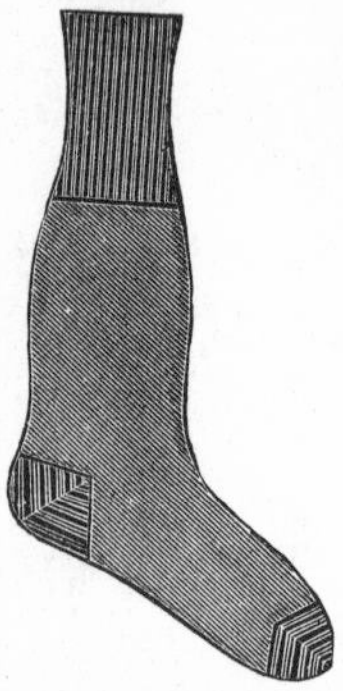

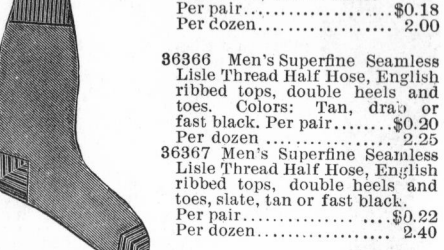

36365 Men's Super Stout, 3-Ply Lisle Finished Half Hose, 4-ply heels and toes, seamless; made of fine combed yarn. Colors: Fast black, tan or slate.
Per pair....................$0.18
Per dozen.................. 2.00

36366 Men's Superfine Seamless Lisle Thread Half Hose, English ribbed tops, double heels and toes. Colors: Tan, drab or fast black. Per pair........$0.20
Per dozen.................. 2.25

36367 Men's Superfine Seamless Lisle Thread Half Hose, English ribbed tops, double heels and toes, slate, tan or fast black.
Per pair....................$0.22
Per dozen.................. 2.40

36370 Men's Extra Fine Half Hose, made of fine Egyptian cotton, double heels and toes, sanitary gray only. Per pair.................. $0.15
Per dozen.................. 1.60

Men's Imported Lisle Thread Half Hose.

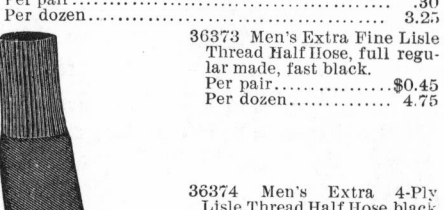

36371 Men's Fine Imported Lisle Thread Half Hose, double heels and toes, fast black.
Per pair....................$0.25
Per dozen.................. 2.85

36372 Men's Imported Lisle Thread Half Hose, heavy, full regular made, fast black.
Per pair.................. .30
Per dozen.................. 3.25

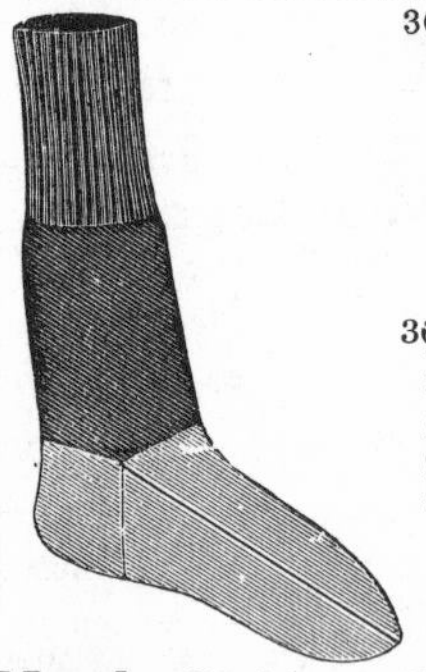

36373 Men's Extra Fine Lisle Thread Half Hose, full regular made, fast black.
Per pair....................$0.45
Per dozen.................. 4.75

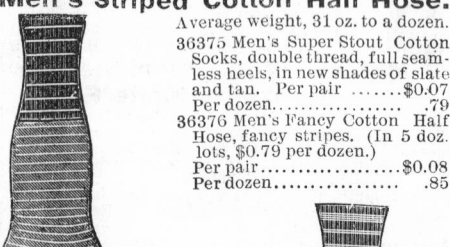

36374 Men's Extra 4-Ply Lisle Thread Half Hose, black tops, with soft unbleached feet, double heels and toes, double soles.
Per pair....................$0.33
Per dozen.................. 3.60

Men's Striped Cotton Half Hose.

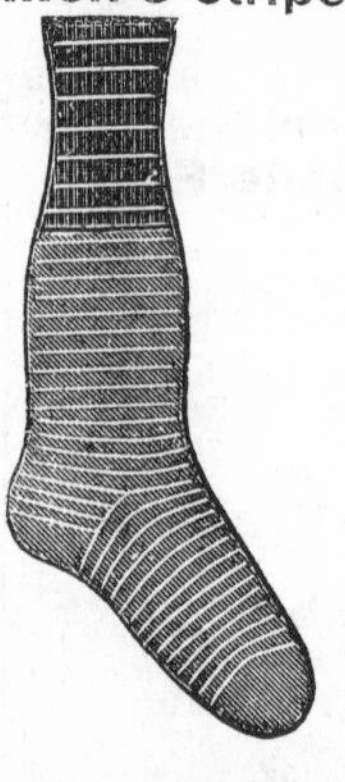

Average weight, 31 oz. to a dozen.

36375 Men's Super Stout Cotton Socks, double thread, full seamless heels, in new shades of slate and tan. Per pair $0.07
Per dozen.................. .79

36376 Men's Fancy Cotton Half Hose, fancy stripes. (In 5 doz. lots, $0.79 per dozen.)
Per pair....................$0.08
Per dozen.................. .85

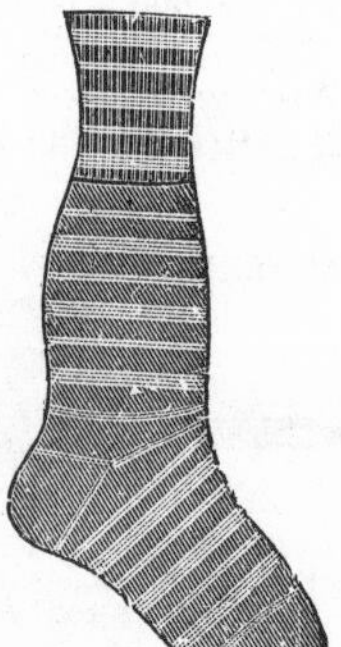

36377 Men's Fancy Cotton Half Hose, full regular made, seamless, imported, stripes of cardinal, blue, brown. See cut. Until sold. Per pair...... $0.11
Per dozen.................. 1.25

36379 Men's Extra Fine Striped Cotton Half Hose, full regular made. Per pair.......... $0.25
Per dozen.................. 2.85

Men's Domestic and Imported Merino Half Hose.

NOTE.—Merino Half Hose are cotton and wool mixed and lighter weight than all wool hose. Merino finished Half Hose are all cotton, with a soft finish like Merino.

36380 Men's Super Stout Merino Finished Half Hose, seamless, double heels and toes, fine, soft and durable. Colors: Gray, tan or drab. Per pr..$0.12
Per dozen...................... 1.35

36382 Men's Extra Super Stout Merino Finished Half Hose, extra soft finish, double heels and toes, full seamless; warranted for durability and comfort. Colors: Dark gray, drab or tan.
Per pair................................. .15
Per dozen................................ 1.60

36384 Men's Superfine Merino Half Hose, ribbed top, seamless, double heels and toes, English mixtures of brown, cinnamon, olive; assorted.
Per pair.................................. .19
Per dozen................................ 2.00

36385 Men's Super Stout Merino Half Hose, assorted tans, seamless, double heels and toes.
Per pair.................................. .19
Per dozen................................ 2.00

36386 Men's Extra Stout Seamless Merino Half Hose, double heels and toes, regular made, tan colors, or fast black,
Per pair....................$0.25
Per dozen.................... 2.80

36387 Men's Superfine Seamless Merino Half Hose, ribbed tops, double heels and toes, English mixtures in olive, gold, brown or cinnamon.
Per pair....................$0.20
Per dozen.................... 2.25

36388 Men's Extra Fine Merino Half Hose, made of extra quality of Australian worsted, warranted for durability and comfort, Oxford mixed or tans.
Per pair..............$0.35
Per dozen.... .... 3.85

36385-88

Men's Ribbed All Wool Shaker Socks.

36389 Men's Heavy Wool Ribbed Leg Shaker Socks, double heels and toes, seamless. sheep's gray, natural gray, or blue mixed, fine quality.
Per pair....................$0.22
Per dozen.................... 2.40

36390 Men's Extra Quality All Wool Ribbed Leg Shaker Socks, seamless. Colors: Scarlet or sheep's gray.
Per pair....................$0.29
Per dozen.................... 3.25

36391 Men's Extra Heavy All Wool Shaker Socks, ribbed legs, seamless, double heels and toes, sheep's gray or natural gray.
Per pair....................$0.25
Per dozen.................... 2.85

36392 Men's Extra Heavy Ribbed Leg Shaker Socks, fine quality lamb's wool, double heels and toes. Colors: Scarlet, gray or indigo blue.
Per pair....................$0.38
Per dozen.................... 4.00

Men's Cashmere Half Hose.

NOTE.—Cashmere Half Hose are made of medium or light weight fine yarn, all wool.
Average weight, 32 ounces to a dozen.

36395 Men's Super Stout All Wool Cashmere Half Hose, seamless, double merino heels and toes. Colors: Sanitary gray, or light or dark olive. Per pair....................$0.20
Per dozen.................... 2.25

36396 Men's Medium Weight Wool Cashmere Half Hose, double heels and toes, full seamless. Colors: Tan, slate, Scotch gray or black.
Per pair.................................. .19
Per dozen................................ 2.00

36397 Men's Super Stout Scotch Wool Half Hose, cashmere finish, medium weight. Colors: Sanitary or natural gray, camel's hair brown or black. Per pair..... .22
Per dozen.................... 2.40

36400 Men's Superfine Natural Wool Scotch and Sanitary Gray Cashmere Half Hose, double heels and toes, English ribbed tops; recommended for wear and warmth. Per pair.........$0.25
Per dozen.................... 2.85

36401 Men's Fine Finish Cashmere Half Hose, double heels and toes, derby ribbed tops. Colors: Gray, tan. Per pair........$0.29
Per dozen.................... 3.25

36402 Men's Medium Weight Half Hose, seamless, black.
Per pair....................$0.30
Per dozen.................... 3.25

36395 to 36402
20—2nd

36403 Men's Extra Fine Silk Finished English Worsted Half Hose, made of 3-ply yarn, full fashioned, seamless, double heels and toes. Colors: Sanitary gray, black, modes, tans.
Per pair....................$0.40
Per dozen.................... 4.50

36405 Men's Extra Fine All Wool Seamless Cashmere Half Hose; no better sock for wear and comfort. Colors: Black or sanitary gray. Per pair............$0.35
Per dozen.................... 3.85

36406 Men's Extra Fine All Wool Seamless Cashmere Half Hose, worsted finish, made of fine Australian wool fine and durable. English mixtures in tan, cinnamon, olive. Per pair......$0.35
Per dozen.................... 3.85

Extra fine 36403-7

36407 Men's Extra Fine Imported Cashmere Half Hose; full regular made. Black or sanitary gray.
Per pair..... 45
Per dozen.............. 5.00

Men's Medium Weight all Wool Half Hose.

36410 Men's Medium Heavy All Wool Socks, derby ribbed tops; double heels and toes, seamless. Colors: Scarlet, blue mixed, sheep's gray or Scotch gray. Weight, per dozen, 48 ounces. Per pair........$0.30
Per dozen.................... 3.25

Men's Heavy Weight English Merino Socks.

36415 Men's Super Stout Seamless Merino Socks, double heels and toes, English mixtures of tan, or brown mixed. Very durable and perfect fitting. Per pair....................$0.25
Per dozen.................... 2.85

36416 Men's Extra Fine English Merino Socks, seamless, double heels and toes, English mixtures in natural gray, pink, or gold. Very comfortable and durable. Per pair............... .35
Per dozen.................... 3.85

Men's Heavy Knit Seamless All Wool Socks, Double Heels and Toes.

36420 Men's Heavy Knit Wool Mixed Socks; weight, per dozen, 32 ounces. Per pair.........$0.14
Per dozen.................... 1.50

36421 Men's Heavy Knit All Wool Socks. Colors: Gray or blue mixed. Per pair............. .19
Per dozen.................... 2.00

36422 Men's Heavy Knit All Wool Socks, ribbed tops, scarlets, blue mixed, sheep's gray; weight, per dozen, about 40 ounces. Per pair...... .20
Per dozen.................... 2.25

36426 Men's Heavy All Wool Socks, ribbed tops, homespun. Colors: Blue mixed or Scotch gray.
Per pair .... .22
Per dozen............................ 2.40

36427 Men's Heavy All Wool Socks, ribbed tops, fancy colors. Per pair............................ .20
Per dozen............................ 2.25

36428 Men's Extra Heavy All Wool Socks, ribbed tops, Homespun. Colors in Scotch gray, blue gray, or sheep's gray; 3½ pounds to a dozen.
Per pair.........$0.25 Per dozen............ 2.85

36430 Men's Heavy Fancy Mixed All Wool Socks. Colors: Blue and white, or red and white mottled. Per pair..$0.25 Per dozen.... .. 2.85

Men's Extra Heavy Knit All Wool Seamless Socks.

36441 Men's Extra Heavy All Wool Seamless Half Hose, ribbed tops, plain legs, double heels and toes. Colors: Blue mixed, sheep's or Scotch gray or scarlet. Per pair....................$0.30
Per dozen.................... 3.25

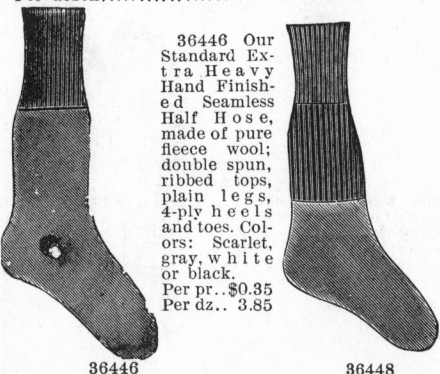

36446 Our Standard Extra Heavy Hand Finished Seamless Half Hose, made of pure fleece wool; double spun, ribbed tops, plain legs, 4-ply heels and toes. Colors: Scarlet, gray, white or black.
Per pr..$0.35
Per dz.. 3.85

36446   36448

36448 Our Arctic Extra Heavy Hand Finished Socks, made of a fine quality of pure fleece wool; double ribbed legs. Heavy, warm and durable; colors: Cardinal, sheep's gray or white. Weight, 4 lbs. Per pair......................... .40
Per pair................................. 4.50

36450 Our Inverness Sock. Made of pure home spun, 4-ply all wool yarn. Ribbed tops, plain legs. Weight, 4½ pounds to the dozen. Per pair....... .45
Per dozen................................ 5.00

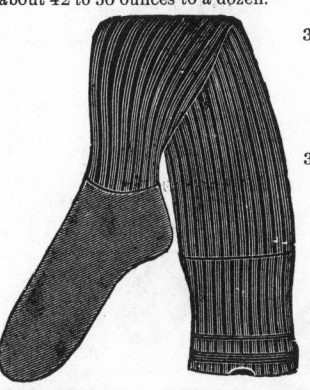

36451 Men's Extra Heavy All Wool Seamless Half Hose, *double soles*, high spliced double heels and toes; colors: Red, gray or white.
Per pair....................$0.33
Per dozen.................... 3.60

Men's Extra Length Bicycle and Athletic Hose.

For all sorts of athletic sports, games, etc. Weight about 42 to 50 ounces to a dozen.

36458 Men's Heavy All Wool Ribbed Hose, double heels and toes; color: Black.
Per pair...$0.40
Per doz.... 4.50

36459 Men's Bicycle Hose, made of extra stout double thread all wool yarn, very durable, extra length, derby ribbed, seamless; colors: black.
Per pair...$0.50
Per dozen. 5.50

36460 Men's Heavy Ribbed Bicycle Hose, cotton, seamless, double heels and toes, fast black.
Per pair.............................. . ...$0.25
Per dozen............................ 2.85

36461 Men's Bicycle Cotton Stockings, extra heavy, ribbed, seamless. Fast black.
Per pair................................. .35
Per dozen................................ 3.85

36462 Men's Extra Stout Ribbed All Wool Bicycle Stockings; the most durable stockings made; black only.
Per pair........ .... .75
Per dozen........ .. .. 8.00

Men's Hunting Stockings.

36473 Men's Royal Norway Hunting Stockings, made of extra heavy all wool 6-ply yarn, in handsomely variegated mixtures of black, brown and gray; black, blue and gray; or black, red and gray. Double feet fleece lined, length, 28 inch leg. No finer snow stocking. Per pair..$1.25
Per dozen..........14.00

Royal Norway.

Heavy Lined All Wool German Socks.

We guarantee every pair of our German socks. Should any prove unsatisfactory after a fair trial return them, and we will refund your money or give you a new pair in exchange. Straps and buckles with every pair.

36478 Our New Patent German Socks or Blizzard Boots, made of a good quality of wool; are put through a special process of fulling and lined all through with wool, solidly spliced into the sock. We guarantee them to be unequaled for wear and warmth. Color: Sheep's gray or brown striped. Length, 19 inch leg; weight, 24 ozs. to a pair. Per pair......$1.10
Per dozen............12.00
36479 The Waukesha All Knit All Wool Boot. Guaranteed to outwear anything of its kind in the market. Heavy, warm and durable. Color: Sheep's gray only. Per pair......$1.10 Per dozen ...$12.00

Men's Extra Long All Wool Hose.

Weight to a pair, 36490–8oz., 36492–7 oz., 36494– 15 oz.

36490
36492
36494
Per dozen....

36490 Men's Polar Long Hunting Stockings, extra heavy, all wool, seamless, ribbed, gartered tops; colors: Scarlet, gray or black. See cut. Per pr ..0.45
Per dz ..5.00
36492 Boys' Extra Heavy Long Polar Stockings; all wool, ribbed legs; very warm; 23-in. legs: Colors: Black, gray or red. Per pair.........$0.40
Per dozen...................... 4.50
36494 Men's Extra Heavy and Extra Long Hunting Stockngs, made of pure Wisconsin wool, all wool tuft lining. Very warm and durable; colors: Red, black or sheep's gray; length of leg, 24 inches.
Per pair.....................$ 1.10
Per dozen. 12.00

Boys' Cotton Half Hose.

Weight, per dozen, 23 ozs.
36495 Boys' Blue or Brown Mixed Seamless Cotton Half Hose, plain tops.
Per pair..................$0.05
Per dozen................... .59
36496 Boys' Cotton Half Hose, blue or brown mixed, 9 in. and 9½ in.
Per pair.... ... .$0.09
Per dozen pairs..... ...... .95

Boys' All Wool Half Hose

36497 Boys' All Wool Half Hose, seamless; Colors: Blue mixed or gray; size, 9 inches. Per pair $0.15
Per dozen 1 65
36498 Boys Extra Fine Cashmere Socks; sizes, 9 and 9½ in.: seamless, double heels and toes; assorted colors. Per pair........... 20
Per dozen...................... 2.25

IN OUR ⁘ ⁘
Wall Paper Department

We are showing the very latest styles of Wall Paper at the lowest prices. . . . .
Send for Samples.

CHILDREN'S CAPS AND BONNETS.

For Spring and Summer Wear.

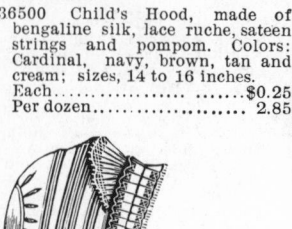

36500 Child's Hood, made of bengaline silk, lace ruche, sateen strings and pompom. Colors: Cardinal, navy, brown, tan and cream; sizes, 14 to 16 inches.
Each.... ....$0.25
Per dozen.................... 2.85

36501 Child's Embroidered Lawn Cap; sizes, 12 to 14 inches.
Each....................$0.05
Per dozen...................
36502 Child's Shirred Cap, white only; sizes, 13 to 16 inches. See cut. Each.............$0.25
Per dozen............... 2.85

36502

36503 Child's Shirred Cap, full pompadour ruche; sizes, 13 to 16 inches. Each........$0.25
Per dozen 2.85

36504 Children's Extra Fine French Shirred Hood, full pompadour ruche; fine lawn ties; sizes, 14 to 16 inches.
Each..................$0.50
Per dozen........ ... . 5.50

36505 Children's Fine Swiss Embroidered Hoods, lace pompon, fine lawn strings, sizes, 13 to 16 inches. Each............$0.25
Per dozen........ ...... 2.85
36506 Children's Extra Heavy Swiss Embroidery Hood, full double lace ruche; sizes, 14 to 16 inches. Each..............$0.35
Per dozen................. 3.85

36507 Extra Heavy French Swiss Embroidered Hood, double lace ruche and pompom, fine lawn ties; sizes, 14 to 16 inches.
Each................. $0.50
Per dozen............ 5.50

36508 Fine Swiss Embroidery Hood, full ruche and cape of fine Swiss edging. All washing material
Each.................. $0.50
Per dozen................ 5.50

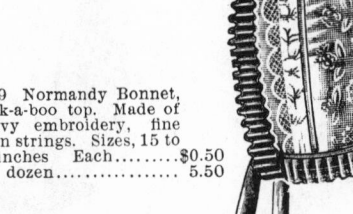

36509 Normandy Bonnet, peek-a-boo top. Made of heavy embroidery, fine lawn strings. Sizes, 15 to 17 inches Each........$0.50
Per dozen.................. 5.50

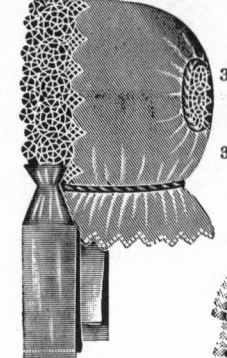

36510 New Patented Washing Caps, can be flattened out like an apron and brought into shape by means of running strings.
No. 1. Plain Lawn Cap or Hood. Each.....$0.25
Per dozen........... 2.85
No. 2. Made of Dotted Swiss, plain lawn strings.
Each................. $0.50
Per dozen.......... 5.50
No. 3. Made of Extra Fine Dotted Swiss, plain lawn strings. Each.....$0.75
Per dozen............ 8.00

36511 Child's Washing Cap, made of fine Swiss embroidery, style of 36512
Each........... .....$0.25
Per dozen.......... 2 85
36512 Child's Washing Cap, made of Irish point, edging, fine quality.
Each................$0.50
Per dozen........... 5.50

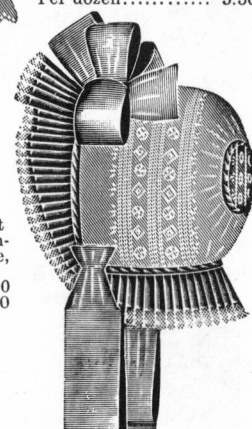

36513 Child's Bonnet made of Swiss embroidery, large ruffle, sizes, 14 to 17 inches.
Each..............$0.50
Per dozen...... 5.50

Children's Sun Bonnets.

36514 Sun Bonnets made of white pique, small sizes
Each $0.15
Per dozen.............. 1.70
36515 Sun Bonnets made of pique, larger, white only. Ages 1 to 3 years.
Each....................$0 24
Per dozen............... 2.75
36516 Children's Sun Bonnets, made of washing gingham. Ages, 2 to 12 years, all colors.
Each................$0.20
Per dozen............... 2.25

36514-16

36517 Child's Sun Bonnet, made of fine Lawn, white only, Nomandy back, peek-a-boo front, 1 to 6 years.
Each..........$0.35
Per dozen..... 3.85
35518 Child's Sun Bonnet, made of printed lawn, peek-a-boo front, Normandy back, extra deep cape, blue and and white, pink and white. Ages 1 to 6 years.
Each..........$0.35
Per dozen..... 3.85

36519 Child's Sun Bonnet, made of fine lawn and Swiss embroidery, peek-a-boo front, and Normandy back, 1 to 8 years (shaped like 36520).
Each...................$0.50
Per dozen................ 5.50
36520 Child's Normandy Sun Bonnet, extra fine lace trimmings, 1 to 8 years.
Each...................$0.75
Per dozen......... ...... 8.00

Ladies' Sun Bonnets.

36521 Ladies' Sun Bonnets, made of printed percale, assorted colors.
Each.............................$0.25
Per dozen.............................2.85
36522 Ladies' Sun Bonnets, indigo blue cloth, with white polka dot. Each.............................35
Per dozen.............................3.85

Children's Bonnets.

36523 Child's Cape Bonnet, made of Bengaline silk, peek-a-boo top; colors: Cream, tan, cardinal, navy or brown. Sizes, 15 and 16.
Each.............................$0.75
Per dozen.............................8.00

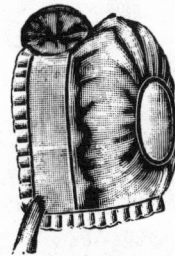

36524 Child's Cashmere Cap, Normandy style, made of fine cashmere; ties of same; rosette and trimmings of velvet. Colors: Cream or tan.
Size, 15 to 17.
Each, until sold.............................$0.50
Per dozen.............................5.50
36525 Child's Novelty Cashmere Cap, richly embroidered sides, fancy top, wide strings. Colors: Cream or tan. Sizes, 15 to 17.
Each.............................$1.00
Per dozen,.............................10 80

Infants' Crocheted Woolen Hoods.

36526 Infants' Heavy Lined, Wool Hoods, white or black.
Each.............................$0.20
Per dozen 2.25
36527 Infants' Hood, made of fine Shetland floss, lined with teaseled yarn; white black or red.
Each.............................$0.25
Per dozen.............................2.85

36528 Infant's Extra Fine Fancy Stitched Hood, made of extra fine Shetland floss, warm lining of fine teaseled yarn, trimmed all round face with eiderdown; color, cream ground; silk floss trimming of pink or blue.
Each.............................$0.95
Per dozen.............................10.00

Children's Fine Silk Caps.

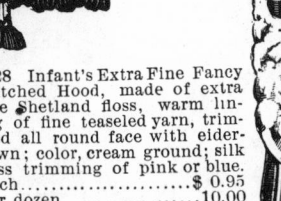

36529 Child's Extra Fine Normandy Cap, richly embroidered, surah silk, fine lace trimming. Peek-a-boo top, cream only. Sizes, 14 to 17 inches. Each.............................1.00
Per dozen.............................10.50
36530 Child's Extra Fine Silk Hood, richly embroidered, extra deep cape, and border of lace. Peek-a-boo top, cream white only. Sizes, 14 to 17 inch. Each.............................$1.50
Per dozen.............................16.00

36531 Child's Mother Hubbard Cap or Hood, made of extra fine silk, neatly trimmed, assorted colors. Sizes, 15 to 17 inches.
Each.............................$1.00
Per dozen.............................10.50
36532 Child's Mother Hubbard Cap, with cape, made of heavy changeable silk, assorted colors; silk lined. Sizes, 15 to 17 in.
Each, $1.25 Per doz $13.50

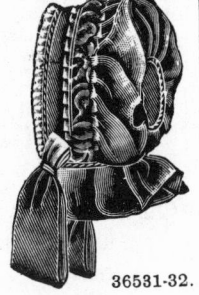

36531-32.

Infants' Fine Silk and Cashmere Caps.

36536 Infant's Silk Embroidered Cashmere Cap. Pompom and strings, lined. Cream or tan. Sizes, 13 to 15 inches.
Each.............................$0.25
Per dozen.............................2.85
36537 Infant's Fine All Wool Silk Embroidered Cashmere Cap. Full lace ruche. Ribbon strings. Cream or tan. Sizes, 13 to 16 inches.
Each.............................$0.50
Per dozen.............................5.50
36539 Infant's Embroidered Silk Hood, with pompon and ruche; cream white; style of 36540. Sizes, 13 to 15 inches.
Each.............................$0.25
Per dozen.............................2.85

36536-39

36540 Infant's Fine Embroidered Silk Hood, cream only. Sizes, 13 to 15. Each, $0.35 Per doz $3.85
36541 Infant's Heavy Silk Embroidered Surah Cap, lace pompon and ruche, cream white. Each $0.50 Per dozen.....5.50

36540-41

36542 Infant's Fine French Shirred Silk Hood, cream only. Sizes, 13 to 15 inches.
Each.............................$0.50
Per dozen.............................5.50

36543 Infant's Extra Heavy Embroidered Sil,k Hood, cream white. Sizes, 13 to 15. Each $0.75 Per dozen $8.00
36544 Infant's Extra Fine Embroidered Pongee Silk Cap, lace pompon and ruche, cream white. Each...$0.90
Per dozen 9.50

36543-44

36545 Infant's Fine French Shirred Hood, made of silk mull in cream, tan, pink or light blue, fine lace pompon. Sizes 14 to 16 inches.
Each. $0.75 Per doz..$8.00

36546 Infant's Extra Heavy Cap, made of richly embroidered silk, large pompon, full ruche, wide surah strings, cream white. (See cut.) Sizes 14 to 16. Each $1.25
Per dozen.............................13.50
36547 Infant's Hand Embroidered extra heavy

36546-47

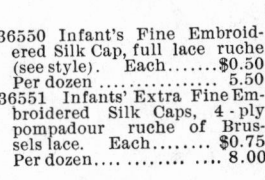

silk Cap, massive silk and lace pompon, silk ties, cream white. Sizes, 14 to 16. Each $1.50   Per dozen ..$16.50

36550 Infant's Fine Embroidered Silk Cap, full lace ruche (see style). Each.............................$0.50
Per dozen.............................5.50
36551 Infants' Extra Fine Embroidered Silk Caps, 4-ply pompadour ruche of Brussels lace. Each.............................$0.75
Per dozen.............................8.00

36550-36551

Children's Lawn and Swiss Hats.

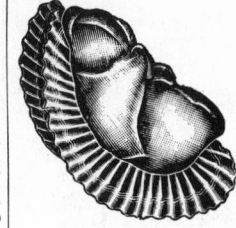

36567 Child's Lawn Hat, shirred brim. Pink, blue white or red. Each $0.15
Per dozen.............................1.65

36568 Child's Lawn Hat, Swiss embroidered crown, shirred brim. Pink, white or light blue.
Each.............................$0.25
Per dozen.............................2.85

36569 Child's Shirred Hat, made of percale in blue and white, or pink and white stripes.
Each.............................$0.25
Per dozen.............................2.85

36570 Child's Lawn Hat, extra shirred brim. Colors: Cardinal, white, pink or light blue.
Each.............................$0.45
Per dozen.............................5.00
36571 Child's Shirred Hat, made of Swiss embroidery shirred brim, trimmed all round with embroidered edging
Each.............................$0.50
Per dozen.............................5.50

Children's Silk Hats.

Ages 1 to 6 years. Colors: Navy blue, brown, tan, drab, cardinal, cream.
36574 Child's Silk Hat, shirred brim.
Each.............................$0.50
Per dozen.............................5.50

36575 Child's Shirred Hat, made of crush silk, extra shirred brim. Each.............................$1.00
Per dozen.............................10.50

36576 Child's Poke Hat, extra shirred brim, all silk
Each.............................$1.25
Per dozen.............................13.50

36584 Child's Tam O'Shanter Hat, made of Swiss embroidery. Each.............................$0.25
Per dozen.............................2.85
36586 Child's Silk Tam O'Shanter Hat, in black, tan and red.
Until sold, each.............................$0.50
Per dozen.............................5.50

RUCHINGS.

Ruching by the Piece or Yard.

Piece Ruching may be ordered in pieces of 12 yards or in a piece of six yards, or by the yard, as desired by the purchaser.

12 yards ruching, with box, weight, 8 to 12 ounces.
12 yards ruching, with box and reel; weight, 20 ounces.

Ladies' Ruching Collarettes.

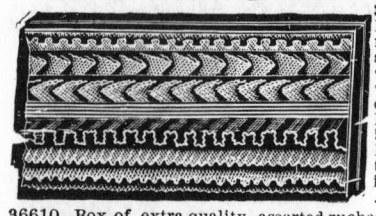

36609—Boxes of 6 ruches, assorted styles; weight, 5 ounces.
Lot 1, per box, $0.15
Lot 2, extra quality, per box $0.25

36610 Box of extra quality, assorted ruches, six styles in box, assorted $0.35

36611 Boxes of Fine Ruching; put up ten ruches, assorted styles in boxes. Weight, 8 ounces. Per box $0.50

36612 Extra fine assorted, 10 ruches in a box. Per box 75

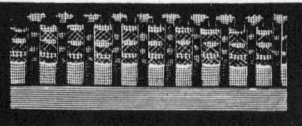

36615 Fancy Fluted French Organdie, with double row lace edge. Per yard $0.09
6 yards.. .50
12 yards. .95

36616 Extra Double Row Ruche lace, and lawn, white only. 12 yards $1.60. 6 yards........$0.90
Per yard 16

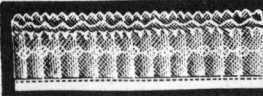

36617 Fine Lace Quilling, for children's caps.
Per dozen...$1.75
6 yards ... .95
Per yard..... .18

36618 Bobinet Quilling, for cap ruching (style of 36617).
12 yards, 75c.   6 yards, 40c. Per yard 8c.

Ruchings—Continued.

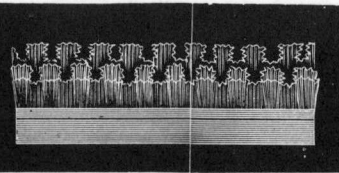

36620—Ruching, two rows of Indian muslin box plaited, cream or white.
12 yds.30c
6 yds.17c.
1 yd... 3c.

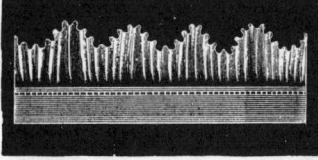

36621 Box Plaited Ruching, 3 rows, Indian muslin, colors, cream or white.

12 yards..........$0.60   6 yards..........$0.35
Per yard..........................07

36624 The Tourist Ruching, made of fine French lawn, single row; white only. Per box....$0.10 Six yards.

36630 Crepe Lisse Ruching, 2 rows corrugated fluting.

cream, white or black; silk finished.
12 yards..........$0.95   6 yards........... $0.50
...........09

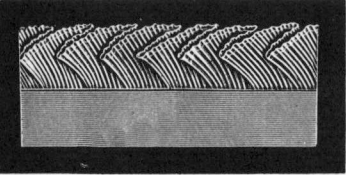

36631—Row Fan Pattern Crepe Lisse Ruching, Silk finished, cream, white or black.

12 yards...........................$0.95
6 yards..........$0.50.   Per yard 09

Ruchings—Continued.

36632 Extra Finish Crepe Lisse Ruching, new style, cream white or black, double row.
12 yds ...$1.25

6 yards..............$0.65.   Per yard..........12

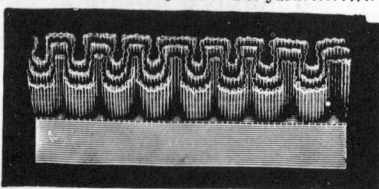

36633 Two Row Crepe Lisse, cream, white or black. 12 yards $1.65
6 yards..........$0.90.   Per yard..........16

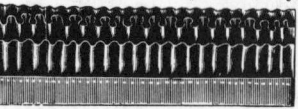

36681 Fine Black Silk Crepe Ruching, extra heavy, 3 rows.
12 yards..$3.75
6 yards... 2.00
Per yard... .35

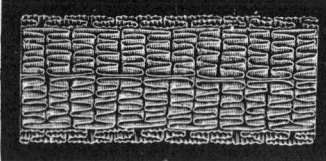

36685 Quaker Ruching, made of Brussels net, six rows of heavy quilling; white only.

Per yard $0.15
Per dozen yards 1.60
36692 Fine Pompadour Ruche, lace and lawn combination; white only. Per yard $0.22
Per dozen yards........................ 2.35

36693 All Lace Pompadour Ruche, heavy plaited, white only.
Per yd. $0.12
Pr dz yd. 1.25

36695 Extra Quality All Lace Pompadour Ruche, white only. Per yard..........................35
Per dozen yards................................. 3.85

Send for Catalogue "E." Ladies' Dresses to Order.

CORSET DEPARTMENT.

In ordering corsets always give size. Take the size from the waist, never from the bust. Deduct about 2 inches from the waist measure for size of corset. No corsets comes in extra size unless so quoted in catalogue. Regular size, 18 to 30. When the dozen price *only* is quoted the price of a single corset is the twelfth part of the price per dozen. All our corsets come in white or drab only, unless otherwise quoted. We will sell one-half dozen corsets, assorted sizes, at dozen rates. Average weight, without box, 12 ounces; with box, 15 ounces; extra sizes, without box, 15 to 18 ounces; with box, 18 to 20 ounces.

NOTE. Our French Form Corsets are light, comfortable, well shaped and very durable. They are soft and pliable. and at the same time give thorough support to the body. Any of these corsets may be returned after 10 days' wear if not satisfactory. A new corset will be given in exchange or the money refunded.

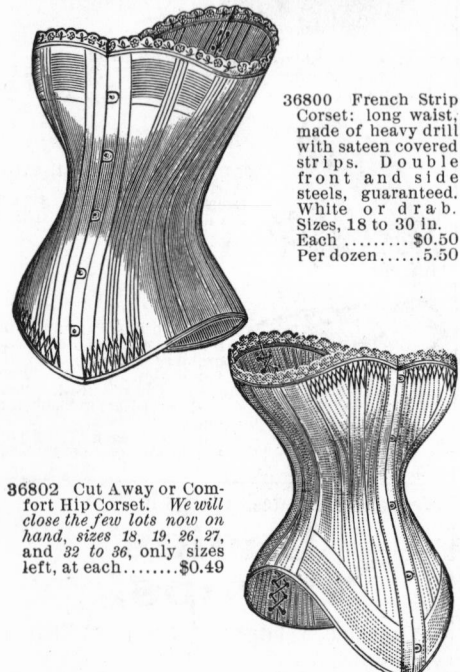

36800 French Strip Corset; long waist, made of heavy drill with sateen covered strips. Double front and side steels, guaranteed. White or drab. Sizes, 18 to 30 in.
Each $0.50
Per dozen......5.50

36802 Cut Away or Comfort Hip Corset. *We will close the few lots now on hand, sizes 18, 19, 26, 27, and 32 to 36, only sizes left, at each.......$0.49*

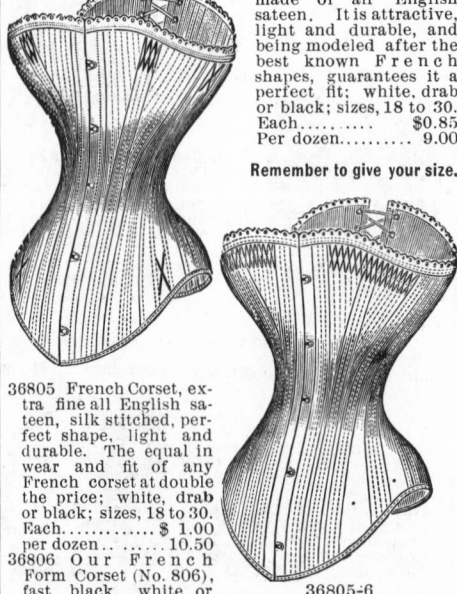

36804 French Corset, is made of all English sateen. It is attractive, light and durable, and being modeled after the best known French shapes, guarantees it a perfect fit; white, drab or black; sizes, 18 to 30.
Each......... $0.85
Per dozen......... 9.00

Remember to give your size.

36805 French Corset, extra fine all English sateen, silk stitched, perfect shape, light and durable. The equal in wear and fit of any French corset at double the price; white, drab or black; sizes, 18 to 30.
Each............. $ 1.00
per dozen.. ......10.50
36806 Our French Form Corset (No. 806), fast black, white or drab; is made of fine French sateen cloth, thoroughly boned, stayed with silk. The most durable and best fitting corset in the market at the price; sizes,19 to 30.
Each.............. $1.25   Per dozen.........$13.50

Venus Back, Correct Shape, Long Waist.

36805-6

36807 Our Paris Model, Venus back, hand finished. Made of the finest French sateen. This corset is very pliable and yields to every motion, thus insuring perfect fit and ease. It has extra strong cushioned bones and double cushioned unbreakable side steels, which give thorough support to the body; every pair guaranteed. Sizes, 18 to 30. Similar goods sold at $4.00 each. Our price, stainless black or drab. Each......$2.00. Per dozen....$22.00

SUMMER DRESS GOODS.

Our lines are way ahead of other seasons. . . .

SEE ......
WHAT WE HAVE
TO OFFER.

Corsets—Continued.

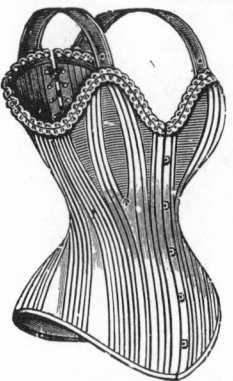

36808 Dress Form Corset, is just the thing for any lady wishing a high bust corset, especially any lady of slender form. The busts are self sustaining and no bosom pads need be worn with them. They also have all the essentials of a perfect health corset. They always improve the form. Colors, white and drab. Sizes, 18 to 30.
Each.............$0.85
Per dozen....... 9.00
Same in fast black, without shoulder straps.
Each.............$1.00

36809 Extra Quality French Shaped Corset, made of the best quality sateen henrietta cloth, thoroughly boned, richly embroidered, black only. Sizes, 18 to 30. Each.............$ 2.85
Per dozen.... .... 29.50
36810 French Strip Corset, made of fine fast black Italian wool cloth, absolutely unbreakable, a most complete and durable corset, extra long waist, black only. Sizes, 19 to 30. Each. $ 3.00
Per dozen.. .... 30.00

36811 Bust Supporter is gotten up for ladies who lead an active life, especially those who engage in out door exercise, as it permits of the freest action of every part of the body; made in white, drab or black sateen or white summer net. Sizes, 18 to 30 waist measure. Order one size larger than regular corset size Each... $ 0.95
Per dozen.............10.50

36812 M. W. & Co.'s Young Ladies Waist. for growing girls 12 to 17 years. Made of white gray or black sateen with soft expanding busts. Sizes, 19 to 28.
Each..................$0.79
Per dozen........... 8.75

Dr. Strong's Celebrated Tricora Corsets.

One-half dozen assorted sizes at dozen rates. We guarantee every pair to give satisfaction or return the money. Don't forget to give your size.

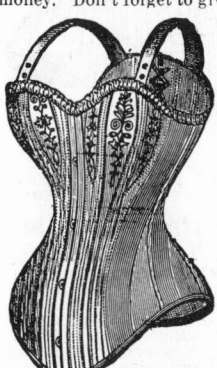

36814 Doctor Strong's Health Supporter, has perfectly formed self-sustaining Tricora busts, which obviate the use of bust pads. It gives every lady wearing it the outline of perfect development and graceful figure. It remedies defects in ordinary figures, making it a most desirable corset to wear jersey over and enable dressmakers to measure and fit perfectly. The best health corset made. Any lady once wearing it will not be without it. Extra long waists. Sizes, 18 to 30. White or drab.
Each..................$0.90
Per dozen........... 9.00

Windsor Cook Stoves
ARE EQUAL TO ANY.
PRICES LOW.

Corsets—Continued.
Remember to give size when ordering Corsets.

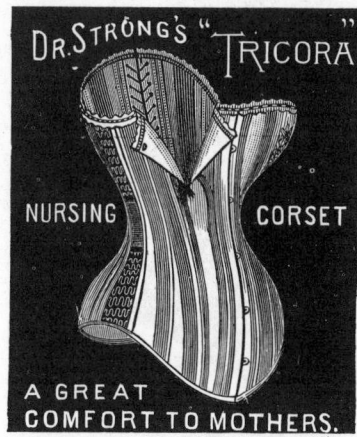

DR. STRONG'S "TRICORA"
NURSING   CORSET
A GREAT COMFORT TO MOTHERS.

36815 "Tricora" Nursing. Dr. Strong's Tricora Nursing Corset has proved a great comfort to mothers, as it affords perfect freedom of action in every position which the body can assume. It is boned with (waterproof) Tricora stays, which will not be affected by moisture, and being tough, pliable and supporting are absolutely unbreakable. Size, 18 to 30. White or drab.
Each $0.90
Per dozen................................. 9.00

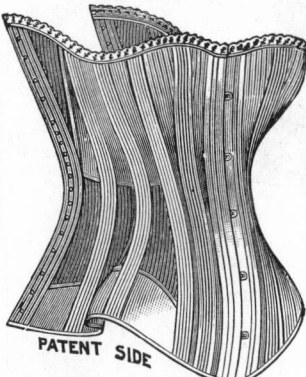

PATENT SIDE
Armourside Unbreakable Hip.
Long Waist.

36816 The "Armourside" Corset will not break at the hips. It has vertical boning on the sides that thoroughly supports the figure. It is made of fine English sateen in drab, black or white. For any that break at the hips we will give a new pair or refund money. Sizes, 20 to 30 only.
Each.. ...$0.89
Per dozen. 9.00

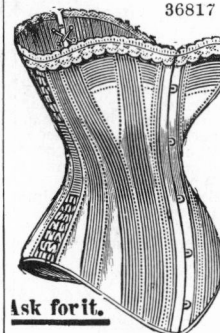

Ask for it.

36817 Dr. Strong's "Tricora" Relief Corset. The most durable, comfortable and healthful corset ever sold for its price. Adapts itself to the various positions of the body in stooping, gives perfect ease in all positions; affords great relief and comfort to the many who find ordinary corsets oppressive. The "Tricora" stays used for boning are pliable, supporting and absolutely unbreakable. Sizes, 18 to 30. White or drab.
Each..................$0.90
Per dozen 9.00

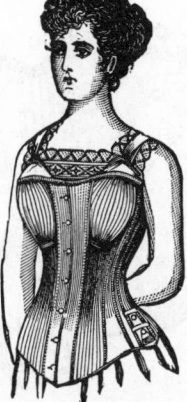

36818 Madam Strong's "Health Bodice." A soft, pliable and delightfully comfortable bodice that supports the figure pleasantly but not rigidly, allowing such freedom of action, in any position, as to have the wearer almost unconscious of a bodice. It is supported chiefly by the celebrated (Waterproof) "Tricora" stays that will not absorb or retain moisture and are famous for their durability and comfort giving qualities. It has perfectly formed self-sustaining "Tricora" busts, which will give to every lady wearing it the outlines of perfect development and stylish figure Sizes, 20 to 30, White, drab or fast black.
Each....................$ 1.15
Per dozen 12.00

The Yatisi Corsets.

We will take back any of the Yatisi Corsets and return the money after 10 days' wear, if not satisfactory. N. B.--Don't forget to give your size.

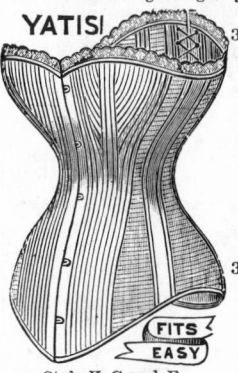

YATISI
FITS EASY
Style H. G and E.,

36820 The New Yatisi Corset, style H, is made of the best quality of English sateen, and shaped after the most approved French model, strongly boned with the best quality of French bones. The shaping parts are made of 6-ply French stockinet; colors: White or ecru. Sizes, 18 to 30.
Each..................$0.85
Per dozen.......... 9.00
36821 New French Form Yatisi Corset, style G, made of extra fine drab sateen and stockinet. All the bones, steel, and clasps are wrapped at the end with linen to prevent them from breaking through the cloth; thus a great annoyance is obviated. Sizes, 20 to 30; every pair guaranteed.
Each...$ 1.50
Per dozen..15.00
36822 The Yatisi Corset, style E, is modeled after the celebrated Fasso Paris made corset, extra long waist, long between the line of the waist and the bust, double side steels, strongly boned; shaping parts are made of 6-ply French stockinet; colors: Ecru or white. Sizes, 18 to 30.$1.15
Per dozen.................................12.00

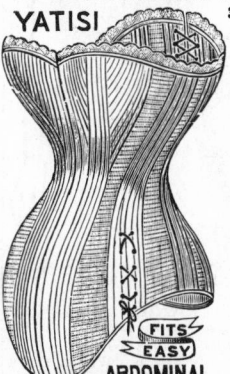

YATISI
FITS EASY
ABDOMINAL

36823 The Abdominal Yatisi Corset was introduced specially for married ladies. It supports the abdomen and prevents the ordinary pressure upon the pelvis organs. It is a most perfect corset for dress purposes, as it has a tendency to increase the length of the waist and lessens the size of the abdomen. Made of a fine quality of English sateen jeans, strongly boned. The shaping parts are made of 6-ply French stockinet; colors: Drab or ecru; sizes, 22 to 30.
Each...... ....$ 1.75
Per dozen.......... 18.00
Extra sizes, 32 to 40.
Each............... 2.00

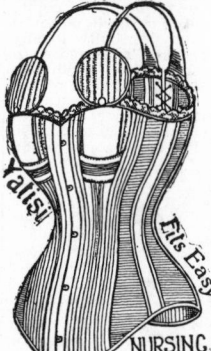

Yatisi   Fits Easy
NURSING

36824 The Yatisi is the latest and most approved, nursing corset. The pivotal bust is its greatest advantage, as it can be removed with ease. It fits perfectly, retains its shape and wears well. It has double front and side steels, and curved shoulder straps; sizes, 18 to 30 only. Each........$ 1.00
Per dozen........... 10.50

M. W. & Co.'s Corsets.

NOTE.—These corsets are made especially for us and bear our name. The most skillful hands are employed to manufacture them. Every corset bearing our brand is guaranteed by us for wear, fit and quality; if any are found unsatisfactory, return them and we will refund your money or give you a new corset.

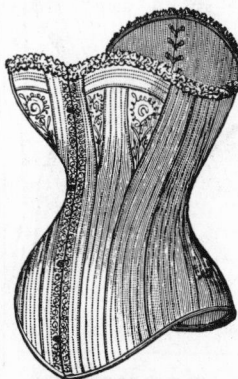

Our Absolutely Fast Black Corset.

36827 M. W. & Co.'s Corset, No. 827, is made in fast black only; is modeled after the French C. P. Corset, long waist, full busts, side and double front steels.
Each........... ..$0.85
Per dozen... . . 9.00
Sizes, 18 to 30

M. W. & Co.'s Stainless Black Corset.

Corsets—Continued.

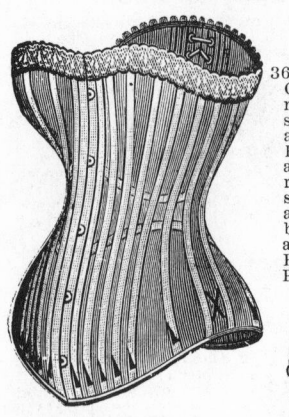

36828 M. W. & Co.'s Corset, No. 828, is made of fine English sateen, shaped exactly like the P. D. French Corset, fits and wears well. We recommend this corset as being comfortable and very durable. Colors: Ecru and drab.
Each $0.85
Per dozen...... 9.00

M. W. & Co. Corset, No. 828. Extra Long Waist.

36829 The Columbian *Dress Reform Waist*, extra length, fluted bust, adjustable to any required size. Made of fine satin finished jean, drab only, shoulder straps. Sizes, 20 to 30; style of 36830.
Each $0.75
Per dozen. ... 8.00
36830 M. W. & Co.'s Extra Long Waist, made expressly for us and guaranteed by us. It is the most original, best fitting, easiest and durable waist in the market. Once try a pair you will never wear any other kind. The busts are so designed they can be made any size. Colors: White, drab or black sateen; also made in summer net; are made with clasps or buttoned front. Sizes, 20 to 30.....................$0.95
Per dozen.... ....10.00
Extra sizes, 31 to 36. Each.................. 1.25

M. W. & Co.'s Extra long Waist. No. 36829-30.

36831 M. W. & Co.'s French Strip Corset, No. 831, made expressly for us. This corset is equal in fit, material and durability to any French corset now in the market at double its price. Try one. Colors: Drab, ecru or fast black.
Each............$ 0.99
Per dozen...... 10.50

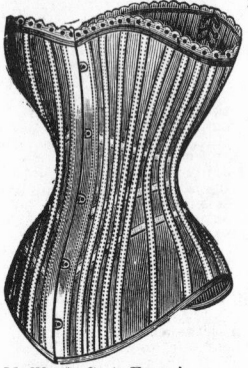

M. W. & Co.'s French Strip Corset No. 831.

Please give your size.

36832 M. W. & Co.'s High Bust Dress Form Health Corset has an extra long waist. The bust pads are flexible but always retain the shape. White or drab. Sizes 18 to 30.
Each.........$ 0.99
Per dozen..... 10.50
Absolutely fast black.
Each.........$ 1.19
Per dozen 12.00
Extra Quality, All English Sateen and French Staying, white, black or drab. Sizes, 18 to 30.
Each.........$ 1.35
Per dozen..... 15.00

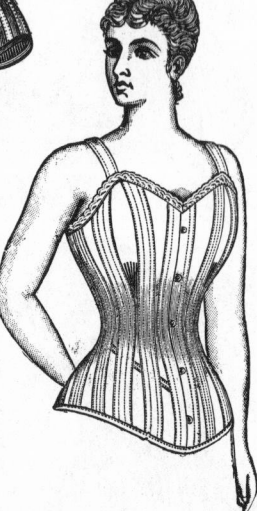

High bust, extra long waist.

INSURE MAIL PACKAGES.

See page 1.

Corsets—Continued.

36833 M.W.&Co.'s Nursing Corset, (No. 833), made expressly for us, is the most convenient ever introduced. The bust pieces have patent clasp fasteners and can be removed or replaced without any trouble, the front is softly corded and the back is regular French strip style. Colors: Fast black or drab only.
Each.....$ 1.25
Per dozen 13.75

M. W. & Co.'s Nursing, style 833.

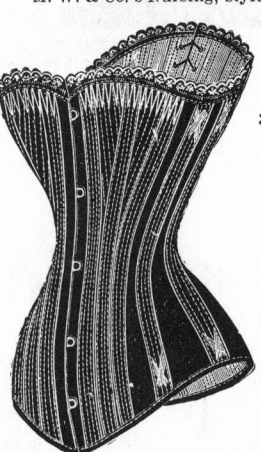

36834 M. W. & Co.'s Corset No. 834 is the longest waist corset made; suitable only for tall, slim figures. It is made to measure. It has a 14½ inch unbreakable steel, is made of the best English sateen elaborately flossed; comes in black, white or drab; the same sold everywhere for $3.50. Our price.
Each.........$ 2 19
Per dozen.... 24.00

36835 M. W. & Co.'s 6-Hook Columbia Corset No. 835 (Same style as 36834), made of fine jeans with sateen covered strips. Colors, drab only.
Sizes, 18 to 30, Each.....................$1.00
Per dozen...11.00
Black is all sateen. Each........................ 1.39
Per dozen..15.00

Madam Foy's Improved Corset.

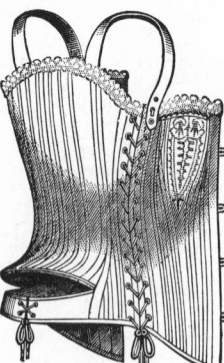

36836 These are the only skirt supporting corsets with shoulder brace and side lacing, and are without exception the best of their kind in the market. White or drab only.
Sizes, 18 to 30. Improved.
Per dozen $12.00
Each, including extra sizes..............$1.25

Madam Foy Corset.

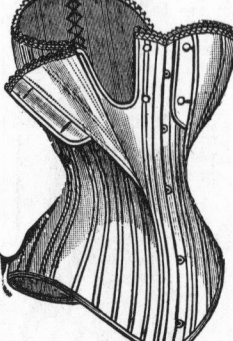

36837 Is a Perfect French Form and Nursing Corset thoroughly boned; soft and pliable busts; made of fine corset jean, with French sateen covered strips, white or drab; sizes, 18 to 30.
Each................$0 89
Per dozne............ 9.50

Nursing.

Corsets—Continued.

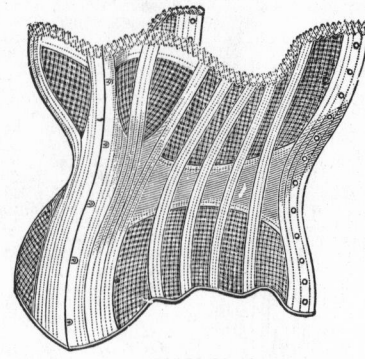

36838-39-40

36838 Ladies' Summer Corset. made of openwork material, very light and cool. White only; sizes, 18 to 30. Each......$0.40 Per dozen....$4.50
36839 Our M. W. & Co.'s Guaranteed Summer Corset, made of extra quality openwork material. Guaranteed not to rip or tear, or money refunded. White or drab; sizes, 18 to 30. Each..... .50
Per dozen.................................. 5.50
Extra sizes, 31 to 36. Each.................. .75
36840 French Form Long Waist Ventilating summer corset. Made of extra fine open work material, thoroughly boned and stayed; guaranteed not to rip or tear or money refunded. White only.
Sizes 18 to 30
Each $0.95
Per dozen....10.50
Extra sizes, 31 to 36.
Each.... .....$1.25
36841 Our "Jersey" Corset, made of good serviceable jean. The best in the market at the price. White or drab. Sizes, 18 to 30. Each.....$0.35
Per dozen. .. 3.75
36842 Corset is Perfect Fitting French Strip Corset. Colors: White, drab, ecru.
Each...........$0.45
Per dozen..... 5.00

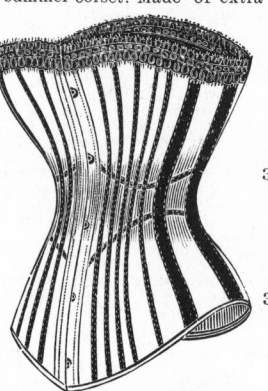

NOTE—We cannot ship corsets if you neglect to give your size.

36843 This finely finished 5-hook corset is made of good sateen, double steel. It has a double section lined with two series of buttons, giving extra strength, where it is most needed. White drab or black. Sizes, 18 to 30.
Each.............$0.50
Per dozen......... 5.00

36843

36844 Corset, made of extra heavy coutile, long waist, double side steels, guaranteed to outwear any corset in the market at the price, or the money refunded. Sizes, 18 to 30.
Colors; White or gray, Each.. ....$ 0.99
Per dozen................................... 10.50

36844

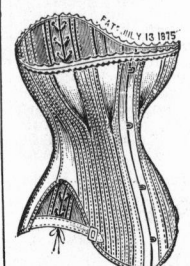

Bortree's Duplex Corset.

36847 Bortree's Perfect Fitting Duplex Corset, double bone, double seam, warranted not to rip. It can be adjusted to fit any form by means of the adjusting straps; sizes, 18 to 30.
Each.................$0 85
Per dozen........... 9.00
Extra sizes, 31 to 36.
Each.................. 1.15
Colors: White or drab.

Dr. Warner's Abdominal Corsets.

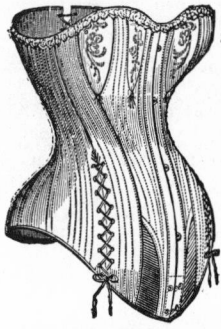

36849 Dr. Warner's Abdominal Corset, with extension front, boned with coraline, made with a 13-inch steel, the corset extending below the steel in front from 2 to 3 inches. On each side a silk elastic gore is inserted. Ladies who cannot wear the ordinary abdominal corset can wear this one with case. White or drab; sizes, 20 to 30.
Per dozen............$ 16.50
Extra sizes, 31 to 36.
Per dozen·····........21.00

Black, sizes, 20 to 30. Per dozen...............$18.00
Black, sizes, 32 to 36. Per dozen............... 22.00

36850   36851

36850 Dr. Warner's Coraline Corset, made of French cloth, 96 coraline stays, which are superior to bone or whalebone. Side steels *removable*, double front steels, a fine shaped bust; white, drab or, black; sizes, 18 to 30.
Per dozen. ....$ 9.00
Extra sizes, 31 to 36. Per dozen.............. 12.00
36851 Dr. Warner's Health Corset, boned with coraline flexible coraline, bust; sizes, 18 to 30.
Per dozen, white or drab.......................$12.00
Extra sizes, 31 to 36. Each..................... 1.50
Black, sizes 18 to 30. Per dozen................16.50

Misses' Corsets.

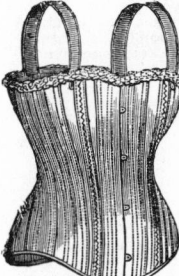

36854 Misses' Corsets, ages, 12 to 15 years. White or drab jeans, sizes, 18 to 26, with shoulder straps. Each...$0.50
Per dozen................ 5.25

36855 Young Ladies' Corset, ages, 13 to 18 years, without shoulder straps. Can also be worn by ladies' with short waists and small bust development. Sizes, 18 to 26; white or drab sateen. Each...............................$0.75
Per dozen................ 8.00
36856 Ladies' Short Corset, 12-inch steel, white or black sateen, embroidered bust; sizes, 18 to 30. Each......$1.00.   Per dozen $10.50

36857-7-12    36858-3-7
36857 Our Misses' Waist, ages. 7 to 12, made of finest washing silesia, white or drab, sizes, 19 to 26. Each.......$0.70. Per dozen $7.50
36858 Our Child's Waist, ages, 3 fo 7 years, finest washing silesia. Each .... .50
Per dozen...................................... 5.65

Ferris' Good Sense Corset Waists.

FOR CHILDREN, MISSES, YOUNG LADIES AND LADIES.
Always give the size. Age does not determine waist measure correctly.
36860 Ferris Waist, white or drab; No. 247, baby's style 1 to 4 years. No. 248,child's, 4 to 8 years.
Each.............. ....$0.25
Per dozen......................... 2.50
36864 Style Misses' Waists, ages, 7 to 12 years. White or drab.; sizes, 20 to 28. Each...........$0.50
Per dozen..................... 5.00
36865 Misses' Styles 223; ages, 12 to 17 years: white or drab; sizes, 20 to 28. Each............. 1.00
Per dozen................ .... 9.50

36867 Ladies' Good Sense Waist, Style 220, white drab or black; sizes, 20 to 30; button front, lace back. Each $1.00
Per dozen 10.00
36868 Ladies' Good Sense Waist, Style 230, medium form, long waist, side lacing, white or drab, buttoned front, laced back. Sizes, 20 to30.
Each $1.25
Per dozen 12.00
Extra sizes, 31 to36.
Each $1.50
Per dozen 16.50
36869 Ladies' Good Sense Waist, Style 219, medium form, long waist buttoned front, laced back and sides, extra fine pearl buttons, superfine material, white or drab.
Each..................$1.50
Per dozen..........15.50
36870 Same as above Style 264; fast black, horn buttons; sizes, 20 to 30.
Each..................$1.75
Per dozen..........16.50

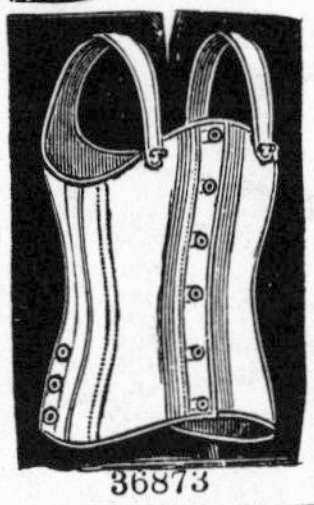

36871 "The Florence," children's double stitched corded waists with adjustable shoulder straps, fine sateen, white or gray. Sizes, 21 to 28. Ages, 2 to 8 years.
Each $0.25
Per dozen.................... 2.85
36873 Child's Waist. made of extra quality washing material, tape fastened horn buttons. Ages, 2 to 10 years. Sizes, 20 to 28. White or gray.
Each..................$0.40
Per dozen 4.50

36873

Child's Ribbed Seamless Waist.

Healthful, Durable, Economical.

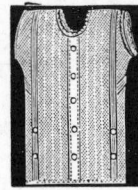

Child's Seamless Knit Ribbed Waist is a shirt and waist combined. Can be worn with or without undershirt; has shoulder straps; tape stays support all the buttons, two rows of waist buttons for underclothes. A complete comfort and health garment. Ages, 1 to 12 years. Age represents size. Price quoted is for all or any size. Give age of child.
36874 Medium weight, with metal buttons, guaranteed not to rust. Each $0.15
Per dozen..................................... 1.50
36875 Heavy weight, linen buttons. Each.... .19
Per dozen..................................... 2.00
36876 Extra heavy weight, horn buttons. Ea.. .22
Per dozen..... .... 2.35

Tampico Dress Form.

(Weight, 2 to 3 ounces each.)

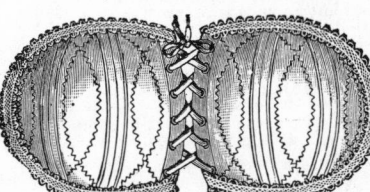

36881 These Dress Forms are made of Tampico grass cloth, cover'd with sateen or ventilated; they are light, soft and flexible and yet so elastic that they will retain their shape; separable or inseparable: cut shows the separable.
No. 1, each......$0.25   No. 2, each..........$0.35

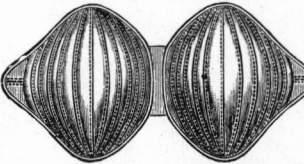

36886 New and Adjustable Dress Form, ribs of featherbone. Two extra reinforcing strips with each form.
Each $0.30
Per dozen. 3.00

Bustles.

Weight, 3 ounces.
36888 Solid Comfort Coil Wire Bustle; until sold, each...$0.01

HARNESS DEPARTMENT.

Single Pony Harness.

Russet Leather Only.

This harness is made of Fair Russet Leather of the best oak tanned skirting.
It can be adjusted to fit a pony weighing 500 lbs or a small horse weighing 900 lbs. It is not suitable for anything larger or smaller than we mention.
We make it in *one style only*, and we insure satisfaction to every purchaser.
It is well made and well finished; is complete in every respect, and is decidedly nobby in appearance.
37000 Single Pony Harness, all fair russet leather; breast collar, 1⅜ inch wide, folded with layer, box loops for traces; traces 1 inch, double and stitched, to buckle to breast collar; blind bridle with overcheck and round winker stays; breeching, 1¾ inches wide, folded with layer; saddle, 3½ inch with leather pad and leather covered seat; round dock, flat back and hip straps; folded bellyband with Griffith's patent buckles; flat lines; full nickel mountings. Per set....$13.50
Weight, per set, packed in box, 19 pounds.

When ordering goods to be shipped by mail, have them insured   See page 1.

37002 Single Russet Pony Harness, single strap; imitation hand sewed; bridle, ½ inch, box loops; round winker stay, layer on crown; breast collar, 1½ inch; traces, 1 inch, stitched to breast collar; breeching, 1⅜ inch; side straps, ¾ inch; hip strap, ½ inch; turnback, ⅝ inch; scolloped, round crupper; saddle, 2½ in.; "Strap," leather jockey, skirts and bottom, leather covered seat; bellyband, "Griffith." Lines, ⅝ inch to loop in, 1 inch hand parts; No hitch strap; full nickel mounting. Per set...$10.00
Weight, per set, wrapped in paper, 11 lbs.

Single Buggy Harness.

Per set.

37004 Single Buggy, Breast Collar Harness, mountings; bridle, ⅝ inch overcheck, flat winker stay; breast collar, folded; traces, 1 inch, doubled and stitched to breast collar; turn-back ⅝ inch, folded crupper; saddle, 2½ inch, enamel cloth lined; lines, ¾ inch; hip straps, ½ inch. We cannot furnish above harness in any other style than as described.........................$3.98
Weight, per set, wrapped in paper, 10 pounds.
37006 Single Buggy Harness, breast collar, double stitched layer, 1 inch double traces, sewed to breast collar, ⅝ inch blind bridle, flat cheeks and flat side or overcheck, ¾ inch flat lines, 2½ inch gig saddle, folded breeching with layer, ¾ inch side straps, ⅝ inch hip straps, folded crupper, no martingale. XC plated mountings.. 4.75
Weight, per set, wrapped in paper, 11 lbs.
We do not furnish hitch straps with single harness at quoted price

Harness—Continued.

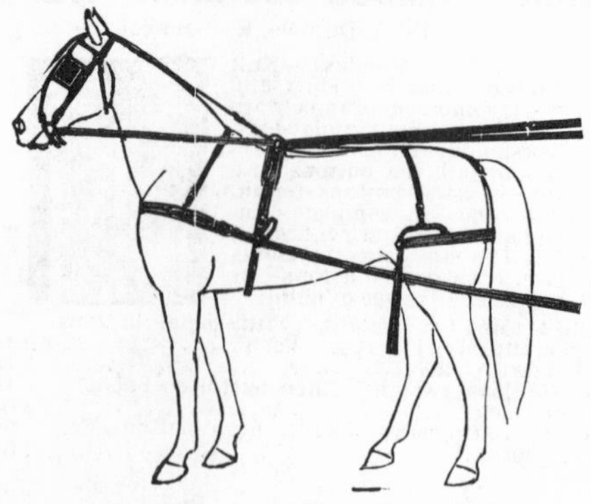

37008 Single Buggy Harness, breast collar, folded with layer and box loops, traces, 1 inch, double and stitched to buckle to breast collar, 2½ inch saddle, breeching folded with layer; bellybands folded Griffith's style, bridle ⅝ inch, box loops, patent leather winkers, flat side or over check, turnback, plain, with round crupper, hip strap ⅝ inch, lines ¾ inch, white mounting. Per set..$6.00
Hames and collar in place of breast collar, extra 1.25
Round lines in place of flat .... .90

37008 Harness with breast collar weighs 12 lbs.; wrapped in paper and with hames and collar, about 16 lbs.

37010 Single Buggy Harness, saddle, 2½ inch japanned jockey patent leather skirts, enamel cloth lined; bridle, ⅝ with box loops, patent leather winkers, round winker braces, overdraw or round side checks; traces, 1 inch, doubled, raised and stitched to buckle to breast collar; lines, ⅞ inch flat, to loop in bit; breast collar folded with layer and box loops; breeching, folded with layer; bellybands, folded Griffith's style; side straps, ¾ inch; turn back, plain with round crupper; hip straps, ⅝ inch; no martingales; all black mountings......................$7.00
37011 Same in XC mounting.................................. 7.25

37012 Same with half nickel mountings......... 7.50
Hames and collar in place of breast collar, extra. 1.50
Round lines in place of flat, extra.............. .90
When ordering single buggy harness, mention whether side or over check bridle is wanted.

37010 11, 12 Breast Collar Harness, wrapped in paper, weighs 12½ lbs. per set; with hames and collar, 17 lbs.

37015 Single Buggy Harness; imitation hand sewed. Saddle, 3 inch; single strap harness leather skirts, leather lined pad; bridle, ⅝ inch box loops, patent leather winkers, round winker braces, overdraw, with nose band or round side checks; traces, 1⅛ inch, doubled, raised and stitched to buckle to breast collar; lines, ⅞ with 1 inch hand parts; breast collar, folded with straight raised layer and box loops for traces and neck straps; breeching, folded with straight raised layer; bellybands, folded, Griffith's style; side straps, ¾ inch; turn back, waved with round crupper; hip straps, ⅝ inch; no martingales; all black mountings............$8.65
37016 Same, full nickel mounting................ 9.00

37017 Same, imitation rubber, gilt lined 9.25
Hames and collar in place of breast collar, extra. 1.50
Round lines in place of flat lines, extra..... .... .90
Either over check or round side check bridles.
No. 37015-6-7 Harness with breast collars weighs 14 lbs. per set, wrapped in paper; and about 19 lbs. with hames and collar.
No hitch straps with single harness at quoted prices.
We furnish our harness with open bridles, when desired, at same price.

37019 Extra Heavy Single Buggy Harness. Saddle, 3½ inch; single strap skirts, leather lined pad; bridle, ⅝ inch, box loops; patent leather winkers, round winker braces, overdraw or round side checks; breast collar, folded, extra wide, with wide raised layer, box loop ends and safes under trace buckles; traces, 1¼ inch, doubled raised and stitched, breeching, folded, extra wide, with wide raised layer, 3 ring stays, box loops; lines, 1 inch to buckle in; turn back, scalloped, round dock; heavy hip straps; bellyband, Griffith's style, with wide raised layer, heavy shaft straps.
Full nickel mountings. Per set................$10.00
Hames and collar in place of breast collar, extra 1.75 Round lines in place of flat, extra. 1.00

Beaded Harness.

37020 Single Buggy Harness, imitation hand sewed; beaded breast collar and breeching; bridle, ⅝-inch, box loops, patent leather blinds, overdraw checks; saddle, 3-inch, hand laced, full padded skirts, covered seat, ⅞-inch bearer straps; shaft tugs, with dees and bellyband billets, box loops; breast collar, folded, solid leather, fine raised beaded layer, box loops, safes under trace buckles, neck strap with wide fold layer; breeching, folded, solid leather, fine raised beaded layer, three-ring round leather stays; traces, 1⅛-inch, doubled, raised and stitched; lines, ⅞-inch fronts, 1⅛-inch hand parts; hip straps, ¾-inch; side straps, ⅞-inch; no hitch strap; full nickel mountings. Per set.......................$10.00
Weight, per set, packed in a box, 20 pounds.

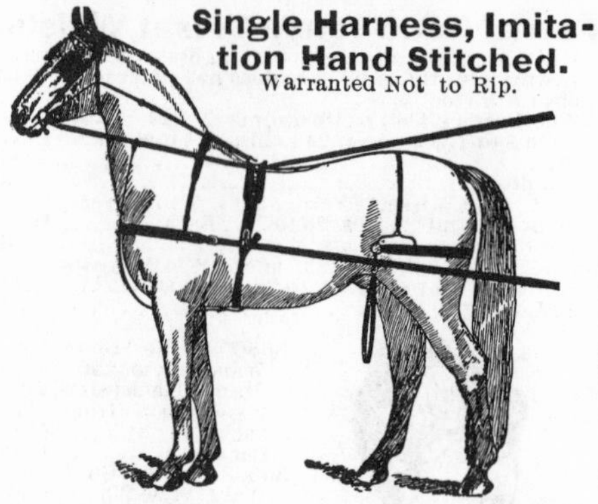

Single Harness, Imitation Hand Stitched.

Warranted Not to Rip.

37022 Single Buggy Harness, imitation hand stitched; bridle, ⅝ inch, box loops, patent leather blinds, or without blinds; over check with nose band or round side check, half cheek bit; saddle, 3 inch, single strap, with leather lined pad or patent leather saddle with full padded skirts; box loops on shaft tugs; breast collar, folded, oiled fold leather, with extra wide raised layer, safe under trace buckles, box loops; neck strap with oiled leather fold; breeching, folded, oiled fold leather, extra wide raised layer, 3 ring stay; traces, 1⅛-inch, doubled, raised and stitched; bellyband, Griffith's style, with wide raised layer; lines, 1 inch, ⅝-inch hip straps; ⅞-inch side straps; flat fork martingale.
All black mountings. Per set....................$10.50
37023 Same, full nickel mounting................ 11.00
37024 Same, imitation rubber, gilt lined....... 11.25
Hames and collar in place of breast collar, extra 1.60
Round lines in place of flat lines, extra........ 1.00
Side checks or over check bridles.
No. 37022-3-4 Breast Collar Harness weighs 15 lbs. per set, wrapped in paper; and about 20 lbs. with hames and collar. Prices do not include hitchs traps.

Hand Made Single Harness.

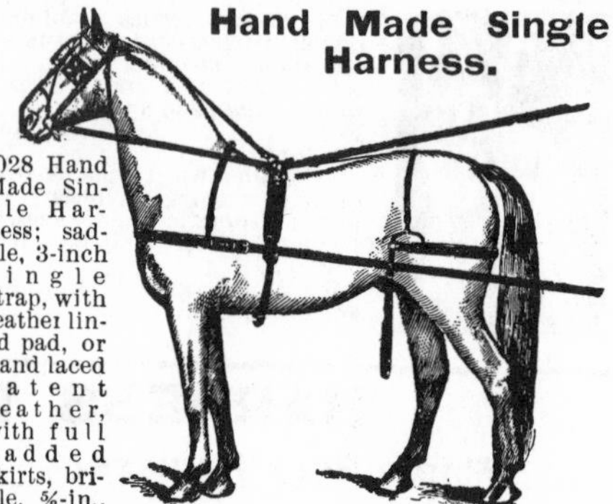

37028 Hand Made Single Harness; saddle, 3-inch single strap, with leather lined pad, or hand laced patent leather, with full padded skirts, bridle, ⅝-in., box loops, patent leather blinds or without blinds, overcheck with nose-band or round sidecheck; traces, 1⅛-inch, doubled, raised and stitched to buckle to breast collar; breast collar, folded, oiled fold leather, extra wide raised layer, safes under trace buckles, box loops; breeching, folded, oiled fold leather, extra wide raised layer, 3-ring stay; bellyband, folded, Griffith style, wide layer; turn back, scolloped, stuffed dock; lines, 1-inch throughout, steel spring billets; side straps, ⅞-inch; hip straps, ⅝. inch; box loops all through. Made from strictly first-class stock in good style. All black japan mountings. Set.$12.50
37029 Same as 37028, full nickel mounting....$13.00
37030 Same as No. 37028, imitation rubber, gold lined.. 13.25
Collar and hames in place of breast collar, extra 1.75
Round lines in place of flat lines, extra.......... 1.00
Either overcheck or round side check bridles.
Nos. 37028-9-30 Breast Collar Harness weighs 15 lbs. per set, wrapped in paper; and about 20 lbs. with collar and hames. Prices do not include hitch straps.

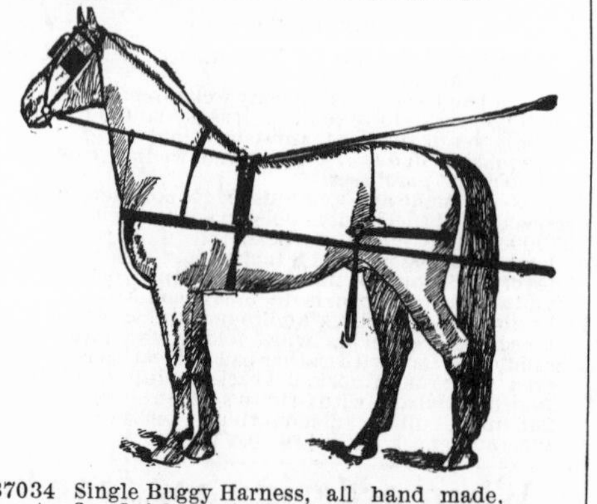

37034 Single Buggy Harness, all hand made, extra fine finished, stitched 9 to the inch, and made of the very best material; ⅝ inch bridle, with box loops, round side or overcheck, round winker braces, fine half cheek bit, 3 inch hand lace patent leather saddle, breeching and breast collar folded with scalloped and raised layers and box loops; traces, 1⅛-inch, doubled, raised and stitched: round hip straps, scalloped back strap; lines flat, 1 inch, with 1⅛-inch hand parts; martingale folded, round forks with celluloid rings, full nickel mountings.........$19.75
37035 Same, full imitation rubber, gilt lined.. 20.00
37036 Genuine rubber mountings..................... 22.50
Hames and collar in place of breast collar, extra.. 2.50
Round lines in place of flat lines, extra........ 1.00
Nos. 37034-5-6 Breast Collar Harness, weighs 24 lbs., packed in box for shipping.

Single Strap, Single Breast Collar Harness.

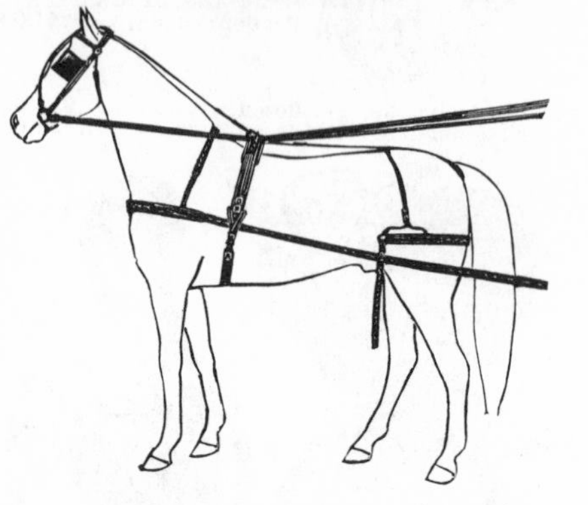

37040 Special Single Strap Track Harness. Bridle, ⅝ inch, box loops, square blinds, round winker braces, overdraw check, nickel front and rosettes; saddle, 2½ inch, single strap, with ⅞-inch shaft tugs, 1½-inch bellyband and ¾-inch shaft straps; breast collar, 1⅝ inch, 1-inch neck strap; breeching, 1⅜ inch, 3-ring stays; lines, ⅞ inch, all black, to loop in bit; side straps, ¾ inch; hip straps, ⅝ inch; breast collar, traces, neck straps, breeching and hip straps, all fancy wave, creased. Nickel mountings. Per set.....$7.00
37041 Same as 37040, with imitation rubber mountings. Per set 7.00
Nos. 37040 and 37041 Harness weighs 12 lbs. per set, wrapped in paper; prices do not include hitch straps.
37042 Single Strap Track Harness, imitation hand sewed; bridle, ⅝-inch, box loops, overcheck round winker stays; breast collar, 1⅞ inch; traces, 1¼ inch, stitched to breast collar; breeching, 1⅝ inch; side straps, ⅞ inch; hip straps, ¾ inch; turnback, ¾ inch; scalloped, round crupper; saddle, 3 inch, single strap, harness leather skirts, iron jockeys, leather pads, bellyband, Griffith's style; lines, 1 inch to loop in bit, edge creased; no hitch strap; full nickel mounting.
Per set.... ....$8.00
Weight, per set, in paper, 14 lbs.

37044 Single Strap Track Harness, imitation hand sewed. Fancy wave, creased.
Bridle, ⅝ inch, overcheck, box loops, round winker stay, layer on crown.
Breast Collar, 1¾ inch.
Traces, 1⅛ inch, stitched to breast collar.
Breeching, 1⅝ inch, side straps ⅞ inch.
Hip Strap, ⅝ inch.
Turnback, ¾ inch, scolloped, round crupper.
Saddle, 2½ inch, "Strap," leather jockey, harness-leather skirts, leather bottom.
Bellyband, "Griffith."
Lines, 1 inch throughout, to loop in.
No hitch strap.
Fancy creased throughout.
Full nickel mountings. Per set.................$9.00
37045 Same harness as No. 37044 with imitation rubber mountings. Per set.................. 9.10
Nos. 37044-5 harness weighs about 13 lbs. per set, wrapped in paper.
37050 Single Strap Track Harness, imitation hand sewed, single crease, round edge finish, oak tanned leather, saddle, 2½ inch, No. 4½ Excelsior; bridle, ⅝ inch, box loops, patent leather winkers, round winker stays and round side or double overdraw checks; traces, 1⅛ inch, stitched to breast collar with scolloped splice; lines, ⅞ inch, with 1 inch hand parts; breast collar, with scolloped layer, box loops for neck straps; breeching, with scolloped layer, stitched stays, with 3 rings; bellybands, Griffith style; side straps, ¾ inch; turn backs, scolloped and round crupper; hip straps, ⅝ inch. No martingale.
Full nickel mounting. Per set.....................$10.00
Weight, per set, wrapped in paper, about 13 lbs.
37052 Single Strap Harness. Bridle, ⅝ inch, box loops, with or without blinds, overcheck with nose band or round side check, round winker braces; saddle, 3 inch, single strap or patent leather, with full padded skirts; breast collar, 1¾ inch, heavy, single strap; neck strap, 1¼ inch; traces, 1¼ inch, sewed to breast collar; breeching, 1½ inch, scalloped points, 3 ring stays, ⅞ inch side straps; lines, 1 inch, to buckle in; bellyband, Griffith style, extra wide; hip straps, ⅝ inch. Plain round edge finish all through and made from good oak-tanned leather. Full nickel mountings. Per set.11.00
37053 Imitation rubber mountings. Per set......11.25
Prices do not include hitch straps. Weight, per set, wrapped in paper, 14 lbs.

Shaped Center Breast Collar Harness.

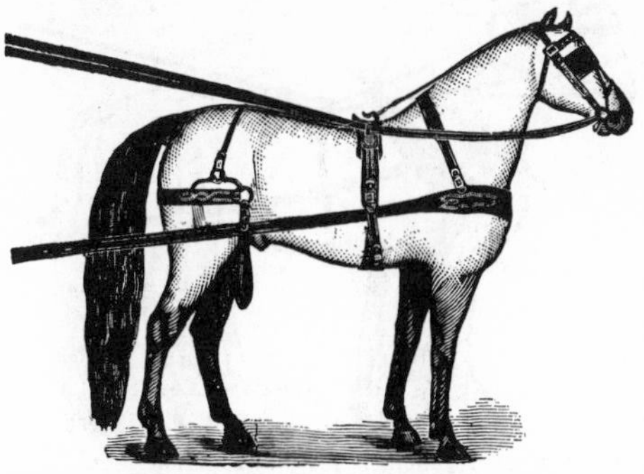

37054 Shaped Center Breast Collar Single Strap Harness, imitation hand sewed. Bridle, ⅝-inch box loops, patent leather blinds, round winker stays, overcheck with nose piece, nickel front and rosettes; breast collar, 3-inches wide, single strap, shaped or "V" center; traces, 1¼-inch, single strap, sewed to breast collar, scolloped and raised points; breeching, 1¾-inch, single strap, scolloped points, three ring stays, ⅞-inch side straps; saddle, 3-inch, single strap harness leather skirts, leather lined pad; shaft tugs, with dees, box loops; belly bands, single strap, looped together, turn back, scolloped and lined, round dock; lines, 1-inch, to loop in bit. All cut from No. 1 oak tanned leather, smooth round edge finish. Full nickel mountings. Per set $11.00
Weight per set, backed in box, about 20 pounds.

37056 Single Strap Harness, imitation hand sewed, choice oak tanned leather throughout. Bridle, ⅝ inch, box loops, patent leather winkers, round stays and overdraw checks; saddle, 3 inch, single strap, with leather lined pad; breast collar, 1¾ inch; breeching, 1½ inch, stitched stays; traces, 1⅛ inch, sewed to breast collar; girth, Griffith's style, heavy folded, with double stitched layer; lines, ⅞ inch; hip straps, ⅝ inch; round crupper.
Genuine rubber mountings. Per set............11.75
Weight, per set, wrapped in paper, 13 lbs.

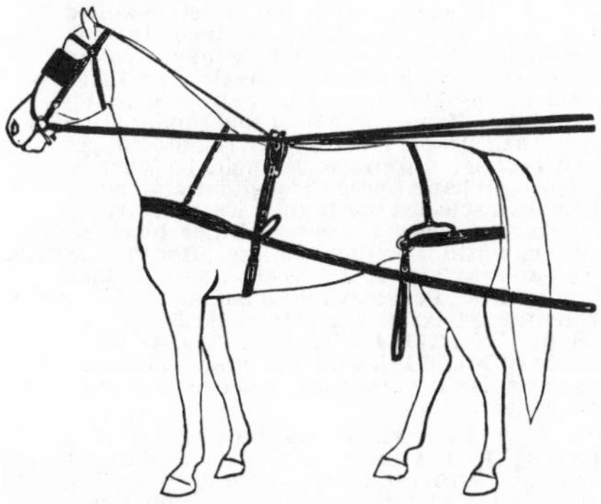

37058 Single Strap Track Harness, imitation hand stitched; saddles 3 in., leather pad; bridle; ⅝ inch, box loops, patent leather winkers, round winker braces, round side or overdraw checks; traces, 1¼ inch, stitched to breast collar with scalloped splice; lines, 1 inch to buckle in; breast collar, 2 in., scalloped points; breeching, 1¾ in., doubled and stitched stays; bellyband, 1¾ in , Griffith's style; side straps, ⅞ in.; hip straps, ¾ in.; turnback, scalloped, round dock; no martingale, all fancy wave creased. Full nickel mounting. Per set $11.00
We can furnish this harness promptly with imitation rubber mountings for 25 cents extra.

37060 All Hand Made Single Strap Harness, stitched 7 to an inch and first-class stock throughout. Saddle 2½ inch, hand laced, patent leather skirts and jockeys; bridle ⅝ inch, box loops, patent leather winkers, round winker braces, over draw or round side checks; traces 1⅛ incn, stitched to breast collar with scalloped splice. Lines, ⅞ in. fronts, 1 inch hand parts; breast collar, scalloped lay, with box loops for neck strap; breeching, scolloped lay, three ring stay; bellyband, Griffith's style, side straps ⅞ inch, hip strap ⅝ inch; turn back, scalloped, round dock; no martingale; genuine rubber mountings.
Per set.......................................13.50
Weight, per set, packed in box for shipping, about 20 lbs.
We will put up No. 37060 Harness to order with 3-inch single strap saddle in place of hand laced saddle for 50c. less on each set.

37062 All Hand Made Single Strap Harness, made of best oak tanned leather and finely finished, stitched 10 to the inch, box loops all through. Traces, 1¼ inch, sewed to breast collar with scalloped splice; 3-in. gig saddle, ⅞-inch bearer and shaft tugs; 2½-in. bellyband, with Griffith's patent buckles; 1¾-in. breeching with turn-back scalloped; doubled and stitched braces, round dock; bridle ⅝ in. with either overcheck with padded nose band or round side checks, half cheek snaffle bit; martingale with rubber rings. All fancy wave creased. Flat lines, 1 in. fronts, 1⅛ in. hand parts, with full nickel mounting.............................16.00

37063 Same as 37062, full imitation rubber gold lined mountings. Per set.......................16.25

37064 Same as No. 37062, with full genuine rubber mountings. Per set 18.50

37067 All Hand Made Single Strap Harness, genuine hand lace, 3 in. patent leather saddle: ⅞-in. bearer and shaft tugs; 1¾-in. bellyband with Griffith's patent buckles; 1¾-in. breast collar: 1⅛-in. traces, sewed to breast collar with scolloped splice; 1½ in. breeching, scalloped turn-back and doubled and stitched stays; round dock; flat hip straps; fine quality blind bridle, either overcheck with padded nose band or round side check reins; flat lines; full genuine rubber gold lined mounting.... Per set..........................$18.00

37068 Same as above, but full imitation rubber "Park" mountings gold lined. Per set..........15.50
Weight per set, packed in box, about 25 lbs.

Collar and Hame Harness.

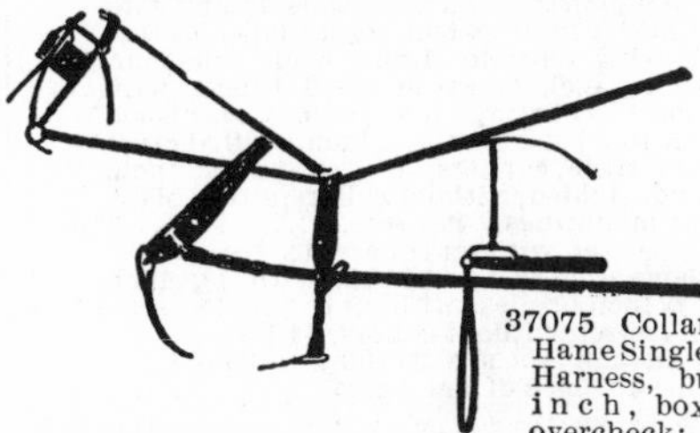

37075 Collar and Hame Single Buggy Harness, bridle ⅝ inch, box loops, overcheck; saddle 2½ inch, iron jockeys, enameled cloth lined; hames 3½ lbs., iron XC plated, collar special heavy, gig style; traces 1 inch doubled and stitched, clipped to hames, three holes for singletrees; breeching folded with layer, turn-back, ¾ inch, plain, folded crupper; hip straps, ⅝ inch; lines, ⅞ inch; mountings "XC" plate. Per set.......................................$6.50
Weight, per set, wrapped in paper, about 16 lbs.
Mention size of collar wanted.

Single Barouche Harness.

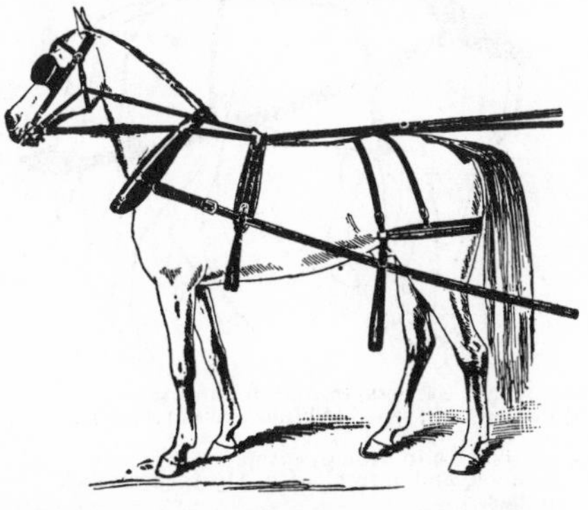

37078 Single Collar and Hame Barouche Harness; bridle, ¾ inch, flat rein and winker stay, box loops, sensible blinds; hame tugs, box loops, 3½ lb. iron hames; traces, 1¼ inch, double and stitched; breeching, folded with layer, side straps ⅞ inch; hip straps, double, ⅝ inch. turn-back, ¾ inch, round crupper to buckle; saddle, 3½ inch, iron jockey enamel cloth lined. belly band, folded cart; lines, ⅞ inch, buckle and billet 1 inch hand parts; collar, kip leather, buggy style. Mention size wanted. Mountings "XC" plate. Price, per set.......................$9.00
Weight per set, wrapped in paper, including collar, about 21 lbs.

37079 Single Barouche Harness, imitation hand-sewed; bridle ⅝-inch throughout, box loops, round rein and winker straps, sensible blinds; Hame tugs, box loops. 3½ pound iron hames; traces, 1¼-inch, doubled and stitched; round edge; breeching folded with layer, ¾-inch double hip straps, 1-inch side straps, back strap ⅞-inch, round crupper to buckle; saddle 3½-inch, iron jockey, leather lined; bellybands inside folded, outside single; shaft tugs with dees; lines, 1 inch; collar half patent leather; mention size; no hitch straps; nickel or brass mountings; weight, per set 22 pounds.
Per set.......................................$11.50

Single Coupe Harness.

37080 Single Harness, bridle, ⅝ in., box loops, round side check, 3½ in. heavy leather strap saddle with leather pad and swell skirts; belly band folded, with Griffith's buckles; breeching folded with raised layer, ¾ in. heavy side straps, turn-back scalloped, round dock, double hip straps, hames full nickel plated; hame tugs with box loops; traces, 1¼ in., raised doubled and stitched to buckle to short hame tugs; choke strap 1 in.; lines, 1 in.; No. 37193 collar. Well made from No. 1 stock and well finished throughout; full nickel mounting. Per set.....$13.25

Single Surrey Harness.

37082 Single Surrey Harness, imitation hand-sewed; bridle, ⅝ inch, round rein and winker stay, box loops, layer on crown, nose band; hame tugs, patent leather, box loops, safe under buckle, 4 lb. full plated hames; traces, 1¼ inch, double and stitched, raised, round edge, with or without cockeyes; breeching folded with scalloped layer, ⅝ in. double hip straps, 1 in. side straps; turn-back double reversed, round crupper to buckles; saddle, 4 in. hand laced, leather lined, leather covered seat; shaft tugs with dees; bellybands inside folded, outside single; lines, ⅞ in. fronts, 1⅛ in. hand parts; choke strap, 1 in.; collar full patent leather surrey, either closed or open on top; full nickel mountings; center bar wire buckles throughout. Per set...$24.00
Mention size of collar.

Bitting Harness.

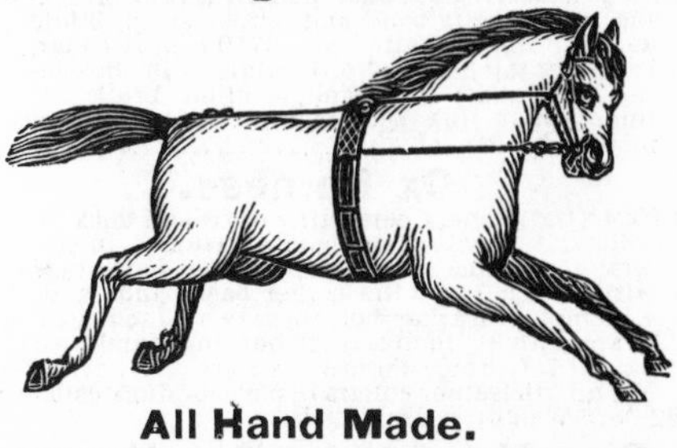

All Hand Made.

37085 Bitting or Breaking Harness, 3½ inch leather surcingle, padded; ⅞ inch open bridle, round check reins, with 38738 XC bitting bit (see cut); ⅞ inch side straps to buckle from bit to surcingle, with heavy crupper. All black leather.
Per set.....................................$6.25

Goat Harness.

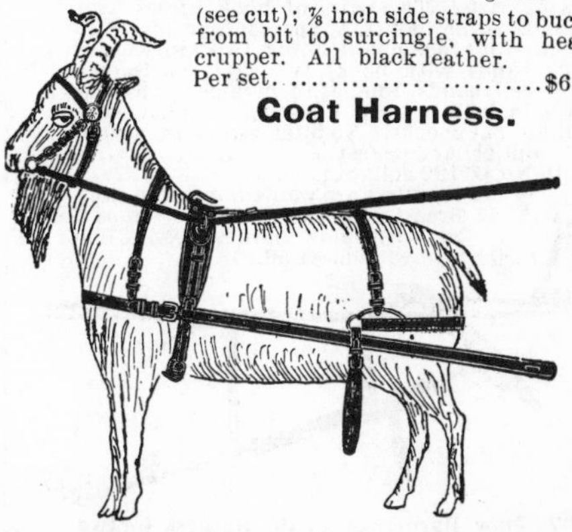

37087 Single Goat or Dog Harness. All made of red leather.
Saddle, 2 inch, full pad, tufted, with belly bands and shaft tugs.
Bridle, open face, with bit.
Traces, 1 inch, single strap, buckle to breast collar.
Lines, ⅝ inch.
Breast collar, flat, with scalloped layer and neck strap.
Breeching, flat, with scalloped layer, round breeching stays.
Turn back, plain, with scalloped chafe. Weight, per set, 4½ lbs. Per set..............................$4.25

Single Express Harness.

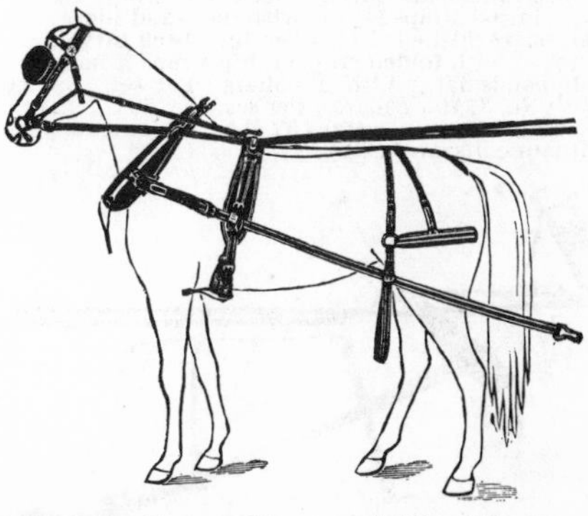

37090 Single Express Harness; bridle, ¾ inch, box loops, Concord blinds, round winker stays and round side check; hame tugs, box loops, champion trace buckles, red ball top hames; traces, 1¼ inch, doubled and stitched; breeching, folded with layer, ¾ inch double hip straps, 1 inch side straps; back straps, 1 inch, round crupper to buckle; saddle, 4 inch express, long pad, harness leather skirts, wool kersey lined, 1¼ inch bearer straps; bellybands, one folded, one solid; lines, 1 inch, to buckle to bit; choke strap, 1 inch, without collar; full solid brass mountings. Per set..............................$15.75

Dump Cart Harness.
Hand Made.

37092 Consisting of collar, hames, saddle, breeching, shaft belly band and choke strap, bridle and line, back chain, No. 37190 draft collar, iron over top hames, No. 1 saddle, 3 in. breeching, 2 in. shaft bellyband, ⅞ blind bridle, ⅞ line, single link back chain. All japanned mounted. Per set. $15.25

Ox Harness.

37094 Ox Harness, consisting of two all duck ox collars; two pair of ox hames fastened to collars; four hame straps; two pair of hame tugs with hooks; two 3 in. leather back bands with 4 inch plain leather housings: two 1 inch neck straps with 3½ inch leather housings, and two pair of 7 ft. trace chains. Per set............$6.75
For all kip leather collars in place of duck collars add $2.00. Weight, per set, 40 lbs.

Plow Harness for Two Horses.

Weight, per set, 40 to 45 lbs.

37096 Double Plow Harness, made up of the following parts: Two pairs of hook hames, two pairs of seven foot trace chains, four pieces of twenty-four inch chain piping, two 3 in. leather back bands with hooks, two 1¼ inch leather loop bellybands, four ⅞ inch hame straps, one set ⅞ inch 18 ft. team lines, two pigeon wing bridles, flat checks. No hitch straps or snaps.
Without collars, per set........ ....$9.00
With No. 37199 collars, per set................. 10.00
If collars are wanted, mention size.
Breast straps or neckyoke straps: do not go with plow harness No. 37096; if wanted, add $1.56.

37097 Plow Harness or Chain Harness for two horses. Bridles,⅞-inch, Jenny Lind blinds,hook hames, varnished over top; back band, 4-inch leather, with loops; bellybands, 1½-inch; back straps, 2½-inch, hip straps 1¼-inch with snaps; traces. 7 feet chains, 30-inch leather piping; lines, ⅞-inch, 15 feet with snaps; breast straps, 1½-inch with slides and snaps. No pole straps or hitch straps. Without collars. Per set......$11.00
Weight, per set, without collars, 45 pounds.
See our quotations on horse collars.

Short Tug Farm Harness.
FOR TWO HORSES.

37098 Short Tug Farm Harness, traces, 1½ inch, 4 feet long, with 3½ feet stage chain, pads, folded, with loop for back strap; lines, ¾ inch, 18 feet long, with snaps; bridles, ¾ inch, pigeon wing winkers, flat checks, neckyoke straps 1¼ inch, breast straps 1¼ in., with snaps and slides; hames, varnished, iron over top, back straps, ⅞ inch, with folded crupper, hip straps ⅞ inch, bellybands flat. Without collars. Per set.....$12.00
With No. 37195 collars. Per set................. 14.00
No 37098 Harness weighs 37 lbs. per double set without collars or casing.

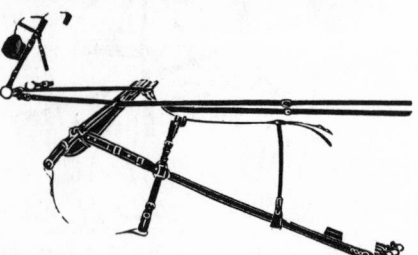

37099 Flat Pad Team Harness; for two horses, imitation hand sewed. Bridles, ⅞ inch, sensible blinds; hames red, iron over top; pads flat, folded, 1¼ inch billets; back straps 1¼ inch, hip straps 1 inch; traces, 1½ inches wide, 5 ft. 10 inches long, double and stitched, clip cockeyes; lines, ⅞ inch 15 feet with snaps; breast straps 1¼ inch, with slides and snaps; pole straps, 1½ inch. No hitch straps. Without collars. Per set............................$14.00
Weight, per set, without collars, 40 lbs.

Long Tug Farm Harness.

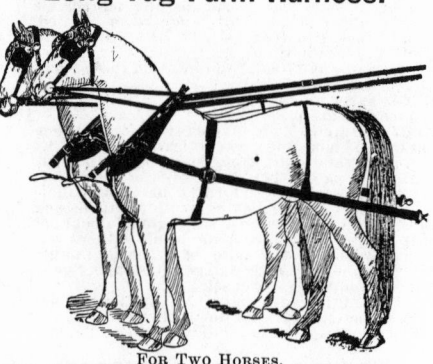

FOR TWO HORSES.

37100 Traces, 1½ inch, 6 ft. long with hame tugs, Champion trace buckles; hads, folded with loop; lines, ⅞ inch 18 feet, with snaps; bridles, ¾ inch, with sensible blinds; neck yoke martingales, 1½ inch; breast straps, 1½ inch, with snaps and breast strap slides; hames, varnished iron over top; back straps, 1 inch, stuffed cruppers and trace carriers; hip straps, ⅞ inch; bellybands, folded; without collars; either black or white mountings. Per set.................$16.00
Weight, per set, without collars, 41 lbs.
37101 Same style as No. 37100, with 1¾ inch traces, ⅞ inch bridles, without collars.Per set 17.50
Weight, per set, without collars, 44 lbs.
EXTRAS FOR NOS. 37100 AND 37101.
Round lines in place of flat, extra................. 1.25
Breeching, extra..................................... 3.50
Above styles are the best value on low priced farm harness that money can buy.
For Horse Collars see following pages.

TEAM HARNESS.

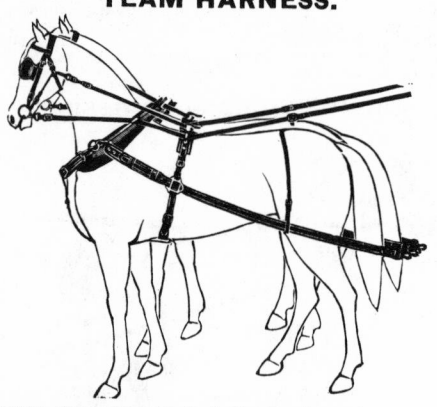

37104 Team Harness, imitation hand sewed. Bridles, ¾ inch, sensible blinds, round reins and winker stay.
Hames, black clip, iron over top.
Pads, hook and terret, with 1¼ inch market strap tugs.
Back Straps, 1 inch, hip straps ⅞ inch.
Traces, 1½ inch. 6 feet, double and stitched. Clip cockeyes.
Lines, ⅞ inch, 18 feet, with snaps.
Breast and pole straps, 1½ inch, "XC" plate (white) mountings.
Without collars, per set.........................$15.00
Weight, per set, about 40 lbs.
See our quotations on horse collars.
37106 Special Hook and Terret Farm Harness, "X C" trimmed only.
Pads, hook and terret, "Medway," folded skirts, 1 inch back straps with round cruppers and trace carriers.
Bridles, ¾ inch, Concord blinds, round check reins, fancy fronts and rosettes.
Traces, 1½ inch, 6 feet long, two rows stitching, clip cockeyes.
Lines, ⅞ inch, 18 feet long, with snaps.
Hames, black clip X C trimmed, combination loops, long hame tugs with Champion trace buckles.
Bellybands, folded, 1¼ inch billets.
Breast Straps, 1½ inch, with snaps and slides.
Neck Yoke Straps, 1½ inch,with ⅞ inch collar straps.
Hip Straps, ⅞ inch.
Without collars, per set.........................$17.00
Weight, per set, about 43 lbs.
We can save you money on horse collars and sweat collars. See our prices.
37108 Team Harness. Imitation hand sewed. Bridles, ¾ inch, with blinds, round reins and winker stay.
Hames, varnished, iron over top,⅝ inch spread straps.
Pads, hook and terret.
Back Straps, 1 inch; hip straps, ⅞ inch.
Traces, 1½ inch 6 feet, double and stitched.
Lines, ⅞ inch; 18 feet with snaps.
Breast Straps, 1½ inch, with slides and snaps.
Pole Straps, 1½ inch; collar straps, ⅞ inch.
Without collars,
White mountings, per set....................$18.50
Weight, per set, without collars, 48 lbs.

Harness—Continued.

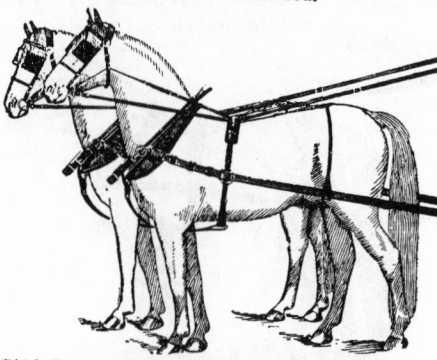

37110 Traces, 1½ inch, 6 feet long, hame tugs, champion trace buckles, pads, hooks and terrets, folded with layer and fancy housing. Lines, ⅞ inch, 18 feet, with snaps; bridles, ¾ inch with harness leather winkers, round side checks and nose bands. Neck yoke martingales, 1½ inch; breast straps, 1½ inch, with snaps and breast strap slides. Hames, iron over top, combination loops; back straps, 1 inch; round crupper, hip straps, ⅞ inch, sewed in ring; bellybands, folded. Without collars.
Very choice stock used throughout. Either black or white mountings. Per set............$21.00
Weight, per set, without collars, 48 lbs.
37111 Same style as No. 37110, with 1¾ in. traces and ⅞ in. bridles. Without collars. Either black or white mountings.
Per set... 22.50
Round lines, in place of flat, will cost $1.50 extra. For breeching add $3.50.
Weight, per set, without collars, 50 lbs.
We carry a large line of horse collars at low prices See our quotations.
37112 Farm Harness, same weight and quality as No. 37110, but made "slip tug" in place of "long tug," either blind bridles or open bridles, either black or white mountings, without collars. Per set (two horses)................ .. ..$21.00

Long Tug Farm Harness.
Hand Made.

37114 Traces, 1½ inch, hame tugs, champion trace buckles, pads, hooks and terrets, swelled with fancy housings. Lines, ⅞ inch, 18 feet, with snaps; bridles, ¾ inch, winkers, round side checks. Neck yoke martingales, 1½ inch; breast straps, 1½ inch, with snaps and breast strap slides. Hames, iron over top, combination loop; back straps, 1 inch, with round crupper trace carrier; hip straps, ⅞ inch; bellybands, folded. All hand sewed throughout and made of the best selected oak tanned leather; strictly first-class in every respect. Either black or white mountings, without collars. Per set...$23.50
37115 Same as 37114; 1¾ inch traces, ⅞ inch blind bridles. Per set, without collars..........25.00
Breeching, $4 extra; round lines, $1.50 extra.
Weight of No, 37114, without collars, 48 lbs.
Weight of No. 37115 without collars, 50 lbs.
We keep a large variety of horse collars which we sell cheap.
37116 Farm Harness, same weight and quality as No. 37114, but made "slip tug" in place of "long tug," either blind bridles or open bridles, either black or white mountings, without collars. Per set (two horses)......................$23.50

Breeching Team Harness.

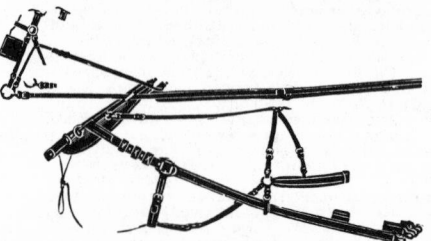

37117 Team Harness, imitation hand sewed. Bridles, ¾ inch, box loops, short round reins, round winker stays, square blinds; Hames, No. 5 Concord, long staples,⅝ inch spread straps, no back pads; breeching, folded, 1¼ inch layer, ⅞ inch double back straps running to rings in hames, ⅞ in. double hip straps, ⅞ inch side straps; traces, 1½ inch, 6 feet, double and stitched; lines, 1 inch. 20 feet, with snaps; breast straps, 1½ inch, with slides and snaps; pole straps, 1½ inch, with rings, white mountings, without collars. Per set.................$21.00
Weight of No. 37117 Harness, without collars, 45 lbs.
37118 Farm Harness with breeching; bridles, ¾ inch Concord blinds, box loops on cheeks, flat winker braces and nose piece covered with nickel spots, fancy front with nickel rosettes, short check rein; lines, 1 inch 18 feet long with snaps; hames, No. 5 Concord clip, long hame tugs, three loop champion trace buckles; traces, 1½ inch, 6 feet long, two rows stitching and

Harness—Continued.

cockeyes, folded bellybands, 1¼ inch billets; back-bands, folded with loops and eight large nickel concord spots; no hooks or terrets, 1 inch back straps with trace carriers and round cruppers; breeching, folded, 3 feet 6 inches long, with 1⅛ inch layer, ⅞ inch hip straps, ⅞ inch side straps with snaps; breast straps, 1½ inch with snaps and slides; neck yoke straps, 1¼ inch with ⅞ inch collar straps and rings for snaps on breeching side straps. Made in good style of first class stock; without collars.

Per set....................................$23.00

We sell horse collars very cheap; look up our prices on following pages.

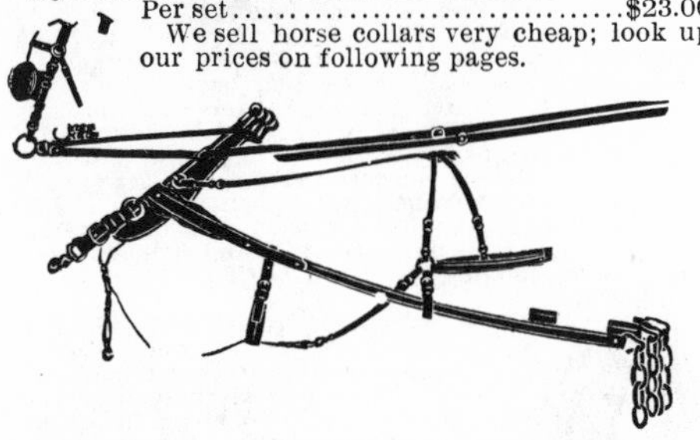

37119 Double Truck Harness, imitation hand sewed; bridles, ¾-inch sensible blinds, flat winker stays, brass fronts and rosettes, Hames, No. 8, red, Concord bolt, brass ball top; breeching, folded, 1¼-inch layers, side straps 1-inch; back straps, 1-inch, double, running to rings in hames; hip straps, ⅞-inch; traces, 1½-inch, double and stitched with heel chains; lines, 1-inch, 18 feet, with snaps; breast straps, 1½-inch, with rollers and snaps and extension straps; martingales, 1½-inch, with 1-inch collar straps; spread straps, ¾-inch. Without collars. Per set....................$26.50
Weight, per set, without collars, 60 pounds.

Lumber or Heavy Truck Harness.

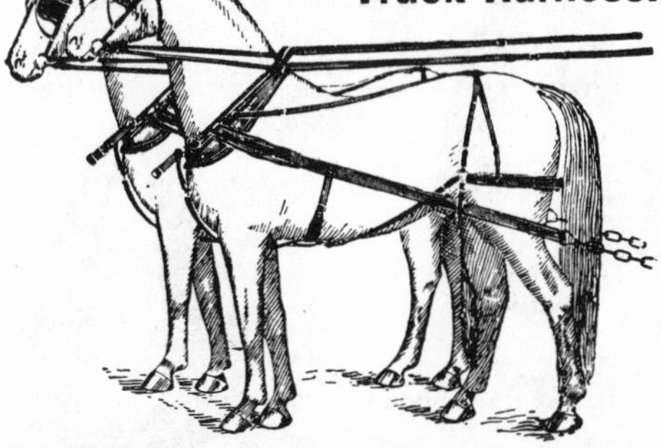

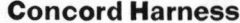

37120 M. W. & Co.'s Heavy Truck Harness. Bridles, ⅞ inch, with Concord winkers, round winker braces, 1 inch brass points, large brass rosettes, short check rein to check over hame tops; lines, 1 inch, 18 feet long, with snaps; hames, No. 8 red Concord bolt, brass ball tops, 1 inch hame straps, ¾ inch spreader straps with brass rings; traces, 1¾ inch, 6 feet long, two rows of stitching, four link and dee butt chain, folded bellybands, 1¼ inch billets on each side, 1 inch double back straps running to sides of hames (no back pads), 1 inch double hip straps sewed in ring with large chafe on rump; breeching, folded, 3 feet 6 inches long from ring to ring, 1¼ inch layer, 1 inch side straps with snaps, 1 inch lazy straps; breast straps, 1¾ inch with snaps and roller snaps; 1½ inch martingales with rings and 1 inch choke straps, 1¼ inch pole spreader. All made strong and substantial from No. 1 selected oak tanned leather; without collars. Per set...............$28.00

Concord Harness.

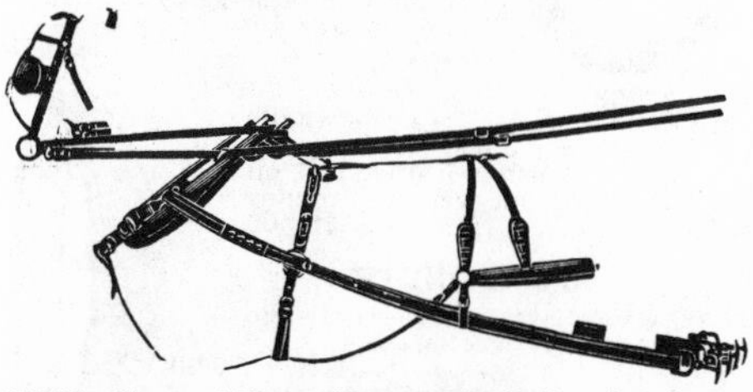

37121 Concord Team Harness, imitation hand sewed. Bridles, ⅞-inch, Concord blinds, fancy face pieces; hames, No. 6 Concord bolt, black; Hame tugs, with box loops; Pads; Concord style, 1½-inch in billets; traces, 6 feet long, 2¼-inches wide, 1¾-inch fronts; either cockeye or toggle ends; breeching, folded, 1½-inch layer, 1½-inch back straps 1-inch double hip straps, 1-inch double side straps: lines, 1⅛-inch, 18 feet with snaps; breast straps, 1¾ inch, with slides and snaps; pole straps; 1¾-inch. Without collars. Per set............................$29.00
For above harness with 2¾-inch traces, with 2-inch fronts add............................... 1.00
Weight, per set, without collars, 65 pounds.

M. W. & Co.'s Heavy Concord Harness.

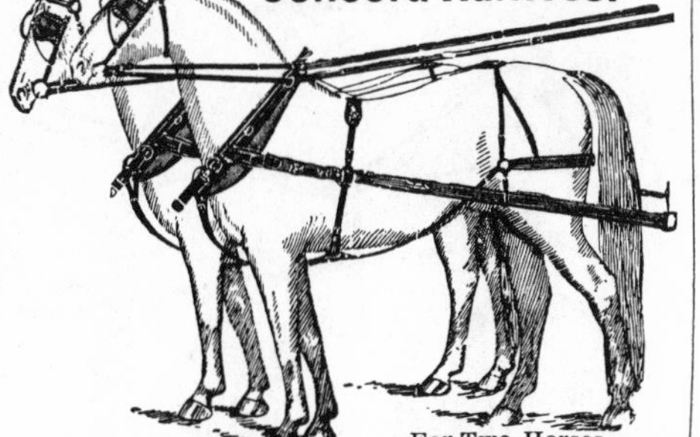

For Two Horses.

37122 Hand Made Concord Wheel or Breeching Harness; traces, 2½-inch single strap, with doubled and stitched points, and either Concord toggles or cockeyes; hame tugs, 1¾ inch, doubled and stitched: pads, Concord style, round loops; lines, 1 inch, 18 feet long, with snaps; bridles, ⅞ inch, with patent leather winkers, flat checks, fancy face piece; choke straps, 1½ inch; breast straps, 1½ inch, with snaps and breast strap slides; hames, polished Concord, bolt No 6; back straps, 1¼ inch, running to ring on rump, with safes; hip straps, ⅞ inch, double and split, bellybands folded; side straps, 1 inch, with snaps; breechings, extra heavy, folded with 1¼-inch layer. All hand made from No. 1 selected oak tanned leather. Without collars, per set......................$32.00
37122 Harness, without collars, weighs about 63 lbs. Please examine our prices on horse collars

Chicago Truck Harness.

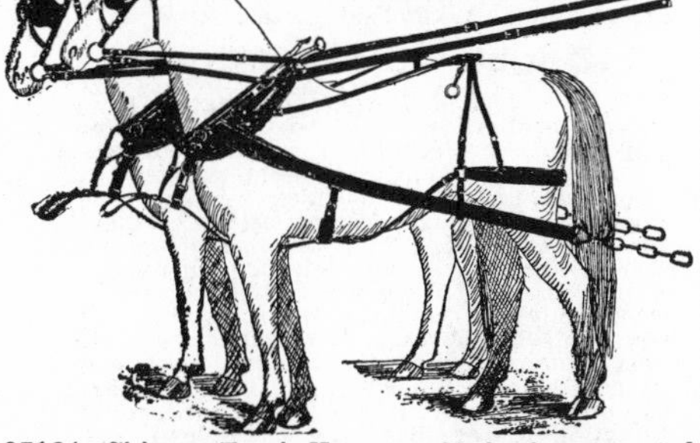

37124 Chicago Truck Harness. Made from selected oak tanned leather, and in keeping with the best custom work. Hames, No. 10 red Concord bolt, with brass plates and balls; traces, 1¾ inch, 6 feet long, three rows of stitching, 4 link and dee butt chain; bridles, ⅞ inch, Concord blinds, round winker braces, fancy face piece with brass spots; 1¼-inch brass fronts and large brass rosettes, short check reins; lines, 1 inch, 18 feet long, with snaps; back straps, 1⅛ inch, double, running to sides of hames; 1-inch double hip straps sewed in rings on rump, padded safes under rings, brass buckle shields; breeching, folded, 3 feet 8 inches from ring to ring, 1¼ inch layer, 1¼-inch side straps with snaps; 1-inch lazy straps; breast straps, 1¾ inch, 6 feet long, with 1¾-inch breast strap spreader 2 feet long: snaps and breast strap rollers; martingales, 1½ inch, doubled and stitched; 1½-inch collar straps; 1½-inch pole spreaders 30 inches long, and rings for breeching, side straps, hame straps, 1 inch; spreader straps, ⅞ inch, with brass rings. Without collars, per set.....$35.00
Weight, per set, about 60 pounds. Our quotations on horse collars follow our harness quotations

Double Hack or Spring Wagon Harness.

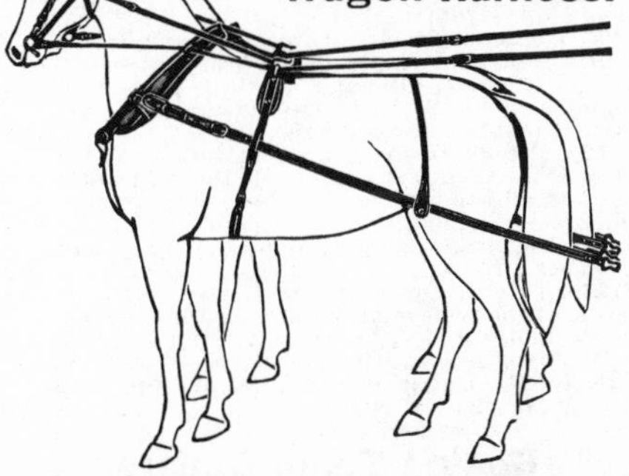

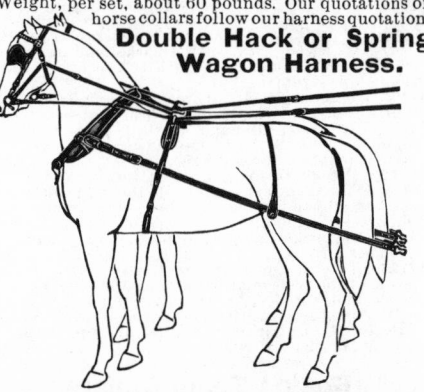

37130 Double Hack or Spring Wagon Harness, imitation hand sewed. Bridles, ¾ inch, box loops, flat reins and winker stays, sensible blinds; hame tugs, box loop, oval iron wood coach hames, ½ inch spread straps; pads, hook and terret, with 3½ inch swell housings, single skirts, double and stitched bearers: turnbacks, ⅞ inch, round cruppers to buckle; hip straps, ¾ inch, with patent leather ornaments; bellybands folded; traces, 1¼ inch, 5 feet 10 inches long double and stitched. with or without cockeyes; lines, round, 1 inch russet hand parts; breast straps, 1¼ inch, with snaps and slides; poles traps, 1¼ inch; "XC" Mountings only. Without collars, per set $16.00
Weight, per set, without collars, 32 pounds.

Road Harness.

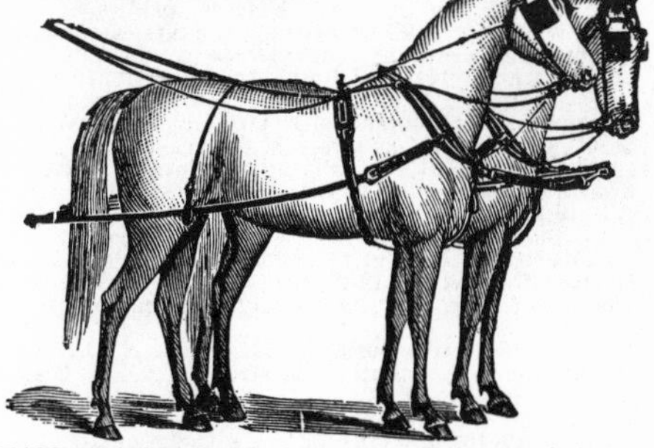

37132 This is a double harness and is intended for a light work harness, or for driving in a family spring wagon; it is well made of oak tanned leather and well finished throughout. Low top wood hames, spread straps and rings, short hame tugs with box loops; traces, 1¼ inch heavy, with cockeyes to buckle to tugs; saddles with leather pads; folded bellybands; blind bridles with patent leather coach blinds and box loop; round side check reins and winker stays; breast and neck yoke straps, 1¼ in.; stuffed crupper docks, flat back and hip straps, flat lines, 1 in., 18 ft. long, with snaps; all XC mountings. Without collars. Per set..........$20.00
With No. 37187 collars. Per set......... .... 23.50
Breeching extra..... .... 3.75
We will make No. 37132 harness to order in either full brass or full nickel mountings for $3.00 extra.
No. 37132 harness weighs 40 lbs. per set without collars or extras.

Double Buggy Harness.

FOR TWO HORSES.

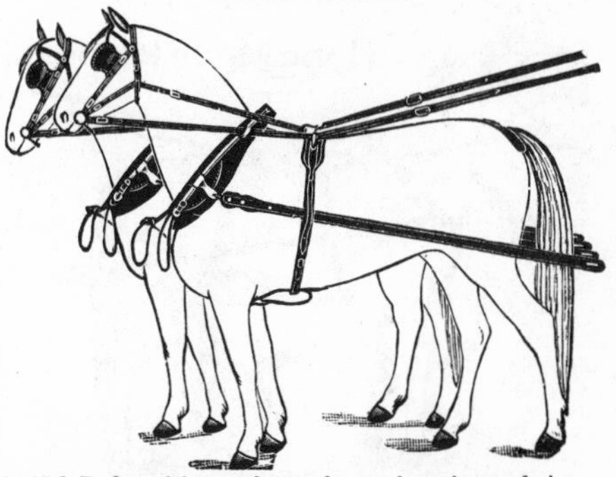

37136 Pads, without plates, fancy housings; bridles, ⅝ inch, patent leather winkers, flat winker braces, traces 1⅛ inch, doubled and stitched, clipped to hames; 7 lb. iron hames; lines, flat, ¾ inch fronts, 1 inch hands; bellybands folded; choke straps and breast straps, 1 inch, turnbacks plain, no hip straps, folded cruppers, with buggy collars, all white (XC) mountings.
Per set...$12.50
Weight, per set without collars, 23 lbs.
When ordering Double Buggy Harness, state size of collars wanted.

37138 Double Buggy Harness, special "XC" only. Bridles, ⅝-inch, patent leather winkers, box loops on cheeks, round winker braces ⅝-inch overchecks, white rosettes; lines, ¾-inch, russet leather hand parts; hames, 7-lbs. XC plated, ⅝-inch hame straps, ½-inch spreader straps, hame tugs with box loops; traces 1⅛-inch, 6 feet 4 inches long, doubled and stitched; coach pads, with iron plates, ¾-inch turn backs with folded crupper docks, folded bellybands; breast straps, 1-inch, 3 feet 8 inches long; choke straps, ¾ inch; no hip straps, with No. 37192 buggy collars. Mention size.
Per set..$14.00

37140 Double Buggy Harness, bridles, ⅝-inch, patent leather winkers, box loops on cheeks, round winker braces, round side checks or flat overdraw checks; lines, ¾-inch cross reins, 1-inch hand parts; hames, 7 lbs., 1-inch hame tugs with box loops, ⅝-inch hame straps, ½-inch spread straps; traces, 1-inch, 6 feet 4 inches long, doubled and stitched; coach pads, No. 2 "O. K." doubled and stitched bearers, ⅞-inch turn-backs with stuffed docks, folded bellybands; breast straps, 1 inch, 3 ft. 8 in. long; choke straps ⅝-inch from belly-band to collar; no hip straps. All black (japanned) mountings, with No. 37192 collars. Mention size.
Per set...16.00
Breast Collars in place of Hames and Collars on Nos. 37138 and 37140 harness will cost $1.00 extra.

HARNESS.

Our prices are very low, but our goods are the very best. Chicago is headquarters for leather, so we are able to do more than ordinarily well in such goods.

Buggy Harness—Continued.

37142 Double Buggy Harness, pads No. 2, O. K flat doubled and stitched bearers; bridles, ⅝ inch, box loops, patent leather winkers, round winker brace, double overdraw or round side check; traces, 1⅛ in., doubled and stitched; lines, ⅞ inch, 1 inch hand parts; hames iron, 7 pounds; hame tugs, with box loops; belly-bands folded; choke straps and breast straps; turn backs plain with round crupper; no breeching or hip straps; with No. 37193 collars, full nickel mountings. Per set.................$19.00

37143 Same as No. 37142, with full imitation rubber mountings, gilt lined. Per set........ 19.50

Extras for Nos. 37142 and 37143, breast collars in place of hames and collars, same price.

Round lines in place of flat....................... 1.50

Breeching, with hip and side straps............. 4.50

For hip straps only add........... .... .75

Nos. 37142-3 Harness with breast collars weighs 28 lbs. and with hames, without collars, 29 lbs.

37146 Double Buggy Harness, pads No. 3 "O. K." doubled and stitched bearers; bridles ⅝-inch, box loops, square patent leather winkers, round winker braces, overdraw or round side checks; traces 1¼-inch, 6 feet 4 inches long, doubled and stitched; lines ⅞-inch to cross reins, 1-inch hand parts; hames iron, 8 lbs. to the set, 1¼-inch hame tugs with box loops, ¾-inch ame straps, ⅝-inch spreaders traps; breast straps 1¼-inch, 3 feet 8 inches long; martingale choke straps, 1 inch from belly-band to buckle on throat of collar; no hip straps; with No. 37193 collars. Mention size of collars. Full nickel mountings. Per set.............................20.00

37147 Same as No. 37146 with full imitation rubber mountings. Per set...........................20.50

Extras for Nos. 37146-7, breast collars in place of hames and collars. Same price.

Round lines in place of flat, extra.............. 1.50

Breeching with side and hip straps, extra........ 4.50

For hip straps only, add........................... .75

Nos. 37146-7 Harness weighs 30 lbs. per set with breast collars, and 32 lbs. with hames without collars.

Hand Made Harness.

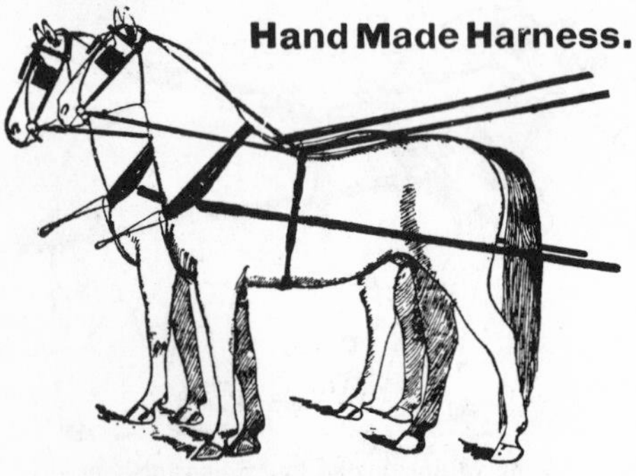

37150 Hand-Made Double Buggy Harness, stitched 7 to an inch, selected oak tanned leather, and first class in every respect; pads No. 2 O. K., with underhousings, straight skirts with round bearers; bridles, ⅝ inch, box loops, patent leather winkers, round winker braces, double overdraw or round side check; traces, 1⅛ inch, doubled and stitched; lines ⅞ inch, 1 inch hand parts; hames iron, 7 lbs; hame tugs, with box loops; bellybands folded; choke straps and breast straps; turn backs, single strap, scalloped, with round crupper; with No. 37193 collars (mention size of collars); full nickel mountings. Per set...$25.00

37151 Same as 37150, with imitation rubber mountings. Per set.............................. 25.50

Extras for 37150 and 37151:

Flat hip straps with patent leather drop......... 1.50

Round hip straps.. 2.00

Breast collar in place of hames and collars, same price.

Round lines in place of flat......................... 2.00

Breeching with hip and side straps................ 5.00

We will put up No. 37151 Harness to order with genuine rubber mountings for $30.00.

37154 Hand Made Double Buggy or Carriage Harness, stitched 9 to an inch, first-class stock and finely finished; pads No. 2 O. K. with underhousings, shaped skirts and scalloped raised bearers; bridle, ⅝ inch, box loops, patent leather winkers, round winker braces, overdraw or round side checks; traces, 1 inch, doubled, raised and stitched; lines, ⅞ inch, with 1⅛ in. hand parts; hames iron, 7 lbs; hame Tugs, with box loops, swelled patent leather ends; belly-bands folded; choke straps and breast straps; turn backs scalloped, doubled, raised and stitched, round crupper; with No. 37193 collars. Mention size of collars; full nickel mountings. Per set.............................. 29.50

37155 Same as 37154, with imitation rubber mountings. Per set.................................. 30.00

Extras for Nos. 37154 and 37155: Breast collars in place of hames and collars. Same price.

Round lines in place of flat, extra.................. 2.00

Breeching with hip and side straps, extra....... 5.25

37154 or 37155 with 1⅛-inch traces, extra.... ... 1.00

Weight about 30 lbs. with breast collars or with hames, without collars.

We will make 37155 Harness to order with genuine rubber mountings for $35.00, complete with collars.

Single Strap Double Buggy Harness.

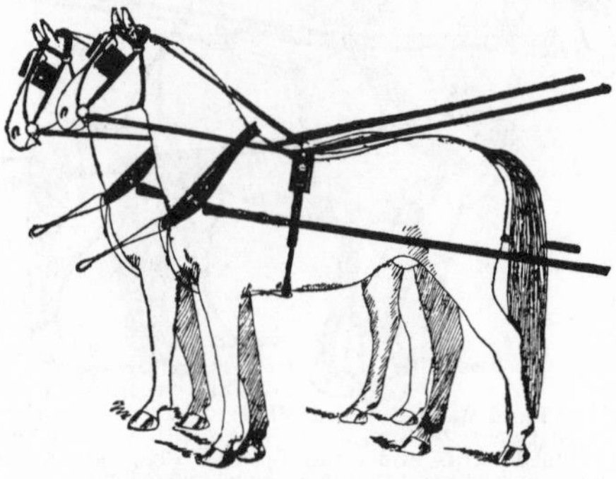

37158 Single Strap Double Buggy Harness, pads. No. 2 with chain trimming, single strap skirts, swelled bearers; bridles, ⅝ inch, box loops, patent leather winkers, round winker stays, either over draw or round side checks; traces, 1¼ inch, single strap attached to hames, doubled and stitched ends, with three holes; lines, ⅞ inch fronts, 1⅛ inch hand parts; hames, iron, 7 lbs.; bellybands. single strap, 2 inches wide, choke straps, 1 inch; breast straps, 1¼ inch, with box loops, turnbacks, scalloped, with round crupper, collars, No. 37193 (mention size), Campbell lock stitched, selected oak tanned leather. Full nickel mountings. Per set......................$22.00

37159 Same as No. 37158, with imitation rubber mountings, gilt lined. Per Set..................$22.50

Round lines in place of flat, extra.......... 1.75

Breeching with hip and side straps, extra 5.00

Double Surrey Harness.

37164 Double Surrey Harness, imitatation hand sewed. Bridles, ⅝-inch, box loops, round winker stays, overchecks or round sidechecks, layer on crown; hametugs, patent leather, box loops, safes under trace buckles, 8-pound iron hames; pads, straight, patent leather bottoms, 4 inch beaded edge housings, single skirts, bearers raised, double and stiched; turnbacks, ⅞-inch, scalloped and wave stiched, round cruppers; bellybands, folded; traces, 1¼-inch, 6½ feet, doubled and stitched, raised round edge; lines, 1-inch, 1⅛-inch hand parts; neckyoke, straps, 1¼ inch; chokestraps, 1 inch; collars, half patent leather, kip face. Either Nickel or Imitation Rubber Mountings. wire or band patterns. Per set.............................$30.00

For ⅞-inch hip straps, with patent leather drops, add.. 1.00

If collars are not wanted, deduct................. 3.50

Horse and Mule Collars.

When ordering horse or mule collars be sure and mention size wanted. Prices given here are for collars from 17 to 21 inches. Collars 22 to 23 inches in size cost 25 per cent. more; collars 24 inches and larger cost 40 per cent. extra. To get the size of a collar in inches, measure in a straight line from top to bottom *on the inside.*

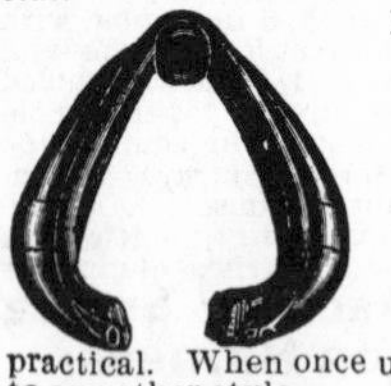

M. W. & Co.'s Open Throat Horse Collars. Experience has proven the wisdom and convenience of having horse collars to open at the throat instead of unbuckling at the top, when you wish to remove them from your horses. These collars are made with the best separable fastener on the market, and are entirely practical. When once used or tried they are preferred to any other style.

37170 Patent Open Throat Heavy Case Horse Collar, hair faced, made of the best selected collar stock, all hand stitched, projecting shoulders, finished with one buckle and peak, with patent fasteners. Each....................$2.80

37172 Patent Open Throat Concord Wool Faced Horse Collar, made of the best collar leather, all hand made, stitched with leather thongs throughout, whole shoulders, outside seam, one buckle and peak on top with patent fastener. Each 2.30

37173 Patent Open Throat Horse Collar, is made of the best collar leather, medium heavy, made and stitched by hand throughout. All stitching is done with leather thongs or whangs; broad welt, one buckle and peak on top, with patent fastener. Each.......................... 2.00

Boston Team Collars.

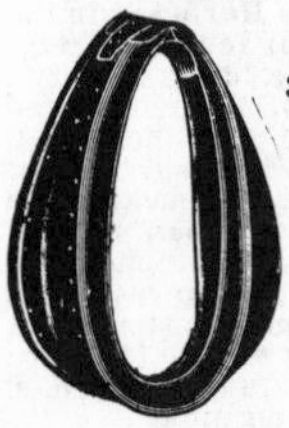

37174 Boston Team Collars, extra heavy cased collars, double capped, thong sewed and made of the best material all through. This style is more popular in the western states than any other.

Sizes, 17, 18, 19, 20 inch. Each.$2.40

Size, 21 inch. Each........... 2.65

Size, 22 inch. Each........... 3.00

Cork Faced Collars.

Cork Faced Horse Collars are now past the experimental stage, and are such an assured success that we can recommend them to our customers with perfect confidence. When properly fitted Cork Faced Collars not only prevent galling and sore shoulders, but will actually cure them with the horse continually working. They are faced with a thickness of one inch of clean, live granulated cork, which gives them an even, smooth-bearing surface.

37175 Cork Faced Horse Collars, imitation Scotch, solid rim, hame chafe, thong sewed, russet bellies, all hand stuffed. Sizes, 17, 18, 19, 20, 21 inches only. Each $1.75

37177 Cork Faced Horse Collars, Imitation Scotch, heavy, solid rim and back, thong sewed, hand stuffed. Made entirely out of selected and fancy collar stock. These collars will wear to the satisfaction of any man, and will give the horses comfort when in use. Sizes, 17, 18, 19, 20, 21 inches only. Each........... 2.20

37179 Dray Collar, is a cased collar, hair faced, made of the best stock, all hand stitched, projecting shoulders, finished with one buckle and peak. Each.................................... 2.50

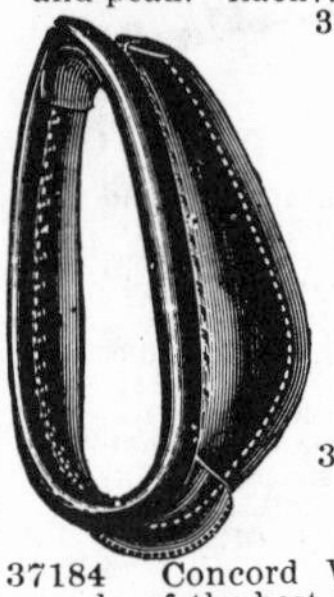

37181 M. W. & Co.'s World's Fair Horse Collar, wool stuffed, patent double grip stitched rim, adding double strength and more hame room than any collar made. It has a housing throat, which makes it the most perfect collar ever placed on the market. The double grip stitched rim and body of collar is all hand thong stitched; the collar embodies every good and practical principle a horse collar can have. Sizes, 17 to 21 inches, Each....................................$2.15

37182 M. W & Co.'s World's Fair Horse Collar, in large sizes, 22, 23 or 24 inches. Each $2.50

37184 Concord Wool Collars, wool stuffed, made of the best collar leather, all hand made, stitched with leather throngs throughout, whole shoulders, outside seam. Each................ 2.00

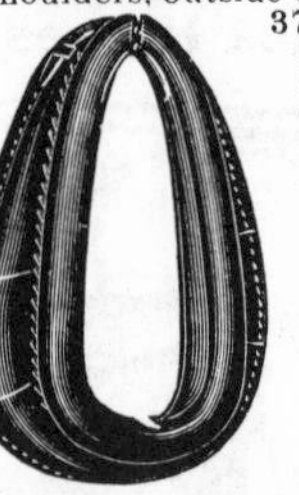

37185 Imitation Scotch Collars, wool faced, all thong stitched, made of choice kip collar stock, with hame chafes, one buckle on top; sizes, 17 to 21 inches. Each $1.50

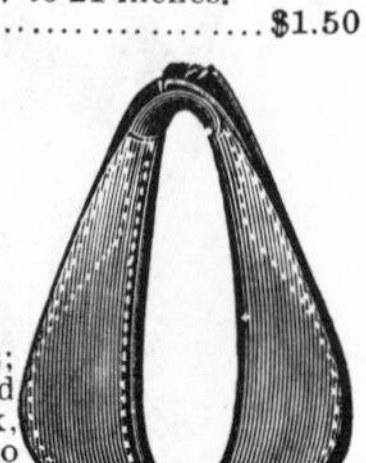

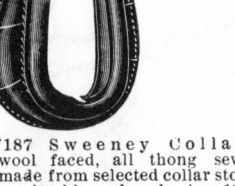

37187 Sweeney Collars; wool faced, all thong sewed made from selected collar stock, one buckle and peak; sizes, 17 to 21 inches. Each..........................$1.75

37188 Draft Collar, is made of best collar leather. medium heavy; made and stitched by hand throughout; all stitching is done with leather thongs or whangs; broad welt, one buckle and peak on top. Each....................... $1.75

37190 Draft Collar, made of the best collar leather, partially stitched with leather thongs and thread; broad welt, finished with one buckle and peak. Each.................................. 1.65

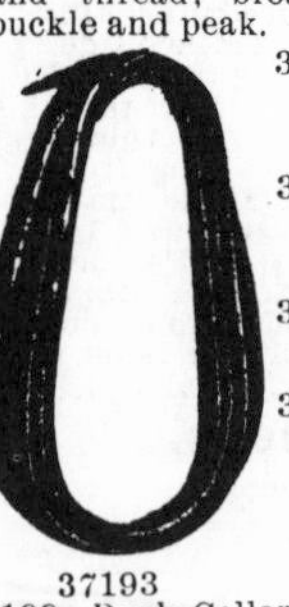

37193

37192 Buggy Collars, common grade, all black leather, spliced shoulders; one buckle on top. Sizes, 17 to 22 inches. Each...... $1.00

37193 Buggy Collars, made of the best kip leather, light and neat; will outwear three patent leather collars. Each................ $1.35

37195 Draft, Welted Collar, kip back, split rim, Baker kersey lined. Each................$1.00

37196 Collar, is made with split leather rim and shoulders, heavy cotton duck liners, leather chafes and top pads. Each................................$0.75

37199 Duck Collar, is made wholly out of cotton duck, with leather chafes on side and leather pad on top, and leather welt all around. Each..........................$0.50

Ox Collars.

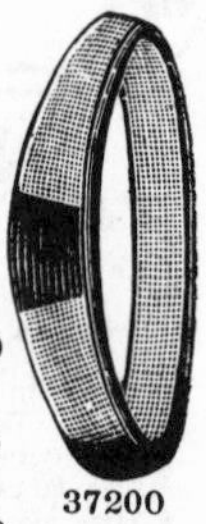

37200

37200 Ox Collars, extra heavy, made wholly of heavy cotton duck. Each.......................$0.50

With split leather rim and cotton duck, back and belly. Each.............. .65

Made of all kip leather, extra heavy. Each.... .... 1.50

Sweat Collars.

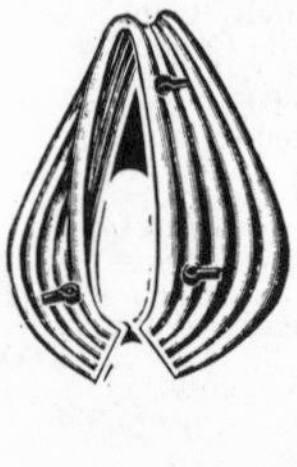

37203 Sweat Collars, made of good drill, one side white, the other brown, open at bottom, closed on top, three hooks, stuffed with goat hair. Sizes, 17 to 23 inches. Each............................. $0.25

Per dozen.................................. 2.70

Collars—Continued.

37204 Patent Sweat Collars, made of heavy white drill, lower ends open, closed on top, stuffed with goat hair, sizes, 17 to 23 inches.
Each $0.32
Per dozen...................................... 3.60

37205 Patent Sweat Collars, made of heavy brown drill, open at bottom, closed on top, three hooks. Stuffed with goat hair. Sizes, 17 to 23 inches. Each $0.35
Per dozen................................. 4.00

37206 Patent Sweat Collars, made of extra heavy white drill and stuffed with pure deer hair, open at bottom, closed on top, three hooks. The best and cheapest sweat collar for the farmer to buy. Sizes, 17 to 23 inches. Each.......45
Per dozen.................... 4.75

Top Collar Pads.

The different styles of collar pads quoted below are to be used on top of the horse's neck, under working collars. They effectually prevent pinching or galling. If your horse has a sore neck, the use of one of these collar pads will heal it rapidly.

37214 Collar Pads, made of heavy harness leather, lined with deer skin tanned, with the hair on, 12½ inches long, 6 inches wide, two ⅝-inch straps, 18 inches long to buckle around collar. Each.....$0.60
Per dozen............. 7.00
Weight, each, 9 oz.

37216 The "O. K." Collar Pads are the best and most practical on the market. They are neat looking, well made, can be put on or taken off in a moment, and will fit any size collar. Each.....$0.50
Per dozen. 5.65
Weight, each, 15 oz.

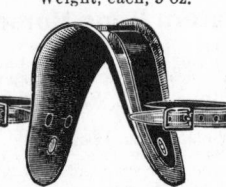

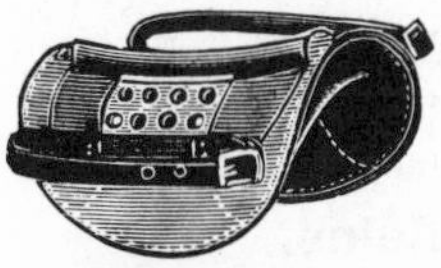

37217 Mishawaka Perforated Collar Pads. These pads are made of heavy sole leather, perforated in the center and padded at each end. The perforated part is clear of the neck of the horse, avoids all friction, allows a free current of air, and effectually prevents any chafing or soreness on the top of a horse's neck. Each $0.50
Per dozen 5.40

37218 Pad, sheepskin lined, stuffed with deer hair, medium.
Each......................$0.40
Per dozen................4.70

37219 Pad, sheepskin lined, stuffed with deer hair, large.
Each....................$0.45
Per dozen............. 5.25

Sole Leather Collar Pads.

37221 Pad, for light team collars.
Each $0.20
Per dozen 2.16
37222 Pad, for heavy team collar. Each, $0.22
Per dozen........................ 2.40 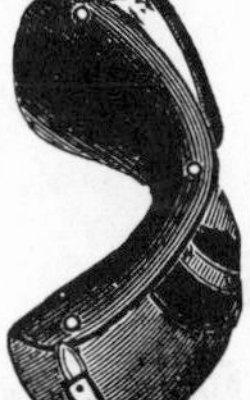
37223 Pad, for heavy truck and Scotch collars. Each...............$0.25
Per dozen... ... . 2.70

Collar Housings.

37225 Brass Trimmed Hames or Collar Housings. To be used on top of horse collars. Made of black leather, shaped center; size. 7½ x14 inches.Per pair$1.75
Weight, per pair, 32 oz.

Gig Housings.

37227 Gig Housings, patent leather, felt lined, fancy bound, strapped. Weight, 4 oz. Each....$0.30

37228 Housing or Gig Sweats, patent leather, fancy bound.strap, ped. kersey lined,stuffed pad. Can be used under saddle on any single or double buggy harness. Each......................$0.40

37230 Gig Sweats, extra quality, patent leather, new style. fancy inlaid,

round corners, wool lined. Each..................$0.60

Mueller's Saddle Pads.

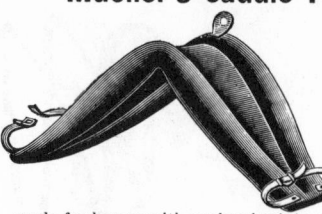

37231— Mueller's Patent Gig Saddle Pads, prevents all sores and relieves all pressure from old sores, allowing them to heal rapidly. Style No.1 is made for horses with sunken back bone, or what is called "round back," which can only be relieved or cured by this pad. Each...........$0.50
Per dozen.... .... 5.40
Weight, each, 6 ounces.

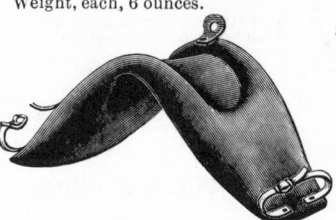

37232— Mueller's Patent Gig Saddle Pads. Style No. 2 is made for horses with sharp, extended backbone, or what is called "high bone," which becomes sore from the weight of the gig saddle. and can only be relieved or cured by removing the pressure from that point. All Mueller pads are filled with the best quality of curled hair.
Each...$0.50
Per dozen.. 5.40
Weight, each, 8 ounces.

Gig Sweats.

37233 Fancy Felt Gig Sweats, common or standard grade, strapped; size, 4½ x14 ins.
Each $0.14
Per dozen 1.50

37235 Fancy Felt Gig Sweats, common or standard grade, strapped. Size, 5x14 inches. Each..$0.15
Per dozen................................ 1.62

37237 Fancy Felt Gig Sweats, strictly first quality, strapped. Size, 5x14 in. Each..........$0.20
Per dozen.............................. 2.25

37238 Fancy Felt Gig Sweats, strapped, strictly first quality. Size, 4½ x14 inches. Each......$0.25
Per dozen........................... 2.75
Weight, each, about 4 ounces.

37239 Powell's Patent Gig Sweats. Heavy fawn felt, covered on one side with patent leather and trimmed with patent hooks in place of straps, which holds them securely in place. Made straight. Size, 3½ x18 inches. Weight, each, 5 ounces.
Each...$0.30
Per dozen...................................... 3.25

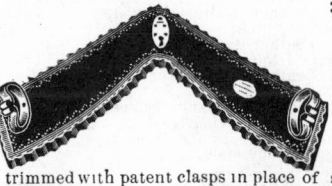

37240 Powell's Patent Gig Sweats, heavy fawn felt covered on top with good heavy patent leather, made with shaped center and trimmed with patent clasps in place of straps, which prevents moving. Can be used on saddles from 2½ to 3½ inches in width. Weight, each, 6 ounces.
Each... .36
Per dozen...................................... 3.90

Breast Collar Housings.

37241 Fancy Felt Breast Collar Housings, common or standard grade: sizes, 3½ to 36 inches, five straps on each. Each.........   ....$0.25
Per dozen........................... 2.70

37242 Fancy Felt Breast Collar Housings, strictly first quality, fawn color; sizes, 3½ x36 inches. Weight, each, 7 ounces. Each.................   .35
Per dozen........................... 4.00

37243 Fancy Felt Breast Collar Housings, pinked, patent leather covered, best quality made; sizes, 3½ x36 inches. Weight, each, 8 ounces. Each .... .45
Per dozen.... .... 4.85

Housings—Continued.

37244 Patent Breast Collar Housings, fawn felt covered with patent leather on the outside, three patent hooks to hold them in place, and leather loops on each end for the traces to pass through; can be used on any straight breast collar on single harness; size, 3½ x42 inches. Weight, each, 10 ounces.
Each $0.48
Per dozen............................ .... 5.25

Double Lines.

FLAT, BLACK LEATHER FOR FARM HARNESS, PER PAIR FOR TWO HORSES.

All hand sewed and made from No. 1 selected stock.

	⅞ inch.	15 ft.	18 ft.	22 ft.	25 ft.	28 ft.
37245	⅞ inch.	15 ft.	18 ft.	22 ft.	25 ft.	28 ft.
Price, per pair..		$1.80	$2.00	$2.35	$2.60	$2.90
Wt., per set...		2¾ lb.	3½ lb.	3¾ lb.	4 lb.	4¼ lb.
37246	1 inch.	15 ft	18 ft	22 ft.	25 ft.	28 ft.
Price, per pair..		$2.00	$2.25	$2.60	$2.85	$3.10
Wt., per set...		3½ lb.	3¾ lb.	4¼ lb.	4¾ lb.	5¼ lb.

37248 Extra Heavy Double Team Lines, 1⅛ inch wide, 20 feet long, choice selected stock and hand made. Per set.....................$3.35
Weight, per set, 5¼ lbs.

Double Driving Lines.

FLAT, FOR DOUBLE BUGGY HARNESS.
Weight, per set, 3½ lbs. Per Set.

37251 Flat Double Driving Lines, ⅞ inch fronts, with one inch russet or black hand parts, spliced on cross rein, nickel buckles. Length, 14 feet...$2.70

37252 Flat Double Driving Lines, ⅞ inch fronts with 1⅛ inch russet or black hand parts to buckle on cross rein; nickel or imitation rubber buckles. Length, 14 feet.................... 3.25

Single Driving Lines.

FLAT, FOR SINGLE BUGGY HARNESS.
Weight, per set, 1¾ lbs.

37254 Single Flat Driving Lines, ⅞ inch front with billets to buckle in bit, 1 inch russet or black hand parts. Length, 12 feet, 6 inches... 1.40

37255 Single Flat Driving Lines, 1 inch fronts with billets to buckle in bit, 1⅛ inch russet or black hand parts. Hand made................. 2.00

Hand Loops.

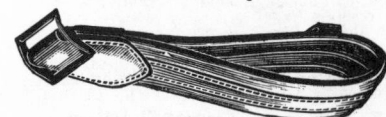

37258 Russet Leather Hand Loops, folded, double stitched layer, nickel loops; can be attached to any driving lines. Per pair....,.............$0.75
Weight, per pair, 5 ounces.

Traces for Single Buggy Harness.

37260 Imitation Hand Stitched Traces, 6 feet long. Good sound stock. Flat, round edge.

	1 inch.	1⅛ inch.	1¼ inch.
Per pair...	$1.10	$1.25	$1.45

37261 Imitation Hand Stitched Traces, 6 feet long. Raised, round edge: selected stock.

	1 inch.	1⅛ inch.	1¼ inch.
Per pair.........	$1.40	$1.55	$1.75.

Traces for Double Buggy Harness.

37263 Imitation Hand Stitched Traces. 6 feet 4 inches long. Flat, round edge.

	1 inch.	1⅛ inch.	1¼ inch.
Per pair.........	$1.30	$1.45	$1.65

37264 Imitation Hand Stitched Traces, 6 feet 4 inches long. Raised, round edge.

	1 inch.	1⅛ inch.	1¼ inch.
Per pair.........	$1.60	$1.75	$2.00
Weight, per pair, 1½ lbs.		2 lbs.	2½ lbs.

Traces for Double Team Farm Harness.

Made straight and intended to buckle to hame tugs on clip hames. Cockeyes sewed in.

	Per set of four.	
	1½ in.	1¾ in.
37267 Machine stitched, 6 ft. long........	$4.70	$5.25
37268 Hand stitched, 6 ft. long..........	5.75	6.40
Weight, per set....	8 lbs.	10 lbs

Breast Collars.

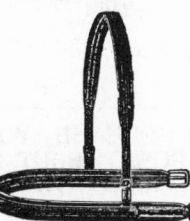

37270 Breast Collar for single buggy harness, machine made, including neck strap, all black buckles, for one horse. Each, 1 in., $1.25; 1⅛ in., $1.35; 1¼ in.$1.45

37272 Same, with nickel buckles, 1 in., $1.40; 1⅛ in., $1.50; 1¼ in., $1.60.

Breast Collars –Continued.

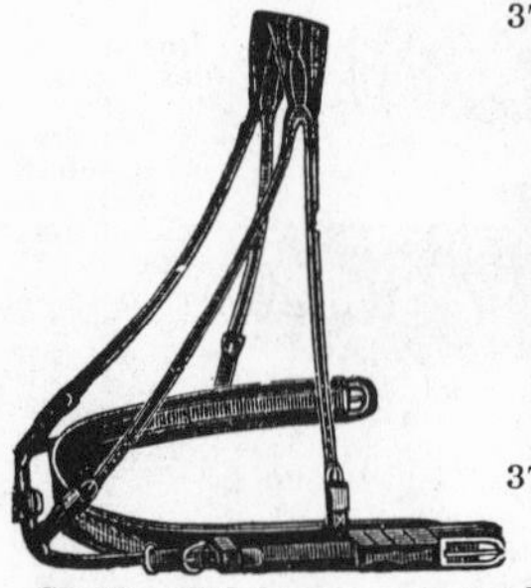

37274　This cut represents breast collar to be used in place of hame on double buggy harness. See quotations under each harness. When ordering breast collars be sure to give size of buckles, as they come in three sizes. Price of breast collars with black buckles. Per pair, 1 in., $6.25; 1⅛ in., $6 30; 1¼ in, $6.35.

37276　Same as above, with nickel buckles. Per pair, 1 in., $7.25; 1⅛ in, $7.30; 1¼ in, $7.35. Weight, per pair, 7½ lbs., 8 lbs., 8½ lbs.

Breeching.

37277　Breeching for single ·hip strap farm harness, including side straps, machine made. Per double set for two horses.............$3.50

37278　Breeching for single hip strap farm harness, including side straps, all hand made. Per double set for two horses.................. 4.00

Buggy Bridles.

37280 Open Buggy Bridles, extra quality, round cheek pieces, good leather brow band, fancy glass rosettes half check nickel bit, either overcheck with nose-band, or round side check reins. Can be used with any buggy harness. Each...............$1.75

37282 Buggy Blind Bridles, ⅝ inch cheeks, patent leather winkers, flat checks and winker braces, ring bit, either side

37280
or over check reins. Each.......................$1.20

37284 Buggy Blind Bridles, ⅝ inch cheeks with box loops, patent leather winkers and round winker braces, either over check or round side check; half cheek, nickel bit, nickel brow band and rosettes. Each............................. 1.85

37286 Round Cheek Pieces for buggy bridles, ⅝ inch ends, with nickel buckles. These cheeks are used to change a blind bridle into an open one. They can be used on any buggy bridle. Per pair... .60

Team Bridles.

37290 Pigeon Wing Blind Bridles, ¾ in. cheeks, ¾ inch flat check reins, plain winkers and front, flat winker braces. Each.............................. $0.80 Weight, each, 2 lbs.

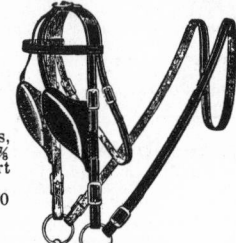

37292　Blind Bridles, Jenny Lind blinds, ⅝ in. cheeks and short reins, ring bits. Each..............$0.90 Weight, each 2¼ lbs.

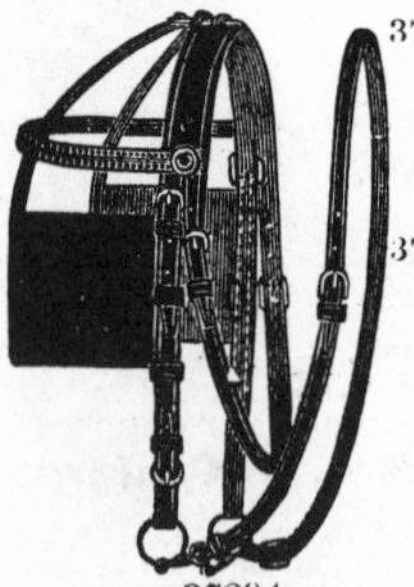

37294　Blind Bridles, ¾ inch cheeks with either square or sensible blinds of plain leather, and ¾ inch short flat check reins sewed in ring bit. Each.............. $1 40 Weight, each. 2½ lbs.

37296　Blind Bridles, ¾ inch flat cheeks with either square or sensible leather blinds, full length round check reins to buckle in ring bit. short cheeks with nose band and bit strap connecting cheeks with bit. Each...... ......$1.75 Weight, each, 3 lbs.

37294

Bridles –Continued.

37298　Team Bridles, sensible blinds, ¾ inch cheeks, round reins and winker stays, plain leather fronts, XC bits and buckles. Each.........................$1.60 Weight, each, 2¾ lbs.

37300　Open Bridles for team harness, ¾ inch cheeks with extra scolloped chafe sewed on, long round check reins. Each.........................$1.50 Weight, each, 2½ lbs.

37301　Open Bridles for team harness, ¾ inch cheeks with extra scolloped chafe sewed on, short flat check reins. Each.........................$1.00 Weight, each, 1¾ lbs.

37300

Stallion Bridles.

37304　Stallion Bridles, heavy cherry red leather, solid crown, 13 feet reins, fancy leather fronts, XC buckles, 1¼ inch all through, without bits. Each ....$1.65 For XC bits, add 25 cents.

37305　Black Leather, 1⅝ inch head piece, 1 inch cheeks, ⅝ inch throat latch, fancy leather front, large nickel rosettes, 18-inch steel stallion lead chain swivel, 1 inch lead line 12 feet long with 3 inch stopper on end. Heavy bit, either stiff or jointed. Each..... ... $2.75 Weight, each, 3½ lbs.

Rawhide and Leather Lead Halters.

Our leather halters are made of the best quality of harness leather, and we know our prices are right. Our rawhide halters are cut from the choicest oil tanned stock.

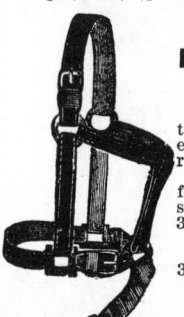

37310　5-Ring Sewed Black Leather Halters, 1½ inch head with leather stale. Each.$1.40

37311　5-Ring Sewed Black Leather Halters. 1½ inch head, no stale. Each..............$1 15

37310

	Each	
	1 in.	1¼ in.
37312　5-Ring, sewed, with black leather stale	$1.00	$1.10
37314　Sensible, riveted, with leather stale	.80	.95
37316　Black Leather Halters, sewed, 5-ring, no stale, 1 inch	.75	
37317　Black Leather Halters, sewed, 5-ring, no stale, 1¼ inch		.85
37318　Black Leather Halters, sensible, riveted, no stale, 1 inch	.60	
37319　Black Leather Halters, sensible, riveted, no stale, 1¼ in		.68
37320　Rawhide Halters, hand riveted, 1 inch, with rawhide stale	.78	
37322　Rawhide Halters, hand riveted, 1¼ inch, with rawhide stale		.98

Weight, each, 1½ to 2¾ lbs.

	Each.	Per doz.
37323　Rawhide Halters, with economy trimmings, 1 inch, without stale	$0.50	$5 40
37325　Rawhide Halters, with economy trimmings, 1¼ inch, without stale	.63	6.75
37326　Colt Halters, black leather, 1 inch, 5-ring, riveted, without stales	.55	6.00

Web and Rope Halters.

	Each.	Doz.
BOSS.　37328　Best English Tube Web Halters, fancy colors, leather filled, without stale	$0.50	$5.75
37329　Same style as above, with heavy russet leather stale	.75	8.75
37330　Heavy 13 Cord Web Halters, leather corners securely sewed on; leather chin strap, no stale	.17	1.95
37331　Same as above, with good rope stale	.20	2.25
37332　Pony Halters, heavy 11 cord web, rope stale, leather chin strap	.16	1.85
37333　Colt Halters, heavy 11 cord web, rope stale. Boss style	.16	1.85

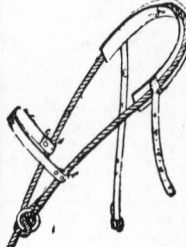

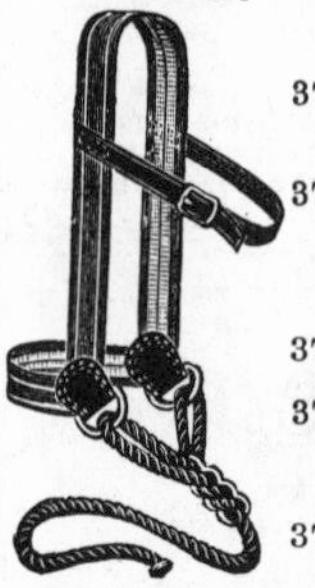

Averill Adjustable Halter.

37335　The "Averill Adjustable Halter, tie and all in one piece; made of ½ inch sisal rope with leather head shield, leather throat latch, and leather nose band; will fit any horse or colt and warranted to hold any puller. Each ....$0.40 Per dozen.............. 4.50

Neck Halters.

Neck halters can be used either in the barn or out side. They are more secure than any other. Can be adjusted by buckle to fit any horse's neck. Good strong tie straps.

37337　1¼ inch neck 1 inch stale. Each........$0.50

37338　1½ inch neck 1¼ inch stale....... .... .65

Adjustable Rope Halters.

37340　Rope Halters, made of nine feet of one-half inch strong sisal rope, which is much stronger than the jute rope generally used. Adjustable to fit any size horse, colt or mule. Each................$0.11　Per dozen............$1.20 Weight, each, 8 oz.; weight, per dozen, 6 lbs.

Patent Rope Horse and Cattle Tie.

37341　Horse Ties, made of 10 feet of ½-inch strong sisal rope, with one snap and ring for the neck, and another snap to use in the bridle bit. Much safer and more convenient than a hitching strap. Each.........................$0.15 Per dozen .... 1.62 Weight, each, 12 oz.; weight, per dozen, 8 lbs.

37342　Cattle Ties. Eight feet of strong sisal rope, with snap and ring. To be used instead of chains. Each.......... .... .09 Per dozen.. .... 1.00 Weight, each, 8 oz.; weight, per dozen, 6 lbs.

37343　Halter Leads. Eight feet of strong ½-inch sisal rope, with spun loop on one end. Each.............$0.07　Per dozen........... .75 Weight, each, 7 oz.; weight, per dozen, 5 lbs.

Check Reins.

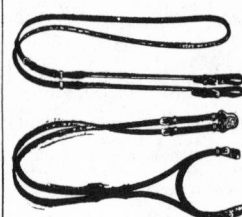

37345　Round Side Check Reins for buggy bridles, ⅝-inch billets. Either nickel or imitation rubber buckles. Each $0.50

37347　Overcheck Reins for buggy bridles, with nose piece. Either nickel or imitation rubber buckles. Each........ ...$0.65 Weight, each, 8 ozs.

Martingales.

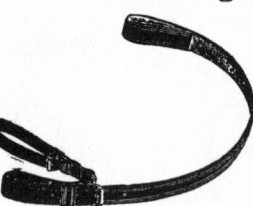

37350　Neck Yoke Martingales for heavy team harness, buckled loop at one end, ring at the other end, choke ring stitched on 24 inch collar strap with buckle. Width, 1½ inches. Each .... $0.55 Weight, each, 18 oz.

Breast Straps.

37352　Breast Straps. Cut from heavy No. 1 selected stock; made up 4 feet 8 inches long.

No snaps or slides.

	1½ inch.	1¾ inch.	2 inch.
Each........	$0.40	$0 46	$0.52

Weight, each, 12 to 16 ounces.

Pole or Neck Yoke Straps.

37354　Pole Straps or Neck Yoke Straps. Buckled loop at one end, sewed loop at the other end, with ring for breeching side straps. No collar straps.

	1½ inch.	1¾ inch.	2 inch.
Each	$0.40	$0.45	$0.50

Weight, each, 12 to 16 ounces.

Hame Straps.

37356　Hame Strap, hand sewed, buckles and leather loops, made up 21 inches long.

	⅞ inch.	1 inch.
Each.........	$0.08	$0.10
Per dozen ..	.90	1.10

37357　Rawhide Hame Straps, best quality of oil tanned rawhide.

	⅞ inch	1 inch.
Each.....	.10	.12
Per dozen	$1.08	$1.30

Spreader Straps.

Without rings or loops.

37359 Leather Spreader Straps with ⅝ in. buckle, 24 inches long, black leather.
Per dozen $1.00
Each .... .09

37360 Same as 37359, but ¾ inch buckle.
Per dozen 1.08
Each .... .10

Halter or Hitching Straps.

Black Leather.

37362 Hitching Straps, 7 feet long, ¾-inch wide, with German snaps riveted on. Each $0.17
Per dozen 1.84

37363 With loops	⅞ in.	1 in.		
Each	23c.	27c.		
37364 With buckles	¾ in.	⅞ in.	1 in.	1¼ in.
Each	23c.	27c.	32c.	38c.

Weight, each, 6 to 10 ounces.

Folded Bellybands.

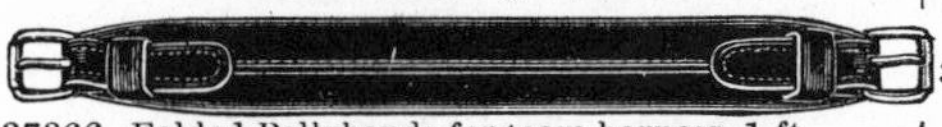

37366 Folded Bellybands for team harness, 1 ft. 9 in. long, with 1¼ inch buckle on each end. Each $0.45

Leather Bellyband with Loop.

37367 Bellybands with leather loop on each end to go over chain traces.

	1¼ in.	1½ in.
Each	$0.35	$0.42
Per dozen	3.95	4.50

Weight, each, 10 to 14 ounces.

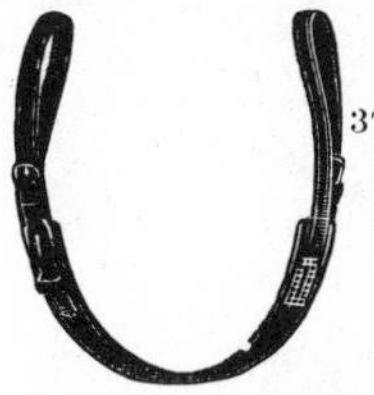

37368 Bellybands for single harness, Griffith's style. Single strap, all hand made, long billets. Either nickel or imitation rubber buckles.
Each $0.60

Leather Plow Back Bands.

37369 Leather Back Bands, with patent hooks to fasten in trace chains for horse or ox plow harness.

	3 in.	3½ in.	4 in.
Each	50c.	56c.	62c.

Weight, each, 20 to 26 ounces.

Cotton Back Bands.

37370 Cotton Back Bands, with patent hooks to fasten in trace chains for horse or ox plow harness.

	3 in.	3½ in.	4 in.
Each	25c.	28c.	33c.

Weight, each, 10 to 14 ounces.

Chain Piping.

37372 Leather Pipes 24 in. long, to cover trace chains for plow harness. Per set of four for two horses $1.35

Side Straps.

37374 Side Straps for breeching on double team harness, length, 6 feet.

	⅞ in.	1 in.	1¼ in.
Per pair	55c.	70c.	85c.
Weight, per pair	14 oz.	16 oz.	22 oz.

37375 Side Straps for single buggy harness 4 feet long, either nickel or imitation rubber buckles.

	¾ in.	⅞ in.	1 in.
Per pair	40c.	50c.	60c.
Weight, per pair	8 oz.	10 oz.	12 oz.

Harness Leather, Etc.

37377 Hemlock Tanned Black Harness Leather; common or "B" grade, whole sides only. Sides weigh from 15 to 20 pounds. Per pound $0.28

37379 Oak Tanned Black Harness Leather; common or "B" grade; whole sides only. Sides weigh from 15 to 22 pounds. Per pound .... .31

37381 No. 1 Hemlock Tanned Harness Leather, black; weight, per side, from 15 to 20 pounds. Per pound, in full sides .... .30

37383 No. 1 Oak Tanned Harness Leather, black; weight, per side, from 15 to 22 pounds. Per pound, in full sides .... .34

37385 No. 1 Rawhide Lace or Whang Leather, oiled and tanned, side measures from 7 to 18 square feet. Per square foot .... .20
Weight, per foot, 4 oz.

37387 Belt Lacings or Saddle Strings, cut from No. 1 oil tanned rawhide or whang leather: put up in bunches of 50 feet.

Width	⅜ in.	½ in.	⅝ in.
Per bunch	$0.50	$0.65	$0.80

37389 Russet Leather Sheepskin, good medium size. Each $0.70
Weight, each, 16 oz.

37390 Russet Leather Sheepskins, good large size for blacksmiths' and lumbermens' aprons, etc.
Each $1.00
Weight, each, 24 oz.

37391 Sheepskins, tanned with wool on, used for lining saddles and harness, large size.
Each .... .99
Weight, each, about 2 pounds.

Prices of leather subject to market change without notice.

Buggy or Carriage Whips.

37395 Straight Rattan, well finished. The best value ever offered for the money. Length, 6 feet. Each $0.10
Per dozen 1.00

37396 Black, platted through, Japan cap, one 1½-inch beaded nickel ferrule, loop snap: made with Overin's patent lining, strongest and best. Superior to any other whip made for the money. Practically unbreakable: a first-class livery whip; length, 6 feet.
Each .... .18
Per dozen 2.00

37398 Black, straight rattan, platted through, linen lined, smooth finish, 1⅛ inch beaded nickel head and 1½ inch beaded nickel ferrule, Philadelphia snap.

Length	5½ ft.	6 ft.
Each	$0.20	$0.25
Per dozen	2.15	2.70

37399 Black, straight rattan, terra cotta painted handle, metal and linen lined, textile head button, two 2¼ inch beaded C gilt ferrules and one 1½-inch center ferrule, English snap; length, 6 feet. Each 0.40
Per dozen 4.50

37400 Stocked Java Whip, black platted through, smooth finish, metal and buck lined, 1¾ inch, chased nickel head, and one 1½ inch nickel ferrule, English snap; length, 6 feet.
Each 0.50
Per dozen 5.50

37401 Full Buck Top, smooth finish, wove handles, metal lined, two English textile buttons, English snap.

Length	6 ft.	6½ ft.
Each	$0.55	$0.60
Per dozen	6.00	6.50

37403 Patent Solid Rawhide center, one-half length, water proof lined, smooth finish platted through double cover, rubber cap, six stitch head, and 30-ring patent buttons, English snap.

Length	5½ ft.	6 ft.	6½ ft.
Each	$0.60	$0.70	$0.80
Per dozen	6.48	7.56	8.64

37405 Stocked Java Whips, buck and metallic lined, smooth finish, black, platted through, seven ½ inch plain nickel ferrules between two 3¼ inch chased nickel ferrules, English snap; length, 6½ feet. Each 0.75
Per dozen 8.10

37406 One-half Whalebone, metal and buck lined, smooth black finish, platted through, English textile head and button. English half silk snap. Length, 6 ft.
Each $0.85
Per dozen 10.00

37408 Whale Bone Whips. Extra quality. One piece of extra heavy regular cut bone running from snap to handle, 12 inches from the butt. Black, German finish, double cover throughout, rubber cap, English silk snap.

Length	6 ft.	6½ ft.	7 ft.
Each	$1.40	$1.65	$1.90
Per dozen	15.00	17.75	19.50

37410 Cart or Sulky Whip, solid rawhide, double covered, one long butt button. Length, 4 feet. Each .... .50
Per dozen 5.75

37412 Ladies' Riding Whips, 25 cents, 50 cents, 75 cents, $1, $1.25, and $1.50 each, according to style and quality.

Riding Crops.

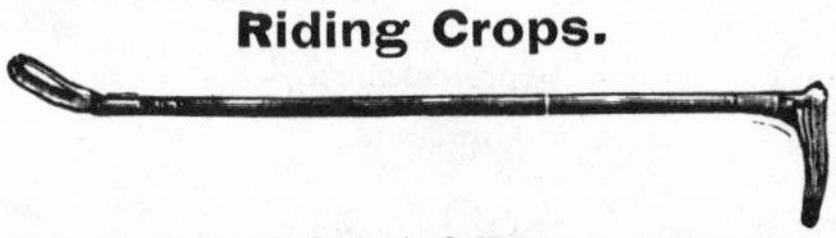

37416 Gentlemen's Imported Hunting or Riding Crops, made of Malacca with English buckhorn hooks and elkskin loops. Each $2.00

37417 Ladies' Imported Hunting or Riding Crops, Malacca stocks with English buckhorn hooks and elkskin loops. Each 1.60

Express Whips.

37419 Express Whips, Java stock handle, black thread cover, one nickel ferrule; white horse-hide braided drop top. Length, 6 ft.
Each .... .40
Per dozen 4.50

Solid Leather Team Whips.

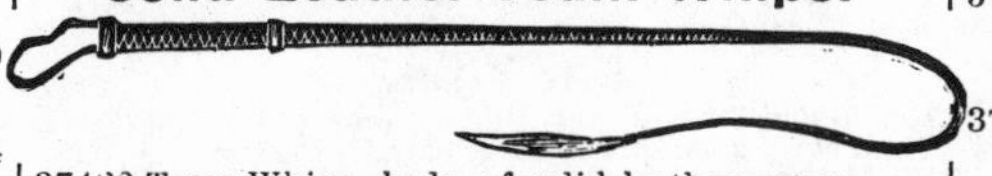

37420 Team Whips, body of solid leather, cover of oil tanned leather, thong stitched, snake style (XX). Length, 5 feet. Each $0.54

37421 Team Whips, body of solid leather, cover of oil tanned leather, thong stitched, snake style (XX). Length, 5½ feet. Each .... .62

37422 Team Whips, body of solid leather, cover of oil tanned leather, thong stitched, snake style (XX.) Length, 6 feet. Each .... .70

Colorado Team Whips, Shot Loaded.

37424 Colorado Team Whips, made of oil tan kip, double covered, sewed with buckskin, one-half kip and one-half 8-plait buckskin, shot loaded, 6½ feet long. Each $1.50
Weight, each, 28 oz.

37425 Colorado Team Whips, made of oil tan kip, double covered, sewed with buckskin, one-half kip and one-half 8-plait buckskin, shot loaded, 7 feet long. Each 1.70
Weight, each, 32 oz.

Mule or Hog Whips.

37427 12 Plait Calf, shot loaded, 5 feet, revolving handle. Each $0.95
Weight, 18 ounces.

37428 Mule or Stallion Whip; 4 plait braided whip leather, colored handle wired, buck cracker. Length, 4½ feet. Each .... .35
Per dozen 3.90

Drovers' Whips.

We are headquarters for drovers' whips, and sell more than all other dealers combined. All hand made and well finished.

Weight, 10 to 25 ounces. Each.

37430 Boys' Drovers' Whips, 6 plait, kip lash, 6 feet long, wired on 9-inch revolving handle, California style $0.40

37431 Boys' Drovers' Whips, 6 plait, 7 feet long, 9-inch handle. California style, lash fastened securely .... .50

37432 Boys' Drovers' Whips, 8 feet long, 9-inch revolving handle, 6 plait, lash firmly attached to handle .... .65

37433 Drovers' Whips, revolving handle, Jacksonville knot, 8 plait kip, buck point, length, 9 feet .... .90

37434 Drovers' Whips, 10-inch revolving handle, lace fastener, 6 plait kip buck point; length, 10 feet 1.00

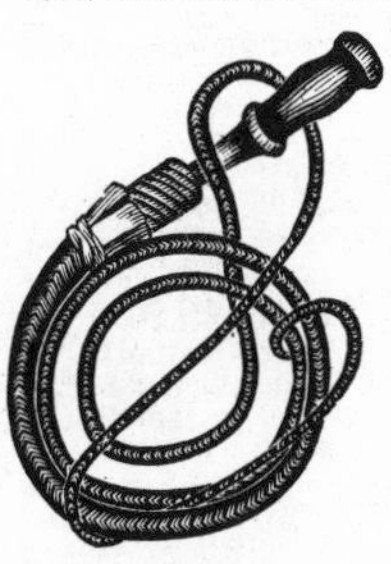

37435.

37435 Drovers' Whips, 8 plait oiled kip, buckskin point, full Jacksonville knot and revolving handle. Length, 10 feet. Each $1.25

37436 Drovers' Whips, 8 plait oiled kip, buckskin point, full Jacksonville knot and revolving handle. Length, 12 feet. Each $1.50

37438 Drovers' Whips, 8 plait oiled kip, buckskin point, revolving handle and full Jacksonville knot. Length, 14 feet. Each $1.75

37440 Drovers' Whips, shot loaded, 12 plait, genuine buckskin, full Jacksonville knot, revolving handle. Length, 10 feet. Nothing neater, finer or better made. Each $3.00

37442 Drovers' Whips, shot loaded, 7 inch spike butt, covered with 12 plait rawhide, body of whip is 12 plait oiled calfskin with buckskin point, no wooden handles. This is as serviceable a whip as can be made. Length, 10 ft. Each 2.00

37443 Drovers' Whips, shot loaded, 7 inch spike butt covered with 12 plait rawhide; body of whip is 12 plait oil calfskin with buckskin point. Length, 12 feet. Each 2.50

37445 Drovers' Whips, shot loaded, 8 plait oiled calfskin with buckskin point, revolving handle, full Jacksonville knot. Length, 10 feet. Each 1.75

37446 Drovers' Whips, shot loaded, 12 plait oiled calf lace leather with long buckskin point, full Jacksonville knot and revolving handle. Length, 10 feet. Each 2.25

Quirts.

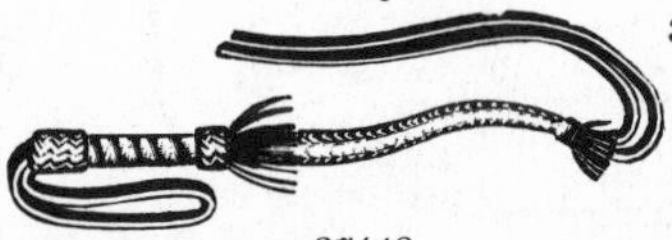

37448

37447 Braided rawhide, shot loaded, 12-plait, no tassel. Each. $1.50

37448 Braided Buckskin, shot loaded, with three tassels, 12 plait 1.25

37449 Braided Calf Strand, shot loaded, 12 plait 1.00

37450 All Leather Covered, buckskin stitched, shot loaded, three tassels. Weight, each, 16 oz. .... .50

37451 Oiled Leather Cover, buckskin stitched, two tassels, not loaded. Weight, each, 8 ounces.
Each .... .35

Whip Lashes.

Weight, 3 to 6 ounces.

37453 Six-plait Genuine Buck Lashes.

Length	5 ft.	6 ft.	7 ft.	8 ft.	9 ft.	10 ft
Per doz	$4.30	$5.10	$5.85	$6.70	$8.30	$9.75
Each	.40	.45	.50	.60	.75	.87

37454 Four-plait Genuine Buck Lash.

Length	5 ft.	6 ft.	7ft.
Per dozen	$3.64	$4.20	$4.90
Each	.32	.36	.44

37456 Eight-plait California Stage Lashes, genuine buck.

Length	10 ft.	12 ft.	14 ft.	16 ft.
Per dozen	$12.36	$14.95	$17.00	$19.50
Each	1.10	1.35	1.55	1.75

37457 Four-plait Imitation Buck Lashes.

Length	4 ft.	5 ft.	6 ft.
Per dozen	$1.08	$1.40	$1.70
Each	.10	.13	.16

37459 Six-plait Imitation Buck Lashes.

Length	5 ft.	6 ft.	7 ft.	8 ft.
Per dozen	$2.00	$2.50	$2.85	$3.60
Each	.18	.22	.25	.32

37460 White Hickory Whip Stocks.

Length	3½ ft.	4 ft.	4½ ft	5ft.
Per dozen	$1.30	$1.50	$1.70	$1.90
Each	.12	.14	.16	.18

37461 Whalebone Whipstocks, with 5 nickel ferrules, 4 feet long. Each $0.90

37462 Whalebone Whipstocks with 5 nickel ferrules, 4½ feet long. Each 1.10
Weight, 8 to 10 oz.

37464 Nickel Ferrules for whipstocks in sets of assorted sizes. Per set of four for one stock .... .14

Whip Crackers.

We do not break dozens.

37466 Cotton Whip Crackers, 7 inches long. Per dozen..$0.10

37467 Whip Crackers, half silk and half cotton, 7 inches long. Per dozen........................ .25

37468 Whip Crackers, all silk, best quality, 7 inches long. Per dozen........................ .40

Waterproof Horse Covers.

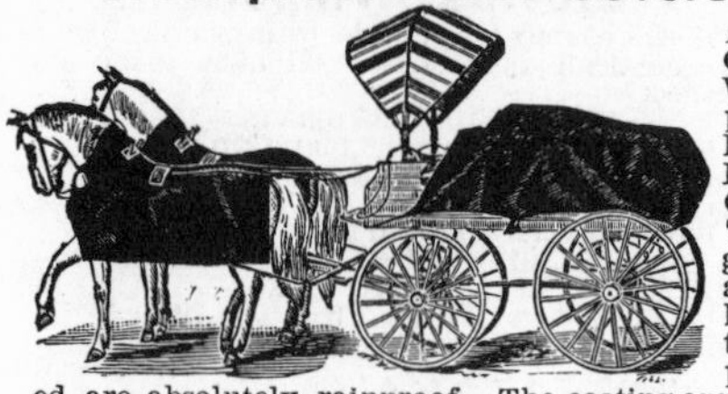

Black Oiled Waterproof Hame Horse Covers. These goods, as we have them prepared, are absolutely rainproof. The coating applied to the canvas contains nothing that will in any way injure the fabric, but is rather a preservative. Our covers extend on the neck twelve inches in front of the collar and can be used over either single or double harness. They are made with hame leathers, trace straps, and straps across the breast.

37476 Made of black oiled 8 oz. duck in sizes from 5 feet to 5 feet 6 inches from collar to tail. Each..$2.00
Weight, each, about 8 lbs.

37477 Made of black oiled drill in sizes from 4 feet 8 inches, to 5 feet 4 inches, from collar to tail. Each.. 1.75
Weight, each, about 5 lbs.

Rubber Horse Blankets.

37480 "Pure Gum" Rubber Horse Covers or Blankets. Dull finish, all seams both gummed and stitched, to neck only. The best made; small, medium or large sizes. Weight, 4 to 5 lbs. Each.. $3.25

37481 Luster Sheeting Rubber Horse Covers or Blankets, to collar only. Small, medium or large. Weight, 3 to 4 lbs. Each........................ 2.50

37482 Long Luster Sheeting Covers, to head. Made in one piece, with holes for ears. Strapped for holding securely in place, small, medium or large. Each.. 3.50
Weight, about 5 lbs. each.

White Duck Rain Covers.

37486 Team Rain Covers, made of heavy 10 ounce white duck. They are 78 inches long and 66 inches wide, all one piece. Have trace leathers with patent hook snaps, line pockets on the back and 3 inch by 11 inch hame leathers. Only made in one size. Per pair (two horses).. $3.50
Weight, per pair, 8 pounds.

Fly Nets.

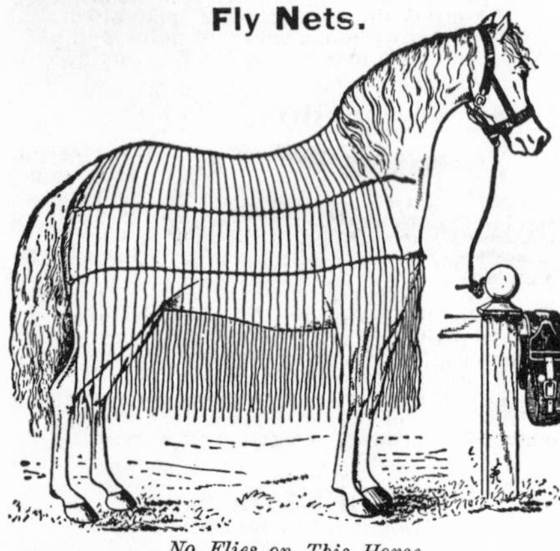

No Flies on This Horse.

Cut shows styles of nets quoted as "Body and Breast" nets.

NOTE.—Our quotations for fly nets are not by the pair, but for one single net for one horse.

37490 Upper Leather Team Nets, to head, standard weight, 5 bars, 84 lashes, body and neck. Weight, each net, 3¼ lbs. Each........................$1.85

37492 Heavy Upper Leather Team Nets, to head, 5 bars body and neck, with heavy hame bars.

No. of strings	60	72	84	100
Price, each	$1.65	1.90	2.20	2.50
Weight, each	3½ lbs.	4 lbs.	4½ lbs.	5 lbs.

37493 Extra Heavy Upper Leather Team Nets, to head, 5 bars, 84 lashes, body and neck; bars are ⅝-inch; lashes are extra heavy, good length and cut from best stock obtainable. Each....$ 2.40
Weight, each, 5 pounds.

37494 Heavy Upper Leather Team Nets, body and breast, 5 bars with 60 lashes in body. Each. 2.00
Weight, each, net, 3½ lbs.

37495 Extra Heavy Upper Leather Team Nets, body and breast; 5 bars with 60 lashes in the body, not counting breast piece; extra heavy lashes; the best body and breast net in the market. Each.. 2.35
Weight, each 4¼ lbs.

37496 Oiled Russet Leather Team Nets, 5 bars, 50 lashes in body, and breast piece. Bars are ¾ inch wide, lashes are very heavy, cut 5 to an inch and 7 feet long. Each........................ 2.15
Weight, each net, 3¼ lbs.

Nets—Continued.

37497 Extra Heavy Round Leather Team Nets, body and breast; 5 bars, 60 lashes; bars are ⅝ inches wide, cut 4 feet 9 inches long, extra heavy round leather lashes cut 7 feet long; breast piece buckles in the center; made from oak tanned leather. Each........................$2.00
Per dozen.. 21.60
Weight, each, 3 lbs.

37498 5 Bar, 40 Lash Team Nets, to breast; blacked and polished. Bars are ¾ inch wide, lashes are extra heavy and 7 feet long. Each.. 1.35
Weight, each, 3½ lbs.

37499 Patent Cover Nets, body, neck and breast; the center of the body is made of one piece of dark cotton duck, 36 inches wide and 58 inches long; the neck piece is 29 inches long, of same duck, and can be attached to the body in a moment; upper leather strings are fastened to the edges of the body and neck and hang as low as the lashes on ordinary nets; upper leather breast piece with strings; made only in one style and one size. Each........................ 1.00
Weight, each, 2¾ lbs.

RUSSET LEATHER FLY NET, HEAVY.

37504 5 Bar, 60 Strings, All Leather Team Nets, with metallic fasteners on bars; the cheapest all leather net in the market, made in body, neck and breast, 5 bar, 60 strings, not counting breast strings. Each........$1.10 Per doz.... 12.50
Weight, each, 53 oz.

37505 Russet Leather Team Nets, body and breast with metallic fasteners on bars. 5 bars, 42 lashes in the body and breast piece. Each.....1.00
Per dozen..10.80
Weight, each, 44 oz.

Buggy Fly Nets.

The "Boss" Fly Nets. These nets are made with leather bars and cord lashes. The lashes are treated with a chemical process which renders them water and acid proof and they are guaranteed not to fade or tangle up.

37507 The Boss Fly Nets, body and breast, 5 black leather bars; 48 black cord lashes on each side and a breast piece. Bars are ⅜ inch wide, lashes are 7 feet long. Weight, each, 20 ounces.$1.20

37508 The Boss Fly Nets, body and breast, 5 russet leather bars, 70 russet cord lashes on each side and a breast piece, Bars ⅜ in wide. lashes 7 feet long. Weight, each, 28 ounces. Each... 1.40

37509 The Boss Fly Nets, body, neck and breast, 5 black leather bars, 72 black cord lashes and breast piece. Bars are ⅜ inch wide and body lashes are 7 feet long. Weight, each, 24 ounces. Each.. 1.50

Leather Buggy Fly Nets.

37510 Fine Bound Black Leather Fly Nets, for buggy or carriage use. 5 bars, body and breast, braided ends. Made from pure oak tanned leather and well finished.

No. strings	50	60	75	90
Each	$1.55	$1.80	$2.25	$2.75
Weight, each net	24 oz.	26 oz.	30 oz.	35 oz.

37511 Extra Fine Calfskin Fly Nets. Body and breast. 5 bars, 80 lashes in the body and a breast piece. Lashes are extra long and are cut from the choicest oak tanned calfskin. Nothing better made. Weight, each, 20 ounces. Each 3.25

37512 Fine Round Black Leather Fly Nets to head. 5 bars, 72 lashes made from pure oak tanned leather and well finished. Weight, each, 32 ounces. Each........................ 2.00

37514 Fine Round Leather Flank Nets. These nets are intended to protect the hips and flanks of a horse, and do not reach further forward than the harness pad or saddle.

No. of strings	40	50	60
Price, each	$1.00	1.25	1.50

Weight each, net, 14 to 18 ounces.

Combination Nets.

37518 Indestructible Nets, body and head, leather tops, extra large bottoms, heavy cotton cord meshed; color: Black with canary bottoms. Each................$1.20 Per dozen.........$13.00

37519 Triumph Team Nets, body and head, 5 heavy cotton bars, 72 all leather lashes, russet in color. Each......$1.12 Per dozen........ 12.75

37520 Non-Tangler Team Nets, 5 bar, 72 strings, body, neck and breast, web bars, with leather strings hanging from lower bar, thus preventing the tangling of strings. Each........................ .90
Per dozen.. 9.72
Weight, each net, 42 oz

Ear Tips.

37522 Ear Tips or Ear Nets. Color old gold. Hard cord, good quality. Per pair for one horse.$0.30

37523 Ear Tips or Ear Nets. Color white. Fine hard twisted cord, close mesh, extra quality. Per pair for one horse........................ .50

Cotton Mesh Nets.

37524 White Cotton Mesh Nets, body, neck and ear tips. Common or standard grade. Each..$0.60
Per dozen.. 6.60

37525 Cotton Mesh Nets, body, neck and ear tips; all new combinations of fancy colors. Common or standard grade. Each........ .65
Per dozen.. 7.00

37527 Heavy Cotton Mesh Fly Fets, white, with colored trimmings, body, neck and ear tips. Exceptional value. Each........................ .70
Per dozen.. 7.75

37528 Heavy Cotton Mesh Fly Nets. All fancy colors with contrasting colored trimmings, body, neck and ear tips. All mesh nets hand made. Each.. .80
Per dozen.. 8.75

Nets—Continued.

37529 Double Cord Fly Nets, body, neck and ear tips. The body of the net is made with two cords knotted together at each mesh. One of these cords is black, the other orange colored, the two together forming a pleasing effect. Black border and orange tassels. Each...$0.95
Per dozen..10.25

37530 Extra Heavy Cotton Mesh Nets, to head, body, neck and ear tips. Colors: Steel, ecru and black. The heaviest mesh net in the market. Each..........$1.00 Per dozen..........10.80

37531 Improved Clipper Nets, to head; have gold brown meshed bottoms, which cannot tangle, and lashes at the top which will not catch in the harness. Each..$0.90 Per dozen.......10.25

37533 White Shaft Nets, to head, 1 inch meshes, white with blue trimmings. Longer and deeper than ordinary shaft nets. Each........ .87
Per dozen.. 9.85

37534 Fancy Shaft Nets to head, all solid colors, Extra size. The most popular grade of shaft nets. Each..........$1.00 Per dozen..........10.80

37536 Fancy Shaft Nets, to head, woven back bands, all one pattern, a combination of drab and ecru colored cord with ecru trimmings. Each..............$1.10 Per dozen............12.00
Weight, each on shaft nets, 18 ounces.

37537 Shaft Nets, to head, 1 inch meshes, woven backbands; a combination of black and canary color cord, canary tassels. Each............ 1.10
Per dozen..12.00

37538 Fancy Shaft Nets, to head, body, neck and ear tips, 1-inch meshes; the body of the net is black with lemon color border and red tassel. Each..........$1.00 Per dozen................10.80

Horse Fly Covers.

Horse Fly Covers are made to cover a horse from head to tail, and made with hame holes and line pockets so as to be used over harness.

37539 Horse Fly Covers, fancy plaided scrim, common or standard length. Each.............$0.32
Per dozen.. 3.50
Weight, each, 8 ounces.

37541 Horse Fly Covers, striped burlap, heavy and strong. 90 inches long. Each.............. .38
Per dozen.. 4.10
Weight, each, 2 pounds.

37543 Horse Fly Covers, plain white netting, hard twisted cord, close mesh, neat and strong, length, 90 incnes. Each........................ .55
Pey dozen.. 6.00
Weight, each, 22 ounces.

37544 Horse Fly Covers, fancy brown or blue plaid apron gingham, assorted colors, 90 inches long. A really good cover, light in weight, but close and strong. Each........................ .60
Per dozen.. 6.50
Weight, each, 16 ounces.

37545 Horse Fly Covers, made of plain white heavy cotton sheeting; firm and close and can be washed like any cotton goods; 90 inches in length.
Each..............$0.65 Per dozen..........$7.00
Weight, each, 26 ounces.

37546 Horse Fly Covers, fancy black and gold plaid netting, strong, hard cord, close mesh; very handsome strong and durable; 90 inches long, 36 inches deep on each side from center.
Each................$0.75 Per dozen........... 8.10
Weight, each, 24 ounces.

Stable Sheets.

Horse sheets, used in the stable, keep horses smooth and clean and ready for driving. They are strongly sewed down the back, stayed in the neck and have straps securely fastened.

37550 Stable Sheets, striped burlap, hemmed, web stays, button front, one surcingle attached; 72 inches long, 34 inches wide on each side.
Each................$0.50 Per dozen...........$5.40
Weight, each, 30 ounces.

37552 Stable Sheets, best quality of plain burlap, flat bound, web stays, sewed strap reinforced, one surcingle; 40 inches deep, 72 inches long.
Each...............$0.62 Per dozen.......... 6.70
Weight, each, 2¾ pounds.

37553 Stable Sheets, white ground, chocolate plaids, fancy border, hemmed all around, web stays, one surcingle; 72 inches long.
Each...............$0.75 Per dozen......... 8.10
Weight, each, 26 ounces.

37555 Stable Sheets, Scotch plaids in assorted patterns of small checks, all handsome and very desirable, web stays and pockets, one surcingle attached; flat bound, 72 inches long, 34 inches deep.
Each...............$0.90 Per dozen......... 9.75
Weight, each, 20 ounces.

37556 Stable Sheets, a limited quantity of excelsior duck stable sheets; fawn grounds, black plaids, well made. Former price, $1.20 each. To close out this lot, each........................ .85
Make second choice in case they are all sold before we receive your order. Weight, each, 32 ounces.

37557 Stable Sheets, heavy plain fawn color duck, flat bound all around and well stayed, reinforced in front under the straps, one surcingle attached; excellent value; 72 inches long, 36 inches deep.
Each...............$1.00 Per dozen.......... 10.80
Weight, each, 30 ounces.

37558 Stable Sheets, heavy duck, diagonal buff grounds, black plaids, hemmed all around and reinforced in front, one surcingle attached; very handsome, strong and well made sheets; 72 inches long, 38 inches deep.
Each.............$1.15 Per dozen.......... 12.42
Weight, each, 30 ounces.

Baby Fur Lap Robes.

37560 White China Goat Baby Carriage Robes, with plain white wool eider-down lining and felt border. Each.......................$2.60
With embroidered eider down lining............ 2.75
Size, 27x32 inches.

37561 White Angora Sheep Baby Carriage Robes, with plain white wool eider down lining and felt border. Each............................ 3.00
With embroidered eider-down lining. Each..... 3.25
Size, 27x32 inches; weight, each, 2 to 3 pounds.

Linen Carriage Robes.

We import our Linen Carriage Lap Robes direct from the manufacturers in Belgium, and can furnish them in any quantity as cheap as the largest jobbing houses sell them in large lots.

Each.

37562 Linen Lap Robes; ground is of natural linen color, with fancy stripes, plain fringe.....$0.45

37563 Linen Lap Dusters, medium grade; ground is of natural linen color, with fancy stripes and checks, fringe on each end........................ .60

37564 Linen Lap Robes, extra quality, fancy checks and stripes, with border and fringe; size, 48x60 in.; weight, about 12 oz.................. .75

37565 Linen Lap Robes, all plain, momie style, very heavy for this kind of goods, heavy knotted fringe; size, 52x62 in.; weight, about 16 oz..... 1.00

37566 Linen Lap Robes, plain body, with cluster of fern leaves embroidered in center; weight, 16 oz. 1.25

Momie Lap Robes.

All our summer lap robes are new and fresh as our large stock of last season was completely sold out. Robes this season are of better quality than last year for same price, and the embroidering is more elegant and varied.

37567 Fancy Dusters. In a variety of handsome and fancy plaids, not embroidered. Each...... $0.35

37569 Fancy Dusters, heavy novelty cloth, knotted fringe, double border, not embroidered, Weight, 20 ozs. Each........................ .50

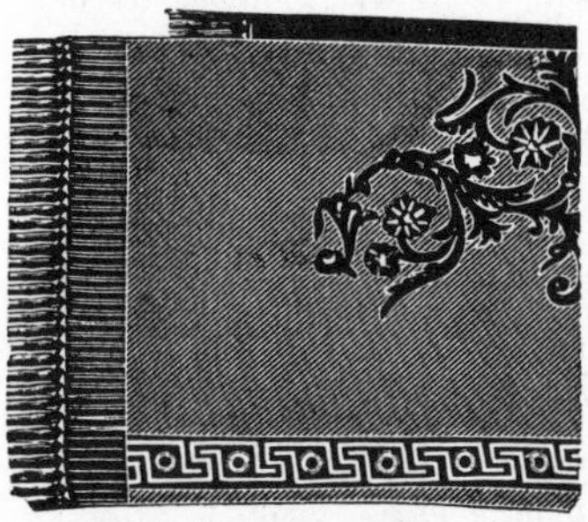

One design among many.
Price governs quality.

37570 Momie Lap Robes, with embroidered center piece designs. Each..$0.40

37572 Momie Lap Robes, with embroidered center piece designs. Each. $0.50

37574 Momie Lap Robes, with embroidered center piece designs. Each.....$0.60

37576 Embroidered Dusters, novelty momie cloth with handsome patterns of new designs embroidered in center. Each.............. 0.75

37578 Embroidered Dusters, novelty momie cloth, assorted colors, 21 inch designs, all new patterns, knotted fringe. Each...................... .90

37580 Momie Lap Robes with embroidered center and fancy border, all new goods and new patterns... 1.00

37582 Momie Lap Robes with embroidered center and fancy border, all beauties in this lot. . 1.25

37584 Elberon Lap Robes, mottled grounds with white plaids; worsted finish; three rows of stitching; not embroidered; superior value. Each.. 1.40

37586 Carriage Lap Robes, with jacquered borders and knotted fringes and embroidered center.. 1.50

37588 Embroidered Dusters, heavy, 18 ounce, novelty cloth, assorted fancy colors, knotted fringe, large, 32 inch peacock design, in colors as natural as life. Each........................ 2.00

37590 Imported Lap Robes, dark brown ground with light brown stripes from end to end, close and firm, knotted fringe. Weight, each, 16 ounces. Each.. .90

37592 Imported Lap Robes, light brown ground with dark brown stripes, knotted fringe. Size, 48x62 inches. Weight, each, 16 ounces. Each. .95

37594 Imported Lap Robes, light or slate color grounds, woven in a herringbone pattern, with a narrow stripe of another color every 2 inches. Size, 48x62 inches. Weight, 16 ounces. Each 1.00

Green Cloth Summer Lap Robes.

This class of goods is becoming very fashionable.

37600 Green Cloth Lap Robes, all wool plain Nassau cloth, pinked edge. Size 48x6 inches. Weight, each, 12 ounces. Each..................$1.00

37602 Green Cloth Lap Robes, all wool Nassau cloth, fine quality, fast color, pinked edge. 32-inch scroll and tulip embroidered design. Size, 48x60 inches. Weight, each, 10 ounces. Each.. 1.25

37604 Green Cloth Lap Robes, single face fabric cloth, pinked edge, large embroidered Corean star in old gold and tinsel cord. Size, 48x-60 inches. Weight, 16 ounces. Each.......... 1.50

37606 Green Cloth Lap Robes, single face fabric cloth, pinked edges, large rustic floral square of worsted emboridery; sizes, 48x 60 in. weight, 16 ounces. Each...................................... 1.75

21—2nd

Lap Robes—Continued.

37608 Green Cloth Lap Robes, single face fabric cloth, hemmed all around edge, silk bird and butterfly on worsted branch of flowers; sizes, 48x 60 inches; weight, 16 ounces. Each............ 2.00

37610 Green Cloth Lap Robes, all wool Nassua cloth, pinked edges, 30 inch. panel design, of three star flowers and ferns; sizes, 48x60 inches; weight, 16 ounces. Each.................. 2.00

37611 Green Beaver Lap Robes, fine quality heavy beaver cloth, with an overlay border 1 in. wide; size, 52x60 in.; weight, 50 oz.................. 3.90

37612 Green Beaver, extra heavy quality of fine grade beaver cloth, with wide worsted braid binding; has a colored silk braid inlay 3 in. from edge, with fancy corners of the same; size, 56x62 in.; weight, 58 oz........................ 6.35

Waterproof Lap Robes.

RUBBER ON ONE SIDE ONLY.

37620 Embroidered Gossamer Lap Robes. The latest robe out. Absolutely dust, wind and waterproof. In a variety of shades with the latest fancy designs embroidered in the center. Can be used in all seasons of the year; weight, each, 16 ounces. Each..........................$1.25

37622 Gossamer Waterproof Lap Robes. This style is reversible, being made with a silk finish rubber cloth on one side, and a pepper and salt colored cloth on the other, producing a modest, yet rich and elegant, protection against dust, wind or rain. Weight, 20 ounces. Each.. 2.00

37624 Heavy Rubber Face, lined with good quality plain black plush. This line will keep you warm and dry in the most inclement weather; size, 48x60 inches; weight, 4¼ lbs.....3.50

Wool Lap Robes.

37630 Media Wool Lap Robes, brown color with stripes, very superior goods for the money; size, 48x60 inches; weight, 3 lbs. Each.............$1.00

37632 Bengal Wool Lap Robes, brown and gray ground with border and colored stripes; bound all around. A popular brand; size, 52x62 inches; weight, 3 lbs. Each.................................. 1.35

37634 Peerless Wool Lap Robes, brown gray ground with three rows of various colored stripes across the length, neat and nobby. bound all around; size, 56x68 inches; weight, 3½ lbs. Each.. 1.60

37636 Scotland Wool Lap Robes, fancy block weave patterns, good quality of stock, bound all around; size, 54x62 inches; weight, 3 lbs. Each.. 2.00

37638 Premier Wool Lap Robes, made from fine selected lamb's wool in assorted patterns which are rich and handsome without being loud or gaudy; principally dark grounds; bound all around; size, 50x62 inches; weight, 3 lbs. Each.. 3.00

37640 Alpine Wool Lap Robes. These are very handsome fine wool lap robes, made in a combination of fancy stripes and block weave, any one of which will be sure to please. They are also reversible having patterns on each side; size, 58x60 inches; weight, 4 lbs. Each......... 3.50

Plush Lap Robes.

We can save you money on Plush Lap Robes.

We receive them direct from the manufacturers, who value our large orders and give us the best goods they have.

We can sell them to our customers, in any quantity, as cheap as dealers can buy them.

You do not pay any jobbers' profits. All new, fresh goods as perfect as they can be made.

37645 Pacific Plush Lap Robes. Each robe is made plain, in one solid color and is alike on both sides. Colors: Green, old gold and scarlet. Size. 46x60 inches; weight, 4 lbs. Mention color wanted. Each..............................$2.00

37647 Palisades Plush Lap Robes. These robes are made with plain backs and fancy fronts, a variety of colors and designs. The lowest priced fancy plush robe on the market. Size, 48x60 inches; weight, 4⅛ lbs. Each..................... 2.65

37649 "Prairie" Double Plush Lap Robes. This style has large animal pattern on either scarlet or canary color ground; size, 48x60 in.; weight, 5½ lbs. Each...................................... 3.20

37650 "Pilgrim" Double Plush Lap Robes, plain backs. New patterns on canary, cream, scarlet or brown color grounds Very handsome goods for the price; sizes, 50x60 in,; weight, 6 lbs. Each.. 3.90

37652 "Puritan" Double Plush Lap Robes; very handsome patterns on either canary, cream, tan or scarlet grounds. All new goods and new patterns, exceptional value; size, 50x60 in.; weight, 6½ lbs. Each.................. 4.50

37654 "Paragon" Double Plush Lap Robes. We have a large variety of new and handsome designs in this grade, on light, medium or dark color grounds. The quality of plush will surprise you; size, 52x60 in.; weight, 7 lbs. Each..5.30

37656 "Premium" Double Plush Lap Robes. This is an entirely new grade, which we have been induced to handle, tempted by the richness of the colorings. They are made in handsome floral and striped patterns on dark grounds. Plain backs. Size, 52x66 inches; weight, 7½ lbs. Each.. 6.45

37657 "Peerless' Plush Lap Robes, double and reversible, finest quality of plush, brilliant colorings, beautiful designs, sure to please. The best plush robe in the market; extra large; size, 52x68 in.; weight, 8 lbs. Each..................7.75

American Buffalo Robes.

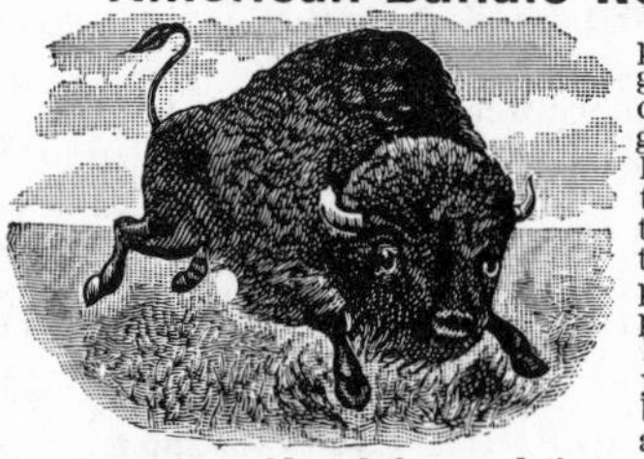

We do not present these goods to our customers as genuine buffalo hides, but as the best substitute for them that has yet appeared. This production has had several years trial, has been tested in all kinds of weather—wet, cold and dry—and the verdict to-day is that five years of rough general usage does not affect them any more than it would have done the old buffalo skin. They are a woven fabric, which much resembles the hide which gives them their name, and are handsome, durable, warm and waterproof.

37659 American Buffalo Robes, strong as any leather, handsome, soft and pliable, warmer than any skin robe, impervious to wind and moths, and are easily dried after having been wet. Made in dark brown color, suitably bordered, with lambskin cloth lining and an inside rubber lining. Size, 54x62 inches. Each. $11.25

Deodorized Goat Robes.

37660 Gray Japanese Goat Robes, deodorized, lined with medallion felt, scalloped border, size 48x60 inches. Weight, about 6½ lbs. Each... $3.30

37662 Gray Japanese Goat Robes, deodorized, lined with ruby plush, scalloped border; size 48x60 inches. Weight about 8 lbs. Each...... 4.00

37664 Gray Japanese Goat Robes, deodorized, lined with fancy medallion plush, scalloped border. Size, 48x60 inches. Weight, about 8 lbs. Each.. 5.25

37666 Large Gray Japanese Goat Robes, deodorized, lined with fine plain plush, double scalloped border; size, 52x64 inches; weight, about 9 lbs.. 5.75

37668 Large Gray Japanese Goat Robes, deodorized, lined with a fine grade of plush in medallion designs, double scalloped border; size, 54x-66 in; weight, about 10 lbs...................... 6.60

37670 Extra Large Gray Japanese Goat Robes, lined with heavy ruby plush, double scalloped border; size, 58x68 in.; weight, about 12 lbs... 7.00

37672 Extra Large Gray Japanese Goat Robes, lined with extra fine grade of plush in fancy patterns of novel design. This is the largest, heaviest and best gray robe made; size, 60x70 in. 8.25

Black Goat Robes are commonly sold as genuine bear. We sell them for what they are.

37674 Black Japanese Goat or Imitation Bear Robes, with new style Saratoga lining; size, 48x60 inches; weight, about 7 lbs.................. 4.90

37676 Black Japanese Goat or Imitation Bear Robes, green plush lined, double scalloped border; size, 48x60; weight, about 9 lbs. 5.75

37678 Black Japanese Goat or Imitation Bear Robes, plush lined, double scalloped border; 54x66 inches; weight, about 10 lbs. 7.00

37680 Large Black Japanese Goat or Imitation Bear Robes, lined with a heavy fancy plush in medallion designs, double border; size, 54x66 inches; weight, about 11 lbs...................... 8.25

37682 Extra Large Black Japanese Goat or Imitation Bear Robes, lined with a superior quality of medallion plush. These are the largest, heaviest and best black goat robes made. Only the very choicest skins are used; size, 60x70 in. 9.50

Dogskin Robes.

37684 Large Fawn Dog Robes, green plush lined, double scalloped border; size, 54x66 inches; weight, about 8½ lbs. Each...........$10.00

37686 Dyed Black China Dog Robes. These robes are choice goods, have fine close fur, are guaranteed free from injury in the dyeing, and are absolutely fast black; plush lined. Size, 54x66 ins. Weight, about 7½ lbs. Each.........11.00

37688 Gray Siberian Dog Robes, green plush lined, double scalloped border; size, 48x60 inches; weight about 7½ lbs. Each................ 8.25

37690 Gray Siberian Dog Robes, large size, green plush lined, double scalloped border; size, 54x66 inches; weight, about 9 lbs. Each.........10.50

Prairie Wolf Robes.

37693 Prairie Wolf Robes, 8 skins to the robe, selected stock. Green plush lined and double border. Size, 54x66 ins. Weight, about 7 lbs.$15.00

37694 Prairie Wolf Robes, very choicest skins, 8 skins to the robe, fancy plush lined and double border. Size, 54x66 ins. Weight, about 8 lbs...16.25

Galloway Robes.

37696 Black Galloway Fur Robes, natural color, strictly first quality. Each robe is made of the hide of one animal; the skins are soft and glove-like, but very tough. They are the best wearing fur robes at present on the market. Green plush lined, scalloped border. Size, 54 inches square. Weight, 10 lbs. Each..............................$13.50

37697 Black Galloway Fur Robes, strictly first quality, natural color. Each robe is made of the hide of one animal, green plush lined, scalloped border. Size, 60 inches square. Weight, 12 lbs. Each..15.00

37699 Black Galloway Fur Robes, common or standard quality. Each robe is the hide of one animal, green plush lined. Size, 54 inches square. Weight, each, 10 lbs. Each............11.25

37700 Black Galloway Fur Robes, common or standard quality, extra large size. Each robe made from one hide; green plush lined. Size, 60 inches square. Weight, each, 12 lbs. Each..12.75

Surcingles.

Weight, each, 10 oz. to 18 oz. Each

37702 Super Cotton Web, 3 inches wide, 1 inch strap and buckle, regular size $0.20

37703 Extra Cotton Web, 3¼ inches wide, 1 inch buckle and strap, regular size .... .25

37704 Extra Fancy Union Web, 3½ inches wide, 1⅛ inch buckle and strap, regular size .... .35

37705 Padded Surcingles, super cotton web, 3 inches wide, 1 inch strap .... .35

37706 Padded Surcingles, twilled cotton web, 3¼ inches wide, 1¼ inch strap .... .45

37707 Padded Surcingles, extra cotton web, 4 in. wide, 1¼ inch strap .... .55

37708 Extra Cotton Web, 4 inches wide, 1¼ inch strap and buckle, 8 feet long. Extra length for large horses .... .40

37709 Padded Surcingles for large horses, extra cotton web, 4 inches wide, 1¼ inch strap and buckle, 8 feet long .... .60

HORSE BLANKETS.
Shaped Horse Blankets.

Please note that horse blankets are not sold by the pair. Price quoted is for single blanket.

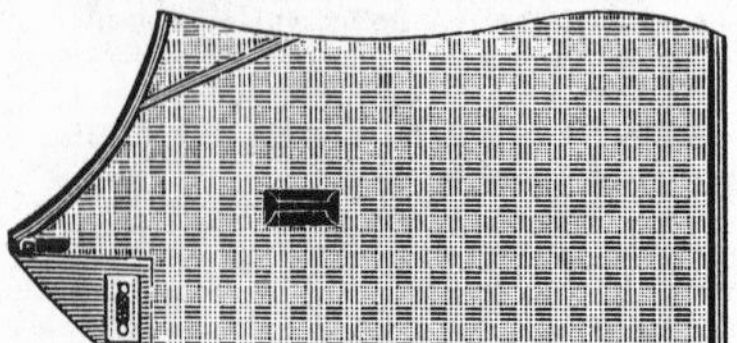

37712 Shaped or Stable Blankets, common size, ruby and gray checks, bound all around, doubled in front, one strap. Weight, 4 lbs. Price, each $0.85

37714 Eastern Shaped or Stable Blankets, gray plaids, new patterns; strapped in front, bound all around. Weight, 4¼ lbs. Price, each. .90

37716 "Hilltop" Shaped or Stable Blankets, dark blue and dark gray plaids, web bound, one strap on front. Standard size. Weight, each, 5½ lbs. Price, each 1.00

37718 Wayside; Shaped or Stable Blankets, 72 inches long, 36 inches deep, flat bound, leather pockets, figure 4 stay; double weave in handsome dark checks; will fit horses from 1,000 to 1,300 lbs. Weight, each 6 lbs. Price, each...... 1.25

37720 Old Honesty; Shaped or Stable Blankets, gray and blue plaids, 74 inches long; contain miles of heavy warp; boot web trimmed and heavy flat binding. Weight, about 7 lbs. each. Price, each 1.50

37722 5-A Eight Mile Shaped Blankets. This well known and popular style has over eight miles of strong warp threads to each blanket; leather surcingle pockets; figure four stay; flat bound; 75 inches long; 40 inches deep; and weighs 7½ lbs. Each 1.80

37724 Ontario Stable Blankets. These are fine grade goods, have checker-board pattern, are strongly made, well bound and strapped, and will give satisfaction; weight, about 7 lbs. Each .. 1.75

37726 Beaver Shaped Blankets. This style is made with double warps, gray and gold mixed grounds with fancy stripes, superior quality, extra size, is bound over the edge and is well stayed, has leather surcingle keepers, and is doubled where buckles and billets are sewed on; weight, about 7½ pounds 1.85

37728 Chicago Stable Blankets are new goods, made for us from our own designing; are very handsome, have double warps, are well bound and full size, and will prove splendid value: weight, about 7 lbs. Each 2.00

37730 5-A Philadelphia Blankets, fit a horse like a tailor-made coat, and have two surcingle attachments which hold the blanket securely on the horse. Blankets sold on this number are all cut 80 inches long and are shaped like a hood at the back so as to cover the horse's tail and protect it. Heavy brown duck outside, ribbed woolen lining inside. Weight, 7 lbs. Each.... 2.25

37732 5-A Philadelphia Blankets, made of same material and in same style throughout as No. 37730 blankets, but are for large horses, being cut 90 inches long. This is the largest size in which these blankets are made. They are intended to fit horses weighing from 1,200 to 1,500 lbs. Weight, 7½ lbs. Each 2.50

37736 Newmarket Stable Blankets. These blankets are made especially for Montgomery Ward & Co. and are as strong as horse blankets can be made. A horse cannot tear them. If you want a stable blanket that will stand hard wear you cannot do better than order one or more of this style. They are made in small checks, known as the "Baker" plaid; are full standard size and weight 7½ lbs. Each 2.50

37738 5-A Extra Test Shaped or Stable Horse Blankets, 72 inches long, 40 inches deep, two swell sewed straps, boot web bound, leather pockets, warm woolen lining made strong by the face. A handsome, well-known and popular blanket. Will fit average horses from 1,000 to 1,300 lbs. Weight, each 6 lbs. Price each..... 3.00

Men of Medicine...

Send 2 cents for our Catalogue of Medical and Scientific Works. We can save you something.

Square Horse Blankets.

Please note that Horse Blankets are not sold by the pair. Price quoted is for single blanket.

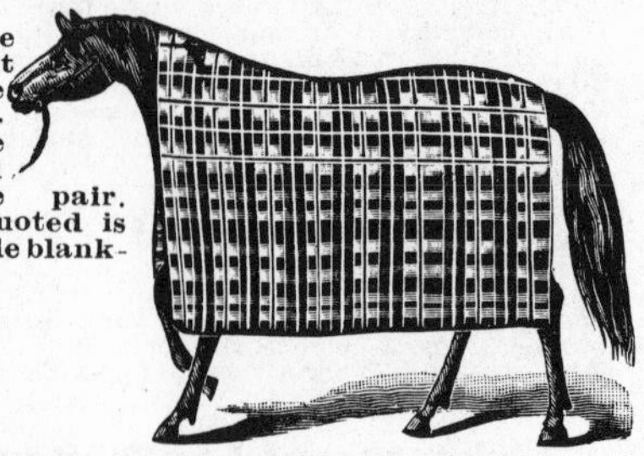

37742 Peru Square Horse Blankets, brown, gray ground, fancy headings, cloth finish, Size, 72x76 inches. Weight, 4¼ lbs. Price, each.... $0.75

37744 Emporia Square Horse Blankets. New fancy print, large blue plaids, stayed strap, common size. Weight, each about 4¾ lbs. Price, each .... .90

37746 Fernwood Square Horse Blankets. Red mixed ground, large fancy headings, one strap, standard size; a very superior blanket for the money. Price, each 1.00

37748 5-A Traders' Square Blankets. The cheapest 5-A square blanket ever sold. Very strong; woven with extra quantity of warps. Fancy stripes, fancy borders. Each 1.25

37752 Syrian Square Blankets. These blankets are made of good stock, have strong warps and a woolly face, and are woven in bright stripes; excellent value for the price; 76x80 in.; weight, 5 pounds, each 1.50

37754 Storm King Square Blankets. The old reliable, fancy stripes, crowded warps, improved finish, extra large and heavy; sewed straps, extra stay at straps; size, 84x90 inches; weight, about 8 pounds. Each 1.75

37756 5-A Trojan Wool Square Horse Blankets. Gray ground, large fancy plaids, extra strong; sewed straps with 5-A stay; the cheapest, strongest and most popular scoured and fulled, plaided wool, square blanket on the market; size, 76x80 inches; weight, each, 5 lbs. Each. 1.90

37760 Mascot Square Blankets. Light gray and dark gray stripes alternating, with wide fancy borders; sewed straps; size 80x84 inches; weight, 6 pounds. Each 2.00

37762 Hamiltonian Square Blankets. These blankets are large size, made of good stock, three different colored stripes, three inches wide and extra wide, bright colored borders, sewed straps. Size, 84x90 inches; weight, 7 lbs. Each 2.20

37764 Caledonia Plaid Square Blankets. Made with double warps, gray ground, large fancy plaids, bright borders, sewed straps, and altogether a very attractive and serviceable line. Size, 84x90 ins.; weight, 7 lbs. Each 2.50

37766 5-A Russian All Wool Square Horse Blankets. All bright, attractive colors. The strongest, best and cheapest all wool fancy plaid blanket in the market, sewed straps. Size, 76x80 ins.; weight, 5 lbs. Each 2.75

37768 Genuine "J. I. C." Square Wool Horse Blankets, brown, gray ground with bright narrow stripes, and wide fancy border, sewed straps; size, 84x90 inches; weight, 7 pounds. Each.... 2.90

37770 Alaska Square Horse Blankets, extra large size, extra heavy, fine quality of stock, light and dark gray stripes, with fancy border; just the blanket for the wind-swept prairies of the West or the lumber districts in the Northwest; size, 90x96 inches; weight, 10 lbs. Each 2.98

37772 "Success" All Wool Square Horse Blankets, dark grounds, large plaids. Size, 76x80 inches Weight, 5 lbs. Each 3.00

37774 Enterprise All Wool Square Horse Blankets, large size, woven in black and scarlet checks and plaids, sewed straps; size, 80x84 ins.; weight, 6 lbs. Each 3.50

37776 5-A Royal All Wool Square Horse Blankets, large size, all bright colors, assorted fancy plaids, sewed straps. One will make a good lap robe as well as a street blanket; size, 84x90 ins.; weight, 7 lbs. Each 4.25

37778 "Nancy Hanks," extra fine square, wool horse blankets, woven in large plaids, box weave patterns, six colors in each blanket, sewed straps. A very attractive street blanket. Size, 80x84 in. Weight, 6 lbs. Each 4.60

Storm Blankets.

All our lumbermen's storm blankets are as perfect as skilled labor can produce them. They are shaped by goring on the neck, and the parts that receive the most strain are carefully strengthened.

37784 Storm Blankets, made of fine brown canvas, lined with a heavy part wool gray lining, well made, with close and strong stitching. Size, 72x80 inches. Weight, each, 6 pounds. Price, each $1.50

37785 Storm Blankets, fine brown canvas, lined with a heavy brown rib wool lining, a very superior blanket for the price. Size, 76x80 inches. Weight, 7½ pounds. Price, each...... 1.75

37787 Storm Blankets, very fine salmon and black plaid canvas, with a very heavy brown rib wool lining; edges turned up at the bottom, giving extra strength. Size, 80x76 inches. Weight, about 6½ pounds. Price, each 1.85

37788 Storm Blankets, very fine brown canvas, lined with extra heavy rib wool lining, well made with strong close stitching and re-enforced at the gore on the neck. Size, 80x80 inches. Weight, about 8 pounds each. Each.. 2.00

Blankets—Continued.

37790 Storm Blankets, very fine 12 ounce brown canvas, lined with a heavy brown rib wool lining; one of the largest and best storm blankets on the market. Size, 84x90 inches. Weight, each 8½ pounds. Price, each $2.50

37791 Storm Blankets, special, extra fine brown canvas with a 6 pound square blanket for lining, two straps on front, and made with three extra rows of stitching on each side, by which the strength and service is greatly increased. Size, 84x86 inches. Weight, 9 pounds. Each. 3.00

Burlington Blankets.

The Burlington Stable Blankets are the most perfect in construction of anything in the blanket line yet placed on the market. They are made to fit: will remain in position; require no surcingles, and can be used in all seasons of the year.

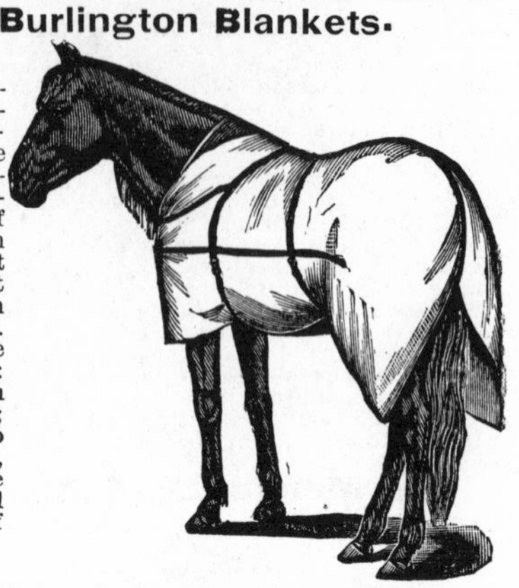

Size 24 will fit a horse weighing from 900 to 1,050 lbs.
Size 26 will fit a horse weighing from 1,050 to 1,250 lbs.
Size 28 will fit a horse weighing from 1,250 to 1,400 lbs.
Size 30 will fit a horse weighing from 1,350 to 1,500 lbs.

Extra sizes made to order at an additional cost of 25 cents each. Be sure and mention size wanted.

37794 Burlington No. 6; made of very heavy and fine 12 ounce bright Hessian, mangled finish burlap, the best made. Without lining. The best and strongest burlap stable blanket on the market. Please state sizes wanted. Each..... $1.00

37795 Burlington No. 73; made of heavy duck, buff grounds, black plaids. A very handsome stable blanket. Please state sizes wanted. Each 1.45

37797 Burlington No. 0; made of heavy 11 ounce brown canvas, without lining, well stayed with heavy and strong corded webbing and equipped with the best and most easily adjusted fastenings. Please mention sizes wanted. Each 1.75

37799 Burlington No. 8; made of same material as No. 6, and in same style, with heavy brown ribbed wool lining. Please mention sizes wanted. Each 2.00

37800 Burlington No. 60; made of fawn color canvas in the well-known Burlington "Stay-On" style, with a heavy brown ribbed wool lining. Please mention sizes wanted. Each...... 2.25

37802 Burlington No. 10; made of same material as No. 0, and in same style, but with a heavy ribbed wool lining. Please mention sizes wanted. Each 2.70

Chase's Adjustable Blankets.

For stable use. Being adjustable are an improvement on common stable blankets. Fit closely. Have two attached surcingles with snaps, and cannot be pulled off. Regular size is adjustable to fit a horse weighing from 900 to 1,400 lbs.

37806 Made of cream plaid burlap. Each $1.00

37807 Made of 9 oz. plaid duck. Each 1.60

Horse Suits.

Blankets with folded breast to button. Hoods with jowl to button.

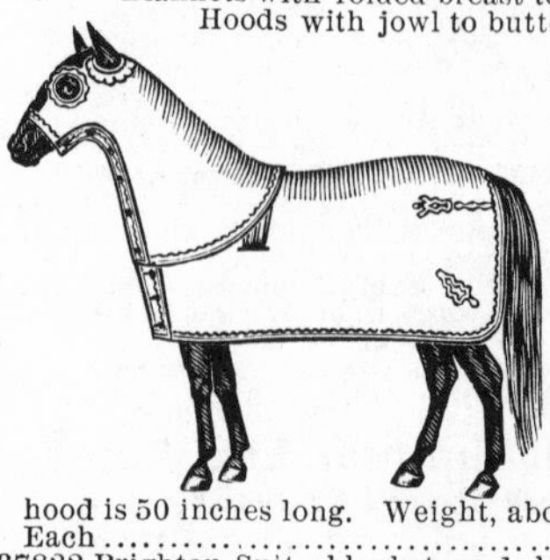

37820 Belmont Suit, blanket and long hood to button, warranted to be extra superfine, *all wool*, woven in bright fancy plaids of a new pattern in drab and scarlet grounds Chinese bindings over edge, size of blanket, 38x72 inches hood is 50 inches long. Weight, about 6 lbs. Each $8.00

37822 Brighton Suit, blanket and long hood to button, superfine *all wool* in red and blue fancy plaids, Chinese binding over edge; size of blanket, 38x72 inches, hood is 50 inches long; weight, about 6½ lbs. Each 6.25

37824 Linsey-Woolsey Horse Suits, square blanket and long hood, both to tie. Blanket is 40 inches deep, 72 inches long. Whole suits, blue and red stripes, scarlet bound. Per suit.... 5.50 Weight, per suit, 4 lbs.

37826 Linen Horse Suits, fancy plaid, shaped blanket, extra deep, to buckle over the breast; long hood to tie. Flat web bound and well stayed. Price, per suit .... 2.67 Weight, per suit, 2¾ lbs.

Sweat Blankets.

37830 Extra Superfine All Wool Sweats, fancy plaids, in handsome drab grounds. Nothing better made; size, 90x96 inches; weight, from 5 to 5½ lbs. Each.............................. 5.25

Cooling Blankets.

37832 Extra Superfine All Wool Coolers, in fancy plaids of assorted colors. First-class goods in every respect; size 84x90 inches, weight, 2½ lbs. Each.. 3.00

37834 Union Cooler, fancy plaids, with brown grounds, medium grade, full value; size, 84x90 inches; weight, 2¾ lbs. Each..................... 2.25

37836 Imitation Wool Coolers; these are really cotton stock, but have a nappy surface and fine finish and closely resemble all wool goods. Assorted grounds and plaids in small checks; size, 84x90 inches; weight, 2½ lbs. Each........... 1.35

Sweat Hoods.

Long Hood.   Throat Hood.

Long and short hoods made to button. Throat hoods made to strap.

37838 Plain White Sweat Hoods warranted all wool, finely bound.

	Long.	Short.	Throat
Each	$3.35	$1.65	$0.90
Weight	35 oz.	18 oz.	8 oz.

37840 Fancy Plaid Sweat Hoods, warranted all wool.

	Long.	Short.	Throat.
Each	$3.75	$1.90	$1.00
Weight	35 oz.	18 oz.	8 oz.

Turf Goods.

We have the cheapest, strongest, most practical and best line of horse boots in this or any market.

Ankle Boots.

37842 Ankle Boots, molded russet leather, one strap; weight, per pair, 3 ozs.
Per pair.... .... $0.30
Per doz. prs 3.25

37844 Ankle Boots, heavy pressed leather ankle, calfskin wrap, machine stitched, 2 straps.

Per pair $0.60
Weight, per pair, 9 ozs.

37846 Ankle Boots, can be used on either front or hind ankles. Heavy leather shield, kersey lining and wrap, chamois bound, two straps.
Per pair................... $1.00
Weight, per pair, 7 ozs,

37848 Front Leg Shin and Ankle Boots, kersey wrap, chamois bound; leather cap, three straps; length, 9½ ins. Weight, per pair, 9 ozs. Price, per pair.............$1.20

37850 Hind Leg Shin and Ankle Boots, kersey lined, chamois bound, leather cap, three straps; length, 11½ inches. Weight, per pair, 13 ozs.

37848-50   Price, per pair. $1.50

Boots—Continued.

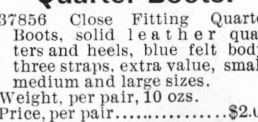

37852 Straight Shin Boots, front or hind, kersey wrap, chamois bound, leather cap, three straps; length, 8½ inches. Weight, per pair, 10 ozs.
Price, per pair.................$1.50

37854 Front Shin and Ankle Boots, wool kersey wrap and wide elastic, chamois bound, 3 straps; length, 10 inches. Weight, per pair, 11 ozs
Price, per pair $1.80

Quarter Boots.

37856 Close Fitting Quarter Boots, solid leather quarters and heels, blue felt body, three straps, extra value, small, medium and large sizes. Weight, per pair, 10 ozs.
Price, per pair................$2.00

37858 Close Fitting Quarter Boots, elkskin lined, solid leather quarters and heels, three straps. The most serviceable boot in the market, small, medium and large. Weight, per pair, 11 ozs.
Price, per pair $3.25

37860 Hinged Quarter Boot, side action, elkskin lined California style, hand made, small, medium or large.
Per pair.....................$3.75

37862 Quarter Boots, solid leather body and quarters, elkskin lined, chamois bound at top, two straps. Weight, per pair, 12 ozs.
Price, per pair...,....... $2.35

37864 Bell Quarter Boots, solid black leather body, wool lined, with wool roll around the top; small, medium and large sizes. Weight, per pair, 14 ozs.
Price, per pair............$2.40

Swabs or Soaking Boots.

37866 Soaking Boots, to buckle over horses hoofs to keep them soft. Made of six thicknesses of Baker kersey with four rows of stitching. Soak well with water and apply in the evening. They will keep wet all night. Per pair $1.00

Weight, per pair, 20 oz.

Knee Boots.

37870 Knee Boots, made of solid black leather, chamois lined all through, strong and substantial, sure protection for horses that knock their knees.
Per pair. $2.40
Weight, per pair, 12 oz.

Scalping Boots.

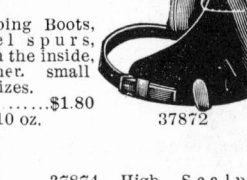

37872 Plain Scalping Boots, made with steel spurs, padded at top on the inside, solid russet leather. small medium or large sizes.
Price, per pair... ....$1.80
Weight, per pair, 10 oz.

37872

37874 High Scalping Boots, made with heel extensions and steel spurs. Top padded inside, solid russet leather, small, medium or large sizes.
Price, per pair.......$1.85
Weight, per pair, 11 oz.

Toe Weights.

37876 The Stick Fast Toe Weight, the best in the market. These weights have an improvement which consists of a small spur resting on the shoe. The weight and spur being one piece prevents jar on the hoof and relieves the screws of all strain. Weight, 2, 3, 4, 6, 8 and 10 oz. each. When ordering give weight wanted.
Price, per pair.........$1.25

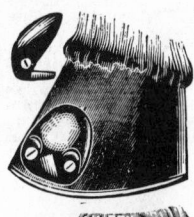

37878 Fenton's Security Toe Weights, with detachable spurs. The best known weights and the most popular, with all horsemen. Weight 2, 3, 4, 5, 6, 8 and 10 ounces each.
Price. per pair....$1.25
Be sure and mention weight desired.

Rubbing Cloths.

37880 Genuine Imported Ashton Salt Sacks for rubbing cloths; full size, best quality.
Each.............$0.40.   Per dozen...........$4.50

Interfering Device.

37882 This device has been in use for some time, and has never failed to stop the most obstinate case of interfering, and in most cases can be dispensed with after using from 10 days to three weeks. They will spread the colt's gait and make him a wide traveler. Every horseman will understand the merits of them when seen.
Price, per pair..................... $1.25
Each........................ .65
Weight, per pair, 12 oz.

Derby Bandages, Cotton.

Full length, 6 feet, with strings.
37884 White Bandages, 4 to the set, per set.....$0.40
37885 Brown Bandages, 4 to the set, per set...... .45
Weight, per set, 14 oz.
37886 Fine Wool Derby Bandages, fawn colored, per set of 4 .... 1.45
Weight, per set, 12 oz.

Trotting Balls.

37888 Rubber Trotting Balls
Per string.............$0.16
Per doz. strings........ 1.75
Weight, per string, 7 oz.

Whip Spurs.

37890 Whip Spurs. To be used on a whip to rub on a horse's hips when speeding.
Each $0.90
Postage.................. .03

Horse Tooth Rasps.

37892 House's Patent Horse Tooth Rasps, with handles (handle not shown in cut), fine, polished, complete and ready for use.
Each $1.20
Weight, each, 24 oz.
37893 Extra Steel Files, 3½ inches long, for horse tooth rasps. Each........................ .. .20
Weight, each, 4 oz.

Horse Tail Holder.

37895 For clasping and holding together the hair of the "horse's tail," protecting it from the mud.
Each $0.18
Per dozen.................. ...... 2.00

Common Sense Horse Tail Clasp.

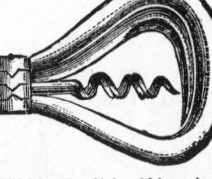

37896 This is a simple device for holding the hair of a horse's tail. It is made of one piece of spring brass, without buckles or other contrivances.
Each....................$0.14
Per dozen 1.50
Weight, each, 2 oz.

Hoof Picks.

37898 Hoof Pick and Corkscrew, combined.
Each................. $0.35
37899 Hoof Pick, single instrument.
Each............. $0.25
Weight, each, 4 oz.

37902 English Clipping Shears, with leather covered bows, 7½ inches long.
Each................$1.10

Weight, each, 6 oz.

Combs—Continued.

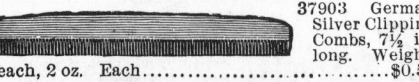

37903 German Silver Clipping Combs, 7½ in. long. Weight, each, 2 oz. Each.....................$0.50

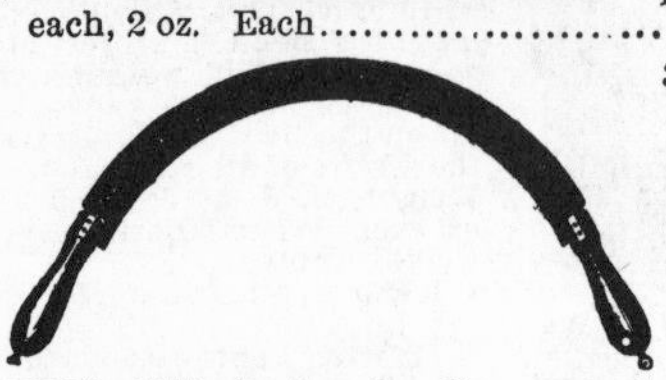

37906 Brass Sweat Scrapers, 1½ in. wide, 20 in. long, with wood handles on each end. Each ..$0.40 Per doz. 4.50

37907 With leather handles on each end. Each ....$0.55 Per dozen..........6.00 Weight, each, 12 oz.

Wood Sweat Scraper.

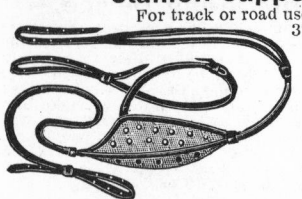

37908 Wood Scrapers. Each......$0.15 Weight, each, 4 oz.

Horse Blanket Pins.

37910 Blanket Pins, protected points; size, 3½ in. Per dozen..............$0.40 Weight, per doz., 8 oz.

Stallion Support.

For track or road use.

37912 This support is manufactured from the purest quality of rubber made, and has met with universal success with all horsemen and stallion owners. Weight, each, 10 oz Each........$2.00

DIRECTIONS.

When not in use keep in a cool, dark place. Before applying wring out pouch in water. When ordering, state size, small, medium or large.

Cribbing Muzzles.

37915 Cribbing Muzzles, made entirely of leather, 1-inch head piece, ⅝-inch throat latch. The sections are held in place by copper rivets, which are fastened by hand. Each.......................$1.10 Weight, each, about 15 ounces.

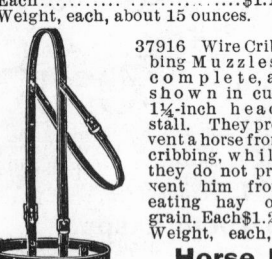

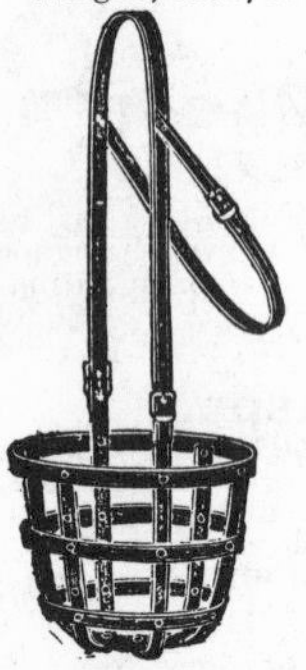

37916 Wire Cribbing Muzzles, complete, as shown in cut, 1¼-inch headstall. They prevent a horse from cribbing, while they do not prevent him from eating hay or grain. Each $1.25 Weight, each, about 30 ounces.

Horse Muzzles.

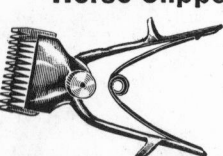

37918 Leather Horse Muzzle, made of No. 1 russet leather, having 1¼ inch halter attachment and ⅝ inch throat latch. Each.............$1.40 Weight, each, 25 oz.

37920 Wire Horse Muzzle, is made of woven wire, and bound with woolly sheepskin, having 1¼ in. halter attachment, and ⅝ inch throat latch Each...........$1.50 Weight, each, 36 oz.

37920

Horse Clippers.

37921 Spring Clippers, "One Hand" Horse or Dog Clippers, well made, keen cutting, with a strong elastic spring, made for trimming about the ears and fetlocks of horses, and will give perfect satisfaction for clipping dogs; nickel plated. Each.....................$2.00 Weight, 12 ounces.

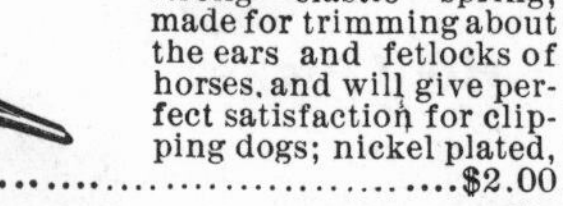

37923 American Horse Clippers, extra fine finish, oval handles, detachable plates; the cutting knives are highly tempered and each clipper is guaranteed to be in perfect order when packed. Each ....$1.75 Weight, each, 20 ounces.

Clippers—Continued.

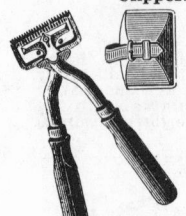

37924 The Genuine Newmarket Horse Clippers (imported), are the most popular in the market; cutting plates of best refined steel. Each...............$2.00 Weight Per pair, 18 oz. Extra top plates, each 75 Extra bottom plates, each...............$1.05 Postage on extra plates, 4c.

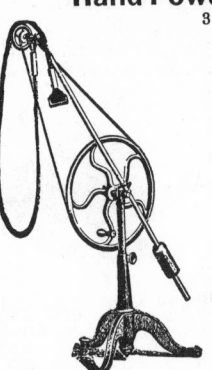

37926 French Horse Clippers, These are imported goods. which we can sell for about the price of a single cutting plate. They have self-adjusting set screws. We positively cannot furnish any extra parts. Length, 10⅝ in.; weight, 14 ounces. Each..........$1.15 *See Index for Toilet Hair Clippers.*

Hand Power Machine.

37928 This Hand Power Clipping Machine is the most substantial, powerful, light running, noiseless machine on the market. The base is of such design and proportion that the machine stands perfectly firm at all times, whether the floor is even or not. The balance wheel is 24 inches in diameter and runs on a turned steel shaft. All bearings are of steel, perfectly fitted and interchangeable. The connection for conveying power from head to cutting knives is by means of an improved flexible shaft, which can be curved and bent in any direction, insuring perfect freedom of motion and extensive range. The knives are of the finest steel, and tempered by an improved process. Every one is tested before leaving the manufacturers and is warranted to be in perfect cutting condition. Full directions for setting up and operating sent with each machine. Weight, boxed ready for shipment, 100 pounds. Price of machine, complete.........$32.50 Extra handles, each, $3.00 Extra knives, per set, 4.00

Singeing Lamps.

37930 Singeing Lamps for removing hair from horses' ears and other places where clippers can not be used to advantage; use kerosene oil; wick furnished with lamp. Each...$2.50

Feed Bags.

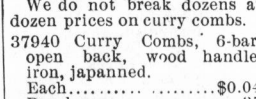

	Each	Per doz.

37934 Cotton Duck Body, soft leather bottom, leather ventilator; weight, each 12 oz...............$0.55 $6.00

37936 Extra Heavy Cotton Duck Body, heavy sole leather bottom, leather ventilator on side and leather bound top....... .75 8.25

Curry Combs.

We do not break dozens at dozen prices on curry combs.

37940 Curry Combs, 6-bar open back, wood handle, iron, japanned. Each.................$0.04 Per dozen.............. .35 Weight, each, 4 oz.

37942 Curry Comb. The standard 7-bar open back, extra refined, well riveted best malleable iron frames, heavy knockers, hardwood handle.

37942   37944

Each................$0.09 Per dozen..........$0.90 Weight, each, 10 oz.

37944 Curry Comb, 8-bar, heavy iron, closed back, heavy wrought iron shank; brace runs through handle and riveted, heavy iron knockers, all well riveted, black enameled. Each..... .13 Per dozen ..... 1.35 Weight, each, 13 oz.

Curry Combs—Continued.

37946 Curry Comb, Climax, 8-bars, fine steel, closed back, japanned, malleable iron, tinned frame, iron knockers, all well riveted, black enameled handle. Each.....................$0.15 Per dozen....................1.55 Weight, each, 10 ounces.

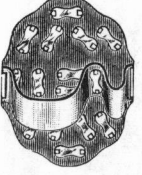

37948 The "Magnetic" Curry Comb. This comb, as its name implies, is made of a magnetic metal; it will not cut the hide or skin of the animal; is a positive self-cleaner; will not rust, and is absolutely unbreakable. Each.................$0.25 Per dozen.........................2.70 Weight, each, about 13 ounces.

Back View. 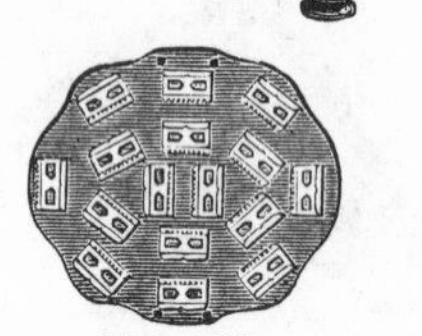   Front View.

37950 The "Perfect" Horse Cleaner. The construction of these cleaners is the adjusting of small sections of metal plates, with teeth and scrapers at different angles, to a flexible back in brush form. While rough team or farm horses and thin coated roadsters or drivers can be cleaned with equal facility, it is impossible to scratch or mark a horse with them. Each.....$0.25 Per dozen.........................2.70

37952   37954

37952 Curry Comb, warranted steel, 8-bar, extra heavy steel, blued, black enameled handle pinned to wrought iron shank. Each....................$0.18 Weight, each, 15 oz. Per dozen.................1.95

37954 Curry Comb, the Climax, all steel 8-bar, closed back, extra heavy steel shank passing through handle and riveted; steel knockers. ☞ We call your special attention to this comb. It is undoubtedly the best for the money in this market. Each....$0.22 Per dozen........$2.40 Weight, each, 15 oz.

Combination Mane and Curry Comb.

37956 Closed Back, 2-bar, japanned iron. Each................$0.05 Per dozen..............$0.50 Weight, each, 6 oz.

37960 Mane and Curry Comb combined, new pattern, extra heavy 6 bar, tinned iron. Each.............$0.15 Per dozen.....1.62 Weight, each, 12 oz.

37960

37962 Imported English Curry Combs, 7 rounding bars, closed back, strong and durable. The finest comb in the country. Each....$0.30 Per dozen..........3.25 Weight, each, 10 oz.

37963

37963 The "Humane" Curry Comb. This is the only comb fit to use on horses' legs or on clipped or short haired horses. it is impossible to hurt a horse with it. It is also the best thing ever produced for a cattle cleaner. Each.......$0.15 Per dozen...............$1.62 Weight, each, 6 ounces.

37965

37965 Circular Steel Spring Curry Combs. Three complete circles of steel working independent of each other, attached to an iron back by a hinged joint, wood handles. A good solid comb. Each..............$0.17 Per dozen...................1.82 Weight, each, 10 ounces.

TRUNKS AND TRAVELING BAGS.—We are decidedly IN IT on these goods.

Curry Combs—Continued.

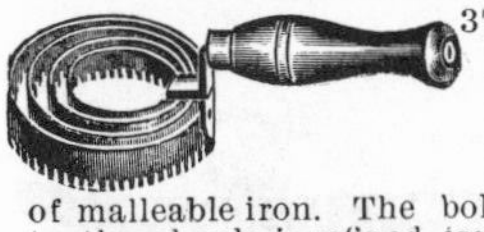

37966 South Bend Spring Curry Comb. This comb is made out of a clock spring and is the best and finest steel. The shank is the best quality of malleable iron. The bolt holding the blade to the shank is refined iron. The handle is turned from seasoned wood and is well finished. Each............$0.16 Per dozen.............$1.75
Weight, each, 8 ounces.

Horse Curry Cards.

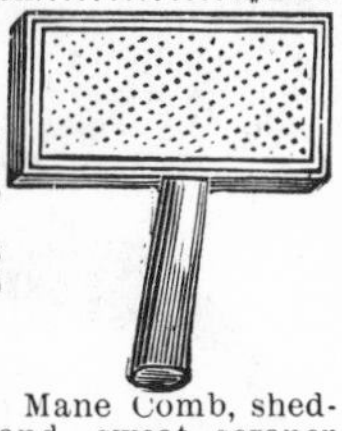

37968 Large, 3½x8¼ inch, first quality. Each..............$0.09
Per dozen.......................... .95
37969 Small, 3½x5½ inch. Each.......................... .08
Per dozen........................ .85
Weight, each, 8 ounces.

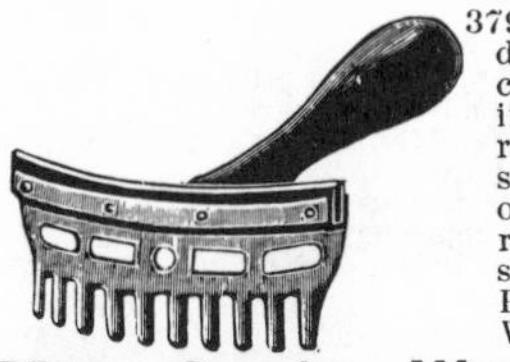

37970 Mane Comb, shedder and sweat scraper combined. A good,strong iron mane comb, with a rubber shedder or sweat scraper, 5½ inches long on the back. Far superior to a wooden sweat scraper. Each.....$0.15
Per dozen.......... 1.62
Weight, each, 8 ozs.

Mane Combs, Warranted Not to Warp or Split.

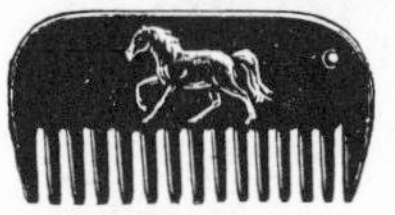

37974

37974 Black Rubber Mane Combs, figure of horse on one side; extra-quality; size, 2¾x5 inches. Each..........$0.15
Per dozen................. 1.65
Weight, each, 2 ounces

37975 Black Rubber Mane Combs, good quality, plain; size, 2½x4½ inches. Each................$0.09
Per dozen.......................................1.00

Horse Brushes.

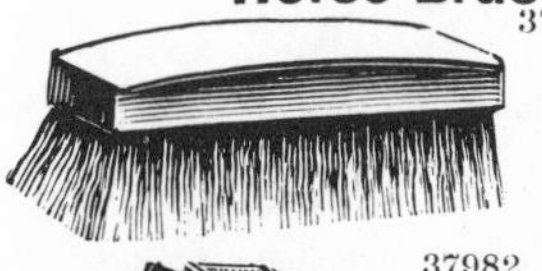

37980 Horse Brushes' Mexican rice root, 2 row, 8 inches. Each.......$0.10
Per dozen...... 1.10
Weight, each, 10 oz.

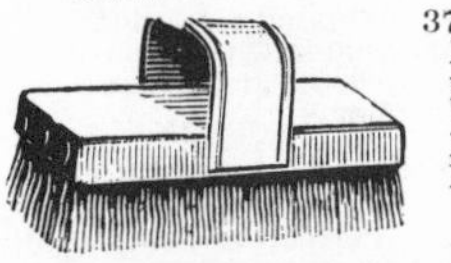

37982 Mexican Rice Root Horse Brushes, solid strapped back: size, 2¾x7 in Weight, each, 7 oz. Each.................$0.12
Per dozen............ 1.35

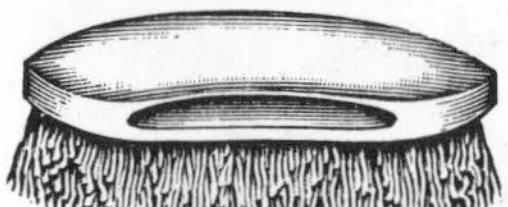

37984 Mexican Rice Root, round back, pointed ends. Size, 2½x11 inches. Each............$0.15
Per dozen........ 1.65

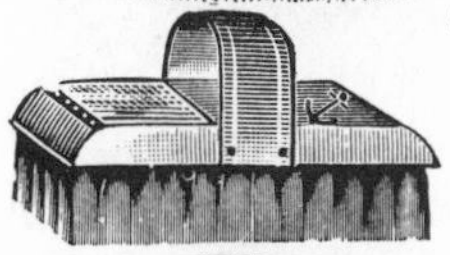

37986 The Famous "Anchor" brand horse brush. All Palmetto fiber, solid back, with hand strap (see cut); size, 2¾x7 in. Each...............$0.20
Per dozen.......... 2.25
Weight, each, 10 oz.

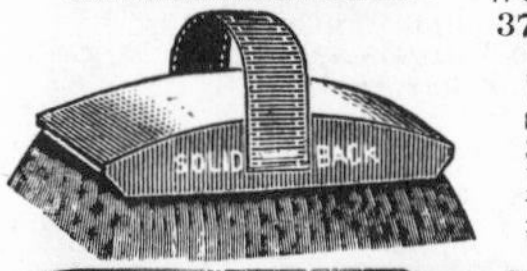

37988 All Palmetto, rounded solid back, beveled ends, hand strap (see cut); size, 3¼x6½ inches. Each............$0.25
Per dozen........ 2.75
Weight, each, 11 oz.

37990

37990 "Pug" Horse Brushes. All Palmetto, solid back, face size, 2¾x10 inches. This is the same grade of goods as the well known "Anchor" and "Ruf and Redy" brushes.
Each $0.25
Weight, each, 13 oz. Per dozen............... 2.65

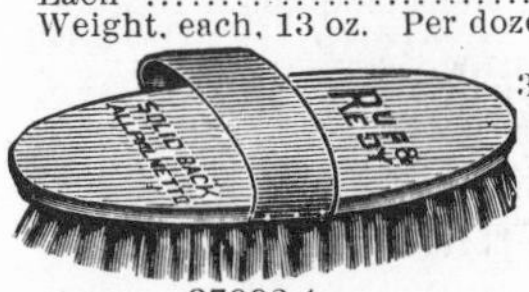

37992-4

37992 The Celebrated "Ruf and Redy" solid wood back, all Palmetto horse brush. Size, 4½x10 inches. Each............$0.30
Per dozen...... 3.25
Weight, each, 15 oz.

37994 Italian Rice Root, solid back, hand strap, same shape as 37992, size, 5x10 inches, excellent value Each..........$0.25 Per dozen..........$2.75
Weight, each, 10 oz.

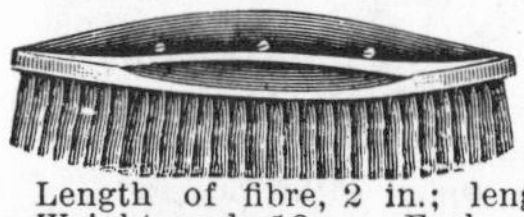

37996 Dandy Brushes. Fine imported dandy horse brushes, made of the best selected Italian rice root, with English wood backs. Length of fibre, 2 in.; length of brush, 10½ in. Weight, each, 12 oz. Each.....................$0.60
Per dozen.................. 6.48

Brushes—Continued.

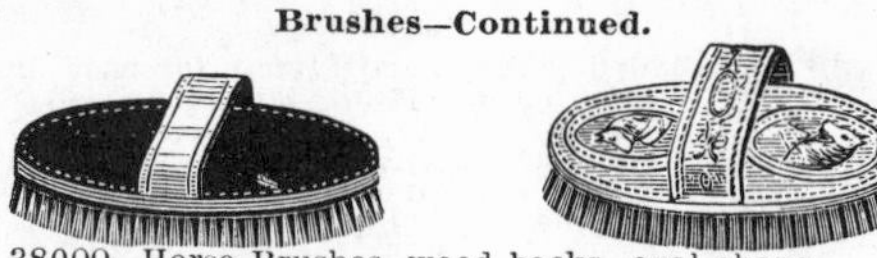

38000 Horse Brushes, wood backs, oval shape, all tampico-gray, center with white row outside. A large and well filled brush. Each. $0.15
Weight, each, 11 oz. Per dozen....... 1.62

38001 Horse Brushes, leather backs, oval shape, gray tampico stock with white outside row. Weight, each, 7 oz. Each.. .20
Per dozen.................... 2.16

38003 Horse Brushes, leather backs, oval shape gray tampico center, with an outside row of black bristles. Weight, each, 9 ozs. Each..... .25
Per dozen.... 2.70

	Each.	Per doz
38004 Horse Brushes, leather back, army pattern, gray center, outside row of white bristle. Weight, each, 10 ounces	$0.33	$3.60
38006 Horse Brushes, leather back, oval shape, flat face, all black bristle. A large sightly brush that will give good service. Weight, each, 12 oz	.40	4.35
38007 Horse Brushes,grain leather back, army pattern, best grade of gray tampico center, with an outside row of white bristles. Weight, each, 10 oz	.50	5.40
38009 Horse Brushes, grained russet, leather back, oval shape, all white American bristles. Weight, each, 12 ounces	.60	6.50
38010 Horse Brushes, oval face, solid leather backs, 15 rows all black bristles. Weight, each, 10 oz	.80	8.65
38012 Horse Brushes, oval shape, leather backs, warranted all gray Russia bristles; splendid value. Weight, each, 10 oz	1.00	10.80
38013 Horse Brushes, oval face, solid leather backs, all brown bristles. Weight, each, 10 oz	1.25	13.60
38015 Horse Brushes, solid leather backs, oval shape, 15 rows, all white Russia bristles, oval face. Weight, each, 11 oz	1.50	16.20
38016 Horse Brushes, oval face, solid leather backs, 19 rows, extra length, brown Russia bristles. Weight, each, 11 oz	2.00	21.60
38018 Horse Brushes, solid leather backs, oval shape, 19 rows of natural yellow Russia bristles. This grade will wear as well as anything money can buy. Weight, each, 13 oz	2.50	27.00

Gig Saddles.

FOR SINGLE HARNESS.

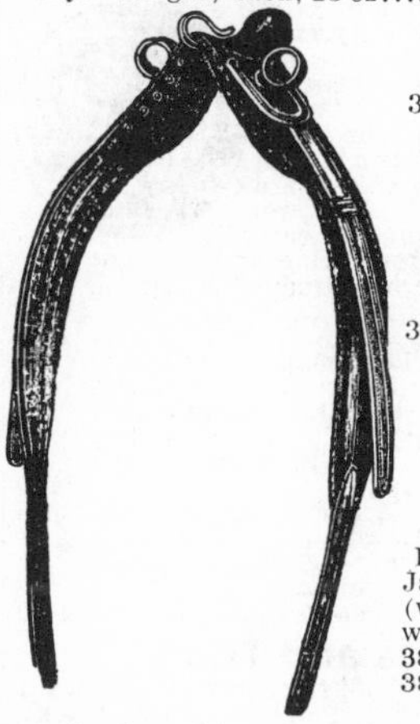

38024 Gig Saddles, made of patent leather, japanned metal seats, enameled cloth pads, 2½ ins. wide with ⅞ in. shaft bearer straps and ⅞ in. bellyband straps. Japan or XC trimmed. Each..............$1.15

38026 Gig Saddles, made of patent leather, japanned metal seats, enameled cloth pads 3 ins. wide, with 1 inch shaft bearer straps and ⅞ in. bellyband straps. Japan or XC trimmed. Each.. ....$1.25
Please mention whether Japan (black) or XC (white) trimming is wanted on 38024 and 38026.

38028 Gig Saddles, Hand laced patent leather skirts, patent leather jockeys, japanned seat, full quilted leather pad, 2½ in. Saddles with ⅞ inch shaft bearer straps and ⅞ inch bellyband straps; trimmed in either nickel or imitation rubber. Each.....................$2.55

38030 Same style as No. 38028 with 3-inch saddles, 1 inch shaft bearer straps and ⅞ inch bellyband straps; trimmed in either nickel or imitation rubber. Each.......................... 2.75
Please state which mounting is wanted.

Patent Gig Saddles.

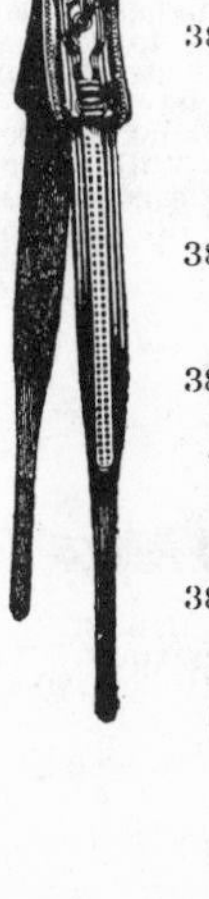

38034 Gig Saddles, harness Leather Skirts, long patent tree, leather lined pads; the most serviceable pad made. 2½ inch saddles with ⅞ inch shaft bearer straps and ⅞ inch bellyband straps. Japan or XC mountings. Each.........$1.75

38036 Same style as No. 38034, but 3-inch saddles, 1 inch shaft bearer straps and ⅞-inch bellyband straps. Japan or XC mountings..... 2.00

38038 Gig Saddles, harness leather skirts, patent leather stitched jockeys' fancy shaped leather lined pads, 2½ in. saddles; ⅞ in. shaft bearer straps, and ⅞-inch bellyband straps. Either nickel or imitation rubber mountings. Each.. 3.05

38040 Same style as No. 38038, but 3 inch saddles, with 1 inch, shaft bearer straps and ⅞-in. bellyband straps. Nickel or imitation rubber. Each. 3.30

Team Harness Pads.

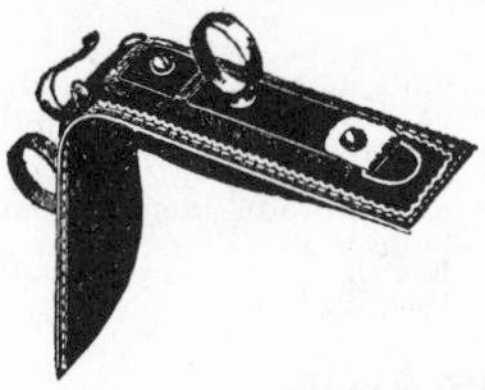

38044 Summit City Team Pads, made with plates. Pads stuffed, with housings and dee rings. This makes a good repair pad, as you can use a strap with a buckle for the skirt or flap. Japan or XC trimmed, for two horses Per pair..........$1.80
Please mention whether black or white trimming is wanted.

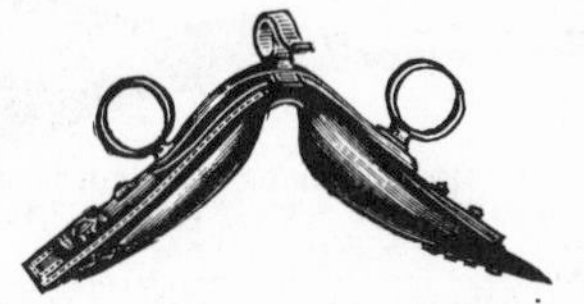

38046 Perfection Team Pads, with patent leather housings and stuffed leather pads to be used where skirts or flaps are screwed on. Japan or XC trimmed.
Per pair. for two horses............................$1.90

Harness Mending Outfit.

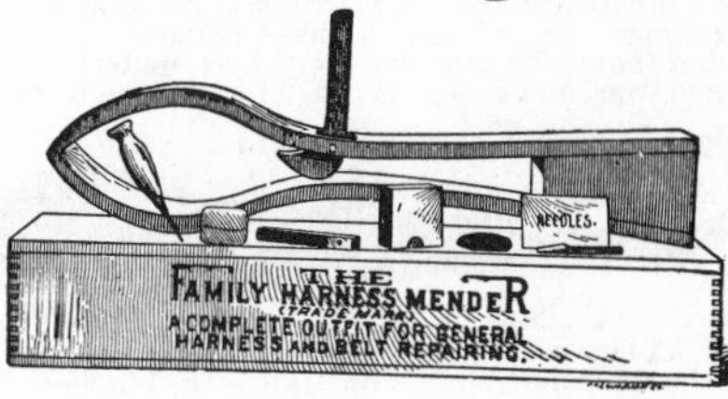

38048 Harness Mending Outfit. A complete outfit for general harness and belt repairing. Contains the following articles: Lever clamp, sewing awl and handle, round punch, rivet set, ball of thread, ball of wax, package of needles, package of copper rivets and burrs. All sets are exactly alike and we do not break sets. Each outfit securely packed in wooden box with hinged lid. Each.......................................$1.50
Weight, about 10 lbs.

Leather Splitters.

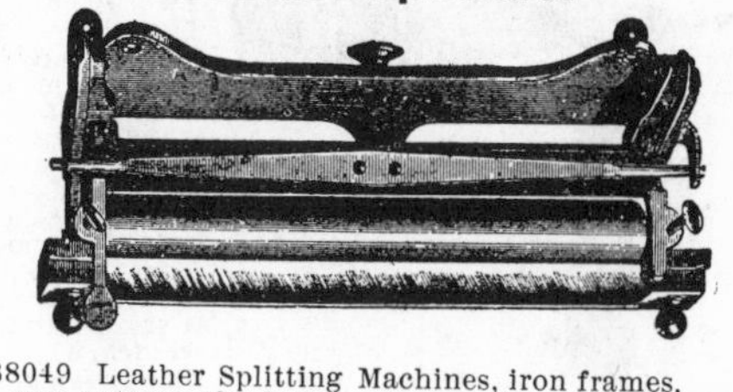

38049 Leather Splitting Machines, iron frames, new pattern, the best made, can be set to any gauge desired and can be fastened to any table or work bench.

Sizes.	5 inch.	6 inch.	7 inch.
Price, each	$4.75	$5.25	$5.75
Weight, each	6 lbs.	7 lbs.	8 lbs.

Harness Horse.

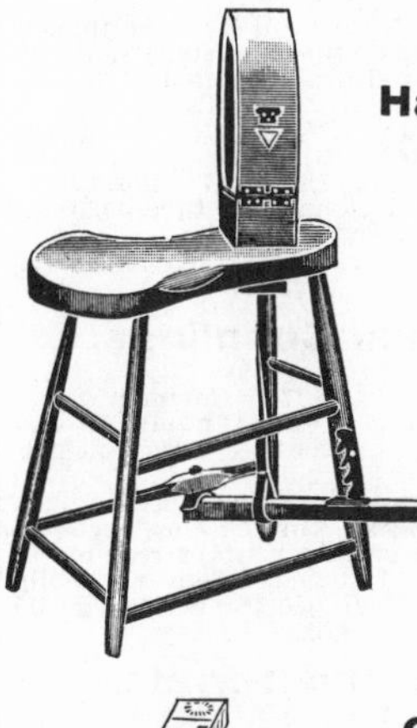

38050 Harness Makers' Stitching Horse. This is something every horse owner should have. Any man can do his own repairing and save his time, as well as his money. Made of good sound wood. Without jaw strap. Each......$2.50
Weight, 18 lbs.
If jaw strap is wanted, add 25c.

Guage Knives.

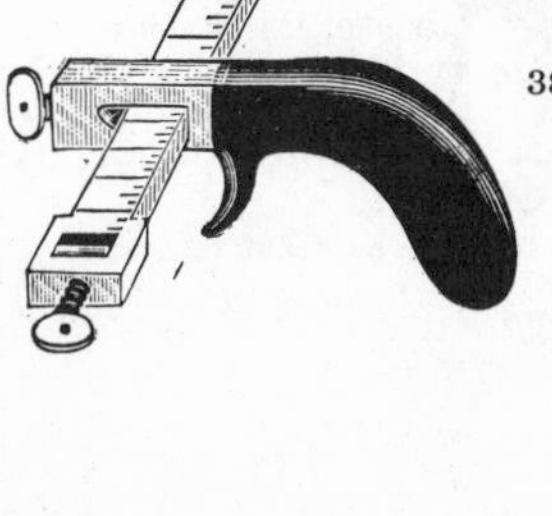

38052 Gauge Knife, hollow iron handle. Will cut from ⅛ to 4 in. Same as used by harness makers, Each..........$1.15
If sent by mail, postage extra,15c.

Harness Knife.

38053 Round Knives, made of best quality steel, oval rosewood handles. Every one guaranteed. Blades measure 5 in. across from point to point.
Each....................$1.20
Weight, 4 oz.

Thong Awls.

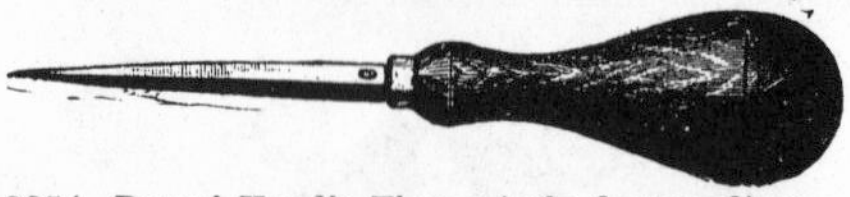

38054 Round Handle Thong Awls, for mending harness, repairing belts, etc. Length, 7 inches.
Each..........................$ 0.25
Per dozen.......................... 2.70
Weight, 3 ounces.

Collar Awls.

38056 Collar Awls or Drawing Awls, made with large eye for sewing horse collars with leather thongs or whangs; very best material, turned wood handles. Length, 9 inches. Each..$0.40

Edge Tool.

38057 Common Edge Tool, used for removing the sharp corners from new strap work, 5 inches long. Each........$0.16 Per dozen.........$1.75
Weight, each, 2 ozs.

Harness Needles, Awls, Handles.

38058 Harness Needles, put up in papers of twenty-five needles, assorted sizes, 0 to 4.
Per paper.........$0.12 Per dozen..........$1.30
38060 Straight Harness Awls, small, medium and large sizes assorted. Per dozen........$0.24
38061 Common Turned Sewing Awl Handles.
Per dozen.............................$0.16

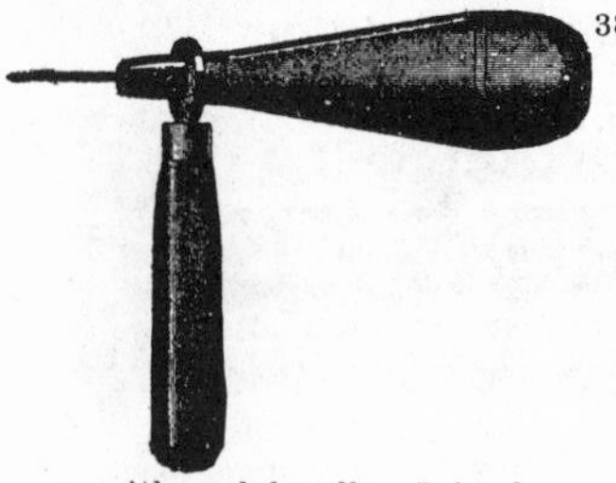

38062 Patent Awl Handles. The awls are held securely in place by a metal cap, which screws on to the awl socket. You can change the awls in a moment without breaking them, A small iron wrench, which fits the cap, goes with each handle. Price does not include an awl. Each........$0.30 Per dozen..........$3.25
Weight each 4 ods.

38063 Wax, per ball, 1c.; per dozen...........10
38064 Harness Thread, No. 10 "H B" thread, natural linen color, 2 oz. balls.
Per ball......... $0.12. Per lb. (8 balls).... .90

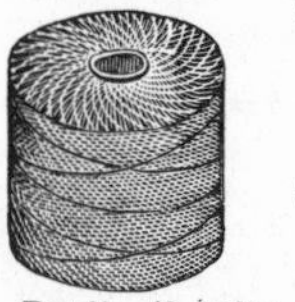

38066 No. 10 "H B" super thread, wound on tubes; waste by snarling, or tangling prevented. Natural linen color, 2 oz. balls.
Per ball..... .... $0.15
Per lb (8 balls).............. 1.05
38067 No. 12 "H B" Devonshire thread, wound on tubes, natural linen color, 2 oz. balls.
Per ball................. $0.16
Per lb. (8 balls). 1.15

Horse Collar Couplings.

38072 Common Sense Collar Couplings. Can be used either on new collars or on old collars that have been broken through constant handling. No springs or straps required to keep them fastened. They are easily adjusted. Each..$0.18 Per doz. $1.95
Weight, each, 8 ozs.

Pad Hooks and Terrets.

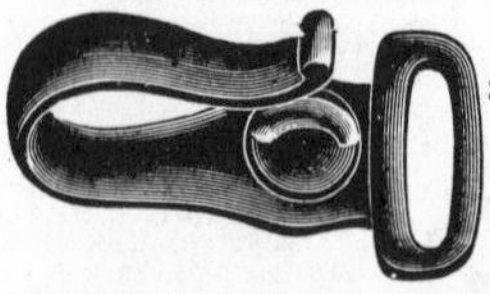

38080 Check Hooks, for pads on team harness, japanned finish.
Each............ ....$0.06
Per dozen......... .65

38082 Check Hooks, for pads on team harness, XC plated. Each................................07
Per dozen.................................75
Weight each, 3 oz.

Terrets—Continued.

38086 Heavy Band Terrets, for pads on team harness, 1¾ in., japanned finish.
Each...........................$0.07
Per dozen............................. .75
38087 Heavy Band Terrets, for pads on team harness. 1¾ inch, XC plate.
Each....................... $0.08
Per dozen.............................. .85
Weight, each, 4 oz.

38090 Heavy Band Bolt Hooks, for buggy harness, made from rolled steel plates. Every hook guaranteed against straightening out or breaking. Japanned finish.
Each........................$0.10
Per dozen.................... 1.00

38091 Same as No. 38090, but XC plated. Each $0.11
Per dozen..................... 1.10
Weight, each, 3 ozs

Safety Check Hooks.

38095 Safety Post Check Hooks, XC plated. Each........$0.20
Per dozen 2.16
38096 Safety Post Check Hooks, wire ball pattern, finely finished and nickel plated.
Each. $0.30
Per dozen..................... 3.24
Weight, each, 3 oz.

Axle Washers.

38100 Adjustable Leather Axle Washers, are made from the best oak tanned stock, durable and satisfactory; can be cut to fit any nut or collar, have been thoroughly tested, and are superior to all others. Put up one hundred washers in a box.

Size.....	⅞ in.	1 in.	1⅛ in.	1¼ in.	1½ in.
Per 100.......	$0.15	$0.18	$0.22	$0.26	$0.32
Per doz. boxes..	1.62	1.95	2.40	2.80	3.45
Weight, per box.	4 ozs.	6 ozs.	8 ozs.	10 ozs.	12ozs.

Crystal Rosettes.

38104 Pflueger's Fancy Crystal Rosettes, for bridles, 1¾ inches in diameter. Put up six pairs on a card especially for Montgomery Ward & Co. No two pair on one card alike; all being of different colors and different designs. All new patterns. Ornamental, strong and durable. Per pair............................$0.18
Per card of six pairs................................. 1.00
Postage, per pair, 3c. Postage, per card, 20c.
38106 Sterling Silver Rosettes, solid metal (18 per cent silver), ⅛ inch thick, hard brazed loop, absolutely non-pull-of, mirror finish, smooth plain surface, 2 inches in diameter. One pair on card. Per pair............................30
38108 Black Terraloid Bridle Rosettes, commonly called rubber; neat and tasty and nothing to soil or tarnish; requires no cleaning. Diameter, 1⅝ inches. Weight, per pair, 2 oz.
Per pair..........$0.10 Per doz. pair.......... 1.00

Iron Hames and Tugs.

38112 Iron Hames. No. 1 full japanned (black), 3½ lb. iron hames with hame straps; box looped hame tugs and 1 inch trace buckles; per pair $1.20,1⅛ in. trace buckles per pair $1.25; 1¼ in, trace buckles, per pair $1.30. Sizes, 17 to 21 inches; mention length.
38114 Iron Hames, No. 1 full XC plated (white), 3½ lbs. iron hames, any size from 17 to 21 ins., with hame straps, box looped hame tugs and 1 in. trace buckles, per pair $1.20. With 1⅛ in. trace buckles; per pair $1.25. With 1¼ in. trace buckles, per pair $1.30

38112-14

Hook Hames.

38120 Hook Hames, iron over-top hook Hames. varnished, with line and breast strap rings.
Per pair of two hames for one horse...........$0.40
Weight, per pair, 4 lbs.

Hames—Continued.

38122 Polished Steel Bound Concord Hook Hames, with line rings and breast strap rings (No. 8). Weight, per pair, 5½ lbs. Per pair.... .80

Clip Hames.

38124 Clip Hames, iron over-top clip hames, varnished, with line and breast strap rings. Per pair of 2 hames for one horse..............$0.45
Weight' per pair, 4 pounds.
38126 Iron Over-top Clip Hames: painted black with XC plated spot, combination loop, line rings and breast strap rings. Per pair........ .65
Weight, per pair, 4¾ lbs.

38128 Low Top Clip Hames; hames are painted black with XC plated spot, line rings and breast strap rings. Per pair................. $0.50
Weight, per pair, 3¾ lbs.

38130 Ball Top Clip Hames; hames are painted black, with white or "C" plate mountings, combination loop, line rings and breast strap rings. Per pair of 2 hames for one horse........$0.75
Weight, per pair, 5 lbs.
38132 Ball Top Clip Hames; Hames are painted red, with white or "C" plate mountings, combination loop, line rings, breast strap rings. Per pair of 2 hames for one horse .... .80
Weight, per pair, 5 lbs.
38134 Brass Ball Top Steel Bound Concord Clip Hames (No. 6), painted red, fitted with line rings and breast strap rings. Per pair 1.35
Weight, per pair, 5¾ lbs.

Bolt Hames.

38136 Polished Steel Bound Concord Hames, 2¼ inch patent screw bolt, with breast rings, back strap rings, line rings (No. 5). Per pair of 2 hames for 1 horse................................$0.90
Weight, per pair, 5 pounds.
38138 Polished Steel Bound Concord Hames, same as above, but are 3 sizes heavier; used for heavy lumber and truck harness (No. 8). Per pair of two hames for one horse................. 1.05
Weight, per pair, 5½ pounds.

38140 Brass Ball Top Concord Steel Bound Bolt Hames (No. 6), with line ring, back strap rings and breast strap rings.
Per pair..$1.40
Weight, per pair, 5½ pounds.
38142 Brass Ball Hame Tops, can be used on any Concord hames.
Per pair.. .33
Weight, per pair, 7 ounces.

38142

Hame Trimmings.

38144 Hame Line Rings, with studs and burrs.

38146   38144
Per dozen....... ....$0.20
Weight, per dozen, 18 ounces.
38146 Hame Breast Strap Rings, with studs and burrs. Per dozen.............................35
Weight, per dozen, 30 ounces.

Hame Trimmings—Continued.

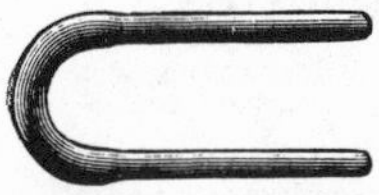

38148 Hame Staples, with burrs, made of best quality malleable iron.
Per dozen........$0.20
Per gross......... 2.00

Weight per dozen, 30 ounces.

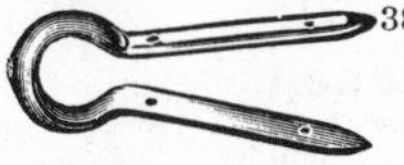

38149 Hame Clips, made of the best quality wrought-iron without rivets.
Per dozen..............$0.20
Per gross 2.00

Weight, per dozen, 38 ounces.
38150 Hame Rivets put up in one pound packages. We do not break packages. Per lb...... ...... .15

Hame Loops.

38154 Screw Hame Bottom Loops; loop will admit 1 inch strap.
Per dozen.........................$0.35
Weight, per dozen, 14 oz.

Success Hame Fasteners.

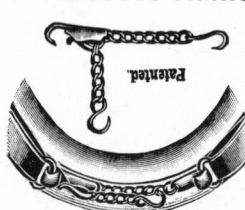

38155 Success Hame Fasteners. Stronger and more easily adjusted than any strap or other fastener. Easily put on and cannot get out of working order. Indestructible, will last as long as the hames. Place the heavy end into the loop of the off hame and hammer down the hook, so that the fastener cannot become detached. We have given these fasteners weeks of successful trial on our own teams. Each...... ....$0.25
Per dozen.............. - 2.70
Weight, each, 13 ounces.

Star Hame Fastener.

38156 No more broken hame straps; it holds your hame always in position, firm and sure. No straps or buckles to open.
Each............$0.18
Per dozen...... 2.00
Weight, each, 5 oz.

Cockeyes.

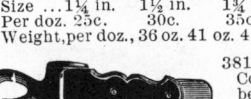

38158 Japanned Screw Cockeyes.
Size ... 1¼ in.   1½ in.   1¾ in.   2 in.
Per doz. 25c.   30c.   35c.   50c.
Weight, per doz., 36 oz. 41 oz. 45 oz. 56 oz.

38160 Patented Clip Cockeyes, made of the best malleable iron. The cockeye is made heavy at the shoulder, and the eye is large. Size, 1½ in.
Per dozen...........$0.40   Weight, per dozen, 70 oz.

Breast Strap Rollers with Snap.

              Per doz.   Each.
38162 Breast Strap Roller, with snap, 1½ in. tinned... $1.70 $0.16
38163 Breast Strap Roller, with snap, 1¾ in. tinned.. 1.80 .17
38164 Breast Strap Roller, with snap, 2 in. tinned...... 2.00 .19
Weight, per pair, 18 oz., 20 oz., 22 oz.

Combined Neck Yoke Snap.

38167 Combination Neck Yoke Snap and Breast Strap Slide. The strongest, safest and most durable snap made. It is indispensable to the farmer, as it is the only snap that can be used successfully on farm machinery. Tinned finish.

Sizes ....1½ in.   1¾ in.   2 in.
Each... ....$0.18 $0.19 $0.20
Per dozen............. 2.00 2.10 2.25
Weight, each.............10 oz. 11 oz. 12 oz.

Breast Strap Slides.

38169 Breast Strap Slides, japanned iron.

Size ....1½ in.   1¾ in.   2 in
Each 5c.   6c.   8c
Per dozen 54c.   65c.   75c
Weight, per pair........10 oz. 12 oz. 15 oz

Breast Chains.

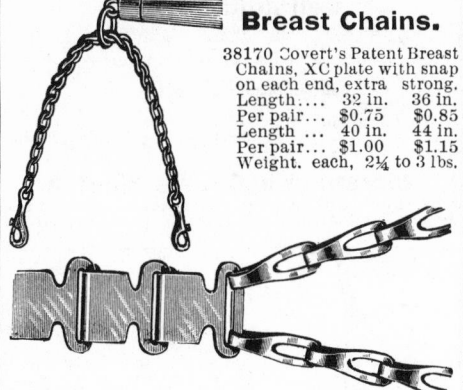

38170 Covert's Patent Breast Chains, XC plate with snap on each end, extra strong.
Length.... 32 in.   36 in.
Per pair... $0.75 $0.85
Length ... 40 in.   44 in.
Per pair... $1.00 $1.15
Weight, each, 2¼ to 3 lbs.

38172 M. W. & Co.'s Fancy Chain Martingales, for buggy or carriage use. Cut shows style of link at intersection of body and forks, finely nickel plated. Length, 42 inches. Each $1.00
Per dozen $11.50
38173 M. W. & Co.'s Fancy Chain Martingales, all steel, style of cut, brightly polished. Length 42 inches. Each ... ... .50
Per dozen.... .... 5.75
Weight, each, 6 oz.

Heel Chains.

38176 Heel Chains for ends of traces, four links and dee, 5-16 in. wire
For 1½ in. traces, per set of four................$0.35
For 1¾ in. traces, per set of four........ .... .38
For 2 in. traces, per set of four..................40
Weight, per set, 3 lbs. to 3¾ lbs.

Trace Chains.

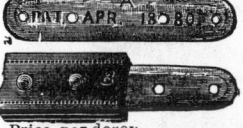

38178 Trace Chain, made of size 2 iron, 7 ft. long. Per pair of two chains for one horse. .. $0.50
Weight, per pair, 6½ lbs.

Stage Chains.

38179 Stage Chains, 3½-feet long: hook on one end, clip on the other end. Per pair $0.36
Weight, per pair, 4 pounds.

Trace Splicers.

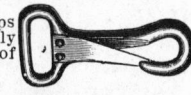

38180 Malleable Iron Trace Splicers for mending traces, simple, quick, cheap and durable. They can be used for buggy, express or farm harness.
Price, per dozen.........................$0.40
Weight, per dozen, 16 oz.

Whip Racks.

1 HALL'S PAT. WHIP RACK

38184 Hall's Whip Racks, japanned sheet iron, 6 inches long; two nails or screws will hold one in position, and each rack will hold a dozen whips. Weight, 2 oz. Each...................$0.08
Per dozen.... .... .85

Harness Snaps.

By size of snap we mean the width of strap that can be used.

38186 German Harness Snaps bronzed finish. We handle only the heaviest and best snaps of this style made.

Size......⅞ in. 1 in. 1¼ in. 1½ in. 1¾ in. 2 in.
Per doz.$0.18 $0.20 $0.32 $0.42 $0.54 $0.60
Weight per doz.—
     13 oz. 18 oz. 26 oz. 32 oz. 48 oz. 50 oz. 
38188 Coverts' Banner Bolt Snaps. The principle feature of this snap lies in the spring being entirely covered, shutting out all foreign substance.
Size ......⅞ in. 1 in. 1¼ in. 1½ in. 1¾ in. 2 in.
Per dozen $0.24 $0.26 $0.40 $0.44 $0.48 $0.52

Harness Snaps—Continued.

38190 Bristol's Patent Snaps, strictly first quality. Every snap is throughly tested in the factory before being packed.

Size... ⅞ in. 1 in. 1¼ in. 1½ in. 1¾ in. 2 in.
Per doz..$0.38 $0.40 $0.48 $0.56 $0.65 $0.78 
38192 The American Wrought Steel Harness Snaps are strong competitors for public favor. All made with swivel strap eye.

38192
Size........ ⅞ in. 1 in. 1¼ in. 1½ in. 1¾ in.
Per dozen.. $0.35 $0.37 $0.45 $0.52 $0.60
38194 The American Wrought Steel Snap for rope halters or cow ties; the strongest made.
Each..................$0.04 Per dozen...........$0.45 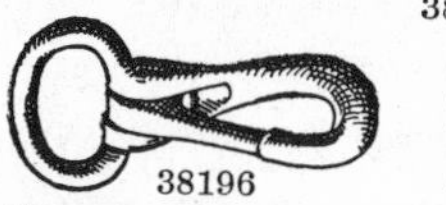
38196 Bristol's Patent Round Eye Snaps for rope, tinned finished. Polished on the loop and milled at the nose of the hook. Every snap is thoroughly tested.

38196
Size .... ⅝ in.   ¾ in.
Per dozen $0.45 $0.50
Weight, per dozen...........15 oz. 25 oz.

38198 Bag Snaps, nickel plated bag or baby snaps. Will take strap ½ inch.
Per dozen..................$0.25

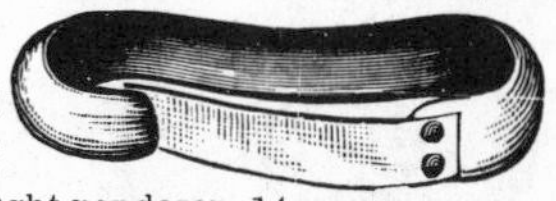

38200 Buffalo Patent Snap, 2 in. long-japanned: can be used for halter bridle and bit. Weight per dozen, 14 ounces.
Each............$0.05 Per dozen............$0.50

California Belt Buckles.

                 Each.   Per doz
38202 California Nickel Plated Belt Buckles, 1¼ inch ....''''' $0.07 $0.75
Weight per dozen, 12 oz.

Trace Buckles.

38204 Three-Loop Champion Trace Buckle, made of best malleable iron, japanned finish.
               Each.   Per doz.
1½ in...... ..$0.06 $0.65
1¾ in...... .07 .75
38205 Three Loop Champion Trace Buckles XC plate.
               Each.   Per doz.
1½ in...... ..$0.06 $0.65
1¾ in...... .07 .75

Harness Buckles.

(Black.)

38210 Japanned Iron Center Bar Harness and Halter Buckles for straps.
Size......½ in. ⅝ in. ¾ in. ⅞ in. 1 in. 1¼ in. 1½ in.
Per doz.. 6c 8c 10c 12c 14c 18c 25c
Wt.pr.dz. 2 oz. 4 oz. 6 oz. 9 oz. 12 oz. 16 oz. 22 oz.
38211 "XC" plated (white) Iron Center Bar Harness and Halter Buckles for straps.
Size........ ½ in. ⅝ in. ¾ in. ⅞ in. 1 in. 1¼ in. 1½ in.
Per doz.... 6c 8c 10c 12c 14c 18c 25c
Wt.per doz. 2 oz. 4 oz. 6 oz. 9 oz. 12 oz. 16 oz. 22 oz.

38214 Japanned (Black) Iron Barrel Roller Buckles.

Size, inches...........½ ⅝ ¾ ⅞ 1 1¼ 1½ 1¾ 2
Per dozen............4c 6c 8c 10c 12c 14c 16c 18c 20c
Weight per doz.,in oz.3 5 6 8 10 12 15 18 22
38215 "XC" plated (white) Iron Barrel Roller Buckles.
Size, inches...........½ ⅝ ¾ ⅞ 1 1¼ 1½ 1¾ 2
Per dozen............4c 6c 8c 10c 12c 14c 16c 18c 20c
Weight per doz.in oz.3 5 6 8 10 12 15 18 22

Harness Rings.

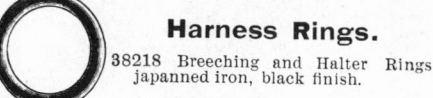

38218 Breeching and Halter Rings, japanned iron, black finish.

Diameter, inches......½ ⅝ ¾ ⅞ 1 1⅛ 1¼
Per dozen...... ....4c 4c 5c 5c 6c 8c 10c
Weight, pr.doz.,in oz.3 4 5 6 7 8 10
Diameter, inches..... 1½ 1¾ 2 2¼ 2½ 3
Per dozen 12c 14c 20c 24c 30c 35c
Weight, pr. doz., in oz. 16 18 22 32 35 37
38219 "XC" Plated (white) Iron Breeching and Halter Rings.
Diameter, inches......½ ⅝ ¾ ⅞ 1 1⅛ 1¼
Per dozen..............4c 4c 5c 5c 6c 8c 10c
Weight, per doz. in oz..3 4 5 6 7 8 10
Diameter, inches........1½ 1¾ 2 2¼ 2½ 3
Per dozen..............12c 14c 20c 24c 30c 35c
Weight, per doz. in oz. 16 18 22 32 35 37

Harness Rings—Continued.

38221 Halter Squares, japanned malleable iron.
Sizes.. 1x1¼in. 1¼x1½in. 1½x1¾in.
Pr doz.   10c.   12c.   15c.
Wt.pr.doz.10 oz.   14 oz.   18 oz.

38222 Halter Dees, japanned malleable iron.
Sizes............1¼ in. 1½ in. 1¾ in.
Per dozen..... 10c.   15c.   20c.
Weight per doz. 10 oz. 14 oz. 18 oz.

38223 Halter Bolts, japanned iron
Sizes .... 1 in. 1¼ in. 1½ in
Per dozen...... 6c.   8c.   10c.
Weight,per doz. 5 oz. 7 oz. 9 oz.

Martingale Rings.

These are inside measurements.
          Per doz.
38225 Genuine Black Rubber Rings, plain, light in weight but strong.................$0.50
38226 Genuine Black Rubber Rings, imitation stitched edge, light but strong, diam., 1½ in.; weight , per doz., 7 oz. .... .65
38228 Red Duranoid Rings, 1⅝ inches........ .30
38229 White Duranoid Rings, 1⅝ inches........ .30
38230 Blue Duranoid Rings, 1⅝ inches........ .30
Weight, per doz., 14 oz.
38234 Bone Rings, red, 1 inch in diameter...... .40
38235 Bone Rings, white, 1 inch in diameter... .40
38236 Bone Rings, blue, 1 inch in diameter..... .40
Weight, per doz., 3 oz.

38238 Celluloid Spreaders, composed of 3 solid celluloid rings in assorted fancy colors.
Per string..........$0.60
Per doz. strings.... 6.75
Weight, each, about 4 oz.

Celluloid Rings.

Red, white or blue.
Unless color is mentioned we invariably send white.
Diameter, inches.
38240....... 1¼   1⅜   1½   1⅝   1¾   2   2¼
Each......$0.10 $0.13 $0.16 $0.19 $0.22 $0.25 $0.28
Per doz... 1.00   1.40   1.75   2.15   2.50   2.80   3.15

White Zylonite Rings.

Diameter, inches.
38242 ...... 1¼   1⅜   1½   1⅝   1¾   2   2¼
Each......$0.09 $0.11 $0.13 $0.16 $0.19 $0.22 $0.25
Per doz... .90   1.15   1.45   1.75   2.10   2.40   2.65
Weight on celluloid and zylonite rings, 5 to 17 oz.,
Per dozen, according to size.

Celluloid Loops.

38244 Celluloid Loops, red,   Diameter ⅝ in.   ¾ in.
Per dozen......... ....$0.33 $0.35
38245 Celluloid Loops, white, diameter,   ⅝   ¾
Per doz............................... .33   .35
38246 Celluloid Loops, blue, diameter,   ⅝   ¾
Per dozen........ .... .33   .35
Weight per doz., 2 oz.
The above loops are used for connecting any size rings for making spreader straps.

Morsman's Buckle Shields.

Buckle Shields are very ornamental on harness and protect the horse's tail from being pulled out on the buckle tongues.

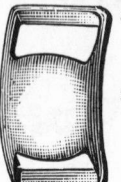

38248 Brass.
Size............½in.   ⅝ in.   ¾ in.
Per doz.... ... $0.70 $0.80 $0.90
Size... ⅞ in.   1 in.   1⅛ in.   1¼ in.
Per doz $1.00 $1.10 $1.45 $1.70
38250 Same, in nickel.
Size............ ½ in.   ⅝ in.   ¾ in.
Per doz... ... $0.75 $0.85 $0.95
Size.... ⅞ in.   1 in.   1⅛ in.   1¼ in.
Per doz $1.05 $1.15 $1.50 $1.75
Weight, per doz., 6, 8, 10, 12, 14, 16, 18 oz.

Bridle Plumes.

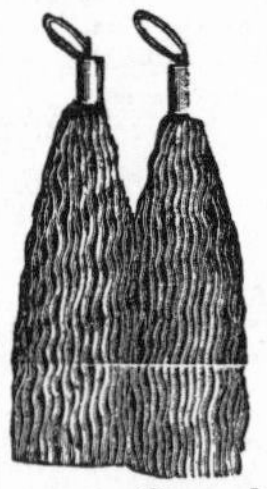

Bridle Plumes, curled horse hair Plumes, or Tassels for team harness.
38254 Bridle Plumes, colors, red or yellow, 9 inches long.
Per pair................... .. .$0.25
38256 Bridle Plumes, colors, red or blue, 11 inches long.
Per pair...................$0.32
38258 Bridle Plumes, colors, red or green, 13 inches long.
Per pair...................$0.40
Mention color wanted. Weight, per pair, 3, 4, 5 ounces.

Carriage Top Dressing.

38260 Frank Miller's Dressing for buggy and carriage tops. Gives an elastic, durable, jet black, waterproof gloss. Can be safely used on the finest stock. Directions on each can.
Pint cans. each........ $0.60 Per dozen.....$6.50

Harness Dressing.

38262 Frank Miller's Harness Dressing, for harness, saddles, fly nets, etc. Gives a beautiful finish, does not lose its luster. Directions for use on every package.
Pint cans, each.................................$0.25
Quart 42

Waterproof Blacking.

38264 Frank Miller's Leather Preservative and Waterproof Oil Blacking. This blacking is designed to render leather soft, pliable, waterproof and durable.
Directions on each package.
            Small size.   Large size.
Each,.................$0.09 $0.12
Pe. doz.........................1.00   1.35

Harness Soap.

38266 Frank Miller's Harness Soap. This is without question the best harness soap made. By using it your harness will wear longer and look better.
Weight, per cake, 12 oz. $0.12
38268 Crown Soap. The Chiswick pure English crown soap. Pint jars. Each.................... .45
Quart jars....................................... .65

Harness Oil.

38270 Arabian Night Harness Oil, for oiling, blacking and preserving leather. Warranted entirely free from any injurious substance, lithographed can, screw tops.
Pint cans, each........................$0.18
Per doz.................................. 2.00
Quart cans, each.......................... .27
Per dozen.............................. . 3.00

Axle Oil.

38272 English Coach Axle Oil, an axle lubricant of unequalled quality, will not gum or corrode, works in winter as well as summer, lithographed cans. Spout tops.
           Each.   Per doz.
Pint cans........................$0.17 $1.95
Quart cans............................ .26   2.95

Chicago Hoof Remedy.

38274 The Chicago Hoof Remedy. This remedy is a sure cure for all ailments of horses' feet; and for healing cuts, wounds, galls, soreness over the kidneys, etc., it can not be excelled. It is specially effective in healing barb wire scratches. Thrush or Foot Rot cured in three applications. It is easily applied, and does the work quickly and surely. Full directions on each package.
           Each.   Per doz.
Quart cans............................$0.55 $6.00
Half gallon cans...................... .85   9.20
Gallon cans........................• 1.60   17.25
Five gallon cans..................... 7.15   77.25
38276 Neatsfoot Oil, quart cans........ .35   4.00
38278 Gladding's Hoof Dressing, quart cans, with brushes. Each. .... .56
38280 Continental Hoof Ointment, ¼ lb. cans.
Each .... .18
Per dozen 2.00
For other oils, see Index.

SADDLE DEPARTMENT.

Children's Side Saddles.

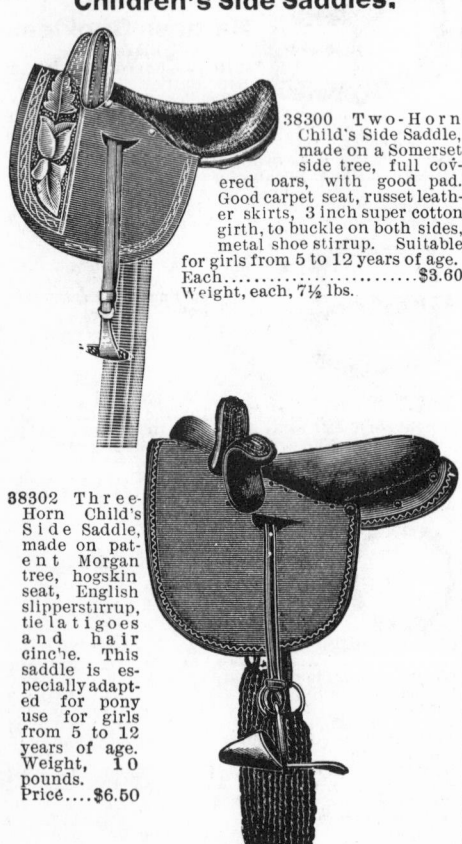

38300 Two-Horn Child's Side Saddle, made on a Somerset side tree, full covered oars, with good pad. Good carpet seat, russet leather skirts, 3 inch super cotton girth, to buckle on both sides, metal shoe stirrup. Suitable for girls from 5 to 12 years of age.
Each..........................$3.60
Weight, each, 7½ lbs.

38302 Three-Horn Child's Side Saddle, made on patent Morgan tree, hogskin seat, English slipper stirrup, tie latigoes and hair cinche. This saddle is especially adapted for pony use for girls from 5 to 12 years of age. Weight, 10 pounds.
Price....$6.50

Ladies' Saddles.

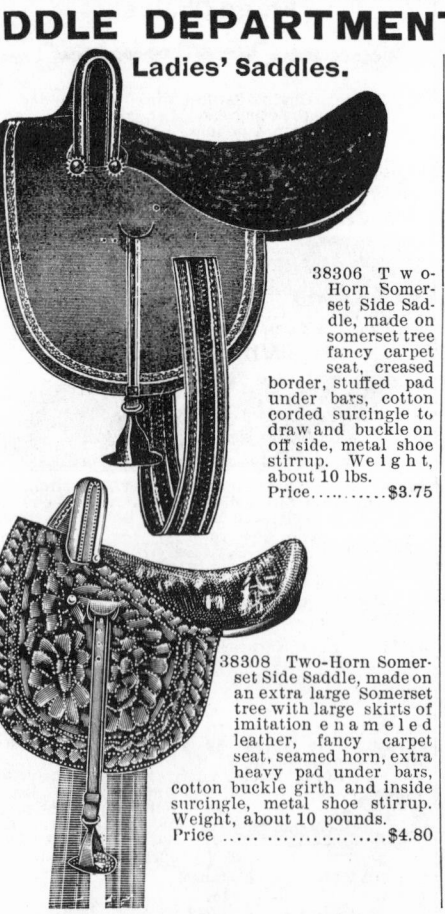

38306 Two-Horn Somerset Side Saddle, made on somerset tree fancy carpet seat, creased border, stuffed pad under bars, cotton corded surcingle to draw and buckle on off side, metal shoe stirrup. Weight, about 10 lbs.
Price...........$3.75

38308 Two-Horn Somerset Side Saddle, made on an extra large Somerset tree with large skirts of imitation enameled leather, fancy carpet seat, seamed horn, extra heavy pad under bars, cotton buckle girth and inside surcingle, metal shoe stirrup. Weight, about 10 pounds.
Price $4.80

Side Saddles.

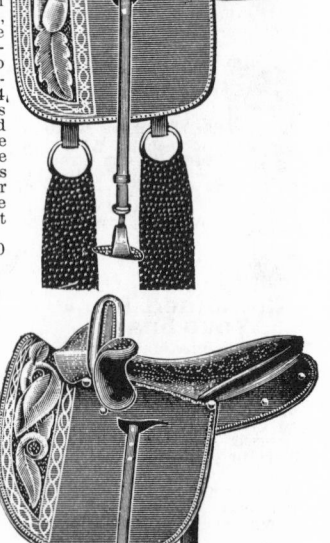

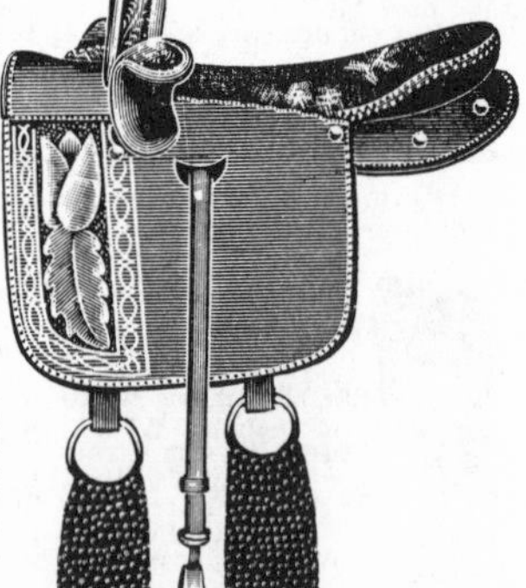

38312 Made on Morgan Tree, plush seat; bars are covered with leather and padded; ¾ in. stirrup strap, with XC iron shoe stirrup, double cinche rigged, leaping horn, two 4-inch hair cinches; weight, 14½ pounds. This is the lowest priced double cinche rigged saddle ever sold. It is of much finer quality than one would expect at the price.
Price $6.50

38314 Side Saddle, made on Morgan tree, quilted leather seat with leaping horn; bars are covered with leather and padded; russet leather skirt, with raised flower ornamentation, double cinche rigged with two 4 in. common hair cinches, ¾ in. leather stirrup strap with XC plate, patent shoe stirrup; weight, 15½ pounds.
Price.....$8.00
For slipper stirrup in place of shoe stirrup, add 75 cents.

Saddles—Continued.

38316 Three-Horn English Style Side Saddle, made on somerset tree; genuine hogskin seat; large russet leather skirts and jockeys; leap horn covered with buckskin and seamed, full stuffed pad, making it comfortable for both horse and rider, best white cotton girth and surcingle, ¾ in. stirrup strap, metal shoe stirrup, weight, 14 lbs. Price $8.50

38317 Two-Horse Side Saddle, made on large size Ruwart side tree. Seat covered with velvet carpet, large enamel leather quilted roll. Bars covered with leather and padded. 13 cord cotton girth, fancy cotton surcinge, metal shoe stirrup. Patent leather binding on skirt and housing; Weight, 15 pounds. Each..........$8.75 We can furnish No. 38317 saddle with leaping horn for $10.00.

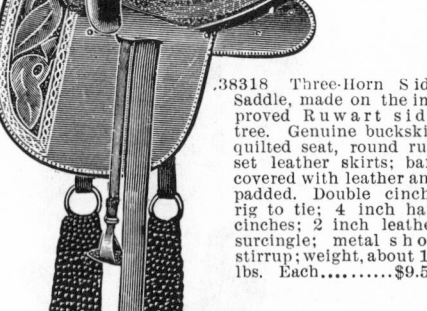

38318 Three-Horn Side Saddle, made on the improved Ruwart side tree. Genuine buckskin quilted seat, round russet leather skirts; bars covered with leather and padded. Double cinche rig to tie; 4 inch hair cinches; 2 inch leather surcingle; metal shoe stirrup; weight, about 15 lbs. Each..........$9.50

38320 Side Saddle, made on the patent Ruwart side tree, fine quilted leather seat and roll, leaping horn, raised ornamental flower work on skirt, cotton surcingle, ¾ in. stirrup straps and slipper stirrups, double cinche rigged, one 4-inch and one 5-inch hair cinche; weight, 16 lbs. Price each.... $10.00

Saddles—Continued.

38324 "Park" Three-Horn Side Saddle, made on Somerset tree, quilted buckskin seat and forepiece, russet leather skirts and jockeys with hogskin impression, slipper stirrup, skirt surcingle, two girths, full pad, buckskin faced. A very superior style which we sell at a very moderate price. Weight, about 18 lbs. Each...........$11.50

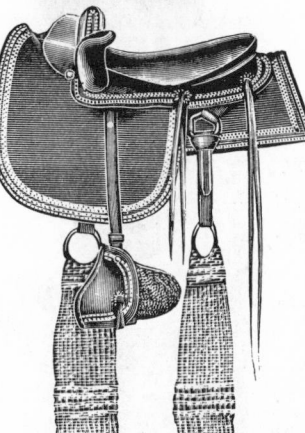

38326 Side Saddle, made on a patent Ruwart tree, with leaping horn, fine moquette seat, hogskin roll around seat; bars are covered with leather and padded with deer hair, leather surcingle on outside, double cinche inside and slipper stirrup, all made of No. 1 material, and in good style. This is a large, roomy saddle, and skirts are extra large; we can recommend this saddle as being comfortable, presentable and substantial. Weight, 18 lbs. Each.............$12.00

38328 Three Horn Western Style Side Saddle; plain genuine buckskin-covered seat; seamed horns, buckskin covered; large, square wool lined underskirts on both sides, entirely covering the bars of the tree; round russet leather outer skirt, extending well forward; double cinche rig to tie; heavy tie straps; exposed rings are leather covered; two 6 inch Mexican string cinches; tapideroe stirrup, leathered on bottom; long wool-lined chafe. All made strong and substantial of good material. Weight, about 17 pounds. Each ...$12.00

38330 Three-Horn Mountain Side Saddle, made on patent Ruwart side tree, genuine buckskin seat, leather covered cantle, extra large leather housing, extra large skirts, stamped and ornamented. Bars covered with leather and padded, seamed jockey and horns, outside leather surcingle. double tie rig, hair cinches, hooded stirrup, with long chafe and leather on bottom. Price, each........$12.50 Weight, 19 pounds.

Saddles—Continued.

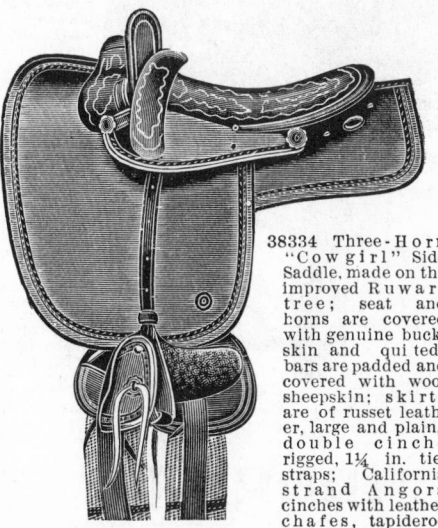

38331 Three-Horn Side Saddle, made on the Ruwart side tree, all dark russet skirting leather. Seat covered with heavy stamp skirting, large plain roll round the outside. Skirts 24 inches long, wool lined: tie straps 1½ inches 5½ feet long: buckle strap, 1⅜ inches. California strand Angora hair cinches, tongues on one end; tapidero stirrup, wool lined cover and chafe, covered rings, sings, seamed horns. A large and substantial saddle. Weight, 20 pounds. Each...$12.65

38332 Western Style Three-Horn Side Saddle, made on the improved Ruwart side tree; russet leather skirts and housings; genuine buckskin seat: seamed horns, buckskin covered; bars covered with wool sheepskin; double tie cinche rig; Mexican string cinches with wool lined chafes and connecting strap; tapideroe stirrup; wool lined chafe, long lace strings. A really good saddle, well made and finished. Weight, 18 pounds. Each.......................................$13.00

38334 Three-Horn "Cowgirl" Side Saddle, made on the improved Ruwart tree; seat and horns are covered with genuine buckskin and quilted; bars are padded and covered with wool sheepskin; skirts are of russet leather, large and plain, double cinche rigged, 1¼ in. tie-straps; California strand Angora cinches with leather chafes, tapideroe stirrup, wool lined. Weight, 20 pounds. Each.................................$15.00

OUR... SADDLES Are the Best Possible Value For the Money.

Don't Make Any Mistake About That.

Saddles—Continued.

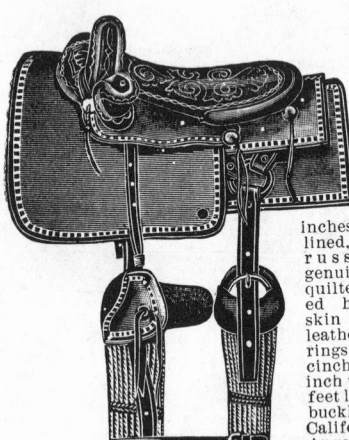

38336 Three-Horn Western Style Side Saddle, made on large size patent Ruwart side tree. Genuine buckskin quilted seat and roll; buckskin quilted knee piece and seamed horns, buckskin covered; large fair russet leather skirts and facings; bars covered with leather and padded with deer hair; double cinche rigged; two 20-strand white hard hair cinches with connecting strap and wool lined leather chafes; pocket on off side; 2-inch leather outside skirt surcingle; victoria stirrup. Weight, 21 lbs. Each $21.00

38338 Imported English Side Saddle, made on straight head Somerset tree, with leaping horn. All pigskin seat, pigskin fancy quilted forepiece, small pigskin pocket on right side, and horns are also covered with pigskin. Full pad of best English all wool serge. Two English white worsted girths with leather balance girth. 1 in. English oak leather stirrup strap, Victoria stirrup with padded pigskin instep facing. Weight, complete, 15½ pounds. Each $25.50

38339 Extra Heavy Three-Horn, "Cowgirl" Side Saddle, made on 18-inch rawhide covered Ruwart side tree, skirts 25 inches long, wool lined, best dark russet skirting, genuine buckskin quilted seat, seamed horns, buckskin covered, leather covered rings; double cinche rig, 1½-inch tie straps, 5½ feet long; 1¾ inch buckle straps; California strand Angora hard hair cinches with wool lined leather chafes, tongues and connecting strap. Tapidero stirrup, wool lined chafe. Each.,................$22.50 Weight, each, 27 pounds.

ERRORS We make them; so does everyone, and we will cheerfully correct them if you will write to us. Try to write us good-naturedly, but if you cannot, then write us anyway. Do not let an error pass unnoticed, or complain to your friends or neighbors about it. We want an early opportunity to make right any mistakes that may occur.

Saddles—Continued.

38340—"Ranche Cowgirls' Saddles," especially adapted for mountain riding, made extra strong. Made on a rawhide covered Morgan tree, with a leaping horn, buckskin lined. buckskin seat and one-half forepiece bound with leather, extra large outside skirts extending back of cantle; jockey and skirt in one piece properly laced on; underbar skirts are wool lined and large enough to protect the cinche rigging from coming in contact with the horse; large pocket on the right hand skirt, extra leather surcingle, stirrup straps 1 inch wide, with slipper stirrup, two 14-strand white hair cinches with wool lined chafes and connecting strap. Weight, 25 lbs. Price........$27.00

Boys' Saddles.

38350 Boys' Saddle, Morgan tree, skeleton, rawhide covered, russet or black leather; weight, 4½ lbs. Price..$2.25 For covered stirrups, add 50c.

38350

38352 Boy's Saddle, made on a raw-hide covered Morgan tree, boy's size, russet leather trimmings, 1 in. stirrup straps with fenders and covered stirrups, cotton back band girth. Weight, 6 pounds. Each $3.50

38354 Boy's Saddle, made on a Kilgore tree. Full covered with fair russet leather, solid seamless seat, stamped skirts, bars covered with leather and padded; 3-inch super cotton girth to buckle; wood stirrups; weight, 6¼ pounds. Each........$4.00 For covered stirrups, add 50c

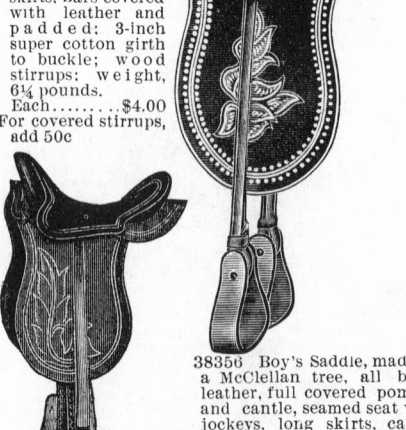

38356 Boy's Saddle, made on a McClellan tree, all black leather, full covered pommel and cantle, seamed seat with jockeys, long skirts, carved border; bars covered with leather and padded; 3-inch super cotton girth to buckle; wood stirrups; weight, 7½ pounds. Each.............................$4.50 For covered stirrups, add 50c.

Saddles—Continued.

38358 Boy's Saddle, Texas style, made on a rawhide-covered Morgan tree. Fair russet leather seat and skirts; bare horn and cantle; leather-covered bars, fenders and tapideroe stirrups, all fancy stamped; tie latigoes, hair cinche; strong and neat; weight, 8 pounds. Each.................$4.75

38360

38358

38360 Boy's Saddle, California style, made on a rawhide covered western tree. All black leather, nicely carved and ornamented; round skirts extending under and covering the bars of the tree, bare horn and cantle, leather seat, fenders and covered stirrups, single tie rig, hair cinche. Weight, 8 pounds. Each.......$5.00

38362 Full Covered Single Cinche Rigged Boys' Saddle, drovers' style; made on rawhide covered Shoshone tree, oiled oak skirting leather, roll cantle, steel strainer in seat, horn full covered, large square skirts extending back of cantle, long tie strings; stirrup straps 1½ inch to buckle, fenders and covered stirrups, hair cinche. Weight, 10 lbs. Price..........$7.80

38362

38363 Boy's Saddle, made on 13-inch, rawhide covered, steel fork, Steininger tree, skirts 20 inches long, oiled russet skirting leather, roll cantle, steel seat plate, stirrup straps, 1½ inch to buckle, fenders attached, 2½ inch wood stirrups, covered rings, double hair cinches, tie straps, 1¼ inch, 4 feet long. Weight, about 16 lbs. Each.. ....$9.00 For wool lined skirts, add $1.00.

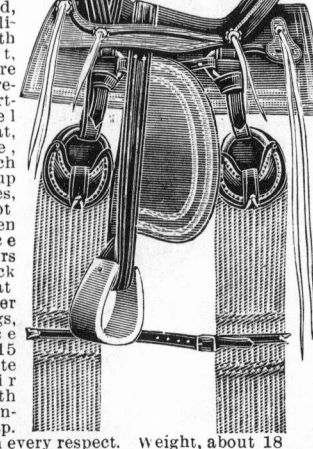

38364 Full Covered Double Cinche Rigged Youth's Saddle, made on a rawhide covered, steel fork, California tree with 14-inch seat, large square skirts of Oregon oiled skirting, steel strainer in seat, roll cantle, jockeys on each side, stirrup strap 1¾ inches, double at bottom, to fasten with lace strings, fenders attached. Block stirrups, tie latigoes, leather covered rings, long lace strings, 15 strand white hard hair cinches with chafes and connecting strap. First class in every respect. Weight, about 18 pounds. Each..............................$11.48 For wool lined skirts, add $1.00.

Race Saddles.

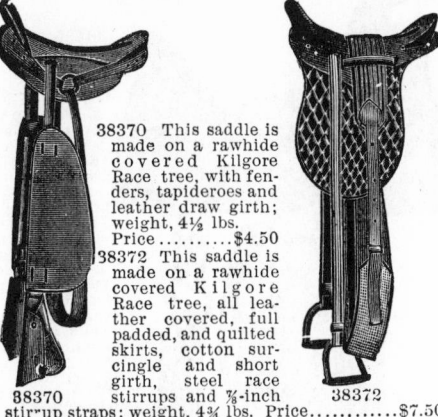

38370 This saddle is made on a rawhide covered Kilgore Race tree, with fenders, tapideroes and leather draw girth; weight, 4½ lbs. Price.........$4.50

38372 This saddle is made on a rawhide covered Kilgore Race tree, all leather covered, full padded, and quilted skirts, cotton surcingle and short girth, steel race stirrups and ⅞-inch stirrup straps; weight, 4¾ lbs. Price..........$7.50

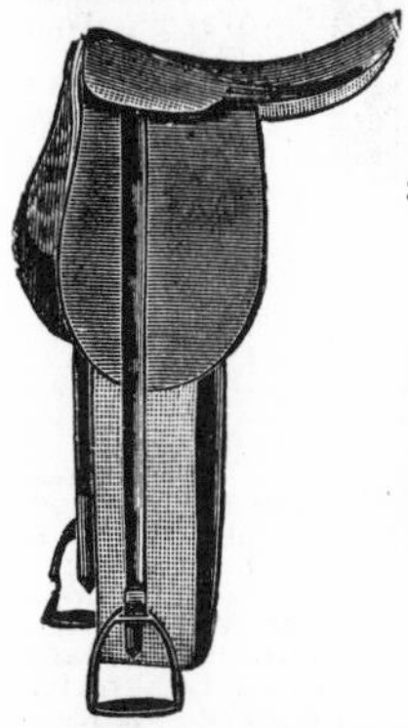

38374 English Race Saddle, made on imported English tree, all fair leather, hogskin seat, full pad; weight, 3½ lbs., complete; worsted girth and outside surcingle over seat; steel race stirrups; ⅞ in, russet stirrup straps. There is surprising value in this saddle at our price. Each $12.00

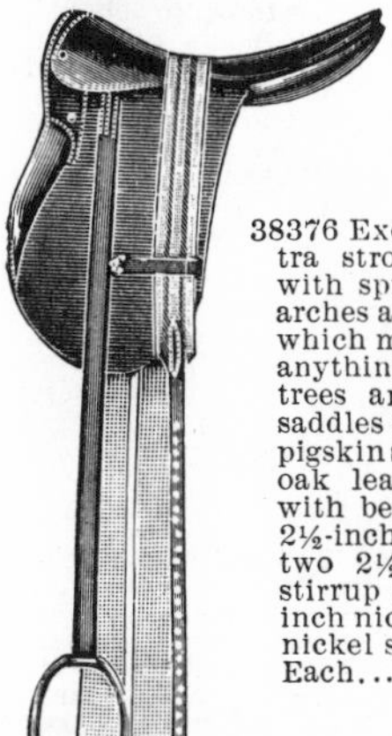

38376 Exercising Saddle, made on extra strong imported cut-back tree with spring bars; cantle, bars and arches are covered with steel plates, which makes these trees as strong as anything of the style produced; trees are 17 inches in length and saddles have 10-inch seats; genuine pigskin seat and knee puffs; stamped oak leather skirts; full stuffed pad, with best English wool serge; one 2½-inch fine worsted surcingle and two 2½-inch fine worsted girths; stirrup straps, extra strong, with 1 inch nickel safety buckles; imported nickel stirrups; weight, about 8 lbs. Each...........................$20.00

Men's Saddles.

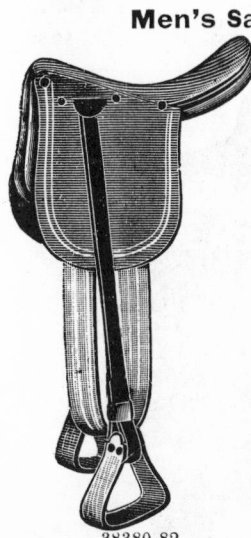

38380 Plain English Style Saddle, made with russet leather seat, pressed split leather skirts and padded bars; 2½ inch fancy cotton buckle girth, light wood stirrups. This is as cheap a saddle of this style as we can produce. They can be used by boys as well as men, as the stirrup leathers can be buckled up to any length desired. Weight, 5½ pounds. Each .. ..$ 2.25 Per dozen...... 24.30

38382 English Style Saddle. (See cut). Made on men's Somerset tree, solid russet leather seat, russet leather skirts with hogskin impression. Full heavy underpad, covered with white drill; 3-inch super cotton girth to buckle; wood stirrups. Weight, 6¾ pounds. Each...$3.00 For covered stirrups, add 50 cents.

38380-82

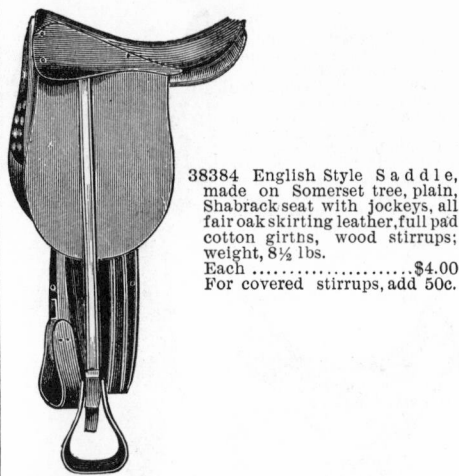

38384 English Style Saddle, made on Somerset tree, plain, Shabrack seat with jockeys, all fair oak skirting leather, full pad cotton girths, wood stirrups; weight, 8½ lbs. Each ....$4.00 For covered stirrups, add 50c.

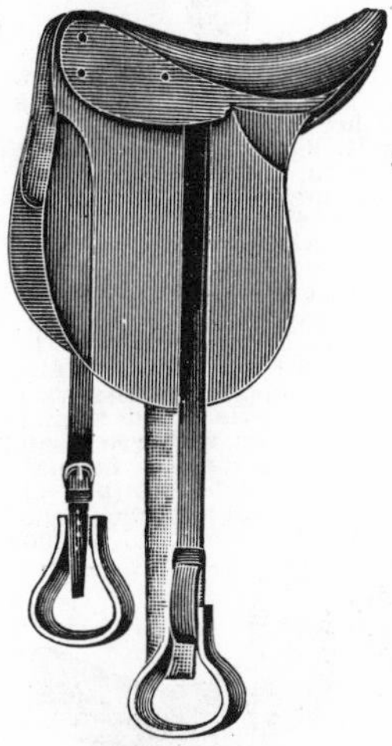

38386 English Style Saddle, made on a 15½-inch Somerset tree. Bars, full padded, heavy leather skirts with hogskin impression, genuine hogskin seat, knee and thigh puffs, stirrup leathers, 1-inch stirrups, 2½-in. wood, cotton corded girth to buckle on both sides; weight, 9 pounds Price $5.50

38388 English Cutback Shaftoe Saddle, made on Somerset tree, genuine hogskin seat, knee and thigh puffs. Skirts and puffs are of solid oak skirting leather with hogskin impression. Full pad of best material, two girths, 1⅛ inch stirrup straps, stirrups bright plate; weight, 11½ lbs. Each................$13.00 We can furnish above saddle in "straight head" Shaftoe style, when desired, at same price. Order No. 38388½.

38390 Imported English Light Park Saddle, manufactured by C. C. Bartley, London, Eng. Made on Shaftoe tree; seat and skirts all over pigskin; knee and thigh puffs; full pad of best English wool serge. Spring stirrup bars, 1¼ inch super English leather stirrup straps. Best forged steel stirrups, nickel plated. English white worsted girths. All made in best style and of best material; weight, 11 lbs. Price..................$25.00

38392 French Shaftoe Saddle; made on an all leather French cut-back tree, with spring steel plates and spring stirrup bars. Made of the best imported hogskins, knee and thigh puffs; best serge pads with hogskin facings; stirrup straps are best English leather with English buckles, Fitzimmon girth, nickel stirrups with rubber bottoms. This is a high grade gentleman's saddle. It is indorsed by all the leading professors of the equestrian art, is used by them in the best riding schools, and is also used in the parks and on the famed boulevards of Chicago more than any, or all other styles. Weight, 15 lbs. Each...$35.00

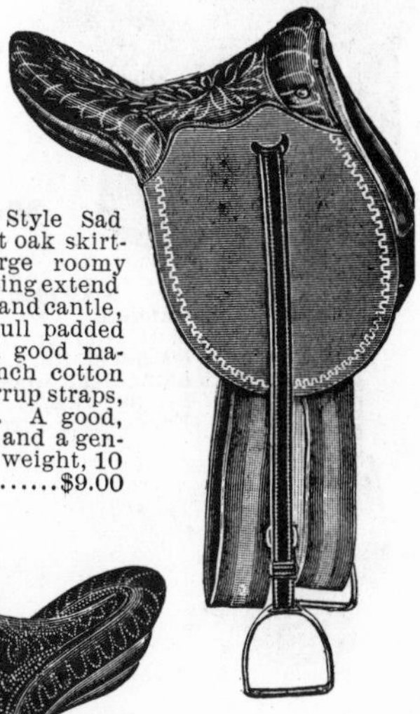

38398 Kentucky Style Saddle, made of best oak skirting leather, large roomy quilted seat, quilting extending over pommel and cantle, under bars are full padded and covered with good material; two 3-inch cotton girths, 1-inch stirrup straps, English stirrups. A good, comfortable seat and a gentleman's saddle; weight, 10 pounds. Price.......$9.00

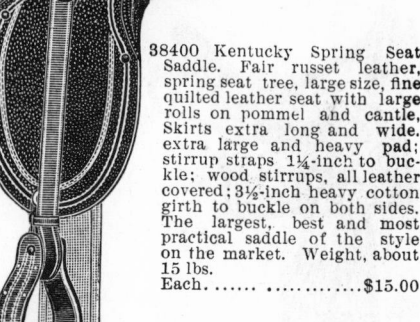

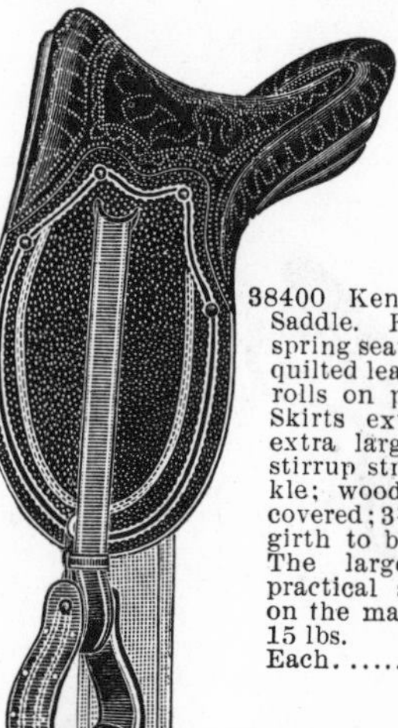

38400 Kentucky Spring Seat Saddle. Fair russet leather, spring seat tree, large size, fine quilted leather seat with large rolls on pommel and cantle, Skirts extra long and wide, extra large and heavy pad; stirrup straps 1¼-inch to buckle; wood stirrups, all leather covered; 3½-inch heavy cotton girth to buckle on both sides. The largest, best and most practical saddle of the style on the market. Weight, about 15 lbs. Each...... ....$15.00

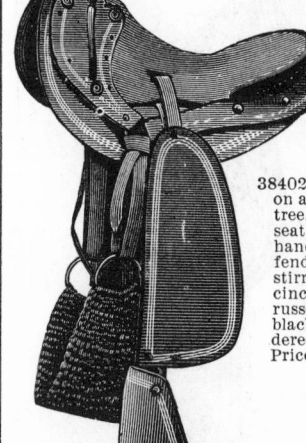

38402 Batesville made on a Muley Morgan tree, solid seamless seat, round leather handle on near side, fenders and covered stirrups, with one hair cinche girth. Made of russet leather unless black is especially ordered; weight, 11 lbs. Price............$6.00

We Believe in Ourselves and Our Methods.

Saddles—Continued.

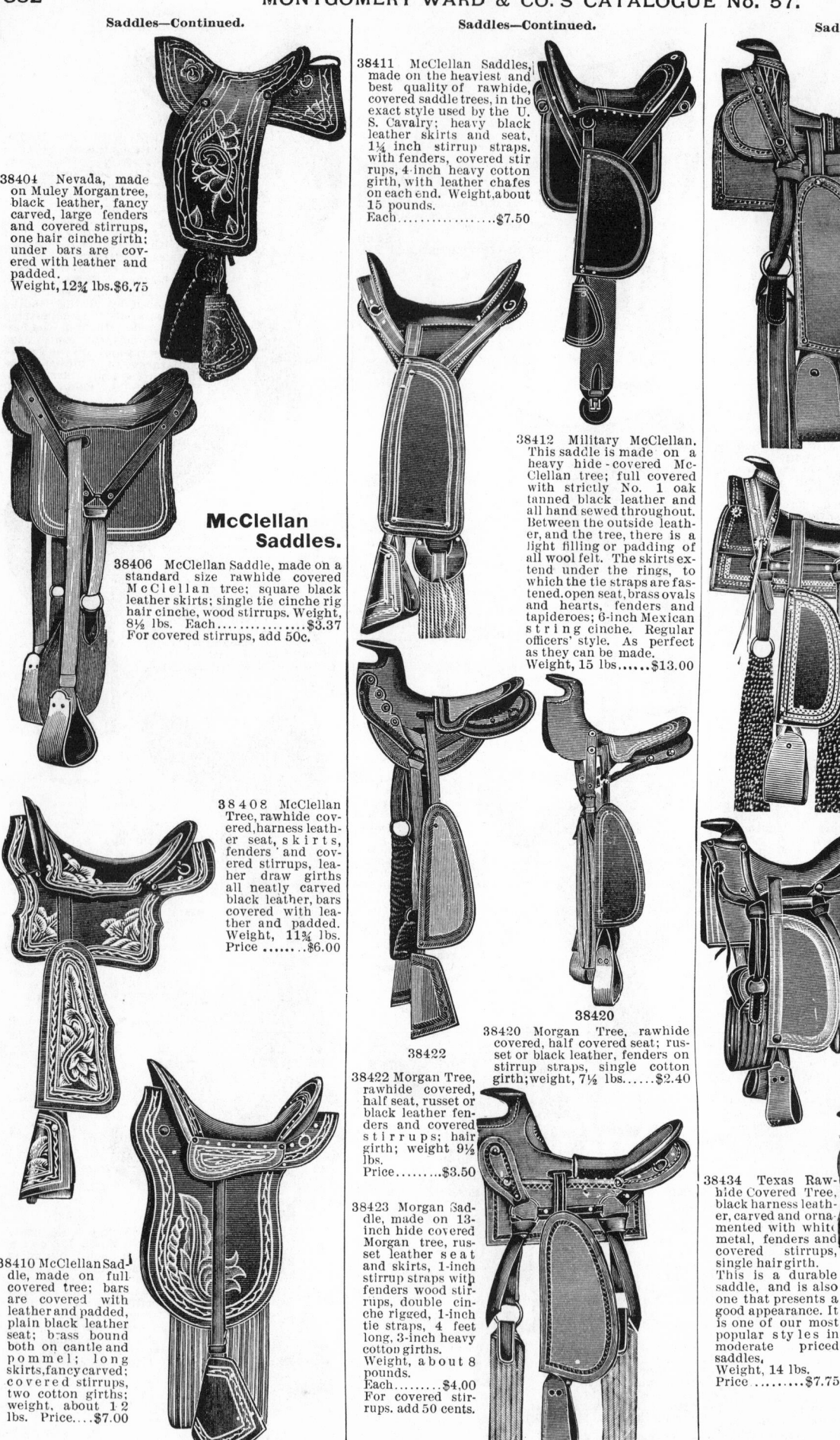

38404 Nevada, made on Muley Morgan tree, black leather, fancy carved, large fenders and covered stirrups, one hair cinche girth; under bars are covered with leather and padded. Weight, 12¾ lbs. $6.75

McClellan Saddles.

38406 McClellan Saddle, made on a standard size rawhide covered McClellan tree; square black leather skirts; single tie cinche rig hair cinche, wood stirrups. Weight, 8½ lbs. Each............$3.37 For covered stirrups, add 50c.

38408 McClellan Tree, rawhide covered, harness leather seat, skirts, fenders and covered stirrups, leather draw girths all neatly carved black leather, bars covered with leather and padded. Weight, 11¾ lbs. Price........$6.00

38410 McClellan Saddle, made on full covered tree; bars are covered with leather and padded, plain black leather seat; brass bound both on cantle and pommel; long skirts, fancy carved; covered stirrups, two cotton girths; weight, about 12 lbs. Price....$7.00

Saddles—Continued.

38411 McClellan Saddles, made on the heaviest and best quality of rawhide, covered saddle trees, in the exact style used by the U. S. Cavalry; heavy black leather skirts and seat, 1¼ inch stirrup straps. with fenders, covered stirrups, 4-inch heavy cotton girth, with leather chafes on each end. Weight, about 15 pounds. Each................$7.50

38412 Military McClellan. This saddle is made on a heavy hide-covered McClellan tree; full covered with strictly No. 1 oak tanned black leather and all hand sewed throughout. Between the outside leather, and the tree, there is a light filling or padding of all wool felt. The skirts extend under the rings, to which the tie straps are fastened, open seat, brass ovals and hearts, fenders and tapideroes; 6-inch Mexican string cinche. Regular officers' style. As perfect as they can be made. Weight, 15 lbs......$13.00

38420

38422 Morgan Tree, rawhide covered, half seat, russet or black leather fenders and covered stirrups; hair girth; weight 9½ lbs. Price........$3.50

38420 Morgan Tree, rawhide covered, half covered seat; russet or black leather, fenders on stirrup straps, single cotton girth; weight, 7½ lbs......$2.40

38423 Morgan Saddle, made on 13-inch hide covered Morgan tree, russet leather seat and skirts, 1-inch stirrup straps with fenders wood stirrups, double cinche rigged, 1-inch tie straps, 4 feet long, 3-inch heavy cotton girths. Weight, about 8 pounds. Each........$4.00 For covered stirrups. add 50 cents.

Saddles—Continued.

38426 Half-Covered Double Cinche Rigged Saddle, made on a hide covered "Prairie" tree. Russet leather seat and skirts. Skirts are 20 inches long, and extend under, covering the bars of the tree. Stirrup leathers, 1¼ in, to buckle. Tie straps 1½ inch, 4 feet long. Girths 3-inch cotton back band; stirrups. 4 in., wood bolted. Weight, about 13 pounds. Each....$5.40

38430 Full Covered Double Cinche Saddle, made on a 14-inch solid fork tree; oiled russet skirting, roll cantle, steel seat plate, 1¼-inch stirrup straps to buckle, fenders attached, 3-inch long wood stirrups, tie latigoes, hair cinches. Weight, 13 lbs. Each........$7.00

38432 Fort Worth Saddle, made on a rawhide covered Jackson tree, full covered with russet skirting leather, solid seamless seat, square skirts covering bars, round after housing; 1½ inch stirrup straps, large fenders, wood stirrups, tie latigoes, two 3½-in. cotton back band cinches with leather chafes under the rings. Weight, 13 lbs. Each...........$7.50

38434 Texas Rawhide Covered Tree, black harness leather, carved and ornamented with white metal, fenders and covered stirrups, single hair girth. This is a durable saddle, and is also one that presents a good appearance. It is one of our most popular styles in moderate priced saddles. Weight, 14 lbs. Price $7.75

Saddles—Continued.

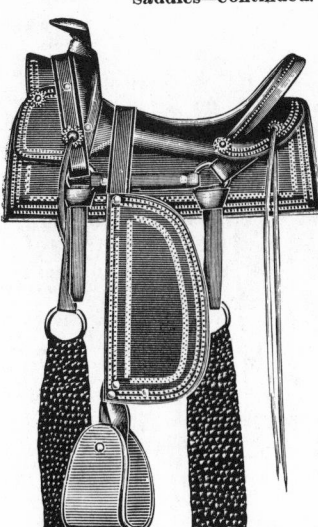

38436 Full Covered Double Cinche Rigged Saddle, made on a rawhide covered steel fork tree, oiled russet skirting, roll cantle, steel seat plate. Stirrup straps 1½ in., fenders attached; 4-in. Texas bolted wood stirrups, tie latigoes on both sides, 4-inch common gray hair cinches. Well made of good stock and a serviceable saddle. Weight 15 lbs. Each ...$8.00

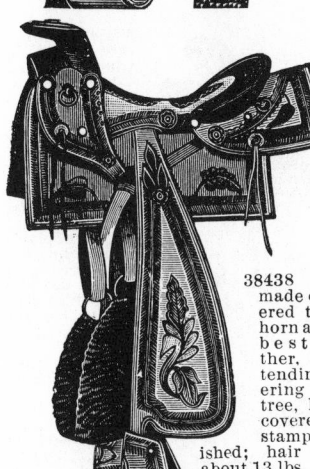

38438 Denver Saddle, made on a rawhide-covered tree, full covered horn and cantle, made of best oak skirting leather, square skirts extending under and covering the bars of the tree, long fenders and covered stirrups; nicely stamped and well finished; hair cinche. Weight, about 13 lbs. Price, single cinche rig...$8.25

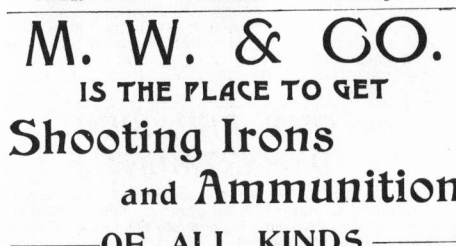

38440— Double Cinche Rigged Saddle, made on full size hide-covered steel fork tree; leather-prime oiled stock; square skirts covering bars of tree; cantle bound and stitched; stirrup straps and cinche support 1½ in.; 20 strand cotton Texas cinches: heavy bolted stirrups. This saddle has been much improved for this season without change of price. They are now better value than ever. Weight, about 16 lbs.... $8.50 For wool lined skirts on No. 38440 saddle, add $1.00 to above price.

Saddles—Continued.

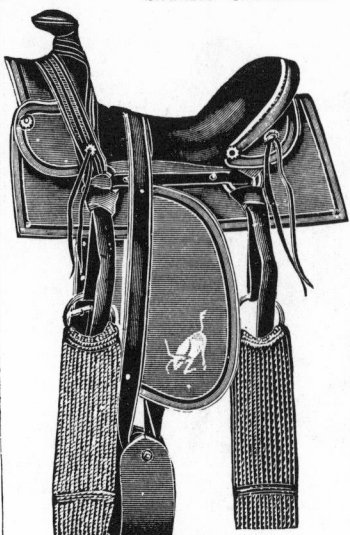

38444 Mexican Full Covered Saddle, made on a rawhide covered tree, choice black saddle leather; under bars are also leather covered. Fenders and skirts are hand carved and skirt corners are finished with white metal ornaments. Covered stirrups and hair cinche. Weight about 16 lbs. Price single cinche rig. $9.50

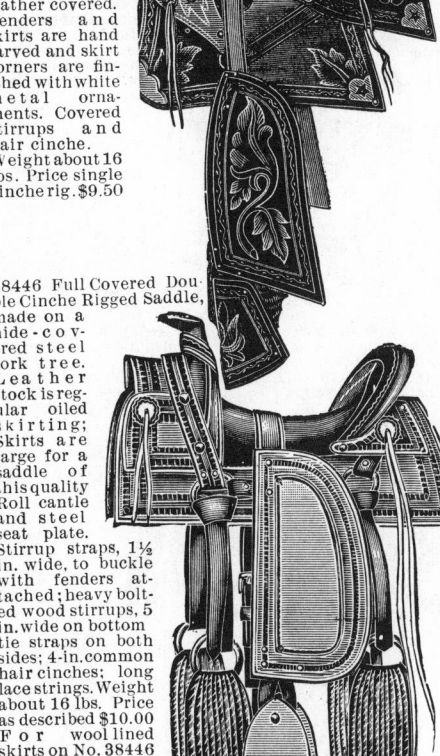

38446 Full Covered Double Cinche Rigged Saddle, made on a hide-covered steel fork tree. Leather stock is regular oiled skirting; Skirts are large for a saddle of this quality. Roll cantle and steel seat plate. Stirrup straps, 1½ in. wide, to buckle with fenders attached; heavy bolted wood stirrups, 5 in. wide on bottom tie straps on both sides; 4-in. common hair cinches; long lace strings. Weight about 16 lbs. Price as described $10.00 For wool lined skirts on No. 38446 saddle, add $1.00 to above price.

Saddles—Continued.

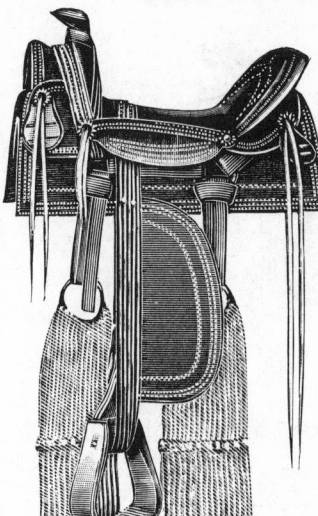

38442 Double Cinche Rigged Saddle, made on a hide-covered steel fork "Daisy" tree; oiled saddle leather; horn and cantle full covered; large square skirts, covered bars; roll cantle; tie straps 1⅛ in., leather covered rings, stirrup leathers 1½ inch; 4-inch bolted wood stirrups. Texas cotton strand cinches. Weight about 18 pounds. Price...$9.25 For wool lined skirts on No. 38442 saddle, add $1.00 to above price.

38448 Full Covered Texas Saddle, made on a rawhide covered steel fork Friesecke tree; best dark russet oiled skirting leather; seat has steel seat plate, square wool lined skirts, jockeys on each side, roll cantle, beaded rolls on pommel, stirrup straps, 1½ inch, with fenders attached; long wood stirrups, leathered on bottoms; leather covered rings; double cinched rigged, to tie on one side; strong tie straps, 6-inch Mexican string cinches. Weight, 20 pounds. Each......$10.50

38450 Full Covered Double Cinche Rigged Saddle, made on a steel fork, hide covered Steininger tree; skirts, 22½ inches long, oiled saddlestock. Stirrup leathers, 1¾ inches to buckle, fenders attached; tie straps, 1¼ inches, 4½ feet long; girths, cotton strand Texas cinches; stirrups, 4-inch wood, bolted; roll cantle, steel seat plate, jockeys and covered rings. Price......$11.00 Weight, about 20 pounds. For wool lined skirts on No. 38450 saddle add $1.00 to quoted price.

38452 Cowboy Saddle, with long black Angora housings, made on steel fork Frisco tree, full covered horn and cantle, Oregon oiled skirting, skirts unlined, roll cantle, steel strainer in seat, double cinche rig to tie on both sides; covered rings, 6-inch Mexican string cinches, stirrup straps, 1¾ inches wide, double at bottom, with fenders, 3 inches long, wood stirrups. This is a very showy and substantial saddle, on which we have made a low price. Weight, 21 pounds. Each............$12.00

CORKERS

Is the word frequently used in connection with our 17 Special Catalogues. Certainly they are above the ordinary, excepting as to prices—they are below the ordinary.

See Index for Wagon and Plow Singletrees. It is good policy to keep a few extra on hand. Only first-class articles carried.

Saddles—Continued.

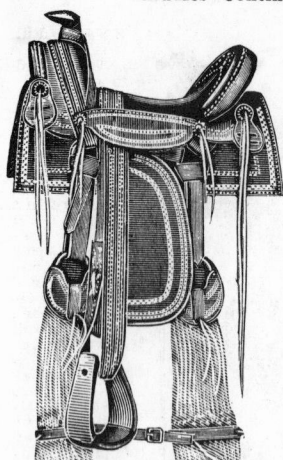

38454 Stockman's Full Covered Double Cinche Rigged Saddle, made on 15-inch rawhide covered steel fork tree; skirts, 24 ins. long, well wool lined; steel strainer in seat, roll cantle, jockeys on each side; stirrup straps, 2 in. wide, double at bottom, fasten with lace strings; fenders attached; 3-inch long wood stirrups, leathered on bars and bottoms; leather covered rings. Tie straps 1½ inches wide, on off side, 1¾ in. to buckle; two 6-inch Mexican string cinches with wool lined chafes and connecting strap; long lace strings; well made of oiled russet skirting. A good plain saddle, strong and durable and at a moderate price. Wgt. 22 lbs. **$13.00**

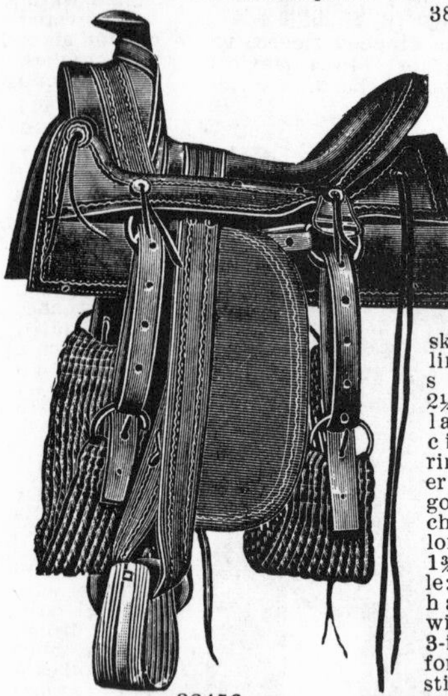

38456 Cowboy Saddle, made on hide covered California "steel Fork" tree; choice oiled skirting leather; horn full covered; seat has steel strainer and roll cantle; skirts are wool lined; stirrup straps, 2¼ inches to lace, double cinche rig; rings are leather covered, latigoes are 1½ inches, 7 feet long, on off side, 1¾ in. to buckle; two 6-inch hair cinches with tongues; 3-in. long California wood stirrups. This saddle will

38456
prove a perfect competition-killer, and an excellent wearer. Weight, 22 pounds. Price...........**$13.50**

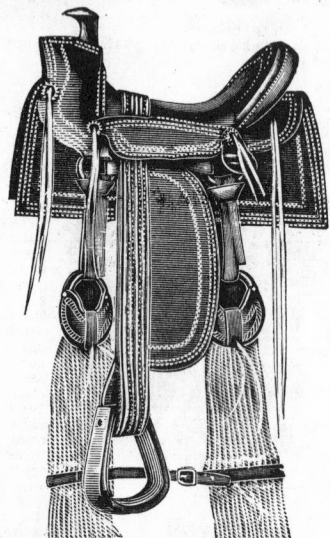

38458 Montana Full Covered Stock Saddle, made on 15½-inch guaranteed steel fork tree, rawhide covered, full covered horn and fine hand sewed extended roll cantle, made of the best oiled skirting in the style known as underrigged; skirts, 24 inches long, wool lined; seat with steel seat plate, jockeys on each side, stirrup straps 2-inch to lace, double at bottom; long wood stirrups leathered bottoms and bars; covered rings, double cinche rig to tie, heavy tie straps, two 6-inch Mexican string cinches, with wool lined chafes and connecting strap. A high class job, very cheap at the price. Weight, 23 pounds. Each...................**$14.00**

Saddles Continued.

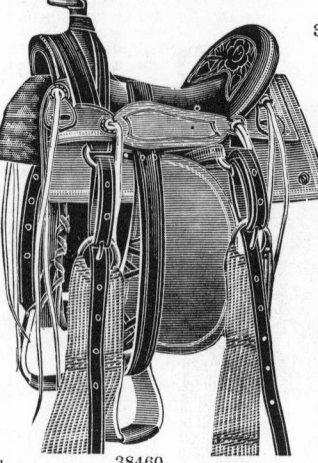

38460 Full Covered Double Cinche Rigged Saddle, made on large hide-covered Cheyenne tree, best oil skirting leather, square skirts, wool lined, concave seat, with steel plate; lace ties on each side stirrup, leathers 2 inch to lace, doubled at bottom; tie straps 1½ inch, on off side, 1¾ inches to buckle, Cheyenne roll cantle. rings leather covered, 5-inch hair cinches, heavy bolted stirrups, leathered bottoms. Weight, about 24 lbs.

38460
Price..........................**$15.00**
We will make No. 38460 saddle to order with single cinche rig for $14.50.

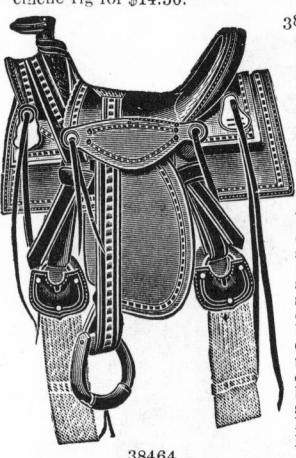

38464 Full Covered Double Cinche Rigged Saddle, made on Cheyenne steel fork, hide-covered tree; prime oiled skirting leather; California style "Loop Seat" with steel seat plate; large square wool lined skirts; large jockeys on side; beaded edge roll on front gullet; stirrup leathers 2 in. to lace, double at bottom; tie straps, 1½ in. on off side, 1¾ in. to buckle; extra fine Colorado roll cantle; rings leather covered; 1½ in. bolted hickory stirrups with leather bottoms laced on; two 15-strand gray California cinches

38464
with large leather chafes. This saddle is made with checker stamped border, and is well finished. Weight, about 28 pounds. Price..........**$17.00**
We will make No. 38464 saddle to order with single cinche rig for $16.50.

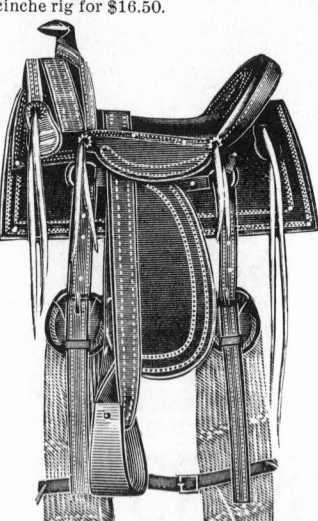

38466 Cowboy Saddle, made on hide covered steel fork, Friesecke tree, fine oiled oak saddle stock, large wool lined skirts, bound at top; seat has steel plate, Colorado cantle, hand stitched. Stirrup leathers 2¼ in. wide to lace, extra large fenders attached to stirrup leathers. Leather covered rings; double tie rig; ties, 1½ in. wide. 7 feet long, off side 1¾-inch. Hair cinches, connected and tongued with wool lined chafes. Long bent wood stirrups, bolted and leathered on bottoms; weight, about 25 lbs. Price, as described.....**$17.50**
We will make No. 38466 saddle to order with single cinche for $16.75.

Saddles—Continued.

38467 "Creole" Tree Saddle. Full covered, double cinche rigged saddle, made on 15½-inch rawhide covered, steel fork "Creole" tree. Skirts 27½-inches long, California oiled skirting leather, wool lined. Seat with plate, fine beaded roll cantle and large jockeys. Stirrup straps, 2¼-inch, fenders attached. Tie straps, 1½-inch, 6 feet long; 2-inch buckle straps on off side, covered rings, Western style Angora strand cinches with leather chafes and tongues. Ox-bow stirrups, leather bottoms laced on. Jockey and fenders are ornamented with fine raised stamped figures. Weight, about 28 pounds. Each...................**$18.50**

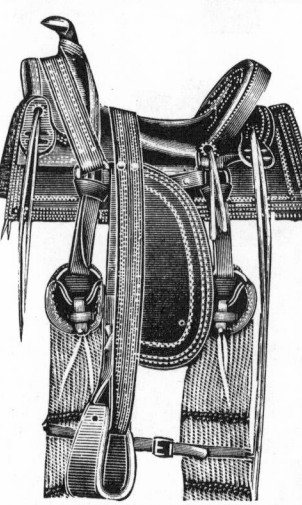

38468 Full Covered Double Cinche Rigged Cowboy Saddle, made on a rawhide covered steel fork, "Visalia" tree. Leather is all the best Oregon oiled skirting; large skirts, wool lined; seat has steel plate; roll cantle; 2½ inch stirrup straps, doubled to lace, tie straps 1½ inch; on off side 1¾ inch to buckle. Leather covered rings, hard hair cinches with wool lined chafes and connecting strap. Solid block stirrups. leathered on

38468
bars and bottoms. We recommend this style to those who want a first-class stock saddle at a moderate price. Weight, about 27 lbs. Price..........**$20.00**

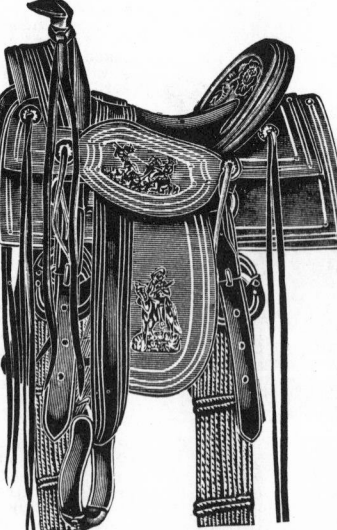

38469—Pueblo Tree Saddle, full covered cowboy saddle, made on 15½ inch rawhide covered, steel fork, "Pueblo" tree, skirts 27½ inches long, best oiled skirting leather, wool lined; fine beaded roll cantle and beaded pommel, steel seat plate, double cinche rig, covered rings, large jockeys, stirrup straps, 3-inches wide, double at bottom, fastened with lace strings, large fenders attached, stamped figures on jockeys, and fenders; tie straps, 1¾ inch, 6 feet long, 2-inch buckle straps on off side; hard hair cinches with leather chafes and tongues, leather covered iron stirrups. Weight, about 30 pounds. Each.............................**$21.00**

Saddles—Continued.

38471 "Creole" Tree Saddle, full covered Texas saddle, made on 15½-in. steel fork, "Creole" tree, rawhide cov-

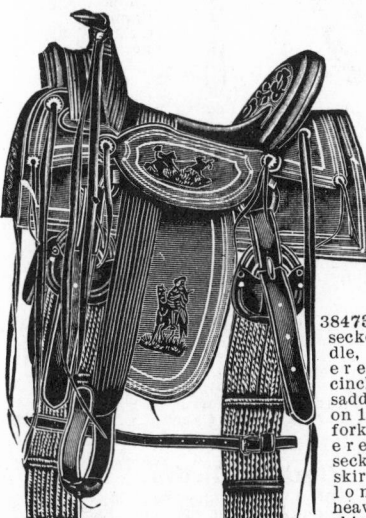

ered, skirts, 27½ in. long, wool lined, and made of best oiled skirting; roll cantle with two raised beads, steel seat plate, large stamp'd jockey on each side, stirrup straps, 2¼-inch, large stamped fenders attached; tie straps, 1½-inch, 6 feet long, 2-inch buckle straps on off side; white Angora hair cinches with leather chafes and tongues, ox-bow stirrups, leather bottoms laced on, large saddle pockets with long black Angora flaps. Weight, about 30 pounds. Each........................$22.00

38472 Extra Large Cowboy Saddle, made on hide covered "Steel fork," long Friesecke tree; out-side of California oiled skirting leather, selected stock. Seat has steel plate seat and jockey made in one piece, hand stitched Colorado cantle, horn full covered with horn cap, beaded edge rolls on pommels, large skirts, wool skin lined and bound, 2½-inch stirrup leathers doubled to lace; extra large fenders attached to stirrup leathers, niggerheads on front and back jockeys, double tie rig, ties, 1⅜ inches wide, 7 feet long, on off side 2 inches to buckle, hair cinches, leathered, wool lined and tongued, long bent wood stirrups, bolted and leathered on bottom. Weight, about 30 lbs. Price...........................$22.50

38473 Friesecke Tree Saddle, full covered, double cinche rigged saddle, made on 16-in., steel fork, hide covered "Friesecke" tree, skirts, 29 in. long, extra heavy oiled skirting, wool lined, seat with plate, stamped jockeys on each side, roll cantle with large oval bead and large bead on pommel covered rings, stirrup straps,

3-inches wide, double at bottom, fasten with lace strings, extra large stamped fenders; tie straps, 1¾-inch, 6½-feet long, 2-inch buckle straps on off side; hard hair strand cinches with wool lined leather chafes, tongues and connecting straps, iron stirrup leather covered. Weight, about 35 pounds. Each........................$25.00

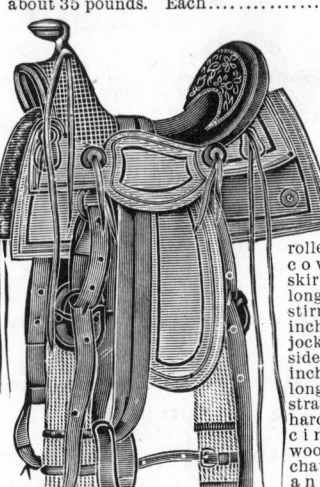

38475 "White River" Tree Saddle, heavy double cinche rigged stock saddle, made on 16-inch steel fork, hide-covered, White River tree; full covered, underrigged, rolled cantle and covered rings; skirts, 30 inches long, wool lined; stirrup straps, 3 inch, large fenders, jockeys on each side; tie straps, 1¾ inches, 6½ feet long; 2-inch buckle straps on off side; hard hair strand cinches, with wool lined leather chafes, tongues and connecting straps; iron stirrup, leather covered, Weight, about 35 lbs. Each........................$27.50
For fine hand-stamped border add $1.50.

Wyoming Saddle.

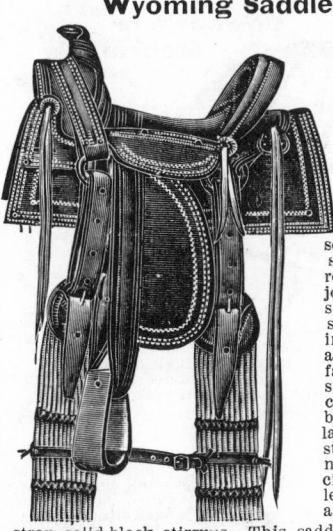

38476 Wyoming Cowboy Saddle made on 16-inch solid fork, beef hide covered, Friesecke tree, large square wool lined skirts, solid concaved seat with steel strainer and roll cantle, large jockeys on each side, stirrup straps 2¾-inch, doubled at bottom, to fasten with lace strings; double cinche rig to buckle, 2-inch latigoes; two 20-strand, California white hair cinches with leather chafes and connecting strap, solid block stirrups. This saddle is all hand made and we guarantee every tree. All leather used is the best quality of California oiled saddle leather. Weight, about 35 lbs.
Price, with solid block stirrups...................$29.00
We will make No. 38476 saddle to order with single cinche rig for $1.00 less than quoted price.

White River Saddle.

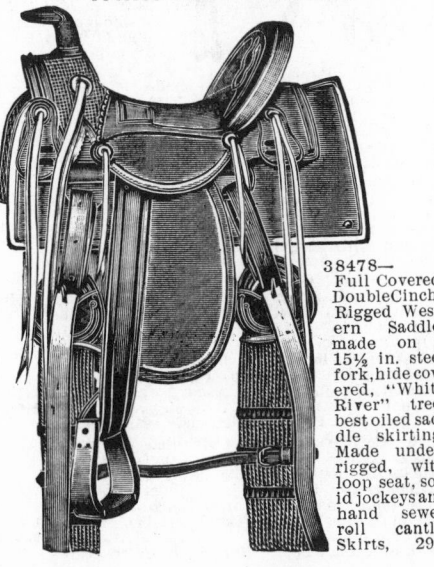

38478—Full Covered, Double Cinche Rigged Western Saddle, made on a 15½ in. steel fork, hide covered, "White River" tree, best oiled saddle skirting. Made underrigged, with loop seat, solid jockeys and hand sewed roll cantle. Skirts, 29½

in. long, wool lined. Stirrup leathers, 3 inches wide, double at bottom, fasten with lace strings, with large fenders attached. Stirrups, 2 in. wood, brass bound, leathered on bars and bottoms. Tie straps, 1¾ inches wide, 7 feet long, on off side, 2 inch to buckle. Leather covered rings. Cinches. California strand, white hard hair, with wool lined chafes and connecting strap. Long lace strings all around. A first-class job in every respect. Weight, about 3? lbs.
Price........................$32.00
We can furnish above saddle made on "Los Angelos" tree, if preferred at same price. For fine hand stamped border add, $1.50.

"Visalia" Tree Saddle.

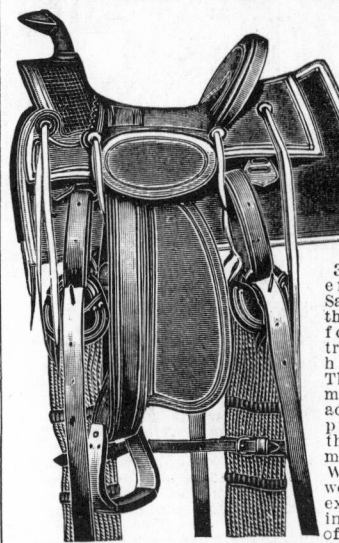

38480 Full Covered Western Saddle, made on the genuine steel fork "Visalia" tree, heavy rawhide covered. These saddles are made in the exact style of the productions of the best saddlemakers of the West and Northwest, and are not excelled by them in either quality of workmanship, material, durability or general appearance. Skirts, 30 inches long, wool lined; stirrup leathers, 3 inch, large fenders; tie straps, 1¾ in., 7 ft. long, on off side 2 inch to buckle; girths, white hard hair, wool lined chafes and connecting strap; stirrups, 2-inch wood, brass bound, laced leather bottoms; roll cantle, solid jockeys, loop seat, covered rings, long lace strings. Choicest oiled saddle leather stock all through. Weight, about 40 lbs.
Price........................$33.00
For fine hand stamped border, add $1.50.

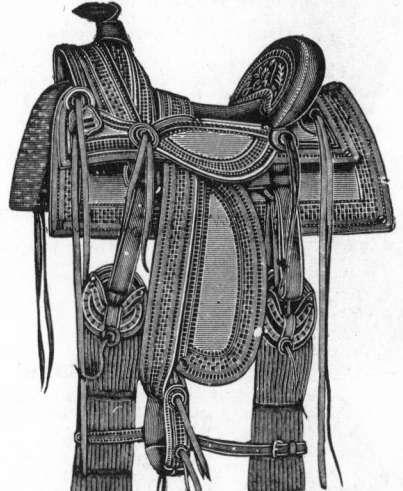

38482 Full Covered, Double Cinche Rigged Cowboy Saddle, made on a 16-inch hide-covered steel fork, long Friesecke tree. Leather used is best oiled skirting. Skirts are 30 in. long and well wool lined. Stirrup leather, 3-inches wide, double at bottom, and have large fenders attached. Large jockeys on each side over stirrup leathers. Seat has steel seat plate. Tie-straps, 1¾ inches wide, 6½ feet long; on off side 2 in. to buckle. Cinches, California strand white hard hair, with wool-lined chafes and connecting straps. Stirrups, 1½ inch steel, leather covered, fine extended roll cantle, leather covered rings, fine raised stamped border and seat. *Weight, about 40 lbs.* Price..........$35.00
We will make this saddle to order with single cinche rig for $33.75.
We can furnish No. 38482 saddle on "Visalia" tree, when desired, at same price.

Our New "Pride of the West."

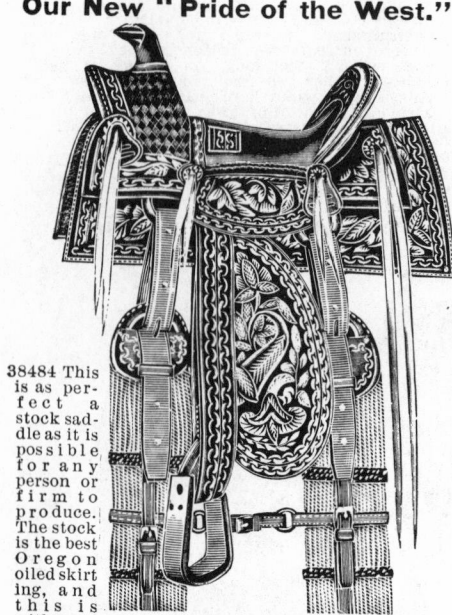

38484 This is as perfect a stock saddle as it is possible for any person or firm to produce. The stock is the best Oregon oiled skirting, and this is without question the best saddle leather tanned. The sewing, stamping and carving is all done by hand by men who are artists as well as the most expert saddle makers. We absolutely guarantee these saddles to be made on the best and strongest trees, to be made of the very best saddle leather by skilled workmen, and that there is nothing better to be obtained. Tree, 16 inches, "Steel Fork," genuine Visalia, rawhide covered; skirts, 30 inches long, wool lined extending well back of cantle, all hand stamped "T" rail border; seat made concave or dished, loop in front, steel seat plate, solid jockeys, fine, hand sewed roll cantle; stirrup straps, 3 inches wide to fasten with whangs, large fenders attached; "T" rail border, hand stamped: stirrups, 2¼-inch heavy wood, brass bound, 3-inch roller bars; double cinche rig to buckle; covered rings 2-inch latigoes; two 20-strand white, hard hair cinches, with wool-lined leather chafes, connecting strap and martingale brace from ring to ring. Weight, as described, 40 lbs.

Price, as described............$37.25
Price, without stirrups..... 36.00

38486 23 inch Eagle Bill Tapideros, put on 2½-inch brass bound stirrups, hand stamped and made to exactly match our "Pride of the West" saddles. Per pair......$9.00
Without stirrups............. 7.75
Weight, per pair, complete, 6½ lbs.

Cantanas.

38487 Cantanas to match our "Pride of the West" saddle. To be hung on horn. Outside size, 10x13 inches on each side; size of bags, 9½ in. each way. Weight, per pair, 2½ lbs.
Per pair..............$5.40

Saddle Bags.

38488 Saddle Bags to match our "Pride of the West" saddle. To be fastened to skirts of saddle behind cantle; length from center to bottom, 15 inches; width of flaps, 9½ inches, size of bags, 9 ins. wide, 7 ins. deep. Weight, per pair, 2¼ lbs.
Per pair........ .. ....$4.60
We will attach any of these parts to any saddle for quoted prices. No charge for extra labor.

HARNESS AND RIDING SADDLES.

We have the largest and most complete "Horse Goods" department on the face of the globe. All kinds of Harness and Parts of Harness and the largest variety of Saddles ever handled by one house.

Saddle Trees.

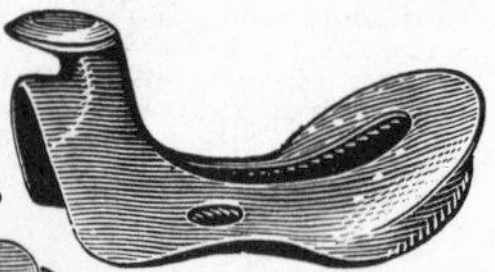

38492 Morgan Saddle Tree, rawhide covered; weight, 3¼ lbs.
Each.............. $1.25

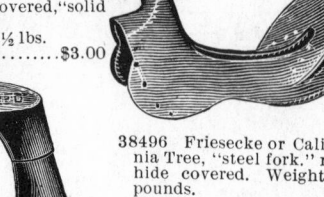

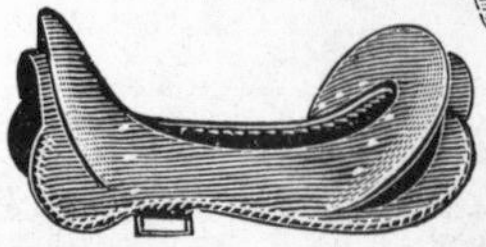

38493 McClellan Saddle Tree, iron arches, rawhide covered. Weight, 4¼ lbs.
Each.............$1.50

38495 Friesecke or California Tree, heavy rawhide covered, "solid fork." Weight, 6½ lbs.
Each......$3.00

38496 Friesecke or California Tree, "steel fork," rawhide covered. Weight, 9 pounds.
Each $4.00

Repair Forks.

38498 Best Malleable Steel Forks for repairing saddles with broken or damaged horns. Can be fitted to any tree.
Each.................$0.80
Postage............... .20

Riding Bridles, Cowboy's or Stockman's Bridles.

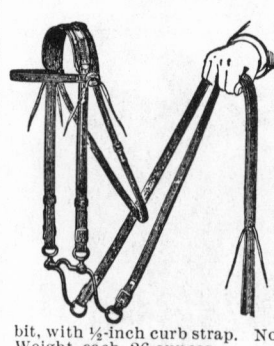

38500 Russet leather, all hand braided, made of 8-plait braided calfskin, fine, all round, with double cheeks and head piece; single reins, made with fancy braided loops and slides, in place of buckles, with leather tassel and curb strap; no martingales; without bit. Each.................$5.25

38502 Double Head stall Bridle, made of oiled stock russet leather only; heavy fringed front, one inch cheeks; fringed slide loops on cheeks, throat and reins; 1 inch 6½ feet quirt reins; nickel buckles, port bit.
Each........$2.25
Without bit.. 2.15
Weight, each, 38 ounces.

38504 No 1 Cowboy Bridles, made from the best Oregon oiled stock ⅞ in. all through, double head buckling on top, 6-foot reins. Box loops on crown, checks and reins, ½-inch curb straps, nickel rosettes and all nickel buckles. Without bits, each................ 1.80

38506 Made of oiled russet California leather. Headstall cut in one piece, one inch wide with one buckle on top of bridle; reins, ⅞ inch to buckle in bit; are six feet long, laced together on end with buckskin strand; curb straps, ⅝ inch wide, nickel rosettes, XC plated port bit.
Each........$1.40 Without bit 1.30
Weight, each, 32 oz. Martingale, extra. Each .50

38508 (No. A.) Cowboys' Bridles, made of the same stock as No. 38506, with ¾-inch head stall cut in one piece to buckle on top; ¾ inch rein 6 feet long to loop in bit, laced together on end with buckskin; ⅝ in. curb strap, with XC plated port bit, nickel rosettes. Each.................. 1.15
Without bit.................. 1.05
Weight, each, 26 ozs. Martingale, each, extra. .50

38510 Cowboys' Bridles, of oiled California black leather; headstall cut in one piece one inch wide with one buckle on top of bridle; ⅞-inch reins 6 feet long, laced together on end with buckskin to buckle on bit; curb strap, ⅝ in.; nickel rosettes and XC plated port bit. Each.. 1.40
Without bit................. 1.30
Weight, each, 32 ozs. Martingale, extra, each. .50

38512 Oiled Bridles, 2-inch solid crown with layer; ⅞-inch double cheeks to buckle from bit to crown; ⅞-inch reins, 6½ feet long with quirt end, nickel buckles, port bits.
Each $1.20
Without bit.. 1.10
Weight, about 30 ounces.

38514 Round Russet Bridles ⅞-inch single cheeks, ⅞-inch double reins; all buckles are leather covered; 4-ring nickel plated curb bit, with ½-inch curb strap. No martingale.....$3.00
Weight, each, 26 ounces.
Martingale to match, with round forks and neck strap, and leather covered rings................. 1.00

38516 Round Bridles, ¾-inch single cheek, and ⅞-inch single reins, leather covered buckles, 2-ring nickel plated curb bit with ½-inch curb strap. No martingale...................... .. 2.25
Martingale to match above...................... 1.00

38517 Round Bridle, ¾-inch single cheeks and ¾-inch single reins, imitation covered buckles, 2-rings, nickel plated curb bit with ½-inch curb strap. No martingale.................... 1.80
Weight, each, 24 ounces.
Martingale to match above................ .75

38519 Flat Bridles, ¾-inch single cheek, and ¾-inch double reins, 4-ring, XC plated curb bit and buckles, ½-inch curb strap. No martingale 1.50
Weight, about 30 ounces each.
Martingale to match above. .... .50

38520 Flat Bridle, ⅞-inch single cheeks. ⅞-inch double reins, XC center bar buckles, 4-ring XC plated curb bit with ½ inch curb strap........... 1.65
Weight, about 32 ounces each.
Martingale to match above...................... .50

38522 Flat Bridles, ¾-inch single cheeks, ¾ inch single reins, full cheek, XC plated snaffle bit and buckles. Each............................ 1.00
Weight, about 19 ounces each.
Martingale to match above.................. .50

38523 Round Bridles, round cheeks, fronts and reins, solid crown, ¾-inch nickel buckles, curb strap, XC bit. Each........................ 1.25
Weight, bout 22 ounces each.

38526 Flat Bridles, ⅞-inch cheek, ⅞-inch single rein, full cheek XC, plated snaffle bit and buckles; all riveted....................... .70
Weight, about 18 ounces each.
Martingales to match above .... .35

38527 Flat Bridles, ¾-inch cheeks, ¾-inch reins, cheeks and reins sewed in XC, jointed ring bit.. .55
Weight, about 16 ounces each.
Martingale to match above..................... .35

38528 Rawhide Bridles. These bridles are all made of the best oil tanned rawhide, ⅞-inch cheeks, ⅞-inch reins, 5 feet long, with curb bit; no martingales................................... 1.35
Weight, about 26 ounces each.

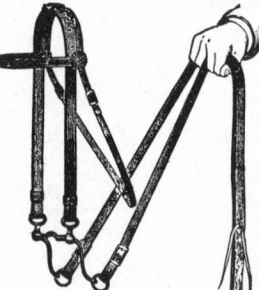

38530 Double Head Stall Bridles, made of oiled stock; ¾-in. double cheeks to buckle on top; ¾-inch reins, 5 feet long with quirt end; XC buckles; port bit. Each.
With bit......$0.75
Without bit.... .65
Weight, about 24 ounces.

38532 Genuine Imported English "Weymouth" Riding Bridles, made in England of English russet leather. Double head and double reins; one head has two-ring English nickel bit with curb chain, the other head has nickel snaffle ring bit. All hand sewed. Each....................$4.25
Weight, each, 2½ pounds.

38533 Genuine Imported English "Pelham" Riding Bridle. Hand made. Best English russet leather. Single head and double reins; four ring, English short port, nickel plated bit. Each. 3.25
Weight, each, 1¾ pounds.

38535 Black Web Riding Bridles, adjustable for any size horse or pony, 1¼-inch head piece, ⅞-inch reins, 5 feet long, with bit and curb strap. Not sold without bit. Each....................... 0.60
Per dozen............................. 6.48

38536 Fawn Web Riding Bridles, adjustable for any size horse or pony, 1¼-inch head piece, ⅞-inch reins, five feet long, with bit and curb strap. Not sold without bit. Each.............. .60
Per dozen................................... 6.48
Weight, each, 22 ounces.

Saddle Cirths.

38540 Super Cotton Web, 3 inches wide, 3½ feet long, with 1¼-inch buckle on each end. Each..$0.20
38541 Extra Fancy Union Web, 3¼ inches wide, 3½ feet long, with 1½-in. buckle on each end.
Each............................ .30
Weight, each, 7 ounces.

Cotton Web Cinches.

38544 Heavy Cotton Web Cinches, 3½ in. wide, with leather chafes on each end.
Each...$0.30
Weight, each, 10 ounces.
38546 Heavy Cotton Web Cinches, 3½ in. wide, with leather chafes and connecting strap.
Per pair.. .70
Weight, per pair, 21 ounces.

Hair Cinches.

38551 Each
38548 Hair Cinches, 4-inch, plain gray..........$0.25
38549 Hair Cinches, 5-inch, plain gray............ .30
38550 Hair Cinches, 6-inch, plain gray............ .35
38551 Hair Cinches, Mexican string, 6-inch....... .40
38552 Hair Cinches, Mexican string, 9-inch....... .60
Weight, each, 12 oz. to 24 ounces.

Cotton String Cinches.

38555 4-inch Cotton String Cinche, colored......$0.20
38556 5-inch Cotton String Cinche, colored...... .25
38557 6-inch Cotton String Cinche, colored...... .30
For tongues on any of the above cotton cinches, add 3c. to each. Weight, each, 10 ounces. to 12 ounces.

California Cinches.

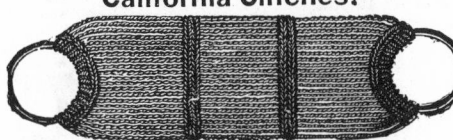

38560 32-strand, 6-cord, 2-bar, white hair, weight each, 20 ounces...........................$1.25
38562 24-strand, 8-cord, diamond center, white hair; weight, each, 30 ounces............. 1.45
38564 20-strand, 6 cord, 2-bar fancy white and black hair; weight, each, 10 ounces. Each...... .60
38566 Connected Cinches, two 6-inch California white hair cinches, 20-strand, 2-bar, with leather chafes, tongues and connecting strap. Weight per pair, 3 pounds. Per pair................. 2.00
38568 Connected Cinches, 4-inch cotton back band, front cinche, 6-inch Mexican string back cinche, with leather chafes, tongues and connecting strap. Weight, per pair, 2¾ pounds.
Per pair... 1 40

Ladies' Saddle Blankets.

38574 Side Saddle Blankets, of heavy brown felt, long on one side; has wide fancy waved binding, with braid inlay. Figure of crossed whip and stirrup worked in corners. Weight, 16 oz. Each........$1.25

38576 Side Saddle Blankets, same style as above, but made of blue felt. Weight, 16 oz. Each.. 1.25
38578 Side Saddle Blankets, same style as 38574; color is green. Each................. 1.25

Men's Saddle Blankets.

38580 Men's Saddle Blankets, made of dark felt, light in weight, but good value.
Each................$0.40
Weight, each, 15 oz.
38582 Men's Felt Cloth Saddle Blankets, medium grade, have fancy colored braid border. Weight, about 10 oz. Each..$0.60

38584
38584 Men's Saddle Blankets, good weight felt, in dark colors, fancy borders and bound all around; extra quality. Each...................$0.90
Weight, each, 12 ounces.

Graduated Saddle Blankets.

Thickest in parts where the hardest wear comes.

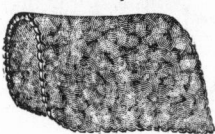

38586 Blue Heavy Graduated Felt, scolloped and pinked edge.
Each..............$1.10
38587 Yellow, Heavy Graduated Felt, scolloped edge.
Each..............$1.15

38586-7-8
38588 Red Heavy Graduated Felt, scolloped and pinked edge. Each....................... 1.20
38590 Spencer's Graduated Felt, plain gray, plain edge. Each............................. 1.25
38592 Spencer's Graduated Felt, plain gray, medium weight. Each........................... 1.65
38594 Spencer's Graduated Felt, plain gray, extra heavy. Each.... .... 2.00
Weight, from 1½ to 2½ lbs.

Woven Hair Saddle Blankets.

38596 Woven Hair Saddle Blankets, 25x36 in., web bound; weight, 3 lbs. Each..............$1.35
22—3d

Stirrup Straps.

38600 Stirrup Straps, 4 ft. 6 in long, with buckle, either black or russet leather.
Width	1 in.	1¼ in.
Per pair	$0.50	$0.65
Weight	14 oz.	17 oz.

38602 California Style Stirrup Straps, cut from the best Oregon oiled skirting leather, 5 ft. 6 in long. with lace strings.
Width	2 in.	2¼ in	2½ in.	2¾ in.	3 in.
Per pair	$1.25	$1.40	$1.85	$2.30	$2 80
Weight	28 oz.	32 oz.	36 oz.	40 oz.	44 oz

Latigoes.

38604 Latigo Straps, 2 inches wide, for buckle cinche rig, cut from the best Oregon oiled skirting, with lace strings to fasten.
Length for draw side, 5 ft. 6 in., per pair.......$1.25
Length for off side, 2 ft. 8 in., per pair.......... .65
Weight, per pair, 24 oz., 12 oz.
38606 Latigoes, for tie cinche rig, with lace strings to fasten to saddle rings.
1¼ in. 5 ft. long, per pair............................$0.75
1½ in. 5 ft. long, per pair.......................... .90
Weight, per pair, 12 oz., 15 oz.

Stirrups.

38610 Metal Shoe Stirrups for side saddles, "XC" plated, Each, $0.15. Per dozen, $1.62
Weight, each, 6 ounces.

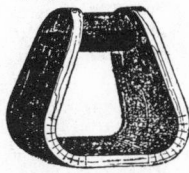

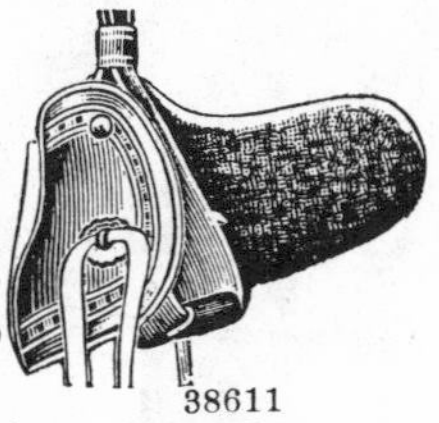

38611 Tapidero Stirrups for ladies' saddles, made of russet leather with long wool lined chafe, and attached to 2 inch wood stirrup, leathered on bottom.
Each.................$0.60
Weight, each, about 12 oz.

38611

38612 Slipper Stirrups, for side saddles; sole or shank is of steel, covered with leather stitched on, heavy hogskin vamp, strong iron swing, comfort and security combined.
Each.................$0.90
Weight, 14 ounces.

38612

38616 Texas Bolted Wood Stirrups, 5 inch bottoms. Bars are 2 inches long and suitable for stirrup leathers from 1½ to 2 inches wide.
Per pair...................$0.17
Per single dozen......... .95
Weight, per pair, 1¾ lb.

38618 2½ inch Brass Bound Heavy Bolted Wood Stirrups, with 3 inch rollers.
Per pair............ .....$1.00
Per single dozen........ 5.50
Weight, per pair, 2¼ lbs.

38618

38620 Ox Bow Stirrups, 1½ inch wood stirrups, ox-bow shape, 2¾ inch bar bolted through.
Per pair.......................$0.35
Per single dozen.................. 2.00
Weight, per pair, 1¾ lbs.

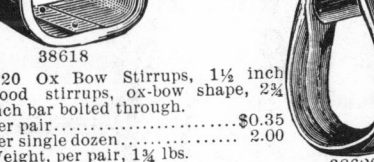

38620

38622 Two-inch Steel Stirrups, covered with oiled California leather, California pattern; bars will admit 3-inch California stirrup strap. Per pair..............$1.50
Weight, per pair, 2½ lbs.

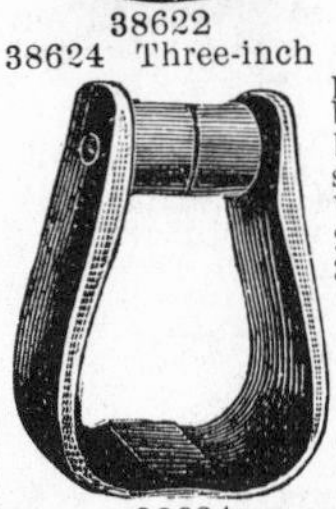

38622

38624 Three-inch Wood Stirrups, long California pattern, with one bolt. Per pr. 30c. Per dozen single stirrups...$1.65
Weight, per pair, 21 ounces. 
38625 Cuban Stirrup, made of heavy forged steel, blued finish; will take 1¼ inch straps.
Per pair...$1.25

38624   38625

Tapideros or Covered Stirrups.

Taps or covers are made of Oregon oiled skirting; are put over good wood stirrups with bars suitable for stirrup straps from 1¼ to 2½ inches wide.

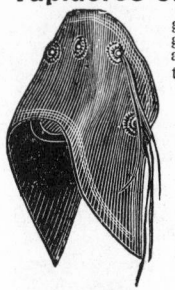
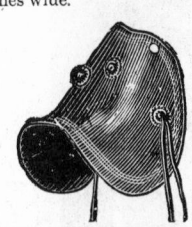

38627 $2.00 per pair.
Weight, per pair, 4 lb.

38628 $1.65 per pair.
Weight, per pair, 2¾ lbs.
Cow Boy Stirrups. California Pattern, Regulation Size.

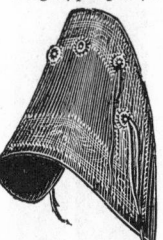

38629   38630
38629 $1.80 per pair. Weight, per pair, 3 lbs.
38630 Made of solid aluminum, strong as steel, light as a feather, weight, only 8 oz. each. Only made with 3-inch stirrup bars.
Per pair.............. .... $1.75

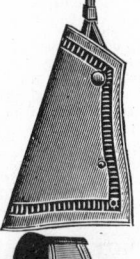

38632 Covered Stirrups, light wood stirrup, fair leather cover, embossed border. Will take stirrup straps from ⅞ to 1¼ in. wide.
Per pair......................$0.65

Cowboys' Saddle Bags.

38636 Large Size "Cow Boys' Saddle Bags; pockets on each side. Size, 7½x8 inches. Outside flaps are covered with long black Angora fur; length, from center to lower edge of fur, from 26 to 28 inches. Per pair............$3.25
Weight, per pair, 3½ lbs.

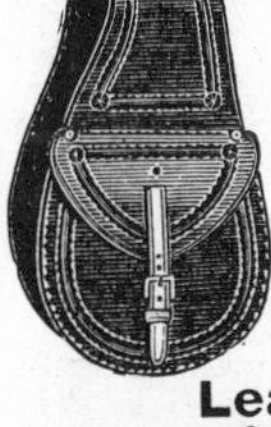

38638 Cowboys' Saddle Bags, to be tied on back of cantle. Pockets, 7½x8 inches, made of Oregon oiled skirting leather. Postage, 30 to 35 cents. Per pair...............$2.60

38639 Cowboys' Saddle Bags, extra large size, made of best oiled skirting. Size of pockets, 10x14 inches on each side.
Per pair..................... .. $4.50
Weight, per pair, 4 lbs.

Leather Cantanas.

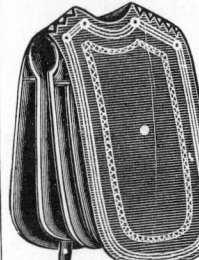

This bag is to be hung on horn of saddle; size of pockets, 9x14 inches on each side. Made of Oregon oiled skirting. Weight, each, 3 lbs.
Each.
38642 Plain cover.....$3.75
38643 Stamped cover 4 20
38644 Angora goat cover.................. 5.00

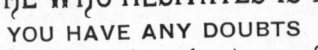

Chaparejos.

Cowboys' Riding Pants.

38646 Chaps, or Cowboys' Riding Pants, made of oiled chaparejos leather, stock being specially prepared for this purpose; solid leather waistband, laced together, fringe on outside of each leg, two pockets; made for service. Sizes, 28 to 33 inches in length of leg. Waist measurement not necessary.

Per pair.....................$8.50
Sizes longer than 33 inches.
Per pair.....................$9.00
Weight, per pair, 5½ to 6½ lbs., according to length.

38647 Chaps or Cowboys' Riding Pants, made of a flexible grained russet leather. Pockets on each side; waist band is both lined and faced, making three ply of leather. Sizes from 28 to 34 ins. inside seam.
Plain legs, per pair.....$5.40
Fringed legs, per pair.... 6.00
Average weight, per pair, 4 lbs.

Horse Hobbles.

38650 Front Hobbles, two leather anklets connected by short swivel chain. To be attached to the two fore legs of a horse to prevent running or straying away when loose.
Per pair.................$0.60
Per dozen pairs......... 6.50
Weight, per pair, 1½ lbs.

38651 Side Hobbles, with chain and snap. To be attached from one foreleg to one hindleg.
Per pair $0.70
Per dozen pairs. 7.60
Weight, per pair, 2¼ lbs

Lariats.

38653 Rawhide Lariats, four plait, best quality of oil tanned rawhide, cable cord center, all hand plaited and whole strands from end to end without splicing. Rawhide hondas.

Length	40 ft.	43 ft.	45 ft.
Each	$6.25	$6.75	$7.25
Weight	2¼ lbs.	2½ lbs.	3 lbs.

38655 Cotton Lariats, extra quality braided cotton rope, ½ inch in diameter; honda of the same, securely fastened.

Length	35 ft.	50 ft.
Each	$1.50	$2.00
Weight	3 lbs.	4½ lbs.

38656 Linen Lariats, extra quality braided linen rope, ⅜ inch in diameter, with rawhide honda. Have been boiled in oil, which keeps them soft and pliable and renders them waterproof; will not kink or snarl and will hold anything that runs on hoof. Ends are patent grip fastened. Length, 40 feet; weight, 2½ pounds.
Each $2.50
50 ft long; weight, about 3 lbs. Each......... 3.00

Lariat Hondas.

38658 Hondas for lariats; firmly pressed rawhide Each, 20c. Per dozen, $2.00.

Bit Burnishers.

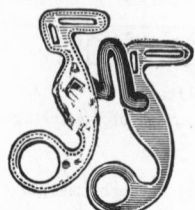

38659 Steel Chain Bit Burnishers, with buckskin back, 4x4 inches. Used for cleaning bits, spurs and buckles.
Each $0.25
Per dozen 2.70
Weight, each, 6 ounces.

Bridle Bits.

We always carry a large stock of bits on hand, as we do probably the largest business in bits, spurs, saddles, etc., of any house in America selling direct to the consumer.

38670 Fine Blued Mexican Curb Bits, with short port on mouth bar.
Each $0.18
Per dozen............... 1.95
Weight, each, 11 ounces.

Bits—Continued.

38671 Fine Nickel Plated Texas Port Bits, small copper roller on port bar. Large rings for bridle straps. Each........ ....$0.30
Per dozen......... 3.35
Weight, each, 9 ounces.

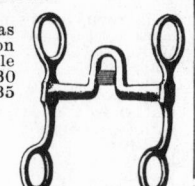

38673 Fine Dead Smooth Filed Mexican Curb Bit, with large ring and rein chains; weight, 19 ounces.
Each...... $0.75
Per dozen.. 8.10

38673

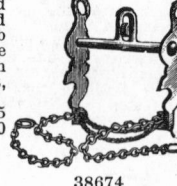

38674

38674 XC Plated Cowboys' Curb Bits, with roller and rein chains; weight, 24 ounces. Each... .....$0.50
Per dozen.................... 5.50
38676 Fine Dead Smooth Filed and Chased California Spoon Curb Bits, with rollers and rein chains. Weight, 18 ounces. Each... ....$0.75
Per dozen................ 8.10

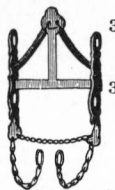

38678 Fine Nickel Plated Colorado Port Bit, plain finish. Heavy mouth bar, 2-inch port with large copper roller. Large rings.
Each $0.80
Per dozen.................. 9.00
Weight, each, 7 ounces.

38680 Nickel and Chased Patent Long Port Mouth, with roller; weight, 15 ounces.
Each...... ...$1.00
38681 Same as above, hand forged steel, not chased. Weight, 15 ounces.
Each.......... ......$2.50

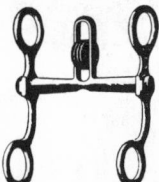

38682 Mexican Curb Bits. Patent filed and chased with trinkets, rein chains and roller. Weight, 18 ounces. Each...........$1.75
Per dozen.....................19.50
38684 The Patent Durable Hand Forged Bit, with roller, fine nickel steel curb bits, and chased, with swivels and rings for reins; weight, 17 ounces. Each...........$5.00
Per dozen.................57.00

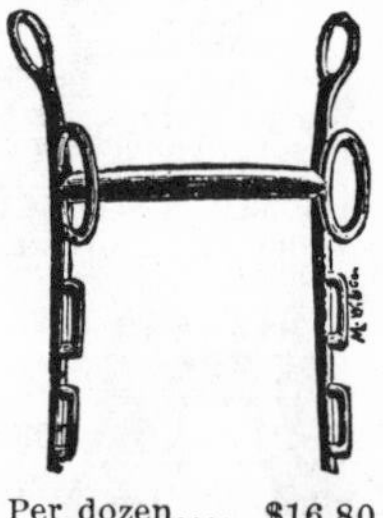

38686 The Military Bit, popular pattern, half plated, with curb chain; weight, 17 ozs.
Each....................$1.50 Per dozen.....$16.80
38687 Hanoverein Fine Nickel Plated Curb Bit, with wrought mouth and stiff cheeks. This bit is used largely in fine carriage, coach or double buggy harness; weight, 15 oz. Each...... .... .75
Per dozen.......................... 8.00

38690 XC Plated Kentucky Short Cheek Racking Bits; with short port on mouth bar.
Each..........................$0.10
Per dozen 1.08
38691 Two Ring XC Plated Riding Bits, with straight round cheeks and short port. Each .... .11
Per dozen................ 1.20
Weight, each, 8 ounces.

38690

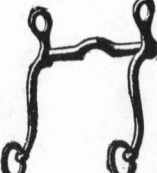

Bits—Continued.

38693 Fine Nickel Plated Leg Patter Bit, patent port mouth, with roller in port, 9-inch rein chains.
Weight, 22 oz. Each.............$2.40
Per dozen.. .... 27.50

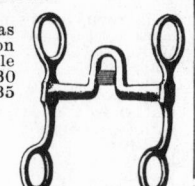

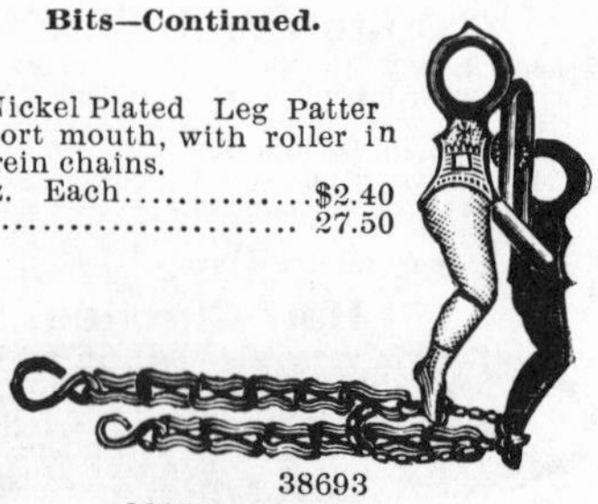

38693

38695 English Riding Bits, two rings, port mouth, fine nickel plated; weight, 10 ounces.
Each...$0.75
Per doz. 7.50

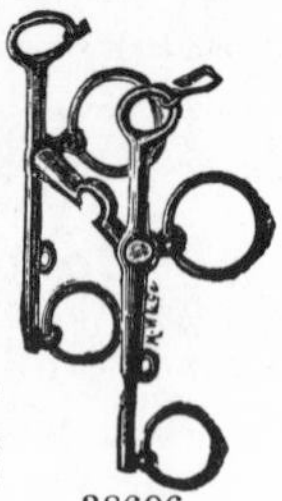

38695
38696 English Riding Bits, 4 rings, port mouth, fine nickel plated.
Each.......................$1.25
Per dozen................. 13.50
Weight, 12 ounces.

38696

38698 Fine Nickel Plated Leg Pattern Bit, port mouth with roller in port.
Each.. .$1.25
Per doz, 13.50
Weight, 16 oz. 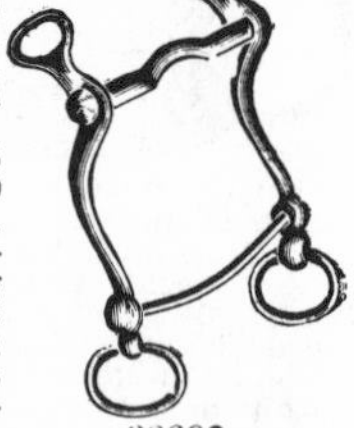
38699 Kentucky Racking Bits, short cheek pattern with bar at bottom to prevent from spreading.

38698

38699

Each ....$0.50 Per dozen $5.25
Weight, each, 10 ounces.

38700 Spanish Curb Bits, nickel plated.
Each.....................$0.60
Per dozen 6.30
Weight, 14 ounces.

38702 XC Plated Driving Bits, stiff mouth.
Each $0.10
Per dozen.............. 1.08
38703 All Black Driving Bits, stiff mouth.
Each.....................$0.10
Per dozen.............. 1.08
38704 Nickel Plated Driving Bits.
Each.......$0.18 Per dozen.............. 2.00
38706 Par Silver or Solid Nickel Driving Bits, half cheek snaffles, very strong and are non corrosive. Absolutely will not soil or tarnish. Mention whether stiff mouth or jointed mouth is wanted.
Each......... ....$1.50

38708 All Black Driving Bits, jointed mouth.
Each.......... ....$0.10
Per dozen.... .... 1.08
38709 XC Plated Driving Bits, jointed mouth.
Each.....................$0.10 Per dozen.........$1.08
38710 Nickel Plated Driving Bits, jointed mouth.
Each.......$0.18 Per dozen.......... 2.00
Weight, 10 ounces.

38712 Bridle Bits for team bridles; heavy, for work harness, 2¾-inch rings, XC plated.
Each $0.08 Per dozen...........$0.85
Weight, each, 8 ounces.

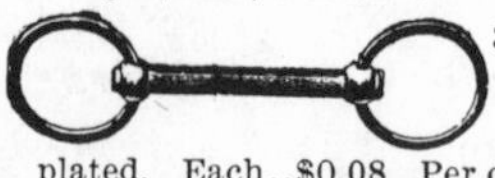

38713 Bridle Bits, with stiff mouth for use in bridles of work harness, 2¾-inch rings, XC plated. Each..$0.08 Per dozen.........$0.85
Weight, each, 8 ounces.

38715 Squires' Flexible Rubber Mouth, Nickel Half Cheek Snaffles, driving bits, No. H.
Each.... ....$0.50
Weight, 10 ounces.

38717 Race Bits, 3½ in. rings, all steel nickel plated.
Each................$0.85
Weight, 10 ounces.

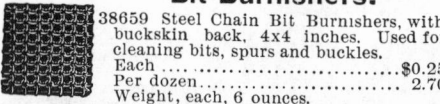

Use Wall Paper and Paint.

Bits—Continued.

38719 Double Twisted Wire Bits, jointed mouth (see cut), XC plated.
Each................$0.12
Per dozen.......................... 1.30
Weight, 10 ounces.
38720 Single Twisted Wire Bits, XC plated.
Each .... .09
Per dozen...................... 1.00
Weight, 10 ounces.

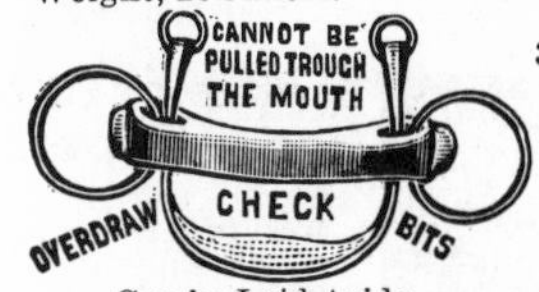

CANNOT BE PULLED TROUCH THE MOUTH — CHECK — OVERDRAW — BITS
Can be Laid Aside.

38722 The Lindsey Humane Bit, No. 1. This bit is made of solid leather; the strongest bit made, and of the best material; are finished oval; mouthpiece has straight spring bedded in center, rein rings, wrought steel, hand forged and heavily nickel plated; check-rein rings are either nickel or Davis rubber; chinpiece of the best material and all hand stitched, and are finished in keeping with the best custom work made. Each..................$1.60
Weight, each, 7 ounces.
38723 Humane Bit, No. 2. Par silver mouth bar and rings with extra fine finish, absolutely non-corrosive. Positively will not soil or tarnish. Padded leather chin strap. Each............... 1.55

38725 Springsteen's Patent Bit, as shown in cut. Extra fine finish, nickel plated.
Each.........$1.75
Weight, 20 ounces.
Size of bits in mouth, 4¼ in. 4½ in. 4¾ in., 5 in. When ordering be sure to give size.
38726 Springsteen's Bits, same grade bits as above, but XC plated instead of nickel.
Each $1.00
Weight, each, 16 ounces.
In Springsteen's Patent Bit, there is comfort and control; you go as you please. It is a positive cure for the worst side-puller.

38728 "Success" Bit; the latest thing out; most practical, humane and safest driving bit in the market. Used either as safe and ordinary bit. XC.
Each $0.50
Weight, 13 ounces.

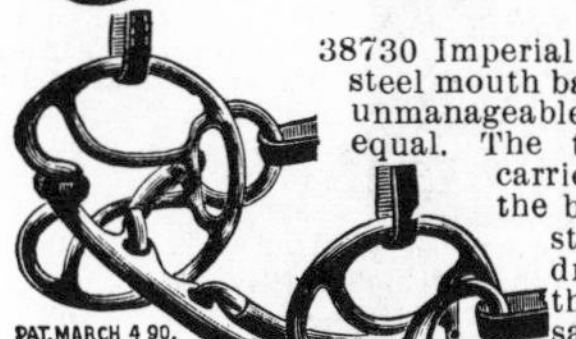

38730 Imperial Driving Bit, forged steel mouth bar. For vicious and unmanageable horses it has no equal. The tongue cannot be carried over the top of the bit. Its peculiar construction gives the driver such leverage that he is absolutely safe behind the most treacherous horse.
XC plate........$0.80
Fine nickel pl... 1.35
Weight, each, 12 oz.
PAT. MARCH 4 90.
38730

J.I.C. BIT — PATENTED

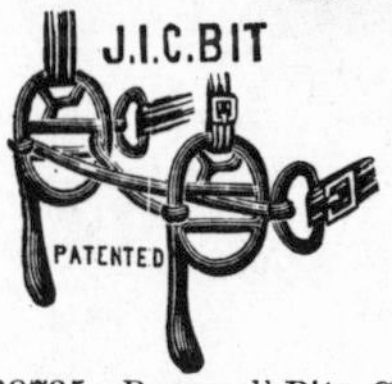

38732 The J. I. C. Bit; for pullers and vicious horses it is unexcelled. Fine XC plate. Each.......$0.75
38733 Same as 38732, but fine nickel plated.
Each............. $1.00
Weight, 13 ounces.

38735 Rockwell Bits. Genuine Rockwell XC plate, jointed bits.
Each.............$0.18
38736 Genuine Rockwell nickel plate.
Weight, 11 ounces. Each.................$0.35

38738 Mouthing Bits, double cheek, XC plate, jointed. Each.....$0.35
Used for breaking colts.
Weight, 17 ounces.

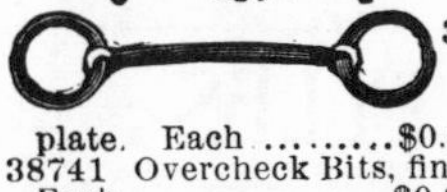

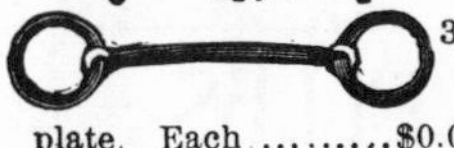

38740 Overcheck Bits: to be used as a separate bit on overdraw check reins, XC plate. Each ....$0.05. Per dozen.......$0.40
38741 Overcheck Bits, finely nickel plated.
Each.................$0.08. Per dozen.......... .75
Weight, each, 2 ounces.

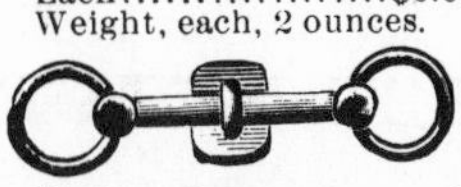

38743 Loose Ring Tongue or Lolling Bit. XC plated. Each $0.40
Weight, 15 ounces.
Used to break horses of the habit of hanging the tongue out of the side of the mouth.

Safety Bridle Rein Chains.

Weight, 6 ounces to 10 ounces.
38750 Safety Bridle Rein Chain, nickel plated, with snaps, 11 in. Per pair.......................$0.90
38751 Regular Bridle Rein Chain, nickel plated, with snaps, 10 in. Per pair........................ .50
38752 Regular Bridle Rein Chain, polished, with snaps, 10 in. Per pair....................... .35
38753 Covert's Bridle Rein Chain, XC plated, with snaps, 11 in. Per pair .... .25

Stallion Lead Chains.

38756 English Steel Lead Chains, 3-16 wire, 18 inches long, polished, with snap and swivel.
Each ....$0.55. Postage........$0.12
38757 American Company Steel Stallion Lead Chain, steel snap, swivel and "D" ring.
Each.................$0.25. Weight, 7 oz.

Spurs.

Spurs are quoted by the dozen (12 spurs to the dozen) and by the pair (2 spurs to the pair). Make no mistake. Single spurs will cost just one-half the price given per pair.

38760 Fine Steel Spurs, nickel and chased, 1⅜-inch malleable rowels, without straps. Per pair........$0.45
Per single dozen... 2.50
Weight, per pair, 6 oz.

38761 "OK" Spurs, fine blued finish; heavy heel band, one button and chain; 1½-inch steel plate rowels, without straps. Per pair.....$0.55
Per single dozen.... 3.00
Weight, per pair, 12 oz
38761

38763 Fine Steel Spurs, polished and chased, one button and chain, 2-inch malleable rowels; a very popular spur, without straps. Per pair....$0.40
Per single dozen......... 2.20
Weight, per pair, 4 oz.
38763

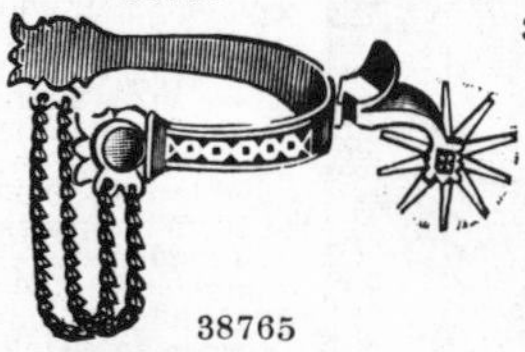

38765 New Patent Steel Spurs with chains, burnished and engraved, solid, medium weight, heel band, 1⅜-in. rowel, very rapid sellers, without straps. Per pair.$1.00
Per single doz... 5.50
Weight, per pair, 13 oz.
38765

38767 Eureka Spurs, wide steel heel band, nickel plated, 1¼-inch malleable rowels. Two buttons, without straps. Per pair. $0.30
Per single dozen.............. 1.65
Weight, per pair, 5 oz.
38767

38769 Stock Spurs, modern style, good weight band, imperial finish, one button and chain, 1⅛-inch steel rowels, without straps. Per pair.............$0.50
Per single doz........ 2.75
Weight, per pair, 11 oz.
38769

38770 Excelsior Steel Spurs nickel plated and engraved, very finely finished. Extra wide, fancy shaped heel band, 1½-inch malleable rowel, one button and chain, without straps.
Per pair. $1.40
Per single dozen........... 7.75
Weight, per pair, 10 oz.

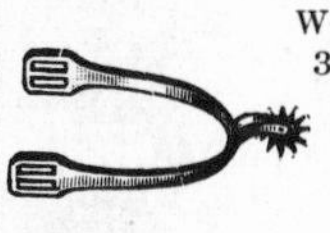

38772 Solid Brass Spurs (No. 9), medium weight, ¾-inch steel plate rowels, without straps.
Per pair......................$0.20
Per single dozen............ 1.10

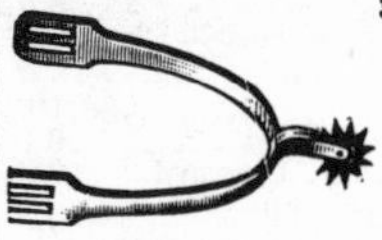

38773 Extra Heavy Solid Brass Spurs (No. 11). Heavy oval heel band, 1⅜-in. rowel shank, ⅞-inch steel plate rowel. Regular military style, without straps. Per pair....$0.50
Per single dozen............ 2.75
Weight, per pair, 8 oz.
38773-4

38774 Extra heavy malleable spurs No. 11. XC plate; see cut 38773. Heavy oval heel band, ⅞-inch steel plate rowels. Without straps.
Per pair.............................$0.30
Per single dozen............................ 1.65
Weight, per pair, 7 oz.

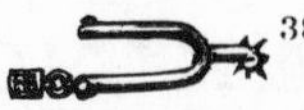

38776 Fine Imported English Park Spurs, nickel plated, light oval band, ⅜-inch steel rowel. One button and strap buckle, with over and under straps.
Per pair......$1.00 Per single dozen............$5.60
Weight, per pair, 5 oz.

Spur—Continued.

38778 Paragon Spurs, wide steel heel band, plain nickel plated finish, two buttons, 1¾-inch blued steel plate rowels, without straps.
Per pair.................$0.50
Per single dozen........ 2.70
Weight, per pair, 8 oz.
38778

38780 Thompson's Pocket Spurs, made of best material and nickel plated. Can be attached or detached in a moment and can be carried in a vest pocket when not in use. No straps required. Per pair.................$1.25
Weight, per pair, 2 oz.

38782 California Spurs, hand forged steel, nickel and chased leather lined, 1¾-inch rowel, without strap, 1 button and chain.
Per dozen.... ...... $14.00
Per pair............. 2.50
Weight, per pair, 16 oz.

38783 California Spur, hand forged steel, nickel and chased, leather lined 2⅜-inch rowel, without strap; 1 button and chain.
Per dozen.........$16.80
Per pair............. 3.00
Weight, per pair, 18 oz.

38785 California Spurs, hand forged steel, silver inlaid, blued finish, medium weight heel band, 1 button and chain, 2¼-inch rowel with steel bells or danglers, without straps. Per pair.........$3.00
Per dozen.................... 18.00
Weight, per pair, 16 oz.

38786 California Spurs, hand forged steel, silver inlaid, blued finish, extra heavy heel band, 1 button and chain, 2¾-inch rowel with steel bells or danglers, without straps.
Per pair...........................$5.00
Per dozen..........................30.00
Weight, per pair, 24 oz.

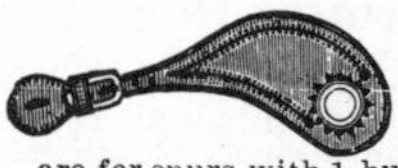

38792 Spur Straps, Texas pattern, made of oiled California stock, with nickel ornaments on sides and nickel buckles. These spur straps are for spurs with 1 button and chain.
Per dozen, single straps..................$4.05
Per pair.......................... .75
Weight, per pair, 7 oz.

38794 Eureka Straps for spurs with 2 buttons.
Per pair......$0.25

38796 Mexican Spur Straps, 2 in. wide, 12 in. long, for spurs with 1 button.
Per pair............$0.15
38796

38797 Spur Straps, ½ in. wide, 17 in. long, for spurs without buttons. Per pair...........$0.07

38798 Texas Spur Straps, made of oiled skirting, stamped border and outside. Four buttonholes on inside end. For spurs with one button.
Per pair............$0.50
Weight, per pair, 4 oz.

WALL PAPER DEPARTMENT.

Wall paper is an article upon which a large profit is made by the ordinary merchant who has to buy in small quantities. We buy in carload lots and pay spot cash consequently we are in position to sell you goods at the lowest possible prices.

Cheapness, style and *perfection* are what we aim to give.

The days of wall paper as a luxury have certainly gone by when 65 cents will buy enough paper (side wall, ceiling and border) to cover an ordinary size room. *Our aim is not only to sell you wall papers 50 per cent. less than other dealers*, but also to give you the latest designs and colorings.

We only ask you to send to us for samples to be convinced that we can save you money.

Wall paper should be shipped by freight when the value of same warrants. Small shipments of small value should be included with other goods to make the purchase profitable. We do not ship wall paper by *Express C. O. D. under any circumstances*, and often decline to ship same by express (when paid for) because the transportation charges are generally in excess of the shipment when compared to the value.

Wall paper is manufactured in 16-yard lengths which are put up in one double roll. Our prices are for double rolls of 16 yards each.

"The Hanging of It."

Paint new walls with glue water before hanging paper. Dissolve one pound of ground glue to one bucket of hot water. Use wheat flour made into a paste and scalded with a little alum for paste Never boil paste. Paste the length of paper you wish to hang, fold each end toward the center, taking care to have the edges perfectly even and trim, thus insuring paste up to the extreme edge, making a better job and taking but half the time, as you cut two thicknesses at once. The laps are to show when paper is cut before pasting, as the paste does not cover the edge.

Sheathing paper or cheese cloth is often used as a background where there is no plaster.

We have bought for the coming season a special line of Wall Paper, designed and colored expressly for churches, halls, etc., samples of which will be sent upon application.

Samples.

Always State What Price Paper You Want.

We will send samples of wall paper and border when requested, but desire that if a selection is made the order be sent in at once, as we are unable to keep long in stock any one pattern, but can usually send as a substitute something similarly colored, and of about the same design. If possible always select a *first* and *second* choice. Should you not care to have samples sent, state whether you have any preference for light, medium or dark colorings, or for small or large figure; what room the paper is for and if you wish any color to predominate. Hanging wall paper is not difficult, and does not require an expert. Anyone who is careful can do it.

Paper Hangers' Samples.

We will send any *Paper Hanger* or *Dealer*, upon receipt of $1.00, three sample books (18x24 inches), containing a larger variety of rare and desirable samples of wall paper than all the stores in any small town combined can show. We will credit the $1.00 when orders for wall paper to the amount of $10.00 have been received. When paper is ordered in *full bundles* or *25 double rolls of one color and design*, we will make a special discount from catalogue prices.

Rules for Measuring a Room.

Measure every side of the room and add the number of feet; multiply the sum obtained by height in feet. To allow for doors and windows, multiply the height of each by the width; add all and deduct from amount. Then divide by 72. The result is the number of double rolls required for side walls.

Sufficient allowance should be made for matching and waste.

EXAMPLE.—Room 15 feet long, 12 feet wide, 9 feet high. One window, 6x4 feet: one door, 7½x4 feet.

```
15 plus 15 plus 12 plus 12=54x9=486
1 Window,     6x4=24        54
1 Door,       7½x4=30            72 ) 432
              ──              ─────
              54              6 rolls.
```

Number of rolls required for ceiling is ascertained in the same manner, dividing the number of square feet by 72, which will give number of rolls.

A double roll of wall paper, when trimmed, contains 72 square feet, excepting 38902, which contains but 63 square feet.

Wall paper weighs about 1¾ pounds per double roll.
State what room paper is for. This is important.

We do not trim wall paper because the edges are exposed to rough usage during transit, and the pattern thus destroyed prevents perfect matching.

WE CALL YOUR **SPECIAL ATTENTION**

TO OUR PRICES

ON **CARPETS . . .
CURTAINS,
TABLE COVERS**
AND **WINDOW SHADES.**

WE have made large contracts for the above goods for the coming season; have taken unusual care in selecting the same, and confidently recommend them, both in quality and price. Samples of all goods (that can be sampled) will be sent free upon request.

Wall Paper is Usually Sold by the Single Roll.

OUR PRICES ARE FOR DOUBLE ROLLS.
All papers have Match Borders and Ceilings.
We do not sell paper by the Single Roll, nor sell half Double Rolls.

Notice Our Low Price on Borders.

Color Papers and Borders.

38902 Brown Back Papers, grounded and printed in colors and illuminated ink. The paper is thin but tough, the designs are splendid, and the price the lowest; colors: Light blue, tan, red, pink, brown or blue, printed in harmonizing colors. Designs are bouquets, scrolls, autumn leaves or squares, making it suitable for chambers, kitchens, dining rooms, etc. Rolls are but 14 yards long.
Pr double roll $0.07

Borders to match above side wall paper. They are made in 2 widths only, 6 and 9 in. wide.
38905 Color Border, 6 in. wide, per yd. $0.01
38907 Color Border, 9 in wide, per yd .... .01½
38909 Color Border, either width, per double roll .... .30

38911 White Back Paper, printed in colors. Small and medium designs in blocks, leaves, vines, etc. Colors are light, medium and dark. Per double roll. $0.09
38913 White Back Ceiling Paper. Per double roll. $0.09
38915 9-inch Color Border, to match. Per yard .. $0.01½
38917 6-inch, as above. Per yard .. $0.01
38919 White Back Colored Border, any width, Per roll $0.30

38921 Better Grade White Back Paper printed in colors (all have illuminated ink) scrolls, wild rose, oak leaf, fern leaf, delicate stripe with roses, tile pattern, etc., in tan, stone, light blue, pink, olive, gray, terra cotta or ecru. All the above are the very latest designs and colorings. Per double roll.... ......$0.10

38923 White Back Ceiling Paper to match above.
Per double roll $0.10
38925 18-inch Color Border. Per yard .... .03
38927 Color 9-inch Matched Border. Per yard .. .01½
38931 White Back Colored Border, any width.
Per double roll .... .30

Bronze or Gilt Parlor Paper.

38933 Gilt Side Wall Paper. Printed best quality of white back paper in gold and colors. Some have two metals, some opalescent colorings. Ecru, pearl, gray, mode, olive, red or tan grounds. Designs are sprays, flowers, geometrical, or set figure, bouquets or hall patterns. Per double roll....... $0.11
38935 Gold Border, 9 inches wide, to match.
Per yard $0.02

38937 Gold Border, 6 inches wide, to match, only two widths, per yard .... .01½
38939 Gold Border, either width, per roll ... .. .50
38941 Gold Ceiling Paper, either open or covered ground, per double roll 11

Liquid Gilt Parlor Paper.

The paper is white and clear, the patterns new, and the gold is artistically laid, Colors are: Pearl, olive, pale blue, pink or tan. Designs are sprays, bouquets, with fine stripe (very handsome), leaves, roses, scrolls and geometrical.
38943 Per double roll $0.14
38945 Gold Ceiling Paper, to match in color and design $0.14

38947 18-inch Gilt Border, per yard $0.04
38949 Gilt Border, 9 in. wide, per yard .... .02
38951 Gilt Border, per double roll .... .50

Varnished and Liquid Gilt High Grade Parlor Papers.

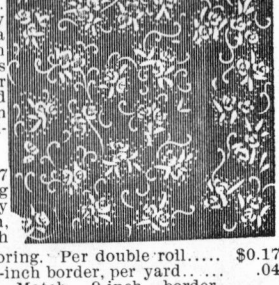

38957 These papers we recommend as being the most perfect in color and design of any we have ever offered for the price. French gray cream, light terra cotta, pearl or flesh tones prevail as ground work, over which are printed choice designs in the very latest colorings.
Per double roll $0.17
38959 Gilt Ceiling paper, equally handsome design, and made to match in pattern and coloring. Per double roll..... $0.17
38960 Plain Gilt, 18-inch border, per yard...... .04
38961 Plain Gold Match, 9-inch border. Per yard .... .02
38963 9 or 18-inch border. Per roll .... .50

Varnish Gold Parlor Paper.

38969 Varnish Gold looks like gold leaf; will not tarnish or grow dull. They are especially rich and heavy looking papers. Designs are scrolls, leaves, buds, blossoms and wreaths in medium and light colorings. Especially adapted to dining rooms, drawing rooms and parlors.
Per double roll. ..$0.21

38971 Varnish Gold Ceiling to perfectly match.
Per double roll. $0.21

38973 Varnish Gold Border, 18 in. wide ..$0.04

38975 Varnish Gold Border, 9 in. wide. Per yard .02

38977 Varnish Gold Embossed Border, 9 or 18 in. wide. Per double roll .50

Gilt Embossed Papers.

OUR LEADER.

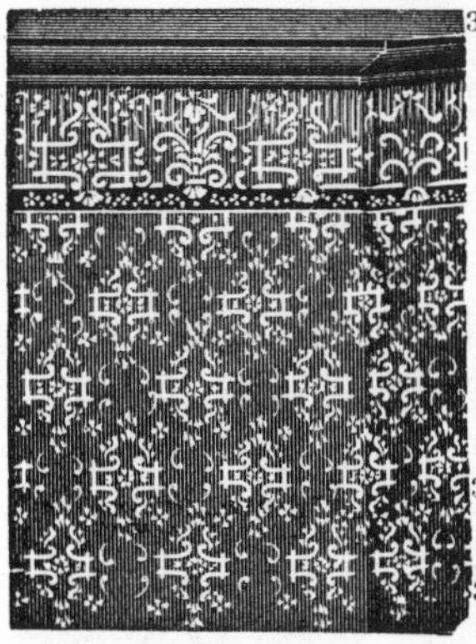

38987 Embossed Gilt Papers in artistic designs. Under this number the papers are very attractive this season. Some are light, some medium; colors are: Cream, mauve, terra cotta, salmon, light green, etc. We have colorings and designs in this grade suitable for any room. The price speaks for itself.
Per double roll..... $0.20

38989 9-in. Embossed Gold Border to exactly match.
Per yard...$0.02½

38991 Embossed Gold Border, 18 in.
Per yard ...$0.04½

38993 Embossed Gold Border, 9 in. or 18 in
Per double roll .65

38995 Gilt Ceiling, to exactly match. Per double roll .20

Embossed, Luminous, Color Gilt Paper.

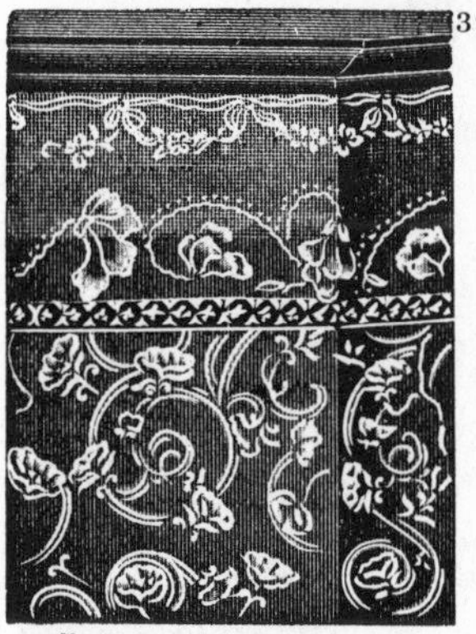

39001 So called because the figures are produced by using gold, luminous and colored inks. They are expensive papers to make and the work put on them shows off to advantage when they are on the wall. Colors are light blue, light olive, pale pink. French gray, tan or nile green, with designs of roses scroll wreath and buds, set or hall designs; Some of the designs have solid luminous grounds which produces the effect of silk draperies. Per double roll $0.25

39003 Gold Ceiling Paper, to match.
Per double roll .25

39005 Embossed Gold, 18-in. border. Per yard. .04½

39007 Embossed Gold, 9 in. border. Per yard.. .02½

39009 Embossed Gold Border. Either width.
Per double roll .65

Best Varnish Gold Embossed Papers.

39011 This is the best grade of wall paper made. The colorings are rich and heavy; the paper weighs 16 oz., and the bronzes used are the highest priced in the market.
Patterns are scroll work, autumn leaves, roses, colonial stripe, geometrical designs, etc. Colorings are olive, mauve, blue, cream, etc
Per double roll $0.32

39013 Varnish Ceiling, to match.
Per double roll .32

39015 Gold Embossed, 18-in. border, to match.
Per yard .04½

39019 Gold Embossed 9-in. or 18-in. Border, to match. Per double roll .65

High Art Varnish Gold Paper.

Note reduction in prices of 22-inch papers.

Weight of paper 16 oz. Printed on 22-inch stock.

39021 For our customers who want a high class paper and are willing to pay what it costs we make this offering. The patterns are all large, exquisitely colored and designed. Color combinations are ivory with nile green, cream with pink, cream with gobelin blue, lead color with tan, terra cotta with olive shadings. Figures are cactus and roses, scrolls and lilacs, or magnolia, all registered private designs, confined to us alone. Samples cannot do the designs justice; rolls will. Price, per double roll......$0.30

39023 High Art Gold Border, 18 in. wide to exactly match in coloring and design, (only width made). Per yard .05

39025 Border, 18 in, as above. Per roll .72

39027 High Art Gold Ceiling, printed on 20-inch stock, made to match and with this paper no other should be used Per double roll .30

High Art Embossed Paper.

39031 Same quality, width and grade of paper as above. Colors and designs are the same, with the addition of Louis XIV designs. We unhesitatingly recommend this as the nearest approach to hand-made goods ever brought out.
Price, per double roll $0.45

39033 High Art Ceilings, to exactly match (no other should be used). Per double roll .30

39035 High Art Embossed, 18-in. border.
Per yard .06

39037 High Art Embossed, 18 in. border.
Per double roll .80

Embossed Leatherettes.

Very Rich and Durable.

39041 Imitation of Embossed Leather, elegant paper for halls, dining rooms and libraries: colors are brown, green, fawn and tan.
Price, per double roll $0.40

39043 Ceiling Paper, to match. Price, per double roll .35

39045 18-inch border, to match. Per yard .06

39047 Same. Per double roll (16 yards) .80

20-inch Ingrain.

39051 These papers are also called Cartridge or Felt paper. They are plain, but properly used with our 18-inch borders produce very satisfactory results. They are two inches wider than ordinary wall paper. Colors are light and dark terra cotta, olive, gobelin, straw or ecru.
Per double roll $0.17

39053 18-in. Flitter Border Per yard .07

39055 Flitter Border 18-in. Per double roll .90

39059 Ingrain or Cartridge Paper, 30 in. wide; colors, same as No. 39051, 16 yards to the double roll .35
Borders to match, same as No.'s 39053 and 39055.

Varnished Tiles.

39061 Sanitary, Varnished or Washable Wall Paper, printed in imitation of tiling, on 12 oz. stock, in colors only. Comes 18 inches wide and is used for waterclosets, bathrooms, kitchens, vestibules, halls and dados. Can be washed. Does not spoil. 16 yards to a roll $0.50

39063 Tinted Paper, 10 oz. stock, 20 in. wide, made to represent tinted walls, in 34 different tints, including solid dark colors .35

39065 Colors: Red, blue, olive green and maroon 60

39067 Flock or Velvet Paper, heavy; paper covered with ground wool, in all solid colors in imitation of cloth. Made in single rolls only, 8 yards long, 18 inches wide. Per roll 1.00

Ceiling Paper.

A ceiling can be covered better and cheaper with paper than with calcimine or paint, and if the ceiling is cracked it will cover the defects, which nothing else will do. In ordering, say whether ceiling is in good condition or cracked. Ceiling paper is made in special designs to serve the purpose, and cannot well be used for other purposes.

We have had all our ceiling papers this year made to match our side wall paper and borders, but sell them separately should you want only that.

Before hanging, be sure all the smoke and dirt has been brushed from the ceiling. If ceiling had several coats of calcimine or whitewash, either wash it off or glue size it, else the paste will not make the paper adhere. Per double roll.

39071 White Back Ceiling Paper .09

39073 White Back Ceiling Paper, better grade... .10

39075 Gilt Ceiling Paper .11

39077 Gilt Ceiling Paper .14

39079 Gilt Ceiling Paper .17

39081 Varnish Bronze Ceiling Paper, better and heavier .21

39083 High Art Gold Ceiling .30

Borders

No paper, however handsome, can look at its best capped by narrow border. Wide borders do not lower the apparent height of the room as formerly thought. Narrow borders are as a sign reading, "I am a low ceiling, that is why I am here." Use nothing less than a 9 or 18-inch border if you would produce the best results, 18-inch border where possible, the wider the border the less side wall paper is required. Our borders all match the paper bearing the same name, but are sold separately if desired. Per yard.

39091 Colored Borders, 18 inch wide $0.03

39093 Colored Borders, 9 inch wide .01½

39095 Colored Borders, 6 inch wide .01

39097 Colored Borders, 4 inch wide .00¾

39099 Colored Borders, any width, per roll..... .30

39101 Gold Borders, 18 inch wide .04

39103 Gold Borders, 9 inch wide 0.02

39105 Gold Borders, 6 inch wide .01½

39107 Gold Borders, any width, per roll .50

39109 Embossed Gold Borders, 18 inch wide... .04½

39111 Embossed Gold Borders, 9 inch wide... .02½

39113 Embossed Gold Borders, 6 inch wide.... .02

39115 Embossed Gold Borders, any width, per roll .65

39123 Ingrain Flitter Border, 18 inch wide...... .07

39125 Ingrain Flitter Border, 18 inch wide, per roll .90

Ceiling Decorations.

Consist of centerpieces, corners and extension or ceiling border. Four corners make one centerpiece. The extension or ceiling border is used to connect the corners and should be used where corners are.

We do not sell less than four corners or one center. Prices are for 4 (or 1 set) of corners.

39129 Color Corners, better. Per set .35

39133 Color Extension or Ceiling Border, 9 in. wide, only width, to match above. Per yard..$0.01½

39135 Color Extension or Ceiling borders, 9 in. wide, only width, to match. Per roll $0.40

39139 Gilt Corners, better. Per set .65

39145 Gilt Extension, 9 in. Per yard .03

39147 Gilt Extension, 9 in. Per roll $0.80

39149 Dado Paper. The dado is that part of the wall between baseboard and chair rail. Block or geometrical figures should be used. Per double roll
In white back quality $0.11
In white back, gilt grade .20
In gilt paper, best quality .30

39151 Wainscoting Paper, same as dado, only made in imitation of natural wood, and should be hung in vertical strips; can be varnished to advantage $0.15
Per yard.

39153 Chair Rail Border is put at bottom of side wall, and just above dado, to prevent the back of chair from marring the wall, 6 inches wide $0.02
Made in colors and gilt, 6 inches wide .03

39155 Binders or Edgings, used for finishing or trimming and to separate the two different colors of paper; one to four inches wide.
Colors, cost, per yard $0.01½
Gilt, cost per yard .02

Room Moldings.

Room Moldings that match the wall paper give a complete finish to a well-papered room, besides the convenience for hanging pictures is worth more than the cost.

Our Moldings are all first-class goods. The prices speak for themselves. Weight, about 3½ ounces per foot.

NOTE.—All room mouldings come in 12-foot lengths. *We do not cut.*

39161 Imitation Oak, Cherry or Georgia Pine, full polish. 1⅛ inch wide. Per foot $0.01¼

39163 Genuine Oak, antique finish, full polish, 1⅛ inch. Per foot .01¾

39165 Genuine Oak, same as above, 2 inches wide. Price per foot .02½

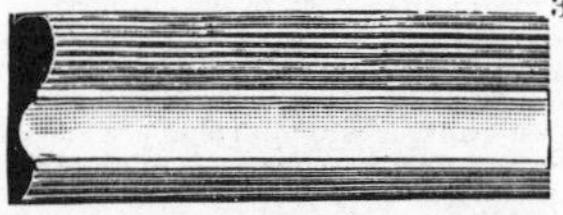

39166 White enamel top and bottom, with, either pink or blue center. Very pretty for bedrooms. 1½ inches wide.
Per foot $0.02

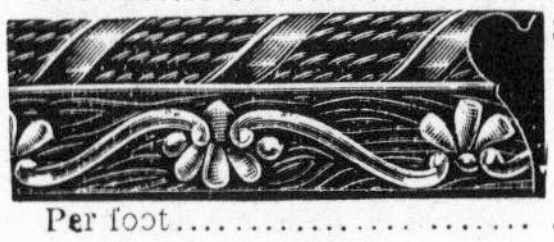

39167 Ground work light cream, with lower edge in light terra cotta pattern in gold relief, 1½ inch.
Per foot $0.03¼

Mouldings – Continued.

39168 Cream top, shaded to light blue, with wreath design in gold relief, 1½ inch wide. Per foot.... $0.03½

39168½ Light and dark blue blended ground, same design as 39168. 1½ inches wide. Per foot.................................... $0.03½

39169 Ground work white with lower edge in blue tint, raised parts in gold relief, 1½ inch. Per foot.... $0.03½

39170 Cream and light terra cotta, blended ground, with gold relief design. 1½ inches wide. Per foot.... $0.03½

39171 Ground work cream and blue, with figure in gold relief, a beauty. 2 inch. Per foot...... $0.04

39172 Light and terra cotta blended ground, gold relief. 2 inches wide. Per foot.... $0.04½

39173 Light buff and pink ground work, raised parts in gold, lower edge cut into the shape of ornament, 2 inch. Per foot.... $0.05½

39174 White enamel top, cream and blue blended center, with raised ornaments in gold. Handsome molding for parlor. 2 inches wide. Per foot...... $0.06

CARPET AND RUG DEPARTMENT.

If you have any doubt about our saving you money on carpets, send for samples and compare quality and price.

Our carpet department is now recognized as one of the best in the West, and is fast growing better. Greater sales (we have sold this season about 80,000 yards of carpet) give us greater purchasing power, experience teaches us how to avoid errors, how to present the matter plainer to you and also how to fill your orders more to your liking.

Carpets will not be sent C. O. D.

Samples.

Our experience of several years teaches us it is not necessary to send for samples before ordering to be satisfied with your carpet; your giving quality, color, size of design, what room is used for that it is to cover, etc., being all that is necessary to get what will suit (*we have never failed to please our customers when the above instructions were given*) but in some cases, samples seem necessary; to such we say: We will send you small samples of carpet from which you can judge quality, color, etc., free upon request. Should larger samples be wanted, we will send you ¼, ½ or 1 yard samples as ordered, to cover the amount of money you allow for their payment, in the design, coloring or quality wanted, and refund you what you paid upon their return if the transportation charges are paid. *We must know what price carpet you want sample of, also size of design and color.* Make these points clear.

Sewing Carpets.

It will usually require a day or two longer to fill an order when carpet is ordered made.

Our charges for sewing carpets are: All grades except velvets and moquettes, 5 cents per yard for plain work; fitting borders, 5 cents per yard extra; sewing borders, 5 cts. per yard; sewing velvets and moquettes, 10 cents a yard. When you want carpets sewed, write "*Make*" on the order, and allow from one to two yards (according to size of room) for waste in matching.

All ingrain carpets are sewed by professional carpet sewers with the herringbone stitch, which makes a flat, turnable, elastic seam.

Brussels and all three-quarter wide carpets are sewed with a machine made for the purpose. It sews them much better than can be done by hand, and then the seams are all ironed. All three-quarter yard goods especially should be ordered sewed here, as it is often difficult to make them by hand so they will lie smooth.

For carpet thread, see Index.

In ordering mention the predominating color wanted, and state whether a plain or fancy pattern is preferred, or whether you want large or small figure. We will use our best judgment in making selections. *Carpets cut and sewed to order cannot be returned if sent as ordered.*

Rules for Measuring Carpets.

Ascertain the *width* of room in inches; divide that product by the width of carpet (27 or 36 in.); the answer will give the number of breadths required. Multiply the number of breadths by the *length* of room (allowing 12 to 18 inches on each breadth for possible waste in matching) the answer will give approximate number of feet required. Divide that number by 3 to find the number of yards.

Measures for bordered carpets must be very exact. Give diagram of all odd-shaped rooms.

Hemp Carpets.

For a cheap carpet this does nicely, as it lies smooth, is easily swept, does not retain dirt and looks neat. All hemp carpets are 36 inches wide, except No. 39203, which is but 32 inches. Per yard.

39203 Hemp Carpet, made only in stripes, no figured patterns. Colors: Red, green, ecru and yellow; 32 in. wide... $0.11
Weight, 6 ounces per yard.

39205 Hemp Carpet, better quality, colors as above... .14
Weight, 8 ounces per yard.

39207 Oriental Plaid Hemp, woven in red and green, red, brown and white and red and brown. .17½
Weight, 16 ounces per yard.

39209 Extra Striped Hemp; colors, weaving and width same as 39205, but of superior quality.... .19
Weight, 16 ounces per yard.

39211 Best 3-ply Hemp Carpet, extra heavy, striped or mottled, 36 inches wide. Just the carpet for an office, hall or stair, also makes very durable covering for a room that is much used, cleans easily and don't show or hold dirt. An immense seller... .26
Weight, 24 ounces per yard.

Irish Brussels or Erin Tapestry.

Per yard

39213 Printed Hemp Carpet, made of a very heavy twilled hemp thread, printed in patterns and colors on one side only in exact imitation of Brussels carpet, 36 in. wide. Combination of colors are: Red and green, ecru, red and yellow; ecru, red and green; ecru, red and bronze. Patterns are block or geometrical; also flowered, Price.. $0.24
Weight, 16 ounces per yard.

39215 Cottage Carpet, 36 in. wide, made in mottled and variegated stripes only. Colors: Green, olive, or red mixed with stripes of gold, red, pearl, or green. Splendid value................. .25
Weight, 15 ounces per yard.

Rag Carpet.

Weight, 20 to 25 ounces per yard.

Many of our customers will call for the old stand-by and as usual we can supply their wants. The rags are all bright and clean, the colors good and the patterns hit or miss as they have always been made. Per yard.

39217 Rag Carpet, fair quality.................... $0.30
39219 Rag Carpet, better rags and more warp... .40
39221 Rag Carpet, really a good article.......... .49

Ingrain Carpets.

All ingrains are 36 inches wide
For a cheap carpet ingrains are most used, and they have never been so cheap, as the following prices will prove. We show a cut of one pattern in each grade. 2-ply ingrains weigh from 15 to 20 ounces per yard.

COTTON INGRAIN.

39231 2-Ply Cotton Ingrain, double warp, double felling. Both sides can be used. Colors are oak ground with wine figure. Medium design. Ecru red and green, block and leaf pattern. Medium dark mottled ground with small leaf design (like cut.) Wood ground well covered with wine and black design. Price, per yard.............. $0.19

EXTRA UNION INGRAINS.

39241 Extra Union are 2-ply extra heavy, reversible, one side as good as the other. Colors are ecru ground with wine and brown figures (like cut). Oak and green. medium design. Chintz ground, colors oak and brown in leaf pattern. Oak ground with small wine figures. Tan ground with brown and wine floral design, medium large. Price, per yard...................... $0.36

Extra Super Ingrains.

39253 Extra Super 2-Ply Ingrains, very heavy. The filling is half wool and we recommend this carpet as it is the best value for the price we ever offered. Colors are, ecru and wine, small figure. (Very pretty for bedrooms.) Oak and brown medium floral design (like cut). Ecru and light olive fern leaf pattern. Red, green and black geometrical design. Ecru and brown with mottled ground, small design. Wood ground with small wine figure. Tan ground with wine and green design in ferns and flowers. Price, per yard.............................. $0.40

All Wool Extra Super Ingrains.

We guarantee the wool used in our extra supers to be well cleaned. The colors are the best and the weaving perfect. We do not offer for sale the cheap loosely woven Ingrains.

39261 The Best All Wool Filled Ingrain with a cotton warp or chain. Some of the colors are ecru ground with bright floral effects, wood ground with wine figure, ecru, red and green and all the late colorings and designs. Price, per yard....... $0.46

39263 All Wool (both warp and filling) Extra Super Ingrain Carpet; we can furnish all of the standard colors and designs in this grade. A few of the colorings are as follows: Scarlet and green with ecru ground; cream and wood combination, ecru ground, gobelin blue figure, wood and green and many other colors and combinations too numerous to mention. Price, per yard....... $0.53

39269 This number we guarantee to be as good if not the best quality of all wool 2-ply ingrain in the market. We can furnish colors and designs as follows: Wood ground, with fern leaf like cut pattern, cream, chinty, ground with oak leaves; ecru, ground with small blue figure; brown ground with gold design; light and dark red in small leaf effects. We can suit all tastes in this grade. Notice the price. Price, per yard......... $0.57

English Art Carpet.

Per yard

39273 English Art Carpet, 36 inches wide, all wool, imported stock, English weave, very heavy, well knit together; warranted to wear equal to best body brussels. The yarns are hard twisted, and they are firm and close; they are reversible. We have: Wood ground, old gold figure, brussels effect; drab ground bright scarlet leaves; ecru ground, brown figure, brussel pattern; ecru ground old gold and brown figure, medium dark blue ground, light green and drab scroll. Large scroll in old gold and olive effects, etc., etc........ .... $0.78

Hartford Three-Ply Carpet.

39277 This carpet is so called because there are three thicknesses of carpet knit into one. The trouble with the large patterns were produced one thickness would wear through, showing the next and making an ugly hole. We have avoided this by selecting smaller patterns, well knit designs and closely woven patterns. By weaving carpets this way, three times as many threads are used; better patterns can be produced, richer and deeper designs made, and a softer floor covering had. We have both light and dark effects, small and large designs, and all colors..................$0.81

Tapestry Brussels Carpets.

Tapestry Brussels Carpets are made to look like the body brussels, but the threads which form the pattern do not form the body of the carpet. It is a good carpet and wears well. All tapestry carpets are 27 inches or ¾ yard wide.

To our customers who wish a strictly first-class carpet at a low price we would recommend our Tapestry Brussels, especially Nos. 39287 and 39289. The designs and colorings are all new and elegant, and wearing qualities are the best.

39283 Tapestry Brussels Carpet, with an all worsted face; great variety of patterns. We have hall and stair patterns that match. Stair carpet has a pretty 6-inch border, with center same as hall; this grade has no border made to match. No very light colors in this quality. Small, medium and large designs; some set, others flowered. All harmonious combinations we have. Per yard.......................$0.50

39285 Tapestry Brussels. No match borders in this grade; hall and stair carpet that match. Grounds are ecru, drab, dark brown, tan, olive, cream, red or gray, and designs are harmonious colors in flowers, leaves, blocks, sombre effects, etc. In some the background is most prominent, others the figures are the distinct feature; some are small patterns, others large; an infinite variety to choose from. Per yard.................. .54

39287 Tapestry Brussels, better quality. This grade has border of ⅝ of a yard wide; should you wish bordered carpet, order it bordered or not, as you choose. Should you want this quality for the stairs or hall, or both, we have them to match; hall carpet has the same color as the center of the stair, which has a dark 6-inch border on both edges. Running vines, bouquets, roses, leaves, mottled effects, with some set figures, are a few of the designs; some are soft and subdued, others bold and startling. Colors never before put in carpets. Queen olive, old rose, gobelin, heliotrope and salmon are found here. Per yard.................. .63

39289 Tapestry Brussels, with hall and stair to match, also 22½-inch border if desired. This will be found a very superior carpet, and if the rows of worsted on the face are counted it will be found to contain 10 rows to the inch, in place of 9, the best grade formerly made. All colors, as in the preceding grades; we can furnish and have all styles. The new colorings are well represented. Per yard.................. .75

Body Brussels.

Body Brussels are so called because the threads which form the face and figure go through to the back and form the body, giving an almost all worsted carpet. Body Brussels are all 27 inches wide. Per yard.

39291 Body Brussels, a fair quality; no border made for this quality; hall and stair designs colored to match; we have small, medium and large patterns; light medium and medium dark colors.$0.89

Leicestershire Three-Thread Brussels—The Highest Grade Made.

39297 Body Brussels, extra quality, with hall and stair designs and colors to match; also 22½-inch border can be furnished to match many of the patterns. Most of the patterns are private. Some colorings are very light, some are medium and others quite dark. Many artistic combinations. Per yard..................................$1.12

Velvet Carpets.

Notice our reduced prices.

Velvet Carpets are made same as Body Brussels, with pile cut. The best worsted has to be used. Effects can be produced that are not possible in any other carpet. They lie smooth and are very durable, rich and soft looking. Per yard.

39300 Wilton Back Velvets, borders to match, also halls and stairs. Medium colors, fern leaves, scroll pattern, flowers, etc., etc. A thoroughly good carpet. Value in the goods rather than in the colors and patterns, though they are good.$0.95

39301 Velvets, Wilton back, with hall and stairs; also borders 22½ inches wide to match or harmonize. All the patterns are medium or large. Colors, medium and dark: shadings very soft, and colors blended. Very rich.................. 1.06

Moquettes.

Please notice our price.

Hartford or Smith's Axminster Moquettes. These carpets are well known as the best Moquettes made. These two grades rank the same—both the highest. Moquettes are woven the same as velvets, but the pile is longer and the thread softer. Very luxurious. Per yard

39307 Hartford or Smith's Axminster Moquettes, with hall and stair to match; borders are 22½ inches wide; moquettes are almost always made in light colors and large or medium patterns; they are richly colored in half tones and soft shades rather than in strong effects..................$1.00

Terry.

39309 Terry is woven the same as an extra super ingrain, but in plain or solid colors, 36 inches wide, and, because plain, very durable; used as entire carpet, also as a center to a carpet or rug. Colors: Navy, cardinal, wine, old gold, olive or tan. Price, per yard..................................$0.65

Carpet Binding.

39311 Cotton and Wool Carpet Binding, 1 inch wide, assorted colors, 12 yards in a roll. Price, per roll..$0.12

Stair Carpets.

Notice reduction in prices of hall and stair carpets.

We have hall and stair carpets to match in most of the different grades of carpets, but many times to match them is unnecessary or too expensive, hence this quotation.

Hemp Stair Carpets.

Per yard.

39321 Hemp Stair, with bright colored border and striped or mottled center, made in two widths. Colors: Combination of green, gold, red and ecru or black, red, blue and gold mottled. State width wanted.
Hemp Stair, 18 in. wide..............................$0.12
Hemp Stair, 22½ in. wide.............................. .16

39323 Venetian Stair, heavy cotton warp, jute filling, bordered with striped or figured center in green, buff, red, brown and drab combined; also mixed small patterns; made in two widths.
Venetian Stair, 18 in. wide.............................. .14
Venetian Stair, 22½ in. wide.............................. .18

39325 Aubusson Stair, similar to 39321, but heavier, better colors, nicer patterns. Center colors correspond to colors in ingrain carpets, and borders are either light or dark; made in three widths. State when ordering which is wanted.
Aubusson Stair, 18 in. wide.............................. .23
Aubusson Stair, 22½ in. wide.............................. .30

Extra Super Hall and Stair.

39327 Union Extra Super Hall and Stair Carpet, cotton warp; half wool filling. We have colors that will match any Ex-Super we quote, except red and green. Hall carpets do not have borders.
22½ in. Stair Carpet..............................$0.30
36 in. Hall Carpet, to match.............................. .40

39331 All Wool Best Extra Super Stair and Hall Carpets, made to match in color and designs.
22½ in. wide.............................. .45
36 in. wide, Hall Carpet, to match.............................. .62

Stair Oil Cloth.

Per yard.

39333 Stair Oil Cloth, made in light slate or tan color only, and two widths.
15 in...............$0.10 18 in...............$0.13

Scotch Drill Stair Linings.

Used to protect stairs that are carpeted with expensive carpet and also to conceal worn places in the center when sides are good; made in the natural linen color and striped with red or red and white. They are all bordered, some centers plain, some striped. State width wanted.

39335 Width,	14 in.	18 in.	20 in.	27 in.
Price, per yard	16c.	20c.	22c.	30c.

Carpet Linings.

Every carpet should be lined; the tread will be softer; the carpet will look richer and will wear at least one-third longer. We do not sell less than a roll.

39337 Cedar Felt Lining, 1 yard wide, 50 yards in a roll. Weight, 46 pounds. Price, per roll..$0.65

Sewed Linens.

39339 Sewed Carpet Lining, 36 in. wide, jute filled, good paper, 5 rows stitching. Per bale, 200 yards. Weight, 120 pounds per bale..........$4.50
Per yard.. .02½

39341 Sewed Carpet Lining, made of two strips of strong 36-inch paper filled with cotton and jute, and sewed with five rows of stitching. Put up in 200 yard bales, Weight, 130 pounds per bale.
Price, per bale, of 200 yards 5.50
Price, per yard.. .03

39343 Sewed Carpet Lining, made of heavier paper, cotton filled, five rows of stitching. Weight, 140 pounds per bale. Price, per bale of 200 yards.. 9.00
Price, per yard.. .05

39349 Sewed Carpet Lining, all cotton filled, more cotton than above, better paper. Weight, 185 pounds per bale.
Price, per bale of 200 yards..............................14.00
Price, per yard.. .08

Stair Pads.

Stair pads weigh about 5 pounds per dozen

39361 Stair Pads, plain pad or cushion, cotton filled and tufted, made for 22½, 27 and 32-inch carpet, all widths same price. Per dozen.........$1.10

39363 Stair Pad, patented; pad extends over and clasps around the nosing of the stair, protect ing where the most wear comes; made in three qualities.
Price per dozen.............................. 1.20
Price, per dozen, better grade,.............................. 1.30
Price, per dozen, best made, double filled.............. 1.60

Brass Stair Rods.

Average weight, about 5 pounds per dozen.

Per doz.
39365 ⅝ inch wide, 22 inch long..............$0.60
39367 ¾ inch wide, 24 inch long.............. .72
39369 ¾ inch wide, 26 inch long.............. .79
39371 ¾ inch wide, 30 inch long.............. .94

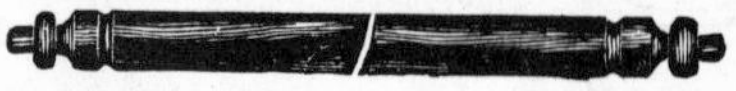

39373 Black Walnut or Oak Stair Rods, with bronzed screw eye fastenings. Average weight of stair rods per dozen, 2½ lbs.

Length..............	27 in.	30 in.
Price each..............	$0.04	$0.04
Per doz..............	.42	.42
39375 Black Walnut or Oak Stair Rods, with nickel ends, with fancy	27 in.	30 in.
nickel fastenings. Each..............	$0.06	$0.06
Per dozen..............	.60	.60

Stair Buttons.

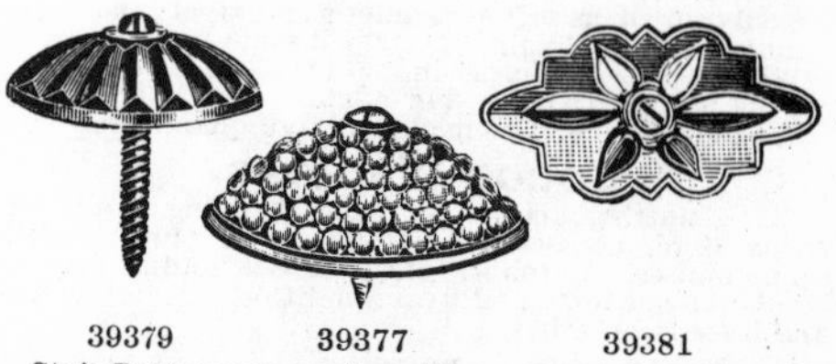

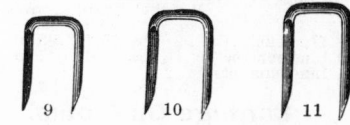

39379 39377 39381

Stair Buttons are preferred by many to the stair rods. They are screwed through the carpet to the raise of the stair at the bottom.

Per dozen.
39377 Brass Stair Buttons, like cut, with screw $0.18
39379 Stair Buttons, like cut, nickel, brass or bronze with screw.............. .25
39381 Stair Buttons, like cut, very heavy, brass or nickel with screws.............. .50

Japanese Straw Mattings Chinese.

Our own Importation.

Japanese and Chinese Straw Mattings are to a large extent, taking the place of cheap carpets, and give the best of satisfaction. All straw mattings are 36 inches wide, and come 40 yards in original package.

Close buyers will notice to their advantage the following prices.

36383 Plain White China Matting. Per yard..$0.12
Full piece of 40 yards weighs 1½ pounds.
Per yard.. .10

39385 Plain White Jointless Mattings, both sides alike, giving two wearing surfaces. Extra close weave and heavy, Per yard.............. .22
Full piece of 40 yards (weighs 2 pounds).
Per yard.. .19

39386 Fancy China Matting, in light and medium dark colors. Per yard.............. .10
Full piece of 40 yards: (weighs, 1½ pounds).
Per yard.. .08½

39388 Fancy China Matting, very heavy in light and dark colors. Per yard.............. .17
Full piece of 40 yards (weighs, 1¾ pounds).
Per yard.. .15

39390 Fancy Jointless China Matting, both sides alike, giving two wearing surfaces: close weave, extra value. Per yard.............. .19
Full price of 40 yards (weighs, 2 pounds).
Per yard.. .17

39390 Fancy Japanese Matting, woven with a cotton warp, making it more flexible and more durable; both sides alike; a very handsome floor covering. Per yard..............$0.21
Full price of 40 yards (weight, 1½ pounds, per yard).. .19

39391 Fancy Japanese Matting, cotton warp, better quality than above; some are mottled, others have plain ground. with Japanese designs; usually sold for 40c. Per yard.............. .26
Full piece of 40 yards (weight, 1¾ pounds, per yard).. 24

39393 White Japanese Matting, cotton warp; the finest matting made; the weave is as fine as carpet. If you have any doubt about the quality, send for samples. Per yard.............. .35
Full piece of 40 yards.. .32

Double Pointed Steel Carpet Tacks.

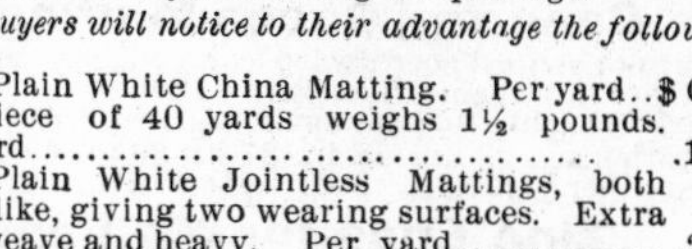

9 10 11

Average weight, 1 pound per dozen boxes.

39395 The only tack suitable for fastening mattings to the floor, and are much better than the common tack for carpets, 100 in each box. Full size cuts. boxes.
Price.............. 15c. 20c. 25c per dozen

Engineers, Electricians, Mechanics, etc., can save money by buying books on their respective trades from us.

Carpet Tacks—Continued.

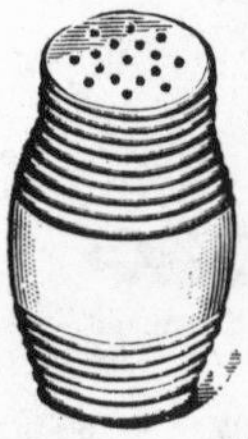

39396 Glass Salt and Pepper Shakers filled with coppered carpet tacks, will answer for pepper and salt cellar when tacks are used.
Price, each $0.05
Per dozen .... .50

Napier Mattings.

Best Quality. Note Reduction in Prices.

Weight, 1½ pounds per square yard.
39397 Napier Mattings are very heavy twilled jute, and are plain or striped as desired. Colors: Tan or tan with stripes of red, black or brown, 9 inches apart, in all widths. Especially adapted to offices, vestibules and lodge rooms; not easily soiled, as soft and quiet as a carpet, and more durable. Plain or striped same price.

Width	18 in.	27 in.	36 in.	45 in.	54 in.
Price, per yard	16c.	24c	32c.	40c.	48c.

Special prices will be made on large quantities.

Cocoa Mattings.

Cocoa Matting, also called rope matting, made of cocoa fibre, coarse and strong. For public halls, schoolhouses, churches, etc., there is nothing better. Made in five widths and two qualities. State width and price in ordering.

PLAIN.

39401 Weight, 2½ pounds per square yard.

Width	18 in.	27 in.	36 in.	45 in.	54 in.
Price, per yard	18c.	27c.	36c.	45c.	54c

PLAIN—BETTER GRADE.

39403 Weight, 3 pounds per square yard.

Width	18 in.	27 in.	36 in.	45 in.	54 in
Price, per yard	23c.	34c.	45c.	56c.	68c.

STRIPED.

39405 Weight, 2½ pounds per square yard.

Width	18 in.	27 in.	36 in.	45 in.	54 in.
Price, per yard	20c.	30c.	40c.	50c.	60c.

STRIPED—BETTER GRADE.

39407 Weight, 3 pounds per square yard.

Width	18 in.	27 in.	36 in.	45 in.	54 in.
Price, per yard	25c.	37c.	51c.	62c.	76c

Cane and Cocoa Matting.

Plain or striped cocoa warp cane filling, heavy and durable. A 3-inch stripe every 9 inches.
39409 Weight, 3½ pounds per square yard.

Width	18 in.	27 in.	36 in.	45 in.	54 in.
Price, per yard	30c.	41c.	57c.	71c.	87c.

Zinc Ends for Matting.

Price includes rivets and burrs.
39411 Weight, each, about 13 ounces.

Width	18 in.	27 in.	36 in.	45 in.	54 in.
Price, each	10c.	13c.	19c.	24c.	27c

Floor Oil Cloth.

Oil cloth is made of a mixture of mineral, earth and oil applied to jute cloth.
The colors are somber or bright, light or dark, as desired. Block patterns prevail, and are small, medium or large, to suit all tastes.

We are Headquarters for Floor Oil Cloths.

The following are the lowest prices ever quoted for first-class good wearing goods, with fine patterns and colors. Send for samples.
39421 Weight, 2 pounds per square yard.

Width	1 yd.	1½ yds.	2 yds.
Price, per yard	20c.	30c.	40c.

FLOOR OIL CLOTH—BETTER QUALITY.

39423 Weight, 3 pounds per square yard.

Width	1 yd.	1¼ yds.	1½ yds.	2 yds.
Price, per yard	24c.	30c.	36c.	48c.

FLOOR OIL CLOTH—BEST QUALITY

39425 Weight, 3½ pounds per square yard.

Width	1 yd.	1¼ yds.	1½ yds.	2 yds.	2½ yds.
Price pr. yard	36c.	45c.	54c.	72c.	90c.

Linoleums.

Note reduction in prices.

Linoleum is but another name for an oil cloth of superior quality, and is made of ground cork and oil. Patterns are the same as in oil cloth. Linoleums are made in three widths only, other widths cannot be furnished.

	Weight, sq. yd.	1 yard wide.	2 yards wide.	4 yards wide.
39427 Linoleum	2 lbs.	$0.45	$0.90	.....
39429 Linoleum, better	4¼ lbs.	.65	1.30	......
39431 Linoleum, best grade	5 lbs.		1.75	$3.50

Carriage Oil Cloths.

Average weight, 2½ pounds per yard.
Made for floor of carriages. Background is black, and patterns are all small designs in light and dark colors.

39441 Width	22½	27 in.	32 in.	36 in.
Price, per yd.	20c.	24c.	29c.	31c.

...WE SELL...
Andrew Dougherty's Playing Cards.
—BEST MADE.—

Oil Cloth Stove Squares.

Made of good material. Assorted designs.

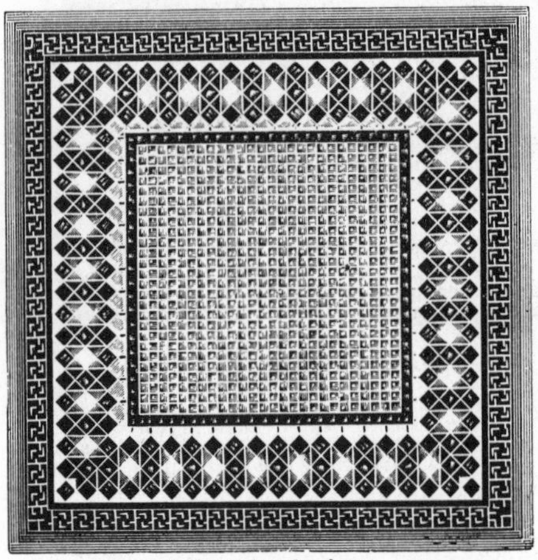

Notice reduced prices.

39443 Sizes	1¼x1¼ yds.	1½x1½ yds.	2x2 yds. square
Price, each	49c.	71c.	$1.26
Weight, each	3¼ lbs.	4½ lbs.	8 lbs.

BEST GRADE.

39445 Sizes	1¼x1¼ yds.	1½x1½ yds.	2x2 yds. square
Price, each	71c.	$1.00	$1.75
Weight, each	5¼ lbs.	7¾ lbs.	14 lbs.

Metallic Oil Cloth Binding.

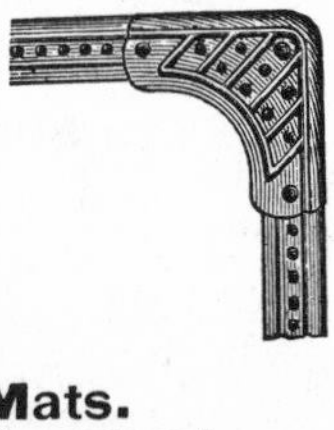

39447 Metallic Oil Cloth Binding for fastening down the edges of the oil cloth; per set of following number of yards, with corners and tacks complete.
Weight, about 6 ounces per set.

	Zinc.	Brass.
4 yards, per set	$0.09	$0.15
5 yards, per set	.13	.19
6 yards, per set	.16	.22
8 yards, per set	.21	.27

Cocoa Door Mats.

Cocoa Mats weigh from 3 to 8 pounds each.

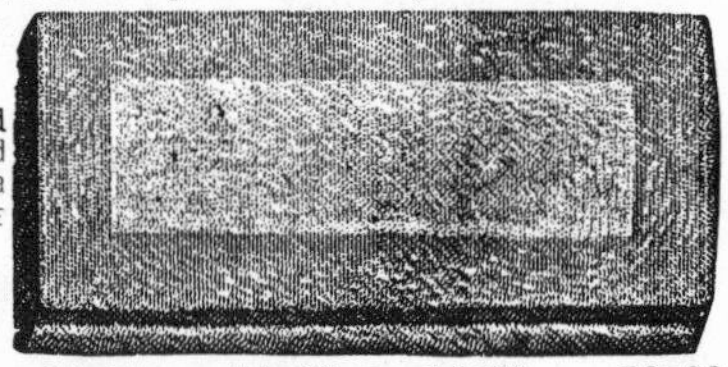

39453 Red Bordered Cocoa Mats (like cut).

Sizes—	14x25	16x27	18x30	20x33
Price, each—	33c.	40c.	54c.	78c.

39455 Mats, finer and softer than above; very durable, all sizes, plain.

Sizes—	14x25	16x27	18x30	20x33	22x36
Price, each—	38c.	50c.	63c.	75c.	94c.

39457 Cocoa Mats, better grade, plain.

Sizes—	14x26	16x27	18x30	20x32	22x36
Price, each—	56c.	68c.	87c.	$1.06	$1.31

Motto Mats.

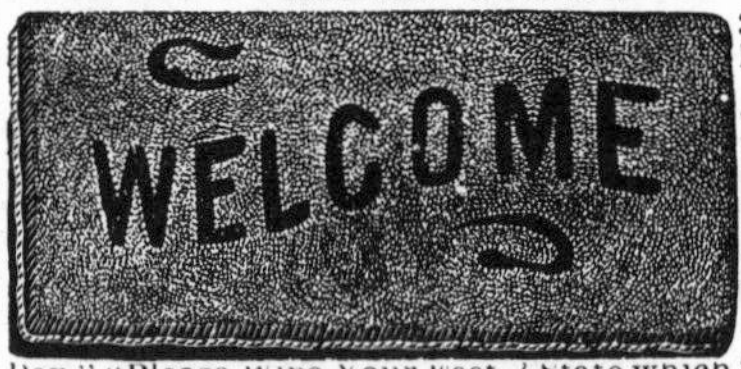

39459—Improved Cocoa, with red lettering in center; mottoes are: "Welcome," "Use Me." "Good Day." "Please Wipe Your Feet." State which is wanted.

Size—	16x27	18x30	20x33
Price, each	80c.	$1.06	$1.25

National Wire Mats.

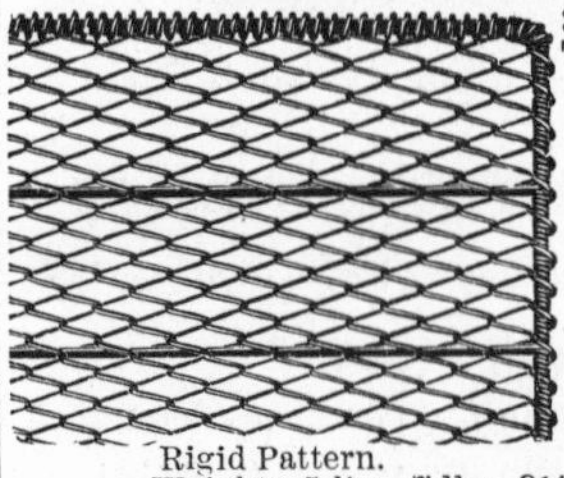

Rigid Pattern.

39461—These mats are made of steel wire, are thin enough to permit any door having a threshold to pass over them; are alway clean, catch the dirt but do not clog.
Every front door should have a wire mat in front of it.

Weights, 5 lbs., 7 lbs., 9½ lbs., 12 lbs.

Size	16x24	18x30	22x36	26x48
Price	$0.75	$1.00	$1.50	$2.50

WE CHARGE NOTHING FOR
CASES, CRATES OR CARTAGE

Rubber Door Mats.

Notice Our Reduced Prices.

These mats wear well, look neat, don't retain dirt, easily cleaned, etc.

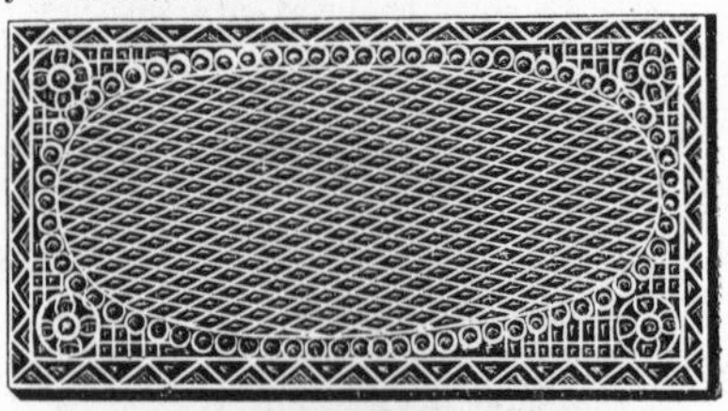

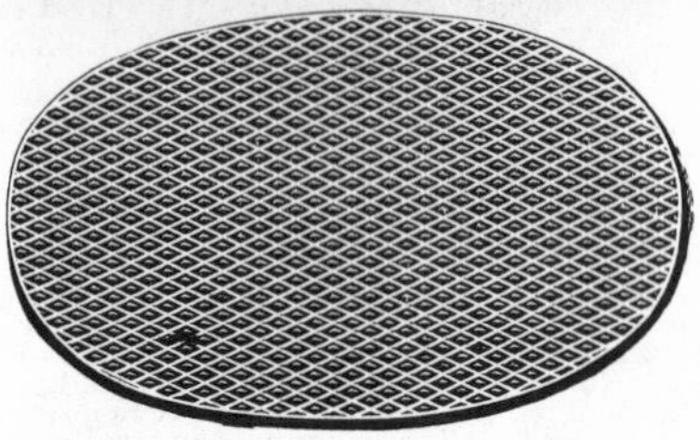

OVAL MATS

Weight, 5 pounds.
39465 Size, 17x31. Price, each..................$1.36

OBLONG MATS.

Weights, 5 lbs., 6 lbs., 7½ lbs.

39467 Size—	17x31	18x36	20x40
Price, each—	$1.47	$1.75	$2.40

The $1.75 and the $2.40 oblong mats have no fancy border. The $1.47 grade is similar to first cut.

Rugs.

This is an age of rugs. It has become the fashion and because of slow growth will stay. In many homes carpets have been abandoned and rugs substituted. The effect is rich. A partly worn carpet can be made to look very presentable with rugs. A new carpet can be saved by them. They are made all sizes, all colors, all designs. We have them all.
Rugs make splendid Birthday, Wedding or Christmas presents, as they are elegant and useful.

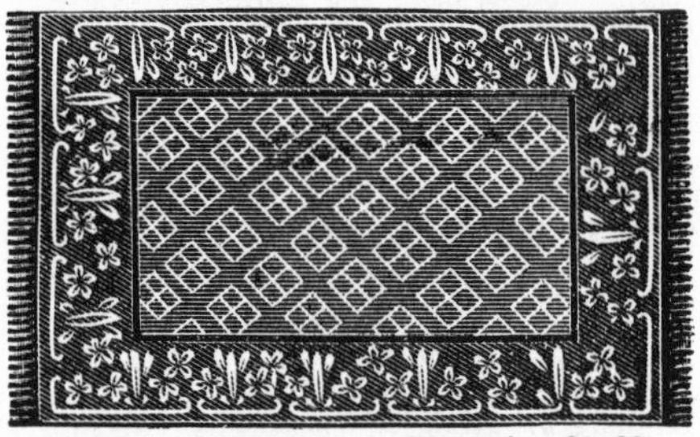

39500 Hemp Body Brussels Rugs; size, 21x39 inches. Colors are light, medium or dark, and geometrical or floral figures in bright or sober colors, fringed on both ends; splendid for rough wear. Each..................$0.25

Reversible Madras Rugs.

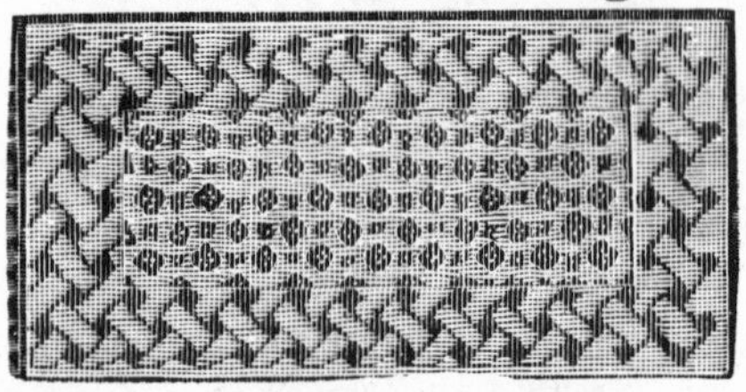

39501

39501 A handsome pattern on both sides. Fringed on both ends and colors bright and pleasing. They are the most serviceable and practical rug we have ever offered.
Think of a rug like the above, size, 30x60 inches, at this price..................$0.69

THIS CATALOGUE
PLACES BEFORE THE BUYER THE LOWEST PRICE ON THE CHOICEST VARIETIES OF GOODS.
Selections May be Made at Home
After mature consideration, and with our full assurance that goods will equal representation or money will be refunded.

Aubusson Rugs.
A New Thing in Rugs.

39503

Known as the Aubusson Art Rug. These rugs are in appearance on the order of an ingrain carpet, but the designs are especially suited for rugs, designed with a bordered edge in keeping with a figured center with a fringe on each end. Colors are cream, old gold and brown, ecru and wine, olive and crimson, etc,
The point most interesting to the customer is the price.

39503 Size 26x54   30x60
     Price .... $0.45   .80

Chenille Rugs.

39505 Mottled Chenille Rugs, made same as curtains of same name, but much heavier. Size, 35x62 inches, fringed on both ends, colors are mixed and are light or medium dark as preferred. They are soft and pliable, wear well, and the price is used as a means of introducing you to our growing carpet department, rather than to make any profit. Price, each $1.00

Smyrna Rugs.

Smyrna Rugs are similar in appearance to velvet carpet, but are much more durable. They are reversible and fringed on both ends. The colors are soft and subdued, or bright and attractive, as desired. Sizes given do not include fringe.

Victoria Smyrna Rugs.

Smyrna Rugs weigh from 1½ to 8 pounds each, according to size.
39507 These Rugs we recommend with confidence, knowing that they are the best, Smyrna Rug ever offered for the price. The patterns are all new in floral, geometrical and animal designs.

18x36 Dog, Lion, Peacock, Floral............. $0.81
21x45 Dog, Lion, Peacock, Floral............... 1.19
26x54 Lion, Dog, Peacock, Floral.. .... 1.69
30x60 Floral, Dog, Peacock, Lion. 1.98
36x72 Dog, Lion, Peacock, Floral........ ..... 2.99
48x84 Floral 4.99

Royal or Imperial Smyrna Rugs.

The best quality of Smyrna Rugs, made in the latest colorings and designs, either floral or geometrical. The following prices are the lowest ever offered on this grade of goods.

39509	Inches.	inches.	inches.	inches.	inches.
Size....	18x36	21x45	26x54	30x60	36x72
Price..	$1.44	$2.05	$2.85	$3.45	$5.12
	Feet.	feet.	feet.	feet.	feet.
Size...	4x7	3x12	3x15	6x9	7½x10½	9x12
Price..	$8.12	$11.65	$13.81	$18.69	$28.40	$40.63
Size				9x15	12x15	12x18
Price				$52.81	$69.07	$89.40

Low Priced Smyrna Mats.

15x28 inches.   Each........................... $0.31

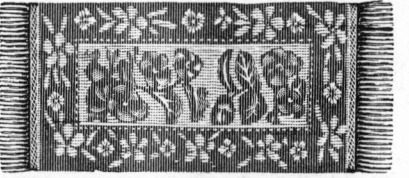

39512 Fancy, like cut, size, about 16x34 inches.
Each.. $0.75

Burmah or Body Brussels Rugs.

These Rugs are made same as the best quality of body Brussels carpet. *Double faced* (both sides alike) and lay smooth. The colors are light, medium or dark, in elegant effects. One of the most durable rugs on the market. Size does not include the fringe.

39514 Size..................... 27x54   36x63
     Price $3.43 $6.00

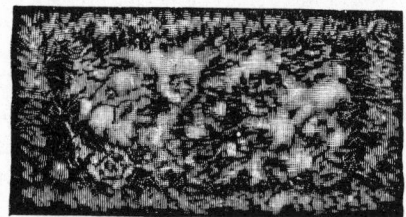

Do not pass this rug at the price offered.
39516 Moquette Rugs are the acme of perfection from a colorist's standpoint. They are softly shaded in colors, toned low and æsthetic, nothing bright or striking. Designs are floral or geometrical; colors mostly light, construction same as carpet bearing same name. No fringe. They are very heavy.

Sizes 18x36   27x60   36x72
Price, each................. $1.00 $2.70 $3.75

French Wilton Rugs.

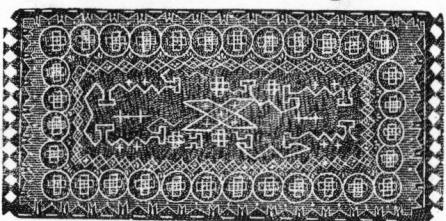

To those who wish something elegant we would recommend our French Wilton Velvet Rugs. They are very handsome, in light or dark colors with blended shadings that are exquisite. The above cut does not do the rug justice.

39518 Size........ 27x54   36x36   36x68   36x72
     Price.......... ... $3.95 $3.95 $6.00 $7.00

Angora Lamp or Vase Mats.

39520 Wavy Angora Vase or Lamp Mats. Hair is long and silky. Colors delicate and lasting; odorless: Colors: Gold, yellow, orange, cream, white, scarlet, cardinal, nile or sapphire. They are round as cut shows. Different lengths of hair make them vary in size about 12 in. in diameter.
Price, each..... $0.10

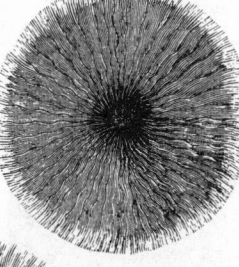

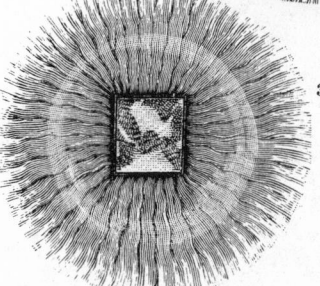

39522 Angora Mats, same as above, but larger. Colors: Old gold, cardinal, gray, lemon, orange, tan, blue, crimson, green or cream.
Each..... $0.20

Combination Fur Rugs.
LINED AND ODORLESS.

A   B

39524 These are elegant goods and fine enough for any parlor. The combinations are black and white, black and gray, gray and white, gray and grizzly bear, gray and red fox, and gray and blue fox. The designs are like cuts A and B. We also have solid colors in white black, and gray. Size. 28x64 in. Each.................... $ 3.75

Unlined Fur Rugs.

39525 Same quality as No. 39524, in solid colors, white, black, gray or red fox. Size 30x60 inches.
Price, each.................................... $2.90

Cashmere Angora Rugs.

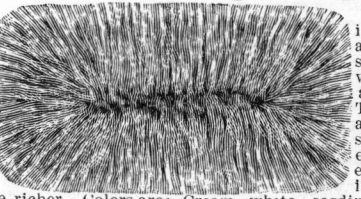

The hair is soft and glossy as silk, very long and fine. The colors are exquisite. Properly placed nothing could be richer. Colors are: Cream, white, cardinal, black, lemon, orange, light green, dark green, old gold, blue or canary. Lined or unlined, as wanted.
39527 Sizes given are measurements of rugs including overlapping hair. Size of skin is always less.

Size, including hair, about 20x32   26x38   24x58   24x62
Price, each...... ....$2.50 $3.50 $7.00 $8.00

Plush Mats, Wool Fringed.

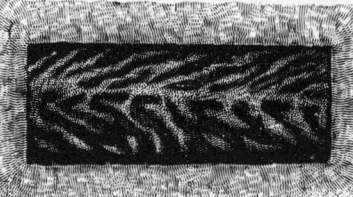

39529 The center is mohair plush, padded cushion like and fringed with bright colored wool that matches or contrasts nicely. Centers are plain or mottled. Colors are: Yellow, red, orange, black or cream. Size, 15x24 inches.
Price, each.................................. $0.39

Japanese Rugs.

Good Quality

Japanese rugs are very popular, as they have good wearing qualities, are very heavy (do not have to be tacked to the floor), and are very cheap. They are made in *oriental designs.*

39530 Sizes, in feet....	2½x5	3x6	4x7	6x9
Each.................	$1.50	$2.00	$3.15	$6.00
Sizes, in feet.........	7½x10½	9x12	12x12	12x15
Each.................	$9.00	$12 00	$16.00	$20.00

Liecestershire Art Squares.

Notice reduction in price of Art Squares.

Art Squares are large extra super carpets woven in one piece, bordered and fringed, and very popular. All wool. Should you have a room they will fit, or nearly so, you can have an artistic covering at small cost, having great wearing qualities and looking as though it were made for the room that it covers. As crumb cloths under a dining room table, they save the carpet and are easily removed and cleaned. Colors are quiet and subdued; no very bright shades. Art squares weigh 20 ounces per square yard.

39535 Sizes, feet..	7½x9	9x9	9x10½	9x12	9x13½
Price, each.......	$5.50	$6.92	$7.75	$8.85	$9.95
Sizes, feet...	9x15	10½x12	12x12	12x13½	12x15
Price, each.	$11.05	$10.35	$11.85	$13.40	$15.00

Jute Art Squares.

A new departure in floor coverings, at less than half the price of the cheapest ingrain carpet. They are made of strong jute, are printed in attractive patterns and colorings, with a 12-in. border, which either contrasts or harmonizes with the color in the center. The leading colors are: Red, green, gold and orange; two colors used in the center, three in the border. Red and green are dark shades, the others medium. Please give choice in ordering.

They can be used as crumb cloths, druggets or as rugs to partly cover a worn carpet. It is not necessary to have them fit a room exactly, as the sides are usually taken up with furniture any way. Think of carpeting a room nicely for this price!　Each.
39539 6x9 feet, weight, 4 lbs.....　............$1.20
39541 9x13 feet, weight, 8 lbs.....................　2.70

Weavers' Supplies.

Our Eureka Loom and Reed have given such universal satisfaction and sales have been so great that we have still further enlarged our list of weavers' supplies.

39571 Kynnett's Eureka Hand Carpet Looms, improved, like cut; outfit sent with loom consists of 1 steel reed (state number of dents, splits or spaces wanted to inch or to whole length of reed), 1 set harness, 1 quill wheel, 48 spools, 18 shuttles, 1 wrench and hammer combined, 1 tape measure, 1 swift

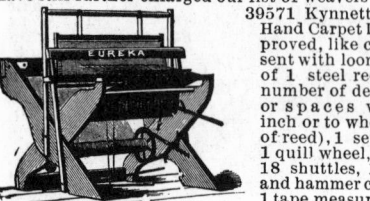

and seat combined, 1 crank, 1 wheel band, 1 temple, and all the fixtures for putting the warp on the beam and through the harness and reed.
Weight, ready for shipping, 280 pounds.
Price, each, including all attachments........$37.00

Instruction Book Free.

Upon request we will send free a 50-page book of instruction regarding carpet looms, spinning wheels, etc.

Warp Measuring Machine.

39577 The Eureka Warp Measuring Machine, measures the warp as it runs from the skein on to the spool; it can be used on any kind of a quill wheel by simply boring an inch hole into the bench of the wheel into which to place the post on which the machine hangs. It can also be used with the wheel attached to the loom.

Every weaver who spools his warp needs this machine, no matter what kind of a loom or quill wheel he uses. Price, each $4.00

Wool Cards.

39579 Wool Cards, No. 30 wire; length, 10 inches; good and strong. Per pair $0.50

Carpet Reeds.

39581 Steel Carpet Reeds, 45 inches long, with 9, 10, 11, 12, 13 or 13½ dents or spaces to the inch. Each $2.25
Weight, about 2¼ pounds each.

Prices for reeds shorter or finer than the above will be furnished on application. No reeds sent C. O. D. Carefully state number of spaces wanted. Reeds made to order will require about ten days' extra time

Spinning Wheels.

39583
39583 Quill or Spooling Wheel, like cut. Each.$3.60
39585 German or Flax Spinning Wheel, with foot power.
Price, each............$4.00

39585

Our Hosiery Department

÷　Prides itself on the fine
÷　quality of its goods.

Spinning Wheels—Continued.

39587 Spinning Wheels, like cut. Each......$4.65
39589 Spools, 6½ inches long, 2 inches in diameter, holds about ¾ pound warp. Per doz.... $0.45

39587

39590 Small Spools, 6½ inches long, 1¼ inches in diameter Per dozen........................$0.30

Shuttles.

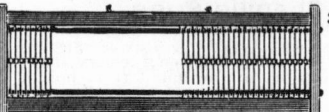

39591 Shuttles, 2 feet long, hold 1 pound filling. Per dozen............ ....$0.55

Harness Frames, Etc.

39593 Harness Frames with hooks for hanging. Per pair. $1.40

39595 Harness Frames, including two frames and 600 heddles. Each..........................　2.35
39597 Temples. Each.......................　.37

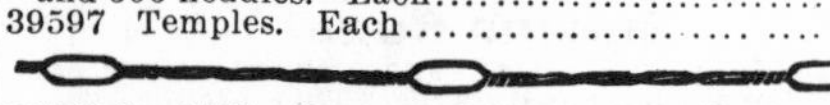

39598 Steel Wire Harness Heddles, No. 22 wire, 12 inches long. Per 100.........................$0.16

39599 Bobbin Shuttles, made of hard maple, 12 inches long; wire protected. Each $1.00

All the above loom fixtures can be used on the old-style looms.

Page 262.

What Some Kind Friends have to say about M. W. & Co.'s

High Arm Sewing Machines.

CURTAIN AND SHADE DEPARTMENT.

Our Curtain and Shade Department has been entirely reorganized. *Prices have been greatly reduced.* The quality and style of goods will be equally as good and many numbers will be much better than heretofore. Any information wanted in regard to curtains, shades or upholstery goods will be cheerfully given.

Portiere Curtains.

All Chenille Curtains (except 39607) have Dados and Fringe similar to cut in colors to harmonize with body of curtain.

Note the great reduction on Chenille Curtains.

39601 Portiere Curtains, made of chenille, 3 yards long, 36 in. wide, tassel drapery fringe on top and bottom. Colors: Light wine, camel's hair, olive or sapphire. Weight, 4 lbs. Per pair......$2.00
39603 Portiere Curtains, made of chenille, 3 yards long, 36 in. wide, tassel drapery, fringe on top and bottom. Colors: Terra cotta, light wine, camel's hair, olive, steel blue or sapphire. Weight, 5 lbs. Per pair. $2.40
39605 Portiere Curtains, made of chenille, 3 yards

long, 40 in. wide, tassel drapery, fringe on both ends. Colors: Terra Cotta, bronze, light wine, camel's hair, steel blue or sapphire. Weight, 6 lbs. Per pair..........................　3 50

39607 Portiere Curtains, made of chenille, plain solid colors, 3 yards long, 50 in. wide, tassel drapery, fringe on both ends. Colors: Light wine, camel's hair, olive or bronze. Weight, 6 lbs. Per pair..............................　4.15

39609 Portiere Curtains, made of chenille, 3 yards long, 50 inches wide, tassel drapery, fringe on both ends. Colors: Light wine, camel's hair, olive or bronze. Weight, 6½ lbs. Per pair..$4.15
N. B.—We do not sample or sell single portiere curtains.
39611 Portiere Curtains, made of chenille. Extra heavy goods with very handsome dado and fringe, 3 yards long, 49 in. wide, tassel drapery fringe, on both ends. Colors: Dark terra cotta, camel's hair, light blue or bronze. Weight, 7 lbs. Per pair.......................................　5.00

Cotton Derby Curtains or Portieres

These portieres are largely taking the place of chenilles, as they wear well and do not catch the dust.
39612 Cotton Derby Cloth Portieres, or curtains, all over design like cut. Fringe only at bottom. Reversible. Colors are: Gold, steel blue, olive, terra cotta and sage. Weight, per pair, about 4¾ pounds. Size, 50 in. wide, 3 yards long. Price, per pair. $3.25

39614 Derby Cloth Curtains, better quality than 39612; all over design like cut; silk finish. Fringed at tops and bottom. Colors same as No. 39612. Weight, per pair, 5 pounds. Size, 50-inches wide, 3 yards long Price, per pair...$4.50

HOUSEKEEPERS

Will be interested in our reduced prices and improved qualities of

House Keeping Linens.

Window Shades.

Window Shades are all mounted on spring rollers with stick at bottom; anyone can put them up. Lengths given on all shades except 39631 are for cloth before hemming or mounting on rollers.

39617 Plain Opaque Felt Shades, made of best rope manilla paper, excellent goods for the price; complete with patent spring rollers. Colors: Buff, stone, light olive, dark olive and nile green. Size, 3 feet wide, 6 feet long.
Price, each........ ....$0.16
Per dozen........ .... 1.80

39619 Holland Shades, best grade, mounted on patent spring rollers. Colors are: spanish olive green, brown, light slate and buff. Size, 3 feet wide, 6 feet long. Weight, 18 ounces.
Each .... .25
Per dozen.... .... 2.85

39621 Plain Holland Shades, made to order, best quality, 3 feet wide by 7 feet long, 40c. each; 3 feet by 8 feet, 45c. each. We cannot furnish Holland wider than 36 inches. Smaller than 3x6. 40c. each.

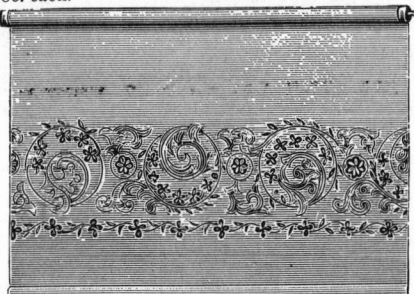

39622 Window Shades, best Holland, complete with fixtures, plain, with elegant dado at bottom. Colors: Spanish olive, pea green, dark green, brown, dark blue, light slate, pale buff or cardinal. We cannot furnish any size except 3 feet wide by 6 feet long in dado Holland shade. Mention color wanted. Each.....$0.31 Per doz.$3.60

Opaque Cloth.

39624 Opaque Cloth Window Shades, machine made, mounted on spring rollers, complete. Colors: Terra cotta, light olive, dark olive, nile green, buff or robin's-egg blue. Plain colors only.
Size, 3 ft. wide, 6 ft. long. Price, each........ .33
Size, 3 ft. wide, 6 ft. long. Price, per dozen.... 3.85
Size, 3 ft. wide, 7 ft. long. Price, each.......... .39
Size, 3 ft. wide, 7 ft. long. Price, per dozen..... 4.50

39625 Window Shades, complete, machine made, opaque cloth, 3 feet wide by 6 feet long. Colors: light olive, dark olive, nile green, slate, ecru or robin's egg blue, with elegant dado at bottom Exactly like cut, printed in Flock and gold.
Each.................................$0.42
Per dozen........................... 4.75

Oiled Opaque Cloth Window Shades.

39627 Best quality of goods. These shades come mounted on spring rollers complete, in plain colors, as follows: Light olive, dark olive, ecru, light slate, Robins egg blue, terra cotta or nile green.
Size, 3 ft. wide, 6 ft. long. Price, each.........$0.40
Size, 3 ft. wide, 6 ft. long. Price, Per dozen.... 4.60
Size, 3 ft. wide, 7 ft. long. Price, each......... 0.46
Size, 3 ft. wide, 7 ft. long. Price, per dozen.... 5.10
Shades smaller than the above will have to be made to order and will cost 70 cents each. For sizes larger than 3x7, see No. 39631.

FOR...

House Cleaning:

BROOMS, AMMONIA, DUSTERS, VARNISH, GASOLINE, SOAP, PAINT, BRUSHES, BORAX, ...WALL PAPER...

WE HAVE THEM ALL.

Everything, Except the Elbow Grease.

Window Shades—Continued.

39629 Opaque Cloth (machine made) window shades. **With Fringe** like cut, mounted on patent spring rollers complete. Colors are buff, light olive, dark olive, Nile green and robbins-egg blue.

	Each.	Per doz
Size, 3 ft. wide, 6 ft. long. Price..$0.42		$4.50
Size, 3 ft. wide, 7 ft. long. Price.. .48		5.00

Store, Office and House Shades.

Colors: Light or dark olive, Nile green, blue, stone, Spanish olive, ecru or old gold. All the following special shades made to order will take from 3 to 5 days extra time to make; no special shades will be sent C. O. D. and cannot be exchanged. In ordering use care in giving the exact size you want the shades to be, when finished; also state whether inside or outside bracket is wanted. By inside measure we mean the space between the jambs of the window casing facing each other; outside measure the space between the brackets when facing the room. If the exact size of shade is not given in the following schedule, then the next larger size will be charged. Mounted on Hartshorn's patent spring stop roller to roll from top or bottom. Lettering in shaded gilt letters, 40c. per running foot extra.

39631 PRICES ARE FOR SINGLE SHADES.
Note the reduction.
Sizes given below are Cloth Measure.

Length in Feet.	Width in inches.										
	38	40	42	45	48	54	63	72	81	90	100
5 ft	$.66	$.90	$.96	1.02	1.28	1.50	2.15	2.55	3.00	3.38	3.80
6 ft	.70	1.00	1.07	1.14	1.40	1.62	2.35	2.79	3.25	3.63	4.16
7 ft	.85	1.12	1.20	1.26	1.64	1.85	2.65	3.00	3.53	3.90	4.50
8 ft	.98	1.24	1.38	1.38	1.76	2.05	2.95	3.30	3.78	4.17	4.85
9 ft	1.09	1.34	1.50	1.55	1.86	2.45	3.20	3.55	4.05	4.50	5.25
10 ft	1.20	1.44	1.60	1.73	2.12	2.75	3.40	3.70	4.31	4.85	5.58
11 ft	1.30	1.64	1.71	1.87	2.34	2.95	3.60	3.95	4.50	5.18	5.93
12 ft	1.40	1.90	2.06	2.18	2.60	3.05	3.85	4.35	4.79	5.40	6.30

Window Curtain Holland and Opaque Cloth.

Weight of Holland, per yard, 4 ounces. Opaque cloth, 8 ounces.

39632 Window Curtain Holland, best grade, 36 in. wide only; colors: Spanish olive, pea green, cardinal, navy blue, green, brown, slate or ecru.
Per yard $0.10

39633 Window Curtain, Opaque Cloth, best grade, 38 inches wide only; Colors: Light olive, greenish tint, light slate, brown or stone.
Per yard. 0.16

39635 The "Hartshorn" Patent Spring Rollers complete with fixtures and slats (cut show, section of end rollers), adjustable to fit any window except unusually wide ones.
Each..............$0.15
Per dozen...... 1.52

39637 Patent Spring Rollers, complete with fixtures and slats. Each........................... .10
Per dozen..................................... 1.08

A GLANCE

AT THIS CATALOGUE

IS NOT ENOUGH

IT IS TOO BIG AND CONTAINS TOO MUCH OF INTEREST TO YOU.

Our Money-Saving Methods

Are Worth a Study.

Lace Curtains.

Lace Curtains and Lambrequins.

NOTE—An entirely new line, manufactured expressly for us, and of exceptionally good values. Sold in pairs only. Weight of lambrequins 3 to 5 ounces, on curtains 14 to 40 ounces. *We do not sample lace curtains* as it would require from ⅛ to ¼ of a curtain to show the border and pattern; width, length and quality governs price on all lace curtains.

39651 Nottingham Lace Curtains, white only; each curtain 3 yds. long, 6 yds to the pair, 36 in. wide, single border, taped all round; sold in pairs only. Per pair.........................$0 59

39653 Nottingham Lace Curtains, white or ecru; each curtain 3 yds. long, 6 yds. to the pair. 40 in. wide, single border, taped all around; sold in pairs only. Per pair.........................$0.75

39655 Nottingham Lace Curtains, white only; each curtain 3 yds. long, 6 yds. to the pair, 45 in. wide, single border, taped all around; sold in pairs only. Per pair.... ....$1.05
We do not sample lace curtains.

Lace Curtains—Continued

39656 Nottingham Lace Curtains, white or ecru; each curtain 3½ yds. long, 7 yds. to the pair, 47 in. wide, single border, taped all around; sold in pairs only. Per pair................................$1.38

39658 Nottingham Lace Curtains, white or ecru; Brussels net effects, each curtain 3½ yds. long, 7 yds. to the pair, 57 in. wide, single border, taped all around; sold in pairs only.
Per pair................................$1.80
We do not sample lace curtains.

39660 Nottingham Lace Curtains, white or ecru; each curtain 3½ yards long, 7 yards to the pair, 56 inches wide, single border, taped all around; sold in pairs only; *point D' Esprit centre,* with beautiful Brussels effect. Per pair........$2.50

Bicycling for Ladies.

A few years ago a lady on a bicycle was looked upon as a freak.

The exercise was good and pleasure was great, so the wheel constantly grew in favor until today all progressive people believe in the silent steed as a splendid means of exercise for women.

Lace Curtains—Continued.

Cut shows only part of curtain.
39662 Nottingham Lace Curtains, white or ecru only, very fine Brussels net effect: each curtain 3½ yards long, 7 yards to the pair, 60 inches wide, taped all around. Sold in pairs only.
Per pair................................$5.50
We do not sample lace curtains.

Combined Lace Curtains and Lambrequins.
NEW AND STYLISH.

39663 These Curtains and Lamberquins are woven in one piece like cut. They are practical and pretty, made of Nottingham lace, 3½ yards long and 60 inches wide, white or ecru
Price, each................................$1.15

Irish Point Lace Curtains.
Never before have Irish Points, full width, full length and standard quality, been offered at the following low prices:

39665 Cut shows only part of curtain. Size, 50 inches wide, 3½ yards long; exactly like cut.
Price, per pair................................$2.35

Do You Use Paint Brushes? Our line is new and carefully selected for practical purposes. Prices right. Try them.

Lace Curtains—Continued.

Cut shows only part of curtain.
39667 Size, 50 inches wide, 3½ yards long, exactly like cut; ecru only. Price, per pair.......$4.00

Brussels Net Lace Curtains.
This quality of curtain has always been too expensive for people of moderate means. We have secured a large importation at prices that will enable us to place them within the reach of anyone.

39693 Brussels Net Lace Curtains, very fine net: come in white only, exactly like cut; size, 48 inches wide, 3½ yards long. Per pair.....$4.75

39695 Brussels Net Lace Curtains, finer net than the above, beautiful design (like cut); white only; size, 48 in. wide, 3½ yards long. Pair. $5.85

Lambrequins similar to cut.

	Each.	Per doz.
39697 Lace Lambrequins, white......	$0.35	$3.80
39699 Lace Lambrequins, white.....	.50	5.40
39701 Lace Lambrequins, white.....	.74	8.07

Bed Spreads and Pillow Shams.

39703 Nottingham Lace Bed Spread, and two pillow shams to match, white only, latest designs: size of spread, 70x85 in.; weight, 20 oz. Per set of 3 pieces....................................$1.50

39705 Nottingham Lace Spread, and two pillow shams to match, white only; size of spread, 70x 90 in.; weight, 26 oz. Per set of 3 pieces.......$2.00

Lace Pillow Shams.

39709 Nottingham Lace Shams, 32x34 inches, taped all around, white only.
Per pair...$0.35
Per dozen pair...3.75
39711 Nottingham Lace Shams, 33x34 inches, taped all around, white. Per pair...............45
Per dozen pair...4.55
39713 Nottingham Lace Shams, 34x34 inches. Brussels effect, ecru or white, taped all around.
Per pair...68
Per dozen pair...7.25

Curtain Draperies.

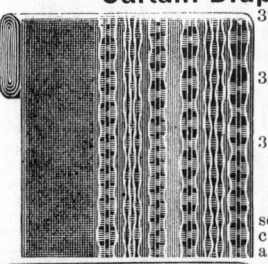

39715 Union Lace Scrim, 38 inches wide.
Per yard...........$0.05
39716 Union Lace Scrim, extra quality, 42 inches.
Per yard........$0.12
39718 Plain Scrim, extra quality, 42 inches wide.
Per yard.......$0.20
NOTE— The above scrims are used for curtains, draperies, aprons and fancy work.

39719—
Union Lace Scrim, with colored stripe in blue, gold or red, 40 inches wide.
Per yard........$0.07
39721 Point D'Esprit Net, like cut, very pretty for sash curtains at a very low price. Width, 30 inches.
Per yard........$0 16

Mosquito Nettings.

Per piece.
39725 Mosquito Netting, white....................$0.40
39727 Mosquito Netting, blue, pink, green, buff or corn color...45
Mosquito Netting is put up in pieces of about 8 yards each by the manufacturers. Weight, per piece, 14 ounces. Quotations on mosquito netting are liable to fluctuations. We shall always bill at lowest market rates.
For wire window screens, etc., see Index.

Cotton Plush for Curtains, Portieres or Lambrequins.

39729 Cotton Plush; double face, nap on both sides, 30 inches wide; colors: Wine, old gold, peacock green, navy or olive. Weight, per yard, 6 ounces. Price per yard................................$0.15
39731 Cotton Plush; double face, two toned or different colors on each side, 30 inches wide; colors: Old gold and black, old gold and cardinal, old gold and wine, or peach and olive.
Per yard...20
39733 Cotton Plush; double face and double width; colors: Wine, cardinal, light and dark olive, peacock blue or old gold. Width, 50 in.
Per yard...45
39735 Cotton Plush; single face, oriental designs; colors of ground work: Gold, peach or ecru, 28 inches wide. Per yard.................16
39737 Cotton Plush; double face rich Paisley designs; colors of ground work: Olive, gold, blue or cardinal, 28 inches wide. Per yard...........19
39739 Cotton Plush; "Fleur de Lis" figured French designs; colors of ground work: Gold, ecru, peach or cardinal, 28 inches wide.
Per yard...22
39741 Cotton Plush; best grade, large flower designs, colors of ground work: Cardinal, gold, wine or black, 28 inches wide. Per yard........27

Plain Chenille.

39743 The same as used in Chenille Portieres. Colors are: Steel blue, wine, olive, tan or peach. Width, 50 inches. Per yard....................45

Furniture Coverings, Upholstery, Drapery, Portieres and Lambrequins.

39747 Jute Furniture Coverings. New designs; colors: Mahogany with gold flowers; red with gold flowers or bluish green with gold flowers; width, 50 inches. Per yard.....................$0.47

39749 Petite Point Tapestry, close, hard weave, interwoven with tinsel. Colors: Light olive with dark olive and black figures, light olive with garnet and black figures; bluish green with olive and black figures; width, 50 inches; weight, per yard, 19 ounces. Per yard.....................$0.72

39851 Callon Tapestry, best quality, is used mostly for medium priced furniture covering. Colors are: Brown, steel blue, red, olive, terra cotta and peach, with beautiful designs in colors to harmonize. Width, 50 inches. Per yard.......68

39753 Silk Tapestry, furniture covering, elegant goods; colors same as No. 39751. Width, 50 inches. Per yard....................................2.00

Plush For Furniture Covering.

39755 Crushed Mohair Plush for furniture coverings, 24 inches wide; colors: Cardinal, terra cotta, peacock blue, medium and light olive, gold brown, bronze, sea green or steel blue. Per yard.$1.00
39757 Marbleized Silk Plush for furniture coverings, 24 inches wide, same colors as above.
Per yard...1.00
39759 Plain Silk Plush for furniture coverings, 24 inches wide; same colors as 39755. Per yard. 1.00

Stand Covers.

Notice reduced prices on Stand Covers.

39765-67-69.

39763 Stand Covers, double face cotton plush, with printed designs; colors: Black and gold, wine and gold, or olive and cardinal. Size, 36x36 in. Each $0.30 Per dozen.........$3.25
39764 Cotton Damask Table Covers, silk finish. Colors are: Olive and mahogany; ecru and olive; cardinal and olive; olive and wine; and Nile green and old rose. They are fringed on all sides and are good value. Size, 52 inches square. Each...$1.00
39765 Chenille Stand Covers, 30x30 inches, fringed borders, new designs, assorted combination colors. Each...................................65
Per dozen..7.50
39767 Chenille Covers, 54x54 inches, fringed borders, new designs, assorted combination colors. Each $0.98 Per dozen 11.25
39769 Chenille Covers, 72x72 inches, same as above. Each $2.50 Per dozen....................29.00

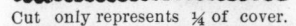

39785 Felt Table or Stand Cover, with applique flowers embroidered with shaded silk floss in contrasting colors, as follows: Green ground with gold flowers; wine with light olive, garnet with dark olive; light olive with dark olive, and dark olive with wine. Scalloped edge; weight, 8 oz.; size, 36x36 in.
Cut only represents ¼ of cover. Each.......$0.85

39787 Felt Table or Stand Cover, with applique velvet stars on each corner, shaded embroidery used for flowers. Embroidered all round with silk floss, scalloped edge. Colors: Green, wine, garnet, dark olive and light olive, with contrasting stars; weight, 8 oz.; size, 36x36 in........$1.20

* * * * * * * * * * * * * *

The Mail Order Business ~ ~ ~

Now Embraces all that is desirable to induce every one, and especially dwellers in sparsely settled and remote districts, to trade directly with an establishment handling every variety of merchandise ordinarily not obtainable in less than half a dozen stores.

* * * * * * * * * * * * * *

Stand Covers—Continued.

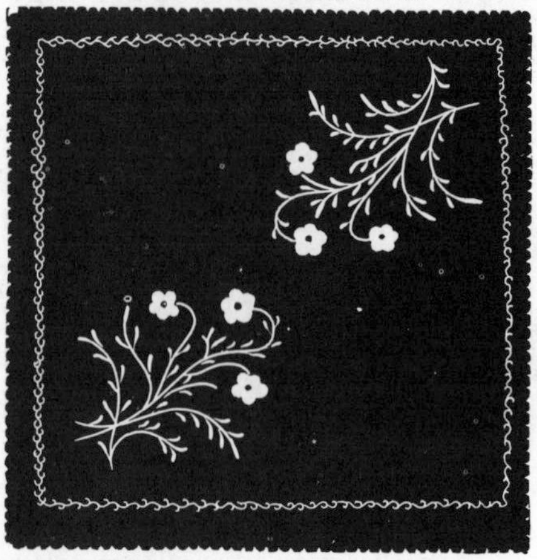

Cut represents style of embroidery.

39789 Felt Table Cover, shaded silk. embroidered flowers and vines, silk embroidered border, scalloped edge, same colors as above. Embroidered on four corners; weight, 18 ounces; size, 54x54 inches (2500). Each..............................$2.70

39791 Felt Table Cover, applique flowers, elegantly embroidered with shaded silk floss on the four corners, scalloped edge. Colors: Green, wine, garnet, dark olive and light olive with contrasting flowers; 17 oz; size, 54x54 inches. Each....$2.25

Cut represents only ¼ of cover.

Felt Scarfs, for Mantels, Stands and Decorating.

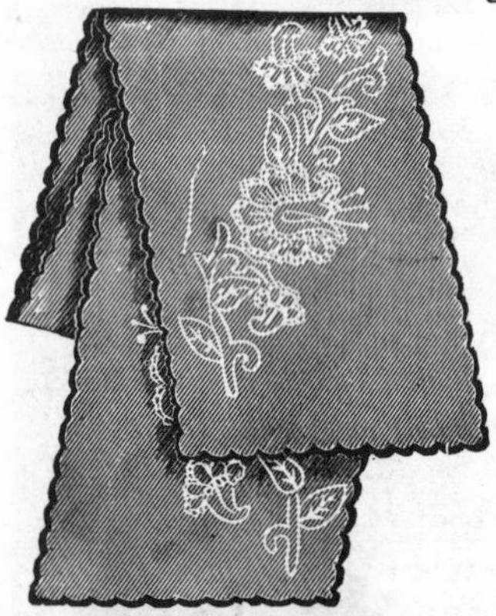

39793 Felt Scarfs, scalloped edges, silk embroidered design on end, size, 14x54 inches. Colors: Wine, garnet, light or dark olive and green; weight 4 oz. Each....$0.52

39795 This is a beautiful scarf, exactly like cut with designs worked in tinsel and silk floss. Size, 17x52 inches. Colors are: Wine, garnet, light or dark olive; weight, 5 oz. Each....$0.95

Scarfs—Continued.

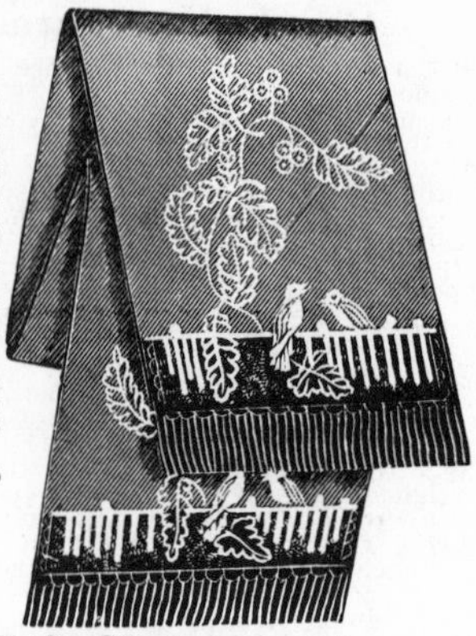

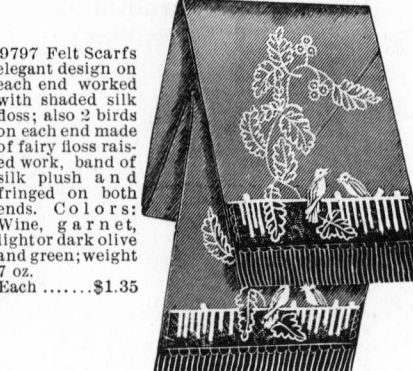

39797 Felt Scarfs elegant design on each end worked with shaded silk floss; also 2 birds on each end made of fairy floss raised work, band of silk plush and fringed on both ends. Colors: Wine, garnet, light or dark olive and green; weight 7 oz. Each.......$1.35

Felt Cloths.

39801 Felt Cloth, best made, for working stamped patterns and embroidering mantel and table ornamentations, etc. Colors: Wine, garnet, gold light and dark olive, peacock blue, green, black, white,orange,yellow, light blue, pink, tan brown or Nile green; 72 inches wide. Per yard..........$0.98

Shelf Oil Cloth.

39803 Shelf Oil Cloth, scalloped edges, 12 inches wide. Marble and wood colors with fancy borders. Weight, 3¼ lbs. per piece of 12 yds. Sold in full pieces only. Per piece.....................$0.60

Table Oil Cloth

These goods are guaranteed to be first quality.

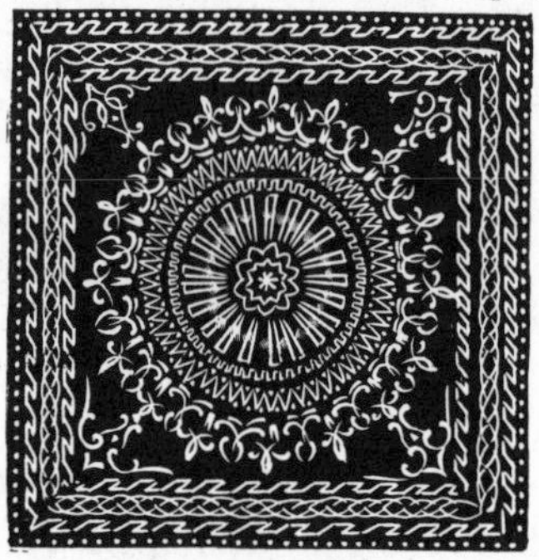

39805

Table Oil Cloths were never before sold as cheap.

39805 Table Oil Cloth Patterns,size, 53x46 inches. Wood colors. Per pattern..........................$0.28
Per piece of 8 patterns............................. 2.18

Table Oil Cloth by the Yard or Piece.

The following have 12 yards in each piece. Weight, 45 inch, 19 ounces; 54 inch, 21 ounces. per yard.

	Per piece.	Per yard
39807 Table Oil Cloth, marble patterns, 45 inches wide	$1.75	$0.16
39809 Table Oil Cloth, marble patterns, 54 inches wide	2.35	.22
39811 Table Oil Cloth, wood colors, 45 inches wide	1.60	.15
39813 Table Oil Cloth, wood colors, 54 inches wide	2.35	.22
39815 Plain Black Oil Cloth, 45 inches wide	2.30	22
39816 Plain Black Oil Cloth Drill, 45 inches wide	3.40	.31

Child's Oil Cloth Table Mats.

39817 These mats are used for placing beneath children's dishes at table thereby protecting the table linen. They are made in handsome designs and colorings and are very popular. Size, 17 x 20 inches. Price, each.................$0.10
Per dozen.. 1.00

Drapery Fringes.

Used for lambrequins, sash curtains, mantels, brackets, chair scarfs, table and stand covers, all kinds of curtain draperies and fancy work. They are made in all the leading colors and combinations. When ordering mention predominating color of material and we will send color that will harmonize best; weight of fringes, ½ to 2 ounces per yard.

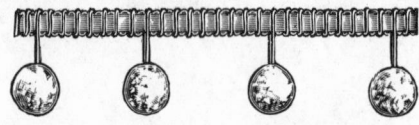

39818 Cotton Ball Fringe, like cut, ⅜ inch heading; full width, 1¾ inch. Not made in any dark colors.
Price, per yard.......$0.05. Per doz. yds.......$0.50

Fringes—Continued.

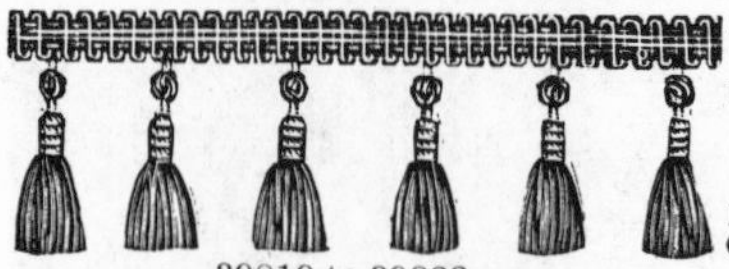

39819 to 39823

39819 Cotton Drapery Fringe ⅜ inch heading; full width, 1⅞ inch. Colors are: White, cream, red, tan, pink, light blue or brown
Per dozen yards.......................................$ .55
Per yard...05

39821 Silk Drapery Fringe, ¼ inch heading; full width, 1⅞ in. in colors same 39819.
Per dozen yards........$1.08 Per yard.......... .10

39823 Silk Drapery Fringe, ¼ inch heading; full width, 2¼ in. in combinations.
Per dozen yards.........$1.50 Per yard......... .14

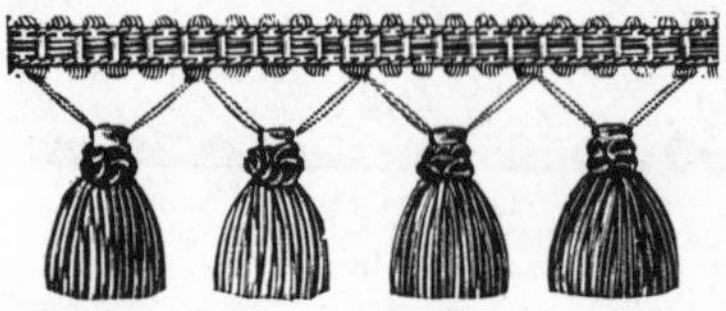

39825 Silk Drapery Fringe, ⅜ inch heading; full width, 3¼ in.; colors: Light blue pink, olive, gold or Nile.
Per doz. yards.........$2.25 Per yard..........$0.21

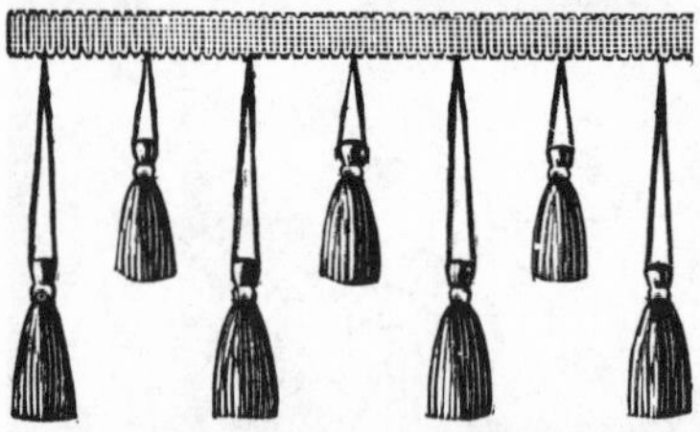

39827 Silk Drapery Fringe, ¼ inch heading; full width, 4 inches in combinations.
Per doz. yds..$2.25
Per yd .21

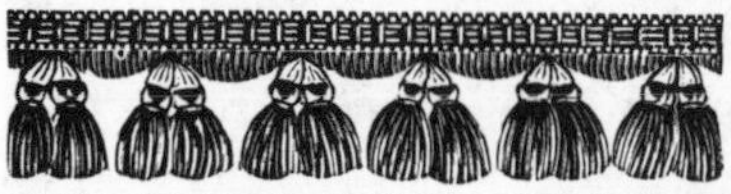

39831 Silk Drapery Fringe, full width, 1⅞ inch; very pretty for side draping; in light materials, in combinations.
Per dozen yards........$3.35 Per yard...........$0.31

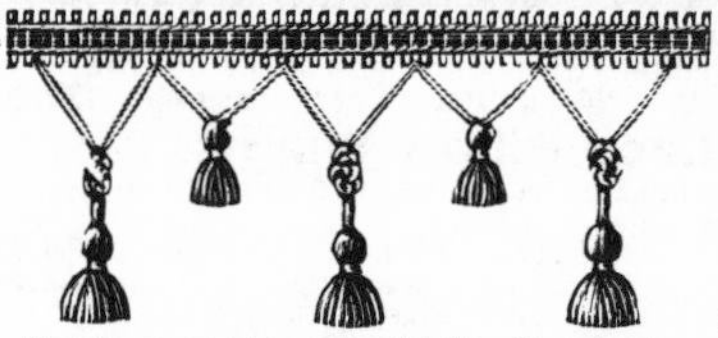

39833 Silk Drapery Fringe, ½ inch heading; full width, 4¼ inches, combinations or plain colors.
Per dozen yards........$4.65 Per yard..........$0.43

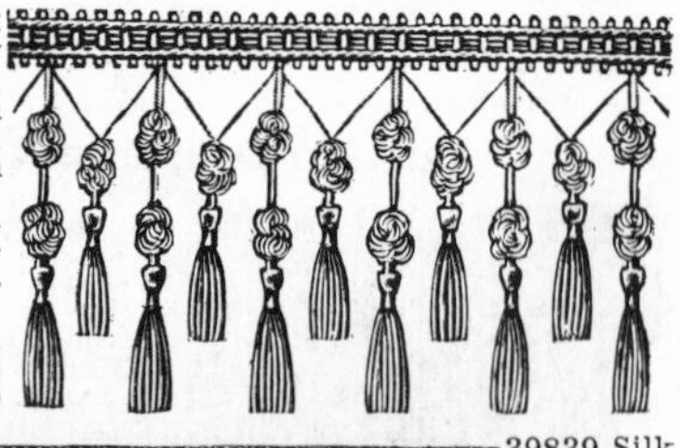

39835 Silk Drapery Fringe, ½ inch heading; full width 6 inches, combinations or plain colors.
Pr. dz. yds. $6.48
Pr. yd.. 60

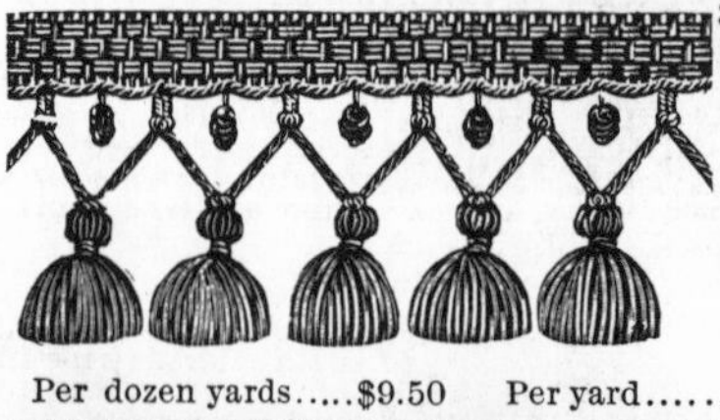

39839 Silk Drapery or Furniture Fringe, ½ in. heading, full width 4½ in. Combination or plain colors.
Per dozen yards.....$9.50 Per yard...........$0.85

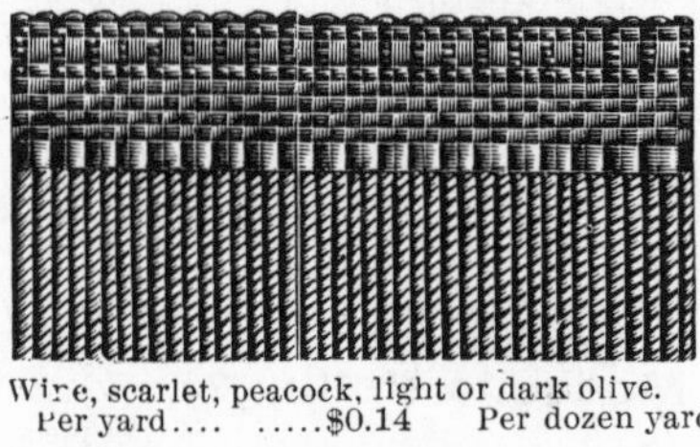

39841—Drapery or Furniture Bullion Worsted Fringe, 1½ in., combination heading; full width, 4 inches. Colors: Wire, scarlet, peacock, light or dark olive.
Per yard.... .....$0.14 Per dozen yards $1.50

Fringe—Continued.

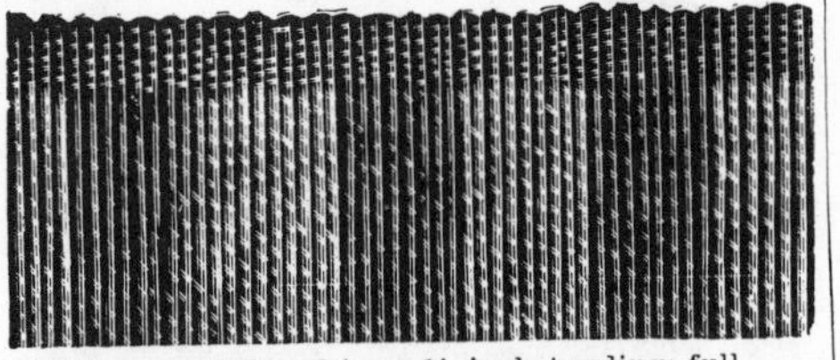

39843 Worsted Rug Fringe, ½ inch heading; full width, 3 inches, combinations or plain colors. Per yard..........$0.06 Per dozen yards....$0.65

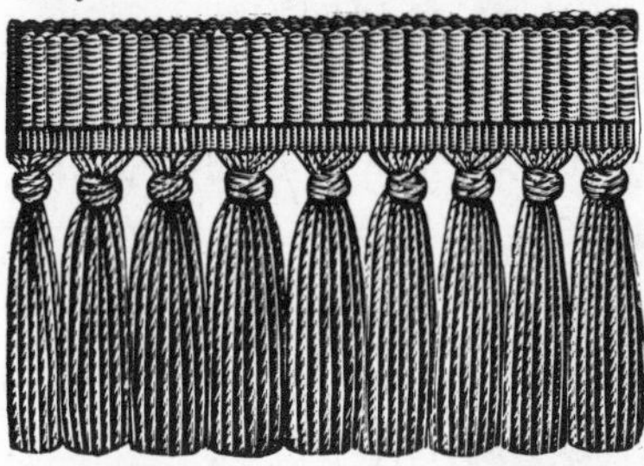

39845—Worsted Rug Fringe, double heading, 1¼ inch wide; full width, 4½ in, combinations or plain colors.
Per yard....................$0.15
Per dozen yards.............1.62

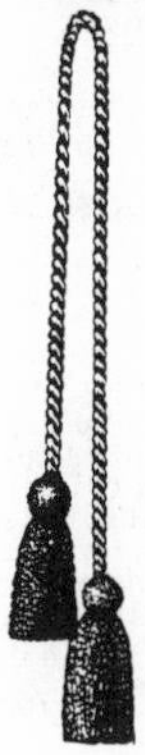

Curtain and Sash Loop.

39847 White Cotton Loops, circumference ⅝ inch; full length, 36 inches. Each....$0.05
Per dozen..........................40
39849 White or Ecru Cotton Loops, circumference 1 inch; full length, 55 inches.
Each...............................$0.07
Per dozen..........................75
39851 Chenille Drapery Loops, colors to match chenille curtains. Lengt , 60 inches.
Price, each........................$0.20
Per dozen..........................2.25

39853 Silk Loops, ½ inch circumference, full length, 50 inches, all staple colors. Each......................$0.15
Per dozen..........................1.62

Furniture Gimp and Cord.

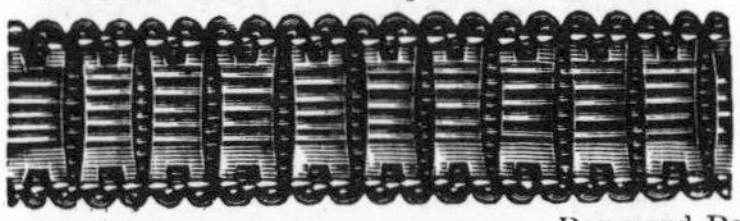

	Per yard.	Per doz yards.
39857 Furniture Gimp, cotton, ½ inch wide; in all staple colors...... Per piece of 36 yards..........$0.30	$0.01	$0.10
39859 Furniture Gimp, silk mixed, ½ inch wide; in all staple colors...... Per piece of 36 yards..........$0.50	.02	.20
39861 Furniture Gimp, extra quality silk mixed, ½ inch wide; in all staple colors.......... Per piece of 36 yards..........$0.80	.04	.30

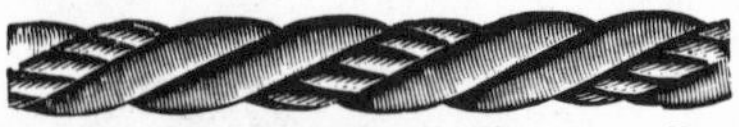

	Per yard.
39863 Furniture Cord, small, all silk covered; in all staple colors...... Per piece of about 18 yards.....$0.60	$0.04
39865 Furniture Cord, medium, all silk covered; in all staple colors.... Per piece of about 18 yards.....$0.75	.05
39867 Furniture Cord, large, all silk combination covered; in all staple colors.......... Per piece of about 18 yards.....$1.40	.09
39869 Silk Plush Upholstery Buttons, size, 22 line; all staple colors. Per dozen..........	.05
Per gross..........	50

Wood Curtain Poles.

33870

Curtain poles weigh from 2½ to 6 pounds according to length.
Prices include pole, two turned wooden ends, two brackets for ends, and two wooden rings for each foot of pole. One set is one pole with trimmings complete.
Be sure and mention which *finish* you want.

39870 1⅜ in. poles. *Finished* in California walnut, Antiqe oak, ebony or mahogany, with wood trimmings complete, like cut.

Length	5 ft.	6 ft.	7 ft.	8 ft.	10 ft.
Price	$0.25	$0.32	$0.40	$0.45	$0.50

Brass Trimmed Curtain Poles.

We do not handle the cheapest brass pole trimmings; ours are all good solid goods.

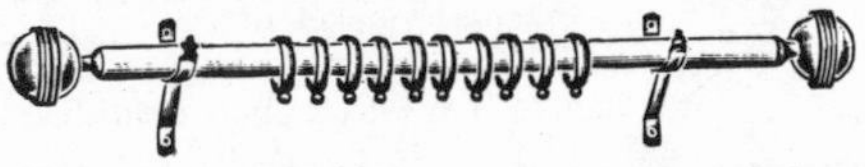

Cut shows Trimmings of Nos. 39871 to 39875, inclusive

39871 1⅜-inch Poles, finished in antique oak, ebony, Mahogany or California walnut, with brass trimmings, complete.

Length	5 ft.	6 ft.	7 ft.	8 ft.	10 ft.
Price	$0.20	$0.30	$0.35	$0.40	$0.45

39873 1⅜-inch Poles, corrugated, *white*, enameled finish, *very handsome*, with brass trimmings, complete.

Length	5 ft.	6 ft.	8 ft.	10 ft.
Price	$0.30	$0.36	$0.45	$0.55

39875 1⅜ inch *Brass* Poles, with brass trimmings, complete.

Length	5 ft.	6 ft.	8 ft.	10 ft.
Price	$0.50	$0.60	$0.75	$0.95

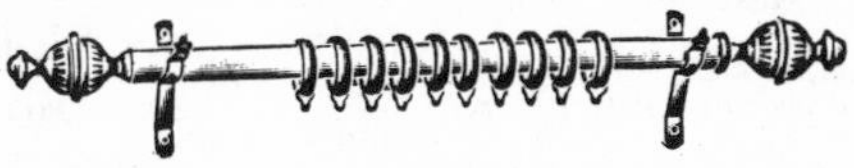

Cut shows Trimmings of Nos. 39887 to 39891, inclusive.

39887 1⅜-inch Poles, finished same as No. 39871, with brass trimmings, complete, like cut.

Length	5 ft.	6 ft.	7 ft.	10 ft.
Price	$0.28	$0.36	$0.40	$0.56

39889 1⅜-inch Poles, like No. 39873, with brass trimmings, complete, like cut.

Length	5 ft.	6 ft.	10 ft.
Price	$0.34	$0.40	$0.60

39891 1⅜-inch Poles, *brass*, with brass trimmings, complete, like cut.

Length	5 ft.	6 ft.	10 ft.
Price	$0.54	$0.65	$1.00

The Telescope Vestibule Rod.

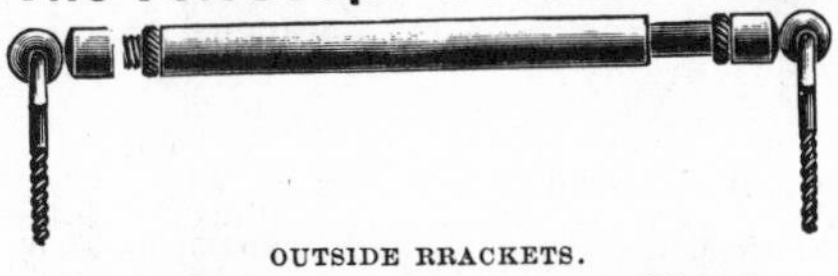

OUTSIDE BRACKETS.

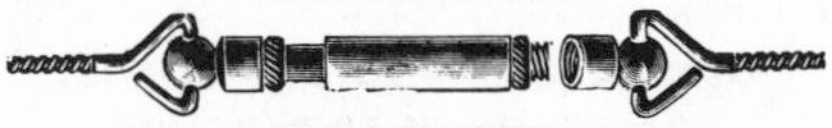

INSIDE BRACKETS

39899 These Rods are made of two brass tubes, one sliding closely inside of the other in telescope style. They are the most practical device for hanging sash curtains in the market, fit any window from 24 to 40 inches wide, No screws needed to put them up. Price Each..........$0.18
Per dozen..........1.90

Brass Rods and Brackets.

Suitable for sash curtains of vestibule doors. Sold by foot. One-half foot will be charged as one foot. Weight, 2 ounces per foot.
39905 Vestibule Rods, brass filled solid; ¼ inch in diameter. Per foot..........$0.04
Weight of brackets and sockets, 2 ounces per pair.

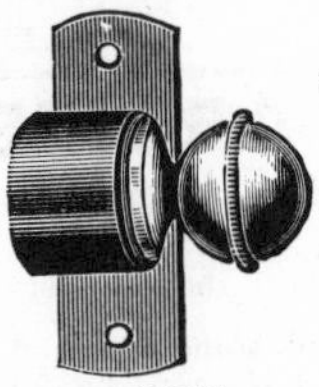

39907 Outside Brackets, ¼ inch. Per pair......$0.07
Single........ .04
39909 Inside Brackets, ¼ inch. Per pair.........$0.10
Single....... .06

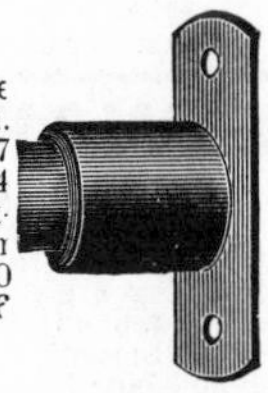

39907 39909

39913 Brass Rings, for vestibule rods, ⅝ inch in diameter. Per dozen.......... .18
39915 Brass Sockets, for all kinds of poles, 1½ inch. Per pair.......... .07
39917 Brass Sockets, for all kinds of poles, 2 inch. Per pair.......... .10

Picture Hooks, Nails, Etc.

Weight, about 3 ounces per dozen for hooks and per 100 nails.

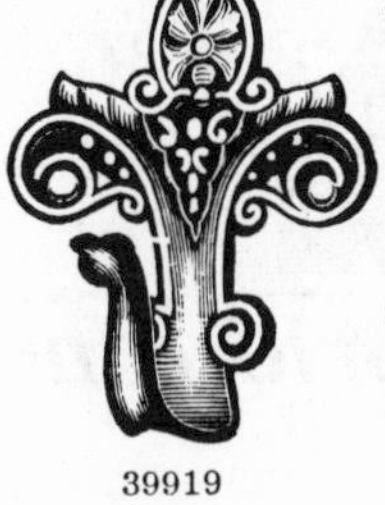

39919

39919 Niles Patent Picture Hooks, made of brass. Pins for fastening come with each. Can be tacked to plaster.
Per doz..$0.25
39921 Gilt Finish Patent Picture Hooks for attaching to moulding, 1¼ in.
Per dozen..........$0.20

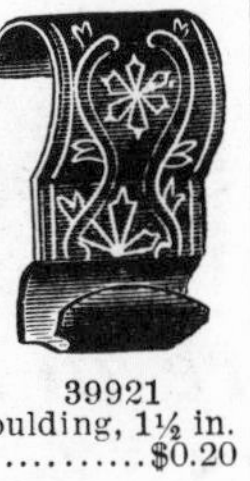

39921

Picture Hooks—Continued.

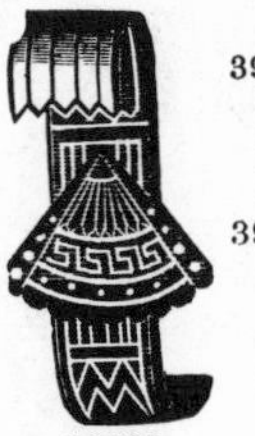

39925

39925 Burnished Brass Moulding Picture Hooks, Grecian design, 2½ in.
Each..........$0.10
Per dozen..........1.20
39927 Patent Picture Hooks, 1½ in., gilt finish, for attaching to moulding.
Per dozen........$0.07
Per gross.......... .75

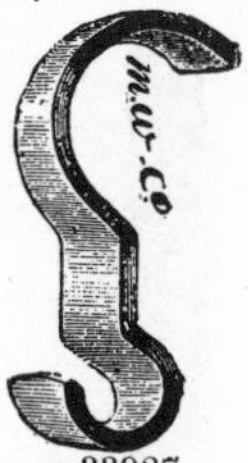

33927

Picture Knobs, with Screws.

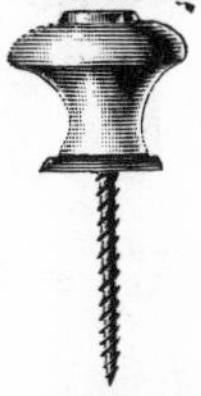

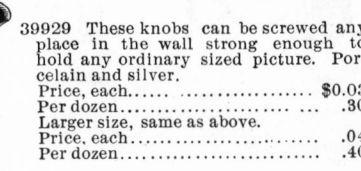

39929 These knobs can be screwed any place in the wall strong enough to hold any ordinary sized picture. Porcelain and silver.
Price, each..........$0.03
Per dozen.......... .30
Larger size, same as above.
Price, each.......... .04
Per dozen.......... .40

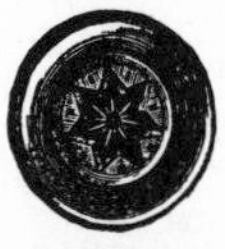

39931 Picture Nails, like cut, assorted colored heads.
Per dozen.......$0.25
39933 Picture Nails, porcelain heads, gilt rims. Per doz..$0.15

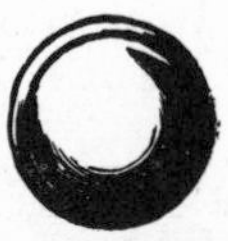

39931 39933

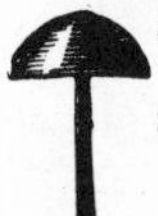

39935 China Headed Nails,
Per 1,000..........$0.65
Per 100.......... .07
39937 Disks for China Headed Nails.
Per 1,000..........$0.50
Per 100.......... .06

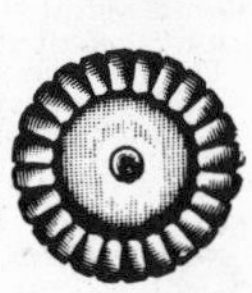

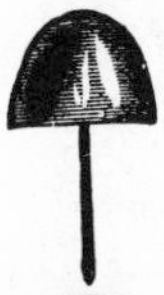

39939 Gilt Furniture Nails.
Large size, per 1,000..........$0.75
Large size, per 100.......... .10
Small size, per 1,000.......... .60
Small size, per 100.......... .07

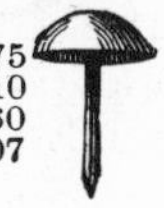

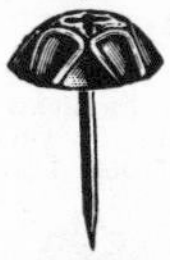

39941 Antique Brass Furniture Nails, fancy designs.
Per 1,000..........$2.10
Per 100.......... .23

Tassel Hooks.

Used also for curtains, portieres, lambrequins.

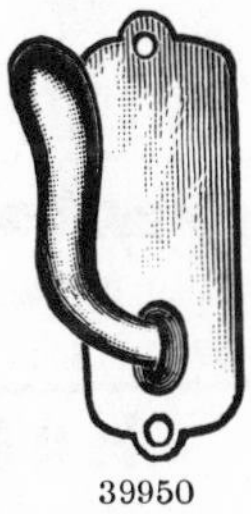

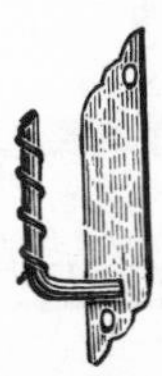

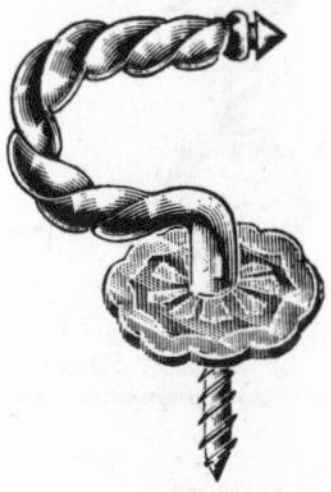

39950 39952-53 39946

	Each.	Per dz.
39946 Brass Tassel Hooks, with screw.	$0.03	$0.30
39950 Tassel Hooks, silver plated, burnished; length, 2 inches..........	.03	.35
39952 Tassel Hooks, brass, with a copper spiral twist, small..........	.07	.72
39953 Tassel Hooks, silver, with a copper spiral twist, medium..........	.08	.80

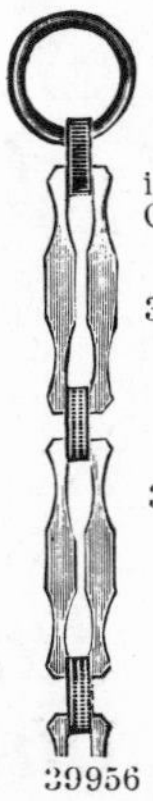

Brass Drapery Chains.

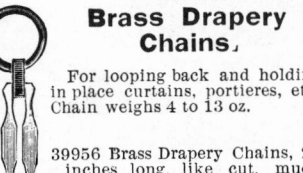

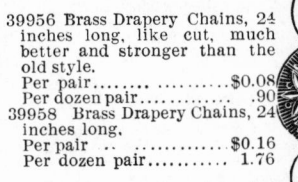

For looping back and holding in place curtains, portieres, etc. Chain weighs 4 to 13 oz.

39956 Brass Drapery Chains, 24 inches long, like cut, much better and stronger than the old style.
Per pair..........$0.08
Per dozen pair.......... .90
39958 Brass Drapery Chains, 24 inches long.
Per pair..........$0.16
Per dozen pair.......... 1.76

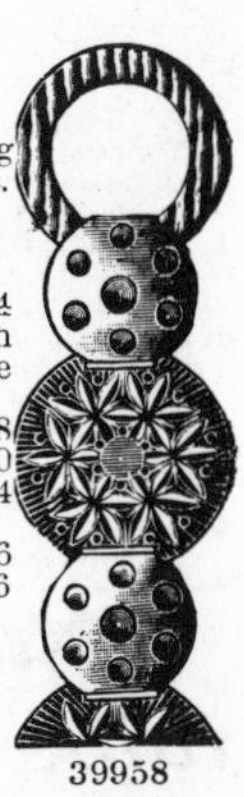

39956 39958

Drapery Chains—Continued.

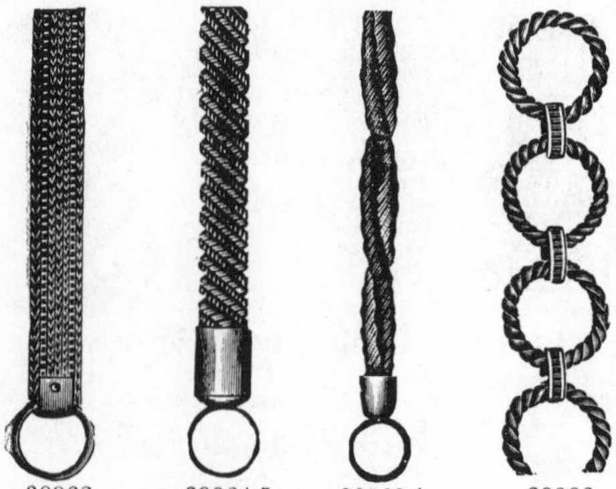

39962 39964-5 39960-1 39966

The effect of these chains is almost entirely *due to the coloring.* The cuts fail to do them justice. They have a *beautiful silky appearance* and are all made of brass wire.

39960 Drapery Chains, spiral wire, silver and pink, 24 inches long. Per pair....$0.18
Per dozen pair....2.10

39961 Drapery Chains, spiral wire, copper and gold. Per pair......$0.18 Per dozen pair.....2.10

39962 Gold Plated Band Drapery Chains, ½ inch wide, 24 in. long. Per pair....40
Per dozen pair....4.50

39964 Spiral Drapery Chains, cut large gilt strand and two small strands of steel blue and Nile green. Each.......$0.28 Per dozen pair.. 3.25

39965 Spiral Drapery Chain, 1 large silver strand and 2 small strands of pink and gold. Per pair....28
Per dozen pair....3.25

39966 Drapery Chains, gold plated, brazed rings, 23 inches long. Per pair....50
Per dozen pair....5.50

Drapery Hooks.

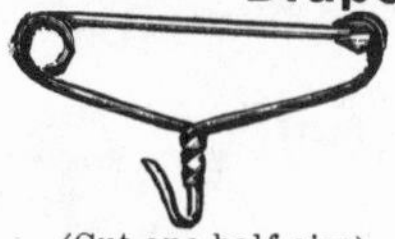

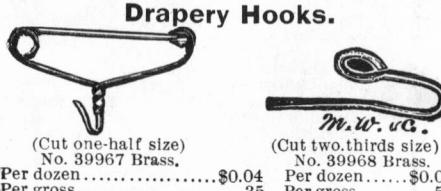

(Cut one-half size)
No. 39967 Brass.
Per dozen....$0.04
Per gross....35

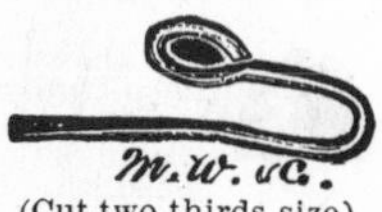

(Cut two-thirds size)
No. 39968 Brass.
Per dozen......$0.05
Per gross.......54

Brass and Nickel Shade Pulls.

FOR ATTACHING TO BOTTOM OF CURTAINS.

Fastened on with brass pins, in addition to the screw eye, which prevents the clasp from catching on the sash in running up. Weight on shade pulls, from 1 to 5 ounces.

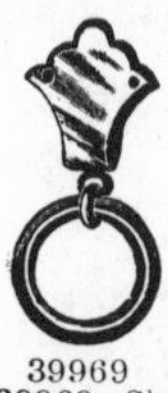

39969

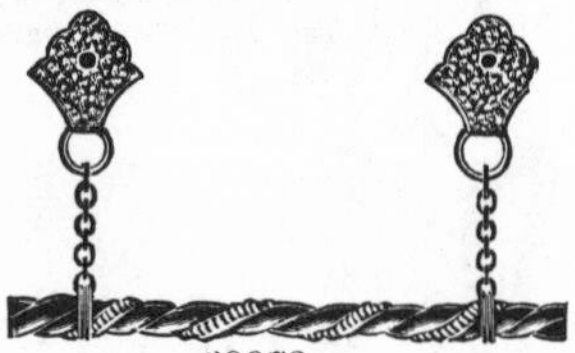

39972

	Each	Per doz.
39969 Shade Pulls, finished in brass, or nickel, diameter of ring, 1¼ inch...	$0.02½	$0.25

Shade Pulls—Continued.

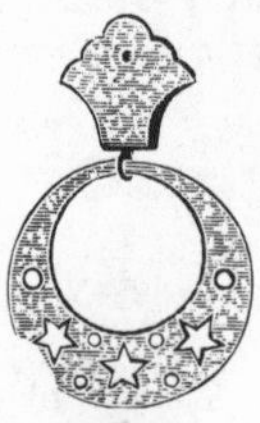

39971 Crescent Shape Pulls, finished in brass or nickel, like cut.
Each....$0.02½
Per dozen....25

39972 Bar Shade Pulls, finished in silver or brass.
Each....$0.05
Per dozen....54

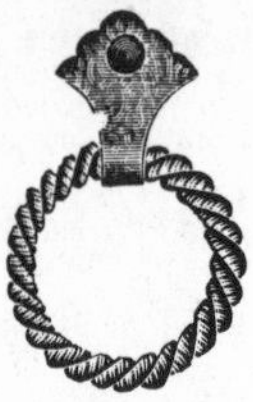

39974-5

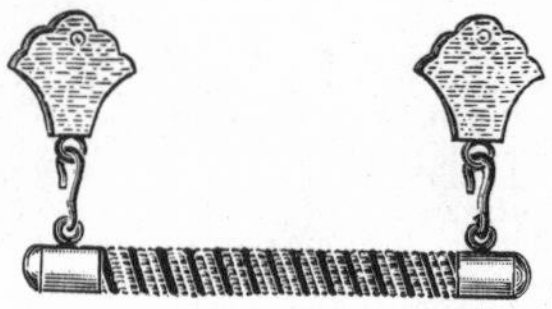

39977-88

	Each.	Per dz.
39974 Shade Pulls, silver finish, spiral rings. Diameter, 1¾ inch....	$0.05	$0.54
39975 Shade Pulls, Nile green finish, spiral rings. Diameter, 1¾ in....	.05	.54
39977 Bar Shade Pulls, copper spiral bar	.08	.85
39978 Bar Shade Pulls, black and copper twisted spiral bar (122)....	.08	.85

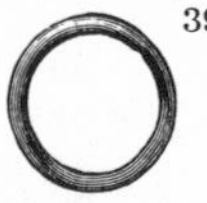

39980 Curtain Rings, small, brass, like cut.

Sizes, diameter....	⅜-inch	½-inch.
Per gross....	15c.	18c.
Sizes, diameter....	⅝-inch.	¾-inch.
Per gross....	20c.	25c.

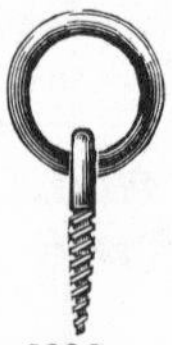

39981 Brass Screw Rings, like cut.

Sizes....	⅜-inch	½-inch.
Per gross....	$0.24	$0.40

39981

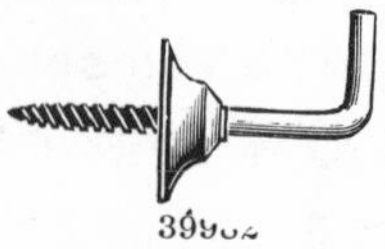

39982

39982 Brass Shoulder Hooks, like cut.

Sizes....	½-inch.	¾-inch.
Per dozen....	$0.05	$0.07
Per gross....	.55	.75

Curtain and Picture Cords.

We do not cut curtain or picture cord.

39983 Curtain Cord. Colors: Green, blue, slate, scarlet, put up in balls said to contain 30 yards; sold only in balls. Each....$0.06
Per dozen....65

39984 Curtain or Picture Cord, hemp covered with worsted; for piece of about 36 yards.......34

39985 Picture Cord, large size, per piece of about 36 yards, same as 39982....50

39986 Bright Braided Picture Wire, per piece of 25 yards, No. 0....05

39987 Bright Braided Picture Wire, larger, No. 3, per piece of 25 yards....14

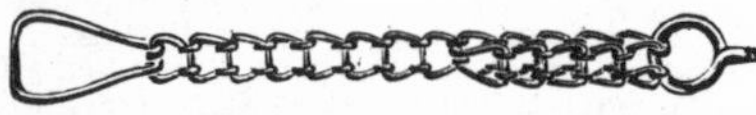

39988 *Brass Picture Chains*, with loop like cut, or with *hook* to hang on moulding; 36 inches long. Per pair....$0.15

Picture Cords—Continued.

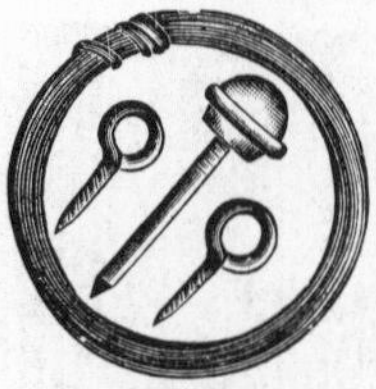

39987-88

39989 Braided Picture Wire, No. 1, 2½ yards; 2 screw eyes and 1 picture nail on card. Per set 04
Per dozen sets....43

39990 Braided Picture Wire, No. 3, 2½ yards; 2 screw eyes, and 1 picture nail hook on card. Per set....06
Per dozen sets....65

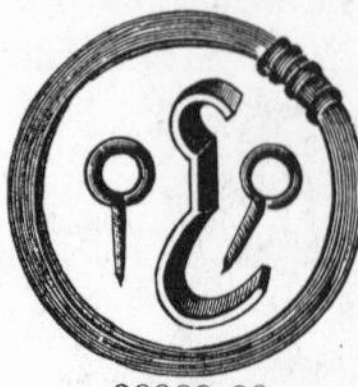

39989-90

39991 Braided Picture Wire, No. 1, 2½ yards; 2 screw eyes and 1 picture molding hook on card. Per set....04
Per dozen sets....43

39992 Braided Picture Wire, No. 3, 2½ yards; 2 screw eyes and 1 picture molding hook on card. Per set....06
Per dozen sets....65

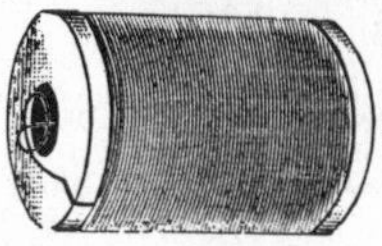

39993 Black Hair Wire on spools. Per spool...04
Per dozen spools....38

39994 Plaited Hai Wire, on spools.
Per spool....05
Per dozen spools.......40

Brass Banner Rods and Stands.

39995 Rustic Banner Rods, with suspending chain and movable ring on rod. Weight 2 to 6 ounces, according to size.

Length, in.	6	8	10	12	14	16	18	20	22	24	30
Each, cts.	9	10	11	13	15	17	19	21	20	25	30

39996 Brass Banner Stand, without cross bar, 16 in. high; weight, 8 oz. Each....$0.15

Pillow Sham Holders.

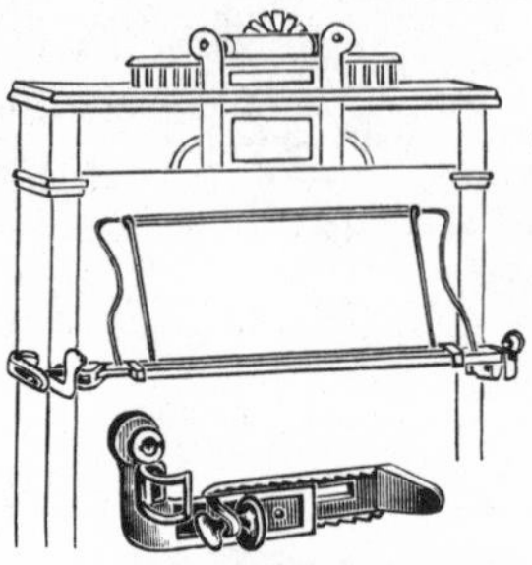

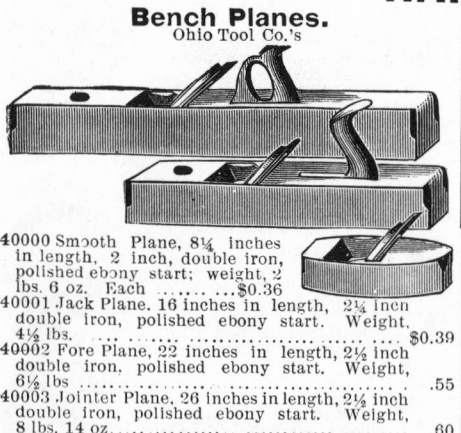

39997 This Sham Holder requires no screws, will not mar or deface the bed; adjustable nickel brackets, adjustable frame, spring friction and will not get out of order.
Each.........$0.75

Lace Curtain Stretcher.

39998 A new stretcher with an iron joint holder, can be adjusted to fit any size curtain; it has tinned pins which will not rust; it is indispensable in drying and stretching lace curtains after being washed. Each....1.50

REMEMBER

That we want a chance to correct any mistakes which may occur.

HARDWARE DEPARTMENT.

Bench Planes.

Ohio Tool Co.'s

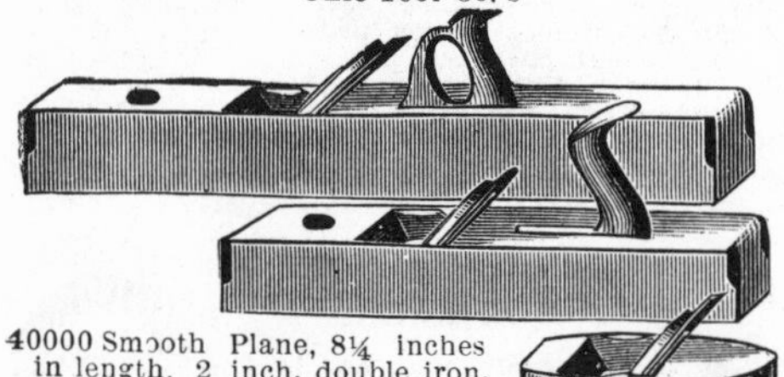

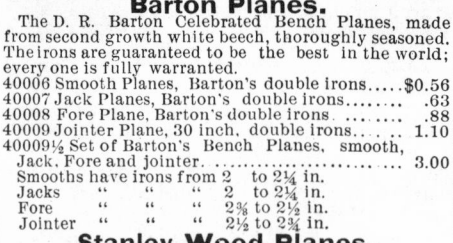

40000 Smooth Plane, 8¼ inches in length, 2 inch, double iron, polished ebony start; weight, 2 lbs. 6 oz. Each $0.36

40001 Jack Plane, 16 inches in length, 2¼ inch double iron, polished ebony start. Weight, 4½ lbs....$0.39

40002 Fore Plane, 22 inches in length, 2½ inch double iron, polished ebony start. Weight, 6½ lbs....55

40003 Jointer Plane, 26 inches in length, 2½ inch double iron, polished ebony start. Weight, 8 lbs. 14 oz....60

40004 A set of 4 planes, one smooth, one jack, one fore and one jointer. Weight, 22¼ lbs.....1.80

Barton Planes.

The D. R. Barton Celebrated Bench Planes, made from second growth white beech, thoroughly seasoned. The irons are guaranteed to be the best in the world; every one is fully warranted.

40006 Smooth Planes, Barton's double irons.....$0.56
40007 Jack Planes, Barton's double irons....63
40008 Fore Plane, Barton's double irons....88
40009 Jointer Plane, 30 inch, double irons....1.10
40009½ Set of Barton's Bench Planes, smooth, Jack, Fore and jointer....3.00

Smooths have irons from 2 to 2¼ in.
Jacks " " " 2 to 2¼ in.
Fore " " " 2⅜ to 2½ in.
Jointer " " " 2½ to 2¾ in.

Stanley Wood Planes.

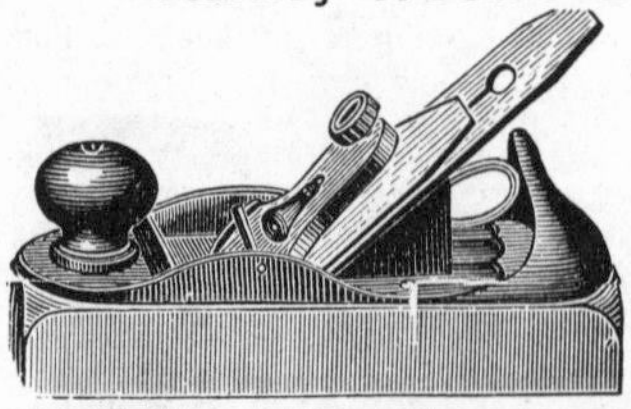

40010 Smooth Planes, adjustable irons, 8-inch, 1¾ inch cutter, No. 122.
Each ..$0.65
Weight, 2 lbs. 2 oz.

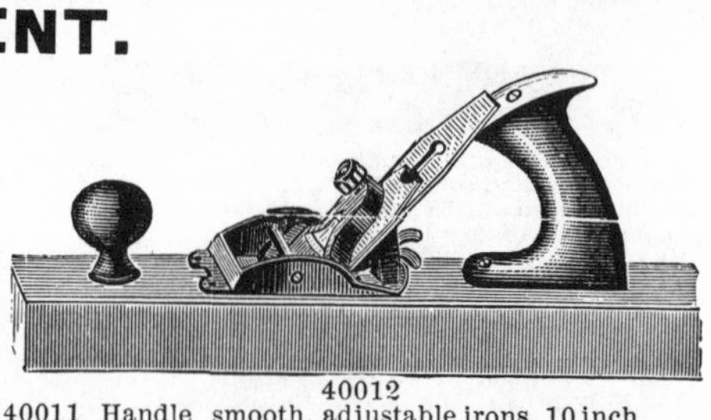

40012

40011 Handle smooth, adjustable irons, 10 inch, 2⅛ cutter, No. 135. Each....$0.85

40012 Jack Planes, adjustable irons, 15 inch 2⅛ inch cutter, No. 127 Weight, 3lbs 8 oz. Each. .85

40013 Fore Planes, adjustable irons, 20 inch, 2⅜ inch cutter, No. 129. Weight, 5 lbs. Each.....95

40014 Jointer Planes, adjustable irons, 26 inch, 2⅝ inch cutter, No. 132. Weight, 6 lbs Each.. 1.05

40015 A Set of Planes, adjustable irons, consisting of the smooth, jack, fore and jointer; four planes in all. Weight, 14¼ lbs.... 3.25

40015½ Set of Planes with handled smooth plane 10-inch, with 2⅛ inch cutter, instead of 40011, for.... 3.50

Extra Parts of Stanley Planes.

No....	40010	40012	40013	40014
Stocks....	$0.36	$0.42	$0.60	$0.75
Top Casting....	.40	.40	.40	40
Levers....	.10	.10	.15	.15
Knobs....	.15	.15	.15	.15
Irons, double....	.30	.35	.39	.42
Irons, single....	.17	.20	.22	24

No hardware store in the world contains as much as ours.

The Bailey Pattern Adjustable Wood Planes.

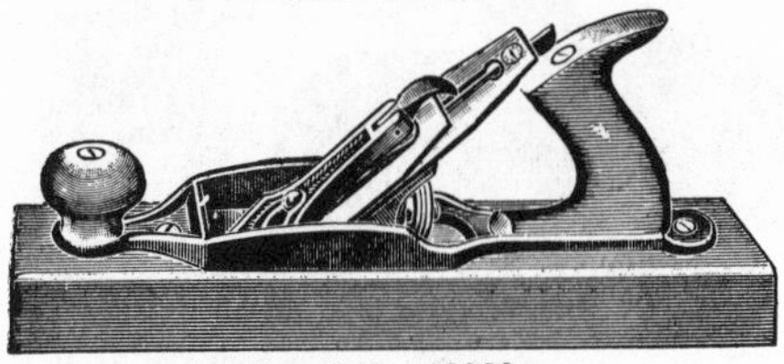

Cut of No. 40020.

Cutters Adjusted by a Lever.

40016 Smooth Plane (adjustable iron), 8 inch in length, 1¾ inch cutter; weight, 2½ lbs. Price, each $0.80

40017 Handle Smooth Plane (adjustable iron), 10 inches in length, 2⅜ cutter. Price, each 1.10

40018 Jack Plane (adjustable iron), 15 inches in length, 2⅛ inch cutter, weight, 4⅛ lbs. Price, each .... .98

40019 Fore Plane (adjustable iron), 20 inches in length, 2⅜ inch cutter, weight, 5½ lbs. Price, each 1.10

40020 Jointer Plane (adjustable iron), 24 inches in length, 2⅜ inch cutter, weight, about 5½ lbs. Price, each 1.20

40021 Jointer Plane, 26 inches in length, with adjustable iron, 2⅝ inch cutter, weight, about 7 lbs. Price, each 1.26

40021½ Jointer Plane, 28 inches in length, with adjustable iron, 2⅝ inch cutter, weight. 7¾ lbs. Price, each 1.26

Parts of Bailey Pattern Plane.

No.	40016	40017	40018	40019	40020
Stocks	$0.36	$0.42	$0.42	$0.60	$0.75
Top Casting	.15	.20	.25	.25	.25
Levers	.20	.20	.20	.25	.25
Knobs	.15	.15	.15	.15	.15
Double Irons	.30	.35	.35	.35	.35
Single Irons	.17	.23	.19	.23	.23
Handles	.15	.15	.15	.15	15

Chaplin's Iron Plane.

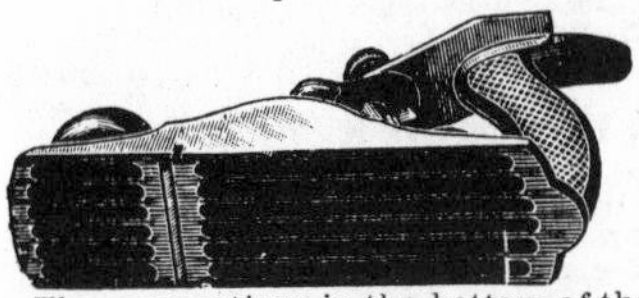

Chaplin's Patent Adjustable Iron Planes. with corrugated bottom, checkered hard rubber handles, nickel finish The corrugations in the bottom of these planes are divided by a series of ribs through the bottom, which gives strength without adding weight. The corrugations are air chambers which relieve the suction which is sometimes urged as an objection to planes. Each.

40022 Smooth Plane, 9 inches long, 2 inch cutter $1.89

40023 Jack Plane, 15 inches long, 2⅛ inch cutter 2.30

40024 Fore Plane, 18 inches long, 2¼ inch cutter 2.70

40025 Jointer Plane, 24 inches long, 2⅜ inch cutter 3.55

40026 A Set of Chaplin's Patent Adjustable Iron Planes, consisting of smooth, jack, fore and jointer. Per set 9.95

40027 Plane Irons for Chaplin's Plane.

Inch	2	2⅛	2¼	2⅜
Each	30c.	35c.	35c.	40c.

40028 Handles for Chaplin Planes. Each .... .30

Bailey Wood Planes.

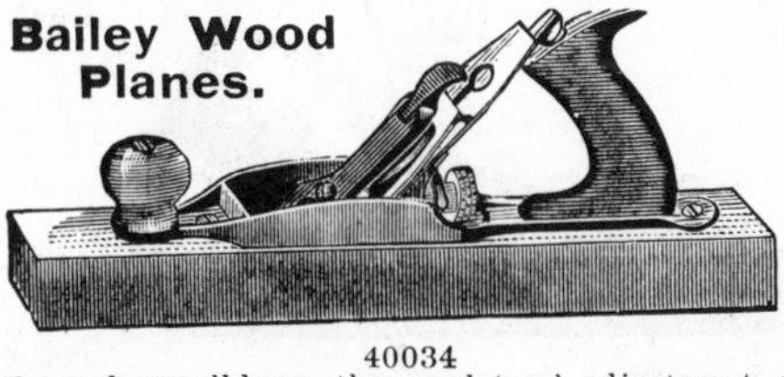

40034

These planes all have the new lateral adjustment, a new method of setting a plane iron side wise to set the cutting edge exactly square with the face of the plane.

40030 Smooth Plane, without handle, adjustable irons, 8 in. in length, 1¾ inch cutter. Weight, 2¾ lbs. No. 22 .... $0.85

40031 Smooth Plane, 9 in. length, with handle, adjustable irons, 2 inch cutter, No. 35 .... 1.05

40032 Jenny Smooth Plane, 13 inches in length, with handle, adjustable irons, 2⅜ inch cutter. No. 37 .... 1.30

40033 Jack Plane, No. 27, adjustable irons, 15 in. in length, 2⅛ inch cutter. Weight, 4 lbs.. 1.10

40034 Fore Plane, No. 29, adjustable irons, 20 in. long, 2⅜ inch cutter. Weight, 5¾ lbs 1.15

40035 Jointer Plane, No. 32, adjustable irons, 26 in. in length, 2⅝ inch cutter Weight, 7¼ lbs.. 1.38

40036 A Set of Adjustable Wood Planes, with No. 40030 smooth, jack, fore and jointer, four in all 4.35

40037 A Set of Adjustable Wood Planes, with No. 40031 smooth instead of No. 40030. Per set of four 4.50

40038 A Set of Adjustable Wood Planes, with 40032 smooth instead of No. 40030. Per set of four 4.80

Every Tool We List is of Standard Make

23--2d

Extra Parts to Bailey Planes.

No.	40030	40031	40032	40033	40035	40034
Stock	$0.36	$0.38	$0.45	$0.42	$0.75	$0.60
Top casting	.15	.25	.25	.20	.25	.25
Levers	.25	.25	.25	.25	.25	.25
Knobs, beech	.15	.15	.15	.15	.15	.15
Handles, beech	.15	.15	.15	.15	.15	.15
Screw and nut		.15	.15	.15	.15	.25
Irons, double.	.30	.33	.42	.36	.42	.39
Iron, single..	.17	.18	.24	.19	.24	.23

Bailey Adjustable Iron Planes.

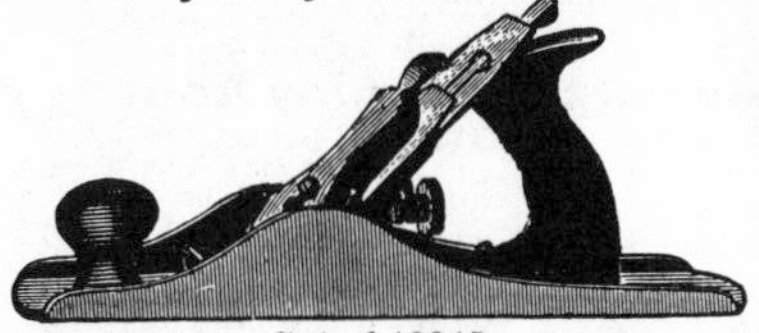

40042½ Smooth Planes, iron, 8 inches long, No 3 cutter, 1¾ in. Weight, 3 lbs 2oz ...$1.30

Cut of 40045.

40043 Smooth Plane (iron), 9 inches long, 2 inch cutter. Weight, 3½ lbs , No. 4. Price, each...$1.40

40044 Smooth Plane (iron), 10 inches long, 2⅜ inch cutter. Weight, 5 lbs., No. 4½. Price, 1.55

40045 Jack Planes, iron, 14 in. long, No. 5, cutter, 2 in. Weight, 4¾ lbs 1.66

40046 Fore Planes, iron, 18 in. long, No. 6, cutter, 2⅜ in. Weight, 7 lbs 2.00

40046½ Jointer Plane (iron), 22 inches long, No. 7 with cutter 2⅜ inch. Weight, 6 lbs. Each 2.35

40047 Jointer Planes, iron, 24 in. long. No. 8, cutter, 2⅝ in. Weight, 9¾ lbs 2.80

40048 A Set of Iron Planes, consisting of the 40042½ smooth jack, fore and jointer, 40046½ four planes in all, Weight, 24 lbs. 6 oz 7.00

40048½ A Set of Iron Planes, consisting of smooth plane 40043, jack plane, fore plane, jointer plane 40047. Four planes in all. Per set. 7.60

Repairs for Bailey Iron Planes.

No.	40042½	40045	40046	40047
Levers	$0.30	$0.30	$0.35	$0.35
Handles, rosewood	.30	.30	30	.30
Knobs, rosewood	.15	.15	.15	.15
Irons, single	.17	.18	.23	.24
Irons, double	.30	.33	.39	.42

No.	40043	40044
Levers	$0.30	$0.35
Handles	.30	.30
Knobs	.15	.15
Irons, single	.18	.23
Irons, double	.33	.39

Baily Pattern Adjustable Iron Planes.

Cutters adjusted by a lever. In buying the Bailey Pattern Planes you can depend upon getting a first-class plane.

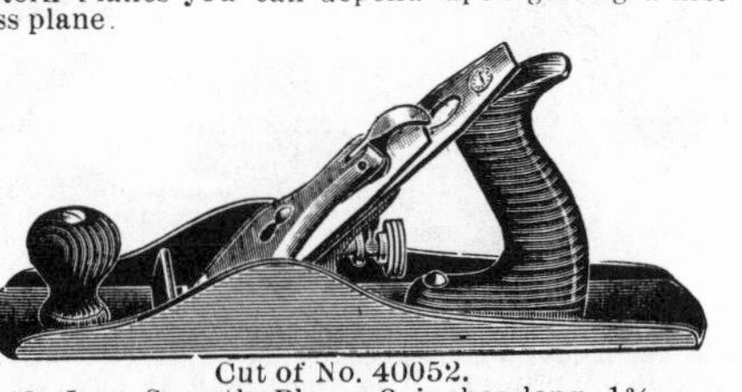

Cut of No. 40052.

40049 Iron Smooth Plane, 8 inches long, 1¾-inch cutter; weight, 3 pounds. No. 3. Each.$1.15

40050 Iron Smooth Plane, 9 inches long, 2-inch cutter; weight, 3½ pounds. No. 4 Each....... 1.33

40052 Iron Jack Plane, 14 inches long, 2-inch cutter; weight, 4½ pounds. No. 5. Each...... 1.50

40053 Iron Fore Plane, 18 inches long, 2⅜-inch cutter; weight, 6½ pounds. No. 6. Each...... 1.85

40054 Iron Jointer Plane, 24 inches long, 2⅝-inch cutter; weight, 9¼ pounds. No. 8. Each. 2.50

40055 A Set of Iron Planes, consisting of No. 4 smooth, jack, fore and jointer; four planes in all; weight, about 24 pounds. Price, per set.... 6.82

Repairs and irons for the Bailey Pattern lanes cost the same as repairs for Nos. 40042½. 40045, 40046. 40047.

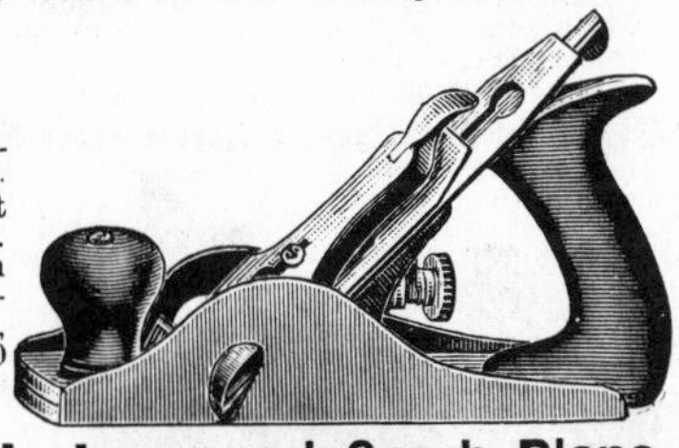

40056 Carriage Makers' Rabbet Plane, 9 in. long with 2⅛ in. cutter. Price, each..$1.60

Stanley's Improved Scrub Plane.

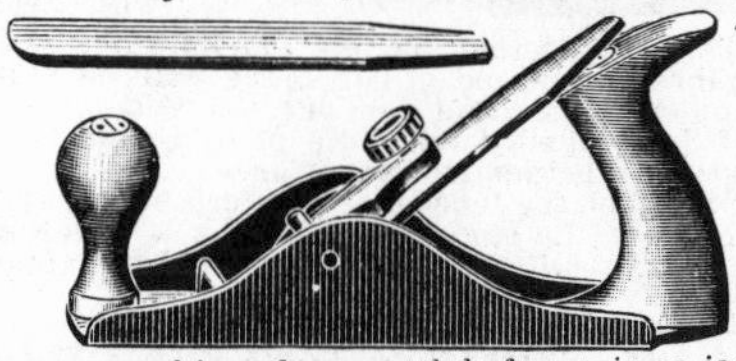

40057 This tool has a single iron with the cutting edge rounded. It is particularly adapted for roughing down work before using a jack or other plane. It has iron stock 9½ inches long with 1¼ inch cutter; made only in this one size. Price, each $0.68

Rabbet Planes.

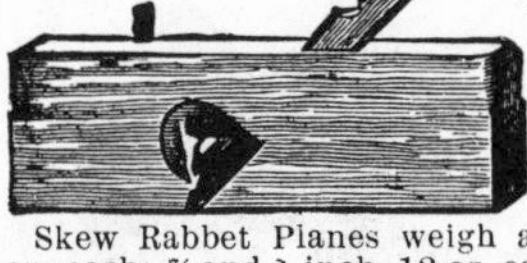

40058 Skew Rabbet Planes, ½, ⅝, ¾, ⅞, or 1 inch Each....$0.33

1¼ inch..	".....	.36
1½ inch..	".....	.38
1¾ inch..	".....	.44
2 inch....	".....	.49

Skew Rabbet Planes weigh as follows; ½ and ⅝, 10 oz. each; ⅞ and 1 inch, 12 oz. each; 1¼ inch, 1 lb. 3 oz.: 1½ inch, 1 lb. 8 oz.; 1¾ inch, 1¾ lbs.; 2 inch, 2 pounds.

40059 Jack Rabbet Planes, 1½ and 2 inch with handles and 2 cutters $0.85

Stanley's Improved Rabbet Planes.

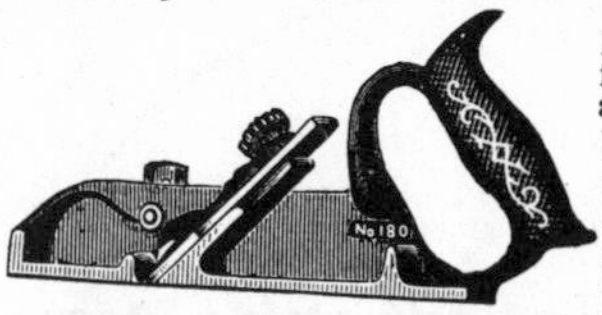

This plane will lie perfectly flat on either side and can be used with right or left hand equally well, while planing into corners or up against perpendicular surfaces.

40060 Rabbet Plane. iron stock, 8 inches in length, 1½ inches wide; weight, 3 pounds 8 oz. Each $0.68

40061 Rabbet Plane, iron stock, 8 inches in length, 1½ inches wide, with spur; weight, 3 pounds 8 oz. Each .... .76

Extra parts of Stanley Improved Rabbet Planes.

Nos	40060	40061
Stocks	55c	60c.
Cutters	20c.	20c.
Levers	10c	10c.

Siegley's Patent Combination Plane.

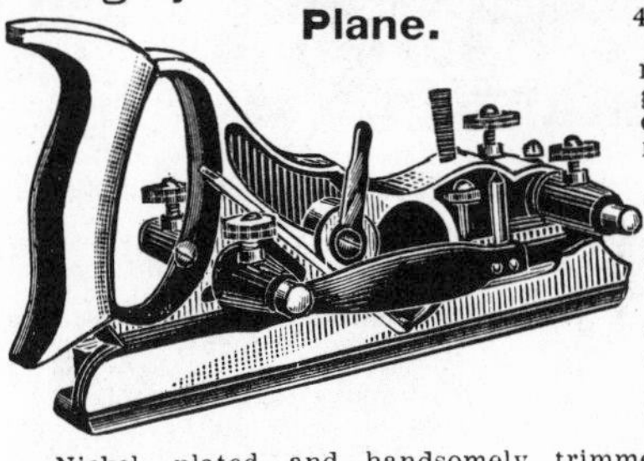

40062 This most ingenious combination of a common carpenter's plow, dado, side and center bend.

Nickel plated and handsomely trimmed. Plane, making in all the most serviceable and cheapest tool in the world.

As a Plow, it has advance cutters on each side of the blade, thus saving the work of setting and running a gauge, is very easy to adjust; is more durable and cuts clean in any cross grain wood

As A Dado, it is adjustable from ⅜ of an inch to any width. The advance cutters are fastened by set screws holding the cutter firmly in its place, and secured to the blades in slanting position, giving a free clearing to the blades.

No. 2 COMBINED PLOW AND DADO includes the following size cutters: 3-16, ¼, 5-16, ⅜, 7-16, ½, ⅝, ¾, and ⅞ inch match plane cutter, ...$6.00 Also includes the following size Bead Plane Cutters: 3-16, ¼, 5-16, ⅜, 7-16, ½; weight, complete, 6 lbs.

PARTS FOR SIEGLEY'S PATENT.

40063 Single Cutters for above plane, 26c. each; Cluster Bea Bits, 2 cluster. 30c.; 3 cluster, 35c.; 4 cluster, 40c.; Sash Molding Cutter, working 1¼ to 1½ in., 50c.

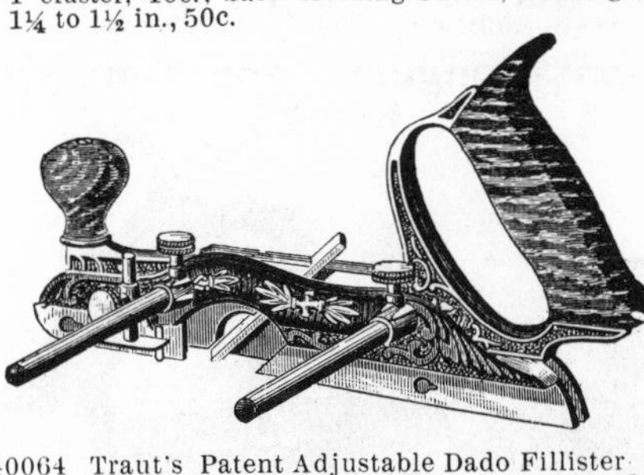

40064 Traut's Patent Adjustable Dado Fillister Plow, etc. $4.62

The tool here represented consists of two sections: A main stock with two bars or arms, and a sliding section, having its bottom or face level with that of the main stock.

It can be used as a dado of any required width by inserting the bit into the main stock, and bridging the sliding section up to the edge of the bit.

The tool is accompanied by eight plow bits, 3-16, ¼, 5-16, ⅜, ½, ⅝, ⅞ and 1¼, a Fillister cutter, a slitting tool and a tonguing tool. These tools, when fastened in stock, are in a *skew*; weight, complete, 5 lbs. 3 oz.

Extra Parts.

Extra parts of 40064 Traut's Patent Adjustable Fillister Plow, etc. Stock, $2.00; Gates or Fences, $1.50; Guard Plate, $1.25; Spurs and Screws, 5 cts. each; Depth Gauge, Brass, 25c.; Iron, 20c.; Long Arms, 50c. pair; Short Arms. 25c. pair; Cutters, in sets, $1.65; Singly, 3-16, ¼, 10c. each; 5-16, ⅜, ½, ⅝, ⅞. 15c. each; 1¼. 20c; Fillister Cutter, 25c.; Tonguing Tool, 35c.; Slitting Tool, 30c.

Circular Plane.

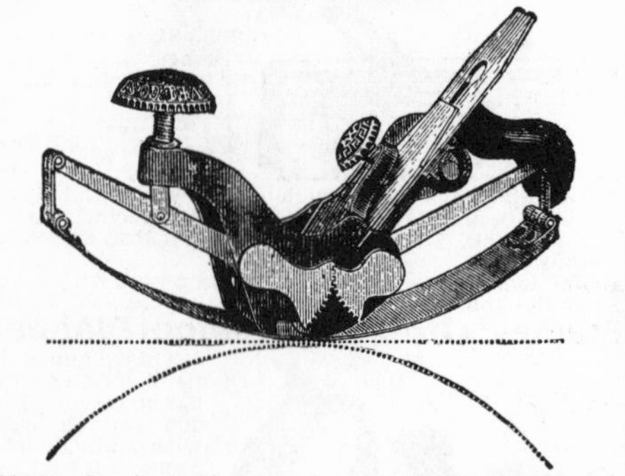

40065 Stanley's Circular Plane, 1¾ inch cutter, concave or convex surfaces; can be worked as easily as straight ones. Weight, 3¾ lbs. Each. $1.75

Traut's Patent Adjustable Beading, Rabbet and Slitting Plane.

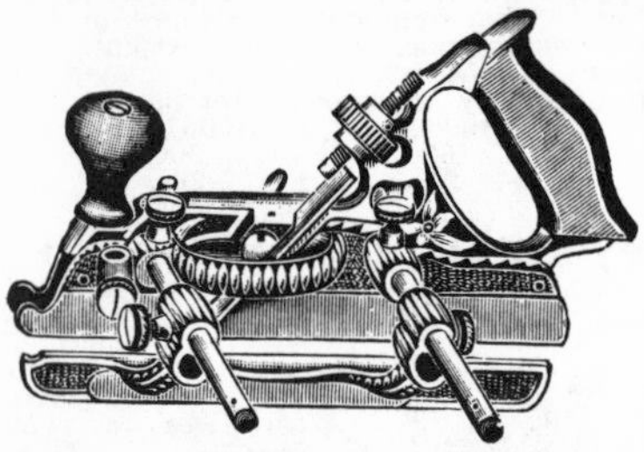

This plane embraces in a compact and practical form. (1) Beading and Center Beading Plane; (2) Rabbet and Fillister, (3) Dado (4) Plow (5), Matching Plane and (6) a superior Slitting Plane.

For center beading the face may be adjusted to allow of making a bead five inches from the edge of the board if desired.

☞ Each plane is accompanied by seven beading tools (⅛, 3/16, ¼, 5/16, ⅜, 7/16 and ½ inch); nine plow and dado bits (⅛, 3/16, ¼, 5/16, ⅜, 7/16, ½, ⅝ and ⅞ inch), a slitting blade and a tonguing tool. Weight, complete, 6¼ lbs.

40066 Price, each...... $5.05

EXTRA PARTS.

Extra parts of Traut's Patent Adjustable Beading, Rabbet and Slitting Plane.

Stocks, $1.95; Gates or Fences, 75 cents; Sliding Section, $1.50; Spurs or Screws, 5 cents each; Depth Gauges, 20 cents; Slitting Tool, 30 cents; Brass Thumb Screw, 15 cents; Arms, 50 cents; Short Arms, 25 cents per pair, Irons in sets, $2.65; Singly, ⅛, 3/16, ¼, 5/16, 20 cents each; ⅜, 7/16, ½, ⅝, ⅞, 25 cents each; 1, 1⅛, 1¼, 1½, 30 cents each; 1¾, 2, 30 cents each. Beading Irons, ⅛, 3/16, ¼, 16 cents each; 5/16, ⅜, 20 cents each; 7/16, ½, 25 cents each. Reeding Irons, 2 reeds, 20 cents; 3 reeds, 30 cents each.

40067 Nosing Tool, 1¼ inch cutter.......... $0.66

Hollows and Rounds.

40068 With Cast Steel Bits to adjust to No. 40066 Plane.

No.	6	8	10	12
Width of Cutter	½	⅝	¾	1 inch.
Works	¾	1	1¼	1½ in. circle
Price, per pair	$0.88	$0.88	$0.88	$0.88

Cutters for Hollow and Round, 20 cents each.

Patent Tonguing and Grooving Plane.

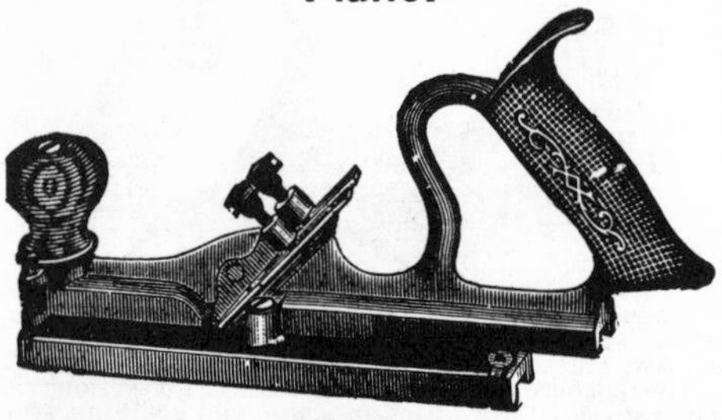

40069-40070.

The stock of this tool is made of metal, and it has two cutters fastened into the stock by thumb screws. The guide or fence, when set as shown in the above engraving, allows both of the cutters to act, and the cutters being placed a suitable distance apart, a perfect tongue plane is made. The guide or fence, which is hung on a pivot at its center, may be easily swung round end for end; thus one of the cutters will be covered and the guide held in a new position, thereby converting the tool into a grooving plane. A groove will be cut to exactly match the tongue which is made by the other adjustment of the tool. Weight, 2¾ lbs.

40069 Iron Stock and Fence for ¾ to 1¼ inch boards. Each........ $1.60

40070 For ⅜ to ¾ inch boards. Each.. ...... 1.60

Extra parts of Nos. 40069 and 40070 Patent Tonguing and Grooving Plane: Stocks, $1.50; cutters, 17 cents; levers, 10 cents; fence, 50 cents.

Hand Beader.

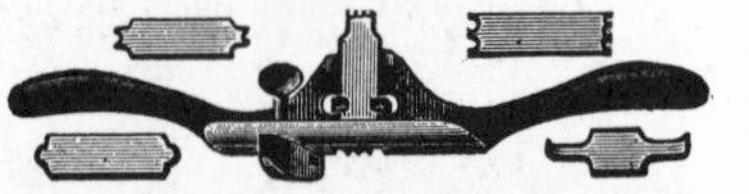

40071 Stanley Universal Hand Beader for beading, reeding or fluting straight or irregular surfaces; is invaluable to wood workers. Iron stock with six steel cutter; complete weight, 1 pound, 10 ounces. Price........ $0.68

Extra cutters for 40071, each........ .05

Woodworker's Handy Router Plane.

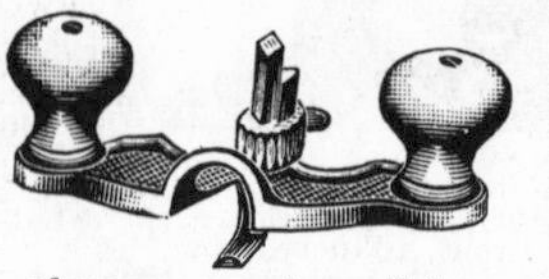

40072 This Tool should be added to the kit of every skilled carpenter, cabinet Maker, stair builder, pattern maker or wheelwright. It is perfectly adapted to smooth the bottom of grooves, panels or all depressions below the general surface of any woodwork. The bits can also be clamped to the backside of the upright post, and outside of the stock. In this position they will plane into corners, will router out mortises for sash-frame pulleys, or will smooth surfaces not easily reached with any other tool. No. 71. Iron stock, with steel bits (¼ and ½ inch). Price, each........ $0.95

Adjustable Scraper Plane.

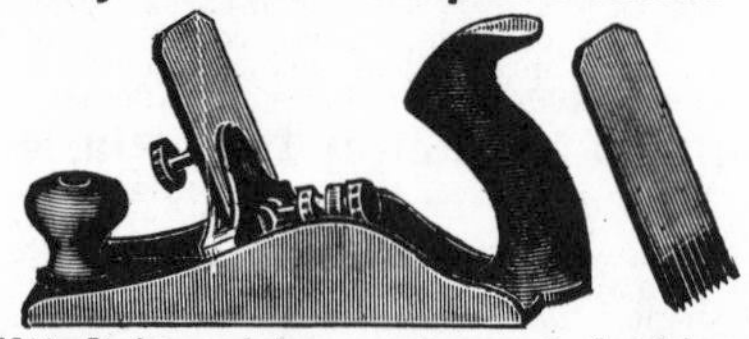

40072½ It is used for scraping and finishing veneers or cabinet work. It can be used equally as well as a tooth plane and will do excellent work in scraping off old paint and glue; 9 inches long, 3-inch cutter. Price, each.......... $1.28

Cutter for veneer scraping........ .15

Cutter for toothing (22, 28, 32 teeth per inch).. .18

Stanley's Adjustable Chamfer Plane.

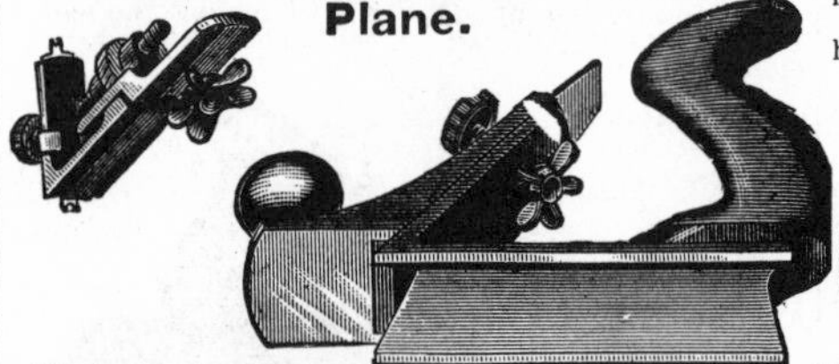

The front section of the plane to which the cutter is attached is movable up and down. It can be firmly secured to the rear section of the plane at any desired point by means of a thumb screw. Without the use of any other tool this plane will do perfect chamfer or stop chamfer work of all ordinary widths.

When the two sections are clamped together so as to form an even base line, the tool can be used as an ordinary bench plane.

40073 Iron Stock, 9 inches in length, 1⅝ inch cutter. Weight, 3 lbs. Price........ $1.28

40073½ Same as above, with beading and molding attachments........ 1.90

Adjustable Beading Plane.

40074 Patent Adjustable Beading Plane. This tool for ordinary beading or for center beading cannot be surpassed. By adjustment of the fence center beading can be done up to 5 ins. from the edge of a board.

Price, including bits, ⅛, 3/16, ¼, 5/16, ⅜, 7/16, ½........ $2.60

Duplex Rabbet Plane and Fillister.

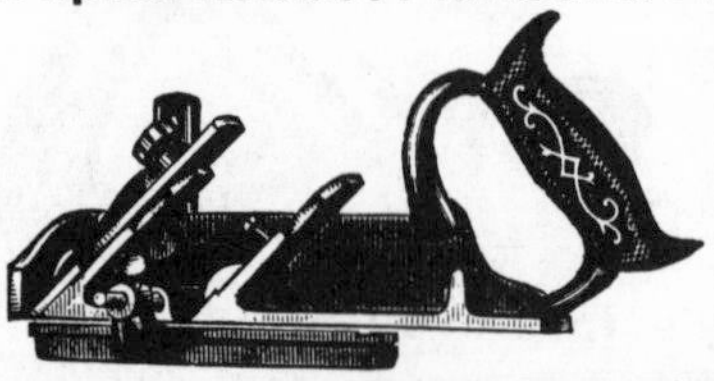

Remove the arm to which the fence is secured, and a handle rabbet plane is had, and with two seats for the cutter so that the tool can be used as a bull nose rabbet if required. The plane will lie perfectly flat on either side, and can be used with either right or left hand equally well while planing into corners or up against perpendicular surfaces.

The arm to which the fence is secured can be screwed into either side of the stock, thus making a superior right or left hand fillister, with adjustable spur and depth gauge.

40075 Iron Stock and Fence (78), 8½ inches long 1½-inch cutter. Weight, 3 lbs. 3 oz. Each.... $1.00

Extra parts of No. 40075, Duplex Rabbet Plane and Fillister: Stocks, 75c., cutters, 20c., levers 10c., fence, 25c each.

Planes—Continued.

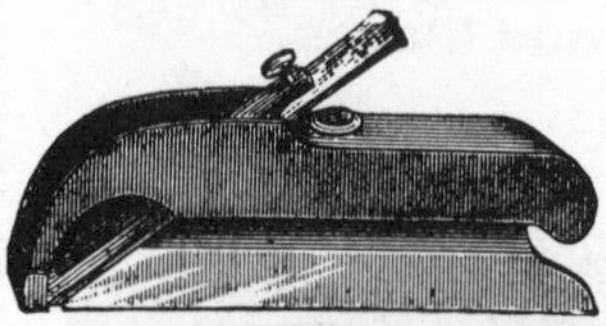

40076 Bull-Nose Rabbet Planes, iron stock, 4 ins. long, 1-in. cutter. Weight, 15 oz. Each...... $0.23

Iron Block Planes.

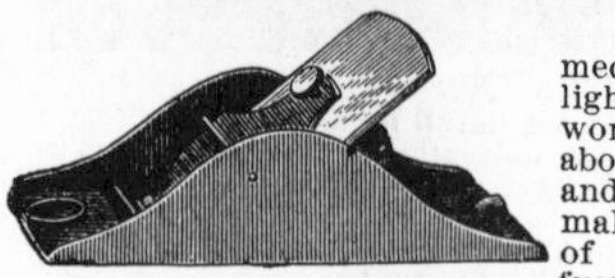

Are valuable to mechanics in all the lighter kinds of wood working, and useful about offices, stores and dwellings for making slight repairs of windows, doors, furniture, etc.

40077 Block Plane, 3½ ins. in length, 1-in. cutter. Weight, 9 oz. Each........ $0.08

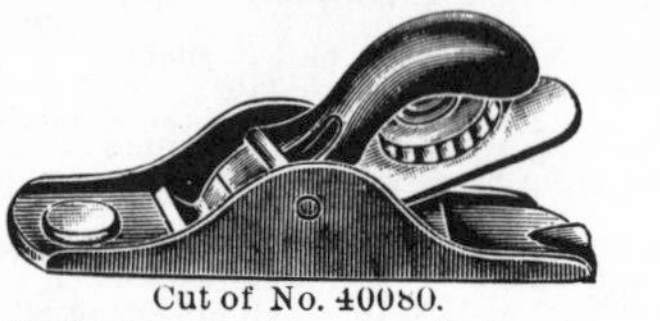

Cut of No. 40080.

40078 Block Plane, 5½ in. long, 1¼ inch cutter. This plane is not adjustable. Each.... $0.17

40079 Block Plane, 5½ inches long, 1¼ inch cutter, *adjustable*, like cut 40078. Each........ $0.25

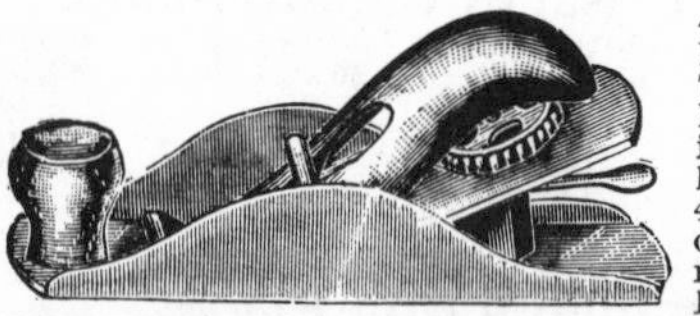

40080—Block Plane 7½ inches long, 1¾ inch cutter, like cut 40081, without adjustment. Each.. $0.25

40081 Block plane, adjustable, 7½ inches in length, 1¾ inch cutter. Each........ $0.35

Adjustable Block Planes.

These block planes are adjusted by a screw and lever movement, and the mouth can be opened wide or be made close as the nature or the work may require.

Weight of block planes without handle, 1¾ lbs., with handle, 2¼ lbs.

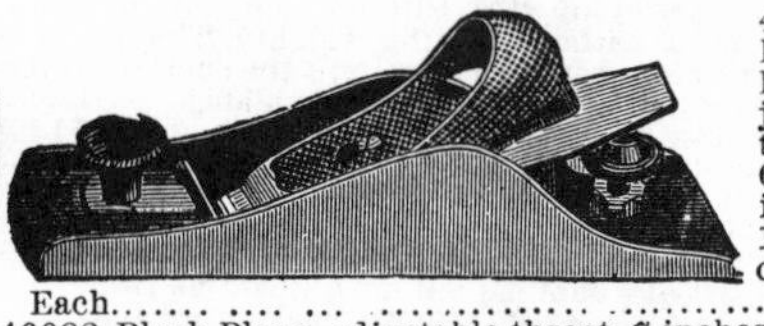

40081½ Block Plane adjustable throat, 6 inches in length 1¾ inch cutter. Each........ $0.60

40082 Block Plane, adjustable throat, 7 inches in length, 1¾ inch cutter. Weight, 1 lb. 14 ounces. Each........ .65

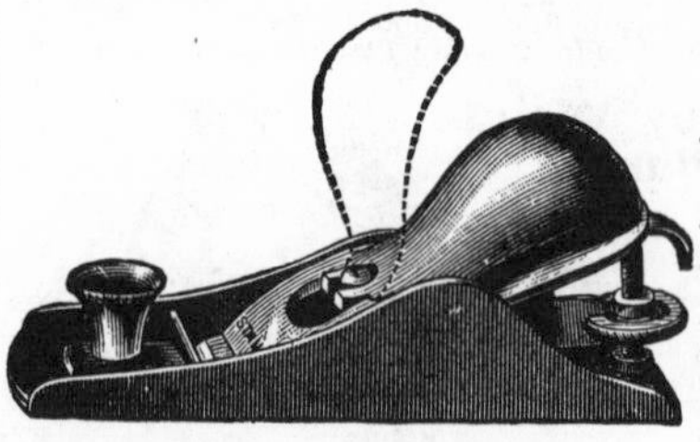

Block Plane, with knuckle joint in cap. The knuckle joint in cap makes it a lever, too, and placing the cap in position will also clamp the cutter securely to its seat.

40083 Knuckle Joint Planes, adjustable throat, 6 inches in length, 1¾ inch cutter, Stanley's lateral adjustment, nickel plated trimmings. Each........ $0.66

40084 Knuckle Joint Planes, adjustable throat, 7 inches in length, 1¾ inch cutter, Stanley's lateral adjustment, nickel plated trimmings. Each........ .75

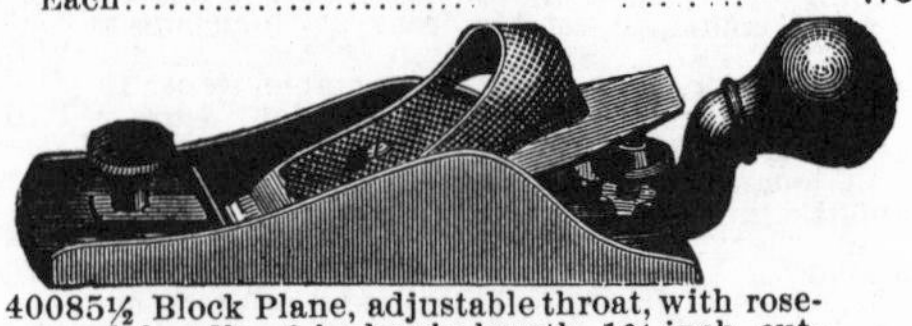

40085½ Block Plane, adjustable throat, with rosewood handle, 6 inches in length, 1¾ inch cutter. Each........ $0.80

40086 Cast Steel Cutters for above planes. Weight, 6 oz. Each........ .18

A GOOD WORKMAN REQUIRES GOOD TOOLS.

Planes—Continued.

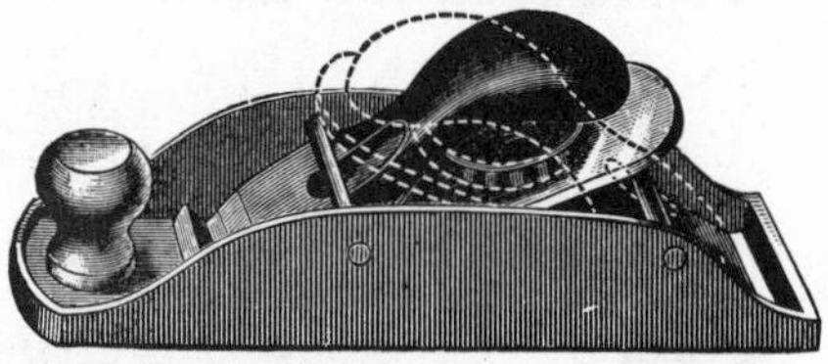

40088 Block Plane (Double Ender), 8 inches in length, 1¾ inch cutter. This plane has two slots and two cutter seats. It can be used as a block plane or by reversing the position of cutter it can be used to plane close up into corners or places difficult to reach with any other plane; not an adjustable mouth plane. Each........ $0.36

Repairs for Block Planes.

No....	40078	40081	40082	40084	40083
Stocks	$0.12	$0.18	$0.60	$0.66	$0.60
Levers	.10	.10	10	.20	.20
Irons	.10	.10	.12	.12	12
Finger rests			.10		
Adj. nut				.10	
Mouth piece					.15

No.............................40085½
Stock............................$0.60
Levers............................ .10
Brass adj. nut.................... ....
Irons............................. .12
Knob.............................. .10

Hollows and Rounds.

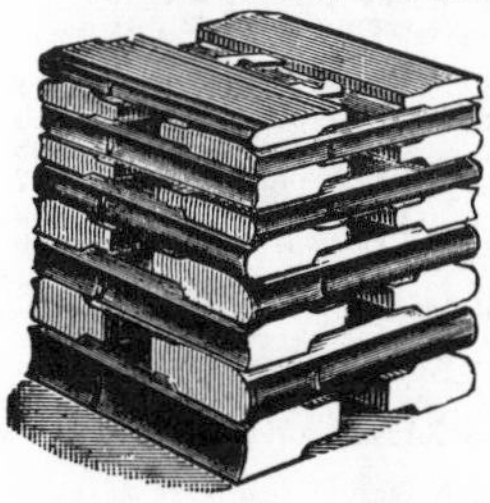

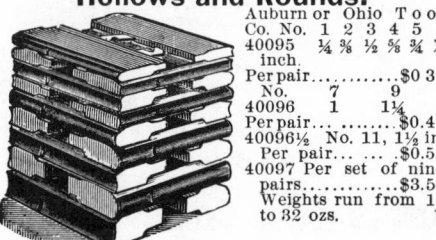

Auburn or Ohio Tool Co. No. 1 2 3 4 5 6
40095 ¼ ⅜ ½ ⅝ ¾ ⅞ inch.
Per pair...........$0 39
No. 7 9
40096 1 1¼
Per pair.........$0.44
40096½ No. 11, 1½ in. Per pair...... $0.55
40097 Per set of nine pairs............$3.50
Weights run from 15 to 32 ozs.

Nosing Plane.

40098 Nosing Plane for steps, two irons, ⅞, 1, 1⅛ and 1¼ inch. Each size...........$0.55
1⅜ and 1½ inch. Each size........... .60

Bead Plane.

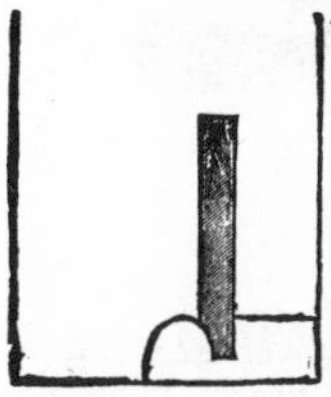

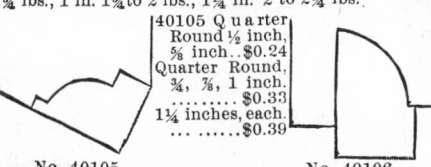

40099 Side beads, single boxed, ⅛, 3/16, ¼, 5/16, ⅜ and ½ inch, each size............$0.24
⅝ and ¾, each size......... .28
⅞ and 1 inch, each size..... .35
40100 Center beads, double boxed, ⅛, 3/16, ¼, 5/16, ⅜, ½ in. Each size.................. .30
⅝ and ¾, each size......... .40
Weights run from 15 to 23 ounces.

Molding Planes.

Cuts show shape of plane, iron and molding.
Weights about as follows: ½ in. 1¼ lbs., ¾ in. 1½ to 1¾ lbs., 1 in. 1¾ to 2 lbs., 1¼ in. 2 to 2¼ lbs.

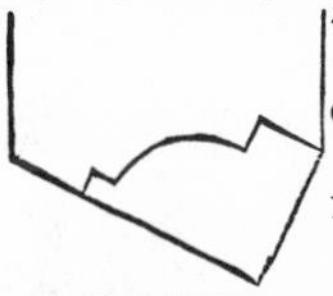

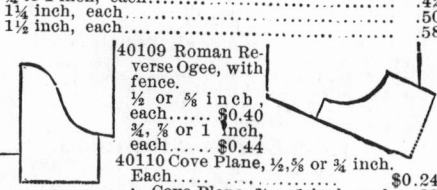

40105 Quarter Round ½ inch, ⅝ inch..$0.24
Quarter Round, ¾, ⅞, 1 inch. $0.33
1¼ inches, each. $0.39

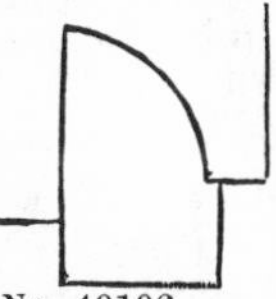

No. 40105. No. 40106.

40106 Quarter Rounds, with fence, ½ to ¾ inch, each $0.39
⅞ or 1 inch, each................ .44
1¼ inch.......................... .50

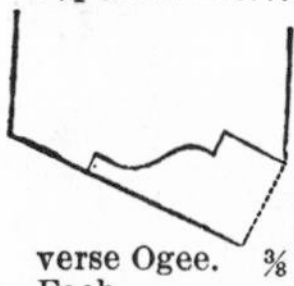

40107 Ogee Plane, ⅜ to 1 inch, each. $0 33
1¼ to 1½ inch, Each.........$0.42
1¾ inch...... .50

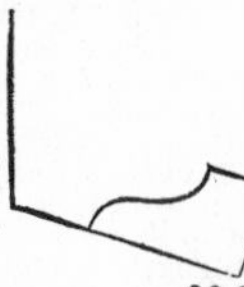

40108 Roman Reverse Ogee. ⅜ to ⅝ inch. Each.................................$0.39
¾ to 1 inch, each................. .42
1¼ inch, each..................... .50
1½ inch, each..................... .58

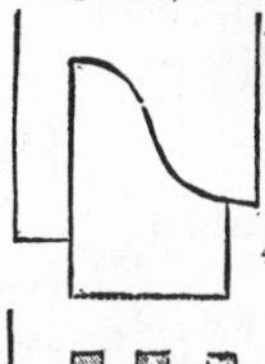

40109 Roman Reverse Ogee, with fence.
½ or ⅝ inch, each...... $0.40
¾, ⅞ or 1 inch, each...... $0.44

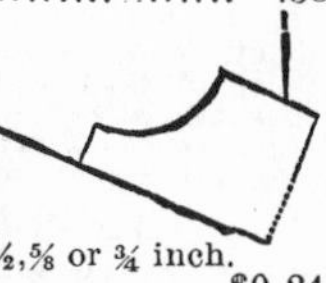

40110 Cove Plane, ½, ⅝ or ¾ inch. Each.................. $0.24
Cove Plane, ⅞ or 1 inch, each .33

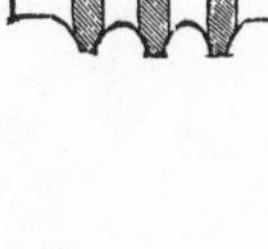

40111 Reeding Plane, ¼, 5-16 or ⅜ inch, two bead. Each.......................$0.72

Dados.

40112 With brass side stop, ¼ to 1 inch. Each..................................$0.55
40112½ With screw side stop, ¼ to 1 inch. Each.................................. .75

Match Planes.

40113 Twins or separate plated, ⅜ to 1 inch. Per pair................................$0.75

Plane Irons.

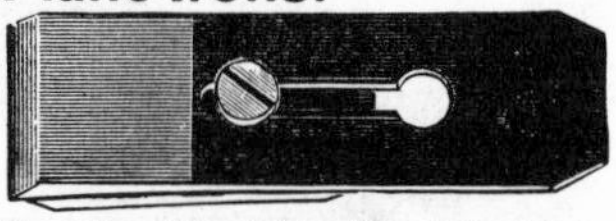

40114 Plane Irons, Ohio Tool Company's single or cut irons.
Sizes...1¾ 1⅞, 2, 2⅛, 2¼, 2⅜, 2½, 2⅝ 2¾ in.
Each.$0.10 .12 .13 .13 .15 .16 .18 .20 .22
40115 Plane Irons, Ohio Tool Company's double irons.
Sizes 1¾, 1⅞, 2, 2⅛, 2¼, 2⅜. 2½, 2⅝, 2¾in.
Each.$0.24 .24 .25 .25 .27 .28 .32 .33 .35
The D. R. Barton plane irons are guaranteed to be the best made. They are carefully ground and are bright all over. The double plane irons have a cast steel cap.
40116 DOUBLE IRONS.
Size..1½, 1¾, 1⅞, 2, 2⅛, 2¼, 2⅜, 2½, 2⅝, 2¾ in
Each$0.40 .43 .45 .46 47 .50 .53 .60 .65 .72
40116½ Plane Irons, Barton's single or cut irons.
Size... 1½, 1¾, 1⅞, 2, 2⅛, 2¼, 2⅜, 2½, 2⅝. 2¾in.
Each.$0.18 .20 .21 .23 .24 .27 .29 .32 .35 .40

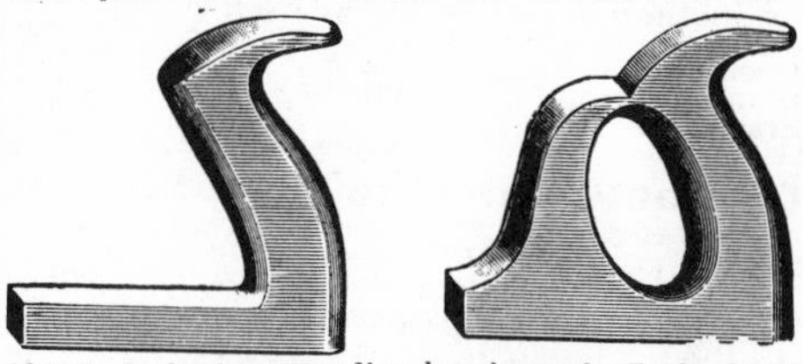

40117 Jack Plane Handles, beech wood. Each..$0.03
Per dozen..................................... .33
40118 Fore or Jointer Plane Handles, beechwood. Each...............$0.05 Per dozen.......... .54

Jointer Gauge.

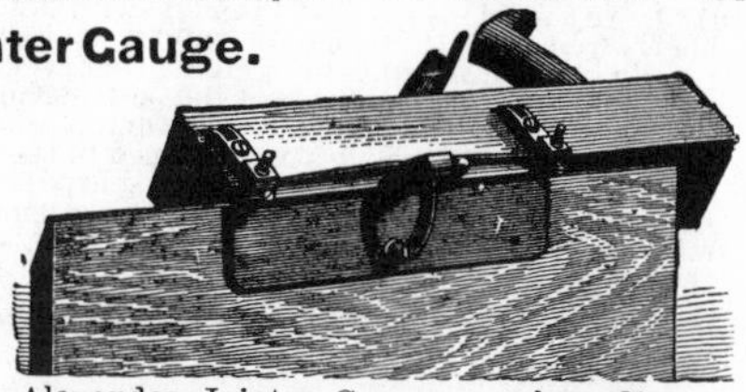

40120 Alexander Jointer Gauge, no plane, 2¼ pounds. Price, each........................$1.25

Veneer and Cabinet Scrapers.

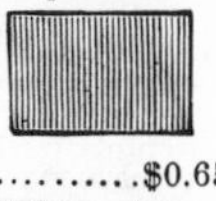

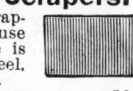

40121 Hand Cabinet or Veneer Scrapers. A very handy article for use where any smooth wood surface is desired. Made of polished saw steel. Assorted sizes up to 6 inches long.
Each, any size...... $0.06 Per dozen..........$0.65

New Langdon Improved Mitre Box

Weight, 25 to 32 pounds.

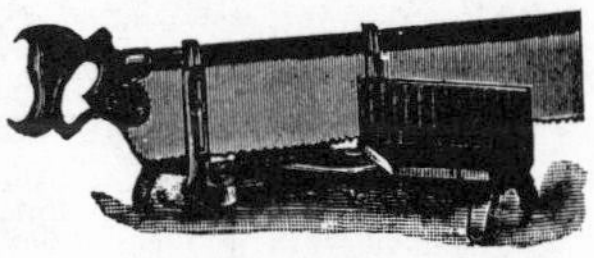

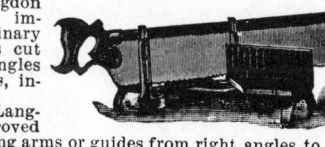

New Langdon Mitre Box, improved; ordinary mitre boxes cut from right angles to 45 degrees, inclusive.
The New Langdon Improved cuts by using arms or guides from right angles to 75 degrees on 2½ inch stuff. The only box adjustable for mitreing circular work in patterns and segments of various kinds.
40124 Langdon New Improved Mitre Box, complete, with 22x4 inch saw.............$8.45
40125 Langdon New Improved Mitre box, complete, with 28x5 inch saw..................12.75

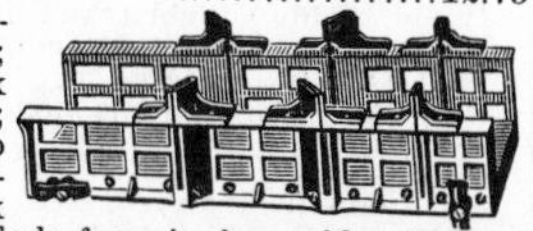

40128 Olmstead's Improved Mitre Box; frame of this box made entirely of iron; a board is secured to the bottom of the inside. When a back saw is used with a blade four inches wide, the back will serve as a stop by striking the top of the adjustable saw guides. Will take work 2½x4 inches. Any kind of a saw may be used. Price, each.........$1.75

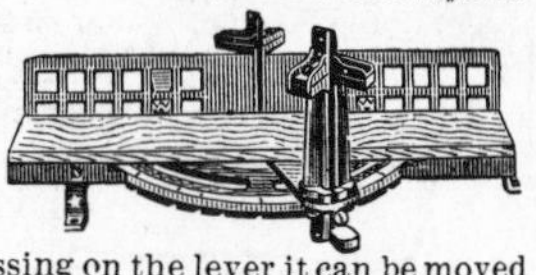

40129 Olmstead's Improved Mitre Box. This box is made entirely of steel and iron; a board is fastened to the bottom. The swinging bar can be placed at any angle desired. By pressing on the lever it can be moved to any of the fixed notches, which are right angle, 1/16, ⅛ and ¼; it can be held at any point between the notches by tightening the screw. The pointed steel springs on the back are used to press into the work to hold it fast while sawing. Any saw can be used. No. 6 will take work 4 inches wide at mitre and 6 inches wide at right angle. Price, each................$5.00

Saws.

Henry Disston & Sons, Wheeler, Madden & Clemsen's and Woodrough & McParlin's Hand, Rip, Cross Cut, Back, Panel, Keyhole, Compass, Butcher, Pit and Circular Saws.

NOTE.—Saws are frequently returned to us which have had teeth broken by prying over on the plate when setting, or which have been cracked by a cold chisel or punch.

We refuse positively to take back a saw injured in any of above ways.

(Saws weigh about 2½ lbs. each).

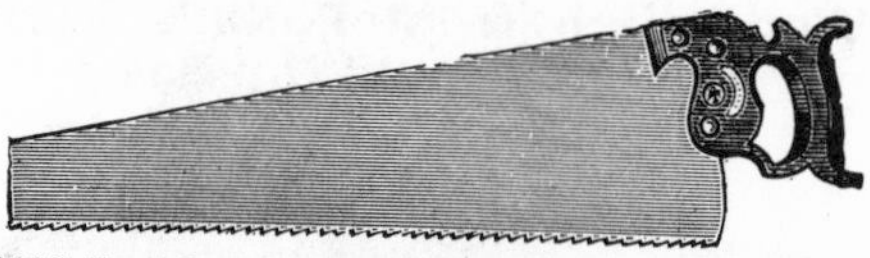

40130 Hand Saw, beech handle, polishec edge, 3 rivets, 26 inches, 6, 7, 8 points; not warranted..$0.35
40131 Hand Saw, cast steel, black walnut handles with steel plates; a very handsome and popular saw; 26 inches, 6, 7, 8 points; not warranted.. .55
40132 Rip Saw, 28 inch, same description as No. 40131, 4, 4½ and 5 points; not warranted...... .68
40133 Hand Saw, 26 inch, C. E. Jennings & Co.'s No. 1½, extra refined London spring steel, skew back, carved apple handles, 5 brass screws. hand smithed and hand filed, set ready for use. This is a very fine saw, fully warranted. 8, 9 and 10 points. Price, each.............................. 1.75
40134 Rip Saw, same description as No. 40133, 4 to 6 points....................................... 2.00
40136 Hand Saws, Wheeler, Madden & Clemsen's Skew Back, improved patent handle—
No. 24, 16 inch.............................. .70
No. 24, 18 inch.............................. .75
No. 24, 20 inch.............................. .76
No. 24, 22 inch.............................. .80
No. 24, 28 inch, rip......................... 1.10

Henry Disston & Sons' Saws.

We are now handling a full line of this celebrated make of saws, and can recommend them to all mechanics and others who need a strictly first class article; they are the best goods in the market and have the best reputation of any saw made. You can buy cheaper saws but they will not prove as good or give you the satisfaction as saws made by Henry Disston & Sons.

40138 Henry Disston & Sons' Hand Panel and Rip Saw No. 7 It has beech handle, polished edges, grained blade, and etched.

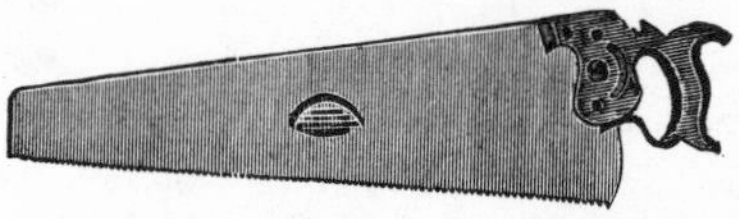

Price, each
16 inch Panel, 8 to 12 pts.......................$ 0.85
18 " " " 0.90
20 " " " 1.00
22 " " " 1.15
26 " Hand, 6 to 12 " 1.30
28 " Rip, 4 to 6 " 1.55

40139 Henry Disston & Sons' D 8 Saw; skew back, apple handle, ground back, 5 improved brass screws with the hand and rip saws. For beauty, finish and utility these saws cannot be excelled.

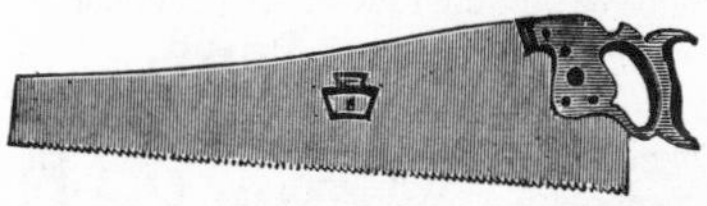

Price, each.
16-inch Panel, 8 to 12 pts.......................$0.97
18 " " " 1.05
20 " " " 1.15
22 " " " 1,22
26 " Hand, 6 to 12 pts.................... 1.36
28 " Rip, 4 " 6 " 1.65

40140 Henry Disston & Sons' No. 12, made from extra refined spring steel, carved handles, 4 brass screws. This is one of their best make of saws and fully warranted.

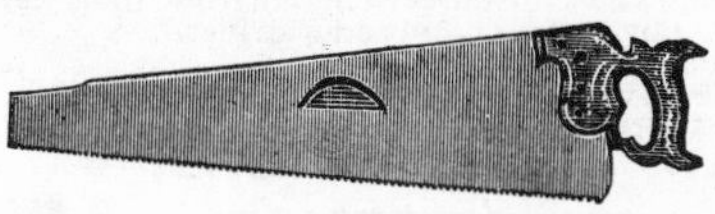

Price, each.
16-inch Panel, 8 to 12 pts.......................$1.25
18 " " " 1.36
20 " " " 1.50
22 " " " 1.61
26 " Hand, 6 to 12 pts.................... 1.86
28 " Rip, 4 " 6 " 2.10

40141 Henry Disston & Sons, Acme, No 120, Saw, made from extra London spring steel; polished spring steel, polished apple handle, with 5 rivets, skew back. This saw is designed for first-class workmen. It runs entirely without set in dry lumber. Do not attempt to set this saw, for it is so highly tempered the teeth will break out. If you are not a first-class mechanic and do not know how to use tools of this grade, don't buy it, for we positively refuse to take back any No. 120 saws when the teeth have been broken out.

NOTE OUR QUOTATIONS ON DAIRY SUPPLIES. WE HANDLE A FULL LINE.

Saws—Continued.

Price, each.
20-inch Panel, 8 to 12 pts......................$1.65
22 " " " 1.75
24 " " " 1.87
26 " Hand, 6 to 12 pts................. 1.92
28 " Rip. 4 " 6 " 2.22

Woodrough & McParlin's Warranted Hand and Rip Saws.

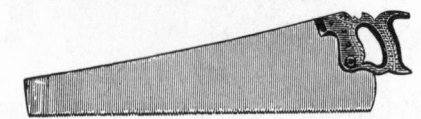

40144 Woodrough & McParlin, Extra Refined London Spring Steel Blade Carved Applewood handle Rip Saw, 28-inch blade, 4 to 6 pts. each.$2.25

40145 Combination Saw, 26 inches in length, beech handle, 4 rivets, cast steel, comprising a 24-inch square and rule, straight edge and scratch awl. Each.....................$0.75

Back Saws.

40146 Henry Disston & Sons Back Saw. It has apple handle, 2 rivets polished edges, blue back.

Size, inches.......... 10 12 14 16
Each................. 96 $1.10 $1.25 $1.38

Compass Saws.

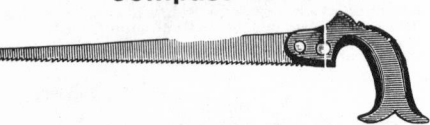

40147 Compass Saw, cast steel.
Size.......................10 in. 12 in. 14 in.
Each..................... $0.16 $0.18 $0.20

Nests of Saws.

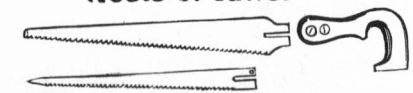

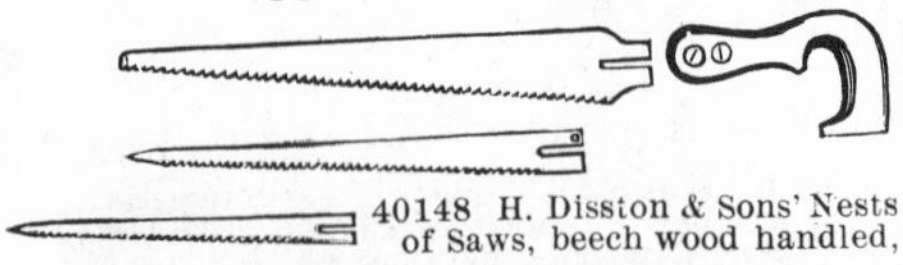

40148 H. Disston & Sons' Nests of Saws, beech wood handled, with one keyhole saw, one compass saw, and one table or pruning saw. Nest, complete......$0.85

Pruning Saws.

40156 Pruning Saw, "The Duplex," with convex and concave cutting edges; a very handy tool.
18 inches. Each......................$0.55
16 inches. Each...................... .50

Keyhole Saws.

40158 Keyhole Saw, with iron pad. This is a cheap and convenient combination of a keyhole saw, saw pad and screw driver.
Each....................................$0.18
40159 Extra saw blades for keyhole saw. Each.. .10
Postage, 6c. each.

Kitchen Saws.

40161 Kitchen Saws, oval back, 12 inches. Each.$0.28

Butchers' Saws.

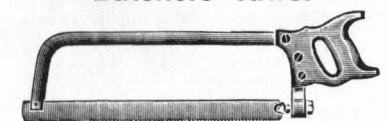

40164 Henry Disston & Sons'. No. 1, oval back polished blade butcher saws.
Size..........20 in. 22 in. 24 in.
Each........$1.22 $1.28 $1.35

Butchers' Saws—Continued.

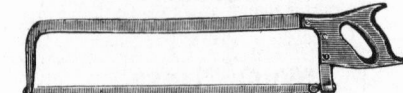

40165 Henry Disston & Sons, No 7, flat steel back.
Size.........24 in. 26 in.
Each........$1.30 $1.35

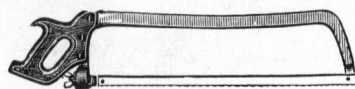

40166 Star Butcher Saw. The blades in these saws are sharpened at the factory and tempered very hard. After cutting bone for six weeks, one of these blades will cut off a ½ inch rod of iron twenty times. Saves the butcher much trouble and expense. The backs of the frames are made of crucible steel. Beech handles, with three brass screws.
Length....18 in. 20 in. 22 in 24 in. 26 in.
Each......$0.90 $0.95 $1.05 $1.15 $1.25

40167 Star Butcher Saw Blades. These blades are sharpened and tempered at the factory where they are made. They cannot be filed. Will last a long time; are so cheap that it would not pay to file them, even if they were soft enough.

Length.	Width.	Teeth to in.	Each.	Per doz
14 and 16 in.	¾	9½	$0.08	$0.91
18 and 20 in.	¾	9½	.09	1.00
22 and 24 in.	¾	9½	.10	1.12
26 in.	¾	9½	.11	1.22

Disston's Butchers' Saw Blades.

40168 Length. 20 22 24 26 inches.
Each........$0.42 $0.44 $0.46 $0.50
Per dozen........ 4.54 4.66 4.97 5.40

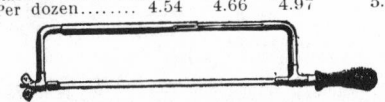

40169 Adjustable Hack Saw Framers. with hold blades from 8 to 12 inches in length; is very readily adjusted, light in weight, but very stiff and durable. It is made of the best spring steel; tempered, seamless steel tubing and mallable iron The blades can be faced in four different directions. Adapted for all purposes, and suitable for cutting iron, steel, brass, bone etc. We can guarantee this frame equal to the best in the market Each.................$ 0.67

Extension Hack Saw Frame.

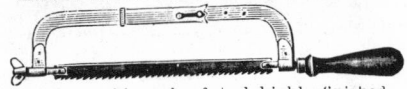

40170 This tool is made of steel, highly finished and so constructed that it can be easily extended from 8 to 12 inches, and when saw is inserted in position, it is as firm as a solid frame. Complete with one blade, as shown in cut.
Price, each............................$0.80

Hack Saws.

40171 Patent Star Hack Saw, wooden frame made of second growth ash, is strong and substantial and carries a 9 inch blade. facing it only one way. It will do good work and costs but little. Complete with 9 inch blade. Each............$0.15

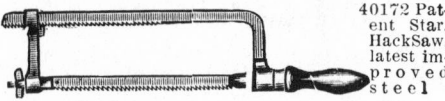

40172 Patent Star, Hack Saw, latest improved steel frame, highly polished and nickel plated; will hold blades from 3 to 12 inches. Complete with 9 inch blade. Price, each.....................$0.50
The frame of this saw is made of steel, and as seen in cut is adjustable so as to face the blade in four different directions. The blades are very much harder than a file, and will cut iron or steel as readily as wood. As it cuts everything, farmers and mechanics will find it indispensable.

Star Hack Saw Blades.

40175 Length..6 in. 7 in. 8 in. 9 in. 10 in. 12 in.
Per dozen....45c. 48c. 54c. 59c. 74c. 89c.
Postage, 1c. each; 4 to 10c. per dozen.

Turning Saw.

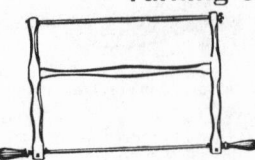

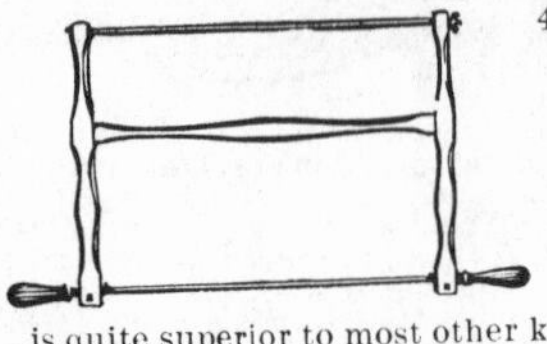

40176 This frame is made of birchwood with ebonized handles. There is an index on each handle to show the operator just how far to turn each. The friction is regulated by screws. It is quite superior to most other kinds in market.
Frame, with one blade, each......................$0.85
40176½ 18 inch blades 15c. each. Per dozen.. 1.69

Felloe Wed Saw Blades.

40177 Length. 12 14 16 18 20 22 24 in.
Width..¼to⅜ ¼to⅜ ¼to½ ¼to½ ¼to⅝ ¼to⅝ ¼to¾
Each... 14c. 16c. 18c. 20c. 22c. 25c. 27c.
Doz....$1.42 $1.62 $1.95 $2.16 $2.38 $2.70 $2.92

Butting and Drag Saws.

40180 Henry Disston & Sons' Warranted Cast Steel Tapered Butting or Drag Saw.

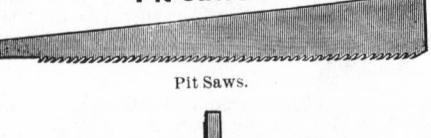

10 in. butt	8 in. point	8 gauge	per foot,$0.88
9 in. butt	7 in. point	8 gauge	per foot, .82
8 in. butt	6 in. point	10 gauge	per foot, .69
7 in. butt	5 in. point	10 gauge	per foot, .65

40181 Drag Saw, equal width, full length of saw. made only to order, and requires from 10 to 15 days.

8 in. wide	10 gauge	per foot, $0.80
9 in. wide	10 gauge	per foot, .86
10 in. wide	10 gauge	per foot, .92
12 in. wide	10 gauge	per foot, 1.10

No extra charge for patent or improved teeth. In ordering saws, state whether Mill or Cross-Cut Teeth are wanted. If set and sharpened we charge 9 cents per foot extra.

Mill Saws.

40182 Henry Disston & Sons' Extra Tempered, Patent Ground Mill Saws.
When ordering, give length, width and thickness or gauge of saw, also space from point to point of teeth, and distance from end of saw to point of first tooth.

8 in. wide	No. 5 gauge	Price, per foot,	$1.21
8 in. wide	No. 6 gauge	Price, per foot,	1.16
8 in. wide	No. 7 gauge	Price, per foot,	1.05
8 in. wide	No. 8 gauge	Price, per foot,	.97
8 in. wide	No. 9 gauge	Price, per foot,	.92
8 in. wide	No. 10 gauge	Price, per foot,	.86

Pit Saws.

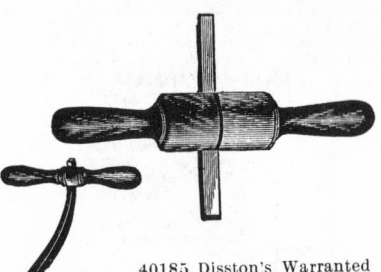

Pit Saws.

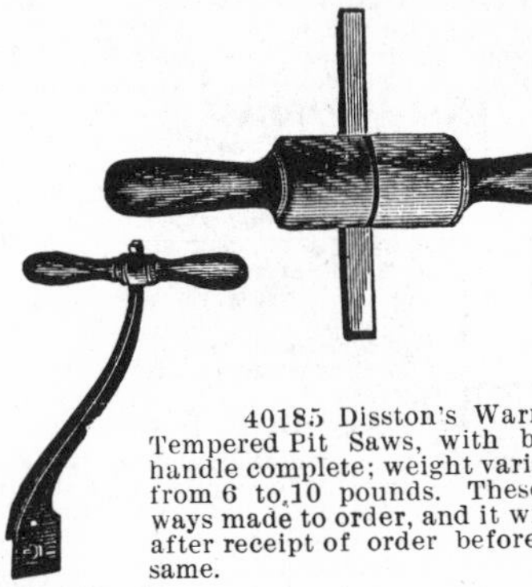

40185 Disston's Warranted Extra Tempered Pit Saws, with box and tiller handle complete; weight varies with length from 6 to 10 pounds. These saws are always made to order, and it will take a week after receipt of order before we can ship same.

Tiller Handle.
Length.....5 ft. 5½ ft. 6 ft. 6½ ft. 8 ft.
Each. complete.$4.28 $4.56 $4.86 $5.15 $6.00

40188 *Disston's Narrow Champion* Two Man Cross Cut Saw, with handles.
Length, 5½ feet; weight, 5¼ lbs..............$1.45
Length, 6 feet; weight, 5¾ lbs............... 1.55
40189 *Disston's Plain Tooth No.2 Cross Cut Saw*, two men.
Length, 6 feet; weight, 7½ lbs.............. 2.45
Length, 7 feet; weight, 9¾ lbs.............. 2.80
40190 *Disston's Champion Tooth*, Two Man Cross Cut Saw with handles
Length, 5 feet; weight, 6 lbs............... 1.90
Length, 5½ feet; weight, 7 lbs.............. 2.20
Length, 6 feet; weight, 8 lbs............... 2.35
Length, 6½ feet; weight, 8¾ lbs............. 2.55
Length, 7 feet; weight, 9 lbs............... 2.75
40191 *Disston's Diamond Tooth*, Two Man Cross Cut Saw -with handles.
Length, 4½ feet; weight, 5 lbs.............. 1.90
Length, 5 feet; weight, 6 lbs............... 2.10
Length, 5½ feet; weight, 7 lbs.............. 2.25
Length, 6 feet; weight, 8 lbs............... 2.43

Cross Cut Saw Handles.

40193 Cross Cut Saw Handles, patent loop. Per pair.............. $0.15 Per dozen............ 1.65
40194 Cross Cut Saw Handles, No. 11, reversible.
Per pair.............$0.20 Per dozen......... 2.25

REMEMBER that in trading with us you pay but ONE PROFIT, as we buy everything direct from the makers.

Cross Cut Saws, One and Two Men.

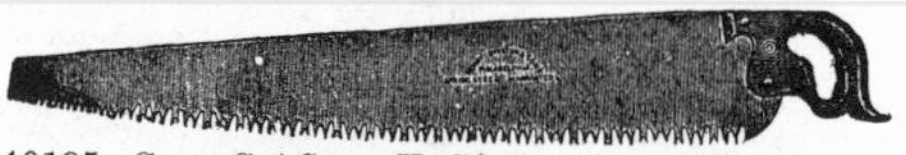

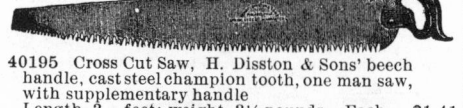

40195 Cross Cut Saw, H. Disston & Sons' beech handle, cast steel champion tooth, one man saw, with supplementary handle

Length, 3 feet; weight, 3½ pounds. Each....$1.41
Length, 3½ feet; weight, 4 pounds. Each.... 1.56
Length, 4 feet; weight, 4¾ pounds. Each ... 1.85
Length, 4½ feet; weight, 5¾ pounds. Each.... 2.00

Ice Saws.

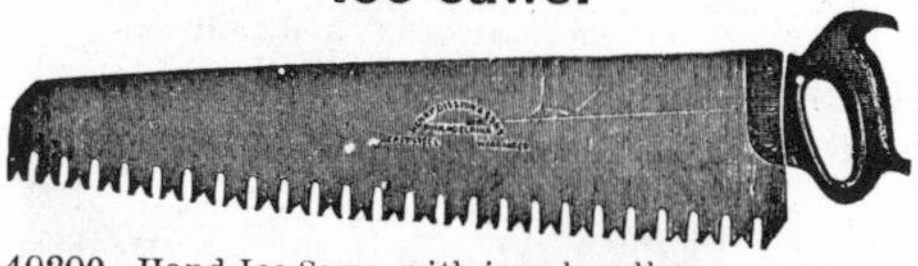

40200 Hand Ice Saws, with iron handles.

Inches	24	26	28	30
Each	$1.10	$1.15	$1.20	$1.25

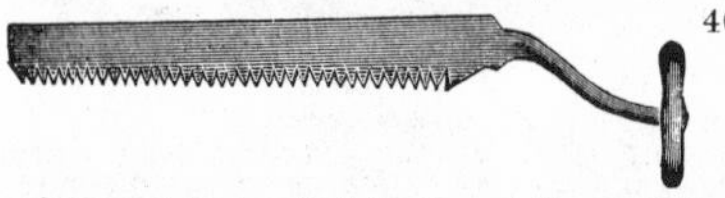

40201—Pond Ice Saws, set and sharpened, tapered from 7 inches to 5 inches at the point; complete with tiller handle, 4 feet long. Each.....$2.40
4½ feet long, each 2.70
5 feet long, each 3 00

Bracket Saw Blades.

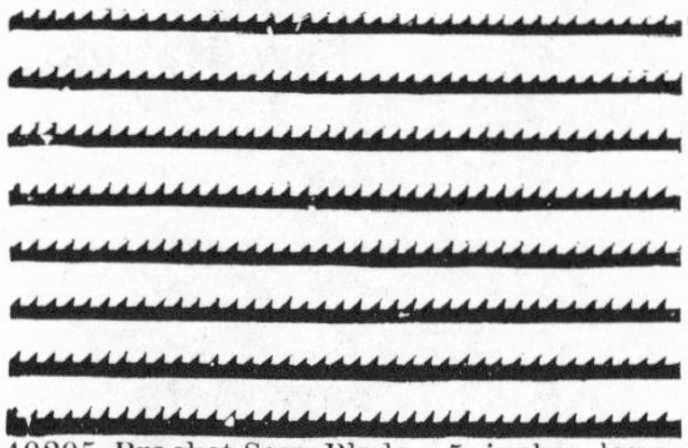

00
0
1
2
3
4
5
6

40205 Bracket Saw Blades, 5 inches long. Any number. We do not sell less than a dozen of any one size. Per doz., No. 0 to 6..........$0.07
Per gross, No, 0 to 6.......... .75
" dozen, No. 7 and 8.......... .08
" gross, " " .... .85
" dozen, 9 10 .... .10
" gross, " " .... .95

Hand Bracket Saw.

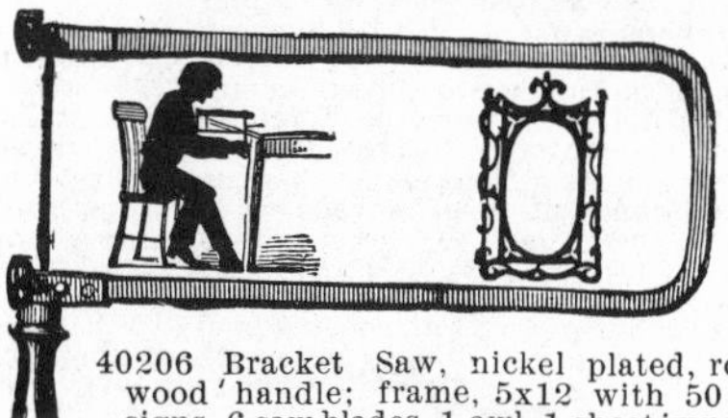

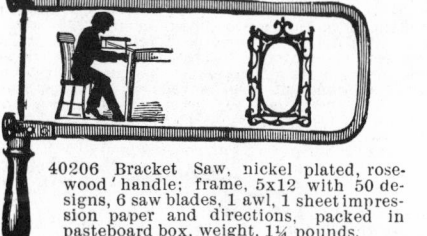

40206 Bracket Saw, nickel plated, rosewood handle; frame, 5x12 with 50 designs, 6 saw blades, 1 awl, 1 sheet impression paper and directions, packed in pasteboard box, weight, 1¼ pounds.
Price for outfit, each..........$0.90

Buck Saws.

The weight of Buck Saws from 3 to 4 pounds.

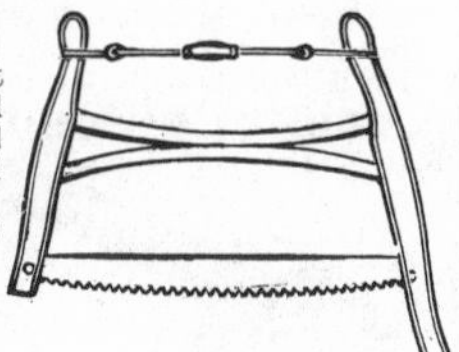

40210 Buck Saw with vermilion red frame. It has 30 inch polished round breasted steel blade set and sharpened ready for use.
Price, each..........$0.60

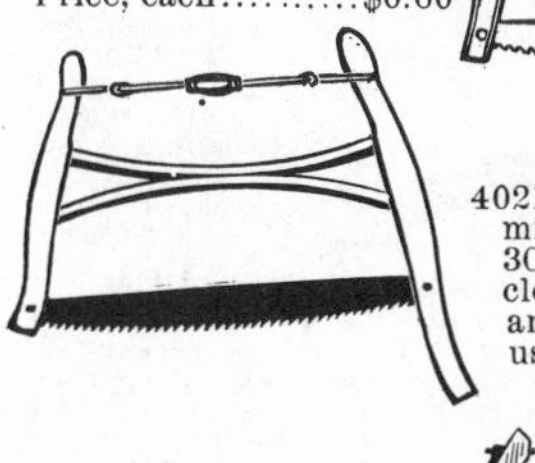

40211 Buck Saw with vermilion red frame. It has 30 inch round breasted clock spring blade set and sharpened ready for use. Price, each..$0.65

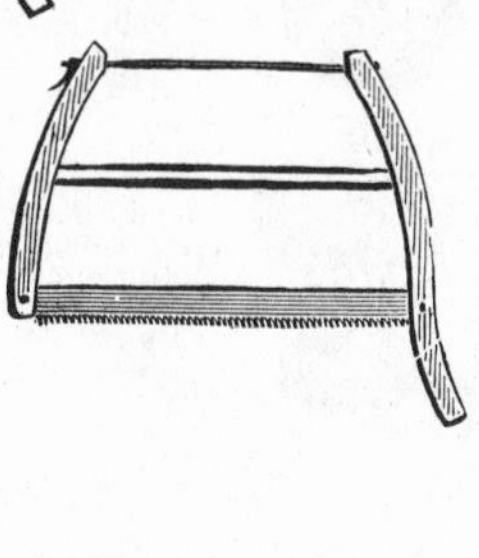

40212 Wood Saw, common frame, Jackson blade, straight rod.
Each..........$0.40

Wood Saw Blades.

40212½ Wood Saw Blades, Henry Disston & Sons' cast steel, 30 inches, set and sharpened.
Each..........$0.40
40213 Wood Saw Blades, cast steel, 30 inches, set and sharpened, not warranted. Each...... .30
Per dozen 3.00

Buck Saw Rods.

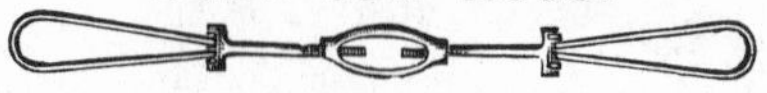

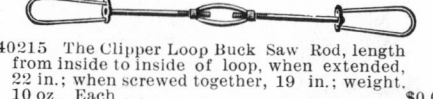

40214 Smith's Heavy Loop Rods; length from inside to inside of loop, when extended, 21 in.; when screwed together, 18¾ inch.; weight, 10 oz. Each..........$0.06
Per dozen .... .65

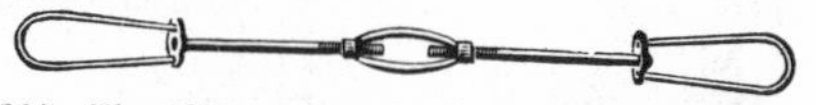

40215 The Clipper Loop Buck Saw Rod, length from inside to inside of loop, when extended, 22 in.; when screwed together, 19 in.; weight, 10 oz. Each $0.05
Per dozen .... .54

Hand Saw Handles.

40216 Hand Saw Handles, for 40140, carved handles. Each..........$0.50

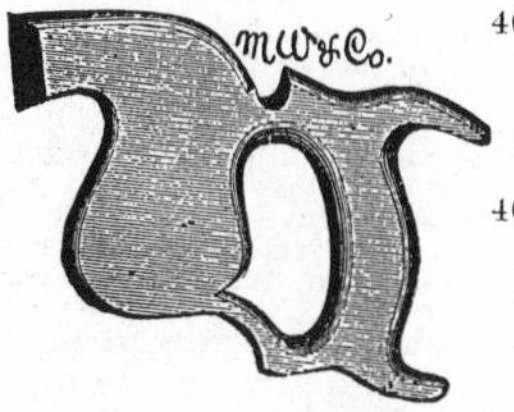

40217 Hand Saw Handles, common beech wood; varnished edges.
Each..........$0.08
Per dozen.......... .87

40218 Hand Saw Handles, for 40139 saw. Apple wood, varnished edges; weight, 10 oz.
Each..........$0.28

	Each.	Per doz
40219 Back Saw Handles, for 40146 back saw, beechwood, varnished edges; weight, 7 oz..........	$0.08	$0.87
40220 Disston's One Man Saw Handles, beechwood, varnished edges; weight, 12 oz..........	.22	2.38

Circular Saws.

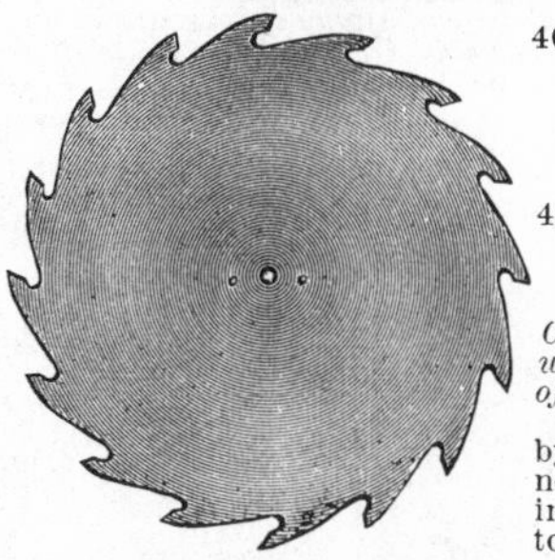

40221 H. Disston & Sons' Patent Ground and Tempered Solid Tooth Circular Cross Cut Saws.

40223 Circular Rip Saws, same price as Cross Cut.

Say whether Cross Cut or Rip Saw is wanted, and give size of hole.

Do not order saws by telegraph. We never have been able in a single instance to fill an order sent us this way, as complete specifications are never given and we never send special or saws made to order C. O. D. Money must accompany the order in all cases.

Diameter.	Thickness.	Size of Hole.	Price, each
4 inches.	19 gauge.	¾ inch.	$0.55
5 inches.	19 gauge.	¾ inch.	.65
6 inches.	18 gauge.	¾ inch.	.77
7 inches.	18 gauge.	¾ inch.	.95
8 inches.	18 gauge.	⅞ inch.	1.10
9 inches.	17 gauge.	⅞ inch.	1.38
10 inches.	16 gauge.	1 inch.	1 65
11 inches.	16 gauge.	1 inch.	1.95
12 inches.	15 gauge.	1 inch.	2.10
14 inches.	15 gauge.	1⅛ inch.	2.47
16 inches.	14 gauge.	1⅛ inch.	3.00
18 inches.	13 gauge.	1¼ inch.	3.85
20 inches.	13 gauge.	1 5/16 inch.	4.68
22 inches.	12 gauge.	1 5/16 inch.	5.50
24 inches.	11 gauge.	1⅜ inch.	6.60
26 inches.	11 gauge.	1⅜ inch.	7.75
28 inches.	10 gauge.	1½ inch.	8.80
30 inches.	10 gauge.	1½ inch.	9 90
36 inches.	9 gauge.	1⅝ inch.	14.00
40 inches.	9 gauge.	2 inch.	17.50
50 inches.	7 gauge.	2 inch.	40.00
54 inches.	7 gauge.	2 inch.	50.00
60 inches,	6 gauge.	2 inch.	72.50

Be sure to say whether cross cut or rip saw is wanted; there is no difference in price. Those ordering circular saws will save themselves much trouble by exercising care in making out their orders. We furnish blanks to facilitate this, which can be had on application. An extra charge will be made for saws of heavier gauge than those as listed above. Other sizes of circular saws quoted on application. We charge extra for each additional gauge heavier than those mentioned above. Saws beveled one gauge without extra charge up to 44 inches.

Saws other than sizes and gauges quoted above are not kept in stock. It will take from one week to ten days to make saws to order. Any saw made to order will not be taken back or exchanged.

NOTE OUR QUOTATIONS on Belting, Saw Machines and General Mill Supplies.

Henry Disston & Son's Patent Chisel Point Circular Saw.

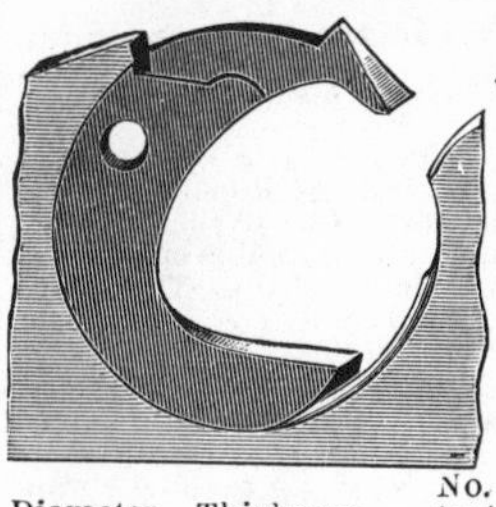

40224 We do not carry these saws in stock as they are made to order and shipped direct from factory at Philadelphia, Pa. Ten extra sets of points in accordance with the number of teeth on this list given with each saw. Parties must allow about two weeks time to complete orders for these saws.

Diameter.	Thickness	No. of teeth.	Size of hole.	Price each.
30 inch.	10 gauge.	20	1½ inch.	$30.25
32 inch.	9 gauge.	22	1⅝ inch.	33.00
34 inch.	9 gauge.	22	1⅝ inch.	36·00
36 inch.	8 gauge.	24	1⅝ inch.	39.60
40 inch.	8 gauge.	26	2 inch.	42.00
50 inch.	7 gauge.	34	2 inch.	65.00
60 inch.	5 gauge.	42	2 inch.	127.50

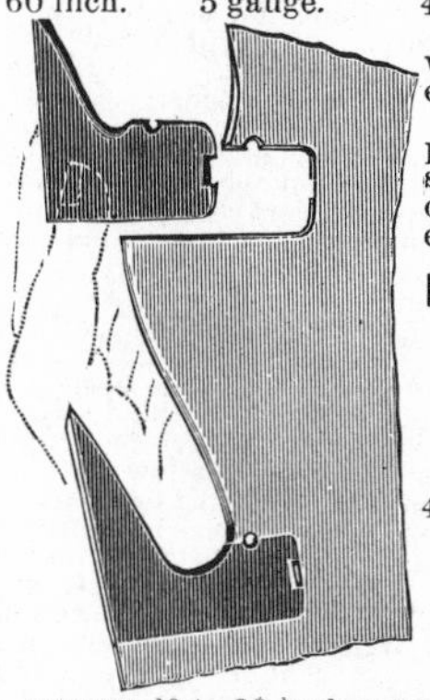

Any saw made as ordered will not be taken back or exchanged.

We can furnish duplicate points for the above No. 3 saw at 3 cents each. Duplicate holders at 30 cents each.

Henry Disston & Son's Inserted Tooth Circular Saw.

40224½ Extra Quality, Superior Workmanship. We do not carry these saws in stock. They are made to order and shipped direct from factory at Philadelphia, Pa.

In saws 20 to 30 inch diameter we insert No. 3 teeth.
In saws 32 to 50 inch diameter we insert No. 2 teeth.
In saws 52 to 72 inch diameter we insert No. 1 teeth.

Dia.	Thickness.	No. of teeth.	Size of hole.	Each.
30 inch.	9 gauge.	16	1½ inch.	$ 27.50
32 inch.	9 gauge.	18	1⅝ inch.	29.70
34 inch.	9 gauge.	18	1⅝ inch	31.90
36 inch.	8 gauge.	20	1⅝ inch.	32.50
38 inch.	8 gauge.	20	1⅝ inch.	34.00
40 inch.	8 gague.	22	2 inch.	37.50
50 inch.	7 gague.	26	2 inch	65.00
60 inch.	5 gague.	34	2 inch.	120.00
70 inch.	4 gaugc.	44	2 inch.	195.00

Duplicate teeth for above saws 40 cents.

Circular Saw Mandrels.

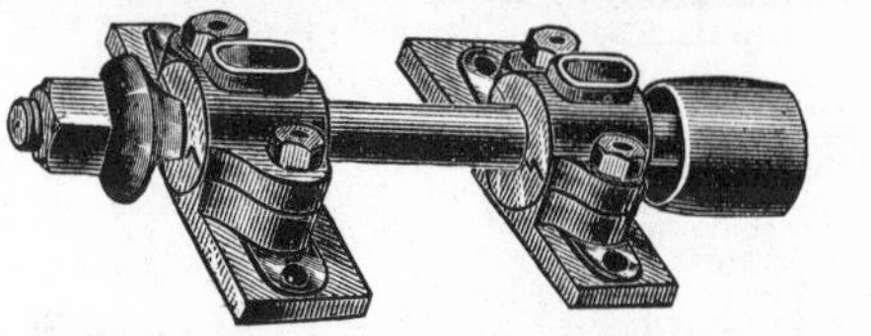

40225 Circular Saw Mandrels with pulley on end. Of the latest and most improved pattern.

Diam. of Pulley.	Face of Pulley.	Diam. of Flange	Length of Shaft.	Diam. of Shaft.	Size of Hole in Saw.	Price of each c'mp'e
2½ in.	3½ in.	2½ in.	16 in.	1 1/16 in.	1 in.	$ 5.50
3 in.	4½ in.	3 in.	19 in.	1 3/16 in.	1⅛ in.	6.40
3¼ in.	4½ in.	3½ in.	20 in.	1 5/16 in.	1¼ in.	6.80
4 in.	5 in.	4 in.	24 in.	1 7/16 in.	1 5/16 in.	7.80
4½ in.	5½ in.	4½ in.	26 in.	1 7/16 in.	1 5/16 in.	8.80
5 in.	6 in.	5 in.	28 in.	1 7/16 in.	1⅜ in.	10.00
5½ in.	6½ in.	5½ in.	30½ in.	1 7/16 in.	1⅜ in.	11.00
6 in.	7 in.	6 in.	32½ in.	1 9/16 in.	1½ in.	12.40
7 in.	8 in.	6 in.	37 in.	1 11/16 in.	1⅝ in.	17.20
8 in.	8 in.	6 in.	41 in.	1 13/16 in.	1⅝ in.	20.60

The "Eaton."

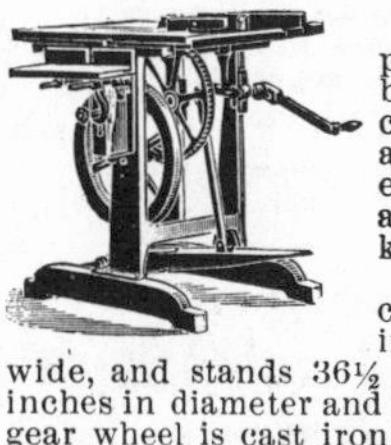

An Improved Hand and Foot power Sawing Machine, with boring attachment. This machine has been in use for years, and has been found practical in every part and is the superior of any machine now on the market.

DESCRIPTION.—The frame is of cast iron. Table is 2 feet 10 inches long by 2 feet 2 inches wide, and stands 36½ inches high. Fly wheel is 20 inches in diameter and weighs 60 pounds. The large gear wheel is cast iron, the other pinions being hard brass, and all are cut true by machine. The saw arbor runs in babbitted boxes, the others in solid bearings. The rip and cross cut saws are 7 inches in diameter and project 2 inches above the table, which has an iron top with two grooves for the cross cut gauges, and the rip-

"Eaton" Saw Machines—Continued.

ping gauge slides in the iron bar in front. The table is hinged at the back and is raised by the hand screw in front.

The saw makes nine revolutions to one of the crank, or treadle, and takes less power to run it than others. Grooving saws can be used in this machine for rabbeting, grooving, etc.

The Boring Table is raised and lowered by an eccentric slide, quick and positive, and has stop on slide for any depth. The arbor is bored for ⅜ shank. The whole making a most complete and durable machine.

Crated for shipping, weight, 300 lbs. The usual guarantee goes with every machine.

40226 Price, with boring attachment, each....$50.00
40226½ Price, without boring attachment, each 45.00

The "Eaton."

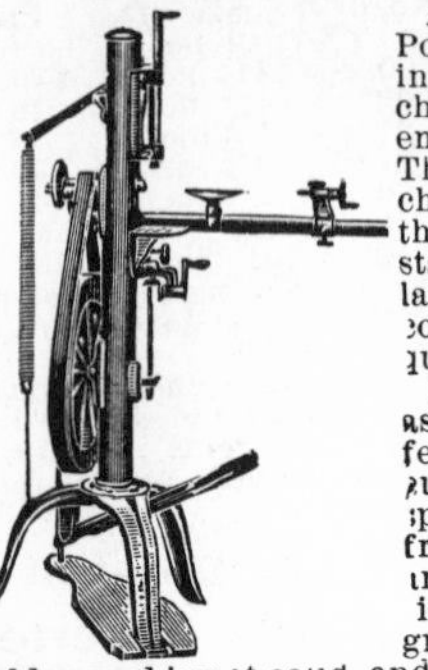

A New and Improved Foot Power Mortising and Tenoning machine, with boring machine, turning lathe and emery wheel attachments. The best combination machine on the market. Strong, thoroughly built and substantial. Is adapted to a large variety of work. No complications. Easily and quickly adjusted.

The combination machine, as shown in cut, stands five feet two inches high and occupies twenty-six inches floor space. The plunger reverses from top, the as shown in cut, and has a feather on the ides working in perfect grooves in each side of the holder, making it solid and cannot get out of position. The pull on the plunger is direct and straight, connected by iron rod insipe column to the treadle, which is made of wood and will not break or allow the foot to slip off. The table is raised and lowered by a screw, run by brass pinions and is held in place by a strong locking handle and will take an 8-inch piece under the chisel. The plunger has a full 4⅝-inch stroke, something no other machine has. The lathe-bed is made of 1-inch cold-rolled shafting and is long enough to turn an ordinary table leg. The spindle extends through the column, as shown in cut, and has a 5-inch emery wheel and is also drilled to take ⅜-inch shank bit for boring machine. The fly wheel is 20 inches in diameter and weighs 60 pounds and is connected with treadle, as shown, giving good speed and great power with easy treading. Every mortising and tenoning machine is so constructed that boring machine, turning lathe and emery wheel can be attained when wanted.

Weight, crated for shipping.

40227 Mortising and Tenoning Machine, 100 pounds. Each..........................$22.00
40227½ Combination Machine for Mortising, tenoning, boring with a lathe attachment and emery wheel. 185 pounds. Each..............40.00

Foot Power and Power Band Saw.

With Dana's Patent Friction Clutch Attachment.

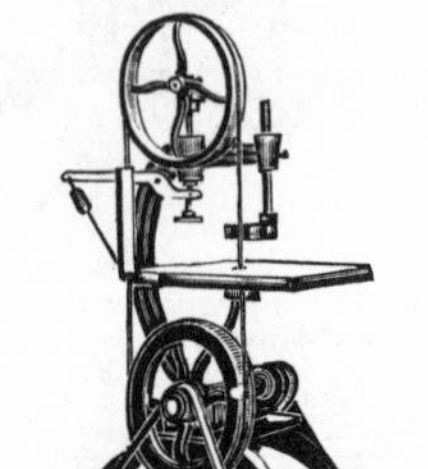

For wagonmakers, carpenters and wood-workers in general. This is a strong, substantial machine, with double treadle, so that two persons can operate it in heavy work. Each treadle is independent of the other. When desired to run by power, we furnish tight and loose pulleys instead of the back treadle. The power pulleys do not interfere with the front treadle. There is no gear, no extra pulleys, and no noise, as the clutches work on the shaft. The wheels are 16 inches in diameter, 1⅛ inch face. The table is 3 feet and 7 inches from the floor. Its size is 21x24 inches. Distance from table to guide, when later is raised its full height, 7 inches. The upper saw pulley can be tilted by means of a hand wheel, and can also be raised and lowered with the hand wheel to change tension of saw. Adjustable brass guide for saw, both above and below the table. We furnish two French steel saws with every machine—your choice of widths $\frac{3}{16}$, ¼, ⅜, ½, filed and set ready for use. We also furnish brazing clamps, with full directions for brazing saws. This machine meets a long felt want among wagon makers, carpenters, pattern makers, and wood-workers in general. Shipping weight, 350 pounds.

40228 Price, with double treadle................$37.50
40228½ Price, with single treadle, and with power pulley..37.50

Foot Power and Power Band Saw Machine.

With Patent Friction Clutch Attachment.

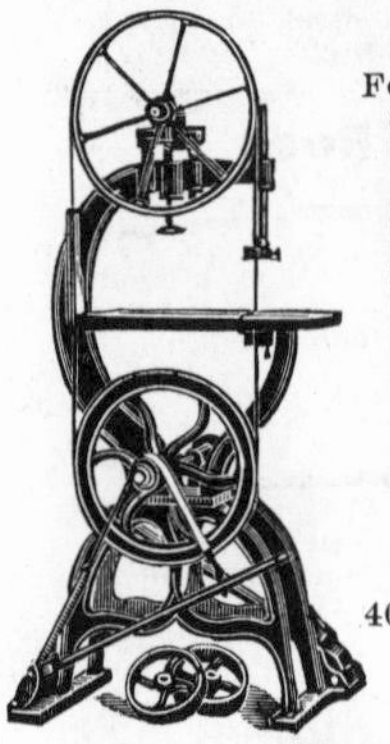

For wagonmakers, carpenters, and wood-workers in general. Same description as 40228½ Band Saw Machine, except that its full height is 6 feet; space, between saw and frame, 20 inches; floor space required, 32x36 inches; power pulley, 8 in., 3-inch face. The wheels are 20-inch in diameter, 1⅛-inch face. The table is 3 feet and 7 inches from the floor. Its size is 18¾x27 inches. Distance from table to guide, when latter is raised its full height, 10 inches. Weight, 300 pounds, not crated.

40229 Price, each.........$54.00

Band Saws.

HENRY DISSTON & SONS.

40230 In using band saws always keep the correct pitch upon the tooth, so as to give the saw a proper lead into the cut. This will take the friction entirely off the stay-pin. By the use of a round edge file the saw will be kept from galling and breaking. We furnish the saws SET AND FILED at the following prices. We keep in stock up to 1 inch wide; anything wider than 1 inch will have to come from the factory and will require from 10 days' to 2 weeks' time. We cannot allow parties to return the saws if sent as ordered, or countermand after order has gone to the factory from us.

Width.	Gauge.	Extra for joining each saw	Price, per foot.
¼ in.	21	$0.20	$0.10
⅜ in.	21	.20	.11
½ in.	21	.20	13
⅝ in.	21	.25	.15
¾ in.	20	.25	.16
⅞ in.	20	.25	.17
1 in.	20	.30	.18

If saws are not filed and set, 4 cents per foot may be deducted from above price. Under no circumstances will we send band saws C. O. D. We can furnish band saws up to 12 inches wide.

Saw Gummers.

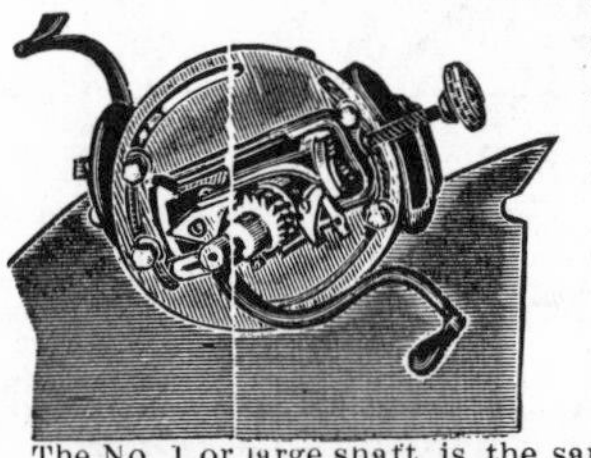

40231 Disston's Patent Self-Feeding Saw Gummer.

Showing the Victor in position for work on a 60-inch circular saw.

In ordering gummers state size of cutter wanted.

We make three sizes of cutter shafts for this gummer.

The No. 1 or large shaft is the same diameter as is used in our No. 1 gummer, and is suitable for 1, 1⅛, 1¼, 1⅜ and 1½ inch cutters.

The No. 2 or medium size shaft is same diameter as is used in our No. 2 gummer, and is suitable for cutters ½, ⅝, ¾ and ⅞ inch.

The No. 3 or small shaft is made specially for ⅜ inch cutters. Price, each..................................$14.25

Saw Tools and Swages.

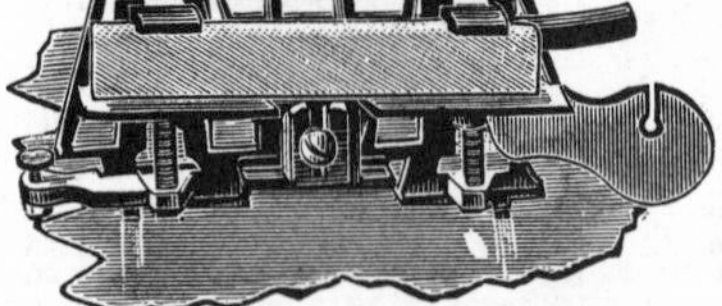

40232 Improved Combination Saw Tool for fitting up cross cut saws.

This very handy tool includes a jointer, a side dress, a cleaner, a tooth gauge, a saw set and a set gauge for testing, the amount of set. To properly fit up a cross cut saw, it is necessary first that the teeth should be uniform in length. To accomplish this, place the file edgeway in the frame and by means of the two screws adjust to the curve of the saw, pass it lightly over the teeth until it touches the shortest cutting tooth, then place the gauge over the cleaner teeth as shown in cut No. 2 and file them down to the required length.

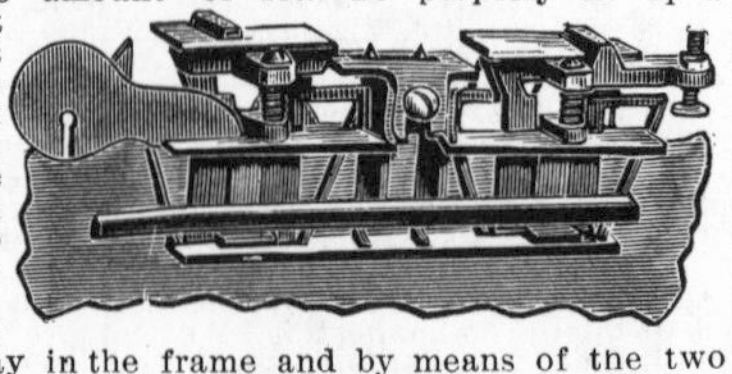

If the saw requires setting use the saw set on the end of the tool. Give the first tooth the required amount of set, and by adjusting the stop bar under the saw set each tooth will be given the same amount of set.

Price, each..$0.80
Per dozen...9.00

The Conqueror Swage, Jumper or Upset.

Special attention is called to the Conqueror Swages. The Conqueror has given entire satisfaction, and we have the most flattering testimonials of its worth. It is indispensable to any sawyer who uses the spread set. Every swage sold by us is warranted perfect and to give satisfaction. The sets themselves shall bear their own recommendation.

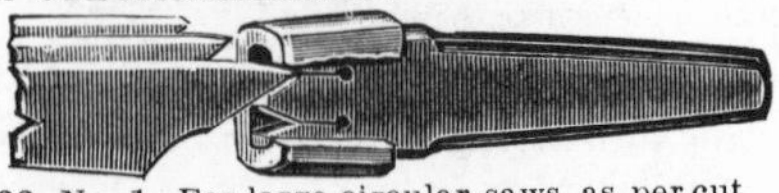

40233 No. 1. For large circular saws, as per cut. Price, each...$2.50
40234 No. 2. For small circular and mill saws. Price, each...2.00
40235 No. 3. For small circular saws. Price, each 1.65

Patent Improved Saw Tool.

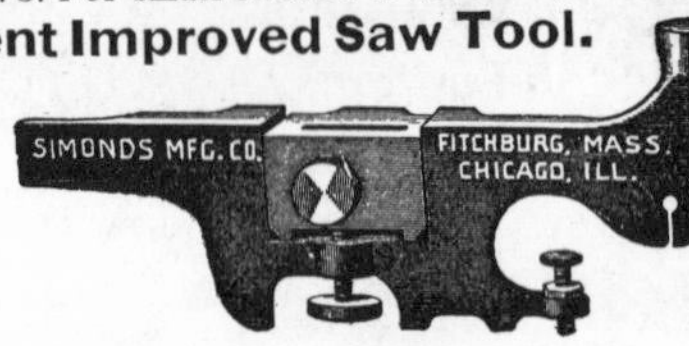

40236 For use in fitting *Cross Cut Saws.* It combines in one tool a perfect *Saw Set, Jointer, Raker Gauge, Set Gauge,* and *Swaging Hammer* in a convenient and compact form. A saw can be fitted up much more quickly and much better with this tool than with any other tools or sets of tools. It takes an 8-inch mill file we do not furnish, except at an additional charge. For price of files see No. 40305.

Price, each..........$0.60. Per dozen..........$6.00

Saw Handle Screws.

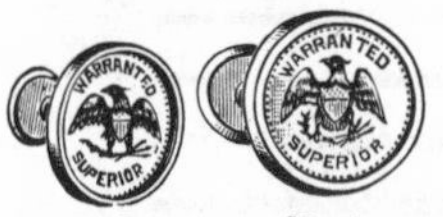

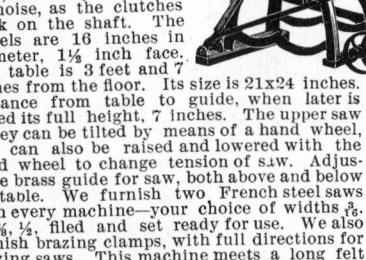

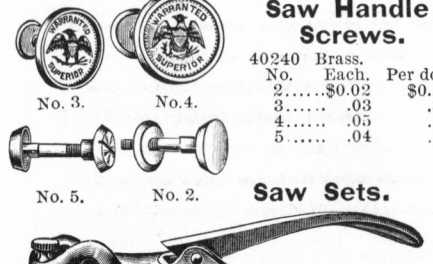

No. 3. No. 4.

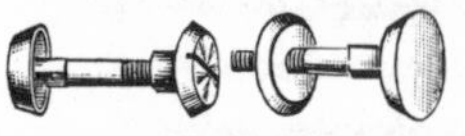

No. 5. No. 2.

40240 Brass.

No.	Each.	Per doz.
2	$0.02	$0.22
3	.03	.33
4	.05	.54
5	.04	.44

Saw Sets.

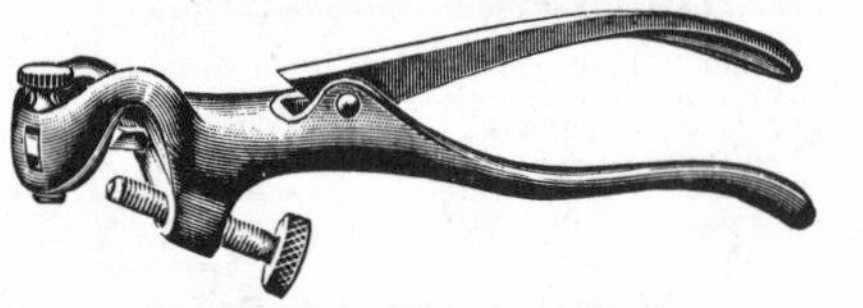

40241 Morrill's Perfect Saw Set No. 1, setting all kinds of hand saws; weight, 13 ounces.

Hold the saw on any level place, teeth upward. Place the set on the saw, as shown in cut. The anvil, movable up and down, must be regulated to suit the distance the operator desires to set his saw teeth down from their points. The guard, when moved forward, increases the amount of set, moved backward, decreases it. When made fast to the screw, compress the handles and the plunger goes forward and takes effect on the saw tooth.

On no account pry over on the saw blade. When the set is properly adjusted simply compressing the handles is all that is necessary. This is for hand saws from 32 to 16 gauge only. Each.................................$0.65

40242 Morrill's Perfect Saw Set, No. 3, for single tooth, cross cut and circular saws, from 20 to 14 gauge. Weight, 1 pound 6 ounces. Each 1.10
40243 Morrill's Perfect Saw Set, No. 4, for Champion or M-tooth cross cut saws, from 22 to 14 gauge; weight, 1½ lbs. Each.......................$1.1..
40244 Extra parts for Morill saw sets.
No. 1, Anvils and Plungers each.................. .10
No. 4, Anvils and Plungers, each.................. .12
No. 4, Anvils and Plungers, each.................. .15

Taintor's Positive Saw Set, 93.

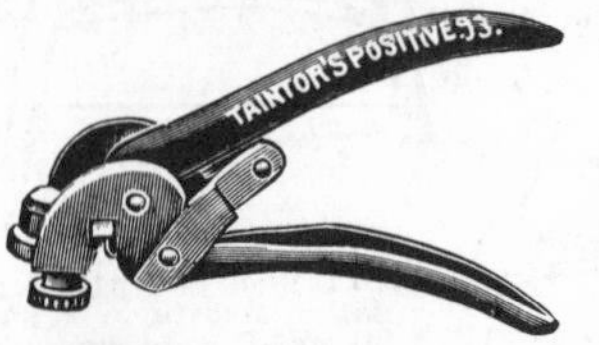

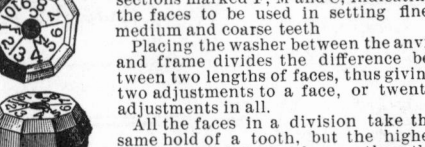

40245 Full directions sent with each saw set.

Description—The face of the anvil opposite the punch determines the set of the saw

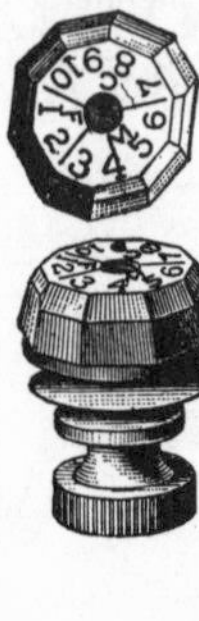

The anvil has ten faces, divided into sections marked F, M and C, indicating the faces to be used in setting fine, medium and coarse teeth

Placing the washer between the anvil and frame divides the difference between two lengths of faces, thus giving two adjustments to a face, or twenty adjustments in all.

All the faces in a division take the same hold of a tooth, but the higher numbers bend the tooth more than the lower ones.

Face No. 4 will set a medium saw about right for general work, and can be used as a trial face.

Price, each $0.65

Saw Sets.—Continued.

40247 Lever Saw Sets, wood handles; weight, 7 oz. Each..$0.10

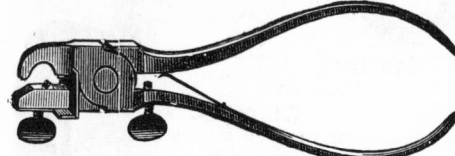

40249 Nash's Saw Sets, new lever; weight, 12 oz. Each..$0.35
40250 Nash's Saw Sets, No. 3, for setting cross cut saws. Price. each........................... .85

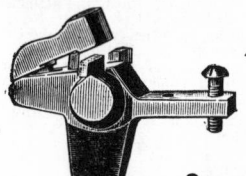

40253 Aiken's Patent Hammer Saw Sets, made of the highest grade of cast steel and warranted genuine. Price. each........$0.60

Saw Vises.

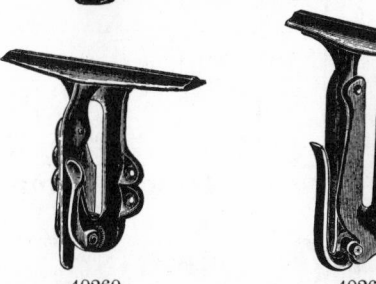

40260    40261

40260 Stearn's Patent Saw Clamp. Length of jaws, 9½ inches. Japanned. Weight, 3 lbs. 7 oz. Each.....................................$0.30

40261 Silent Saw Clamp. By one movement of the lever the saw is firmly clamped, after which a third jaw faced with solid rubber is pressed against the saw, preventing all noise of vibration. Weight, 3¾ lbs. Each..............................$0.90

40262 Patent Saw Clamp. The jaws are so constructed as to prevent the vibration of the saw in filing, lessening the noise and causing a great saving in files; the jaws are planed to match precisely. Weight, 4¾ lbs. Price, each.....................$0.93

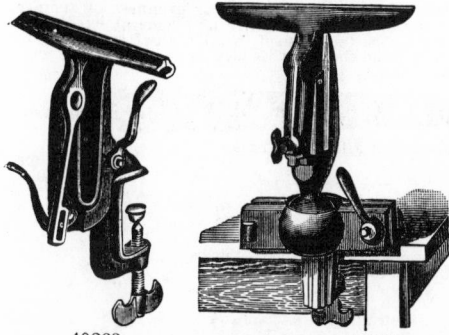

40263   40264

40263 Patent Saw Clamp (3). This vise has a malleable iron screw clamp for attaching it to the work bench, and a lever and cam for holding it in any position. Weight, 5 lbs. Japanned. Each..........................$0.45
40264 Adjustable Ball and Socket Saw Clamp. By the use of this vise a saw can be filed any angle or square as the operator may desire. Weight, 10½ lbs. Price, each......................... .68

Prices of Merchandise are now lower than they have been for 20 years. There was never a better time to buy.

Saw Clamp and Sharpener.

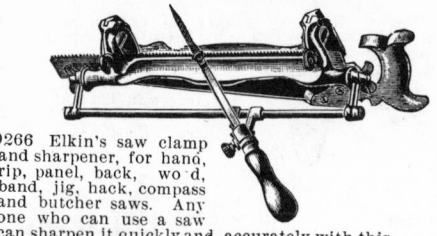

40266 Elkin's saw clamp and sharpener, for hand, rip, panel, back, wood, band, jig, hack, compass and butcher saws. Any one who can use a saw can sharpen it quickly and accurately with this invention. Weight, 5½ pounds. Each........$2.29

Saw Jointer.

40267 The Practical Saw Jointer. By its use perfect accuracy is attained in jointing the teeth squarely and to equal lengths. The file can be adjusted in the slot until the surface has been used on both sides. Each....................................$0.35

Tanite Emery Wheel.

When ordering emery wheels, give diameter, thickness, size of hole and also be sure to state the nature of your work, kind of metal you intend to use wheel on, etc. This is absolutely necessary in order for us to send you a wheel suitable, as there are about 15,000 different kinds, sizes, classes and shapes of wheels; we haven't the space to quote them all, but will quote prices and furnish any kind or size upon application.
40270 Emery Wheel, flat face.
40271 Emery Wheel, bevel edge, for gumming saws.

	40270		THICKNESS.		40271	
	¼	⅜	½	⅝	¾	1
Diameter.			Price, each.			
1½	$0.24	Not made in these sizes.	$0.25	Not made in these sizes.	$0.28	$0.32
2	.27		.32		.35	.38
2	.40		.45		.48	.52
3	.43		.52		.58	.65
4	.60	$0.62	.68	$0.75	.85	1.00
5	.79	.78	.84	.96	1.08	1.32
6	.84	.96	1.02	1.25	1.44	1.84
7	1.10	1.27	1.38	1.80	1.93	2.32
8	1.28	1.42	1.56	1.95	2.63	2.65
10	1.72	1.98	2.23	2.65	3.10	3.95
12	1.80	2.11	2.40	2.90	3.40	4.42

The Eagle Emery Wheel.

In ordering emery wheels the diameter, thickness and size of hole must be given and and the purpose for which they are to be used. *The wheel must be kept very dry in all cases.* Parties must be very particular in this respect to insure perfect satisfaction. Every wheel guaranteed if kept free from dampness.
Wheels less than ½ inch in thickness, same price as ½ inch.
40272 Flat face.
40273 Bevel edge.

				THICKNESS.				
diameter.	½	⅝	¾	1	1¼	1½	1¾	2
3	$0.30	$0.34	$0.38	$0.44	$0.50	$0.54	$0.58	$0.64
4	.44	.48	.54	.64	.76	.88	1.00	1.10
5	.56	.64	.72	.84	1.04	1.20	1.48	1.52
6	.70	.84	1.00	1.20	1.48	1.72	2.00	2.24
7	.92	1.08	1.26	1.58	2.00	2.24	2.56	2.90
8	1 04	1.24	1.40	1.80	2.28	2.56	3.00	3.32
9	1.24	1.40	1.54	1.96	2.72	3.20	3.68	4.20
10	1.48	1.76	2.04	2.64	3.24	3.80	4.40	4.96
12	1.60	2.00	2.40	2.96	3.60	4.28	5.08	5.60
14	2.48	2.98	3.48	4.28	5.28	6.08	7.00	7.80

DOLLARS...
...and SENSE..

Are You Entirely Satisfied with your present facilities for purchasing your ordinary household wants with the varieties at your disposal and the prices which you have been paying? We feel confident that we can save you time, trouble and money. Freight or express rates to any point quoted upon application.

A Great Success. Shop Saw, With Automatic Feed.

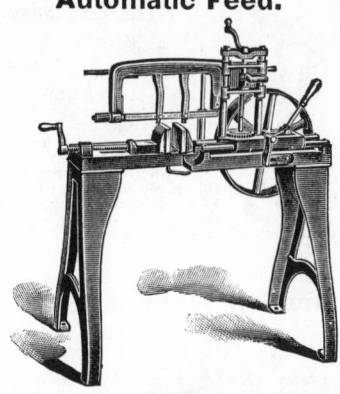

40274

For cutting all kinds of metal, iron, steel, brass and castings, including tool steel. Capacity, 5 inches and less.

The "Q & C" shop saw is a great improvement over the gravity feed, or hack saw; has positive feed, entirely automatic, and speed can be instantly changed to accommodate all classes of work.

The common hack saws depend entirely upon gravity to feed the saw through the work, and, as the weight of saw frame cannot be increased, the cutting speed diminishes as the size of work increases, whereas with the "Q & C" shop saw, having automatic screw feed, the same cutting speed is maintained throughout.

The old style machines drag the blades backward on the return stroke with nearly, if not quite, as much pressure as when cutting, destroying the keenness of the edge as well as the blade itself in a short while. The "Q & C" shop saw clears the metal on return stroke, effecting an actual saving of 50 per cent. of wear; a single blade lasting from three days to two weeks. Our special saw blades are superior to all others.

The "Q & C" shop saw was specially designed to overcome the known weaknesses of the old style machines, which are very slow and very expensive to keep supplied with saw blades; one of our special blades will outwear several dozen of the old style.

These machines are supplied with movable vise, allowing use of entire blade, also double adjustable guards to hold the blade firmly, insuring true work.

Actual Comparative Cutting Speed.
OLD STYLE MACHINE.

Size of Work	
1-inch round steel..	9 minutes
2 " " "	36
3 " " "	2 hours 30
4 " " "	3

THE "Q & C" MACHINE.

Size of Work	
1-inch round steel	3 minutes
2 " " "	9
3 " " "	27
4 " " "	45

The above test was actually made, using a new saw blade on each cut made on the old style machine, and a single blade for the four tests on the "Q & C" shop saw.
The price of the "Q & C" shop saw includes six special saw blades. Each machine fully guaranteed. Shipping weight...... Price each........$20.00
We can also furnish larger machines for beams, channels, T's. rail, all kinds of heavy work. Prices furnished on application.
40274½ Extra Saw Blades for the "Q & C" shop saw. Per dozen.....................................$1.50

Bracket Saw.

Has tilting table drilling attachment and dust blower. Height of table above floor, 32 inches.
Diameter of belt wheel, 12 inches.
Diameter of balance wheel, 5 inches.
Length of arms in the clear, 18 inches.
With each machine we furnish 3 drills, 6 saw blades, wrench, sheet of designs and directions.
Machine, boxed, weighs 36 pounds.
40275 Price of No. 2 Rogers' saw complete...................$3.37

The new Rogers is altogether superior to any machine offered at the same or less price.
40276 Extra Saw Clamps for new Rogers. Per pair...$0.30
We do not sell designs other than furnished.

Send for a copy of our BICYCLE CATALOGUE. High Grade Wheels can now be had for a little money.

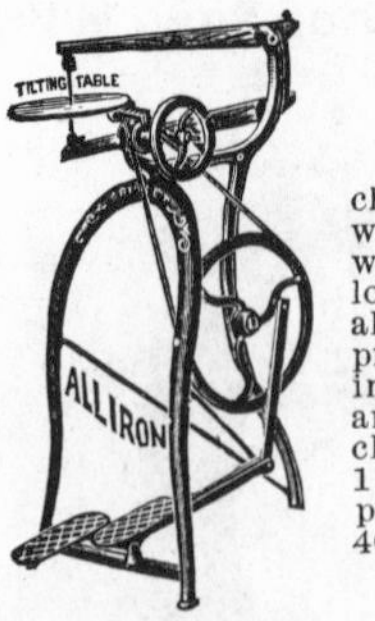

Bracket Saw.

To meet the demand for a cheap and good Foot Power Saw we have made an all-iron machine which we are offering at a very low figure. For scroll sawing alone it is about as good as higher priced saws. It has an iron tilting table, second growth ash arms, 18 inches long, improved clamp, etc. Weight of saw, about 17 pounds, shipping weight, 35 pounds.
40277 Price, each.........$2.50

Goodell Turning Lathe.

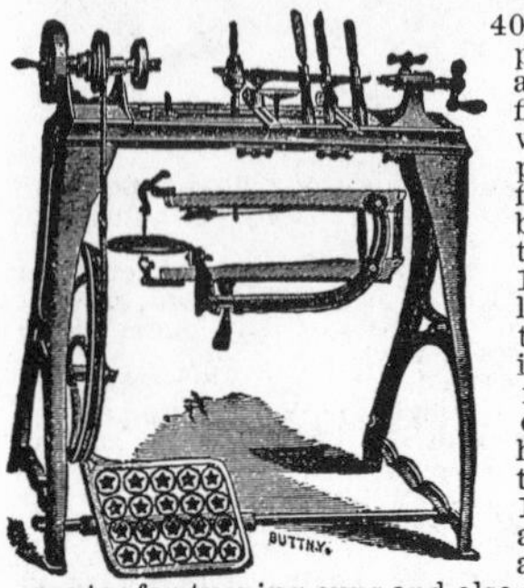

40280 This lathe is provided with a long and short tool rest, five turning tools, wrench and drill points. Swing of lathe five inches, length of bed 24 inches, distance between center 15½ inches. The large drive wheel has two grooves of varying depths on its face to give it a change of speed: the higher speed is 11 to 1; the lower 7 to 1; the lathe head has a two inch face plate, a spur center, a screw center for turning cups and also a drill chuck to hold from 1-32 to ¼ inch round twist drills for drilling wood or iron. The lathe is thoroughly built and highly finished, the plain and polished parts being nickel plated. Price.................$8.55
40280½ Goodell Lathe with scroll saw attachments.. 10.80

Champion Turning Lathe.

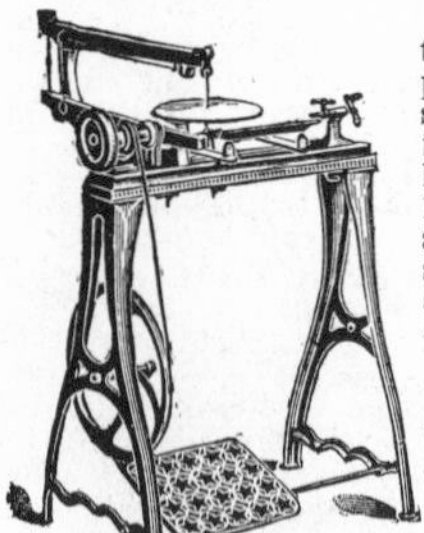

This lathe is large enough to do good work, and is supplied with all tools and instructions needed for putting it into successful use. The lathe bed is 24 inches long, 15 inches between centers, and 5-inch swing. The scroll saw can be taken off by loosening one bolt.
40281 Price of lathe with scroll attachment. Each...................$7.55
40281½ Price of Lathe without scroll attachments. Each................. 6.30

Bench Lathe.

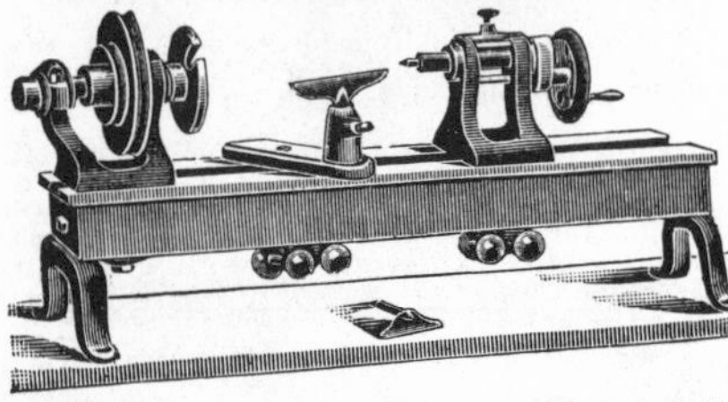

The above cut represents our small Bench Lathe, which will be found a most useful tool for light turning, drilling and polishing, and will take the place in many cases of the large and more expensive tools in general use. This lathe is made in two sizes, 24 inch and 36 inch bed; both have 6½ inch swing. The distance between centers of the 24 inch bed is 14 inches, and the distance of the 36 inch bed between centers is 26 inches.

		Price, each.
40283	Lathe, with 24 inch bed	$12.00
40284	Lathe, with 36 inch bed	14.00

PRICE OF EXTRAS FOR ABOVE LATHE.

40285	Foot Wheels	5.00
40286	Counter Shaft	2.50
40287	Spur Center for Wood	1.00
40288	Crotch Center for Drilling	1.00
40289	Drill Pad for Tail Stock	.75
40290	Extra Face Plate	.75
40291	Screw Chuck for Wood	1.00
40292	Drill Chuck fitted to lathe to hold drills from ⅜ inch down	4.00

Note Our Prices and Assortment of

-:- Disston Saws.

We carry the largest stock of these saws to be found in the west and can fill orders as promptly as anyone.

Countershafts.

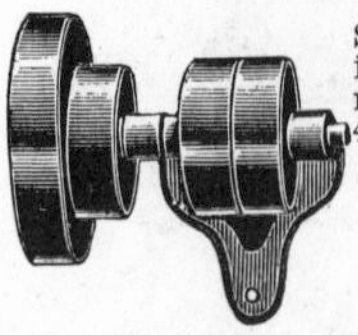

Fig. 1.

Suitable for running the preceding lathes or any other small machinery by power.
40293 Fig. 1 has fast and loose pulleys, 3 inch in diameter, 1⅛ inch face, and flat cone pulley, 5 inch and 3 inch diameter, 1⅛ inch face. Price, each....$2.50

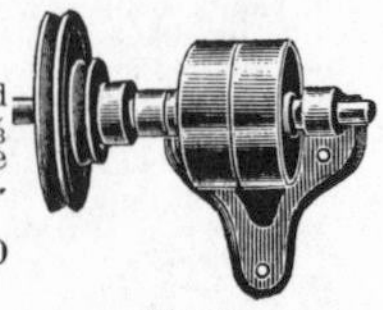

Fig. 2

40293½ Fig. 2 with fast and loose pulley 3 in. diameter, 1⅛ in. face, and grooved cone pulley, 4 and 2 inches diameter.
Price.....................$2.00

Lathe Head.

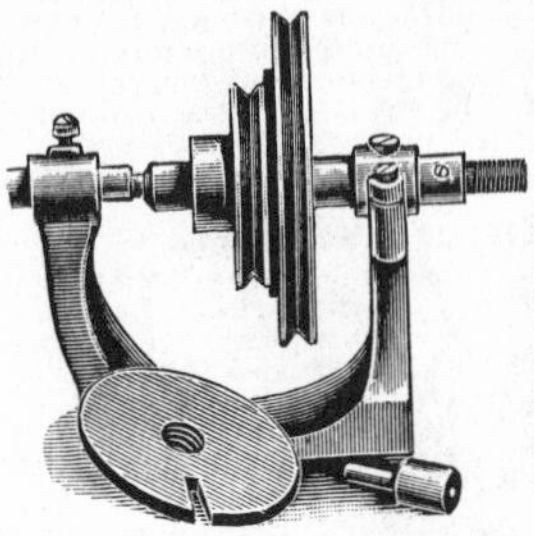

40294 Has castiron adjustable bearings and steel spindle; swings 3 inches and will take a stick of wood 6 inches in dimaeter; is furnished with face plate and arbor.
Price.......... $3.00
40295 Head and tail stock complete. $6.00

Foot Power Emery Wheel Grinding Machine.

Speed, 2,600 to 2,800 Revolutions Per Minute.

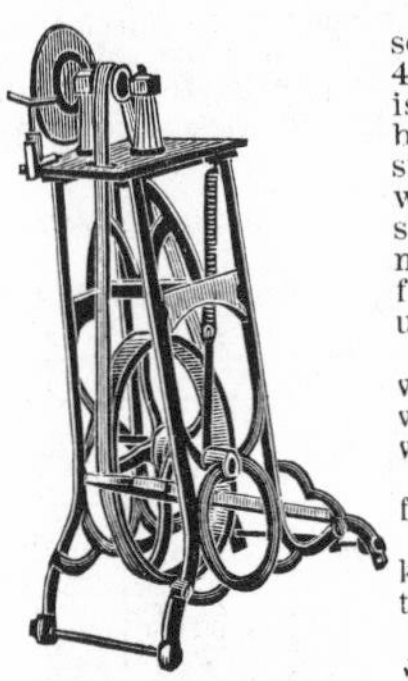

40295½.

For price of Emery Wheels, see Nos. 40270, 40271, 40272, 40273. This machine is designed for the use of blacksmiths, carpenters, gunsmiths, and marble granite workers. It will save a blacksmith a great deal of time and many files. It will do three-fourths of all the work he usually does with a file.

For ordinary tool grinding we use an 8x¾-inch emery wheel, which is furnished with each machine

A narrow wheel can be used for gumming saws.

This machine will do all kinds of tool grinding in less than one-fourth of the time equired on a grindstone, and will do the work much better. It is a light machine, and can be moved around easily.
40295½ Weight, 190 lbs. Price, each.........$10.50

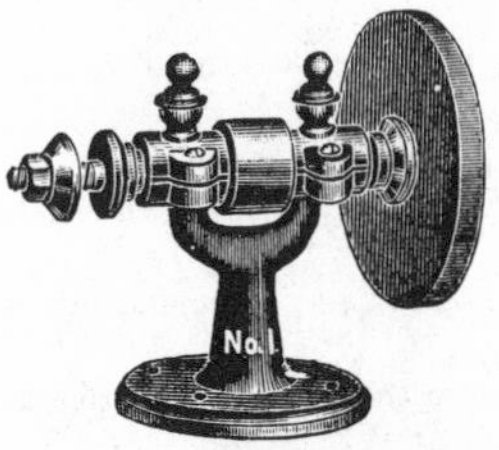

40296 Emery Grinding Machine, for power. Will run two 6-inch emery wheels, 1 inch thick, has ⅜ inch steel spindle, ½ inch between flanges, pulley 2 inches in diameter, 1⅜ inch face. Weight, 9 lbs.
Price, each.....$4.00

Polishing Heads.

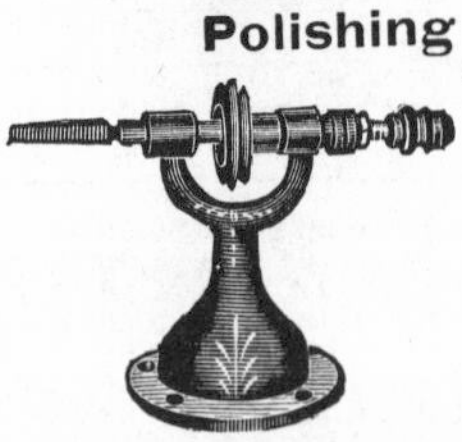

40298 Stands 6 in. high and has a spindle 9 inches long, one end of which is a taper screw the other end is fitted to hold emery wheels, buffers, polishing wheels, and small circular saws. It is also fitted with chuck for holding drills. We furnish the head only, as shown in the cut. Each..................................$1.00

Polishing Head.

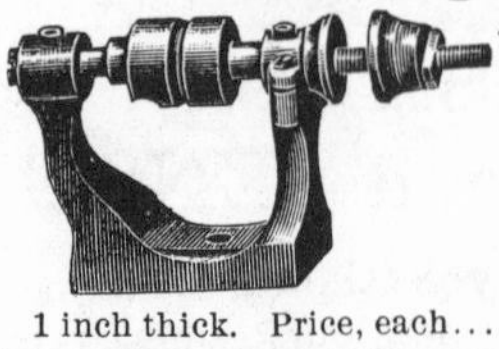

40299 For running emery wheels, circular saws, etc. Has castiron adjustable bearings and steel spindle, and is made to run with round or flat belts; will hold wheels 6 inch in diameter, and 1 inch thick. Price, each.......................$3.25

Write Down What You Want, put it in an Envelope with the Money,

... WE DO THE REST.

No easier way to buy was ever invented.
If the goods don't suit, the money is at your call.

Iron Clamps.

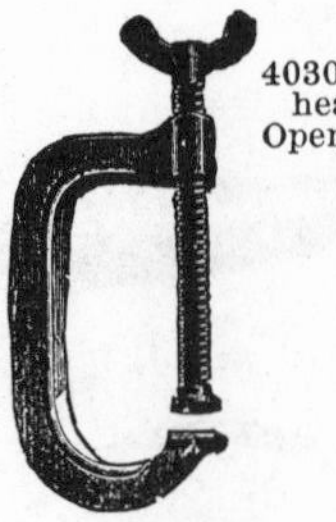

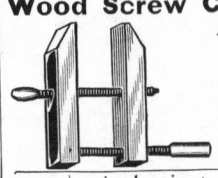

40300 Malleable Iron Clamps, swivel head.

Opens inches.	Weight.	Price, each.
4	1½ lbs.	$0.15
5	1¾ "	.20
6	2 "	.25
7	3 "	.30
8	3¼ "	.35
10	5¼ "	.42

Quilting Frame Clamps.

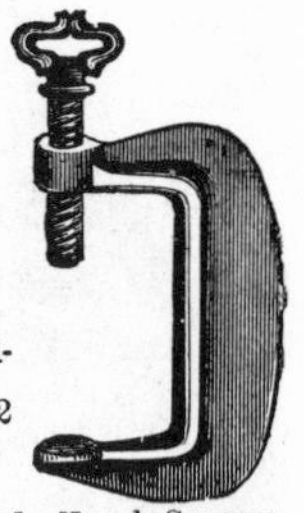

40301 Quilting Frame Clamps, malleable iron, 2¼ inch opening.
Per set of four.................$0.12

Wood Screw Clamps.

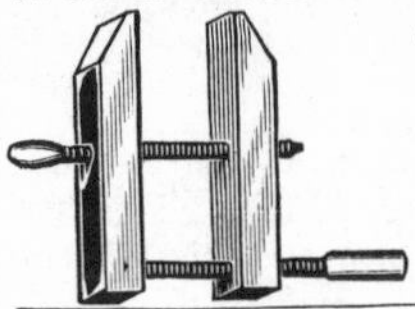

40302 Wood Hand Screws, the Grand Rapids Pattern. This make is unexcelled; the spindles are made of second growth hickory; the jaws are of hard maple or birch thoroughly seasoned; the threads are cut deep enough to prevent stripping.

Diameter of Screw. Inches.	Length of Screw. Inches.	Length of Jaw. Inches.	Size of Jaw. Inches.	Opens. Inches.	Price Each.	Price, per doz.
⅝	11	8½	1⅜x1½	5	16c	$1.63
¾	13	10	1⅝x1⅝	6½	20c	2.16
⅞	14	12	1⅞x1⅞	6½	23c	2.50
1⅛	20	16	2¼x2¼	10½	35c	3.78
1¼	22	20	2½x2¾	12	43c	4.65
1¼	24	24	2¾x3	13½	50c	5.40
1¼	26	24	2¾x3	15½	55c	5 95

Iron Clamp Head.

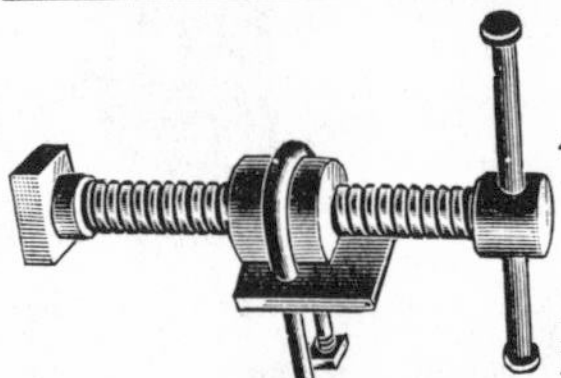

40303 With wrought iron screw, single nut, iron handle; made only in three sizes.

Dia. of screw each—			
Inch	1	1⅛	1¼
Price,	$0.60	.90	1 00

Stearn's New Door Frame Clamp.

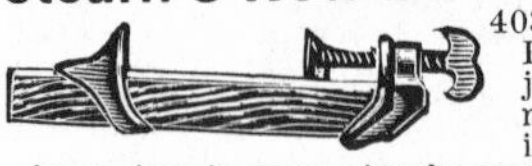

40304 Stearn's New Door Frame Clamp. The jaws are mounted on maple bars, 1¼ x 1½ inches; 4 feet long; the loose jaw is very simply operated, being supported with a spring which holds it at any point required. The stationary jaw has a malleable iron thumb screw with a ball and socket joint, making an adjustable washer. It is unrivaled for ease and rapidity of adjustment, cheapness and strength. Each.......$0.45
Per dozen....................................... 4.86

Kerney & Foote and Arcade Files.

Our Files are unexcelled for evenness of temper, cutting qualities, durability and general excellence. They are used exclusively by all of the largest machine and railroad shops. This fact alone is worthy of consideration.

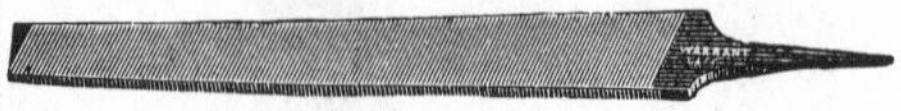

40305 Mill Files, no handle:

	Weight.	Each.	Per doz.
6 inch	6 oz.	$0.07	$0.66
8 inch	7 oz.	.10	.85
10 inch	10 oz.	.12	1.10
12 inch	16 oz.	.17	1.60
14 inch	31 oz.	.25	2.30
16 inch	2 lbs.	.33	3.35

40306 Flat Bastard Files:

4 inch	2 oz.	.07	.63
5 inch	4 oz.	.07	.65
6 inch	4 oz.	.08	.75
8 inch	7 oz	.11	1.00
10 inch	12 oz.	.15	1.40
12 inch	1¼lb.	.21	2.00
14 inch	29 oz	.30	2.85
16 inch	39 oz.	.40	4.00

40307 Round Bastard Files:

	Weight.	Each.	Per doz.
4 inch	2 oz.	06	.52
5 inch	4 oz.	.07	.60
6 inch	5 oz.	.07	.65
8 inch	6 oz.	.10	.85
10 inch	8 oz.	.12	1.12
12 inch	12 oz.	17	1.60

40308 Half Round Files, same shape as mill files.

6 inch	4 oz.	.10	1.00
8 inch	8 oz.	.14	1.30
10 inch	11 oz.	.19	1.75
12 inch	18 oz.	.25	2.30

Taper Files.

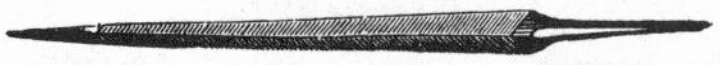

40310 Taper or Saw Files, 3 square sides:

	Weight.	Each.	Per doz.
3 inch	2 oz.	$0.04	$0.36
4 inch	3 oz.	.04	.38
5 inch	4 oz.	.06	.54
6 inch	5 oz.	.08	.76
7 inch	6 oz.	.10	.95
8 inch	7 oz.	.12	1.20

40310½ Slim Taper Files:

3 inch	2 oz	.04	.35
3½ inch	2 oz.	.04	.35
4 inch	3 oz.	.05	.40
4½ inch	3 oz.	.05	.42
5 inch	4 oz.	.06	.52
5½ inch	4 oz.	.06	.55
6 inch	4 oz.	.07	.63
7 inch	4 oz.	.08	.75
8 inch	6 oz.	.10	.90

Taper Files.

40311 Stubbs' Taper Files:
An English hand-cut file of superior quality.

	Weight.	Each.	Per doz.
3 inch	3 oz.	$0.12	$1.30
3½ inch	3 oz.	.13	1.35
4 inch	3 oz.	.15	1.50
4½ inch	4 oz.	.19	2.10
5 inch	4 oz.	.22	2.35
6 inch	4 oz.	25	2.65

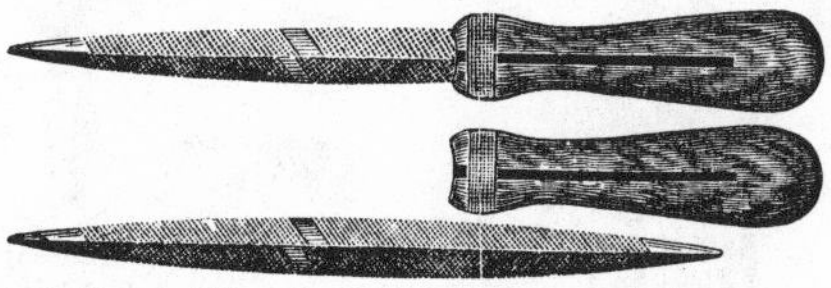

40312 Taper Files, double enders

	Weight.	Each.	Per doz.
7 inch	2 oz.	$0.08	$0.80
8 inch	2 oz.	.09	.80
9 inch	3 oz.	10	1.00
10 inch	4 oz.	.12	1.15

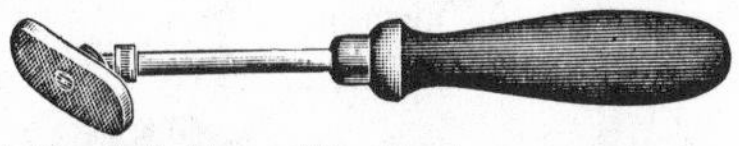

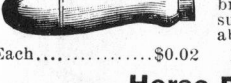

40313 Goodell Shoe File, made expressly for family use. It will readily clear any part of the shoe of nails and pegs. The file is made of the best quality of steel finely tempered and so attached to the shank as to make it adjustable to any position, or can be held stationary if desired. Price, each......$0.12 Per dozen.........$1.35

File Handles.

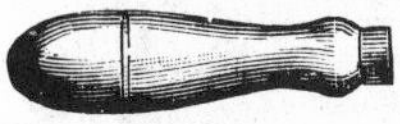

40314 File Handles. with brass ferrule, assorted sizes, suitable for files quoted above. Weight, 2 oz.
Each...............$0.02 Per dozen...........$0.22

Horse Rasps.

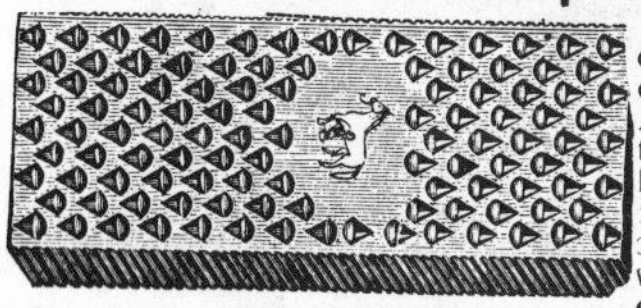

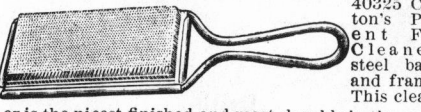

Cut by hand; can furnish either the Arcade. Disston's, or the Kerney & Foote makes at prices quoted. weight, 18 to 42 ounces.

40318 Horse Rasps:

Size	12 in	14 in.	16 in.
Price, each	28c	40c	56c
Price, per dozen	$3.16	$4.32	$6.18

40319 Heller's Horse Rasps are cut by hand acknowledged by all blacksmiths to be the best in use.

Size	12 in.	14 in	16 in
Price, each	32c	50c	65c
Price, per dozen	$3.60	$6.25	$7.20

Wood Rasps.

40320 Half Round.

Size	6 in.	10 in.	12 in.	4 in.
Price, each	13c	28c	40c	54c
Price, per doz	$1.47	$3.07	$4.32	$5.93

File Cleaners.

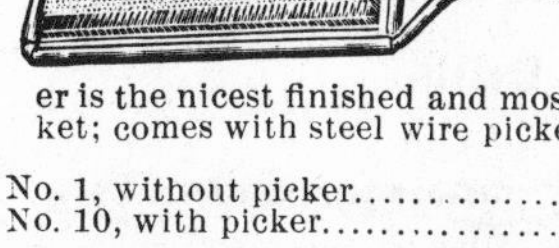

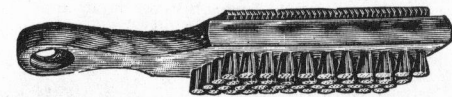

40325 Colton's Patent File Cleaner, steel back and frame. This cleaner is the nicest finished and most durable in the market; comes with steel wire picker and without.

	Each.	Per doz.
No. 1, without picker	$0.12	$1.30
No. 10, with picker	.15	1.62

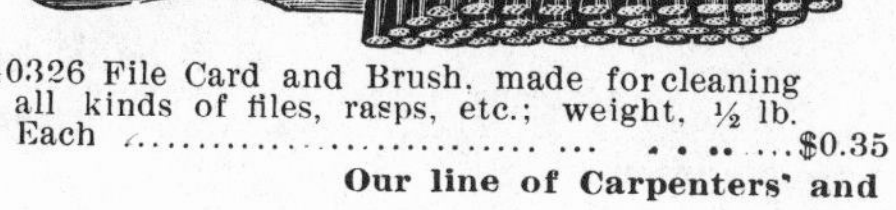

40326 File Card and Brush. made for cleaning all kinds of files, rasps, etc.; weight, ½ lb. Each $0.35

Drills.

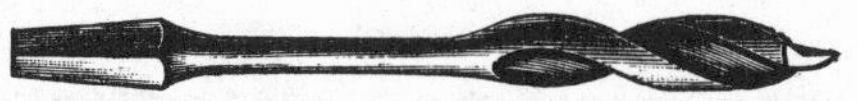

40327 Syracuse Short Wood Brace Drills, for dowels, casters, tire bolts, sugar bits, etc.; blades from 4 to 10, 2½ inches long, from 11 to 20, 4½ inches long. The numbers indicate the sizes in 32ds of an inch.

Sizes	4	4¼	4½	5	5¼	5½	6	6¼
Each	9	.9	.10	.10	.10	.12	.12	.12
Sizes	6½	7	7¼	7½	8	8¼	8½	9
Each	15	15.	.15	.18	.18	.18	.20	.20
Sizes	10	11	12	13	14	16	18	20
Each	20	24.	.24	.27	.27	.30	.33	.30

30 inches in length.

40328 Syracuse Long Wood Brace Drills, for bell hangers, telephone and telegraph work; they will go through plaster, nails, and even brick walls, and can be sharpened when dull; are 30 inches in length. The numbers indicate the sizes in 32ds of an inch.

Sizes	8	10	12	14	16	18	20	22
Each	.65	.65	.72	.72	.78	.83	.89	.90	.95

Sizes	24	26	28	30	32
Each	$1.00	$1.07	$1.13	$1.18	$1.20

Bit Boxes.

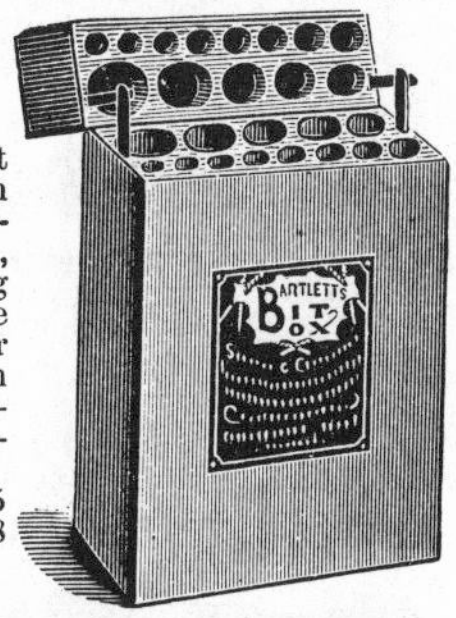

40329 Bartlett's Patent Bit Boxes. The best thing in the market for the purpose. Every mechanic, farmer or any one using auger bits should have one of these; a place for every bit and every bit in its place; made of hardwood, is strong and durable, holds 13 bits.
Price, each..........$0.35
Per dozen............ 3.78

Auger Bits.

40330 C. E. Jenning's Extra Quality Double Spur Auger Bits.

Sizes		3/16	¼	5/16	⅜	7/16	½	9/16
Price, each		13	.12	.12	.13	.13	.13	.15
Sizes	⅝	11/16	¾	13/16	⅞	15/16	1	1⅛
Each	16	.19	.21	.23	.25	27	.31	.38

40331 Price, per set of 15 bits....................$2.62
40332 Price, per set of 8 bits, 3/16, ¼, ⅜, ½, ⅝, ¾, ⅞, 1.................... 1.33

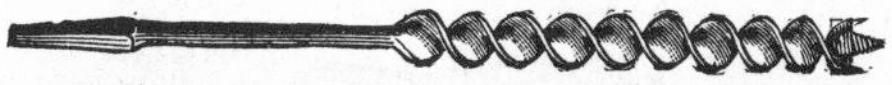

40333 Extra Cast Steel Auger Bits, double spur; Every bit fully warranted and any proving defective may be returned and perfect goods will be sent in place; you will make no mistake in buying this bit.

Sizes	3/16	¼	5/16	⅜	7/16	½	9/16	⅝	11/16
Price each	$0.10	.09	.09	.09	09	.10	.11	.12.	.13
Per doz	$0.95	.81	.81	.88	.98	.95	1.08	1.22	1.35

Sizes	¾	13/16	⅞	15/16	1	1⅛
Price, each	$0.14	$0.15	$0.17	$0.20	$0.21	$0.25
Price, per doz	1.49	1.62	1.76	1.96	2.16	2.70

40333½ We put this bit up in sets of 32½ qrs. (13 bits) in nice wooden box. Price, per set...$1.80

AUGER BITS IN CANVAS ROLLS.

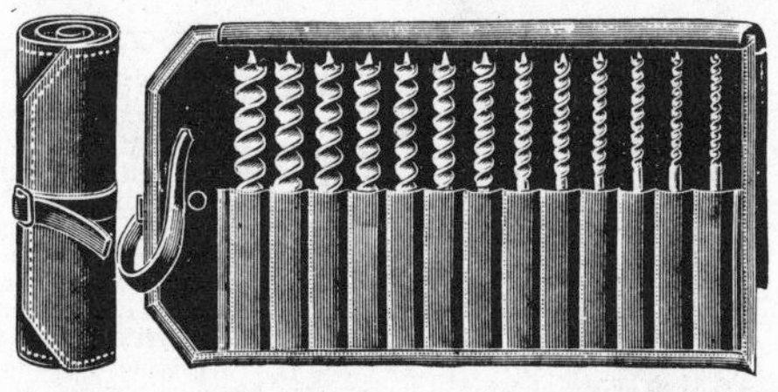

A very convenient methodof keeping bits safe from injury, and a handy way for the mechanic to convey them wherever needed. The case is made of dark colored canvas, nicely lined with canton flannel, having a receptacle for each bit. Shank and points protected by extra canvas. The case rolled up with bits complete, measures 3x11 inches. We positively cannot sell the case without the bits.

40334 With Jennings' patent extension lip bit, 1 set of 13 bits (32½ qrs.) 1 each 4/16 to 16/16 inclusive. Price, complete with case as shown in cut......$3.95
40335 With 40330 Bits. One set of 13 bits (32½ grs.), with case.................... 2.80

Russell Jennings' Auger Bits.

40337 Genuine Russell Jennings' Auger Bits.

Sizes	¼	5/16	⅜	7/16	½	9/16	⅝
Each	19	.22	.25	.28	.30	.33	.35
Sizes	11/16	¾	13/16	⅞	15/16	1 in
Each	.40	.42	.45	.50	.55	.58

40338 Russell Jennings' bits, sets of 7, viz; ¼, ⅜, ½, ⅝, ¾, ⅞, 1 in., complete.............. $2.75
40339 Russell Jennings' Bits, full sets of 13, one each of every size. Packed in a patent three-section box 4.69

Perfection Auger Bit.

40340 A strictly first-class Auger Bit, same pattern as the genuine Russell Jennings' auger bits. We guarantee this bit in every particular, and that it will bore equal to the very best bit made.

Size	4/16	5/16	6/16	7/16	8/16	9/16	10/16	11/16
Each	$0.10	$0.12	$0.13	$0.14	$0.16	$0.18	$0.20	$0.22
Per doz	1.08	1.23	1.37	1.59	1.73	1.96	2.00	2.20

Size	11/16	13/16	14/16	15/16	16/16	18/16	20/16
Each	$0.23	$0.24	$0.25	$0.28	$0.30	$0.38	$0.40
Per dozen.	2.38	2.60	2.81	3.03	3.24	3.68	4.10

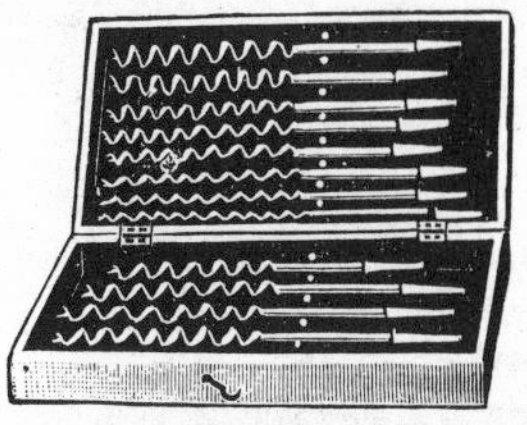

40344 C. E. Jennings' Extra Quality Double Spur Auger Bits, in set , put up in handsome wood boxes with rack to hold each bit in place. This is a great convenience, as the bits can be put away immediately after using. These boxes alone are worth 50 cents.
The set consists of 13 bits of the following sizes: ¼, 5/16, ⅜, 7/16, ½, 9/16, ⅝, 11/16, ¾, 13/16, ⅞, 15/16 and 1 in.
Price, per set.............................$ 2.65

40345 The Perfection Bit Set, Russell Jennings' pattern, not made by Russell Jennings, but same pattern and considered just as good. Every bit fully warranted and any proving defective may be returned and perfect goods will be sent in their place. Same number and same size as No. 40344 set, in nice wood box. Per set.......$3.00

Cook's Patent Auger Bits.

40346 Cook's Genuine Patent Auger Bits, single twist from ¼ to 7/16; double twist from ½ to 1 in.

Sizes	4/16	5/16	⅜	7/16	½
Price, each	$0.16	$0.17	$0.18	$0.20	$0.22
Sizes	9/16	⅝	11/16	¾	13/16
Price, each	$0.24	$0.27	$0.29	$0.32	$0.35
Sizes	⅞	15/16	1		
Prices, each	$0.40	$0.40	$0.43		

40347 Per set of 13 Cook's Bits, without box...$3.54

Handy Set.

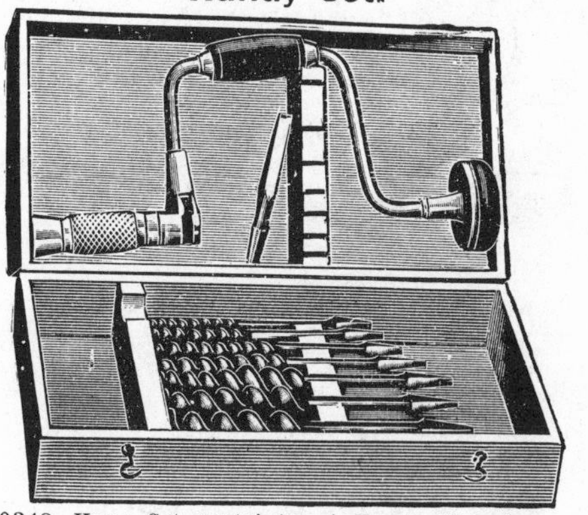

40348 Home Set, containing 1 Fray's 10-inch nickel plated ball-bearing brace, 1 first quality auger bit of each of the following sizes: ¼, ⅜, ½, ⅝, ¾, ⅞, 1 inch, also 1 brace screw driver bit, put up in a nice wood box like cut.
Price, complete, per set.......................$2.60

Ship Auger.

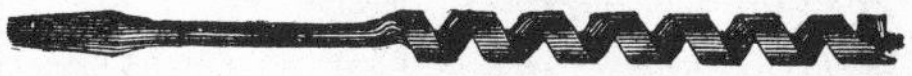

40349 D'Hommedieu Ship Auger Bits, 5 to 6 in twist

Sizes	4/8 and under.			9/16	⅝
Price, each	$0.43			$0.54	$0.54
Sizes	11/16	¾	13/16	⅞	15/16
Price, each	$0.65	$0.65	$0.75	$0.75	$0.85
Sizes	1	17/16	18/16	19/16	1¼
Price, each	$0.85	$0.97	$0.97	$1.08	$1.08

40350 Price, per set, of 32½ quarters, 1 each from 4 to 16-15ths (13 bits), Price, per set....$8.00

Expansive Bits.

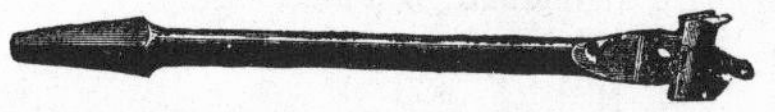

Clark's "Pattern" Expansive Bit. It is made of steel and warranted; complete in three pieces. The spring cap formed by a cut separating, but detaching the face of the stock, secures important advantages. The shank is graduated for depth.

40352 Cuts from ½-inch to 1½-inch; weight, 7 ounces. Each.................................$1.00
40352½ Cuts from ⅞-inch to 3-inch weight, 12 ounces. Each.................................. 1.35

Expansive Bits have two cutters and can be made to cut any size between the sizes mentioned above by loosening the screw and sliding the bit in or out.

40353 EXTRA CUTTERS FOR BITS No. 40352, The No 1 and 2 are for bit 40352. The No. 3 and 4 are for bit 40352½.

No. 1 cuts from ½ to ⅞-inch. Each.............. .18
No. 2 cuts from ⅞ to 1½-inch. Each.............. .23
No. 3 cuts from ⅞ to 1¾-inch. Each.............. .32
No. 4 cuts from 1¾ to 3-inch. Each.............. .36

Our line of Carpenters' and Mechanics' Tools are all of superior quality; the best obtainable at the price.

Steers' Patent Expansive Bit.

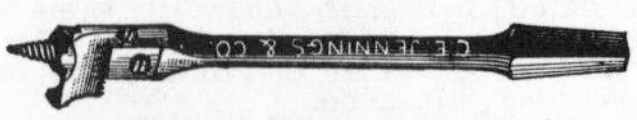

This bit is dropped-forged from selected cast steel, and is finished in a most thorough manner. The cutter is adjusted by means of a micrometer screw, which holds the cutter firmly, preventing any possibility of slipping or creeping.

40354½ No. 1, with 2 cutters, will cut any size from ⅞ to 3 inches. Price, each................$1.45

40355 No. 2, with 2 cutters, will cut any size from ⅝ to 1¾ inches. Price, each............ 1.00

40355½ Extra Cutters for Steers' Expansive Bits. The Nos. 1 and 2 are for the No. 2 bit; the Nos. 3, 4, 5 are for the No. 1 bit.

No. 1 cutter, cutting from ⅝ to 1⅛ in. Each..$0.18
No. 2 cutter, cutting from 1⅛ to 1¾ in. Each.. .23
No. 3 cutter, cutting from ⅞ to 1⅝ in. Each.. .32
No. 4 cutter, cutting from 1⅝ to 3 in. Each .36
No. 5 cutter, cutting from 3 to 4 in. Each.. .75

Center Bits.

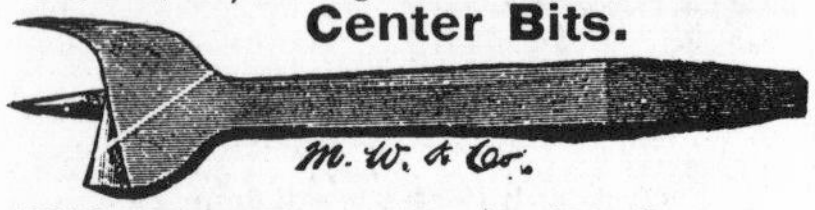

40356 Center Bits, cast steel, polished.

Sizes...	⅜	½	⅝	¾	⅞	1	1¼	1½	1¾	2
Each..	5c.	5c.	5c.	5c.	5c.	6c.	8c.	10c.	15c.	19c.

Price, per set, 10 center bits.........................$0.80

Gimlet Bit.

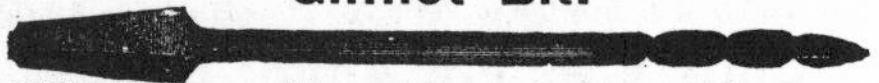

40357 Extra quality cast steel, double cut bits. State size wanted.

Sizes............	0	1	2	3	4	5	6
Price, each......	3c.	3c.	3c.	3c.	3c.	3c.	3c.

40358 Price, per set of 7 bits, one of each size....$0.20

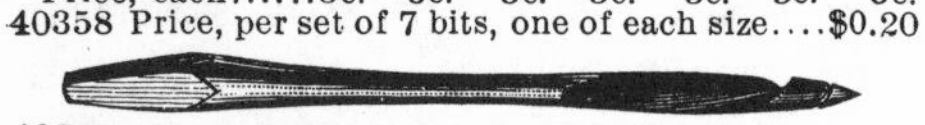

40359 German Gimlet Bits, extra quality.

Sizes...	2/32	3/32	4/32	5/32	6/37	7/32	8/32	10/32
Price, each..	6c.	6c.	6c.	6c.	6c.	6c.	6c.	7c.
Price, doz.	60c.	60c.	60c.	60c.	60c.	60c.	60c.	70c.

40360 Price, per set of 7 bits, one of each size..$0.38
German Gimlet Bits, up to No. 4, weigh 4 ounces; from No. 5 to 8, 5 ounces; a set weighs 10 ounces. Sizes on German bits are given in 32ds of an inch.

The Forstner Bit.

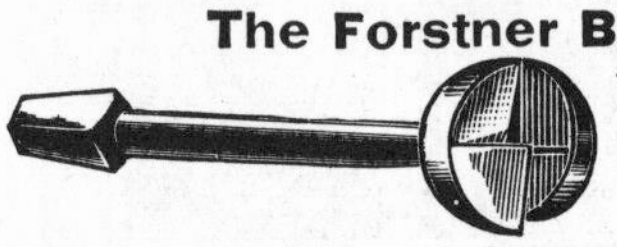

40362 The Forstner Brace Bit, for smooth round, oval or square boring scroll, and twist work.

Unlike other bits, it is guided by its periphery instead of its center. It will bore any arc or circle and can be guided in any direction regardless of grain or knots. Send for circular showing cuts of the work it will do and directions how to operate.

Sizes.......	⅜	7/16	4/8	9/16	⅝	11/16	6/8
Price, each.	40c.	50c.	50c.	62c.	62c.	70c.	72c.
Sizes	13/16	⅞	15/16	8/8	9/8	10/8	11/8
Price, each.	80c.	83c.	90c.	95c.	$1.00	$1.04	$1.22

Ship Augur Pattern Car Bits.

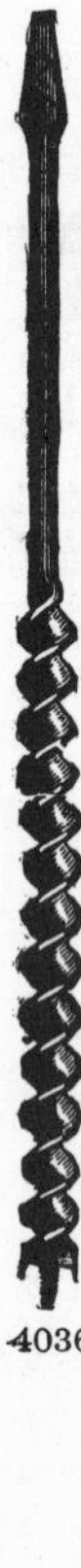

40364 Ship Augur Pattern Car Bits, 12-inch twist designed especially for hard wood and rough boring, are very strong; designed for car, boat and bridge building. Same pattern as No. 40349.

Sizes	5-16	⅜	7-16	½
Price, each....	60c.	65c.	68c.	72c.
Sizes	9-16	⅝	11-16	¾
Price, each....	75c.	80c.	83c.	86c.
Sizes...........	3/16	⅞	15/16	1
Price, each ...	90c.	93c.	95c.	$1.25
Sizes	16/17	1⅛	19/16	1¼
Price, each...	$1.10	$1.15	$1.22	$1.25

40365 Price per set 16 ship auger pattern car bits, 12-inch twist, 1 each of the above size. Weight, 16 pounds.........................$13.37

Car Bits.

TWELVE INCH TWIST.

40367 C. E. Jennings' Double Spur Pattern Car Bits, 12-inch twist. These are not the poor, cheap articles sold ordinarily by retail dealers, but are extra quality, high grade, good tools.

Sizes,	¼	5/61	⅜	7/61	½	7/16	⅝	11/16
Each,	26c.	26c.	30c.	36c.	41c.	46c.	51c.	52c.
Sizes,	¾	13/16	⅞	15/16	1	17/16		18/16
Each,	62c.	66c.	71c.	75c.	82c.	96c.		$1.08

40368 Price per set of 15 C. E. Jennings' car bits.......................................7.80

Angular Boring Attachment.

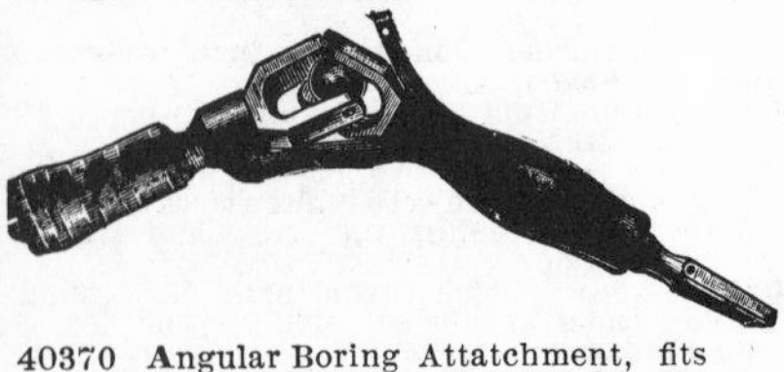

40370 Angular Boring Attachment, fits any brace, nickel plated. Weight, 4½ pounds Each..................................$1.20

40367

Bit Gauge.

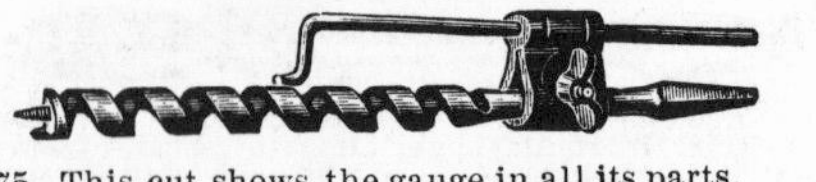

40375 This cut shows the gauge in all its parts. It will be seen that one bolt with thumb screw tightens the clamps on the gauge spindle and auger bit at the same time. It will fit any size bit and exactly gauge the depth of hole to be bored. Price, each, no bit.......................$0.25

Extra Quality Warranted Boring Machine Augers

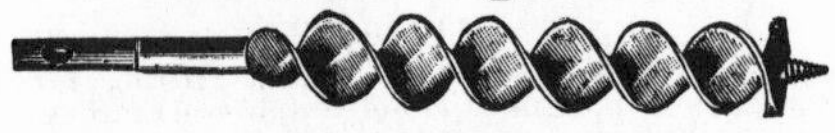

40376 Sizes......	1	1¼	1½	2
Prices, each........	$0.30	$0.35	$0.40	$0.60

Carpenter's Augers.

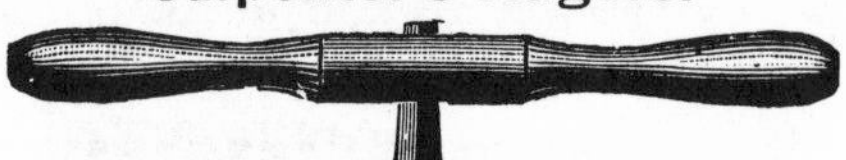

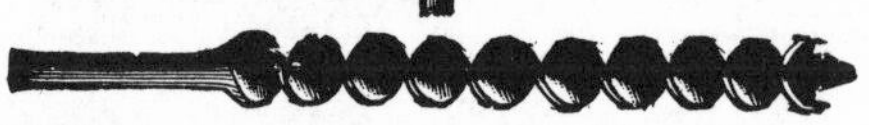

40377 Augers, solid cast steel, full polished shrauk brass nut, price includes handle. These augers are not a cheap grade, but warranted to be first-class tools.

Size..................	⅝ in.	¾ in,	⅞ in.	1 in.
Each..................	$0.18	$0.20	$0.25	$0.28

Size..	1¼ in.	1½ in.	1¾ in.	2 in.	2¼ in.	2½ in
Each..	$0.30	$0.35	$0.45	$0.50	$0.60	$1.00

Adjustable Auger Handles.

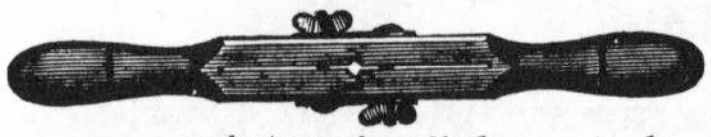

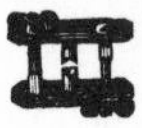

40379 Will fit any size auger; very convenient as but one handle is required to a full set of augers. No carpenter's tool chest is complete without one. Weight, about one pound Price, each.....$0.18 Per dozen.....$1.85

Auger Handles.

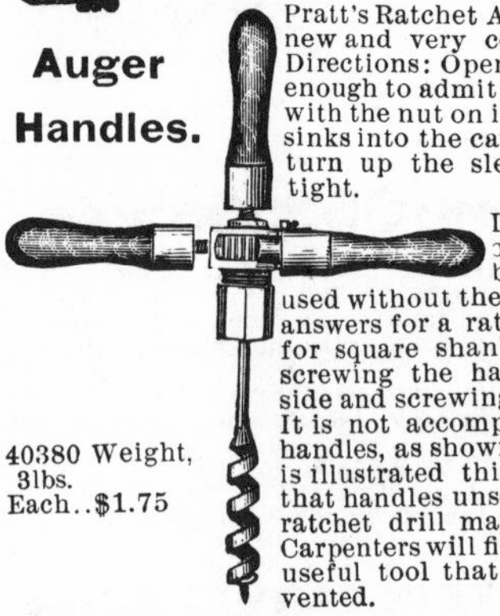

Pratt's Ratchet Auger Handle, a new and very convenient tool. Directions: Open the chuck wide enough to admit the auger shank with the nut on it; when the nut sinks into the cavity of the jaws, turn up the sleeves until it is tight.

It ratchets with one handle or both, or may be used without the ratchet; it also answers for a ratchet drill stock for square shank drills, by unscrewing the handle from one side and screwing it into the top. It is not accompanied by three handles, as shown in the cut, but is illustrated this way to show that handles unscrew and how a ratchet drill may be made of it. Carpenters will find this the most useful tool that has yet been invented.

40380 Weight, 3lbs. Each..$1.75

Angular Boring Machines.

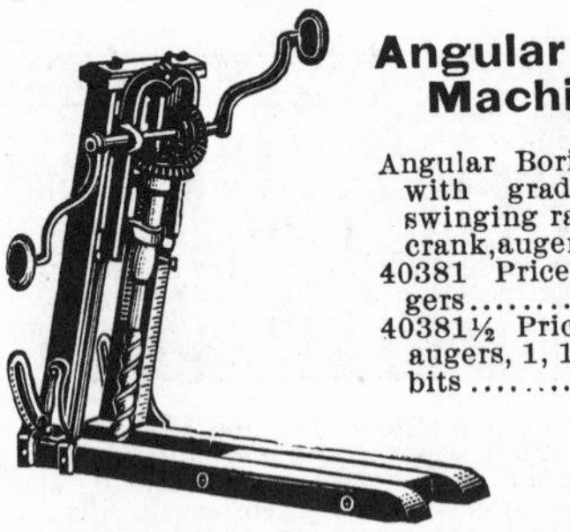

Angular Boring Machines, with graduated ways, swinging rack, malleable crank, augers and pointer.

40381 Price, without augers.................$3.00

40381½ Price, with set of augers, 1, 1½ and 2 inch bits.......................$4.25

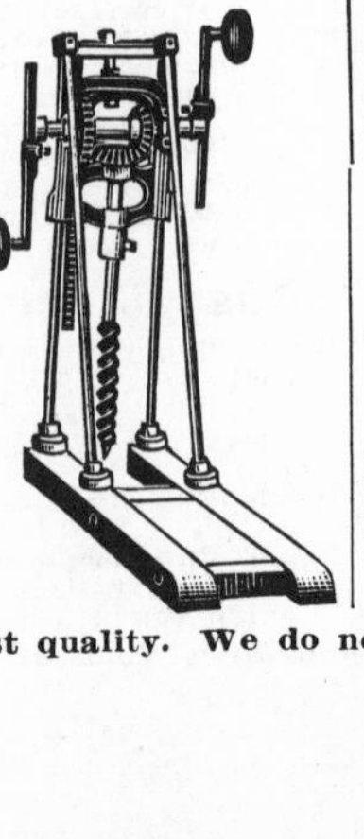

The Millers Falls Boring Machines. This machine has been fully perfected in all its parts and is now sold with full warrant that it will do better work and give better satisfaction than any other kind in use; the frame is made of one-half inch round steel rods; the braces are the same as attached to the rods at the top by a set-screw; when this set-screw is loosened the frame falls over so as to bore at any desired angle. Weight, 42½ lbs.

40382 Price, each, without augers................ $6.50

40382½ With 1, 1½, 2-in augers 7.75

Patent Adjustable Hollow Augesr.

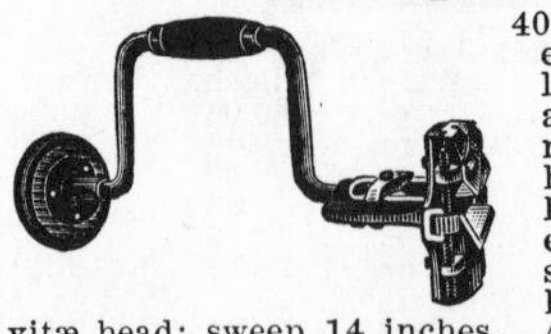

40383 Goodell's Patent Adjustable Hollow Auger. This auger is an improvement on anything hitherto in use, as it has fitted to it a nickel plated bit brace sweep, with rosewood handle and lignum vitæ head; sweep, 14 inches. As the brace sweep is fitted to it, it will always work true, which is not the case when the ordinary kind is used in an ordinary bit brace; besides, it often happens that the bit brace on hand is not large enough to drive a spoke auger. The auger is adjustable to cut from ¼ to 1¼ inch. Price, each, complete with sweep $3.42

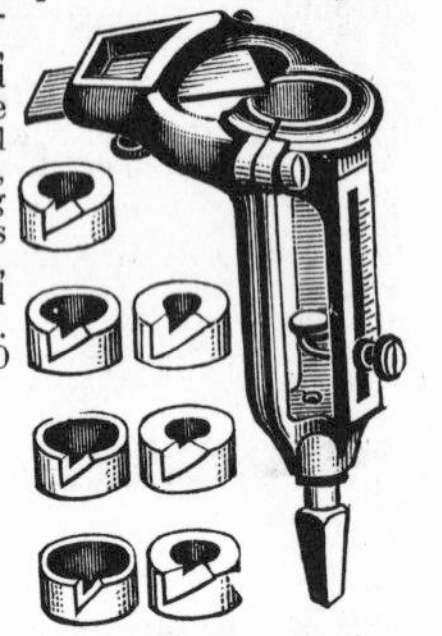

40384 Stearn's Patent Adjustable Hollow Auger, made of malleable iron, and nicely finished. The knife is made of the best tool steel, has adjustable stop, with scale for regulating length of tenon. It cuts eight sizes, as follows: ⅜, 7/16, ½, 9/16, ⅝, ¾, ⅞ and 1 inch. Weight, 1 lb. 9 oz. No. 1, complete $3.00

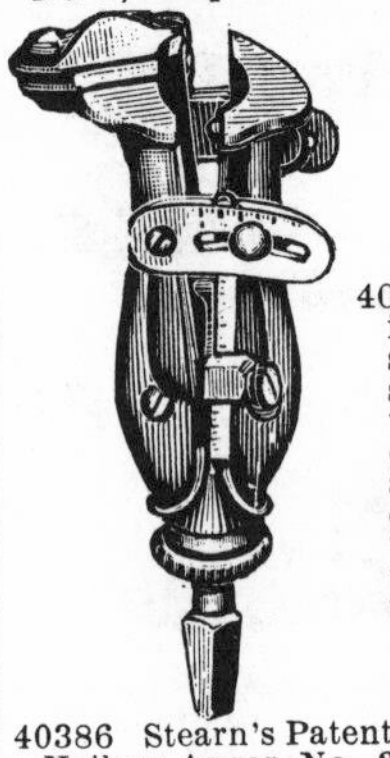

40385 Made entirely of malleable iron and steel; has adjustable stop and scale with rulings to sixteenths for length, also graduated strap to indicate the diameter of tenon. The jaws or sides are pivoted and are opened and closed by means of a conical nut upon the shank. Cuts any sized tenons, ⅜ to 1 inch and 3 inches in length. Price, each....$3.00

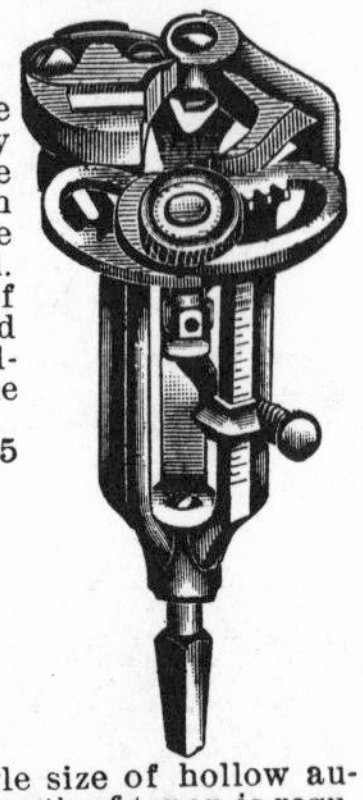

40386 Stearn's Patent Adjustable Hollow Auger, No. 3; cuts any size tenon from ¼ to 1¼. The pivoted jaws are provided with a graduated scale by which the size of the tenon is regulated. To secure required length of tenon, a movable stop is operated upon a graduated scale with rulings to sixteenths. This is the finest tool of the kind made. Each..........................$3.75

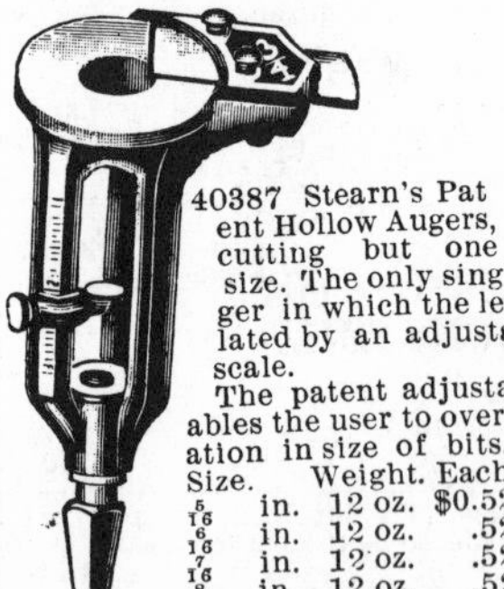

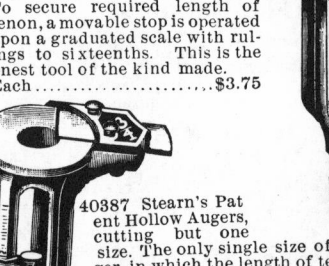

40387 Stearn's Patent Hollow Augers, cutting but one size. The only single size of hollow auger in which the length of tenon is regulated by an adjustable stop and graded scale.

The patent adjustable cap and knife enables the user to overcome any slight variation in size of bits. (No bit furnished.)

Size.	Weight.	Each.	Size.	Weight.	Each.
5/16 in.	12 oz.	$0.52	¾ in.	18 oz.	$0.58
6/16 in.	12 oz.	.52	⅞ in.	18 oz.	.84
7/16 in.	12 oz.	.52	1 in.	18 oz.	.84
8/61 in.	12 oz.	.52	1⅛ in.	23 oz.	.90
9/16 in.	12 oz.	.58	1¼ in.	23 oz.	.90
10/16 in.	15 oz.	.58	1¾ in.	23 oz.	1.00
			1½ in.	32 oz.	1.00

Spoke Pointers.

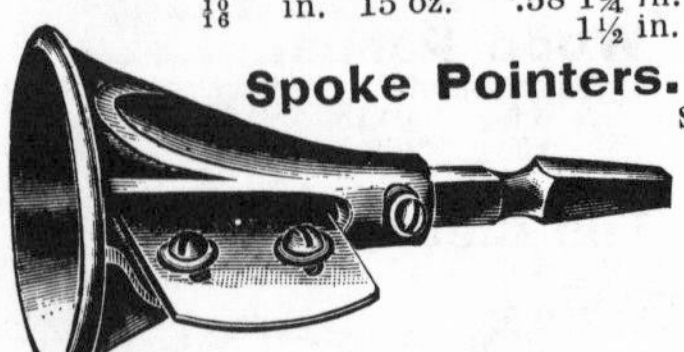

Stearn's Patent Spoke Pointer with graduated adjustable shank. Points 1⅞ inches in diameter.

40388 No. 1, weight, 12 oz. Each..............$0.58

40388½ No. 2, weight, 18 oz. (large). Each.... .97

Drills.

Drills and bits weigh from 5 to 9 ounces, according to size.

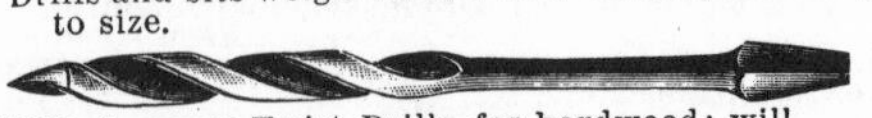

40390 Syracuse Twist Drills, for hardwood; will cut through a nail in boring without injuring. The bits are tempered so they will bore iron and stone equally as well as wood.

Sizes....................	⅛	5/32	3/16	7/32	¼	9/32	5/16	11/32
Each, in cents........	10	11	12	15	18	21	22	24

Sizes....................	⅜	13/32	7/16	15/32	½
Each, in cents........	25	27	28	29	30

Price Per Set 13 Drills, 1 each of the above size..................................$2.58

You can feel sure that our tools are of the best quality. We do not handle trash.

Drills—Continued.

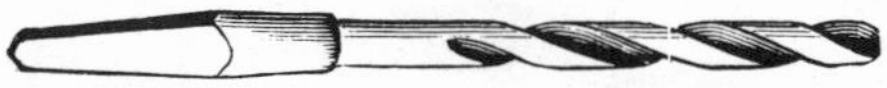

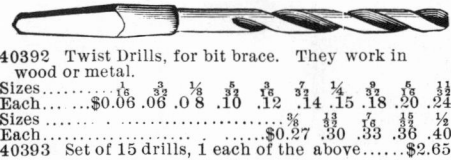

40392 Twist Drills, for bit brace. They work in wood or metal.

Sizes	1/16	3/32	1/8	5/32	3/16	7/32	1/4	9/32	5/16	11/32
Each	$0.06	.06	.0 8	.10	.12	.14	.15	.18	.20	.24

Sizes	3/8	13/32	7/16	15/32	1/2
Each	$0.27	.30	.33	.36	.40

40393 Set of 15 drills, 1 each of the above......$2.65

ROUND SHANK DRILLS.

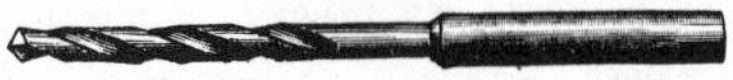

40395 Twist Drill, round shank, for drill machine for wood or metal; shank ½ inch in diameter, 2½ inches long.

Sizes	1/8	5/32	3/16	7/32	1/4	9/32	5/16	11/32	3/8	13/32
Each	$0.21	.22	.23	.25	.27	.30	.32	.34	.35	.37

Sizes	7/16	15/32	1/2	17/32	9/16	19/32	5/8	21/32
Each	$0.38	41	42	44	46	48	50	52

Sizes	11/16	23/32	3/4	25/32	13/16	27/32
Each	$0.53	54	.57	.60	.65	.70

Sizes	7/8	29/32	15/16	31/32	1 inch.
Each	$0.73	.75	.80	.85	.90

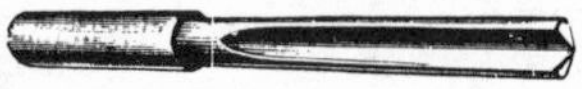

40396 Straight Fluted Drills, for drill machines, ½ inch round shank; the best drill made for blacksmiths' and brass workers' use; no blacksmith should be without a set of these drills; made of the finest steel.

Diameter.	Length.	Price, each.
1/8 inch.	4⅞ inch.	$0.25
5/32 inch.	4⅞ inch.	.25
3/16 inch.	5⅝ inch.	.25
7/32 inch.	5⅝ inch.	.28
1/4 inch.	6 inch.	.30
9/32 inch.	6 inch.	.33
5/16 inch.	6 inch.	.35
11/32 inch.	6 inch.	.38
3/8 inch.	6 inch.	.40
13/32 inch.	6 inch.	.41
7/16 inch.	6 lnch.	.42
15/32 inch.	6 inch.	.43
1/2 inch.	6 inch.	.44
17/32 inch.	6 inch.	.45
9/16 inch.	6 inch.	.46
19/32 inch.	6 inch.	.48
5/8 inch.	6 inch.	.55
21/32 inch.	6 inch.	.58
11/16 inch.	6 inch.	.59
23/32 inch.	6 inch.	.60
3/4 inch.	6 inch.	.63
25/32 inch.	6 ihch.	.65
13/16 inch.	6 inch.	.68
27/32 inch.	6 inch.	.70
7/8 inch.	6 inch.	.73
29/32 inch.	6 inch.	.75
15/16 inch.	6 inch.	.80
31/32 inch.	6 inch.	.85
1 inch.	6 inch.	.90

The above drills have shanks 2¼ inches long and ½ inch diameter.

Increase Twist Drills for machinists' use. We guarantee our drills to be equal in quality and workmanship with the best made in the world.

Jobbers' Drills.

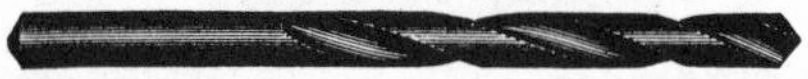

40397--

JOBBERS' AND MACHINISTS' SETS.

Diameter.	Length.	Price, per Dozen.	Price, each.
1/16	2½	$0.50	$0.05
5/64	2⅝	.55	.06
3/32	2¾	.60	.06
7/64	2⅞	.65	.07
1/8	3	.73	.08
9/64	3⅛	.80	.09
5/32	3¼	.90	.10
11/64	3⅜	1.00	.11
3/16	3½	1.10	.12
13/64	3⅝	1.20	.13
7/32	3¾	1.33	.15
15/64	3⅞	1.45	.16
1/4	4	1.58	.18
17/64	4⅛	1.70	.19
9/32	4¼	1.83	.20
19/64	4⅜	1.95	21
5/16	4½	2.10	.22
21/64	4⅝	2 25	.23
11/32	4¾	2.40	.25
23/64	4⅞	2.55	.27
3/8	5	2.70	.28
25/64	5⅛	2.85	.30
13/32	5¼	3.00	.32
27/64	5⅜	3.20	.34
7/16	5½	3.40	.36
29/64	5⅝	3.60	.40
15/32	5¾	3.75	.42
31/64	5⅞	3.88	.44
1/2	6	4.00	.45

INSURE MAIL PACKAGES.

See page 1.

Taper Square Shank Drills Fitting Rackets.

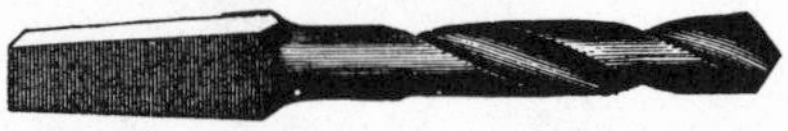

40400

Price with shanks ⅝ inch by ⅜ inch and 1½ inches long, and shanks ¾ inch by ½ inch and 1¾ inches long.

Diameter.	Length.	Price, each.
1/4 inch.	5 inch.	$0.65
9/32 inch.	5 inch.	.68
5/16 inch.	5 inch.	.75
11/32 inch.	5 inch.	.78
3/8 inch.	6 inch.	.80
13/32 inch.	6¼ inch.	.83
7/16 inch.	6¼ inch.	.83
15/32 inch.	6¼ inch.	.83
1/2 inch.	6½ inch.	.87
9/16 inch.	6½ inch.	.90
5/8 inch.	6½ inch.	.95
11/16 inch.	6½ inch.	.97
3/4 inch.	6½ inch.	1.00
13/16 inch.	7 inch	1.17
7/8 inch.	7½ inch.	1.37
15/16 inch.	8 inch.	1.53
1 inch.	8½ inch.	1.70
1⅛ inch.	9 inch.	2.10

Improved Drill Chuck.

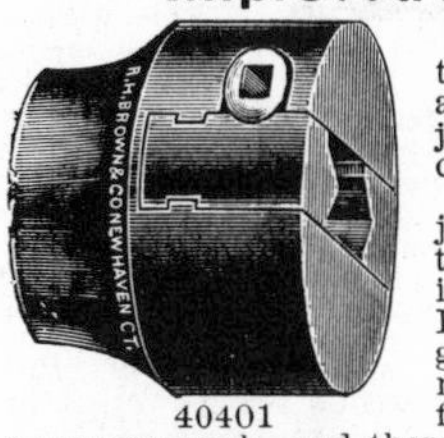

40401

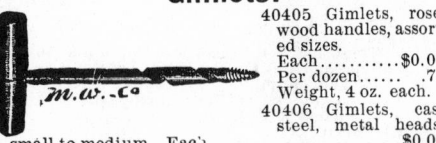

This Chuck has no projections. The jaws and screws are all within the body. The jaws are of the best tool steel, carefully hardened.

A guard ring prevents the jaws from being opened so as to take in larger work than is designed for the chuck. It is very powerful, and is guaranteed to hold true and not to injure or shear the finest drill. It holds round or square work, and there is no chuck equal to it for holding wood-boring tools.

The jaws are guided by three strong gibs, which prevent their canting when taking a short bit.

PRICES OF LITTLE GIANT IMPROVED.

Number.	Holding Drills.	Price, each.
0	0 to ½ inch	$4.00
1	0 to ¾ inch	5.00
2	0 to 1 inch.	6.50

Machinists' Hand Tap.

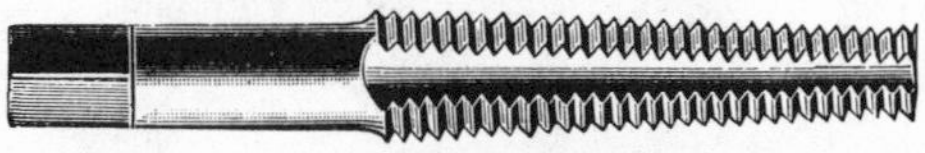

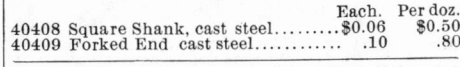

Taper Tap.

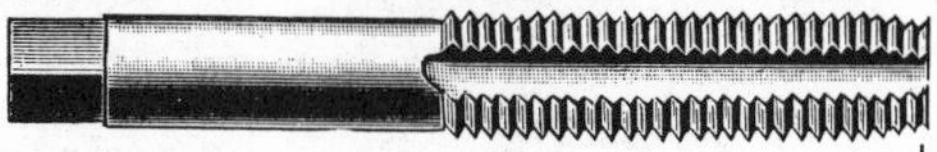

Plug Tap.

40404 Made standard sizes with standard V thread; right hand.

Diameter.	Number of Threads to the inch.	Price, each.
1/4	16, 18 and 20	$0.22
5/16	16 " 18	.23
3/8	14, 16 " 18	.25
7/16	14 " 16	.26
1/2	12, 13 " 14	.32
5/8	10, 11 " 12	.42
3/4	10 " 12	.55
7/8	9 " 10	.76
1	8 " 10	.95

Gimlets.

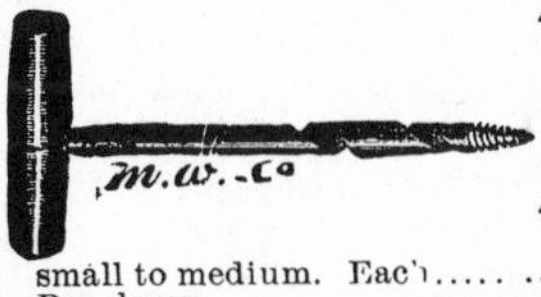

40405 Gimlets, rosewood handles, assorted sizes.
Each..........$0.07
Per dozen...... .78
Weight, 4 oz. each.

40406 Gimlets, cast steel, metal heads, small to medium. Each..... ....$0.02
Per dozen.. .17

Screw Driver Bits.

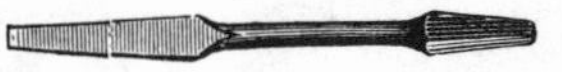

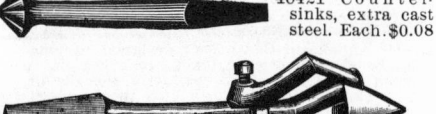

		Each.	Per doz.
40408	Square Shank, cast steel.........	$0.06	$0.50
40409	Forked End cast steel............	.10	.80

* * * * * * * * *

IT WILL BE A FAVOR TO US (and perhaps to your friends) if you will place, where they will do the most good, any duplicate catalogues or advertising matter received from us.

Reamers.

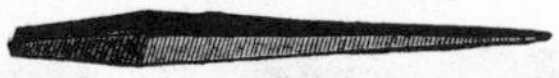

		Each.	Per doz.
40413	Reamers, square, extra cast steel....................................	$0.09	$1.00
40414	Reamers, octagon, extra cast steel	.12	1.25

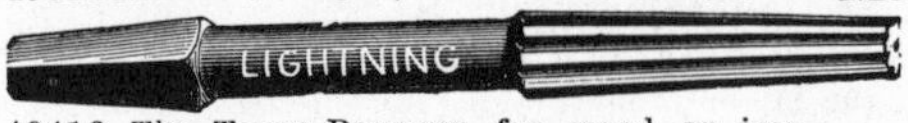

40416 The Taper Reamers for wood or iron. These reamers are made of the finest steel and will make true, smooth holes for bit braces.

Sizes,	1/4	5-16	3/8	7-16	1/2	9-16	5/8	11-16	3/4
Each.	27c.	30c.	33c.	36c.	42c.	48c.	54c.	64c.	72c

Countersinks.

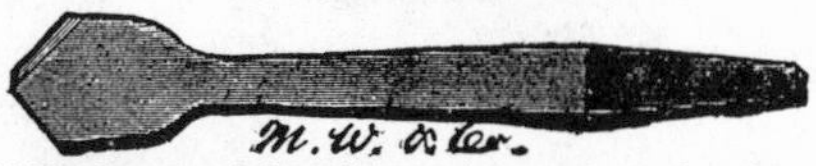

40420 Countersinks, flat, extra cast steel, polished, for metal. Each.............................$0.08

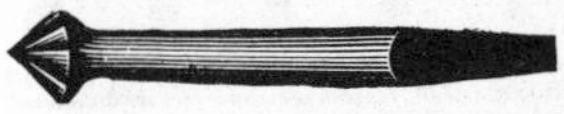

40421 Countersinks, extra cast steel. Each.$0.08

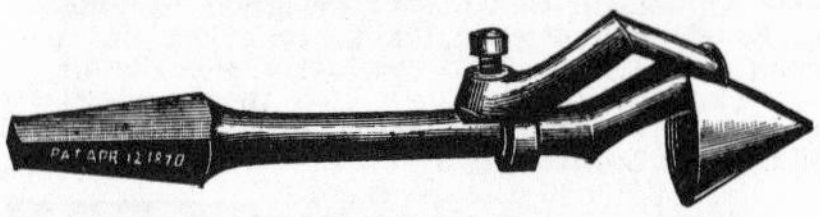

40425 Wheeler Countersink, for wood, with gauge.$0.23

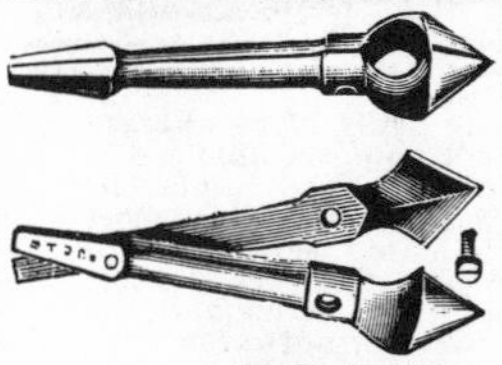

40426 Clark's Patent Double-cut Countersink; makes the smoothest work of anything sold; can be kept as sharp as a plane; cuts show it closed for service and open for sharpening. Weight, 5 ounces. Each............$0.25

Prick Punches.

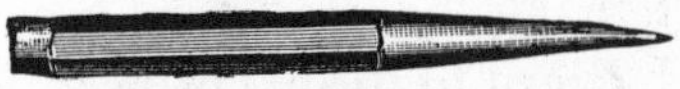

40430 Prick Punches, made of ⅜ octagon steel; weight, 5 ounces. Price, each..................$0.07

Whitney Geared Hand Drill.

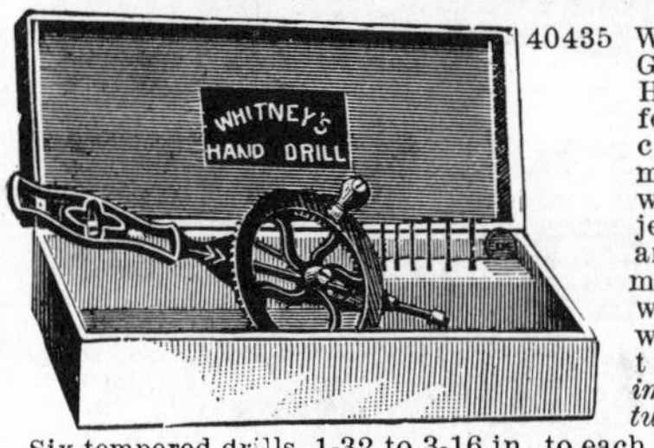

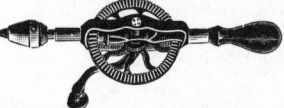

40435 Whitney's Geared Hand Drill for machinists, metal workers, jewelers, and ornametal wood workers with new tempered *improved twist drills.* Six tempered drills, 1-32 to 3-16 in. to each set. Each set packed in a hardwood box, with brass hinges and catch; weight, 1¼ lbs. Each........$0.75

40436 Extra Drills, per set of 6 drills........ .... .12

Hand Drills.

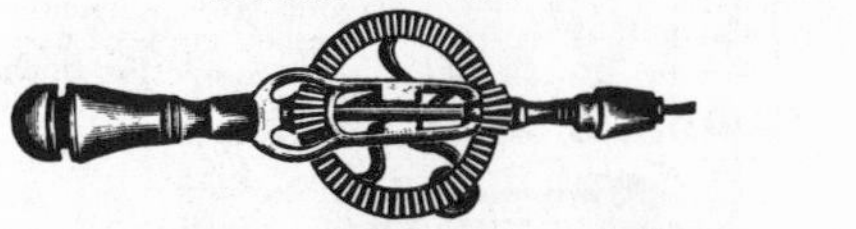

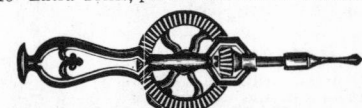

40437 The No. 1 Hand Drill, single gear, hollow, handle jaws, made of forged steel; complete, with six drill points. Each.....................$1.10

40438 Extra drill, per set.............................. .25

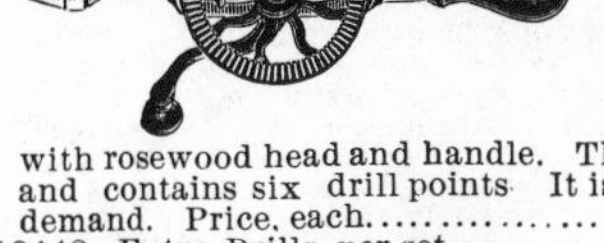

40439 The No. 2 Hand Drill. The chuck of the drill stock is the same as No. 1. It has cut gears, is heavily nickel plated, with rosewood head and handle. The head is hollow and contains six drill points. It is a tool much in demand. Price, each.............................$2.20

40440 Extra Drills, per set............................ .25

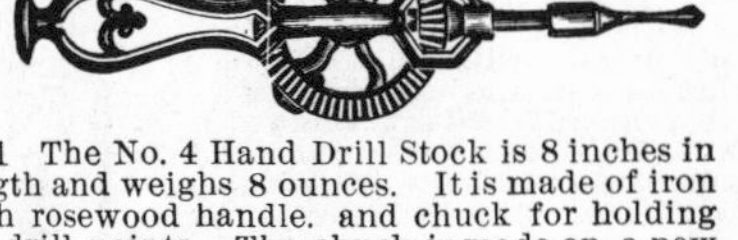

40441 The No. 4 Hand Drill Stock is 8 inches in length and weighs 8 ounces. It is made of iron with rosewood handle, and chuck for holding the drill points. The chuck is made on a new plan, and it centers and holds the drill perfectly. With each drill stock we send a box containing six superior drill points of various sizes. Price, each.......................................$0.45

40442 Extra Drills, per set.............................. .25

Lightning Brace.

Lightning Brace, nickel plated. lignum vitæ and rosewood trimmings, is especially designed for light boring and screw driving; it may be used running the bit back and forward or turn the bit only one way, as it is necessary; the movements are regulated by the head; very rapid in its work; strong and durable.

40445 Like cut.....................................$1.40
40446 Small size, principle same as 40445...... 1.15

Automatic Hand Drills

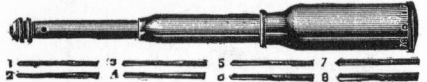

40450 Automatic Hand Drill, designed for boring wood, for setting brads, finishing nails, screws, etc. Eight bits or drills, the size of which are indicated by the dots in the above cut, accompanying each tool. Price, each......$1.00
40451 Extra Points, 8 cents each.

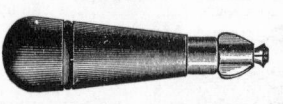

40452 Goodell's Automatic Drills, made of brass, nickel plated, with 8 drill points complete. The drill points are all contained in the handle. The exact location of each is designated by a number on the outside of handle. To remove the drill press slightly upon the pin which fills the hole from which the drill points are taken out; the cap can be taken backwards or forwards until the hole is opposite the desired number, when the point can readily be removed.
Price, each, complete....................... $1.30
40453 Extra Points, 8 cents each.

Combination Tools.

40457 The handle is cocobolo, a handsome hardwood, resembling rosewood. The tools consist of a chisel, gouge, screw driver, tack puller, gimlet, scratch awl and four brad awls, different sizes. All solid steel, hand forged, of good size; the most practicable and serviceable tool of its kind offered; weight, 9 ounces. Each........$0.40
40458 The handle is cocobolo, and extra large. The tools are all contained in the receptacle in the handle and are warranted the highest grade of cast steel. It has superior thumb nut and grip nickel-plated. Price, each...........$0.85

Crispin's Awls.

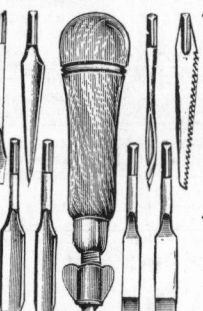

40459 This is a tool for everybody. It is a hollow handle made of hardwood, 5 inches long and weighing 3 ounces. It contains inside, on a spool, 50 feet of best waxed linen shoe thread. The spool is also hollow and contains 3 awls and 3 needles of various shapes and sizes. The thread fits the needles and the awls fit the handle, and are held by a set screw, as seen in the cut. It is for use in the house, stable, field, camp, or on the road, for making immediate repairs, where one use of it will be worth more than its whole cost. Weight, 6 ounces. Each $0.18

Breast Drill.

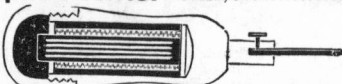

40460 Breast Drill. This is a very powerful drill; the breast plate is 12 inches long, has very heavy cut gears speeded about two to one and double cranks which are adjustable to any length; the hole in the spindle which receives the drill is ½ inch in diameter; weight, 9½ pounds. See 40395 and 40396 for bits to fit this machine.
Price...........................$4.25

Breast Drills—Continued.

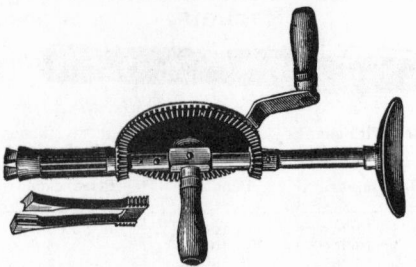

40461 **Geared Breast Drill.** *With Peck's Patent Adjustable Chuck.* Nickel plated with cut gears. Rosewood handles and adjustable steel jaws, which will hold equally well; round and square shank boring instruments in every size. Weight, 4 lbs. Price.....................$2.75

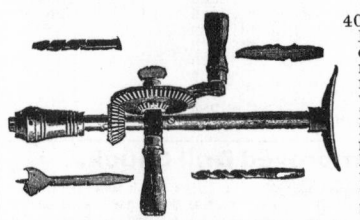

40462 Breast Drill. This drill is made of round wrought iron ⅝ of inch in diameter. The handles are rosewood, the head, malleable iron, and the chuck jaws of steel. It has a changeable gear, one even and the other speeded 3 to 1. The change from one to the other can be made in one second. The chuck will hold any shaped shank, round, square or flat, as seen in the cut. It has been improved lately with what is called second grip; after the nut has been screwed down on the bit, as tight as can be done by hand, grasp the nut firmly with the left hand and give the crank a turn from you; this forces the jaws upward, increasing the power of the grip. Weight, 4½ pounds.

☞ **These tools are not sold with the drill stock, but are illustrated simply to show the shape of the shank which the chuck will hold.**
Drill stock is heavily nickel plated and has cut gear. An extra set of steel jaws goes with each drill stock for holding small round drills. Price...........$2.50

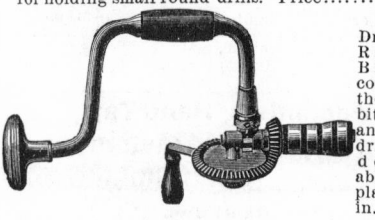

40463— Drill and Ratchet Brace, combining the regular bit brace and breast drill detachable, nickel plated. 10 in. sweep
Price.............................$2.30

Ratchet Bit Braces.

40465 First-class goods in every respect and fully guaranteed to be equal to the very best made; the sweep, pawls, jaws and ratchet are steel. Mahogany stained wood, head and handle; all metal parts are nickel-plated, blued jaws with cane ring to operate the pawls; will take any shape bit or tool shank. 8 inch. Each. $1 00
10 inch 1.10
12 inch 1.20
40466 *These Ratchet Bit Braces* are the same as No. 40465, except that they are plain polished, and not nickel plated; head and handle black enameled wood, with every part durable and reliable. 8 inch. Each............................ .75
10 inch .... .80
12 inch .... .85
40467 These Ratchet Braces are not unlike in appearance and finish to No. 40465, but the jaws and socket are not milled. It makes a most excellent brace for farmers to use; made only in 2 sizes. 8 inch sweep. Each .... .60
9-inch sweep.............................. .65
8-inch sweep, nickel plated................ .70
9-inch sweep, nickel plated. .... .75

Patent Corner Brace.

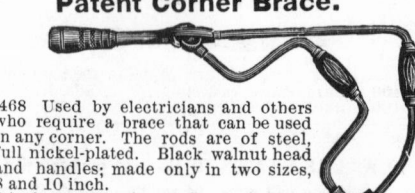

40468 Used by electricians and others who require a brace that can be used in any corner. The rods are of steel, full nickel-plated. Black walnut head and handles; made only in two sizes, 8 and 10 inch.
8-inch sweep, price, each........$2.25
10-inch sweep price, each........ 2.50

Bit Braces—Continued.

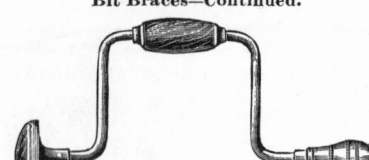

Patent Bit Braces, hardwood head and handle, patent bit fasteners. Each.
40470 10-inch sweep...... ....$0.30
40470½ 8-inch sweep............................ .25

Peck's Adjustable Rachet Brace.

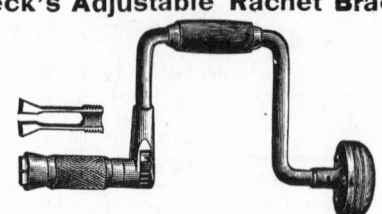

40471 Nickel plated, lignum vitae head, rosewood center. This is unquestionably the finest brace made; will hold either round or square shank bits. Mechanics who desire a handsome and durable brace should buy this one. Each.
8-inch sweep, nickel plated.....................$1.35
10-inch sweep, nickel plated..................... 1.47
12-inch sweep, nickel plated..................... 1.60

Improved Adjustable Ratchet Brace.

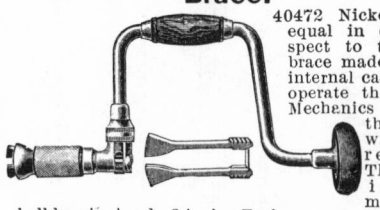

40472 Nickel plated, equal in every respect to the best brace made. It has internal cam ring to operate the pawls. Mechanics who buy this brace will never regret it. This brace is now made with ball bearing head. 8-inch. Each............ $1.20
10-inch. Each 1.30
12-inch. Each 1.45

Barber's Bit Braces.

Barber's Patent Brace, rolled steel sweep, rosewood handle, lignum vitae head; nickel plated. Each.
40473 14-inch sweep.............................$1.25
40474 Bit Brace, not so high priced as Barber's, but a very good brace. Same description as Barber's. 12-inch sweep..................... .80

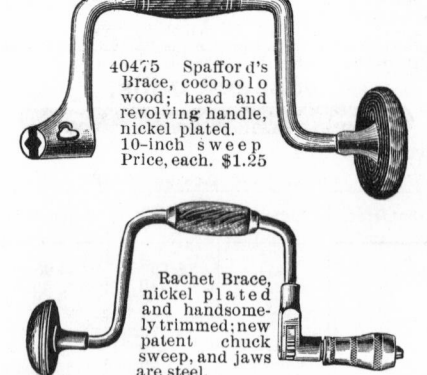

40475 Spafford's Brace, cocobolo wood; head and revolving handle, nickel plated. 10-inch sweep Price, each. $1.25

Rachet Brace, nickel plated and handsomely trimmed; new patent chuck sweep, and jaws are steel.
40476 10 in. sweep......................$0 65
40477 12 in. sweep...................... .75

Nail Sets.

Weight, about 4 ounces.
40480. Nail Set, solid cast steel, round, common. Each ....$0.04. Per dozen... .... $0.38

40481 Cannon's Diamond Point Nail Sets, made of the finest steel and pointed on nail end, which prevents slipping off nail head. Each, 8c. Per dozen..................... $0.87

40482 Hunter's Cup Point Nail Set; will set at any angle, and not split the head. Screws with worn or broken heads easily backed out with this set. Price....$0.06. Per dozen $0 56

We can now guarantee lowest prices on all leading makes of Guns, Rifles, Revolvers, Ammuntion, Etc.

Bench Screws.

Iron Bench Screws, wood handle, movable collar; entire length, 15 inches, double thread.

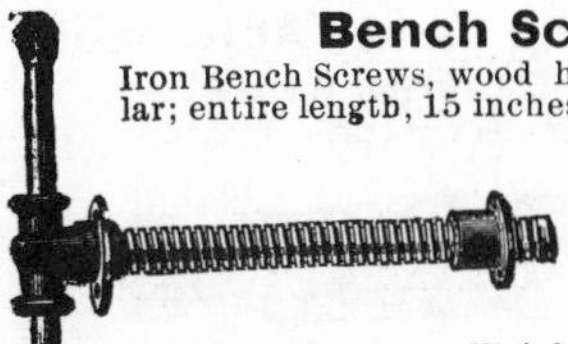

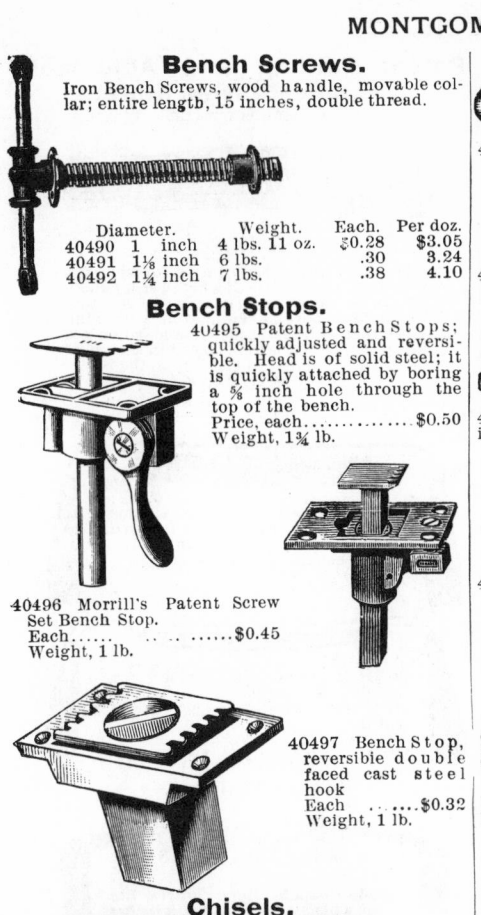

	Diameter.	Weight.	Each.	Per doz.
40490	1 inch	4 lbs. 11 oz.	$0.28	$3.05
40491	1⅛ inch	6 lbs.	.30	3.24
40492	1¼ inch	7 lbs.	.38	4.10

Bench Stops.

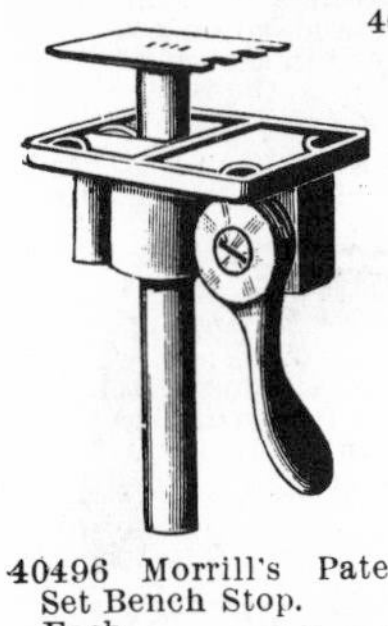

40495 Patent Bench Stops; quickly adjusted and reversible. Head is of solid steel; it is quickly attached by boring a ⅝ inch hole through the top of the bench.
Price, each.............$0.50
Weight, 1¾ lb.

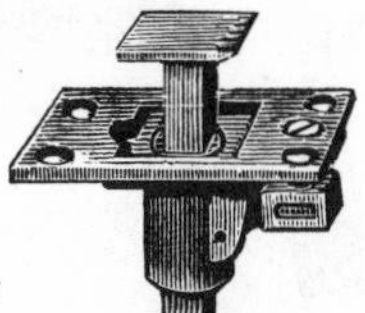

40496 Morrill's Patent Screw Set Bench Stop.
Each.................$0.45
Weight, 1 lb.

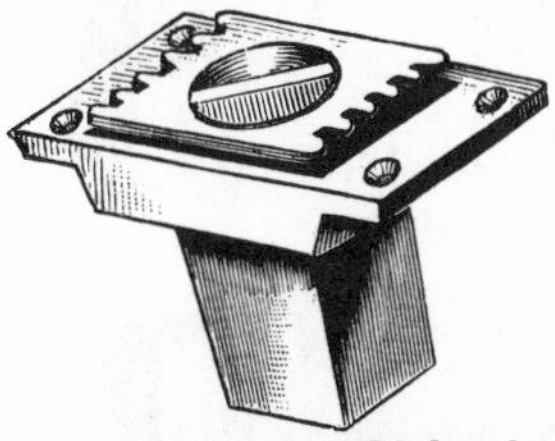

40497 Bench Stop, reversible double faced cast steel hook
Each $0.32
Weight, 1 lb.

Chisels.

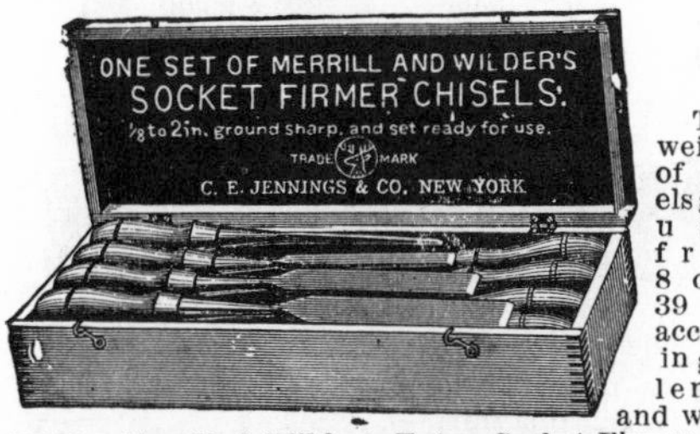

The weights of chisels graduate from 8 oz. to 39 oz., according to length and width.

40550 Merrill & Wilder's Extra Socket Firmer Chisels; solid cast steel; fully warranted to be perfect, so far as material and workmanship are concerned. Put up in sets in fancy wood box, 12 chisels in a set. ⅛, ¼, ⅜, ½, ⅝, ¾, ⅞, 1, 1¼, 1½, 1¾ and 2 inch, sharpened ready for use. Weight, 8½ pounds. Per set of 12............$3.75

40551 Swan's Socket Firmer Chisels, beveled edges, sharpened and honed ready for use; *fully warranted;* put up in hardwood box. 12 chisels to set, from ⅛ to 2 inch. An important feature of this set is the handles, which have an iron ferrule inserted in the end of all except the two smaller sizes; this prevents their splitting and makes them practically indestructible.
Price, per set 5.00

40552 Merrill & Wilder's Extra Socket Firmer Chisels, beveled edges, solid cast steel polished, applewood handles, in sets of 12 chisels in wood boxes, same as No. 40550. For a fine tool this chisel is unexcelled, and the bevel edges add greatly to its appearance and cutting qualities 12 chisels: ⅛, ¼, ⅜, ½, ⅝, ¾, ⅞, 1, 1¼, 1½, 1¾ and 2 inch, sharpened ready for use. Weight, 7¾ pounds. Price, per set of 12 .... 4.69

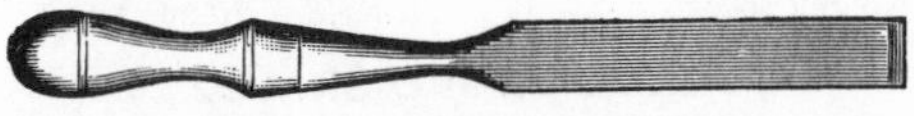

40553 Socket Firmer Chisels (price includes handles). These chisels are of the very best make, and we guarantee them to give satisfaction.

Sizes	¼ in	⅜ in.	½ in.	⅝ in.	¾ in.	⅞ in.
Price, each	20c	20c	21c	23c	25c	27c
Sizes		1 in.	1¼ in.	1½ in.	1¾ in.	2 in.
Price, each		30c	33c	35c	38c	40c

40554 Price, per set of 11 socket firmer chisels, one of each size $3.00

Beveled Edge Chisels

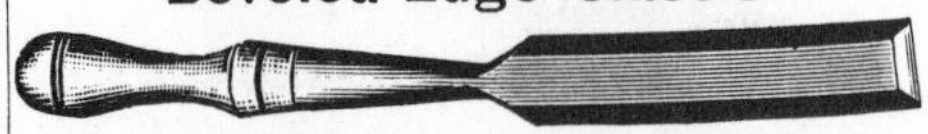

40555 Socket Firmer Chisel, beveled edge (price includes handles), These are high grade tools, made in the best manner of the best materials. Bevel Blade, 6 inches long; applewood handles.

Size	⅛	¼	⅜	½	⅝	¾	⅞
Price, each	30c	30c	30c	32c	38c	41c	42c
Size	1	1¼	1½	1¾	2		
Price, each	45c	48c	53c	56c	60c		

40557 Price, per set of 12, Beveled Edge, Socket Firmer Chisels, one of each size. Weight, 5¼ lbs......................................$4.25

Socket Framing Chisels.

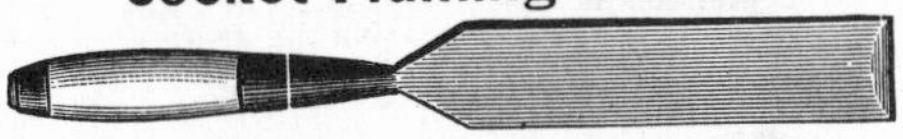

40560 Framing Chisels, socket handles (price including handles).
Size, ⅜ in..$0.28 Size, 1 in $0.36 Size, 1¾ in..$0.53
Size, ½ in.. .30 Size, 1¼ in. .40 Size, 2 in.. .55
Size, ¾ in.. .32 Size, 1½ in. .45

Corner Chisels.

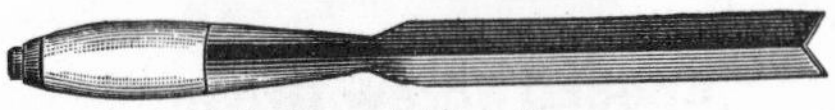

40561 Corner Chisels, socket handles.

Size	¾ in.	1 in.	1¼ in.
Each	$0.63	$0.75	$0.82

Carpenters' Slick.

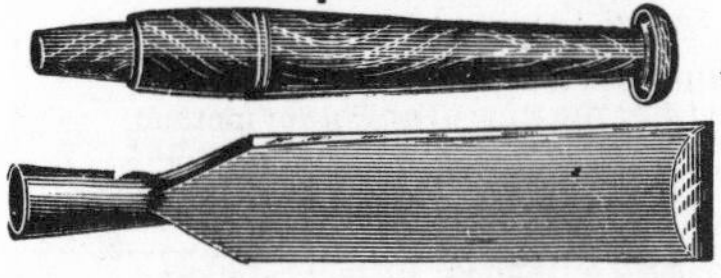

40562—Socket Slicks, best cast steel blade.

Width of blade	2½	3	3½	4
Price, each	$0.85	$0.93	$1.10	$1.27

Barton's Chisels and Gouges.

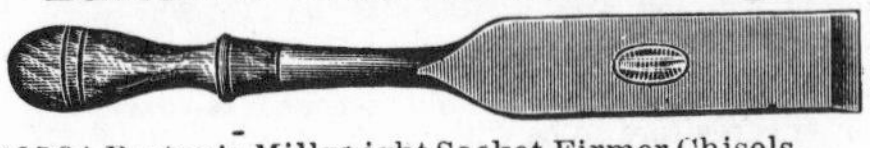

40564 Barton's Millwright Socket Firmer Chisels. 8 in. heavy solid cast steel blades, with hickory handle.

Sizes	¼	⅜	½	⅝	¾
Each	$0.56	$0.62	$0.65	$0.68	$0.72
Sizes	1	1¼	1½	1¾	2
Each	$0.75	$0.85	$0.97	$1.12	$1.32

40565 Price per set of Barton's Millwright Socket Firmer Chisels, from ¼ to 2 in.; 9 chisels, one of each, ¼, ⅜, ½, ⅝, ¾, 1, 1¼, 1½ and 2 in. $7.50

40566 Barton's Millwright Socket Firmer Chisels, with 10 inch heavy cast steel blades, with hickory handles.

Sizes	⅛	¼	⅜	½	⅝	¾
Price, each	$0.68	$0.68	$0.72	$0.75	$.78	$0.82
	⅞	1	1¼	1½	1¾	2
	$0.88	$0.92	$1.00	$1.10	$1.35	$1.57

40567 Price per set of Barton's Millwright Socket Firmer Chisels, with 10 inch blades. from ⅛ to 2 inch. 12 chisels..............................$11.25

40568 Barton's Millwright Socket Firmer Gouges, 8 in., heavy solid cast steel blades, with hickory handles, inside bevel.

Sizes	¼	⅜	½	⅝	¾
Each	$0.62	$0.65	$0.70	$0.75	$0.80
Sizes	1	1¼	1½	1¾	2
Each	$0.88	$0.95	$1.06	$1.10	$1.50

40569 Price per set of Barton's Millwright Socket Firmer Gouges, from ¼ to 2 in.: 10 Gouges, one of each size..........................$9.34
Weight, 12½ lbs.

Barton's Paring Chisels.

40572 Barton's Long Paring Socket Firmer Chisels, 10 blades, with apple wood handles.

Sizes	⅛	¼	⅜	½	⅝	¾	⅞
Each	$0.58	$0.72	$0.75	$0.80	$0.85	$0.90	$0.98
Sizes		1	1¼	1½		1¾	2
Price, each	$1.05	$1.13		$1.20	$1.31		$1.42

40573 Price per set of Barton's Long Paring Socket Firmer Chisels, with 10 inch blades from ⅛ to 2 inches, 12 chisels.................. 11.42

40574 Barton's Socket Firmer Chisels, solid cast steel, 6½ inch blades, apple wood handles, in sets of 12 chisels, in the following sizes; ⅛, ¼, ⅜, ½, ⅝, ¾, ⅞, 1, 1¼, 1½, 1¾ and 2 in.; weight, 11½ lbs. Per set (we do not sell less than a set)........................ 5.13

Tanged Firmer Chisels and Gouges.

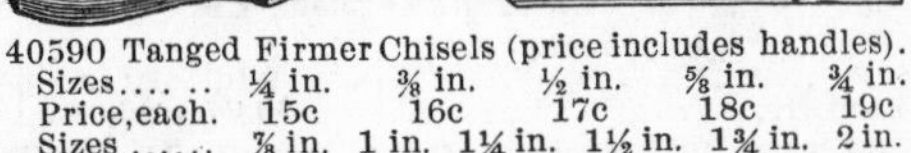

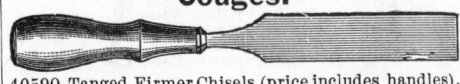

40590 Tanged Firmer Chisels (price includes handles).

Sizes	¼ in.	⅜ in.	½ in.	⅝ in.	¾ in.	
Price, each.	15c	16c	17c	18c	19c	
Sizes	⅞ in.	1 in.	1¼ in.	1½ in.	1¾ in.	2 in.
Price, each.	20c	23c	30c	35c	42c	50c

Gouges—Continued

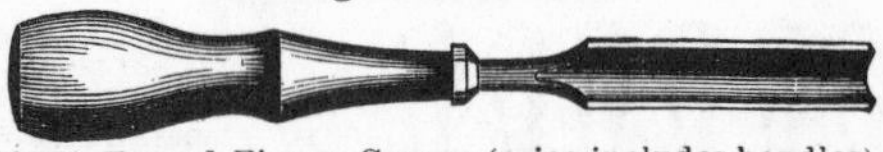

40591 Tanged Firmer Gouges (price includes handles). Extra quality warranted.

Sizes	¼ in	⅜ in.	½ in.	⅝ in.	¾ in.	
Price, each	18c	19c.	20c	21c	22c	
Sizes	⅞ in.	1 in.	1¼ in.	1½	1¾ in.	2 in
Price, each	23c	28c	35c	43c	55c	65c

Turning Chisels and Gouges.

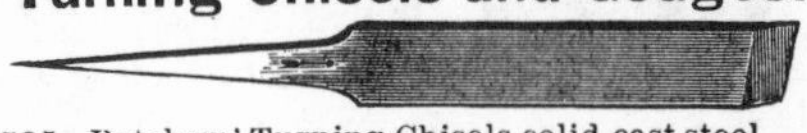

40595 Butchers' Turning Chisels, solid cast steel. Price does not include handle

Size		¼	⅜	½	⅝	¾
Price, each.		15c	15c	18c	21c	23c
Sizes	⅞	1	1¼	1½	1¾	2
Price, each.	28c	32c	41c	52c	63c	75c

40596 Price, per set of 12 Butchers' Solid Cast Steel Turning Chisels, from ¼ to 2 in., one of each size..$3.74

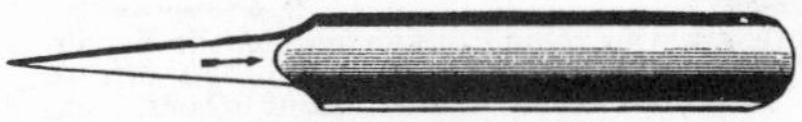

40597 Butchers' Turning Gouges, solid cast steel. Price does not include handles.

Sizes	¼	⅜	½	⅝	¾	⅞
Price each.	22c	25c	27c	30c	35c	40c
Sizes	1	1¼	1½	1¾	2	
Price each.	45c	58c	75c	88c	$1.08	

40598 Price per set of 11 Butchers' Solid Cast Steel Turning Gouges, from ¼ to 2 inches, one of each size $4.98

Carving Tools.

Order No. 40600.

Addis' Pattern Carving Tools, made of the best English steel and are the equal of any made. These are not amateur tools but are for professional carvers', carpenters' and wood workers' use generally. No carpenter shop should be without this set of tools. We do not furnish handles at this price. For price of Carving Tool Handles, see No. 40601.

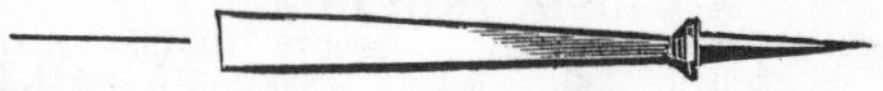

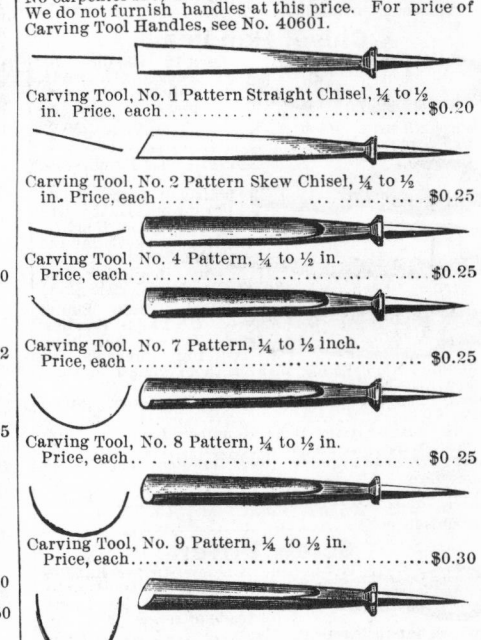

Carving Tool, No. 1 Pattern Straight Chisel, ¼ to ½ in. Price, each..................................$0.20

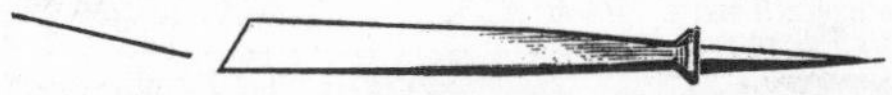

Carving Tool, No. 2 Pattern Skew Chisel, ¼ to ½ in. Price, each..................................$0.25

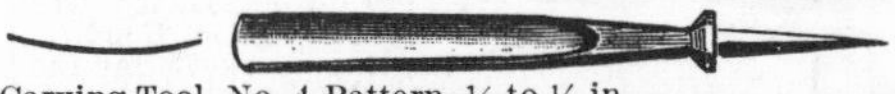

Carving Tool, No. 4 Pattern, ¼ to ½ in. Price, each.......................................$0.25

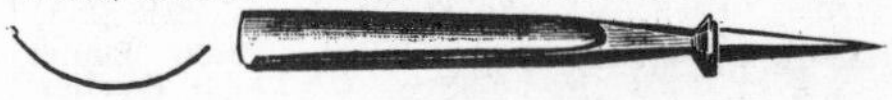

Carving Tool, No. 7 Pattern, ¼ to ½ inch. Price, each.......................................$0.25

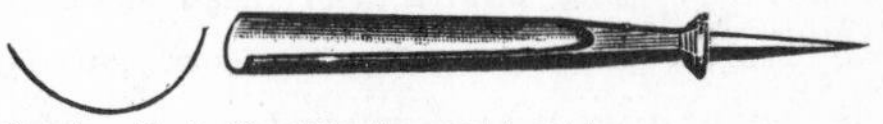

Carving Tool, No. 8 Pattern, ¼ to ½ in. Price, each.......................................$0.25

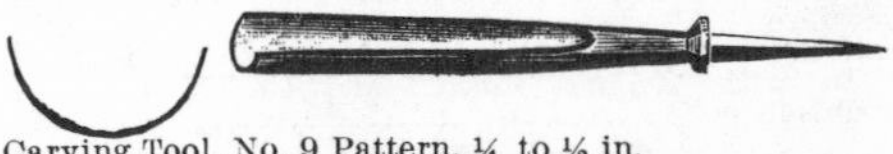

Carving Tool, No. 9 Pattern, ¼ to ½ in. Price, each.......................................$0.30

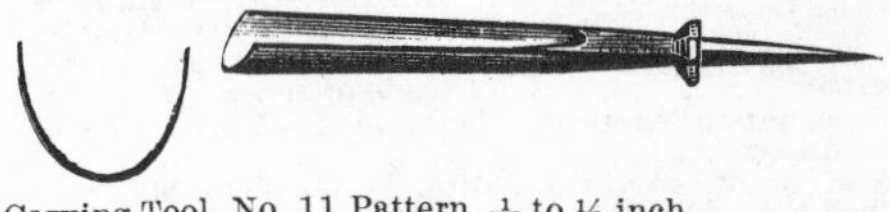

Carving Tool, No. 11 Pattern, 1/16 to ½ inch. Price, each.......................................$0.30

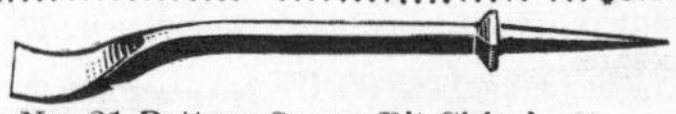

Carving Tool, No. 21 Pattern Spoon Bit Chisel, ⅜ inch. Price, each..............................$0.40

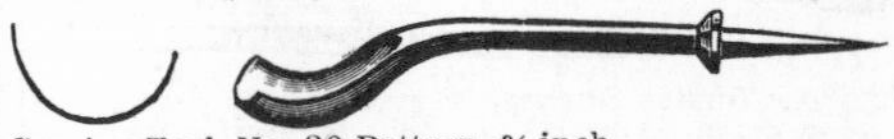

Carving Tool, No. 30 Pattern, ⅜ inch. Price, each.......................................$0.35

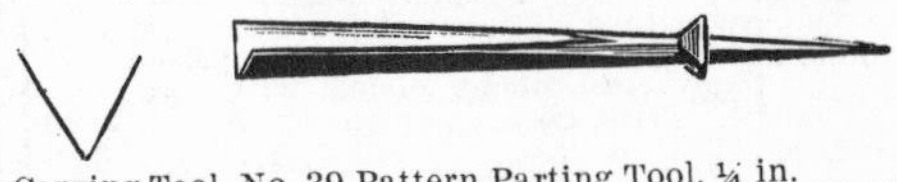

Carving Tool, No. 39 Pattern Parting Tool, ¼ in. Price, each.......................................$0.40

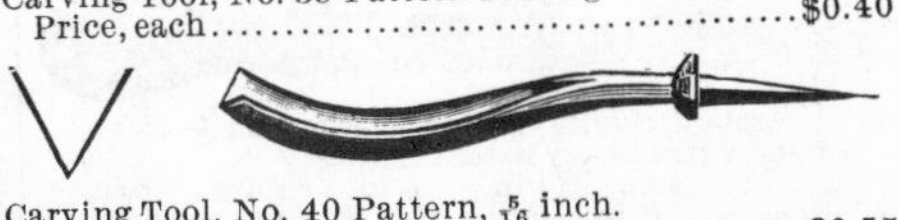

Carving Tool, No. 40 Pattern, 5/16 inch. Price, each.......................................$0.55

40601 Apple Wood Carving Tool handles. Each .08
Per dozen.. .75

Carving Tools—Continued.

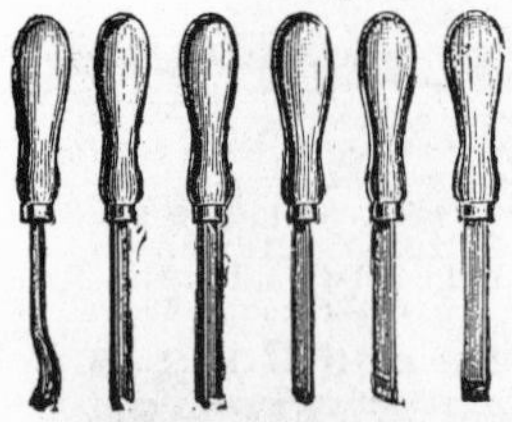

40610 Amateurs' Carving Tools, extra cast-steel, rosewood handles; weight, 10 ozs. Per set of 6 assorted tools in a wood box.
Per set..........$0.85

Chisel Grinder.

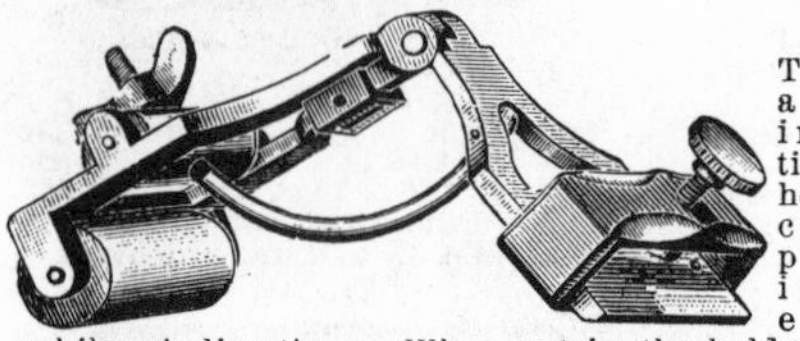

40612 This is a new invention for holding chisels, plane irons, etc., while grinding them. When put in the holder and brought to the right bevel with the adjusting screw, nothing is left to do but to bear it on the stone, and it will grind all right without further care. Price each $0.64

Chisel Gauge.

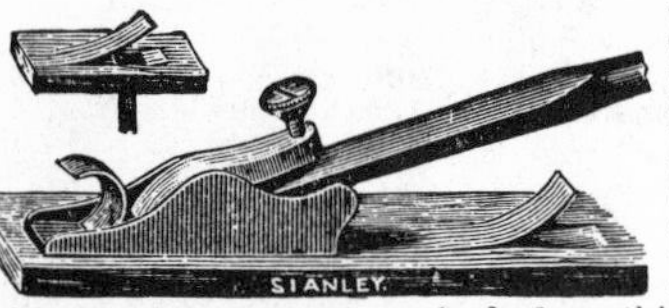

40614 Chisel Gauge for use in finishing work where blind nailing is required. By attaching the gauge to a ¼ inch chisel, a shaving can be raised of any thickness with precision, and when glued down again the shaving will fit its recess perfectly; weight, 3 oz. Made for ¼ inch chisel only.
Price, each, no chisel.............................$0.15

Chisel Handles.

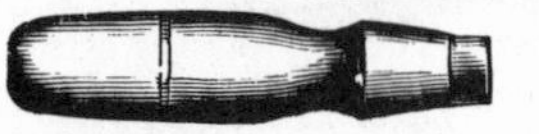

40616 Handles for Tanged Chisels, polished hickory-brass ferrules, assorted, 6 sizes. Each.........................$0.02
Per dozen...22

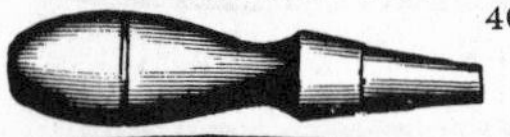

40617 Chisel Handles, for Socket Firmer Chisels, polished. Each....$0.02
Per dozen.........18

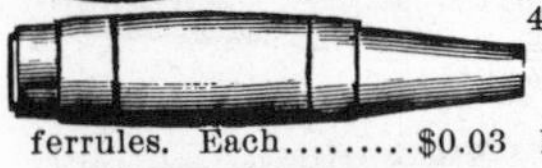

40618 Chisel Handles, for socket framing chisels, polished hickory, malleable iron, ferrules. Each.........$0.03 Per dozen.........$0.25

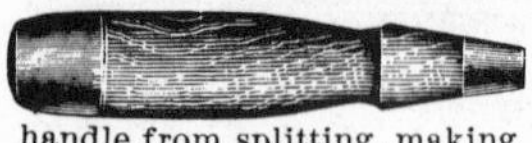

Raw Hide Bound Chisel Handles. The raw hide binding prevents the handle from splitting, making them almost indestructible.

40620 Tanged Firmer Chisel Handles. Each....	$0.08
Per dozen....	.75
40621 Socket Firmer Chisel Handles. Each.....	.07
Per dozen....	.65
40622 Socket Framing Chisel Handles. Each.,	.08
Per dozen....	.68
Can furnish raw hide bound handles instead of plain with 40550, 40551, and 40552, set of chisels for....	.50

Screw Driver.

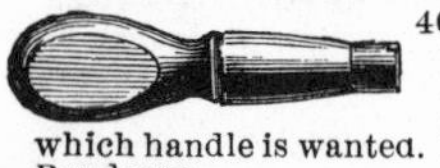

406 3 Screw Driver Handles beechwood, polished brass ferrule, assorted. Give length of blade of screw driver for which handle is wanted. Each...........$0.03
Per dozen.........................33

40624 screw driver Handles, beechwood, polished brass ferrules large size. Give length of blade of Screw Driver for which handle is wanted Each... $0.04 Per dozen.......... .38

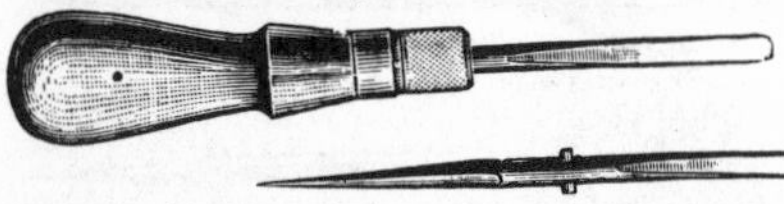

40630 The Duplex Screw Driver. Generally when a screw driver is used some tool is wanted to make a hole for the screw. On the reverse end of the screw driver is a square reamer, better for the purpose than a gimlet; it can be turned around instantly so as to use either end. Made of hand forged steel, nickel plated, with cocobolo handle. Price, each, complete, one bit.....$0.36
Per dozen.............................3.90

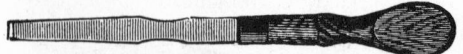

40631 Screw Drivers, cast steel patent metallic fasteners, extra heavy brass ferrules.

Size	3 in.	4 in.	5 in.	6 in.	8 in.
Whole length	7½ in.	9 in.	10½ in.	12½ in.	15 in.
price, each	5c.	6c.	8c.	10c.	12c.

Screw Drivers—Continued.

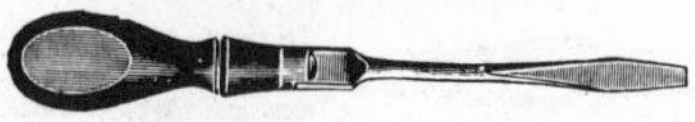

40633 Round Forged Blade, Warranted, Screw Driver. Highly finished with nickel plated capped ferrule, black handle.

Length of blade	3	4	5	6	8 inch
Price, each	8c.	10c.	12c.	13c.	16c.

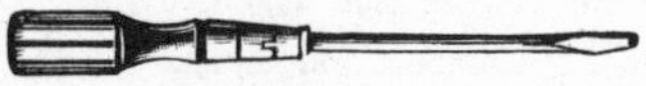

40637 The Champion Screw Driver, undoubtedly the finest made. The blade is forged from the toughest steel, and is fastened securely into a fluted applewood handle; every blade is tested to split a screw head before leaving the factory.

Size	3 in.	4 in.	6 in.	8 in.	10 in.
Price	20c.	24c.	34c.	46c.	57c.

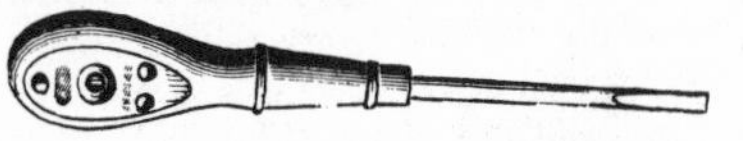

40639 Gay & Parsons' Double Action Ratchet Screw Drivers.

Size	4 in.	5 in.	6 in.	8 in.	10 in.
Price	51c.	57c.	68c.	76c.	85c.

Special Screw Driver.

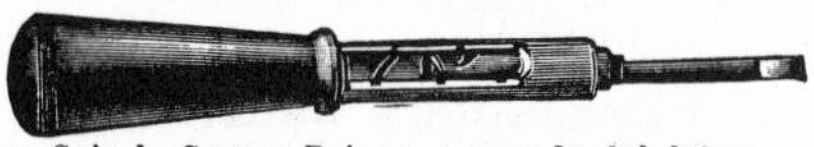

The Spiral Screw Driver, a wonderful labor-saving tool, an entire revolution in driving screws; it will drive a screw into wood, soft or hard, in one-third the time of any other method. Pressure on the handle turns the blade and drives the screw. Hand does not turn at all.
40640 No. 1, length extended, 14 inches; closed, 9 inches; blade, ¼ inch. Each....................$0.70
40641 No. 2, length extended, 19 inches; closed, 13 inches; blade, $\frac{5}{16}$ inch.................... .82
40642 No. 4; the most wonderful spiral screw driver on the market; it has all the merits of the most perfect drivers and has also the addition of a chuck and double bits; length, when extended. 20 inches, closed, 13 inches. We guarantee it in every particular; it saves two-thirds of the time of the old method. No carpenter can afford to be without it. Each........$1.10

Goodell Brace Screw Driver.

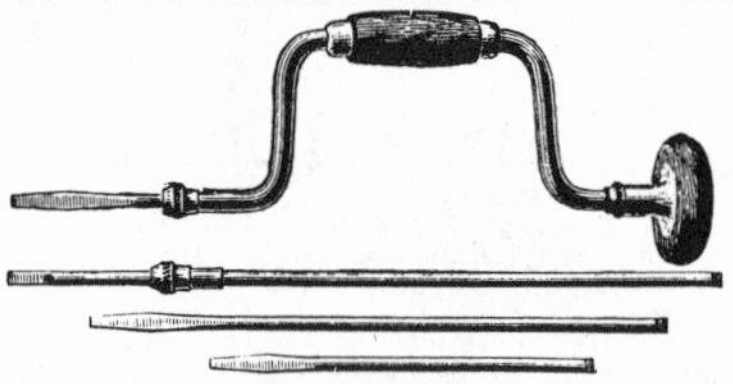

40643 The brace has a nickel plated 6 inch steel sweep, cocobolo head, and handle with patent adjustable collar for taking up the wear. The brace is packed one in a box with four blades, 2-4 inch, 1-8 inch, 1-12 inch, also 1-12 inch extension which gives a variety in lengths of 48 inch, 24-inch, 20-inch, 16-inch and 12-inch. The chuck on this brace is very strong and compact. The tool is designed for carpenters, machinists, electricians, cabinet, carriage, organ and piano makers.
Price, each, complete with 12-inch extension....$1.35

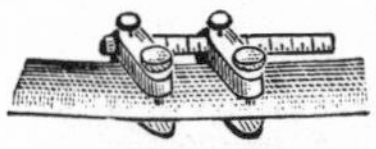

40644 Improved Draw Knife. Chamfer Gauge, with graduated scale; with this attachment there is no stopping to measure the work for fear of getting off too much; made of iron, nickel plated.

Sizes	1 in.	1⅛ to 1¼ in.	1⅜ to 1½ in.	1¾ in.
Fits blades,	⅞ to 1 in.	1⅛ to 1¼ in.	1⅝ to 1¾ in.	
Price, each, any size				$0.55

Drawing Knives.

Weight, 1¼ to 1¾ lbs.

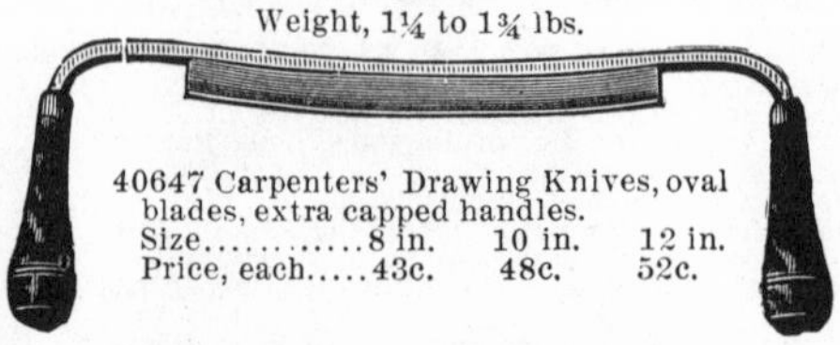

40647 Carpenters' Drawing Knives, oval blades, extra capped handles.

Size	8 in.	10 in.	12 in.
Price, each	43c.	48c.	52c.

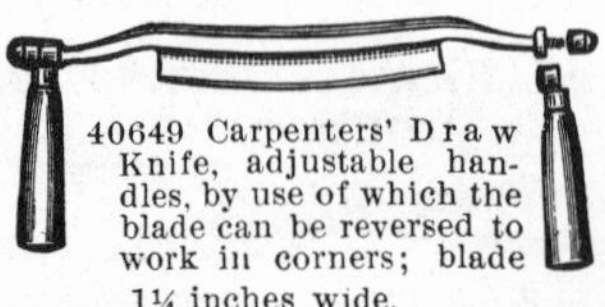

40649 Carpenters' Draw Knife, adjustable handles, by use of which the blade can be reversed to work in corners; blade 1¼ inches wide.

Size	8 in.	9 in.	10 in.
Each	$0.75	$0.87	$0.94

Patent Folding and Adjustable Handle Drawer Knife.

LOCKS AUTOMATIC.

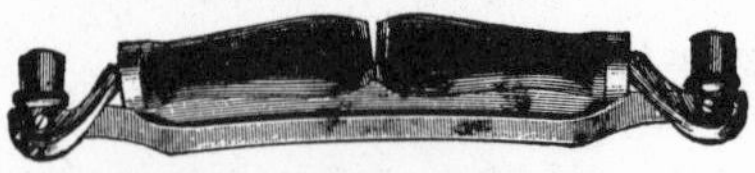

Showing Knife Closed.

40650 Handles can be adjusted for wide, flat surfaces, and can be used where a stiff handle cannot be used. The mechanic will be quick to see the many advantages of a drawing knife that can be adjusted, and when not in use can be folded and placed in the kit of tools without danger of injury to the blade.
Every Blade Warranted.

Size	7	8	9	10 inch
Price, each	$1.10	$1.25	$1.30	$1.40

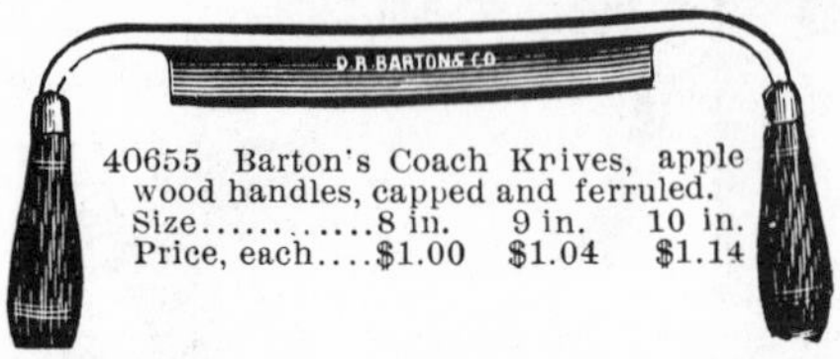

40655 Barton's Coach Knives, apple wood handles, capped and ferruled.

Size	8 in.	9 in.	10 in.
Price, each	$1.00	$1.04	$1.14

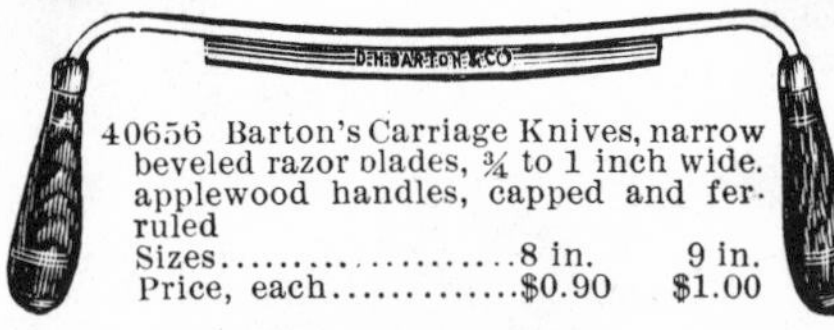

40656 Barton's Carriage Knives, narrow beveled razor blades, ¾ to 1 inch wide. applewood handles, capped and ferruled

Sizes	8 in.	9 in.
Price, each	$0.90	$1.00

Hoop Knives.

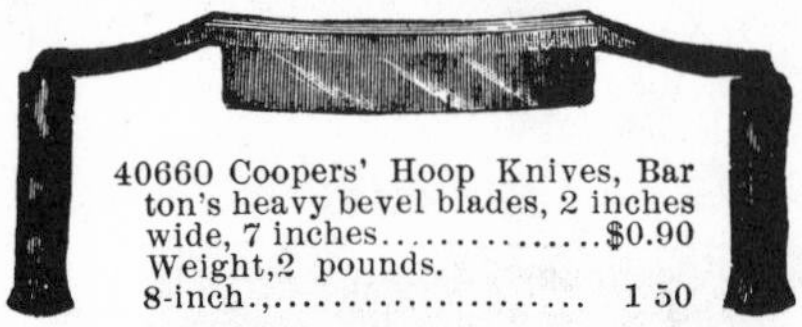

40660 Coopers' Hoop Knives, Barton's heavy bevel blades, 2 inches wide, 7 inches...............$0.90
Weight, 2 pounds.
8-inch...................... 1 50

Froes.

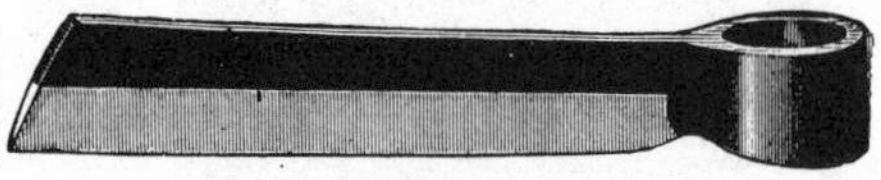

Weight, 2⅛ pounds.

40662 Coopers' Froes, polished steel edge, 12 to 14 inch cut, used by coopers for making staves, and in sections of the country where lumber is scarce for splitting shingles. Each..............$0.75
Per dozen.................. 8.10

Spoke Shaves.

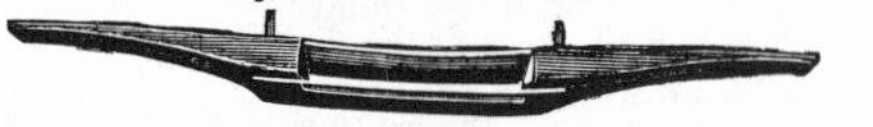

40663 Spoke Shave, beechwood handle, one 2½ cast steel cutter; weight, 8 oz...................$0.22

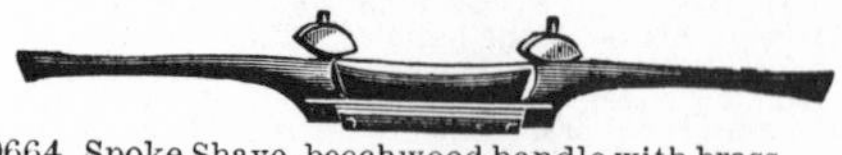

40664 Spoke Shave, beechwood handle with brass set screws, one 3-inch cast steel cutter; weight, 9 ozs..$ 0.54

40665 Spoke Shave, iron handle, two cutters, best English cast steel (like cut). Weight, 16 oz..........................$0.20 (Each) $2.16 (Per doz.)

Goodell Spoke Shave.

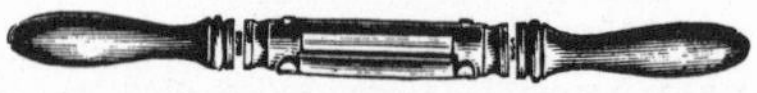

40670 Goodell's Spoke Shave, owing to its circular shape, will work in smaller circle than any other shave. The angle of the knife is such that it cuts instead of scraping the grain of the wood. Either handle can be removed to work in cramped places. Each...........................$ .68
Per dozen.................................. 7.75

40673 Patent Chamfer Spoke Shave, raised handles, 1½ in. cast steel cutters, adjusted by means of thumb screw attached to the guides. Will chamfer an edge any width up to 1½ inches; weight, 14 oz.
Each...$0. 3
Per dozen.. 3.65

Remember-- That it would be Poor Policy for us to misrepresent any of our goods. We want every sale made to bring us in two or three new customers. This is the secret of our success.

Hatchets.

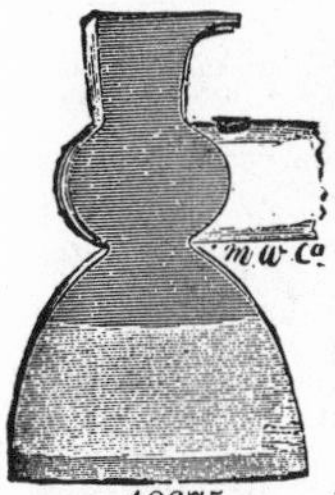

All of our hatchets have handles, but the weights given do not include handles.

40675 Hatchets, cast steel, with claw (see cut). Y.& P. brand, are considered by all first

40675   40676

class mechanics to be the best goods in the market. Great care is taken in the manufacturing, and tempering warranted.

	No. 1.	No. 2.	No. 3.
Weight	1 lb. 3 cz	1 lb. 9 oz.	1 lb. 15 oz.
Width	3½ in.	4 in	4½ in.
Each	$0.40	$0.45	$0.50
Per dozen	4.65	4.85	5.40

40676 Broad Hatchets, extra cast steel, wide, heavy and fine quality, bronzed. Y. & P. brand warranted. Weight, 1 lb. 12 oz.; width, 4½ in.
Each..$0.54
Per dozen... .6.00
Weight, 2 lbs. 2 oz; width, 5 in. Each........... .63
Per dozen... 6.85
Weight, 2 lbs. 8 oz.; width, 5½ in. Each........ .75
Per dozen... 8.10
Weight, 2 lbs. 14 oz.; width, 6 in. Each........ .82
Per dozen... 8.85

40680— Lathing Hatchet, Underhill Star pattern warranted. Solid cast steel, full polished, extra thin blade, width

of blade   40680   40681   40685

2 in.; weight, 1 lb. Each..................$0.83
Per dozen..................................... 8.97
40681 Lathing Hatchet, Yerkes & Plumb's Adz Eye Bell Pole, solid cast steel, thin blade, full polish, cut 2¼ in. Fully warranted. Weight 1 lb. Each..................................... .80
Per dozen..................................... 8.64
40685 Shingling Hatchet, Yerkes & Plumb's Adz Eye Bell Pole, solid cast steel, thin blade, full polished; weight,1 lb. 4 oz.Fully warranted.
Each... .80
Per dozen.................................... 8.64

40686 Lathing Hatchet, cast steel, Vulcan brand. Weight, 10 oz. Width, 2 in.
Each..................$0.34
Per dozen.,........ 3.68
40687 Weight, 14 oz. Width, 2¼ in.
Each... .38
Per dozen.................................... 3.68
40690 Shingling Hatchet, common pattern, cast steel. Y. & P. brand, warranted. 

No.	0	1
Weight,	13 oz.	1 lb., 1 oz.
Width of bit,	3¼ in.	3½ in.
Each,	34c.	38c.
No.	2	3
Weight,	1 lb., 7 oz.	1 lb., 13 oz.
Width of bit,	4 in.	4½ in.
Each,	41c.	43c.

40691 Hatchet Handles.......$0.05

Adzes.

40695 Carpenters' Adze, English cast steel, bronzed 3½ to 4 in. cut; weight, 3¾ lbs. Y. & P. brand. Fully warranted.
Each........$1.15
40696 Barton's Ship Adze, 4 to 4½ in. cut. Each 2.10
40699 Adze Handles. Each..................... .40

CHICAGO IS NOW THE

Commercial Center of America

and is recognized as the Largest Market for Manufactured Articles, Hardware, Tools, Etc., in the world.

Axes.

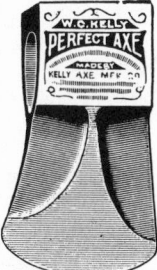

40700 The Celebrated Kelly Perfect Ax. This ax is made of the finest steel and is hand hammered tempered and tested before leaving the shop. The blade is so shaped that it will cut very deep, but will not bind in timber. It will burst the chip, and it will not become stubbed after grinding. It has a taper eye which binds handle. Try one and you will use no other. We can furnish the Western pattern like cut, or Michigan pattern, which has rounded head. Comes assorted weight, from 3½ to 5 lbs. each
Each..........................$0.60
Per dozen...................... 6.50

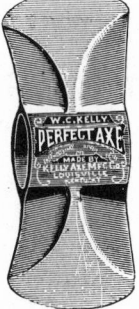

40702 The Celebrated Kelley Perfect Double Bitted Ax, made of the finest steel and hand hammered; will cut deeper than any other ax, and will not bind in timber. Comes in assorted weights, from 3½ to 5½ lbs.
Price, each.................... $1.00
Per dozen 11.00

40705 Carpenters' Broad Ax, Western pattern, extra cast steel; weight,6 to 7½ lbs.; 9 to 11 in. cut. Each.....................................$1.50
40706 Broad Ax Handle, extra quality, right or left hand, 26 inches long. Each.......... 18
Per dozen............................. .... 1.77

40710 Montgomery Ward & Co.'s Phantom Bevel, solid silver steel, full polished ax. This is a new pattern that promises to give good satisfaction. The peculiar bevel of the bit has the tendency to free it from the wood, besides giving the ax a very neat appearance; weight, 3, 3¾ to 4¾ lbs.
Each $0.69

40711 Montgomery Ward & Co.'s solid SilverSteel Ax, full polished, like cut, a handsome pattern; has a longer and thinner bit than ordinary, is made of best quality of steel, and handsomely finished. We can also furnish the same ax with rounded head, if preferred; both the same price; weight, 3¾ to 4¾ lbs. Each.......$0.60
40712 Red Warrior Ax, Western pattern, wide bit, heavy poll, inserted steel, manufactured by Wm. Mann, Jr., & Co.; weight, 3½ to 4¾ lbs; no handles. Each.....................
40713 Axes, Northwestern pattern; Hunt's narrow bit, heavy poll; inserted steel; weight, 3½ to 4¾ pounds; no handle. Each.................. .65
Per dozen, selected assortment.................. 6.00
40714 Hunters' Axes, with handle, extra cast steel, steel poll; weight, 1¾ pounds; this is a very convenient tool; it makes a light ax or a heavy hatchet.. .52
40715 Boys' axes, hickory handle, 27 inches long, highly polished and bronzed.............. .65

Ax Handles.

	Each	doz.
40720 Ax Handles, New York J pattern No. 1 turned xx quality.....	$0.10	$1.00
40721 Ax Handles, clipper pattern, hand shaved oval xxx quality..................	.20	1.85
40722 Ax Handles, octagon pattern, hand shaved, xxx quality.................	.25	2.55
40723 Ax Handles for double bit ax, extra shaved quality...	.16	1.50

Wood Wedges.

40724 Wood Wedges,solid cast steel; weight, 3½ to 5 pounds. Per pound, 4c.

Please observe that wood wedges are quoted by the pound and cost 18 to 25 cents each.

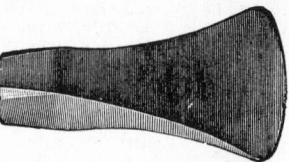

40726 Wood Wedges, Oregon pattern, made of the highest grade of tool steel, oil finished, 4 to 10 pounds.
Per pound, $0.12

Mauls.

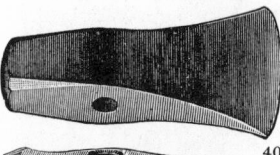

40728 Wood-Choppers' Mauls, Oregon pattern,made of the best tool steel,oil finished; no handle;weighs from 4 to 12 pounds.
Per lb......$0.12

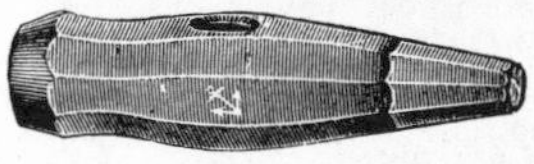

40729 Ship Spike Maul, solid cast steel, oil finished, polished faces, no handle.
Weight, 4 to 12 lbs. Per pound.... ....$0.09
40730 Railroad Spike Maul, solid cast steel, oil-finished, polished face, no handle; from 6 to 12 pounds. Per pound...............$0.07

Beetle Rings.

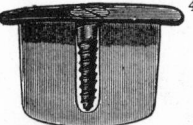

40735 Beetle Rings, made of 1x3x16, 4½ in. weight, 1 lb. Price each.		$0.10
5 in. " 1½ lbs. "		.15
6 in. " 2¾ " "		.20

40736 The Hub Malleable Iron Ax Wedges. The only practical ax wedge, because it is the only one that can be taken out easily; the screw holds the wedge in its place; take out the screw and the wedge can be easily removed allowing the handle to be withdrawn from the ax; weight, 5 oz.
Each ....$0.03 Per dozen..........$0.33

Adze Eye Nail Hammer.

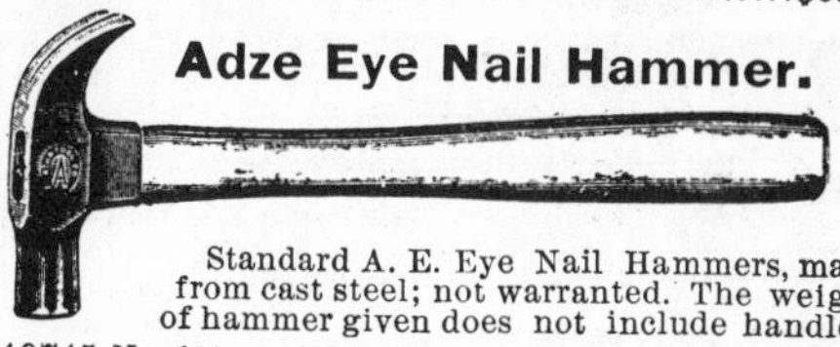

Standard A. E. Eye Nail Hammers, made from cast steel; not warranted. The weight of hammer given does not include handles.
40745 No. 1½; weight, 1 lb. Price, each...........$0.28
Per dozen... 2.90
40746 Hammer Handles.................................. .05
Quaker City. Adze Eye Nail Hammers, made from the best cast steel and fully warranted. If they prove too hard or, too soft or are defective in the steel, a new one will be given in exchange.
40747 No. 1, weight, 1 pound 4 oz. Price, each..$0.35
Per dozen.. .... 3.50
40748 No. 1½, weight, 1 pound. Price, each ..... .30
Per dozen... 3.25
40749 No. 2, weight. 13 ounces. Price, each .... .28
Per dozen... 3.00

Adze Eye Bell Face. Nail Hammer.

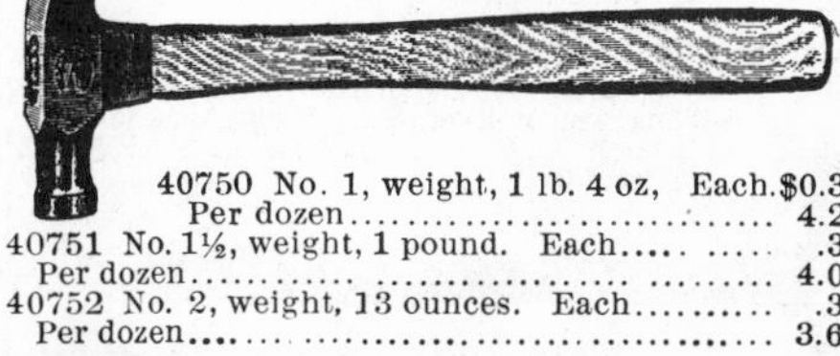

40750 No. 1, weight, 1 lb. 4 oz, Each.$0.38
Per dozen.. 4.25
40751 No. 1½, weight, 1 pound. Each..... ..... .35
Per dozen... 4.00
40752 No. 2, weight, 13 ounces. Each............ .32
Per dozen... 3.60

Hammers.

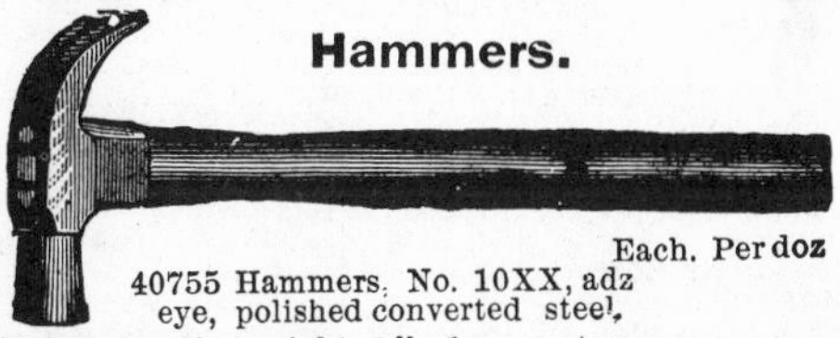

	Each.	Per doz
40755 Hammers, No. 10XX, adz eye, polished converted steel, hickory handle; weight, 1 lb. 1 oz., not intended for mechanics' use. Price.........	$0.15	$1.25

Hammers—Continued.

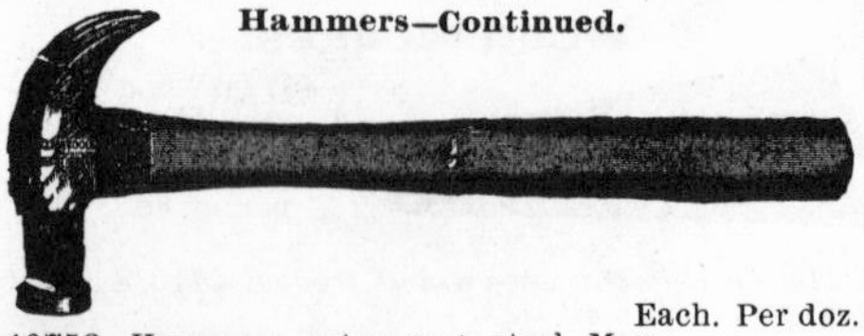

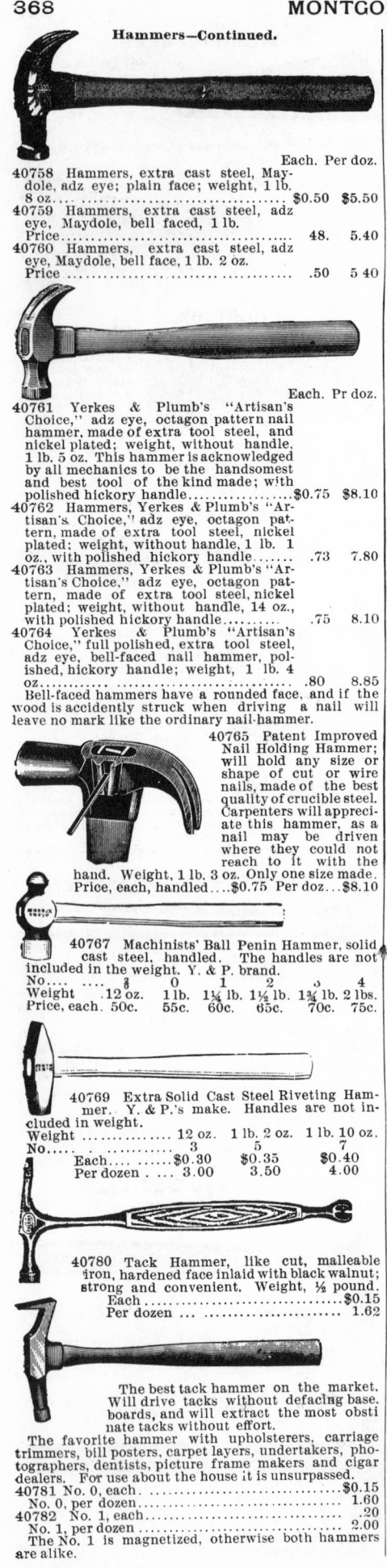

Each. Per doz.

40758 Hammers, extra cast steel, Maydole, adz eye; plain face; weight, 1 lb. 8 oz. $0.50 $5.50

40759 Hammers, extra cast steel, adz eye, Maydole, bell faced, 1 lb. Price 48. 5.40

40760 Hammers, extra cast steel, adz eye, Maydole, bell face, 1 lb. 2 oz. Price .... .50 5 40

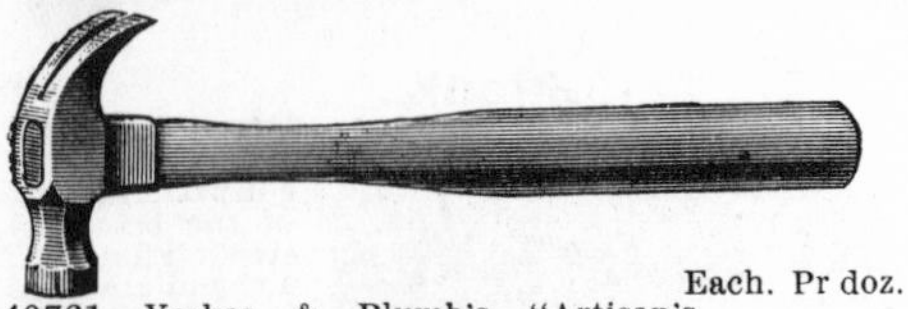

Each. Pr doz.

40761 Yerkes & Plumb's "Artisan's Choice," adz eye, octagon pattern nail hammer, made of extra tool steel, and nickel plated; weight, without handle, 1 lb. 5 oz. This hammer is acknowledged by all mechanics to be the handsomest and best tool of the kind made; with polished hickory handle $0.75 $8.10

40762 Hammers, Yerkes & Plumb's "Artisan's Choice," adz eye, octagon pattern, made of extra tool steel, nickel plated; weight, without handle, 1 lb. 1 oz., with polished hickory handle .... .73 7.80

40763 Hammers, Yerkes & Plumb's "Artisan's Choice," adz eye, octagon pattern, made of extra tool steel, nickel plated; weight, without handle, 14 oz., with polished hickory handle .... .75 8.10

40764 Yerkes & Plumb's "Artisan's Choice," full polished, extra tool steel, adz eye, bell-faced nail hammer, polished, hickory handle; weight, 1 lb. 4 oz. .... .80 8.85

Bell-faced hammers have a rounded face, and if the wood is accidently struck when driving a nail will leave no mark like the ordinary nail-hammer.

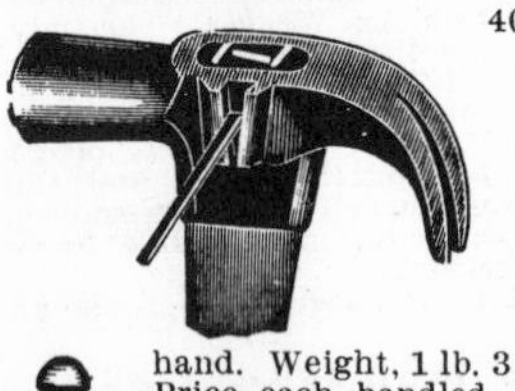

40765 Patent Improved Nail Holding Hammer; will hold any size or shape of cut or wire nails, made of the best quality of crucible steel. Carpenters will appreciate this hammer, as a nail may be driven where they could not reach to it with the hand. Weight, 1 lb. 3 oz. Only one size made. Price, each, handled....$0.75 Per doz...$8.10

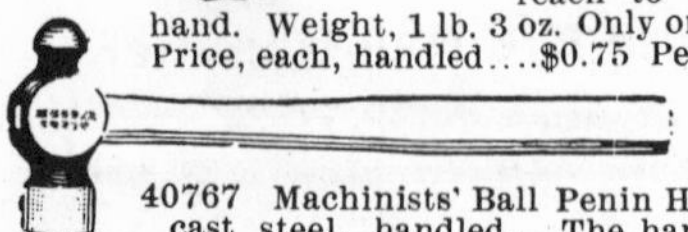

40767 Machinists' Ball Penin Hammer, solid cast steel, handled. The handles are not included in the weight. Y. & P. brand.

No....	3/8	0	1	2	3	4
Weight	12 oz.	1 lb.	1¼ lb.	1½ lb.	1¾ lb.	2 lbs.
Price, each.	50c.	55c.	60c.	65c.	70c.	75c.

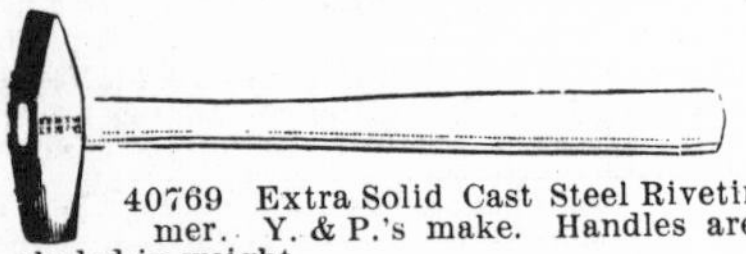

40769 Extra Solid Cast Steel Riveting Hammer. Y. & P.'s make. Handles are not included in weight.

Weight	12 oz.	1 lb. 2 oz.	1 lb. 10 oz.
No.....	3	5	7
Each	$0.30	$0.35	$0.40
Per dozen	3.00	3.50	4.00

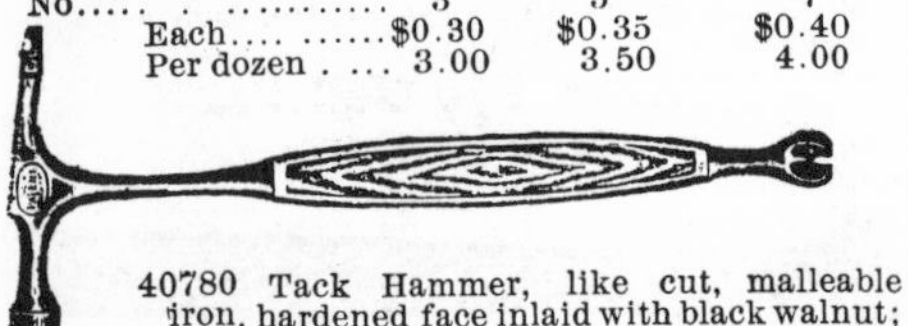

40780 Tack Hammer, like cut, malleable iron, hardened face inlaid with black walnut; strong and convenient. Weight, ½ pound.
Each $0.15
Per dozen 1.62

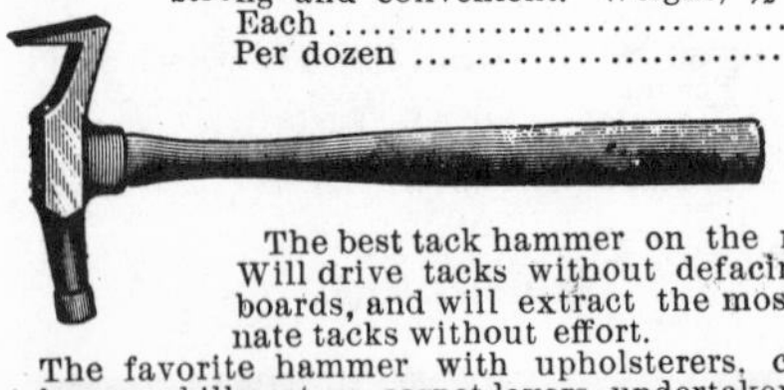

The best tack hammer on the market. Will drive tacks without defacing base. boards, and will extract the most obstinate tacks without effort.

The favorite hammer with upholsterers, carriage trimmers, bill posters, carpet layers, undertakers, photographers, dentists, picture frame makers and cigar dealers. For use about the house it is unsurpassed.

40781 No. 0, each $0.15
No. 0, per dozen 1.60
40782 No. 1, each .... .20
No. 1, per dozen 2.00

The No. 1 is magnetized, otherwise both hammers are alike.

Hammers—Continued.

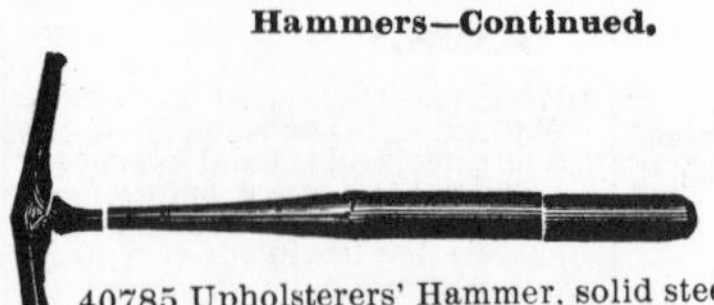

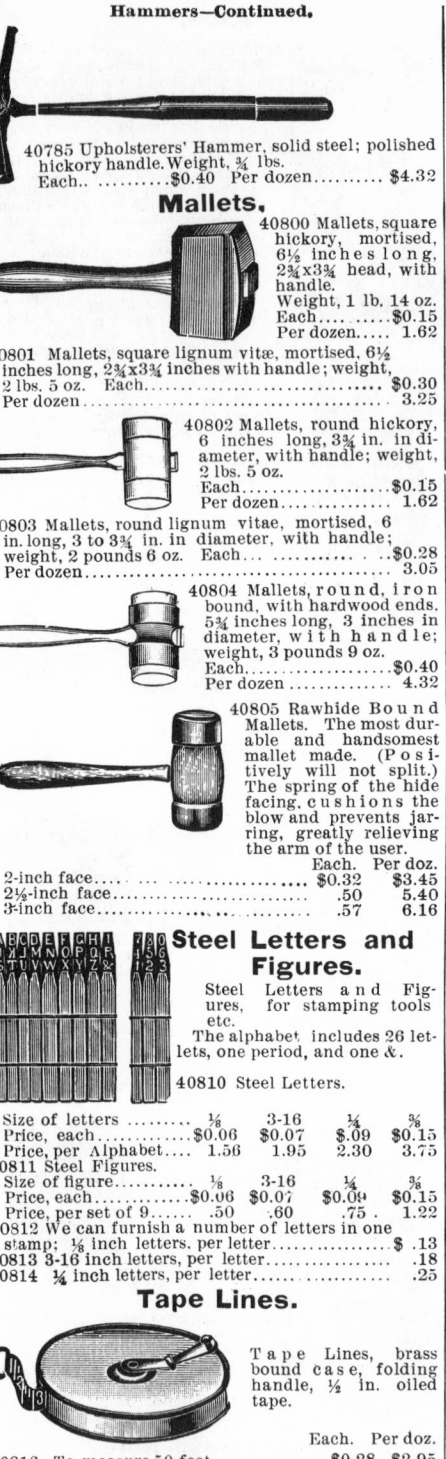

40785 Upholsterers' Hammer, solid steel; polished hickory handle. Weight, ¾ lbs.
Each.. ....$0.40 Per dozen $4.32

Mallets.

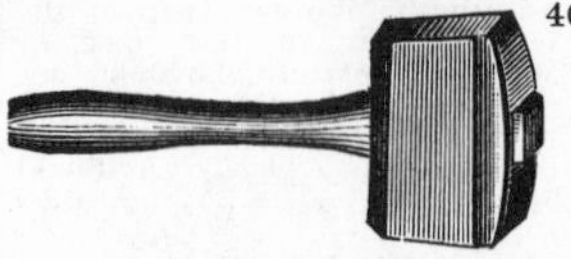

40800 Mallets, square hickory, mortised, 6½ inches long, 2¾x3¾ head, with handle.
Weight, 1 lb. 14 oz.
Each $0.15
Per dozen 1.62

40801 Mallets, square lignum vitæ, mortised, 6½ inches long, 2¾x3¾ inches with handle; weight, 2 lbs. 5 oz. Each $0.30
Per dozen 3.25

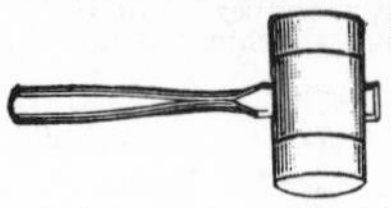

40802 Mallets, round hickory, 6 inches long, 3¾ in. in diameter, with handle; weight, 2 lbs. 5 oz.
Each $0.15
Per dozen 1.62

40803 Mallets, round lignum vitae, mortised, 6 in. long, 3 to 3¾ in. in diameter, with handle; weight, 2 pounds 6 oz. Each $0.28
Per dozen 3.05

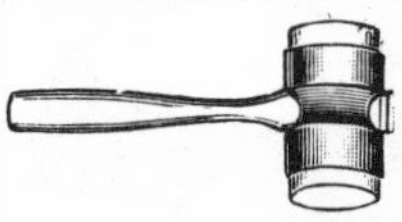

40804 Mallets, round, iron bound, with hardwood ends, 5¾ inches long, 3 inches in diameter, with handle; weight, 3 pounds 9 oz.
Each $0.40
Per dozen 4.32

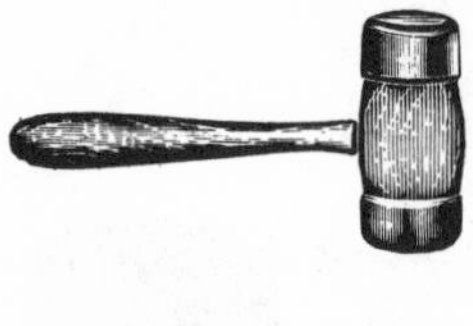

40805 Rawhide Bound Mallets. The most durable and handsomest mallet made. (Positively will not split.) The spring of the hide facing, cushions the blow and prevents jarring, greatly relieving the arm of the user.

	Each.	Per doz.
2-inch face	$0.32	$3.45
2½-inch face	.50	5.40
3-inch face	.57	6.16

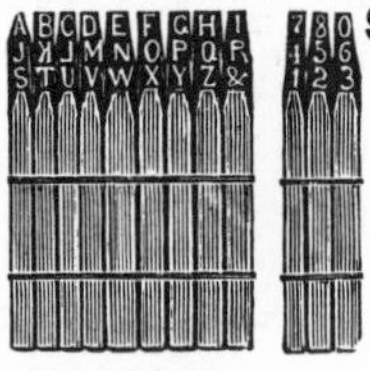

Steel Letters and Figures.

Steel Letters and Figures, for stamping tools etc.

The alphabet includes 26 letters, one period, and one &.

40810 Steel Letters.

Size of letters	⅛	3-16	¼	⅜
Price, each	$0.06	$0.07	$.09	$0.15
Price, per Alphabet	1.56	1.95	2.30	3.75

40811 Steel Figures.

Size of figure	⅛	3-16	¼	⅜
Price, each	$0.06	$0.07	$0.09	$0.15
Price, per set of 9	.50	.60	.75	1.22

40812 We can furnish a number of letters in one stamp; ⅛ inch letters, per letter .... $ .13
40813 3-16 inch letters, per letter .... .18
40814 ¼ inch letters, per letter .... .25

Tape Lines.

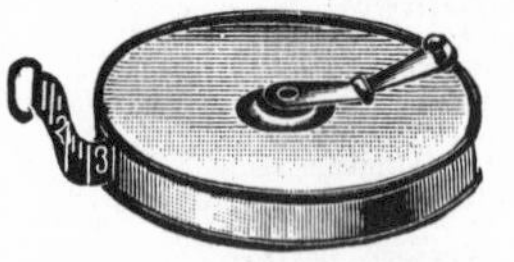

Tape Lines, brass bound case, folding handle, ½ in. oiled tape.

		Each.	Per doz.
40816	To measure 50 feet	$0.28	$2.95
40817	To measure 75 feet	.40	4.50
40818	To measure 100 feet	.50	5.40

Tape Lines, Best.

Tape Lines in best leather cases, ⅝ inch heavy Holland tape, making a very serviceable line for all kinds of work. *Warranted.*

		Each.	Per doz.
40819	To measure 50 feet	$1.00	$10.80
40820	To measure 75 feet	1.15	13.00
40821	To measure 100 feet	1.25	13.50

Chesterman's Tape Line.

With heavy red leather case; the tape has metallic woven in with the linen, which makes the strongest and most accurate linen tape made.

40822 To measure 50 feet, each $1.87
40823 " " 66 " " 2.38
40824 " " 100 " " 3.00

Tallying Register or Counting Machine.

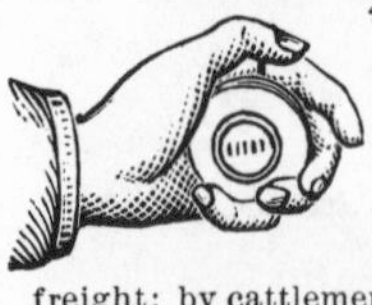

40831 This little register tallies from 1 to 1,000 and can be set at zero at will, can be carried in the pocket; weighs about 8 ounces. It is used by railroad, telegraph and steamboat men for checking or tallying ties, telegraph poles, and passengers, and all kinds of freight; by cattlemen for counting cattle and sheep, and at places of amusement, for counting the people going in and out. Has a glass dial in front, through which the figures may be plainly seen as they appear. Nickel plated. Price, each $2.50

Ivory Rules.

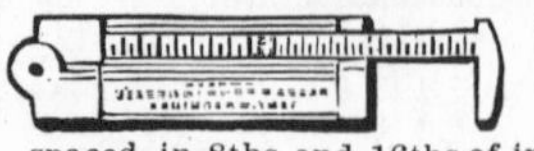

40832 Ivory Caliper Rule, six inch German silver trimmed. two fold, ⅝ wide, spaced in 8ths and 16ths of inches. Price, each $0.60

40833 Ivory Caliper Rule, one foot, German silver edge plates; four fold, spaced in 8ths. 10ths, 12ths, and 16ths of inches. ⅝ inch wide. Price, each 1.70

40834 Ivory Two-foot Rule, 4-fold German silver edge plates; spaced 8ths, 10ths, 12ths and 16ths of inches. Price, each 2.00

Architects Rules, 4-fold.

40838 Has arch joints, edge plates; 8ths, 10ths, 12th and 16ths of inches, with inside beveled edges and architects' drafting scale; 1 inch wide. Price, each $0.30

Boxwood Rules.

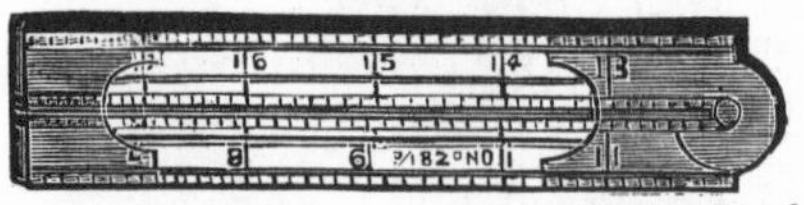

	Each.	Per doz.
40840 Carpenters' 1 Foot Rules..	$0.04	$0.45
40841 Carpenters' Boxwood Rules, 1 foot, 4-fold, double brass bound, ⅝ inch wide..	.15	1.75
40842 Carpenters' Boxwood Rules, 2 feet, 4-fold, 1 inch wide	.08	.70
40843 Carpenters' Boxwood Rules, 2 feet, 4-fold, half brass bound, 1 inch wide	.18	2.00
40844 Carpenters' Boxwood Rules, 2 feet, 4-fold, double brass bound, 1 inch wide	.27	2.92
40845 Carpenters' 2 feet, 4-fold, Broad Boxwood Rules, has joints spaced in 8ths, 10ths and 16ths of inches, drafting scales, 1⅜ in. wide, double brass bound	.40	4.32
40846 Carpenters' 2 feet, 4-fold, Broad Boxwood Rules, has board measure, and is spaced in 12ths and 16ths of inches; drafting scales, arch joint brass bound on ends, 1⅜ inches wide	.23	2.50

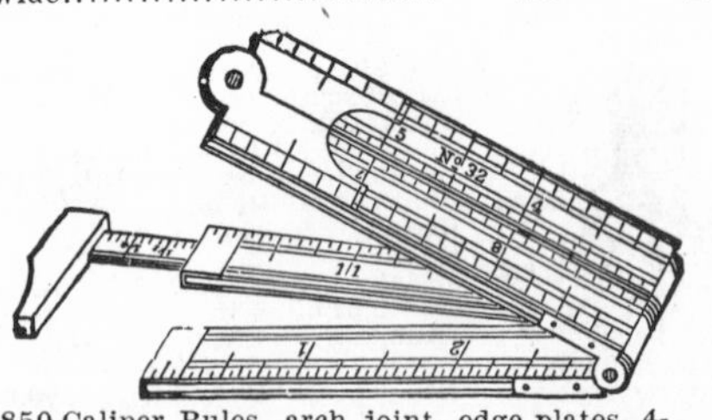

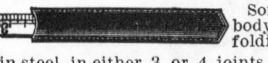

40850 Caliper Rules, arch joint, edge plates, 4-fold, 12 inches, in 8ths, 10ths, 12ths, and 16ths. 1 inch wide. Each $0.20

40851 6-inch Boxwood Caliper Rules, square joint, 2 fold, 8ths, 10ths, 12ths and 16ths, ⅞ in. wide. Each .... .10

Pocket Rule.

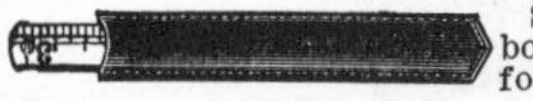

Something for everybody's vest pocket. A folding rule, made of thin steel, in either 3 or 4 joints, in a nice stitched leather case. The 3 jointed ones, when folded in the case, are 4 inches long, and the 4 jointed 3 inches long. They are as accurate as the most expensive boxwood rules made, and more convenient; spaced in 16ths.

40855 3 joints. 40855½ 4 joints.
Price, each .... $0.23 Per dozen $2.50
Postage, 3c.

Some goods look better than they are, while others are really better than they look. You must make a good many allowances for the latter kind as we do not flatter our goods either by illustration or description.

Log and Board Rules.

Log Rules, either Scribner or Doyle scale.
40856 Scribner's scale. **40856½** Doyle's scale.
No. 14, 4 feet square head $1.15
No. 15, 3 feet square head....................... 1.00
No. 16, 4 feet solid steel head...................... 1.15
In ordering log rules give scale wanted; also required measurement.

WALKING CANE LOG AND BOARD RULES.

40857 Walking cane log or board rule, octagon shape, 3 feet long, 8 lines, Doyle's scale only, brass head and end. Price, each..$0.70 Per dozen..$7.50

40858 Board Rules, hand shaved, second growth, No. 1, 3 tier, 3¼ feet; inspectors' board, extra heavy brazed heads, steel caps and brass shoulders. Each..........................$1.15
40859 Board Rules. No. V, 3 tier, 3 feet, extra heavy brazed heads. Each.................. 1.00

Plumbs and Levels.

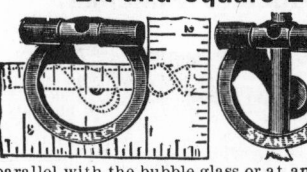

40860 Stanley's Improved Level Sighting. Leveling from one given point to another at a long distance away can be accomplished with these devices; when not in use can be detached and put away for further use; can be attached to any level. Price, per pair............$0.58

40863 Pocket Levels; brass top plate, japanned; weight, 6 oz.
Each.....$0.08
Per doz.. .87

40864 Pocket Level, all brass, very handsome; weight, 6 oz. Each................................$ .20
Per dozen.. 2.25

Bit and Square Level.

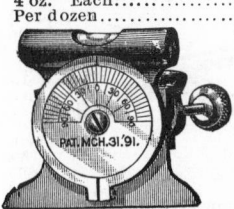

The frame of this level has 3 pairs of V-slots on its back and edges. The shank to a bit will be in these slots, either parallel with the bubble glass or at an exact angle of 45 degrees. A thumb screw secures the level to the bit in either position, and boring can be done with perfect accuracy as to perpendicular, horizontal or angle of 45 degrees, by observing the bubble glass while turning the bit.

This level can with equal facility be attached to a carpenter's square, thus making an accurate plumb or level for all ordinary use.
40866 Bit and Square Level, brass frame; weight, 4 oz. Each................................$0.25
Per dozen.. 2.70

40867 The Unique Pocket Level and Plumb Inclinometer, Bevel, etc., can be applied to rule, steel square, straight edge, auger bit, drill, etc.; is well made and is the most complete and convenient article of its kind made. Come nickel plated or plain brass.

	Each.	Per doz.
Brass	$0.60	$6.48
Nickel plated	.80	8.64

40868—Goodell's Right Angle Triangle, Iron Level, 4 inch.
Each, 67c.
Per doz.,
$6.75

40870—Goodell's Patent Iron Level, with double plumb, made in four sizes. Each.
6 inch...$1.15
12 inch.. 1.35
18 inch.. 1.45
24 inch.. 1.88

40872 Machinists' Level, iron frame, with inclinometer; length, 12 inches. Each $2.15
40873 Length, 18 inches. Each.................. 2.55

24—3d

Levels—Continued.

40875 Patent Improved Adjustable Plumb and Level, arch top plate, two side views, polished and tipped, 26, 28 or 30 inches, all sizes; weight, 3½ lbs. Each..............................$0.57
40876 Patent Adjustable Plumb and Level, made of three pieces of wood, joined together, arch top plate, two ornamental brass-lipped side views, polished; length, 26, 28 or 30 inches. Each.. .90
40877 Level Glasses, assorted sizes. Each........ .05

Stratton Bros.' Levels.

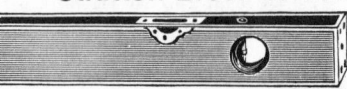

40880—Stratton Bros.' Improved Spirit Levels. Without doubt these are the finest levels made, are more accurate, durable and reliable than any other; made of rosewood and mahogany, selected wood, adjustable level and two ornamental brass lipped side views, brass corner rods, heavy brass top and end plates, polished; all of the edges protected by heavy brass rods. (see cut.)

Length	22	24	26	28	30
Rosewood	$5.50	$5.90	$6.00	$6.10	$6.48
Mahogany, each	3.98	4.10	4.22	4.35	4.55

40881 Stanley's Patent Handy Plumb and Level made of cherry, arch top plate, two side views; lengths, from 24 to 30 inches. The shallow grooves along each side afford an excellent grip on the tool, and if used on a ladder or high staging there is less liability of slipping from the hand than with the ordinary pattern, and is especially desirable for house framing, bridge building, etc., for this reason. Price, each............................$0.90

Cook's Patent Plumb and Level.

40882 Cook's Patent Level, mahogany, nickel trimmings. We can furnish 24-inch only......$1.95
40883 Cook's Patent Level, mahogany, made of three pieces glued together, nickel trimmings. We can furnish 24-inch only 2.20
40884 Cook's Patent Level, cherry, nickel trimmings. We can furnish 24, 26, 30-inch only.... 1.65
40885 Cook's Patent Level, cherry, made of three pieces glued together, nickel trimming. We can furnish 24, 26, 30-inch only...................... 1.95
40886 Cook's Patent Level, cherry, brass trimmings. We can furnish 24, 26, 30-inch only... 1.44
40887 Level Glasses, assorted sizes. Each........ .05

Socket Scratch Awls.

40895 Cast Steel, with cherry handle, Norway iron socket; length of awl and socket, 5 inches. This is a very fine tool. Each...........................$0.10
Per dozen... 1.08

Chalk Line Reels.

40900 Chalk Line Reels, beechwood, with scratch awls (like cut); weight, 6 oz. Each............$0.08
40901 Same, without scratch awls, 4 oz. Each... .05
40902 Scratch awls only, 5 oz. Each............ .05
NOTE.—For Cha.k Lines, see Fish Lines in Index.

Shingling Bracket.

40905 Elmer's Shingling Bracket is adjustable and absolutely safe; made entirely of malleable iron and is very strong; adjustable to any pitch of roof; the more weight the stronger the grip. Directions: In adjusting to roof throw back the top of the bracket as far as it will go, then slide the under jaw under and between two shingles, then rock the can backward and forward according to the pressure required for different thickness of shingles and bring down the top part to the required position and lock the brace with the button. Price, per pair....................$0.48
Per single dozen...................................... 2.82

Shingling Brackets—Continued.

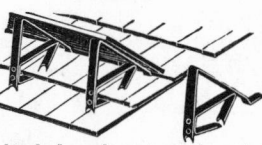

40906 Stanley's Patent Roofing Bracket is an efficient device used in connection with shingling roofs. Every carpenter is employed more or less in doing this kind of work and needs suitable staging for his security. This bracket not only is secure, but may be put in position quicker than any other without the waste of lumber, as in the old way. Each......$0.25
Per dozen... 2.70

Trammel Points.

40909 Trammel Points, small, with steel points; weight, 6 oz. Per pair............$0.70
40910 Trammel Points, medium, with steel points; weight, 6 oz. Per pair.................$0.90

Rule Trammel Point.

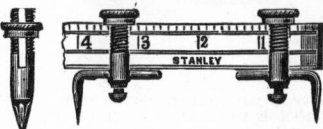

40915 Adapted for convenient use to a carpenter's rule; can be attached to folding rules of any ordinary width, and in many kinds of work will take the place of regular trammel points, calipers or divider. A convenient marking gauge can be made by using the rule for a gauge bar. Complete set consists of two brass-trimmed heads, with movable steel points, and one head with a pencil socket; weight, 3 ounces.
Price, each, no rule............ ....$0.38
Per dozen........................ . ... 4.10

T Bevels.

Weight, 7 to 9 oz. each.

40918 Sliding T Bevel.

Size...	6 in.	8 in.	10 in.	12 in.
Each..	$0.18	$0.20	$0.22	$0.25
Doz..	1.98	2.15	2.34	2.52

Bevels and Squares.

40920 Patent Eureka T Bevels, iron handle, steel blade, with parallel edges. The blade is secured at an angle by turning the thumb screw at the lower end of handle.

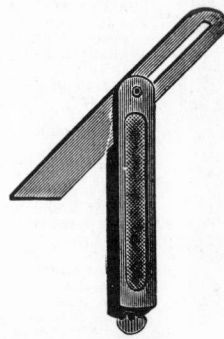

Sizes	6 in.	8 in.	10 in.
Each	$0.30	$0.33	$0.40
Doz..	3.24	3.42	4.00

Try Square.

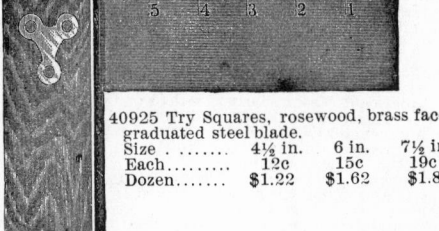

40925 Try Squares, rosewood, brass face, graduated steel blade.

Size	4½ in.	6 in.	7½ in.
Each	12c	15c	19c
Dozen	$1.22	$1.62	$1.87

Try and Miter Square.

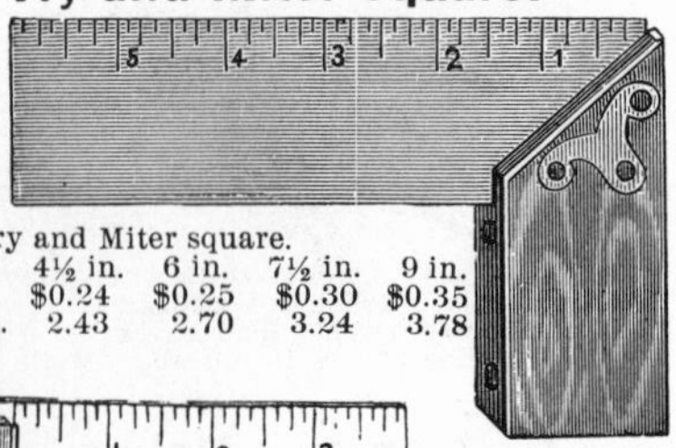

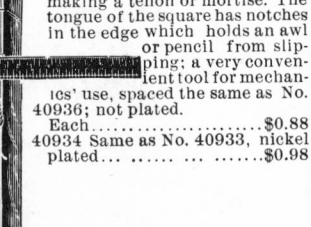

40926 Try and Miter square.

Size	4½ in.	6 in.	7½ in.	9 in.
Each	$0.24	$0.25	$0.30	$0.35
Per doz.	2.43	2.70	3.24	3.78

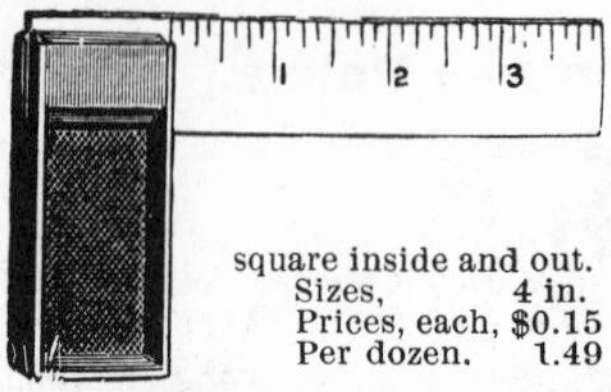

40927 Patent Improved Try Squares, iron handle, graduated steel blade, square inside and out.

Sizes,	4 in.	6 in.	8 in.
Prices, each,	$0.15	$0.20	$0.25
Per dozen.	1.49	1.89	2.43

Topp's Framing Tool.

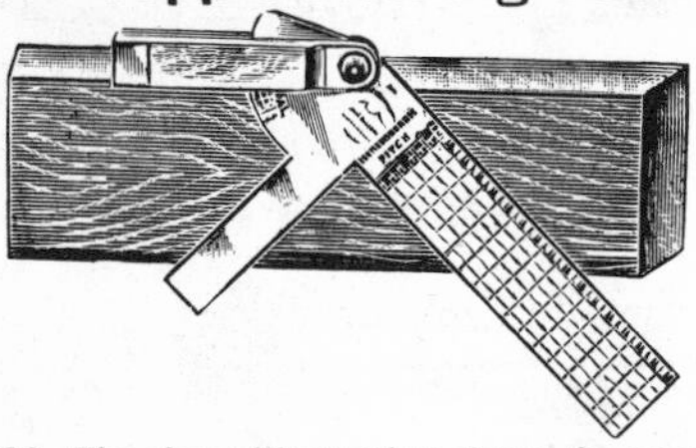

40928 The above illustration shows the manner in which the tool is used when marking out rafters.

A Perfect Tool and the only tool for the purpose ever invented. Endorsed by architects, contractors and mechanics everywhere. Saves from 3 to 24 hours in laying out a shingle roof. Saves time for the skilled mechanic, and enables the ordinary workman to frame the most difficult roof with absolute certainty. Price, each.......$1.50

Steel Squares.

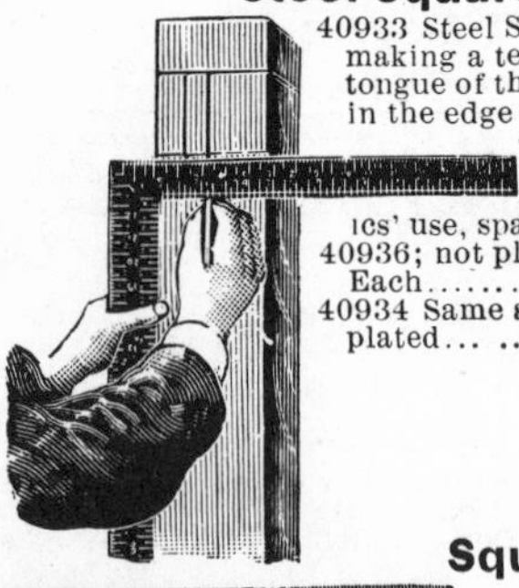

40933 Steel Square calculated for making a tenon or mortise. The tongue of the square has notches in the edge which holds an awl or pencil from slipping; a very convenient tool for mechanics' use, spaced the same as No. 40936; not plated.
Each......................$0.88

40934 Same as No. 40933, nickel plated... ....$0.98

Squares.

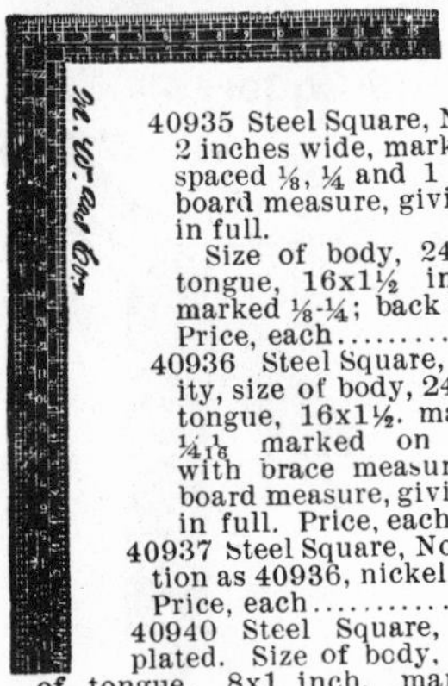

These squares are the very best made and we fully warrant them.

40935 Steel Square, No. 7, extra quality, 2 inches wide, marked on both sides, spaced ⅛, ¼ and 1 inch. Essex new board measure, giving feet and inches in full.
Size of body, 24x2 inches; size of tongue, 16x1½ inch. The face is marked ⅛-¼; back is marked ¼-1¼-¼.
Price, each.............................$0.45

40936 Steel Square, No. 3, extra quality, size of body, 24x2 inches, size of tongue, 16x1½, marked on face, 1/16-1/4-1/8, marked on back, 1/12-¼-2-¼, with brace measure and Essex new board measure, giving feet and inches in full. Price, each..................... .50

40937 Steel Square, No. 03, same description as 40936, nickel plated.
Price, each............................... .60

40940 Steel Square, No. 112, nickel plated. Size of body, 12x1½ inch, size of tongue, 8x1 inch, marked on face, 1/8-1/16-1/8, marked on back 1/12-1/8-1/12-1/8. This square will be found very convenient, as it may be put in an ordinary tool chest. Price, each... .50

40942 Steel Square, No. 14, size of body, 24x2 inch, size of tongue, 16x1½, with brace measure and Essex board measured, marked on face, 1/8-1/4-1/8-1/4, marked on back, 1/4-1-1/4-1/4, giving feet and inches in full. Price, each................... .40

40944 Steel Square No. 100, extra quality, body 24x2 inches; tongue, 16x 1½; brace measure, 8 square and Essex's board marked on face, 1/16-1/8-1/16-1/8, marked on back 1/2 and 100-1/32 1/2-1/16 giving feet and inches in full. Price, each ....$ 0.90

40945 Same square as No. 40944 only nickel plated. Price, each 1.00

40947 Iron Square, size of body, 24x1½ inches; size of tongue, 12x1 inch, marked in ⅛ths on both sides. Price, each........................ .18

40950 Iron Square, size of body, 24x2 inch; size of tongue, 12x1½ inch; marked in ⅛ths on both sides. Price, each......................... 25

Plumb Bobs.

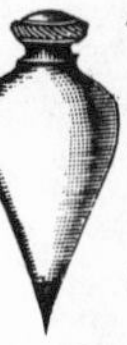

40951 Plumb Bob, iron japanned; weight 9½ ounces.
Each......................................$0.05
Per dozen...... .... .54

40953 Plumb Bob, brass, steel point; weight, 6 ounces.
Each .... .25
Per dozen.................................. 2.70

40955 Plumb Bob, brass, steel points, screw caps.
Weight, 1 lb............ .... .85
Weight, 2 lbs.. 1.00
Weight, 4 lbs.. 1 35

Stanley's Odd Jobs.

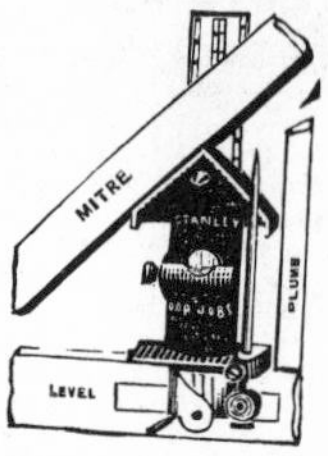

40957 This tool embraces within itself, and when in combination with an ordinary carpenter's rule, a try-square, mitre square, T-square, marking gauge, depth gauge, mitre, level, spirit level and plumb, beam, compass, inside square for making boxes and frames; weight, 10 oz.
No. 1, Odd Job, nickel plated with level.
Each.........................$0.58

Gauges.

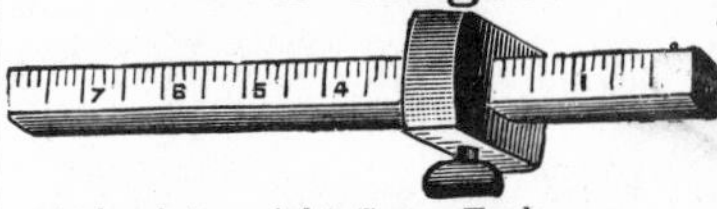

40960 Marking Gauge, beech-wood, oval bar, steel point; weight, 7 oz. Each............ .... $0.04
Per dozen.. .44

40962 Stanley's Butt and Rabbet Gauge for hanging doors, mortising, marking, etc. This without question is the most ingenious as well the most convenient tool for carpenters' use ever invented. No carpenter should be without one. Each.........................$1.00

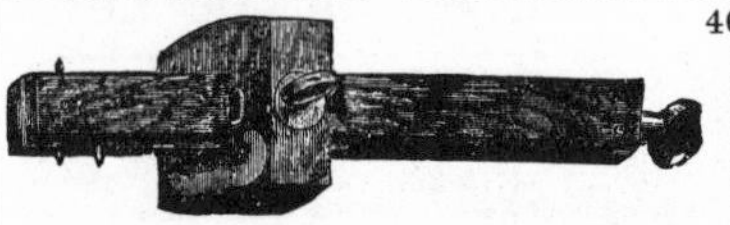

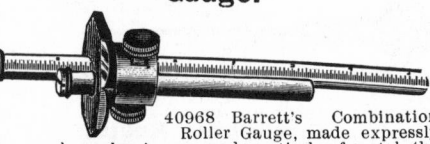

40963 Marking Mortise Gauge, rosewood, plated, head, improved screw slide, brass thumb screw and shoe, oval bar, marked, steel points; weight, 9 oz. Each.........$0.34
Per dozen.......... .... 3.68

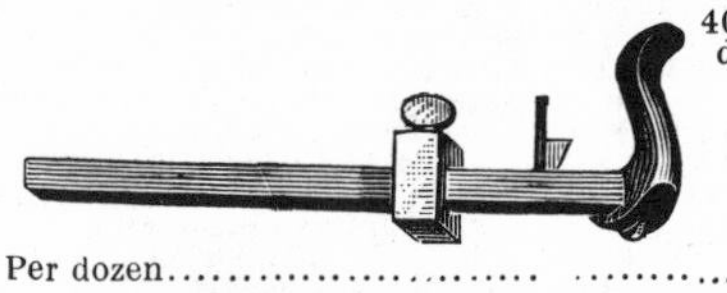

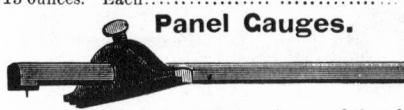

40965 Handle Slitting Gauge, with roller and 17 in. marked bar. Each$0.34
Per dozen.. 3.68

Barrett's Combination Roller Gauge.

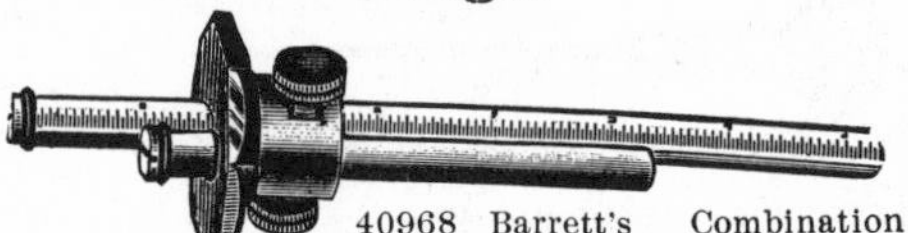

40968 Barrett's Combination Roller Gauge, made expressly for wood workers' use, made entirely of metal; the most perfect tool of the kind ever invented; weight, 15 ounces. Each.......................... $0.65

Panel Gauges.

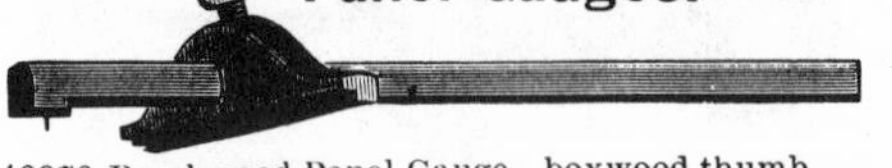

40970 Beechwood Panel Gauge, boxwood thumb screws, 17 inches oval bar. Each.................$0.15
Per dozen 1.62

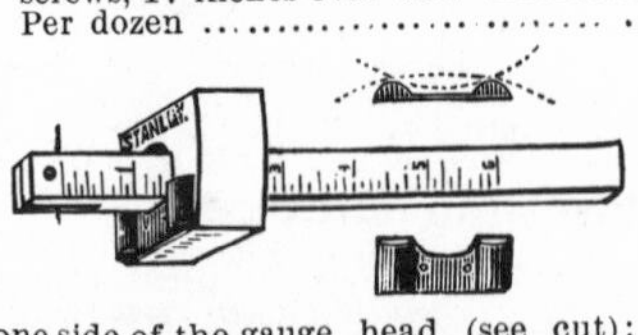

Stanley's Patent Improved Marking Gauges have brass face, with two ribs or projectors attached to one side of the gauge head (see cut); will enable the operator to run a gauge line with perfect steadiness and accuracy around curves of any degree and either concave or convex. The opposite side of the gauge head remains flat and can be used for all ordinary work.
40972 Beechwood, boxwood thumb screw. Each.$0.07
40973 Boxwood, brass thumb screw and shoe, plated head, adjusting steel point. Each...... .20

EVERYTHING WE SELL YOU IS *WORTH* THE *MONEY*.

We will not handle trash at any price; not if we know it.

Clapboard Marker.

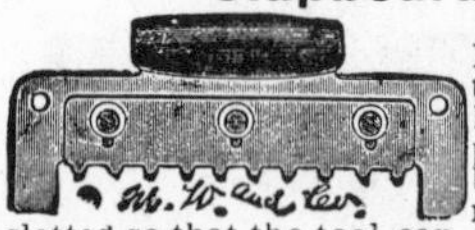

Adjustable Clapboard Marker. This ingenious tool can be used with one hand while the other is employed in keeping a clapboard in position. The marking blade is properly slotted so that the tool can be easily adjusted to any thickness of clapboard. The sharp edge of the teeth on marking board are just parallel with the other edges of the legs when placed against the corner board, and by moving the tool half an inch it will mark a full line across the clapboard exactly over and conforming to the edge of the corner board. There is then no difficulty in sawing for a perfectly close joint

40978 Adjustable Clapboard Marker, iron stock, with wooden handles, steel blade. Each........$0.40

Clapboard Gauge.

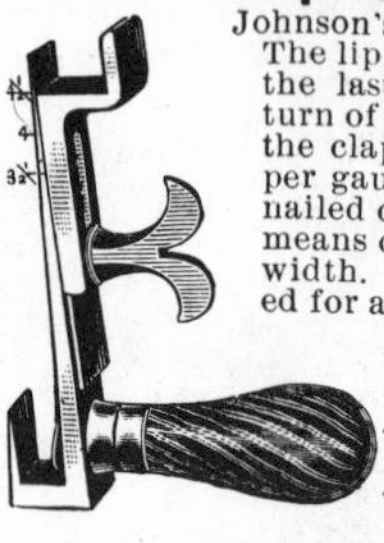

Johnson's Patent Clapboard Gauge. The lip on the bottom is slipped under the last clapboard; nailed on, a slight turn of the handle clamps it to its place; the clapboard can be placed on the upper gauge where it is held fast until nailed on. The upper gauge is set by means of a thumb screw to any desired width. The edge of the gauge is stamped for a short distance to facilitate setting. Once set it does not need moving.

	Each.	Per doz.
40979 No. 1 Plain, polished	$0.25	$2.92
40980 No. 2 Nickel plated	.35	3.78

Stanley's Clapboard (Sliding) Gauge.

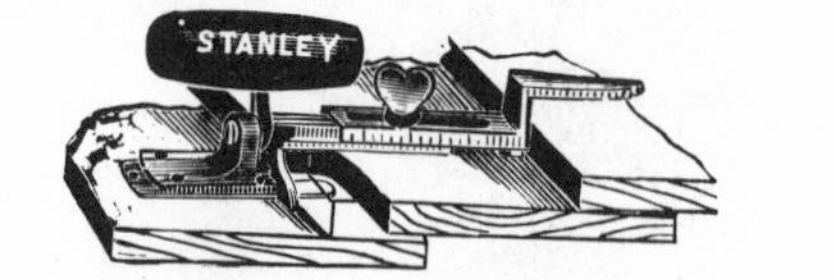

40981 Metal Stock, with wood handle, steel blades. Price, each...... ....$0.35

Conductors' Punches.

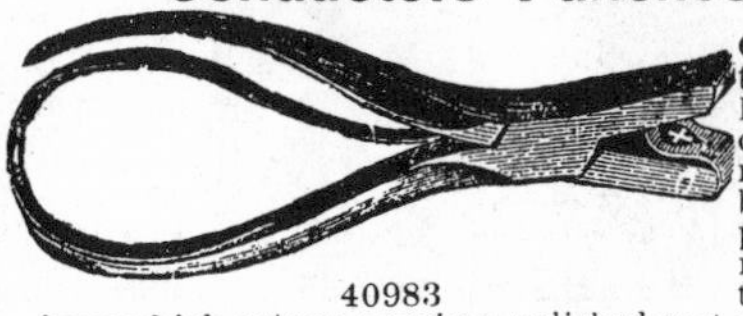

40982—Conductors' Punches, common, not like cut but have a piece of rubber between the jaws which acts as a spring; polished cast steel, Round die only. Weight, 5 ounces. Each $0.50
Per dozen.. 5.40

40983

40983 Conductors' Punches, like cut, extra cast steel, nickel plated, assorted fancy dies. Each. 1.00
Per dozen.. 11.00

40984 Conductors' Punches, nickel plated, with letter die; made only to order. Weight, 6 ounces.
Each, any letter.. 2.00

Spring Punches.

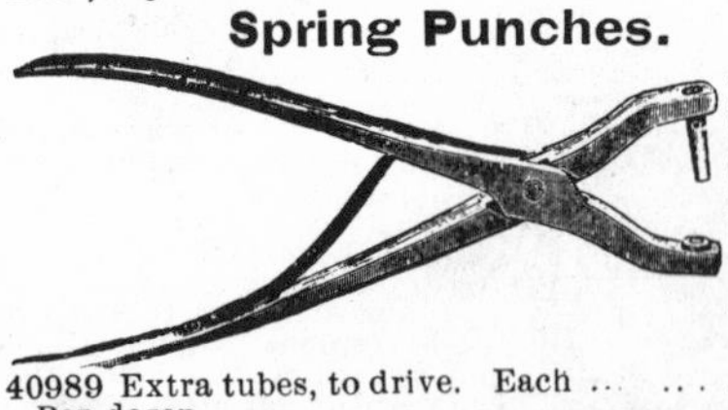

40988—Spring Punch, 6 inch, cast steel, polished. Each.... .... $0.20 Weight, 13 oz.

40989 Extra tubes, to drive. Each $0.06
Per dozen.. .65

40990 Revolving Spring Punch, extra cast steel, 4 tubes. Each..........$0.50 Per dozen....... 5.25

40991 6 tubes. Each............. .... .60
Weight, 14 ounces. Per dozen........ .... 6.25

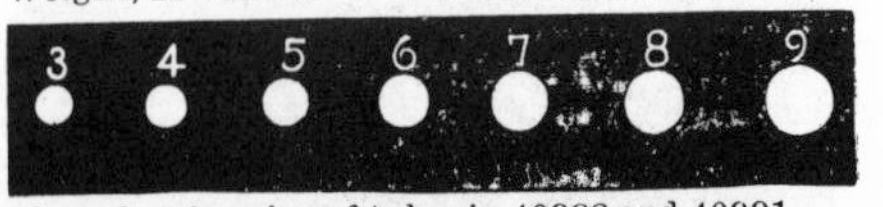

Plate showing size of tubes in 40988 and 40991.

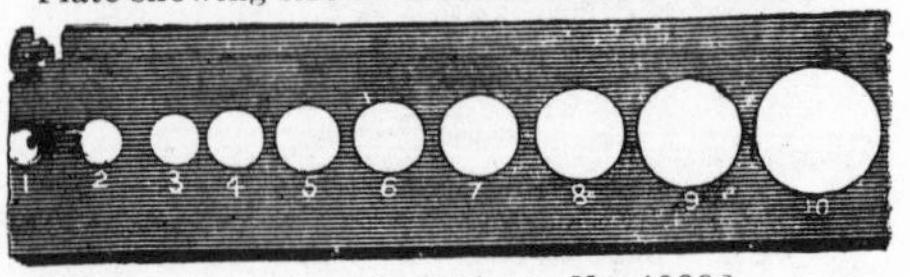

Plate showing size of punches. No. 40992.

40992 Hollow Saddlers' Punches.

Nos.	1, 2, 3, 4, 5	6, 7, 8, 9,	10.
Price, each	10c	12c.	15c.

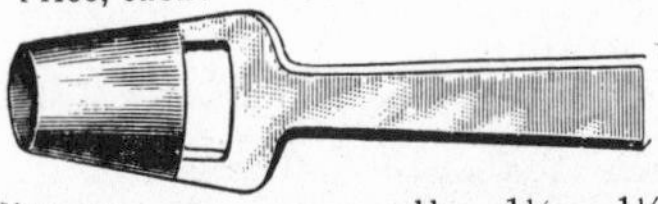

40993 Round Punches, cast steel, hand forged, very fine.

Sizes	1/16	1¼	1½	1¾	2⅛
Price, each	45c	75c.	$1.00	1.50	1.75
Sizes	2¼	2⅜	2½	2¾	3 in.
Price, each	$2.00	2.25	2.50	3.00.	3.50

Pliers.

40995— Flat Nose Pliers, made of a fine quality of steel.

Do not buy a small size to do the work that the large sizes are intended for.

Length, inches	3	3½	4	4½	5	5½	6
Price, each...	13c.	13c.	13c.	13c.	15c.	15c.	20c

40996 Flat Nose Pliers, made of the best quality of steel and are fitted with a spiral spring between the handles back of the jaws, which holds the jaws open when not in use. This is a great convenience, as the pliers are always ready for use.

Length, inches	3	3½	4	4½	5	5½	6
Plain, each ..	28c.	29c.	30c.	32c.	33c.	35c.	40c

40996½ Round Nose Pliers, polished jaws, 6 in.
Each.............................$0.40

Key's Patent, All Solid Steel Pliers, flat nose.

Length, inches	4	5	6	7 in.
40997 Plain, each.....	7c.	9c.	12c.	14c.
40997½ Nickel, each....	10c.	12c.	14c.	15c.

Wire Cutters and Pliers.

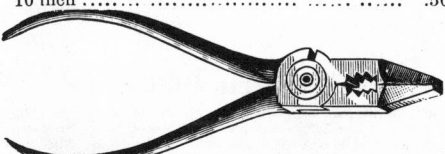

40998 Hall's Patent Compound Lever Nippers. These are without any exception the finest cutting nippers in the market. The most important feature about them is that all the parts are interchangeable.

If you accidentally break a handle, jaw, screw, etc., they can be replaced and you do not have to buy an entire new tool; made of the finest quality of steel.

Length, inches	4	5	7	8
Price, each	$0.60	$0.68	$1.00	$1.50

40999 Extra jaws 1 and 2 30c; 4, 45c; 5, 50c each.
41000 Extra handles, 1 and 2, 30c; 4, 45c; 5, 50c each.
41001 Extra screws 10c. each.
41002 Extra springs, 10c each.

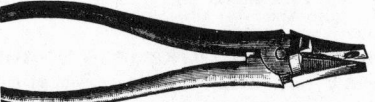

41005 Buttons Plier, made of the best quality of tool steel and guaranteed to be the strongest plier in the market. It is better and stronger than the old Buttons Pattern, as the cutting surfaces between the jaws are left out. This was the weak spot in the old make and caused the jaws to break easily.

Size.	Price, each.
6 inch..	$0.30
8 inch..	.40
10 inch.......................................	.50

41007 Combination Plier is a wire cutter, gas and flat nose plier in one tool, the most useful article in the market for the money; 5½ inches in length. Price, each, $0.20 Per dozen.. $2.00

41009 Cronk's Pliers and Wire Cutters, combined, the most ingenious and useful tool made for handling wire. A variety of articles may be made with it, such as hog rings and cage springs, wire springs, hooks, etc. Wire may be held in the jaws of pliers, and the wire cut without releasing it. Very handy to have about the house or shop; 8 inch. Weight, 17 ounces.
Each, $0.55 Per dozen.....................$6.00
41010 Same as above, 10 inches long. Each... .75
Per dozen 8.50

Wire Cutters—Continued.

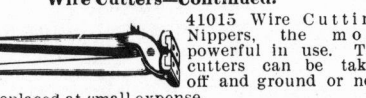

41015 Wire Cutting Nippers, the most powerful in use. The cutters can be taken off and ground or new ones replaced at small expense.

Size.....	8 in.	10 in.	11 in.	12 in.	13 in.
Each.....	70c	80c	90c	$1.00	$1.35

Extra jaws or cutters for Todd's nippers, any size, 25c per pair. Send sample when ordering.

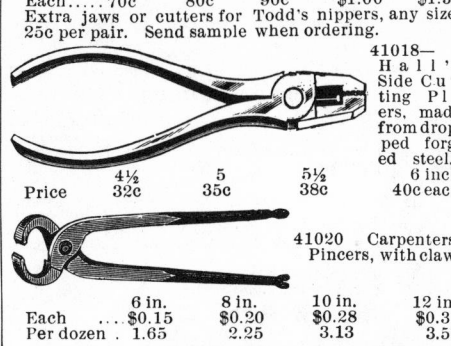

41018— Hall's Side Cutting Pliers, made from dropped forged steel.

	4½	5	5½	6 inch
Price	32c	35c	38c	40c each

41020 Carpenters' Pincers, with claw

	6 in.	8 in.	10 in.	12 in.
Each	$0.15	$0.20	$0.28	$0.35
Per dozen	1.65	2.25	3.13	3.50

Tack Claw.

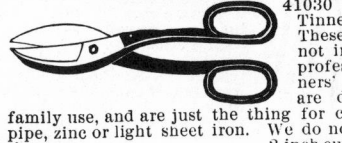

41025 Tack Claw, forged steel blade, finished handle. Each....$0.06 Per dozen $0.65

Nail Puller.

41028 The Improved Nail Puller, made of the best tool steel and so constructed that it cannot break or get out of order. Iron or steel nails can be pulled without being bent.
Price, each $1.00
Price, per dozen 10.00

Tinners' Shears.

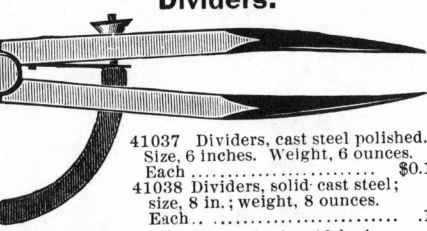

41030 The Ajax Tinners' Shears. These shears are not intended for professional tinners' use. They are designed for family use, and are just the thing for cutting stove pipe, zinc or light sheet iron. We do not guarantee them. 2 inch cut. 3 inch cut.
Each...............................$0.22 $0.35
Per dozen........................ 2.28 3.50
41031 Same as No. 41030, extra quality, for professional tinners' use; 3 in. cut. Each......... 1.35
Weight, 1 lb. 12 oz.
41032 Same as 41031, extra quality and equal to the best in the market; 3-in. cut. Per pair... 1.00

Compasses.

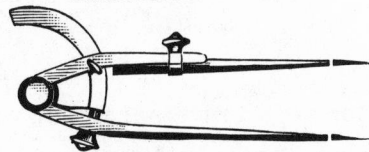

41035 Compasses, cast steel, polished.

Inches	3	4	5	6	7	8
Each	8	9	10	12	13	15
Per dozen...	$0.70	$0.75	$0.88	$1.00	$1.10	$1.31

Dividers.

41037 Dividers, cast steel polished. Size, 6 inches. Weight, 6 ounces.
Each......................................$0.13
41038 Dividers, solid cast steel; size, 8 in.; weight, 8 ounces.
Each........................... .18
41039 Dividers, solid cast steel; size, 10 inches; weight, 12 ounces. Each.................. .24

Extension Dividers.

41040 Cast Steel Polished, Single Leg Extension Dividers, as shown above, a common lead pencil can be used in place of the movable point. The 6-inch size will scribe a 17-inch circle, the 7-inch a 20-inch circle, the 8-inch a 22-inch circle and the 10-inch a 30-inch circle.

Size, inches	6	7	8	10
Per dozen...	$4.50	$5.00	$5.50	$6.00
Each.........	.45	.50	.55	.60

Calipers.

41045 Calipers, self registering, for outside or inside; length, 4 in., to caliper, 2 in., nickel plated; weight, 4 oz.
Each.... $0.40
Per doz. 4.25
41046 Self Registering Calipers, 6 in. long, will caliper 4 inch.
Each.....$0.60
Per doz... 6.50

41047 Wing Calipers, with spring and set screw.
6 inch; weight, 6 oz. Each..$0.25 Per doz.... 2.70
41048 8 inch; weight, 12 ounces..$0.30 Per doz 3.24

41050 Fancy Caliper; 2½ inches weight 3 ounces.
Each, $0.09
Pr.dz. .98

41052 Double Calipers cast steel; weight, 4 oz.; 4 in.......$0.11
Per dozen.......... 1.14
41053 Double Calipers, cast steel, weight; 5 oz.; 6 in. Each.......$0.15
Per dozen......... 1.62

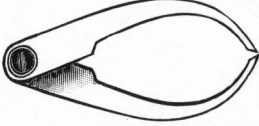

41054 Inside Calipers, cast steel, polished.

Size, inch	3	4	5	6
Each	$0.07	.08	.10	12

41055 Outside Calipers, cast steel, polished.

Size, inch.	4	5	6	8
Each.	$0.08	.10	.12	.15

Pencil Holders.

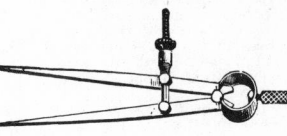

41060 Excelsior Pencil Holder, can be attached to any divider; weight, 3 ounces.
Each.......$0.18
Per dozen.. 1.95

MACHINISTS' TOOLS.
Spring Dividers.

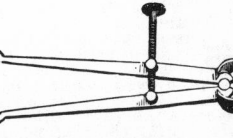

41068 Yankee Spring Dividers. These dividers are very finely made goods, are perfectly made and nicely finished.

Length	Each.
3 inches	$0.57
4 inches.......................................	.65
5 inches.......................................	.70
6 inches.......................................	.75

Inside Calipers.

41069 Yankee Inside Calipers, like the Yankee spring dividers are fine tools made on scientific principles the spring being so applied that a firm joint is always maintained and an even tension is secured, whether the legs are closed or opened to their full extent. Back lash in these calipers and dividers is impossible. 4 inch...........................$0.55
5 inch.. .60
6 inch.. .65

Calipers and Dividers.

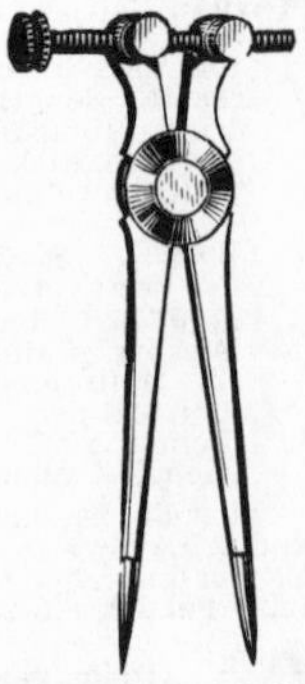

41070 Stevens' Reliable Divider, forged from heavy stock and operated with a right and left hand screw, also provided with two tension screws which remove all back lash. All machinists pronounce this a perfect tool; is 5 ins. in length.
Each....$1.20
Per doz..12.96

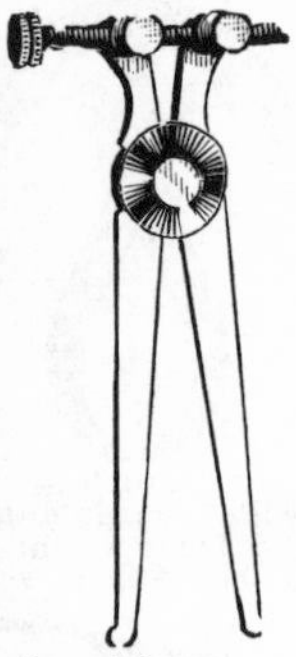

41071 Stevens' Reliable InsideCaliper,forged from heavy stock and operated with a right and left handscrew,also provided with two tension screws which remove all back lash: pronounced by all machinists to be perfect; length, 5 inches.
Price, each.......$1.00. Per dozen.......... $10.80

Scriber.

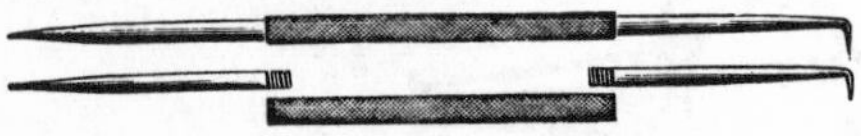

41072 Stevens' No. 80 Scriber for mechanics' use, made in three pieces, the center piece being heavily knurled, into which is screwed the two points which are made of fine steel, nicely tempered; is 7 inches in length. Each..........$0.35
Per dozen.......... 3.78

Depth Gauge.

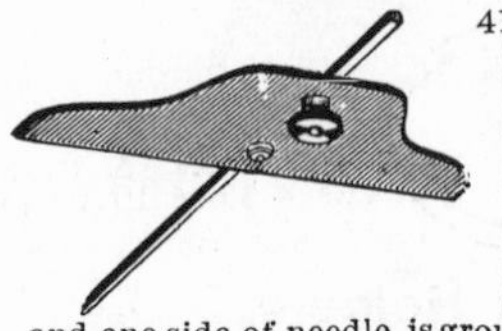

41073 Stevens' Depth Gauge for machinists' use. The back is made from sheet steel, nicely polished; the edge is ground straight so that by removing the needle it may be used as a straight edge, as one edge of back is beveled and one side of needle is ground away, bringing the point of needle directly under edge of back; it may be rocked, thus determining the depth of hole or slot more accurately than can be done with a tool having a broad base. Price, each...$0.45
Per dozen.......... 4.86

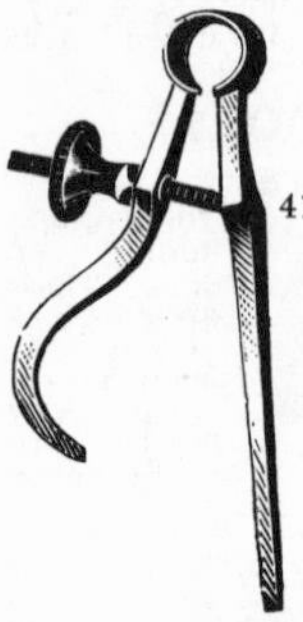

Keyhole Calipers.

41075 Spring Keyhole Calipers, with patent washer, an indispensable tool for calipering work from center when a seape caliper could not be used; a fine tool for wood turners. Two sizes. 3 inch, each...... $0.95
Per doz.......... 10.25
4 inch, each.......... 1.20
Per dozen.......... 12.95

Combination Inclinometer.

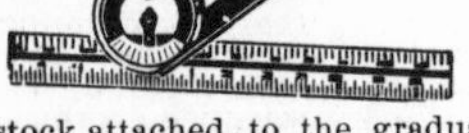

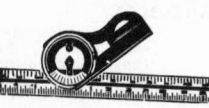

41077 Starrett's Patent Inclinometer, Try Square and Bevel Protractor. Combined steel stock and disk, both slotted to receive the blade, which folds in the stock attached to the graduated rotary disc; it may be secured at any angle from 0 to 90 degrees; by loosening the clamp screw it may be shortened or extended full length or removed for a straight edge; at 90 degrees the blade brings up against the case-hardened screw, accurately adjusted, thus forming a try square; by holding the blade perpendicular (the level in the stock being at right angles) a plumb, by folding the tool at level. Each.
12 inch blade.......... $4.30
18 inch blade.......... 5.10
24 inch blade.......... 6.00

Starrett's Double Square.

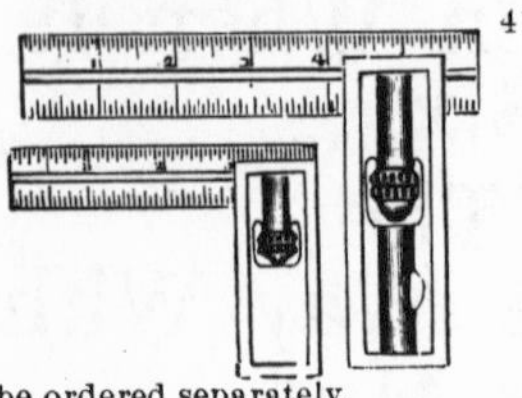

41079 Starrett's Patent Double Square. The most practical one for machinists' and fine tool makers' use in the market; with the extra bevel blades quoted below you have both the hexagon and octagon angles; this blade does not come with the square but must be ordered separately.
4 inch, each..........$1.10 6 inch, each..........$1.80

Bevel Blades.

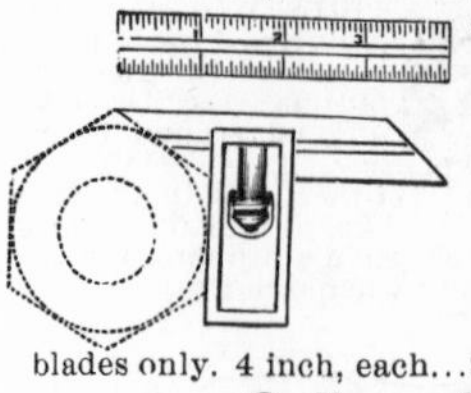

41081 This cut represents Starrett's Patent Double Square with an extra blade, one end of which is beveled to an octagon and another to a hexagon, the most simple and practical tool for obtaining these angles made. These prices below are for the bevel blades only. 4 inch, each...$0.32. 6 inch, each..$0.42

Caliper Square.

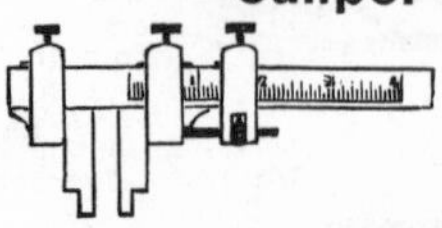

Starrett's Patent Caliper Square. The jaws are made independent and accurately ground; can be reversed for inside caliper of larger scope or used for depth gauge, etc. The beam is nicely graduated, 64 on one side, 100 on the other, for close work. This is an indispensable tool. Each.
41083 4 inch, with adjusting screw..........$3.20
41084 4 inch, without adjusting screw.......... 2.50

Screw Pitch Gauge.

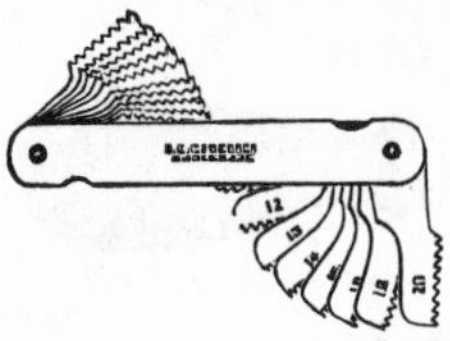

41086 Improved Screw Pitch Gauge, has 20 pitches. Size, 9, 10, 11, 12, 13, 14, 15, 16, 18, 20, 22, 24, 26, 28, 30, 32, 34, 36, 38, 40 to the inch. Can be used inside a nut as well as on the outside of a screw or bolt
Each.......... $0.75

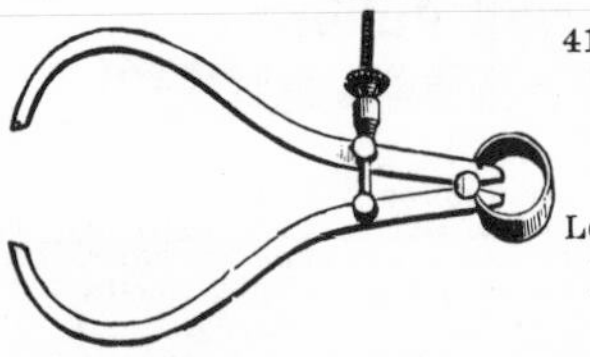

41088 Yankee Outside Calipers. Same description as No. 43075 Yankee Inside Calipers.

Length.	Each.
3 inch	$0.56
4 inch	.60
5 inch	.65

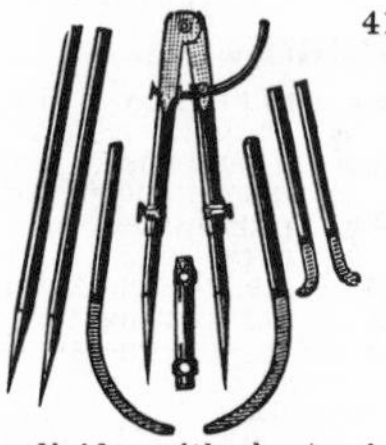

41090 Starrett's Improved Bronze Divider. The head and socket legs of this tool are made of drawn bronze metal, are tough, strong and finely finished; it is fitted with a patent locking nut, which is a valuable feature. After the fine adjustment is made the nut may be turned back, locking spring and arms firmly. A common pencil fits either socket leg. The auxiliary head fits the reversed end of short points. The divider with short points is 8 inches long; outside caliper, 10 inches long; inside caliper, 12½ inches. With short points will scribe a 24 inch circle, with long points, 34 inch circle. Complete with long and short points, outside and inside caliper legs and auxiliary pencil holder. Each..........$3.00

Combination Square.

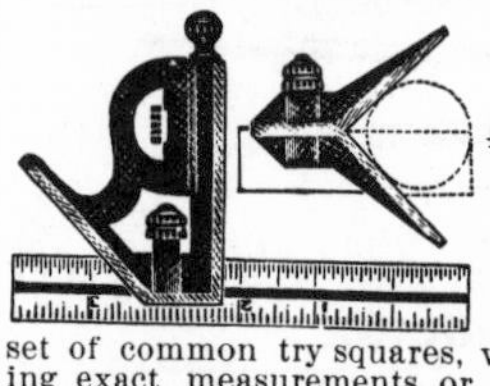

41093 Combination Square, Starrett's Patent Square with the adjustable scale. This is a very convenient and useful tool, a complete substitute for a whole set of common try squares, very useful for transferring exact measurements or laying out work for a miter. With the auxiliary center head it forms a centering square both inside and outside; every tool warranted accurate; made in three sizes with center head and level. Each,
6 inch...$1.70 9 inch....$2.15 12 inch....$2.30

Bevel Protractor.

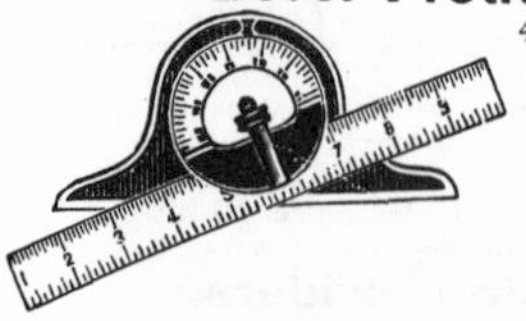

41095 Starrett's Improved Bevel Protractor and Adjustable Rule, held firmly at any point by a thumb nut, which passes through a revolving turret, is nicely graduated in degrees from 0 to 90, both right and left. The best and most accurate tool of its kind ever invented. Each.
9 inch Rule, 5 inch head..........$2.15
12 inch Rule, 7 inch head.......... 2.30
18 inch Rule, 7 inch head.......... 3.25
24 inch Rule, 7 inch head.......... 4.25

Starrett's Universal Bevel.

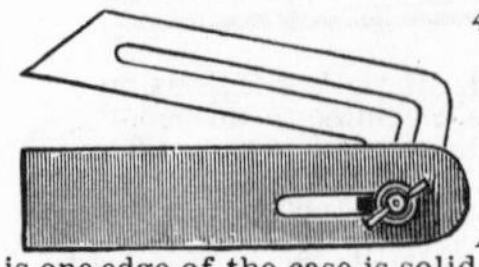

41098 Improved features. The set-off in the blade increases its capacity and usefulness for bevel gear work, etc., so that any angle, however slight, may be obtained. Another valuable feature is one edge of the case is solid, forms a rest directly under the blade, where thin templets may be placed and accurately fitted. Each..........$1.30

Tool Chests.

These Chests are all made of well seasoned oak, finely finished with dovetail corners. The locks, handles and trimmings are strong and made for wear.

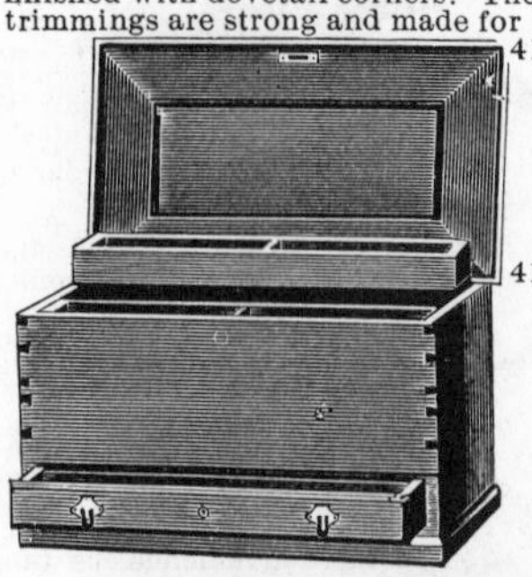

41203 **No. 1 Machinists' Chest.** This is exactly like cut, with 1 bottom drawer. Length, 20 in.; width, 11 in.; height, 11½ in.
Price..........$3.75

41205 **No. 2 Machinists' Chest.** This is the same as cut but has two separate lower drawers. Yale lock and fancy panel in lid. Length, 20 inches; width, 11 inches; height, 11½ inches.
Price..........$4.75

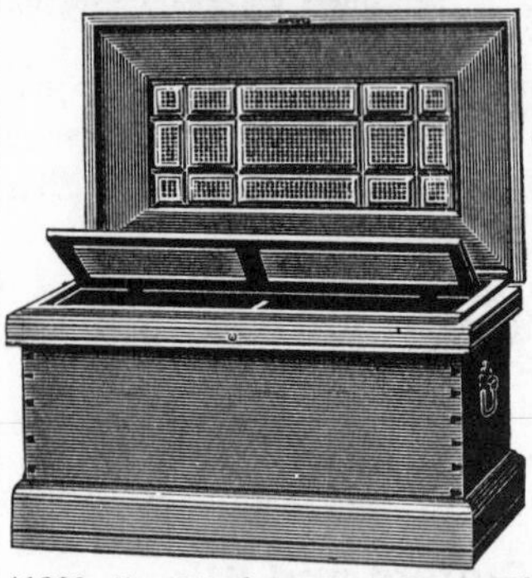

41208 **No. 4½ Carpenters' Chest.** This is the same as cut; it is a medium-sized chest with two sliding trays, rack in bottom for three saws, has fancy panel in lid and bronze handle. Length, 28 in.; width, 15 in.; height, 12½ in.
Price.....$6.85

41209 **No. 5½ Carpenters' Chest.** The same as above but considerably larger. Length, 31 in.; width, 18 in.; height, 17 in. Price..........$8.90

41210 **No. 6½ Carpenters' Chest.** The same as number 4½, except in size. Length, 36 in.; width, 21 in.; height, 19 in. Price..........10.60

Oil Stones.

Best quality White Washita Oil Stones, green label brand. We make a specialty of this brand of Washita stone, which is carefully selected with reference to its cutting qualities, and is much superior to the quality ordinarily kept for sale; it is softer, has a more even grain and is not liable to glaze with proper usage. Never use kerosene oil on any kind of oil stone.

Unmounted Washita Stones.

Each
41215 Washita Oil Stones, about 1 lb..........$0.30
41216 Washita Oil Stones, 1½ lbs.......... .45

Mounted Washita Stones.

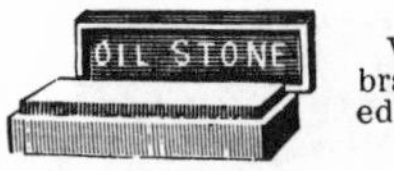

Washita Oil Stones, green label brand, very fine qualities; mounted in mahogany cases.

			Each
41218	Size, 5x1¾x1⅛,	weight, 16 oz..........	$0.42
41219	Size, 6x1⅞x1⅛,	weight, 22 oz..........	.47
41220	Size, 7x1⅞x1,	weight, 25 oz..........	.52
41221	Size, 8x1¾x1,	weight, 30 oz..........	.60

Washita Slips.

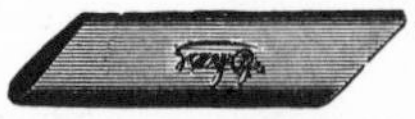

41225 Round Edge Washita Slips, 3½ to 5 inches.
Each..........$0.15
41226 Round Edge Slips, *extra quality*.......... .20
41227 Pen Knife Pieces, 3 to 5 inches in length, 1x¾ cut, expressly for sharpening pen knives.
Price, each.......... .40

Soft Arkansas Oil Stones.

Soft Arkansas Oil Stones are very fine. They are very much liked by mechanics generally. They cut fast, do not glaze, produce a very keen cutting edge and are especially desirable for use in sharpening fine tools.

Unmounted Soft Arkansas Stones.

41230 Soft Arkansas Oil Stones, about 1 pound..$0.80
41231 Soft Arkansas Oil Stones, about 1½ pounds.......... 1.25

Mounted Soft Arkansas Stones.

Mounted Soft Arkansas Oil Stones in mahogany cases.
41235 Size, 5x1¾x1⅛.......... $0.70
41236 Size, 6x1⅞x1⅛.......... .90

Soft Arkansas Slips.

41237 Round Edge Slips, Soft Arkansas..........$0.50
41238 Pen Knife Pieces, Soft Arkansas.......... .50

INSURE YOUR MAIL PACKAGES.
. . SEE PAGE 1 . .

Oil Stone Wheels.

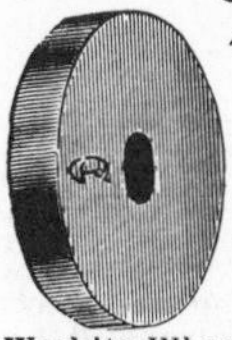

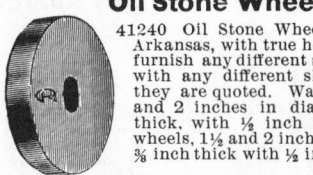

41240 Oil Stone Wheels, Washita and Arkansas, with true holes. We cannot furnish any different sizes of wheels or with any different size holes than as they are quoted. Washita wheels, 1½ and 2 inches in diameter by ⅜ inch thick, with ⅛ inch holes. Arkansas wheels, 1½ and 2 inches in diameter by ⅜ inch thick with ½ inch holes.

Washita Wheels, 1½ inch diameter, each	$0.90
" " 2 " " "	1.20
Arkansas " 1½ " " "	1.80
" " 2 " " "	2.40

Genuine Turkey Oil Stones.

Each.
41241 Genuine Turkey Oil Stones, about 1 pound. $0.40
41242 Genuine Turkey Oil Stones, about 1½ pounds .60

Chest Handles.

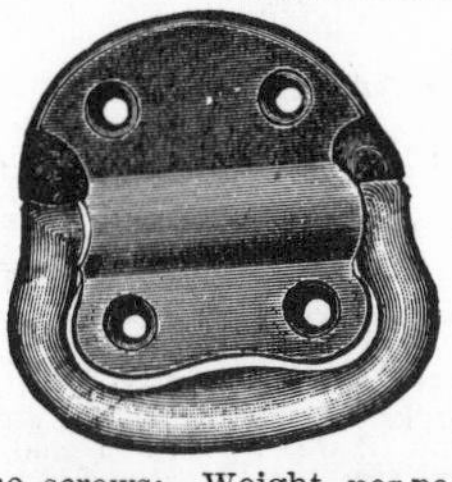

41245 Chest Handles, 3½ inch, japanned, heavy; weight, per pair, 1 pound 5 ounces. No screws.
Price, per pair $0.07
Per dozen .78

41246 Chest Handles, 4 inch, japanned heavy; weight, per pair, 1¾ lbs. No screws.
Price, per pair $0.10
Per dozen pair 1.08

41247 Chest Handles, 4½ inch, japanned, heavy; no screws; Weight, per pair, 2 lbs. 6 oz.
Price, per pair $0.13 Per 12 pair $1.40

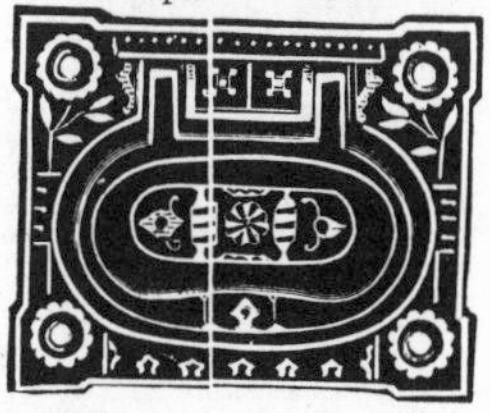

41248 Flush Chest Handles, iron. Kahala bronzed; packed with screws. Sizes: 3¼x2½, 4x3½, 5x4½. Weight, per pair, 14 oz., 1 lb., 5 oz, 2½ lbs.

Per pair	$0.12	$0.16	$0.23
Per 12 pairs	1.30	1.73	2.50

Strap Hinges.

Nearly everyone has screws that will fit these hinges. We do not furnish screws with hinges at prices quoted below. For screws see Index.

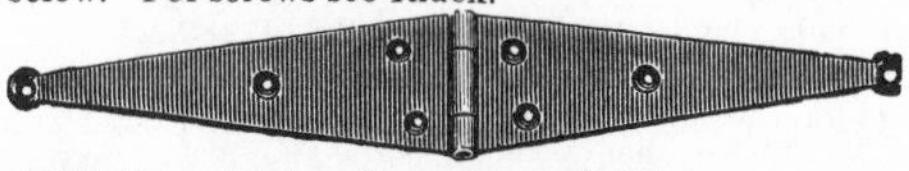

41255 Wrought Iron Strap Hinges, light.

Size	3 in.	4 in.
Weight, per pair	4 oz.	5 oz.
Sizes of screws used	7	7
Price, per pair	3c.	4c.
Price, per 12 pair	17c.	33c.

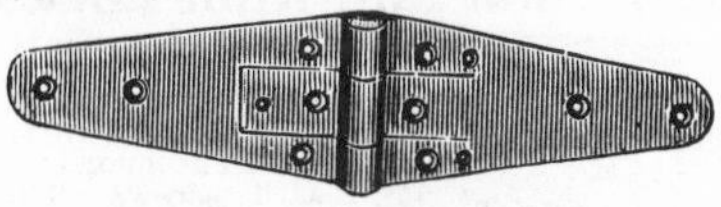

41257 Well's Patent Heavy Strap Hinges are superior to the common, from the fact that they are much stronger in the joint and will last much longer for that reason.

Size	6 in.	8 in.	10 in.	12 in
Weight	31 oz.	3¼ lbs.	4 lbs.	7 lbs.
Per pair	$0.12	$0.19	$0.28	$0.40
Per 12 pair	1.20	1.80	2.65	3.80

T-Hinges.

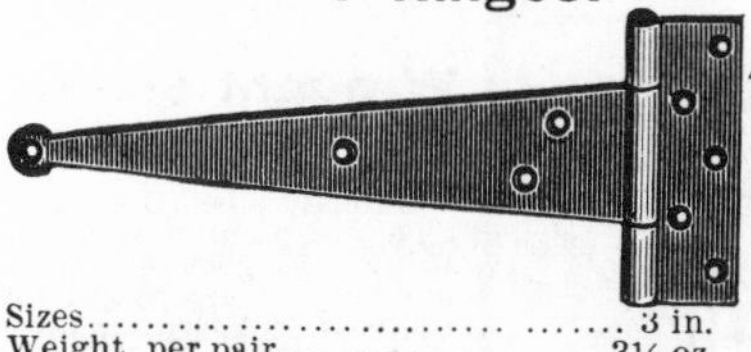

41258 T Hinges, wrought iron, light.

Sizes	3 in.	4 in.
Weight, per pair	3¼ oz.	5 oz.
Size of screw used	7	8
Price, per pair	$0.03	$0.04
Price, per 12 pair	.17	.33

41259 T Hinges, wrought iron, extra heavy.

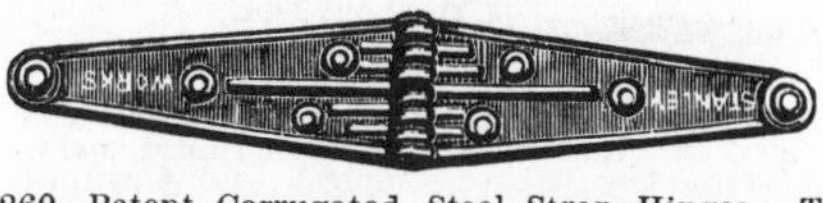

41260 Patent Corrugated Steel Strap Hinges, The principle of corrugation as applied to these hinges gives them great strength and rigidity at the joints, besides improving the general appearance. They are much lighter than the ordinary hinge and at the same time are capable of sustaining much greater weight,

Sizes	5 in.	6 in	8 in	10 in
price, per pair	$0.04	$0.06	$0.09	$0.15
price, 12 pair	.38	.55	.85	1.40

Hinges—Continued.

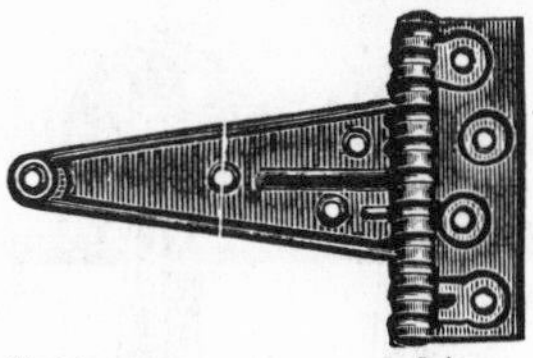

41261 Patent Corrugated Steel T Hinges, stronger and lighter than the common kind.

Sizes	5 in.	6 in.	8 in.	10 in.
Price, per pair	$0.06	$0.08	$0.12	$0.18
Price, 12 pair	.60	.70	1.10	1.50

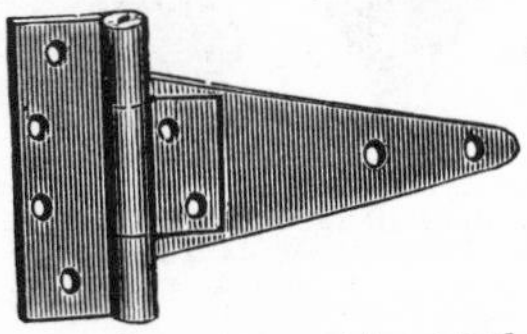

41262 Well's Patent Heavy T Hinges are better than the common T Hinge, being much stronger in the joint; will last twice as long as the ordinary kind.

Screws are not furnished at these prices.

Sizes	6 in.	8 in.	10 in.	12 in.
Weight	2¼ lbs.	3¼ lbs.	4⅛ lbs.	6¼ lbs.
Per pair	$0.14	$0.21	$0.31	$0.46
Per 12 pairs	1.40	2.30	3.10	4.60

Hinge Hasps.

41263

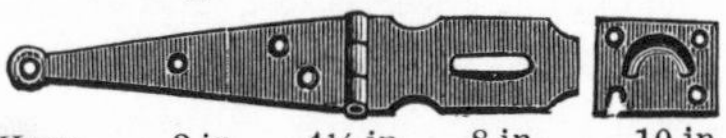

Length of Hasp	3 in.	4½ in.	8 in.	10 in.
Whole length	5¾ in.	7 in.	12½ in.	15 in.
Weight of pair	7 oz.	8 oz.	10 oz.	14 oz.
Size of screw used	8	9	10	10
Price, per set	5c	6c.	10c	12c
Per dozen set	40c.	50c.	85c.	$1.10

Screw Strap Hinges.

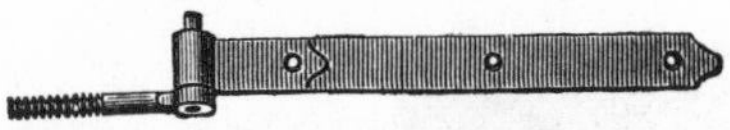

41264 Heavy Wrought Iron Strap.

Size	10 in.	12 in.	14 in.
Weight, per pair	3½ lbs.	4½ lbs.	5½ lbs.
Price, per pair	16c.	20c.	28c.
Per dozen pairs	$1.73	$2.16	$3.05

Screws not furnished.

Gate Hinges and Latches.

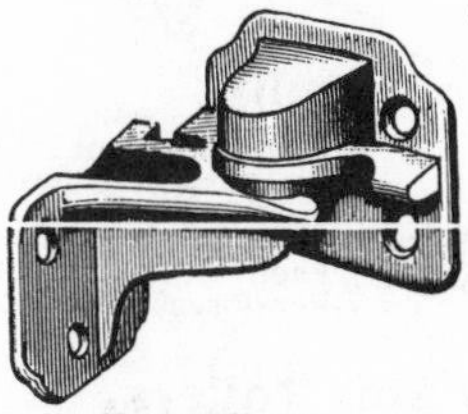

Upper Hinge

41269 Gate Hinges and Latches, Patent Double Swing (self-closing) Gate Hinges and Latches.
Weight, 3½ lbs.
Screws not furnished.
Gate Hinges and Latch complete.
Weight, 3½ lbs.
Each $0.25
Per dozen 2.70

41270 Gate Hinges only.
Weight, 2½ lbs.
Per set $0.18

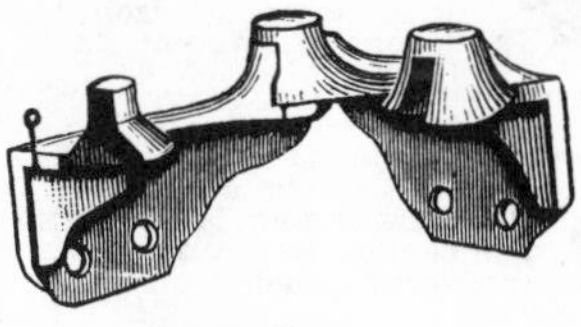

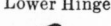

Lower Hinge.

41271 Gate Latch only. Weight 1¾ lbs. Each $0.08
Per doz .87

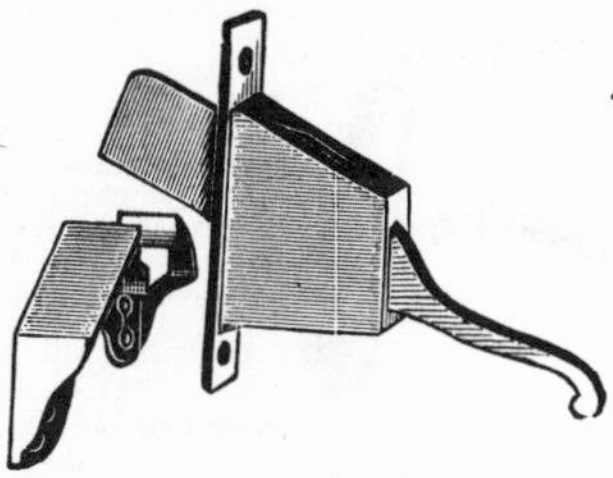

41272 Reversible Gate Hinge and Latch, to swing one way, reversible for either right or left hand gates, a new improved pattern that is very well liked.

Gate Latch.
Price, complete, each $0.18
Per dozen 1.95

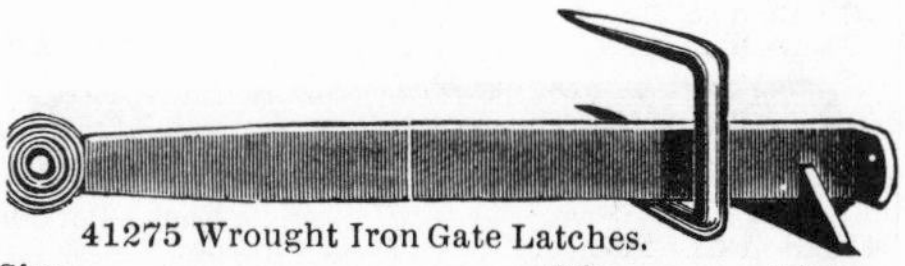

41275 Wrought Iron Gate Latches.

Size	8 in.	10 in.
Weight	10 oz.	12 oz.
Price, each	$0.10	$0.12
Price, per dozen	.85	1.10

Wrought Hasps and Staples.

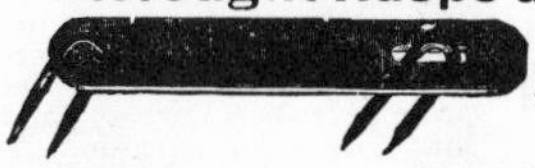

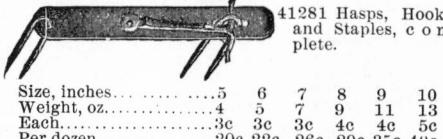

41280 Hasp and staple, complete.

Size, inches	5	6	7	8	9	10
Weight, ounces	3	3	3	3	4	5
Each	2c	2c	3c	3c	4c	4c
Per dozen	15c	16c	18c	21c	27c	30c

Wrought Hasps, Hooks and Staples.

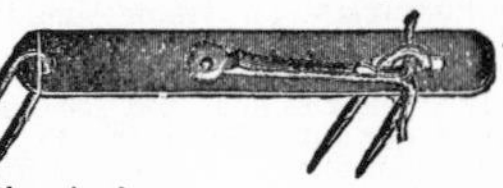

41281 Hasps, Hooks and Staples, complete.

Size, inches	5	6	7	8	9	10
Weight, oz	4	5	7	9	11	13
Each	3c	3c	3c	4c	4c	5c
Per dozen	20c	22c	26c	29c	35c	40c

Combination Hasp and Padlock.

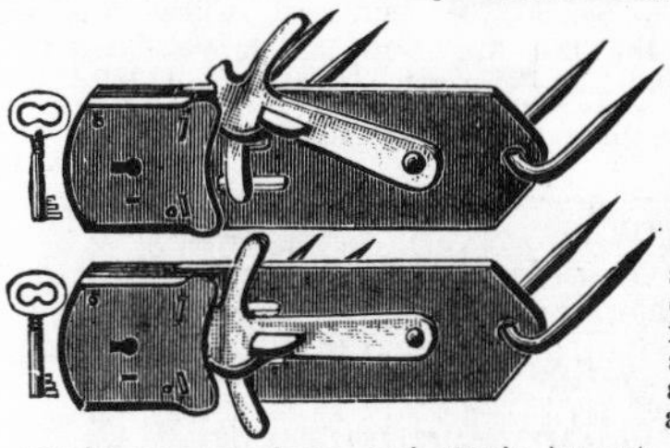

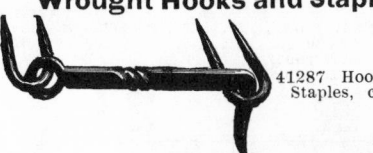

41285—Combination Hasp and Lock, self-locking; is cheaper and more convenient than a padlock, and just as secure; can be used as a hasp and staple by putting the staple in the upper slot, with the staple in the lower slot; it is self-locking, the key being required only to unlock it; complete with one key and two tinned staples.

	Each	Per doz.
Size, 6 inches; weight, 10 ounces	$0.25	$2.75
Size, 8 inches; 12 oz	.38	4.00

Wrought Hooks and Staples.

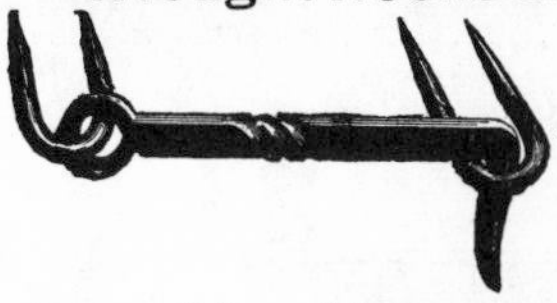

41287 Hooks and Staples, complete.

Size	3 in.	3½ in.	4 in.	4½ in.	5 in.	6 in.
Weight	3 oz.	3 oz.	4 oz.	4 oz.	4 oz.	5 oz.
Each	2c	2c	2c	3c	3c	3c
Per doz.	12c	14c	16c	18c	19c	22c

Wrought Staples.

41288 Staples only.

Sizes	1½ in.	2 in.	2½ in.	3 in.	3½ in.
Weight	2 oz.	5 oz.	8 oz.	10 oz.	14 oz
Per doz	2c	3c	4c	5c	6c
Per gross	18c	23c	32c	43c	50c

Gate Hooks and Eyes.

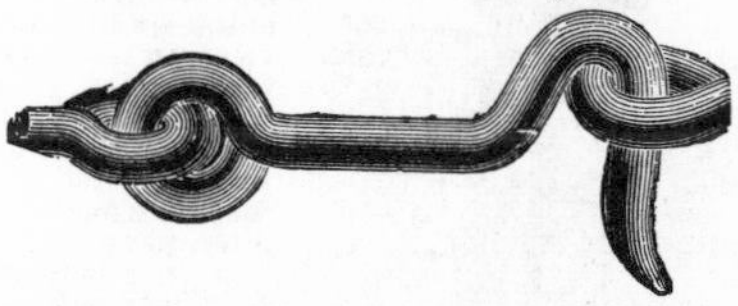

41295 Bright Iron Wire Gate Hooks and Eyes.

Inches	2	2½	3	3½	4 in.
Weight	2	2	2	3	3oz.
Each	2c.	2c.	3c.	3c.	3c.
Per dozen	10c.	10c.	12c.	15c.	15c,
Per gross	75c.	85c.	$1.00	1.15	1.25

Safety Gate Hooks.

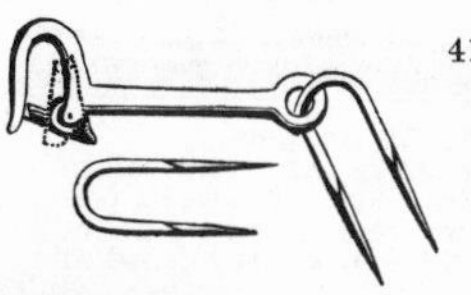

41296 Tinned Malleable Iron Hooks, wrought iron staples; two sizes.

Length	4 in.	6 in.
Weight	4 oz.	5 oz.
Each	5c.	6c.
Per dozen	49c.	64c.

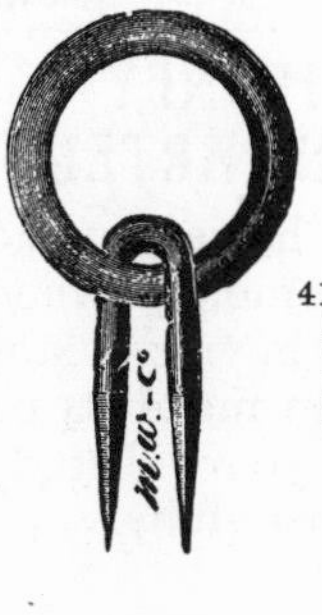

Wrought Ring and Staple.

41298 Wrought Ring and Staple.

Inches	2	2½	3
Weight	2oz.	3oz.	4oz.
Each	2c.	3c.	3c.
Per dozen	19c.	28c.	30c.

Barn Door Hangers and Rails.

41300 The Perfection Anti-Friction Barn Door Hangers. This is a new-pattern which promises to become very popular. The steel channel that axle of wheel revolves in is rolled in one piece, and is very strong. The axle is loose in the wheel and when working the wheel revolves on axle and axle revolves in channel, making it a perfect anti-friction hanger. The wheel cannot jump the track. The frame is made in such a shape that it can be fastened securely to the door, which is a great advantage. Use 5-16 bolts to fasten hangers to door (see 43366.) No screws or bolts furnished at price quoted.

		Per pair	Doz pair
1	For doors having run of 6 ft.	$0 50	$5.50
1½	For doors having run of 8 ft.	.60	6.50
2	For doors having run of 10 ft.	.70	7.84

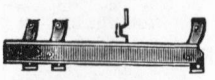

41301 Steel Bracket Barn Door Rail. For the Perfection Anti-Friction barn door hanger, having a grooved wheel. For putting up the rail use 5-16 lag screws (see 43384), or No. 12 wood screws (see 41980). No. Lag screws or wood screws furnished at prices quoted; is very strong, 3-16x1 inch.
Per foot............$0.03½

41302 Cronk's Steel Covered Anti-Friction Barn Door Hangers. With these hangers you will not have trouble with ice or snow or breakage. They are the strongest in the market.

		Per pair.	Per doz
1	For 5 ft run	$0.50	$5.50
1½	For 8 ft. run	.60	6.50
2	For 10 ft. run	.70	7.84
3	For 15 ft. run	.85	9.50

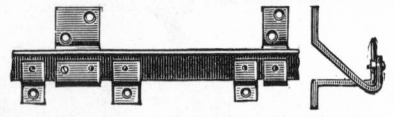

41303 Braced Steel Rail, for No. 41302 Cronk's Hanger. Being braced both ways it will not sag; the joint is made so that it is perfectly solid, guaranteed to hold a door weighing 2,000 lbs. No screws furnished. Per ft............$0.03½

41310 Check Back Barn Door Hangers. Use 5-16 bolts (see 43366) or No. 18 screws (see 41980) to fasten hangers to doors. No bolts or screws furnished at prices quoted.
Size of wheel—
3 in., per pair....$0.22
4 in., per pair.... .25
5 in., per pair.... .35
6 in.. per pair.... .45
Weight per pair, 4 in.. 5½ lbs.; 5 in., 8¼ lbs.; 6 in., 10¼ lbs.

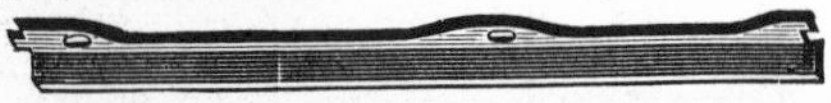

For No. 41310 Hangers.
41311 Iron Rail, double flange barn door rail in two feet lengths. Use No. 12 screws (see 41980) for the rail. Two screws required for each foot of rail. No screws furnished at prices quoted. Per foot, in 2 feet lengths....$0.02½

"A FOOL AND HIS MONEY=== ===ARE SOON PARTED."

There are some folks, however, who won't part with their money when they should. Judicious buying means a great saving. You can make $4.00 do the work of $5.00 if you will study our various catalogues carefully.

Common Barn Door Hangers.

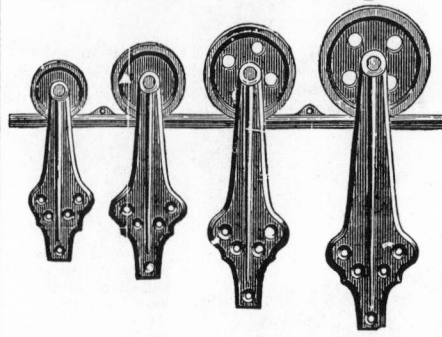

41312 Common Barn Door Hangers. Use 5-16 bolts (see 43366) to fasten these hangers to doors. No bolts or screws furnished at prices quoted.

Size of wheel	3 in.	4 in.	5 in.	6 in
Price, per pair	12c	17c	21c	26c.

41313 Iron Rail for No. 41312 hangers. No screws furnished, (see 41980). No. 12 screws for this rail. Price, per foot, in 2 feet lengths.$0.02½

Door Handles.

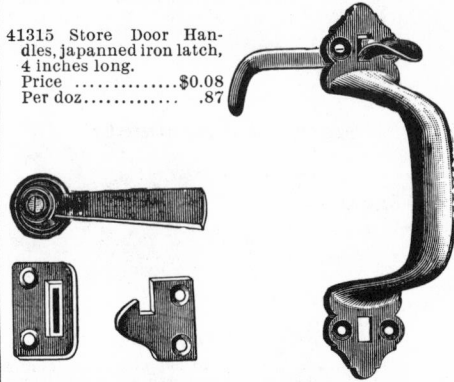

41315 Store Door Handles, japanned iron latch, 4 inches long.
Price............$0.08
Per doz............ .87

Barn Door Pulls.

41316 Barn Door Pulls, japanned, extra heavy, weight, 10 oz. No screws furnished.
Each............$0.04
Per dozen........ .40

Barn Door Stay Rollers.

41320 Barn Door Stay Roller, to screw, wrought iron shank, japanned. Weight, 14 oz.
Each............$0.07
Per doz............ .65

41321 Adjustable Hinge Stay Roller. Can be adjusted to any thickness of door, is extra strong and cannot get out of place. No screws furnished.
Each............$0.10
Per dozen............ .95

Box Hooks.

41325 Box Hooks. Blades made of steel, forged and very carefully tempered. Handles fastened by a new method. No pains have been spared to make these hooks as good as can be produced; made in five sizes.

Size.	Each.	Doz.
6 inch	$0.10	$1.00
9 inch	.12	1.35
10 inch	.15	1.50
12 inch	.17	1.80
14 inch	.20	2.00

Each. Per doz.
41328 Box Chisel, solid cast steel forged, 15 inches long, very handy for opening berry crates, and by using hammer or mallet with it the largest size of boxes may be opened easily............$0.50 $5.50

Phillips' Patent Key Guard.

The best thing for the purpose ever invented. It makes a common lock burgular proof, as it is impossible to open the lock when the key guard is in its place. Supt. of police Breman of Chicago says it is a good thing. Made from bright sheet metal.
41329 Price, each..$0.10
Price, per dozen... 1.00
Price, per 100..... 8.00

Door Locks.

Our door locks are the best for the price in the market; nicely finished and fitted, substantially made and easy working.

All door locks quoted by us are for right or left hand doors.

Please note that all locks are quoted with and without knobs. In ordering be sure and state what is wanted.

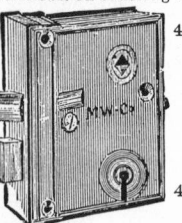

41375 Reversible Upright Rim Locks, like cut, with stop iron bolts, tinned malleable iron key, japanned escutcheons, complete with screws; size, 4x3¾ in. This price does not include knobs. Weight. 2 lbs. 4 oz.
Each............$0.12
Per dozen............ 1.15
41376 The above No. 41375 lock, with No. 41480 brown mineral knob, japan mountings. Each.........$0.18 Per dozen............ 1.80
41377 The above No. 41375 lock, with No. 41482 white porcelain knob, japan mountings. Each............$0.20 Per dozen............ 2.00
41378 Reversible Upright Rim Lock, same as No. 41375, with stop, brass bolt and nickel plated steel key; size, 4¼x3½, with screws, japanned escutcheons. This price does not include knobs; weight, 2 lbs. 8 oz. Each............ .20
Per dozen............ 2.20
41379 The above lock No. 41378, with No. 41480 brown mineral knobs, japan mountings. Each .26
Per dozen............ 2.85
41380 The above lock, with No. 41482 white porcelain knob, japan mountings. Each...... .28
Per dozen............ 3.07
41400 Upright Reversible Rim Front Door Lock, 6x4 inches, heavy brass bolts and hub, brass key. To reverse the lock pull latch bolt forward and turn half round. This is an elegant strong lock. Price, each, with white porcelain knob, japanned mountings and japanned escutcheon. .50
Weight, 3 pounds 3 ounces.

Horizontal Rim Knot Locks.

41403 Reversible Horizontal Rim Locks, like cut, with stop, iron bolt and key; size, 4½x3⅛; japanned escutcheons, complete with screws. This price does not include knobs. Weight, about 1 lb. 5 oz.
Each............$0.12
Per dozen............ 1.25
41404 The above No. 41403 lock with No. 41480 brown mineral knobs, with japan mountings. Each............18c. Per dozen............ 1.90
41405 The above No. 41403 lock with No. 41482 white porcelain knobs, japan mountings. Each .20
Per dozen............ 2.12

Wrought Steel Door Locks.

Wrought Steel Door Locks are comparatively a new thing, are a good deal lighter and very much stronger than the cast lock, are almost indestructible, and will not get out of order, like the common kind. The rim locks have an ivory black finish, the mortise a bright finish. Weight, about 2 lbs.

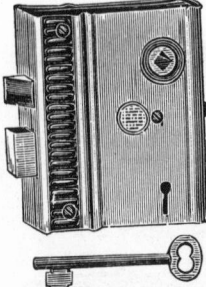

41410 Reversible Wrought Steel Upright Rim Lock, 4x3, iron bolts, 4 changes, tinned malleable iron key, packed complete with japanned escutcheons and screws. This price does not include knobs. Each............$0.15
Per dozen............ 1.55
41411 The above No. 41410 lock with No. 41480 brown mineral knobs, japan mountings. Each. .21
Per dozen............ 2.20
41412 The above No. 41410 lock with No. 41482 white porcelain knob, japan mountings. Each, .23
Per dozen............ 2.42

Locks—Continued.

41413 Reversible Wrought Steel Horizontal Rim Lock, 5x3¼, 12 changes, nickel plated, malleable iron key, packed complete, with screws, japanned escutcheon. This price does not include knobs; weight, about 2½ lbs. Each... .25
Per dozen... 2.25

41414 The above No. 41413 lock with No. 41480 brown mineral knob, japan mountings. Each... .31
Per dozen... 2.90

41415 The above No. 41413 lock with No. 41482 white porcelain knob, japan mountings. Each, .33
Per dozen... 3.12

41416 Reversible Wrought Steel Upright Rim Lock, 4x3, brass bolts, nickel plated, malleable iron key, 4 changes, packed complete, with screws; japanned escutcheons. This price does not include knobs. Each... .28
Per dozen... 2.81

41417 The above No. 41416 lock with No. 41480 brown mineral knob, japan mountings. Each.. .34
Per dozen... 3.46

41418 The above No. 41416 lock with No. 41482 white porcelain knob, japan mountings. Each, .36
Per dozen... 3.68

41419 Reversible Wrought Steel Mortise Lock, 3½x3, plain front, nickel plated, malleable iron key, packed complete with screws, japanned escutcheons. This price does not include knobs. Each... $0.16 Per dozen... 1.56

41420 The above No. 41419 lock with No. 41480 brown mineral knobs, japan mountings. Each, .22
Per dozen... 2.20

41421 The above No. 41419 lock with No. 41482 white porcelain knob, japan mountings. Each, .24
Per dozen... 2.43

41422 Reversible Wrought Steel Mortise Lock, 3½x3, brass front and striking plate, nickel plated steel key, packed complete, with screws, japanned escutcheons. This price does not include knobs. Each...$0.30 Per dozen... 3.44

41423 The above No. 41422 lock with No. 41480 brown mineral knob, japan mountings. Each.. .36
Per dozen... 4.09

41424 The above No. 41423 lock with No. 41482 white porcelain knob, japan mountings. Each, .38
Per dozen... 4.31

Mortise Knob Latch.

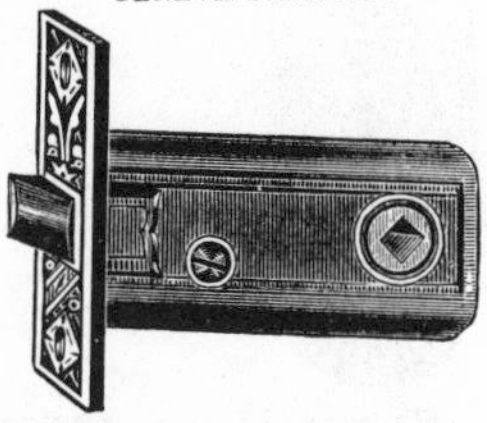

GENEVA BRONZED.

41430 Geneva Bronze Mortise Knob Latches, round edges; size, 1¾x3¼; Geneva bronzed front and strike, brass bolt, complete with ebony knobs. Geneva bronze mountings and screws; weight, 13 oz.
Each... $0.35
Dozen... 3.60

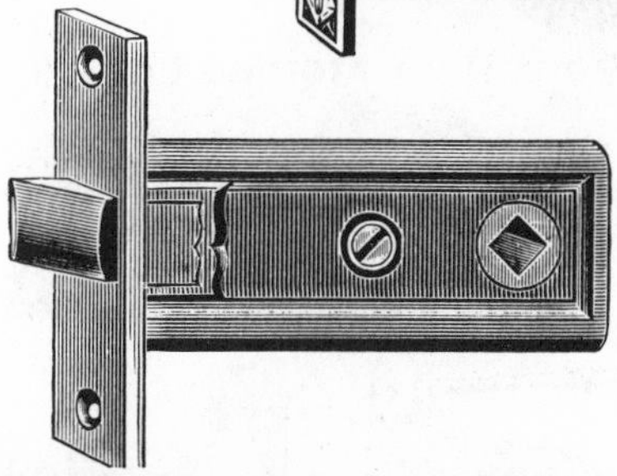

41432 Mortise Knob Latch; size, 1¼x3⅛; has iron face, iron bolt and iron strike-plate. Price named is for latch without knobs; for price of knobs see Nos. 41480 to 41490. Price, each... $0.08
Price, per dozen... .65

41433 Mortise Knob Latch, same style as cut 41432; size, 1¾x3¼, with brass front and strike-plate; bronze bolt. No knobs furnished at this price. For price of knobs see Nos. 41480 to 41490. Price, each...$0.15 Price, per doz.. 1.50

Door Latches.

41435 Wrought Steel Mortise Latch for closet doors, etc., 3x13-16, plain front, packed, with screws. Without knobs. Price, each... $0.15
Per dozen... 1.40

41436 The same latch with No. 41480 brown mineral knob, japan mountings. Each... .21
Per dozen... 2.05

41437 Same as above, with white porcelain knobs. Each... $0.23 Per dozen... 2.27

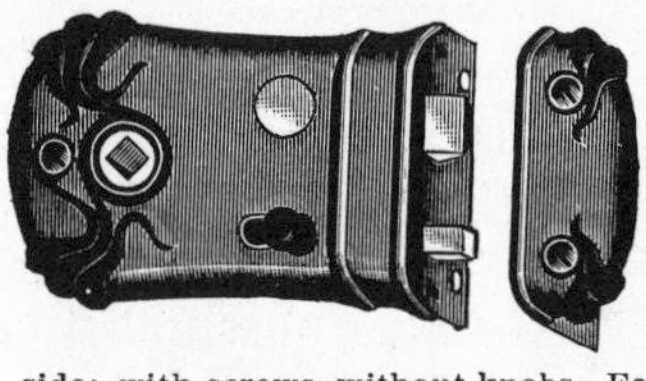

41438—Wrought Steel Rim Latch, ivory black finish, for small doors, for closets and bedrooms; has bolt by which door may be securely locked from the inside; with screws, without knobs. Each... $0.15
Per dozen... 1.40

41439 The same latch with No. 41480 brown mineral knobs, japan mountings, each... .21
Per dozen... 2.05

41440 The same latch with No. 41483 white porcelain knobs, japan mountings. Each... .23
Per dozen... 2.27

RIM DEAD LOCKS.

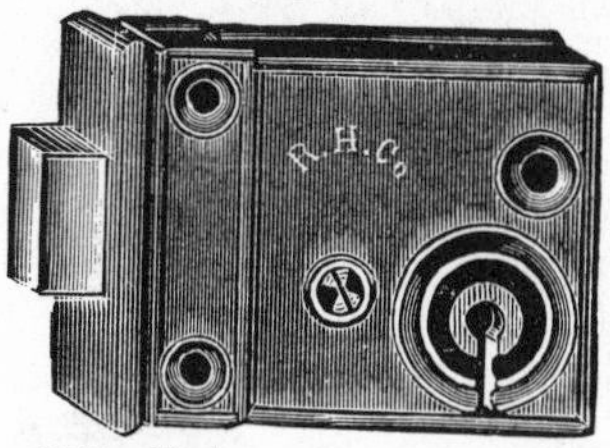

41450 Horizontal Rim Dead Locks; size, 2x2¾, for closets or cupboard, iron bolt, 1 iron key.
Notice.—This lock cannot be used with knobs. Complete with screws and japanned escutcheons. Each... $0.10
Per dozen... 1.00

41453 Rimmed Dead Lock (cannot be used with knobs), like cut No. 41450. Size, 2¾x3⅛ in.; with iron bolts, coppered iron key, 1 tumbler, complete with screws and escutcheons.
Price, each... $0.10. Per dozen... 1.07

41454 Rim Dead Lock (cannot be used with with knobs), like cut No. 41450. Size, 2½x3½ in; with iron bolts, tinned malleable iron key, 1 tumbler, 12 changes, complete, with screws and escutcheons. Price, each... .12
Per dozen... 1.25

41455 Rim Dead Lock (cannot be used with knobs), like cut No. 41450. Size, 2¾x4; with tinned malleable keys, 1 tumbler, 12 changes complete, with screws and escutcheons. Each.. .15
Per dozen... 1.56

Yale Pattern Night Lock.

Warranted to be Perfect and Equal to Any in the Market

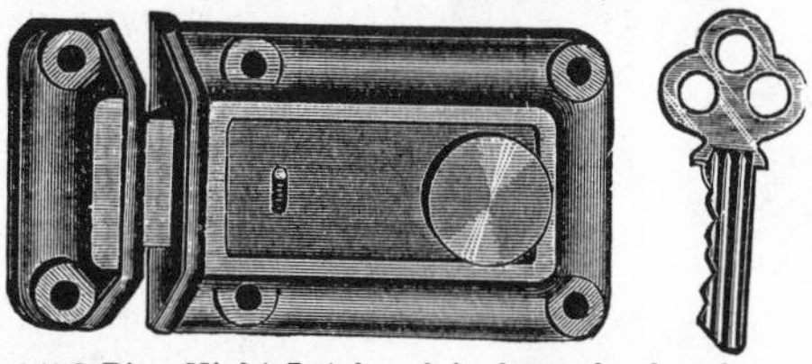

41458 Rim Night Latch, plain brass knob and escutcheon, japanned iron case; size, 3⅝x2⅝ inches; 3 steel keys. This latch is operated from the outside by the key only and on the inside by the knob, and the bolt may be fastened back at will by the spring catch on the inside of case; suitable for doors from ⅞ to 2¾ inches thick.
Complete... $1.25

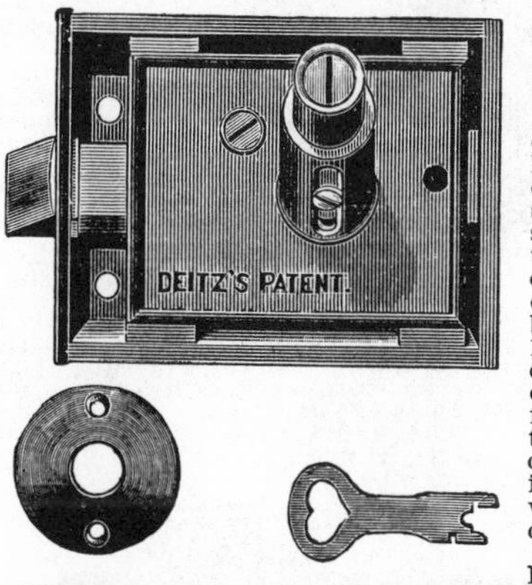

41461 Rim Night Latch, for right or left hand doors; heavy iron case, brass side and stop knob, two steel double notched tumblers for 1¼, 1½, 1¾ or 2 inch doors; state for what thickness door lock is wanted when ordering. Weight, 1 lb. 3 oz.
Each... $0.50

Store Door Lock.

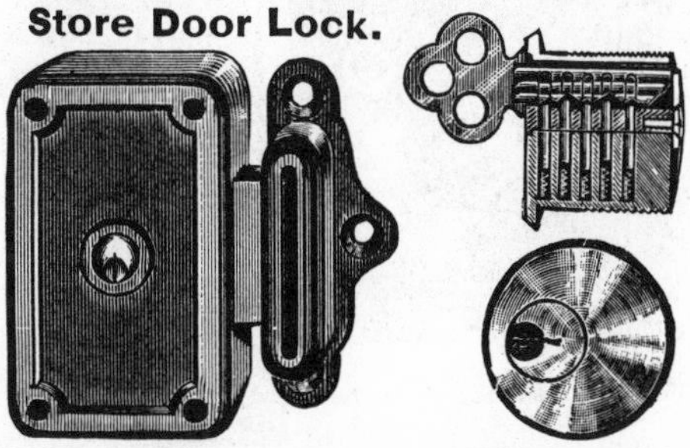

41462 Upright Dead Lock for store doors; size, 5x3, or doors 1⅛ to 4 inches thick, operated by key from both sides of door; has heavy japanned iron case, with bronze bolt 2½x½ inch, plain brass escutcheons, 3 corrugated steel keys with each lock; no two sets of keys made alike; complete; weight, 3 lbs. 5 ounces... $2.75

Our Hardware Department is without doubt the most complete under any one roof. Our prices are right; our goods are right.

Locks—Continued.

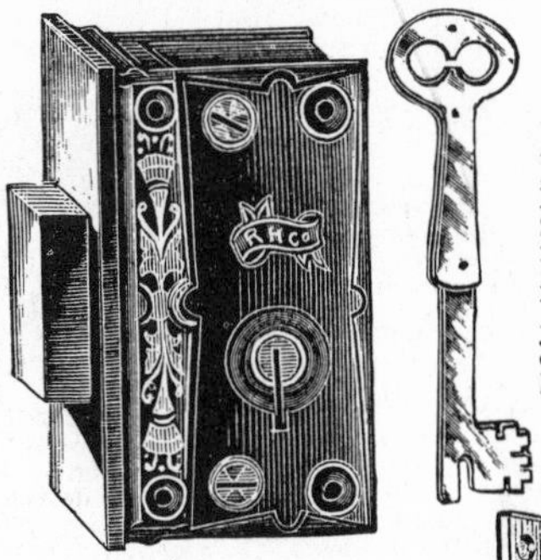

41465 Store Door Rim Dead Lock; 5x3; heavy iron bolt, 2 nickel-plated folding steel keys, complete, with screws and japanned escutcheon.
Each... $0.60

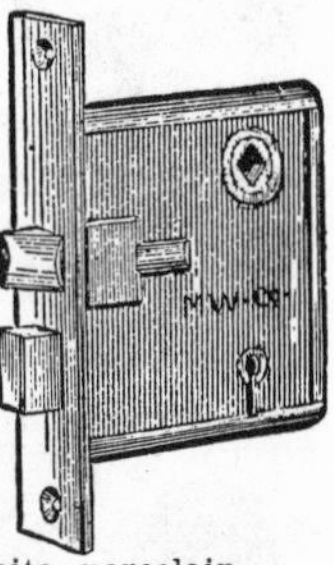

41466 Reversible Mortise Lock, like cut, lacquered iron front, iron bolt, wrought iron striking plate, tinned malleable iron key; size, 3½x3¼, with japanned escutcheons. Price is without screws or knobs. Weight, about 1 lb
Each... $0.12
Per dozen... 1.15

41467 Same lock, with No. 41480 brown mineral knobs, Japan mountings. Each... $0.18
Per dozen... 1.90

41468 Same as above, with white porcelain knobs, japanned mountings. Each... $0.20
Per dozen... 2.16

41469 Reversible Mortise Lock, similar to cut of 41466, brass front, brass bolts, nickel plated steel keys size, 3½x3¼; weight, 1 lb. 3 oz. Each... .20
Per dozen... 2.20

41470 Same lock, with No. 41480, japanned mineral knobs, japanned mountings. Each... .26
Per dozen... 2.87

41471 Same as above, with white porcelain knobs, japanned mountings. Each... .28
Per dozen... 2.99

Mortise Knob Locks.

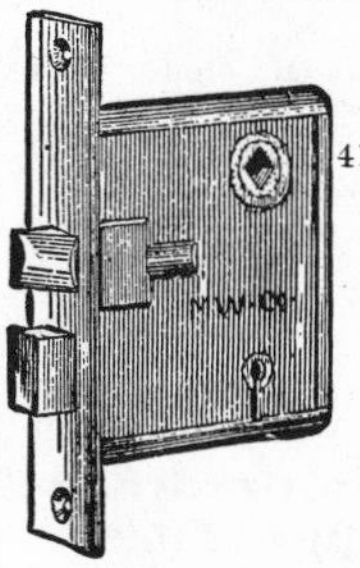

41472 Size, 3½x3⅛ inch, with iron front, bolts and strike plate with steel key; 12 changes. The price of the lock is without the knob; for price of knobs, see No. 41480 to 41490.
Each... $0.20
Per dozen... 1.60

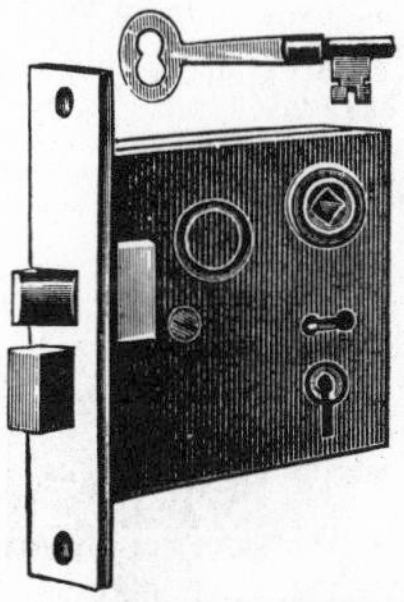

41473 Mortise Knob Lock: size, 3½x3¼ inch, with plain bronze metal front and bronze bolt, brass strike plate, nickel plated steel key, with 1 tumbler, 12 changes. The thickness of case is ⅝ inch, width of face, 1⅛ inch. The distance from front of lock to center of hub and keyhole, 2⅜ inches. The price of this lock is without knobs: for price of knobs, see No. 41480 to 41490.
Price, each... $0.30
Per dozen... 3.12

Door Knobs.

Weight, 1 lb.

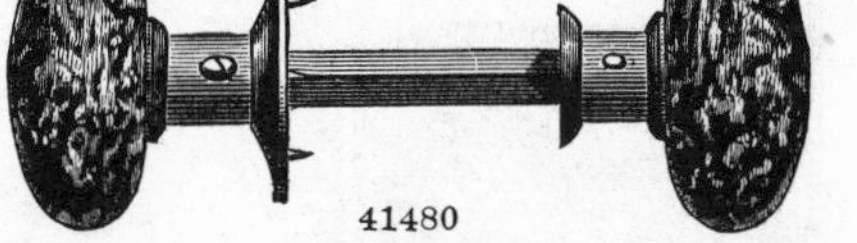

41480

No screws furnished.

See Index for screws.

	Each	Per doz.
41480 Brown Mineral Door Knobs, with 5-16 inch spindles, japanned mountings, for rim locks; no screws furnished...	$0.06	$0.65
41481 Brown Mineral Door Knobs, with 5-16 inch spindles, japanned mountings for mortise lock; no screws furnished...	.06	.65
41482 White Porcelain Door Knobs, with 5-16 inch spindles, japanned mountings for rim locks...	08	.87
41483 White Porcelain Door Knobs, 5-16 inch spindles, japanned mountings, for mortise locks; no screws furnished...	.08	.87
41484 Ebony Door Knobs, 5-16 inch spindles, japanned mountings, for rim locks.	.08	.87
41485 Ebony Door Knobs, with 5-16 inch spindles, japanned mountings, for mortise locks; no screws furnished...	.08	87

Door Knobs—Continued.

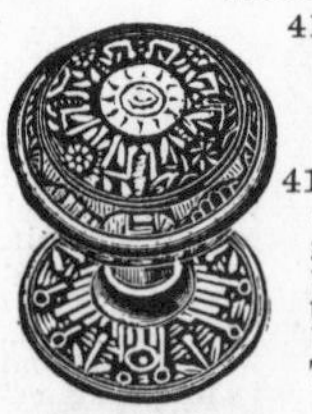

41486 Geneva Bronzed Iron Knob, 5-16 inch spindles, Geneva bronzed mountings for mortise locks. Each....$0.25
Per dozen....2.70

41487 Ebony Door Knobs, with 5-16 inch spindle, ornamental gold bronze mounting, for mortise locks, packed with screws to match mountings. Each.....25
Per dozen....2.70

This cut shows only one-half of the knob.

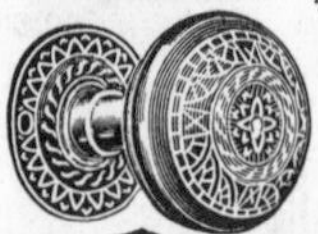

41489 Bronze Metal Door Knob, 2¼ in. size with $\frac{5}{16}$ in. spindle for mortise locks; this knob is made of bronze metal, has polished surfaces, with black background; a new and very handsome design. Each....$0.40
Per dozen....4.10

This cut only shows one-half of the knob. The price includes two knobs and spindle, like cut 41480.

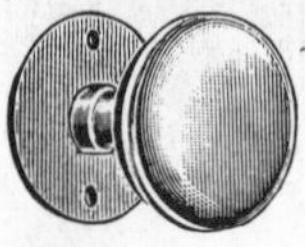

41490 Antique Copper Bronze Metal Knob, 2¼ in. size with $\frac{5}{16}$ spindle for mortise locks. This is the latest in antique copper.
Each....$0.50
Per dozen....5.00

This cut shows only one-half of the knob. The price includes two knobs and one spindle, like cut 41480.

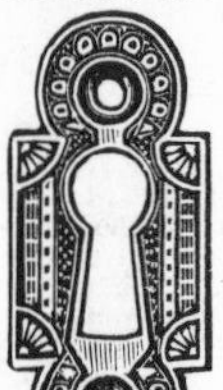

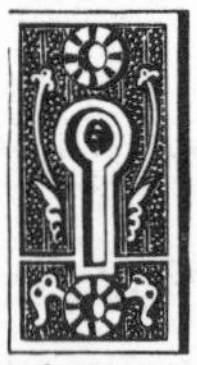

41496 Keyhole Plate or Escutcheon, japanned iron, for iron key.
Each....$0.02
Per dozen.....20

41497 Keyhole Escutcheon, ornamental bronze metal, with screws for steel key.
Each....$0.03
Per dozen.....33

41498 Keyhole Escutcheon, ornamental bronze metal, with screws for iron or brass key.
Each....$0.05
Per dozen.....54

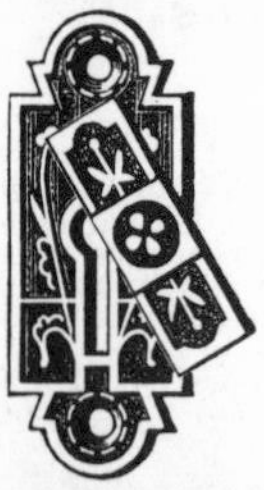

41499 Keyhole Escutcheon, with drop; ornamental bronze metal, packed, with screws for steel key.
Each....$0.08
Per dozen....87

Escutcheons weigh from 8 to 15 oz. to the dozen.

Locks, Etc. Geneva Bronzed, Royal Bronze and Old Copper Finish.

Geneva bronzed goods are iron made in imitation of royal bronze. The background is finished in black, the raised surfaces (the white lines seen in cuts) are finely polished and then electroplated with bronze metal. They are handsome goods, and such a good imitation of the genuine bronze that an expert can hardly tell them apart, and being much lower in price must naturally become very popular.

Front Door Locks.

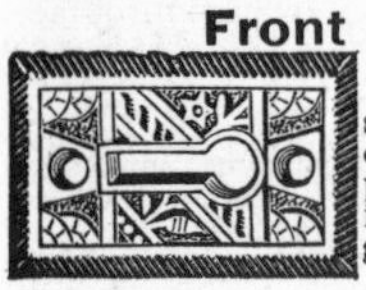

We will always send you the latest and most popular designs in Geneva bronz goods.

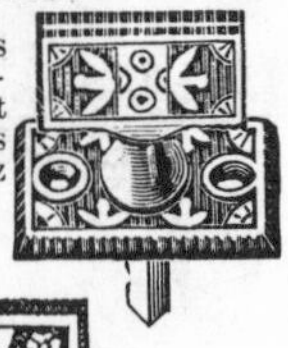

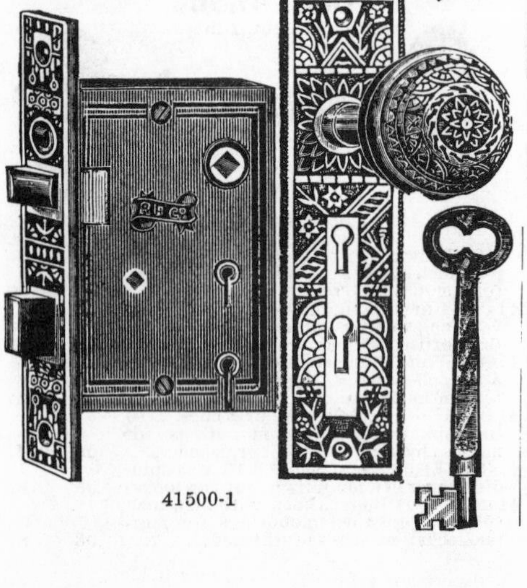

41500-1

Locks—Continued.

41500 Front Door Mortise Lock, royal bronze front and strike knobs and escutcheon; has bronze bolts, royal bronze turn knobs, plated steel lock key, 2 plated steel night keys. Size of lock, 4¾x3½; size of knobs, 2¼. Packed one set in a box complete, with screws, per set....$1.25

41501 Front Door Mortise Lock, same description as No. 41500; plain bronze, old copper finish; an entirely new, elegant and very popular finish. Complete, packed with knobs, escutcheons and screws, per set....1.55

Bronze Metal Front Door Lock.

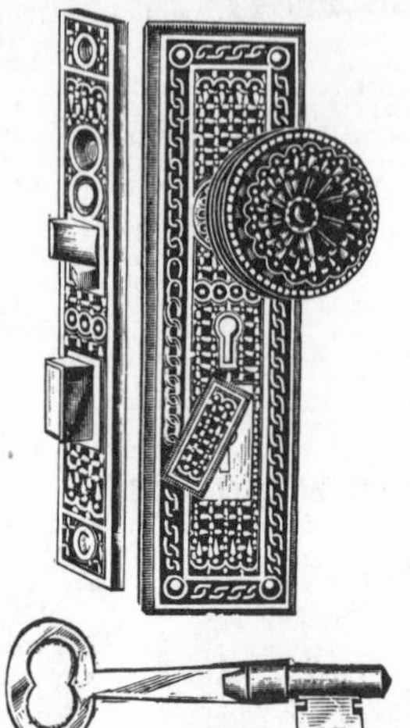

41502-3.

The preceding cuts, showing lock, front door knob, escutcheon and pair f butts, represent the handsomest pattern of real bronze goods made. The finish is extremely handsome; the raised surfaces are a light polished bronze; the background a dark color, making a durable and elegant finish.

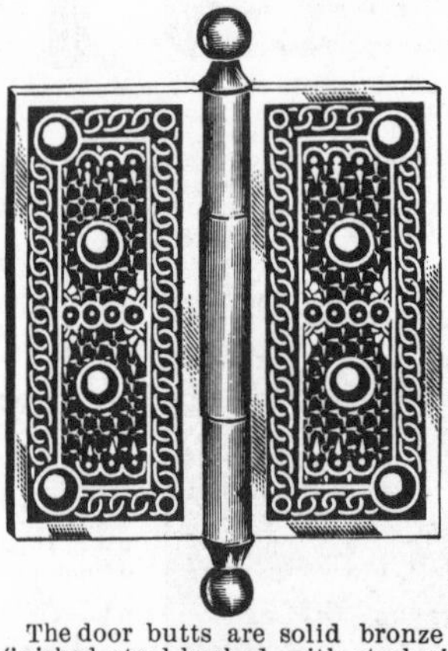

Front Door Lock Mortise Knob, with patent anti-friction latch ornamental bronze front (see cut of front); 2 bolts, bronze thumb-piece and rose, 1 nickel plated steel bolt key, 2 nickel plated steel night keys, ornamental solid bronze knobs, an escutcheon for outside (see cut), 1 escutcheon for inside; size of lock, 5¾x4 inches. This lock is finely made and will last for years. When ordering, state whether right or left hand is wanted.

The door butts are solid bronze metal, handsomely finished, steel bushed, with steel pin; 4x4 butts weigh 1 lb. 15 oz., the 5x5 butts, weigh 3 lbs. 3 oz. We furnish the above with 4x4 or 5x5 butts.

41502 Set complete, with 4x4 butts....$4.06
41503 Set complete, with 5x5 butts....4.55

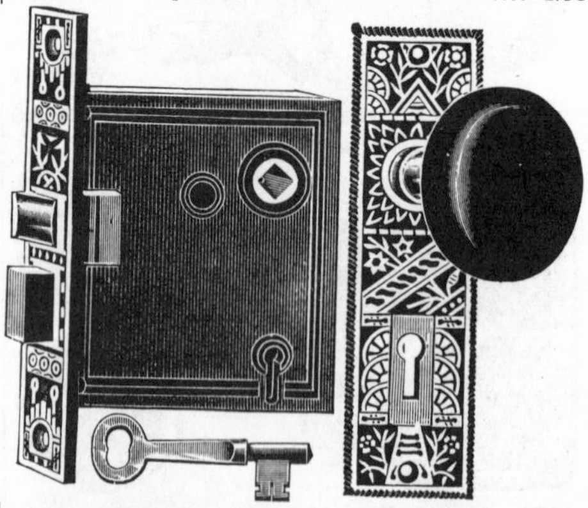

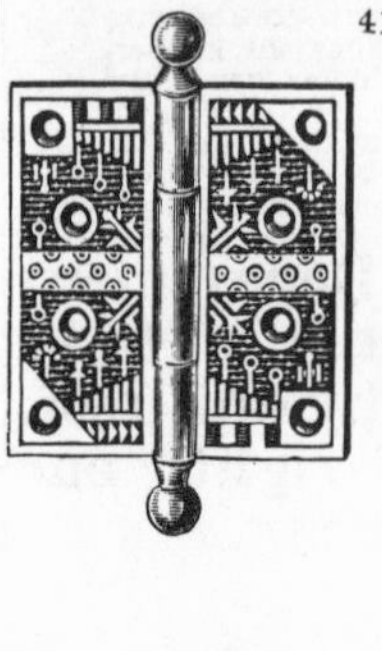

41504 Set of furnishings, for single door, consisting of one reversible mortise lock, 3½x3½, with bronze plated front and striking plate, brass bolts, ebony knob, bronze plated mountings and two 6-inch bronze plated escutcheons, one nickel plated steel key and a handsome pair of 4x4 bronze-plated cast butts; all packed in paper box, complete with screws. The lock alone is worth the price we ask for the set.
Weight, 4¾ pounds.
Price, per set, complete.$ 1.00
Per dozen sets....10.65

Trimmings for Front Doors.
Front Door Set.

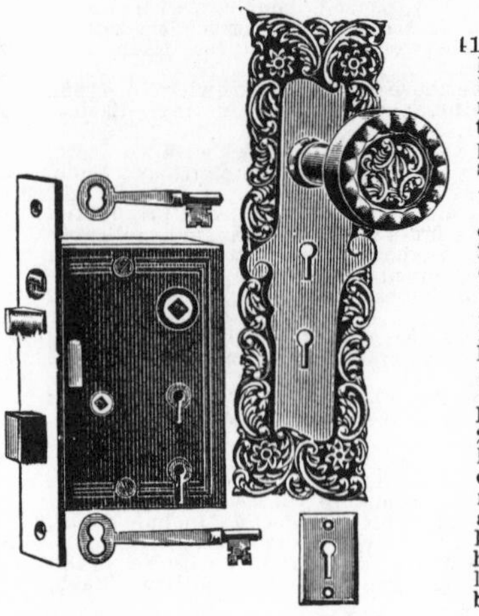

41507 Eulalia Design, bronze metal, antique copper finish, size of lock 4¾ x 3½, thickness of case ⅝ inch, width of front 1$\frac{1}{16}$ inch, distance from front of lock to center of hub and key holes, 2⅝ inch; it has 2 plated steel night keys and 1 lock key; lock has 1 tumbler on each bolt.

Price, per set, as shown in cut....$1.40
Price, per dozen sets....15.75

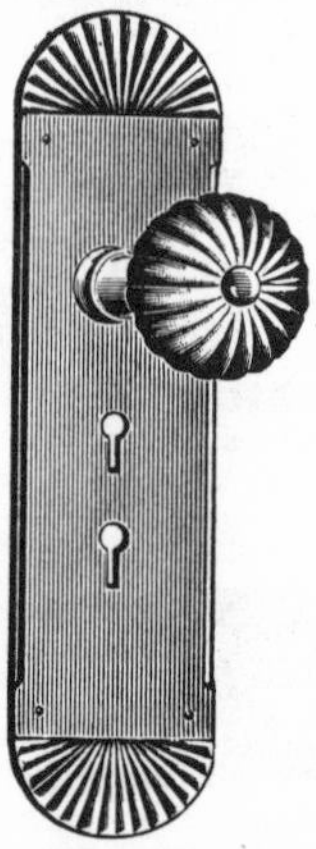

41508 This set comprises 1 lock 4¾x3½, the same as shown in cut 41507. Circular fluted pattern, wrought bronze knob and escutcheon, as shown in cut.
Price per set....$1.40
Price, per dozen sets....15.75

Front Door Mortise Lock Set,

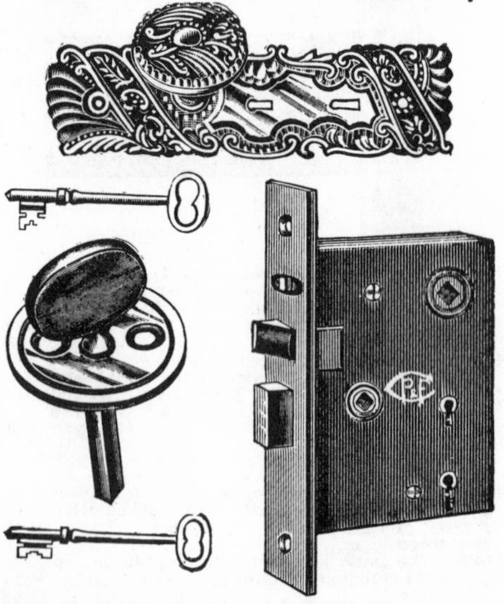

41509 Reversible Easy Springs, with Turn Knob; size of lock, 4½x3½, plain front, in old copper finish, an entirely new and very elegant design, weight per set, 3¼ lbs. Price per set, complete.$1.75
Price, per dozen sets, complete....20.00

IT IS ASTONISHING HOW MUCH DEEPER A HOLE SEEMS AFTER ONE GETS INTO IT.

Write us for prices or information on any article which you don't find in this book. We have 25 typewriters always ready to wait on you.

Address all letters
MONTGOMERY WARD & CO.,
111 to 116 Michigan Avenue. CHICAGO.

Locks—Continued.

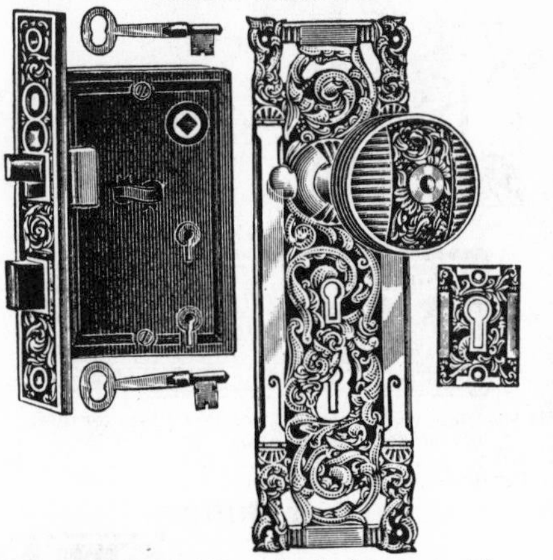

41510 Mortise Front Door Lock, bronze metal antique finish. Brass and wrought iron inside work, with night works. Size of lock, 5¼x3½. Knob and escutcheon of bronze metal, antique finish; a new and handsome design; has plated steel key with one tumbler on each bolt.
Price, per set complete, as shown in cut........$3.25

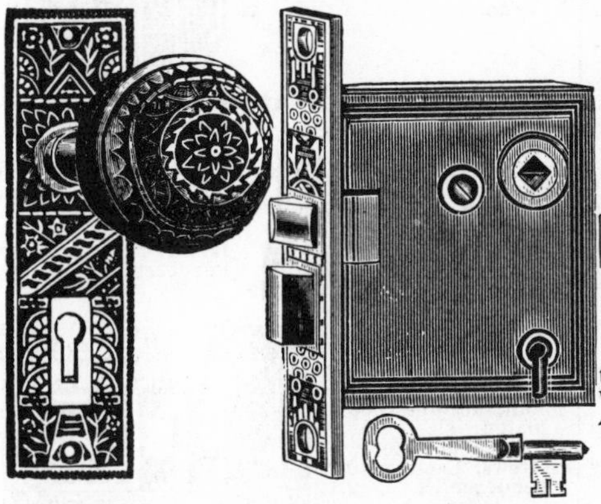

41515 Royal Bronze Mortise Knob Lock (reverse by taking off cap); size of lock, 3½x3¼; size of knobs, 2¼ inches. Has plated steel key, complete with screws. With Geneva Bronze Knob, price each complete..$0.70 Per dozen..$8.12

41516 Plain Bronze Mortise Knob Lock, old copper finish, an entirely new, elegant and popular finish. Knobs and inside escutcheons same as No. 41515. Packed, complete, with knobs, escutcheons and screws. Price, each, complete. 0.90
Per dozen.. 10.00

MORTISE KNOB LOCKS AND KNOBS.

For inside doors.

Consists of 1 mortise lock, 1 pair knobs, and two escutcheons.

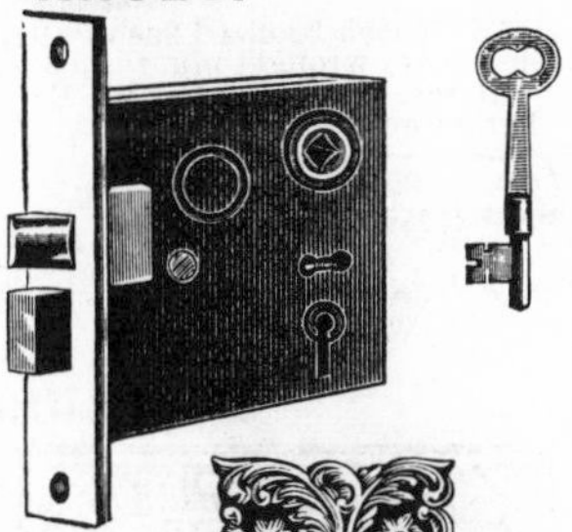

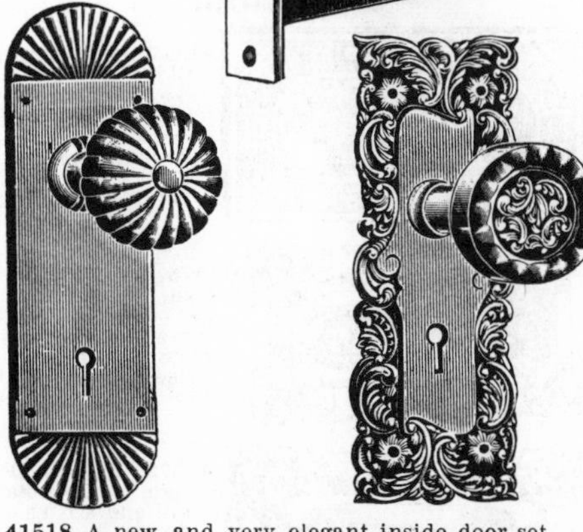

41518 A new and very elegant inside door set of Eulalia design. It has bronze metal front, antique copper finish with bronze metal antique copper finish knob and escutcheons. Size of lock, 3½x3¼ inches, nickel steel key, one tumbler, 12 changes. Price, per set complete.......$0.85
Price, per dozen sets.................................. 9.38

FLUTED DESIGNS.

41519 We can furnish the above lock, No. 41518, with knob and escutcheons of fluted design like cut. Price, per set, complete.......$0.85
Per doz sets, complete.......................... 9.38

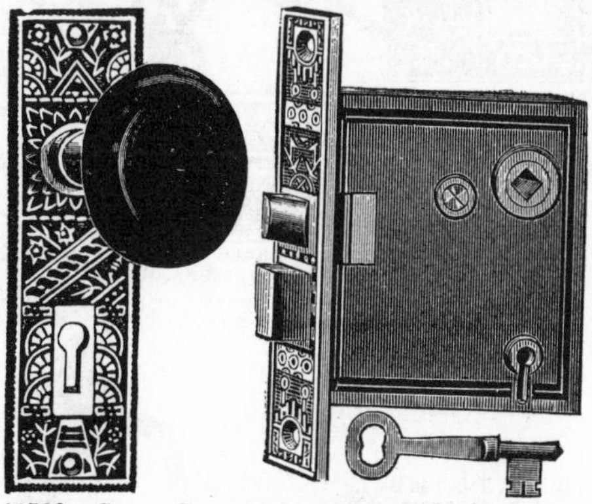

41520 Geneva Bronzed Mortise Knob Lock, reversible by taking off cap. Size of lock. 3½x3¼; size of knobs, 2¼ inches; has bronze plated bolts, plated steel key; packed, complete, with screws; has an ebony knob with Geneva bronzed escutcheons, which makes a pleasing contrast.
Price, per set, complete....$0.40 Per dozen....$4.20

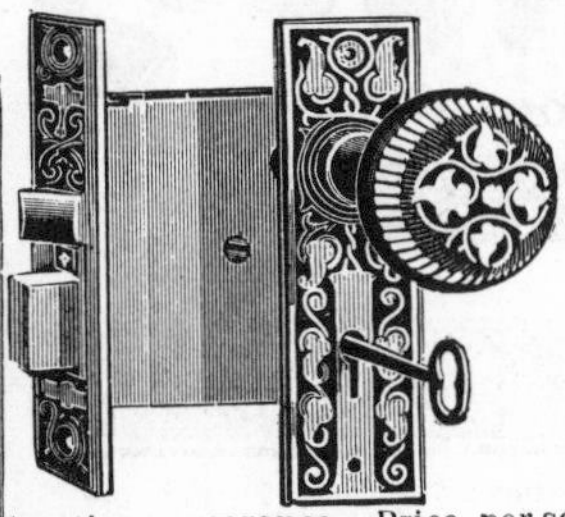

41525 Wrought Steel Mortised Lock, 3½ inch, with ornamented real bronze front, knob and escutcheons and nickel plated steel key. This is an entirely new pattern and is extremely handsome. The surfaces are polished bronze, the background a dark finish, making a very effective and attractive appearance. Price, per set, packed, complete, with screws.................................$0.88

41526 Wrought Steel Mortise Lock, 3½ inch, bronze plated knob and escutcheon, same pattern as No. 41525, but is bronze plated on iron, in place of being solid bronze metal. A very good lock for inside doors. Price, per set, with knob and escutcheon.......................... .67

Inside Lock Sets.

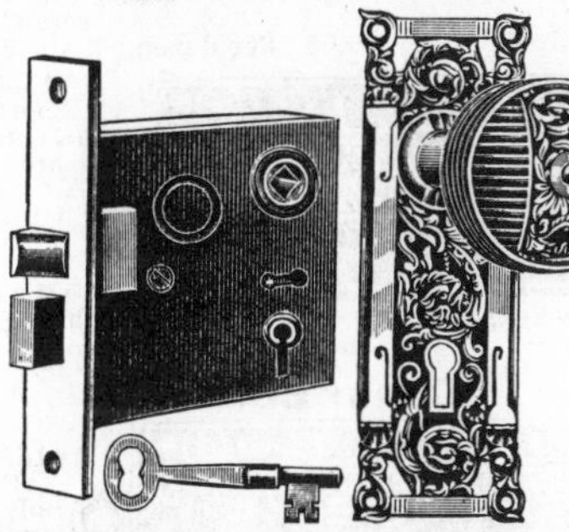

41527 The above set is bronze plated in the best possible manner and finished in antique copper, closely resembling genuine bronze in appearance. They are made from entirely new patterns and are offered with the full assurance that they are superior to any goods of this kind on the market. The size of the lock is 3½x3¼ inch, has nickel steel key, one tumbler, 12 changes.
Price per set (consisting of one mortise lock, 2 escutcheons and 1 pair of knobs, as shown in cut).... $0.90 Price, per dozen sets..........$10.00

Store Door Handles and Locks.

41533 **Geneva Bronzed Extra Heavy, Oblique Double Handle,** 3-tumbler, mortise lock, 4½x3 inches; bronze metal bolts; patent anti-friction latch; 2 nickel-plated flat steel keys; flat front reversible latch.
Price, per set, as shown in cut, with flat front lock....
.........................$1.75

41534 Same as above, with full rabbet front lock, ½-inch rabbet. In ordering parties must state if RIGHT, or LEFT hand is wanted, as this latch is not reversible. Price, per set, as shown in cut, with rabbet front lock.....................$2.00

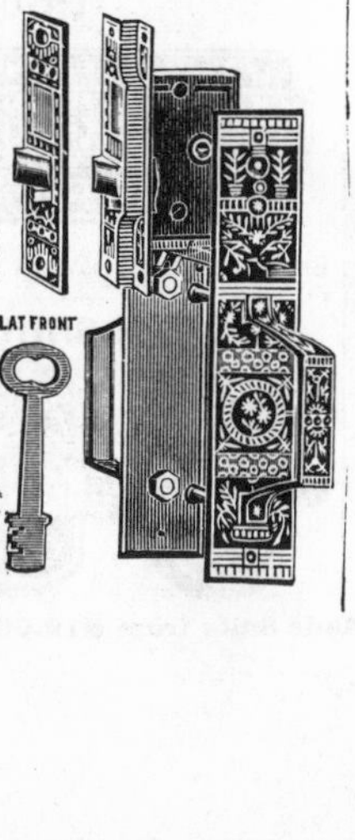

Store Door Handle.

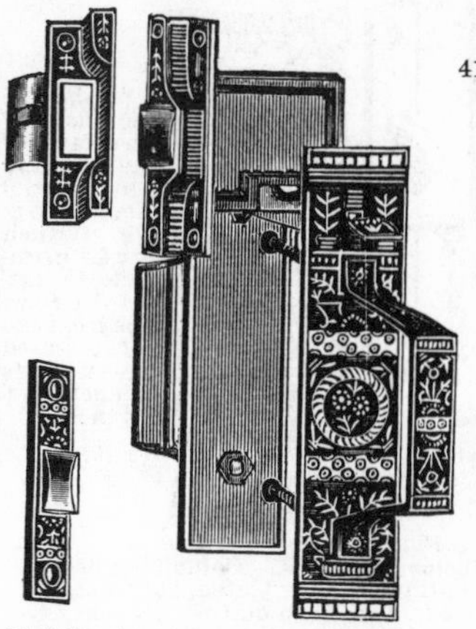

41535 Store Door Handle with latch, rabbet front, ½ inch rabbet, like cut, oblique double handle, Geneva bronze finish. Size of latch, 2¾x3¼; bronze metal bolt with anti-friction roller strike. In ordering state whether right or left-hand is wanted. Complete with screws. Per set..$1.00

Flat Front.

41536 Store Door Handle with mortise latch, same as above, reversible flat front, either right or left hand, complete with screws, per set .... .80

Oblique Store Door Handles.

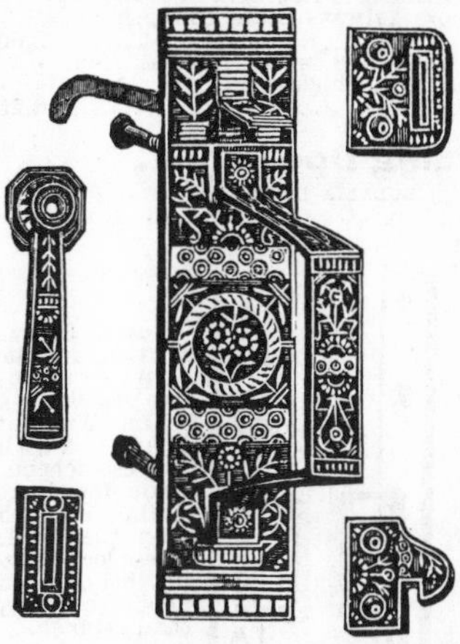

41538 Store Door Handle, a new pattern, Geneva bronzed, with oblique handle, either for right or left hand, complete with screws.
When ordering above store door handle, be sure to state whether for right or left hand, or we shall be obliged to omit it. Price, per set.......$0.30

Sliding Door Latch.

GENEVA BRONZED.

41540 Geneva Bronzed Sliding Door Latch, flat fronts; for double doors; size, 3¼x3¼ inches. Geneva bronze front and strike, bronze bolt, complete with 4 elongated flush Geneva bronzed escutcheons, one set in a box; weight, 4½ pounds.
Per set..........$0.80

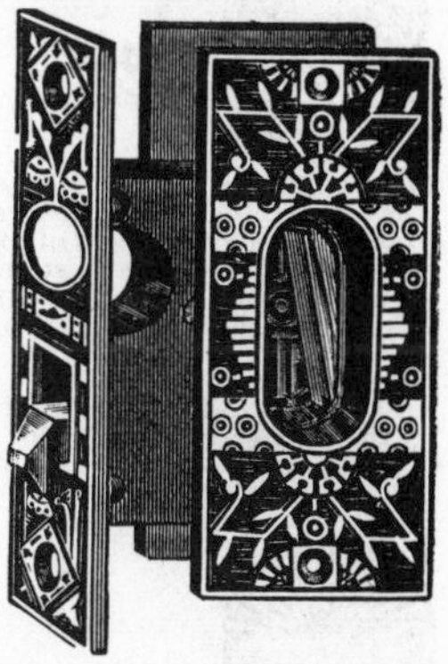

Sliding Door Lock.

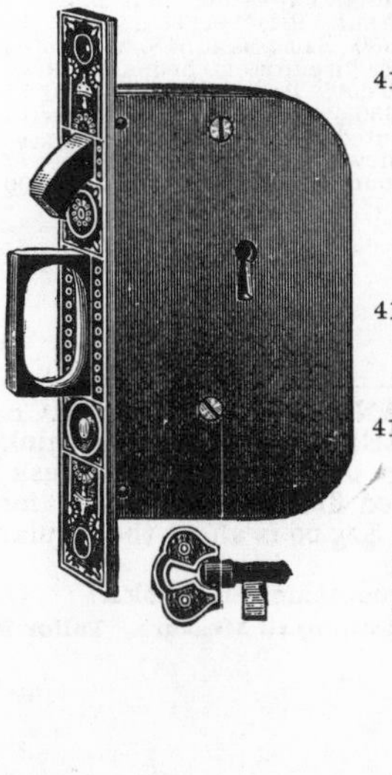

41542 Sliding Door Lock; size, 5½x3½; Geneva bronzed, flat front, brass bolt and pulls, bronze metal drop key, complete with 4 elongated flush Geneva bronzed escutcheons; weight, 4¼ lbs. Per set.......$1.20

41543 Sliding Door Lock, 5½x3¾, same description as above, only astragal front; weight, 4¼ lbs. Per set $1.40

41544 Sliding Door Lock, flat front, 5½x 3½, same description as No. 41543 for single door; has two elongated escutcheons. These locks cannot be used on doors thicker than 1½ in. Price, complete. $0.85

Sliding Door Locks.

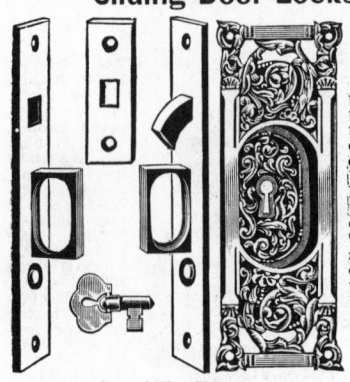

We show in the cuts only the face of the locks and one cup escutcheon. We furnish locks complete as stated below. The locks can not be used on doors thinner than 1½ inch.

Cut of Flat Front.

41545 Single Sliding Door Lock. Columbian design in iron, antique copper plated, flat front, with single lock; two flush cup escutcheons. Size of lock, 5½x3½ inches. In ordering always state thickness of your door. This is very important, as keys are made for 1½-1¾ to 2-2¼ inch doors. Price, per set, complete for single door.................$1.25

41546 Sliding Door Lock for double doors, same as 41545, except that it has double locks with 4 flush cup escutcheons. Price, per set, complete, for double doors (always state thickness of your door)..........2.00

41546½ Same as 41546 with astragal front locks. (Always state thickness of your door.) Price, per set, complete...........2.25

Sliding Door Lock.
EULALIA DESIGN.

Heavy Bronze metal, antique copper finish. Size of lock, 5½x3½ in. Wrought bronze flush cup escutcheons made for doors sliding in flush with the wall. These locks cannot be used on doors thinner than 1½ inch.

41547 Sliding Door Lock for single door, with flat front lock, 5½x3½ inch; two flush cup escutcheons; thickness of lock ½ inch; width of front, 1 inch. Always state thickness of your doors. Price, complete, for single door.........$1.10

41548 Sliding Door Locks (for double door), same as 41547, except that it has double lock with four flush cup escutcheons. State thickness of your door. Price, per set, complete, for double doors.......$1.75

41548½ Same as above, with astragal front locks. Per set, complete..................2.00

41549 Same as 41547, with fluted design cup escutcheons, as shown in cut. Price, per set.........$1.10

41550 Same as 41548, with fluted design cup escutcheons, as shown in cut. Price, per set.......$1.75

41550½ Same as 41548½, with fluted design cup escutcheons, as shown in cut. State thickness of your door. Price, per set....$2.00

EVER HAVE ANY USE FOR A NICE OFFICE DESK? What do you think of a Rolling or Flexible Top Desk, made of oak, rubbed finish, all complete, for less than $15.00? $25.00 is about the regular price for this desk.
See Index for Quotations of Desks.

Chain Door Fasteners.
GENEVA BRONZED.

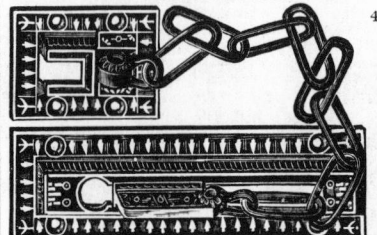

41551— Geneva Bronzed Chain Door Fasteners, a very neat device. The door may be left slightly ajar and no one can effect an entrance from the outside. Size, 6 inches, complete with screws. Weight, 15 oz. Each.................$0.22

41552 Thumb Latches, enameled. Weight, 15 ounces. Per set, ...$0.08 Per dozen sets, ...$0.65

Door Pulls.

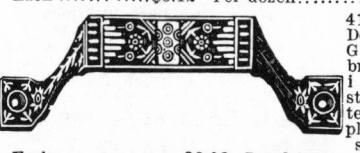

41553 Door Pull, Geneva bronzed, 7 inch, oblique pattern, packed, complete with screws. Each ....$0.12 Per dozen.............$1.30

41554— Door Pulls. Geneva bronzed, 6 inches, straight pattern, complete with screws.
Each..... .$0.08 Per dozen.. ....$0.60

41556— Foot Bolt Geneva bronzed, 6 inch extra heavy, with strike plate. Packed, complete, with screws. Each....$0.25 Per dozen..................2.40

Chain Bolts.

41557— Chain Bolt for top of door: Geneva bronzed, 6-in., extra heavy, with strike plate.
Each...............................$0.25 Per dozen.....................2.75

Door Bolts.

41558 Geneva Bronzed Door Bolt, with bronze metal knob; size of bolt, 3 inch; packed with screws. Weight, 9 oz.
Each.................... $0.15 Per dozen......................1.45

Shutter Bars.

41560 Geneva Bronzed Shutter Bars, reversible, 2½ in.; complete with screws, weight, per doz.; 12 oz. Each.........$0.08 Per dozen..........60

41561 Columbian Design, antique copper plated; complete with screws. Price, each..$0.12 Per dozen...... ....1.35

Letter Box Plates.

41564 Geneva Bronzed Letter Box Plate for door, 7¼ in.; packed with screws. Weight, 12 oz.
Each ....$0.20 Per dozen......................1.80

Door Button.

41566 Geneva Bronzed Door Buttons, on plate, size, 2 in.; complete with screws. Weight, per doz., 1 lb. 9 oz.
Each.....................$0.05 Per dozen..................40

Cupboard Bolts.

41568 Geneva Bronzed Flat Cupboard Bolt, with bronze metal knob; complete with screws. Weight, each, 5 oz.
Each...... ....$0.07 Per dozen........85

Cupboard Turns.

41569 Columbian Design, antique, copper plated, size, 2¾x2¼ inch; complete with screws. Each....$0.20 Per dozen......2.12

Sash Pulleys.

41575 Geneva Bronzed Sash Pulley, 2¼ in. noiseless heavy wrought pin, turned wheel, complete with screws. Weight, 1 lb. Each.............$0.12 Per dozen.........................1.00

41576 Common Iron Sash Pulleys; 2 inches. Per dozen.........$0.20

Sash Lifts.

41577 Geneva Bronzed Flush Sash Lift; size, 3 inches over all; complete with screws. Weight, 6 oz. Each.........$0.05 Per dozen....45

41578 Columbian Design, antique, copper plated; has side screw holes; complete with screws. Price, each...$0.12 Per dozen......1.06

41579 Eulalia Design, bronze metal, antique copper finish; has side screw holes; complete with screws. Price, each...$0.08 Per dozen....70

Sash Lifts—Continued

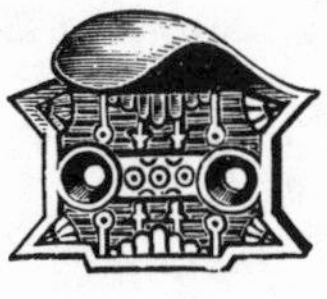

41580 Geneva Bronzed Sash Lift 1⅝ inches wide; complete with screws; weight, per doz., 1 lb. Each .... $0.03 Per doz .... .25

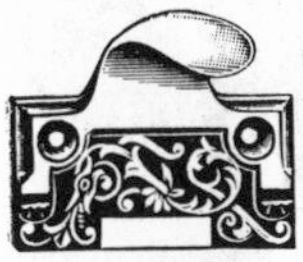

41581 Columbian Design, antique copper plated; size, 2x1¾ inches. Complete with screws. Price, each .... $0.07 Price, per dozen .... .67

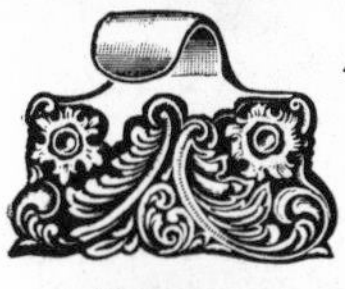

41582 Eulalia Design, bronze metal, antique copper finish. Complete with screws. Price, each .... $0.07 Price, per dozen .... .60

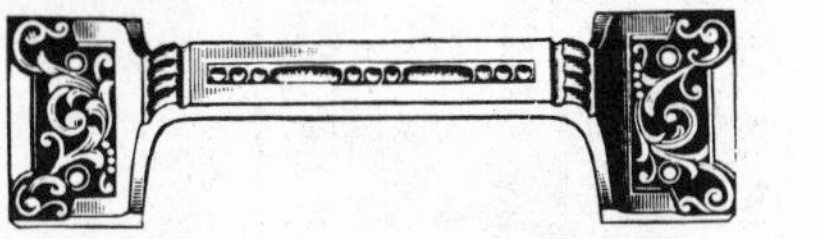

41583 Bar Handle Window or Sash Lift, Columbian design, antique copper plated. Complete with screws. Price, each .... $0.17 Price, per dozen 1.70

Sash Pull Plates.

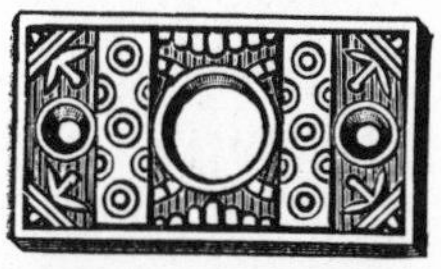

41584 Geneva Bronzed Sash Pull Plates, used in connection with pull-down hook; size, 2½ inches; complete with screws, plates only; weight, 1 lb. 15 oz. to the dozen. Each .... $0.04 Per dozen .... .31

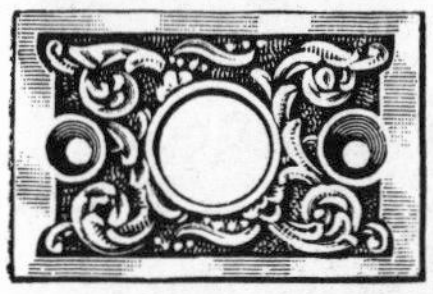

41584½ Columbian Design, antique copper plated, used in connection with pull-down hook; size, 2 inches. Complete with screws. Each .... $0.08 Per dozen .... .75

Sash Pull Down Hooks.

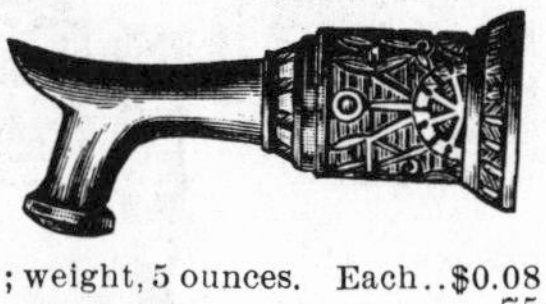

41585 Geneva Bronzed Sash Pulldown Hooks, to fasten on long pole, used in connection with No. 41584, sash pull plates, for closing high windows; complete with screws, no pole; weight, 5 ounces. Each .. $0.08 Per dozen .... .75

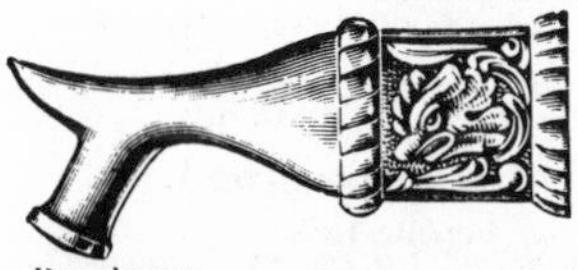

41585½ Columbian Design, antique copper plated, used in connection with No. 41584½ We do not furnish the pole with these hooks. Each .... $0.12 Per dozen 1.20

Window Catches.

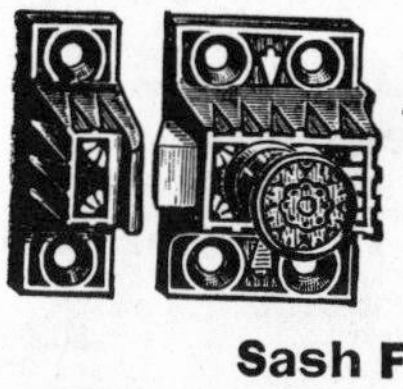

41586 Geneva Bronzed French Window Catcher; size, 1½ inch, with bronze metal knob, complete with screws; weight, 5 ounces. Each .... $0.07 Per dozen .... .62

Sash Fasteners.

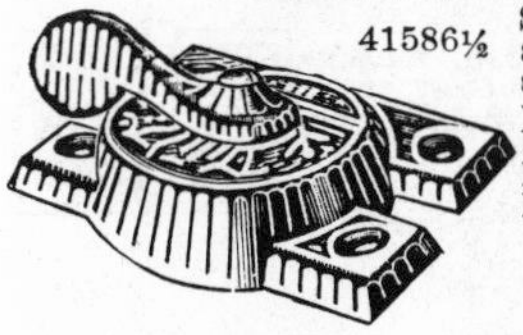

41586½ Sash Fastener, lever and arm movement, a very secure pattern. Packed with screws, Geneva bronzed. Each .... $0.12 Per dozen 1.30

41587

41587 Defiance Sash Fastener, bronze metal; plain, highly polished, packed with screws to match. Each .... $0.25 Per dozen 2.70

41587½ Wardrobe Hooks; bronze metal; plain, highly polished, packed with screws to match. Weight, each, 4 oz. Per doz. $2.10 Weight, per doz. 1¾ lbs.

Sash Fasteners—Continued.

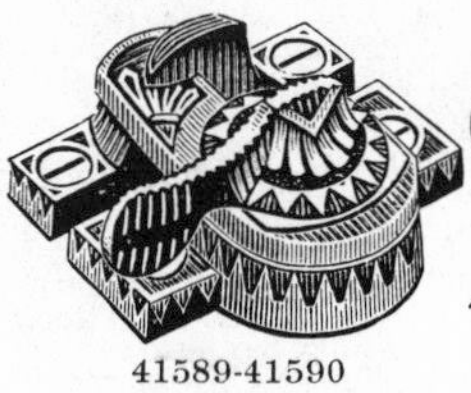

41589-41590

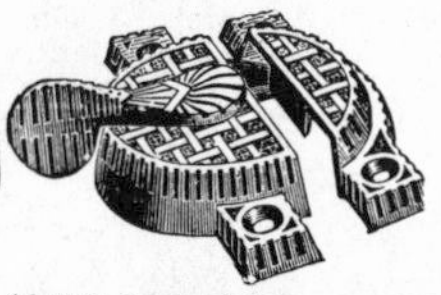

41588 Sash Lock, a new pattern, enameled iron finish. Each .... $0.05 Per dozen .... .40

Ives' Burglar Proof Sash Locks are pronounced by architects and builders to be the best in use. When locked they draw the two sashes tightly together, which prevents their rattling. They are ornamental and easily put on. Packed with screws.

41589 Ives' Burglar Proof Sash Locks, Ogee tipped, ornamental iron. Each .... $0.05 Per dozen .... .40

41590 Ives' Burglar Proof Sash Locks, ornamental iron, bronzed, with bronze metal knob. Each .... 7c. Per dozen .... .78

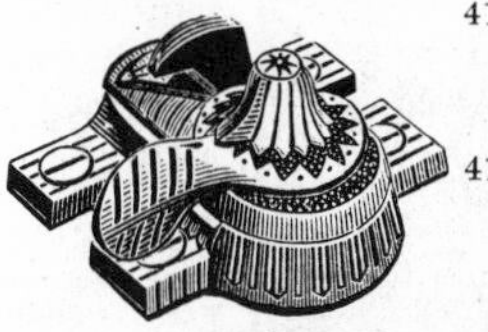

41592

41591 Ives' Burglar Proof Sash Locks, ornamental iron, bronzed bell tip. Each .... $0.05 Per dozen .... .54

41592 Ives' Burglar Proof Sash Locks, ornamental iron, bronzed with bronze metal bell tip. Price, each .... $0.08 Per dozen .... .75

Window Springs.

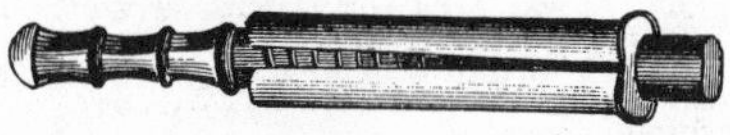

41593 Window Spring Bolts, japanned, silvered tip, tin case. Per dozen .... $0.12 Per gross 1.00

41594 Window Spring Bolts, japanned tip, tin case: weight, per dozen, 14 ounces. Per dozen .... 10c. Per gross .... .80

Transom Plates.

41595 Sash Centers or Transom Plates, iron, japanned.

Length	1⅞	2¼	2⅞
Weight, per set	3 oz.	7 oz.	10 oz.
Per set of two	$0.03	$0.04	$0.05
Per ½ doz. sets	.17	.22	.27

Sash Cord.

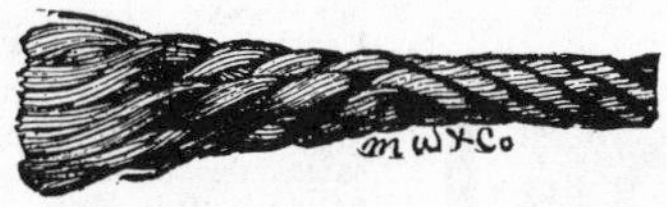

Braided sash cord is put up in bundles of 100 feet. We do not sell less than a bundle.

	Size.	Length Per lb.	Per lb.
41596 American Hemp Unbleached	8-32	38 ft.	$0.18
41597 Indian Hemp Bleached	7-32	46 ft.	.20
41598 Silver Lake Braided	7-32	55 ft.	.30
41599 Silver Lake Braided	8-32	46 ft.	.26
41600 Silver Lake Braided	9-32	40 ft.	.26
41601 Silver Lake Braided	10-32	30 ft.	.26

7-32 weighs about 2¼ lbs to the bundle.
8-32 " " 2½ " " "
9-32 " " 2½ " " "
10-32 " " 2¾ " " "

Sash Balances.

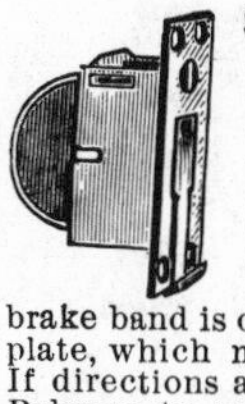

The Pullman Sash Balance, for use instead of weights, can be applied to old houses where weights cannot be used; is easily put in and operates almost noiselessly. This style of balance is becoming very popular, is very neat in appearance, works smoother and lasts longer than sash cord. The tension or brake band is operated by an adjusting screw in face plate, which makes it adjustable to varying weights. If directions are fully carried out we will warrant the Balance to work perfect. Where there is not room enough to use a Side Balance we make a special Balance for the top of the window, and can also be used in Mullen windows.

41610 Side Balance.

No.	Length.	Weight.	Per set of 4.
0—for sash 30 in.		4 to 5 lbs	$0.80
1—for sash 30 in.		5 to 7 lbs	.80
2—for sash 30 in.		7 to 9 lbs	.85
3—for sash 38 in.		9 to 11 lbs	.90
4—for sash 46 in.		11 to 13 lbs	1.05
5—for sash 46 in.		13 to 15 lbs	1.15
6—for sash 46 in.		15 to 17 lbs	1.22
7—for sash 46 in.		17 to 19 lbs	1.35
8—for sash 46 in.		19 to 21 lbs	1.55
9—for sash 48 in.		21 to 24 lbs	1.65
10—for sash 48 in.		24 to 27 lbs	1.75
11—for sash 48 in.		27 to 30 lbs	1.82

41611 Top Balance.

No.	Length.	Weight.	For set of 4.
3—for sash 38 in.		9 to 11 lbs	$0.90
4—for sash 46 in.		11 to 13 lbs	1.05
5—for sash 46 in.		13 to 15 lbs	1.15
6—for sash 46 in.		15 to 17 lbs	1.22

Transom Lifters.

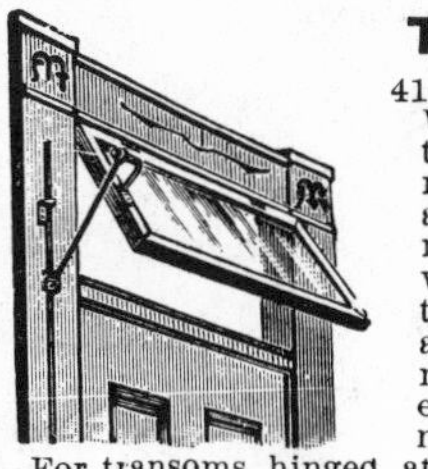

41612 Transom Lifters. With this device transoms may be lowered or raised at will with great ease and locked in any position; no other fastenings required; when ordering give size of transom and whether hinged at bottom or top They are made from round iron rods, electro copper plated and nicely finished.

For transoms hinged at top or hung in the middle.

Length.	Diameter, ¼ inch. Bronzed iron.	Diameter, $\frac{5}{16}$ inch. Bronzed iron.	Diameter, ⅜ inch. Bronzed iron.
3 feet, each	$0.21	$0.38	
4 feet, each	.21	.45	$0.53
5 feet, each		.53	.60
6 feet, each		.60	.68
7 feet, each			.83

41613 To hang on bottom.
4 feet $\frac{5}{16}$, iron. Each $0.60
5 feet ⅜, iron. Each .... .75
6 feet ⅜, iron. Each .... .80

Door Hangers.

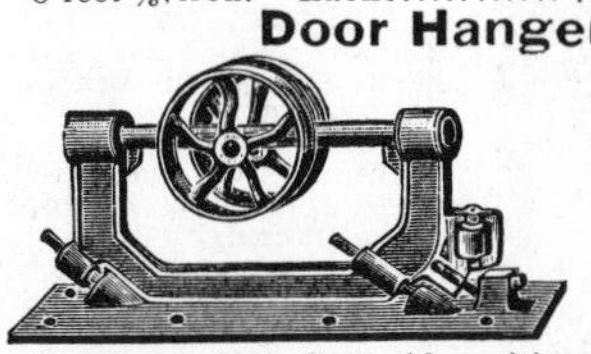

41615 Anti-Friction Drawing Room Door Hanger. This hanger is positively the best sliding door hanger on the market. Each set will carry two doors up to 4½ feet wide, without friction. One set consists of 4 hangers, 1 patent overhead stop, 4 lengths (7 feet each) hard maple rail. Full directions for putting up track and hanging double doors sent with every set hangers. Per set for double doors. $3.00

Drawer, Cupboard, Chest, Box and Wardrobe Locks, Etc.

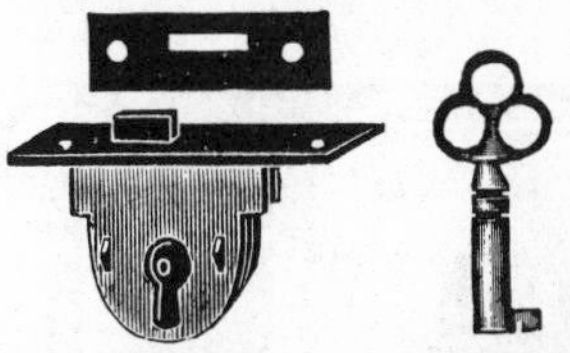

41620 Mortise Lock, for small writing desk or work box, ⅞ wide, ¾ deep, $\frac{3}{16}$ thick, brass selvedge bolt and striker, one key. Each .... $0.06 Per dozen .. .45

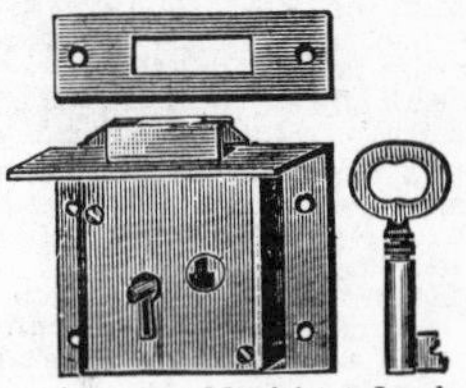

41621 Desk Lock, all iron, 2 inch, 3 secure levers, fine flat bow keys, all different in doz. Each $0.30 Per dozen 3.12

41622 Desk Lock, same as No. 41621 only all brass. Each .... $0.40 Per dozen 4.00

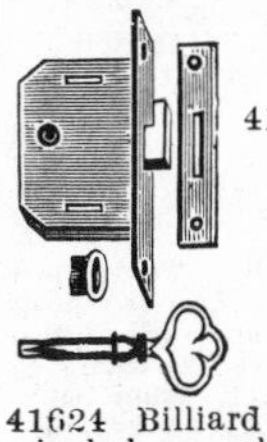

41623 Piano or Sewing Machine Lock, mortise, brass face, triangular key, silvered escutcheon; size of lock, 2¼ selvedge; body of lock, 1⅜ x1⅛ x $\frac{3}{16}$ thick, ⅞ inch from selvedge to middle of keyhole. A well-made lock. Each .... $0.10 Per dozen .... .84

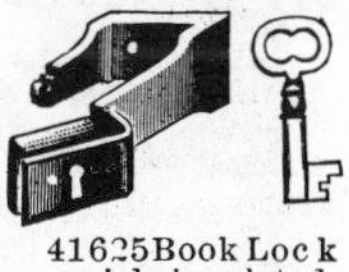

41624 Billiard Cue Lock, 1¾ inch, brass, self-locking, 2 keys, all different in a dozen; very convenient for securing billiard cues. Each .... $0.90 Per dozen 9.62

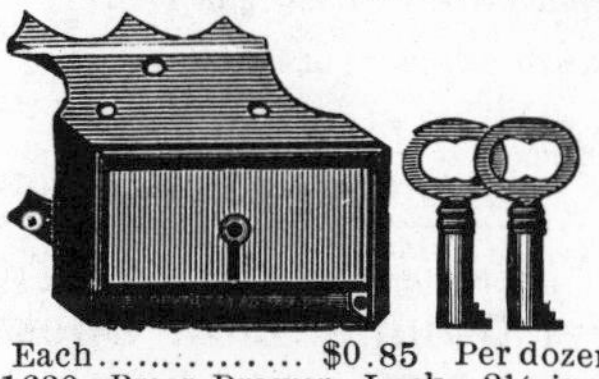

41625 Book Lock nickel plated, adjustable locking double lock, 2 fine flat bow keys with each, 6 changes in a dozen. Adjustable for a book ¾-inch to 1¼ inch thick. Each .... $0.85 Per dozen $8.40

41630 Brass Drawer Lock, 2¼ in. wide; from selvedge to key pin, ⅞ inch; has two secure levers, with fine flat bow key. Price, each .... $0.25 Per dozen 2.66

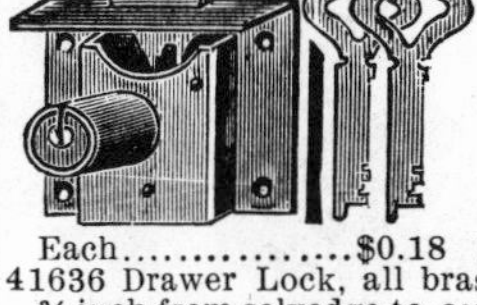

41635 Drawer Lock, iron, 1¾ inches, broad, heavy bolt, ¾ inch from selvedge to center of key cylinder; two nickel plated flat steel keys with each lock, all different in a dozen; made for ⅞ inch wood only. Each .... $0.18 Per dozen $1.75

41636 Drawer Lock, all brass, 2-inch, iron bolt, ¾-inch from selvedge to center of key cylinder, 2 nickel plated flat keys with each lock, all different in a dozen. Each .. $0.25 Per dozen 2.55

41637 Drawer Lock, all brass, 1⅝ inch wide, 1⅞-inch long, 1½ inch from top of lock to center of key cylinder, made for ⅞ inch wood, 2 nickel plated flat steel keys with lock, all different in a dozen. Each ...... $0.20 Per dozen 2.00

Locks—Continued.

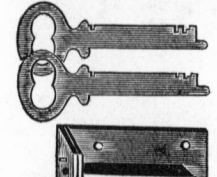

41650 Box Lock, for small work box, etc., brass, 1¼x¾ in.
Each.............$0.05
Per dozen........ .35

41651 Single Link Iron Chest or Box Lock, made of brass, like cut No. 41650. Size, 1½ inch; ⅜ inch from selvedge to key pin. Each $0.05
Per dozen............................ .33
41652 Like cut No. 41650. Size, 2 inches; made of iron; ½ inch from selvedge to key pin. Each, .05
Per dozen....................... ... .35

Chest Locks.

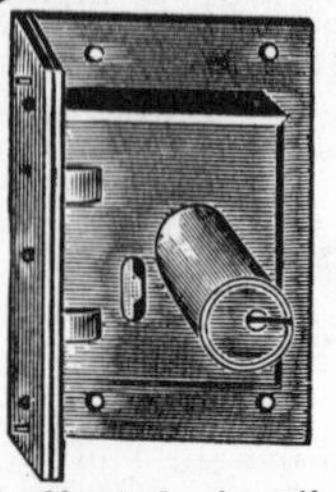

41655 Chest Lock, all brass, 3 inch, square selvedge; solid square box, screwed. 4 secure levers, 1⅛ inch from selvedge to center of key cylinder. Double link, 2 nickel plated flat steel keys with each lock, all, different in a dozen. Cylinders in 3 lengths, for 1½, 1¼ and 1 inch wood. Say for what thickness of wood when ordering.
Each... .... $0.50
Per dozen............ 5.60

41656 Chest Lock, all brass, like No. 41655 with 3 secure levers, ¾ inch from selvedge to center of key cylinder, with two nickel plated flat steel keys with each lock; width of lock, 1½ inches. Each................$0.25
Per dozen....................... 2.80

41657—Chest Lock all iron, four inch, square selvedge; self locking, double link, screwed, one double bitted key with lock, all different in a dozen; has secret wards and brass escutcheons. Each................................. $0.25
Per dozen......................... 2.50
41658 Chest Lock, 2½ inch, all iron, double link, secret wards, brass escutcheons, double bitted key, self locking, all different in a dozen
Each...................................... ..... .20
Per dozen................................ .. 2.40

Double Link Chest Locks.

41669 For small chests or box; made of brass; size, 1½ inch; ½ inch from selvedge to key pin.
Each...... $0.12
Per dozen. 1.13

41670 Same style as 41669, made of iron; size, 2 inches; ¾ inch from selvedge to key pin.
Each..............10c. Per dozen.......$0.95
41671 Same as 41670, but made of brass.
Each..............12c. Per dozen........ 1.13
41672 Same style as 41669; size, 2½ inch; made of iron; 1 ward, 6 changes in the dozen; ⅞ inch from selvedge to key pin. Each............... .12
Per dozen........................... 1.10
41673 Same as No. 41672, but made of brass.
Each...............15c. Per dozen........ 1.30

Secure Lever Double Link Chest Lock.

41674 A good substantial lock for a carpenter's tool chest. Made of iron, has two secure levers; flat bar keys, all different in a dozen. Size of lock, 3 inches; 1⅛ inch from selvedge to key pin. Each..................$0.20
Per dozen..... 2.00
41675 Same as 41674, but made of brass.
Each........ ....22c. Per dozen......... 2.25

Wardrobe Locks.

41676 Wardrobe Locks, iron bolts, shoots right or left, for either right or left hand doors, 3x1¾; weight, 5 oz. Each $0.07
Per dozen.......... .... .50

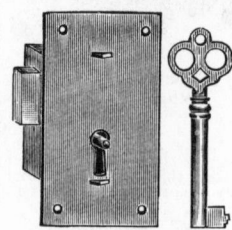

41677 Wardrobe Lock, all iron, solid square box, broad, heavy bolt, shoots right and left, can be applied to either right or left hand doors. Fancy flat bow keys, all different in a dozen. Size of lock 3x1¾. Price each....................$0.17
Per dozen......... 1.56
41678 Wardrobe Lock, same description as No. 41677, only all brass. Each $0.25
Per dozen 2.65

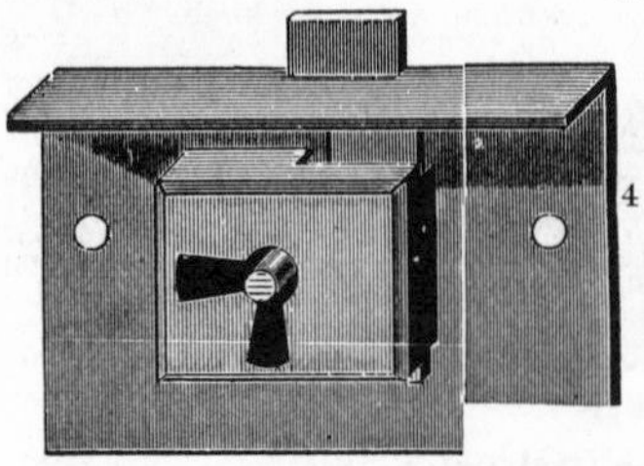

41685 Cupboard Locks, polished iron; size, 1½ x 2½ in. Each. ..$0.05
Per doz. .33
41686 Cupboard Locks, brass, 2¼ in., solid box, 3 secure levers, fine flat bow keys; weight, 5 oz. Each... $0.20
Per doz.. 1.80

41687 Till Lock, back spring with broad bolt and double keyhole, from selvedge to key pin, 1¼ inch, 2½ inch wide, like cut 41686. Brass selvedge. Price, each.............................13
Per dozen................................... 1.05

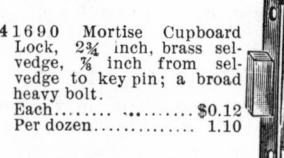

41690 Mortise Cupboard Lock, 2¾ inch, brass selvedge, ⅞ inch from selvedge to key pin; a broad heavy bolt.
Each........ ....$0.12
Per dozen.............. 1.10

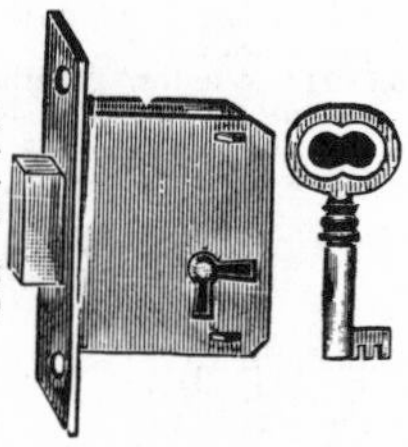

41691 Cupboard Latch Lock, all iron, 2½x¾, solid square box, 4 patent Ward's fancy bow keys, brass strikers. Keys all different in a dozen.
Each.....................$0.15
Per dozen.............. 1.45
41692 Cupboard Latch Lock, same description as No. 41691, iron lock, only all brass. Each............$0.17
Per dozen................ 1.70

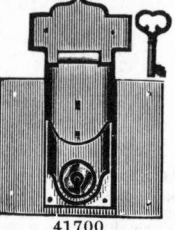

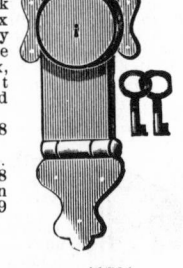

41700 Trunk Lock, 4x 3, heavy iron plate and box, patent japanned hasp. Weight, 8 oz.
Each.....
....$0.18
Per dozen 1.89

41701

41701 Excelsior Trunk Lock, cast brass, for wood frame trunk, complete with two keys.
Each $0.50
Per dozen.. 5.40

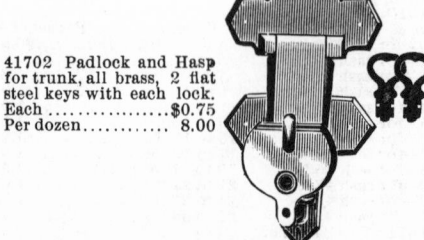

41702 Padlock and Hasp for trunk, all brass, 2 flat steel keys with each lock.
Each $0.75
Per dozen............ 8.00

41703 Padlock and Hasp for trunk, same as No. 41702, but all iron instead of brass. Red japanned. Each $0.25
Per dozen.. 2.00

Loose Pin Butts
COLUMBIAN DESIGN.

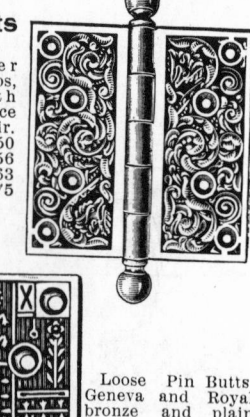

41709 Antique copper plated with ball tips, packed complete with screws.

Sizes.	Pr. pair.
3½x3½	$0.50
4x4	.56
4½x4½	.63
5x5	.75

Loose Pin Butts, Geneva and Royal bronze and plain bronze, old copper finish; packed complete with screws.

41710 Geneva Bronze. We always send the latest designs in Geneva bronze goods.

Sizes	3x3	3½x3½	4x4	4½x4½	5x5
Per pair.	$0.25	$0.28	$0.32	$0.35	$0.40

41711 Royal Bronze.

Sizes	3x3	3½x3½	4x4	4½x4½	5x5
Per pair.	$0.65	$0.75	$0.92	$1.06	$1.25

41712 Plain Bronze Old Copper.

Sizes	3x3	3½x3½	4x4	4½x4½	5x5
Per pair.	$0.75	$0.88	$1.00	$1.19	$1.38

Door Butts.

41720 Cast Butts, plain, loose pin; can be used for both right and left hand doors. No screws furnished at these prices.

Sizes	2x2	2½x2½	3x3	3½x3½	4x4
Weight, per pair	9	12	15	18	23 oz.
Per pair	3c.	3c.	4c.	7c.	8c.
Per dozen pair	28c.	38c.	44c.	60c.	75c.

Door Butts, Japanned.

41721 Cast Door Butts, japanned, right or left hand steeple tips, drilled holes. No screws furnished at these prices. Same pattern as 41720.

Sizes	2x2	2½x2½	3x3	3½x3½	4x4
Weight, per pair	9	12	15	18	23 oz.
Per pair	5c.	6c.	8c.	10c.	11c.
Per dozen pair	54c.	65c.	87c.	$1.08	$1.12

Inside Shutter Butts.

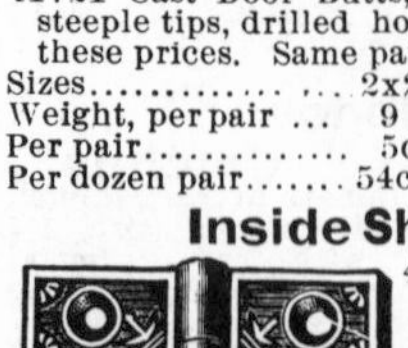

41725 Geneva Bronzed Inside Shutter Butts, fast joint; size, 1¼x2; complete with screws. Weight, per pair, 4 oz.
Per pair....... ... .$0.10
Per dozen. 1.08

41726 Columbian Design, antique copper plated inside shutter butts, fast joint, size, 1¼x2 inches. complete with screws.
Per pair......................$0.17
Per dozen pair................. 1.80

41728 Geneva Bronzed Inside Shutter Butts, fast joint; size, 2¼x1¾; complete with screws; weight, per pair, 6 oz.
Per pair.... ....$0.15
Per dozen pair.............. 1.62

Shutter Butts—Continued.

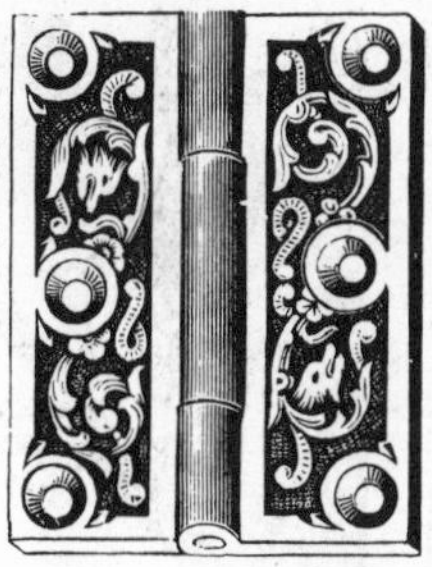

41729 Columbian Design; antique copper plated, inside shutter butts, fast joint 2¼x1¾ inches, complete with screws.
Per pair.......... ....$0.25
Per dozen pair....... 2.30

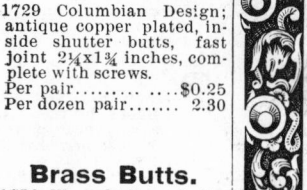

Brass Butts.

41736 Wrought Brass Butts. No screws.

Sizes..................	¾x¾	1x¾	1¼x⅞	1½x1
Weight, per pair......	2	3	4	4 oz.
Per pair..............	2c.	3c.	4c.	5c.
Per dozen pair.... ..	9c.	11c.	14c.	18c.
Sizes......	1¾x1⅛	2x1⅛	2½x1⅜	3x1½
Per pair..............	6c.	06c.	07c.	10c.
Per dozen pair........	24c.	28c.	47c.	75c.

We do not furnish screws at the above prices.

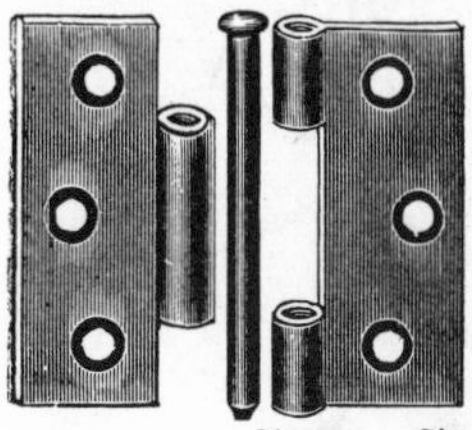

41740 Wrought Steel, loose pin, light narrow butts. No screws furnished.

Size.	Size open.	Size of screw.	Per dozen.	Per pair
1½ in	1 7/16	No. 5	$0.19	$0.03
1¾ in	1 7/16	No. 5	.22	.03
2 in..	1 9/16	No. 6	.24	.04
2¼ in	1 11/16	No. 6	.27	.04
2½ in	1 11/16	No. 6	.30	04
3 in	2	No 6	.39	05

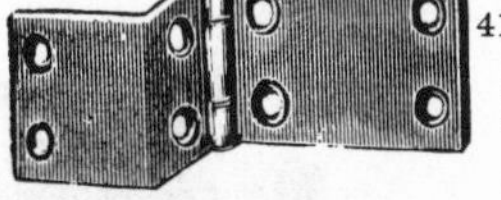

41744 Wrought Steel Chest Hinges, patent riveted. No screws furnished.

Size.	1½ inch.	2 inch.
Inside of bend to center of pin...	15/16	1
Size of screw used............	No. 8	
No. of screw-holes in each........	8	8
Price, per pair................	$0.05	$0.08
Per dozen pair................	.45	.61

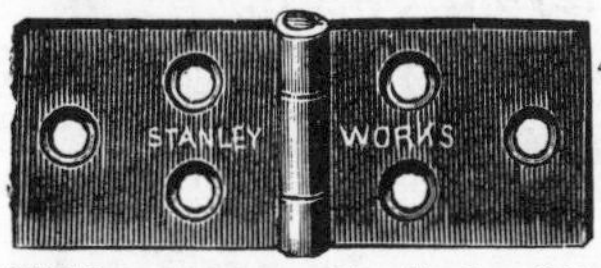

41746 Wrought Steel Back Flaps, patent riveted, 6 screw holes. No screws furnished.

Width.............	¾	⅞	1	1⅛	1¼	1⅜	1½	2
Length, open.	2¾	2¾	2⅞	3	3¼	3¼	3½	4⅜
Size of screw used	6	6	6	6	7	7	8	8
Price, per pair....	3c.	3c.	3c.	3c.	4c.	4c.	4c.	5c.
Price, pr dz pair	16c.	18c.	20c.	22c.	24c.	27c.	30c.	35c.

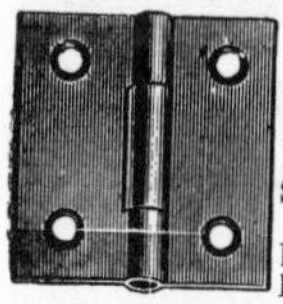

41748 Wrought Iron Butts, fast joint. (No screws furnished.)

Size	1 in.	1¼ in.	1½ in.	1¾in.
Wgt, pr pair	2	3	4	4 oz.
Per pair.......	2c.	2c.	3c.	3c.
Per dozen... .	12c.	14c,	17c.	20c.
Size.........	2 in.	2¼ in.	2½ in.	3 in.
Wgt. pr pair	4	5	7	8 oz.
Per pair......	4c.	4c.	4c.	4c.
Per dozen. .	21c.	22c.	25c.	32c.

41749 Wrought Steel Reversible Butts, much stronger and better than iron, with planished surface. Same as 41740, but much heavier.
The price given is without screws.

Size open,	Size of screw.	Price per dozen pairs.	Per pair.
3x2½.............	No. 10	$0.51	$0.06
3x3.............	No. 10	.57	.07
3½x3½...........	No. 11	.81	.09
4x4.	No. 11	1.00	.10
4½x4½.....	No. 12	1.29	.12

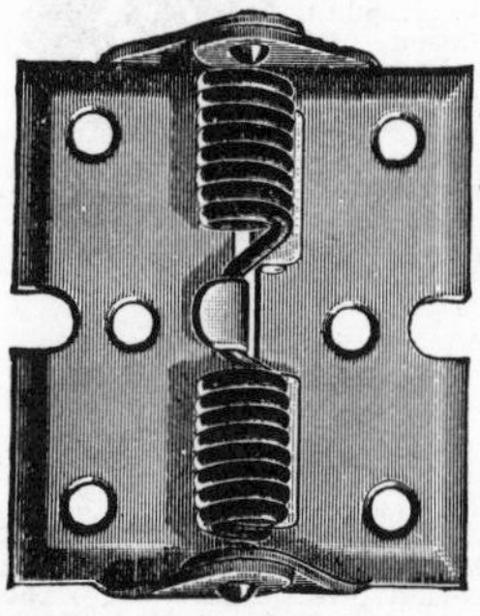

Wrought Steel Spring Hinges.

41755 Stearns' Unbreakable Steel Spring Hinge; the only wrought steel hold-back screen door hinge in the market; japanned, packed, with screws.
Price, each.......$0.12
Per dozen........ 1.30

Hinges—Continued.

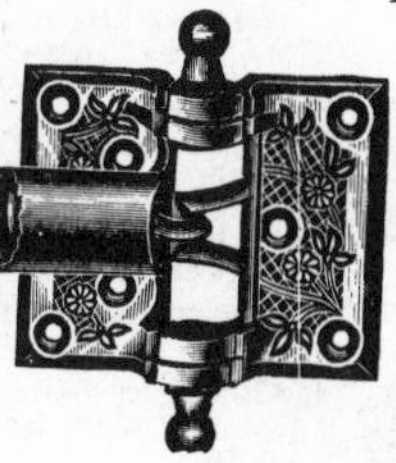

41756 Stearns Matchless Hold-Back Spring Hinge, with covered spring, for screen doors, either right or left hand. This hinge is made extra heavy, with no light parts to break and get out of order. The spring being covered, is protected from the weather and will last longer than any other spring hinge made. It will hold the door either open or closed. Per pair, no screws furnished. $0.10
Per doz. pair........ 1.00

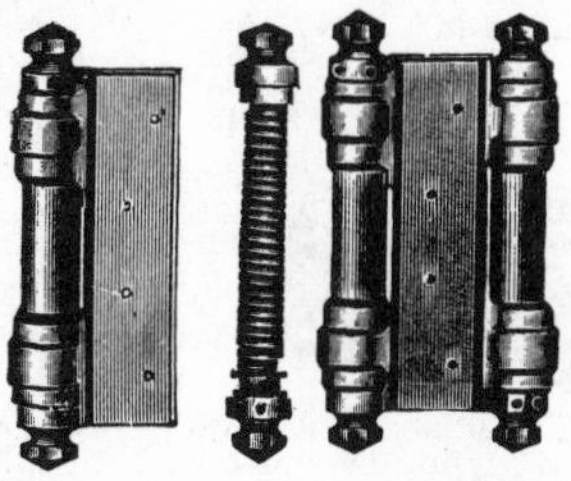

The Gem Screen Door Spring Butt, japanned, with spiral spring, reversible, for right or left hand doors; weight, 2¾ to 3¾ lbs. per pair.

SINGLE ACTION, TO SWING ONE WAY.

41757 3½-inch for doors ¾ to 1 inch, per pair..$0.55
41758 4-inch for doors ⅞ to 1⅜ inch, " .. .65
41759 5-inch for doors 1 to 1½ inch, " .. .85

DOUBLE ACTION, TO SWING BOTH WAYS.

41760 3½-inch for doors ¾ to 1 inch, per pair..$1.10
41761 4-inch for doors ⅞ to 1⅜ inch, " .. 1.25
41762 5-inch for doors 1 to 1½ inch, " .. 1.60

Door Springs.

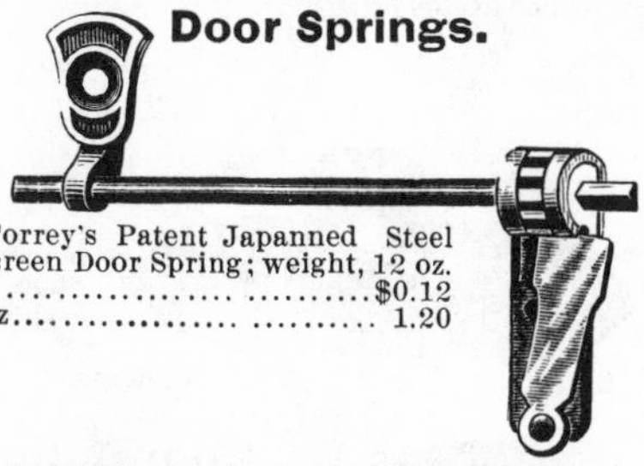

41763 Torrey's Patent Japanned Steel Rod Screen Door Spring; weight, 12 oz.
Each. $0.12
Per doz.............................. 1.20

41764 Spiral Spring, made of No. 9 steel wire, japanned; weight, 11 oz. Each, 8c. Per doz...$0.87

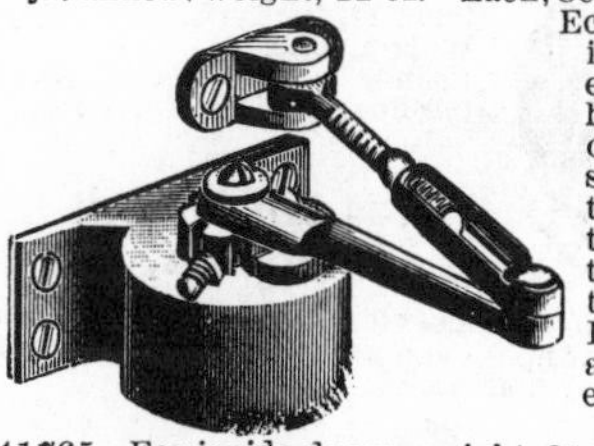

Eclipse Door Spring is suitable for either right or left hand doors. To change the doors, simply withdraw the pin at the bottom of the case and turn the spring the other side up. Directions how to apply packed with each one.

	Tuscan bronze	Nickel plated.
41765 For inside doors; weight, 3¼ lbs. Each..............................	$0.90	$2.40
41766 For heavy outside doors; weight, 5¾ lbs. Each	1.25	2.85

Eclipse Door Check.

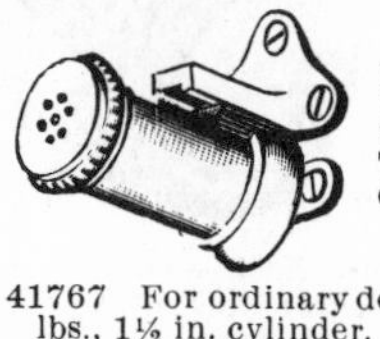

Eclipse Door Check, used to prevent doors with springs attached from slamming. Always put cylinder indoors if possible. To regulate the draft turn cap at end of cylinder.

	Tuscan bronze.	Nickel. plated.
41767 For ordinary doors; weight, 3¼ lbs., 1½ in. cylinder. Each...........	$1.50	$3.00
41768 For heavy doors; weight, 4½ lbs., 2 in. cylinder. Each...........	1.98	3.50

Base Knobs.

Weight, per dozen, 1¾ lbs.

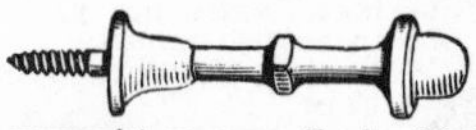

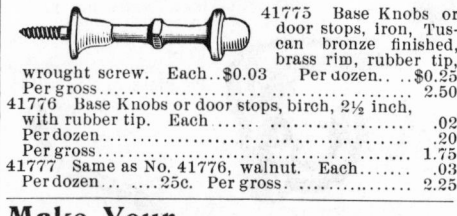

41775 Base Knobs or door stops, iron, Tuscan bronze finished, brass rim, rubber tip, wrought screw. Each..$0.03 Per dozen...$0.25
Per gross................................ 2.50
41776 Base Knobs or door stops, birch, 2½ inch, with rubber tip. Each .... .02
Per dozen.. .20
Per gross.. 1.75
41777 Same as No. 41776, walnut. Each....... .03
Per dozen... ....25c. Per gross. 2.25

Make Your
HARDWARE ORDER
Come to 100 lbs.
And go by Freight. It is the Way to Save.

Padlocks.

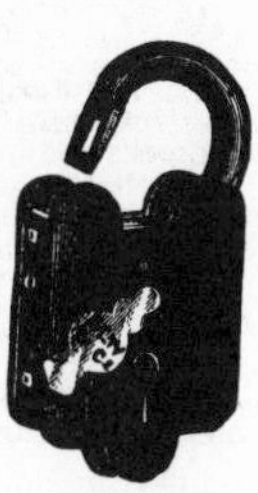

41790 Japanned Iron, square, 1 wheel ward, self locking, spring shackle, brass, keyhole cover; width, 2½ inch, a strong lock, 2 keys; weight, 7 oz,
Each........................ .$0.12
Per dozen... .... 1.25

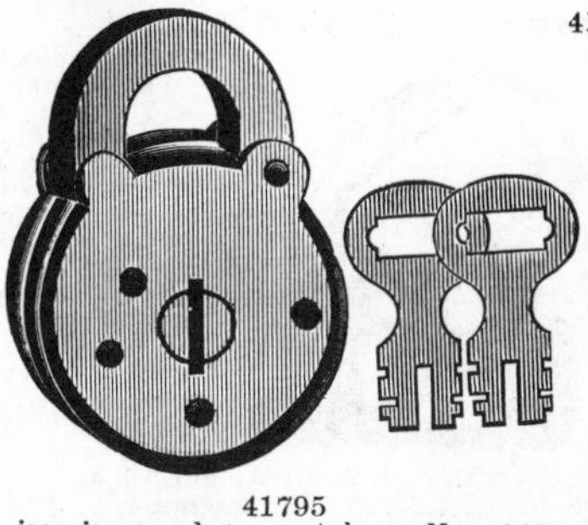

41795 Eagle Padlocks. brass, plain finish, self-locking two double bitted flat steel keys with each lock, all different in a dozen.
Each.$0.50
Per dozen, ...$5 40
41795
41796 The Eagle Padlock, made of wrought iron japanned, same style as No. 41795, self-locking, two fancy double bitted keys with each, a very stong and good lock.
Each................$0.40 Per dozen $4.40

Solid Bronze Metal.

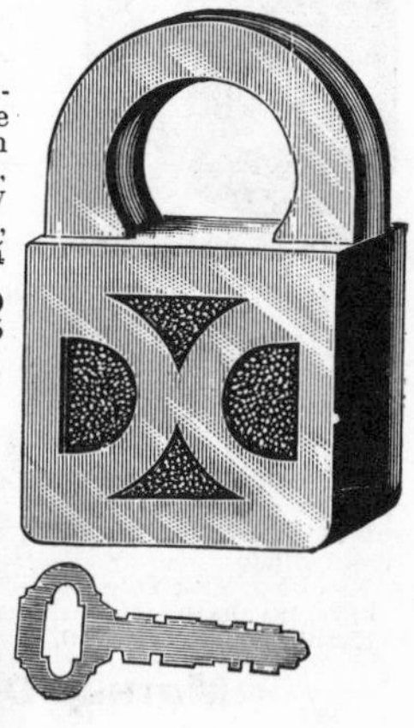

41797 Self-locking Unpickable Padlock, the best in the market, with two rolled steel keys, with keyhole covered by revolving brass cylinder, size, 2½x1¾; weight 5¼ oz.
Price, each........$0.20
Price. per dozen... 2.25

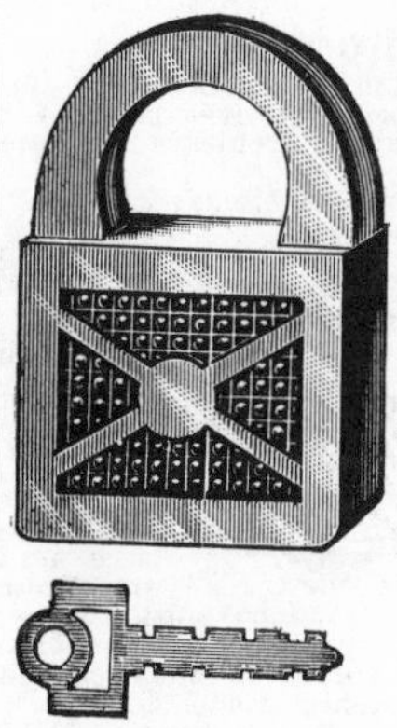

41798 Something new—Alumnium Bronze Spring Padlock, with automatic self-acting hinged shackle, one key; weight 3¼ oz. size, 2⅜x1¾ inches
Price, each........... $0.12
Price, per dozen..... . 1.25

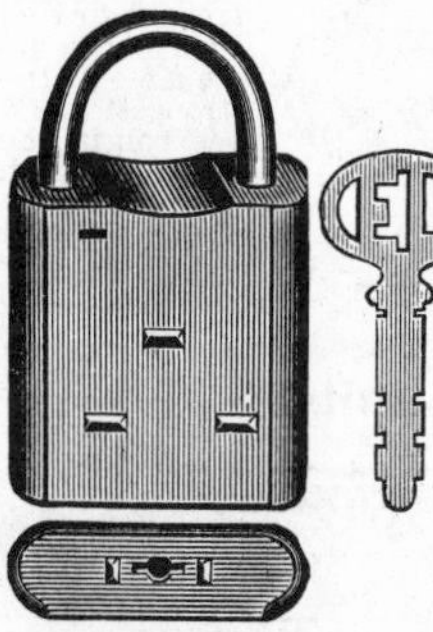

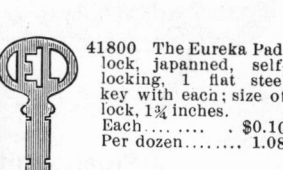

41800 The Eureka Padlock, japanned, self-locking, 1 flat steel key with each; size of lock, 1¾ inches.
Each... .... . $0.10
Per dozen........ 1.08

6-Lever Padlock.

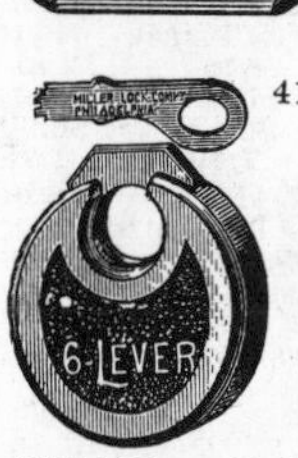

41803 6-lever Padlock made entirely of cast bronze, with interior parts of brass, warranted not to give out or rust in any climate; springs made of the celebrated phosphor bronze, keys of steel, nickel plated, no two locks take same keys, most secure and durable self-locking padlock in the market; 3½ inches, 2 keys, hasp will pass through ⅜ inch hole. Weight, 12 ounces.
Each.......................$0.42
41804 6-lever Padlock, same as 41803 with chain; weight, 14 ounces. Each. .. ..$ 0.50

"4-Lever Automatic" Padlock.

For *security, durability* and *convenience* these Padlocks are unequaled. Made of steel and brass.
41805 Steel, dark finish. Price.each $0.16
Per dozen ... 1.75
41806 Brass, bright finish.
Price, each ... $0.20
Per dozen 1.90

Screw Lock Padlocks.

41807 Padlock, iron japanned, and self-locking, screw key; this padlock is very novel and secure, after inserting the key into the keyhole it has to be turned 3 or 4 times, or screwed into the padlock before it will unlock; two keys with each lock. Weight, 10 oz.
Price, each.........$0.25 Per dozen.........$2.70

Scandinavian Padlocks.

Padlock, iron case, painted red, detached shackle, two keys. good substantial lock, like cut, excepting has open keyhole and nearly square key.
41809 Size, 1⅝x2½.
Each $0.07
Per dozen.... ......$0.50
Extra, by mail. Each 07
41810 Size, 2½x1½.
Each ....$0.08 Per dozen.......... .70
Extra, by mail. Each........................... .11
41811 Size, 3x1¾.
Each.... ...$0.10 Per dozen............. .80
Extra, by mail. Each.......................... .15

Yale Padlocks.

For design, construction and finish these are undoubtedly the best line of padlocks ever made; for solidity, security, durability and convenience they are unexcelled.
41812 No. 813, Yale padlock: size, 1 inch; 2 flat keys, no chain; weight, 5 ounces.
Each ....$0.70 With chain $0.90

Mortise Door Bolt.

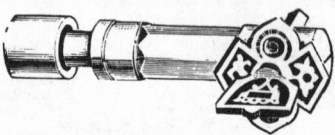

41820 Iron Mortise Front Door Bolts, ¾x3, with real bronze thumb-piece and rose. These bolts are preferable to the common outside barrel bolt, as they are not unsightly, being mortised into the door. Nothing shows but the thumb-piece, and they are the most secure fastening made.
Weight, 9 oz. Each.......$0.12 Per dozen....$1.15
41825 Wrought Iron Barrel Door Bolts, japanned; the strongest and best bolt in the market, with best staple, which gives it greater resisting power; price is without screws.

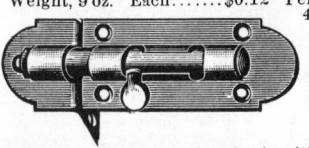

	Price, each		Per dozen
4 inch	$0.07		$0.60
5 inch	" " .08		" " .75
6 inch	" " .09		" " .85

Flush Bolts.

41828 Geneva Bronzed Flush Bolts, 1 inch wide; packed with screws.

	6 in.	8 in.	12 in.
Weight	10 oz.	11 oz.	14 oz.
Price, each	$0.12	$0.15	$0.20
Per dozen	1.25	1.40	1.75

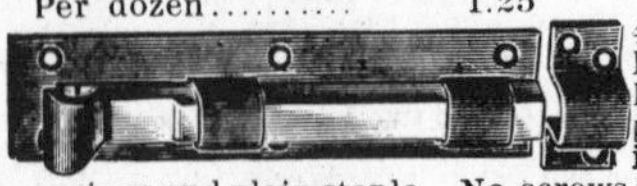

41831 Wrought Iron Square Door Bolts, with japan plates and polished bolts. steel springs and plain staple. No screws furnished at this price.

Size.	4 in.	5 in.	6 in.
Bolts,	⅜ in. sq.	⅜ in. sq.	½ in. sq.
Per dozen,	$0.40	$0.70	$0.75
Each	.06	.08	.08

Barn Door Bolts.

41832 Barn Door Bolts, japanned iron. This bolt is very handy; can be operated from both sides of the door: has heavy bolt 8 inches long; weighs 2 lbs.
Each........ ... $0.15 Per dozen.... ...$1.60

41833 Door Bolts. japanned, with brass knobs.

Sizes	4 in.	5 in.	6 in.
Weight, each...	8 oz.	10 oz.	12 oz.
Price, each	$0.03	$0.05	$0.06
Price, per dozen	.33	.45	.60

41836. Barrel Bolts, dark bronzed; packed with screws, weight 7 oz.

3-inch, Each	$0.06	Per dozen	$0.60
4-inch, Each	.07	Per dozen	.75
5-inch, Each	10	Per dozen	.90

41839— Wrought Iron Bottom Bolt, with japanned plates, polished bolts, steel springs and floor plates. No screws furnished at this price.

Size.	5 in.	6 in.	7 in.	8 in.
Bolts,	⅜ in. sq.	⅜ in. sq.	½ in. sq.	½ in. sq.
Per doz.	$0.79	$0.85	$1.15	$1.20
Each.	.10	.12	.15	.16

41845 Cupboard Catch (ab), japanned iron, porcelain knob.
Weight, 4 oz.
Each.... ... $0.04 Per dozen.. ....$0.44

Door Buttons.

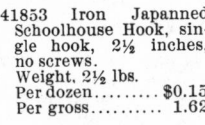

41850 Door Buttons, japanned iron, 1¾ inch.
Weight, 4 oz.
Each $0.02
Per dozen................ .22

Hat and Coat Hooks.

School house hooks are heavier and stronger than the ordinary hat or coat hooks and are sometimes preferred for wardrobe use for that reason.

For screws see Index.

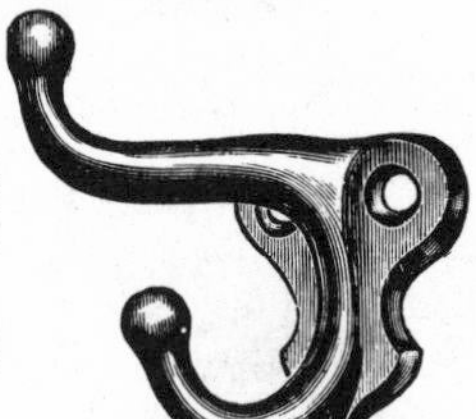

41853 Iron Japanned Schoolhouse Hook, single hook, 2½ inches, no screws.
Weight, 2½ lbs.
Per dozen........ $0.15
Per gross.......... 1.62

41854 Iron Japanned Schoolhouse Hook, double hook, 2½ in., no screws. Weight, per dozen 3 lbs. 13 oz.
Per dozen............................$0.25
Per gross.................................... 2.50

41855 Iron Japanned Schoolhouse Hook, triple hook, extra heavy, 2½ inches, no screws, Weight, per doz., 3 lbs. 13 oz.
Per dozen.........$0.20
Per gross.......... 2.16

41858 Iron Japanned Hat and Coat Hook, 4 inch. Weight, per doz., 1 lb. 13 oz.
Per dozen. $0.10
Per gross 1.05

Hat and Coat Hooks—Continued.

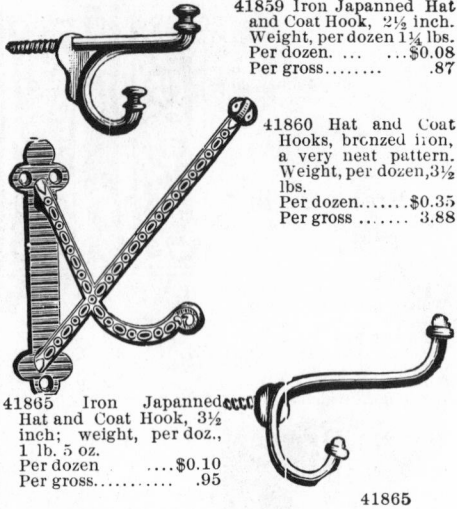

41859 Iron Japanned Hat and Coat Hook, 2½ inch. Weight, per dozen 1¼ lbs.
Per dozen. $0.08
Per gross........ .87

41860 Hat and Coat Hooks, bronzed iron, a very neat pattern. Weight, per dozen, 3½ lbs.
Per dozen......$0.35
Per gross 3.88

41865 Iron Japanned Hat and Coat Hook, 3½ inch; weight, per doz., 1 lb. 5 oz.
Per dozen $0.10
Per gross.......... .95

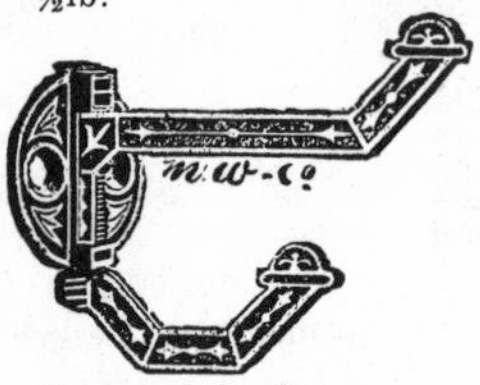

41865

41866 Adamantine bronzed Hat and Coat Hook, 4 inch. Weight, per dozen, 2 lbs. 10 oz.
Per dozen..........$ 0.20
Per gross........... 2.16
(Screws furnished.) 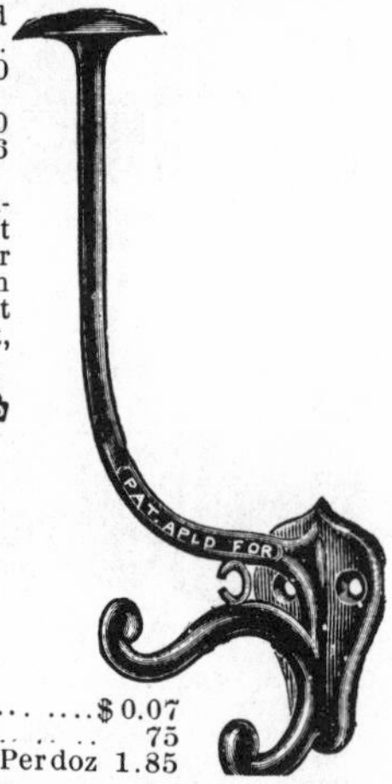
41867 Hat, Coat and Umbrella Rack. The short hook 4 inches long, for coat; whole length from lower hook to top of hat hook, 10 inches; weight, ½ lb.
Japanned. Each ....$ 0.07
Per dozen.................. 75
Nickel plated, each $0.17. Per doz 1.85

Geneva Bronzed.

41868 Hat and Coat Hook, Geneva bronzed complete with screws; a very handsome pattern; size, 3¼ in. weight per doz.. 2 lb. 10 oz.
Per dozen.....$ 0.45
Per gross..... 4.80

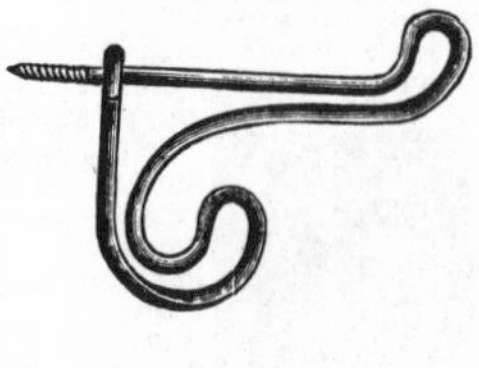

The Gem Wire Hat and coat hooks having gimlet screw points; they are easily put up or removed, no extra screws or tools being required.
41869-Coppered.
41870-Japanned

Size	2½	3	3½
Japanned per dozen.....	$0.08	$0.10	$0.10
Japanned, per gross.....	.87	1.08	1.08
Coppered, per dozen.....	.07	.08	.09
Coppered, per gross......	.75	.87	.98

Furniture Handles.

41880 Furniture Handle, ring pattern, gilt. Weight, per doz., 1 lb. 4 oz
Each....$0.06
Per dozen. .67
41881 Furinure Handle, ring pattern, gilt finish: weight, per dozen 15 oz.
Each.... $0.03
Per doz.. .33

41883 Flush Brass Pulls for small drawers.

Size	1	1¼	1½	2 in.
Weight	2 oz.	2 oz.	3 oz.	3 oz.
Price, each	7c.	8c.	9c.	15c.
Per doz	$0.60	$0.80	$0.90	$1.62

Trap Door Rings.

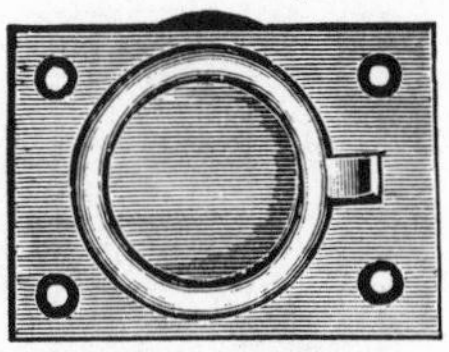

41885 Flush Trap Door Rings, iron, japanned. Diameter of rings—

	2¼	2½	2¾
Each—	$0.05	$0.06	$0.08
Per dz.	.54	.65	.87

Drawer Pulls.

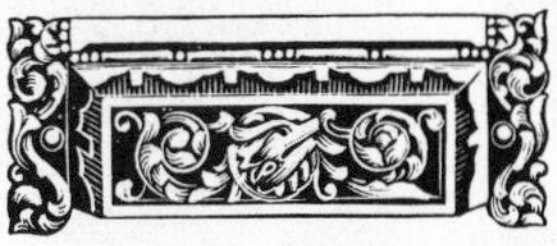

41890 Columbian Design Antique Copper Plated, size, 4x1⅜ inches; complete with screws.
Per doz......$0.65
Per gross.... 7.20

MW&Co.

41895 Drawer Pulls, iron Tuscan bronzed, with screws; weight, each, 4 oz.
Each....$0.03
Per doz. .20
Per gross. 2.16

WE CHARGE NOTHING FOR CASES OR CARTAGE

Drawer Pulls—Continued.

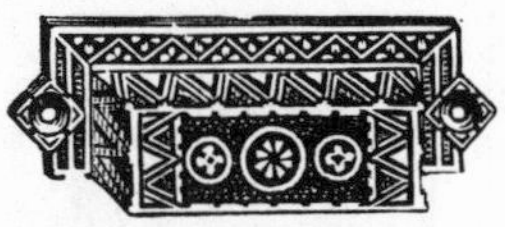

41900 Drawer Pull, Iron bronze plated, a very handsome pattern; weight, 4 oz.
Per dozen.......$0.35
Per gross........ 3.78

Drawer Knobs.

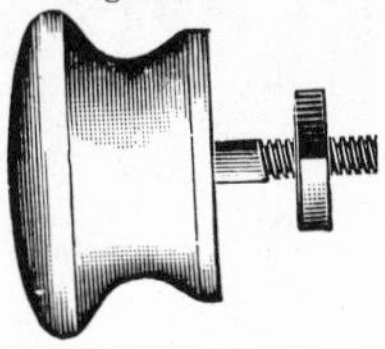

41905 Porcelain Knobs.

Inches	1	1¼	1½	1¾	2
Weight, per doz	15 oz.	20 oz.	27 oz.	39 oz.	45 oz.
Per dozen	20c.	25c.	30c.	35c.	40c.
Each	2c.	3c.	3c.	4c.	4c..

Drawer Drop Handles.

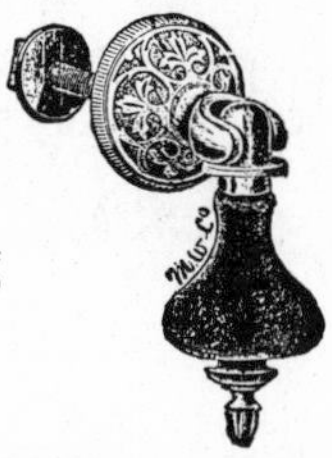
MW&Co

41908 Ebony and Gilt.
Each.................... $0.04
Per dozen .... .35
Weight, per doz. 1 lb. 1 oz.

Brass Lifting Handles.

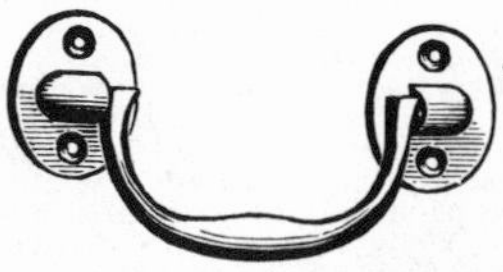

41912 Brass Lifting Handles.

Size.	Weight.	Per pair.
2½ in	5 oz.	$0.15
3 in.	8 oz	.18

Hooks and Eyes.

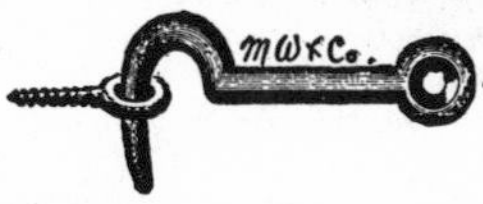
MW&Co.

41915 Brass Hooks and Eyes.

Size	1 in.	1¼ in.	1½ in.	2 in.
Weight, per doz.	4 oz.	4 oz.	5 oz.	6 oz.
Per dozen	7c.	8c.	9c.	11c.

HARDWARE FITTINGS...

WHERE ELSE CAN YOU FIND SO MANY THINGS WHICH YOU WANT DAILY

SCREWS.

41980 SCREWS.—These screws are cold forged: stronger than a cut screw; inserted easier; increased holding power; centralized point.

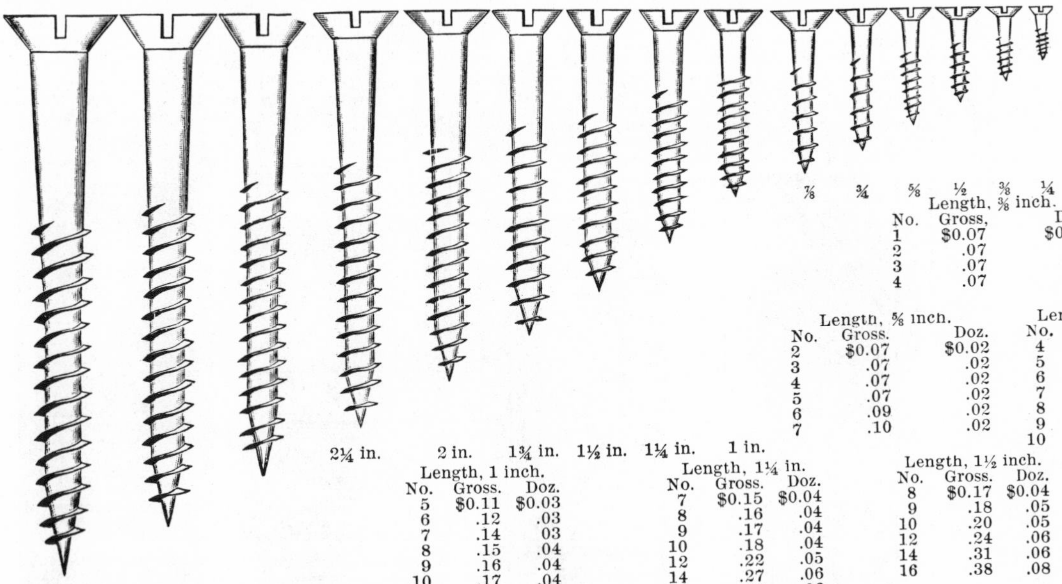
Diam. No. 20
18
16
14
12
10
9
8
7
6
5
4
3
2
1
⅞
¾
⅝
½
⅜
¼
2¼ in.
2 in.
1¾ in.
1½ in.
1¼ in.
1 in.
Length, 3 in.
2¾ in.
2½ in.

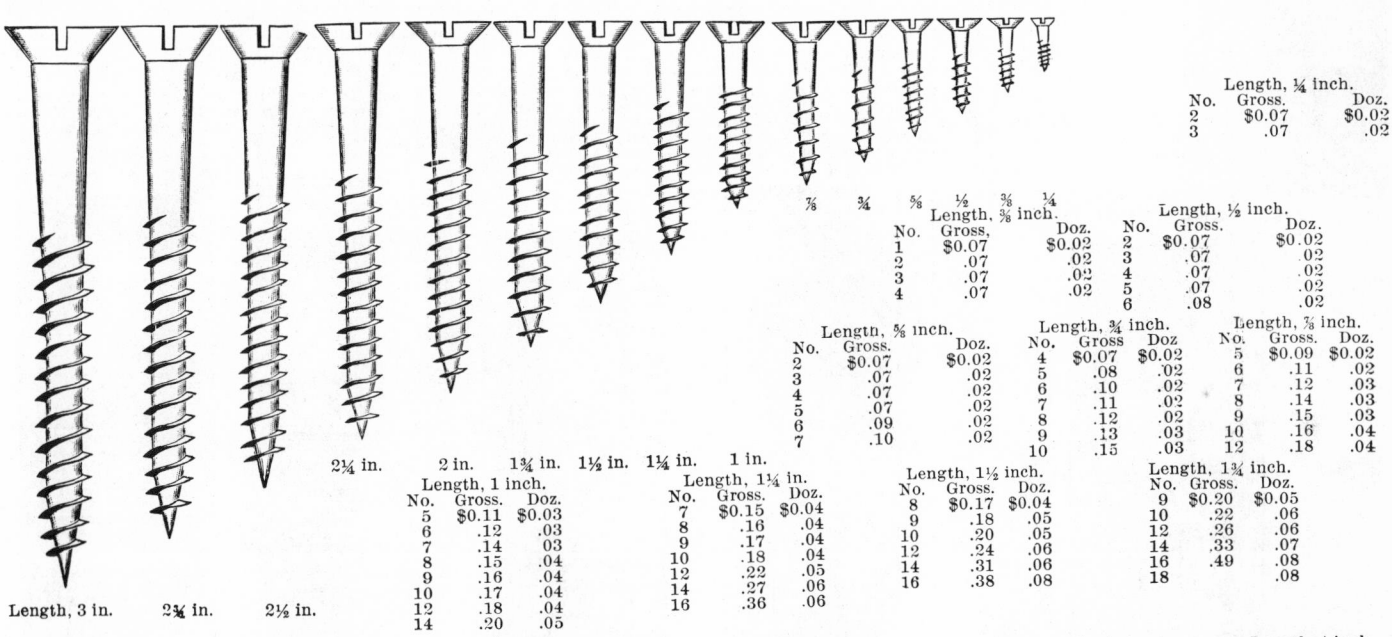

Length, ¼ inch.

No.	Gross.	Doz.
2	$0.07	$0.02
3	.07	.02

Length, ⅜ inch.

No.	Gross,	Doz.
1	$0.07	$0.02
2	.07	.02
3	.07	.02
4	.07	.02

Length, ½ inch.

No.	Gross.	Doz.
2	$0.07	$0.02
3	.07	.02
4	.07	.02
5	.07	.02
6	.08	.02

Length, ⅝ inch.

No.	Gross.	Doz.
2	$0.07	$0.02
3	.07	.02
4	.07	.02
5	.07	.02
6	.09	.02
7	.10	.02

Length, ¾ inch.

No.	Gross	Doz
4	$0.07	$0.02
5	.08	.02
6	.10	.02
7	.11	.02
8	.12	.02
9	.13	.03
10	.15	.03

Length, ⅞ inch.

No.	Gross.	Doz.
5	$0.09	$0.02
6	.11	.02
7	.12	.03
8	.14	.03
9	.15	.03
10	.16	.04
12	.18	.04

Length, 1 inch.

No.	Gross.	Doz.
5	$0.11	$0.03
6	.12	.03
7	.14	03
8	.15	.04
9	.16	.04
10	.17	.04
12	.18	.04
14	.20	.05

Length, 1¼ in.

No.	Gross.	Doz.
7	$0.15	$0.04
8	.16	.04
9	.17	.04
10	.18	.04
12	.22	.05
14	.27	.06
16	.36	.06

Length, 1½ inch.

No.	Gross.	Doz.
8	$0.17	$0.04
9	.18	.05
10	.20	.05
12	.24	.06
14	.31	.06
16	.38	.08

Length, 1¾ inch.

No.	Gross.	Doz.
9	$0.20	$0.05
10	.22	.06
12	.26	.06
14	.33	.07
16	.49	.08
18		.08

Length, 2 inch.

No.	Gross.	Doz.
10	$0.24	$0.06
12	.28	.06
14	.36	.07
16	.44	.08
18	.52	.08

Length, 2¼ inch.

No.	Gross.	Doz
12	$0.31	$0.06
14	.38	.08
16	.47	.08
18	.55	.08

Length, 2½ inch.

No.	Gross.	Doz.
12	$0.34	$0.06
14	.37	.08
16	.50	.08
18	.60	.09
20	.70	.10

Length, 3 inch.

No.	Gross.	Doz.
14	$0.48	$0.08
16	.60	.09
18	.72	.10
20	87	.12

Length, 3½ inch.

No.	Gross.	Doz.
16	$0.71	$0.10
18	.86	.12
20	1.00	.15

Length, 4 inch.

No.	Gross.	Doz.
18	$1.00	$0.15
20	1.16	.18

Round Head Blued Screws.

41981 Sizes same as No. 41980.

Length	½	½	½	¾	¾	¾	⅞	⅞	⅞	⅞
No.	3	4	5	5	5	6	5	6	7	8
Gross	$0.14	.14	.15	.15	.17	.19	.19	.21	.24	.26

Length	1	1	1	1	1¼	1¼	1¼	1¼	1½	1½	1½
No.	6	7	8	10	7	8	9	10	10	12	14
Gross	$0.24	.26	.28	.33	.28	.31	.33	.35	.39	.46	.60

Length	1¾	1¾
No.	12	14
Gross	$0.51	.65

Flat Head Brass Screws.

41982 Sizes same as No. 41980.

Length	⅜	⅜	⅜	⅜	½	½	½	½	⅝	⅝	⅝	⅝
No.	2	3	4	5	2	3	4	5	3	4	5	6
Gross	$0.25	.25	.28	.30	.25	.25	.30	.30	.29	.30	.35	.39

Length	¾	¾	¾	¾	1	1	1	1¼	1¼
No.	5	6	8	10	7	8	10	8	10
Gross	$0.39	.42	.55	.70	.57	.59	.85	.75	.95

Diamond Point Drive Screws.

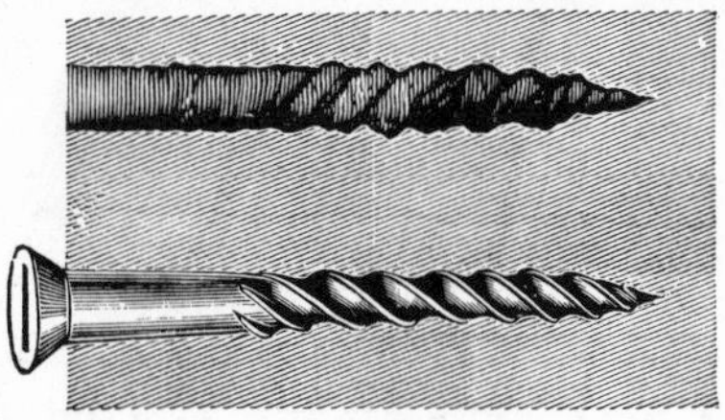

41985.

Driven with a hammer its entire length. It turns like a screw as it goes in, and does not break the fibers of the wood. Holds stronger than a common screw as ordinarily inserted. They can be easily removed with a screw driver. We do not sell less than a gross.

L'gth	⅞	⅞	1	1¼	1½	1	1¼	1½	1¾	1¼	1½	2	2½
No.	7	8	8	9	9	10	10	10	10	12	12	21	12
Per gross.	$0.13	.16	.16	.20	.20	.20	.20	.20	.24	.21	.26	.30	.38

Nails.

Quotations of nails will be found in our Grocery List, sent free upon request.

Sash Weights.

41987 Sash Weights. Per lb......................$0.01¼
Subject to change of market without notice. Sash weights are sold as they are marked and not by actual weight.

FOR **Groceries**

... REFER TO OUR ...

GROCERY LIST

Which is issued every month and mailed free to any address upon application.

Sash Doors and Blinds.

We handle clean, well manufactured stock, and aim to fill orders promptly. Goods made to order, of some special size, requires from seven to ten days to complete the order. When ordering this class of goods it is IMPORTANT that you send us all measurements *correctly*, as we will not exchange mill work when sent as ordered. In sending orders for doors always state the height, width thickness and number of panels, if they are to be all wood doors or sash doors. We give below a list of sizes of doors in general use, but we can make to order any size that you may require.

O. G. Sash Doors.

41990 One light, double strength glass; raised panel. Thickness of door, 1⅜ inches.

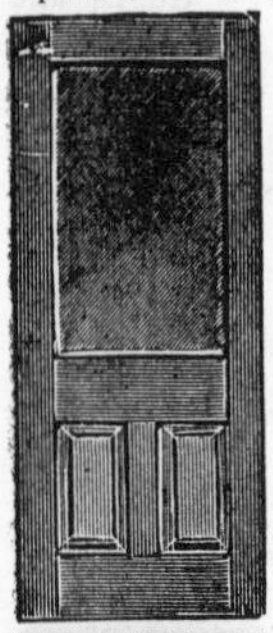

Size. ft. in. ft. in.	Price, each, unglazed.	Price, each, glazed.
2 6x6 6	$1.65	$2.75
2 8x6 8	1.80	3.15
2 6x6 10	1.90	3.20
2 10x6 10	1 95	3.50
2 6x7 ...	1.90	3.45
3 ...x7 ...	2.05	3.95
2 6x7 6	2.05	3.75
3 ...x7 6	2.25	4.50
2 6x8 ...	2.20	4.20
3 ...x8 ...	2.40	4.85

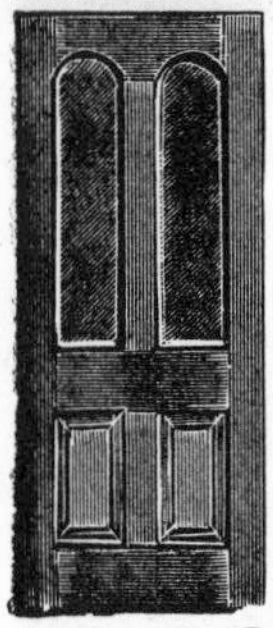

O. G. SASH DOORS.

41991 Two lights, raised panel in both sides. Thickness, 1⅜ inches.

Size. ft. in. ft. in.	Price, each, unglazed.	Price, each, glazed.
2 6x6 6	$2.00	$3.10
2 8x6 8	2.25	3.15
2 6x6 10	2.30	3.20
2 10x6 10	2.40	3.65
2 6x7 ...	2.35	3 40
3 ...x7 ...	2.50	3.75
2 6x7 6	2.45	3.85
3 ..x7 6	2.70	4.35
2 6x8 ...	2.65	4.45
3 . x8 ...	2.90	5.00

O. G. Four Panel Door.

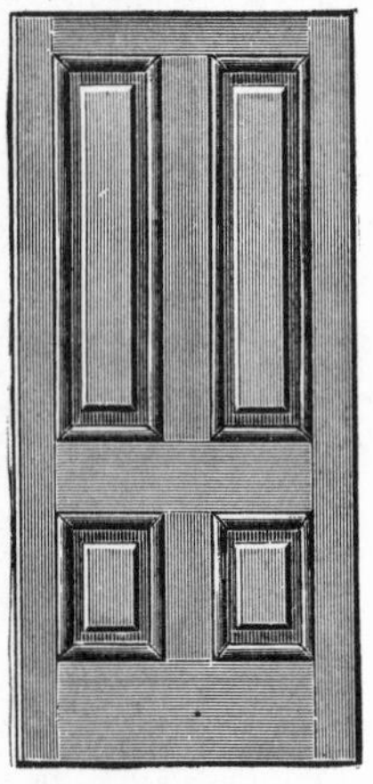

Order No. 41992.

Size. ft. in. ft in.	Thickness.	Price, each, 1st quality	Price, each, 2d quality.
2 ...x6 ...	1⅛	$1.05	$1.00
2 6x6 6	1⅛	1.25	1.20
2 6x6 8	1⅛	1.35	1.30
2 8x6 8	1⅛	1.42	1.35
2 10x6 10	1⅛	1.50	1.45
2 6x6 6	1⅜	1.55	1.40
2 8x6 8	1⅜	1.60	1.45
2 10x6 10	1⅜	1.75	1.65
2 6x7 ...	1⅜	1.75	1.65
3 .. x7 ..	1⅜	1.90	1.80
3 ...x7 6	1⅜	2.05	1.95

Front Doors.

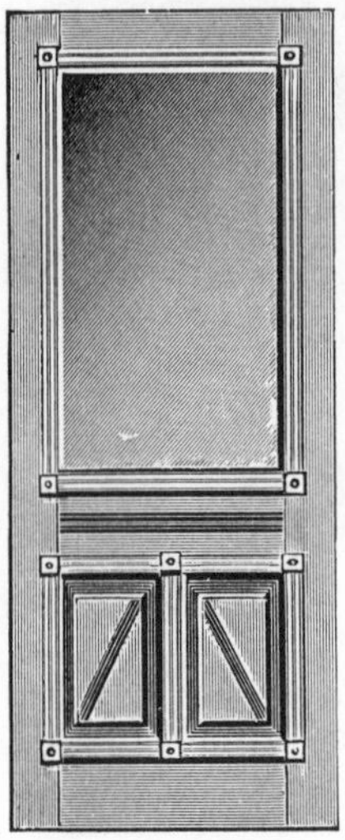

Garfield.

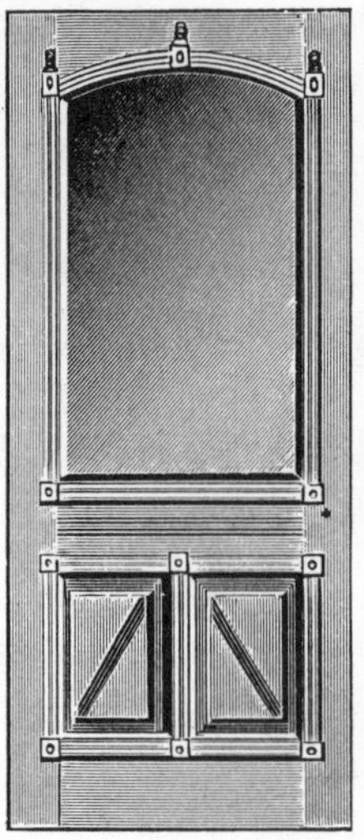

Jenny Lind.

41994 1⅜ thick. The price of glazed doors as given below is based in all cases on glazed with plain double strength glass.

Size. ft. in. ft. in.	One light square top. Price, Un-glazed.	Glazed. D. S. Plain.	One light seg. top. Price, Un-glazed.	Glazed. D. S. Plain.
2 6x6 6	$2.75	$3.82	$3.11	$4.35
2 8x6 8	2.85	4.20	3.25	4.70
2 8x6 10	2.85	4.20	3.25	4.70
2 10x6 10	3.10	4.70	3.55	5.20
2 8x7 0	3.20	4.85	3.70	5.30
2 10x7 0	3.30	5.15	3.75	5.70
3 0x7 0	3.35	5.36	3.85	5.90

EXTRAS.-We can furnish the Garfield and Jenny Lind 3 ft. x 8ft 6 in. Prices for same will be quoted on application. We can glaze the above doors with *Colored, Cathedral*, Enamel or Chipped Glass at an additional cost to the above prices of 75 cents to each door. For do r 1¾ inch, add $1.50 to above prices.

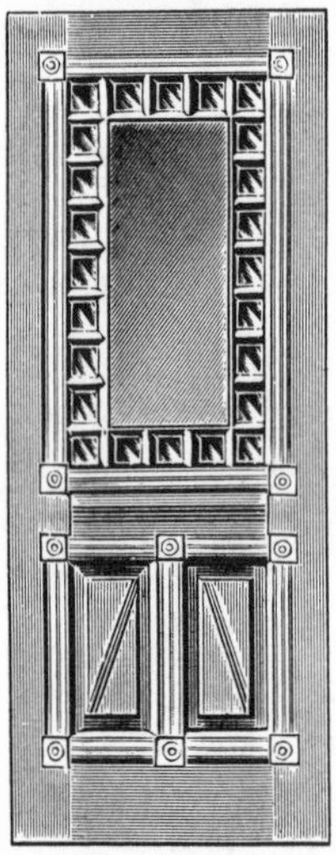

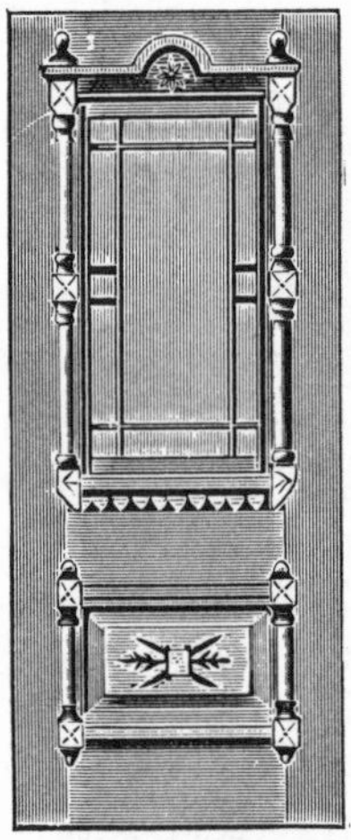

41995 1⅜ inch thick. The price of glazed doors as given below are based in all cases on glazed with plain double strength glass.

Sizes, ft. in. ft. in.	Garfield Marginal. Price, Unglazed.	Glazed, D.L. Plain	Queen Anne. Price, Unglazed.	Glazed, D.L. Plain.
2 6x6 6	$3.15	$4.97	$4.37	$5.90
2 8x6 8	3.75	5.48	4.55	6.15
2 8x610	3.75	5.48	4.55	6.25
2 10x610	4.80	5.95	4.81	6.65
3 0x7 0	5.10	6.68	5.10	7.20

Extras.

We can furnish the above doors, glazed, assorted colored border lights, with cathedral, enamel or chipped center light, at an additional cost of 75 cents to the above price of each door. For doors 1¾ inch thick add $1.50 to above prices.

Front Doors—Continued.

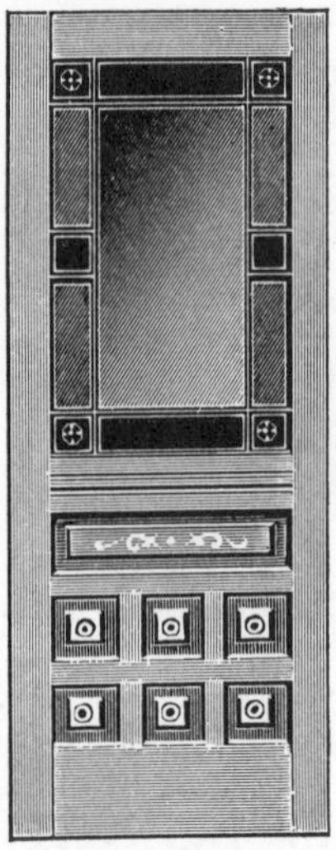

Fig. 305

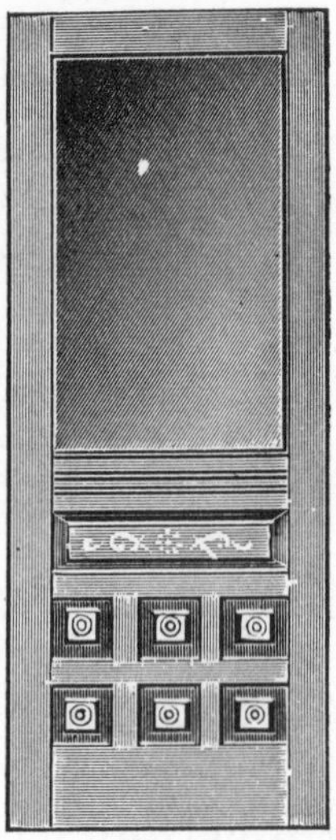

Fig. 486.

41996 Front Doors, 1⅜ inches thick, World's Fair style. This price is based on glazed, with plain, double strength glass.

Sizes ft. in. ft. in.	Unglazed.	Glazed.	Unglazed.	Glazed.
2 6x6 6	$2.85	$4.40	$2.40	$3.80
2 8x6 8	2.90	4.50	2.40	3.80
2 10x6 10	3.15	5.00	2 65	4.20
3 0x7 0	3.45	5.50	2.89	4.75

We can furnish colored border lights, assorted colors, with cathedral, enamel, or chipped center lights at an additional cost of 75 cents to the above price of each door.

For doors 1¾ inch thick, add $1.50 to above prices. We can furnish the figured glass, as in Door Quaker A41997, with the above doors at an extra charge of $2.25 each to the above price.

Quaker A.

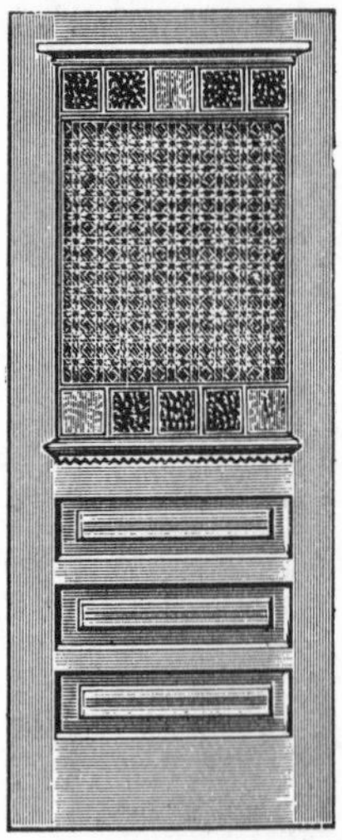

Quaker C.

41997 Quaker pattern; something handsome and very reasonable. Glass in A door cut by the old process would cost you more than we are charging for door and glass.

Sizes, ft. in. ft. in.	Un-glazed.	Glazed, Cut.	Un-glazed.	Glazed Colored and Enamel.
2 6x6 6	$2.50	$3.75	$2.81	$3.65
2 8x6 8	2.71	3.85	3.00	3.75
2 10x6 10	2.85	4.20	3.10	4.10
3 0x7 0	3.00	4.65	3.45	4.45

For doors 1¾ inch thick add $1.50 to above. The above light of cut glass, which is cut by a new process, is of very handsome design and can be used in any of our front doors by adding $2.25 to the price of each door.

PAINTS, OILS AND VARNISHES.

IT is not enough for us to say that our prices are low because poor paint is sold at prices which seem low, but it is a great deal for us to say that we sell the BEST PAINT at the prices quoted. A million people have learned that when we say best, it is best. See last pages.

Doors—Continued.

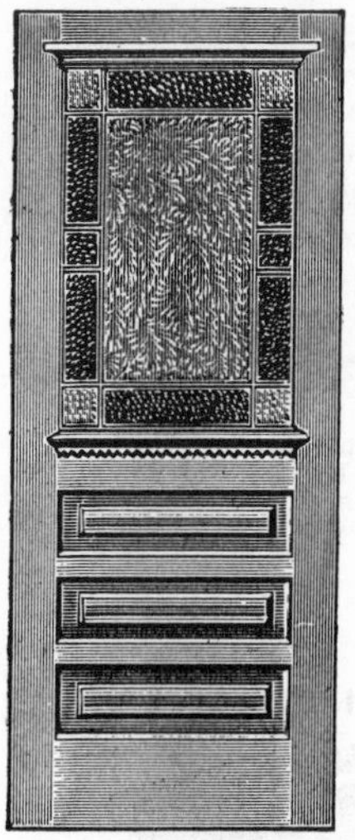

41997½ Front Door, 1⅜ inch thick; glazed with chipped center lights and colored border lights. Quaker B. style.

ft. in. ft. in		Glazed.
2 6x6 6	Each	$3.65
2 8x6 6	"	3.75
2 10x6 10	"	4.10
3 0x7 0	"	4.40

Plain Rail Sash.

41998 Plain rail sash are made 1⅛ inch thick and are not arranged to operate with weights. In ordering give number and size of lights and see if outside dimensions as given below correspond with size of your frames. By an *open sash* is meant a sash without glass, while a *glazed sash* is one complete with glass. Prices given are for one window which consists of one top and one bottom sash. Always state whether you want open or glazed sash.

Size of glass.	No. of lights in window.	Price pr window, open.	Price pr window, glazed.	Size of window. ft.	in.	ft.	in.
7x 9	12	26c.	55c.	2	1x	3	4½
8x10	12	32c.	60c.	2	4x	3	9¼
8x12	12	38c.	70c.	2	4x	4	6
8x14	12	40c.	85c.	2	4x	5	2
8x16	12	45c.	95c.	2	4x	5	10
9x12	12	39c.	80c.	2	7x	4	6
9x13	12	42c.	85c.	2	7x	4	10
9x14	12	43c.	88c.	2	7x	5	2
9x15	12	48c.	95c.	2	7x	5	6
10x12	12	44c.	85c.	2	10x	4	6
8x10	8	34c.	50c.	1	8½x	3	9¼
9x12	8	37c.	60c.	1	10½x	4	6
9x14	8	41c.	70c.	1	10½x	5	2
10x12	8	40c.	65c.	2	0½x	4	6
10x14	8	43c.	70c.	2	0½x	5	2

CHECK RAIL SASH.

Check rail sash are made 1⅜ inches thick and are intend to be used with box frames and sash weights. In ordering give number and size of lights in frame, and see if outside dimensions as given below correspond with your frames. By an open sash is meant a *sash without glass*, while a glazed sash is one *complete with glass*. Prices given are for one window, which consists of one top and botton sash. You must be particular and state whether you want open or glazed sash. Sash weigh as follows: Eight lights, glazed, from 18 to 27 pounds; four lights, glazed, from 20 to 35 pounds; two lights, glazed, from 20 to 26 pounds.

41999 Size of glass.	No. of Lights in window.	Price, per window open.	Price, per window glazed.	Size of window. Ft. in. ft. in
10x12	8	$0.34	$0.75	2 1 x4 6
10x14	8	.39	.80	2 1 x5 2
10x16	8	.45	1.00	2 1 x5 10
12x14	8	.42	1.05	2 5 x5 2
12x16	8	.48	1.10	2 5 x5 10
12x18	8	.54	1.10	2 5 x6 6
12x24	4	.35	.85	2 5 x4 6
12x28	4	.40	.95	2 5 x5 2
12x32	4	.46	1.25	2 5 x5 10
12x36	4	.52	1.40	2 5 x6 6
14x24	4	.44	.95	2 9 x4 6
14x28	4	.47	1.25	2 9 x4 10
14x32	4	.53	1.40	2 9 x5 10
14x36	4	.58	1.60	2 9 x6 6
16x24	2	.32	.70	1 8 x4 6
16x32	2	.43	.95	1 8 x5 10
18x28	2	.38	.97	1 10 x5 2
18x32	2	.44	1.07	1 10 x5 10
18x36	2	.50	1.20	1 10 x6 6
18x40	2	.58	1.35	2 10 x7 2
20x28	2	.39	1.00	2 0 x5 2
20x30	2	.41	1.05	2 0 x5 6
20x32	2	.45	1.15	2 0 x5 10
24x28	2	.42	1.10	2 4 x5 2
24x30	2	.46	1.08	2 4 x5 6
24x34	2	.51	1.40	2 4 x6 2
24x38	2	.59	1.60	2 4 x6 10

25—2d

Pantry Sash.

42000 Pantry Check Rail Sash, 1⅜ inch thick, made like 41999 but are only one light wide. Prices are for one window complete, consisting of one bottom and one top sash. Average weight of glazed pantry sash is from 20 to 30 lbs.

Size of glass.	Number of lights in window.	Price, per window, not glazed.	Price, per window, glazed.	Size of window. ft. in. ft. in.
9x12	4	$0.34	$0.49	1 1⅛x4 6
9x14	4	.38	.60	" 5 2
9x16	4	.45	.68	" 5 10
12x14	4	.39	.70	1 4⅛x5 2
12x24	2	.35	.63	" 4 6
12x28	2	.40	.78	" 5 2
12x32	2	.46	.94	" 5 10

Cellar Sash.

42001 Cellar Sash up to 10x14 are 1⅛ in. thick, above 10x14 are 1⅜ in. thick. Prices are for one sash only; weight from 7 to 15 lbs., glazed.

Size of glass.	No. of lights.	Price, ea., open.	Price, ea., glazed.	Size of Sash. ft.in. ft.in
8x10	3	$0.14	$0.34	2 4x1 2
9x12	3	.17	.38	2 7x1 4
9x14	3	.19	.44	2 7x1 6
10x12	3	20	.45	2 10x1 4
10x14	2	15	.36	2 1x1 6
12x14	2	22	.46	2 5x1 6
12x16	2	.23	.48	2 5x1 8

Transom Sash.

Order No. 42002

Size of Sash ft. in. in.	Price, each, open.	Price, 1 light, glazed.	Price, 2 light, glazed
2 6x12	$0.17	$0.39	$0.36
2 6x14	.18	.42	.39
2 8x14	.21	.47	.42
2 10x14	.22	.50	.44
2 10x16	.24	.53	.48
3 0x14	.25	.58	.52

See Index for Transom Lifters and Centers.

Porch Trimmings, Etc.

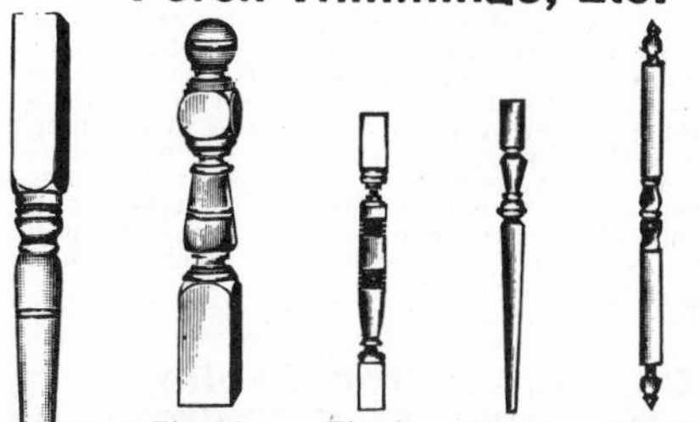

Fig. 10 Fig. 8 Fig. 9 Fig. 7

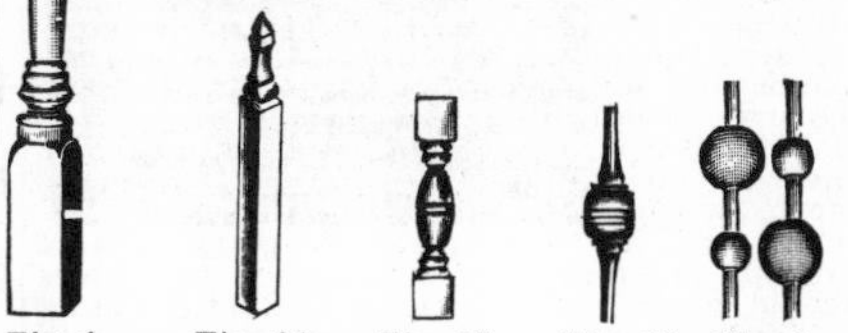

Fig. 1 Fig. 11 Fig. 12 Fig. 13 Fig. 6

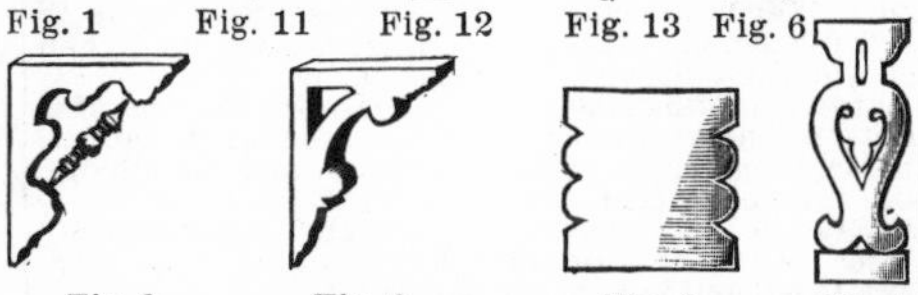

Fig. 3 Fig. 2 Fig. 5 Fig. 4

Fig. 1. **Selected Poplar Porch Columns,** smooth turned. *Bored center*, avoids check. *Steam dried*, prevents mill-dew. Order No. 42004.

Size.	Length.	Each.	Size.	Length.	Each
4x4 in.	8 feet	$0.72	6x6 in.	8 feet	$1.32
4x4 "	9 "	.77	6x6 "	9 "	1.49
4x4 "	10 "	.83	6x6 "	10 "	1.60
5x5 "	8 "	.94			
5x5 "	9 "	1.05			
5x5 "	10 "	1.21			

Fig. 2. Brackets 1⅜ thick, 10x12 inch. Each...10c
" " " " " 12x14 " " 12c
Fig. 3. " " " 10x12 " " 11c
" " " " " 12x14 " " ...14c
Fig. 4. **Baluster,** made of pine, ⅞ inch thickness, 6 inch wide, 18 to 20 inches long. Each.. 9c
Fig. 5. **Beaded Porch Rail,** 2x2 inch. Per foot.. 2¼c
Fig. 6. **Ball Spindles,** 1¼ inch ball spindles, 8 to 10 inches long. Each.... 4c
Fig. 7. Corner Bead, made of pine, 4 feet long 1⅛ inch in diameter. Each.... 7c
1⅜ " " " 8c
1¾ " " " 11c
Fig. 8. Baluster, made from pine, 20 to 24 inches long, 1¾ inch diameter, each.... 10c
Fig. 9. Stair Baluster, 1¾ inch diameter, 20 to 24 inches long, made from oak or ash. Each..... 12c
Made from walnut or cherry. Each.... 17c
Fig. 10. Outside Newell, made from white wood, 4 ft. long. Size, 4x4. Each.... 45c
" 5x5 " 55c
" 6x6 " 77c
Fig. 11. Base Angle Bead, 1⅜ inch, 12 to 14 inches long (saves mitering base).. Each.... 3c
Fig. 12. Spindle, 1¾ inch, 8 to 10 inch long. Each.... 6c
Fig. 13. Spindle, 1¾ inch, 8 to 10 inch long. 4c

Outside Blinds with Roller Slats.

42005 Outside Blinds measure same as No. 41356; check rail windows, with the addition of 1 inch to the bottom rail for sub sill window frames, which can be cut off if necessary. Outside blinds are 1⅛ inch thick, and prices are for a pair of blinds. **The size of glass and number of lights given below are to show what blinds to order for windows with No. 41999 check rail sash.** Blinds weigh, for 8 light windows from 15 to 26 lbs. per pair; for 4 light windows, from 18 to 30 lbs.; 2 light windows, from 21 to 26 lbs. per pair. See Index for blind fixtures

Size of glass.	No. of lights.	Per pair.	Size of glass.	No. of lights.	Per pair.
10x12	8	$0.72	12x36	4	$1.05
10x14	8	.82	14x32	4	1.06
10x16	8	.87	14x36	4	1.10
12x14	8	.84	14x40	4	1.20
12x16	8	.92	16x24	2	.75
12x18	8	1.05	16x32	2	.95
12x24	4	.73	18x36	2	1.05
12x28	4	.83	18x40	2	1.22
12x32	4	.93	20x40	2	1.30

Blind Fixtures.

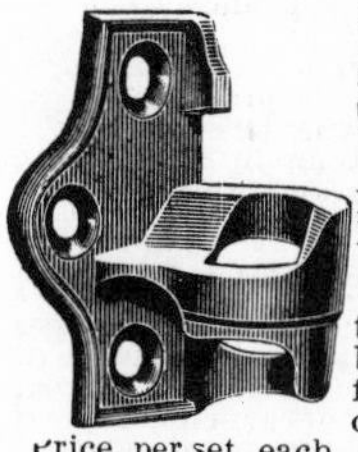

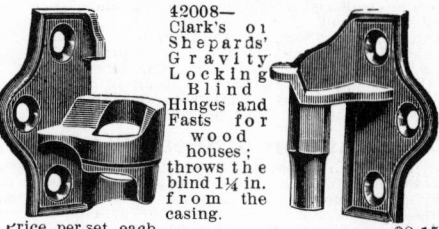

42008—Clark's or Shepards' Gravity Locking Blind Hinges and Fasts for wood houses; throws the blind 1¼ in. from the casing.

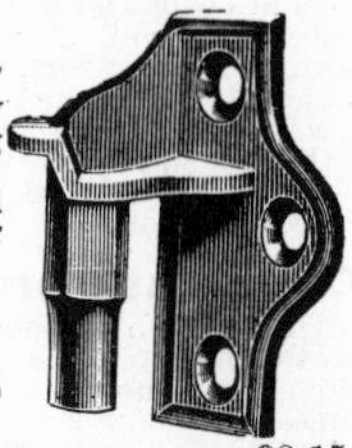

Price, per set, each.... $0.15
Per dozen.... 1.25

42009 Clark's or Shepard's Gravity Locking Blind Hinges and Fasts, for brick houses; throws the blind 3¼ inches from the casing.
Per dozen sets.... 1.50

Wrought Steel Gravity Blind Hinge.

FOR WOOD.

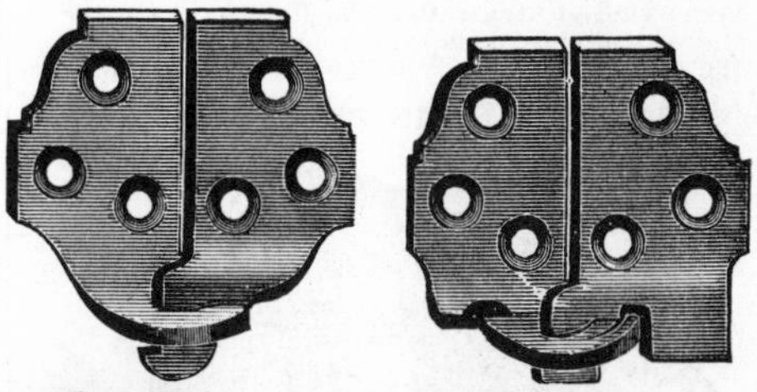

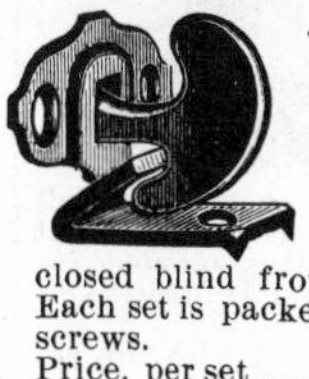

42010 These hinges lock the blind by the action of gravity, and being made of heavy wrought steel will not break. The blind is securely locked when open and the hinge cannot be unlocked without lifting the blind. The improved sill catch prevents the closed blind from being opened from the outside. Each set is packed in a box complete with 1 inch screws.
Price, per set.... $0.15
Price, per dozen set.... 1.25

Window Glass.

42013

Window glass is packed at the factory by experienced packers. As we could not safely repack we will not sell less than a box, and will make no allowance for breakage or shortage.

"A" Grade.	Lights in box.	Single Th'k. per pox.	Dbl. Th'k. per box.
6x8	150	$1.98	......
7x9	115	1.98	......
8x10	90	1.98	......
9x12	67	1.98	......
9x14	57	1.98	......
10x12	60	1.98	$2.75
10x14	52	1.98	2.75
10x16	45	2.25	3.35
12x16	38	2.25	3.35
12x18	34	2.25	3.35
12x24	25	2.25	3.35
12x28	22	2.25	3.35
12x32	19	2.98	4.30
12x36	17	2.98	4.30
14x32	16	2.98	4.30
14x36	14	2.98	4.30
14x40	13	3.10	4.65
16x20	23	2.25	3.35
16x24	10	2.25	3.35
16x32	14	2.08	4.30
18x36	11	3.10	4.65
20x30	12	2.98	4.30
20x30	9	3.60	4.95
24x30	10	3.10	4.65

Other sizes upon application.

The above prices are subject to the change of market without notice. [See grocery list.]

Sheathing and Building Papers.

We handle the very best grades of sheathing and building papers and our arrangements with the largest manufacturers enable us to make very low prices.

Our sheathing papers are *not* suitable for roofing purposes but are intended to use under shingles, clapboards, floors, etc., and aid greatly in keeping a building warm and dry. They are much more economical and serviceable than plain or tarred straw board, and their additional cost can be saved in one winter in economy of fuel. *We send samples on application.*

42020 **"Diamond Brand" Red Resin-sized Sheathing.** A strong, durable paper with a smooth finish and clean to handle. Put up in rolls of 500 square feet, 36 inches wide and weighing about 40 pounds. Price, per roll.... .$1.20

42021 **"Union Brand" Red Resin-sized Sheathing.** This is a fine grade of paper similar to the "Diamond," but not quite so strong and durable. Put up in rolls of 500 square feet, 36 inches wide and weighing about 35 pounds. Price, per roll.. 1.05

42022 **"Peerless Brand" Gray Resin-sized Sheathing.** Waterproof, strong and durable; no waste or shrinkage in weight and clean to handle. Put up in rolls of 500 square feet; 36 inches wide and weighing about 35 pounds. Price, per roll.......... .85

42023 **"Beaver Brand" Sheathing.** A strong, clean paper, lays smooth and is practically waterproof. At our price this paper is cheaper than common strawboard. Put up in rolls of 500 square feet, 36 inches wide and weighing about 40 pounds. Price, per roll.... .75

O.K. Waterproof Sheathing Paper.

This paper is composed of two sheets of strong paper between which is a layer of waterproof bitumen or asphaltic cement. The whole is united under great pressure, making it a waterproof article of great toughness and strength. It is vermin proof, odorless and inexpensive.

Made in two grades, No. 1 being a trifle heavier than No. 3. Put up in rolls, 36 inches wide, containing 500 square feet.

42027 No. 1, per roll.......... $1.45

42028 No. 3, per roll.......... 1.20

42029 **Plain Straw Board.** Put up in rolls weighing from 50 to 75 pounds, 32 inches wide. Runs about 16 pounds to the 100 square feet. Price, per pound.......... .01

42030 **Tarred Straw Boards.** Put up the same way as plain board and runs about 15 pounds to the 100 square feet. Price, per pound.......... .01¼

Roofing Felts and Papers.

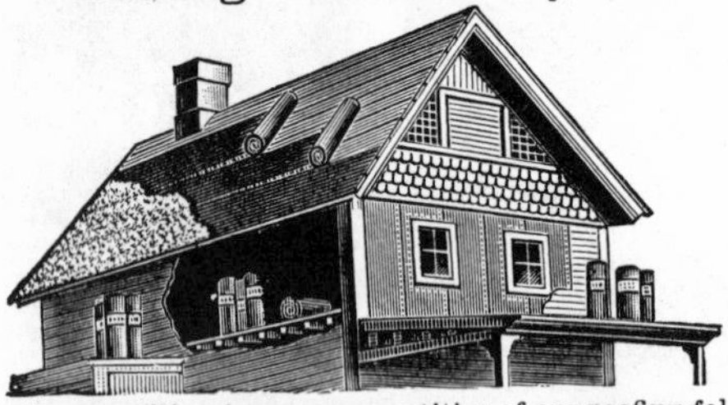

We are selling immense quantities of our roofing felt and papers and they are everywhere giving excellent satisfaction. Our prepared roofing felt is adapted for either flat or steep roofs, is suitable for all climates and not affected by severe winters.

It is easy to apply, and when coated with our asphaltum cement is not injured by steam, acids or gases, which are so destructive to tin and metal roofs. It is used extensively for covering roofs of factories, warehouses, barns, residences and all farm buildings. In fact everywhere where a good roof is required at a low price. No other tools than a jack knife, hammer and a brush are necessary to apply it. Complete directions with each roll. We put in 2 gallons cement with each roll, which is enough for two coats. Our 2 and 3-ply felt is 32 in. wide, about 40 feet long and put up in rolls containing 108 square feet. Every roll, allowing for lap, will cover 100 square feet, or a space 10 feet by 10 feet. Price includes, with each roll, 2 gallons cement, 1½ pounds tin caps, 1½ pound barbed roofing nails.

42035 2-Ply Roofing Felt. Weight, about 75 pounds per roll. Price, with cement, caps and nails. Per roll.......... $1.60

42036 3-Ply Roofing Felt. Weight about 100 pounds per roll. Price, complete with cement, caps and nails. Per roll.......... 1.90

42037 Roofing Brushes. Made expressly for applying the cement

2-Knot Brush, each.......... .70

3 " " " .... .90

42038 Tin Roofing Caps, per pound.......... .07

42039 Barbed Roofing Nails, per pound.......... .04

42040 Roofing Cement. The price on this varies according to the quantity desired, the cost of the cask being included in the price of the cement.

50 gallon lots or more	14 cts. per gal.
21 to 40 gallon lots	16 " "
11 to 20 gallon lots	18 " "
6 to 10 gallon lots	20 " "
5 gallons	25 " "
2 gallons and less	30 " "

ALWAYS Put Felting under Shingles and siding. Keeps a house dry and warm.

Neponset Red Rope Roofing Fabric.

This is an air-tight and waterproof roofing paper and makes a good permanent covering for roofs and sides of buildings at one quarter the cost of shingles. A coat of good paint adds to its durability. It is also used extensively in place of plaster. Made in one grade only. Put up in rolls of 250 and 500 square feet each. Prices per roll include roofing nails and caps sufficient to apply the same.

	250 square feet		500 square feet.
42043 No. 1, per roll	$2.55	42044	$4.60

Tarred Roofing Felt.

42046 Used extensively for roofing lumber camps and temporary buildings. Put up in rolls of about 50 pounds, 32 in. wide and runs about 16 pounds to 100 square feet. Price, per lb..... $0.01¾

Steel Pressed Brick Siding.

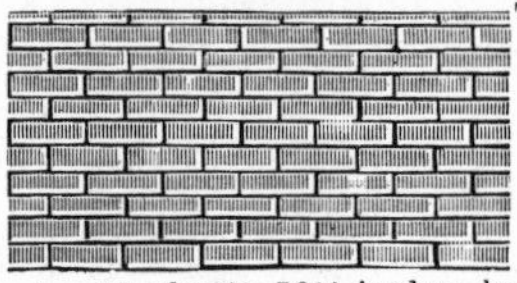

This is an excellent imitation of pressed brick. It is made of the best grade of annealed sheet steel, painted on both sides with the best iron ore paint. It is put up in squares, containing 11 sheets, 50½ inches long by 26 inches wide (or its equivalent), with sufficient nails to put it on, and dry paint for second coat. Weight, per square, 75 pounds.

42047 Price, per square, for less than 5 squares..$3.10

Price, per square, for more than 5 squares...... 2.90

We do not sell less than one square.

V Crimped Roofing.

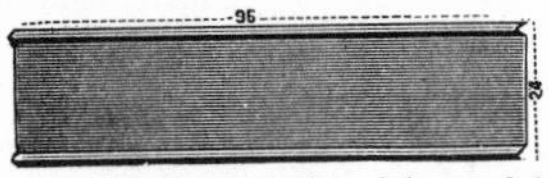

Made from mild sheet steel and is used for the same purpose as our Corrugated Iron Roofing, No. 42049. This crimped roofing can be laid over sheathing, old shingle or direct to the rafters, and is suitable for a roof having a pitch of *two inches* or more to the foot. It can be applied by any one who knows how to drive a nail. A square consists of 6 sheets, 24 inches wide, 96 inches long, or its equivalent, and is packed with 1½ pounds of dry paint, one pound of wire nails and sufficient wooden V strips for laps. Weight, when crated, per square, 90 pounds.

42048 Price, per square, for *less* than 5 squares $2.80

Price, per square, for *more* than 5 squares.. .... 2.58

Corrugated Iron Roofing.

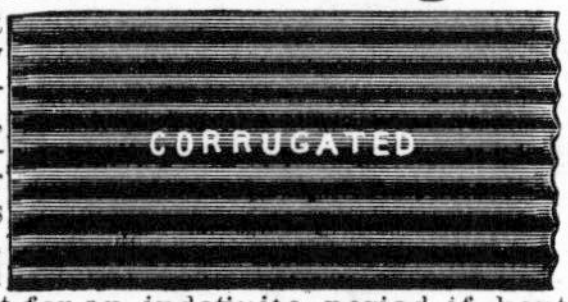

Corrugated sheet iron is used largely for covering warehouses, barns, sheds, etc., and has the advantage over other material in that it is absolutely fireproof. It is cheap, light and durable; and will last for an indefinite period if kept well painted. It is already painted red on both sides but should receive an additional coat after being laid. When ordering state whether you wish to use it for roofing, siding or ceilings, as we shall then send you the proper size corrugation.

Our iron roofing is put up in squares consisting of 6 sheets, 96 inches long by 26 inches wide (or its equivalent), with sufficient nails to put it on, and enough dry paint for second coat.

42049 Price, per square, for less than 5 squares.$2.80

Price, per square, for more than 5 squares...... 2.58

We do not sell less than 1 square.

Corrugated Conductor.

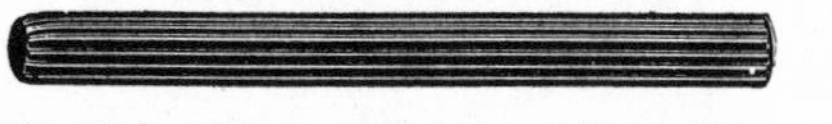

42051 Made of same grade iron as the gutters and corrugated to allow for expansion and contraction. Made in 8-foot lengths without a cross seam. It will not burst if full of ice. When ordering state if round or square is wanted. Both the same price.

We do not furnish cut lengths.

Size.	2	3	4	5	6 inch.
Price, per foot,	4½c.	6c.	7½c.	9c.	11c.

Galvanized Iron Elbows.

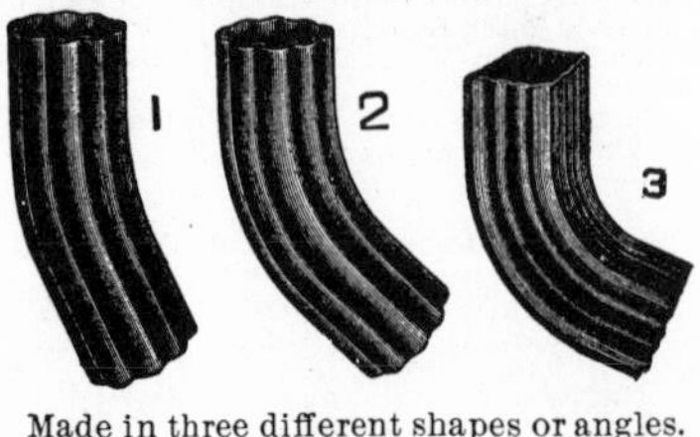

42053 Made in three different shapes or angles. You must always state which angle is wanted. Can be furnished square or round.

	Price, each, round.	Price, each, square.
2 inch.	11c.	14c.
3 "	14c.	17c.
4 "	18c.	26c.
5 "	25c	30c.
6 "	28c.	

Galvanized Eave Troughs.

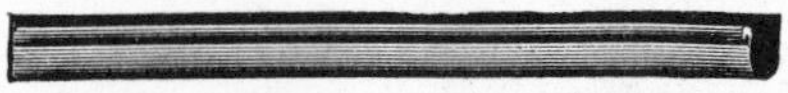

42054 Made of the best galvanized iron, which is much more durable than tin and easier put up. It is made in 8-foot lengths, and we do not furnish cut lengths. Sizes are measured inside of bead.

Size	3½ inch	4 inch	5 inch	6 inch
Price, per foot,	4c.	4½c.	5c.	6½c.

Galvanized Ridge Roll.

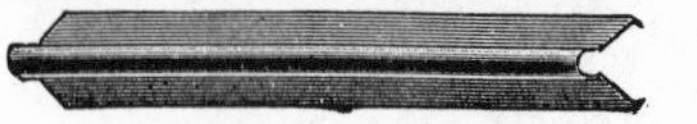

42055 Makes a neat waterproof cap for the ridge of roofs. It is made in 8-foot lengths. We do not furnish cut lengths.

Size of roll.	Width of apron.	Girt.	Price, per ft.
1¼ inch	2 inch	7 inch	4¾c.
1½ "	2 "	8 "	5c.
2 "	2½ "	10 "	6c.
2½ "	2½ "	12 "	7c.
3 "	3½ "	15 "	7½c.

Eave Trough Corners.

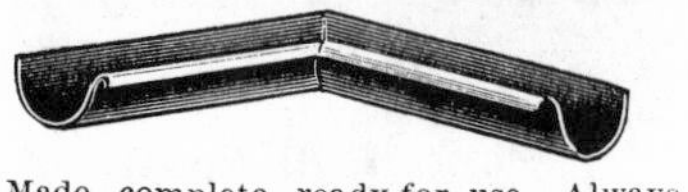

42056 Made complete, ready for use. Always state if bead is to be inside or out.

Size,	3½ inch	4 inch	5 inch	6 inch
Each,	32c.	35c.	38c.	42c.

Wire Eave Trough Hangers.

42057—

	Per dozen.		Per dozen.
Price, 3½ inch	$0.32	Price, 6 inch	$0.42
Price, 4 inch	.37	Price, 7 inch	.46
Price, 5 inch	.40	Price, 8 inch	.50

Conductor Hooks, Tinned.

42058 For fastening conductor to side of house

2 inch	Per doz. $0.40	5 inch	Per doz.	$1.10
3 inch	" .50	6 inch	"	1.35
4 inch	" .70			

This catalogue places before the buyer the lowest prices on the choicest varieties of goods. Selections may be made at home after mature consideration, and with our full assurance that goods will equal representation or money will be refunded.

Fence Looms.

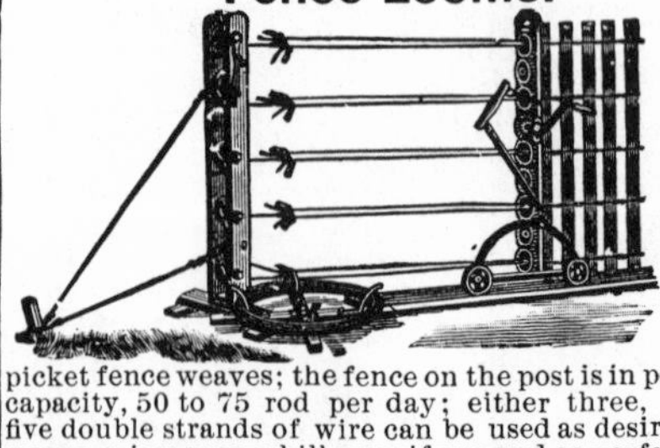

42065—The Little Giant portable Fence Loom, for making combination wire and picket fence weaves; the fence on the post is in position; capacity, 50 to 75 rod per day; either three, four or five double strands of wire can be used as desired; will weave going over a hill as uniform and as perfect as on level ground. Save money by building your own fences; in most cases we will ship the machine direct from our factory in Richmond, Ind. Style A weaves 5 strands: style B 3 strands; weight of machine, in shipping order, about 100 lbs.

	Price.
Complete, Style A, with reel	$11.87
Style A, without reel	10.95
Style B, with reel	11.75
Without reel	10.00

CORRUGATED IRON costs less than Shingles in many sections, and beats it all to pieces for a roof.

Woven Wire Fencing.

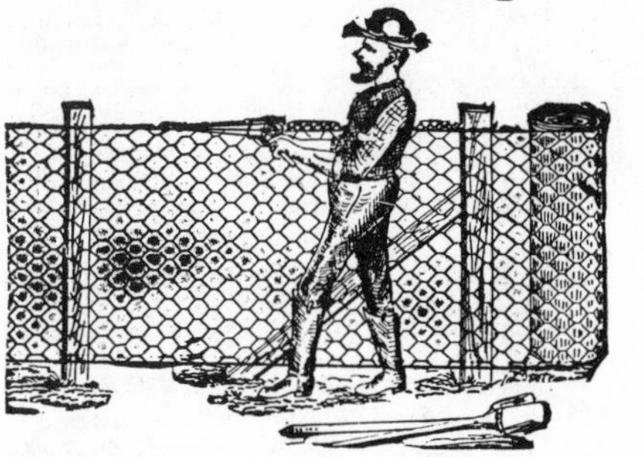

Made of galvanized steel wire, three-strand selvedge No. 13 wire, mesh of No. 14 wire. For fencing farms, plantations, ranches, corrals, cemeteries, railroads, etc. A harmless fence for horses or cattle, sufficiently strong for vicious stock, a reliable protection against dogs for sheep. A legal fence everywhere. Excellent for grape vine trellises.

	Price per bale of 20 rods long.	Cut bales, price per rod.
42070 Mesh, 5½x10½ inch.		
25 inch or 4½ mesh wide,	$5.04	$0.34
36 " 6½ " "	6.12	.41
47 " 8½ " "	7.20	.48
42071 Mesh, 4x8 inch.		
26 inch or 6½ mesh wide,	$6.12	$0.42
34 " 8½ " "	7.20	.50
42 " 10½ " "	8.28	.55
50 " 12½ " "	9.36	.65
62 " 15½ " "	10.98	.76
70 " 17½ " "	12.06	.80
42072 Mesh, 3x6		
26 inch or 8½ mesh wide,	$7.38	$0.50
32 " 10½ " "	8.56	.55
38 " 12½ " "	9.54	.60
50 " 16½ " "	11.70	.75

Sheep and Hog Fencing.

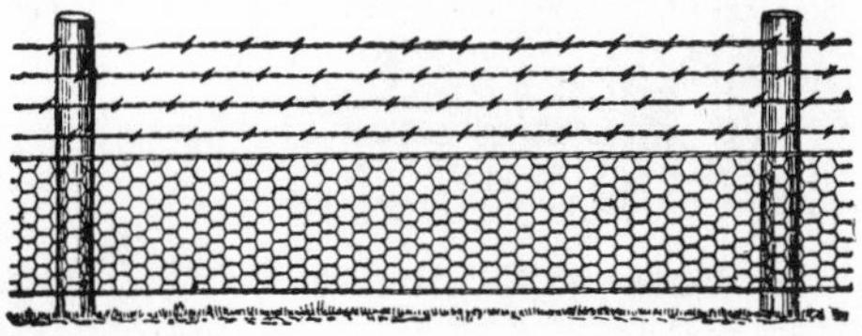

42075 Made of No. 16 Galvanized Steel Wire; three-strand selvedge, 3x6 inch mesh. It is extensively used for sheep and hogs. Where it is used with barbed wire, as shown in cut, it can be stretched up at bottom and animals cannot get through; being a fabric the wire cannot be spread apart. We do not furnish the barbed wire unless at an extra price; for price see *Grocery List*. The fencing is illustrated above to show how it can be used in connection with barbed wire. Put up in bales of 20 rods long; sold only in full bales.

26 inch wide; price, per bale.....................$5.40
50 " " " " 8.64

COTTAGE, LAWN AND GARDEN FENCING.

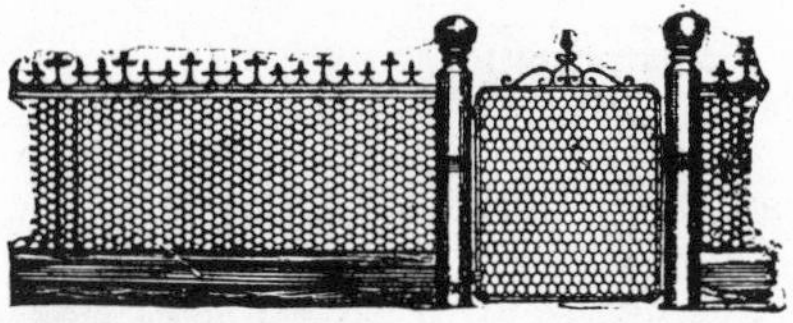

We do not furnish top pickets as shown in cut. For price of top pickets see No. 42077.

Inexpensive, substantial, attractive, durable. Adapted for front and division fences, inclosing gardens, orchards, orange groves, cemeteries, parks, etc. It is a heavy STEEL wire web of two inch meshes, No. 14 wire, and has three-strand hard steel selvedges at top and bottom. After weaving it is heavily galvanized, which protects the wires from rust and solders them firmly where twisted. It is strong enough to resist all large animals, and small ones cannot pass through its fine meshes. It is also difficult to climb. For lawn fencing it is without an equal. It is strong, offers little or no obstruction to the view, requires no paint or repairs, and at its low cost all can afford to use it. For gardens it is excellently adapted, as it occupies the smallest amount of space, casts no shade, and forms a perfect barrier for both large and small animals.

PUT UP IN BALES OF TEN RODS (165 FEET) LONG.

42076	Price per Bale of 10 rods long.	Cut Bale. Price, per rod.
24 inch	$6.25 per bale	$0.90 "
30 "	7.90 "	1.13 "
36 "	9.25 "	1.35 "
42 "	10.75 "	1.57 "
48 "	13.75 "	1.80 "
54 "	14.25 "	2.02 "
60 "	15.50 "	2.25 "
72 "	18.00 "	2.50 "

Fence Ornaments or Pickets.

42077

Made of malleable iron japanned, about 12 inches long, can readily be screwed to the top rail of fence.

Price, each (12 in. long) $0.10
In lots of not less than 100. Price, each....... .09
In lots of not less than 500. Price, each...... .08

COTTAGE, LAWN AND GARDEN GATES.

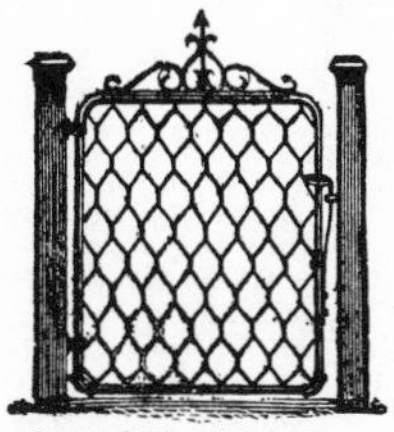

Galvanized wire, 2-inch mesh steel frame, painted brown, complete with latch, hinges and screws. All small gates provided with self-closing hinges, ornamental top, light in weight, strong and durable.

Cut of Single Gate.

42080 Width of frame	Space between posts.	Height of frame.	Price, each.
36 inch	40 inch	30 inch	$2.55
36 "	40 "	36 "	2.60
36 "	40 "	42 "	2.75
36 "	40 "	48 "	2.85

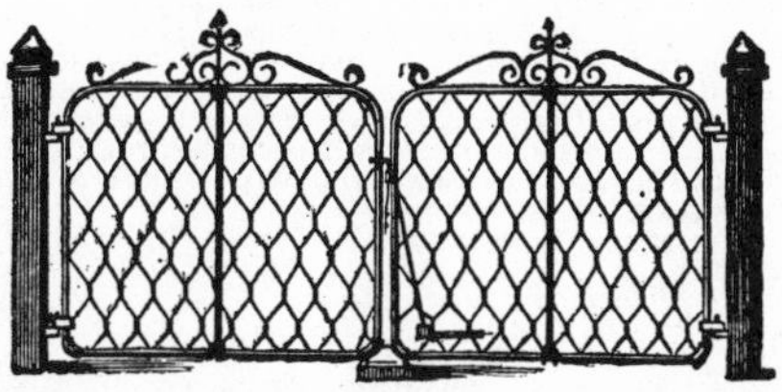

42081— Cut of Double Gate. Price, per pair, Ornamental Top.

Size of Gates.	
10 ft.x36 inch	$8.45
10 ft.x42 inch	9.00
10 ft.x48 inch	9.60

SINGLE DRIVING GATES.

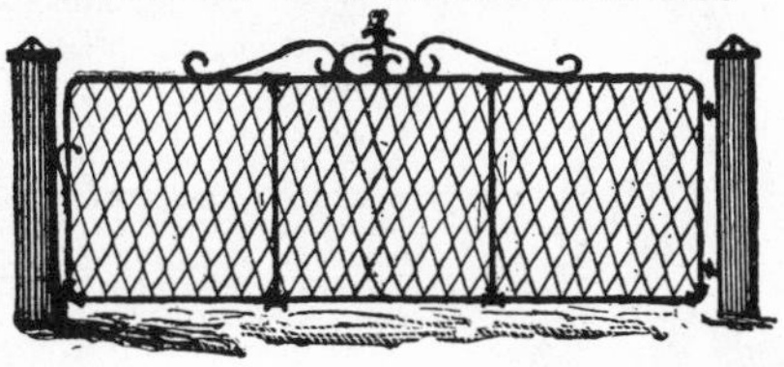

42082 With Ornamental Top.

Size of Gates.	Price, each.
10 ft.x30 inches high	$7.35
10 ft.x36 " "	7.35
10 ft.x42 " "	7.90
10 ft.x48 " "	8.40

Galvanized Steel Wire Poultry Netting.

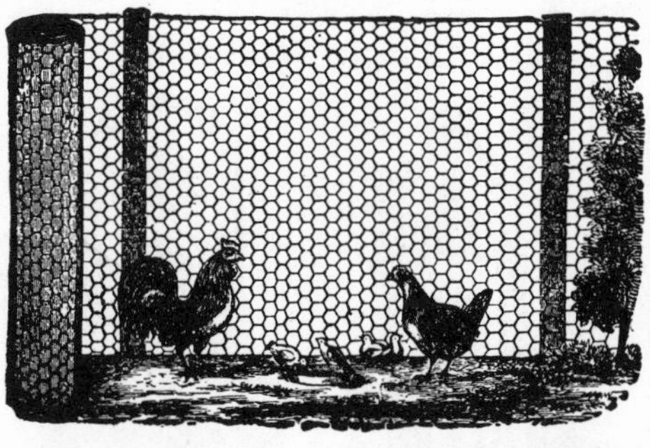

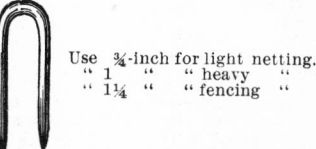

Can be used for poultry fence, bird and game cages, vine trellises, pea brush, tree guards, lawn borders, etc. Our netting is made from best wire and galvanized after being woven, making it more durable than if made of plain galvanized wire. Made of No. 19 wire with 2-inch mesh, and has a 3-standard twisted selvedge.

42085 Width.	Bale of 150 running feet	Less than bale, per running foot.
12 inches	$0.60	$0.01
18 inches	1.00	.01½
24 inches.	1.35	.02
30 inches.	1.75	.02½
36 inches.	2.00	.02¾
42 inches.	2.40	.03
48 inches.	2.70	.03½
54 inches.	3.05	.04
60 inches.	3.50	.04½
72 inches.	4.10	.05

Galvanized Steel Wire Netting.

For lawn, garden and farm fencing; 1-inch mesh No. 20 wire; excellent for bottom of poultry fence to keep young chickens in.

42086	Price per bale of 150 running feet.	Cut bales. Price per running foot.
12 inch wide	$1.65	$0.02
18 " "	2.48	.03
24 " "	3.30	.04
30 " "	4.12	.05
36 " "	4.95	.06
42 " "	5.77	.07
48 " "	6.60	.08

42087 1½ in. mesh, No. 19 wire.

	Price per bale of 150 running feet.	Cut bales. Price per running foot.
12 inch wide.	$0.90	$0.01½
18 " "	1.35	.02¼
24 " "	1.80	.03
30 " "	2.05	.03¼
36 " "	2.70	.04½
42 " "	3.15	.05¼
48 " "	3.60	.06
60 " "	4.50	.07½
72 " "	5.40	.09

Galvanized Staples.

FOR FENCING—SHARP POINTED.

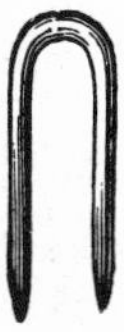

Use ¾-inch for light netting.
" 1 " " heavy "
" 1¼ " " fencing "

	Per pound.
42090 ¾-inch long, No. 14 wire, 550 to a pound	$0.06½
1 inch long, No. 12 wire, 230 to a pound....	.06
1¼ inch long, No. 19 wire, 100 to a pound....	.03

Galvanized Twist Wire Cloth.

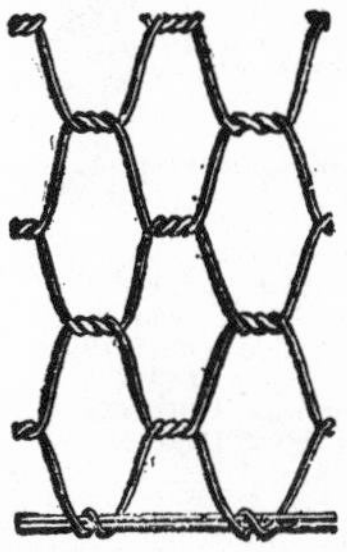

1x½ Inch Mesh, No. 19 wire; can be used as window guards for churches, cages for birds and small animals. Can furnish 12, 14, 16, 18, 20, 24, 28, 30, 32, 36, 42, 48, 54, 60 and 72 inch wide; put up in bales of 100 running feet. We will sell any quantity.

42091— Width.	Per Bale.	Per running foot of ½ bale or more.	Per running foot of less than ½ bale.
12 inches	$ 4.50	$0.04¾	$0.06¼
14 inches	5.26	.05½	.07
16 inches	6.03	.06¾	.08¼
18 inches	6.75	.07¼	.08¾
20 inches	7.52	.08¼	.09¾
24 inches	8.50	.09½	.11
28 inches	9.76	.10½	.12
30 inches	11.25	.11¾	.13¼
32 inches	12.01	.13¼	.14¾
36 inches	13.50	.14¼	.15¾
42 inches	15.75	.16¾	.18¼
48 inches	18.00	.19	.20½
54 inches	20.25	.21½	.23
60 inches	22.50	.23¾	.25¼
72 inches	27.00	.28½	.30

Galvanized Wire Cloth.

SQUARE MESH.

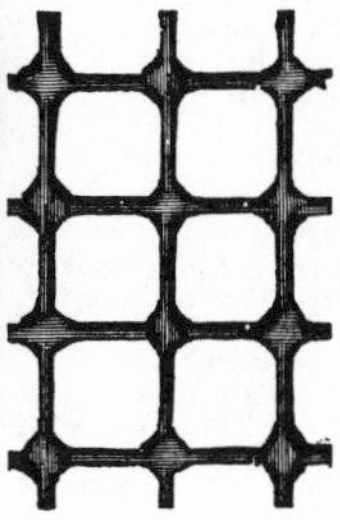

Useful for window guards, cages, fruit evaporators, screens and hundreds of purposes where heavier cloth is wanted than ordinary fly screen. We can furnish ½-inch, ⅓-inch, ¼-inch, ⅕-inch, ⅙-inch mesh, and carry in stock the following widths: 18, 24, 30, 36, 42, 48. Put up in rolls of 100 feet long. We sell any quantity.

42092— Width.	Per Bale.	Per running foot of ½ bale or more.	Per running foot of less than ½ bale.
12 inches	$ 4.50	$0.04¾	$0.06¼
14 inches	5.26	.05½	.07
16 inches	6.03	.06¾	.08¼
18 inches	6.75	.07¼	.08¾
20 inches	7.52	.08¼	.09¾
24 inches	8.50	.09½	.11
28 inches	9.76	.10½	.12
30 inches	11.25	.11¾	.13¼
32 inches	12.01	.13¼	.14¾
36 inches	13.50	.14¼	.15¾
42 inches	15.75	.16¾	.18¼
48 inches	18.00	.19	.20½
54 inches	20.25	.21½	.23
60 inches	22.50	.23¾	.25¼
72 inches	27.00	.28½	.30

Wire Nests.

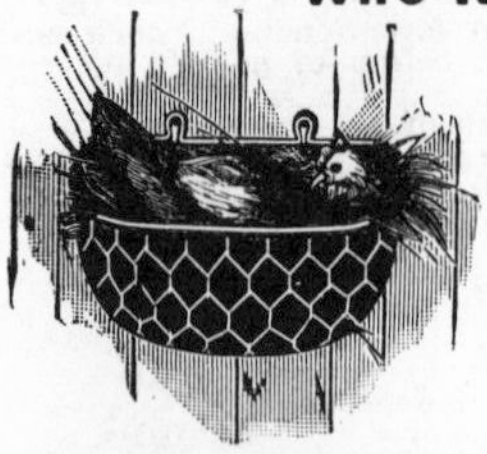

42095 Wire Hens' Nests, made of steel wire japanned; are clean, afford no place for vermin, are durable and cheap. Intended to fasten to wall by two screws, no screws furnished.
Each.... ....$0.08
Per dozen........ .75

42096 We also make wire nests with finer mesh, which prevents the eggs from falling through, and prevents the waste of straw. Each........$0.12
Per dozen.... .... 1.00

Wire Fence Ratchet or Tightener.

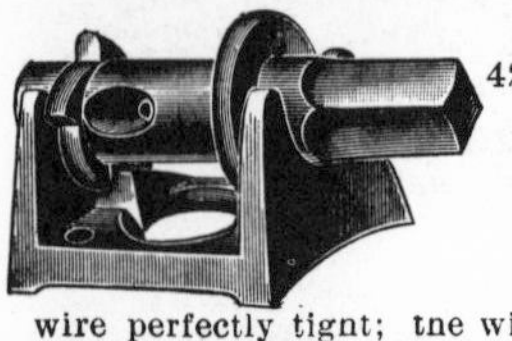

42098 A very handy tool for every one using wire fence. The ratchet is designed to be put on the end post of each 50 or 60 rods stretch of any make of fence wire, to draw and keep the wire perfectly tignt; tne wire can be stretched at any time by turning the square part on the ratchet with an ordinary wrench, thus keeping it from sagging. To overcome the contraction of wire during cold weather the pawl can be thrown back and the wire slackened, to prevent breaking. It saves time, labor and fence posts. Price, each.......$0.06
Per dozen.......... $0.65 Per 100............ 5.00

Caskin's Tackle Block Wire Stretcher.

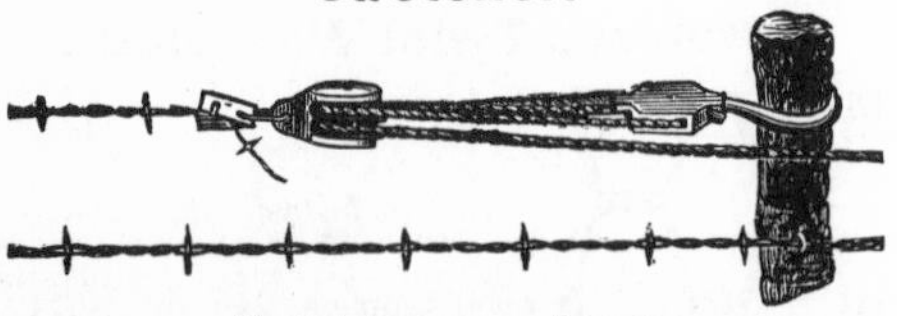

Useful for every farmer.

42100 This stretcher is provided with all grapples necessary for stretching "Barb Wire" strand and woven fencing quickly. It is also complete for use as a tackle block, being made of malleable iron; it is strong enough for any ordinary use. We furnish with each stretcher 16 feet of ⅝-inch manilla rope. Price, each...... ......$1.00
Per dozen..11.00

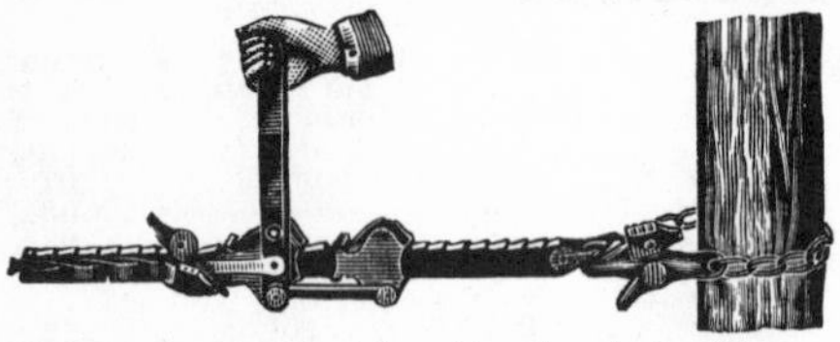

42101 Fence Wire Stretcher. Dean's patent. The only lever stretcher with an automatic take-up.
Each.......... .... $0.45

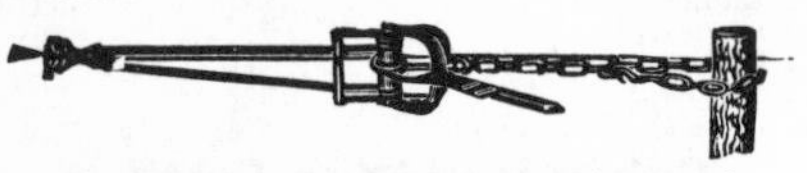

42102 The Perry Wire Stretcher, the only stretcher that winds with a rope and works with a lever, is made of malleable iron, and is extra strong where the most strain comes. The chain is wrought iron and is long enough to reach around a post 9 in. in diameter. Has an attachment which holds the wire for splicing. Will stretch plain or barb and netting fences; weight, 8 pounds. Each.....................................$0.85

Wire Cloth for Screens.

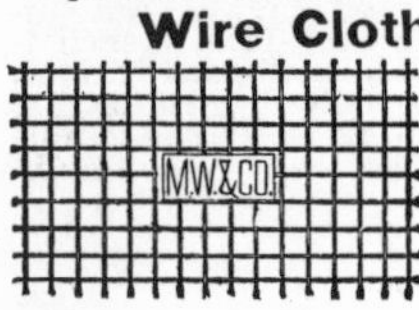

Green Wire Cloth for window screens, doors, safes, etc.

42105 Wire Cloth, 24 to 36 in. wide, standard mesh. Put up in rolls of 100 lineal feet. Note our low price per roll. See cut for exact size of mesh.

Width.	Per yard.	Per roll.
24 in	$0.12	$3.20
26 in	.13	3.45
28 in	.14	3.79
30 in	.15	4.06
32 in	.16	4.34
34 in	.17	4.60
36 in	.18	4.88

42106 Pearl Wire Cloth for window screens, doors, etc. This cloth is entirely new, made of steel wire, and instead of being painted has a bright metallic silver finish that will not rust. It does not intercept the vision like painted wire, and dust and dirt do not adhere to it. Standard mesh

Width.	Per yard.	Width.	Per yard.
24 in	$0.27	32 in	$0.35
26 in	.29	34 in	.37
28 in	.31	36 in	.38
30 in	.33		

Wire Cloth—Continued.

42107 Pearl Wire Cloth. Extra heavy grade; made especially for panels of doors, which are likely to be pushed out.

Width.	Per yard.	Width.	Per yard.
24 in	$0.42	32 in	$0.57
26 in	.44	34 in	.60
28 in	.49	36 in	.63
30 in	.52		

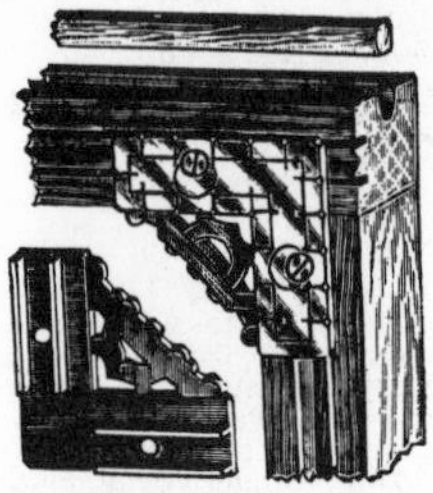

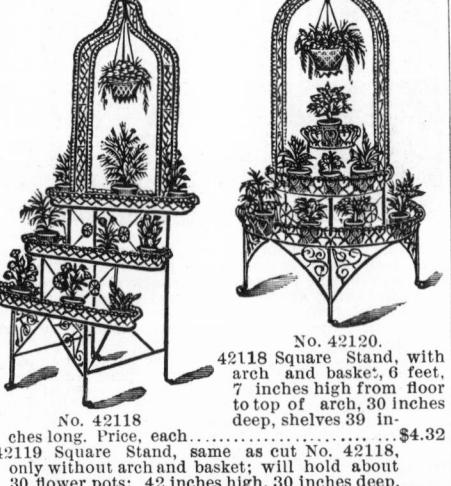

42108 The Gem Window Screen Frame, made of handsomely molded sticks ⅝x1 in. and finished in black walnut stains; sticks grooved on surface; a raised surface on the corner; irons fitting into grooves, making the frame when put together very strong. The side pieces are grooved to receive the slide that attaches to the window casing and are furnished with set. These frames do not come put together, but everything is furnished, sticks, iron and screws, so that they may be made according to size of your window. Size, 36x36, per set of four pieces molding, 2 slide pieces, 4 corner irons and screws.
Per set........ .... $0.20
Per 12 sets.. 1.95
Size 42x42, per set.............................. .28
Per 12 sets.. 2.25
Observe that if your window is wider than 42 in. or your sash higher than 42 in. we cannot fit you, but for any size smaller the sticks may be sawed off.

WITH PATENT CORNERS.

42110 Door Screen Frame, finished in black walnut stain. No carpenter work is required. Simply saw the strips the required length and attach the patent corner. A set comes complete with corner irons, knobs and bead molders to tack over wire. No wire cloth furnished at prices quoted.

Length of stick.	Size of stick.	Per set.	Per 12 sets.
3 x7 ft.	⅞x2 in.	$0.70	$8.00
3½x8 ft.	⅞x2 in.	.70	8.00
3 x7 ft.	⅞x2½ in.	.75	8.25
3½x8 ft.	⅞x2½ in.	.75	8.25

We cannot furnish screen door frames of any different sizes than those quoted above.

Wire Flower Pot Stands.

FREIGHT NOTICE.

Flower pot stands take a high rate of freight, and it is not profitable to the buyer for us to ship them unless with other goods, making shipment 100 lbs. or more.

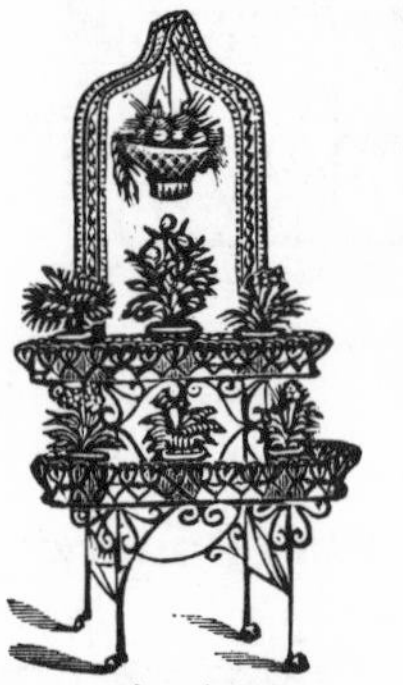

No. 42115

For strength, beauty of design and superior finish our stands are unexcelled if equaled. The legs are heavy round iron, well braced; good strong casters are used; the wires are heavy, well woven in and clinched. They are nicely finished with green paint and bronze; they are ornamental and durable, and weigh from 15 to 25 pounds.

42115 Semi-Circle Stand, with arch and basket, like cut; size, 5 feet 8 inches from floor to top of arch, 42 inches wide and 26 inches deep.
Price, each... ....$3.78

42116 Semi-Circle Stand, like cut No. 42115, except that it does not have the arch or basket. Size, 36 inches high, 42 inches wide and 26 inches deep. Price, each $3.00

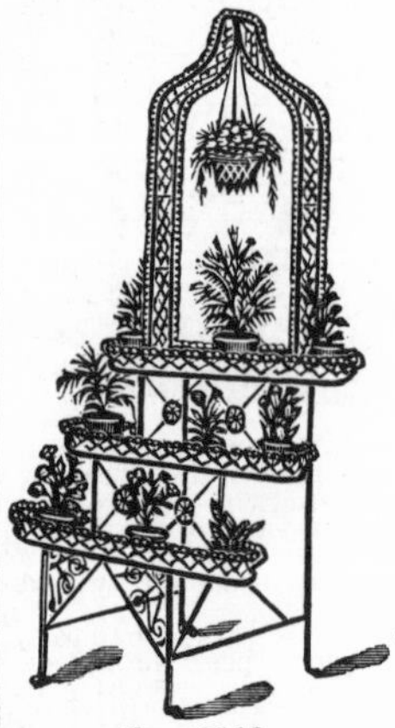

No. 42118

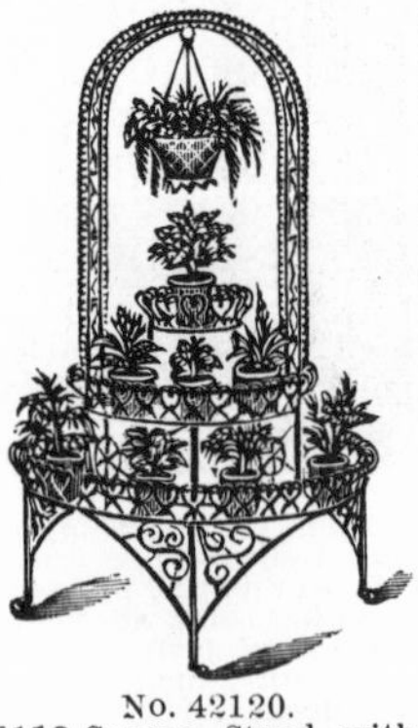

No. 42120.

42118 Square Stand, with arch and basket, 6 feet, 7 inches high from floor to top of arch, 30 inches deep, shelves 39 inches long. Price, each.......................................$4.32

42119 Square Stand, same as cut No. 42118, only without arch and basket; will hold about 30 flower pots; 42 inches high, 30 inches deep, with shelves 39 inches long. Price, each....... 3.50

42120 Square Stand, with arch and basket, 5 ft. 8 inches high, 18 inches deep, with shelves 33 inches long. Price, each......................... 3.00

Window Shelves.

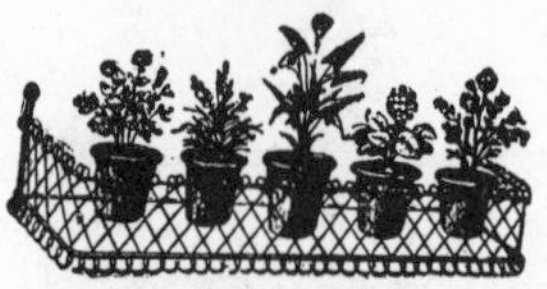

42123 Wire Window Shelves for flowers. Can be fastened either to the inside or outside of window. The border is 5 inches high; green and bronze finish; made in three sizes 33, 36 and 39 inches long; 7 inches wide.
33 and 36 inches, each.... ....$0.80
Per dozen.... .... 8.50
39-inch, each.............. .. .. .90
Per dozen 9.00

Screen Door Catches.

42130 Screen Door Catches, Geneva bronzed, 2¼x1⅞, for doors ⅞ to 1⅜ in. thick; complete with knob. This pattern has a reverse bevel. Be careful and examine cuts when ordering and not order the wrong one. Packed complete with screws.

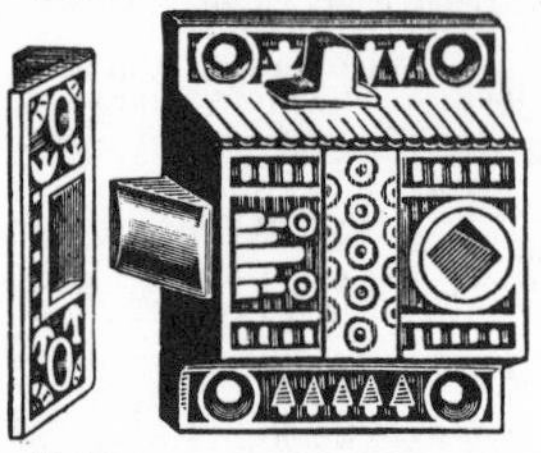

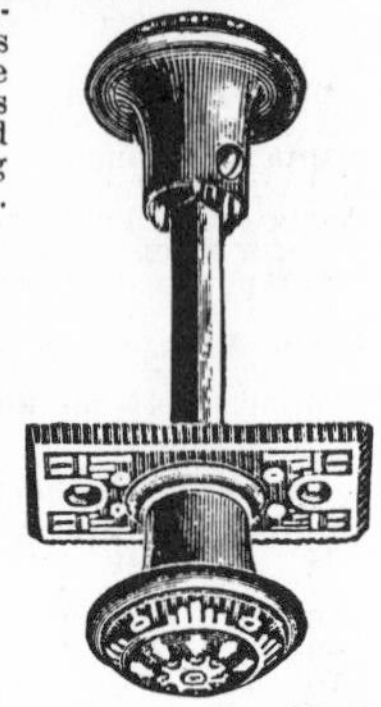

Price.. ....$0.15

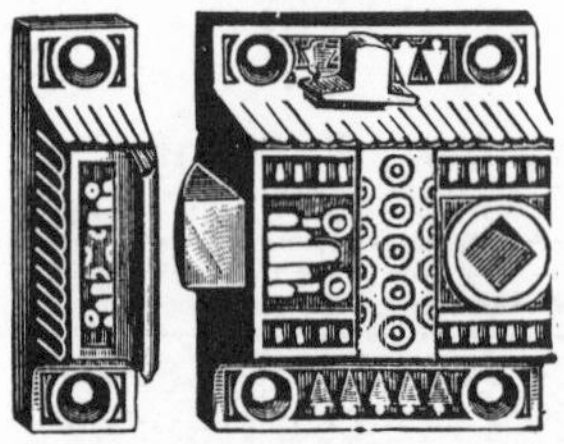

42131 Screen Door Catch, Geneva bronzed, 2¼ x 1⅞, for doors ⅞ to 1⅜ in. thick: complete with knobs and packed with screws.
Each.........$0.15

Screen Doors.

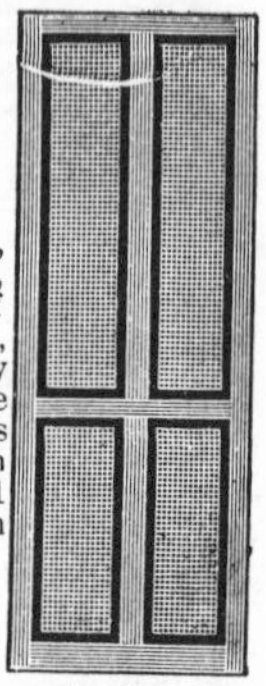

42135 Screen Doors made up complete, four panel, molded on under edge, molding flush with the face of frame; wire cloth runs the full length, which strengthens the door very much; frame stained walnut, wire painted green. No hinges or latches included at prices quoted. Each frame is made ⅝ inch wider and 1 inch longer than the measures given in the list.

SIZES AND PRICES.

	Price, each.	Per doz.
2 ft. 6 in.x6 ft. 6 in.x ⅞ thick	$0.75	$ 8.00
2 ft. 8 in.x6 ft. 8 in.x ⅞ thick	.75	8.00
2 ft. 8 in.x6 ft. 10 in.x ⅞ thick	.75	8.00
2 ft. 8 in.x7 ft. 1⅛ in. thick	.90	9.00
2 ft. 10 in.x7 ft. 1⅛ in. thick	.90	9.00

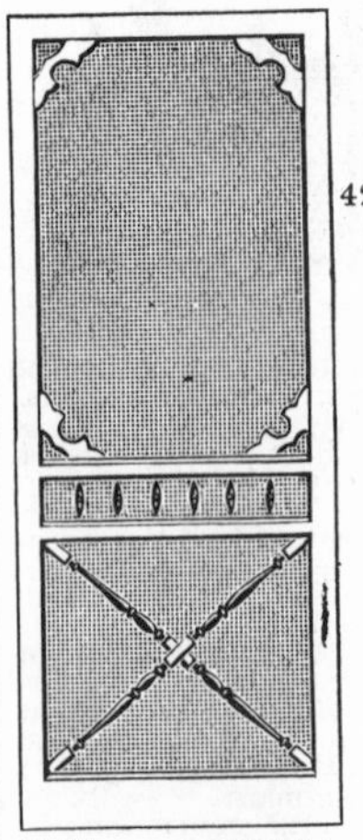

42136 This is a very popular screen door; it is made from clear dry stock finished in oil and hard oil finish, presenting a handsome and durable appearance. This door is made one half inch wider and one inch longer than sizes given. We advise our customers to place their orders early for screen doors and window screens. This door is 1⅛ inch in thickness.

Width.	Height.	Each.	Per dozen.
2 ft. 6 in.	6 ft. 6 in.	$1.15	$13.00
2 ft. 8 in.	6 ft. 8 in.	1.15	13.00
2 ft. 8 in.	6 ft. 10 in	1.15	13.00
2 ft. 8 in.	7 ft.	1.25	14.00
2 ft. 10 in.	7 ft.	1.25	14.00

You can buy SCREENS cheaper than you can make them. Take measure carefully.

Screen Doors—Continued.

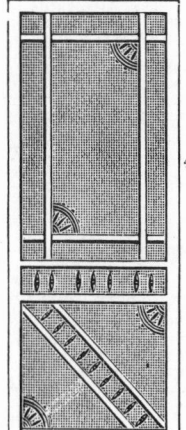

42137 This is the best screen door we make, and for style and finish cannot be excelled. It is made from clear dry stock 1⅛ inch thick, finished in oil and hard oil finish. It is made ½ inch wider and one inch longer than sizes given below.

Width.	Height.	Each.	Per dozen.
2 ft. 6 in	6 ft. 6 in.	$1.50	$16.67
2 ft. 8 in.	6 ft. 8 in.	1.50	16.67
2 ft. 8 in.	6 ft. 10 in.	1.50	16.67
2 ft. 8 in.	7 ft.	1.65	18.00
2 ft. 10 in.	7 ft.	1.65	18.00

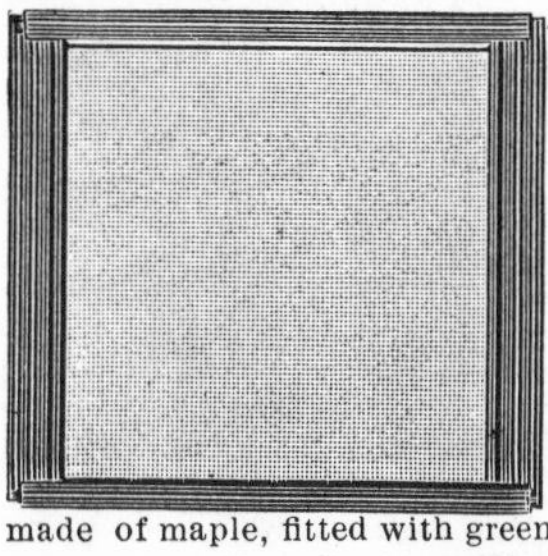

42138 Adjustable Window Screen, so constructed as to form a perfect joint with the parting strip, so that it is not necessary to remove the screen in order to close the window; the wings or adjustable parts are pressed up against the window by a very stiff cast steel spring; frame made of maple, fitted with green wire cloth complete.

	High.	Extends.	Each.	Per doz.
No. 1	24 in.	21 to 26 in	$0.25	$2.75
No. 2	24 in.	25 to 30 in	.26	2.85
No. 3	24 in.	29 to 34 in	.27	2.95
No. 23	32 in.	29 to 34 in	.30	3.40
No. 32	36 in.	25 to 30 in	.35	3.75
No. 33	36 in.	29 to 34 in	.37	3.87
No. 34	36 in.	34 to 39 in	.40	4.00

Wire Rope.

42140 Standard Wire Hoisting Rope. This is the kind of wire in common use; it is made of six strands of nineteen wires each, laid around a hemp heart; this makes very pliable rope, which will wind on moderate sized drums.

Size.	Weight, per Foot-Pounds.	Safe Working Load Iron.	Safe Working Load Steel.	Price per foot. Iron.	Price per foot. Steel.
⅜ in.	26	¼ Ton.	....	$0.05	$0.07
½ in.	35	½ Ton.	1 Ton.	05½	.08
⅝ in.	60	1¼ Ton.	2½ Ton.	.08	.09
¾ in.	88	1¾ Ton.	3½ Ton.	.10½	.12½
⅞ in.	120	2½ Ton.	5 Ton.	.13	.16
1 in.	150	3 Ton.	6 Ton.	.17	.20

BUTCHERS' SUPPLY DEPARTMENT.

Butcher Knives.

Weight, 6 to 12 ounces.

See "Cutlery Department" for other quotations of butchers' knives, etc.

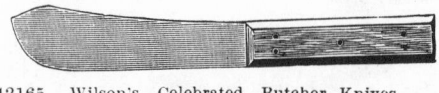

42165 Wilson's Celebrated Butcher Knives, beechwood handles.

Sizes	5	5½	6	6½	7	8	10	12 in.
Each	20c.	25c.	27c.	32c.	37c.	48c.	75c.	$1.05
Doz.	$2.00	2.45	2.80	3.40	4.00	5.25	8.10	11.25

42166 Wilson's Celebrated Sticking Knives, beechwood handles.

Sizes	6	6½ in.
Each	27c.	32c.
Per dozen	$2.80	$3.40

42167 Wilson's Celebrated Skinning Knives, beechwood handles.

Sizes	6	6½	7 in.
Each	27c.	32c.	37c.
Per Dozen	$2.80	$3.50	$4.00

Lee's Celebrated Butchers' Steels.

The best in the market. Mr. Lee commenced to make this steel in 1851, and the machine which gives the steel the peculiar cut that is the distinguishing feature of the Lee steel was contrived by Mr. Lee himself. It is made from a special high priced steel made expressly for the purpose. It has been adopted by all the large Chicago butchers.

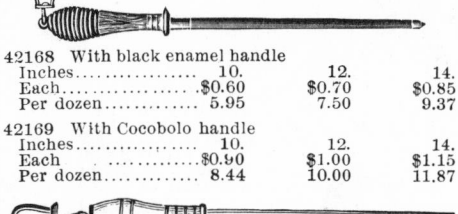

42168 With black enamel handle

Inches	10.	12.	14.
Each	$0.60	$0.70	$0.85
Per dozen	5.95	7.50	9.37

42169 With Cocobolo handle

Inches	10.	12.	14.
Each	$0.90	$1.00	$1.15
Per dozen	8.44	10.00	11.87

42170 Wilson's Celebrated Butcher Steels, stag or rosewood handles, weight about 1 lb. each.

Sizes	10 in.	12 in.	14 in.
Each	$1.05	$1.25	$1.50
Per dozen	10.80	13.60	16.50

Butchers' Saws.

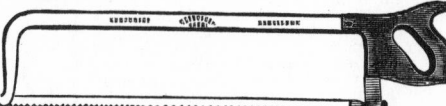

Weight, 2½ to 3 lbs.

42172 Disston's Butcher Saws, No. 1, oval back, polished blade.

Sizes	20 in.	22 in.	24 in.
Each	$1.22	$1.28	$1.35

42173 Disston's Butcher Saws, No. 7, flat steel back. 24 inch, each............$1.30
26 inch, each............1.35

Cleavers.

42175 Family Cleavers, with improved malleable iron shanks riveted through handles into heavy iron caps, very strong and durable; 7 inch cast steel blades forged and hardened; is a very handy household article and should be in every one's kitchen. Each............$0.35
Per dozen............3.78

Beatty's Butchers' Cleavers.

Extra Cast steel, hickory handles.

	Each	Per doz.
42176 Choppers, 7-in. cut 1½ lbs	$0.60	$6.90
42177 Choppers, 8-in. cut 1¾ lbs	.70	8.10
42178 Cleavers, 9-in. cut 3¼ lbs	1.00	11.00
42179 Cleavers, 10-in. cut, weight, 4 pounds	1.12	12.00
42180 Cleavers, 12-inch cut, weight, 5 pounds	1.40	16.20

Wire Fencing.

In these days it is sheer nonsense to build a fence of anything but wire. Our Woven Wire is galvanized after weaving, so that the joints won't rust. Our Barbed Wire is the best made, and is sold at the lowest prices. See Grocery List.

Skewers.

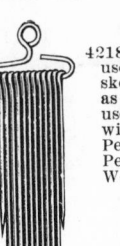

42185 Tinned Iron Skewers for kitchen use. These are superior to wooden skewers for putting up roast meat, etc., as they can be easily withdrawn and used over again. Come in sets of 12, on wire hook with eye for hanging on nail.
Per set $0.15
Per dozen set............ 1.50
Weight, 9 oz.

Block Scrapers.

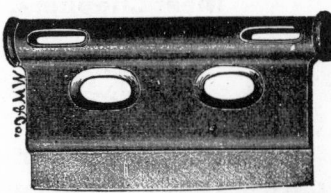

42188 Butchers' block scrapers, cast steel blades, oil tempered; weight, 1 lb., 7 oz. Each........$0.38
Per dozen............ 4.90

Hog Scrapers.

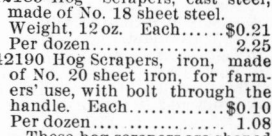

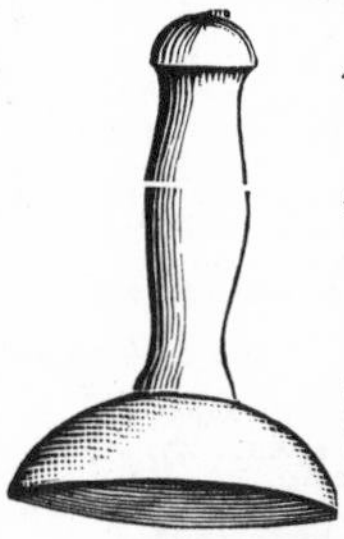

42189 Hog Scrapers, cast steel, made of No. 18 sheet steel. Weight, 12 oz. Each......$0.21
Per dozen 2.25
42190 Hog Scrapers, iron, made of No. 20 sheet iron, for farmers' use, with bolt through the handle. Each............$0.10
Per dozen............ 1.08
These hog scrapers are shaped something like the bottom of an iron candlestick, and are considered the best instruments in use for the purpose.

Meat Cutters.

The Little Giant Meat Cutters. They combine the best qualities of all the latest improved machines, and are without doubt the fastest cutters ever made.
42196 The No, 205 size, like cut, for family use, with clamp for fastening to kitchen table; weighs 5¼ lbs.
cuts 1½ lbs. per minute. Each............$1.50
Per dozen............16.20
42197 Little Giant Meat Cutter, No. 310, for family or hotel use, with clamp for fastening to table; weighs 8¾ lbs., cuts 3 lbs. per minute. Each............ 2.00
42198 Little Giant Meat Cutter, No. 220, for hotel or butchers' use, with clamps for fastening to table; weighs 12½ lbs., cuts 4 lbs. per minute. Each............ 3.00
Per doz............33.00
42199 Extra plates for 42196............ .20
" knives " 42196............ .18
" plates " 42197............ .40
" knives " 42197............ .20
" plates " 42198............ .50
" knives " 42198............ .30

Sausage Stuffer, Fruit and Lard Press Combined.

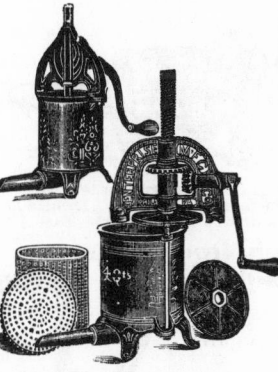

The Enterprise Combined Sausage Stuffer, Fruit and Lard Press; unexcelled for butchers' and farmers' use for stuffing sausages, and will be found useful for many purposes in every family. Directions will be found in catalogue that comes with each press.

Each.
42204 2-Quart Size, japanned, rack movement. Weight, 21 lbs............$2.40
42205 4-Quart Size, japanned, screw movement. Weight, 30 lbs............ 4.10
42206 8-Quart Size, japanned, screw movement. Weight, 44 lbs............ 4.95

Sausage Filler.

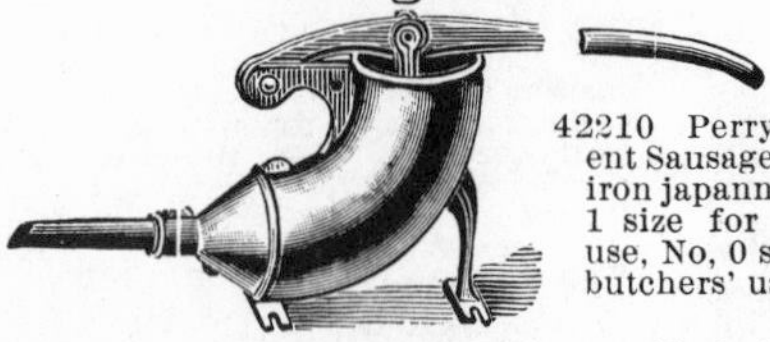

42210 Perry's Patent Sausage Filler, iron japanned, No. 1 size for family use, No, 0 size for butchers' use.

	Each.	Per doz
No. 1	$0.70	$8.10
No. 0	.92	9.94

Meat Choppers.

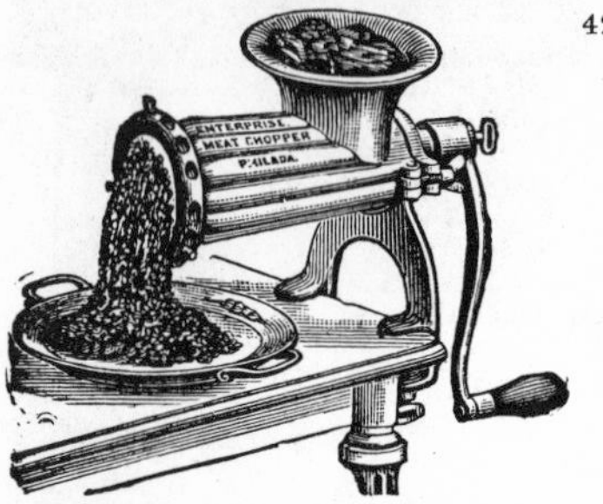

42212 Enterprise Meat Chopper will not tear the meat, but chops it precisely like the snipping process of a pair of shears. It is particularly adapted for family use being so constructed that it can be clamped to the table by means of thumb-screws, making it very convenient.

By means of an attachment Meat Choppers No's 10. 12 and 22 may be converted into excellent sausage stuffers. When in use the plate and knife are taken out and attachment secured by screwing the ring over it.

Enterprise Meat Chopper, family size No. 10, chops one pound per minute. Price, each $2.50
42214 Price of attachment for No. 10, each...... .30
42215 Extra knives for 42212. Each.......... .25
42216 Enterprise Meat Chopper, No. 12. This chopper is exactly like 42212, only has legs instead of clamps, and is required to be screwed to the table. It is of the same capacity as 42212, and is precisely like it in all other respects. Each 2.00
42219 Price of attachment for No. 12, each...... .30
42220 Extra knives for 42216. Each.......... .25
42222 Enterprise Meat Chopper, No. 22. This size is especially suited to butcher, market men, farmers, hotels and restaurants. It does not fasten to table with clamps like 42212, but has legs, and screws down tight. Weight, 12 lbs; chops 2 lbs. per minute. Each 3.10
42223 Price of attachment for No. 22. Each.. .45
42224 Extra knives for 42222. Each...... .45

The Star Raisin Seeder.

For Bakers, Caterers, Confectioners, Hotels and Family Use.

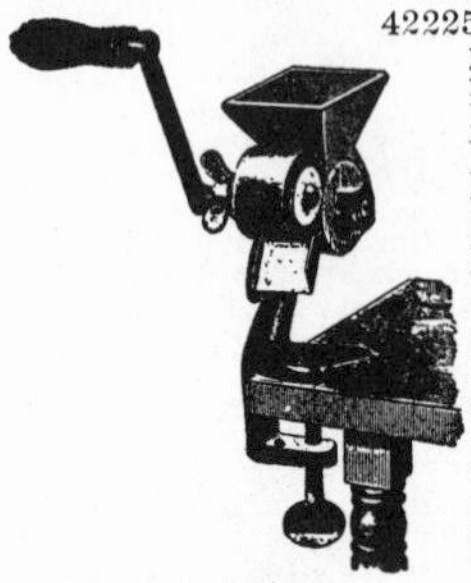

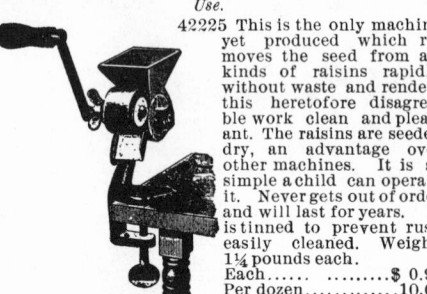

42225 This is the only machine yet produced which removes the seed from all kinds of raisins rapidly without waste and renders this heretofore disagreeable work clean and pleasant. The raisins are seeded dry, an advantage over other machines. It is so simple a child can operate it. Never gets out of order and will last for years. It is tinned to prevent rust, easily cleaned. Weight, $1\frac{1}{4}$ pounds each.
Each...... ....$ 0.90
Per dozen............10.00

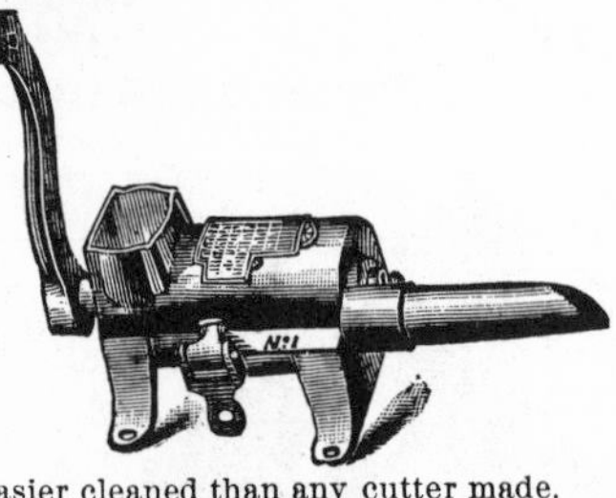

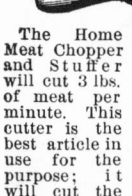

The Home Meat Chopper and Stuffer will cut 3 lbs. of meat per minute. This cutter is the best article in use for the purpose; it will cut the meat more rapidly and is easier cleaned than any cutter made.
42229 No. 1, japanned, 6 inch cylinder. Each..$0.85
42230 No. 21, galvanized, 6 inch cylinder Each.1.25

Wrought Iron Hooks.

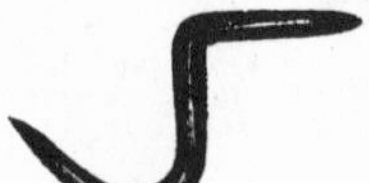

42236

42236—Wrought Iron Tinned Meat Hooks, to drive.

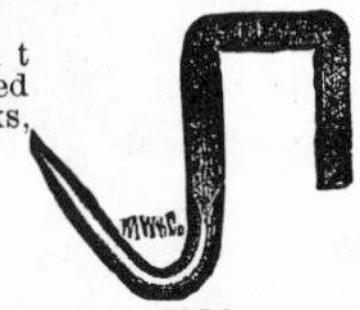

42238

Nos.	1	2	3	4	5	6
Size of iron	¼	¼	$\frac{5}{16}$	⅜	⅜	⅜
Per dozen	8c	9c.	10c.	14c.	19c.	25c.

Hooks—Continued.

42237 Wrought Iron Tinned Meat Hooks, to screw in.

Nos.	1	2	3	4	5	6
Size of iron	¼	¼	$\frac{5}{16}$	⅜	⅜	⅜
Per dozen	10c.	12c.	16c.	21c.	30c.	35c.

42238 Wrought Iron Tinned Mutton Hooks, for 2 inch bar, made of $\frac{5}{16}$ square iron. Per dozen.$0.45
Per gross 5.15
42239 Wrought Iron Tinned Beam Hooks, same shape as mutton hook, very heavy, for 2 inch bar, made of 7-16 square iron: weight, per doz., 3 lbs. 15 ounces. Per dozen 0.70
Per gross 7.56
42240 Wrought Iron Tinned Beam Hooks, with large round bend; very heavy, for 2 inch bar, made of ½ inch iron; weight, per doz., 9¾ lbs. Per dozen..........$0.80. Per gross 8.64

Spring Balances.

42245 Circular Spring Balance, for butcher's use, weighs 30 pounds by 1 oz., has glass sash and white enameled front, tin pan, tinned iron bows and swivel: shipping weight, 5 pounds 14 oz.
Each..........$3.35

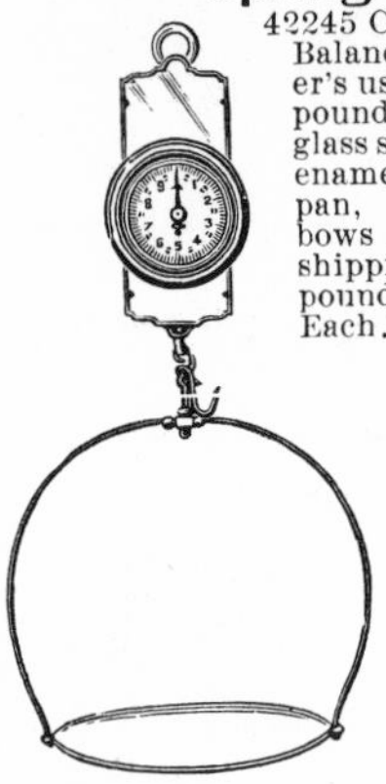

42245

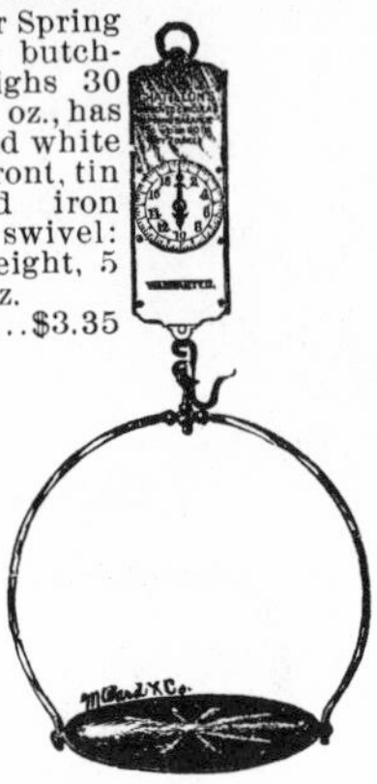

42249

42249 Circular Spring Balance, for meat market; brass front, tinned iron bows and swivel, tin pan, to weigh 30 lbs.; shipping weight, 5 lbs. Each $3.00
42250 Spring Balances, to weigh 24 lbs. by ½ lb.; shipping weight, 9 oz. Each..$0.08
Per dozen .... .87
42251 Spring Balances, to weigh 50 lbs.; shipping weight, 13 oz. Each.......$0.16
Per dozen 1.73

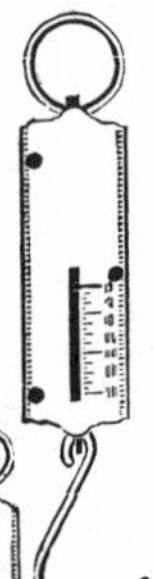

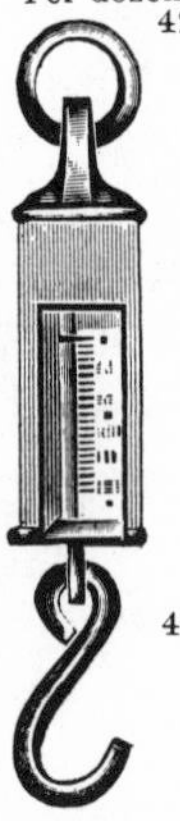

42254 Spring Balance with round tin dish, very convenient for family use, for weighing butter, etc.; weighs 24 lbs. by ½ lb.; shipping weight, 2 lbs.
Each..........$0.20
Per dozen........ 2.00
42257 Same as above, to weigh 50 lbs. by lbs; shipping weight, 1¾ lbs.
Each..........$0.35
Per dozen........ 3.88

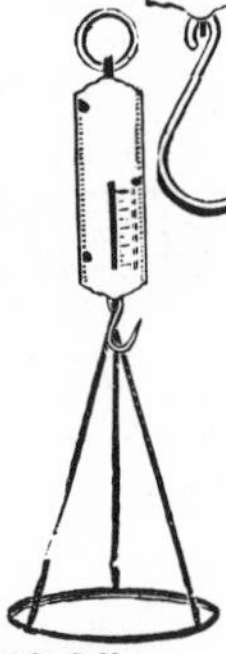

42260 Ice Balances. The most durable in the market. Weight, 4¾ lbs.

To weigh:	200x50 lbs.	300x5 lbs	400x5 lbs.
Each..	$2.15	$2.56	$3.00

Butchers' Scales.

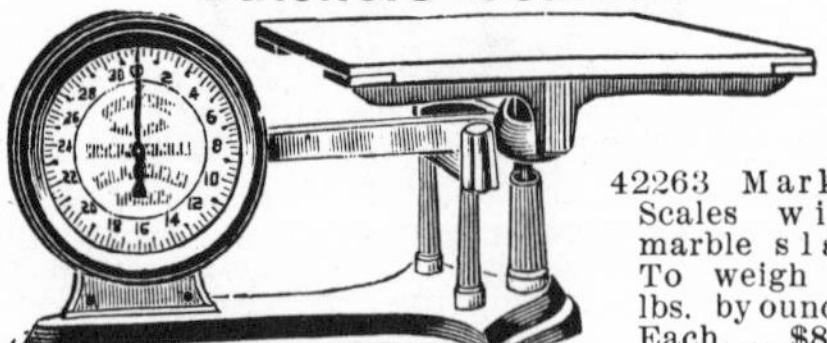

42263 Market Scales with marble slab. To weigh 32 lbs. by ounces. Each.... $8.75
To weigh 64 lbs. by 2 ounces. Each $10.00
Weight, boxed for shipment, 40 lbs.

Steelyards.

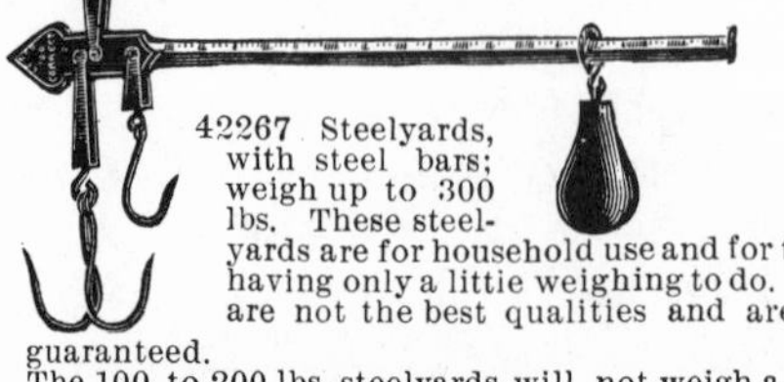

42267 Steelyards, with steel bars; weigh up to 300 lbs. These steelyards are for household use and for those having only a little weighing to do. They are not the best qualities and are not guaranteed.

The 100 to 200 lbs. steelyards will not weigh a quantity less than 6 pounds, the 250 and 300 lbs. will not weigh a less quantity than 10 lbs.

Capacity	50	100	150	200	250	300 lbs.
Price, each	27c.	37c.	47c.	53c.	60c.	65c.

Steelyards—Continued.

42268 Steelyard with steel bars. These steelyards are guaranteed to weigh absolutely correct. They weigh up to the 50 lbs. size by ¼ lbs.; above this size by ½ lbs. The 100 and 150 lbs. Steelyards do not start at zero and are not intended to weigh any quantity weighing less than 10 lbs. If you wish to weigh a smaller quantity than 10 lbs. use a 50 lb. steelyard, as all others start at the 8 lb. point, and are accurate in weighing above 10 lbs.

Capacity.	50	100	150	200	250	300 lbs.
Each....	45c.	50c.	58c.	72c.	86c.	$1.00

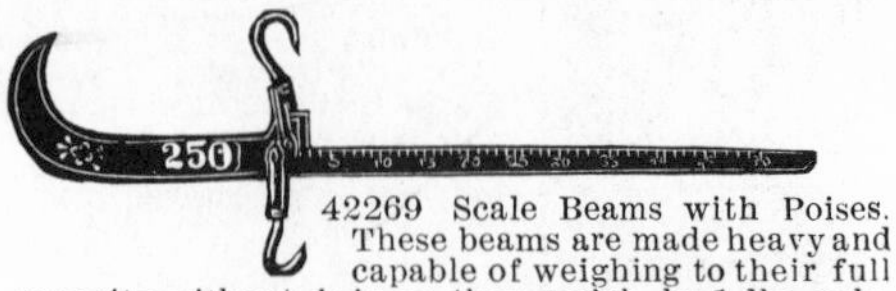

42269 Scale Beams with Poises. These beams are made heavy and capable of weighing to their full capacity without injury; they weigh by 1 lbs. only.

To weigh.	250	400	600	1,000	1,200 lbs.
Price, each.	$1.10	$1.50	$2.00	$3.50	$4.00

We furnish poises for scales beams as follows:
The 250 lbs. beam have each a 2 lb. and 8 lb. poise.
The 400 lbs. beam have each a 3 lb. and 12 lb. poise.
The 600 lbs. beam have each an 8 lb. and 16 lb. poise.
The 1,000 lbs. beam have each an 8 lb. and 32 lb. poise.
The 1,200 lbs. beam have each a 16 lb. and 32 lb. poise.

The Standard Family Scales.

These scales are warranted correct. Are very convenient, and the best scales for family use made There are no weights to get lost, are light and easy to handle, and do not take up much room, are japanned and beautifully ornamented in assorted colors.

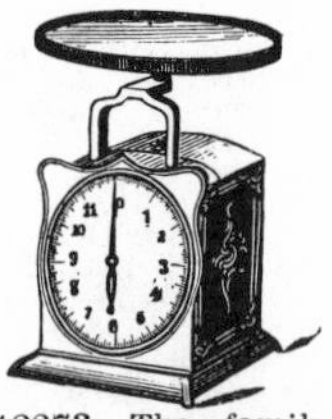

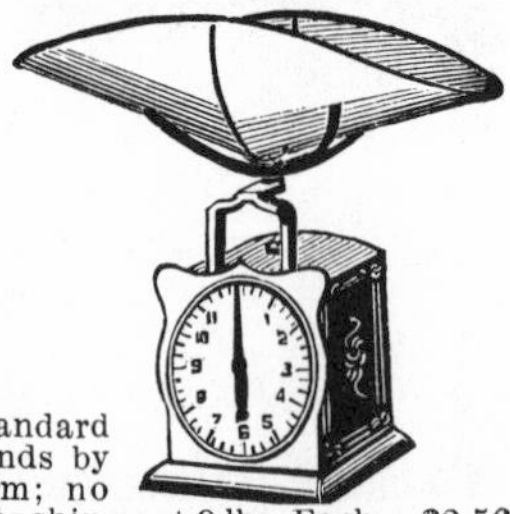

42273 The family Standard Scale, to weigh 48 pounds by 2 ounces, with platform; no scoop. Weight, boxed for shipment, 9 lbs. Each...$2.56
42274 The Standard Family Scale, to weigh 12 pounds by ounces, with tin scoop. Each.. .... 2.25
42275 The Standard Family Scale, to weigh 48 pounds by 2 ounces, with tin scoop. Each..... 2.75

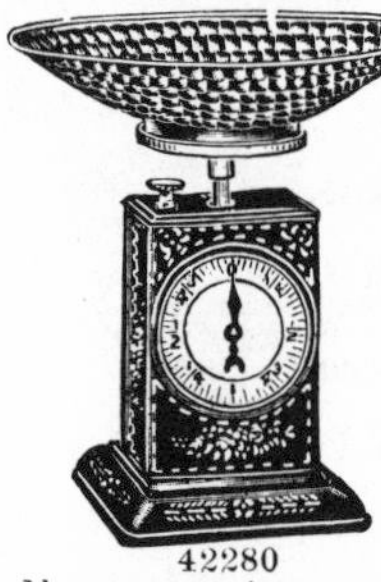

42280

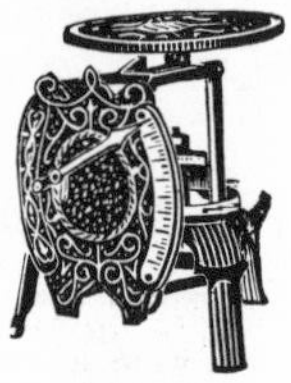

42278 The Novelty Family Scale, no weights needed. Weighs 12 lbs. by 2 ozs. With platform; no scoop.
Each...$1.30

42279 42278-79

With platform and tin scoop $1.40
42280 Candy Scale; weighs up to 2 pounds by ½ oz. Hammered brass scoop. A very neat and convenient article $1.35

U. S. Postal Scale.

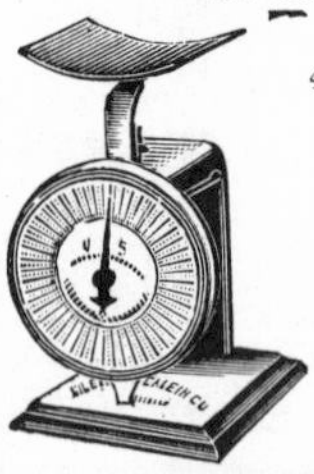

42282 A necessity in every office. It computes and indicates accurately and instantly the amount of postage required for letters, books, newspapers and merchandise, to any part of the Untted States and Canada. It is easily regulated by an adjustable screw at top. Gives amount of postage in cents on any package from one ounce to four pounds. Price, each..........$2.50

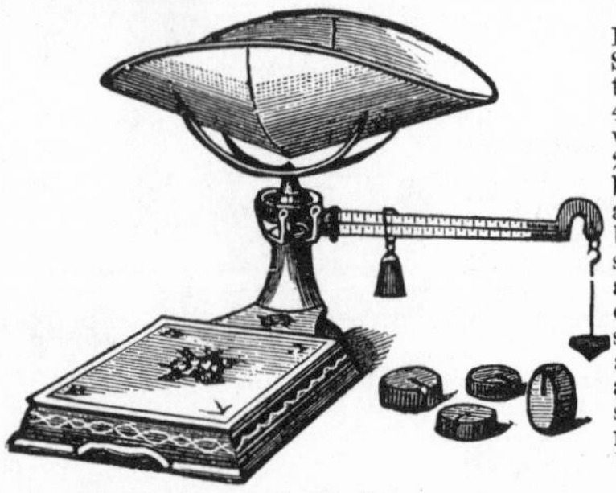

42286—Platform Scale better than 42287; weight 240 lbs,, by ounces all steel bearings, scales and wgts, officially scaled and each and every scale warranted. Weight, boxed for shipment, 35 lbs $4.00

INSURE MAIL PACKAGES.

See page 1.

M. W. & Co. Scales.

42287 The Montgomery Ward Co. Platform Counter Scales, steel bearings, tin scoop, brass beam; weighing ½ oz. to 240 lbs. Warranted reliable (See cut). Weight, boxed for shipment, 39 lbs. Price, each........................$2.43

42288 The Housekeeper's Friend, price with platform, no scoop; shipping weight 15 lbs. Weighs from ⅛ oz. to 25 lbs. Each.....................$1.68

42289 With tin scoop 2.00

Our scales are all packed ready for shipment. We have some of these scales, which have been in constant use for several years, and they answer our purpose as well as those sold for $14.

Garden Trowels.

42292 Garden Trowels: extra quality, cast steel; made in four sizes.

Length, inches	5	6	7	8
Price, each	$0.04	$0.05	$0.06	$0.07
Price, per dozen	.44	.54	.65	.75

Weeding Hooks.

42294 Weeding Hook, wood handle, entire length, including handle, 10 in. This pattern is the most popular style of hand weeder; each..............$0.07
Per dozen..................... .75

Strawberry Forks.

42296 Strawberry Forks. Japanned iron fork wood handle, length, including handle, 11 in. Made in two patterns, light and heavy.
Light pattern, each....$0.08 Per dozen.......$0.87
Heavy pattern, each .... .12 Per dozen....... 1.30

Garden Line Reel.

42299 Garden Line Reel. Malleable iron, japanned; no line furnished with reel. Each $0.37
Per dozen..................... 4.00

42304 Garden Rake and Hoe combined, very nice for weeding purposes 4 and 6 teeth. Polished steel.

4 teeth.
Each, $0.25
Per doz.
$2.70
6 teeth.
Each, $0.35
Per doz.
$3.85

42305 Garden Rake and Hoe combined, malleable iron, cast steel blade, 4 and 6 teeth.
4 teeth. Each.....................$0.18
Per dozen..................... 1.95
6 teeth. Each .... .20
Per dozen..................... 2.16

Scuffle Hoe.

42307 Scuffle Hoe, malleable socket, steel blade, 6 foot handle. Each..$0.40
Per dozen...................... 4 25

Onion Hoe.

42310 Onion Hoe, polished, solid shank; a very convenient shape.
Each. $0.25
Per doz. 2.70

Hoes.

42313 Garden Socket Hoes, blued.
Each.....................$0.30
Per dozen.................. 3.00
42314 Garden Shank Hoes, blued. Each.......... .25
Per dozen..................... 2.75
42315 Warren Garden Hoes, extra cast steel, polished. Garden size. Each .... .40
Per dozen.................. 4.55
Field sizes. Each .... .50
Per dozen.................. 5 40

Garden Rakes.

42320 Garden Rake, malleable iron, polished, 12 teeth. Each.. ....$0.20
Per dozen..................... 2.15
42321 Garden Rake, cast steel polished, 12 teeth. Each................... .35
Per dozen................... 3.55
42322 14 teeth Garden Rake, cast steel. Each.... .40
Per dozen..................... 3.90

Garden Rakes—Continued.

42323 The Gibbs Lawn Rake. Improved for 1891. The teeth are made of No. 9 coppered steel spring wire, and so formed as to comb the lawn, taking up the loose grass or leaves without tearing the sod; 24 inches wide, 30 teeth. Each.............. $0.50
Per dozen..................... 5.40

42324 The favorite Lawn Rake, strong and durable steel. Head 24 inch with 24 tinned No. 9 steel wire teeth. To unload rake simply push backward without raising it. Each.... $0.38
Per dozen..................... 4.10

42324½ Hay Rakes, wood, made of ash; mortised head. Each........$0.15 Per dozen....... 1.62

42330 Floral Set. Ladies' Favorite, same size tools as are in No. 42328 set, but are fitted with polished hardwood handles. In place of the rake it has a 5 prong weeder set consisting of four pieces as shown in cut. The fork and weeder are tinned. All packed in a pasteboard box.
Price, complete.....$0.40 Per dozen sets.....$4.32

42336 Garden Hoe, Southern Queen, the gem of garden hoes. Blade, 11 in. long by 3½ in. wide. Handle, 5 feet long by 1¼ inches in diameter. This hoe is made of an extra quality crucible steel; the eye and blade is solid, being forged from one piece of steel.

Each. Per doz.
Complete with handle....$0.38 $4.10

Hazel Hoes.

42337 Hazel Hoes, weight, 3 pounds, length, 10 in.
Each.. ....$0.38
Per dozen.. 4.00
42338 Hazel Hoe Handles.
Each........$.15

Grub Hoes.

42339 Grub Hoes, cast steel oval eye, ax finish, 3 lbs.
Each....$0.35
42340 Grub Hoe, cast steel, oval eye, ax finish, 3½ lbs. Each...................$0.38

Bush Hooks.

42343 Bush Hook, bronzed and handled.
Each..........$0.62
Per dozen..... 6.75

42345— Pruning Shears, or Sheep Toe Clippers, Henry's pattern, steel blade, malleable handle, brass springs. Each....................$0.25
Per dozen..................... 2.75

Cronk's Pruning Shear.

Forged from solid steel and made strong so it will last a lifetime. It is in all respects a strictly first-class tool and is only intended for use where a good shear is needed. All vineyard men claim that it cuts much easier and smoother than any shear ever made, and we guarantee it to be superior to any shear costing double the money. Made only in one size, 9 inch. It is made with a straight blade and draw cut.
42346 Price, each $0.75
Price, per dozen.................... 8.00

Cronk's Pruning Shears, Solid Steel Blade, Malleable Handle.

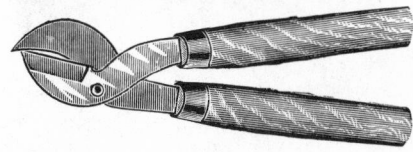

42347 It is made with straight blade, draw cut and will do the work much easier than the old style pruning shear. The price is low, considering the quality. Price, each $0.40
Price, per dozen 4.00

Cronk's Wood-Handle Pruning or Hedge Shear.

This pruner, being made with the shear cut, will work with double the ease of any other pruner of this style on the market. The blades are forged from best tool steel, 26-inch handle.
42348 Price, each............................$0.75
Price, per dozen......... . ... 8.00

Pruning Shears.

42349 Buckeye Pruning Shears, 26-inch handle.
Each. $0.60

Hedge Shears.

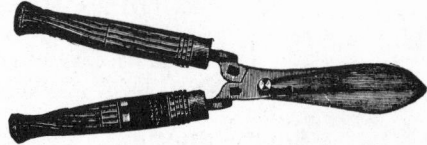

42350 Wilkinson's Hedge Shears. notched blades, hardwood handles.

Sizes	8	9	10	12
Each	$1.15	$1.25	$1.40	$2.00

Tree Pruner.

42351 Waters' Improved Tree Pruner is the best yet offered for sale. The blade being thin offers slight resistance to the wood in cutting, and does not injure the bark. It is supported on both sides by the hook which guides it and prevents its turning from a straight line. For this reason it will cut the smallest twig. With it pruning can be done standing on the ground, without climbing or using ladder.

Length.	Weight.	Each.
4 ft	2¼ lbs	$0.45
6 ft	3 lbs	.50
8 ft	3½ lbs	.55
10 ft	4 lbs	.58
12 ft	4½ lbs	.63

42351½ Extra knives for above pruners, each... .20

Pruning Hooks and Saws.

42352 Disston's Pruning Hook and Saw; can be used with or without pole; the saw can be detached when the hook alone is to be used.
Each, without pole.......................$1.20

Scythes.

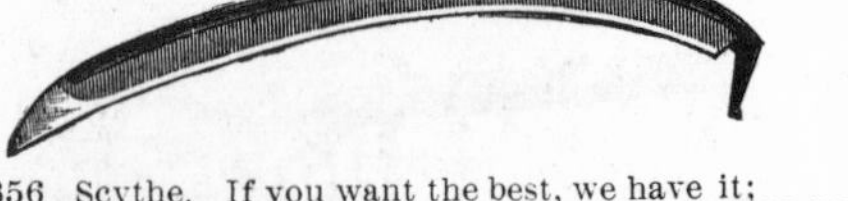

42356 Scythe. If you want the best, we have it; polished solid steel scythes. Each............$0.57
Per dozen.......................... 6.16

42357 Scythe, extra polished web, bronzed, polished back, ground sharp. Each...........$0.50
Per dozen.......................... 5.40

42358 Scythe, the Western Dutchman, bronzed; polished back, ground sharp.
Each $0.45
Per dozen........................... 4.85

42359 Scythe. the Western Dutchman, solid steel.
Each 50
Per dozen........................... 5.40

42360 Scythe, railroad or weed scythe, extra cast steel, green ribbed.
Each $0.45
Per dozen....................... 4.85

42363 Scythe, cast steel bush scythe.
Each.....$0.50
Per dozen 5.46

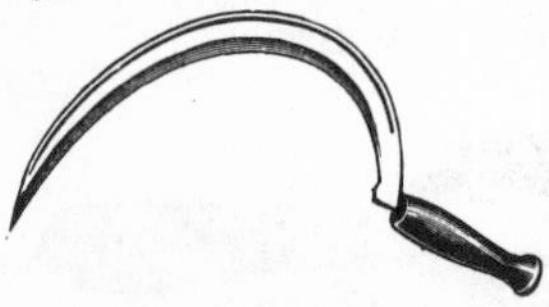

Grass Hook or Sickle.

42366 Grass Hook or Sickle.
Small size.....$0.25

Scythe Snaths.

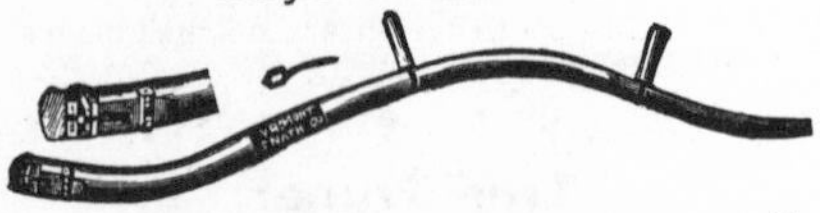

Each.
42369 Scythe Snath, patent loop.................$0.50
42370 Scythe Snath, for bush scythe............ .52

Scythe Stones.

42375 Scythe Stones, "Nova Scotia." Each ... $0.05
Per dozen....................................... .54
42376 Scythe Stones, "Ragg." Each............. .08
Per dozen.. .87
42377 Scythe Stones, "Indian Pond." Each.... .06
Per dozen.. .65
42378 Scythe Stones, "Vienna." Each.......... .10
Per dozen....................................... 1.08

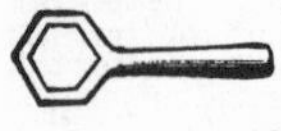

42379 Wrench for Patent Loop Snath. Each. .... .04
Per dozen.................. .... .44

42380 Loop for Patent Loop Snath.
Each............................. .07
Per dozen. .... .75

Hay Knives.

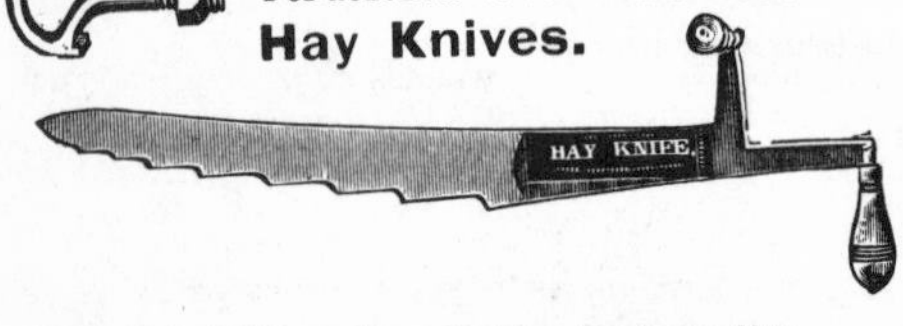

42385 Lighting Hay Knife Best quality.
Weight, 4¼ pounds...........................$0.62
42386 Spear Point Hay Knife; weight,4½ pounds. .70

Corn Knives.

42387 Corn Knives, new pattern. Excelsior pattern, cast steel blade, length of blade 18 inches.
Price, each..........$0.35 Per dozen 3.78

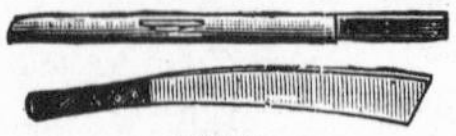

42388 Corn Knife, Excelsior pattern, cast steel blade, Length of blade, 15 inches; width of blade, 2½ in.

42388

Price, each..............$0.25 Per dozen 2.70

Hay Forks.

Our hay forks, rakes, hoes, etc., are the very best quality; we guarantee them.   Each. Per doz.
42392 Hay Fork, 3 tine, oval, cast steel, plain ferrule, straight handles, 4½ feet in length. Weight, 3 pounds...........$0.30 $3.32
42393 Same as above, only strapped ferrule. Weight, 3 pounds.................. .35   3.75
42394 Hay Fork, 3 tine, oval, cast steel, bent handle, plain ferrule. Weight, 2 pounds 9 ounces...................... .30   3.40
42395 Same as above, only strapped ferrule, handle, 4½ to 5½ feet.......... .35   3.90
Weight, 3 pounds.

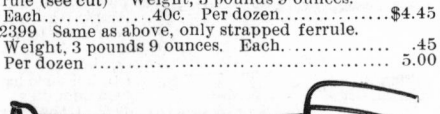

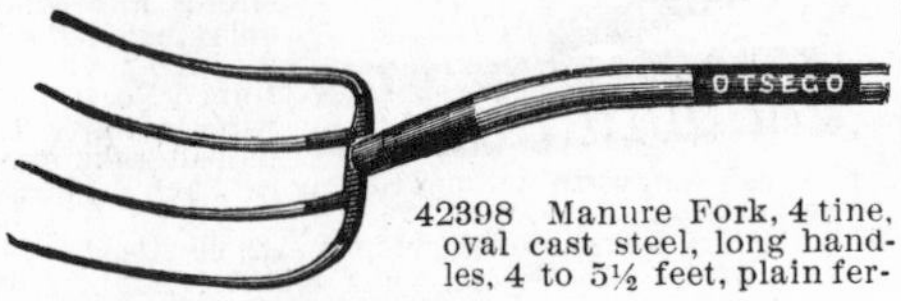

42398 Manure Fork, 4 tine, oval cast steel, long handles, 4 to 5½ feet, plain ferrule (see cut) Weight, 3 pounds 9 ounces.
Each............40c. Per doz..............$4.45
42399 Same as above, only strapped ferrule. Weight, 3 pounds 9 ounces. Each. .... .45
Per dozen 5.00

42400 Manure Forks, D handle, solid steel shanks.
                Price, each. Per doz.
4 tine, Common Ferrule..............$0.45 $4.80
4 tine, Strapped Ferrule............. .48   5.10
5 tine, Common Ferrule............. .60   6.75
5 tine, Strapped Ferrule............. .65   7.42
6 tine, Common Ferrule............. .75   8.38
6 tine, Strapped Ferrule............. .78   8.90

Manure Hooks.

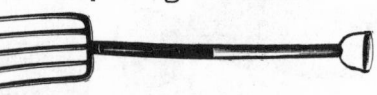

42403 Manure Hooks; weight, 3½ pounds.
Each $0.35
Per dozen....................... 3.90

Spading Forks.

42406 Spading Fork, four heavy flat tines, common ferrule, D handle. Each $0.50
42407 Spading Fork, four heavy flat tines, strapped ferrule, D handle   Each............... .55

42410 Potato Hooks, four flat tines
Each... ....$0.30
Per dozen.... 3.20

Heads for Fork and Shovel Handles.

42414 Malleable D heads for fork or shovel handles.
Each.... ....$0.08
Per dozen .... .85

Fork Handles.

42415 Hay Fork Handles, XX, second growth ash, straight, 5 feet.
Each $0.08
Per dozen.... .... .87
5½ feet, each................................... .09
Per dozen... .98
6 feet, each.................................... .12
Per dozen....................................... 1.20
                Each. Per doz.
42418 Hay Fork Handles, XX, second growth, bent; 4½ feet.................$0.09 $0.98
5 feet .... .12   1.30
5½ feet .... .13   1.41
42420 Manure Fork Handles, XX, second growth, bent; 4 feet............. .11   1.19
4½ feet................................. .12   1.20

.. KEEP ..
YOUR GRASS CUT
And Make Things Look Attractive.

Grass Carrier.

42422 Grass Carrier for Lawn Mower. This is a great convenience, as you do not have to use a rake. Raking a lawn is more than double the work of cutting, and this carrier catching all the grass as it is cut saves this extra work and leaves the lawn smooth and clean. It is adjustable to any size or make of lawn mower; has a strong iron frame covered with strong sail duck and enameled drill.
Price, each.......................................$1.85

Grass Catcher.

Improved.

42423 This Catcher is now made with sheet steel bottom, heavy cotton duck body, and has new device for attaching to lawn mower. Will catch all the grass and fit any make of lawn mower.
No. 1 fits 10, 12, and 14 in. mowers.
No. 2 fits 16, 18 and 20 inch mowers.
Price, each $0.67

Lawn Mowers.
The "New York."

This Mower is made to meet the demand for a good, substantial lawn mower at a medium low price. It has several of our latest improvements in *ratchet, back roller hanger, handle, adjustment, etc.,* and has ready sale to the large class of trade who wish to buy a first-class mower at lower price than heretofore. It has steel shafts ⅝ inch in diameter, double rachet. The knife is adjusted by one screw at each end of the knife bar, which is more simple and durable than the old plan. Its noiseless and light draft are very pleasant features with this mower, and there is more in it for the dollar than any other mower on the market. It is made in medium sizes only.
42424 12 inch, price, each...................... $3.60
42425 14 inch, price, each...................... 3.85
42426 16 inch, price, each...................... 4.00

Imperial Lawn Mower.

This is our "Best Goods," and is not surpassed by any lawn mower in the market. The principal feature of this machine is that the bottom knife-bar is bolted to the sides, thus making the frame perfectly rigid, while by a new patent hanger the revolving cutter is adjusted to the bottom knife. This is the reverse of the adjustment in all other mowers, When the knives are properly adjusted a lock screw secures them in position.
The *Positive Triple Ratchet* is the simplest and most durable made. The *Gears* will wear much longer than those in other mowers, as they do not move when the machine is reversed. Our patented *Terrace Mowing Attachment* has proved a valuable addition, being very simple and effective. It is the only mower made with an arrangement for cutting terraces. This mower has been built with special reference to its durability, and we can safely say that we believe it will outwear any mower made. We make this mower with high and low wheel.

Imperial High Wheel Mower.

42427 14 Inch Cut.........Price each, $7.20
42428 16 " " .... " 7.92
42429 18 " " .... " 8.64
42430 20 " " .... " 9.36
Price of Horse Lawn Mowers furnished on application. Send for special circular.

Imperial Low Wheel Mower.

42431 12 Inch Cut..............Price each, $5.40
42432 14 " " .... " 6.15
42433 16 " " .... " 6.85
42434 18 " " .... " 7.56
42435 20 " " .... " 8.28

Shovels and Spades.

All Shovels branded "Montgomery Ward & Co." are guaranteed to be as fine as any made at any price. Shovels weigh from 4½ to 8 lbs.

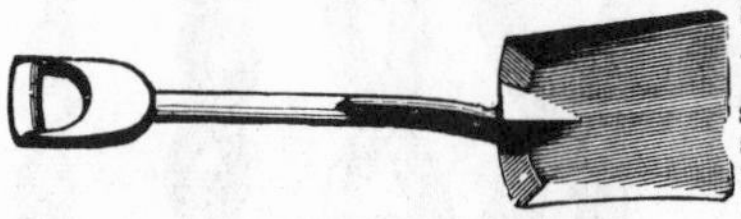

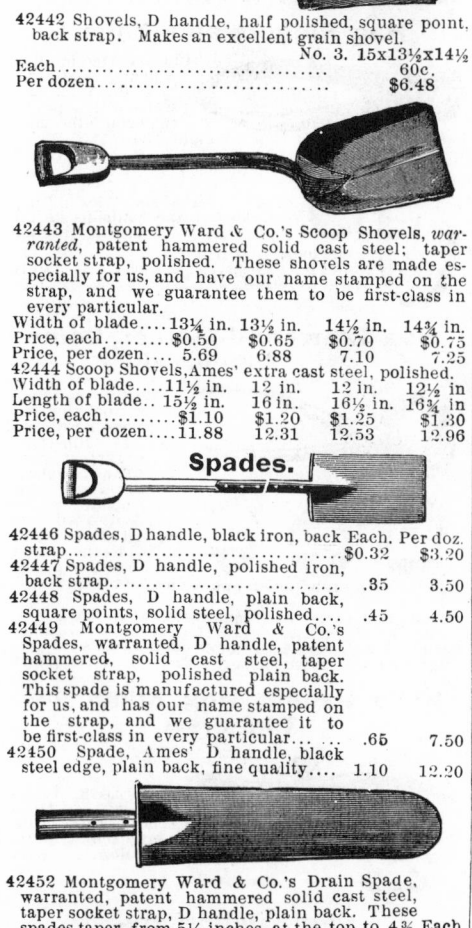

42436—Shovels, D handle, back straps, square points, black iron. Each....$0.30. Per dozen..........$3.25

	Each.	dozen.
42437 Shovels, D handles, back straps, square points, polished iron..........	$0.35	$3.50
42438 Shovels, D handle, plain back, solid steel, square points, polished.....	.45	4.50
42439 Montgomery Ward & Co.'s Shovels, *warranted*, D handle, plain back, square points, pat. polished, solid steel	.65	7.50
42440 Shovels, Ames' D handle, plain back, square points, best quality, patent solid black steel..........	1.00	11.85
42441 Shovels, Ames' D handle, plain back, square points, best quality, patent solid polished steel..............	1.10	12.54

42442 Shovels, D handle, half polished, square point, back strap. Makes an excellent grain shovel.

No. 3. 15x13½x14½

Each.................................... 60c.
Per dozen.................................. $6.48

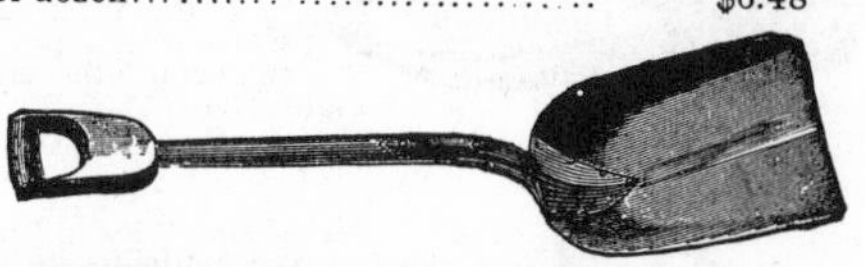

42443 Montgomery Ward & Co.'s Scoop Shovels, *warranted*, patent hammered solid cast steel; taper socket strap, polished. These shovels are made especially for us, and have our name stamped on the strap, and we guarantee them to be first-class in every particular.

Width of blade....	13¼ in.	13½ in.	14¼ in.	14¾ in.
Price, each.........	$0.50	$0.65	$0.70	$0.75
Price, per dozen....	5.69	6.88	7.10	7.25

42444 Scoop Shovels, Ames' extra cast steel, polished.

Width of blade....	11½ in.	12 in.	12 in.	12½ in
Length of blade..	15½ in.	16 in.	16½ in.	16¾ in.
Price, each..........	$1.10	$1.20	$1.25	$1.30
Price, per dozen....	11.88	12.31	12.53	12.96

Spades.

	Each.	Per doz.
42446 Spades, D handle, black iron, back strap..................................	$0.32	$3.20
42447 Spades, D handle, polished iron, back strap..................	.35	3.50
42448 Spades, D handle, plain back, square points, solid steel, polished....	.45	4.50
42449 Montgomery Ward & Co.'s Spades, warranted, D handle, patent hammered, solid cast steel, taper socket strap, polished plain back. This spade is manufactured especially for us, and has our name stamped on the strap, and we guarantee it to be first-class in every particular... ...	.65	7.50
42450 Spade, Ames' D handle, black steel edge, plain back, fine quality....	1.10	12.20

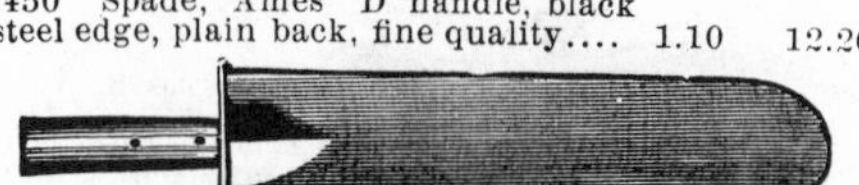

42452 Montgomery Ward & Co.'s Drain Spade, warranted, patent hammered solid cast steel, taper socket strap, D handle, plain back. These spades taper from 5½ inches at the top to 4⅜ inches at the point. 18 inches long............ Each $0.78
20 inches long. Each..$0.85 22 inches long .. .90

Coke Forks.

42454 Coke or Coal Forks, 8 diamond tines, D handle, strapped ferrule. Each.............$1.50

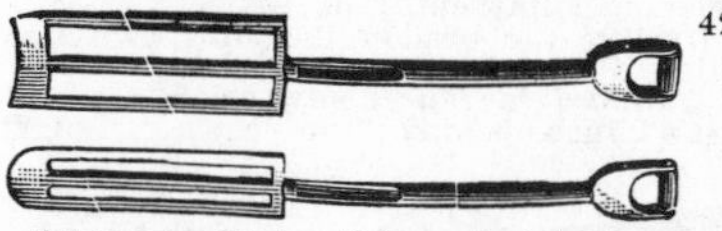

42455 The Boss Tilling spade, made of first quality cast steel. Resistance in driving this spade into the earth is greatly reduced, while the suction and scraping of ordinary spades is entirely avoided. Trenching and ditching can be done with greater ease than with any other spade. Made in 4 sizes.

Sizes, inches......	4½x18	4½x20	6½x18	6½x20
Price, each........	$1.70	$1.70	$1.85	$1.85

Drain Cleaner.

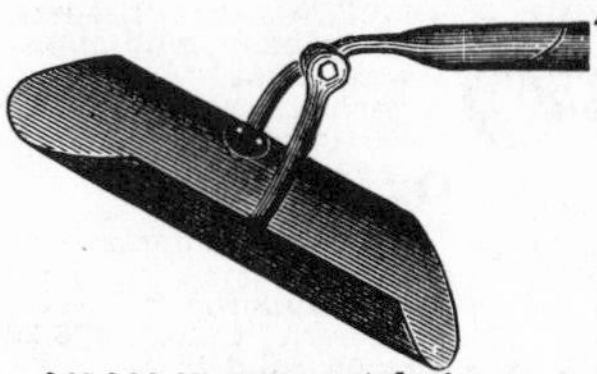

42457 Champion Adjustable Drain Cleaner, made to push or pull; can be adjusted to any angle. The most convenient and substantial tool on the market for making the oval groove in the bottom of the ditch. It is the only perfect drain cleaner made. The blade is made of solid cast steel, polished.

Size of blade, 4x15, concave. Price, each.......$1.00
" " 5x15, " " 1.10
" " 6x15, " " 1.20

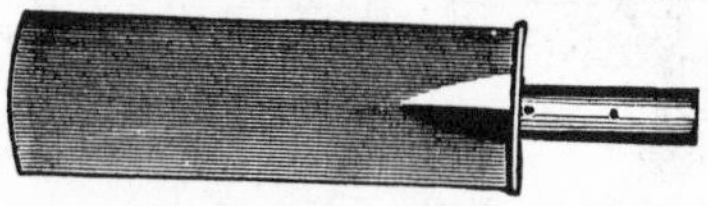

42459 Montgomery Ward & Co.'s Post Hole Spade, warranted; patent hammered, solid cast steel, taper socket strap, D handle, plain back and polished. This spade is also used for drainage purposes; 5½ inches at the step and 6 inches at the point 18 inches long..................$0.75
20 inches long... .80

Mining Shovels.

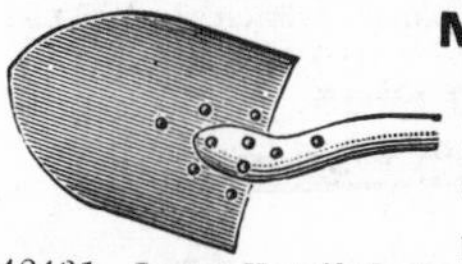

	Each.	Per doz.
42460 Long Handled Round Point Mining Shovels, stiff polished. Price.......	$0.65	$7.00
42461 Long Handled Round Point Mining Shovels, half spring, polished	.65	7.00
42462 Long Handled Round Point Mining Shovels, full spring, polished	.65	7.00
42463 Long Handled Square Point Grading Shovels..................	.75	8.45

Our facilities for filling orders for mining supplies are unlimited. We guarantee to furnish the best of goods at the lowest possible price and will supply anything wanted not found in our catalogue if obtainable in Chicago.

Wire Clothes Lines.

Twisted Galvanized Wire Clothes Lines

	Each.	Per doz.
42468 100 feet, No. 20 wire............	$0.17	$1.85
42469 100 feet, No. 18 wire............	.20	3.00

For manilla, jute or cotton lines, see Grocery List.

42470 Solid Annealed Galvanized Wire Clothes Line, preferred by a great many because they are smooth. Made of No. 9 wire, and in coils of 100 feet. We do not sell less. Per coil. $0.50
Per dozen coils.. 5.00

Mining Tools.

For Miners' Shovels, etc., see Index.

Railroad Picks.

42479 Picks, cast steel, ax finish; weight, 5½ to 6½ lbs. Each.. $0.35 Per dozen..........$3.75
42480 Pick Handles, hickory, 36 inches. Each... .12
Per dozen.. 1.03

Drifting Picks.

42481 Drifting Picks, adz eye; natural finish.

No............	1	2	3	4
Weight..............	3 lbs.	4 lbs.	4½ lbs.	5 lbs.
Each................	$0.35	$0.40	$0.45	$0.50
Per dozen..........	3.75	4.00	4.35	4.56

42482 Drifting Pick Handles, second growth; length, 35 inches; size of eye, 3x1. XXX quality. Each......$0.25 Per dozen........$2.70

Pole Picks.

42483 Pole Picks, adz eye.

Nos.	1	2	3
Weight......	3½ lbs.	4 lbs.	4½ lbs.
Each........	$0.47	$0 50	$0.52
Per dozen....	6.16	6.70	7.00

42484 Pole Pick Handles, second growth: length, 34 inches; eye, 3x1, XXX quality. Each.......$0.20
Per dozen.. 2.16

Mattocks.

42485 Mattocks, cast steel, adz eye, ax finish, long cutter.
Weight, 6 pounds. Each...........................$0.55
42486 Mattocks, cast steel, adz eye, ax finish, short cutter: weight, 5½ pounds. Each......... .50

Post Hole Diggers.

42489 Eureka Post Hole Digger, steel blades, 9 in.; wgth. 1¾ pounds.
Each.........$1.00

42490 The National Post Hole Digger, the best and cheapest tool of its kind in the market. Blades and shanks are dropped out of single pieces of steel. Every digger fully warranted.
Price, each...$1.00

Post Hole Augers.

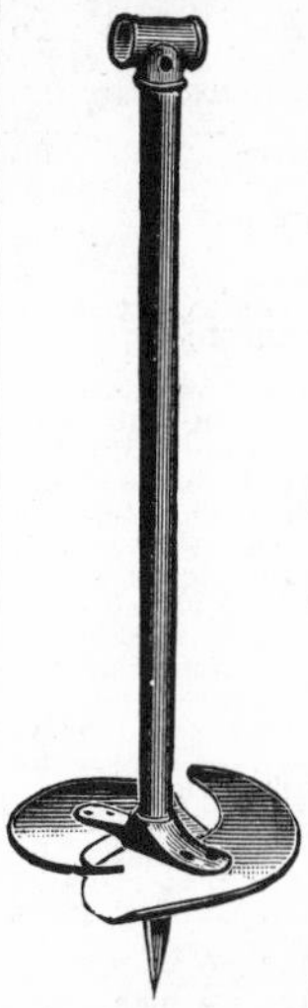

42491 Vaughan's Post Hole Augers, with steel blades. The manufacturers claim that it is the most popular of any post hole augur ever invented. The blades are riveted to the bottom and can be replaced if one becomes broken. It is made in the following sizes: 6 inch, 7 inch, 8 inch and 9 inch. We send any size desired at the same price.
Each....$0.50 Per dozen..$5.50

Post Mauls.

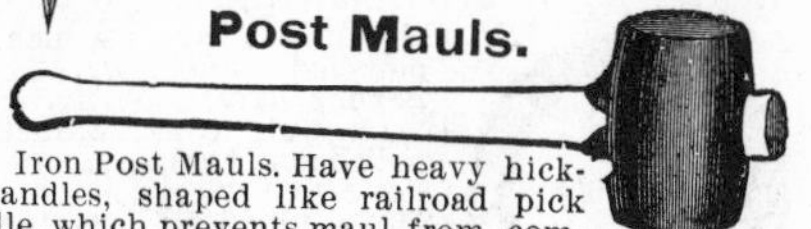

42493 Iron Post Mauls. Have heavy hickory handles, shaped like railroad pick handle, which prevents maul from coming off.

10 pounds. Each....	$0.30	18 pounds. Each.....	$0.45
13 pounds. Each....	.35	20 pounds. Each....	.50
16 pounds. Each	.40		

42494 Maul Handles. Price, each............... .12

Sheep Shears.

42495 Sheep Shears, common German, bent handles; known as grass shears.....$0.20
Per dozen........ 2.00

Wilkinson & Son's Sheep Shears.

	Each.	Per doz.
42499 Wilkinson & Son's Sheep Shears, polished blades, swaged, single spring.		
5-inch..	$0.70	$8.10
5½-inch..	.70	8.10
6-inch..	.75	8 70
42500 Wilkinson's Sheep Shears, full polished and etched, swaged, single spring, 5-inch..........	.90	10.26
5½-inch..	.90	10.26
6-inch..	1.00	11.34

The Hero Sheep Protector.

Before Taking.

42505 is made of steel galvanized wire formed into links. Each link has two sharp projections. Each collar consists of thirteen links, which will reach around the ordinary sheep's neck. Links can be removed or more added in a moment's time; by this means you adjust the colars to the sheep's neck. These protectors are made of galvanized wire to prevent them from rusting. They will last for ten years or more. This collar adheres close to the sheep's neck and is not noticeable except for a short time after shearing. What the manufacturers claim and will guarantee: First, that sheep can not hurt themselves on these protectors. Second, that by the use of this protector 95 per cent. of the sheep killed by dogs, wolves, etc., would be saved. You say that a dog does not always catch a sheep by the neck. We say, right you are; but when they catch them elsewhere it is done to check the sheep so that they can get to its neck, and in some instances they do not lacerate the neck to speak of but the object in catching the sheep is to cut the throat and drink the blood. In many instances one dog has killed 30 sheep in one night. In their wrestle with the sheep they are sure to come in contact with this protector. This closes the chase; they will not give blood for blood. If you will put the Hero Protector on your sheep, you can pasture them in your remotest field, and you need not lay awake at night for fear of them being molested.

After Taking.

Price, per dozen collars $0.85
" " gross " 8.50
" " 1000 " 54.60

The Nebraska Calf Weaner.

FULLERS.

42508 For calves four to eight months old.
Each.............$0.25
Per dozen. 2.70
42509 For calves eight months to two years old.
Each..............$0.28
Per dozen........ 3.05
42510 For cows (without wire bits).
Each..............$0.35
Per dozen......... 3.78
Calf weaners, extra by mail, 25 to 40c.

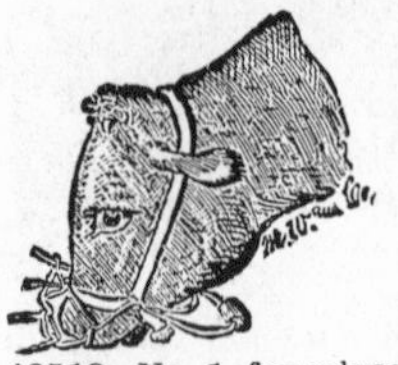

Hoosier Calf Weaners, so made that when the animal's head is lowered in the act of feeding the barbed muzzle is raised by a weight under the jaw. When the head is raised in position to suck, the weight forces the muzzle over the mouth. The most effectual and humane weaner in the market.

42513 No. 1, for calves, each.....................$0.40
Per dozen................................... 4.55
42514 No. 2, Range Weaner, for large calves and colts. Each........................... .68
Per dozen............................... 7.35
42515 No. 3, for cows 1.17
Per dozen.................................12.64

Bull Rings.

42518 Bull Rings, 2½ inch, steel polished. Each............$0.10
Per doz......................... 1.08
42519 Bull Ring, 3 inch steel polished. Each............$0.12
Per dozen.................... 1.30
42520 Bull Rings, 2½ inch, polished copper, with screw driver.
Each...........................$0.12
42521 Bull Rings, 3 inch, polished copper, with screw driver...$0.15

Bull Snaps.

42522 Patent Bull Snap, tinned with 3 feet of chain and ring on end and three screw eyes; is used in connection with bull ring in leading vicious cattle; there is no handle comes with it, but a rake or hoe handle can be used.
Each.. .... $0.25

Cow Ties.

42523 Cow Ties, with toggler; weight, per dozen, 24 pounds. Price, each.....................$0.18
Price, per dozen.............................. 1.90

42525 Cow Ties, closed ring, with toggle; weight, per doz, 18¾ lbs. Each.........................$0.17
Per dozen.................................. 1.80

Newton's Improved Cow Ties.

42526 The boss of all other ties. No feed is wasted. Better than swinging stanchions. The tie is made of wood, and bent in the shape of a bail or three sides of a square. It is provided with a swivel that is fastened in the center by two iron pins, and made so that one part turns with the neck piece, and the other part revolves around the wooden tie, making it impossible for the animal to get it twisted. The end of the wooden tie is riveted, so that it will not split where the bolts go through that fasten it to the manger. It will keep the cows cleaner than any other mode of fastening, because it pushes them back when standing, and draws them forward while lying down. We furnish the wooden tie, with neck piece, complete, and bolts to put it up. Full directions for making the manger and putting up furnished with each tie.
Price, in lots of 1 to 5 ties, complete. each.. ......$1.65
Price, in lots of 6 or more ties, complete, each... 1.50

Cattle Leaders.

42527 Cattle Leaders, malleable iron, brass wire spring.
Each $0.05
Per dozen......... .54

Ox Balls.

Ox Balls are put on the tips of horns of vicious cattle.
42529 Ox Balls, octagon, hollow.
Each $0.32
42530 Ox Balls, octagon, solid.
Per dozen.................. .35

Cattle Tie Irons.

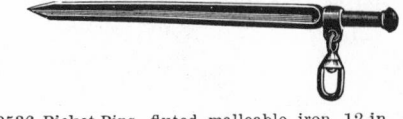

42534 Cattle Tie Irons, japanned, for ½ in. rope, with patent covered snap, very convenient, as ordinary rope can be used and renewed at small expense when worn out; weight each, 7 ounces. Each $0.05
Per dozen................................. .55

42535 Cattle Tie Irons, tinned, ½ in. rope, or smaller; with patent covered spring snap; very convenient, as ordinary rope can be used and renewed when worn out; weight, each, 6 ounces. Each........$0.07
Per dozen.................. .75

Picket Pins.

42536 Picket Pins, fluted malleable iron, 12 in. long, weight, 1½ lbs. Each.....................$0.08
Per dozen................................ .87

42537— Picket Pins, spiral, ½ in., wrought iron, 14½ in. long, weight, 1 lb. 6 oz. Each, $0.13 Per dozen......$1.40

Lariat Swivels.

42538 Lariat Swivels malleable iron, ⅝ and ⅜ eye, 4½ in. long.
Each............$0.03
Per dozen..... .33
42539 The American Wrought Steel Lariat Swivel, the strongest and easiest working swivel in the market.

Each..............$0.04 Per dozen......... $0.44

Chains.

42540 Cable Log Chains, made of self-colored coiled chain, with large hook, one hook on each end, 12 and 14 feet long. The sizes given below do not indicate the size of the chain across the link, but the size of the iron in the link is made of. Prices are for either 12 or 14 feet.

Size	¼	5/16	⅜	½
Price, each...	$1.25	$1.50	$1.75	$2.50

42542 Straight Link, hand made.

	3/16 in.	¼ in.	5/16 in.	⅜ in.	7/16 in.	½ in
Weight, Per foot.	8 oz.	1 lb.	1 lb. 4 oz.	1 lb. 8 oz.	2 lb.	2 lb. 8oz.
Price, per pound..	10c.	7c.	6¼c.	5c.	4¾c.	4½c.

American Halter Chains.

American Halter Chains are made wholly of steel and are the strongest made, as there are no welds to give way.
42543 American Halter Chains 4½ feet long, links 1¼ in. long, ⅜ in. wide. Each............$0.10
Per dozen............................... 1.00
42544 American Halter Chains, 6 ft. long, links 1⅜ in. long, 7-16 in. wide. Each................ .15
Per dozen................................ 1.60
42545 American Halter-Chains, 6 ft. long, links 1⅜ in. long, ½ in. wide. Each.............. .25
Per dozen... . ... 2.45

Jack Chains.

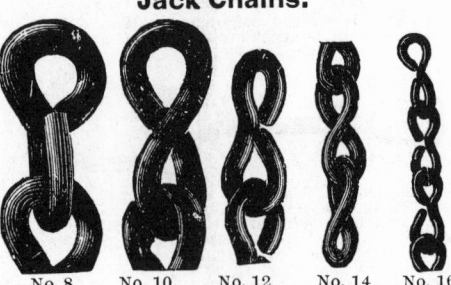

No. 8   No. 10   No. 12   No. 14   No. 16

42549 Iron Jack Chains. Cuts are exact size of chains.

Nos.	8	10	12	14	16
Per yard.........	$0.08	0.07	0.05	0.04	0.03
Per dozen yards.	.40	.36	.20	.18	.15

42550 Brass Jack Chains. Cuts are exact size.

Nos.	8	10	12	14	16
Per yard.....	$0.20	0.15	0.10	0.08	0.06
Per doz. yds.	2.10	1.40	.90	.60	.50

Glaziers' Points.

42555 Glazier's points in ¼ lb papers. Postage, 5c. per paper.
Per paper.....................$0.08
Per dozen papers............. .85

Hog Ringers and Rings.

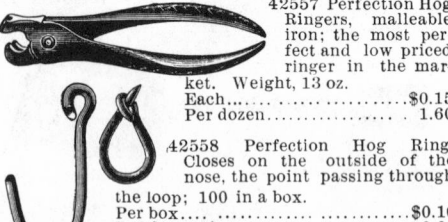

42557 Perfection Hog Ringers, malleable iron; the most perfect and low priced ringer in the market. Weight, 13 oz.
Each......................$0.15
Per dozen................. 1.60
42558 Perfection Hog Ring. Closes on the outside of the nose, the point passing through the loop; 100 in a box.
Per box.... ....$0.10
Per dozen rings.................. 0.03

Hog Tamer and Marker, Combined.

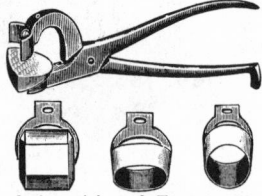

We illustrate a combination tool for cutting hogs noses, and dies, as illustrated above, for ear marking. The cut shows the Hog Tamer. The lower plate can be detached and the ear dies are easily attached to the Tamer. We furnish one steel knive with each Tamer, and ear markers, as given below.
42559 Hog Tamer, with square die, for ear marking. Price, each....... ....$3.00
42560 Hog Tamer, with round or oval dies, for ear marking. Price each.......................$2.50

Hiil's Pattern Hog Rings and Ringers.

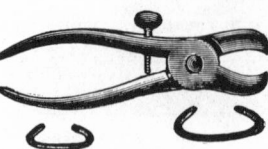

42561 Hog Rings. Per box... ..$0.07
42562 Hog Ringers, each.....$0.10
Per doz..... 1.10

Cattle Dehorners.

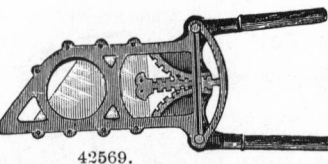

Big Thing for Cattle Raisers. Newton's lately improved dehorning knife, revolving and sliding shear, each one making a draw cut. Cuts perfectly smooth, does not fracture the head or the horns; causes to heal quickly.

42569.

42567 No. 1, *Intended for Calves* only, weighs 4½ lbs, and has a 2 inch opening. Price, each.......$3.00

42568 No. ½, intended for young or medium aged cattle, with revolving cut knife. Price, each...$4.40

42568

42569 No. 3, intended for young or old cattle, has a 4¼ inch opening, weighs 17 lbs. Price, each.......................................$6.88

Hog Tamer.

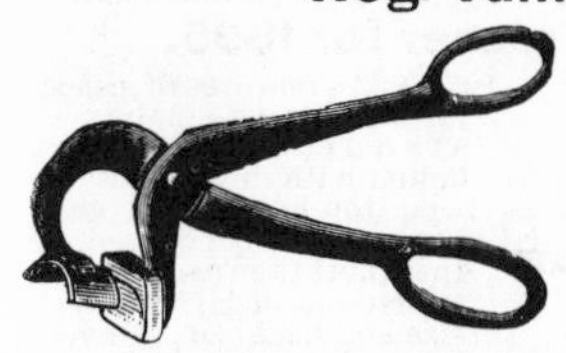

42570 Hurd's American Hog Tamer, to keep hogs from rooting; made from malleable iron; three tempered steel knives, assorted sizes, furnished with tamer. Each.........$0.55
Per dozen.... 5.95

BELLS IN GREAT VARIETY.

Open Polished Bells.

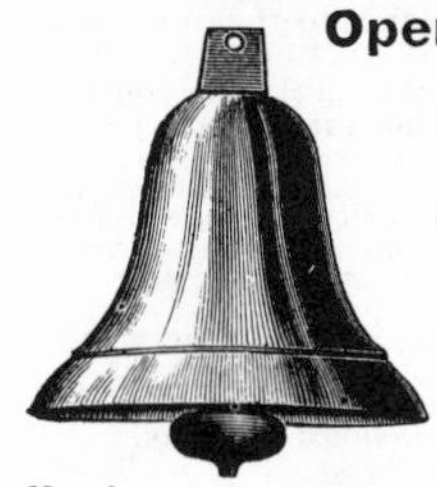

42575 Open Polished Bells may be used for a variety of purposes; make good sheep bells, a harness bell for milk wagons, drays, etc.

Numbers	1	2	3	4	5	6
Diameter of mouth in inches	2¼	2½	2¾	3	3¼	3½
Each	7c	9c.	11c.	13c.	15c.	18c.
Per dozen	76c.	98c.	$1.10	$1.41	$1.62	$1.95

Hand Bells.

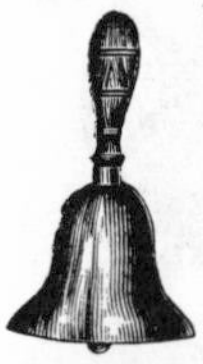

42576—

No.	Weight.	Diameter.	Each.
1	5 oz	2	$0.07
3	10 oz	2 13/16	.13
5	15 oz	3 11/16	.22
7	18 oz	4⅛	.35
9	1 lb. 9 oz	5	.60
13	3 lb. 15 oz	6⅞	1.05
14	5 lb.	7¼	1.20

Farm Bells.

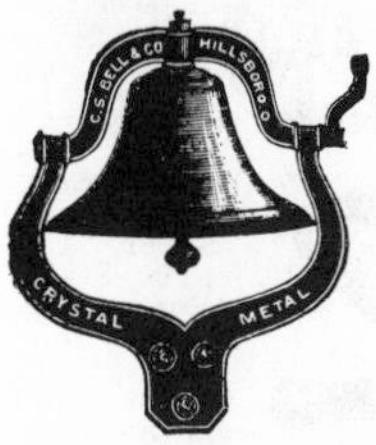

Bronzed, with iron frame.
Our customers need have no fear in buying this bell. Do not think because we sell it at such a low figure that it is a cheap bell for it is not. We caught the manufacturer when he wanted money; we had the money to buy a year's supply. This is why you do not have to pay us more.

42579 Diameter at mouth.

	15 in.	17 in.	19 in.	21 in.
Weight	40 lb.	50 lb.	75 lb.	100 lb.
Each	$0.93	$1.18	$1.75	$2.33

Steel Alloy Bells

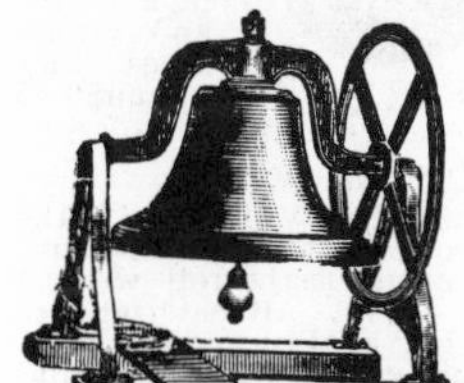

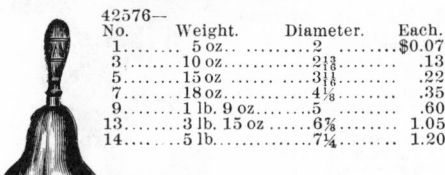

42580 Steel Alloy Church Bells, made of an alloy of cast steel and crystal metal and are of superior tone, finished and warranted against breaking with ordinary use *for two years*. For complete description send for our Special Bell Catalogue. Mailed free.

School House or factory Bells.

BELLS ARE NUMBERED BY THE DIAMETER IN INCHES.

Number.	Bell only.	Complete.	Price.
20	105 lbs.	150 lbs.	$ 7.50
22	125 "	175 "	9.25
24	155 "	225 "	11.50
26	220 "	325 "	18.50
28	255 "	425 "	25.50

42581

Church Bells.

BELLS ARE NUMBERED BY THE DIAMETER IN INCHES.

Number.	Bell only.	Complete.	Price.
30	335 "	550 "	$29.25
32	380 "	600 "	33.75
34	465 "	725 "	40.50
36	570 "	850 "	49.50
40	780 "	1,200 "	67.50
44	1,100 "	1,600 "	90.00
54	2,100 "	3.000 "	168.75

The weights and prices above named are for complete bells, and include wood sills, iron wheel, and for Nos. 30, 32, 34, 36, 40, 44 and 64, tolling hammer, without extra charge.
Tolling hammers for Nos. 24, 26 and 28, when so ordered, $5.00 each extra.
These bells are cast from an alloy of cast steel and crystal metal, and can be relied on under all circumstances and in all seasons. Nos. 20 to 28 are school or factory bells, and are not suitable for churches. Nos. 30 to 54 inclusive are recommended for churches.
Send for our Special Bell Catalogue, gives full information and numerous testimonials.

Trip Gong Bells.

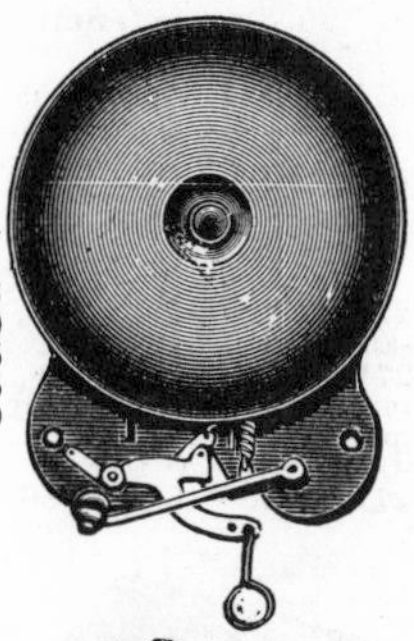

42582 Trip Gong Bells. Genuine bell metal.
3-in...wgt., 1 lb. 5 oz..$0.66
4-in....wgt., 1½ lb ...... .70
6-in....wgt., 2 lb. 13 oz 1.35
8-in....wgt., 6 lb. 2.65
10-in...wgt., 9¾ 4.00

Door Gongs.

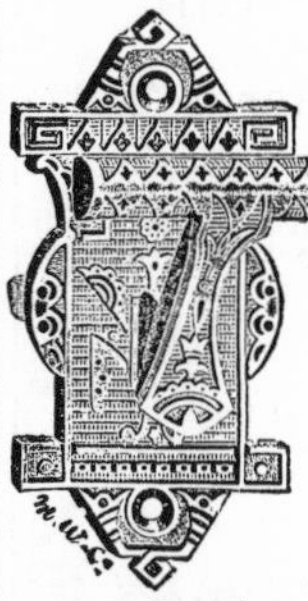

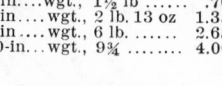

Knocker.

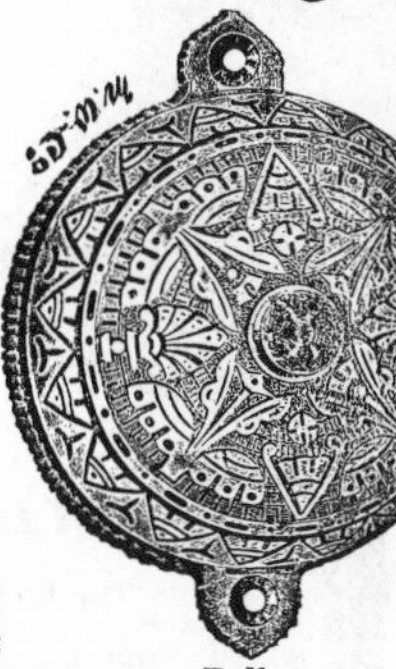

Bell.

42584 Geneva Bronzed Door Bell (Weight 2 lb. 2 oz., size 4 in.). Each.$0.42
Crank door gongs are no longer made.

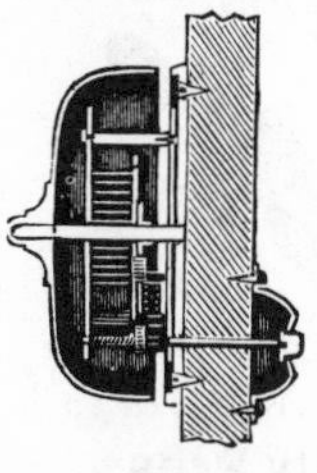

42590 The New Departure Electric Action Door Bell; winds up like a clock by turning the gong; when wound simply pushing the button will cause it to ring; will give from 400 to 500 calls at one winding, is strongly made and cannot get out of order; the most perfect and novel electric action door bell yet invented. Directions how to apply it come with each bell. Weight, 5 lbs.
4 inch, with plain bronze rosette..................$1.75
5 inch, with plain bronze rosette.................. 2.35

New Departure Rotary Door Bells.

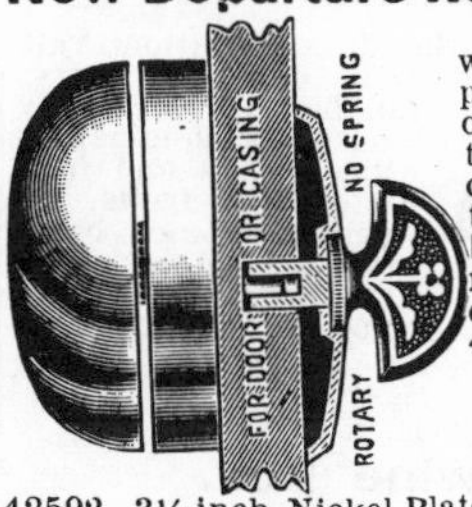

With electrical results. It winds up like a clock. Simply turning the knob about one fourth in either direction produces about ten clear full tones, which, though not startling, can be better heard than any bell made to immitate electrical results.
42591 3-inch Nickel Plated Bell with nickel plated turn knob. Price, each.........$0.75
42592 3½-inch Nickel Plated Bell with nickel turn knob. Price, each 0.85

Cow Bells.

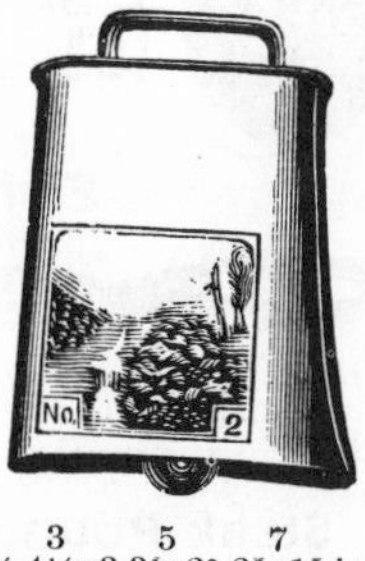

42594 The shape of these is designed to produce the loudest sound possible.

No.	0	2	3	5	7
Size of mouth	6x4½	5½x3½	4½x3	3¼x2⅜	2⅜x1¾ in
Height	6½	5	4¾	3¼	2⅜ in.
Price, Each	$0.40	$0.25	$0.20	$0.15	$0.10
Per dozen	4.00	2.65	2.00	1.50	1.00

42595 Cow Bell Straps, made of leather.

Width	1½ in.	1¾ in.
Per dozen	$2.50	$2.75
Each	.25	.28

Sheep Bells.

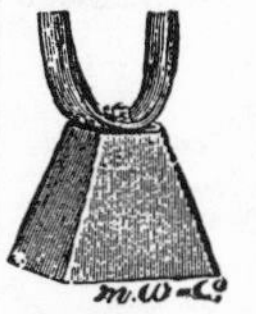

Sheep Bells, complete with straps. These bells are made of extra quality of metal and emit a sharp, tinkling sound that can be heard a greater distance than the small sized cow bell that is sometimes used.

42599 Length, 1½ inches; size across mouth of bell, 1⅛x1¼, with straps complete. Each......$0.15
Per dozen 1.60
42600 Length, 2 inches; size across mouth of bell, 1½x1¾, with straps complete.
Each...............$0.20 Per dozen............ 2.00

Ice Tongs.

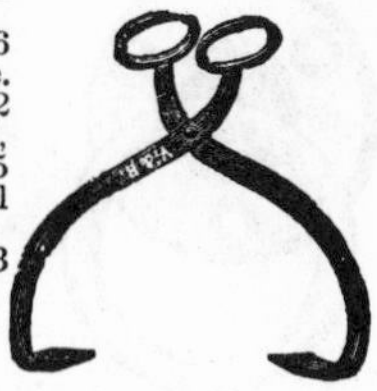

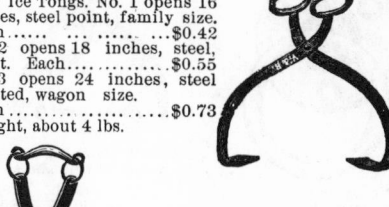

42673 Ice Tongs. No. 1 opens 16 inches, steel point, family size. Each......................$0.42
No. 2 opens 18 inches, steel, point. Each..............$0.55
No. 3 opens 24 inches, steel pointed, wagon size.
Each.........................$0.73
Weight, about 4 lbs.

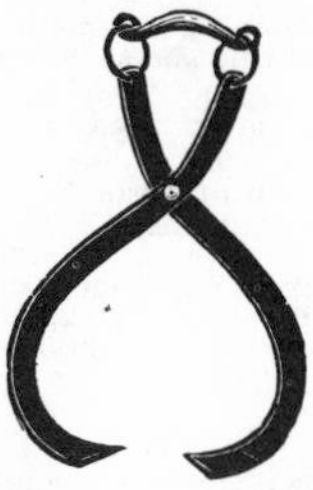

42674 Ice Tongs. No. 6 opens 14 inches, with bale top, family size; weight, about 2¾ lbs.
Each $0.45

Harness Hooks.

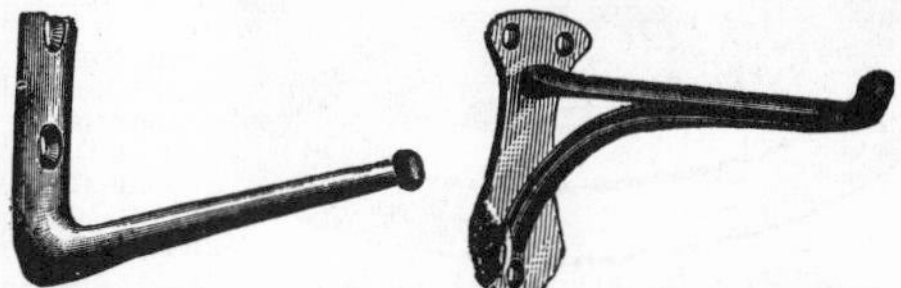

42675 Harness Hooks, japanned iron, 6 inches in length. Weight, per dozen, 6 lbs. Each.........$0.04
Per dozen.............. .45
42676 Harness Hooks, japanned iron, 8 inches long; weight, per dozen, 10½ lbs. Each.......... .07
Per dozen.............. .75

Collar Hooks.

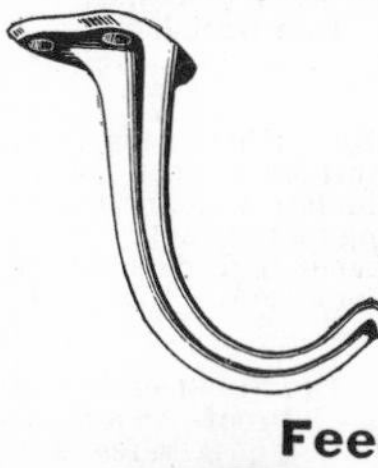

42680 Collar Hooks, japanned iron, to hang from the ceiling. Weight, per dozen, 12 lbs.
Each.........................$0.15

Feed Boxes.

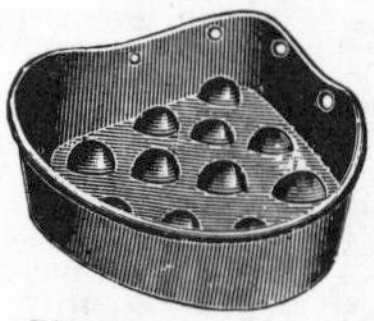

World's Fair highest award given to Smith's Perfection Feed Box. Patented April 5, 1892.

If it does not do all claimed for it return it and get your money back.

What is claimed.

First—It obliges the animal to eat its feed slowly, because it has to work to get its feed. While doing this it is masticating what it already has in its mouth, consequently no food goes to its stomach not properly masticated. It therefore produces better results with less feed.
Second—The animal cannot plow through it and waste food.
Third—Being of metal, it will not sour, and admits of feeding any kind of food.
Fourth—With all of these advantages it costs no more than any other metal box.
42681 Price, each.................................$1.25

Hay Rack.

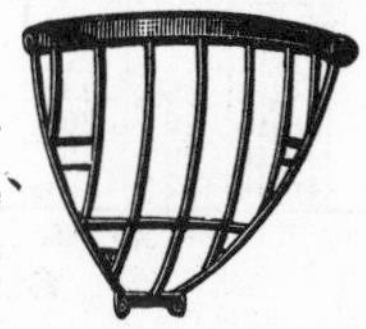

42683 Cast Iron Hay Rack, for horse stall. Weight, 29 lbs., neat and convenient; can be put up in 5 minutes.
Each......................$1.10

42685 Steel Hay Racks, same style as No. 42683, but made of bent steel rods.
½ inch steel, each...................................$2.00

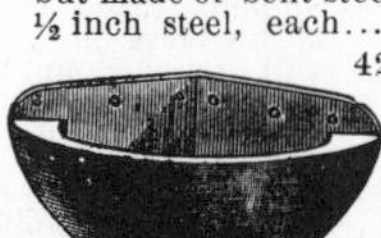

42687 Castiron Feed Box, for horse stall; is 16 inches on each side, 10 inches deep and weighs 28 lbs.; is easily put up; fastened with screws.
Each, no screws.... .....$0.90

Riding Saddles

In all Shapes, Styles and Prices. We sell more Saddles than all other Catalogue Houses combined.

Examine our numerous quotations, which are made on guaranteed "Steel Fork" Trees.

Hitching Rings.

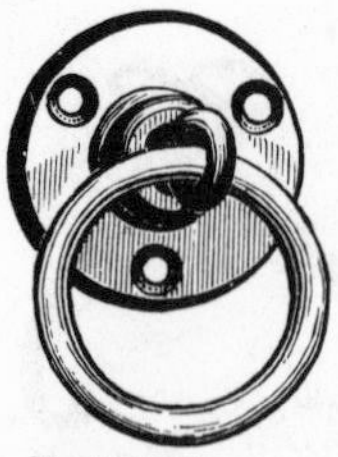

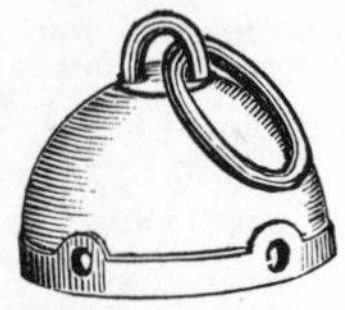

42689 Hitching Rings, wrought ring and swivel,

No screws.	Each.	Per doz
Japanned	$0.05	$0.54
Galvanized	.08	.87

42690 Post Caps, for fastening over top of posts to hitch horses to. Very neat and convenient; made of iron, japanned, no screws.

Size	4⅞ inches.	5¼ inches
Each	$0.20	$0.28
Per dozen	2.16	3.00

Oat Sieves.

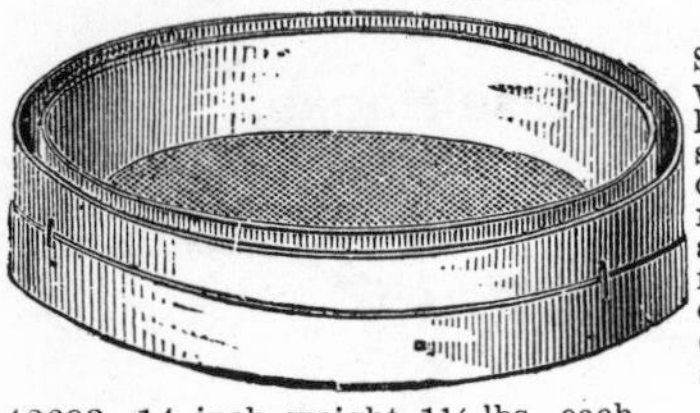

Oat Sieves made with extra heavy blued steel wire cloth. No. 12 mesh; hoops are oak; used for sifting dirt and dust out of oats and grain.

42693 14 inch, weight, 1¼ lbs., each $0.27
42694 16 inch weight, 1½ lbs., each .... .32
42695 18 inch, weight, 2 lbs. each .... .35

Boot Jacks.

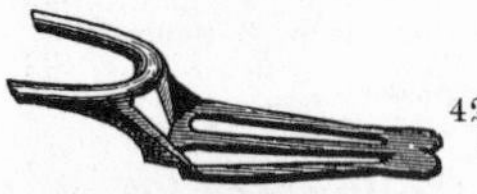

Weight, 1¼ pounds.
42698 Iron Boot Jack.
Each $0.08

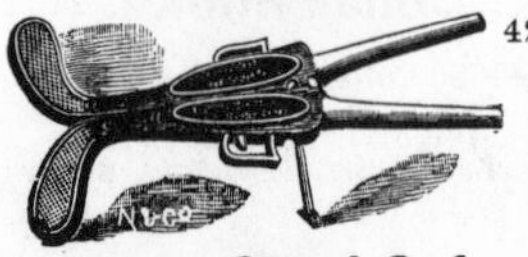

42700 The American Bull Dog Boot Jack, the latest and best selling novelty out.
Lacquered, each..$0.15
Per dozen 1.50

Steel Safes.

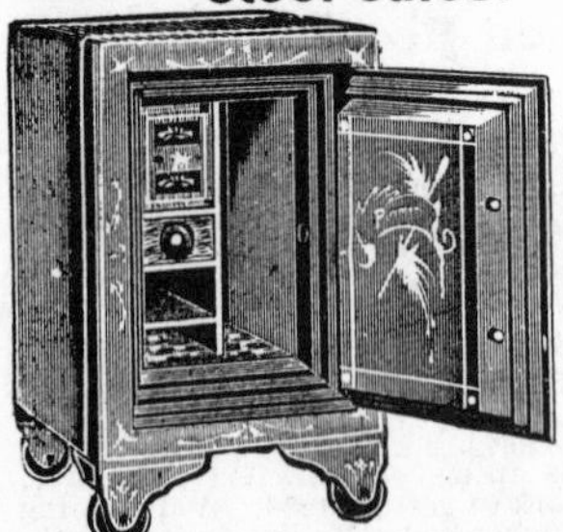

42705 Steel Fire Proof Safes. These safes are made in the best material, have combination locks, are handsomely decorated and are fire proof. Satisfaction, ease of mind, a feeling of security, etc., is attained by possessing one of our safes. In all cases they will be shipped direct from the factory. Name will be put on above the door, shaded in bronze, free of charge, when specified. Allowance for slight delay in shipping must be made when this is done. Write name wanted on safe plainly, so that no mistake will be made.

	Outside Measure.			Inside Measure.			Appx Wt., lbs	Price.
	High	Wide	Deep	High.	Wide	Deep		
3	28 in	18½	19	15	10	12	445	$20.00
4	31 in	21½	21¼	17	13¾	13½	625	26.00
5	34¼in	22¾	23¼	19¾	14¼	14½	840	34.00
6	38¾in	26	26	22	16	15½	1,210	50.00
7	42½in	29	29	23½	17½	18	1 610	55.00
9	46½in	32	29½	27¾	21	18	1,925	90.00

No 9 isa Double Door Safe.

Stencils.

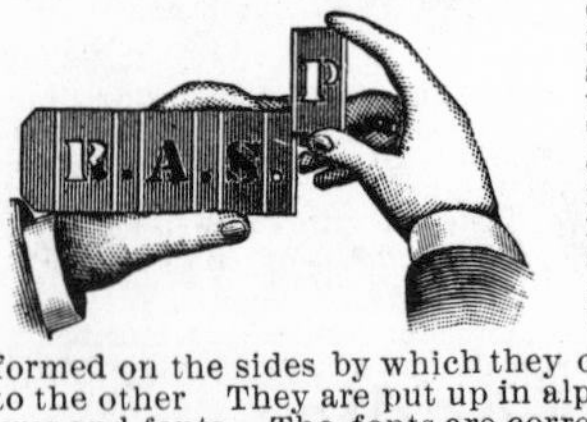

Improved Interchangeable Lock Stencils, made of spring brass. They will not curl up. The letters and characters are perfect in design and finish, cut in spring brass on separate plates, having a lock formed on the sides by which they can be joined one to the other They are put up in alphabets, sets of figures and fonts. The fonts are correctly assorted as to vowels, consonants, periods, etc., by printers' rules for printing names and general use. Are especially useful to farmers for marking crates and boxes, etc.

42708 Font No. 1, 55 pieces only.

Size, inch	½	¾	1	1½
Per font	$0.55	.57	.65	.83

42709 Font No. 2, 70 pieces, letters and figures.

Size, inch	½	¾	1	1½
Per font	$0.70	.75	.80	$1.05

No ink on brush furnished with font No. 1 and 2.

Stencils—Continued.

42710 Ink for interchangeable stencils. Large cans, price each $0.30
42711 Small Cans, price, each $0.12
42712 Stencil Brushes, large. Each $0.12
42713 Stencil Brushes, large Each $0.10
42714 House Numbers, 3 inch made of brass and nicely nickel plated, each. per doz. per 100. Oval.....$0.10 $0.80 $8.40
42715 Flat .08 60 6.25

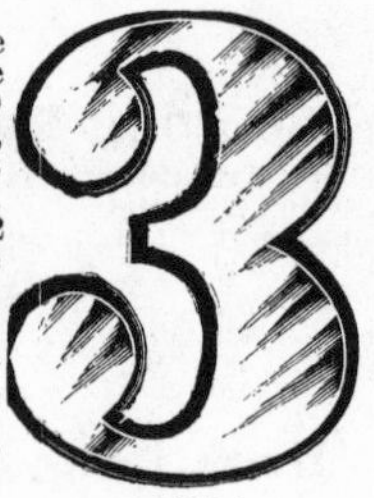

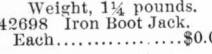

42714

Alarm Till.

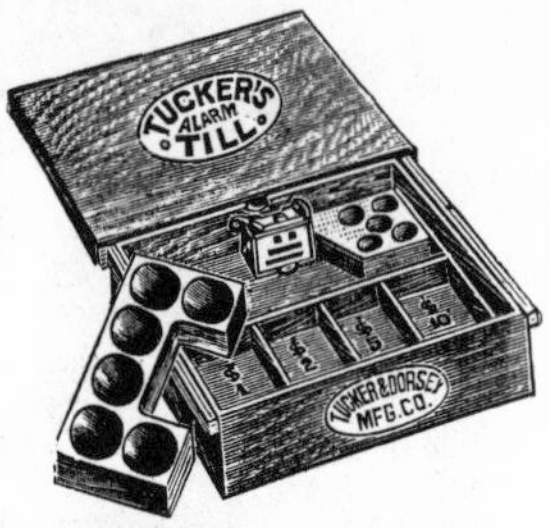

42721 Tucker Patent Alarm, Till Lock and Drawer. Hardwood, strongly dove-tailed, combination quickly changed. No keys required.
Price, each..$1.45

Tap Borers.

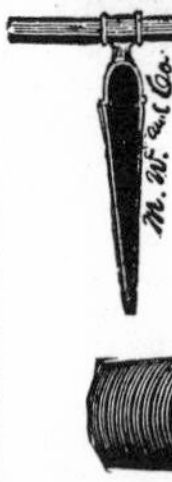

42723 Tap Borer, weight, 1¼ lbs.
Each $0.55
Per dozen 5.95

Molasses Gates.

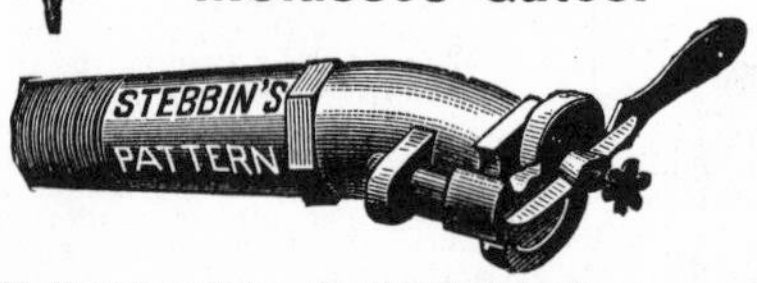

42725 Molasses Gates, Stebbins' Patent.

No.	1	2	3	4	5
Bores, inches	1	1⅛	1¾	1⅝	1$\frac{13}{16}$
Each	$0.12	$0.15	$0.16	$0.18	$0.20

Fruit, Wine and Jelly Press Combined.

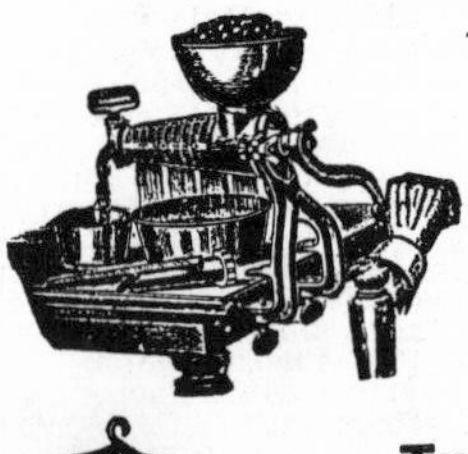

42730 Combination Fruit Wine and Jelly Press; can be used for many purposes, such as making wines, jellies and fruit butter from fruits, the entire substance being extracted in one operation. Weight, 12½ lbs., Price, each........ $2.35

Twine Box.

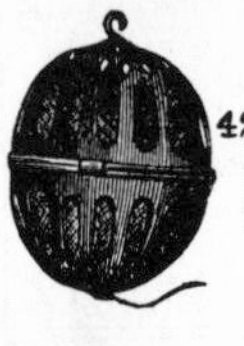

42736 Improved Hanging Twine Box; bronzed iron; weight, 15 ounces.
Each $0.12
Per dozen 1.30

Fish Scaler.

42737 Fish Scaler iron, japanned, 9 inches in length, removes the scales from fish in much shorter time than it can be done in any other way. Weight, 9 ounces.
Each $0.05
Per dozen .... .54

Steak Pounder and Ice Pick.

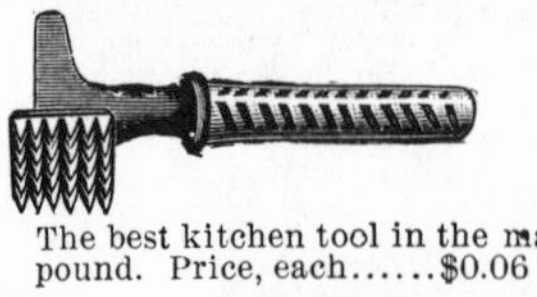

42738 The Diamond Beef Steak Pounder and Ice Pick combined, made of gray iron, cast in one solid piece, nicely japanned. The best kitchen tool in the market; weight, 1 pound. Price, each......$0.06 Per dozen......$0.55

Easy Can Opener.

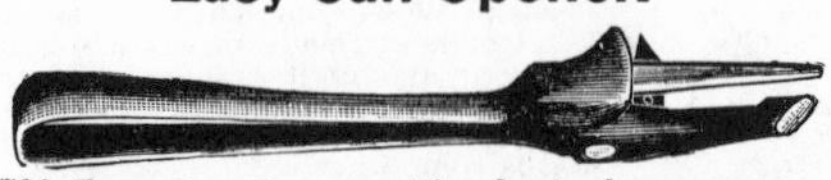

42739 Easy Can Opener. The best cheap can opener made; cuts the entire top off the can and leaves a smooth edge. Try one. Each..... $0.08
Per dozen .... .87

NO CHARGE For Cases Or Cartage.

The Improved White Mountain Ice Cream Freezer for 1895.

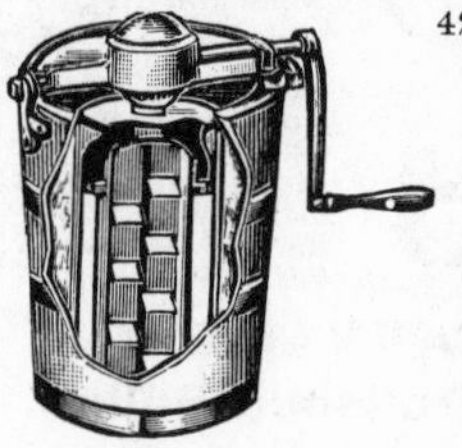

42740 As features of especial merit, we claim: A strong waterproof tub, bound with heavy, galvanized iron hoops; the gearing completely covered, so that nothing can get between the cogs; cans full size and made of the very best quality of tin-plate; beaters of malleable iron and tinned; all castings attached to the tub nicely galvanized to prevent rusting. It is the only freezer in the market having the **celebrated duplex dasher, with double self-adjusting wood scraping bar,** by the use of which cream can be frozen in one-half the time, yet finer and smoother than can possibly be produced in any other freezer now in use. Positively the best freezer in the world, and guaranteed if properly used to make ice cream in 3 MINUTES.

Size	2-qt.	3-qt.	4-qt.	6-qt.	8-qt.
Each	$1.50	$1.85	$2.20	$2.80	$3.75
Size	10-qt.	......	15-qt.	20-qt.	25-qt.
Each	$5.00	......	$6.80	$9.20	$11.20

42741 Extra Fly Wheel for 25 quart Freezers.
Each $3.50

Extra Cans for White Mountain Freezers.

42743—

Quarts..	6	8	10	12	15	20	25
Each...	$0.90	$1.10	$1.50	$1.75	$2.00	$2.85	$4.00

Apple Parers.

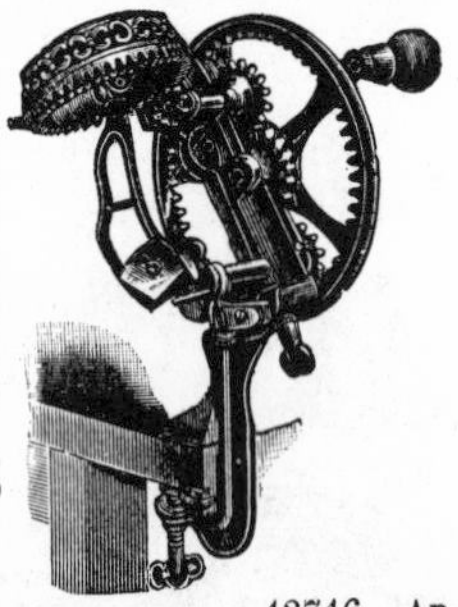

42745 The '78 Parer, with improved curved knife still maintains its reputation as the best in the world. All parings fall clear from the machine, and do not become mixed up in the gears. The Automatic "push off" never fails to "push off" the apple every time after it is pared.
Price. each $0.75
Price, per dozen.... 8.00

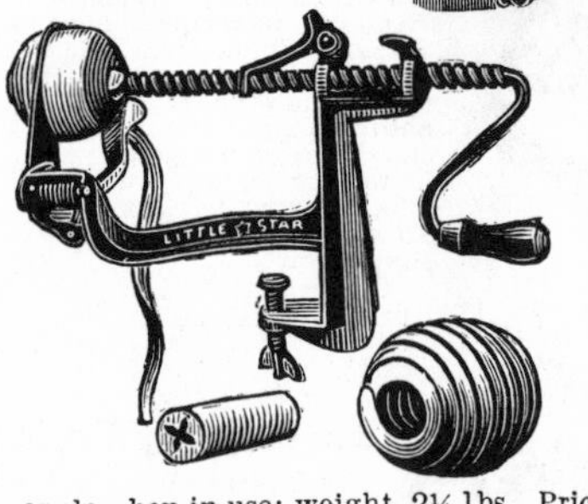

42746 Apple Parer, Corer and Slicer, "Little Star." For paring, coring and slicing; the Little Star is the simplest and best machine in use. The knife arm works on a swivel, and always faces the apple when in use; weight, 2¼ lbs. Price, each $0.45
Per dozen 4.86

Wringers.

We use the Genuine Patent Rolls. Vulcanized to the shaft; the very best rolls known to the wringer business, except the old-fashioned elastic roll wringer which we quote under No. 42771. All material used in our wringers are of the best quality, and the workmanship and finish are not surpassed by any similar goods in the market. We aim to have the best goods.

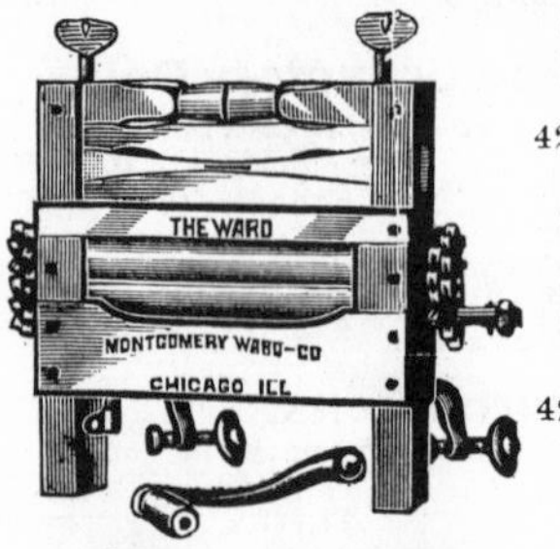

42763 Improved Montgomery Ward & Co. Wood Frame Wringer. No. 2½, like cut. Length of rolls, 10 inches, diameter, 1¾ in.
Price, each.... $2.00
Per dozen..... 21.00
42764 With rolls, 11 inch long, 1¾ in. diameter, large size.
Price, each.... $2.50
Per dozen.... 26.50

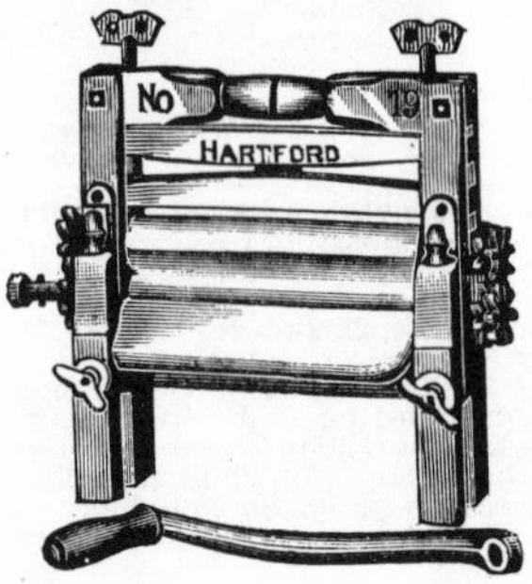

42766 The Hartford Wringer, a splendid wringer for the money, and one that will give satisfaction and good service. Length of roll, 10 inches; diameter, 1¾ inches.
Price, each... $1.75
Per dozen.... 18.00

Wringers—Continued.

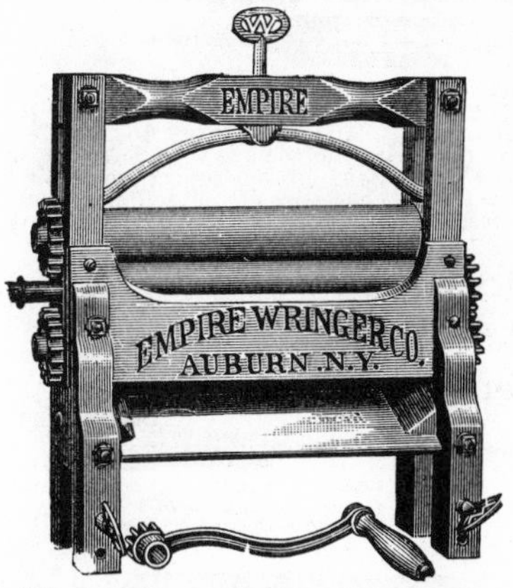

42768 The Geneva Wringer, purchase gear. Turns with half the labor that other wringers do; has solid white rubber rolls; made of the best material throughout; length of rolls, 10 in.; diameter, 1¾ inches.
Price $3.00

Old Reliable Wringer.

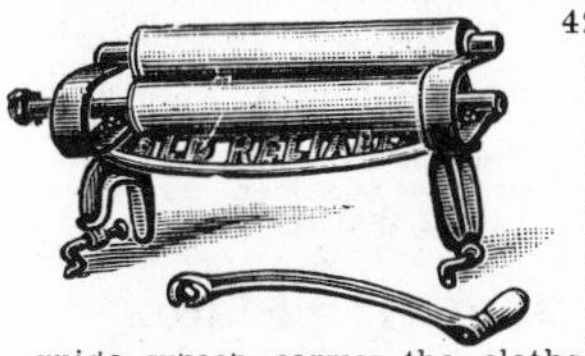

42770 The Old Reliable Wringer, like cut. Has white rubber rolls, 10 inches long and 1¾ inches in diameter, best steel springs, warranted; has a malleable iron crank that will not break, an apron clothes guide which carries the clothes over the edge of the tub. Weight, about 10 lbs. Price, each.....$1.65
Per dozen...17.50

Lovell Guarantee Wringer.

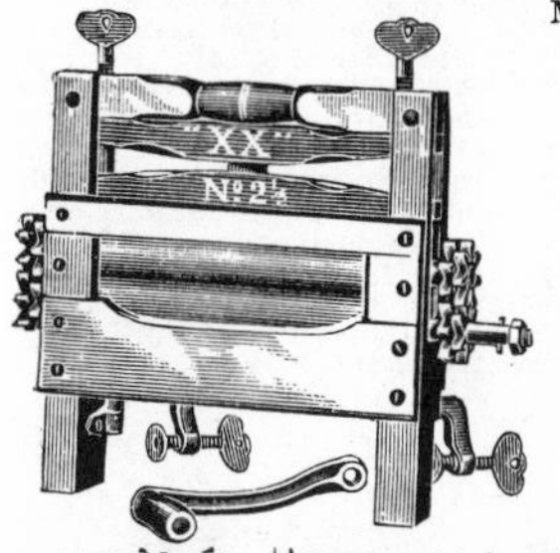

Made with those *old-fashion* Elastic *rolls*, such as were put in wringers 20 YEARS ago, many of which did good service in family from six to twelve years. The manufacturers making this wringer today is the same company that made it 20 years ago, and they claim they are making them better now than they were at that time, for they are using all fine Para rubber in the roll, which makes a better roll than was ever made before, as nothing in the world equals Para rubber for durability and toughness. Any roll in these wringers proving defective within FIVE YEARS we will replace free of charge.

42771 **Improved Guarantee Wringer**, with wood frame, like above cut; length of roll, 10 inches; diameter, 1¾ inches. This ringer has the old-fashioned elastic rubber roll. Price, each...$4.00

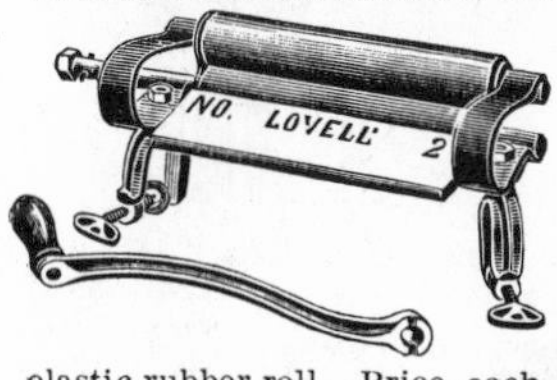

42772 **Lovell Guarantee Iron Frame Wringer**, with wood apron clothes guide, which carries the clothes over the edge of the tub: length of roll, 10 inches; diameter, 1¾ in. This wringer has the old-fashioned elastic rubber roll. Price, each.................................$3.25

Mrs. Potts' Sad Irons.

This cut represents a full set of three irons one stand and one detachable walnut handle.

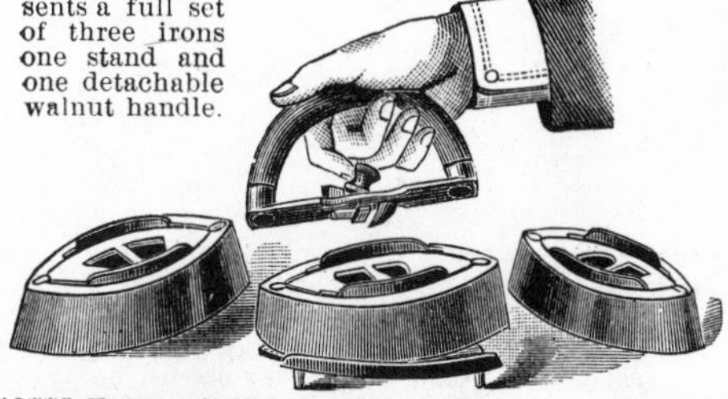

42775 Extra polished, No. 55: weight, per set, 15¾ lbs. (This price is subject to change of market without notice.)..............$0.65 Per set.
42776 Nickel plated, No. 50. (This price is subject to the change of market without notice.).... .70
42778 Extra handles for Mrs. Potts' Irons:
Japanned. Price, each..................................... .15
Tinned. " " .... .20
Iron Stands.. .05
42779 Mrs. Potts' Nickel Plated Smoothing Iron, perforated handle, No. 70; weight, each, 5¾ lbs. Each ....$0.35. Per dozen.......... 3.90

Chinese Polisher.

42780 Mrs. Potts' Chinese Polishing Iron, with detachable handle; all round edges, nickel plated. No. 80, 4½ lbs. Each...................$0.65
No. 82, 3 lbs. Each.. .50

The Ideal Sad Iron.

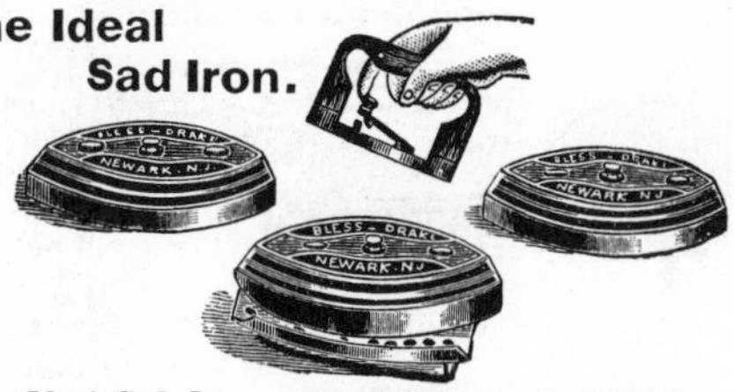

The Ideal Sad Iron, with detachable handle; three irons, one handle and one stand to a set. The Ideal has the strongest handle of any made and will hold tighter, and is very much easier on the hands than any shape yet made; weight, per set, 16 lbs. Per set.
42783 The Ideal Sad Iron, double pointed, plain, polished...$0.75
42784 The Ideal Sad Iron, double pointed, nickel plated... .80
42785 Extra Handles for Ideal Sad Irons........ .25
Iron Stands.. .05

Sad Iron Stands.

42788 Sad Iron Stands, bronzed iron.
Each $0.05
Per dozen.. 54

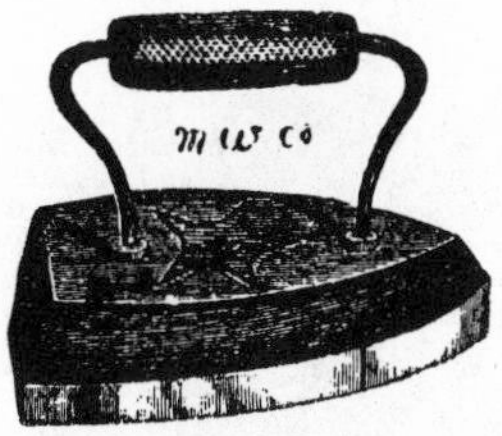

Common Sad Irons.

42790 Extra polished, from 5 to 9 pounds each.
Per lb.........$0.02½

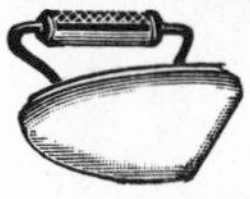

Laundry Irons.

42792 Laundry Irons, round edge, nickel plated; weight, 5 and 6 lbs.
Each.........................$0.55 $0.58
Per dozen............. 6.00 6.25

Troy Polishing Irons.

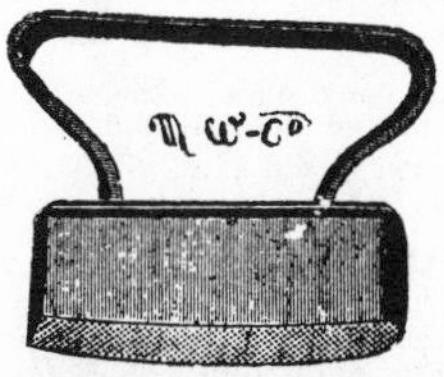

42793 Troy Polishing Iron, extra polished, perforated bottom, 4 lbs.
Each..............$0.42
42794 Nickel Plated, plain bottom
Each...............$0.50

Charcoal Irons.

42797 Charcoal or Self-Heating Irons, wood handle, with shield, plain polished, one flue. Weight, 6½ lbs.
Each $0.75
Per dozen.. .... 7.90
42798 Tailor's Charcoal Iron, double flue, adjustable chimney. Wt. 17 lbs.
Price, each.... ..$2.50

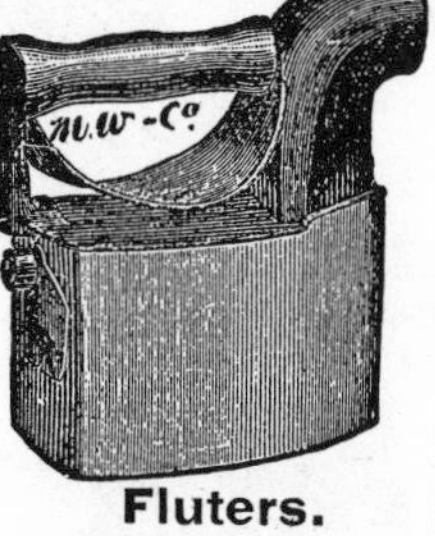

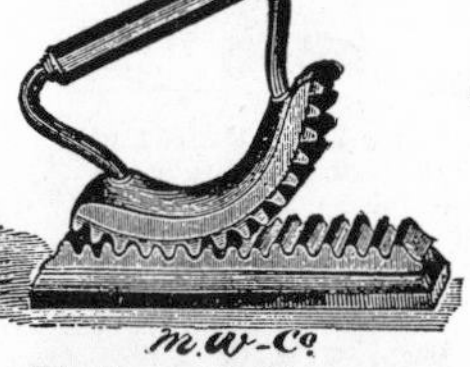

Fluters.

42803 Geneva Hand Fluters, white metal base, with metal rocker: weight, 4¾ pounds.
Each $0.80

Tailors' Goose.

42805 Tailor's' goose, extra polished; weighs 16, 18, 20 and 22 pounds. Per pound......$0.04

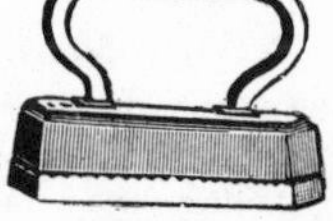

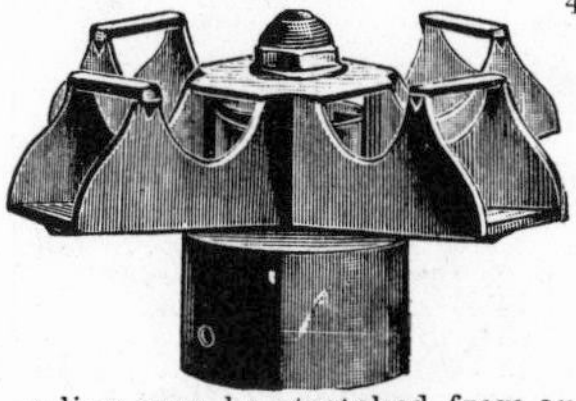

42810 Clothes Line Reels, japanned iron, for making a clothes dryer; has socket that fits over and is fastened on to end of post standing upright on the ground; has places in top for 4 rails or bars. When in position a line may be stretched from one end to the other in continuous rows to the outer end of bars, thereby affording a great deal of drying surface in as compact a form as possible. No bars or posts are furnished. Weight, 13¼ lbs.
Price of reel only $0.55
Per dozen 5.94

Line Cleat.

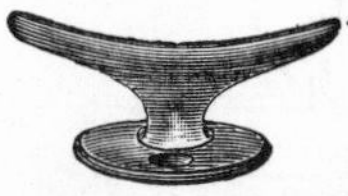

42815 Line Cleats. Length from tip to tip of horn, 2 in japanned. Each .... .03
Per dozen.............................$0.25
Galvanized. Each......... .05
Per dozen................... .25

Clothes Line Pulleys.

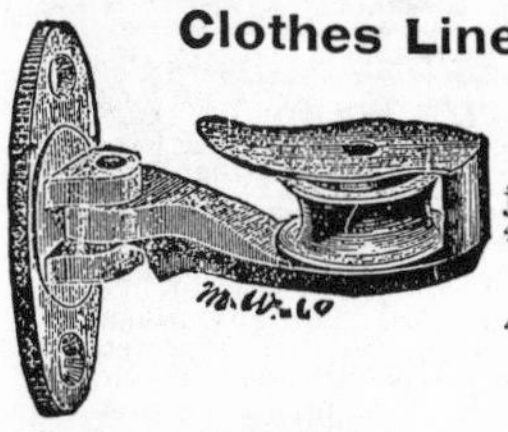

Clothes line pulleys, jointed on plate.
42817 Japanned.
Per dozen.......$0.54
Each........... .05
42818 Galvanized.
Per dozen....... .75
Each........... .07

Clothes Line Hooks.

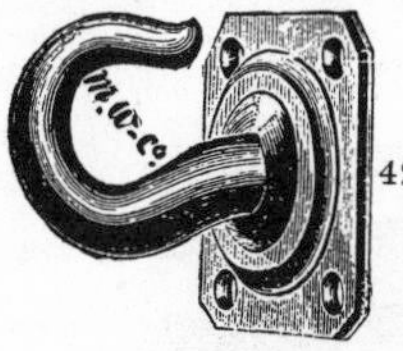

42820 Clothes Line Hooks, japanned, heavy. Weight. 6 ounces. Each.... ......$0.03
Per dozen.......... .30

Hammoch Hooks.

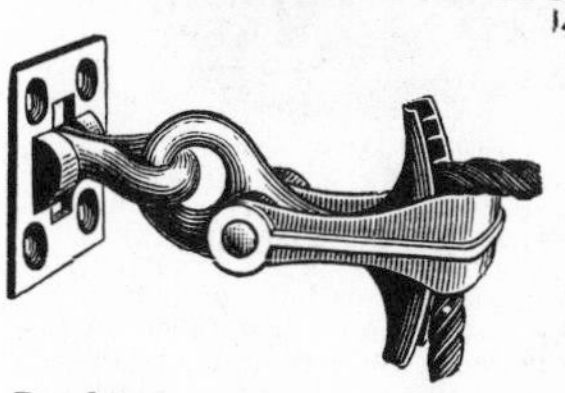

42823 Hammock Hook, a new pattern. The heavier the weight the more firmly it holds. No tying, no fastening. The hammock can be removed in an instant. Price, each, tinned with plate like cut.....$0.10
Per dozen.... ... 1.10

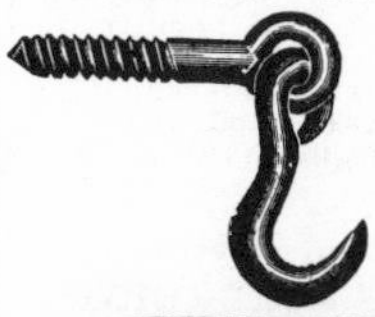

42826 Hammock Hook tinned to screw, 7-16 in.
Each $0.06
Per dozen.......... .... .65
Weight, 8 ounces.

Family Nail Box.

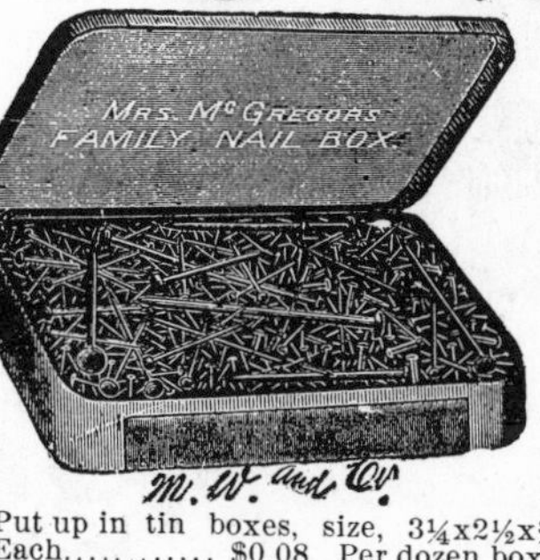

42828 Mrs. McGregor's Family Nail Box contains about 700 steel wire nails, assorted sizes, for repairing furniture, brackets, picture frames, in fact a nail for every purpose required in or about a house. Invaluable to housekeepers.
Put up in tin boxes, size, 3¼x2½x¾.
Each............ $0.08 Per dozen boxes........$0.85
Extra by mail, per box........ .. .. .10

Sand Paper.

Weight, 2 ounces per sheet
42830 Extra Flint Sand Paper, Nos. 00, 0. ½ 1 and 1½, 2. Per quire, 18c. Price, per sheet.....$0.01

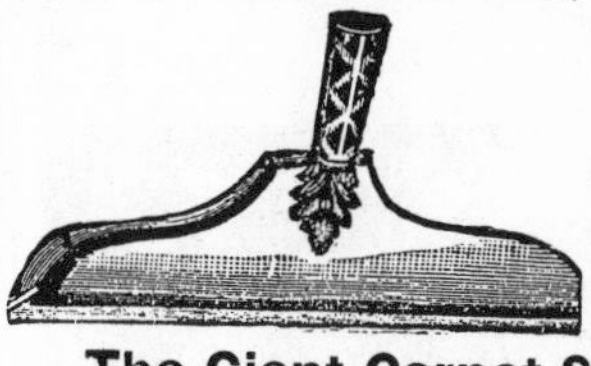

Rubber Scrapers.

For cleaning and drying floors and windows.
42833 12 inches wide, weight. 12 oz. Each...$0.30

The Giant Carpet Stretcher.

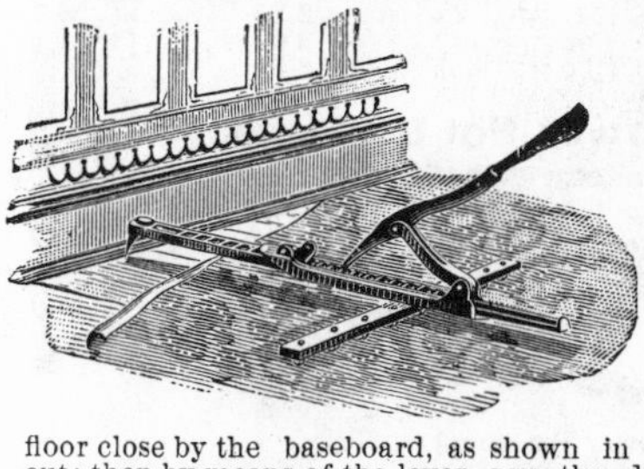

42835 Tack the carpet firmly at one corner, set teeth of the drawbar through the carpet, drive the hook into the floor close by the baseboard, as shown in the cut; then by means of the lever pry the draw bar forward until the carpet is sufficiently stretched, where the gravity drop will hold it until tacked. Set the stretcher at intervals until the carpet is laid. Weight, 1 lb. 11 oz.
Each ....$0.40 Per dozen..............$4.32

Carpet Sweepers.

42838 The Ward Carpet Sweeper, a superior machine made expressly for us. The advantages possessed over other makes: are first, a perfect friction which never wears out; second, the dust pans are easier opened, requiring no pressure, and remain open until thoroughly cleaned. Has a rubber band around the outside of case to protect furniture. The case is finished in antique oak, handsomely decorated. Price, each..$2.00

42840 Bissell's Grand Rapids is the most famous of the Bissells, generally accepted as the standard of the line. It contains the Bissell Broomaction—the only device invented which makes a sweeper self-adjusting to every kind of carpet. Its spring dumping device opens both pans by a single light pressure. It has our automatic reversible bail, which holds the sweeper always firmly on the carpet, rubber frictions, rubber furniture protector, and our pure bristle everlasting brush. The cases are made of popular woods handsomely hand decorated. The construction is as perfect as care and skill can make it. Each sweeper is carefully tested and fully guaranteed. Weight, 6 lb. Price, each........$2 35
Per dozen........ ....,, ...24.00

Shelf Brackets.

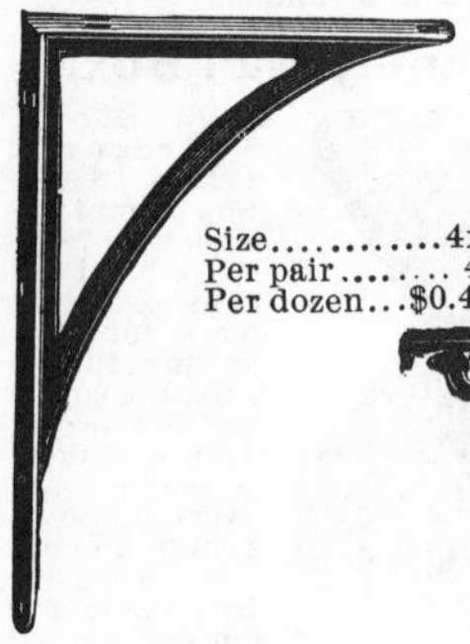

42842 Japanned Iron Shelf Bracket, plain,

Size	4x5	6x8	7x9	8x10
Per pair	4c	10c.	11c.	12c.
Per dozen	$0.44	$1.08	$1.19	$1.30

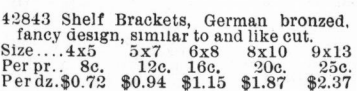

42843 Shelf Brackets, German bronzed, fancy design, similar to and like cut.

Size	4x5	5x7	6x8	8x10	9x13
Per pr.	8c.	12c.	16c.	20c.	25c.
Per dz.	$0.72	$0.94	$1.15	$1.87	$2.37

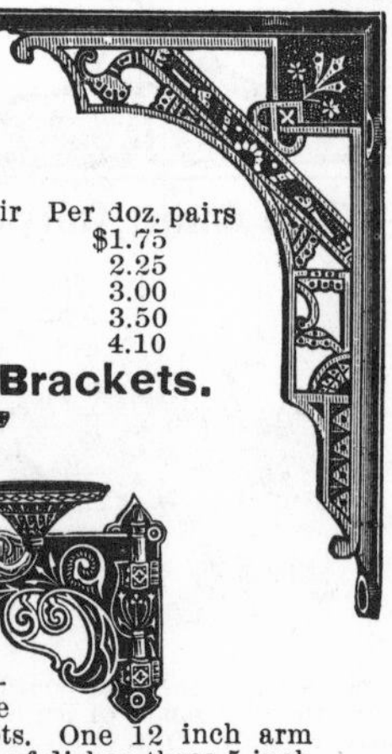

42845 Geneva Bronzed Shelf Brackets, complete with screws .

Size	Weight.	Per pair	Per doz. pairs
4x5 in.	11 oz.	$0.18	$1.75
5x7 in.	1¼ lbs.	.22	2.25
6x8 in.	1 lb. 7 oz.	.32	3.00
7x9 in.	1 lb. 13 oz.	.35	3.50
8x10 in.	2 lb. 5 oz.	.38	4.10

Flower Pot Brackets.

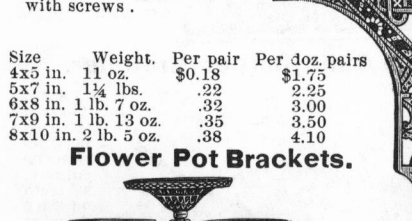

42850 Flower Pot Brackets, iron antique verde finish; will hold four pots. One 12 inch arm and two 6-inch; diameter of dishes, three 5-inch and one 5½ inch. Weight, 5 lbs.
Price each, complete. 70c. Per dozen.........$7.56
For flower pots see Index

Flower Pot Brackets—Continued.

42851 Japanned iron, 5-inch arm shelf, 4 inches in diameter Weight,12. oz.
Each $0.10
Per dz. 1.00

42852 Dark Antique, bronzed iron, 12-inch arm, 1 5½ inch shelf and one 4-inch shelf; weight, 25 oz.
Each $0.35
Per doz..... 4.00

Match Safes.

42855 Fry Pan Match Safe, a very unique receptacle for matches, to hang on wall; made of brass. Fry Pan enameled black egg and handle of fry pan oxidized silver finish. Price, each $0.08
Per Dz. 87

42856— Owl Match Safe made of brass oxidized silver finish. Price, each...7c. Per dz 75c.

Household Tool.

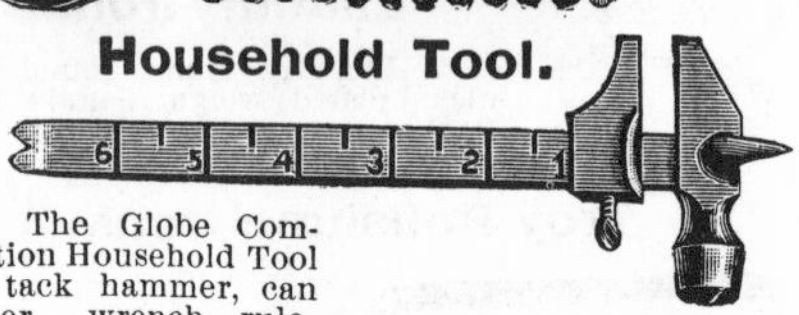

42858 The Globe Combination Household Tool is a tack hammer, can opener, wrench, rule, square, caliper, box opener, tack claw, stove lifter and ice pick. Full nickeled and polished.
Price, each............$0.18 Per dozen..........$1.88
Per gross...18.75

Glass Cutters.

42872 Revolving Wheel Glass Cutter, Regular 25c cutter.
Price, each $0.08
Per dozen.. .87

42874 Glaziers' Diamonds; genuine diamond, at $4, $5 and $7 each, according to size and quality.

42875 Combination Glass Cutter, Putty Knife and Glazier's Point Driver. This tool embraces a glazier's kit in itself. The ease with which it can be used with a straight edge insures a better cut and adds life to the wheel. Price, each.....$0.05
Per dozen... .54

Metal Polish.

42880 Putz's Pomade Metal Polish. A thick red paste, which when applied to any polished surface and rubbed off will leave a luster obtained in no other way. Will take off dirt, grease or tarnish quicker than any known substance.
Per box..$0.05

Babbitt Metal and Solder.

	Per lb.
42883 Babbitt Metal	$0.25
42884 Babbitt Metal, hard	.27
42885 Babbitt Metal, No. 1, tin, copper, antimony and lead	.12
42886 Babbitt Metal, No. 2, tin copper, antimony and lead	.14
42887 Tinners' Solder in 1¼ lb. bars, per lb	.18
42888 Plumbers' Solder in 1¼ lb. bars, per lb	.16
42889 Sheet Lead, 6¼ cents per lb., any thickness	

Thickness... ....1-32 1-25 1-16 ⅛ 3-16 ¼
42890 Bar Tin, per lb ....28c.
As the price of babbitt metal and solder are constantly changing, we cannot guarantee above prices, but will at all times make the lowest prices the market affords.

Soldering Coppers.

42898 Soldering Coppers, square points, for common use. Weight, per pair.1½   2   3   4   5   6   8 lbs.
Price, each.......... 16c. 25c.28c,38c.48c.58c. 78c.
42899 Price, per pair. 32c.45c.52c.75c.95c.1.15 1.52
Owing to the fluctuations of the copper market we can not guarantee the above prices of soldering coppers for the season, but will make the lowest prices at all times.

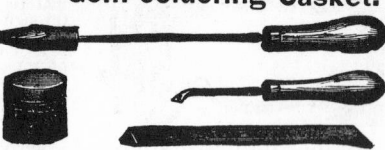

42900 Soldering Copper Handles, basswood, wire ferrules. Each...... $0.03
Per dozen.. 25

Gem Soldering Casket.

42904 The Gem Soldering Casket. The above useful article is intended for family use, also farmers, mechanics and every one using tin, brass or copper ware. The casket contains soldering iron, scraper, large bar of solder, box of soldering salts and full directions all inclosed in a neat wooden box with sliding cover, 1 lb. Each........ .... $0.70
42905 The Gem Soldering Casket, containing soldering iron, scraper and large bar of solder. This casket is the same as 42910, except that the tools are not as nicely finished. Each... .... $0.35

Electric Soldering Plate.

42910 It mends copper, lead brass pipe, tinware, electric wire, in fact every thing that solder will mend. Always ready for use; no acid, no soldering iron required. Full directions come with each sheet of the Electric Soldering Plate. Guaranteed to do the work if directions are followed. Each plate contains 192 quarter inch squares, which is equal to over $5.00 at only 5c a mend. Price, each........$0.07
Postage.....................02
Price, per 100 sheets....... 6.50
The cut shows the manner of mending a leak in a tea pot.

Cork Screws.

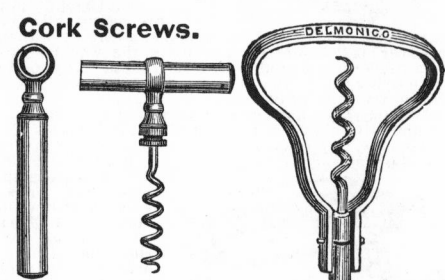

42917 Cork Screws, folding. Weight, 2 oz.
Each $0.10
Per dozen... 1.10
42918 Pocket Cork Screw, nickel plated. Weight, 2 ounces. Each........ .... .12
Per dozen.. 1.30

42920 Cork Screw, extra heavy hand forged steel. This is an excellent cork screw, and can be relied upon every time. While the price is higher than some others, any one using a cork screw much will appreciate its worth. Weight, 5 oz. Each............................. .20

The Hawkeye Corn Huskers.

42928 The Hawkeye Corn Husker, the best and cheapest; is provided with strap adjusted to any size hand ready for use.
Price, each..........$0.05. Per dozen.........$0.54

Corn Huskers—Continued.

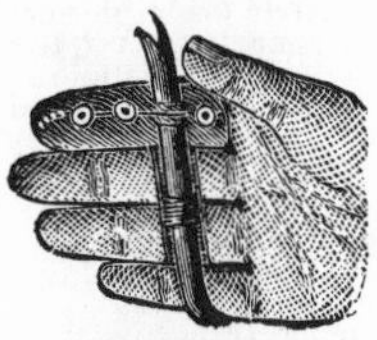

42929 The Hawkeye Corn Husker, with finger cot protector for forefinger. Can be worn on bare hand or over glove. Made of hogskin. Price, each, complete with husker.......$0.08
Per dozen.......... .87

The Universal Corn Huskers.

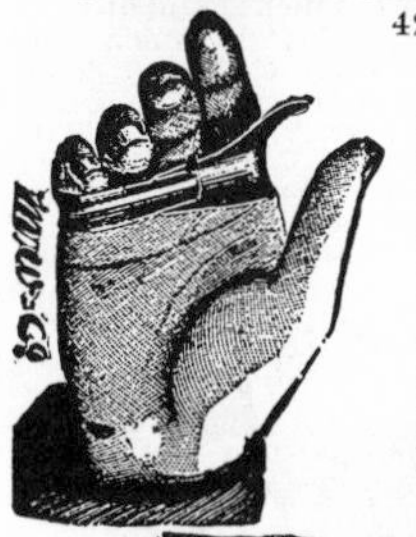

42930 The New Universal Corn Husker has concave hooks, which project beyond the palm of the hand; just the right position for rapid work. It is made entirely of steel, nickel plated, and will not wear out. It is adjustable and will fit any hand. It may be worn over gloves or mittens. All well made and superior to anything of the kind ever before offered; weight, 4 oz. Each, right hand........$0.10
Per dozen.............. 1.08

See Index for husking gloves

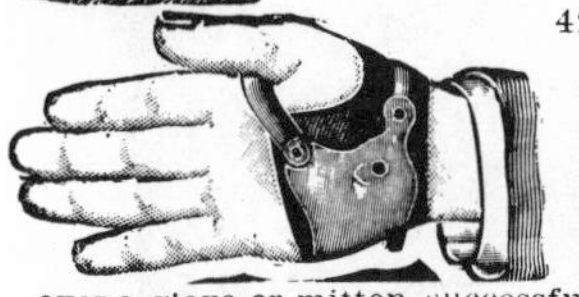

42931 **The Standard Corn Husker.** Superior to any husker in the market, for you can husk more corn; you can husk corn more easily. You will never get a sore hand. You can use it over a glove or mitten successfully, and the user has full use of every joint in the hand. A trial of the husker will convince you.... Price, each $0.40
Per dozen.......... 3.78

The Perkins Boss Husker.

The Perkins' Boss Husker. This is a new pattern, and is without question the finest finished and most complete and convenient husker in the market. It is forged from the finest steel, nickel plated, brass trimmed with strappings of the best yellow calf.

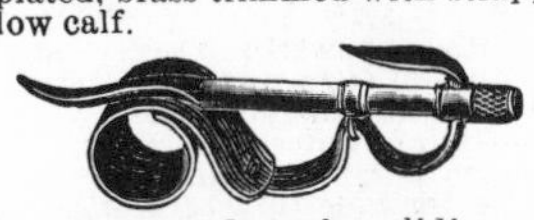

42932 Perkins' No. E Husker is strapped so that it can be worn with gloves or bare hand; the slack is adjusted by means of clamp and nut, has sliding center sleeve, can be adjusted to light or heavy glove.
Each ....$0.25 Per dozen.............$2.70

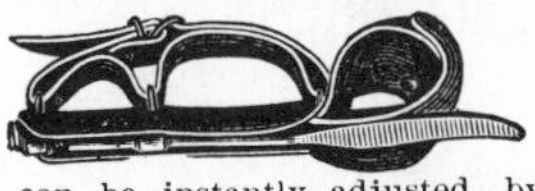

42933 Perkins' B Husker, is double strap buckle husker with patent detachable finger guard and hand pin; slack can be instantly adjusted by tightening the buckle. Each.. ..$0.30 Per dozen $3.25

Sacking Needles.

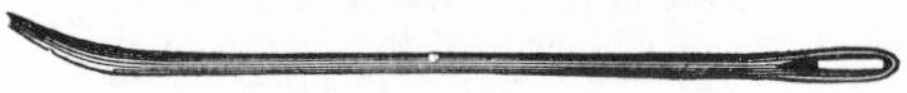

42944 Sacking Needles, 4, 4½, 5, 5½ inches in length. Price, each, any size..............$0.03
Per dozen .33

42945 Sail Needles, Best English.

Length, inches	2½	2⅝	2¾	3
Each	$0.02	$0.02	$0.02	$0.02
Per dozen	.18	.19	.20	.22

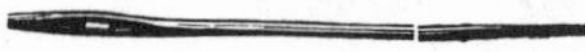

42946 Best English Upholsterers' Needles, double point.

Length, inches	6	8	10	12	14	16
Each	$0.06	.07	.08	.09	.10	.10
Per dozen	.65	.75	.87	.98	1.08	1.08

42947 Best English Mattress Needles, single point.

Length	6	7	8	9	10	12	14	16
Each	$0.03	.04	.05	.06	.07	.08	.09	.10
Dozen	.33	.44	.54	.65	.76	.87	.98	1.00

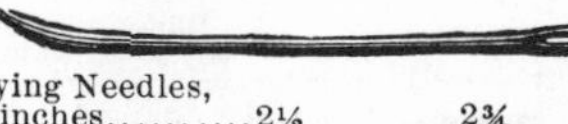

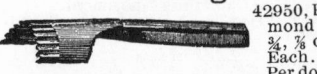

42948 Spaying Needles,

Length, inches	2½	2¾	3
Each	$0.02	$0.02	$0.02
Per dozen	.22	.22	.22

Pinking Irons.

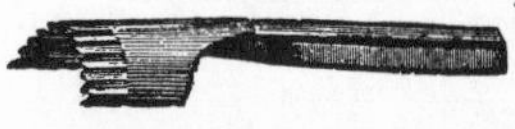

42950, Pinking Iron diamond tooth, ⅜, ½, ⅝, ¾, ⅞ or 1 inch.
Each.............$0.06
Per doz., assorted. .65

Lamp Trimmers.

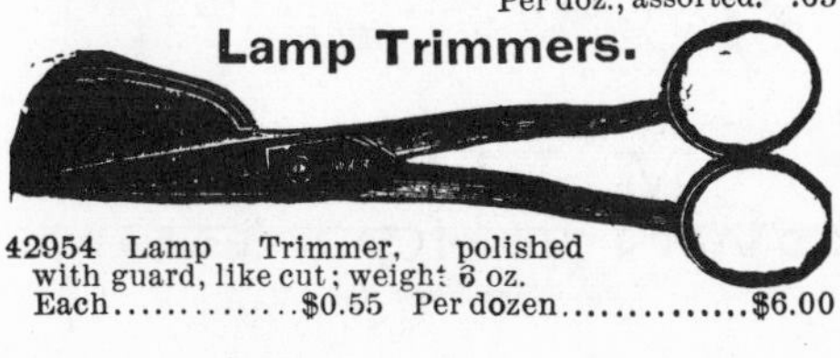

42954 Lamp Trimmer, polished with guard, like cut; weight 6 oz.
Each..............$0.55 Per dozen..............$6.00

Foot Scrapers.

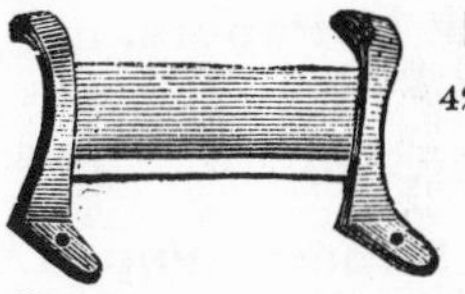

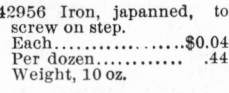

42956 Iron, japanned, to screw on step.
Each..................$0.04
Per dozen............ .44
Weight, 10 oz.

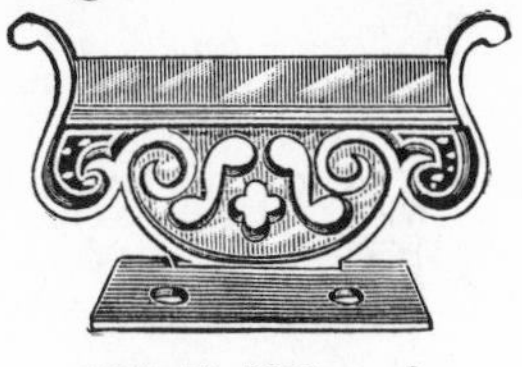

42958 Foot Scraper, fancy pattern, japanned iron.
Each...........$0.08
Per dozen..... .87

Well Wheels.

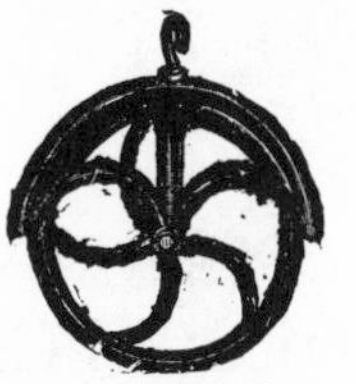

Weight, 3 to 6 lbs

42960 Well Wheels, japanned.

Diameter	8 in.	10 in.	12 in
Each	20c.	25c.	30c.
Per doz	$2.16	$2.70	$3.24

Well Wheel Hooks and Chains.

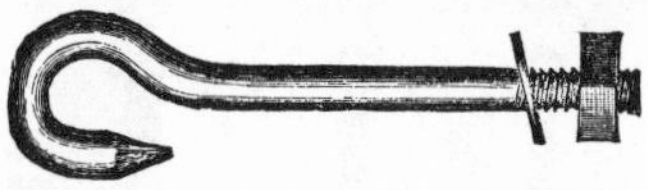

42962 Well Wheel Hooks, ⅜-inch wrought iron, length, 6½ inches, with screw and nut. Each.. $0.07
Per dozen.......... .75
42963 Well Chains, with hook and ring; length, 2 feet. Each....... $0.10 Per doz.............. 1.00

Ladder Sockets.

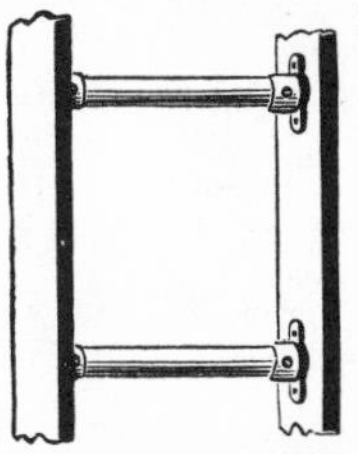

42965 Ladder Sockets, made of iron. A useful invention whereby a ladder may be made half the usual weight and of equal strength. To make a ladder with these sockets make the rounds of equal length, fitted in and wedged, then screw the socket to the side pieces. A broken round may be replaced without taking the ladder apart. Diameter of hole, 1 inch.
Per dozen.................$0.25
Per 100........ 1.50
Weight, per 100, about 14 lbs.

Iron Storm Threshold.

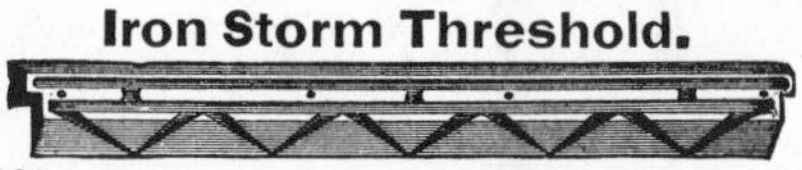

42968—
No matter how exposed your doors may be, or how severe the rain may beat against them, no rain will beat under them if you use Wood's Iron Storm Threshold.
From 30 to 36 inches, inclusive, are cast in one piece; above 36 inches the sizes are made with a center piece 30 inches in length and ends to make any size desired.

Sizes	30	32	34	36 in.
Price, each	$0.90	$0.96	$1.00	$1.10
Sizes	38	40		
Price, each	$1.52	$1.60		

Weights range from 7 pounds up, according to size.

Weather Strips.

42970 All rubber, no wood, no sawing. Flexible. Put up in rolls of 50 feet. Any one can apply them with tack hammer and shears.

Width.	Per foot.
⅜ inch, for sides of windows	$0.01½
½ inch, for sides of windows and doors	.02
¾ inch, for sides and bottoms of doors	.02¼
1 inch, for bottoms of heavy doors	.03

[Order any quantity you wish.

Bird Cage Springs.

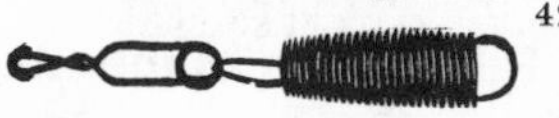

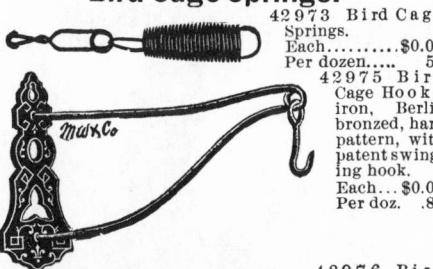

42973 Bird Cage Springs.
Each.........$0.05
Per dozen..... 54

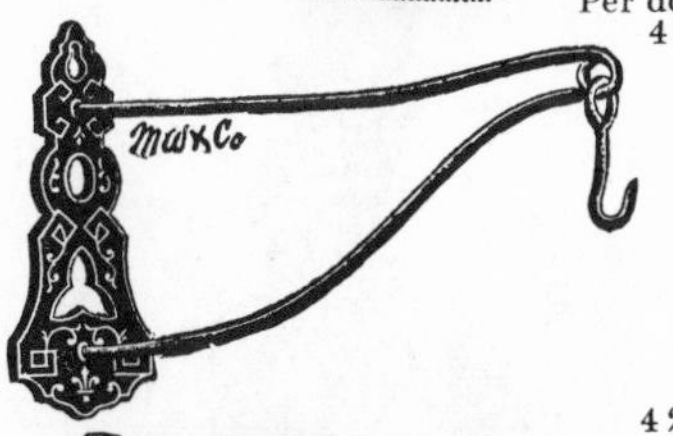

42975 Bird Cage Hooks, iron, Berlin bronzed, harp pattern, with patent swinging hook.
Each...$0.08
Per doz. .87

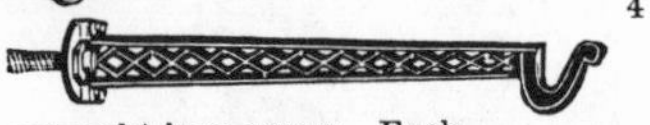

42976 Bird Cage Hooks, iron Berlin bronzed, with wrought iron screw. Each..............$0.04
Per dozen... .44

42977—Swinging Bird Cage or Hanging Basket Hook. 10 inches, iron, Kahala bronzed, a very pretty pattern. Each.......$0.10
Per dozen...... 1.08

Spool Wire.

42981 Shellac Coated Soft Copper Wire on Spools.

Gauge of Wire	18	20	22	32
Per Spool of 1 lb	$0.35	$0.38	$0.40	$0.65

42982 Annealed Shellaced Steel Wire on spools.

Gauge of wire	16	17	18	19	20
For spool of 1 lb	$0.09	$0.10	$0.11	$0.12	$0.13

42983 Soft Brass Wire, shellac coated, on spools.

Gauge of wire,	16	17	18	19	20
Per spool of 1 lb.	$0.28	$0.28	$0.28	$0.30	$0.30

42984 Brass Spring Wire, shellac coated on spools.

Gauge of wire,	16	17	18	19	20
Per spool of 1 lb	$0.32	$0.32	$0.32	$0.33	$0.33

Wire Gauges.

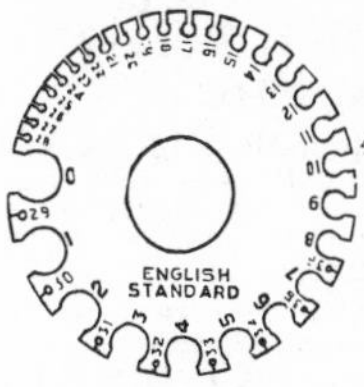

42985 Wire Gauge, English Standard Round Polished Cast Steel. The No. 1 will gauge wire from No. 0 to No. 36. The No. 2 from No. 6 to 36.
Each.
No. 1.....................$1.50
No. 2..................... .95

Bedstead Irons.

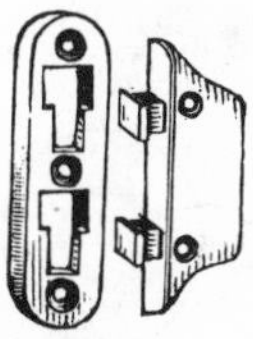

42990 Bedstead Irons double hook; Weight, per set, 2 lbs., 6 oz. and 4 lbs.

Size	4½ in.	6 in.
Per set	$0.15	$0.25
Per doz. sets	1.62	2.70

Bed Casters.

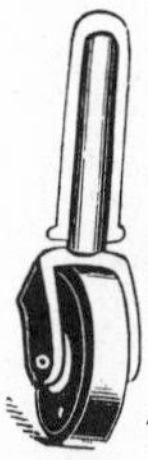

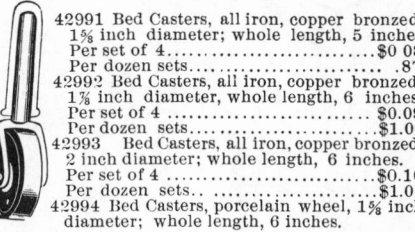

42991 Bed Casters, all iron, copper bronzed 1⅝ inch diameter; whole length, 5 inches
Per set of 4..........................$0 08
Per dozen sets.......... .87
42992 Bed Casters, all iron, copper bronzed, 1⅞ inch diameter, whole length, 6 inches.
Per set of 4 ....$0.09
Per dozen sets.....................$1.00
42993 Bed Casters, all iron, copper bronzed, 2 inch diameter; whole length, 6 inches.
Per set of 4 ....$0.10
Per dozen sets.. ....$1.08
42994 Bed Casters, porcelain wheel, 1⅝ inch diameter; whole length, 6 inches.
Per set of 4 ....$0.09
Per dozen sets............ .98
42995 Bed Casters, porcelain wheel, 2 inch diameter
Per set of 4 ....$0.10
Per dozen sets.............. 1.08
42996 Bed Casters, apple wood wheel, 2 inch diameter
Per set of 4 ....$0.10
Per dozen sets.................... 1.08

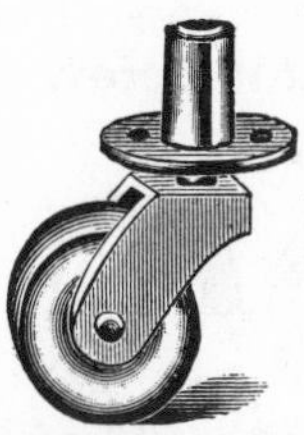

42997 Plate Casters, all iron, copper bronzed, ⅞ inch wheel, depth of socket, ⅝ inch; whole length, 2 inch.
Per set of 4..... ....$0.06
Per dozen sets.................$0.65
42998 Plate casters, all iron, copper bronzed, 1 inch wheel, depth of socket ¾ inch; whole length, 2¼ inches.
Per set of 4..................$0.06
Per dozen sets.......... .65

42999 Plate Casters, porcelain wheel, diameter of wheel, ⅞ in., depth of socket, ⅝ inch; whole length, 2 in.
Per set of 4... ....$0.06
Per dozen sets........... .65
43000 Plate Casters, porcelain wheel, diameter of wheel, 1 inch: depth of socket, ¾ inch; whole length, 2¼ in. Per set... .... .07
Per dozen sets.......... .75

Payson Anti-Friction Casters.

This Caster revolves upon a series of steel rollers or disks, placed in an annular chamber, and carries the weight outside the center of the main wheel. This gives an even bearing upon the circle of disks and relieves all friction upon the pivot. They have been thoroughly tested in the past five years on all classes of work, and are pronounced by all who have used them to be the best caster ever made.

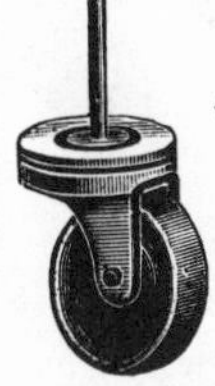

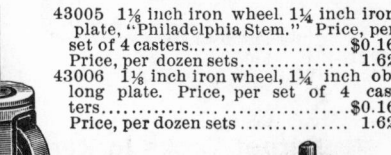

43005 1⅛ inch iron wheel. 1¼ inch iron plate, "Philadelphia Stem." Price, per set of 4 casters.................$0.16
Price, per dozen sets........ 1.62
43006 1⅛ inch iron wheel, 1¼ inch oblong plate. Price, per set of 4 casters..................$0.16
Price, per dozen sets 1.62

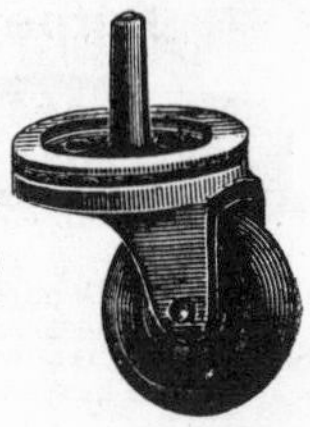

43007 1⅝ inch iron wheel, common stem, 1⅝ inch plate.
Price, per set of 4 casters....$0.22
Price, per dozen sets......... 2.34

Casters—Continued.

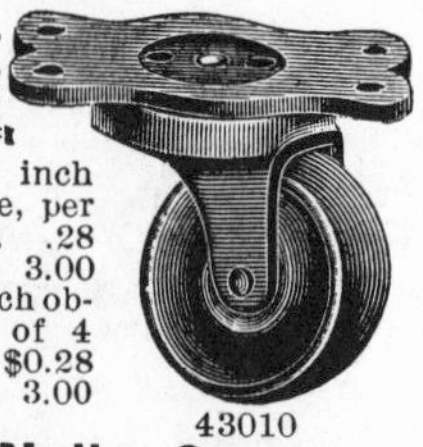

43010

43008 1⅜ inch iron wheel, 1⅝ inch oblong plate. Price, per set of 4 casters....$0.22
Price, per dozen sets. 2.34

43009 1⅝ inch wheel, 1⅞ inch plate, common stem. Price, per set of 4 casters.............. .28
Price per dozen sets........ 3.00

43010 1⅜ inch wheel, 1⅞ inch oblong plate. Price per set of 4 casters......................$0.28
Price per dozen sets........ 3.00

Carpet Tacks, Nails, Screw Hooks, Eyes, Etc.

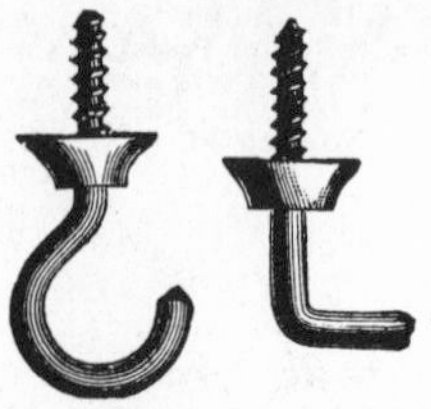

For quotations of iron and steel nails, wire nails, etc., etc., see our Grocery List, published monthly (copy sent free).

43014 Brass Screw Hooks, for bangle boards.

Size	½ in.	⅝ in.	¾ in.
Per doz.	4c.	5c.	6c.

43015 Brass Cup Hooks,

Size,	⅝ in.	¾ in.	⅞ in.	1 in.
Pr dz	6c.	7c.	8c.	9c.

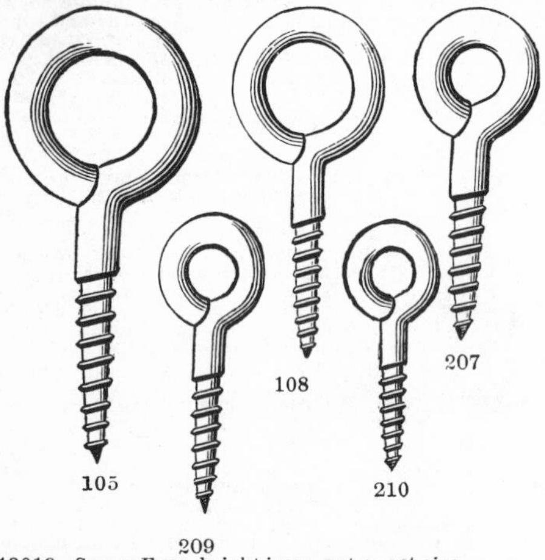

43019 Screw Eyes, bright iron; cut exact size.

Nos	105	108	207	209	210
Per doz	5c.	5c	5c.	3c.	3c.
Per gross	30c.	25c	25c.	17c.	15c.

Bright Iron Wire Blunt Screw Hooks.

Order No. 43020.

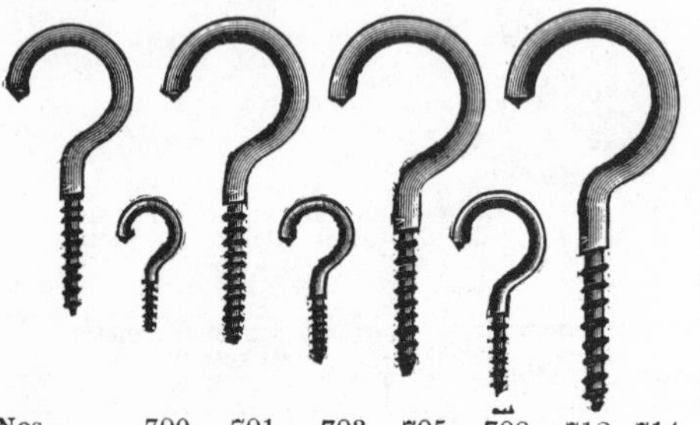

Nos.	700	701	703	705	708	712	714
Size of wire	0	1	3	5	8	12	14
Length	4 in.	3⅞ in	3 in.	2⅞ in.	2¼ in.	1⅝ in.	1½ in.
Each	$0.02	$0.02	$0.02	$0.02	$0.02	$0.02	$0.02
Dozen	.18	.16	.12	.10	.08	.05	.02
Gross	1.44	1.20	.84	.60	.50	.25	.25

Bright Wire Screw Hooks.

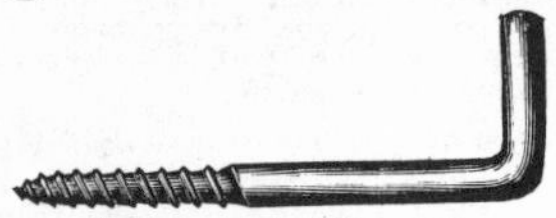

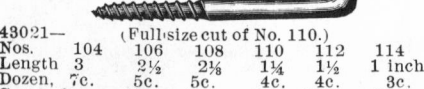

43021— (Full size cut of No. 110.)

Nos.	104	106	108	110	112	114
Length	3	2½	2⅛	1¼	1½	1 inch
Dozen,	7c.	5c.	5c.	4c.	4c.	3c.
Gross	67c.	45c.	42c.	25c.	22c.	20c.

Carpet Tacks in Kegs.

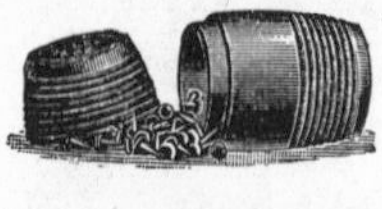

43022 Put up in neat wooden kegs, which when empty can be used for a variety of purposes. We can furnish only two sizes put up in this way about 4 ounces of tacks in a keg.

Sizes, 8 and 10 ounces. Polished, per keg $0.04
Per dozen kegs.. .40
Sizes, 8 and 10 ounces. Tinned, per keg.......... .05
Per dozen kegs.. .50

Carpet Tacks in Papers.

(Polished.)

43023 100 tacks in each paper.

Ounce	4	6	8	1(	12
Length	7/16	8/16	9/16	10/16	11/16 inch.
Per paper	$0.02	.02	.03	.03	.03
Per doz. paper	.18	.20	.22	.26	.28

Carpet Tacks in Papers (tinned.)

43024 100 tacks in each paper.

Ounce	4	6	8	10	12
Length	7/16	8/16	9/16	10/16	11/16 inch.
Per paper	$0.02	.02	03	.03	.04
Per doz. papers.	.20	.22	.26	.30	.35

Sweeds' Iron Cut Tacks (in bulk.)

43025 In 25 pound boxes. We do not sell less than 25 pounds under any circumstances.

Ounce..	2	2½	3	4	6	8	10	12	14	16
Per lb.	$0 24	.23	.22	.20	.17	.15	.14	.14	.13	.13

See Grocery List for Market prices on Glass and Nails.

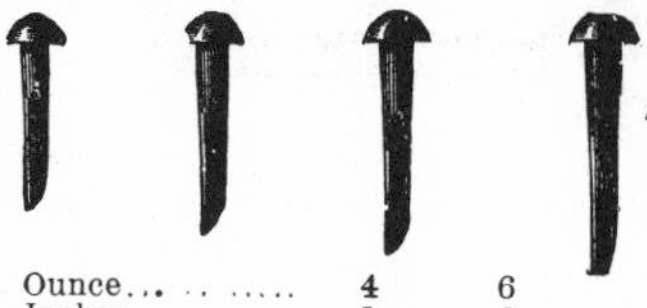

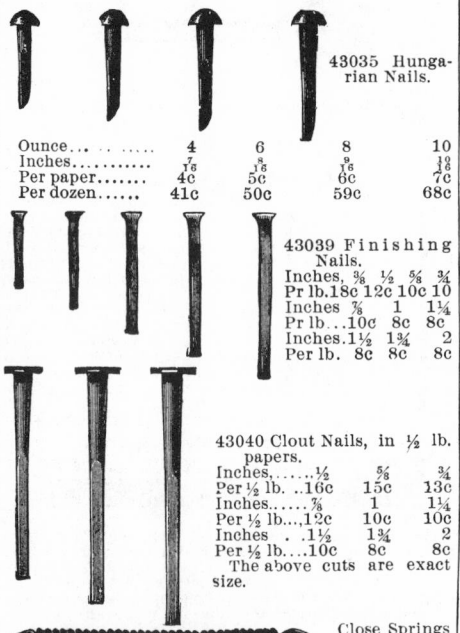

43035 Hungarian Nails.

Ounce	4	6	8	10
Inches	7/16	8/16	9/16	10/16
Per paper	4c	5c	6c	7c
Per dozen	41c	50c	59c	68c

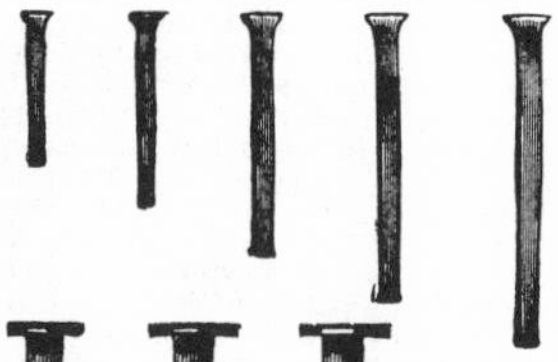

43039 Finishing Nails.

Inches,	⅜	½	⅝	¾
Pr lb.	18c	12c	10c	10

Inches	⅞	1	1¼
Pr lb...	10c	8c	8c
Inches.	1½	1¾	2
Per lb.	8c	8c	8c

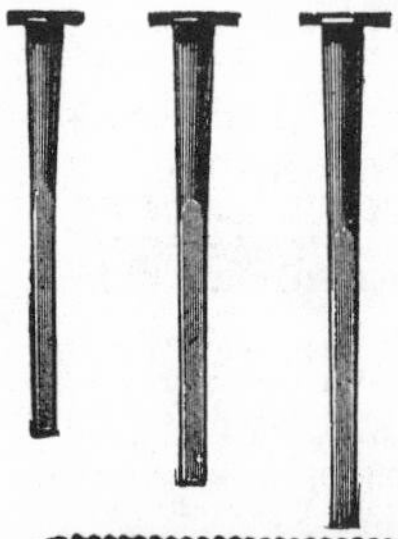

43040 Clout Nails, in ½ lb. papers.

Inches,	½	⅝	¾
Per ½ lb.	16c	15c	13c
Inches	⅞	1	1¼
Per ½ lb.	12c	10c	10c
Inches	1½	1¾	2
Per ½ lb.	10c	8c	8c

The above cuts are exact size.

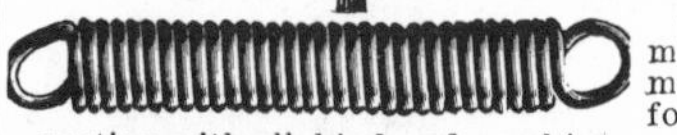

Close Springs made of Bessemer steel wire for use in connection with all kinds of machinery, cannot be furnished any other length or sizes. These springs when stretched half their length will pull: ¼ in., 4 lbs.; ⅝ in., 8 lbs.; ½ in., 12 lbs.

43047 ¼ INCH DIAMETER.

Length	2	3	4	5 inches.
Price, each	3c	4c	4c	5c
Per dozen	33c	44c	44c	54c

43048 ⅜ INCH DIAMETER.

Length	3	4	6	8 inches.
Price, each	3c	4c	5c	7c
Per dozen	33c	44c	54c	76c

43049 ½ INCH DIAMETER.

Length	4	6	8	10	12 inches.
Price, each	6c	7c	10c	12c	14c
Per dozen.	$0.65	$0.75	$1.08	$1.30	$1.52

The Aurora Punching Machine.

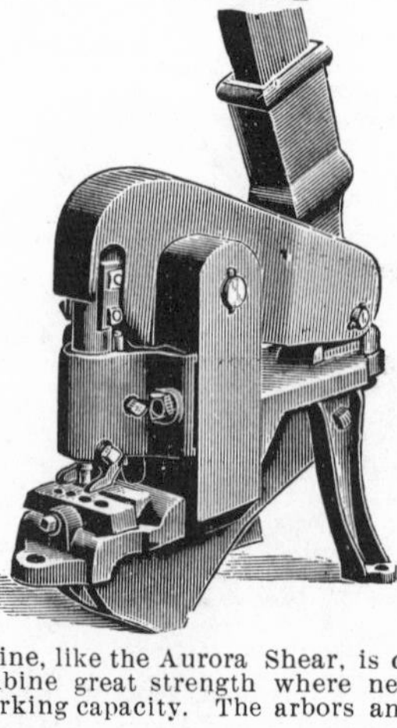

This machine, like the Aurora Shear, is constructed so as to combine great strength where needed, with immense working capacity. The arbors and plungers are of turned steel, and work in accurately bored and reamed bearings. The double eccentric principle enables one man to do easily what other machines require the strength of two men to accomplish. The die and punches are made from best imported tool steel, and tempered by an expert. All adjustments and changes can be accurately and quickly made.

TWO SIZES.

43050 No. 5.—Will punch ½ inch hole in ⅜ inch iron, and is furnished with four punches and dies—¼, 5/16, ⅜ and ½, all 1/32 full, unless otherwise ordered. Will punch 2¾ inches from edge of iron. Price, each.............................$24.00
No. 6.—Is furnished with same punches and dies as No. 5; will do the same work, and will punch six inches from edge of iron. Price, each 32.00
Price of punches and dies, per pair...............1.50
Square punches and dies, per pair................ 2.00

For special sizes of punches under ½ inch diameter add 20 per cent. to above price. For special sizes of punches over ½ inch diameter add 20 per cent. and $1.00 additional for extra caps to fit them. No punches made over ¾ inch diameter.

The Aurora Shear.

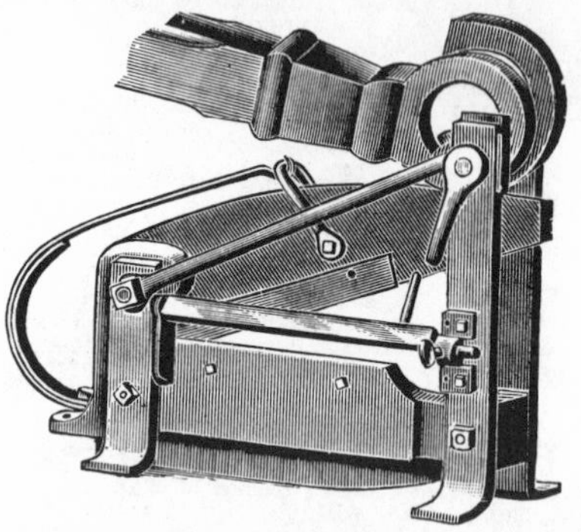

As now improved this is the best machine in the market. It not only works to the capacity given, but does its work easily and neatly.

It is compact, simple and very powerful. Every part, from the heavy steel castings of frame to the tool steel knives, is of first quality, and thoroughly tested.

1st. Double eccentric—Giving immense power and quick action for heavy bar cutting, and full length of stroke of knife for wide thin bars or plow shovels, the shift from one to the other requiring less than ten seconds time.

2d. Bar holder—Instantly adjusted to hold bar of any thickness, level and square with the machine, enabling one man to operate.

3d. Knives are in plain sight, so that operator can cut to a pencil mark exactly.

4th. All parts interchangeable—New knives and repairs, if ever needed, will fit perfectly.

5th. One man can do work below, at *one pulling down of lever*. Not necessary to hitch iron forward two or three times to complete work with *this* shear.

MADE IN FOUR SIZES, AS FOLLOWS:

43051 No. 3—Will cut cold iron, ½x1½, ⅜x3, ¼x4 and ⅝ round or square, and will trim corn-plow shovels. Price, each........................$18.80
No. 4—Will cut ½x3, ⅜x4, ¼x7 and ¾ round or square iron, and will trim corn-plow shovels. Price, each.. 20.00
No. 5—Will cut ⅝x2, ½x3, ⅜x5 and ⅞ round or square iron. Price, each.... .... 24.00
No. 8—This shear will do the same work as No. 3, and is especially constructed for trimming corn-plow shovels, where long points are required, It will trim both edges from the face side, without straightening the shovel. Price, each.. .... 20.00

EXTRAS

Knives for Shears Nos. 3, 4 and 8. Per pair. . 1.75
No. 5. Per pair.................................... 2.25

Forges.

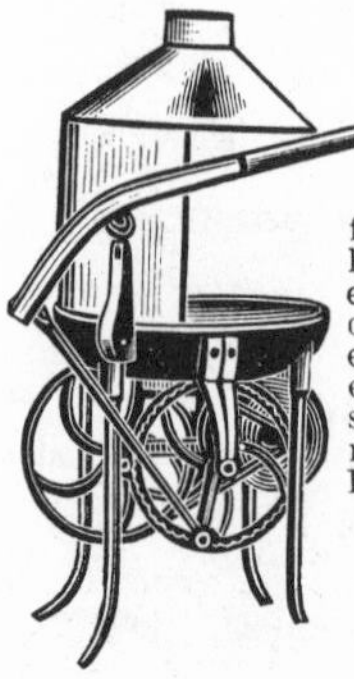

43054 Buffalo Forge. Height, 29 in.; fan, 10 in.; hearth, 21x27; weight, 140 lbs. This forge is guaranteed to produce a welding heat on 2¼ to 3 inch iron in from 5 to 10 minutes, and on heavier work if required. It is especially adapted for all kinds of tool work—machinists, plumbers, miners, marble works, millers, railroad repair shops, locksmiths, farmers, and repairs for manufacturers in general.
Price.......................$15.00

M. W. & Co.'s OWN SHOT GUN.

.... See Page 449 ....

Forges—Continued.

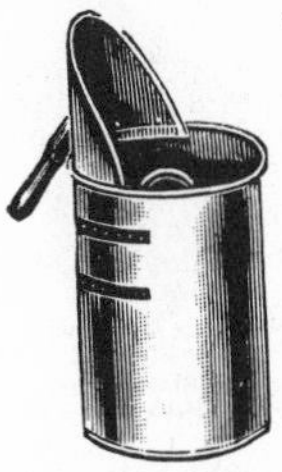

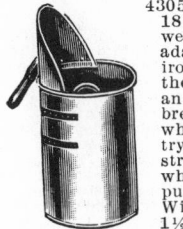

43056 Buffalo Forge. Size of hearth, 18 in. diameter; height, 32 in.; weight, 110 lbs. It is especially adapted for railroad repair work, iron bridge and tank builders. All the machinery being protected by an iron drum, there is no danger of breaking or getting out of order when transporting around the country. In short, it is entirely indestructible by the rough handling to which forges in use for the above purposes are usually subjected. Will produce a welding heat on iron 1½ inches in diameter in 5 minutes. Price $12.00

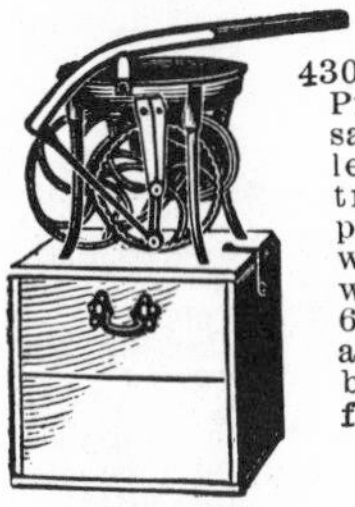

43057 The Champion Miners' and Prospectors' Forge. This forge is same size as 41384, but with shorter legs, making it more compact for transportation. It is of large capacity, allowing a great variety of work to be done in a short time and with but little labor; weighs but 60 pounds, with case. The case affords ample room for full line of blacksmith tools. Price, complete, forge and case $15.50

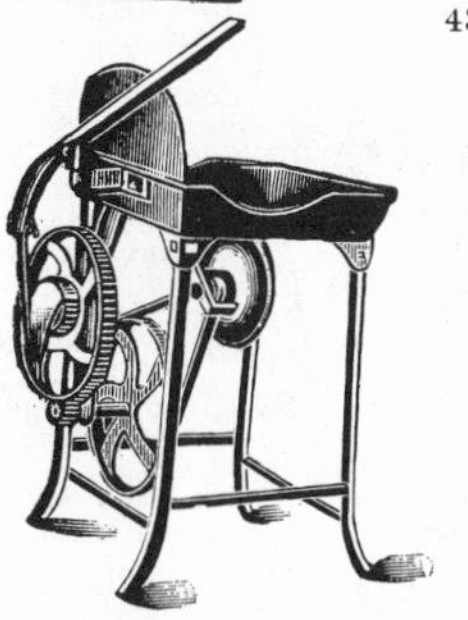

43060 Portable Forge. The same as cut, except the gear for driving the fan, which is tne ratchet principle used on all Champion forges. This is a decided improvement. By a special arrangement with the manufacturers, by taking a large quantity, we have secured a much lower price. This is now the cheapest good forge in the market. This is not the small forge sold with sets of cheap blacksmiths' tools suitable for farm work. A tire can be welded with it and it will do heavier work than the smaller one is capable of doing. Stands up high on legs, has 7 inch size of fire pan, 15x19; is 33 inches high and weighs 95 pounds. Each..$8.00

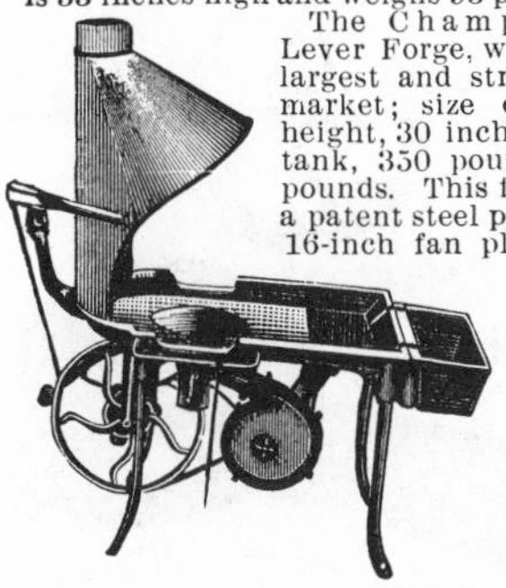

The Champion Blacksmith's Lever Forge, with half hood. The largest and strongest forge in the market; size of hearth, 32x45; height, 30 inches; weight, without tank, 350 pounds; with tank, 370 pounds. This forge is supplied with a patent steel pressure blower, with 16-inch fan placed in positions so that the blast discharges directly into the fire; elbow turns done away with. Is also provided with a coal box with sloped bottom that will hold one-half bushel of coal; it extends underneath the bottom of the hearth and is out of the way. This is a great convenience. This forge will heat a 4½-inch iron to a welding heat in 10 minutes. Price.

43063 Without tank......$19.00
43064 With tank......... 20.50

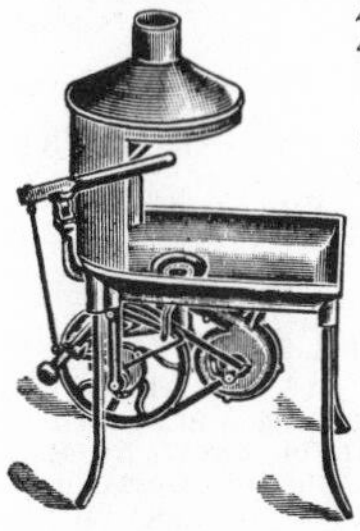

43065 The Champion No. 2 Lever Forge has 12-inch fan; size of hearth, 23x35; weight, 120 pounds. Guaranteed to produce a welding heat on 3-inch iron in five minutes; has a ball tuyere iron; nothing like it in the market for the money. Price, each, without hood $12.50

43066 With hood, like cut......................$14.40

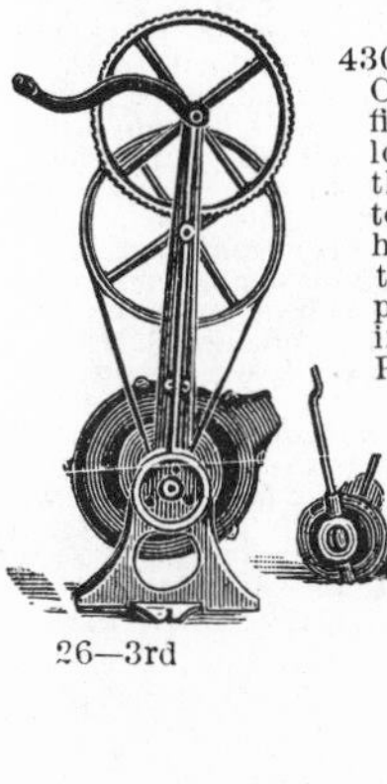

43072 The Champion Cog Geared Crank Blower can be set to any fire, right or left hand, by simply loosening three screws and throwing the outlet of the fan to the opposite side; turning the handle either way will produce the blast; has 14-in. fan; complete with tuyere iron and piping; shipping weight, 100 lbs. Price.............................$8.00

26—3rd

Blowers—Continued.

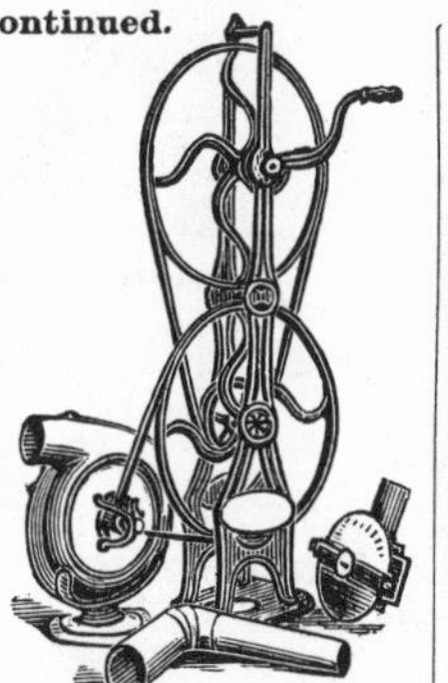

43074 The Centennial Crank Fan Blower can be placed to a right or left hand fire; has 14-inch fan; complete with ball tuyere iron and piping; shipping weight, 160 lbs. Price......$10.00

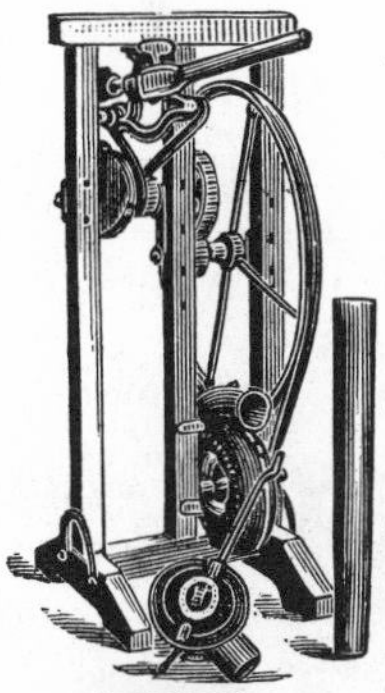

43075 The Champion 1890 Blower, the king of all blowers. The largest hand blast producer in the world, double that of any other blower or bellows; is noiseless and has the world-renowned Champion lever motion; has 16-in. fan, 25-in. fly wheel; weighs 160 pounds; complete with tuyere iron piping.....$13.00

43077 We can furnish the Champion 1890 Blower with steel frame; complete with tuyere iron and piping.$14.00

The Champion Lever Blacksmith Blower.

OUR 1894 LEADER.

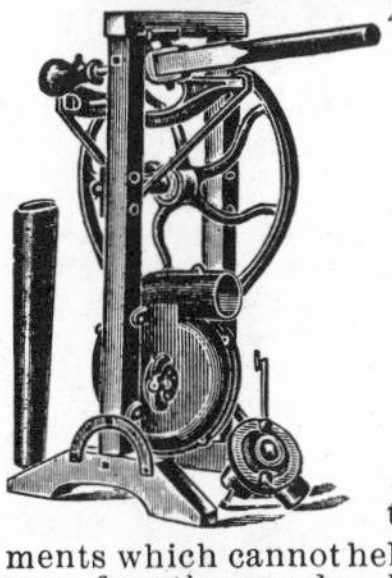

43078 Has 16-in. fan and 25-in. fly wheel with, a capacity of a 50-in. bellows. Neither skill, money nor labor has been spared to make this a strictly first-class blower. The mechanical. self-acting and simple lever motion has nothing to get out of order and is absolutely perfect in its construction; it is light running with a continuation of momentum between strokes, keeping the blast regular and powerful. By selling this blower at the low price will enable us to place thousands of working advertisements which cannot help but pay us by bringing customers for other goods. Every blower warranted. Price, complete with tuyere iron and piping f.o.b. cars. $9.00

Bench Drills.

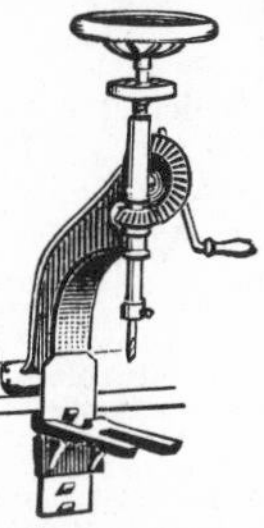

New Model Bench Drill. This drill is 24 inches high, weighs 31 lbs., drills ⅛ to ¾ inch hole. Squares with bed plate; run of screw, 3½ inches; drill stock, 13-16 inch in diameter, crank has extension for large drilling; is fitted with chuck for square or round shank drills; has no self-feed attachment, weight, 35 lbs.

43080 New Model Drill for square shank drills only. Each...$4.40

43081 New Model Drill for ½ inch around shank drills only...$4.40

Champion Upright Post Drills.

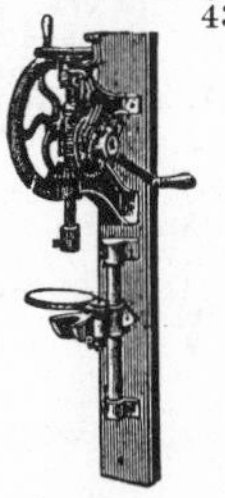

43083 Every drill guaranteed. (O.S.3.) Blacksmith drill, as we here illustrate, is a complete tool in every respect, made from the best procurable material, and finished equal in polish and accuracy to drills costing double the money.

The Swing Table will be found useful in many ways, and much more convenient than driving them in and out with a hammer. It is out of the way when not in use, and may be quickly swung into position when wanted.

No. O.S-3 Upright Self-Feed Drill, length 50 inches, will drill to centre of a 14-inch circle. Spindle bored to take ½ inch straight shank drill. Drills from ⅛ to 1-inch hole. Weight, 100 lbs. No drills included in this price. Price, each $6.50

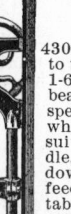

Champion Post Drill, 1893 Pattern.

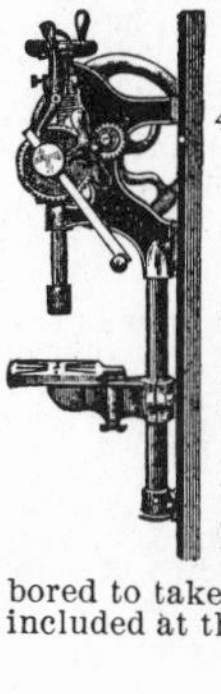

43084 (No. 3) Weight. 120 pounds. Drills to the center of a 15-inch circle, and from 1-64 to 1¼ inch hole. Has double journal bearings with full back gear, also two speeds on the right hand side of the drill, which can be changed in an instant to suit all kinds of work. Diameter of spindle, 1¼ inches. The screw has an up and down run of 4½ inches. The automatic self-feed is of the latest improved pattern. The table is large and slotted so the operator can securely bolt work on for drilling, which is very convenient for many kinds of work. This drill is mounted on a hard wood plank 2 inches thick. The spindle is bored to take in ½ inch straight shank drills. No drills included at this price........ ....$7.50

Champion Post Drills No. 4.

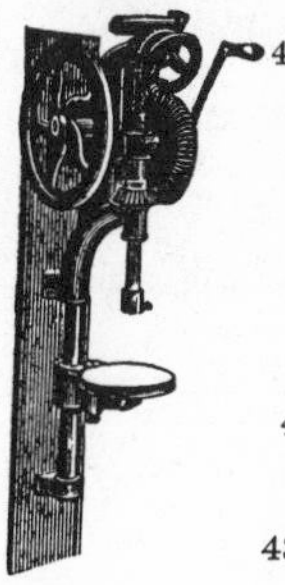

43085 The Champion (No. 4) Upright Self-feed Drill. This machine has nearly a continuous feed, which may be quickly adjusted by a thumb-screw for two rates of speed. Has swing table which is very convenient, is out of the way when not in use, and may be quickly swung into position when wanted; will drill to the center of an 18 inch circle; spindle bored to take drills with ½ inch round shank; will drill from ⅛ to 1½ inch hole; length, 450 inches; weight, 185 lbs. No drill bits furnished with this machine at prices quoted. See Nos. 40395 and 40396 for bits. Price, each, $12.00

43086 **With Quick Return Attachment** (4½). Price, each...............$13.50

43087 The No. 43086 Post Drill, with pulley to be used with power. Each.......................$15.00

Post Drill.

The $10.00 Mechanical Wonder.

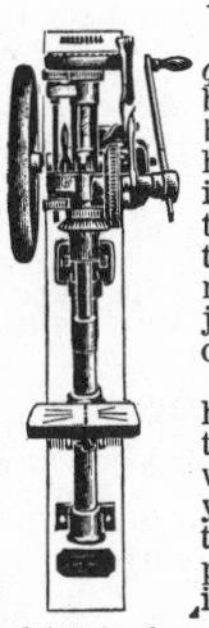

This drill is supplied with our *patent quick-return* attachment, by which the drill bit is removed from the work in an instant by simply pushing a lexer with the left hand, while the right hand continues turning the hanle or crank which raises the bit to any height desired, and at the same time cleaning the hole bored, as the bit revolves while being raised. It has two journal bearings which are double, as in our 1893 pattern.

The drill is supplied with two true and honest speeds on the right hand side of the drill. First speed for light and medium work and second speed for heavy work, you simply change the hub from first speed to second speed. Actual weight, 130 pounds. Will drill to a center of 15½ inch. The spindle has a run up and down of 4½ inches and will bore from 0 to 1¼ inch hole. Spindle is bored to take in ½-inch shank drills. No drills furnished at this price.

43088 *Price, each*......... ....$10 00

Champion Fan Blower.

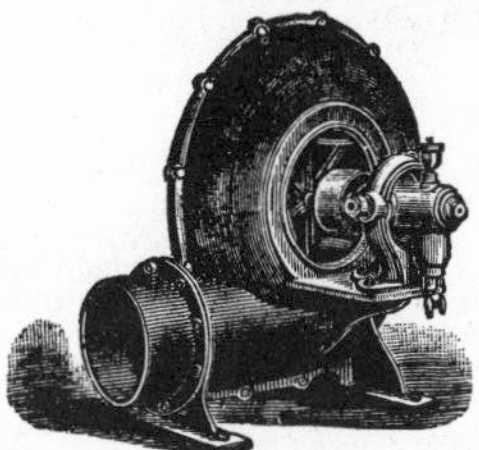

43090 The Champion Fan Blower is especially adapted for blowing forge fires, boiler fires, steam boiler furnaces, puddling and heating furnaces, dry rooms, refrigerators or or for ventilation, etc., where a larger volume of air is required. It is made either horizontal at the bottom or top, or vertically upward direction; also, right hand or left hand.

No. of Exhauster.	Price.	Height.	Diameter of Inlet.	Diameter of Pulley.	Face of Pulley.	Revolutions per min. 4 oz. Blast for Forge Fires.
1	$ 8.25	15 in.	5	2 9/16	2	4,000
2	11.00	18 "	5¾	3	2½	3,600
3	14.30	21½ "	6⅛	3½	2½	3,200
4	18.15	25½ "	7½	4¼	3½	2,682
5	24.20	29¼ "	9	5⅛	4	2,279
6	30.25	34 "	10½	6	4¾	1,961
7	36.22	40 "	12	6¾	5¼	1,662
8	46.50	45 "	14	8	6½	1,417
9	77.62	50 "	16	9	8	1,234
10	103.50	57 "	18	10	9	1,065
11	129.37	65 "	21	12	10½	932

All sizes from 5 to 11 we ship from factory. When ordering state whether right or left hand is wanted.

Blacksmiths' Bellows.

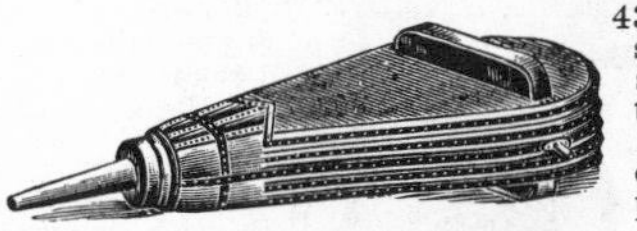

43095 Blacksmiths' Bellows, standard patterns. We use *Cow Hide* leather prepared especially for our use, and we guarantee it to wear equal to any made. We use Whitewood, Basswood and Pine in the woodwork, which is kiln dried, making it perfectly dry, that it may not be effected by the change of climate. We aim to use nothing but the best and most suitable materials in their construction. The weight of our bellows are about as follows. They may vary a little, but not much.

Width......	20 to 24 in.	26 in.	28 in.	30 in.	32 in.
Weight......		30 lbs.	40 lbs.	50 lbs.	60 lbs
Price, each..	$3.40	$3.75	$4.10	$4.40	$4.75
Width		34 in.	36 in.	38 in.	40 in.
Weight..................		70 lbs.	80 lbs.	90 lbs.	100 lbs
Price, each..............		$5.40	$6.10	$6.75	$7.75

Moulders' Bellows.

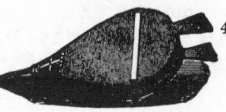

43099 Moulders' Bellows, weight, 3¾ lbs. Width, 12 inches. Each..............$1.10

Hand Bellows.

43100 Same shape as 43099, width 10 inches. Price, each..$0.65

Little Giant Tire Upsetter.

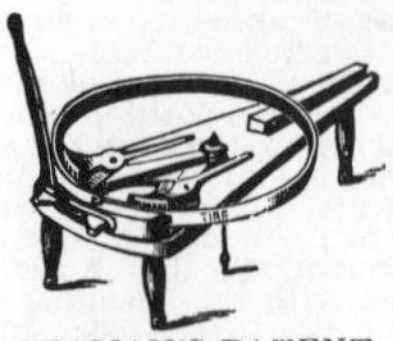

SEAMAN'S PATENT.

43102 No. 1 Little Giant will upset any size or diameter of tire, from the light buggy to the heavy tire ½ inch thick to 2 in. wide. Weight, 100 lbs. Price.................. $8.00

43103 No. 2 is heavier than No. 1, and lies on the floor. Both jaws move. Will upset any tire from the light buggy tire to a truck tire 4 inches wide, or bars of square or round iron up to 1¼ inch in diameter. Weight, 160 pounds. Each..$11.00

Champion Tire Shrinker.

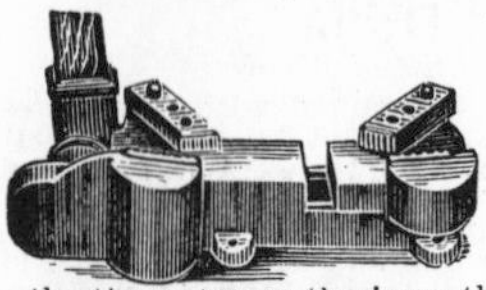

43106 The Champion Tire Shrinker is a very simple and inexpensive machine, which saves all cutting and welding of tires. Works equally as well on the lightest steel tire, and on wagon tires 4x1 inch. Place the tire between the jaws, than draw the cams against the tire, then with but little pressure on the handle you can shrink the tire to suit. Weight, 140 lbs., floor space required for it, 18x10 inches; will shrink tire 1x4, and axles 1¼x1¼. Price, each............$7.50

The Mole Tire Shrinker.

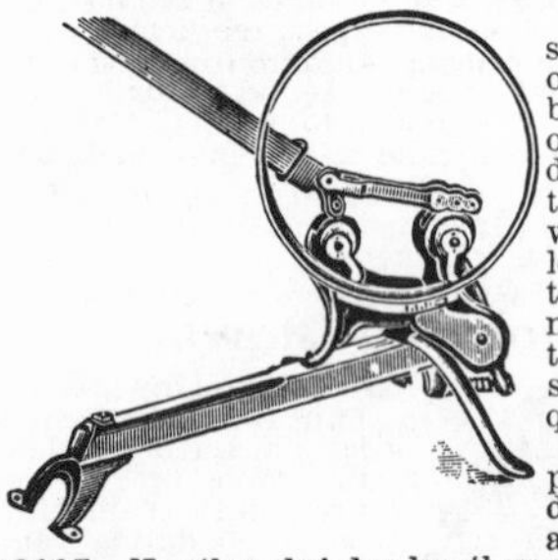

It is the only tire shrinker that can be operated successfully by one man. The operation of bringing down the lever grasps the tire and does the work; raising the lever opens it. By this means it is not necessary to remove the tire until it is upset as much as required.

These machines are provided with an index finger showing amount of shrinkage.

43107 *No other shrinker has these advantages.*

No. 1 is adapted to general custom work. No. 2 will do all but the heaviest work with ease. No 3 made for heavy wagon and truck tires. It is very powerful, having a long lever. It does heavy work easily.

Our new No. 3½ is made especially for heavy truck tires; it will work on tires 30 inches and over.

No. 1, 2, 3, 3½ will work equally well on light and medium tires. The shrinkers are made from good, strong iron, and only first-class material.

No. 1 Shrinker, bed 2¼-inch, weight, 150 pounds. Price..$ 8.00
No. 2 Shrinker, bed 3-inch, weight, 225 pounds. Price..10.67
No. 3 Shrinker, bed 4-inch, weight, 300 pounds. Price..13.50
No. 3½ Shrinker, bed 4-inch, weight, 300 pounds. Price..13.50

Tire Benders.

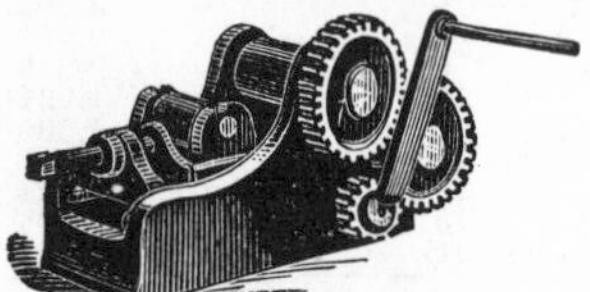

43108 The Champion Tire-Bender. The frame is one solid piece, is double back geared, and worked with two cranks. The height of the tire is regulated by a screw; its bending capacity is 3x⅜ inches to the lightest tire; it will take in 5 inches in width; it will bend fifth wheels as well as tires. Price, each..............................$6.50

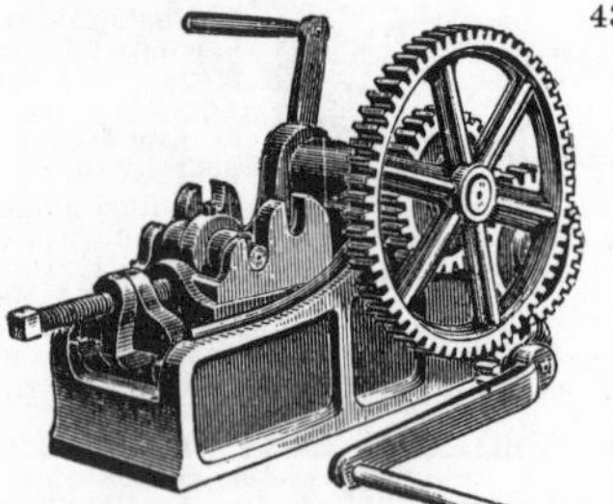

43110 The Eureka Tire Bender is strong and powerful; the two end rolls are provided with wrought iron collars in order to keep the tire from twisting; the height of the tire is regulated by a screw. The No. 1 size will bend 4x1 tire; the No. 2, 6x1½ inches to the lightest tire.

No. 1, price, each..$10.00
No. 2, price, each..15.50

Engineers, Electricians, Mechanics, etc., can save money by buying books on their respective trades from us.

Combination Vise.

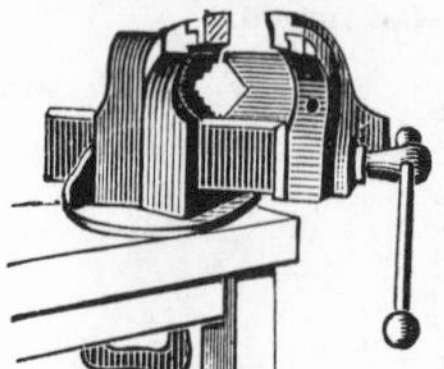

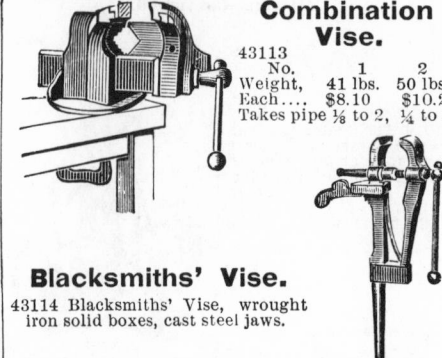

43113

No.	1	2
Weight,	41 lbs.	50 lbs.
Each....	$8.10	$10.20

Takes pipe ⅛ to 2, ¼ to 3.

Blacksmiths' Vise.

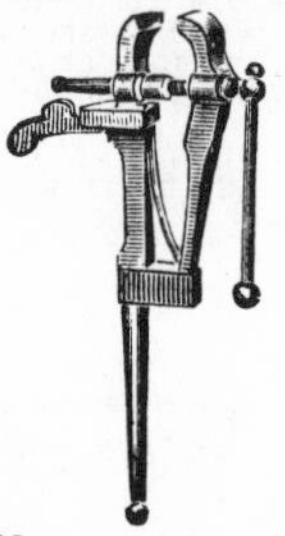

43114 Blacksmiths' Vise, wrought iron solid boxes, cast steel jaws.

Weighs, lbs.	35	40	45	50	55	60	65	70	75
Each.....	$4.00	4.20	4.40	4.60	5.15	5.25	5.70	6.00	6.40

Vise Screw Only.

43115 Vise Box and Screw, 1⅛ in. for blacksmiths' vises. Each..$2.97

Jewelers Vises.

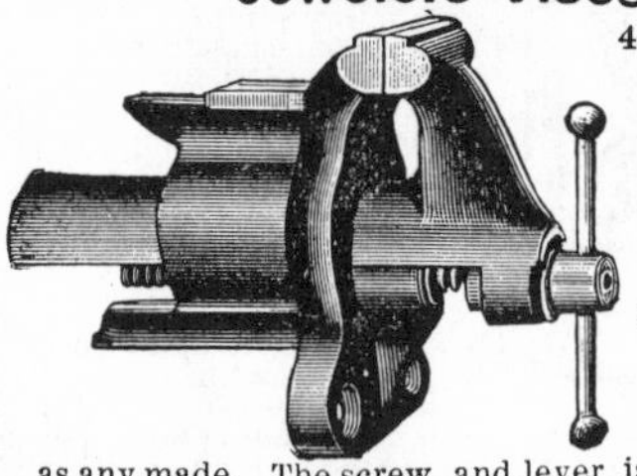

43119 Anvil and Vise for jewelers, mechanics, farmers or amateurs. This vise is made in the finest manner by means of special tools and machinery and every part is as accurately fitted and as finely finished as any made. The screw and lever is made of Bessemer steel. Jaws, anvil and horn are ground and polished, and the body is neatly japanned; jaws are 1½ inches wide, and open 1¾ inches. Weight, 1¼ lb. Price, each...........$0.25 Per dozen..........$2.70

43120 Anvil and Vise, same as above, only 2 inch jaws, open 2½ inches. Weight, 3 lbs., 15 oz. Price, each............$0.60 Per dozen.......... 7.00

Bench Vise.

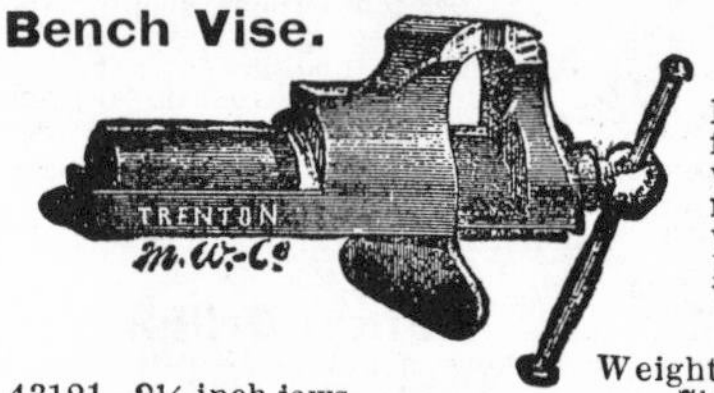

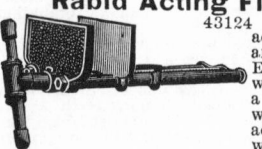

Paralles Bench Vises for light work in metal or wood—"The Farmers' Vise."

		Weight, lbs.	Each.
43121	2¼ inch jaws....	7½	$1.10
43122	3 inch jaws....	17½	1.70
43123	4 inch jaws....	38½	2.85

Rapid Acting Flush Vise.

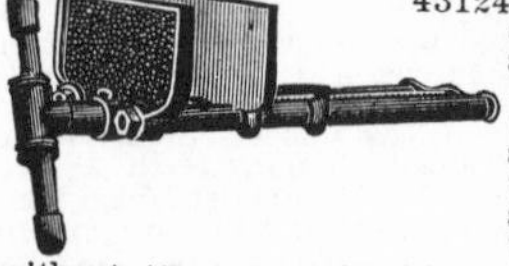

43124 This vise especially adapted for carpenters' and cabinetmakers' use. Equally valuable to all wood workers prefering a vise having jaws flush with the bench. The adjustment of jaws to work is instantaneous, without the use of triggers, catches, cams or devices. We use only a powerful screw and nut. This vise is fully guaranteed. Has 10-inch jaw and opens 12 inches. Price..$ 6.50

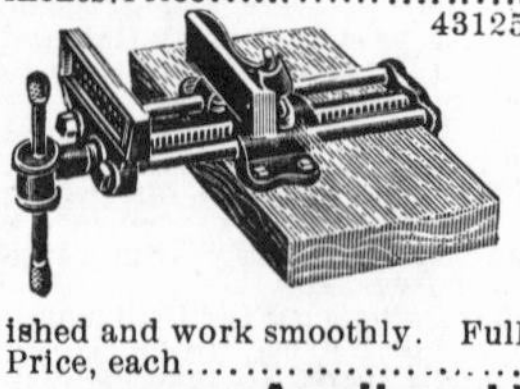

43125 This cut shows the vise as fastened to the bench. This vise is especially valuable to all wood workers preferring a high vise. The back jaw is swiveled, holding taper as well as straight work. All parts of vise are finished and work smoothly. Fully guaranteed. Price, each..$7.50

Anvil and Vise.

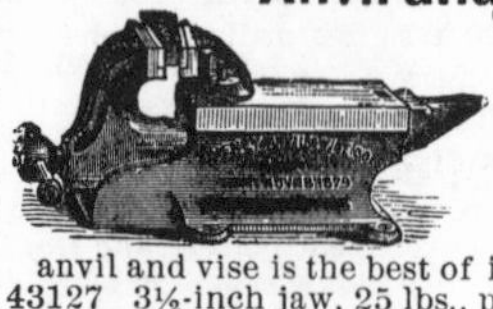

The Vise is adjustable By removing a pin the inner jaw can be swung round so as to hold and wedge or irregular shape. The anvil has a chilled, hardened and polished surface. This anvil and vise is the best of its kind made.

43127 3½-inch jaw, 25 lbs., price, each..........$3.40
43128 4 -inch jaw, 35 lbs., price, each.......... 4.10
43129 4½-inch jaw, 40 lbs, price, each.......... 4.70

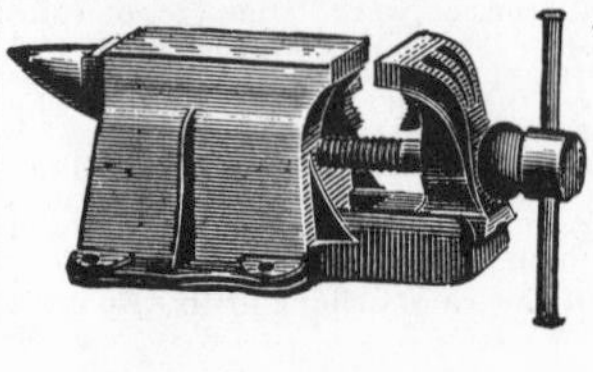

43130 Anvil and Vise combined, with jaws for holding pipes; has chilled face and jaws; jaws are 3 inches wide; opens 5 inches; weighs 33 lbs. Price, each $1.65

Hand Vise.

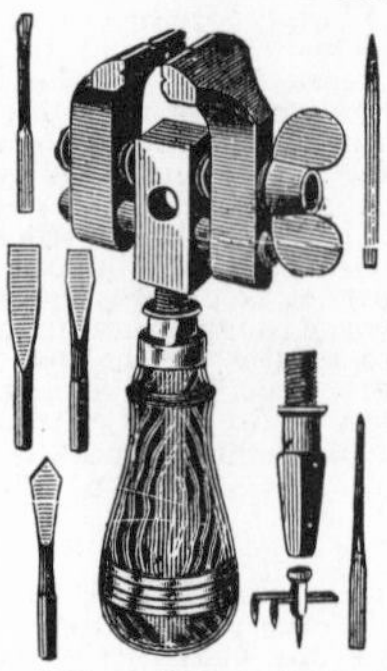

43135 The Alford Hand Vise; jaws are forged and tempered steel, rosewood handle, with lignum vitæ cap. It is hollow, and the tools seen in the cut are placed inside; the vise jaws are 1¼ inches wide and open 1½ inches. The handle can be unscrewed from the vise and the bit stock put in its place; the handle can also be screwed into the vise at right angles, which is desirable for many kinds of work. Each........................$1.50

Blacksmiths' Drills.

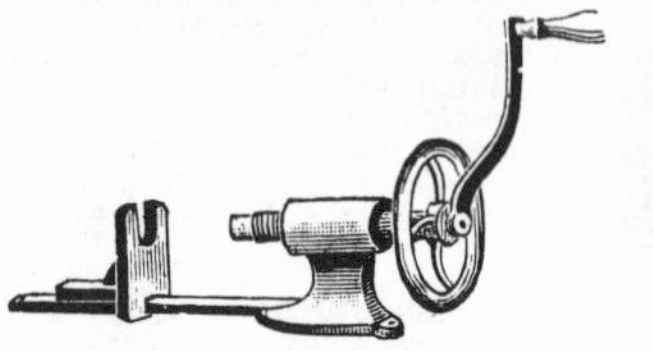

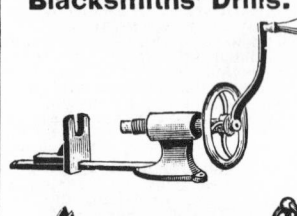

43137 Blacksmiths' Horizontal Drill, solid standard; 29 in. long; weight, 29 lbs. The drill is fitted for ½-inch square shank drills. We do not furnish drills. Each.....$1.75

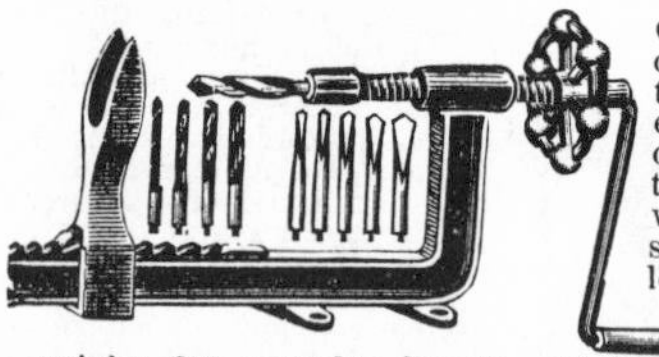

Combination clamp and drill; the lowest priced good article of its kind on the market; has wrought iron screw feed, malleable frame, sliding clamp; weighs 6½ pounds; length, 17 inches; height, 7 inches.

43139 With Diamond pointed drills. Price, each. $1.75
43140 With Syracuse Twist drills. Price, each... 2.35
Extra drills for 43139. Per set............ .40
Extra drills for 43140. Per set............ 1.12

Graduated Tire Measuring Wheel.

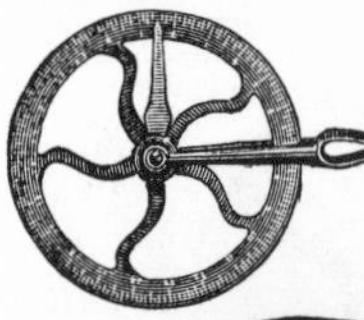

43143 A drop forging is made so that the figures and lines are raised above the surface of the wheel and cannot be filled or defaced with rust or dirt. It is exactly 24 in. in circumference, with index hand. Price, each....$1.25

Tuyere Irons.

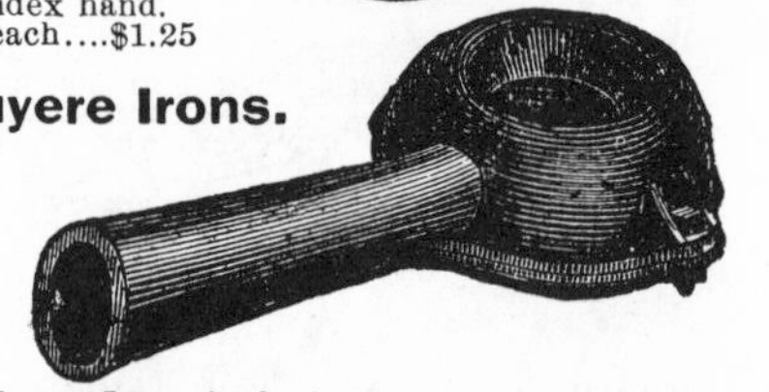

43144 Tuyere Iron, single duck's nest; weight, 14 pounds. Each..............................$0.35

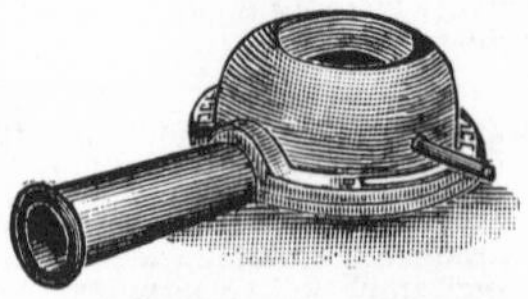

43145 Clark's Tuyere Irons. No. 2. Price, each....$0.82
No. 3. Price, each...... .95

Champion Iron Cutter.

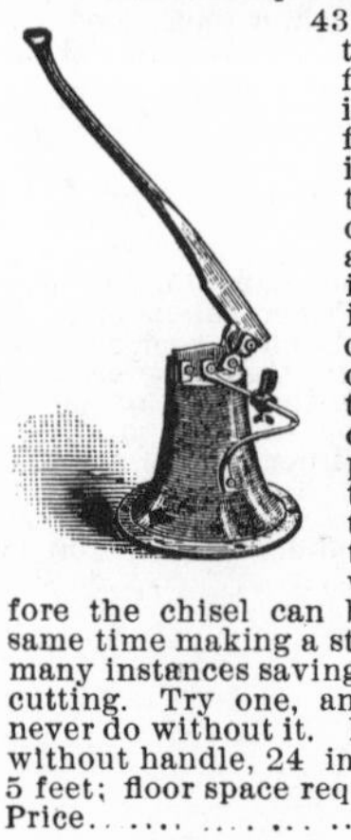

43146 The greatest labor-saving tool of the age. Will earn its first cost in 60 days. No anvil in any blacksmith shop can afford to be without one, if saving of time and hard work is taken into consideration. It will cut cold iron up to ½-inch round and hot iron up to ⅝x1⅝-inch in an instant and with ease. It is only intended to be used in connection with all work done on the anvil, instead of using the chisel to cut both hot and cold iron. This tool must be placed on the right-hand end of the anvil, close and convenient to same, as nine out of ten cuttings can be made with this tool while working on the anvil before the chisel can be put in its place, and at the same time making a straight and smooth cut, and in many instances saving a heat by the gain of time in cutting. Try one, and we feel confident you will never do without it. It weighs 120 pounds; height, without handle, 24 inches; length of handle, about 5 feet; floor space required, about 20 inches. Price..$10.00

The "Fisher" Horseshoer's Anvil, with Detachable Vise.

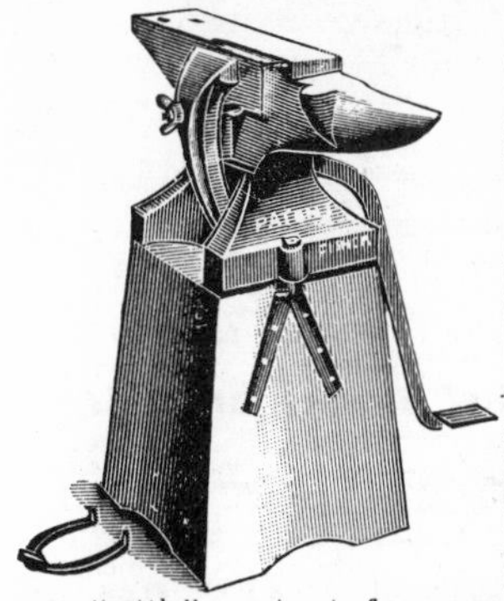

Weight of anvil, 170 pounds; length of face, 16½ inches; width of face, 4 inches; length of horn, 10½ inches; width of horn, 3 inches; width of face at end next horn, 3 inches; cutter hole, 1 inch square; clip on the horn is 1¼ inches projection.

This has also the "*Fisher*" *double-thick-edge face of best tool cast steel*, warranted to be in one piece, perfectly welded, and never to come loose or break off. It will never "settle" or get out of shape as do the faces of all the foreign-made anvils after a few years of use. It is planed to a true, straight surface and given a fine temper, hard and uniform. The *solid steel horn* with side clip is long and slim, the best shape for horseshoers' work, and it will not break or bend. It is an inch below the face, giving that depth of shoulder which most blacksmiths like. The cutter hole is always true and square with the face, and is chamfered all around to fit the tools. The tail of the anvil is long and thin, being only *seven-eights* of an inch thick at the end. A perfect arrangement for bolting the anvil to the block is provided by the heavy lug at each end.

This pattern of anvil has been gotten up expressly for horseshoers. It is altogether better than the Peter Wright anvils or any of the other imported anvils, is cheaper and is the only one that is *fully warranted* against failure in any way.

Should an anvil made by us prove imperfect upon using, we will replace it by another without charge. There is no other make of anvil that gives such a guarantee.

The hardened steel jaw hinges, with a blind joint in special socket at the base, and is closed by means of a bolt with slotted head from the other side. This bolt pases through the body of the anvil, its extremity holding the jaw by the thumb screw. The lever pivots with a knife edge on that side of the anvil, its upper end entering the bolt's slotted head, and extending downward it terminates in a treadle of convenient height for the foot. A plain spring on the inner side of the jaw throws it open when the foot is off the treadle, leaving it ready to insert the shoe for turning calks of toe or heel. The whole arrangement is attached to the anvil itself without any connection on the block. The jaw, bolt, treadle and thumb screw, only four pieces in all, can be detached instantly by simply unscrewing the thumb nut, leaving the anvil free for any work required, as shown in the small cut. They can be put back again ready for vise work in *one minute*, thus saving the time and money of a separate vise.

About 5 inches of the front edge is beveled off and rounded for drawing down work. Also the face for a couple of inches in length is reduced to 3 inches, sometimes a convenience for narrow work on the face.

43147 Price of anvil, with vise, complete.......$20.00

Wrought Anvils.

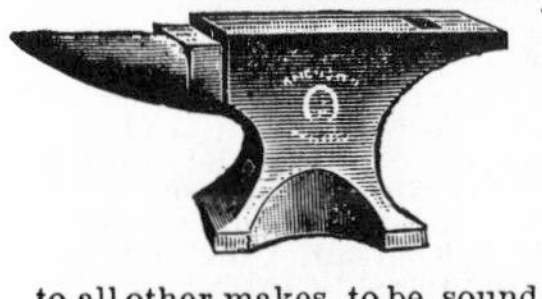

43150 The American Wrought "Horse Shoe" Brand Anvil, *fully warranted*, made of the best American wrought iron, and faced with the best crucible steel, are guaranteed superior to all other makes, to be sound, free from flaws and to have faces hard and true. Try one: if not satisfactory, return at our expense. Any weight from 85 lbs. and upward. Per pound....................$0.11

43151 The American Wrought Horseshoe Brand Anvil up to 85 lbs. Per pound..........$0.11½

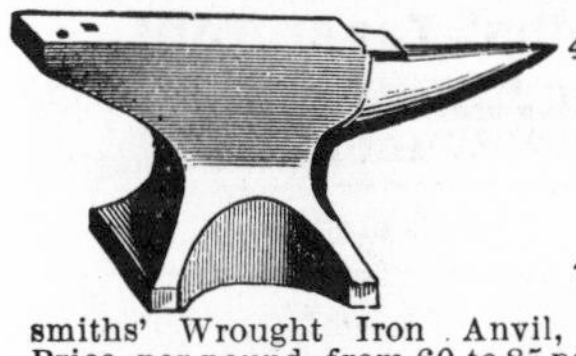

43152 Peter Wright's Blacksmiths' Wrought Iron Anvil, steel face. Price, per pound, from 85 lbs. and upwards...$0.10½

43153 Peter Wright's Celebrated Blacksmiths' Wrought Iron Anvil, steel face.

Price, per pound, from 60 to 85 pounds.........$0.11
Price, per pound, from 50 to 60 pounds.............12

Cannot always furnish exact weights wanted in anvils. Make second or third choice in weights when ordering

Cast Iron Anvils.

43154 With steel face; is only intended for light work and is not guaranteed, as we do not take back or exchange if they prove defective.

No.	2	3	4	5	6	7	8	9
Weight	20	30	40	50	60	70	80	90 lbs.
Each	$2.70	3.04	3.54	4.05	4.39	4.82	5.40	6.08

Plow Anvil.

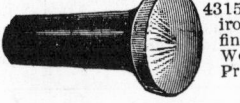

43155 Plow Anvil, not cast iron, but solid cast steel; oil finished, polished face. Weight, from 4 to 4½ lbs. Price....................$0.50

Ratchet Drills.

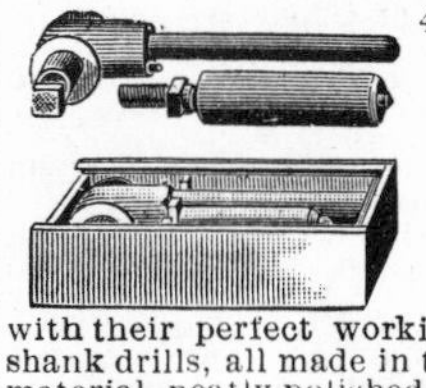

43157 Whitney's New Combined Double Acting Ratchet Drill; stock is two ratchets in one, boiler and common at the price of one. Is reversible, which is convenient in light drilling to turn on and not move drill. The ratchets are all encased, so that no dirt will interfere with their perfect working; socket fitted for square shank drills, all made in the best manner, of the best material, neatly polished nickel plated head.

Price, each	$3.60	$4.50	$5.40	$6.75	$8.10	$10.00
Wt., boxed	2½	7½	12	15½	18	22 lbs.
Length	8 in.	10 in.	12 in.	16 in.	18 in.	24 in.

Farriers' Hammers.

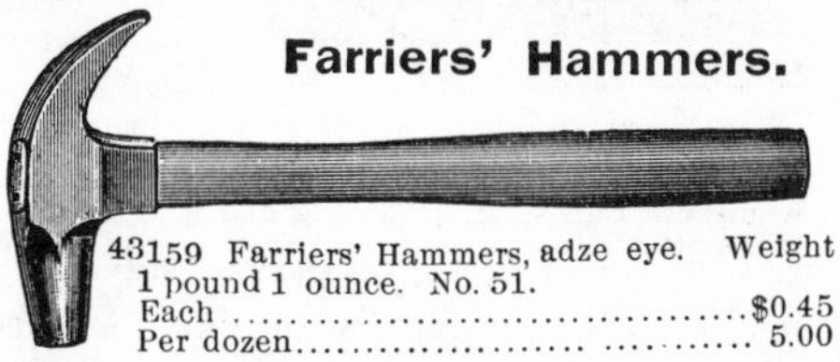

43159 Farriers' Hammers, adze eye. Weight 1 pound 1 ounce. No. 51.
Each....................$0.45
Per dozen....................5.00

Blacksmiths' Hand Hammers.

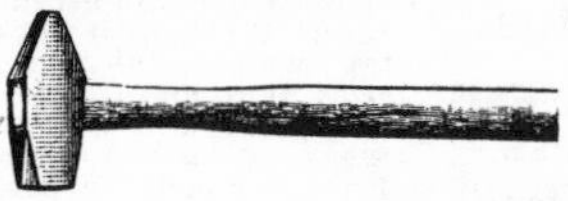

43162 Blacksmiths' Hand Hammers, handled, extra fine steel. Y and P brand, fully warranted.

No	1	2	3
Weight	2 lbs.	2 lbs. 10 oz.	3 lbs
Each	60c.	65c.	70c.

43164 Plow Hammers, solid cast steel, polished and handled.
Each, 1 pound 2 ounces....................$0.40
Each, 2 pounds.....................45

Horseshoers' Turning Hammers.

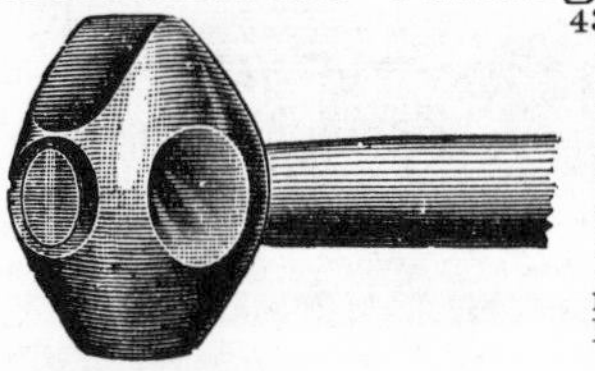

43166 Horseshoer's Turning Hammer, Chicago pattern, with handles, solid cast steel; 2, 2½ and 3 lbs.; weight does not include handle. Y and P brand, fully warranted.
Each..........$1 35

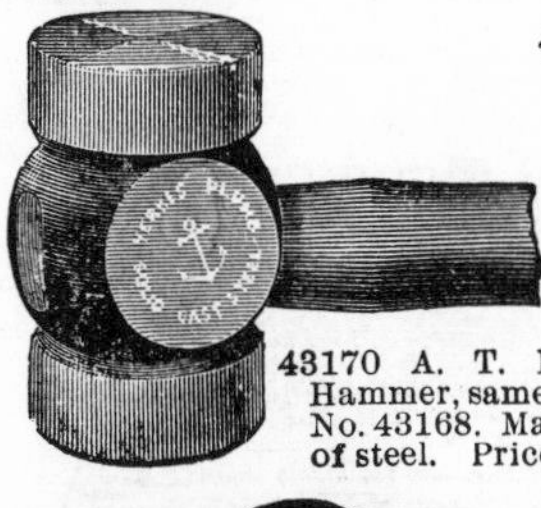

43168 Horseshoer's Turning Hammer, New York Pattern, with handle; solid cast steel, 2, 2½ and 3 pounds; weights do not include handle. Price, each $1.40

43170 A. T. Horseshoer's Turning Hammer, same style and weight as No. 43168. Made of superior quality of steel. Price, each..........$1.25

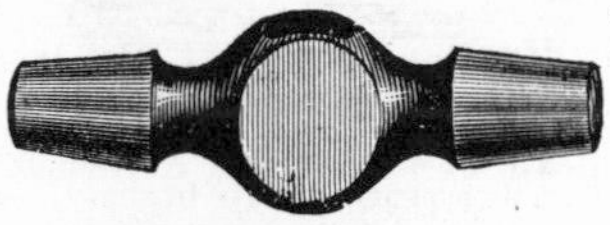

43173 Boiler-maker's Hammer, solid cast steel, oil finished, polished faces, no handle; weight, 2 and 3 lbs. Per lb. $0.20

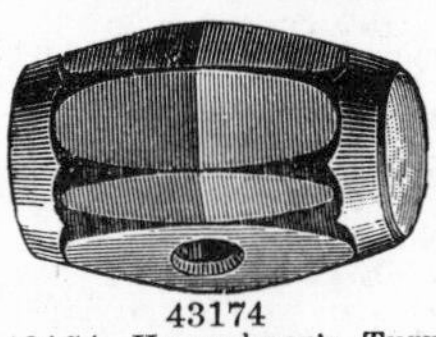

43174

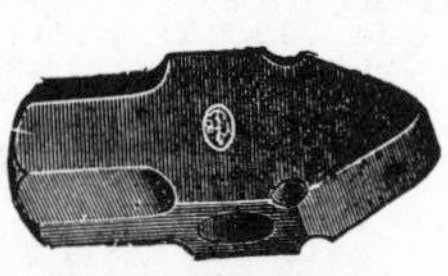

43175

43174 Horseshoer's Turning Sledge, solid cast steel, oil finish, polished faces, from 6 to 10 pounds. Price, per lb....................$0.09

43175 Blacksmiths' Sledges, solid cast steel, weight, from 8 to 17 pounds. The increase is by pounds. Per pound....................07½

Flatters and Hardies.

These tools are of the very best quality procurable, and are not the cheap kind sold with cheap blacksmiths' sets.

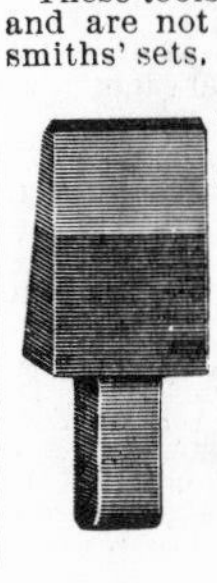

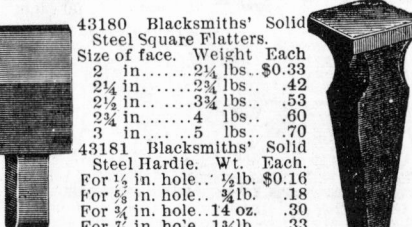

43180 Blacksmiths' Solid Steel Square Flatters.

Size of face.	Weight	Each
2 in.	2¼ lbs.	$0.33
2¼ in.	2¾ lbs.	.42
2½ in.	3¾ lbs.	.53
2¾ in.	4 lbs.	.60
3 in.	5 lbs.	.70

43181 Blacksmiths' Solid Steel Hardie.

	Wt.	Each.
For ½ in. hole	½ lb.	$0.16
For ⅝ in. hole	¾ lb.	.18
For ¾ in. hole	14 oz.	.30
For ⅞ in. hole	1¾ lb.	.33
For 1 in. hole	2 lb.	.40

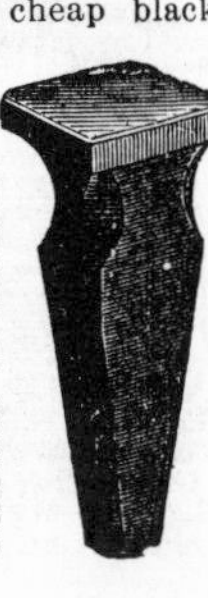

Fullers and Swages.

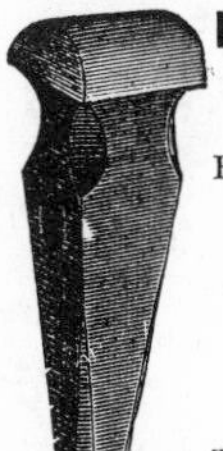

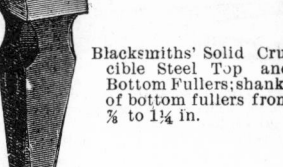

Blacksmiths' Solid Crucible Steel Top and Bottom Fullers; shanks of bottom fullers from ⅞ to 1¼ in.

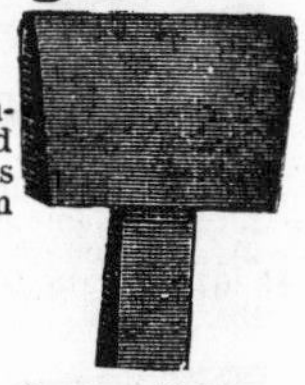

Top Fuller. Bottom Fuller.

43182 Top Fullers.

Size	¼	⅜	½	⅝
Weight	2 lbs.	2 lbs.	2¼ lbs.	2¼ lbs.
Each	30c	30c	40c	40c
Size	¾	⅞	1	1⅛	1¼
Weight	3 lbs.	3 lbs.	3¼ lbs.	3¼ lbs.	4¼ lbs.
Each	45c	45c	50c	50c	65c

43183 Bottom Fuller.

Size	¼	⅜	½	⅝	¾	⅞
Weight	2¼ lbs.	2¼ lbs.	2¼ lbs.	2½ lbs.	2¾ lbs.	2¾ lbs.
Each	35c	35c	35c	38c	42c	42c
Size	1		1⅛		1¼	
Weight	3¼ lbs.		3¼ lbs.		3¼ lbs.	
Each	50c		50c		50c	

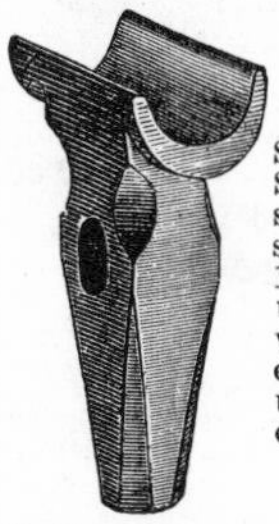

Blacksmiths Solid Crucible Steel Swages, shanks of bottom swages from ⅞ to 1¼ in. Top swages up to ⅝ inch, weight 2 lbs. 6 oz. each; from ⅝ and upward, 2 lbs. 15 oz.

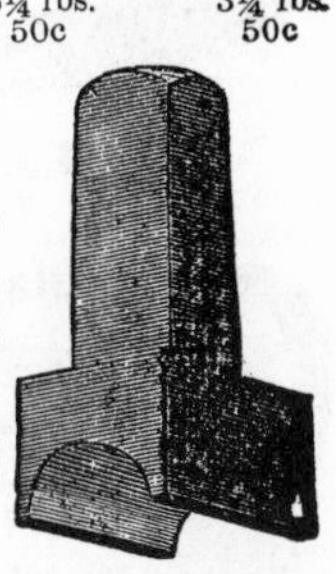

Bottom Swage Top Swage.

43184 Top Swage.

Size	¼	5/16	⅜	7/16	½	⅝	¾-in.
Weight	1½ lb.	1½ lb.	2 lb.	2 lb.	2 lb.	2 lb.	2¾ lb.
Each	25c	25c	30c	30c	30c	30c	42c
Size	⅞	1	1⅛	1¼	1½	2-in.	
Weight	2¾ lb.	2¾ lb.	3 lb.	3 lb.	4 lb.	4 lb.	
Each	42c	42c	45c	45c	60c	60c	

43185 Bottom Swage.

Size	¼	5/16	⅜	7/16	½	⅝-in.
Weight	2¼ lb.	2¼ lb.	2¼ lb.	2¼ lb.	2¼ lb.	2¼ lb.
Each	34c	34c	34c	34c	34c	34c
Size	¾	⅞	1	1⅛	1¼-in.	
Weight	2½ lb.	2¾ lb.	3 lb.	3 lb.	3¼ lb.	
Each	38c	42c	45c	45c	50c	

Cold Chisels.

Cold Chisels, cast steel, octagon, half polished.

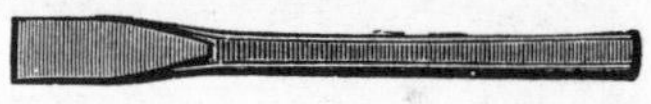

		Each.	Per doz.
43186	½ inch; weight, 5 oz.	$0.08	$0.85
43187	¾ inch; weight, 1 lb. 2 oz.	.15	1.65

Hot and Cold Chisels.

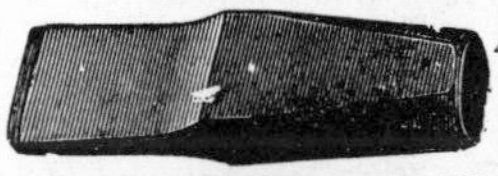

43188 Hot Chisel, 1⅜ inch cut; weight, 2 lbs. 2 oz.
Price, each..........$0.38

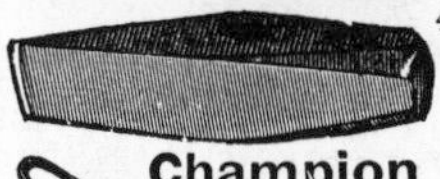

43189 Cold Chisel, 1⅜ in. cut; weight, 2 lbs. 14 oz.
Each....................$0.38

Champion Bolt Clipper.

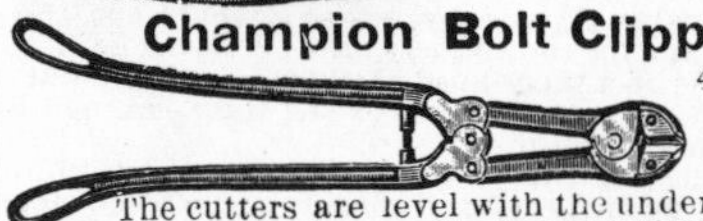

43195 This Clipper has solid steel head. The cutters are level with the under bar, which is a great advantage, as the bar is entirely out of the way, and a bolt can be cut level in any place where a bolt clipper can be used. The adjustment is simple and effective, and is accomplished by steel set screws. The material is of the very best and is forged and tempered with great care; made in two sizes only. No. 1 cuts up to ⅜ inch bolts in the threads only. Each, $3.60
No. 2 cuts up to ½ inch bolts in the thread only. 4.50

Keystone Bolt Clipper.

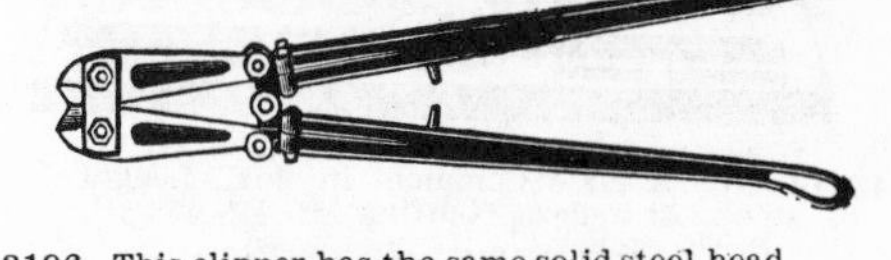

43196 This clipper has the same solid steel head as the Champion. The handles are of the best malleable iron and very strong. The adjustment is simple, being accomplished by a shim which can be put in place by simply loosening the bolts in the handles. We do not hesitate to recommend this clipper. Made in four sizes.

No. 0 cuts ¼ in. bolts in the thread only. Each..$2.50
" 1 " ⅜ " " " " " " 3.25
" 2 " ½ " " " " " " 4.25
" 3 " ⅝ " " " " " " 8.45

Blacksmiths' Tongs.

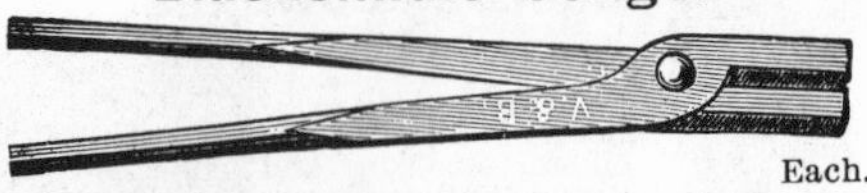

Each.

43200 Blacksmiths' Tongs, straight lipped, drop forged; all one piece, no weld. Weight, per pair, 2¼ lbs., length, 20 inches. Price $0.28
43201 Length, 22 inches. Weight, per pair, 2¾ lbs. Price .... .32

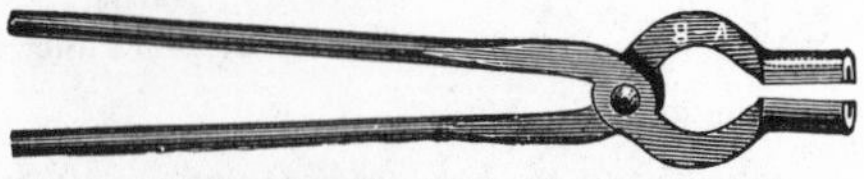

Blacksmiths' Round Bolt Tongs, length, 20 inches. When ordering bolt tongs be sure and give size of bolts they are wanted for.
43202 For bolts 5-16 to ½ inch, weight from 1¾ to 2¼ lbs. Price $0.45
43202½ For bolts ⅝ to ¾ inch, weight 2¾ lbs. Price .... .55
43203 For bolts ⅞ to 1 inch, weight 3½ lbs. .60

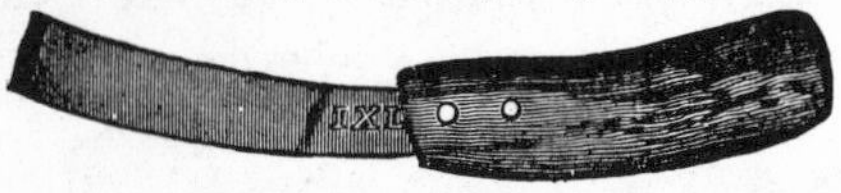

Farriers' Knife.

43205 Farriers' Knife, Wostenholm; weight, 7 oz. Each..........$0.30

Blacksmiths' Pincers.

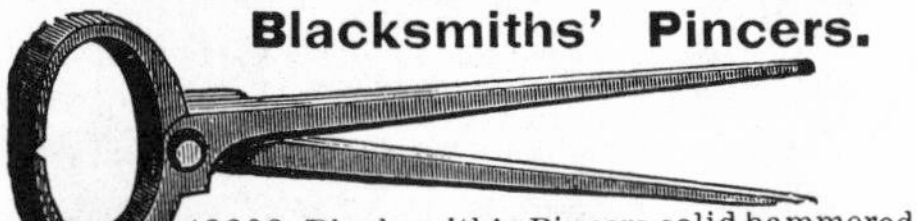

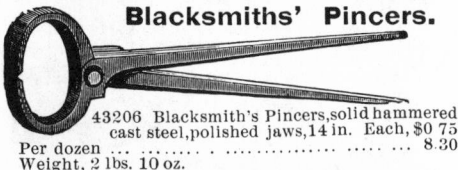

43206 Blacksmith's Pincers, solid hammered cast steel, polished jaws, 14 in. Each, $0 75
Per dozen 8.30
Weight, 2 lbs. 10 oz.

Hoof or Cutting Nippers.

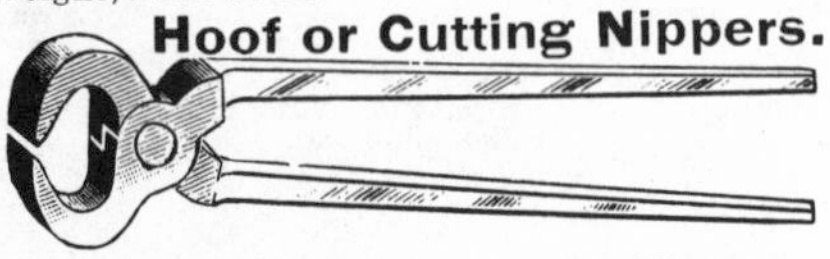

43207 Blacksmiths' Hoof or Cutting Nippers, solid steel; finely polished. These nippers are the finest made, are full polished and made of the best material.

	Each.	Per doz.
10 inch	$0.70	$ 8.00
12 inch	.95	11 00
14 inch	1.10	12.00

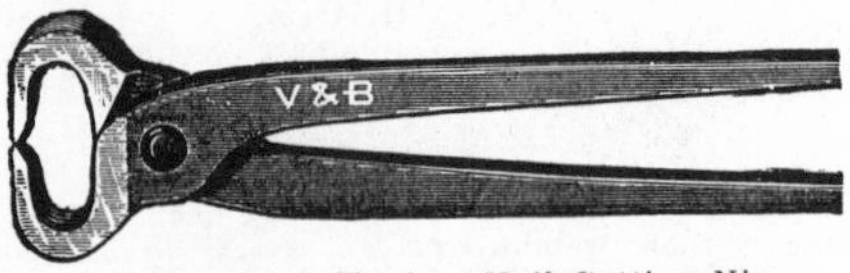

43208 Blacksmiths' Hoof or Nail Cutting Nippers, solid steel, 14 inch; weight, 2 lbs. 5 oz. Each ....$0.75 Per dozen..........$8.55

Buttress.

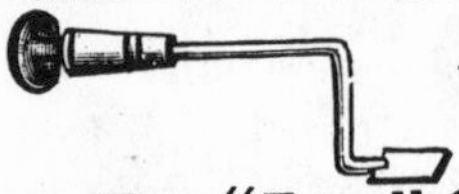

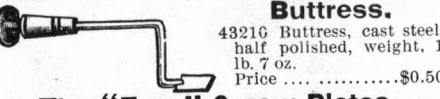

43210 Buttress, cast steel, half polished, weight, 1 lb. 7 oz. Price $0.50

The "Easy" Screw Plates.

For simpleness in construction, compactness and neatness in design, with every improvement in a screw plate which makes a perfect screw at a single cut, the EASY ranks among the highest, the die being adjustable by the use of a taper-head screw with a taper-nut, thus being braced on both sides of the die, making it perfectly rigid and solid.

The simpleness of the plate in manufacturing, in connection with the great demand already established for it, enables us to produce the tool at a price which astonishes all, meeting the long felt want of a first class screw plate for a small amount of money.

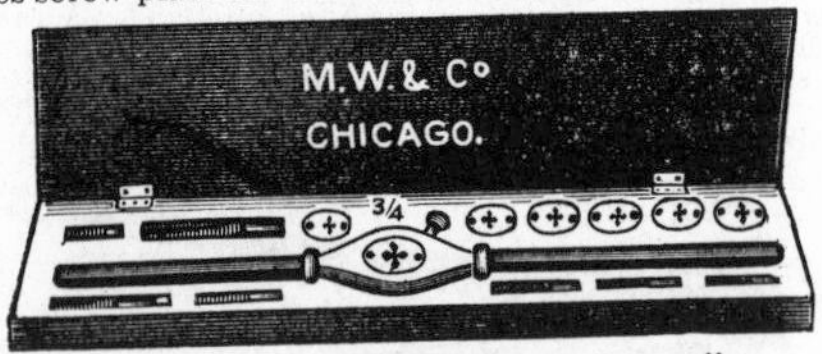

PRICES AND DIMENSIONS OF THE "EASY."

43213 No. 2a, Plate Complete in Box. Length of stock, 23 inches. Cutting $\frac{1}{4}^{20}$, $\frac{3}{8}^{16}$, $\frac{1}{2}^{12}$, $\frac{5}{8}^{11}$, $\frac{3}{4}^{10}$. Price, each $6.64
43215 No. 4a, Plate Complete in Box. Length of Stock, 26 in. Cutting $\frac{1}{2}^{12}$, $\frac{5}{8}^{11}$, $\frac{3}{4}^{10}$, $\frac{7}{8}^{9}$, 1^{8}. Each . 8.59
43216 No. 5a, Plate Complete in Box. Length of Stock, 23 inches. Cutting $\frac{1}{4}^{20}$, $\frac{5}{16}^{18}$, $\frac{3}{8}^{16}$, $\frac{7}{16}^{14}$, $\frac{1}{2}^{12}$, $\frac{5}{8}^{11}$, $\frac{3}{4}^{10}$. Price, each 7.78
43218 No. 5½a, Plate Complete in Box. Length of Stock, 23 inches. Cutting $\frac{1}{4}^{20}$, $\frac{5}{16}^{18}$, $\frac{3}{8}^{16}$, $\frac{7}{16}^{14}$, $\frac{1}{2}^{12}$, $\frac{9}{16}^{12}$, $\frac{5}{8}^{11}$, $\frac{3}{4}^{10}$. Price, each 9.39
43219 No. 7a, Plate Complete in Box. Length of Stock, 26 inches. Cutting $\frac{1}{4}^{20}$, $\frac{5}{16}^{18}$, $\frac{3}{8}^{16}$, $\frac{7}{16}^{14}$. $\frac{1}{2}^{12}$, $\frac{5}{8}^{11}$, $\frac{3}{4}^{10}$. $\frac{7}{8}^{9}$, 1^{8}. Price, each 12.63

Screw Plates--Continued.

43221 No. 8a, Plate Complete in Box. Has two Stocks 14½ inches long for first four sizes, 26 inches for the larger sizes. Cutting $\frac{1}{4}^{20}$, $\frac{5}{16}^{18}$, $\frac{3}{8}^{16}$, $\frac{7}{16}^{14}$, $\frac{1}{2}^{12}$. $\frac{5}{8}^{11}$, $\frac{3}{4}^{10}$. Price, each 9.10
43222 No. 9a, Plate Complete in Box. Has stocks same as No. 8. Cutting $\frac{1}{4}^{20}$, $\frac{5}{16}^{18}$, $\frac{3}{8}^{16}$, $\frac{7}{16}^{14}$ $\frac{1}{2}^{12}$, $\frac{5}{8}^{11}$, $\frac{3}{4}^{10}$, $\frac{7}{8}^{9}$, 1^{8}. Price. each 13.93
All plates supplied $\frac{1}{32}$ oversize for rough iron, unless otherwise ordered. All our plates warranted.

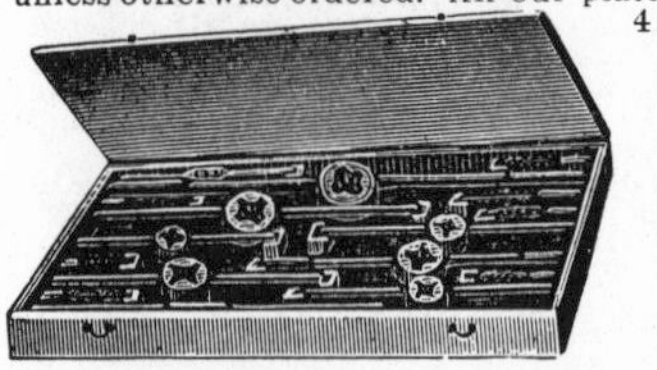

43223 The Ever Ready Screw Plate. No more changing or adjusting of dies, a stock with each size of die and of a proportionate size. This allows several sizes to be in use at one time. Each set furnished with two tap wrenches. Set complete, consisting of 7 taps, 7 dies, 7 stocks and two tap wrenches. Cuts ¼, 5/16, ⅜, 7/16, ½, ⅝ and ¾. Price, per set $12 50

43224 Ever Ready Stocks, Dies and Tap, cutting one size.

Size	¼	5/16	⅜	7/16
Price, Stock, Die and Tap ..	$1.50	1.67	1.85	2.00
Size	½	⅝	¾	
Price, Stock, Die and Tap	$2.33	2.60	3.10	

Screw Plates.

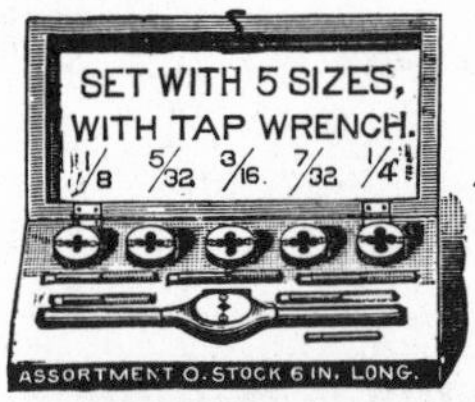

43225 The Lightning Screw Plate, with stock tap wrench and five sizes taps and guides, ⅛, 5/32, 3/16, 7/32 and ¼ inch. Stock, 6 inches long. Price, complete in case $4.55
43226 The Lightning Screw Plate, set C, cutting from ¼ to 1 inch. Stock 29 inches long, will cut sizes, ¼, 5/16, ⅜, 7/16, ½, ⅝, ¾, ⅞ and 1 in. 9 sizes. Price complete in case..........$20.40

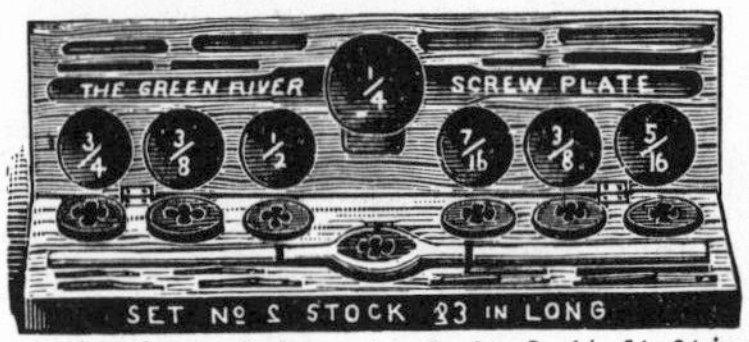

43227 The Green River Screw Plate, set No. 1½, cuts from ¼ to ¾ in., stock 22 inches long, 7 sizes; ¼, 5/16, ⅜, 7/16, ½, ⅝, ¾ inch. Taps; dies and guides complete in case. Per set.....$10.50
43228 The Green Riv r Screw Plate, set No. 3, from ¼ to 1 inch; stock, 29 inches in length, 5 sizes: ½, ⅜, ¾, ⅞, 1 inch. Taps, dies and guides complete in case per set; weight, 18 lbs.......$14.25

Electric Full Mounted Screw Plates.

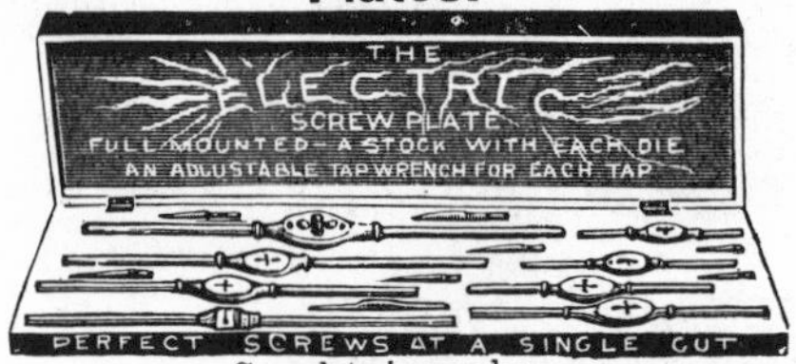

Complete in one box.

Every set supplied with our Patented Adjustable Electric Tap Wrench. The best screw plate in the market.

43229 Electric Screw Plate, No. 102, cutting ¼-20 ⅜-16, ½-12, ⅝-11, ¾-10 threads. Price, each.$ 11.62
43229½ Electric Screw Plate, No. 104, cutting ½-12, ⅝-11, ¾-10, ⅞-9, 1-8 thread. Price, each.... 14.62
43230 Electric Screw Plate, No. 105, cutting ¼-20, 5/16-18, ⅜-16, 7/16-14, ½-12, ⅝-11, ¾-10 thread. Price, each 13.50
43231 Eleatric Screw Plate, No. 107, cutting ¼-20, 5/16-18, ⅜-16 7/16-14, ½-12, ⅝-11, ¾-10, ⅞-9, 1-8 thread. Price, each 22.25

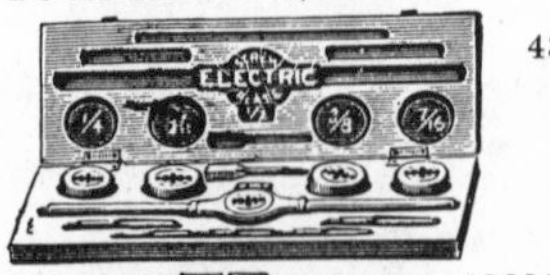

43232 The Champion Electric Screw Plate, No. 4. Length of stock; 26 inches, cuts ½x12, ⅝x11, ¾x10, ⅞x9, 1x8 threads......$12.00

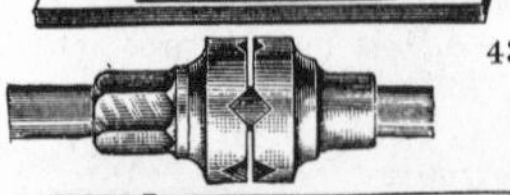

43232½ We furnish Tap Wrench with 43232 screw plate at an extra cost of $1.00 each.

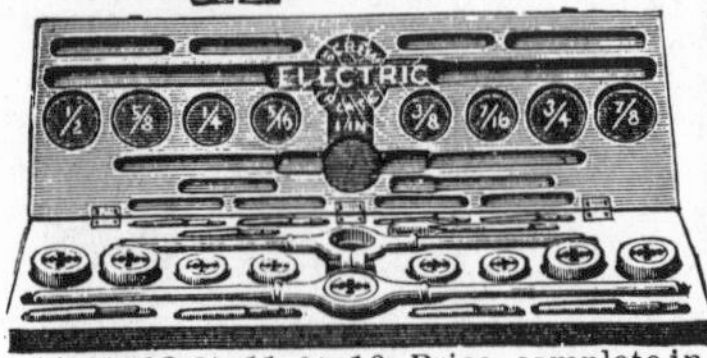

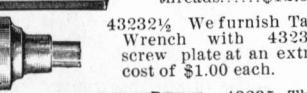

43235 The Champion Electric Screw Plate, No. 5. Length of stock, 23 inches, cuts ¼x20, 5/16x18, ⅜x16, 7/16x14, ½x12, ⅝x11, ¾x10. Price, complete in box.$11.00
43235½ We furnish Tap Wrench with 43235 screw plate at an extra cost of $1.10 each.

Screw Plates—Continued.

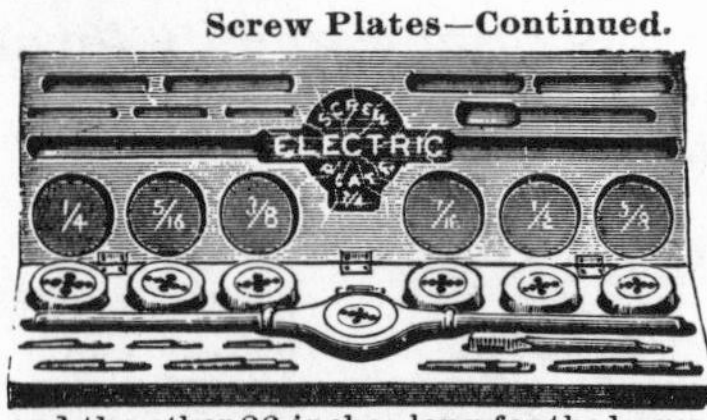

43236 The Champion Electric Screw Plate, No. 9, has two stocks, one 14½ inches long for the first four sizes and the other 26 inches long for the larger sizes; cuts ¼x20, 5/16x18, ⅜x16, 7/16x14, ½x12, ⅝x11, ¾x10, ⅞x10, 1x8. Complete in case..........$18.14
43236½ We furuish Tap Wrench for 43236 Screw plate at an extra cost of $1.50 each.

Blacksmiths' Stocks and Dies.

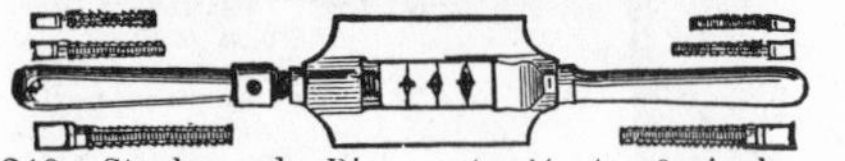

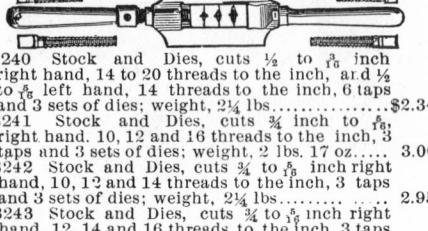

43240 Stock and Dies, cuts ½ to 3/16 inch right hand, 14 to 20 threads to the inch, and ½ to 5/16 left hand, 14 threads to the inch, 6 taps and 3 sets of dies; weight, 2¼ lbs..........$2.34
43241 Stock and Dies, cuts ¾ inch to 5/16, right hand. 10, 12 and 16 threads to the inch, 3 taps and 3 sets of dies; weight, 2 lbs. 17 oz..... 3.00
43242 Stock and Dies, cuts ¾ to 5/16 inch right hand, 10, 12 and 14 threads to the inch, 3 taps and 3 sets of dies; weight, 2¼ lbs.......... 2.95
43243 Stock and Dies, cuts ¾ to 5/16 inch right hand, 12, 14 and 16 threads to the inch, 3 taps and 3 sets of dies; weight, 2¼ lbs.......... 2.95
43245 Stock and Dies, cuts ⅝ to 3/16 inch right hand, 14, 18 and 22 threads to the inch, 6 taps and one set of 3 dies; weight, 3 lbs. 5 oz.. 2.90
43246 Stock and Dies, cuts ½ inch to ⅛ inch, right hand, 16, 20 and 26 threads to the inch, 6 taps and one set of three dies; weight, 2¼ lbs.......... 2.30
43247 Stock and Dies, cuts 5/16 to 1/16 inch, right hand, 16, 20, 24 and 32 threads to the inch, 4 taps and 1 set of 4 dies; weight, 1 lb.. 2.00
43248 Stock and Dies, cut 1 inch to ⅜ inch right hand, 9, 10 and 14 threads to the inch, 3 taps and 3 sets of dies, complete; weight, 4 lbs. 2 oz.......... 3.15
43249 Stock and Dies, cut 5/16 to 1/16, right hand, 18, 24 and 32 threads to the inch, 4 taps and 3 sets of dies, complete; weight, lb.......... 1.70

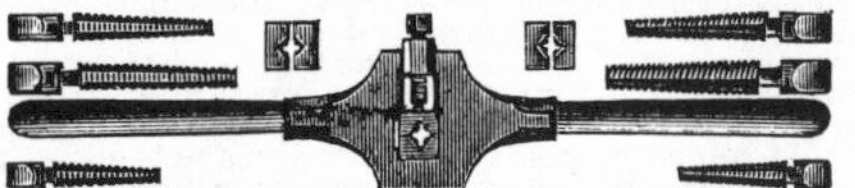

43250 Stock and Dies, cut ¾ to ⅛ inch right hand, 10, 12. 14 and 18 threads to the inch, 4 taps and 4 pairs of dies. Price, per set $4.50
43251 Stock and Dies, cuts ¾ in. to ⅜, right hand, 10, 12 and 16 threads to inch, 6 taps and 3 pairs of dies; weight, 5 lbs.......... 4.50

Combination Axle Cutter.

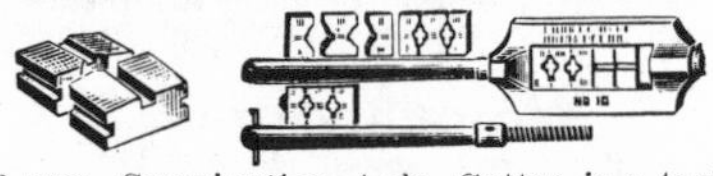

43252 The Combination Axle Cutter is a tool designed for cutting back the nut shoulder on carriage and wagon axles that have become worn, to allow the nut to be brought sufficiently close to the wheel to prevent the wobbling of the latter. It consists of one screw plate, with right and left hand dies, cutting as follows: 1⅛ inch and less 9 thread; 1 inch and less, 10 thread; ¾ inch and less, 12 thread; one pair each right and left hand cutters, for cutting back the nut shoulder of axle, also one pair cutters and two collars for cutting down axle from top, and one hack saw for cutting off end of axle when necessary. Price of axle cutter, complete..........$13.35

Blacksmiths' Taper Taps.

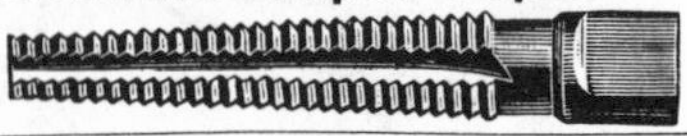

Order No. 43253.

Size.	Hand	Threads to the inch.	Price each.
1½ inch	R	6 7 & 8	$1.50
1½ inch	L	6 7 & 8	1.50
1¼ inch	R	6 7 8 & 9	.90
1¼ inch	L	8 & 9	.90
1 inch	R	7 8 9 & 10	.65
1 inch	L	8 & 9	.65
⅞ inch	R	8 9 10 & 12	.45
⅞ inch	L	9 & 12	.45
¾ inch	R	7 8 9 10 11 12 & 14	.33
¾ inch	L	10 12 14	.33
⅝ inch	R	10 11 12 14 & 16	.25
⅝ inch	L	10 11 12 14 & 16	.25
9/16 inch	R	10 12 14 & 16	.25
9/16 inch	L	12	.25
½ inch	R	10 12 14 16 & 18	.20
½ inch	L	12 & 14	.20
7/16 inch	R	10 12 14 16 & 18	.20
7/16 inch	L	14	.20
⅜ inch	R	10 12 14 16 18 & 20	18
5/16 inch	R	14 16 18 20 & 22	.16
¼ inch	R	16 18 20 22 24 & 26	.16
3/16 inch	R	24 26 & 28	.16
⅛ inch	R	30 & 32	.16

Blacksmiths' Dies.

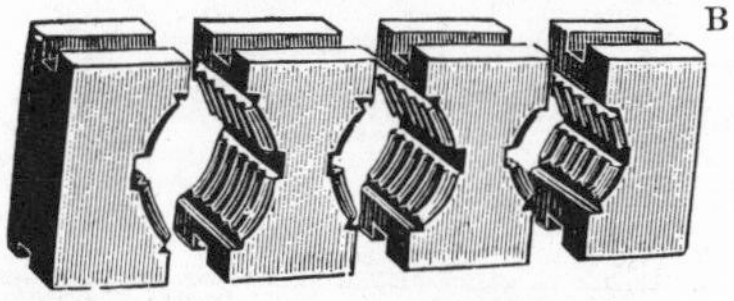

Blacksmiths' Dies, in sets only, to fit stocks as given on previous page.

We can not furnish extra dies to fit every No. of stock as they are not all interchangeable.

		Per set.
43254	For No. 43240 Stock and Die	$1.20
43255	For No. 43241 Stock and Die	1.50
43256	For No. 43243 Stock and Die	1.20
43257	For No. 43245 Stock and Die	1.20
43258	For No. 43247 Stock and Die	1.20
43259	For No. 43249 Stock and Die	1.50
43260	For No. 43250 Stock and Die	1.50
43261	For No. 43251 Stock and Die	1.65
43261½	For No. 43252 Stock and Die	1.65

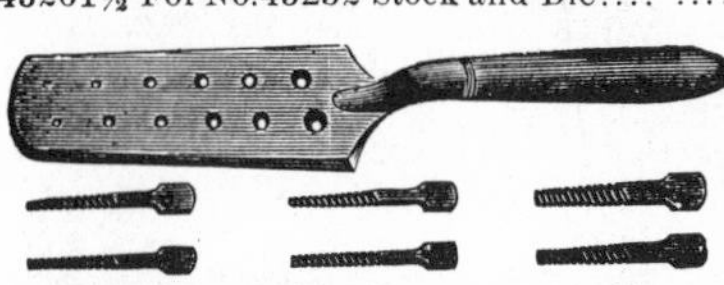

43262—Screw Plates, iron handles, will cut 14 different sizes from ⅛ to $\frac{3}{16}$; intended for gunsmiths', jewelers' or model makers' use. (The illustration shows only 12 holes.) Weight, 10 oz. Each............$ .90
Per dozen............10.50
By mail, 10c. extra.

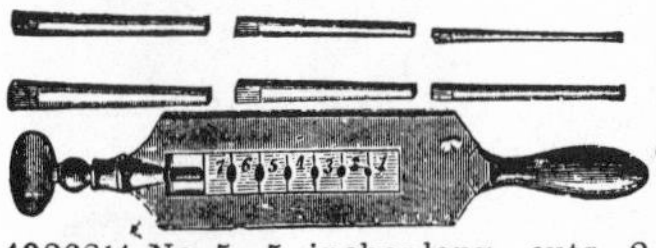

Gunsmiths' Stock and Dies. Being an imported article we cannot warrant them.

43262½ No. 5, 5 inches long, cuts 2-32, 3-32, 4-32 inch. 5-32, 4 taps and 4 dies............$1.68
43263 No 5½, 5½ inches long, cuts 3-32, 4-32, 5-32, 6-32 inches, 4 taps and 4 dies............ 1.73
43264 No. 6, 6 inches long, cuts 4-32, 5-32, 6-32, and 7-32, 4 taps and 4 dies............ 1.84
43265 No. 6½, 6½ inches long, cuts 4-32, 5-32, 6-32, and 7-32, 8-32, 5 taps and 5 dies............ 1.95
43266 No. 7, 7 inches long, cuts 5-32, 6-32, 7-32 and 8-32, 9-32, 5 taps and 5 dies............ 2.00
43267 No. 8, 8 inches long, cuts 6-32, 7-32, 8-32, 9-32 and 10 32 in. 5 taps and 5 dies.. 2.20
43268 No. 9, 9 inches long, cuts 6-32, 7-32, 8-32 9-32, 10-32, and 11-32 inches, 6 taps and 6 dies............ 2.60
43269 No. 10, 10 inches long, cuts 7-32, 8-32 9-32, 10-32, 11-32, 12-32 6 taps and, 6 dies..... 3.00
Weights vary from 10 oz, to 1 lb. 10 oz.

Bicycle Screw Plate.

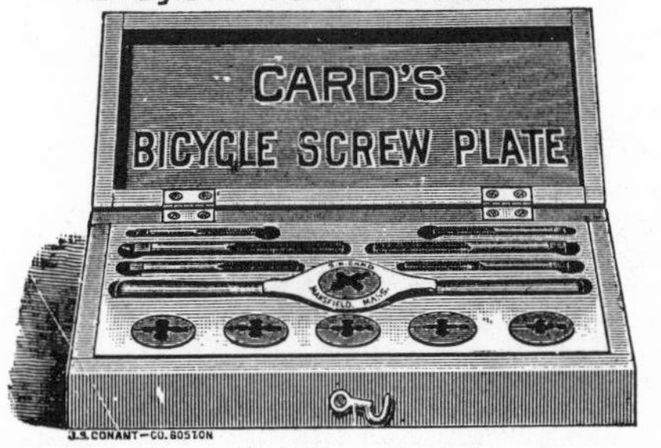

These plates will be found very convenient as they are especially adapted to bicycle work. The dies are adjustable for making tight or loose fits. Plug taps are furnished with these plates.

43270 Set No. 1. Stock 5 inches long, dies ⅝ of an inch in diameter, 6 dies and 6 taps.
Cutting 3-32, 54; ⅛, 40; ⅛, 42: 3, 48; 3, 56; 6, 38 -or an equal number of regular sizes.
Price, complete, in hardwood case............$ 5.00

43271 Set No. 2. Stock 5 inches long, dies ⅝ of an inch in diameter, 6 dies and 6 taps.
Cutting 3-32, 56; 7-64, 56; 9-64, 40; 1, 64; 1½, 56; 2, 48, or an equal number of regular sizes.
Price, complete, in hard wood case............ 5.00

43273 Set No. 3. Stock 5 inches long, dies ⅝ of an inch in diameter, 14 dies and 14 taps.
Cutting 3-32, 52; 3-32, 54; 3-32, 56; 7-64 56; ⅛, 40; ⅛, 42; 9-64, 40; 1, 64; 1½, 56; 2, 48; 3, 48; 3, 56; 4, 42; 6, 38; or an equal number of regular sizes.
Price, complete, in hard wood case............10.00

Do you own A Horse?

Then examine the prices we make on harness and horse supplies generally. We can supply your wants if any house can, and all our goods are exceptional value for the prices.

Wood Screw Cutter.

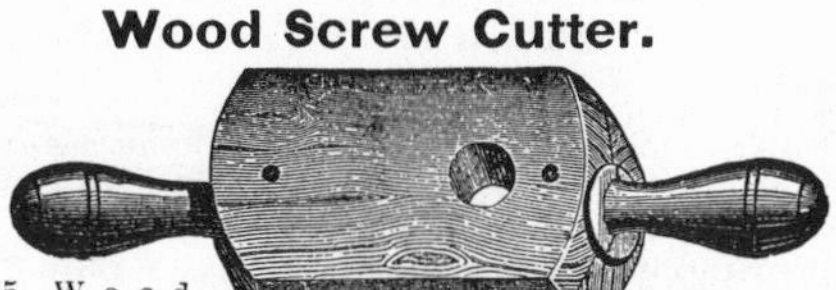

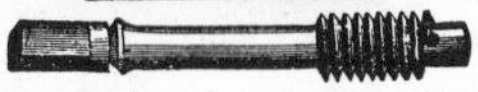

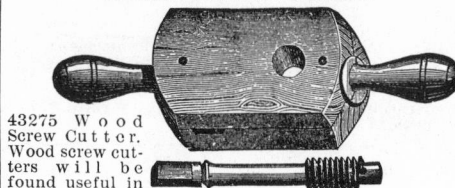

43275 Wood Screw Cutter. Wood screw cutters will be found useful in cutting wood screws for hand screws, and in jointed wood work, furniture, etc.

Cuts	¼	⅜	½	⅝	¾	1	1⅛
Each	.63c.	63c.	72c.	80c.	90c.	$1.05	1.25
Weight	8	9	10	13	15	22	32 oz

Cuts	1¼	1⅜	1½	1¾	2 in.
Each	$1.42	1.67	2.00	2.57	3.23
Weight	2¼ lbs.	3 lbs.	3 lbs.-3oz.	4½ lbs.	

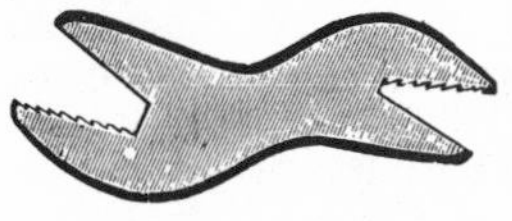

The "Always Ready" Wrench, the "Farmer's Friend." Forged from prepared steel, tempered in oil and nickel plated. The most convenient and durable wrench made, as it can be used on several sizes of nuts and gas pipes as well without adjusting it to fit. It is superior to and more durable than any monkey wrench or any other style of wrench made.

		Weight.	Each.
43277	Takes nut or pipe ¼ to ¾ in.	11 oz.	$0.30
43278	Takes nut or pipe ¼ to 1 in.	17 oz.	.40
43279	Takes nut or pipe ¼ to 1¼ in.	3 lbs.	.60

Monkey Wrenches.

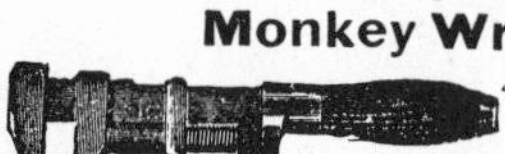

43281 Coe's Genuine Screw Wrenches, best wrought iron bar, head and screw, warranted.

Size	8 in.	10 in.	12 in.	15 in.
Weight	1 lb. 6 oz.	2 lbs. 3 oz.	2 lbs. 15 oz.	4 lbs. 5oz
Each	47c	56c	65c	$1.10

43283 Agricultural Screw Wrench, wrought iron bar, head and screw; same as cut of 43281.

Size	8 in.	10 in.	12 in	15 in.
Weight	1 lb. 6 oz.	2 lbs.	2½ lbs.	3½ lbs.
Each	20c	23c	27c	45c

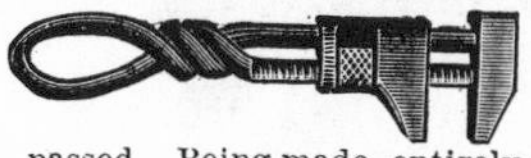

43285 The Acme Wrench. For strength, durability and easy action this wrench is unsurpassed. Being made entirely of iron, it will stand more hard usage than any monkey wrench made.

Sizes	5 in.	6 in.	8 in.
Weight	9 oz.	14 oz.	1 lb.
Each	30c	35c	40c.
Sizes	10 in.	12 in.	15 in.	18 in.
Weight	2 lbs. 2 oz.	4 lbs. 6 oz.	6 lbs.	8 lbs.
Each	45c	50c	90c	$1.10

The 5 or 6 inch sizes are the best wrenches made at a reasonable price, for bicycles, light machinery, etc.

A Leader.

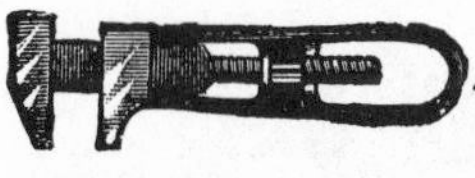

43289 Skeleton Monkey Wrench, all iron, tin finish. Good enough for common work. Weight, 7 oz.; length, 3¾ inch.
Each............$0.09
Per dozen............ .95
43290 Same style wrench, larger and better made, bright steel finish. Takes 1½ inch nut, weight, 11 oz.; length, 5 in. Each............ .17
Per dozen............ 1.75

Malleable Wrenches.

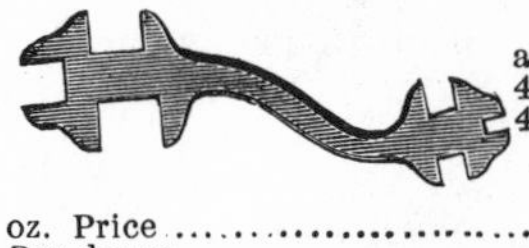

"S" wrenches, malleable iron.
43296 9 in.
43297 11 in.
9 inch weighs 1 lb. 11 inch weighs 1 lb. 9 oz. Price............$0.08
Per dozen............ .87

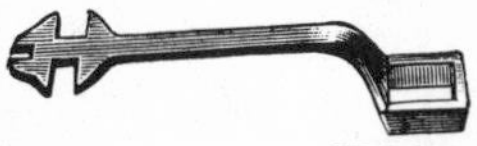

43298 Carriage Wrenches, malleable iron.

Size.	Weight.	Price each.
⅞ in.	9 oz.	$0.05
1 in.	12 oz.	.07
1⅛ in.	14 oz.	.08
1¼ in.	15 oz.	.10
1½ in.	16 oz.	.12

Per dozen, assorted as desired............1.00

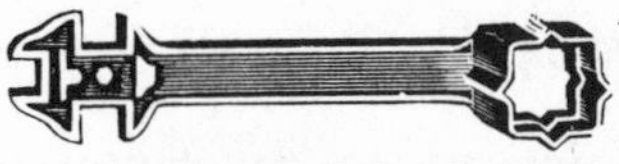

43299 Miller's Vehicle Axle Wrench, a new and very convenient article; one wrench does the work of four; made of malleable iron, japanned.

	Each.	Per doz.
1. Fits axle nuts, square or hexagon, from ⅞ to 1¼	$0.08	$0.87
2. Fits axle nuts, square or hexagon, from 1¼ to 1½	.12	1.30
3. Fits axle nut, sq. or hex., from 1½ to 2.	.15	1.50

Jack Screws.

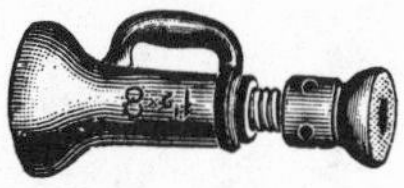

43300 Jack Screws, wrought iron screws, cast iron stands. We do not furnish levers with these screws.

Diameter of screw.	Height of stand.	Height over all.	Price each.	Price per doz.
1½ inches.	8	12	$1.12	$12.00
1½ inches.	10	14	1.27	14.25
1½ inches.	12	16	1.40	15.75
1¾ inches.	10	14	1.50	17.25
1¾ inches.	12	16	1.67	18.00
1¾ inches.	14	18	1.80	20.00
2 inches.	8	12½	1.60	18.00
2 inches.	10	14½	1.80	20.00
2 inches.	12	16½	2.00	22.00
2 inches.	16	20½	2.40	27.00

Slotted Rivets.

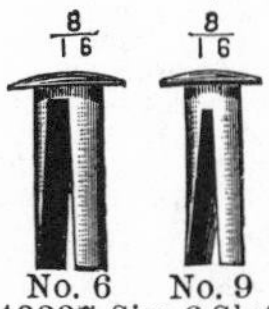

No. 6 No. 9

Slotted Clinch Rivets for general repair work. No tools except a common hammer required to set them; made of annealed steel coppered. Put up in wood boxes containing 100 rivets.

43337 Size 6 Slotted Rivets
Lengths...... $\frac{5}{16}$ $\frac{6}{16}$ $\frac{7}{16}$ $\frac{8}{16}$ $\frac{9}{16}$ $\frac{10}{16}$ $\frac{11}{16}$ $\frac{12}{16}$ inch.
Price per 100 rivets, any length............$0.20
43338 Size 6 slotted rivets assorted per 100.... .20
43339 Size 9 slotted rivets.
Lengths...... $\frac{3}{16}$ $\frac{4}{16}$ $\frac{5}{16}$ $\frac{6}{16}$ $\frac{7}{16}$ $\frac{8}{16}$ inch.
Price per 100 rivets, any length............$0.12
43340 Size 9 slotted rivets, assorted, per 100.... .12

Copper Rivets with Burrs.

Sizes 8, 9, 10 and 12 refer to the diameter of the wire. It will be observed that we quote different lengths in each size. *We sell them by the pound only.* There are about one-fourth more burrs than rivets in each pound.

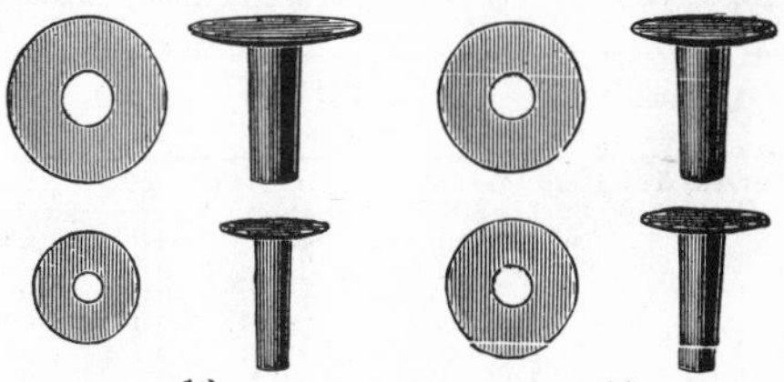

Burrs. 12 Rivets. Burrs. 10 Rivets.

43343 Size 8, Copper Rivets, with Burrs to fit.
Length, ¼ in., ⅜ in., ½ in., ⅝ in., ¾ in.
Price per pound, any length up to ¾ in............$0.23
43344 Assorted, from ⅜ in. to ¾ in. in pound boxes. Per box............ .23
43344½ Assorted, from ⅜ in. to ¾ inch in ½ lb. box. Per box............ .13
43345 Size 9, Copper Rivets, with Burrs to fit.
Length, ¼ in., ⅜ in., ½ in., ⅝ in., ¾ in.
Price per pound, any length up to ¾ in............ .25
43346 Assorted, from ⅜ in to ¾ inch in pound boxes. Per box............ .25
43346½ Assorted, from ⅜ in. to ¾ inch in ½ lb box. Per box............ .15
43347 Size 10, Copper Rivets, with Burrs to fit.
Length, ¼ in., ⅜ in., ½ in., ⅝ in., ¾ in.
Price per pound, any length up to ¾ inch............ .28
43348 Assorted, from ⅜ in. to ¾ inch in pound box. Per box............ .28
43348½ Assorted, from ⅜ in. to ¾ inch in ½ lb. box. Per box............ .16
43349 Size 12, Copper Rivets with Burrs to fit.
Length, ¼ in., ⅜ in., ½ in., ⅝ in., ¾ in.
Price per pound, any length up to ¾ in............ .30
43350 Assorted, from ⅜ in. to ¾ inch in pound boxes. Per box............ .30
43350½ Assorted, from ⅜ in. to ¾ inch in ½ lb. boxes. Per box............ .17

Rivet Sets.

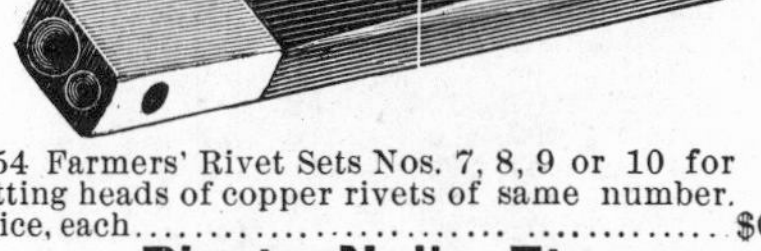

43354 Farmers' Rivet Sets Nos. 7, 8, 9 or 10 for setting heads of copper rivets of same number.
Price, each............$0.20

Rivets, Nails, Etc.

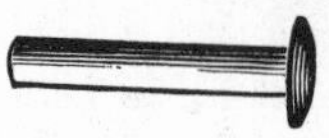

43355 Rivets, oval head. The number of rivets to the pound is approximated, ¼ inch in diameter, any length.
Per lb............$0.07

¼ INCH DIAM.

Length		1	1⅛	1¼	1⅜	1½	1½
No. rivets to lb.		56	54	52	50	48	46
Length	1¾	1⅞	2	2⅛	2¼	2¾	2½
No. rivets to lb.	44	40	37	35	33	30	28
Length				2⅝	2¾	2⅞	3
No. rivets to lb.				25	23	22	20

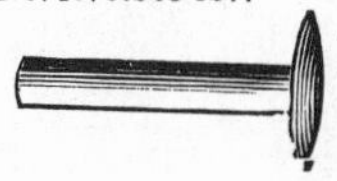

43356 Rivets flat head. The number of rivets to the pound is approximated, ¼ inch in diameter, any length.
Per lb............$0.07

Rivets—Continued.

Length	1	1⅛	1¼	1⅜	1½	1⅝
No. rivets to lb.	58	56	54	53	50	48
Length	1¾	1⅞	2	2⅛	2¼	2⅜
No. rivets to lb.	46	44	42	40	38	36
Length		2½	2⅝	2¾	2⅞	3
No. rivets to lb.		34	32	30	28	26

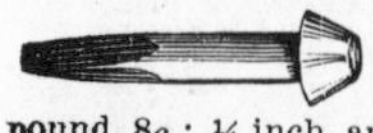

43357 Wagon Box Nails, 3-16 and ¼ inch in diameter, lengths 1¼, 1⅜, 1½, 1⅝, 1¾ 1⅞ and 2 inch, any length per pound, 8c.; ¼ inch, any length, per lb $0.07

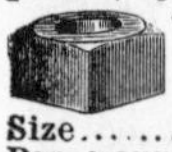

43358 Threaded Square Nuts. We furnish Standard Thread only.

Size	¼	5/16	⅜	7/16	½	⅝	¾
Per pound	25c.	17c.	13½	12c.	11c.	9c.	9c.
Av. No. in lb	74	30	22	13	12	6	3

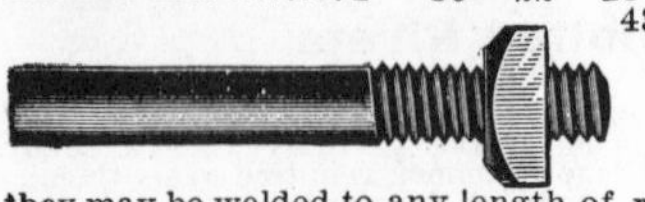

43359 Bolt ends, square nuts, very convenient when extra long bolts are required, as they may be welded to any length of round iron same size.

Diameter of iron	½	⅝	¾	⅞	1 in
Length of ends	8	9	10	11	12
Price, per doz	25c.	28c.	45c.	84c.	$1.20
Av. weight, per doz.	6	8	13	25	48 lbs.

Carriage Bolts.

43364 Patent Reverse helecoid agricultural bolts. These bolts are something new, and are giving great satisfaction. The advantages over the ordinary kind are that having no square shoulder under the head avoids the necessity of mortising a square hole in the better grades of work, or heating the bolt to burn out the hole as is done in ordinary practice, and owing to the thread or ribs they will not turn when the nut is being screwed up. Besides giving them great strength, they are very symmetrical and nicely finished goods.

¼ inch.			5/16 inch.			⅜ inch.		
	Per doz.	Per 100		Per doz.	Per 100		Per doz.	Per 100.
1	$0.06	$0.36	1	$0.07	$0.43	1	$0.10	$0.63
1½	.06	.38	1½	.07	.43	1½	10	.63
1¾	.07	.39	1¾	.08	.45	1¾	.10	.63
2	.07	.40	2	.08	.47	2	.10	.63
2¼	.07	.41	2¼	.08	.50	2¼	.10	.63
2½	.07	.41	2½	.08	.51	2½	.11	.68
2¾	.08	.43	2¾	.09	.54	2¾	.11	69
3	.08	.45	3	.09	.54	3	.12	.72
3¼	.08	.47	3¼	.09	.57	3¼	.12	.76
3½	.08	.48	3½	.10	.60	3½	.12	.79
3¾	.08	.49	3¾	.10	62	3¾	.15	.81
4	.10	.50	4	.10	.63	4	.15	.84

Carriage Bolts.

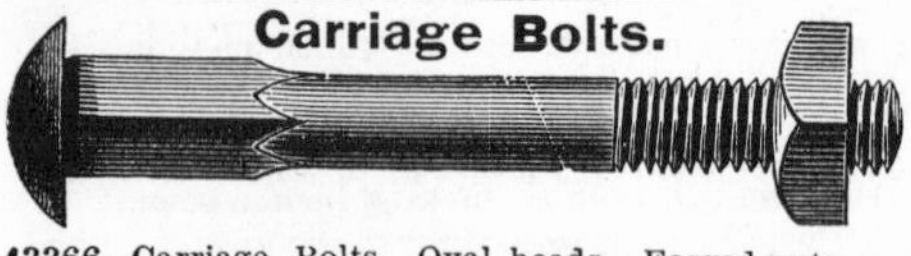

43366 Carriage Bolts, Oval heads. Forged nuts. These bolts are not a cheap, poorly made article. We guarantee them to be first class. They are made by one of the largest and best known manufacturers of this class of goods in the world.

WEIGHT OF CARRIAGE BOLTS PER 100.

Carriage bolts ¼ inch from 1¼ to 6 inches in length, weigh from 2 lbs, to 9¾ lbs.; ⅜ from 1¾ to 12 inches weigh from 9½ lbs, to 45 lbs;. 5-16 from 1¼ to 8 inches in length, from 6½ to 20 lbs.; ½ inch from 2 to 16 inches, from 20 to 98 lbs. per 100.

¼ inch.			5/16 inch.			⅜ inch:			½ inch.		
Length.	Per Doz.	Per 100.	Length.	Per Doz.	Per 100.	Length.	Per Doz.	Per 100.	Length.	Per Doz.	Per 100.
	$	$		$	$		$	$		$	$
1¼	0.05	0.30	1¼	0.06	0.35	1¼	0.09	0.50	2	.15	0.90
1½	.05	.30	1½	.06	.35	1½	.09	.50	2¼	.15	.90
1¾	.05	.31	1¾	.06	.37	1¾	.09	.50	2½	.15	.92
2	.05	.32	2	.07	.39	2	.09	.50	3	.15	.97
2¼	.05	.33	2¼	.07	.40	2¼	.10	.53	3½	.16	1.05
2½	.06	.34	2½	.07	.42	2½	.10	.55	4	.17	1.12
2¾	.06	.35	2¾	.08	.43	2¾	.10	.57	4½	.18	1.18
3	.06	.36	3	.08	.45	3	.10	.59	5	.20	1.25
3¼	.07	.38	3¼	.08	.47	3¼	.10	.61	5½	.22	1.32
3½	.07	.39	3½	.09	.49	3½	.10	.63	6	.23	1.40
3¾	.07	.40	3¾	.09	.50	3¾	.11	.66	6½	.24	1.47
4	.07	.41	4	.09	.52	4	.11	.68	7	.25	1.54
4½	.08	.43	4¼	.09	.53	4¼	.11	.70	7½	.26	1.60
5	.08	.45	4½	.10	.55	4½	.11	.72	8	.26	1.68
5½	.09	.47	5	.10	.58	4¾	.12	.75	8½	.27	1.75
6	.10	.50	5½	.10	.62	5	.12	.77	9	.28	1.83
7	.10	.56	6	.10	.65	5½	13	.82	9½	.30	1.92
8	.10	.63	6½	.11	.68	6	.13	.86	10	.31	2.00
			7	.12	.72	6½	.14	.90	10½	.32	2.07
			7½	.13	.75	7	.14	.95	11	.33	2.15
			8	.15	.78	7½	.15	1.00	11½	.34	2.25
			9	15	.85	8	.16	1.05	12	.35	2.32
			10	.15	.95	8½	.17	1.10	13	.36	2.40
						9	.18	1.12	14	.37	2.51
						10	.20	1.21	15	.40	2.66
						11	.22	1.30	16	.45	2.80
						12	.24	1.38			

Tire and Iron Work Bolts.

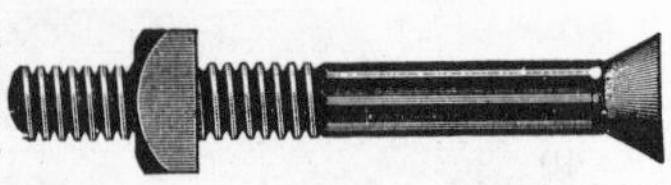

43368 This pattern of bolt is entirely new. The thread prevents bolt from turning in the wood when nut is turned, which is a decided advantage.

3/16 inch.			¼ inch.			5/16 inch.		
Lgth.	Per doz.	Per 100	Lgth.	Per doz.	Per 100	Lgth.	Per doz.	Per 100
1¼	$0.03	$0.17	1¾	$0.04	$0.23	1¼	$0.05	$0.30
1½	.03	.17	2	.04	.25	1¾	.05	.30
1¾	.03	.18	2¼	.04	.26	2	.05	.32
2	.03	.19	2½	.04	.27	2¼	:05	.34
2¼	.04	.21	2¾	.05	.29	2½	.05	.36
2½	.04	.22	3	.05	.31	2¾	.05	.38
2¾	.04	.23				3	.06	.46
3	.04	.25						

43369 Common Tire Bolts, not fluted; like cut No. 43368 Same sizes and price as No. 43368.

Iron Washers.

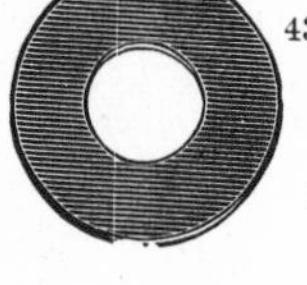

43370 Iron Washers.

	Per doz.	Per 100
For ¼ in. bolt	1c.	$0 06
For 5/16 in. bolt	2c.	.15
For ⅜ in. bolt	3c.	.22
For ½ in. bolt	4c.	.30

43371 By the pound.	Number of washers in a pound.	Price, per pound.
For ¼ in. Bolt	139	$ .07½
For 5/16 " "	113	.08
For ⅜ " "	55	.07½
For ½ " "	20	.07
For ¾ " "	10	.07
For ⅞ " "	9	.07
For 1 " "	8	.07

Stove Bolts.

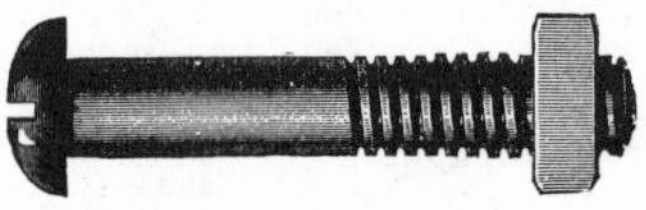

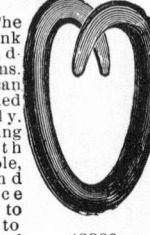

43373 3/16 INCH ROUND HEAD.

Length.	½	⅝	¾	⅞	1	1¼	1½	1¾	2	2½	3
Per doz.	$ 0.05	.06	.06	.06	.06	.06	.07	.07	.07	.08	.08
Per 100.	.31	.31	.31	.33	.33	.35	.36	.38	.40	.44	.47

¼ INCH ROUND HEAD.

Length.	½	⅝	¾	⅞	1	1¼	1½	1¾	2	2½	3
Per doz.	$0 06	.06	.06	.06	.06	.07	.07	.07	08	.08	.08
Per 100	.35	.35	.35	.36	.36	.38	.38	.42	.44	.50	.52

5/16 INCH ROUND HEAD.

Length	¾	⅞	1	1¼	1½	2	2½	3
Per doz	$0.08	.09	.09	.09	.10	.10	.11	.12
Per 100	.50	.52	.53	.56	.60	.63	.67	.72

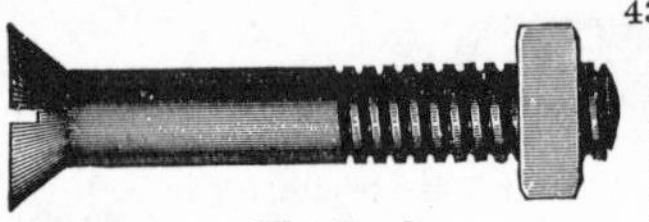

Flat Head.

43374 Stove bolts. Stove Bolts are very useful; are used for a variety of purposes--for repairing and manufacturing machinery, etc. Be sure and state whether round or flat head is wanted. If no kind is stated will send flat head.

3/16 INCH FLAT HEAD.

Length	½	⅝	¾	⅞	1	1¼	1½	2	2½	3
Per doz	$0.04	.04	.04	.04	.05	.05	.05	.06	.06	.07
Per 100	.22	.22	.22	.24	.25	.26	.27	.32	.35	.38

¼ INCH FLAT HE&D.

Length	⅝	¾	⅞	1	1¼	1½	2	2½	3
Per doz	$0.05	. 05	.05	.05	.05	.05	.06	.06	.07
Per 100	.24	.24	.26	.26	.28	.29	.33	.36	.40

5/16 INCH FLAT HEAD.

Length	¾	⅞	1	1¼	1½	2	2½	3
Per doz	$0.06	.07	.07	.07	.07	.07	.08	.08
Per 100	$0.36	.40	.40	.42	.44	.47	.51	.54

Bolts—Continued.

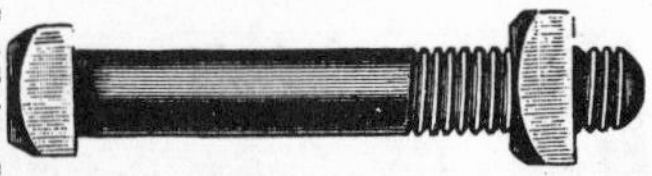

43375 Machine Bolts, with square heads and nuts, finished points. Machine bolts do not have a square shoulder near the head like carriage bolts, but are round all the way up to the head.

¼-inch.— L'gth Up to	Per dz.	Per 100	⅜-inch.— L'gth Up to	Per dz.	Per 100	½-inch.— Length, Up to	Pr dz.	Per 100
1½	$0.10	$0.56	1½	$0.13	$0.72	1½	$0.21	$1.20
2	.10	.59	2	.13	.74	2	.22	1.27
2¼	.10	.59	2¼	.13	.78	2¼	.23	1.31
2½	.10	.60	2½	.14	.80	2½	.24	1.34
3	.10	.62	3	.15	.84	3	.25	1.41
3½	.10	.64	3½	.16	.88	3½	.26	1.48
4	.11	.66	4	.17	.92	4	.27	1.55
4½	.11	.68	4½	.18	.96	4½	28	1.62
5	.11	.70	5	.20	1.00	5	.30	1.69
5½	.12	.72	5½	.21	1.04	5½	.33	1.76
6	.12	.74	6	.22	1.08	6	.35	1.83
6½	.12	.76	6½	.22	1.12	6½	.37	1.90
7	.13	.78	7	.23	1.16	7	.38	1.99
5/16-inch.— L'gth,	Pr dz.	Per 100	7½	.23	1.20	8	.39	2.12
1½	$0.10	$0.64	8	.23	1.24	9	.40	2.26
2	.12	.67				10	.43	2.40
2½	.13	.69				11	.46	2.54
2½	.13	.70				12	.48	2.68
3	.13	.73				14	.58	2.96
3½	.14	.76				16	.63	3.24
4	.15	.79				18	.65	3.52
4½	.15	.82				20	.68	3.80
5	.16	.85						
5½	.18	.88						
6	.19	.91						
6½	.20	.94						
7	.21	.97						

Repair Links for Chains.

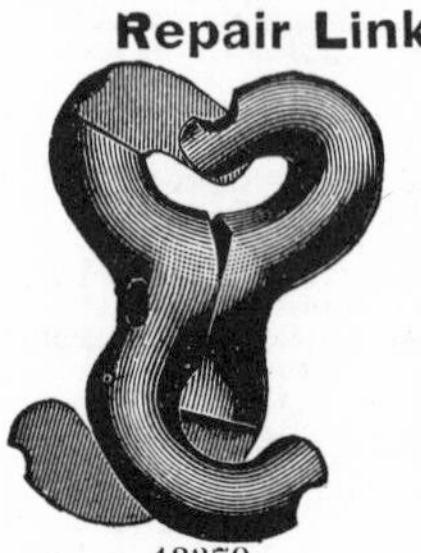

43379

43379 The Baker Link for Mending Chains. A chain can be mended instantly, thus doing away with the trouble, delay and annoyance of having to take it to shop and have it mended. Made four sizes.

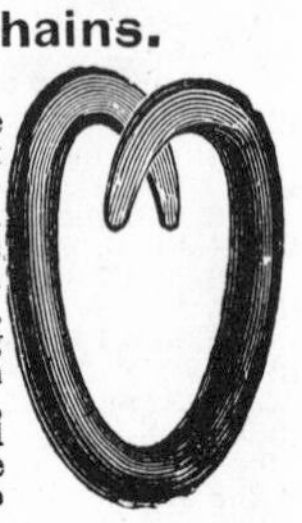

43380

Sizes	5/16	⅜	7/16	9/16
Each	7c	8c	9c	11c
Per dozen	.75c	87c	98c	$1,19

43380 Repair Links for connecting or repairing chains.

Sizes	3/16	¼	6/16
Weight per dozen	12 oz.	14 oz.	1 lb. 7 oz.
Per dozen	12c	20c	25c.
Sizes	⅜		
Weight	2½ lbs.		
Per dozen	28c.		

Lag or Coach Screw.

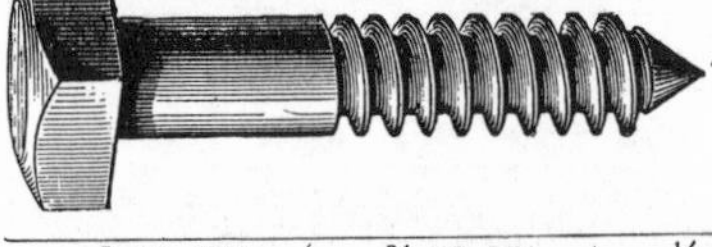

43384 LAG OR COACH SCREWS, SQUARE HEADS.

5/16 IN. DIA.			⅜ IN. DIA.			½ IN. DIA.		
Length	Per doz	Per 100	Length	Per doz	Per 100	Length	Per doz	Per 100
1½	$0.10	$0.54	1½	$0.11	$0.62	1½	$0.14	$0.86
2	.10	.58	2	.11	.66	2	.15	.93
2½	.11	.62	2½	.12	.70	2½	.18	1.00
3	.11	.66	3	.12	.74	3	.19	1.07
3½	.12	.70	3½	.13	.78	3½	.19	1.14
4	.12	.74	4	.13	.82	4	.19	1.21
4½	.13	.78	4½	.14	.86	4½	.20	1.28
5	.13	.82	5	.15	.90	5	.20	1.35
5½	.14	.86	5½	.16	.94	5½	.20	1.42
6	.15	.90	6	.17	.98	6	.22	1.50
						7	.24	1.64
						8	.25	1.78
						9	.26	1.92
						10	.28	2.06
						11	.30	2.20
						12	.32	2.34

Skein Screws.

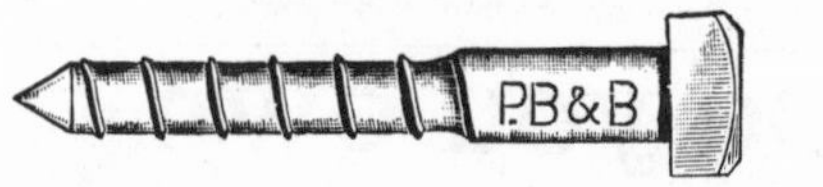

43385 Skein Screws, square heads.

Length	6	7	7½	8
Diameter	½	9/16	⅝	⅝
Per dozen	32c	35c	38c	42c

Horseshoes.

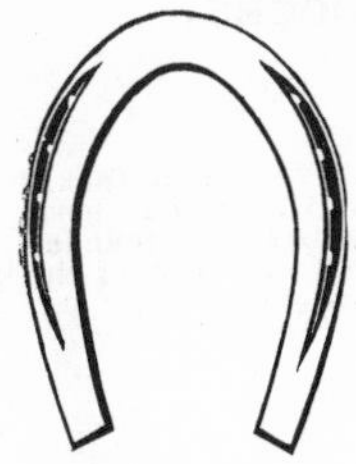

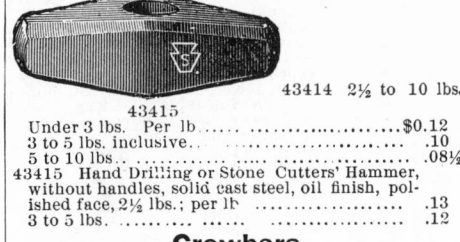

43386 Horse Shoes. Perkins' pattern patent machine, steam hammered, front and hind. The shoes are not ready to put on as they are not finished, but are for blacksmiths who finish them.

Number	1	2	3	4	5	6
Length from outside of front shoe	5½	6	6½	6⅞	7¼	7⅜ in
Width from outside to outside of front shoe	4½	4¾	5⅛	5⅝	6	6¾
Price, per set, front and hind	18c	20c	30c	35c	40c	50c
Price, per keg of 100 lbs. front and hind	$4.50	4.50	4.50	4.50	4.50	4.50

Toe Calks.

43388 Toe Calks, admitted to be the best in the market, made of Bessemer steel.

No.	1	2	3	4	5	6
No. of calks to lb.	20	12	8	6	5	4

Price, per lb. 6c.

Horse Nails.

43389 Au Sable Horse Nails are forged hot from the end of the rod on precisely the same principle that a nail is made by hand. No acids used in polishing.

No.	Size.	Per lb.	Per box.
5	1⅞	$0.19	$4.50
6	2	.17	4.05
7	2¼	.16	3.81
8	2⅜	.15	3.57
9	2½	14	3.42
10	2⅝	.11	2.70

The above sizes are the average, as they may run 1-16 of an inch shorter or longer; in boxes of 25 pounds.

Washer Cutters.

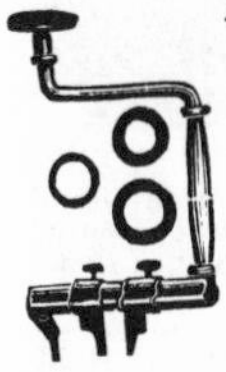

43394 Universal Washer Cutter, for cutting out rings or washers of leather, wood, rubber, etc. In form of a brace, all complete. Malleable, with steel cutters. Cuts a circle up to 8½ inches diameter. Size 10¼ x4⅞. The most perfect washer cutter in existence.

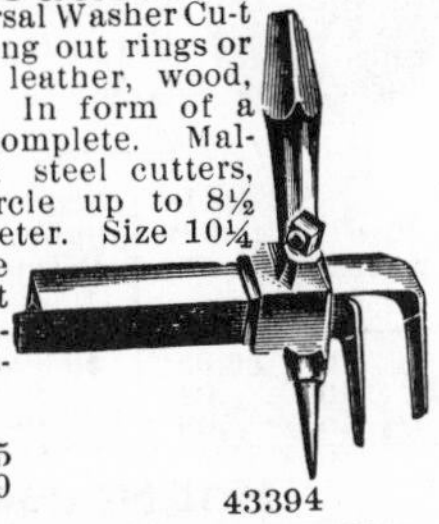

Weight, 21 ounces.
Each $0.75
Per doz 8.10

43394

43395 Washer Cutter, extra fine steel knives, is adjustable so that several sizes of washers may be cut with it; cuts the washer and the hole in the center with one operation; intended to be used in ordinary bit brace. Price, each ...... $0.50. Per dozen $5.40

Oil Trough.

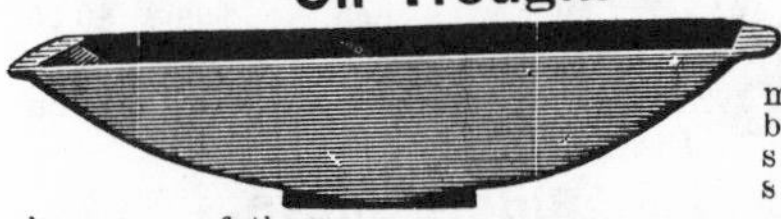

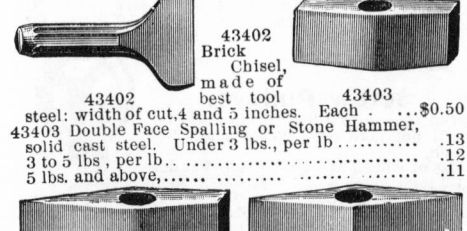

Every wagon-maker or black-smith should have one of these.

43399 Oil Trough, for oiling wagon wheels, for 2-in. tire; made of cast iron; weighs 10 lbs. Each. $0.45

43400 Oil Trough, larger size than 43399, for wheels with tire as wide as 4 inch. Weight, 15 pounds. Each 65

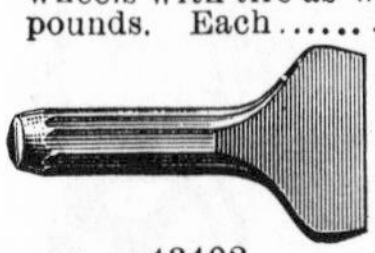

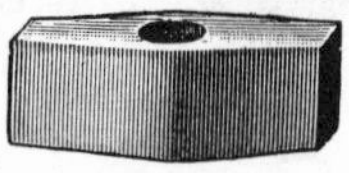

43402   43403

43402 Brick Chisel, made of best tool steel: width of cut, 4 and 5 inches. Each $0.50

43403 Double Face Spalling or Stone Hammer, solid cast steel. Under 3 lbs., per lb ...... .13
3 to 5 lbs, per lb ...... .12
5 lbs. and above ...... .11

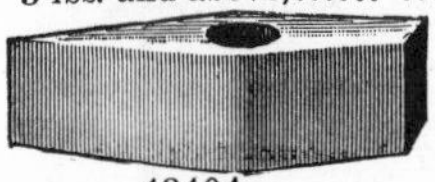

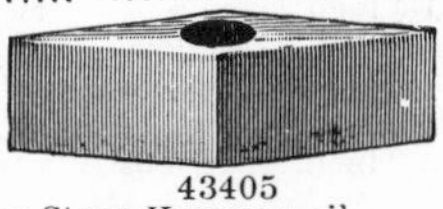

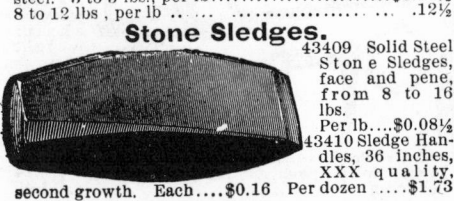

43404   43405

43404 Single Face Spalling or Stone Hammer, oil finish, polished face and pene, solid cast steel.
Under 3 lbs., per lb $0.13
3 to 5 lbs., per lb ...... .12
5 lbs. and above, per lb ...... .11

43405 Stone Axes, oil finished, made of best tool steel. 3 to 5 lbs., per lb $0.13½
8 to 12 lbs, per lb ...... .12½

Stone Sledges.

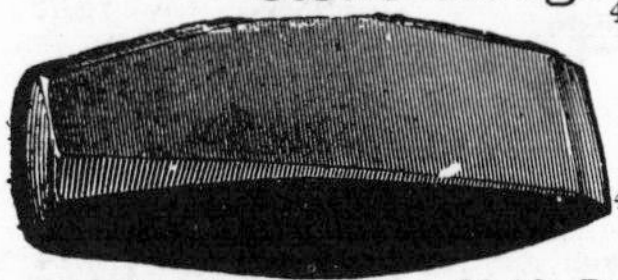

43409 Solid Steel Stone Sledges, face and pene, from 8 to 16 lbs.
Per lb.... $0.08½

43410 Sledge Handles, 36 inches, XXX quality, second growth. Each .... $0.16 Per dozen $1.73

Drilling or Striking Hammers.

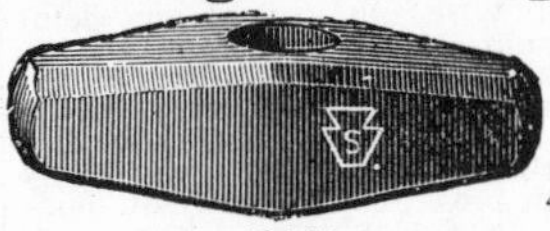

43415   43414 2½ to 10 lbs.

Under 3 lbs. Per lb $0.12
3 to 5 lbs. inclusive ...... .10
5 to 10 lbs ...... .08½

43415 Hand Drilling or Stone Cutters' Hammer, without handles, solid cast steel, oil finish, polished face, 2½ lbs.; per lb ...... .13
3 to 5 lbs ...... .12

Crowbars.

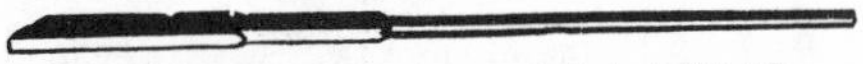

43419 Pinch Point Crowbars, solid steel, 12, 13, 14, 15, 16, 17, 18, 19 and 20 lbs. Per lb $0.03½

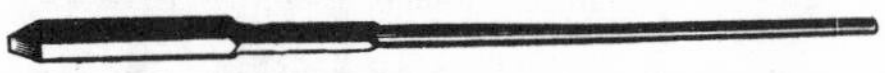

43420 Wedge Point Crowbars, solid steel, 12, 13, 14, 15, 16, 17, 18, 19 and 20 lbs. Per lb $0.03½

Trowels.

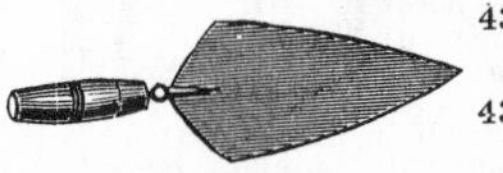

43423 Masons' Brick Trowel, 10 in.
Each $0.40

43425 Masons' Brick Trowel, 11 in.
Each $0.50

43427 Brade's English Crown Brick Trowels, London pattern.

Length	11 in.	12 in	13 in.
Price, each	90c	$1.00	$1.10

Plastering Trowels.

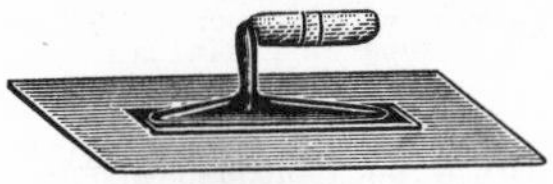

43429 Plastering Trowels—
10in. 11in. 12in.
Ea. 66c 71c 81c

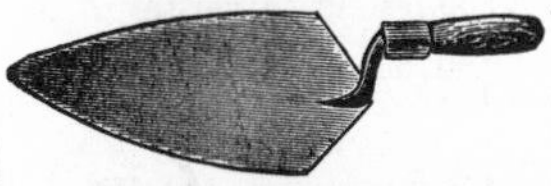

43430 Brick Trowels, celebrated make, Philadelphia pattern.
10½ inch ...... Each. $1.20
12 inch 1.30

Corner Trowels.

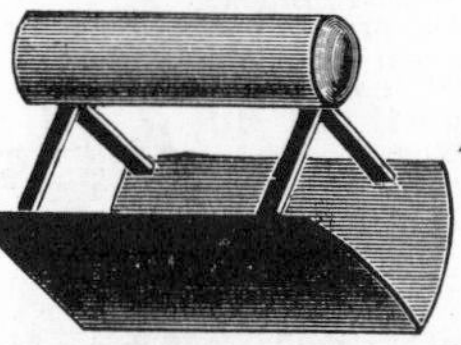

43434 Corner Trowels, 6 inch, cast steel.
Each $0.60
Per dozen 6.48

Pointing Trowels.

43435 Pointing Trowels, like 43423.

Length	4in.	4½in.	5in.
Each	20c	22c	25c

Masons' Lines.

43439 Masons' Cotton Lines, put up in hanks of 48 feet, several connected in one length, No. 4½.
Per hank of 48 feet. Each $0.23
Per dozen 2.50

43440 Garden Lines, braided Italian hemp, in hanks of 100 feet, 2 lines connected. Per hank of 100 feet ...... .38
Per dozen 4.20

Wheelbarrows.

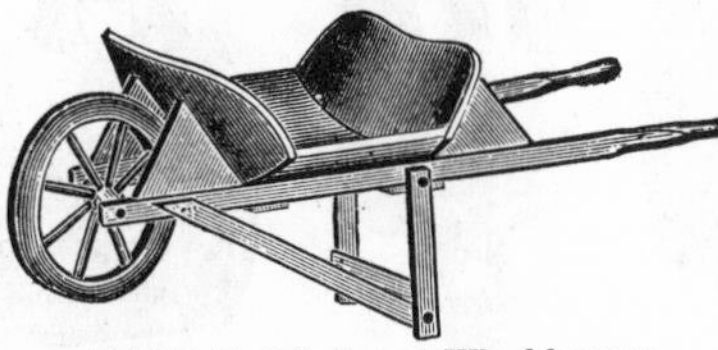

Half Bolted Railroad Wheel barrow.

The best low priced wheelbarrow made. Has full size tray; wood or steel wheels. Diameter of wheels, 16 in. Packed for shipment, tray is fastened to handles, legs are folded on side of handles, and wheel bolted on inside of tray. Can be easily and quickly set up.

		Each.	Per doz.
42442	With wood wheels	$1.15	$12.00
43442½	With steel wheels	1.25	13.00

OUR BUSINESS

Is to keep on hand, at reasonable prices, all those things which you require in your business.

Garden Wheelbarrow.

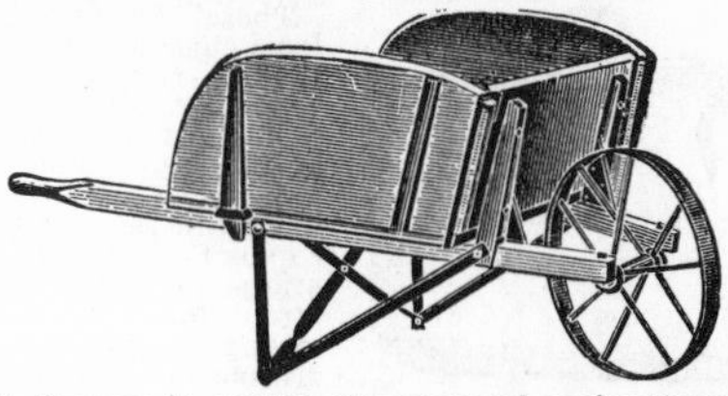

This Barrow is neater, stronger and easier to put together than any other garden barrow made. It is folded for shipping, including wheel it takes a space 5x24x60 inches; weight 40 pounds. The frame is made of japanned steel, body and handles are of wood, nicely painted. Size of bottom 21x27 inches, sides 12x28 inches, size of front 12x19 inches. It has a steel wheel 16 inches in diameter, with tire ¼x1½ inches.

43443 Price, each.. $2.25 Per dozen 26.00

Steel Frame Barrow.

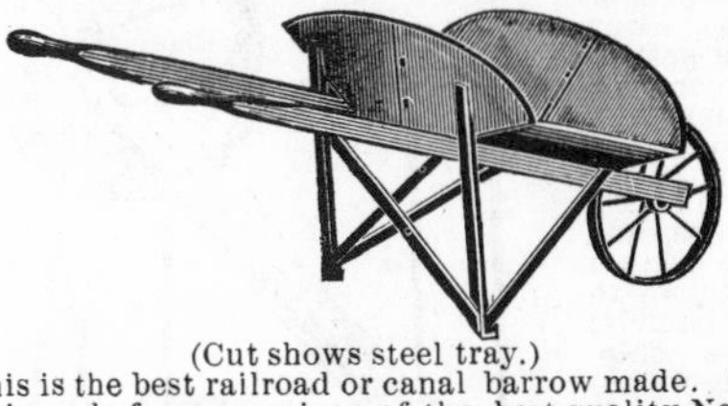

(Cut shows steel tray.)

This is the best railroad or canal barrow made. The tray is made from one piece of the best quality No. 16 steel, the frame is of steel and bolted to handles. It is folded for shipment, in a space 3x5x60 inches. Furnished only with 16 steel wheel. Weight, 45 pounds.

43444 Price, each, with steel tray $2.50

43445 We can furnish the above wheelbarrow with full size best quality wood tray.
Price, each, with wood tray 1.75

Mortar Barrow.

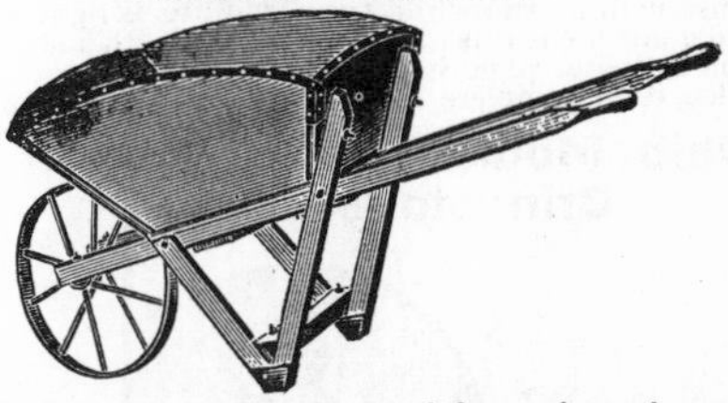

This barrow can also be used for coal, sand, gravel, etc. Our patent malleable shoe bolted on combines the legs, braces and cross bar, so that we have simplicity and great strength. Edges of tray are iron strapped; painted brown, size of tray, 10 inches deep at handles, 15 inches deep at wheels; top 27 inches wide by 30 inches long. Furnished with 16 inch steel wheels. Packed for shipment, weight, 50 pounds.

43446 Price, each $2.00

Stone Barrow.

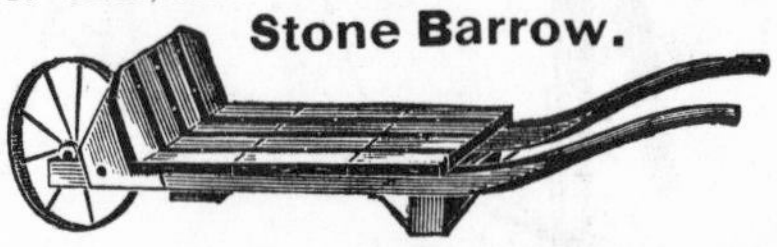

Made very strong and especially adapted to heavy work. Bent handles, thoroughly bolted, well ironed, painted brown; size of bottom, 28x28 inches, front, 9x28 inches; weight, 65 pounds.

43447 Price, each $2.50

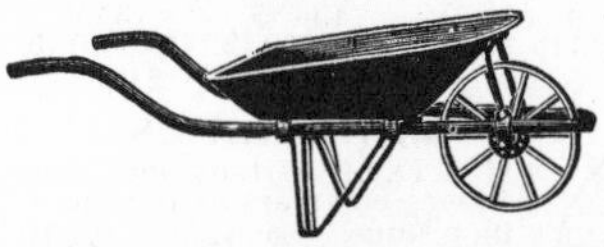

43449 Columbus tubular steel mining and general purpose barrows. No. 6 size, tray made of No. 14 steel: capacity 3 cubic feet of earth. Weight of barrow, 80 lbs.
Price each ...... $5.82 Per dozen $63.00

Sand Screens for Masons' Use.

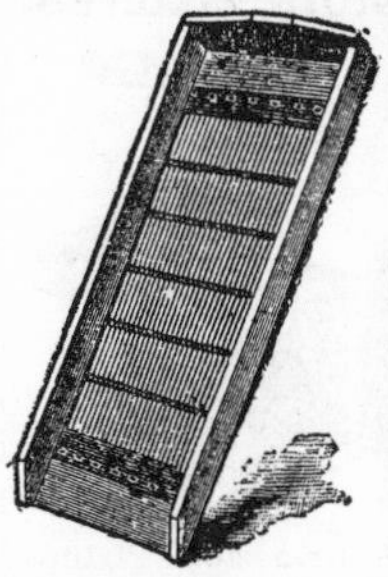

Made of heavy parallel wires, looped to pass through the slots punched uniformly in narrow strips of sheet steel. The supporting rods are passed through the loops at the back of the sheet steel and firmly hold the wires in place. At the top and bottom wide steel plates are connected in the same manner. Weight, large size, about 42 lbs.; small size, about 35 lbs. Made in three sizes of mesh.

No. 2, about ⅜ inch between wires.
No 3, about ¼ inch between wires.
No. 4, about 3.16 inch between wires.

In ordering always state size of mesh wanted.

43450 Small size, 60 inches long, by 22 inches wide. Each $3.75

43451 Large size, 66 inches long, by 26 inches wide. Each 4.69

Mason Tool Bag.

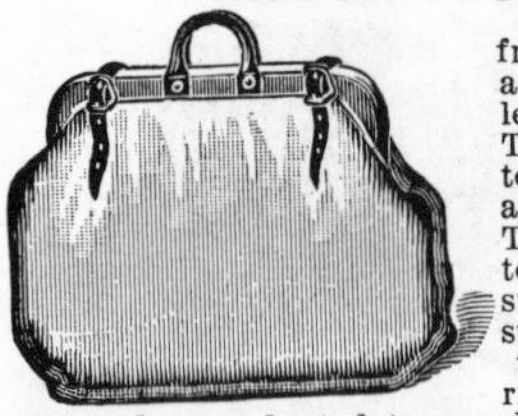

These bags are made from close woven canvas, and are reinforced with leather in all the seams. The bottoms are protected by metal studs and are well stiffened. They are secured at the top by two riveted russet straps in addition to a strong lock. They have trong leather handles, riveted on, are made with care, and are adapted to rough usage. Have them in two sizes only.

43452 20-inch. Price, each $1.60
24-inch. Price, each 2.00

Quick Edge Grindstone.

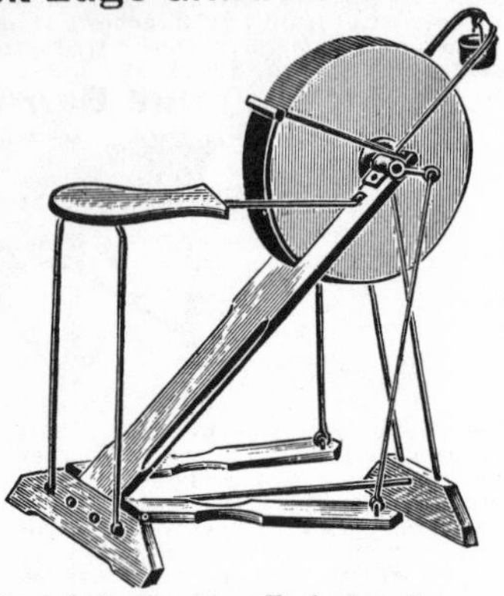

43453 For the use of the farmer, butcher, carpenter, cabinet maker and pattern maker. The diameter of the stone is 17 inches, width 2¼ inches, and weighs from 45 to 50 pounds; the shipping weight is 70 lbs. It is packed for shipment, but it is a very small matter to set up the grinder for use. Each stone is plugged and center-bored true, and faced to fit the mandrel plate. Hard wood is used in its construction, and while the structure is light and convenient it is of wonderful strength and firm in operative position.
Price, each, complete, as shown in cut.........$3.50

Ohio Mounted Grindstones.

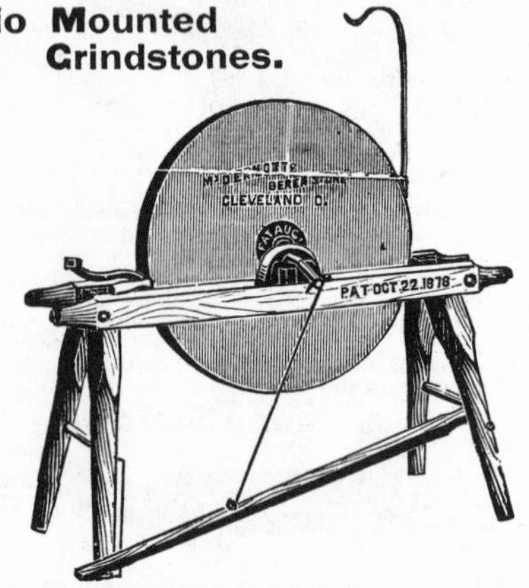

OAK FRAME, FOOT POWER.

Comes knocked down ready for shipping, c n be put together in a few minutes. This is a ver, practical, honest machine, and for general use abcut a farm or shop cannot be excelled.

	43454	43455	43456
Weight of stone,	1\ ) to 110 lb.	60 to 70 lb.	40 to 50 lb.
Each..................	$2.00	$1.75	$1.60

Grindstones.

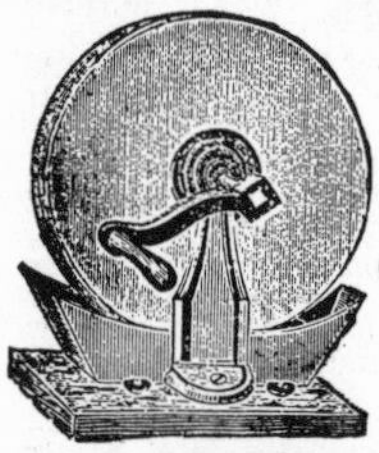

43457 Family Grindstones, with frames complete as per cut, 8-inch stone. Each.... ...$0.70
These are very convenient for sharpening knives and small tools, and take up little room.

Grindstone Fixtures.

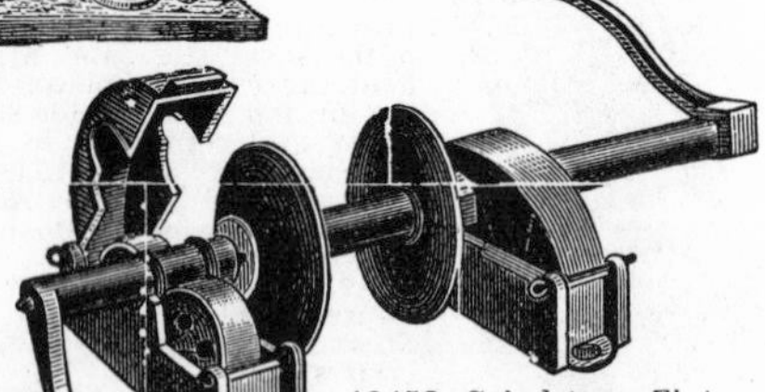

43458 Grindstone Fixture, similar to cut, except top bolts down instead of hinged.

	15 in.	17 in.	19 in.	21 in.
For	40-lb.	60-lb.	80-lb.	100-lb. stones.
Each	25c.	28c.	30c.	35c.

Sure-Grip Steel Tackle Block.

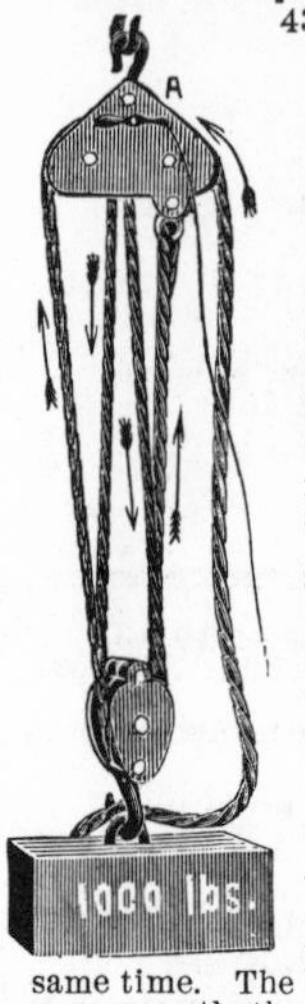

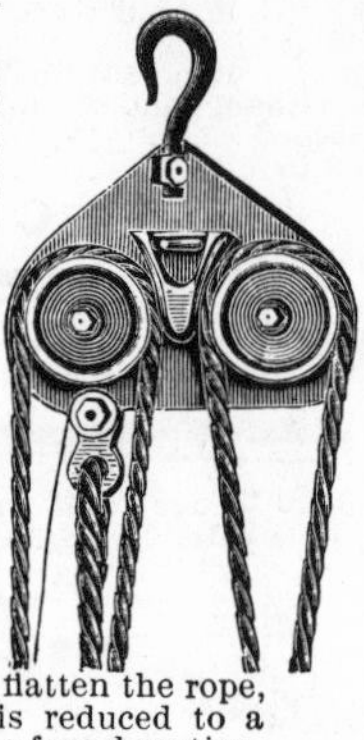

43460 Will hold load at any point without fastening the rope; the brake is absolutely automatic; the heavier the load the better the grip. At the same time the brake is susceptible of being disengaged by very slight pressure. The body of block is made of steel plates. The pins are cold rolled steel. The essential castings are malleable iron, making the strongest and safest possible combination of materials, thus affording immunity from accidents in the highest degree. The brake is a fluted wedge, dropping between two ropes in such a manner that the load' is brought on all the strands of the rope at same time. The brake does not flatten the rope, consequently the wear upon it is reduced to a minimum. This machine will be found particularly valuable by boat and ship builders, contractors, dealers in hardware and machinery, grocers, truckmen, butchers, machine shops, founders and roofers in stringing heavy electric wires, handling barrels, baled hay, safes, in fact any place where hoisting blocks are used it will be found SAFE, SURE and ECONOMICAL.

No. 5. To be used with ⅝ rope; one man can lift 400 lbs; capacity, 1,800 lbs. Price, per set..$4.50
No. 6. To be used with ¾ rope: one man can lift 450 lbs.; capacity, 2,500 lbs. Price, per set. 5.38
No. 4½. To be used with ½ rope; one man can lift 600 lbs.; capacity, 3,000 lbs. Price, per set. 6.00
No. 5½. To be used with ⅝ rope; one man can lift 700. lbs; capacity, 3,500 lbs. Price, per set, 7.20
The price as given above does not include rope or the weight as shown in cut, but it does include one upper and one lower block.

Tackle Blocks.

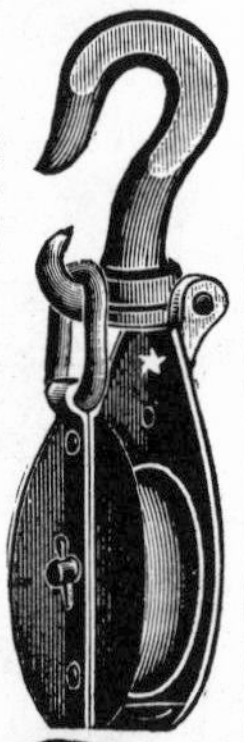

43462 Improved Steel Snatch Block, edges of plates rounded to protect the rope with Ford's Patent Self Lubricating Shears, needs no oil, cost but a trifle more than iron bushed, and will do nearly double the service.

For Dia. rope	Size of shell	Price. Each.
⅞ in.	6 in.	$2.25
⅞ "	7 "	2.37
1 "	8 "	2.87
1⅛ "	9 "	3.38
1¼ "	10 "	4.05
1½ "	12 "	4.95
1¾ "	14 "	6.30
2 "	16 "	8.55

Iron Strapped.

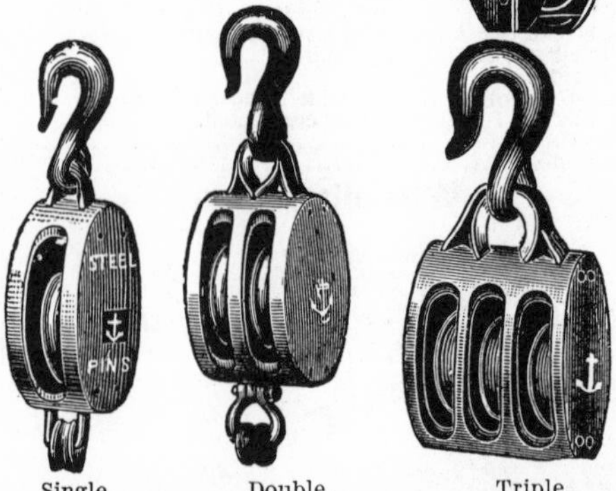

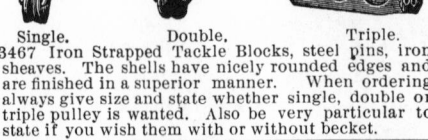

Single. Double. Triple.

43467 Iron Strapped Tackle Blocks, steel pins, iron sheaves. The shells have nicely rounded edges and are finished in a superior manner. When ordering always give size and state whether single, double or triple pulley is wanted. Also be very particular to state if you wish them with or without becket.

For Rope.	Size of shell.	Single pulley each.	Double pulley each.	Triple pulley each.
5/16 in......	3	$0.28	$0.50	$0.70
⅜ in......	3½	.30	.60	.80
½ in.....	4	.35	.65	.85
⅝ in......	5	.38	.70	.90
¾ in... .	6	.45	.80	1.20
⅞ in	7	.55	.95	1.40
1 in......	8	.70	1.15	1.80
1⅛ in......	10	1.25	1.90	2.50
1¼ in.. ...	12	2.00	3.00	4.25

Single pulleys weigh from ¾ to 18 pounds. Double pulleys, from 1¼ to 32 pounds. Triple pulleys, from 2 to 64 pounds.

Steel Tackle Blocks.

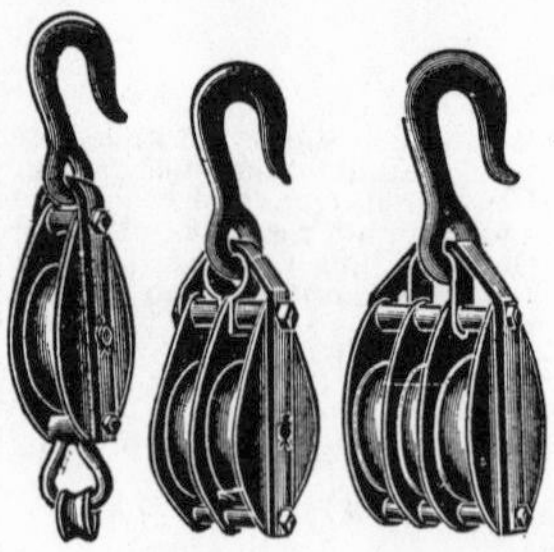

43470 Steel Tackle Block with loose hooks and rounded edge to protect the rope.

For Rope.	Size of shell.	Single pulley	Double pulley.	Triple pulley.
½ inch....	4 inch	$0.40	$0.80	$1.20
⅝ inch....	5 inch	.45	.86	1.32
¾ inch....	6 inch	.56	1 05	1.56
⅞ inch....	7 inch	.68	1 25	2.00
1 inch....	8 inch	.83	1.45	2.28
1⅛ inch....	9 inch	1.08	1.80	2.64
1¼ inch....	10 inch	1.40	2 30	3.25
1½ inch....	12 inch	2.30	3.75	5.88

Awning Pulleys.

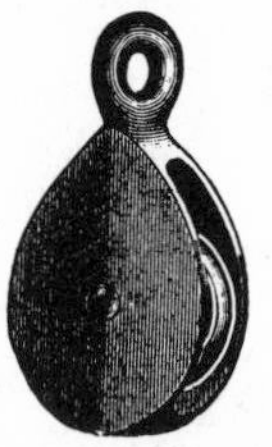

43473 Awning Pulleys, galvanized iron; will not take rope larger than 5-16 inch. Single pulleys weigh 3 5 and 8 ounces, double pulleys weigh 6, 8 and 12 ounces.

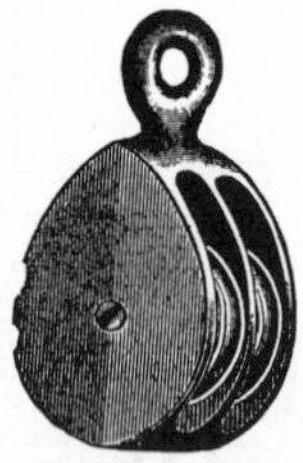

Size wheel.	Single pulley Each.	Single pulley Dozen.	Size of wheel.	Double pulley Each	Double pulley Dozen.
¾ in.	$0.03	$0 30	¾ in.	$0.05	$0.50
1 in.	.04	40	1 in.	06	.60
1½ in.	.08	.80	1½ in.	.11	1.15

Hot House Pulleys.

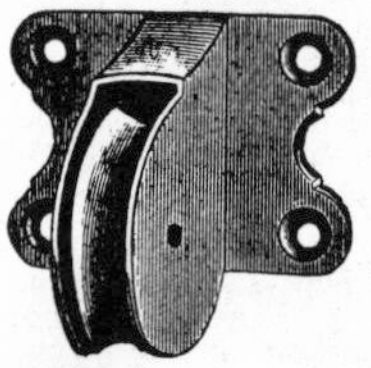

Hot House Pulleys, japanned iron, takes small rope, 5-16 or ⅜ each. Single pulleys, 13 ounces; double pulleys, 1 pound 2 ounces.
43475 Single Pulley.
Size of wheel. Each. Doz.
2 inch. $0.08 $0.65
43476 Double Pulley.
Each. Doz.
Size of wheel, 2 in. $0.12 $1 06

Side Pulleys.

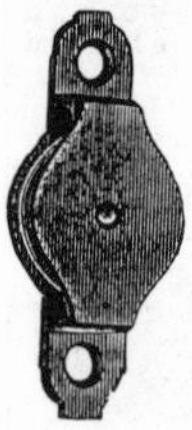

43478 Japanned Iron Side Pulleys; will not take larger than 5-16 inch rope.

Size of wheel.	Weight.	Each.	Per doz.
1½ inches.	5 oz.	$0.04	$0.30
1¾ inches.	7 oz.	.05	.40
2 inches.	10 oz.	.06	.48
2½ inches.	14 oz.	.07	.70
3 inches.	18 oz.	.10	1.C0

Screw Pulleys.

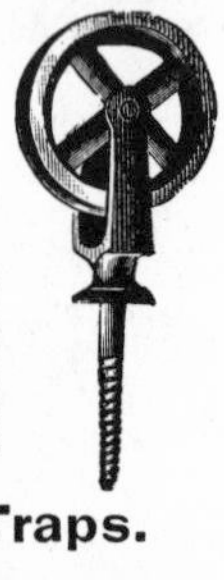

43480 Screw Pulley, japanned iron, will not take rope larger than 5-16 inch.

Size of wheel.	Weight.	Each.	Per doz.
1½ inch.	4 oz.	$0.03	$0.20
1¾ inch.	5 oz.	.03	.28
2 inch.	6 oz.	.04	.35
2¼ inch	7 oz.	.05	.45
2½ inch.	8 oz.	.06	.48
3 inch.	9 oz.	.07	.65

Imitation Newhouse Traps.

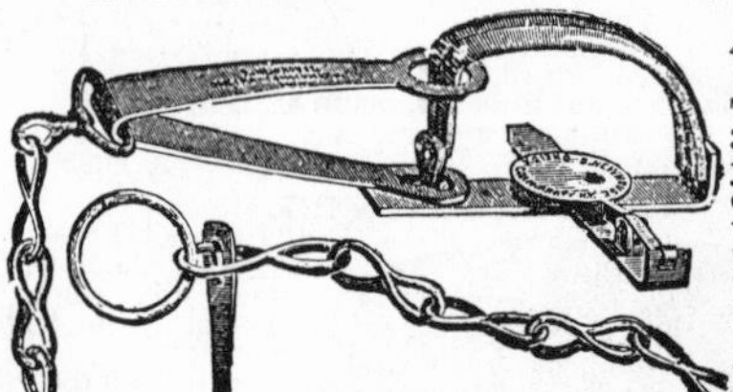

43484 — Rat Traps, 3½ inch jaw with chain; weight 14 oz. No. 0. Each $0.11
Per doz. $1.25

43485 Rat Traps, 4-inch jaw, with chains; weight 14 oz. No. 1. Each........ .14
Per dozen 1.45

Newhouse Traps.

WITH CHAINS.

The Newhouse Traps are the best in the world. They have held first place in the estimation of trappers for the last fifty years, are reliable and are sure to hold the game every time.

43490 No. 0 size. This trap is used mostly for catching the gopher (a little animal which is very troublesome to western farmers) and also rats and other vermin. It has a sharp grip, and will hold larger game, but should not be overtaxed. Spread of jaws, 3½ inches; weight 13 oz. Each $0.25 Per dozen....$2.37

43491 No. 1 size This trap is used for catching muskrats and other small animals, and is sold in greater numbers than any other size. We recommend it to the farmer, as the most serviceable size for catching skunks, weasels, rats and such other animals as may visit his poultry houses and barns. Spread of jaws, 4 inches; weight, 17 ounces. Each $0.28 Per dozen.... 2.75

43492 No. 1½ Trap. This size is called the Mink Trap. It is however suitable for catching the woodchuck, skunk, etc. Professional trappers often use it for catching foxes. It is very convenient in form and is strong and reliable. Spread of jaws 4⅞ inches; weight 1 lb. 6 oz. Each $0.40 Per dozen.... 4.10

43493 No. 2 size. The No. 2 trap is called the Fox Trap. Its spread of jaws is the same as the No. 1½, but having two springs is, of course, much stronger; weight, 1 lb. 10 oz. Each.... .55
Per dozen.... 5.75

43495 No. 3 size. Otter Trap, very powerful, will hold almost any game smaller than a bear. Spread of jaws 5½ inches. Double spring; weight 2 lbs. 8 oz. Each $0.70 Per dozen.... 7.75

43497 No. 4 size. This is the regular form of beaver trap. It is longer than the No. 3 trap and has one inch greater spread of jaws. It is a favorite with those who hunt and trap for a living in the far West and Canada. Spread of jaws 6½ inches; weight 3 lbs. 2 oz. Each.... .80
Per dozen.... 9.00

Wolf Traps.

43498 No. 4½ size, especially adapted to catching wolves. This trap has 8 inch spread of jaws, with the other parts in proportion, and is provided with a pronged "drag," a heavy snap and an extra heavy steel swivel and chain, 5 feet long, warranted to hold two thousand pounds. The trap, complete with chain and "drag," will weigh about 9 lbs.
Price, each.... $2.00
Per dozen.... 22.00

43499 No. 5 size with offset jaws. This trap weighs 17 lbs. and has a spread of jaws of 11¾ inches. It is used for taking the common black bear, and is furnished with a chain and swivel sufficiently strong. Double spring. Each.... 6.25

43502 No. 6 Trap for grizzly bear. This is the strongest trap made. It will hold lion, cougar, tiger or moose, as well as the great grizzly bear. Spread of jaws 16 inches; weight, 42 lbs. Each. 12.00

Setting Clamps.

43506 For setting game traps.	Each.	Per doz.
No. 4 for setting No. 4 trap	$0.15	$1.25
No. 5 for setting No. 5 traps	.30	3.15
No. 6 for setting No. 6 trap	.50	5.25

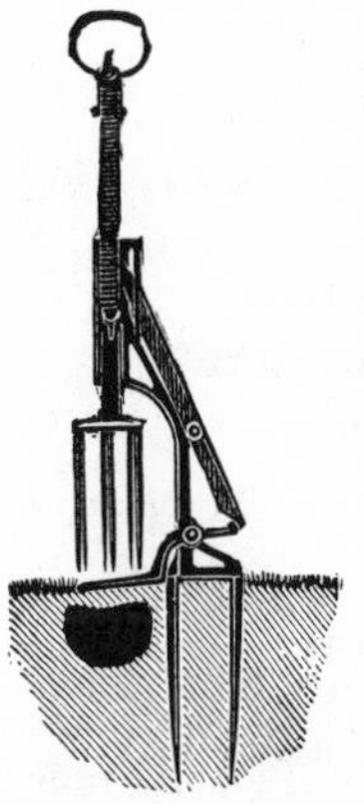

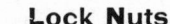

43510 The Wherry Mole Trap. This is an entirely new pattern and is a decided improvement on all other makes; is more simple and less liable to get out of order. The frame is strong and terminates in one point which has a cross piece to anchor it firmly in the ground. The principal feature about it is its setting device: Simply pulling up on the handle sets it. Being much more simple as to construction it can be sold at a much lower price than any other make.

DIRECTIONS FOR SETTING TRAP.

Press the dirt down across the trail; push the trap down before setting till the pan rests within ½ inch of top of run; put foot on cross piece and pull up on handle a few times to loosen dirt about the fork tines, then set it; lay a weight on end of cross piece to keep it firm in the ground; oil plunger rod.
Price, each.... $1.00

We can furnish almost anything made in pipe fittings. Write us for prices on goods you do not find quoted. The sizes of pipe fittings are determined by the size of pipe over which they fit; thus, ¼ inch tee or elbow, etc., fits over ¼ inch pipe.

Lock Nuts.

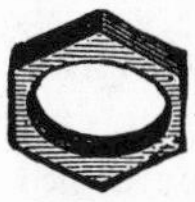

43580—

For Pipe, in.	¼	⅜	½	¾	1	1¼	1½	2
Each	2c	2c	3c	3c	4c	5c	6c	8c

Pipe Caps.

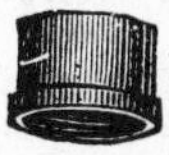

43581— For Pipe, in.	¼	⅜	½	¾	1	1¼	1½	2
Black, each	2c	3c	3c	4c	5c	7c	10c	12c
43581½— Galv'd, each	3c	3c	4c	5c	7c	10c	14c	18c

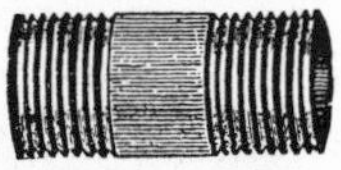

Nipples.

43582 Size, inches,	¼	⅜	½	¾	1	1¼	1½	2
Black, short, price ea.	2c	3c	3c	4c	4c	5c	6c	8c
43582½— Galv'd, short, price ea.	3c	4c	4c	4c	5c	6c	7c	10c
43583— Black, long, price ea.	3c	4c	4c	4c	5c	6c	8c	10c
43583½— Galv'd, long, price ea.	4c	5c	5c	6c	6c	7c	9c	12c

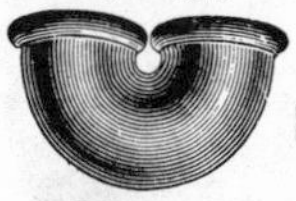

Malleable Return Bends, Open Pattern.

43585 For Pipe, in.	¾	1	1¼	1½	2
Black, each	9c	12c	15c	23c	38c

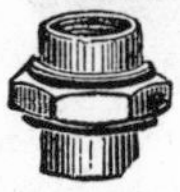

MALLEABLE UNIONS.

43586 For Pipe, in.	¼	⅜	½	¾	1	1¼	1½	2
Black, each	7c	8c	10c	11c	14c	17c	23c	29c
43586½— Galvanized, each.	9c	10c	11c	15c	19c	25c	32c	40c

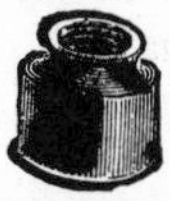

MALLEABLE REDUCERS.

43587 For Pipe, in.	¼	⅜	½	¾	1	1¼	1½	2
Black, each	3c	3c	3c	5c	6c	9c	12c	17c
43587½— Galvanized, each.	4c	4c	5c	6c	10c	13c	17c	26c

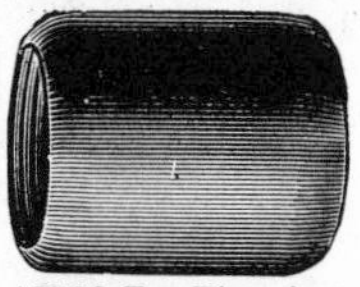

WROUGHT IRON COUPLINGS.

43588 For Pipe, in.	¼	⅜	½	¾	1	1¼	1½	2
Black, each	3c	4c	4c	5c	7c	8c	9c	12c
43588½— Galvanized, each,	4c	5c	5c	7c	8c	10c	13c	16c

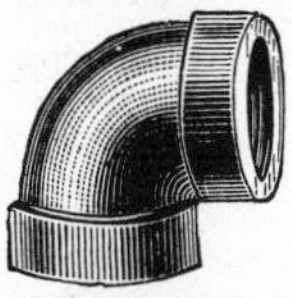

MALLEABLE ELBOWS.

43589 For Pipe, in.	¼	⅜	½	¾	1	1¼	1½	2
Black, each	3c	4c	5c	6c	8c	9c	15c	18c
43589½— Galvanized, each.	4c	5c	6c	9c	12c	15c	22c	30c

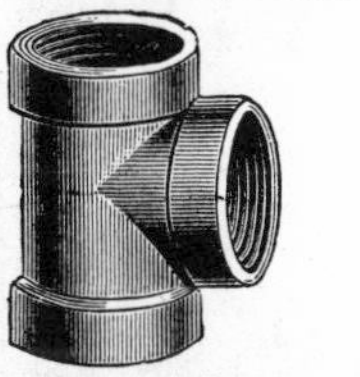

MALLEABLE TEES.

43590 For Pipe, in.	¼	⅜	½	¾	1	1¼	1½	2
Black, each	4c	5c	6c	7c	10c	12c	17c	23c
43590½— Galvanized, each.	5c	5c	7c	10c	15c	18c	25c	35c

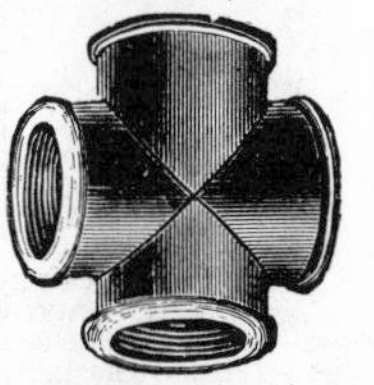

MALLEABLE CROSSES.

43591 For Pipe, in.	¼	⅜	½	¾	1	1¼	1½	2
Black, each	5c	5c	6c	9c	12c	15c	23c	35c
43591½— Galvanized, each.	6c	7c	8c	10c	17c	23c	32c	50c

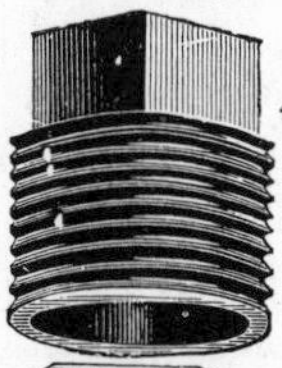

Plugs.

CAST IRON PLUGS.

43592 For Pipe in. ¼ ⅜ ½ ¾ 1
Black, each.... 2c 2c 3c 3c 4c
For Pipe, in.... 1¼ 1½ 2
Black, each.... 4c 5c 6c
43592½ Galvanized, each—
3c 3c 4c 4c 5c 6c 7c 10c

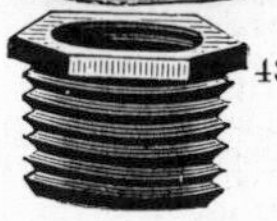

Bushing.

43593 For pipe, in. ⅜ ½ ¾ 1
Black, each.... 3c 3c 4c 4c
For Pipe, in.... 1¼ 1½ 2
Black, each.... 5c 6c 8c
43593½ Galvanized, each—
3c 4c 5c 5c 6c 9c 12c

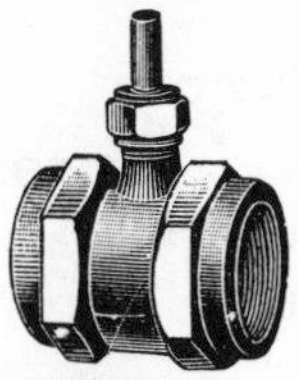

Butterfly Valves.

43608 Iron Body Brass Trimming, screwed.

Size—	1½	2	2½
Price, each	$1.65	$2.15	$2.80
Size	3	3½	4
Price, each.	$4.10	$5.15	$6.65

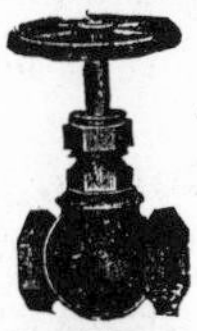

Globe Valves.

BRASS.

43609 For pipe—

....in.	¼	⅜	½	¾
Price, each..	$0.20	$0.25	$0.32	$0.40
For pipe, in....	1	1¼		
Price, each....	$0.52	$0.75		
For pipe, in....	1½	2	2½	3
Price, each....	$1.15	$1.50	$2.90	$4.00

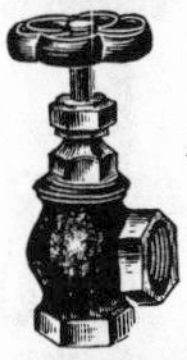

Brass Angle Valves.

Order No. 43610.

43610 For pipe—

in.	¼	⅜	½
Price, each....	$0.20	$0.26	$0.35
For pipe, in.	¾	1	1¼
Price, each	$0.42	$0 55	$0.80
For pipe, in.	1½ 2	2½	3
Price, each..	$1.25 $1.65	$3.10	$4.30

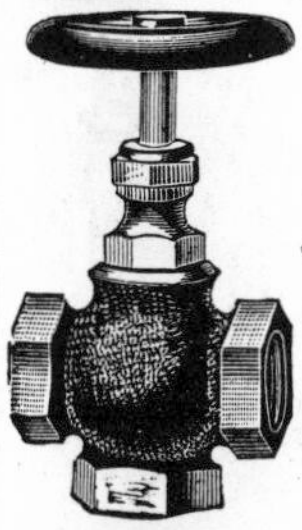

Brass Cross Valves.

43612—

For pipe in.	¼	⅜	[½	¾
Price, each..	$0.25	.32	.48	.60
Pipe, in.		1	1¼	1½
Price, each....		$0.75	1.00	1.55
Size....		2	2½	3
Price, each....		$2.50	4.80	7.10

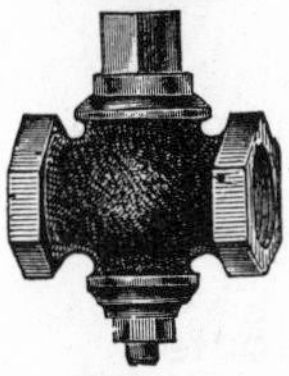

Brass Steam Cocks.

Flat heads.

43614—

For pipe in.	¼		⅜	½
Price, each...	$0.25		.26	.45
Pipe, in.	¾	1	1¼	1½
Price, each...	$0.55	.80	1.45	1.85
Size	2		2½	3
Price, each....	$2.68		4.95	6.90

436014

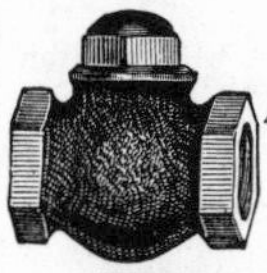

Horizontal Check Valves.

43616 For pipe—

in.	¼	⅜	½	¾	1	1¼
Price, each	$0.18	.22	.28.	.35	.48	.65
For pipe, in.	1½	2	2½	3		
Price, each	$0.85	$1.40	$2.80	$3.90		

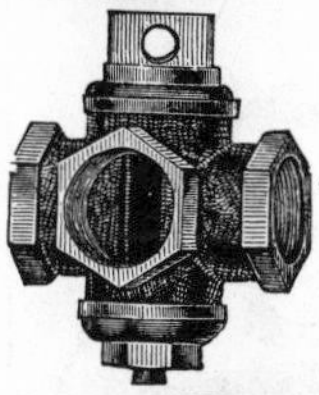

Brass Three-Way Cocks.

43618 For pipe—

in	½	¾	1	1¼
Price. each	$0.65	.85	$1.30	$2.10
For pipe, in.	1½	2	2½	3
Price, each	$2.70	$3.65	$6.50	$8.95

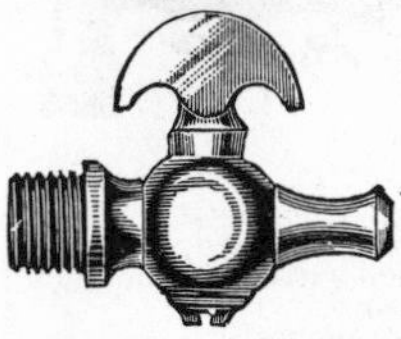

Brass Air Cocks.

Finished.

43620 Size...	⅛	¼	⅜	½
Price, each.	15c	17c	20c	24c

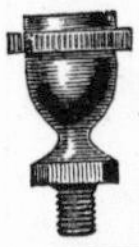

Brass Oil Cups.

Finished.

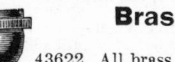

43622 All brass, with screw top.

Diameter of body	¾	1	1¼	1½	2
Pipe size of shank	⅛	¼	¼	⅜	⅜
Price, each....	13c	16c	25c	32c	65c

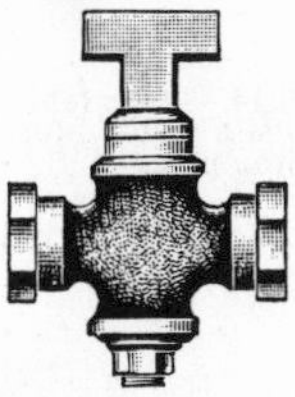

Pipe Stops.

43625 Brass Rough Stop. T handles round way nut and washer, screwed for iron pipe.

Size, inches....	½	¾	1
Price, plain....	$0.40	$0.63	$0.93

THE TOOLS WE HANDLE ARE THE BEST OBTAINABLE ANYWHERE.

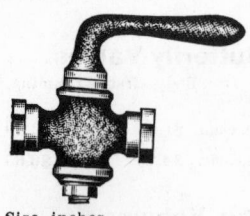

Water Pipe Stops.

43626 Brass Rough Stop lever handle, screwed for iron pipe.

Size, inches	½	¾	1
Price, plain, each	$0.41	$0.65	$0.95

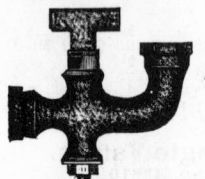

Hydrant Cocks.

43627 Brass Hydrant Cock, with T handle for iron pipe. Size, ¾ in. 1in. 1¼ in. Price, each, 62c. 85c. $1.30

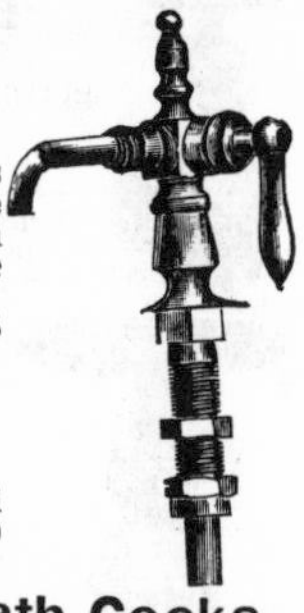

Hydrant Clamps.

43628 Hydrant Clamps malleable iron, with square hole. When ordering you must always give us the size of hydrant cock. Price, each..........$0.15

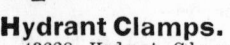

Basin Cocks.

43630 Fuller Pattern, nickel plated. Price, each........$1.20

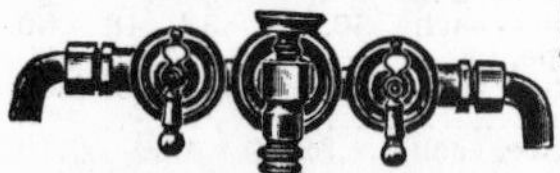

Bath Cocks.

43631 Combination Fuller Pattern, complete with sprinkler. nickel plated. Price, each...$3.40

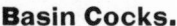

Bath Cock.

43636 Compression Valve, double nickel plated. Price, each.$2.20

Brass Bibs or Faucets.

43638 Hose Bibs for iron pipe. Lever handle. Size, inches, finished. ½ ⅝ ¾ 1 Price, each, $0.48 .62 .80 1.30

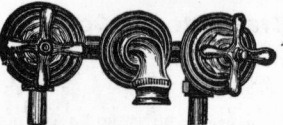

43640 Compression Hose Bibs, screwed for iron pipe with shoulder, finished Size, inches— ⅜ ½ ⅝ ¾ 1 Price each— $0.37 .40 .45 .68 1.25

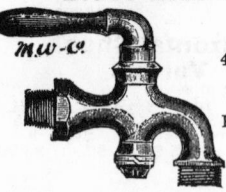

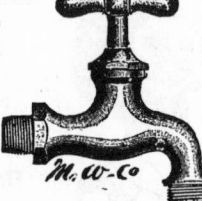

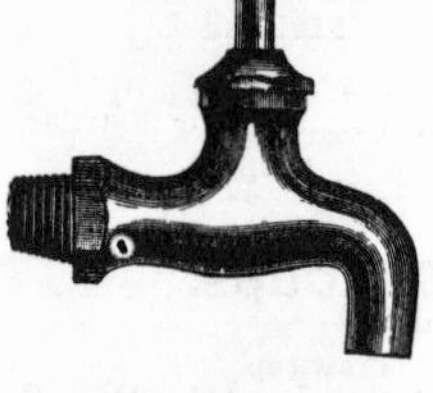

43642 Compression Plain Bibbs, screwed, for iron pipe, with shoulder, finished. Size, inches— ⅜ ½ ⅝ ¾ 1 Price, each— $0.35 .40 .45 .62 1.15

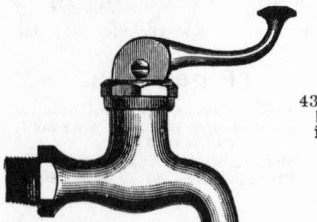

43644 Telegraph Plain Bibs for iron pipe.

Size, inches	⅜	½	⅝	¾
Price, each, brass	$0.70	$0.80	$0.90	$1.25
Nickel plated	.80	.90	1.05	1.35

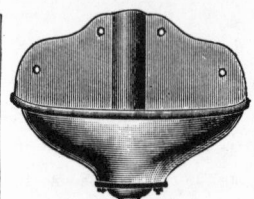

Urinals.

43650 Iron Corner Urinal, enameled; size, 9 inches; fitted for lead pipe. Price, each......$1.70

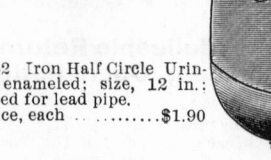

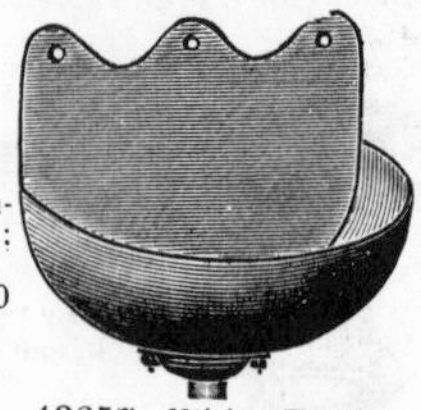

43652 Iron Half Circle Urinal, enameled; size, 12 in.; fitted for lead pipe. Price, each $1.90

Wash Basins.

43657

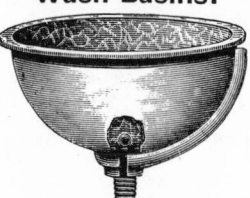

43657 White Earthen Patent Overflow Wash Basin, for rubber plug for stationary wash stand, complete with chain and plug. Diameter outside.

Inches	12	13	14
Each	$0.90	$1.05	$1.10
Inches	15	16	
Each	$1.40	$2.00	

43658 Stopper with chain, for 43657 basin.
Each $0.25
Per dozen.....................................2.70
Prices on marble slabs for washstands on application.

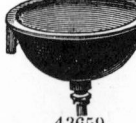

43659

43659 Iron Wash Basins, enameled; common overflow; diameter, 14 in., complete with stopper. Price, each..................$2.10

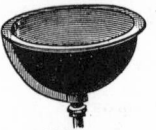

43660

43660 Iron Wash Basins, enameled, patent overflow; diameter, 14 inches, complete with stopper: fitted for either iron or lead pipe. Price, each.....................$2.67

Bibs.

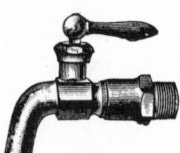

43665 Fuller Pattern, Plain Bib, for iron pipe, finished brass. Sizes... ½ ⅝ ¾ 1 inch Price ea.$0.55 $0.62 $0.82 $1.05

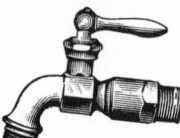

43666 Fuller Pattern Hose Bib for iron pipe, finished brass. Sizes ½ ⅝ ¾ 1 inch Price, ea. $0.62 .70 .85 1.20

Oil Faucet.

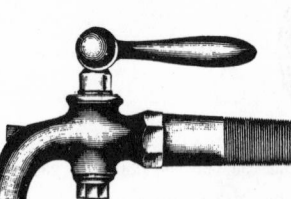

43667 The original and only genuine Frary's Patent Oil Faucet, made of iron, japanned key, bushed, with brass lever handle, screw shank; for oil barrel.
½ in.....$0.30
⅝ in .... .32
¾ in .... .40
1 in .... .50

Oil Faucet.

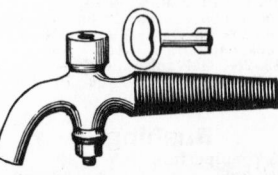

43668 Loose Key Faucets to screw, brass. These faucets are very convenient. The key may be withdrawn and the contents of the barrel cannot be drawn easily without the aid of the key to open the faucet. It is a guard against accident, as the faucet cannot accidentally be opened, as is often the case with the ordinary kind. One size, ½ inch. These faucets cannot be used for kerosene. Each........$0.54

Sinks.

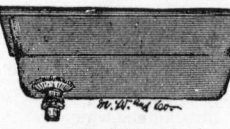

Wrought Steel Kitchen Sinks. These sinks are made from one plate of steel and are superior to cast iron sinks in every particular, being lighter, stronger and more durable, are fitted for 1¼ in. lead or 1½ inch iron pipe, and come painted or galvanized in the following sizes:

Order No. 43669 PAINTED.

Size.	Weight.	Each.	Size.	Weight.	Each.
16x24x6	13 lbs.	$1.35	20x30x6	22½ lbs.	$2.30
18x30x6	15¼ lbs.	1.87	20x36x6	23 lbs.	2.77
18x36x6	18½ lbs.	2.25	20x40x6	25½ lbs.	3.00

Order No. 43670 GALVANIZED.

Size.	Weight.	Each.	Size.	Weight.	Each.
16x24x6	13¼ lbs.	$2.00	20x30x6	21¾ lbs.	$3.12
18x30x6	18¾ lbs.	2.55	20x36x6	28 lbs.	3.75
18x36x6	24½ lbs.	3.25	20x40x6	30 lbs.	4.25

Bath Tubs.

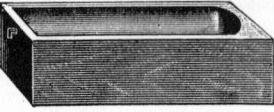

43675 Stationary Copper Bath Tub, 5, 5½ or 6 feet long, made of 12 oz. copper. Outside width at head and foot, 24 in.; outside depth, 19 inches. Prices subject to fluctuation of copper market. Price, each, for 5, 5½ or 6 feet.......$ 9.45

Stationary Zinc Bath Tubs.

43676 Same as above but lined with zinc instead of copper. Made in three sizes, 5 ft., 5½ ft. and 6 ft.
Price, each..$5.95

Iron Bath Tubs.

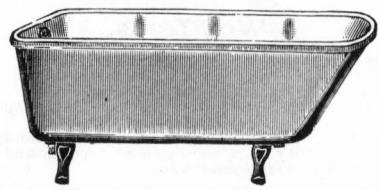

French Pattern.

43677 the most durable and satisfactory Bath Tubs made. They are made of heavy cast iron. *white enameled* inside and painted outside. They are neat and handsome in appearance, can never rust or leak, and the white enameled inside surface is easily kept clean and pure. Prices below include nickel plated overflow and strainer, waste plug and rubber stopper.

Size of Tub	4 ft.	4½ ft.	5 ft.	5½ ft.	6 ft.
Length inside	48 in.	54 in.	59 in.	65 in.	71 in.
Width "	23 "	23 "	23 "	23 "	23 "
Depth "	19 "	19 "	19 "	19 "	19 "
Height on legs	25 "	25 "	25 "	25 "	25 "
Price	$22.50	24.25	27.10	29.40	32.25

In ordering state whether you wish tub tapped for bath cock or with plain end. See 43631 and 43636 for suitable bath cock.

43678 For hardwood rim around top, oak or cherry, add $3.50 to above prices

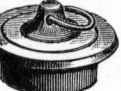

43680

43680 Sink or Bath Plugs. Size ....1¼ 1½ Price, each...........$ 0.10 $0.15

Iron Float Valve.

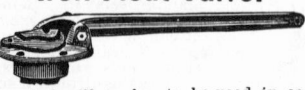

43681 For wind mill tanks: to be used in connection with our No. 43682 copper float.

Size	¾	1	1¼
Price	$ .38	.40	.50

Copper Float.

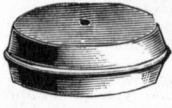

43682 Can be bolted to a lever attached to tank valve, to open and close automatically. Size, ...9½ in. x 2¾ in. Price, each.................$0.72

THE CELEBRATED

H. H. Taylor Elgin Watch

Has been discontinued by the manufacturers. We bought the last lot the Elgin Company turned out, and of course we bought them very cheap.

WHILE THIS LOT LASTS

We will sell H. H. Taylor full jeweled adjusted Watches at about the price of the lower grades. See quotations on pages 130 to 138.

The Mosley Self-Heating Folding Bath Tub and Water Heater.

FOR GAS OR GASOLINE.

Is a handsome piece of furniture, of modern style, complete in all mechanical appointments, and is perfect in operation as a folding bed, giving the full equivalent of a modern bath room, as far as the bath is concerned, with the advantage of quick and independent heating, and comprises a full-sized 9-oz zinc, or 14-oz. copper-lined bath tub, water tank, heater, and waste water outlet. The cases are of modern designs, excellent quality of cabinet work and thoroughly seasoned hard lumber. The style and finish corresponds with the latest and most popular in furniture. The material used in the finish is impervious to moisture, hot or cold water, insuring a durable and permanent lustre. All burners, gas or gasoline, are made expressly for the requirements of these tubs, and are unequaled. Each tub is fitted with a flexible outlet with brass couplings, one of which fastens permanently to the tub, the other may be connected to ordinary gas or lead pipe, or tubing, leading to any waste water outlet in the building, or to make an independent exit, or the contents of the tub may be emptied by means of the connecting tube into any convenient recepticle in the apartment. Having a fixed journal bearing, this tub has a positive action in raising or lowering, thus avoiding all use of casters and slides. The adjustable back supporting the water tank forms a counterbalance to the tub, rendering its manipulation sufficiently easy for a child to operate. This tub is made in two lengths, and measures 2 feet wide, 18 inches deep, and 5 feet and 5 feet 6 inches long, respectively, and occupies a floor space when closed about 26x28 inches. Weight crated for shipment about 250 pounds. This tub does not require fastening to the wall. It is an independent article of furniture, complete in itself. No cutting of carpets necessary.

GASOLINE BURNER WITH HEATER WILL BE SHIPPED UNLESS OTHERWISE ORDERED.

Tubs are lined with best quality No. 9 zinc or 14 oz. copper.

EXTREME OUTSIDE MEASUREMENTS.

Five-foot tub, height when closed, 5 feet 8 inches Length over all when open for use, 5 feet 9 inches. Five-foot 6-inch Tub, height when closed, 6 feet 4 inches. Length over all when open for use, 6 feet 5 inches.

No, 10½. Panel fron oval top, antique finish Length 5 fet 6 in.

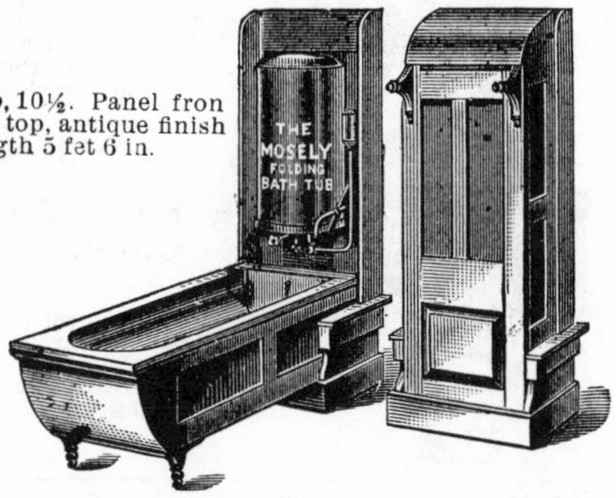

43685 A, Zinc-lined Tub with enameled iron heater, like cut, each $27.60
B, Enamel Tub with enameled iron heater, like cut, each 31.59
C, Copper-lined Tub with enameled iron heater, like cut, each 34.50
43686 A, Zinc Tub without heater 15.69
B, Enamel " " " 19.79
C, Copper " " " 21.68

No. 12½ Panel Front, natural, antique, or XVI Century. Polished finish, length, either 5 feet or 5 feet 6 inches. Folding legs supplied for $2.00 extra.

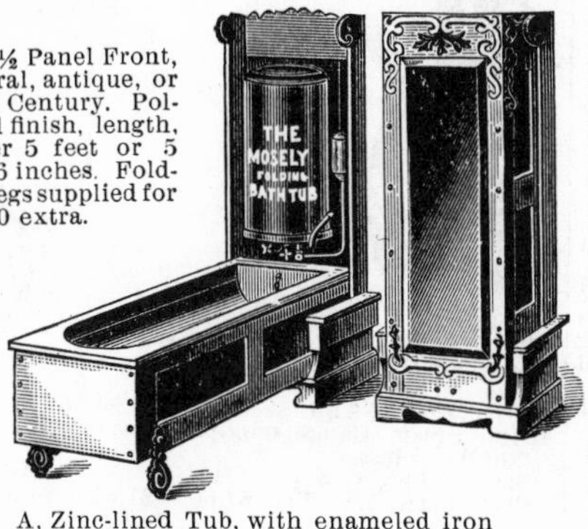

43687 A, Zinc-lined Tub, with enameled iron heater, like cut. Each $33.60
B, Enameled-lined Tub, with enameled iron heater, like cut. Each 37.59
C, Copper-lined, with enameled iron heater, like cut. Each 40.40
43688 Zinc-lined Tub, without heater 20.83
B, Enameled Tub, without heater 25 00
C, Copper Lined Tub, without heater 27.91

EXAMINE...

THE BATH TUBS QUOTED ABOVE. THEY ARE FINE THINGS.

Water Heaters—Continued.

No. 15 Beveled French Plate Mirror, 34x16, imitation drawers, natural, antique or XVI Century, polished finish, zinc lined. Length, 5 feet 6 in. With folding legs.

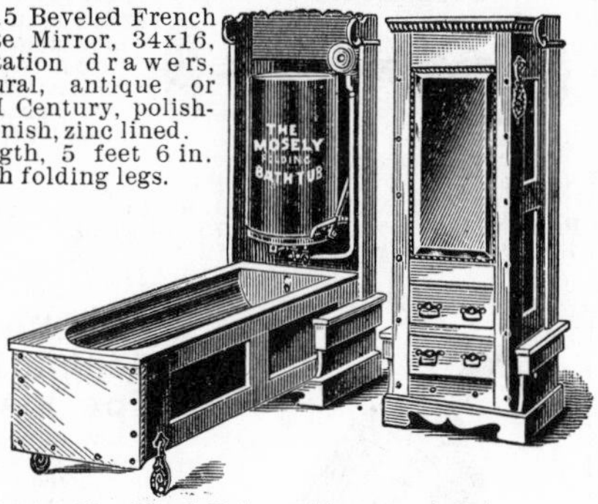

43689 A, Zinc-lined Tub, with enameled iron heater, like cut. Each $40.80
B, Enameled Tub, with enameled iron heater, like cut. Each 44.80
C, Copper-lined Tub, with enameled iron heater, like cut. Each 47.60
43690 A, Zinc-lined Tub, without heater 27.20
B, Enameled Tub, without heater 31.20
C, Copper Lined, without heater 34.00

No. 23. Full Beveled French Plate Mirror, 54 x16, fine raised carvings, natural, antique or XVI Century, polished finish, zinc lined. Length 5 feet 6 inches.

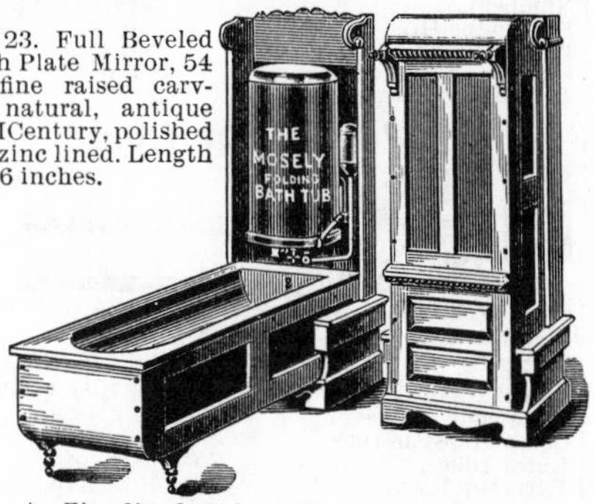

43691 A, Zinc-lined Tub, with enameled iron heater like cut. Each $52.19
B, Enameled Tub, with enameled iron heater, like cut. Each 57.20
C, Copper-lined Tub, with enameled iron heater, like cut. Each 60.00
43692 A, Zinc-lined Tub, without heater 39.60
B, Enameled Tub, without heater 43.59
C, Copper-lined Tub, without heater 46.40

The Mosley Improved Water Heater No. 3.

WITH GAS OR GASOLINE BURNER.

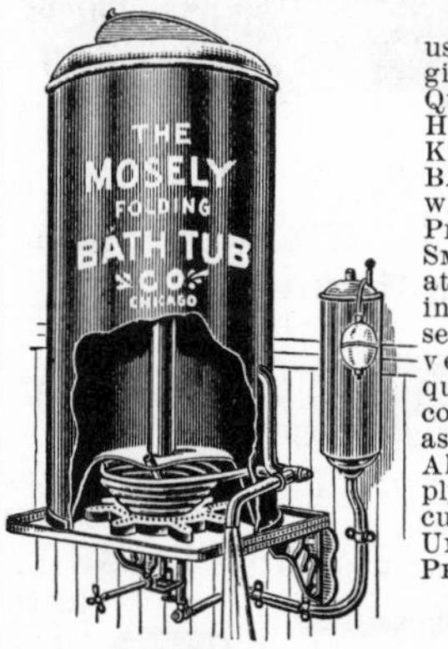

Especially adapted for use with stationary baths, giving the advantage of QUICK AND INDEPENDENT HEATING, also for KITCHENS, LAUNDRYS, BARBER SHOPS, etc., with minimum fuel cost. PERFECT COMBUSTION. NO SMOKE. All parts clean at all times; may be used in connection with water service or otherwise. No ventilating flue required. Water tank is constructed with lid, so as to fill with bucket. Also has opening for supply pipe connecting with cut-of valve. NOT USED UNDER WATER OR STEAM PRESSURE.

Gasoline Burner.

43695 A, Enameled Galvanized Iron Heaters, with bracket $15.00
B, Copper heaters, with bracket 18.60
C, Nickel Plated Copper Heaters 22.40

Experienced Dressmakers

Are employed in our new Dress Making Department. Save money by letting them make your dresses.

Shower Bath Ring.

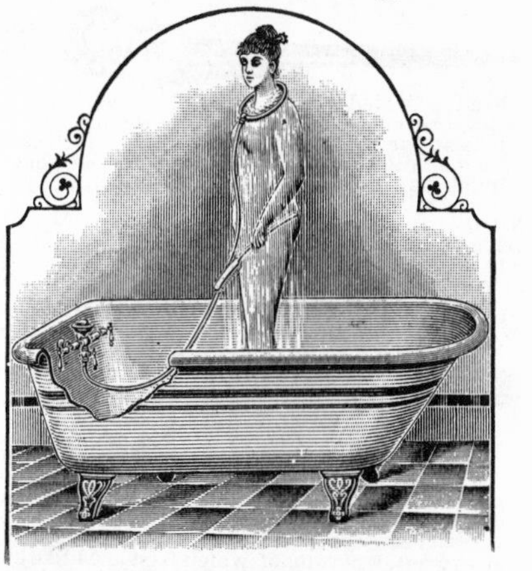

43696 This cut shows one of the many ways this shower may be used. A lady can use it without wetting her head. Each limb can be showered separately. The ring resting on the shoulders as shown in cut allows the free use of both arms. There is no splashing of walls or floor. The bath ring is made of brass tubing, nickel plated. The extra cock is used only when a person wishes to regulate the temperature of water befoie placing it over the head, and can be fastened onto the combination cock by any plumber. For bath tubs fitted with double cocks we have an extension slip joint connection that converts two single cocks into a combination cock. No skill is required. In ordering this connection, state outside diameter of cocks and distance apart.
Nickel Plated Shower Bath Ring, with tubing .. $2.05
Nickel Plated Cock, each 1.25
Extension Slip Joint Connection, each 1.80

Brown's Adjustable Pipe Tongs.

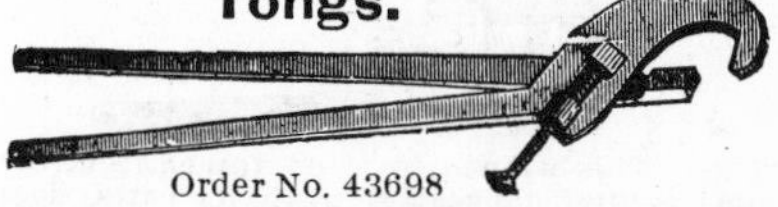

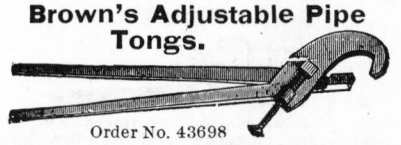

Order No. 43698

Number	1	1½	2	3	4
Takes pipe from	½ to ¾	⅜ to 1	½ to 1¼	1 to 2	1¼ to 3
Price, each......	$0.42	$0.48	$0.60	$0.90	$1.87

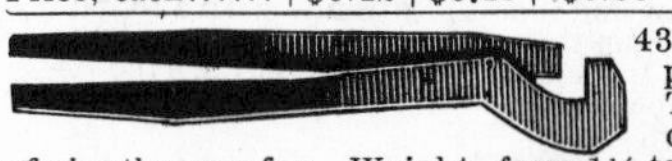

43699 Common piP Tongs. The size indicates the size of pipe they are for. Weight, from 1½ to 4 lbs.

Size......	⅛	¼	⅜	½	¾	1
Each......	$0.25	$0.29	$0.30	$0.35	$0.45	$0.50
Size......	1¼	1½	2	2½	3	
Each......	$0.60	$0.70	$0.75	$1.15	$1.57	

Pipe Lifter.

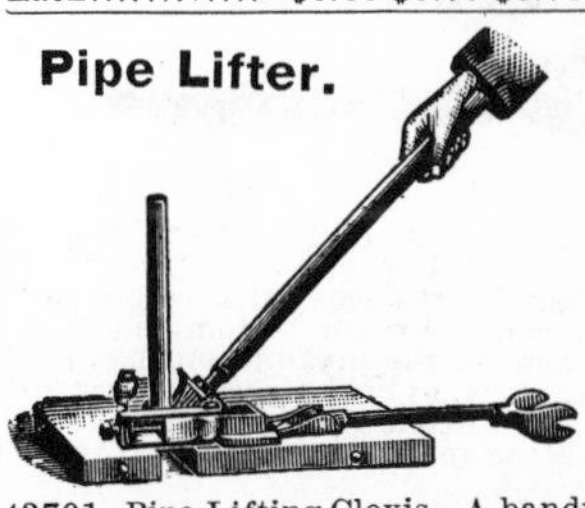

43700 Babcock Pipe Lifter and Holder complete. For well drillers; a simple yet complete tool. Price, each $6.10

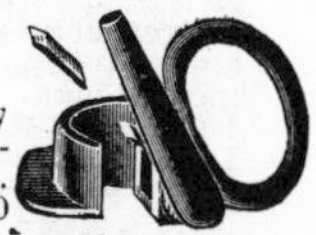

43701 Pipe Lifting Clevis. A handy device to prevent pipe from slipping when being taken from well. Price, each $1.10

Gas Pliers.

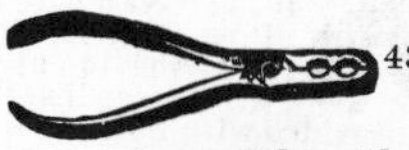

43703
Length, inches 6 8 10.
Each 25c. 35c 40c

Combination Gas Pliers.

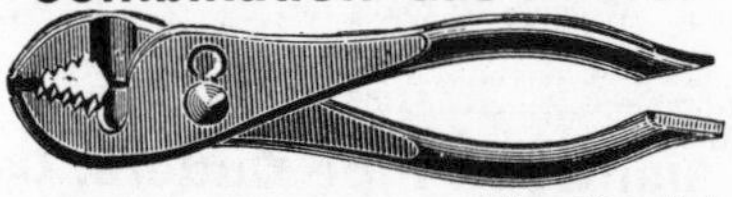

43704 These pliers are a strong, well made article, and will take several sizes of pipe. Price, each ... $1.25

Alligator Pipe Wrench.

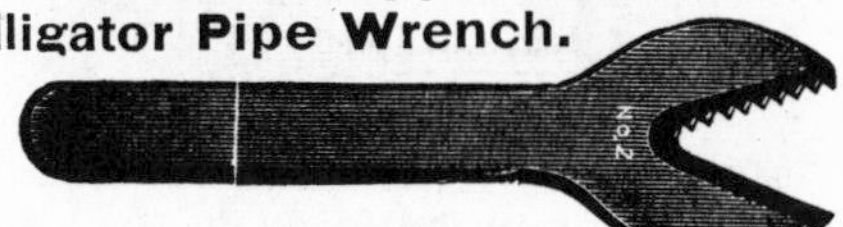

Order No. 43705

Length, inches	5¾	10	16	22	27
Takes pipe....	⅛ to ⅜	⅜ to ¾	½ to 1¼	1¼ to 2	2 to 3
Price, each ...	$0.20	$0.50	$1.00	$1.50	$2.15
Weight........	¼	¾	2¾	6¼	13

Trimo Chain Pipe Wrench.

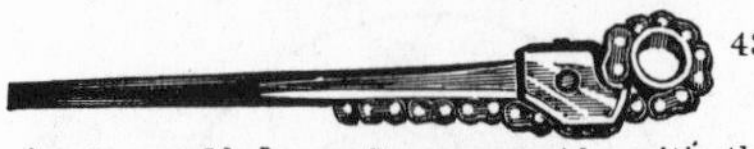

43706—Has a solid head provided on its upper side with three slots or grooves to admit and hold the projecting pins on the chain, giving six bearing surfaces. To the head is attached a forged steel jaw, having a racking movement, enabling it to grip firmly without slipping.

Number	1	2	3
Length, in inches....	20	27	37
Size of pipe..........	1 to 2½	1 to 3½	1¼ to 6.
Price, each..........	$2.10	$3.30	$4.50.

Engineer's Wrench.

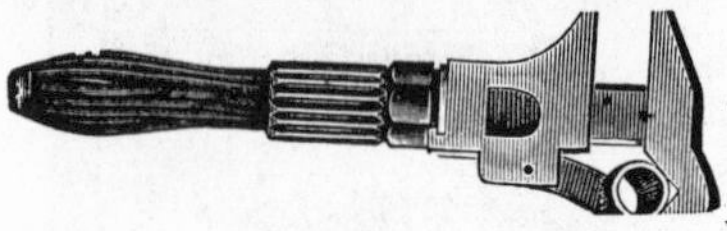

43707 A Combined Nut and Pipe Wrench, for engineers and mechanics generally. All parts interchangeable. Made from drop steel forged bars. By referring to cut it will be seen that the adjustment is a long sleeve nut, a portion of which is shaped like an octagon nut, permitting the application of another wrench when extra power is required, which is a great advantage. The 10-inch size takes pipe ½ to 1 inch, the 12-inch takes ½ to 1¾ inch, 15 takes ½ to 2½.

	Each
10 inch..........	$1.40
12 inch..........	1.60
15 inch..........	2.15

Bemis & Call's Pipe Wrench.

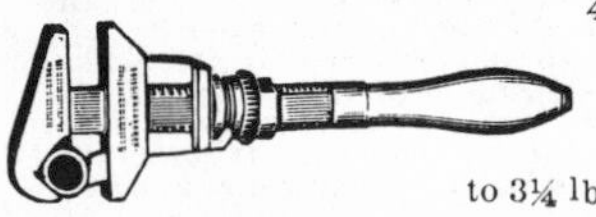

43708 Bemis & Calls' Combination Nut and Pipe Wrench, bright finish. Weight, 2¼ lbs. to 3¼ lbs. With long nut.

	Each.
10 inch takes pipe ½ to 1 inch..........	$1.60
12 inch takes pipe ½ to 1¾ inch..........	1.80
15 inch takes pipe ½ to 2 inch..........	2.65

Trimo Pipe Wrench.

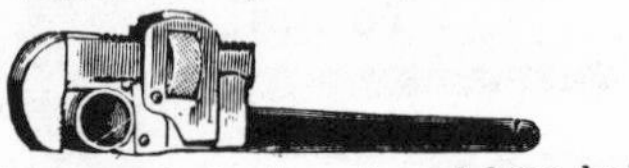

43709 This wrench is drop forged from bar steel, is interchangeable in all its parts, does not lock upon the pipe, but releases its hold readily, grips the pipe firmly without lost motion; does not crush the pipe or slip. The movable jaw and the nut are made with a round top and bottom thread, guaranteed not to strip or burr. An inserted jaw is placed in the handle, which can be renewed for little expense when dull or worn.

Length, open, in inches.	10	14	18	24
Takes pipe from	⅛ to ½	¼ to 1½	¼ to 2	¼ to 2½
Price, each,	$1.25	$1.75	$2.30	$3.50

Martini's Patent Wrench.

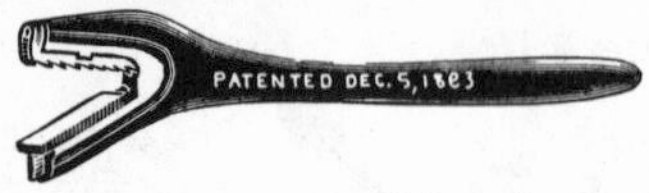

43710 This wrench is made of drop forged steel, the jaws are made of the best tool steel, hardened and tempered, and can be replaced with very little expense. The movable jaw on bottom causes it to tighten as you increase the pressure on the handle. *It will not slip.* It takes hold and lets go instantly. No lost motion and no time lost in adjusting. It is always ready. Made in two sizes only, 10 and 16 inches long.

10 inch, capacity from ¼ to 1 inch, each....... $1.30
16 inch, capacity from ⅜ to 1¾ inch, each...... 1.75

Saunder's Pipe Cutter.

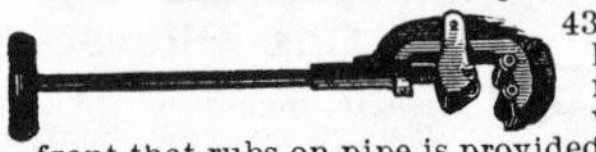

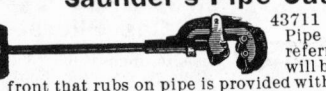

43711 Saunder's Pipe Cutters. By referring to cut it will be seen that the front that rubs on pipe is provided with rollers which reduce the friction, making it a very easy cutting tool. Weight, 3¾ to 6¾ lbs.

No..........	1	2	3
Cuts pipe..........	⅛ to 1	1 to 2	2 to 3
Complete..........	$1.65	$2.50	$7.87
Wheels..........	.24	.32	.50

Stanwood Pipe Cutters, Case Hardened.

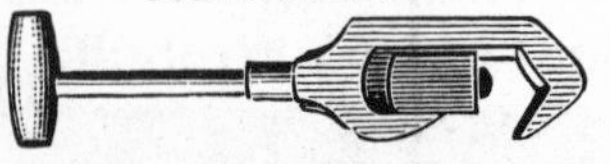

Order No. 43712. Weight, 3¾ lbs., 8½ lbs., 24 lbs.

Number..........	1	2	3
Fits pipe from..........	⅛ to ¾	1 to 2	2 to 3
Price, each..........	$1.10	$1.65	$5.00
43713 Cutter wheels, price each..........	.12	.18	.25
43714 Cutter Bl'ks and Wheels, price..........	.40	.60	1.00

One Wheel Pipe Cutter.

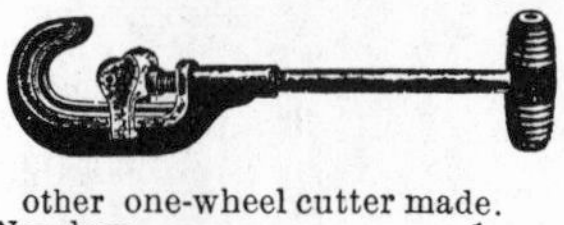

43715 Made of malleable iron with steel rod and tool steel cutter; lighter and stronger than any other one-wheel cutter made.

Numbers..........	1	2	3
Cut pipe from..........	⅛ to 1 in.	1 to 2 in.	2 to 3 in.
Price, each..........	$0 75	$1.38	$2.00
43715½ Extra wheels.	.12	18	.25

Open Hinge Malleable Iron Pipe Vise.

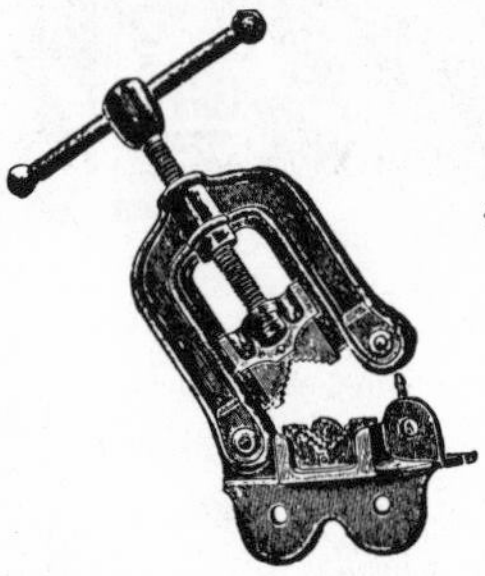

43716 Has interchangeable cut steel jaws, and is constructed to do the heaviest work. Great care has been taken in manufacturing the various parts, putting the strength where most desired. Jaws are warranted.

Number..........	1	2
Holds pipe from..........	¼ to 2 in.	¼ to 3 in.
Weight, pounds..........	20	26
Price, each..........	$3.00	$4.00
43716½ Extra jaws..........	1.25	1.88

Pipe Stock Dies.

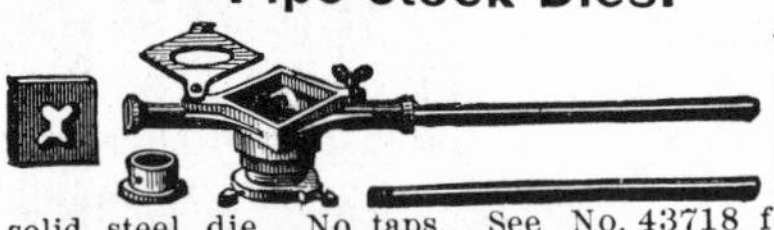

43717—Malleable Iron Pipe Stock, with solid steel die. No taps. See No. 43718 for taps. Weights range from 15 to 35 pounds.

Numbers..........	0	1	1½
Pipe Sizes of Dies..........	⅛, ¼, ⅜, ½.	¼, ⅜, ½, ¾, 1	¾, 1, 1¼
Dimension of Dies..........	2x½	2½x¾	3x¾
Complete with Dies..........	$2.55	$3.75	$3.50
Extra Dies..........	.75	.85	.90
Extra Guides..........	.12	.15	.22
Numbers..........	1¾	2	3
Pipe Sizes of Dies..........	1, 1¼, 1½,	1¼, 1½, 2,	2½x3
Dimension of Dies..........	3x3¾	4x⅞	5x1¼
Complete with Dies..........	$3.50	$5.00	$10.00
Extra Dies..........	.95	1.40	3.35
Extra Guides..........	.30	.30	.45

Pipe Taps.

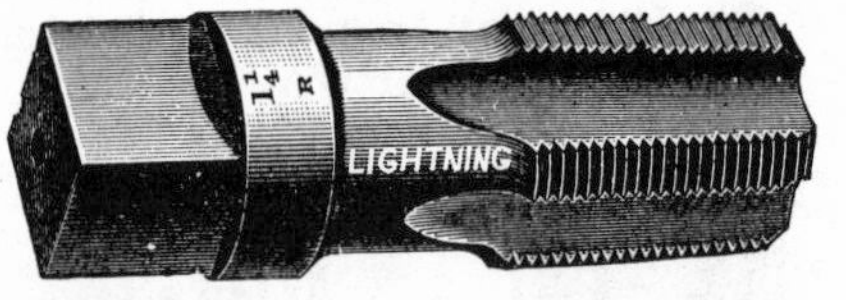

43718 Pipe Taps.

Size..........	⅛	¼	⅜	½	¾	1
Each..........	30c	35c	40c	50c	65c	80c
Size..........	1¼	1½	2	2½	3	
Each..........	90c	$1.10	$1.44	$2.53	$3.42	

Pipe Reamers.

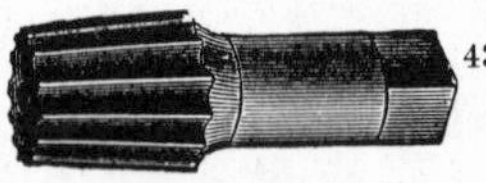

43719 Pipe Reamer for reaming out the ends of pipe.

Size, Inches.	⅛	¼	⅜	½	¾	1	1¼	1½	2
	30c	35c	40c	50c	65	80c	90c	$1.10	$1.44

Lightning Tap and Dies.

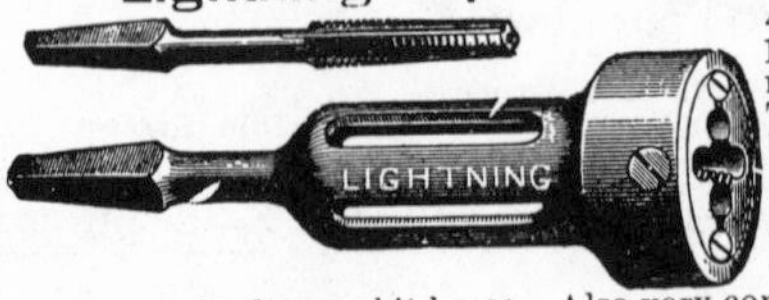

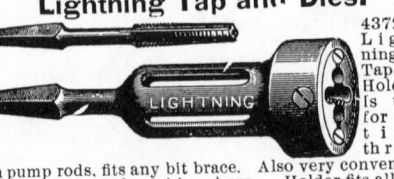

43720—Lightning Die Tap and Holder. Is used for cutting thread on pump rods, fits any bit brace. Also very convenient in blacksmith and machine shops. Holder fits all size dies.

Size.	Die Tap and Holder.	Die Only.	Tap Only.
3-16	$1.80	$0.90	$0.45
¼	1.80	.90	.45
5-16	1.85	.90	.50
⅜	2.00	1.05	.54
7-16	2.35	1.05	.63

DON'T Let an error pass unnoticed. We want a chance to correct all our mistakes.

Lightning Screw Plate.

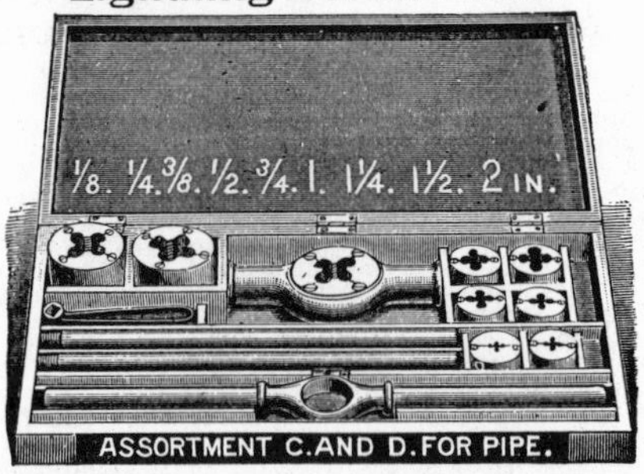

43725 The Lightning Screw Plate, for pipe, cuts 9 sizes with dies, right or left hand; cut from ¼ to 2 inches. Weighs 62 pounds. Price, complete for set in wood case.......... $21.60

Spring Tube Expander.

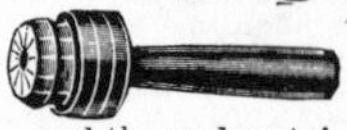

43727 Tubes put in with this tool are expanded on both sides of the tube plate, which makes a brace of the most efficient kind and the ends retain their original thickness. The dimensions given refer to outside diameter of tubes or flues,

Size ins..	1¼	1½	1¾	2	2¼	2½	2¾	3
Price...	$5.20	5.85	7.10	7.85	8.30	9.45	11.25	13.60

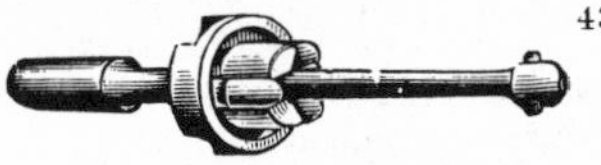

43728 The Tonkin Tube Expander, made entirely of Jessop's English cast steel, except the head, which is first quality wrought iron, case hardened. It costs nothing to keep in repair and will outlast a dozen of the expanders in common use; when ordering, state thickness of tube sheet for which they are required.

Size....	1	1¼	1½	1¾	2	2¼	2½	3
Price.	$3.50	3.60	3.70	4.00	5.00	6.00	7.00	9.00

Wire Flue Brushes.

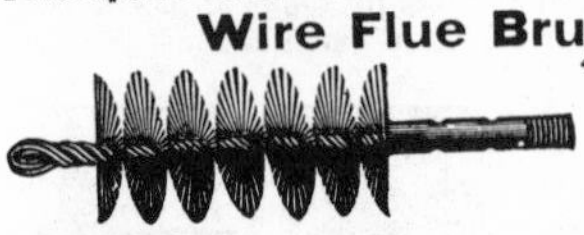

43730 Flat Wire Flue Brushes. When ordering, give outside diameter of the tube, the brushes are wanted for.

Outside diameter of tube	2	2¼	2½	3
Price, each..........	$0.58	$0.72	$0.78	$0.95

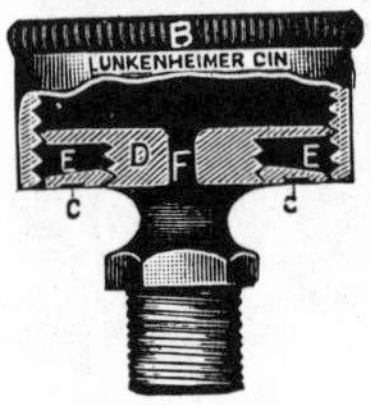

Screw Feed Grease Cups.

43731 This cup is unsurpassed where a simple and efficient one is wanted. Is specially adapted for jarring machinery, traction engines, etc.

Nos..........	00	0	1	2	3	4
Inside diameter..........	1 in.	1¼	1½	2	2½	3
Pipe thread..........	⅛ "	¼	¼	⅜	½	½
Finished brass. Price	25c.	35c.	48c.	58c.	78c.	1.05

Steam Whistles With Valve.

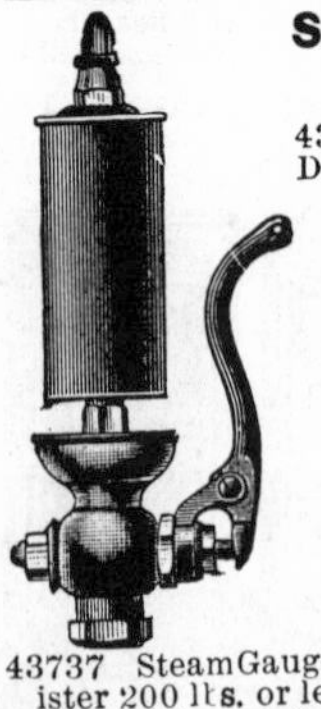

43735—

Diameter of bell.	Size of pipe.	Price, each.
1	⅜	$1.40
1¼	½	1.50
1½	½	1.60
2	¾	2.10
2½	¾	2.60
3	1	3.20
3½	1	4.40

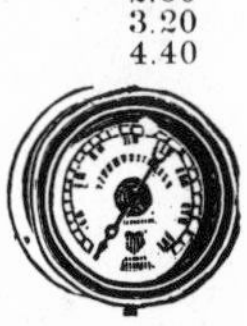

43737 Steam Gauges, BRASS CASE, to register 200 lbs. or less.

Size, inches.	3	3½	4½	5	5½	66
Price, each..	$2.50	$3.15	$3.50	$3.75	$5.50	$6.25

43738 Steam Gauge, IRON CASE, japanned, to register 200 lbs or less.

Size, inches...	3½	4½	5	5½	56
Price, each....	$1.75	$1.80	$1.85	$4.50	$5.25

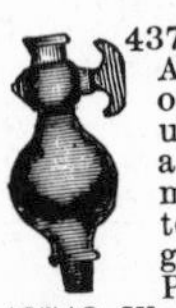

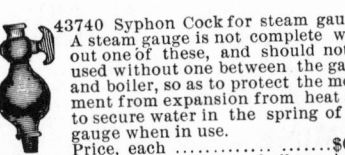

43740 Syphon Cock for steam gauges. A steam gauge is not complete without one of these, and should not be used without one between the gauge and boiler, so as to protect the movement from expansion from heat and to secure water in the spring of the gauge when in use.
Price, each.......... $0.80

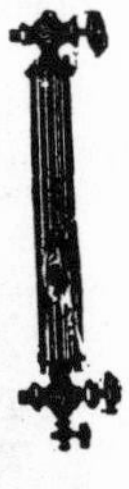

43742 Water Gauges for steam boilers; size of glass, ⅝x12 inches; size of pipe, ½ inch.
Price, each, rough finish.......... $1.10

Glass Tubes.

43745 Scotch Glass Tubes for water gauges, ½ or ⅝ inch in diameter.

Length	10	11	12	13	14	15	16
Price, each	10c.	10c.	12c.	12c.	12c.	14c.	15c.
Price, per doz.	$1.00	1.00	1.15	1.15	1.25	1.35	1.50

Compression Gauge Cocks.

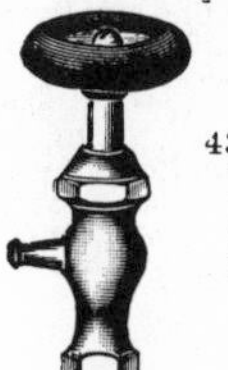

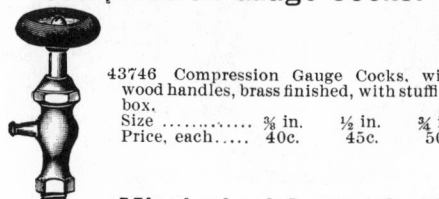

43746 Compression Gauge Cocks, with wood handles, brass finished, with stuffing box.

Size	⅜ in.	½ in.	¾ in.
Price, each	40c.	45c.	50c.

Mississippi Gauge Cock.

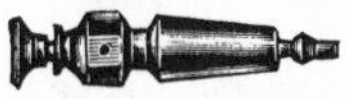

43747 The most simple and efficient gauge cock made. Reliable and safe.

Cut for pipe thread	⅜ in.	½ in.	¾ in.	1 in.
Price, finished brass	28c.	40c.	72c.	85c.

The "Detroit" Lubricator.

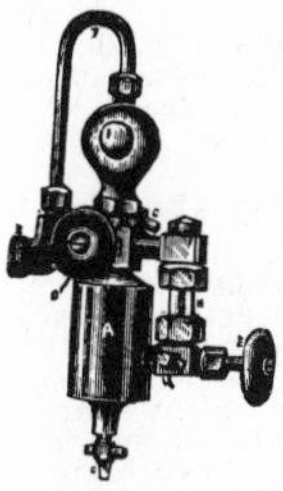

43748 Single connection, for traction engines, steam pumps, etc. Description: A, oil reservoir; C, filler plug; D, water feed valve; F, condensing chamber; G, drain valve; H, sight feed glass; K, connection to steam pipe or steam chest; Q, drain valve for sight feed glass. This lubricator is designed for use on traction engines, where it is desirable to discharge the oil either into steam pipe below the throttle or into steam chest or cylinder. Its construction is such that the oil cannot be syphoned out; a regular and steady stream is obtained. Size of glass in sight feed, ¾x2⅛ inch.

Size.	Price, brass finish.
¼ pint	Each, $2.37
⅓ "	" 2.63
½ "	" 2.95

Detroit Sight Feed Lubricator.

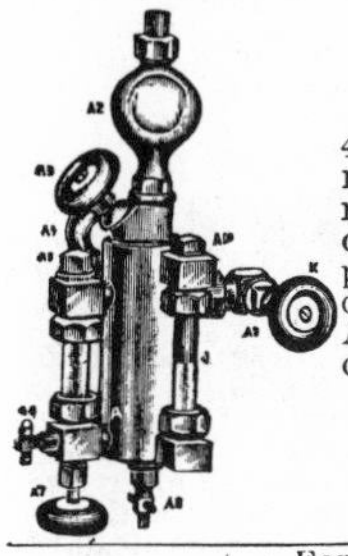

43749 The most popular and most reliable Sight Feed Lubricator made. Is simple in construction, contains no piston, springs or plunger, and as the body is cast in one piece it cannot get out of order. Adapted to feed any clean oil, light or heavy.

Size	For cylinder diameter.	Price, brass.
⅓ Pint	Up to 8 in.	$2.80
½ "	8 to 10 in.	3.30
1 "	10 to 18 in.	4.40
1 Quart	18 to 30 in.	6.60
2 "	30 and over.	8.50

The Metropolitan Automatic Injector.

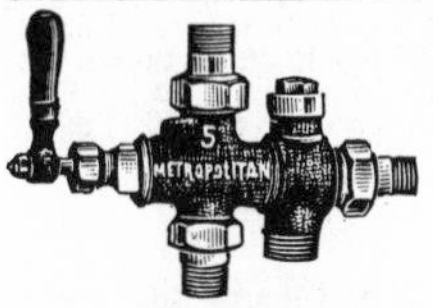

43750

Size.	Price.	Size of dipe connection.	Gallons per hour, 65 lbs. Pressure.	Horse power.
2	$4.90	⅜	40	1 to 4
3	5.10	⅜	60	4 to 8
3½	5.70	½	90	8 to 12
4	6.35	½	120	12 to 16
5	7.92	¾	220	16 to 28
6	9.50	¾	300	28 to 40
7	12.67	1	420	40 to 57
8	14.25	1	540	57 to 72
9	17.45	1¼	720	72 to 93
10	19.00	1½	900	93 to1 20
11	30.00	1¼	1,260	120 to1 68
12	36.00	1½	1,740	168 to2 32
13	44.00	2	2,240	232 to2 98
14	50.00	2	2,820	298 to3 82

SAVE COAL

By putting Sheathing Paper under Shingles and Sidings. It keeps out cold and keeps in heat

Le Count's Pattern Light Steel Lathe Dog.

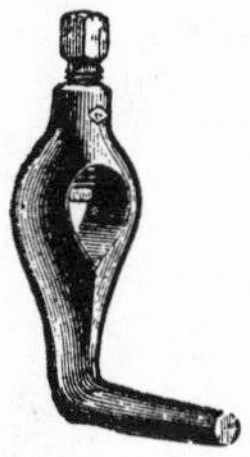

43752 With hardened steel screw turned in lathe.

No.	Opening, Inch.	Price, each.
1	⅜	15c.
2	½	15c.
3	¾	20c.
4	1	25c.
5	1¼	30c.
6	1½	35c.
7	1¾	40c.
8	2	45c.

Ejector or Jet Pump.

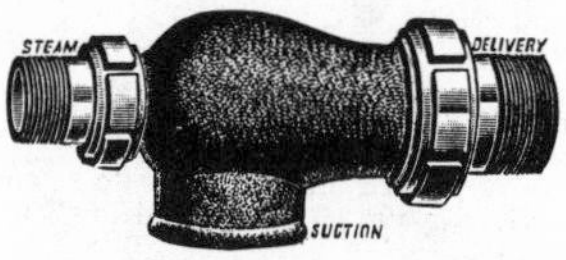

MADE WITH INDEPENDENT COUPLINGS AND TUBES.

These ejectors are used for lifting and conveying water and other liquids from one level to another in mines, pits, wells, tanneries, paper mills—in fact in every place where it is desired to transport liquids of any kind. These ejectors are especially adapted for use as a bilge pump for steam boats.

They are made with independent couplings and tubes, which can be replaced, when worn or damaged, at a small cost. The ejector can be taken off for cleaning without disconnecting the pipes.

The H-D Ejector will lift 24 feet. When it is desired to raise the liquid to a greater distance, place the ejector near the liquid and elevate it. With a steam pressure of 65 pounds it will elevate from 50 to 60 feet and with 100 pounds steam from 70 to 80 feet.

43753—

Size.	Pipe Connections. Steam.	Suction and delivery.	Capacity, per hour.	Price.
1 Brass.	⅜	½	250 Gals.	$1.80
2 "	½	¾	500 "	2.25
3 "	¾	1	960 "	3 65
4 "	1	1¼	1,300 "	4.60
5 "	1¼	1½	2,000 "	5.90
6 Iron.	1¼	2	3,500 "	8.32
7 "	1½	2½	5,000 "	9 50
8 "	2	3	8,000 "	11.96

Size No. 6 has iron body, balance brass.

Sizes Nos 7 and 8 have iron bodies and delivery connections, balance brass.

Safety Valves.

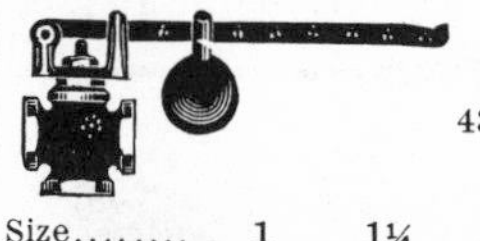

43754 Iron Body, brass mounted, with brass disks, screwed.

Size	1	1¼	1½	2	2½	3
Price, each	$1.00	1.40	1.60	2.10	3.25	4.45

Pop Safety Valves.

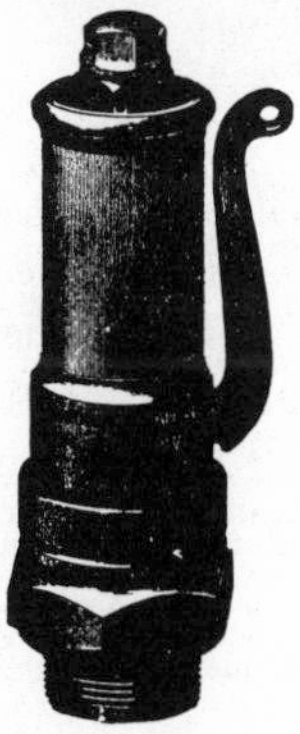

Made of finished brass and warranted accurate, durable and reliable. Has full relieving capacity and very sensitive.

Each valve is carefully tested.

43755 Pipe size.	Horse power.	Price, each.
¾	Under 5	$2.95
1	5 to 10	3.50
1¼	10 to 20	4.10
1½	20 to 30	5.25
2	30 to 40	7.25

Rubber Belting.

We handle two grades of Rubber Belting, *Standard* and *Extra* Quality. Our Standard quality is a fair quality, but we do not recommend it where a large belt would have to be used. It is sold by many dealers as a first-class article, but it is not, and we will not guarantee it if used as a *Thresher Belt*. Our *Extra Quality* we guarantee and it can be used for Thresher belts with satisfaction, but it is not as reliable as No. 43851. We can furnish endless belts in the *Extra* quality only. Parties ordering endless belts must give us from two to three weeks, time for filling the order, as it requires that length of time to properly make an endless belt. When ordering endless belt always allow three feet of the belt you are ordering for the cost of making the lap. Do not include this three feet in the length of belt, but simply allow money to pay for it. For example, if you wanted endless belt 100 feet long, allow for 103 feet.

43834 Standard Quality, not guaranteed.
43835 Extra Quality guaranteed.

2-Ply Rubber Belting.

Size.	Standard, per ft.	Extra, per ft	Size.	Standard, per ft.	Extra, per ft.
1 - inch..	$0.02	$0.03	2½-inch..	$0.05½	$0.07½
1¼-inch..	02¾	.03¼	3 - inch..	.06½	.09
1½-inch..	.03¾	.04½	3½-inch..	.07½	.10½
2 - inch..	.04½	.06	4 - inch..	.09	.12

3-Ply Rubber Belting.

43836 Standard Quality, not guaranteed.
43837 Extra Quality, guaranteed.

Size.	Standard, per ft.	Extra per ft.	Size.	Standard, per ft.	Extra, per ft.
2 - inch..	$0.05	$0.07	8 - inch..	$0.21½	.28
2½ inch..	.06½	.10	9 - inch.	.23½	.32
3 - inch..	.07½	.10½	10 - inch..	.26½	.36
3½-inch..	.09	.12	11 - inch..	.29	.40
4 - inch..	.10	.13½	12 - inch..	.31	.43
5 - inch..	.12½	.17	13 - inch..	,35	.47
6 - inch..	.15	.21	14 - inch .	.38	.51
7 - inch..	.18	.24			

4-Ply Rubber Belting.

43838 Standard Quality, not guaranteed.
43839 Extra Quality, guaranteed.

Size.	Standard per ft.	Extra, per ft.	Size.	Standard, per ft.	Extra, per ft.
3 - inch..	$0.09	$0.12½	10-inch..	$0.34	$0.43
3½-inch..	.11	.15	11-inch..	.38	.47
4 - inch..	.12	.17	12-inch..	.42	.52
4½-inch..	.14	.19	13-inch..	.44	.57
5 - inch..	.15	.21	14-inch..	.49	.62
6 - inch..	.18	.25	15-inch..	.53	.66½
7 - inch..	.20	.29	16-inch..	.57	.71
8 - inch..	.23	.34	18-inch..	.64	.81
9 - inch..	.26	.38			

When ordering endless belts always allow the price of 3 feet for the lap.

Leather Belting.

We handle two grades of leather belting, Standard and Extra Standard. The Standard belting is a medium quality and is not made wider than 4 inches. It is usually used in connection with light agricultural machinery and in machine shops. It must not be used as a thresher belt. Extra Standard leather belting is made from selected stock, with one long and one short lap, riveted together with copper rivets. It is recommended for thresher belts, and we guarantee it to be the best leather belting in the market for the money. We also have what is called a SHORT LAP belt. Prices on this belting we will quote on application; it is much higher in price.

43840 Standard.
43841 Extra Standard.

Width.	Standard, per ft.	Extra Standard, per ft.	Width.	Extra Standard per ft.
1 - inch...	$0.03	$0.04	4½-inch......	$0.22
1¼-inch...	.03½	05	5 - inch......	.25
1½-inch...	.04½	.07	5½-inch......	.28
1¾-inch...	.05½	.08	6 - inch......	.31
2 - inch...	.06	.09	6½-inch......	.33
2¼-inch...	.07	.10½	7 - inch......	.36
2½-inch...	.08	.12	8 - inch......	.41
2¾-inch...	.09	.13	9 - inch......	.46
3 - inch...	.10½	.14½	10 - inch......	.52
3½-inch...	.11½	.17	11 - inch......	.57
4 - inch...	.13½	.20	12 - inch......	.62

Gandy Cotton Belting.

On account of the peculiar construction of this belting it is unaffected by atmospheric changes, uninjured by water or steam, and may be subjected to a degree of heat ruinous to other belting. It is therefore the best belt known for outdoor use and for wet, damp or hot places. When ordering endless belt allow the price of 3 feet for the lap, but do not include this 3 feet in the length of belt you order.

43844 4-ply Cotton Belting.

Width.	per foot.	Width.	Per foot.	Width.	Per foot.
1½ in.....	$0.07	3 in	$0.13½	8 in......	$0.36
		3½ in.....	.16	9 in......	.40½
2 in.....	.09	4 in.....	.18	10 in......	.45
		5 in.....	.22½	11 in......	.50
2½ in.....	.12	6 in.....	.27	12 in......	.54
		7 in.....	.31½		

43845 6-ply Cotton Belting.

Width.	Per foot.	Width.	Per foot.	Width.	Per foot
3 in.....	$0.18	7 in......	$0.42	14 in......	$0.84
3½ in.....	.21	8 in......	.48	15 in......	.90
4 in.....	.24	9 in......	.54	16 in.....	.96
4½ in.....	.27	10 in......	.60	17 in.....	1.02
5 in.....	.30	12 in......	.72	18 in....	1.08
6 in.....	.36	13 in......	.78		

Thresher Belts.

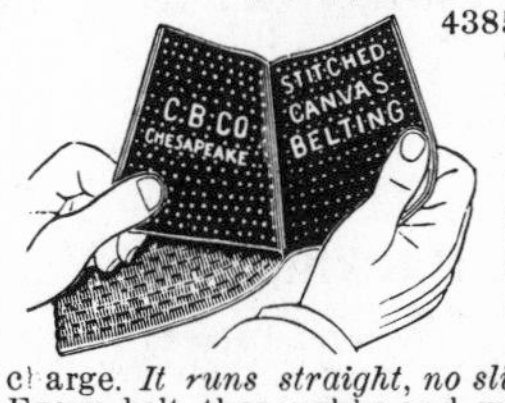

43850 Chesapeake "Stitched Canvas Belting." We do not furnish any size of the belt but that which is quoted below; warranted to give satisfaction with fair usage. Should any prove defective they may be returned and a new belt will be sent in place free of charge. *It runs straight, no slipping, does not get hard.* Every belt thoroughly and well stretched by special machinery. The holes for lacing straight belts should be made with a pointed awl, and well back (not a hollow punch which cuts the thread and weakens the belt). We keep only the following sizes of endless belts in stock: 120, 130, 140, 150, 160 feet, 4 ply, which is equal to 4 ply rubber. It requires 3 feet of belt to make the lap, therefore the above belts will measure just 3 feet short. For example, 150 feet endless belt will measure 147 feet; we charge for 150 feet.

4 ply, 6 inch, price per foot $0.25
4 ply, 7 inch, price per foot .... .29

CERES THRESHER BELT.
Strongest and Most Durable Endless Rubber Thresher Belt Manufactured.

43851 It is a well established fact that cotton belting is far superior to rubber belting in a great many respects, but rubber belting excells because it does not stretch. In the "Ceres" we have combined the good qualities of the cotton belting with the superior qualities of the rubber, and produced the *only* belt that will meet all the requirements of a good thresher belt. This belt is adhered together with rubber friction, and is also sewed together by our celebrated "Cross-Stitch," which, of itself, is a guarantee of the superiority of this belt.

This is the only rubber belt that we will guarantee for thresher purposes, and, in fact, is the only rubber belt yet made that will stand the abuse that thresher belts get.

The "Ceres" will convey much more power than the cotton belt, as it has a surface that will not slip. Send for sample of the "Ceres." We keep only the following sizes in stock, 120, 130, 140, 150, 160 feet.

4-ply. 6-inch, 4-ply. Price, per foot..........$0.28
7-inch, 4-ply. Price, per foot .... .33
8-inch, 4-ply. Price, per foot.................... 0.36

Packing.

43854 Arrow Brand Braided Flax Packing, is manufactured from long fibre flax on the most improved machines and saturated with an excellent lubricant. It is used in the water end of pumps, hydraulic elevators. We carry in stock the following sizes: ¼, ½, ¾, 1, 1¼ inch.
Price, per pound, any size............ . ...$0.33

Red Cross Piston Packing.

43855 Is similar to Empire and Eureka, and made from the very best material on the most improved machinery. It has a rubber core covered with the best cotton fibre, saturated with an excellent lubricant, and is guaranteed to be equal to any in the market. Made for steam, principally. Made both in round and oval shape; the cut represents the oval shape, made in the following sizes: ¼, ⅜, ½, ⅝, ¾, ⅞, 1 inch. Price, per pound, any size........$0.27

Skull and Bones.

43856 Steam Piston Packing. We call it this because it is death to delays. This is a special quality of round rubber core piston packing lubricated entirely with the best quality *Dixon's Graphite* and will outrun other packing three fold; made in the following sizes: ¼, ⅜, ½, ⅝, ¾, ⅞, 1 inch. Price, per pound, any size...... ....$0.45

Steam Packing Cloth Insertion.

43857 There is one ply of cloth to every 1-16 thickness. Each cloth, whether insertion or on outside, to count as one ply.

Thickness.	Weight	Price, per pound.
¾ inch	1¾ lbs.	$0.15
⅜ inch	3¼ lbs.	.15
⁷⁄₁₆ inch	6½ lbs.	.15
½ inch	9¼ lbs	.15
⅝ inch	12½ lbs.	.15
⅜ inch	18 lbs.	.15
¼ inch	24 lbs.	.15

Garlock Packing.

43860 This packing is more generally in use than any other and gives universal satisfaction; put up in twelve foot lengths. We give below the weight per 12 feet of each size.

Sizes	³⁄₁₆	⅛	¼	⁵⁄₁₆	⅜	⁷⁄₁₆	½	⅝
W't per 12 ft	⅜	¼	¹¹⁄₁₆	1	1⁹⁄₁₆	2³⁄₁₆	2⅝	3¹³⁄₁₆
Sizes	¹¹⁄₁₆	¾	⅞	1	1⅛	1¼	1⅜	
W't pr 12 ft	4⅝	5⅜	6⁷⁄₁₆	9⅜	10¹⁄₁₆	8¼	10⁷⁄₁₆	5⅜

Price, per pound, any size...............$0.85

Sheet Packing.

43861 Unsudurian Sheet Packing self vulcanizing, ¹⁄₁₆ inch thick, weighs 6 pounds to the square yard, ⅛ 10 pounds, ¼ 16 pounds; price, per pound, any size................................$0.50

Pure Rubber Packing.

43862 Pure Rubber Sheet Packing runs the same to the yard as No. 42926; per pound, any thickness.................................$0.65
43863 Italian Hemp Packing, per pound........ .18
43864 Asbestos Wick and Rope Packing, any size, per pound................................... ...... .38

Belt Studs.

43865 Belt Studs for fastening the ends of rubber or leather belting together; made of the best quality of brass. The only really good fastener made.

Nos.....	00	0	1	2	3	4	5
Length between shoulders......	⅞	¹¹⁄₁₆	¾	⁹⁄₁₆	½	⁷⁄₁₆	⅜
Per dozen........	12c	10c	8c	6c	4c	4c	3c
Per 100	90c	71c	60c	45c	30c	30c	23c

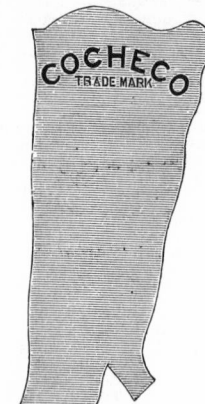

COCHECO
TRADE MARK

Raw Hide Lace Leather.

We have the very best grade of raw hide lacing and furnish it either cut or in sides. It is much tougher than tanned lacing; always remains pliable and will never rot.

We do not sell less than a side or a full package of 100 feet.

43868 Cut lacing in packages of 100 ft.
¼ in.$0.50 per 100 ft.
⅕ in. .60 per 100 ft.
⅜ in. .70 per 100 ft.
½ in. .90 per 100 ft.
⅝ in. 1.25 per 100 ft.
¾ in. 1.45 per 100 ft.

43869 Lacing in sides, 16c per square foot.
43870 Lace Leather Cutters, 40c each.
A side of lacing will average 15 square feet.

Hose Nozzles.

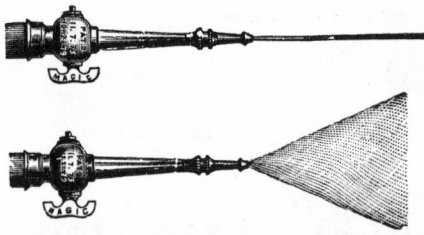

The Magic Hose Nozzle can be regulated to produce a variety of sprays, from a fine mist to a solid stream.

Each.
43879 For ¾-in. hose $0.54
43880 For 1-inch hose .... .65

Rubber Hose.

We can furnish in 25 and 50 foot lengths only.
Montgomery Ward & Co.'s Rubber Hose. The standard quality is as good as what dealers sell ordinarily as extra quality; good enough for ordinary use but will not wear as well nor stand the pressure that the extra will. Our extra is the best hose made. Two-ply hose is suitable for conducting under a moderate pressure only: 3-ply stands 75 lbs. to the square inch; 4-ply from 100 to 150 lbs. pressure

Montgomery Ward & Co.'s Rubber Hose.
Standard Quality. Not Warranted.

43883 ¾ inch, 3 ply, per foot.......... ... .$0.08
43884 ¾ " 4 " " .... .10
43885 1 " 3 " " .... .11
43886 1 " 4 " " .... .13

Montgomery Ward & Co.'s Rubber Hose.
Extra Quality.

43887 ¾ inch, 3 ply, per foot.....................$0.10
43888 ¾ " 4 " " .... .12
43889 1 " 3 " " .... .12
43890 1 " 4 " " .... .16

Suction Hose.

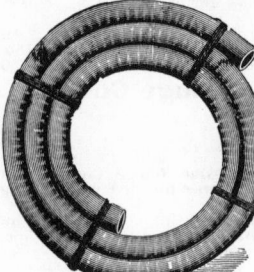

Suction Hose, wire lined. We can recommend this hose as being of very fine quality; made only in lengths of 15-20-25 feet.
43893 2 in Price, per ft. $0.45
43894 2 in. Couplings. Each. ....75.
43895 2 in. Clamps Each...........$0.15

Garden Hose Reels.

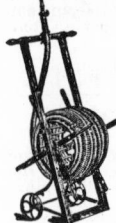

43898 Has iron wheels, 6 in. diameter, and the reel will hold 100 feet of ¾ in. rubber hose; weight, about 10 lbs. Price of reel without hose. Each$0.75
43899 Fountain Reel will carry150 feet of ¾ in. hose, has 7 in.iron wheels, weight about 12 lbs. Price of reel without the hose, each...................$1.10
43900 Columbia Reel, will carry 200 feet of ¾ inch hose, has 7 inch iron wheels; weight, about 15 lbs. Price of Reel without the hose.... . ...$1.60

All Iron Hose Reels.

Made in three sizes. It is a good, strong, handsome and convenient reel, being constructed entirely of wrought iron pipe and malleable iron; it is indestructible. The reels are light in weight; wheels are high. It forms a splendid nozzle holder for lawn sprinkling.

	Height of wheel.	Weight.	Capacity, ¾-in. hose.	Price, each.
43901......	21 in.	18 lbs.	100 ft.	$1.87
43902......	24 in.	22 lbs.	150 ft.	2.20
42903......	30 in.	32 lbs.	500 ft.	3.50

Hose Couplings.

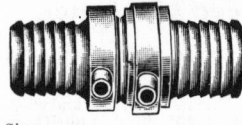

43912 Hose Couplings, for standard steam or hydraulic hose.

Size......	¾	1	1¼	1½
Each	$0.08	$0.20	$0.40	$0.55
Per dozen	.80	2.00	4.50	6.00

Hose Splicers.

43913 Hose Splicer for mending hose; very convenient. If hose gets damaged any place or is worn the bad place may be cut out and the two ends joined together with this device.

Size...	½	¾	1 in.
Price, each.....................	$0.05	$0.05	$0.05
Per dozen	.35	.30	.35

Hose Clamps.

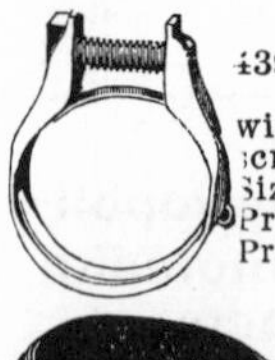

43915— Made of brass, never rusts, cheap as a wire band and very much better. A small screw driver will put it on or take it off.

Size....	¾ in.	1 in.
Price, each.................	$0.06	$0.10
Price, dozen	.50	1.00

43917 Hose Clamps for securing coupling in rubber or canvas hose.

Size..	½	¾	1	1¼ in
Each..........	$0.06	$0.06	$0.08	$0.10
Per dozen	.60	.60	.75	0.85
Size........	1½	2	2½	3 in.
Each..........	$0.12	.15	.22	.30
Per dozen	1.25	1.50	2.55	3.50

Rubber Tubing.

43920 Rubber Tubing is used for a variety of purposes, nursery bottles, syringes, bath-rooms, etc. Inside 1-16 inch 3-32 inch. Inside 1-16 inch 3-32 inch

measure.	thick.	thick.	measure.	thick.	thick.
⅛ in.pr.ft.	$0.03½	$0.04	⅜ in.pr.ft.	$0.09	$0.10
³⁄₁₆ in.pr.ft.	.04½	.05	½ in.pr.ft.	.10	.11
¼ in.pr.ft.	.07	.07½	⅝ in.pr.ft.	.11	.12
⁵⁄₁₆ in.pr.ft.	.08	09½	¾ in.pr.ft.	.14 •	.15

Lawn Sprinkler.

43927 Will spray the water perfectly and covers a surface of 25 to 40 feet, according to amount of pressure. Made of brass, nickel plated.
Price, each $0.30
Price per dozen 3.25

Arc Lawn Sprinkler.

43930 This Sprinkler is instantaneously changed from a circular to an arc sprinkler by simply removing the small screw on the outside of disk to the opposite side. By moving screw back a c rcular spray is again ob tained. Made in brass, handsomely finished, and nickel plated.
Price, each.....................$0 65
Price, per dozen................. 7.25

Eclipse Lawn Sprinkler.

43931 This little article is made of cast iron handsomely japanned in bright vermilion. It has no revolving parts, cannot be demolished when stepped on. It will distribute the water evenly. covering a surface of thirty-six feet, with proper pressure. Made only for ¾ inch hose.
Price, each...........................$0.20
Per dozen.......................... 2.00

Mystic Lawn Fountain

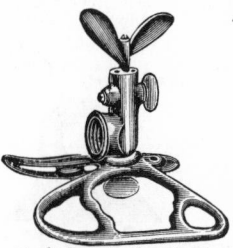

43932 The strongest and best sprinkler made Throws either whole or half circle by simply turning thumb piece. It is constructed on scientific principles so the wings will not choke or clog, and very little pressure is required to revolve them, ¼ or ⅓ is sufficient to throw a full circle; have thumb piece stand perpendicular as shown in cut, for ½ circle set thumb piece horizontal. The slide enables the sprinkler to be moved about the lawn by the hose, or by a cord attached. Should the holes get clogged, from impurities in the water, the thumb piece can be taken out so as to get at the holes more readily. Price, each...........................$0.75
Per dozen...............................8.00

Rainmaker Sprinkler.

43933 Which is the same as the above except that it has no thumb piece and throws a *full circle only*. It is the finest sprinkler of this class on the market. Price, each...........................$0.50
Per dozen......................................4.75

Fitting Out Door Pumps.

To enable those not familiar with iron Pumps to understand their construction and working, we show in the cut a "Set Lengh"or a pump standard with cylinder connected one-half, represented as cutaway to show the inside. The Cylinder D, which contains the valve and suction, is connected by 4 feet of pipe, C, with the Pump Standard A; B is the connecting rod which connects the handle with the suction in the cylinder. They are fitted this way so that they will not freeze in winter; the cylinder which contains the working parts is below the frost line, and will not freeze.

We receive all of our pumps from factory, fitted with cylinder, 4 feet of pipe connecting same with base of pump, when other pipe is attached. They are ready to draw water from wells up to 30 feet in depth; notice—for well deeper than this they have to be refitted, which necessitates an extra charge for the labor of doing this. Fitting pumps *does not include pipe*, but merely covers the cost of extra labor and the necessary *rods* and *rod couplings*, the cost of which will be as follows:

PRICES CHARGED FOR FITTING PUMPS.
Fitting Pumps for wells 25 to 35 feet,$1.50 each
"   "   " 35 to 50 feet, 2.00 each
"   "   " 50 to 75 feet, 2.50 each
"   "   " 75 to 100 feet, 3.75 each
Jn ordering pumps for deep wells be sure and state how far down you wish the cylinder put, otherwise we will use our own judgment.

WE COULD NOT AFFORD TO MAKE ANY FALSE STATEMENTS. EVERYTHING WE SAY IS SO TO THE BEST OF OUR KNOWLEDGE AND BELIEF.

Anti-Freezing Well Pump.

43936 With 4 feet set length as in cut. This is a light but durable pump for use in well of ordinary depth. The set length is wrought iron and connected under spout. Prices are for pump with iron cylinder. Average weight, 60 lbs.

No.	Cylinder.	For pipe.	Price.
1	2¼ in.	1 in. each	$2.95
2	2½ in.	1¼ in. each	3.15
3	2¾ in.	1¼ in. each	3.25
4	3 in.	1¼ in. each	3.40

Anti-Freezing Force Pump.

WITH 4 FOOT SET LENGTH.

43938 This is a good medium priced force pump, with air chamber in top of stock. It is adapted for wells about 30 feet deep, but with the cylinder placed within 15 to 20 feet from the bottom it will do good work in wells 50 to 60 feet deep. Prices are for pumps with iron cylinders. Average weight, 85 lbs.

No.	Clylinder.	For pipe.	Price.
3	2¾ in.	1¼ in.	$4.95
4	3 in.	1¼ in.	5.00
5	3¼ in.	1¼ in.	5.30
6	3½ in.	1½ in.	5.80

Anti-Freezing Force Pump.

WITH 4 FOOT SET LENGTH.

43940 This is a good strong force pump, with air chamber on spout. It is especially adapted for use around gardens, yards and stables, and when located near the house is quite efficient protection against fire. When used as a lift pump, the cap on the air chamber should be unscrewed. With the cylinder properly placed, the pump will work to advanage in wells up to 75 feet deep. Prices are with iron cylinder. Average weight, 100 lbs.

No.	Cylinder.	For pipe.	Price.
3	2¾ in.	1¼ in.	$5.30
4	3 in.	1¼ in.	5.35
6	3¼ in.	1¼ in.	5.85
5	3½ in.	1½ in.	6.10

Double Acting Force Pump.

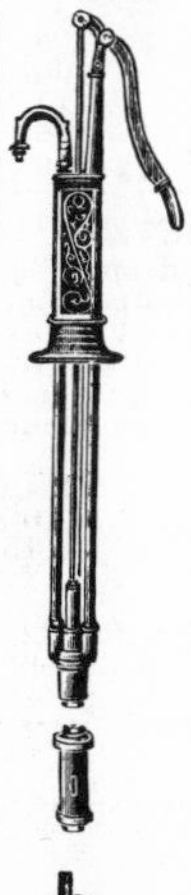

43941 The easiest double acting pump on the market. It can be used either in deep or shallow wells by attaching the lower cylinder for deep wells, or detaching the lower cylinder for shallow wells, as shown in cut. For wells 25 feet deep or less the lower cylinder is not required. In deeper wells it must be placed near the bottom of the well and connected to upper cylinder with pipe and rod. This pump is supplied with brass lined cylinder, rubber valve seat, strainer and hose attachment.

No	Cylinder	pipe	Price for shallow well	Price for deep well
2	2½ in.	1¼		$8.10
4	3 "	1¼	$8.00	8.50

Anti-Freezing Windmill Pump.

WITH 4-FOOT SET LENGTH.

43942 This is a substantial pump for wind mill or hand use. The flat rods fit the top tightly, thus preventing stones and dirt from falling into the pump. It is adapted for either open or dug wells not exceeding 30 feet in depth, but with the cylinder placed within 15 to 20 feet from the bottom, it will do the work in a 75 foot well. Price is with iron cylinder Average weight, 80 lbs.

No.	Cylinder.	For Pipe.	Price.
2	2½ in.	1¼ in.	$3.60
3	2¾ in.	1¼ in.	3.70
4	3 in.	1¼ in.	3.90
5	3¼ in	1¼ in.	4.10
6	3½ in	1½ in	4.20

Windmill Force Pump.

ANTI-FREEZING, WITH 4-FOOT SET LENGTH.

43944 A very desirable tank pump. The windmill top gives it a direct vertical motion to the plunger, thus wearing the cylinder evenly. It is provided with a brass stuffing box, hose coupling and back outlet. When used as a lift pump, loosen the screw in the air chamber. It has a cock spout, so that water can be forced in tank or discharged at spout. The length of stroke is 6 in. and the average weight is 95 lbs.

No.	Cylinder.	For Pipe.	Price.
2	2½ in.	1¼ in.	$5.80
3	2¾ in.	1¼ in.	5.90
4	3 in.	1¼ in.	6.00
5	3¼ in.	1¼ in.	6.20
6	3½ in.	1½ in.	6.45

We can furnish above pump without cock spout for 50 cent lsess.

Windmill Force Pump.

ANTI-FREEZING, WITH IMPROVED VERTICAL DISTRIBUTING VALVE.

43945 One of the most popular windmill pumps made and can be used in either open, drilled or tubular wells. Its construction insures a heavy stream of water; it is easy of operation, durable and handsome in appearance. Price includes three way cock, hose coupling, and lower elbow coupling. Average weight, 55 pounds.
Price. with 6 inch stroke, each..$7.85
Price, with 10 inch stroke, each 8.65

Hand Force Pump.

EXTRA HEAVY.

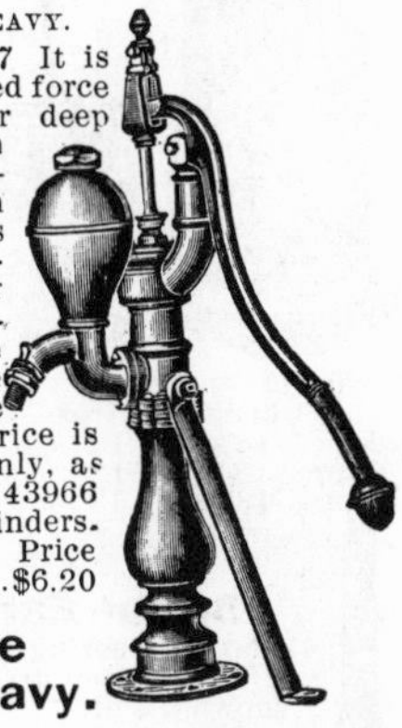

43947 It is an improved force pump for deep wells with air chamber on spout. It is very desirable for yard or street use. To prevent freezing, a drip hole should be drilled in the pipe 3 or 4 feet below the base of the pump. The price is for the pump standard only, as shown in cut. See cut No. 43966 and 43968 for price of cylinders. Average weight, 110 lbs. Price with 7 inch stroke, each...$6.20

Windmill Force Pumps, Extra Heavy.

43950 A very strong, solid pump with double braces, and is adapted for hand or windmill use. It is used mostly for very deep wells, and where a pump receives hard usage. The price is for pump standards only, as shown in cut. See Nos. 43966 and 43968 for cylinders. 6 in. stroke, height 55 in., for pipe 1½ in. Price $9.60
10 in. stroke, height 59 in., for pipe 2 in. Price...... .....$10.20

Hydraulic Ram.

43951 The "Deming" Hydraulic Ram is made entirely of iron and bronze, and is practically indestructible. Send for special circular, giving full description of these wonderful machines and table showing their efficiency.

No.	Quantity furnished by reservoir to which ram is adapted.	Size of Pipe.		Price
		Drive.	Discharge.	
2	½ to 2 gal. per min.	¾	½	$4.80
3	1½" 4 " " "	1	½	5.80
4	3 " 7 " " "	1½	¾	7.40
5	6 " 14 " " "	2	1	11.55
6	12 " 25 " " "	2½	1¼	21.00
7	20 " 60 " " "	4	2	39.50
8	30 "120 " " "	6	2½	65.75

Irrigating Lift Pump.

43952 This pump is capable of raising a large quantity of water by means of a wind mill or other power having a vertical motion. The No. 4, has a 10-inch stroke, 8½-inch cylinder, and a capacity of 2½ gallons per stroke. A wind mill having 40 revolutions per minute would raise with this pump 100 gallons per minute, 6,000 gallons per hour, 144-000 per day, supposing the wind to be blowing steadily at the proper speed. Four acres of land could be irrigated per day with such an outfit at the rate of 36,-000 gallons to the acre. This pump is not suitable for lifting over 25 feet vertically. In deeper wells would suggest the use of our *Irrigating Cylinders.*

No.	Dia. of Cylinder	Capacity Per stroke.	Price. each.
2	6	1½ gal.	$10.75
4	8½	2½ gal.	12.25

Irrigating Cylinders.

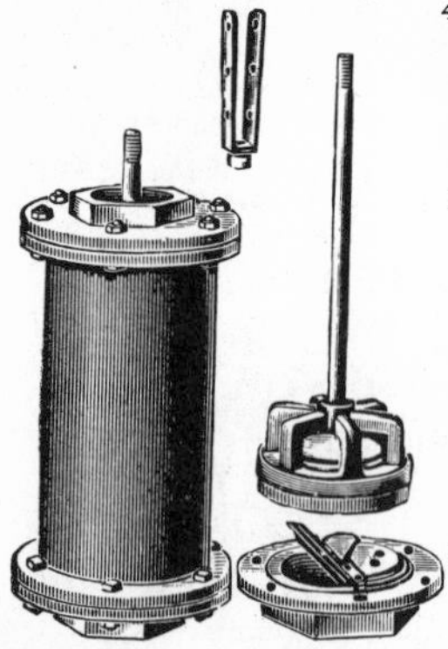

43953 This is a new iron cylinder which was recently designed for pumping large quantities of water from either shallow or deep wells. It can be operated by wind mill or other power and is adapted for any stroke up to 12 inches. When used as a lift pump only, no pump head is required; it is only necessary to place a TEE at end of discharge pipe, which will allow the water to flow to the irrigating ditches. Prices are for cylinder complete, with forked rod coupling, for wood rod as shown in cut.

Inside Dia.	Length.	Stroke.	Fitted for	Cap. for Stroke.	Price.
6 in.	18 in.	12 in.	3 in.	1¼ gal.	$ 6.75
8 in.	18 in.	12 in.	4 in.	2¼ gal.	10.25
10 in.	18 in.	12 in.			13.80

Spiral Earth Augers.

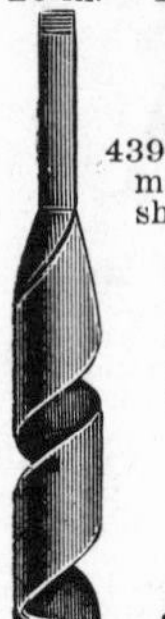

43955 For boring wells. Strong and well made. Prices given are for either style shown in cut.

Size.	Price, each.
2½ in.	$2.75
3 in.	3.10
4 in.	4.25
5 in.	6.10
6 in.	11.20

Pitcher Spout Pumps.

43959 This pump is extra heavy and well finished, polished cylinders and patent closed top, which prevents the water from flying up when pumped; is anti-freezing, and fitted for 1¼ inch pipe; either lead or iron.
No. 1, 2½ inch bore. Weight, 21¼ lbs., for 1-inch pipe. Price, each......... $1.05
No. 2, 3-inch bore. Weight 23½ lbs., for 1¼-inch pipe. Price, each $1.20
No. 3, 3½-inch bore. Weight, 26¾ lbs., for 1¼-inch pipe. Price, each......$1.25
No. 4, 4-inch bore Weight, 31 lbs., for 1½ inch pipe. Price, each..............$1.45
Average weight, 30 lbs.

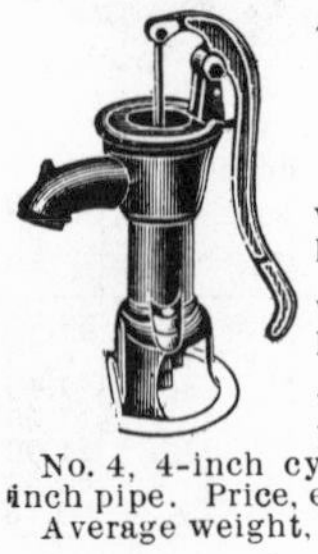

43960 Pitcher Spout Pump, with closed top and spout; can be used either right or left handed and is fitted with couplings for iron or lead pipe.
No. 1, 2½-inch cylinder; weight, 21 lbs., for 1 inch pipe. Price, each................$1.25
No. 2, 3-inch cylinder; weight, 23 lbs., for 1¼ inch pipe. Price, each............. 1.35
No. 3, 3½-inch cylinder; weight, 26 lbs., for 1¼ inch pipe. Price, each 1.50
No. 4, 4-inch cylinder; weight 31 lbs. for 1½ inch pipe. Price, each............... .. 1.75
Average weight, 35 pounds.

Standard Wrought Iron Pipe.
Black and Galvanized.

FOR STEAM, GAS AND WATER.

The following prices are for pipe coupled and threaded in random length; that is, in pieces as they come from the mills, which range from 16 feet to 20 feet each. When ordering pipe cut to exact lengths, always make allowance for cutting and threading. Prices subject to change of market without notice. Orders will be filled at all times at correct market rates.
43964　Black Iron Pipe.
43965　Galvanized Iron Pipes.

Size inside diameter	Black, Price per foot.	Galvanized, Price per foot.	For cutting extra threads per cut.	Approximate weight, per foot. Pounds.
⅛ in.	$0.02½	..	$0.04	.24
¼ in.	.03	$0.03¼	.05	.42
⅜ in.	.03	.03½	.04	.56
½ in.	.03¼	.04½	.04	.84
¾ in.	.03½	.05	.05	1.12
1 in.	.05	.07	.05	1.67
1¼ in.	.06	.09	.06	2.24
1½ in.	.07½	.12	.08	2.68
2 in.	.10	.14	.10	3.61
2½ in.	.15	.22	.10	5.74
3 in.	.18	.28	.15	7.54
3½ in.	.24	.35	.20	9.00
4 in.	.26	.45	.30	10.64

Iron Well Cylinders.

43966 Always state for what size pipe you wish cylinders fitted. In case you mention no size we will send them for 1¼ inch pipe. The 10 and 12 inch cylinders have 6-inch strok, and the 14-inch cylinder has an 8-inch stroke.

Diameter.	10 inches long.	12 inches long.	14 inches long.
2 in	$0.85	$1.00	$1.35
2¼ in	.93	1.35	1.45
2½ in	1.00	1.40	1.50
2¾ in	1.10	1.45	1.60
3 in	1.20	1.60	1.75
3¼ in	1.25	1.75	1.85
3½ in	1.30	1.85	2.00
4 in	1.50	2.10	2.45

Seamless Brass Well Cylinder.

43967 Made with seamless brass body, iron caps and plunger. The 10-inch cylinders have 6-inch stroke; the 12 and 14-inch cylinders have 8-inch stroke.

Diameter.	10 in. long. Each.	12 in. long. Each.	14 in. long. Each.
2¼ in	$2.20	$2.50	$2.70
2½ in	2.40	2.60	2.85
2¾ in	2.60	2.70	2.90
3 in	2.70	2.85	2.00
3¼ in	2.90	3.00	3.15
3½ in	3.10	3.20	3.35
4 in	3.85	4.10	4.20

Tubular Well Cylinders.

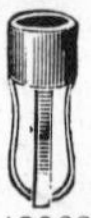

43968 This cylinder is used chiefly in deep wells, and is intended to slip inside of the pipe after the well is completed. It can be fastened at any point desired and is easily withdrawn for repairs. Prices given are for brass body cylinders and valves complete as shown in cut. Not made smaller than for 2-inch pipe.
Sizs, 2-inch. Each.. .. .. $2.40
" 2½-inch. Each............. 4.00
" 3-inch. Each............. 5.75

43968

43970 Foot Valve and Strainer, for 1¼ inch pipe. Weight, 2 pounds, 15 ounces. Each...................... $0.45
43971 Foot valve for 1½ inch pipe; weight, 4½ lbs. Each..............$0.55

Bicycle Prophets

State that in a few years everybody will be riders. Indications certainly point that way, if we may judge from the tremendous demand. More than half a million were sold last year in the United States. Get in line!

Drive Well Points.

43972 Made of wrought iron pipe, perforated and galvanized; covered with a brass jacket of No. 60 GAUZE. This is the point in common use; we can furnish points with finer GAUZE for quicksand, etc. Prices on same will be furnished on application.

Diameter.	Length.	Each.
1¼ in.	24 in.	$0.95
1¼ in.	30 in.	1.10
1¼ in.	36 in.	1.30
1¼ in.	42 in.	1.50
1½ in.	30 in.	1.35
1½ in.	36 in.	1.70
2 in.	36 in.	2 30
2 in.	48 in.	3.30

43974 Lead pipe. Price per pound...........$0.06½
We can furnish lead pipe any size at the above price. In ordering always give the diameter and length wanted, not the weight.
Average weight, per foot, 1 inch, 2 lbs., 8 oz.
Average weight, per foot, 1¼ inch, 3 lbs.
Average weight, per foot, 1½ inch, 4 lbs.
43975 Sheet Lead. Price, per pound..........$0.06½

Rubber Bucket Chain Pumps.

43981 Rubber Bucket Chain Pump, complete for well 10 feet deep...............$3.50
43982 Rubber Bucket Chain Pump, complete for well 12 feet deep..... ....$3.60
43983 Rubber Bucket Chain Pump, complete for wells 18 feet deep...............$4.00
43984 Rubber Bucket Chain Pump, complete for wells 18 feet deep...............$4.35
43985 Rubber Bucket Chain Pump, complete for well 20 feet deep.... ....$5.50
We would not advise the use of chain pumps for deeper wells than 20 feet.

43986 Rubber Buckets for chain pumps.
Each.......................$0.08
Per dozen... 69

Wood Pumps.

Made of good selected stock, neatly painted and decorated Outside measurement of pumps is 6x6 inches with 3½-in bore.

43987—

Length.	Price with plain cylinder.	Price with porcelain lined cylinder.
6 feet....	$ 2.50	$ 3.25
7 "	3.75	3.50
8 "	3.00	3.75
10 "	3.50	4.25

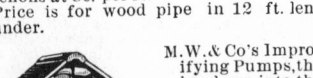

43988 **Wood Suction Pipe.** Steam tested—to fit above pumps: 4x4-in. pipe, 1¾-in. bore, 3½ tenons at 8c. per ft.
Price is for wood pipe in 12 ft. lengths and under.

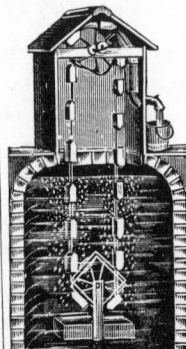

M.W.& Co's Improved water Purifying Pumps, the buckets passing down into the water full of air aereates and purifies it. It always furnishes the water from the bottom of the well, as no water enters the cups until they begin to rise at the bottom. No suckers or valves or wooden tubing to rot or get rusty; buckets are made of galvanized iron: only good for dug wells.
43993 Complete for 10 foot well...................$6.00
43994 Complete for 15 foot well.................. 7.00
43995 Complete for 20 foot well................. 8.20
43996 Complete for 25 foot well................. 9.30
43997 Complete for 30 foot well................ 10.53

Myers' Brass Spray Pump.

WITH 8 GALLON TANK.

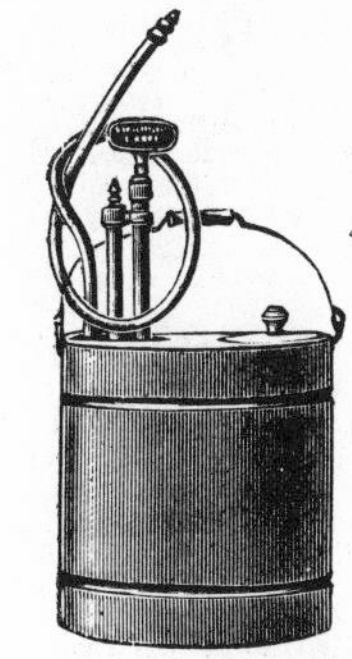

43998 The tank is made of galvanized iron and is equipped with one of Myers' powerful brass spray pumps, as shown in cut 44000 Price, complete with 8 gallon tank, each. $4.80

The "Model" Hand and Garden Pumpor Fire Extinguisher.

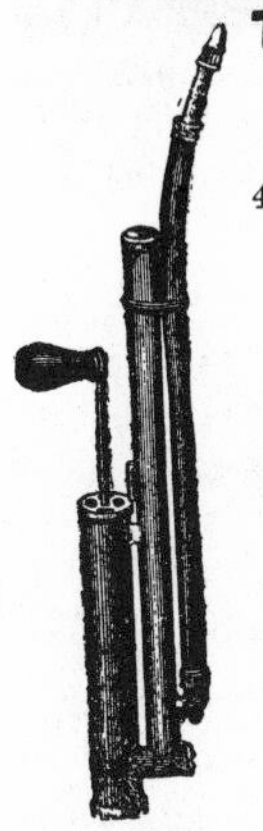

43999 For pumping from pail or tub for spraying fruit trees and bushes, sprinkling lawns and flowers, washing windows and carriages; will force a ¼-inch stream from 40 to 60 feet; is furnished with a spraying attachment in the shape of a flat piece of brass; when attached to nozzle may be twisted so as to spray or to convert the stream into small drops. It is not intended for heavy work, such as extinguishing large fires, etc., but may often prove useful in putting out small blazes, thereby preventing large fires. The piece of hose which comes with pump is 28 inches long and ½ inch in diameter; cannot attach any more than this; is plenty long enough to do the work mentioned; weight, 5 pounds.
Price, each $2.00

The Meyers' Bucket Brass Spray Pumps.

AND FIRE EXTINGUISHER, WITH AGITATOR.

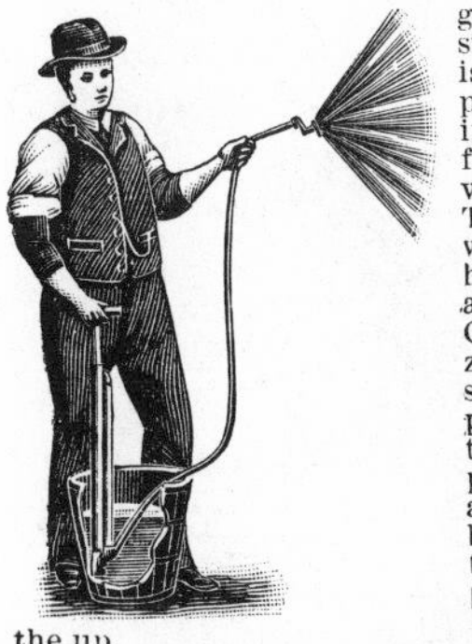

Farmers' and fruit growers' friend. Is constructed of material that is not affected by the poisonous arsenites used in the different formulas for spraying fruit trees, vines and shrubbery. The cylinder and all the working parts are brass: has rubber ball valves and is equipped with our Combination Spray Nozzle, and will throw a spray as fine as mist. The pump differs in construction from the old-line pumps of this class and is arranged so that the heavy work is done on the down stroke of the plunger and nothing on the up.

The operator is enabled to keep a constant pressure on the nozzle of from 50 to 100 lbs. with very ordinary exertion. It will throw a solid stream 50 feet, and is of unusual value for washing windows, etc. For spraying it is arranged so it discharges a fine jet in bottom of bucket to keep the solution thoroughly mixed and agitated, a feature peculiar to this pump. Will throw a solid stream 50 feet.

44000 Price of Brass Spray Pump, with agitator, complete with hose, combination, fire and coarse spray and solid stream nozzles, each $2.65

The Myers' Fountain Spray Pump.

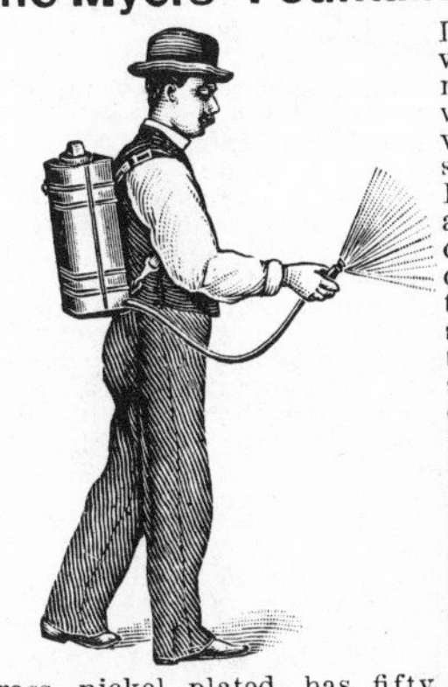

Is constructed of galvanized iron, with round corners, built with tight lid to prevent liquid from splashing on operator. It is fitted with adjustable straps so as to be carried on the back, or it may be carried by the bail. The hose and bulb are made of the best white rubber and protected at each end by coiled wire to prevent breaking. The valves are made of brass and will not corrode, have large openings, which permit the free flow of water and shut off instantly when under pressure. The nozzle is made of brass, nickel plated, has fifty small openings, and throws a spray six feet wide at a distance of twelve feet.

OPERATION.—The pump is operated by grasping the bulb in the hand and compressing it, which causes a spray to be thrown any distance from three to fifteen feet, as desired, on relaxing the pressure on bulb it expands, refilling instantly, when the same operation can be repeated. To shut off flow of water entirely, use valve on hose for that purpose. The operator can cover one or two rows of plants or vines as desired, and do the work at a rapid walk, thus covering a large amount of territory in a very short time.

CAUTION.—Always mix Paris green or London purple in a separate vessel, forming into a paste before adding water. In this way everything will be dissolved and will not need to be agitated. Holds 5 gallons. Weight, 52 lbs., when full.

44001 Price, each, complete, with 1 tube, rubber bulb and rose $3.00

44002 Price, each, complete, with 2 tubes, rubber bulb and roses to work with both hands. 4.00

Dry Cold Air Refrigerators.

Our sales of refrigerators last season were way beyond our expectation, and we were compelled to disappoint some of our customers. This year we are prepared for a still larger increase in the trade and feel confident we can at all times make prompt shipments, as we have ample stock of dry hardwood lumber, with the latest improved machinery, the best of dry kilns, and the most skilled workmen. We **Guarantee** our refrigerators to give **Perfect Satisfaction**. The capacity of the factory is over two hundred complete refrigerators per day.

Points of Superiorty—Scientific Insulation.

The walls of the refrigerators are constructed as follows. First, the outside case: second, a layer of wool felt; third, a dead-air space: fourth, a charcoal sheathing; fifth, inside case; sixth, a charcoal sheathing which is non-odorous, waterproof and a first class insulator; seventh, a zinc lining, making complete seven walls to preserve the ice. The result is a great saving of ice and lower temperature than can be obtained in other refrigerators.

Ice being placed on the false bottom in the upper compartment, the air under the false bottom becomes very cold and heavy, and falls through the opening into the provision chamber below, forcing the warm air up through the flues, where it strikes the ice, is condensed and cooled. Our refrigerators will keep crackers and ginger snaps crisp and dry. We advise our patrons to buy as large a refrigerator as possible, to get the benefit of **cold storage.** Each size has a special design of great beauty.

The Metallic Ice Rack.

Is a very important feature of our goods, as the under side acts as a moisture condenser, while the arched center prevents the moisture from dropping through the opening into the provision chamber below. The **shelves** are made of heavy galvanized iron with wide slats and rolled edges, making them very strong.

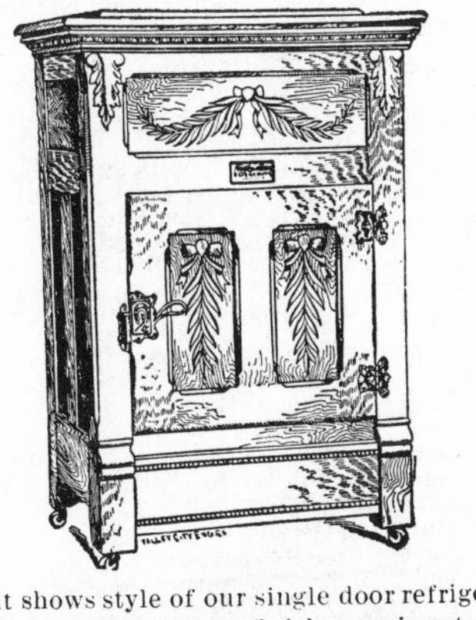

This cut shows style of our single door refrigerator.

44003 Hardwood, Antique finish, empire style. Richly carved panels and ornaments; single door. Holds 35 lbs. ice.; Length, 26½ in.; Depth, 18in.; Height, 40 in. Price, each $7.26

44004 Same as No. 44003, except that it holds 30 lbs. of ice. Has porcelain lined water cooler. The faucet is nickel plated and the tumbler holder bronzed. We do not advise the use of melted ice for drinking water, as it is frequently impure and always has condensed on its surface the smells from the food below, so we get rid of it as soon as possible and provide a separate place for drinking water. Price each 9.05

44005 Hardwood Antique Finish, richly carved panels and ornaments. Flap in front lifts up for waste pan; single door. Size of opening of provision chamber 17½ in. high, 16½ in. wide, 11½ in. deep.

Holds lbs. ice.	Length.	Depth.	Height.	Price, each.
40	28 in.	20 in.	44 in.	$8.36

44006 Same as No. 44005, except that it holds 35 lbs. of ice. Has porcelain lined water cooler. The faucet is nickel plated and the tumbler holder bronze. Price each 10.34

44007 Solid Ash, Antique Finish, elegant hand carved ornamentation; single door. Size of opening of provision chamber 18 in. high, 20½ in. wide, 13¾ in. deep; single door.

Holds lbs. ice	Length.	Depth.	Height.	Price.
45	32	21½	46½	10.12

44008 Same as No. 44007 except that it holds 40 pounds of ice, has porcelain lined water cooler with nickel plated faucet and bronze tumbler holder. Price, each $12.10

Refrigerators—Continued.

44009 Solid Ash, Antique Finish, hand carved, raised ornaments. This refrigerator is deep enough to hold two rows of dishes, one behind the other; single door. Size of opening of provision chamber 20 in. high. 21½ in. wide, 17½ in. deep.

Holds Ice.	Length.	Depth.	Height.	Price.
40 lbs.	33 in.	24½ in.	49 in.	$11.66

44010 Same as No 44009, except that it holds 35 pounds of ice, has porcelain lined water cooler, flap in front, lifts up for water pan.
Price, each $14.10

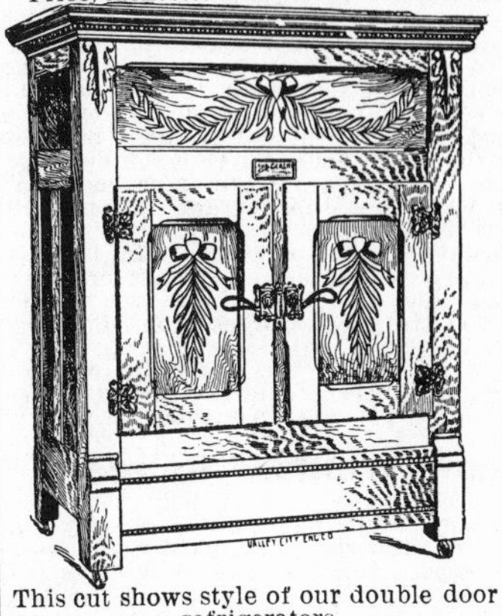

44011 Solid Ash, Antique Finish, rich hand carvings, **double doors,** movable flues. Size of opening of provision chamber 18½ in. high, 22½ in. wide, 13½ in. deep. Holds 45 lbs of ice. Length 34 in.; depth 22 in.; height 47 in.

This cut shows style of our double door refrigerators.

Price, each 12.32

44012 Same as No 44011 except that it will hold 40 pounds of ice, has porcelain lined water cooler. All goods are warranted to give perfect satisfaction. Price, each $14.30

44013 Solid Ash, Antique Finish, elegant hand carving, double door, patent arch center, false bottom, and interior circulation of pure, dry, cold air. Size of opening of provision chamber 20 in. high, 25 in. wide, 14½ in. deep. OUR BEST FAMILY SIZE.

Holds ice.	Length.	Depth.	Height.	Price, each.
70 lbs.	36½ in.	23 in.	50 in.	$14.10

44014 Same as No. 44013, except that it holds 60 lbs. of ice. Has porcelain lined water cooler
Price, each 16.28

44015 Solid Ash, Antique Finish, double doors. This style has a partition between the doors, making two separate provision chambers. A most excellent family size. Size of opening of each provision chamber 20½ in. high, 13½ in wide, 17½ in. deep.

Holds ice.	Length.	Depth.	Height.	Price.
125 lbs.	41½ in.	25½ in.	52 in.	$16.72

44016 Same as No. 44015, except that it holds, 115 lbs. ice. Has porcelain lined water cooler. The large ice chamber affords room for bottles, pitchers, etc. 19.20

44017 Solid Ash. Four Doors. Antique Finish, rich hand carvings. Ice doors open in front; size of opening, 14x29 inches. Two provision chambers below. Size of each provision chamber, 23½ in. high 13 in. wide, 19 in. deep.

Holds ice.	Length.	Depth.	Height.	Price.
150 lbs.	41½ in.	26 in.	60 in.	$18.92

44018 Same as No. 44017, except, that it holds 140 pounds ice, has porcelain lined water cooler, Price, each 21.34

Sideboard Style Refrigerators.

As we furnish refrigerator sideboards on orders it requires from 7 to 10 days before we can ship.

44019 Same as No. 44003, with the addition of a sideboard top. It has beveled plate glass mirror, 12x18, and convenient shelf on which things can be placed when the cover is raised; 72 inches high. Price, each $11.88

44020 Same as No. 44005, with the addition of a sideboard top, beveled plate glass mirror 12x18 inches. Height, 75 inches. Price, each 13.30

44021 Same as No. 44011 with the addition of a sideboard top. The glass is bevel plate, 16x20 inches. Price, each 19.00

Hardwood Ice Chests, antique ash finish. Made double with inside boxes with lining between. This makes them triple walled and the best ice boxes in the market. They are lined throughout with zinc and furnished with metal shelves. We have an opening in the back for ventilation. We cannot guarantee them not to sweat, as we do our Dry Air Refrigerators.

	Length.	Depth.	Height.	Price.
44022	30 in.	18 in.	25 in.	$4.50
44023	33 in.	20 in.	27 in.	5.50
44024	36 in.	22 in.	31 in.	6.75
44025	40 in.	24½ in.	34 in.	8.25
44026	44 in.	29 in.	36 in.	10.50

Table of shipping weights for the Dry Cold Air Refrigerators and Ice Chest:

Catalogue No.	Weight.	Catalogue No.	Weight
44003	120 lbs	44015	265 lbs
44004	125 "	44016	275 "
44005	145 "	44017	300 "
44006	150 "	44018	310 "
44007	170 "	44019	145 "
44008	175 "	44020	170 "
44009	170 "	44021	210 "
44010	175 "	44022	100 "
44011	180 "	44023	130 "
44012	185 "	44024	160 "
44013	200 "	44025	200 "
44014	210 "	44026	250 "

27—2nd

STOVE DEPARTMENT.

The Windsor Stoves and Ranges.

Montgomery Ward & Co., Manufacturers.

We manufacture all of our Windsor stoves from the very best brands of iron, and with sufficient flue capacity for soft coal, and with fire boxes, flue plates and damper arrangements of sufficient strength to be durable. We claim them to be the very best in the market, and, having confidence in our claim, we fully guarantee every Windsor Stove. Our Reservoirs as constructed are *right*, for we secure an abundance of heat under and around the tanks. All of our ranges are also arranged for *water fronts.* We use the best of iron with polished edges, nickel and tile trimmings, towel rods, pedal attachments, outside nickel oven shelf, deep ash pan, etc. Our cheap stoves are made of the same material as our higher priced stoves, and we fully guarantee each and every one.

All ranges are fitted with revolving oven bottoms. The illustrations show only complete ranges, but prices are arranged for any desired combination of low closets, reservoir, or pipe shelf with the body of the range.

Let us give you a few suggestions for operating a stove. Remember, a stove possesses no power in itself to force smoke up a chimney, that the pipe and chimney give the draft, and if these are defective, no matter how good the stove may be, it will not work satisfactorily. If the stove smokes or the soot adheres to the covers and sides of the flues, then something is wrong with the pipe or chimney, which prevents the smoke from taking its natural course up and out through the chimney. When this occurs your stove will not bake. Your fire will not burn or the reservoir will not heat, and you can be sure that the whole trouble lines in the obstruction to the draft. Therefore, to secure proper and satisfactory results with our stoves, first be sure and secure proper draft and then see that the products of combustion are not cooled off by the admission of cool air over the fire or into the flues; see that the pipe fits closely on the stove and in the chimney, and is well jointed. See that no accident has befallen the stove in transit, that every part is in its proper place; see that you understand the dampers so that you can throw the heat under the reservoir or under the oven at pleasure; see that the front grate and linings are in place. If you will follow these simple directions you will have no trouble in securing satisfactory operations in our stoves and ranges.

Our facilities for prompt shipment are now perfect, and we can also furnish without delay repairs for any of our stoves. *In ordering repairs,* state plainly what you want, giving the full name of the stove, the number and the date, and in ordering a part for the right or left side of the stove always stand in front of the fire-box and consider all parts on your right hand as the right side, and all parts on your left hand as the left side. If the part wanted is in connection with the back of the stove, specify if it is for a square or one with a reservoir.

We give you the measurements of the oven near to the floor of the oven; if we measured as other manufacturers, at the greatest swell of the oven doors, we could increase the size of our ovens from three to five inches. We measure our fire-boxes, first giving the length at the top; second, width at top; third, width at bottom; fourth, depth.

Remember, we guarantee every Windsor stove to give perfect satisfaction if the chimney is clear and has a good draft. Try one and be convinced that you save money by buying direct from the manufacturers. Cuts show but few of the forms of our ranges, but the lists indicate other forms. The closets, the reservoir and pipe shelf can be arranged in any desired form with the body of the range. Our stoves are not blacked but are as they leave the foundry.

The Grand Windsor Range.

We make this range with sufficient flue capacity for soft coal, and with properly constructed fire boxes, flue plates and damper arrangements to be durable.

We can furnish wood fixtures for the Grand Windsor Range (any size), which includes front and bottom grates, at an extra charge of $1.00. We do not furnish any cooking utensils, stove boards, or the first joint of pipe, with any of our ranges, at prices quoted.

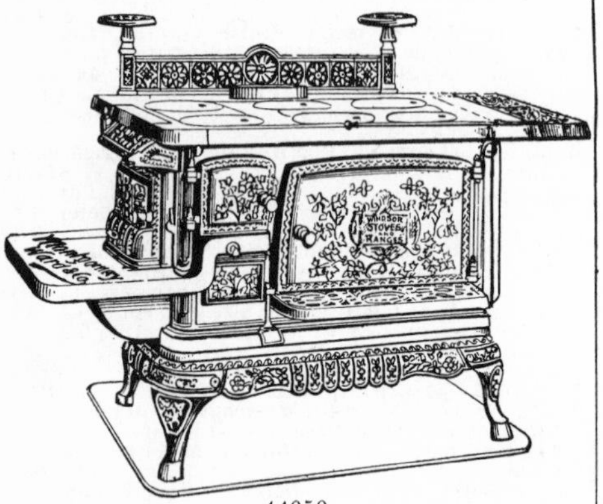

44050

44050 Grand Windsor Range, 6 hole, like cut. Square Plain for hard or soft coal, coke or wood.

Size.	Covers.	Fire box.	Shipping weight.	Size of oven.	Price.
8-19	8 inch.	16x10 7x6½	360 lbs.	19x18x11	$20.50
8-21	8 inch.	17½x10 7x6½	405 lbs.	21x20x12	23.76
9-21	9 inch.	17½x10 7x6½	405 lbs.	21x20x12	24.30

We can furnish wood fixtures for the above range at an extra charge of $1.00.

Water fronts, brass couplings, ground joints, all sizes: weight, 20 lbs. Price, each, $4.00 extra.

44051 Grand Windsor Range, 6 Hole, with reservoir.

Size.	Covers.	Fire box.	Shipping weight.	Size of oven.	Price.
8-19	8 inch.	16x10 7x6½	420 lbs.	19x18x11	$26.46
8-21	8 inch.	17½x10 7x6½	475 lbs.	21x20x12	29.77
9-21	9 inch.	17½x10 7x6½	475 lbs.	21x20x12	31.65

Water fronts: weight, 20 lbs. Price, each, extra. 4.00

We can furnish wood fixtures for the above range at an extra charge of $1.00.

44052 Grand Windsor Range, 6 hole, without reservoir, but with low closet.

Size.	Covers.	Fire box.	Shipping weight.	Size of oven.	Price.
8-19	8 inch.	16x10 7x6½	410 lbs.	19x18x11	$24.62
8-21	8 inch.	17½x10 7x6½	465 lbs.	21x20x12	28.10
9-21	9 inch.	17½x10 7x6½	465 lbs.	21x20x12	28.62

Water fronts: weight, 20 lbs. Price, each, extra. 4.00

We can furnish wood fixtures for the above range (any size), which include front and bottom grates, at an extra charge of $1.00.

OUR GUARANTEE IS AS GOOD AS GOLD.

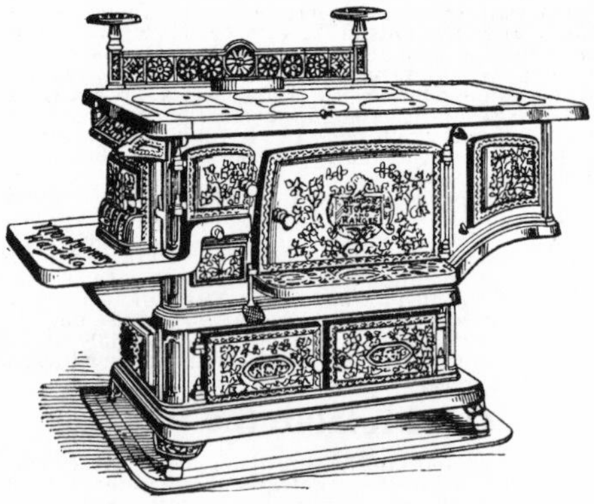

44053

44053 Grand Windsor Range, 6 hole, with low closet and reservoir.

Size.	Covers	Fire box.	Shipping weight.	Size of oven.	Price
8-19	8 inch.	16x10 7x6½	470 lbs.	19x18x11	$30.67
8-21	8 inch.	17½x10 7x6½	535 lbs.	21x20x12	34.15
9-21	9 inch.	17½x10 7x6½	535 lbs.	21x20x12	36.00

Water fronts; weight, 20 lbs. Price, each, extra. 4.00

We can furnish fixtures for burning wood in the above range, at an extra charge of $1.00.

44054 Grand Windsor Range, 6 hole, with high shelf and reservoir.

Size.	Covers	Fire box.	Shipping weight.	Size of oven.	Price.
8-19	8 inch	10x10 7x6½	470 lbs.	19x18x11	$29.87
8-21	8 inch.	17½x10 7x6½	525 lbs.	21x20x12	33.27
9-21	9 inch.	17½x10 7x6½	525 lbs.	21x20x12	33.80

Water fronts: weight, 20 lbs. Price, each, extra. 4.00

We can furnish wood fixtures for the above range (any size), at an extra charge of $1.00

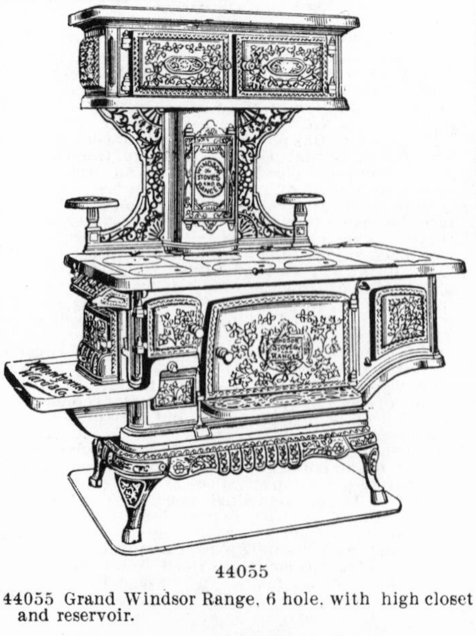

44055

44055 Grand Windsor Range, 6 hole, with high closet and reservoir.

Size.	Covers.	Fire box	Shipping weight.	Size of oven.	Price.
8-19	8 inch.	16x10 7x6½	520 lbs.	19x18x11	$35.11
8-21	8 inch.	17½x10 7x6½	575 lbs.	21x20x12	38.76
9-21	9 inch.	17½x10 7x6½	575 lbs.	21x20x12	39.13

Water fronts; weight 20 lbs. Price, each, extra. 4.00

We can furnish wood fixtures for the above range, which include front and bottom grates, at an extra charge of 1.00

44056 Grand Windsor Range, 6 hole, with high and low closets and reservoir.

Size.	Covers.	Fire Box.	Shipping weight.	Size of oven.	Prices
8-19	8 inch.	16x10 7x6½	575 lbs.	19x18x11	$39.50
8-21	8 inch.	17½x10 7x6½	635 lbs.	21x20x12	43.20
9-21	9 inch,	17½x10 7x6½	635 lbs.	21x20x12	43.77

Water fronts; weight, 20 lbs. Price, each, extra. 4.00

We can furnish fixtures for burning wood in the above range (any size), at an extra charge of... 1.00

Separate Parts for making any combination desired in the Grand Windsor Range.

44057 Price of high closet only.................. 8.00

44058 Price of high shelf only.................. 3.95

44059 Price of low closet only $4.25

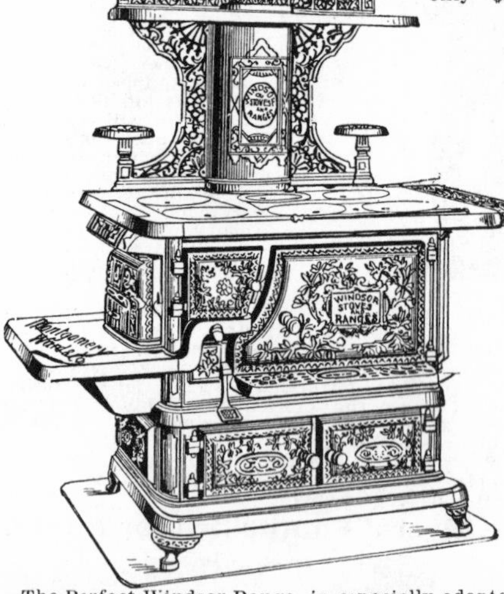

The Perfect Windsor Range is especially adapted to soft coal. The flues are very large, and the firebox is one of the best constructed. The linings are protected by air currents. The oven is thoroughly ventilated by hot air currents. Has outside nickel shelf, nickel ornaments, towel rod, ground edges, and made of the best of iron. We guarantee quick baking and quick heating of the reservoir; in fact, perfect operation with perfect draft. We furnish water fronts for all Perfect Windsor Ranges at $4.00 each extra. We can furnish wood fixtures for the Perfect Windsor Ranges, which includes front and bottom grates, at an extra charge of $1.00. We do not furnish any cooking utensils, stove boards or the first joint of pipe with any of our ranges at prices quoted.

44060 The Perfect Windsor Range, 6 hole, plain, for hard or soft coal, coke or wood. Stove *without high shelf and low closet as shown in cut.* In finish it is the same as our Grand Windsor.

Size.	Covers.	Fire box.	Shipping weight.	Size of oven.	Price
8-19	8 in.	16x10 6½x7	360 lbs.	19x19x11	$18.73.
8-21	8 in.	17½x10 6½x7	385 lbs.	21x21x12	22.14
9-21	9 in.	17½x10 6½x7	385 lbs.	21x21x12	22.68

We can furnish wood fixtures for the above range, which include front and bottom grates, at an extra charge of $1.00. Water front, extra, $4.00.

Stoves—Continued.

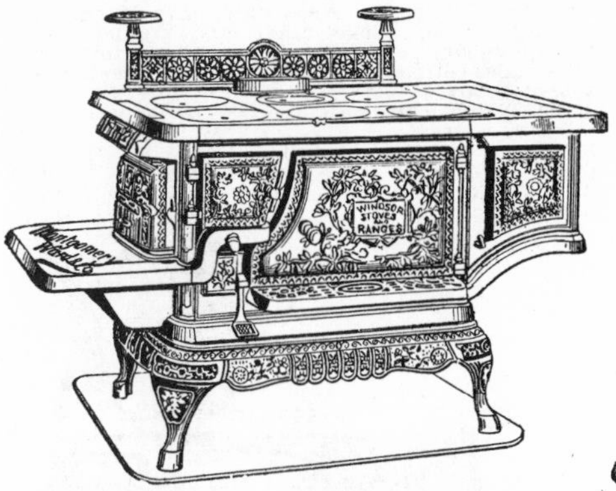

44061

44061 The Perfect Windsor Range, 6 hole, with reservoir.

Size.	Covers.	Fire box.	Shipping weight.	Size of oven.	Price.
8-19	8 in.	16x10 6½x7	405 lbs.	19x19x11	$24.84
8-2	8 in.	17½x10 6½x7	460 lbs.	21x21x12	28.18
9-21	9 in.	17½x10 6½x7	460 lbs.	21x21x12	28.73

We can furnish wood fixtures for the above range (any size), which include front and bottom grates, at an extra charge of $1.00.

44062 The Perfect Windsor Range, 6 hole, plain, square, with low closet only.

Size.	Covers.	Fire box.	Shipping weight.	Size of oven.	Price.
8-19	8 in.	16x10 6½x7	390 lbs.	19x19x11	$22.68
8-21	8 in.	17½x10 6½x7	445 lbs.	21x21x12	25.54
9-21	9 in.	17½x10 6½x7	445 lbs.	21x21x12	26.00

We can furnish wood fixtures for the above range (any size), which include front and bottom grates, at an extra charge of $1.00.

44063 The Perfect Windsor Range, with reservoir and low closet.

Size.	Covers.	Fire box.	Shipping. weight.	Size of oven.	Price.
8-19	8 in.	16x10 6½x7	455 lbs.	19x19x11	$28.19
8-21	8 in.	17½x10 6½x7	530 lbs.	21x21x12	31.59
9-21	9 in.	17½x10 6½x7	530 lbs.	21x21x12	32.13

We can furnish wood fixtures for the above range (any size), which include front and bottom grates, at an extra charge of $1.00.

44064 The Perfect Windsor Range, with high shelf and reservo r.

Size.	Covers.	Fire box.	Shipping weight.	Size of oven.	Price.
8-19	8 in.	16x10 6½x7	455 lbs.	19x19x11	$28.00
8-21	8 in.	17½x10 6½x7	510 lbs.	21x21x12	31.59
9-21	9 in.	17½x10 6½x7	510 lbs.	21x21x12	32.23

We can furnish wood fixtures for the above range (any size), which include front and bottom grates, at an extra charge of $1.00.

44065 The Perfect Windsor Range, with high closet and reservoir.

Size.	Covers.	Fire box.	Shipping weight.	Size of oven.	Price.
8-19	8 in.	16x10 6½x7	505 lbs.	19x19x11	$31.49
8-21	8 in.	17½x10 6½x7	560 lbs.	21x21x12	34.99
9-21	9 in.	17½x10 6½x7	560 lbs.	21x21x12	35.25

We can furnish wood fixtures for the above range (any size), which include front and bottom grates, at an extra charge of $1.00.

EVERY WORD = = =

WE SAY ABOUT THE...

Windsor Stoves

HAS BEEN THOROUGHLY PROVEN.

You Can't Buy a Better Stove at any Price or Under Any Name.

Stoves—Continued.

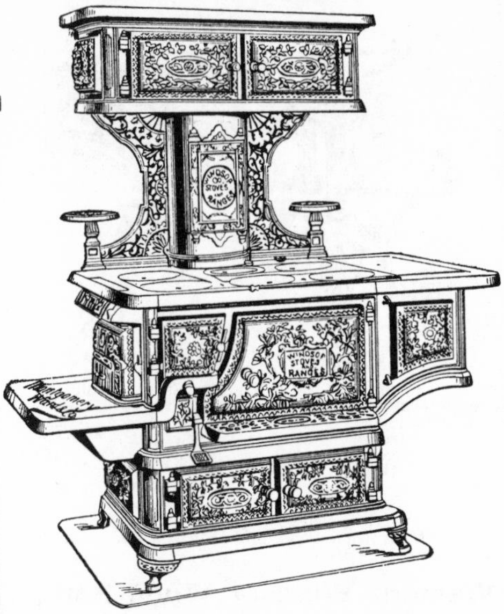

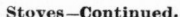

44066

44066 The Perfect Windsor Range, with high and low closets and reservoirs.

Size.	Covers.	Fire box.	Shipping weight.	Size of oven.	Price.
8-19	8 in.	16x10 6¼x7	555 lbs.	19x19x11	$34.79
8-21	8 in.	17½x10 6½x7	600 lbs.	21x21x12	38.44
9-21	9 in.	17½x10 6½x7	600 lbs.	21x21x12	38.93

We can furnish wood fixtures for the above Range (any size), which include front and bottom grates, at an extra charge of $1.00.

Water Front with brass couplings, $4.00 extra.

SEPARATE PARTS for making any combination desired in Perfect Windsor Range.

44067 High Closet. Price, each $8.00
44068 High Shelf " " 3.95
44069 Low Closet " " 4.25

This range is made with special hard coal features, yet has ample flues for soft coal. The grate is composed of two triangular bars lying side by side, and which can be revolved one-third of a revolution at a time, which brings their flat surface up and drops the ashes and clinkers into the ash pan below. A hard coal fire in the Prize can be run continually night and day and always be as good as a new fire. The fire box is lined with IRON OR ANTI-CLINKER BRICK AS ORDERED. Handsomely ornamented with ground edges, outside nickel arm shelf, towel rod, nice castings and perfect mountings. We can furnish wood fixtures for the Prize Windsor Ranges, which includes front and bottom grates, at an extra charge of $1.00.

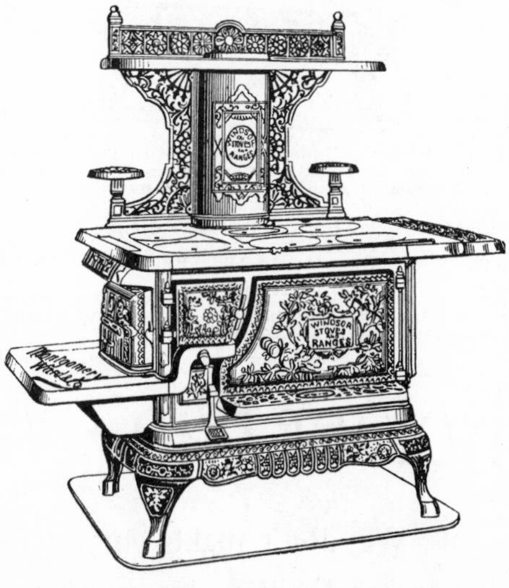

44070 The Prize Windsor Range; 6 holes, plain square, for hard or soft coal, coke or wood. Same size, weight and measurements as 44060. (Stove has not high shelf as shown.)

Price, each.
No, 8-19 .... $17.25
No. 8-21 .... 21.00
No. 9-21 .... 21.60

We can furnish wood fixtures for the above range, which includes front and bottom grates, at an extra charge of $1.00.

Water Fronts, extra, $4.00.

Stoves—Continued.

44071 The Prize Windsor Range; 6 holes with reservoir. Same size, weight and measurements as 44061.

No. 8-19 .... $23.60
No. 8-21 .... 26.78
No. 9-21 .... 27.16

We can furnish wood fixtures for the above range, which include front and bottom grates, at an extra charge of $1.00.

Water Fronts, extra, $4.00.

44072 The Prize Windsor Range; 6 holes with low closet. Same size and weight as No. 44062.

No. 8-19 .... $21.60
No. 8-21 .... 24.28
No. 9-21 .... 25.00

We can furnish wood fixtures for the above range, which include front and bottom grates, at an extra charge of $1.00.

Water Fronts, extra, $4.00.

44073 The Prize Windsor Range; 6 holes, reservoir and low closet. Same size and weight as No. 44063. No. 8-19 .... $26.95
No. 8-21 .... $30.00 No. 9-21 .... 30.65

We can furnish wood fixtures for the above range, which include front and bottom grates, at an extra charge of $1.00.

Water Fronts, extra, $4.00.

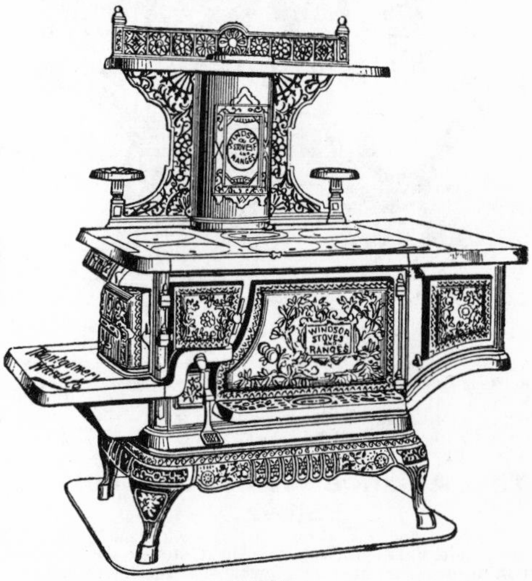

44074

44074 The Prize Windsor Range; 6 holes with reservoir and high shelf. Same size and weight as No. 44064. No. 8-19 .... $26.95
No. 8-21 .... $30.00 No. 9-21 .... 30.65

We can furnish wood fixtures for the above range, which include front and bottom grates, at an extra charge of $1.00.

Water Front, extra, $4.00.

44075 The Prize Windsor Range; 6 holes with high and low closet and reservoir. Same size and weight as No. 44066.

No. 8-19 .... $33.25
No. 8-21 .... 36.52
No. 9-21 .... 37.00

We can furnish wood fixtures for the above range, which include front and bottom grates, at an extra charge of $.100.

Water Fronts, extra, $4.00.

SEPARATE PARTS for making any combination in Prize Windsor Ranges.

44076 High Closet. Price each $8.00
44077 Low Closet, " " 4.25
44078 High Shelf. " " 3.95

The Famous Windsor Range.

Many people prefer a range to a cook stove. The Famous Windsor is a desirable range with good sizes, excellent shaped oven, large top, large flues, excellent fire box, with sectional linings, flues ventilated, of first class construction and ornamentation. It is sure to please in use. We do not furnish any cooking utensils, stove boards, or the first joint of stove pipe with any of our stoves at prices quoted. We can furnish wood fixtures for the Famous Windsor Range, which include bottom grate and fireback, at an extra charge of $1.00

Water fronts, with brass couplings, furnished extra 4.00

44079 The Famous Windsor Range; 4 holes, plain square, without reservoir, for hard or soft coal, coke or wood.

Size.	Covers.	Fire box.	Shipping weight.	Size of oven.	Price, each.
88-19	8 inch	16x8 5½x6	290 lbs.	19x18x12	$14.58
99-19	9 inch	16x8 5½x6	290 lbs.	19x18x12	15.12

44080 The Famous Windsor Range; 4 holes with reservoir.

Size.	Covers.	Fire box.	Shipping weight.	Size of oven.	Price, each.
88-19	8 inch	16x8 5½x6	365 lbs.	19x18x12	$20.62
99-19	9 inch	16x8 5¼x6	365 lbs	19x18x12	21.16

We can furnish wood fixtures for the stove, which includes a bottom grate and fireback, at an extra charge of $1.00.

NO CHARGE For Cases Or Cartage.

The Modern Windsor Cooking Stove.

44081 Plain Square, 4-hole, *for coal or wood.* Will bear the most critical examination. You will find in this stove the best coal box you ever saw, the most practical common sense construction in every respect. A reservoir that will boil 5 gallons of water in less than 30 minutes, flues that are ample for soft coal. It has a large ash pan, in fact every part is large and good, and will meet all requirements of a first class stove.

Size.	Weight.	Size of oven.	Covers	Price, each.
8-19	325 lbs.	19x18x13	8 inch.	$18.00
8-21	370 lbs.	21x20x14	8 inch	21.38
9-21	370 lbs.	21x20x14	9 inch	22.25

We can furnish wood fixtures for the above stove, which includes a bottom grate and fireback, at a n extra charge of $1.25.

The Modern Windsor Cooking Stove.

44082 With Reservoir, 4 holes; for coal or wood.

Size.	Weight.	Size of oven.	Covers	Price.
8-19	415 lbs.	19x18x13	8	$25.30
8-21	435 lbs.	21x20x14	8	29.33
9-21	435 lbs.	21x20x14	9	29.90

Cast Pipe an l shelf will cost extra............$3.95
Wood Fixtures will cost extra..................1.25

The Alliance Windsor Cooking Stove.

Here is a cooking stove just as well made, of the same material as our higher priced stoves, has nickel trimmings, ground edges, towel rods, oven door kicker, automatic oven shelf, a nice leg base, cemented oven top, cut center, ventilated oven, sectional back linings, ventilated, curved front grate, tin lined doors. We can furnish a grate for burning wood at an extra charge of 50c.

44084 The Alliance Windsor: 4 holes; for hard or soft coal, coke or wood, square, without reservoir.

Size.	Covers.	Fire box.	Shipping weight.	Size oven.	Price, each
8	8 inch	14½x8 5x6	225 lbs.	17x17x10	$12.54
80	8 inch	16x8 5x6	245 lbs.	18x18x11½	14.25
9	9 inch	16x8 5x6	245 lbs.	18x18x11½	14.82

44085 Alliance Windsor with reservoir.

Size	Size of fire box.	Shipping Weight.	Size of oven.	Price.
80	16x8	320 lbs.	18x18x12	$20.40
9	5x6	320 "	18x18x12	20.97

We can furnish a grate for burning wood at an extra charge of 50 cents.

Farmers' Windsor Cooking Stove, 4 Hole.

44086 For coal or wood. Plain square, without reservoir.

Size.	Covers.	Size of fire box.	Shipping weight.	Size oven.	Price.
8	8 inch	14½x8 5x6	225 lbs.	17x17x11	$12.54
80	8 inch	16x8 5x6	245 "	18x18x11½	14.25
9	9 "	16x8 5x6	245 "	18x18x11½	14.82

We can furnish wood grate at an extra charge of 50c.

Cooking Stoves—Continued.

44087   Farmers' Windsor Cooking Stove. 4 holes, with large gray enamel reservoir that you can boil water in.

Size.	Size of fire box. 16x8	Shipping weight.	Size of oven.	Price.
80	5x6	320 lbs.	18x18x12	$19.33
9	16x8 5x6	320 "	18x18x12	19.87

We can furnish a wood grate for the above stove at an extra charge of 50c.

Western Windsor Wood Range.

Western Windsor Range, 4 holes, for wood only; first class in every respect and fully guaranteed; nickel trimmings, ground edges, nickeled outside, oven shelf, revolving oven bottom, heavy false fire bottom and fireback, deep ash pit.

We do not furnis l any cooking utensils, stove boards or the first joint of stove pipe at prices quoted.

44088 Plain Square, without reservoir, for wood only.

Size.	Covers.	Size of fire box. 26x10	Shipping weight.	Size of oven.	Price.
8-22	8	7½x6	335 lbs.	22x22x13	$18 52
9-22	9	26x10 7½x6	335 "	22x22x13	19.10

44089 Western Windsor, for wood, with gray enamel reservoir, with heating flues below it. The below prices do not include high shelf, as shown in cut.

Size.	Covers.	Size of fire box. 26x10	Shipping weight.	Size of oven.	Price.
8-22	8	7½x6	410 lbs.	22x22x13	$24.84
9-22	9	26x10 7½x6	410 "	22x22x13	25.38

44089½ Cast Iron Pipe Shelf to fit above stove. Weight, 50 lbs. Price, each, $3.75, extra.

Not for Fun.

We don't make our guarantees for fun, nor do we try to crawfish when a claim is made.

We mean exactly what we say everytime.

Cook's Windsor for Wood.

Cook's Windsor, for wood only, has a door on each end of fire box, nickel ornaments, ground edges, large fire box, patent oven door opener, towel rod, heavy false bottom in fire box, a swing fender and outside nickel oven shelf.

44090 Plain Square, without reservoir, for wood only.

Size.	Oven.	Fire box.	Weight.	Price.
8-20	18x21x12	24x10 in.	275 lbs.	$14.00
9-20	20x21x12	24x10 "	275 "	14.58
8-22	20x22x12	26x11 "	300 "	16.20
9-22	22x23x12	26x11 "	300 "	16.75

44091 Cook's Windsor Stove with gray enamel reservoir.

Size.	Oven.	Fire box.	Weight.	Price.
8-20	18x21x12	24x10 in.	355 lbs	$19.45
9-20	20x21x12	24x10 "	355 "	21.00
8-22	20x23x12	26x11 "	380 "	22.80
9-22	22x22x12	26x11 "	380 "	23.37

The above prices do not include pipe shelf, as shown in cut.

44091½ Pipe Shelf to fit above stove (weight 35 lbs.). Price, extra............................$3.25

Lake Windsor for Wood Only.

Four hole, with door on each end of fire box, automatic oven shelf that fits both sides of the oven, flush swing hearth, mica front with cut off; oven doors are lined with tin nickel trimmings, castings smooth and well mounted; the best working stove in the market.

44092 Plain square, without reservoir.

Size.	Oven.	Fire box.	Shipping weight.	Price.
8	19½x17	23 in.	220 lbs.	$11 40
80	21x18	25 in.	240 lbs.	13.68
88	23x19½	26 in.	280 lbs.	15.96
9	21x18	25 in.	240 lbs.	14 25
90	23x19½	26 in	280 lbs.	16.53

44093 Lake Windsor, with copper reservoir which heats perfectly, being incased and with flues under it.

Size.	Oven.	Fire Box.	Shipping Weight.	Price.
8	19½x17	23 in.	315 lbs.	$17.55
80	21x18	25 in.	340 lbs.	19.44
88	23x19½	26 in.	385 lbs.	22.68
9	21x19½	25 in.	350 lbs.	19.98
90	23x19½	26 in.	390 lbs.	23.22

The above prices do not include pipe shelf as shown in cut.

44093½ Cast Pipe Shelf for above, weight 35 lbs. Extra, $3.90.

Ward Windsor.

Hard coal, self feeding, base heating. We claim that there has been great care given to every detail of construction to secure durability and the greatest heating capacity with greatest economy of fuel, that it is a solid, substantial STOVE, adapted to the business for which it is intended, and that it will outlast a half a dozen of the ordinary stoves on the market. The magazine is placed at the back of the fire pot to give a large surface fire and is guaranteed to outlast any other in the market. The length of the front main base of the stove is 24 inches, and of the side 22 inches. Height, with top ornament, 62 and 66 inches. Height, without top ornament, 50 and 54 inches.

44094—

Size.	Shipping weight.	Fire box.	Price.
2	400 lbs.	13x10x8	$26.90
3	450 lbs.	15x10x8	30.00

Ward Windsor with Oven.

44095 The oven on this stove is guaranteed to work perfectly; it is placed close to the fire box, and the top oven plate is on a line with the top of the fire pot, so that there is an abundance of heat for baking and boiling with an ordinary fire. We claim that we have secured a practical one without destroying the beauty of the stove. We do not furnish tea kettle as shown in cut. Height, with top ornament, 62 inches. Height, without top ornament, 50 inches.

Size.	Shipping weight.	Fire box.	Price
2	465 lbs.	13x10x8	$32.00

The Thorne Windsor.

44096— A hard coal, self - feeding, base heating stove with all modern devices; 2 sizes. The leg base, foot rails, top rim, swing top, name plate, upper front mica frame, knobs, hinge pins are nickeled. The flues extend around the entire bottom; the hot air flues are in the back corners and unite at the top for double heating, beautifully ornamented and a perfect stove of the first class, and we guarantee it in every respect. Height given includes top ornament; height of ornament, 12 in.

44096

Size.	Height.	Shipping weight.	Firebox.	Price. each.
11	54	290 lbs.	11x10x7	$19.40
13	60	340 "	13x11x7	22.88

Home Windsor for Wood.

44097— A first - class wood heating stove, direct draft, or with revertible flue which extends under the entire base: nicely covered surface, ornamented with nickel. The grade is of the latest pattern and gives perfect control of the fire; large ash pan, hot air flues in rear corners extending the whole length of the upright flues. It is the best wood burner in the market. Height, with top ornament, 50 in. Height, without top ornament, 43 in.

Size.	44097	Shipping weight.	Fire box	Price. each.
24	Direct Draft	250 lbs.	24 in.	$15.12
24	Base Heater	270 "	24 in.	17.28

Star Windsor for Wood Only.

44098 Has a false bottom and back lining, deep ash pit, double end door. An excellent stove and one that will give satisfaction. Pilasters, panel, urn, rail, etc., nickeled *No* ash pan furnished with this stove. Height of No. 22 and No. 24, without top ornament, 38 and 40 inches; height of ornament, 10 inches.

44098--

		Fire box.	Shipping weight.	Price.
22	Direct Draft	22 in.	190 lbs.	$10.25
24	"	24 in.	210 "	11.79
22	Base Heater	22 in.	220 "	13.33
24	"	24 in.	250 "	14.83
22	Parlor Cook	22 in.	210 "	12.82
24	"	24 in.	235 "	14.53

Size of oven for the above Parlor Cook.

No.	Length.	Height.	Depth.
22	10 1-2 inches.	8 inches.	12 inches.
24	11 1-2 "	8 3-4 "	13 1-2 "

Star Windsor for Coal.

44099 Large feed door in upper section, heavy iron linings, two covers in top under the swing top, nickeled trimmings. *No* ash pan furnished with this stove. A very durable stove.

		Fire box.	Shipping weight.	Price.
22	Direct Draft	14x9 7x9½	210 lbs.	$11.80
24	"	8x7½ 16x10	230 "	13.96
22	Parlor Cook	7x9½ 14x9	265 "	14.82
24	"	8x7½ 16x10	285 "	16.53

Size of oven for the above Parlor Cook.

No.	Length.	Height.	Depth.
22	10 1-2 inches.	8 inches.	12 inches.
24	11 1-2 "	8¾ "	13 1-2 "

Heat and Cold.

The Refrigerators we quote are as good for cooling as our Stoves are for heating. It don't pay to get a small one. See page 417.

The Windsor Oak.

Our plates are of the very best and our mountings are first class. Special attention has been given to controlling the supply of air to the fire. Our gas burning features are excellent. Our ash pan is twice the size of any other Oak, and it goes in the stove where it belongs. With the best shaking and dumping grate we have confidence in saying we offer you the best Oak in the market. Height, without top ornament, 42, 45 and 48 in.; height of ornament, 10 inches

For Hard Coal, Soft Coal, Coke or Wood.

	Weight.	Price.
44100 Body 14 in. diameter for wood.	160 lbs.	$11.59
Body 16 in. diameter for wood.	200 lbs.	13.95
Body 18 in. diameter for wood	255 lbs.	16.60

44101 The Windsor Oak for Coal, same price as No. 44100.

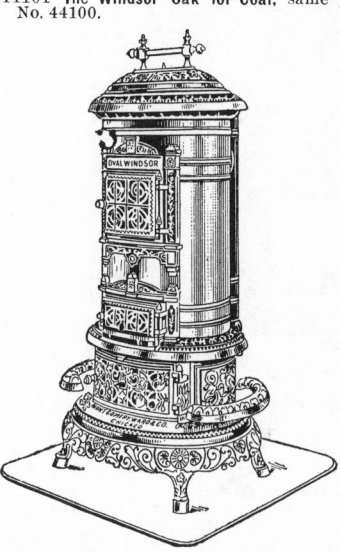

44102 The Oval Windsor. This Stove embodies every feature of excellence known in such Stoves —the flues are large, and pass down the sides and under the entire base, thus securing more heat than from any Stove with different flues. The hot air pipes extend from the bottom up through the side flues to the top, and give all the advantages of such pipes in stoves. Has draw center shaking grate; mica door above poke hole, anti-clinker brick linings; and large ash pan. Mounted with Russian iron and crated.

No.	Weight.	Price, each.
110	225 lbs.	$16.20
112	290 lbs.	19.44
114	325 lbs.	22.68

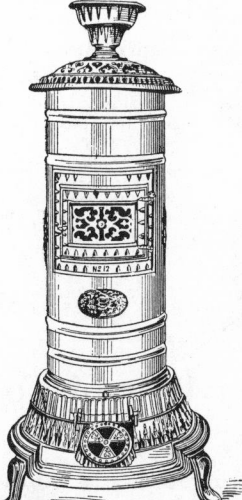

44103 Gem Windsor. The specialty in this stove is in the grate which can be removed without dismounting the stoves. The grate shakes and dumps. The Gem has a large sheet-iron ash pan. brick linings, anti-clinker shaking and dumping grate. mica door and is an excellent cheap cylinder stove. Mounted and crated.
Height, 44, 45 and 46 inches.

No. 10. weight, 110 lbs. Price, each, $6.00
No. 12. weight, 125 lbs. Price, each, $7.00
No. 14, weight, 140 lbs. Price, each, $8.00

Stoves—Continued.

44104 Daisy Windsor. This stove embodies every feature of excellence possible to put into this kind of stove. It has a large ash pit with large sheet iron ash pan, a beautiful leg base, a draw-center, anti-clinker, grate with poke hole; is a new, original pattern, ornamented in the latest fashion, and it will sell. Mounted and crated. Height, 45, 46½ and 50 inches.

No.	Weight.	Price, each.
10	120 lbs.	$6.50
12	140 lbs.	7.80
14	160 lbs.	9.00

44105 Cannon Windsor. (The number indicates the inside diameters in inches of the fire pot.) The Cannon Windsor is not a "Paper Stove." The fire pot is from 20 to 100 per cent. heavier than in other stoves of similar form; the whole stove is made to be durable and to render good service to the user. There are no rods to burn off and no bolts exposed to the fire. The top is made to receive a drum, if desired.

No.	Weight	Height	Price each
10	85 lbs.	35 inches	$4.25
12	100 "	37 "	4.85
13	120 "	39 "	5.94
14	145 "	42 "	7.00
16	195 "	47 "	9.15
18	255 "	51 "	11.80

We can furnish repairs for any stove we make at not over a day's delay because if the plate is not in stock we can make it any day, and without sending 1,000 miles or more to some foundry, or some stove repair dealer after it, and when you get it from us *it will fit the stove.*

Laundry Stove.

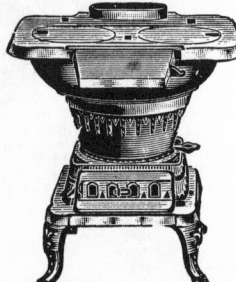

See our special catalogue for other LAUNDRY STOVES.

44110 Laundry Stove for hard or soft coal; has two holes, swing feed door and dumping grate. Made in two sizes only.

No.	7	8
Height	24 in.	24 in.
Weight	55 lbs.	75 lbs.
Price	$3.25	$3.55

Box Stoves.

ENTIRELY NEW AND VERY HANDSOME.

44113—   Price, each.
22 inches, with one 7 inch boiler holes, 75 lbs. $3.25
25 inches, with two 7 inch boiler holes, 100 lbs. 3.65
28 inches, with two 8 inch boiler holes, 120 lbs. 4.80
30 inches, with two 8 inch boiler holes, 125 lbs. 5.33
34 inches, with two 9 inch boiler holes, 165 lbs. 7.50

The Windsor Steel Ranges.

The Windsor Steel Ranges are without exception the most economical and durable steel range on the market today. These steel ranges are made with a heavy cast top, covers and centers. There are two thicknesses of steel plate around the sides and back with an asbestos lining in between. By this patent device the steel plate will not warp, and it will force all possible heat to oven. For baking the Windsor Steel Ranges are unequaled. Water fronts are generally used in cities where people use hot water throughout the house. The hot water is heated by passing through water front, which is placed in front or back of fire box in range.

We do not furnish any cooking utensils or stove pipe with any of our ranges at prices quoted.

In order to obtain steel fixtures at prices quoted with the following steel ranges, same must be ordered with range, or there will be a charge of 9 cents per pound for same.

All Steel Ranges ordered with **Water Front** will in all cases be fitted in the range, ready for use, before leaving the factory, unless otherwise ordered, as the front lining has to be taken out and a flange on the back broken off in order to admit the water front in its proper place. We make no charge for this work, therefore would advise all of our customers to allow us to do the work, as it will save them time and expense. NEVER start a fire in your range until water has been connected to your boiler or tank, as it will certainly damage the water front if you do.

44115 Windsor Steel Range, 4-hole. It is the most complete steel range in the market. Price of plain range only.

No.	Size of Oven.	Size of Top.	Weight.	Price.
8-60	17x22x13½	29x33 inch.	430	$20.63
High closet for above range, weight, 65 lbs.				5.00
High shelf for above range, weight, 40 lbs.				2.65
Water front, for above range.				2.50
Wood fixtures for above range, weight, 30 lbs.				1.00

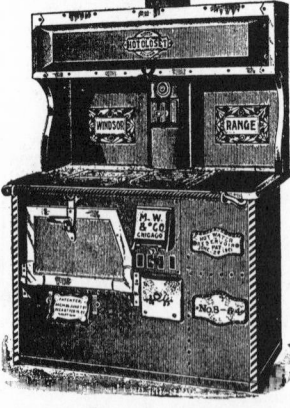

This cut represents our 4-hole Windsor Steel Range, with an incased cast iron reservoir. The reservoir in this range is placed against steel plate which fire box linings rest against; it being placed in this manner, receives sufficient heat to heat water satisfactorily. Hard or soft coal or wood. Prices do not include high closet, as shown in cut.

44116 Price of Range, with reservoir.

No.	Size of Oven	Size of Top.	Weight	Price
8-64	17x22x13½.	29x42 inch.	575 lbs.	$26.88
High closet for above range, weight, 75 lbs.				6.25
High Shelf for above range, weight, 45 lbs.				4.00
Wood fixtures for above range, weight. 30 lbs.				1.00

This Windsor Steel Range has 6 cooking holes. It is the same style range as No. 44118, but without the incased reservoir. It has heavy covers and centers; made from the best brand of iron; with two thicknesses of steel plate with an asbestos lining in between, so as to prevent steel from warping, and which forces all possible heat to oven. This is a first-class range in every respect.

44117 Price of range, only.

No.	Size of Oven.	Size of Top.	Weight.	Price.
8-62	19x22x13½.	29x34 inch.	435 lbs.	$23.13
High closet for above range, weight 65 lbs.				5.00
High shelf for above range, weight, 40 lbs.				2.65
Water front for above range.				2.50
Wood fixtures for above range, 30 lbs.				1.00

Ranges—Continued.

44118 This cut represents our 6-hole Windsor Steel Range, with cast iron enameled reservoir. This reservoir being enameled makes it sweet and clean and it will last a lifetime if properly taken care of. It should not be allowed to run dry. This reservoir is heated by the same patent device as our 4-hole range No. 44116. This is a first-class range and it is a good family size. See description under No. 44117. For hard coal, soft coal or wood. Prices do not include high closet, as shown in cut. Price of this range with incased reservoir:

No.	Size of oven.	Size of top.	Weight	Price.
8-66	19x22x13½	29x43 inches.	600 lbs.	$29.38
High closet for above range, weight, 75 lbs.				6.25
High shelf for above range, weight, 45 lbs.				4.00
Wood fixtures for above range, weight, 30 lbs.				1.00

44119 This Windsor Steel Range we guarantee to give best of satisfaction in cooking, baking and for durability. It has two thicknesses of steel plate with an asbestos lining in between, around sides and back, so as to prevent the steel plate from warping. It is the same style range as No. 44120 but without reservoir attachment. Size of cooking surface, 30x37 inches. For hard or soft coal and wood. Price of plain stove only.

No.	Size of oven.	Weight.	
8-37	20x22x14	565 lbs.	$31.25
9-37	20x22x14	565 lbs.	31.88
High closet for above, weight, 70 lbs.		Extra.	$6.25
High shelf for above, weight, 45 lbs.		"	4.00
Water front for above		"	2.65
Wood fixtures, for above, weight, 50 lbs		"	1.00

44120 This Windsor Steel Range is the same as our No. 44119, with the exception of a planished copper reservoir as shown in cut. The water is heated in reservoir by two pieces of ¾-inch pipe passing from reservoir into fire box of stove. (Notice—in connecting this pipe to reservoir see that pipe extends at least 1½ inches in fire box.) Size of cooking surface 30x37 inches. Prices do not include high closet, as shown in cut. Price of stove with planished copper reservoir.

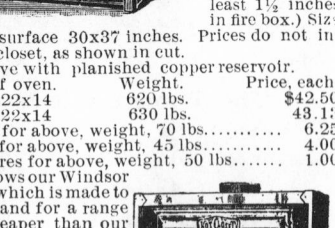

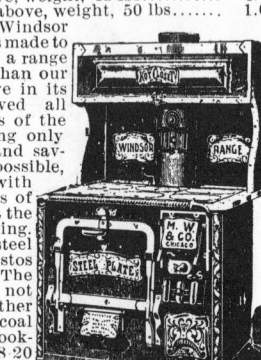

No.	Size of oven.	Weight.	Price, each.
8 37	20x22x14	620 lbs.	$42.50
9-37	20x22x14	630 lbs.	43.13
High closet for above, weight, 70 lbs.			6.25
High shelf for above, weight, 45 lbs.			4.00
Wood fixtures for above, weight, 50 lbs.			1.00

This cut shows our Windsor Steel Range, which is made to meet the demand for a range somewhat cheaper than our best grade. We have in its construction preserved all the principal features of the regular line, changing only the ornamentation and saving labor, wherever possible, without interfering with the working qualities of the range. It has not the double steel plate lining. It has one sheet of steel plate with an asbestos lining attached to it. The lids and centers are not as heavy as our other ranges. Hard or soft coal and wood. Size of cooking surface of No. 8-20 and 9-20, 30x36 inches. Size of cooking surface of No. 8-25 and 9-25, 30x37 inches. Prices do not include high closet, as shown in cut.

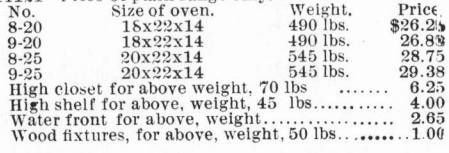

44121 Price of plain range only.

No.	Size of oven.	Weight.	Price
8-20	18x22x14	490 lbs.	$26.2½
9-20	18x22x14	490 lbs.	26.88
8-25	20x22x14	545 lbs.	28.75
9-25	20x22x14	545 lbs.	29.38
High closet for above weight, 70 lbs.			6.25
High shelf for above, weight, 45 lbs.			4.00
Water front for above, weight.			2.65
Wood fixtures, for above, weight, 50 lbs.			1.00

Ranges—Continued.

44122 Windsor Steel Range, with planished copper reservoir, same style reservoir as our No. 44120. This range is the same style as No. 44121, with the addition of reservoir. Price of range, with planished copper reservoir:

Size	Size of oven.	Weight.	Price.
8-20	18x22x14	575 lbs.	$36.25
9-20	18x22x14	575 "	36.88
8-25	20x22x14	630 "	38.75
9-25	20x22x14	630 "	39.38

High closet for above, weight, 70 pounds....... 6.25
High shelf for above, weight, 45 pounds 4.00
Wood fixtures for above. weight, 50 pounds.... 1.00

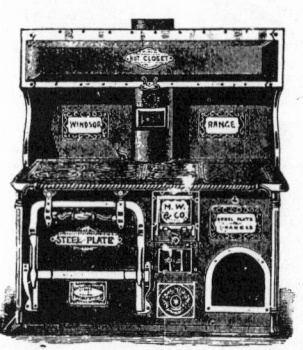

44123 Windsor Steel Range, with incased cast iron enamel reservoir, which holds about 12 gallons. We warrant every range to be perfect and made of the best material. They are without exception the most economical and durable range on the market to-day. It is made with a heavy cast top, covers and centers. It has two thicknesses of steel with a lining of *asbestos* between, around the sides and back. You can pay double what we ask for this range and then not get one as good. The space under reservoir can be used as a fruit dryer, or a receptacle for hot flatirons, pokers, etc. In order to obtain wood fixtures at prices quoted, same will have to be purchased with range, or there will be a charge of 9 cents per pound for same Size of cooking surface, 30x50 inches. Prices do not include high closet as shown in cut.
Price of range, with incased reservoir.

No.	Size of oven.	Weight.	Price.
8-50, 6-8-in. covers	20x22x14	740 lbs.	$40.00
9-50, 6-9-in. "	20x22x14	740 "	40.62

High closet for above, weight, 80 pounds 7.50
High shelf for above, weight, 50 pounds...... 5.00
Wood fixtures for above, weight, 50 pounds... 1.00

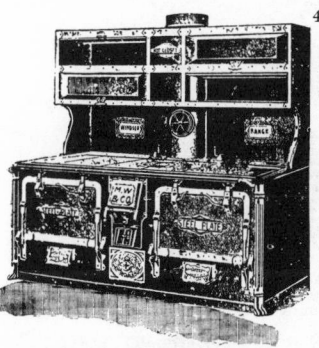

44124 This cut represents our Windsor Steel Range with double oven and fire box in center. This range is just the thing for hotels, restaurants, boarding houses, etc. We make this range from the best of material and guarantee them to be the most economical and durable range in the market. The sides and back have two thicknesses of steel with an asbestos lining in between thus preventing the steel plate from warping, and by this patent device all possible heat is forced to ovens The top, lids and centers are of extra heavy cast iron cast from new iron of the best material (not from scrap iron.) The doors have a patent spring drop. Combined dumping and shaking grate. These ranges are equaled by few, surpassed by none.
Prices do not include high closet as shown in cut.
Size of cooking surface of No. 9-16, 36x48; No. 9-18, 36x60; No. 9-22, 36x66 in. For hard coal, soft coal and wood.
Price of range only:

No.	Size of oven	Weight	Price.
9-16	8 9-inch lids	16x24x15	980 lbs.	$66.25
9-18	8 9 "	18x26x15	1215 "	67.50
9-22	8 9 "	22x26x15	1350 "	95 00

High closet for No. 9-16 Range, $8.75; for No. 9-18 Range, $10.00; for No. 9-22 Range, $11.25; weight 125, 150 and 175 pounds.,
Water front for above ranges, any size, extra $2.65
Wood fixtures " " " " " " 1.25

Range Boilers.

44130 Made of galvanized iron and tested at 160 pounds per square inch. Prices are for boilers complete with couplings and inside tubes.

Gallons.	Height.	Weight.	Price each.
30	60 in.	72 lbs.	$8.40
35	60 in.	76 lbs.	9.20
40	60 in.	85 lbs.	10.25
52	60 in.	120 lbs.	12.80
60	60 in.	150 lbs.	17.46

44163 Plain Boiler Stands for above. Price each, $1.20.

Gas Range.

44131-- This range, despite its low price, is well built in every particular. It has four top burners, operated by our new needle point and is fitted with movable ovens. It has two side shelves 5¼ inches wide

	Height.	Width.	Depth
Range	35 in	21½ in	16½ in.
Baking oven	11½ "	18 "	15 "
Broiling	11½ "	18 "	15 "
Top plate		24½ "	21½ "

Price each $18.00

GASOLINE STOVES.
1895 Reliable Process.

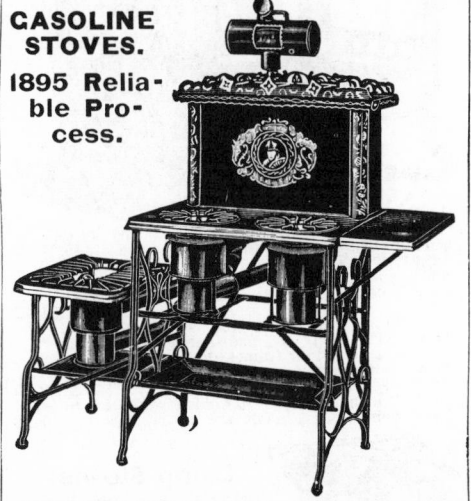

Two burners on top and one on half low step. This stove has no equal in points of finish, design and durability. Hot air and vaporizing tubes are connected with removable iron elbows, easily taken apart, so that the vaporizers can be taken out and cleaned. Vaporizers are made of perforated brass. Drums are made of sheet brass, with cast iron tops and bottons. Cone seats have iron flanges to protect the drums from heat, grease and dirt. Burners are fastened together with two bolts, easily taken apart. Needle points on valves are German silver wire. They will never rust or corrode. The tanks cannot be removed for filling until all valves have been closed. Reliable Process Stoves will run perfectly in cold weather. Weight, crated with oven, 146 pounds.
44135 Price, with Russia oven.............. $17.52
44135½ Price, with tin oven.............. 16.75
Same description as No. 44135, except that it has three burners on top and one on half-low step.
Weight, crated, 164 pounds.
44136 Price, with Russia oven...............$19.92
44136½ Price, with tin oven................... 19.20

This is our No. 13 Cabinet Process, which has two burners on top, with step attachment, making 3 cooking frames; also oven under top, making stove of large capacity, and taking up small floor space. All Reliable Process stoves are so constructed that our burner drums and hot air tubes are indestructible from heat or rust. Weight, crated, 222 pounds.
44137 Price, each.....$22.31

Reliable Juniors.

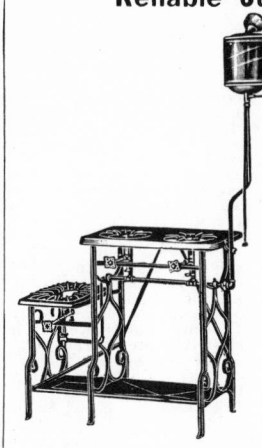

This cut represents our new Reliable Step Junior with lay-down tank. This is by all odds the best stove ever offered for the money. They have same cooking capacity as any $16 or $18 store on the market. The main top is fitted with reliable burners, step attachment is furnished with our powerful Giant Burner. This burner will furnish sufficient heat for the large Russia or tin ovens, and will be found more desirable than the double cone burner for cooking utensils.

Height.	Crated weight.	Size of main top.	Size of step top.	Each.
44138 27-inch	51 lbs.	22½x15½	16x14	$6.76
44139 27-inch	60 lbs.	32½x15½	16x14	8.25

The No. 44139 has three burners on main top.

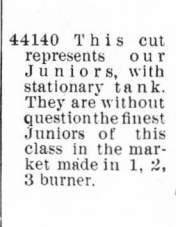
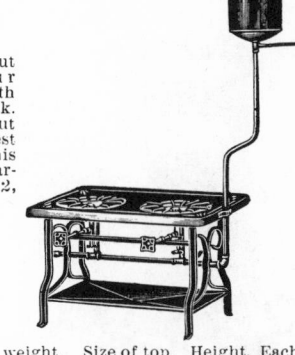

44140 This cut represents our Juniors, with stationary tank. They are without question the finest Juniors of this class in the market made in 1, 2, 3 burner.

Burners.	Crated weight.	Size of top.	Height.	Each.
1	17 lbs.	15½x11½ in.	14 in.	$2.50
2	26 lbs.	22½x15½ in.	14 in.	3.00
3	39 lbs.	32½x15½ in.	14 in.	4.27

44141 The above cut represents our Reliable Juniors, 24 inches high, with stationary tank.

Burners.	Crated weight.	Size of top.	Height.	Each.
2	36 lbs.	22½x15½ in.	24 in.	$3.60
3	45 lbs.	32½x15½ in.	24 in.	4.86

Oil Heaters (44).

44163 Height from floor to top of ornament, 31 inches; diameter of heating drum, 7 inches; circumference of wick, 6½ inches. This stove is a very powerful heater for its size and is as well made as our larger stoves. It has cast iron reservoir, Russia iron drum, brass burner. Reservoir holds 3 quarts and will burn from 10 to 12 hours. It is suitable for rooms 12 feet square, and will warm even larger rooms in moderate weather. Weight, 25 lbs. Our heaters have a grate under the swinging top for heating or cooo king.
Price, each............. 4.25

Oil Heaters (54).

44164 Height from floor to top of ornament, 35 inches; diameter of heating drum, 8 inches; circumference of wick, 8 inches. This stove is similar to No. 44163, but is larger in every way and is suitable for rooms 12 to 15 feet square. It has brass burner, Russia iron drum, cast iron reservoir, enameled inside and out. They will never leak or rust out and are not affected by the acids in the oil. We have a safety feature in this stove which absolutely prevents any communication between the fire and the main body of oil in the reservoir.
Price, each $6.00

Oil Heater, No. 74.

44165 Height. from floor to top of ornament, 39 inches. Diameter of heating drum, 9 inches; size of wick, in circumference, 10 inches. Cast iron reservoir, holding five quarts and will burn 10 to 12 hours. A roller base furnished with each stove without extra charge. The heating drum has the same circulating feature as No. 64, described on preceding page. This stove is a good "general purpose" heater, as it can be used with a low fire for small rooms in moderate weather, or will comfortably warm a large room in very cold weather if run to its full capacity. All of our oil heaters are provided with our improved brass burners and the stoves are mechanically and thoroughly made. The wickraising device used in all our heaters, raises and lowers the wick with absolute certainty.
Price, each $8.50

Oil Heater, No. 84.

44166 Height from floor to top of ornament, 39 inches; diameter of heating drum, 9 inches; size of wick, in circumference, 15 inches. Globe fire box, circulating drum, cast iron reservoir holding six quarts and will burn 10 hours. Roller base furnished with each stove. This stove is recommended for halls or very large rooms or where it is desired to heat several adjoining rooms with one fire. Each stove is provided with a grate under the swing cover for heating water or cooking.
Price, each $9.50

Wicks.

It is very important that the wick in an oil heating stove be of the correct weave and texture and also of the proper thickness to suit the burner for which it is intended. The Puritan Oil Heaters, when sent out from the factory, are supplied with proper wicks and are warranted to give satisfaction only when wicks furnished by the Cleveland Foundry Company are used. We will send extra wicks by mail, postage prepaid, at the following prices:

44167—	Each.	Per doz.
No. 44 Wicks for No. 44 stove	$0.10	$1.00
No. 54 " " 54	.10	1.00
No. 74 " " 74	.10	1 00
No. 84 " " 84	.15	1.50

Full directions for trimming, adjusting or renewing wicks sent with each stove.

Oil Heater.

44168 Ornamental, Useful, Convenient. Contains more radiating surface than any other oil heater, Cast iron reservoir, consequently no leakage. Capacity one gallon, burns 10 hours. It is the most economical oil heater as one, two, three or four burners can be used, according to heat required. It has two holes on top for cooking purpose. It has perfect combustion; on casters and can be readily moved about. Height, 25½ inches, weight, 40 pounds; but onesize made. Price, each......$8 60

Grand Oil Cook Stove.

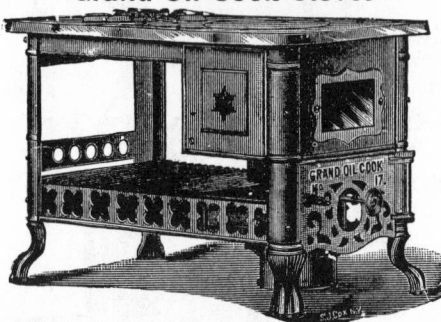

44170 The Grand Oil Cook Stove; burns kerosene oil, has a 12-inch circular wick. Size of top, 12x21, with two cooking holes. Is finished in nickel and japan, except the top, which has burnished edges; is very substantial and neat.
Each $4.75
44171 Russia Iron Oven for Grand Oil Cook Stove. The body is made entirely of Russia iron, cast iron door frames, double tops and deflector bottoms and are excellent bakers.
Price, each 2.40
44172 Wicks for Grand Oil Cook Stove. Each.. .10
Per dozen........ .... 1.08

Lamp Stoves.

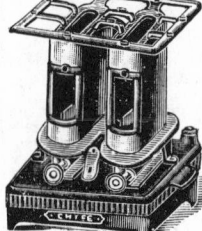

44173 Has one 4-inch burner, with solid castiron reservoir. It has moveable mica frames and is well made in every particular. We consider it one of the best stoves on the market for the price. Weight, about 7 lbs.
Price, each............$0.50

44174
44174 Like cut, with 2 burners. Weight about 11 pounds. Price, each...... .. ..$1.00
44175 Extension top to fit 44174 Each........... .85
44176 Oven to fit 44174, made of tin; size 10½x 12x12 inches, Each.......................... 1.25
44177 Lamp Stove, style of 44174 with three 4-inch burners. Weight about 13 pounds
Price, each............................... 1.40
44178 Extension top to fit No. 44177. Price, each. .90
44179 Oven made of tin; size 10½x12x12 inch to fit oil stove No. 44177. Each................. 1.25

Round Wick Oil Stoves.

44180 The burner used in this stove having a round wick (No. 2, Rochester) and center draft. The combination is better and the capacity is greatly increased over the flat wick stoves. Weight about 10 pounds; has movable mica frames. Price, each.....$1.75
44181 Two Burner Round Wick Oil Stove. The construction of this stove is the same as 44180, but having two burners it has double the capacity; weight, about 16 pounds.
Price, each............ $3.00

Extension Tops.

44182 For Oil Stove, No. 44180. Price. each.$ .50
44182½ For Oil Stove, No. 44181. Price, each. .75

Summer Queen Oil Stoves.

44185 Summer Queen Oil Stove, one burner with 3-inch wick. Weight 2½ lbs. Price, each.$1 00
44186 Oil Stove like cut; has two burners with two 3-inch wicks. Weight 6 lbs. Price, each.$1.35
44187 Oil stove, two burners, with 4-inch wicks. Weight, 7½ lbs. Price, each.$1.85

44187½ Summer Queen Oil Stove, with three burners, each 4 inches wide. Price, each.$2.40
44189 Russia Iron Oven, double lined, to fit 44186 stove. Size, 11x 12x10 inches. Price, each.......$1.78
44190 Russia Iron Oven, to fit above stove 44187½; doubled tinned; size, 14½x17½x 13¾ inches. Price, each.. ...$2.95
44191 Russia Iron Oven. to fit 44187 stove; size, 13x14x12.
Price, each...... ....$2.40

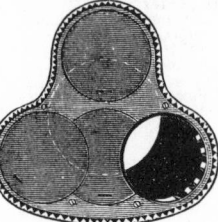

44192 Extension Top, like cut to fit 44187 and 44197 stoves, with three cooking holes. Price, each....... $1.25
44193 Extension Top, to fit 44187½ and 44199 stoves, with three cooking holes. Price, each........ $1.30

44192

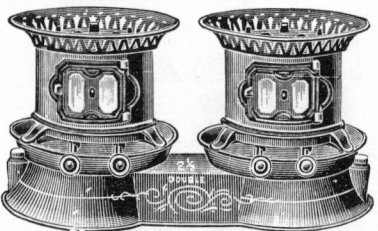

44197 Summer Queen Oil Stove, double, with four burners each; 4 inches wide. Price, each. 3.86
For extension top to fit above see No. 44192.
For Russia iron oven to fit above stove see No. 44191.
44199 Summer Queen Oil Stove, double; has six brass burners with six 4-inch wicks. Price, each. 4.90
For extension top to fit above see No. 44193.
For Russia iron oven so fit 44199 stove see No. 44190.

Oil Stove Wicks.

44200 Cotton Oil Stove Wicks.

Width, inches..........	3	3½	4	4½	5
Price, each...............	2c	2c	3c	3c	4c
Price, per dozen........	20c	22c	25c	28c	30c

44201 Felt Oil Stove Wicks.
4 inch. Price, each....4c. Price, per dozen....40c.
5 inch. Price, each....5c. Price, per dozen. ...45c.

Queen Oil Stove Iron Heaters.

Will hold Mrs. Potts' Irons.

44205 Iron Heaters like cut, will fit No. 44187 and No. 44197 stoves. Price, each............$0.60
44206 Iron Heaters, same as cut, but will hold three irons and fits No. 44187½ and 44199 stoves. Price, each ....$ .90
44207 Flat Iron Heater in use on a Two Burner Lamp Stove. Price, each.......................$0.60

OVER 200 STYLES OF NEW
LAUNDRED SHIRT WAISTS FOR LADIES.
Perfect Fitting.   Fast Colors.
Prices that talk. -   -   See quotations.

Sad Iron Heaters for Gasoline or Gas Stoves.

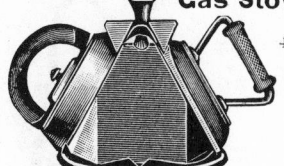

44208 Sad Iron Heaters, made of cast-iron, will hold four irons; measures at bottom 9¼ inches. Price, each...$0.60

Broilers for Gasoline or Gas Stoves.

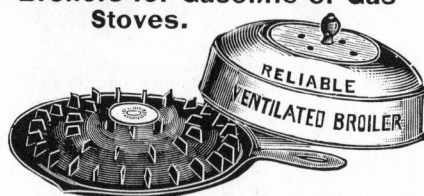

44209 Broilers, made of cast iron, with tin cover. 10 inches diameter. Price, each $0.65

Divided Sauce Pans.

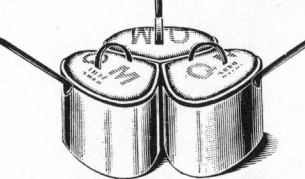

44210 Divided Sauce Pans, made of tin. Two pans, price each...$0.90 Three pans (like cut), price each $0.75

Lamp Stove Ovens.

44212 This Oven fits our single burner lamp stoves. Dimensions, 10½ inches long, 9½ inches wide, 6 inches high. Price, each............$0.75

44213 This oven, like cut, will fit all of our two and three burner oil stoves. They are provided with japanned cast-iron door frames, cast-iron racks or shelves and adjustable cast-iron rack supports.

Dimensions, 12 inches long, 12 inches wide, 12 inches high. Price, each....................$1.25

Climax Stove.

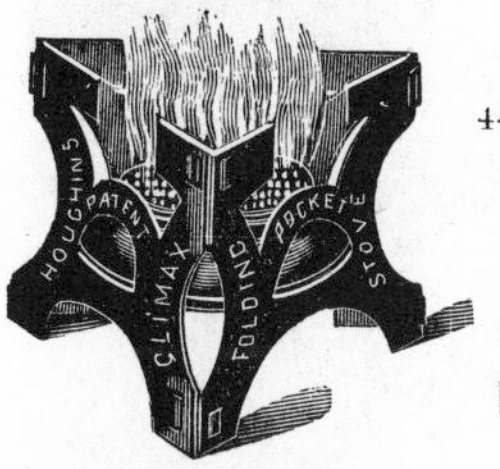

44220 The Best Folding Pocket Alcohol Cook Stoves ever invented for the price, with boiler, cover and gridiron, complete. Each.$0.25

Pocket Stoves.

Burns Alcohol.
44221 The preceding cut shows the "Multum in Parvo Stove," with boiler. Water can be boiled in 5 minutes to make tea, coffee or other hot drinks, boil eggs, make oyster stews, etc. Packed in a box 1¾ inches high and 4 inches square. Each ....$0 50 Per dozen....... $5.25

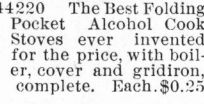
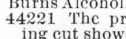

The "Multum in Parvo."

The Excursionist's Stove.

44222 A new style stove and stand; boiler holds 3 pints, has a lip strainer, folding handle and cover. The stove will hold sufficient alcohol to burn one hour full flame or two hours small flame; will boil 3 pints of water in 15 minutes. The stand and stove fit inside the boiler, packed in a box 5 inches square.

6 inches high. There is room enough left to hold a gridiron, cups, spoons, knives and forks, and canteen to hold a pint of alcohol; weight, 1¾ pounds. Price of Excursionist, with gridiron, each.........$0.85 Per dozen........ 9.50

Canteens.

44223 Canteens; nickel plated canteens for pocket cook stove; holds ½ pint of alcohol......$0.15

Lamp Chimney Stoves.

44225 Lamp Chimney Stove, very convenient for warming food, boiling water, etc. It is a cast iron device that can be attached to the top of any size chimney (as shown in the cut). No one should be without one of these handy little articles. Price, each....$0.05 Per dozen...... .54

Gasoline Torches.

44250 Gasoline Torches; full one hundred thousand in use; can be used in a high wind without going out. Just the thing for campers, shows, fishing, etc.; is used extensively for fishing in boat at night; burns gasoline. ... $1.25

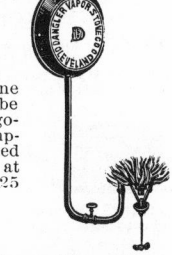

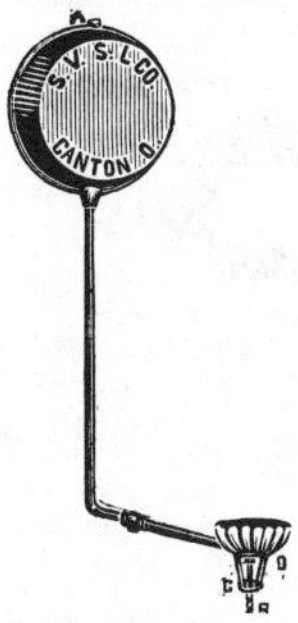

Out-Door Torch.

44251 For foundries, machine shops, street salesmen, mills, in fact, for any out-door use. Requires no protection, and will burn in any kind of weather. Reservoir will hold one gallon and will burn six hours; burns gasoline. Price, each.................$1.30

Gasoline Blow Pipe.

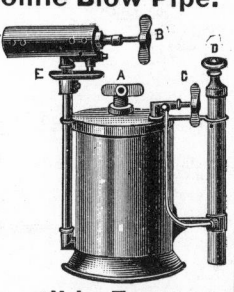

44255 The best pipe for lighting street lamps, softening paint on cars, coaches, carriages, houses, signs, furniture, etc., also for tempering drills, light brazing, thawing out frozen water pipes and for every purpose where a hot, smokeless flame is required. Made entirely of brass and warranted. Price, each........$3.75

The "Sun" Convertible Furnace.

44256 The "Sun" Convertible Furnace is the best on the market. It will heat soldering coppers, and melt lead or solder quicker than any other furnace. It can be used as successfully on roofs as in-doors, and will positively not blow out. The burner is made with large passages, is powerful and will not clog up. Has heavy jig drilled cap; will not warp or burn out like a sawed cap. Casing is made of Russian sheet iron and malleable iron fittings. Reservoir has tinned malleable iron bottom and top, while the body is made of heavy sheet steel. The top casing being detachable, it is a great convenience for unsoldering pipes, brazing, etc. It is converted from a tinner's to a plumber's furnace in a moment. Cannot be filled while burning, and cannot explode. It is the strongest and most durable furnace on the market. Every furnace thoroughly tested before shipping. Height, 15 inches; with top casing off, 10½ inches. Weight, 30 lbs., boxed. Price, each.............. ....$5.40

Tinners' Stoves.

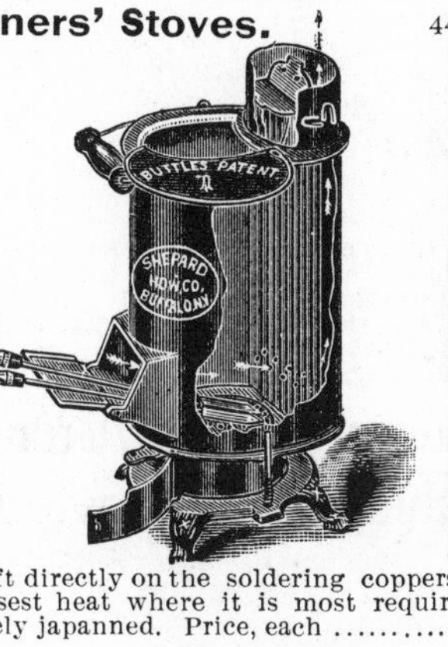

44258 Tinner's Stove or Fire Pot with shaking grate, side oven, hinged hearth door. The only double damper, base burning, reversible flue, tinner's stove made. To start the fire open front damper; after the fire is well started, the front damper is closed and the back damper is opened; this causes a downward draft directly on the soldering coppers, creating the densest heat where it is most required. Each pot nicely japanned. Price, each $2.00

Acme Stove Pipe.

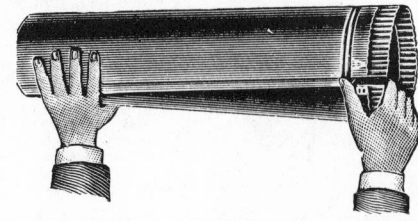

(Cut shows manner of putting pipe together.)

The only practical loose pipe made. No rivets, no malleting of seams necessary. The pipe is made from No. 26 smooth iron, and covered with a coating to prevent rust. It is a better quality of iron than has ever been used in ordinary pipe. A length of pipe properly put together cannot possibly collapse. Length of joint, 24 inches.

44260 Diameter...........	5-inch.	6-inch.
Price, per length.............	$0.10	$0.12
Price, per crate of 25 lengths.	2.25	2.35
Price, per crate of 50 lengths.	4.50	4.70

Universal Stove Pipe.

Patent Universal Stove Pipe. This pipe is not complete, but the seam is made and edges turned over, and one with a mallet or hammer can put together in a few minutes' time. It is left this way to facilitate shipping, as a dozen joints do not occupy any more space than one joint put together; it is packed in crates of fifty joints, but we will sell any quantity ordered. It is made from Planished or American Russia Iron. Length of joint, 30 inches.

Diameter...........	5-inch.	6-inch.
Price, per length....	$0.38	$0.45

Ready Made Stove Pipe.

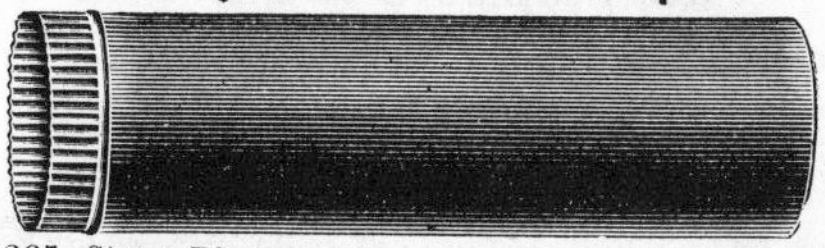

44265 Stove Pipe made up complete, ready to adjust to stove. Pipe shipped this way takes up considerable room, and we would advise the purchase of the patent pipe when convenient, as it can be put together very quickly; can furnish in No. 27 iron only. Length, 24 inches.

Diameter.	5 in.	6 in.	7 in.
Price, per length.........	$0.08	.09	.17

44266 Planished or American Russia Iron Stove Pipe, same style as 44265; length, 30 inches.

Diameter...................	5 in.	6 in.	7 in.
Price per length..............	30c.	32c.	45c

44266½ Planished Iron Elbows, corrugated, made from one piece of iron.

Diameter.....	5 in.	6 in
Price, each...	25c	30c

44267 Planished Iron Elbows, common.

Diameter...	5 in.	6 in.	7 in.
Price, each..	16c	18c	28c

Common Iron Elbows.

44269 Common Iron Elbows, four pieces, same style as 44267.

Diameter.......	5 in.	6 in.	7 in.
Price, each	$0.05	$0.06	$0.12
Price, per dozen..	.55	.65	1.20

Stove Boards.

44275 Crystalized Stove Boards, wood lined, square. The above cut does not represent the exact pattern or finish, but only the general character.

Size, inches	Each.	Size, inches	Each.
26x26	$1.00	30x30	$1.18
26x32	1.10	33x33	1.25
28x28	1.15	30x38	1.30
28x34	1.20	36x36	1.45

Stove Pipe Shelf.

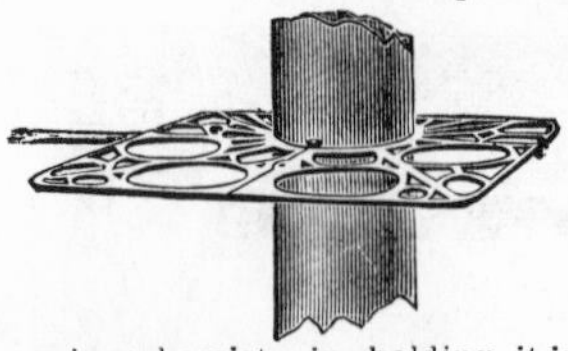

44300 Cast Iron Sapanned; is 18 inches square: made for 6 inch pipe. This shelf is very complete in itself and is easily applied or raised and lowered. A heavy weight upon it strengthens its grip and assists in holding it in place, forcing the shelf farther over the wedge-shaped tin and making the grip on the pipe tighter.
Price, each ....$0.50 Per dozen..........$5.40

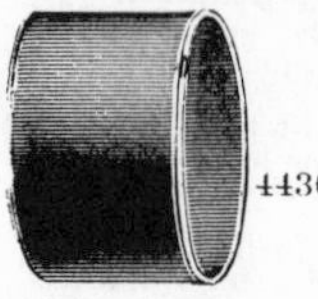

Chimney Thimbles.

	Diam.		Length.	Each.	Per doz.
44305—	6	x	4	$0.05	$0.50
	7	x	4	.07	.70

Stove Pipe Dampers.

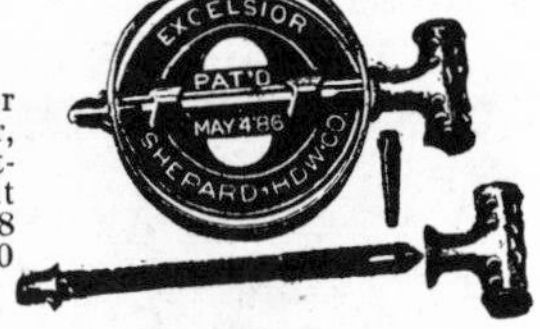

44306 The Excelsior Stove Pipe Damper, 6 inch, cool, ventilated handle, easily put in. Each......$0.08
Per dozen..... .80
Weight, 12 oz.

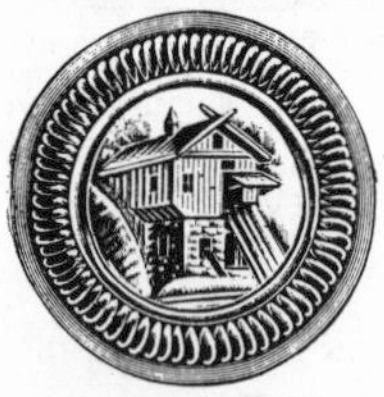

Flue Stopper.

44310 Flue Stopper, brass finished, with decorated center; very handsome. Diameter, $8\frac{3}{16}$ inches. Fits all size flues.
Each................ $0.06
Per dozen.......... .60

Flue Stoppers—Common.

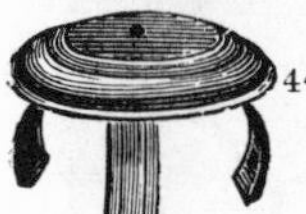

	Size.	Each.	Per doz.
44311	6 inch	$0.05	$0.54

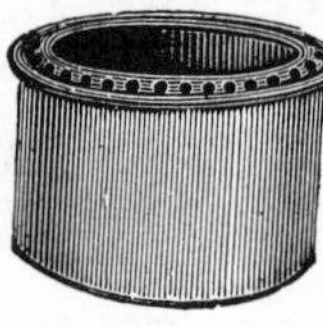

Ventilators.

	Length.	Diam.	Wt.	Each.
44315	6x4	2 lbs.	10 oz.	$0.25
	6x6	2 lbs.	10 oz.	.30
	6x10	3 lbs.	4 oz.	.38

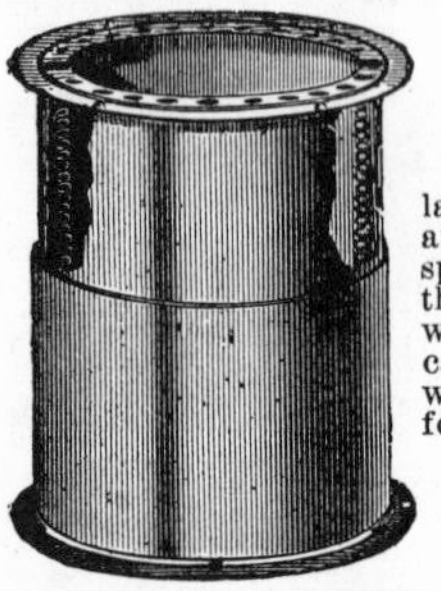

The Star Adjustable Ventilator or Register. The heads are connected by spiral steel springs, whose tension adjusts them to anythickness required with register plate they can be used in connection with our double heating stoves for conducting heat over head

No.	Size.	Extends from	Weight.	Each.
44316	5 inch...	4 to 8 inches.	2¼ lbs.	$0.36
44317	5 inch...	6 to 12 inches.	2¾ lbs.	.40
44318	6 inch...	4 to 8 inches.	2¼ lbs.	.41
44319	6 inch...	6 to 12 inches.	3¼ lbs.	.45
44320	7 inch...	4 to 8 inches.	2 lbs. 15 oz...	.47
44321	7 inch...	6 to 12 inches	3¼ lbs.	.55

44322 Register Plates for above ventilator or register, that can be opened and closed. Price, per set, 6 in., 27c; 7 in., 35c.

Stove Shovels.

The IXL Steel Stove Shovels, made extra strong, unlike the cheap article ordinarily sold; the handle cannot be broken; it is hollow and of an oval shape and fits the hand nicely; it will outwear any other shovel,

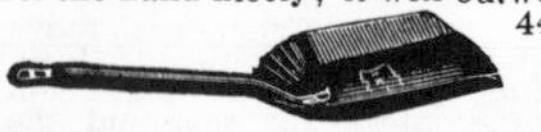

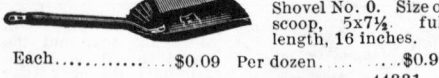

44330 The IXL Steel Shovel No. 0. Size of scoop, 5x7½. full length, 16 inches.
Each...............$0.09 Per dozen..........$0.90

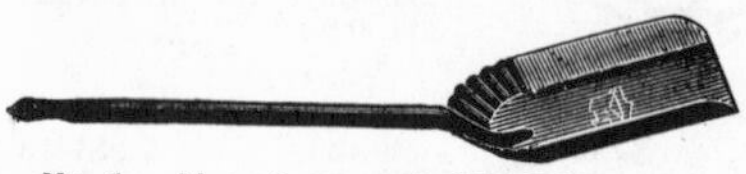

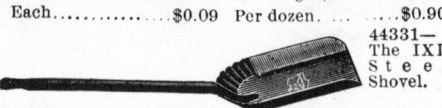

44331—The IXL Steel Shovel.
No. 1. Size of scoop, 5x8½; full length, 22 inches.
Each .... $0.10 Per dozen............$1.05

Stove Shovels—Continued.

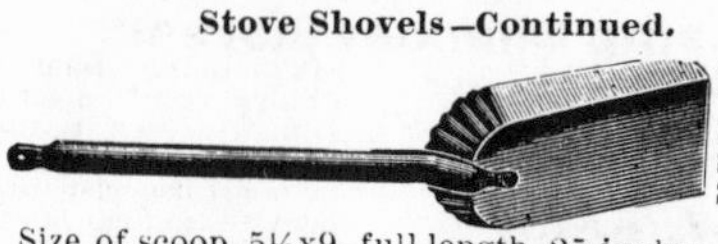

44332—The IXL Steel Stove Shovel No. 2.
Size of scoop, 5½x9. full length, 25 inches.
Each............$0.11 Per dozen $1.20

Stove Lid Lifters.

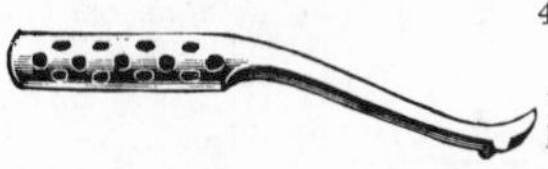

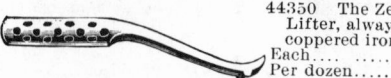

44350 The Zero Lid Lifter, always cool, coppered iron.
Each.... ......$0.05
Per dozen...... .54

Alaska Stove Trimmings, Shovel, Poker and Tongs.

These are very elegant goods. The handles consist of spirally coiled wire which admits of a circulation of air through them, keeping them always cool. All of the implements *are handsomely nickel plated.*

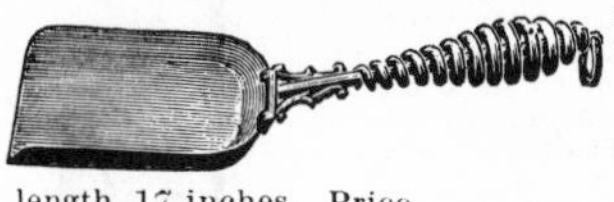

44351 Alaska Fire Shovels, cool handles, nickel plated and handsomely finished; length, 17 inches. Price $0.18
Per dozen................................... 1.85

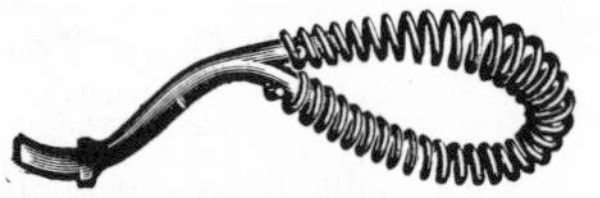

44352 Alaska Stove Lid Lifters, always cool handles, handsomely nickel plated. Price each.... $0.08
Per dozen.................................. .90

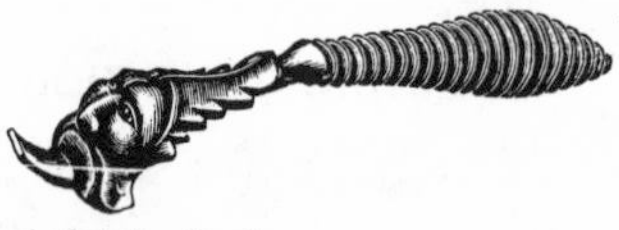

44353 Alaska Stove Lid Lifters, always cool handle; a unique and very popular pattern, nickel plated. Each $0.08
Per dozen.................................. 90

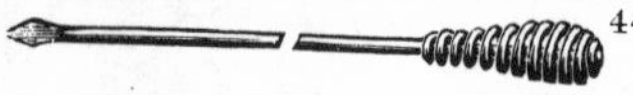

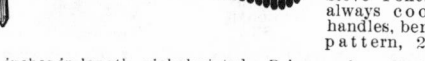

44355 Alaska Stove Poker, always cool handles, straight pattern, nickel plated, length 20 inches. Price, each..........................$0.08
Per dozen.................................. 0.90

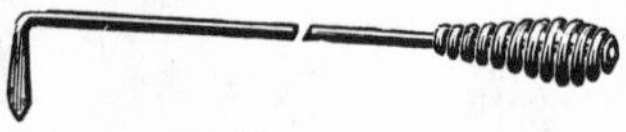

44356 Alaska Stove Poker, always cool handles, bent pattern, 22 inches in length, nickel plated. Price, each....$0.08
Per dozen.................................. 0.90

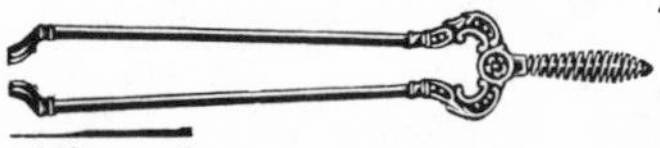

44357 Alaska Coal Tongs Nickel plated, 26 inches long.
Price each.. ....$0.15
Price, per dozen...............................1.69

Adjustable Firebacks.

Readily adjusted to fit all sizes of cook stoves; made in two sizes. Send depth of fire back and fuel used. The only fireback that will adjust itself in both length and width. This fireback is so constructed that when contracted it will fit the smallest size cook stove, and when extended it will fit the largest size stove.

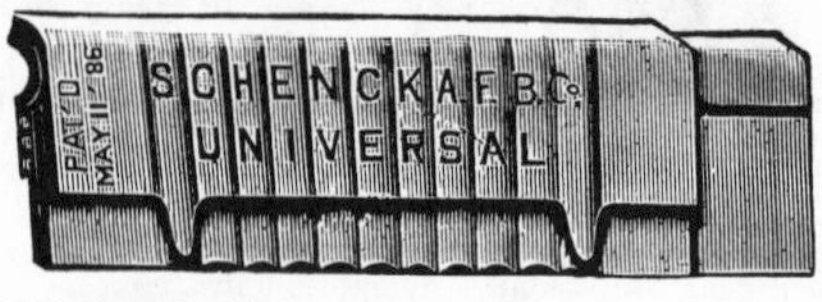

44366 Length, 14½ to 21 in.; width, 5 to 6 in.; weight, 10 lbs. Each..............................$0.60
Per dozen.................................. 6.50
44367 Length, 17½ to 24 in.; width, 6½ to 7⅝ in.; weight, 15 lbs.
Each ....$0.85 Per dozen.......... 9.10

Adjustible Grates.

TO DUMP AND SHAKE.

Something new; will adjust to fit any ordinary cook stove.
No. 1 will adjust from 9 to 14½ in. in length.
No. 2 will adjust from 13 to 17½ in. in length.
Both sizes are adjustable from 5½ to 7 in. in width.
44368½ (No. 1.) Price each.................$0.70
44369 (No 2) Price, each.................. .75

Aluminum Cooking Utensils are fine things; beat any other kind.

Coal Hods.

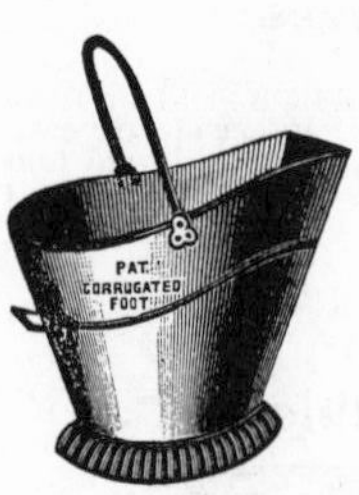

44380

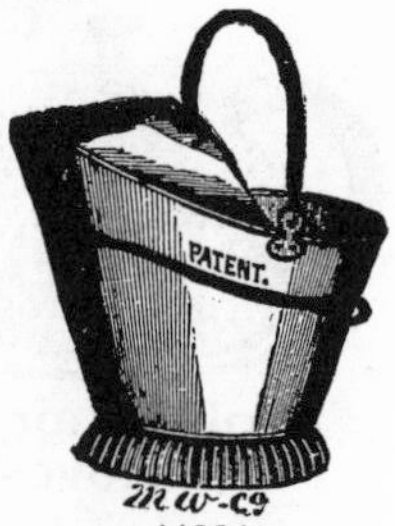

44384

44380 Open Coal Hods, japanned. We do not sell less than one dozen at dozen price. 16 in..
Each $0.18
Per doz... 1.80
17 inch, each.................................... .20
Per doz... 2.10
18 inch, each..................................... .25
Per dozen... 2.50
44382 Common Open Coal Hods, galvanized. We do not sell less than one dozen at dozen prices.
16 inch, each..................................... .25
Per dozen... 2.76
17 inch, each..................................... .28
Per dozen... 3.00
18 inch, each..................................... .30
Per dozen... 3.30
44384 Funnel Coal Hods, japanned. We do not sell less than one dozen at dozen prices; 17 in., each... .25
Per dozen... 2.55
44386 Funnel Coal Hods, galvanized. We do not sell less than one dozen at dozen prices. 17 inches Each...................................... .32
Per dozen... 3.50

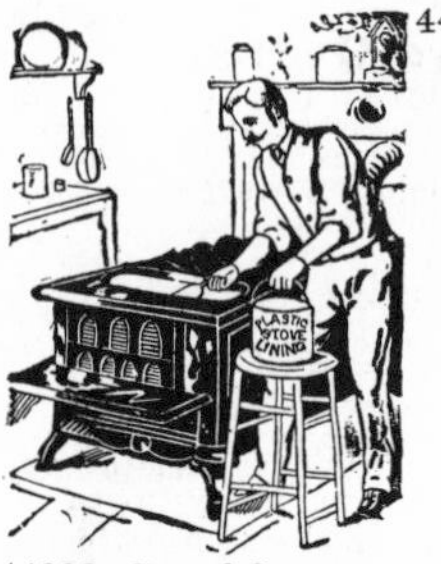

44390 Asbestos Plastic Stove Lining, composed of asbestos and other fireproof materials; is easily applied with a trowel and makes a durable and economical lining for cook stoves; useful for repairing broken brick or iron lining. Put up in 5 and 10 lb. pails.

	Each.	Doz.
5 lb. pails	$0 45	$4.50
10 lb. pails	.60	6.50

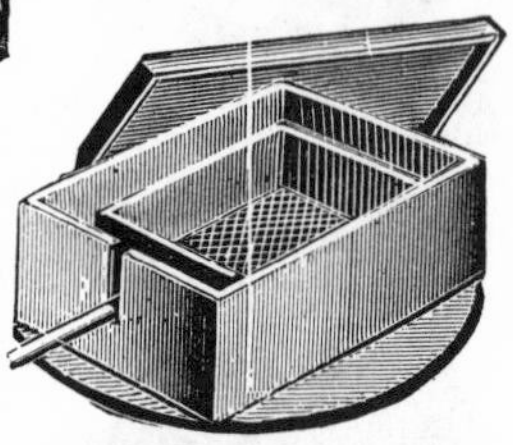

44393 Barrel Cover, Ash Sifter with cover; will fit a 21 inch barrel. Inside box measures 12 x 14; outside box has cover; made of pine stained: a good serviceable sifter at a low price; each.$0.30

Asbestos Stove Mat.

Diameter, 9 inches.

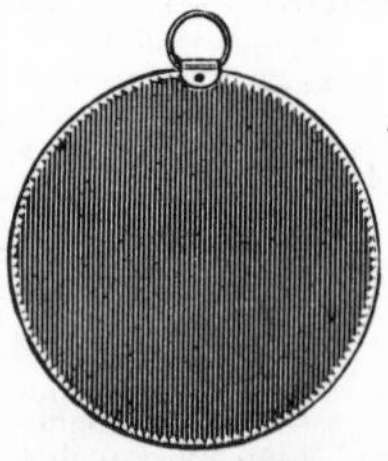

44395 A household necessity. This mat is made of asbestos of superior quality, and is scorch-proof as well as fireproof. Any cooking utensil used upon it becomes absolutely scorch-proof.

Price each.	Per doz.	Per gross.
$0.06	$0.50	$5 30

Coffee Pot Stands.

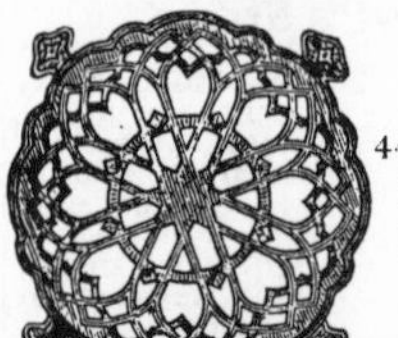

44398 Iron Coffee Pot Stand, 4¾ ins. in diameter.
Each.............................$0.05

Soap Dishes.

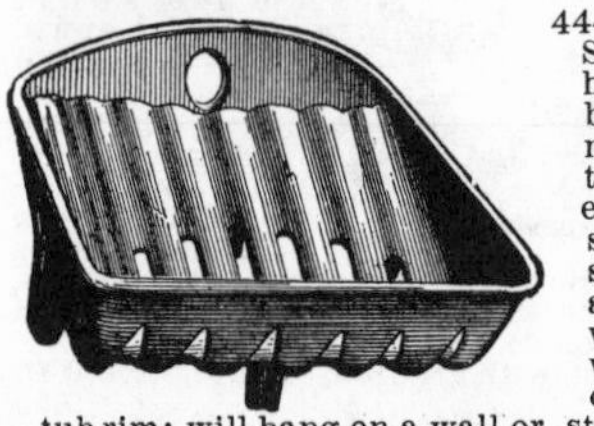

44400 Galvanized Soap Dish, 6 in. long. holds a one-pound bar of soap. By its novel construction the air circulates entirely around the soap, keeping the soap dry and firm and preventing waste. This cup will rest securely on a bucket or wash tub rim; will hang on a wall or stand on a table. It has more uses than any other soap dish. Each..$0.09
Per dozen.. 1.08

Iron Tea Kettles.

44410 Iron Tea Kettles, wood handle. Each.
No. 7, weight, 8 lbs....$0.28
No. 8, weight, 9 lbs.... .36
No. 9, weight, 11 lbs.. .41

Schofield's Patent Cake Griddle.

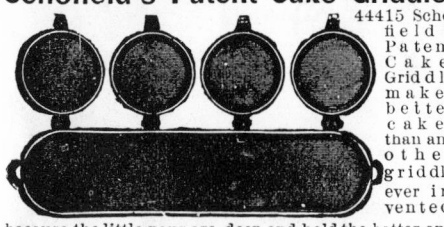

44415 Schofield's Patent Cake, Griddle makes better cakes than any other griddle ever invented, because the little pans are deep and hold the batter and prevent it spreading out, getting thin and drying out. The round pans being hinged are filled first; each cake can be turned into a large pan as soon as it is sufficiently done; the round pan is returned for another cake; in this way it bakes more cakes in less time than any cake griddle sold. Small size will bake six cakes per minute. Each.$0.50
Per dozen.. 5.40
Large size will bake eight cakes per minute. Each .65
Per dozen. 7.00

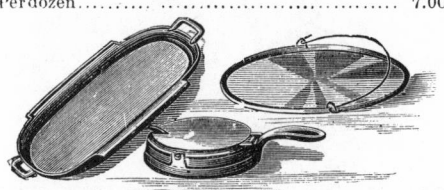

44417 Large Round Cake Griddle, ground and bailed, No 14............$0.30
No. 16. .40
44418 Sad Iron Heaters, deep pattern.
No. 7. .25
No. 8. .29
No. 9. .36
44420 Waffle Irons, new pattern, Nos. 8 to 9. Weight, each, 8 lbs. .70

Waffle Iron.

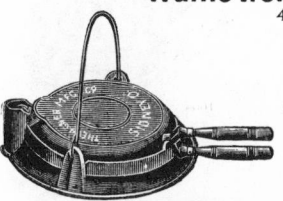

44421 It is the most simple in construction, the most convenient to handle and the easiest to clean; can be used on any size stove; also on gas or gasoline stoves.
Price, each.. $0.67

Frying Pans.

44430—

BLACK IRON	Each.	Per doz.
8 inch	$0.11	$1.19
9 inch	.12	1.24
10 inch	.16	1.65
12 inch	19	2.20

44430

44431—Acme Frying Pans, polished, with patent handle.

Always cool.

Nos	3	4	5	6
Inches	9½	10	11	12
Price, each	$0.12	$0.14	$0.15	$0.17

44435 Potato or Cruller Friers, made of bright iron; weight, 4 to 7 lbs.
Sizes, inches—
9 10 12 14
Each—
$0.80 $1 05 $1.25 $1.42

Gem Pan.

44440 Iron Gem Pan, new pattern.
Each.
10 cups, shallow....... $0.16
Weight 3 lbs. 5 oz.

44441 Iron Gem Pans, deep. Weight, 5 pounds.
Price, each......$0.20

Gray Enameled Hollow Ware.

Gray enameled ware is superior to the common hollow ware for the reason that, being enameled on the inside, it will not rust and is easier cleaned.

Stove Pot.   Stove Kettle.
Nos. 7 8 9
44445 Gray Enameled Stove Pot.
Weight................ 7 lbs. 10¼ lbs. 11 lbs
Price, each...........$0.35 $0.42 $0.50
44446 Gray Enameled Stove Kettle.
Weight................ 6 lbs. 7½ lbs. 9 lbs.
Price, each............. $0.32 $0.35 $0.43

44449 Gray Enameled Round Cake Griddle, with bail. Diameter
10 12 14 in.
Each.. 45c. 50c. 60c.

Bake Oven.

44450 Bake Oven, deep pattern with bails and covers. These ovens are designed for camp use; can be set in center of wood fire without injury to contents; cover fits down snug, so that nothing can get inside. Each.
No. 0, 14 inch, weight 27 lbs....................$1.22
No. 1, 12 inch, weight, 14 lbs .... .95
No. 2, 11 inch, weight, 13 lbs .... .76
No. 3, 10 inch, weight, 11 lbs .... .70

Miner's Gold Pan.

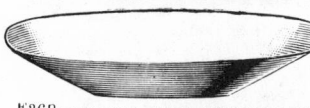

44500 Miners' Gold Pans. Polished iron, 15¼x 2½; weight, 2 pounds.
Each............................$0.30

Broilers.

44521 The American Broiler, with cover made of sheet iron. This broiler is superior to any in the market, as meat may be broiled in it without getting your stove covered with grease, as is the case with all others, and having a cover, the smoke and odor cannot escape into the room; weight, 2 lbs.; each.....$0.55 Per dozen.....$6.38

The Never-Break Wrought Steel Hollow Ware.

Each vessel stamped complete from one piece of steel, heavy retinned inside, will not break, rust or absorb grease and will last forever, being made of homogeneous cold rolled steel; they are much lighter than the clumsy cast goods, which fact alone, aside from their durability, makes them much more preferable. 
44525 Never-Break Wrought Steel Stove Kettle, flat bottom.
No.... 7 8 9
Diameter,... 8¾ 9¾ 10¾ in.
Weight, lbs.. 4¾ 5¼ 6½
Each, no cover,
$0.72. $0.80. $0.93

44526 Never-Break Wrought Steel Stove Kettles, with rounded bottom.
No. 7 8 9
Diameter.. 8¾ 9¾ 10¾ in.
Weight, each 4 lbs. 5¼ lbs. 5¾ lbs.
Each, no cover,
$0.73 $0.81 $0.94

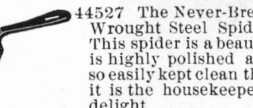

44527 The Never-Break Wrought Steel Spider. This spider is a beauty, is highly polished and so easily kept clean that it is the housekeeper's delight.
No. 8 9 10 12
Weight. lbs ... 2½ 3¼ 3½ 4 5
Each........... 25c. 30c. 35c. 45c. 50c

Hollow Ware—Continued.

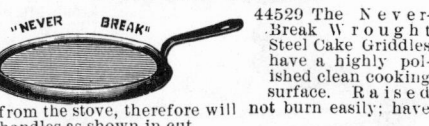

44529 The Never-Break Steel Cake Griddles have a highly polished clean cooking surface. Raised from the stove, therefore will not burn easily; have handles as shown in cut.
No........ 8 9 10
Cooking surface........... 8¾ 9¾ 10¾
Weight, each, lbs.......... 2½ 2¾ 3
Each.................... 25c. 30c. 35c. 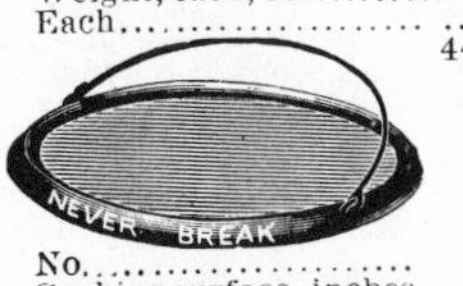
44530 The Never-Break Round Wrought Steel Cake Griddle with bail, has a highly polished clean cooking surface, with cooking surface raised from the stove.
No........ 12 14 16
Cooking surface, inches ... 11¾ 12¾ 13¾
Weight, each, lbs.......... 3½ 4¼ 4¾
Each.................... 40c. 45c. 55c.

Nickel-Plated Iron Tea Kettle.

44535 High grade and extra finish.
Price each.
No. 7 .... $0.98
No. 8............ 1.10
No. 9 .... 1.32

Nickel-Plated Spider.

44536 This spider is highly polished and then nickel plated, and the highest grade goods in the market. An article that will surely please.
No......... 7 8 9 10
Price each.. $0.35 $0.45 $0.50 $0.65

Nickel-Plated Scotch Bowl.

44537 It is highly polished inside and out, making it the handsomest ware in the market.
No......... 3 4 5
Size, inches. 10 11 12
Price, each. 70c. 80c. 90c.

TINWARE DEPARTMENT.

Strainer Pails, Tin.

For Dairy Supplies, see Index.

44575 Strainer Pails, pieced; will not hold as much as represented. Weight, 1½ and 1¾ pounds. 10 qt. each $0.25
14 qt., each............. .30

The Dairyman's Favorite.

44576 This cut represents an article having all the essential points of a perfect strainer pail. Among its points of excellence we mention the breast and front half of the pail being formed in one piece, making but two up and down seams in the body. It will be noted that the breast is tunnel-shaped and will not slop over in pouring. Besides the wire gauge strainer there is a brass spring clamping around the mouth to hold a cloth, thus making a double strainer without extra labor or loss of time. Another important feature is—there is no part but what can be thoroughly washed, and no rough and unsoldered seams in which dirt can accumulate and sour. Weight, 2¼ and 2¾ pounds.
12 quarts, per doz.... $5.40 Each............ ......$0.50
14 quarts, per doz .. 6.05 Each..... .... .56

AGRICULTURAL IMPLEMENTS ON THE NO AGENT BASIS.

Baking Dish.

44580 Baking Dishes, nickel plated, hard metal. A handsome article, with blue and white enamel pan for serving dishes direct from the oven; for scolloped oysters, meat pies, macaroni, beans, puddings, etc. The removal pan is protected by a hard metal band spun piece over the edge and nickel plated.

Size.	Actual capacity.	Price, each.
4 pints	2½ pints	$0.90
6 pints	3¼ pints	1.00
7 pints	4¼ pints	1.25

Chafing Dishes.

44581 Height, 9½ inches; weight, 4¼ pounds; can be used stewing, frying and making all kinds of fancy dishes. A book of fine recipes comes with each dish. It is nicely nickel plated, plated, 9¼-inch diameter, holds 3 pints, with hot water pan; has an asbestos lamp, which burns alcohol. Price, each...............$3.47

44582 For a cheap Chafing Dish, this will equal anything on the market. You can obtain the same results as from a higher priced dish. It has hot water pan, 9¼-inch diameter, nickel plated. Price, each............................$2.90

44583 Aluminum Chafing Dish, with water bowl. Price, each..$4.50

Tea Kettles.

44615 Flat Bottoms, retinned. Weight, from 1 to 1¾ lbs.

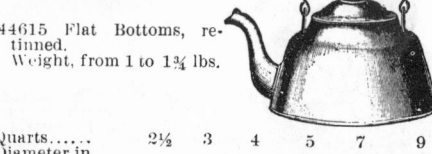

Quarts	2½	3	4	5	7	9
Diameter in in. of bottom	7¾	8¼	9	10	11	12
Each	30c	32c	40c	45c	54c	58c.

Tea Kettles.

Tin with copper bottom. Weight, from 1¼ to 2 pounds,
44621 Flat Bottom.
44621½ Pit Bottom.
No. 7. Each....$0.30
No. 8. " ..... .33
No. 9. " ... .36

Copper Rim Tea Kettles.

Tin, with copper bottom and rim. Weight, 1¾ to 2¼ pounds
44622 Flat Bottom.
44622½ Pit Bottom.
No. 7. Each....$0.48
No. 8. " .... .53
No. 9. " .... .60

All Copper.

44623 Flat Bottom. Weight, 2 to 3 lbs.
44623½ Pit Bottom.
No. 7. Each....$0.65
No. 8. " ... .74
No. 9. " .80

44623½-24½

All Copper, Nickel Plated.

44624 Flat Bottom.
44624½ Pit Bottom. Like above cut.
No. 7. Each. $0.80
No 8 " ...... .85
No 9 " ...... .90

Agate Iron Tea Kettles.

44625½ Pit Bottom.

For Stove No		7	8	9
Holds quarts		5	7	8
Price, each		$1.06	$1.23	$1.40

44626 Flat Bottom,

holds quarts	2	3	4	5	7	8	11
Price, each	$0.69	.85	.90	1.05	1.20	1.40	1.70

Range Kettle.

44630 All Copper Polished.
6½ inch diameter.
Price each.....$0.40
7½ inch diameter.
Price each.....$0.50
8½ inch diameter.
Price each... .$0.55
44631 All Copper Nickel Plated.
7½ inch diameter. Price, each................... .62
8½ inch diameter. Price, each ..... .68

Planished Tea Pots.

Will not hold as much as represented.

With Copper Bottom.
44635
3 pints..........$0.22
4 pints........... .25
5 pints........... .28
6 pints........... .32

Octagon Tea Pots

Tin Fluted Spouts and Britannia handles. Will not hold as much as represented.

Each.
44636 3 pints........$0.15
4 pints .... .18
5 pints............. .20
6 pints........... ... .22

Tea Steepers--Tin.

44639 1 quart.. Each.......$0.08

44639

44640 Agate Ironware Tea Steepers, with agate cover; holds 1½ pints. Size, 4⅜x3⅛. Each...$0.35

44640

Table Tea Kettles.

44641 The Table Tea Kettle has become as great a necessity as the Chafing Dish, and a most pleasant finale of a social evening at home is the serving of a cozy supper with the aid of these little utensils, and a most useful article in the sick room. A book of recipes is sent with each kettle. This very handsome tilting kettle and stand is made of highly polished brass, capacity, 2¾ pints, with new vapor lamp which burns alcohol. Price, each........$6.25

Table Tea Kettles—Continued.

44642 Kettle Stand and Lamp, is made of polished brass, but is not a tilting kettle. Capacity, 3 pints, with vapor lamp. Each...................... $4.50

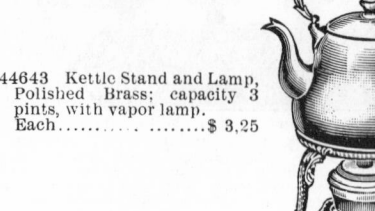

44643 Kettle Stand and Lamp, Polished Brass; capacity 3 pints, with vapor lamp. Each.......... ....$ 3.25

44644 Kettle Stand and Lamp, Polished Brass. Capacity, 3½ pints, with asbestos lamp. Each.............. $ 2.70

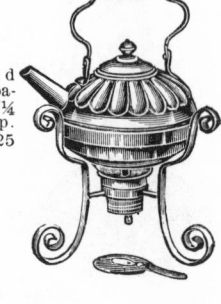

44645 Kettle Stand and Lamp, Polished Brass, capacity, 4½ pints; diameter 7¼ inches, with asbestos lamp. Each $2.25

44646 This Lamp has wrought iron stand, finished in antique iron, kettle and lamp polished brass, capacity, 2 pints, with asbestos lamp. Price, each.......... $2.00

New England Tea and Coffee Pot.

44650   44651

Nickel plated on polished copper. Something very handsome.
44650 Tea Pots, Nickel Plated.
3 pints, each.......$0.50 4 pints, each........$0.55
5 pints, price each .... .60
44651 Coffee Pots, Nickel Plated.
3 pints, each.......$0.50 4 pints, each........ .55
5 pints, price each................................. .60

Decorated Tea and Coffee Pots.

44655   44656

44655 Patent Decorated Pearl Agate Tea and Coffee Pots, white metal mountings and protection bands, white porcelain inside, decorated on the outside with leaves and flowers in their natural colors. These pots are very handsome and strong.

TEA POTS.	Each.	COFFEE POTS.	Each.
3 pints	$2.65	4 pints	$3.08
4 pints	2.88	5 pints	3.27
5 pints	3.08	6 pints	3.50

44656 Pearl Agate Tea Pots, porcelain lined, with patent enameled wood handle and hard metal nickel plated cover.

	Each.		Each.
3 pints	$1.25	5 pints	$1.45
4 pints	1.30		

44657 Pearl Agate Coffee Pots, porcelain lined, with patent enameled wood handles and hard metal nickel plated cover

4 pints	$1 25
5 pints	1.40
6 pints	1.50

44660 Elliott's Perfection Filter Coffee Pot. Two tablespoonfuls of pulverized coffee make five breakfast cups of perfect coffee, clear as amber; no eggs required. This coffee is made in one minute, either at the table or in the kitchen, as may be desired. Directions come with each pot. Has not a tip on spout as shown in cut.

| 1 quart, 5 cups | $0.35 | 3 quarts, 15 cups | $0.45 |
| 2 quarts, 10 cups | .40 | 4 quarts, 20 cups | .50 |

Planished Coffee Pots.

Copper Bottoms. Will not hold as much as represented.

		Each.
44662	3 pints	$0.23
	4 pints	.25
	5 pints	.28
	6 pints	.32

Solid Lip Coffee Pots.

TIN, WITH BAIL.

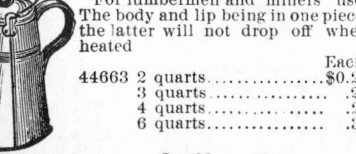
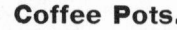

For lumbermen and miners' use. The body and lip being in one piece, the latter will not drop off when heated

		Each.
44663	2 quarts	$0.20
	3 quarts	.25
	4 quarts	.28
	6 quarts	.35

Coffee Pots.

Manufacturers' measure. They will not hold as much as represented. All tin.

		Each.
44665	2 quarts	$0.10
	3 quarts	.12
	4 quarts	.15
	5 quarts	.18

44666 Tin Coffee Pots, same style as 44665, but has copper bottoms.

	Each.		Each.
2 quarts	$0.20	4 quarts	$0.25
3 quarts	.22	5 quarts	.30

Coffee Pots—Continued.

44668 COPPER BOTTOM AND RIM.

Quarts	3	4	5
Price each	33c	35c	38c

Agate Iron Coffee Pots.

44670 Agate Iron Lipped Coffee Pots, black enameled handles, retinned covers.

Quarts	2	3	4	5
Price each	$0.40	$0.65	$0.75	$0 85

Agate Iron Tea Pots.

44671 Agate Iron Tea Pots black enameled handles retinned covers, curved spouts.

Quarts	1½	2
Price, each	$0.37	$0.42
Quarts	3	4
Price, each	$0.63	$0.73

Agate Iron Coffee Boilers.

With bail and agate iron cover.
44672   Flat bottom.
44672½   Pit bottom.

No.	7	8	9
Quarts	6	8½	11
Each	$1.00	$1.16	$1.37

Coffee Boilers.

Pit Bottom.

44675 Tin. I C.

	Each.
Size 7	$0.35
Size 8	.40
Size 9	.48

Camp Coffee Boilers.

Copper Bottom IXX Tin
44676 Same as 44675 but has flat bottom. Price each

Gallons 3	11 inches.	$0.84
" 4	11½ "	.92
" 5	13 "	1.08
" 6	13½ "	1.35

Tea or Coffee Strainers.

44680

44680 Tea or Coffee Strainers; with wood handle.

Each, small	$0.08
Medium	.10
Large	.12

44681 Tea or Coffee Strainers, patent (like illustration in lower right hand corner of cut); each $0.05

44681

CAMPERS.—We can fit you out completely look over our sporting goods department.

Aluminum Cooking Utensils.

CLEAN, EVERLASTING, LIGHT.

Aluminum is a beautiful white metal similar in appearance to sterling silver, as strong as steel and will never tarnish or change color. The heat-conducting power of aluminum is about double that of wrought iron and of tin. The cooking utensils made from aluminum are highly recommended by many prominent people who have used them, as fruits or other food can be cooked in these vessels without danger of their burning or sticking to the vessel. All aluminum cooking utensils bought from us are guaranteed to be as represented, and we have not the slightest hesitation in stating that aluminum provides us with cooking utensils which are practically everlasting. Aluminum has a few enemies which are met with in cooking and we believe it is well to mention them. Caustic alkalies consume aluminum rapidly. Muriatic acid acts slowly upon it but pure sulphuric or nitric acid does not affect it, except the nitric acid be at high temperature. We are certain that a fair trial will convince any one that aluminum has come to supplant the use of heavy and poisonous copper in the kitchen.

Aluminum Sauce Pan.

Milk or food will not scorch or stick to the pan.
44683 Made of pure aluminum, always bright like silver; no scouring required.

Quarts	1	2	3	4	5
Price each	32c	65c	90c	$1.10	$1.25

Aluminum Fruit Kettle.

44685 Made of pure aluminum with lip handle and bail. No cracking, flecking like agate ware; will not rust or corrode.

Price	3 quarts	$0.82
Price	4 quarts	1.00
Price	5 quarts	1.20
Price	6 quarts	1.37
Price	7 quarts	1.50
Price	8 quarts	1.70

Aluminum Fry Pan.

The great advantage of the Aluminum Fry Pan lies in the fact that food in cooking does not adhere to the bottom or side of the vessel.

44686—7-inch, price, each	$0.58
7½-inch, price, each	.67
9-inch, price, each	1.08
10-inch, price, each	1.20

Aluminum Milk or Baking Pan.

44688 Made of pure aluminum, always bright and clean.

Price, 7½ in. dia., each	$0.50
Price, 8½ in. dia., each	.60
Price, 9½ in. dia., each	.70
Price, 10 in. dia., each	.92
Price, 10½ in. dia., each	1.15

Aluminum Wash Basin.

44690 Pure aluminum, always bright.

10½ in., price, each, 40c
11½ in., price, each, 65c
13 in., price, each, 75c

Aluminum Dippers.

44691 Aluminum dippers, always bright and clean; will not rust. Tinned iron handles.

Price, each, 1 pt	22c.
Price, each, 2 qt	30c.
Price, each, 2 qt	60c.

Aluminum Dippers will not hold as much as represented; manufacturers' measure.

Aluminum Drinking Cups.

WITH HANDLE.

	1	2
Pints.		
Each.	$0.25	$0.38

44693.

Child's Drinking Cup.

MADE FROM PURE ALUMINUM.

One half pint, each $0.23

44695.

Aluminum Lemonade Shaker.

44696

6 inch, each.....................$0.60

44696.

Aluminum Tea or Coffee Cup and Saucer.

44697

Price for 1 Cup and Saucer...$0.65
Price for 12 Cups and 12
Saucers.....................$7.00

44697.

Aluminum Soup Ladle.

44699   Price, each..$0.33

44699

Aluminum Funnels.

44700 Size, ½ pint, each.$0.48
1 Pint, each............ .50

With Strainer.

44701 Size, ½ pint, each.$0.60
1 Pint, each............ .65

Aluminum Fruit Jar Fillers.

44702   Size, 5x4¼ inch.
Each.....................$0.75

Aluminum Dinner Plates.

44703
Size, 8 inches. Each...$0.60
Per doz............. 6.70
Size, 9 inches. Each.... .65
Per doz............., 7.20

44703

Aluminum Braising Pan and Cover.

Spun from one piece of metal.

44705 Size, 12 inches in diameter, 3½ inches deep.
Each.....................$ 0.45

Aluminum Hotel Pans.

Spun from one piece of metal.

44707 Size, 16x12 inches. Each .... $ 11.45
Size, 9¾x9½ inches. Each.................. 5.33
Size, 8½x8½ inches. Each.................. 4.40
Lids with long handles, for hotel pan, Each... .72

Aluminum Stock Pots.

44709—
Size, 16x12. Each..$ 12.20
Size, 9¾x6½.. Each.. 5.96
Size, 8¾x8¾. Each.. 4.98

Aluminum Gold Miners' Pan.

44711—
Size, 12x2¾ inches.
Each ....$ 1.32
Per dozen.............14.87

Aluminum Cuspidors.

44712--
Size, 7x3 inches. Each.$ 1.20
Per doz..................13.56

44712

Aluminum Spun Tea Pots.

(Seamless.)

44713

Size, pints........	2	3	4	5	6
Price, each....	$ 1.85	1.95	2.05	2.15	2.28

Aluminum Tea Steepers.

44716 Only one size made.
1 quart, with cover. Price,
each.....................$0.65

44716

Aluminum Coffee Boilers.

(Seamless.)

44718
Size, 6½ quarts. Each..$ 3.69

44718

Aluminum Milk or Rice Cookers.

44720

Quarts, inside pot.. ..	1	2	3	4
Price, each.............	$ 1.70	2.05	2.83	3.70

Aluminum Water Pails.

44721 Spun from one piece
of metal.

Size, in...9½x6¾.	10½x7¾.
Quarts... 8	10
Each.... $2.56	$2.82

44721

Cast Aluminum Tea Kettles.

44722—		
No. Quarts.		Each.
7	6	$3.40
8	7	3.69
9	8	3.85

44722

Spun Aluminum Tea Pots.

(Seamless.)

44723—

Pints.	3	4	5
Each	.$1.60	$1.88	$2.00

Aluminum Coffee Pots.

44724 Aluminum Coffee Pots,
with wood handles.
3 Pints, price, each......$1.50
4 Pints, price, each...... 1.63
5 Pints, price, each...... 1.75
6 Pints, price, each 1.80
8 Pints, price, each 2.00

Aluminum Afternoon Tea Kettle

44727—
Each........$7.45

Aluminum Camping Outfit for Six Persons.

44728 Each piece spun from a single piece of
metal without seams; no solder used. *Will
never rust.* Outfit consists of outside pan, with
cover and handle, 10½ diameter, 7¼-inch deep;
second pan, 10¼ diameter, 7-inch deep; third
pan, 10 diameter, 6¾-inch deep; fourth pan, 9¾
diameter, 6½-inch deep. 1 coffee pot, 2 fry
pans, 6 cups, 6 plates. All the above are aluminum goods and weigh 12 pounds. 6 knives,
6 forks, 6 spoons, 1 pepper and salt are of usual
material, *not* aluminum.
Total weight of outfit, 13½ pounds,
Price, complete...... ....$26.56

Aluminum Is The Coming Metal,
TIN WILL BE DISPLACED.

Aluminum has merits which tin has not, and also all the merits of tin.

Camping Outfit.

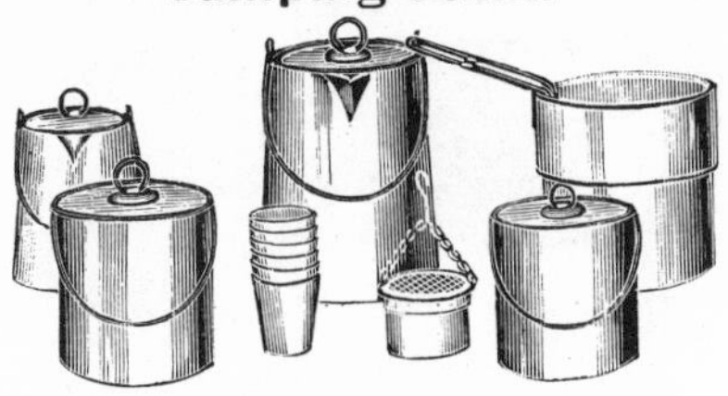

44729 The whole outfit is carried in two parts, viz.: In the coffee boiler and the stew-pot.
Weight, 6 pounds.
The outfit consists of 1 coffee boiler, 6 quarts, with strainer attached to cover by chain; strainer will steep half pound of coffee at once, has strong carrying bail. 1 stew pot, 5 quarts, with cover and strong carrying bail; 1 vegetable cooker, 3 quarts. *Cooks on top of stew pan* and nests in coffee boiler; 1 soup or fruit pan, 3 quarts, nests in stew pot; 1 soup or fruit pan, 2 quarts, nests in soup pan; 6 cups nested carried in coffee boiler. Each piece spun from a single piece of metal without seams, no solder used. *Will never rust.* They are always pure, healthful and clean, and will last a lifetime.
Price for outfit, complete, as above............$17.00

Galvanized Iron Ware.

Galvanized iron ware is growing more in popular favor every day. It is more durable than tin ware and not so expensive as granite or agate ware, and is just as strong. As it is galvanized after it is made it will not leak or rust.

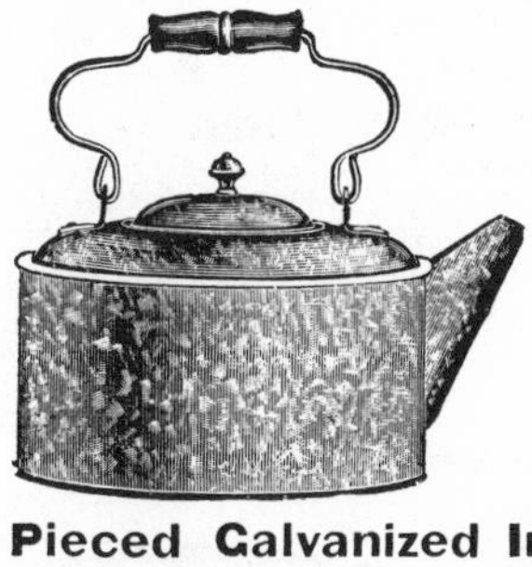

44730 Galvanized Iron Tea Kettle. Flat bottom only.

No.	Weight.	Each.
7	1¼ lbs.	$0.33
8	2¼ lbs.	.39
9	2¾ lbs.	.44

Pieced Galvanized Iron Dippers.

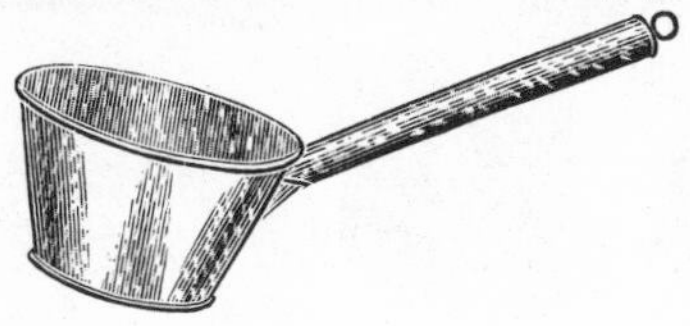

44735—	Each.
1 quart	$0.08
2 quarts	.10
3 quarts	.15

Galvanized Iron Wash Bowls.

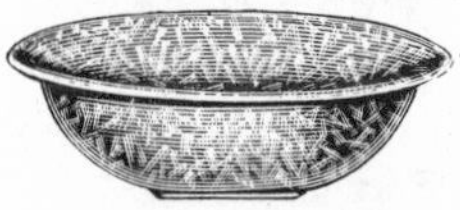

44740 Galvanized Iron Wash Bowl.
10 inches...........$0.05
10½ inches......... .08

Galvanized Iron Measures.

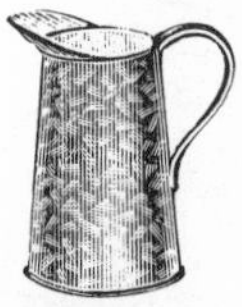

44742 Galvanized Iron Measures.
Pint..............................$0.12
Quart.............................. .15
Gallon.............................. .23

Galvanized Iron Water Pails.

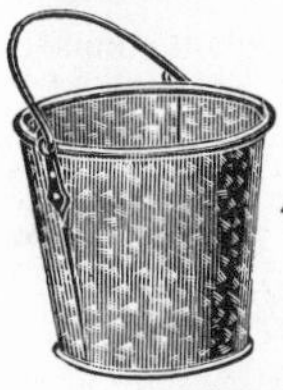

44745—

	Each.
12-quart	$0.25
14-quart	.30

Refrigerator Pans.

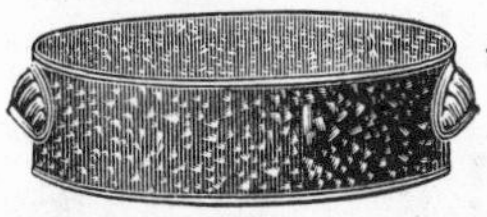

44746 Made of Galvanized Iron, and especially adapted for placing under the refrigerator to catch the water from the melting ice.

Diameter, inches	12	14	16
Depth, inches	5	15	5
Price, each	21c.	26c.	35c.

Perfection Cake and Pie Tins.

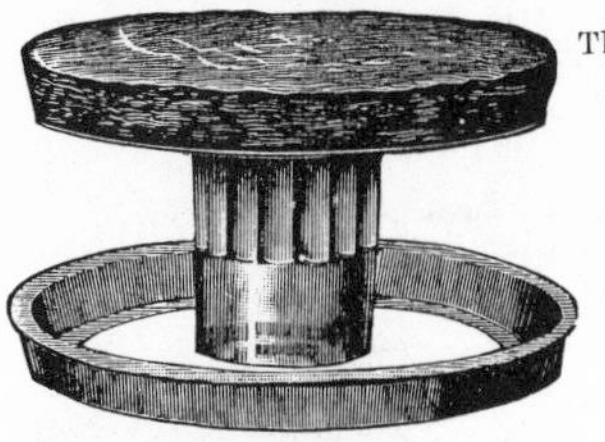

The side cut shows the method of removing the cake from a "Perfection" Tin by placing the tin upon a tumbler or bowl, the removable bottom supporting the cake while the rim drops to the table.

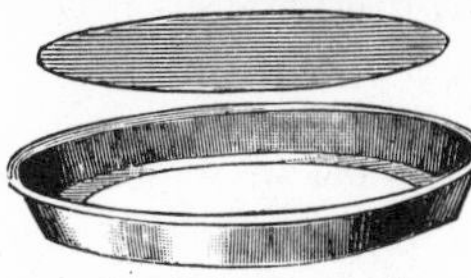

44750 "Perfection" Tins for pies and layer cakes.

	Price, each.	Per doz
7½x1 inch deep, round	$0.08	$0.80
9 x1 inch deep, round	.10	1.00
10 x1 inch deep, round	.12	1.25

No more broken cakes or pies.

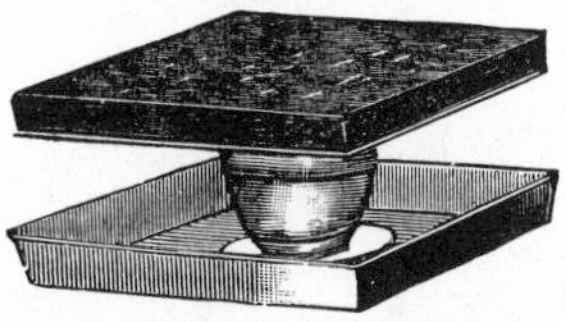

44755 "Perfection" Tins for layer cake.

	Price, each.	Per doz.
8 inches square, 1½ inches deep	$0.15	$1.68
8 inches square, 2½ inches deep	.20	1.94

No more paper to grease for tins.

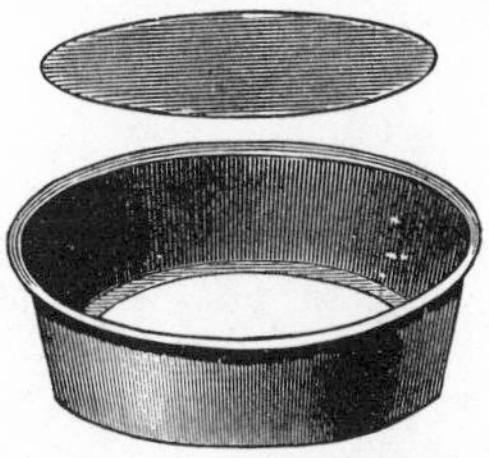

44756 "Perfection" Cake Tins, for pound, fruit and cup cakes. 9⅛x2⅞ in., round.
Price.............$0.20
Per doz............ 1.94

Perfection Tin for Bread and Loaf Cake.

It is just the thing for pressing meat into bars convenient for slicing.

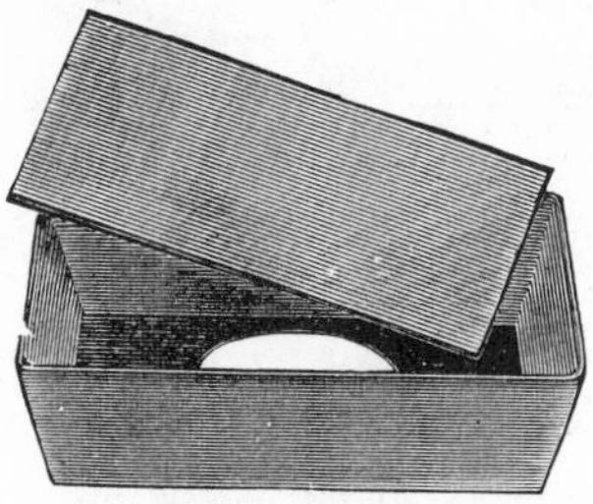

44757 Width.	Length.	Depth.	Each.	Per dozen.
5	9	2⅝	$0.15	$1.60
6	10	2⅝	.20	1.87

The cake is never baked too hard on the bottom.
The Perfection Tins are surely a **Good Thing.**

For Loaf or Angel Cake.

WITH TUBE.

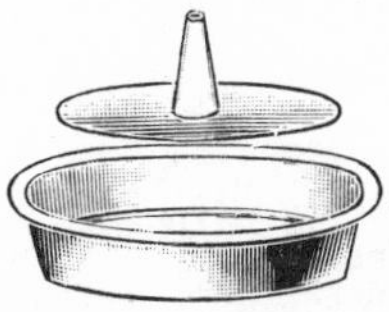

44758	Each.	Per doz.
8½x2⅞ in. deep.	$0.15	$1.60
9½x2⅞ in. deep.	.20	1.87

AGATE IRON WARE.

Known as Granite and Agate Ware. We are now prepared to offer this justly celebrated kitchen ware at unheard-of prices. It is guaranteed to be absolutely pure and safe to use and is the most durable ware in the world. It is especially desirable, as it is so easily cleaned. Quotations will be found scattered through the following pages.

Agate Iron Water Pails

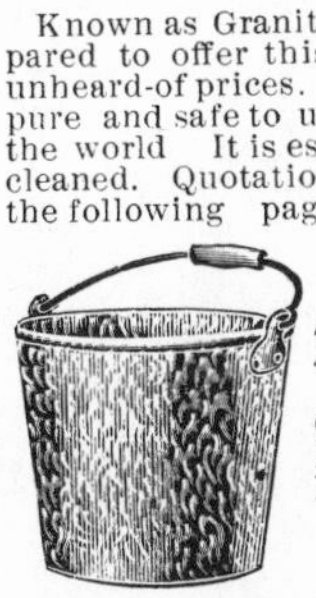

44760 Agate Iron Straight Water Pails, flat bottom.

Quarts.	8	10	12	15	20
Price— Each	$0.60	.70	.78	.90	1.05

Agate Iron Ware—Continued.

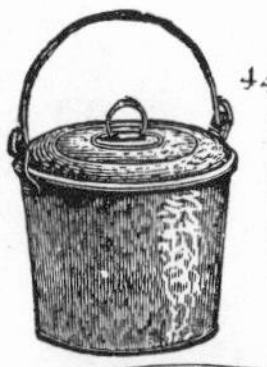

44761 Agate Iron Straight Seamed Covered Buckets, with retinned covers. Will not hold as much as represented.

Quarts	½	1	2	3	4
Price, each..	13c	21c	25c	30c	40c
Quarts		6	8	10	12
Price each..		47c	58c	70c	77

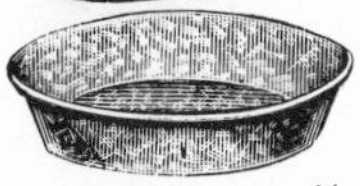

44765 Agate Iron Straight Milk pans. We sell any quantity at dozen rates. Will not hold as much as represented.

Quarts..	¼	½	1	1½	2	3	4
Per doz..	$1.00	1.32	1.65	1.98	2.31	2.64	3.30
Quarts..	5	6	8	10	12		
Per dozen..	$3.63	3.96	4.30	4.62	5.28		

Agate Iron Sauce Pans.

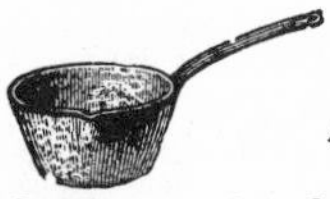

44775 Will not hold as much as represented.

Quarts......	1	2	3	4	5	6	7½	10
Price........	17c	22c	33c	39c	45c	50c	60c	70

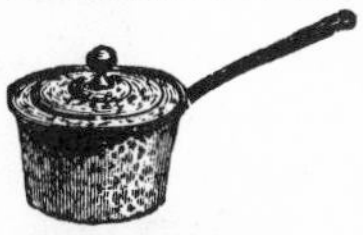

44776 Agate Iron Covered Windsor Sauce Pans with tin covers. Will not hold as much as represented

Quarts.........	1	2	3½	4½	5½	6½
Price each.....	25c	36c	47c	52c	58c	66c

Tubed Cake Pans.

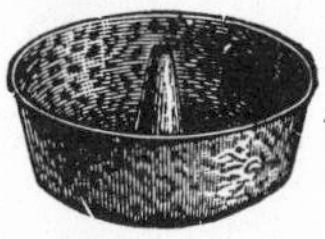

44780 Agate Iron, Extra Deep Tubed Cake Pans.

Quarts.	2	3	4	5	6
Size.	8½x3	8¾x3¼	9¾x3⅜	10½x3½	11¼x3¾
Price each,	27c	30c	36c	42c	48c

Pudding Pan, Extra Deep.

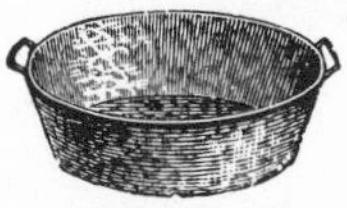

44781 Agate Iron Pudding Pans, flat edge, without handle. Will not hold quite as much as represented.

Quarts	1	2	3	4	5	6
Size..	7⅛x2½	8⅝x3	9⅜x3¼	10¼x3⅝	11x3½	11⅞x3⅝
Price.	17c	22c	25c	28c	31c	36c

44785 Agate Ironware Bake Pans Seamless.

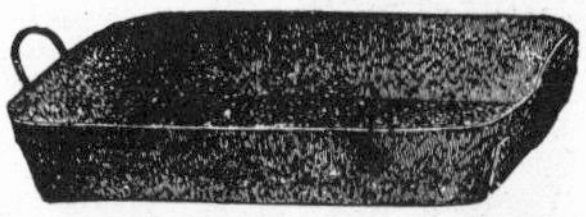

Size..	13x9x2½	14x9½x2½	15x10½x2½	16x11x2½
Price each	40c	45c	50c	55c

Agate Fry Pans.

44787 Agate Lipped Fry Pans, with patent handle.

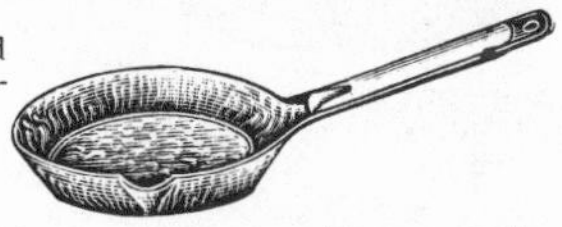

Diameter at top	9 in.	9½ in.	10 in.	11 in
Price each	33c	35c	42c	45c.

Dish Pan.

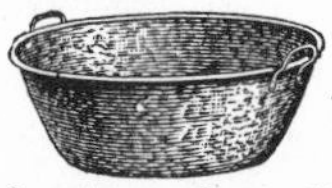

44790 Agate iron improved deep dish pan.

Quarts	8	10	14	17	21	30
Size	14¼x4¾	14½x5	15¾x5½	17¾x5¾	19½x6	21x7
Price each	60c	69c	83c	96c	$1.10	$1.65

Pie Plates.

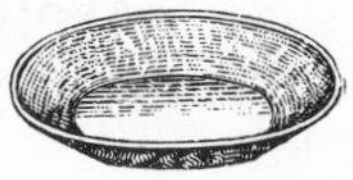

44791 Agate iron pie plates. We sell any quantity at the dozen price.

Size	7x⅝	8x⅝	9x⅞	10x1	11x1
Per dozen.	$1.15	$1.32	$1.50	$1.81	$2.15

Dinner Plates.

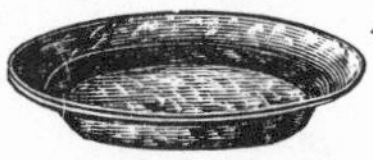

44792 Agate iron dinner plates, round bottom.
Size ....9x1 in
Price, per doz $5.28

Jelly Cake Pans.

44793 Agate Iron.

No.	9	10
Size	9x½	10x½
Per doz	$1.48	$1.81

We sell any quantity at dozen price.

Lipped Preserving Kettles.

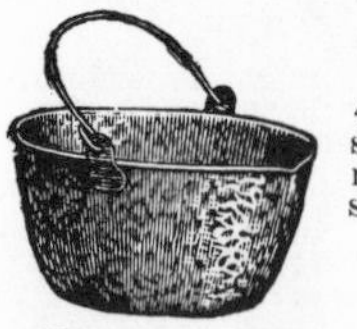

44795 Agate Iron Lipped Perserving Kettles, with bail. Will not hold quite as much as represented.

Size	7x3½	8¼x3¾	9½x4	9¾x4½	10¾x5
Quarts	2	3	4	5	6
Price, each	22c	33c	39c	45c	50c
Size	11¼x5½	12x5½	13x5¾		
Quarts	8	10	12		
Price each	58c	70c	$0.83		

Agate Iron Soup Stock Pot.

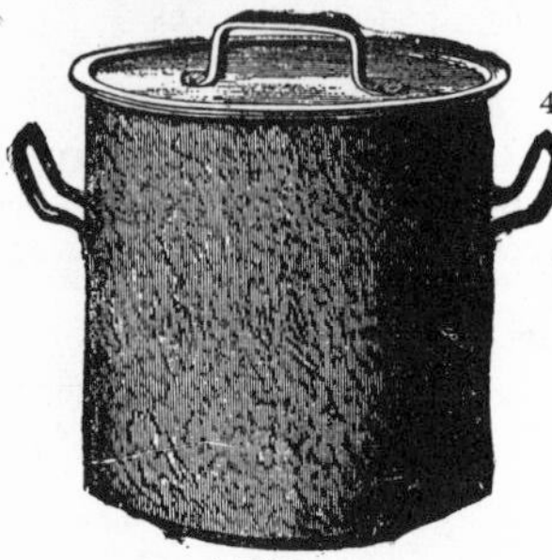

44796

44796 With agate cover. These stock pots are used in hotels and restaurants for the keeping of soup stock and are also used for boiling hams.

Gallons	3	6	9
Inches	10½x10¼	13x14¾	15x14
Each	$2.09	2.85	3.57

Agate Iron Rice Boiler

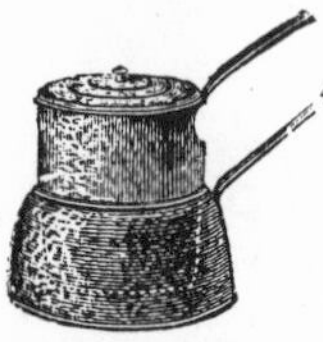

44797 Agate Iron Seamless Milk or Rice Boiler, with tin cover which fits both vessels. Will not hold quiet as much as represented

Inside boiler holds	1qt	2qt	3qt
Price, each	$0.55	$1.00	$1.60

Climax Cooking Pots.

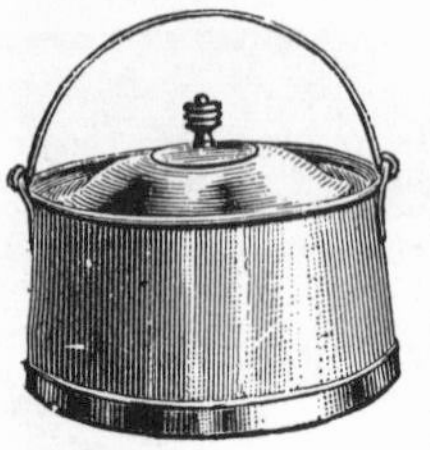

44798 Something new. Agate Enameled Ironware Covered Seamless Climax Cook Pots. These pots have a second bottom of copper, arranged so as to form an air chamber, which prevents the burning of or scorching of milk or any kind of delicate food, and also affords protection to the portion of the vessel that gets the most wear, besides adds to its attractiveness. Will not hold quiet as much as represented.

Quarts	2	3	5	7
Size	6¾x4	8x4½	9x5	9⅝x6
Each	58c	70c	.80	.90

Water Pitchers.

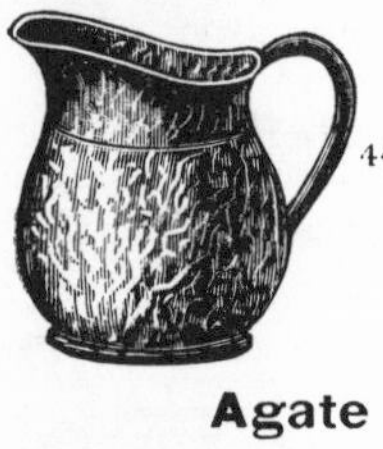

44799 Agate Iron Water Pitchers.

Pints	2	3	4	5
Price, each	50c	60c	66c	75c

Agate Iron Dipper.

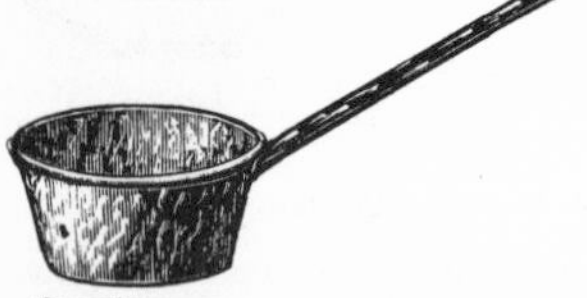

44800 Agate Iron Dippers, the most durable made. Will not hold as much as represented.

Quarts	1	2
Price, each	$0.30	$0.38

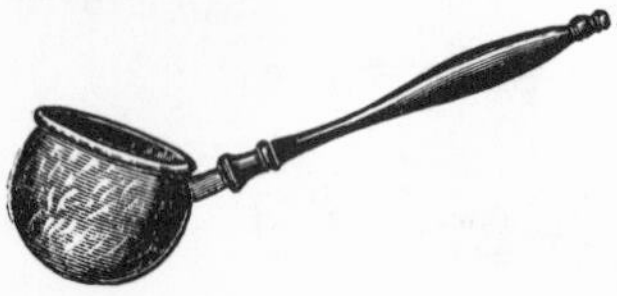

44801 Agate Iron Ware Cocoa-shaped Dipper, black enameled wood handle. Size, 1 pint. Price, each $0.30

Agate Iron Milk Skimmers.

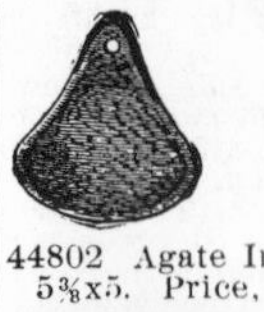

44802 Agate Ironware Milk Skimmers, pierced, 5⅜x5. Price, each $0.10

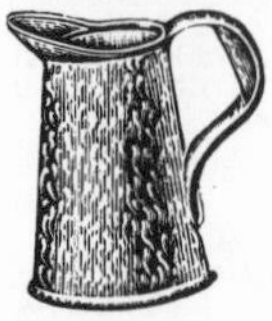

44805 Agate Iron Measures.

Size	½pt.	1 pt.	1qt.	2 qt.	4qt.
Price, each	22c.	31c.	36c.	45c.	66c.

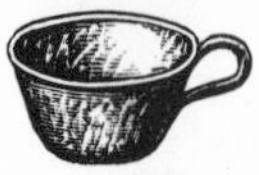

44808 Agate Iron Straight Drinking Cup.

No.	14	16	18
Size	3½x2¼	4¼2⅝	5¼x2½
Price, ea.	10c.	13c.	17c.

Agate Cups and Saucers.

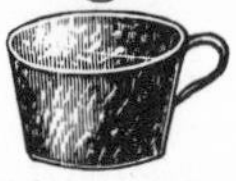

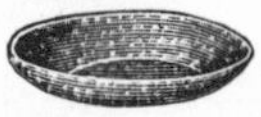

44809 Agate Cups. Size, 4½x3. Price, each $0.14
Price, per dozen 1.50
44809½ Agate Saucers to match 44809 cups. Size 6¾x1 inch. Price, each .... .13
Price, per dozen 1.35

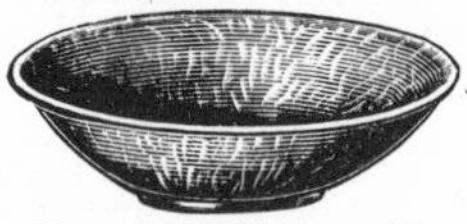

44810 Agate Iron Wash Basins, with rings.

No.	26	28	30	32
Size	10⅜x2¾	11⅜x2⅞	12¼x3⅛	13x3⅜
Price, each	25c.	28c.	33c.	38c.

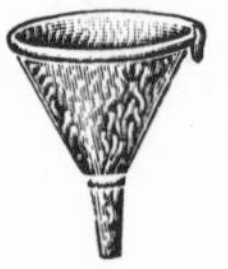

44811 Agate Iron Funnels

No.	02	03	04	05	06
Capacity	½ pt.	1 pt.	1 qt.	2 qt.	4 qt.
Each	17c.	20c.	25c.	33c	50c

Seamless or Stamped Ware. Water Pails.

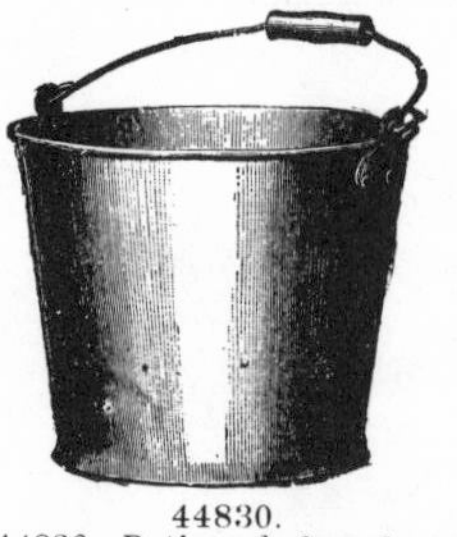

44830.

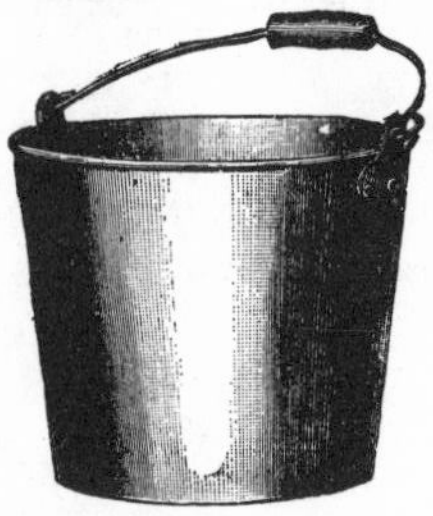

44831.

44830 Retinned Seamless Flaring Water Pail, made of heavy tin with patent seamless foot.

Quarts	6	8	10
Each	40c.	50c.	59c.
Quarts	12	15	20
Each	68c.	75c	95c.

44831 Retinned Seamless Water Buckets, flat bottom, made of heavy tin.

Quarts		8	10
Each		52c.	62c.
Quarts	12	15	20
Each	70c.	80c.	95c.

Retinned.

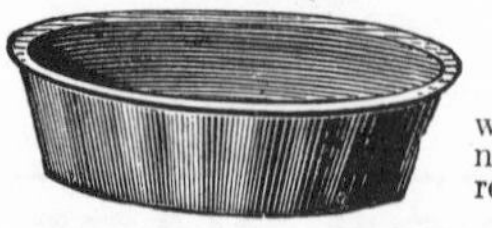

Dairy pans, stamped ware, flat edge. They will not hold as much as represented.

44835—

Quarts.	Inches.	Weight, per doz.	Price, per doz.
¼	5¼x1⅜	1 lb. 10 oz.	$0.29
½	6x1⅜	2 lbs. 2 oz.	.34
1	7x1⅝	2 lbs. 14 oz.	.42
1½	7½x1¾	3 lbs.	.48
2	8½x2	3 lbs. 6 oz.	.52
3	9¼x2¼	4 lbs. 10 oz.	.74
4	10⅝x2½	6 lbs. 3 oz.	.81
6	12⅝x2¾	7 lbs. 11 oz.	1.04
8	13¼x2⅞	8 lbs. 12 oz	1.18
10	14¼x3	9 lbs 8 oz.	1 38
12	15x3⅛	11 lbs. 9 oz.	1.56

Dairy Pans, holding, 8, 10 and 12 quarts, are made of heavier tin than the smaller sizes.

Round Pudding Pans.—I. C. Tin.

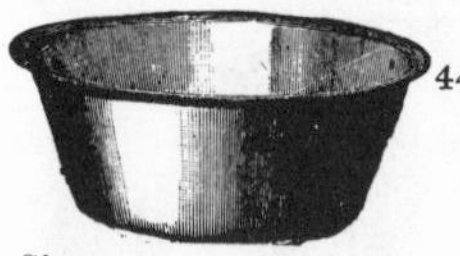

44838 Extra deep. Plain. Manufacturer's measure will not hold quite as much as represented.

Size.	Each.	Per doz.
1 quart	$0.04	$0.36
2 quarts	.05	.48
3 quarts	.07	.65
4 quarts	08	.75
5 quarts	.09	.86

Muffin Pans.

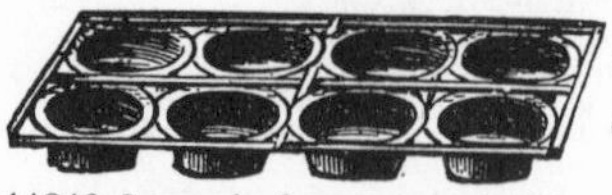

Stamped Ware, shallow.

	Per dozen.	Per frame.
44840 8 cups in frame, cups 3x1 in.	$0 12	$1.25
12 cups in frame, cups 3x1 in.	.18	1.90
44841 Muffin Pans; deep; stamped ware. Same style as 44840.		
8 cups in frame, cups 3x1¼ in.	.20	2.00
12 cups in frame, cups 3x1¼ in.	.22	2.52

Turk's Head Pans.

Plain on frame.

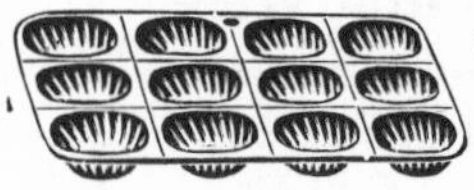

44842 Turk's Head Pans, plain stamped ware.

8 heads on frame, size, 3¼x1½ inch. Each.... $0.17
12 " " " 3¼x1½ " " ..... .25

Lady-Finger Pans.

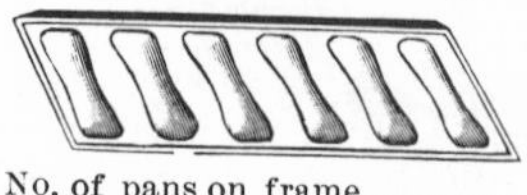

44843 Lady-Finger Pans, plain, stamped seamless.

No. of pans on frame	6	6
Inches	11¾x4⅜	12x6
Each	$0.06	$0.07
Per dozen	.65	.75

Hotel Sauce Pans.

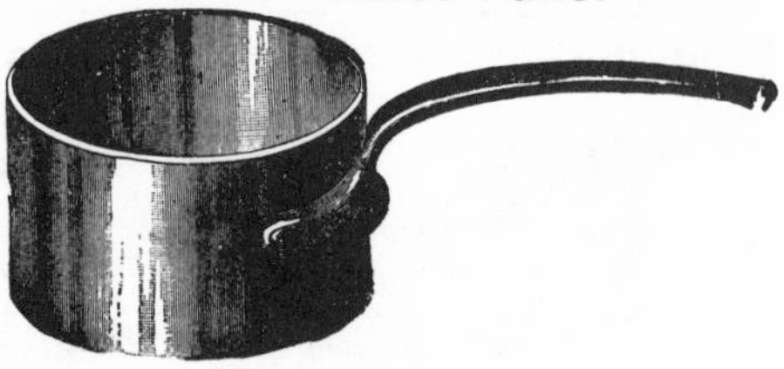

44844 Made of wrought steel. extra heavy, retinned with long handle.

Quarts	6½	10	16½	20
Inches	9¾x5½	11⅜x6	13¼x7⅛	14x8
Each	$1.38	$1.75	$2.19	$3.00

Hotel Sauce Pan Cover.

44844½ To fit pans No. 44844, with same length of handle as on the pans.

Size	6½	10	16½	20
Each	$0.33	.47	.60	.73

Sauce Pan—Tin Lipped.

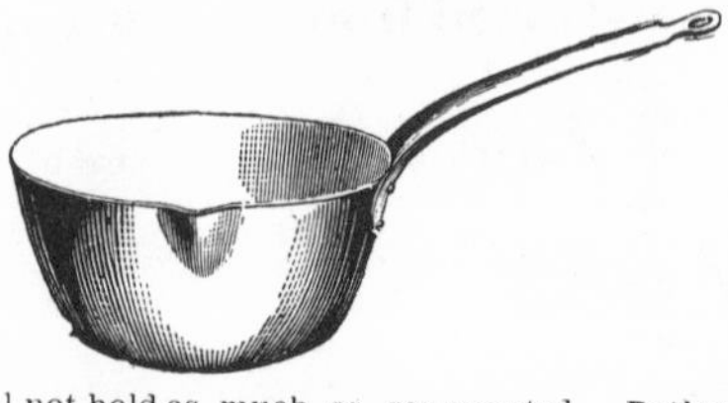

Will not hold as much as represented. Retinned stamp ware.

	Each	Per doz
44845 1 quart	$0.06	$0.60
2 quarts	.09	.80
3 quarts	.10	1.08
4 quarts	.12	1.30
5 quarts	.14	1.50
6 quarts	.16	1.73

Egg Fry Pans.

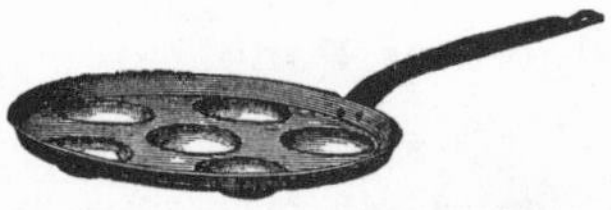

44848 Egg Fry Pans, retinned

Each
For 4 Eggs. $0.20
For 6 Eggs .25

Colored Novelties in Summer Wash Goods.

A beautiful line shown in our White Goods Department.

Send for Samples.

Buffalo Steam Egg Poachers.

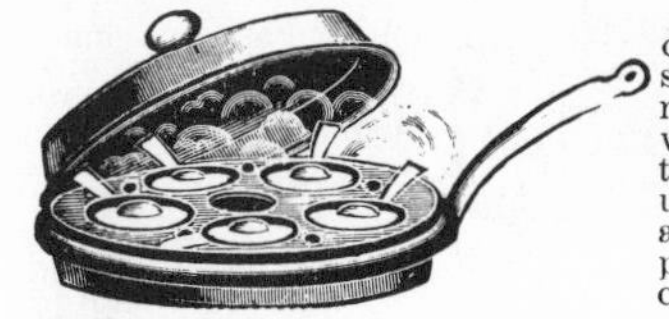

The eggs are cooked by steam in two minutes, and when ready for the table are of uniform shape and inviting appearance. Only one size made.

44850 Retinned. for 5 eggs. Price, each..........$0.53

Patty Pans.

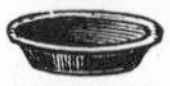
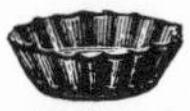

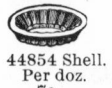

44852 Plain. Per doz.		44853 Washington Scalloped. Per doz.	
3 inches	$0.05	3 inches	$0.07
4 inches	.08	4 inches	.10

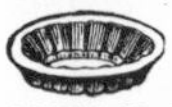
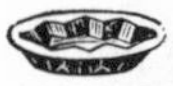
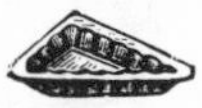

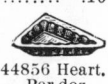

44854 Shell. Per doz. 7c. 44855 Star. Per doz. 7c. 44856 Heart. Per doz. 7c.

Windsor Sauce Pans.

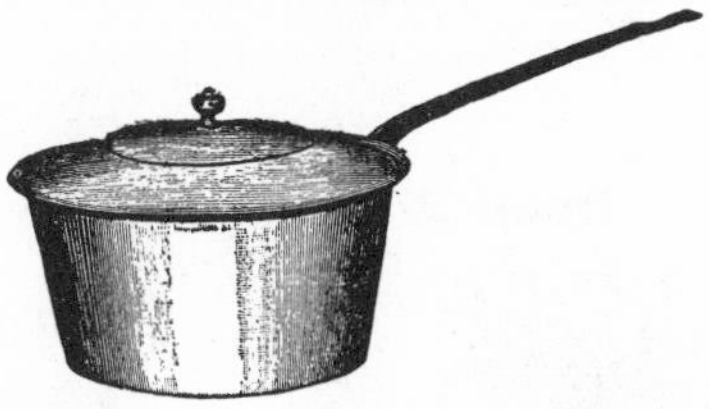

Flaring, with cover. Retinned. Will not hold quite as much as represented.

	Each.
44860 2 pints	$0.16
3 pints	.18
4 pints	.25
5 pints	.28

Retinned Octagon Cake Molds.

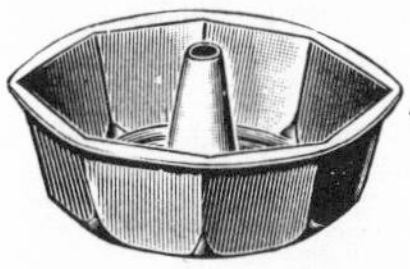

44861 Octagon Cake Molds, retinned.

		Each.	Per doz.
2 quarts,	8¼x2⅞ inches	12c	$1.15
3 "	8½x3¼ "	13c	1.25
4 "	9¼x3½ "	15c	1.45

Tubed Cake Pans—Retinned.

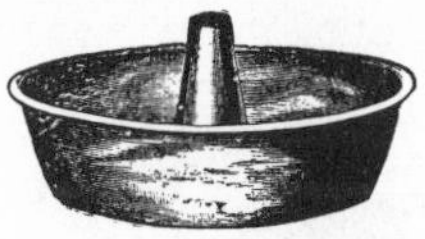

44862—Size.	44862 Each.	Per doz.
9¼x2¼	$0.07	$0.80
11 x2⅝	.09	1.00
11⅝x2⅝	.11	1.25
8¾x3¼	.10	1.10

Tubed Cake Pans—Scalloped.

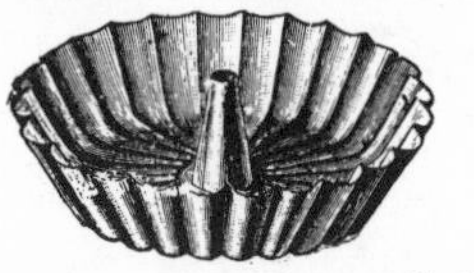

	Each.	Per doz.
44863 Size 8 inches	$0.04	$0.40
Size 10 inches	.07	.78

Scalloped Cake Pans.

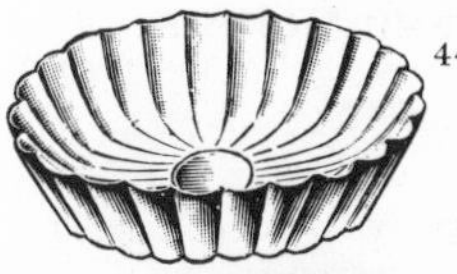

44864 Scalloped Cake Pans plain.

	Each.	Per doz.
8 inch	3c	.32
10 "	4c	.43

Bread Raisers.

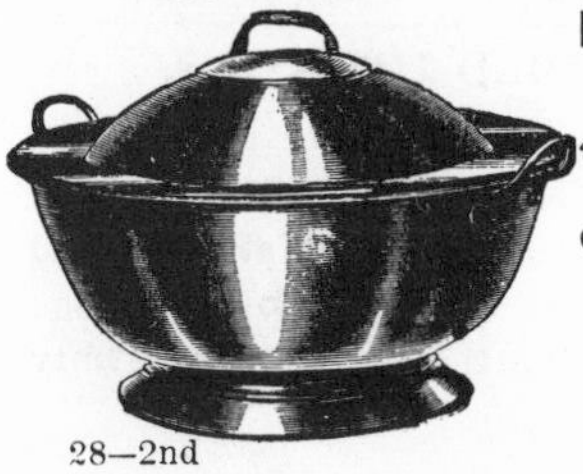

44865 Bread raisers, stamped, retinned.

Quarts.	Wght.	Each.
10	2½ lbs.	$0.50
14	3 lbs.	.62
17	3½ lbs.	.72
21	4 lbs.	.82

28—2nd

Dish Pans—IXX Tin.

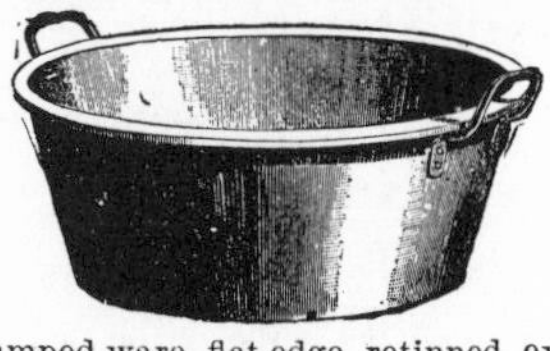

44866 Stamped ware, flat edge, retinned, extra heavy.

Quarts.	Weight.	Each.	Quarts.	Weight.	Each.
10	1½ lbs.	$0.24	14	1¾ lbs.	$0.28
17	3	.33	21	3¼	.39

Pie Plates—Extra Deep.

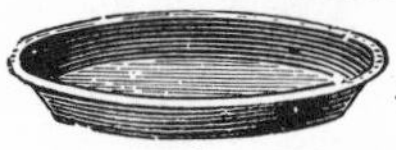

		Dozen.
44868	Size, 9x1⅛	$0.35
	Size, 10x1⅛	.45

Pie Plates—Plain—Tin.

	Per doz		Per doz.
44869 Size, 6x⅝	$0.20	Size, 7x⅝	$0.22
Size, 8x⅝	.25	Size, 9x⅞	.30
Size, 10x⅞	.40		

Pie Plates—Scalloped.

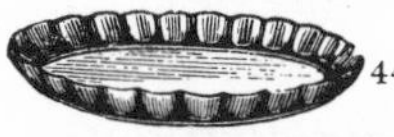

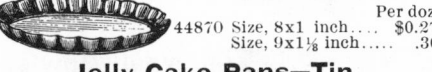

		Per doz.
44870	Size, 8x1 inch	$0.27
	Size, 9x1⅛ inch	.30

Jelly Cake Pans—Tin.

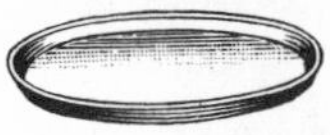

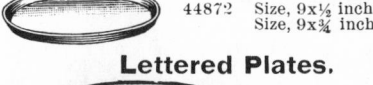

		Dozen.
44872	Size, 9x½ inch	$0.32
	Size, 9x¾ inch	.47

Lettered Plates.

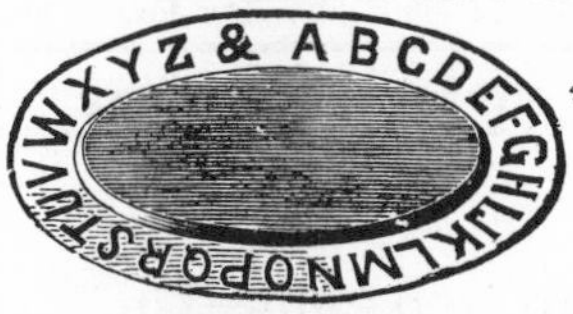

44874—Size. 6 inch. Each. $0.02. Per doz. .20

Pot Covers.

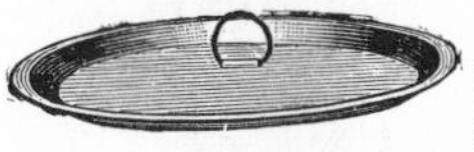

44875 Hemmed Pot Covers, with rings made of tin.

Size.	8 in.	10 in.	10½ in.	11 in.	12 in.	13½ in.
Each	3c	4c	4c	5c	6c	8c
Per doz.	33c	44c	44c	50c	65c	85c

Tin Preserving Kettles.

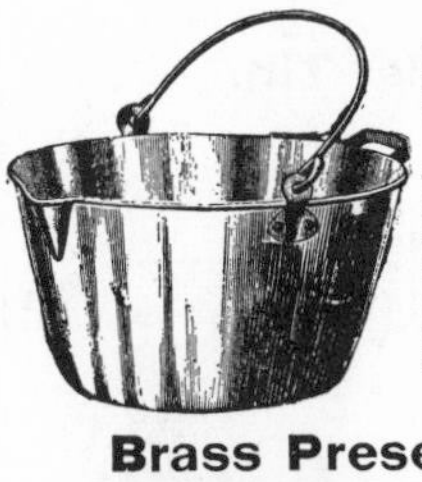

Lipped with bail. They will not hold as much as represented. Retinned. Stamped ware.

44876	Each.	Per doz.
2 quarts	$0.10	$1.00
3½ quarts	.12	1.20
4½ quarts	.13	1.38
5½ quarts	.15	1.56
6½ quarts	.18	1.85
8 quarts	.20	2.10

Brass Preserving Kettles.

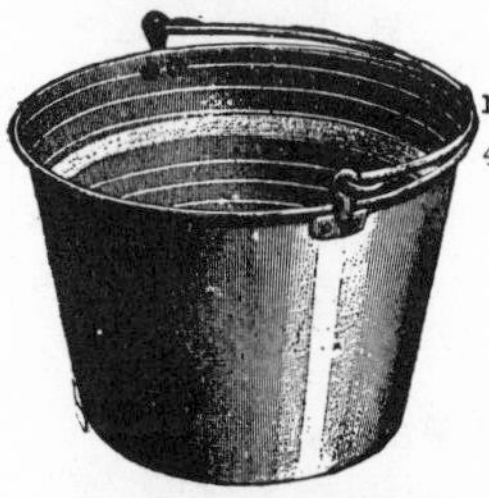

Will not hold quite as much as represented.

44878	
1½ gallon, 10 in	$0.84
2 gallons, 11 in	.95
3 gallons, 13 in	1.17
4 gallons, 14 in	1.62
5 gallons, 15 in	1.80
6 gallons, 16 in	2.10

Hotel Soup Stock Pots.

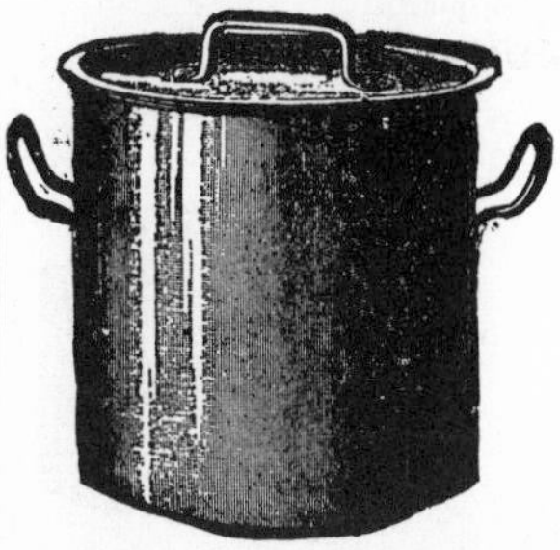

44879 Hotel Soup Stock Pots, made from wrought-steel heavily retinned, with retinned cover. These pots are used for keeping soup stock in and are used for boiling hams.

Gallons	3	6	9
Inches	10½x10¼	13x11¾	15x14
Price	$1.57	$2.25	$2.93

Porcelain-Lined Cast Preserving Kettles—No. 44880.

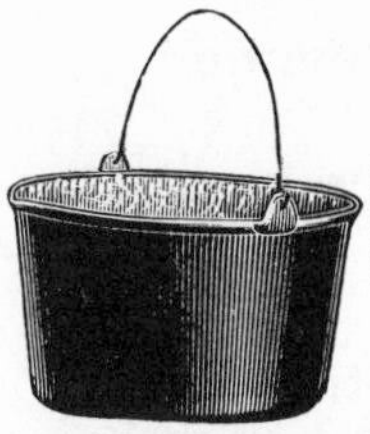

	Each		Each
3 quarts	$0.20	8 quarts,	$0.40
4 quarts	.23	10 quarts,	.43
5 quarts	.28	12 quarts,	.50
6 quarts	.32	14 quarts,	.60
7 quarts	.36		

Porcelain-Lined Steel Preserving Kettles.

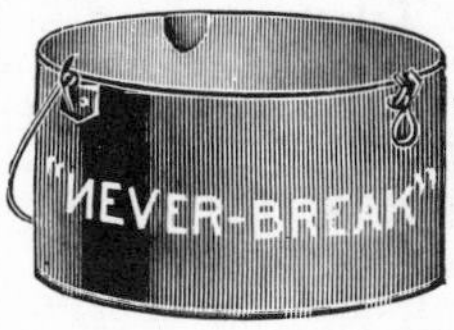

44883 Never-Break Wrought Steel Porcelain Lined Preserving Kettle; the strongest preserving kettle in use; light, strong and durable.

Quarts	7	8	9
Price, each	$1.15	$1.25	$1.35

Retinned Rice Boilers.

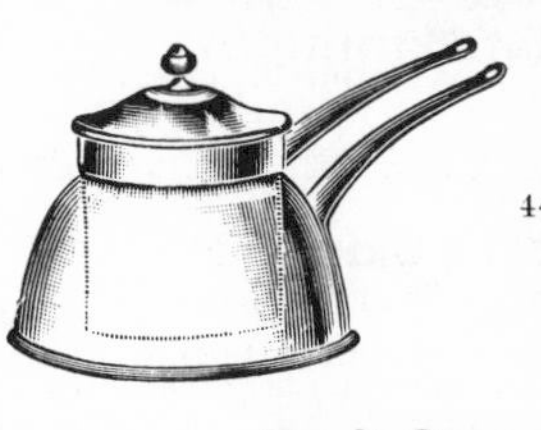

Retinned Stamped Tinware. Will not hold as much as represented.

44888—	Each
2 pints	$0.50
3 pints	.60
4 pints	.75
6 pints	.80

Fruit Steamer.

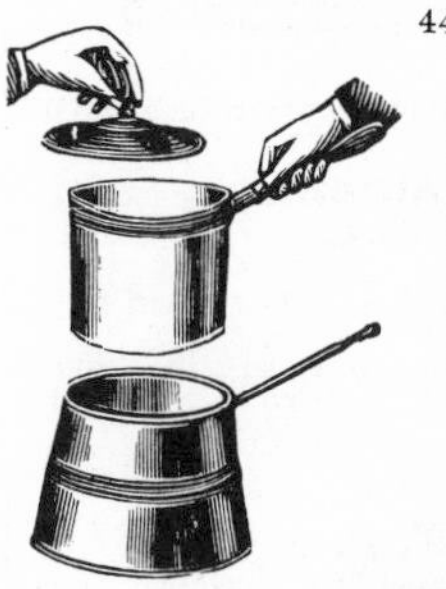

44890 Pure White Porcelain Cereal and Fruit Steamers, with enameled wood handle on food jar, and tinned iron handle on half planished tin boiler; for cooking oat meal, rice, or any kind of fruit, they are unexcelled; nothing can burn in them. Capacity of food jar.

3 pints	$0.62
4 pints	.80
5 pints	.90

Scoops.

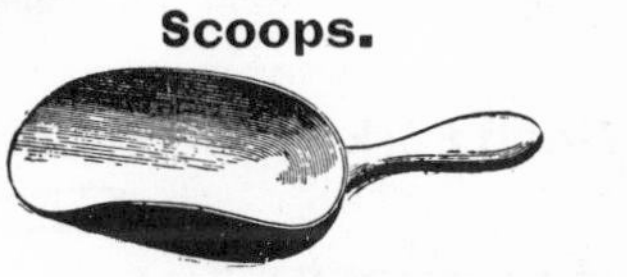

44891 Tin Scoops, retinned; weigh from ½ to 2 lbs.

Size	6¾x4¾	8x5½	10x6½	11¼x7
Price, each	$0.10	$0.12	$0.15	$0.20
Per dozen	.90	1.20	1.45	1.80

Water Dippers—Stamped.

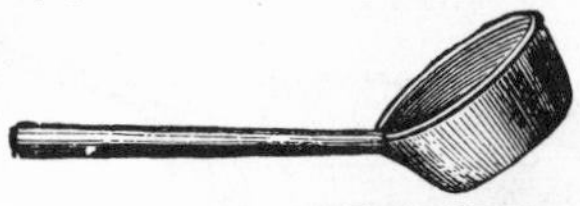

44892—Will not hold as much as represented. Bossed handles.

Size	Each	Per doz.
1 pint	$0.04	$0.36
1 quart	.05	.45
2 quarts	.06	.56

Cocoa-Shaped Dippers.

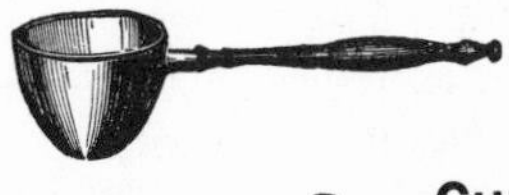

44893 Retinned Cocoa-Shaped Dipper, with wood handle.
Each..........$0.06
Per dozen....... .65

Cup Dippers.

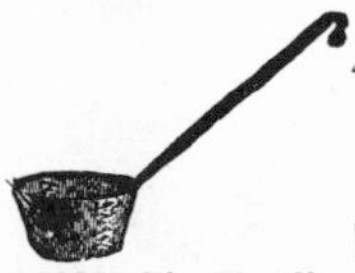

44894 Flat Handles, stamped tin, with tinned iron handle.

	Each.	Per doz.
Size, 3¾x2 in	$0 05	$0.54
Size, 4x2¼ in	.06	.65

Ladles.

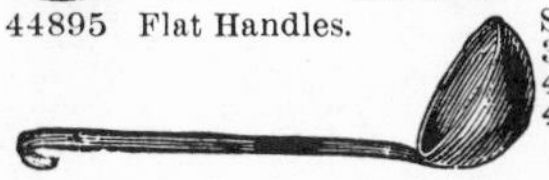

44895 Flat Handles.

Size.	Each.	Per doz.
3¾x1½ in.	$0.05	$0.55
4⅛x1¼ in.	.06	.70
4⅝x2 in.	.07	.80

Hotel Ladles.

44896 Made from steel, heavy, retinned like No. 44895.

Inches	6x2¾	7¾x4⅛
Each	$0.23	$0.32

Soup Ladles—Retinned.

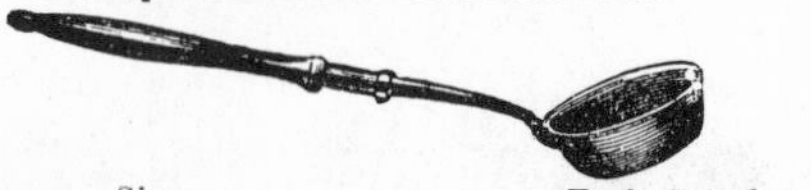

	Sizes.	Each.	Per. doz.
44897	3¾x1¼ in.	$0.06	$0.60
	4x1½ in.	.08	.75

Cake Turners, Retinned.

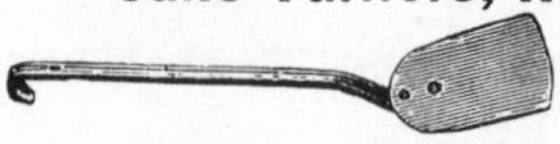

Flat Handles.

	Size.	Each.
44903	2¾x3¾ in.	4c
	3¼x4½ in.	5c

Hotel Cake Turners.

44904 Same style as 44903, made with steel blade, retinned: length, 18 inches. Price, each..$0.20

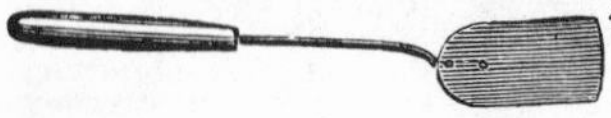

44905 Russia Iron, wood handles, 2¾ inches. Each..... $0.06

Skimmers.

Flat Handles—Retinned.

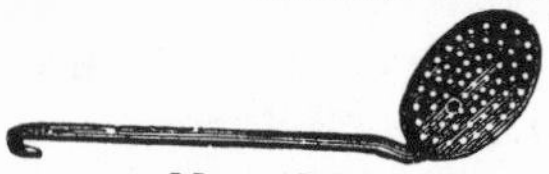

44908—

Size.	Each.	Per doz.
4 in.	4c	$0.44
5 in.	5c	.54
5½ in.	6c	.65

Hotel Flat Skimmers.

44909 Pieced, extra heavy, retinned. Same style as 44908.

Inches	6⅛	7¾
Price	$0.19	$0.24

Milk Skimmers.

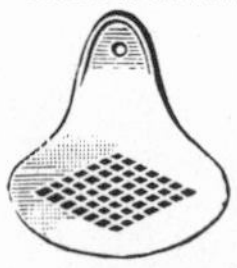

44910 5⅜x5 in., plain, each, 3c.; per dozen, 30c.
44912 Milk Skimmers, pierced, 5⅜x5 in.: price, each, 4c.: per dozen, 45c.

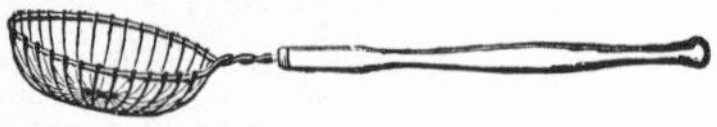

44914 Wire Handled Vegetable Skimmer, each..$0.05
Per dozen .38

Gravy Strainers.

Seamless—Retinned.

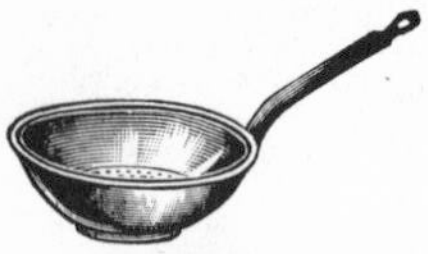

44915
Each, 4⅜x1⅝ in....$0.07
Per dozen .75

Hotel Meat Forks.

44916 Made of wrought iron, 2-frog, retinned, same style as 44917.

Inches	20	24
Price	$0.28	$0.34

Flesh Forks, Two Prong.

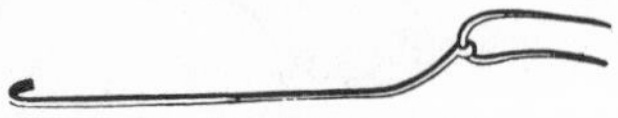

44917 Tinned Iron Flesh Forks, all iron prongs.

Length	15 in.	18 in.
Price, each	6c.	7c.
Price, per dozen	65c.	87c.

Hotel Chinese Strainers.

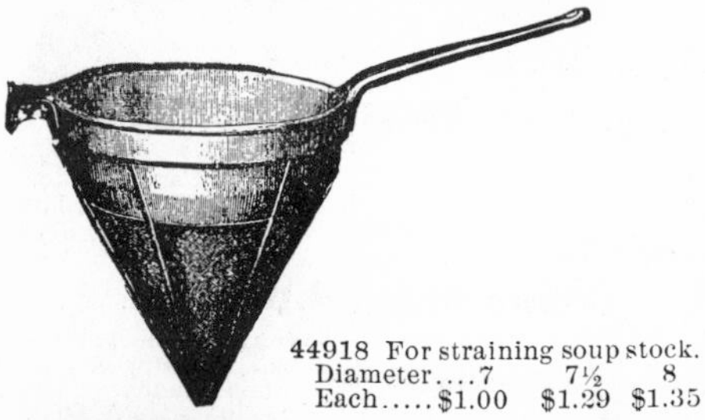

44918 For straining soup stock.

Diameter	7	7½	8
Each	$1.00	$1.29	$1.35

Milk Strainers.

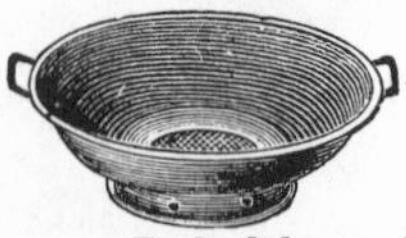

44919 Size, 9¼x2⅝, each $0.12
Size, 9¾x3, each .... .15

Drinking Cup.

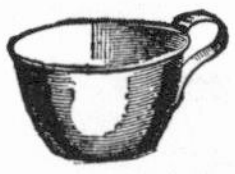

44920 Stamped Ware, light retinned cup.

Size.	Each.	Per doz.
3¾x2	$0.03	$0.35
4x2⅛	.04	.40
4⅜x3½	.05	.45
5x2⅝	.06	.55

Miners' Drinking Cups.

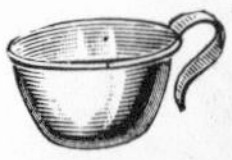

44922 Stamped Miners' Drinking Cups, with hook handle, retinned

Size	4¼ inch to	4½ inch.
Each	4c.	5c.
Price, per doz.	40c.	50c.

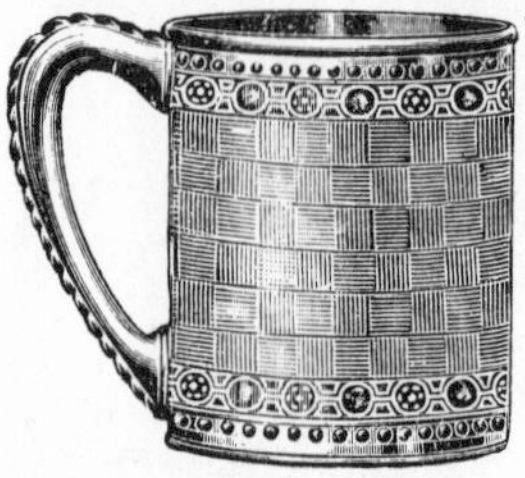

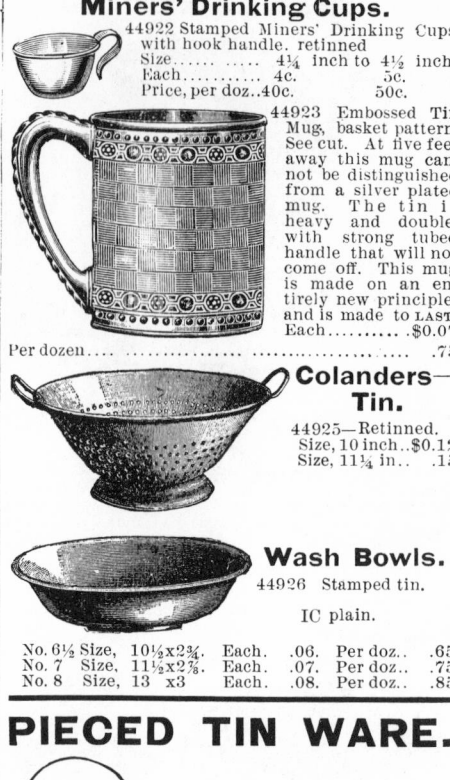

44923 Embossed Tin Mug, basket pattern. See cut. At five feet away this mug cannot be distinguished from a silver plated mug. The tin is heavy and double, with strong tubed handle that will not come off. This mug is made on an entirely new principle, and is made to LAST. Each..........$0.07
Per dozen .75

Colanders—Tin.

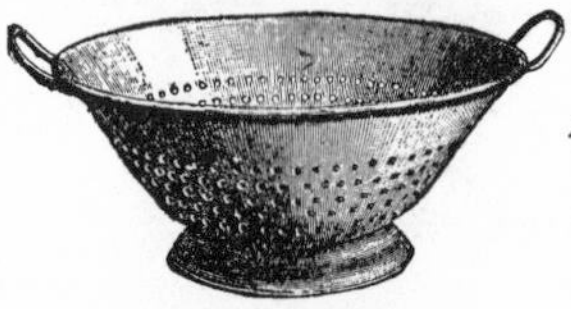

44925—Retinned.
Size, 10 inch..$0.12
Size, 11¼ in.. .15

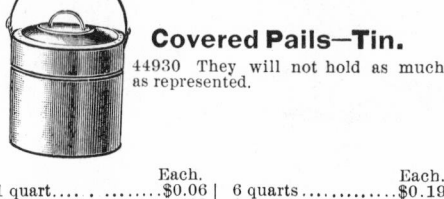

Wash Bowls.

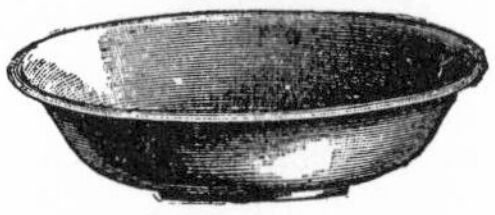

44926 Stamped tin.

IC plain.

No.	Size	Each.		Per doz..	
No. 6½	10½x2¾.	Each.	.06.	Per doz..	.65
No. 7	11½x2⅞.	Each.	.07.	Per doz..	.75
No. 8	13 x3	Each.	.08.	Per doz..	.85

PIECED TIN WARE.

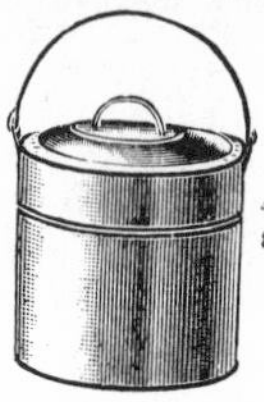

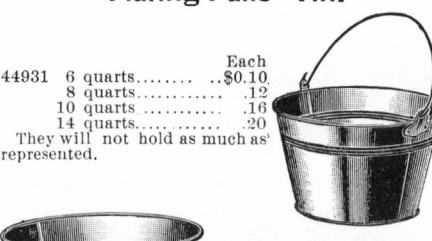

Covered Pails—Tin.

44930 They will not hold as much as represented.

	Each.		Each.
1 quart	$0.06	6 quarts	$0.19
2 quarts	08	8 quarts	.24
3 quarts	.11	10 quarts	.29
4 quarts	12		

Flaring Pails—Tin.

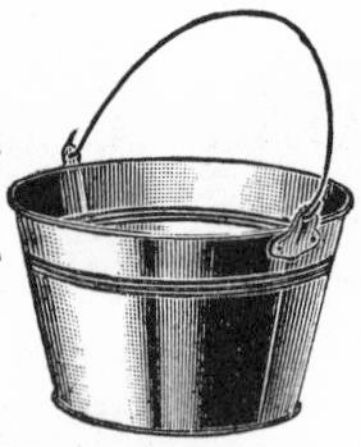

		Each
44931	6 quarts	$0.10
	8 quarts	.12
	10 quarts	.16
	14 quarts	.20

They will not hold as much as represented.

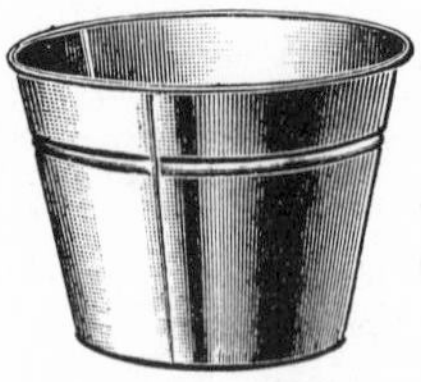

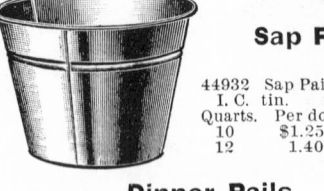

Sap Pails.

44932 Sap Pails made from I. C. tin.

Quarts.	Per doz.	Per gross.
10	$1.25	$13.15
12	1.40	14.38

Dinner Pails.

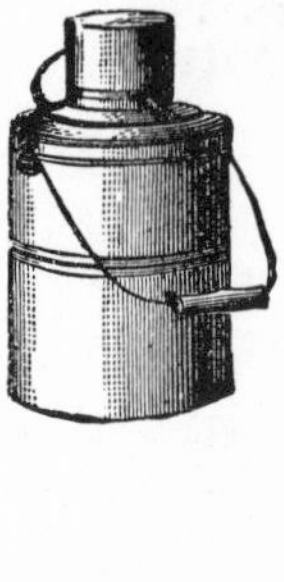

		Each.
44935	3 quarts	$0.17
	4 quarts	.18
	5 quarts	.25

Oblong Dinner Pails.

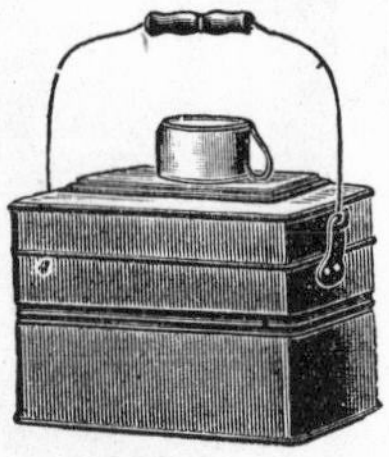

44936 With cup, tin I c.

2 quarts, 7½x5x5½ in.	Price each	$0 25
3 quarts, 8¼x5¾x6 in.	Price each	.30
4 quarts, 9x6¼x6¾ in.	Price each	.35

Lunch Boxes.

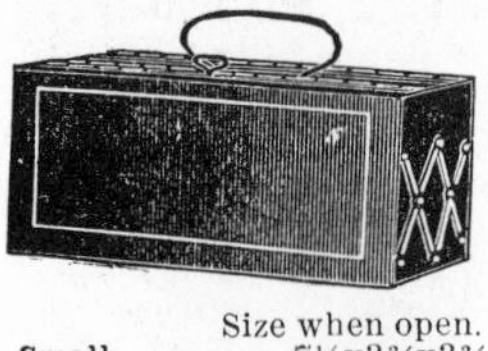

44941 Folding lunch box, made of tin, nicely japanned. With handle.

	Size when open.	Size closed.	Each.
Small	7½x3¾x3¾	7½x3¾x1½	$0.17
Large	9x4x4	9x4x½	.40
Large, with flask	9x4x4	9x4x1	.60

Milk Pans.

Will not hold as much as represented.

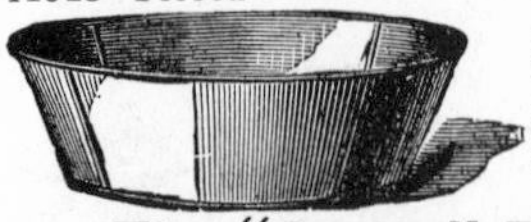

44945 Pieced—

Quarts.	Per doz
2	$0.72
3	.85
4	1.05
6	1.20
10	1.73

The "Crusty" Bread Pan.

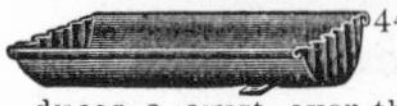

44946 Owing to its peculiar form is the most perfect bread baker ever produced. Its produces a crust over the entire surface of the loaf, bottom as well as top. Slices are perfect in shape and size for sandwiches. Made only in one size.
Each $0.12
Per dozen 1.25

Deep Bread Pans.

44948 Tin—

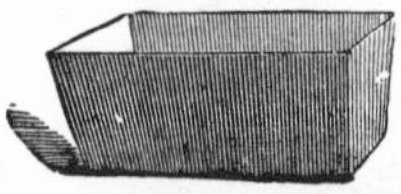

Sizes.	Each	Per doz.
4⅝x 9¾x3	$0.07	$0.70
5½x10¾x3	.09	.80
6 x11¾x3	.10	.90

Common Square Pans.

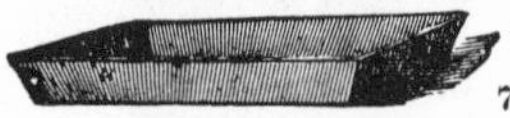

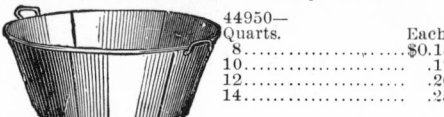

44949—

	Each.	Per doz.
7¾x11¾x1⅜	6c.	60c.

Dish Pans.—I. C. Tin.

Pieced—Will not hold as much as represented.

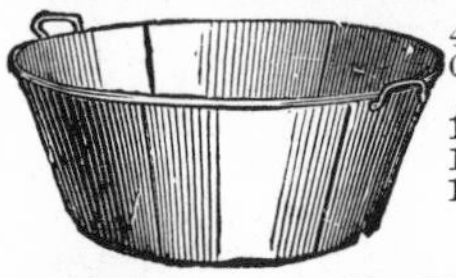

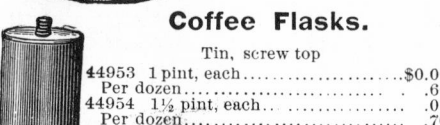

44950—

Quarts.	Each.
8	$0.15
10	.17
12	.20
14	.25

Coffee Flasks.

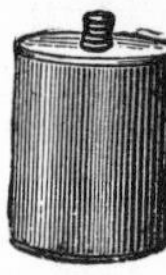

Tin, screw top

44953 1 pint, each $0.06
Per dozen .60
44954 1½ pint, each .07
Per dozen .70

Sauce Boilers.

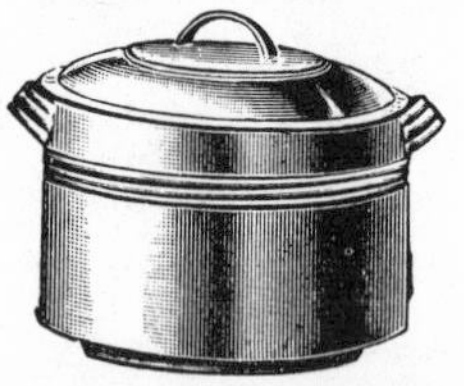

I. C. TIN.—Pit.

Copper bottoms.
44956 Size 7........$0.30
Size 8 .40
Size 9 .45

Wash Boilers.

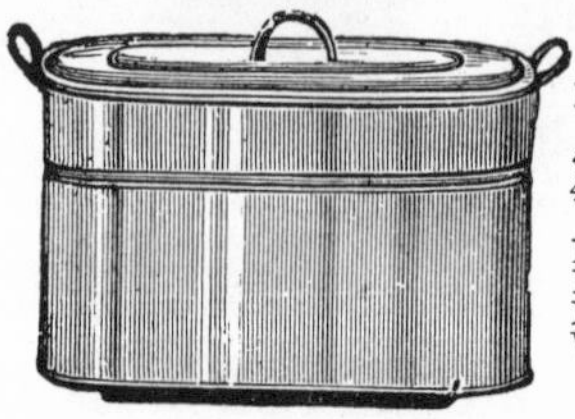

Heavy IX Tin, with copper bottom.
44960 Flat Bottom.
44960½ Pit Bottom.

	Each
No. 7	$0.85
No. 8	.90
No. 9	1.05

Weight, 5¼ to 7 lbs.

All Copper Wash Boilers.

We guarantee all of our copper boilers to be made of 14-ounce copper.
44961 Flat Bottom.
44961½ Pit Bottom.

Nos.	7	8	9
Price, each	$1.70	$1.80	$2.00

Weight, 6¼ to 8½ lbs.

HOUSEHOLD UTENSILS.

There is no line in which deception can be practiced better than this. Only an expert can tell a first from a second quality at first. You will soon find out the difference however when you come to use the articles. We handle only first-class goods.

Heavy Copper Bottom and Rim.

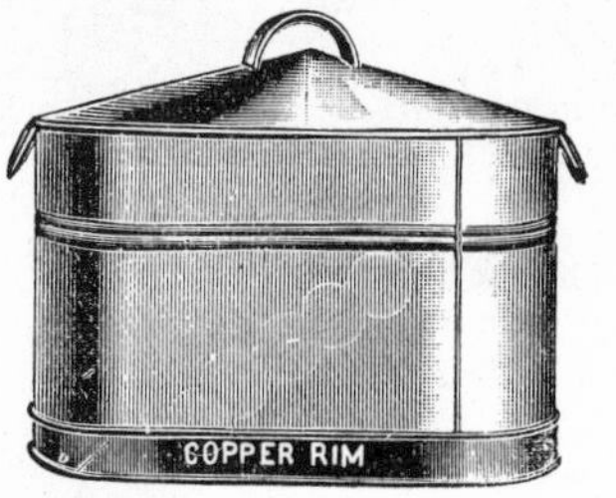

44962 Flat Bottom.
44962½ Pit Bottom.

No.	8	9
Price, each	$1.20	$1.35

Weight, 5¾ to 7½ lbs.

Milk Dipper.

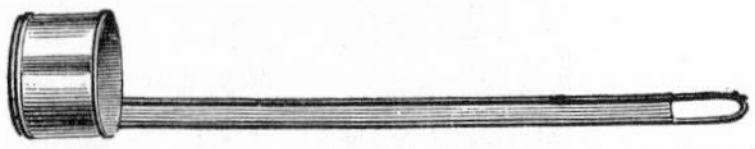

44970 Milk Dippers, made of tin, with long handles: weight. 1 lb. to 2½ lbs.

Quarts	½	¾	1	2
Price, each	$0.10	.15	.20	.25

Tin Horns.

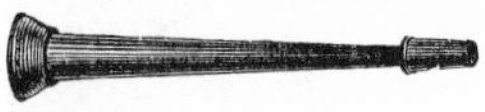

44971 Tin Dinner Horns.

Length	13	22
Each	6c	15c

Measures—Tin.

FOR LIQUIDS.

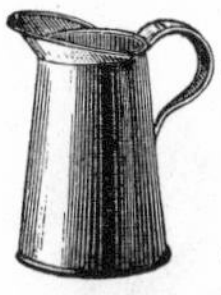
44972

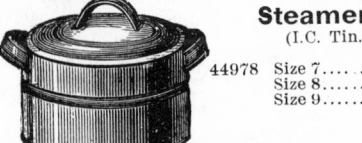

44972	Each.	Per doz.
½ pint	$0.04	$0.44
1 pint	.05	.54
1 quart	.06	.65
2 quarts	10	1.08
4 quarts	.16	1.73

44973 Milk measures, graduated, tin. Each. Per doz.
1 quart $0.08 $0.87

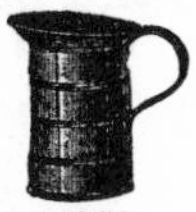
44973

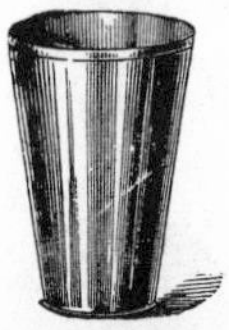

44975 Liquor Mixers or Lemonade Shakers of tin; size, 5⅛x2¾. Weight, 5 oz. Each. $0.05 Per doz. $0.54
See Index for lemonade glasses.

Tin Cups.

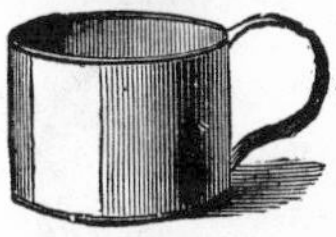

44976— Size	Each.	Per doz.
½ pint	$0.02	$0.20
1 pint	.03	.25
1 quart	.04	.45
2 quarts	.07	72

Steamers.

(I.C. Tin.)

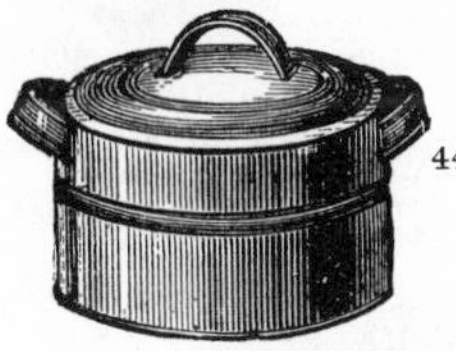

44978	Each.
Size 7	$0.18
Size 8	.20
Size 9	.25

Watering Pots.

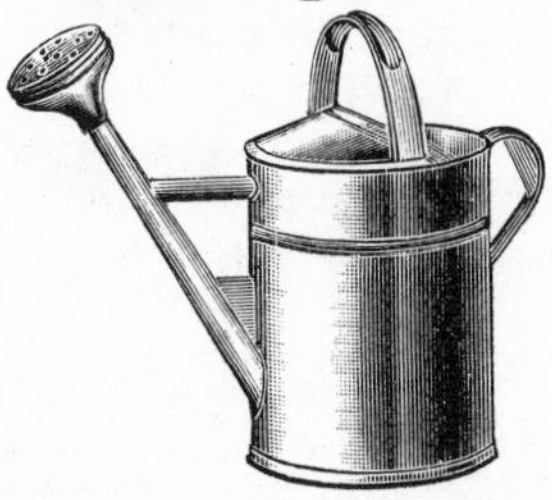

44979 Watering Pots, made from IC tin.

Quarts	1	4	6	8	10
Inches	4⅜x4⅝	6¼x6½	7¼x7¾	8¼x8¾	8¾x10½
Price, each	$0.15	.23	.27	.35	40

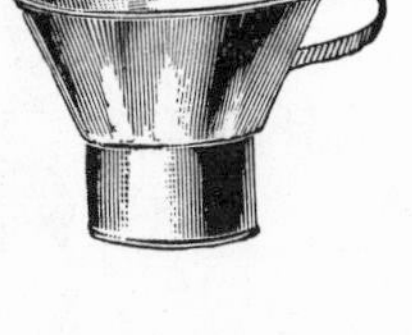

44982 Fruit Jar Fillers made of tin. No one putting up fruit should be without one of these Measures across lower end 2 in. Weighs 5 oz.
Price, each $0.06
Per doz. .54

Funnels—Tin.

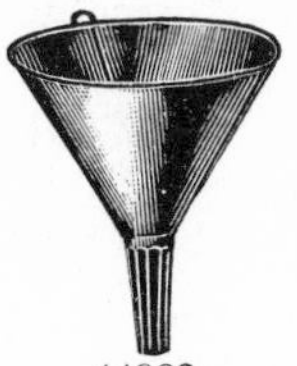
44983

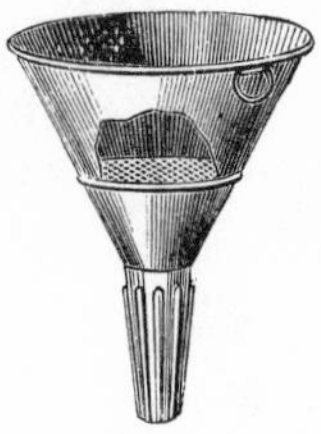
44984

		Each.	Per doz.
44983	½ pint	$0.03	$0.34
	1 pint	.04	.45
	1 quart	.06	.67
	2 quarts	.07	.77

44984 Funnels, made of tin, with brass wire cloth strainer. These funnels are very convenient.

	Weight.	Each.
½ pint	5 oz	$0.04
1 pint	6 oz	.05
1 quart	8 oz	.06
2 quarts	12 oz	.10

Box Graters.

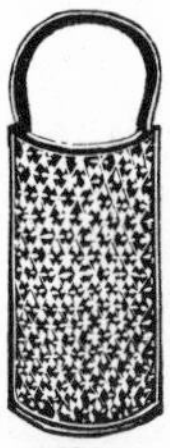
44986

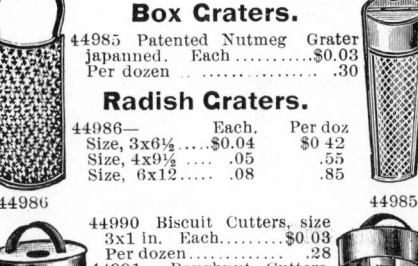

44985 Patented Nutmeg Grater japanned. Each $0.03
Per dozen .30

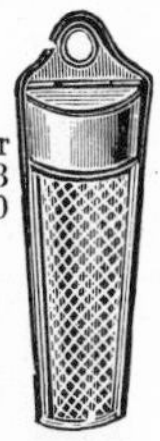
44985

Radish Graters.

44986—	Each.	Per doz
Size, 3x6½	$0.04	$0 42
Size, 4x9½	.05	.55
Size, 6x12	.08	.85

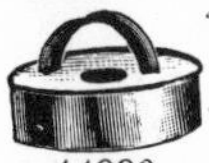
44990

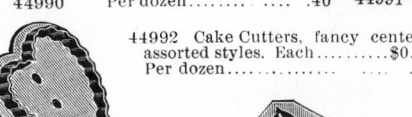

44990 Biscuit Cutters, size 3x1 in. Each $0.03
Per dozen .28

44991 Doughnut Cutters, size 3x1 in. Each $0.04
Per dozen .40

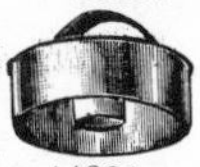
44991

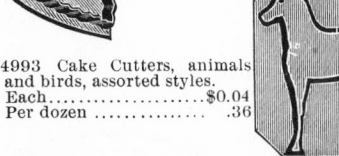

44992 Cake Cutters, fancy centers, assorted styles. Each $0.04
Per dozen .40

44993 Cake Cutters, animals and birds, assorted styles.
Each $0.04
Per dozen .36

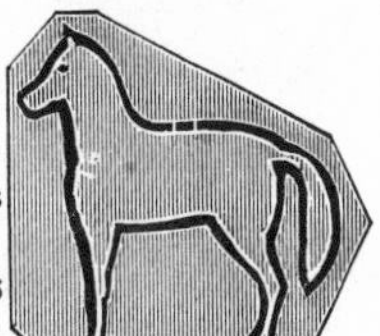

Pieced Muffin Rings.

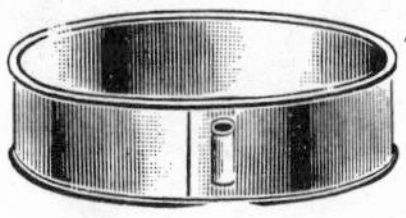

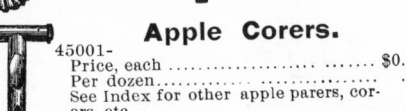

44995 Pieced Muffin Rings' size 3 in. Price, each $0.02
Per dozen .15

Pieced Water Dippers.

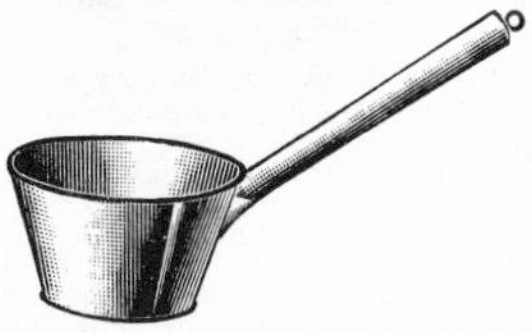

44998 Pieced Water Dippers, with copper bottom; size 2 quarts. Each..$0.10
Per dozen 1.10

Paste Jaggers.

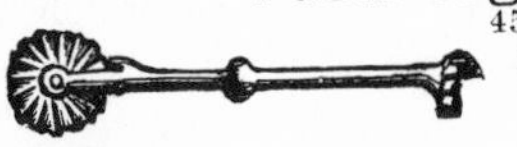

45000 Tinned Paste Jaggers. Each $0.05
Per dozen .... .54

Apple Corers.

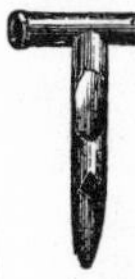

45001-
Price, each $0.04
Per dozen .40
See Index for other apple parers, corers, etc.

Jelly Molds.

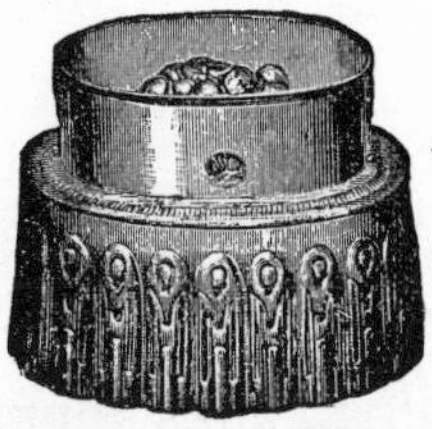

45002 Oval Jelly Molds, assorted patterns, ear of corn bunch of grapes, rose, etc. It is not always possible for us to send just the pattern ordered; we will substitute unless you say not to.

Size, pints	½	1	1½	2	3	4
Each	18c.	25c.	30c.	37c.	44c.	53c

Pudding Molds.

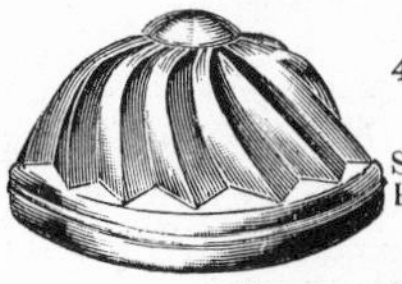

45002½ Retinned Pudding Molds.

Quarts,	2	4	5
Size, in.	7x4	8⅝x4⅛	9¼x4⅛
Price ea.	$0.23	.29	.34

Dripping Pans.

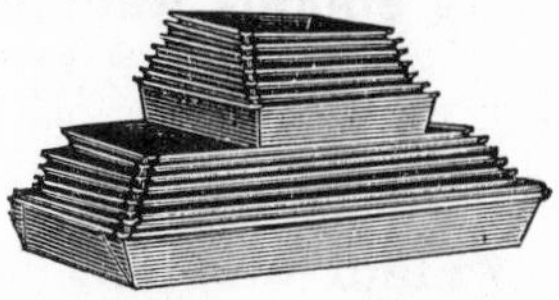

45003 Patent Improved Sheet Iron Dripping Pans. These pans have a raised bottom and do not bulge down in the center like the ordinary dripping pan. They wear longer for this reason, and are always straight, never getting out of shape; just as cheap as the common.

Size.	Each.	Per doz.	Size.	Each.	Per doz.
7x10	$0.08	$0.87	10x14	$0.13	$1.42
7x14	.09	1.06	10x16	.15	1.62
8x12	.10	1.08	12x19	.19	2.06
10x12	.12	1.34	14x17	.20	2.16

The Perfection Roasting Pan.

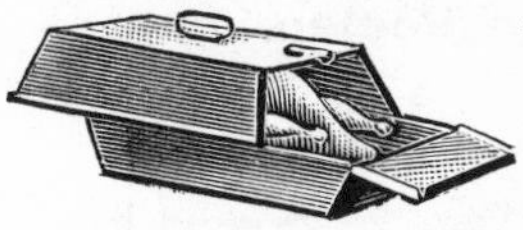

45004 This pan is one of the finest things for roasting fowls or meats, baking biscuit or Boston baked beans. It has a sliding cover and open end. You can see how things are getting along inside by just dropping the end of the cover, without removing the pan from the oven. No basting of the meat is required, as when the pan is closed the steam and moisture are retained inside, thus preventing the meat from becoming dry. Made of sheet iron.

Length.	Width.	Height.	Weight.	Each.	Per doz.
13 ins.	9 ins.	7 ins.	3lb, 6 oz	$0.68	$ 7.20
15	10	8	4lb, 6 oz	1.82	9.00
16	11	9	4lb, 12 oz	1.05	10.85
18½	13	10	6lb, 6 oz	1.20	13.55

The Economic Roasting Pan.

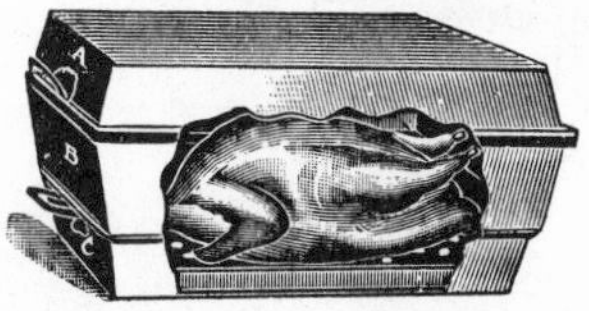

45005 The Economic Self Basting Roaster will cook oat meal, fruit, etc., as well as roasting meat. As a steamer it is unsurpassed. Directions accompany each one. Made in three sizes. Sizes of dripping pans that make the top and bottom of the No. 1, 9x14 and 10x15; and No. 2, size 10x15 and 11x16; No. 3, 10x17 and 11x18. These may be used as dripping pans in the ordinary way if desired. Made of sheet iron.

No.	Weight.	Each.	Per doz.
1	4½ lbs.	$0.57	$6.10
2	5 lbs.	.65	7.10
3	6¾ lbs.	.75	8.10

Tea and Table Spoons, Etc.

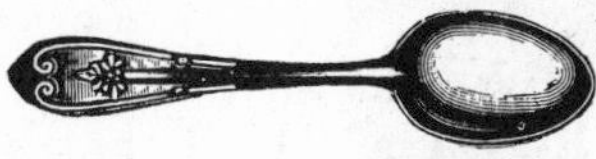

45020 Tea Spoons. tin, retinned Per dozen.... $0.08
Per gross.. .75

45021 Table Spoons, same pattern. Per dozen..$0.10
Per gross 1.10

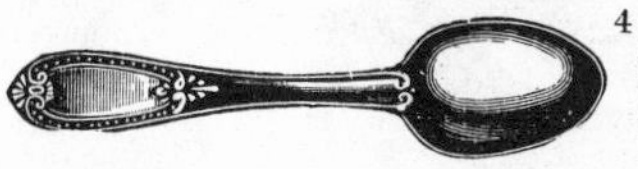

45022 Tea Spoons tin, retinned. Per dozen....$0.15
Per gross 1.62

45023 Table Spoons, same pattern. Per dozen.. .25
Per gross 2.70

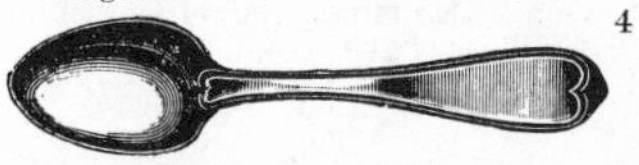

45024 Tea Spoons, tin, retinned. Per dozen ..$0.15
Per gross, 1.65

45025 Table Spoons, same pattern as above, steel, retinned. Per dozen.....$0.32. Per gross.... ..3.00

45026 Forks, steel, same pattern as above. Per doz...........$0.26 Per gross 2.75

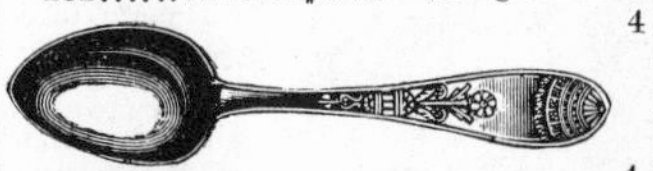

45027 Tea Spoons, steel, retinned. Per dozen....$0.28
Per gross 3.00

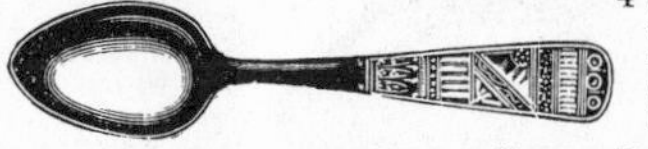

45028 Tea Spoons, steel, retinned. per dozen $0.25
Per gross 2.67

45029 Table Spoons, same pattern. Per dozen.. .60
Per gross 4.80

45030 Forks, same pattern as 45028. Per doz.... .50
Per gross 5.50

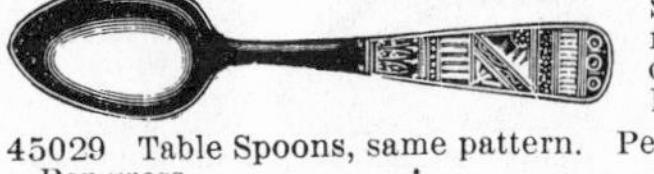

Basting Spoons, Agate Iron Ware.

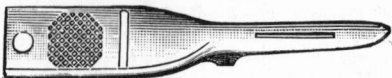

45040 Agate Basting Spoons.	Each.
10 in	$0.10
12 in	.12
14 in	.13
16 in	.14
18 in	.18

Basting Spoons Retinned.

45041—	Weight per doz.	Each.	Per doz.
10 in	1 lb. 7 oz.	$0.04	$0.35
12 in	1 lb. 15 oz.	.05	.40
14 in	2¼ lbs.	.06	.45
16 in	2½ lbs.	.07	.60
18 in	4½ lbs.	.08	.75

Potato Chipper.

45045 Saratoga Potato Chipper, can be used as a peeler for vegetables and fruits, corer for apples and pears, slicer to make Saratoga chips of potatoes, apples, carrots, etc., nutmeg grater, chopper for potatoes. The point can pick out potato eyes and the edge can scale fish. Made from sheet steel. Each...........................$0.06
Per dozen...........$0.50 Per gross.........5.60

Potato Peelers.

45046 The Peerless Potato Peeler. This is an entirely new and novel article for peeling and slicing potatoes and other vegetables.
Each............$0.06 Per dozen.............$0.50

Fruit Presses.

45050 Fruit and Vegetable Press and Strainer, can be used for a variety of purposes; is especially recommended for mashing potatoes. Potatoes after being forced through the strainer have a delicious creamy taste that no other method of mashing will impart. Weight, 1 lb. 4 oz.
Each............$0.35 Per dozen..........$3.78

Revolving Craters.

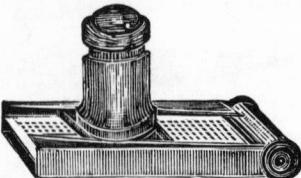

45055—Revolving Grater for grating horse radish, cocoanut, pumpkins, squash, lemons, crackers, cheese, etc. The cylinder is three inches in diameter and three inches long. No family should be without one. Weight 1 lb. 10 oz. Each.................$0.35
Per dozen...........................3.78
45056 Revolving Grater, larger than No. 45055, has a cylinder 6 inches in diameter, 5 inches in length. Weight 7 lbs. 7 oz. Each.............1.25

Unique Nutmeg Crater.

45058 Unique Nutmeg Grater, the only grater that reduces the nutmeg to a fine powder, with no small pieces wasted; has an automatic *cleaner* which *prevents clogging.* No waste, no clogging, no scratched fingers, no grating finger nails in your pies or pudding; will save its price in a short time. Weight, 5 ounces. Each.... ....$0.05
Per dozen..............................50

Revolving Slicer.

45060 Revolving Slicer, for slicing apples, Saratoga potatoes, pumpkins, cucumbers and other vegetables; weighs 1 lb. 13 oz. Each, $0.35

Chopping Knives.

45068 Chopping Knives, braced shank, wood handle, cast steel blade; weight, 8 oz. Each.... .....$0.03

45068

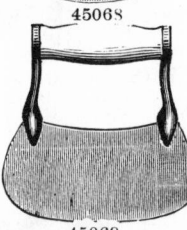

45069 Chopping Knives (as per cut), iron handle and frame, extra cast steel blade. Weight, 12 ounces.
Each.................$0.10
Per dozen.... ......1.08

45069,

45070 Chopping Knives, extra cast steel, double blades; tinned with malleable iron frame, wood handle. Weight, 8 ounces.
Each..................$0.06

45070

Metallic Sieves.
Tinned Rims.
ANNEALED WIRE BOTTOM.

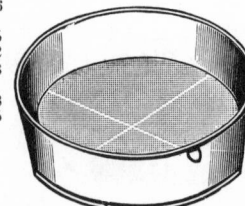

45075 Size of mesh, 16 to the inch.
Each........... $0.15
Per dozen... .. 1.62
45076 Size of mesh, 18 to the inch.
Each...........$0.18
Per dozen.......1.95

Flour Sifters.

45080 The Improved Rotary Flour and Meal Sifter, scoop, measure, weigher, mixer, rice washer, tomato, pumpkin, starch strainer, wine and fruit or jelly press combined. This is the most convenient kitchen utensil ever sold, combining, as it does, ten necessary articles for the culinary department. For mixing baking powder, etc., through flour it is almost indispensable.
Each...........................$0.10
Per dozen.... ....1.00

45081 Similar to No. 45080 but larger and with a round handle. Size, diameter, 4¾ inch. Height at front, 6½ inch. Height at back, 5¼ inch.
Price, each...............$0.12
Per dozen....... ......1.35

GINGHAMS...

AT PRICES THAT WILL ASTONISH EXPERIENCED BUYERS. SEE OUR QUOTATIONS UNDER DEPARTMENT HEADING. WE CARRY THE LARGEST OPEN STOCK IN CHICAGO.

Ice Shave.

45085—Something new The Gem Ice Shave, constructed like an ordinary plane, having in front of the knife a receptacle closed by a lid in which the ice shaved off collects as the tool is shoved forward over a block of ice. Shaved ice can be used for making water ices or for cooling liquors, and is also very valuable as a cooling medium in the sick room. The shave is made of galvanized iron. Price, each.............. ....$0.40
Per dozen............. ....4.32

"Magic" Milk Shake Machine.

45086 "Magic" Milk Shake Machine is a counter machine, made to do the work as effectively and satisfactorily as the famous A. & W. floor machines. It has a direct up and down movement, thoroughly mixing the contents of the tumblers, and there is no swinging motion which leaves the ingredients unmixed. Diameter of fly wheel, 11¾ in. Machine, with four tumblers and four glass tops, price, $6.00

Egg Beaters.

45087 Easy Egg Beater. It consists of a spirally coiled wire, which in use opens and closes with exceeding rapidity, and instead of cutting the egg, as most beaters do, thoroughly ærates it, which is acknowledged by all experienced cooks to be the only correct way of beating an egg. For whipping cream it is just the thing. This egg beater is having the largest sale of any yet made; try it and you will like it.
Each........ ....$0.08
Per dozen........................87

45088 Dover Egg Beaters. Each $0.10
Per dozen....................................1.08

45089 Surprise Egg Beater, retinned.
Each...................$0.05
Per dozen..... .35

45090 Spoon Egg Whip, with wood handle. Ea. $0.05
Per dozen. .40

Ice Chippers.

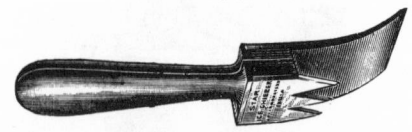

45100 The Star Ice Chipper, iron handle. By the use of this chipper ice can be chipped into small and nearly uniform pieces, the guard projecting beyond the knife making it impossible to cut off thicker pieces than the space between. Only a minute's time is required to reduce a 15 or 20 pound block of ice; cuts small pieces.

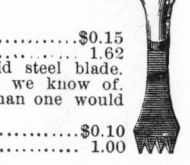

Weight, 1¼ pounds. Each $0.15
Per dozen. 1.62
45101 Ice Chisel, 4 prongs, solid steel blade. The very best ice cutter that we know of. Will cut a much larger block than one would suppose; weight 9 oz.
Each $0.10
Per dozen.... ....1.00

Boss Lemon Squeezer.

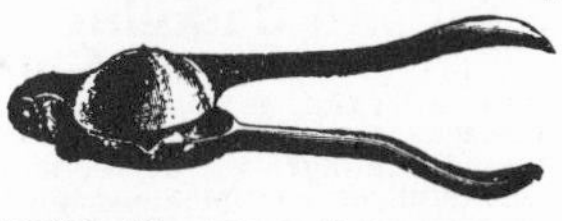

45105 Made of fine malleable iron, heavily tinned. Each.......$0.15 Per dozen... 1.62

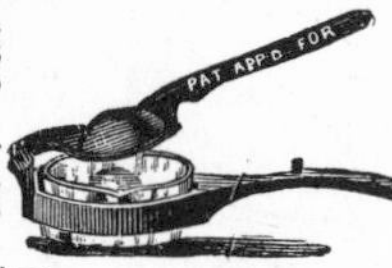

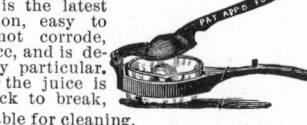

45106 The "King" Lemon Squeezer. This is the latest modern invention, easy to handle, will not corrode, saves all the juice, and is desirable in every particular. The receiver for the juice is of glass too thick to break, and is removable for cleaning. Weight, 2 lbs. 7 oz. Each...... ....$0.25 Per dozen.. 2.70

Measures.

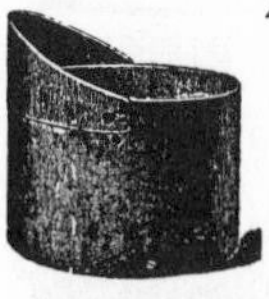

45110 The Raymond funnel measures; made of steel, japanned; a boon to farmers and storekeepers and anyone having use for a measure. The peculiar scoop shape facilitates pouring into paper bag or basket; made in five sizes, 1qt., 2qt., 4qt., 8 qt., ½ bushel, Price per nest of five measures, $1.45.

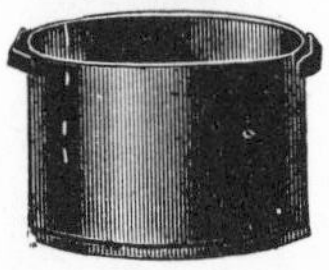

45111 Patent Iron Measures, japanned.

Size	Weight.	Each.
½ bushel.....	3 lbs. 15 oz.	$0.33
Pecks.....	2 lbs. 11 oz.	.25

Pantry Cabinet.

The Raymond Pantry Cabinet; a place for everything and everything in its place. Bread, crackers, dried fruit, rice, etc. Made of tin, japanned, antique oak frame. Pull down the glass front of the case, take out what you want and it closes itself; contents kept free from dust, damp air, etc.

45112 No. 2, 7 cans, size of cabinet, 48 inches high, 22 inches wide; 11 inches deep...........$6.50

45113 No. 3, 9 cans; size of cabinet, 58 inches high, 22 inches wide, 11 inches deep.......... 8.00

Flour Bin and Sieve.

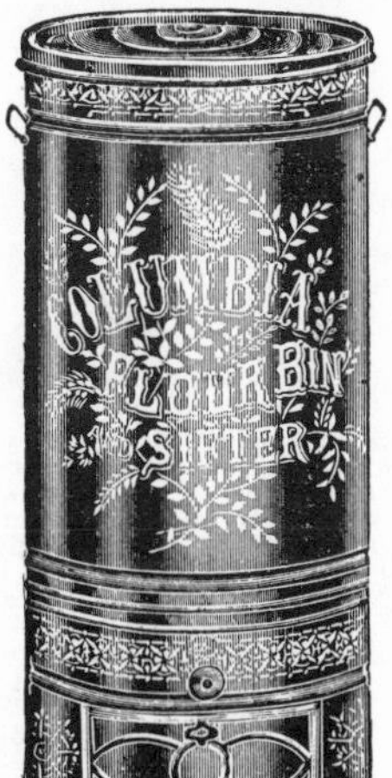

The flour saved pays the cost. Keep your flour in the Columbia Flour Bin, secure from moisture, dust, dirt and vermin. This flour bin and sieve must not be confounded with others upon the market. It is unlike any other—an improvement over all. It is made of the best material, handsomely finished. It has a patent slide sieve which will do its work faster and better than any other in the market. All good cooks know the value of clean, dry-sifted flour. How to Use: Put the flour in at the top—pull the rod and sifted flour will be found in the drawer underneath.

45114 50 lbs. capacity. Each...............$1.30

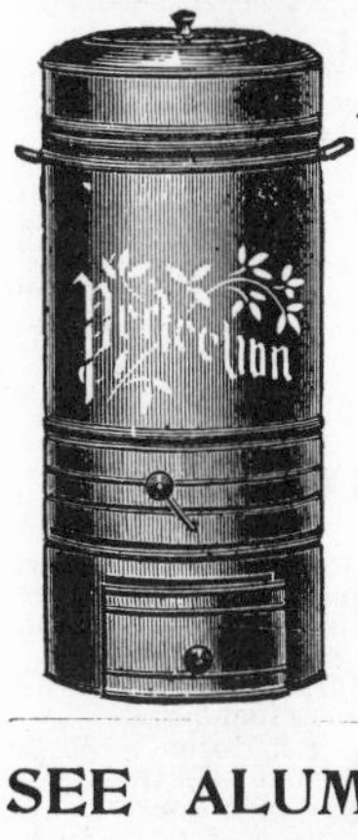

45115 The Perfection Combination Flour Bin and Sieve, a very convenient household article, made of tin, japanned. It will keep flour or meal dry and free from dust, mice, rats and cockroaches, as it contains a sieve, which, by turning a crank, sifts the flour into the movable pan at the bottom; it avoids the necessity of reaching into barrels or sacks.

100 lb, size weighs 25 lbs. Each.......................$2 10

50 lb. size weighs 16½ lbs. Each........................ 1.50

25 lb. size weighs 13¼ lbs Each..... .. .. 1.30

Dust Pans.

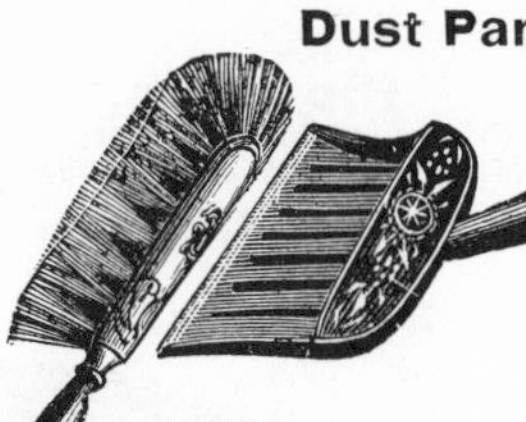

45122

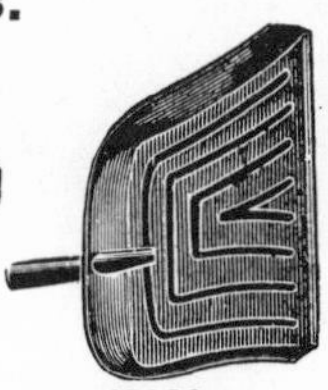

45120

45120 Dust Pan, Corrugated, not covered. Each..........$0.08 Per dozen..........$0.90

45121 Dust Pan, Plain Brown, covered. Each. .12 Per dozen... 1.38

45122 Dust Pan, Fancy assorted colors, with brush. Each..... ......$0.52 Per dozen....... 5.60

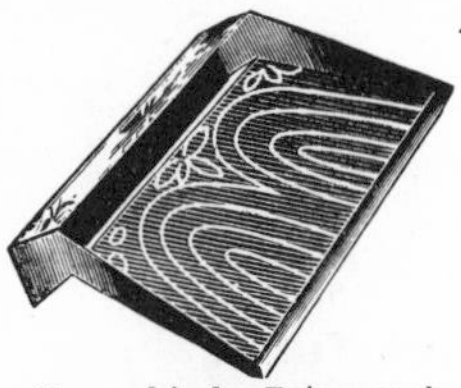

45123 The Downing Dust Pan It rests firmly on the floor and is perfectly smooth on the bottom. It has a receiving box at the back into which the dust is swept, and can be moved from one place to another with the foot without danger of spilling the contents, which is a great improvement on the ordinary kind. Price, each, $0.12 Per dozen....$1.25

Crumb Pans and Brush.

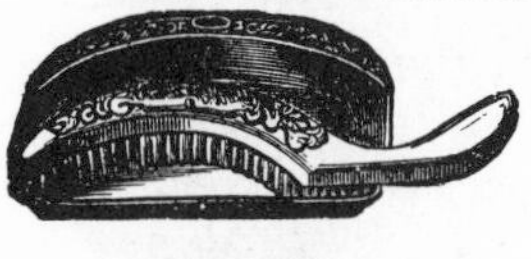

45125-26

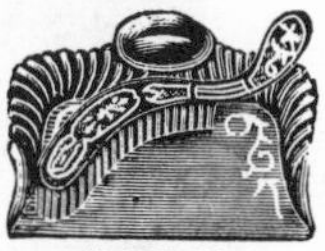

45127-28

45125 Crumb Pan, with brush, plain japanned...$0.20

45126 Fancy Japanned Pan, with brush, finished nicer than 45125 Each.................. .40

45127 Brass Crumb Tray and brush. Each...... .69

45128 Polished Brass, nickel plated. Each...... .80

Candlesticks.

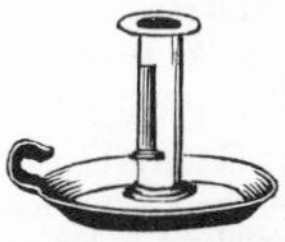

45135 Candlesticks, japanned.

	Each.	Per doz.
Size, 5 in.........	$0.03	$0.33

Tea Tray.

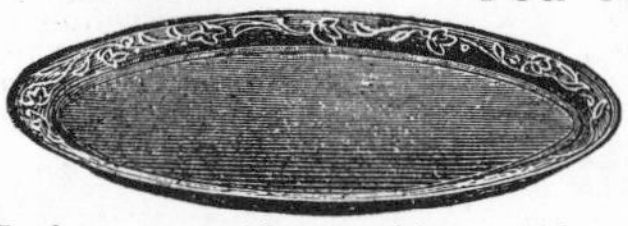

45136 Tea Trays, oval, japanned.

Inches.......	12	14	16	18	20
Each..........	$0.12	$0.15	$0.18	$0.23	$0.25
Per doz......	1.25	1.60	1.90	2.25	2.50
Inches.......	22	24	26	28	
Each	.30	.37	.47	.57	
Per doz......	3.25	3.75	4.75	5.75	

CHILD'S TRAYS.

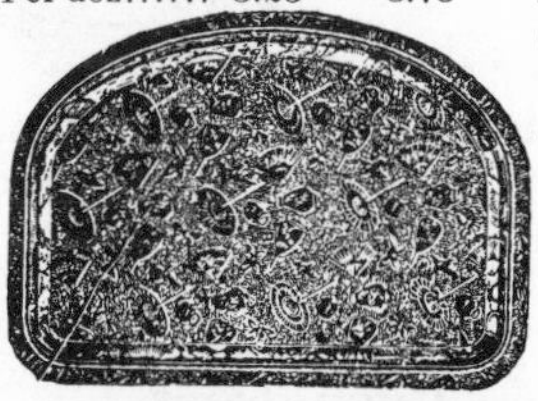

45137 The Crown Child's Tray, silver finish, the best and cheapest child's tray made; complete with springs Ready to adjust to table or high chair. Price, each ...$0.18

Knife and Fork Boxes.

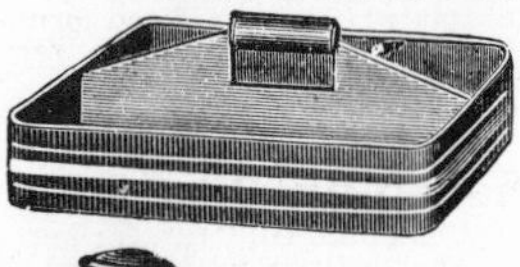

45140 Knife and Fork Boxes, open top, size, 12x8............$0.35

Canisters.

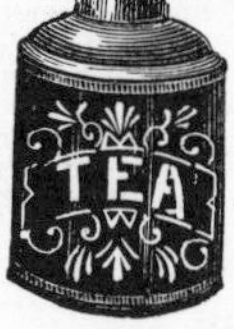

45145-46

Japanned Tea or Coffee Canister.

45145 Tea Canister.

45146 Coffee Canister.

	Each.	Per doz.
1 pound........	$0.07	$0.76
2 pound.........	.09	1.05

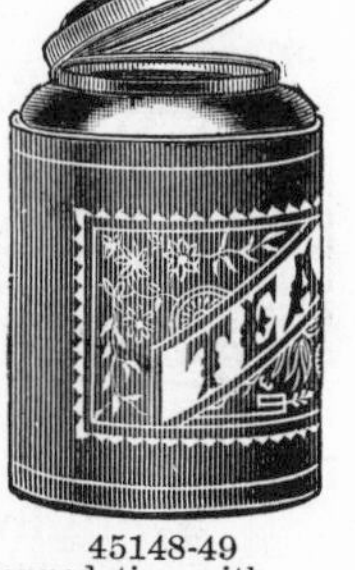

45148-49

Tea and Coffee Canisters, japanned tin, with hinged covers. These canisters are preferable to the ordinary kind, as the covers cannot get lost.

45148 Tea Canisters.

45149 Coffee Canisters.

To hold—	Each.	Per doz.
2 pounds......	$0.10	$1.08
4 pounds......	.15	1.50

Dredge Boxes.

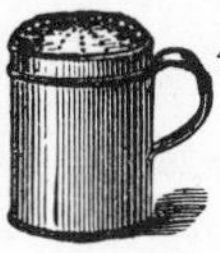

45156 Japanned, large, size, 2½x3¼. Each............................$0.04 Per dozen.............................. .44

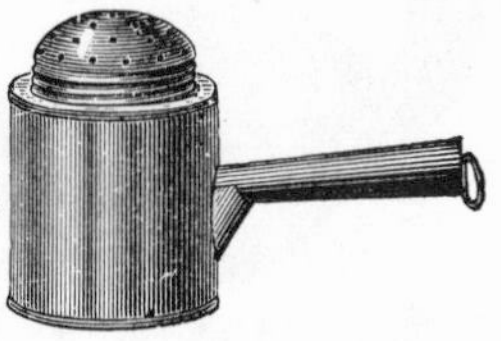

45158 Clothes Sprinkler, with screw cover and handle. This is a new and very convenient article, used for sprinkling clothes before ironing. Each............ $0.12 Per dozen........ 1.30

Round Spice Boxes.

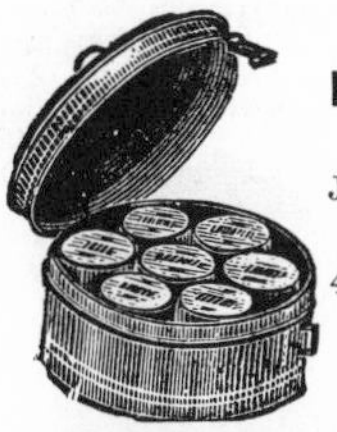

Japanned, containing five small boxes and grater. Price, per set.

45160 Size, 6¼x3½ in.......$0.35

Bread Boxes.

JAPANNED.

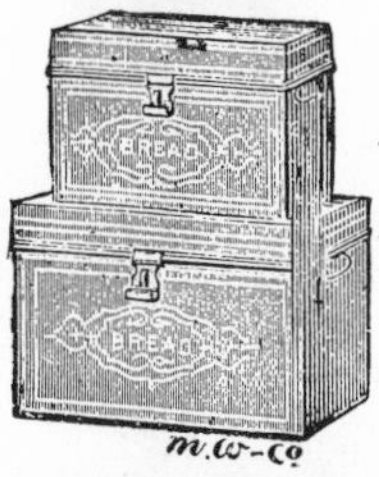

45165 Medium; size, 15x11¼ x10¼; weight, 4¼ lbs. Each $0.60

45166 Large; size, 19x13½x x14½; weight, 4¾ pounds. Each $0.75

Cash Boxes with Lock and Key.

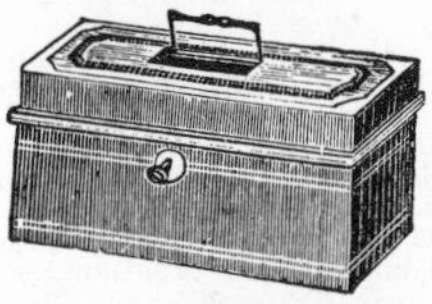

Weighs 1¼ pounds, 1½ pounds, 2 pounds; japanned.

		Each.
45168	Size, 8x5½x4	$0.50
45169	Size, 10x7x4½	60
45170	Size, 11x8x5½	.68

Folding Cash Boxes.

Open, 9½x8¼x2¾ inches; closed, 9¼x4½x4⅝ inches.

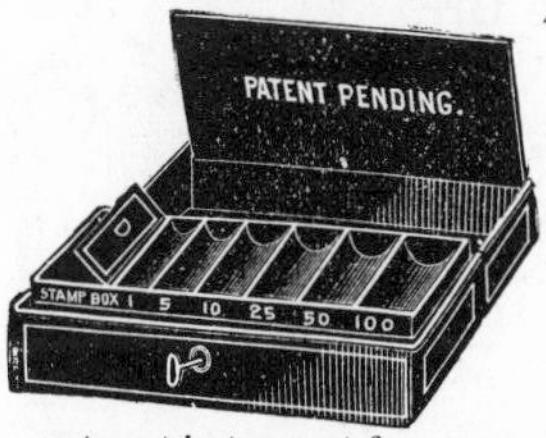

45175 The Folding Cash Box. It is made of heavy tin, well enameled, good lock. It saves time in making change and in verifying the cash. It may be used on a table or in a drawer; locked, put in a safe or vault and be ready for use the next day. It has a compartment in top part for currency, and a place under the tray for checks, drafts, money orders, postal notes, etc. It also has a tray with compartments for 31 silver dollars, 50 halves, 64 quarters, 85 dimes, 51 nickels, and 65 cents, and a box for postage stamps. The stamp box is often used for gold coin. Note our reduced price. Weight, 2¼ pounds. Each.....$1.40 Per dozen.................................. ....15.96

Deed Boxes.

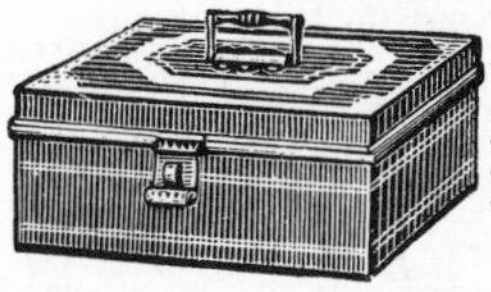

Weight, 1¼ to 2 pounds.

Japanned.		Each.
45176	Size, 8½..	$0.30
45177	Size, 10....	.40
45178	Size, 11....	.45

Chamber Pails.

Will hold 12 quarts each.

45185 Painted, assorted colors. Each $0.30

45186 Galvanized Iron Chamber Pail, made of heavy iron. 12 quarts. Each.................. .35

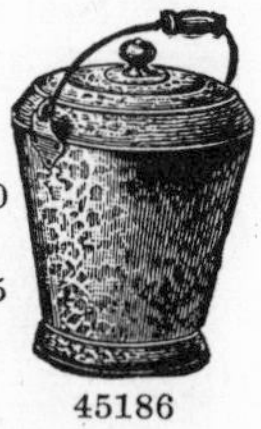

45186

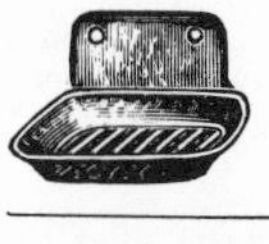

45190 Agate Iron Ware Soap Dish 6½x4x1¼ Price, each.....$0.22

SEE ALUMINUM KITCHEN WARE QUOTATIONS.

REPORT ANY ERRORS.

WE WANT TO CORRECT THEM.

Chambers.

45191 Chambers, Agate Iron Ware.
Size 7x4⅛   8½x4⅞   9¾x5½
Each 53c.   68c.   85c.

Agate Iron Bed Pans.

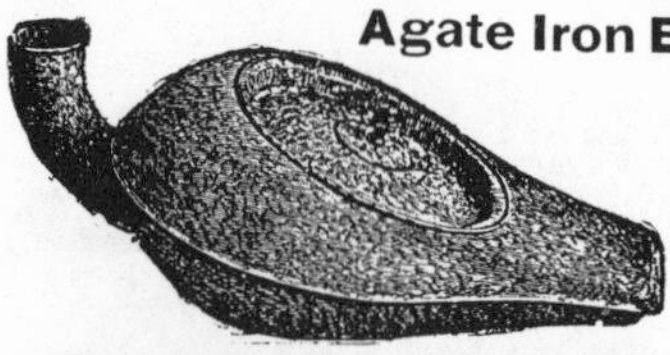

45192 Agate Iron Bed Pans, like cut.
Each..$2.04

Wash Bowls and Pitchers.

45193 Fancy Japanned Wash Bowl and pitcher; weight, 2½ lbs. Bowl, 11¼x3¾, pitcher, 6¼ x10¾. Per set........$0.62

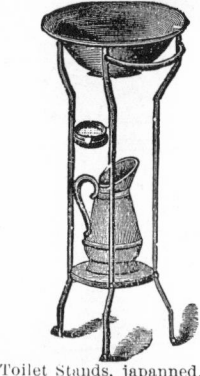

45195 Toilet Stands, japanned, 30½ inches high, with japanned tin wash bowl and pitcher and soap cup, assorted colors; weight, 2¾ lbs.
Each, complete..........$1.50
45196 Japanese Toilet Stand, with basin, slop jar, water carrier and reservoir; reservoir holds about 2 gallons; all nicely japanned and ornamented; weight, 18 lbs. Price, complete $5.95

Coffee Urn.

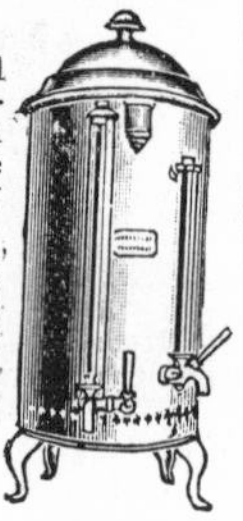

45199 Made of Copper and Nickel Plated, with water gauge, and so constructed that they can be easily taken apart for cleaning and repairing. The faucets and inside couplings screw together. The inside jars are enameled.

	Price, each.
Capacity, 10 gallons	$33.75
Capacity, 8 gallons	32.00
Capacity, 6 gallons	30.00
Capacity, 4 gallons	28.00
Capacity, 3 gallons	26.00

Water Coolers.

45200 Japanned Water Coolers, wrought iron body and base, stamped tin breast, stamped tin plate cover, corrugated galvanized iron reservoir, plated self-closing faucet, charcoal filled, assorted colors; artistic decoration.

45200
Sizes, gals....	2	3	4	6	8
Price, each..	$1.28	$1.39	$1.72	$2.05	$2.73

Water Filters.

45201 The Jewett Water Filter, for rain, river and hydrant water. The long tested and proved reliable filtering medium is natural gravel and sand combined with expressly prepared recarbonized charcoal. This filter removes all impurities in the water and renders it chemically pure. It should be cleaned out as often as once a week. Complete with faucet and cover.

Capacity, gallons	4	6	9	14
Extreme height, inches.	20	21	22½	27
Diameter of top, ins.	13¼	15	17	18¼
Weight, crated, lbs	60	80	100	1.35
Price, each	$4.65	$5.62	$6.00	$7.00

Hip Baths.

45203 Japanned Hip Baths.
Diameter 22½ in. Each..$3.50
" 27 " " .. 4.20

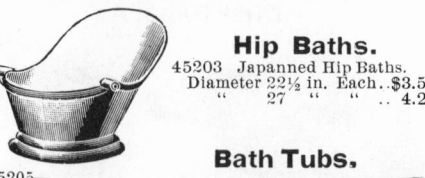

Bath Tubs.

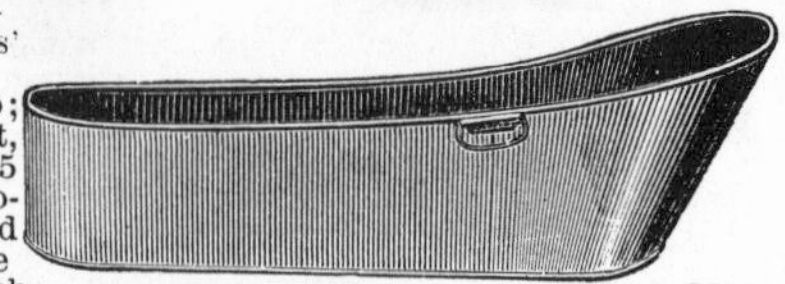

45205— Infants' Bath Tub; weight, 10 to 25 lbs; japanned tin. Size
27 inch	$0.95
30 inch	1.05
33 inch	1.25
36 inch	1.45

45206 Plunge Baths; same shape as cut, made of heavy zinc and tin, with wooden bottoms and handles at each end; japanned, blue inside, drab outside; trimmed with black, blue and gilt stripes; weight, 50 lbs. Prices include crating.
4 feet........$4.00   6 feet........$5.50
For Bath Tubs see No. 43685 to 43692.

Japan Foot Tubs.

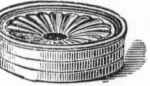

45208—
Size,	Weight.	Price each.
17x13½x7½	2 lbs	$0.45
18½x14½x8¼	2 "	.50

Spittoons.

45210 Spittoons, japanned, assorted colors........$0.16
See Index for other spittoons.

Protection Cuspidors

45212 Handsomely ornamented and secured to a mat 12 inches in diameter; cannot be tipped over; can be detached from the mat for cleaning. Three colors, blue, green and red; japanned.
No. 1. Each............$0.24
Per dozen........ 2.60

Nickel-Plated Cuspidors.

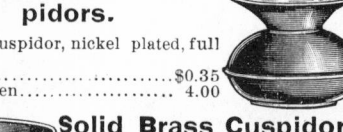

45214 Cuspidor, nickel plated, full size.
Each........$0.35
Per dozen........ 4.00

Solid Brass Cuspidors.

45216 Cuspidor, solid brass, has broad bottom, large opening in top; cannot be tipped over easily; is heavy; full size (86). Each........$0.95
Per dozen........10.26

Polished Brass Cuspidors.

45218 Cuspidor, polished brass, not nickel plated; has oxidized ornamental band around base; a very handsome pattern; is full size.
Each........$0.60
Per dozen........ 6.48

Champion Oil Cans.

45222 Champion Oil Cans, for kerosene or gasoline; made from galvanized iron, with brass faucet, nickel plated and screw top. We can recommend this can, as it is an established fact that galvanized iron is the best material that can be put together to hold kerosene or gasoline. Every can warranted not to leak.
5-gallon, price, each........$0.75

The Sterling Swinging Can.

45223 The Sterling Swinging Can, for kerosene or gasoline; has spring valve spout and is made of galvanized iron. The frame-work is made from heavy steel and is separable from can. To fill lamp, swing can in position, then push the button.
5-gallon, price, each........$0.90

New Ironsides Oil and Gasoline Pump Can.

45224 This can is made from galvanized iron, with brass valves, brass trimmings; valve is removable; plunger rod comes out; steady stream force pump; is the most reliable and rapid worker; screw cap covers the entire pump; any part of pump or can is so constructed that repairs can be made if necessary.
3-gallon, price, each........$0.90
5 " " 1.10
10 " " 1.50

Kerosene Cans.

Glass with tin jacket Oil Can. This cut does not represent the exact pattern, but only the general character.
45231 One gallon, weight, 3 lbs.
10 oz. Each........$0.28
Per dozen........ 2.50

Tin Oil Cans.

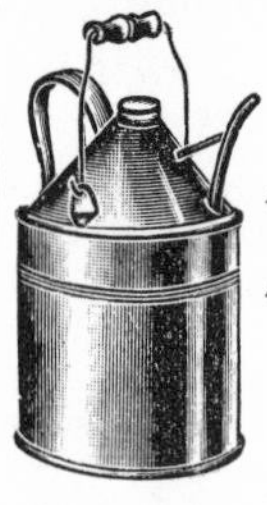

45233 One gallon; weight, 1 lb.
Each........$0.20
Per dozen........ 2.00
45234 Two gallons; weight, 1¾ lbs.
Each........ .30
Per dozen........ 3.25

Wood Jacket Oil Cans.

45235 Wood Jacket Oil Cans, made of IC tin.
Gallons	1	2
Price, each	20c	25c
Price, per dozen	$2.00	$2.62
	3	5
	30c	40c
	$3.35	$4.00

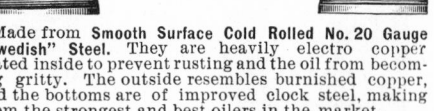

Copperized Anti-Rust Oilers.

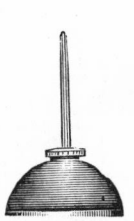

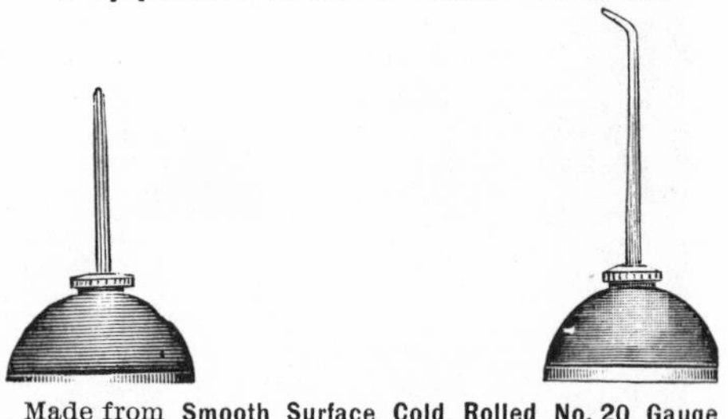

Made from Smooth Surface Cold Rolled No. 20 Gauge "Swedish" Steel. They are heavily electro copper plated inside to prevent rusting and the oil from becoming gritty. The outside resembles burnished copper, and the bottoms are of improved clock steel, making them the strongest and best oilers in the market.

					Each.	Doz.
45236 No. 13—	3⅜ in. dia.,	3 in. nozzle			$0.20	$1.85
" 13A—	3⅜ in. dia.,	5 in. nozzle			.25	2.00
" 14—	3⅜	"	9	" (bent).	.26	2.15
" 14A—	3¾	"	3	"	.28	2.56
" 14AA	3¾	"	5	"	.30	2.67
" 14B—	3¾	"	9	" (bent).	.31	2.83
" 15—	4⅛	"	3	"	.32	3.08
" 15A —	4⅛	"	5	"	.35	3.25
" 16—	4⅛	"	9	" (bent).	.37	3.50

Extra Nozzles.

45237 Copperized Steel Nozzles, from 3 to 12 inches; are interchangeable and will fit any size of No. 45236 oilers.

				Each.	Doz.
3 inch nozzles				$0.10	$1.10
5 "	"			.12	1.30
9 "	" (bent)			.16	1.70
12 "	"			.25	2.30

Railroad Oilers.

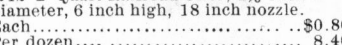

Also an excellent traction engine oiler: have seamless drawn bodies and are indestructible. They are heavily nickel plated on electro copper plate.
45241 1 Pint Railroad Oiler; 3⅜ inch diameter, 5 inches high, 12 inch nozzle.
Each........$0.75   Per dozen .. $7.20
45242 1 Quart Railroad Oiler; 4⅛ inch diameter, 6 inch high, 18 inch nozzle.
Each........$0.80
Per dozen.... .... 8.40

Oil Cans.

45243—
Sizes....... 0 1 2 4 5
Each........ 4c. 5c. 6c. 8c. 10c.
Per dozen.. 40c. 50c. 60c. 80c. $1.10
No. 0 is small, 2 inches across bottom and holds about ⅛ pint. No. 5 is 4¾ inches across bottom and holds about 1 pint. The others are graduated between The weights vary from 4 to 7 ounces

45244 Automatic Zinc Oiler. This oiler cannot be tipped over like the ordinary zinc oiler. When accidently over-thrown it will immediately resume an upright position because of the rounding shape of sides and very heavy bottom, consequently no oil can be accidentally spilled from this oiler
Nos............. 1 2 3
Holds......... 3 oz. 4 oz. 6 oz.
Each .... 15c. 17c. 19c.
Per dozen....... $1.62 $2.16 $2.38

45245 Malleable Iron Oiler; very strong; has patent elliptic steel spring; weight 10 oz. Each...... $0.25
Per dozen 2.70
Mowing Machine Oilers, tin, bent or straight spout; weight, 7 oz.
45246 Bent Spout.
45247 Straight Spout.
Each $0.07
Per dozen............ .78
45245   45246-7

WHITE LUSTRAL WIRE GOODS.

Wire Comb and Hair Brush Cases.

45250—
                    Each. Per doz
6 inch..... $0.15 $1.60
9 inch........ .25 2.70

Wire Sponge Baskets.

45251—
Size   Each.   Per doz.
5x3 .. $0.16 $1.73
7x4 ..   .20   2.16
8x5½ .. .24   2.60
10x6½ .. .28   3.00

Wire Brush Broom Holders.

45252 Adapted to all varieties of small brooms and brushes.
Each...................... $0.12
Per dozen..................... 1.30
See Index for other broom holders.

Wire Soap Brackets.

45253—
Each..... ....$0.17
Per dozen.... 1.80

Tea or Coffee Pot Stands.

45260 6¼ inch.
Each...............$0.07
Per dozen.......... .75

Coat Hangers.

45263 Wire Coat or Garment Hanger, 17 inch. Garments when hung on this device do not lose their shape as when hung on hook or nail.
Price, each, tinned.................$0.06
Per dozen.......................... .65
45264 Price, each, copper finish...... .... .05
Per dozen.... .... .50

Fruit Jar Holder.

45265 Fruit-Jar Holder, for holding jar while hot or when taking off caps.
For 1 quart jars, each.... ....$0.15
Per dozen.. 1.65
45266 For 2 quart jars, each.. $0.17
Per dozen... 1.85
For price of fruit jars, see Grocery List.

Plate Lifter.

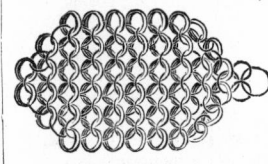

45267 Triumph Plate Lifter, for lifting hot plates from oven.
Each..... ....$0.13

Pot Cleaners.

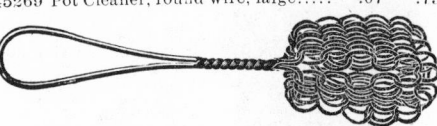

Pot Cleaner or Wire Dish Cloth, the most convenient and popular utensil extant; pots and kettles can be cleaned of grease easily, and when done there is no dirty dish rag to wash out. Each. Per doz
45268 Pot Cleaner, round wire, small.....$0.05 $0.54
45269 Pot Cleaner, round wire, large..... .07 .75

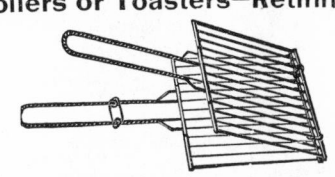

45270 Handled Pot Cleaner, tinned wire handle, bright wire rings; total length, 9½ inches.
Each ....$0.08 Per dozen $0.85

Broilers or Toasters—Retinned.

45275—
Long. Wide.   No. bars. Each.
9 x 6...........................9.... $0.12
9 x 7½.........................11.... .14
9 x 9..........................11.... .15
9 x 10½........................15.... .16
9 x 12.........................17 .. .18
9 x 13½........................19 .20

Vegetable Boilers.

45278 Made of wire. Can also be used for boiling eggs.
Size   6 in.   7 in.   8 in.   9 in.
Each   14c.   17c.   19c.   21c.

Corn Popper.

45280 Corn Poppers, tin top. 1 quart. Each....$0.08
Per dozen........................ .87
45281 Corn Poppers, wire top, 2 quarts.
Each .... .15
Per dozen........................ 1.62
45282 Corn Poppers, 4 quarts, each.............. .75
45283 " " 8 " " 2.75
The 4 and 8 quart poppers are such used by confectioners, street venders, etc.

Wire Toasters.

45285 Wire Toaster, wood handle.
Each........................ $0.05
Per dozen.................... .45

Dish Cloth Holder.

45288 Dish Cloth Holder. Lamp Chimney Cloth Holder, or for pulling corks from bottles.
Each ....6c. Per dozen $0.56

Potato Masher.

45292 Tinned wire Potato Masher, wood handle.
                    Each. Per doz.
Large $0.09 $0.90

Fly Traps.

45295 The Champion Fly Trap, made of fine wire cloth; a very strong and well made trap, with a high cone; will catch flies faster than any other.
Each.............. ....$0.15
Per doz 1.62

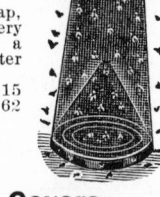

Dish Covers.

45296 Round Dish Covers, made of blued wire cloth.
Size..... 6 7 8 9 10
Each $0.04 $0.05 $0.06 $0.07 $0.09
Per doz..40 .50 .60 .70 .90
45297 Round Dish Covers, made of blued wire cloth, in sets of 5, one of each size, 6, 7, 8, 9, 10.
Per set..... .... $0.28

Bird Cages.

45300 Bird Cage, round, all brass, 8½ inches in diameter, with seed cups, perch, etc.; has bell bottom.
Each..................................$1 00

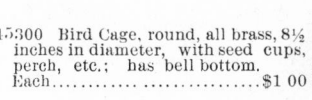

45305 Squirrel Cages, for red or chip squirrels, made of wire, japanned; size, over all, 18 in. long; 10 in. wide, 13 in. high; size of body, 10 in. long, 9 in. wide, 12 in. high; size of wheel, 6½ in. long, 9 in. in diameter.
Price, each............$1.60

Climax Rat Trap.

45306 A Self-Setting Rat Catcher. Convenient bait box, novel tilting platform. This trap is made with a bait box that is supplied through a lid at the top. It holds the bait alluringly to the rat, yet he cannot readily withdraw it through the fine meshes. The trap is made of heavy double crimped steel wires which cannot be displaced or broken. The trap will maintain its original shape and can be shipped compactly and will always reach destination in good condition. Size of trap, 20 inches long, 8 inches wide, 7 inches high. Price, each................$1.00
Per dozen........................ 10.50

Combination Rat and Mouse Trap.

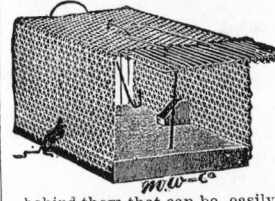

45307 This is made of retinned wire cloth and may be used to catch either mice or rats. When set for mice, the end is closed, the mice entering at the hole inside the trap; small wire door drops behind them that can be easily opened by the mice on the outside but not from inside; as one mouse will act as a decoy for another, quite a number may be caught at once. When rats are to be caught it is set as seen in cut. Weight, 1 lb. 13 oz. Each $0.35
Per dozen........................ 3.60
N. B.—Rat traps are often sprung by mice who go out between the wires and leave no track behind them. This trap will catch them every time.

Rat Traps.

45308 National Rat Traps Weight, 1 lb. 3 oz
Each..
......$0.25
Per doz
.... $2.70

Genuine Marty's French Trap for Catching Rats Alive.

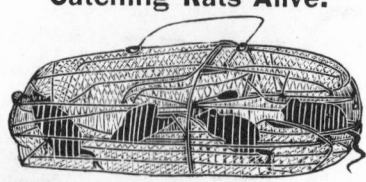

45309 The Marty trap is made only in France, and was patented in the United States in December, 1893. It is a wonderful effect trap, and is used by the leading hotels, public institutions and market houses. Many testimonials proving that they will catch their full capacity night after night as long as the rats hold out. No. 3, family size, 17 inches long, capacity, 20 rats. No. 1, hotel and stable size, 27 inches long, capacity, 50 rats. No. 3. Each....................$0.75
Per dozen................................7.20
No. 2. Each...............................1.75
Per dozen................................20.00

The Grip Self Setting Animal Trap.

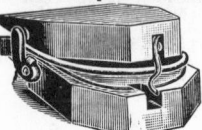

45310 For rats and all small game. Made of hard wood and best spring steel wire.
Each.....................$0.10
Per dozen.... ....1.00

This is the way to set the trap.

45315 Round Wire Rat Traps wood bottom.
13 inch, each............$ 0.25
Per dozen................2.70

Mouse and Rat Traps

Choker Mouse Trap, round pattern, easy to set, and will catch a mouse every time:

	Each.	Per doz.
45316 4 holes	$0.03	$0.33
45317 5 holes	.05	.54

The Choker Mouse Trap, oblong pattern, very easy to set and can be depended upon to go off at the proper time; 1, 2 and 3 holes.

	Each.	Per doz.
45319 1 hole	$0.02	$0.15
45321 2 holes	.03	.20
45322 3 holes	.04	.30

45323 The Mascotte Mouse Trap, the most successful mouse catching device ever invented; one mouse sets the trap for another; will hold several. When several are caught, put the trap in a pail of water. Each..$0.10
Per dozen......................1.00

45324 The Erie Rat Trap; a trap that can always be depended upon to catch rats. There is nothing suspicious looking about it to scare them, and it kills instantly without drawing blood or otherwise scenting the trap; a great number of rats can continually be caught in it. Weight, 1½ lbs. Each............................$0.12
Per dozen.........................1.30

Sheet Metals.

SHEET ZINC.
45340 This is the ordinary stock Zinc, about 26 gauge, 36 inches wide, 7 feet in length, weighs 14 lbs. Per sheet...........................$1.15
Per one-half sheet.........................65

SHEET IRON.
45341 Common Black Sheet Iron, such as stove pipe is made of, etc.; size of sheet 24x101 inches.

No.	Wt. per sheet.	Whole sheet.
24	17 lbs.	$0.75
26	14 lbs.	.65
27	13 lbs.	.60

GALVANIZED SHEET IRON.
45342 Size of sheet, 28x96 inches.

No.	Wt. per sheet.	Whole sheet.
24	24 lbs.	$1.30
26	18 lbs.	1 25
27	16½ lbs.	1.20

We do not sell any less than a box at box prices.

BRIGHT TIN.
45343 IC Bright Charccal.

Inches.	14x20	20x28
No. sheets in box.	112	112
Weight, lbs.	120	240
Per box.........	$8.00	$15.67
Per sheet.........	.07	.15

Sheet Metals—Continued.

IC ROOFING TIN.
45344 IC Charcoal.
We carry two grades of roofing tin.

Inches	14x20	20x28
No. of sheets in a box	112	112
Weight of box	120 lbs.	240 lbs.
Per box	$6.60	$12.65
Per sheet	.07	.12

IX ROOFING TIN.
45345 IX Charcoal.
The IX quality is heavier than the IC.

Inches	14x20	20x28
No. sheets in a box	112	112.
Weight per box	150 lbs.	300 lbs
Per box	$8.25	$15.95
Per sheet	.08	.15

IC COKE TIN.
Used for making Gutters, etc.
45346 Size of sheets, 10x20. No. sheets in box 225. Weight per box, 110 lbs.
Per box..............................$10.72
Per sheet...............................05
Owing to the constant fluctuations of the price of tin the box price is subject to change of market.

SHEET COPPER.
45347 Soft Sheet Copper, soft rolled, not polished. For sheets tinned on one side add 8 cents per sheet.

Size of sheet.	Weight of sheet	Per sheet.
14 oz.. 14x48 in.	4 5-16 lbs.	$1.20
16 oz.. 14x48 in.	4¾ lbs.	1.30

The above prices of above metals subject to market changes, but will always bill them at the lowest price ruling. We do not sell less than one sheet of copper.

Improved Farmers' Boilers.

For Wood or Coal

For cooking feed for stock, heating water, making soap and sugar, rendering lard, washing clothes, as well as all other kinds of boiling. Give our boilers a trial and you will never buy any other.

45365 Price with cover and feet as shown in cut.

Gallons	Weight with cover and feet.	With Wood Fixtures.	With Coal Fixtures.
15	200 lbs.	$12.25	$15.00
20	235 "	14.00	17.28
30	305 "	17.64	20.52
45	395 "	22.68	25.66
60	434 "	29.52	31.80

We can furnish wheels in place of feet at an extra cost of $2.70 per set of 4 wheels.

Copper Kettles.

45366—

Size.	Weight, about	Diameter on top inside.	Deep.	Price, each.
40 Gallon	48 lbs.	27 inch	19¼ inch	$11.04
36 Gallon	46 lbs.	26 inch	19 inch	10.58
30 Gallon	39 lbs.	24½ inch	17½ inch	8.97
25 Gallon	32 lbs.	23½ inch	15 inch	7.35
20 Gallon	29 lbs.	22 inch	14½ inch	6.67

45367 Sugar or Wash Kettles, with bails milled and painted. No. 7, 30 gal. kettle is the largest cast iron kettle with bail made. Average weights of kettles are given below.

Actual Measure.	Weight. Each.	Actual Measure.	Weight. Each.
No. 1, 8 gal.	25 lb.$0.93	No. 5, 21½ gal.	52 lb.$.200
No. 2, 10 gal.	30 lb. 1.19	No. 6, 25 gal.	65 lb. 2.35
No. 3, 15 gal.	42 lb. 1.40	No. 7, 30 gal.	85 lb. 2.80
No. 4, 18 gal.	48 lb. 1.70		

M. W. & CO.'S HAMMERLESS GUN.

❧ ❧   **$65.00 GRADE FOR $35.00.**

None Genuine Unless Stamped on Top Rib, Montgomery Ward & Co., Chicago.

See Page 449.

CUTLERY DEPARTMENT.

Our knives are selected from the most reliable manufactories, and are warranted as represented. The blades of our knives are ground as thin as a good cutting blade should be ground. If the edge gets dull sharpen by holding on the "stone" at an angle of about 40 degrees.

Ladies' Knives.
Extra by mail for Ladies' Knives, 3 cents.

46000 One blade, white handle, good steel blades.
Each..............$0.10 Per dozen.............$1.10

46002 Ladies' Pearl Handle Knife, one blade and glove buttoner; best quality, finely finished, 2½ in. long. Each....$0.34 Per dozen.......$3.60

46003 Ladies' Knife, inlaid shell handle, two blade, 2¾ in, well finished and a good article.
Each..............$0.12 Per dozen.............$1.25

46004 Two blades, with white handle. Each....$0.12
Per dozen 1.25

46005 Pearl Handle. Each $0.18 Per dozen....$1.65

46006 Two blades, pearl handle. Each.........$0.15
Per dozen.................................1.50

46007 Ladies' two blade fancy pearl handle.
Each.........$0.18 Per dozen..............$1.00

46008 Two blades, finest pearl handles and best finish, highest grade steel blades; an elegant article.
2½ in. handle. Each.........$0.70 Per dozen, $7.56
2¾ in. handle. Each.......... .75 Per dozen. 8.10

46009 Ladies' two blade fancy pearl handle; a fine knife. Each......$0.20 Per dozen ... $2.00

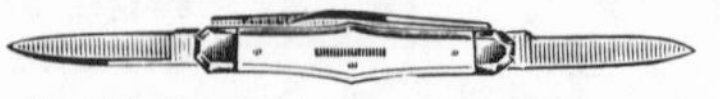

46010 Four blades, 2½ in., pearl handle, German silver bolster, finest finish, best of steel blades, warranted Each......$0.60 Per dozen....$6.90

46011 Two blades, scored pearl handle. Each.$0.18
Per dozen........ ....1.95

46012 Three blades, pearl handle; a fine knife.
Each.......$0.49 Per dozen...............$5.00

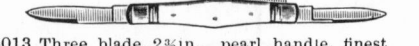

46013 Three blade, 2⅜in., pearl handle, finest finish, best quality, warranted. Each........$0.75
Per dozen.... ....8.20

46014 Four blades, pearl handle. Each.........$0.45
Per dozen.................................4.27

Cutlery—Continued.

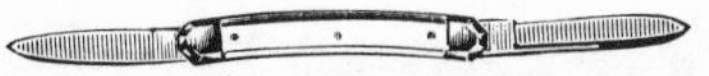

46015 Two blade, 2½ in., pearl handle, fine finish, warranted. Each..................$0.45
Per dozen.. 4.80

46016 Two blade, 2⅜ in., pearl handle, brass lined, milled edges; a neat article. Each..... $0.30
Per dozen...................................... 3.20

46017 Four blades, 2⅝ inch shell handle, 1 large, 1 manicure and 2 small blades; a neat little knife. Each..............................$0.25

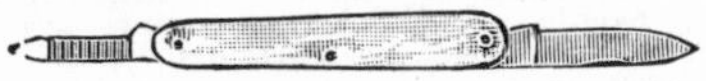

46018 Two blade, 2¾ in., fine pearl handle, finely finished, and warranted finest steel blades. Each........$0.47 Per dozen.........$5.00

Men's Knives.

All of our knives are warranted. If not found as represented can be returned at our expense. Knives by mail, 3 to 5 cents extra.

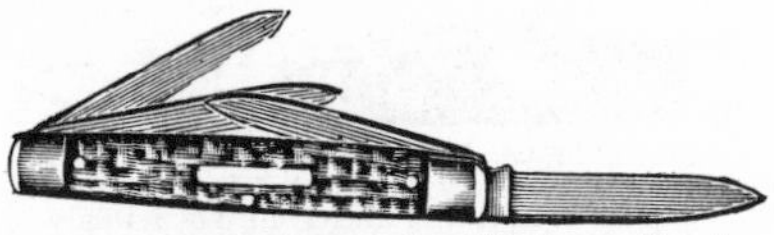

46019—Four blades, stag handle, brass lined. Each..............$0.27 Per dozen........ $2.90

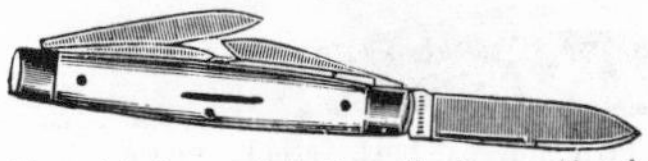

46021 Four blades, white handle, brass lined, a good seller. Each....$0.30 Per dozen........$3.00

46022 Two blades, fine ivory handle 3¼ inch long, handsome in design and finish, the very best quality steel blades; retail price $1.00. See our price: warranted. Each..$0.50 Per doz..$4.90

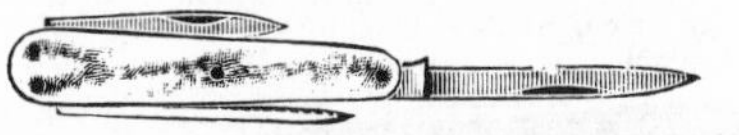

46023 Two blades, finest pearl handle, 3 in. long manicure file blade on back, very best quality and finish; a beauty: retail price $2.00. See our price, warranted. Each... $.90 Per doz.$ 9.00

46027 Three blades, ebony handles, brass lined, warranted ....$0.30 Per dozen........$3.25

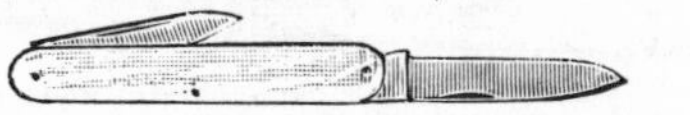

46028 Two blades, 3 in., fine pearl handle, finely finished, warranted best quality steel blades; a very desirable article; our big seller. Each......................$0.60 Per dozen........$6 50

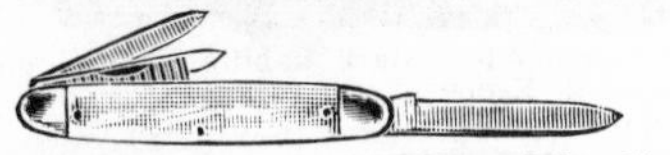

46029 Three blades, 3 in., finest pearl handle, German silver bolsters, finely finished; every one warranted best steel blades. Each..............$0.70 Per dozen..........$7.90

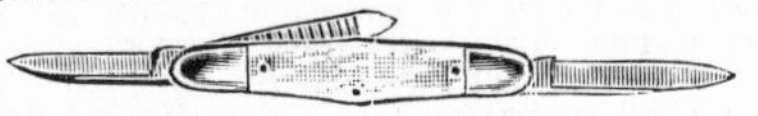

46030 Three blades. 2⅞ in., pearl handles, German silver bolsters. 1 file blade; well made and durable: every one warranted best steel blades. Each...................$0.35 Per dozen........$3.60

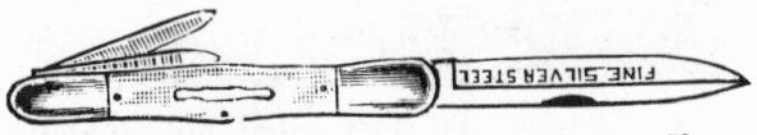

46031 Three blades, 3½ in., fine pearl handles German silver bolsters, well finished. A good, strong durable article. Each........$0.50 Per dozen..........$5.50

46035 Three blades, fine buck horn handle, brass lined. German silver bolster, best quality blades, warranted, 3½ in. handle. Retail price, $1.50. Our price, each....$0.90 Per dozen.......$9.50

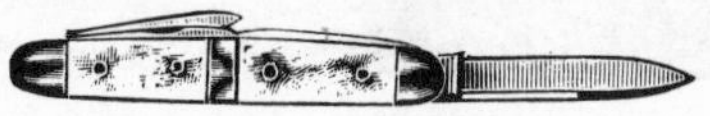

46038 Three blades, pearl handle, brass lined, German silver bolster, warranted. Each.......$0.50
Per dozen...................................... 5.40

Cutlery—Continued.

46044 Three blades, fancy pearl handle, brass lined, finely finished and warranted. Each...$0.40
Per dozen...................................... 4.25

46045 Two blades, 3¼ in., dark horn handle, brass lined milled edges, crocus polished; a good office or vest pocket knife. Each..$0.35 Per dozen..$3.60

46047 Six blades, pearl handle. Each $0.40
Per dozen...................................... 4.40

46050 Three blades, 3½ in., fine pearl handle; German silver lined, German silver bolsters; a beauty; warranted. Retail price, $1.75. (See our price until sold.) Each..$0.85 Per dozen............$9.00

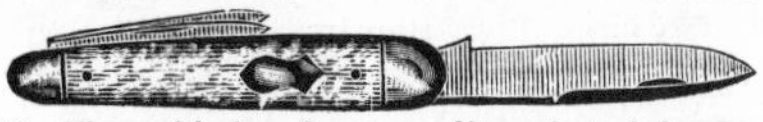

46053 Three blades, finest quality of steel, brass lined, 3½ in. pearl handle, German silver bolsters, nail blade, good, strong, large blade; no better knife made for durability and cutting quality. Every one warranted. Retail price, $2.00. Our price, each....$1.50 Per dozen..........$15.00

46054 Three blades, stag horn handle, otherwise same as No. 46053. Every one warranted. Each............ $1.00 Per dozen..........$11.00

46056 Three blades, 3½ in. ebony handle, otherwise same as 46053, every one warranted; just the right size for a pocket knife for general use. Each.........$0.79 Per dozen..............$8.40

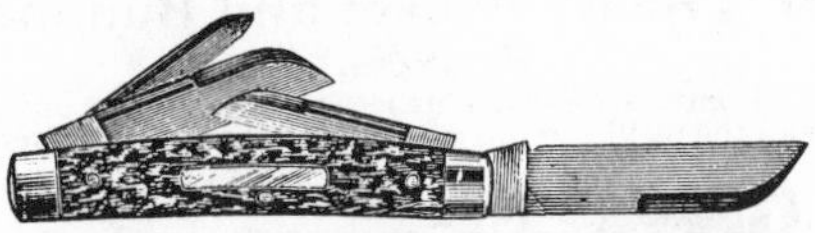

46058 Four blades, "Congress" style, 3¾-inch stag horn handle, German silver bolsters, brass lined, best steel blades; a good strong article; warranted. Each...$0.87 Per dozen $9.00

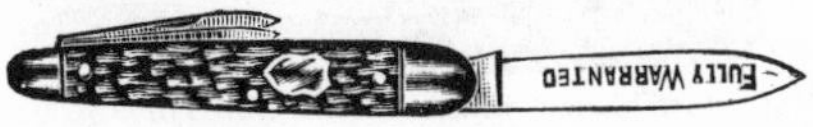

46059 Three blades, fine 3½ inch buck horn handle brass lined, German silver bolsters, brass lined; warranted. Each.. $0.54 Per dozen....$5.75

46060 Four Blade Congress buck horn handle, best steel, warranted. Each. $0.55 Per dozen.... $5.50

46061 Four blades Congress, 3½ inch buck horn handle, genuine IXL Wostenholm make. Each. $1.35
Per dozen...................................... 13.90

46062 Three blades, fine pearl handle, German silver bolsters, warranted, a fine knife. Each. $0.48
Per dozen...................................... 4.50

46063 Genuine IXL George Wostenholm, four blades, 3-inch pearl handle. It is a large size ladies' knife or a medium size for gentlemen, and a fine knife for any one. Retail price, $2.25. See our price, Each..$1.60 Per dozen...... 15.95

46064 Genuine IXL George Wostenholm, 3⅜ in., pearl handle, four blades. Is just right size for gentlemen's use. No better knife made at any price. Each.......$1.65 Per dozen $19.00

Cutlery—Continued.

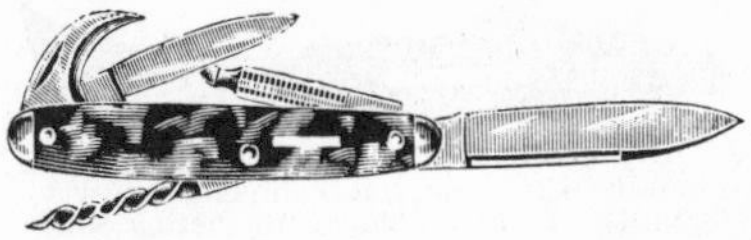

46065 Champagne Knife, German silver lined and bolsters, best 3¾ in. shell handle. A beauty; warranted. Each...........................$1.00
Per dozen......................................10.50

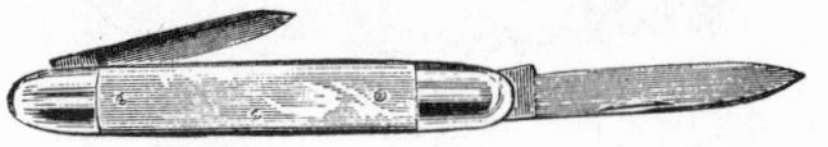

46066 Two blades, German silver bolsters, 2¾ inches, best warranted steel; a fine little article. Each..............$0.56
Per dozen...................................... 5.75

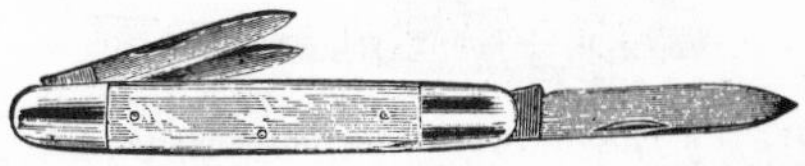

46067 Three blades, German silver bolsters, 2¾ inches, finest pearl handle, fine finish, highest quality steel blades; warranted. Each........$0.80
Per dozen...................................... 8.40

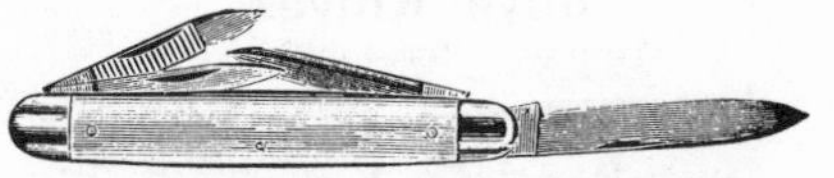

46068 Four blades, German silver bolsters, 2¾ inches, finest pearl handle, finest finish, highest quality steel blades; vest pocket size; warranted. Each......................................$1.00
Per dozen......................................10.95

46069 Three blades, German silver bolsters, 2⅞ inches, finest quality pearl handles, best steel blades, best finish; handsome and desirable; warranted. Each............................$0.80
Per dozen...................................... 8.64

46070 Three blades, German silver bolsters, 3⅜ inches, fine pearl handles, finest finish, best steel blades, good and strong; warranted. Each..$0.98
Per dozen......................................10.80

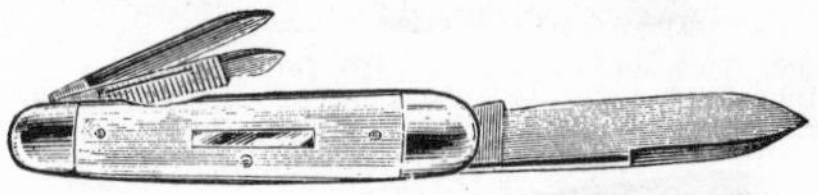

46071 Three blades, German silver bolsters, 2⅞ inches, finest pearl handles, finest finish, good, strong and durable; warranted. Each......$1.15
Per dozen......................................12.00

46072 Three blades, brass lined, German silver bolsters, 3⅜ in. pearl handle, finest steel blades, finely finished, a good strong knife; warranted. Retail price, $2.50. See our price, each $1.20
Per dozen......................................13.00

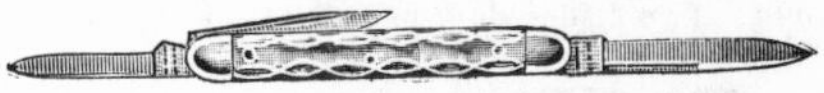

46073 Three blades, 3⅜ in. fine pearl handle, German silver bolsters, warranted best of steel. A beauty. Each...................$0.75
Per dozen...................................... 7.50

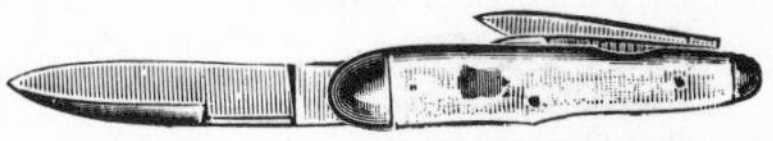

46074 Three blades, pearl handles, brass lined, German silver bolsters, a good strong knife, finely finished and warranted; best of steel blades. Retail price, $2.50. See our price. Each......................................$1.40
Per dozen......................................14.50

46075 Two blades, 3 in. pearl handle, brass lined, German silver bolsters, fine finish, best of steel blades; warranted. Each...................$0.80
Per dozen...................................... 9.00

Cutlerp—Continued.

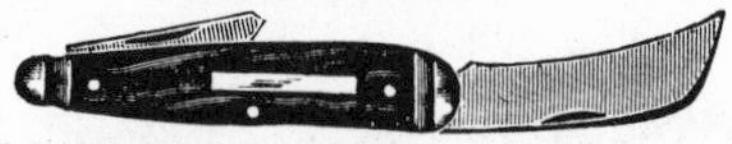

46076 Two blade Pruner and Budding Knife, stag horn handle, 4 in. long, finely finished and very best quality of steel blades; no better knife made: every one warranted.
Retail price. $1.25. Our price, each $0.85
Per dozen 9.00

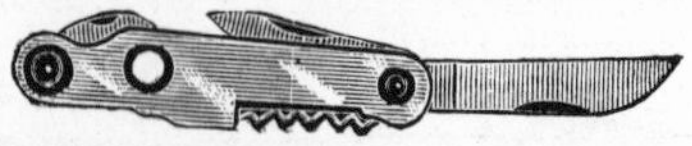

46076½ Champagne Knife, German silver handles, 3¼ inch long, cork screw and cigar cutter, well finished and a good strong, durable article; warranted. Retail price, $1.00.
Our price, each $0.45
Per dozen 4.80

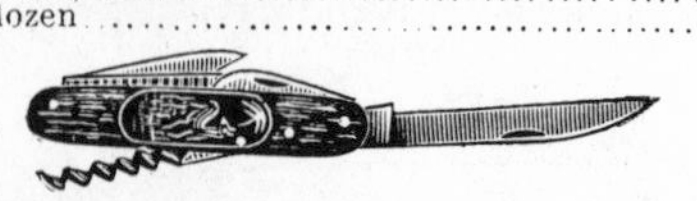

46077 Champagne Knife, stag horn handle, 2⅞ inches long, manicure blade and corkscrew; a general utility knife, finely finished, good and strong: warranted. Each $0.70
Per dozen 8.00

Boys' Knives.

Postage, extra, 3 to 5 cents.

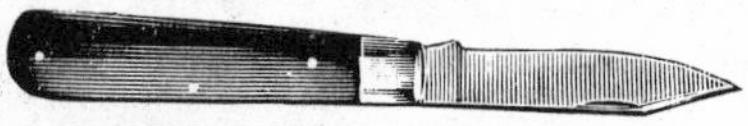

46078 One blade Boys' Knife, clip blade, 3⅜ in. cocoa handle. Each $0 15
Per dozen 1.65

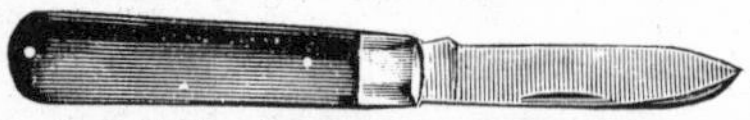

46079 One blade Boys' Knife, 3⅜ inch, cocoa handle. Each $0.14
Per dozen 1.63

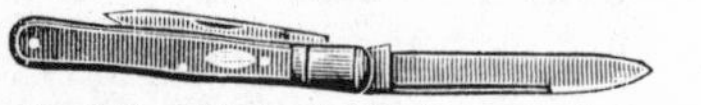

46080 Boys' Two-blade Knife, fancy dark horn handle. brass lined, fancy bolsters, a very fine article. Each $0.20
Per dozen 2.20

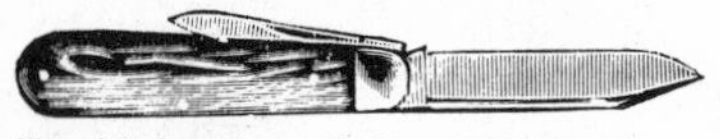

46081 Two blades, Boys' Knife, clip blade. 3¼ in., cocoa handle. Each $0.24
Per dozen 2.40

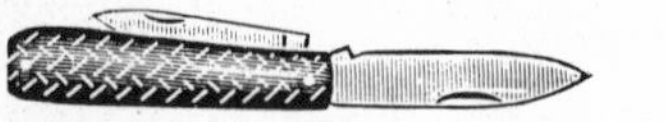

46082 Two blades, Boys' Knife, fancy metal handle. Each $0.07
Per dozen .... .60

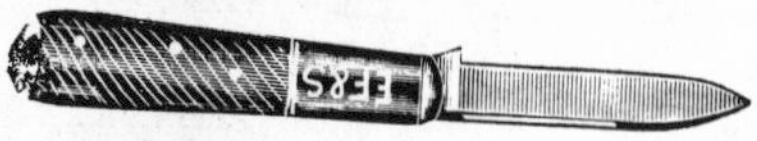

46084 One blade, Boy's Barlow. Each $0.08
Per dozen .... .86

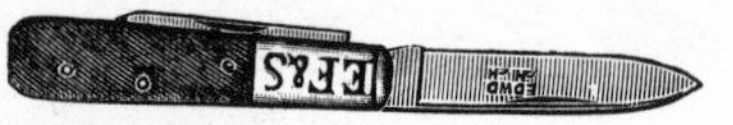

46085 Two blades, Boy's Barlow, horn handle.
Each .... $0.12 Per dozen $1.30

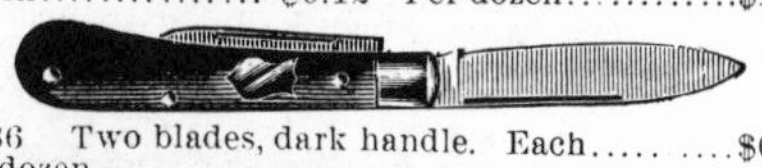

46086 Two blades, dark handle. Each $0.12
Per dozen 1.30

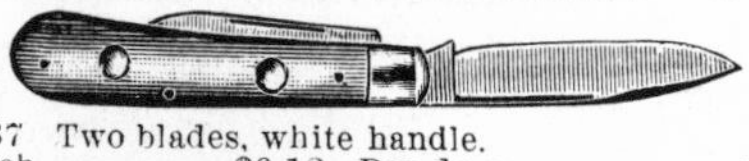

46087 Two blades, white handle.
Each .... $0.12 Per dozen $1.25

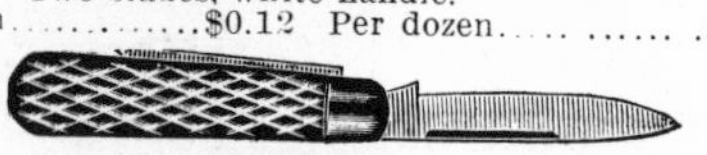

46088 Two blades, scored wood handle.
Each .... $0.12 Per dozen 1.25

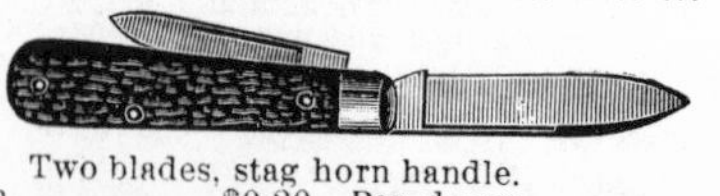

46090 Two blades, stag horn handle.
Each .... $0.20 Per dozen 2.00

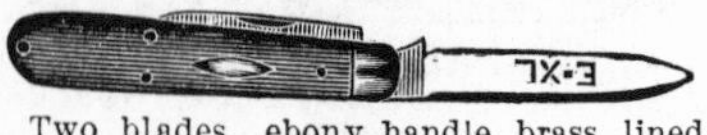

46092 Two blades, ebony handle, brass lined, German silver bolsters; warranted finest quality blades. Each .... $0.39 Per dozen 3.95

Cutlery—Continued.

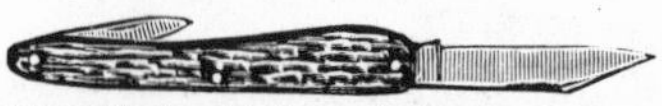

46093 Two blades, 3¼ inch, imitation stag horn handle, brass lined. Each $0.15
Per dozen 1.40

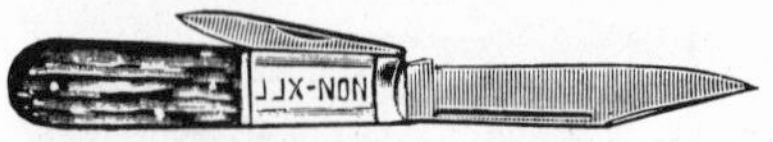

46094 Two blade Barlow, 3¼-inch, stag horn clip handle, point blade, English make: warranted. Each $0.29
Per dozen 3.20

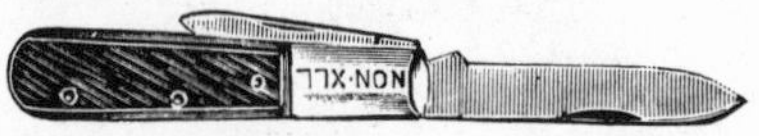

46095 Two blades, Barlow, 3⅛-inch, stag horn handle, spear point blade, English make, warranted. Each ..... $0.25 Per dozen $2.50

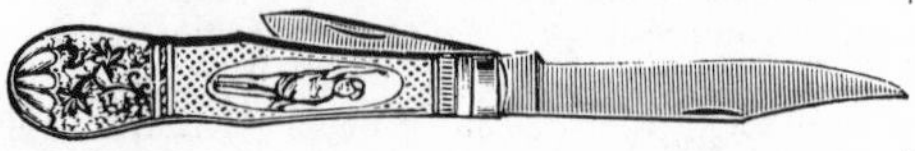

46096 Two blades, Boys' Hunting Style Knife, clip point blade, fancy nickel plated handle. Each. $0.12
Per dozen 1.25

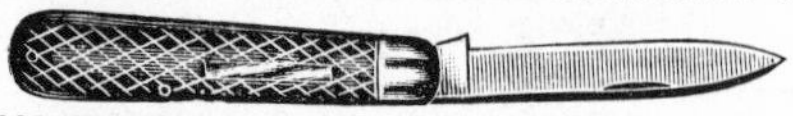

46097 Boys' iron handle, in imitation of buck horn, good steel blades. A strong knife; warranted. Each ..... $0.09 Per dozen $0.75

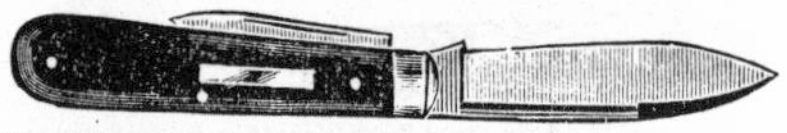

46099 Two blades, ebony handle, better quality: warranted. Each ..... $0.28 Per dozen $3.00
46099½ Two blade, dark handle, a good strong knife. Each .... $0.25 Per dozen 2.20

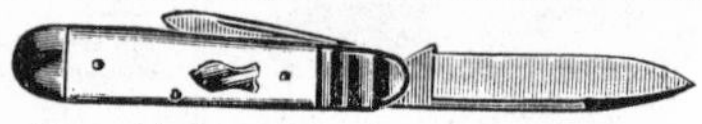

46100 Two blades, white bone handle, better quality; a good knife.
Each .... $0.35 Per dozen $3.60

Men's Heavy Pocket and Hunting Knives.

All our knives are warranted. Our prices are about one half the regular retail price. Extra by mail, 5c. each.

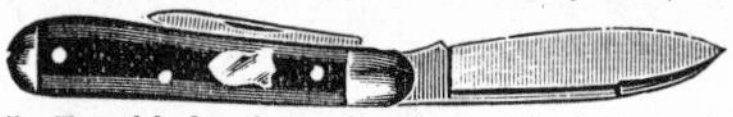

46105 Two blades, brass lined, double bolstered, fine cocoa handle; warranted.
Each .... $0.40 Per dozen $4.00

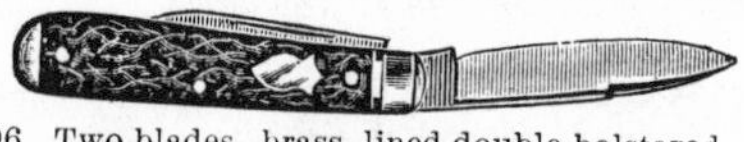

46106 Two blades, brass lined double bolstered, fine stag horn handle, warranted.
Each .... $0.35 Per dozen $3.60
46107 Two blade, finest quality, brass lined, German silver bolsters, 3½ in. stag horn handle; a good strong article; warranted.
Each .... $0.60 Per dozen $6.50

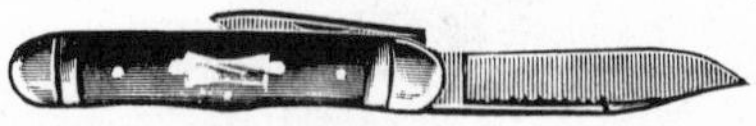

46108 Two blades, 3½-inch, ebony handle; brass lined, fancy Germain silver bolsters, clip blade.
Each .... $0.55 Per dozen $6.00

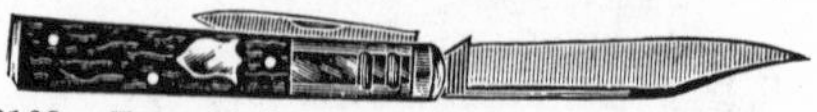

46109 Two blade, fancy clip barlow, heavy capped end, 4-in handle· a good article.
Each .... $0.40 Per dozen $4.00

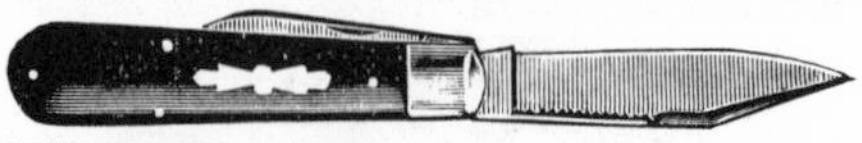

46110 Two blades, 3⅞-inch ebony handle; clip blade, brass lined, German silver bolster. Warranted. Each .... $0.55. Per dozen $6.00

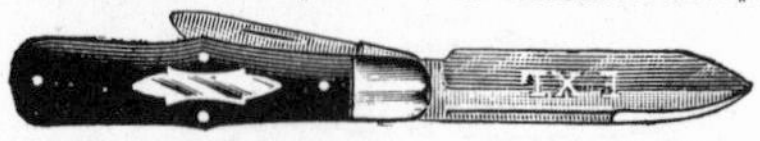

46112 Two blades, 3¾-in. ebony handle Swedish shape blade: well made and durable. Every one warranted. Each $0.50
Per dozen 5.30

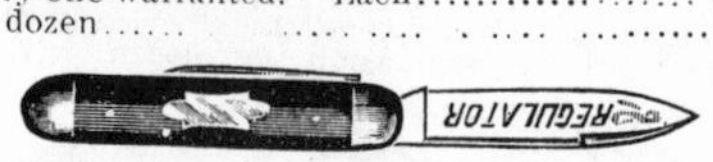

46116 Two blades, 4⅛ in, fine ebony handles, best quality steel blades, brass lined, German silver bolsters. A large, strong and durable article. Retail price, $1.25
See our price. Warranted. Each $0.70
Per dozen 7.20

Cutlery—Continued.

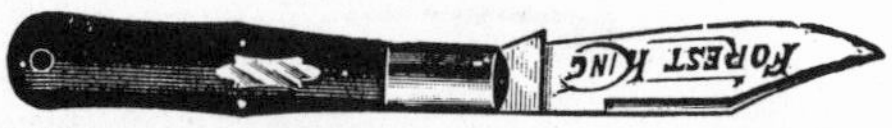

46118 One blade, clip hunting style, best quality steel, 5 inch ebony handle; warranted.
Retail price, $1.00.
Our price, each $0.69
Per dozen 7.20

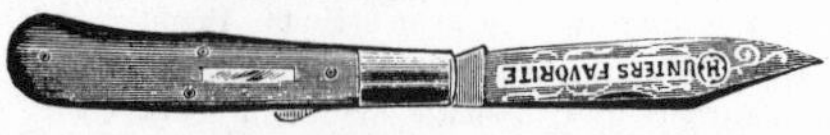

46119 One blade, clip hunting style, 5½ inch cocoa handle, spring back, brass lined, heavy and strong, best steel and warranted. Each ... $1.00
Per dozen 11.00

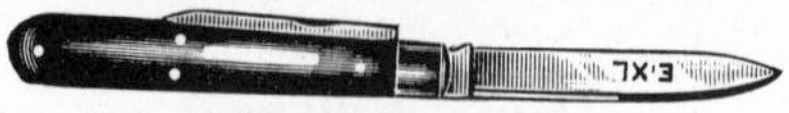

46122 Two blade, 3⅝ in. ebony handle, brass lined, German silver bolsters, narrow large blade, best steel and warranted. Each $0.50
Per dozen 5.40

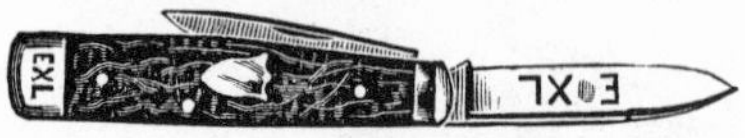

46123 Two blades, brass lined, fine buckhorn handle; German silver lined, 3⅝ inch handle: very best quality and finest finished blades, warranted. Retail price $1.25
Our price, each .... $0.70 Per dozen $7.80

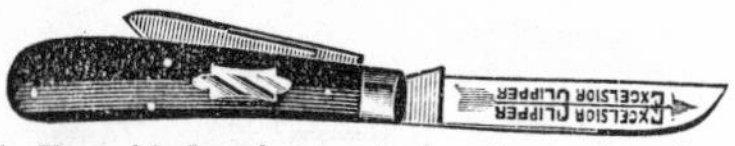

46127 Two blades best steel, ebony handle, brass lined, German silver bolsters, finest quality and finish, 3½ inch handle; warranted.
Retail price, $1.00.
Our price, each ..... $0.45 Per dozen $4.70

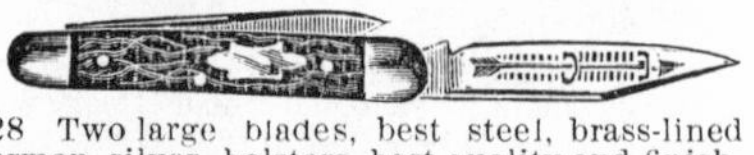

46128 Two large blades, best steel, brass-lined German silver bolsters, best quality and finish, 3⅞ inch stag horn handle: warranted.
Retail price, $1.25. Our price. Each $0.80
Per dozen 8.50

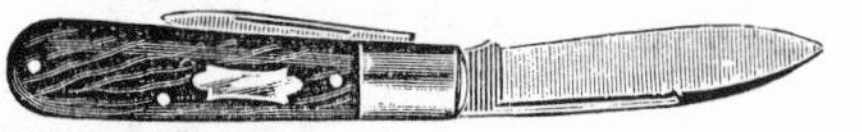

46131 Two blades, brass lined, cocoa handle: warranted. Each .. $0.40 Per dozen $4.20
46132 Two blades, 3⅞ in. ebony handle, good, strong, heavy blade. Every one warranted. The "Farmers Favorite" and one of our best sellers
Each .... $0.48 Per dozen $5.00

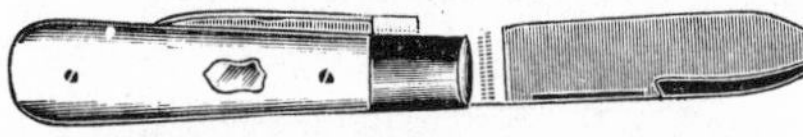

46140 Two blades, white bone handle, good and strong; warranted. Each $0.45
Per dozen 5.52

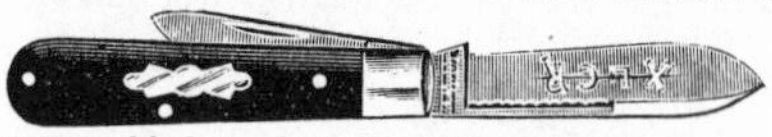

46141 Two blades, dark handle, extra heavy, warranted. Each $0.47
Per dozen 5.00

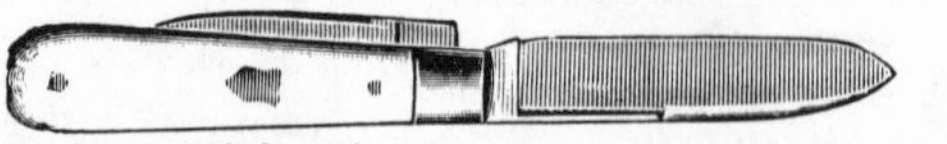

46142 Two blades, 4 in. white bone handle, extra heavy, fine finish, brass lined, German silver bolsters; every one warranted. Each $0.60
Per dozen 6.00
46142½ Two blades, same as 46142, with ebony handles; a fine large knife; every one warranted.
Each 0.60
Per dozen 6.00

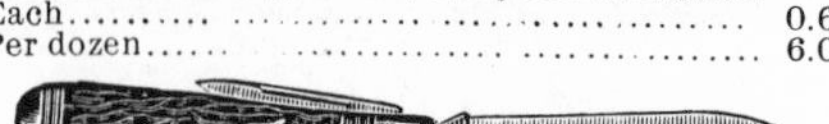

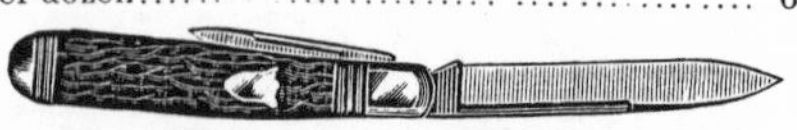

46143 Two blades, 3¾ inch stag horn handle, brass lined, German silver bolsters, long, narrow large blade, best quality; warranted. A big bargain. Each .... $0.40 Per dozen $4.00

46146 Two blades and corkscrew, white bone handle, brass lined. A handy knife to have in your pocket. Each ..... $0.49 Per dozen ... $5.52

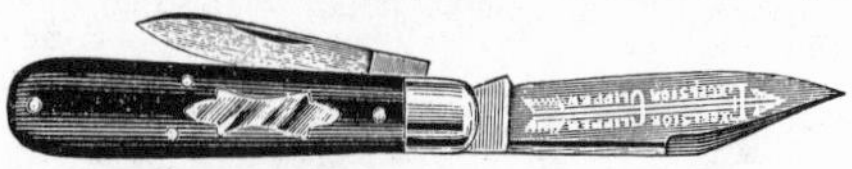

46147 Two blades, 3¾ in ebony handle, German silver bolsters, best steel blades; warranted. Each $0.65
Per dozen 7.00

Cutlery—Continued.

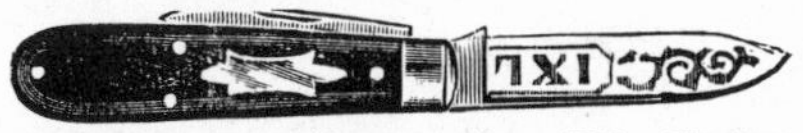

46149 Farmers' Knife, genuine IXL Wostenholm, two blades, black horn handle, heavy and strong; every knife warranted; 4-in. handle, the best grade manufactured. Each....$0.90
Per dozen 9.75
3½ inch handle. Each....$0.65. Per dozen..... 7.00

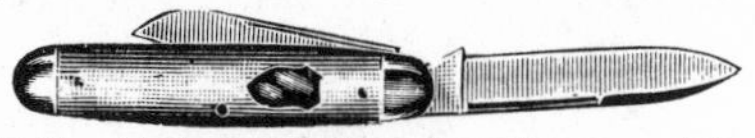

46150 Two blades white bone handle; warranted. Each..............$0.37 Per dozen............$3.75

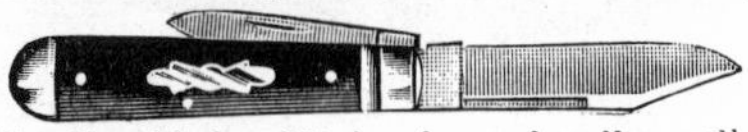

46151 Two blades, 3⅝ in. ebony handle, well made and durable. Every knife warranted. Each $0.45
Per dozen..$4.80

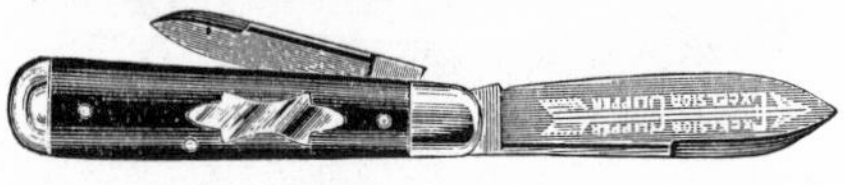

46154 Two blades, finest quality steel, brass lined, German silver bolsters, 3⅝ in. ebony handle; warranted. Each......$0.60 Per doz..$6.74

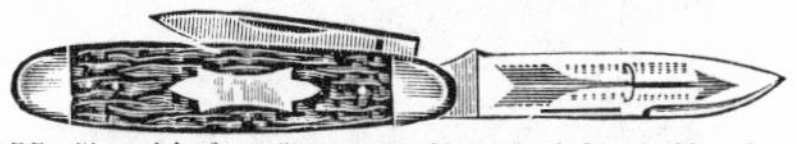

46155 Two blades, finest quality steel, brass lined, German silver bolsters, 3⅝ in. stag horn handle; warranted. Retail price, $1.00.
Our price, each.........$0.60 Per dozen......$6.30

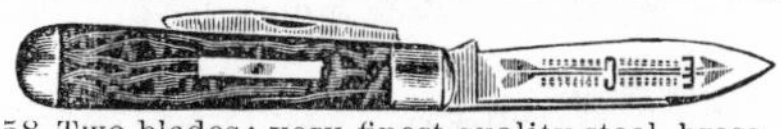

46158 Two blades; very finest quality steel, brass lined, German silver bolsters, 3¾ inch stag horn handles; warranted. Each $0.70 Per doz.$7.00

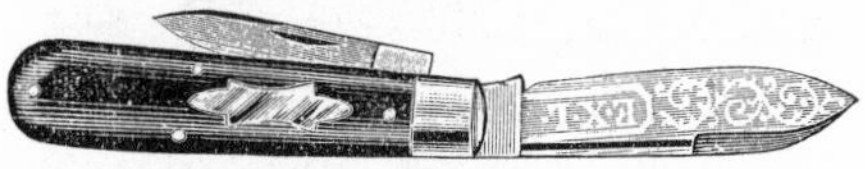

46160 Two blades 3¾-inch ebony handle, brass lined German silver bolsters. "Our big seller." Warranted finest quality steel blades.
See our price, each......$0.60 Per dozen......$6.75

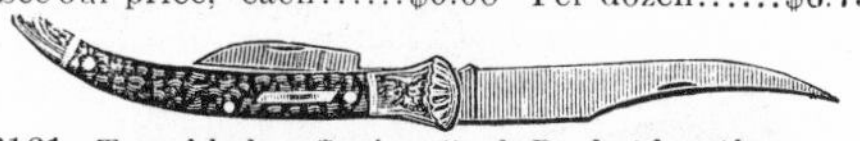

46161 Two blades, Spring-Back Pocket hunting knife: large blade can be closed by pressing on small blade; buck horn 4 inch handle, brass lined; large blade 3 inches long. best quality steel. Each...........$0.79 Per doz $9.19

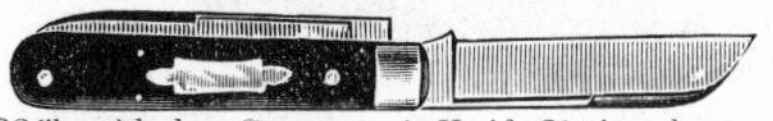

46162 Two blades, Carpenter's Knife 3¼ in. ebony handle, both blades are large; one of the most useful knives around the shop or mill. Best quality steel blades and warranted. Each.......$0.55
Per dozen.. 5.87

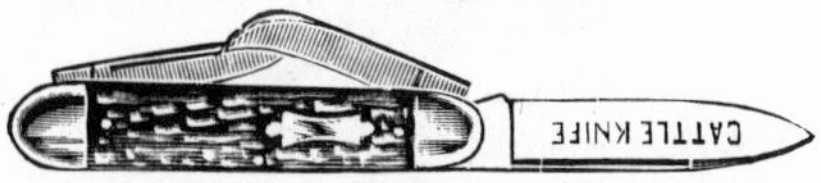

46168 Three blades, buckhorn handle cattle knife, 3⅝ inch handle; brass lined, German silver bolsters. Each..........$0.84 Per dozen. $9.00

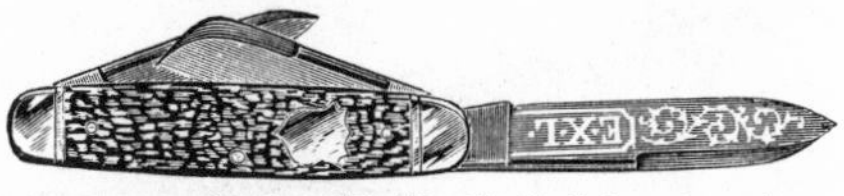

46169 Three blades, "Cattle Knife," finest quality steel, brass lined, German silver bolsters. 4¼ in. stag horn handle: warranted. Each.........$1.49
Per dozen 15.75

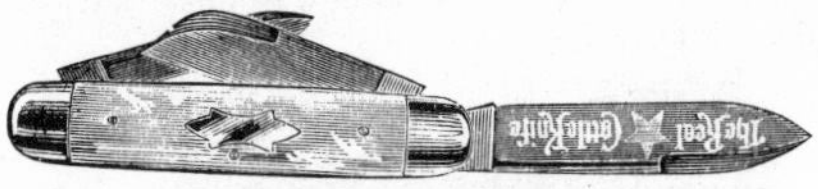

46171 Three blades, "Cattle Knife," finest quality steel, extra fine finish, brass lined, German silver bolsters, 3⅝ in. pearl handle, best quality; warranted. Retail price, $2.50.
Our price, each ...$1.60 Per dozen...........18.00

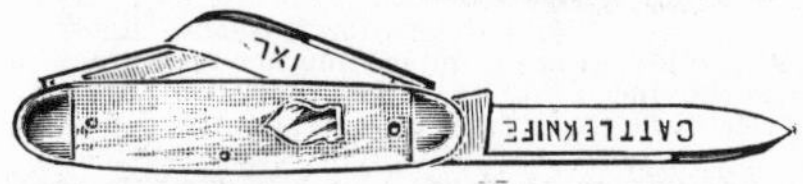

46173 Three blades, Genuine IXL George Wostenholm Cattle Knife, heavy and strong, 3⅝ in., pearl handle, the best knife of this kind in the market. Each $2.50

Cutlery—Continued.

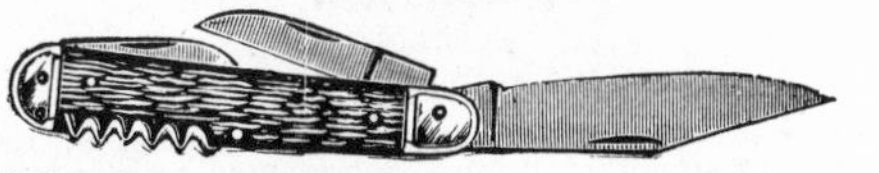

46174 Three blades and corkscrew, spring back, large blade closed by pressing on small blade; 4½ inch stag horn handle. Each...................$1.30
Per dozen 14.00

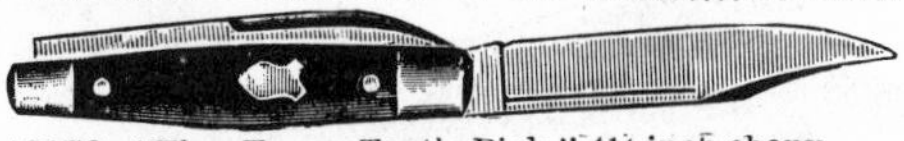

46176 "The Texas Tooth Pick," 4¼ inch ebony handle, 1 large clip point blade, 1 large spear point blade; a handy hunting knife; warranted; steel blades. Each.........$0.70 Per dozen.. $7.50

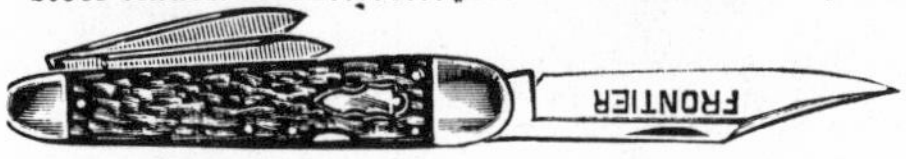

46177 Three blades Frontier Hunting Knife: spring back on large blade to prevent closing while in use. 4¼ inch stag horn handle, German silver bolster: brass lined, crocus polished, heavy, strong and durable; warranted. Each...$1.25
Per dozen 12.50

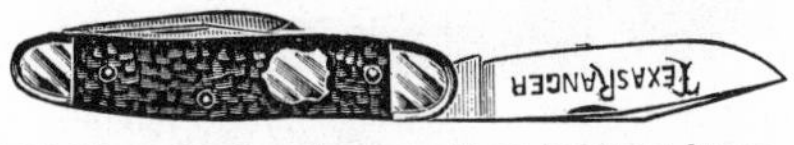

46180 Three blades, German silver bolsters, brass lined, 4½ inch stag horn handle; a fine knife. Each.............$1.50 Per dozen.......... $16.00

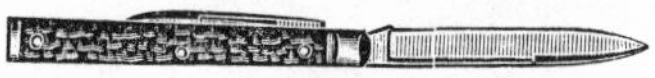

46186 Two blades, stag horn handle, 3½ inches; physician's knife. Each..$0.48 Per dozen.....$4.80
46188 Same as above, with pearl handle, finest quality and finish; warranted. Each.......... .80
Per dozen 8.87

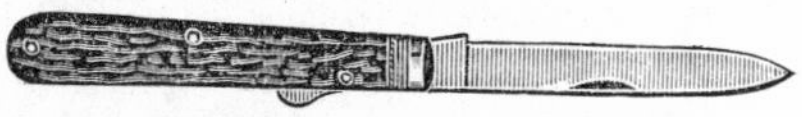

46190 One blade, spring back, stag horn handle, 4 inch blade. Each......$0.48 Per dozen........$4.80
46191 One blade, spring back, stag handle. 4 inch blade. Same as 46190, except has "clip point" similar to 46192. Each...................$0.50
Per dozen 5.00

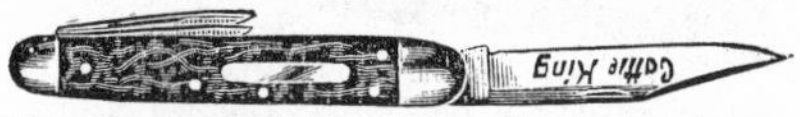

46192 Cowboy's Pride, brass lined, stag horn handle; a fine article, spring back. Each......$ 1.00
Per dozen 11.00

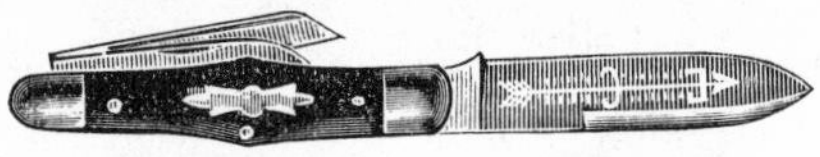

46193 Three blades, 4 inch ebony handle, heavy and strong, 1 large short wide blade, 2 small blades. Very best steel in blades; every one warranted; brass lined, German silver bolsters.
Each.................$0.90 Per dozen.......... $10.00
46194 Three blades, same style as 46193, but smaller, 3½ inch ebony handle, strong and durable, finest steel blades; warranted. Each.......$0.75
Per dozen 8.00

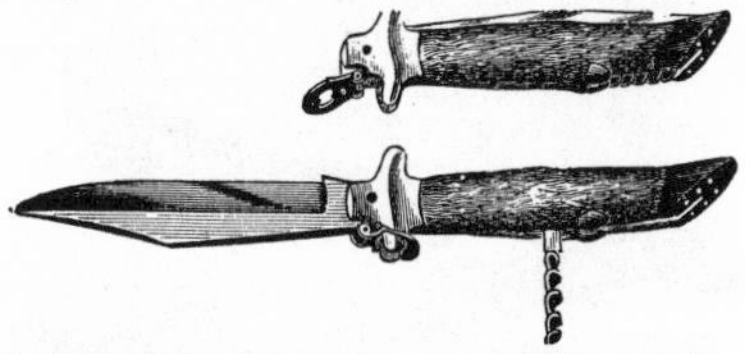

46195 One blade and corkscrew, hunting style, deer-foot handle. Each....$1.50 Per doz....$15.00
46196 Three blades, 3¼ inch, stag horn handle; spear marker and spay blades.
Each $0.60
Per dozen 6.00

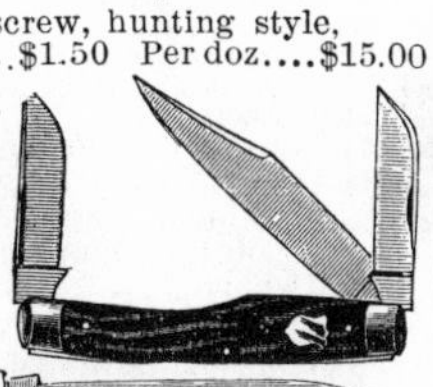

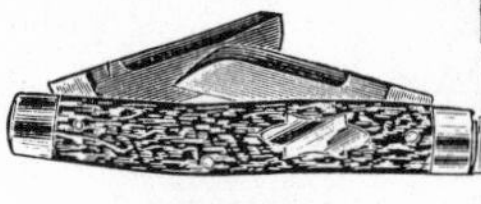

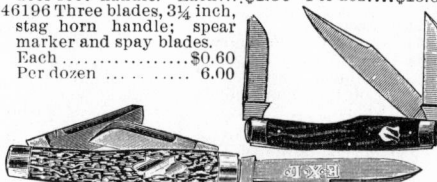

46197 Three blades, 4 inch stag horn handle, brass lined German silver bolstered, best steel. spear, marker and spay blades; warranted. Each.$0.90
Per dozen 9.29

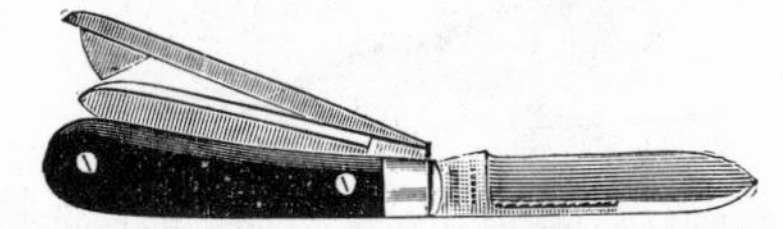

46198 Spay, fleam and spear blades, 3⅝ inch ebony handle; warranted best of steel. Each....$0.75
Per dozen 8.00

Cutlery—Continued.

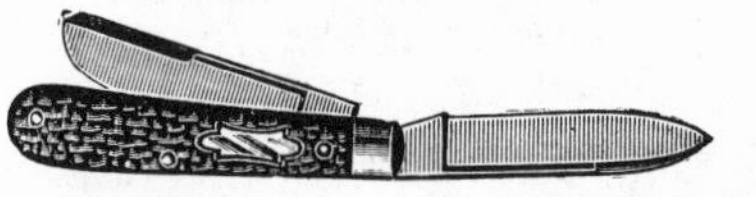

46200 Two blade, 3½ in. stag horn handle, spaying knife. Each..............................$0.50
Per dozen 5.78

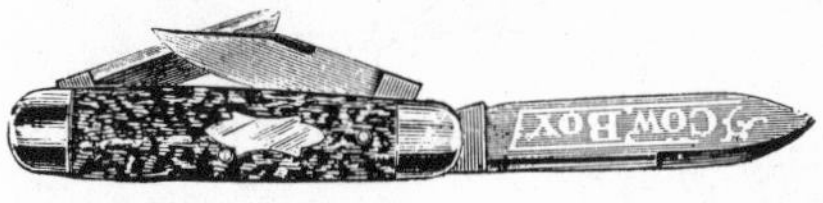

46201 Three blades, 3½-inch stag horn handle, German silver bolsters, brass lined; fine finish, best steel blades; warranted. Each.............$0.84
Per dozen 9.40

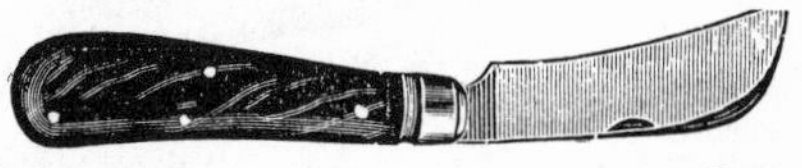

46205 One blade, pruning, 4-inch cocoa handle. Each...............$0.40 Per dozen.........$4.00

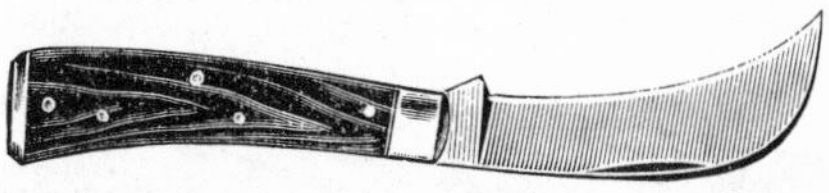

46206 One blade, pruning, 4½-inch cocoa handle. Each...............$0.65 Per dozen..........$6.50

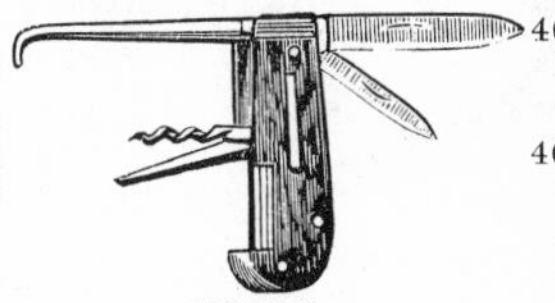

46207-8

46207 Combination Knife, genuine IXL Wostenholm.
Each $2.50
46208 Combination Knife, genuine IXL Wostenholm, same as No. 46207, with addition of a saw blade.
Each..............$2.25
46209½ Sportsmen's Knife. Same as 46207 in shape; stag handle, 3½ inches long: neat and handy. Each.......$0.75 Per dozen...........$8.00

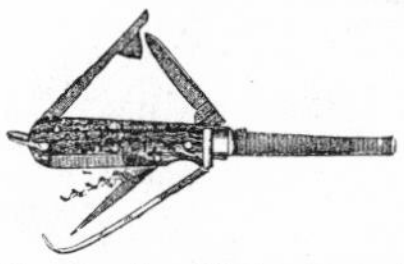

46211 A horseman's pocket knife. Among the new patterns in cutlery recently got up is the Horseman's Friend, intended for the use of a gentleman or veterinarians. The chief feature is the farrier's blade for paring the hoof. Highest grade steel, 3½ inch, stag horn handle. Each..............................$2.00

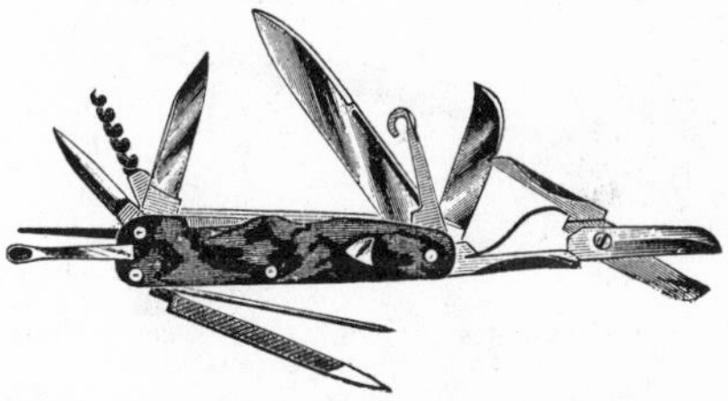

46213 Combination Knife, fine shell pearl handle. An elegant article. No sportsman's outfit complete without it. Retail price, $5.00.
Our price, each 3.00

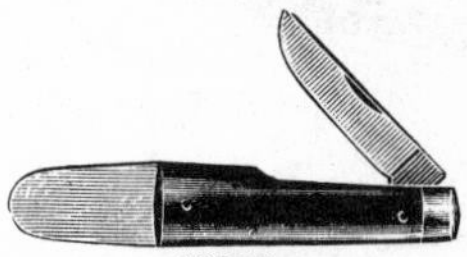

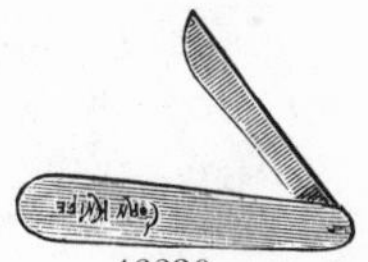

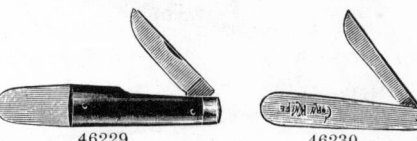

46229 46230

46229 Budding and Grafting Knife, black horn handle, 4 inches long, finely finished, best quality. Warranted. Each.......$0.50 Per dozen........$5.40
46230 Corn Knife, white handle, 3½ inches long, well finished, best steel blade and warranted Each..............$0.50 Per dozen.........$5.40

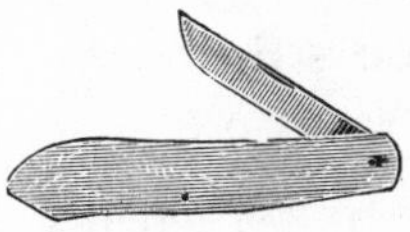

46231 Pocket Eraser and Paper Cutter, ivory handle, 4 inches long, finely finished, best steel blade. Warranted.
Each $0.86
Per dozen.................. 9.26

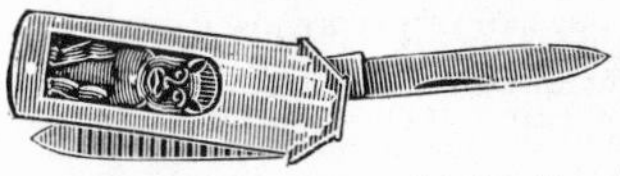

46233— Novelty Vest Pocket Knife, antique ivory handle, nicely finished and a good one. Each......$0.25 Per dozen $2.95

EVERY HORSE OWNER MUST BUY HORSE GOODS.
We can save him money on everytbing he needs. Examine our prices, and be convinced of this fact.

Toilet Hair Clippers.

Postage, 13 cents extra.

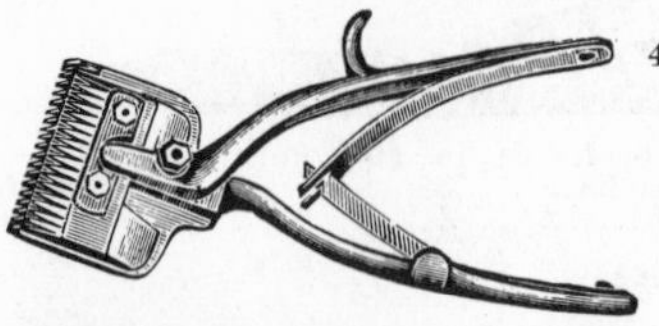

46234 The Imported French Toilet Hair Clipper, cuts one length only. Each....$1.20

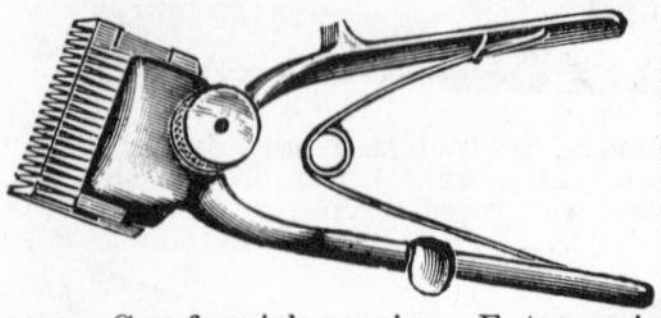

Do not use these clippers on dogs or horses. They are intended for clipping human hair only and not suitable for any other purpose. Can furnish repairs. Extra springs, 15c. each; top or bottom plates, $1.00 each. When ordering only one spring, say which is wanted—the one with the notch in or not. Weight. Price,
46236 Plain, each........................12 oz. $1.50
Extra combs that can be attached to bottom plates to cut hair, 3/16 of an inch longer than the regular cut of clipper. Each................ ....$0.50

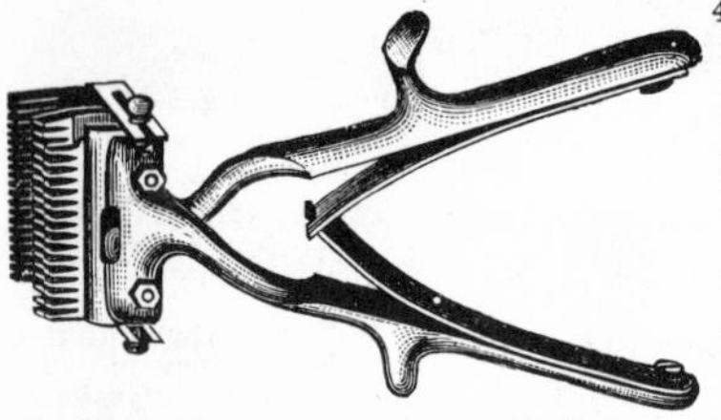

46238—Toilet Hair Clipper, with adjustable plate, for cutting hair two different lengths; plate can be easily removed and adjusted; remove plate entirely for cutting shortest length. Each...... ....$3.00
Extra top or bottom plates. Each................ 1.30
Extra springs... .15

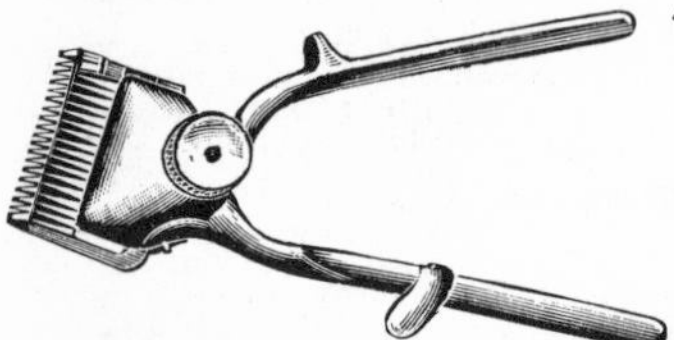

46239 The Columbia Toilet Hair Clipper, a high grade will finished article. Warranted. Cuts hair one length only. Each..$1.87
Extra adjustable combs to make the Columbia Clipper cut hair 1/16 or 3/16-inch longer. Each..... .90

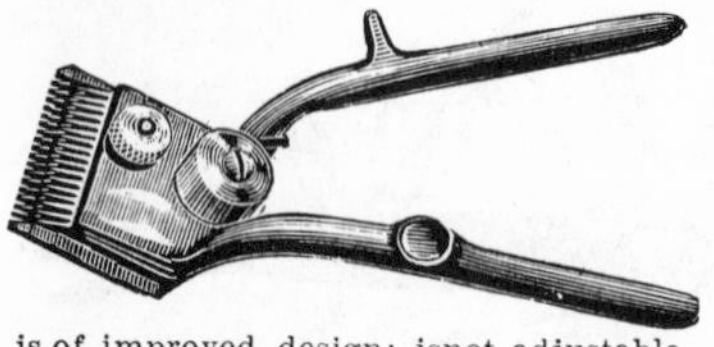

46240—The King Hair Clipper. This is a higher grade of clipper than 46236 or 46238 is of improved design; is not adjustable. We especially recommend this clipper for professional barbers' use. Each..... ....$2.75
Extra adjustable combs to make the King Clipper cut 1/16 or 3/16-inch longer than regular cut of clipper. Each........... .... .75

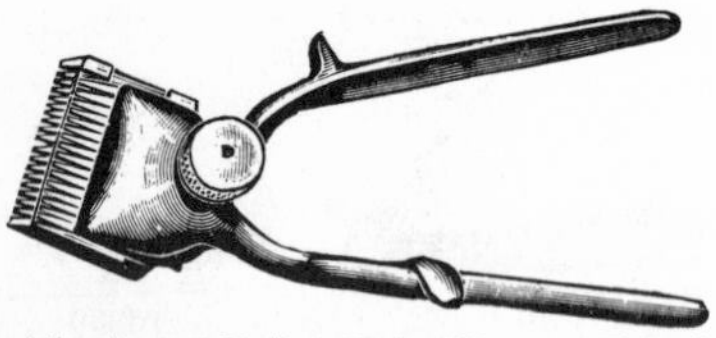

The Aluminum Toilet Hair Clipper. This is the lightest clipper made, finely finished and warranted. Very best quality in every respect.
Weight, clipper only, 4 ounces.
46241 No. 0, razor cut. Each...................$3.75
46242 No. 1, ⅛-inch cut. Each......... ...... 3.90
Repairs. Regrinding old clipper plates. Each.. .60

Brown and Sharpe's Barbers' Clippers.

Brown and Sharpe's Clippers are very finely made and are intended more especially for professional barbers' use. The very best hair clipper in the market.
46243 No. 0, to cut hair very short, about equal to shaving. Each.................................$3.00
46244 No. 1, to cut hair ⅜ of an inch long. Each 3.00
46245 No. 2, to cut hair ¼ of an inch long. Each 3.50
46246 No. 3, to cut hair 5/16 of an inchlong. Each. 3.75
Postage, extra, 15 cents.

Barbers' Jackets---
SEE INDEX.

RAZORS.

Razors sent by mail, 3 to 6 cents extra.
Our razors are fully warranted by *us*, and if *properly* used and *stropped* on a *good smooth* strop they can be returned at our expense and money refunded or exchanged for another, if not as represented.

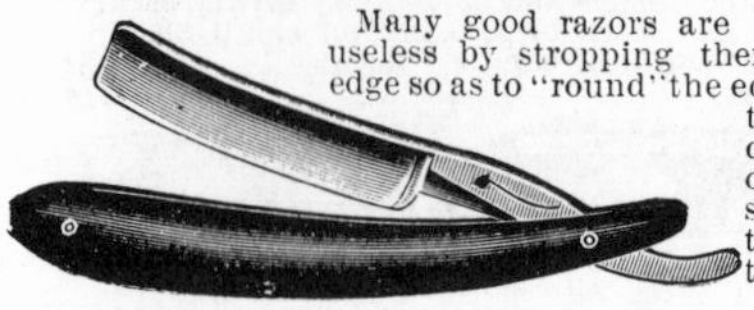

Many good razors are rendered useless by stropping them on the edge so as to "round" the edge. Lay the razor down flat on the strop, and turn on the back. Never strop a razor by turning with the edge on the strop.
46249 Wostenholm's New Pipe. ½-inch finest quality, hollow ground. A little gem, and a dandy shaver; no better steel put in a razor. Every one likes them. Our biggest seller; warranted. Each...................................... $1.00

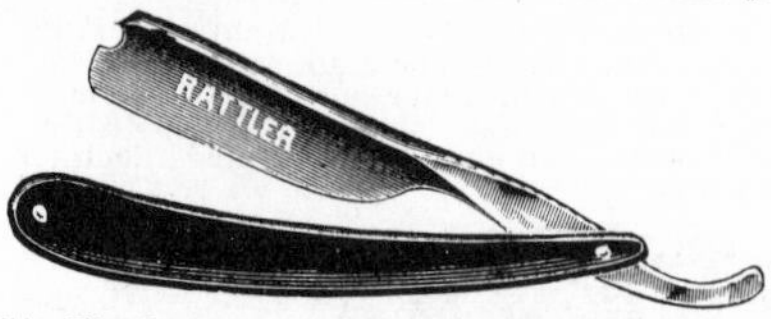

46250 The Improved "Rattler" Razor, hollow ground, set ready for use; finely finished and warranted. ⅝-inch wide. Each................$0.95

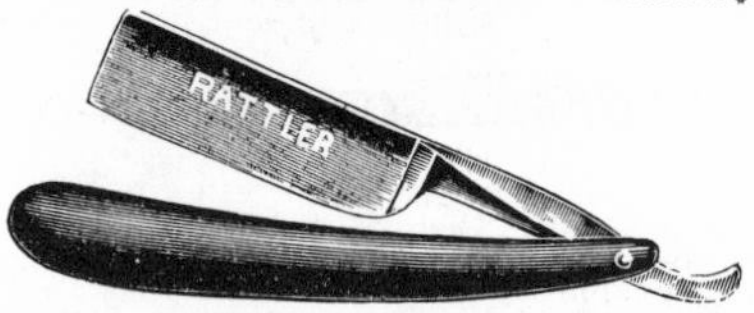

46251 The "Hamburg Ground Rattler" Razor, full hollow ground, square point, best of steel, finely finished, and a good one. Warranted.
Each.................⅝-inch, $1.25 ¾-inch, $1.40

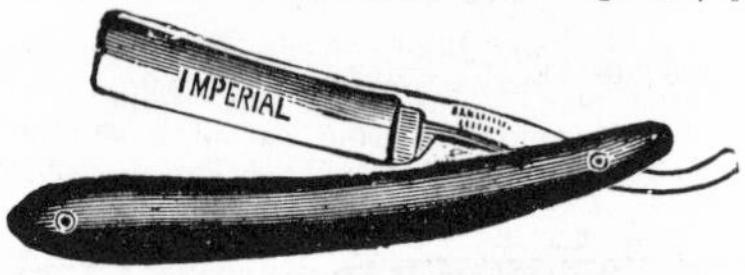

46252 The Imperial Razor, extra hollow ground, made from the best double refined English razor steel. If you want a thin ground razor it will please you. Sent ready for use and every one warranted a keen cutter. Try one of these razors. Price, ½ inch blade. Each..... ....$1.20
Price, ⅝ inch blade. Each.. .... 1.30
Price, ¾ inch blade. Each......................... 1.50

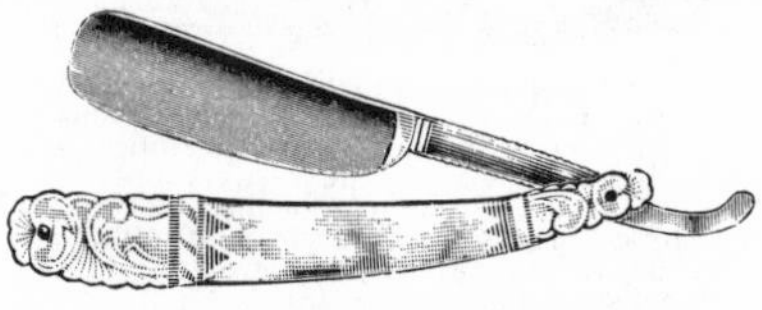

46253 High Grade Fancy Pearl Handle Razor, beautifully finished, hollow ground, round point, very best grade of steel; warranted.
Each.... ....⅝-inch, $3.60

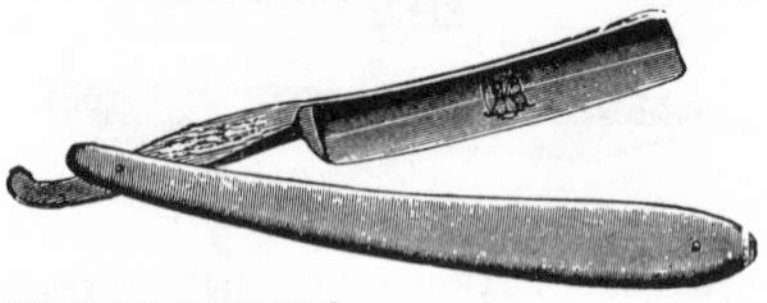

Every razor warranted.
46254 Razors, Torrey, plain ground, ⅝ inch blade. Each.... ....$0.60
46255 Razors, Torrey, hollow ground, ¾ inch blade. Each...... .... .87
46256 Celluloid Imitation Bamboo Handles, square point, ⅝-inch hollow ground. Warranted. Each................................$1.00
46257 Razors, Torrey, extra hollow ground, ⅝ inch blade; warranted. Each................ 1.25
46259 Razors Wostenholm, straight ground, for stiff beards, square end, ⅝ inch blade. Each.... .68
46260 Razors, Wostenholm, best hollow ground pipe razor, ¾ inch blade. Set for use and warranted. Each.............. .... 1.65

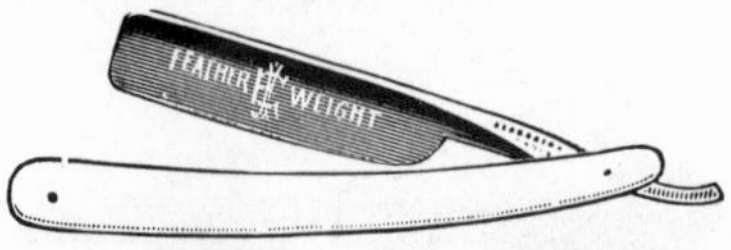

46261 The Celebrated Joseph Elliot's Sheffield Razor, ivory handle, ⅝-inch silver steel, finest finish. Each.....................................$2.25

Razors—Continued.

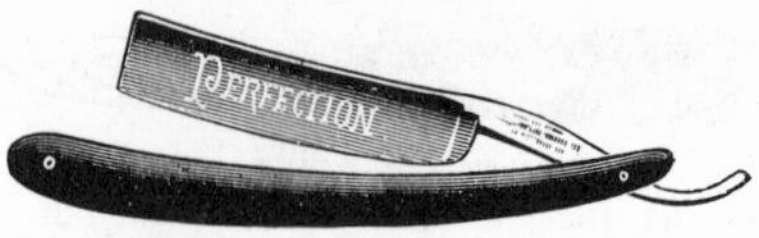

46262 The Celebrated Joseph Elliot's Sheffield Razor, Perfection, hollow ground, ⅝-inch, every one warranted. Each............................$1.25

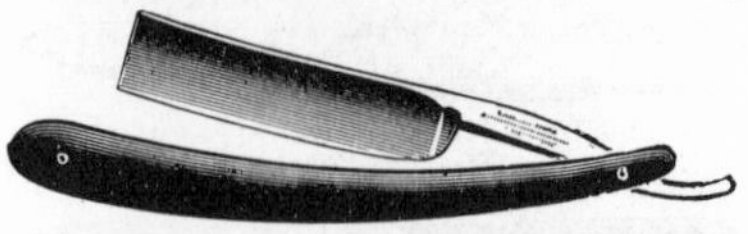

46263 The Celebrated Joseph Elliot's Sheffield Razor, ⅝-inch, hollow ground, best steel. Each.$1.00

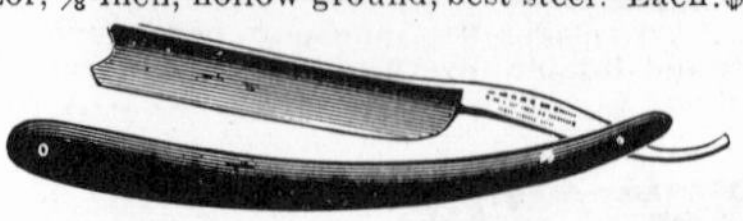

46264 The Celebrated Joseph Elliot's Sheffield Razor, medium, hollow ground, ½-inch, every razor warranted. Each........ . ...$0.95

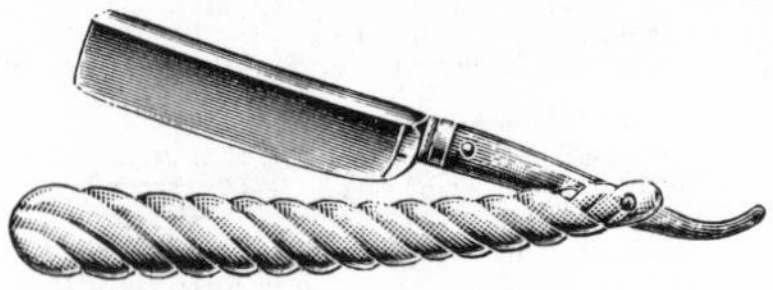

46266 Razor, hollow ground, fancy celluloid handle, antique finish, ivory tang, a fine article, every one warranted. Each, ⅝-inch............$2.25

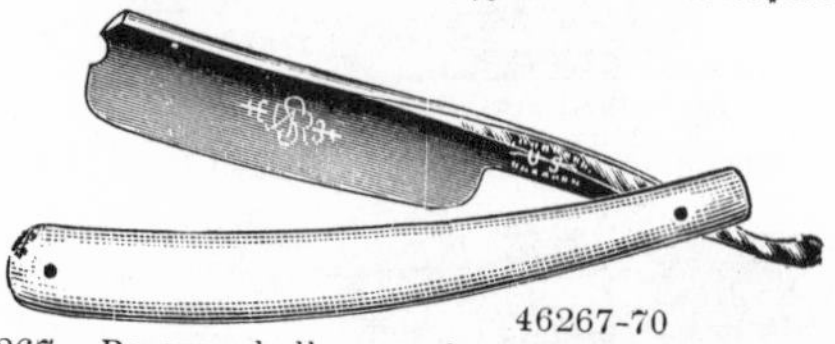

46267-70

46267 Razors, hollow point, ivory handle, hollow ground, finest finished, best made; warranted, ¾ inch blade. Each $3.00
46269 Razor, hollow point, hollow ground, fine finish, best steel; warranted; ¾ inch blade, same shape as No. 46267, black handle, warranted... 2.00
46270 Razor, same as 46269, only ⅝ inch blade; warranted. Each...... 1.75

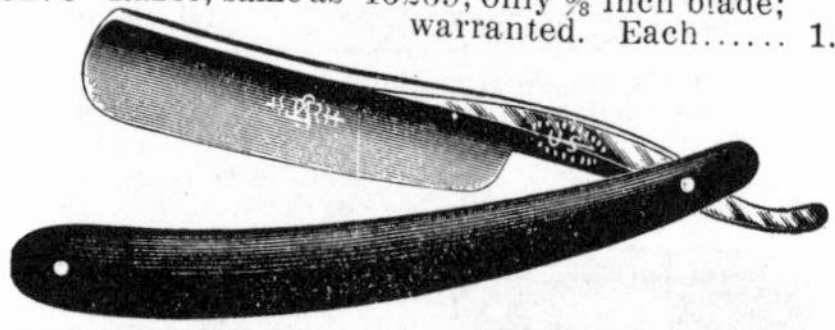

46271 Razors, full concave finish, best make, black rubber handle; warranted; ¾ inch blade.$2.35

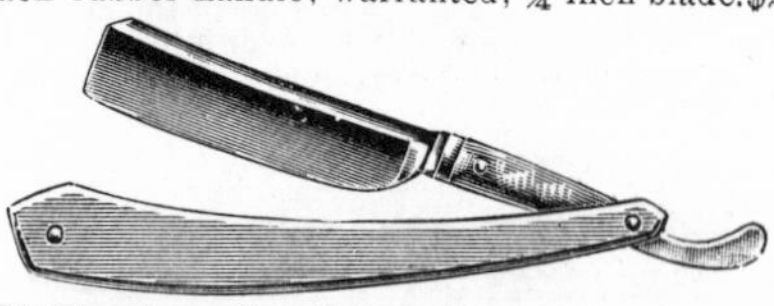

46272 Fine Ivory Handle Pearl Tong Razor, beautifully finished, hollow ground; every razor warranted. Each, ⅝-inch...........................$3.00

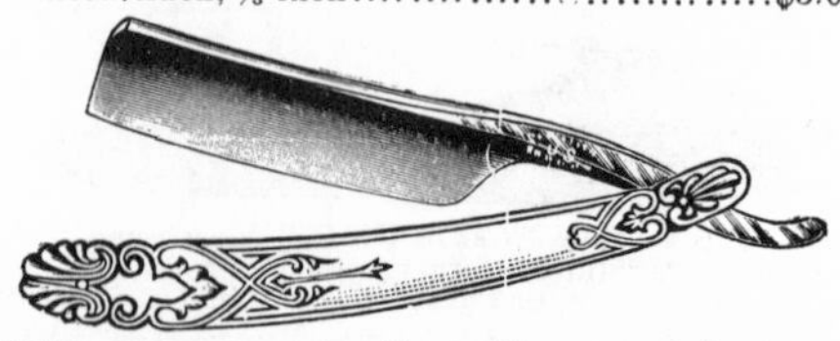

46273 Razor, fancy handle, hollow ground, best make, warranted, ⅝ inch, white handle. Each...$2.00

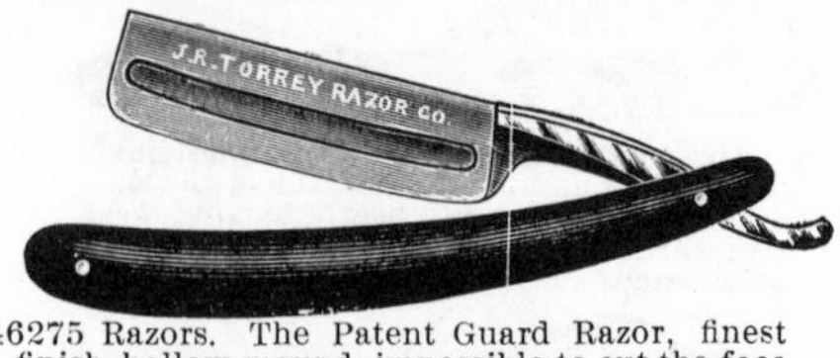

46275 Razors. The Patent Guard Razor, finest finish, hollow ground, impossible to cut the face while shaving if you keep the guard on blade. Just the thing for new beginners, or timid people, or nervous men who cannot shave without cutting their faces; shaves closer, cleaner, more evenly than any other guard razor on the market; the best guard razor on the market, of the very best of steel; warranted; ⅞ in blade. Each $1.70

Razors—Continued.

46276 Little Dandy Razor, same as No. 46275, except blade is only 3¼ inches from rivet to point, Try one once and you will be pleased with it... 1.65

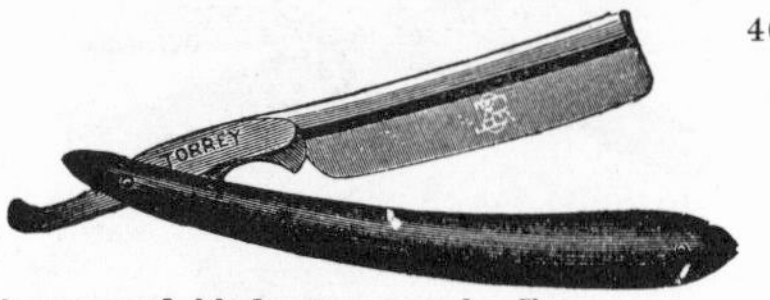

46277—Razors, Swedish pattern, ⅝ inch blade, fine hand hammered blade; warranted. Each.............$ 2.50

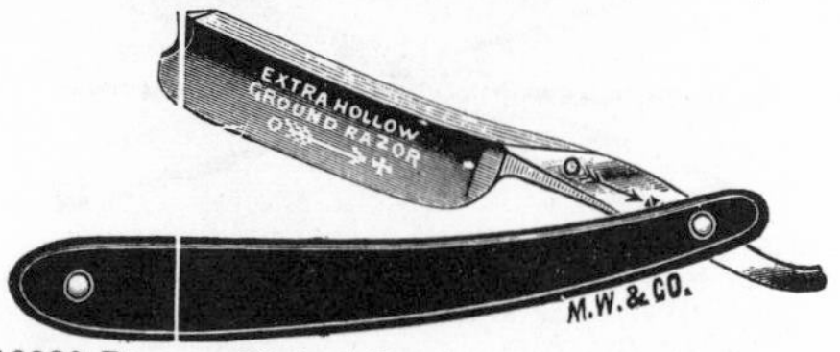

46280 Razors. Wade & Butcher, best Each. ¾ inch bevel edge, warranted,...... $1.75

46281 Razors. Wade & Butcher's best, hollow ground, 1$\frac{1}{16}$ inches wide, extra heavy; warranted. Each.................................. $1.50

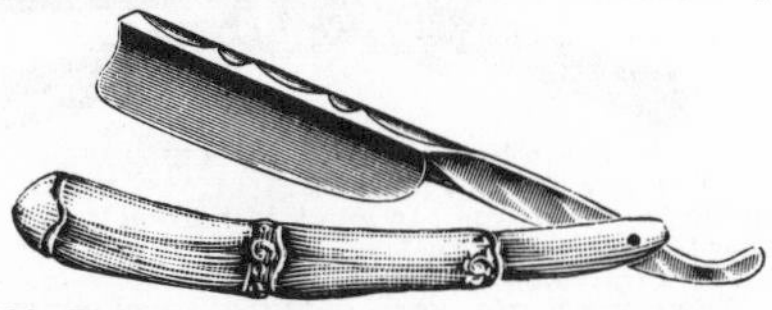

46282 Razor. celluloid handle, imitation bamboo finish, hollow ground, set ready for use and warranted. Each, ⅝-inch $1.50

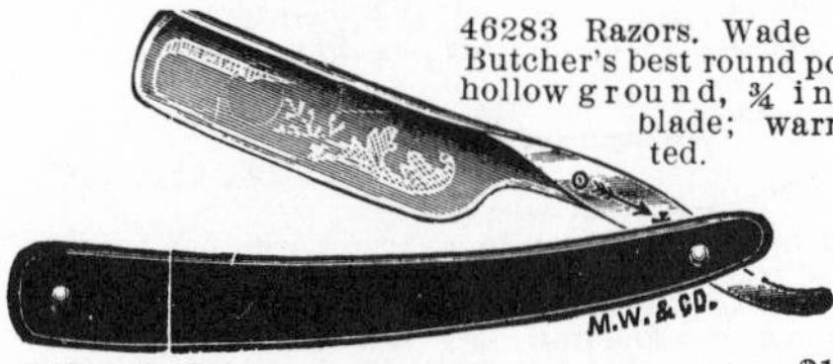

46283 Razors. Wade & Butcher's best round point hollow ground, ¾ inch blade; warranted.

Price, each $1.50

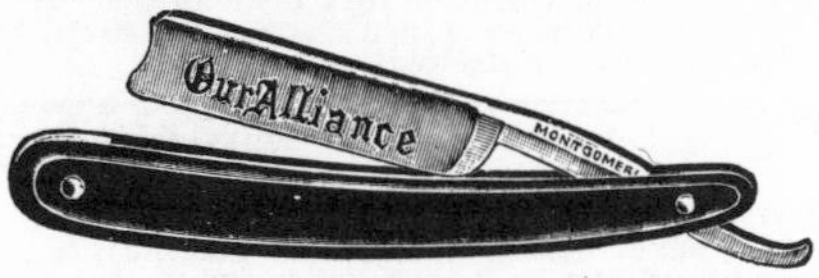

Keen Cutter.

46284 M. W. & Co.'s Improved Alliance Razor, full hollow ground, finely finished, very best steel, set ready for use and every one warranted; a keen cutter, the best hollow ground razor in the market; try one. Price, ½ in........$1.00 ⅝ inch..............$1.20. ¾ inch...............$1.30

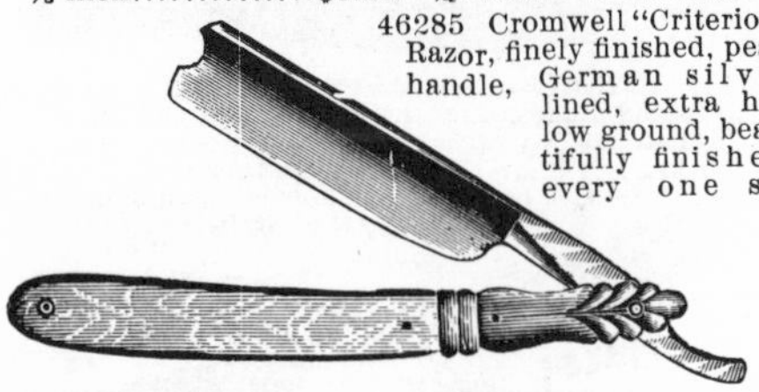

46285 Cromwell "Criterion" Razor, finely finished, pearl handle, German silver lined, extra hollow ground, beautifully finished every one set ready for use, and warranted; ¾ in. Each........$3.50

Repairs. Regrinding old razor, plain ground, for 35 cents. Hollow ground, for 50 cents per razor.

The Star Safety Razor.

Patented April. 1887.

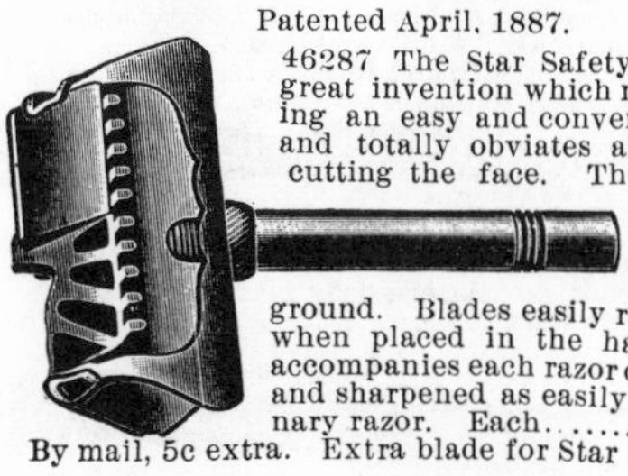

46287 The Star Safety Razor is a great invention which renders shaving an easy and convenient luxury and totally obviates all danger of cutting the face. The blades are made of the finest steel, and are fully concave ground. Blades easily removed, and when placed in the handle which accompanies each razor can be honed and sharpened as easily as an ordinary razor. Each...............$1.50
By mail, 5c extra. Extra blade for Star Razor.. 1.00

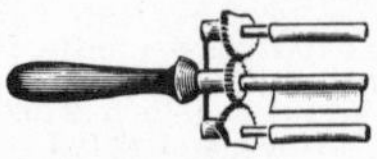

46288 Stropping machines for Star Safety Razor. Postage. extra, 8 cents Each..................... 1.75
46289 Strops, for Star Safety Razors. Each.... .40

The Star Safety Gem Case.

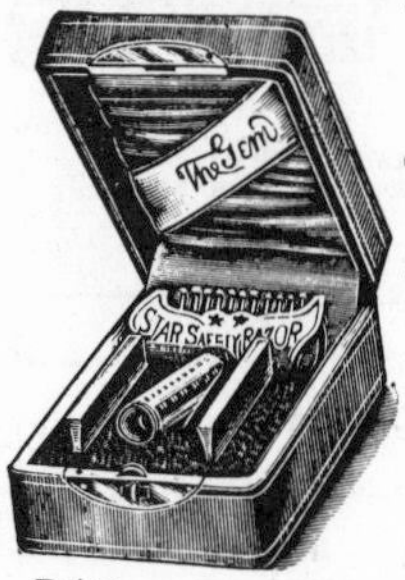

46291 Contains one safety frame with two blades, elegantly gotten up in morocco, and is a gem in the full sense of the word. Price.....$3.37

The Star Safety Favorite Case.

46294 Contains one safety frame and seven blades—one blade for each day in the week. This case is specially adapted to the wants of those who find that a razor works easier by frequent changing. It is a very elaborate and handsome affair, put up in morocco and lined with satin.
Price $9.50

The Star Safety Traveling Case.

46295 Put up in elegant satin-lined morocco case, and contains one safety frame with two perfectly adjusted blades of fine silver steel; box of finely perfumed shaving soap, holder for stropping and honing blades; shaving brush, comb and cosmetique—in fact, everything requisite for an easy, quick and luxurious shave. Price.$ 5.50

Razor Strops.

Weight, 8 to 10 ounces
Postage is 1 cent per ounce.

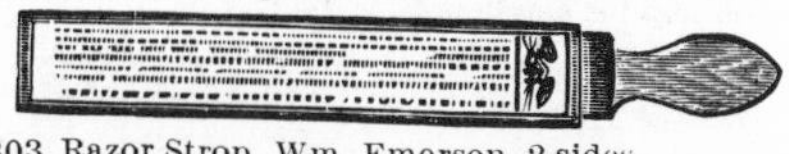

46303 Razor Strop, Wm. Emerson, 2 sides. Each...........$0.25 Per dozen...............$2.70
46304 Razor Strop, Genuine Chas. Emerson, 2 sides. Each.......$0.30. Per dozen......... 3 00

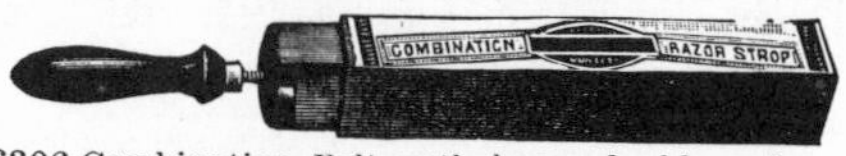

46306 Combination Belt with hone, double rod and screw, 4 sides. Each.........................$0.30

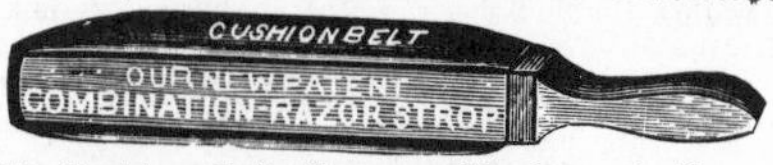

46307 Cushion Belt Strop, with hone, 4 sides. This is the latest improvement. Each...........$0.50

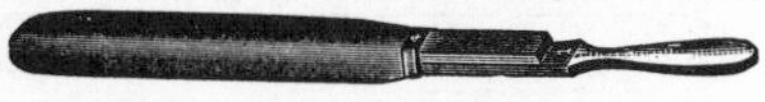

46308 Combination Elastic and Flat Strops, with best quality stone hone; an elegant and handy article. Each...................................$1.75

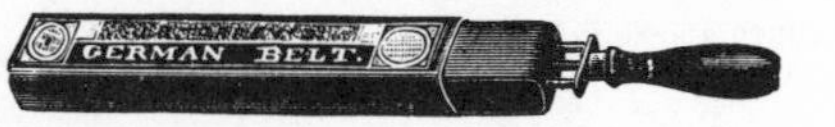

46309 German Belt Razor Strop, double rod and screw handle, 2 sides. Each........................$0.50
46310 Genuine Russian Leather German Belt Strop, double rod, screw handle. Each .... .75

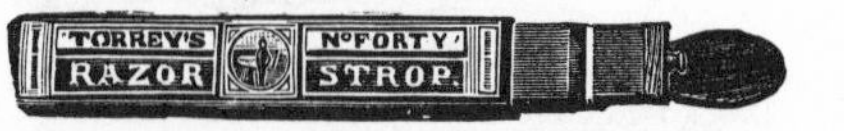

46311 Razor Strop, 2 sides leather, with drawer for razor; the old reliable strop. Each......... $0.50
Swing Strop, by mail, 3c extra.
Give our strops a trial and you will use no other.

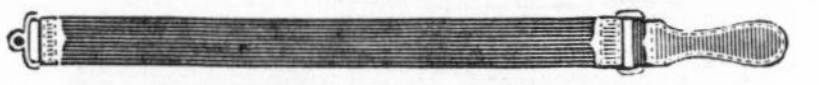

46312 The "Boar Skin" Barbers Swing Strop. All leather, one side boar skin, the other side satin finish leather; a good heavy strop. Stropping surface 20x 2¼ inches. Each......................$0.65
Extra by mail, 5 cents.

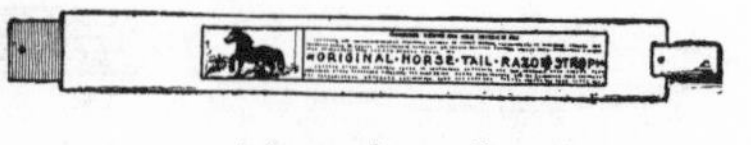

"A good one."

46313 The Magnetic Horse Tail Razor Strop. Satin finish one side. Entire length, 20 in. Each..$0.25
Width, 2 inches.

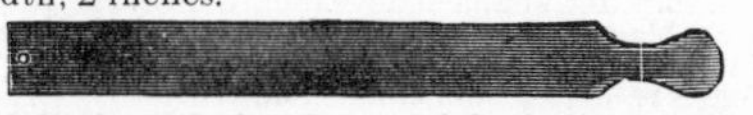

46314 Barbers' Swing Strop, plain leather, satin finish one side, light weight. Each........ $0.10
46315 Barbers' Swing Strop, plain leather, satin finish, one side, heavy weight. Each........... .25
46317 Barbers' Swing Strop, prepared leather, heavy weight. Postage, extra, 5 cents. Each.... .37

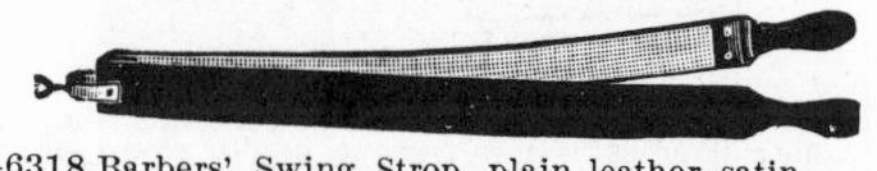

46318 Barbers' Swing Strop, plain leather, satin finish, one side, and canvas with swivel. Each.$0.48
46319 Barbers' Swing Strop, prepared leather and canvas with swivel; closed ends; very best quality. Postage, extra, 6 cents. Each............. .84

Razor Hones.

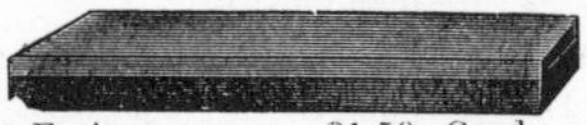

46320 German Razor Hones, best selected.
Each ....$1.50 Good......................$1.00
Medium.. .75
N. B.—These hones are all the same quality stones, but some are chipped off on sides or ends, which prevents them from being SELECTED stones.

Table Cutlery.

Six knives and six forks constitute a set. Extra by mail, 25 to 40c per set.

All forks have three tines. ALL BLADES AND TINES WARRANTED STEEL.

Our table cutlery is acknowledged to be the best, and at the lowest prices that any dealer in this country can show. YOUR RETAIL DEALER pays more for same quality of goods than we ask YOU for OURS, unless he purchases of us.

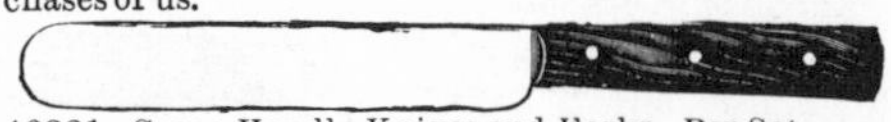

46321 Cocoa Handle Knives and Forks. Per Set, 6 knives and 6 forks $0.40
Knives only, per dozen.................................. .50

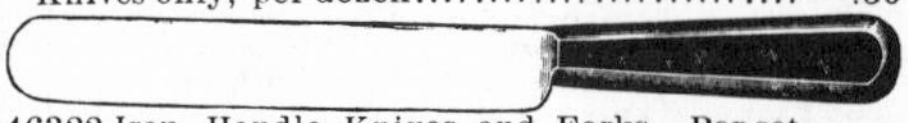

46322 Iron Handle Knives and Forks. Per set, 6 knives and 6 forks..................................$0 39

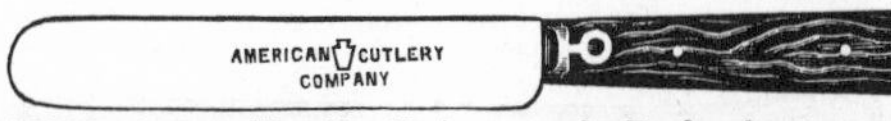

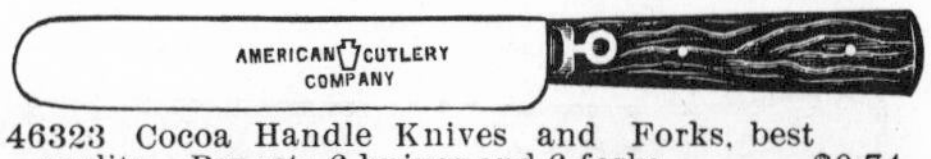

46323 Cocoa Handle Knives and Forks. best quality. Per set; 6 knives and 6 forks $0.74

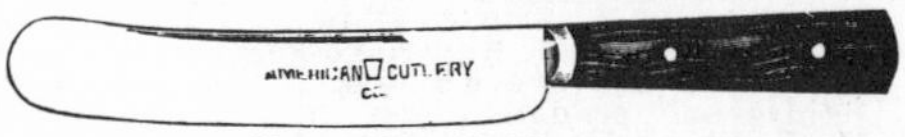

Nos. 46324-25-26.

46324 Cocoa Handle Knives and Forks. Per set of 6 knives and 6 forks $0.74
Knives only, per dozen.................................. .90
46325 Ebony Handle Knives and Forks. Per set of 6 knives and 6 forks................................ .80
Knives only, per dozen.................................. 1.00
46326 White Bone Handle Knives and Forks. Per set of 6 knives and 6 forks............................ .95
Knives only, per dozen.................................. 1.25

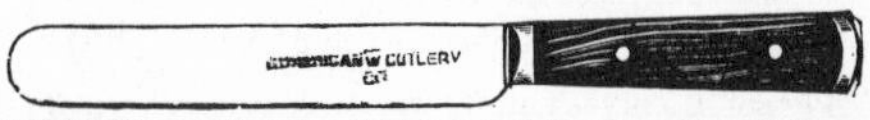

46327 Ebony Handle Knives and Forks. Per set of 6 knives and 6 forks $0.78
Knives only, per dozen.................................. 1.03
46328 White Handle Knives and Forks. Per set of 6 knives and 6 forks 1.06
Knives only, per dozen.................................. 1.30

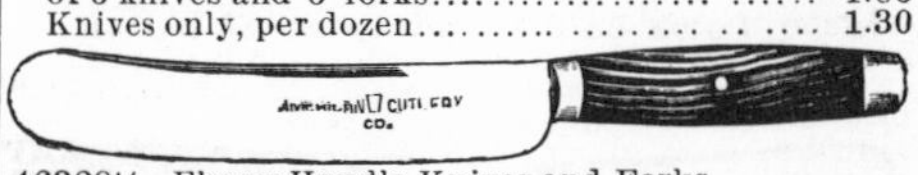

46328½ Ebony Handle Knives and Forks.
Per set of 6 knives and 6 forks.. .... $1.22
Knives only, per dozen................................ 1.48
46329 White Handle Knives and Forks.
Per set of 6 knives and 6 forks.......................... 1 75
Knives only, per dozen.................................. 2.00

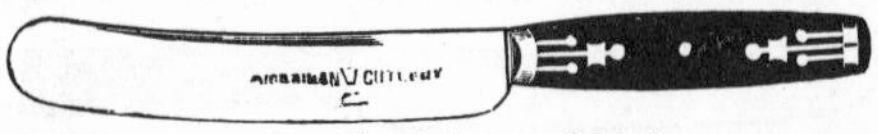

46329½ Cocoa Handle Knives and Forks.
Per set of 6 knives and 6 forks........................$1.23
Knives only, per dozen.................................. 1.48
46330 White Handle Knives and Forks.
Per set of 6 knives and 6 forks 2.00
Knives only, per dozen.................................. 2.25

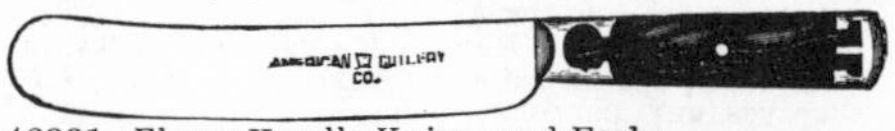

46331 Ebony Handle Knives and Forks.
Per set of 6 knives and 6 forks..........................$1.32
Knives only, per dozen 1.57

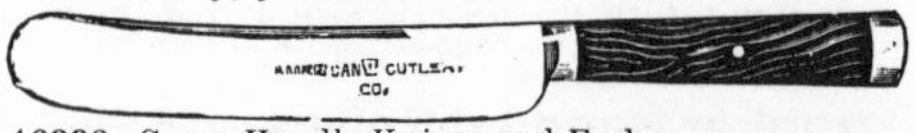

46332 Cocoa Handle Knives and Forks.
Per set of 6 knives and 6 forks $1.15
Knives only, per dozen 1.40

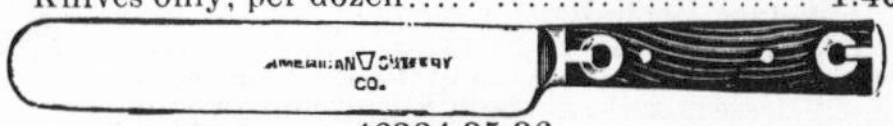

46334-35-36

46334 Cocoa Handle Knives and Forks.
Per set of 6 knives and 6 forks..........................$0.84
Knives only, per dozen.................................. 1 09
46335 Ebony Handle Knives and Forks.
Per set of 6 knives and 6 forks.......................... .95
Knives only, per dozen.................................. 1.20
46336 White Handle Knives and Forks.
Per set of 6 knives and 6 forks.......................... 1.20
Knives only, per dozen.................................. 1.45

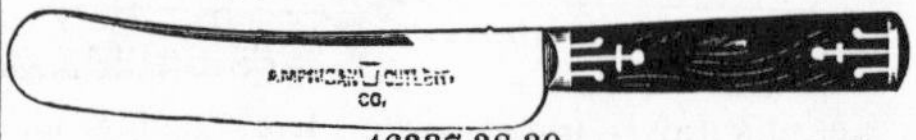

46337-38-39.

46337 Cocoa Handle Knives and Forks.
Per set of 6 knives and 6 forks $1.35
Knives only, per dozen.................................. 1.60

Table Cutlery—Continued.

46338 Ebony Handle Knives and Forks.
Per set of 6 knives and 6 forks 1.40
Knives only, per dozen 1.65
46339 White Bone Handle Knives and Forks.
Per set of 6 knives and 6 forks 1.90
Knives only, per dozen 2.12

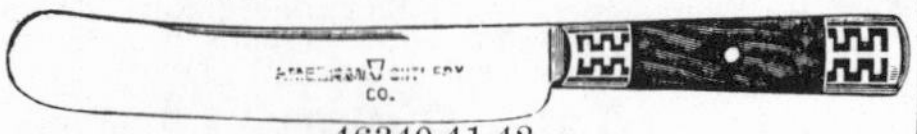

46340-41-42.

46340 Cocoa Handle Knives and Forks.
Per set of 6 knives and 6 forks. $1.40
Knives only, per dozen 1.65
46341 Ebony Handle Knives and Forks.
Per set of 6 knives and 6 forks. 1.50
Knives only, per dozen 1.75
46342 White Handle Knives and Forks.
Per set of 6 knives and 6 forks 1.95
Knives only, per dozen 2.10

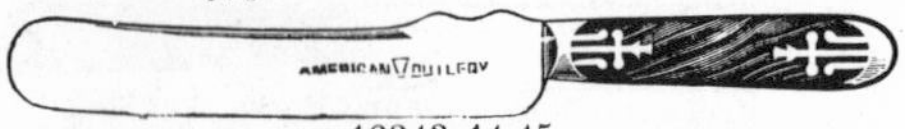

46343-44-45.

46343 Cocoa Handle Knives and Forks.
Per set of 6 knives and 6 forks $1.70
Knives only, per dozen 1.90
46344 Ebony Handle Knives and Forks.
Per set of 6 knives and 6 forks 1.85
Knives only, per dozen 2.00
46345 White Bone Handle Knives and Forks.
Per set of 6 knives and 6 forks 2.30
Knives only, per dozen 2.47

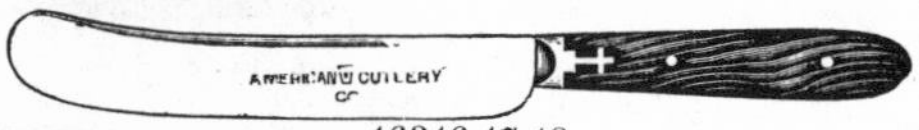

46346-47-48.

46346 Cocoa Handle Knives and Forks.
Per set of 6 knives and 6 forks $1.00
Knives only, per dozen 1.25
46347 Ebony Handle Knives and Forks.
Per set of 6 knives and 6 forks 1.33
Knives only, per dozen 1.58
46348 White Bone Handle Knives and Forks.
Per set of 6 knives and 6 forks 1.67
Knives only, per dozen 1.92

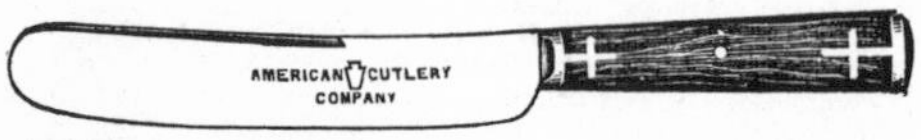

46349 Cocoa Handle Knives and Forks, best quality steel blades.
Per set, 6 knives and 6 forks $0.95

46350 Cocoa Handle Knives and Forks, best quality steel blades.
Per set, 6 knives and 6 forks $0.93

46351 Cocoa Handle Knives and Forks, best quality steel blades.
Per set, 6 knives and 6 forks $0.99

46354-55-56.

46354 Cocoa Handle Knives and Forks.
Per set of 6 knives and 6 forks $1.25
Knives only, per dozen 1.50
46355 Ebony Handle Knives and Forks.
Per set of 6 knives and 6 forks 1.28
Knives only, per dozen 1.63
46356 White Bone Handle Knives and Forks.
Per set of 6 knives and 6 forks 1.90
Knives only, per dozen 2.15

We have no "trashy" goods. Our knives and forks are all steel tines and blades. Handles fitted evenly and rivets filed down smoothly.

We can furnish dessert size knives at same prices and styles as regular table knives from No. 46324 to No. 46356.

Rubber Handled Knives and Forks.

Handles will stand hot water and never crack or come off. Finest steel blades.
Weight, per dozen knives...... ... .35 oz.
Weight, per dozen forks....................25 oz.
A medium knife is about 9¼ in. long.
A dessert knife is about 8¼ in. long over all.
All forks have 3 tines.

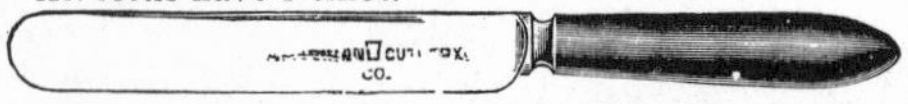

46357 Black Hard Rubber Handled Knives (no forks), oval swell handles, best steel.　Per doz.
Medium size $3.00
46358 Dessert size 2.75
46359 Forks to match 2.95

46359½ Knives, white handles, ivory grained, never crack or turn yellow.　Per doz.
Medium knives $4.34
Dessert knives.............................. 4.00
Forks...... .... 4.30

Table Cutlery—Continued.

Per doz.
46360 Black Hard Rubber Handled Knives (no forks), flat handle, best of steel, medium size ..$2.70
46361 Dessert size 2.24
46362 Forks to match 2.60

46362½ Knives, white celluloid handles, medium size (9¼ in.) Per dozen $3.67
Dessert size (8¼ in.) Per dozen................. 2.30
Forks to match. Per dozen................. 3.60
All our table knives and forks have fine steel tines and blades.

Children's Knives and Forks.

Made just as fine as the large knives.
Postage, per set, 5 cents.

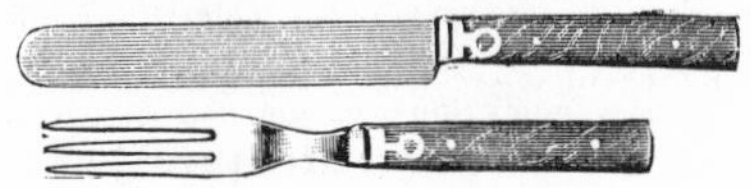

46363 Child's Set, one knife, one fork, cocoa wood handle, single bolster, best steel ....$0.14　Per set.

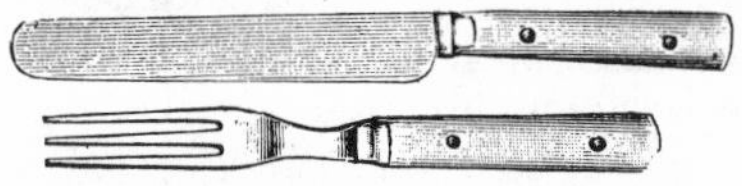

46364 Child's Set, one knife, one fork, white bone handles, single bolster, best steel... ....$0.16

Extra, by mail, 6 cents.
46365 Child's Set, one knife, one fork, white bone handles, double bolster, scimiter-shaped blades, finest quality. Per set...........................$0.24

Carving Sets.

Our carving sets are all well made, and only the best of steel is used in blades and forks, and all warranted

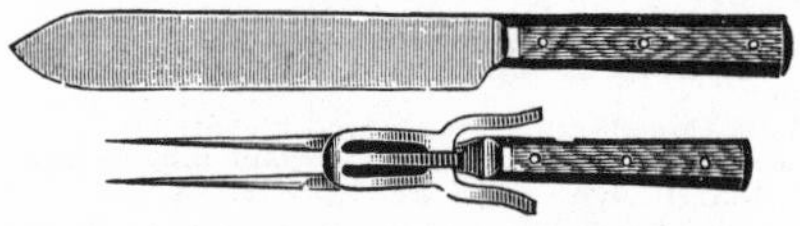

46367 Carving Knife and Fork, cocoa handles, good steel blade for........ ....$0.60
Extra, by mail, 12 cents.

46367½ Carving Knife and Fork, buckhorn handles, guard on fork, good steel blade for.... $0.60
Extra, by mail, 18 to 23 cents.

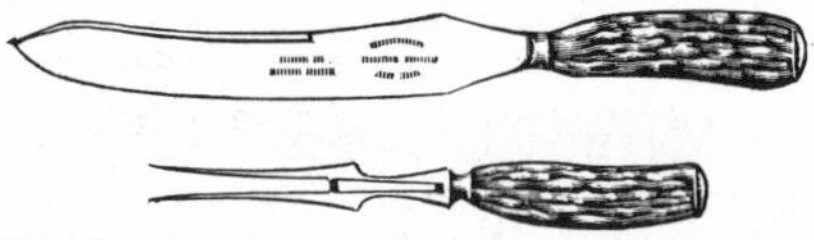

46369 Carving Knife and Fork, stag handles, steel capped end, guard on fork, good steel blade, English make; for...........................$0.90

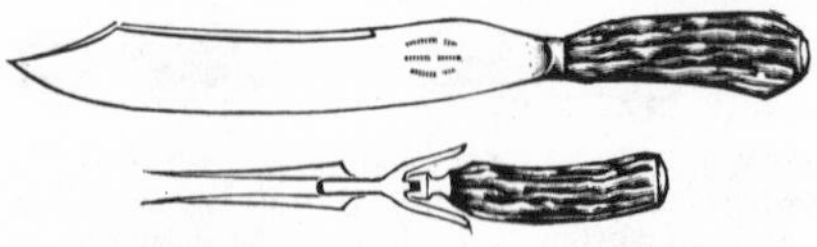

46370 Carving Knife and Fork, stag horn handles, scimiter shape blades, guard on fork, good steel blades and tines, English make, and warranted. Knife and fork for.....................$1.15
Steels to match, 35 cents, each.

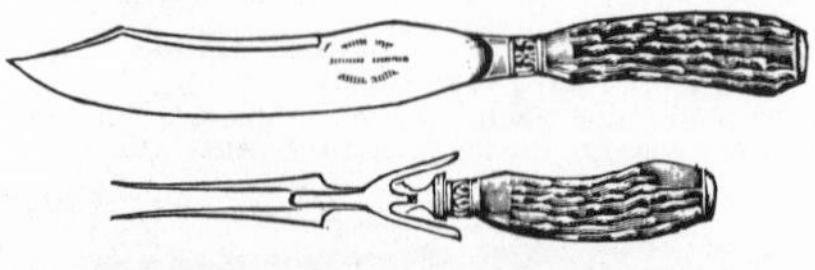

46372 Carving Knife and Fork, fine large stag horn handles, scimiter shape blade, guard on fork, German silver bolster, capped ends, best English steel blades and tines, well finished throughout, English make; warranted.
Knife and fork for.............................$1.65
Steel for sharpening knife, 49 cents, each.

Table Cutlery—Continued.

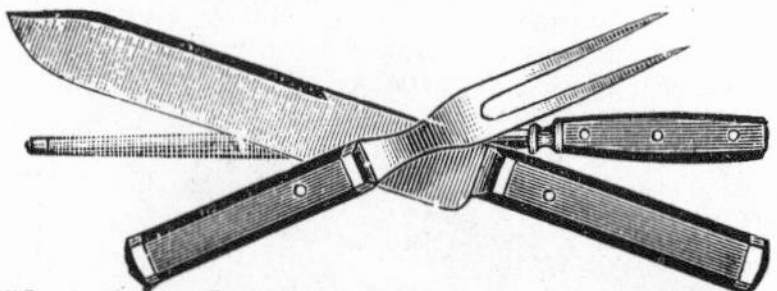

46373 Carving Knife, Fork and Steel Sharpener, guard on fork, fine steel, cocoa handles, warranted, for............. .... $1.27

Weight, 26 ounces.

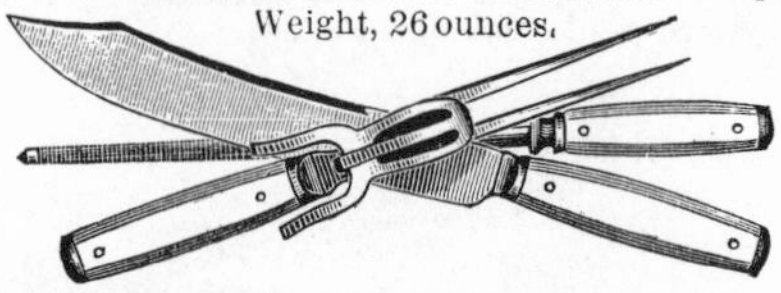

46374 Carving Knife, Fork and Steel, flat oval white bone handles, double nickel bolstered, best of steel; warranted (knife and fork only)..$1.60
Steel, 47 cents extra.

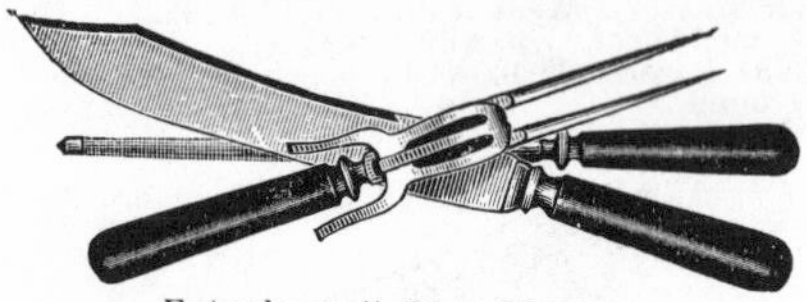

Extra by mail, 20 to 25 cents.
46375 Carving Knife, Fork and Steel, oval rubber handle; warranted not to crack in boiling water, saber blade, best of steel, an elegant set (knife and fork only $1.87, steel, 58c). Per set........$2.40
46376 Carving Knife, Fork and Steel, oval white celluloid handles, saber blade, best of steel; a good set; warranted. Handles never crack, 8 inch blade. Per set.......................... 3.00
46377 Carving Knife and Fork, white celluloid handles; guard on fork, scimiter blade, best steel, for......... .. .. 2.00

46378 Carving Knife and Fork, with finest celluloid ivory grained handles; resembles ivory so closely that it takes an expert to tell them from genuine ivory and will outlast the best ivory. Handles never crack or turn yellow, guard on fork, knife and fork made of the best steel, finely finished, 9 inch blade. Per pair ...$2.60
Steels to match, if desired, each .... .60

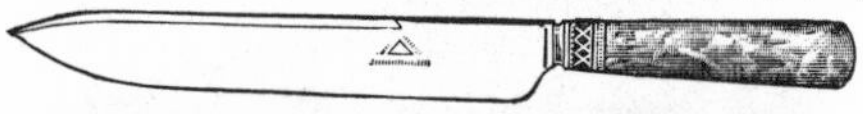

46379 Pearl Handle Carving Knife and Fork, with silver ferrules; length of pearl, 3½ in.; length of ferrules, 1 inch; knife and fork made of the best steel, finely finished, guard on fork, a handsome set.
8-inch blade. Per pair................. $5.67
Steel to match, if desired 3.00
Extra, by mail, 10 cents per pair.

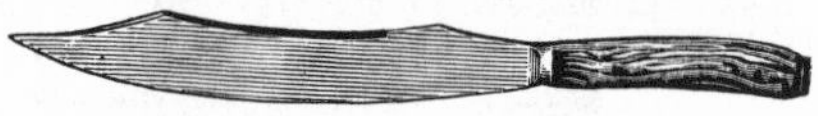

46380 Carving Knife and Fork, best quality steel tines and blades, fine stag handles, capped ends, English pattern, strong and durable, 9-inch blade. Per set...........$1.70　Steel to match....... $.49
Send for our special catalogue of cutlery, free for the asking.

46381 Carving Knife and Fork, Turkish blade, English stag horn handle, German silver bolster and cap; very best of steel, 9 inch blade, handsome and durable. Knife and fork.............$2.00
8-inch blade. Knife and fork.............. 1.90
Steel sharpeners to match set, each.... 75

46382 Carving Set, knife, fork and steel, English stag handle, fancy silver bolster and capped end; no better goods made with stag handles. Per set................................. $6.67

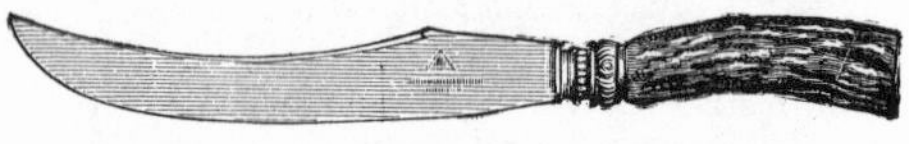

46383 New Style Carving Set, knife, fork and steel to match, very large, fine quality stag handles, heavy silver ferrules, 9-inch Turkish scimiter blade; finely finished, warranted very best quality throughout. Per set..........................$4.90
Extra case for carving sets for any sets, we quote $1.56, $2.25, $3.50 each. Prices govern quality and finish.

Table Cutlery—Continued.

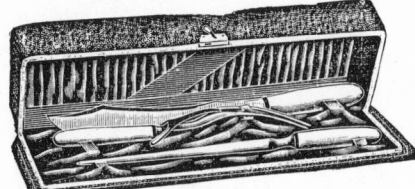

46384 Carving Sets, knife, fork and steel, in beautifully finished, plush covered, satin lined case, with nickel fastenings, celluloid ivory grained handles, better than ivory to wear and quite as handsome in appearance, because they do not crack; best of steel blades and tines, neatly finished in the best, substantial manner, 9 inch blade. Per set, with case.........$4.87 Weight, 44 ounces.
Our carvers are the highest quality and finish and every pair is warranted.

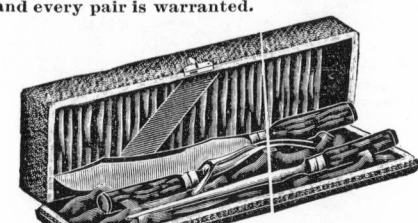

46385 Highest Quality Carving Sets, knife, fork and steel, in finely finished, plush covered, satin lined case, stag horn handles, with German silver ferrules and capped end, scimiter shaped blade, guard on forks, best of steel, finely finished and warranted, 9 inch blade. Weight, 54 ounces. Per set, in case..$4.75
Knife and fork, without case 2.30
Steel to match...................................... .78
All of our carving sets are warranted as represented, and if not satisfactory, can be returned at our expense and money refunded.

46386 Carving Knife and Fork, stag handles, Turkish blades, best steel, 9-inch blade, guard on fork Warranted. Per pair.....$2.40 Weight, per set, 22 ounces. Steel to match... .89

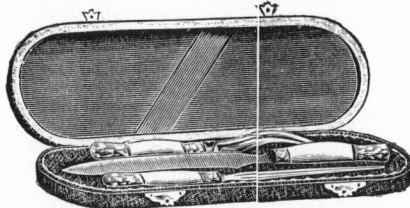

46387 Highest Quality Carving Set, knife, fork and steel in round cornered, plush covered, satin lined case, artistically finished, celluloid, ivory grained handles, with beautifully finished silver ferrules and cap on ends, highly finished blades, and best of steel in all pieces; one of the most attractive sets in the market; if not satifactory can be returned at our expense. Poorer sets are sold at $18.00 at retail in many stores. 10-inch blades, guard on fork. Weight, 64 ounces. Per set, in case.........$12.50

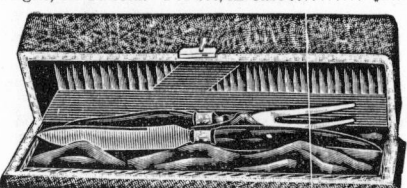

46388 Bird Carving Set, knife and fork in plush covered case, satin lined, and finely finished, stag horn handles, German silver ferrule, blade and fork best of steel; a handsome set; blade, 5 inches long. Per pair, in case (25 oz.).$4.00

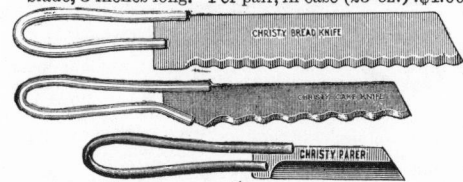

6⅞ IN

46389 The "Genuine Original Christy Set," finest finish, best quality, consisting of 1 bread knife, 1 cake knife and 1 paring knife. Per set.......$0.90

Table Cutlery—Continued.

COMET HOUSE SAW

46390 The Comet Kitchen Saw, best steel, nickel finish, metal handle: the handiest article in the house. Blade, 12 inches long, 2 inches wide at the handle, 1 inch at end. Each..............$0.35 By mail, 6 cents extra.

Butcher Knives.

Our butcher knives are all the highest quality of steel; we do not handle the cheap trashy 5 cent counter goods, that are worse than nothing. Ours are all warranted to hold an edge.

46391 Butcher Knives, 6 in. steel blades, plain riveted cocoa wood handles, a good article. Each.............$0.09 Per dozen.....$1.00 Postage, extra, 6 cents.

Each.   Per doz
46392 Butcher Knives, Sheffield make, heavy steel blades, cocoa wood handles, well riveted, good and strong.
6 in. blade. $0.15 $1.50
7 in. blade .... .20   1.75
8 in. blade........... .... .27   2.20
Postage, extra, 7 cents.

AMERICAN CUTLERY COMPANY

46393 Butcher Knife, cocoa redwood handles, scale tang, bolstered and riveted, best quality. Each...............6 inch, $0.25   8 inch, $0.49

46394 Butcher Knives, 6 in. blade, hunting style, best of steel. Each...... ....$0.35
Per dozen........................... 3.70
Postage, 6 cents extra.
46395 Butcher Knives, cocoa handle, one bolster, 8 in. blade. Each....................... .45
Per dozen......................... 4.85
Postage, 6 cents extra.
Our beech handled goods are the best in the world.

46396 Butcher Knives, beech handles, best steel, 6 in. blade, each......................$0.12
Per dozen 1.30
8 in. blade, each .... .23
Per dozen......................... 2.49
10 in. blade, each ......$0.45 Per dozen...... 4.50
No better cutters in the market. Handles warranted not to come off. Try one. Postage, 6c. extra.

46397 Sticking Knives, beech handles, best steel, 6 in. blade. Each........$0.15 Per dozen.....$1 62
Postage, 5 cents extra.
No better cutters in the market. Handles warranted not to come off. Try one.

46398 Skinning Knives, beech handles, best steel. 6 in. blade. Each..$0.18 Per dozen............$1.95 Postage, 5 cents extra. No better cutter in the market. Handles warranted not to come off.

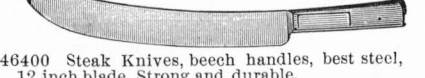

46399 Slicing Knives, cocoa handles, fancy bolster, best steel, 8 inch blade, each.............$0.35
Per dozen................................... 4.00
Postage, 5 cents extra.

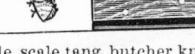

46400 Steak Knives, beech handles, best steel, 12 inch blade. Strong and durable.
Each............$0.55 Per dozen....... ......$6.00
Postage, 10 cents extra.
No better knives in the market. No butcher shop would be without them after a trial.

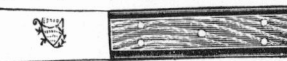

46401 Beech handle, scale tang, butcher knives; best quality, heavy and durable.
Each, 6-inch $0.20
8-in. .... .28

Table Cutlery—Continued.

46402 Sticking knives, beech handle, scale tang, riveted, very best quality. Each, 5½-inch.....$0.20
6-inch......................... 0.25

46403 Skinning Knives: beech handles, scale tang, riveted, Chicago Stock Yards shape, very best quality. Each, 5½-in....................$0.22
6-inch........................ .23
7 inch .... .25

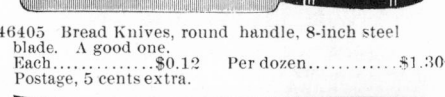

46404 Butcher or Bread Knives, cocoa handles, one bolster, 8-inch blade, best steel.
Each..... $0.40 Per dozen $4.00
6-inch blade.
Each..... $0 27 Per dozen 2.60
Postage, 5 cents extra.

46405 Bread Knives, round handle, 8-inch steel blade. A good one.
Each...........$0.12   Per dozen...........$1.30
Postage, 5 cents extra.

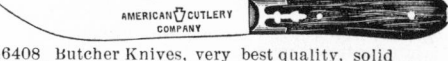

46406 Bread Knives, oval cocoa handles, 8-inch blade, single bolster, finest steel. (Retail price. 50 cts.) Each.......$0.28 Per dozen........$3.00 Postage, 5 cents extra.

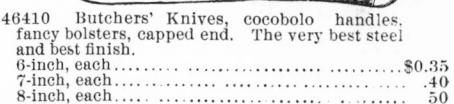

46407 French Cook Knives, ebony wood handles, best steel blades. The best slicer in the market.
8-inch blade, each.........................$0.60
10-inch blade, each......................... .75
12-inch blade, each......................... .85
Postage, 7 cents extra.

AMERICAN CUTLERY COMPANY

46408 Butcher Knives, very best quality, solid and durable. Each, 6-inch...................$0.28
8-inch 39

46410 Butchers' Knives, cocobolo handles, fancy bolsters, capped end. The very best steel and best finish.
6-inch, each...........................$0.35
7-inch, each........................... .40
8-inch, each........................... .50
Postage, 7 cents extra.

46411 Tinned Cheese Knives, cocobolo handles.
10-inch, each. $0.40
12-inch, each......................... .50
14-inch, each......................... .75

46413 Ham Slicers, long narrow slim blades, solid rubber handles, highest quality steel blades. No better goods made at any price.
10-inch blade, each...................$0.65
12-inch blade, each.................. .78
Postage, extra......................... .05

46414 Hotel and Kitchen Fork, best steel, with guard the very best quality. Entire length, 12 inches.
Each $0.68
46415 Hotel and Kitchen Fork, best steel, without guard. Entire length, 12 inches.
Each......................... .57
Postage, extra................... .05

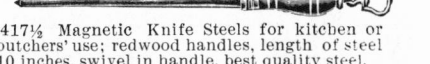

46416 The Magnetic Butcher's Steel, for sharpening knives; stag horn handle, swivel in end. Steel 12 inches long, each..... ....$0.95
Extra by mail 15 cents

46417½ Magnetic Knife Steels for kitchen or butchers' use; redwood handles, length of steel 10 inches, swivel in handle, best quality steel. Each $0.75
By mail 13 cents extra.

Table Cutlery—Continued.

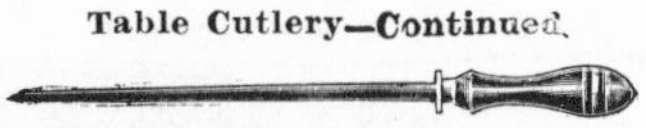

46418 Magnetic Kitchen or Table Steel; light and handy, best quality steel. Steel 8 inches long. Each $0.30
By mail 6 cents extra.

Kitchen Knives.

Our kitchen knives are all good steel and not the cheap iron affairs generally sold at these prices.

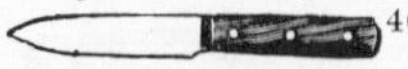

46420 Kitchen Knives, beech wood handles.
Each .... $0.05 Per dozen $0 50

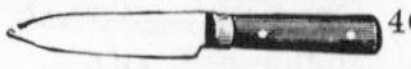

46421 Kitchen Knives, cocoa handles, cap bolster.
Each .... $0.06 Per dozen $0.60

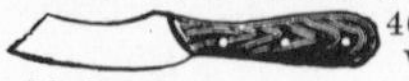

46422 Kitchen Knives, cocoa wood handles, best steel blade. Each .... $0.09 Per dozen $0.98
Postage, extra .... .03

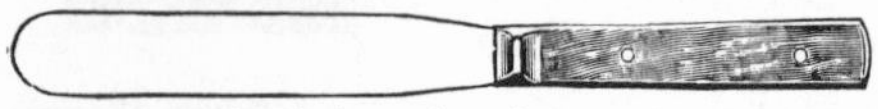

46423 Spatulas, balanced lap bolstered cocobolo handles.
6-inch, each $0.24
8-inch, each .... .37
10-inch, each .... .55

Shoe Knives.

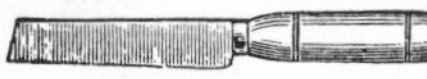

		Each.	Per doz.
46425	Best Steel Shoe Knives, square. point, 3 inches	$0.06	$0.60
46426	Shoe Knives, square point, 4 in.	10	1.00
46427	Shoe Knives, round point, 3½ in.	.08	.87
	Postage, extra		.03

Family Knife Sharpener.

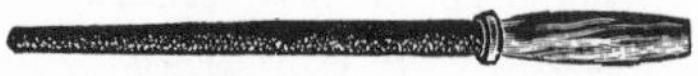

Blade, 7 in.; total length, 12 in.; weight, 5½ oz.
46428 Patent Sharpener, plain wood handle, for kitchen and general use. Each $0.11
Per dozen 1.10
Better than a whetstone, because not so easily broken and will not become glazed and useless. Better than a steel, because it will sharpen a tool without spoiling it.

Putty Knives.

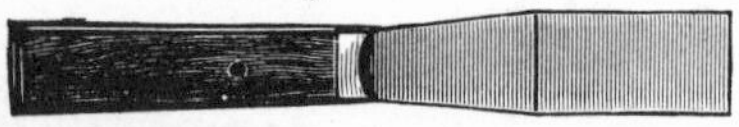

46429 Putty Knives, solid cocobolo handles, 3¾ inch blade, square point, best steel. Each $0.20
Weight, 4 oz.
46430 Same, beech handle, no bolster. Each .... .12

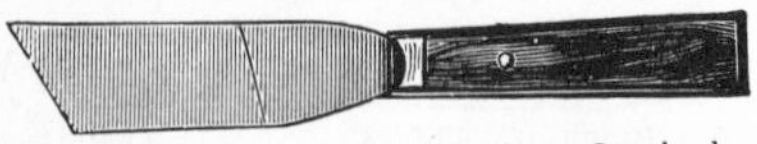

46431 Putty Knives, cocobolo handles, 3¾ inch blade, beveled point. Each $0 20

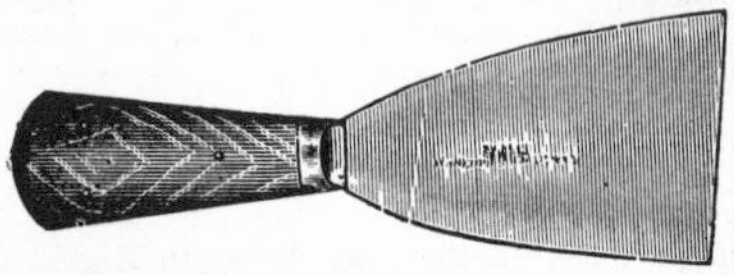

46432 American Cutlery Co.'s Scraping Knives, for painters' and glaziers' use, cocobolo handles.

Width of blade	2½ in.	3 in.	4 in.
Each	35c.	38c.	50c.

Postage, extra, 6c.

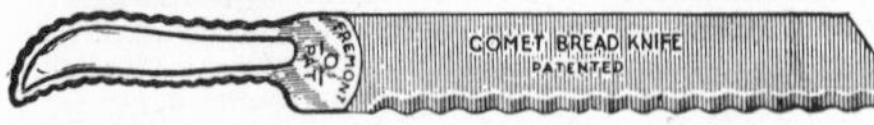

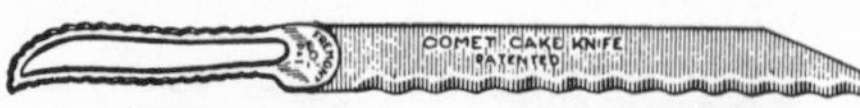

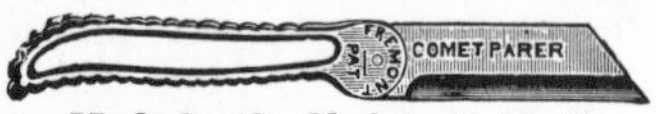

Made by the Christy Knife Co.

46433 The Complete Set, "Christy" style, consisting of 1 bread knife, 1 cake knife, 1 paring knife, made of the very best sheet steel, with iron handles, nickel finished and scolloped edges. Postage, 15c. extra. Per set $0.50

We have an expert Traffic Manager. He can tell you all you want to know about rates or cost of goods laid down at your station. Write, and points which seem difficult, will be made plain to you.

Traveling Cases—Continued.

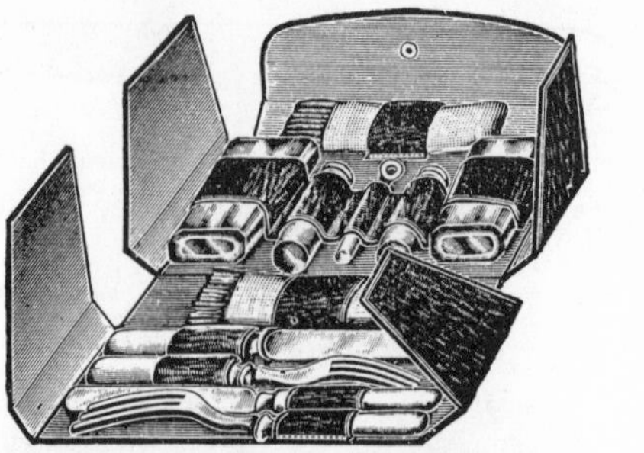

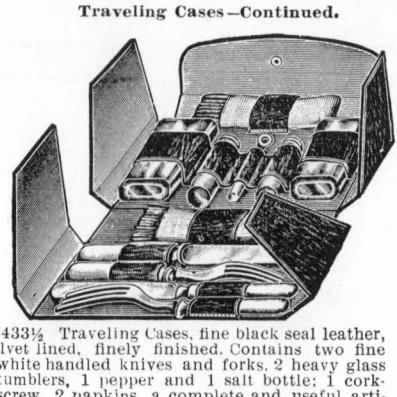

46433½ Traveling Cases, fine black seal leather, velvet lined, finely finished. Contains two fine white handled knives and forks, 2 heavy glass tumblers, 1 pepper and 1 salt bottle; 1 corkscrew, 2 napkins a complete and useful article, 8¼x4x2 inches. Weight, 1¼ pound. Each. $4.38

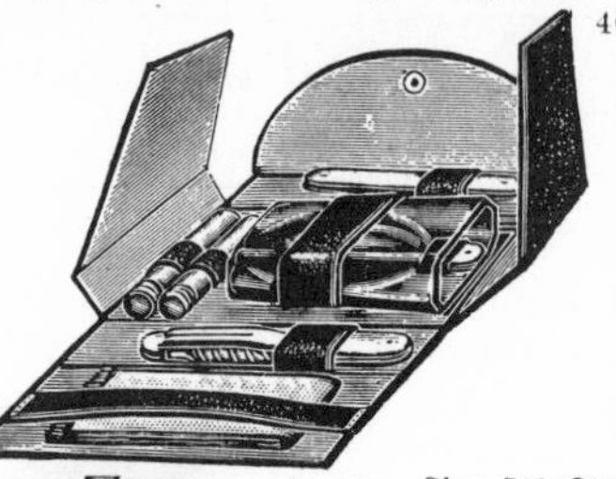

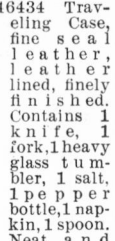

46434 Traveling Case, fine seal leather, leather lined, finely finished. Contains 1 knife, 1 fork, 1 heavy glass tumbler, 1 salt, 1 pepper bottle, 1 napkin, 1 spoon. Neat and handy. Size, 5½x3¼x1½ inch. Weight, ¾ lb. Each $2.75

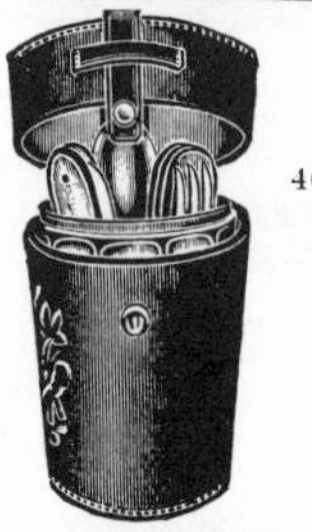

46435 Pocket Traveling Case, heavy black leather. Contains heavy glass tumbler and folding knife, fork and spoon; well made and durable. Size, 4¼x2½. Weight, ½ lb. Each $2.00

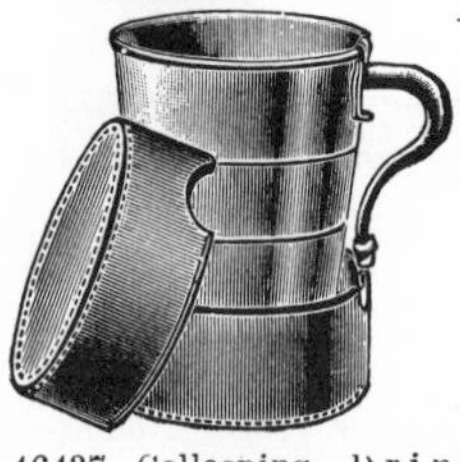

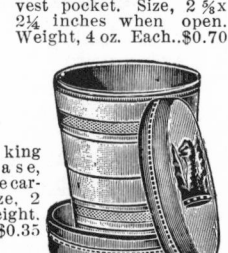

46436 Collapsing Drinking Cups, heavy white metal, nickel plated, finest finish, in neat leather cases; can be carried in vest pocket. Size, 2⅝x 2¼ inches when open. Weight, 4 oz. Each.. $0.70

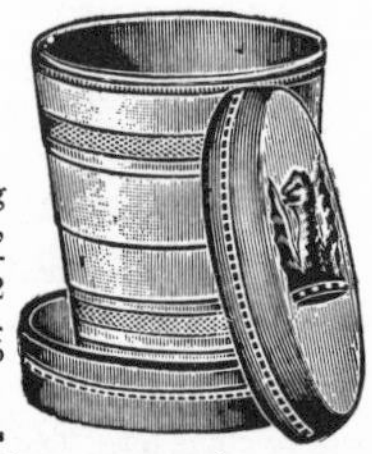

46437 Collasping Drinking Cup, in neat leather case, strong and durable; can be carried in vest pocket. Size, 2 ⅝x2⅜ in. when open. Weight, 4 oz. Each $0.35

Shears and Scissors.

Weights vary from 3 to 20 ounces each.
Our Shears and Scissors are the best in the market and are celebrated for THEIR GOOD CUTTING QUALITIES AND DURABILITY.
Lengths mentioned are the full dimensions from end to end.

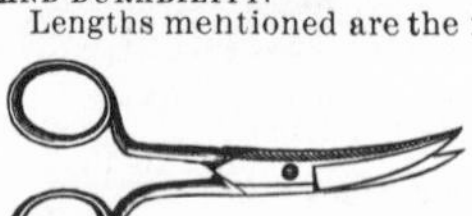

46439 Nail Scissors, used in manicuring the nails on hands or feet, 4 inch best steel, fine finish. Each $0.42

46439

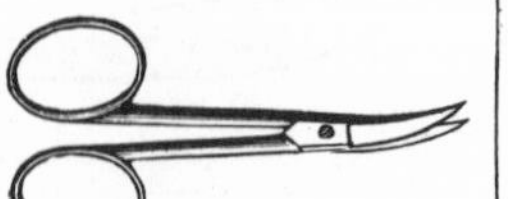

46440 Manicure Scissors, for trimming around the finger nails. Best steel, finely finished, best quality. Long narrow bent points.

46440

Each .... 3½ in. length, 45c.; 4 in. length, 55c.

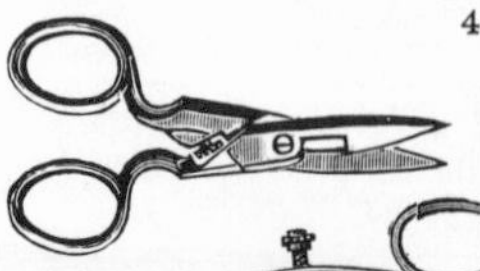

46441 Button Hole Scissors, with inside set screw, to adjust the blades for different size button holes, 4½ inch, best steel, fine finish. Each $0.50

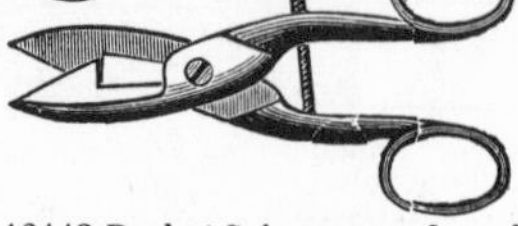

46442 Buttonhole scissors, polished steel blade, adjusted by thumb screw to cut any size buttonhole. Price, pair. $0.39
Per doz 4.25
Postage. extra.. .04

46443 Pocket Scissors, good quality, 4 in. Each. $0.20

Shears and Scissors—Continued.

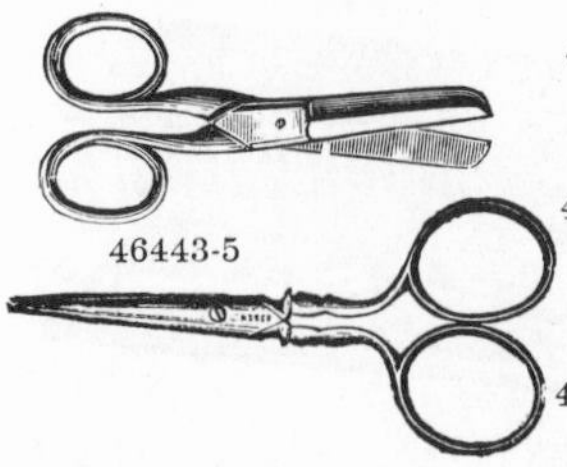

46443-5

46444 Better quality. Rogers' pattern warranted. heavy and strong, 4 in. Each.. $0.35
46445 Best quality, finest finished Rogers' pattern: warranted, heavy and strong, 5-in. Each $0.60
46446 Embroidery Scissors, good quality steel.
Each $0.30
Per doz .... .40

46447 Fancy Embroidery Scissors finest steel. Each $0.40

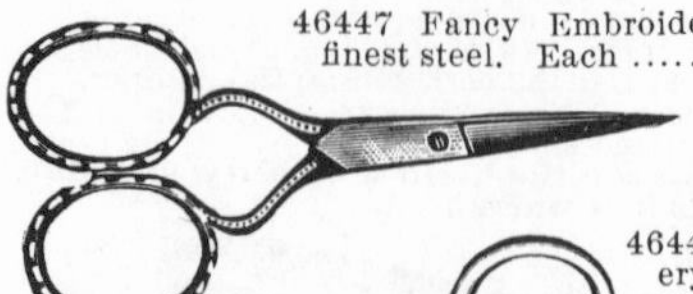

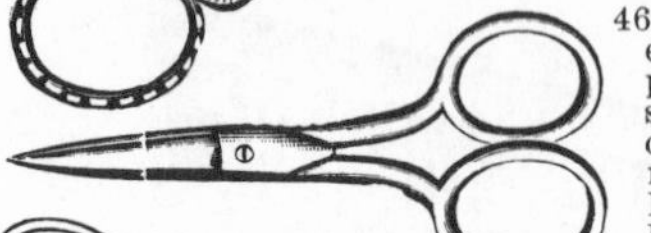

46448 Embroidery Scissors, polished laid steel and good cutters; warranted. Each. .. $0.25
Postage ext. 4c

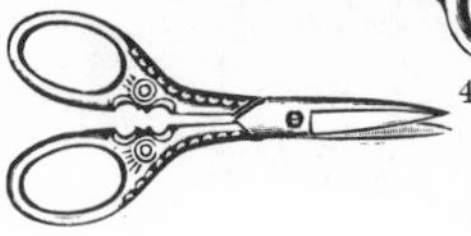

46449 Fancy Embroidery Scissors, gilt and nickel finish, best quality of steel blades; every pair warranted; 3½ inch. Each $0.40

46450 Scissors, the best laid steel, nickel plated, best quality and finest finish.

Inches	4½	5	6	6½	7
Each	$0.35	$0.40	$0.45	$0.50	$0 55

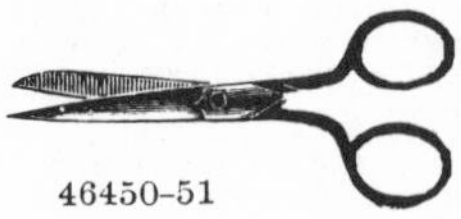

46450-51

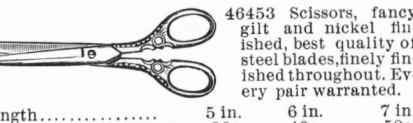

46451 Scissors, good polished laid steel blades, round bows: every pair warranted

Length	5 in.	5½ in.	6 in.	6½ in.	7 in.
Each	$0.20	$0.25	$0.27	$0.30	$0.35

Postage, extra, 5 to 10 cents.

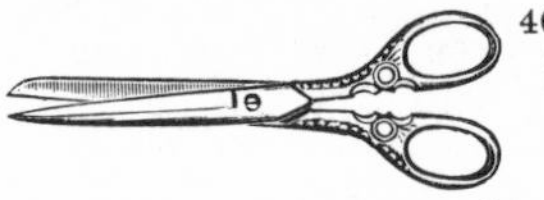

46453 Scissors, fancy gilt and nickel finished, best quality of steel blades, finely finished throughout. Every pair warranted.

Length	5 in.	6 in.	7 in.
Each	36c.	40c.	50c

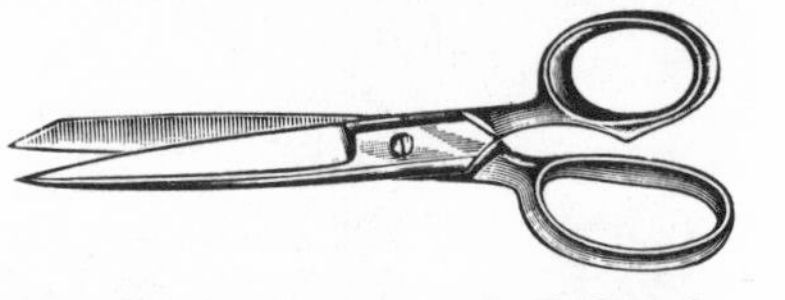

46454 Shears, straight trimmers, with the celebrated "brass bolt and nut" for taking up wear; full nickel plated, best steel. Every pair warranted.

Length	8 in.	9 in.	10 in.
Each	50c.	56c.	68c.

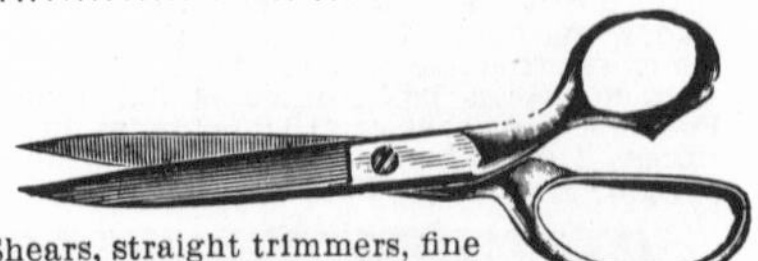

46455 Shears, straight trimmers, fine laid steel blades, full nickel plated blades and handles, a good article, warranted.

Length	6in.	7in.	7½ in.	8 in.	9 in.	10 in.
Each	$0.29	$0.33	$0.39	$0.44	$0.50	$0.60

Postage, extra, 5 to 10 cents.

46456 Shears, straight trimmers, japanned handles, maroon color, polished laid steel blades. Every pair warranted good cutters and good wearing qualities. The best low-priced shear on the market.

Length	6 in.	7 in.	8 in.	9 in.
Each	21c.	23c.	26c	33c.

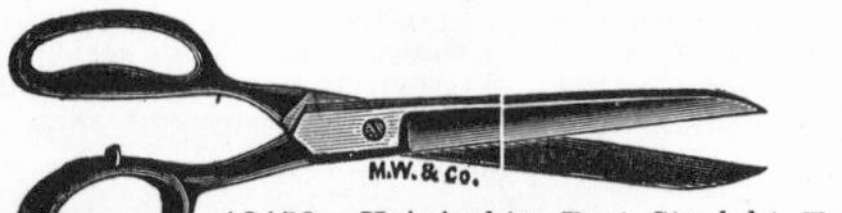

46459 Heinisch's Best Straight Trimmers, finest laid steel, japanned handles.

Inches	6	7	8	9	10
Each	35c.	38c.	40c.	49c.	78c

46460 Heinisch's Shears, best straight trimmers, finest laid steel, nickel plated. No better made.

Inches	6	6½	7	7½	8	8½	9
Each	45c.	50c.	55c.	60c.	65c.	70c.	75c

46461 Heinisch's Shears, left hand only, nickel plated, finest laid steel, 8½ inch. Each $1.00
Postage, extra, 5 to 10 cents.

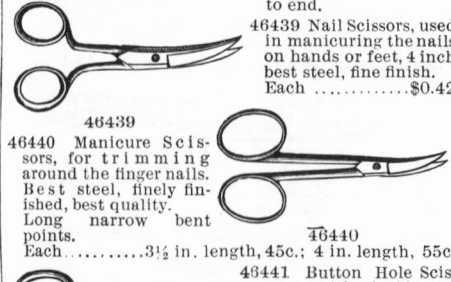

Shears—Continued.

46462 Shears, bent trimmers, R. Heinischs Sons, nickel plated, best made: warranted.

Weight....	½ lb.	¾ lb.		¾ lb.	1 lb.
Inches.....	8	8½	9	10	12	13
Each.......	70c	75c	85c	$1.15	$1.25.	$1.70

46463 Shears, bent trimmers, R. Heinisch's Sons best make, black Japanned handles. Every pair warranted.

Length......	8 in.	9 in.	10 in.	12 in.	13 in.
Each........	56c.	74c.	90c.	$1.10	$1.20

Bent trimmers are large and strong, and made for heavy work.

Shears—Continued.

46464 Paper Hangers' or Bankers' Shears, best steel; no better made. Postage, extra 5c.
Each, 12-inch.........$0.95   Each, 14-inch....$1.20

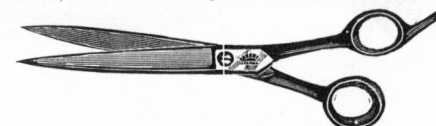

46465 Barbers' Shears, Heinisch's best japanned handles, laid steel; warranted. Each, 8½ inch... ....$0.50   Each, 9 inch $0.60

Shears—Continued.

46466 Left Hand Barbers' Shears, Heinisch's best, japanned handles. 9 inch only. Each.... .80

46466½ Barbers' Shears, R. Heinisch's best nickeledhandles, laid steel, warranted. No better goods made.

Length............	7½ in.	8 in.	8½ in.	9 in.
Each.	70c.	75c.	78c.	85c.

R. Heinisch & Sons' shears have a wide wide reputation and are acknowledged to be the best goods manufactured. No factory in the world can make better shears.

Length of shears and scissors are for the entire length over all, from point to end of bow.

46467 The Novelty Shear and Scissor Sharpener. Any one can sharpen the dullest shear or scissors in a few seconds. Each.................$0.10 Postage, 5 cents extra.

GUN DEPARTMENT.

All guns are guaranteed as represented, and if not found so they can be returned at our expense if FULL AMOUNT OF MONEY is sent with order, and if returned within three days from time taken from express office, properly cleaned and packed as received and in as good order as when received. If gun is as represented by us, return charges and all expenses must be paid by purchaser. Guns and rifles can be sent C. O. D. subject to examination, ONLY when $5.00 is sent with ORDER, anywhere this side of the Missouri River. Beyond this point full money, or $15.00, must accompany order. Send CASH with order and you run no risk and save money if you want a gun, as you then have three days for trial and examination, and also save your cash discounts and return charges on C. O. D. envelope.

Guns subject to same discount as other goods. See pages 1 and 2 for discounts.

Do not return us DIRTY and RUSTY guns and expect us to take them back, or guns that have been used until the finish has been worn off, for we cannot do so. Prices quoted on any make of gun in the market. Send full description of gun wanted, and if possible to obtain we can furnish it.

A NEW HAMMERLESS SHOT GUN.

M. W. & CO.'S NEW HAMMERLESS DOUBLE BARREL SHOT GUN. NONE GENUINE UNLESS STAMPED ON TOP RIB, MONTGOMERY WARD & CO., CHICAGO.

A $65.00 List Gun for $35.00.   **A $50.00 List Gun for $29.00.**

CROSS BOLTED, HANDSOME IN DESIGN AND FINISH, AUTOMATIC SAFETY BLOCK TO TRIGGER.

EASY COCKING, BORED FOR NITRO OR BLACK POWDER.

Damascus. $35.00.

Twist Barrel. $29.00.

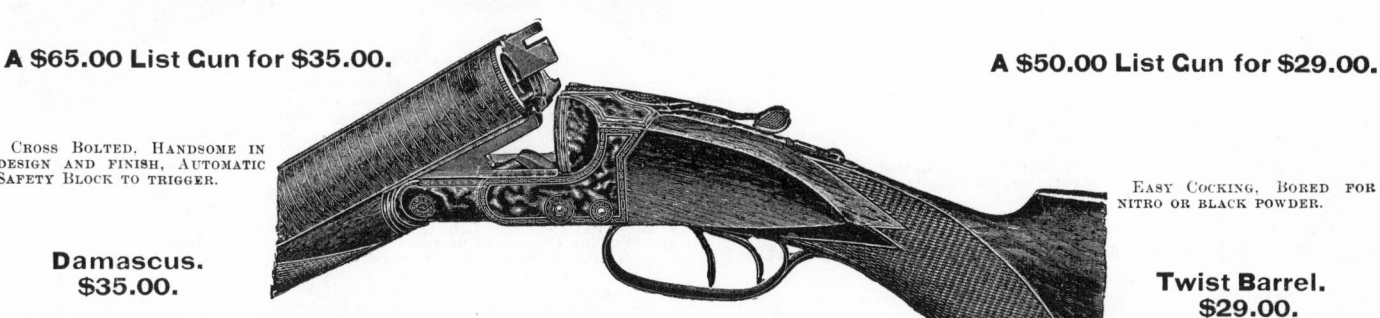

M. W. & CO.'S HAMMERLESS GUN.

A High Grade Gun, with all the best features of the "High Priced" Guns. Made of best material, handsome in design and finish, "well balanced;" easy cocking (the weight of barrel doing the work). For beauty of "out-line," "hang and balance," it has no superior at any price. Top lever, cross-bolted, pistol grip, English walnut stock patent compensating snap fore-end, case hardened lock-plates and action, finely matted tapering concave rib, wide heavy breach, narrow at muzzle, neatly engraved, bored for nitro or black powders (will shoot either kind). Good at the "trap" or in the field, in fact a first-class all around gun, for a small amount of money. No better shooting guns at any price. Made in two grades only, both grades being the same in design and finish, the only difference being in the grade of barrels. The twist barrels are just as good shooters as the Damascus. ALL CHOKE BORED UNLESS OTHERWISE ORDERED. Every gun tested and target accompaning each gun.

46468 Fine Damascus Steel Barrels, 10 or 12 gauge..$35.00
46469 Finest Laminated Twist Steel Barrels, 10 or 12 gauge............................... 29.00

10 Gauge, 30 or 32 inches 8½ to 9¾ pounds. 12 Gauge, 28, 30 or 32 inches, 7 to 9 pounds.

The Celebrated Chas. Daly Hammerless Guns.

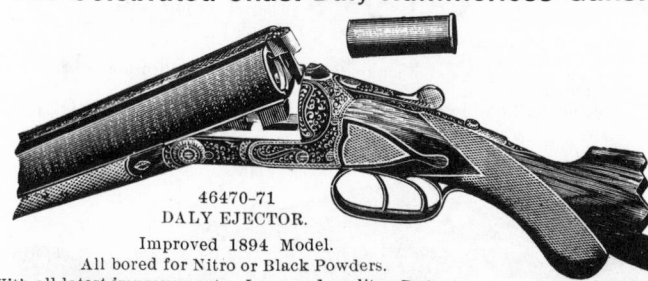

46470-71 DALY EJECTOR.

Improved 1894 Model.
All bored for Nitro or Black Powders.

With all latest improvements. Improved quality. Reduced prices. Quality the best. 46470 No 250, Diamond Quality Automatic Ejector, highest grade Damascus barrels, automatic lock, trigger safety, pistol grip, beautifully engraved Turkish walnut stock. There is no gun in the world superior to it. Will bear comparison with the finest Purdy—the highest-priced gun made; 12 and16 gauge. Each,$210.00
46471 No. 150, Damascus Barrels, Automatic Ejector, fine plain engraving, selected stocks, matted rib, 12 and 16 gauge. A perfect ejector. Each...........$140.00

Weight, 12 gauge, 28 and 30 in., 7¼ to 7¾ lbs.

The Daly Ejectors are the handsomest, strongest and most perfect ejectors made at any price. They are perfect in every respect. No gun in the world surpasses them in shooting or wearing qualities. Can be returned if not as represented.

Daly   Hammerless.

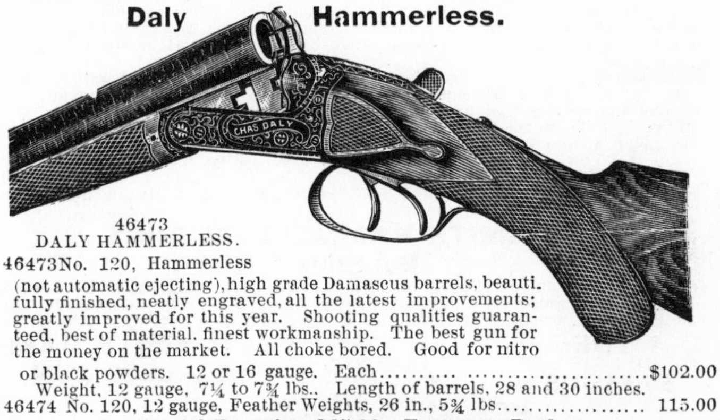

46473 DALY HAMMERLESS.

46473No. 120, Hammerless (not automatic ejecting), high grade Damascus barrels, beautifully finished, neatly engraved, all the latest improvements; greatly improved for this year. Shooting qualities guaranteed, best of material, finest workmanship. The best gun for the money on the market. All choke bored. Good for nitro or black powders. 12 or 16 gauge. Each...........$102.00

Weight, 12 gauge, 7¼ to 7¾ lbs. Length of barrels, 28 and 30 inches.
46474 No. 120, 12 gauge, Feather Weights, 26 in., 5¾ lbs................... 115.00

Special Bargains, $65.00.—Every one Perfect.

46475 Daly Hammerless Gun, same as No, 120, except not so finely engraved. Subject to previous sale. Built for service, and are long range, close, hard shooters. 10 gauge, 30 in., 9¼ to 10 lbs. Ea., $55.00; 10 gauge, 32 in., 9 to 10¼ lbs. Ea.,$65.00 All new and in perfect order. Warranted good shooters.

THE WORLD RENOWNED W. W. GREENER EJECTOR GUNS.

WORKS, BIRMINGHAM, ENGLAND.

The Greener Gun is made as a fine gun; in fact, is the highest development of the sporting gun in every particular. Workmanship and material the very best. The ejector gun only throws out the case that is fired or both shells when both are fired. Breech action is self fastening; the lock is self-cocking and the extractor is self-ejecting. Beautiful in design and finish. The Greener is so well known that it is not necessary to mention all of its superior qualities.

46478 No. 3 Quality Greener Ejector, hammerless, finely engraved, fine Damascus barrels, treble wedge, fastening self-acting ejector. Has all the improvements of the higher cost guns, but more plainly finished, still a very high grade gun; 12 gauge, $250.00 list. 10 gauge, $260.00 list; 12 gauge, 30 inch, 7¼ to 8 lbs. Our price... 210.50
10 gauge, 30 and 32 in., 8½ to 9 lbs. Our price.. 215.50

The "Facial Princeps" grade is the most popuar gun of the Greener's. More of them are in use by noted trap shooters and sportsmen, than of any other high grade gun in the world. They are made for downright hard service, and are long range, close shooters.

Facile Princeps Greener.

46479 "Facile Princeps" Quality, Greener cross bolt, treble wedge-fast, hammerless gun, made of best material, neatly finished, well balanced, light and strong, fine Damascus barrels, matted ribs and a good one. Made especially to our order for trap shooting. No better shooting gun at any price.
12 gauge, 30 in. barrels, 7¼ to 8¾ lbs., $125.00 list   Our price........$100.00

THE IMPROVED LEFEVER HAMMERLESS AND EJECTOR GUNS.

Model 1894

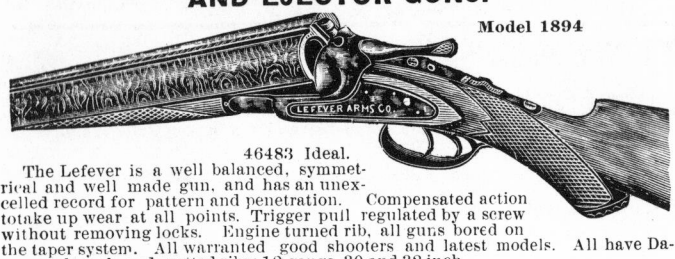

46483 Ideal.

The Lefever is a well balanced, symmetrical and well made gun, and has an unexcelled record for pattern and penetration. Compensated action to take up wear at all points. Trigger pull regulated by a screw without removing locks. Engine turned rib, all guns bored on the taper system. All warranted good shooters and latest models. All have Damascus barrels and matted ribs; 12-gauge, 30 and 32 inch.
46483 Ideal or G Grade Damascus. English walnut stocks, full pistol grip, rubber butt, 12 gauge Weight, 7¼ to 9 lbs......$42.50
46484 F Grade Damascus, pistol grip, horn or steel butt plate, engraved; 12-gauge. 7¼ to 9 lbs......$57.50
46485 **Lefever Automatic Ejector**, Damascus barrels, pistol grip, beautifully checkered and engraved. Weight, 7½ to 8¾ lbs; 30 or 32-inch barrels; 12-gauge only......$93.75
46486 Automatic Ejector. Damascus steel barrels, English walnut stock, checked and well engraved, rubber butt plate. full pistol grip, full compensated action, 12 gauge......$74.82
46487 Automatic Ejector; the new medium priced gun, Damascus Barrels, walnut stock, rubber butt plate, full pistol grip with rubber cap, checkered, line engraving, full compensated action. 12 guage......$62.00
Higher priced guns to order on short notice. The Lefever is a high grade gun, and warranted good shooter with either nitro or black powder.

COLT'S NEW HAMMELESS BREECH LOADING GUN.

MADE BY THE COLT'S PATENT FIRE ARMS CO., HARTFORD, CONN.

Improved Model.

46488 Colt.

The 10-bore is the long range Duck Gun. $60.00
"The best gun in the world for the money;" best material, best workmanship, beautifully finished. No better shooting gun AT ANY PRICE.
Safer than a hammer gun. Simple and few parts. No better gun made for durability and shooting qualities. All have pistol grip. All are choke bored. All have extension rib. All are warranted as represented. or can be returned at our expense and money refunded. Long range, hard shooters. All warranted highest quality to the grade.
46488 Fine Damascus steel barrels, neatly engraved, fancy imported walnut stock, pistol grip, fancy rubber butt, checkered grip and fore-end, case-hardened lock plates and actions, and finely finished; 12 gauge, 30 and 32 inch barrels; 7½ to 9 lbs. $80.00 grade. Our price......$60.00
10 gauge, 30 and 32 inch barrels, 8½ to 10 lbs. Our price......60.00
46489 $125.00 Grade, finest Damascus, beautifully finished and engraved, 12 or 10 gauge. Our price......95.00
Higher priced guns made to order. All have the automatic safety, and every one a beauty at the trap or in the field.

L. C. SMITH HAMMERLESS GUNS.
Bargains.

46490 10 guage only. 30 inches only, 9½ to 10½ pounds only, $80.00 grade for $47.50 each. Same style as No. 46497. Made for heavy charges and long range hard shooting. 'Bran' new and in perfect order. Every gun warranted.

THE FAMOUS.
L. C. SMITH HAMMERLESS GUN.

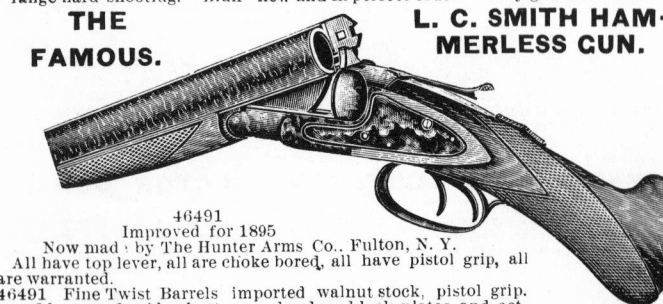

46491
Improved for 1895

Now made by The Hunter Arms Co., Fulton, N. Y.
All have top lever, all are choke bored, all have pistol grip, all are warranted.
46491 Fine Twist Barrels imported walnut stock, pistol grip, and bore, and rubber butt case hardened lock plates and action. Plain finish, but a good gun. Everyone warranted, 10 or 12 gauge. 30 or 32 inch barrels......$35.00-
46496 No. 1 quality, fine, laminated steel barrels, imported watnut stock, pistol grip, checkered grip and fore-end, rubber butt case hardened, lock plates and actions; no fancy engraving, but well made and desirable, and just as good a shooter as a higher price gun; 10, 16, or 12 gauge, 30 and 32 inch barrel, 7¼ to 8¾ pounds......$40.80

Guns—Continued.

46497 No. 2 quality, good Damascus steel barrels, imported walnut stock, pistol grip, checkered and finely engraved, finely finished, $80.00 grade: 10, 12 or 16 gauge, 28, 30 and 32 inch barrels. Our price......$57.50
46498 No. 3 quality, $100.00 grade. Our price......70.00
Weights, 12 gauge, 7¼ to 9 lbs; 10 gauge, 8½ to 10¾ lbs. Higher grade guns to order. The Smith Hammerless has won more prizes than any other gun on the market. Circulars showing working parts of any hammerless guns sent on application.

L. C. Smith Pigeon Gun.

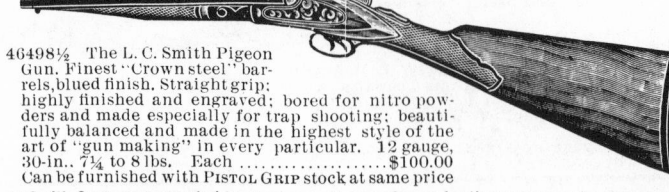

46498½ The L. C. Smith Pigeon Gun. Finest "Crown steel" barrels, blued finish. Straight grip: highly finished and engraved; bored for nitro powders and made especially for trap shooting; beautifully balanced and made in the highest style of the art of "gun making" in every particular. 12 gauge, 30-in. 7¼ to 8 lbs. Each......$100.00
Can be furnished with PISTOL GRIP stock at same price

All Smith Guns are warranted to shoot any nitro powder made; they never can be shot loose.

Baker Hammerless Gun With Positive Automatic Block to Firing Pin. Cross Bolted.

No better shooting gun at any price.

EVERY GUN WARRANTED.
Bored for Nitros or Black Powder

No. 46500

GREATLY IMPROVED FOR 1894.
All accidental discharge of either barrel or *simultaneous* firing of both barrels is rendered impossible. There is no condition, position or situation that this gun can be discharged other than by a pull of the triggers. The gun is locked by solidly cross-bolting the extension rib. There are no retracting bolts, in consequence of which the frame is not cut away. but is left intact, solid and strong. Beautiful in design and finish, wide breech; made for down-right hard service; not liable to get out of order; one of the best American guns on the market, and stands the "RACKET" OF ALL NITRO *Powders* EVERY TIME: 10 gauge, same price as 12 gauge.
46499 Fine Damascus Barrels, beautifully engraved; finely finished; equal to many $150.00 grade guns; 12 gauge, 28, 30 or 32 in. barrels; 7¼ to 9½ lbs. $60.00
10 guage, 30 and 32 in. barrel, 8¾ to 10½ lbs......60.00
46500 Fine Four-Blade Damascus Barrels, beautifully engraved, choke bored for best possible shooting. Every gun warranted. Handsome, well made and durable. 12 gauge, 28, 30 or 32 in.barrels, 7¼ to 9 lbs.; 10 gauge, 8 to 10 lbs...$37.95
46501 Finest Twist Barrels, neatly engraved, choke bored for best possible shooting. Every gun warranted, perfect and a good shooter. 12 gauge, 30 or 32 in. barrels, 7¼ to 8½ lbs., or 10 gauge, 30 and 32 in. barrel, 8 to 10 lbs. Each......$33.00

Forester Grade Greener.

46502 No. 6 Greener "Forester's" Hammerless Gun, Anson & Deely action, treble wedge-fast, cross-bolted, matted ribs, laminated barrels, finely finished, well balanced, choke bored, made for service, and a good shooter. The value of these guns is in the barrels and lock work and are made especially for us. They shoot just as well as the higher costing guns, and wear just as long.
12-gauge, 30 in. barrels, 7½ to 8 lbs......$80.00
12 gauge, 30 to 32 in., 8½ to 9½ lbs......84.00
Prices on hammer guns and other grades furnished on application. Correspondence solicited.

Ejector and Non-Ejector.

New Hammerless Double Gun.

Manufactured by Forehand Arms Company, Worcester, Mass.
$33.00

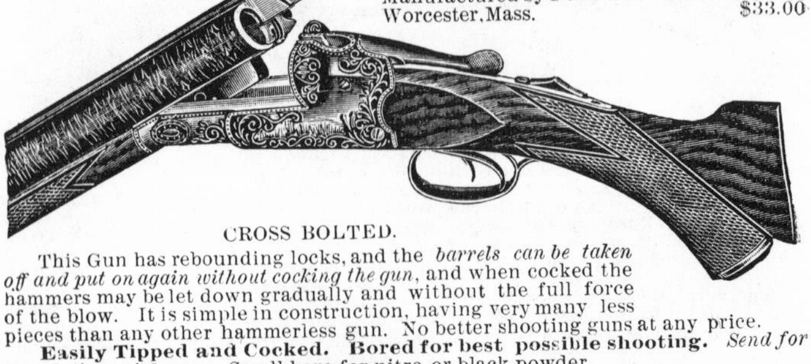

CROSS BOLTED.
This Gun has rebounding locks, and the *barrels can be taken off and put on again without cocking the gun*, and when cocked the hammers may be let down gradually and without the full force of the blow. It is simple in construction, having very many less pieces than any other hammerless gun. No better shooting guns at any price.
Easily Tipped and Cocked. Bored for best possible shooting. *Send for descriptive catalogue.* Small bore for nitro or black powder.
46503 Finest twist barrels, no engraving, but finely finished, 12 ga., 30 or 32 inch barrels 7½ to 8½ lbs. Each......$33.00
46504 Fine Damascus Barrels (dark-finish), Italian walnut stock, full pistol grip, checkered grip and fore-end, engraved action and mounting, handsome; well made and durable. Every gun warranted a good shooter. 12 gauge, 30 inch barrels, 7½ to 8½ lbs. Each......$37.50

Forehand Automatic Ejector Guns.

46506 Finest twist barrels, style of No. 46503......$53.00
46507 Fine Damascus barrels, style of No. 46504......57.50
46508 Extra fine Damascus barrels, extra fine finish, beautifully engraved. 75.00
The automatic ejectors are made in 12 gauge only, 30-inch barrel, 7 to 8 lbs weight.
The F. & W. gun is made for down, right hard service, and is a first-class gun in every particular.

THE L. C. SMITH AUTOMATIC EJECTOR,
Hammerless.

Always   **Ejects.**

ALL SMITH GUNS ARE GUARANTEED NOT TO GET LOOSE OR SHAKY WITH ANY NITRO POWDER. IMPROVED MODELS. BORED FOR BEST POSSIBLE SHOOTING.

46510 No. 1 Ejector, pistol grip, laminated steel barrels, line engraving, neatly finished, well made and durable, warranted, full choke bore, unless otherwise ordered, 12 gauge, 30 or 32 inch barrels, 7½ to 8½ lbs....................$56.25

46511 No. 2 Ejector, Damascus barrels, finely engraved, pistol grip, English walnut stock, warranted, 12 gauge, 30 or 32 inch, 7¼ to 8¾ lbs...............74.75

46512 No. 3 Ejector, fine Damascus barrels, pistol grip, handsomely engraved, beautifully finished, 12 gauge, 30 or 32 inch barrels, 7¼ to 8½ lbs.........89.50

46513 Quality A 1 Ejector, very fine Damascus steel barrels, very fine imported English walnut stock, fine checkering and engraving. Choke bored on the multi-plied system, and all warranted close hard shooters. 12 gauge, 28, 30 and 32 in. barrels, 7¼ to 8½ lbs............ ....$117.00

Catalogue or circulars showing working parts sent on application.

The Smith Ejector guns are PERFECT and POSITIVE in their working parts and never fail to eject the empty shell. They are not liable to get out of order.

THE PARKER HAMMERLESS GUN.
"The Long Range Hard Shooters."

Cut shows style of engraving on $150 grade, $120 Net cash.

AMERICA'S BEST-KNOWN GUN —ALL TOP LEVER—ALL CHOKE BORED—MADE BY PARKER BROS., MERIDEN, CONN.

Fine Damascus Steel Barrels, fine figured American or imported walnut stock pistol grip; checkered, handsomely engraved, hard rubber butt plates, beautifully finished throughout. Every gun warranted; highest quality to the grade. Matted ribs.   Our price.

46515 "E. H." Grade, 10 gauge, $85.00 list $62.75
46516 "G. H " Grade, 12 gauge, 16 gauge, 28, 30 and 32 inch, $80.00 list 57.50
46516½ "D. H." 10, 12, 16 gauge, $100.00 list........... .. .. 72.00
46517 Fine Twist Barrels, 12 and 16 gauge, $65.00 list................ 44.95

Weight, 12 bore, 7½ to 9 pounds; weight, 10 bore, 8½ to 10 pounds; length of barrel, 28 to 32 inches, "drop" of stock 2½ to 3¼ inches. "Stocks" (measured from center of first trigger to center of butt plate), 14 to 14¼ inches. We can make shorter or longer barrels and different stocks to special orders and prices according to extra amount of labor. Circulars with illustrations of working parts sent on application. Higher priced guns made to order. Send for prices. ·

MODEL 1894. THE IMPROVED ITHACA HAMMERLESS.

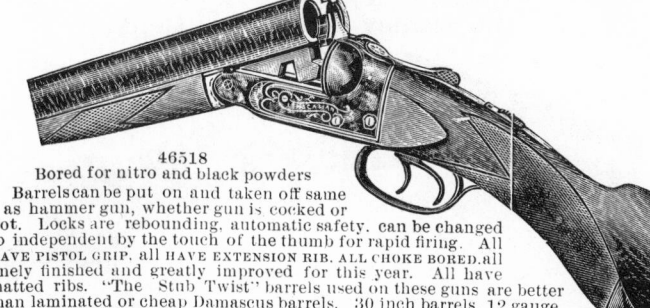

46518

Bored for nitro and black powders

Barrels can be put on and taken off same as hammer gun, whether gun is cocked or not. Locks are rebounding, automatic safety, can be changed to independent by the touch of the thumb for rapid firing. All HAVE PISTOL GRIP, all HAVE EXTENSION RIB. ALL CHOKE BORED, all finely finished and greatly improved for this year. All have matted ribs. "The Stub Twist" barrels used on these guns are better than laminated or cheap Damascus barrels. 30 inch barrels, 12 gauge, 7½ to 8½ lbs; 32 inch, 7¾ to 9½; 30 inch barrels, 10 gauge, 8½ to 9½; 32 inch, 8¾ to 11 lbs.

12 gauge, 7½ to 9½ lbs.; 10 gauge, 8½ to 11 lbs.; 16 gauge, 6½ to 7½ lbs.

46518 Fine English Stub Twist Barrels, American walnut stock, pistol grip, checkered line engraving, No. 10, 12 or 16 gauge..................$32.50

46519 Fine Damascus Steel Barrels, English walnut stock, pistol grip, checkered, neatly engraved, No. 10, 12 or 16 gauge $38.75

NEW MODEL. ITHACA HAMMERLESS.

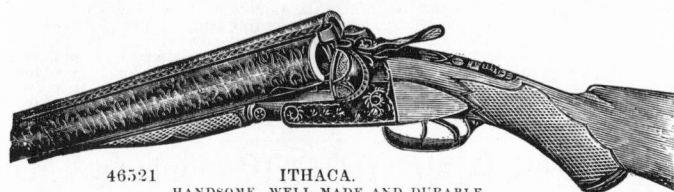

46521   ITHACA.

HANDSOME, WELL MADE AND DURABLE.

Bored for nitro and black powders.

46521 Fine Damascus Steel Barrels, selected English walnut stock, pistol grip, checkered, fancy finished breech action, neatly engraved. A handsome, finely finished gun. All warranted for shooting qualities and wear.

10 and 12 gauge, 28, 30 and 32 inch barrels....................................$52.00
Higher priced guns to order, $65.00, $75.00, $115.00 to $150.00, on short notice.

THE WELL-KNOWN PARKER GUN.
Latest Improved.

See that your Parker guns are stamped Parker Bros.—All others are only IMITATIONS, and cheap grade of common guns.

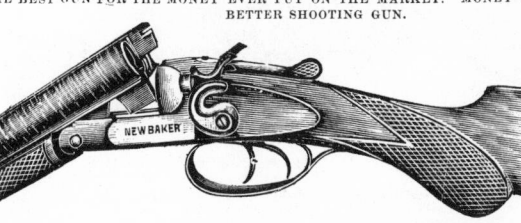

Cut shows "D" grade.

Breech loading, double gun, top lever, made by Parker Bros., Meriden, Conn. All grades of this gun, as quoted below, are breech loading. All have the top lever action, double bolt and improved check-hook and pin, fore-end lock, solid head plunger, extension rib, rebounding locks and low hammers. In ordering guns, give first and second choice on weights and dimensions. We shall always do our best to give the "first choice," and generally will be able to do so. All Parker guns are choke bored for close shooting, and are accompanied by target made at factory. 12 gauge, 7½ to 9½ pounds: 10 gauge, 9½ to 10½ pounds. Length of barrel, 30 to 32 inches. Our guns are the very best made in these grades. Every gun warranted. All bored for long range, and the cheapest will shoot as well as the most expensive.

	12 gauge.	10 gauge.
46522 Parker, twist barrels, American stock, engraved and checkered pistol grip	$40.00	$44.00
46523 Parker, fine Damascus steel barrels, fine figured American or imported stock, engraved rubber butt plate, checkered pistol grip	57.50	62.75

REMINGTON AUXILIARY RIFLE BARRELS.

46525 These barrels extend the entire length of the breech-loading shot gun barrels, and are held firmly in place by a thumb nut at muzzle. They shoot accurately. Can be inserted in any shot gun. Each barrel has an extractor. For 30 and 32 in. barrels, 10 or 12 gauge, calibre 32, W. C. F., 32-40, 38-55, 45-70. Price..$8.00

THE IMPROVED NEW BAKER GUN--Breech.
Loader. $19.90

Manufactured by The Baker Forging and Gun Co., Batavia, N. Y. Just the gun you have been asking us for—plain, but a good one.

THE BEST GUN FOR THE MONEY EVER PUT ON THE MARKET. MONEY WILL NOT BUY A BETTER SHOOTING GUN.

CROSS BOLTED.   LIST $30.00.—$19.90

The makers claim for this gun" even pattern, powerful shooter, and challenge any gun in the market to equal it for durability and simplicity." Best English steel twist barrels, extension ribs, checkered pistol grip, English walnut stocks, rubber butt plate, low circular hammer, solid strikers, rebounding locks, top snap action, interchangeable parts, choke bored, unless otherwise ordered. No better shooting guns at any price. A plain, well balanced, neatly finished gun, made of best material, compensating fore-end, cannot get loose and shaky in hinge joint. In fact just the gun for business at a moderate price. Every gun warranted. All have matted ribs.

46527 $30 grade, 12-gauge, 30 and 32-in. barrels, 7¼ to 8½ lbs........ .. ....$19.90
46528 10-gauge, 30 and 32 in.-barrels 8½ to 11 lbs.................... 19.90
Every gun warranted.

THE NEW BAKER   BAR LOCK GUN.
A New   Model Gun.

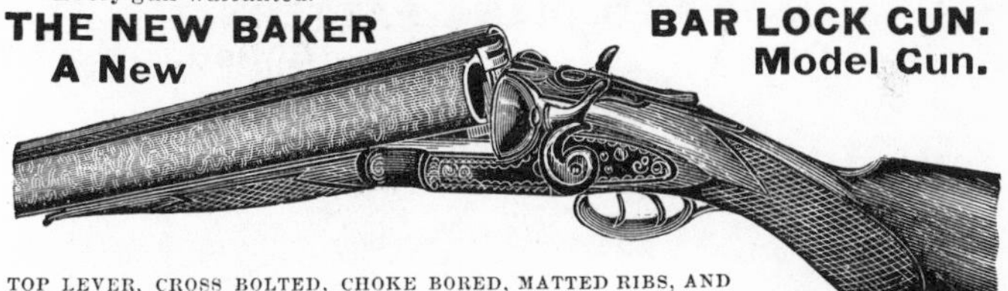

TOP LEVER, CROSS BOLTED, CHOKE BORED, MATTED RIBS, AND EVERY GUN WARRANTED.

A good shooter, made of best material, and finely finished. A high grade gun for a little money. List..$50.00

46529 Fine Damascus Barrels, finely finished, engraved, fine case-hardened lock plate and action, choke bored for nitro or black powder. 12-gauge, 30 and 32-inch barrels, 7½ to 9 pounds.....................................$26.00
10-gauge, 32-inch barrels 8½ to 10½ pounds...................... 26.50

N. B. The "Baker" is well-known as the "long range Duck Gun."

THE NEW ITHACA GUN. Improved Model.

(Manufactured by the ITHACA GUN COMPANY, Ithaca, N. Y.)

$23.00

Made of best materials. Simplest and best locks. Low hammers, top lever swinging over them when cocked. Self - compensating, taking up wear at every point. Never gets loose and shaky. Matted rib, and all have walnut pistol grip, stock checkered, case hardened lock plates and blued mountings.

All guns are choke bored to shoot the closest pattern. No extra charge for a No. 10-gauge over a No. 12-gauge, or a heavy weight over a light gun. Only the best English twist and Damascus steel barrels are used.

All have Rubber Butt. All have Top Lever. All have Extension Rib. All are Choke Bored. Every gun warranted. All have Matted Rib.

46531 Fine English Stub Twist Barrels; American walnut stock, pistol grip, checkered, No. 10, 12 or 16-gauge, neatly engraved............... ....$23.00
46532 Fine Damascus Steel Barrels, selected American walnut stock, pistol grip, checkered, No. 10, 12 or 16-gauge, engraved $33.00

10-gauge, length of barrel, 30 and 32 inches; 12-gauge, 30 and 32-inch barrel; 12-bore, weight, 7¼ to 10½ lbs ; 10-bore, weight, 8½ to 11 lbs.; 16-gauge, 28, 30 and 32-inch barrels, 6¾ for 28 inch, up to 8 lbs. for 32 inch.

N. B.—No better shooting gun at any price. The "Boss" Duck Gun.

SEE PAGE 449. M. W. & CO.'S OWN SHOT GUN.

New Model Machine Made Breech Loaders.
(Made by H. Pieper.)

HERE YOU HAVE IT. A GOOD GUN FOR A LITTLE MONEY,
Handsome, well made, finely balanced, good shooting, machine made gun, at popular prices by a well-known maker. The machine made gun has come to stay, and is vastly superior in every way to the old-style hand made article.

Modified Diana Pattern Machine Made Breech Loading Shot Guns.

The barrels are screwed in the breech; they remain perfectly round and straight and are not pinched together, as is the case in the old way of manufacture. The lumps and the steel breech are one solid piece. thus avoiding lumps becoming loose.

The barrels being independent of each other, the expansion is even, and the penetration and shooting qualities in general are thereby increased. The steel breech is level with the barrels; in this it differs from the Diana Gun, where the breech projects, and the new system is therefore called the "Modified Diana."

Top Lever.   Barrels are choked after the most approved system.

Back Action.

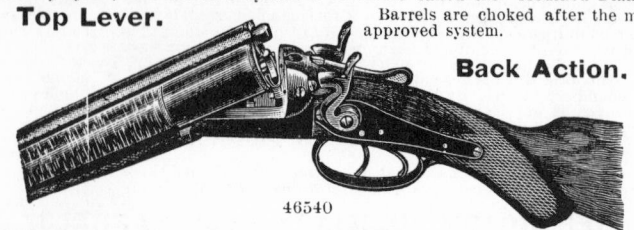

46540

46540 Top Snap, Modified Diana Pattern, back action, two spring rebounding locks, pistol grip, matted rib, rubber butt, extension rib, left barrel choke bored, genuine twist barrels. Warranted. Locks are polished inside, and are as good and will wear as long as the bar locks. Low circular hammers.
12-gauge, 30 or 32 in., 7¼ to 8¾ lbs $14.95
10-gauge, 30 or 32 in., 8¾ to 9¾ lbs 15.45

Top Lever.   **Bar Locks.**

46541

Every One Good.

46541 Top Snap, Modified Diana Pattern, genuine laminated twist barrels, bar rebounding locks, extension rib, low circular hammers, pistol grip, rubber butt, matted rib, left barrel choke bored. A good one. Warranted.
12-gauge, 30 or 32 in. barrels, 7¼ to 8¾ lbs., each $16.90
10-gauge, 30 or 32 in. barrels, 8½ to 9¾ lbs., each 17.45
16-gauge, 28 or 30 in., 6½ to 6¾ lbs. 19.00
46542 Top Snap, genuine laminated twist steel barrels, double bolt, bar rebounding locks, extension rib, matted rib, low circular hammers, pistol grip, rubber butt, Deely & Edges' fore-end, fine engraving on barrels, best finish, rubber cap on pistol grip, both barrels full choke bored. A fine gun.
12-gauge, 30 and 32 in. barrels, 7¼ to 8½ lbs., each $20.25
10-gauge, 30 and 32 in. barrels, 8¾ to 9½ lbs., each 21.00
16-gauge, 28 and 30 in. barrels, 6½ to 7 lbs., each 21.50
20-gauge, 28 inch barrels, 6½ to 6¾ lbs., each 21.75

MODIFIED DIANA PATTERN.
Cross   **Bolted.**

46543

A Fine Gun.

46543 Modified Diana Pattern, Greener cross bolt, top snap, Damascus barrels, bar rebounding locks, extension rib, matted rib, double bolt, Deely & Edges, fore-end, new style low circular hammers, nicely engraved, pistol grip with rubber cap, rubber butt, full choked both barrels, fine finish. Built for service and a fine gun in every particular.
12-gauge, 30 and 32 in., 7¼ to 8¾ lbs., each $24.50
10-gauge, 30 and 32 in., 8¾ to 9¾ lbs., each 25.00
16-gauge, 30 inches, 6½ lbs 25.25
20-gauge, 28 inches, 6¼ to 6¾ lbs 25.30

L. C. SMITH HAMMER GUN.
Cross Bolt.   **Choke Bored**

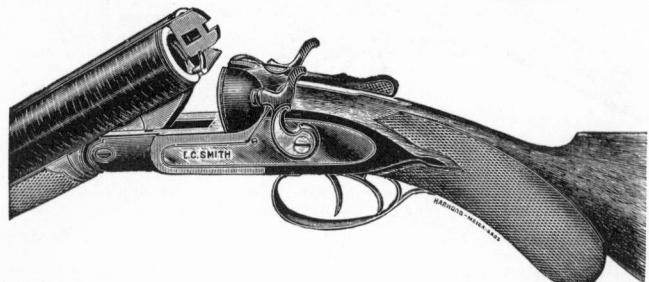

Factory Price, $55.00.

The New L. C. Smith Hammer Gun, cross bolted, pistol grip, circular hammer, matted extension rib, choke bored, good for nitro or black powder. A long-range, hard-shooting gun, not liable to get "loose or shaky" in the joints. Finest stub twist barrel.
46544 12-gauge, 32 inch barrels, 7¾ to 9½ lbs., each $23.76

Belgian Double Barrel Breech Loader.

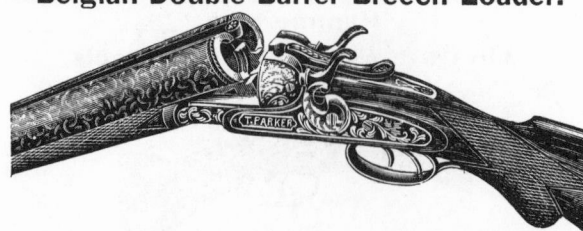

46547 Belgian Double Barrel Breech Loader, top lever, bar action locks, rebounding hammers, extension rib, pistol grip, patent fore-end, matted rib, circular hammers, engraved lock plate and action, steel barrels, finished in imitation of Damascus; can hardly be told from genuine Damascus. A showy gun for the money.
12-gauge, 30 or 32 inch barrels, 7¼ to 8½ lbs., each $13.50
10-gauge, 30 and 32 inch, 8¾ to 9¾ lbs., each 13.75

A Complete Back Action Gun.

EXTENSION RIB.

46548 Special Complete Double Barrel Breech Loader, extra engraved, top snap back action locks, pistol grip, walnut stock, checkered grip and fore-end, extension matted rib, low circular hammers, patent fore-end, genuine laminated steel barrels, left barrel full choke bored, well made, a good shooter, safe and reliable.
12-gauge, 30 and 32 inch, 7½ to 8¾ lbs $11.75
10-gauge, 30 and 32 inch, 8¾ to 9¾ lbs 12.50

THE RICHARDS.—Double Barrel Gun.

Left Choke.   **Extension Rib.**

46550.

46550 Richards' Breech Loaders, double barrel, back action locks, top lever, low hammers, pistol grip, checkered grip and fore-end, and brass studded on grip and fore-end, both lumps through frame, nickel-plated locks, *extension rib;* guard and butt plate; neatly engraved: a showy gun and a good one. Blued steel barrels, left barrel choke-bored for close shooting. 10-gauge, 30 or 32 inch, 8½ to 9¾ pounds $9.35
12 gauge, 30 or 32 inch, 7¼ to 8¾ pounds 9.00

The Stanley Arms Co.'s Guns.

46551-2

46551 Stanley Arms Co.'s, Double Barreled Breech Loader, Greener treble wedge fast cross bolt, top lever, bar rebounding locks, pistol grip, solid strikers, double bolt extension matted rib, rubber butt, circular hammers, patent fore-end, nicely engraved, left barrel full choked, well made, well balanced, and a handsome gun, fine Damascus steel barrels. All good shooters, and made for service in the field or at the trap. (List price $30.00.)   Our price.
12 gauge, 30 and 32 inch, 7 to 8½ lbs $18.75
10 gauge, 30 and 32 inch, 8¾ to 9¾ lbs. 19.45
Elegant gun for the money. Each gun tagged with record of shooting.
46552 The Stanley Arms Co.'s Breech Loading Double Barreled Shot Gun, Greener cross bolt top lever, bar rebounding locks, patent fore-end, solid head strikers, double bolt, extension matted rib, pistol grip, rubber butt, new style circular hammers, laminated steel barrels, made of good material, well finished, well balanced, choke bored, and a good gun at a moderate price. All good shooters. The best material and finish. (List price $28.00). Our price. 12-gauge, 30 and 32 inch 7¼ to 8¾ lbs $16.75
10-gauge, 30 and 32 inch, 8¾ to 9¾ lbs 17.50

IN ORDERING GOODS Sent by Mail or prepaid Express, always allow sufficient money to cover charges as it saves both time and trouble.

COMPLETE BAR LOCK.—Double Guns.

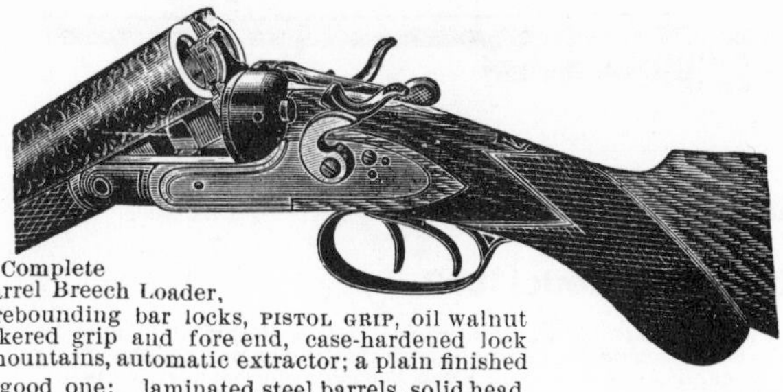

46558 The Complete Double Barrel Breech Loader, top lever, rebounding bar locks, PISTOL GRIP, oil walnut stock, checkered grip and fore end, case-hardened lock plates and mountains, automatic extractor; a plain finished gun, but a good one; laminated steel barrels, solid head strikers, extension rib, low circular hammers out of line of sight, patent snap fore-end; well balanced. (List price $23.00.) Our price.
12-gauge, 30 and 32 inch, 7¾ to 8¾ lbs. $12.50
10-gauge, 30 and 32 inch, 8¾ to 9¾ lbs. 12.95
16-gauge, 28 and 30 inch, 6¼ to 7 lbs. 13.25
Left barrel choke bored, 75 cts. extra Both barrels choke bored, $1.25 extra.
46559 Same as 46558, steel barrels, a good imitation *twist finish*, giving them the appearance of *genuine twist* barrels. The browning will wear as long as on a genuine twist barrel, and they are just as good shooters, and sold by many as genuine laminated steel. A well-made gun for the money.
12 gauge, 30 and 32 inch barrels, 7½ to 8¾ lbs. Each .... $ 9.80
10 gauge, 30 and 32 inch barrels, 8¾ to 9¾ lbs. Each 10.30
46559½ Complete Double Barrel Breech Loader, bar locks, patent fore-ends, pistol grip, extension rib, solid large firing pins, rebounding locks, top lever, case-hardened lock plates and action; imitation Damascus barrels, sold by many for genuine Damascus. Strong, safe and reliable; good shooters.
10 and 12 gauge, 30 and 32 inch, 12 gauge, 7½ to 8¾ pounds; 10 gauge, 8½ to 9¾ pounds; 12 gauge, each $10.70; 10 gauge, each $11.00

N. B.—Prices on guns have evidently reached "bottom" and are subject to market changes. We look for an advance in prices before Septemher, on the low priced goods.

Special Complete. Bar Lock Guns.

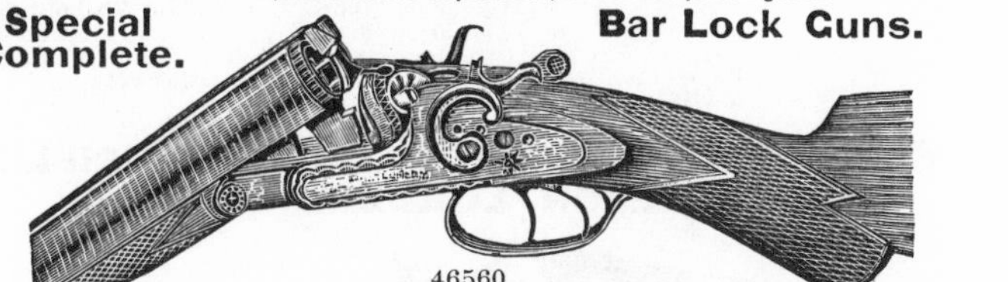

46560

46560 Special Machine Finished Complete Double Barrel Breech Loader, Top Lever, Bar Rebounding Lock, locks polished inside, pistol grip, oiled walnut stock, checkered grip and fore-end, case-hardened lock, plates and mountings, laminated steel barrels, large head firing pins, extension rib, low circular hammers out of line of sight, patent snap fore-end, well balanced, well made, finely finished locks and action. The best gun for the money ever put on the market. Good shooters. 12-gauge, 30 and 32 inches, 7¼ to 8¾ lbs. $17.00
10-gauge, 30 and 32 inches, 8½ to 9¾ lbs., choke bored 17 50
46560½ Special Complete Double Barrel Breech Loader. Bar rebounding locks, pistol grip, solid head firing pins, patent fore-end, extension rib, case-hardened lock plates and action, top lever. Well made and a good gun; left barrel full choke-bored, laminated steel barrels.
12 gauge, 30 and 32 inch, 7¼ to 8¾ lbs. Each $15.00
10 gauge, 30 and 32 inch, 8½ to 9¾ lbs. Each 15.50

SEE PAGE 449.

THE MONTGOMERY WARD & CO. SHOT GUN.

HAMMERLESS.

$65.00 grade Damascus barrels, finely engraved. $35.00

$50.00 grade fine steel twist barrels, otherwise same. $29.00

10 or 12 gauge.

TOP LEVER, BACK ACTION.

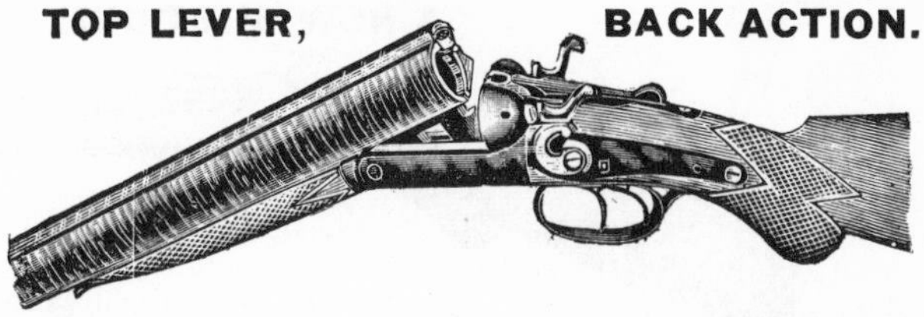

46561 Special Complete Double Barrel Breech Loader, top lever, snap action, fine rebounding back action locks, walnut stock, checkered grip and fore-end, fine case, hardened lock plates and mountings, automatic shell extractor. A good, honest, well made gun, and a good shooter, well balanced. Fine laminated steel barrels extension rib, patent fore-end. (List price, $18.00) Our price.
12 gauge, 30 and 32 inch barrel, 7½ to 8¾ lbs. .... $ 9.95
10 gauge, 30 or 32 inch barrel, 8½ to 9¾ lbs. 10.40
16 gauge, 28 and 30 inch barrel, 6¼ to 7¼ lbs. 11.00
With one barrel full choked, 75 cents extra. With both barrels full choked, 1.25 extra, and shooting qualities guaranteed.
46561½ Same style as 46561, Imitation twist barrels, not as finely finished as the genuine twist, cannot be told from genuine and the browning will wear just as long. A good gun for the money.
12 gauge, 30 and 32 inch, 7¼ to 8½ lbs. Each $8.65

Top Lever, Back Action, High Grade.

46562 Machine Finished, Complete Double Barrel Breech Loader, fine polished rebounding back action locks, top lever, extension rib, pistol grip, patent fore-end, case hardened lock plates and action, low circular hammers, well balanced, finely finished for the grade, strong, well made and durable, safe and reliable. A good all-around gun. (List price, $20.00.) Left barrel full choked. Our price.
12 gauge, 30 and 32 inch, 7¼ to 8½ lbs. $12.25
10 gauge, 30 and 32 ineh, 8½ to 9¾ lbs. 12.95

BLUED SIDE LEVER. Double Barrel.

$7.50 **$7.95**

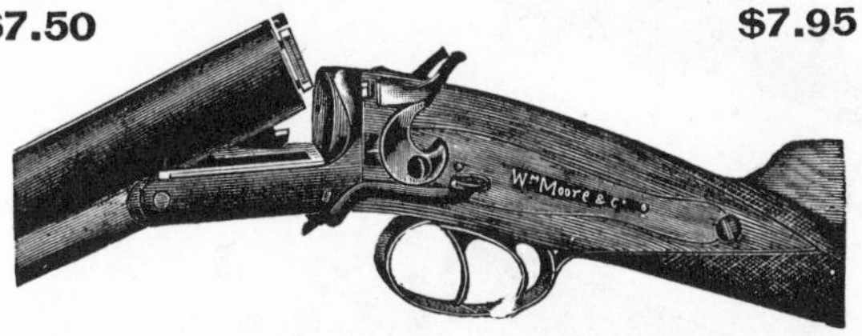

46563 Double Barrel Breech Loader, side lever, snap action, automatic shell ejector, walnut stock, checkered grip, patent fore-end, case-hardened mountings, BLUED BARRELS, low hammers out of line of sight, well balanced. A good, safe gun. 12 gauge, 30 or 32inch barrels, 7½ to 8½ lbs. Each $7.50
10 gauge, 30 and 32 inch barrels, 8½ to 9¾ lbs. Each 7.95
One barrel full choked, 75 cents extra; both barrels, $1.25 extra.

OUR SPECIAL SIDE LEVER. Double Barrel.

$9.00 **$9.40**

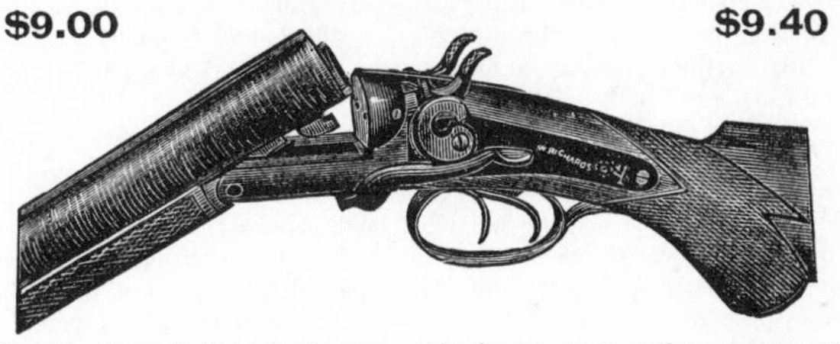

46564 Double Barrel Breech Loader, side lever, snap action, automatic shell ejector, case-hardened mountings, PISTOL GRIP, patent fore-end, walnut stock checkered grip, GENUINE TWIST BARRELS, safe and reliable and a good gun for the money. Low circular hammers out of line of sight, well balanced. Good shooters. (List price, $18.00.) Our price
12 gauge, 32 or 30 inch, 7¼ to 8½ lbs. Each .... $ 9.00
10 gauge, 30 and 32 inch, 8½ to 9¾ lbs. 9.40
16 gauge, 28 and 30 inch, 6 to 6¾ lbs 9.50
With one barrel full choked 75 cents extra. With both barrels, full choked, 1.25 extra.

THE CELEBRATED LEFAUCHEAUX ACTION GUNS.

CENTER FIRE BRASS OR PAPER SHELLS ARE USED IN ALL OF OUR LEFAUCHEAUX GUNS.

$6.50 **$6.57**

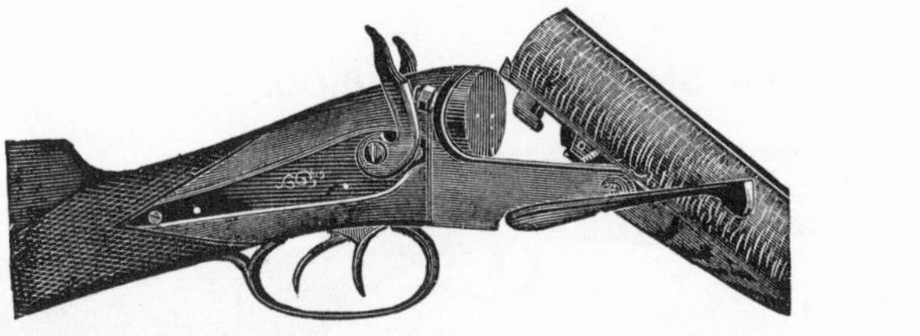

Celebrated Lefaucheaux Action. **BREECH LOADERS.**

N. B.—Observe Price.

46565 The Celebrated Lefaucheaux Action, double barrel, breech loading shot gun, blued decarbonized steel barrel, back action lock, checkered grip, bottom lever, (not pistol grip), 12 gauge automatic shell ejector, 30 and 32-inch barrel, weight, 7½ to 8¾ lbs. List price, $12.00. Our price $6.50
10 gauge, 8½ to 9½ lbs 6.57
16-gauge, 30 and 32-inch 6.90

$8.50 **$8.75**

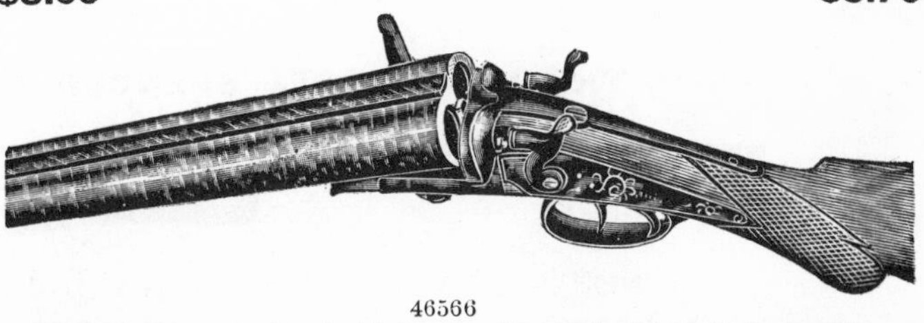

46566

46566 Lefaucheaux Action, double barrel, rubber butt, pistol grip, laminated steel barrels, rebounding locks, double key, 12 gauge, 30 and 32 inches, 7¼ to 8½ lbs $8.50
10 gauge, 30 and 32 inches, 8¾ to 9¼ lbs. 8.75
16 gauge, 30 and 32 inches, 6½ to 7 lbs 9.00
N. B.—Any gun purchased of us not described as choke bored, we will full-choke bore one barrel for 75 cents, or both barrels for $1.25; and warrant them to be close shooters. All Breech Loaders use brass or paper shells, center fire.

A NEW SHOT GUN.—WINCHESTER, MODEL 1893. $16.88

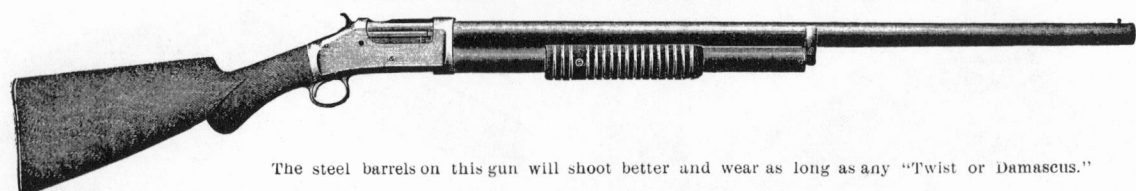

The steel barrels on this gun will shoot better and wear as long as any "Twist or Damascus."

Winchester Repeating Shot Gun, Model 1893.

The arm is operated by a sliding fore-arm below the barrel. When the hammer is down, the backward and forward motion of this slide unlocks and opens the breech-lock, ejects the cartridge or fired shell and replaces it with a fresh cartridge. The construction of the arm is such that the hammer cannot fall, or the firing-pin strike the cartridge until the breech-lock is in place and locked fast. While the hammer stands at the full cock notch, the gun is locked against opening. In this position the firing-pin must be pushed forward to open the gun. When the hammer stands at half-cock, the gun is locked both against opening and pulling the trigger.
To Load the Magazine.—Turn the gun with the guard upward. Lay the cartridge on the underside of the carrier and push it into the magazine.

12 Gauge only, no other gauge made.

46568 Rolled Steel Barrels, plain walnut pistol grip stock. Length of stock, 13 inches; drop of stock, 2¾ inches, 7¾ lb. weight; 6 shot. 12 gauge only; 30 or 32 inch barrels. $16.88
All guns choke-bored for best possible shooting unless otherwise ordered. This new gun has few parts and not liable to get out of order.

The Burgess Repeating Shot Gun. $28.00

46569 The Burgess Single Barrel Repeating Shot Gun, walnut stock, Damascus barrels, bored for long range close shooting. This gun has the sliding pistol grip movement for loading and ejecting shell. Made of best material, has few parts and not liable to get out of order. Barrel can be separated from stock in an instant. 12 gauge, 30 or 32 inch, about 7½ pounds weight; 6 shot. $28.00
Circulars giving full description of Burgess Gun sent free on application.

THE DALY THREE-BARREL BREECH LOADER.

46570 Damascus barrels, selected English walnut stock, extension rib, open sights and fine folding rear sight. (The plunger for rifle barrel is set by pushing the lever slightly to the left, and is fired by the right hand hammer.) The rib is matted, and locks and body neatly engraved.
12 bore. 30 inch, 8 to 9 lbs., 45–70 and 38–55 and 32–40 caliber rifle.......$75.00
10 gauge, 45–70 caliber, 30 inch barrels, 9½ lbs...........................80.50
This is the most attractive three-barrel breech-loader yet produced.
It is a marvel of beauty; the rifle barrel is made of such a quality of steel that the addition to the weight is not noticed at all. The putting together of the three barrels is perfect, so that the utmost accuracy with shot and bullet is guaranteed. The sight on the tang can be used the same as the Lyman sight. The demand has surpassed our expectations. We have never bought any thing which achieved such marked success in so short a time.

PIEPER'S COMBINED SHOT GUN AND RIFLE BREECH LOADER.

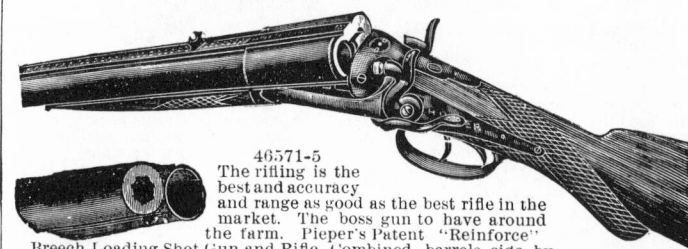

46571-5
The rifling is the best and accuracy and range as good as the best rifle in the market. The boss gun to have around the farm. Pieper's Patent "Reinforce" Breech Loading Shot Gun and Rifle Combined, barrels side by side, finest blued steel barrels and steel butt plate, sporting rear sight, sliding to right or left, white metal front knife sight, shot gun stock, checkered pistol grip. This is without doubt the handsomest and strongest shooting, most accurate and combined arm ever offered for sale in this or any other market.
46571 12 gauge and 44 W. C. F caliber, 30 in. barrels, weight about 8½ lbs. $23.45
46573 Pieper's Patent Combined Shot Gun and Rifle, 12 gauge and 38 caliber; 55 grains powder, 255 grains lead; barrel, 30 inches; 8½ lbs., using cartridge 47222 side lever.... .... $23.45
46574 Pieper's Patent Combined Shot Gun and Rifle, side snap lever, blued barrel, good on game up to 300 yards; accurate and reliable. 12 gauge and 32 W. C. F. caliber, using cartridge 47193; 30 inch; 8½ lbs $23.45
46575 Pieper's Combined Shot Gun and Rifle, side lever, blued barrels, 12 gauge and 40-60 caliber (using No. 47232 cartridge) 30-inch, 8½ to 9 lbs. Each $23.45

BEST RIFLING. MERWIN, HULBERT & CO.'S COMBINED SHOT GUN AND RIFLE. A GOOD GUN.

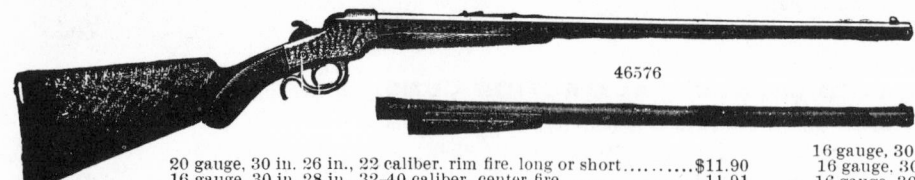

46576

46576 Merwin. Hulbert & Co.'s Rifles with interchangeable shot gun barrels; barrels changed easily and quickly. Rebounding locks, shell ejected by throwing trigger guard down smartly. Solid vertical breech block. Case hardened frame, checkered pistol grip, walnut stock. A1 shooter. Choke bored shot barrel. Made of best material, perfectly safe and reliable; no better shooting rifle made.

20 gauge, 30 in. 26 in., 22 caliber. rim fire. long or short.........$11.90
16 gauge, 30 in. 28 in., 32-40 caliber. center fire 11.91

16 gauge, 30 in., 22 caliber, rim fire, 28 in......................$11.95
16 gauge. 30 in. 26 in., 32 caliber. rim fire..................... 11.93
16 gauge. 30 in. 26 and 28 in., 32-73 Model Winchester..........11.94
Weight, with shot barrel, 6½ lbs.; with rifle barrel, 6½ to 7 lbs.

THE NEW MODEL SPENCER REPEATING SHOT GUN. $28.00.

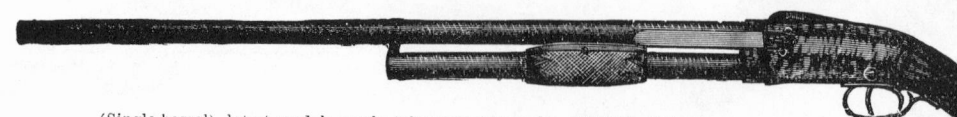

(Single barrel). latest model: can be taken apart to pack. **1890 Model.**

46577 The magazine is located under the barrel and will hold 5 cartridges. Damascus barrels. walnut pistol grip stock, checkered, beautifully finished throughout, and is superior to any double barrel shot gun in precision and penetration. Has few parts and is solid and substantial. Can be used as a single loader and cartridges in magazine held in reserve. 30 and 32-inch barrels, 7¾, 8¼ pounds. weight; 12 gauge. Each $28.00
46577½ The Spencer Gun, same as 46577, except twist barrels and wood slide and not checkered grip; iron butt plate, 12 guage, 30 and 32-inch, 7½ to 8½ lbs; drop stock. 3-inch: length stock, 13¼, 14 inch. Each $18.75

THE WINCHESTER REPEATING SHOT GUNS.

Price, $16.88.

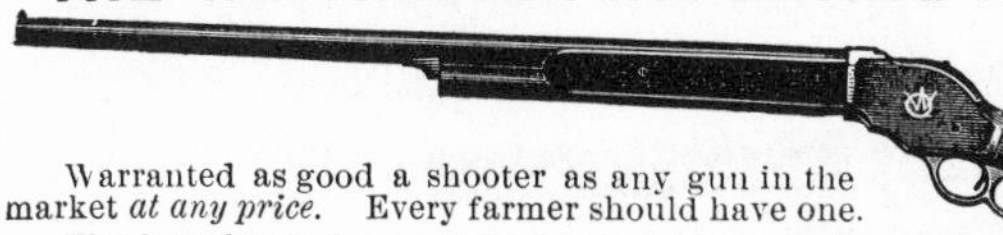

Warranted as good a shooter as any gun in the market *at any price.* Every farmer should have one.

The barrel can be examined and cleaned from the breech. The magazine and carrier hold five cartridges which, with the one in the chamber, makes six at the command of the shooter. The forward and backward motion of finger lever, which can be executed while gun is at shoulder, throws out empty shell, raises a new cartridge from magazine and puts it into the barrel. The gun is then ready to be fired. Rolled steel barrel, case-hardened frame and pistol grip, stock of plain walnut, not checked. All guns are full choked, and no gun will be sent out that will not make a good target. The standard gun will have a stock 12¾ inches in length and 2⅝ inches drop, and any variation from standard length or drop will be charged for extra.

46578 Winchester Repeating Shot Gun, rolled steel barrel, with plain pistol grip stock, 30 and 32 inch barrel, 12 gauge; weight, 7¾ lbs. Factory *net cash* price, $25.00; Our price.... ....Net cash $16.88
For 10 gauge, 30 and 32 inch, 9 lbs. weight.... .... .Net cash 16.88
For 10 gauge, 2⅞-inch paper shells. 12 gauge, 2⅝ inch paper shells.

This gun has the largest sale of any gun on the market. Buy one; you will like it. Everybody does who tries one. N. B. The blued steel barrels used on this gun are made by the Winchester Arms Company, and will wear as long and shoot as well as any Damascus or twist barrel.

BREECH LOADERS—Single Barrel. FOREHAND AND WADSWORTH GUNS.

$6.40 **Manufactured at Worcester, Mass.**

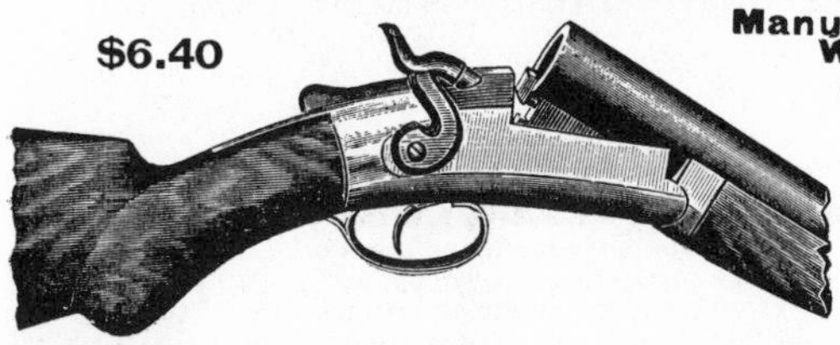

46579 The F. & W. Top Snap Single Barrel Breech Loading Gun, rebounding locks, pistol grips, snap fore-end, solid block strikers, choke bored. Finest blued steel barrels, just as durable as twist steel barrels, just as strong and just as good shooters, using paper or brass center fire shells.
12 guage, 30 and 32 inch barrels, 7 lbs. weight. Each. $6.40

BREECH-LOADERS.

The Great Long-Range Duck and Goose Gun.

Single Barrel.

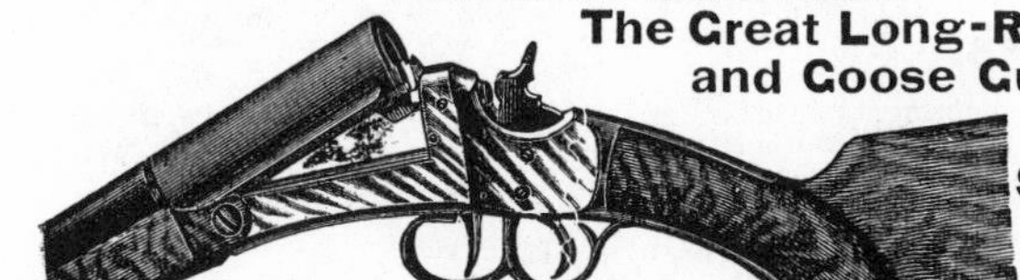

American Trigger Action.

46580 American Trigger Action, Single Barrel Breech-Loader, pistol grip, fine twist barrel, rebounding lock, case hardened mounting, *choke bored,* oiled walnut stock; front trigger throws the barrel open, self-acting shell ejector, strong, simple and durable action; 8 gauge, 36-inch barrel, weight about 12 to 13 lbs. The 8 gauge is the long-range goose gun. The 10 and 12 gauge are made in the same style as the 8 gauge, but of course will not shoot as far. Price............$24.25
46581 10 gauge, pistol grip, 32 to 34-inch barrel, 8 to 9½ pounds... .... 14.00
46582 12 gauge, pistol grip, 32-inch, 7 to 7½ pounds.... .... 10.90

This gun (46580, 8 gauge) is without doubt the "best and most substantial long-range single breech-loader ever built." It is made with a special view to hard service, with heavy charges of ammunition and long range shooting. No. 3 or larger shot should be used, for an 8 gauge is not good with smaller shot using paper or brass shells, center fire. See "Remarks" about ammunition, and how to load.

THE FOREHAND HAMMERLESS. $12.50.

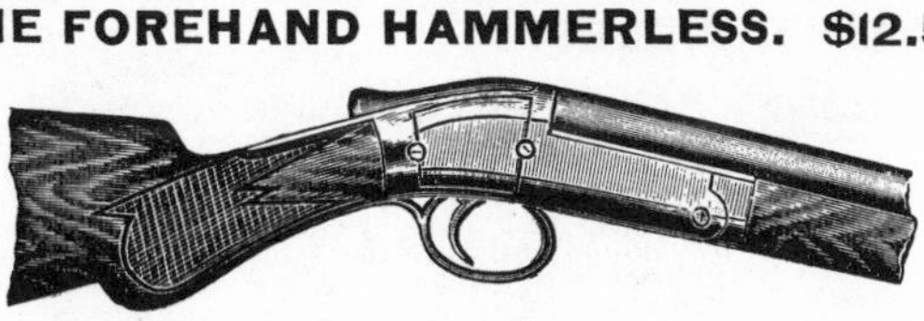

Finely Finished. Good Shooter.

The Hammerless Gun is the coming gun, and is safer and more durable than the *hammer gun.*

46584 The F. & W. Hammerless Single Barrel Breech Loading Shot Gun, top snap, pistol grip, snap fore-end. Automatic action, with an absolute safety catch to lock the trigger to prevent accidental discharge, simple in construction, perfectly safe, and made of best material. Choke bored, twist steel barrels, using brass or paper shells, center fire, 12 gauge, 30 inch barrel, 7 lbs. weight. Each............$12.50

THE PERFECTION BREECH-LOADER.

Single Barrel. **Price, $7.50**

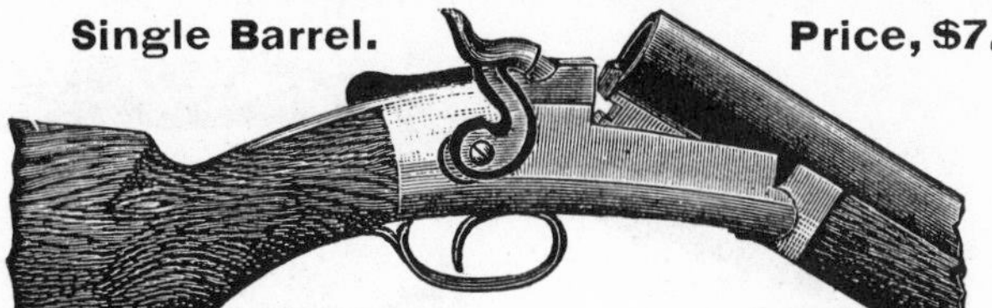

46585 The Improved Perfection Single Barrel Breech-Loading Shot Gun, walnut stock, pistol grip, improved fore-end, rebounding lock, plated frame, twisted steel barrel, medium *choke bored,* shell extractor, center fire, top lever; as good a shooter as any double barrel gun of the same caliber. This gun is all that its name ("Perfection") implies, and in its manufacture the best ideas of years of experience have been embraced, and *it is* the most perfect single barrel breech-loader *ever produced.* Its *simplicity* and *perfection* of action render it almost equal to a *double* breech-loader. For strength, beauty, penetration, and *general* shooting qualities it is without a rival. Using paper or brass shells, center fire; 30 and 32 inch barrels, 6½ to 7½ lbs., 12 gauge. Each..................$7.50
16 gauge. Each.. .... 7.40
46586 The Victor Single Barrel Breech Loader, same as 46585, with fine decarbonized steel barrels; 12 gauge, 30 and 32 inch barrels, 6½ lbs. weight. A fine gun and a good shooter. Each....... ....$5.85

Top-Snap Champion Single Breech-Loading Shot Gun.

MANUFACTURED BY JOHN P. LOVELL'S SONS.

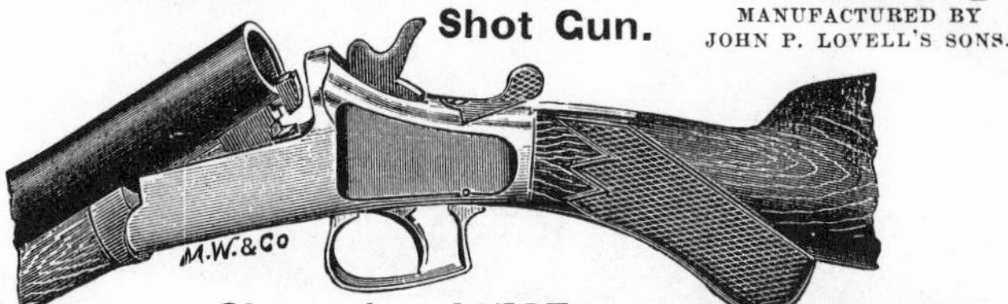

Champion 46587.

46587 Champion Single Breech-Loader, top lever (that can be operated either to right or left), choke bore, rebounding lock, patent fore-end fastening, pistol grip, oiled walnut stock, nickel-plated frames, a fine shooter and a well-made and durable gun. Fine twist barrel, 12 gauge, 32 inch, 6¼ pounds; 30 in., 6 lbs ... $8.40

Every gun warranted a good and reliable shooter. Just as long range as the double guns.

The Boys' American Side Snap. $5.85. The Boss Single Gun. Big Bargains.

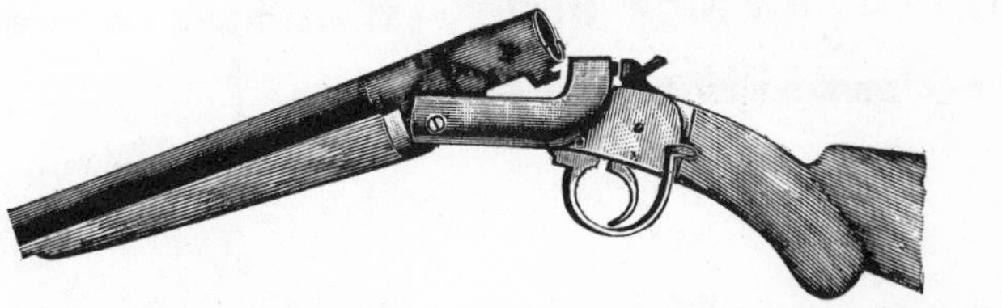

46588 The New American Side Snap. Pistol grip, fine quality, plain blued barrels, nickel plated mountings, rubber butt plate, choke bored, 12 gauge only, 30 inch barrel, weight, 6½ pounds, using paper or brass shells, center fire. Each...$5.85

This is not a *toy gun,* but a handsome, well-made, safe, reliable, accurate shooting gun, and made of the best material. Every gun warranted. Order one, and if not found as represented can be returned at our expense both ways and money will be refunded.

IDEAL. SINGLE GUN.

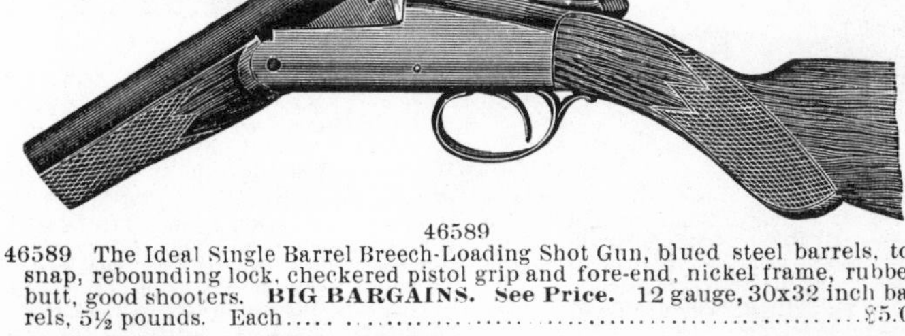

46589

46589 The Ideal Single Barrel Breech-Loading Shot Gun, blued steel barrels, top snap, rebounding lock, checkered pistol grip and fore-end, nickel frame, rubber butt, good shooters. **BIG BARGAINS. See Price.** 12 gauge, 30x32 inch barrels, 5½ pounds. Each $5.00

THE NEW HOPKINS & ALLEN SHOT GUN. $6.50.

46590 The New Hopkins and Allen Shot Gun, a perfectly safe and good shooting gun, that can be taken apart without tool and put into very small compass. It has a rebounding lock and a vertical sliding breech block operated by the guard as a lever, which when thrown down ejects the empty shell from the chamber, and with sufficient force to carry it 6 to 8 feet from the shooter. The barrel is fastened to the frame by a tapering screw key, easily removed by the hand, which passes through the frame and section of the barrel laterally, keeping the barrel always in its proper position. Finest blued steel barrel, case-hardened mountings, choke bored. The barrels are bored out of solid metal; oiled walnut pistol grip stock, double bolt. One of the strongest and best made guns in the market. 12 guage only, 30 inch barrels, 6½ to 7 pounds
Each $6.50

HOPKINS & ALLEN MFG. CO'S SINGLE SHOT GUN, 12 GAUGE

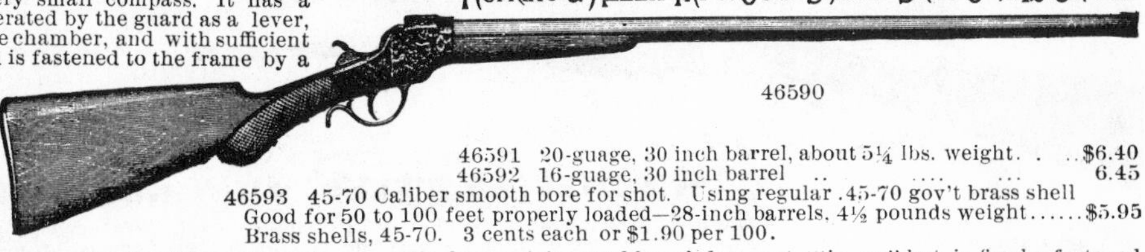

46590

46591 20-guage, 30 inch barrel, about 5¼ lbs. weight. . . .$6.40
46592 16-guage, 30 inch barrel 6.45
46593 45-70 Caliber smooth bore for shot. Using regular .45-70 gov't brass shell Good for 50 to 100 feet properly loaded—28-inch barrels. 4½ pounds weight......$5.95
Brass shells, 45-70. 3 cents each or $1.90 per 100.

The H. & A. gun never gets loose and shaky in the hinge joints like the "tip up" barrel guns, as it has no joints and barrel does not "tip up" but is firmly fastened in the breech action.

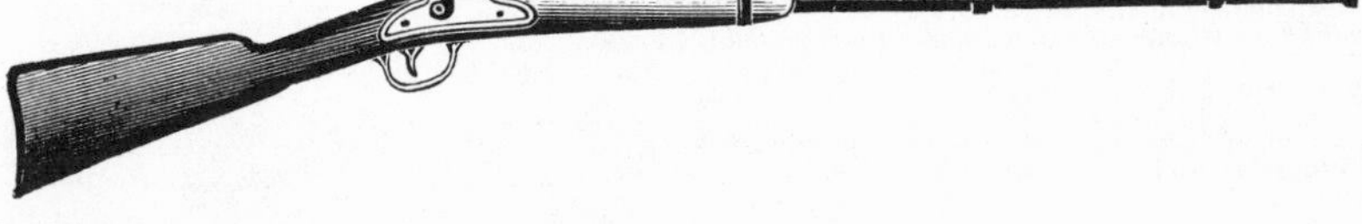

46595 Cut Down Muskets, 32 in. barrels, 16 gauge, walnut stocks blued finish, muzzle-loading single barrel, weight, about 6¼ lbs.
Each...$2.90

Boys' Muzzie Loader—Single Barrel.

46596 The Boys' Muzzle Loader, single barrel, wood ramrod, pistol grip, blued barrels, a good, safe gun, small nipple for G. D. or E. B. caps, 31 inch barrels, 4½ lbs. weight, 16 gauge. Each..$2.75

MUZZLE LOADERS—Double Barrel.

This cut represents as near as possible a Double Barrel Muzzle Loader, with back action locks.
46597 Imitation Twist Barrels, back action lock, plain breech, guage, 11, 12, 13 and 14, Belgian manufacture. Price $5.40
46598 Double Barrel Muzzle Loader, Belgian manufacture. genuine twist steel barrels, oiled walnut stock, patent breech and break of back action locks, checkered grip, 12 to 14 bore; weight, 7 to 8½ pounds; length, 30 to 34 inches. A good, safe and reliable gun.$8.00

46599 Double Barrel Muzzle Loader, pistol grip, blued barrels. The barrels are made from new musket barrels, and are perfectly safe and reliable. A good strong, durable gun in every particular, about 14 to 15 gauge, 34 inch barrels; about 8 pounds weight............$5.00

46599

DOUBLE BARREL MUZZLE LOADERS.

With bar lock. All have patent breech and break off.
46600 Double Barrel Muzzle Loader, laminated steel barrel, bar locks, oiled walnut stock, patent breech and break off, checkered pistol grip, German manufacture, 12 to 14 gauge. 7 to 8½ pounds, 30 to 34 inch barrels. Price..............$9.00
46603 Genuine Twist Barrels, bar locks, walnut stock. checkered grip, gauge, 13 to 15, English manufacture. Length of barrel 30, 32, 34 to 36 inches, weighs 7½ to 8½ lbs. Pistol grip..................................$9.75

46600-3.
Cut showing Bar Locks,
Pistol Grip.

BIG BARGAINS IN GUNS.

46604 We have a consignment of *big double barrel muzzle loaders*, straight grip, for duck, goose and deer shooting. Bar locks, finely finished, 10 and 11 gauge, 34 and 36 inch, 10 to 11 pounds. Just the thing for buckshot. Price, $11.00 each, until sold. Made by Ed. Middleton, Birmingham, England.

STEVENS' LADIES' RIFLE.—Warranted Accurate.

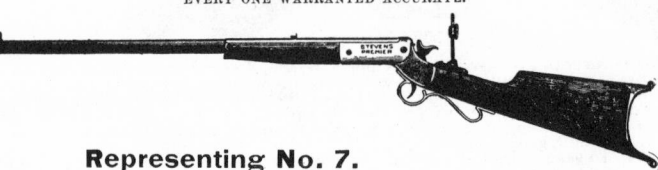

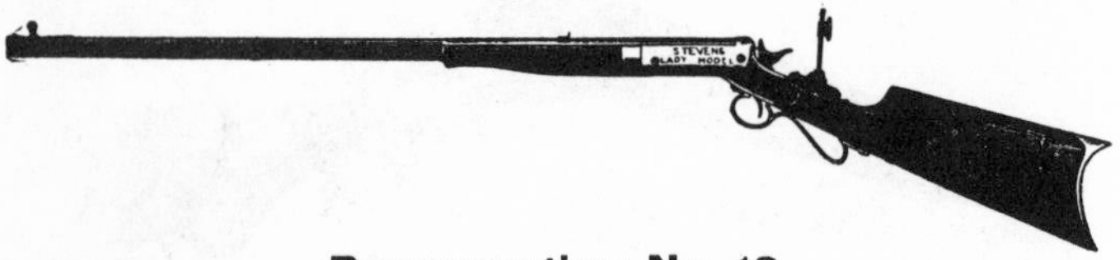

Representing No. 13.

46610 Half Octagon Barrel, beach front sight, open back sight on barrel and vernier peep sight on frame, fore-end and stock varnished, nickel plated frame and butt plate. Using 22 rim-fire cartridges, splendidly balanced, light weight and especially adapted for ladies' use. 22 *rim-fire*, chambered for the long rifle cartridge No. 47160. or 47155. Both can be used when chambered for the long rifle cartridge. 24-inch barrel; 5½ pounds. No better rifle manufactured.$16.80

STEVENS' PREMIER RIFLE.

EVERY ONE WARRANTED ACCURATE.

Representing No. 7.

46611 Half Octagon Barrel, beach front sight, open back sight, on barrel, vernier peep sight on frame, Swiss butt plate, varnished fore-end and stock, nickel plated frame and butt plate, 22 caliber rim-fire, using No. 47160 long rifle cartridge, or any 22 short or long rim-fire cartridge, 26-inch barrel, 7¼ pounds......$18.95
Other lengths and caliber can be furnished if desired in the Premier rifle.

COLT'S NEW LIGHTNING MAGAZINE RIFLES.

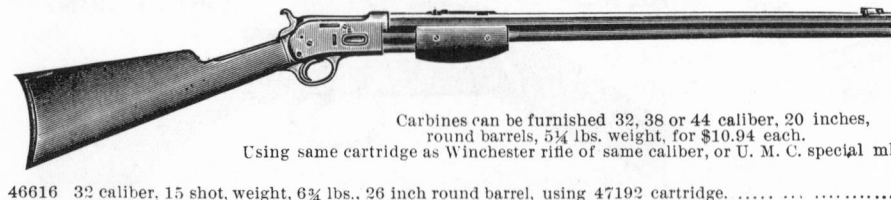

Manufactured by Colt's Patent Fire Arms Manufacturing Co., Hartford, Conn. Constructed upon entirely new principles. The workmanship is of the same high standard as that of the other arms manufactured by this company. Old shell ejected and new cartridge inserted by sliding motion of the forearm, and as it can be done with the left hand it is at once convenient and rapid. Every rifle warranted. ALL CENTER FIRE.

Carbines can be furnished 32, 38 or 44 caliber, 20 inches, round barrels, 5¼ lbs. weight, for $10.94 each.
Using same cartridge as Winchester rifle of same caliber, or U. M. C. special mke.

		Reduced Prices.	Factory Price.	Our Price.
46616	32 caliber, 15 shot, weight, 6¾ lbs., 26 inch round barrel, using 47192 cartridge.		$16.50	$10.94
46617	32 caliber, 15 shot, weight, 7¼ lbs., 26 inch octagon barrel, using 47192 cartridge		18.00	11.86
46618	38 caliber, 15 shot, weight, 6¾ lbs., 26 inch round barrel, using 47201 cartridge.		16.50	10.94
46619	38 caliber, 15 shot, weight, 7¼ lbs., 26 inch octagon barrel, using 47201 cartridge.		18.00	11.86
46620	44 caliber, 15 shot, weight, 6¾ lbs., 26 inch round barrel, using 47214 cartridge.		16.50	10.94
46621	44 caliber, 15 shot, weight, 7½ lbs., 26 inch octagon barrel, using 47214 cartridge.		18.00	11.86

N. B.—Factory is out of No. 38-56, 40-60 and 45-85 Rifles and will not make any more.

COLT'S LIGHTNING RIFLE—22 Caliber. $9.72.

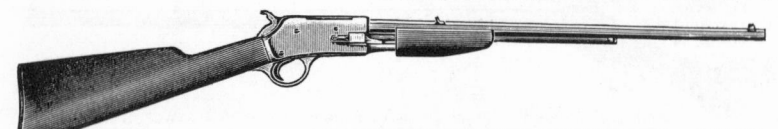

46629 Colt's Magazine Rifle, 22 caliber, 15 shot, rim'fire, long or short, weight, 5¾ lbs., 24 in. octagon barrel. Each........$9.72
Using 47155-59 cartridge.
Extra for Colt Rifles. Fancy pistol grip stock, checkered grip and fore-end, $12.00 extra. Extra length barrels, $1.00 per inch.

WINCHESTER RIFLES. All Warranted. Highest Grade Made.

These Rifles are all perfectly new and direct from the factory, and are fully warranted by the Winchester Company and by us. They are among the very best sporting and target rifles manufactured in the world. There are no poor ones. Every one is perfect. The extremely low prices at which we are now offering them place them within the reach of every man and boy in the land. There are no later models in any grade than those we have listed. The 1873 and 1876 models are exactly the same in design; the only difference is caliber, length and weight.
For additional length of barrel and magazine add to price $0.75 per inch. For set triggers on models 1873, $2.00.
Extra for set trigger case hardened mountings and lock plates and extra finished plain stocks, $3.75.
Extra for plain walnut, pistol grip, stocks not checkered.$4.75. Extra for fancy walnut pistol grip, stocks checkered, $11.00.
All have oiled walnut stocks. Sling strap and swivels, $1.50 per set.
Prices on extra parts and fancy styles and cuts of same furnished on application.
For Cartridges see Index. For Reloading Tools and Sights see Index.
46736 Winchester Carbine, 32 caliber, center fire (model 1873), 20-inch round barrel; 12 shot; using No. 47193 cartridge. Each....................................$10.94
46737 Winchester Carbine, 38 caliber, center fire (model 1873), 20-inch round barrel; 11 shot; using No. 47200 cartridge. Each 10.94

WINCHESTER RIFLES—Continued.

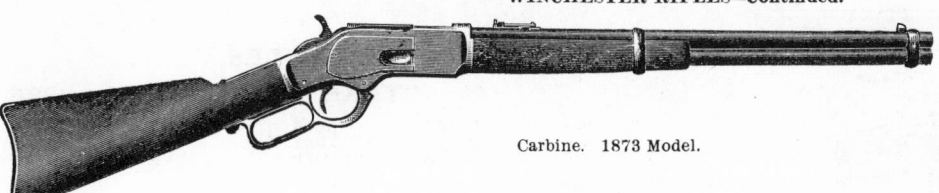

Carbine. 1873 Model.

46738 Winchester Carbine, 44 caliber (model 1873), center fire, 20-inch round barrel, 12 shot, weight 7¼ lbs., using No. 47208 cartridge.
Price..... .... $10.94
46739 Winchester Carbine (model 1876), 22-inch round barrel, stock full length of magazine, number of shots 9, weight, 8¼ lbs.,45-60 caliber, using No. 47240 cartridge. Price................$13.00
46740 40-60 caliber, using No. 47230 cartridge.
Price 13.00

WINCHESTER RIFLES—MODEL 1873.

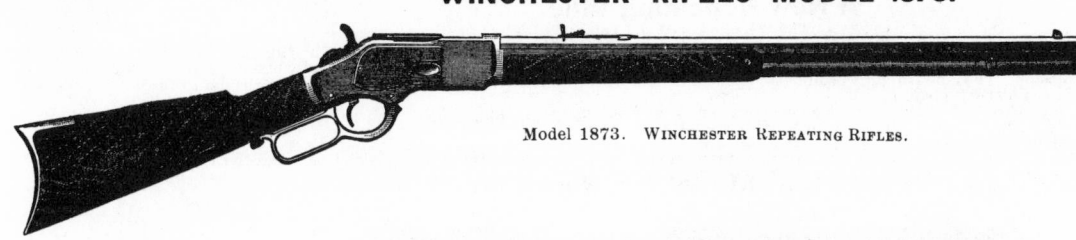

Model 1873. WINCHESTER REPEATING RIFLES.

46744 Winchester Sporting Rifle (model 1873), repeating, round barrels: length of barrel, 24 inches; center fire: caliber, 44; number of shots, 15; weight, 8¾ lbs.; using 47208 cartridge
Price $10.94
46745 Octagon Barrel: length of barrel,24 inches; center fire; caliber, 44; number of shots, 15; weight, 9 lbs.; using No. 47208 cartridge. Each $11.86
46746 Octagon Barrel, 24 inches, 15 shot; weight, 9 lbs.; 38 caliber; using No. 47200 cartridge only (model 1873). Each.$11.86

Sporting Rifles.

46747 Round Barrels, 24 inches, 15 shot; weight, 8¾ lbs.; 38 caliber, using No. 47200 cartridge only (model 1873)). Each.. 10.94
46748 Octagon Barrels, 24 inch, 15 shot; weight, 9 lbs.; 32 caliber, using No. 47193 cartridge only (model 1873). Each.... .. . . 11.86
46749 Round Barrels, 24 inch. 15 shot; weight, 8¾ lbs.; 32 caliber, using No. 47193 cartridge only (model 1873). Each.... .. .. 10.94
46750 Octagon Barrels, 24 inch, 25 shot; weight, 9 lbs.; 22 caliber, rim fire short, only, using No. 47156 cartridge only (model 1873). Each........................ 11.86

NEW—WINCHESTER REPEATING RIFLES—1894.—NEW.

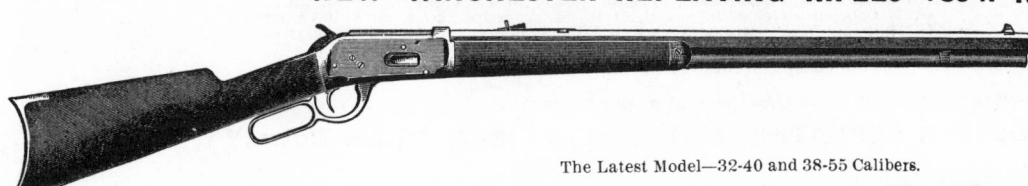

The Latest Model—32-40 and 38-55 Calibers.

46751 Octagon Barrels, 26 inches, 10 shots, 7½ lbs., 32-40 caliber, using No. 47222½ cartridge. Each........$11.86
46752 Octagon Barrels, 26 inches, 10 shots, 7½ lbs., 38-55 caliber, using No. 47224½ cartridge. Each.... ...$11.86
46753 Round barrels, 26 inches, 7¼ lbs., either caliber; no other lengths or styles can be furnished at present.
Each.. . . .. $10.94

WINCHESTER 22-CALIBER REPEATING RIFLE—Model '90. "Take Down."

Winchester, Model 1890 Repeating Rifle. Loads and ejects the shell by the sliding motion of the forearm. All 24-inch octagon barrels, all 5¾ pounds weight.

46757 For 22 Caliber Rim Fire Short, only 15 shot, using No. 47156 Cartridges.
.....................................$9.72

46758 For 22 Caliber Rim Fire Long, 12 shot, using No. 47159 cartridges.$9.72

46759 For 22 Caliber Rim Fire Special Winchester Lubricated Bullet cartridge, using No. 47165 cartridges.......$9.72
The same rifle will only load the one length of shell.
All warranted accurate and reliable.

46757-9 Taken apart.

All Rim Fire.
Model 1890.
Factory price........ ....$16.00
Our price...................... 9.72
New model, stock and barrel can be separated by removing a screw.

TESTING GUNS FOR ACCURACY.

In testing guns for accuracy, sit down when firing, resting the muzzle on some solid object, and if possible securing a solid rest for the arms and body. In this way extreme accuracy can be obtained—sufficient for the testing of the gun. Do not in any case attempt to get accuracy by screwing the gun in a vise. No reliable resul can be had in this way.

WINCHESTER REPEATING RIFLES—Model 1886.

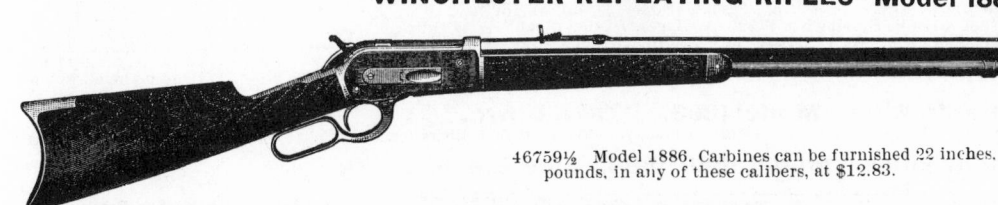

All have case-hardened lock plates and mountings.
Prices on longer or shorter barrels on application.

46759½ Model 1886. Carbines can be furnished 22 inches. round barrels, 8 pounds, in any of these calibers, at $12.83.

		Factory prices.	Our prices.
46760 Octagon Barrel, 26 inches or under, 9½ lbs., 40-82 caliber, 260 grain bullet, 8 shot, using No. 47234 cartridge...............................		$21.00	$14.18
46761 Round Barrel, 40-82 caliber.................		19.50	13 16
46762 Octagon Barrel, 26 inches or under, 9¼ lbs., 45-70 caliber, 405 grain bullet (using a regular Government cartridge), 9 shot..............		21.00	14.18
46763 Round Barrel, 26 inches or under, 9 lbs., 45-70 caliber........................		19.50	13.16
46764 Octagon Barrel, 26 inches or under, 9¼ lbs., 45-90 caliber, 300 grain bullet, 8 shot, using No. 47249 cartridge...........................		21.00	14.18
46765 Round Barrel, 26 inches or under, 9 lbs., 45-90 caliber, using No. 47249 cartridge...		19.50	13.16
46766 Octagon Barrel, 26 inches, 9½ lbs., 38-56 caliber, 8 shot, using No. 47225 cartridge.....		21.00	14.18
46767 Round Barrel, 26 inches, 9¼ lbs., 38-56 caliber...		19.50	13.16
46768 Octagon Barrel, 26 inches, 9½ lbs., 40-65 caliber, using No. 47231 cartridge		21.00	14.18
46769 Round Barrel, 26 inches, 40-65 caliber........		19.50	13.16
46770 Octagon Barrel, 26 inches, 50-110 Express, using No. 47262 cartridge.................		21.00	14.18
46771 Octagon Barrels, 26 inches, 9½ lbs., 38-70-255 caliber, using No. 47226 cartridge..................		21.00	14.18
46772 Octagon Barrels, 26 inches, 9½ lbs., 40-70-330 caliber, using No. 47228 cartridge.......		21.00	14.18

The standard length of barrel will be 26 inches. Guns taking the 45-70 cartridge will have the Sporting Leaf Sight, and all others the Sporting Rear Sight.
Plain walnut pistol grip stocks not checkered, $4.75; extra barrels can be made any length from 20 to 36 inch; add $1.00 per inch for barrels over 26 inch.
Cleaning Rods will not be put in butt stocks, but each gun will be accompanied by a slotted hickory rod, without charge.
All extras same as other Winchester Repeating Rifles.
Set Triggers, $2.25 extra. Fancy Walnut Pistol, Grip Stock,Checkered Grip and Fore End, $12.00 extra.

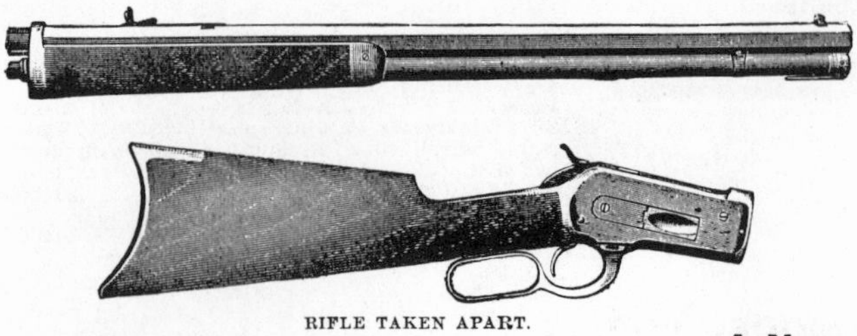

RIFLE TAKEN APART.

WINCHESTER REPEATING RIFLES, "TAKE DOWN"—Model 1886.

46772½ Winchester Repeating Rifles, model 1886, "Take Down," 26 inches, octagon barrels, any caliber from No. 46760 to [illegible] $17.60
No other lengths made in the "Take-Down" style.

A New Repeating Rifle.

The Winchester Model 1892.

The system is the same as the model of 1886. Loaded and discharged by a finger lever. The firing pin is first withdrawn, the gun unlocked and opened, the shell ejected, and a new cartridge presented and forced into the chamber of the barrel. The locking bolts are always in sight, and when the gun is closed support the breech bolt against the force of the explosion. The rifle is light, strong, handsome and simple in construction. Cleaning rods *will not* be put in the butt stocks, but each rifle will be accompanied with a slotted hickory cleaning rod.

They will only be made with 24 inch barrel. (Factory price on octagon barrel) $19.50. } SEE OUR PRICES.
They will only be made with plain triggers. (Factory price on round barrel) $18.00.
They will only be made with straight grip stocks.
They are only made as quoted below, using the same tools and cartridge as the model 1873. See index for quotations on Tools and Cartridges.

Winchester, Model '92, Repeater.

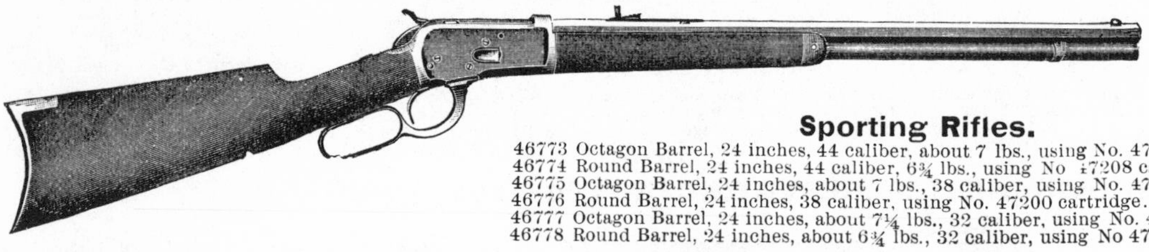

Sporting Rifles.

		Our price, Each.
46773	Octagon Barrel, 24 inches, 44 caliber, about 7 lbs., using No. 47208 cartridge	$11.86
46774	Round Barrel, 24 inches, 44 caliber, 6¾ lbs., using No. 47208 cartridge	10.84
46775	Octagon Barrel, 24 inches, about 7 lbs., 38 caliber, using No. 47200 cartridge	11.86
46776	Round Barrel, 24 inches, 38 caliber, using No. 47200 cartridge	10.84
46777	Octagon Barrel, 24 inches, about 7¼ lbs., 32 caliber, using No. 47193 cartridge	11.86
46778	Round Barrel, 24 inches, about 6¾ lbs., 32 caliber, using No 47193 cartridge	10.94

Winchester Model '92 Carbine.

46779 Carbines, with 20 inch round barrels, full magazine, in 32, 38 or 44 caliber, 6¼ lbs. weight. Each $10 40

THE WINCHESTER REPEATING RIFLE. Model 1892. "Take Down."

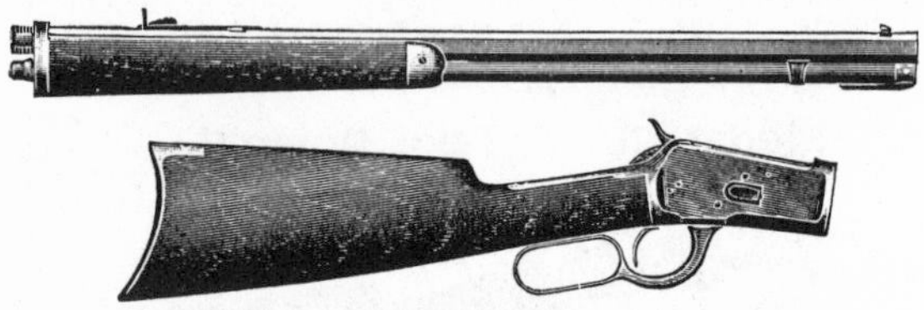

Rifle Taken Apart.

No better Rifle made.

46779½ Winchester model '92—Take Down Repeating rifle. 24-inch Octagon Barrels, made in 32 W. C. F. Caliber, 38 W. C. F. Caliber, and 44 W. C. F. caliber. Each $15.00
Operates same as No. 46773-75-77, and takes same cartridges. No other length of barrels or style of rifle made in this model "Take Down."

Marlin Safety Rifle. Model 1893. Side Ejector.

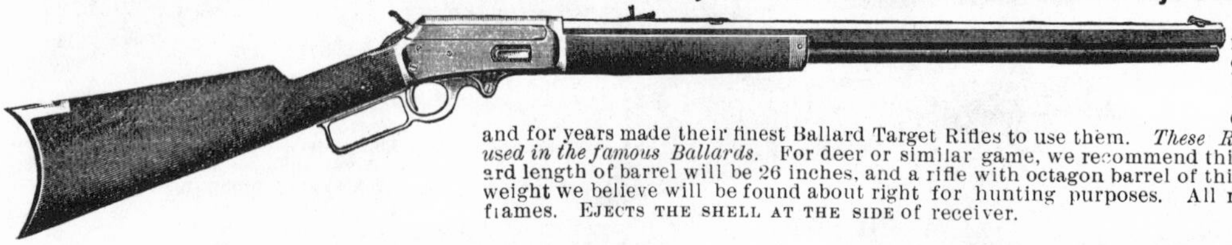

This model is similar in principle to the 1889 model, and is made in response to the many demands for a rifle in 32-40 and 38-55 calibers. It is the only repeater on the market using these cartridges. The Marlin Fire Arm Co. were the originators of these cartridges, and for years made their finest Ballard Target Rifles to use them. *These Rifles are to have exactly the same barrels as were used in the famous Ballards.* For deer or similar game, we recommend this model above any in the market. The standard length of barrel will be 26 inches, and a rifle with octagon barrel of this length will weigh about 7¾ pounds. This weight we believe will be found about right for hunting purposes. All rifles of this model will have case hardened frames. EJECTS THE SHELL AT THE SIDE of receiver.

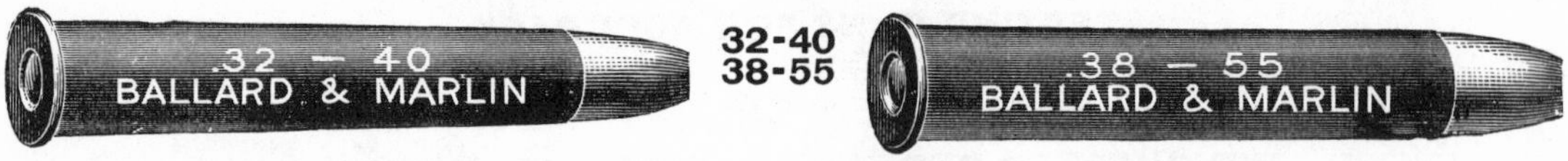

46780	Marlin Rifle, 26-inch octagon barrel, 10 shot, 32-40 caliber (using No. 47220 cartridge), 7¾ lbs. weight	$12.87
46781	Marlin Rifle, 26-inch round barrel, 10 shot, 32-40 caliber (using No. 47220 cartridge), 7½ lbs. weight	11.86
46782	Marlin Rifle, 26-inch octagon barrel, 38-55 caliber (using No. 47222 cartridge), 10 shot, about 7¾ lbs. weight	12.87
46783	Marlin Rifle, 26-inch round barrel, 38-55 caliber (using No. 47222 cartridge), 10 shot, about 7½ lbs. weight	11 86

We can furnish either the 32-40 calibre or 38-55 caliber with 28 inch octagon barrels, at $14.37 each; with 30 inch octagon barrels, $15.87. If not on hand, would take a few days to have them made.

Marlin Rifle. Model 1893. "Take Down."

46783½ Marlin Rifle, Model 1893, made to separate barrel from stock easily, 26-inch octagon, 32-40 and 38-55 calibers. Each $15.92

Marlin Rifles. Model 1889-1894. Side Ejector.

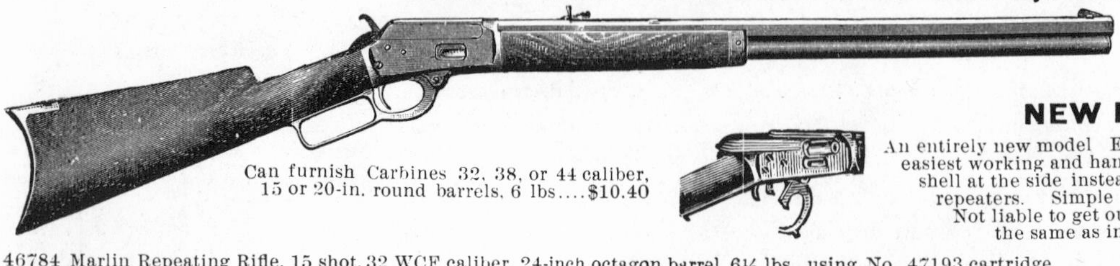

New 25-20 Caliber. See Price Below.

Can furnish Carbines 32, 38, or 44 caliber, 15 or 20-in. round barrels, 6 lbs.... $10.40

NEW MARLIN RIFLE

An entirely new model Every rifle warranted. Model 1889 and '94. The easiest working and handiest rifle in the market. Ejects the empty shell at the side instead of at the top. The newest feature in repeaters. Simple in construction, and accurate shooters. Not liable to get out of repair. The system of rifling is the same as in the world-renowned Ballard rifles.

46784 Marlin Repeating Rifle, 15 shot, 32 WCF caliber, 24-inch octagon barrel, 6¼ lbs., using No. 47193 cartridge $11.86
46785 Marlin Repeating Rifle, 15 shot, 38 WCF caliber, 24-inch octagon barrel, using No. 47200 cartridge, weight, 6½ lbs 11.86
46786 Marlin Repeating Rifle, 15 shot, 44 WCF caliber, 24-inch octagon barrel, using No. 47208 cartridge, weight, 6½ lbs 11 86
26-inch barrel, octagon, either caliber .... $13.50 | 28-inch barrel, octagon, either caliber 14.50
46786½ Marlin Repeating Rifle, 25-20 caliber, 14 shot, 7¼ pounds weight, 24-inch octagon barrel, using No. 47187½ cartridge 11 86
Catalogues of fancy styles of finish on Marlin's free.
Model 1889 Rifle not made with set trigger. Extra for plain walnut, pistol grip stocks, checkered grip and fore-end $4.00 on Marlin 1889 or 1894 model.
Extra for selected walnut stock, checkered grip and fore-end, $12.00.
46787 24-inch, round barrel .... $10.95 26-inch, round barrels. Each 12.96

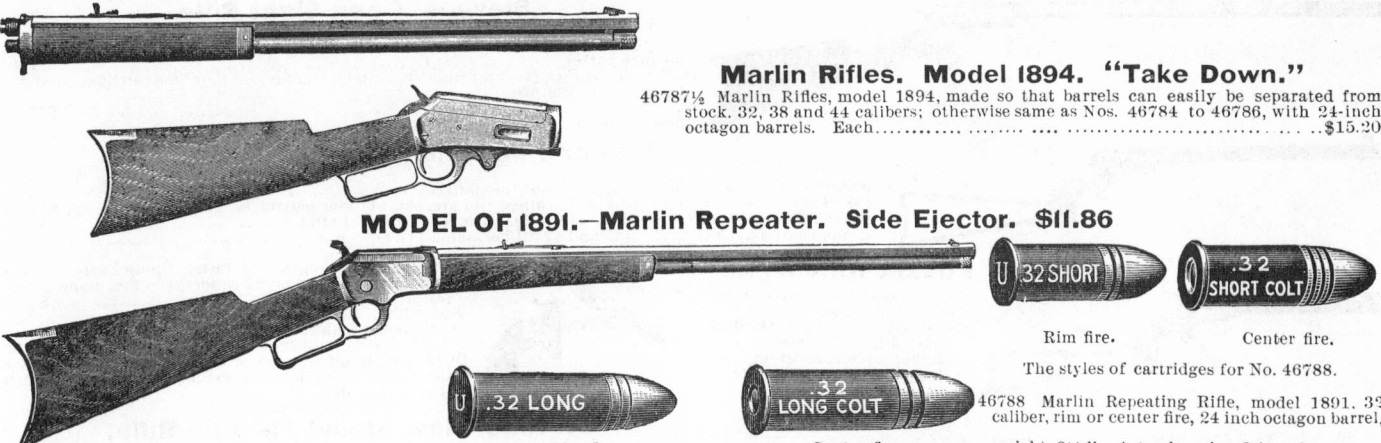

Marlin Rifles. Model 1894. "Take Down."

46787½ Marlin Rifles, model 1894, made so that barrels can easily be separated from stock. 32, 38 and 44 calibers; otherwise same as Nos. 46784 to 46786, with 24-inch octagon barrels. Each..$15.20

MODEL OF 1891.—Marlin Repeater. Side Ejector. $11.86

Rim fire. Center fire.

The styles of cartridges for No. 46788.

No. of shots: short cartridge 18, long 15. Using Nos. 47170, 47171, 47189 and 47190 cartridges

Rifle will be shipped with rim fire, firing pin in rifle. An extra firing pin for center fire will be sent with each gun.

46788 Marlin Repeating Rifle, model 1891, 32 caliber, rim or center fire, 24 inch octagon barrel, weight, 6½ lbs, interchanging firing pins. 24-in. $11.86 ; 26-in. $13.80 ; 28-in. $14.80. Rifle is loaded same as the 22 caliber, by drawing out magazine.

MARLIN MODEL 1891. 22 Caliber Repeater. $11.86.
Full length magazine.
SIDE EJECTOR.

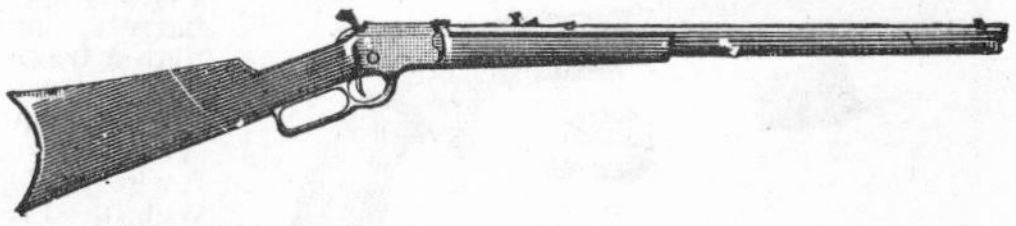

46789 Marlin Repeating Rifle, model 1891, 20 to 25 shot, 22 caliber, rim fire. 24-inch octagon barrel, side ejector, magazine full length of barrel, using Nos. 47155 to 47160 cartridges; weight, 6 lbs...................................$11.86

Same rifle, model 1891, will use both short and long rim fire, 22 caliber cartridges without any changes. 20 long or 25 short cartridges can be put in magazine. Accurate and reliable.

DISMOUNTED TO CLEAN.

THE FAMOUS WINCHESTER SINGLE SHOT RIFLE. $10.13.

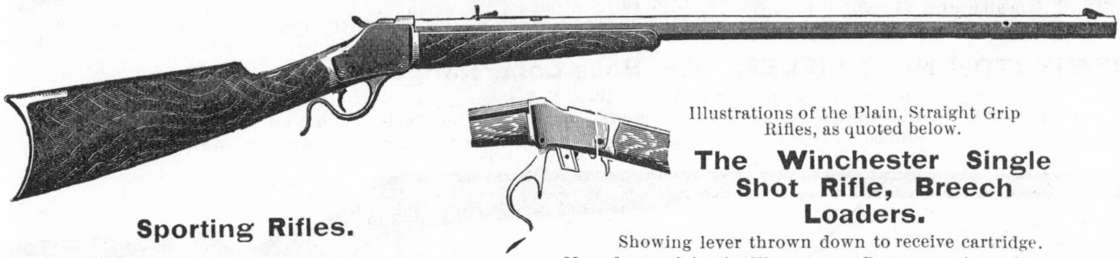

Although this rifle is a recent production it has become almost as famous as the "Winchester Repeater," and stands in the "front rank" with the very best target rifles of this and other countries.

This gun has the old Sharp's breech block and lever, and is as safe and solid as that arm. The firing pin is automatically withdrawn at the first opening movement of the gun and held back until the gun is closed. The hammer is centrally hung, but drops down with the breech block when the gun is opened, and is cocked by the closing movement. It can also be cocked by hand. This arrangement

Illustrations of the Plain, Straight Grip Rifles, as quoted below.

The Winchester Single Shot Rifle, Breech Loaders.

Sporting Rifles.

Showing lever thrown down to receive cartridge.
Manufactured by the WINCHESTER REPEATING ARMS Co.,
New Haven, Conn.

allows the barrel to be wiped and examined from the breech. In outline everything has been done to make the gun pleasing to the eye. All of these rifles have case-hardened lock plates and dark walnut stocks. Other styles and calibers made to order.

Every rifle warranted perfect and accurate. These rifles are not made with *double trigger*. The set locks are adjusted by a little screw in rear of trigger, and can be set to pull as desired or not used at all. Pushing the trigger *forward* places it in the "hair pull" notch, same as working a double trigger. All rifles have sporting rear sights. CAN BE RETURNED AT OUR EXPENSE if not found as represented.

WINCHESTER SINGLE SHOT RIFLES.

		Each
46790	22 caliber, *rim fire*, BB caps, short or long cartridge, 24-inch octagon barrel; weight, 7 lbs., plain trigger	$10.13
46791	22 caliber, *rim fire*, BB caps, short or long cartridge, 26-inch octagon barrel; 7 lbs. weight, plain trigger	11.00
46794	32 caliber, *rim fire*, extra short, short or long cartridges, 26-inch octagon barrel; 7 lbs. weight, *plain trigger*	10.13
46796	22 caliber, *center fire*, using No. 47186 cartridge, 26-inch octagon barrel; 7 lbs. weight, *plain trigger*	10.75
46797	25 caliber, *center fire*, using No. 47187 cartridge, 28-inch octagon barrel; 7 lbs. weight, *plain trigger*	10.13
46798	32 caliber, *center fire*, using No. 47193 cartridge, 28-inch octagon barrel; 8½ lbs. weight, *plain trigger*	10.40
46799	32-40 caliber, *center fire*, using No. 47220 cartridge, 30-inch octagon barrel, 9 lbs. weight, *plain trigger*	10.13
46800	32-40 caliber, *center fire*, using No. 47220 cartridge, 30-inch octagon barrel; 9 to 9½ lbs. weight, *set trigger*	12.13
46801	38 caliber, *center fire*, using No. 47200 cartridge, 28-inch octagon barrel; 8½ lbs. weight, *plain trigger*	11.00
46802	38-55 caliber, *center fire*, using No. 47222 cartridge, 30-inch octagon barrel; 9 lbs. weight, *plain trigger*	10.13
46803	38-55 caliber, *center fire*, using No. 47222 cartridge, 30-inch octagon barrel; 9½ lbs. weight, *set trigger*	12.75
46804	40-60 caliber, *center fire*, using No. 47230 cartridge, 30-inch octagon barrel; 9½ lbs. weight,	10.13
46805	40-82 caliber, *center fire*, using No. 47234 cartridge, 30-inch octagon barrel; 9½ lbs. weight, *plain trigger*, long range	10.13
46806	40-90 caliber, *center fire*, using No. 47237 cartridge, 32-inch octagon barrel; 9½ to 11 lbs., *set trigger*	14.75
46808	45-70 caliber, *center fire*, using No. 47243 cartridge, 30-inch octagon barrel; 9½ lbs. weight, *plain trigger*, long range	11.00
46810	40-65 caliber, *center fire*, using No. 47231 cartridge, 30-inch octagon barrel; 9½ lbs., a good target rifle	11.00
46812	45-90 caliber, *center fire*, using No. 47249 cartridge, 30-inch octagon barrel; 9½ lbs., long range. The "Boss" *Bear and Deer Rifle*	11.00
46813	40-70 caliber, using No. 47233 cartridge, 30-inch octagon barrel; 9½ lbs., *plain trigger*	10.13
46813¼	30, U. S. caliber, using No. 47219 cartridge, 30-inch special round barrel; 9¼ lbs., *plain trigger*	23.00

Extras on Winchester single shot rifles. Barrels can be furnished up to 36 in. Extra for longer barrels than quoted, $1.00 for every two inches. Barrels making gun weigh 1 to 1½ lbs. more, $2.00 extra. Barrels making gun weigh about 12 lbs., $8.00 extra. Set trigger, $2.00 extra.

It may take 10 to 20 days to have guns made extra lengths or otherwise different from our regular quotations. Fancy walnut pistol grip stock, checkered, extra $11.00; plain pistol grip stocks, $4.75 extra; 22 and 25 caliber not made over 28 inches.

Keep Your Rifles Bright and Clean Inside or They Will Not Shoot Well.
NEW MODEL STEVENS' RIFLE.—"Sure Shot."

46814 The "Sure Shot" is an entirely new model. The barrel swings to extract the shell instead of "tipping up" as in the old models. Barrels are rifled same as in the higher grades, and is a wonderful shooter. Frame nickel plated, walnut stock, rebounding lock, German silver front sight, finely finished throughout. Stock and barrel easily separated to clean or pack. Barrel 20 inches, entire length, 34 inches, weight, 3½ lbs., 22 caliber, rim fire short, long, or long rifle cartridge. Every rifle warranted as long range and as accurate as any 22 caliber rifle in the market. Each..................$6.49

J. Stevens & Co.'s Single Breech Loading Rifles.

Manufactured at Chicopee Falls, Mass. In all styles the barrel "tips up" at the breech the same as a breech loading shotgun. Stock and barrel can be easily separated and packed in a trunk or case. All have nickel-plated frame and mountings, oiled walnut stock, blue barrels and are finely finished throughout. Every rifle is rigidly tested at the factory and warranted perfectly accurate and reliable. There are no better shooting rifles in the market. There are more of these rifles in the shooting galleries than of any other make. There are no better ones.

Stevens' "Expert" Rifles No. 5, Vernier and Open Back Sight and each Front Sight.

Weight of Rifles boxed for shipment, 15 to 25 pounds, each; 25 caliber rim or center fire same prices as the 22 calibers.

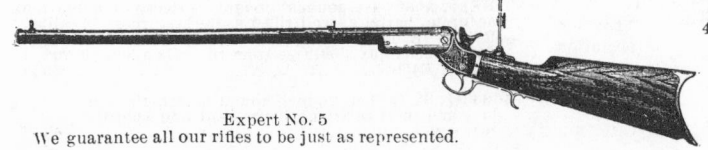

46815 Stevens' Rifle No. 5, 22 caliber, rim fire, weight, 6¼ to 7¼ for 24 in.; 7 to 7¾ lbs. 28 in.

	Each.
24-inch barrel	$15 00
28-inch barrel	17.49

Expert No. 5
We guarantee all our rifles to be just as represented.

Stevens' Open Sight Rifle.

46816 Stevens' Open Sight Rifle, 22 caliber, rim fire, short or long cartridges
Weight, 6½ to 7½, 24 in., 7½ to 8 lbs. 28 in. 24-inch barrel............ .$12.00
28-inch barrel.. 14.40
46817 Stevens' Open Sight Rifle, 32 caliber, rim fire, short or long cartridges and 25-
20 caliber center fire
24-inch barrel...$12.00
28-inch barrel.. 13.20

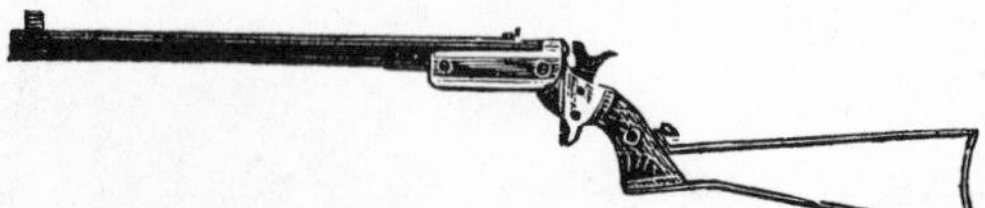

Hunter's Pet Rifle.

Weight of 18 inch, about 5¼ lbs., and good for 40 rods.   Each.
46818 Stevens' Hunter's Pet Rifle, 22 caliber rim fire, short or long cartridges, 18-inch barrel. . . .$12.15
46819 Stevens' Hunter's Pet Rifle, 32 caliber, rim fire, 18-inch barrel........ .... 12.15
20-inch barrel............... ....(22 and 32 caliber, same price) 13.00

The Stevens' New Model Pocket Rifles.

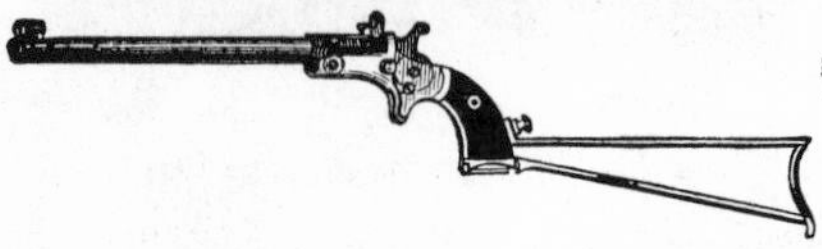

A fine target or squirrel rifle,
good for 100 yards.
46820 Stevens' New Model
Pocket Rifle, 22 caliber, rim
fire, short or long cartridge, and
BB cap cartridges, 22 caliber.

	Each.
12-inch barrel, 2¼ lb. weight	$8.95
15-inch barrel, 2½ lb. weight	10.13

46821 Stevens' Diamond Model
Pistol, single shot, tip-up, blued
barrels, long plain grip stock,
plated frame, chambered for 22
rim fire short or long rifle cartridges, plain open sights.
Weight, 10 oz., 6 inch barrel, good
for 50 yards, each..........$4.75
Weight, 12 oz., 10 inch barrel,
good for 20 to 100 yards...$6.75
The Stevens' pistols are all
made of the very best material, and
are all warranted accurate shooters.

Cut of sights, plain open, such as
will be sent on rifle.

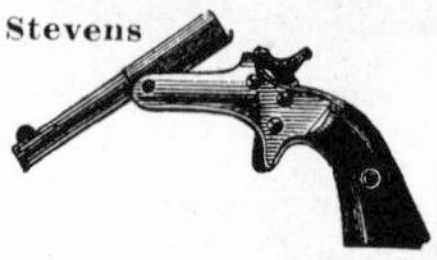

46822 Stevens' Single Shot Pistol, tip-up barrel, plated
finish, 3½-inch barrel, 22 caliber, rim fire, a fine target
pistol...$2.10
30 caliber, rim fire, short................................ 2.15
No better material put in rifles; weight, 8 oz.
Stevens' 25 Caliber Rifles, rim or center fire, can be
furnished at same prices as the 22 caliber styles. See
"Cartridges" for prices on ammunition. Can furnish
any style to order .

Stevens' New Model Favorite Rifle.

As well rifled as
the higher cost
rifle.

STEVENS' FAVORITE TAKEN APART

46823 The Favorite is an entirely new
model Stevens' rifle. The barrel is
held to stock by a set screw, and
easily separated or put together.
Rifling and quality of barrel same
as the higher cost rifle, case-harden-
ed frame, walnut stock, finely finished, warranted accurate,
rim fire, 22 caliber; using long or short cartridges. Each
22 in. barrel, about 4½ lbs. weight...............$6.95
46823½ Steven's Favorite Rifle, 25 calibre, rim fire, 22 inch barrel. Weight,
4½ lbs. Each.................. .. ..$6.95

REMINGTON No. 3 RIFLES.   The Boss Long Range Rifle.

Made by Remington Arms Company, Ilion, N. Y.
Over a Million Sold, Pretty Good Recommendation.   Latest Model, and Every One Perfect and New.
No better target rifle in the market.   We have full octagon only in stock.   All Warranted.

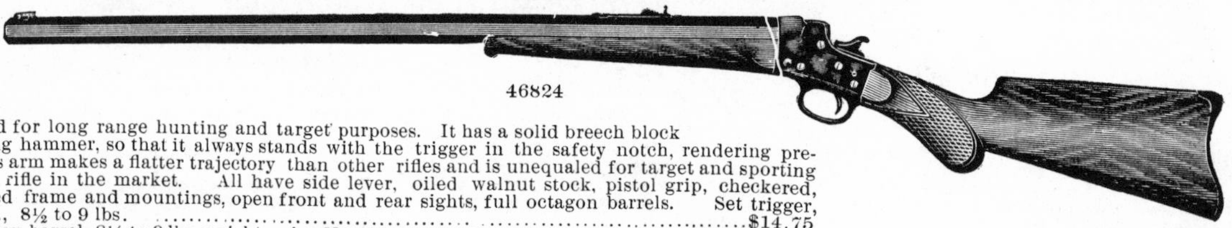

46824

This rifle is especially designed for long range hunting and target purposes. It has a solid breech block
with direct rear support, rebounding hammer, so that it always stands with the trigger in the safety notch, rendering premature discharge impossible.   This arm makes a flatter trajectory than other rifles and is unequaled for target and sporting
use.   No better or more accurate rifle in the market.   All have side lever, oiled walnut stock, pistol grip, checkered,
rebounding hammer, case-hardened frame and mountings, open front and rear sights, full octagon barrels.   Set trigger,
2.75 (extra). 32-30 Caliber, 30 in., 8½ to 9 lbs.   The Boss 200 yd. off hand.
46824 32-40 caliber, 30-inch octagon barrel, 8½ to 9 lbs. weight, using No. 47220 cartridge *only*. The Boss 200 yd. off hand.......................$14.75
46825 38-55 caliber, 30-inch octagon barrel, 8¾ to 9½ lbs. weight, using No. 47222 cartridge *only*. Good for 100 to 500 yards...............$14.75
46826 40-65 caliber, 30-inch octagon barrel, 8¾ to 10 lbs. weight, using No. 47268 cartridge *only*.   Good for 150 to 600 yards............ 14.75
46827 40-90 caliber, 32-inch octagon barrel, 10 to 11 lbs. weight, using No. 47237 cartridge.   Long range............. .... 14.75
46828 45-70 caliber, 30-inch octagon barrel, 10 lbs., using No. 47244 cartridge. Good for 200 to 1,000 yards............................... 16.75
Our Remington rifles are the best, and every one warranted.   Can be returned at our expense if not found as represented.   14.75
Remington Match and Fancy Target Rifles made to order.   The Remington Rifle is used by many of the best shots in the world.   The system of rifling is the
best and material finest.

REMINGTON SINGLE SHOT RIFLES.—Elegant Shooters.

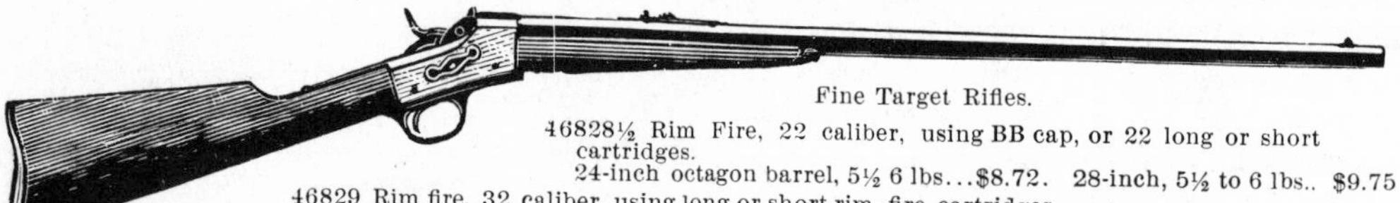

Fine Target Rifles.

46828½ Rim Fire, 22 caliber, using BB cap, or 22 long or short
cartridges.
24-inch octagon barrel, 5½ 6 lbs...$8.72. 28-inch, 5½ to 6 lbs.. $9.75
46829 Rim fire, 32 caliber, using long or short rim, fire cartridges.
28-inch octagon barrel, 5¾ to 6 lbs...... .... 8.75
28-inch octagon barrel, 7 to 7½ lbs., 32 W. C. F. caliber.... ...... 8.80
46830 Remington No. 4 Rifle, 22 caliber, rim fire, long or short cartridge, 22½-inch octagon barrel, 4½ lbs. weight, rifle butt, a fine little rifle and an accurate
shooter, each..$5.00
46830½ Remington No. 4, 32 caliber, rim fire, long or short cartridge, 24-inch barrel............... 5.00

Remington Rifles, No. 4, oiled walnut
stocks, case-hardened frames and mountings,
open front and rear sights. As finely rifled
as any rifle in the market, and made of the
very best rifle material, perfectly accurate,
and every one warranted. No better or
longer range rifles made of these calibers.
Warranted as represented.

MERWIN HULBERT & CO.'S RIFLE.

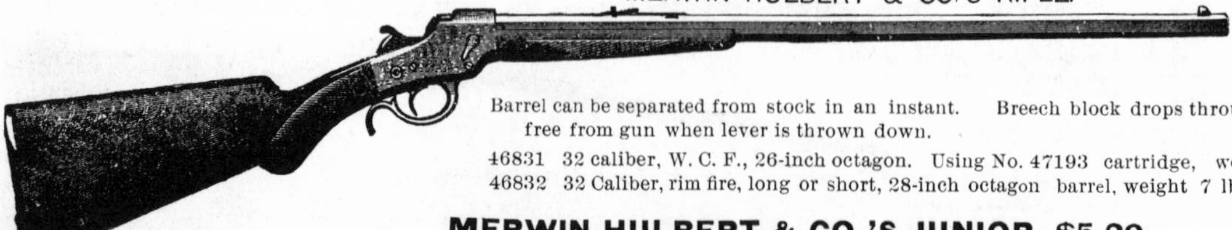

FINE TARGET RIFLES.

Barrel can be separated from stock in an instant.   Breech block drops through frame to load, and ejects the shell
free from gun when lever is thrown down.

46831 32 caliber, W. C. F., 26-inch octagon. Using No. 47193 cartridge, weight, about 7 lbs...............$8.75
46832 32 Caliber, rim fire, long or short, 28-inch octagon barrel, weight 7 lbs........ ... . 8.90

MERWIN HULBERT & CO.'S JUNIOR, $5.20.

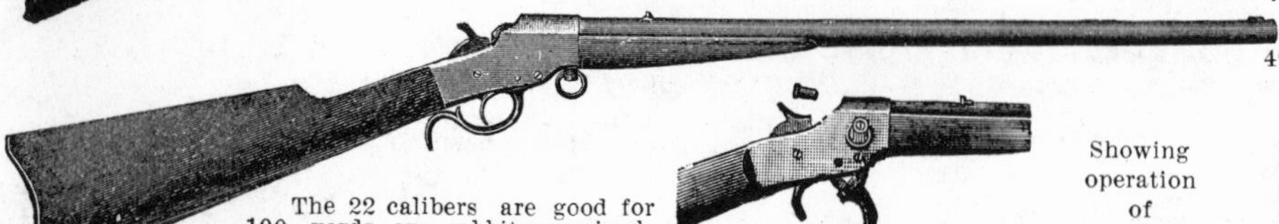

The 22 calibers are good for
100 yards on rabbits, squirrels
and small game. Elegant shooters.

Showing
operation
of
lever.

46833 M. H. & Co.'s Junior Target Rifle, single shot, barrel
easily removed from stock for packing or cleaning, blued
barrels; case-hardened lock plates, 22-inch ROUND BAR-
RELS, about 4½ pounds' weight, perfectly reliable and
accurate, barrel as well rifled as the best rifles; 22 caliber,
RIM FIRE, using BB caps and 22 long and short cartridges.
Ejects the empty shell free from gun, when lever is *thrown
down.* Each.................................$5.20
46833¼ 32 caliber, 26-inch round barrel, rim fire,
long and short cartridge, ivory bead and sporting
rear sights................. .... $6.75

NO. 3 REMINGTON MATCH RIFLE.
THE LONG RANGE TARGET RIFLE.

46833½ A quality, ½ octagon barrel, rebounding hammer, oiled walnut stock, pistol grip, checkered, nickel plated Swiss butt plate, case-hardened frame, Beach combination front and tang graduated rear sights, 32-40 caliber, using No. 47220 cartridge, 28-inch barrel; weight, 8½ to 9 lbs........ ..$18.75
38-55 caliber, using No. 47222 cartridge, 30-inch barrel, weight, 9 to 10 lbs.....................................$19.50
There are no better Target Rifles.

FLOBERT—Remington Action. $2.25.

A cleaning rod is sent with each rifle quoted in this catalogue
Short cartridges are better than long for any 22 caliber rifle, and Flobert's are not made for 22 long cartridges.
Don't expect a Stevens or Winchester in a Flobert rifle.
46835 Flobert Gallery Rifle, Remington action, 22 caliber, BB caps, round and conical, and 22 short *rim fire cartridge*, 24-inch octagon barrel; weight, 6 to 6½ lbs.; is a good short range target or squirrel rifle, oiled walnut stock, shell extractor, rifled barrels, PISTOL GRIP...$2.80
We do not guarantee any Flobert rifle in the market with a long cartridge. They shoot the short cartridge the best.

46834 Flobert Gallery, Rifle Remington action; shoots 22 caliber cap cartridge or 22 short. *rim fire cartridge*; oiled walnut stock, pistol grip, octagon barrel, well rifled and a good shooter. Shell extractor Weight, 4½ lbs.; length of barrel, about 22 inches, Price....................$2.25

RIFLES, $3.25.

New Model Solid Breech.
The Best Model.
46836–38

46837 Flobert Rifle, new model; Warnant action, oiled walnut stock, checkered pistol grip, 24-inch octagon barrel, 6 lbs. weight, shell extractor, 22 caliber, RIM FIRE, short or long cartridge, rifled barrels.... ....$3.40
N. B.—In ordering any 22 caliber rifle we advise only using the short cartridge for accurate work.

46836 Flobert Rifle, Warnant action, new model, oiled walnut stock, checkered pistol grip, 24-inch barrel, 32 caliber, SHORT rim fire, shell extractor. A good, strong shooting rifle, heavy octagon barrel, 6½ lbs., rifled barrel.....$3.25
Prices subject to market changes on Flobert rifles.

STEVENS' IDEAL RIFLE, NO. 107.

46838 Half Octagon Barrel, Beach front sight, open back sight on barrel, vernier peep sight on frame, swiss butt plate nickeled, varnished fore-end and Stock, case-hardened frame. This style rifle can be supplied with Lyman sights, if preferred, at same price.
.22-caliber, long rifle, rim fire 24-inch barrel, 6½ pounds.....................$17.40
25-20 caliber center fire, using 47187 cartridge, 28-inch barrel, 8 pounds weight.....................................$19.80

No. 109

46838½ Ideal Rifle, No. 109, half octagon barrel, wind gauge front and mid-range vernier back sight, no rear barrel sight, fore-end and stock varnished. Frame case hardened and Swiss butt plate nickel plated. Stock easily separated from barrel when desired.
28-inch, 7 lbs., 25-20 caliber, using No. 47187 cartridge...$21.30
30-inch barrel, 8¼ lbs., 32 Ideal caliber, center fire, using No. 47195 cartridge.................................... 20.70
Other calibers and lengths, can be furnished in the Ideal rifles. Prices on application.

FLOBERT RIFLES. $2.55.

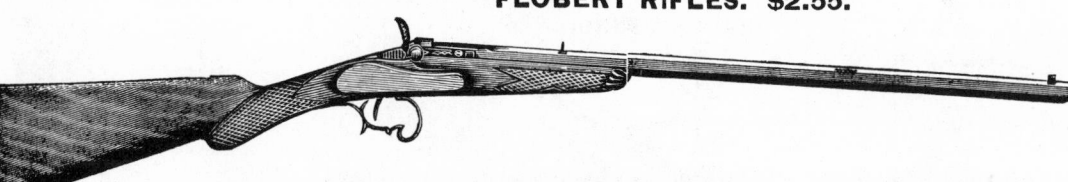

46839 Warnant Action, Flobert Rifle, oiled walnut pistol grip stock, checkered, octagon barrels, blued finish and rifled, safe and reliable, good shooter, 22 caliber, rim fire, shoots BB cap, or 22 short or long cartridges, 22-inch barrels, 4 to 4½ lbs. weight. Each $2.55

H. M. Quackenbush's Safety Cartridge Rifle—A Fine Target Gun, $4.75.

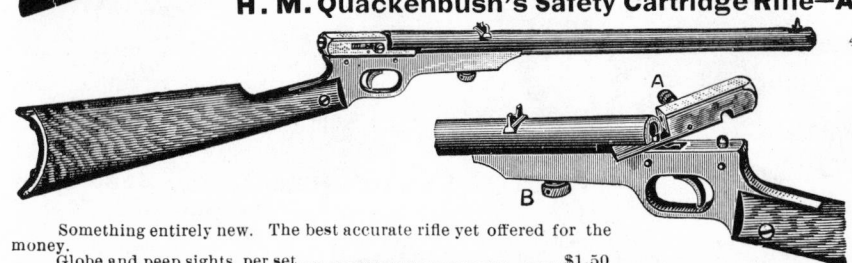

Something entirely new. The best accurate rifle yet offered for the money.
Globe and peep sights, per set...................$1.50

46840 It has a rifle steel barrel, automatic cartridge extractor, and adjustable rear sight; stock is of black walnut handsomely finished, and so fastened to the barrel that the two may be easily and quickly separated, making the arm handy to carry in a trunk, valise or package. The barrel and parts are well and durably nickeled, except the breech block, which is case hardened in colors. Whole length, 33 inches; 18-inch barrel; weight, about 4½ pounds; 22 caliber for regular *rim fire*, "BB" or long and short cartridges. Plain open sights, as shown in cut. Price. 18-inch barrel........ .. ..$4.75
22-inch barrel.. 5.00

THE CHICAGO AIR RIFLE. "OLD RELIABLE." $0.85.
It is not a Spring Gun.
The ball is thrown by compressed air.

46841 The Chicago Air Rifle shoots common BB shot and darts; will kill small game at 50 feet, with the BBs, costs 1 cent to shoot 100 times; the stock and frame are maple, nicely varnished and stained, representing rosewood. The air chamber and inserted barrel are made of drawn brass, accurately bored and polished. The ball is held tight in place in barrel. Plunger and piston made of best steel. Made to stand hard usage. Not liable to get out of order. No smoke, no noise, no caps, death to sparrows and rats, etc. Entire length, 33 inches. Each..... ....$0.85
Postage, extra, 25c. BB shot, 5 pounds for 40c. Darts, per dozen, 35c. Mainsprings, each, 10c.

SOMETHING NEW, BOYS.
A Repeating Air Rifle That Shoots 65 Times Without Reloading. $1.75.

46842 Hart's Repeating Air Rifle. Don't expect these guns to shoot like a first-class rifle. Blue finish metal barrel, black walnut stock, adjustable sights. Just the thing for old or young for amusement and practice. No smoke, no noise, no smell; easy to handle, effective at short range on sparrows, rats and other small game. Shoots "BB" shot, and 65 shot can be placed in the magazine at one time. Only one shot can be discharged at one time. Entire length, 35½ inches, weight, 2¾ pounds Full directions for loading and handling, with 65 shot and 10 paper targets, accompanies rifle Price, $1.75.
BB shot per bag of 5 pounds, 40 cents. Mainsprings, 25 cents. Do not snap these guns unless you have shot in the barrel.

THE DAISY AIR RIFLE, IMPROVED. $0.75.

46845 The Daisy Air Rifle has been improved in many parts and is now one of the best of all metal air rifles in the market. It shoots BB shot, one at a time. All of the parts are made of good strong metal and are not liable to get out of order.
Each..$0.75
BB Shot per sack of 5 lbs., 40 cents.

THE KING AIR RIFLE, $0.90 EACH.

46846 The King Air Rifle. The barrel is made of one continuous piece of Brass, with no soldered joints or levers to break. Neatly nickel plated. Working parts can easily be removed when desired to clean or repair. The latest thing in air guns. Shoots BB shot. One of the strongest and most durable on the market.
Each..$0.90
BB shot per sack of 5 lbs.,................40

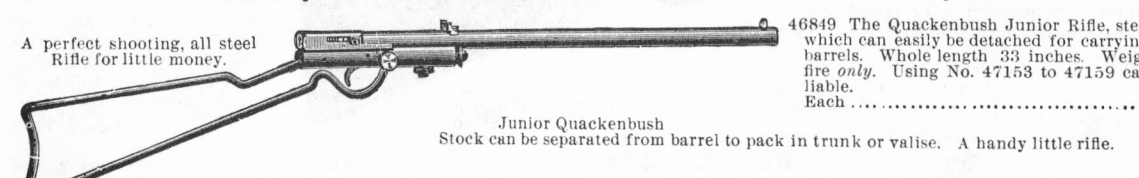

THE QUACKENBUSH JUNIOR SAFETY RIFLE—Finely Rifled—$4.00

A perfect shooting, all steel Rifle for little money.

46849 The Quackenbush Junior Rifle, steel nickel plated, skeleton stock which can easily be detached for carrying in small space. Nickel plated barrels. Whole length 33 inches. Weight, about 4 lbs. 22 caliber, *rim fire only*. Using No. 47153 to 47159 cartridges. Safe, accurate and reliable.
Each..$4.00

Junior Quackenbush
Stock can be separated from barrel to pack in trunk or valise. A handy little rifle.

M. H. & CO.'s FANCY JUNIOR RIFLE—Highest Grade Rifling. Accurate.

46851 Merwin, Hulbert & Co., octagon barrel, fancy Junior rifle, rebounding locks, case hardened frame, solid breech block, polished and checkered walnut stock and fore-end, sporting rear sight, Lyman ivory beadfront sight, nickel plated butt plate, 22 caliber, rim fire, short or long cartridge, 22-inch octagon barrel, 4½ lbs. weight. Safe, accurate and reliable. Barrels easily separated from stock in a moment. Each........ $6.80

THE NEW YORK CLUB RIFLE.

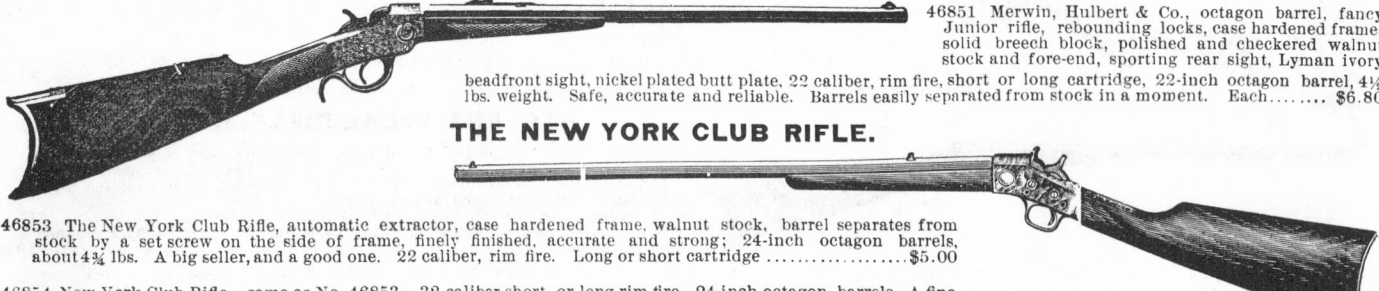

46853 The New York Club Rifle, automatic extractor, case hardened frame, walnut stock, barrel separates from stock by a set screw on the side of frame, finely finished, accurate and strong; 24-inch octagon barrels, about 4¾ lbs. A big seller, and a good one. 22 caliber, rim fire. Long or short cartridge...................$5.00

46854 New York Club Rifle, same as No. 46853. 32 caliber short or long rim fire, 24-inch octagon barrels. A fine shooter, accurate and reliable. Each..$5.00

The Boys' Delight Snip Snap.

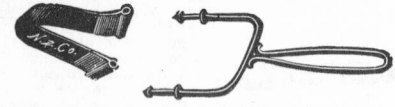

46855 The most accurate and durable Snip Snap ever manufactured.
Each, complete, 5 in. handle.....................$0.09
Per dozen complete......................98
46856 Extra Rubbers, each, 6c; per dozen.........65
Postage on Snip Snap, 5 cents each.
46857 Snip Snap, 2½-inch iron handle and rubber. Each...................................$0.05
Per dozen......................40
Extra rubber, each....................04
Per dozen....................36

Rifle Sights.

When ordering sights for Winchester or other Rifles, mention caliber and model, as the same sights will not fit all calibers. Sights by mail 1 to 4 cents extra.

Lyman's Patent Rifle Sights.

The optical principle involved in these sights is entirely new in its application. When aiming, this sight has the appearance of a ring or hoop, which shows the front sight and the object aimed at, without intercepting any part of the view.

The cut gives an approximate idea of how the sight appears when aiming. It will be noticed that the top of rifle barrel and front sights are seen as distinctly as if no rear sight was used.

46857¼ Lyman's New Front Target Sight, with globe or aperture combination.
Each............$1.35

As Globe.

WHEN sending us an order, be sure to sign your name, and also to give postoffice, county and state, and thus avoid all delay in filling order.

Lyman's Patent Combination Rear Sight on Rifle.

Anyone can attach these sights to a rifle in a few minutes. Lyman sights of all kinds can be furnished for almost every kind of rifle on the market.

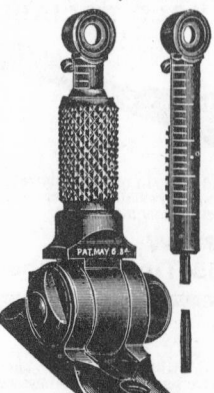

Lyman's Patent Combination Sight.

46858 Showing "point blank" stop pin in the sight stem. Price of this sight...................$2.45
These sights more than double the value of a rifle, either for hunting or target shooting, for instantaneous aim can be taken with great accuracy. The sights are made in all sizes. When ordering, give the make and gauge of rifle.

46858

Lyman's Patent Wind Gauge Sight

46859 Used without the large disk, the principle of this Sight is the same as the Combination Sight. For target shooting it is unequaled, and it is an improvement on the Combination Sight for hunting. Price.......$4.00

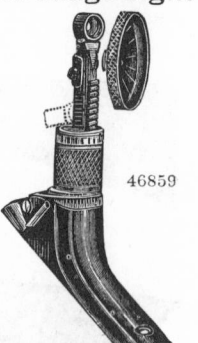

46860 A good sight for quick shooting, also in poor light or with the Jack at night. It will surprise many to find that this large sight is very accurate and that fine target shooting can be done if used with the tang sight. Price.....$0.90

46859

Lyman's Patent Ivory Bead Front Sight.

46861 This Sight gives the sportsman a clear, white bead, which can be seen distinctly against any object in the woods, or in bright sunlight.
Price......................$0.80

Lyman's Patent Improved Ivory Front Sight.

46862 This Sight is better than the Bead Sight for a hunting rifle. The ivory is so well protected by the surrounding metal that there is no danger of its being injured. Price...............$0.42

46863 Blank Piece to replace the rear Crotch Sight, which is usually on the barrel when the rifle is purchased. This Sight should always be removed when Peep Sights are used.
Price......................$0.23

46864 An excellent Spirit Level, which can be used in place of blank piece. Price....................$0.85

WE AIM TO PLEASE . . .
Our customers, and we Guarantee Satisfaction.

ANY ERROR WHICH WE MAY MAKE
we will always gladly rectify.

Lyman's Leaf Sight (Rear).

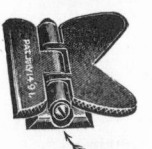

Both leaves folded down.   Using the straight bar.   Using the crotch.

46865 Each $0.75

One leaf is a bar with a triangular ivory center, the other is a wide open V crotch.

Many sportsmen who use the Lyman rear sights do so with the ordinary crotch sight on the barrel. This is much in the way and the shooting is done at a great disadvantage. Lyman's leaf sight can be put in place of it. It folds down close to the barrel, allowing the shooter to use the combination sight in an unobstructed manner, and the result is that the shooting is twice as good as when the ordinary crotch sight is on the barrel. Although the shooter should in any case use the Lyman tang sights for nearly all shooting, he has the satisfaction of knowing that if he wishes to use this leaf sight that it is the best form of crotch and bar sight in use.

The bar leaf is excellent as a twilight sight or when used at night with a jack.

The right-hand screw, as indicated by arrow, adjusts the leaves to fold as tightly as desired.

(Front) Wind-Gauge Target Sight.

Showing Aperture.   Showing Globe.

46866 Each........................ ....$2.40

This is the best wind-gauge ever made for a match rifle. It has a reversible globe and aperture which can be changed quickly. It is compact in form, being close to the barrel. When set for a given point of wind it is locked by a spring clamp firmly in position.

Notice.

The front sight, blank, spirit level and leaf sight should be driven into the barrel slot from the right-hand side.

Combination Rear Tang Sight, With Cup Disk.

46867 ....$2.65

This sight has a large detachable disk and is intended for match rifles and gallery rifles. It is not as good for "all around" shooting as the 46858 combination sight. Many target shooters like it, as it is much better than the vernier peep sight.

The disk is easily removed, and for most work is not needed.

For gallery practice the aperture in the disk can be enlarged to advantage.

When ordering give the make and size of rifle.

Sporting Wind-Gauge Sight.

46868

A good sight for general shooting. It is the combination front sight on the wind-gauge base.

Price $2.27

Lyman's Patent Combination Ivory Front Sight.

46870 One cut shows the Sight with the ivory open part in use, and the other with the globe turned up

Each $0.80

46877 Knife Blade Front Sight, German Silver. Price. $0 48

46877

46879

46878 Knife Blade. Front Sight, Ivory. Price...$0.45

46879 Sporting Front Sight. Price............. .30

GENTLEMEN ~ ~ ~

We Have the Latest and Most Tasty Styles in

LADIES' SHIRT WAISTS.

See that your family does not overlook them.

Sights—Continued.

46880 Sporting Leaf Rear Sight.
Price $1.30

46885 Sporting Rear Sight.
Price.................... $0.78

46880

46886 Wind Gauge Sight, with spirit level and 3 disks.
Each........$3.85

46887 Without spirit level..$2.95

ALWAYS MENTION NAME AND CALIBER OF RIFLE WHEN ORDERING SIGHT.

46890 Beach Combination Sight.
Price........$0.75

As Open. 46890   As Globe. 46890

46891

46891 Globe Sight with interchangeable disk. Price $1.20

46892 Graduated Peep Sight, complete, with screws to fasten to stock of rifle. Each.... ...$2.25

46893 Mid Range Vernier Peep Sight, complete with screws to fasten to stock of rifle.

Each $3.90

The Lyman, Vernier and Graduated Peep Sights can be put on rifle in five minutes by any person with screw driver.   46893

46892

In ordering sights state caliber and maker's name of rifle, as the sights are made to fit only one special rifle and the same base will not fit all rifles.

46896 Winchester Express Front Sight.
Each $0.45

46897 Winchester Express Rear Sight. Each........... .....$1.48

Ballard and Marlin Sights.

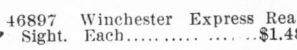

46898 Rocky Mountain Front Sight (knife edge).
Each.. .. .. $0.43

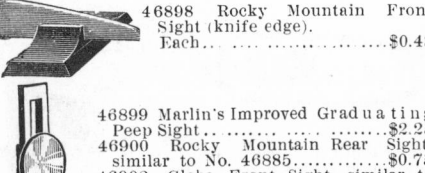

46899 Marlin's Improved Graduating Peep Sight $2.25

46900 Rocky Mountain Rear Sight, similar to No. 46885............$0.75

46902 Globe Front Sight, similar to 46891. No extra disks.

Each $0.95

Always give name and caliber of rifle when ordering parts.

Lyman's Patent Ivory Shot Gun Sights.

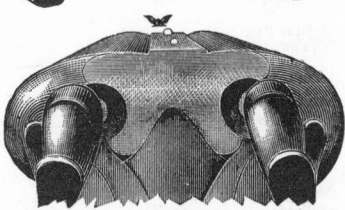

A New System of Sighting Shot Guns.

Postage, extra, 11 cents.

46904 The left hand cut shows the large muzzle or front sight. The right hand cut, the small rear sight. This sight is placed 18 inches from the muzzle sight.

The first engraving gives the appearance of the sights when aiming at a straight-a-way bird. The second engraving shows the effect of these sights when the gun is held correctly for a quartering bird.

The elevation of the gun is right, but the rear sight shows that the gun is out of line, which would not be discovered if these sights were not used. This system is a great help both in the field and at the trap. Price, per set.$0.85

Gun Repairing Department.

We have the largest jobbing gun repair shop in the country. None but experienced workmen employed, and each one an expert in his line. We have one of the best stockers and one of the best barrel borers in the world, and can guarantee the highest grade work in every particular on the finest guns. Give us a trial. We guarantee satisfaction. All kinds of repairing done; fine work a specialty. Price as low as first-class work can be done.

We do not change muzzle loaders to breech loaders, for it costs more to do it than you would have to pay for a first-class breech loader ready-made.

Stocks bent, stocks straightened; new stock made same drop as old one, or changed any way you may desire.

When you send us a gun, rifle or parts, send us a letter at the same time, giving full description of the article, name of the gun, style, etc., and also state plainly what you want done.

Gun Material and Gun Repairing.

N. B.—These parts are not fitted or case hardened and are for hand-made guns only, and require fitting. We cannot fit them unless we have the gun here, and then we would have to make an extra charge for the labor. Always send the old part you wish duplicate for, if possible, as no two guns have parts just alike, and a part that would fit one gun would not fit another of the same make and cost. Hammers, etc., for American machine made guns cost much more than those quoted here. Parts for all American made shot guns and rifles, in stock, are furnished on short notice.

Flobert Rifle Parts.

By mail, 2 to 4 cents extra.

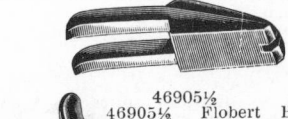

These parts are soft iron in the rough, and not fitted, but plain as shown in cuts. They are blocked out large, and require a great deal of filing to fit them to the rifle. We cannot fit them unless we have the rifle here, and then we would have to make an extra charge for the labor.

No two rifles are just alike, and all Flobert rifles are hand made, and all are imported from Europe.

46905 Flobert Hammers, Remington action, cut nose, not fitted. Each........................$0 50

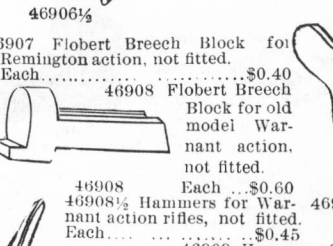

46905½

46905½ Flobert Breech Block for new model Warnant rifles, filed, just blocked out.
Each $0.80

46906½ Flobert Hammer, for new model Warnant, not fitted.
Each $0.50

46906½

46907 Flobert Breech Block for Remington action, not fitted.
Each....................$0.40

46908 Flobert Breech Block for old model Warnant action, not fitted.

46908   Each ...$0.60

46908½ Hammers for Warnant action rifles, not fitted.
Each.... ....$0.45

46909 Hammers for Warnant 6 lb. rifles..............$0.70

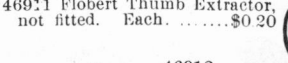

46908½   46909½

46909½ Flobert Trigger, not fitted.
Each........................ $0 25

46910 Flobert Extractor for Remington action, not fitted. Each. $0.20

46911 Flobert Thumb Extractor, not fitted. Each. $0 20

46912— Flobert Mainspring, not fitted.
Each.. $0.25

46912   46911

Rifle Parts—Continued.

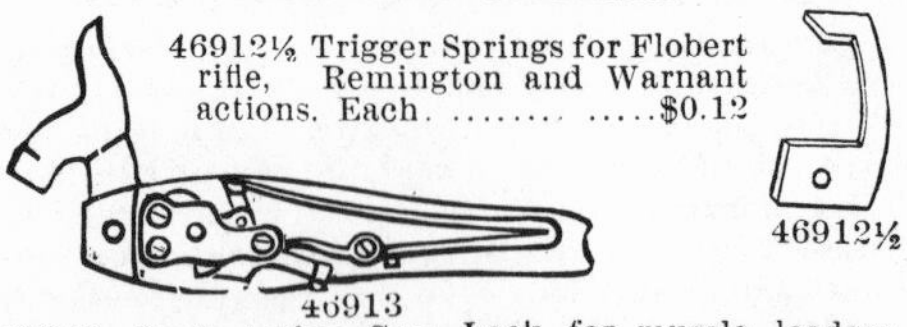

46912½ Trigger Springs for Flobert rifle, Remington and Warnant actions. Each..............$0.12

46912½

46913

46913 Back Action Gun Lock, for muzzle loaders. Each..........$0.75 Each, better grade.... $1.50

Postage on locks, 6 cts. extra.

46913½ Bar Locks, for muzzle-loading shotguns. Each...... $1.25 And according to quality Each. $1.50

46913½ 46914½

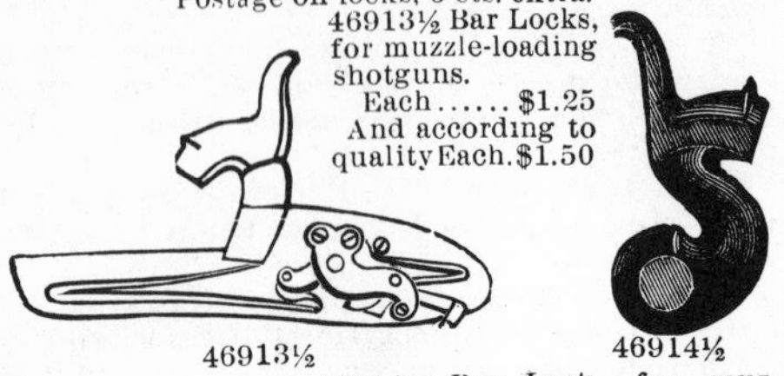

46914 Bar Lock, for muzzle-loading rifles. Each..........................$1.25

46914½ Hammer, for breech loading shotguns, plain stamped.........................$0.23

Polished and filed (not fitted) $0.50, .75, 1.00. 1.50.

Hammers and parts, 2 to 4 cents extra by mail

46914

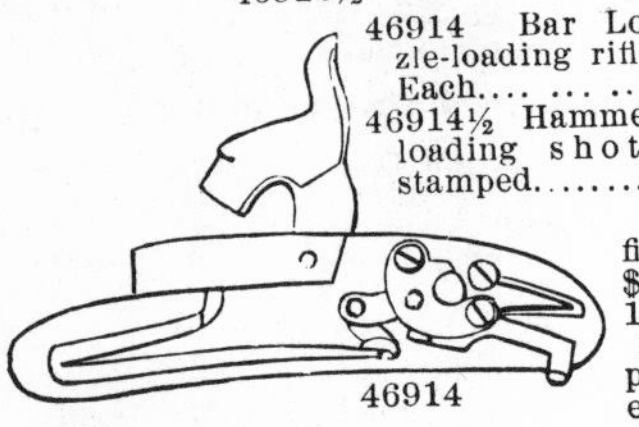

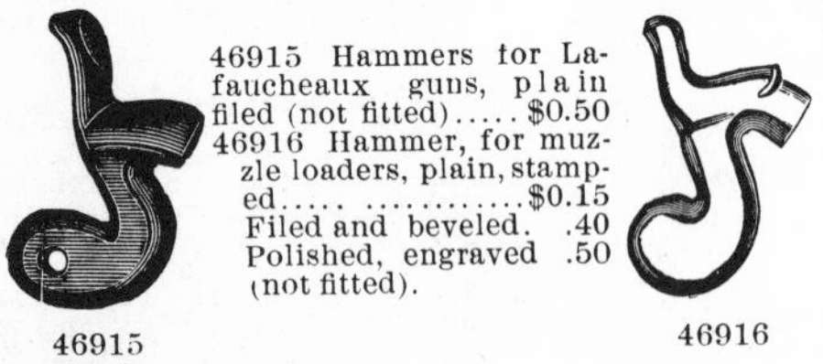

46915 Hammers for Lafaucheaux guns, plain filed (not fitted)..... $0.50

46916 Hammer, for muzzle loaders, plain, stamped.....................$0.15

Filed and beveled. .40

Polished, engraved .50 (not fitted).

46915 46916

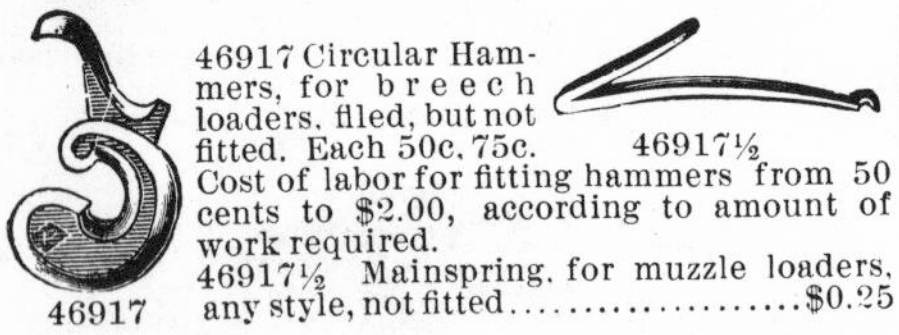

46917 Circular Hammers, for breech loaders, filed, but not fitted. Each 50c, 75c.

46917½

Cost of labor for fitting hammers from 50 cents to $2.00, according to amount of work required.

46917 46917½ Mainspring, for muzzle loaders, any style, not fitted.........................$0.25

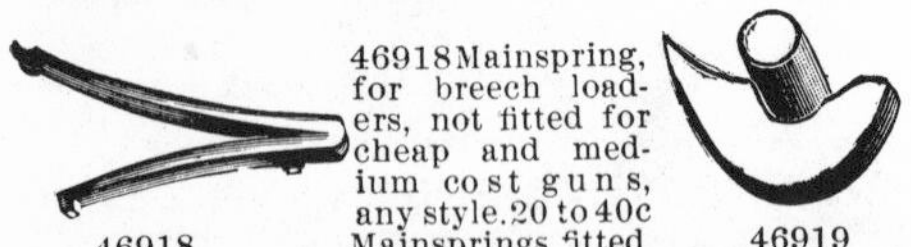

46918 Mainspring, for breech loaders, not fitted for cheap and medium cost guns, any style. 20 to 40c

46918 Mainsprings fitted 46919

25 cents to $1.25 extra, according to quality and how much labor is required.

Always state whether right or left hand parts are wanted.

46919 Hook Tumblers for back or front action locks, not fitted. Each..............................$0.15

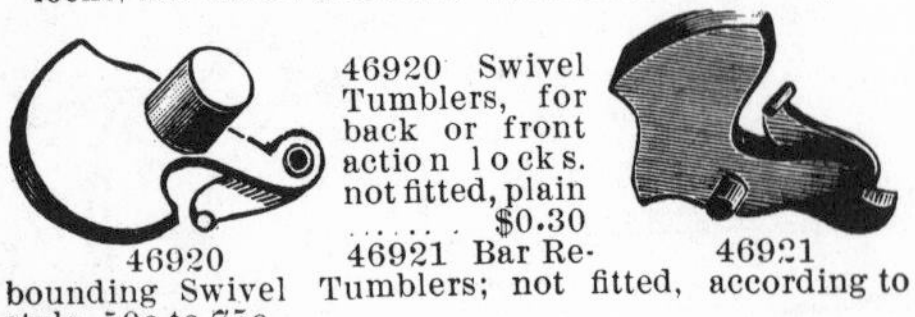

46920 Swivel Tumblers, for back or front action locks, not fitted, plain..........$0.30

46920 46921 Bar Rebounding Swivel Tumblers; not fitted, according to style, 50c to 75c. 46921

Cost of labor for fitting tumblers, $1.50 to $2.50, according to work done. If you send too much money we will refund the balance.

Send your old parts, or the whole lock is the better way, when it needs repairing.

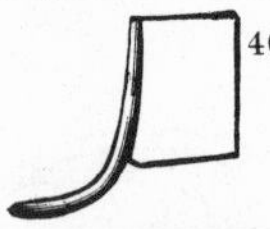

46925 Triggers, malleable iron, not fitted..............................$0.20

Cost of fitting, extra, 35c to...... .75

Always state whether right or left hand parts are wanted.

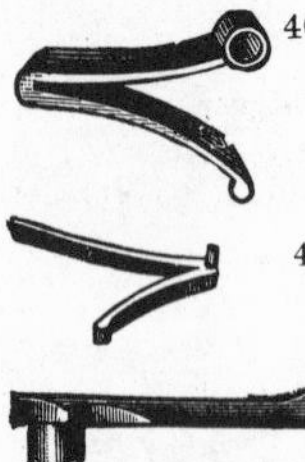

46926 Top Lever Springs, not fitted, 40c. and 75c. and $1.00, according to style and quality. Send old part for sample. If too much money is sent, will refund the balance. Cost of fitting, 25c. to 50c. extra

46926½ Top Lever Springs for breech loaders.................. $0.40

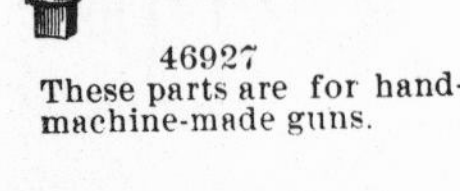

46927 Top Snap Levers, filed and blue. Each.................. $0.89

46927

These parts are for hand-made guns, not American machine-made guns.

Rifle Parts—Continued.

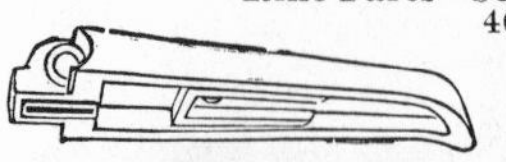

46929 Lefaucheux Fore-end Irons, filed, not finished, single key. Each..............$1.50

Postage, extra, 8 cents

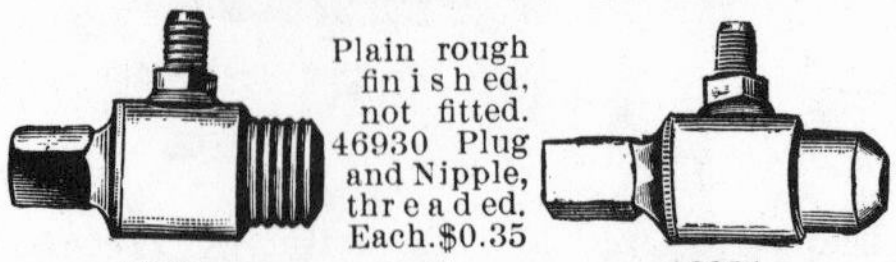

Plain rough finished, not fitted. 46930 Plug and Nipple, threaded. Each. $0.35

46930 46931

46931 Plug and Nipple, plain, each.............$0.25

Postage on parts, 3 to 6 cents extra.

46932 46933.

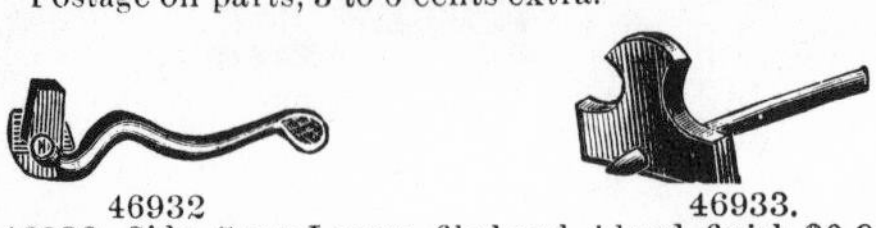

46932 Side Snap Levers filed and blued finish. $0.90

46933 Extractors, milled, not fitted, Each..... .50

Cost of fitting $2.00 to $2.50 extra; cannot fit extractors, unless we have barrels.

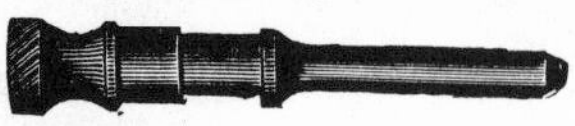

46934 Zulu Plungers or firing pins. Each...$0.35

46935 Zulu Plunger Springs, Each................................ .05

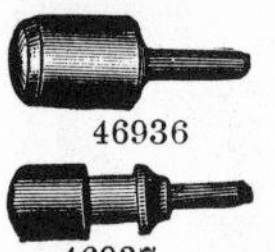

46936 46936 Solid Head Plunger for firing pins, plain iron, not fitted, each............................. .18

46937 Solid Head Plunger or firing pins, not fitted........ .30

46937 Cost of fitting firing pins, 25c. to 50c. extra, according to size.

46938 Plain Plunger or firing pin.......................... .08

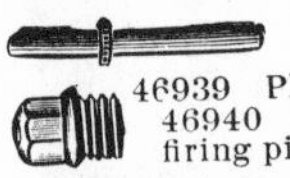

46939 Plunger Springs.................. .05

46940 Nipple Seats, for guns using firing pins, like 46938.................. .35

Gun Tubes.

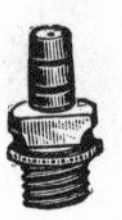

46941 Gun Tubes, common muzzle loaders, 5, 8, 10, 15 and 20 cents each; 50c, 75c.. $1.00 $1.50, $1.75 and $2.00 per dozen, according to quality.

	Each.	Per doz.
46942 Musket Tubes.............	$0.06	$0.63
46943 Musket Tubes, small top.	.08	.84

Always send old parts with your order, as no two guns are just alike.

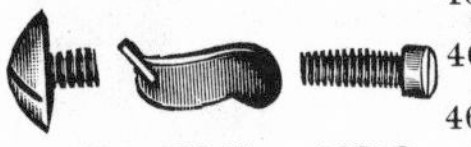

46946 Tumbler Pins, threaded...........$0.05

46947 Swivels, malleable..................$0.10

46948 Inside Lock Screws...............$0.05

46946 46947 46948

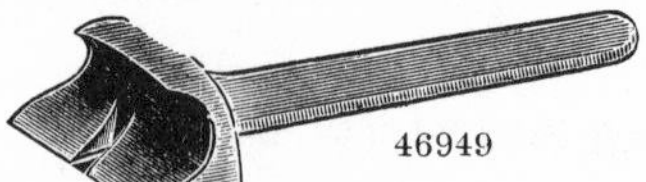

46949 Fore-end Irons, milled. $0.35

46949

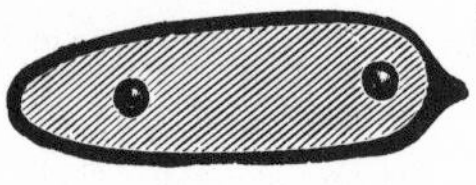

46950 Rubber Butt Plates finished and fancy patterns.............$0.75

46952 Bolt Loop Breech Loaders. $0.10

46953 Bolt Loop Muzzle Loaders .10

46952

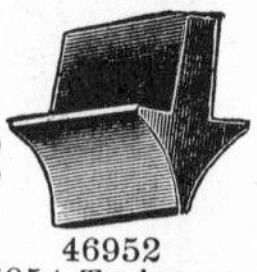

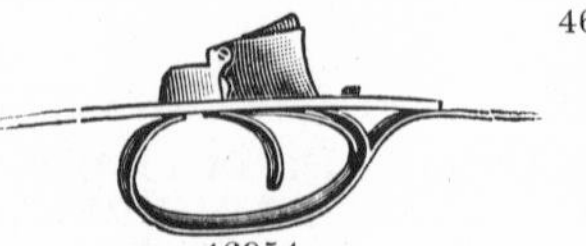

46954 Trigger Guards, complete for breech loaders, wrought iron-spring triggers. Per set... $1.80

46954

46955 Belgium Fring Pins.. $0.15

46956 Break-off for muzzle loaders, forged.................................$0.30

46957 Sear Spring, for back action locks...$0.18

46955 46956

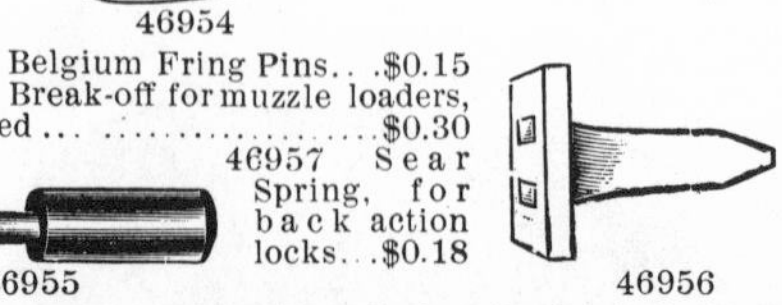

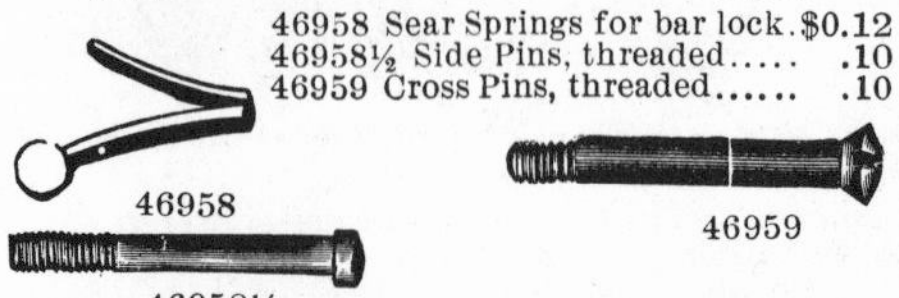

46958 Sear Springs for bar lock. $0.12

46958½ Side Pins, threaded..... .10

46959 Cross Pins, threaded...... .10

46958 46959

46958½

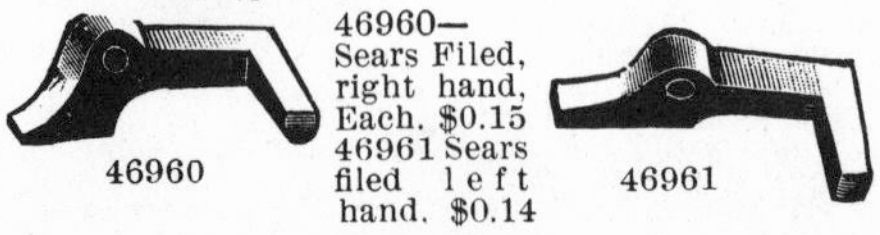

46960—Sears Filed, right hand, Each. $0.15

46961 Sears filed left hand. $0.14

46960 46961

Rifle Parts—Continued.

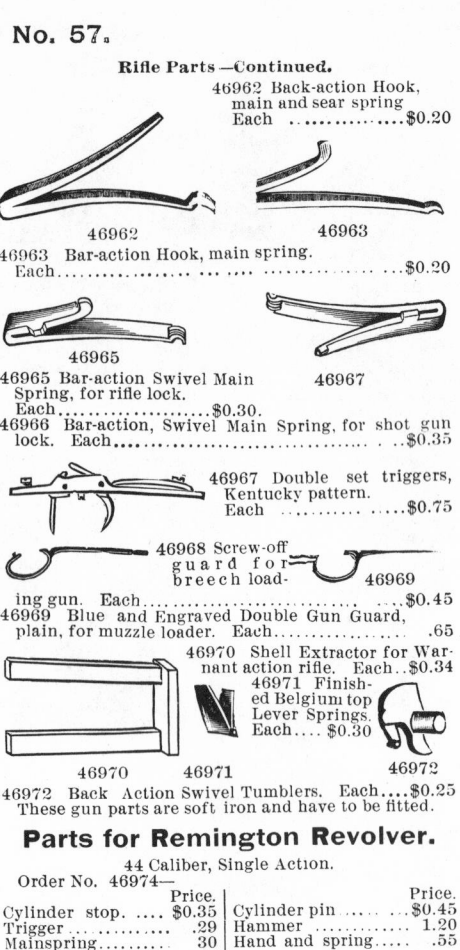

46962 Back-action Hook, main and sear spring Each.....................$0.20

46962 46963

46963 Bar-action Hook, main spring. Each...$0.20

46965 46967

46965 Bar-action Swivel Main Spring, for rifle lock. Each......................$0.30.

46966 Bar-action, Swivel Main Spring, for shot gun lock. Each...$0.35

46967 Double set triggers, Kentucky pattern. Each..................$0.75

46968 Screw-off guard for breech loading gun. Each...............................$0.45

46969

46969 Blue and Engraved Double Gun Guard, plain, for muzzle loader. Each.................. .65

46970 Shell Extractor for Warnant action rifle. Each..$0.34

46971 Finished Belgium top Lever Springs. Each.... $0.30

46970 46971 46972

46972 Back Action Swivel Tumblers. Each....$0.25

These gun parts are soft iron and have to be fitted.

Parts for Remington Revolver.

44 Caliber, Single Action.

Order No. 46974—

	Price.		Price.
Cylinder stop.	$0.35	Cylinder pin..........	$0.45
Trigger..............	.29	Hammer..............	1.20
Mainspring..........	30	Hand and spring.....	.55
Sear and bolt........	.20		

Parts for Remington Shot Gun.

Order No. 46975—

	Price.		Price.
Extractor..	$0.75	Sear spring...........	$0.25
Hammer..............	1.50	Solid head plungers..	.15
Lever spring........	.25	Tumblers..............	.50
Mainspring........	.75	Tumbler pins.........	.15
Sear..................	.30	Tumbler stirrup	.15
Triggers, right and left hand..........	.25	Trigger plates........	1.00
Joint Check and Extractor.............	.25	Guard bow............	1.00

Parts for Remington Rifle.

Order No. 46976—

	Each. Nos. 1, 1½, 2 Rifles.	Each. No. 3 Rifles.
Extractor..........................	$0.30	$0.30
Extractor spring...................	.20	
Firing pin..........................	.20	.20
Hammer............................	1.00	1.00
Lever...............................	.30	1.25
Lever spring.......................	.20	.40
Mainspring.........................	.40	.40
Rocker..............................	......	.75
Trigger.............................	.40	.40
Butt stock, straight grip........	2.00	......
Butt stock, pistol grip..........	......	4.00

Parts for Colt's Revolver.

Order No. 46977—	Army double.	38 and 41 double.	Army single action.
Cylinder..............................	$3.00	$2.25	$3.00
Hammer...............................	1.50	1.10	.97
Hand..................................	.30	.20	.25
Rear sear.............................	.60	.30	......
Front sear............................	.30	.25	......
Trigger................................	.55	.50	.35
Rear sear and bolt spring....	......	.20	...
Cylinder pin.........................	.49	.50	.49
Trigger spring......................	.49	.25	......
Mainspring...........................	.50	.50	.35
Ejector rod and head..........	.70	.50	.70
Ejector tube........................	1.55	1.25	1.50
Ejector spring......................	.15	.10	.15
Hand spring........................	......	.10	......
Front sear spring.................	......	.10	......
Cylinder pin bushing...........	.45	......	.45
Trigger guard......................	1.75	1.50	1.75
Barrel, blued or plated	3.00	1.50	3.00
Cylinder pin catch complete	.30	.25	......
Screws, each.......................	.10	.05	.10

Hunting Boots. We are right in line; best goods at low prices.

Component Parts of the H. & R. Automatic Double Action Revolvers. 32 and 38 Calibers. Harrington & Richardson Arms Co.

Always mention the caliber of revolver when ordering, and return broken or worn parts when possible.

Order No. 46980—

Guard	$0.60	Lever Spring	$0.15
Cylinder	1.75	Cylinder Catch	.15
Cylinder Ratchet or Extractor	.60	Trigger	.45
Barrel Catch Bolt	.20	Trigger Spring	.20
Barrel Catch Bolt Spg	.04	Trigger Pin	.04
" Catch Bolt Screw	.06	Sear	.20
Barrel Catch	.60	Sear Spring	.05
Barrel Catch Spring	.15	Guard Pin	.04
Barrel Catch Spring Screw	.05	Friction Spring	.05
Barrel Catch Screw	.05	Hinge Screw	.15
Quill	.45	Main Spring	.20
Quill Pin	.04	Stock, right	.35
Center pin	.30	Stock, left	.35
Center Pin Spring	.15	Escutcheons, nut	.05
Hammer	.55	Escutcheons, head	.05
Hammer Screw	.05	Stock Screw	.05
Sight	.05	Stock Pin	.02
Lifter	.35	Hook for Auto	.85
Lifter Pin	.05	Hook Bushing	.20
Lever	.20	Frame Catch	.55
		Frame Catch Spring	.05

Component Parts of American, Young America and Safety Hammer Double Action Revolvers. Harrington & Richardson Arms Co.

Always mention the caliber of revolver when ordering, and return worn or broken parts when possible.

Order No. 46981—

Cylinder	$0.60	Friction Pin Spring	$0.02
Center Pin	.15	Guard	.50
Center Pin Catch	.15	Guard Pin	.05
Center Pin Catch Spg	.05	Stock, right	.15
Center pin Catch Pin	.05	Stock, left	.15
Hammer	.50	Stock Screw	.06
Safety Hammer	.50	Stock Pin	.04
Hammer Screw	.05	Escutcheons, head	.06
Lifter	.25	Escutcheons, thread	.06
Lifter Pin	.05	Sear	.15
Lever	.15	Sear Spring	.04
Lever Spring	.15	Sear Pin	.04
Trigger	.35	Sight	.10
Trigger Spring	.15	Gate for 44 cal. only	.25
Trigger Pin	.02	Gate Spring	.05
Main Spring	.20	Gate Spring Screw	.05
Friction Pin	.05	Gate screw	.05

Parts for American Side Snap Gun.

Order No. 46982—

Main Springs	$0.25	Plungers	$0.15
Triggers	.18	Hammers	.45
Extractors	.30	Side Levers	.45
Lever Springs	.15	Butt Stocks	2.00

Send old parts when possible.

Parts for American Trigger Gun.

Order No. 46983 State gauge of gun.

Front Trigger	$0.45	Main Springs	$0.20
Rear Trigger	.25	Barrel Screw	.25
Trigger Springs	.15	Guards	.40
Extractors	.35	Butt Stocks	2.25
Plungers	.15		

Send old parts when possible.

Parts for Champion Top Lever Gun.

Order No. 46984—

Butt Stocks	$3.35	Firing Pins and Nut	$0.23
Triggers	.20	Main Springs	.65
Trigger Springs	.20	Top Lever Springs	.15
Hammers	.40		

Send old parts when possible.

Parts for the Perfection Breech Loader.

State gauge of your gun.

Order No. 46985—

	Each.		Each.
Tumblers	$0.40	Firing Pins & Springs	$0.40
Locking Bolts	35	Triggers	.40
Main Springs	.20	Hammers	.35
Extractors	.20	Top Lever Springs	.15
Top Levers	.30	Guards	.35
Stirrups	.10	Butt Stocks	2.50
Screws	.05	Fore-Arms	1.50
Trigger Springs	.15		

Send old parts when possible.

Parts for Merwin & Hulbert Junior Rifle.

State caliber of your rifle.

Order No. 46986—

	Each.		Each.
Main Springs	$0.50	Hammers	$0.80
Lever Springs	.50	Extractors	.80
Extractor Screws	.30	Guard Levers	1.50
Trigger Springs	.20	Barrel Key, with ring	.40
Firing Pins	.40	Butt Stocks	4.00

Send old parts when possible.

Parts for Forehand & Wadsworth Revolvers.

Order No. 46987—

	Each.		Each.
Extractors, complete	$0.60	Hammers	$0.48
Barrel Catch, automatic	.35	Main Springs	.15
		Base Pins	.25
Barrel Catch (hammerless)	.60	Guards	.55
		Triggers	.50
Cylinder Catcher	.15	Hand or Lever	.15

State caliber and send old parts when possible.

Parts for Forehand & Wadsworth Shot Gun.

Order No. 46988. Single Barrel.

	Each.		Each.
Hammers	$0.40	Extractors	$0.35
Plungers	.20	Top Levers	.40
Triggers	.15	Main Springs	.15
Top Lever Springs	.12	Fore-Arms	1.40
Tumblers	.30	Butt Stocks	2.00
Tumbler Pins	.06		

State caliber and send old parts when possible.

30--2nd

Parts for Marlin Safety Repeatiug Rifle.

Order No. 46989—Model 1891.

	Each.		Each.
Barrel (round)	$4.69	Main Spring	.30
Barrel (octagon or ½ octagon)	6.00	Main Spring Screw	.05
Beech Bolt	2.00	Magazine Tube (outside)	1.50
Butt Stock	1.50	Magazine Tube (inside)	1.50
Butt Plate	80	Magazine Tube Spring	.20
Carrier	1.30	Magazine Tube Spring Follower	.15
Carrier Rocker	.35	Magazine Tube Plug	.25
Carrier Rocker Spring	15	Magazine Tube Plug Pin	.05
Carrier Rocker Spring Screw	.05	Magazine Tube Stud	.15
Extractor	.30	Magazine Tube Stud Screw	.05
Ejector	.30	Receiver	6.00
Ejector Screw	.05	Trigger	.30
Firing Pin	.60	Sear	.30
Finger Lever	1.50	Sear Spring	.10
Finger Lever Spring	.25	Sear Spring Screw	.05
Finger Lever Spring Screw	.05	Tang Screw	.10
Cartridge Stop (22 caliber only)	.30	Safety Catch	.30
Cartridge Stop Screw	.05	Safety Catch Pin	.04
Fore-Arm	.60	Side Plate	1.50
Fore-Arm Tip	.60	Side Plate Screw	.20
Hammer	.60		
Hammer Screw	.10		

The 22 caliber was at first made to load through a gate in the side of the receiver and if parts for this old style are wanted please so specify, otherwise parts for rifle as now made will be sent. In case the carrier *complete* is desired please so specify, otherwise the carrier will be sent without rocker, etc. State caliber and send old part when possible.

Marlin Safety Repeating Rifle.

Order No. 46990—Model 1889.

Barrel, carbine, 20-inch	$3.60	Forearm Tip Tenon Screws (2)	$0.10
Barrel, round rifle, 24 inch	4.30	Hammer	.60
Barrel, octagon or ½ oct., rifle, 24 inch	5.40	Hammer Screw	.10
Breech Bolt	1.50	Locking Bolt	.60
Butt Stock	1.30	Main Spring	.30
Carrier	1.30	Main Spring Screw	.05
Carrier Screw	.05	Magazine Tube	1.50
Carrier Rocker	.35	Magazine Tube Spring	.20
Carrier Rocker Pin	.04	Magazine Tube Spring Follower	.10
Extractor	.30	Magazine Tube Plug	.10
Extractor Pin	.04	Magazine Tube Stud	.15
Ejector	.30	Magazine Tube Stud Screw	.05
Ejector Screw	.05	Receiver	6.00
Firing Pin	.60	Loading Spring Cover	.30
Firing Pin Pin	.04	Loading Spring Cover	
Finger Lever	1.50	Trigger	.30
Finger Lever Screw	.05	Sear Spring	.10
Finger Lever Catch	.14	Sear Spring Screw	.05
Finger Lever Catch Pin	.04	Tang Screw	.10
Firing Lever Catch Spring	.06	Trigger Plate	1.60
Fore-Arm	.60	Trigger Plate Screw	.05
Fore-Arm Tip	.60	Sear	.30
		Safety Catch	.30

In ordering any of the above parts, state what kind of rifle, whether Carbine, Plain Rifle or Pistol Grip, parts are wanted for, and caliber.

Above prices for barrels are for rifles 24 inch. For additional length of barrels, add $0.75 for each additional inch.

Parts for Marlin Safety Repeating Rifle. Model 1893.

Order No. 46991—

Barrel, Carbine, 20-inch	$4.50	*Magazine Tube Spring Follower	.10
Barrel, Round Rifle, 26-inch	5.40	*Magazine Tube Plug	.10
Octagon or ½ Octagon Rifle, 26-inch	6.00	*Magazine Tube Stud	.15
Breech Bolt	2.50	*Magazine Tube Stud Screw	.05
*Butt Stock	1.50	Receiver	6.00
*Butt Plate	.80	Loading Spring Cover	.50
*Butt Plate Screws (2)	.10	*Loading Spring Cover Screw	.05
Carrier	2.00	*Trigger	.45
*Carrier Screw	.05	*Trigger Pin	.04
Carrier Rocker	.35	*Trigger Spring	.15
Carrier Rocker Spring	.05	*Trigger Spring Screw	.05
Carrier Rocker Pin	.04	Trigger Plate	2.00
*Extractor	.30	*Trigger Plate Screw	.05
*Extractor Pin	.04	*Tang Screw	.10
*Ejector	.36	*Front Band for Carbine	.35
*Ejector Screw	.05	*Front Band for Carbine Screw	.05
Firing Pin (2 pieces)	.60	*Rear Band for Carbine	.35
Firing Pin Spring	.05	*Rear Band for Carbine Screw	.05
Firing Pin	.04	*Magazine Tube Plug Screw for Carbine	.05
Finger Lever (with friction plunger)	2.00	*Butt Plate for Carbine	.80
*Finger Lever Screw	.05	*Sling Ring and Staple for Carbine	.30
*Forearm	.60	*Stock Swivel and Screw	.40
*Forearm Tip	.60	*Tip Swivel	.40
*Forearm Tip Tenon	.35	*Dummy Screw (to fill sight screw holes in tang)	.04
*Forearm Tip Tenon Screws (2)	.10		
*Hammer	.60		
*Hammer Screw	.10		
*Locking Bolt	.75		
Main Spring	.30		
*Main Spring Screw	.05		
*Magazine Tube	1.50		
*Magazine Tube Spring	.20		

Parts marked thus * are interchangeable with parts of the Model 1894 rifle 38 and 44 calibers. Send old parts if possible and state caliber of your rifle.

Parts for Marlin Rifle, Model 1894.

25, 32, 38 and 44 caliber.

Send old part when possible. Give caliber when ordering.

Order No. 46992--

Barrel, Carbine, 20-inch, round	$3.60	Finger Lever, with friction plunger	$1.30
Barrel, round, 24-inch	4.30	Magazine Tube	1.13
Barrel, octagon, 24-inch	5.40	Magazine Tube Spring	.20
Breech Bolt	1.50	Magazine Tube Spring Follower	.10
Carrier	1.20	Magazine Tube Plug	.10
Carrier Rocker	.35	Magazine Tube Stud Screw	.05
Carrier Pin	.04	Receiver	5.00
Ejector	.30	Trigger Plate	1.20
Firing Pin, 2 pieces	.60		
Firing Pin Spring	.05		
Main Spring	.30		

Parts for Remington No. 4 Rifle.

22 and 32 caliber,

Order No. 47016—

			Each.
Extractor	$0.50	Firing pin	.20
Trigger block and extractor pin	.25	Main spring	.40
		Trigger	.50
Hammer	.60	Butt stock	1.25

Parts for Smith & Wesson Revolvers.

Postage, 2 to 3 cents extra.

Order No. 47017.	32 Single Action.	32 Double Action.	32 Hammer-less	38 Single Action.	38 Double Action.	38 Hammer-less.	44 Single Action.	44 Double Action.	32 and 38 Target.
Barrel Catch	$0.40	.40	.30	.40	.40	.15	.60	....	1.10
Cylinder Stop	.30	.30	.45	.35	.35	.45	.35	1.35	.25
Extractor	.87	.85	.85	.85	.85	.85	1.10	1.10	1 00
Extractor Spring	.10	.10	.10	.10	.10	10	.10	.15	.10
Front Sear	....	.40	.45	....	.35	.45	....	.45	....
Guard	...	.60	.60	....	.60	.55	.55	.85	.55
Hammer	.50	.55	.55	.55	.55	.40	.85	.85	.85
Hand	.30	.30	.30	.30	35	.35	.40	.40	.46
Hand Spring	.12	.12	.12	.15	.15	.15	15	.15	.15
Main Spring	.30	.30	.30	.35	.35	.35	.35	.35	.35
Rear Sear	....	.30	....	..	.40	....	...	.30	....
Rear Sear Spring	....	.45	....		.25	....	...	25	...
Side plate	.30	.35	.30	.45	.45	.35	.40	.40	.35
Triggers	.30	.30	.30	.40	.30	.40	.30	.60	.30
Trigger spring	.12	.12	.12	.12	.12	.12	.30	.30	30

State caliber and our catalogue number on guns when ordering parts.

Parts for Ballard.

Order No. 47018.

	Each.		Each.
Trigger, plain	$0.50	Front Set Trigger spring, No. 5 rifle	$0.25
Front Set Trigger, No. 5 rifle	.65	Rear Set Trigger spring, No. 5 rifle	.35
Rear Set Trigger, No. 5 rifle	.65	Mainsprings	.40

State caliber and number of rifle in ordering parts.

Parts for Stevens' Rifles.

32 and 22 Caliber.

Order No. 47020—

	Price.		Price.
Hammer	$0.70	Mainspring	$0.19
Trigger	.45	Sear Spring	.19
Barrel Catch and Spring	.36	Barrel Screw	.13
Barrel Catch Nut	.15	Firing Pin	.29
Extractor	.39	Firing Pin Screw	.38
Extractor Bar	.40	Extractor Spring	.39

Parts for Stevens' Tip-up Pistol.

Order No. 47021—

	Price		Price
Hammer	$0.39	Barrel Catch Nut	$0.15
Mainspring	.17	Extractor	30
Trigger Spring	.35	Extractor Spring	.25
Barrel Catch and Spring	.27		

Parts for Winchester Shot Guns.

Lever Action.

Order No. 47022—

	Price.		Price.
Mainspring	$0 50	Magazine Tips	$0.50
Firing Pin	.25	Magazine Tubes	.90
Firing Pin Spring	.10	Cartridge lifter	25
Extractor, single	.30	Trigger Spring	.15
Extractor Pin and Spring	.15	Trigger	.45
		Carrier Screws	.05
Hammer	.75	Breech Block Stud	.20
Extractor, left hand	.30	Butt Stock	2.50
Extractor, right hand	.30	Carrier, right	1.00
Breech Block Pins	.10	Carrier, left	.60
Tang Screw	.10	Blued Steel, 10 or 12 ga.	7.50
Magazine Followers	.45		

Component Parts of the Winchester Repeating Rifle, Model 1892.

Order No. 47022½—

	Price.		Price.
Barrel, Round	$4.30	Cartridge Guide, right hand	.30
Barrel, Octagon	5.40	Cartridge Guide, left hand, 32 caliber	.60
Barrel, Carbine	4.20	Cartridge Guide Screws (2), each	.05
Breech Bolt	2.75	Cartridge Stop	.30
Butt Stock	1.40	Cartridge Stop Pin	.02
Butt Plate	80	Cartridge Stop Spring	.15
Butt Plate Screws (2), each	.05	Ejector, with Collar and Spring	.45
Carrier	.90	Extractor	.25
Carrier Stop	.10	Extractor Pin	.02
Carrier Stop Pin	.02	Finger Lever	1.40
Carrier Stop Spring	.05		
Carrier Screws (2), each	.05		

Order No. 47022½—Continued.

	Price.		Price.
Finger Lever Pin....	.20	Locking Bolt Screw.	.05
Finger Lever Pin		Mainspring	.30
Stop Screw	.05	Mainspring Screw...	.05
Friction Stud........	.10	Mainspring Strain	
Friction Stud Spring.	.05	Screw	.05
Friction Stud Pin....	.02	Magazine............	1.40
Firing Pin..........	.50	Magazine Follower..	.10
Firing Pin Stop Pin.$0.05		Magazine Spring.....	.20
Fore-arm	.60	Magazine Plug......	.10
Fore-arm Tip........	.80	Magazine Plug Screw	.03
Fore-arm Tip Screws		Magazine Ring ...	.40
(2), each..........	.03	Magazine Ring Pin..	.02
Fore-arm Tip Tenon.	.40	Receiver, complete	
Hammer.............	.50	with Tang........	5.40
Hammer Stirrup.....	.15	Receiver Tang......	1.10
Hammer Stirrup Pin.	.02	Spring Cover........	.30
Hammer Screw.....	.05	Spring Cover Screw.	.03
Locking Bolt, right		Trigger	.45
hand............ ..	.60	Trigger Pin........	.02
Locking Bolt, left		Trigger Spring.....	.10
hand...........	.60	Trigger Spring Screw	.05
Locking Bolt Pin....	.20	Tang Screw	.10

Parts for Winchester Single Shot Rifles.

Order No. 47023—

	Price.		Price.
Mainspring.........$0.40		Fore Arm.... ....$1.00	
Extractor	.40	Knock Off........	.40
Sear Spring........	.30	Sear Set Lock	.30
Hammer, plain lock.	.90	Finger Lever........	1.50
Firing Pins........	.30	Trigger	.50
Ejector Springs (22		Receiver Tang, separ-	
cal. only)........	.30	ate from receiver	1.20
Hammer Set Lock...	1.00	Sears..............	.30
Breech Blocks	1.00	Knock-Off Spring, for-	
Butt Stocks........	1.40	set lock...........	.30
Catch hook Set Lock	.30		
Catch Hook Spring.	.05		

Parts for Winchester Repeating Rifle, Model '90, Take-Down.

Order No. 47023½—

	Price.		Price.
Carrier...... ...$1.00		Magazine Tube, in-	
Firing Pin..........	.50	side, complete....$2.00	
Mainspring...........	.30	Extractor	.25
Trigger.	.45	Hammer	.50
Magazine Spring....	.20	Firing Pin-stop......	.10
Magazine Tube, out-		Butt Stock..........	1.40
side..............	1.00		

In ordering Carrier state if for 22 caliber short, 22 long, or 22 W. R. F. cartridge.

Parts for Winchester Model '86 Rifle.

Order No. 47024—

	Price.		Price.
Cartridge Stop $0.35		Hammer Stirrups.... $ .15	
Cartridge Guide	80	Finger Lever Pin....	.10
Carrier Spring	.20	Hammer Screws.....	.10
Extractor	.25	Fore Arms..........	.60
Carrier Hook	.55	Ejector Spring......	.10
Trigger............	.45	SpringCover,complete	1.15
Trigger Spring.....	.10	Set Sear	.60
Lower Tang	2.00	Butt Stock..	1.40
Hammer, plain lock.	.50	Finger Lever........	1.50
Hammer, set lock..	.90	Mainspring...........	.30
Ejector............	.35	Carrier............	2.00
Spring Cover Leaf..	.40	Firing Pin..........	.50
Spring Cover Bases.	.60	Magazine Springs...	.20
Spring Cover Leaf		Screws, each..........	.05
Springs...........	.10		

Winchester Repeating Shot Gun Parts.

Order No. 47024½—Model 1893, 12 ga. only.

	Price.		Price.
Action Slide.........$1.50		Magazine Band......$0.70	
Action Slide Stop Pin.	.05	Magazine Band Screw	.05
Action Hook.......	.30	Magazine Follower...	.45
Action Hook Screws.	.05	Magazine Plug........	.50
Barrel, plain.. ......7.50		Magazine Plug Screw	.05
Breech-block.......	3.00	Magazine Spring.....	.20
Butt Plate.........		Mainspring...........	.30
Butt Plate Screws, ea.,	.05	Mainspring Strain	
Butt Stock..........2.00		Screw............	.05
Carrier.............1.75		Receiver, complete,	
Carrier Pin...........	.05	with Guard........7.50	
Cartridge Stop, right		Receiver Bolt........	.40
or left hand, each...	.35	Receiver Bolt Washer	.05
Cartridge Stop Base..	.20	Receiver Shank......	.25
Cartridge Stop Screw.	.05	Sear...............	.45
Cartridge Stop Spring.	.10	Sear Pin............	.05
Extractor............	.30	Sear Spring.........	.15
Extractor Pin........	.05	Sear Spring Screw...	.05
Extractor Spring......	.05	Slide Handle........	.85
Firing Pin.	.50	Slide Handle Escutch-	
Firing Pin Lock	.50	eons, 2, each.........	.05
Firing Pin Spring.....	.05	Slide Handle Screws,	
Front Sight...........	.25	2, each..............	.05
Guard Bow...........1.25		Stirrup..............	.15
Hammer..............	.50	Trigger.............	.45
Hammer Pin..........	.05	Trigger Pin.........	.05
Magazine............	.90		

Parts for Colt's Rifle.

Order No. 47025—

	22 Cal	32 to 44 Cal.	38-56 to 45-85 Cal.
Magazine Cartridge Stop.	$0.75	$0.55	$0.75
Mainspring	50	.36	.40
Hammer............. .	1.10	.92	.97
Firing Pin..............	.80	.44	.55
Trigger	.45	.40	.45
Carrier Levers...........	.75	.52	.75
Shell Extractor.........	.30	.28	.33
Trigger Spring	.20	.16	.20
Tang Screws	.15	.10	.10
Butt Stock.............	2.75	2.15	2 25
Magazine Spring...........	.30	.35	.40

Parts for Winchester Rifle. Model 73 and 76.
Order 47028.

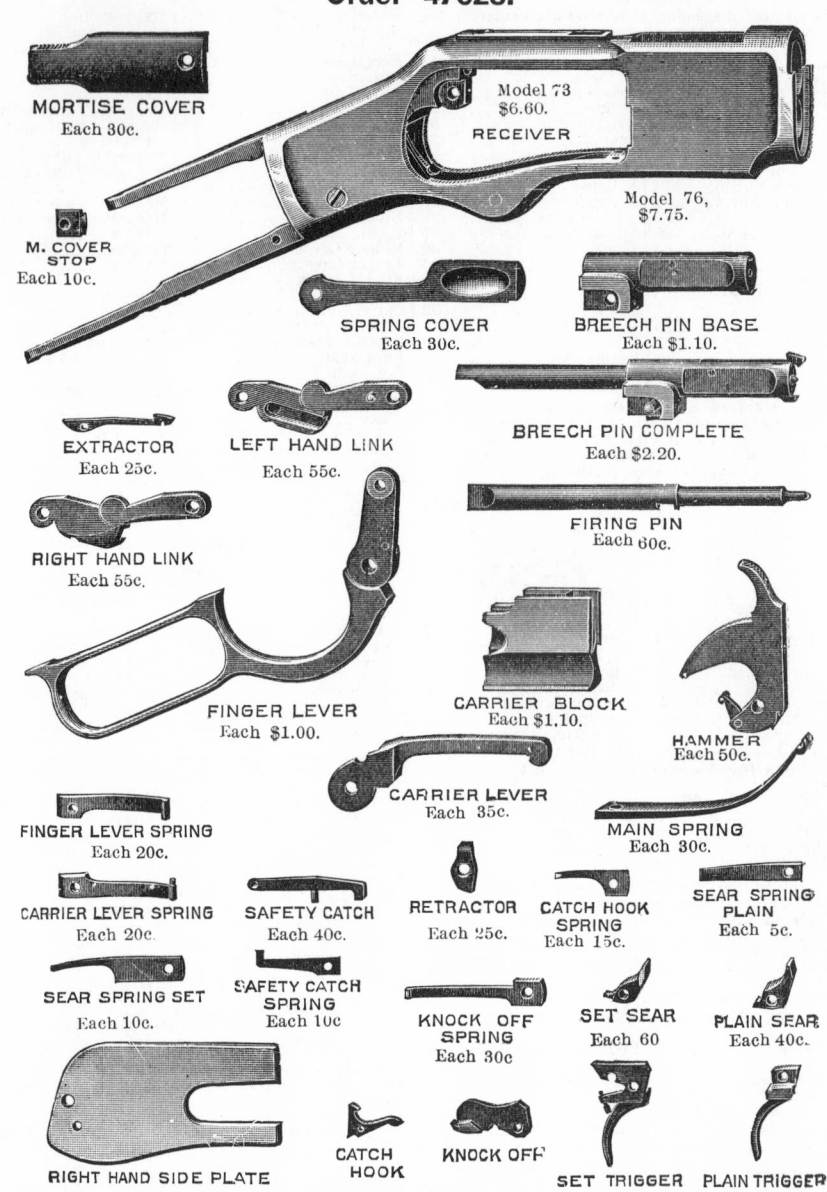

MORTISE COVER
Each 30c.

M. COVER STOP
Each 10c.

Model 73 $6.60. RECEIVER

Model 76, $7.75.

SPRING COVER
Each 30c.

BREECH PIN BASE
Each $1.10.

EXTRACTOR
Each 25c.

LEFT HAND LINK
Each 55c.

BREECH PIN COMPLETE
Each $2.20.

RIGHT HAND LINK
Each 55c.

FIRING PIN
Each 60c.

FINGER LEVER
Each $1.00.

CARRIER BLOCK
Each $1.10.

HAMMER
Each 50c.

CARRIER LEVER
Each 35c.

FINGER LEVER SPRING
Each 20c.

MAIN SPRING
Each 30c.

CARRIER LEVER SPRING
Each 20c.

SAFETY CATCH
Each 40c.

RETRACTOR
Each 25c.

CATCH HOOK SPRING
Each 15c.

SEAR SPRING PLAIN
Each 5c.

SEAR SPRING SET
Each 10c.

SAFETY CATCH SPRING
Each 10c.

KNOCK OFF SPRING
Each 30c.

SET SEAR
Each 60

PLAIN SEAR
Each 40c.

RIGHT HAND SIDE PLATE
Model 73, 80c.   Model 76, 90c.
Hammer, Set Lock, 90c each

CATCH HOOK
Each 50c.

KNOCK OFF
Each 60c.
Screws, each, 5c.

SET TRIGGER
Each 60c.

PLAIN TRIGGER
Each 30c.
Magazine Springs, 20c. each.

In ordering parts state caliber of rifle and send old part for sample when possible to do so, and mention model of rifle. Parts by mail, 1c. to 5c. extra.

PARTS FOR QUACKENBUSH SAFETY RIFLE.

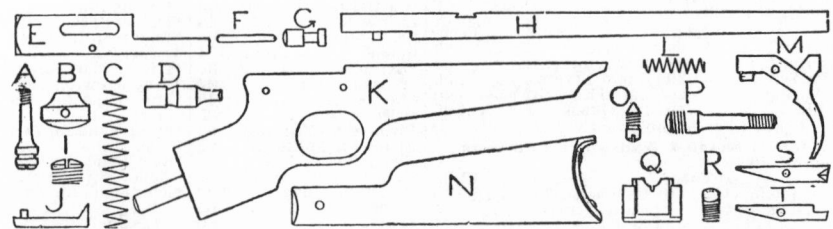

Order No. 47029

	Each.		Each.
A. Cocking Screw......$0.15		G. Friction Stud. $0.06	
B. Stud Nut	.15	H. Barrel only, plated	
C. Main Spring.......	.15	or blued finish....	2.00
D. Firing Pin..........	.20	I. Breech Screw.......	.08
E. Breech Block, with		J. Extractor	.15
lock work.........	1.70	K. Frame.............	1.25
Breech Block, with-		L. Friction Stud or	
out lock work......	1.00	Sear Springs........	.05
F. Trigger Sear and			
Friction Stud Pin .	.05		

Order No. 47029—Continued.

	Each.		Each.
M. Trigger $0.15		Wiping Rod, jointed...$0.15	
N. Stock with butt plate,	1.35	Breech Block, extra for	
O. Adjusting Screw....	.08	postage.............	.08
P. Barrel Stud.........	.10	Barrel, postage, extra..	.35
Q. Rear Adjustable		Frame, postage, extra..	.25
Sights............	.30	Stock, postage, extra..	.14
R. Front Sight.........	.08		
S. Sear...............	.15		
T. Sear, old pattern....	.15		
wiping rod	.10		

Postage on other parts, 3c. extra.

REVOLVERS.

In accordance with the following extract we cannot sell a *minor* resident of the State of Illinois a revolver. This law does not apply to any State except Illinois.

Extract from Illinois State Laws.

PAR. 2D. Whoever, not being the father, guardian or employer of the minor herein named, by himself or agent, shall sell, give, loan, hire or barter to any minor within this State, any pistol, revolver, derringer, bowie knife or dirk or other deadly weapon of like character capable of being secreted upon the person, shall be guilty of misdemeanor and shall be fined in any sum not less than twenty-five dollars nor more than two hundred dollars.

NOTICE.

TO RESIDENTS OF ILLINOIS ONLY.

If you live in any other State you do not have to send the "Sample Letter."

Orders for revolvers to residents of the State of Illinois must be accompanied with a letter embracing all the points contained in the following "SAMPLE LETTER." The purchaser will of course substitute his own name, residence, age and purpose for which the arm is required, and also obtain two witnesses. Attention is called to the extract from the Illinois State Law above. A minor cannot buy a revolver, but his father, guardian or employer can buy it for him. This law applies to the residents of Illinois only.

"SAMPLE LETTER."

Sept. 1, 1890.

MESSRS. MONTGOMERY WARD & Co., CHICAGO, ILL

Gentlemen: I wish to purchase a revolver of you, and to enable you to comply with the laws of the State of Illinois, I make the following statement: My name is JOHN DOE. I reside at Windsor Park, Ill. My age is 24 I want the revolver for self-protection.

JOHN DOE.

This is to certify that we, the undersigned, legal voters of the State of Illinois, are personally acquainted with the aforesaid John Doe and believe the above statement made by him to be correct in every particular.

JOHN BROWN, Witness.
ALBERT JONES, Witness.

REVOLVERS.—The following quotations do not include cartridges.

All revolvers can be sent by mail when so ordered. Postage, 1 cent per ounce in weight.

47032

Defender, wood stock, full nickel plated, plain cylinder, 7-shot, 22 caliber, rim fire, long or short, 2½ inch barrel; weight, 7 ounces. Safe and reliable. Each.....$0.74

Postage, extra, 10 cents.

47033 Eclipse, vest pocket single shot pistol, nickel plated wood stock, 2½ inch barrel; weight, 5 ounces; for BB and conical caps and 22 caliber short cartridge, safe and reliable barrel swings to the right to load.
Each....................$0.50
By mail, extra........................05

47034 Rosewood stock, 7-shot, full nickel plate, 22 caliber long or short, rim fire; weight, 7 oz., 2½ in. barrel; entire length, 5½ in., safe and reliable.
Each..........................$0.79
Using No. 47155-59 cartridges.

47035 Rubber Stock, 7-shot, 22 caliber, long or short, 2½ inch barrel, rim fire, entire length, 5½ inches, full nickel plated, weight, 7 ounces, rifled barrels (See cut 47034.)
Each....................90c   Extra by mail....   10c
Using No. 47155-59 cartridge.

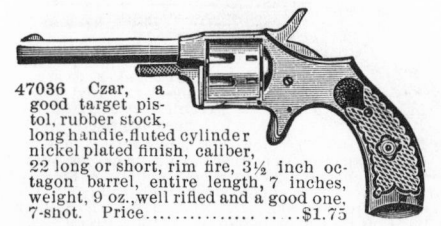

47036 Czar, a good target pistol, rubber stock, long handle, fluted cylinder nickel plated finish, caliber, 22 long or short, rim fire, 3½ inch octagon barrel, entire length, 7 inches, weight, 9 oz., well rifled and a good one. 7-shot. Price.............$1.75
Using 47155-59 cartridges. Extra by mail.......11c.

Revolvers—Continued.

47037 Blue Jacket, No. 1½, a fine shooter, 22 caliber, long or short cartridges, round barrel, rubber stock, full nickel plate, saw handle, length of barrel, 2½ inches; entire length, 6 inches; weight, 9 oz., using No. 47155-59 cartridge, well rifled, and a good one.
Price, each, 7 shot, $1.35.   By mail, extra, 12c.

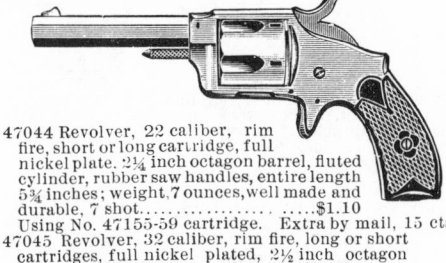

47039 Wood stock, plain cylinder, 5 shot, 32 caliber, long or short, rim fire, 2½ inch barrel, weight, 12 oz., full nickel plate, entire length, 6½ inches, rifled barrels. Price....   ....$1.00
Using No 47169-70-71 cartridge.
Extra by mail, 15c. Safe and reliable.

Rifled Barrel.

47044 Revolver, 22 caliber, rim fire, short or long cartridge, full nickel plate, 2¼ inch octagon barrel, fluted cylinder, rubber saw handles, entire length 5¾ inches; weight.7 ounces, well made and durable, 7 shot....................$1.10
Using No. 47155-59 cartridge. Extra by mail, 15 cts
47045 Revolver, 32 caliber, rim fire, long or short cartridges, full nickel plated, 2½ inch octagon barrel, fluted cylinder, rubber saw handles; entire length, 6¾ inches; weight, 10 ounces, Price, $1.25. Using 47169-70-71 cartridges.   Extra by mail, 15 cents.

47046 Forehand & Wadsworth's New Double Action Self-Cocking Revolvers, full nickel plated, rubber stocks, rifled barrel, safe, reliable and accurate Rebounding

47046-47 locks and parts are interchangeable. 32 caliber, 2½ in. octagon barrel, 6 shot, 12 oz. weight, using No. 47188 cartridge..............   ......$1.40
47047 38 caliber, 2½ in. octagon barrel, 5 shot, weight about 15 oz., using No. 47194 cartridge. 1.40
Postage, extra, 17c.

47048 Forehand & Wadsworth Safety Hammer Double Action Revolvers, full nickel plated, rubber stocks, rifled barrels, rebounding lock; safe, reliable and accurate, 32 caliber, 2½ in. octagon barrel, using No. 47188 cartridge, 6 shot, about 12 oz. weight $1.40
47048½ 38 caliber, 2½ in. octagon barrel, 5 shot, about 15 oz. weight, using No. 47194 cartridge.. 1.40
Postage, extra, 17c.

Big Bargains.

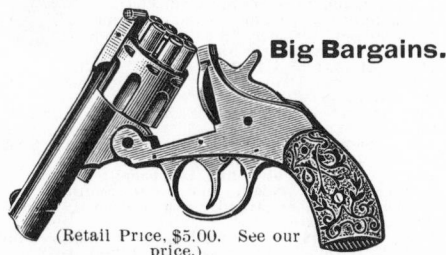

(Retail Price, $5.00. See our price.)

Harrington & Richardson's Improved Automatic Shell Extracting Double Action Self-cocking Revolver (modeled on the Smith & Wesson pattern), beautifully nickel plated, rubber stocks, as accurate and durable as any revolver in the market, equal to a Smith & Wesson in shooting; weight, 18 to 20 ounces; 3¼ inch barrel.
47049   6 shot, 32 caliber, center fire, using 47188 cartridge. By mail, 21 cents extra.... $2.90
47050   5 shot, 38 caliber, center fire; using 47194 cartridge. By mail, 23 cents extra...... 2.90

Revolvers—Continued.

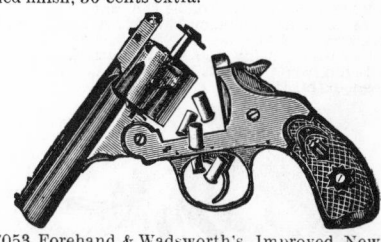

Forehand & Wadsworth's New Hammerless Revolver. Automatic shell ejector double action, self-cocking, rebounding lock, absolute safety catch to lock hammer, made of best material, beautifully finished throughout; accurate and reliable, no better shooters in the market, all center fire. Length of barrel, 3¼ inches; entire length, 7¾ inches. Weight, 17 ounces, nickel plated, 38, 5 shot, 32-6 shot.
47051 32 S. & W., center fire..............$4.75
47052 38 S. & W., center fire. Each............ 4.75
Either caliber, 5 inch barrel....   .... 5.40
Blued finish, 50 cents extra.

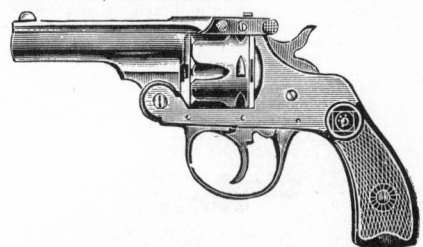

47053 Forehand & Wadsworth's Improved New Model Revolver. Automatic shell extracting, rebounding locks, double action, self cocking. simple and accurate; interchangeable parts made from *drop forgings*; the frame is cast steel; *no malleable iron about it.* Nickel plated, rubber stocks. WARRANTED. Length of barrel, 3¼ in. Weight, 17 oz.; entire length, 7¾ in. This is the best selling revolver in our stock, having contracted for several thousand. 32 Caliber, S. & W., center fire cartridge. Each, 6 shot.$2.50
47054 38 caliber, S. & W. center fire cartridge. Each, 5 shot...........   .... 2.50
Either above calibers with 5 in. barrel. Each.. 4.00
Blued finish, 50 cents extra.

47056 The H. & R. Premier Automatic Double Action Self Cocking Revolver. Full nickel plated, rubber stocks, weight, 11½ ounces, 3-inch barrels, well made, finely finished and accurate. 32 S. & W. center fire, using No. 47188 cartridge. Each....................   ....$4.00

47058 Hopkins & Allen Automatic Hammerless Double Action Revolver. High grade finish. fine adjustment. Its trigger locking device makes it one of the safest revolvers to carry in the pocket. Automatic shell ejector, rebounding lock, safety trigger, locking device, chambered cylinder, rifled barrel, nickel plated, 32 caliber, S. & W. small frame, 5 shot, weight, 13 oz.: length of barrel, 3 inches, using cartridge 47188. (Retail price, $7.50.) Our price $4.90
47059 38 S. & W. large frame, weight 18 oz., length of barrel, 3¼ in. Price, $4.90. Using cartridge 47196. Either of above calibers in blued finish same price. Pearl stocks. $3.00 extra. Postage, extra, 22 cents.

47061 Frontier Bull Dog for home protection, beautifully nickel finished, 6 shot, double action self-cocking revolver, rifled barrels, 44 Winchester center fire, cartridge No. 47208, 4¾ in. barrel; weight, 32 oz. Good, strong and durable. Each........$3.85
Postage, extra. 35 cents.

Revolvers—Continued.

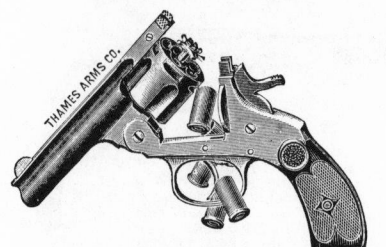

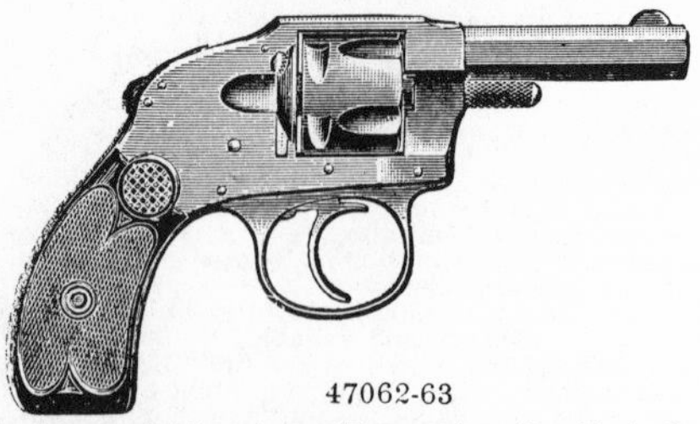

47062-63

Hopkins and Allen Acme Hammerless Double Action Revolver. Rebounding lock, safety trigger, locking device, chambered cylinder. Safe, reliable and accurate. (Retail price, $5.00.)
47062 32-caliber, using No. 47188 cartridge, 5 shot, 11 oz., 2¾ in. octagon barrel..............$2.65
Postage, extra, 13 cents.
47063 38-caliber, using No. 47194 cartridge. 3 in. octagon barrel 5 shot, 17 oz..................2.65
Postage, extra, 19 cents.

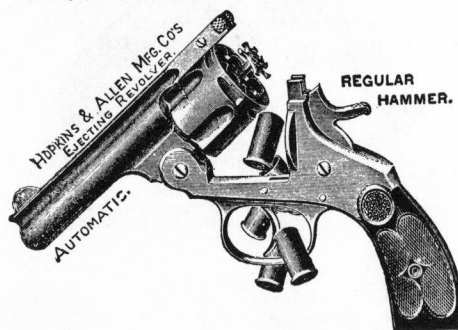

REGULAR HAMMER.

Hopkins & Allen Automatic Shell Ejecting Revolvers. Forged steel barrels and cylinders, in all respects of the best material and finish. Guaranteed accurate, safe and reliable. Nickel plated, rubber stock. A high grade revolver at a popular price.
47065 32 caliber, 5 shot, 12 oz., 3-inch barrel, using No. 4718 cartridge.....................$3.90
47067 38 caliber, 5 shot, 17 oz, 3½ inch barrel, using No. 47194 cartridge...................3.95
47069 38 caliber, 5 shot, 19 oz. 5½ inch barrel, using No. 47194 cartridge.................4.75
Blued finish, same price as nickel plated.

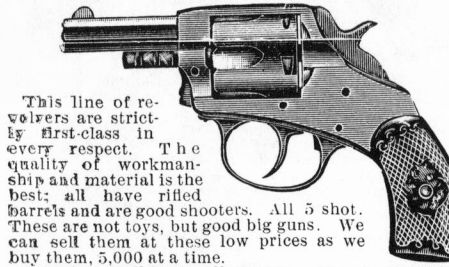

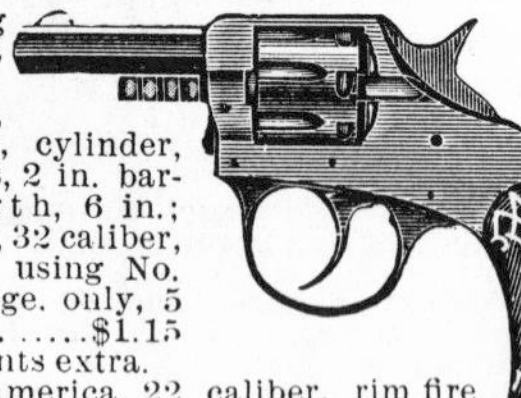

47073 Young America double action, full nickel plated fluted, cylinder, rubber handles, 2 in. barrel, full length, 6 in.; weight, 9½ oz., 32 caliber, center fire, using No. 47188 cartridge only, 5 shot. Each $1.15
By mail, 12 cents extra.
47074 Young America, 22 caliber, rim fire, length of barrel, 2 in., entire length 6 in., 8 oz.; using No. 47155-59 cartridge, 7 shot, double action. self-cocking. Each...............$1 15
By mail, 8 cents extra.

Big Bargains. American Bull Dog Revolvers.

This line of revolvers are strictly first-class in every respect. The quality of workmanship and material is the best; all have rifled barrels and are good shooters. All 5 shot. These are not toys, but good big guns. We can sell them at these low prices as we buy them, 5,000 at a time.
American Bull Dogs, all double action, self-cocking all have rubber stocks, all beautifully nickel plated, all have saw handles, all have fluted cylinders, all have octagon barrels, all warranted new and in perfect order.
47075 32 caliber, center fire, 2½ in. barrel, 13 oz. weight..........................$1.20
47078 32 caliber, center fire, 4½ in. barrel, 16 oz. weight.........................1.55
47079 32 caliber, center fire, 6 in. barrel, 17 oz. weight. All 32 caliber use No. 47188 cartridge 1.89
47080 38 caliber, center fire, 2½ in. barrel, 16 oz. weight.......................1.20
47081 38 caliber, center fire, 4½ in. barrel, 17½ oz. weight.......................1.55
47082 38 caliber, center fire, 6 in. barrel, 18 oz. weight........................1.89
All 38 caliber use No. 47194 cartridge
Postage, when sent by mail, 18 to 20 cents extra.
Revolvers of all kinds can be sent by mail; postage is 1 cent per ounce in weight.

Revolvers—Continued.

The Thames Arms Co.'s Double Action Self Cocking Revolver. Automatic shell ejecting, rebounding hammer, rubber stock, finely finished, well rifled barrels accurate and reliable, every one warranted, full nickel plated, 5 shot, 38 caliber, 3¼-inch barrels, 18 oz. weight, 6 shot, 32 caliber.
47083 32 caliber, using 47188 cartridge, ...$3.00
47084 38 caliber using No. 47194 cartridge 3.00

A New Revolver.

The Universal Double Action Revolver, Self Cocking, nickel plated, rubber stock, rebounding locks, well made and durable. This revolver meets the demand for a good article for a little money. 16 oz. weight either caliber.
47085 32 caliber, 2½ inch barrel, using 47188 cartridge $1.25
47086 38 caliber, 2¾ inch barrel, using 47194 cartridge 1.25
The 32 caliber is 6 shot, the 38 caliber 5 shot.

HOPKINS & ALLEN MFG. CO.

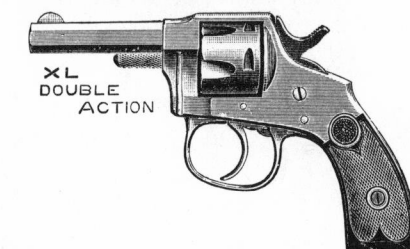

XL DOUBLE ACTION

The H. & A. Double Action, Self-Cocking Revolver, nickel plated, rubber stock, finely finished, accurate and reliable, rifled barrels; a good one; 16 oz. weight.
4,087 32 Caliber, 3 inches, using No. 47188 cartridge. Price.....................$2.30
47088 38 Caliber. 3 inches, using No. 47194 cartridge. Price....................2.30

X. L. Double Action.
WITH FOLDING HAMMER.
GOOD ONES.

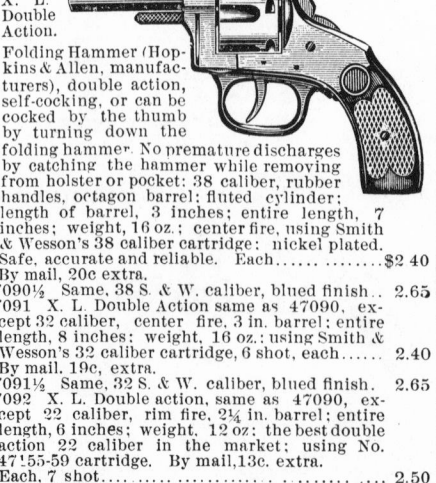

47090— X. L. Double Action.
Folding Hammer (Hopkins & Allen, manufacturers), double action, self-cocking, or can be cocked by the thumb by turning down the folding hammer. No premature discharges by catching the hammer while removing from holster or pocket: 38 caliber, rubber handles, octagon barrel; fluted cylinder; length of barrel, 3 inches; entire length, 7 inches; weight, 16 oz.; center fire, using Smith & Wesson's 38 caliber cartridge: nickel plated. Safe, accurate and reliable. Each.........$2 40
By mail, 20c extra.
47090½ Same, 38 S. & W. caliber, blued finish.. 2.65
47091 X. L. Double Action same as 47090, except 32 caliber, center fire, 3 in. barrel; entire length, 8 inches; weight, 16 oz.; using Smith & Wesson's 32 caliber cartridge, 6 shot, each...... 2.40
By mail, 19c, extra.
47091½ Same, 32 S. & W. caliber, blued finish. 2.65
47092 X. L. Double action, same as 47090, except 22 caliber, rim fire, 2¼ in. barrel; entire length, 6 inches; weight, 12 oz: the best double action 22 caliber in the market; using No. 47155-59 cartridge. By mail, 13c. extra.
Each, 7 shot.......................2.50
47092½ Same, 22 caliber, blued finish 2.65

Horse Goods, we have all you will require.

Handsome Revolvers.

ACCURATE.   RELIABLE.

47093 Hopkins & Allen Automatic Shell Ejecting Center Fire, Double Action, Self-cocking. Folding Hammer Revolvers, 38 caliber, 3¼ inch barrel, nickel plated, rubber stocks, using 47194 cartridges, finely made and accurate, rifled barrels. Each 5 shot, 17 oz $4.40
47095 Same, 38 S. & W. caliber, blued finish.. 4.40
47096 Hopkins & Allen Revolver, same as No. 47093, except 5½ inch barrel, plated, rubber stock, 38 caliber, using No. 47294 cartridge. weight, 19 ozs. By mail, 23 cents extra. Each, $5.00
47097 32 caliber, 3 inch barrel, 11 ozs, using S. & W. cartridge. Each........ 4.65
47098 Same, 32 S. & W. caliber, blued finish.... 4.68

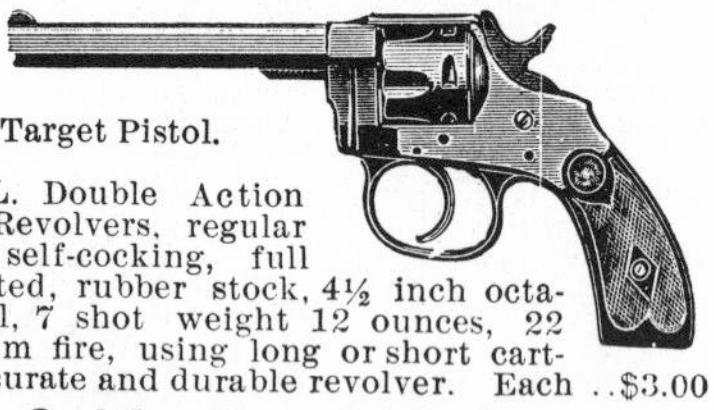

A Fine Target Pistol.

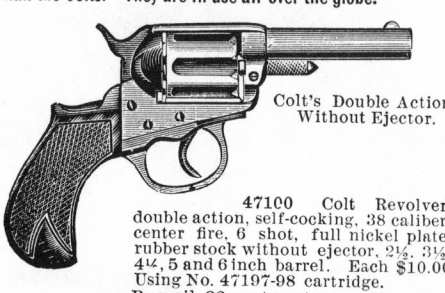

47099 X. L. Double Action Target Revolvers, regular hammer, self-cocking, full nickel-plated, rubber stock, 4½ inch octagon barrel, 7 shot weight 12 ounces, 22 caliber, rim fire, using long or short cartridges, accurate and durable revolver. Each ..$3.00

Colt's Revolvers.

Manufactured by the Colt's Patent Fire Arms Co. Hartford, Conn. No better revolvers manufactured in the world than the Colts. They are in use all over the globe.

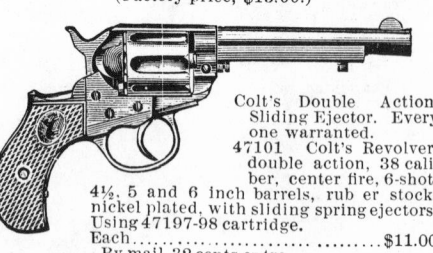

Colt's Double Action Without Ejector.

47100 Colt Revolver, double action, self-cocking, 38 caliber, center fire. 6 shot, full nickel plate, rubber stock without ejector, 2½, 3½, 4½, 5 and 6 inch barrel. Each $10.00
By mail, 32 cents extra.
47100½ Same as 47100, except blue finish. 10.00
(Factory price, $15.00.)

Colt's Double Action, Sliding Ejector. Every one warranted.
47101 Colt's Revolver, double action, 38 caliber, center fire, 6-shot, 4½, 5 and 6 inch barrels, rub er stock, nickel plated, with sliding spring ejectors. Using 47197-98 cartridge. Each...................$11.00
By mail, 32 cents extra.
47101½ Colt's Revolver, same as 47101, except blued finish. Each...................11.00
47102 Colt's Revolver, double action, 41 caliber, center fire, rubber stock, nickel plated frames and barrels, 6 shot with sliding spring ejector, 4½,5 or 6 in. Using No. 47203 cartridges. Each............................11.00
By mail, 32 cents extra.
Extra for pearl stock on either of above numbers. Each 4.25
47102½ Colt Revolver; same as No. 47102, except blued finish. Each.................11.20
Postage, extra, 32 cents.

New Single Action Frontier and Peacemaker. Every one warranted. (Regular price $16.00.)
See our price.
47103 Colt Revolver, single action, sliding ejector, 38 caliber. using 38 caliber Winchester rifle cartridge, model '73, 4¾, 5½ and 7½ inch barrels, rubber stocks, nickel plated. 6 shot. Our price $12.00
47103½ Colt Revolver, same as 47103, except blued finish. Our price 12.00

Revolvers—Continued.

47104 Colt Revolver, single action, sliding ejector, rubber stocks, 32 caliber, using Winchester rifle cartridge, 32 caliber, model '73, 4¾, 5½ and 7½ inch, nickel plated, using 47192-93 cartridge 12.00

47104½ Colt Revolver, same as 47104, except *blued* finish, 6 shot. Our price 12.00

47105 Colt Revolver, "Frontier," 44 caliber, single action, sliding ejector, using Winchester 44 caliber, model 1873 cartridge, central fire, nickel finish, rubber stocks, 6 shot, 4¾, 5½, 7½ inch barrel. Each.................. 12.00
Postage, extra, 54 cents.

47105½ Colt Revolver, same as 47105, except blued finish.... .... 12.00

47106 Colt Revolver, "Peacemaker," single action, sliding ejector, rubber stocks, 45-caliber, central fire, nickel plated, 6 shot, 4¾, 5½ and 7½ in. barrel. Using No. 47216 cartridge. 12.00

47106½ Colt Revolver, same as 47106, except blued finish.......................... 12.00

47107 Colt Revolver, single action, sliding ejector, 41 caliber, center fire, 4¾, 5½, and 7½ inch, nickel plated, rubber stocks, using 47203-cartridge...$12.00 Extra for plain pearl stocks. 8.00
Extra for pearl stocks, carved ox head or eagle 13.00

47107½ Colt Revolver, same as 47107, except blued finish ....$12.00 By mail, extra... .52

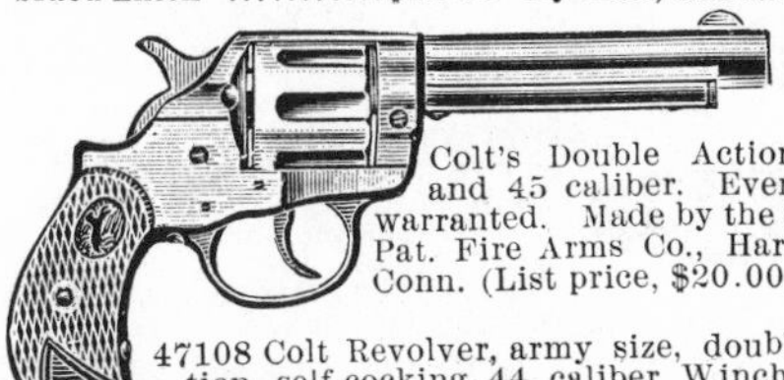

Colt's Double Action, 44 and 45 caliber. Every one warranted. Made by the Colt's Pat. Fire Arms Co., Hartford, Conn. (List price, $20.00.)

47108 Colt Revolver, army size, double action, self-cocking, 44 caliber Winchester, center fire, case-hardened, NICKEL plated, rubber stock with sliding spring ejector, 4¾ inch, 5½ inch or 7½ inch barrel, 6 shot.... $13.00

47110 Colt Revolver, 44 caliber, same description as No. 47108, except BLUED finish......... 13.00

47112 Colt Revolver, army size, double action, self-cocking, 45 caliber, center fire, case-hardened, 4¾, 5½ and 7½ inch barrel, NICKEL plated, 6 shot, rubber stock, with sliding spring ejector 13.00

47114 Colt Revolver, 45 caliber, same description as No. 47112, except BLUED finish........ 13.00

47115 Colt Revolver, double action, self-cocking, 4¾, 5½ and 7½ inch barrel, 38 caliber, using 38 Winchester rifle cartridge, model '73, NICKEL plated 13.00

47116 Colt's Revolver, same as No. 47115, BLUED finish........................ 13.00

47117 Colt Revolvers, double action, self-cocking, 32 W. C. F. caliber, using cartridge No. 47193, NICKEL PLATED, 4¾ inches; 5½ inches; 7½ inches................... 13 00

47117½ Colt's Revolver, same as 47117, except BLUED FINISH.. .... 13.00
Extra for plain pearl stock on 44 or 45 caliber, double action, $4.50. By mail, 50 cents extra.

Smith and Wesson Revolvers.

Lookout for imitations. There are many on the market All genuine Smith & Wesson revolvers are stamped on the barrel, "Smith & Wesson, Springfield, Mass."

Genuine Smith & Wesson Hammerless.

47118 Smith & Wesson's Hammerless Revolver, automatic ejector, 32 caliber center fire, 3½ inch barrel, nickel plated, double action, self-cocking; weight, 16 ounces, 5 shot. Each............ $11.50
By mail, extra.............................. .19

47119 Smith & Wesson's Hammerless Revolver, automatic ejector, double action, self-cocking, 32 caliber, center fire, using No. 47188 cartridge, blued finish, double action; weight, 16 ounces, 5 shot......... $11.65. By mail, extra....... $0.19

47120 38 caliber, 3¼ inch barrel, nickel plated, double action; weight, 20 oz., 5 shot...... .... 12.00
By mail, extra .... .23

47121 38 caliber, 3¼ inch barrel, blued finish, using No. 47194 cartridge; weight 20 oz., 5 shot.
By mail, extra, 23c. Each.......12.50

Genuine Smith & Wesson Single action 32 caliber. Manufactured at Springfield, Mass.

32 CALIBER, CENTRAL FIRE, 3½ INCH BARREL, AUTOMATIC EJECTOR, LATEST MODEL WITH HAMMER.

47125 32 caliber, 5 shot, blued, rubber stock, single action: weight, 13 oz.... . ... $8.95
By mail, extra .... .18

47126 32 caliber, 5 shot, blued, double action, self cocking, 32 caliber; weight, 13 oz........ 10.65
By mail, extra .... .18

Revolvers—Continued.

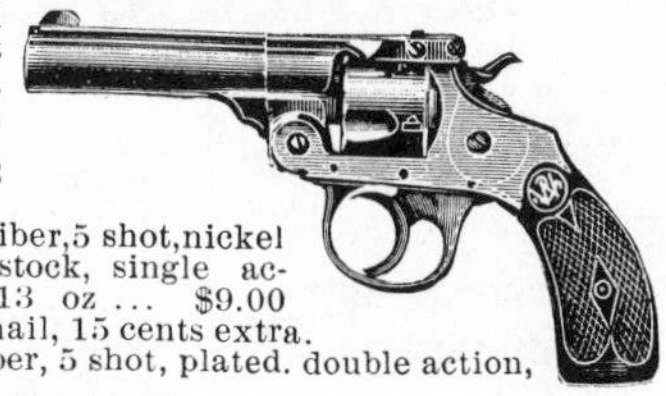

Manufactured by Smith & Wesson, Springfield, Mass.

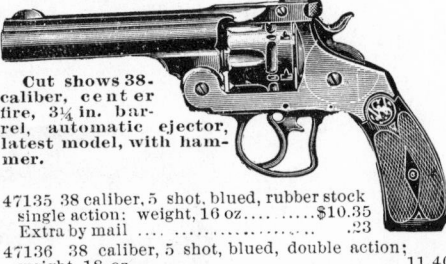

S. & W. 32 D. A.

47127 32 caliber, 5 shot, nickel plate, rubber stock, single action; weight, 13 oz ... $9.00
By mail, 15 cents extra.

47128 32 caliber, 5 shot, plated, double action, self-cocking; weight, 13 oz $10.65
By mail, 18c. extra.

47129 32 caliber, 5 shot, blued or plated, 6 in. barrel, rubber stock, double action, using 47188 cartridge; weight, 15 oz...... .... 12.00
Extra, for pearl stock... .... 2.00

47130 The Lord Model Stevens Target Pistol, nickel plated frame and butt, blue barrels, open sights, heavy butt, spur trigger guard, 10 inch barrel, weight, 3 pounds, 22 caliber, rim fire. Each........... $14.85

47131 The Gould Model Stevens Target Pistol, nickel frame and butt, blued barrels, 10 inch barrels, weight, 3 pounds, 22 caliber, rim fire. Each...... .... $13.50

47132 The Conlin Model Target Pistol, nickel frame, blued barrels, 10 inch barrels, weight, 2 pounds. Each...................... $13.50

Smith and Wesson Target Revolvers.

Made at Springfield, Mass.

WITH SPECIAL SIGHTS FOR FINE SHOOTING

47133 Single Action. 38-44 and 44 Russian caliber, center model, 6½ in. barrel, automatic ejector, full nickel plated. rubber stock, 6 shot, weight, 2 pounds, 11 ounces, using 47273-4 and 47204 cartridge............ .... $15.50

47134 Single action, 32-44 caliber, center fire, 6½ in. barrel, automatic ejector, full nickel plated, rubber stock, 6 shot; weight 2 pounds, 11 ounces; using 47271-2 cartridge $15.50

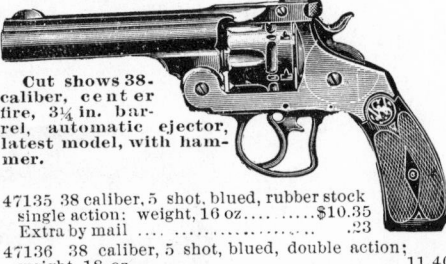

Cut shows 38-caliber, center fire, 3¼ in. barrel, automatic ejector, latest model, with hammer.

47135 38 caliber, 5 shot, blued, rubber stock single action: weight, 16 oz.... .....$10.35
Extra by mail .... .23

47136 38 caliber, 5 shot, blued, double action; weight, 18 oz...... .... 11.40

47137 38 caliber, 5 shot, nickel plate, rubber stock, single action; weight, 16 oz 10.40

47138 38 caliber, 5 shot, plated, double action; weight, 18 oz...... .... 11.40

47140 38 caliber, 5 shot, blued or plated, 4 or 5 in. barrels, rubber stocks, double action; weight, 18 oz., using 47194 cartridges..........12.00
Extra for pearl stocks. 3.25
Extra by mail.............................. .23

Parties desiring an article not quoted in our Catalogue, we will purchase for them if it can be obtained in Chicago.

Smith & Wesson.

47141 44 caliber, 6 shot, blued, rubber stock, single action; 6½ in. only; using 47208 cartridges; weight, 40 oz.. $12.50 Extra by mail..$0.52

47142 44 caliber, 6 shot, blued finish, rubber stock, double action, 6, 5 or 4 in.; using 47208 cartridges; weight, 40 oz. $14.40. Extra by mail .48

47143 44 caliber, 6 shot, nickel plate, rubber stock, single action, 6 in. only; using 47208 cartridges; weight, 44 oz.....................12.60
Extra by mail........... .... .52

47144 44 caliber, 6 shot, Smith & Wesson, plated, rubber stock, double action, 6, 5 or 4 in.; weight, 40 oz., using 47208 cartridge..........14.75

47145 44 caliber, Russian model, double action or self cocking, 4 in., 5 in., 6 in. barrel; weight, about 40 oz., using No. 47204 cartridge. Each...........$14.55 Extra by mail.......... .48
Extra for pearl stock... .... 4.00

Colt's New Navy.

Made by the Colt's Pat. Fire Arms Co., New Haven Connecticut.

This revolver has been adopted by the U. S. Navy and every one has to pass a rigid inspection.

47146 Colt's New Navy, Double Action, Self-Cocking, Shell-ejecting Revolver, nickel plated or blued finish, rubber stock, beautifully finished, finest material; length, about 12½ in., 6 shot, weight, 2 lbs.; 4½ or 6 in. barrels, 38 caliber, using No. 47198 cartridges, 6 shot. Each........................$12.00
41 caliber, using No. 47203 cartridge, 6 shot. Each..........................$12.00
By mail, 35 cents extra.

Colt's Special Target Pistol.

47147 Colt's Special Target Pistol, single action, six shot, solid frame; the best quality and finish; warranted accurate and perfect in every detail. Nickel plated or blued finish. Barrel, 7½ in., length, 12½ in.; 32-44 S. & W.................$15.80

Weight, 2 lbs. 5 oz., 38-44 S. & W. target caliber 15.75
44 S. & W. Russian caliber........ .... 15.75

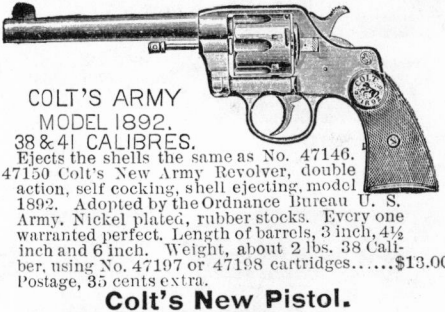

COLT'S ARMY MODEL 1892. 38 & 41 CALIBRES.

Ejects the shells the same as No. 47146.
47150 Colt's New Army Revolver, double action, self cocking, shell ejecting, model 1892. Adopted by the Ordnance Bureau U. S. Army. Nickel plated, rubber stocks. Every one warranted perfect. Length of barrels, 3 inch, 4½ inch and 6 inch. Weight, about 2 lbs. 38 caliber, using No. 47197 or 47198 cartridges......$13.00
Postage, 35 cents extra.

Colt's New Pistol.

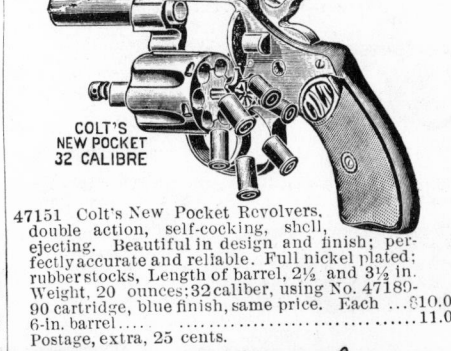

COLT'S NEW POCKET 32 CALIBRE

47151 Colt's New Pocket Revolvers, double action, self-cocking, shell ejecting. Beautiful in design and finish; perfectly accurate and reliable. Full nickel plated; rubber stocks, Length of barrel, 2½ and 3½ in. Weight, 20 ounces; 32 caliber, using No. 47189-90 cartridge, blue finish, same price. Each ...$10.00
6-in. barrel.......................... 11.00
Postage, extra, 25 cents.

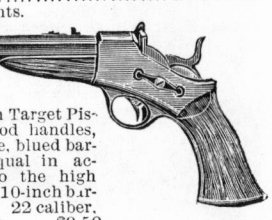

47152 The Remington Target Pistol, single shot, wood handles, case hardened frame, blued barrels. Guaranteed equal in accuracy and finish to the high priced target pistols. 10-inch barrel, 3 poundsweight. 22 caliber. short rim fire............. $9.50
32 S. & W. center fire........ 9.50

LOADED METALLIC CARTRIDGES.

We do not send cartridges C. O. D. Cartridges cannot go by mail. We can furnish all kinds of cartridges not in this list at lowest market price.

CARTRIDGES CAN BE SHIPPED WITH OTHER GOODS BY EXPRESS OR FREIGHT.

Prics subject to changes without notice. U. M. C., U. S., Lowell and Winchester Makes, all the same price and kept in stock.

RIM FIRE CARTRIDGES.

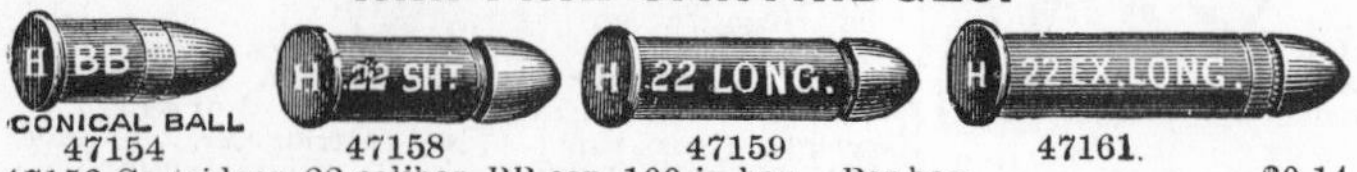

CONICAL BALL 47154 47158 47159 47161.

47153 Cartridges, 22 caliber, BB cap, 100 in box. Per box.......... $0.14
Per 1,000.......... $1.27 Weight, ¼ lb. per box.
47154 Conical Ball Cap Cartridge, 22 caliber, rim fire, box of 100.......... $0.22
Per 1,000.......... $2.00 Weight, ¼ lb. per box.
47154½ Conical Ball Cap Cartridge U. M. C. make, powder loaded. 22 caliber, per 100.......... $0.22 Per 1,000.......... 2.00
47155 Cartridges, 22 caliber, short, rim fire, U. M. C. make, "U," 50 in box .12
Per 1,000.......... 2.25
47156 Cartridges, 22 caliber, short, rim fire, Winchester make, "H," 50 in box .12
Per 1,000.......... 2.25
47157 Cartridges, 22 caliber, short, rim fire, U. S. make, 50 in box.......... .12
Per 1,000.......... 2.25
47158 Cartridges, 22 caliber, short, rim fire, 50 in box.... $0.12 Per 1,000.... 2.25
47159 Cartridges, 22 caliber, long, rim fire, 50 in box.......... .15
Per 1,000.......... $2.85 Weight, ¾ lbs. per box
47160 Cartridges, 22 caliber, long rifle, rim fire, 50 in box.......... .15
Per 1,000.......... 2.85
47161 Cartridges, 22 extra long, rim fire, 100 in box.......... .47
Per 1,000.......... $4.30 Weight. 1¼ lbs. per box.

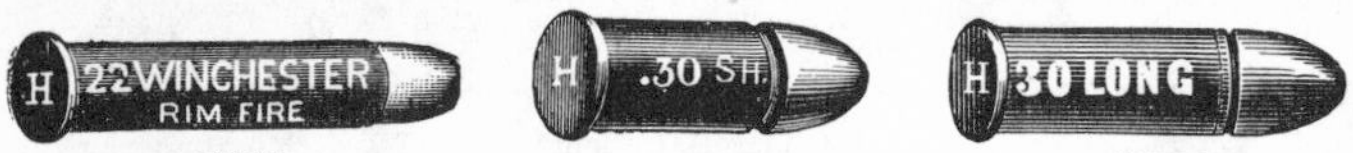

47165 47167 47168

47165 Cartridges, special 22 caliber, for Winchester model '90, repeating rifle, 7 grains powder, 45 grains lead. Per 50.... $0.24 Per 100.......... $0.46
47166 Cartridges, 25 caliber, for Stevens, Maynard and Winchester single shot rifles, 11 grains powder, 65 grain ball, rim fire, 50 in box, $0.40 Per 100 .70
47167 Cartridges, 30, short, rim fire, 50 in box, $0.23 Per 100.......... .44
Weight, ¾ lb. per box.
47168 Cartridges. 30, long, rim fire, 50 in box, $0.28 Per 100.......... .51
Weight, ¾ lbs.

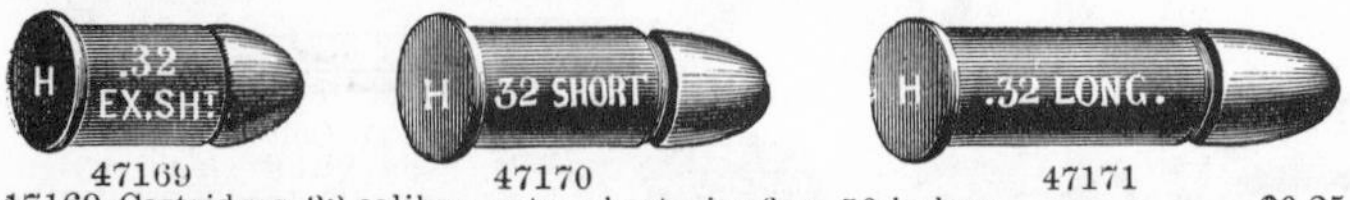

47169 47170 47171

47169 Cartridges. 32 caliber, extra short, rim fire 50 in box.......... $0.25
Per 100.......... $0.46 Weight, ½ lb. per box.
47170 Cartridges, 32 caliber, short, rim fire, 50 in box $0.26 Per 100.......... .48
Weight, ¾ lb.
47171 Cartridges, 32 caliber, long, rim fire, 50 in box $0.30 Per 100.......... .56
Weight, 1 lb.

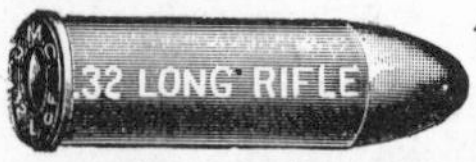

47171½ Cartridge, 32, long, rifle rim fire, for Marlin Rifle model '91, rim fire.
Per box of 50.......... $0.35
Per 100.......... .65

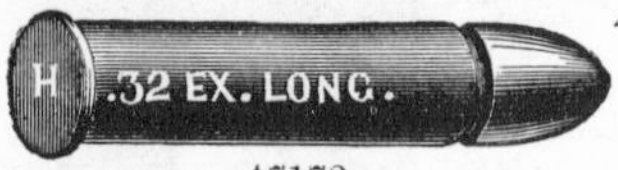

47172

47172 Cartridges, 32 caliber, extra long, rim fire 50 in box, 48c

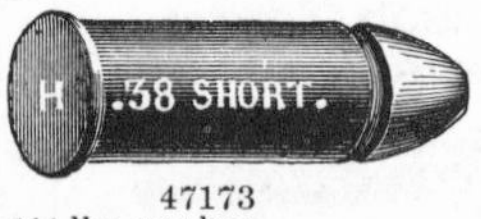

47173

Per 100.......... $0.80 Weight, 1¼ lbs. per box.
47173 Cartridges, 38 caliber, short, rim fire, 50 in box.......... $0.42
Per 100.......... $0.79 Weight, 1¼ lbs.

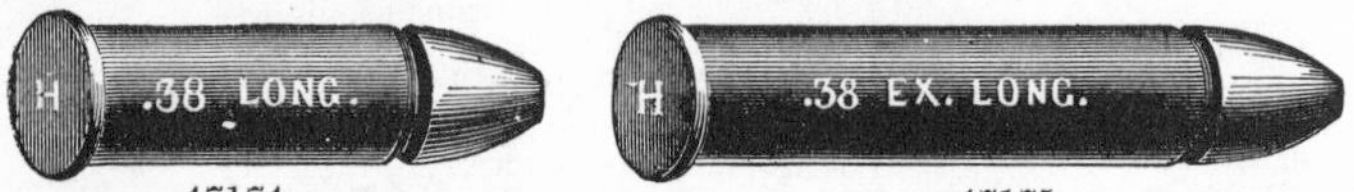

47174 47175

47174 Cartridges, 38 caliber, long, rim fire, 50 in a box.......... $0.47
Per 100.......... $0.87 Weight, 1½ lbs.
47175 Cartridges, 38 caliber, extra long, rim fire, 50 in box.......... .65
Per 100.......... $1.20 Weight, 1¾ lb.

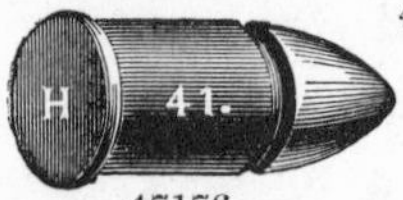

47176

47176 Cartridges, 41 caliber, rim fire, for Remington Derringer pistol.
Per box of 50...... $0.40
Per 100.......... .72
Weight, 1¼ lbs.

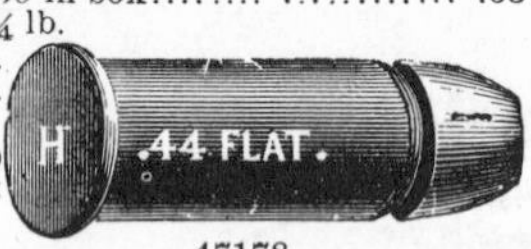

47178

47177 Cartridges, 41 caliber, long, rim fire, 50 in box. Weight, 2 lbs.......... $0.45
Per 100.......... .85
47178 Winchester, model '66, rim fire, 28 grains powder, 200 grain ball, 50 in box.......... $0.62 Per 100.......... 1.17
Weight, 1¼ lbs. per box.

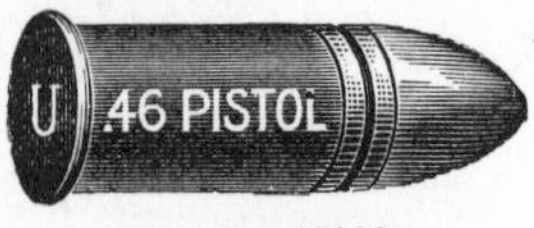

47180

47180 Cartridges, 46 caliber, rim fire, short, for Remington revolvers and Kentucky Ballard rifles. Box, 50 in box.......... $0.65
Per 100.......... 1.20
Weight, 2¼ lbs.

47181 Cartridges, 46 caliber, long, rim fire, for Remington revolvers and Kentucky Ballard rifles, 50 in box... $0.86
Per 100.......... 1.61
Weight, 3⅛ lbs per box.

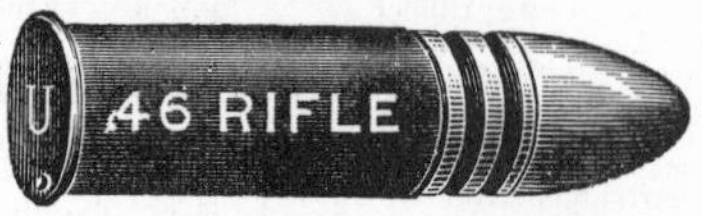

47181

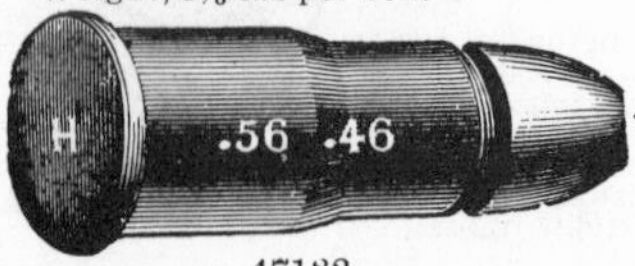

47182

47182 Cartridges, 56-46, Spencer Carbine, rim fire, 25 in box.......... $0.52
Weight, 2 lbs. Per 100.......... 1.94

47183 Cartridges, 56-50 Spencer carbine, rim fire, 25 in box.......... $0.52
Weight, 2½ lbs. per box. Per 100... 1.94

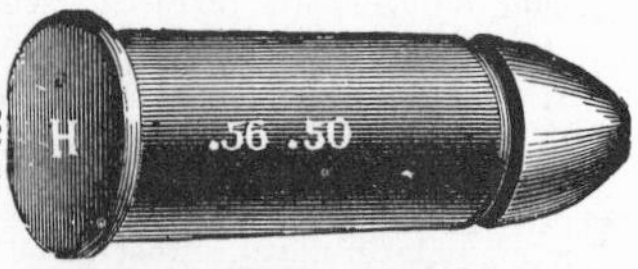

47183

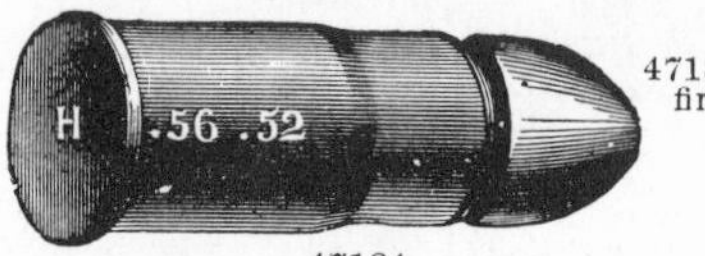

47184

47184 Cartridges, 56-52, Spencer rifle, rim fire, 25 in box.. $0.52 Per 100..... $1.94

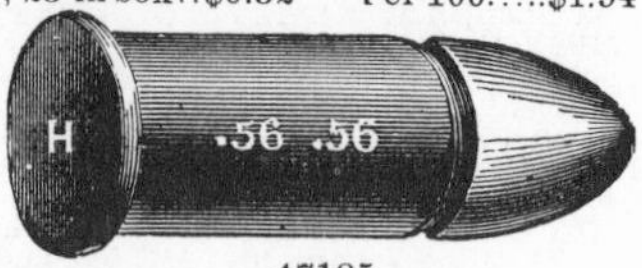

47185

47185 Cartridge, 56-56, Spencer carbine, rim fire, 25 in box.......... $0.52
Per 100.......... 1.94
Weight, 2½ lbs. per box.

Center Fire Pistol and Rifle Cartridges.

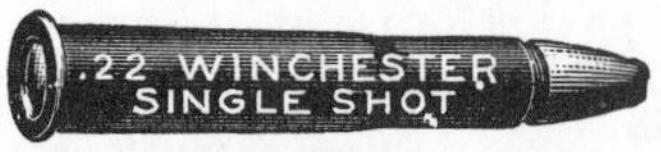

47186 Cartridges, 22 caliber, center fire, 15 grains powder, 45 grain bullet for Winchester *single shot* rifle, box of 50.. $0.58
Per 100.......... 1.10
Weight, 1 lb. per box.

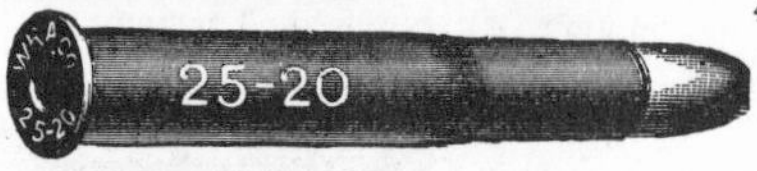

47187 Cartridges, 25-20 caliber, center fire, 19 grains powder, 86 grain ball, for Stevens, Maynard and Winchester single shot rifles, box of 50.......... $0.75
Per 100.......... 11.35
Weight, 1¼ lbs.

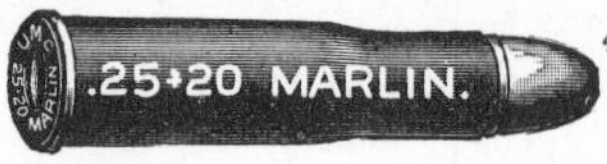

47187½ Special Cartridge, 25 and 20 caliber, 86 grain ball, for Marlin repeating rifle.
Per box of 50, center fire.......... $0.64
Per 100.......... 1.10

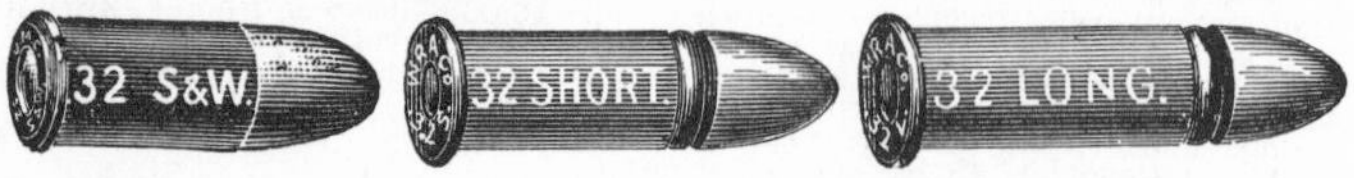

47188 47189 47190

47188 Cartridges, 32 caliber, Smith & Wesson, center fire, 50 in box.......... $0.44
Weight, 1¼ lbs. Using No. 1 primers if made by W. R. A. Co Using No. 0 primer if made by U. M. C. Co. Per 100.......... .80

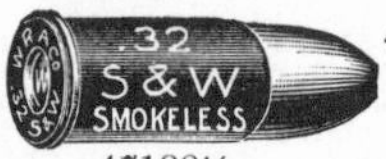

47188½

47188½ Cartridge, 32 S. & W. smokeless powder loaded: for Smith & Wesson revolvers of this caliber.
Per box of 50.......... $0.50
Per 100.......... .92
47189 Center fire, 32 caliber, short, for Colt's revolver, 50 in box.......... .44
Weight, 1¼ lbs. Per 100.......... .80
47190 Center fire, 32 caliber, long, Colt's or Ballard, 50 in box.......... .48
Weight, 1½ lbs. per box. Per 100.......... .88

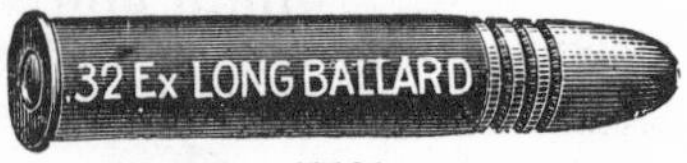

47191

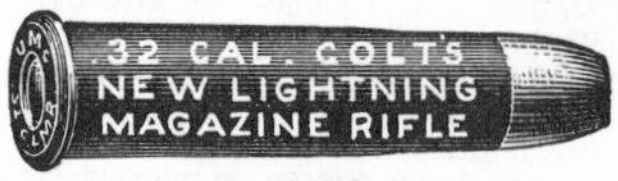

47192

47191 Cartidges, 32 caliber, extra long, center fire, 50 in box.......... $0.72
Per 100.......... $1.32 Weight, 1¾ lbs.
47192 Cartridges, center fire, 32 caliber, for Colt's lightning repeating rifle. 20 grains powder, 100 grains lead, box of 50.......... .64
Per 100.......... $1.16 Weight, 1¾ lbs. per box.

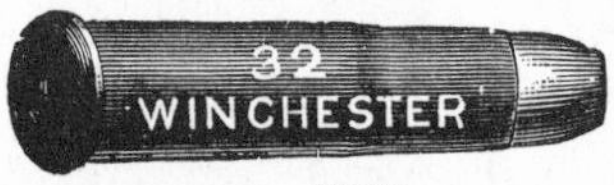

47193

47193 Cartridges for Winchester rifle, 32 caliber, center fire,

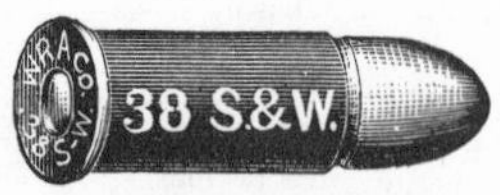

47194

20 grains powder, 115 grains lead. Weight, 1¾ lbs. Per box of 50, using No. 1 primer.......... $0.64 Per 100.......... $1.16
47194 Cartridges, 38 caliber, center fire, Smith & Wesson, 50 in box.......... .54
Per 100.......... $0.98 Weight, 2 lbs. per box.

47194½ Smokeless Powder Cartridges, for '92 model Winchester rifle also for single shot rifles of this caliber, 32 W. O. F.
Per box of 50.......... $0.94
Per 100.......... 1.75

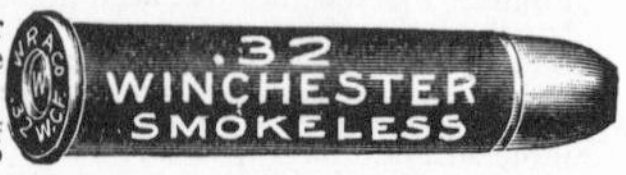

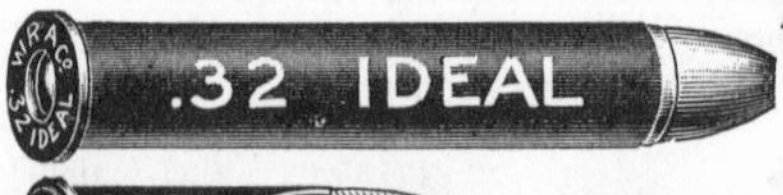

47195 32 Ideal Cartridge, 1¾ in. straight shell, 25 grains powder, 150 grains lead.
Per box of 50.......... $0.75
Per 100.......... 1.40

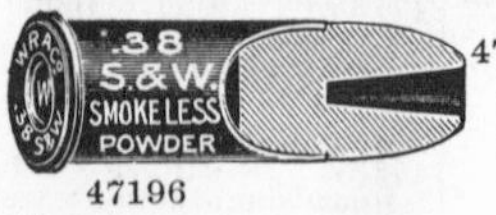

47196

47196 Smokeless Powder, 38 S. & W., 7 grain powder, 135 grains lead adapted to Smith & Wesson revolvers. Per box of 50 cartridges.......... $0.58
Per 100.......... 1.05

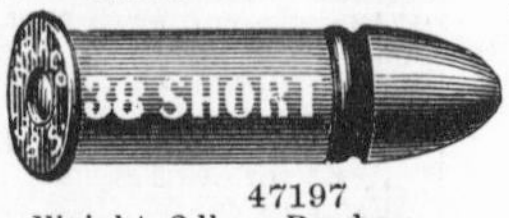

47197

47197 Center fire, 38 caliber, short, for Ballard rifles and Colt's and Remington revolvers, 50 in box.

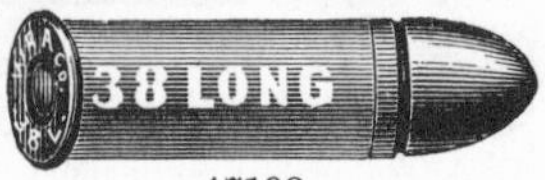

47198

Weight, 2 lbs. Per box.......... $0.54 Per 100.......... $0.98
47198 Center fire, 38 caliber, long, for Ballard rifle and Colt's revolvers, 50 in a box.......... $0.58 Per 100.......... 1.05
Weight, 2¼ lbs. per box
47198½ Cartridges, for Colt New Navy and New Army Revolvers, 38, long, inside lubricant, 50 in box. Per box.......... $0.59. Per 100.......... $1.05

Cartridges—Continued.

38 EXTRA LONG

47199 Center fire, 38 caliber, extra long, 38 grains powder, 148 grains lead, for Ballard rifle No. 2 50 in a box. Per box....$0.92
Per 100.....................1.67
Weight, 2½ lbs.

38 WCF.
47200

47200 Winchester (model '73), center fire, 38 caliber, 40 grains powder, 180 grains lead, 50 in a box, using No. 1 primer.
Per box............ ....$0.69
Per 100..........................1.38
Weight, 2¾ lbs. per box.

47200½ Smokeless Powder Cartridges. 38 and 40 caliber for Winchester rifles', 92 model, '73 model and single shot of this caliber.
Per box of 50 ....$1.16 Per 100.......................$2.25

.38 CAL. COLT'S NEW LIGHTNING MAGAZINE RIFLE
47201

47201 Cartridges, center fire, 38 caliber for Colt's lightning repeating rifle, 40 grains powder, 180 grains lead, per box of 50. ....$0.70
Per 100..........................1.37
Weight, 2¾ lbs. per box.

47203 Colt's Revolver, caliber 41, center fire, (long DA), 50 in a box. Per box........$0.70
Per 100..........................1.28
Weight, 1½ lbs.

.41 LONG COLTS, D.A.
47203

47203½ Cartridges, Colt's Revolver, 41 caliber, center fire (short DA), 50 in a box.
Per box $0.60
Weight, 1½ lbs. per box. Per 100.....$1.15

47204 Cartridges, 44 caliber, Smith & Wesson, center fire, No. 3 Russian, 50 in a box.
Per box $0.80
Per 100......................1.42
Weight, 2½ lbs

44 S.&W. RUSS.
47204

47205 Smith & Wesson, American model, 44 caliber, center fire, 50 in a box.
Per box $0.76
Per 100......................1.38
Weight, 2½ lbs.

44 S.& W.AM
47205

47207 Cartridges for Colt's Pistol, 44 caliber, center fire, 50 in a box. Per box..... ....$0.80
Per 100..... ....$1.45 Weight, 2½ lbs. per box

47208 Cartridges for Winchester Rifle, model 1873, 44 caliber, center fire, 40 grains powder, 200 grains lead, 50 in a box, using No. 1 primer. Per box..$0.70
Per 100......................1.38
Weight, 1¾ lbs.

.44 WINCHESTER MODEL 1873
47208

47209 Cartridges, 44 caliber, long, center fire, for old Ballard rifles, 50 in a box.
Per box................$0.88 Per 100..............$1.60. Weight, 2½ lbs.

47210 Cartridges, Evans' New Model Repeating Rifle, 44 caliber, 42 grains powder, 280 grains lead, 50 in a box. Per box............$1.00
Per 100..........................1.89
Weight, 3¼ lbs. per box.

.44 EVANS. N.M.
47210

47211 Cartridges, Evans' Old Model Repeating Rifle (34 shot), shell 1 inch long. 33 grains powder, 220 grain bullet, 50 in a box.
Per box...................$0.88
Per 100......................1.60
Weight, 2½ lbs.

44 EVANS, O.M.
47211

47213 Cartridges, 44 caliber, Webley. center fire, for bull dog revolver, 50 in a box. Per box........$0.68
Per 100..........................1.20
Weight, 2¼ lbs. per box.

.44 WEBLEY
47213

47214 Cartridges, center fire, 44 caliber, for Colt's lightning repeating rifle, 40 grains powder, 217 grains lead, per box of 50....
.................$0.70
Per 100......................1.37
Weight, 2¾ lbs.

.44 CAL. COLT'S NEW LIGHTNING MAGAZINE RIFLE
47214

47216 Colt's Army and DA Revolvers, 45 caliber, center fire, 50 in a box.
Per box............$0.84
Per 100......................1.57
Weight, 3¼ lbs. per box.

.45 COLTS
47216

Center Fire Cartridges for Target and Sporting Rifles.

Five per cent. discount for CASH in case lots if 1,000 of one kind are ordered.

.30 U.S.ARMY

47219 U.S. Army Cartridge, smokeless powder, steel jacketed bullet.

40 grains powder, 220 grain bullet. Per box of 20...............   ......$0.90
For Winchester single-shot rifle, per 100 .... 4.25

32 — 40 BALLARD & MARLIN

Per 100.

47220 Cartridges, for Ballard, Marlin and Winchester single shot rifles, center fire, 32 caliber, 40 grains of powder, 165 grains lead. Weight, 1¼ lbs. Per box of 20 ....$0.47 $2.29
47221 Cartridges, for Ballard, Marlin and Winchester single shot, short range, 32-40 caliber, 13 grains powder, 98 grains lead. Weight, 1¼ lbs. Per box of 20...................48 2.33
47221½ Cartridges, 32-40-165 for model '94 Winchester repeating rifles and single shot rifles. Per box of 20.....$0.47. ....Per 100............$2.29

Cartridges—Continued.

.38 — 55 BALLARD & MARLIN

47222 Center Fire 38-55 caliber, powder 55 grains, lead 255 grains, for Ballard and Marlin and Winchester single shot rifles

of this caliber; 20 in a box. Weight, 1½ lbs...........$0.60   Per 100...$2.72
47223 Cartridges 38-55 Express for Marlin and Winchester rifles, 38-55 caliber. Box of 20............$0.63. Per 100.......................$2.96
47224 Cartridges, for Ballard, Marlin and Winchester single shot, 38-55 caliber. SHORT RANGE, 20 grains powder, 155 grains lead; same length shell as No. 47222. Per box of 20.$0.60. Per 100. ..   2.72
47224½ Cartridges, 38-55-255, for model 94 Winchester repeating rifles and single shot rifles. Per box of 20.............$0.63......Per 10..................2.96

.38 – 56 – 255 WINCHESTER MODEL 1886

47225 Cartridges, for Winchester rifle, models 1886, 38-56 caliber, 255 grains. Weight, 1¾ lbs. 20 in box.

Per box..... ....$0.60   Per 100......................$2.70

.38 – 70 – 255 WINCHESTER MODEL 1886

47226 Cartridge for Model, 86, Winchester rifle, 38-70-255. 20 in a box.
Per box.   Per 100
$0.60 $2.85

.40 – 60 COLT'S NEW LIGHTNING MAGAZINE

47227 Cartridges, center fire for Colt's lightning rifle, 40 caliber, 60 grains powder, 260 grains lead. Weight, 1¾lbs. Box of 20.

Per box..... ....$0.55   Per 100..... ....$2.62

.40 – 70 – 330 WINCHESTER MODEL 1886

47228 Cartridges for Winchester rifle, model '86, 40-70-330, 20 in a box.
Per box...$0.65
Per 100.   3.00

40 — 60 WINCHESTER

47230 Cartridges, for Winchester rifle, 40-60 caliber, 60 grains powder, 210 grains lead. 20 in box.
Per box....... ....$0.54
Per 100........................2.62
Weight, 1⅝ lbs.

40 – 65 – 260 WINCHESTER MODEL 1886

47231 Cartridges, for Winchester repeating rifle, model 1886, 40-65-260 caliber, center fire. 20 in box.
Per box.......$0.59
Weight, 1½ lbs.
Per 100........ 2.70

.40-60 MARLIN

47232 Cartridges, for Marlin rifle, 40-60 caliber, center fire, 60 grains powder, 260 grains lead, 20 in a box.
Per box........$0.59
Weight, 1½ lbs.
Per 100....   2.70

.40 – 82 – 260 WINCHESTER MODEL 1886

47233 Cartridges, 40-70-330 sharps, straight shell, grooved ball, 20 in box.
Per box......$0.64
Per 100....   2.95
Weight, 1¾ lbs.
Per 100
$2.97

47234 Cartridges, 40 caliber, 82 grains powder, 260 grain bullet, center fire, for Winchester rifle, model 1886. Per box of 20, $0.64
47235 Cartridges, 40-75-260, hollow point express bullet, for Winchester Rifle, 40-82 caliber. Per box of 20........ ....$0.75   3.20

.40-85 BALLARD

47236 Cartridges, 40-85 caliber, center fire, straight shell, for Ballard Rifle; this caliber, 85 grains powder, 370 grains lead. Per box of 10..........$0.45
Per 100
$4.12
47237 Cartridges, for Sharp's rifle, 40-90, Sharp's, Remington and Winchester single shot rifles, center fire, 3¼ inches, straight shell, 90 grains powder, 370 grains lead. For shape of shell see 40-85 Ballard. Per box of 10..................$0.45   4.12
47239 Cartridges, 40-110 Express, 3¼ inch shell, 110 grains powder, 260 grains lead. Per box of 10 ....$0.72   6.80

WINCHESTER 45-60

47240 Cartridges, for Winchester rifle, model 1876, 45 caliber, center fire, straight shell, 60 grains of powder, 300 grains of lead. 20 in box.
Per box..................$0.60
Per 100... ....   2.72

Weight per box, 1⅝ lbs.

WINCHESTER CENTENNIAL MODEL 1876 45

47242 Cartridges, for Winchester rifle, model '76, 45 caliber, center fire, '75 grains powder, 350 grains lead, 20 in box.
Per box............$0.63
Per 100............ 3.00
Weight per box, 1⅛ lbs.

Cartridges—Continued.

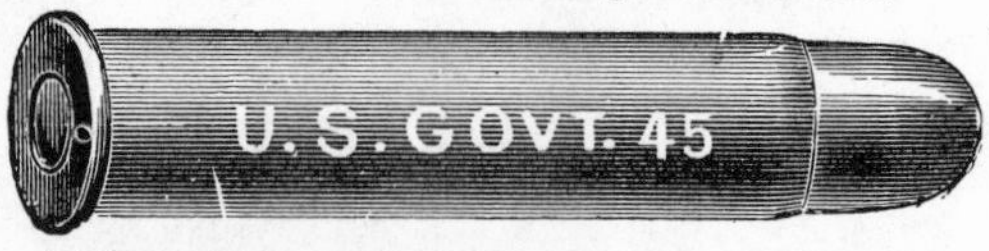

47243 Cartridges, 45 caliber, center fire, for Winchester rifle, model 1886, 70 grains powder, 405 grains lead, 20 in box. Weight, per box, 36 oz.
Per box...................$0.67 Per 100..........................$2.98

47244 Cartridges, for Marlin rifle and Winchester Model '86 rifle, 45 caliber, center fire, 70 grains powder, 405 grains lead, 20 in box.
Per box...............$0.67 Per 100...............$2.98. Weight, per box, 36 oz.

47245 Cartridges, for single shot rifles, 45-70 caliber, for armory practice, 5 grains powder, 140 grains lead, round ball, per box of 20.
Per box...............$0.67 Per 100...............$2.98 Weight, per box, 20 oz.

47246 Cartridges, for Marlin rifle or any other 45-70 caliber rifle, 45 caliber, 85 grains powder, 285 grain bullet, per box of 20.......................$0.67
Weight, per box, 30 oz. Per 100...............................2.98

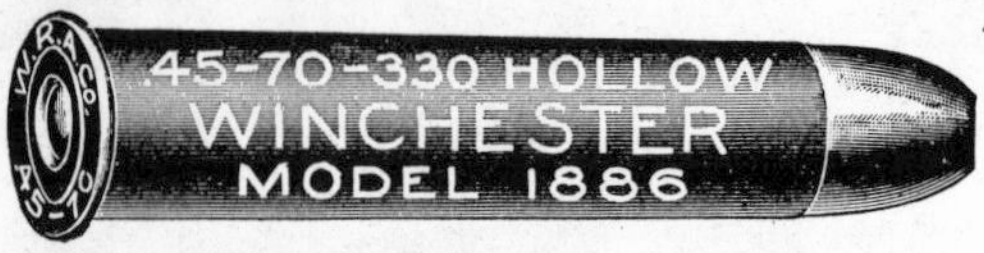

47247 Cartridges, 45-70-330, hollow bullet, (Gould bullet) for Winchester rifles, 45-70 caliber.
Per box of 20...$0.70
Per 100......... 2.97

47248 Cartridges 45-70-350, solid ball, for any 45-70 caliber rifle.
Per box of 20....$0.70
Per 100......... 2.97

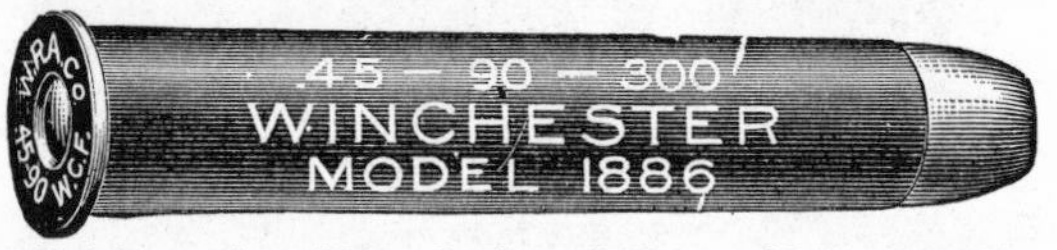

47249 Cartridges for Winchester repeating rifle model 1886, 45 caliber, 90 grains powder 300 grain bullet.
Weight, per box, 28 oz. Per box of 20 ......$0.70 Per 100 ....$3.17

47250 Cartridges 45-90-300, hollow point express bullet, for Winchester Rifle, 45-90 caliber. Per box of 20...............$0.75 Per 100.......................$3.25

47254 Cartridge, Sharp's only, 2¼ in. necked shell, 44-77-405. Per box of 20 .80
Per 100...3.62
Weight, per box 30 oz.

47255 Cartridges, U. S. Government 45 caliber, 70 grains powder, 2$\frac{1}{10}$ inch shell, 500 grain ball, special long-range target, for Winchester and other 45-70 caliber rifles, 20 in box..$0.72
Weight, per box, 36 oz. Per 100..3.23

Cartridges—Continued.

	Per box.	Weight.	Per 100
47257 Cartridges, 50 caliber, U. S. Government center fire, 70 grains powder, 1¾ inch shell, per box of 20	$0.80	44 oz.	$3.62
47258 Cartridges, Regular and Remington, 44-77-470, necked 2¼ inch shell, patched ball per box of 20	.80	44 oz.	3.62
47259 Cartridges, Sharp's straight 2⅞ inch shell, 45-105-550, per box of 20	1.08	55 oz.	4.84

47261 Cartridges, 50 95 Winchester Express Rifle, 95 grains powder, 300 grains bullet, 20 in box.
Price, per box, $0.76 Per 100 $3.35

47262 Cartridges. 50-110-300, Winchester Express, per box of 20 .87 3.92

Cartridges for Remington Rifle.

	Per box.	Weight, per box.	Per 100
47264 32 caliber, center fire, 30 grains powder, 125 grains lead, per box of 50	$0.90	36 oz	$1.70
47265 38 caliber center fire, 1¾ inch, 40 grains powder, 245 grains lead, straight shell, per box of 20	.60		2.65
47266 38 caliber, center fire, 2¼ inch straight shell, 50 grains powder, 245 grains lead, per box of 20	.63		2.88
47267 40 caliber, center fire, 45 grains powder, 265 grains lead, 1⅞ inch straight shell, per box of 20	.62	24 oz.	2.88
47268 40 caliber, center fire, 65 grains powder, 330 grains lead, 2¾ inch straight shell, per box of 20	.71	38 oz.	3.30

47271 32-44 caliber, center fire, S. & W. target cartridges, grooved ball, 19 grs. powder, 83 gr. ball; per box of 50...$0.71

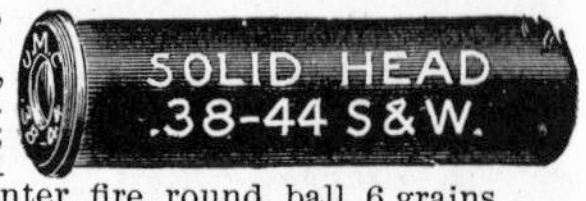

47272 32-44 S. & W gallery cartridges, center fire, round ball, 6 grains powder, 50 grain bullet, per box of 50...$0.68

47273 38-44 caliber, center fire, S. & W. target cartridges, grooved ball, 23 grains powder, 140 grain ball, per box of 50................................ .87

47274 38-44 caliber, center fire. S. & W. gallery, round ball, 6 grains powder, 70 grain ball, per box of 50.. .70

Patent Metal Patch Bullet Cartridges.

These Cartridges are made up with the regular shell, and vary only in charge of powder and weight and kind of bullet. The Patent Metal Patched Bullet gives increased accuracy, penetration and cleanliness. The bullet has a covering of copper.

47275 Metal Patch Cartridge, 38-56-255 for Winchester Mod. '86 rifle.
Per box of 20...................$0.65 Per 100.............................$3.00

47276 Metal Patch Cartridge, 40-65-245 for Winchester Rifle Mod. '86.
Per box of 20...................$0.65 Per 100.............................$3.00

47277 Metal Patch Cartridge, 40-82-245 for Winchester Rifle Mod. '86.
Per box of 20...................$0.68 Per 100.............................$3.20

47278 Metal Patch Cartridge, 45-90-295 for Winchester Rifle.
Per box of 20...................$0.75 Per 100.............................$3.73

Blank Cartridges.
Order No. 47280.

Primed and regular powder charge, but without ball.
Weight, per box of 50, ¾ to 1¼ lbs.

22 caliber, rim fire, per box of 100	$0.18
32 caliber, rim fire, per box of 50	.22
32 caliber S. & W. Blanks, per 100	.75
38 caliber, S. & W. Blanks, per 100	.91
44 W. C. F. Model '73 Blanks, per 100	1.35
45-70 caliber, per box of 25	.57
50-70 caliber, per box of 25	.72

Empty Rifle and Pistol Shells.
Order No. 47281.

Sold in any quantity from one shell to a thousand. All center fire. Shells can be sent by mail.

	Weight.	Per 100.
22 caliber, Winchester	1 lb.	$0.77
25-20 caliber	1 lb.	1.02
32 caliber, for Smith & Wesson	1⅛ lb.	.55
32 caliber, for Winchester, 1873 model	1⅜ lb.	.75
32-44 S. & W., gallery	¾ lb.	.90
32-44 S. & W., target	¾ lb.	91
32 caliber, for Colt's rifle	1⅜ lb.	78
38 caliber, for Smith & Wesson	1⅛ lb.	.64
38 caliber, for Colt's pistol	2 lb.	.63
38 caliber, for Winchester, model 1873	1¾ lb.	.85
38-44 S. & W., gallery	1⅛ lb.	1.08
38-44 S. & W., target	1⅛ lb.	1.08
41 caliber, for Colt's long D. A. pistol	2 lb.	.63
44 caliber for Smith & Wesson, Russian	2 lb.	.85
44 caliber, for Winchester, model 1873	1¾ lb.	.85
44 caliber, for Colt's Lightning rifle	1¾ lb.	.86
44 caliber, for Evans' rifle, new model	1$\frac{1}{8}$ lb.	1.00
44 caliber, Webley	⅞ lb.	.68
45 caliber, for Colt's revolvers	1$\frac{1}{8}$ lb.	.90
32-40 caliber, Ballard and Marlin	2 lb.	1.30
38-55 caliber, Ballard and Marlin	2½ lb.	1.50
40-60 caliber, Winchester, model 1876	2¾ lb.	1.68
40-85 caliber, Ballard	2¾ lb.	2.20
40-65 caliber, Winchester, model 1886	2¾ lb.	1.55
45-60 caliber, Winchester, model 1876	2½ lb.	1.68
40-82 caliber Winchester, model 1886	2¾ lb.	2.00
45-70 caliber, U. S. Government	2¾ lb.	1.90
45-75 caliber, Winchester, model 1876	2¼ lb.	1.75
44-77 caliber, Sharp's only, necked	2¼ lb.	2.00
40-90 Ballard	2¾ lb	2.20
45-90 Winchester	2⅞ lb.	2.00
50-70 Government	2¾ lb.	1.80
40-70 Remington, straight	2⅛ lb.	1.85
40-90 Sharp's, straight	3¼ lb.	2.26
38-56 Winchester	2⅞ lb.	1.60
40-90 Sharp's necked	2⅝ lb.	2.20

Prices of cartridges, shot and ammunition in general are subject to market change without notice.

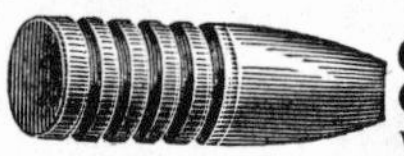

Grooved Bullets.
Order No. 47285.

Weight, per 100, 1¾ lbs. to 4 lbs., according to size.

Sizes.	description.	Weight, grains.	Price, per 100.	Weight, per 100.
22	Winchester	45	$0.21	1 lbs.
32	Short Pistol	80	.30	......
32	Long Pistol	90	.35	......
32-40	Short Range	98	.45	2 lbs
38-55	Short Range	155	.63	2¼ lbs
25-20	Stevens'	86	.35	1¾ lbs.
32	Smith & Wesson	85	.25	1¾ lbs.
32-73	Winchester	115	.35	2 lbs.
32-40	Ballard & Marlin	165	.60	2½ lbs.
32-40	Ballard & Marlin	185	.81	4 lbs.
32-44	S. & W.	83	.47	1 lb.
32-44	S. & W. round ball	50	.36	1½ lbs.
38-44	S. & W., target	146	.48	1¾ lbs.
38-44	S. & W., round	70	37	1 lbs.
38	Smith & Wesson	146	.38	3 lbs.
38-73	Winchester	180	.42	4 lbs.
38-55	Ballard & Marlin	255	.78	4 lbs.
40-60	Winchester	210	.66	3½ lbs.
40-60	Marlin	260	.75	3½ lbs.
45	Marlin or Colt Rifle	285	.94	4½ lbs.
44-73	Winchester	200	.50	3¼ lbs.
44	Smith & Wesson, Russian	256	.54	4 lbs.
45	Colt DA	260	.58	4¼ lbs.
45-60	Winchester	300	.75	4½ lbs.
45-75	Winchester	350	.79	5¼ lbs.
45-70	Government	405	1.00	6 lbs.
45-70	Government	500	1.25	7¼ lbs.
50-70	Government	450	1.15	6¾ lbs.
50-95	Hollow Ball Express	300	.90	5¼ lbs.
50-95	Solid Ball Express	312	.76	....
45-70	Solid Ball	350	.86	....
45-70	Hollow Ball (gould bullet)	330	.99	....
50-110	Winchester	300	.99	....
32	Ideal	150	45	....

Patched Bullets.

Order No. 47286.

Size.	Description.	Weight, grains.	Weight, per 100.	Price, per 100.
32-40	B. & M.	165		$0.90
32-40	Ballard.	185	3¼ lbs.	.95
38-55	Ballard.	255	4¼ lbs.	.95
40-85	Ballard.	370	5¾ lbs.	1.05
40-90	Sharp & Winchester, straight	370	5¾ lbs.	1.05
44-77	Remington.	470	7 lbs.	1.34
44-90	Remington.	550	8 lbs.	1.40
45-70	Sharp's	420	6¼ lbs.	1.25
45-105	Sharp's	550	10¼ lbs.	1.89
45	....	500	7½ lbs.	1.48
45	....	330	5 lbs.	.96

Metal Patched Bullets.

Order No. 47287.

	Price, per 100.
38-56--245 grains	$1.00
40-65--245 grains	1.00
40-82--245 grains	1.00
45-90--295 grains	1.00

The metal patched bullet is adapted to Winchester rifles of above calibers.

Everlasting Shells.

No.	Size.	Description.	Each.
47294	45-70	Ballard Everlasting Shells	$0.08
47295	45-100	Ballard Everlasting Shells	.07

By mail, 1 cent extra.

Shot Cartridges.

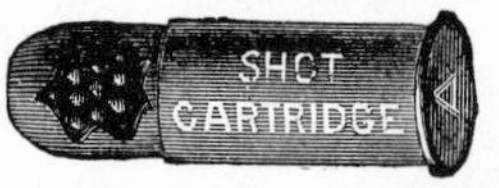

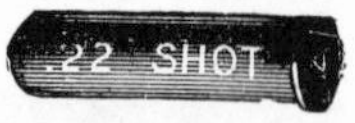

Loaded with shot instead of ball. For use in rifles and revolvers.

	Weight, per 100.	Price, per 100.
47300 22 caliber, rim fire, 50 in box.	¾ lbs.	$0.55
47301 32 caliber, long rim fire, 25 in box	2 lbs.	1.15
47303 32 caliber, S. & W., center fire, 50 in box	2 lbs.	.98
47304 38 caliber, S. & W., center fire, 50 in box	4 lbs	1.30
47305 44 caliber, Winchester, model 1873, center fire, 50 in box	5 lbs.	1.64
47307 32 caliber, center fire, Winchester model 1873, 50 in box	2½ lbs.	1.36
47308 38 caliber. center fire. Winchester model 1873, 50 in box	4 ½ lbs.	1.65
47309 56-52 caliber, Spencer rim fire		2.50
47309½ 56-56 caliber, Spencer rim, 25 in box		2.50

Pin Fire Pistol Cartridges.

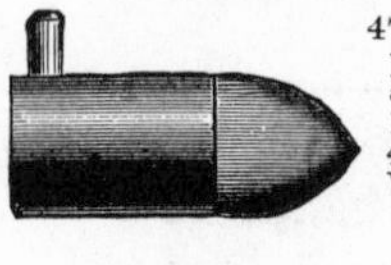

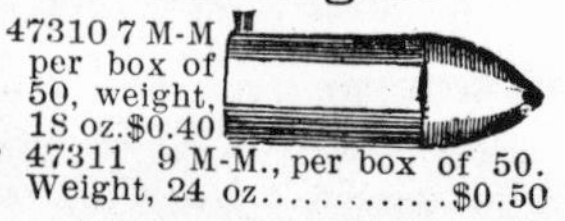

47310 7 M-M per box of 50, weight, 18 oz. $0.40

47311 9 M-M., per box of 50. Weight, 24 oz..............$0.50

In sizes 7 M-M 32 calibeer, 9 M-M is 38 caliber, 12 M-M is 44 caliber.

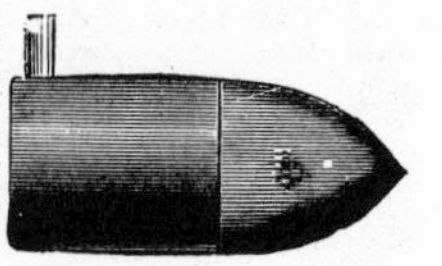

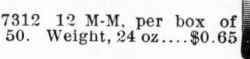

47312 12 M-M, per box of 50. Weight, 24 oz....$0.65

Machine-Loaded Paper Shot Shells.

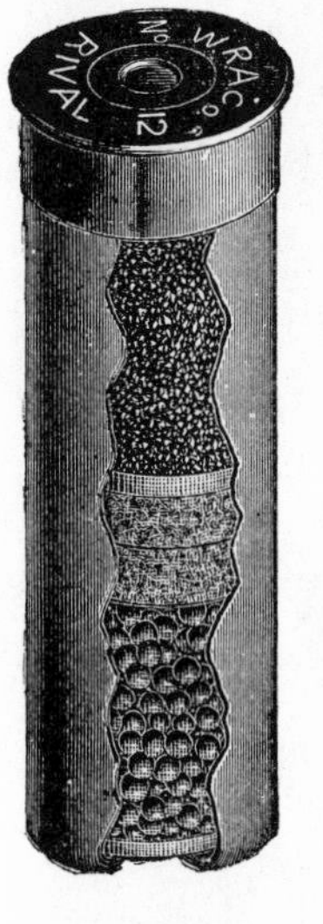

Every Shell warranted. Loaded Shells can go by freight or express, alone or with other goods.

The shells used are the celebrated WATERPROOF RIVAL and Club, U. M. C. and Winchester make. (Waterproof paper shells.) Put up in boxes of 25 shells, 20 boxes or 500 shells to the case. These shells are loaded with two thick black edge wads, and one CARDBOARD wad over the powder, and one thin cardboard wad over the shot.

NO BETTER MADE.

The uniformity of the material used and the regularity of the machine work, insure level seating of wads and even pressure of powder, the compression being such as to secure the *highest explosive force*, thereby giving absolute perfection of loading, and becoming at once the most salable form of fixed ammunition. We ean usually furnish these goods, loaded with Dupont, Laflin & Rand, or Hazzard American dead shot powder.

PRICES SUBJECT TO CHANGE WITHOUT NOTICE.

Weight, per case, 12 gauge, 65 lbs.; 10 gauge, 77 lbs. 500 shells in a case.

5 per cent. discount for cash on 1,000 lots or over.

Order No. 47315. 12 Cauge.

Black Powder.

Load No.	Am't of powder	Am't of shot	Size shot	Adapted to shooting.	Price per box 25	Price per 100
701	3 dr.	1 oz	10	Woodcock	$0.34	$1.22
703	3¼ dr.	1⅛ oz	9	Snipe	.35	1.25
705	3¼ dr.	1 oz	8	Quail	.34	1.24
707	3¼ dr.	1⅛ oz	8	**Quail & Prairie ch'ks**	.36	1.25
709	3½ dr.	1⅛ oz	8	Prairie chicken	.37	1.31
711	3 dr.	1¼ oz	8	Inanimate Targets.	.37	1.31
713	3¼ dr.	1¼ oz	8	Inanimate Targets.	.38	1.34
715	3½ dr.	1¼ oz	8	Live Pigeons	.38	1.34
717	3¼ dr.	1¼ oz	7	Clay Pigeons	.38	1.34
719	3¼ dr.	1⅛ oz	7	Ruffed Grouse	.3	1.25
721	3½ dr.	1⅛ oz	7	Teal	.37	1.32
723	3½ dr.	1¼ oz	7	Live Pigeons	.39	1.37
725	3¼ dr.	1⅛ oz	6	Bluebill	.36	1.29
727	3½ dr.	1⅛ oz	6	Pintail	,37	1.32
729	3½ dr.	1⅛ oz	5	Mallard	.36	1.32
731	3¾ dr.	1⅛ oz	4	Red-head	.38	1.34
733	3¾ dr.	1⅛ oz	3	Canvas-back	.38	1.34
735	4 dr.	1⅛ oz	2	Turkey	.38	1.37
737	4 dr.	1⅛ oz	1	Brant	.38	1.37
739	4 dr.	1⅛ oz	BB	Goose	.45	1.54
741	3 dr.	1⅛ oz	9		.34	1.22
743	3 dr.	1⅛ oz	8		.34	1.23
745	3 dr.	1⅛ oz	8		.36	1.27
747	3 dr.	1⅛ oz	7		.34	1.22
749	3 dr.	1⅛ oz	6		.34	1.22
751	3¼ dr.	1⅛ oz	5		.36	1.29
755	3 dr.	1⅛ oz	7		.35	1.27
757	3 dr.	1½ oz	7		.35	1.30

NO CHARGE For Cases Or Cartage.

Order No. 47316. 10 Gauge.

Machine Loads. Black Powder.

Load No.	Am't of powder	Am't of shot.	Size shot.	Adapted to shooting.	Price per 25	Price per 100
700	4 dr.	1⅛ oz.	10	Woodcock	$0.40	$1.41
702	4 dr.	1⅛ oz	9	Snipe	.40	1.41
704	4 dr.	1⅛ oz.	8	Quail [en	.38	1.42
706	4¼ dr	1⅛ oz.	8	**Quail & Prairie Chick-**	.40	1.44
708	3¾ dr.	1¼ oz.	8	Inanimate Targets.	.40	1.44
710	4 dr.	1¼ oz.	8	Inanimate Targets.	.41	1.46
712	4¼ dr.	1¼ oz.	8	Inanimate Targets	.42	1.49
714	4½ dr.	1¼ oz.	8	Live Pigeons	.42	1.51
716	4¼ dr	1¼ oz	7	Clay Pigeons	.42	1.49
718	4¼ dr.	1⅛ oz.	7	Ruffed Grouse	.40	1.44
720	4½ dr.	1⅛ oz.	7	Teal	.41	1.46
722	4½ dr.	1¼ oz.	7	Live Pigeons	.42	1.51
724	4¼ dr.	1⅛ oz.	6	Bluebill	.42	1.44
726	4½ dr.	1⅛ oz.	6	Pintail	.41	1.46
728	4½ dr.	1⅛ oz.	5	Mallard	.41	1.46
730	4½ dr.	1⅛ oz.	4	Red-Head	.41	1.46
732	4¾ dr.	1⅛ oz.	3	Canvas-Back	.42	1.49
734	5 dr.	1⅛ oz.	2	Turkey	.42	1.51
736	5 dr.	1⅛ oz.	1	Brant	.42	1.51
738	5 dr.	1⅛ oz.	BB	Goose	.55	1.66
740	3½ dr.	1¼ oz.	8		.40	1.41
742	3½ dr.	1⅛ oz.	7		.39	1.37
744	3¾ dr.	1⅛ oz.	6		.39	1.39
746	4 dr.	1⅛ oz.	6		.40	1.41
748	4 dr.	1⅛ oz.	7		.40	1.41
750	4¼ dr.	1⅛ oz.	5		.40	1.44

See our quotations of Books on Hunting and Sporting Subjects.

Order No. 47318. 16 Gauge.

Machine Load Black Powder.

Load No.	Am't of powder	Am't of shot.	Size shot.		Price per 25	Price per 100.
800	2½ dr.	⅞ oz.	10		$0.33	$1.20
802	2¾ dr.	1 oz.	10		.37	1.27
804	2½ dr.	⅞ oz.	9		.35	1.20
806	2¾ dr.	1 oz.	9		.37	1.27
808	2¾ dr.	1 oz.	8		.37	1.27
810	2¾ dr.	1 oz.	7		.37	1.27
812	2¾ dr.	1 oz.	6		.37	1.27
814	3 dr.	1 oz.	6		.38	1.30
815	2½ dr.	1 oz.	8		.37	1.25
816	2½ dr.	1 oz.	7		.37	1.25

M. W. & Co.'s Prices for Hand-Loaded Shells.

USE OUR HAND-LOADED SHELLS AND IMPROVE YOUR SCORES 10 TO 20 PER CENT.

A MILLION LOADED IN 1894 AND NOT A MIS-FIRE OR A RETURNED SHELL.

EVERY LOAD WARRANTED.

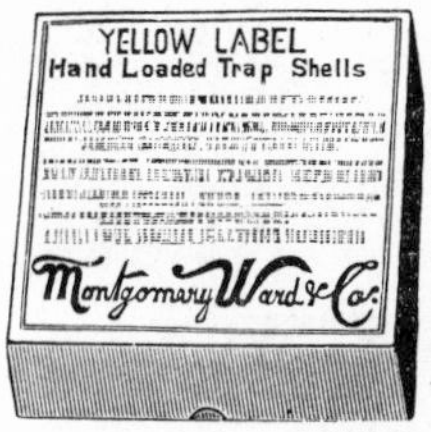

Your ammunition is only second in importance to your gun. Your gun may be of the highest grade, but with improper ammunition a cheaper gun properly loaded might prove more effective at the trap or in the field. Knowing this to be a fact we have added this new department and placed it under the supervision of a well-known trap shooter who has had long experience in loading shells for the most prominent trap shooters in the West. Shooting and testing all kinds of guns and experimenting with all kinds of powder for years, assures us that we can guarantee our hand loaded shells to be as good as it is possible to obtain anywhere in the world. A trial will convince you that our claim is good.

Our Famous $2.00 Load.

S. S.", "E. C." OR DUPONTS SMOKELESS POWDER.

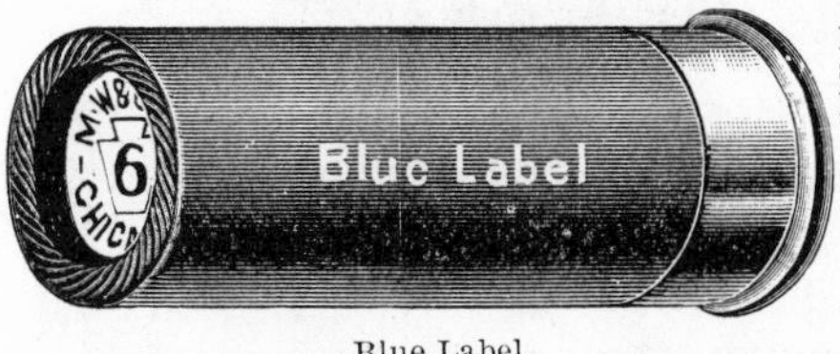

Blue Label.

Loaded with "S S" Smokeless "E. C." powder or Dupont smokeless powder. No other powder will be loaded under the BLUE LABEL BRAND. Loaded into U. M. C. Nitro Club or Climax or W. R. A. Nitro Blue Rival Paper Shells. These shells have the new strong primers.

47322 12 or 16 gauge, 3 drams or less powder; ten gauge 3¾, drams or less powder: any size of Drop Shot. Per 100, 12 or 16 gauge $2.00

Per 100, 10 gauge 2.35

Our World-Beater $2.40 Load.--(Yellow Label).

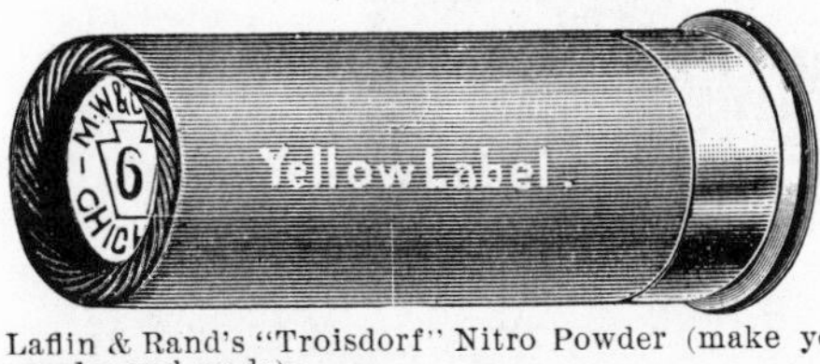

47323 Loaded into "Nitro Club," "Nitro Blue Rival No.3 W Primer," or "Climax Paper Shells. Any quantity of powder, any quantity or size of drop or chilled shot. (S. S.) NITRO POWDER or WOOD POWDER, trap grade, or SCHULTZE POWDER, or E. C. "Dupont's Smokeless," or Laflin & Rand's "Troisdorf" Nitro Powder (make your own selection of shell and powder and wads).

12 or 16 gauge, per 100 .... $2.40 10 gauge $2.85

Our Yellow Label $2.85 Load.

47324 Loaded in the new U.M.C. Red Color "Smokeless" Grade Shells with the No. 3 long quick primer, or Winchester "Leader," or U. S. "Rapid" Nitro Shells. These shells are made especially for nitro powders. Any quantity of Wood, Schultze, E. C. (SS) Smokeless, or "Dupont's Smokeless," or Laflin & Rand's "Troisdorf" powder. Any quantity of chilled or soft shot. Wadded and loaded in the most scientific manner, by a well-known trap shooter.

12 gauge per 100 .... $2.85. 10 gauge .... $3.35.

No "hang fires" when you use our S. S. Loads. Every shell warranted.

Our Trap Shooters' Delight $3.40 Load - (Yellow Label).

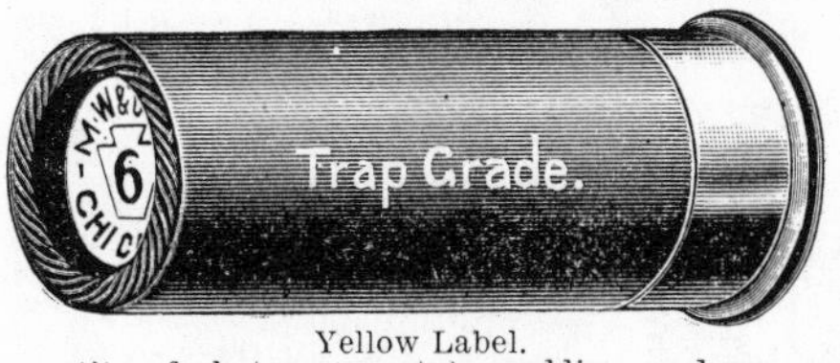

Yellow Label.

47325 Schultze, E. C., S. S. Wood or Black (any grade) or "Dupont's Smokeless," or Laflin & Rand's "Troisdorf" powder loaded into U. M. C. Trap metal-lined shells or Eley gas tight or Red Smokeless Paper Shells or WINCHESTER TRAP OUTSIDE REINFORCED paper shells, with high-grade wadding. Any size or quantity of shot, or any style wadding, and any quantity of powder. Price, per 100, 12 gauge $3.40. 10 gauge $3.90

Every one of our hand-loaded shells are warranted the best possible to furnish. No two guns will shoot exactly alike, whether made and bored by the same man or not. This being a fact your only safe way is to test your gun with different loads until you find the load or the loads it will shoot the best.

Black Powder Hand Loaded Shells.

47326 Black Powder, Dupont, Laflin & Rand, American Dead Shot F. G., F. F. G., F. F. F. G., loaded into Club, Climax or Rival paper shells.

Drams	2½	3	3½	4	4½	5
Per 100, 12 gauge., 16 gauge	$1 80	1.90	2.00	2.10	2.20	2.30

10 gauge loads, 20 cents per 100 higher than 12 gauge.

If your gun don't shoot to suit you, order some of our hand-loaded shells.

Try (SS) Smokeless Powder. It's the best nitro on the market.

Price for Shells Loaded with "Walsrode" Powder and Wads Only, Without Shot.

47327 Climax Shells or Blue Rival, primed, 12 bore, $1.90 per 100, per M net, $16.00; Climax Shells or Blue Rival, primed, 10 bore, per 100, $2.25, per M net, $20.00; U. S. or U. M. C. No. 3 primer, "Walsrode" Shells, 12 bore, per 100, $2.50, per M net, $22.50; U. S. or U. M. C., No. 3 primer, "Walsrode" Shells, 10 bore, per 100, $2.75; per M net, $25.50.

Load—12 gauge, 29 or 31 grains; 10 gauge, 35 or 38 grains.

Add for shot to all above shells $0.60 per 100, $6.00 per M net.

Shot Spreaders—Patented.

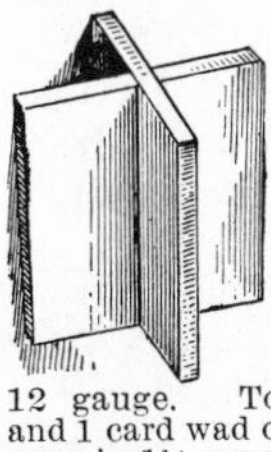

47329 Full Chokes made to spread MORE than cylinders. SHOT SPREADERS do it. A FULL CHOKE makes a circle of only 12 inches at 15 yards. Shot Spreaders make the same gun scatter from 24 to 30 inches. No use of carrying two sets of barrels on a hunting trip. They are made of pasteboard, and pass loosely through the choke. Very successful in the bushes where shooting is done at short range. Just right for quail, woodcock, partridge and rabbits. Do not mangle the game at close quarters. No trouble to load them.

12 gauge. To load: In a 2⅝ inch shell use 2¾ drs. powder; 1 B. edge and 1 card wad on powder. Drop the spreader down onto the powder wads, and then pour in 1⅛ ounces shot. 1⅛ ounce fills the spreader and a little over. Lay on an ordinary card wad and turn over the shell. If your shell is more than 2⅝ inches long use any load of powder and wads you have room for. All 12 gauge will work O. K. in 10 gauge also.

Price, per hundred .... 50c. Box of fifty .... 25c.

Empty Paper Shot Gun Shells.

Pin-Fire.

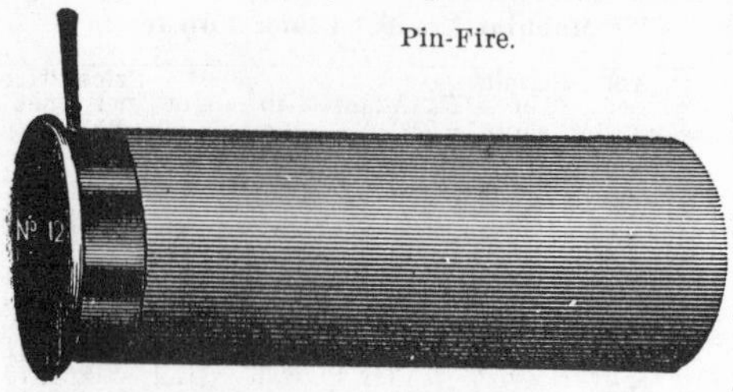

Pin-Fire

47335 Pin-fire Paper Shells, 20 gauge; per box of 100 weight, 2 pounds, ...$0.70

47336 Pin-fire Paper Shells, 14 gauge; per box of 100, weight, 2 pounds, ...$0.70

47337 Pin-fire Paper Shells, 16 gauge; per box of 100, weight, 2 pounds, ...$0.70

47338 12 gauge: per box of 100, pin-fire, weight, 4¼ pounds.........$0.90

47339 10 gauge, pin-fire, paper shells, per box of 100..........$1.45

U. M. C. "Walsrode" Paper Shell.

(Salmon.)

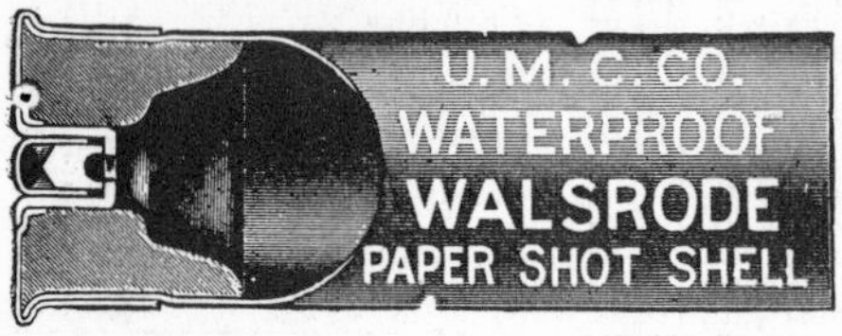

47350 U. M. C. Walsrode Paper Shell, Salmon Color No. 3, primer and battery cup, made especially for any proper charge of "Walsrode" powder. It is not adapted to any other powder.

—100 in a box—

	Per box.	Per 1,000.
12 Gauge, 2⅝ in	$0.90	$7.98
12 Gauge, 2¾ in	.97	9.50
10 Gauge, 2⅞ in	.97	9.50
16 Gauge, 2 9/16 in	.90	8.75

U. M. C. Smokeless Paper Shells.

(Salmon.)

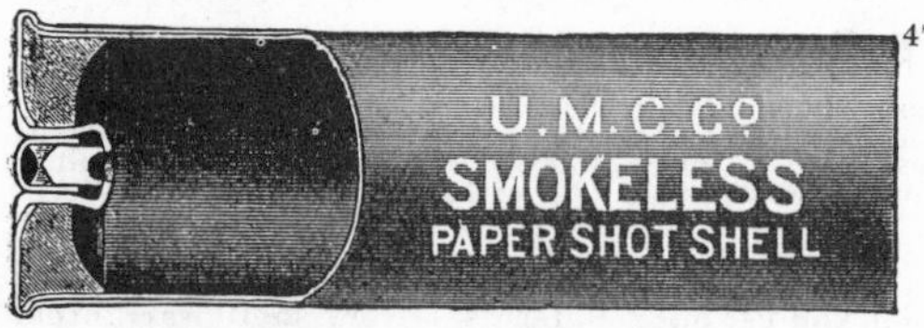

The Smokeless Shell is the Boss Paper Shell.

47361 The New U. M. C. Smokeless Red or Salmon Color Paper Shell, made expressly for (SS) smokeless powder' and the best low-priced shell for E. C. Schultze and Wood powders, using the LONG, STRONG No. 3 primer made by the U. M. C. Company. only. With "Nitro" powder of any kind this is much the *quickest* and strongest shell now upon the market for the price. See that your shells take the LONG No. 3 PRIMER, for they are *much* the *best*. (The long No. 3 primer is twice as long as other primers.)

		Per 1,000.
12 gauge, 2⅝ in., per box of 100, Weight 2¼ lbs.	$0.83	$7.80
12 " 2¾ in., " " " " 2½ "	.89	8.50
10 " 2⅞ in., " " " " 2¾ "	.89	8.50
16 " 2⅝ in., " " " "	.87	8.60

Green Trap U. M. C. Paper Shell.

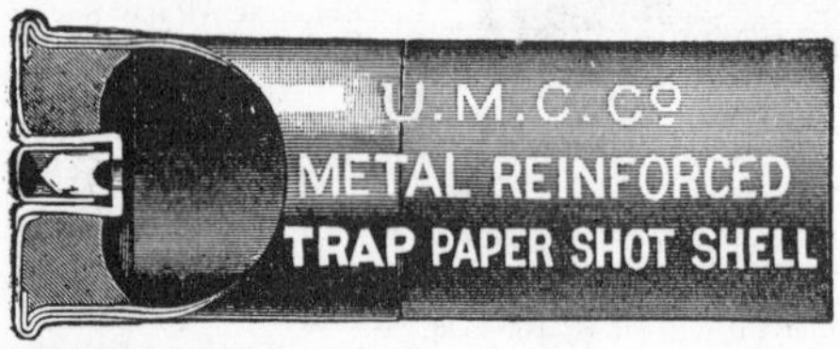

Prices subject to change without notice (Empty shells, not loaded.)

All center fire.

Weight, per box, 12 gauge, 2½ lbs.: 10 gauge, 3¼ lb.; 8 gauge, 4¼ lb.

The Trap Shell is the best and strongest paper shell made, and is used by all experts in live-bird "matches," and where heavy charges are required, and are warranted gas-tight.

47362 Paper U. M. C. Trap Shell, metal reinforced, green colored paper, gas-tight especially adapted to E. C. Schultze, Wood and all nitro powders; crimp same as any paper shell; reloadable, using No. 3 long, quick, strong primer.

		Per 1,000
10 Gauge, 2⅞ in. Per 100	$1.32	$12.57
12 Gauge, 2⅝ in. Per 100	1.25	12.00
12 Guage, 2¾ in. Per 100	1.32	12.55
12 Guage, 2⅞ or 3 in. Per 100.	1.32	12.57

U. M. C. "Salmon" Paper Shell.

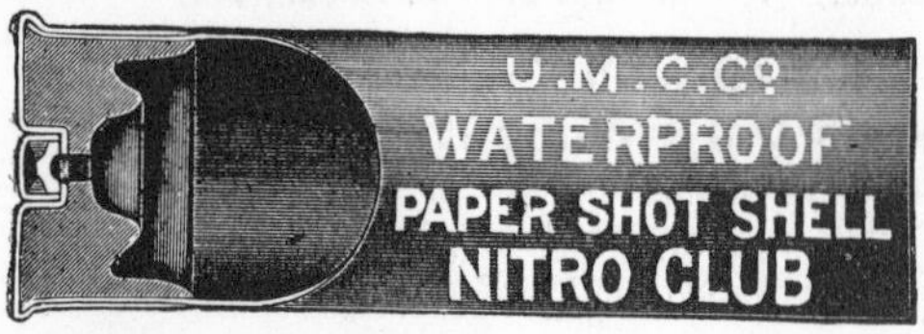

47364 U. M. C. Salmon Paper Shell for black and nitro powder, using No. 4 primer. Can be reloaded.

	Per 100.	Per 1,000.
12 gauge, 2⅝ in	$0.49	$4.65
12 gauge, 2¾ in	.55	5.40
10 gauge. 2⅞ in	.55	5.30
16 gauge, 2 9/16 in	.56	5.39
20 gauge, 2½ in	.56	5.40

Black Club Paper Shell.

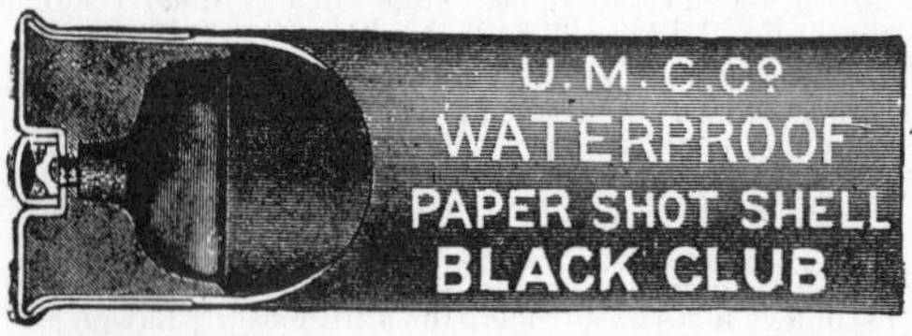

47366 The New Club Nitro or Black Powder Shell, with special strong primer. Strong and quick. No. 2. Can be reloaded.

	Per 100.	Per 1,000
12 gauge, 2⅝ in.	$0.49	$4.65
12 gauge, 2¾ in.	.55	5.30
10 gauge, 2⅞ in.	.55	5.30

Winchester Green Trap Shell.

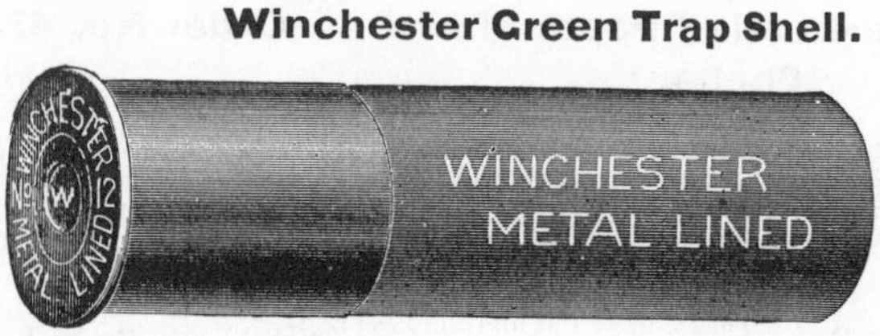

47367 The New Trap Paper Shell made by the W. R. A. Co. Reinforced inside and outside with brass, as shown in cut, for nitro or black powder new, strong.

No. 3 W. primer.

		Per 1,000
12 gauge, 2⅝ in., per box of 100	$1.25	$11.50
12 gauge, 2¾ in., per box of 100	1.33	12.60
10 gauge, 2⅞ in., per box of 100	1.33	12.60

Winchester "Leader" Paper Shell.

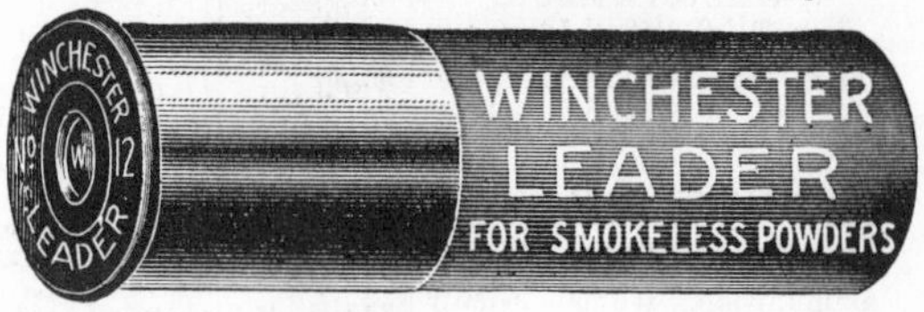

47368 Winchester Leader Smokeless Paper Shells: can be reloaded; for nitro or black powders; using No. 3 W nitro primer.

	Per 100.	Per 1,000
12 gauge, 2⅝ in.	$0.83	$7.80
12 gauge, 2¾ in.	.89	8.50
12 gauge, 3 in.	1.00	9.60
10 gauge, 2⅞ in.	.89	8.50
10 gauge, 3 in.	1.00	9.65
16 gauge	.85	8.25

Winchester "Blue" Rival Paper Shells.

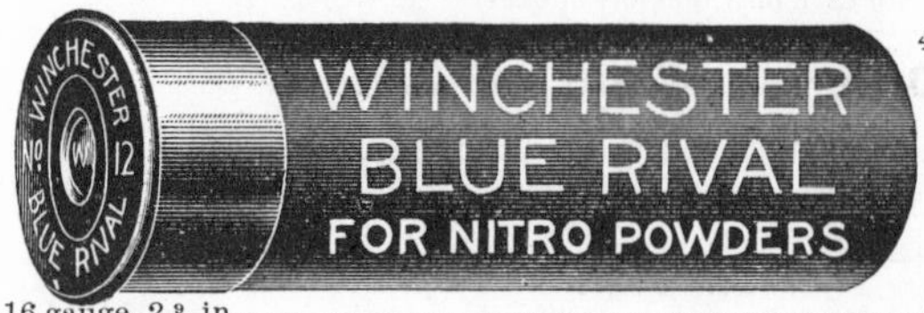

47369 Winchester Blue Rival Paper Shells, waterproof, quick and reliable, using No 3 W primer; can be reloaded; for black or nitro powders.

	Per 100	Per 1,000
16 gauge, 2 9/16 in	$0.56	$5.39
12 gauge, 2⅝ in	.49	4.65
12 gauge, 2¾ in	.54	5.30
12 guage, 3 in	.65	5.90
10 guage, 2⅞ in	.54	5.30

Rival Paper Shells.

47371 Winchester "Rival" Paper Shells, warranted perfect; a good shell, waterproof, U. M. C. or Winchester; No. 2 primer: can be reloaded.

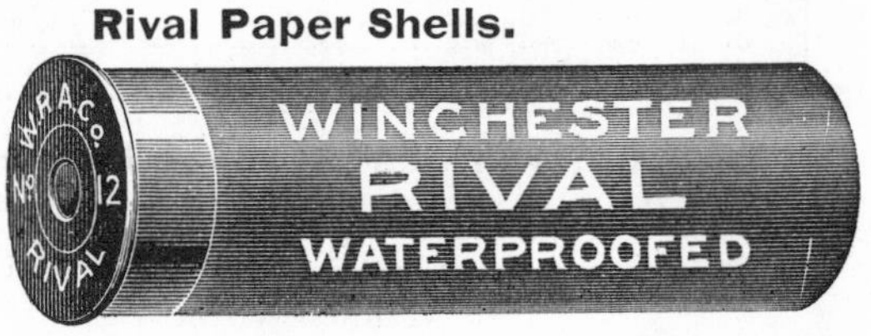

	Per box.	1.000
12 gauge. 2⅝ in Weight 2¼ lbs.	$0.49	$4.65
12 gauge, 2¾ in	.54	5.30
10 gauge, 2 ⅞ in	.54	5.30
14 gauge, 2 9/16 in	.56	5.40
16 gauge. 2 9/16 in	.56	5.40
20 gauge, 2½ in	.56	5.40

U. S. Climax.

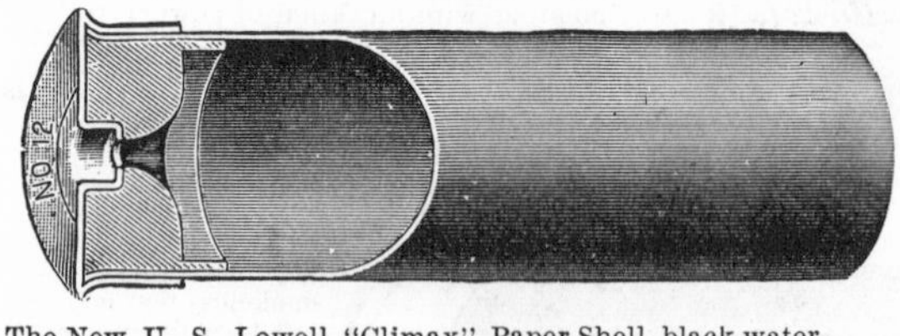

47373 The New U. S. Lowell "Climax" Paper Shell, black waterproof, conical base, re-enforced base, gas-tight, extra strong, quick primer, for E. C. Wood, Schultze or black powders; can be reloaded, using any No. 2 primer.

	Weight.	Per .100	Per 1,000
12 gauge, per box of 100, 2⅝ in.	2¼	$0.49	$4.65
12 gauge, per box of 100, 2¾ in.	2 5/16	.54	5.30
12 gauge, per box of 100, 2⅞ in.	2⅜	.54	5.30
10 gauge, per box of 100, 2⅞ in.	2⅞	.54	5.30
14 gauge, per box of 100		.56	5.30
16 gauge.		.56	5.40
20 gauge		.56	5.30

U. S. "Rapid" Paper Shell.

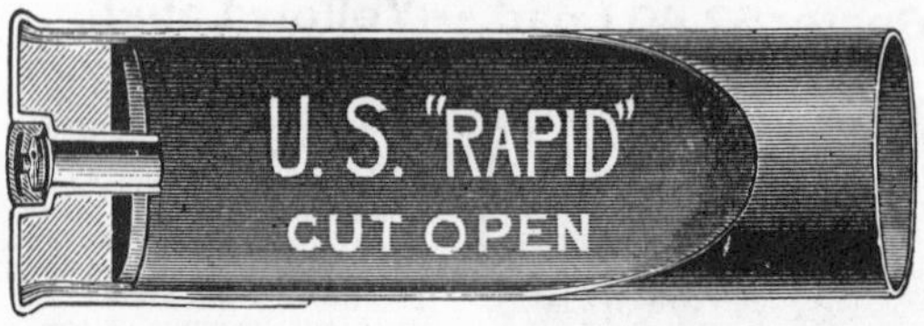

47374 U. S. "Rapid" Paper Shells, a new nitro powder shell; new primer

	Per 100.	Per 1,000.
12 gauge, 2⅝ in	$0.83	$7.80
12 gauge, 2¾ in	.89	8.50
10 gauge, 2⅞ in	.89	8.70
16 gauge	.85	8.25

U. S. "Walsrode" Paper Shell.

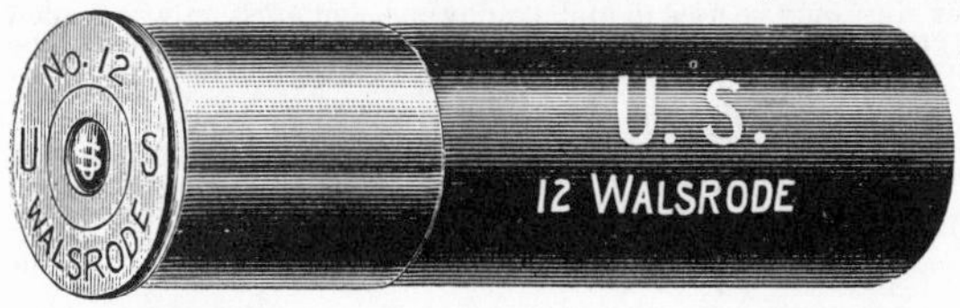

47375 U.S. "Walsrode" Paper Shells, for Walsrode powder only; not suitable for any other powder.

	Per 100.	Per 1,000.
12 gauge, 2⅝ in	$0.90	$7.98
12 gauge, 2¾ in	.97	9.50
10 guage, 2⅞ in	.98	9.50

First Quality 8 Gauge Paper Shells.

47377 Winchester or U. M. C. First Quality Paper Shells, using No. 2 primers, any make.
8 gauge, 3¼ in. Per 100 ... $1.90. Per 1,000 ... $18.75
8 gauge, 3½ in. Per 100 ... 2.10. Per 1,000 ... 19.95

Empty Brass Shells.

Give gauge and length when ordering shells.

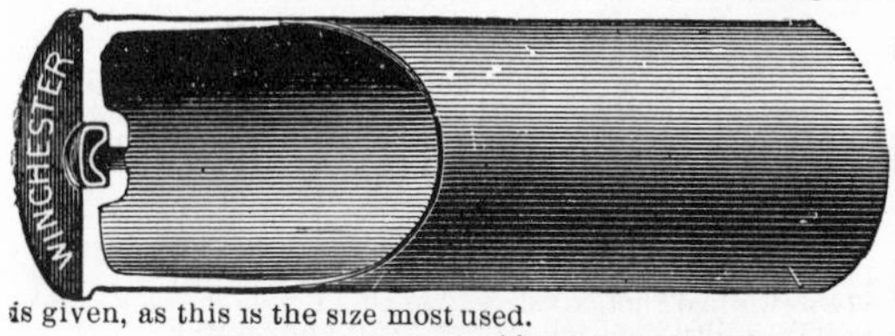

Weight, per box of 25 shells, about 1¾ lbs.

Don't forget to give gauge wanted when ordering shells.

We always send 2½ inch in 12 gauge and 2⅞ inch in 10 gauge unless length is given, as this is the size most used.

Winchester "Rival" Brass Shells.

47380 Brass Shells, "Rival," using any No. 2 primer. A good, strong shell, but lighter than the first quality, 12 gauge, 2½ and 2⅝ inches long, each, 4½c. per box of 25 ... $0.80
47381 Brass Shells, "Rival," 10 gauge, 2⅝ or 2⅞ inches long, each 4½ c., per box of 25 ... .80

N. B.—The Rival Shells are sold by many dealers as "The very best quality." Don't be fooled. Send to us for samples at box rates.

Winchester 'Best' Brass Shells. Order No. 47385.

Winchester Brass Shells, first quality, using Winchester No. 2 primer
20 gauge, 2½ inches long, per box of 25 ... $1.15
16 gauge, 2½ inches long, each 5c.; per box of 25 ... 1.16
14 gauge, 2⅝ inches long, each 5c.; per box of 25 ... 1.17
12 gauge, 2½ and 2⅝ inches long, each 5c.; per box of 25 ... 1.18
12 gauge, 2¾ and 2⅞ inches long, each 5c.; per box of 25 ... 1.19
10 gauge, 2⅝ inches long, each 5c.; per box of 25 ... 1.20
10 gauge, 2⅞ and 3 inches long, each 5½c.; per box of 25 weight, 1¾ lbs. ... 1.21
8 gauge, 3 inches long, each 9c.; per box of 25, weight, 2¼ lbs ... 2.10

In ordering shells, be careful to give gauge of gun for which you wish the shells.

U. M. C. Brass Shells. Order No. 47387.

Give gauge and length when ordering shells.

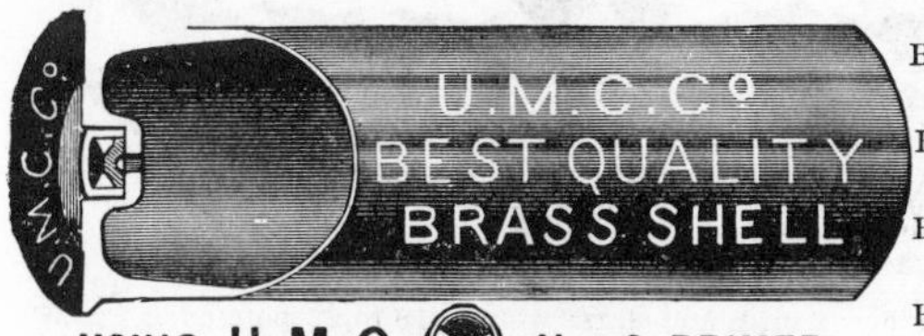

Brass Shells, 20 gauge, 2⅝ inches, each 5c. Per box of 25 .. $1.15
Brass Shells, 16 gauge, 2½ inches, each 5c. Per box of 25 .. $1.16
Brass Shells, 14 gauge, 2⅝ inches, each 5c. Per box of 25 .. $1.17
Brass Shells, 12 gauge, 2½ or 2⅝ inches long. Per box of 25 .. $1.18
Brass Shells, 12 gauge. 2¾ or 2⅞ inches long, Per box of 25 .. $1.19

USING U. M. C. 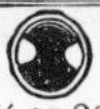 **No. 2 PRIMER.**

Brass Shells, 10 gauge, 2⅝ or 2¾ inches long, per box of 25 ... 1.20
Brass Shells, 10 gauge, 2⅞ inches long, per box of 25 ... 1.22
Brass Shells, 10 gauge, 3 inches long, per box of 25, weight, 1¾ lbs ... 1.25
Brass Shells, 8 gauge, 3 inches long, per box of 25, weight, 2¼ lbs ... 2.10

Gun Caps and Primers.

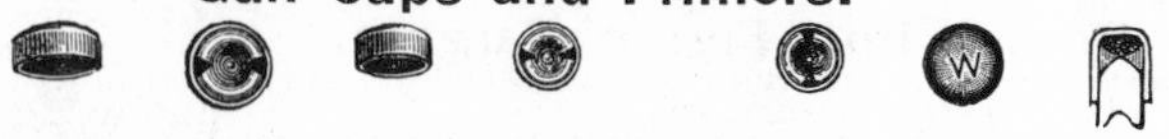

Showing size of No. 2 and 2½. Showing size of Primer No. 1. 1½ and No. 3. Cannot go by mail.

	Per box.	Per 1,000
47390 Primer, for pin-fire paper shell, per box of 250	$0.60	$2.00
47391 Primer, for pin-fire pistol cartridges, per box of 250	.50	1.80
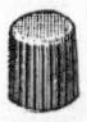 47392 The W. R. A. Waterproof Gun Caps for muzzle loaders	.05	.45
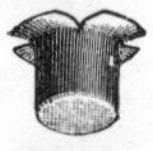 47393 U. S. Musket Caps, 10 boxes (1,000 caps)	.06	57
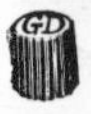 47394 Gun Caps, G. D. percussion	.04	.35
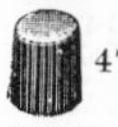 47396 Gun Caps (E.B.), water proof. 10 boxes (1,000)	.07	.65
47397 Primers, center fire, for shot gun shells and cartridges, U. M. C. No 2½, 2, 1, 1½, 0, per box of 250	.35	1.20
47398 Primers for Winchester cartridges and shot gun shells, Nos. 1, 1½, 2 and 2½, per box of 250	35	1.20
47399 Primers, No. 3, for U. M. C. Trap and "Smokeless" grade paper shells. These primers are twice as long as the regular primers and are the only No. 3 primer known to the trade. They are much stronger and quicker than any other primer. Per box of 250	.35	1.20
47401 Primers, No. 4, U. M. C.	.35	1.20
47405 Winchester, No. 3, W Primer, for Rival paper shells, when nitro powder is used	.35	1.20

When ordering *Primers* be sure to give *manufacturer's name* of shell or *our* catalogue number. *Primers cannot go by mail.*

Wads for Shot Guns.

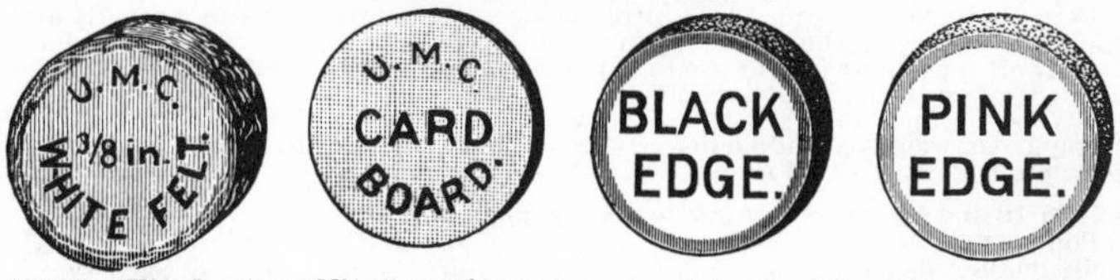

47407 **Winchester "Nito"** powder wad, made of elastic felt, soft and pliable, unlubricated, perfectly dry and free from all greasy matter, covered both sides with thin, soft blue paper. 125 in a box.

	⅛ in. Per box.	⅛ in. Per 1,000.	¼ in. Per box.	¼ in. Per 1,000.	⅜ in. Per box.	⅜ in. Per 1,000.
11 or 12 gauge,	$0.05	$0.48	$0.13	$0.88	$0.27	$1.92
9 or 10 gauge,	.10	.66	.15	1.00	.30	2.16

47408 **Winchester Field ad,** elastic white felt, covered with black waterproof material on one side and blue paper on the other, unlubricated, for use over powder.

	Per box.	Per 1,000.
10 gauge, 250 in box	$0.26	$1.00
12 gauge, 250 in box	.24	.80

47409 **"Nito Card" Wad,** extra thick cardboard, covered both sides with thin paper, for use over powder. The claim for this wad is improved pattern and preventing balling of shot, when used in combination with the Winchester "Nitro" and Field wad.

	Per box.	Per 1,000.
9 or 10 gauge, 250 a box	$0.08	$0.28
11 or 12 gauge, 250 in a box	.07	.24

47410 **The New Thin Top Shot Wad.** For trap shooting, made of specially prepared paper, less than ¼ as thick as regular card wads. Advantages of this wad: Evener distribution of shot; closer pattern; more space for powder wads and shot; blows to pieces when "fired," and offers less resistance to the shot, and yet stiff enough to hold shot in place when crimped, and does not "bulge" in crimping.

		Per 1,000
10 gauge, per box of 500	$0.20	$0.35
12 gauge, per box of 500	.10	.20

Weight, per box, about 4 oz.

Top Shot Wads

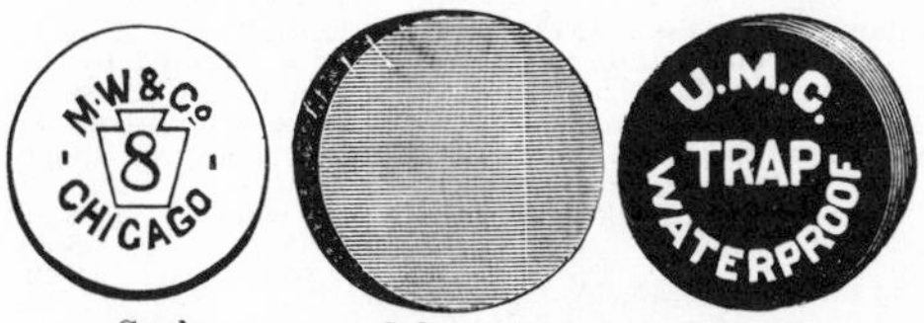

Card Salmon 47419

47411 **Engraved 'Thin' Top Shot Wad.** THE BEST YET. Try them once and be convinced. Size of shot engraved on BOTH SIDES. Sizes of shot. Nos. 5, 6, 7, 8 and 9.

		Per 1,000
12 gauge. per box of 500 (weight, 6 oz. per 1,000)	$0.15	$0.25
10 gauge, per box of 500, (weight, 7 oz. per 1000)	.18	.30

47412 **Salmon Felt Wads, "soft,"** for use over ni tro powder. Gives the best satisfaction of any wad in the market for "top powder" use. Has soft hair on one side, thin salmon colored paper glued on the other side.

		Per 1,000
12 gauge, package of 250 (weight, per 1,000, 1 lb)	$0.18	$0.60
10 gauge, package of 250 (weight, 1¼ lbs. per 1,000)	.20	.70

WADS—U. M. C. AND WINCHESTER MAKE.

47413 Shot Felt, a thin black edge wad for overshot; preferred by many to the card wad. 250 in a box.

	Per box.	Per 1,000
8 gauge	$0.18	$0.60
9 or 10 gauge	.15	.53
11 or 12 gauge	.14	.48

47414 **Pink Edge Wads,** ¼ inch thick, 250 in a box.

	Per box.	Per 1,000
11 or 12 gauge	$0.33	$1.20
9 or 10 gauge	.38	1.40

47415 **Cardboard Wads** for use over shot. Wt., per 1,000, 1¼ lbs.		
7 gauge, per box of 250	$0.07	$0.21
8 gauge, per box of 250	.07	.20
9 or 10 gauge, per box of 250	.06	.17
11 to 20 gauge, per box of 250	.05	.15
47416 **Black Edge Wads** for use over powder. Weight, per 1,000, 2 to 3½ lbs., according to size.		
6 gauge, per box of 250	.28	1.12
7 gauge, per box of 250	.19	.65
8 gauge, per box of 250	.18	.64
9 or 10 gauge, per box of 250	.15	.56
11 to 20 gauge, per box of 250	.13	.48
47417 **Pink Edge Wads,** for use over powder. Weight per 1,000, 2 to 3½ lbs. 6 gauge, pink edge, per box of 250	$0.40	$1.40
7 gauge, pink edge, per box of 250	.34	1.21
8 gauge, pink edge, per box of 250	.33	1.20
9 to 10 gauge, pink edge, per box of 250	.27	1.00
11 to 20 gauge, pink edge, per box of 250	.22	.80
47418 **White Felt Wads,** ⅜ inch thick, for use over powder. Weight per 1,000, 5 to 6 lbs.		
7 gauge, per box of 125	.47	3.60
8 gauge, per box of 125	.41	3.20
9 or 10 gauge, per box of 125	.33	2.37
11, 12, 14, 20 gauge, per box of 125	.29	2.18
47419 **The new "Trap" Wool Felt Wad,** one side black waterproof reverse side salmon color paper; sometimes called express or field, wads; about the same thickness as a pink edge, for over powder, not as hard "finish" as most wads of this kind, and consequently better than any other wad of this kind on the market; weight, 1½ to 1¾ lbs. per 1,000.		
10, gauge, per box of 250	.25	.80
11, 11½ and 12 gauge, per box of 250	.24	.80
47420 **Black Edge. ¼ Inch Wads;** weight, per 1,000, 2¼ to 3 lbs.		
9 or 10 gauge, per box of 250	.24	85
11 and 12 gauge, per box of 250	.20	.72
47420½ **Black Edge Wads,** ⅜ in. thick, 125 in abox, 9 and 10 gauge.	.29	2.16
11 and 12 gauge; weight per 1,000, 3¼ to 4¼ lbs	.26	1.92
47422 **Express Wads,** ⅛ inch thick, White Felt; a lubricated White Felt Wad covered with black grease proof material. Specially adapted for use over nitro powder.		
9 or 10 gauge, per box of 125	.45	4.00
11 or 12 gauge, per box of 125	.40	3.50

N. B.—In 12-gauge brass shells, use 10-gauge wads; in 10-gauge brass shells, use 8 gauge wads. In paper shells use wads the same size as shell. Always put the wad down to place flat and evenly, otherwise the shooting quality of your gun will be greatly impaired.

Wad Cutters. Order No. 47424.

Be sure and give gauge wanted. Postage, 5 cents extra.

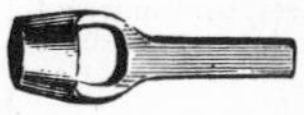

Wad cutters, 6, 7 and 8 gauge ... $0.35
9 and 10 gauge ... .20
11 to 20 gauge ... .15
Any size pistol or rifle 32 to 50 caliber ... .45

American Wood Powder.

Care must be used in loading nitro powders. Measure your load properly and follow directions on the can, and you will never go back to using "black powder."

All nitro powders are for use in paper shells only, as the shell must be crimped about ¼ of an inch for good results.

Wood powder does not weigh as much as black powder, bulk for bulk. A 1-pound can weighs about 8 ounces. Recoil much lighter than when using black powders, and little or no smoke.

47425 10 and 12 gauge, trap grade. Very quick and strong.

Pound can (bulk)	$0.65
6¼ pound can (bulk)	3.65
"E" grade, for revolvers; 1 lb	.54
"C" grade; 1 lb. can	.54
"C" grade; 6¼ lb. cans	3.15
Rifle grade, for rifles; 1lb.	.90

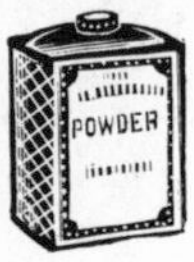

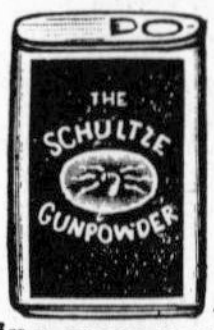

Schultze Powder.

These powders are made for first-class guns.

47426 Schultze Powders for shot guns, very little smoke.

1-pound (bulk) cans	$0.68
10-pound (bulk) drums	6.50

Follow directions on cans for loading.

E. C. Powder.

47427 E.C. Shot Gun Powder, little or no smoke. It is becoming more popular every year.

1-pound (bulk) cans ....$0.68 10-pound (bulk), per can $6.50

Great care must be taken in loading these powders to obtain best results. Directions for use on each can.

N. B.—Wood, S. S. Schultze or E. C. Powder can go by express or freight, as is will not explode unless confined. The great advantage of Wood, Schultze, S. S. and E. C. powders over common powder is the fact that there is much less recoil and no smoke to prevent seeing game or target for second shot.

Dupont Smokeless Powder.

One of the best powders on the market.

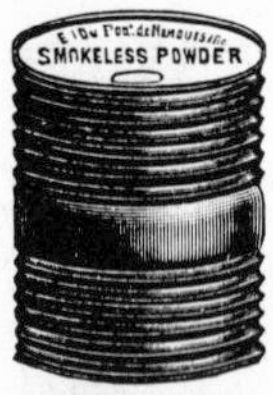

47428 Dupont Smokeless Nitro Powder is a hard, fine grain powder and is quick, clean and smokeless. It is not affected by the extremes of heat, cold or moisture. It may be loaded the same as black powder, except the quantity should be less; use paper shells only; load measured in a regular powder measure. 16 ga. 2 to 2½ drams; 12 ga. 2½ to 3 drams; 10 ga. 2¾ to 3½ drams.

12½ lb. cans, equal in bulk to	25 lbs.	black powder		$16.50
6¼ " " " "	12½ lbs.	"	"	8.44
3½ " " " "	6¼ lbs.	"	"	4.30
½ " " " "	1 lb.	"	"	.75

Directions for loading with each can.

N. B.—All nitro or smokeless powders can be shipped by express or freight, either alone or with other goods.

THE NEW GRADE (S. S.) Smokeless Powder.

THE BEST.

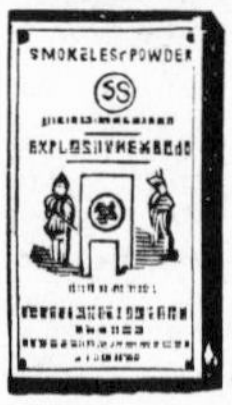

47429 The New Smokeless (S. S.) Shot Gun Powder; does not weigh as much bulk for bulk as black powder.

1 pound can (bulk). Price	$0.65
10 pound cans (bulk)	5.80
100 pound cans (bulk)	58.00
"S. V." Smokeless Powder for revolvers, 1-pound can	1 00
"S. R." Powder for rifles, 1 pound can	1.00

The superiority of the (S. S.) powder consists in its high velocity, long range, reduced recoil, reduced smoke, reduced fouling and more regular patterns. (S. S.) is the highest development in "Nitro" compounds. In consequence of the absence of "jar" and the reduced recoil it is the most agreeable of powders to shoot.

A trial of 500 of our hand loaded shells, will convince the most pronounced advocate of any other powder that the (S. S.) is all we claim for it.

(S. S.) The Best Smokeless or Nitro Powder Yet Produced.

Comparative Table of Nitro-Powders.

		Wood or Schultze.	"S. S"	"E. C"
2½ drs.	(Black Powder measure) equal	35 grains.	34 grains.	36 grains.
2¾ "	" " " "	38 "	36 "	40 "
3 "	" " " "	42 "	38 "	44 "
3¼ "	" " " "	45 "	40 "	47 "
3½ "	" " " "	48 "	43 "	50 "
3¾ "	" " " "	51 "	46 "	53 "

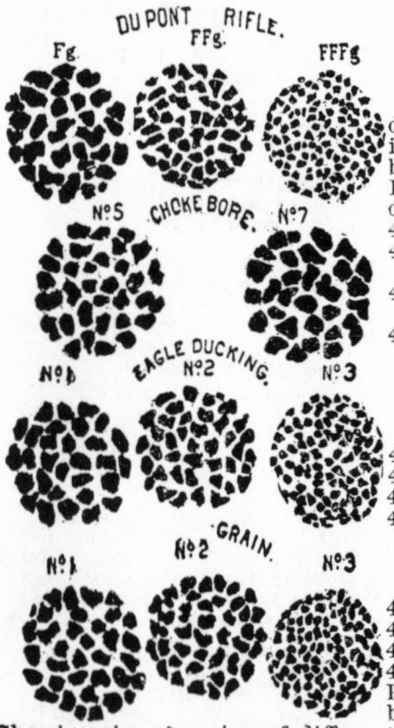

Showing size of grains of different powders. Hazard Powder same price as Dupont.

Dupont Rifle and Shot Gun Powder (Black.)

The Messrs. Dupont & Co. are the oldest powder makers and have the most extensive works in the country. We consider their powder the best. Every pound warranted *good* and clean. In air-tight metallic kegs; Fg, coarse; FFg, medium; FFFg, fine.

47430 Kegs, Fg, FFg, FFFg, 25 pounds,	$3.25
47431 ½ Kegs, Fg, FFg, FFFg, 12½ pounds	1.90
47432 ¼ Kegs, Fg, FFg, FFFg, 6¼ pounds	1.15
47433 1-pound cans, Fg, FFg, FFFg, per can	.30

Choke Bore.

47438 Kegs, Nos. 5 and 7, 25 lbs	$4.86
47439 ½ kegs, Nos. 5 and 7, 12½ lbs	2.70
47440 Kegs, Nos. 5 and 7 6¼ lbs.	1.50
47441 1 pound cans, Nos. 5 and 7	.40

Dupont Eagle Duck.

47444 Kegs, Nos. 1, 2, 25 pounds	$11.00
47445 ½ kegs, Nos. 1, 2, 12½ pounds	5.75
47446 ¼ kegs, Nos. 1, 2, 3, 6¼ pounds	3.00
47447 1-pound cans, Nos. 1, 2 and 3	.60

Powder cannot be shipped by express, but must be sent in separate kegs or cases, and marked "gunpowder," and sent by freight. Freight charges are double first-class rates on powder

Walsrode Smokeless Shot Gun Powder, Nitro.

47450 This powder must only be used in high grade guns, and must only be loaded according to directions on each package; in no case must a larger quantity be used than the directions specify. Don't guess at the quantity but use the measure made expressly for the work.

SINGLE CANISTERS ....$0.80 DRUMS $7.50

A single canister will load 120 12-gauge shells; a drum will load 1,200 12-gauge shells. Use "Climax" or "Blue Rival," or "Walsrode," U. M. C. paper shells. The Climax or Blue Rival should be primed with about ⅓ grain of black powder.

47451 "Walsrode" Special Powder Measures $0.30
10 or 12 gauges; mention gauge wanted and grain. 29 or 31, 12-gauge; 35 or 38 grain, 10 gauge.

47454 Laflin Rand's "Troisdorf" Smokeless Shot Gun Powder, nitro,
1 pound cans (bulk), each........$0.68 6½ pound drums (bulk), each... $3.95

"V. C. P." Dupont's "V. C. P."

47455 The New Trap Powder--black, moist, quick, clean and strong (not a nitro). 12½ pound kegs $2.00
6¼ pound kegs 1.15

Prices Quoted on Any Make of Powder in the Market.

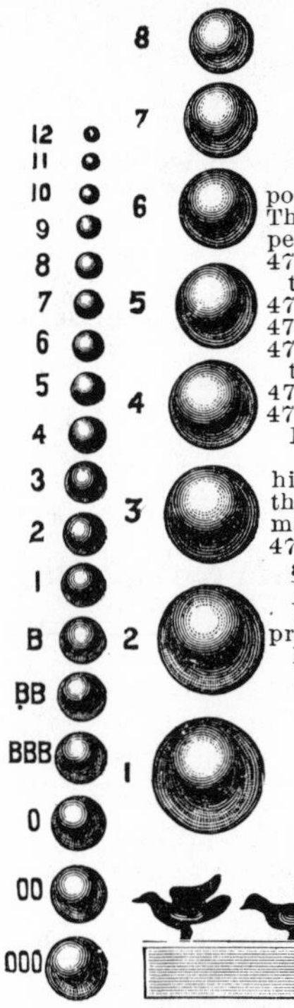

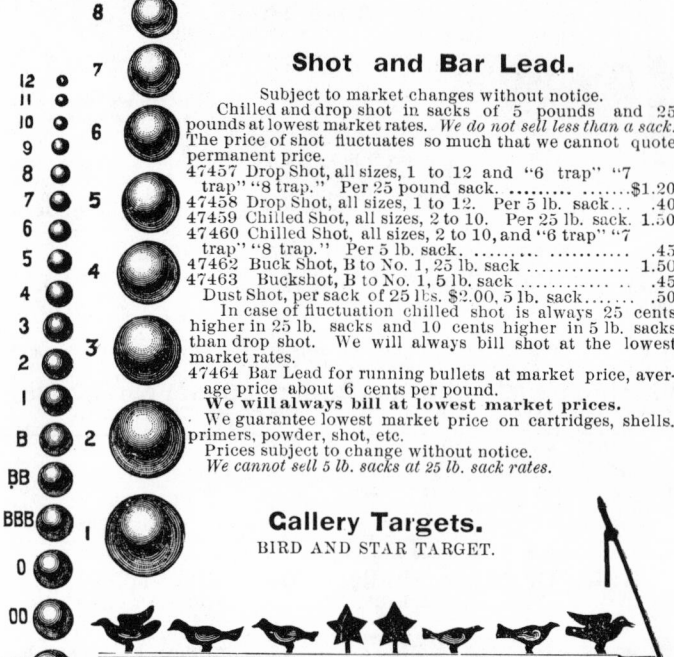

Shot and Bar Lead.

Subject to market changes without notice.

Chilled and drop shot in sacks of 5 pounds and 25 pounds at lowest market rates. *We do not sell less than a sack.* The price of shot fluctuates so much that we cannot quote permanent price.

47457 Drop Shot, all sizes, 1 to 12 and "6 trap" "7 trap" "8 trap." Per 25 pound sack.	$1.20
47458 Drop Shot, all sizes, 1 to 12. Per 5 lb. sack	.40
47459 Chilled Shot, all sizes, 2 to 10. Per 25 lb. sack.	1.50
47460 Chilled Shot, all sizes, 2 to 10, and "6 trap" "7 trap" "8 trap." Per 5 lb. sack.	.45
47462 Buck Shot, B to No. 1, 25 lb. sack	1.50
47463 Buckshot, B to No. 1, 5 lb. sack	.45
Dust Shot, per sack of 25 lbs. $2.00, 5 lb. sack	.50

In case of fluctuation chilled shot is always 25 cents higher in 25 lb. sacks and 10 cents higher in 5 lb. sacks than drop shot. We will always bill shot at the lowest market rates.

47464 Bar Lead for running bullets at market price, average price about 6 cents per pound.

We will always bill at lowest market prices.

We guarantee lowest market price on cartridges, shells, primers, powder, shot, etc.

Prices subject to change without notice.

We cannot sell 5 lb. sacks at 25 lb. sack rates.

Gallery Targets.

BIRD AND STAR TARGET.

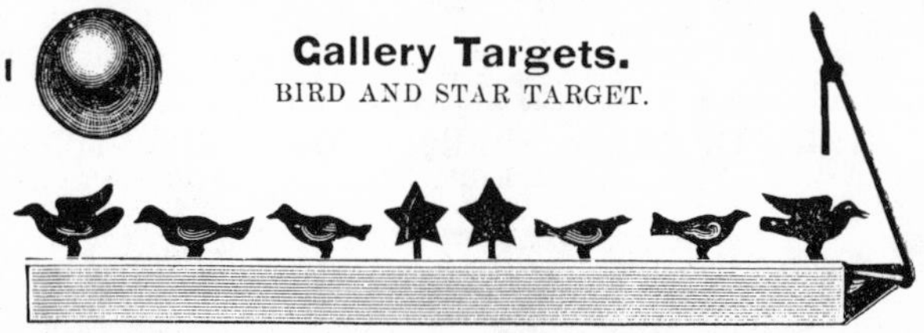

The birds and stars fall back out of sight when hit, and are reset by rope from shooting stand. It is one of the most satisfactory targets in the market, and is made to last. Heavy wrought iron face plate.

47465 Target, of 6 extra heavy birds and stars; weight, 14 to 18 pounds. Each $2.30

47466 Target, of 8 extra heavy birds and stars; weight, 18 to 22 pounds 2.65

Round Iron Targets.

Bell rings when bullseye is hit, and self setting, round iron; no figure.

47468 12-in. diameter, for Flobert ball caps; weight, 12½ pounds $0.90

47470 12-in. diameter, heavy, for 22 cartridges 1.35

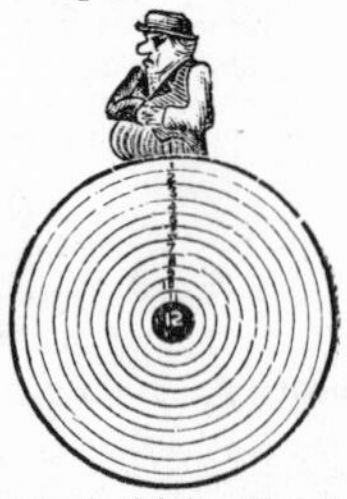

Round Iron Figure Targets.

Figure springs up and rings bell when bullseye is hit; reset with rope from shooting stand.

47471 12-inch diameter, for Flobert ball caps; weight, 15 lbs $1.95

47473 12-inch diameter, heavy, for 22 cartridges; weight, 15 to 18 lbs $2.25

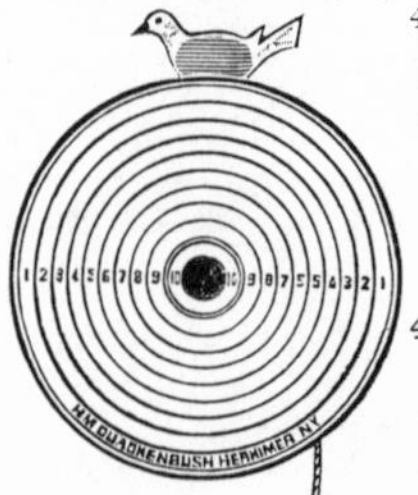

47474

47474 12-inch diameter, steel faced, ¼ inch thick. Bird is thrown up and bell rings when bulls eye is hit For air guns or cartridges not larger than 22 long; weight, 12½ lbs. Each $2.90

Paper Targets for rifle and pistol practice furnished. Write for prices.

Empire Targets and Traps.

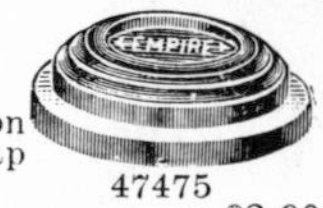

47475

47475 The New Empire Composition Target, can be thrown for any trap except the "Old Peoria."

Per Barrel of 500 targets	$2.90
Per 1,000 targets	5.75
Per 5,000 targets (per 1,000)	5.50

Weight, per barrel, about 135 pounds.

 See Page 473.

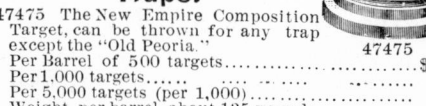

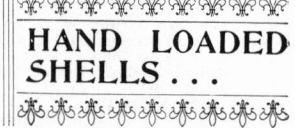

Targets and Traps—Continued.

47476

47477 The Empire Expert Trap, no better trap made. Can be changed instantly to any angle required. Weight, boxed, 26 pounds. Each........................$6.50

47476 The Empire Amateur Trap, can be changed instantly to throw any angle. Each...$4.50 Weight, 12 pounds.

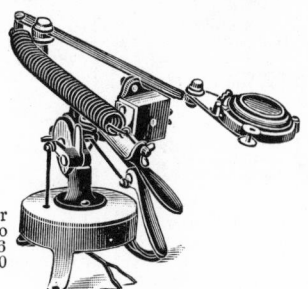

47477

47478 The Empire Electric Puller, complete for 5 traps. Each...........$25.00

47479 The Cleveland Blue Rock Targets. Can be thrown from any trap except the "Old Peoria."
Per barrel 500 targets.......................$2.90
Per 1,000 targets........................ 5.75
Per 5,000 targets (per 1,000)................5.50
Weight per barrel about 148 pounds.

Blue Rock Extension Trap.

47481 Blue Rock Extension Traps Each.......................... $4.50

We Furnish Score Cards Free.

Peoria Black Birds same price as other targets.

Il. Blue Rock and Trap. 47484

Traps—Continued.

47482 The New Blue Rock "Expert" Traps. Each $6.50
47483 Paul North's Electric Trap Pulls, complete with wire and battery. Weight, 35 lbs.
For One Trap.........................$10.00
For Three Traps......................... 25.00
For Five Traps......................... 30.00
47484 The Blue Rock Compression Spring Trap, good and strong. Each.......................$3.75
SHOOTING CLUBS are being formed all over the country, even among the farmers. They find it pays in the increased amount of "work" the boys and "hired" men perform.

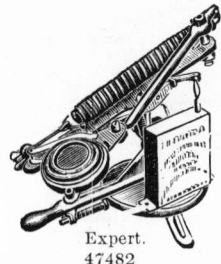

Expert. 47482

Midget Traps.

47485 U. S. Midget Traps. The smallest trap made; will throw U. S. pigeons, Blue Rocks, or Empire 40 yds. Weight, 13 lbs.
Each............................$2.50
Prices on targets are subject to market changes.

Ruoldph's Ground Pigeon Trap.

47488—closed.

47488 Rudolph's Ground Pigeon Trap, for live pigeon match shooting. The most satisfactory trap for the purpose and used by many of the State Associations for 8 years. Made of heavy galvanized sheet iron. This trap has filled a long felt want for a good trap at a reasonable price. Every club should have a set.
Each.......................$2.15
Weight, 6½ lbs. each.

Standard American Paper Targets.

—On good White Paper—

47490 Paper Target Centers.
200 yard centers. Per dozen....$0.60
100 yard centers. Per dozen 0.27
50 yard centers. Per dozen.....0.12
25 yard centers. Per dozen.....0.10
200 yard rest bull's eye. Per dozen..$0.15
50 yard full size targets. Per dozen.. 0.25
25 yard full size targets. Per dozen .. 0.13
12½ yard targets. Per dozen..........0.14

Directions for pistol practice.
Use the 200 yard at 50 yards. Use the 100 yard at 30 yards.
Use the 50 yard at 20 yards, Use the 25 yard at 10 yards,

We can Furnish Score Cards Free.
THE GUN CLUB SCORE BOOK.
COPYRIGHTED.
100 sheets ruled with 25x25 spaces; alternate sheets perforated to tear out and mail for publication or otherwise. Pocket with three sheets of carbon paper in rear. Bound in cloth, with gold side stamp. Price, per copy,............................$0.75

Winchester Make Reloading Tools, Including Bullet Molds, Complete Set.

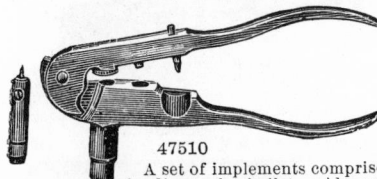

47510

A set of implements comprises the reloading tool, a bullet mold and charge cup. The reloading tool removes the exploded primer and fastens ball in the shell, at the same time swaging the entire cartridge to the exact form and with absolute safety. Wood handles on bullet molds. Blued finished and polished. Perfect in every respect.

47510   Extra by mail 42 and 45 cents.   Per set
22 caliber, center fire, Winchester.......... $1.70
25-20 caliber, center fire, Winchester.......... 1.71
32 caliber, center fire, Winchester model '73... 1.76
38 caliber, center fire, Winchester model '73... 1.77
44 caliber, center fire, Winchester model '73... 1.78
32 caliber, center fire, S. & W 1.68
38 caliber, center fire, S. & W............ 1.69
38-90 Winchester Express...................... 2.75
44 caliber, center fire, Webley cartridge....... 1.80
40-90 caliber, Sharps's Patched Straight.... ... 2.80
40-70 Ballard Patch Ball...................... 2.81
40-110 caliber, Winchester Express............. 2 40
40-60 caliber, Winchester.................. 2.15
44 S. & W. Russian....................... 1.80
44 S. & W. American....................... 1.80
45 75 caliber, Winchester...... .... 2.26
50-95 caliber, Winchester Express......... ... 2.70
50-70 caliber, U. S. Government.............. 2.50
45-60 caliber, Winchester................ 2.22
50-110 Express....................... 2.40
47511 Reloaders, only 22 to 44 caliber...... 1 45
Reloaders, only from 40-90 to 45-60 caliber.
Each 1.85
47512 Bullet Molds, any caliber. Each......... .75
47512½ Brass Charge Cups................ .10
Mention caliber when ordering tools.
WINCHESTER NEW MODEL TOOL, including bullet mold with wood handles. A complete set. Reloads and resizes the shell. Weight, 3¼ lbs. Polished blued finish. Perfect in every respect.

Reloading Tools—Continued.

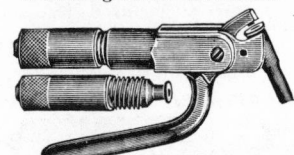

47514

                                                    Per set.
32-44 caliber, Winchester.......................$2.10
38-55 caliber, Winchester....................... 2.11
38-56 caliber, Winchester....................... 2.12
38-70 caliber, Winchester....................... 2.13
40-65 caliber, Winchester....................... 2.14
40-70 caliber, Winchester....................... 2.15
40-82 caliber, Winchester....................... 2.16
40-70 caliber, Winchester....................... 2.17
45-70 caliber, Government 405.................. 2.18
45-70 caliber, Government 500.................. 2.19
45-90 caliber, Winchester....................... 2.20
50-110 Winchester Express...................... 2.22
45-70 330 Hollow Ball (Gould bullet)....... .... 2.25
45-70-350 Solid Bullet......................... 2.24

Ideal Combined Reloading Tools.
IDEAL RELOADING TOOLS.
These tools will reload shells using patched balls, but to run smooth balls you require an extra bullet mold.

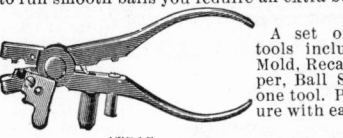

47515
IDEAL RELOADING TOOLS.
47515 State caliber wanted.
                                                    Per set.
22 caliber, center fire U. M. C................$1.59
32 caliber, short....................... 1.59
32 caliber, long, U. M. C................ 1 59
32 caliber, Smith &. Wesson.... .... 1.59

A set of reloading tools includes: Bullet Mold, Recapper, Decapper, Ball Seater, all in one tool. Powder Measure with each set.

Reloading Tools—Continued.
32 caliber, extra long........................... 1.59
38 caliber, short................................ 1.59
38 caliber, long, outside lubricator............. 1.59
38 caliber, extra long........................... 1.59
38 caliber, Smith & Wesson. 1.59
41 caliber, Colt's D. A. pistol................... 1.59
41 caliber, long, Colt's D. A. pistol............. 1.59
Postage on above tools about 25c. extra
Don't order a "short" or a "long" caliber to load Smith & Wesson cartridges, for they will not do the work.

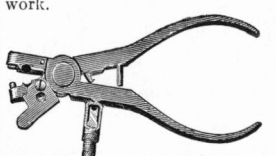

47517 Ideal Tools. State caliber when ordering.
32-44 S. & W. grooved ball.
Per set........$3.50
32-44 S. & W. gallery round ball.
38-44 S. & W. target grooved.......$3.50

38-44 S. & W. gallery round.................... 3.50
38 Long Colt Pistol, inside lubricator, per set... 3.00
Postage on above tools about 40c. extra.

47518 Ideal Tools.
25-20 caliber, U. M. C. make for Stevens rifle.
Per set........$1.70
32 caliber, Colt's lightning rifle.
Per set...... $1.71
                                                    Per set.
25-20-77 Ideal.............................$1.70
25-20 Marlin Repeater 1.75
32-25-150 Ideal.......................... 1.75
32 caliber, Winchester Rifle.................. 1.72
32-20 caliber, Marlin....................... 1.73
32-30 caliber, Remington.................... 1.75
38-40 caliber, Winchester model '73............ 1.74
38-40 caliber, Colt's Rifle................... 1.75
38-40 caliber, Marlin Rifle.................. 1.76
44-40 caliber, Colt,s Rifle................... 1.77
44-40 caliber, Winchester model '73........... 1.78
44-40 caliber, Marlin....................... 1.79
44 caliber, S. & W. Russian model.............. 1.80
44 caliber, American model........ .... 1.80
45 caliber, Colt's Pistol.................... 1.70
Postage on above tools about 30 cents extra.

M. W. & CO.'S SHOTGUN = = = = Page 449.

Reloading Tools—Continued.

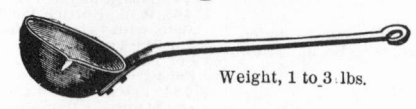

47519 Ideal Reloading Tools. State caliber wanted.
32-40 Ballard and Marlin. Per set........$2.10
32-40 caliber, Remington. Per set....$2 11

Per set.
38-40 caliber, Remington.... ....$2 12
38-50 caliber, Remington............ 2.13
38-55 Marlin.......................... 2.14
38-56 Winchester and Colt............ 2 15
40-60 Winchester..................... 2 16
40-60 Colt and Marlin...... .... 2.17
40-65 Winchester..................... 2.18
40-70 Sharp's straight grooved 2.70
40-82 Winchester..................... 2.19
44 Evans' new model 2.30
45-60 Winchester 2.20
45-70 405 Government................. 2.12
45-70 500 Government................. 2.24
45-70 Marlin......................... 2.14
45-85 285 Ballard and Marlin.. .. .... 2.25
45-90 Winchester 2.22
50-70 Government 2.24
40-90 Sharp's straight 3¼ in. shell... 3.00
Postage on above tools about 35c. extra.
Can furnish any other caliber in the Ideal Tools that are made, including those for Winchester rifles, etc.

47534 Shell Reducer and Resizer for any size, from 32-40 and larger. Each, $1.75 Order size wanted.
Every good rifle shooter needs these tools.
Postage, extra, 15c.

47535 Ideal Bullet Sizer, for making bullets to exact size, and one standard die.
Each.......................... $1.50
Extra dies.................... .50
You require a die for each style of bullet. Postage, extra, 18c.

47536 Ideal Re-and-De-capper for pistol cartridges. One tool will only re-and de-cap the one size shell. Each .$1 00 Postage, extra, 8c.

47538 Ideal Loading Flask. Holds ¾ of a pound of black powder; accurate and reliable for either black or nitro powder. Directions for using with each flask.
No. 1 for Rifle, 38 to 50 caliber........ $2.25
No. 2 for rifles and pistols, 38 to 22 caliber..... 2.20
Extra shell receiver from 22 to shot gun size... .50
Postage, extra, 20c.

Bullet Molds Only.

Be sure and give size wanted.
For all sporting and military sizes of cartridges.
Extra by mail.....16c
Each
47540 To make Grooved Balls. $0.85
47541 To make Express Balls................ 1.25
47542 To make Round Balls................ 1.15
47543 To make Smooth Balls for cartridges made only with patched bullet........... 1.00
47543½ Cut Paper Patches, per 1,000....... $0.55
47544¾ Lubricating Material for bullets, in sticks. Per stick........................ .15
47545 Patch Paper for cartridges, using patched ball. Per quire.................... .55
Per sheet.............................. .07

PERFECTION MOLD 17545½ The Perfection Grooved Bullet Mold, for running balls of different lengths and weights of same caliber.
32-40 Caliber, 75, 109, 125, 175, 200, 225 grains.
38-55 Caliber 135, 170, 205, 245, 285, 325 grains.
45-Rifle Caliber,305, 365, 405, 465 grains. Price, each.$3.00
Bullet Molds, with wood handles, to run any one size ball of above calibers...................... 1.50

47546 Ideal Dipper for running bullet. Each.........$0.40 Postage, extra, 10c.

Ideal Melting Pot.

47547 Ideal Melting Pot for melting lead......$0.38 Postage, extra, 15c.

47548 Adjustable Cover to fit any stove for Ideal melting pot, 38 cents. Postage, extra, 24c.

Melting Pot, Cut ½ size.

IDEAL Cover

SEE LIST OF **Mercantile Publications** ON INSIDE of REAR COVER.

Melting Ladles.

Weight, 1 to 3 lbs.

47550 Melting Ladles, for melting lead, etc.   Each
3-inch diameter bowl.........................$0.22
4-inch diameter bowl........ .... .25
5-inch diameter bowl......................... .40
6-inch diameter bowl......................... .45

Loaders, 10 and 12 Gauge.

Extra by mail, 4c.

47600 Cocobolo Loader, complete, 10 and 12 gauge. Each.................$0.15
47601 Common Loader, complete. Each.................$0.08
47602 Loader, without tube, 10 and 12 gauge. Each .... .06
All with extracting pin Be sure and give gauge wanted. **47604—** Barclay Loader, with inside spring wad starter: 10 and 12 gauge. Each.....$0.40

8 gauge .... .75

47605 Nitro Powder Loader, cocobolo rammer and base, nickel tube, spring equal to 10 lb. pressure in rammer, 10 or 12 gauge only. Each. $0.35

B. C. I. Co. NITRO RAMMER

Reloading Tools.

For 14, 16, and 20 gauge only. These are the only styles and prices we have in these gauges.
In ordering state size wanted.
47610 Cocobolo Loader with nickel tube and extracting pin, 14, 16 or 20 gauge only............$0.18
Extra by mail, 3c.
47611 Recapper, bronzed iron, for 14, 16 or 20 gauge only.................................. .15
Extra by mail, 3c.
47612 Shell Crimper, best quality for 14, 16 or 20 gauge only.................................. .70
Extra by mail, 10c.
47613 Ring Shell Extractor, for 14, 16 or 20 gauge only.................................. .10
Postage, extra, 1c. (State gauge wanted.)

8-Gauge Reloading Tools.

These tools are of the very best quality, and are the only style made for this gauge.
47615 Cocobolo Loader with tube and extracting pin; weight, 4 ounces, 8 gauge only. $0.50
47617 Shell Crimper, best quality, 8 gauge only: Weight, 24 oz................................. 1.50
47618 Recapper, red japanned, polished joints, 8 gauge only. Weight, 5 oz................... .84
47619 Ring Shell Extractor, 8 gauge only......... .20

Re-Capper & De-Capper.

IDEAL

Shell Extractor & Rammer.

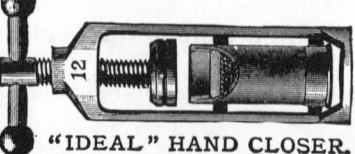

FUNNEL   BASE

47620 The Ideal Shell Loader, including funnel and base, bronze finish, compact and handy to carry in the pocket, re-and de-caps and seat wads. Weight, 4 oz.
Each, 16 gauge.................................$0.42
Each, 12 gauge............................... .40
Each, 10 gauge............................... .40

47621—The Ideal Handshell Closer for paper shells, handy to carry in the pocket, always ready for

"IDEAL" HAND CLOSER. use. Weight 5 oz. Each, 16 gauge............$0.28
Each, 12 gauge........$0 29. Each 10 gauge.... .30

47622 Ideal Powder and Shot Measure combined, nickel plated cap, wood handle. Postage, extra, 2c. Each......... $0.09

POWDER SHOT   IDEAL

10 and 12 Gauge Reloading Tools.

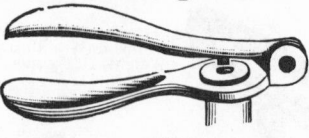

47625 Red Japanned Recapper, neat and handy, 10 and 12 gauge. Weight, 2 ounces. Each.. .$0.06

Weight, 3 ozs.
16 or 20 gauge .... .12
47626 Recapper, with flat automatic spring in handle, 10 and 12 gauge. Each.............. .10

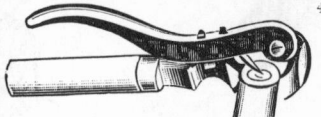

47630 Remington De- and Re-capper 10 or 12 gauge. Each....$0.50 Be sure and give *gauge wanted* when ordering de and re-cappers or implement sets.
Postage, extra, 11c.

If you haven't got Mann's De and Re-capper, don't find fault if your gun misfires.

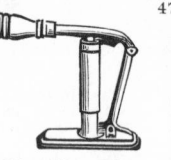

47631 Mann's De and Re-capper, is first-class in every respect, nickel-plated shell-post, cocobolo handle. A simple, convenient and effective implement, de-capping and re-capping the cartridge shell without removing from the shell post or reversing the lever, doing its work easily,
When Decapping. rapidly and perfectly. Misfires will be avoided by its use. 12-gauge..$0.90 Weight, 8 oz. 10-gauge..... .95

47632 Paper Shell Crimper, bronzed iron, 10 and 12 gauge. State gauge wanted; a crimper will only crimp 1 gauge. Weight, 10 ounces. Each...................$0.27
16 gauge.............................. .40

47634 Paper Shell Crimper, bronzed and brass, with expelling pin 10 and 12. State gauge wanted. Weight, 12 ounces. Price, each, 10 or 12 gauge $0.36
16 gauge or 20 gauge.......... .45

47635 The B. G. I. Paper Shell Closer red japanned, brass and ebony trimmings, expelling pin; a good strong closer. Gauge 10 or 12, each...........................$0.54
Gauge, 16 or 20, each....... .64
Weight, 13 oz.

47636 The New Improved Spangler Square Crimper. New straight feed lever with steel grip. The only tool that will crimp every shell alike, no matter what the variations of load may be. The only tool having an automatic plunger, that prevents the end of shell from spreading over the wad. All wearing parts are of steel. The best crimper ever made; 10 or 12 gauge only. Weight, 30 oz. Each...............$1.75

SQUARE CRIMP

Showing style of crimp.

47637 The New No. 3 B. G. I. Crimper with reversible crimp, making either the oval or the square crimp with the same tool; a good, strong and durable article, 10 or 12 gauge.....................$1.29
Postage, extra, 32c.
N. B.—Order by gauge or shell you wish to crimp. A 10 gauge will not crimp a 12 gauge.

Cleaning Rods.

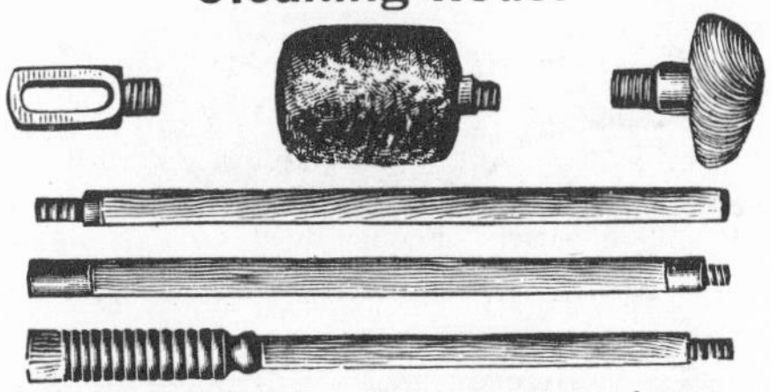

47638 Cleaning Rods, hardwood, patent brass joints and three implements, swab, scratch brush and wiper, 10, 12, 16 gauge. Wt., 7 oz., per set. .$0.25
47639 Cleaning Rod, 3 joints, lancewood, nickel trimmings, four implements, swab, scratch brush, wormer and wiper; 10, 12 and 16 gauge. Weight, 7 ounces; each .50
47640 Cleaning Rod, three joints, ebony wood, nickel trimmings, four implements, swab, scratch brush, wormer and wiper; a fine rod, 10, 12 and 16 gauge; weigh, 7 oz. Each .75
47642 Snake Wood Cleaning Rod, nickel trimmings and implements, 10 or 12 gauge 1.00

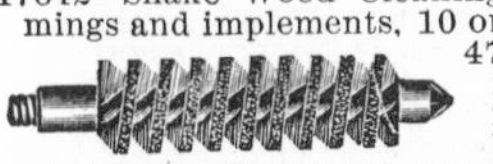

47643 Brass Wire Brush, for removing lead caking and rust spots; can be attached to any joint rod; 10, 12, 16 and 20 gauge. Order by gauge, as one brush will fit but one gauge. Each $0.45
Postage, extra, 2 cents.

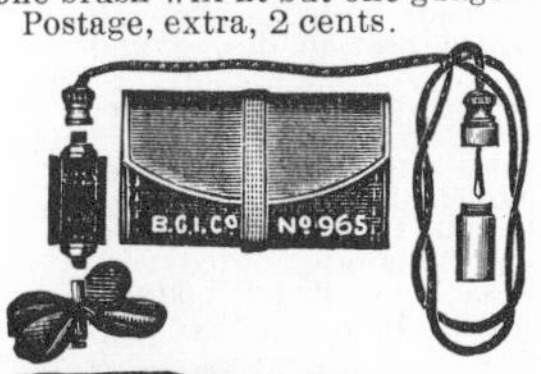

47644 Field Cleaner, large bristle brush, slotted wiper, string and oil bottle weight, fine leather pouch with clasp; 10 and 12 gauge. Weight, 3 ounces. Each $0.90

47649

47650

47649 Expansion Felt Swab, to fit jointed rod, 10 or 12 gauge; weight, 2 ounces. Each $0.35
47650 Three Row Wire Brush, to fit jointed rods. 10 and 12 gauge. Each .30
Weight, 3 oz., 16 and 20 gauge. Each .45

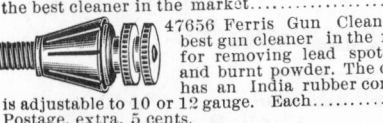

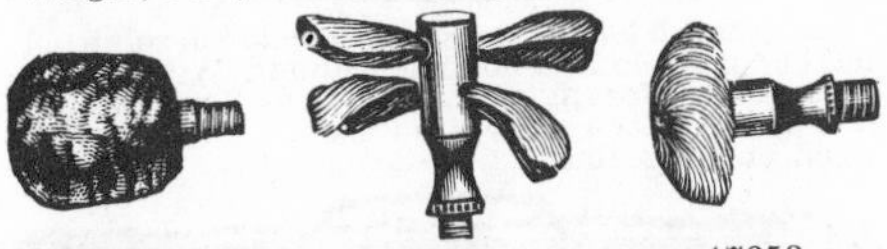
47651 47652 47653

47651 Wool Swab, to fit jointed rods, 10 and 12 gauge; weight, 2 ounces. Each $0.08
47652 Flannel Wiper, to fit jointed rods, 10 and 12 gauge; weight, 1 oz. Each .06
47653 Wire Scratch Brush, to fit jointed rods, 10 and 12 gauge; weight, 1 oz. Each .06
By mail, 3c. extra.

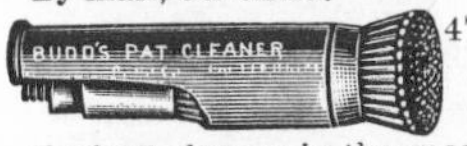

47655 Budd's Improved Petmecky Gun Cleaner, 10 or 12 gauge; screws onto all jointed rods; the best cleaner in the market $0.65

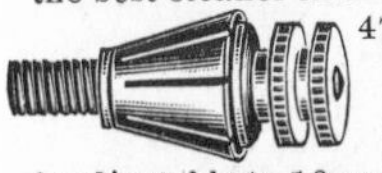

47656 Ferris Gun Cleaner, the best gun cleaner in the market for removing lead spots, rust and burnt powder. The cleaner has an India rubber cone, and is adjustable to 10 or 12 gauge. Each $0.70
Postage, extra, 5 cents.

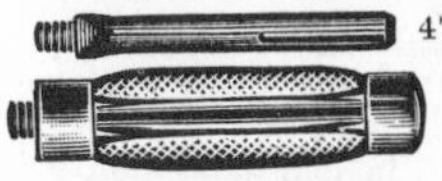

47657 The Tomlinson Gun Cleaner, for shot gun. Wire gauze cleaner. Fits any standard jointed cleaning rod. Each, $0.80

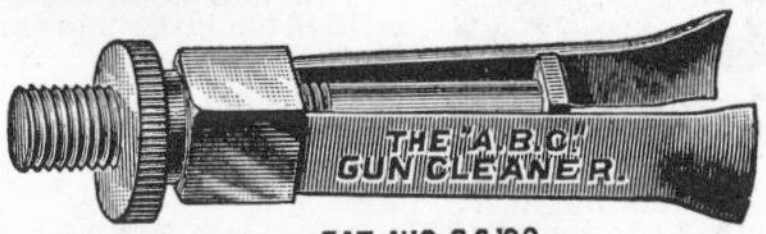

PAT. AUG. 30,'92.

Postage, extra, 4 cents.
47658 The A, B, C Gun Cleaner, nickel-plated metal, for use with jointed rods, adjustable from 8 to 16 gauge; a good one. Each $0.33
By mail, 2 cents extra.

Shell Extractor.

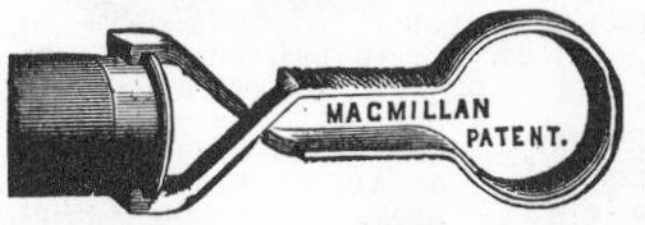

47659 The Universal Shell Extractor will extract any shell from 8 to 22 caliber; 15c. By mail, 1c. extra.

47660

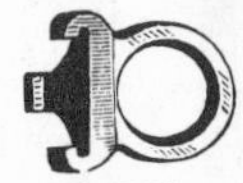
47661

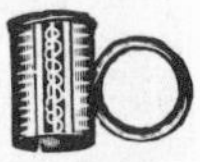
47665

47660 Wormer's to fit jointed rods, 10 and 12 gauge. Weight, 1 ounce. Each $0.06

Shell Extractors—Continued.

47661 Ring Shell Extractor, polished, 10 and 12 gauge, nickel finish. Weight, 1 oz. Each .08
47665 Powder and Shot Measure, combined, ring handle, polished nickel finish. Weight, 1 oz. Each .15

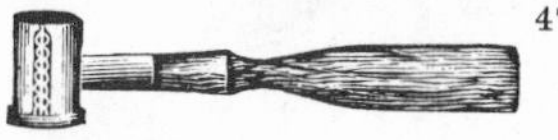

47666 Powder and Shot Measure, combined, cocobolo handles, polished, nickel finish, weight, 2oz. Each $0.12
47667 B.G.I. Standard Nitro Powder Measures, 2½, 2¾, 3, 3¼, or 3½ drams; will only measure one size charge. Each .20
47668 Standard Shot Measures, graduated from 1 to 1½ ounce. Each .20

Rifle Cleaning Rods.

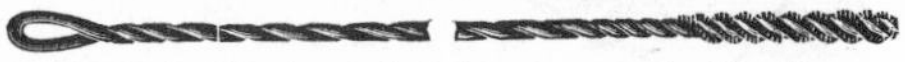

47670 Twisted wire, bristle brush on end; 22 caliber. Weight, 2 ounces $0.04

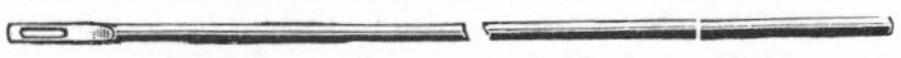

47671 Plain Brass Wire, slotted, for 22 caliber. Weight, 4 ounces $0.12

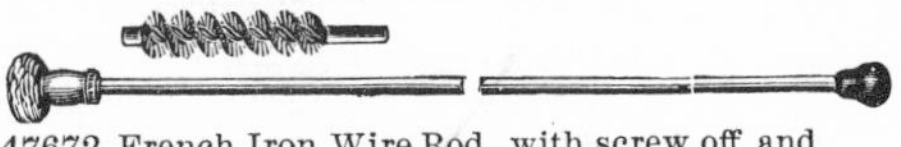

47672 French Iron Wire Rod, with screw off and bristle and wire scratch brushes, 22 caliber, 19c; 32 caliber, weight, 4 ounces $0.18

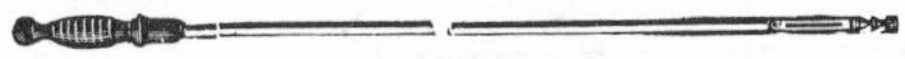

47673 Cocobolo Handle, brass wire jagged, slotted and knob for 32 and 22 caliber; weight, 4 oz. Each $0.35

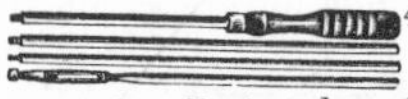

47675 Four Jointed Brass Cleaning Rods; can be carried in the pocket. The best and handiest rod on the market, about 30 inches long. If you wish a longer rod, you can order 2 rods, as they are interchangeable.

22 Caliber	$0.35	32 Caliber	$0.35
40 Caliber	.35	45 Caliber	.35
38 Caliber	.35	44 Caliber	.35
50 Caliber	.35	Postage, extra, 6 cents.	

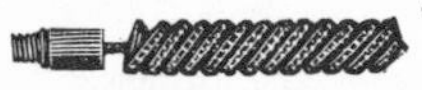

47676 Brass Wire Brush to fit 47675 Rods, 22, 32, 38, 40, 44, 45 and 50 calibers. Each $0.19
Postage, extra, 2 cents.

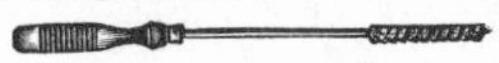

47677 Revolver Cleaners, brass rod, snake wood handle, brass wire brush. Order caliber wanted. Same brush only good for one caliber. Each $0.38
Postage, extra, 3 cents.

Gun Implement Set.

State gauge wanted.

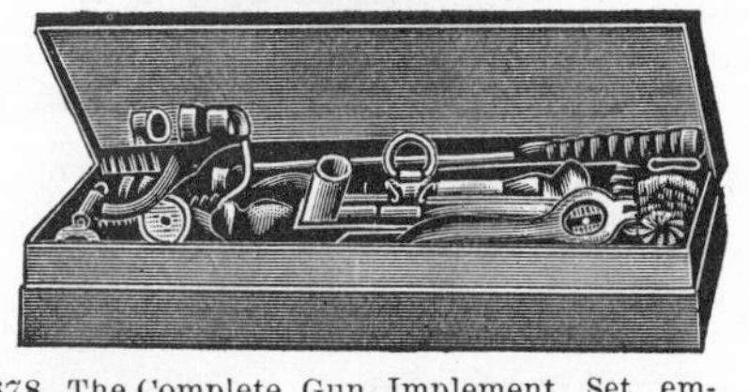

47678 The Complete Gun Implement Set, embracing Loader, Paper Shell Crimper, Re and De-capper, Shell Extractor, Powder and Shot Measure, and Cleaning Rod with implements. This set comes in a strong pasteboard box, neatly divided into compartments for each article, and each implement is made of *good material*, and recommends itself to every owner of a breech-loading shot gun. The best ever offered for the money. Size of box, 5x13 inches. Price, per set, best quality, 10 or 12 gauge, with 20 hole loading-block; weight, 3 pounds $1.60
47679 Price per set, medium quality, 10, 12, 16 and 20 gauge, with loading block with 20 holes. .98
47681 Price, good every day quality, 10, 12, 16 and 20 gauge; weight, 2 pounds .70
State gauge wanted.

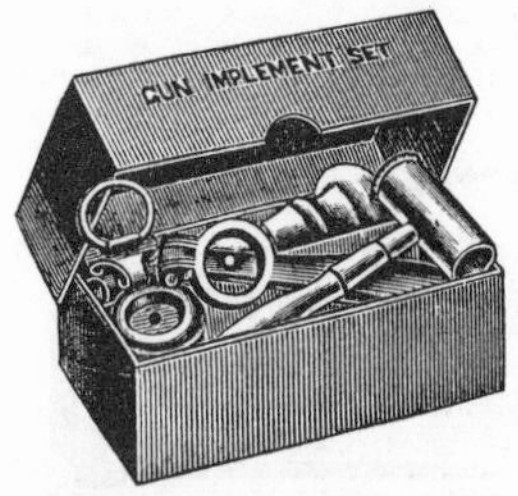

47683 Reloading Set, consisting of rammer and de-capper, with base block, nickel loading tube and re-capper, ring extractor, and patent paper shell crimper, graduated powder and shot measure, all inclosed in a strong paper box, making a neat and convenient set of tools.
Per set, 16 or 20 gauge, weight, 1 lb. $0.50
47684 Per set, 10 or 12 gauge .45
47685 Per set, for brass shells only, no crimper, 10 or 12 gauge only, weight, 12 ounces .15
16 or 20 gauge 20
Weight, packed, 16 ounces.

Loading Machines—Continued.

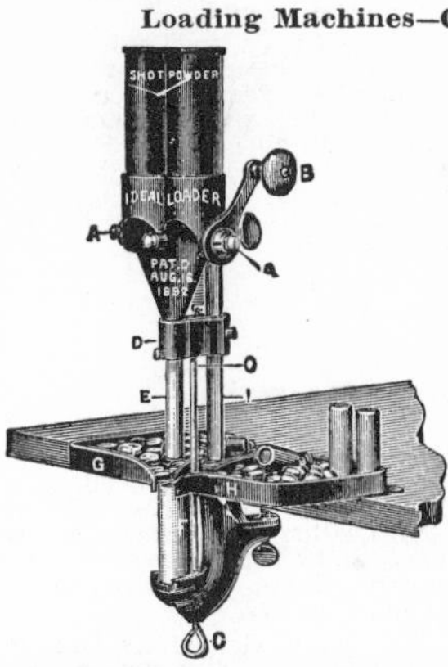

47689. Ideal Hand Loading Machine; will load black or nitro powders. The best machine of this kind on the market 10, 12 or 16 gauge; can be loaded. Loader fitted for 12 gauge. Each $6.50
Extra chamber for any gauge. Each $1.00
Full instructions with each machine.
No. 1 Funnels for 38 to 50 caliber. Each $0.50
No. 2 Funnels for 22 to 38 caliber, Each $0.50

Ideal Universal Powder Measure.

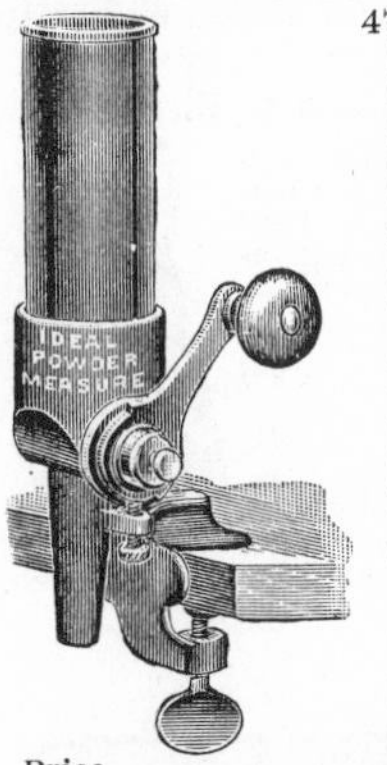

47690 As the name implies, this little implement *is universal*, for it can be set instantly for any charge of powder, for rifle, pistol or shot gun. Gunsmi hs, dealers in arms who load various kinds of ammunition, rifle clubs, gun clubs, or individuals have not a complete outfit without the "universal" measure. The measuring device and graduations are for drs. and grs. The range of work is from a 22 caliber up to an eight gauge shot gun; it will handle all varieties of powder now made. It can be clamped on the table or bench conveniently, there is no tipping over or spilling, there is no dipping and striking off measure. It conducts the powder into all sizes of shells without spilling.
Price $2.50

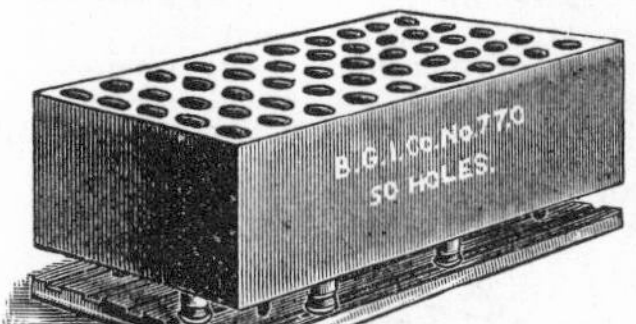

New model, made of white wood, holes bored with shoulder to fit entire length of shell; top of hole reamed out in place of wad-starter; shell does not come within ½ inch of top of block; shells cannot "bulge or break down." Just the thing to load shells for Smith or Parker guns, or where wads larger than shell are required. Weight, 3 lbs.
47700 Holding 50 12-gauge shells $0.85
Holding 50 10-gauge shells .85
Holding 50 16-gauge shells .95
47701 Metal-lined Block, 10 or 12 gauge Each 5.55
Weight, 6¾ lbs.

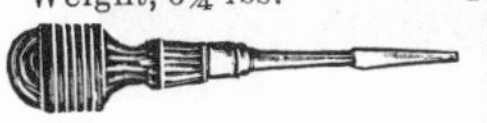

47702 Gun Screw Driver, entire length, about 6 inches; made of best steel. Each $0.32
Postage, extra, 3c.

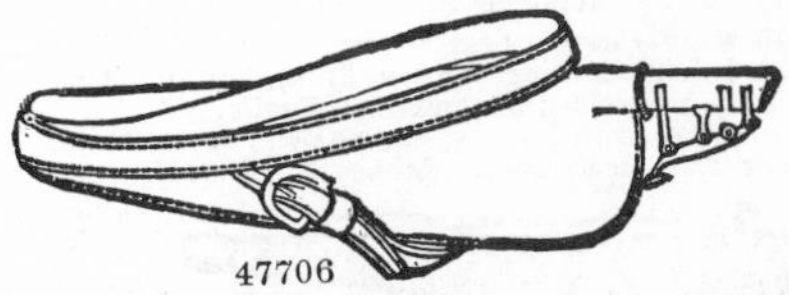
47706

47705 Single Belts, with Irish charger $0.35
47706 Single Belts, with lever charger .70
47707 Double Belts, with patent charger 1 00
By mail, 3 to 5c extra. Each.
47708 Pouches, 2½ lbs, with common Irish charger, not illustrated $0.30
47709 Pouch, 2½ lbs., with lever charger $0.60
Extra, by mail, 3 to 5 cents.

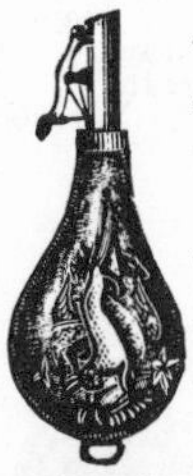
Pouch.

Powder Flasks.

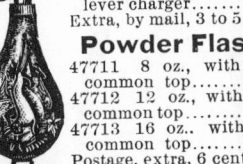

47711 8 oz., with cord, common top $0.29
47712 12 oz., with cord, common top $0.48
47713 16 oz., with cord, common top $0.50
Postage, extra, 6 cents.

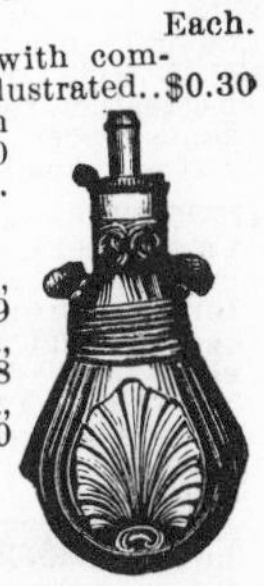

Shell Bags.

47715 Brown Canvas Bags, leather bound, with pocket; wt., 12 oz.
50 shells $0.28
75 shells .30
100 shells .33
150 shells Weight, 15 oz. .70
47717 Leather Bags, extra finished. Weight, 16 to 20 oz.
300 shells $2.65
200 shells 2.20
100 shells 1.18
75 shells 1.06
50 shells .93

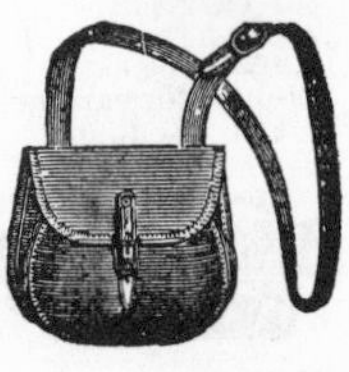

Shell Bags—Continued.

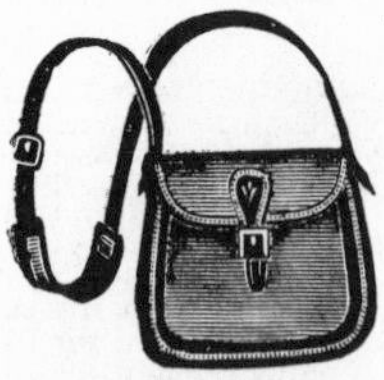

47718 Heavy Drab Colored Canvas Shell Bag, bound with red leather, 2 pockets, extra shoulder piece, handsome and durable. Each.
50 shells $0.58
75 shells................ .65
100 shells................ .79
200 shells 1.05

Weight, 9 to 20 ounces.

Game Bags.

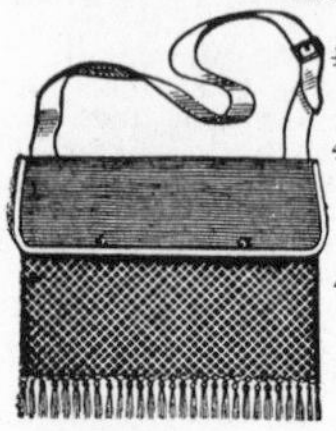

47721 Brown Canvas Game Bags, leather bound, with pockets. No. 100. Weight, 8 oz. Each..$0.80
47722 Leather Game Bags, leather flaps and backs, canvas pockets, square corners. No. 3. Each $1.12 Weight, 12 oz.
47723 Leather Game Bags, leather flaps and back, large pocket and small ,canvas pocket, round corners, with fringe. Weight, 16 oz. Each.................$1.95

Bedell's Patent Game Skirts.

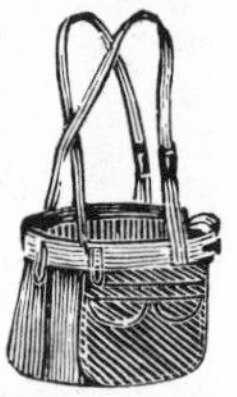

47724 Bedell's Patent Game and Cartridge Holder, heavy russet leather belt with game hooks, double leather shoulder straps, heavy brown canvas skirt with pocket to carry 100 shells. The best game and cartridge holder for field shooting in the market.
Each $2.00
Postage, extra, 26 cents.

Gun Covers.

By mail, 15 to 20 cents extra.

N. B.—When ordering covers state whether gun is "single" or "double barrel," "repeater" or "single shot," "rifle" or "shot gun."

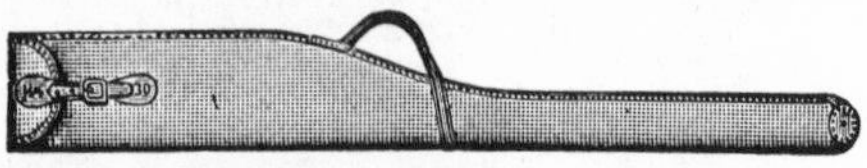

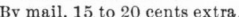

Gun Covers, Nos. 47725-26.

47725 Brown Canvas, leather bound, leather handle and muzzle protector, cotton flannel lining, 30 to 40 inch barrel. Each. $0.50 Per doz....$5.50
47726 Brown Canvas, same style as 47742 but lighter material, for single barrel shot guns and small rifles, 24 inch to 34 inch. Each.......... .38

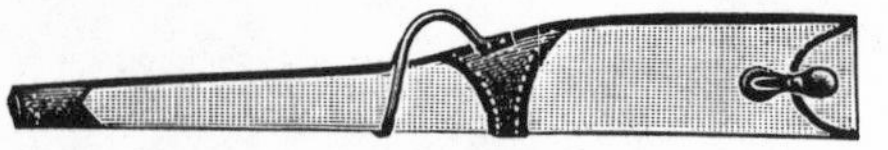

47727 Best Quality Brown Canvas, leather bound, with leather lock and muzzle protector and handle, cotton flannel lined. Each..$0.70 Per doz 7.50
N. B.—Give length of barrel and style of rifle when ordering covers. State whether "single shot" or "repeater."

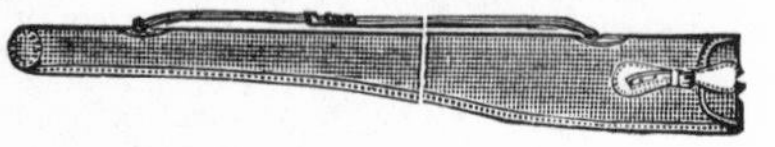

Rifle covers—Waterproof.

47729 Rifle Cover, best brown canvas, leather bound, leather sling, cotton flannel lined, best quality, 24 to 36 inch barrel. Each.............$0.45
47730 Shot Gun Covers, same as 47729 in shape, 30 or 32 inch barrels. Each..................... .50

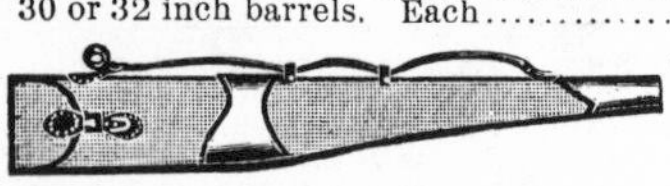

47732 Rifle Cover, same as 47729, with heavy leather lock and muzzle protector. Each.... .... $0.75
47734 Shot Gun Covers, same as 47932 in style, 30 or 32 inch barrels. Each..................... 0.80
47735 Rifle Cover, with sling straps, all heavy bag leather, russet color, made same style as the canvas covers. Waterproof and a good one. ... 1.50
Extra, by mail, 24 cents.

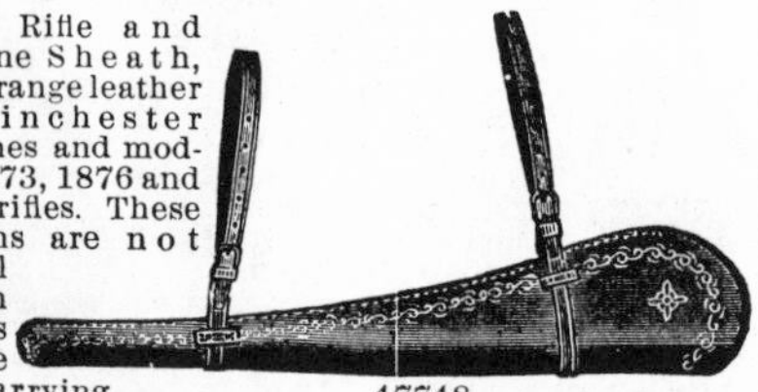

47748

47737 Rifle and Carbine Sheath, best orange leather for Winchester carbines and models 1873, 1876 and 1886 rifles. These sheaths are not full length covers but are for carrying rifle on saddle, leaving the stock of rifles exposed to be easily grasped. Each................$1.15
Weight for carbines, 13 oz., model '73, 16 oz., model '76 and '86, 26 oz.

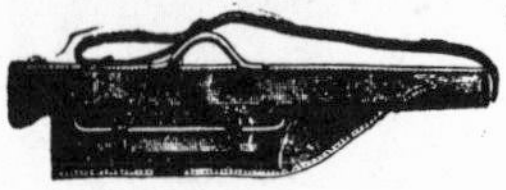

47738 Victoria Gun Case, heavy brown canvas, reinforced on ends with leather, with shoulder sling strap. Each....$1.00

Gun Covers—Continued.

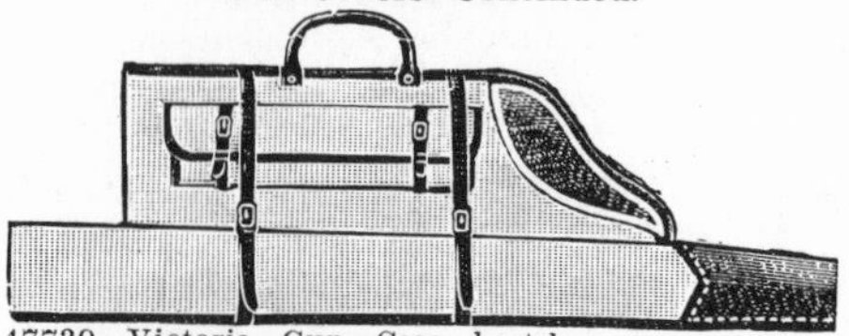

47739 Victoria Gun Case, best brown canvas, leather bound, with, leather handle, lock and muzzle protector, with heavy leather and with tool pocket on outside. Weight, 32 oz. Each...$ 1.00
Per dozen...11.00

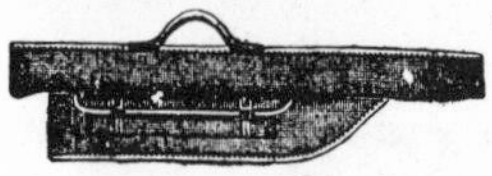

47740 Victoria Gun Case, heavy brown canvas, well made and durable; leather bound. Each.... ....$0.48

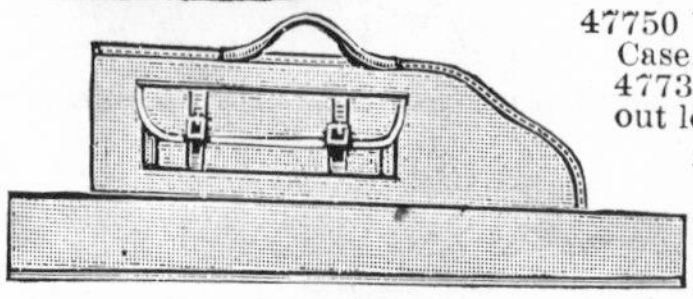

47750 Victoria Gun Case, same as 47739, but with. out lock and muzzle protector. Weight, 25 ounces Each. $0.65 Per dz. 7.20

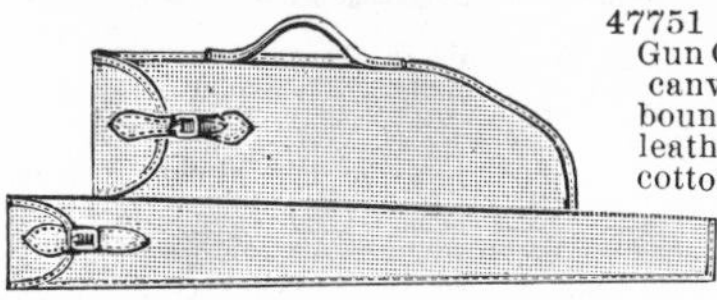

47751 Victoria Gun Case, brown canvas, leather bound, with leather handle, cotton flannel lined, no tool pocket, a good cover.
Weight, 20 oz. Each..$0.44 Per dozen.........$4.80
We can furnish any style Victoria Gun Case, either canvas or leather, for "Take Down Rifles."

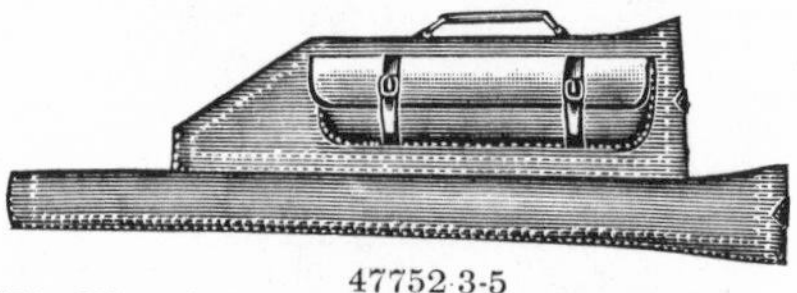

47752-3-5

47752 Victoria Gun Case, extra heavy russet leather, good, strong and durable, 30 and 32 inch barrels, with tool pocket outside................$2.40
47753 Victoria Gun Case, heavy russet sole leather, cotton flannel lined, tool pocket outside, 30 and 32 in. barrels. Weight, 36 oz. Each........ 2.63
Sling straps on leather gun cases, 50 cents extra.

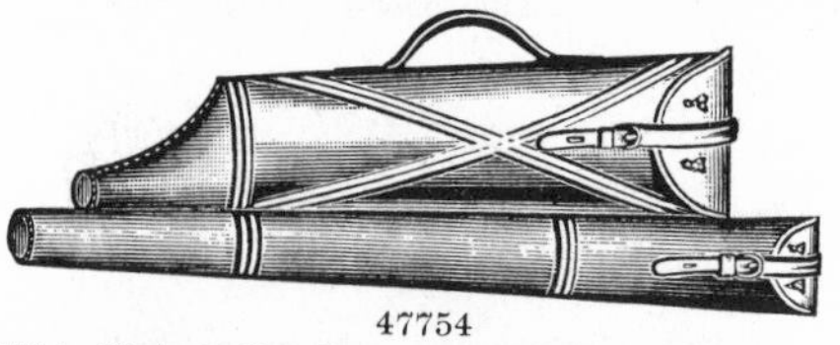

47754

47754 Victoria Gun Case, extra heavy leather, good, strong and durable, no outside pocket, 30 and 32 in. barrels. Each............................ 1.75
47755 Victoria Gun Case, extra heavy russet colored sole leather, highly finished, with tool pocket, flannel lined, 30 and 32 inch barrels. Weight, 44 oz. Each...................................... 2.75

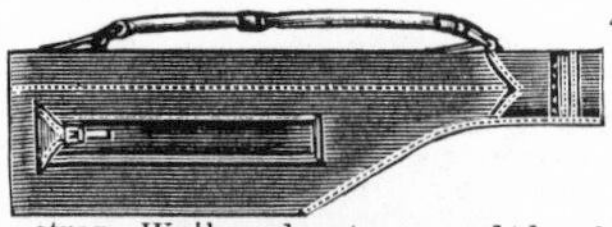

47755½ California Style Gun Case. Heavy brown canvas, leather muzzle protector, tool pocket and sling strap. Well made, strong and durable. Each...$0.75
Postage, extra, 25 cents.

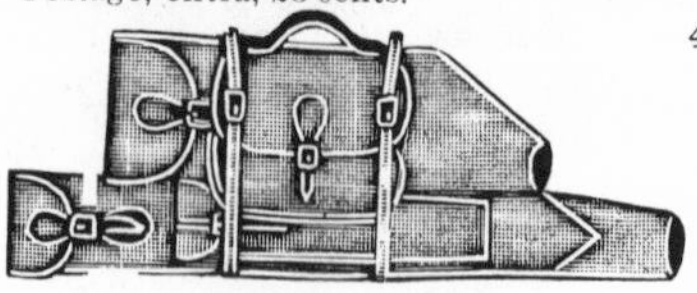

47756½

47756—Victoria Gun Case, heavy waterproof canvas, reenforced on stock and barrel with pocket for cleaning rod, also shell bag to hold 50 shells. The most complete cover offered to sportsmen and trap shooters. Each..............................$1.27
Postage, extra, 35 cents.

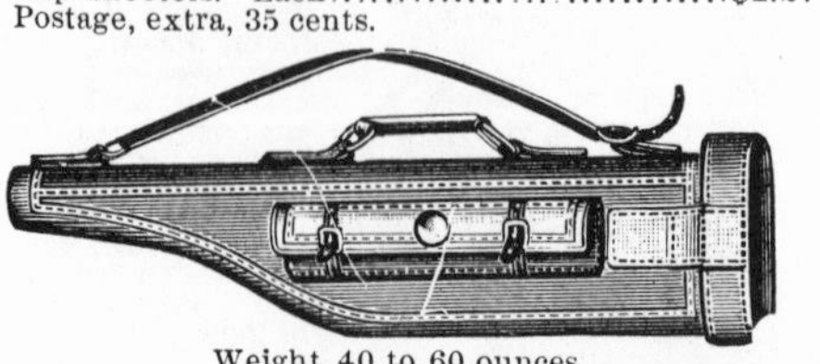

Weight, 40 to 60 ounces.

47757 English Victoria Gun Case, extra heavy oak tanned russet leather, embossed, nickel plated trimmings, patent fastening, staple for lock. A fine case, well made and very durable; 30 and 32 inch barrel. Each... ....$4 00

Gun Covers—Continued.

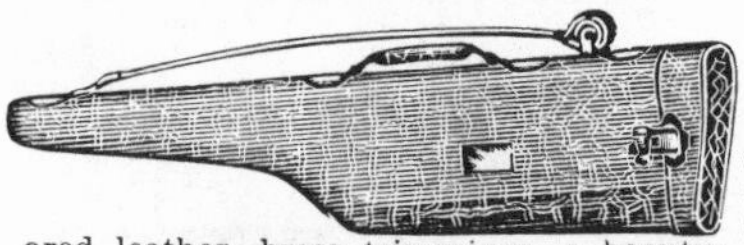

47758 English Victoria oak tanned russet colored leather, brass trimmings, a beauty; 28, 30 or 32 in. barrels. Flannel lined, each $4.75
47758½ Same as 47758 with tool pocket on outside. Each.. 5.25

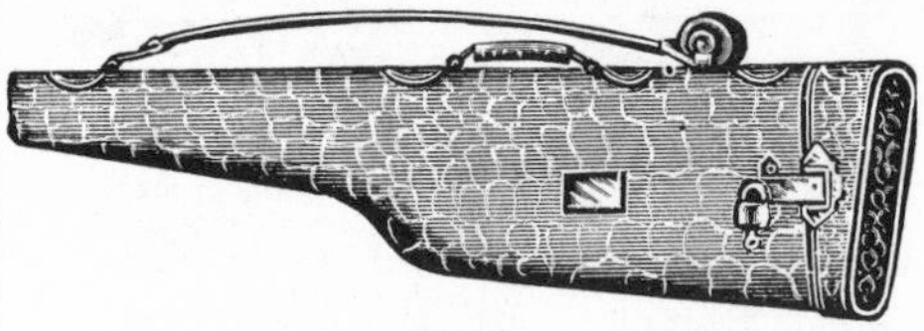

47759

47759 English Victoria, imitation alligator, chestnut colored leather, heavy and strong, a fine case: leather covered buckles; Each........$4.40
Any of above cases lined with lambskin with the wool left on for $1.50 extra; to order chamois lined $1.50 extra.
47759½ English Victoria Gun Case, same as 47759, except has tool pocket on outside. Each, 4.80
47760 English Victoria Gun Case, made of the very best orange color finish sole leather, burnished brass trimmings, made up in the very best style; no tool pocket; elegant in design and finish. Each 5.50
47761 Victoria Case, same as 47760, with tool pocket on the outside. Each.... .... 6.00
All leather Victoria cases are the best and handsomest covers for guns. The leather being thick and heavy protects the guns from being injured or getting rusty. These cases are called sole leather and are almost as heavy as sole leather. (Mention length of gun barrels.)

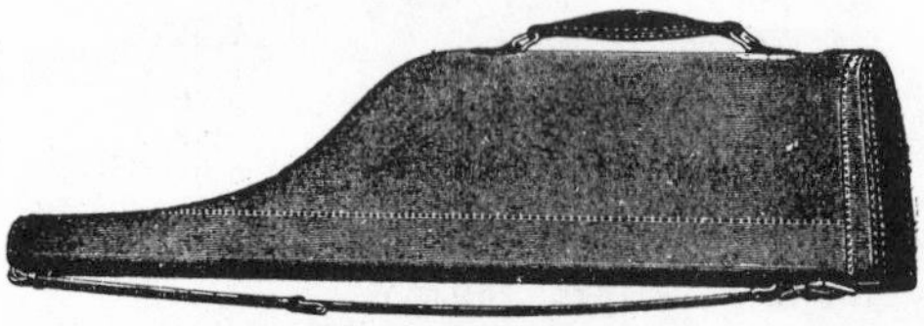

47762 English Style, finest cream colored, solid leather, made in best possible manner, 28 or 30 inch barrels for light 12 gauge guns, 8 pounds and under. Each, moleskin lined...................$6.30
Each, chamois lined...................... ...... 6.40

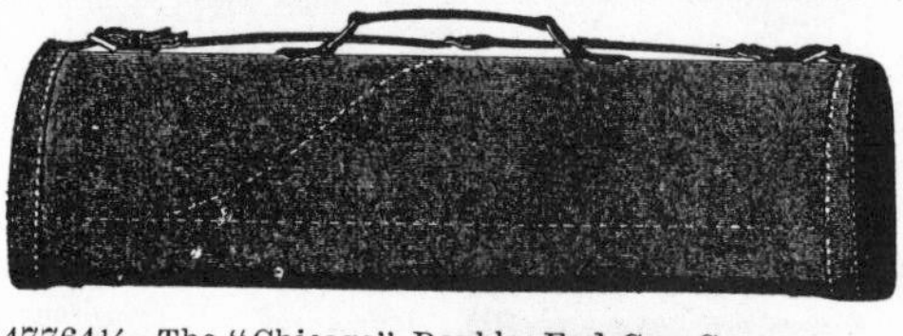

47764½ The "Chicago" Double End Gun Case, fine russet sole leather, all hand made. 30 or 32 inch barrels, light and handy. Flannel lined.
Each $7.50
Chamois lined, each.............................. 8.50

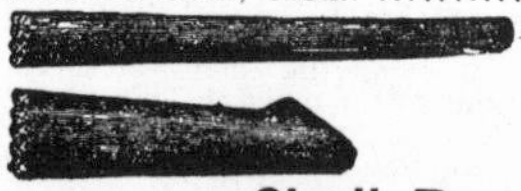

47765 Chamois Skin Stock and Barrel Covers, 30 or 32-inch barrels.
Per set........$0.75

Shell Boxes.

Weight, 5 lbs.

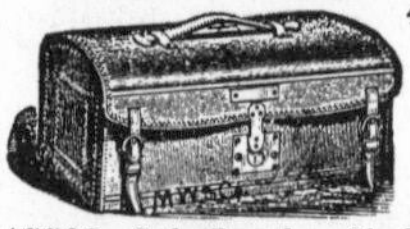

47767 Sole Leather Shell Boxes, tin lined, with compartments, nickel plated trimmings. Dimensions: 12¾ in. long, 6 in. wide, 7½ in. high; holding 200 shells. Each..... ....$2.95
47768 Sole Leather Shell Boxes, same as 47767 dimensions: 13¾ in. long, 8½ in. wide, 8 in. high; holding 300 shells, each 3.50

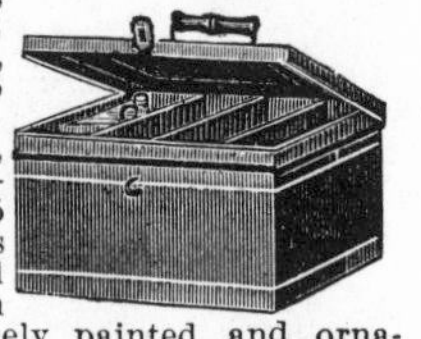

47769 Metallic Shell Box; length, 11 in.; width, 6½ in.; depth, 5 in.; capacity 100, No. 12. Each..........$1.75
Weight, 3 lbs.
47769½ Length, 13 in.; width, 8½ in.; depth, 7½ in.; capacity, 400 No. 12. Each.$2.75
The material of this box is very heavy, so it could be used for a seat or a stool to sit upon without damage. All are nicely painted and ornamented. Weight, about 4 lbs.

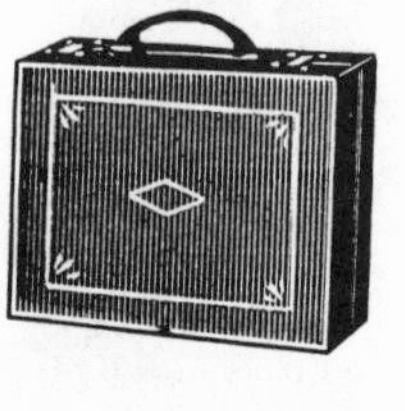

47770 Trap Shooters' Leather Ammunition Cases, heavy russet sole leather, tin lined, partitioned for 25 shells in each space; tray for cleaning rod and three partitions for sundries; holds 150 shells.
Each.........................$4.96
Weight, 5 lbs.

Shell Boxes—Continued

47770½ Trap Shooters' Shell Cases, heavy russet leather, tin-lined, partitioned for 25 shells in each space, well made, and durable for 100 shells. Each......$2.75 For 150 shells, each 3.40

Pistol Holsters.

47771 Russet Leather Pocket Holster (as adopted by police officers), heavy russet leather, for 3½ in. barrel, 32 and 38 caliber. Made to wear in the hip pocket; sweat proof. The best pocket holster in the market, made to fit the hip pocket, and not necessary to remove it when you take out the revolver. Each......$0.30 Per dozen......3.24

47771½ Russet Leather Pocket Holster, 32 or 38 caliber, for 3 to 3½ inch barrels only. Each......40

Holsters, chamois lined, will cost 35 cents extra each.

47772-73 Holsters, by mail, 5 cents extra.

47772 Pistol Holster with loop similar to cut, heavy russet leather, 32 caliber. Each......$0.25
47773 Pistol Holster, with loop similar to cut, russet leather, 38, 44 and 45 caliber. Each......38

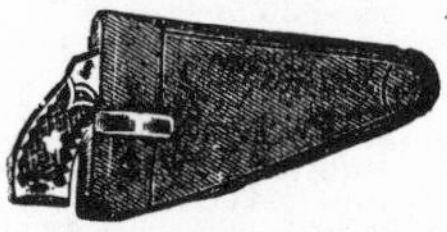

47774 Rubber Pocket Holster, with steel hook. 32 caliber......$0.50 38 caliber......60 44 caliber......80 Postage, 4 cents extra.

The rubber holster is rust proof, and being soft and pliable, it is the best and most convenient holster ever made to carry a revolver in the pocket. Will hold revolvers with 3½ in. barrel or shorter.

47776 Pocket Pistol Holster, soft russet leather (no loop for belt), for pocket use only, 22, 32 and 38 calibers. Each.$0.15 Per dozen......1.65 Postage, 3 cents.

Pistol Holsters.

(By mail, 5 cents extra.)

47777 Pistol Holster with loop for belt, heavy russet leather, 22 and 32 caliber. Each......$0.20

47778 Pistol Holster, with loop for belt, best russet leather, 38 caliber......Each $0.25
47779 Pistol Holster, with loop for belt, best russet leather, 44 caliber......30
47780 Pistol Holster, with loop for belt, best russet leather, 45 caliber......35

47782 Mexican Holster, best russet leather, heavy and durable, 32 and 38 caliber......40 44 caliber......47 45 caliber......50 By mail, 6c. extra. For chamois lined holsters add 35 cents each extra.

Leather Belts.

Our Leather Goods are the Best in the Market.

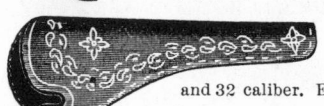

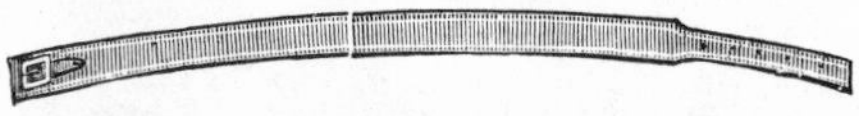

47783 Belts only, russet leather, without loops for cartridges. By mail, 5c. extra. Each......$0.15

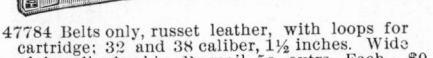

47784 Belts only, russet leather, with loops for cartridge; 32 and 38 caliber, 1½ inches. Wide plain roller buckle. By mail, 5c. extra. Each...$0.30

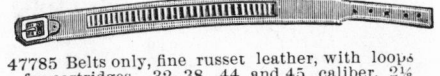

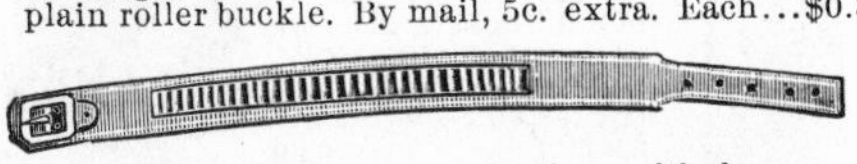

47785 Belts only, fine russet leather, with loops for cartridges, 32, 38, 44 and 45 caliber, 2⅛ inches wide, large nickel plated buckle. By mail, 10c. extra. Each......$0.45

31—2nd

Rifle Cartridge Belts.

By mail, 5 cents extra. Be sure and mention caliber of cartridge you wish to carry.

47787 Leather Rifle Belt, 32, 38, 44, 45 caliber, 2⅛ inches wide, best quality, heavy......$0.45

Cartridge and Shot Belts.

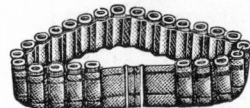

47788 The Woven Cartridge Belt, invention of Col. Anson Mills, U. S. A. The main body of the belt, as well as the loops which hold the cartridge, is woven in one solid piece. The belt is soft and pliable, particularly adapted to rifle cartridges. In ordering be sure to give caliber and name of cartridges you wish to carry. 32 to 50 caliber. By mail, 20 cents extra. Each......$1.46

47789 The Anson Mills Woven Shot Shell Belts, 10-gauge and 12 and 16 gauge, with shoulder strap and game hooks. By mail, 22 cents extra.$1.50

Shell Belts.

47790 Anson Mills Hunter's Belt. The loops are woven, closed at the bottom, protecting the crimped end of shell, no sewing on the belt whatever; weight, 5 oz. 10 or 12 gauge. Each...$1.20
47790½ Light Web Shell Belts, no shoulder straps or welt on bottom, 10, 12 or 16 gauge; weight, 4 oz......18 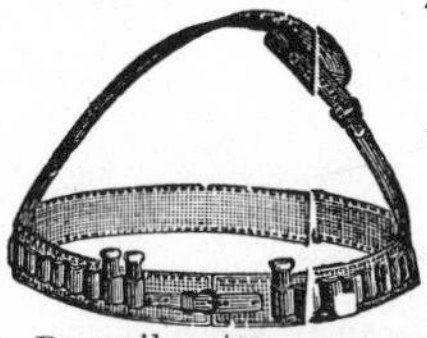
47791 Canvas Shell Belts, 10, 12, 16 and 20 gauge, with shoulder strap; weight, 15 oz......$0.40
47792 Russet Leather Shell Belt, with shoulder strap, 10, 12, 16 and 20 gauge Each......$0.46
47793 Russet Leather Shell Belt with shoulder strap, 8 gauge only. Each...$1.00 By mail, extra......16

47795 Mexican Combined Cartridge and Money Belt, made of the very best russet leather; belt 3 inches wide, soft and pliable and will not get hard and crack; neatly embossed 32 and 38 caliber......$0.75 44 caliber......$0.80 45 caliber......85 By mail, 13c. extra. Don't forget to state caliber wanted.

47796 "The Pop" Shoulder Holster, with breast and shoulder strap to wear under coat on left side, as shown in cut. Made of fine soft russet leather, any caliber or length of barrel. Each......$0.60 Extra by mail, each 7c. *Always forget to state caliber if you are in a hurry for your goods, and then it will be necessary to write you for size.*

Money Belts.

By mail, 3 cents extra.
47797 Money Belts, chamois skin, with 3 compartments, width, 3 inches; to be worn around waist under clothing. Each....$0.40 Per dozen......$5.00
47798 Money Belts, soft, pliable leather, 3 compartments, sweat proof, never get hard or stiff, the best thing in the world. Each......$0.75 Per dozen......7.70

47799 Heike's Hand Protector, for shot gun barrels, a protection from cold barrels or hot barrels, made of spring steel leather covered. A necessity to trap shooters. Each...$0.69 By mail, 3c. extra.

MEDIUM CUT.

Recoil Pads.

By mail, 5c. extra.

 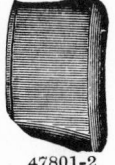

47800 Rudolph's Popular Recoil Pad, leather, with lacing; will not become loose. Each......$0.95 Postage, extra....10
47801 The Rubber Recoil Pad, made entirely of rubber, well padded and will fit any gun, its elasticity keeping it in position, and preventing the shock of the recoil doing injury to the shoulder. Price, each ....$0.35 Per dozen......$3.95
47802 Pure Red Rubber Recoil Pad, the best pad in the market. Two sizes, Nos. 3 and 4. No. 3 smallest. Give length of heel plate on gun for which you want the pad. Each......75 Postage extra......07

47803 Silver's Patent Recoil Pad and Butt Piece combined, making a hard rubber butt plate and a flexible rubber pad; for 10 or 12 gauge gun. The screws from old butt plate can be used to hold it on. Each......$3.70 By mail, 10 cents extra.

47804 The "Cowboy" Holster, made of heavy red, oiled leather, raised embossed work; made to match in color and style our Cowboy Saddles. The best holster on the market. 38 caliber......$1.40 44 caliber......$1.50 45 caliber......1.60 Postage, extra......11

47805 The "Cowboy" Combined Cartridge and Money Belt; made of heavy red, oiled leather, strong and durable, designed to match our Cowboy Saddles. 38, 44 and 45 caliber. Each, $2.25 Postage, extra.....$0.08

Hunting Knives.

All these knives are of very best quality steel.

47807 Deer Foot.

47807 Hunting Knife, deer's foot handle, 7-inch clip blade, best steel leather sheaths, with loops to attach to belt, nickel bolstered (see cut)......$1.85

Spear point

Clip blade

47809 Hunting Knife, buckhorn handle, 6-inch steel clip blade, leather sheath, with loop to attach to belt; entire length, 11 inches. By mail, 8c. extra......$0.90
47811 Hunting Knife, same description as No. 47809, 6 inches, spear point. By mail, 8c. extra. .95

By mail, 8c. extra.
47813 Hunting Knives, scored ebony handle bolstered with guard, best steel blade, 6-inch blades. Each......$0.50 6½ in. blades. Each, $0.60 7-in. blades. Each, .70

47814 Hunting Knife, extra heavy blade, hand forged, ebony handles, 6 inch clip blade. Each. .70

Sheaths and Belts.

By mail, 8c. extra.

47815 Leather Knife Sheaths.
6 in.   7 in.   8 in.   9 in.
$0.10   .12   .15   .18

47816 Leather Belts for knife sheaths, 1¼ in. wide......$0.15

Hunter's Ax.

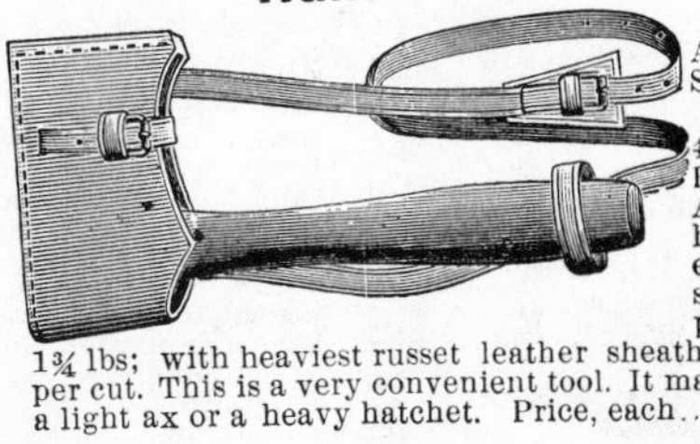

Hunters' Ax and Sheath.

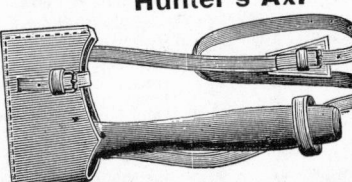

47818—Hunters' Ax, with handles, extra cast steel, steel poll; wt., 1¾ lbs; with heaviest russet leather sheath, as per cut. This is a very convenient tool. It makes a light ax or a heavy hatchet. Price, each.....$1.40

Pocket Oilers.

47819 The C. & D. Perfection Gun Oiler, the best and handiest gun and revolver oiler in the market. Each $0.23

47820 The Pocket Oiler, flat, nickel plated with brass screw on top, 'entirely preventing the escape of oil, can be carried in the vest pocket; about the size of a watch. Each.. ....$0.12
Extra, by mail, 2c.

Gun Oils, Etc.

Winchester Gun Grease, put up by the Winchester Repeating Arms Company.

47821 The Winchester Gun Grease is the best rust preventer manufactured. It has been in use in this factory for years. For any steel or polished iron surface and for inside or outside of gun or rifle barrels it has no equal. Put up in neat metallic tubes. Per tube..$0.12
Postage 12c, extra, per 10 tubes. Box 10 tubes. 1.10

47821½ Gunoleum Lubricant, for protecting and preserving all metals from rust and tarnish. Especially adapted to guns, revolvers and fine machinery. Put up in metallic tubes. Per tube..$0.12
Per dozen..$1.15 One-half-pound cans, each.. .40
One-pound cans, each....... .... .60

47822 Parafine Gun Oil, put up exclusively for guns, gun locks, and fine machinery and furniture: removes rust and will not gum, 2 oz. bottles. Price, per dozen....$0.50 3 bottles for.. .15

47823 Montgomery Ward & Co's Popular Lubricating Oil, best oil in the market for guns, locks, sewing machines, bicycles and any small machines: will not freeze, gum, rust, or corrode or become rancid. Per bottle................... .08
Per dozen (Unmailable)........................ .80

47825 Rust Remover, coarse, for removing rust from iron, steel, brass or any metal where cutting properties are desired. Per bottle........ .20
47826 Rust Remover, medium.................. .18
47827 Rust Remover, fine. (Postage, 5c extra). .19
47830 Wood Polish. Nothing like it for bright, clean and lustrous polish on furniture, desks, gun stocks and all walnut, oiled or varnished furniture Per bottle. (Unmailable)............ .20

47833 Cook's Black Fly and Mosquito Paste. It is the nicest, most pleasing and effectual mosquito and fly starter in the country. A little rubbed on the face and hands will positively keep them off, as well as keep off fleas, wood ticks, forest, sand and house flies, and all similar pests. Per bottle $0.20
Postage, 10c. extra.

Bird Calls.

By mail, 2 to 3 cents each.

47835 Grubb's Improved Illinois River Duck Call. The most natural toned call made; easy to blow: not easy to get out of repair, having a fine tempered reed; makes it so you can call teal, woodduck and bluebill, as well as mallard. This is the only call you can do this with. Each.... ....$0 50

47836 The Perfection Duck Call, made of red cedar, silver mounted, with silver reed which gives it perfect tone. This is the finest duck call made, perfect, similar in style to the Grubb's call, and is warranted. Each.......$1.00

47841 Allen's Improved Wood duck Caller, the most natual toned, easiest blowing. Used in the field by all the best duck shooters in America. Each $0.45

47842 Duck Calls, horn, with rosewood mouth piece. Each.........$0.25
47843 Turkey Calls, horn, with rosewood mouth piece. Each....$0.27
Extra by mail, 3c.
47844 Snipe Calls (no cut) Each.............$0.18
Postage, 2c. extra.
47845 Fuller's Metallic Wild Goose Caller. Each ....80c.
Extra by mail 5c.

Allens' Duck Call.   Turkey Call.

Barnum's Patent Game Carrier.

Barnum's.   Rudolph.

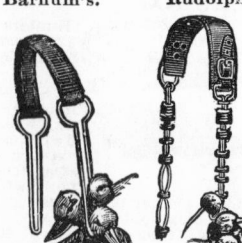

By mail, 3c extra.

47848 Worth its weight in gold; a blessing to feathered game shooters; weight, 2½ ozs. folded, 8½ inches long; ½ inch thick; can be carried in the pencil pocket, yet holds securely 18 ducks, balanced on the shoulders, on the belt, gun barrel, or in the hand. Price, each....$0.14
Per dozen....... 1.40

47849 Rudolph's Compact Game Carrier, with leather shoulder strap. Each $0.30
Per dozen 3.00
By mail, 3c extra.

Decoys.

In making these decoys great care has been used to select only sound white cedar for their construction and to secure a perfect balance. They are light, substantially and naturally painted. Assortments; Mallard canvas back, red head, blue bill, teal, pin or sprig tails. Weight, per dozen, 35 to 40 pounds.
47850 No. 1 Best Decoy Ducks (glass eyes). Per dozen $3.75
47851 No. 2 Good Decoy Ducks (metallic eyes). Per dozen 2.00
47852 Cords and Anchors for Decoys. Per dozen. .75
We do not handle the No. 3 decoy, as they are too poorly finished.

The Brinkop Metal Duck Decoy.
It's the best.

Decoy as it appears on the water.

The body is stamped in one piece, and the head and neck in another, from thin sheet metal, and can be connected firmly in an instant, then thrown into the water. They always assume and hold their proper position; can be used with or without the board float, being open underneath. If perforated with holes its buoyancy is not affected. They are neatly painted, and on the water closely resemble a live duck, being so light the least wind gives them an easy, graceful motion. A dozen of these decoys do not weigh much more than two wooden ones, and occupy, when nested, about as much space, cheaper and better than wooden decoys.
47855 Per dozen (all mallards), with board float and anchors, complete........................$4.95
Each, weight, 17 oz .... .45
Mallard decoys are good for decoying almost any kind of ducks.

Folding Canvas Decoys.

47862 Folding Canvas Decoys. The best imitation of the natural duck in the market. Made of best canvas, beautifully painted in natural colors, waterproofed. Weight 4 oz. each. Packed 1 dozen in a neat wooden box 2¾x9 inches. We do not sell less than a dozen. Mallards, red heads, canvas backs and blue bills. Per doz.....$6.50
Weight, per dozen, packed, 9 lbs.
47863 Folding or Collapsible Canvas geese, packed in boxes of one dozen. Sold in ½ dozen lots at dozen prices; not less than ½ dozen sold. Per dozen........................ ....$11.90
Weight, per dozen, packed, 11½ lbs.

Crass Suits.

47864 For wild goose, duck and all kinds of shore bird shooting; made of long, tough marsh grass into cape cloth with hood. Weigh less than four pounds; are convenient to wear and shoot from. Make good waterproofs in rainy weather, are easily packed and carried. Hunters appreciate the value of these suits, as no blind or bough house is necessary when shooting on marshes.
Single suits, each $2.25

Hunters' Clothing.

Also good for Farmers, Teamsters and Mechanics. Finest quality and the best made goods in the market. All double stitched and never rip. Extra by mail, 40 to 50 cents on canvas coats. Hunting Coats and Vests not made in "odd sizes."

47867 Hunting Coat made of heavy 10 oz. dead army duck, lined throughout with 8 oz. duck, dead grass color, otherwise same as 47869. Leather bound, made in the best possible mann r, heavy and durable.
Each $3.50

47869 (No. 1) Hunting Coat is made of heavy 8 oz. double filling duck, dead grass color and waterproof, bound with leather to prevent wearing out of edges, has 6 pockets, entrance to game pocket from outside; shoulders re-enforced, corduroy collar, corduroy lined cuffs; no better coat in the market, sizes. 36 to 46.
Price, each.... ....$2.50
47871 Coat, same as No. 1, without leather binding; sizes, 36 to 46.
Price, each $2.35
47872 Coat, lighter duck, 6 pockets outside, full game pocket inside, corduroy collar; sizes, 36 to 46; a good coat.
Each...............$1.50

47873 Coat, same as, No. 47872, except leather bound all around. Each. $1.75
47874 Hunting Jacket, 8oz., dead grass color, duck, 6 outside pockets, full skirt, game pockets, single stiched, metal button, corduroy collar. Each .... .90
Extra, by mail, 25 cts.
47875 Hunting Suit, greenish drab color, 8 oz. duck, for hunting or fishing, before the foliage is dead, or in the south, 6 outside pockets, full inside game pocket, entrance on the outside, shoulders re-enforced. Made in first-class manner; a good suit; coat, pants and vest........... 4.50
Coat only, $2.40 Vest only, $0.95 Pants only 1.27
Caps and hats, any hunting style, same prices as the DEAD GRASS colored.
N. B—We can furnish the above coats heavy flannel lined, $1.50 extra. No other coat is needed where No. 1 coat is lined.
47876 Drill Hunting Coat, dead grass color, 6 outside pockets, 2 skirt game pockets inside. Each.$0.60

47876½ The 10-oz. Army Duck Hunting Coat, best quality water proof canvas, dead grass color, corduroy collar, leather bound; wrist lined with corduroy, and made to button close if desired. Sizes, 36, 38, 40, 42, 44 and 46. Each....$3.00

47877½ The 10-oz. Army Duck Hunting Coat, same as No. 47876½, not leather bound. Each.............................$2.75
Coats, flannel lined, $1.50 extra.

47878 (No. 1) Vest, made of best 8 oz., duck, waterproof, color to match coat, with four pockets, which will carry forty shells or more; sizes, 36 to 44. Price, each............. 0.75
20 cents extra by mail.

47879 Vest, same as above, but with shell bands instead of pockets; sizes, 36 to 44.
Price, each $1.00
Extra by mail 15 cts.
Give chest measure for coat and vest.

47880 Hunting Pants, made of heavy 8 oz. waterproof duck to match coat and vest, with two long pockets in front, one hip pocket, full length, regular make, double stitched, never rip until worn out.
Each....................... ....$1.30
47880   Extra by mail 25 cts.
47878   47879

Hunting Clothing —Continued

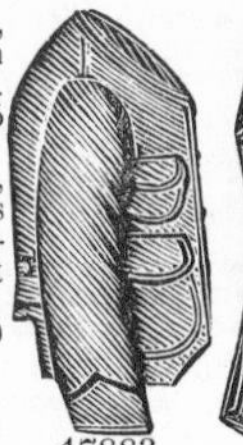
47883

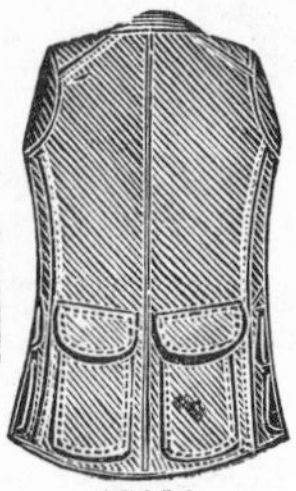
47884

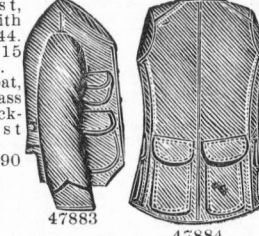

47883 Canvas Vest, dead grass color, with sleeves; sizes, 36 to 44. Each $1.15
Extra by mail 16 cts.
47884 Skeleton coat, canvas, dead grass color with game pockets. Sizes, breast measure, 36 to 44. Each.. .... $0.90
Extra by mail 16 cts.

Best Imported Corduroy Suits.

DRAB OR DARK BROWN, PLAIN COLORS.

We can furnish suits made of mottled or "Partridge" brown and white mixture. Coats, $8.75, pants, $6.50, vest, $4.50.

Weights, coat, 42 oz; pants, 33; vest, 16 to 20 oz.

47885 Corduroy coat, size, 36 to 44............. $6.15
47886 Corduroy Vest, size, 36 to 44. .... 2.93
47887 Corduroy Pants; give waist and inside seam measure; full length, regular make........ 4.45
47888 Corduroy Hunting Coat, dark drab color, not as heavy as 47885, but well made and durable. (Many prefer them to the heavier goods.) $3.95
47889 Corduroy Pants, same.................... 3.00
47889½ Corduroy Vest, same.................. 1.80

Our corduroy clothing is made of IMPORTED goods, and is free from any objectionable "odor," such as is found in some "so-called" imported corduroys. They are well made and nice fitting goods, and all warranted as represented. Coats are all sack style, similar to our hunting coats in design and finish.

Oil-Tanned Horsehide Suits.

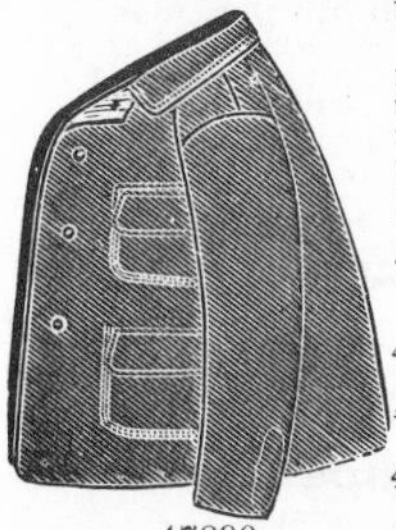
47890

Weight, coats, 56 to 60 oz. Positively the best garment made in this or any other country for those exposed to rough weather. They are water and wind proof, pliable and soft as kid, and will always remain so. Made with outside pockets.

47890 Horsehide Coat, reversible with corduroy; sizes, 36 to 44 .... $11.65
47891 Horsehide Coat, heavy cassimere lined $9.79
47892 Vest, cassimere lined, horsehide.............. $3.90
47892½ Vests, reversible, with corduroy.................. $5.60
47893 Pants, horsehide, cassimere lined; weight about 3 lbs., full length regular make $6.95

Our horsehide clothing is genuine horsehide, and not "goatskin" or "sheepskin" or "dogskin" (which is another name for "sheepskin" in most cases), and will never "peel off" or get rough, no matter how sharp the thorns or how thick the brush and trees are, and can be oiled like a boot or harness; grows softer and more pliable the longer it is worn; keep well oiled with neatsfoot oil.

Sweaters.

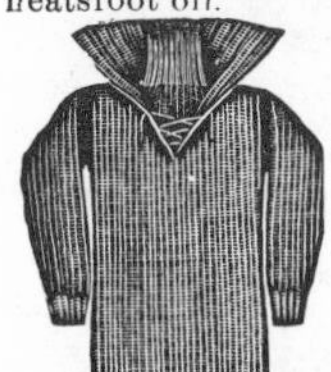

47896 The Turtle Neck Shirt or Sweater, double from waist up; one of the most desirable garments ever invented for cold-weather shooting. Made of the best wool in tan and dark navy blue colors. Sizes, 34, 36, 38, 40, 42, 44. Each.............. $4.25

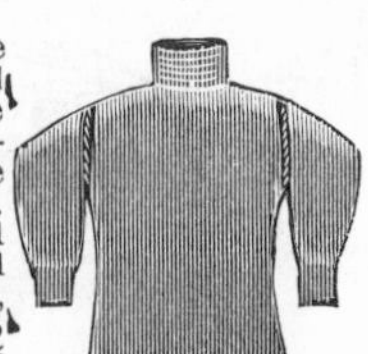

47897 The Hunters' Shirt, made of lamb's wool. They pull down over the head and make a close fitting, wind-proof garment. Being elastic they are also good for trap shooters. Colors: White, tan, black and navy blue. Extra heavy (Retail price, $6.00). Sizes, 34, 36, 38, 40, 42, 44. Each...... ..$3.75
Medium heavy. Each.... 2.75
Weight, 22 to 30 ounces.

Shooting Blouse.

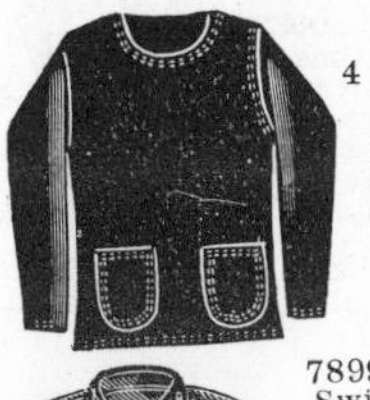

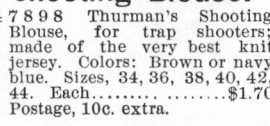

47898 Thurman's Shooting Blouse, for trap shooters; made of the very best knit jersey. Colors: Brown or navy blue. Sizes, 34, 36, 38, 40, 42, 44. Each.. .... $1.70
Postage, 10c. extra.

Chamois Shirt.

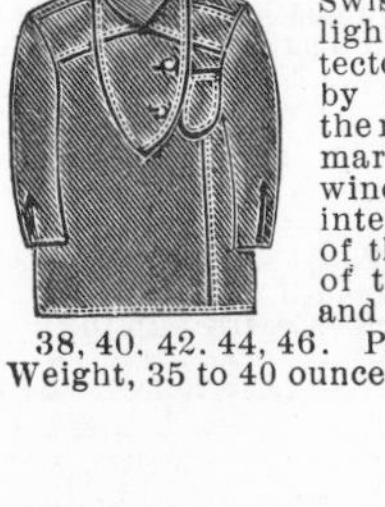

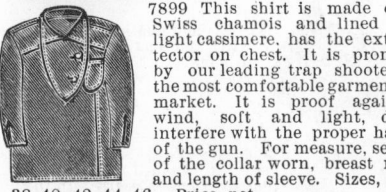

7899 This shirt is made of fine Swiss chamois and lined with a light cassimere, has the extra protector on chest. It is pronounced by our leading trap shooters to be the most comfortable garment on the market. It is proof against the wind, soft and light, does not interfere with the proper handling of the gun. For measure, send size of the collar worn, breast measure and length of sleeve. Sizes, 34, 36, 38, 40, 42, 44, 46. Price, net................ $6.25
Weight, 35 to 40 ounces.

Hunting Hats and Caps.

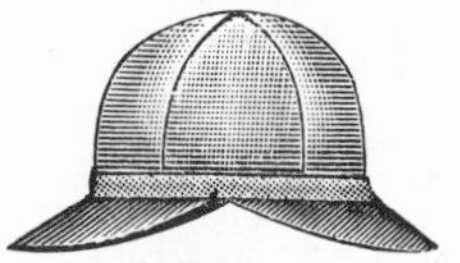
47900

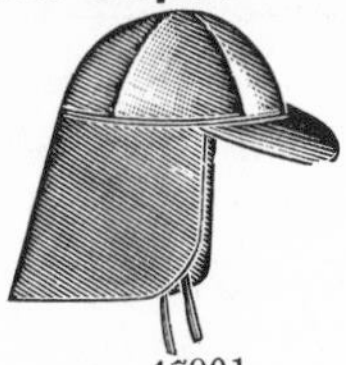
47901

47900 Hunting Cap, made of heavy dead grass colored duck, with double visor. Give size of hat worn. Weight, 5 ounces. Each.........$0.38
47901 Hunting Cap, same as above, one visor; has havelock cape to protect the neck from storm or sun, taped seams, light flannel lined; weight, 12 ounces. Each .... .48

Our canvas goods are the best in the market. We do not handle the cheap stuff.

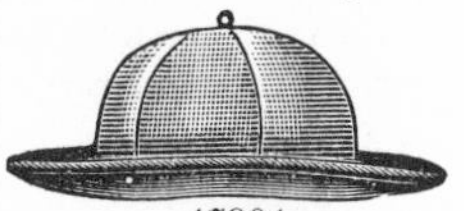
47904

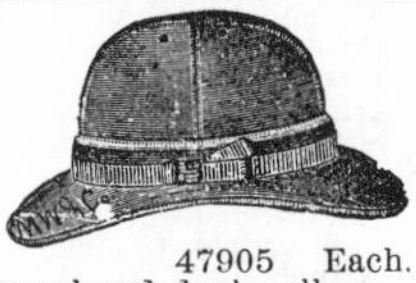
47905 Each.

47904 Hunting Hat, dead grass colored duck, all around rim, taped seams; weight, 10 ounces .. $0.38
47905 Solar Hunting Hat, duck, dead grass color, with ventilated sweat band inside.... 60
47906 Corduroy Hats, round top, light drab color, taped seams .... .85
47907 Corduroy Hat, square top, light drab color, taped seams.................................. .85
47908 Corduroy Cap, double visor, light drab color, taped seams.. .... .75
47909 Corduroy Cap, with short cape, to protect the neck, light color, taped seams.............. .75
Postage, extra, 12c.

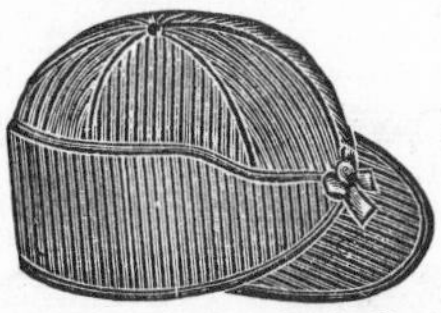

47910 Corduroy Cap. Each $0.75
Postage, extra, 12c.

For lined duck clothing see "Clothing Department."

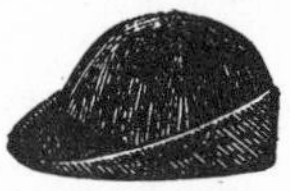
47911

47911 Windsor Style Corduroy Cap, green silk lined. Each $1.00

Clothes Bags.

47912 Made of heavy white duck, with drawing strings fastened on the top, with round bottom; weight, 2 pounds.......................... $0.50
Postage, extra, 35c.

Leggings.

FOR HUNTING BOOTS AND SHOES, SEE INDEX.

When ordering leggings, be sure and give size of calf of leg outside of pants.

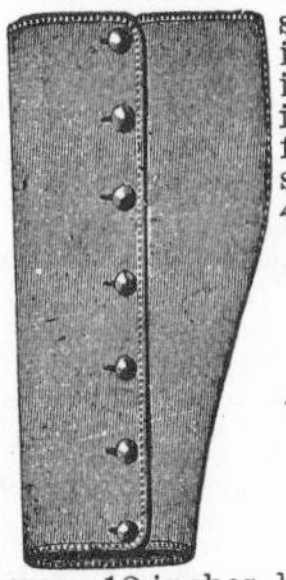

Leggings are not made in half sizes. The size of calf measurement is 12-inch, 13-inch, 14-inch, 15-inch, 16-inch, 17-inch, 18-inch, 19-inch; allowance is made in manufacture for half-inch variation in size, except in "Side Spring" style.

47915 English Style Riding Leggings, fine russia calf, leather bound, silk stitched, 7 leather covered buttons; a fine article. Per pair.............................. $3.00

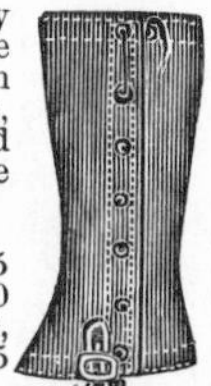

47918 Reynolds' Army Style Leggings, made of heavy 10 oz. brown waterproof canvas, with eyelets and hooks to lace all the way; 12 inches long. In ordering send size around calf of leg.
Per pair....... .... $0.75
Per dozen 8.00
47919 Men's Knee Leggings, to buckle, brown canvas. Per pair $0.45
Postage, extra, 4c.

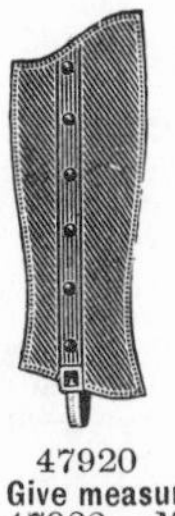
47920

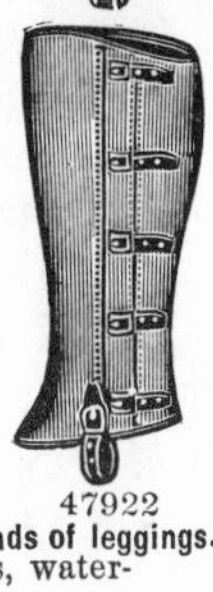
47922

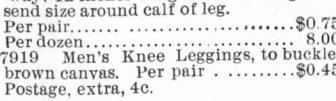

47920 Men's Leggings, brown waterproof canvas, leather facings, to button on side, 16 inches long.
Postage, extra, 12c.
Per pair. $0.45
Per dozen 4.80
47920½ Men's Leggings, brown waterproof canvas, leather facings, to lace on side.
Per pair. $0.75
Per dozen.......... 8.00
Postage, extra, 15c.

Give measurement around calf of leg for all kinds of leggings.

47922 Men's Leggings, brown canvas, waterproof, leather facings, to buckle.
Like cut, 16 inches long. Per pair.............. $0.55
Per dozen.. 6.00
Postage, extra, 21c.
47922½ Men's Leggings, same as 47922, except has steel spring fastening on side instead of buckles or buttons. Per pair, $9.82 Per doz... 9.00
Postage, extra, 25c.

Leggings—Continued.

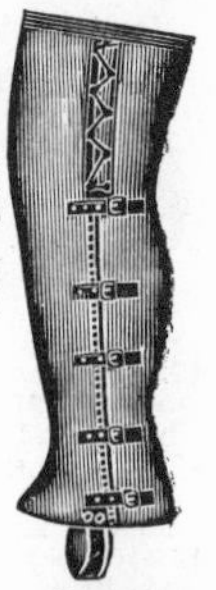

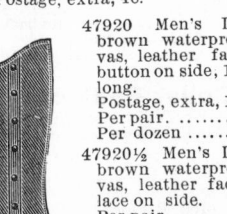

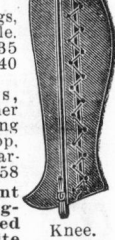

47923 Men's Leggings, brown canvas, waterproof, leather facings, to lace and buckle. Like cut, extra long, 25 inches long.
Per pair $0.93
Per dozen.. .... 10.00
Postage, extra, 25c.

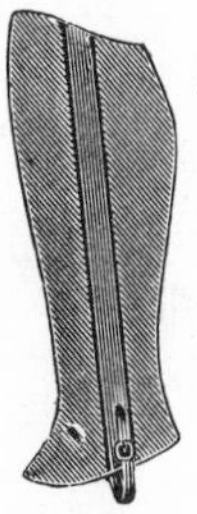
47924-5

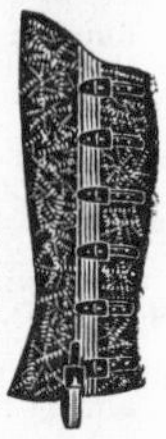
47926

47924 Men's Leggings, black grain leather, with steel spring stiffener on side, the new and convenient fastening, like cut; 19 inches long.
Per pair $1.72
Postage, extra, 25c.
47925 Men's Leggings, russet grain leather, with steel spring stiffener on side, the new and convenient fastening, like cut; 18 inches.
Per pair.................. $1.75
Postage, extra, 26c.
47926 Men's Leggings, black grain leather to buckle all the way up, 18 inches long.
Per pair .... $ 1.60
47927 Men's Leggings, russet grain leather, like cut 47926; to buckle all the way up; 18 inches long. Per pair.................................. 1.65
47927½ Leggings, same as 47927, except to lace; russet leather. Per pair.................... 1.70
Postage, extra, 25c.

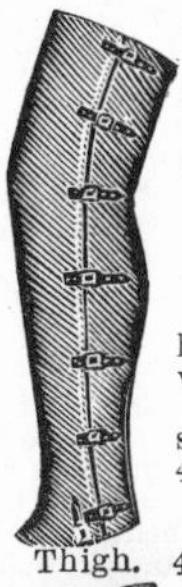
Thigh.

Horsehide Leggings, either "Knee" or "Thigh" lengths. To lace all the way. Same price as to buckle.
47928 Men's Knee Leggings, russet, tanned horsehide, to lace. Per pair......... $2.35
47929 Men's Thigh Leggings, russet tanned horsehide, to buckle and lace; weight, 36 oz. Per pair........ .... $3.20
Postage, extra, 30c.

Showing shape of thigh legging, all buckle.

N. B.—The horsehide leggings are the handsomest and best in the market; are always soft and pliable.

Horsehide leggings to lace; all same price as buckle.

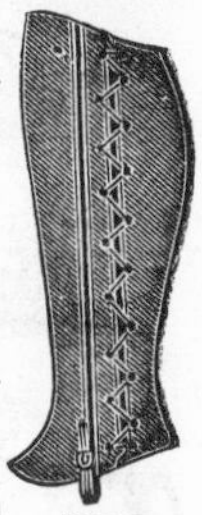
Knee.

47930 Men's Knee Leggings, imported corduroy, to buckle. Each.................. $1.35
47931 To lace. Per pair.. 1.40
Postage, extra, 23c.

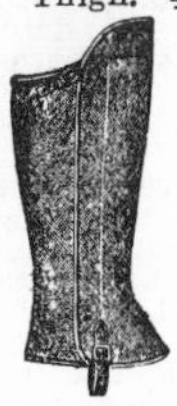

47931½ Men's Leggings, heavy black leather, leather bound all around, side spring fastening and buckle at top, cavalry style; a very fine article. Per pair......... $2.58

Always send measurement around calf of leg for leggings, or we will be obliged to hold the order and write you for size.

Dog Collars—Big Bargains.

Our prices "to lock" are for collars alone and do not include lock. Collars "to lock" usually have 3 spaces or holes to change the length; this varies the length about 1 inch. Our lengths as given are for the outside space, consequently the collar can be made about 1 inch smaller when desired.

By mail, 5 to 14c. extra.

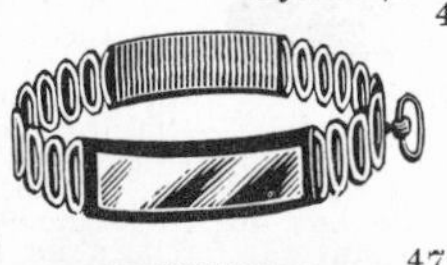

47932 Dog Collar, nickel, wide, flat links, nickel name plate, with staple for padlock. The most popular and a big seller; very attractive; 14, 16, 17 and 18 in.; width, 1 inch. Each. $0.20

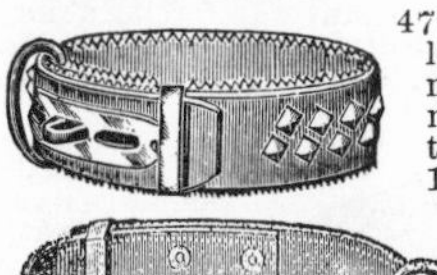

47933 Dog Collar, fine orange leather, chamois lined, large nickel plated studs, nickel name plate and trimmings, to lock; length, 15, 17 and 19 in.; 1 in. wide. Each. $0.50

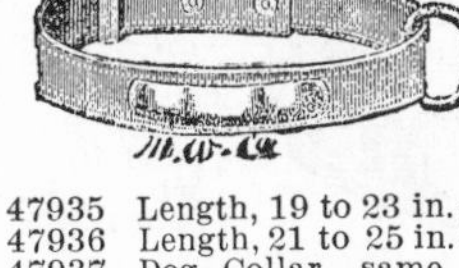

47934 Dog Collar, double harness, leather, black stitched edges, nickel trimming, ring, name plate, with staple to lock; length, 17 to 21 inches; width, 1 in.
Each $0.45
47935 Length, 19 to 23 in.; width, 1¼ in., each. .50
47936 Length, 21 to 25 in.; width, 1½ in., each. .55
47937 Dog Collar, same as 47934, except to buckle; length, 17 to 21 in.; width, 1 in., each.. .38
47938 Length, 19 to 23 in.; width, 1¼ in., each. .44
Length, 21 to 25 in; width, 1½ in., each......... .47

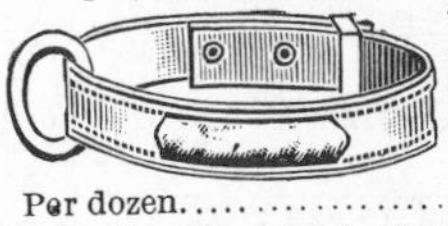

47941 Dog Collar, fancy leather, assorted colors, nickel trimmings and name plate; length, 8 and 9 in.; width, ⅝ in.
Each................ $0.18
Per dozen................................ 1.60
47942 Length, 13, 14, 15 or 16 in.; width, ⅞ in.
Each.................. $0.27 Per dozen. 2.75

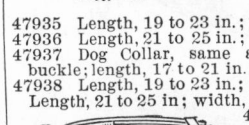

Dog Collars—Continued.

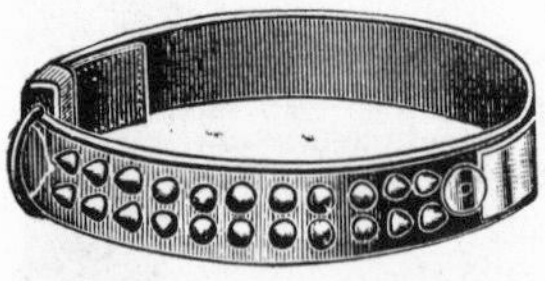

47943 Dog Collar, best English single russet harness leather, studded, nickel name plate and ring to buckle; length, 14, 15, 16, 17, 18 and 20 in.; width, 1 in.; all collars have nickel name plates. Each..........$0.30

47944 Dog Collar, same as 47943; double row, heavy plated studs, is 1¼ to 1½ inches wide; to buckle, 21 inches; 22 and 25 inches long. Each .35

47945 Dog Collar, same as No 47943; 3 rows fine nickel plated studs, 1½ inches wide, to buckle: 15, 16, 17, 18 and 20 inches long. Each .40

47946 Dog Collar, same as 47943, except to lock; 1¼ in. wide, 2 rows, heavy nickel plated studs, fine russet leather, 16, 17, 18, 19, 20, 21, inches long. Each.......... .50

47947 Dog Collar, extra quality, single harness leather, studded, to lock (locks not included in price named), 1 inch wide, 17, 19, and 21 inches long. Each.......... .40

47948 Three rows studs, with staple to attach lock, 1¼ to 1½ inches wide, 14, 15, 17, 19, 21 and 23 inches. Each.......... .55

47949 Dog Collar, same as No. 47947, with staple to attach lock, 2¼ inches wide, four rows nickel plated studs, 15, 16, 17, 18, 19, 20, 21, 22 and 24 inches long. Each.......... .89

Postage, extra, 12c.

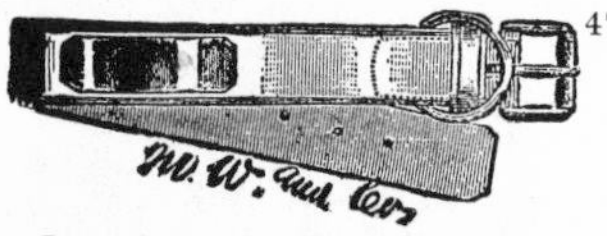

47950 Dog Collar, russet leather, nickel name plate and ring to buckle; length, 14 to 18 in.; width, 1 in. Each........$0.15

Length, 9 to 12 in., ½ in. wide. Each.......... .12

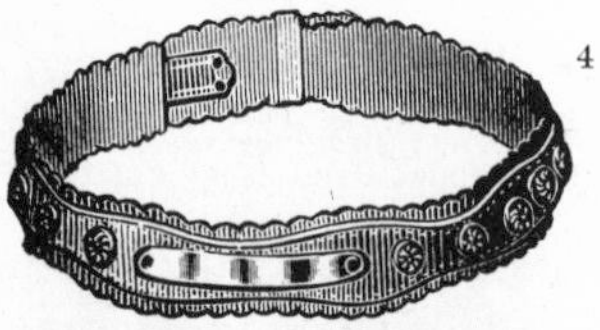

47951 Scalloped russet leather (to lock), chamois lined, new style ornaments. Width, ¾ in.; length, 13, 15 or 17 inches. Each........$0.30

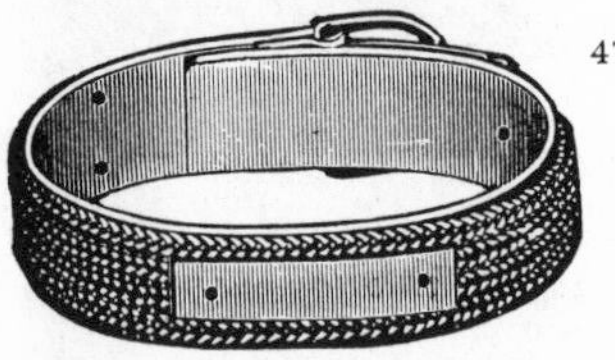

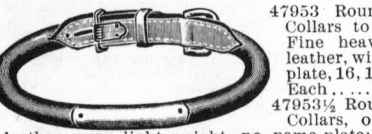

47952 Nickel plated, woven, steel wire chain, leather and chamois lined, handsome and stylish, 1 in. wide, staple to lock. Lengths, 17, 19, 21 inches. Each.........$0.56

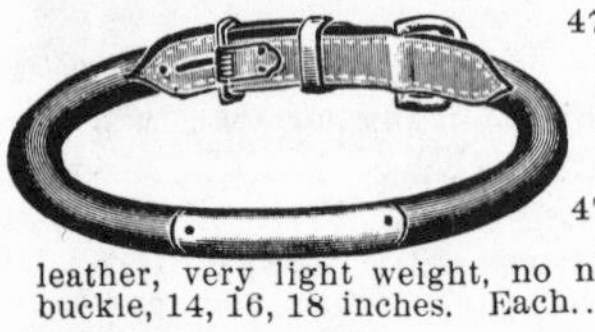

47953 Round Dog Collars to buckle. Fine heavy black leather, with name plate, 16, 18, 20 in. Each........$0.55

47953½ Round Dog Collars, orange leather, very light weight, no name plate; to buckle, 14, 16, 18 inches. Each.......... $0.55

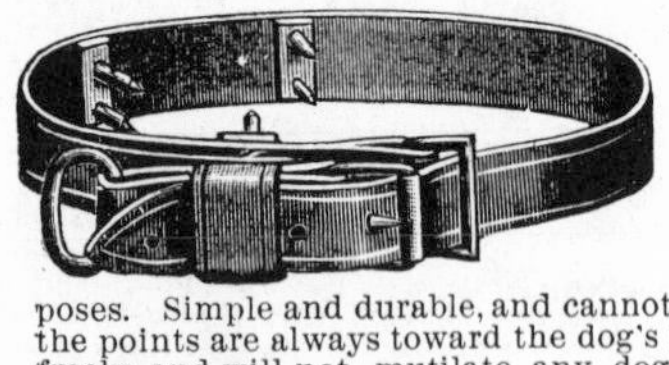

47954 D. Watter's Spike Collar, pronounced by all dog trainers the best collar ever made for training purposes. Simple and durable, and cannot twist. Hence the points are always toward the dog's neck. It works freely, and will not mutilate any dog. Punishment can be applied or ended instantly in forcing a dog to retrieve. Every owner of a dog should have one. Made of *good* black leather Each..........$1.40
Extra by mail.......... .10

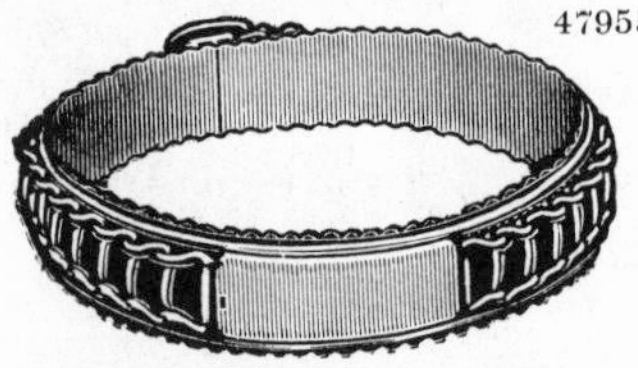

47955 Nickel plated, ladder link chain, leather and chamois lined, a big seller (to lock); width, ¾ in., length, 13, 15 17 and 19 in. Each... ..$0.30
Per doz... 3.00

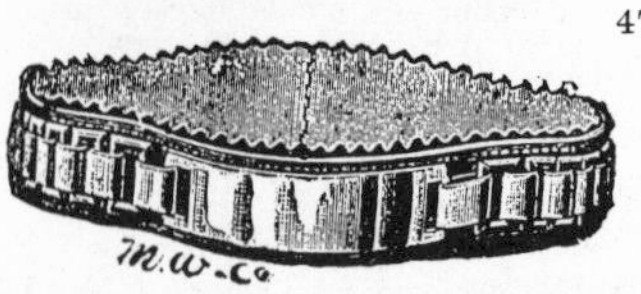

47956 Dog Collar, lined with fancy colored leather, making a handsome and durable collar; width, ½ inch. Length, 9, 10, 12 and 14 indhes.
Each..........$0.30
Width, ¾ in.; length, 13, 15 and 16 in.......... .40
Width, 1 in.; length, 14, 15, 16, 17, 18 and 20 in.
Each.......... .50

Dog Collars—Continued.

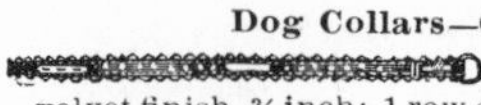

47957 Ooze Calf, velvet finish, ⅜ inch; 1 row studs, chamois lined, nickel trim; to lock. 7, 9, 11 inches. Each..... .25

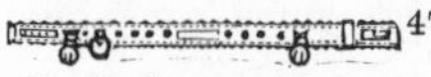

47959 Fancy Leather, assorted colors; felt lined, fancy nickel trim; 2 bells; to lock; ½ inch. 7, 9 and 11 inches. Each.......... .35

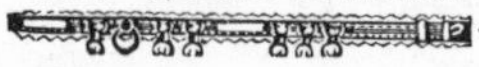

47960 Glazed Finish Leather, chamois lined, fancy nickel trim; 5 to 8 bells, according to length of collar; ½ inch; to lock. 9, 11 and 13 inches. Assorted colors. Black, each... .49
Orange, each.......... .53
Russet, each.......... .55

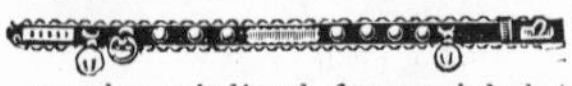

47961 Glazed Finish Leather, chamois lined, fancy nickel trim; 2 bells, ⅝ inch; to lock. A very fine article. 10, 12 and 14 inch. Assorted colors. Black, each.......... .45
Orange, each.......... .50
Russet, each.......... .55

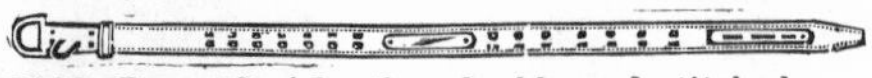

47962 Russet Seal Leather, double and stitched, smooth inside, fine finish, nickel trim; an elegant article; to lock.
½ inch, 7, 9 or 11 inch, 1 row studs. Each....$0.45
⅝ inch, 9, 11 or 13 inch, 2 row studs. Each.... .55
¾ inch, 12, 13 or 15 inch, 2 row studs. Each.... .69
⅞ inch, 16, 15 or 17 inch, 2 row studs. Each.... .80
1 inch, 15, 17 or 19 inch, 3 row studs. Each.... .98

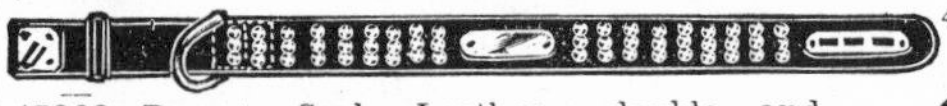

47963 Russet Seal Leather, double and stitched, finest finish, polished, smooth inside, nickel trim, large round studs; one of the finest collars made; to lock.
1¼ inch, 17, 19 or 21 inch, 2 row studs. Each..$1.70
1½ inch, 19, 21 or 23 inch, 3 row studs. Each.. 1.95
2 inch, 21, 23 or 25 inch, 2 row studs. Each.. 2.50
2½ inch, 23, 25 or 27 inch, 3 row studs. Each.. 2.90

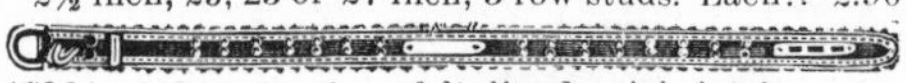

47964 Russet Leather, felt lined, nickel trim, to lock; 2 row studs. 1 inch, 15, 17 or 19 inch. Each..........$0.50

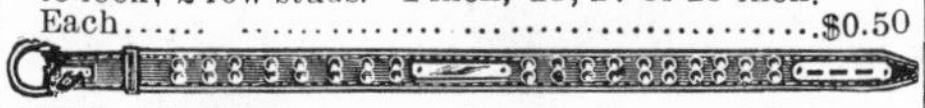

47965 Black Leather, good and strong, nickel trim; 3 rows fancy studs; to lock. 1½ inch. 19, 21 or 23 inch. Each.......... 1.00

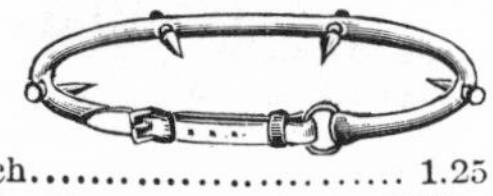

47966 Round Russet Choke Collar, nickel trim, best finish, good and strong. 18, 20 or 24 inch. Each.......... 1.25

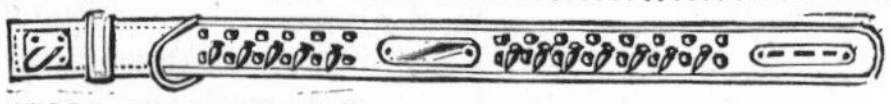

47967 Protector Collar, russet leather or black leather, double and stitched, finest finish, nickel trim, 1 row spikes and 2 rows pointed studs; to lock 1½ in.; 15, 17 or 19 inch. Each..........$2.00

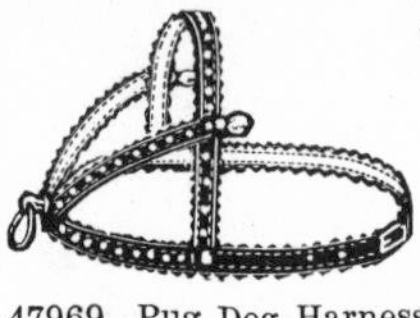

47968 Pug Dog Harness, black or russet leather, chamois lined, 2 bells, nickel trim, 21 in body, 13 in. breast, 12 in. shoulder (can buckle 3 in. smaller body), ½ inch straps. Each, black..$0.90
Russet.......... 1.00

47969 Pug Dog Harness, cream colored leather, blue felt lined, blue stitched, square stud, 2 bells, nickel trim, a beauty, 23 in. body, 13 in. breast, 12 in. shoulder, ½ in. straps. Each... .$2.00

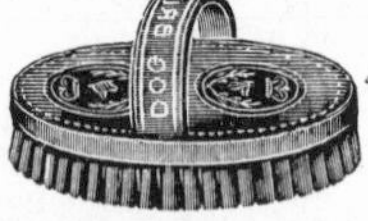

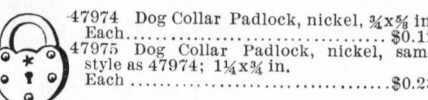

47970 Dog Brush, good stiff bristles, sole leather back, stitched, well made and durable. Each..........$0.90

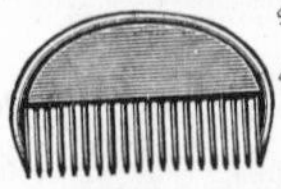

47971 Dog Comb, rubber, best quality. Each..........$0.25

47972 Dog Combs, metallic back and teeth, solid white metal. Each..........$0.50

Dog Collar Padlocks.

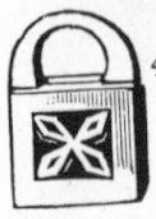

47973 Dog Collar Padlock, made of aluminum, almost as light as a feather, ¾ in. by 1⅛ in. Each..........$0.20
Per dozen.......... 2.25

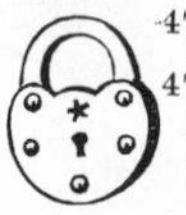

47974 Dog Collar Padlock, nickel, ¾x⅝ in. Each..........$0.12

47975 Dog Collar Padlock, nickel, same style as 47974; 1¼x¾ in. Each..........$0.23

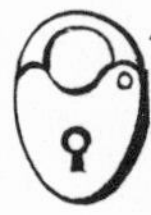

47976 Padlock, 1x¾ in., all nickel plated, with key: each..........$0.20
Per dozen.......... 2.20

47977 Padlock, 1x¾ in., brass, with key. Each..........$0.20
Per dozen.......... 2.20
Extra by mail.......... .10

Dog Collar Padlocks—Continued.

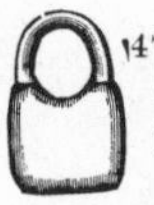

47978 Scandinavian Padlock for dog collar.
Small..........$0.15
Large.......... .20
Postage, extra.......... .02

Dog Leads.

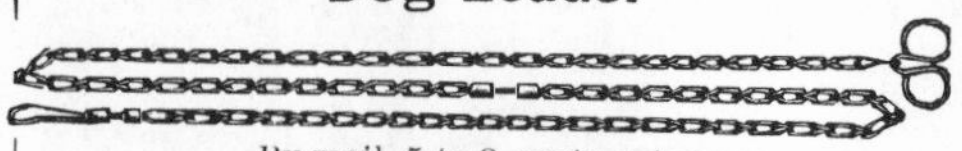

By mail, 5 to 8 cents extra.

47979 Dog Leads, polished steel, cable link, very light weight, snap on end. Each..........$0.25

47980 Dog Leads, fancy silver link, light weight, but strong and durable, 4½ feet. Each.......... .35

47981 Dog Lead, polished steel, cable link, large size, with swivel and snap, 4½ feet. Each..... .30

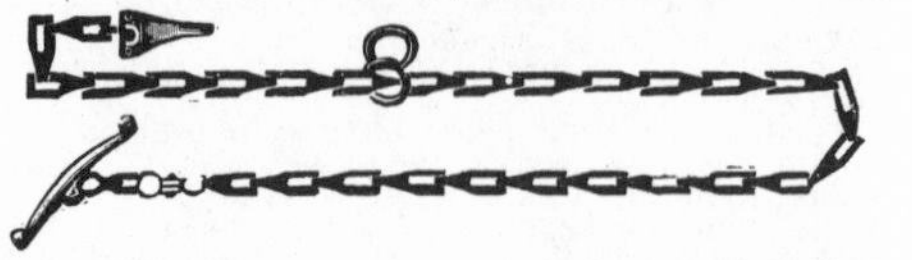

47982 Dog Lead, polished iron, flat safety link, neatly polished, and very strong and durable, also makes the best of halter chains. 4½ feet.
Small. Each..........$0.15
Medium, each.......... .18
Large, each.......... .25

47983 Dog Leads, hand braided leather, round, with loop and snap, 40 in. Each.......... .40

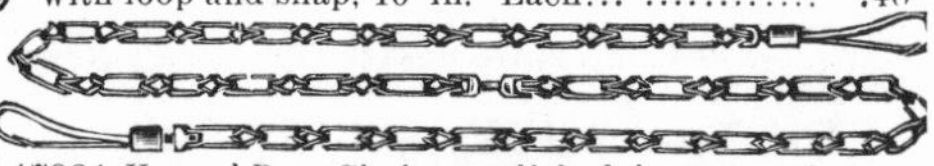

47984 Kennel Dog Chains, polished iron, round link 6 feet, with snap and swivels. Weight, 16 oz. $0.44

47985 Kennel Dog Chains, polished steel, round wire, new style safety links, 3 swivels, 2 hooks, well made and durable; no dog can break it, 9 feet. Each.......... .65
Weight, 16 oz.

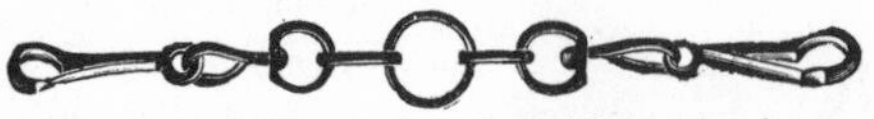

47986 Dog Couplings, polished steel, large ring in center, snap hook on each end, two swivels. Weight, 5 oz. Each..........$0.40

Dog Whips.

By mail, 8 cents extra.

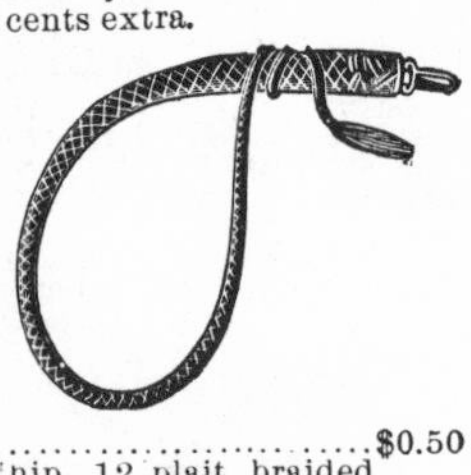

47987 Whips, hand braided russet leather, whistle on handle, heavy and durable. Each....$0.73

47988 The Never Break Whip, same as 47987, with snap on end instead of whistle, making a good lead as well as whip; can be folded into small compass and carried in pocket.
Each..........$0.50

47989 The Never Break Whip, 12 plait braided leather, with leather loop on end, loaded butt, strong and durable. Each.......... .80

47989½ Rawhide Dog Whip, hand braided; the most durable whip in the market. Swivel snap on end. Can be folded and carried in the pocket. Each.......... 1.25

Dog Muzzles.

By mail, 4 to 6 cents extra.

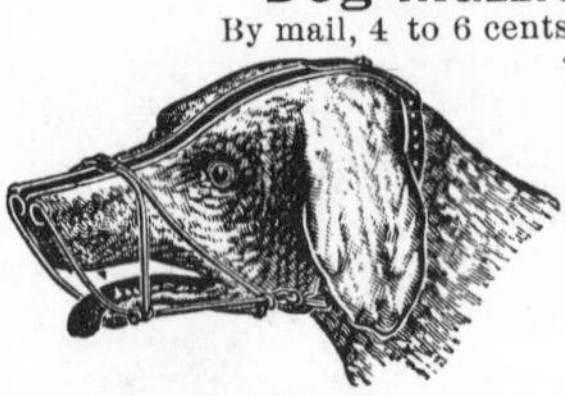

47990 Dog Muzzles, common iron wire, with strap to buckle around the neck. Basket style to cover nose and mouth. Each........$0.25

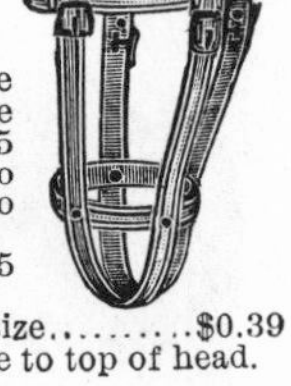

Safety.

47991 The Safety Dog Muzzle, made of iron wire with strap to buckle around neck. Each..........$0.25

47992 Leather Strap Dog Muzzle, to buckle around neck and buckle to take up around head if too large.
Small size..........$0.15
Medium size.........$0.30 Large size..........$0.39
Give measurements from tip of nose to top of head.

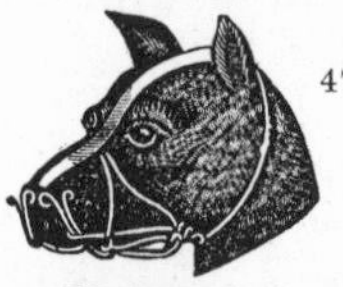

47993 Automatic Dog Muzzle, wire and leather. Permits dog to open mouth to drink or eat. Each..........$0.70

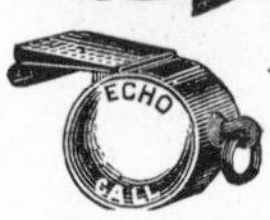

47996 The Echo Call, the loudest yet, beautifully nickel-plated. Can be carried in the vest pocket. Each..........$0.15

The Surprise Whistle.

By mail, 1c. extra.

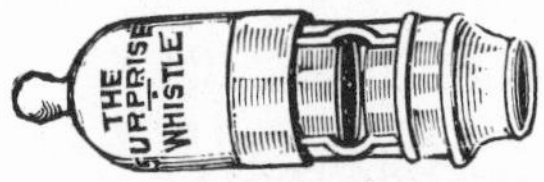

47998 The Surprise Whistle, the loudests and best dog call in the market. By squeezing in the bulb at the end you can regulate the sound and produce any effect, from purling, or muffled notes up to a great swelling, booming, two mile piercing note. A good snipe or plover call also.
Each $0.20
Per dozen 2.00
Postage, extra, 2cts.

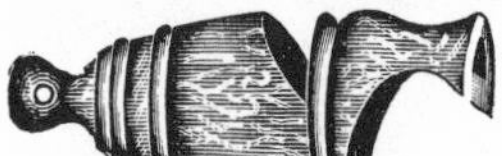

47999 Celluloid Dog Call or Whistle. A loud one.
Small, each $0.15
Large, each 19
Postage, extra 2 cents.

Drinking Cups.

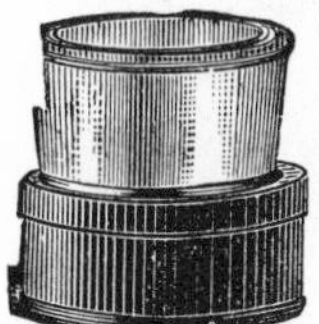

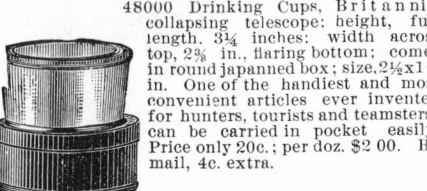

48000 Drinking Cups, Britannia collapsing telescope; height, full length, 3¼ inches; width across top, 2⅜ in., flaring bottom; comes in round japanned box; size, 2½x1⅜ in. One of the handiest and most convenient articles ever invented for hunters, tourists and teamsters; can be carried in pocket easily. Price only 20c.; per doz. $2 00. By mail, 4c. extra.

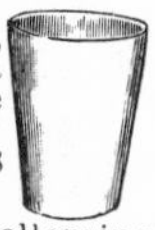

48002 Soft White Rubber Drinking Cup, tumbler shape, will hold about as much as a common table tumbler, flexible and can be folded and put in pocket.
Each $0.18
By mail, 3c. extra.

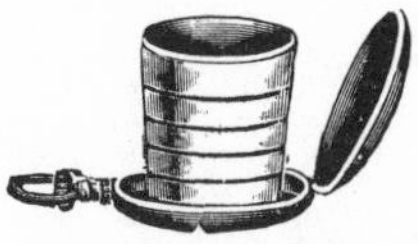

48008 Patent Collapsing Pocket Cup, in nickeled tin watch case. Cup stands about 2 inches high when open. Case exact size of a watch. One of the best novelties ever invented. Price, each $0.25; by mail, 4c. extra.

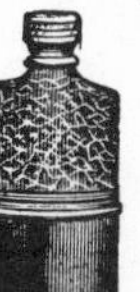

48009 Olry Pocket Flasks, leather covered, with metal drinking cup on bottom, and white metal screw-off top or stopper. Almost a household necessity.

	¼ pt.	½ pt.	¾ pt.	1 pt.	1 qt.
Each..	$0.75	$0.87	$1.10	$1.25	$2.10

Dog Remedies.

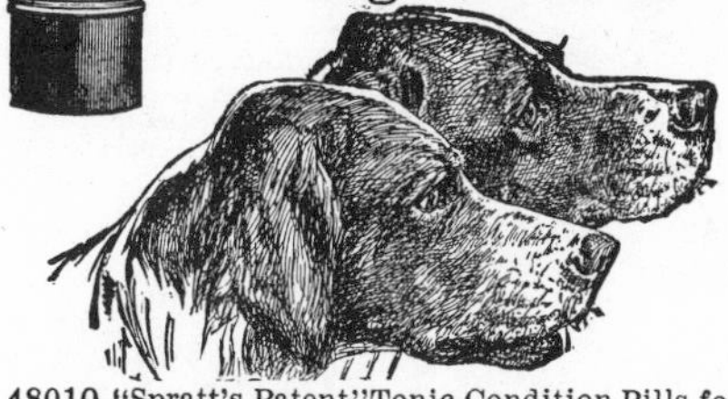

48010 "Spratt's Patent" Tonic Condition Pills for debility arising from disease, and of great value in preparing dogs for work requiring endurance. Unequaled in preparing dogs for bench shows.
Price, per box $0.35
Postage .... .04

48011 "Spratt's Patent" Mange Cure, which rarely fails to speedily cure mange in every form, and the destruction of fleas, lice, ticks, etc., in the dog, horse, ox, pig and other animals; it is non-poisonous. Full directions wrapped around each bottle. Price .... .40
Postage .... .10

48012 "Spratt's Patent" Worm Cure. A speedy and sure destroyer of these troublesome parasites, which are the source of so many forms of canine disease. Price, per box .... .35
Postage .... .04

48013 "Spratt's Patent" Distemper Cure, the new antiseptic remedy; an effective cure for the scourge of the kennel; each packet contains very minute directions for the treatment of dogs suffering under distemper. Price, per box .... .70
Postage .... .04

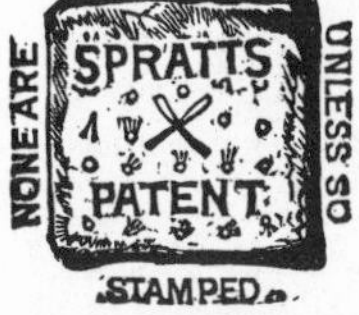

48014 "Spratt's Patent" Fibrine Dog Cakes (with beetroot); these celebrated biscuits are supplied to all the leading kennels and are used at the principal dog shows in America and England, and have been before the public for more than a quarter of a century. 100 lb. bag $5.75
Price, per 50 lb. bag 3.00
25 lb. boxes, per box 1.70
5 lb boxes, per box ...... .40

48015 "Spratts Patent" Dog Soap. This is of the greatest value to dog owners, as it is entirely FREE FROM POISON and at the same time most effective in the destruction of lice, fleas and ticks; it is the only soap that should be used in preparing dogs for exhibition, as it leaves the coat smooth and glossy. Printed directions for using the soap on each wrapper.
Price, per cake $0.20
Extra, by mail .... .07

Dog Remedies—Continued.

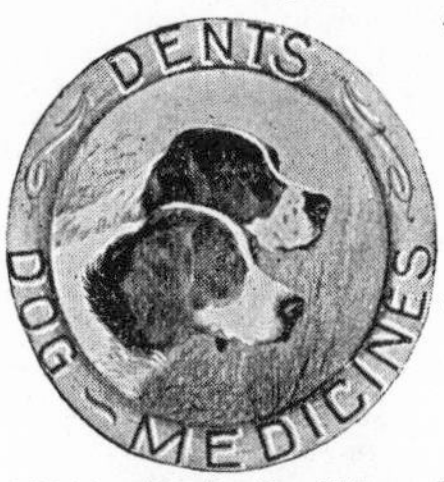

48016 Dent's Dog Biscuit is pronounced the most wholesome and nutritious dog food on the market.
Price, 25 lbs $1.70
Price, 50 " 3.00
Price, 100 " 5.75
Try a 5 pound box for .40

48017 *Dent's Distemperine* is a positive preventive of distemper and if used in time will cure the worst case. Price $0.45

48018 *Dent's Condition Pills*—for run down or debilitated systems, promote appetite and digestion, and return life and animation .... $ .45

48019 *Dent's Skin Cure* is an unfailing cure for all skin diseases. Contains no carbolic acid, oil or tar. Price .... .45

48020 *Dent's Worm Medicine* destroys all intestinal parasites, is easily administered and can be used without danger to life of patient. Price .. .45

48021 Dent's Canker Lotion, guaranteed to cure canker of the ear and all inflammation. Price. .45

Send for Book on "*Dogs, Their Management in Health and Treatment in Disease*" free. Profusely illustrated

Plaited Billy.

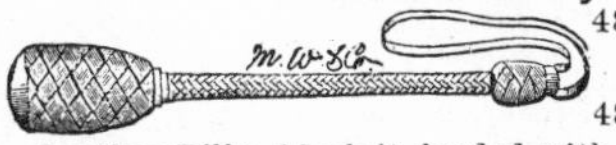

48025 Plaited Billy, black leather.
Each $0.30

48026 Braided Leather Billy, 12 plait, loaded with shot, made of the best material and cannot be broken. 9½ inches; Weight, 6 oz. Each $0.95
Postage, extra .... .06

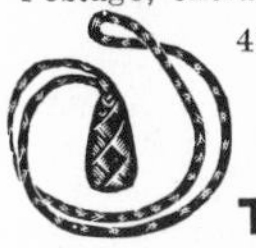

48027 Braided Leather Pocket Billy made of the best material; cannot be broken.
Each $0.50
Postage, extra .... .05

The Duplex Police Call or Bicycle Whistle

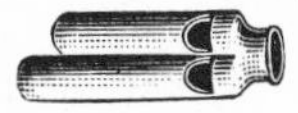

48033 Duplex Call, nickel plated.
Each $0.13
48034 Duplex Call, with guard chain. Each .... .18
Extra, by mail, 3c.

Lawn Tennis Goods, Poles, Etc.

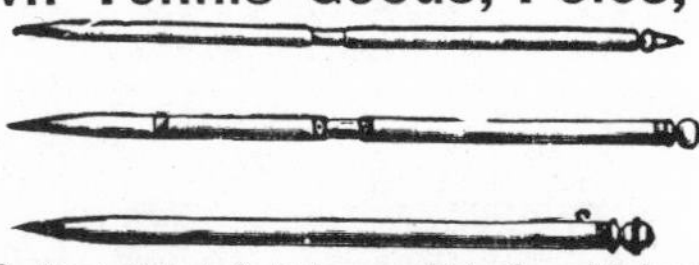

48060 Best Jointed Poles, polished, with brass ferrules, ornamented. Per pair $1.70
48062 Ordinary Jointed Poles. Per pair .... .90

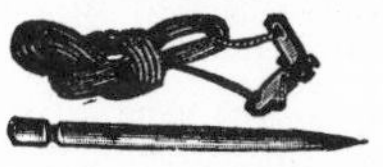

48063 Lawn Tennis Guy Ropes and Pins; complete, 2 ropes, 4 guys and 4 pins; per set, 25c, 50c, 75c., according to quality.

48064 Tennis Marking or Boundary Tapes for marking out the court with pins and staples with sufficient webbing to lay out a court correctly. Price, single court, $3.35; double court. $3.75

48065 Dry Powder Court Marker, cylinders and

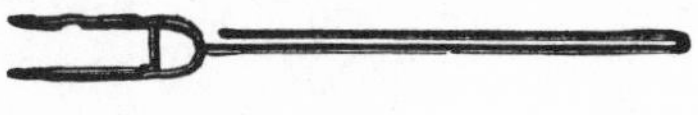

handle, complete $1.70

48067 Tennis Fork to hold net up in center, made of smooth iron. Each .... .75
Weight, 2¼ lbs.

48068 Tennis Marking Plates for marking angles of court. Made of iron; per set of 8 plates and two T pieces with pins for fastening in ground. Painted white .... .90

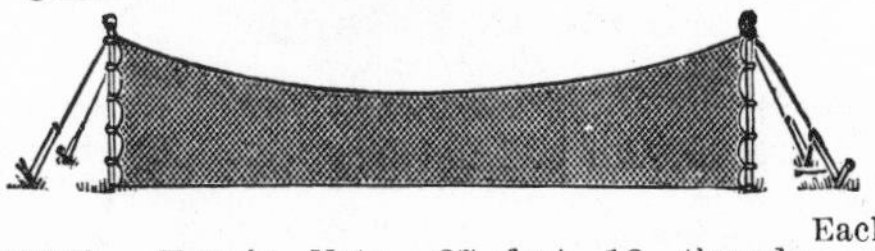

Each.
48070 Tennis Nets, 27 feet, 12 threads, weight, 27 oz $0.90
48074 Tennis Nets, 36 feet, double court, 15 thread, weight, 32 ozs 1.35
48075 Tennis Nets, 42 feet, 15 thread, double court, weight, 32 ozs 1.55
48076 Back stop Nets, 50x7 feet, No. 12 thread. Each 2.90
48077 Tennis Nets, white, canvas bound, 36 feet, 15 thread, double court. Each.. .... 1.96
48078 Tennis Nets, white, canvas bound. 42 feet, double court 2.25

Lawn Tennis Is a game for everybody. The best athletes find it requires all their energy, and yet the weakest girl can play the game.

Lawn Tennis Ooods—Continued.

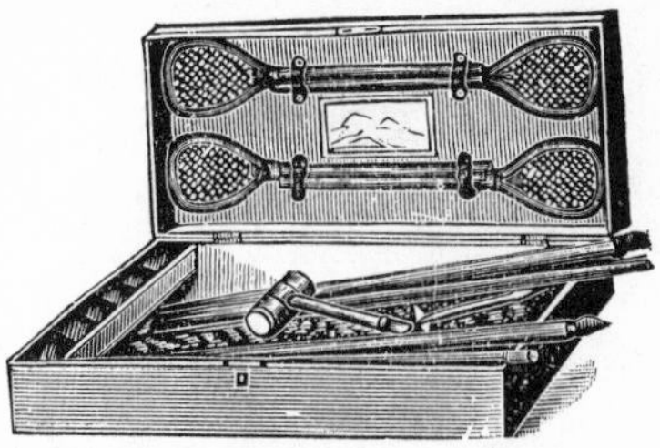

40880—Popular Lawn Tennis set; contains 4 strung gut bats, 4 balls, portable poles, net, 3x27 feet, lines and runners, mallet and book complete in box, a good plain set; small bats. Per set $7.67

48081 Popular Lawn Tennis Set, contains 4 regulation bats, 4 balls, good net, 3x33 feet, portable poles, lines and runner, mallet and book of instructions, complete in box 10.00

48082 Picnic Lawn Tennis Set; contains 4 regulation racquets, regulation net, 4 regulation balls, painted poles, jointed guys, ropes, pegs and mallet, with book of instructions, complete in case. 13.00
Better sets, complete $18.00. $20.00, $25.00, $30.00

Lawn Tennis Balls.

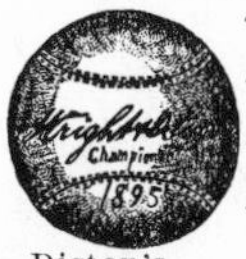

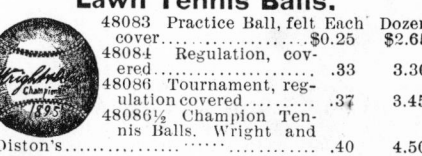

	Each	Dozen
48083 Practice Ball, felt cover	$0.25	$2.65
48084 Regulation, covered	.33	3.30
48086 Tournament, regulation covered	.37	3.45
48086½ Champion Tennis Balls. Wright and Diston's	.40	4.50

Lawn Tennis Bats. "Racquets."

Our Tennis Bats this year are the latest improved.

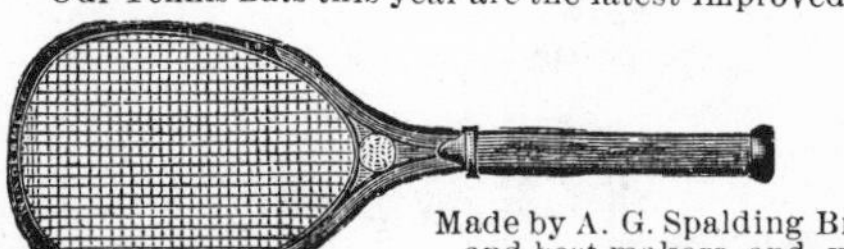

Made by A. G. Spalding Bros. and best makers, and warranted A 1 quality. If not satisfactory for price, can be returned at our expense after examination. These prices are from 30 to 50 per cent. less than regular retail prices. Each.

48087 Boys' Practice Bat, white ash frame, good quality gut, nicely finished. Each $0.75
48088 Boy's and Girl's Favorite Bat, white ash frame, good quality gut, nicely finished 1.10
48089 Medium Size Bat, white ash frame, good quality gut, checkered cedar handles 1.50
48090 Full Size Bat, white ash frame, good quality gut, checkered cedar handles, nicely finished. 1.75
48091 Full Size Bat, white ash frame, good quality gut, checkered cedar handles, nicely finished 2.20

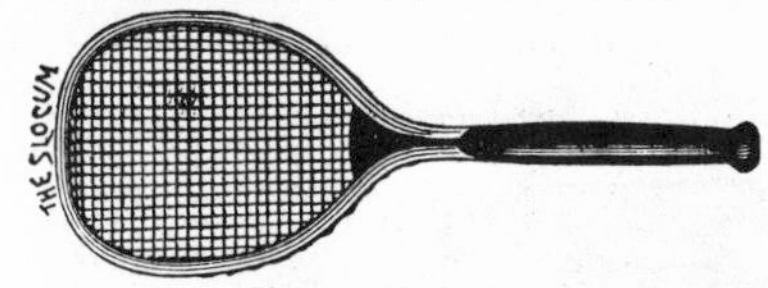

Slocum Pattern.

48092 No. C H— "The Oval," finest white ash frame, strung with finest Oriental white gut, new oval-shaped handle, handsomely polished and finished in antique oak, scored sides. Each 5.75

48093 No. C X—"The Tournament," frame and stringing same as in our No. C H racquet, but handle of regular shape and made of polished mahogany, checkered on all sides and leather capped. Each 5.70

48094 No. O, "The Slocum," frame of selected and polished white ash, Oriental "B" main strings and red cross strings, polished cedar handle, finely checkered and all of superior quality. Each 4.00

48095 No. OC, same as 48094 only with cork handle. Each 4.50

48096 No. P, "The Junior," frame of fine white ash, polished cherry throat-piece, checkered cedar handles, strung with all white Oriental gut. Each 3.00

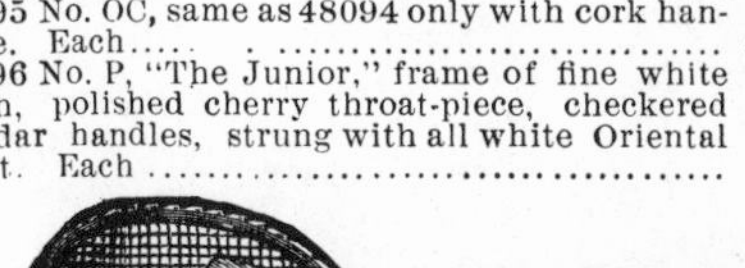

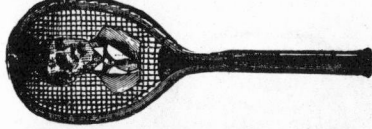

48097 "The Campbell," designed by Mr. O. S. Campbell, and an exact duplicate of the one used in all his championship games, material and construction of the highest quality throughout. Each $6.90

48098 "Sears' Special," finest white ash frame, high grade gut and handsomely finished, checkered handle. Each 5.95

48099 "Sears' Special," same quality as above, cork handle. Each 6.50

Have your Mail Packages insured. See page 1.

Racquet Covers.

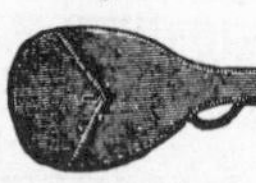

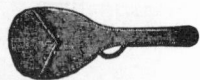

48100 Tennis Bat Covers, made of green felt. Each .45
48101 Tennis Bat Covers, made of canvas, leather bound. Each .... .75

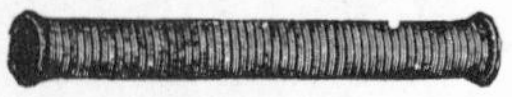

48102 Corrugated Rubber Handle Cover for Tennis Bats, to secure better grip. Each $0.23

The Obear Glove.

Of corrugated rubber.

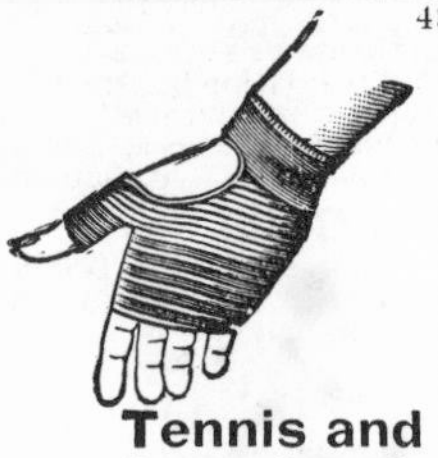

48103 Especially adapted for tennis players. The lightest and coolest glove for polo, hand ball, rowing, etc. It holds with the grip of a vise. It protects the hands and prevents blistering. In ordering, state whether right or left glove is required, and give your kid glove size. Each. $0.85

Tennis and Outing Belts.

COMMON SENSE BUCKLES ON SILK BELTS.

Colors, plain, black, white or navy. Each.
48104 Silk, 2-inch $0.22
48104½ White Duck, adjustable, nickel buckle .. .40
48105 Fine Silk, 2½-inch .... .40

PLAIN LEATHER BELTS.

Colors: Orange, tan and black.

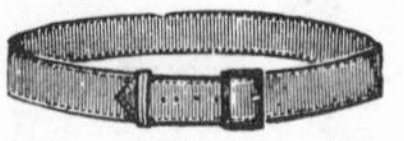

Plain. Each.
48106 Leather, 1½-inch $0.30
48107 Leather Stirrup, 1¼-inch .... .40
48108 Leather, 2-inch, covered buckle .... .47
48109 Pigskin, 2-inch, covered buckle .... .70

LEATHER BELTS, WITH RINGS.

Colors: Orange, tan or black.

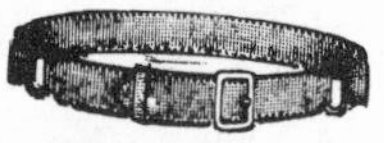

With Rings E ch.
48110 Leather 2-inch, nickel buckle and rings .. $0.45
48111 Leather, 2-inch, covered buckles and rings .50
48112 Monkey Grain, 2-inch, covered buckles ... .75

Croquet Sets.

Weight, 16 to 28 pounds. Per set

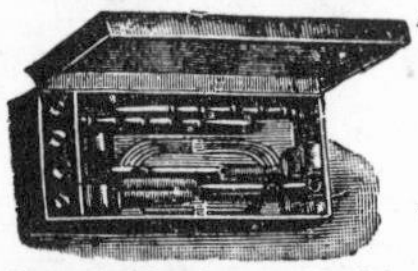

48116 Four-ball Croquet Set, plain mallets, oiled balls and stakes varnished, ten arches, with book, in neat box with hinged cover $0.68
48117 Same as No. 48,-116, with 8 balls in dove tailed box with hinged cover 1.10
48118 Eight-ball Croquet Set, mallets and balls of neat design, painted and striped, 2 large fancy stakes, heavy coppered arches. An excellent set at a low price 1.75
48119 Eight-ball Croquet Set, handsome maple, with fancy striped mallets, handles and balls, 2 elegant beaded stakes, heavy pointed arches, painted, superior workmanship and materials in every part 2.20
48121 Eight-ball Croquet Set, shellac finish, 8 fancy striped 6 inch ebonized and bronzed mallets, handles and balls beautifully finished, painted and striped, 2 elegantly beaded stakes, heavy arches, with sockets, an elegant set 3.40

Base Balls.

At Manufacturers' Prices.

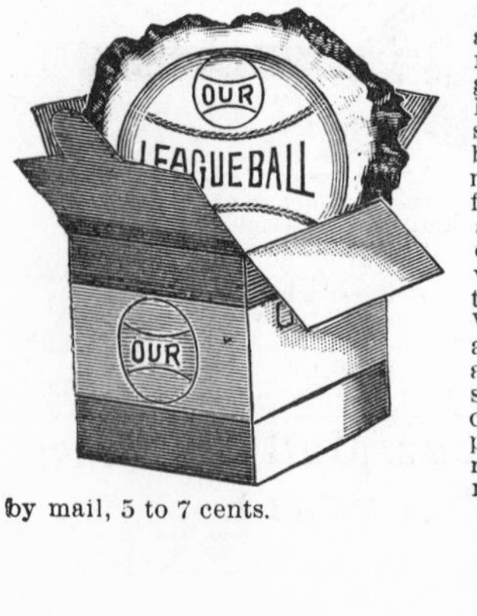

Our base balls are the best in the market and are guaranteed regulation weight and size. Our League balls are all warranted to stand a full game, which is all any maker claims for the very best balls that they make We do not guarantee balls against accidents such as striking sharp corners of home plate or brick corners or sharp rocks, etc. Extra, by mail, 5 to 7 cents.

Base Balls—Continued.

48122 Regular League Ball, warranted equal to the finest league balls. Each ball wrapped in tin foil and packed in separate box and sealed. Each $1.00
Per dozen 11.00
48125 Amateur, regulation size, rubber center, with all wool core, wound with woolen yarn, horsehide cover. This ball will give satisfaction every time. Each .... .65
Per dozen 6.50
48126 King of the Diamond Ball, horsehide cover; each ball in a box. Each .... .40
Per dozen 4.00
48127 Boy's Favorite Ball, horsehide cover, regular make. Each .... $0.25 Per dozen 2.00
48129 Boy's Amateur Ball, horsehide cover, regular make. Each .... $0.15 Per dozen 1.25
The above Nos. 48127 and 48129 are regulation weights and sizes, and no better balls made for the money

Base Balls for Boys.

Cheap and well made, leather covered.

	Each.	Per doz.
48130 Ball, 8⅝ in. Boys' Lively	$0.09	$0.85
48131 Ball, 7½ in. Boss	.04	.35

Base Ball Bats.

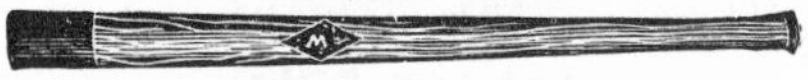

We take pleasure in calling attention to our line of bats, which are made from improved models, and of the best selected timber, and are approved by the best players in the country.

Men's bats, 20 to 40 ounces, length, 30 to 36.

	Each.	Per doz.
48135 Men's Bat, best straight grain, second growth white ash, thoroughly seasoned; broad band on ends, antique finish and lathe polished, warranted equal in quality, style and finish to the best fancy named bats such as "Oriental, Wagon Tongue," etc	$0.50	$5.49
48136 Men's Bats, best selected white ash, highly finished and lathe polished, broad band, regulation sizes, no better bat in the market for service	$0.35	$3.60
48137 Men's Bats, selected, first growth white ash, finished with best shellac and lathe polished, a good one	.25	2.50
48138 Men's Willow Bats, lathe polished, and finished with the best white shellac; the best light bat in the market	.35	3.90
48139 Men's Bat, best white ash, plain finish	.15	1.30
48143 Boy's Bat, best white ash, fine finish, black end	.25	.270
48144 Boy's Bat, best polished maple, gilt stripes	.10	1.00
48145 Boy's Bat, best polished maple, black stripes	.05	.40

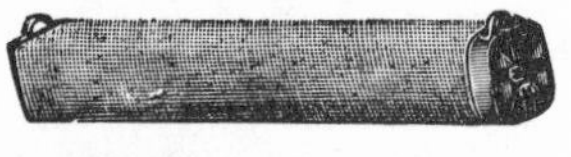

48146 Canvas Bat Bags, heavy waterproof canvas, leather heads to hold 1 dozen bats. Each $3.40

The higher priced bats are those commonly sold from 75 cents to $1.00.

Don't pay fancy prices for the dealer's name on a bat, when we sell the same article, minus the paint, for less than one-half the money. Sold in one half dozen lots or over at dozen prices.

Base Ball Gloves.

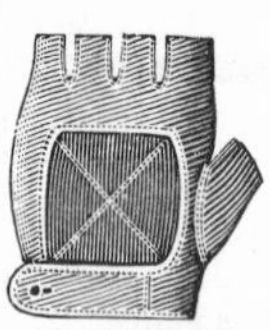

48149 Special Baseman's Glove, heavy oil tanned goat skin, extra heavy padded; full left hand, not tipped, right hand fingerless, hand sewed, warranted.
Per pair $1.50
Extra by mail, 10 cents
48156 Boys' Gloves, fingerless, open backs padded .... .20

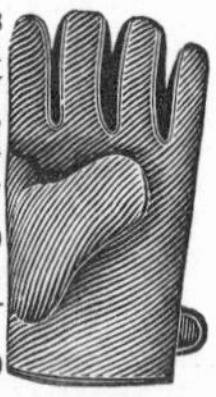

Short Fingers. 48149
Extra by mail, 3 cents.

Base Ball Caps.

Made to Order.

Base Ball Clothing is not carried in stock by any dealer or maker in Chicago, but is made to order only; 3 to 10 days should be allowed to make the goods.

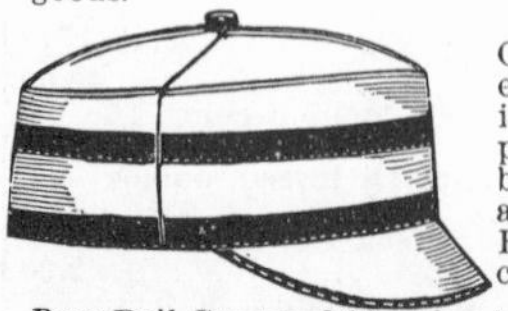

The Chicago Club or College Cap, as represented in accompanying cut, is the most desirable and popular shape, having been adopted by nearly all the leading clubs. Extra by mail, 3 to 5 cents.

Base Ball Caps and Clothing have to be made to order, consequently, in ordering allow as much time as possible.

48160 Cap, white, red, royal blue, navy blue, black, brown, maroon, old gold, and gray colors, with or without one or two stripes. Fine flannel, leather sweat band; best quality. Each $0.65
48161 Cap, white, red, royal blue, navy blue, black, light gray, medium gray, or dark gray, with one, or two stripes. Good flannel, well made leather sweat band .... .55

Base Ball Caps—Continued.

48162 Cap, same colors as No. 48161, well made and durable, with one or two stripes or without stripes .... .45
48163 Cap, all muslin, assorted colors, plain red, plain blue, plain white, no stripes or bands, all plain solid color .... .12

Amateur Shoe Plates.

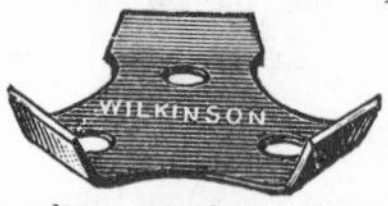

48165 Amateur Shoe Plates. This is made of tempered steel; safe, strong and light, and is positively the best shoe plate made. They are nicely packed, each pair in envelope with suitable screws, all complete, one dozen pairs in a box.
Extra, by mail, 3c. per pair.
Per pair $0.10
Per dozen .... .95
48166 Professional Shoe Plates, large size.
Per pair .... .20
Per dozen pair 2.00

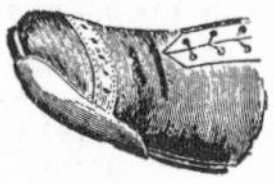

48167 Pitcher's Toe Plates, made of heavy brass, for right shoe.
Each $0.45
For base ball shoes, see index.

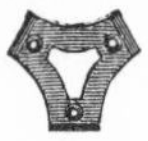

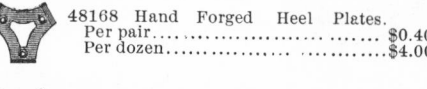

48168 Hand Forged Heel Plates.
Per pair $0.40
Per dozen $4.00

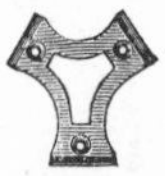

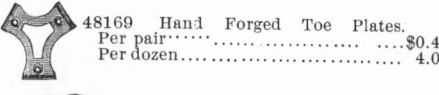

48169 Hand Forged Toe Plates.
Per pair $0.40
Per dozen 4.00

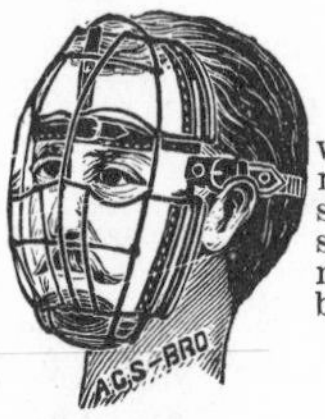

Warranted the best mask made. It is made of the best material, well padded, and by an ingenious arrangement of the wires an unobstructed view is obtained. It is far superior to the old style of wire mask, or the heavy, dangerous steel bar mask.

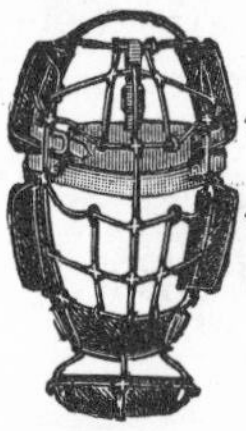

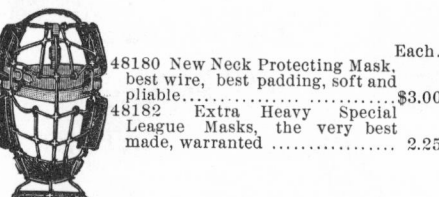

Each.
48180 New Neck Protecting Mask, best wire, best padding, soft and pliable $3.00
48182 Extra Heavy Special League Masks, the very best made, warranted 2.25

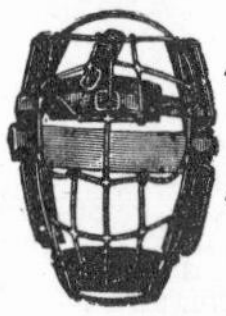

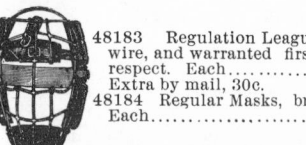

48183 Regulation League Masks, heavy wire, and warranted first-class in every respect. Each 2.10
Extra by mail, 30c.
48184 Regular Masks, bright wire. Each $1.75

Each.
48185 Amateur Men's Masks. We guarantee this mask to be equally as good as many dealers sell for the best league mask 1.35
48186 Amateur Boys' Masks. This mask is the same as the men's masks, only smaller, to fit a boy's face .... .90
Extra by mail, 20c.
48187 Youths' Masks, without head or chin piece. .60
48189 Boys' Masks, light wire, without head or chin piece 22

Base Ball Belts.

Extra by mail, 3 cents.

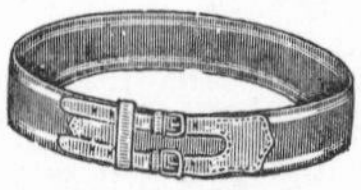

	Each.	Per dz.
48190 Cotton Web Belts, 2¼ in wide, leather mounted, single strap and buckle. Colors: Red, blue, white, maroon, navy blue, red, white edge, blue, white edge, red, white and blue, red and white stripe, blue and white stripe	$0.14	$1.45
48191 Cotton Web Belts, 2¼ inch double strap, nickel buckle (same colors as 48190)	.23	2.30
48192 Worsted Web Belt, 2½ in., single leathered covered buckle, colors: Red, blue, navy brown, black, white, maroon and old gold	.40	4.00
48193 Worsted Web Belt, 2½ in. double leathered covered buckles (same colors as 48192)	.45	4.25
48194 Special League Belt, worsted web, large nickel plated buckle (same colors as 48192)	.45	4.70

Spalding's Base Ball Goods.

Base Balls.

Extra by mail, 10c each.   Net cash.
48219 Spalding's League Base Ball, per dozen.$15.00
48220 Spalding's Double Seam Base Balls.
Per dozen.........................$13.25
Sold in any quantity at the above price.

Bats.

Weight, 22 to 40 ounces.   Per doz.
48225 Spalding's Best Second Growth Ash Bat, new model......................$ 8.00
48226 Spalding's Second Growth Ash Black Band League Bat, polished, rough handle wagon tongue, ash.................. 7.50
48231 Spalding's Trade-Marked Black Band Willow Bat.................... 4.00
Sold in any quantity at above prices.

Catchers' Mitts.

48234 "Decker Patent" Mitt, hand of soft deerskin, back of selected hogskin, laced, and sole leather reinforced on back for additional protection, well made and padded; the original catchers' mitt. Each ...$2.60

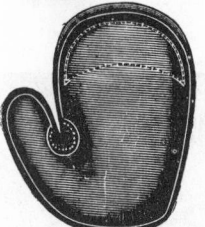

Front   Throwing Glove.

48235 Spalding's Special League Mitt, finest quality drab buckskin, new model, laced. Each ...$5.50
48236 Spalding's League Mitt, hogskin, laced back. Each.................. 4.25
48239 M. W. & Co.'s New League Mitt, best buckskin, padded with extra thick felt, heavy rubber welt around front of fingers, fingers heavy leather tipped, as good as the best; once used you would have no other kind. As well padded and as good quality in every way as the best glove in the market; warranted, with throwing glove........................ 3.85
48240 M. W. & Co.'s Horsehide Back, Buckskin Palm, Laced Fastening, League Mitt and Throwing Glove, same make as No. 48239. Made of good leather, and a good serviceable glove.... 3.00
48241 M. W. & Co.'s Goatskin League Mitt and Throwing Glove, thick felt pad with welt around front of fingers, laced back. A good one...... 2.30
48242 M. W. & Co.'s Boy's League Mitt and Throwing Glove, laced fastening, heavy padded, fingers well protected, the best boy's mitt in the market; buck front.............. 1.75
48243 Men's Goatskin Mitt and Throwing Glove, well padded, laced fastening.......... 1.00
48244 Boy's Mitt and Throwing Glove, padded; good and strong, elastic wrist fastening, a good large mitt, made in best style........... .50
48245 Boy's Mitt (no throwing glove), leather front hand piece, strong and durable. Each... .25
48249 Spalding's Sun-Protecting Base Ball Mask. Each $3.95
48250 Spalding's New Patented Neck Protecting Mask 3.00
48251 Spalding's Special League Mask, used by all the leading professional catchers, extra heavy wire, well padded with goat hair, padding faced with best imported dogskin.......... 2.75
48252 Spalding's Regulation League Mask, made of heavy wire, well padded and faced with horsehide, warranted first-class in every respect. 2.30
Weight, 2¾ to 3½ lbs.

Catchers' and Umpires' Breast Protectors.

Nicely made, and well padded and quilted, and are used by nearly all professional catchers and umpires.
48260 Chamois and canvas Weight, 1 lb. Each.......$2.90
48262 Spalding's League Body Protector, inflated........$8.00
48263 Spalding's Amateur Body Protector $5.00

Indian Clubs.

Sold in pairs only, and made of the best rock maple and finely polished. Weight given is the weight on each club. If you order one pair 1 lb. clubs, you get two 1 lb. clubs, etc.

		Per pair.
48270	1 lb.	$0.25
48271	1½ lbs.	.30
48272	2 lbs.	.35
48273	3 lbs.	.48
48274	4 lbs.	.55
48275	5 lbs.	.60

Boxing Gloves.

Weight, 3 to 4 pounds, packed for shipment. Our Boxing Gloves are the latest designs and are the best gloves in the world for the money.
Average weight, men's sizes, about 7 oz. each.
Prices quoted are per set of 4 gloves.

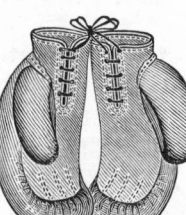

48281

48280 The Champion Boxing Gloves, new shape, finest brown french kid, lined throughout with kid, stuffed with the very best curled hair, ventilated palms, laced wrist; no better glove made of this style. Per set of four gloves (a $7.00 set at retail). Our price... ......$4.75   CHAMPION

48281 Boxing Gloves, the California patent, padded on end of fingers, side heel pads, dark buff color; weight, each glove, 8 oz. Per set of 4....................................$6.00

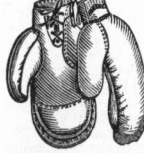

48282 Boxing Gloves, new style, ends of fingers padded inside as well as out, very best quality with kid finish, claret color... ...$5.75
48283 Boxing Gloves, same style as 48282 except dark goat finish, quality not as good, but strong and durable Per set of 4 gloves..........$3.48

48282-89

48286 Boxing Gloves, new style, all claret color, whole palm, elastic wrist fastenings, 6-ounce (retail price $3.75). Our price...............$2.10

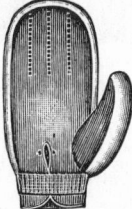

48287 Boxing Gloves, same style as No. 48282, but not as good quality. Color white. Per set.........$1.75
48288 Boxing Gloves, same style as No. 48282, better quality, color black. Per set $2.40
48289 Boys' Boxing Gloves, all white kid, whole palm, elastic wrist fastening. Per set of 4 gloves...... ..... $1.00

48290-98

48290 Boys' sizes, well stuffed white kid, tan colored palms, good size, made of same material and just as well as the men's size. Per set of 4 gloves......$1.50
48291 Men's sizes, same as 48290. Per set of 4 gloves, well made and durable 2.25
48292 Men's sizes, well stuffed and extra tan leather, wrists bound with fancy leather. Per set................................ 2.85
48293 Men's sizes white kid, better quality, heel padded. Per set......................... 3.75
48295 Same as 48292, best quality, heel padded.. 4 85
48297 Finest Kid Gloves with ventilated palm, very best quality. Per set 5.50
48298 Same as 48297, heel padded, welted seams finely finished and durable..................... 5.75
We cannot furnish any better gloves than what we quote above, as there are no better ones in the market at any price

Dumb Bells.

48300 Our Iron Dumb Bells are cast from pure gray iron, and are very much stronger and more durable than those ordinarily sold, which are usually made from scrap iron, tin, etc., and are very brittle and break easily. We make them with weights as follow: 1 lb. 2, 3, 4, 5, 6, 8, 10, 12, 14, 15, 20, 25 pounds each. Sold by the pound. Price, per lb., 4c; 50 lbs. 5c; 75 lbs, 6c.; 100 lbs. 7c. per lb.

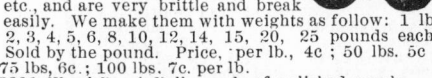

43301 Wood Dumb Bells, made of polished maple.

Weight.........1 lb.	2 lb.	3 lb.	4 lb.
Per pair........ 25c.	30c.	40c.	50c.

Foot Balls.

48302 The Association leather Foot Ball, Bladder, made of best India rubber, with fine leather outside case, hand sewed, laced, round. Postage, about 20c. extra.

	Each.
22-inch circumference	$1.50
24-inch circumference	1.75
27-inch circumference	2.05
30-inch circumference	2.33
33-inch circumference	2.63

48302½ The Association "College Match" Leather Foot Ball, finest quality, with inside rubber bladder, complete. Each.
27-inch circumferance.. .$2.60
30-inch circumfereuce ... 2.90

48303 Rugby Foot Ball, regulation size, oval shape, Bladder, made of the best India rubber, with outside leather case, hand sewed, laced. Best quality.
Each.
22-inch circumference....$1.35
24-inch circumference 1.50
27-inch circumference 1.80
30-inch circumference 2.10
33-inch circumference.... 2.30

48303½ The Rugby "College Match" Leather Foot Ball, finest quality, with inside bladder, complete. Each.
27-inch circumference.
...................$2.60
30-inch circumference.
..................$2.90

Rugby Bladders.   Association Bladders.

48304 Extra Foot Ball Bladders for either Rugby or Association Foot Balls. In ordering state which kind is wanted.   Each.
For 22-inch bail, weight, 8 oz.. .... $0.57
For 24-inch ball .... .69
For 27-inch ball.......................... .73
For 30-inch ball.... .... .76
For 33-inch ball.......................... .79

Rubber Foot Balls.

48305 American Round Rubber Foot Ball. By mail, 7 to 12c. extra.
No. 1, 6 in. diameter......$0.57
No. 2, 7 in. diameter.. ... .68
No. 3, 8 in. diameter...... .79
No. 4, 9 in. diameter...... .90
No. 5, 10 in. diameter..... 1.00
No. 6, 11 in. diameter.. ... 1.15
48306 Extra keys for foot ball...... .10

Foot Ball Inflaters.

48307 Pocket Inflaters, polished brass, length when closed, 7¼ inches (postage, extra, 6 cents).
Each.................. ....$0.37

48308 "Club" Inflaters, extra large, polished brass, length, closed, 13½ inches.
Each................$0.87
Extra by mail, 12 cents.

Foot Ball Suits.

Foot Ball Canvas Jackets.
48310 Best...................$1.35
48311 Medium .... .85
Foot Ball Canvas Pants.
48312 Best, padded................ 2.25
48313 Medium, padded............ 1.50
Moleskin Pants, padded.
48314 Best...... .... 4.50
48315 Medium 3.15
These goods are made to order. Give full measurements when ordering.

Bicycle Clothing Is Quoted with Bicycle Goods. ......SEE INDEX.

GYMNASIUM GOODS.

Improved Striking Bags.

FOR PHYSICAL CULTURE.

Refines, elevates and ennobles; adds to our courage, zeal and health and thereby to our happiness.

The bag is intended to strengthen the arms, wrists, shoulders, back, loins and particularly the muscles of the abdomen, and will teach the striker how to deal a blow. It is of inestimable value to everyone, especially to those whose business requires confinement.

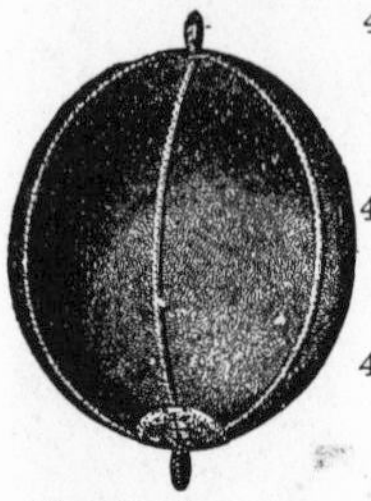

Showing loop, top and bottom.

48320 Canvas Striking, with leather loop on top, complete, with rubber inside bladder, good, durable.
Each, 12 in. diameter....$1.50
Each, 14 in. diameter.. . 1.70

48324 Amateur Striking Bag, soft leather, loop on top, complete, with rubber inside bladder. Each, 12 in. diameter$1.60
Each, 14 in. diameter..... 2.18

48325 Amateur Striking Bag, made of bag leather, loop on top and bottom, complete, with inside rubber bladder.
Each, 12 in. diameter....$2.40
Each, 14 in. diameter..... 3.87

48326 Professional Striking Bag, English grain leather, loop on top and bottom, complete, with inside rubber bladder. Each, 12 in. diameter.. 2.75
Each, 14 in. diameter........................ 3.25

48328 Striking Bag, Russia calf leather, welted seams, finest made, complete, with inside rubber bladder, loop top and bottom. Each, 12 in. diameter....$3.45 Each, 14 in. diameter.... 3.90

48330 Rubber Bladders, for striking bags. Each, 12 in........$0.90........Each, 14 in............ 1.00

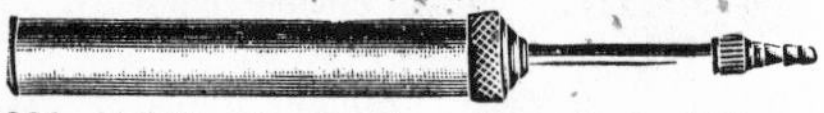

48331 Striking Bag Inflaters, brass, large, 10 in. cylinder. Each..$0.90
48332 Elastic Tubes, for striking bags.......... .50
48333 Large Elastic Tubes, for striking bags, loop on each end... .90
48334 Rawhide Hanging Straps, for striking bags, 3 feet long, with swivel snap on end. Each.. .50
48335 Screw Eyes, to screw in floor and ceiling. 2 for.. .05

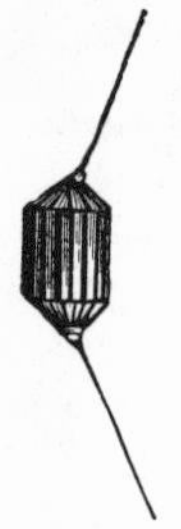

48336 Rumsey's Pattern Striking Air Bag, with cords and screw eyes, complete, ready to set up. Weight, 3 lbs. Each 5.00
48337 Elastic Tubes, for Rumsey striking bag.. .90

Horizontal Bars.

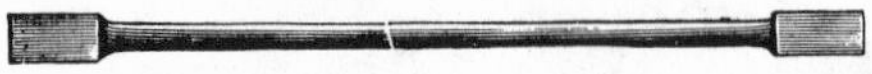

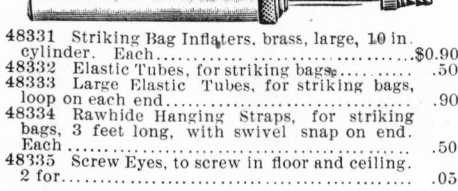

Weight, 4½ to 6 lbs.

Made of best quality second growth straight hickory, square ends.

	Each.
48345 4 ft. long	$0.50
4½ ft. long	.60
5 ft. long	.70
5½ ft. long	.95
6 ft. long	1.20

Trapeze Bars.

Weight, 2 to 3½ pounds.

Made of the best second growth hickory. Without ropes.

	Each.
48346 2 ft. Bar, without ropes	$0.45
2½ ft. Bar, without ropes	.48
3 ft. Bar, without ropes	.55
3½ ft. Bar, without ropes	.60
4 ft. Bar, without ropes	.70

Goodyear's Round Rubber Health Pull.

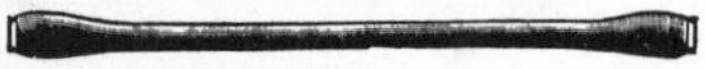

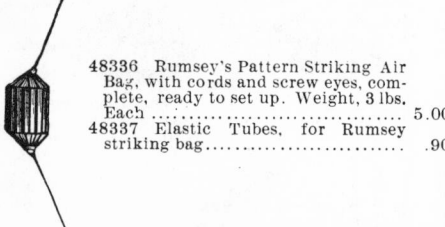

Each

48351 For ladies and children, 14 years and upward.. $1.25
48352 For men of moderate strength............ 1.45
48353 Used by ladies, children or men; is fitted with screw eye to attach to wall or floor......... 1.90
48354 For men of extra strength, made like No. 48353 .... 2.40

Eastman's Calisthenics.

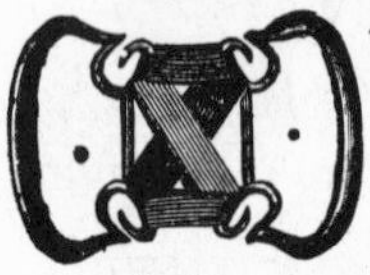

48361 A complete system of calisthenics brought within the compass of a single instrument of not above a pound in weight. The handles are of iron and are connected with rubber bands.
Japanned with book of instructions. Pair................$0.47

Fencing Foils, Masks and Gloves.

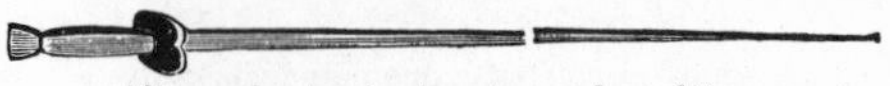

All goods standard make and quality.
Weight, 24 to 32 ounces per pair.

48363 Fencing Foils with steel blades, iron mounted handles. Per pair............................$1.50
48364 Fencing Foils, steel Solingen blades, brass mounted, bell guard. Per pair........... 2.50
48365 Fencing Foils, best steel Solingen blades, brass mounted, wound handles. Pair.......... 3.75

Fencing Masks.

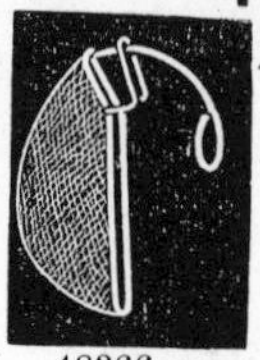

48366

Weight, 24 to 28 ounces.
48366 French pattern, standard quality. Per pair........$2.30
48367 French pattern, standard quality, with ears. Per pair........$2.75

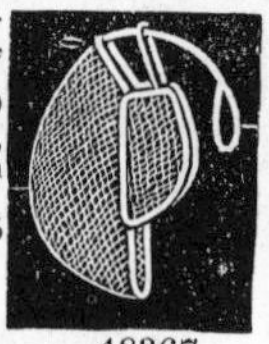

48367

Fencing Gloves, Buckskin.

Weight, 10 to 15 ounces.

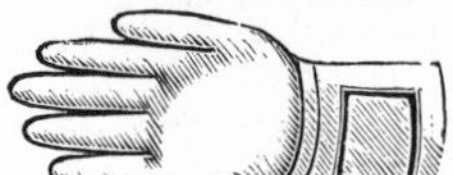

48369

48369 Fencing Gloves, with gauntlet. Per set of 2 gloves.$2.70

Athletic Clothing.

(See Index for Bicycle Clothing.)

Give chest measure when ordering shirts; waist measure when ordering tights.

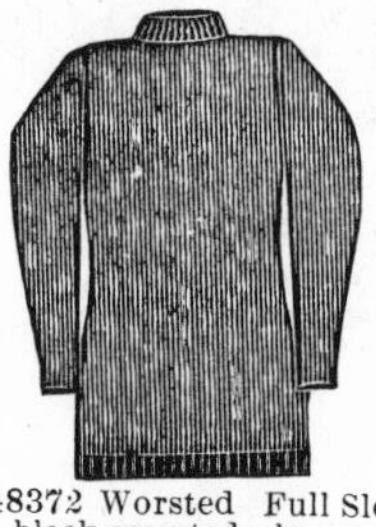

48370 Cotton Sweaters, rib knit, same style as the wool sweaters, cream color, a very handy article, just the thing for a baseball shirt; they are very elastic, 32, 34, 36 and 38 chest measure. Each.................$0.40
48371 Sweaters, made of lamb's wool, the best in the market, full length sleeves, heavy. Colors: Tan, navy, black and white. Sizes, 34, 36, 38, 40, 42, 44......$3.75
Medium heavy...... ... 2.75
Medium wool.......... 1.65
48372 Worsted Full Sleeve Shirts, with collar, black worsted; heavy, good for trap shooters' use also.................................... 2.40
48373 Worsted Full Sleeve Shirts, with collar, black or navy blue, extra heavy.................. 3.25
48374 Shirts, long sleeve, worsted, black or navy blue, light weight, good for trap shooters also... 1.80

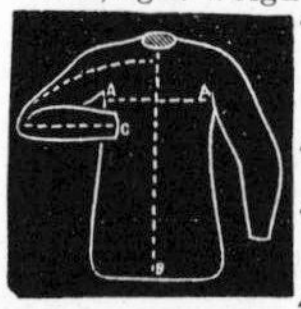

48375½ Boys' Wool Sweaters, good quality. Sizes, 28, 30, 32 and 34. Colors: Navy blue and tan. Each...........................$1.65
48376 Shirts, fast black, silk finish cotton, long sleeve shirts.....$1.30
48377 Shirts, fast black, silk finish cotton, long sleeve, standing collar $1.35
48378 Shirts, black Polo cotton, long sleeve...$1.15

Sleeveless Shirts 30, 32, 34 and 36 Chest.

48379 Worsted, any color, plain, sleeveless.......$3.00
48381 Cotton, white or flesh color.................. .75
By mail, extra.. .10
University or Quarter Sleeve Shirt, 26, 28, 30, 32 and 36 chest measure. Each.
48382 Shirts, worsted, plain, any color, ¼ sleeve.$3.10

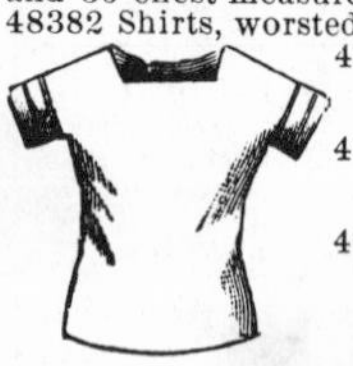

48383 Shirts, worsted, ¼ sleeve, black or navy blue, medium weight..... ...... 1.55
48384 Shirts, cotton, ¼ sleeve, white or flesh color, good weight .... .72
48384½ Shirts, cotton, ¼ sleeve, flesh color or black, fast colors, light weight, but firm and good wearing goods. .55

Full Length Tights.

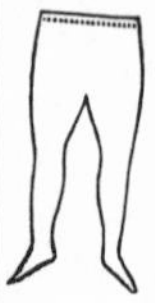

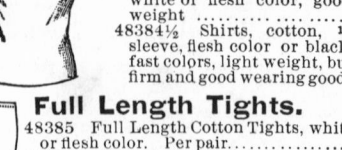

48385 Full Length Cotton Tights, white or flesh color. Per pair.................$1.60
48386 Full Length Tights, worsted, plain colors. Per pair..... .... 3.25
Postage.... .... .15
48387 Full Length Tights, worsted, medium weight, black. Per pair...... 2.40

Knee Tights.

48390 Worsted, plain black, per pair...........................$2.00
48391 Knee Tights, cut Jersey goods, plain black, per pair..........$1.40
48392 Worsted, plain colors, per pair...............................$2.60
48393 Cotton, white or flesh color; also make good bathing trunks, per pair.............................$0.50
By mail, extra............................. .10
48395 Trunks, worsted, black, navy, flesh or maroon, per pair.........$1.50
48396 Trunks, fancy colored cotton, in stripes, assorted sizes....$0.20

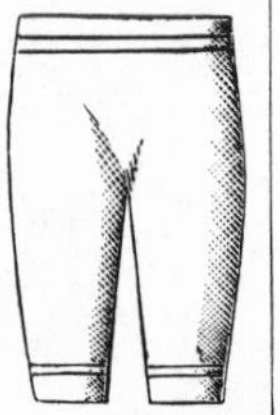

Tights—Continued.

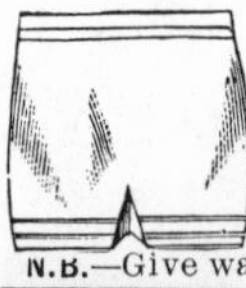

48397 Trunks, fancy colored cotton, in stripes, assorted sizes. Each. $0.30
By mail, extra............ .... .05
48398 Cotton Trunks, red or blue, Trunks. Per pair.................$0.55
48399 Puffed Velvet Trunks, black, red, navy or maroon, per pair..$1.00

N.B.—Give waist measure for gymnasium goods.

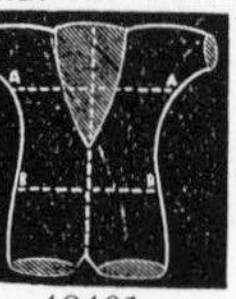

48401

48401 Full Fashioned Leotards, worsted, black or tan color.
Each........$3.75

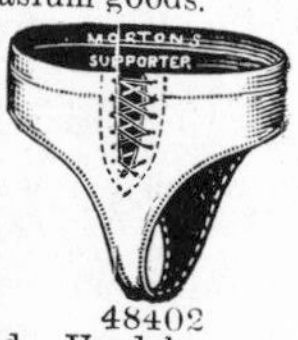

48402

48402 Morton's Perfect Supporter, the best fitting, most comfortable and effective supporter yet devised. Used by ball players, athletes and the theatrical profession generally; made of best quality Canton flannel, laced front, cool and pleasant to wear.
Each.................$0.35 Per dozen.........$3.30

Give waist and hip measure for supporters. Send us your order for anything in the athletic goods line. We will take good care of you both as regards quality and price.

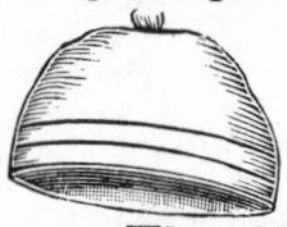

48403 Skull Caps, worsted.
Each $0.50

The Whiteley Exerciser.

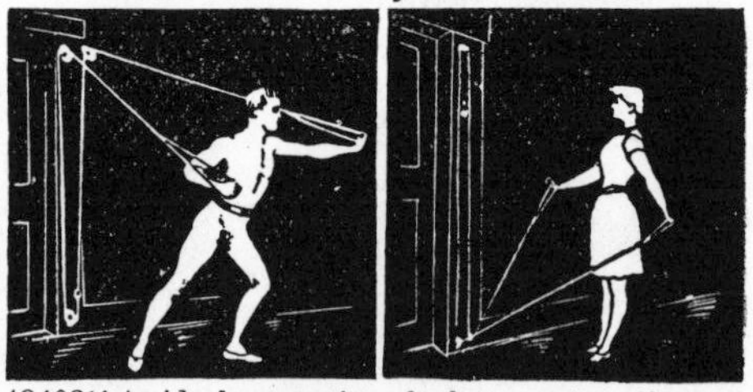

48403½ An ideal gymnasium for home or traveling use; noiseless; warranted to remain so; weighs less than two pounds; can be carried in your pocket or corner of valise and used in hotel, sleeping car or stateroom of steamer; a special attachment enabling travelers to suspend the Exerciser anywhere in a second; can be put up permanently in two minutes without tool of any kind; with a few extra hooks can be used in every room in the house; the hooks are of steel wire, though small, and do not injure the woodwork; no straps to buckle; no weights to change; self-adjusting resistance of two to forty pounds; no jerks, no dead weights—you'll think its alive. Exercises all the muscles, not the upper limbs only; attachment for foot movements; makes all movements that can be made on weight machines, and many others that would break any pulley weight machine all to pieces; a thing of beauty and a hustler forever; equally adapted to ladies, gentlemen or children; written endorsements from the very highest authorities; ask for pamphlet containing them; World's Columbian Exposition medal and diplomas awarded for merit and general superiority; will do the work of several cumbrous machines, aggregating a cost of fifteen to thirty dollars. Price, complete, with illustrated book of instruction, best quality........$3.00
Medium quality, not as well finished, each........ 1.85

Chest Weights.

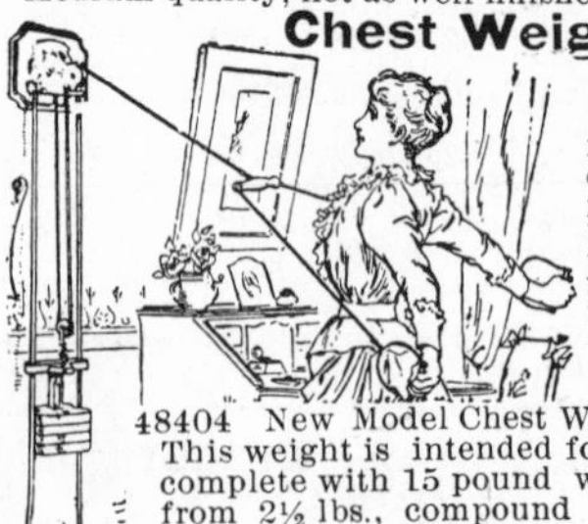

Improved Pattern for development of chest and all the muscles of the body. The most healthful exercise, for indoors, ever invented.

48404 New Model Chest Weights, single pull. This weight is intended for home use. Sent complete with 15 pound weights, adjustable from 2½ lbs., compound rope and floor attachment, enamel finish, complete ready for use; each..$5.00

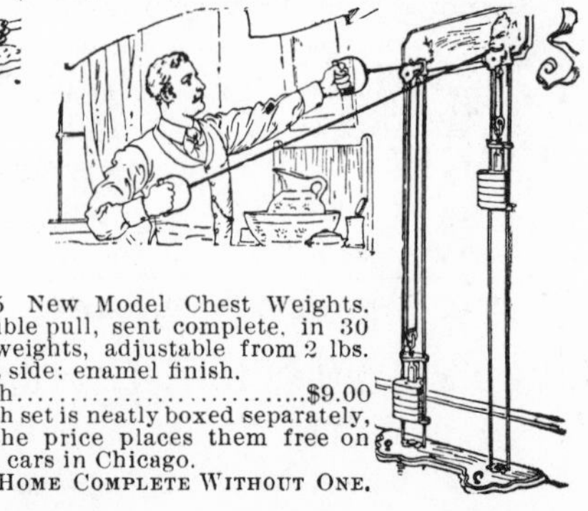

48405 New Model Chest Weights. Double pull, sent complete, in 30 lb. weights, adjustable from 2 lbs. on a side: enamel finish.
Each................................$9.00
Each set is neatly boxed separately, and the price places them free on board cars in Chicago.

NO HOME COMPLETE WITHOUT ONE.

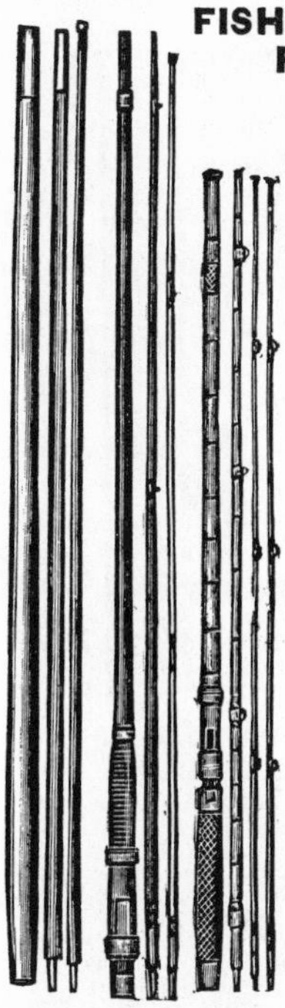

FISHING TACKLE, RODS, REELS, ETC.

In selecting the goods for this department, it has been done with a view of securing standard and reliable goods only, and we know of no single article in the list which follows that is not the best of its grade to be obtained. We have endeavored to so illustrate the various articles in such a manner that it will be possible for you to select intelligently, though you may not be familiar with the goods themselves.

FISHING RODS.

The weights given are for rods alone, and do not include case or wood form. Any rod not found as represented can be returned at our expense and money will be refunded if returned in as good order as when received.

Wood Rods.

Our prices are lowest jobbing prices on fishing tackle. That is why the prices may seem low to you for GOOD goods.

Plain Rod. Fly Rod. Bait Rod.

	Feet.	Each.
48410 Fish Rod, 3 pieces, jointed, single brass ferrule; about	10½	$0.10
48411 3-Piece Jointed Rod, single brass ferrule, ringed for line	10½	.15
48412 4-Piece Jointed Rod, varnished, single brass ferrule, ringed for line, natural color	12	.20
48413 3-Piece Light Bass, stained, double ferrules, rings and reel bands, brass capped butt	10½	.35
48414 Fish Rod, 3 pieces, fly or light bait, stained dark, double ferrule, brass butt cap, ringed for line, brass reel bands	10	.50
48415 4-Piece Bass or Bait Rod, stained lancewood tip, guides and reel bands, brass butt cap, double brass ferrules, finely finished	12	.70
48416 3-Piece Bait Rod, stained ash and lancewood tip, *brass mounted*, guides and reel bands	9½	.65
48421 4-Piece Fine Stained General Rod, covered dowels, reel bands, brass mounted, hollow butt, extra lancewood tip, braided butt	12	1.60

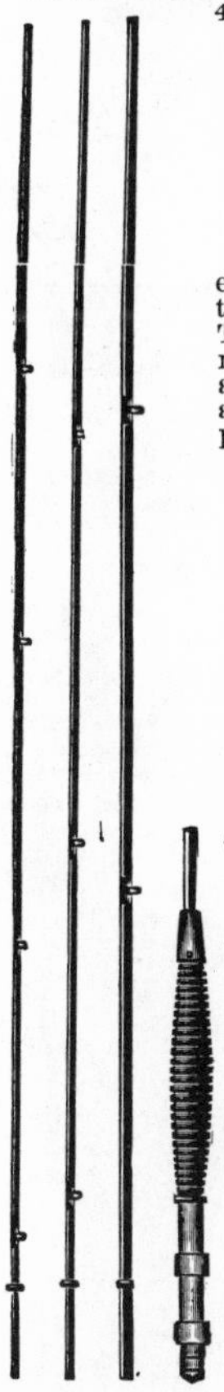

Steel Rods.

The **Bristol Steel Rods**. The toughest wood rod, however heavy, is not so tough as the lightest Bristol Steel Rod. They are a marked departure from all rods of the past, and are the best rods for all kinds of fishing. Every rod is guaranteed against breakage by reason of poor workmanship or poor material.

48423 (1) Bass Rod, telescopic, 9 ft. 6 in., full nickel mounted, with solid reel seat above hand, line runs through the center of the rod; when telescoped the rod is 32 in. in length, all closed within the butt length, with celluloid wound handle. Weight, 12½ oz. Price........$4.25

48423¼ (4) Bass Rod, 10 ft. in length, full nickel mounted, with solid reel seat above the hand. This rod is jointed and has standing guides on outside and 3-ring tip. Does not telescope; celluloid wound handle; weight, 10½ oz. Price.$5.10

48423½ (5) Fly Rod, 9 ft. 6 in., reel seat *below* hand, otherwise same style and description as No. 1. Weight, 11¾ oz. Price........$4.20

48424 (8) Fly Rod, 10 ft., full nickel mounted, with solid reel seat below hand. This rod is jointed, has standing line guides on outside, does not telescope. Weight, 9½ oz., with celluloid wound handle. Price... $5.00

With cork handle........5.25

48424¼ (15) Expert Bait Casting Rod; 6 ft. 6 in. in length, full nickel mounted, with solid reel seat above hand. This rod is jointed and has standing tie guides on outside, and 3-ring tip. This is just *the* rod for a long cast and for heavy work. With celluloid wound handle, weight, 9 oz. Price........$5.15

With cork grip handle, weight, 8 oz. Price........$5.25

Steel Rods—Continued.

48424½ (13) The St. Lawrence Bass Rod 7 ft. 6 in., full nickel mounted with solid reel seat above hand. This rod is jointed, has standing guides and 3 ring tip. This is one of the best bait-casting, or boat rods on the market. Weight, 9¼ oz., with celluloid wound handle.

Price........$5.00

Price, with cork handle........5.25

48424¾ (16) Fly Casting Rod. 9 feet in length, full nickel mounted, with solid reel seat below hand. This rod is jointed, and has standing line guides on outside, is finely balanced. This rod is sure to please any angler who enjoys light tackle for fly casting. Weight, 8 ounces. With cork grip handle only.

Price........5.30

Lancewood Rods.

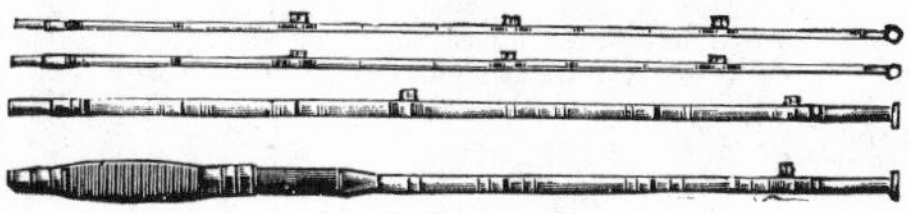

Bait Rod.

	Length feet.	Each.
48425 3-Piece All Genuine Imported Lancewood Fly Rod, finely nickel plated, improved shoulder ferrules, silk wound tie guides, covered dowels, solid nickel reel seat below hand, fancy or corrugated hand grasp, with one extra tip, in cloth bag, partitioned, a BARGAIN. Fly rod, heavy	10½	$1.25
Fly rod, light	10	1.35
48427 3-Piece All Genuine Imported Lancewood Fly Rod, in wood case or form, finely finished, full nickel plated shoulder ferrules, fancy silk wound tie guides, covered dowels, solid nickel reel seat below hand grasp, corrugated zylonite butt with one extra tip. A good one	10½	1.75
Weights on rods may vary 1 to 3 oz.		
48428 3-Piece All Genuine Imported Lancewood Bass Rod, finely nickel plated, improved shoulder ferrules, silk wound tie guides, covered dowels, solid nickel reel seat above hand, cane wound or zylonite butt, with one extra tip, in cloth bag, partitioned; a very fine rod (a bargain)	9	1.25
48429 3-Piece All Genuine Imported Lancewood Bass Rod, in wood form, varnished and polished, nickel plated, solid reel seat, shouldered ferrules, covered dowels, metal plugs, fancy silk wound tie guides for line, wound or fancy butt stock, one extra tip (a bargain). Bass rod	9	1.75
Bait rod	7½	1.85
48430 3-Piece and Extra Tip, all best Jamaica lancewood, carefully selected and thoroughly tested, patent hard rubber butt and extra fine finish, welt ferrules and metal plugs. Each rod in wood form, full nickel plated mountings, fancy silk winding between joints. Fly rod, reel seat below hand	10	2.50
Bass rod, reel seat above hand	9	2.75
Bait rod, extra heavy	7	2.85
48430½ Trout or Black Bass Rod, best Jamaica lancewood, for bait casting. Patent hard rubber butt, which affords many points of superiority over anything now used. They always retain their original shape, being made in one piece and in the form of a hollow tube, they will last longer than any other, and admit the wood of which the butt section of rod is made to be run clear through them, making the rod stronger and giving an "action" not possible in any other hand grasp that has the same appearance. Full nickel plated mountings, fancy silk windings. Two piece, extra tip, in wood form	6½	3.00

Henshall Bass Rods.

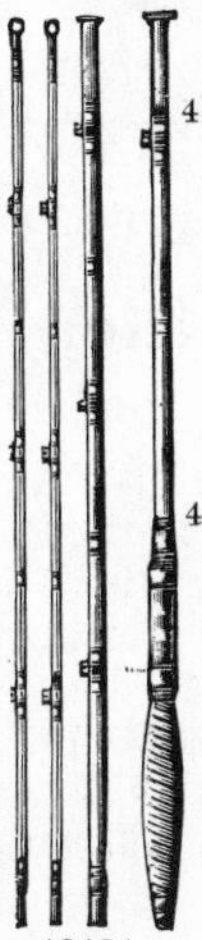

48431

48431 Henshall Bass Rod, all genuine Jamaica lancewood, patent hard rubber butt, German silver mountings, extra fine finish, with welt ferrules and metal plugs, extra fancy silk windings. Each rod put up in lined wood form. The best lancewood rod in the market at any price. No better rod made. Generally retails at $8.00. Our price	8¼	3.75
48431½ Genuine Jamaica Lancewood Short Bait Rod, 3-piece with extra tip, cork butt and aluminum reel seat, extra fancy silk windings, green and red clusters, full German silver ountings, in lined wood form. Bait	8	5.00
Very light fly	9¼	4.00

Combination Lancewood Rod

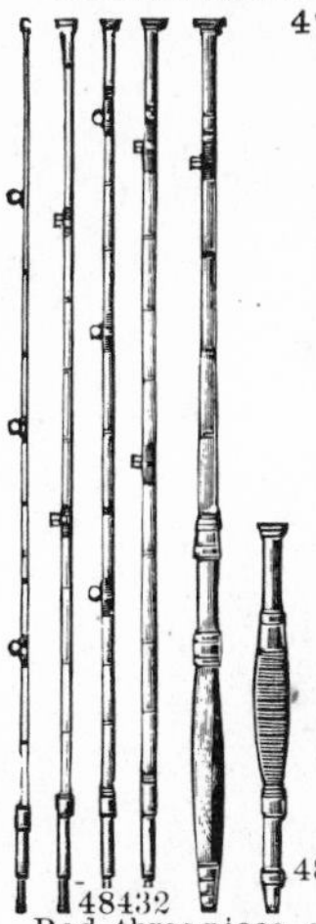

48432

48432 7-Piece Combination Lancewood Rod, for general fishing, has two butts, corrugated black celluloid, with solid reel seat, and one long ash, with solid reel seat, balance of rod all lancewood, shouldered and trimmed ferrules, nickel plated trimmings, silk wound tie guides, makes bass bait, trout bait and trout fly combination. When short butt is used will make a difference of 24 inches in length of rod, in any combination 7 to 10 feet; one of the best and handiest rods in the market. Will make 6 different rods. Each		4.00
48432½ "Double Handed" Salmon Fly Rod, three piece, celluloid wound butt, fancy silk windings throughout rod, welted ferrules, metal plugs, first joint made of second growth ash, balance of rod genuine lancewood, full, solid metal reel seat, patent adjustable locking reel bands, one extra tip. Just *the* rod for the northwestern fisherman	14	6.25
48433 Florida Bass Rod, extra heavy, all lancewood, selected wood; zylonite hand grasp, silk wound throughout; nickel plated mountings, metal plugs 3-piece, extra tip, has double guides	8½	2.60
48434 Tarpon or Florida Bass Rod, combined rod, will make a 3-piece rod, 8½ ft., 18 oz., and a 2 piece rod, 5¾ ft. 16 ounces; Jamaica lancewood, double tie guides, solid nickel reel seat, nickel mounted corrugated zylonite butt, heavy, strong and durable. The 2-piece rod is a good tarpon or Gogebec trolling rod. Everything about this rod is finely finished		3.00

Jointed Bamboo Fishing Rods.

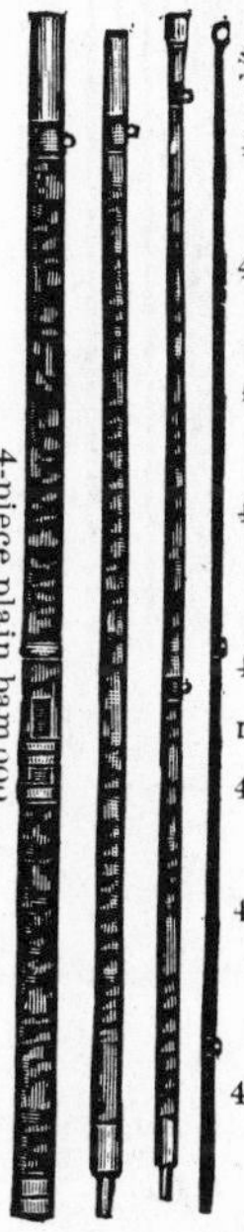

4-piece plain bamboo.

The Bamboo Rods are light, handy and strong, can be used with or without reels The best trolling rods in the market.

	Length feet.	Each.
48435 2-Piece, Japanese bamboo, double ferrules plain straw color	8 to 9	$0.15
48436 3-Piece, Japanese bamboo, double ferrules, plain straw color	14 to 18	.30
48437 4-Piece, Japanese bamboo, double ferrules, ringed, plain straw color	14 to 16	.40
48438 3-Piece, Japanese bamboo, double ferrules, reel bands, ring guides capped and stained wood butt	12 to 16	.60
48439 3-Piece, Calcutta bamboo, double ferrules, ringed, reel bands and capped butt	10 to 12	.45
48440 4-Piece, Calcutta bamboo, double ferrules, ringed and capped butt	14 to 17	.75
48440½ 4-Piece, Calcutta bamboo, jointed with long, heavy double ferrules, ring guides, capped butt, brass mounted	10 to 13	.50
48441 4-Piece, Calcutta bamboo, double ferrules ringed, reel bands, capped butt	14 to 17	.90

MONTGOMERY WARD & CO.'S HAMMERLESS SHOT GUN.

$65.00 Grade, Fine Damascus Steel Barrels, 10 or 12 Gauge, $35.00.

$50.00 Grade, Finest Laminated Twist Steel Barrels, 10 or 12 Gauge, $29.00.

SEE WHAT WE HAVE TO SAY ABOUT IT PAGE 449.

Fishing Rods—Continued.

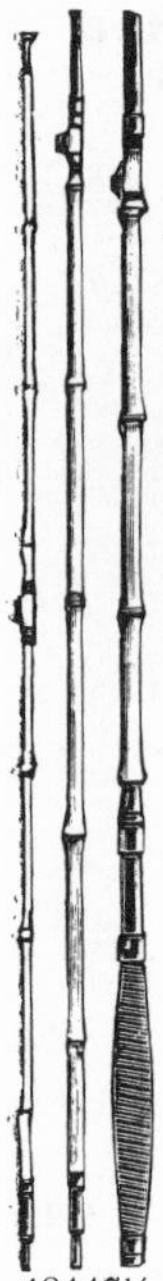

48447½

48441½ 4-Piece. Calcutta bamboo, jointed with long, heavy double ferrules, standing ring guides, reel bands, and capped butt	10 to .13	.75
48442 4-Piece, Calcutta bamboo, double ferrules, reel bands, capped and cane wound butt	13 to 16	1.10
48443 3-Piece. Calcutta bamboo, double ferrules, standing guides, reel bands, capped and cane wound butt, nickel mounted	10 to 12	.95
48444½ 5-Piece, Calcutta bamboo, jointed with long, heavy brass ferrules, standing ring guides, reel bands and capped butt, brass mounted	19 to 21	1.40
48447½ 3-Piece. Japan, fine quality, zylonite butt full mounted, with solid metal reel seat, nickel-plated standing ring guides, capped butt	10 to 13	.85
48448¼ 2-Piece, Japan, fine quality, zylonite butt, full nickel-mounted, solid, metal reel seat, standing ring guides, capped butt, a good boat rod	7 to 9	.60

Split Bamboo Rods.

These rods we believe to be fully equal to any and far better than most makes of split bamboo rods; a saw is not used in splitting the cane, neither cut into strips by machinery, but are split in such a manner as to preserve the grain of the wood which makes the rod far more reliable. All have welted waterproof ferrules and metal plugs. All our rods are guaranteed just as represented, any not found so, can be returned at our expense. On many we use the PATENT HARD RUBBER BUTT, which affords many points of superiority over anything now used; they always retain their original shape being made in one piece and in the form of a hollow tube: they last longer than any other and admit the wood of which the butt section of rod is made to be run clear through them, thus making the rod stronger and giving an "action" not possible in any other hand grasp.

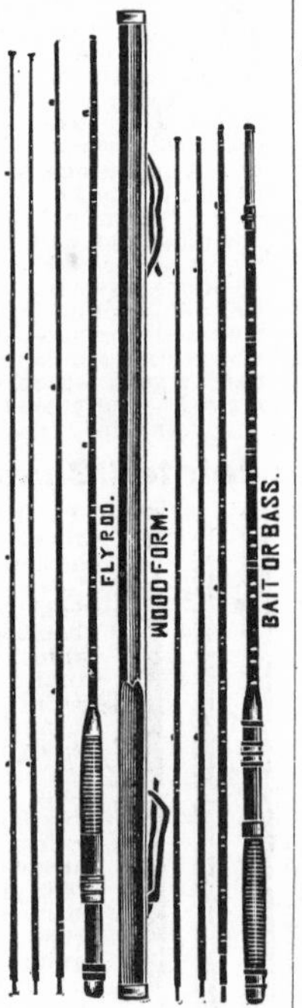

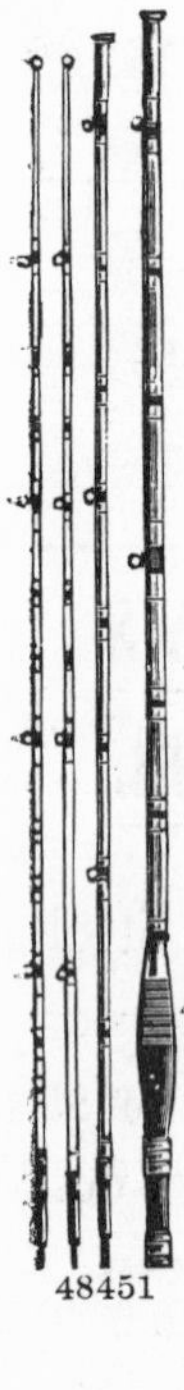

48451

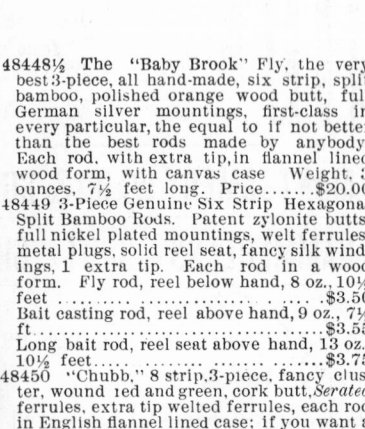

48448½ The "Baby Brook" Fly, the very best 3-piece, all hand-made, six strip, split bamboo, polished orange wood butt, full German silver mountings, first-class in every particular, the equal to if not better than the best rods made by anybody. Each rod, with extra tip, in flannel lined wood form, with canvas case. Weight, 3 ounces, 7½ feet long. Price $20.00

48449 3-Piece Genuine Six Strip Hexagonal Split Bamboo Rods. Patent zylonite butts, full nickel plated mountings, welt ferrules, metal plugs, solid reel seat, fancy silk windings, 1 extra tip. Each rod in a wood form. Fly rod, reel below hand, 8 oz., 10½ feet $3.50
Bait casting rod, reel above hand, 9 oz., 7½ ft $3.55
Long bait rod, reel seat above hand, 13 oz., 10½ feet $3.75

48450 "Chubb," 8 strip, 3-piece, fancy cluster, wound red and green, cork butt, *Serated* ferrules, extra tip welted ferrules, each rod in English flannel lined case; if you want a rod with "*back bone*" and fine action you need look no further, it is a *Dandy*. Retails generally for $30.00, *see our prices*.
10-foot fly $15.00
7-foot bait 14.75

Fishing Rods—Continued.

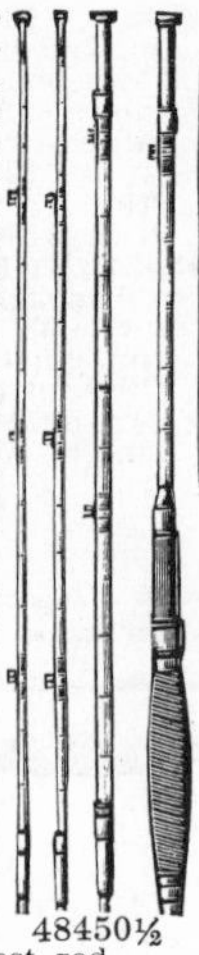

48450½

48450½ Three-Piece Hexagonal Six Strip Bamboo Rods, welted waterproof ferrules, metal plugs, full nickel plated, fancy silk windings, fancy celluloid wound butt, inlaid with cedar, each rod in lined wood form. These rods are beauties. Fly rod, weight, about 7 oz; length, 10 feet $5.00
Bait rod, weight, about 9 oz; length, 8¼ feet $5.10

48451 The Very Best 3-Piece, All Hand-Made Six Strip Hexagonal Split Bamboo Rods. Patent hard rubber butts full German silver mounted, waterproof welted ferrules, metal plugs, fancy silk windings, first class in every particular. Each rod in lined wood form, with canvas bag and extra tip. This is the rod that usually retails at $25.00, and is good value even at that price. It is the best rod that we can get made up. Fly rod, reel seat below hand, 7 oz., 10 feet $16.50
Bait rod, reel seat above hand, 10 oz., 8½ feet $16.55

48452 Three-piece Split Bamboo Rods, genuine six strip hexagonal patent hard rubber butts, full German silver mountings, solid metal reel seats, welt ferrules, metal plugs, fancy silk wound. Each rod in a lined wood form, extra tip. The best rod offered by *anybody* for *anything* like the *price* we name.
Fly rod, reel seat below hand, 8 oz., 10½ feet ... $5.60
Bait rod, reel seat above hand, 11 oz., 8½ feet 5.75

48452½ Trout Fly Rod, 3-piece split bamboo, six strip, cork butt, aluminum reel plate, full German silver mountings, with extra tip, fancy silk windings. Each rod in a lined wood form, the best rod for the price ever offered. Very light; 5 ounces; length, 9 feet. Each 5.65

48453 Three-Piece Hexagonal Six Strip Genuine Bamboo Rods, welted waterproof ferrules, metal plugs, full German silver mounted, fancy silk windings between ferrules, inlaid cedar butt. Each rod in wood form, lined; extra tip. These rods we believe to be better than most $12.00 to $15.00 rods on the market. *They are good ones.* Fly rods, reel seat below hand, 6 oz., 9½ feet 7.50
Fly rods, reel seat below hand, 8 oz., 10½ feet .. 7.55
Henshall bass rod, 9 oz., 8 feet 3 in. long 7.75

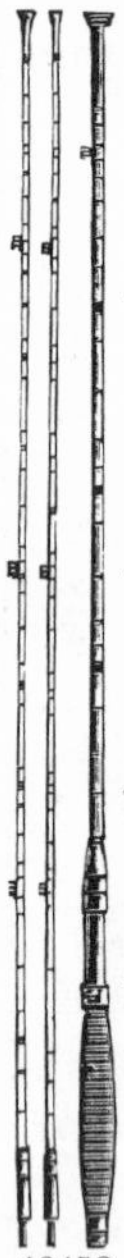

48458

48454 Three-Piece Genuine Six Strip Hexagonal Split Bamboo Rods, full nickel plated mountings, silk wound tie guides, solid reel seats, metal plugs, corrugated zylonite butts, each rod in wood form; 1 extra tip. Fly rod, reel seat below hand, 10 feet $1.25
Bait rod, reel seat above hand, 9½ feet. 1.30

48455 Three-Piece Six Strip Hexagonal Split Bamboo Rods, full nickel plated mountings, silk wound tie guards, solid reel seats, metal plugs, corrugated zylonite butts, each rod in wood form, extra tip, selected stock, a better rod all through than 48454. Fly rod, weight about 8oz; length, 10½ feet $1.80
Bait rod, weight about 12 oz; length, 9½ feet $1.85

48456 Three-Piece Six Strip Hexagonal Split Bamboo Rods, with cork grip, nickel plated mountings, solid metal reel seats and metal plugs in wood form. An extra tip. Fly rod, weight, about 8 oz; length, 10½ feet .. $2.80
Bait rod, weight, about 12 oz; length, 9½ feet $2.85

48457 Four-Piece Six Strip Hexagonal Split Bamboo Rods, with zylonite grips, nickel plated mountings, solid metal reel seat and metal plugs in wood form, without extra tip. Bait rod only, weight, about 13 oz; length 10 feet $1.45

48458 Boat Casting Rod, 2-piece, hexagonal section bamboo, patent *hard rubber grip*, full nickel-plated mountings, solid metal reel seat, welt ferrules, wire ring guides. Extra tip length, 6½ feet, this is the rod for boat casters; rod comes in covered wood form and cloth bag; don't pay others $10.00 for the same rod. Our priceis $3.75

Our prices on Split Bamboo Rods are 50 to 100 per cent. lower than regular retail prices.

We Endeavor...

To Meet Competition Everywhere.

The added cost of transportation to the prices we quote, is nominal when compared with the manifest advantages of our methods and consequent saving effected, as freight rates will average but $1.50 per 100 lbs., while express rates will average $4.00 to $6.00 per 100. Accurate information on this point or on any business subject will be given upon application.

Trunk Rods.

"Trunk Rods" means that they have joints not too long to be carried in an ordinary trunk or a large sized gripsack; the pieces including plugs are about 26 inches long.

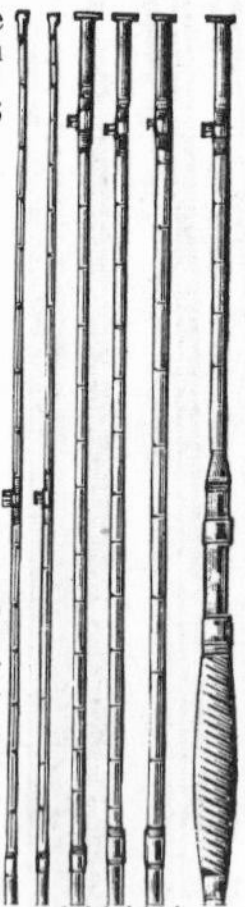

48464½

	Feet.	Each.
48459 Five-Piece Trunk Rod, varnished; long double nickel ferrules, covered dowels, nickel butt cap, ring guides, reel bands above hand, lancewood tips; a very good, handy article	11	$1.00
48460 Five-Piece Wood Trunk Rod, natural finish, varnished, double brass ferrules, lancewood tip, ring guides, reel bands above hand, brass butt, cap, fine little rod	10	.75

48461 Five-Piece Bamboo Trunk Rod, plain brass-finished mounting, ring guides, reel bands above hand; a very neat rod; 11½ to 12 .... .85

48462 5-Piece Bamboo Trunk Rod, improved and rimmed shoulder ferrules, covered dowels, silk-wound tie guides, metal reel seat, extra lancewood tip; a fine rod 1.50

48463 5-Piece Trunk Rod, all genuine lancewood, butt varnished and polished, shouldered ferrules, fancy finish, nickel plated, whole rod made of lancewood, fancy silk windings and tie guides, solid metal reel seat, one extra tip; 10 to 13 oz., a good, honest rod. Fly rod, reel below hand, about 9½ feet 2.10
Bait rod, reel above hand, about 8½ feet 2.15

48463½ Five-Piece Hexagonal Split Bamboo, zylonite butts, nickel plated mountings, solid metal reel seat, adjustable locking reel band, extra tip, in wood form, silk windings, bait rod has standing wire guides. Fly rod, about 8 ounces, 10 feet long 3.75
Bait rod, about 12 ounces, 9½ feet long 3.70
Put up in wood form, about 28 inches long.

48464 Five-Piece Trunk Rod, genuine hexagonal split bamboo, celluloid wound zylonite butts, nickel plated mountings, solid metal reel seat, and metal plugs, fancy silk windings and a handsome rod. Each rod in a wood form. An extra tip with each rod.
Fly rod, reel below hand, about 8 oz, 10 feet ... 3.25
Bait rod, reel above hand, about 12 oz., 9½ feet. 3.30

48464½ Six-Piece Rod, making a five piece rod with extra tip, split bamboo. Patent hard rubber grips, full nickel plated mountings, solid metal reel seats, welt ferrules, metal plugs; these rods are extra fancy wound yellow and black, put up in lined wood form equal to the regular $12.00 rod, our prices:
Fly rod, 8 ounces, 10 feet long 5.25
Bait rod, 12 ounces, 10 feet long 5.15

Rod Cases.

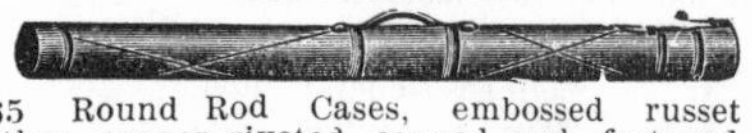

48465 Round Rod Cases, embossed russet leather, copper riveted, capped and fastened with strap and buckle, for single rod 40 to 50 inches. Price $1.50
Double Rod Case, 40 to 50 inches, same description as above 1.75
Heavy *Orange Leather*, same description as above, single rod Price 2.25
Heavy *Orange Leather* Double Rod Case. Price .. 2.50

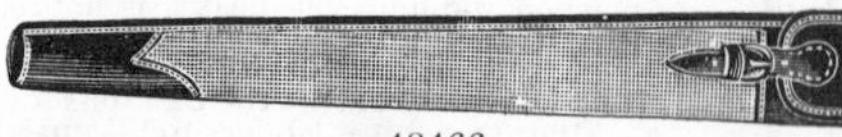

48466

48466 Canvas Rod Cases, leather protected ends, a dandy for the money. Weight, 6 to 8 ozs.—40 to 50 in. long. Each $0.60
48466½ Canvas Rod Case, plain, heavy canvas, with leather straps and handle. Each .... .40

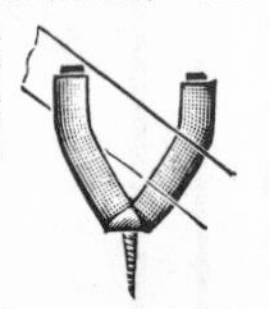

48467 The "Handy" Fish Rod Holder, can be carried in the vest pocket; screws on gunwale of boat; is covered with rubber. Ordinary size, each ... $0.13
Large size, each .... .15

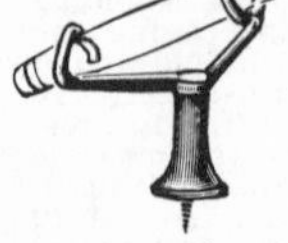

48468

48468 Fish Rod Holder, a good one for the money; screws on any part of the boat; forks covered with rubber. Each $0.30

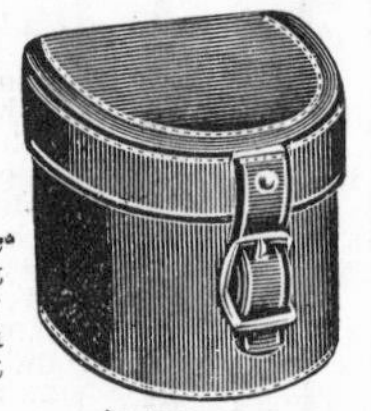

48469

48469 Leather Reel Cases are made of bleached oak, finest leather, felt lined, with leather covered buckles. If you have a good reel, you should have it protected.

No. 11, to hold small single action fly reel $0.55
No. 12, to hold large single action fly reel .... .65
No. 13, to hold small multiplying reel .... .70
No. 14, to hold large multiplying reel .... .90

The Universal Fish Rod Holder.

48510 For trolling and still fishing in a boat. It can be fastened either to the gunwale or seat. It enables a person, if he desires, to go fishing without a guide to row for him, or to have two or three rods in use without their being all over the bottom of the boat to be stepped on and broken. By means of a thumb-screw it can be adjusted to any angle or any direction, as it works on a ball and socket joint. It is neatly and strongly made, it is tinned, and forks are covered with rubber; it will take any rod from ¾ to 2 in. diameter at butt. Weight, 26 oz. Each $1.10

Fishing Reels.

(Reels by mail, 10 tc 15 cents extra.)

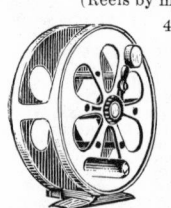

48511 The Expert Reel. This reel has an entirely new device for use in casting or "playing" a fish, whereby the angler may vary the reel from a free running to a delicate drag, heavy drag, or bring it to a complete stop, simply by the pressure of the thumb upon the guard. By this device the line may be stopped instantly at any desired point when casting. This guard is made of extra hard spring metal so that no matter how often used or struck by accident it will resume its original position. These reels, having a large diameter of spool, will reel in a line faster than the best quadruple multiplying reel. All finely polished, heavy nickel plated and well made; 40 yards, 2¼ in. diameter, with click. Each.........................$1.50
Extra by mail, 6c.
70 yards, 3 in. diameter, with click. Each...... 1.65
Extra by mail, 7c.

48512 The Famous Amateur Drag Reel, fine nickel plate, allowing line to dry quickly; can be changed to a free runner in an instant by simply pressing down on spring. Beats the best multiplier in reeling in the line. Very light weight, and fits any reel band. Small..........$0.95
Medium.................... 1.25
Extra by mail, 5c.

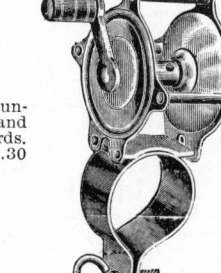

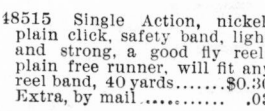

48513 T h e Competitive Reel, brass finish, plain, no click or drag, light and strong. Plain, free runner.
Each $0.10
Extra by mail, 3c.

48513

48514 Brass Free Running Reel, with band to screw on rod, 25 yards.
Each........ ......$0.30

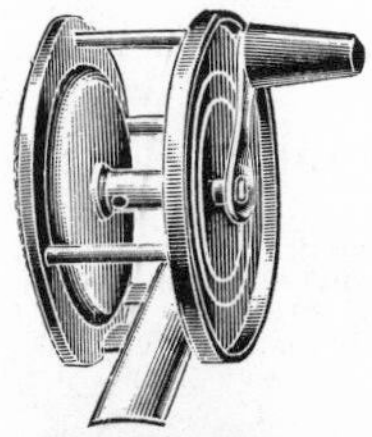

48515 Single Action, nickel, plain click, safety band, light and strong, a good fly reel: plain free runner, will fit any reel band, 40 yards.......$0.30
Extra, by mail .... .03

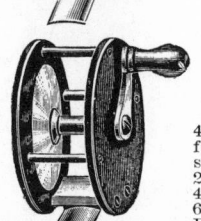

48516 Rubber Side Plate Reel, for light trout fishing, a good and strong reel.
25 yards, each..........$0.45
40 yards, each.......... .50
60 yards, each........... .60
Extra, by mail............. .05

Reels—Continued.

48517

25 yards, each $0.15
40 yards, each .... .20
60 yards, each .... .25
Extra, by mail.... .05

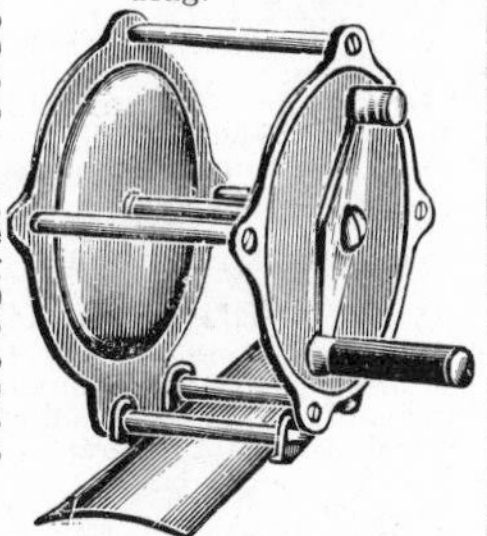

48519 Single Action, screwed raised pillar, with safety band, balance handle, and back sliding click, nickel plated. 40 yards, each $0.50
60 yards, each .... .55
80 yards, each 60
100 yards, each... .65
Extra by mail..... .05

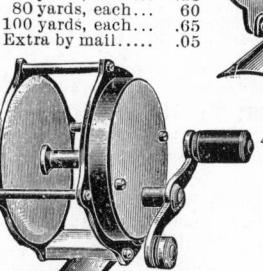

48519

48520 Nickel Plated Raised Pillar Reel, multiplier, balance handle, free running, adjustable sliding click or drag.
40 yards.....$0.55
60 yards..... .65
80 yards..... .70
100 yards...... .75
Extra, by mail .07

48520-21

48521 Nickel Plated Reel, raised pillar, double multiplier, balance handle, free running, adjustable sliding click or drag; same style as 48520. A special heavy reel for large fish; it is a fine tarpon reel. 200 yards, each $1.50
300 yards, each................. 1.90
Extra, by mail................. .16

48522 Nickel Plated Milled Edge Reels, quadruple multiplier, with front sliding drag and back sliding click, steel pivot, springs and ratchet with bushed bearings with removable oil cap and with handle.
Extra by mail 10c.
60 yds., each.$2.10
80 yds., each. 2.20
100 yds., each 2.30
150 yds., each 2.60

48523 Hard Rubber Reel, first quality, with rubber safety band, balance handle and back sliding click, steel springs and ratchet, nickel plated. You do not want a better fly reel.
40 yards, each.....$1.05
60 yards, each..... 1.20
80 yards, each..... 1.30
Extra, by mail..... .05

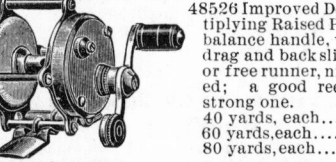

48526 Improved Double Multiplying Raised Pillar Reel, balance handle, with slide drag and back sliding click or free runner, nickel plated; a good reel and a strong one.
40 yards, each......$0.60
60 yards, each......... .75
80 yards, each......... .85
100 yards, each.................... 1 00
Extra, by mail .... .07

48526½ Improved, brass finished, raised pillar, multiplying balance handle, screwed collar, sliding drag. Same shape as No. 48526. A good article for the money and a big seller with us.
40 yards, each.....................$0.50
60 yards, each..... 60
80 yards, each........................ .65
100 yards, each...................... .75

48527½ Aluminum Reels, double multiplying raised pillar, balanced handles, steel pivots, copper screws, swinging oil cap, sliding cover, similar to 48526 in design, with click and drag, 4½ ounces weight, beautifully finished; 100 yards. Each 4.50

48528 Aluminum Reel, quadruple multiplier, otherwise same as 48527½. 80 yards, each.... 4.99

Reels—Continued.

48517 Polished Brass raised pillar, star pattern, with click, 25 yards, 1¾ inches diameter of plates.
Each.......... $0.15
40 yards, 2 inches diameter of plates.
Each.......... $0.20
60 yards, 2 3-16 in., diameter of plates.
Each.......... $0.25
Extra, by mail.. .04

48518 Raised Pillar, polished brass, free running, no click or drag.

48529 Aluminum Reel, single action, finished pivots, back click, front sliding drag, copper screwed swinging oil cap cover, finely finished throughout. Weight, about 3 oz. Just the thing for fly casting; 60 yards.
Each.......... $3.25
100 yards, each. 3.75

48530 Double Multiplier, nickel plated, balance handle, adjustable click and drag, a complete and good reel, steel pivots and made to wear.
40 yards, each....$0.90
60 yards, each... 1.00
80 yards, each.... 1.10
100 yards, each... 1.25
150 yards, each.. 1.35
Extra by mail .10

48532 Extra Fine Double Multiplying Reel, hard rubber, nickel plated sliding click, balance handle. When click is not used is free running; steel bearing, screw-off oil cap. A beauty and made for service.
40 yards, each.......................$2.05
60 yards, each................................. 2.15
80 yards, each................................. 2.40
100 yards, each................................ 2.90
200 yards, each................................ 3.15

48533 Fine Double Multiplier Reel, nickel plated and rubber cap, balance handle, adjustable sliding click, free running when click is not used, steel bearings; a fine reel. Style of 48532.
40 yards, each ....
60 yards each ....$1.00 80 yards. each.... 1.10
Extra by mail .... .07

48533½ J. Vom Hofe's Quadruple Multiplying Patent Hard Rubber German Silver Steel Pivot Reels, backsliding click, steel click cog and ratchet with patent adjustable pivot cap. Finest quality; recommended for long distance bait casting.
60 yards, each....$ 8.25
80 yards, each.... 9.75
100 yards, each.. 12.75

48533½-34-34½

48534 J. Vom Hofe's Quadruple Multiplying Patent Hard Rubber and Nickel Plated Steel Pivot Reels, with back sliding click, steel spring and ratchet, patent adjusting pivot cap. A fine article, good anywhere, same style as 48533½.
60 yards, each....................$4.25
80 yards, each....................... 4.75
100 yards, each........................ 5.25
Extra, by mail .08

48534½ Double Multiplying Reels, same style, quality and make as 48533½. The adjustable attachment on these reels is regulated by a thumb screw, forming the cap to the oil cup. Well made and durable. 60 yards, each............$3.00
80 yards, each............................ 3.25
100 yards, each.......................... 3.50
Extra, by mail........................ .08

48535 Extra Fine Quality Quadruple Multiplying Reel, steel pivots, balance handle, screw-off oil caps, back sliding click and front sliding drag, heavy nickel plated, and a fine reel; warranted equal to any $4.00 to $6.00 reel in the market.

48535

40 yards,......$2.40 60 yards $2.50
80 yards......... 2.65 100 yards 2.90
Extra by mail, 8 cents.

We have experimented with the best reels that we could find and even the celebrated Kentucky hand made reels, but for beauty of finish, ease of action and wearing qualities, we have selected the "Compensator" quoted *on next page* as the *best*. If kept in good order and well oiled they will last longer than any other in the world.

Reels—Continued.

48537 Abbey & Imbrie's Patent Compensating Quadruple, finest quality throughout, beautifully nickel plated, back sliding click and sliding drag. The steel pivots are so made that any wear may be adjusted in a few moments, so that the reel is practically everlasting, and a beauty besides. Easily oiled and re-adjusted. 40 yards $7.25
60 yards......... 7.75
80 yards......... 8.25
Extra by mail, 8 cts.

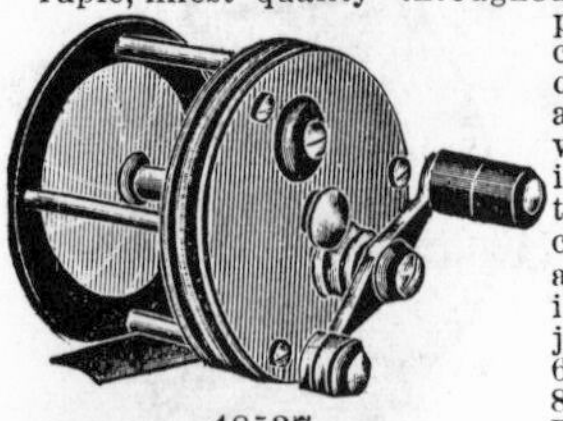

48537

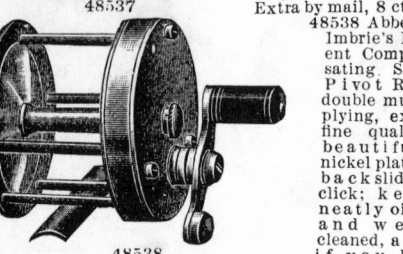

48538 Abbey & Imbrie's Patent Compensating Steel Pivot Reel, double multiplying, extra fine quality, beautifully nickel plated, back sliding click; keep neatly oiled and well cleaned, and if you buy one of these you will have one of the best and most durable "double multipliers" possible to obtain, in our opinion. They are all warranted perfect. You have been asking us for a good reel at a fair price, and here it is
40 yards, each.......$2.70 60 yards, each.......$2.90
80 yards, each ...... 3.15 100 yards, each....... 3.40
Extra by mail, 8 cents

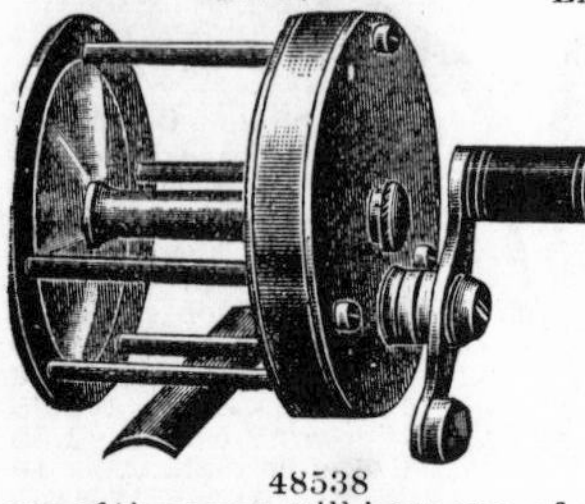

48538

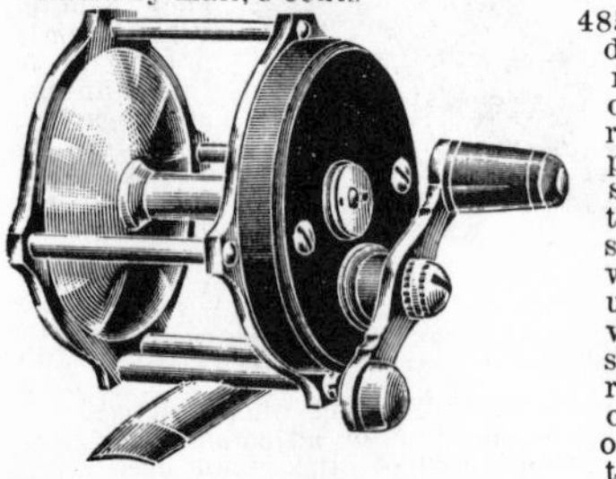

48539½ "President"—these reels consist of the ordinary external appearance, but so constructed that in a few seconds and without the use of any tool whatever the spool may be removed from or replaced in operative position in the frame of the reel. Thus all wearing parts of the reel may be conveniently exposed for cleaning at any moment, whereby not only is the useful life of the reel prolonged, but its operative condition is always at its best. The thumb screw in the center of the plate allows the reel to come apart. Hence there are no mutilated screws or screw heads and no possibility losing them; these reels are multiplying, hard rubber, nickel plated steel pivots, back sliding steel click, cog and ratchet.
60 yards, $6.00. 100 yards, $7.80. 200 yards, $9.80
Extra by mail, 10c.

FISHING LINES.

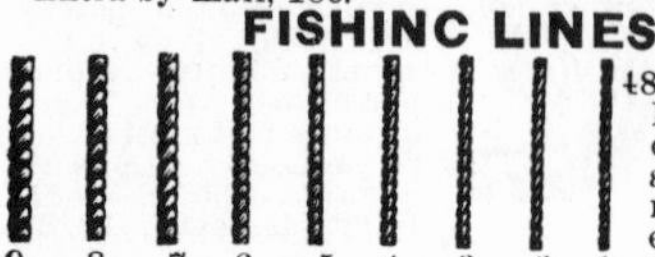

9 8 7 6 5 4 3 2 1

48540 Eureka Fish Lines. colored sea island cotton imination of linen, put up in 15 feet lengths; connected. Price, per dozen pieces of 15 feet each.

No.	Per doz.	Per 12 doz.	No.	Per doz.	Per 12doz.
1	$0.05	$0.45	5	$0.10	$0 80
2	.06	.50	6	.11	0.85
3	.07	.60	7	.12	1.10
4	.08	.70	9	.15	1.30

Linen Lines in Hanks.

48542 Linen Fish Lines, drab or variegated colors, each line 15 ft. long, 180 feet to the dozen. (Numbers correspond to Eureka Fish Lines.)

No.	1	2	3	4
Per dozen	$0.10	$0.11	$0.13	$0.15

48543 Linen Lines, 25 feet or 300 feet to the dozen. (Numbers correspond to Eureka Fish Lines.)

No.	5	6	7	8
Per dozen	$0.20	$0.25	$0.30	$0.35

48546 Drab Linen Fish Lines. Wound on blocks, 50 feet on block. See Eureka lines for sizes. 50 feet on block (6 connected, if desired); fine quality.

Nos	4	5	6	7
Each	$0.07	$0.08	$0.10	$0.11
Per dozen	.75	.80	.90	1.00

White Cotton Chalk Lines.

48547 Chalk Line put up in 18 feet lengths, 12 connected. Illustrations show larger than actual size but are as near as can possibly be shown on paper. These lines make good stagging for trot lines.

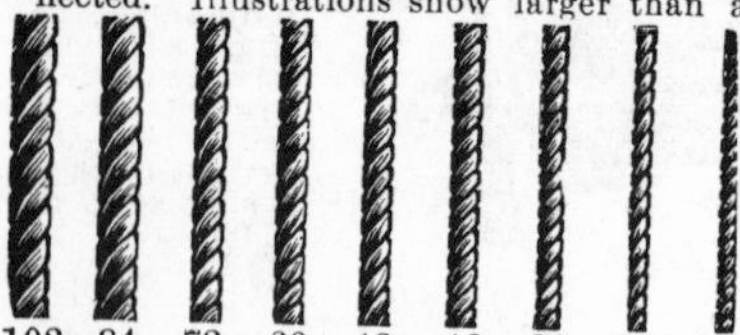

102 84 72 60 48 42 36 30 24 18

Price per dozen pieces (connected) of 18 feet each.

No.	24	30	36	42	48
Per dozen	$0.10	$0.12	$0.15	$0.18	$0.20
No.		60	72	84	1.02
Per dozen		$0.22	$0.25	$0.30	$0.35

Brook Trout Linen Lines.

48548 In coils of 25 feet; 12 connected. A fine line, best quality. Smallest reel line made; silver gray color; in coils of 25 feet, 12 connected, if desired. Each (for 25 feet)..........$0.04
Per dozen coils (12 connected) .... .35

Egyptian Cotton Lines.

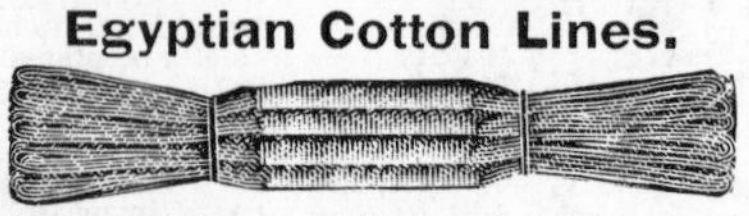

48549 These lines are braided and come in hanks of 12 connected. 25 feet each, all dark drab or mottled colors, sizes same as Eureka Fish Lines. Price for (25 feet) each.

No	1	2	3	4	5
Each	$0.02	$0.03	$0.04	$0.05	$0.06
Per dozen	.26	.27	.28	.30	.35

48549½ Egyptian Braid in coils, 12 connected. 50 feet each, all dark drab or mottled colors, sizes same as Eureka Lines; a good strong line. Price for (50 feet) each.

Nos.	1	2	3	4	5
Each	$0.04	$0.05	$0.06	$0 07	$0.08
Per dozen	.56	.58	.59	.60	65

Sea Island Cotton Fish Lines.

48550 Extra Fine Quality in 25 feet-coils, 12 coils connected; sold in any quantity; a beautifully finished line and good reel or trolling or bass line. (Nos. correspond to Nos. 1, 2, 3, 4 and 5 of "Eureka" Fish Lines)

Nos	9	12	15	18	21
Each	3c	4c	5c	6c	7c
Per dozen	25c	30c	35c	40c	45c

Brown Linen Trolling Lines.

In coils of 84 feet, 3 connected.
Sold in any quantity.

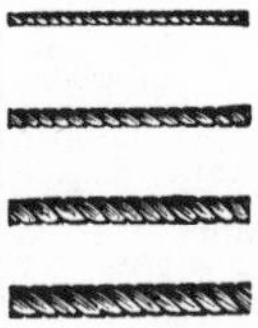

DESCRIPTION.	Each coil.	Per doz. coils.
48551 Size 1, in coils of 84 feet, 3 connected	$0.12	$1.25
Size 2, in coils of 84 feet, 3 connected	.15	1.50
Size 3, in coils of 84 feet, 3 connected	.18	1.75
Size 4, in coils of 84 feet, 3 connected	.20	2.00

Braided Cotton Lines.

In coils.
Strong and durable.

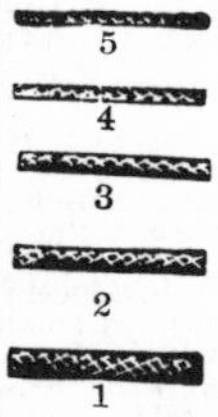

5 4 3 2 1

	Each coil.	Per doz. c oils.
48553 Braided Cotton Lines, No. 1 the largest, Nos. 2, 3, 4, 5 running smaller; in coils of 84 feet. Nos. 5, 4, 3	$0.08	$0.75
Nos. 2, 1	.10	0.85

Braided Linen Lines,

In coils.
Much stronger than twisted or laid lines.
Sizes 1, 2, 3, 4, 5, 6. No. 1 is the largest (4 lines connected if desired).

	Each coil.	Per 100 yards.
48554 Hard Braided Linen Lines, in coils of 25 yards. See illustrations of braided cotton lines for sizes	$0.15	$0.75

Braided Linen Lines.

On boards.
For bass, pike and other large fish. A good trolling line (4 lines connected if disired).

	Each.	Per 100 yds.
48555 Braided Linen Lines on boards. Sizes: 1, 2, 3, 4, 5. No. 1 is the larges on boards of 25 yards. See Illustrations of braided cotton lines for sizes	$0.10	$0.40

Fine Twisted Silk Lines.

In hanks for trout and other small fishing.
48556 Assorted Colors, 15 feet in each hank.

Size	1	2	3	4
Each	4c	5c	7c	10c
Per dozen	42c	54c	76c	$1.00

Our Silk Lines are all Silk and Fine Quality.

In silk lines No. 5 is for brook trout, No. 4 small bass, No. 3 large bass and pickerel, Nos 2 and 1 for large fish.

Braided Silk Lines.

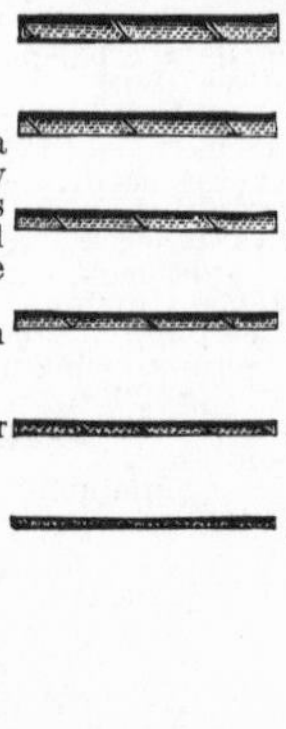

1 2 3 4 5 6

The illustrations of lines appear a little larger than the line, but they are the exact diameter of the lines they represent. This applies to all the illustrations of fish and seine lines.

48557 Braided Dressed Lines on 25 yard block. Four connected.
Nos.....1 2 3 4 5
Prices, 40c. 35c. 30c. 25c. 20c. per 25 yards. No. 5 smallest.

Lines—Continued.

48559 Fine Quality Braided Oil Silk Lines, in coils of 25 yards each; 4 connected. A BIG SELLER and a good one.

Nos.	1	2	3	4	5
Prices	40c,	35c,	30c,	25c,	20c., per 25 yds.

48560 High Grade Raw Braided Silk Lines, on blocks of 25 yards each; 4 connected.

Nos.	1	2	3	4	5
Prices	35c,	30c,	25c,	20c,	15c per 25 yds.

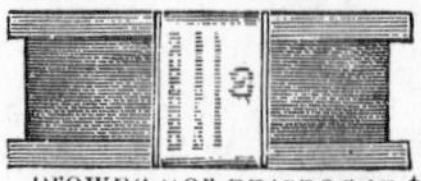

48562 Extra Strength, Waterproof, Finest Quality, Braided Silk, strength tested, label on each 50 yards showing strength, dark browncolor finished in the highest style, put up 50 yards on a block, 2 blocks or lines connected, sold in 50 yard lengths or over. Strongest line made. No. 5 largest.

No.	9	8	7	6	5
Per 50 yards	$1.25	$1.50	$1.75	$2.00	$2.25

No. 9 is tested to a 14 lb. pull.

48563 Extra Strength, strength tested label on each 50 yards showing strength; this is the best line that can be made. No. 9 is tested to a 14 pound pull. No. 5 to 33 pound pull. Finest quality, braided silk lines, dark brown color, finished in the highest style of the art. Put up 50 yards on a block; 2 blocks or lines connected. Sold in 50 yard lengths or over. No. 9 is the smallest silk line made.

Nos	9	8	7	6	5
Per 50 yards.	$1.00	$1.25	$1.50	$1.75	$2.00

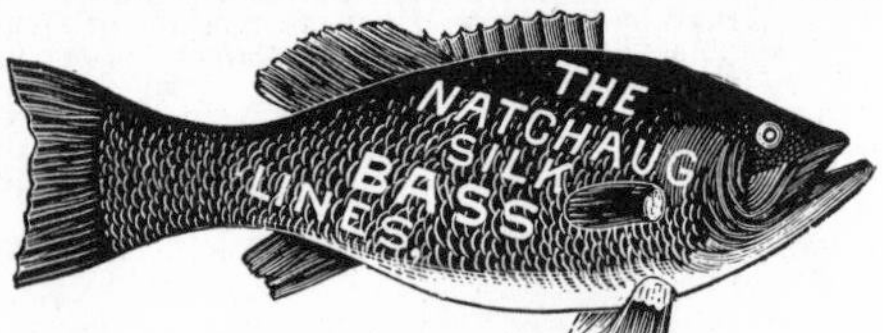

48463½ Natchaug Silk Fish Lines, experts who have used these lines pronounce them superior to any other make, all are braided 16 strand, thereby producing a perfectly round and even cord that is uniform both as to strength and size. Price, per 25 yards, on boards.

Nos.	1½	3	5	40	41
Price	$0.50	$0.60	$0.70	$0.75	$1.00

You can purchase 25, 50, 75 or 100 yards in continous line.

No. 1½ is the smallest line made and is the one usually used by bait casters, numbers 40 and 41 are for large fish and are braided 16 strand over a silk line center which makes it doubly strong. No stronger line made than the Natchaug. No. 1½ will hold the largest bass.

Superior Waterproof Braided Silk Lines.

48564 Mist Color Waterproof Braided Silk, in 25 yard coils, 4 connected; you can order 25, 50, 75 or 100 yards in a line. The best line made for fly fishing that is not enameled.

Nos	4	5	6
Per 25 yard coil	50c	45c	40c

48565 Enameled Waterproof Braided Silk Lines, hard enameled and run free on the reel. In 25 yard coils, 4 connected; can order 25, 50, 75 or 100 yards in one.

Nos	3	4	5	6
Per 25 yard coil	$1.00	$0.75	$0.65	$0.60

48566 Highest Quality Waterproof Braided Silk Luster Finish Fly Lines. The best highly polished line made. No. 6 or G is the smallest, 25 yard coils, 4 connected; can order 25, 50, 75 or 100 yards in a line. Just the line for long distance fly casting.

Nos	6 or G	5 or F	4 or E	3 or D
Price, per 25 yards	$1.00	$1.25	$1.50	$1.75

Irish Linen Line.

48568 Irish Linen, braided, waterproofed, this proofing is not simply put on the outside, but goes clear through; a good line for salt water; is also a fine bass lines; put up in 25 yard coils, four connected, making 100 yards; you can order 25, 50, 75 or 100 yards.

Nos	4	4	6
Per 25 yards	$0.70	$0.60	$0.50

No. 6 is the smallest, 4 the largest.

Cutty Hunk Linen Line.

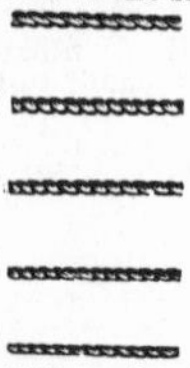

21 18 15 12 9

48570—
Best and strongest line made. Cutty Hunk Linen Lines best quality.
The best linen reel line in the market, runs smooth and even and does not kink.

150 feet blocks.

	9 Thread,	12 Th'd,	15 Th'd,	18 Th'd,	21 Th'd.
Each	25c	30c	35c	40c	50c

48570½ In 300 ft. lengths.

	9 Thread,	12 Th'd,	15 Th'd,	18 Th'd,	21 Th'd.
Each	50c	60c	70c	$ .80	$1.00

Linen Reel Lines.

In coils.

48572 Made of best imported gilling thread. (No. 35), in 50 foot coils, connected. See Cutty Hunk lines for sizes.

Nos	9	12	15	18	21
Each coil	10c	11c	13c	14c	15c

Sea Grass Lines.

48573 Six lines in bunch, 10 to 15 feet in a line. One of the best and strongest lines made, fine as silk.
Nos.........1 for trout, 2 for bass, 3 pike, etc.
Per bunch of 6...   45c.   50c.   55c.

Tarpon Lines.

48573½ Made of No. 27 Irish Flax, 600 feet spool, tested to a pull of 35 lbs.
Price, per spool, for 600 feet....................$2.75

Fishing Line—Rigged.

	Each.	Per doz.
48575 Fishing Lines, rigged with hook and float, a good line............	$0.03	$0 25
Medium laid line......	.04	.35
Silk line........... ..	.20	1.75

48575½ Fishing Lines, braided linen, rigged with Carlisle hook tied to single gut snell with fancy cork float two split shot sinkers, all ready to go-a-fishing.
Each $0.10
Per dozen 1.00

FISH HOOKS.

Weight per box of 100, No. 12 to 2-0, 3 oz.; 4-0 and 5-0, 6 oz.; 6-0, 8-oz.; 7-0, 10 oz.; 8-0, 14 oz.; 9-0, 18 oz.; 10-0, 20 oz.

We do not break boxes at these prices. If you purchase more than you require for yourself you can easily sell enough to pay for your whole purchase, so that those for your own use would cost you nothing.

Limerick Hooks.

48576 Limerick Fish Hooks, spring steel, superfine, ringed; put up in boxes of 100 hooks. Only one size in a box.

Nos.	12	11	10	9	8	7
Per box	6c.	6c.	6c.	6c.	6c.	6c.
Nos.	6	5	4	3	2	1
Per box	6c.	6c.	6c.	6c.	6c.	6c.

Nos.	1-0	2-0	3-0	4-0	5-0	6-0	7-0	8-0	9-0	10-0
Per box	7c	8c.	9c.	10c.	12c.	14c.	16c.	20c.	35c.	45c.

Per 1,000, Nos. 12 to 1...........................$0.50

Kirby Hooks.

48577 Kirby Bent Fish Hooks, spring steel, superfine, ringed. Put up in boxes of 100 each.

Nos.	12	11	10	9	8	7
Per box	6c.	6c.	6c.	6c.	6c.	6c.
Nos.	6	5	4	3	2	1
Per box	6c.	6c.	6c.	6c.	6c.	6c.

Nos.	1-0	2-0	2-0	4-0	5 0	6-0	7-0	8-0	9-0	10-0
Per box	7c.	8c	9c.	10c.	12c.	14c.	16c.	20c.	35c.	40c.

Carlisle Hooks.

48578 Fine Quality English "O. V. B." Blue Spring Steel Kirby Bend, Hollow Point Carlisle Hooks, ringed. Put up in boxes of 100 each. only one size in a box; 100 hooks in a box.

Nos....	8	7	6	5	4	3	2	1
Per box.	25c.	25c.	25c	25c.	25c.	25c.	25c.	25c
Nos....	1-0	2-0	3-0	4-0	5-0	6-0	7-0	8-0
Per box	28c.	30c.	35c.	40c.	50c.	60c.	65c.	70c.

48579 Carlisle Hooks, good quality, blued, not so good as No. 48578, just as strong, but not so nicely blued. Put up 100 in a box, only one size in a box.

Nos....	8	7	6	5	4	3	2	1
Per box	15c.	15c.	15c.	15c.	15c.	15c.	15c.	15c.
Nos....	1-0	2-0	3-0	4-0	5-0	6-0	7-0	8-0
Per box	17c.	18c.	20c.	21c.	25c.	30c.	40c.	50c.

48580 Carlisle Hooks, best steel spring, extra heavy wire, ringed, the very best hook made. They are a little higher in price than the other Carlisle hooks, yet they are worth more, and are worth more than we ask for them. Put up 100 in a box, only one size in a box. Nos

Nos	6	5	4	3	2	1
Per box	30c.	30c.	30c.	30c.	30c.	30c.
Nos...............	1-0	2-0	3-0	4-0	5-0	6-0
Per box........	35c.	40c.	50c.	55c.	70c.	90c.

Aberdeen Hooks.

Superfine Spring Steel English Blued, Spring Steel Round Bend, Aberdeen Hooks, ringed. Put up in boxes of 100 each; only one size in a box.
48584 (100 hooks in a box.)

Size.....	6 to 1	1-0	2-0	3-0
Per box....................	25c.	30c.	32c.	35c.
Size....	.4-0	5-0	6-0	7-0
Per box..................	40c.	50c.	60c.	65c.

H. P. Sproat Hooks.

Superfine English Blued Spring Steel Hollow Point Sproat Hooks, ringed. Put up in boxes of 100 each; only one size in a box.
48585 (100 hooks in a box.)
Size...10 to 1 1-0 2-0 3-0 4-0 5-0 6 0 7-0
Per box 20c. 25c. 35c. 40c. 45c. 50c. 60c.75c.

Something New.

48588 **Warren's Never Strip** Snelled Hooks, put up in wrapper envelopes; the hooks are all in view the moment the package is opened, and can be taken out singly or in any quantity desired without tangling the balance. We carry in stock Carlisle, Sproat and Aberdeen, tied in a good and serviceable manner, at prices and in sizes quoted below. In ordering be sure and state *kind* wanted. If no kind is mentioned we will send Carlisle. One dozen of a size in a package. Price for *single* snelled:

3-0	2-0	1-0	1 to 10
30c.	25c.	22c.	20c. per package.

48589 Warren's Never Strip Hooks, same description as No. 48588, tied to *double* gut. Price per doz.; 1 doz. of a size in a package:

6-0	5-0	4-0	3-0	2-0	1-0	1 to 10
50c.	45c.	39c.	35c.	30c.	29c.	30c.

Snelled Hooks.

Always give size and price, when ordering.
Full length gut; best tied.
48590 Superior Limerick Hooks to single gut, and superior Kirby bent hook to single gut.

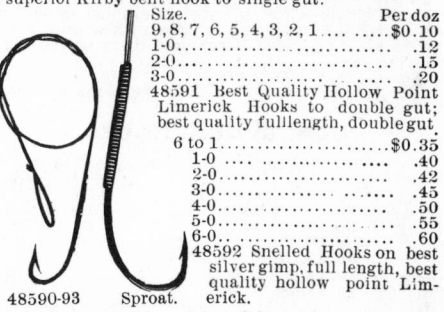

Size.		Per doz
9, 8, 7, 6, 5, 4, 3, 2, 1....	......	$0.10
1-0...............................		.12
2-0...............................		.15
3-0...............................		.20

48591 Best Quality Hollow Point Limerick Hooks to double gut; best quality fulllength, double gut.

6 to 1	....	$0.35
1-0	....	.40
2-0	....	.42
3-0	....	.45
4-0	....	.50
5-0	....	.55
6-0	....	.60

48592 Snelled Hooks on best silver gimp, full length, best quality hollow point Limerick.

48590-93   Sproat.

Size..	..4 to 1	1-0	2-0	3-0	4-0	5-0	6-0
Per doz..	40c.	50c.	55c.	58c.	60c.	65c.	70c.

48593 **Sproat Hooks**, to 9 inch, best quality double gut.

Size.....	2 or 1	1-0	2-0	3-0	4-0	5-0	6-0
Per doz..	35c.	40c.	42c.	55c.	60c.	65c.	70c.

Snelled Hooks or Hooks to gut sold in packages of half dozen or over only, at above prices.
48595 **Aberdeen Hooks**, tied to best quality, full length double gut.

(Sold in ½ dozen lots or over.)

Size......	4 to 1	1-0	2-0	3-0	4-0	5-0	6-0
Per doz..	40c.	50c.	55c.	58c.	60c.	65c.	70c.

Carlisle.
48596 **Carlisle Hooks**, Superior Spring Steel, tied to full length, best quality *single* gut. (Sold in ½ doz. lots or over.)

Sizes..............	8 to 1	1-0	2-0	3-0.
Per dozen.............	15c.	20c.	22c.	25c.

48597 **Carlisle Hooks, Superior Spring Steel**, tied to full length, best quality *double* gut.

Size....	4 to 1	1-0	2-0	3-0	4-0	5-0	6-0
Per doz..	20c.	25c.	28c.	30c.	33c.	35c.	40c.

48598 **Sneck Kendall Hooks**, Spring Steel, tied to full length, best quality *single* gut.
Sizes, 1, 2, 3, 4, 5, 6. Per dozen................$0.25
State size wanted.

48599 **Sneck Kendall Hooks**, spring steel, tied to full length, best quality *double* gut.

Size............	1 to 4	1-0	2-0	3-0	4-0	5-0
Per doz........	40c.	50c.	55c.	58c.	60c.	70c.

FISH HOOKS.—Double Refined Cast Steel.

To determine whether you have the proper size, or to reorder exactly the size you have, lay the hook on the illustration, which it should just cover up. Except that Limerick and Kirby will be short shank.

All best English manufacture. There are cheaper hooks in the market, but we do not carry them in stock, as they are no good for catching fish.

These illustrations show the different sizes of Limerick, Kirby, Carlisle, and all other kinds of hooks as nearly as possible.

The cuts illustrate full size of hooks.

State Kind Wanted.

10/0 1/0 9/0 1½ 8/0 2 7/0 4 6/0 6 5/0 8 10 4/0 3/0 2/0 1 3 5 7 9 11 12

Fish Hooks—Continued.

48599½ Sneck Kendall Hooks, plain ringed.
Put up 100 of a size in a box. Full filed points. This hook, in our opinion, is the best hook to use for black or big mouth bass, being so shaped it keeps your minnow alive longer than any other hook. It is almost impossible for a fish to drive the minnow up on your line or snell as is frequently done with all other kinds of hooks; if you have never used them, try them and be convinced.

Size	10 to 1	1-0	2-0	3-0	4-0	5-0
Per box	20c.	25c.	30c.	35c.	40c.	50c.

Central Draft Hooks.

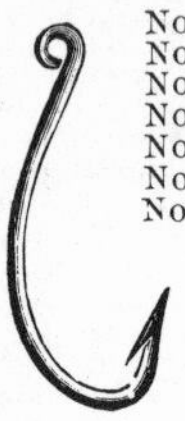

48600 Central Draft Hooks, ringed, filed points.

	Per doz.	Gross.
No. 9, 4⅜ inches long	$0.20	$2.15
No. 10, 4⅛ inches	.18	1.95
No. 11, 3½ inches	.15	1.60
No. 12, 3¼ inches	.10	1.10
No. 13, 2¾ inches	.08	.85
No. 14, 2½ inches	.06	.60
No. 15, 2¼ inches	.05	.50

Sturgeon Hooks.

48604 Sturgeon Hooks, shaped same as No. 48600. Will hold a 500-lb. fish; hook is 6½ inches long.
Per dozen $0.65
Per gross 7.20

Plain Treble Hooks, Ringed.

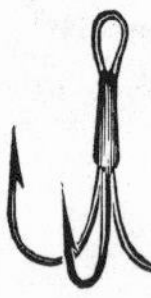

48605 Treble Hooks, plain ringed. Size 9, 8, 7, 6, 5, 4, 3, 2, 1. Each $0.04
Per dozen $0.15

Size	1-0	2-0	3-0	4-0	5-0	6-0	7-0
Per dz	17c.	18c.	21c.	28c.	30c.	35c.	40c.

Sold in any quantity at dozen rates.

Tapered Treble Hooks.

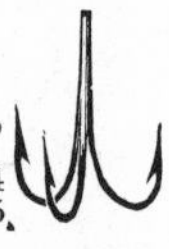

48607 Tapered Treble Hooks. Size, 10, 9, 8, 7, 6, 5, 4, 3, 2 or 1.
Each $0.04
Per dozen ...... .15

Size	1-0	2-0	3-0	4-0	5-0	6-0	7-0	8-0
per doz.	17c.	18c.	21c.	25c.	28c.	35c.	40c.	45c.

Feathered Treble Hooks.

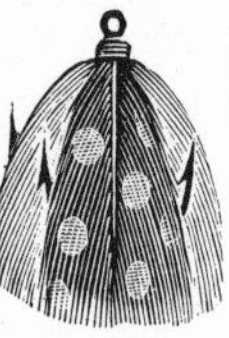

48608

48608 Feathered Treble Hook, don't throw away your spoon bait because the feather is worn out, you can replace the feather treble hook without buying an entire new bait.
Size......10, 9, 8, 7, 6, 5, 4, 3, 2, 1.
Per dozen, 50 cents.

Size	1-0	2-0	3-0	4-0	5-0	6-0	7-0	8-0
Doz.	52c.	55c.	60.	65c.	70c.	75c.	80c.	85c.

Tarpon Hooks.

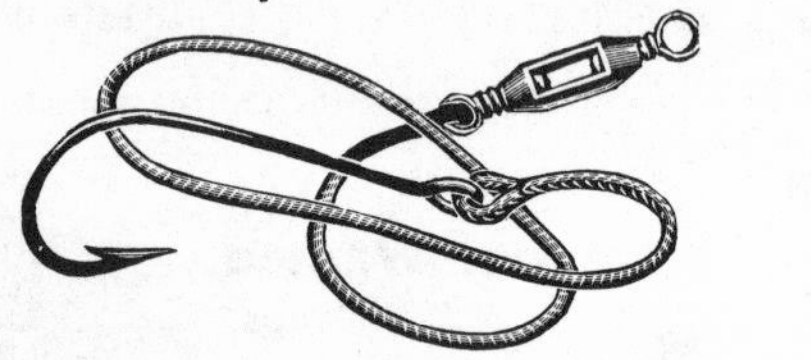

48609 Tarpon Hook, with braided linen snell, wound with copper wire, with improved swivel, forged and bronzed hooks. These hooks are 10-0 in size, are the latest improved patterns for tarpon fishing, and are warranted.
Price, each $0.75

The St. Lawrence Gang.

PATENTED IN ENGLAND AND THE UNITED STATES.

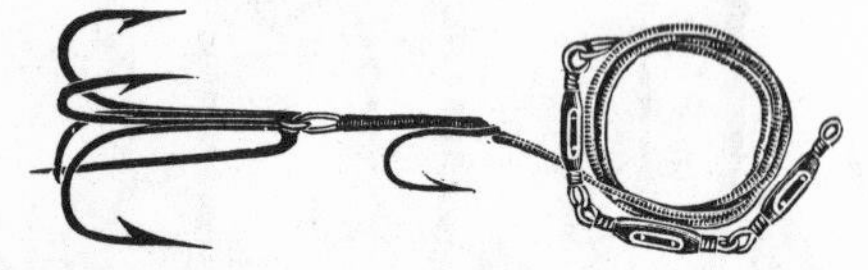

48610—

Nos.	1 to 6,	1-0, 2-0,	3 0
Each	25c	30c	40c

All have patent hooks, with baiting needle, adjustable lip hook and treble swivel, best silk metal wound gimp on hook to attach line to.

This is the most ingenious invention and radical improvement in trolling tackle yet made. Its manifest superiority over all gangs now in use, is evident to every expert angler. A few of the peculiar excellencies are: It is the only gang on which a bait can live. It is the only gang which can be adjusted to any sized minnow instantly and perfectly. It is not only the simplest but also the strongest gang made. It does not scare away the big and wary fish by a long array of treble hooks. The treble swivel insures perfect revolution of bait, and reduces to the lowest possible point the liability of kinking the line.

First Quality of Excelsior Floats.

Wood Floats and Cork Floats. Painted in two colors and varnished, assorted. This is one of the most popular lines of floats.

48611 Egg Shaped Excelsior Wood Float; stick top; painted in two colors and varnished.

	1½ in.	1¾ in.	2 in.	2¼ in.	2½ in.
Each	2c	3c	4c	5c	6c
Per dozen	22c	27c	30c	37c	47c

Cork Floats.

48612 Bound Egg Shape, quill top. Painted in two colors, and varnished.

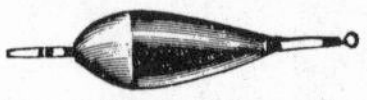

	1¼ in.	1¾ in.	2⅛ in.	2½ in.
Each	4c	5c	6c	8c
Doz.	35c	51c	75c	87c

48613 Barrel Shape, best bound, quill top. Painted in two colors.

	Each.	Per doz
2-inch Float	$0.05	$0.46
2¾-inch Float	.08	.78
4-inch Float	.18	1.75

Brass Box Swivels.

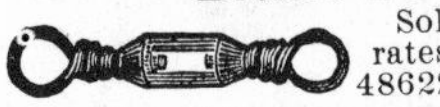

Sold in any quantity at dozen rates.
48622 Brass Box Swivels, No. 8, smallest, ½ inch long; 3-0 largest, 1¾ inch long.

Sizes	1 to 8	1-0	2-0	3-0
Per doz	15c	25c	30c	40c

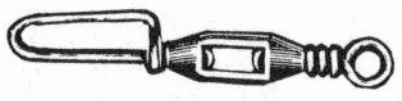

48623 Brass Hook Swivels. Sizes, 1-0, 2, 4, 6, 8. No. 1-0 largest, about 2¼ in. long; 8 smallest, 1 inch long. 1-0 per dozen $0.70
Per dozen, Nos. 2, 4, 6, 8 .... .55

Sinkers.

48627 Patent Adjustable Sinkers. These can be attached or detached by a single turn of the line. No. 1 smallest, ⅞ inches long. No. 7, 2 inches long. No. 10, 3 inches long.

Sizes	1	2	3	4	5	6	7	8	9	10
Per doz.	10c	13c	17c	17c	20c	23c	25c	30c	32c	35c

Sold in any quantity at dozen rates.

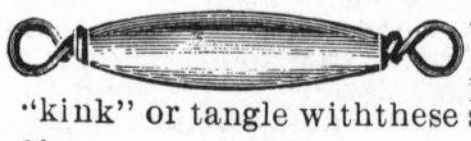

48628 "Pitcher's" Patent Swivel Sinkers. Impossible for your line to "kink" or tangle with these swivels.

Sizes	1	2	3	4	5	6	7	8	9	10
Each	10c	8c	7c	6c	6c	4c	4c	4c	4c	4c
Per doz.	80c	75c	70c	65c	60c	50c	45c	45c	40c	40c

No. 1, largest, is 2½ in. long, weighs 3½ oz.: No. 10, smallest, ⅞ in., weighs ½ oz.

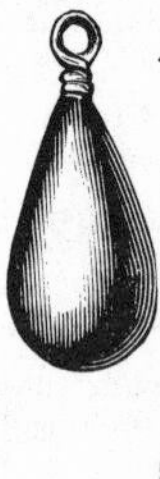

48629 Swivel Dipsey Sinkers. This sinker makes a fine cast sinker; the No. 5 is the size to use when you want to practice bait casting; all experts use this sinker.

Sizes	1	2	3	4	5	6	7	8
Each	6c	7c	8c	6c	5c	4c	4c	4c
Per doz.	70c	65c	60c	55c	50c	40c	35c	30c

No. 1 is the largest, 3½ oz.; No. 8, smallest, ¼ oz.

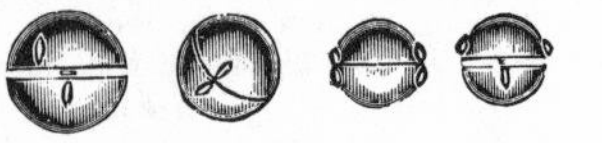

48630 The "Mackinac," sinker is easily adjusted to the line; top and bottom screws together.

Sizes	1	2	3	4
Per dozen	15c	20c	25c	30c

No 1, smallest, ⅛ of an oz; No. 4, ¼ of an oz. Sold in any quantity at dozen rates; postage, 1c per dozen extra.

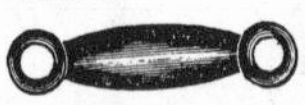

48632 Ringed Sinkers.

No. 1.	Nos.	Per doz.
Smallest	1, 2, 3, 4.	$0.08

Nos	5	6	7	8	9	10
Per doz	9c	10c	15c	18c	20c	25c

No. 1 smallest, ¾ inch long. No. 10 largest, 3 inches long, weight 2¼ oz.

Split Shot.

For light sinkers and fly casting when it is windy. By mail, 1 cent extra per box.

	Per box.	Per doz. bxs.
48635 Split Shot for sinkers, ⅛ gross in wood box	$0.03	$0.20

Gut Leaders.

Always thoroughly soak your leader before you use it. If you do not you are liable to lose not only your leader, but your fish as well. It always pays to carry a leader box made for this very purpose; see description of them under No. 48806. This advice applies equally as well to flies.

48640 Spanish Silkworm Gut.

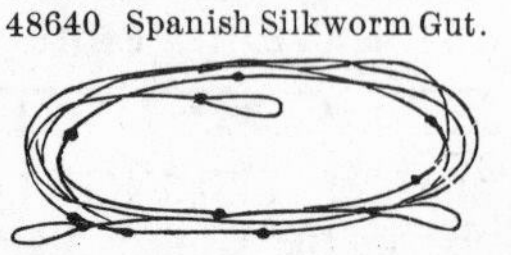

Leaders, 3 ft. single.
Each $0.03
Per doz ...... .20
Leaders, 3 ft. double.
Each $0.05
Per doz ...... .35

Gut Leaders—Continued.

	Each.	Per doz.
48641 Leaders, good heavy.		
3 ft. single	$0.04	$0 30
6 ft. single	.05	.50
9 ft. single	10	1.00
48642 Leaders, good, extra heavy.		
3 ft. single	.06	.65
6 ft. single	.10	1.00
9ft. single	.15	1.50
48642½ Leaders, heavy Bass and Salmon		
3 ft. single	.15	1.50
6 ft. single	.30	3.00
9 ft. single	.45	4.50
48643 Leaders, regular quality.		
3 ft. double	.08	.86
6 ft. double	.14	1.65
9 ft. double	.25	2.70
48644 Leaders, best, heavy, double.		
3 ft. double	.20	2.25
6 ft. double	.37	4.00
9 ft. double	.60	6.50
48645 Special Grade, made for us expressly, from large and heavy selected gut, each leader tied on card.		
3 ft. single	.05	.40
6 ft. single	.10	1.00
9 ft. single	.15	1.50
48646 Special Grade, same as 48645, except double.		
3 ft. double	.10	1.00
6 ft. double	.15	1.50
9 ft. double	.25	2.25
48647 Leaders, spliced knot, twisted.		
3 ft. long	.20	2.00
6 ft. long	.40	3.60
9 ft. long	.75	5.00

Silkworm Gut.

48648 Put up 100 in a bunch.
12 11 inches long, fine, per bunch $0.40
10 11 inches long, heavy, per bunch .... .75
8 11 inches long, heavy, per bunch 1.00
6 11 inches long, heavy, per bunch 1.50

Trout Flies and Hackle.

Our stock of trout flies is made up of the best known and most popular varieties and patterns, and adapted to all waters and seasons. We selected the most popular and best killing varieties made, and carry them in stock in three grades. viz.: A, B and C; grade C being the best fly made; the B grade, the standard fly (sold by many dealers as the *Best*) and the grade A being the same fly with less hackle and wing, and cheaper quality of tying. All of our flies are tied on Harrison spring steel needle pointed sproat hook and guaranteed as such. We list and describe the following most popular styles:

Sizes of hooks, 6, 8 and 10. These are the sizes used by expert fly fishermen. All flies tied on best single gut. Always mention name and grade wanted when ordering flies. *We guarantee our flies to be a better quality grade for grade than any other dealer can furnish at these prices. A comparison is all we ask.*

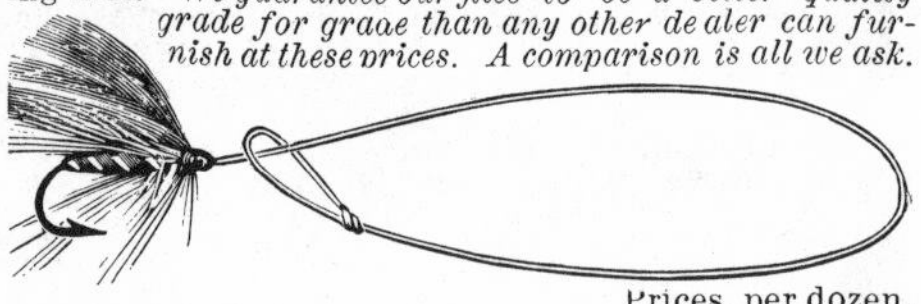

Prices, per dozen, 6, 8 and 10 hooks.

Always mention size of hook, name and grade wanted.	A	B	C
48650 PROFESSOR, yellow body, gold bound and tipped scarlet tongue, ginger hackle, black and white mottled wing	$0.20	$0.35	$0.50
48651 GOVERNOR ALVORD, peacock body, cinnamon hackle, dark gray or mouse colored wing		.35	.50
48652 REUBEN WOOD, white silk plush body, light brown hackle, light mottled wing		.35	.50
48653 BROWN DRAKE, dark brown body, black and gray hackle, brown mottled wing		.35	.50
48654 KINGFISHER, red body, wound and tipped with gold, fawn colored hackle, light gray and white mottled wings		35	.50
48656 MARCH BROWN, light brown body, dark ginger hackle, brown and gray wing	.20	.35	.50
48659 JUNGLE COCK, gold body, black and brown hackle, light brown mottled wing	.20	.35	.50
48660 CARDINAL, silver body, fawn colored hackle, garnet and black mottled wing		.35	.50
48661 YELLOW SALLIE, yellow body, bound with gold, light yellow hackle, yellow tongue, canary wing		.35	.50
48663 TURKEY BROWN, dark brown body, wound with red silk, ginger hackle, gray and brown mottled wing		.35	50
48665 BEE, body black in center, tipped at each end with yellow and white silk, ginger hackle, dove colored wing		.35	.50
48667 ROYAL COACHMAN, royal scarlet body, bound in center with turkey, bronze plush, dark cinnamon hackle, miller white wing		.35	.50
48670 CINNAMON, orange and gold wing, ginger hackle, cinnamon colored, woodcock wing		.35	.50
48671 WHITE MILLER, white silk plush body, white hackle, white wing	.20	.35	.50
48672 GREEN DRAKE, gold body wound with Turkey plush, dark cinnamon hackle, mottled canary bird wing	.20	,35	.50
48673 COACHMAN, peacock silk plush body, ginger hackle, white wing	.20	.35	.50

Tackle—Continued.

Price, per doz. 6, 8 and 10 Hooks.

48674 MONTREAL, purple body bound with gold, royal purple hackle, dark brown wing .... .20 .35 .50
48675 IBIS, scarlet body, bound with gold, red hackle, crimson tongue and wing .... .35 .50
48676 CAPTAIN, black body, gold tipped, dark ginger hackle, white wing .35 .50
48680 EVENING DUN, silk wound scarlet body, gold tipped, dark hackle, light dove colored wing .... 35 .50
48681 SILVER DOCTOR, silver bound body, yellow hackle, variegated colored wing .... .35 .50
48682 SETH GREEN, green body bound with gold, fawn colored hackle, brown dappled wing .... .35 .50
48683 CAPT. SCOTT, turkey bronze body, tipped with red, black hackle, light gray and white dapple wing.... .35 .50
48684 COW DUNG, dark brown body, light brown hackle, dove-colored wing, tied on best single gut $0.20 $0.35 $0.50
48685 QUEEN OF WATERS, large body, silver bound, dark ginger hackle, light mottled black and white wing .... .35 .50
48686 JUNE, body in rings of two colors (white and red) black hackle, brown and black hackled wing...... .35 .50
48690 GRIZZLY KING, green body, bound with silver, red tongue, gray and black hackle, light gray and dark brown mottled wing .... .20 .35 .50
48691 DARK COACHMAN, wings, lead color; body, peacock herl, legs, brown hackle .... .20 .35 .50
48692 BROWN PALMER, wings, red; body, red silk wound with a brown hackle .... .20 .35 .50
48693 BROWN PALMER, green body; body, green silk, wound with brown hackle .... .20 35 .50
48694 BROWN STONE, wings, brown mallard; body, brown mohair; tail, brown mallard legs, dark brown hackle .... .35 .50

48694½ We can furnish any of the above named flies on 3, 4 and 5 hooks in grade "C" only. Price pr dz. $0.50

48695½ **MIDGES**, or small trout flies. Superior midget flies tied on Sproat hooks; Nos. 12 and 14 of which the following is a list: Golden Spinner, Royal Coachman, Abbey, March Brown, Black Hackle, Beaverkill, Coachman, Hare's Ear, Professor, White Miller, Great Dun, Brown Hackle, Dark Coachman, Yellow May, Gray Hackle, Red Spinner, Brown Ant, Governor, Grizzly King, Black Knat, Dark Cow Dung. The above selections are "Killers." Per dozen $0.55

Trout Hackle Flies.

Tied on same quality and size hooks and gut as regular flies.
48696 Black Hackle, Brown Hackle, Gray Hackle Grizzly Hackle, Golden or Yellow Hackle, Ginger Hackle, Peacock Black Hackle, Peacock Brown Hackle, Peacock Gray Hackle, Red Hackle, White Hackle....$0.35

Highest Grade Trout Flies.

48698 High Grade Trout Flies, reversed wing, tied on best spring steel hooks, and the best gut in the best possible manner. Names: Black Palmer, Brown Palmer, Gray Palmer, Black Gnat, Beaver Kill, Bee, Captain, Coachman, Royal Coachman, Cow Dung, Grizzly King, Golden Spinner, Gov. Alvord, Hare's Ear, Scarlet, March Brown, Dark Montreal, Parmachenee Bell, Professor, Queen of Waters, Silver Doctor, Shoemaker, White Miller, 3, 4, 6, 8, 10 and 12 hooks. Each $0.10
Per dozen 1.00
In ordering give catalogue number and name of fly and size of hook.

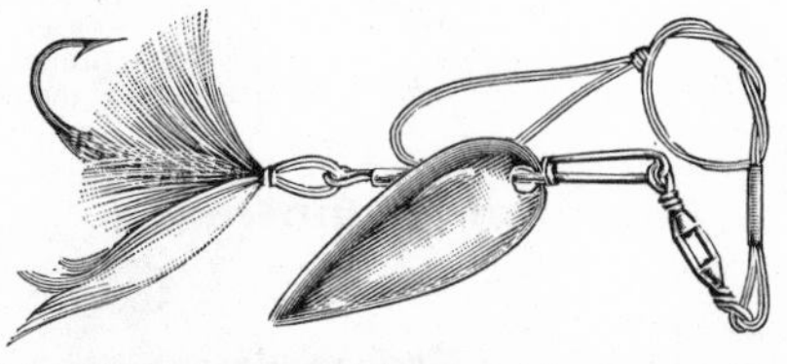

48705 The Spinning Coachman, with spoon and loop combination; the best thing now on the market for black bass and trout. Suitable for all kinds of water; it has swivel and gut leader, and with the loop, if you are not having success you can change your fly instantly, without removing the leader or spoon from the line; three on a card, tied on No. 1 sproat hook, Coachman, Queen of the Waters and Governor, *three on a card*. Per card $0.25
48706 Same description as 48705 with Coachman, Silver Doctor and Lake George, three on a card. Per card .... .25
48707 Same description as 48705 with Coachman, Blue Professor, Gold Brown. Three on a card. Per card $0.25

WE CAN FURNISH ANYTHING YOU WANT IN THE WAY OF FISHING TACKLE, SPORTSMEN'S SUPPLIES, ETC. IF YOU DON'T SEE IT QUOTED HERE WRITE US FOR PRICES.

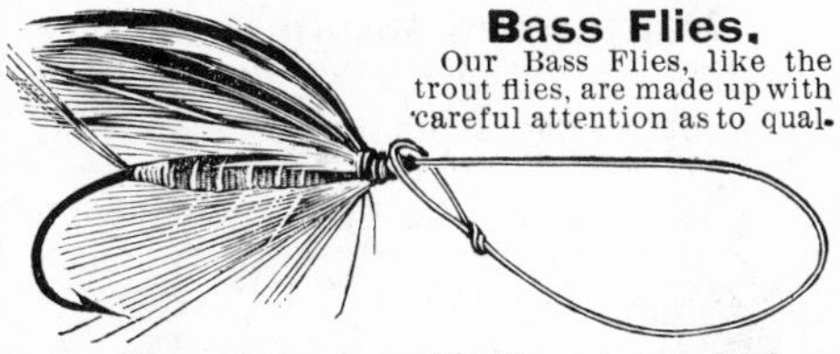

Bass Flies.

Our Bass Flies, like the trout flies, are made up with careful attention as to quality, workmanship and combination of natural colors. They are tied on best spring steel needle, pointed Limerick and Sproat hooks. Sizes 1 and 2 | 1 | 0, 2 | 0, | 3 | 0, hooks, nicely mounted on cardboard. By mail 2 to 4c. per dozen extra. Sold in any quantity at dozen prices.

The Famous Buck Tail.

48715 This fly does not mat when wet; it is one of the best for black bass; it is made (as its name implies) from the tail of a buck deer and has been used with great success. they are Tied to double gut. We can furnish them in No. 1, 1 | 0, 2 | 0 or 3 | 0 hook.
Price, each $0.08
Per dozen .... .75
48716 Bass Flies, consisting of the following styles: Windsor, Sweep, Oak, Olive, Montreal, Professor, Cock Robin, Captain, Governor, Soldier, Snowflake, Polka, Golden Ibis, Lake Huron, White Miller, March Brown, Lake Erie and Scarlet Ibis.
Each ....$0.10 Per dozen $1.00

Extra Fine Special Bass Flies.

Ea. Per dz.

48717 SETH GREEN, tied to finest double gut on best steel spring Sproat hooks, made of the very best material, gold plush body, green neck, silver tipped, mottled tongue, heavy brown hackle, wing of female mallard, brown mottled feather. Sizes, 4-2-1, 1 | 0, 2 | 0 and 3 | 0 hooks...$0.15 $1.25
48718 Tipperlin, silver and scarlet body and tongue, gilt neck, black and gray hackle, guinea hen wing. Sizes, 1 | 0, 2 | 0 and 3 | 0 hooks .... .15 1.25
48719 ROYAL COACHMAN. Sizes, 1 | 0, 2 | 0 and 3 | 0 hooks .... .15 1.25
48720 PROFESSOR. Sizes, 1 | 0, 2 | 0, and 3 | 0 hooks .... .15 1.25
48721 BLACK JUNE, peacock breast body, gold tipped, hair tongue, black hackle, raven wing. Sizes, 1 | 0, 2 | 0 and 3 | 0 hook .... .15 1.25
48722 GRIZZLY KING. Sizes, 1 | 0, 2 | 0 and 3 | 0 hooks .... .15 1.25
48723 MARCH BROWN. Sizes, 1 | 0, 2 | 0 and 3 | 0 hooks .... .15 1.25
48724 SILVER DOCTOR. Sizes, 1 | 0, 2 | 0 and 3 | 0 hooks .... .15 1.25
48725 Good Bass Flies, well made and durable, generally sold by dealers as the best. We have the following styles: Seth Green, Tipperlin, Royal Coachman, Professor, Black June, Grizzly King, March Brown, Silver Doctor. Sizes 4—2—1, 1 | 0, 2 | 0 .... .06 .60

Job.

We have a quantity of fresh new *Bass Flies*, and good ones too, which we will close out at 15 cents per dozen; assortment of *our own selection*, mostly 3 and 4 hook.

Artificial Baits.

We have selected the best and most used baits, all of which we can recommend. Any bait not satisfactory at the price can be returned as soon as examined.

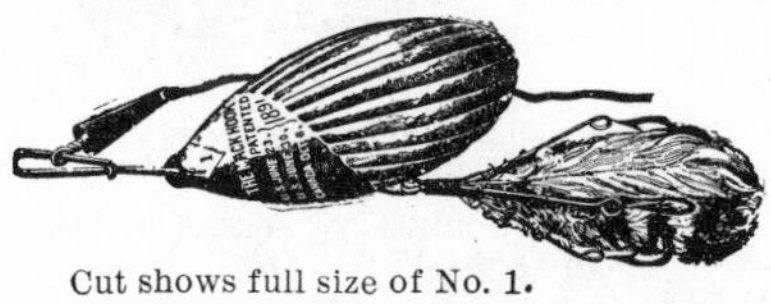

Cut shows full size of No. 1.

The Mack Automatic Trolling Bait.

WEEDLESS HOOK.

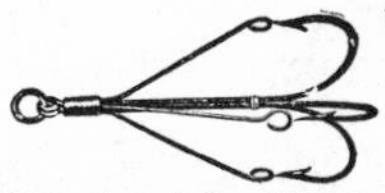

Showing style of hook.

The Mack Automatic Weed Deflecting Trolling Bait. The hook or spring retains its normal or natural position until struck by the jaws of the fish; when so struck the hooks instantly spread and are fastened to the jaws of the fish, and can only be removed after the fish is caught. Hooks are made of the best spring wire, and are so made that the point can not catch weeds. Spoons all nickel plated. Prices are for baits and feathered hooks complete.

48726 No. 1, spoon 1 inch long, each $0.30
No. 3, " 1¼ " " " .... .35
No. 5, " 1⅜ " " " .... .38
No. 7, " 2 " " " .... .42
No. 9, " 2½ " " " .... .46
No. 11, " 3 " " " .... .50

The Hawthorne Bicycle, at $65

Is without doubt the equal of any $100 wheel on the market. Have you our Special Bicycle Catalogue? It will be mailed free upon application.

Rubber Frogs.

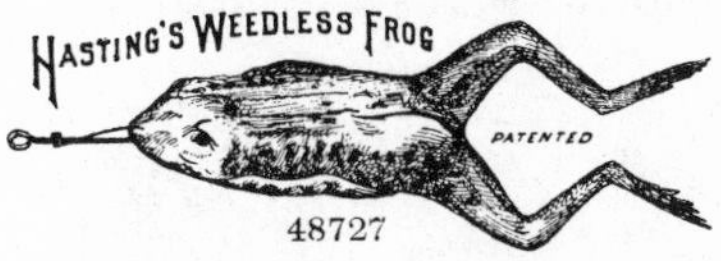

48727

These frogs are made of pure rubber making them indestructible, are painted from life by an artist, and are the most natural artificial bait made. They are about the size of a half-grown frog, and always land in the water right side up, the hook being fully exposed to fish biting. It never fails to hook them in the mouth. This bait will not foul in weeds, being "weedless." Hooks can be replaced if broken. It has no superior. But one size on a 6 | 0 Carlisle hook.
Price, for each, with single hook $0.75
Price, each, for double, with weedless hook...... .85

Payson's Weed Guard Hooks.

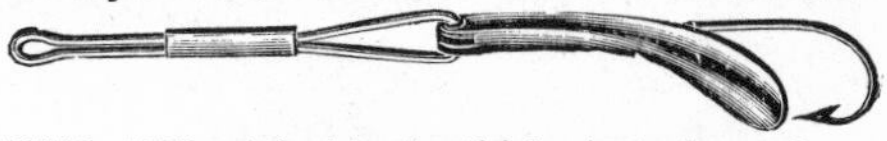

48728 Will not foul in the thickest weeds, will cast a long distance against the wind, will catch more fish than any other device, either in weeds or clear water, casting, trolling, or still fishing; *hooks can be replaced.* Three sizes, 2-0, 4-0 and 7-0. Carlisle, each $0.25

Skinner's New Casting Spoon.

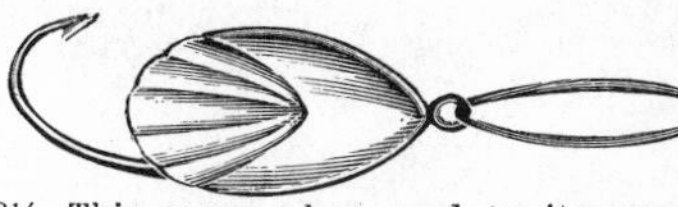

48728½ This spoon when used in its present form is a most killing bass bait; it is equally as good for trout if baited with a small worm. It is tied to Harrison's best Sproat hook on 4-ply gut leader.
No. 1 spoon is 1 inch long. Each $0.25
No. 1-0 spoon is 1¼ inch long. Each .... .25

Skinner's Spoon Bait.

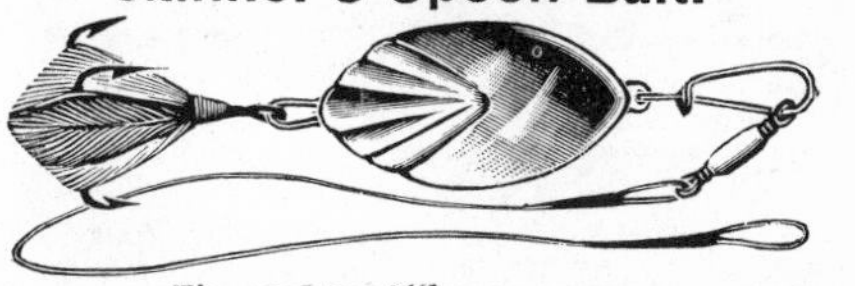

The genuine Skinner spoon.

Skinner's Spoons, Silver Plated.

Each bait is finely plated and mounted with first quality natural color flies. Each spoon has a fine gimp-leader attached to the swivel about 6 inches long. This is the best trolling spoon in the market.
48729 Suitable for black bass, trout, etc.
Nos. 1, 2, 3, 4, 4½, 4¾. Each $0.35
48730 For pickerel, muskallonge, etc.
Nos. 5, 6, medium. Each $0.44
48731 Nos. 7 and 8, large. Each .... .50

Skinner's Spoons, Nickel Plated.

48732 Suitable for black bass, trout, etc.
Nos. 1, 2, 3, 4, 4½, 4¾. Each $0.18
48733 Suitable for pickerel, lake trout, pike and muskallonge; medium. Nos. 5 and 6. Each...... 24
Nos. 7 and 8. Each .... .30

Copper Spoons.

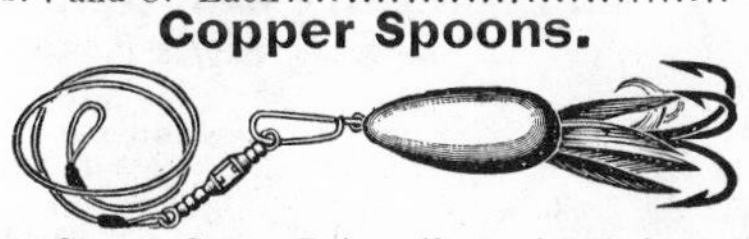

48734 Copper Spoon Bait, silver plated back, oval pattern, for bass, trout, pickerel, pike, etc. One of the best trolling baits. No. 1 is 1 in long, No. 2, 1¼ in., No. 3, 1⅜ in., No. 4, 1⅝ in., No. 5, 1⅞ in., No. 6, 2⅛ in., No. 7, 2¼ in.
Price, each $0.35

Mottled Pearl Spoons.

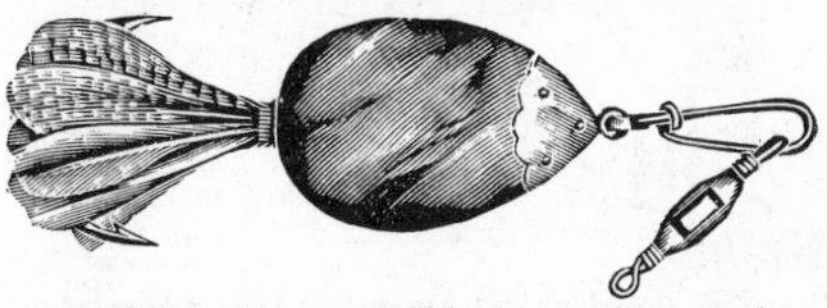

48735 With patent reversible hinge lug, and patent nickel cap which protects the pearl from breaking; without doubt the only practical pearl spoon made.
No. 1 (1 inch pearl) $0.45
No. 2 (1½ inch pearl .... .50
No. 3 (2 inch pearl) .... .60

Black Bass Spinners.

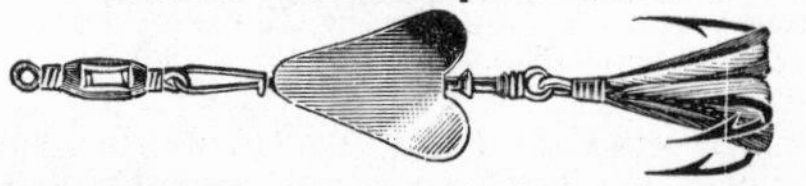

48735½ Black Bass Spinners, finely plated, with swivel, revolving spoon, feathered hooks. Sizes, 1, 2, 3, 4, 5 and 6. No. 6 is smallest. Each.....$0.12
No. 1 is 1⅝ inches long. No. 6 is ⅝ of an inch.

Kidney Spoon Baits.

All good baits.

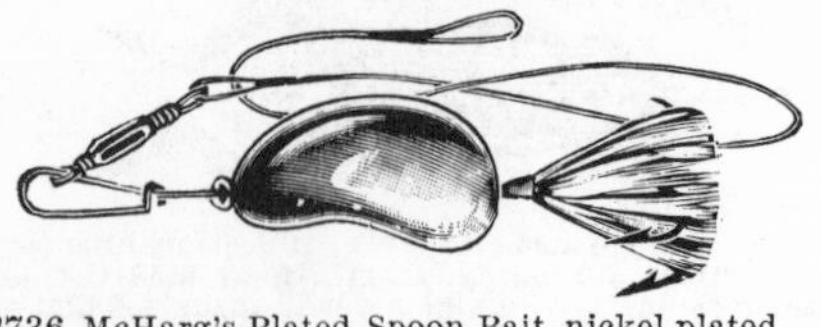

48736 McHarg's Plated Spoon Bait, nickel plated spoons on silver gimp, fine feathered treble hooks. Sizes, 1, 2, 3, 4, 5 and 6. No. 1 spoon is about 1 in. long; No. 2, 1¼ in.; No. 3, 1⅜ in.; No. 4, 1⅝ in.; No. 5 is 1⅞.; No. 6 is 2¼ in. Each $0.15

48739 Pickerel Bait, same shape and sizes of No. 48736, is tinned, with feathered treble hook; box swivel attached without leader; a good one. Each .... .06

48740 Bass, Pickerel or Pike Bait, kidney shape with swivel, without leader attached, same shape and sizes as No. 48736. Each .... .10

Fluted Spoon Bait.

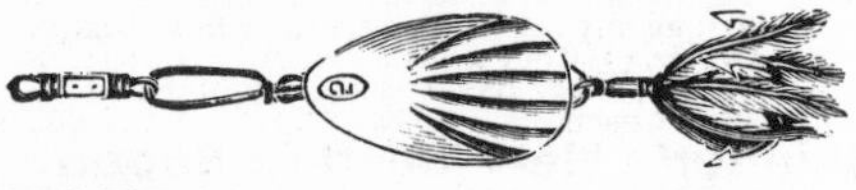

48741 Fluted Trolling Spoons, nickel plate on tin, same shape as Skinner's and same size, treble hook and fly. No. 2 is the smallest. is 1⅛ inch long. No. 8, largest, is 2¾ long. Each $0.07
Per dozen 0.75

48742 Fluted Trolling Spoon, full nickel plate, same shape spoon as Skinner's and same size hook, treble hook and fly, a first-class spoon. No. 2, smallest. 1⅛ inch in spoon; No. 8 spoon 2¾ inches. Nos. 2, 3, 4, 4½, 4¾, 5, 6, 7, 8. Each... $0.10

American Fancy Spinner.

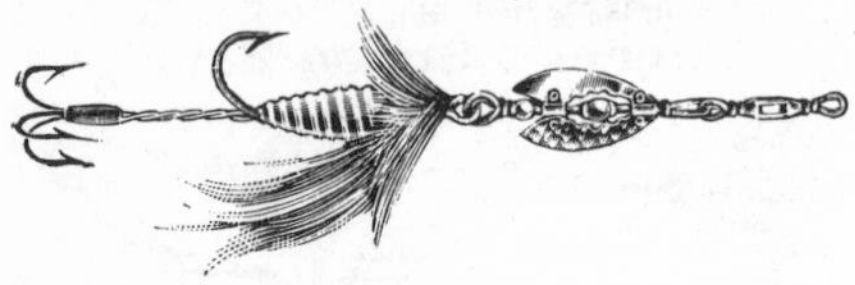

48744 One in a box, brass, nickel plated, fancy flies. They are a very effective bait either for casting or trolling. Spoon is 1⅜ inch. Fly tied on a 3-0 Sproat hook with treble follower....... Each $0.70

American Spinner.

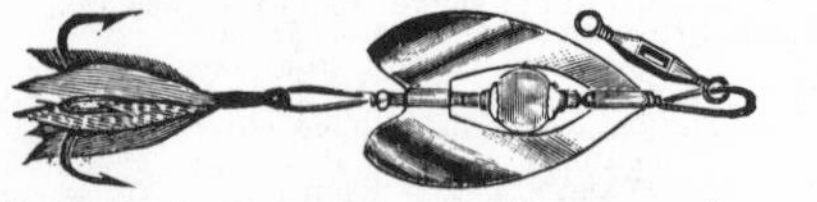

48746 Best Plated Spoon, one-half hammered; best material, and a rapid spinner, for bass, pickerel, etc. Nos. 2, 3, 4, 5 and 6, smallest. Each $0.20

Lightning Ball Bait. A Big Seller.

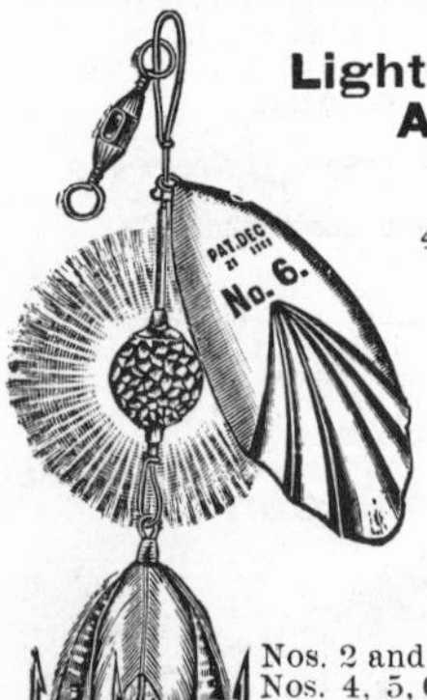

It's a good one.

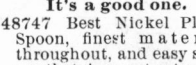

48747 Best Nickel Plated Spoon, finest material throughout, and easy spinner that does not get easily tangled. This is the latest thing out in spoon baits, treble hook and fly; same size spoon and hook as Skinner baits.

	Each
Nos. 2 and 3, Trout, small bass..	$0.20
Nos. 4, 5, 6, Pickerel	.25
Nos. 7 and 8, Muskallonge, etc.	.30

The Admiral Spoon Minnows.

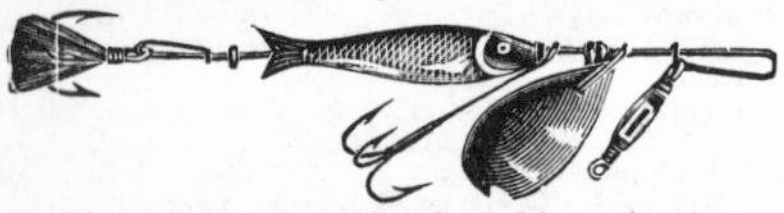

48748 Fine Nickel Plated Spoon, rubber minnows, spoons attached to minnows are assorted fancy metal, best material, treble hook; a good bait for large fish, Nos. 7, 8, 9. Each $0.65

Local dealers and others interested in having you buy at home constantly exaggerate the cost of shipping, to both your and our disadvantage. We will gladly quote both freight and express rates to your town upon request.

Hammered Spoon Baits.

In ordering state kind of fishing wanted for.

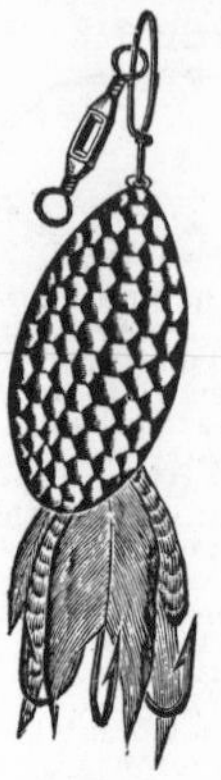

48749

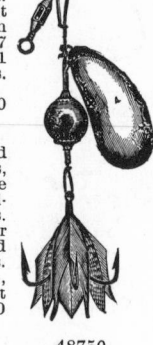

48749 Best Nickel Plated Spoon, feathered treble hook. One of the most successful baits in the market. No. 7 smallest, 1 in.; No. 1 largest, 2½ in. Nos. 1, 2, 3, 4, 5, 6, 7. Each, ... $0.10

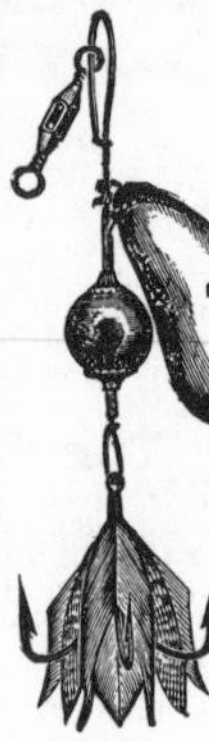

48750

48750 Ball Bait, good nickel plate spoons, feathered treble hook, No. 1 smallest, for small bass. Larger ones for pickerel, pike and muskallonge. Nos. 1, 2, 2½, 3, 3½, 4, No. 1, largest, about 2¾ in. Each. $0.20

Cayuga Lake Spoons.

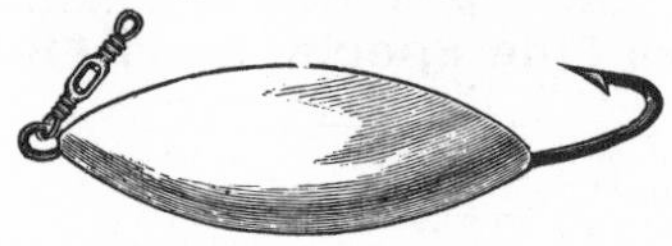

48751 The Salmon Trout Bait, nickel plated, painted red on inside. Sizes, 1, 2-3, 4. No. 1 is the smallest, No. 4 the largest, being 4 inches long. Each $0.25

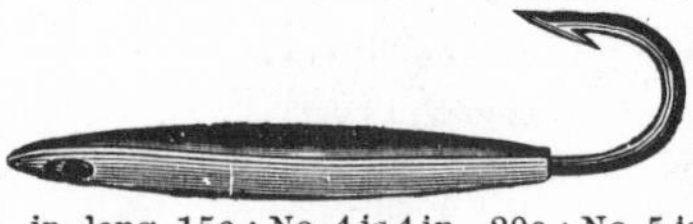

48752 Trolling Squids Diamond Block, tinned, No. 6 smallest, 3 in. long, 15c.; No. 4 is 4 in., 20c.; No. 5 is 3½ in., 25c No. 6 is 3 in., 35c.

The Muskallonge or Tarpon Baits.

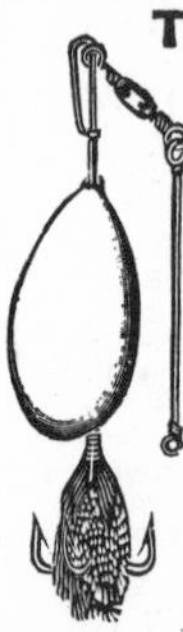

The herculean strength of this bait will tell its own story to the fisherman in the pursuit of large game. For the St. Lawrence, the Western lakes and rivers and the coast of Florida they fill the bill to perfection.

48753 Fine Nickel Plated Spoon, treble hook, feathered, very best material, 2¾ inch spoon for 10 to 25 lb. fish. Each $0.25
3½ inch spoon, for 30 to 100 lb. fish. Each .... .30

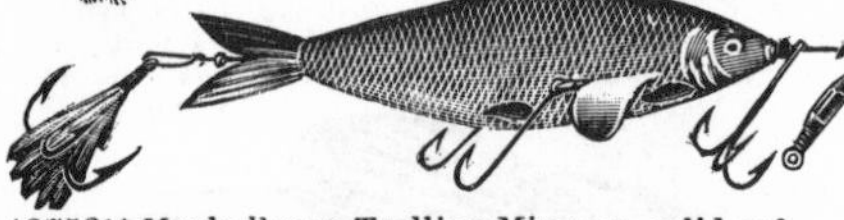

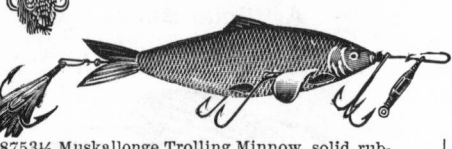

48753½ Muskallonge Trolling Minnow, solid rubber, accurately decorated to represent the live minnow to perfection, the finest bait in the world to capture "Muskey;" entire length of minnow 6½ inches. Price, each $1.25

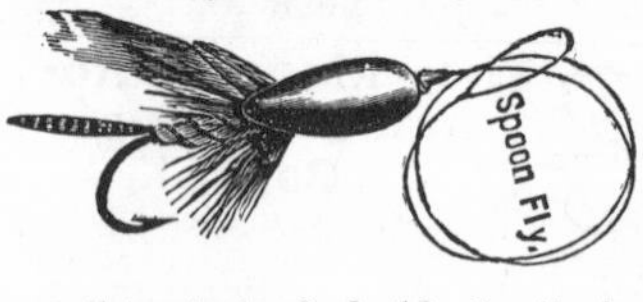

48754 Adirondack Spinner Spoon Fly, smallest nickel spoon, feathered hook for small trout, etc., 8., 9., 10. Small, about ¾ inch spoon; medium, 1 inch; large, 1¼ inch. Each.. $0.15

The Patent Luminous Fish Bait.

The most attractive lure for day fishing and the only successful bait in deep and roily water, and after dark. Every suitable size, style and pattern made for bass, pike, pickerel, muskallonge and other game fish of America. As game fish do most of their feeding by night, luminous bait is the best bait to fish with.

DIRECTIONS.—For day fishing, use same as ordinary baits. For night fishing, expose baits to light during the day.

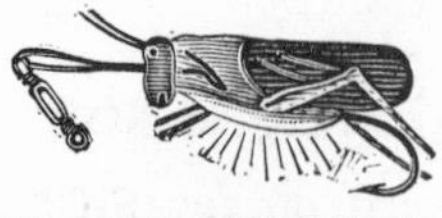

48755 Luminous Soft Rubber Grasshopper. The most natural and most durable article on the market. Each $0.30

IF YOU SEE IT IN THE GUIDE, IT'S SO.

Fish Bait—Continued.

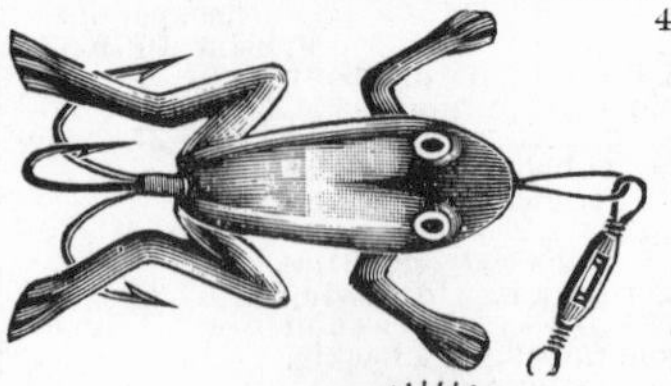

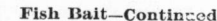

48756 Luminous Soft Rubber Frogs. This bait is a lasting one, combined with luminous qualities. It is a decided improvement over live frogs. Each $0.30

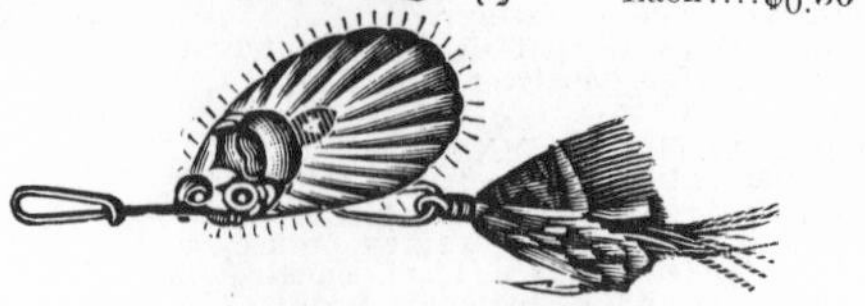

"The Success."

48757 Luminous Fluted Bait, with gimp leader and swivel.

Nos.	5	7	8	9
Each	25c.	35c.	40c.	45c.

Number 5 smallest, about size of Skinner's bait No. 4.

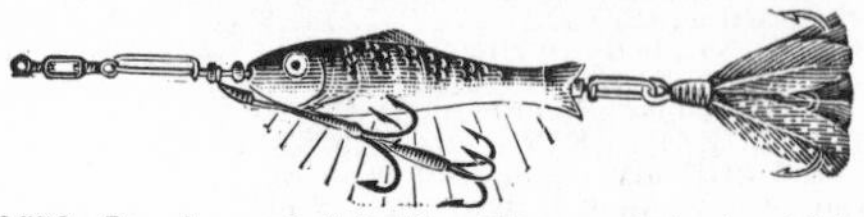

48759 Luminous Soft Rubber Minnow, indestructible. The best imitation of a minnow, finely colored. The "cut" is poor but the bait is the best in the market with single treble gang on side. No. 9 has double treble gang on side, No. 7, No. 8, No. 9. Price, each all sizes, 40c.

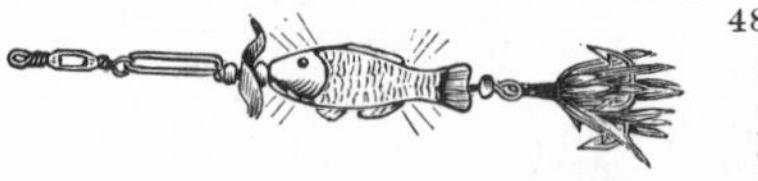

48760—Luminous Crystal Minnow a very attractive lure, and often successful when all kinds fail. Price, each, No. 1 .... $0.30
No. 2 .... .40

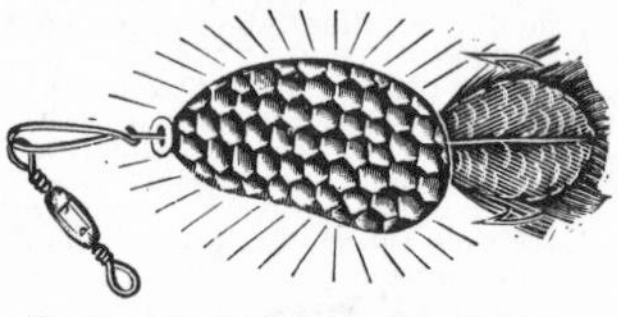

48761 Luminous Kidney Baits. No. 3, small, for trout.... $0.25 No. 4, medium, small bass. Each.... $0.25 Nos. 5 and 6, large, big bass
Each, nickel plated $0.35

Caledonia Minnows.

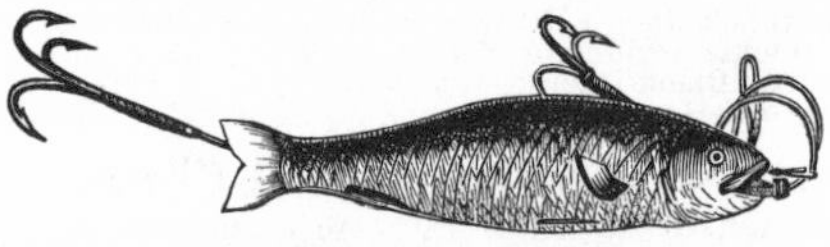

This minnow is made of a hard rubber composition, has glass eyes, is painted to perfection, treble gang on side, and treble gang follower. No. 1 is 1½ inches long. No. 8 is 3¼ inches long.

48762 No. 8, largest, 60c.; No 7, 50c.; No. 6, 45c.; Nos. 5, 4, 3 and 2, 40c. each.

Protean Minnows.

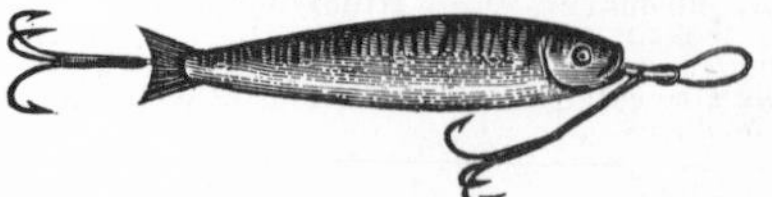

48764 Flexile Rubber. Handsomely painted in colors to represent the live minnow, this minnow is reported, a splendid skittering minnow.

Nos.	1, 2, 3, 4	5	6	7	8
Each	35c	45c	50c	55c	65c

Phantom Minnows.

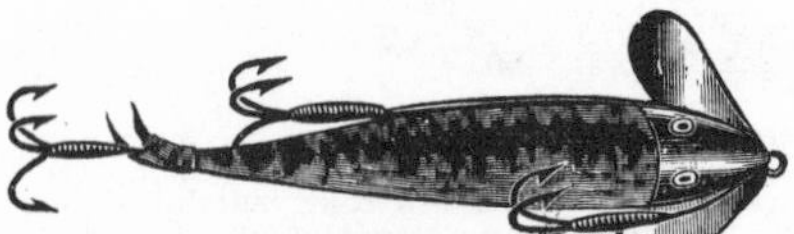

48765 One of the most successful baits made. The body is made of silk, waterproofed, nicely mounted, assorted colors and shades, when put into the water it almost immediately becomes as soft as velvet and as tough as leather, besides having the appearance of a real minnow.

Nos.	2, 3, 4	5	6	7	8
Each		45c	49c	55c	60c

Dobson or Helgamites.

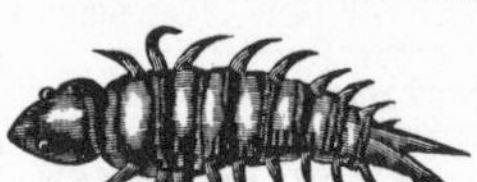

48769 Helgamite, true to nature or Dobson soft rubber, with swivel. Each $0 25

Fish Bait—Continued.

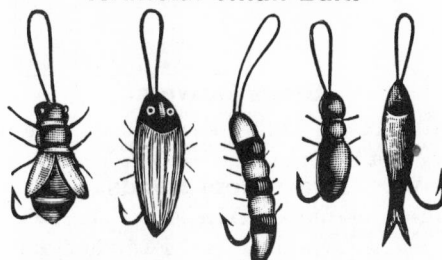

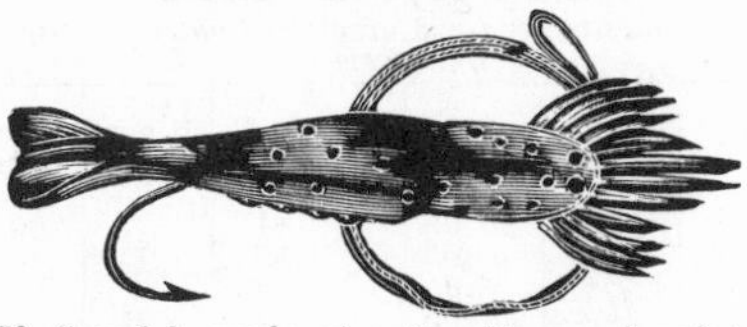

48770 Crawfish, made of soft rubber and painted to imitate the crawfish to perfectiou. Each. .. $0.25
48771 Shrimps, made of soft rubber with hook and snell. Each.................. .... .25

Artiflcial Small Bait.

48773 May Fly, Cricket, Wasp, Grasshopper, Fly Min-now and Froggie. Each.... $0.15
These baits are tied with strong gut loop to a No. 1 Sproat hook

Froggie.

48774 Luminous Small Soft Rubber Frogs. Each................$0.20
48775 Non-Luminous Small Frogs. Each................... ....$0.15

Rubber Angle Worms.

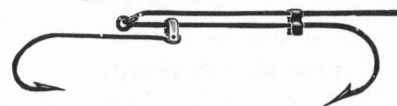

48776 Angle Worms; a perfect imitation, made of soft rubber, no wear out to them, perfect as life. Nos. 1, 2 and 3. Each....................$0.20
Nos. 4, 5 and 6. Each......................... .30
No. 1 is two inches long, No. 6 is 3½ inches long.

Geer's Lever Hooks.

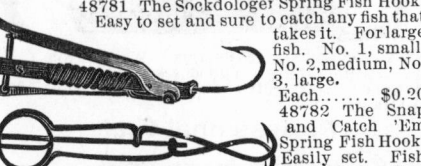

48780 Geer's Patent Lever Fish Hook; no more fish lost and baits to reset: no coming home without your largest fish; a dead sure thing on getting your fish if it bites; it is easily adjusted to all kinds of fishing, by sliding the little clamp on the rod; it is the best hook made for set lines; made on 3-0 Carlisle hooks. Each............. . $0.10. Per dozen.........$1.00

Spring Hooks.

48781 The Sockdologer Spring Fish Hook. Easy to set and sure to catch any fish that takes it. For large fish. No. 1, small, No. 2, medium, No. 3, large. Each........ $0.20
48782 The Snap and Catch 'Em Spring Fish Hook. Easily set. Fish cannot get away once he is hooked.
For small fish
No 20, small, No. 19 medium No 18, large. Each $0.10

Fish Stringers.

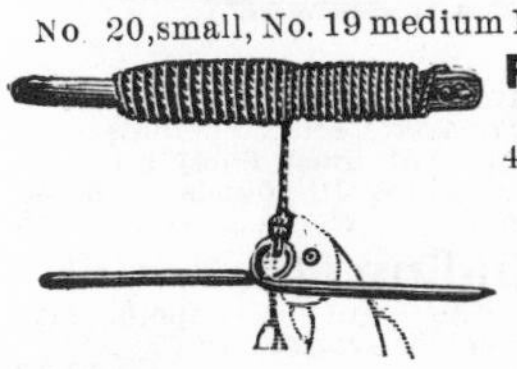

48783 Fish Stringer, No. 1. XC plate, complete with line.
Each.............$0.05
Per dozen. .... .45
By mail, 2c extra.

Cnain Fish Stringer.

48784 Chain Fish Stringers brass links, heavily nickel plated, strong and durable, will hold 100 pounds of fish and not break. Each........$0.25

Nickeled Steel Combined Fish Hook Extractor and Fish Stringer.

RUDOLPH'S STEEL NICKLED

48785 Extracts the hook instantly. Saves time, line, hook and fish. Each.......................$0.18

32--2nd

Fish Hook Disgorger.

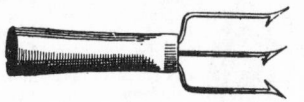

48786½ Fish Hook Disgorger, nickel ptated over steel. Your tackle is not complete without one. Each $0.25

Frog Spear.

48787 Frog Spear, 3 tines, with socket to put pole in. Each...$0.15

48787

Fish Spears.

Lengths given the entire length of prongs; weight, 8 to 12 ounces each

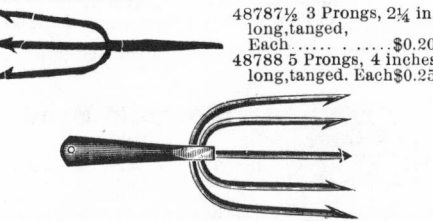

48787½ 3 Prongs, 2¼ in. long, tanged, Each..... .....$0.20
48788 5 Prongs, 4 inches long, tanged. Each$0.25

48789-90.
48789 5 Prongs. 4½ inches, with sockets. Each.$0.50
48790 5 Prongs, 5 inches, with socket. Each.... .65
Lengths given are length of prong.

THE BEST SPEAR on the market

48791 Hand Made Fish Spear, all best steel, except socket and wedge; beards of each tine made on solid shank, screws into socket and makes its own thread in wood (of handle); the outside tines can be removed if smaller spear is wanted at any time by putting in larger wedge: width, about 4¼ to 4½ inches; entire length of tines, about 6½ inches; entire length, 22 inches. Weight, about 1¼ lbs. Each...................$2.25

Fishing Tackle Boxes.

The very best in the market.

Showing comparative sizes of 48793-4.
This is a very practical and ornamental box, made of heavy tin, double seamed and soldered, and will stand hard service.
48793 Single Outfit Tackle Box, 10 spaces, 1 tray and space for small reel; length, 8½; width, 5¼; depth, 2½ in. Each. $0.75
48793½ Double Outfit Tackle Box, 10 spaces, 1 tray space for large reel; length, 10¼; width, 6¼; depth, 4 inches. Each 1.10
48794 Stock Tackle Box, 15 spaces, 2 trays, space for three reels; any amount of lines, hooks, etc. They must be seen to be appreciated. All are made black finish, gilt stripe and ornamen-tation. Length, 12¼; width, 8¼; depth, 6 in....1.88
48795 Pocket size; length, 7¾ inches; width, 4¼ inches; depth, 1 inch; made of tin, well and neatly japanned, gold stripes, has 5 spaces for hooks, lines, etc. Each...... ....$0.50

Borcherdt's Fishing Tackle Box.

48796½ Size, 10¾x7½x 3¾, has 1 tray, space for 2 reels, and any amount of lines, hooks, etc.; has patent pockets in cover. These pockets are made of parchment bond paper, reinforced with tape, and are folded into two pieces of tin, one of which is permanently attached to the cover, the other movably attached by turn buckle. This device adds only ¼ of an inch to the height of box, but practically doubles its capacity. Must be seen to be appreciated.
(Patent Applied For.)
Each $2.85
48797 12½x8x4½; has 3 trays, space for 2 reels, trolling line, etc., and 24 pockets; same description as 48796½; strong as a safe; can use them for a seat. Each 3.00
These boxes were planned by a practical fisherman, and have given satisfaction to all. They are all made of heavy stock, double seamed and soldered, smoothly made and elegantly painted and ornamented.

Pocket Tackle Books.

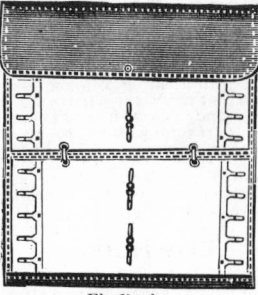

48798 Solid Leather Tackle Books, bound and stitched edges, strap fastening, 6 compartments.
6 inches long..$1.65
7 inches long.. 2.13
48799 Pocket Fly Book, patent celluloid leaves, clip fly holders, morocco leather covered, snap fastening; a good book: 7 inches long. Each......... $1.50

Fly Book.
48800 Pocket Fly Book, made of good, strong morocco colored leather, snap fastening, made of best materials throughout; not a cheap article, but made for service; patent clips; a fine book; 8 leaves, 64 clips, 7 inches. Each...............$1.83
48802 Snake Skin Fly Book, 7 inches long, holds 6 dozen flies, celluloid leaves, celluloid pocket in center, patent clip, pocket front and back, 2 felt leaves in center for keeping flies moist; is handsome and durable. Each...................... 3.50
48803 Pocket Fly Book, leather covered, patent fastenings, well made, patent clips, parchment leaves, 7 inches. Each......................... .75
48804 Pocket Fly Book, leather covered, patent clips, snap fastening, good shape, parchment leaves, but not made of fine material, 6 in. long. .40
48805 "Best South Side" solid leather, fine quality, celluloid leaves, 2 compartment pockets, 2 leather pockets, clips to hold 5 dozen flies, felt pads for keeping flies moist; size of book, 7x4. An elegant book for the money. Price...... 3.00

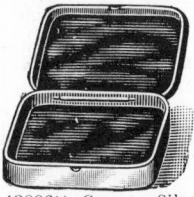

48806 Leader Boxes, heavy nickel plated leader boxes; size, 4½x3¼; has felt pad to keep leaders moist; no more whipping off of leaders or wasting of time trying to get them in shape after you are at your fishing grounds. Each $0.50

48806½ German Silver Fly Box, with pads to moisten flies. Before you start fishing moisten the pads, lay in your flies; by the time you are at your fishing grounds your flies are in perfect shape; will pay its way your first trip; can be used at same time for leaders. Is 6½ inches long and 3 inches wide; it is handsome. Each $1.75

Bait Boxes.

Crescent. Each.
48807 Oval pattern $0.09
48808 Padlock pattern...........................09
48810 Crescent...........................15
48811 Bait Box Straps, leather, ¾ inch wide, 36 inches long......................................20

The Harvard Ice Top Minnow Pail.

48813 Made of tin, neatly japanned. It has perforated ice top cover, to enable one to carry a lump of ice to keep the water cool and minnows fresh.

	6-qt.	8-qt.	10-qt.
Each.....	50c	65c	75c

Rudolph's Celebrated Floating Minnow Buckets.

48816 Handiest, lightest, noiseless and most complete minnow bucket ever put on the market. Will not sink, free circulation of air and water attracts the fish to it, thereby making good fishing around the bucket. No loss of bucket or bait should you drop it overboard. Ice top to carry ice, if desired, to keep the minnows fresh while in transit. When you arrive at the lake drop inside bucket into the water, where it will remain on the surface, the waterproof wire making it so open that it affords a full flow of fresh water all the time, bringing to your minnows the insect food upon which they exist, as well as attracting other fish to it. Weight, 3½ to 5½ pounds.

Quart...	6	8	10	12
Each..............	$1.15	$1 35	$1.55	$1.65

IF YOU SEE it in the Guide, It's So.

Floating Minnow Pocket.

(Rudolph's Patent.)

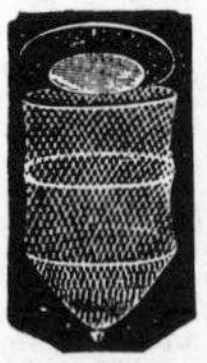

48817
When in use

When several ladies and gentlemen go fishing together, they may provide themselves with Floating Minnow Pocket each, so that when they arrive at the fishing grounds each may have his own minnows, avoiding the necessity of more than one minnow bucket in the party. When not in use are so small that they will go in an ordinary coat pocket and are no thicker than your hand.

48817 Floating Minnow Pocket. Each $0.90

Live Nets.

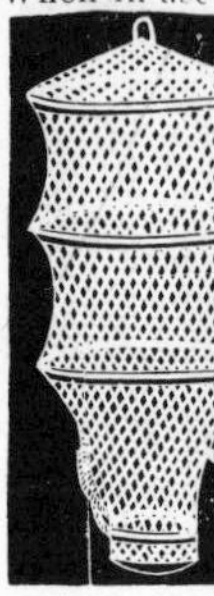

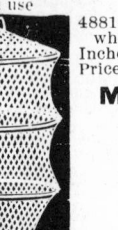

48818 These nets are to put fish in when caught, keeping them alive.

Inches	10	12	14
Price, each	45c.	50c	55c

Minnow Dip Nets.

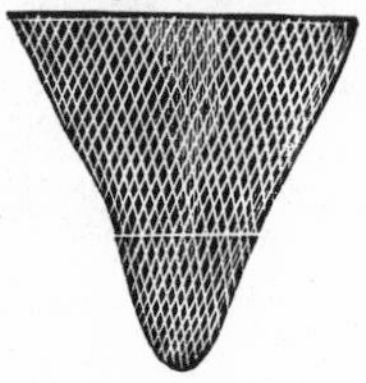

48819-20-21-22

48819 (Linen) Minnow Dip Nets.

Inches deep	16	18	20	24	30	36
Each	35c.	40c.	45c.	50c.	73c.	$1.00

Linen Landing Nets

48820 Inches	20	24	30
Each	25c.	30c.	40c

Braided Waterproof Landing Nets.

(Cotton.)

48821 Inches deep	24	30
Each	60c.	78c.

48822 Crab Nets, made of 12-thread cotton seine twine, regulation meshes.

Inches deep	16	20	24
Each	12c.	15c.	20c.

Landing Net Rings.

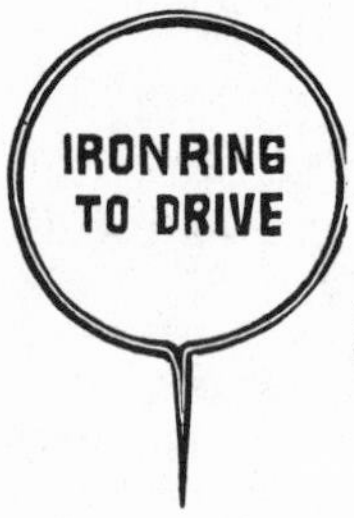
IRON RING
TO DRIVE

48823 Iron Net Rings for landing and crab nets.

Inches, diameter.	12	14	16	18
Each,	15c.	20c.	25c.	30c.

48824 Plain 6 feet Ash Handles for crab and landing nets. Each $0.18

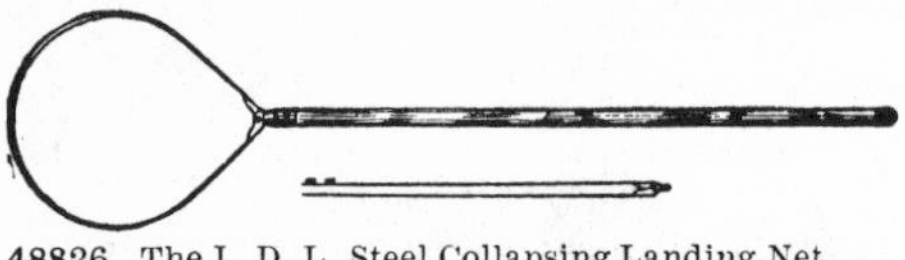

48826 The I. D. L. Steel Collapsing Landing Net and Staff, 30 inch bamboo handle, size of ring, 11¼x13½ inches, packed in a partition bag. This is the lightest collapsing net made. It is simplicity itself and as its name implies I. D. L., it is a net in its most perfect state. Each........$0.95

The "Harrimac" Steel Net Ring.

As good as anybody wants.

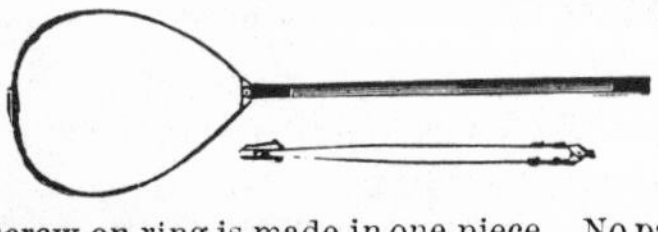

48829 These net rings are very light and strong, made of best tempered steel. The screw on ring is made in one piece. No parts to get lost. Net is left on ring when not in use. Put up in partitioned bag.

No. 9, with 12 inch wood handle. Each........$1.40
No. 10, with 4 foot jointed bamboo handle, each 1.68

Creels.

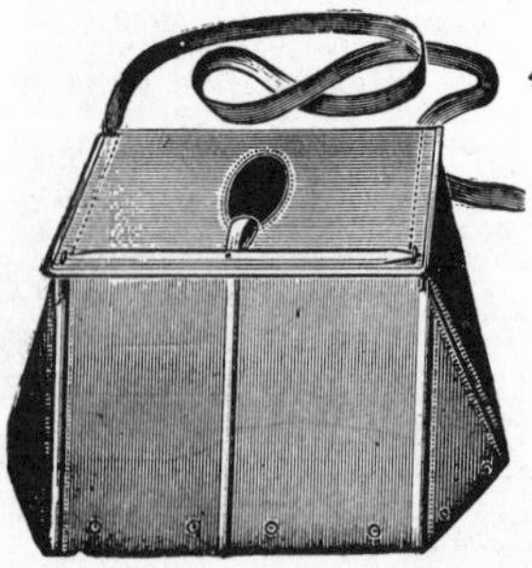

48830 Patent Folding Canvas Creels or Trout Baskets, with shoulder strap, made of heavy brown canvas. Can be folded and carried in large pocket.

(A) Capacity, 12 lbs.........$0.95
(B) Capacity, 20 lbs......... 1.00
(C) Capacity, 25 lbs......... 1.10

Trout Baskets

Weight, 1 to 1¾ pounds.

The baskets have the new patent fastening, instead of the old willow one.

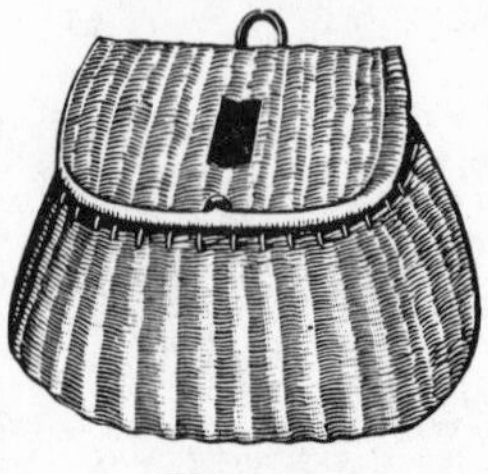

48831 7½x10¾ inches on back..........$0.70
Capacity, 6 lbs.
48832 7½x12 inches on back..............$0.80
Capacity, 9 lbs.
48833 9x13 inches on back $1.00
Capacity, 12 lbs.
48834 9½x14½ inches on back..........$1.25
Capacity, 20 lbs.
48835 16x16 inches on back.............$1.45
Capacity, 25 lbs.

Trout Basket Straps.

48836 Leather Basket Straps. Each..............$0.15
48837 Webbing Basket Straps. Each .... .20
48838 Patent Sliding Straps, leather and web combined.. .25

Mosquito Head Nets.

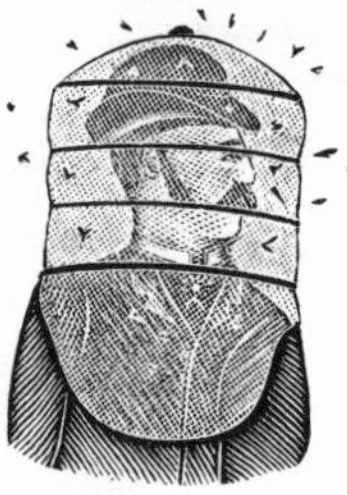

48839 To be worn over the hat or cap. Made of white tarletan. Fitted with five light steel springs. Can be folded up and put in ordinary coat pocket. Weight, 5 oz. Each $0.60

Landing Nets.

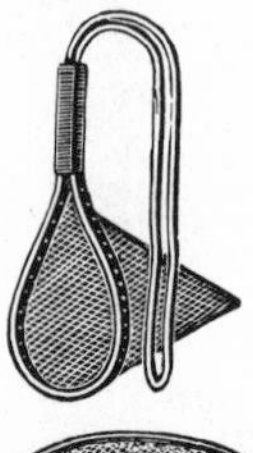

48845 Landing Net, with rubber sling, with light cane frame, with net attached and rubber sling to pass over shoulder. The rubber sling allows the net to be extended towards the fish and when the strain upon the rubber is relieved the net resumes the hanging position at the side. Each $1.00

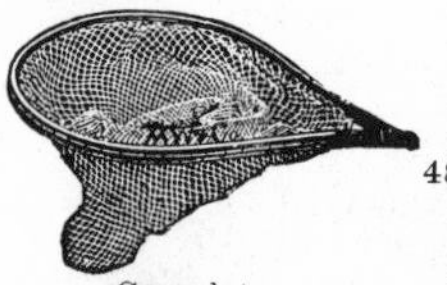

Complete.

This is a fac-simile of our wooden frame landing net, 12 inch screw of handle; a very complete and necessary part of a fishing outfit.

48846 Wooden Frame Linen Landing Net, with 12 inch handle. Weight, about 8 ounces. Each $0.85

48847 Wood Frame Linen Landing Net, with 3 foot screw-off handle, complete with net. Weight, about ¾ pound. Each .... .95
48848 Landing Net, cane bow wound handle, 6 inch handle, bow 9 inch diameter, complete with net. Each.................................... .50

Gaff Hooks.

48849 Gaff Hooks, japanned, with a 3 foot wood handle. Each...................................... .50

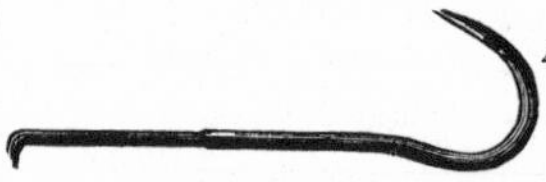

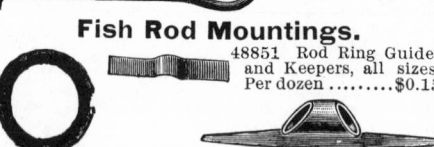

48850 Plain japanned steel. Each..........$0.20

Fish Rod Mountings.

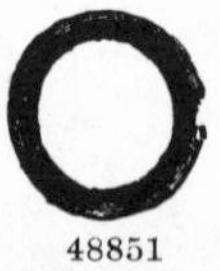

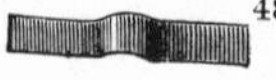

48851 Rod Ring Guides and Keepers, all sizes. Per dozen $0.15

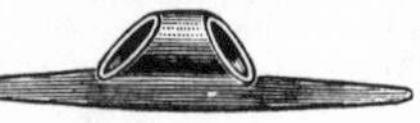

48851 48852

48852 Rod Tie Guides, brass, all sizes. Per doz..$0.25

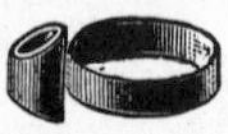

48853 Rod Standing Guide, brass, $\frac{6}{32}$ to 1¼ inch. Per dozen...........................$0.50

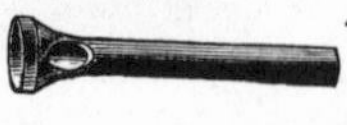

48854 Rod Tips Funnel, brass sizes 6 to 12; No. 6 smallest. Each..... ....$0.10

48855 Rod Butt Caps, solid brass, ¾-inch, ⅞ inch. Each, 8c.; 1-inch, 12c.; 1⅛-inch, 1⅜-inch, 17c.
48856 Rod Screw Butt Caps, brass, ⅞ inch, each, 15c. 1 inch, 18c.; 1⅛ inch, 20c.

The M. W. & Co. Hammerless
SHOTGUN LEADS THEM ALL.
See quotations and description on first page of GUN DEPARTMENT.

Rod Ferrule—Brass.

Measurements are for diameter of *outside* ferrule.

48857-- DESCRIPTION.

No.	Diam. inches.	Plain per pair.	No.	Diam. inches.	Plain per pair.
00	5/32	$0.05	11	11/16	$0.13
0	6/32	.05	12	23/32	.14
2-0	7/32	.05	13	¾	.14
1	¼	.05	14	25/32	.15
1½	9/32	.05	15	13/16	.17
2	10/32	.05	16	⅞	.17
3	11/32	.05	17	15/16	.18
4	⅜	.06	18	31/32	.19
5	13/32	.07	19	1	.19
6	7/16	.07	20	1 1/16	.19
7	½	.08	21	1⅛	.20
8	9/16	.09	22	1 5/32	.20
9	19/32	.10	23	1 3/16	.20
10	10/16	.11	24	1¼	.20

Brass Dowels.

48858 FOR SIZE SEE FERRULE.

Nos. 0, 1, 2, 3............Price, per dozen..........$0.25
Nos. 4, 5, 6, 7, 8.........Price, per dozen.......... .30
Nos. 9, 10, 11,12,13, 14.Price, per dozen.......... .35

Brass Reel Bands.

48859--

Size	¾ in.	⅞ in.	1 in.	1⅛ in.	1¼ in.
Price per set of three,	12c.	12c.	15c.	15c.	20c.
Price per set of three nickeled and polished	18c.	18c.	20c.	20c.	25c.

Brower's Reel Seat Holder.

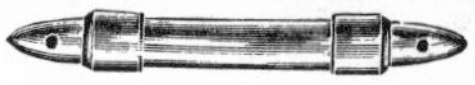

48860 Can be tied to any kind of a rod or pole in five minutes. The best thing in the market, plated. Each...$0.25

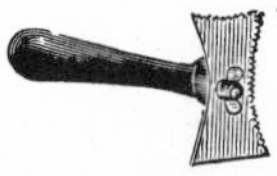

48862 Fish Scale Scraper. Steel plate, iron handle, one end is sharpened to cut off the heads. The best thing out for the purpose. Each...$0.35
Extra by mail, 10c

Fish Rod Mountings.

48863 Lancewood tips, nickel mounted. Each.
For fly rods...$0.50
For bait rods... .75
48863½ Lancewood tips, unmounted,
For fly rods... .35
For bait rods... .50
48864 Split bamboo tips, silk wound, nickel mounted, for fly rods.............................. 1.25
For bait rods... 1.00
48864½ Split bamboo tips, unwound.
For fly rods... .75
For bait rods... .50
In ordering mounted tips you must give size of ferrule.

Fish Rod Cement.

48865 Ferrule Cement for fish rod, in 4 inch stick, waterproof. Per stick..............................$0.15

Fish Rod Varnish.

48866 Fish Rod Varnish, put up in about 2 ounce bottles, best quality, camel's hair brush with each bottle. Per bottle.............................. 0.25

Weigh Your Fish.

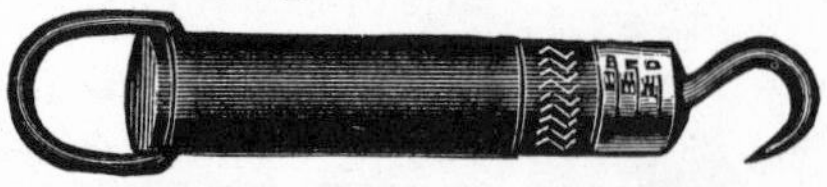

48867 Novelty Spring Balance. Weighs from 1 to 15 pounds, by ¼s. A good scale with tare allowance Every pair warranted perfect. Each..$0.30
Extra by mail 5c.

Professional Scale.

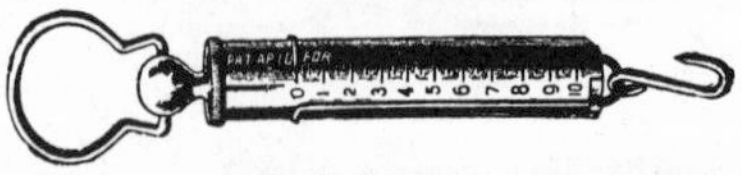

48867½ These scales are made in two sizes, weighing 10 pounds by quarters, and 20 pounds by quarters; they are made of brass finely finished in nickel. Scale weighing 10 pounds.....$0.35
Scale weighing 20 pounds.............................. .45

Rod Winding Silk.

48868 Winding silk, 100 yards on spool, size "A" in black, yellow, green or scarlet.
Price per spool...$0.07

White Ash Oars.

Weight of Oars, 8½ to 15 lbs per pair.

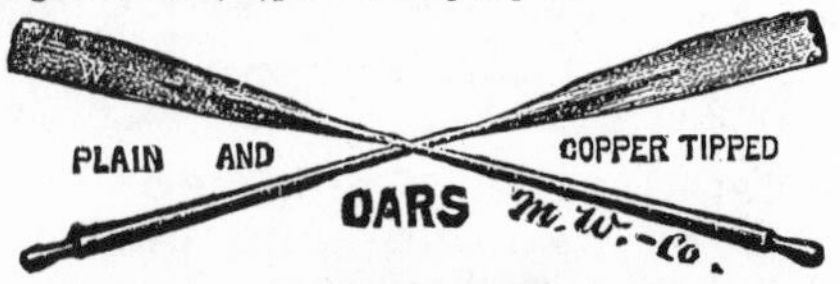
PLAIN AND COPPER TIPPED
OARS
M. W.-Co.

Copper Tipped Ash Oars.

48869 Length,	6 ft.	6½ ft.	7 ft.	7½ ft.	8 ft.
Per pair	$0.88	$0.94	$1.00	$1.12	$1.20
Length		8½ ft	9 ft..	9½ ft.	10 ft.
Per pair		$1.25	$1.32	$1.39	$1.46

Plain Ash Oars.

48870 Length	6 ft.	6½ ft.	7 ft.	7½ ft.	8 ft.
Per pair	$0.78	$0.82	$0 88	$0.95	$1.04
Length		8½ ft.	9 ft.	9½ ft.	10 ft.
Per pair		$1.10	$1.16	$1.19	$1.25

Spruce Oars.

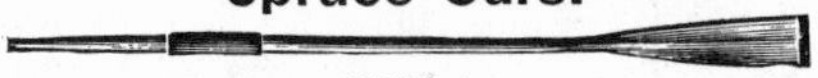

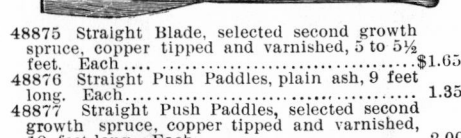

48873-4

48871 Plain Spruce Oars, copper tipped.

Length	6 ft.	6½ ft.	7 ft.	8 ft.
Per pair	$1.20	$1.30	$1.41	$1.60

48872 Spruce Spoon Oars, varnished and copper tipped.

Length	6 ft.	6½ ft.	7 ft.	8 ft.
Per pair	$2.10	$2.25	$2.43	$2.88

48873 Spruce Spoon Oars, copper tipped, leathered and varnished.

Length	6 ft.	6½ ft.	7 ft.	8 ft.
Per pair	$2.35	$2.55	$2.75	$3.15

48874 Regular Straight Spruce Oars, leathered, copper tipped.

Length	6 ft.	6½ ft.	7 ft.	8 ft.
Per pair	$1.80	$1.95	$2.10	$2.40

Straight Blade Single Paddle.

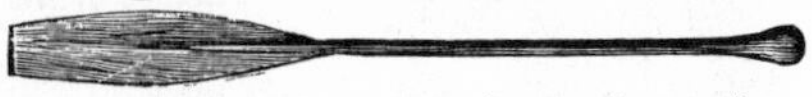

48875 Straight Blade, selected second growth spruce, copper tipped and varnished, 5 to 5½ feet. Each $1.65

48876 Straight Push Paddles, plain ash, 9 feet long. Each 1.35

48877 Straight Push Paddles, selected second growth spruce, copper tipped and varnished, 10 feet long. Each 2.00

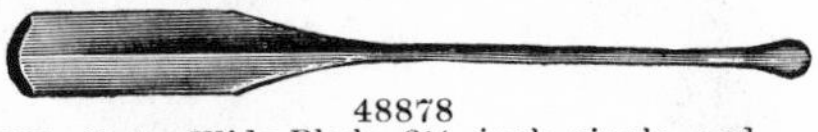

48878

48878 Extra Wide Blade, 6½ inch. single paddle. Single paddles 5 to 5½ feet long. Selected second growth spruce, copper tipped and varnished. Each $2.95

48879 Regular Spoon Blade, single paddle, selected second growth spruce, copper tipped and varnished, 5 to 5½ feet. Each 2.90

Oar Locks.

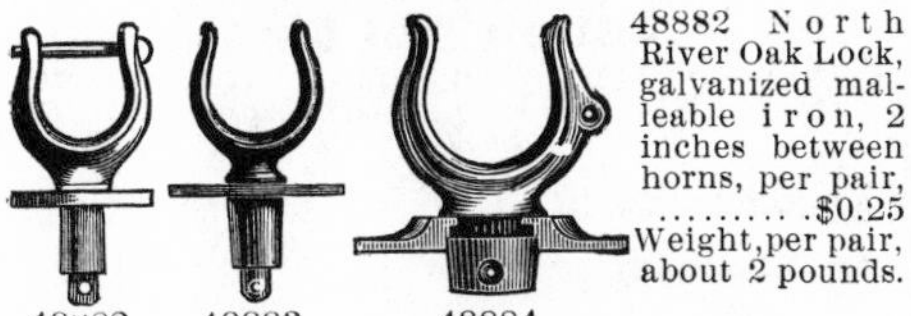

48882 48883 48884

48882 North River Oak Lock, galvanized malleable iron, 2 inches between horns, per pair, ... $0.25 Weight, per pair, about 2 pounds.

48883 Socket Oar Locks, good iron; weight 24 to 50 ounces; width, 1½ inches per pair $0.16
Width 2 inches, between horns, per pair .... .19
Width 2½ inches, per pair .... .25

48884 Patent Swivel Oar Locks, galvanized iron; weight, 48 to 60 ounces per pair, good and strong, one of the best oar locks on the market. Width, 1¾ inches .... .60
Width, 2 inches .... .65
Width, 2¼ inches .... .79
Width, 2½ inches .... .85

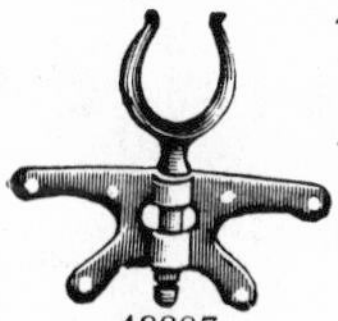

48887

48887 Side Plate Oar Lock, plain, malleable iron. Per pair...$0.35

48888 Round Socket Oar Locks. Per pair...$0.20

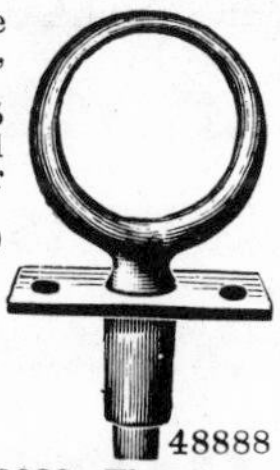

48888

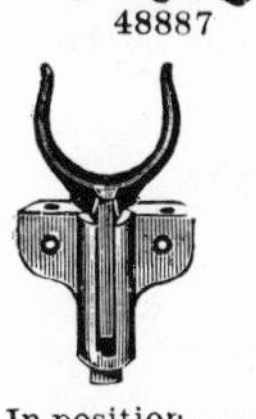

In position. 48889

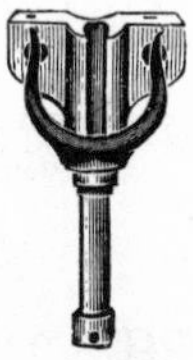

Out of position. Acme.

48889 The Acme Row Lock, galvanized iron. This row lock is designed to be used without a lanyard; and, instead of removing the horns from the sockets when alongside of vessels or wharves, as is required with most other rowlocks, simply turn them half way around, and they fall of their own gravity below the gunwale, obviating the necessity of removal from the sockets, except when it is desired to do so.

Width, between horns, 1¾ inches, per pair $0.70
Width, between horns, 2 in., per pair .... .80
Width, between horns, 2¼ inches, per pair 1.00

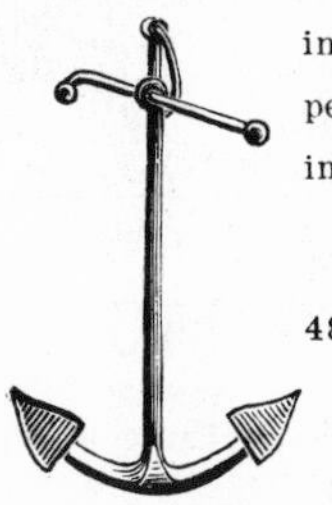

Boat Anchors.

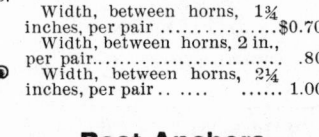

48890 Boat Anchors, black wrought iron, regular shape. Per lb.
6 to 9 lbs $0.12
10 to 18 lbs .... .11
20 to 70 lbs .... .10
75 lbs. or over .... .09

Life Preservers.

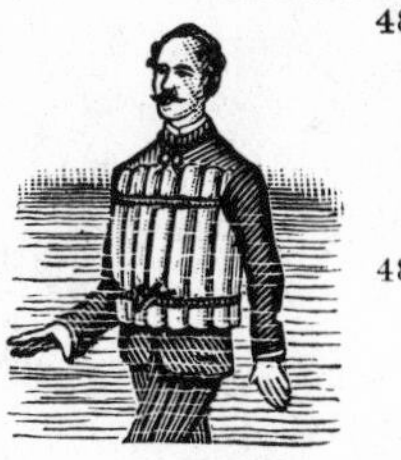

48897 "Never Sink" Cork Jackets, adopted as standard, and the government inspector's stamp on each one, and easily put on, durable and has great buoyancy. Weight, 9 pounds; each $1.25
Per dozen 13.50

48898 Life Belts, in squares, similar to the "Never Sink," and buckles on the same way. One of the best in the market; safe and durable. Weight, 9 lbs. Each ... $1.10
Per dozen 10.20

Lake and River Seines.

Made of the best quality cotton twine, all complete, with buoys, sinkers, etc., except hauling lines. We do not send seines C. O. D.

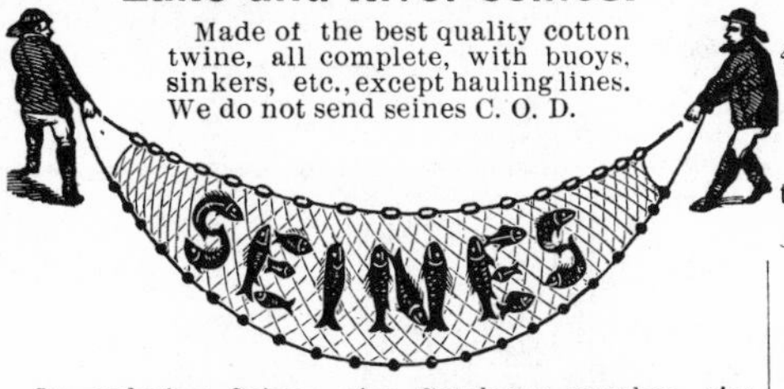

In ordering Seines, give Catalogue number, size wanted and price.

Special prices are given upon request for large Lake Seines and other lengths and depths not in this list.

These Seines all have top line ¼ inch manilla rope tarred, and bottom lines ¼ inch manilla rope tarred, doubled, with reverse twist to prevent rolling. We use new improved cast lead sinkers on all our Seines. Twine, Woodbury's best.

DENNIS--592X

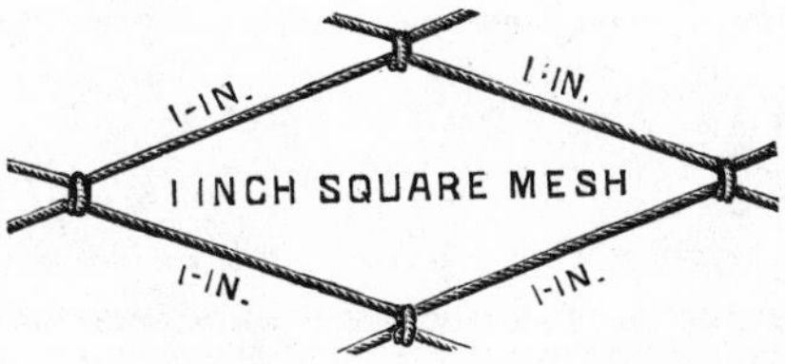

N. B.—A seine mesh is diamond shaped, and a 1 inch square mesh measures 1 inch on each of the four sides. A 1½ measures 1½ on each of the four sides, etc., etc. One inch square mesh is 2 inch stretched mesh; 1½ inch square mesh is 3 inch stretched mesh.

12 THREAD COTTON SEINE TWINE--SQUARE MESH.

No.	Length. Feet.	Depth Center. Feet.	Depth at ends. Feet.	1 Inch Mesh. Pricc.	1¼ Inch Mesh. Price	1½ Inch Mesh. Price.	2 Inch Mesh. Price.
48900	20	4	3	$ 1.40	$ 1.37	$ 1.34	$ 1.30
48901	30	4	3	2.15	2.05	2.00	I.67
48902	40	5	4	3.00	2.82	2.23	2.00
48904	50	5	4	3.75	3.25	2.76	2.44
48905	6C	6	5	4.70	4.56	4.17	3.53
48906	72	7	6	6.10	5.40	5.00	4.30
48907	90	8	7	7.80	7.30	6.70	5.47
48908	100	8	7	8.65	7.70	7.30	5.97
48909	120	10	8	12.00	11.00	10 10	8 50
48910	150	12	10	17.85	15.85	13.40	11.15
48911	180	12	10	21.45	17.55	16.15	13.15
48912	200	14	10	23.90	20.80	18.20	15 10
48913	250	14	10	29.90	26.00	20.30	17.95
48914	300	14	10	35.90	31.20	23 40	21.00

16 THREAD COTTON SEINE TWINE—SQUARE MESH.

No.	Length. Feet.	Depth Center. Feet	Depth at ends. Feet.	1 Inch Mesh. Price.	1¼ Inch Mesh. Price.	1½ Inch Mesh. Price.	2 Inch Mesh. Price.
48915	20	4	3	$ 1.80	$ 1.55	$ 1.50	$ 1.40
48916	30	4	3	2.52	2.27	2.20	2.05
48917	40	5	4	3.25	3 17	3.00	2.84
48918	50	5	4	4.00	3.85	3.65	3.25
48919	60	6	5	5.70	5.27	4.87	4.25
48920	72	7	6	7.43	6.90	6.50	5.65
48921	90	8	7	9.75	8.53	7.80	6.70
48922	100	8	7	11.75	9.22	8.75	7.30
48923	120	10	8	14.60	13.00	12.20	10.15
48924	150	12	10	22.25	19.10	16.45	13.80
48925	180	12	10	26.80	21.55	19.70	15.65
48926	200	14	10	31.20	24.95	22.45	17.95
48927	250	14	10	39.00	31.20	27.95	21.85
48928	300	14	10	46.80	38.25	33.55	25.75

Seines as above quoted are hung with leads, floats and lines ready for use, except hauling lines.

IF YOU SEE It in the Guide, It's So.

Seines—Continued.

48930 **Seines.** In thirty yards (90 feet) lengths or over. No lengths less than 30 yards. The depths given are straight from end to end, and do not taper. Hung with leads, floats and lines. Made of Woodbury's best soft laid twine.

Prices per running yard. 12 Thread—Soft. Prices, per running yard 16 Thread—Soft.

Mesh, Inches	1	1¼	1½	1¾	2&3	1	1¼	1½	1¾	2&3
6 ft. deep	24c	23c	20c	18c	17c	28c	25c	22c	20c	18c
8 ft. deep	28c	24c	22c	20c	18c	33c	28c	26c	24c	22c
10 ft. deep	33c	31c	28c	25c	22c	41c	34c	31c	28c	24c
12 ft. deep	37c	33c	29c	27c	24c	49c	39c	35c	30c	27c
15 ft. deep	45c	37c	33c	30c	26c	54c	46c	41c	37c	32c
18 ft. deep	52c	43c	40c	36c	30c	65c	51c	47c	42c	35c

Straight Seines.

48931 Lake or River Drag Seines, made of Woodbury's best white cotton, soft laid, seine twine. No better seine made at any price. Hung with lead floats and line ready for use. Square mesh.

These Seines are straight from end to end, and do not taper; all complete ready for use.

Length.	Depth.	No. 9 thread. 1 inch Mesh. Price	No. 9 thread. 1¼ inch Mesh. Price	No. 9 thread. 1½ inch Mesh. Price	No. 12 thread. 1 inch Mesh. Price	No. 12 thread. 1¼ inch Mesh. Price	No. 12 thread. 1½ inch Mesh. Price	No. 12 thread. 2 to 3 inch Mesh Price
20 ft.	4 ft.	$1.10	$0.95	$0.86	$1.44	$1.36	$1.34	$1.23
30 ft.	5 ft.	1.93	1.64	1.44	2.25	2.10	2.05	1.94
40 ft.	6 ft.	2.75	2.62	2.34	3.08	2.87	2.67	2.25
50 ft	7 ft.	4.10	3.28	3.08	4.30	3.79	3.49	2.76
60 ft.	8 ft.	4.92	4.30	3.77	5.50	4.71	4.40	3.69
75 ft.	8 ft.	6.15	5.14	4.71	6.75	5.85	5.54	4.41

Cotton Netting (white) only. Just the Netting; no Floats, Leads or Lines.

48941 12 Thread, soft twine, 1 inch square mesh, or larger, per lb $0.48
48942 16 or 20 Thread, soft twine, 1 inch square mesh, or larger, per lb .... .45
48943 12 Thread, medium twine, 1 inch square mesh, or larger, per lb .... .50
48944 15 or 18 Thread, medium twine, 1 inch square mesh, or larger, per lb .... .47

Can furnish any depth required.

When ordering seines or netting give full description of what is wanted, and state if length ordered is just the length wanted, or you want it to hang a net that length.

Creek Seines—Square Mesh.

Half inch Mesh Center. One inch Mesh Ends.

No.	Depth.	4 Ft. Price.	5 Ft. Price.	6 Ft. Price.	7 Ft. Price.
48945	10 ft. long	$ 1.15	$ 1.40	$ 1.90	$ 2.10
48946	15 ft. long	1.70	2.00	2.75	3.10
48947	20 ft. long	2.20	2.70	3.25	4.00
48948	25 ft. long	2.70	3.25	4.00	5.00

Each end of a Creek Seine is of 1 inch mesh; ⅓ the length of seine in center is ½ inch mesh.

When ordering seines give size and price as well as catalogue number.

Minnow Seines.

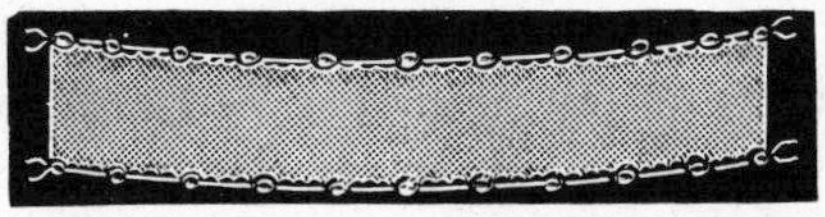

HUNG WITH LEADS AND FLOATS. ⅜ INCH SQUARE MESH.

Minnow seines are the same width from end to end. Runs from 3½ to 5¾ feet to the pound.

No.	Depth.	3 Feet. Price	4 Feet. Price.	5 Feet. Price	6 Feet. Price.
48950..	10 ft. long.....	$2.00	$2.85	$3.40	$3.85
48951..	12 ft. long.....	2.40	2.90	3.55	4.00
48952..	15 ft. long.....	3.00	3.75	4.25	4.85
48953..	20 ft. long.....	4.00	5.00	5.70	6.10
48954..	25 ft. long.....	4.95	5.70	6.70	7.50

Rigged ready for use except hauling line.

When ordering seines, give size and price as well as catalogue number.

The M. W. & Co. Hammerless Shotgun LEADS THEM ALL

THOROUGHLY UP TO DATE.

We sell the $65.00 grade, finely engraved, with Damascus barrels, for $35.00. The $50.00 grade, same engraving, best stub twist barrels, $29.00.

Seines—Continued.

Minnow Seines, hung with floats and leads ready for use except hauling lines, ¼-inch square mesh. Runs 3¼ to 2½ feet to the pound.

No.	Depth.	3 Feet. Price.	4 Feet. Price	5 Feet. Price.	6 Feet. Price
48970..	10 ft. long.....	$2.85	$3.40	$4.35	$5.25
48971..	12 ft. long.....	3.45	4.05	5.30	6.50
48972..	15 ft. long.....	4.25	4.85	6.50	8.10
48973	20 ft. long	5.55	6.50	8.60	10.75
48974..	25 ft. long.....	6.90	8.10	10.75	13.40

48976 **Minnow Netting**, made of cotton twine, just the netting only no sinkers. floats or lines. Price is by the running yard, stretched measure.

	3 ft.deep. Per yd.	4 ft. deep. Per yd.	5 ft.deep. Per yd.
¾ in. square mesh.....	24c.	25c.	29c.
½ in. square mesh.....	27c.	39c.	45c.
⅜ in. square mesh.....	35c.	45c.	55c.
¼ in. square mesh.....	55c.	70c.	85c.

Price is per running yard, stretched. The mesh is described on the square.

The Common Sense Minnow Seine.

48977 **Minnow Seines.** ⅛ inch mesh, made of a light woven netting. Not as strong or as lasting as the regular goods as quoted above, yet a good article for the money. Hung with leads, floats and lines.

Size..	4x10 ft.	4x12 ft.	4x15 ft.	4x20 ft.	4x25 ft.
Each..	$0.80	$0.95	$1.20	$1.50	$1.75

The Peerless Fyke or Hoop Net.

WITH WINGS.

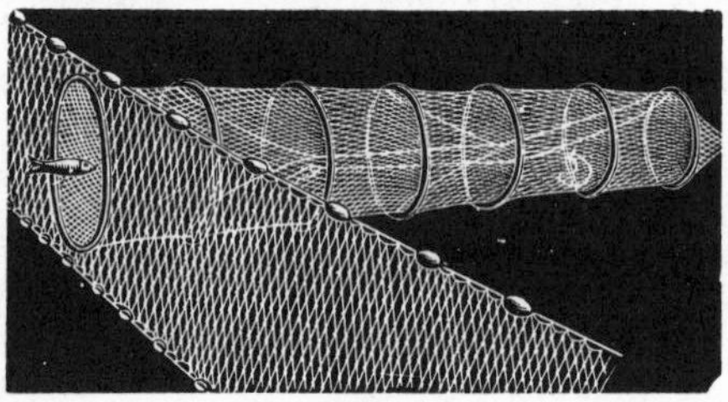

Wts. 2 ft. 10 lbs.
Wts. 2½ ft. 12 lbs.
Wts. 3 ft. 20 lbs.
Wts. 4 ft. 25 lbs.
Wts. 5 ft. 35 lbs.
Wts. 6 ft. 45 lbs.

		Height Mouth.	Number Hoops.	Length Net.	Full Length Wings.	No. Twine.	Size of Mesh, Inches Square. Front.	Middle.	Tail.	White Twine. Price Each.
				ft.	ft.					
48978	Single throat.	2 ft.	4	6	12	9	¾	¾	¾	$3.75
48979	Single throat.	2½ft.	6	8	12	16	1	1	1	3.95
48980	Single throat.	3 ft.	6	10	18	24	1¼	1¼	1¼	4.25
48981	Single throat.	4½ft.	8	18	30	24	1½	1½	1½	6.75
48982	Double throat	2½ft.	6	8	12	16	1	1	1	4.30
48983	Double throat	3 ft.	6	10	18	24	1¼	1¼	1¼	4.45
48984	Double throat	4 ft.	7	16	24	24	2	1¾	1½	5.65
48985	Double throat	4½ft.	8	18	30	24	2½	2	1½	6.95
48986	Double throat	5 ft.	8	18	30	28	2½	2	1½	7 67
48987	Double throat	6 ft.	8	18	40	28	2½	2	1½	9.67

For Fyke Nets made of preservative tarred twine add ⅓ to above prices. Lengths on wings are for both wings from end to end.

Our Peerless has the hoops on the outside of netting, thus greatly saving the netting.

Made of best quality cotton twine. Hung ready for use. Netting only can be furnished without hoops, if desired.

Funnel Nets. Without Wings.

Same style as the Peerless, but has *no wings.* With hoops complete.

No.		Weight.	Height Mouth.	Number Hoops.	Length.	Square Mesh. Front.	Tail.	Each.
		lbs.	ft.		ft.	in.	in.	
48988	Single throat....	7	2	4	6	¾	¾	$2.54
48989	Single throat....	8	2½	6	8	1	1	2.95
48990	Single throat....	10	3	6	10	1¼	1¼	3.15
48991	Single throat....	20	4½	8	18	1½	1½	4.60
48992	Double throat...	9	2½	6	8	1	1	2.65
48993	Double throat...	15	3	6	10	1¼	1¼	3.35
48994	Double throat..	20	4	7	16	2	1½	3.60
48995	Double throat...	25	4½	8	18	2½	1½	4.70
48996	Double throat...	30	5	8	18	2½	1½	4.95
48997	Double throat...	35	6	8	18	2½	1½	5.95

Made of best quality cotton twine.

When ordering seines, give size, price and catalogue number to avoid error.

N. B.—We make all kinds of fish nets to order, if you will fully describe what you want and send diagram of shape. Money must accompany the order, as they cannot be sent C. O. D. or returned when made to order.

Quail or Partridge Nets.

(Weight, 3½ lbs.)

48998 No. 1, 25 feet long, 20 feet wing each side, with funnel. Each $4.75
48999 No. 2, 20 feet long, 20 feet wing each side, with funnel. Each.................. 4.35
49000 No 3, 20 feet long, 20 feet wing each side, without funnel.... .... 3.75
49001 No. 4, 15 feet long, 20 feet wing each side, without funnel. Each.................... 3.35
49002 No. 5, 12 feet long, 15 feet wing each side, with funnel. Each........................ 2.80

Front hoops of our quail nets are of wood. Netting 1¼ inches, square mesh, 12 thread cotton.

Gill Netting.

49004 LINEN NETTING for gill nets or inside of trammel nets, made of best silver gray 3 cord linen twine. Any depth required. This netting is for "gill" or "set" net and not for "drag" seines, the twine being too small for such use.

Order No 49004	Square Mesh.	Price per pound. No. 18. twine.	No. 20. twine.	No. 25. twine.	No. 30. twine.	No. 35. twine	No. 40 twine
	¾ in.	$1.84	$1.95	$2.18	$2.35	$2.60	$2.81
	1 in.	1.67	1.77	2.00	2.16	2.37	2.61
	1¼ in	1.54	1.67	1.87	2.04	2.27	2.50
	1½ in.	1.48	1.59	1.82	2.00	2.22	2.45
	1¾ in.	1.43	1.54	1.77	1.93	2.16	2.38
	2 in.	1.30	1.45	1.65	1.87	2.00	2.20

49005 Cotton netting for outside of trammel nets, from 6 to 8 inch square mesh. Per pound........... $0.45

Improved Perfection Trammel Net.

It has three nets hung upon a single top and a single bottom line. Of the three nets, two have large meshes of cotton seine twine. The inside net is made of best linen gilling twine, which is hung slack, forming a bag in which fish coming from either side are caught, unable to escape. These nets are not "drag seines" but are to be "set" in the water the same as a gill net.

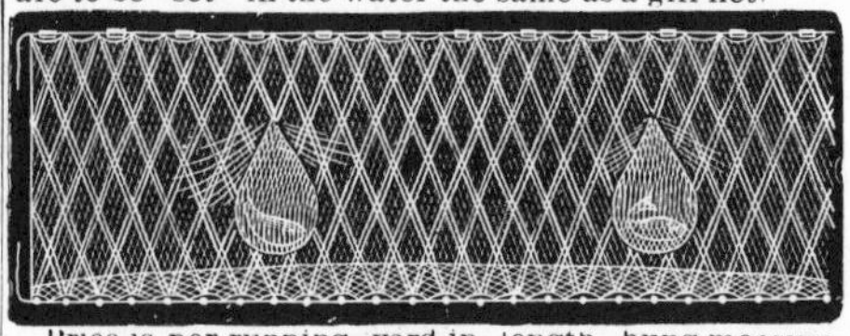

Price is per running yard in length, hung measure. the three nets combined complete with leads and floats. Square mesh. Weigh, per yard, about ½ lb.

No.	Depth.	Outside mesh.	Inside mesh.	Inside linen twine.	Outside cotton twine	Price Per Yard.
49010	3½ ft.	6 in.	¾ in.	No. 25	No.	$ .22
49011	3½ ft.	6 in.	1 in.	No. 25		.21
49012	3½ ft.	6 in.	1¼ in.	No. 25		.19
49013	4 ft.	6 in.	1 in.	No. 25		.24
49014	4 ft.	6 in.	1¼ in.	No. 25		.22
49015	4½ ft.	7 in.	1¼ in.	No. 20		.24
49016	4½ ft.	7 in.	1¼ in.	No. 25		.22
49017	4½ ft-	7 in.	1½ in.	No. 18		.23
49018	4½ ft.	7 in'	1¾ in.	No. 18		.22
49019	4½ ft.	7 in.	2 in.	No. 18		.21
49020	5 ft.	8 in.	1 in.	No. 25		.28
49021	5 ft.	8 in.	1½ in.	No. 18		.24
49022	5 ft.	8 in.	2½ in.	No. 18		.20
49023	5 ft.	8 in.	3 in.	No. 18	All No. 16, Soft Laid.	.19
49024	6 ft.	8 in.	1 in.	No. 25		.34
49025	6 ft.	8 in.	1½ in.	No. 18		.27
49026	6 ft.	8 in,	2 in.	No. 18		.26
49027	6 ft.	8 in.	2½ in	No. 18		.21
49028	6 ft.	8 in.	3 in.	No. 18		.28
49029	7 ft.	8 in.	1½ in.	No. 18		.35
49030	7 ft.	8 in.	2 in.	No. 18		.33
49031	7 ft	8 in.	2½ in.	No. 18		.24
49032	7 ft.	8 in.	3 in.	No. 18		.22
49033	8 ft.	8 in.	1½ in.	No. 18		.39
49034	8 ft.	8 in.	1¾ in.	No. 18		.37
49035	8 ft.	8 in.	2 in.	No. 18		.34
49036	8 ft.	8 in.	2½ in.	No. 18		.26
49037	8 ft.	8 in.	3 in.	No. 18		.24

Other styles made to order. Meshes as given above are diamond square. Hung complete for use except hauling lines. When ordering nets, give SIZE, PRICE and CATALOGUE number.

Gill or Set Net.

A gill net is a single net, hung with floats and leads complete, without hauling lines. Made of best imported linen twine. These nets cannot be used for "drag" seines, the twine being too fine. They are set in the water, and allowed to remain from 5 to 24 hours. Commencing at one end "lift" gently when taking up net. The fish are caught by the gills, hence the name "gill" or "set" net.

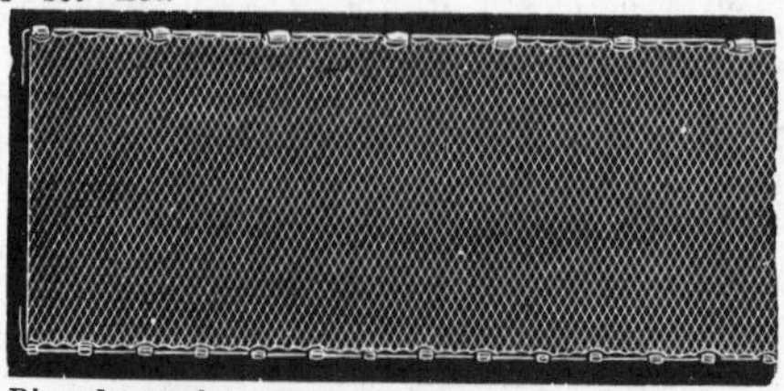

Rigged complete. Ready for use. Made of linen twine. Price is per running yard in length, hung measure. Weight, per yard, about ¼ pound.

Nets—Continued.

No.	Depth.	No. twine. linen.	Size of mesh square	Price per yard.
49045	3½ feet.	40	2 inch.	$0.13
49046	4 feet.	40	1 inch.	.19
49047	4 feet.	40	1¼ inch.	.15
49048	4 feet.	35	1½ inch.	.16
49049	4 feet.	35	1¾ inch.	.14
49050	4 feet.	40	2 inch.	.15
49051	5 feet.	40	1 inch.	.22
49052	5 feet.	40	1¼ inch.	.19
49053	5 feet.	35	1½ inch.	.18
49054	5 feet.	25	1¾ inch.	.17
49055	5 feet.	40	2 inch.	.16
49056	5 feet.	40	2¼ inch.	.15
49057	5 fcet.	40	2½ inch.	.16
49058	6 feet.	40	1 inch.	.25
49059	6 feet.	40	1¼ inch.	.22
49060	6 feet.	35	1½ inch.	.20
49061	6 feet.	35	1¾ inch.	.19
49062	6 feet.	35	2 inch.	.18
49063	6 feet.	40	2¼ inch.	.17
49064	6 feet.	40	2½ inch.	.16
49065	7 feet.	25	1½ inch.	.22
49066	7 feet.	20	1¾ inch.	.21
49067	7 feet.	20	2 inch.	.20
49068	8 feet.	25	1½ inch.	.24
49069	8 feet.	20	1¾ inch.	.23
49070	8 feet	20	2 inch.	.22

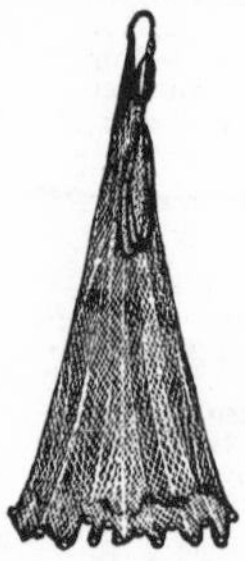

Cast Nets.

49071 Cast Nets Mounted, made of No. 6 thread. without rope.

	⅜-inch square mesh.	⅝-inch square mesh.
3 feet long, each.......	$3.20	$2.50
3½ feet long, each.......	3.75	2 75
4 feet long, each.......	4.50	3.15
4½ feet long, each.......	5.35	3.85
5 feet long, each.......		3.35

Cotton Trot Line.

49089. Cotton Trot Line in 50 feet coils (6 connected). best quality, sold in any quantity at dozen rates.

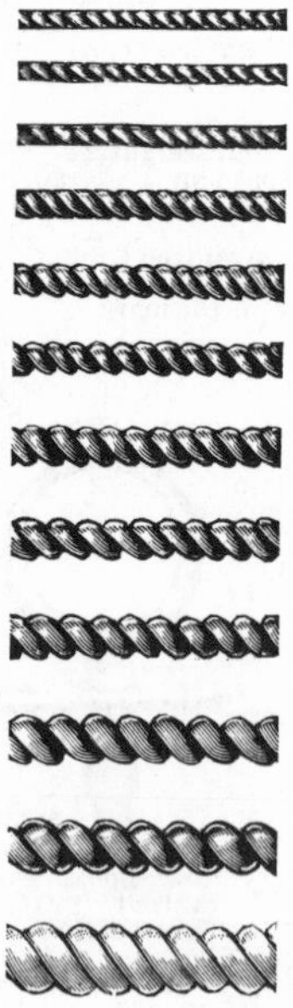

No.	Per doz. coils.	Wt. Per doz
1	$0.38	15 oz.
2	.4	16 oz.
3	.50	19 oz.
4	.65	20 oz.
5	.75	23 oz.
6	.85	24 oz.
7	.95	32 oz.
8	1.05	36 oz.
9	1.20	44 oz
10	1.35	52 oz.
11	1.55	56 oz.
12	1.85	96 oz

Gilling Twine.

The best quality imported.

Gilling twine is a small all linen twine, used for gill or set nets, and cannot be used to make a drag, lake or river net.

No.		Per lb.
49090	Linen Gilling Twine, No. 12, 3 cord......	$ 0.78
	Linen Gilling Twine, No. 16, 3 cord..........	.92
	Linen Gilling Twine, No. 18, 3 cord..........	.96
	Linen Gilling Twine, No. 20, 3 cord..........	.98
	Linen Gilling Twine, No. 25, 3 cord..........	1.10
	Linen Gilling Twine, No. 30, 3 cord..........	1.15
	Linen Gilling Twine, No. 35, 3 cord..........	1.30
	Linen Gilling Twine, No. 40, 3 cord..........	1.50
	Linen Gilling Twine, No. 50, 3 cord..........	1.85

Gilling twine comes in ½ lb. balls.

OUR SALES OF . . .

TENTS, SEINES, ETC.,

Are the largest of any house in America. Our goods and our prices are right. Examine our quotations carefully.

Seine Twine.

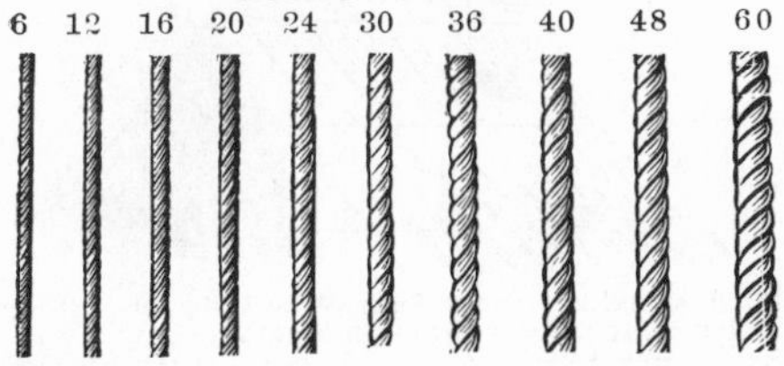

Showing sizes of seine twine as near as possible. These illustrations appear larger than the twine.

Our Seine Twine is the best in the market, laid smooth and even, and uniform in size. We do not handle the loosely laid, bunchy cheap goods.

49091 White Seine Twine, soft laid, in skeins of about 1 to1¾ lb. each. Nos. 6, 9, 12, 16, 20, 24, 28, 32, 36, 40, 44, 48, 60; No. 6. smallest, No. 60, largest; 32 to 48 is the proper size for fly nets; 16 to 24 is the hammock size.
Per lb., in less than 5 lb. lots $0.20
Per lb. in 5 lb. lots and over .... .18

49092 White Seine Twine, medium laid, for Seines and Hammocks, in skeins. Nos. 9, 12, 15, 18, 21, 24, 27, 30, 33, 36, 42, 48, 54, 60. (No. 9 smallest) Per lb .... .24
Per lb., in 5 lb. lots or over .... .20

49093 White Seine Twine, hard laid, in skeins, Nos. 9 to 60, same size as in medium laid.
Per lb., in 5 lb. lots or over .... .22
Per lb .... .24

N. B.—In the small size the hanks weigh about one lb. In the larger sizes they run about 1½ lb. to the skein. We do not break skeins.

In large quantities, write for prices.

Colored Twine for Hammocks and Fly Nets.

49094 Colored Seine Twine, for hammocks and fly nets: colors: Blue, red, brown and orange; Nos. 24 and 32 only. (No. 24 for hammocks and No. 32 for fly nets.) Per lb $0.30

Price on Rope and Seine Rigging quoted on application. We can furnish nearly everything in this line at low prices

Seine Needles.

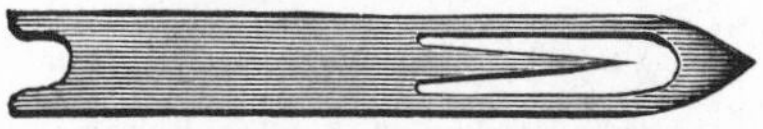

49095 Seine Knitting Needles. Made of white wood.

	½ in.	¾ in.	1 in.	1¼ in.	1½ in.
Each...	10c	12c	15c	16c	17c

For quotations on Sailors' Palms, Needles and Twine, see Index.

Hammocks.

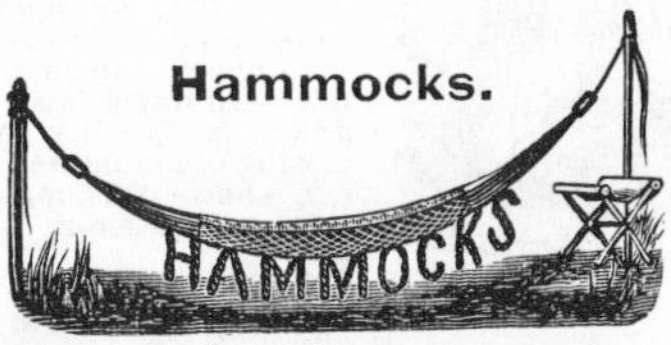

49100 Hammocks for children, open mesh, cotton cord, mixed bright colors, strong and durable, 7 ft. bed by 4 ft wide; weight, 8 oz. Each .. $0.45

49102 Hammocks, full size, made of heavy double seine twine, full width, entire length end to end 14 ft., fancy bright colors; weight, 2 lbs. Each .. .90

49105 Hammocks, Mexican, white, entire length 14 ft., bed 6 ft. 6 in. long; weight 3½ lbs. .... .70

49106 Hammock, Mexican, assorted colors, same size as No. 49105; weight, 3 lbs. .... .85

The Mexican Hammocks are made of a sea grass and are light and strong and among the most durable in the market.

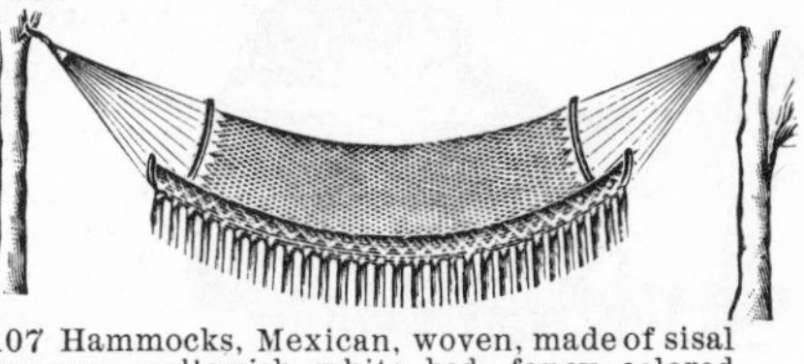

49107 Hammocks, Mexican, woven, made of sisal sea grass, yellowish white bed, fancy colored valance on each side, bright colored end strings, clinch thimble on end, entire length 14 ft., length of bed 6 ft. 6 in., full width: a showy, well made, strong and durable article; weight, 4 lbs. Each $1.45

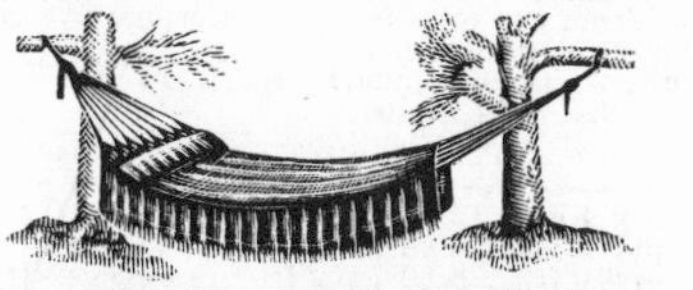

49108 Hammocks, close woven body, cotton weave, in bright fancy mixed colors, canvas weave, wide valance on each side, with pillow, 48x90 in., heavy and strong. 1 long steel spreader, nickel plated; 2 short steel crossbars on each end, to hold hammock in shape; one of the most desirable articles of this kind on the market. Weight about 6 pounds. Each $3.90

Hammocks—Continued.

49109 Hammocks, close woven body, cotton weave, in bright fancy colors mostly red mixed with other bright colors, wide valance on each side, curved spreader on each end, with pillow. One of the most comfortable and showy hammocks, well made, strong and durable, bed 42x84 in., entire length 13 ft; weight, about 5 lbs. Each 2.75

49111 Hammock, close woven body, cotton weave, modest pale colors mixed with white, with valance, pillow and curved spreaders on each end, bed 40x80 in., entire length 12½ ft., well made, strong and durable and much more comfortable than the open mesh style; weight, about 5 lbs. Each 2.40

49112 Hammocks, close woven body, cotton weave, white mixed with pale modest colors, valance on both sides, curved spreaders in each end, no pillow, bed 42x84 in., entire length 13 ft.; weight about 4⅛ lbs., well made and durable. Each 2.25

49113 Hammocks, close woven body, cotton weave, fancy mixed colors (no valance) with pillow, curved spreaders in each end, well made, strong and durable, bed 40x80 in., entire length 12½ ft.; weight about 4½ lbs., strong and durable. Each..... $1.85

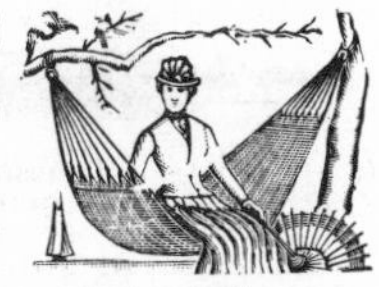

49114 Hammocks, close woven body, cotton weave, fancy bright colors, without pillow, curved spreader in each end, bed 42x84, entire length 13 ft. well made and durable; weight, 3½ lbs. Each 1.50

49115 Hammocks, close woven body, cotton weave, white and pale mixed colors, without pillow, curved spreaders in each end, bed 42x84, entire length 13 ft.; weight, 3¼ lbs, well made, strong and durable. Each 1.30

49116 Child's Hammock, double cord open mesh, bright colors, curved spreaders on each end entire length from end to end 8 ft. 6 in., spreaders, 2 ft. 6 in. long, strong, well made and durable; weight, 1½ lbs. Each .... .45

Peerless Hammock Spreader.

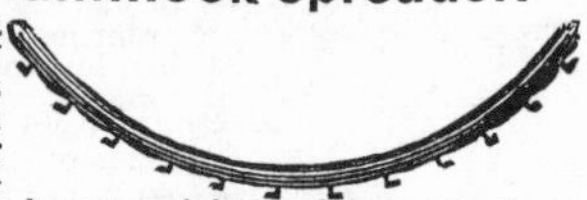

49130 Is made of a solid piece of hard wood, bent bow shape with hooks on its lower edge. It is designed to sustain a heavy weight, and is so simple in its construction and application that all will understand how to use it.
Each .... $0.07 Per doz $0.75
Weight 1 lb. each.

Hammock Ropes and Hooks.

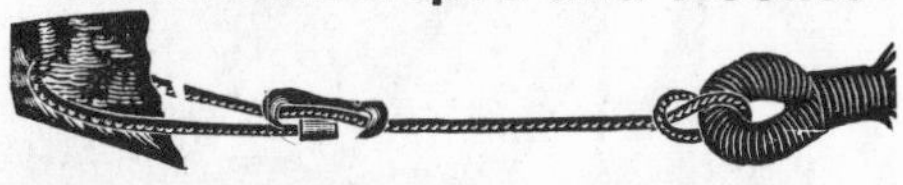

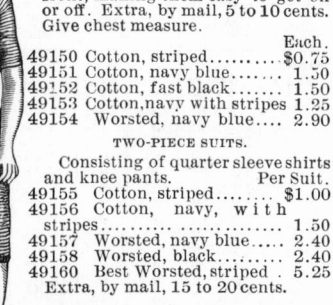

49133 Hammock Ropes, 7 feet long, with galvanized iron anchor fastening that remains where you place it; no knots to tie after attached to hammock, no slipping while in hammock. Hammock can be raised and lowered in an instant. Each $0.07

49136 Screw Hammock Hooks, tinned, 7-16 inch diameter, to screw in. Each $0.06
Per doz .... .65

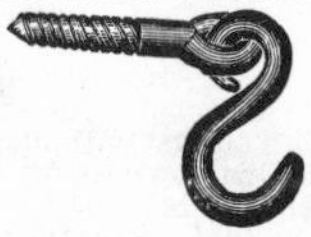

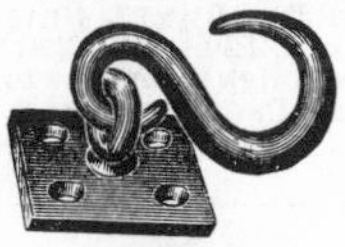

49137 Plate Hammock Hooks, tinned, 7-16 inch in diameter, to screw on. Each $0.09

Bathing Suits.

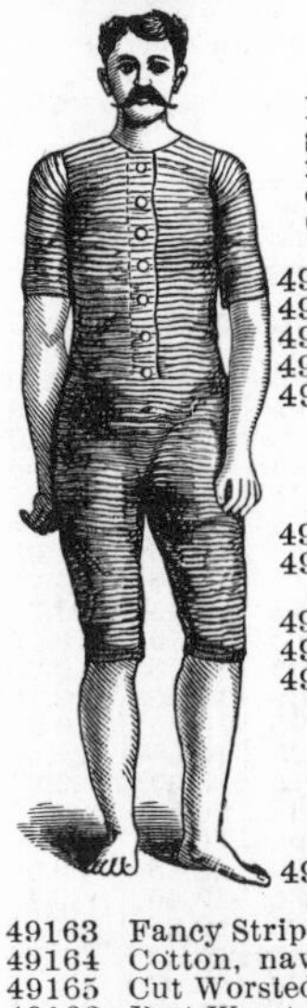

ONE-PIECE SUITS.

Knit goods, very elastic, not cloth goods. Button well down to the front, making them easy to get on or off. Extra, by mail, 5 to 10 cents. Give chest measure.

		Each.
49150	Cotton, striped	$0.75
49151	Cotton, navy blue	1.50
49152	Cotton, fast black	1.50
49153	Cotton, navy with stripes	1.25
49154	Worsted, navy blue	2.90

TWO-PIECE SUITS.

Consisting of quarter sleeve shirts and knee pants.

		Per Suit.
49155	Cotton, striped	$1.00
49156	Cotton, navy, with stripes	1.50
49157	Worsted, navy blue	2.40
49158	Worsted, black	2.40
49160	Best Worsted, striped	5.25

Extra, by mail, 15 to 20 cents.

Swimming Trunks.

Knit goods, very elastic. Extra by by mail, about 5 cents each. Each.

49162 Fancy Stripes, boys' sizes $0.18
49163 Fancy Stripes, all sizes .... .40
49164 Cotton, navy blue .... .40
49165 Cut Worsted, navy and black .... .95
49166 Best Worsted, any color 1.60

Waterproof Canvas Bags.

49167 Fitted with handle and straps around each end; a very desirable article. These bags are made of canvas, lined with rubber, and are thoroughly waterproof; will hold bathing suit, towels, brush, comb, etc. Extra, by mail, 10 cents. Each $0.70

TENTS.

SPECIAL NOTE.—If you are interested in other styles of tents not listed in this catalogue, we invite your correspondence. Quotations given on applications, and at bottom prices. We can meet your expectation.

"A" or Wedge Tents.

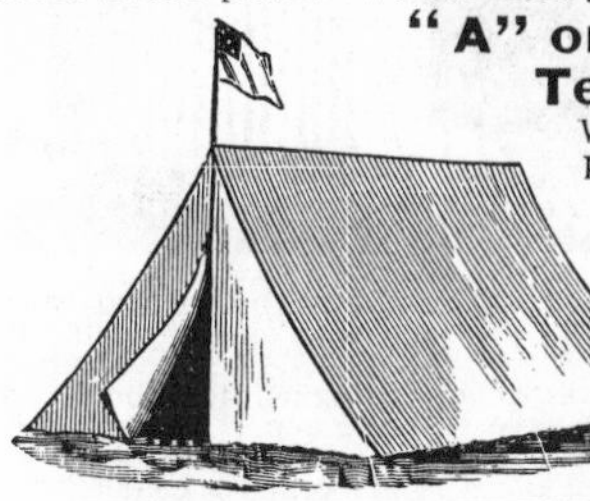

Weight without poles, 18 to 40 lbs.; weight of poles, 14 ounces to the foot in length.

Order No.	Length and Breadth, Feet.	Height, Feet.	Price 8 oz. Duck.	Price, 10 oz. Duck.	Price, 12 oz. Duck.
49190	7x7 ft.	7 ft.	$2.90	$3.40	$4.50
	7x9 ft.	7 ft.	3.50	4.10	5.40
	9x9 ft.	7 ft.	3.85	4.55	6.00
	9½x12 ft.	7½ ft.	4.75	5.60	7.40
	12 x14 ft.	9 ft.	6.80	8.00	10.7(

Miners' Tents.

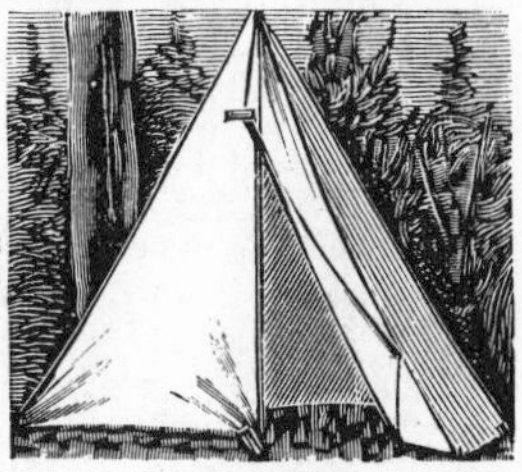

Weights without poles 14 to 30 pounds; poles 13 ounces per foot in length.

49195		Price, Complete.		
Size of Base.	Height.	8 oz. Single Filling Duck.	10 oz. Single Filling Duck.	12 oz. Double Filling Duck.
7 ft.x7 ft.	7ft.	$2.00	$2.35	$3.25
9 ft.x9 ft.	8ft.	3.05	3.50	4.85
12 ft.x12 ft.	9ft.	4.60	5.30	7.35

Refreshment Tents.

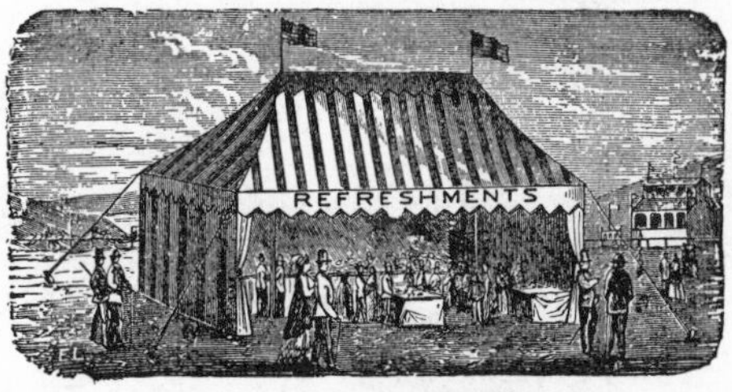

(Plain White Duck.)

Oblong or Refreshment tent, made of PLAIN WHITE DUCK, not striped, as shown in cut. Price includes poles, pins, guys, etc., complete, ready to set up. The cut shows front open, it can be closed, or stretched out in front for an awning or taken off altogether, as it is put on with hooks for these changes.

No. 49197— Size.	Wall.	Center.	8 oz. White Duck.	10 oz. White Duck	10 oz. Double Filling Duck.
9x14	6 ft.	10 ft.	$10.30	$11.70	$12 25
9x16½	6 ft.	10 ft.	11.50	13.05	13.90
9x19	6 ft.	10 ft.	12.75	14.50	15.45
12x19	6 ft.	11 ft.	14.10	16.05	17.50
12x21½	6 ft.	11 ft.	16.90	19.30	21.10
14x21½	6 ft.	11 ft,	17.30	19.75	21.90
14x23½	6 ft.	11 ft.	21.30	24.40	27.40

NOTE.—Where 8 oz. stripe, blue or brown, is wanted, the price will be the same as 10 oz. white duck.

Refreshment Tent Tops.

Order No. 49198 (Without wall)

Size.	Center.	8 oz. White Duck.	10 oz. White Duck.	10 oz. double filling Duck.
9x14	10 ft.	$5.95	$6.45	$ 7.90
9x16½	10 ft.	6.75	7.35	9.15
9x19	10 ft.	7.60	8.30	10.30
12x19	11 ft.	8.50	9.35	11.91
12x21½	11 ft.	10.50	11.50	14 70
14x21½	11 ft.	10.85	12.00	15.45
14x23½	11 ft.	13.60	15.10	19.75

The above prices include everything complete ready for putting up.

Family Compartment Tents.

Oblong, with square ends. Weights without poles, 50 to 150 pounds.

Tents made of 8 oz. double filling, brown and white or blue and white stripe, same as 10 ounce double filling white.

These tents are especially designed for families or parties who must have separate rooms. It is accomplished as perfectly as at home. It is divided into four bed rooms on sides and dining room in center. The awning as shown in this tent is not extra to the tent, but part of the wall lifted up, thus forming an awning affording free circulation of air through the tent, as well as complete shade. The prices include everything complete, ready for putting up.

No.	Size.	Wall.	Pole	White 10-ounce double filling or 8-ounce army duck.	White 12-ounce double filling or 10-ounce army duck.
	9 x16½	6 ft	10 ft	$20.90	$23.70
	9 x19	6 ft	10 ft	22.75	26.00
	12 x19	6 ft	11 ft	26.90	30.60
49199	12 x21½	6 ft	11 ft	29.20	33.35
	14 x21½	6 ft	12 ft	32.20	36.60
	14 x23½	6 ft	12 ft	34.25	38.90
	16½x23½	6 ft	13 ft	38.85	44.40

Dimensions of bed rooms and dining room.

2 bedrooms	5½x9	Dining room	5 x9
2 bedrooms	6 x9	Dining room	6½x9
4 bedrooms	6 x6	Dining room	7¾x12
4 bedrooms	6 x7	Dining room	7½x12
4 bedrooms	7 x7	Dining room	7½x14
4 bedrooms	7 x7	Dining room	7½x14
4 bedrooms	8¼x8¼	Dining room	7½x16½

The above prices include everything complete ready for putting up.

NOTE.—When 8 oz. stripe blue or brown is wanted the price will be the same as 10 oz., double filling.

The Protean Tent.

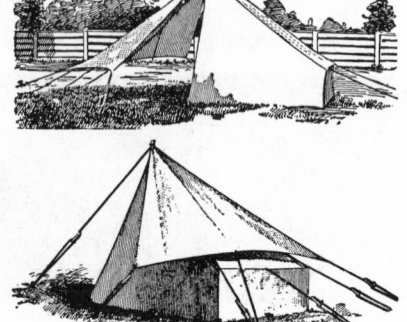

49200

It is the best all 'round tent for camping purposes in the world. It is compact, roomy, easy to put up, and suitable for both hot and cold weather; only one pole required. The tent has a sod cloth 9 inches wide all around to keep out wind and mosquitoes. The tent has also a "fly" that can be used in many ways, as a fly protecting the roof and part of sides or as an awning in front of tent, or as a store house. It has other advantages too numerous to mention here, and circulars showing the different shapes it can be made into with illustrations free.

Prices of Protean tents, including fly, sod cloth, ash pole and pins complete ready to set up.

Order No. 49,200.

Size on Ground.	Height Rear Wall.	Height of Pole.	8-oz. Dock Single Filling.	10-oz. Duck, Single Filling	Additional for 3 Joint Pole.	Additional for Comstock's Carry Bag With Shoulder Straps
6½x6½	2 ft.	6ft.9 in	$ 6 90	$ 7.80	$ 1.25	$ 1.00
7 x7	2 ft.	7ft.3 in	8.00	9.00	1 25	1.00
8 x8	2½ ft.	8ft.9 in	10.00	11.50	1.70	1.10
9 x9	3 ft.	9ft.9 in	13.25	15.10	2.10	1.20

Comstock's Carry Bag.

49201 It is a very simple and inexpensive bag for carrying tent, jointed pole, pegs and blankets or extra clothing. It is light and convenient, and carries the load in comfortable position on the back. The bag can be instantly opened without removing the straps. The straps and cords can be instantly detached and stowed in top of bag for shipment. When ordering these bags for Protean tents, column in tent list above marked "additional for patent carry bags with shoulder straps" will give price of bag for any sized tent. Tent, jointed pole. etc., when packed in this bag can be checked as baggage. Each $1.20

Comstock's Malleable Iron Tent Peg.

49202 One set of these pegs will last a lifetime, as they cannot be broken. They are fully as light as wooden pegs of the same holding power, and will pack in one quarter the space. They save time and labor in putting up any tent.   Doz
Short pegs, 8¾ inches, weigh 4½ to 5 ozs......$0.75
Long pegs. 13½ inches, weigh 7 to 7½ ozs 1.00
Each set of one dozen or more put up in 12 oz. canvas bag. If you own a tent send for a set of these pegs.

Wall Tents.

We can furnish tents in large or small quantities on short notice generally. Our tents are the best quality; they are *all full size*, and all have a *good* "pitch" to roof, to turn rain, and all made in a durable and substantial manner. Prices in lots of 5 or more furnished on application. Tents will not be sent C. O. D., as they have to be made to order.

We warrant them to be exactly as represented. In ordering give catalogue number, length and breadth and price.

We can make to order all kinds of tents, canopies, etc.

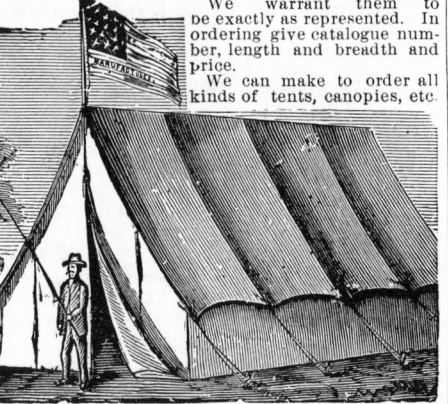

Wall Tent No. 49215

Wall Tents.

Weights without poles, 7x7, 30 lbs.; 9½x12, 40 to 50 lbs.; 14x16, 66 to 76 lbs.; 16x24, 120 to 130 lbs.; 18x32, 147 to 160 lbs. Ridge poles weigh 22 ounces to the foot. Upright poles, 14 oz. to the foot. Pins weigh ¼ to ¾ pounds each. All of our 12 ounce duck tents are double filling, best quality.

No.	Length and Breadth Feet	Height Wall Feet	Height Pole Feet	Price with Poles, Pins, Guys, etc. Complete ready to set up 8 oz. Duck.	10 oz. Duck.	12 oz. Duck.
Order 49215	7 x 7	3	7	$3.70	$4.30	$5.80
	7 x 9	3	7	4.35	5.10	6.70
	9 x 9	3	7½	5.05	5.90	7.50
	9½ x 12	3	7½	5.95	6.95	9.20
	9½ x 14	3	7½	6.75	7.85	10.40
	12 x 12	3½	8	7.05	8.25	10.90
	12 x 14	3½	8	7.95	9.30	12.35
	12 x 16	3½	8	8.85	10.30	13.75
	12 x 18	3½	8	9.80	11.45	15.05
	14 x 14	4	9	9.45	11.10	14.75
	14 x 16	4	9	10.45	12.25	16.30
	14 x 18	4	9	11.65	13.70	18.15
	14 x 20	4	9	12.95	15.05	19.70
	14 x 24	4	9	14.60	17.00	22.10
	16 x 16	5	11	12.95	15.25	20.25
	16 x 18	5	11	14.25	16.65	22.60
	16 x 20	5	11	15.70	18.30	23.95
	16 x 24	5	11	17.85	20.80	27.15
	16 x 30	5	11	21.62	26.00	32.90
	16 x 35	5	11	24.20	28.25	36.90
	18 x 18	5	11	16.30	19.45	25.40
	18 x 20	5	11	17.95	20.95	27.45
	18 x 24	5	11	20.05	23.40	30.60
	18 x 30	5	11	24.00	28.00	36 75
	18 x 35	5	11	26.95	31.20	41.55

Photographers' Tents.

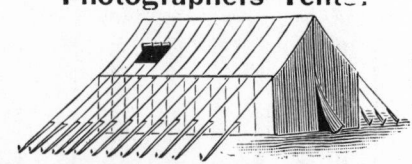

49220 Weight, without poles, 66 to 176 pounds. Ridge poles, 22 to 25 oz. per foot in length.

Size.	Pole.	Wall	Price, complete, without dark room.		
			8 oz. single fill'g duck.	10 oz. single filling duck.	10 oz. double filling duck.
12x16 ft....	11 ft.	6 ft.	$13.55	$15.20	$18.20
12x21 ft....	11 ft.	6 ft.	16.55	19.10	22.54
12x24 ft....	11 ft.	6 ft.	18.40	21.15	24.85
14x16 ft....	12 ft.	6 ft.	15.20	17.95	21.60
14x21 ft....	12 ft.	6 ft.	18.40	21.15	25.55
14x24 ft....	12 ft.	6 ft	20.00	23.25	27.60
14x28 ft....	12 ft.	6 ft.	22.75	26.45	31.30
16x18 ft....	13 ft.	6 ft.	17.95	20.95	25.05
16x24 ft....	13 ft.	6 ft.	22.10	25.75	30.60
16x28 ft....	13 ft.	6 ft.	25.10	29.20	34.75
16x30 ft....	13 ft.	6 ft.	26.90	31.30	37.25

Prices on tents include poles, pins, guys, etc. Tent complete ready to set up.

Dark rooms extra, 6x6 feet, $7.80; 4½x4½ feet $6.50. Our dark rooms are made of same material, same weight and color as the tent—all white. We make the room only, the artist can darken it to suit his own taste. Some use black silesia, some yellow, etc.

The above prices include poles, pins, guys, etc., ready to set up tent. Quotation on other sizes on application and at bottom prices.

Prices on stable tents, stable, tops, Sibley tents, canopy tops without wall, photographers' tents, square hip-roof tents, or any other style, given on application and at bottom prices.

Palmetto, or Lawn Tents.

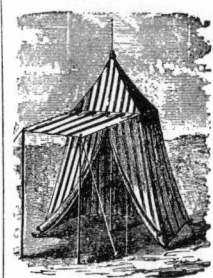

49225 Positively the best tent in use for lawn, croquet or archery parties They are made of 8 ounce awning duck, color, blue and white or brown and white, internate shades. They have but one pole, and that in center. Top is supported by wood frame, umbrella shape. It can be set up in three to five minnutes and taken down as speedily as the closing of an umbrella. The cut shows this tent with awning extension.

Size of Base.	Size of Top.	Heighth in Center.	Heighth at Side.	Price, without Awning.	Price, with Awning.
7x 7	2 ft. 4 in.	7 ft. 6 in.	6 ft.	$4.30	$5.95
8x 8	2 ft. 4 in.	8 ft.	6 ft.	4.95	6.50
9x 9	3 ft. 6 in.	8 ft. 6 in.	7 ft.	6.25	7 95
10x10	3 ft. 6 in.	9 ft.	7 ft. 6 in.	7.00	9.00

Black Oiled Wagon Cover.

These covers are made from 8 oz. duck and although black and called tarpaulins, have no tar in their composition. Our water proof dressing is an oil preparation, and is entirely free from anything calculated to rot or burn the canvas, but adds to the durability of the cover, being impervious to water, and very soft and pliable. It will neither rot nor mildew from damp, nor break from being too hard. They are invaluable to all persons who are shipping and receiving goods which are liable to damage from wet weather. In ordering, give catalogue number, size and price.

Weight 9 to 28 pounds. 6x12, 12 lbs; 6x9, 9 lbs; 7x12, 16 lbs; 7x14, 19 lbs.

No.	Size.	Price.	Size.	Price.	Size.	Price
49227	6x 8 ft	$2.50	7x 9 ft	$3.30	8x10 ft	$4.00
	6x 9 ft	2.85	7x10 ft	3.65	8x12 ft	5.15
	6x10 ft	3.10	7x12 ft	4.40	8x14 ft	5.85
	6x12 ft	3.75	7x14 ft	5.10	8x16 ft	6.65
	6x14 ft	4.35	7x16 ft	5.80	9x14 ft	6.60

TRY AND GET INTO THE HABIT OF THINKING about the goods that you will need two or three weeks hence. This plan will double the advantages of buying away from home.

Wagon Covers.

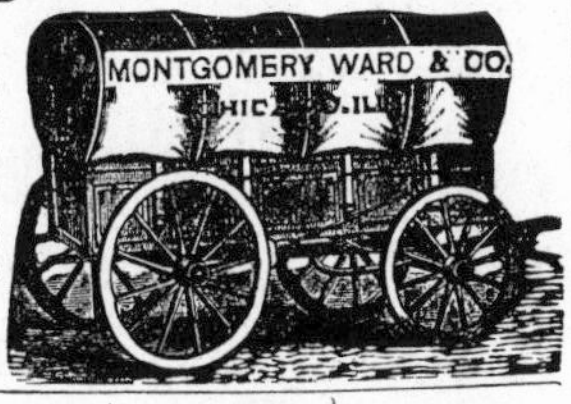
MONTGOMERY WARD & CO.

49228 Wagon Covers, white duck (see cut). Always give size when ordering. Weight, 7 to 50 lbs., 10x10, 8 oz., 7 lbs., 10x13, 10oz., 16 lbs.; 12x22, 40 to 50 lbs.

Size—Feet.	8 oz. Duck.	10 oz. Duck.	12 oz. Duck.
10x10	$1.20	$1.50	$2.33
10x12	1.45	1.85	2.75
10x14	1.70	2.15	3.25
10x15	1.80	2.35	3.50
10x16	1.90	2.45	3.70
11x13	1.75	2.20	3.40
11x15	2.05	2.55	3.90
11x18	2.45	3.10	4.75
12x15	2.30	2.85	4.35
12x16	2.50	3 05	4.65
12x20	3.10	3.80	5.85

Stack, Machine and Merchandise Covers, Called Paulins.

Weight from 15 to 100 lbs.
16x14, 10 to 26 lbs; 14x20, 25 to 30 lbs.
20x20, 38 to 45 lbs.

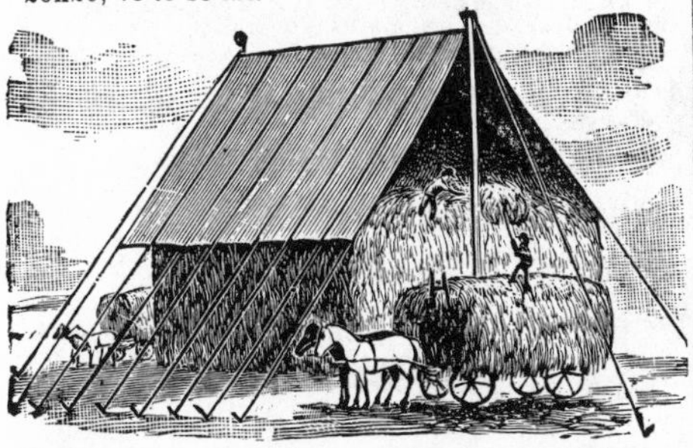

49229 White Duck. Always state size wanted, when ordering. Prices quoted on application, on sizes not mentioned here. Our 12 ounce duck is best double filling. These goods are not tents, but "stack covers" or paulins.

Size.—Feet	8 oz. Duck.	10 oz. Duck.	12 oz. Duck.
10x16	$ 1.95	$ 2.40	$ 3.70
10x18	2.20	2.70	4.20
12x14	2.10	2.65	4.05
12x16	2.50	3.00	4.65
12x18	2.75	3.40	5.25
12x20	3.05	3.75	5.80
14x16	3.50	3.95	5.60
14x18	3.65	4.45	6.30
14x20	4.05	4.95	7.00
14x24	4.85	5.90	8.40
16x16	3.70	4.55	6.40
16x18	4.20	5.15	7.70
16x20	4.65	5.65	8.00
16x24	5.55	6.80	9.60
18x20	5.20	6.40	9.00
18x24	6.25	7.65	10.80
18x28	7 30	8.95	12.60
18x30	7.80	9.60	13.50
20x24	6.90	8.50	12.00
20x36	10.45	12.75	18.00
24x30	10.40	12.70	17.95
24x36	12.50	15.35	21.60
24x40	13.90	17.05	24.00
24x50	17.40	21.30	30.00

Stack covers have short ropes, but no poles, machine and merchandise covers have eyelets around side. Any other size furnished on short notice. Prices on application.

Binder Covers.

49230 Weight, 6½ to 7¼ lbs. Fitted to cover the binder and not the whole machine. Will fit any binder. Made of white duck.

	8 oz.	10 oz
Price, each	$1.85	$2.15

Stockman's Bed Sheets.

Weights, 10 to 22 lbs. Fitted with snap rings or eyelets as may be ordered.
Made of very best heavy white duck.

Order No.	Feet.	13 oz.	15 oz.	18 oz.
49231	6x12	$2.35	$2.85	$3.05
	6x14	2.70	3.30	3.50
	6x15	2.90	3.50	3.80
	6x18	3.45	4.20	4.45
	7x12	2.75	3.25	3.60
	7x14	3.10	3.75	4.15
	7x15	3 35	4.05	4.45
	7x18	3.95	4.75	5.25
	8x12	3.40	4 10	4.40
	8x14	3.90	4.70	5.15
	8x18	5.00	6.05	6.60

Arctic Sleeping Bags.

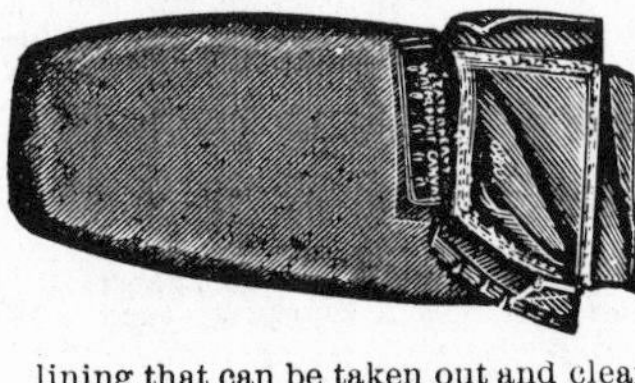

49240 The Improved. Made of heavy waterproof tan-colored duck, lined with sheepskin, with the wool left on, inside of sheepskin lining, is a heavy drill lining that can be taken out and cleaned at any time; large enough to cover any man entirely, can cover up "head and ears" and still have plenty of air. Loops on sides so that it can be hung up with ropes if desired. With these bags all bed and bedding can be dispensed with; it rolls up into small package, so that it can be fastened to a saddle, or "packed on back." The best bed ever invented for outdoor sleeping or tent camping. Weight, about 20 lbs. Each.......$15.50

Camper's Clothes Bag.

49241 These bags are made of heavy white duck, round bottom, drawing string top fastening. Handy for extra clothing, shells, boots and other "truck." Regular sailor's bag. Don't cost much, always useful. Every family needs them. Each....................................$0.50

Campers' "Carry-All" Bag.

(Try one on your next outing trip.)

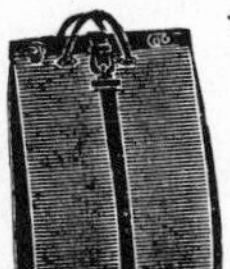

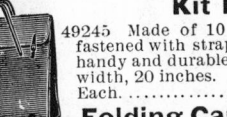

49243 This bag is made of heavy waterproof tan colored duck, with leather lap over mouth, leather lock strap fastening, mail bag style. Durable and strong, large size. The BEST and most USEFUL bag a "cowboy," hunter or camper could suggest. No campers' outfit complete without one; about 20x30 inches. Each.................................$3.00

Kit Bag.

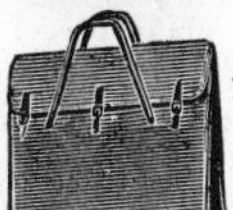

49245 Made of 10 oz, brown canvas, fastened with straps and buckles, neat, handy and durable. Length, 27 inches; width, 20 inches. Each.............................$0.75

Folding Canvas Boats.

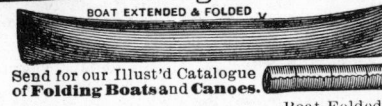

BOAT EXTENDED & FOLDED

Send for our Illust'd Catalogue of Folding Boats and Canoes.

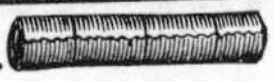

Boat Folded.

The Acme Folding Canvas Boat.

49252 (2) The Acme Folding Canvas Boat. Painted dark green. Length, 12 feet, beam, 45 inches, depth at stem and stern, 22 inches, depth amidships, 14 inches. Weight, light form, 35 pounds, weight complete 46 pounds; capacity, two and three passengers. Complete with 1 pair 6½-foot oars, pair adjustable oar locks, 2 folding seats, 1 adjustable back and shipping case. Price complete..........................$35.00

This is our most popular boat. It is a good general purpose boat. It can be made up in a light form weighing but 35 pounds by leaving out some of the parts which are necessary only when the boat is loaded to its full capacity. It can be made up into two bundles of equal size and weight. For from one to three passengers we would recommend it above any of the other sizes.

The Eureka Canvas Folding Boat.

49255 No. 1.—Length, 10 feet; beam, 36 inches; depth at ends, 20 inches; depth at center, 12 inches; weight, 35 pounds; capacity, one to three passengers. Price, with one pair 6-foot ash oars, malleable rowlocks and two folding seats, Grade A....................$24.00

The No. 1 has a full model, the full beam being carried well up to the ends. It has great carrying capacity for a boat of its length and weight, and is very steady on the water. It is a boat capable of carrying safely two or three persons, yet light enough and compact enough to be easily carried long distances by hand.

The Eureka does not fold as compactly as the Acme, and of course is not as well made, but yet is strong and durable.

The Koshkonong Hunting Skiff.

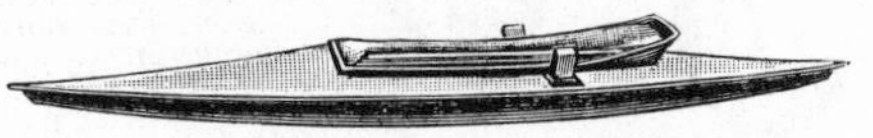

"Sets on the water like a duck."

49260 The Celebrated Koshkonong Hunting Boat is without doubt the best in the world, all things considered. Fifteen feet long, three feet beam, cockpit five feet long, two feet wide, pointed at both ends deck boarded and canvas covered—can walk all over deck. Folding canvas wing around cockpit. Oarlocks not fitted, can put on any kind of locks desired. Water and air tight chamber in each end, good in open rough, as well as shallow water. Cannot be tipped over, easy rowing, foot rack in bottom made espceially for running easily over grass and weeds, sets low on the water. Capacity 1,200 to 1,500 lbs. Just what every hunter and fisherman has been looking for; "easy as a rocking chair." Weight, about 90 lbs. Boat and 1 pair 6 feet ash oars. $25.00

Buzzacott's "Patent" Complete Camp Cooking Outfit.

SPORTING SIZE, EXTREMELY PORTABLE.
Order No. 49270.

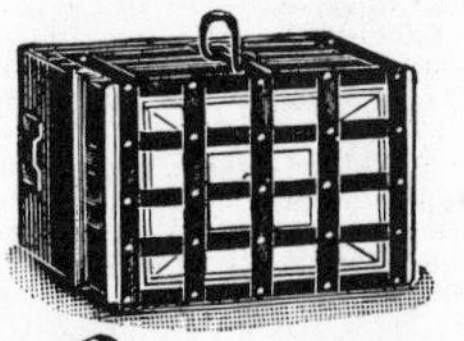

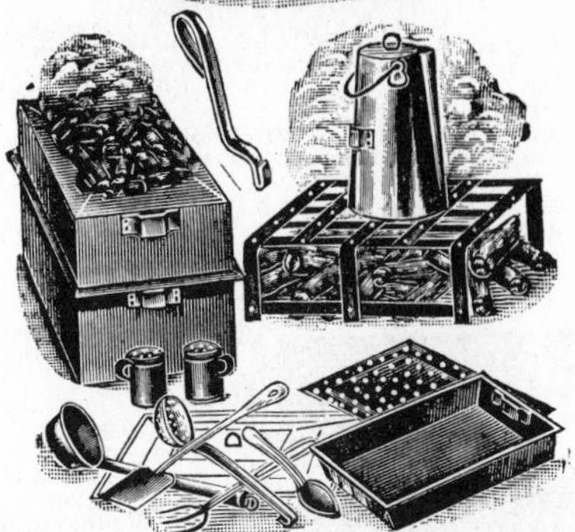

49270 Same style as adopted by the United States Army, every part solid and substantial; description, etc. Top engraving shows the entire outfit, 15 pieces nested and packed forming a package for carrying not a foot square. Below are found the various utensils (15) arranged so as to form an idea of one of the many forms of use contents, etc.

THE OUTFIT INCLUDES.

1 Skeleton Stove, 11x14x6 inches (steel)
1 Large Stew Pot, steel, 8 quart.
1 Medium Stew Pot, steel, 5 quart.

These combined for an excellent oven, 14xx10x10 inches. Capacity for 12 pound roast. 1 Coffee Pot, solid lip, mincers, 3 quart, I Frying Pan, used also for baking and roasting when desired, 12x8x2½, with cover to fit. 1 Boiler, 12x8; used also for pan rest. 1 Ladle Dripper; 1 Ladle Strainer; 1 Spoon; 1 Pancake Turner; 1 Fork, handle 12 inches long; 1 Adjustable handle, a feature so arranged as to fit any utensil for handling in any way when in use; 1 Combination Pan and Pot Cover, 2 Dredges 15 pieces. Price, complete.............. ....$5.50

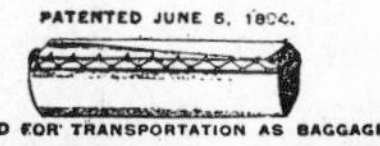
PACKED FOR TRANSPORTATION AS BAGGAGE.

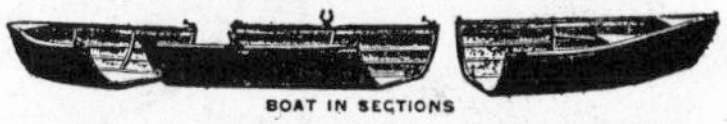
BOAT IN SECTIONS

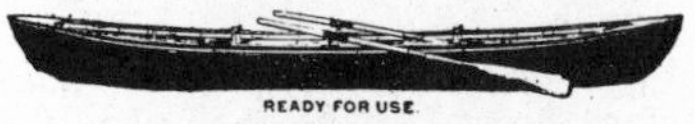
READY FOR USE

The "Kankakee."

A Portable Sectional Boat.

49271. CONSTRUCTION.

The frame of the Boat is constructed of second growth white oak as to ribs, side slats, top rail, and bow and stern Post. Cypress is used for floor, seats, and bow and stern deck. For fastening frame together, brass screws, copper rivets and copper nails are used throughout, which allows no parts to rust or corrode, and makes a very stiff, rigid frame. The outside covering is the best No. 1 galvanized steel, fastened throughout with copper rivets (which adds greatly to the strength) and then soldered over rivets and at all joints. This makes boats water-tight and prevents any action on the different metals when used in salt water.

JOINTS.

The joints are made each with one tongued and one groved brass casting reaching from rail to rail clear across mid section of boat. The grooved casting being milled out to receive a soft rubber gasket $\frac{3}{16}$ by ½ inch. The milled slot holds gasket in place and the pressure of the tongued casting on the rubber makes a perfect and absolutely water-tight joint. The joints are held together each by four brass clamps, two at bottom of boat and one on each rail at top of joint, as shown in foregoing cut. These four fastenings at each joint are very strong and rigid and so far from being a weak point the joints are the strongest part of boat, and we guarantee more than ample strength to carry all the boat will float, not only in smooth water, but in rough water, over shallow parts, sunken logs, rocks or any other obstructions.

This construction makes boat impervious to the weather as there can be no swelling or shrinkage to cause leakage; prevents being snagged, admits of use in heavy ice without damage, makes the use of paint to preserve unnecessary, does away with all bulkheads thus giving free use of entire boat without obstruction.

As parts are made interchangeable, we have two sizes of boats in one by simply leaving out middle section and joining two end sections. This is a very light, handy boat useful for one man in a great many places where a large boat would be inconvenient. See page 504 for prices.

The Kankakee Boat—Continued.

AIR TANKS.

When so ordered, we furnish two air tanks with each boat, amply large enough to float boat when full of water. We always advise the use of these as a matter of safety in case of accident. They are placed one under each deck, bow and stern. They are made of galvanized steel.

CANVAS CASE.

This case is made of heavy canvas, with strong handles and should always be used as a matter of convenience. With it a complete camping outfit can be carried with the boat, and when packed in case is readily accepted as baggage.

OARS AND PADDLES.

These are all jointed, with heavy brass ferrules; are made of best spruce and elegantly finished.
49271 Model No. 1, length, 14 feet, beam, 36 inches, depth 10 inches.
Price, crated, with one pair 6-foot jointed oars..$50.00
With canvas Case, with one pair 6-foot jointed oars.............................. 55.00
With Canvas Case and Air Tanks, with one pair 6-foot jointed oars............................... 60.00

Camping Outfit.
The best in the market.

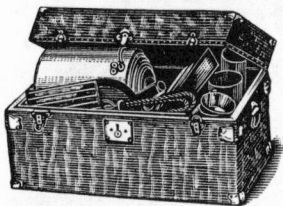

Everything packs in box, including stove. Put up in a strong, well-made, stained wooden box, with metal trimmings and durable lock. Length, 28 in.; depth, 13 in.; width, 19 in., wt. about 77 lbs. and will stand lots of hard usage.

49278 No. A. Contents. 1 stove, 4 lengths pipe, 1 elbow, 1 baking pan, 1 frying pan, 1 wash bowl, 3 camp kettles, 1 coffee pot, 6 knives and 6 forks, 1 carving knife, 1 basting spoon, 6 teaspoons, 6 enameled cups, 6 enameled plates. Price, complete..........................$18.50
49279 No. B Outfit, contents same as No. A, except tin cups and plates in place of white enameled ware. Price, complete.........................15.50
Stove is made of heavy Russia sheet iron, has 4 lids, oven is placed on top of stove when in use. Stove does not knock down; fire is built on ground; fuel door in front. The stove just fits easily into box mentioned above, and of course is just a little smaller than dimensions of box. There are cheaper outfits on the market, but this is a first-class one in every particular.

United States Flags.

Made of Standard Wool Bunting.

Prices are for flags only, without staff or tassels.

Regulation widths.

Fast colors.

49280

Length..	3 ft.	4 ft.	5 ft.	6 ft.	7 ft.	8 ft.	10 ft.
Each....	$0.89	$1.20	$1.45	$1.94	$2.20	$2.60	$3.65
Length..	12 ft.		14 ft.		16 ft.		18 ft.
Each....	$4.52		$5.75		$7.40		$8.76
Length..	20 ft.		24 ft.		28 ft.		30 ft.
Each....	$10.50		$14.00		$18.00		$21.00

N. B.—A 6 ft flag is the smallest that 44 stars can be put on. All flags 6 ft and over have 44 stars.

Procession Flags.
Made of Standard Bunting.

49290 6x6½ feet, with staff, spearhead, tassel and boot; complete ... .$ 9.75
49291 Flag only................................ 4.50

U. S. Muslin Flags on Stick.

To amuse the children and for decorating purposes.

	Per doz.	Per gross.
49295 Size, 2x3 inch.............	$0.03	$0.20
Size, 2½x4 inch.............	.04	.27
Size, 3½x6 inch.............	.05	.43
Size, 4½x7½ inch.............	.09	.60
Size, 6x9½ inch.............	.14	1.15
Size, 9x14 inch.............	.25	2.25
Size, 12x18 inch.............	.40	3.35
Size, 13x23 inch.............	.45	
Size, 18x27 inch.............	.65	
Size, 22x36 inch.............	1.00	

Burgees, Streamers and Campaign Flags furnished on short notice. Prices on application.

SMOKERS' ARTI- CLES PIPES, ETC.

You will find our prices on pipes from 25 to 75 per cent. less than regular retail prices. Moisten your wood pipes with water before smoking to prevent burning the pipes. Postage, 3 to 5 cents extra on pipes

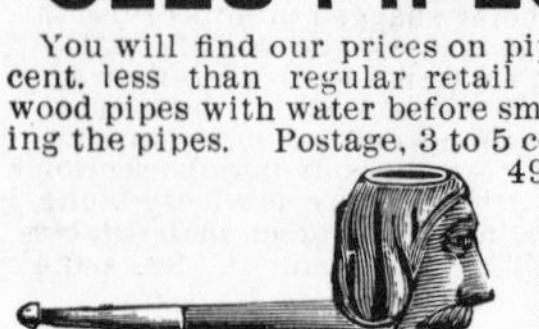

49600 Fancy Carved Brier Pipes, good large bowl, English amber mouthpiece. Entire length, 5 inches.
Each...........$0.38
Per dozen........ 4.00

Pipes--Continued.

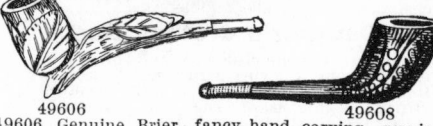

49602 Genuine Brier, hand carved, assorted designs or stems, genuine amber mouthpiece; an elegant pipe. Entire length, about 6 inches. A regular $2.00 pipe at retail.
Each...............$1.13 Per dozen.........$11.00
49603 Genuine Brier, assorted designs, same shape as 49602. English amber mouthpiece. A GOOD PIPE. Generally sold for highest quality for $1.00 to $1.50 each. Our price, each .75
Per dozen.................................... 8.40 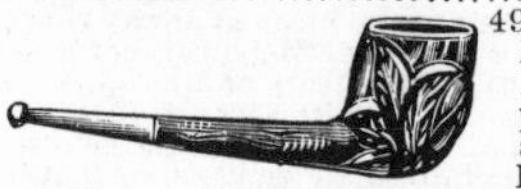
49604 Genuine Brier, hand carved, long. English amber mouthpiece, entire length, about 6 inches, good large bowl.
Each............$0.30 Per dozen............$2.90

49606 Genuine Brier, fancy hand carving, genuine amber mouthpiece, large bowl; a fine pipe.
Each.......$0.75 Per dozen.......$8.00
49608 Genuine Carved Brier. "Woodstock shape," English amber mouthpiece, good heavy bowl, and a desirable pipe; about 5¾ inches entire length, one of our best sellers.
Each...........$0.25 Per dozen....... 2.70
49610 Genuine Brier, carved bowl and stem, good large bowl, genuine amber mouth piece.
Each.......$0.40
Per doz............$4.40
49612 Genuine Brier, English amber mouthpiece, good, thick bowl, length, about 6 in. assorted shapes, all desirable and well made. Each.....$0.35 Per dozen........$3.60 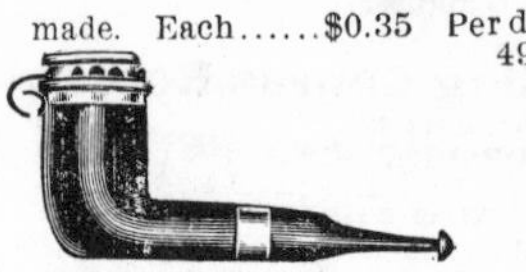
49616 Dark Rosewood Finish, heavy nickel cover, band on stem, good heavy horn mouthpiece, large bowl and stem, a very durable pipe, elegantly finished.
Each...........$0.38 Per dozen.............$4.00
49617 Genuine Brier, self-cleaner, band on stem, fine horn mouthpiece with cleaner.
Each............$0.28
Per dozen........ 3.00

49618 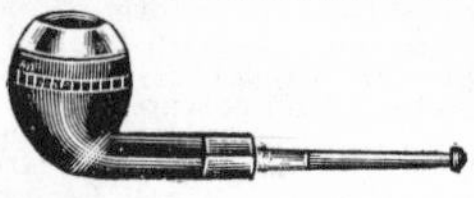   49620
49618 Self cleaner, same as 49617, a French brier bowl, rubber stem, horn cleaner, entire length about 5½ in. assorted shaped bowls, English bull dog and egg shape, in dark colors.
Each...........$0.22 Per dozen......... $2.25
49620 Dark Rosewood Finish, English shape, heavy nickel band on top of bowl and on stem. English amber mouthpiece, entire length about 5¾ inches. A very handsome pipe.
Each...............$0.18 Per dozen.........$1.75 
49624 W. R. Co. brier bowl, long rubber stem and nicotine cup, screw-off bowl and screw-off nicotine cup, nickel and gilt cover, cool smoker.
Each.....................$0.35
Per dozen.................... 3.38

49624   49625
49625 Genuine Brier, fine horn mouthpiece, band on stem nickeled and gilt cover, horn screw-off nicotine cup on end of stem. A handy, cool smoker. Each.............$0.40 ! 4.50
49650 Pipes, polished applewood.
Each $0.05
Per dozen.. 45

49654   49650
49654 Brier Pipes, imported, assorted shapes, and similar to cut, second in quality, but just as good as the best for a good smoke.
Each...............$0.12 Per dozen..........$1.30

Pipes--Continued.

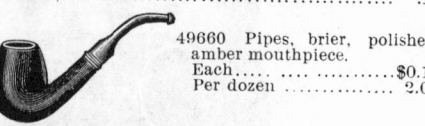

49655 French Brier Pipes, round stem, amber mouthpiece, medium size, straight stem (style 49654). Each....................... .18

49660 Pipes, brier, polished, amber mouthpiece.
Each..... ....$0.18
Per dozen 2.00

49660

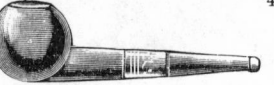

49664    49666
49664 Pipes, applewood, polished, with cover, rubber stem. Per doz....$1.20 Each.........$0.12
49666 Pipes, applewood, with patent adjustable perforated cover, rubber mouthpiece.
Each ....$0.10 Per dozen......... 1.15
49676 English Brier Pipe, finished in dark colors, a large heavy pipe, with light colored horn mouthpiece, nickel band on stem. A very durable pipe.
Each......................................$0.35

49678 French Brier Pipe, finished in natural color of wood; a large heavy pipe. Light colored horn mouthpiece; same shape as No. 49676. Each.. .25
49682 Brier Pipe, egg shape, cannot tip over when laid on table or shelf, English amber mouthpiece.
entire length, 5½ inches. Each.................$0.20
Per dozen.................... 2.25

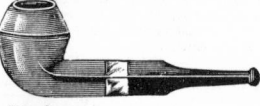

49683 Fine Brier Pipe, nickel cover, band on stem, rubber mouthpiece, "bull dog" style.
Entire length, 5¼ inches. Each..............$0 25
Per dozen 2.85

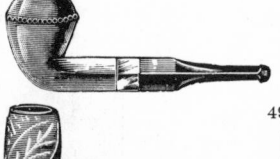

49684 Applewood Pipe, band on stem, "bull dog" style, rubber mouthpiece, strong and durable. Each..........$0.13
Per dozen 1.40
49685 Bull Dog Brier Pipe, nickel band, rubber stem, good large bowl, strong and durable. Entire length, 5¼ inches. Each..........$0.18
Per dozen.... 2.00 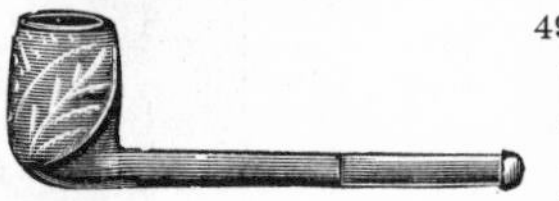
49686 Genuine Brier Pipe, imitation amber mouthpiece, carved bowl, a very neat little pipe.
Each... ......$0.18
Per dozen........ 1.70

49687 Genuine Brier Pipe "The Teamster's Favorite." Large deep bowl, short heavy stem, English amber mouthpiece, made strong and durable, can be carried in the vest pocket, not liable to get broken.
Entire length, 4¼ inches. Each..........$0.35
Per dozen 3.60

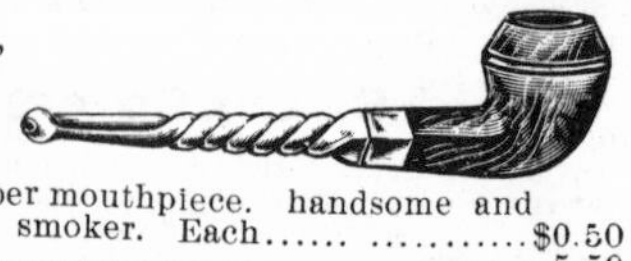

49688 Fine brier, "bull dog" shape, nickel band on stem, 3½ inch twisted English amber mouthpiece. handsome and durable—a fine smoker. Each...... ....$0.50
per dozen... 5.50
49733 Genuine Brier Bowl, 4 inch rubber stem; a neat, tidy little pipe.
Each................$0.08

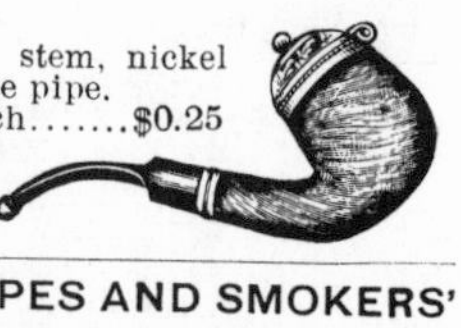

49739 Pipe, brier, rubber stem, nickel cover, a good and durable pipe. Entire length, 5¾ in. Each.......$0.25
Per dozen.........$2.70

Pipes—Continued.

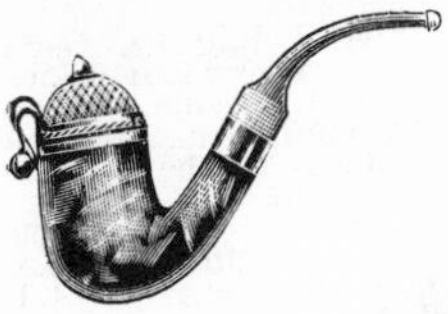

49740

49740 Brier Pipe, nickel band on stem, fancy nickel cover, bent stem, English amber mouthpiece, entire length, 5½ inches.
Each.................$0.38
Per dozen.......... 4.00

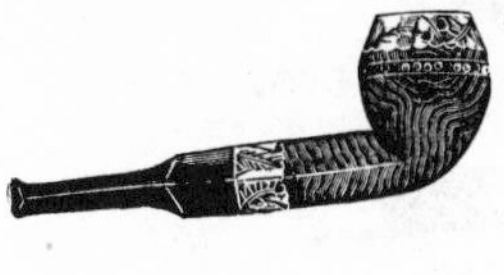

Bull Dog

49753 Real French Brier, English bulldog shape, heavy diamond square stem, horn mouthpiece, fancy silver plated band on stem and top of bowl, entire length 5½ inches. Each..$0.40

49754 Brier Pipe same 49753 in a fine leather covered case.
Each..$1.00

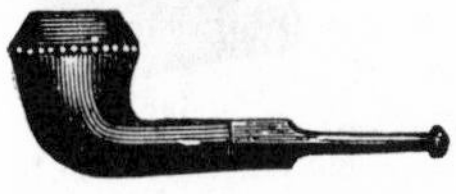

Bull Dog.

49755 Imported Brier Pipe, London shape, heavy and strong, fine horn mouthpiece.
Each.........$0.38
Per dozen....... 4.00

49756 French Brier Bowl, bull dog shape, diamond square stem, fine amber mouthpiece, heavy and durable, English bulldog style.
Each...$1.00

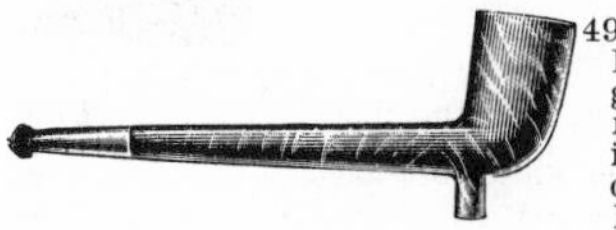

49765 Genuine Brier Pipe with genuine amber mouthpiece, finished in natural color of wood.
Each......$0.59
Per dozen.. 6.00

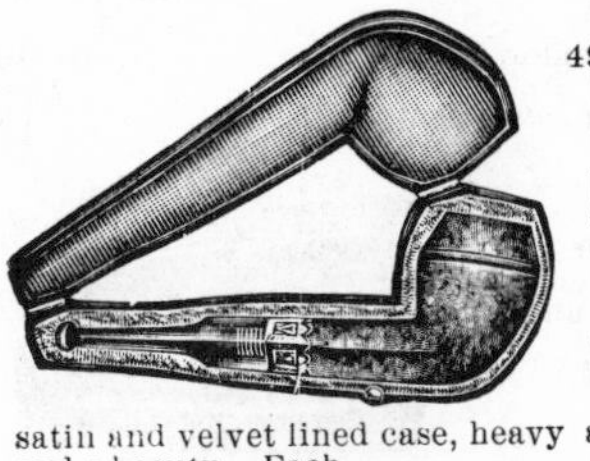

49767 Pipe, warranted finest quality French brier, English shaped bowl, finest finish, diamond square stem, 2½ in., fine amber mouthpiece, silver band on stem. Entire length, 5½ in., in leather covered, satin and velvet lined case, heavy and durable and a beauty. Each $3.00

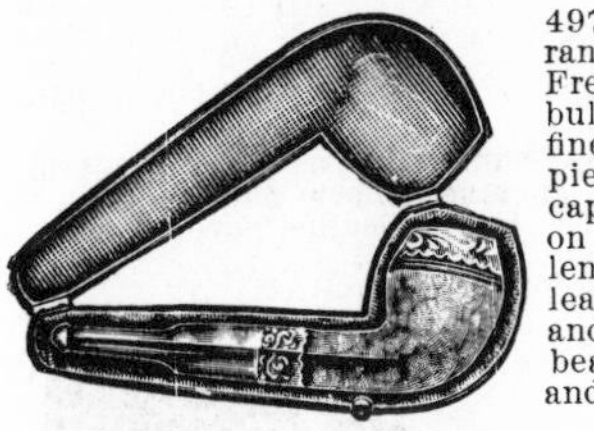

49768 Pipe, warranted fine quality French brier, English bull dog shape, 2½ in., fine amber mouthpiece, German silver cap on bowl and band on stem. Entire length, 5½ in.; in fine leather covered, satin and velvet lined case, beautifully finished and an elegant article.
Each.......................................$2.25

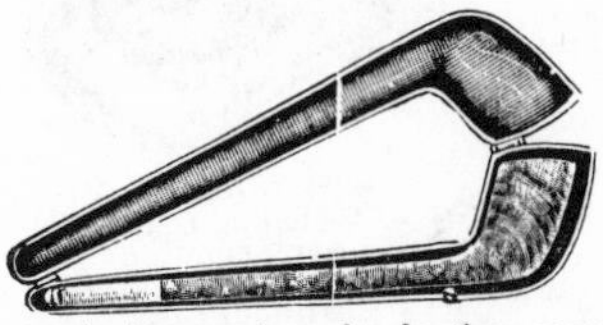

49773 Pipe, warranted, French brier, finely finished, assorted shape, 2 inch oval amber mouthpiece, Entire length, 6 inches, medium sized bowl, a cool nice smoker, in leather covered, satin and velvet lined case. Each.....................$2.00

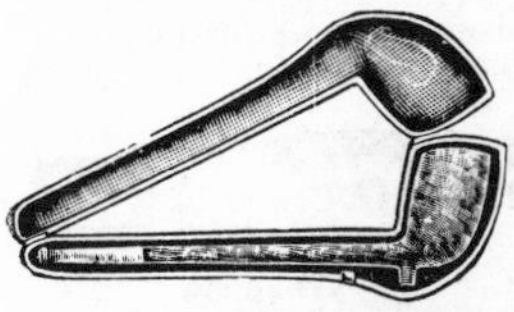

49774 Pipe, warranted French brier, fine finish, round stem, 2 in. fine amberite mouthpiece. Entire length, 5 in. In leather covered, velvet and satin lined case, assorted.
A little dandy smoker.
Each............$1.00

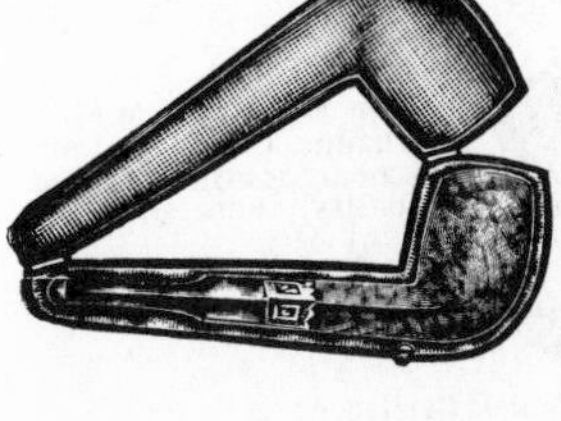

49775 Pipe, warranted finest French brier, diamond square stem, heavy, 2½ inch, fine amber mouthpiece, silver band on stem. Entire length, 6 in. In leather covered, satin and velvet lined case. A handsome and durable article.
Each......... $2.95

Pipes—Continued.

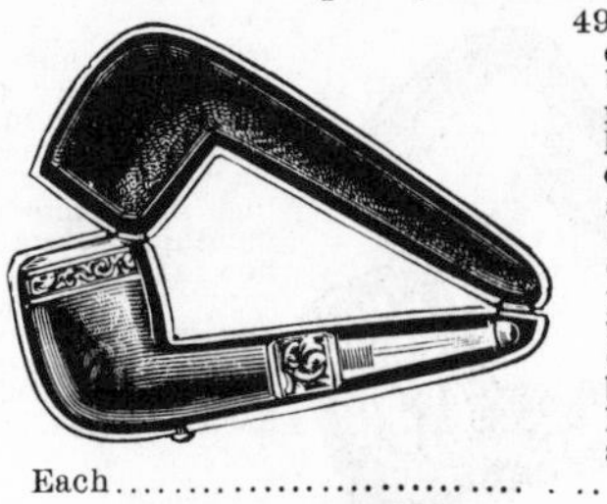

49780 Very finest quality French brier, fine amber mouthpiece, heavy gold plated band on bowl and on stem, in leather covered case, fine silk plush lined, just the thing for Christmas and birthday presents, large, handsome and durable.
Each.......................................$4.75

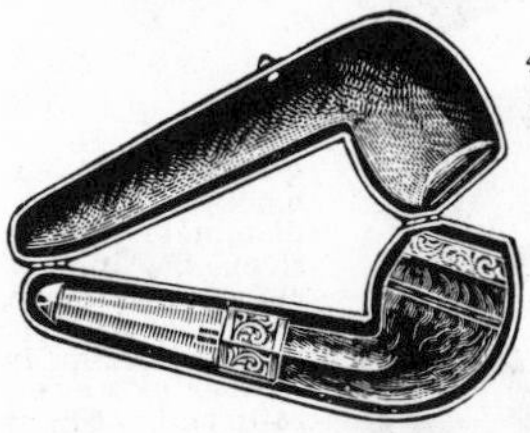

49784 Very finest French brier, fine amber mouthpiece, heavy gold plated band on bowl and stem, highest quality finish, in leather, covered case lined with silk plush, a beauty.
Each $4.50

49785 Fine Chip Meerschaum, same style as 49784, fine amberite mouthpiece, silver plated band on bowl and stem, in leather covered case, silk and plush lined; a good pipe and a handsome one. Each..........................$1.75
Per dozen 18.00

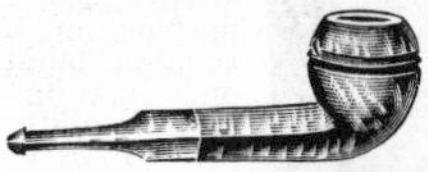

49791 English shape, genuine brier, 2¼ in. imitation amber mouthpiece, entire length, 5 in. Each..$0.18
Per dozen............ 1.90

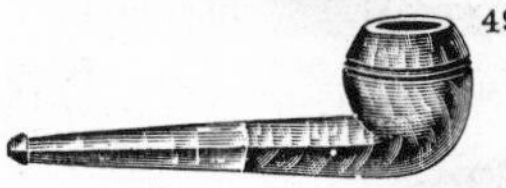

49792 English shape, genuine brier, 2⅝ in. mouthpiece, entire length, 5¾ in.; bargain.
Each $0.37
Per doz.......... 3.95

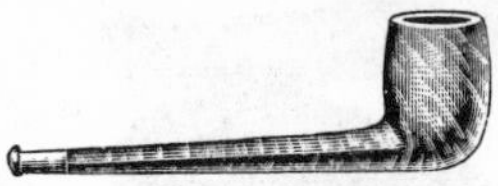

49793 Genuine Brier, genuine amber mouthpiece, entire length 5¼ in., height bowl about 1⅞ in.; big seller. Each.......$0.35
Per dozen.. 3.60

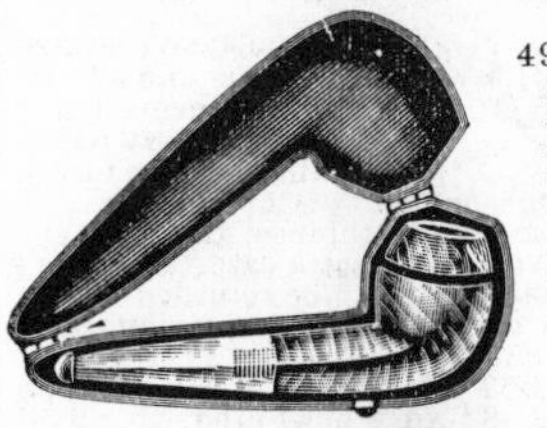

49794 nglish shape, genuine brier, 2¼ in. amber mouthpiece, in fine leather covered case, "just the right size bowl, not too large and not too small," entire length, 5⅛ in.
Each $1.80

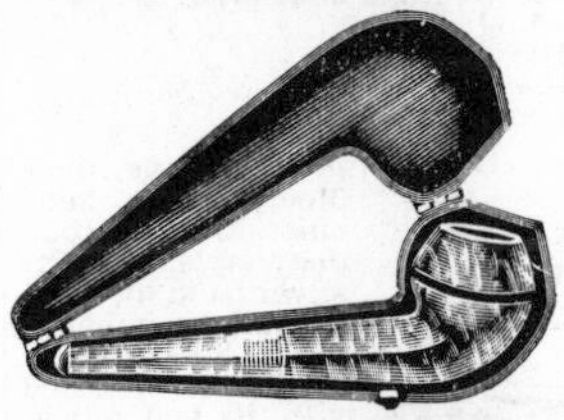

49795 English shape, genuine brier, 3 in. fine amber mouthpiece, in leather covered case, medium size bowl, entire length 5⅝ in.
Each.........$2.10

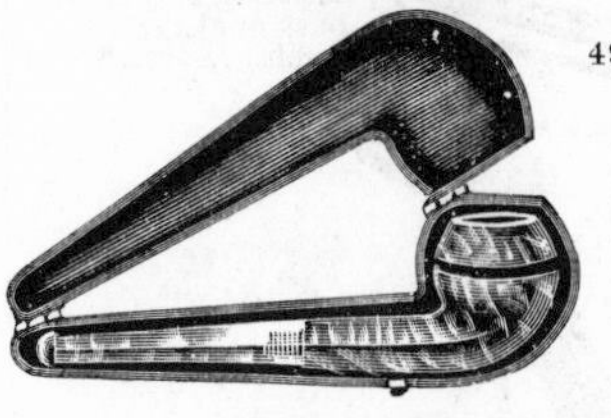

49796 English shape, genuine brier, 3¼ inches, Chinese amber mouthpiece, in fine leather case, entire length, 6 in.; good size.
Each.... .$1.10
Per dozen 12.00

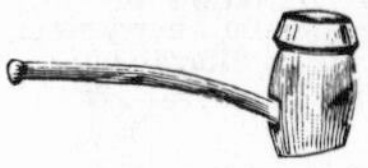

49800 Genuine Weixelwood Pipes, wood stem.
Each.................. $0.08

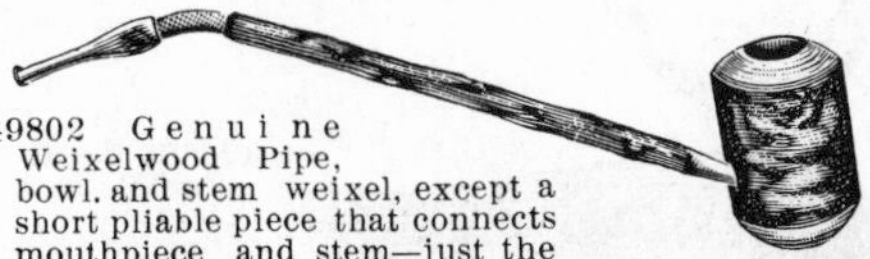

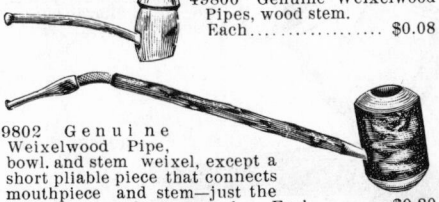

49802 Genuine Weixelwood Pipe, bowl, and stem weixel, except a short pliable piece that connects mouthpiece and stem—just the article for a cool, sweet smoke. Each...........$0.20

Pipes—Continued.

49803 Pipe Bowls (no stems), genuine brier root, with fancy cover, to use stems with cork on the end like Nos. 49810 and 49811. Bowls, each, $0.40

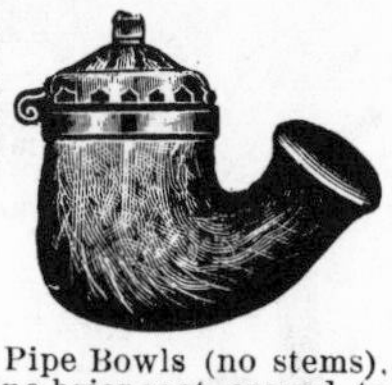

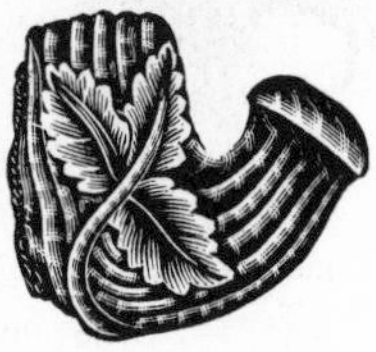

49805 Pipe Bowls (no stems), genuine brier root, carved, to use stem with cork on end like Nos. 49810 and 49811.
Bowls, each.............$0.50

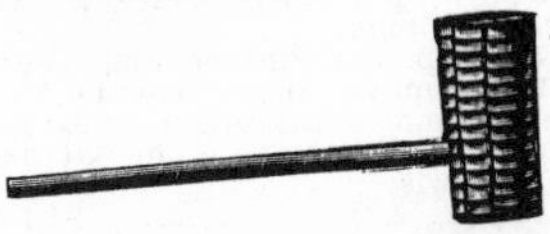

49806 Corn Cob Pipes, reed stem, well made.
Each........$0.03
Per dozen... .25

Pipe Stems.

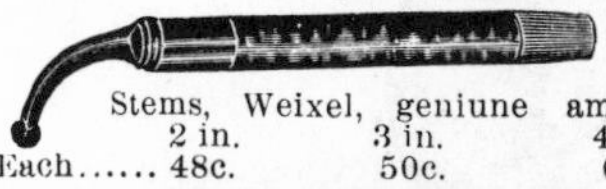

Stems extra by mail, 2 to 4 cts.

49810 Pipe Stems, Weixel, genuine amber mouthpiece

	2 in.	3 in.	4 in.	6 in.
Each......	48c.	50c.	60c.	70c.

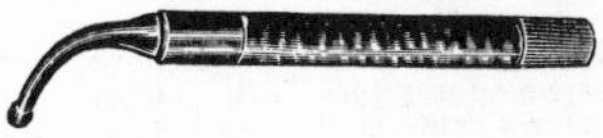

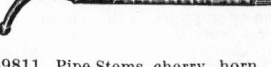

	Each.	Per doz
49811 Pipe Stems, cherry, horn mouthpiece, 2 in. to 6 in..	$0.12	$1.25
49813 German Horn Mouthpiece	.11	1.05

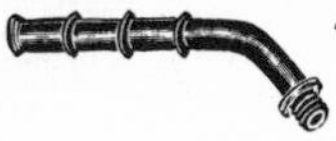

49814 Horn Mouthpiece.

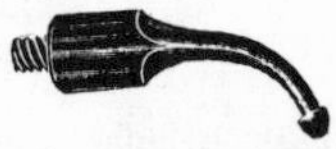

	Small.	Medium.	Large.	Doz. assorted
Each	7c	11c.	16c.	$1.13

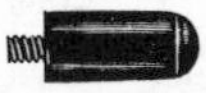

49815 Horn Mouthpieces straight,

	Small.	Medium.	Large.	Doz assorted.
Each....	5c	8c	10c	90c.

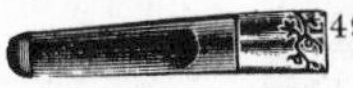

	Each.	Per doz
49816 English Amber Pipe Stem Mounts, assorted sizes, round..	$0.15	$1.25
49817 English Amber Pipe Stem Mounts, bent, assorted sizes, round...	.20	2.00
49818 English Amber Pipe Stem Mounts, assorted sizes, flat....	.15	1.30
49819 Genuine English Amber Pipe, Stem Mounts, assorted sizes, flat	.25	2.40
49820 Rubber Pipe Stem Mounts, with nickel band; straight, round.........	.04	40
49822 Rubber Pipe Stem Mounts; nickel band; bent......	.08	.85

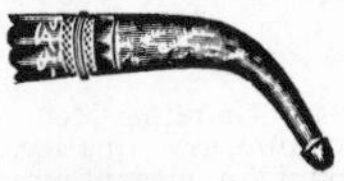

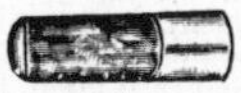

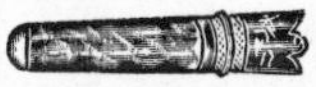

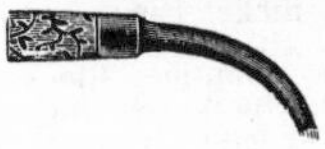

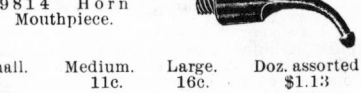

Pipe Stem Mounts are for fitting on stems where the old mouthpiece or a stem has been broken.

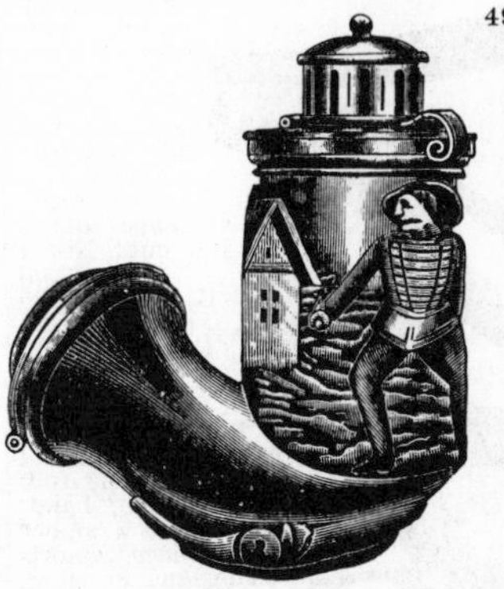

49823 German Antique Pipe, imitation colored meerschaum bowl engraved in different designs, nickel plated, cover 8-inch, cherry stem with horn mouthpiece, bowl about 3¾ in. high; a big pipe and a good one.
Each.... $1.40
Extra by mail 10 cents.

WE CAN NOW GUARANTEE LOWEST PRICES
on all leading makes of Shot Guns, Rifles, Revolvers, Ammunition, etc.

Pipes—Continued.

49830 German Porcelain Pipe with 18-inch wood and flexible rubber stem, horn mouthpiece, porcelain bowl and nicotine cup, fancy figured bowls, different designs; just the pipe for a big long smoke.

Each.................................$1.00
Bowls only. For above pipes......30
Weight, 10 ounces.

49831 Companion Pipe, genuine meerschaum, genuine amber mouthpiece, nickel trimmings, in leather case, silk lined; a neat little pipe; different designs in bowls.
Each...............................$1.50

49836 Chip Meerschaum Pipes with amber mouthpiece, in velvet and satin lined case, bent stem. Each...............$1.20
Pipes by mail, 5c extra.

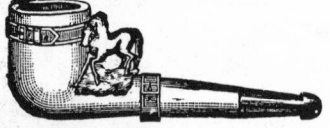

49840 Genuine First Quality Hand Carved Meerschaum Pipe with amber mouthpieces, in fine colored satin case; assorted figures, carved on this pipe. Each..................$4.00

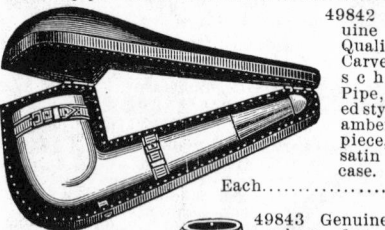

49842 Genuine First Quality Hand Carved Meerschaum Pipe, assorted styles with amber mouthpiece, in satin lined case.
Each...................$3.00

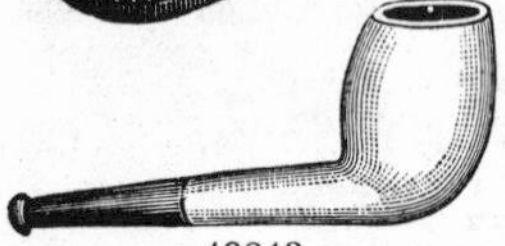

49843 Genuine Meerschaum, first quality, hand cut, elegant amber mouthpiece, assorted shapes; are in satin lined case, good.
Each...........$2.90

49844 Meerschaum Pipes, second quality amber mouthpiece (style of 49843,) in case velvet lined, Each..................$0.75
49845 Imitation Meerschaum Pipe, white and colored, with rubber mouthpiece, nickel band on stem, straight stem. Each...................25 
49846 Genuine Block Meerschaum, 4 inch turkey bone stem.
Each..............$0.20

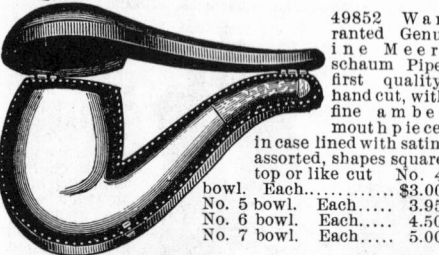

49852 Warranted Genuine Meerschaum Pipe, first quality, hand cut, with fine amber mouthpiece, in case lined with satin, assorted, shapes square top or like cut No. 4 bowl. Each..........$3.00
No. 5 bowl. Each.....3.95
No. 6 bowl. Each.....4.50
No. 7 bowl. Each.....5.00

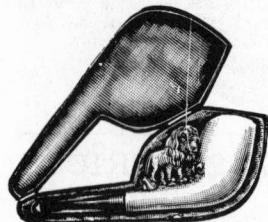

49855 Pipe, finest quality block meerschaum, hand-cut, best amber mouthpiece, assorted designs on stem, large bowl, and a beauty. In fine leather covered, velvet and satin lined case. Each...$4.00

Pipes—Continued.

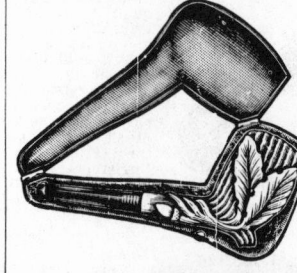

49856 Pipe, finest quality block meerschaum, hand cut and carved, 2½ inch fine amber mouthpiece, large bowl and an elegant article, in fine leather covered satin and velvet lined case.
Each........$4.25

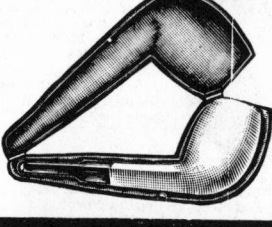

49857 Pipe, finest quality, hand cut block meerschaum, diamond square stem, 2½ in. fine amber mouthpiece, entire length 6 in. A large *fine* pipe in leather covered satin and velvet lined case.
Each........$4.75

49859 Warranted highest quality genuine block meerschaum, hand cut, genuine amber mouthpiece; in satin lined case.

No. 3 bowl......$2.00	No. 5 bowl.......$3.00
No. 4 bowl......2.45	No. 6 bowl.......4.15

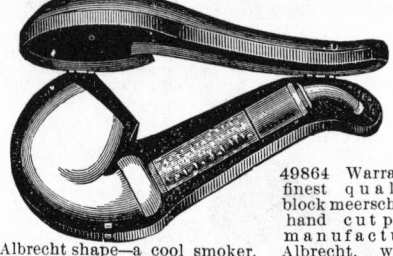

49864 Warranted finest quality, block meerschaum hand cut pipes manufactued.
Albrecht shape—a cool smoker. Albrecht, with Weichsel stem and amber mouthpiece, all in an elegant leather covered velvet and satin case. The very finest goods in the market. Can be returned if not as represented. Can also furnish this pipe in same shape bowl as No. 49858.
No. 2 bowl pipe.....$2.63 | No. 5 bowl pipe.....$4.89
No. 3 bowl pipe.....3.38 | No. 6 bowl pipe.....5.50
No. 4 bowl pipe.....4.00
Extra by mail, 5 to 10c.
Above pipe without case. 75c.less.
Pipes by mail, 3 to 5 cents extra.

49866 Genuine Block Meerschaum, hand cut, English bull dog style, sterling silver band on stem, 2¼ in. fine amberite mouthpiece; in leather case, lined with silk and velvet, best quality.
Each.........$3.75

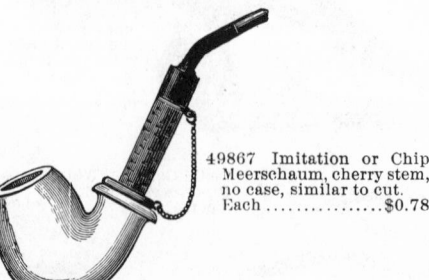

49867 Imitation or Chip Meerschaum, cherry stem, no case, similar to cut.
Each...............$0.78

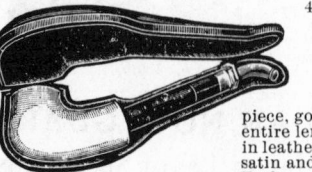

49868 Genuine Block Meerschaum Pipe. Hamburg shape, genuine amber mouthpiece, good large pipe; entire length, 7 inches, in leather covered case, satin and silk lined.
Each..............$4.50

Pipes—Continued.

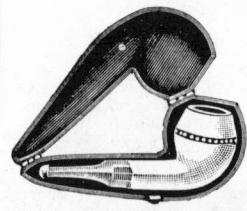

49870 "Bull Dog" Genuine Meerschaum; finest quality, genuine amber mouthpiece, thick and finely finished. Entire length.
                                     Each.
No. 5 4½ in....$3.50
No. 6 5¼ in....4.35
No. 7 5½ in....4.88

Cigar Holders.

(Cigar holders by mail, 3 to 5c. extra.)

49876
49876 Cigar Holder, brier and meerschaum.
Each...$0.15
Per dozen...................................1.60

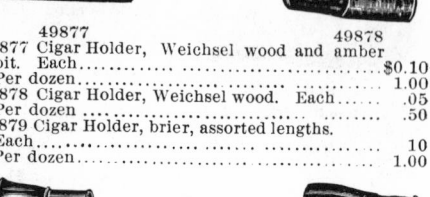

49877   **49878**
49877 Cigar Holder, Weichsel wood and amber bit. Each..$0.10
Per dozen...................................1.00
49878 Cigar Holder, Weichsel wood. Each......05
Per dozen.....................................50
49879 Cigar Holder, brier, assorted lengths.
Each...10
Per dozen....................................1.00

49880   **49881**
49880 Cigar Holder, all horn. Each.......$0.04
Per dozen.....................................40
49881 Cigar Holder, all wood. Each.......05
Per dozen.....................................42

49886   **49884**
49884 Cigarette Holder, brier. Each.......$0.10
Per dozen...................................1.00
49886 Cigarette Holder, brier. Each........08
Per dozen.....................................75

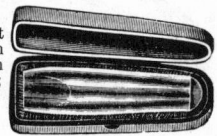

49888 Cigar Holders, finest quality, solid amber in leather covered and satin and plush lined cases; a very fine article.

Holder, 2 in. long........................$1.68
Holder, 2½ in. long.....................2.25
Holder, 3 in. long.........................3.00
Holder, 3½ in. long......................3.35

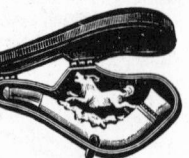

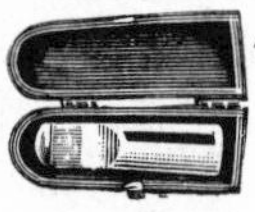

49889 Genuine Meerschaum Cigar Holder, genuine amber mouthpiece 2¼ inches long, in leather covered case.
Each...$0.33
Per dozen....................................3.40

49890 Cigarette Holder, of genuine meerschaum and amber, in silk lined case $1.00

49895-96
49895 Genuine Meerschaum Cigar Holder, genuine amber mouthpiece. without case.
Each.........$0.50

49896 Genuine Meerschaum Cigarette Holder, amber mouthpiece, without case. Each........$0.45

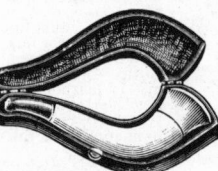

49897   **49899**
49897 Cigar Holders, meerschaum, medium small, in neat case. Each.........................$0.40
49899 Cigar Holder, meerschaum, medium large, extra quality, neat case........................75

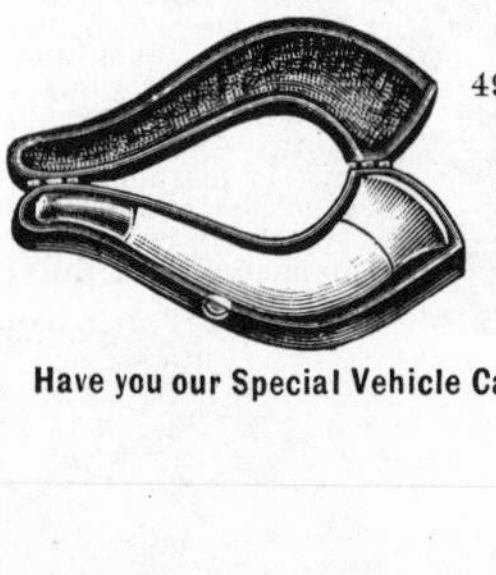

49900 Genuine Meerschaum Cigar Holder, amber mouthpiece, best quality, and just the right size.
Each..............$0.75

Cigar Holders—Continued.

49902 Meerschaum Cigar Holders, assorted designs, similar to cut, in fine velvet lined case.
Each.................$0.80
Per dozen............ 8.00

49902

49902½ Same as No. 49902, without case. Each $0.40
49903 Meerschaum Cigar Holders, hand cut. Amber mouthpiece, similar to cut, assorted styles. in velvet lined case. $0.70
Per dozen........ 7.00

49903

49907 Genuine Fine Quality Cigar Holders, hand carved. Elegant designs assorted, with amber mouthpiece similar to cut, in cases.
Each...............$1.50
Per dozen 15.00

49907

Pocket Match Safes.
Extra by mail, 2 to 3 cents.

   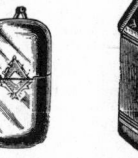

49915.   **49916.**   **49917.**   **49919.**

Each. Per doz.
49915 Pocket Match Safe, all leather, telescope style, a fine case........ ...$0.15 $1.40
49916 Pocket Match Safe, nickel plated, spring cover........... .05 .50
49917 Pocket Match Safe, heavy, nickel plated, patent snap cover........... .20 2.20
49919 Pocket Match Safe, heavy metal, leather covered, with nickel plated ends, an elegant article................. .20 2.00

49920 Pocket Match Safe, finely nickel plated metal, spring cover, embossed raised figures, 2¾x1½x⅜ inch, neat and desirable as it does not take up much room in pocket.
Each.....................$0.20
Per dozen.... .... 2.00

49921 Pocket Match Safe, fine nickel plated metal, plain finish, sliding spring cover, a very handy article, 2¼x1¼x¼ inch.
Each $0.14
Per dozen............................ 1.50

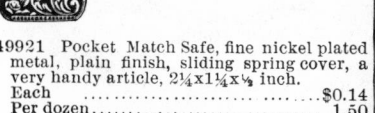

49922 The "Chuck Luck" Pocket Match Safe and Dice Box, combined, finely nickel plated metal, embossed raised figures in center, 5 dice in sliding cover on one end, which forms a neat DICE BOX, when removed. Each $0.25
Per dozen......................... 2.40
Retail price, 50c.

49924 The Handy Pocket Match Safe, "just a little thicker than a match," nickel plated on fine metal, handsomely made, finely finished. By pushing cover slightly it pushes one match out far enough to get hold of it. Illustration shows just how far it pushes the match out. Only one match at a time can be pushed out. The handiest match safe on the market. Each..$0.20

NO CHARGE For Cases Or Cartage.

Cigar Cases, Cigarette Cases, Tobacco Boxes.
Cigar Cases by mail, 3 to 5 cents extra.

49925 Cigar Case, embossed leather, nickel frame.
Each...............$0.23
Per dozen......... 2.40

49930 Cigar Case, fancy leather, nickel plated frame, good plain article.
Each..............$0.39

49931 Cigar Case, fancy embossed leather, nickel frame, leather and satin lined, full size and good case.
Each $0.70

49932 Cigar Case, fine embossed leather, fine nickel frame, satin and leather lined, with embroidered floral design done in silk on the inside, full size, handsome and durable.
Each..............,...$0.93

49933 Cigar Case, seal skin, dark colors, handsome nickel and gilt frame, leather and satin lined. Elegant floral designs done in silk on inside, full size and a good one.
Each.............,,...$1.20

49934 Cigar Case, fine Russia leather, fine nickel frame, leather lined, silk embroidered floral designs on inside, finely finished throughout; a beauty.
Each................$1.55

49935 Cigar Case, finest fancy finished leather, handsome figured bronze and gilt bronze frame, leather and satin lined, elegant floral designs in silk and gilt inside, full sizes, made in best manner; a gem.
Each............ . $3.00

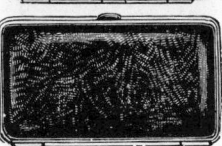

49936 Cigar Case, alligator leather, satin and leather lined, nickel frame, well made and durable.
Each..............$1.15

49937 Cigar Case, genuine lizard leather, drab and buff color, leather lined, nickel frame; a very desirable article.
Each..............$1.30

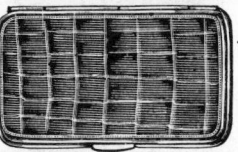

49938 Cigar Case, fine embossed leather cover, nickel frame, satin and leather lined, good size.
Each..............$0.60

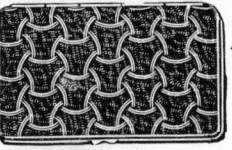

Each. Per doz.
49940 Cigar Case, Turkish leather, telescope style (see cut).......$0.30 $3.00

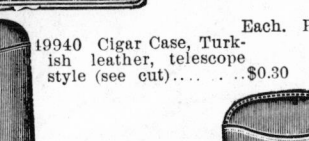

49941 Cigar Case, telescopic style, heavy embossed leather.
Each.....................$0.35
Per dozen................ ...... 3.40

Cigar Cases—Continued.

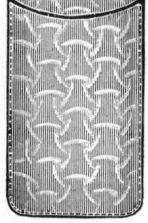

49942 Cigar Case, telescope style, soft leather, embossed finish.
Each.....................$0.23
Per dozen.................... 2.30

49945 Cigarette Case, telescopic style, all leather, vest pocket size, good and durable.
Each.....................$0.18
Per dozen.............. ...... 1.60

Snuff and Tobacco Boxes.

49971 German rustic design wood covered with birchbark buckskin string lift Each.... ....$0.06

49971   **49973**

49973 Snuff or Tobacco Box, fine black colored composition, strong and durable; 3¼x2 inches.
Each.... .... .17

49974 Snuff or Tobacco Box: ebony composition inlaid pearl on cover.

49974   **49975**

3x1½ in. Each $0.25
49975 Snuff or Tobacco Box, composition imitation ebony and tortoise shell, 3¼x1⅞, strong and durable. Each......................... .29·

49977 Tobacco Box, finest nickel plated metal, spring cover, good and strong, keeps tobacco clean and fresh.
Each.....................$0.20
Per dozen... .... 2.25

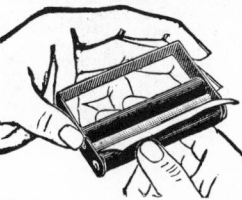

49978 Cigarette Case, fine nickel plated metal, embossed raised figures around sides, metal spring holder; inside, spring cover; keeps the cigarettes fresh and in perfect order. Neat and desirable.
Each.....................$0.25
Per dozen................ 2.40

Cigarette Machine.

49979 The Champion Cigarette Maker. The frame consists of a single piece, nickel plated and polished. There are two rollers, one moves back and forth in a slot and around these is a piece of flexible rubber cloth. It is handsomely made, strong, simple and durable; can be carried in the vest pocket, being but 3 in. long, 1½ in. wide by ¾ in. thick. Each...........................$0.25

BOOT AND SHOE DEPARTMENT.

Over 200,000 pairs sold in 1894.

Our yearly output of boots and shoes is now on a scale of such magnitude that we can still further reduce our well-known moderate percentage of profit without affecting our gross earnings, as the prices below will indicate.

In all cases send the size you want when you know it; otherwise send us the length and shape of the foot, drawn with a pencil while standing on a piece of clean, white paper; instep, ball and other measurements not necessary. From length and shape of this outline we can determine, from our knowledge of measurement, what size and width will fit your foot the best.

We would call special attention to goods in this department marked "warranted." We mean by "WARRANTED" just this: If at any time a pair of WARRANTED boots or shoes give out without just cause, report the fact to us and we will pay for repairing them, replace them with others or refund the money paid for them, according to the circumstances of the case. We do not warrant boots and shoes against fire. We will not allow for damages incurred by wetting and then burning shoes.

We will not warrant "Calf or Light Kip-Boots" to endure usage that only a "Stoga Boot" was designed for.

The meaning of the different letters representing the widths on the inside of ladies' shoes are as follows: (A) extra narrow: (B) very narrow; (C) narrow; (D) medium: (E) wide; (EE) very wide. The same applies to men's shoes. ☞ *Pegged and nailed boots and shoes are not made in half sizes.*

The Feather Weight.

Ladies' Hand Turn Shoes.

52001 This shoe is made from genuine Grisson French Kid, narrow, square toe last, long patent leather tip; very flexible sole, with thin edge. For a fashionable dress-boot there is nothing finer. This shoe we can thoroughly recommend, and equal to any six dollar shoe on the market. Sizes, 2½ to 7. Widths, C, D, E, and EE. Per pair................$4.25

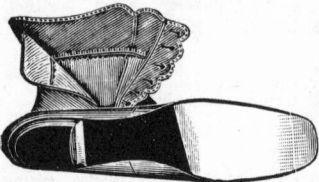

52002 Ladies' Genuine Grisson French Kid Button, made over a perfect common-sense last. The bottom being sewed by hand, turn or slipper sole being very light and fine, and of the best material, will wear equal to a much heavier shoe, at the same time will give a greater amount of comfort. They are now considered a very stylish shoe and are worn by the majority of ladies. Widths, B, C, D, E. Size, 2½ to 7. Per pair $4.25
Weight, 14 ounces.

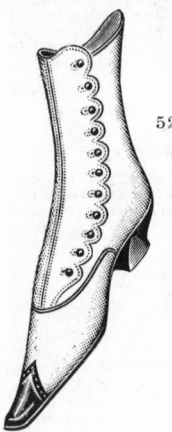

52003 Ladies' Fine French Dongola Button Shoes. The stock in this shoe is a very fine quality, soft satin finish and wears equally as well as French kid. The last is the very latest narrow square toe, with long patent leather tip, light turn sole, feather edge, medium opera heel not high, making in all a very graceful looking shoe when on the foot, fits perfectly and wears well. Sizes, 2½ to 7. Widths, C, D, E and EE. Per pair........... ....$3.00

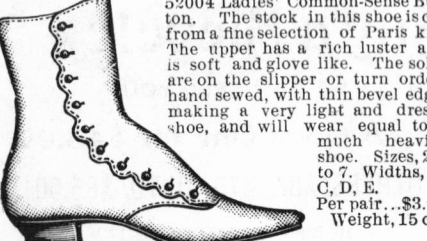

52004 Ladies' Common-Sense Button. The stock in this shoe is cut from a fine selection of Paris kid. The upper has a rich luster and is soft and glove like. The soles are on the slipper or turn order, hand sewed, with thin bevel edge, making a very light and dressy shoe, and will wear equal to a much heavier shoe. Sizes, 2½ to 7. Widths, B, C, D, E. Per pair...$3.00
Weight, 15 oz.

We have a finely equipped Freight and Express Bureau, and will be glad to quote Freight and Express Rates to any point upon application.

52005 This shoe is made from a very fine grade of satin finish dongola. Needle toe last and new cut pointed tip. This style is worn a great deal now as the very pointed toe has a tendency to make the foot appear smaller, and gives it a very graceful appearance; should be worn a trifle longer than the ordinary shoe. This shoe we claim to be equal to many of the four dollar shoes on the market and will give the wearer the same amount of comfort as a high-priced shoe, and will look and wear equally as well. Sizes, 2½ to 7. Widths, C, D, E and EE. Per pair.......$2.50
Weight, 15 ounces.

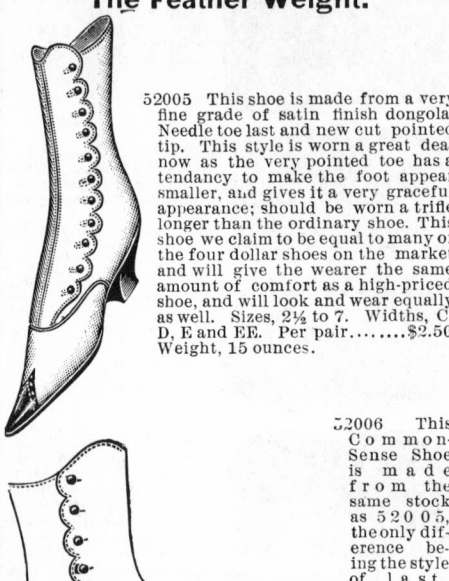

52006 This Common-Sense Shoe is made from the same stock as 52005, the only difference being the style of last, which calls for a low heel and wide toe. This being a very popular style, we claim for it to be equal to any $4.00 turn shoe on the market. Sizes, 2½ to 7; widths, B, C, D, E. Per pair... ....$2.50
Weight, 15 ounces.

Extra High Cut Shoe.

52007 Ladies' Glazed Dongola Kid Button, opera last, high heel and pointed toe, extra high cut tops, with tassel, attractive and dressy, flexible soles, very desirable as a riding boot. Sizes, 2½ to 7. Widths, C, D, E. Per pair..$3.75
Weight, 16 ounces.

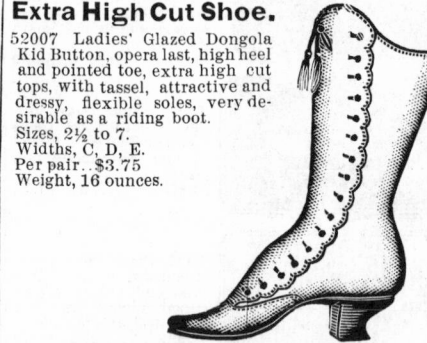

Goodyear Welt Shoes.

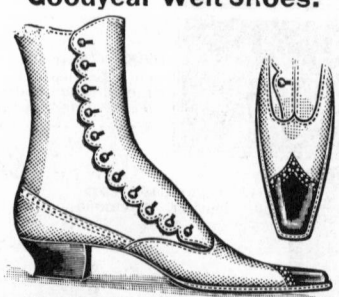

52008 This shoe is made from a very fine selection of Vici kid of high grade finish, much more so than the ordinary dongola stock. The style is the very latest narrow square toe, with long patent leather tip, and medium heel with fair stitch around outside of sole. This shoe is adapted to all kinds of wear, has a very graceful appearance when on the foot. Do not pass this shoe when selecting, for they will give excellent wear. Sizes, 2½ to 7; widths, B, C, D, E, and EE. Per pair................$3.00

52009 Ladies' Genuine Vici Kid Button. Philadelphia square toe last, with patent leather tip and medium Goodyear welt soles, slightly extended, with fair stitch around outside. This style takes the place of a full common sense last, which is not so wide and clumsy looking, and at the same time gives the required width across ball of foot. One of the prevailing styles at present, fits neat and looks well, and will give excellent service for a fall and winter shoe; has no equal. Sizes, 2½ to 8; widths, A, B, C, D, E, and EE. Per pair.............$3.00

Ladies' Walkenfast.

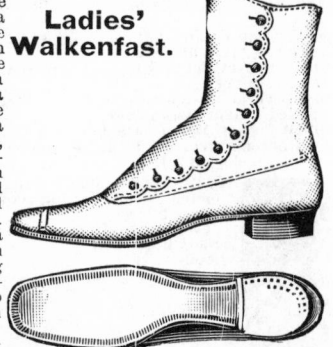

52024 This shoe is made from a very fine grade of satin finish dongola. The tops are also a dongola, but a dull finish. The bottoms are a Goodyear welt, making a perfectly smooth inner sole and free from all imperfections. The toe is a medium width with a long perforated patent leather tip and extension sole; medium weight, becoming very flexible after wearing a few times. This shoe is a perfect beauty, a good fitter and a good wearer, and for ease and comfort in walking it has no equal. Sizes, 2½ to 7; widths, C, D, E, and EE. Per pair................ ....$3.30
Weight, 17 ounces.

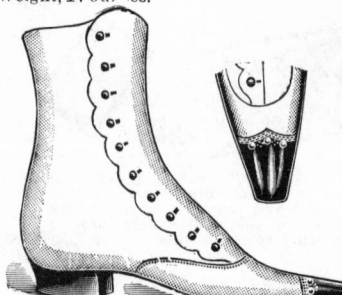

52027 Ladies' American French Kid Button, medium square toe, with long patent leather tip, the heel of a medium height, making a very attractive and dressy shoe. The stock used in the manufacture of this brand has the appearance of a French kid, being soft and glove like, enabling it to readily adjust to the foot, insuring a perfect fit. We think it superior to French kid, being less liable to chip or crack and much more durable. Sizes, 2½ to 7; widths, B, C, D, E, and EE. Per pair................$3.00
Weight, 16 ounces.

52028 Ladies' American French Kid, Button, same as 52027, only made on Common Sense last. Low heel and broad toe, giving ample room across the ball of foot, making a comfortable shoe for tender feet, and will not create corns or bunions; sole light and flexible. Sizes, 2½ to 7. Widths, A, B, C, D, E. Price................ ....$3.00
Weight, 16 ounces.

Our Wonder.

52031 This shoe is made from a very choice selection of dongola kid, with patent leather tip, opera toe and medium heel. This shoe we may well call a wonder, for it contains all of the good qualities of the higher grade shoes both as to style, fit and finish. We have this shoe made special for our own trade, and we claim for it to be the best shoe in the country for the money; do not be afraid to order; they will wear you well. Sizes, 2½ to 7, C, D, E, EE. Per pair..$2.00 Weight, 16 ounces.

Ladies' Dongola Blucherette.

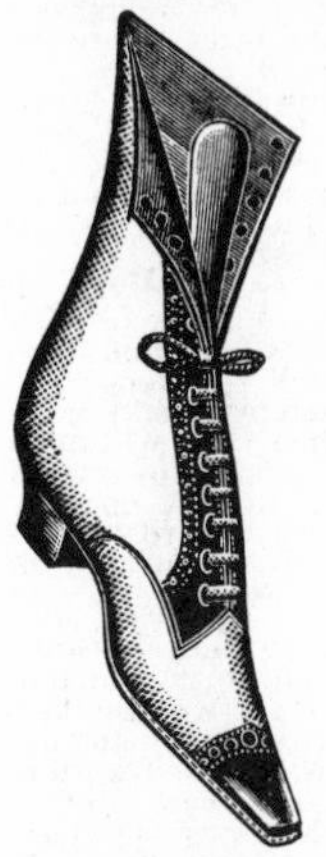

52033 You will notice the novel and very peculiar way in which this shoe is constructed; unlike any other shoe in the book, making one of the newest patterns in ladies' shoes. The uppers are made from fine satin finish dongola kid, handsomely trimmed with patent leather; medium weight soles, making a very neat and stylish dress boot; narrow square toe with long patent leather tip. Sizes, 2½ to 7, B, C, D, E and EE.
Per pair....................$2.75
Weight, 15 ounces.

The Razor Toe.

Weight 15 ounces.

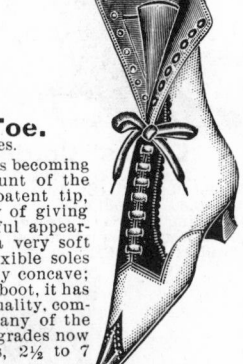

52034 This style shoe is becoming very popular on account of the long narrow toe, and patent tip, which has a tendency of giving the foot a very graceful appearance. The stock is a very soft dongola, with light flexible soles and medium but slightly concave; for a neat stylish dress boot, it has no equal and for the quality, compares favorably with many of the three dollar and a half grades now on the market. Sizes, 2½ to 7 widths, C, D, E and EE.
Per pair....................$2.50

Ladies' Tan or Russet Shoes.

Weight, 17 ounces.

52035 This shoe is made from a very fine quality of russet or tan colored dongola, front lace with light flexible soles. Picadilly toe with long perforated tip. This shoe requires no blacking or dressing and will be all the rage for the coming season. We have taken special pains to secure a shoe that will give good, honest service, and for style and finish will have no equal. Do not fail to order if you want a sightly and stylish shoe at a price that cannot be beaten. Sizes 2½ to 6; widths, C, D and E.

Per pair....................$2.75

M. W. & Co's Wear Resisters.

Weight, 16 ounces.
52043 Ladies Glazed Dongola Kid Button, opera last. The chief feature of this shoe is the perfect fitting qualities, combined with style and finish; equal to any four-dollar shoe. Every pair guaranteed. Sizes, 2½ to 7; widths, C, D, E, EE. Per pair.........$2.75 Weight, 16 oz.

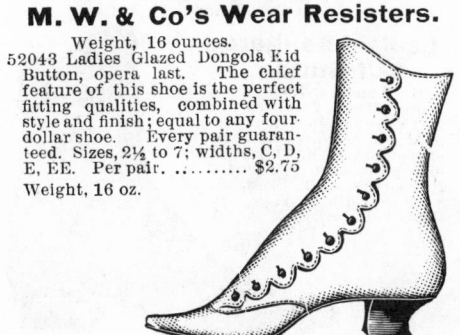

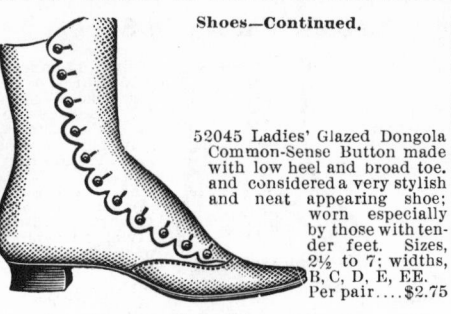

52045 Ladies' Glazed Dongola Common-Sense Button made with low heel and broad toe. and considered a very stylish and neat appearing shoe; worn especially by those with tender feet. Sizes, 2½ to 7; widths, B, C, D, E, EE. Per pair....$2.75

Ladies' Spring Heel.

Weight, 17 ounces.

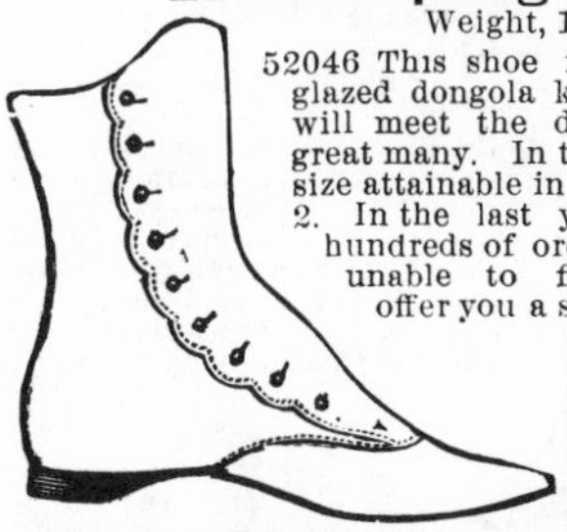

52046 This shoe is made from fine glazed dongola kid and a shoe that will meet the desired wants of a great many. In the past the largest size attainable in this style was No. 2. In the last year we have had hundreds of orders, which we are unable to fill. Now we can offer you a shoe we can recommend, and we trust will be appreciated by those of our customers that could not obtain them heretofore. Sizes, 2½ to 6.
Widths, C, D, E and EE. Per pair..........$2.15

Patent Tip Spring Heel.

52047 Owing to the growing demand for a neat, stylish patent tip spring heel shoe, we have this made special, so as to meet the desired wants of many of our customers who are prejudiced against a heel shoe. The stock is a fine selection of a French Dongola tannage, soft and glove like and readily adjusts itself to the foot. Medium narrow toe, with long patent tip, over-lap quarter, a perfect fitted, flexible sole, and a shoe that will give excellent wear. Sizes, 2½ to 6.
Widths, C, D, E and EE. Per pair............$2.55

The Princess.

52048 Ladies' Glazed Dongola Button, opera last, medium high heel, pointed toe, with fancy patent leather tip, giving an attractive and dressy appearance; beveled edge, single soles, suitable for general wear. Sizes, 2½ to 7. Widths C, D, E. and E E Weight, 16 oz. Per pair...$2.15

The Sunbeam.

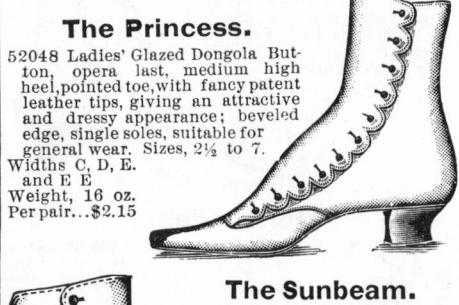

52050 Ladies' Glove Top Button, opera last, popular style heel and toe; flexible, single soles. The vamps or front are of soft, pliable Dongola kid, with dull glove kid tops. A well made and thoroughly reliable shoe of standard value. Sizes, 2½ to 7. Widths, D, E, and EE, only. Weight, 15 oz. Per pair.. $2.25

The Fashion.

(Weight 15 ounces.) 
52053 This shoe is a combination of bright and dull dongola, with patent leather tip. The tip is made from a fine quality of dull finished Dongola, soft and fine, similar to glove kid, the vamps or uppers are of a bright finish, with over-lap quarter. Medium, opera heel, and narrow toe, with long patent leather tip, making a decidedly novel shoe, and one that will wear, and at the same time fit the foot perfectly, and always look neat and dressy. Do not overlook this shoe when ordering, as it will surely please you. Sizes, 2½ to 6. Widths, C, D, E and EE. Per pair..........$2.50

Our Solid Comfort Line.

Weight, 17 oz.

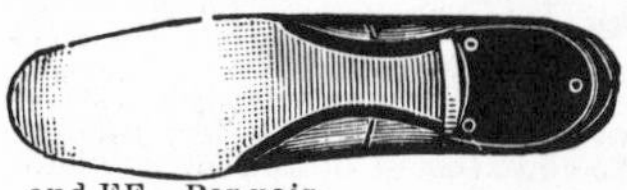

52054 This common sense shoe is made from a fine grade of satin finish dongola, low heel and wide toe. The stock is very soft and recommended for its strength and toughness, making a shoe that is thoroughly reliable. The shoe is very neat in appearance, and a perfect fitter. We can recommend it as being first-class. Sizes, 2½ to 8, C, D, E and EE. Per pair...................$2.50

52056 Ladies' narrow square toe, patent leather tip. This is the very latest style toe, and is a decided success, for the simple reason it looks very dressy on the foot and gives a little more room in the toe than the regular opera last. The stock is a fine selection of dongola kid, and made up in a good, substantial manner; the heel is a trifle lower than the ordinary opera heel, and broader. Will give excellent wear. Sizes, 2½ to 8; widths, C, D, E and EE. Pair.. $2.25
Weight, 16 oz.

The Majestic.

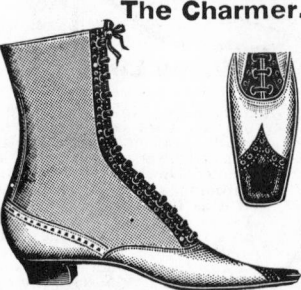

52064 This shoe is made with a fine cloth top, French dongola vamp, medium narrow square toe, and patent leather tip. This style shoe is worn a great deal and considered very stylish. Constructed of the very best material and workmanship; a good fitter and an excellent wearer. Do not fail to try this shoe if you are partial to cloth tops. Sizes, 2½ to 7, widths, A, B, C, D and E. Pair...$2.50

The Charmer.

52066 This shoe is made up of a cloth top, with a fine French dongola foxing, with narrow, square toe, long diamond patent leather tips, medium heel, light sole and flexible, with fancy patent leather stay up the front, all of which goes to make an exceedingly stylish dress or street shoe, Cloth top shoes are very stylish, more so in lace than button, as the former can be adjusted more easily than the latter. We can recommend this shoe to our trade as being first-class and as to *price, quality* and *style* we stand at the head. Sizes, 2½ to 7, A, B, C, D and E. Pair..$2.60

The Trilby.

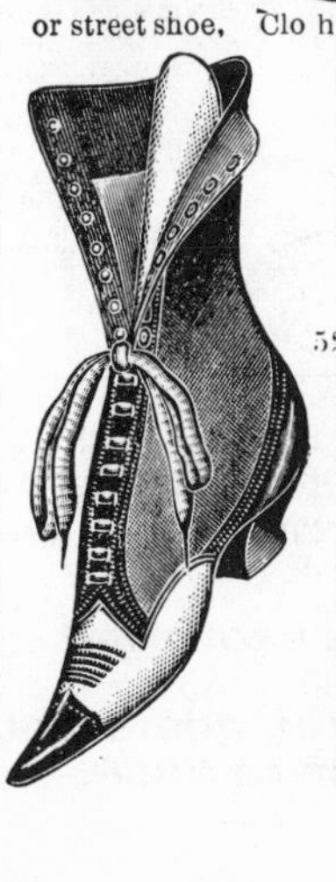

(Weight, 15 ounces.)

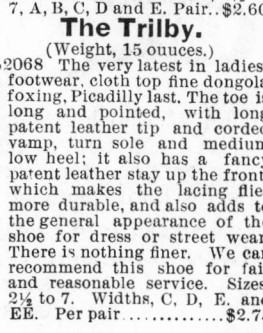

52068 The very latest in ladies' footwear, cloth top fine dongola foxing, Picadilly last. The toe is long and pointed, with long patent leather tip and corded vamp, turn sole and medium low heel; it also has a fancy patent leather stay up the front, which makes the lacing flies more durable, and also adds to the general appearance of the shoe for dress or street wear. There is nothing finer. We can recommend this shoe for fair and reasonable service. Sizes, 2½ to 7. Widths, C, D, E, and EE. Per pair............$2.75

The Derby.

Weight, 17 ounces.

52070 This shoe is a combination of two style lasts, a common-sense and opera. The toe is the same as a full opera, being narrow and pointed, with patent leather tip. The heel is of the common sense pattern. We have taken particular pains to get this shoe up so as to suit those of our trade that are prejudiced against a full opera and a full common sense last. The stock is a fine soft dongola kid, will give excellent wear, and will make a very comfortable walking shoe on account of the low heel; the narrow toe tends to give it a very graceful appearance. Sizes, 2½ to 7. Widths, C, D, E, to EE.
Per pair.............................$2.65

"Stop."

We carry the largest line of ladies' shoes in the United States; almost 100 styles to select from.

The "Tampico" Coat Button.

Weight, 23 ounces.

52071 Ladies' Pebble Goat Button, common-sense last, wide toe and low flat heels, heavy single sole, flexible; the genuine Tampico goat used in this line is a guarantee of durability and satisfaction to the wearer.
Sizes, 2½ to 8, widths, C, D, E, EE. Per pair.....$2.10

52072 Ladies' Tampico Pebble Goat button, opera last, standard heel and toe, heavy single soles. Can be worn for everyday and dress wear, being neat in appearance, yet having strength and serviceable qualities. Sizes, 2½ to 8. Widths, C, D, E, EE.
Per pair.................$2.15
Weight, 20 ounces.

Our Full Value Line.

Weight, 17 ounces

52073 Ladies' Kid Button, made on New York last, the toe is similar to a common-sense last, put narrower and a trifle pointed; heel low and neat in appearance. Sizes, 2½ to 8. Widths, D, E, EE
Per pair...............$2.00
52074 Ladies' Bright Pebble Goat, button, New York last, medium weight, single soles, very flexible, for general street, and house wear. Style comfort and perfect fit are true qualities of this line. Sizes, 2½ to 8; widths, D, E, EE.
Per pair.......$2.00
Weight.., 19 oz.

Ladies' Fat Ankle Shoe.

Weight, 17 ounces.

52075 This shoe we have made to meet the desired wants of our customers, who cannot find a fit in the ordinary cut shoe. It is made extra wide around ankle and through the instep giving abundance of room for extra fleshy ankle and high instep. The style is a medium opera. The stock is a nice soft dongola kid with a medium weight sole, and a shoe that will give good wear and look neat when on the foot. Sizes, 2½ to 8. Width, EE only. Pair.................$2.50

Weight 17 ounces.

52077 This shoe is made from a good plump selection of bright dongola, with a common-sense heel and toe. A shoe designed for service; is neat in appearance and looks as well as a high price shoe. All solid, with a medium weight sole. Sizes, 2½ to 8; widths, C, D, E and EE. Per pair.......$1.75

52077

Weight, 17 ounces.

52079 Ladies' Domestic Kid Button, opera last, good weight, flexible single soles, short vamp or front, with overlap seam, all solid throughout, no shoddy. Sizes, 2½ to 8; widths, D, E, and EE. Per pr. $1.75

52079

52081 Ladies' Bright Pebble Goat Button, opera last, half double soles, short vamps or fronts, solid and serviceable. There is nothing like leather; no imitations used in this shoe. Sizes, 2½ to 8. Widths, D, E, EE.
Per pair... ....$1.75
Weight, 21 ounces.

Our Leaders.

52083 This shoe is made from genuine dongola, solid counters and insoles with patent leather tips, and for the price has no equal. When selecting do not pass this shoe without giving it a thought, as an ordinary house slipper will cost as much. When on the foot they look as well as most any of our higher price shoes, and for the price they will give satisfaction. Sizes, 2½ to 7. Widths, D, E and EE.
Per pair...................................$1.25

Weight, 16 ounces.

52084 Ladies' Genuine Dongola Kid Button, patent leather tip, opera last, shapely, durable and well made, of solid leather. This is unquestionably the best kid shoe in the market at the price; widths, D, E, EE. Sizes, 2½ to 8. Per pair........$1.50

Shoes—Continued.

Weight, 16 ounces.

52086 The stock in this shoe is a very good selection of dongola kid, common-sense last, all solid, very neat and serviceable and at the same time a very comfortable shoe for ordinary wear. Low heel and wide toe. Sizes, 2½ to 8; widths, D, E and EE.
Per pair.... ....$1.50

Field and Farm Brands.

52087 Ladies' Custom Calf Button, machine sewed, worked buttonholes, extra fine quality and finish; nothing better for hard wear; warranted. Sizes, 2½ to 8; widths, D, E, EE.
Per pair $2.10
52088 Ladies' Calf Button, heavy, strong, for rough use, full widths. Sizes, 3 to 8. Per pr. $1.90

Ladies' Glove Grain Button.

52089 This shoe is specially constructed for general wear, with good plump uppers, soft and pliable, and also solid bottoms and counters, thereby making a shoe that will give abundance of service for a little money. Sizes, 2½ to 8; full width. Per pair. $1.25
Weight, 25 oz.

52092 Ladies' Glove Grain Button, oil tanned for wet weather, extra quality and finish, worked buttonholes, half double soles, very serviceable. Sizes, 2½ to 8. Widths, D, E, EE $1.75

Ladies' Cordovan Button.

Weight, 25 ounces.

52093 Ladies' Oil Tanned Cordovan Button, worked buttonholes, half double soles, neat looking and very strong; nothing better for everyday use; warranted all solid. Sizes, 2½ to 8; widths D, E, EE.................................$1.75

Ladies' Bright Grain Button.

52094 Ladies' Bright Grain Button, worked buttonholes, half double soles, all solid leather. The best shoe in the market at the price. Sizes, 2½ to 8; full width.
Per pair.....$1.35

Ladies' Oil Grain Button.

52096 This shoe is made from genuine oil grain leather, with solid bottoms and counters. Designed principally for hard usage; a regular field and farm brand. It is not clumsy nor heavy like most shoes of this class. The stock is soft and pliable, and will give extra good wear. We can recommend this shoe as being first class. Sizes, 2½ to 8. Widths, E and EE. Weight, 25 ounces. Per pair. .$1.25

Ladies' Kangaroo Calf Button.

52097 Women's Kangaroo Calf Button Shoe. This stock is very soft and glove like, does not get hard and crack. Very comfortable on the feet and gives excellent good wear. A good shoe for general wear. Sizes, 2½ to 8. Full width.......$2.00
Weight, 25 oz.

Ladies' Side Lace Shoes.

52099 Ladies' Dongola Side Lace, opera last, very neat and serviceable. Made specially for those prejudiced against button shoes. Stock in this shoe is very soft and glovelike. Sizes, 2½ to 7; widths, D, E. and EE. Per pair..........$2.50

52100 Ladies' Dongola Side Lace, common sense last, low heel and broad toe, a very comfortable shoe, will cause no corns or bunions; neat and durable; Sizes, 2½ to 7, widths D, E and EE. Per pair..$2.50 Weight, 15 oz.

52099

The Nun's Shoe.

52102 This shoe we have taken extra pains with, so as to have it made neat, plain and serviceable for those of our customers who are obliged to wear this style shoe. The stock is of a soft, bright finished daisy kid, medium low heel and flexible sole and will give excellent wear, solid counters and sewed bottoms, no tacks or nails to bother the feet. Sizes, 2½ to 8. Widths, C, D, E and EE. Per pair..........$1.75

Housekeeper's Delight.

52104 Ladies' Dongola Kid Congress. Made on a broad commonsense last and is specially designed for comfort; a shoe that will look neat and dressy; also a very desirable shoe, as no buttoning or lacing required; sizes, 2½ to 8; widths D, E and EE. Per pair.... $1.85 Weight, 16 ounces.

Ladies' Glove Grain Polish.

52105 Ladies' Oil Glove Grain Polish (or front lace), straight last, machine sewed, very desirable for damp and wet weather wear; good style and well made; warranted; sizes, 2½ to 8; widths, D, E, EE. Per pair.... .... $1.50 Weight, 22 ounces.

Ladies' Heavy Pegged Shoes.

52107 Ladies' Custom All Calf Polish, hand-pegged and warranted. The best is the cheapest; sizes, 3 to 8. Per pair.... ....$1.65 Weight, 28 ounces.

52108 Ladies' Calf Polish, pegged, double soles, very strong and well made; sizes, 3 to 8. Per pair.... ...$1.45 Weight, 29 ounces.

52109 Ladies' A Calf Polish, pegged heavy soles, strong and stout, all solid; sizes, 3 to 8. Each, ...$1.10 Weight, 30 ounces.

52110 Ladies' Oil Grain Polish, double soles, pegged; field and farm brands; sizes 3 to 8. Per pair $1.15

Ladies' Serge Foxed Button.

52112 Ladies' Serge Button Shoes, kid foxed, good style and finish, worked buttonholes; sizes 2½ to 8; widths, D, E. EE. Per pair...$2.00 Weight, 17 ounces.

52113 Ladies' Serge Kid Foxed Polish (or front lace) made on straight lasts; half double soles, nothing better made at any price; sizes, 2½ to 8; widths, D, E and EE. Per pair .... $1.85 Weight, 16 ounces.

Old Ladies' Serge Congress.

52114 Ladies' Serge Congress Gaiters, machine sewed, light flexible single soles, fine quality and finish; sizes, 2½ to 8; widths D, E, EE. Per pair $1.35 Weight, 16 ounces

52116 Ladies' Serge Congress Gaiters, hand sewed or turn slipper, soles easy on the feet and very satisfactory to wear; sizes 3 to 8; widths D, E, and EE. Per pair .$1.35 Weight, 14 ounces.

52118 Ladies' Serge Congress Gaiters, machine sewed, single soles, broad toe and heels; sizes, 3 to 8; widths, D, E and EE ....$1.00 Weight, 15 ounces.

Old Ladies' Glove Kid Congress and Bal.

52121 Old Ladies' Glove Kid Congress Gaiters, broad and roomy, with low heels, flexible soles and soft uppers, solid comfort for tender feet; sizes, 3 to 8. Pair .$1.65 Weight, 14 ounces

52123 Old ladies' Glove Kid Bals, front lace, straight last, low heels and broad toes, sole light and flexible, suitable for general wear; sizes, 3 to 8; full width; per pair..........$1.60 Weight, 14 oz.

Ladies' White Canvas Oxfords.

52124 Made from heavy white canvas, with light flexible sole, narrow toe and medium heel, white kid tip and also stayed up the front with same making it strong and durable, and will wear equally as well as the ordinary kid Oxfords, they will be very stylish the coming season, light and cool, also very desirable for a vacation or outing shoe. Sizes, 2½ to 6. Width, C, D, E and EE. Per pair....$1.25

Ladies' Grey Linen Oxfords.

52125 This Oxford is made exactly as the one preceding, the only difference being in the color which will not show the dirt and dust as quickly as the white; the tip is a russet or tan color kid also the stay on the front, the same making a very desirable combination. The uppers are very heavy and genuine linen, closely woven; a very desirable warm weather shoe, neat and dressy. Sizes, 2½ to 6. Widths, C, D, E and EE. Per pair $1.30

Ladies' Dongola Oxford.

52126 Ladies' American French Kid Lace Oxford, hand sewed, turn or slipper soles, late style toe and heels, fancy patent leather tips; neat fitting and stylish, suitable for street or house wear; sizes, 2½ to 7; widths, C, D, E and EE. Weight, 14 ounces. Price........ ....$1.90

52128 The Blucherette Oxford. The very latest novelty in footwear, made from the finest French dongola, with long diamond tip and turnsole; in appearance a perfect beauty, and will give satisfaction as to wearing qualities; sizes, 2½ to 7; widths, B, C, D, E, EE. Weight, 12 ounces. Per pair..............$1.75

Ladies' Tan Colored Oxfords.

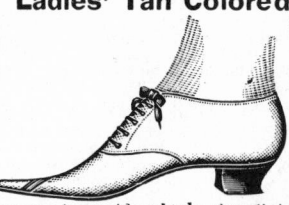

52130 Ladies' Tan Colored Imitation Oxford, made over the Picadilly last; very pointed toe and long perforated tip, fits well and wears well with light turn sole, and for the coming season is considered "the shoe;" sizes, 2½ to 7; widths, C, D, E, EE. Weight, 10 ounces. Per pair....................................$1.75

52133 Ladies' Tan-Colored Oxford. This shoe is very neat in appearance, made over a perfect fitting opera last, light turn sole, opera heel tan tip and sold by the majority of dealers for far more than we ask for it; size, 2½ to 7; widths, D, E and EE. Weight, 11 ounces. Per pair...... ....$1.25

Ladies' Prince Albert.

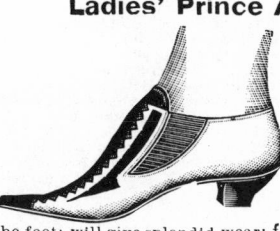

52134 Ladies' Prince Albert; the stock is a fine Vici kid, light sole, flexible medium opera heel, fancy patent leather trimmed up the front, a very graceful and neat appearing shoe when on the foot; will give splendid wear; for a neat summer shoe it has no equal. Sizes, 2½ to 7; widths, C, D, E. and EE. Per pair...... ....$1.60

Ladies' Dongola Oxfords.

52135 Ladies' Bright Dongola Kid Lace Oxford, Picadilly toe, long perforated patent leather tip, very attractive and dressy; flexible soles; sizes, 2½ to 7; width, C, D, E and EE. Per pair.........$1.40 Weight, 12 ounces.

52138 Ladies' Dongola Oxford Patent Leather Tip, with turn sole, all solid, and a very neat and dressy shoe for summer wear. Sizes, 2½ to 8; widths, C, D, E and EE. Per pair...... ....$1.25 Weight, 12 ounces.

Housekeepers' Delight.

52140 In this Oxford we give you better value for the money than any other shoe. It is made from a good plump grade of dongola kid, patent leathr tip, all solid and very good style; made to give excellent wear; sizes, 2½ to 8; widths, D, E and EE. Weight, 14 oz. Per pair.$1.00

Common Sense Oxfords.

52141 Ladies' Common Sense Oxford, made from a good plump dongola kid, with wide toe and sensible heel, flexible sole; neat and dressy, and a very comfortable shoe for ordinary or dress wear. Sizes, 2½ to 8; C, D, E and EE. Weight, 10 oz. Per pair..............$1.25

52143 Ladies' Dongola Oxford, made on common sense last, low, broad heel and wide toe, neat and dressy and bound to insure comfort; slipper or turn sole; sizes, 2½ to 8; widths, D, E and EE. Price, per pair...$1.65 Weight, 13 ounces.

We carry the largest line of Ladies' Shoes in the United States.   Almost 100 Styles to Select from.

The Elite.

52146 This is a new departure in the line of stylish footwear. The stock in this shoe is of a very fine selection of Dongola, French tannage, very soft and durable. This being the first season for this very stylish Congress, we look for a large sale on same. The accompanying cut represents this very accurately. It has a very neat patent leather stay up the front and a light turn sole with thin edge, and a medium heel, which makes a very comfortable and stylish dress shoe. Sizes, 2½ to 7, C, D, E, EE. Weight, 11 ounces. Per pair.........$2.75

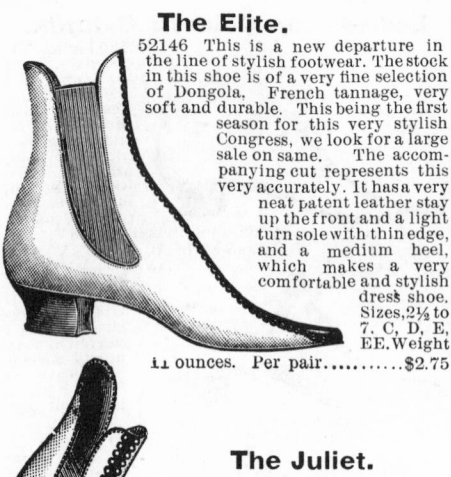

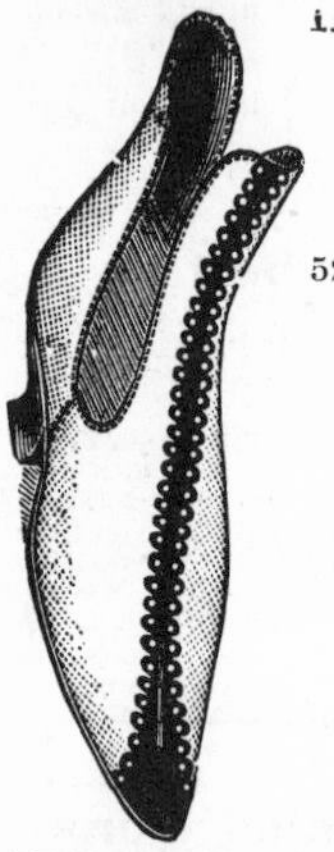

The Juliet.

52148 The stock in this shoe is a very fine French dongola kid, with hand turned soles, fancy patent leather stay up the front, as shown in accompanying cut; the uppers are cut seamless, with elastic sides, making one of the most handsome low shoes to be found; never gets out of shape and always looks neat and gives the foot a long and slender appearance. This is a beauty. Sizes, 2½ to 7. Widths, B, C, D and E. Per pair...................$2.50

The Old Reliable.

52149 Ladies' Pebble Goat Oxford, medium toe and heel, special value; sizes, 2½ to 8; widths, D, E and EE. Weight, 15 ounces.. ....$1.10
52151 Ladies' Dongola Oxford, machine sewed, neat looking, soft and pliable, ladies' favorite; sizes, 2½ to 7; full width. Weight, 14 ounces.. 1.10
52152 Ladies' Pebble Grain Newport Tie, all solid and well made, for rough wear; sizes, 2½ to 8, regular width ....$0.90 Weight, 16 ounces.

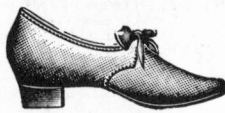

Ladies' Toilet and House Slippers.

52154 Ladies' Kid Strap Sandal Slipper, hand sewed, turn sole, extra quality and finish, very popular for house or dance wear; sizes, 2½ to 7; widths C, D & E. $1.60 Weight, 10 ounces.

Ladies' Common Sense Opera.

52155 Ladies' Common Sense Opera Slipper, made from a light soft dongola stock, common sense heel and toe; light slipper sole, making a very durable and comfortable house slipper. Size, 2½ to 7; widths, C, D and E. $1.25

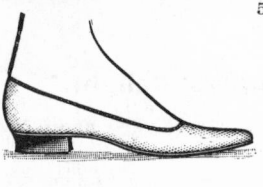

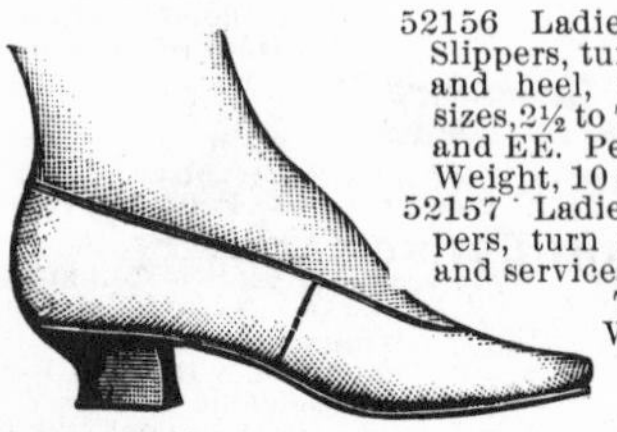

52156 Ladies' Kid Opera Slippers, turn sole, opera toe and heel, soft and pliable; sizes, 2½ to 7; widths, C, D, E and EE. Per pair......$1.35 Weight, 10 ounces.
52157 Ladies' Kid Opera Slippers, turn soles, well made and serviceable; sizes, 2½ to 7, full width $1.00 Weight, 10 oz.

52156

52158 The accompanying cut represents a very stylish slipper made from soft dongola stock, with light turn sole and medium heel; a very attractive and sightly slipper, and one that will give good satisfaction to the wearer. Sizes, 2½ to 7, widths, C, D and E. Per pair......$1.40 Weight, 10 ounces.

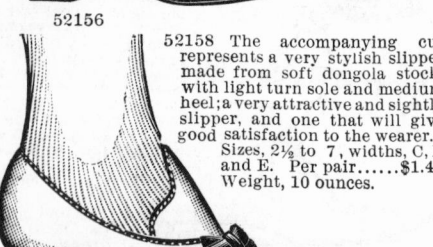

Ladies' White Kid Slippers.

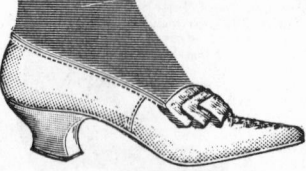

52159 Ladies' White Kid Slippers, hand sewed, turn soles, fine quality and finish; sizes, 2½ to 6, width, C, D and E.......$1.50 Weight, 8 oz.

Ladies' Satin Slippers.

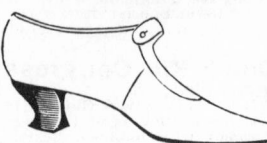

52160 Made from genuine satin; opera toe, hand-turned sole, French heel, with strap buttoning across instep; light and fine; made in assorted colors.

Very appropriate for a dress or a party slipper; very rich in appearance and very sightly when on the foot. Colors: Black, blue, pink, white and red. Sizes, 2 to 6; width, A, B, C, D and E.......$2.00

52161   **52165**
         Per Pair.

52161 Ladies' Glove Kid, 3 point slipper, turn soles, low flat heels, soft and pliable, easy on the feet, and very desirable for house wear; sizes, 2½ to 8; width, D, E and EE. Weight, 12 oz ..$1.00
52162 Ladies' Pebble Goat Buskin Slippers, old ladies' style, best quality; sizes, 3 to 8, full width. Weight, 11 ounces.. .... 1.00
52165 Ladies' Pebble Goat Buskin Slippers, flannel lined; warm and comfortable; sizes, 3 to 8; full width. Weight, 12 ounces.................... 1.00
52167 Ladies' Grain Slippers, damp proof, sewed strong and durable for out or indoor wear, all solid; sizes, 3 to 8; full width. Weight, 15 ounces.......$0.75

52169 Ladies' Serge Buskin Slippers, turn soles, low flat heels, fine quality; sizes, 3 to 8; full width. Weight, 8 ounces..................... .90
52171 Ladies' Serge Buskin Slippers, medium grade; sizes, 3 to 8, full width.................... .65

Ladies' Carpet Slippers.
Weight, 10 ounces.
52172 Ladies' Brussels Carpet Slippers, best quality, bound and stayed; sizes, 3 to 8, full width.. .30

"The German" Slipper.
Weight, 15 ounces.

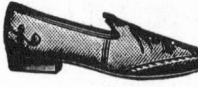

52173 Ladies' German Slipper, heavy cloth, embroidered toe, leather foxing; nothing better for wear and for comfort, no equal; see 52497 for men; sizes, 3 to 8; full width..... ....$0.90

Girls' Wear.
Weight, 14 ounces.

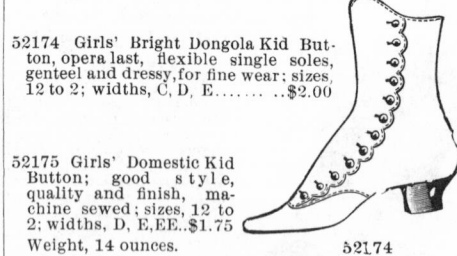

52174 Girls' Bright Dongola Kid Button, opera last, flexible single soles, genteel and dressy, for fine wear; sizes, 12 to 2; width, C, D, E........ ..$2.00

52175 Girls' Domestic Kid Button; good style, quality and finish, machine sewed; sizes, 12 to 2; widths, D, E, EE..$1.75 Weight, 14 ounces.

52174

Misses' Kangaroo Calf Spring Heel.
Weight, 18 ounces.

52176 The stock is a genuine calf skin, made with the grain side and tanned the same as kangaroo, making it very soft and pliable, and a very desirable shoe for school and general wear, single sole, all solid, neat and dressy. Sizes, 11 to 2; widths, D E and EE. Per pair.............$1.25

Misses' and Children's Goat Shoes.
Weight, 11 to 14 ounces.

52177 Misses' and Children's Genuine Tampico Oil Goat, spring heel. These shoes are made of the very best material, with solid leather counters and insoles; the wearing qualities being first-class, and at the same time making a neat, dressy shoe.   Per pair
Sizes 6, 6½, 7, 7½...........$0.90
Sizes, 8, 8½, 9, 9½, 10 10½ 1.15
Sizes, 11, 11½, 12, 12½, 13, 13½ Per pair....$1.50
Sizes, 1, 1½, 2, Per pair....$1.55

52178 Girls' Genuine Dongola Kid Button, opera last, single soles, medium weight, machine sewed, worked buttonholes; a good fitting, serviceable shoe at rock bottom price; sizes, 12 to 2; full width. Weight, 12 ounces $1.25

52179 Girls' Oil Grain Button, standard last, medium weight, suitable for general wear; sizes, 12 to 2; widths, D, E, EE. Weight, 21 oz...$1.15

Misses' and Children's Tan Colored Shoes.
Weight, 11 to 14 ounces

52180 Made from a very fine selection of russet tan-colored goat skin. Spring heel, flexible soles, all solid, and a shoe that will give excellent good service, as the stock is very soft and pliable and at the same time tough, wearing equally as well as a much heavier shoe. Made over a very neat spring heel last.

They require no blacking or oiling, and for light summer wear they are considered cool and very dressy. Sizes, 8, 8½, 9, 9½, 10, 10½. Widths C, D, E.....$1.25
Sizes, 11, 11½, 12, 12½, 13, 13½, 1, 1½ and 2. Widths, C, D, E. 1.65

Misses' Heavy Calf Polish.
Weight, 22 to 25 ounces.   Per pair.
52181 Misses' Oil Grain Polish, pegged, double soles, damp proof; nothing better for wet weather use; sizes, 13 to 2.............................$1.10
52182 Misses' Bright Grain Polish, pegged, double soles, strong and solid; sizes, 13 to 2............. 1.00
52183 Misses' Custom All Calf Polish, hand pegged, double soles, warranted; sizes, 13 to 2.. 1.50
52184 Misses' Calf Polish, pegged, double soles, well made and solid throughout; sizes, 13 to 2 ..1.25
52185 Misses' A Calf Polish, pegged double soles, stout and heavy; for hard wear; sizes, 13 to 2.. 1.00

Misses' Tan Colored Oxfords.

52186 This shoe is made from tan goat skin, is very neat and dressy, with tip, and the prevailing style for the coming season, Spring heel only. Sizes 12 to 2; width C, D, E; per pair. ....$1.25 Weight, 10 oz.

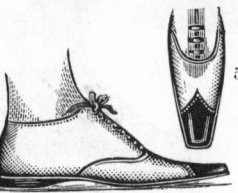

Weight, 10 oz.
52188 Misses' Dongola Spring Heel Oxford, machine sewed, good style and quality; sizes, 11 to 2; widths, D and E $1.25

Misses' Grain Ties.

52189   Misses' Grain Ties, straight last, sewed strong and solid; sizes, 13 to 2 .... $0.80

Misses' and Children's Dongola Spring Heels.

Weight, 11 to 13 ounces.   52190 This shoe is made from a fine selection of dongola kid, with patent leather tip and square toe, which adds greatly to the appearance. The bottoms are of solid sole leather, also the counters, which are a sure guarantee of a good wearing shoe. Misses' sizes, 1, 1½, 2. Widths, C, D and E.

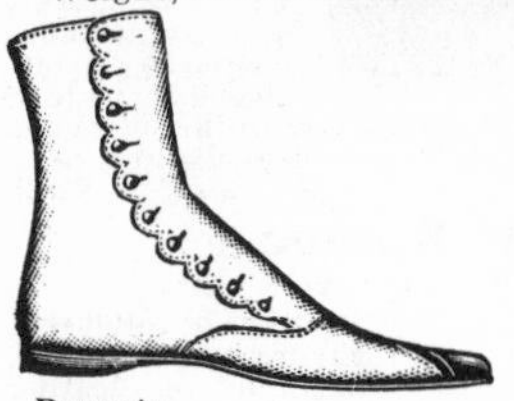

Per pair............................ $1.65
Girls' sizes, 11, 11½, 12, 12½, 13, 13½. Widths, C, D and E. Per pair....................... 1.55
Children's sizes, 8, 8½, 9, 9½, 10, 10½. Widths, C, D and E............................ 1.25

Weight, 9 to 14 ounces.

52191 Misses' and Children's Glazed Dongola Kid, spring heel, plain toe. This shoe is designed for general wear also for dress, being made from a good selection of stock; the bottoms and counters are of solid leather, and in appearance the shoe is perfect; we can recommend this shoe as being a good wearer.

Per pair.
Misses' sizes, 1, 1½, 2. Widths, C,D and E..... $1.55
Girls' sizes, 11, 11½, 12, 12½, 13, 13½ Widths, C, D and E............................. 1.40
Children's sizes, 8, 8½, 9, 9½, 10, 10½ Widths, C, D and E............................. 1.25
Children's sizes, 5, 5½, 6, 6½, 7, 7½. Widths, C, D and E....................................... .95

Misses' Dongola Box Toe, Button.

52192   Made from a good, plump dongola kid, soft and pliable. Medium heavy sole with a genuine sole leather box toe and spring heel; a very good wearing shoe, and durable for school and dress wear, the toe being protected by the sole leather tip, thereby making it wear longer than the plain toe.
Sizes, 1, 1½ and 2. Widths, D, E and EE. Per pair $1.60
Misses', same as above sizes, 11, 11½, 12, 12½, 13 and 13½........................ 1.50
Children's, same as above sizes, 8, 8½, 9, 9½, 10, 10½................................. 1.25
Children's, same as above sizes, 5, 5½, 6, 6½, 7, 7½. 1.00

M. W. & Co.'s School Shoes.

We wish to call your special attention to our celebrated school shoes, numbers 52193, 52194, 52195. These shoes are warranted by us. We have the fullest confidence in their wearing qualities, and our increasing sales for the past 18 years demonstrate that that confidence is shared by our customers.

Weight, 11 to 18 oz.

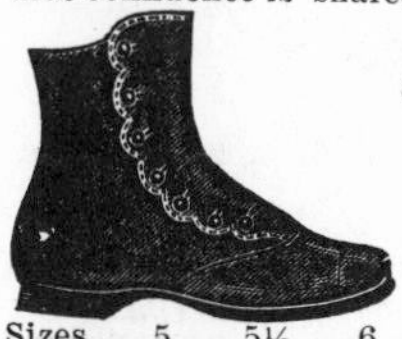

52193 Child's Pebble Grain School Shoe, button, double sole, spring heel, sole leather box tip toe, worked buttonholes; all solid and warranted.

						Per pair.
Sizes,	5,	5½,	6	6½	7	7½........$0.95
Sizes,	8	8½	9	9½	10	10½.... ... 1.15
Sizes,	11	11½	12	12½	13	13½......... 1.30
Sizes,	1	1½	2			.... 1.60

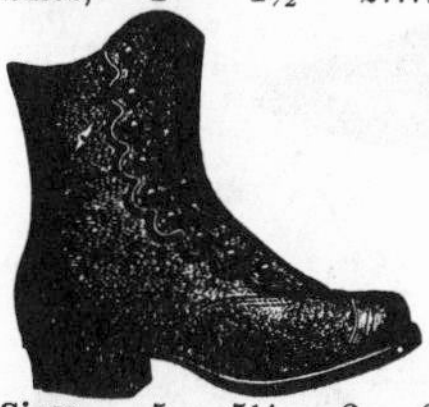

52194 Child's Pebble Grain School Shoe. button, double sole, low flat heels, sole leather box tip toes, worked buttonholes; all solid and warranted.

Weight, 12 to 20 oz.

						Per pair
Sizes,	5	5½	6	6½	7	7½......$0.95
Sizes,	8	8½	9	9½	10	10½......... 1.15
Sizes,	11	11½	12	12½	13	13½......... 1.30
Sizes,	1	1½	2			.... 1.60

33--2nd

Shoes—Continued.

52195   Child's Pebble Grain School Shoe, front lace, double soles, low flat heels, sole leather box tip toe, straight cut top; very desirable, for boys wear. Weight, 16 to 20 ounces

						Per pair.
Sizes, 8	8½	9	9½	10	10½............	$1.15
Sizes, 11	11½	12	12½	13	13½............	1.30
Sizes, 1	1½	2			....	1.60

Children's Dongola and Goat Heel Shoes.

52196   Child's Dongola Kid Button, machine sewed, single sole, worked buttonholes; neat fitting and stylish; sizes, 8 to 11.
Per pair.................... $1.15
Weight, 10 ounces.

Children's Red Goat Shoes.

Weight, 6 ounces.

52198   This shoe is made from genuine red tanned goat, spring heel, turn sole, with tassel: the very latest color in children's shoes, making a very neat and sightly shoe. Sizes, 4 to 8.
Per pair.................... $0.80

Children's Tan Shoes.

Weight, 6 ounces

52199   This shoe is made from tan goat skin, which is very neat and stylish, and at the same time, serviceable; with spring heel, worked buttonholes. Sizes, 4 to 8.
Per pair... .... $0.75
Sizes, 1 to 5, no heel.
Per pair................... .65

Children's Dongola Shoes.

Weight, 6 ounces.
52200 Child's Dongola Kid Button, hand sewed, turn sole, spring heel, worked buttonholes and tassel, six button; sizes, 4 to 8.
Per pair......... ....$0.70

52201   Child's Patent Top Dongola Button Shoe, medium square toe, turned sole, worked buttonholes, and tassel, soft and flexible, spring heel. Sizes, 4, 4½, 5, 5½, 6, 6½, 7, 7½. 8.
Per pair.... .... $0.75

Children's Goat Shoes.

Weight, 6 ounces.
52202 Child's Bright Pebble Goat Button, hand sewed, turn sole, spring heel, worked buttonholes and tassel, neat and serviceable; sizes, 4 to 8..................................$0.70
52203 Child's Pebble Goat Button, spring heel, turn sole with sole leather tip toe, light weight and durable, for every daywear; sizes, 4 to 8.... .75
Weight, 9 ounces.

52204   Child's Bright Grain Button, with heels, single sole, neat and serviceable; sizes, 5 to 8. Price....... ....$0.60

Children's Dongola Oxfords.

Weight, 8 ounces.
52205 Child's Kid Oxford Tie, flexible sole, spring heels, fine quality, sewed; sizes, 8 to 11. Per pair.$0.88
52206 Child's Kid Oxford Tie, fine quality, turn soles, with spring heels, sewed; sizes, 4 to 7½................... .75
Weight, 5 ounces.

Children's Tan Color Oxfords.

Weight, 5 to 8 ounces.

52207   Child's Tan Oxford, made from a genuine goat skin, soft and pliable, with turn sole and spring heel; very dressy for the little ones. Sizes, 8½, 9, 9½, 10, 10½, 11.
Per pair................... $0.90
Sizes, 5, 5½, 6, 6½ 7, 7½, 8. Per pair...... .75

Child's Tan Colored Sandals.

Weight, 4 to 8 ounces.

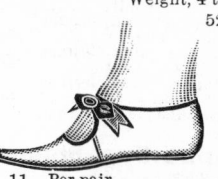

52208   Made from tan or russet colored kid, with strap buttoning over instep, with a nice bow of same, colored satin, ribbon fastened in center with fancy buckle, spring heel and turn sole; very cute and dressy.
Sizes, 8, 8½, 9, 9½, 10, 10½, 11. Per pair......................$0.95

For Hard Knocks.

Weight, 16 ounces. 
52209 Child's Custom All Calf Front Lace Shoes, hand pegged, double sole, warranted; sizes, 8 to 12.
Per pair...................$1.15
52210 Child's Calf Front Lace Shoes, double sole, tipped, strong and heavy, pegged; sizes, 8 to 12.
Per pair....................$1.00
52211 Child's Oil Grain Front Lace Shoes, tipped, double sole, damp proof, pegged; sizes, 8 to 12 Per pair........................$0.90

Infants' Red Shoes.

Weight, 4 ounces.
52212 Infant's Red Shoe, worked buttonhole and tassel, turn sole, no heel, fine quality and latest color. Sizes, 1 to 5.
Per pair.............. $0.65

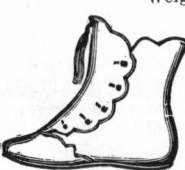

Infants' Dongola Shoes.

Weight, 4 ounces. 
52213 Infants' American French Kid Button, worked buttonholes and tassles; flexible, turn soles, sewed, no heels; sizes, 1 to 5................ .....$0.75

52214 Infants' Kid "Fat Baby" Shoe; button, worked buttonholes and tassel, light and fine, made especially for thick, fat feet; no heels. Sizes, 1 to 5.
Per pair..........$0.65

            Per pair.
52215 Infants' Kid Button. turn sole, sewed, worked buttonholes and tassels, no heels; sizes, 1 to 5....................................$0.60
52216 Infants' Pebble Goat Button, hand-sewed, turn sole, no heels, sole leather tip toe; sizes, 1 to 5.................................... .55
52217 Infants' Kid Button, turn sole, well made, no heels, sizes, 1 to 5...................... .45
52218 Infants' Pebble Goat Button, turn soles, no heels, durable; sizes, 1 to 5.................... .40

Infants' Soft Sole Shoes.

Weight, 2 ounces.
52219 This shoe is made from genuine French kid with kid sole, nothing finer for an infant; sizes, 0, 1, 2, 3. Per pair............$0.35
The same style, only in dongola kid; sizes, 0, 1, 2, 3. Per pair........................... .25

Infants' Moccasins.

52220 Infants' Moccasins, made from soft dongola stock, with silk lace and tassel, very durable for an infant's first shoe. Per pair.................$0.35
Weight, 2 ounces.

Don't fail to send for one of our Special Book Catalogues. You will admit that it excels anything published, both in variety and in prices. Postage, 5 cents

Wigwam Slippers.

Weight, 7 to 16 ounces.

Men's, Ladies', Boys, Misses' and Children's Wigwam Slippers, with sole leather soles and heels. These slippers are made throughout with leather, making the most durable and comfortable foot covering for house, lawn and camping out purposes.   Per pair.

52221 Men's Wigwam Slippers, laced, leather soles and heels; sizes, 6 to 11; full width........$1.00

52222 Boys' Wigwam Slippers, laced, leather soles and heels; sizes, 1 to 5; full width....... .90

52223 Ladies' Wigwam Slippers, laced, leather soles and heels; sizes, 3 to 7; full width. .90

52224 Misses' Wigwam Slippers, laced, leather soles and heels; sizes, 11 to 2; full width........ .80

52225 Child's Wigwam Slippers, laced, leather soles and heels; sizes, 6 to 10; full width........ .65

We are constantly improving and perfecting our styles of shoes.

Child's Ankle-Supporting Shoes.

Weight, 6 ounces.
A Success.

52225½ Made from a good plump dongola kid, with light turn soles that will give good service and at the same time comfort. A high sole leather counter extending to top of shoe to give support to the ankle. It adjusts itself comfortably to the foot. It is on the inside between lining and outside, so when shoe is on the foot it cannot be noticed. They are all made in lace, so they can be adjusted to suit wearer. No child with weak ankles should be without a pair of these shoes. Sizes, 4 to 8, spring heel. Per pair......$1.25
Sizes, 2 to 6, no heel. Per pair................... 1.00

TO THE PUBLIC

We carry a full line of the celebrated Alfred Dolge's felt shoes and slippers, manufactured special for our trade. We guarantee that the felt in these shoes is made of **Pure Live Wool**, which absorbs and disperses the perspiration with its impurities, and so keeps the feet dry and in a healthy condition.

See that every pair is stamped Alfred Dolge & Co.; none genuine without. From Nos. 52220 to 52243.

Men's All Wool Felt Shoes and Slippers.

Weight, 27 ounces.

Men's Beaver Felt Bal with Leather Sole.

52226 Made from our new combination Beaver Felt, more durable than anything we have ever made, Felt innersole, leather outer sole. Leather foxing, is of a fine soft quality. The very best of material all the way through. Every pair warranted. Sizes, 6 to 11. Widths, D. E. and EE. Price................$4.25

52227 This shoe is made with a felt upper, lining and innersole. Outer sole and heel of leather. Stayed in front and back. This shoe is practically adapted for climates where the walks are wet. It is almost a waterproof shoe, as the water runs off the felt. A rubber can be worn over the shoe as well as over a leather shoe. *Every pair warranted.* Sizes, 5 to 11. Widths, D, E and EE. Per pair.... ....$4.25
Weight, 27 ounces.

Men's Felt Bals or Lace.

Weight, 22 oz.

52228 Uppers and heels of solid all wool Felt, soles ⅜ to ½ inch thick, color, black; sizes, 5 to 11. Per pair..$3.85

Men's Felt Creedmore, or Seamless Bals.

Weight, 20 ounces.

52229 Uppers, Sole and Heels of Solid All Wool Felt, sole, ⅜ to ½ inch thick; colors black; sizes, 6 to 11.
Per pair..$2.85

Men's Leather Sole Romeo.

52230 This slipper is made of one piece of black felt, the sole and upper all in one piece, and the leather sole put on after the shoe is made. The sole is sewed to the upper and is of the finest leather consistent with durability. The manner of combining the felt with the leather is entirely new and protected by patent. The sole is very flexible and makes one of the most comfortable and durable slippers on the market; sizes, 6 to 11; widths D, E and EE. Per pair $2.00

Men's Felt Slippers, Plush Bound.

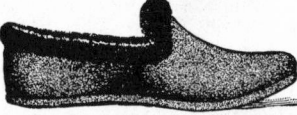

Weight, 13 oz.
52231 Soles of All Wool Felt, no heels; colors dark blue; sizes, 6 to 11; width, D and E.
Per pair...$1.55

Men's Toilet Slippers.

Weight, 12 ounces.

TOILET SLIPPER.

52232 Plain; no heels; upper is fine, all wool felt, ¼ inch thick; sole of extra hard felt, ¼ in. thick; colors, black and blue; sizes, 6 to 11.
Per pair......$1.45

Ladies' All Wool Felt Shoes.

Weight, 20 ounces.

LADY WASHINGTON.

52233 Uppers soles and heels of all wool felt, soles ¼ to ⅜ inch thick; black worked buttonholes, felt heels. This shoe we guarantee to wear longer than any shoe in the catalogue. If you wear felt shoes in the cold weather, do not forget to order this shoe, as we warrant every pair. They fit as neat as any dongola shoe, and are very light. Per pair...$3.15

Ladies' Front Lace Shoes.

Weight, 15 oz.
52234 Without heels, plush bound, seamless linings, upper and soles of all wool felt; soles ¼ to ⅜ inch thick; color black; sizes, 2 to 8.
Per pair...$1.85

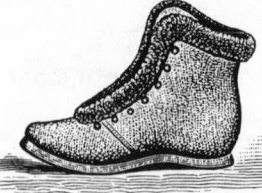

52235 Women's Felt Lace Shoe; uppers, sole and heel of felt. This shoe is made without lining of any kind, but the felt is more than twice as thick as that used in shoes previously described. Being of coarser felt this shoe is very durable. Sizes, 2½ to 8. Widths, D, E and EE. Per pair............$1.85
Weight, 15 ounces.

Ladies' Felt House Slippers.

Plush Bound, Seamless Linings.

Weight, 11 ounces.
52236 Soles of all wool felt, ⅜ inch thick, no heels; color, dark blue; sizes, 2½ to 8.
Per pair.....$1.25

Ladies' Felt Toilet Slippers.

Weight, 8 ounces.

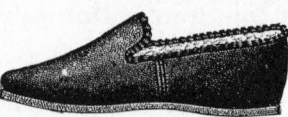

52237 This is one of our most popular slippers. It is made of toilet felt and is shapely and comfortable. Owing to the fact that it is made of toilet felt, and therefore has no extra lining, it is compact, light and neat in appearance. Sizes, 2½ to 8.
Per pair................................$1.25

Ladies' Romeo.

Weight, 11 ounces.

52238 Made of toilet felt, fur trimmed. Seamless, with sole of leather sewed on, making them very soft, warm and light. This is something entirely new in footwear, and as for a house slipper it has no equal. The sole is sewed to the slipper and is of the softest and finest of leather, and at the price will give the required amount of wear. Sizes, 1 to 8; widths C, D and E. Per pair..............$2.00

Child's and Infant's Felt Button.

Weight, 6 ounces.

52242 Child's Felt Button Shoes, uppers and soles of all wool felt with kid tips on toe, no heels; light, fine and warm; sizes, 6 to 8. Per pair.............$1.00
Weight, 5 ounces.

52243 Infant's Felt Button; same style as above; sizes, 1 to 5½. Per pair.... ....$0.85
Weight, 5 ounces.

Felt Shoes and Slippers.

Men's, Ladies', Misses' and Children's Felt Shoes and Slippers. Weight, 15 ounces.

52246 Men's Felt Slippers, brown embroidered, plush trimmed, leather soles and heels; sizes, 6 to 11. Per pair..........$1.40

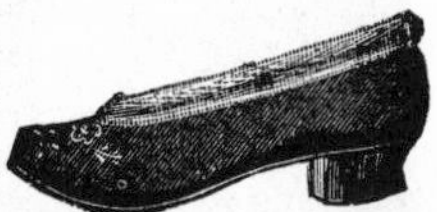

52248 Ladies' Felt Slippers, embroidered, flannel lined, plush trimmed, leather soles and opera cut; sizes, 3 to 7........$1.25
Weight, 11 ounces.

52250 Ladies' Felt Slippers, dark blue, plush trimmed, flannel lined, leather soles, without heels; sizes, 3 to 8.$1.00
Weight, 15 ounces.

52251 Ladies' Felt Slippers, plush trimmed, flannel lined, felt soles, without heels; sizes, 3 to 8 ......$0.90
Weight, 12 ounces.

52254 Misses' Felt Slippers, flannel lined, felt soles, without heels; sizes, 11 to 2. Per pair.......................$0.90
Weight, 9 ounces.

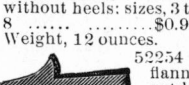

52255 Children's Felt Slippers, flannel lined, felt soles, without heels ; sizes, 8 to 11......... .80

52256 Children's Felt Slippers, flannel lined, felt soles, without heels; sizes, 5 to 8...., ... .70
Weight, 6 to 8 ounces.

Ladies' Beaver Button Leather Foxed.

Weight, 20 ounces.

52257 Ladies Beaver Top Button, bright grain foxed, flannel lined, very desirable, warm shoe; sizes, 2½ to 8; full width. Per pair ..$1.65

52258 Ladies' Beaver Shoes, dark blue, front lace, plush trimmed, leather soles and heels; sizes, 3 to 8. Per pair.... ......$1.15
Weight, 16 ounces.

Ladies' Beaver Polish Leather Foxed.

52259 Ladies' Beaver Polish, with dongola kid foxing, flannel lined, and all solid; a very desirable shoe for winter wear, being soft and warm, and at the same time will give extra good service. Sizes, 2½ to 8; full width............$1.40

52261 Children's Felt Button, foxed around with leather and also flannel lined throughout. Leather sole with spring heel. A good, sensible shoe for winter wear. Sizes, 5 to 8. Wt. 7 oz. Per pair.................$0.85

52262 Same as above, only without heels, leather foxing, flannel lined. Sizes, 2 to 5. Wt. 6 oz. Per pair......$0.65

M. W. & Co.'s Celebrated Custom Made Shoes.

Weight, 32 ounces.

52275 Men's Custom Made Calf Waukenfast Ball or Lace Shoes, made from the finest of calf skin, with hand-sewed inseam and outseam. The style of last is the original and natural shape of the foot, and specially designed for ease and comfort. The bottoms are the finest of California oak sole leather, with low broad heel and medium width toe, with perforated tip and abundance of room across the ball of foot not usually found in other style shoes. Sizes, 5 to 11. Widths, C, D, E and EE. Per pair.... ....$5.00 Weight, 31 ounces.

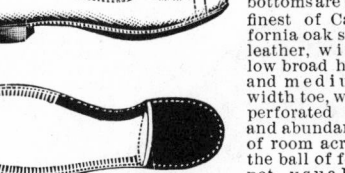

"Waukenfast."

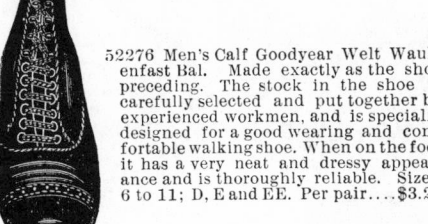

52276 Men's Calf Goodyear Welt Waukenfast Bal. Made exactly as the shoe preceding. The stock in the shoe is carefully selected and put together by experienced workmen, and is specially designed for a good wearing and comfortable walking shoe. When on the foot it has a very neat and dressy appearance and is thoroughly reliable. Sizes, 6 to 11; D, E and EE. Per pair....$3.25

52279 Men's Calf Lace Shoe. The stock in this shoe is carefully selected, one half double sole, not too heavy and sewed with a strong waxed linen thread by experienced shoemakers. Medium width toe, a trifle square, the very latest style. You will find the fit and wearing qualities of this shoe are entirely different from the majority of factory-made shoes. Our experience for the last eighteen years with this line of shoes is such that we can thoroughly recommend them to our trade. Sizes, 5 to 11. Widths, C, D, E and EE. Per pair.........$4.75 Weight, 28 ounces.

52280 Men's Custom Made Calf Congress Gaiter. The stock, style and workmanship are exactly the same as the shoe preceding, and contains all the good qualities that the other shoe does. Every pair warranted for a fair and reasonable amount of service. Sizes, 5 to 11; widths, C, D, E and EE Per pair..$4.75

If you see it in the Guide, its so.

Men's Shell Cordovan Shoes

Weight, 28 ounces.

52282 Cordovan or Horse Hide Shoes. Cordovan leather is made from certain portions of the horse hide, and when properly tanned is the best wearing leather in existence. The stock runs light and is very tough, and stretches very little, consequently the shoe keeps its original shape better than the ordinary calf shoe. It is practically damp-proof, as the texture is much finer than it is on other kinds of leather, also shines much easier than calfskin from ordinary box blacking. The shoe is a Goodyear welt, with solid oak bottoms, medium square toe, and imitation tips. This shoe we can thoroughly recommend. Sizes, 5 to 11. Widths, C, D, E and EE. Per pair........................$5.00

Weight, 26 ounces.

52283 Men's Cordovan Congress, made exactly as the one preceding. The same stock, same style last, and same workmanship. We also thoroughly recommend this as being a first-class shoe, and for style and finish has no equal. Sizes, 5 to 10. Widths, C, D, E and EE. Per pair..$5.00

Men's Kangaroo Welt Shoes.

Weight, 29 ounces.

52284 This shoe is made from the genuine Australian kangaroo, is very soft and pliable and does not get hard and crack as quickly as the ordinary calf shoe. Light uppers and medium heavy soles. The only shoe for real tender feet. Goodyear welt, Yale toe, with tip, which is a medium square, is very stylish; slightly on the foot, and gives excellent wear. Sizes, 5 to 11; widths, C, D E and EE Per pair.$4.00

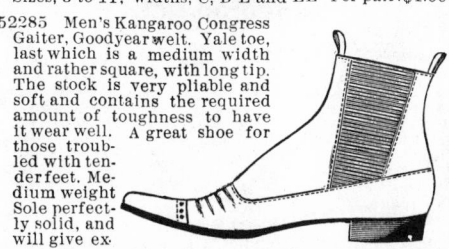

52285 Men's Kangaroo Congress Gaiter, Goodyear welt. Yale toe, last which is a medium width and rather square, with long tip. The stock is very pliable and soft and contains the required amount of toughness to have it wear well. A great shoe for those troubled with tender feet. Medium weight Sole perfectly solid, and will give excellent wear. Sizes, 5 to 11; widths, C, D, E, and EE. Weight, 27 ounces. Per pair.............$4.00

Razor Toe Patent Leather.

Weight, 25 ounces.

52289 This shoe is made from the very finest of patent leather of French tannage. The bottoms are Goodyear welt, which makes a perfectly smooth insole and flexible bottom. much more so than the ordinary machine sewed shoe. The Razor toe last is very narrow at toe, and one of the very popular styles on the market. The tip is very long with large perforations, late style Baltimore edge on outside, slightly extended, making in all a very handsome shoe. Sizes, 6 to 10, C, D, E. and EE. Price, per pair............$4.50

Cloth Top Patent Leather Congress.

Weight, 25 oz.

52290 This shoe is really a full dress shoe, made in the very latest style, with cloth top, imitation button, with narrow toe and long perforated tip, making a very graceful and sightly shoe. The stock is Hyles' patent French calf skin, and made up by the most experienced shoe makers in this city; sole put on by the Goodyear welt process; medium, light and flexible, very desirable for party or dress wear. Sizes, 5 to 10. Widths, C, D, and E. Per pair........................$4.75

Men's Patent Leather Lace Shoes.

52291 Men's Patent Leather Hook Lace Shoe, Goodyear welt, made from the very best grade Hyles' Patent French calf. Patent Leather stay up the front. The Columbia last, which is a medium square toe, plain. This is considered the most stylish shoe for full dress wear. No blacking or oiling required. Sold by all retailers for $7.00. We can say this much, that there is nothing finer made in the line of men's shoes. Sizes, 5 to 10; widths, C, D and E. Weight, 25 oz. Our price, per pair...... ....$4.75

Men's English Enamel.

52292 Made from the best English enamel calf skin. Requires no blacking or polish, can be cleaned by rubbing with an ordinary sponge. The style is the Columbia last. medium narrow toe, square, with long tip, Goodyear welt, with a perfectly smooth inner sole. The surface of the shoe looks like a very fine grain leather, highly enameled. Some prefer it to the patent leather, as water has no effect on it, neither does the mud stick to it like it does to oiled calfskin. This stock wears splendidly. Sizes, 5 to 10; widths, C, D, E, and EE. Weight, 30 oz. Per pair...................$4.50

DOLLARS AND SENSE.

Judicious buying means hundreds of dollars saved. Take the trouble to compare our prices with those of others, write us for Freight and Express rates to your town, and you will find that we can save you something on nearly everything you use,—an average of twenty per cent.

Our Own Invention.

We give you $7 for $5.50 in this shoe.

52293 We have at last got a shoe of our own invention, made from the finest grade of imported English grain, highly enameled. This grain consists of a very fine selection of calfskin, finished on the grain side; made hook lace and large spread eyelets and cork sole, extending from heel to toe, or the entire length of the shoe, thereby protecting the entire bottom of the foot from any moisture. This is entirely different from the ordinary cork sole and a decided improvement. This shoe has the appearance of patent leather; no blacking or oiling required. Water has no effect on the leather—you might say, a waterproof shoe. Do not go without a pair. They will keep your feet dry and in a healthy condition. Made on the globe toe last, with tip; very stylish, and a shoe that will give excellent satisfaction. Sizes, 6 to 11; widths, C, D, E and EE. Weight, 32 ounces. Per pair.........$5.50

Men's Russet and Tan Colored Shoes.

Weight, 25 ounces.

52295 This shoe is made from a fine grade of russet leather; the stock is very soft and pliable and a genuine blucher cut narrow toe and long perforated tip. Our sales on this class of goods went away ahead of our expectations last season, and for this coming season we offer you a more stylish shoe at a less price, as our purchases are much larger and we consequently buy them cheaper, and at the same time giving our customers the benefit. The bottoms are put on by the Goodyear welt process, which makes the sole light and flexible. Thoroughly reliable and all the rage. Sizes, 5 to 11. Widths, C, D and E. Per pair..............$3.25

Yale Toe, Russet Bal.

Weight, 29 ounces.

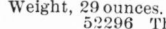

52296 The stock in this shoe is a very fine quality of russet leather; the color is a light tan of a high grade finish, and the prevailing style for the coming season, made over a narrow square toe last with tip. The tip is longer than the ordinary tip used, and tends to give the shoe a very narrow and graceful appearance. Goodyear welt bottoms, made on the same principle as handsewed shoes; will wear as well and will be just as comfortable on the foot. Sizes, 5 to 10. Widths, C, D, E and EE. Per pair 3.00

Russet or Tan Colored Razor Toe Bal.

Weight, 30 ounces.

52297 The stock in this shoe is a good selection of russet leather, made over the very latest Razor toe last. Baltimore edge on outside, slightly extended with long square tip and large perforations, which add to the general appearance of the shoe. This shoe is so constructed as to be as easy on the foot as those made over a wide toe last, as they have abundance of room across the ball and are made longer than the ordinary shoe. There is a very light box in toe to keep same from falling down. Do not fail to order this shoe, as it is a beauty. Sizes, 6 to 11. Widths C, D, E and EE. Per pair.............$3.00

MEN'S CLOTHING TO MEASURE.

We employ our own cutters, buy the cloth by the case, and our prices for good suits, made to FIT you, are as low as the ordinary ready made kind. Send for Custom-Made Clothing Pamphlet, with Samples.

The Blucher.

Weight, 27 ounces.

52300 Men's Blucher made from the finest of calf, Goodyear welt and dongola top, narrow square toe with long tip, making a very stylish shoe, and one that will give excellent wear. See cut. Sizes, 6 to 10. Widths C, D, E. and E. E. Per pair...........$3.00

Chicago Razor Toe.

Weight, 27 oz.

52302 This shoe is made from a fine quality of calf skin of our own selection, with the best of oak sole leather in the bottoms, which is as hard as flint, and will wear much longer than the ordinary cheap sole leather that is used to make cheap shoes. We use nothing but the best of stock, which is a sure guarantee that it will wear well for a fair and reasonable amount of service. Genuine Goodyear welt with long perforated tip, and narrow toe, a very sightly shoe when on the foot. Sizes, 6 to 10. Widths, C, D, E and EE. Per pair......................$2.95

Men's Calf Cork Sole Shoes.

Weight, 32 oz.

52305 Men's Cork Sole, Bal or hook lace, made from the best of domestic stock, with the cork placed between the inner and outer sole, thereby protecting the foot from any moisture and at the same time making a warm and comfortable shoe, and being made over a perfect fitting last has the same style and finish of a light shoe. Bound to give satisfaction; widths, D, E and EE. Sizes, 6 to 11. Per pair...........$3.25

52306 Men's Calf Congress Gaiters, machine sewed; cork sole, plain wide toe. A shoe for general winter wear. The cork being placed between the inner and outer sole keeps the foot warm and dry, and adds comfort in walking. We recommend these goods. Sizes, 6 to 11; widths, D E, and EE. Per pair................................$3.25
Weight, 31 ounces.

Kangaroo Bal.

52307 This shoe is made from the genuine kangaroo skin, which is very soft and glove-like, and at the same time tough, which will wear equally as well as stock much heavier and will give much more comfort to the wearer. We can thoroughly recommend this shoe, and for a light, comfortable and dressy shoe it has no equal. Sizes, 6 to 11; widths, D, E and EE. Per pair........................$3.00

The Tenderfoot.

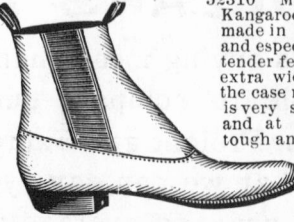

52310 Machine Sewed Kangaroo Congress Gaiter, made in different widths, and especially adapted for tender feet. Can furnish extra wide or narrow as the case may be. The stock is very soft and pliable, and at the same time tough and will wear splendidly. Medium weight, sole plain, broad toe. Sizes, 6 to 11. Widths, D, E and EE. Weight, 26 oz. Per pair.......$3.00

Our Corn Cure.

52313 This shoe we have made for our own trade. The stock is a first selection of calf skin, with Dongola top, Goodyear welt bottoms. The chief feature of this shoe is the toe, as it runs extra wide, being about the same width as it is across the ball of the foot; giving the toes abundance of room to lay in their natural shape without being cramped, as they are in a narrow toe shoe. This shoe will create no corns or ingrowing nails, but on the other hand will cure them if you wear a pair of these shoes. Very neat in appearance, and made of the very best material. If you are after a comfortable and at the same time serviceable shoe, order this one. Sizes, 6 to 11; widths, D, E and EE. Per pair..$3.15

M. W. & Co.'s Special Goodyear Welt Shoes.

Weight, 28 ounces.

52315 This shoe we have made special for our own trade; the stock is our own selection, genuine oak tanned. The bottoms are cut from the finest grade of California oak sole leather, which is very pliable and at the same time as hard as flint; made by first-class workmen; are of a very stylish last, plain, medium width toe; hub goring which never gives out. It contains all we can possibly put in a shoe to make it wear. We claim it to be equal to any five dollar shoe on the market. We can recommend this shoe to our customers to be first-class for any fair and reasonable amount of service. Sizes, 5 to 11, widths, C, D, E and EE. Per pair.....................$3.40

52316 Men's Calf Lace, made exactly as the one above. The same stock in the uppers, and also in the bottoms, and are the same style last, and in fact contain all good points found in the other shoe. Sizes, 5 to 11. Widths, C, D, E and EE. Per pair..$3.40
Weight, 28 oz.

World's Fair Prize Winners.

Weight, 33 ounces.

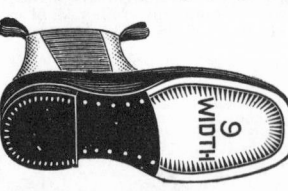

52317 This is a Genuine calf shoe, Goodyear welt, dongola top, with Hub elastic goring; we guarantee them to be the best shoes ever offered by any house in America for the money. The chief feature of this shoe is the width, being made over a nine-width last, wide toe and wide across the ball, and low, flat heel; just the shoe for tender and extra wide feet. Neat and serviceable. (See 52318 for lace in the same shoe.) Sizes, 6 to 12; width, in. 9; price.... $3.00

52318 Men's Genuine Calf Shoe, Goodyear welt, dongola top, hook lace, made on a 9 width, and something entirely new, being neat and serviceable, and at the same time giving the room across the ball of the foot not found in medium width shoes, broad toe and low heel. The same as 52317; sizes, 6 to 12; width, 9; price....$3.00
Weight, 32 ounces.

Our line of Ladies' Shoes is the largest in the United States. Almost 100 styles to select from.

Porpoise Congress.

52320 This shoe is made exactly like 52321 from the genuine North Sea porpoise, and as to wearing qualities there is nothing better known. Made with wide toe, hook lace and double sole, leather lined and high cut, perfectly solid. Sizes, 6 to 11; full widths.
Per pair $2.99
Weight, 46 ounces.

Porpoise Bal.

52321 This shoe is made from the skin of the genuine North Sea porpoise, and as to wearing qualities there is nothing better known. Made with wide toe, hook lace and double sole, leather lined and high cut, perfectly solid. Sizes, 6 to 11; full widths.
Per pair $2.99
Weight, 46 ounces.

M. W. & Co's. World Beaters.

52330 We now place before you for the coming season a shoe that we have been trying to produce for the last year. Never before could we offer a shoe made up in the style this one is. A Genuine Calf Welt Congress, in-seam and out-seam, and has all the style and finish found in a high-priced shoe, made of the best tannery calfskin, solid bottoms and counters, and a shoe that will meet the desired wants of a great many who do not wish to pay the prices asked by retail dealers, when they can get the style and wear out of this shoe. Sizes, 6 to 11; widths, C, D, E and EE.
Per pair $2.90
Weight, 28 ounces.

52330

The Columbia.

Weight, 28 oz.

52331 Men's Calf Goodyear Welt Bal. The tops are of dongola, solid bottoms and counters, and contains all the style and finish of a high price shoe. Made exactly like the one preceding. We predict for these two shoes a big trade for the coming season, as the price comes within the reach of most every one who wants a good wearing shoe, with style and finish combined. Do not overlook them, for they are worthy of your notice. Sizes, 6 to 11; widths, C, D, E and EE.
Per pair $2.90

The Railroad Bal.

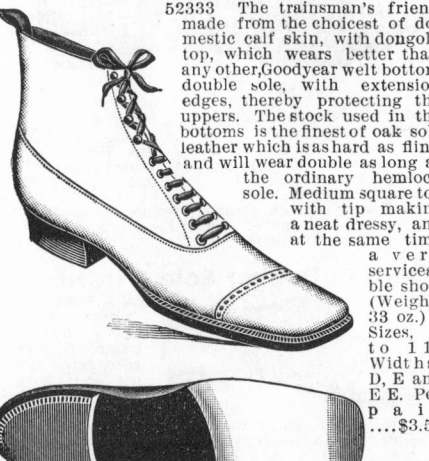

52333 The trainsman's friend made from the choicest of domestic calf skin, with dongola top, which wears better than any other, Goodyear welt bottom double sole, with extension edges, thereby protecting the uppers. The stock used in the bottoms is the finest of oak sole leather which is as hard as flint, and will wear double as long as the ordinary hemlock sole. Medium square toe with tip making a neat dressy, and at the same time a very serviceable shoe. (Weight, 33 oz.) Sizes, 6 to 11. Widths, D, E and E E. Per pair $3.50

The Railroad Congress.

(Weight, 33 oz)

52334 This shoe is made exactly like the one preceding, the only difference being in the elastic sides, which is considered by some railroad men to be much handier than the lace, as they can be taken off and put on in less time than it takes to lace a shoe. Double sole extension edge, a very neat and durable shoe. Sizes, 6 to 10. Per pair $3.50

The Light Weight Bal.

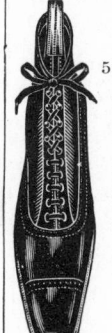

52335 Nothing finer for mid-summer wear Light soft and flexible, and conforms to the foot as a glove does to the hand. Yale toe last with long perforated tip, Goodyear welt bottoms with perfectly smooth inner sole, no nails to bother the foot. This stock is a genuine dongola, dull finish, the same we can guarantee to wear equally as well as any calf skin, and for a light dress shoe we can thoroughly recommend the same to our customers. Per pair...... ......$3.00
Sizes, 6 to 11. Widths, D E and E E

The Light Weight Congress.

52336 This shoe is made exactly as the one preceding, only difference being that one is a lace and the other congress. The stock workmansh p and style of last, exactly the same, and for the price they can not be equaled; you will have lots of comfort if you wear a shoe of this description
Size, 6 to 11.   Widths, D, E and E E Per pair ..$3.00

Our Hard Cash Line.

52340 Men's Machine Sewed Calf Lace, dongola top, globe toe tipped, made with smooth inner sole, free from nails, tacks or wax thread, and are far superior to the class of shoes commonly sold at this price. Sizes, 6 to 11; widths, D, E and EE. Price per pair.$2.75

Weight, 30 ounces.

52341 Men's Machine Sewed Calf Congress Gaiters, dongola top, Globe toe, tipped smooth inner sole, no nails, tacks or wax thread to hurt the feet. Sizes, 6 to 11; widths, D, E and EE ..$2.75
Weight, 29 ounces.

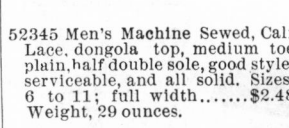

52345 Men's Machine Sewed, Calf Lace, dongola top, medium toe plain, half double sole, good style, serviceable, and all solid. Sizes, 6 to 11; full width......$2.48
Weight, 29 ounces.

52346 Men's Machine Sewed Calf Congress Gaiter, dongola top, medium toe plain, half double sole, good style, serviceable, and all solid. Sizes, 6 to 11; full width.
.........$2.48

M. W. & Co.'s Rock Bottom Line.

52350 Men's Calf, broad toe and extra wide, double soles, and tap nailed; made for hard knocks. Sizes, 6 to 11... ..$1.75
Weight, 47 ounces.

52351 Men's Calf, Congress, broad toe and extra wide double sole and tap. Made for hard knocks, same as 52350. Sizes, 6 to 11. Per pair.. ..$1.75
Weight, 47 ounces.

Men's Low Shoes.

52356 This shoe is made from genuine dongola kid, light and soft, with flexible sole, medium heel and all solid. Just the shoe for light summer wear. Sizes, 6 to 11. Widths, D, E & EE. Weight, 20 ounces. Per pair.................. 1.50

52357 Men's Machine Sewed Calf Oxfords, good value, all solid. Sizes, 6 to 11. Widths, D, E and EE. Per pair$2.50
Weight, 23 oz.

52359 Men's Calf Oxford, Goodyear welt, strictly first class stock and workmanship. Just the shoe for light dress summer wear. Made over the Globe last with tip, and in itself a beauty. Sizes, 5 to 11; widths, D, E, and EE. Weight, 23 ounces. Per pair................$2.75

52360 Men's Patent Leather Oxford, used principally for dancing or dress wear; very neat and serviceable, with light hand turn or slipper sole. Sizes, 5 to 11; widths, D, E and EE. Per pair........ ..$2.00
Weight, 16 ounces.

Satin Oil Line.

52365 Men's Satin Oil Congress Gaiters, crimp, seamless top plain medium toe, half double sole; sizes, 6 to 11; full width. Weight, 34 ounces.......$1.95

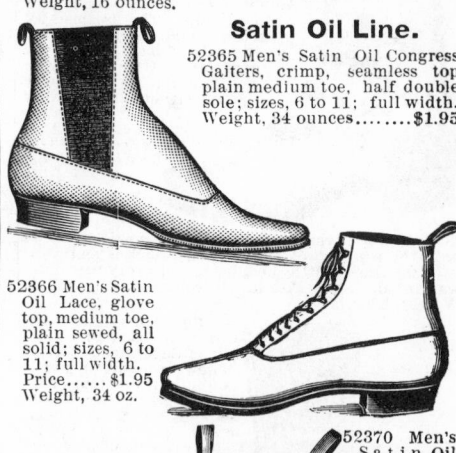

52366 Men's Satin Oil Lace, glove top, medium toe, plain sewed, all solid; sizes, 6 to 11; full width. Price...... $1.95
Weight, 34 oz.

52370 Men's Satin Oil Congress, all solid, half double sole, medium narrow toe; the right shoe at the right price. Sizes, 6 to 11; full width. Per pair $1.50
Weight, 37 ounces.

52371 Men's Satin Oil Bal, half double sole, good style and quality, sole leather counters and insoles; will give excellent service. Sizes 6 to 11; full width. Per pair...$1.50
Weight, 37 ounces.

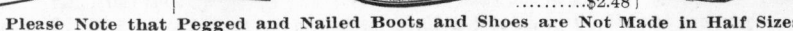

Please Note that Pegged and Nailed Boots and Shoes are Not Made in Half Sizes.

Mining Shoes.

52380 Men's Whole Stock Kip Miners' Shoes, two buckles, dirt excluder, hob nailed, warranted; sizes, 6 to 11, Per pair..$2.00 Weight, 68 ounces.

52381 Men's Whole Stock Kip Miners' Shoes, lace, high cut, dirt excluder, hob nailed; warranted; sizes, 6 to 11. Per pair..........$2.00 Weight, 68 ounces.

52384 Men's "A" Kip Mining Shoe, lace, medium high cut, heavy soles and broad heels to protect uppers. The bottom thoroughly hob-nailed. The shoe will give excellent wear. Sizes, 6 to 11. Per pair. ... $1.50 Weight, 53 ounces.

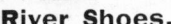

52387 Men's One Buckle Miner, heavy soles, well nailed and made to stand hard knocks. A good shoe for little money. Sizes, 6 to 11. Per pair..........$1.25 Weight, 53 ounces.

River Shoes.

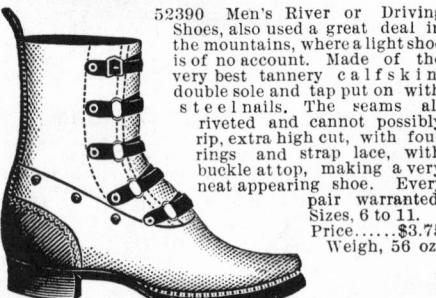

52390 Men's River or Driving Shoes, also used a great deal in the mountains, where a light shoe is of no account. Made of the very best tannery calfskin, double sole and tap put on with steel nails. The seams all riveted and cannot possibly rip, extra high cut, with four rings and strap lace, with buckle at top, making a very neat appearing shoe. Every pair warranted. Sizes, 6 to 11. Price......$3.75 Weigh, 56 oz.

52392 Men's River or Driving Shoe, made exactly the same as 52390, only the stock is veal calf, making a little heavier shoes; every pair warranted. Sizes, 6 to 11. Price, per pair......$3.25 Weight, 56 ounces.

52395 Men's Extra High Cut Calf Lace Drive or River Shoe, made with bellows tongue. Extra double sole and tap. The high tops fit the ankle securely, keeping them warm and dry in the severest kind of weather, This feature will be appreciated by many who are unable to find a comfortable fit in the other style Drive shoes. They are not clumsy in appearance and will give excellent wear. Sizes, 6 to 11. Per pair......$3.75 Weight, 55 ounces.

53395

Farmers' Kip Plow Shoes.

52399 Men's Custom Kip Plow Shoes, 3 buckle, dirt excluder, hand pegged, warranted. Sizes, 6 to 13. Per pair..........$1 75 Weight, 53 ounce.
52400 Men's Whole Stock Kip Plow Shoes, 2 buckle, dirt excluder, hand pegged; warranted. Sizes, 6 to 13. Per pair ......$1.50 Weight, 40 oz.

If you See It in the Guide, Its So.

BUY A BICYCLE! We can sell you a good one for $45.00, or the best $100.00 machine in the market

M. W. & Co.'s Oil Grain Plow Shoes.

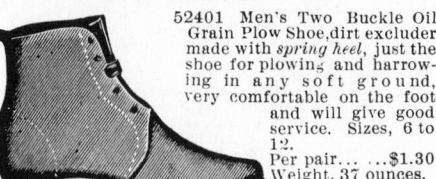

52401 Men's Two Buckle Oil Grain Plow Shoe, dirt excluder made with *spring heel*, just the shoe for plowing and harrowing in any soft ground, very comfortable on the foot and will give good service. Sizes, 6 to 12. Per pair... ...$1.30 Weight, 37 ounces.

52405 Men's Oil Grain Plow Shoes, two buckle, dirt excluder, half double soles, pegged. Sizes, 6 to 12. Per pair $1.25

52407 Men's **Milwaukee** Oil grain Dom Pedro Dirt Excluder. This shoe is made from all solid leather; is soft and pliable, and a shoe that will meet the desired wants of a great many. Very serviceable and not too heavy. Sizes, 6 to 11. Per pair.....$1.30

Weight, 38 ounces.

52409 Men's Oil Grain Congress Plow Shoe made from all solid leather, and will give excellent wear. Sizes, 6 to 11. Per pair..$1.40 Weight, 40 oz.

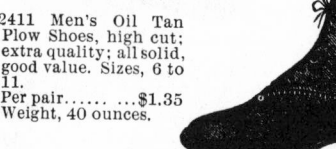

52411 Men's Oil Tan Plow Shoes, high cut; extra quality; all solid, good value. Sizes, 6 to 11. Per pair...... ...$1.35 Weight, 40 ounces.

Kip Brogans.

52415 Men's Whole Stock Kip Brogans, lace, half double soles, pegged, all solid. Sizes, 6 to 11. Per pair...........................$1 15 Weight, 41 ounces.
52416 Men's Whole Stock Kip Brogans, lace, all solid; good value. Sizes, 6 to 11. Per pair...... 1.00 Weight, 41 oz.

M. W. & Co.'s Cotton King.

52420 This shoe is made from Milwaukee oil grain leather, solid counters and insoles with bellows tongue, or dirt excluder. This shoe we claim to be the best on earth for the money. Sizes, 6 to 12. Per pair...............$1.15 Weight, 36 ounces.

Men's Grain Creedmoors.

52425 Men's English Grain "Creedmoor" hook lace extra, high cut, bellows tongue, calf lined, very desirable for hunting or wet weather wear; double soled and tap nailed and as near waterproof as leather can make it. Sizes, 6 to 11; full width. Per pair.....$3.50

Weight, 57 ounces.

Base Ball Shoes.

Weight, 22 ounces.
52430 Men's Heavy Canvas Base Ball Shoes, calf trimmed solid leather soles and counters, extra quality. Sizes 6 to 11. Per pair.................$1.10
52431 Boys' Heavy Canvas Base Ball Shoes, calf trimmed, all solid, best grades. Sizes 1 to 5. Per pair........$1.00 Weight, 20 ounces.

Black Tennis Bals.

(Weight, 20 ouncees.)

52440 Men's Black Canvas Tennis Bals, corrugated rubber soles, with leather insoles. Sizes, 6 to 10. Per pair, $1.00

52441 Boys Black Tennis Bals, corrugated rubber soles, with leather insoles. Sizes, 1 to 5. Per pair.................. ....$0.95 Weight, 17 ounces.
52442 Ladies' Black Tennis Bals, corrugated rubber soles, with leather insoles. Sizes, 2½ to 7. Per pair................ .... .90 Weight, 17 ounces.

Black Tennis Oxfords.

52445 Men's Black Tennis Oxford, corrugated rubber soles, with leather insoles. Sizes, 6 to 11. Per pair..$0.85
52446 Boys' Black Tennis Oxford, corrugated rubber soles, with leather insoles. Sizes, 1 to 5. Per pair............................ .75 Weight, 15 ounces.
52447 Ladies' Black Tennis Oxfords, corrugated rubber soles, with leather insoles. Sizes, 2½ to 6. Per pair................................ .75 Weight, 15 ounces.

Check Tennis Bals.

Weight, 20 ounces.

52450 Men's Check Tennis Bals, corrugated rubber soles with leather insoles. Sizes, 6 to 11. Per pair.$1.00

52451 Boys' Check Tennis Bals, corrugated rubber soles, with leather insoles. Sizes, 1 to 5½. Per pair.................................$0.95 Weight, 17 ounces.
52452 Ladies' Check Tennis Bals, corrugated rubber soles, with leather insoles. Sizes, 2½ to 6. Per pair.................................$0.90 Weight, 15 ounces.

Check Tennis Oxfords.

Weight, 17 ounces.
52460 Men's Check Canvas Tennis Shoes, with corrugated rubber soles, best quality; sizes, 6 to 11. Per pair............................$0.85
52461 Boys' Check Canvas Tennis Shoes, with corrugated rubber soles, best quality; sizes, 1 to 5½. Per pair............................ .75 Weight, 15 ounces.
52462 Ladies' Check Canvas Tennis Shoes, with corrugated rubber soles; best quality; sizes, 2½ to 6. Per pair............................ .75 Weight, 15 ounces.

Canvas Rubber Sole Oxford.

52465 Men's Canvas Tennis Shoes, leather trimmed, heavy corrugated rubber sole, with leather slip sole, and leather sock lining. Keeping the foot from coming in contact with rubber; very popular with tennis clubs, also a good bicycle shoe and for ordinary wear. Neat and durable. Sizes, 6 to 10. Per pair............................ ....$1.50

for $65.00. Send for Special Bicycle Catalogue.

L. A. W. Bicycle Bal.

52467 This shoe is made from a plump grade of dull dongola kid, with light sole, lacing nearly to toe. The stock is light and soft, and will give excellent wear, neat and dressy and can be worn for a regular street shoe as well as for bicycle riding. Sizes, 6 to 10. Width, D, E & EE.
Per pair................................$1.75

Men's Gymnasium Oxfords.

52469 Made from light kangaroo calf, soft and flexible, with extra light sole. No heel can be used, for all kind of athletic exercises. Sizes, 6 to 10.
Per pair................................$1.25

Running Shoes.

Weight, 11 ounces.
52470 Men's English Running Shoes, made of fine cordovan leather, with English steel spikes inserted between the soles, hand sewed; sizes, 6 to 10. Per pair...........................$3.50

Weight, 13 oz.
52471— Men's American Running Shoes, made after the style of the English shoe, cordovan leather, steel spikes, machine sewed; a desirable shoe for amateurs; sizes, 6 to 10. Per pair.................................2.40

Canadian Snow Shoes

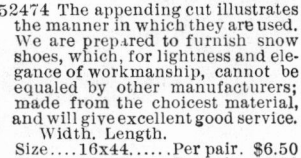

52474 The appending cut illustrates the manner in which they are used. We are prepared to furnish snow shoes, which, for lightness and elegance of workmanship, cannot be equaled by other manufacturers; made from the choicest material, and will give excellent good service. Width. Length.
Size....16x44.....Per pair...$6.50
Size....16x42.....Per pair....4.50

Dancing Shoes.

Weight, 25 ounces.

52475 Men's Song and Dance Shoes, made of calfskin, with extra heavy soles, machine sewed; sizes, 14 to 16 inches long. Per pair...........$4.50

52476 Men's Dancing Clogs, made of red, blue or black morocco leather, wood soles, all one piece; sizes, 6 to 10, full width. Per pair...........$2.50
52477 Brass Jingles for above, per set.........25
52478 Wooden Shoes for clog dancers and comedians, also extensively used in dyeing establishments, laundries, cellars, dairy farms, etc.
Weight, 33 ounces.
Men's sizes, 6 to 11. Per pair...........$0.50
Boys' sizes, 1 to 5. Per pair.............50
Women's sizes, 3 to 7. Per pair...........50

Shoe Pacs.

Weight, 29 ounces.

52479 This Pac is made from and oil tanned Pac, leather uppers and soles with low flat heels, making a very light and serviceable shoe for all kinds of wear. Sizes, 6 to 12.
Per pair..........$1.75

Lumberman's Pacs.

Weight, 41 ounces.

52480 The accompanying cut represents our best hand sewed Pac with ten inch leg of oil grain leather and oil tan Pac leather uppers; the soles are doubled, sewed and inserted with round cone-headed Hungarian nails, which adds to the wearing qualities. The sole is light and flexible, and very easy to walk in, and does not slip. Sizes, 6 to 12. Per pair.$2.35

Wood Shoes with Leather Uppers.

52481 This shoe is made with wooden bottoms and leather uppers They are used in laundries, dairies, and are also very useful on the farm; are very light and durable. Sizes, 5 to 12. Full width. Per pair............$0.80

Weight, 21 ounces.

Wood Sole Clip-Clap Slippers.

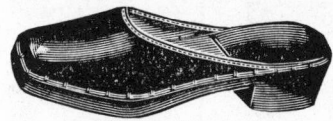

Weight, 20 ounces.
52482 The Old Style Clip-Clap Slipper, wood sole and leather vamp, light and durable and very useful on the farm for out door choring; sizes, 4 to 12. Per pair.................................$0.50

Men's Slippers.

52485 Men's Silk Plush Chenille Embroidered Slippers, fancy shades, opera cut, extra fine quality and finish, hand sewed, turn soles. These are decided novelties in slipper line and cannot fail to please. Sizes, 5 to 11. Weight 13 oz.
Per pair.................................$1.65
52487 Men's Everett Cut Slipper, velvet embroidered. Is very serviceable and stylish. Sizes, 6 to 11.
Per pair..................................$0.75

2488 Men's Velvet Embroidered Slippers, good style and quality, sewed; sizes, 5 to 11.

Weight 15 ounces. Per pair...................$1.00

52489 Men's Genuine Alligator Slippers, opera cut; hand sewed soles, chamois lined throughout, making the most serviceable, stylish and comfortable slipper to be had at any price; sizes, 5 to 11. Per pair.................................$2.15
Weight, 13 ounces.

52490 Men's Tan Color Slippers, made opera cut, very soft and fine; lined, hand sewed, turned sole, flexible; very popular for fine wear; sizes, 6 to 11.
Per pair..................................$1.50

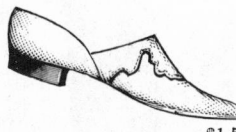

The Romeo (Nullifiers).

52491 This is the most popular and most sensible slipper ever put before the public. Any man who has ever worn a pair will never wear any other kind of a slipper. Its great and principal advantage is in the fact that the ankle and instep being covered protects the health by preventing colds, which arise from drafts that are constantly passing over floors; can be worn as a light summer street shoe. There is no slipper or shoe made which gives so much comfort to the feet; color, black. Sizes, 5 to 11; widths, C, D, E and EE. Per pair.................................$1.65

Slippers—Continued.

52492 This shoe is made exactly as the above, only the stock is of a tan color, morocco calf and a much finer quality, being a turn sole, light and serviceable and on a very stylish last; in fact the very latest in gentlemen's slippers. If you want something fine and for solid comfort they have no equal. Sizes, 5 to 10; widths, B, C, D and E. Per pair.................................$2.50

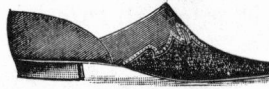

52495 Men's Goat Slippers, dark maroon, patent leather trimmed, turn soles, hand sewed, opera cut; sizes, 6 to 11.
Per pair.................................$1.40
52496 Men's Goat Slippers, black; Everett cut, turn soles, sewed, solid comfort; sizes, 6 to 11..1.25
52497 Men's German Cloth Embroidered Slippers, all solid, broad and roomy, nothing better for wear, with leather foxing (see 52144 for style); sizes, 6 to 11................................1.00
52498 Men's Oil Grain Slippers, machine sewed, damp proof, strong and serviceable, for house or outdoor wear, all solid; sizes, 6 to 11...85

Men's Carpet Slippers.

52499 Men's Brussels Carpet Slippers, best quality; bound and stayed, leather soles and heels, sewed; sizes, 6 to 11.$0.39
We think we sell first class goods. Let us know if your shoes don't wear well and give us an opportunity to make them satisfactory.

Cowboys' or Ranchmen's Boots.

Weight, 53 ounces.

The "Opera."

52500 Men's Calf "Opera Cowboy" Boots, sewed, extra long goat leg, fancy stitched front and back (see cut), 2-inch heel, 20-inch leg; sizes, 5 to 10.
Per pair.................................$5.00

The "Montana."

52501 This boot is made from the very best tannery calf skin, all solid, and after the style of the regular cowboy boot; extra high heel and medium toe; very serviceable, and a boot that is adapted to all kinds of wear. Sizes, 5 to 10.
Per pair.................................$3.25
Weight, 56 ounces.

The Soudan.

Weight, 46 oz.
52502 Men's Soudan Calf "Cowboy" Boots, sewed, 19-inch leg, stitched and ribbed, 2-inch heels; very dressy, fine quality and finish; sizes, 5 to 10.
Per pair.................................$4.75

Cowboys' Pride.

Weight, 56 ounces.

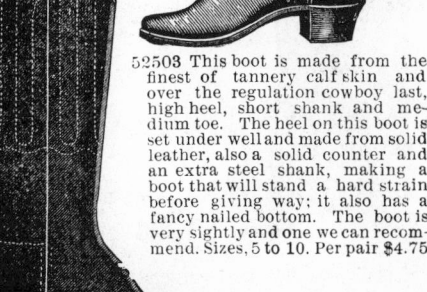

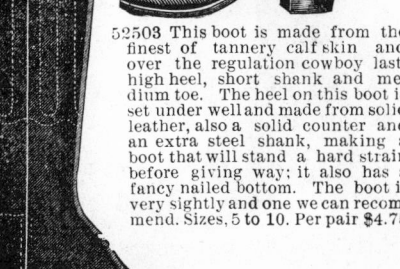

52503 This boot is made from the finest of tannery calf skin and over the regulation cowboy last, high heel, short shank and medium toe. The heel on this boot is set under well and made from solid leather, also a solid counter and an extra steel shank, making a boot that will stand a hard strain before giving way; it also has a fancy nailed bottom. The boot is very sightly and one we can recommend. Sizes, 5 to 10. Per pair $4.75

The "Cattle Trail" Boot.

Weight, 57 ounces.
52504 Men's All Calf "Cowboy" Boots fancy scolloped top, half double soles, hand pegged solid, and serviceable, 15 in. leg, 2 in. heels; sizes, 4 to 11.
Per pair..................... $4.00

Men's Calf Opera Boots.

Weight, 41 oz.
52510 Men's Calf Opera Boot goat leg, single sole, hand welts, low, broad heels, for fine wear; quality guaranteed; sizes, 6 to 11.
Per pair....... ....$4.75

52511 Men's Calf Opera Boots, goat leg, machine sewed, half double soles, low heels, solid and well made; sizes, 6 to 11.
Per pair.....................$4.00
Weight, 56 oz.

52510

Men's Calf Boots, Pegged.

52515 Men's Genuine French Calf Boots, half double soles, medium low heels, custom-made throughout, hand pegged and hand sided This boot we claim to be genuine French calf and no imitation, and our experience for the last 18 years in handling this work is sufficient evidence to convince most any one that the boot must be just what we represent it to be. Every pair warranted for fair and reasonable amount of service. Sizes, 5 to 11. Per pair...$4.10

Tap Sole Calf Boot.

Weight, 54 oz.
5 2517 This is a genuine custom-made calf boot, backs and fronts of the best of calf-skin, half double sole, with an extra tap, making one of the best wearing boots on the market; made over a neat

last, with medium heel and toe. Every pair warranted for reasonable service. Sizes, 5 to 12.
Per pair...........................$3.85

The Farmers' Pride.

"Tested for twenty years."
52519 This boot we have constantly sold for the last eighteen years, and has stood the test so well and has given such good satisfaction that we cannot say too much in its praise. This is what it is made up of: The calf skin is the first selection, the bottoms from first quality sole leather and are hand pegged, with calf backs and fronts and half double sole, making a medium weight calf boot, and from the quality of stock that we use and the workmanship, we cannot hesitate to warrant this boot to give entire satisfaction; not to be used as you would use a common heavy stoga boot. Sizes, 5 to 11; no half sizes.
Per pair.....................$3.75
Weight, 53 ounces

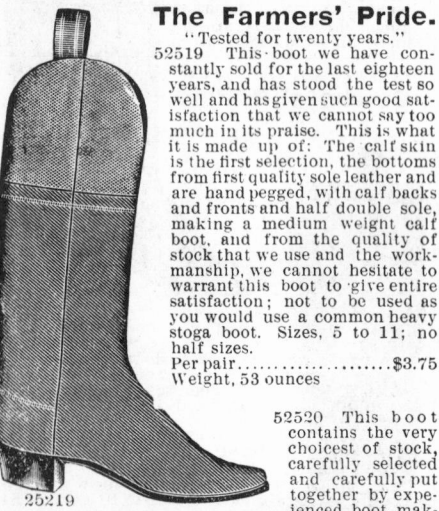

52520 This boot contains the very choicest of stock, carefully selected and carefully put together by experienced boot mak-

25219

ers. We can cheerfully recommend this boot to our customers to give good service; calf backs and fronts and strictly solid. Nothing shoddy used in any of our foot wear. Sizes, 6 to 12 No half sizes. Per pair.............. $3.00
Weight, 60 ounces.

The Tornado.

Weight, 55 ounces.

52521 This boot we claim to be the best boot ever offered by any house in this country for the price. Genuine calf skin, calf backs and fronts, solid counters and inner soles and a regular custom appearance. This boot we have made special for our own trade and can thoroughly recommend it to those wanting a first-class calf boot for a little money. Sizes, 6 to 12.
Per pair...........$2.50

Men's Light Kip boot.

Weight, 70 ounces.
52523 Men's Genuine French Kip Boots, half double sole, pegged, 16-inch leg, all hand made, warranted; sizes, 6 to 11
Per pair...... .... $4.50
Weight, 70 ounces.
52525 Men's Light Veal Kip Boots, half double sole, hand pegged, whole stock and solid throughout, warranted; sizes, 5 to 12. Per pair...........$3.50
Weight, 60 ounces.
52527 Men's Fine Kip Boots, pegged, half double sole, whole stock, well made and durable; sizes, 6 to 11.
Per pair $2.85
Weight, 64 ounces.

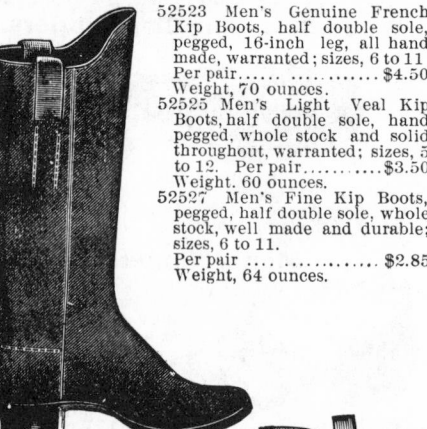

52,523

Our Best Kip.

52530 This boot is made with double sole, kip backs and fronts of extra quality. We have handled this particular boot for the past eighteen years continuously, and our sales are increasing every year. This boot, without exception, is the best custom made heavy kip boot sold in this market or any other market. We can thoroughly warrant this boot as being first-class, and those of our customers who are in need of a strictly custom made boot will do well to order this one. Sizes, 6 to 12. No half sizes.
Per pair $3.50

The Monarch.

52531 This boot we have made special for our own trade. The stock is a genuine California fine kip of a medium weight, solid counters and inner soles, kip backs and fronts. We claim that this is the finest and cleanest boot ever offered by any house in the country, and at a price that defy competition. We can thoroughly recommend them as being first-class for a fair and reasonable amount of service. Sizes, 6 to 11. No half sizes.
Per pair....   ....$2.60
52532 Men's Kip Boots, pegged, whole stock, hand double sole, strong and heavy, warranted; sizes, 6 to 11. Weight, 68 ounces.
Per pair.................$2.92

52531

52534 Men's Kip Boots, whole stock machine sided, double sole, pegged, all solid; sizes, 6 to 11.
Weight, 68 ozs.
Per pair....$2.40

Miners' Boots

Weight, 85 ounces.
52537 Men's Miners' Boots, whole stock light kip, long leg, tap sole, hob nailed, best quality; sizes, 6 to 11.
Per pair $4.00
52539 Men's Miners' Boots, heavy S kip, double sole,

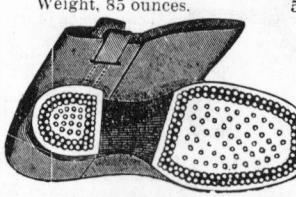

hob nailed, all solid; sizes, 6 to 11. Per pair.....$2.25
Weight, 74 ounces.

River Driving Boot.

Weight, 78 ounces.
52540 This boot is made from the very best grade of calf-skin. The bottoms are of the very finest of oak sole leather. As you know, the quality of this boot must be first class to to stand the test that it is put to. Made with extra heavy double sole and tap, with large broad heel, which is almost impossible to run over. If you want a good durable boot, do not fail to procure a pair, as they are thoroughly warranted for fair and reasonable service; sizes, 5 to 11; no

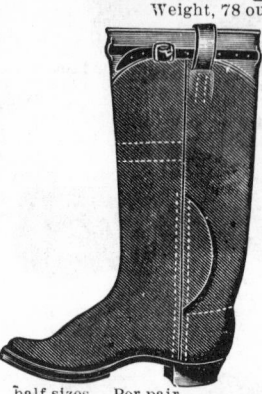

half sizes. Per pair.... ....$4.25

Men's Shooting Creedmoor.

52541 This shoe we have made special for our own trade, in response to the numerous inquiries we have for a light shooting shoe, made from genuine kangaroo calf skin; calf lined throughout, with bellows tongue, and medium weight sole. The stock is light

and soft, and very comfortable on the foot. In fact, making a shoe that is adapted for almost any kind of wear and as near waterproof as a leather shoe can be made. Try a pair; they will stand the test thoroughly; warranted; sizes, 6 to 11.
Per pair. $3.25

The High Water Shoe.

52543 We have this shoe made from the finest selection of Domestic calf, with kangaroo calf top, eleven inches high, the same being very soft and pliable, bellows tongue, calf stayed inside and out, thereby protecting the seam thoroughly. Double sole with extension edges, plain, medium toe, making a shoe suitable for most any kind of wear; very desirable for hunting, prospecting, and also for log driving, can be worn for dress, as the stock is light and made on a neatfitting last. Sizes, 6 to 11.
Per pair..$4.00

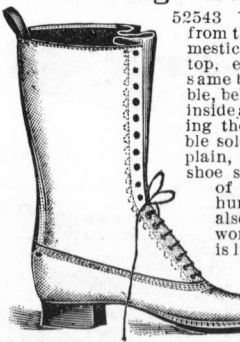

Thompson, Quinby Hunting Boots.

Weight, 72 ounces.
5 2544 This boot combines all the advantages of a top boot, with great ease of adjustment, and the comfort of a lace shoe. Being a *strictly hand made* boot, and is water-tight to the top, and does not wrinkle at ankle. It is held up over the swell of the calf by a nicely adjusted lacing at top, made of a fine finished oil grain leather "Color Russet." Soles broad and projecting, so

as to protect the uppers. This boot we can thoroughly recommend as being first-class in every particular, and those wishing a comfortable, well fitting hunting boot should by all means try a pair, as our price is much lower than any of our competitors on this boot. Sizes, 5 to 11.
Per pair $10.00

The Sportsman's Delight.

52545 This boot is made from Kangaroo Calf, extra soft and light, Goodyear welt bottoms, medium weight sole, lace leg and instep. This boot will be a great favorite, as it is very neat and will be as easy on the foot as a hand sewed shoe. Made o. er a very neat medium toe last, and has not that clumsy appearance always found in the heavy grain sporting boot. Sizes, 5 to 11; widths, D, E & EE.
Per pair....$5.25
Weight, 52 ounces.

52547 This boot is made from genuine oil tan Color Russet Jap kip, lacing all the way up with watertight gusset, 16 inch leg and sewed bottoms, has an extra tap sole put on with cone head nails; also heels put on in the same way, which makes it impossible to slip. The boot is entirely different from the ordinary sporting boot; it is extra light and fits perfectly, is not heavy and ill-shaped like most sporting boots. If you are a hunter, do not be without a pair of these boots. An elegant boot for chicken hunting. Sizes, 5 to 11.
Per pair.............................$4.00
Weight, 58 ounces.

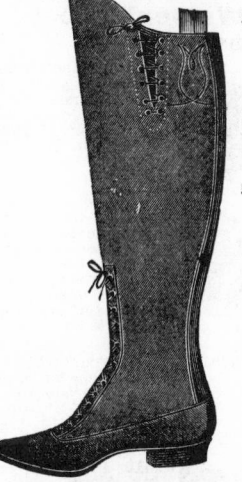

52549 Men's Black English Grain Leather "Hunting Boots," double sole, laced leg and instep, as near waterproof as a leather boot can be made; best quality; warranted; sizes, 5 to 11.
Per pair.........$5.00
Weight, 76 ounces.
52550 Men's Russet English Grain Leather "Hunting Boots," double sole, laced leg and instep; as near waterproof as a leather boot can be made; best quality; warranted; sizes, 5 to 11.
Per pair.........$5.00
Weight, 76 ounces.

The Napoleon.

52552 This boot is made from genuine English oil grain, Napoleon cut, extra long leg, with seam in the back. A very desirable boot for brewers, butchers, drovers and cattle shippers. Will wear well. Sizes, 6 to 11.
Per pair.............$5.00
Weight, 60 ounces.

Kangaroo Grain Protection Seam Boot.

Weight 79 ounces.

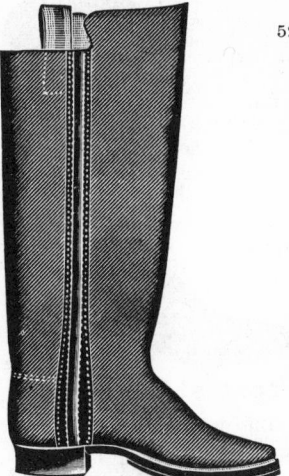

52555 Men's Oil Grain Boot, double sole and tap, with protection seam on inside. This seam is the one that generally gives out, on account of the constant rubbing. We have it protected by a long piece of leather running the full length covering the seam thoroughly and double stitched on each side; another point to mention is that the stock is light and soft, and not harsh and heavy like in the majority of grain boots. This boot we can thoroughly recommend and warrant as being far superior to anything in grain boots in the market.
Sizes, 6 to 11.   Per pair...........................$3.35

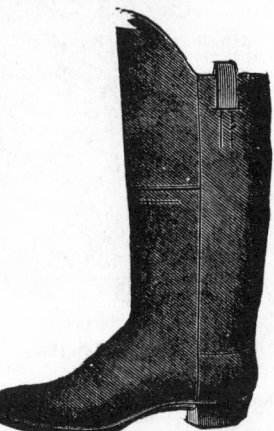

52557 Men's grain leather, double sole pegged, 15 inch leg, good quality and all solid; sizes, 6 to 11.
Per pair.....$2.75
Weight, 65 ounces

Grain Plow Boot.

Weight, 64 ounces.

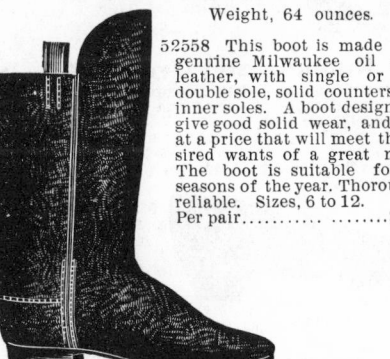

52558 This boot is made from genuine Milwaukee oil grain leather, with single or half double sole, solid counters and inner soles. A boot designed to give good solid wear, and sold at a price that will meet the desired wants of a great many. The boot is suitable for all seasons of the year. Thoroughly reliable. Sizes, 6 to 12.
Per pair.............. ....$2.00

Wool Lined Boots.

Weight, 84 ounces.

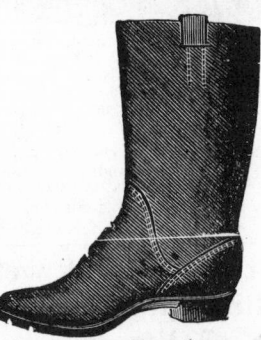

52559 This boot has been out of the market for years, but on account of the many inquiries we have had for a boot of this description we have gone to the trouble to have this made special for those of our customers that need a good warm leather boot; lined throughout with the natural wool sheep skin, made from the best Milwaukee grain leather and thoroughly reliable.
Sizes, 6 to 11. Per pair..... ....$3.25

Wool and Felt Boots.

THE ALPINE.

Order your Felt Boots early.
Note price on Felt Boots Weight, 30 oz.
52560 M. W. & Co.'s Alpine Felt Boot, made from the finest imported wool, calf front and back stay, and is undoubtedly the finest boot in the market, thoroughly warranted. Sizes, 6 to 12.
Per pair........$1.00
Per doz. net.....10.50

The Full Value.

52561 M. W. & Co.'s Full Value Felt Boots, made of extra quality all wool white felt; soft, firm and flexible, and perfectly free from grease. Has calf stays, front and back, and loop at heel for removing. This loop will add greatly to the wear of the boot, as it takes all the strain while the boot is being removed from foot. Sizes, 6 to 13. Per pair.....$0 90
Per doz. net.... 10.00
Weight, 30 oz.

The Empire.

52562 Men's Empire Felt Boots, all wool, gray felt, 16 in. leg, uniform thickness throughout; has calf back and front stay, and strap at heel for removing. These boots are strictly first quality and should not be compared with inferior grades usually sold at this price. Sizes, 6 to 11.
Per pair.................$0.70
Per doz. net, ... 8.00
Weight, 30 oz.

Boys' Dakota Felt Boot.

52563 Boys' Dakota Felt Boot, extra quality, all wool, gray felt, has calf front and back stay and strap at heel for removing. The best boy's boot in the market. Sizes 1 to 5.
Per pair $0.60
Per doz. pairs, net...........6.75
Weight, 24 oz.

Felt Boot Combination.

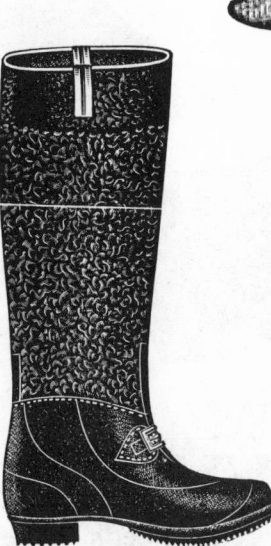

52563
52564 This combination is composed of Felt Boot No. 52562 and the lumberman's rubber ankle boot, with tap sole and solid rubber heel. The number on rubber is "5 2 6 4 4." This combination comes cheaper than if bought separately as you can see from prices under the above numbers. This combination will give excellent wear, as they are both first quality goods.
Sizes 6 to 12.
Per pair..$2.10
Per dozen pairs, net..24.00
Weight, 93 oz.

Boys' and Youths' Wear.
Weight, 24 oz.

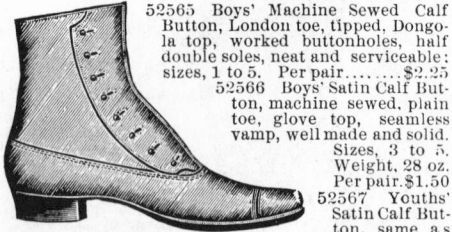

52565 Boys' Machine Sewed Calf Button, London toe, tipped, Dongola top, worked buttonholes, half double soles, neat and serviceable; sizes, 1 to 5. Per pair........$2.25

52566 Boys' Satin Calf Button, machine sewed, plain toe, glove top, seamless vamp, well made and solid. Sizes, 3 to 5. Weight, 28 oz. Per pair.$1.50

52567 Youths' Satin Calf Button, same as above. sizes, 12 to 2. Per pair. $1.40

52569 Boys' Calf Congress Gaiters, machine sewed, London toe, tipped, Dongola tap, seamless, for everyday or dress wear; sizes, 3 to 5. Per pair........$2.10 Weight, 24 oz.

52570 Boys' machine sewed. A calf Lace London top tipped, Dongola top, half double sole, good style and quality; sizes, 1 to 5. Per pair, ...$1.50 Weight, 25 ounces.

52570

Boys' and Youths' Rock Bottom Shoes.

52574 We have this shoe made special for boys, and of an extra quality of light kip, with bellows tongue, Hook lace, seams all riveted, which makes a shoe thoroughly reliable and one to give good solid service. Sizes, 1 to 5....$1.25 Weight, 33 oz.

52575 We have this shoe made exactly as the one preceding. As it has always been a hard matter for customers to get a good, solid, heavy shoe for a youth, this one will give excellent service. Made from light kip skins. Riveted seams; will not rip. Sizes, 10 to 13. Per pair...$1.15

Boys' and Youths' Plow Shoes.

52576 Boys' Oil Grain Two Buckle plow shoes, pegged, strong and heavy; warranted; sizes, 1 to 5. Per pair...$1.15 Weight, 32 ounces.

52577 Boys' Kip Lace Shoes, hip cut, pegged double soles, all solid; sizes, 1 to 5. Per pair... ......$1.15 Weight, 32 ounces.

52577

52579 Boys' Oiled Grain Creole Congress. This shoe is made from the best Milwaukee oil grain leather, with solid counters and solid leather soles, making a very serviceable shoe for general wear.

52579

Size 1 to 5, per pair.............................$1.25 Weight, 28 ounces.

Boys' Calf Boots.

Weight, 40 ounces.
52580 Boys' All Calf Boots, pegged, half double sole, hand made, warranted; sizes, 1 to 5. Per pair....................$2.60

52581 Boys' Calf Boots, split back, pegged, half double sole, all solid; sizes, 1 to 5. Per pair...................$2.00 Weight, 46 oz.

Boys' and Youths' Kip Boots.

52585 Boys' Best Kip Boots, whole stock, pegged, double sole, all hand made, warranted; sizes, 1 to 5. Per pair..........$2.41

52586 Boys' Whole Stock Kip Boots, half double sole, pegged, well made and solid throughout. Sizes, 1 to 5. Per pair... ..$1.70 Weight, 48 oz.

52587 Youths' Best Kip Boots, whole stock, pegged, double sole, all hand made, warranted; sizes, 10 to 13. Weight, 29 oz. Per pair $1.86

52588 Youths' Whole Stock Kip Boots, half double sole, pegged, well made and solid throughout; sizes, 10 to 13. Weight, 29 oz. Per pair.... ....$1.55

52585

Children's Boots.
Weight, 20 ounces.

52589 Child's Light Glove Grain Boots, soft stock, pegged. Extra fine. warranted; sizes, 7 to 10. Per pair............... ....$1.40

52590 Child's S Calf Boots, red tops, pegged, good value; sizes, 7 to 10. Per pair.................. .....$1.00

Rubbers and Overshoes.

NOTE—We quote below a complete line of rubbers which we guarantee to be of first quality. We do not buy second quality rubbers like most country merchants and sell them at prices first should be sold for. We warrant every pair we send out to be strictly first-class, at prices that cannot be duplicated.

52600

52600 Men's Imitation Sandals, net lined, first quality, sizes, 6 to 13. Per pair......$0.59 Weight, 21 ounces.

52601 Boys' Safety Strap Sandals, net lined, first quality; sizes, 1 to 6. Weight, 19 oz. Per pair ... $0.54

52602 Ladies' Imitation Sandals, net lined, first quality, sizes, 2½ to 8; weight, 13 oz. Per pair.$0.38

52603 Misses' Spring Heel Sandals, first quality, net lined; sizes, 11 to 2. Weight, 8 oz. Per pair $0.29

52604 Child's Spring Heel Sandals, net lined, first quality; sizes, 5 to 10½. Weight, 7 oz.

52603

Per pair...................................$0.25

Rubbers—Continued.

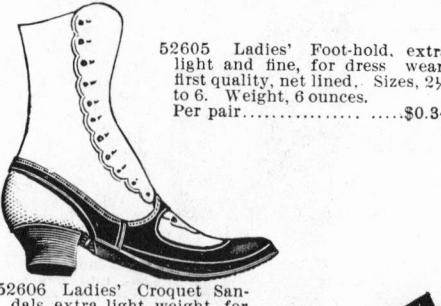

52605 Ladies' Foot-hold, extra light and fine, for dress wear, first quality, net lined. Sizes, 2½ to 6. Weight, 6 ounces. Per pair................ .....$0.34

52606 Ladies' Croquet Sandals, extra light weight, for fine dress wear, net lined, first quality, 2 to 7. Per pair................$0.42 Weight, 10 ounces.

52607 Woman's Storm Rubber; nothing better for wet weather, light and dressy; first quality; sizes, 2½ to 7. Per pair................$0.46 Weight, 10 ounces.

52609 Men's Self-acting Sandals, net lined, first quality. Sizes, 6 to 12. Weight, 20 ounces. Per pair. $0.63

52610 Men's Self-acting Clogs, low cut, light and stylish, net lined, first quality. Sizes, 6 to 11. Per pair...........$0 67 Weight, 15 ounces.

52611 Men's Plain Heavy Overshoes, net lined; first quality; sizes, 6 to 13. Per pair ..... $0.75 Weight, 24 ounces.

52612 Men's Safety Strap Sandal Rubber, for mud, no coming off, can be worn as an ordinary over without strap. See 52601 for boys. Sizes, 6 to 12. Weight, 23 ounces. Per pair.............$0.67

Men's and Women's Wool Alaskas.

52614 Men's Plain Alaskas, wool lined, first quality; sizes 6 to 13. Per pair.....$0.84 Weight, 22 oz.

52616 Ladies' Storm Alaska; differs from the ordinary Alaska, as it protects the front of the foot more. Medium weight, fleece lined, first quality; only it makes a very desirable shoe for cold climates. Sizes, 2½ to 8. Weight, 12 oz. Per pair.......................$0.84

52617 Ladies' Croquet Alaska, extra fine finish, for dress wear, wool fleeced lined, first quality; sizes, 2½ to 7. Weight, 12 oz. Per pair. $0.75

52618 Men's Self-acting Alaska, wool-lined, first quality; sizes, 6 to 12. Per pair ....$0.88 Weight, 18 oz.

52619 Men's Storm Alaska; this is wool lined, first quality. The style is very desirable, as it protects the foot more than the ordinary warm lined Alaska.

They are very desirable and are not clumsy on the foot. Sizes, 6 to 11. Weight, 16 ounces. Per pair..................................$1.05

52620 Men's Alaska, extra light and fine, wool fleeced lined, self acting first quality, sizes, 6 to 11. Per pair.....$0.92 Weight, 16 oz.

NO MAN
Be he ever so robust can stand wet feet. We carry a line of Footwear suitable to the needs of every manner of life.

Arctics and Snow Excluders.

52621 Men's Heavy Buckle Arctics, wool lined, first quality; sizes, 6 to 13. Weight, 39 oz. Per pair...... $1.25

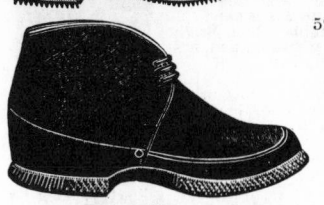

52625 Men's Heavy Buckle Arctic, wool lined, with heavy rolled edge, protecting uppers, and also extra heavy sole and heel. Sizes 6 to 13. Per pair..$1.45

Boys' Buckle Arctics.

52633 Boys' Heavy Buckle Arctics, wool lined, first quality; sizes, 1 to 6. Weight, 24 ounces. Per pair.. $1.00

Youths' Buckle Arctics.

52634 Youths' Heavy Buckle Arctics, wool lined, first quality; sizes, 10 to 13; weight, 22 oz. Per pair...$0.80

Women's and Misses' Buckle Arctics.

52635 Ladies' Buckle Arctics, wool lined, first quality; sizes, 2½ to 8. Weight, 20 oz. Per pair.$0.96
52637 Misses' Buckle Artics, wool lined, first quality; sizes, 11 to 2. Weight, 16 ounces. Per pair.. .75

Child's Buckle Arctics.

52639 Child's Buckle Arctics, wool lined, first quality. Sizes, 5 to 10½. Weight, 10 oz. Per pair. .... $.55

Men's Extra Light Buckle Arctics.

52640 Men's Buckle Arctics, extra light and fine, wool fleeced lined, first quality; sizes 6 to 11. Per pair....$1.35 Weight, 24 oz.

Men's and Women's Snow Excluding Arctics.

52641 Men's Buckle Snow Excluder Arctics, wool lined, first quality; sizes, 6 to 13. Per pair...................$1.35
52642 Ladies' Buckle Snow Excluder Arctics, wool lined, first quality; sizes, 2½ to 8. Per pair. $1.05

52641.

Lumbermen's Ankle Boots.

Weight, 48 ounces.

52643 Men's One-buckle Snow Excluder with rubber vamp or frontwith heels (for socks and wool boots), wool lined, first quality; sizes, 6 to 13. Per pair.$1.60

52644 Men's Lumbermen's One-buckle Ankle Boots, high cut, with tap sole and heel (for socks and wool boots), net lined, first quality; sizes, 6 to 13. Per pair. ...$1.50 Weight, 52 oz.

52645 Boys' Lumbermen's One-buckle Ankle Boots, high cut, heavy sole, with heels, net lined (for socks and wool boots), first quality; sizes, 2 to 6. Per pair............................... $1.25 Weight, 30 ounces.

Many additions have to be made to our Tinware Department which will meet with the approval of homekeepers.

Milwaukee All Wool Knit Boot Combination.

52646 This boot, with Lumbermens' Rubber ankle boot, is composed of first quality goods, which we *warrant*. Made with strap at top to be drawn close around leg, keeping out snow and wind, which is a decided improvement over the old style. It is not a stiff, heavy boot, being soft and pliable, and will give excellent wear. We warrant it to be genuine knit; sizes, 6 to 13, with rubber. Per pair........ ....$2.35 Per doz. net................27.60 Weight, 74 ounces.

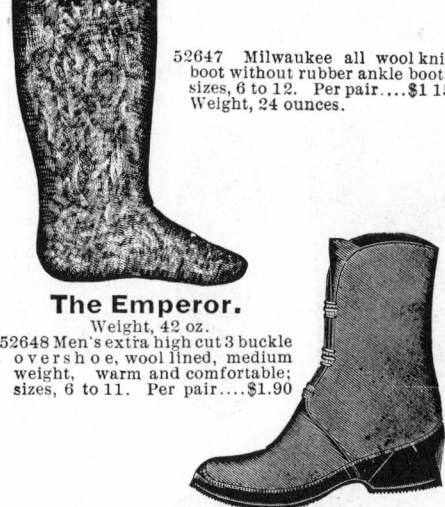

52647 Milwaukee all wool knit boot without rubber ankle boot; sizes, 6 to 12. Per pair....$1 15 Weight, 24 ounces.

The Emperor.

Weight, 42 oz.
52648 Men's extra high cut 3 buckle overshoe, wool lined, medium weight, warm and comfortable; sizes, 6 to 11. Per pair....$1.90

The Portland.

Weight, 50 oz.
52649 This Two Buckle Snow Excluder is made exactly as the one preceding, only the material used is much heavier and is designed for rougher usage; first quality, wool lined, making a very serviceable and comfortable overshoe. Sizes, 6 to 11. Per pair $1.90

52650 This ankel boot, made with strap and buckle tap, sole and heel first quality, and is usually worn over German sock or knit boot. Can be buckled tight around instep. Sizes, 6 to 12. Weight, 42 ounces. Per pair....................$1.25

52651 This ankle boot is made with strap and buckle; extra heavy sole with rolled edge and solid heel; generally worn with socks or knit boot; first quality only Sizes, 6 to 12. Per pair.................... ....$1.45

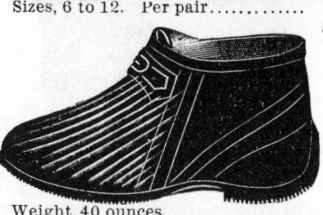

52653 Men's Lumbermen's One-Buckle Ankle Boots, high cut, heavy sole ;no heel; netlined (for socks and wool boots), first quality. Sizes, 6 to 13 Per pair $1.35 Weight, 40 ounces.

The Captain.

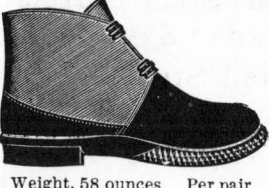

52654 This 2-Buckle Rubber Vamp Snow Excluder, made with rolled edge, extra heavy sole and solid heel, wool lined, first quality, made for rough wear, warm and comfortable for knit boot and socks only. Sizes, 6 to 12 Weight, 58 ounces. Per pair....................$1.85

Shoes—Continued.

52655 Men's Two Buckle Snow Excluder, wool lined, with rubber vamp, tap sole and solid rubber heel, first quality (for socks and wool boots). Very serviceable and warm. Sizes, 6 to 12. Per pair.........$ 1.70 Weight, 54 ounces.

52656 Men's Lumbermen's Extra High Cut Two Buckle Ankle Boots, tap sole and heel, net lined (for socks and wool boots), first quality; sizes, 6 to 13. Per pair...... $1.90

The Empress.

Weight, 17 ounces.
52659 This ladies' overshoe is made after our own ideas, as we are always on the lookout for the wants of our customers. We now offer you one of the handsomest and most comfortable overshoes on the market. Extra high cut with 3 buckles, fleece lined, warm and comfortable. Sizes, 2½ to 8. Per pair.....$1.75

52660 Ladies' Cashmerette High Button Overshoe, wool lined, first quality. Sizes, 2½ to 8. Per pair....$1.60 Weight, 12 to 17 oz.
52661 Misses' Spring Heel Overshoes, button. Sizes, 11 to 2. $1.35
52662 Child's Spring Heel Overshoes, button; sizes, 8 to 10½. Per pair.........$1.15

52660

All Wool Felt Slippers.

Weight, 2 ounces.

52665 For wearing in rubber boots; warm, comfortable and healthy.

Men's sizes, 7 to 11...............................$0.35
Boys' sizes, 2 to 5.................... .30
Women's sizes, 3 to 7............. .30

Men's and Boys' Sheep Skin Slippers.

Weight, 2 ounces.
52666 For wearing in rubber boots, made from standard quality skins.
Men's sizes, 6 to 11, per pair...............$0.15
Boys' sizes. 1 to 5, per pair. .... .12

SPORTING BOOTS.
Hannaford's Ventilated Rubber Boot.

Weight, 66 to 97 ounces.

52667 No more sweaty feet. This boot is constructed with a compressed rubber upper sole, by which at each step the foul air is forced through tube running up the back of boot. A leather slip sole is fitted in each boot, making a thoroughly ventilated waterproof boot, a great sportsman's boot. In ordering, state style wanted.

Short Boot, knit lined; sizes, 5 so 11.......... $3.75
Thigh Boot, knit lined; sizes, 5 to 11............ 4.80
Hip Boot, knit lined; sizes, 5 to 10.............. 4.75

Harness and parts of harness; Riding Saddles and Saddle Supplies; Halters and Whips; Horse Blankets and Stable Sheets; Fly Nets and Lap Robes for summer or winter. Everything you need. All sold in any quantity at wholesale prices.

RUBBER BOOTS.

Weight, 66 ounces.

In ordering rubber goods be sure and state whether wool or cotton lining is wanted, as we send cotton lining unless otherwise ordered.

52670 Men's Pebble Leg Short Rubber Boots, bright finish, light weight, wool net lined, 16 inch leg, finest quality; sizes 6 to 11. Per pair.... .... $2.55

52670

52675 Men's Pure Gum Rubber Boots, short, 16 inch leg, wool or net lined; sizes 6 to 13. Weight, 81 oz Per pair........$3.20

52676 Men's Dull finish Rubber Boots, short, 16 inch leg, wool or net lined, first quality; sizes; 6 to 12. Weight, 81 oz. Per pair.. $2.55

Boys' Rubber Boots.

52677 Boys' Dull Finish Rubber Boots, short, 14 inch leg, wool or net lined, first quality; sizes, 1 to 6. Weight, 58 oz. Per pair. $2.10

52678 Boys' Pebble Leg Short Rubber Boots, first quality, same as above; sizes, 1 to 6. Weight, 50 oz. Per pair.................. ...$2.10

The Vacation Boot.

Weight, 64 ounces.

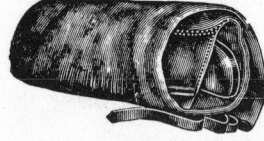

52680 Men's Vacation Thigh Rubber Boots. extra light, dull finish net lined; the only boot for hunting or fishing; sizes, 6 to 10. Per Pair.. . .....$3.85

Miners' Rubber Boots, Leather Soles, Hob Nailed.

Weight, 90 ounces.

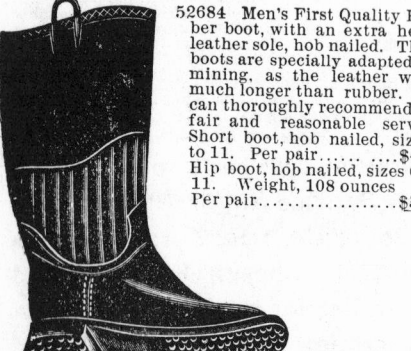

52684 Men's First Quality Rubber boot, with an extra heavy leather sole, hob nailed. These boots are specially adapted for mining, as the leather wears much longer than rubber. We can thoroughly recommend for fair and reasonable service. Short boot, hob nailed, sizes 6 to 11. Per pair...... ....$4.25 Hip boot, hob nailed, sizes 6, to 11. Weight, 108 ounces. Per pair..................$5.25

Pure Gum Hip and Thigh Boots.

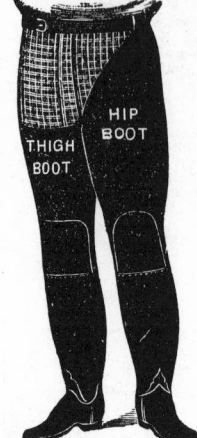

HIP BOOT

THIGH BOOT

52690 Men's Pure Gum Rubber Boots, hip leg, wool or net lined; sizes, 6 to 12. Weight, 114 ounces. Per pair..............$4.5C

52691 Men's Dull Finish Rubber Boots. hip leg, wool, or net lined, first quality; sizes 6 to 12; weight, 114 ounces. Per pair.............. $3.75

52692 Men's Pure Gum Rubber Boots, thigh leg, wool or net lined ; sizes, 6 to 12. weight, 90 ounces. Per pair..............$4.50

52693 Men's Dull Finish Rubber Boots, thigh leg, wool or net lined, first quality; sizes, 6 to 12. Weight, 90 ounces. Per pair..............$3.75

M. W. & Co.'s Snag Proof Boot.

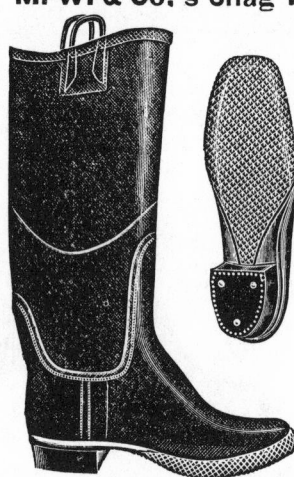

52695 The accompanying cut represents our genuine Snag proof and also Crack proof boot. Owing to the constant enquiry we have had for a boot of this description we have gone to considerable expense to bring out a boot that is so much different from anything on the market in the line of so-called snag proof boots. We are now thoroughly convinced, after experimenting for about one year, that we have at last a boot that will meet the desired wants of the farmer, miner, ditcher and the railroader, and in fact for any one in need of a first-class article Made from imported duck, thoroughly waterproofed, with extra heavy sole and tap, *rolled edge* protecting the uppers. which makes the uppers wear longer than those on the ordinary boot. Give them a trial. We *warrant* every pair for a fair and reasonable amount of service, and also warrant them not to crack or snag. Sizes, 6 to 12. Per pair.................. ....$3.50

Rubber Boots with Leather Soles and Heels.

Weight, 78 ounces.

52698 Men's Dull Finish Rubber Boots, short, 16 in. leg, leather soles and heels, put on with brass screw clinched nails, will not rip, net lined; sizes, 6 to 11. Per pair... ....$4.00

52699 Men's Dull Finish Rubber Boots, hip leg, leather soles and heels, put on with screw clinched nails; will not rip, net lined; sizes, 6 to 11, wt.103 oz. Per pair.$5.00

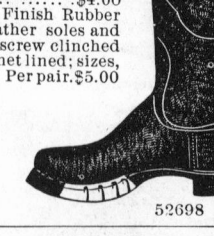

52698

Montgomery Ward & Co.'s Hammerless Shot Gun.

Fine Damascus Steel Barrels ($65.00 grade,) $35.00.

Best Laminated Steel Twist Barrels ($50.00 grade,) $29.00.

See page 449.

Rubber Boots.

LADIES', MISSES', YOUTHS' AND CHILD'S.

Weight, 18 to 38 ounces

52700 Ladies' Rubber Boots, bright finish, pebble leg, wool lined, first quality; sizes, 2½ to 8. Per pair $1.50

52701 Misses' Rubber Boots, bright finish, pebble leg, wool lined, first quality; sizes 11 to 2. Per pair$1.25

52703 Youths' Rubber Boots, bright finish, pebble leg, wool lined, first quality; sizes, 10 to 13. Per pair.................$1.50

52705 Child's Rubber Boots, bright finish, pebble leg, wool lined, first quality; sizes, 6, 6½, 7, 7½, 8, 8½, 9, 9½, 10, 10½. Per pair..................$1.10

McIntosh Wading Pants.

52710 McIntosh Wading Pants, dead grass color, with stocking feet, net lined; sizes, 5 to 11. Weight, 70 oz. Per pair.....$9.00

52712 Dull Finish Rubber Wading Pants, on drill, with stocking feet, best quality; sizes, 5 to 11. Weight, 72 oz. Per pair...............$5.00

52715 McIntosh Wading Pants, dead grass color, net lined, with boots, extension edge; sizes, 5 to 11. Weight, 101 oz. Per pair..$10.00

52710

Baptismal Pants.

52720 Baptismal Pants, made from fine black cashmere, waterproof, with boots. Pants to fit same as ordinary pants over boot; sizes, 5 to 10. Weight, 110 ounces. Per pair................... $11.00

52721 Luster Wading Pants, on drill with boots, best quality; sizes, 5 to 11. Weight, 131 ounces. Per pair $7 00

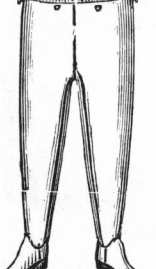

52715

52722 McIntosh Hip Boots, dead grass color, net lined, with straps; warranted strictly waterproof; sizes, 5 to 11. Weight, 79 ounces. Per pair.........................$7.75

Men's Overgaiters.

52722

52725 Made from the best of black cloth and good fitters. When ordering overgaiters, *give size of shoe worn.* Weight, 3 oz.

	Per pair.	Per doz.
Men's 5 Button Overgaiter "Leader"....	$0.65	$ 7.00
" 5 " " Vienna......	1.00	10.00
" 5 " " Paris........	1.25	12.00

Women's Overgaiters.

52729 Made from the finest of imported and domestic cloth, good style and good fitters; when ordering send size of shoe. Weight, 3 oz.

	Per pair.	Per doz.
Ladies' 7 Button Overgaiter "Leader"..	$0.65	$ 7.00
" 7 " " Vienna...	1.00	10.00
" 7 " " Paris..	1.25	12.00

Give the name of the overgaiter wanted when ordering.

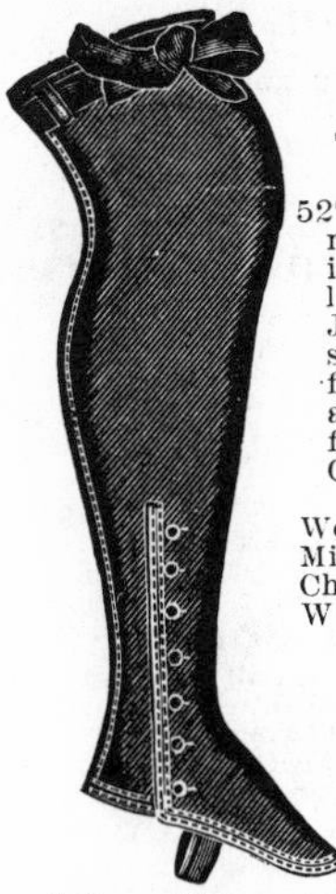

The Combination.

52730 The accompanying cut represents one of our latest designs in the shape of an overgaiter and legging, made from one piece of Jersey cloth. They fit like a stocking and are warm and comfortable, with elastic supporters at top. Do not be without a pair for the cold day coming.
Give size of shoe when ordering.

	Per pair.
Women's, size, 2 to 6	$2.25
Misses', size, 10, 12, 13, 1	1.70
Children's, size, 2 to 8	1.25

Weight, 3 to 9 oz.

The New Improved Stocking Saver.

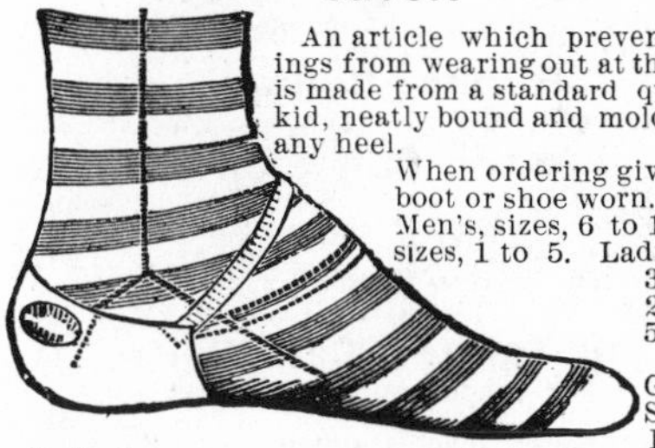

An article which prevents stockings from wearing out at the heel. It is made from a standard quality of kid, neatly bound and molded to fit any heel.
When ordering give size of boot or shoe worn.
Men's, sizes, 6 to 10. Boys', sizes, 1 to 5. Ladies' sizes. 3 to 7; wt., 2 oz.
52735—Heel Guards, or Stocking Protector.
Per pair ... $0.11
Per dozen pairs ... 1.20

Heel Stiffeners.

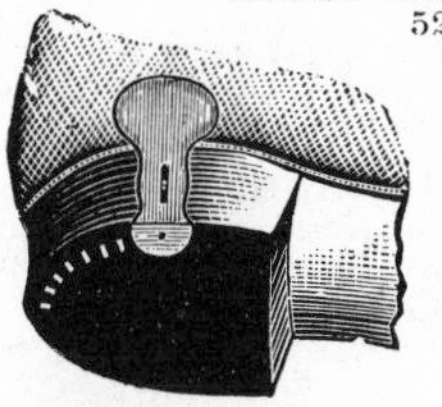

52736 Prevents boots and shoes from running over, wearing off on the sides, and ripping in the seam. Only one size needed to fit any height heel.
No. 1, Men's size, Per pair ... $0.06
No. 2, Ladies' and Boys', Per pair ... .06
Weight, 2 oz.
Per dozen pairs ... .60

Calks.

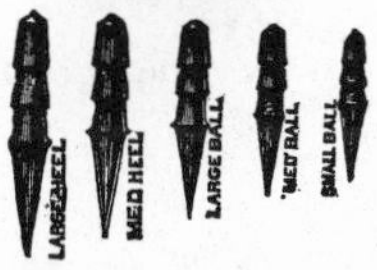

For lumbermen's and loggers' boots and shoes.

	Per 100	Per doz.
52739 Heel Calks, large	$0.60	$0.09
52740 Heel Calks, small	.60	.09
52741 Ball Calks, large	.60	.09
52742 Ball Calks, medium	.60	.09
52743 Ball Calks, small	.60	.09

CALK SET AND PUNCH COMBINED.

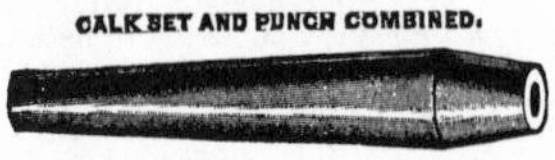

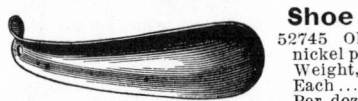

52744 Calk Set and punch for setting calks. Weight, 4 oz. Each ... $0.25
Per dozen ... 2.75

Shoe Lifts.

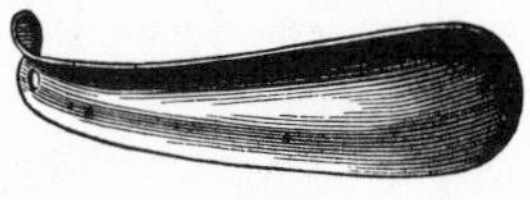

52745 Old Style, nickel plated. Weight, 2 oz.
Each ... $0.07
Per dozen ... .72

Barbours' Shoemakers' Thread.

52746 Barbours' Celebrated Irish Flax Thread, half bleached, for shoemakers' use for hand sewing, 2 ounce balls.

No.	Per lb.	Per ball.
12	$1.30	$0.18
3	1.05	.15
10	.95	.13

American Standard Shoe Thread.

52747 American Standard Shoe Thread, half bleached for shoemakers. 2 ounce balls. Used for hand sewing.
No. 10 only. Per pound ... $0.65 Per ball ... $0.10

Do you see the word
"WINDSOR?"
It refers to our unparalleled
PIANOS AND ORGANS.

M. W. & CO.'S

Family Outfit.

Weight, 18 1-2 pounds.

Every Man His Own Cobbler.

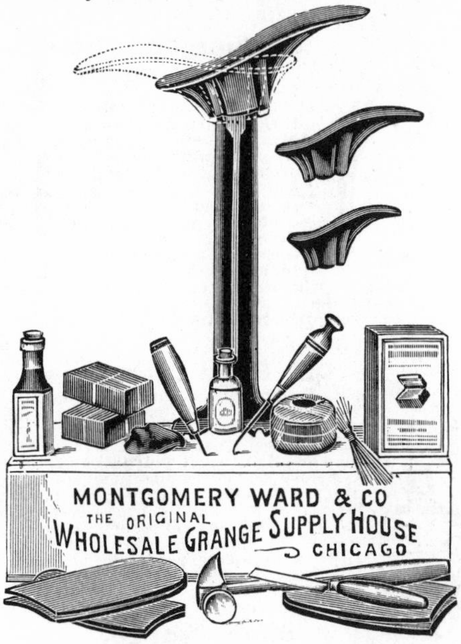

52748 A complete set of shoemakers' tools and all the necessary articles for general shoe repairing. No family should be without one as it saves time and money. Every article contained in same is of the best. We do not try to deceive you; we give you good value for your money. We give below a complete list of tools contained in outfit:

1 Iron Stand.	1 Package Brass Clinch Nails, ⅜.
1 Large Iron Last.	1 Package Brass Clinch Nails, ⅝.
1 Medium Iron Last.	1 Peg Awl Handle.
1 Small Iron Last.	2 Peg Awl Blades.
¼ Dozen Good Tap Soles.	1 Sewing Awl Handle.
1 Harrington Shoe Knife.	2 Sewing Awl Blades.
1 Ball Shoe Thread.	1 Hammer.
1 Ball Wax.	1 Dozen Pair Star Heel Plates.
1 Bunch Bristles.	
1 Can Rubber Cement.	
1 Bottle Leather Cement.	

The above outfit, complete, for $2.00.
Special discounts on dozen and half dozen lots.

Iron Shoe Lasts and Stand.

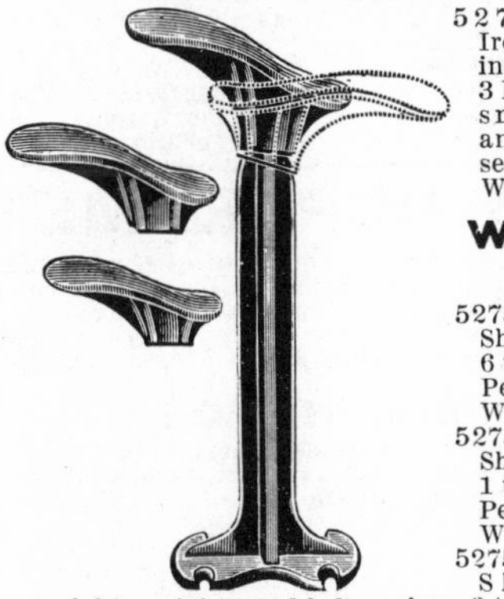

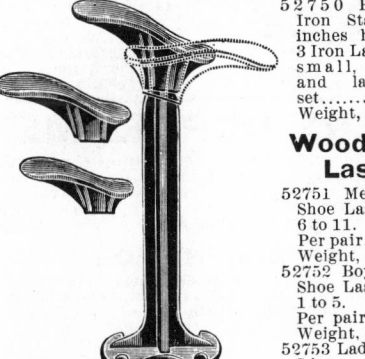

52750 Reversible Iron Stands, 14 inches high and 3 Iron Lasts, sizes, small, medium and large; per set ... $0.65
Weight, 167 oz.

Wood Shoe Lasts

52751 Men's Wood Shoe Lasts; sizes, 6 to 11.
Per pair ... $0.30
Weight, 44 oz.
52752 Boys' Wood Shoe Lasts; sizes, 1 to 5.
Per pair ... $0.30
Weight, 32 oz.
52753 Ladies' Wood Shoe Lasts; straight or rights and lefts; sizes, 3 to 7.
Per pair ... $0.30
Weight, 38 oz.

Heaton's Patent Button Machine.

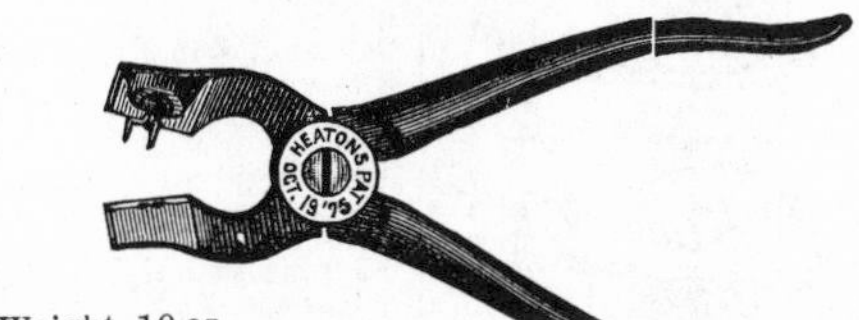

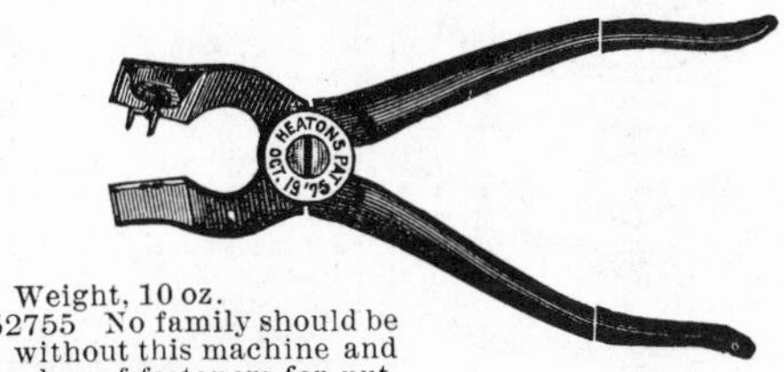

Weight, 10 oz.
52755 No family should be without this machine and a box of fasteners for putting on their own shoe buttons; very simple and will last a lifetime.
1 Machine, same as cut ... $0.55
1 Gross fasteners. Weight, 1½ oz. ... .10
1 Great gross fasteners ... 1.00

Lap Lasts.

52756 Shoemakers' Common Iron Lap Lasts, medium size (for ladies' and child's shoes) ... $0.20
Weight, 48 oz.
Large size, for men's and boys' shoes ... .25
Weight, 63 oz.

Peg Cutter.

52759 Hand Pegged Floats, for cutting pegs from inside of boots ... $0.40
Weight, 12 oz.

HAMMOND'S STEEL SHOE HAMMERS.

Shoemakers' Hammers.

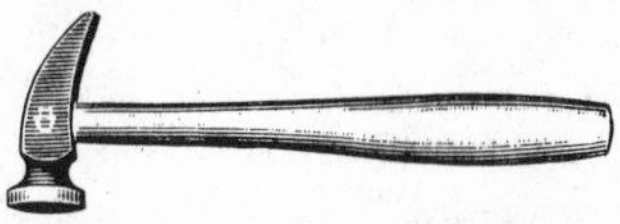

52760 Shoemakers' Hammer, No. 0, 15 oz ... $0.30
52761 Shoemakers' Hammer, No. 1, 17 oz ... .35

Shoemakers' Needles.

52762 Shoemakers' Needles, for sewing leather. Per paper ... $0.10

Shoemakers' Pincers.

52765 Shoemakers' Pincers, for lasting, nailing or pegging boots and shoes, No. H, 14 oz. Each, $0.55
Weight, 12 oz.

Shoemakers' Bristles.

52766 Shoemakers' Bristles, white hair in bunches, from 5c to 25c per bunch.

Shoemakers' Wax.

52767 Shoemakers Wax, per ball ... 1c
Shoemakers' Wax, per dozen ... 10c

Awl Blades and Handles.

52769 Shoemakers' Pegging Awl Blades, assorted sizes. Per dozen ... $0.08
Weight, 2 oz.
52770 Shoemakers' Sewing Awl Blades, assorted sizes. Per doz ... .15
52771 Shoemakers' Pegging Awl Hafts (or handles). Each ... .10
Per doz ... 1.00
52772 Shoemakers' Sewing Awl Handles.
Each ... .03
Per doz ... .25

Oak Calf Skin for Patching.

52775 This stock is used where leather cement is required for patching, as it works better on oak tanned calf than any other, no oil being used in the preparation of oak skin.
Medium skin ... $1.75
Large ... 2.00
Weight, 20 oz.

Oak Sole Leather.

52776 We sell in sides only; medium weight side, 18 to 20 lbs., per lb ... $0.29
Heavy weight side, 20 to 26 lbs., per lb ... 30

Hemlock Sole Leather.

52777 Sole Leather; we sell in sides only.
Light sides weigh 15 to 19 lbs.
Per lb ... $0.23
Medium sides weigh 20 to 22 lbs.
Per lb ... .24
Heavy sides weigh 23 to 26 lbs. Per lb ... .26

Wood Shoe Pegs.

52780 Shoe Pegs; sizes, ⅜ in., ½ in., ⅝ in., ¾ in.
Per quart ... $0.05

Brass Shoe Nails.

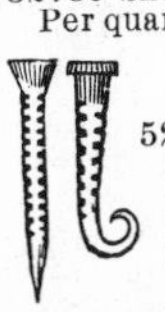

52781 The Improved Brass Clinching Boot and Shoe Nails; sizes, ⅜ in., ½ in., ⅝ in., ¾ in., ⅞ in.
Per ½ pound package ... .13
Per pound package ... 25

52782 Iron Heel Nails, any size from ½ in. to ⅞ in. Per 1 lb. package ... $0.07

Shoemakers' Rasps.

Shoemakers' Rasps, best quality.
52785 Size, 8 inch. Weight, 6 oz ... $0.25
52786 Size, 9 inch. Weight, 8 oz ... .30

Jumbo Oak Soles.

Size, 8½x12½ inches.

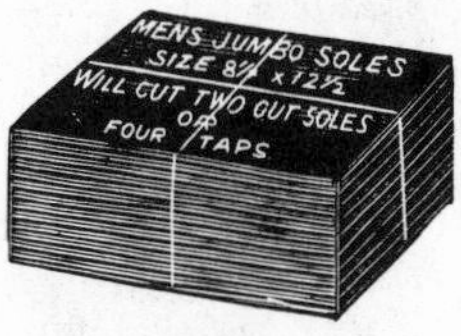

52787 These pieces are cut from choice selection of oak sole and will cut four different size taps.

Grade.	Height.	Lbs., per doz.	Price, per doz
XXXX	5½ inch	10	$5.50
XXX	5 inch	9	4.75
XX	4½ inch	8	3.75
X	4 inch	7	2.75

The above sold in single pieces, 8½x12½ inches.
XXXX 55c. XXX 50c. XX 40c. X 35c.

Complete Bottom Stock.

52788—　　　　　　　　　　　Oak　　Hemlock.
Mens' Heavy Bottom Stock......$1.00　　$0.90
Mens' Medium Bottom Stock.....　.95　　　.80
Ladies' Medium Bottom Stock....　.65　　　.60

Hemlock Tap Soles.

Weight, 4 to 6 ounces.
52789 Men's Tap Soles, sizes, 6, 7, 8; per pair $0.18
　Sizes, 9, 10, 11, per pair....　............　.19
　Per dozen, assorted................　.........　2.10
52790 Boys' Tap Soles, sizes, 1 to 5, per pair.....　.17
　Per dozen, only............　...............　2.00

Slipper Soles.

Weight, 3 ounces.
Slipper Soles, leather covered bottom, bound with braid, wool faced.
52791 Men's sizes, 6 to 11......................$0.25
52792 Ladies' sizes, 3 to 7.......................　.20
Less 10 per cent. if ordered in dozen lots.

Leather Insoles.

Weight, 2 ounces.
Sole Leather Insoles, cemented on bottom, make a smooth, comfortable sole for the foot.
52795 Men's sizes, 6 to 11........................$0.12
52796 Ladies' sizes, 3 to 7........................　.10

Cork Insoles.

Weight, 2 ounces.
52800 Men's Cork Insoles, 6 to 11..............$0.06
52801 Ladies' Cork Insoles, 3 to 7.............　.05

Eyelets.

52802 Eyelets, black or white, B long, put up 1,000 in a box. Weight, 2 ounces. Per box. ...$0.10

Eyelet Sets.

Weight, 10 ounces.
52803 Eyelet Sets, common. .　.........　.....$0.45
52804 Eyelet Sets, with spring..................　.55

Leather Cement.

52810 Best Leather Cement, for patching and cementing all kinds of leather; put up in 1 ounce bottle. Weight, 3 ounces. Per bottle....$0.07
Per doz....................................　.80

Rubber Cement.

52811 Rubber Cement, for repairing and cementing rubber boots, etc. Weight, 4 oz. In boxes..$0.12
Per doz ....　1.35

Wood Shoe Stretcher.

Weight, 30 ounces.
52815 Wood Shoe Stretcher, can be used for ladies' or men's shoes; very useful for stretching shoes across toes or ball of foot, with corn and bunion attachments. Price........　.........$0.80

Leather Laces.

Genuine Porpoise Laces.
52816 36 inch length. Per pair.......　.......$0.05
　45 inch length. Per pair..................　.07

Round Leather Laces.

52817 27 inch length. Per 3 pairs............$0.05
52818 36 inch length. Per 2 pairs.................　.05

Star Heel Plates.

Weight, 2 ounces.
52820 Star Heel Plates, for preventing boots and shoes from wearing off at the heels. No nails or screws required. Any child can put them on. No. 1, small, for child's heels. No. 2, medium, for ladies' heels. No. 3, large, for boys' heels. No. 4, extra large, for men's heels.
Per pair.....　.........$0.02 Per dozen pairs....$0.20

Cobbler's Outfits—Continued.

52822 Revolving Eyelet Set and Punch. This combination is composed of a revolving eyelet set and punch, used for B long eyelets, making almost an indispensable tool in any household; will last a lifetime properly used. Eyelet set and punch combined. Weight, 12 ounces.
Each.........................$0.90

Blacking and Shoe Dressing.

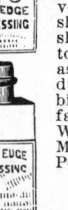

52823　Ladies' Glycerole Shoe Dressing, the only dressing in existence that contains oil which answers the purpose of oiling and dressing the leather at the same time. It is perfect in composition, containing no acids to injure the leather. Put up in fine carton, with brush in each bottle for application. You will find the regular price, which is 25 cents, on each box. Weight, 12 ounces.
M. W. & Co.'s price, per bottle $0.19
Per dozen.........................　2.00

Gilt Edge Dressings.

52824 Ladies' Gilt Edge Shoe Dressing is very useful for a great many things besides shoes. It will make your old rubbers, shopping bags, black kid gloves, look equal to new. Many use it to dye straw hats and as a stove polish, saving time and labor, dust and brushes, as it requires no rubbing. You will find it a necessity in your family. Sold everywhere for 25 cents.
M. W. & Co.'s price, per bottle........$0.18
Per dozen.........................　..1.90

Shoe Bronze.

52825　Used in bronzing white or colored shoes, when soiled. Used as ordinary shoe dressing, covering the surface evenly to gain the desired effect, and then drying before wearing. Bronze. Weight, 2 ounces.
Per bottle...$0.15
Per dozen............　......................　1.50

Unrivaled French Blacking.

52826 This blacking, of superior quality, is recommended to all our customers desirous of preserving the strength and elegance of their boots and shoes. It prevents the leather from getting hard, polishes very quickly, even when the boots and shoes are damp, and has a remarkable dark color which is not tarnished by contact with the air. *Our personal experience is that this is the finest blacking yet produced.* Every box warranted. Weight, 4 oz.
No. 0, small,　per box.....$0.04 Per dozen...$0.45
No. 1, medium, per box......　.08 Per dozen...　.90
No. 2, larger,　per box ......　.12 Per dozen...　1.40

Russet Polishing Paste.

52827 This paste is used for tan or russet colored shoes. Have the leather clean and dry, then apply with a soft woolen cloth, rubbing well into the leather, then rub to a polish, with a dry woolen cloth; apply more of the paste when they do not shine bright enough. Weight, 4 oz.
Russet Paste. Per box . $0.15 Per dozen....$1.25

Rubberine or Waterproof Dressing.

52830 This Rubberine used on boots and shoes, makes the leather thoroughly waterproof and at the same time softens and keeps it very pliable under all conditions; also used on harness and belting. We thoroughly recommend this as an article of merit.
Rubberine, weight, 7 oz. Per bottle $0.20
Rubberine, weight, 32 oz. Per quart can.......　1.00
Rubberine, for harness and belting; weight, 128 ounces. Per gallon....　..................　2.00

Patent Leather Polish.

52831 By rubbing over the surface will give the leather a bright luster, and will again look almost as good as new. Weight, 5 ounces.
Meltonian's Cream for Patent Leather, per bot.$0.25
Whittemore's Patent Leather Dressing, per box....　.25

Rubber Patching and Repair Cloth.

52832 Light Rubber Patching, per square........$0.50
Weight, 9 ounces. Medium and heavy... .. ....　.55

Rubber Repair Cloth.

52835 Rubber repairing cloth, per square $0.30
Weight, 3 ounces. Per yard....................　2.00

Rubber Soling.

52840 Rubber Soling, for boots and shoes, per lb..$0.45

French Calf Skins.

These skins run in weight from 2 to 3½ lbs. each.
52841　Simon Ullmo, first choice, 2 to 3½ lbs.
　Each, per pound ...　..................　.........$1.80
52842　Mercier's, first choice, 2 to 3½ lbs.
　Each, per pound ....　1.80

Oak Tanned Calf Skins.

52844　Crown, extra choice; weight, 2 to 2½ lbs.
　Each, per pound $1.05
52845　Crown, extra choice; weight, 2½ to 3 lbs.
　Each, per pound ....　1.00

Hemlock Calf Skins.

52847　Chicago, a calf, extra selection, 2 to 2¼ lbs.　Each, per pound $0.95
52848　Chicago, a calf, spready, 3½ to 4 lbs.
　Each, per pound..............................　.70
52849　Chicago, a runner, for boot backs. 4 to 5 lbs.　Each, per pound..........................　.65

Alligator Skins.

52850　Large size........................$5.50
　Medium size ....　5.00

Elastic Goring.

52851　Hub Goring, 5 inch; per yard.............$0 50
　Hub Wool Goring, 5 inch; per yard.............　.60

Knives and Skivers.

　　　　　　　　　　　　　　　Each. Per doz.
52852 Square point, T. Harrington's best $0.15　$1.25
　Curve point,　　"　　"　　"　.15　　1.25
　Lip or fore part,　"　　"　　"　.15　　1.25
　Thin Kid Skivers,　"　　"　　"　.25　　　.50
　Sole Leather Skivers,　"　　"　　"　.25　　5.50
Send for our special catalogue of leather and shoe findings.

CROCKERY DEPARTMENT.

We invite a careful inspection of our Crockery Department, in which will be found an attractive line of decorative dinner, tea and chamber sets, all very desirable ware of the best English, French, German and American manufacturers' make. The following advantages to be derived from buying these goods from us are worthy of your consideration. First, you do not have to take the large, expensive, and sometimes superfluous dishes that come in regular made (dinner) sets, as all of our dinner ware is open stock, and you can buy as many or as few dishes as you like. We have eighteen open stock patterns of dinner ware; more than any exclusive crockery house in America. Second, we can supply the missing pieces of sets that are broken within one year from date of purchase. Third, the prices are lower than can be obtained elsewhere.

SPECIAL NOTICE.

We have taken considerable pains in selecting our made-up Dinner and Tea Sets, and cannot change the combination by adding or deducting any pieces. We use every precaution when packing crockery or glassware, "employing none but experienced men for that purpose," and cannot allow claims for breakage. When goods of this character are returned package must contain full amount of straw, otherwise they will be receipted for as "damaged" and allowance made only for such pieces as are taken from package in good condition.

Ravenna Pattern.

MANUFACTURED BY J. H. WEATHERBY & SON, HANLEY, ENGLAND.

Genuine English semi-porcelain ware decorated with neat border design of pansy flowers and leaves in a light brown color. The decoration is put on under the glaze and cannot wash or wear off. It is priced nearly as low as plain white ware of this same quality and is of exceptionally good value.

Order No. 54000.

	Per doz.		Per doz.		Each.
1 Tea Cup and Saucers, handled $1.26		15 Oatmeal Bowls, 1 pint $1.26		33 Covered Dishes, 9 inch $0.63	
2 Coffee Cups and Saucers, handled... 1.47		16 Platters, 8-inch ...　.14		34 Casserole (square covered dish), 9 inch ....　.71	
4 Plates, 5-inch.....　71		17 Platters, 10-inch..　.24			
5 Plates, 6-inch.....　.87		18 Platters, 12-inch..　.39			
6 Plates, 7-inch....　1.02		19 Platters, 14-inch..　.56		35 Soup Tureen with ladle and stand..... 2.85	
7 Plates, 8-inch.... 1.17		20 Platters,16-inch..　.87		36 Sauce Tureen with ladle and stand.....　.78	
8 Soup Plates, 7 inches 1.02		21 Bakers, 7-inch....　.15			
9 Sauce Plates......　.47		22 Bakers, 8-inch....　.24		39 Sauce Boat.......　.21	
10 Individual Butters .32		24 Scalloped Nappies, 7 inch ....　.15		40 Pickle Dish.......　.15	
11 Bakers 3 inch (used as side dishes) 1.10		25 Scalloped Nappies, 8 inch ....　.24		41 Cake Plate.......　.21	
12 Bone Dishes...... 1.10		26 Pitcher, ½ pint..　.14		42 Covered Butter Dish ....　.48	
13 Bowls, 1 pint.... 1.26		29 Pitchers, 1-pint..　.16		43 Teapots ....　.42	
14 Oyster Bowls, 1 pint........ .. 1.26		30 Pitchers, 1-quart..　.18		44 Sugar Bowls ......　.35	
		31 Pitchers, 2-quart..　.32		45 Cream Pitchers...　.15	
		32 Pitchers, 3-quart..　.47			

"READING MAKETH A FULL MAN."

We offer a wide range of Literature for your selection. You must read or degenerate.

Evangeline Pattern.

Manufactured by Johnson Bros., Hanley, Eng.

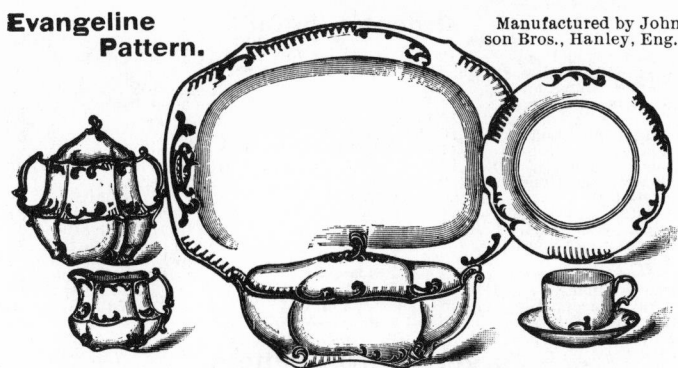

English semi-porcelain ware; thin and pure white. The glaze is burnt on and will not nick or chip with ordinary use. The shape is of the very latest design and the raised scroll work is handsomely ornamented with neat gold decorations. Pure white dinner ware of this quality with gold decoration is unusually attractive and sure to please. We shall be pleased to furnish any quanity you may desire.

Order No. 54004.

	Per doz.		Per doz.		Each.
1 Tea Cups and Saucers, 12 cups and 12 saucers	$1.87	10 Bone Dishes	$1.64	22 Casserole, Square covered dish, 8-in.	$1.06
2 Coffee Cups and Saucers,12 cups and 12 saucers	2.18	11 Bowls, 1 pt	1.87	23 Soup Tureen,Cover and Ladle(no stand)	3.50
		12 Oyster Bowls, 1 pint	1.87	24 Sauce Tureen, complete with cover, ladle and stand,	1.18
		13 Oatmeal Bowls, 1 pint	1.87		Each.
3 Plates, scalloped edge, 5 inches	1.06			25 Sauce Boat	.32
4 Plates, scalloped edge, 6 inches	1.28	14 Bakers, 8-inch	.35	26 Pickel Dish	.25
5 Plates, scalloped edge, 7 inches	1.52	15 Nappies, 8-inch	.35	27 Covered Butter Dish, with drainer.	.71
6 Plates, scalloped edge, 8 inches	1.75	16 Platters, 8-inch	.20	28 Pitcher, pint	.25
		17 Platters, 10-inch	.35	29 Pitcher, 1 quart	.27
7 Soup Plates. 7 inches	1.52	18 Platters, 12-inch	.59	30 Pitcher, 3 quarts.	.71
8 Sauce Dishes, 4-in.	.71	19 Platters, 14-inch	.82	31 Tea Pot and Cover.	.63
9 Individual Butter Plates	.47	20 Platters, 16-inch	1.28	32 Sugar Bowl and cover	.54
		21 Covered Dish, 8-inch	.94	33 Cream Pitcher	26
				34 Cake Plate	.31

Utopian Pattern.

Manufactured by Henry Allcock & Co., Hanley, England.

Superior grade of English Royal semi-porcelian, decoration of small forget-me-not flowers, handsomely put on under the glaze; all the pieces are shapley and have richly gold trimmed edges and handles, plates are scalloped on the edge. This is a very handsome table set and can be furnished in two colors, fawn and pencil, both equally attractive. When ordering be sure to state which color you prefer.

Order No. 54005.

	Per doz.		Per doz.		Each.
1 Tea Cups and Saucers, handled	$2.00	13 Bowls, 1pint	$2.00	30 Pitchers,1-quart	$ .30
2 Coffee Cups and Saucers, handled	2.35	14 Oyster Bowls, 1 pint	2.00	31 Pitchers 2-quart	.51
3 After Dinner Coffee Cups and Saucers, handled	1.67	15 Oatmeal Bowls, 1 pint	2.00	32 Pitchers 3-quart	.75
				33 Covered Dishers,9 inch	1.00
			Each.		
4 Plates, 5 inches	1.12	16 Platters, 8-inch	$0.22	34 Casserole (square covered dish)9-inch	1.12
5 Plates, 6 inches	1 38	17 Platters, 10-inch	.38	35 Soup Tureen and ladle (no stand)	3.75
6 Plates, 7 inches	1.63	18 Platters, 12-inch	.63	36 Sauce Tureen with ladle and stand	1.26
7 Plates, 8 inches	1.88	19 Platters, 14-inch	.87	39 Sauce Boat	.34
8 Soup Plates, 7 inches	1.63	20 Platters, 16-inch	1.38	40 Pickle Dish	.26
9 Sauce Plates	.75	21 Bakers, 7-inch	.26	41 Cake Plate	.34
10 Individual Butters	51	22 Bakers, 8-inch	.38	42 Covered Butter Dish	.75
11 Bakers, 3-inch (used as side dishes)	1.75	24 Scalloped Nappies 7-inch	.26	43 Teapots	.67
12 Bone dishes	1.75	25 Scalloped Nappies 8-inch	.38	44 Sugar Bowls	.56
		29 Pitchers, 1-pint	.26	45 Cream Pitchers	.26

Columbia Pattern.

Manufactured by Johnson Bros., England.

Semi-porcelain ware, thin and very shapely; decoration consists of flowers leaves and fine spray in neutral brown color; warranted not to wash or wear off; scalloped edge plates. This is a very desirable pattern and cannot fail to please. We will sell you as few or many pieces as you wish.

Order No. 54007.

Order No. 54007.

	Per doz.		Per doz.		Each.
1 Tea Cups and Saucers with handles	$1.47	13 Oyster Bowls. 1 pint	$1.47	27 Sauce Tureen,with ladle and stand	$0.92
2 Coffee Cups and Saucers with handles	1.71		Each.	28 Sauce Boat	.26
		14 Bakers, 7 inches	$0.19	29 Pickle Dish	.19
3 Plates, scalloped edge, 5 inches	.83	15 Bakers, 8 inches	.28	30 Covered Butter Dish	.56
		16 Bakers, 9 inches	.38		
4 Plates, scalloped edge, 6 inches	1.02	17 Platters, 8 inches	.16	31 Covered Vegetable Dish	.74
5 Plates, scalloped edge, 7 inches	1.19	18 Platters, 10 inches	.28	32 Casserole (square covered dish)	.83
		19 Platters, 12 inches	.47		
6 Plates, scalloped edge, 8 inches	1.38	20 Platters, 14 inches	.64	33 Tea Pot	.50
		21 Platters,16 inches	1.02	34 Sugar Bowl	.42
7 Plates, scalloped edge, 7-in., soup	1.19	22 Scalloped Nappies, 7 inches	.19	35 Cream Pitcher	.19
8 Fruit Saucers, 5-in.	.55	23 Scalloped Nappies, 8 inches	.28	36 Cake Plate	.26
9 Individual Butters	.38	24 Scalloped Nappies, 9 inches	.38	37 Pitcher, 3 quarts.	.56
10 Bone Dishes	1.28	26 Soup Tureen,with ladle and stand	3.65	38 Pitcher, 2 quarts.	.38
11 Bakers (used for side dishes), 3-inch.	1.28			39 Pitcher, 1 quart.	.22
12 Bowls, 1 pint	1.47			40 Pitcher, 1 pint	.19
				41 Pitcher, ½ pint.	.16

Oregon Pattern.

Manufactured by Mellor, Taylor & Co., Burslem, England,

Genuine English Semi-porcelain ware. A delicate anemone flower spray decoration in a steel gray color put on under the glaze; warranted not to wear off or to crack. The shapes are new and gracefully moulded For a low priced pattern it is unexcelled, as to finish, decoration and durabillty, and is a decided change from the ordinary brown prints.

Order No. 54010.

	Per doz.		Each.		Each
1 Tea Cups and Saucers, handled	$1.40	13 Platters, 8-inch	$0.14	30 Soup Tureen(with ladle and stand)	$3.50
2 Coffee Cups and Saucers, handled	1.64	14 Platters, 10-inch	27	31 Sauce Tureen (with ladle and stand)	.88
		15 Platters, 12-inch	.43		
3 Pie Plates, 5-inch	.78	16 Platters, 14-inch	.61	32 Sauce Boat	.24
4 Plates, 6-inch	.96	17 Platters, 16-inch	.96	33 Pickle Dish	.18
5 Plates, 7-inch	1.13	18 Bakers, 7-inch	.18	34 Covered Butter Dish	.53
6 Plates, 8-inch	1.31	19 Bakers, 8-inch	.27	35 Covered Vegetable Dish	.70
7 Soup Plates, 7-inch	1.13	21 Scalloped Nappies, 7-inch	.18		
8 Fruit Saucers	.53	22 Scalloped Nappies, 8-inch	.27	36 Casserole (square covered dish)	.78
9 Individual Butters.	.35				
10 Bakers, 3-inch (for side dishes)	1.23	25 Pitchers, ½ pt	.14	37 Teapot	.41
10½ Bone dishes	1.23	26 Pitchers, 1 pt	.18	38 Sugar Bowl	.39
11 1 pt. Bowls	1.40	27 Pitchers, 1 qt	.21	39 Cream Pitcher	.18
12 1 pt. Oyster Bowls.	1.40	28 Pitchers, 2 qt	.35	40 Cake Plate	.24
Oat Meal Bowls,5-inch	1.40	29 Pitchers, 3 qt	.54		

Lexington Pattern.

Manufacturered by Johnson Brothers, Hanley, England.

English semi-porcelain, a very pretty shape, decorated with a light brown begonia leaf, enameled with blue forget-me-nots and warranted not to wash or wear off; scalloped edge plates, gold traced handles. We shall be pleased to have your order for any quantity, no matter how small.

Order No. 54011.

	Per doz.		Per doz.		Each.
1 Tea Cups and Saucers with handles	$1.87	12 Bakers (used for side dishes), 3-in.	$1.64	24 Pickle Dish	$0.25
2 Coffee Cups and Saucers with handles	2.18	13 Oyster Bowls, 1 pint	1.87	25 Covered Butter Dish	.71
4 Plates, scalloped edge, 5-inch	1.06		Each.	26 Covered Vegetable Dish, 9-inch	.94
5 Plates, scalloped edge, 6-inch	1.28	14 Bakers, 7-inch	$0 26	27 Casserole (square covered dish)	1.06
		15 Bakers, 8-in	.35		
6 Plates, scalloped edge, 7-inch	1.52	16 Platters, 8-in	.20	28 Tea Pot	.63
		17 Platters, 10-in	.35	29 Sugar Bowl	.54
7 Plates, scalloped edge, 8-inch	1.75	18 Platters, 12-in	.59	30 Cream Pitcher	.31
8 Plates, scalloped edge, 7-in., soup	1.52	19 Platters, 14-in	.82	31 Cake Plate	.31
		20 Platters, 16-in	1.28	32 Pitcher, ½ pt	.20
9 Fruit Saucers, 4-in.	.71	21 Soup Tureen with ladle	3.50	33 Pitcher, 1 pint	.25
10 Individual Butters	.47	22 Sauce Tureen with ladle and stand	1.18	34 Pitcher, 1 qt	.27
11 Bone Dishes	1.64	23 Sauce Boat	.32	35 Pitcher, 2 qts	.47
				36 Pitcher, 3 qts	.71

London Pattern.

Manufactured by Bridgwood & Sons, Longton, England.

Best quality of English semi-porcelain. A very effective decoration of pink and canary roses. All the pieces are handsomely moulded and neatly gold trimmed. The handles to all the covers, and the side handles on the soup tureen and covered dishes are entirely covered with bright gold which produces a very elaborate and pleasing effect, and must be seen to be appreciated. We recommend this pattern as one durable for everyday use and one suitable for all occasions.

Order No. 54012.

	Per doz.		Each.		Each
1. Tea Cups and Saucers, with handles	$2.10	15 Bakers, 7-inch	$0.27	31 Pitchers, ½ pt	$0.22
2 Coffee Cups and Saucers, with handles	2.45	16 Bakers, 8-inch	.39	32 Soup Tureen, and ladle	3.93
4 Plates, 5-inch	1.17	18 Platters, 8-inch	.22	33 Sauce Tureen, complete	1.31
5 Plates, 6-inch	1.44	19 Platters, 10-inch	.39	34 Covered Dish, 9 in.	1.05
6 Plates, 7-inch	1.71	20 Platters, 12-inch	.66	35 Casserole, Square dish	1.17
7 Plates, 8-inch	1.97	21 Platters, 14-inch	.91	37 Pickle Dish	.27
8 Soup Plates, 7-in.	1.71	22 Platters, 16-inch	1.44	38 Sauce Boat	.35
9 Fruit Saucers	.78	23 Scalloped Nappies, 7-inch	.27	39 Cake Plate	.35
10 Individual Butters	.53	24 Scalloped Nappies, 8-inch	.39	40 Tea Pot	.70
11 Bone Dishes	1.83	27 Pitchers, 3 qt	.78	41 Sugar Bowl	.59
12 Bowls, 1 pint	2.10	28 Pitchers, 2 qt	.53	42 Cream Pitcher	.27
13 Oyster Bowls, 1 pint	2.10	29 Pitchers, 1 qt	.31	43 Covered Butter	.78
		30 Pitchers, 1 pt	.27		

Yale Pattern.

Manufactured by Doulton & Co., Burslem, England.

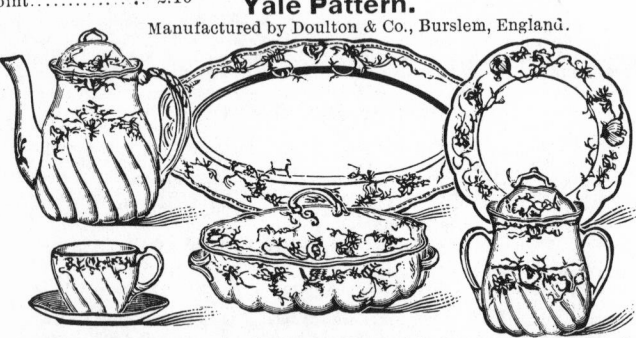

English decorated semi-porcelain, manufactured by Doulton & Co., Burslem England, who are world renowned as makers of the most reliable goods. The decoration is a handsome design of blackberry blossoms and vines in a neutral or slate blue color, put on under the glaze; new graceful shapes, neat gold trimmings, scalloped edge plates. We shall be pleased to be favored with an order for any quantity, no matter how small.

Order No. 54015.

	Per doz.		Per doz.		Each.
1 Tea Cups and Saucers, with handles	$2.00	10 Bone Dishes	$1.75	22 Covered Butter Dishes	$0.75
2 Coffee Cups and Saucers, with handles	2.35	11 3-inch Bakers (used as side dishes)	1.75	23 Sauce Boat	.34
3 Plates, scalloped edge, 5-inch	1.12		Each.	25 Pickle Dish	.26
4 Plates, scalloped edge, 6-inch	1.38	12 Platters 8-inch	$0.22	27 Teapot	.67
5 Plates, scalloped edge, 7-inch	1.63	13 Platters, 10-inch	.38	28 Sugar Bowl	.56
6 Plates, scalloped edge, 8-inch	1.88	14 Platters, 12-inch	.63	29 Cream Pitcher	.26
7 Plates, scalloped edge, 7-in, soup	1.63	15 Platters, 14-inch	.87	31 Cake Plate	.34
8 Sauce Plates, 4-inch	.75	16 Platters, 16-inch	1.38	32 Pitcher, ½ pint	.22
9 Individual Butters	.51	18 Soup, tureen cover, ladle and stand	4.75	33 Pitcher, 1 pint	.26
		19 Sauce Tureen, stand, cover and ladle	1.26	34 Pitcher, 1 quart	.30
		20 Covered Dishes.		35 Pitcher, 2 quart	.51
		9-inch	1.00	36 Pitcher, 3 quart	.75
		21 Casserole, square covered dish	1.12	37 Nappies, 7-inch	.26
				38 Nappies, 8-inch	.38
				39 Bowls, 1 pint	.17
				40 Oyster Bowls, 1 pint	.17
				41 Baker, 7-inch	.26
				42 Baker, 8-inch	.38

Peach Blossom Pattern.

Manufactured by Johnson Bros., Hanley, England.

Best quality of genuine English semi-porcelain, very durable. The decoration is a rich flown blue of peach blossoms and leaves put on under the glaze; the blossoms are illuminated with gold traced outlines burnt on which conduce to make it the handsomest dark blue ever brought out. All the pieces have full gold trimmings. Order any number of pieces desired. Order No. 54018.

Order No. 54018.

	Per doz.		Per doz.		Each.
1 Tea Cups and Saucers, with handles	$2.10	12 Bakers (used for side dishes), 3 inch	1.83	26 Covered Vegetable Dish, 8-inch	1.05
2 Coffee Cups and Saucers, with handles	2.45		Each.	27 Casserole (square covered dish)	1.17
3 After Dinner Coffees	1.75	14 Bakers, 7-inch	.26	28 Tea Pot	.70
4 Plates, scalloped edge, 5-inch	1.17	15 Bakers, 8-inch	.39	29 Sugar Bowl	.58
5 Plates, scalloped edge, 6-inch	1.44	16 Platters, 8-in	.22	30 Cream Pitcher	.26
6 Plates, scalloped edge, 7-inch	1.70	17 Platters, 10-in	.39	31 Cake Plate	.35
7 Plates, scalloped edge, 8-inch	1.97	18 Platters, 12-in	.66	32 Pitcher, ½ pint	.22
8 Soup Coupe Saucer shape 6-inch	1.70	19 Platters, 14-in	.91	33 Pitcher, 1 pnit	.26
9 Fruit Saucers, 4-in.	.78	20 Platters, 16-in	1.44	34 Pitcher, 1 quart	.31
10 Individual Butters	.53	21 Soup Tureen, with ladle	3.93	35 Pitcher, 2 quarts	.53
11 Bone Dishes	1.83	22 Sauce Tureen with ladle and stand	1.31	36 Pitcher, 3 quarts	.78
		23 Sauce Boat	.35	37 Bowls, 1 pint	.18
		24 Pickle Dish	.26	38 Oyster Bowls, 1 pt	.18
		25 Covered Butter Dish	.78	39 O tmeal Bowls, 1 pt.	.18
				40 Nappies, 7-in	.26
				41 Nappies, 8-inch	.39

Forget-Me-Not Pattern.

Manufactured by Johnson Bros., Hanley, England.

English semi-porcelain ware, pure white body, very durable, burnt on glaze, will not crack or chip. The shape is of the very latest pattern. All the pieces are gracefully moulded and artistically decorated with delicate spray of forget-me-not flowers in water green color; warranted not to wash or wear off. The handles and knobs are neatly gold traced. Order any quantity you desire.

Order No. 54023.

	Per doz.		Per doz.		Each
1 Tea Cups and Saucers, 12 Cups and 12 Saucers	$1.64	10 Bone Dishes	$1.64	23 Soup Tureen, Cover and ladle (no stand)	$3.50
2 Coffee Cups and Saucers, 12 Cups and 12 Saucers	2.18	11 Bowls, 1½ pint	1.87	24 Sauce Tureen, cover, ladle and stand	1.18
3 Plates, scalloped edge, 5-inch	1.06	12 Oysters, Bowls 1½ pint	1.87	25 Sauce Boat	.32
4 Plates, scalloped edge, 6-inch	1.28	13 Oatmeal Bowls, 1 pint	1.87	26 Pickle Dish	.25
5 Plates, scalloped edge, 7-inch	1.52		Each.	27 Covered Butter Dish and drainer	.71
6 Plates, scalloped edge, 8-inch	1.74	14 Bakers, 8-inch	$0.35	28 Pitcher, 1½ pint	.25
7 Soup Plates, scolloped edge, 7-inch	1.52	15 Nappies, 8-inch	.35	29 Pitcher, 1 quart	.27
8 Sauce Dishes, 4 in.	.71	16 Platters, 8-inch	.20	30 Pitcher, 3 quarts	.71
9 Individual Butters	.47	17 Platters, 10-inch	.35	31 Teapot and cover	.63
		18 Platters, 12-inch	.59	32 Sugar Bowl and cover	.54
		19 Platters, 14-inch	.88	33 Cream Pitcher	.26
		20 Platters, 16-inch	1.28	34 Cake Plate	.31
		21 Covered Dish, 8-in.	.94		
		22 Casserole (square covered dish) 8 in.	1.06		

Imperial Pattern Carlsbad China.

Superior grade of Imported Carlsbad China. Very thin like French China, a pretty decoration of blue forget-me-nots and small fern leaves in their natural color on nicely shaped pieces, combine to make this a very desirable pattern. The price is lower and decoration more attractive than we have been able to offer heretofore on ware of this high quality; gold traced handles. Order any quantity you may desire.

Order No. 54024.

	Per doz		Per doz.		Each
1 Tea Cups and Saucers, with handles	$2.52	9 Sauce Plates, 5-inch	$1.26	20 Covered Dishes	$1.75
2 Coffee Cups and Saucers, with handles	3.15	10 Individual Butters	.63	21 Casserole (square covered) dish	1.75
3 After Dinner Coffee Cups and Saucers, with handles	2.80	11 Bone Dishes	2.10	22 Covered Butter Dishes	1.12
4 Plates, scalloped edge, 5½-inch	1.40		Each.	23 Sauce Boat	.98
5 Plates, scalloped edge, 6½-inch	1.54	12 Bakers, 8-inch	$ .49	24 Lobster Salad	.98
6 Plates, scalloped edge, 7½-inch	1.75	13 Platters, 10-inch	.77	25 Pickle Dish	.56
7 Plates, scalloped edge, 8½-inch	2.66	14 Platters, 12-inch	1.05	27 Teapot	1.19
8 Soup Plates, coupe shape, 6½-inch	2.52	15 Platters, 14-inch	1.54	28 Sugar Bowl	.84
		16 Platters, 16-inch	1.89	29 Cream Pitcher	.42
		18 Soup Tureen and cover [only (plated ladles are used)	2.80	30 Bowl, 5½-inch	.31
		19 Sauce Tureen and Stand (plated ladles are used)	1.61	31 Cake Plate	.56

Violet Pattern Carlsbad China.

The Superior grade of Imported Carlsbad China, very thin like French china, most pleasing and artistic decoration ever executed on ware of this quality. The design is mixed violets in deep purple and white. The purple predominating. The cups and plates are on the milano shape, having raised scroll work following the edges; all the pieces are neutral gold trimmed. One of the handsomest patterns we carry. We will be pleased to fill your order for any number of pieces desired.

Order No. 54027.

	Per doz.		Per doz.		Each
1 Tea Cups and Saucers, 12 Cups and 12 Saucers	3.57	7 Plates, scalloped edge, 7½-in. Soup	3.50	24 Sauce Tureen, cov. and stand	1.88
2 Coffee Cups and Saucers, 12 Cups and 12 Saucers	4.55	8 Sauce Dishes, 4-in.	1.68	25 Sauce Boat	.98
		9 Individual Butters	.91	26 Pickle Dish	.42
2½ After Dinnercoffees 12 Cups and 12 Saucers	3.15	10 Bone Dishes	$2.66	27 Covered Butter Dish and drainer	1.36
		13 Oatmeal Bowls	2.80	31 Teapot and cover	1.47
3 Plates, scalloped edge, 5½-inch	2.10		Each.	32 Sugar Bowl and cover	.95
4 Plates, scalloped edge, 6½-inch	2.45	14 Bakers, 8-in	.63	33 Cream Pitcher	.53
5 Plates, scalloped edge, 7½-inch	2.80	17 Platters, 10-inch	.84	34 Cake Plate	.66
6 Plates, scalloped edge, 8½-inch	3.57	18 Platters, 12-inch	1.19	35 Bowls, 5½ in	.42
		19 Platters, 14-inch	1.68	36 Salad Dish	1.26
		20 Platters, 16-inch	2.24		
		21 Covered Dish 8in	2.10		
		22 Casserole, square covered dish	1.93		
		23 Soup Tureen and cover	3.22		

Fairy Pattern, French China.
Manufactured by Theodore Haviland & Co., Limoges, France.

This is a very handsome and thin pattern, of very best quality French China, of our latest importation. It is handsomely hand decorated with a very delicate blue forget-me-not spray, and richly gold traced handles. We offer this pattern cheaper than any other ever brought out by this famous maker. We solicit your order for any quantity, no matter how small.

Order No. 54030.

	Per doz.		Per doz.		Each
1 Tea Cups and Saucers, with handles	$3.80	9 Sauce Plates, 5 inch	$2.03	20 Covered Dishes. 8-inch	$2.27
2 Coffee Cups and Saucers, with handles	5.07	10 Individual Butters	1.13	21 Casserole, round covered dish	2.27
		11 Bone Dishes	2.33	22 Covered Butter Dishes	1.13
3 After Dinner Coffee Cups and Saucers, with handles	3.47		Each.	23 Sauce Boat and Stand	2.16
		12 Bakers, 8-inch	$1.00		
4 Plates, scalloped edge, 5½-inch	2.33	13 Platters, 10-inch	1.00	24 Lobster Salad	1.84
5 Plates, scalloped edge, 6½-inch	3.00	14 Platters, 12-inch	1.27	25 Pickle Dish	.43
6 Plates, scalloped edge, 7½-inch	3.47	15 Platters, 14-inch	1.84	27 Teapot	1.40
		16 Platters, 16-inch	3.43	28 Sugar Bowl	1.13
7 Plates, scalloped edge, 8½-inch	3.80	17 Platters, 18-inch	4.93	29 Cream Pitcher	.56
8 Plates, scalloped edge, 8-inch, Soup	3.80	18 Soup Tureen and Cover only (plated ladles are used)	4.93	30 Bowl, 5-inch	.43
		19 Sauce Tureen and Stand (plated ladles are used)	2.27	31 Cake Plate	.79
				33 Celery Tray	1.00
				34 Jelly Dish	.79

Carnot Pattern French China.
Manufactured by Haviland & Co., Limoges, France.

This beautiful pattern is genuine Haviland china, every piece marked Haviland & Co., Limoges. We call special attention to the handsome shape, which is the latest production of this celebrated maker. It is artistically hand decorated with delicate sprays of cornflowers in soft tints of pink and blue. The handles are richly finished in gold clouded effect. This pattern cannot fail to please anyone desiring the best made. We will be pleased to furnish any number of pieces you may select.

34--2nd

Order No. 54032

	Per doz.		Each		Each
1 Tea Cups and Saucers, 12 cups and 12 saucers	$4.40	10 Fruit Saucers, 4½-inch	1.96	21 Sauce Tureen with cover and stand	2.21
		11 Individual Butters	1.23	22 Sauce Boat and stand	1.96
2 Coffee Cups and saucers, 12 cups and 12 saucers	5.88		Each.	23 Pickles	.81
		12 Baker, 8 inch	1.34	24 Salad Dish	2.21
3 After Dinner Coffees	3.92	13 Platters, 10-inch	.98	25 Covered Butters	1.10
		14 Platters, 12-inch	1.47	26 Chocolate Pot	1.96
4 Plates, 5½-inch	2.94	15 Platters, 14-inch	2.10	27 Tea Pot	1.95
5 Plates, 6½-inch	3.30	16 Platters, 16-inch	3.30	28 Sugar Bowl	1.47
6 Plates, 7½-inch	3.92	17 Platters, 18-inch	4.90	29 Cream Pitcher	.85
7 Plates, 8½-inch	4.41	18 Round, Chop Platter, 11-inch	2.03	30 Cake Plate	1.05
8 Plates, soup, 8-inch	4.17	19 Round Covered Dish, 8-inch	2.45	31 Bowl, 5½-inch	.56
		20 Soup Tureen and cover	4.90	32 Pitcher, 1-pint	1.40
9 Plates, soup, coupe shape, 6½-inch	3.30			33 Pitcher, 2-pint	1.96
				34 Olive Dish	.49

Kent Pattern.   (Semi-Porcelain.)
Manufactured by Alfred Meakin, Tunstall, England.

This pattern is entirely new, it is remarkably handsome, both as to shape and decoration, all the pieces are gold lined. We are able to furnish it in dove, a soft gray or in the new flown pearl, a dark blue. Please mention color desired when ordering.

Order No. 54034.

	Per doz.		Each		Each
1 Tea Cups and Saucers, handled	$1.82	13 Platters, 8-inch	$0.19	29 Pitchers, 3 qt	.68
2 Coffee Cups and Saucers, handled	2.12	14 Platters, 10-inch	.35	30 Soup Tureen and cover	1.50
		15 Platters, 12-inch	.56	31 Sauce Tureen (with ladle and stand)	1.19
3 Pie Plates, 5-inch	1.02	16 Platters, 14-inch	79		
4 Plates, 6-inch	1.25	17 Platters, 16-inch	1.24		
5 Plates, 7-inch	1.48	18 Bakers, 7-inch	.22	32 Sauce Boat	.30
6 Plates, 8-inch	1.70	19 Bakers, 8-inch	.33	33 Pickle Dish	.22
7 Soup plates, 7½-inch	1.48	21 Scalloped Nappies 7-inch	.22	35 Covered Vegetable Dish	.91
8 Fruit Plates	.68	22 Scalloped Nappies 8-inch	.33	36 Casserole, square covered dish	1.02
9 Individual Butters	.46	25 Pitchers, ½ pt	.19	37 Teapot	.60
10 Bakers, 3-inch (for side dishes)	1.60	26 Pitchers, 1 pt	.22	38 Sugar Bowl	.50
11 1 pt. Bowls	1.82	27 Pitchers, 1 qt	.26	40 Cake Plates	.30
12 1 pt. Oyster Bowls	1.82	28 Pitchers, 2 qt	.45		

Dove Genoa Pattern.
Manufactured by Smith & Ford, Staffordshire, England.

This pattern is very handsome in shape and decoration: the decoration consists of wild flowers and leaves in soft gray, although it is very low in price, we consider the body of the ware equal to any other pattern sold by us; we recommend it very highly where a cheap and durable set is wanted,

Order No. 54036.

	Per doz.		Per doz.		Each
1 Tea Cups and Saucers, with handles	$1.26	10 Bone Dishes	1.10	23 Sauce Boat	.21
		11 3-inch Bakers (used as sidedishes)	$1.10	25 Pickle Dish	15
2 Coffee Cups and Saucers, with handles	1.47		Each.	27 Teapot	.42
		12 Platters, 8-inch	13	28 Sugar Bowl	.35
3 Plates, scalloped edge, 5-inch	.71	13 Platters, 10-inch	.23	29 Cream Pitcher	.15
4 Plates, scalloped edge, 6-inch	.86	14 Platters, 12-inch	.39	31 Cake Plate	.21
		15 Platters, 14-inch	.54	32 Pitcher, ½ pint	.13
5 Plates, scalloped edge, 7-inch	1.02	16 Platters, 16-inch	.87	33 Pitchers, 1 pint	15
6 Plates, scalloped edge, 8-inch	1.17	18 Soup Tureen Cover, ladle and stand	3.15	34 Pitchers, 1 quart	.18
7 Plates, scalloped edge, 7 in-soup	1.02	19 Sauce Tureen Stand, cover and ladle	.78	35 Pitchers, 2 quarts	.32
8 Sauce Plates, 4-inch	.47	20 Covered Dishes 9-inch	.63	36 Pitchers, 3 quarts	47
		21 Casserole, square covered dish	.71	37 Nappies, 7-inch	.15
9 Individual Butters	.32	22 Covered Butter Dishes	.47	38 Nappies, 8-inch	.23
				39 Bowls, 1 pint	.10
				40 Oyster Bowls, 1 pt.	.10
				41 Baker, 7-inch	.15
				42 Baker, 8-inch	.23

Victoria Pattern.

Manufactured by Johnson Bros., Hanley, England.

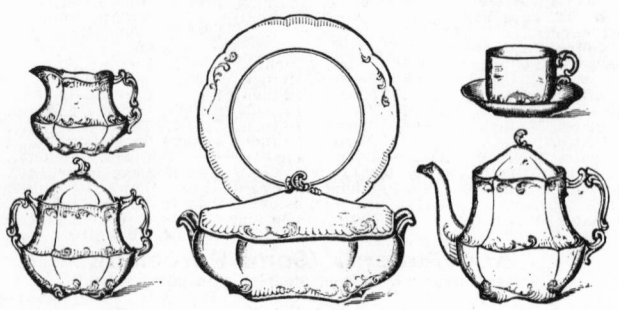

Semi-porcelain resembles pure, white French china. It is thin and has a finish not easily detected from china. For those desiring a service of pure white ware of a better and more modern style than regular ironstone, there is nothing better made. The shapes are pretty and cannot fail to give good satisfaction.

Order No. 54038.

	Per doz.		Each.		Each.
1 Tea Cups and Saucers, handled	$1.20	17 Platter, 18-inch	$1.20	35 Covered Butter Dish	$0.45
2 Coffee Cups and Saucers, handled	1.40	18 Bakers, 5-inch	.11	36 Covered Vegetable Dish, 7-inch	.54
3 Plates, 5-in., scalloped edge	.68	19 Bakers, 6-inch	.14	37 Covered Vegetable Dish, 8-inch	.60
4 Plates, 6-in., scalloped edge	.83	20 Bakers, 7-inch	.15	38 Covered Vegetable Dish, 9-inch	.68
5 Plates, 7-in., scalloped edge	.98	21 Bakers, 8-inch	.23	39 Casserole (square covered dish), 7-inch	.60
6 Plates, 8-in., scalloped edge	1.12	22 Bakers, 9-inch	.31	40 Casserole (square covered dish), 8-inch	.68
7 Soup Plates, 7 in.	.98	23 Scalloped Nappies, 5-inch	.11	41 Casserole (square covered dish), 9-inch	.75
8 Sauce Dishes, 4 in.	.45	24 Scalloped Nappies, 6-inch	.14	42 Sauce Boat	.20
9 Individual Butters	.31	25 Scalloped Nappies, 7-inch	.15	43 Pickle Dish	.15
10 Bone Dishes	1.06	26 Scalloped Nappies, 8-inch	.23	44 Teapot	.40
11 Bakers, 3 in. (used as side dishes)	1.07	27 Scalloped Nappies, 9-inch	.31	45 Sugar Bowl	.33
		28 Pitchers, ½ pt	.14	46 Cream Pitcher	.15
	Each.	29 Pitchers, 1 pt.	.15	47 Cake Plate	.20
12 Platter, 8-inch	$0.14	30 Pitchers, 1 qt.	.18	48 Bowls, ½ pt	.09
13 Platter, 10-inch	.24	31 Pitchers, 2 qt.	.31	49 Bowls, 1 pt.	.10
14 Platter, 12-inch	.38	32 Pitchers, 3 qt.	.45	50 Bowls, 1 qt.	.13
15 Platter, 14-inch	.54	33 Soup Tureen, ladle and stand	2.71	51 Oyster Bowls, 1 pt	.10
16 Platter, 16-inch	.83	34 Sauce Tureen, ladle and stand	.75		

Vitrious Hotel China.

Extra quality of vitrious hotel china, warranted not to crack, and will not turn black when chipped. Our hotel ware is made especially for restaurant and hotel use, being of weight and shape as mostly used by them.

Order No. 54046.

	Per doz.		Per doz.
1 Coffee Cups & Saucers, without handles	$1.52	14 Platters, 5-inch, actual measurement 8 inches	$1.14
2 Coffee Cups and Saucers, with handles	1.73	15 Platters, 6-inch actual measurement 8½ inches	1.25
3 Tea Cups and Saucers, without handles	1.38	16 Platters, 7-inch, actual measurement 9 inches	1.39
4 Tea Cups and Saucers, with handles	1.59	17 Platters, 8-inch, actual measurement 10½ inches	1.73
5 Plates, 5-inch; actual measurement, 6¾ inches	.77	18 Platters, 9-inch, actual measurement 10½ inches	2.18
6 Plates, 6-inch; actual measurement, 8 inches	.96	19 Bakers, 2½-inch, actual measurement 5 inches	1.13
7 Plates, 7-inch; actual measurement, 9 inches	1.12	20 Bakers, 3-inch, actual measurement 5½ inches	1.13
8 Soup Plates, 7-inch	1.21	21 Bakers, 4-inch, actual measurement 6½ inches	1.13
9 Ice Cream Dishes, 4-inch	.51	22 Bakers, 5-inch, actual measurement 7½ inches	1.31
10 Ice Cream Dishes, 4-inch	.51	23 Butter Dish with drainer, 5-inch	4.54
11 Fruit Saucers, 4-inch	.51	24 Oyster Bowls, 1 pint	$1.47
12 Platters, 3 inch, actual measurement 6-inches	1.04	25 Individual Cream Jugs	.96
13 Platters, 4-inch, actual measurement 7-inches	1.04	26 Sugar Bowls covered	2.81
		27 Pitchers, 2-quarts	6.93
		28 Pitchers, 1-quart	4.40
		29 Pitchers, 1 pint	2.16
		30 Pitchers, ½ pint	1.83
		31 Room Pitchers, or Hall Boy's, holds 3 pints	2.60
		32 Ice Pitchers, with lid, 2 quart	11.27
		33 Comports or Cake Stands	8.24
		34 Wash Bowls and Pitchers	14.30
		35 Covered Chambers	9.09
		36 Slop Jars, no cover	15.20
		37 Cone Match Stands	80
		38 Open Sugar Bowls, Round	3.45

Anemone Dinner Set--100 Pieces.

Manufactured by W. H. Weatherby & Son, Hanley, England.

Genuine English semi-porcelain ware, decorated with delicate spray of anemone flowers and leaves put on under the glaze, which prevents it wearing off. Can furnish in two colors, a light chocolate brown or a peacock blue. Be sure and state which is wanted when ordering. Sold only in complete sets as follows:

Order No. 54048.

12 Tea cups with handles.	1 Baker, 7-inch.	1 Sauce Boat.
12 Tea Saucers.	1 Baker, 8-inch.	1 Pickle Dish.
12 5-inch Plates.	1 Platter, 8-inch.	1 Covered Butter Dish.
12 6-inch Plates.	1 Platter, 10-inch.	1 Covered Sugar Bowl.
12 7-inch Plates.	1 Platter, 12-inch.	1 Cream Pitcher.
12 Fruit Saucers.	1 Covered Dish, 9-inch.	1 Slop Bowl.
12 Individual Butters.		

Price, per set $7.50

Weight, packed for shipment, 100 pounds.

Bengal Tea Set, 56 Pieces.

54053   Decorated English StoneChina Set; decorated on ivory-colored body in brown. The decorations are leaves and flowers in their natural colors, put on under the glaze, and will not wear off. Set consists of the following pieces, packed for shipment. Weight, 40 pounds.

12 Tea Cups, handled.	2 Cake plates.	1 Cream Pitcher.
12 Tea Saucers.	1 Tea Pot.	1 Slop Bowl.
12 Plates, 6-inch.	1 Sugar Bowl.	12 Fruit Plates.

Price $3.75

Montrose Dinner Set -- 100 Pieces.

Manufactured by Johnson Bros., Hanley, England.

Genuine English semi-porcelain with under glaze decoration; warranted not to wash or wear off. The shape is very handsome, as is also the decoration, which consists of vines and small flowers in natural colors of pink, blue and yellow, the handles are delicately traced in gold. This set is sold only complete and with the following number of pieces.

Order No. 54055.

12 Tea Cups, handled.	2 Bakers, 8 inch.	1 Covered Butter Dish, with drainer.
12 Tea Saucers.	1 Meat Dish, 8-inch.	1 Covered Sugar Bowl.
12 Pie Plates, 5-inch.	1 Meat Dish, 10-inch.	1 Cream Pitcher.
12 Tea Plates, 6-inch.	1 Meat Dish, 12-inch.	1 Bowl, 1 pint.
12 Breakfast or Dinner Plates, 7-inch.	1 Covered Dish, 8 inch.	12 Sauce Dishes, 4-inch.
12 Individ'l Butter Plates	1 Sauce Boat.	
	1 Pickle Dish.	

Weight, packed for shipment, 100 lbs. Price $12.95

Montgomery Ward and Co.'s Coral Pattern.

Tea and Dinner Sets. American Manufacture.

The Coral Pattern Sets are made expressly for us by one of the largest manufacturers in America. They are made of the best quality pure white granite, and decorated by hand, with leaves and sprays of a natural gray tint and wild blossoms in delicate blue. This is intended for an every day set, and is made strong and substantial. The decorations are put on under the glaze, and will not wash or wear off. They are packed for us by the manufacturers, one set in a box, or barrel, and we cannot change the combination by adding or deducting any number of pieces. Edges and handles are gold lined

54074.   Coral Brand, 56-Piece Tea Set.

12 Tea Cups, handled.	2 Cake Plates.	1 Cream Pitcher.
12 Tea Saucers.	1 Tea Pot.	1 Slop Bowl.
12 Plates, 6 inch.	1 Sugar Bowl.	12 Fruit Saucers.

Weight, 40 pounds.   Price, ... $4.50

54075.   Coral Brand, 98-Piece Dinner Set.

12 Plates, 5-inch.	1 Platter, 10-inch.	1 Nappie, 8-inch.
12 Plates, 6-inch.	12 Tea Cups, handled.	1 Covered Dish, 8-inch.
12 Plates 7-inch.	12 Tea Saucers.	1 Cream Pitcher.
12 Fruit Plates.	1 Cake Plate.	1 Sugar Bowl.
12 Individual Butters.	1 Nappie, 7-inch.	1 Sauce Boat.
1 Platter, 8 inch.	1 Bowl.	1 Tea Pot.

Weight 82 pounds.   Price, ... $7.75

54078.   Coral Brand, 102-Piece Dinner Set.

12 Plates, 5-inch.	1 Platter, 12-inch.	1 Sauce Boat.
12 Plates, 7-inch.	1 Platter, 14-inch.	1 Jug, 2 quarts.
12 Plates, 7-inch, soup.	2 Bakers, 7-inch.	1 Pickle Dish.
12 Individual Butters.	2 Covered Dishes, 8-inch.	12 Tea Cups.
12 Fruit Saucers.	1 Cream Pitcher.	12 Saucers.
1 Platter, 10-inch.	1 Nappie, 8-inch.	1 Soup Tureen, and ladle
		1 Slop Bowl.

Weight, 100 pounds.   Price, ... $11.00

The Daisy Gold Band Tea and Dinner Set.
American Manufacture.

The Daisy pattern is made of a superior granite body, heavily gold banded. The pieces are very elegantly shaped and glazed; it will not chip or crack and can be relied upon as a first-class article. They are made to our order in large quantities, which enables us to offer them at a very low price.

54080.   Daisy Gold Band. 56-Piece Tea Set.

12 Tea Cups, handled.	1 Sugar Bowl.	12 Plates, 6-inch.
12 Tea Saucers.	1 Cream Pitcher.	1 Tea Pot.
2 Cake Plates.	1 Slop Bowl.	12 Fruit Saucers.

Weight, 45 pounds.   Price...$5.10

54082. Daisy Gold Band. 112-Piece Dinner Set.

12 Plates, 5-inch.	1 Platter, 12-inch.	1 Baker, 8-inch.
12 Plates, 6-inch.	1 Platter, 14-inch.	1 Covered Dish, 8-inch.
12 Plates, 7-inch.	12 Tea Cups.	1 Casserole, 7-inch.
12 Fruit Saucers.	12 Tea Saucers.	1 Pitcher, 1 quart.
12 Individual Butters.	12 Oyster bowls.	1 Comport.
1 Platter, 10-inch.	1 Baker, 7-inch.	2 Pickle Dishes.
1 Covered Butter.		

Weight, 100 pounds.   Price...$12.25

MUSICAL INSTRUMENTS TO BEAT THE BAND.

We import our own Musical Goods direct from Germany

We can furnish anything in this line whether quoted or not.

Moss Rose Tea and Dinner Sets, American Manufacture.

Our Moss Rose Tea and Dinner Sets are manufactured expressly for us by the very best factories. The decorations are of a very high order and are put on so that they will neither wash nor wear off. We have them packed one set in a box, and for this reason we cannot change the assortment.

54085. Moss Rose Tea Set, 56 Pieces.

12 Tea Cups.	2 Cake Plates.	1 Cream Pitcher.
12 Tea Saucers.	1 Tea Pot.	1 Slop Bowl.
12 Plates, 6-inch.	1 Sugar Bowl.	12 Fruit Plates.

Weight, 50 pounds. Price..$4.75

54090. Moss Rose Dinner Set, 101 Pieces.

12 Plates, 5-inch.	1 Platter, 12-inch.	1 Covered Dish, 8-inch.
12 Plates, 6-inch.	1 Platter, 14-inch.	1 Casserole, 7-inch.
12 Plates, 7-inch.	1 Sauce Boat.	1 2-quart Pitcher.
12 Fruit Plates, 4-inch.	12 Tea Cups.	1 Comport.
12 Individual Butters.	12 Tea Saucers.	1 Covered Butter Dish.
1 Platter, 10-inch.	1 Baker, 7-inch.	2 Pickle Dishes.
1 Baker, 8-inch.		

Weight, 102 pounds. Price..$11.65

54095. Moss Rose Dinner Set, 131 Pieces.

12 Plates, 5-inch.	1 Baker, 7-inch.	2 Pickle dishes.
12 Plates, 6-inch.	1 Baker, 8-inch.	12 Tea Cups.
12 Plates, 7-inch.	1 Covered Dish, 8-inch.	12 Tea Saucers.
12 Fruit Saucers,	1 2-quart pitcher.	12 Coffee Cups.
12 Individual Butters.	1 Casserole, 7-inch.	12 Coffee Saucers.
1 Platter, 10-inch.	1 Sauce boat.	1 Cream pitcher.
1 Platter, 12-inch.	1 Comport.	1 Tea Pot.
1 Platter, 14-inch.	1 Butter dish.	1 Sugar Bowl.
1 Slop Bowl.		

Weight, 120 pounds Price..$15.75

Plain White English Stone China Tea and Dinner Sets.

Order No. 54106.
WHITE STONE CHINA TEA SET—56 PIECES.

12 Tea Cups, handled.	1 Sugar Bowl.	2 Teapot.
12 Saucers.	1 Creamer.	1 Bowl.
12 Tea Plates, 6-inch.	2 Cake Plates.	12 Sauce Plates, 4-inch.
	Weight, 50 pounds.	

56 pieces in all, boxed for shipping..................................... $3.65

Order No. 54110.
WHITE STONE CHINA DINNER SET—101 PIECES.

12 Dinner Plates, 8-inch.	1 Platter, 10-inch.	2 Oval Covered Dishes,
12 Soup Plates, 7 inch.	1 Platter, -14-inch.	one 7-inch, one 8-inch.
12 Dessert Plates, 5-inch.	2 Bakers, 8-inch.	1 Soup Tureen, cover and
12 Cups.	1 Covered Butter Dish.	ladle, 8 inches round.
12 Saucers.	12 Sauce Plates, 4-inch.	1 Sauce Boat.
12 Individual Butter.	Weight, 122 lbs.	2 Pickle Dishes.

100 pieces in all, boxed for shipping.....................................$8.75

Order No. 54115.
WHITE STONE CHINA DINNER SET--143 PIECES.

12 Dinner Plates, 8-inch.	12 Cups, handled.	1 Soup Tureen, cover and
12 Breakfast Plates, 7-inch.	12 Saucers.	ladle, 7-inch round.
12 Soup Plates, 7-inch	2 Platters, 10-inch.	1 Sauce Tureen, with ladle
12 Dessert Plates, 5-inch.	2 Platters, 14-inch.	and stand.
12 Sauce Plates.	1 Salad Dish, 7-inch.	1 Covered Butter Dish.
12 Cup Plates.	2 Covered Vegetable	2 Pickle Dishes.
12 Individual Butter Plates.	Dishes, one 8-inch, one	2 Bakers, 8-inch.
12 Custard Cups.	9 inch.	Weight, 155 lbs.

142 pieces in all, boxed for shipping..................................$13.00

Our White Stone China Tea and Dinner Sets come all packed from the manufacturer. We cannot make any changes. They are made and packed for us by men who thoroughly understand their trade, and we would not under any circumstances attempt to repack. The risk of breakage must be assumed by the purchaser.

All our crockery is sold for *cash only, money to accompany order.*

N. B.--Under no circumstances will claims be allowed for breakage. Goods, if returned, must be in good order, with full amount of straw. Freight prepaid.

Each and every piece about our crockery department counts one, i. e., teapot and cover count one, dishes with covers count two, etc.

NOTICE.—Measurements for plates, platters, etc., are taken from the outer rim on one side to the inner rim on the opposite side. Measurements for bowls, tureens, oval dishes, etc., are taken from one extreme edge to the other.

Souvenir or After-Dinner Cups and Saucers.

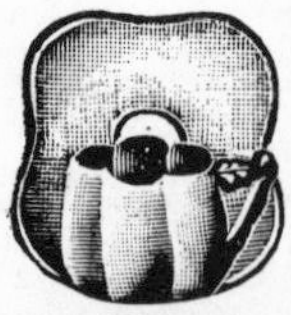

54117 Imported China Thin After-dinner Coffee Cups and Saucers. fancy tulip shape and handsomely tinted. Sold in the following assorted colors: Pink, yellow, blue, Nile green, salmon and heliotrope; gold handles.
Each....................$0.35
Per dozen.................. 4.00

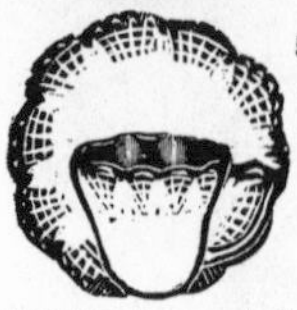

54118 Imported China Thin After-dinner Coffee Cup and Saucer, decorated with vines and small flowers in delicate tints of blue and pink on white body.
Each....................$0.25
Per dozen.................. 2.75

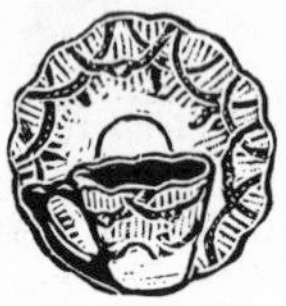

54119 Imported China Thin After-dinner Coffee Cup and Saucer, pure white body, with a rich, gold-stippled border
Each....................$0.20
Per dozen.................. 2.18

Imported Tea and Coffee Cups and Saucers.

Cups and saucers can go by mail; allow 25 cents for postage.

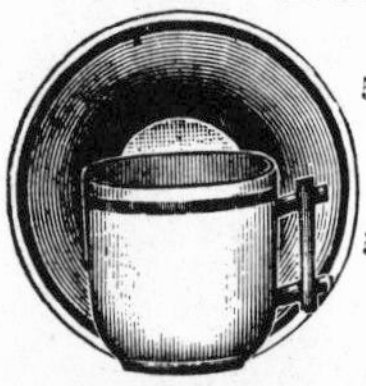

54125 Gold Band Imported China Coffee Cup and Saucer, very neat and of fine quality; good large size. Each.........$0.25
Per dozen.................. 2.70

54126 Same as above, with moustache bar. Each..........$0.27
Per dozen.................. 2.90

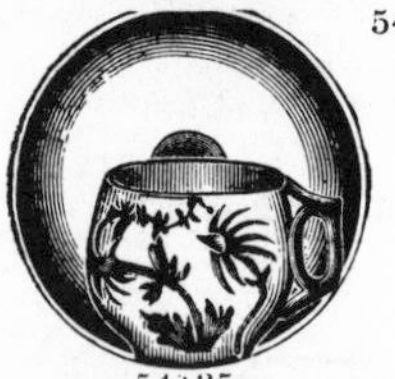

54135

54135 Imported Coffee Cup and Saucer; globe shape, elaborately decorated and tinted in gold and colors. Each........$0.35

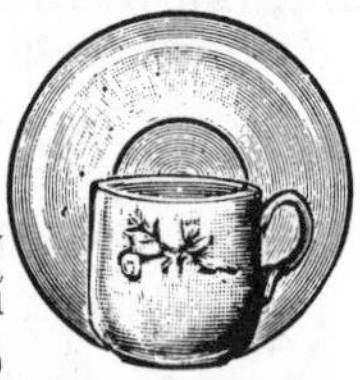

54140

54140 Child's Cup and Saucer, genuine imported china, very pretty and of good size; not a toy; assorted decorations, hand painted and very neat.
Per set....................$0.10
Per dozen sets............ 1.08

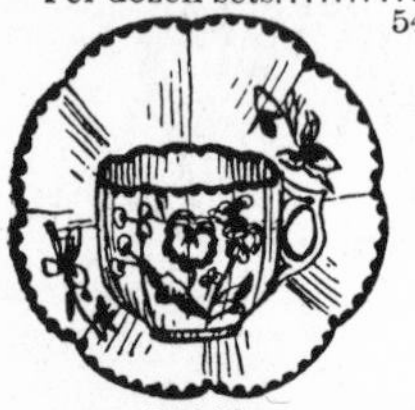

54143

54143 Imported China Cup and Saucer, fluted and stippled gold edges handsomely hand-decorated with flowers, etc. This is a very favorite shape and one which will be sure to please. Price............$0.55
Per dozen.................. 6.00

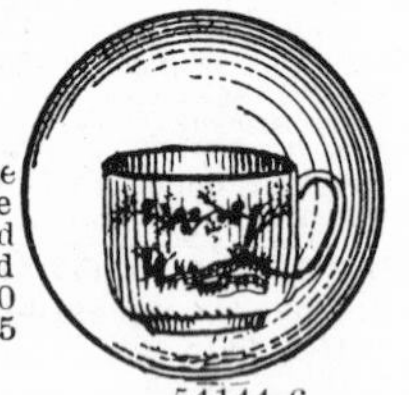

54144-6

54144 Imported China Coffee Cup and Saucer, very large and strong, nicely decorated in colors; has gold lined edges. Price.......... $0.30
Per dozen................ 3.35

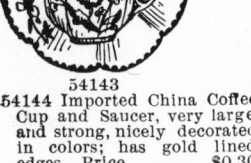

54146 Same as 54144, with moustache bar.
Price....................$0.35
Per dozen.................. 3.75

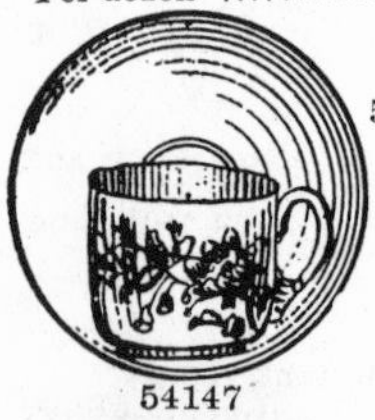

54147

54147 Imported China Coffee Cup and Saucer, large and strong, square shape, hand decorated and gold lined.
Price....................$0.25
Per dozen.................. 2.75

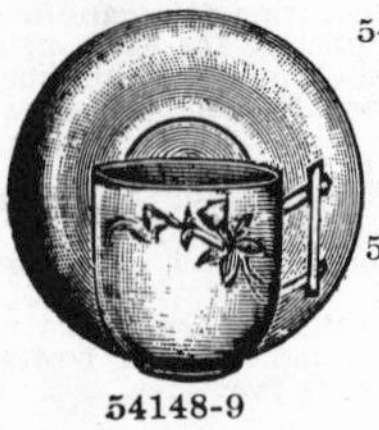

54148-9

54148 Imported China Coffee Cup and Saucer, very large, nicely decorated in colors, edges gold lined; for those desiring an extra large cup this is the very thing. Price....$0.30
Per dozen.................. 3.30

54149 Same as No. 54148, with moustache bar.
Price....................$0.35
Per dozen.................. 3.70

Cups and Saucers—Continued.

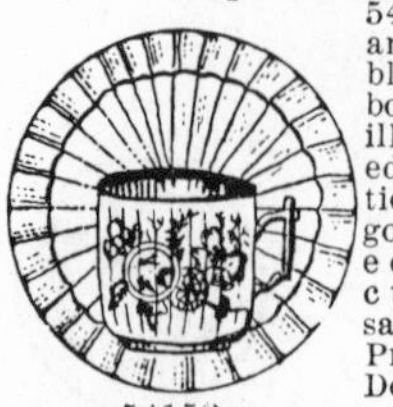

54152

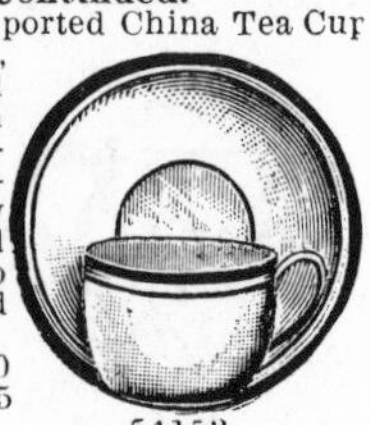

54153

54152 Imported China Tea Cup and saucer, blue tinted body with illuminated decorations heavy gold lined edges to cup and saucer.
Price $0.40
Doz... 4.45

54153 Imported China Tea Cup and Saucer, pure white with gold band and handle; a very neat and desirable article....$0.20 Per dozen.......$2.25

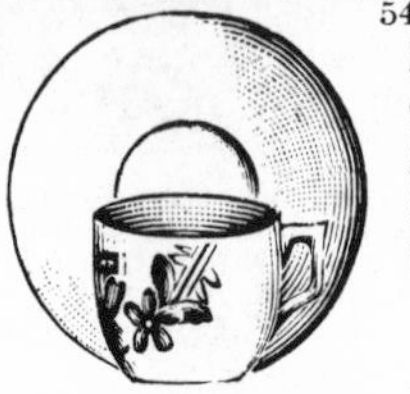

54155 Imported Motto Tea Cups and Saucers, with the words "A Present," "Think of Me," etc., in gold letters across the front of cup, and decorated with flowers; has gold lined edges.
Each....................$0.20
Per dozen.................. 2.16

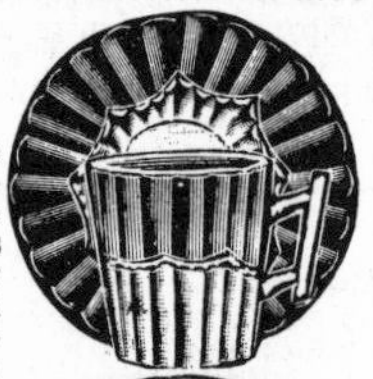

54156 Imported China Coffee Cup and Saucer, solid dark maroon color almost over entire length of cup; the balance is pure white with gold trimming and fluted in the manner shown by cut; this is by far the handsomest cup and saucer for the price we have seen this season.
Each....................$0.60
Per dozen.................. 6.48

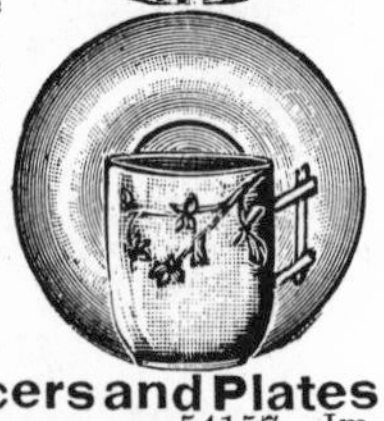

54156½ Imported China Cup and Saucer, medium size; the body is tinted a solid color, and hand decorated with bright colored leaves and flowers; for a medium priced article, it is the best we have to offer.
Price....................$0.20

Imported Cups, Saucers and Plates

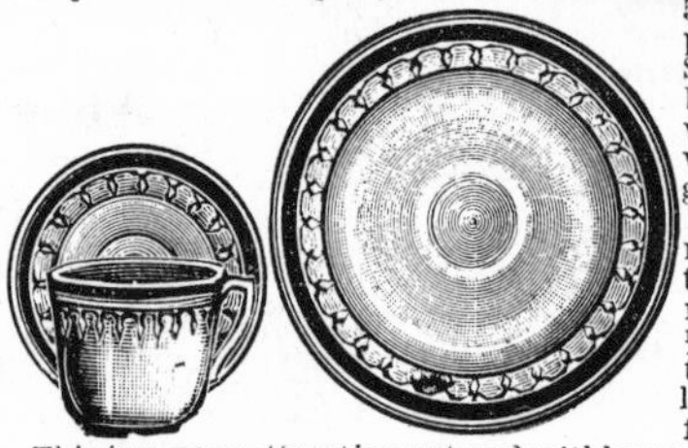

54157 Imported Cup, Saucer and Plate, pure white body with heavy gold and blue lines round edges; the plate measures 8-½ in. across; the cup is large enough for coffee. This is a very attractive set and will be sure to please.
Per set..............$0.40 Per dozen sets......$4.35

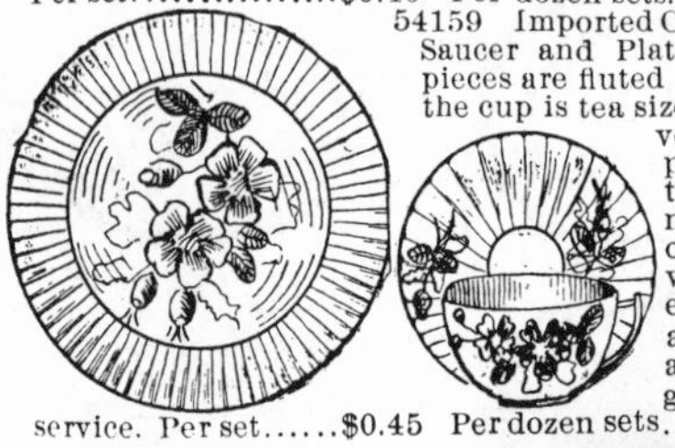

54159 Imported China Cup, Saucer and Plate; all the pieces are fluted or ribbed the cup is tea size and of a very dainty pattern; they are nicely decorated with colored flowers; are strong and will give good service. Per set......$0.45 Per dozen sets......$4.76

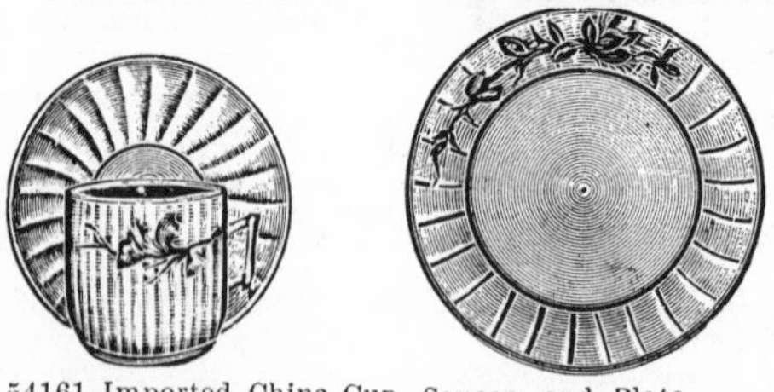

54161 Imported China Cup, Saucer, and Plate, suitable for children; very neatly decorated in colors Per set........$0.30 Per dozen sets.....$3.24

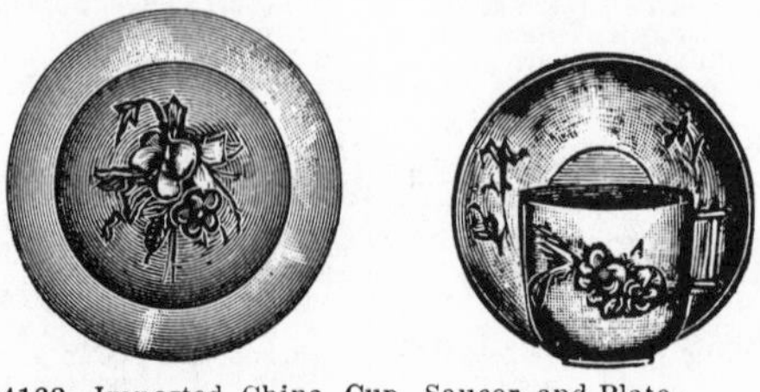

54163 Imported China Cup, Saucer and Plate, medium size, suitable for either tea or coffee. This is a very pretty set and is decorated by hand with pansies and roses in their natural colors. Per set......$0.45 Per dozen sets..... $4.86

Cups and Saucers—Continued.

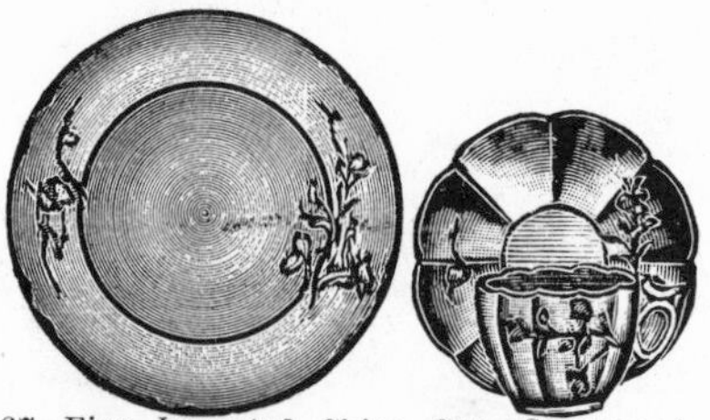

54167 Fine Imported China Cup, Saucer and Plate; all the pieces are tinted in blue and hand decorated with gold and colored flowers; the cup is large and can be used for coffee. If you desire something extra nice, we would strongly recommend this set as being the neatest both in point of shape and decoration that we have ever offered. Per set....................$0.85
Per dozen sets.................. 8.28

China Drinking Mugs.

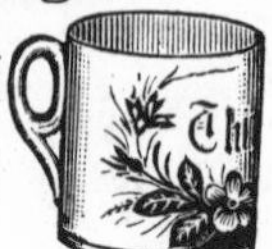

54180 Imported China Drinking Mugs, with mottoes and assorted decorations.
Each....................$.0 10
Per dozen.................. 1.10

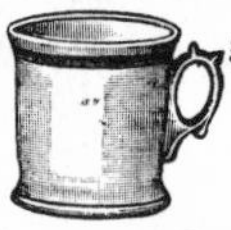

54182 Imported China Drinking Mug, pure white, with heavy gold band running around top and fine gold line inside and around bottom; nice size, holds about an ordinary tumbler full.
Each....... $0.15. Per dozen....$1.60

China Shaving Mugs.

54185 Decorated Imported China Shaving Mugs, with partitions similar to cut.
Each....................$0.22
Per dozen.................. 2.38

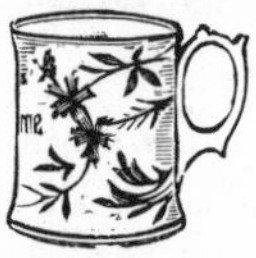

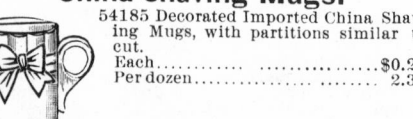

54186 Shaving Mugs, decorated china with partition for soap. Each..$0.25
Per dozen.................. 2.70

54189 Decorated Imported China Shaving Mugs, assorted decorations, similar to cut.
Each....................$0.15
Per dozen.................. 1.68

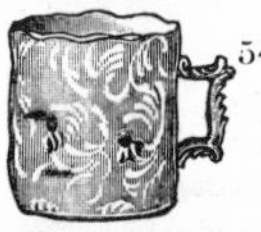

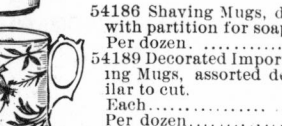

54190 Genuine White China Shaving Mug, very handsomely gold lined and decorated on the outside; has separate partition for soap and brush. The shape is odd and pretty. Each...$0 35
Per dozen.................. 3.78

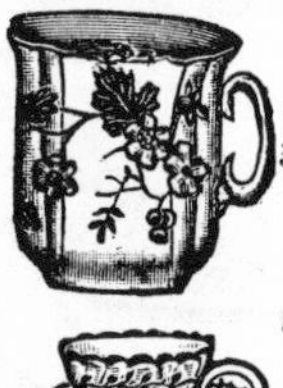

54198 Imported Decorated China Shaving Mug, a little larger than the ordinary size. The top flares out, making it easy to keep clean.
Each....................$0.25

54200 Fancy Shape China Shaving Mug, separate partition on top for soap, leaving the under part for shaving brush and water; it is very desirable on this account, as it is easily kept clean. It is profusely gold-lined and stippled at neck and base with a very rich blue and burnt in so that it cannot possibly wash or wear off. Price..$0.45
Per dozen.................. 4.86

54202 Same as No. 54200, but is pure white with gold trimmings. Each.................... .40
Per dozen.................. 4.32

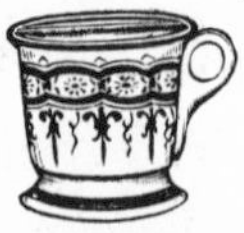

54203 Very handsome China Shaving Mug with partition on top for soap; it is handsomely gold trimmed over the entire surface, and has a broad colored band near the top running all the way around.
Price....................$0.40
Per dozen.................. 4.32

54204 Imported Shaving Mug, without soap partition; the body is tinted a beautiful cream color both inside and out; on this are painted beautiful sprays of pink blossoms, while the base, top and handle are heavily lined with gold; it is of good size and by far the handsomest article of its kind ever offered by us. Each....................$0.45
Per dozen.................. 4.86

Bone Dishes.

54205 Imported Thin China Bone Dish fancy shape, decorated with delicate flower spray work in a neat manner; gold traced edges. Each........$0.25
Per dozen.................. 2.70

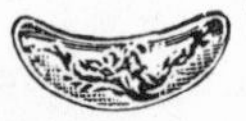

54206 Imported Carlsbad China Bone Dish, crescent shape, decorated with small flowers and spray. For the price this is the best bone dish we ever handled. Each...........$0.12
Per dozen.................. 1.30

Bone Dishes—Continued.

decorated.

54209 Bone Dish. A convenient individual side dish for table use, in which to deposit game or fish bones, parings of fruits, etc.; semi porcelain, nicely decorated. Each.....$0.15 Per dozen.........$1.70

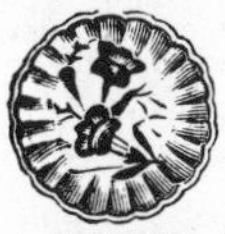

54212 Individual Butter Plates. Cannelle pattern. Thin china floral, decoration, gold trimmed edges.
Per dozen $0.75

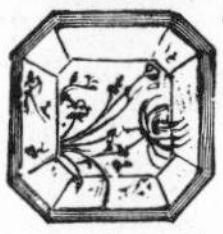

54215 Individual Butter Plates; odd Chinese decoration.
Per dozen $0.40

Decorated Bon Ware.

The following articles of bon ware are all decorated in the same manner, with orchids and pansies in pleasing colors; all the edges are gold trimmed and heavily stippled, giving them a very rich effect; the ware itself is light in weight, but very strong and serviceable. We recommend it highly to those in search of something extra nice in table ware for use on extra occasions.

54237 Bon Ware Butter Dish, with inside drainer, good size, measuring 8 inches across.
Each... ....$0.60
Per dozen........... 6.48

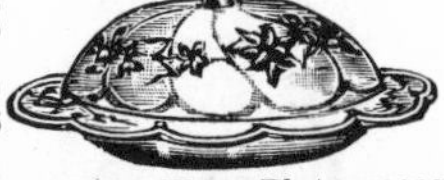

54239 Bon Ware Plate, measures 9 inches across; can be used as fruit, cake or bread plate. Each.............$0.25
Per dozen............... 2.70

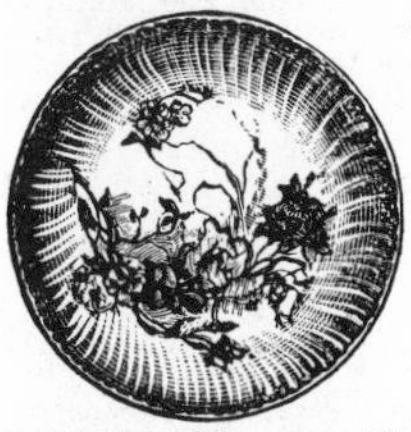

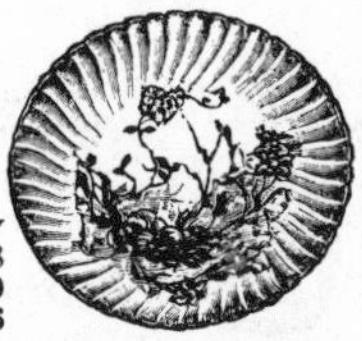

54244 Bon Ware Tea Plate, a very convenient size, measures 8 inches across. Each......$0.20
Per dozen.................. 2.16

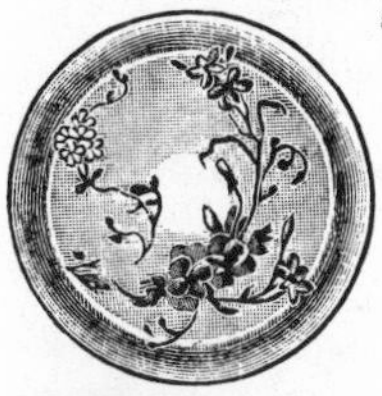

54250 Bon Ware Teapot Stand, measures 7 inches across, made with a ventilated or hollow bottom, so that it cannot become hot or stick to the table.
Each.......................$0.18
Per dozen 1.95

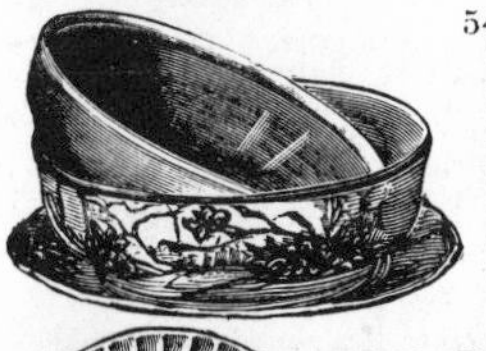

54255 Bon Ware Pudding Set, three pieces; the inside top dish, seen in cut is the one in which the pudding is cooked; the other two are set on the table and receive the pudding dish, which sets inside the larger one; very convenient.
Per set...............$1.25

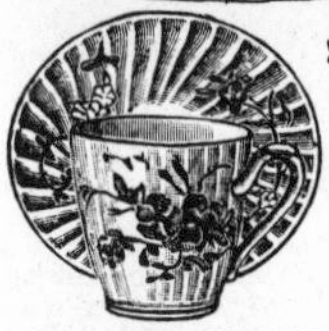

54259 Bon Ware Cup and Saucer, medium size, suitable for either tea or coffee. Each.........$0.22
Per dozen 2.38

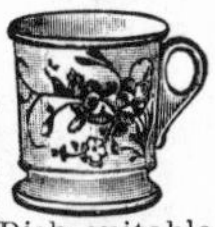

54265 Bon Ware Drinking Mug, very pretty shape; holds about ⅓ pint.
Each.............................$0.15
Per dozen........................ . 1.62

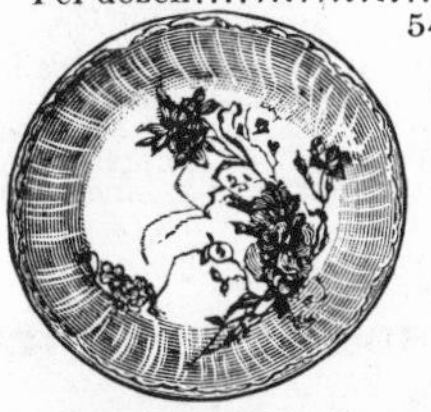

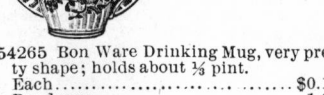

54270 Bon Ware Dish, suitable for a great many purposes, such as salad, berry or fruit bowl; measures 9 inches across. Each...........$0.40
Per dozen 4.32

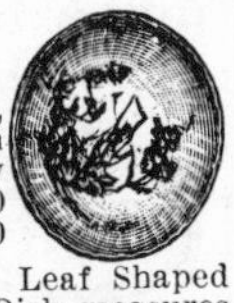

54272 Bon Ware Sauce or Berry Dish, measures 5½ inches across, used with 54270 bowl makes an excellent berry set. Each................$0.10
Per dozen...........................110

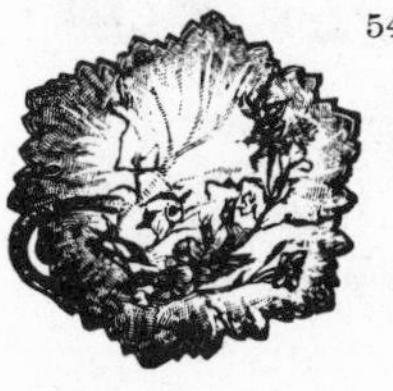

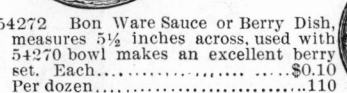

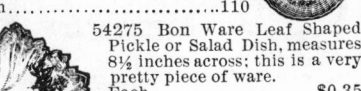

54275 Bon Ware Leaf Shaped Pickle or Salad Dish, measures 8½ inches across; this is a very pretty piece of ware.
Each.......................$0.35
Per dozen.................. 3.78

Bon Ware —Continued.

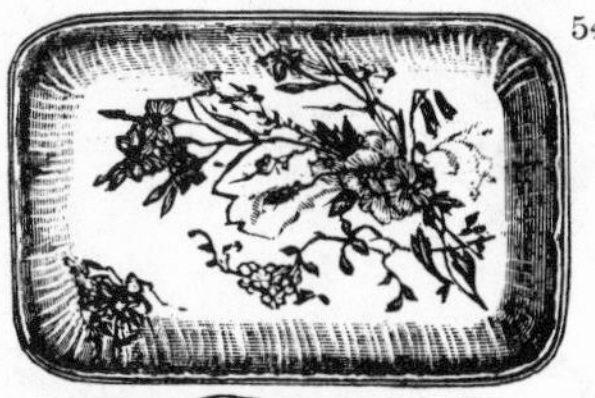

54278 Bon Ware Ice Cream Dish, 12 inches long, 8 in. wide. The small round dishes, No. 54272 are intended to match, and if used with this large dish make an elegant and inexpensive set.
Each.........$0.65

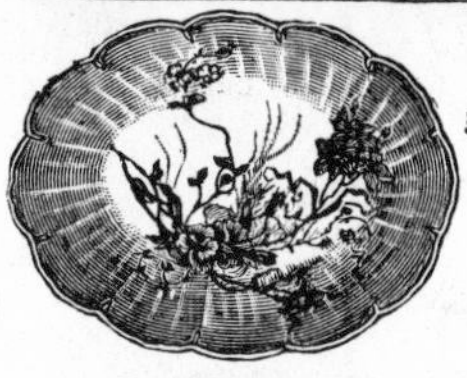

54280 Bon Ware Salad Dish, oblong and scalloped, 7 inches wide and 10 inches long.
Each......... .... $0.55

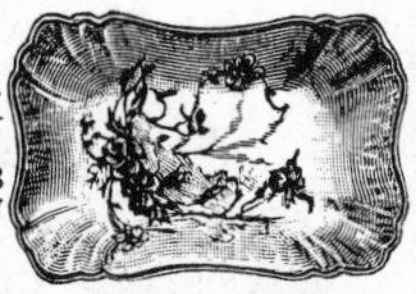

54282 Bon Ware Celery Tray. A very pretty shape; 9 inches long.
Each...... ....$0.33
Per dozen............. 3.57

Imported Cake and Fruit Plates.

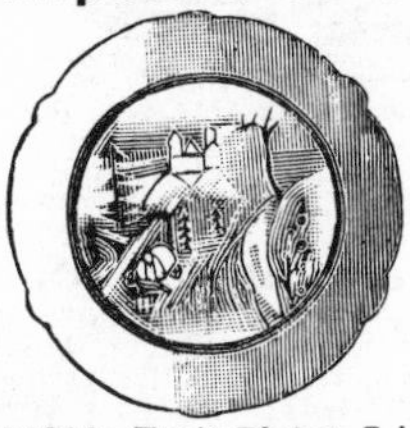

54306 Imported China Fruit Plate, 7½ inches across, fluted edges, tinted borders and hand painted centers; very neat and pretty goods.
Each..... ....$0.17
Per dozen............. 1.84

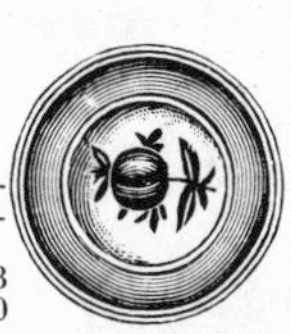

54310 Fruit Plates, 7 inches, Carlsbad china, decorated fruit in center, with assorted colored rims.
Each...........................$0.13
Per dozen........ .... 1.40

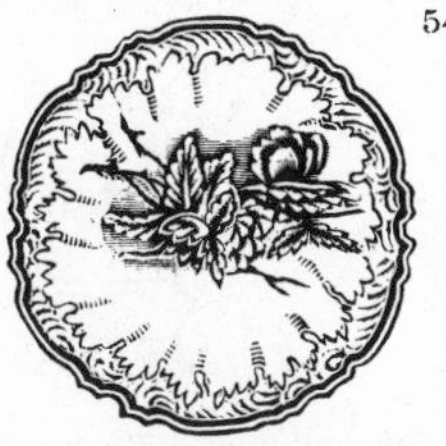

54315 Fine Imported China Fancy Edge Plate, richly gold trimmed, and decorated in the center with a bunch of yellow roses; the body of plate is a rich creamy white and contrasts beautifully with the gold and coloring. It measures 8½ inches in diameter and is large enough for a cake plate.
Each $0.30
Per dozen 3.24

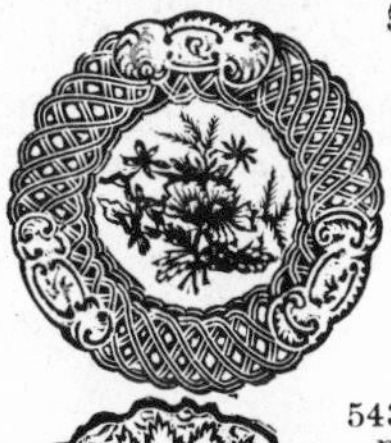

54317 Tea Plate of fine imported china; the edge is perforated and scalloped; it is decorated around the edge and border with gold, and in center with a cluster of flowers and ferns in their natural colors put on under glaze and warranted not to wear off. It measures 7½ inches in diameter. Each.............$0.25
Per dozen 2.70

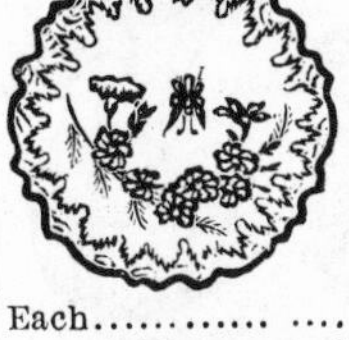

54320 Fancy scalloped Edge Imported China Bread and Butter plate. This is a remarkably handsome piece of ware and must be seen to be appreciated; the edge and border are neatly traced in gold, while the center is decorated by hand with flowers and sprays of grass in their natural colors. Order some; we are sure you will like them. Diameter, 6½ inches.
Each............ .....$0.20 Per dozen..........$2.16

Fancy Japanese Plates.

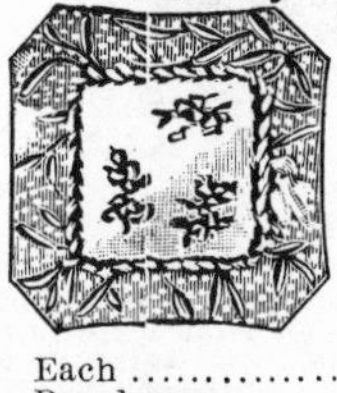

54330 Fine Japanese Fruit, Cake or Tea Plates, tinted and decorated in a very artistic manner. We cannot show these goods to good advantage by cut, as it does not bring out the fine and artistic manner of tinting and odd fashion of decoration. Try one—we are sure it will please. Plate measure, 6½ inches from one extreme edge to the other.
Each $0.40
Per dozen 4.35

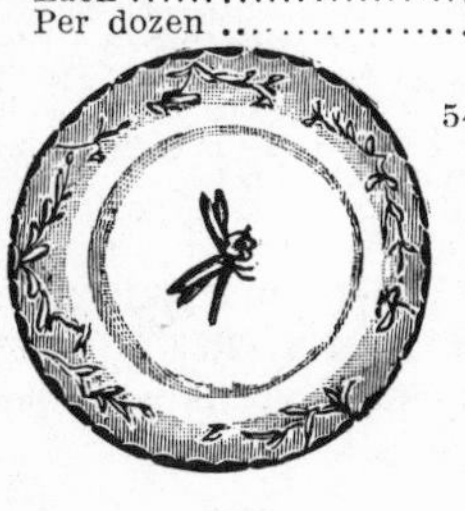

54340 Fancy Scalloped Japanese Cake Plate, very thin and transparent, handsomely tinted and decorated in rich subdued colors; must be seen to be appreciated. Measures 8 inches across.
Each $0.55
Per dozen 6.00

Plates—Continued.

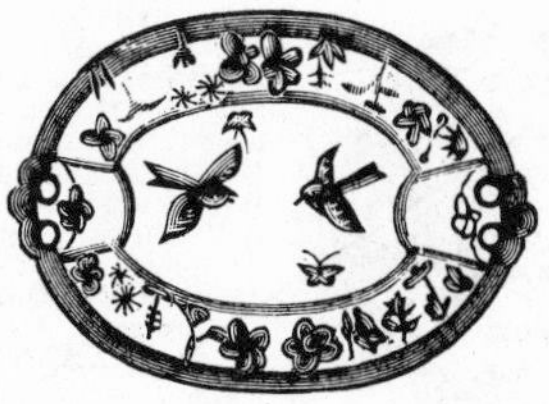

54350 Fancy Japanese Side Dish or Baker, tinted and decorated in a beautiful manner; measures 6 inches long, 4¾ inches wide.
Each $0.35
Per dozen..... 3.75

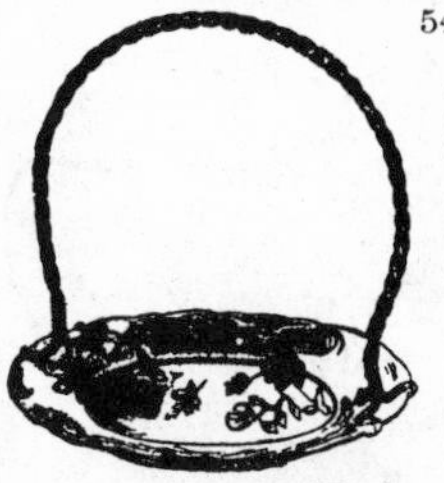

54360 Timberlake's Twisted Wire Plate Handles; fit all sizes of plates. A beautiful effect is produced by trimming with round silk cord (or narrow ribbon) wound in the grooves, with ribbon bows below. The handle is made of the best steel wire, with beautiful finish that holds its brilliancy. Our price is for handle only, no plate.
Each $0.10
Per dozen............. 1.05

Berry Sets.

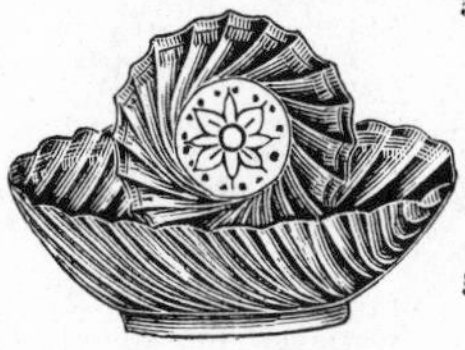

54410 Fine Imported China Berry Set, consisting of one large 8-inch dish and one dozen 4½-inch dishes of pure white china, profusely decorated with gold in a very neat and artistic manner.
Price, per set. $2.90

54412 Same as above, with 1 large and 6 small dishes.
Per set...............$1.75

54414 Fine Imported China Berry Set, very handsome shape; set consists of one 7-inch and one dozen 4½-inch dishes, decorated with pretty flowers and gold.
Price, per set......$2.15

54418 Same as above, with 1 large and 6 small dishes.
Price, per set.....$1.45

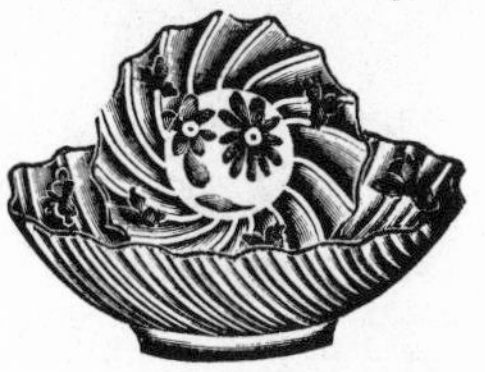

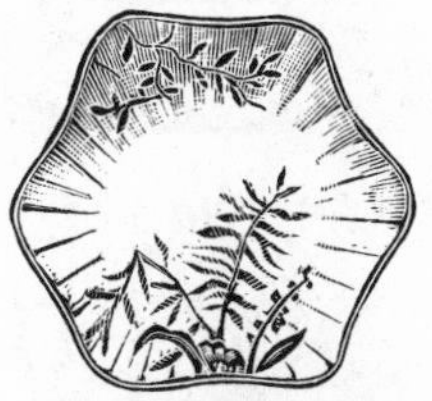

54420 Fine Imported China Salad Bowl, decorated in colors and by hand; measures about 7 inches across. This is a very handy dish, as it can be used for numerous purposes.
Each...................$0.40

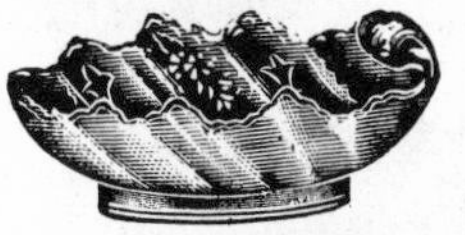

54421 Fine Imported China Salad Bowl, ribbed pattern, hand decorated and tinted: measures 9 inches across. Each......$2.25

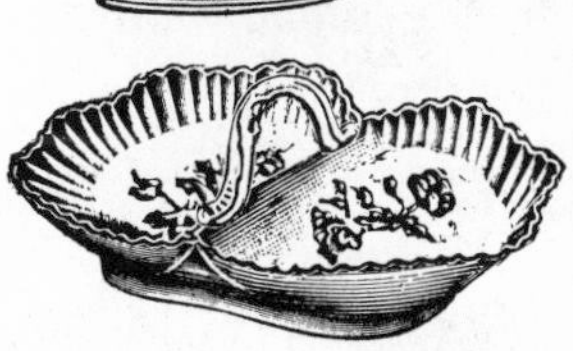

54423 Fine Imported China Hand Decorated and Gold Trimmed Cabaret; can be used for two kinds of cake or fruit; measures 12 inches across.
Each...... $1.50

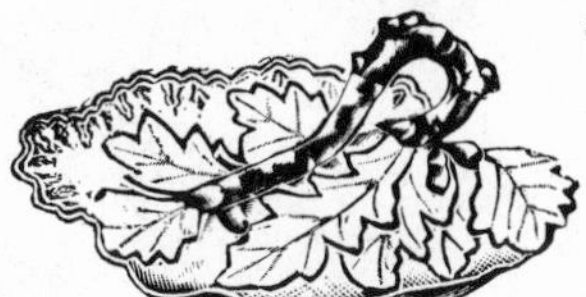

54424 Fine Imported China Richly Decorated and Tinted Cabaret; intended for serving two kinds of cake or fruit; measures 12½ inches across.
Each $2.00

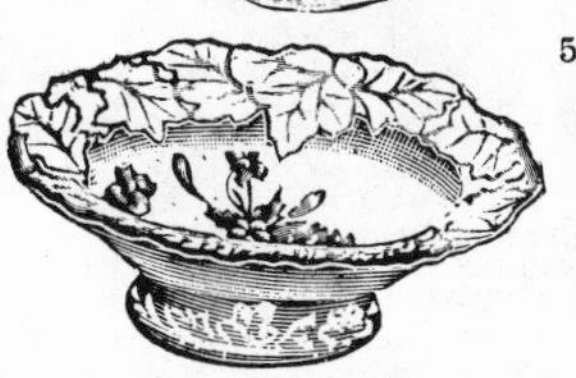

54425 Fine Imported China Fruit or Cake Stand, handsomely tinted and decorated with floral wreath center in natural colors, rich trimmed gold edges; measure 12 inches across and 5½ inches high.
Price $3.25

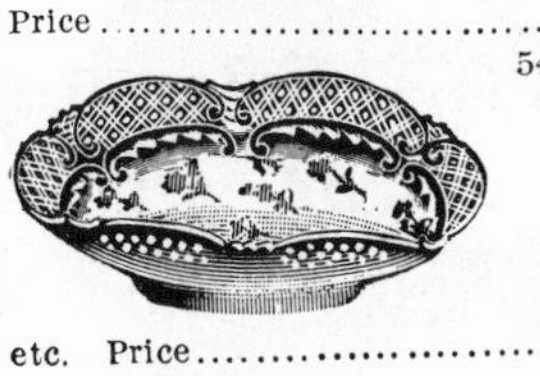

54426 Fine Imported China Comport, neatly tinted and decorated, gold trimmed, openwork edge, measures 10 inches across; can be used for berries, salads, fruit, cake, etc. Price................................$1.50

Tom and Jerry Sets.

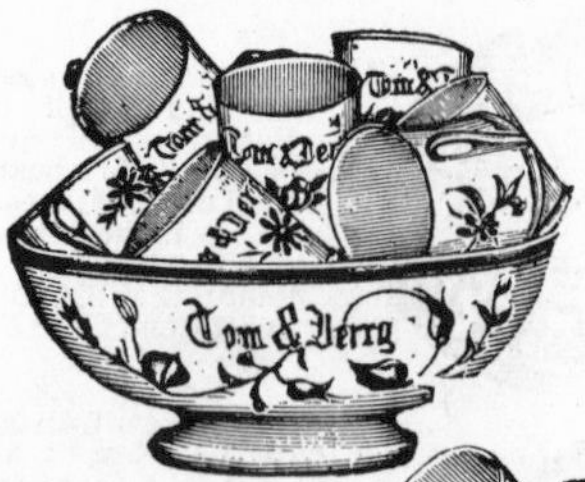

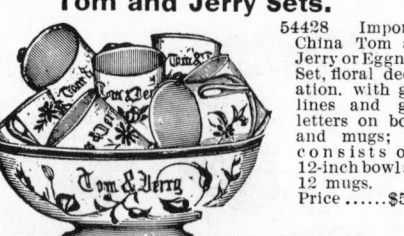

54428 Imported China Tom and Jerry or Eggnogg Set, floral decoration, with gold lines and gold letters on bowl, and mugs; set consists of 1 12-inch bowl and 12 mugs. Price......$5.00

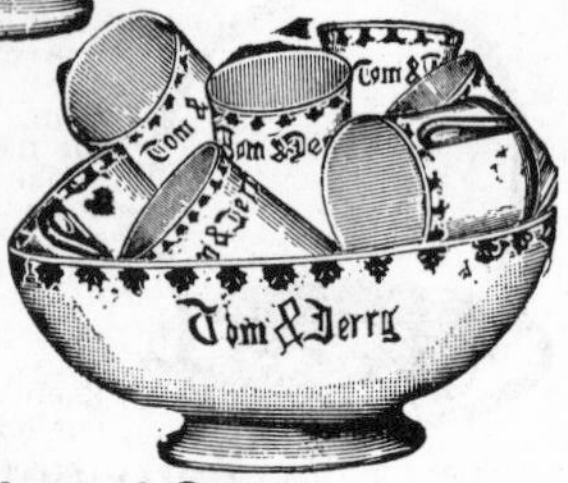

54429 Finest China, pure white body, with a neat scroll work border decoration in bright gold. The mugs and bowl are all decorated and gold lettered to match; set consists of 1 12-inch bowl and 12 mugs. Price........$5.00

Oatmeal Sets.

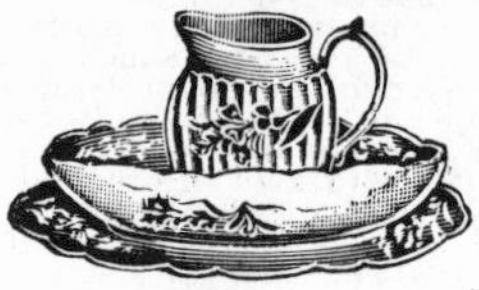

54432 Imported China Oatmeal or Mush and Milk Set; 3 pieces; cream pitcher, bowl and plate, new corrugated shape, decorated with sprays of small flowers and assorted colors. Per set $0.50

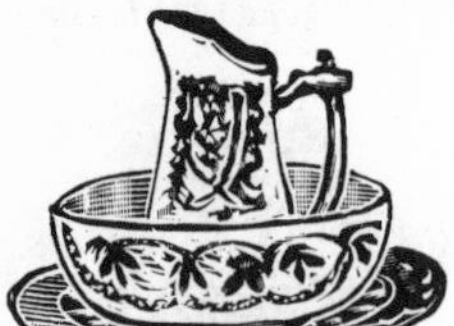

54434 Imported China Oatmeal or Mush and Milk Set, 3 pieces, cream pitcher, bowl and plate, decorated with panel flower design of rose buds in their natural colors. Per set....$0.50

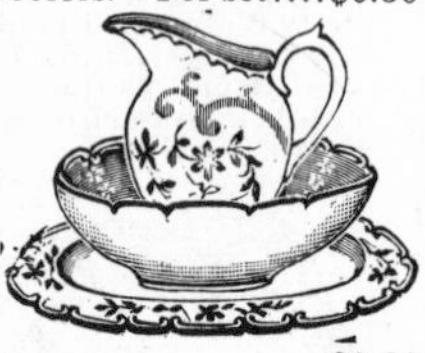

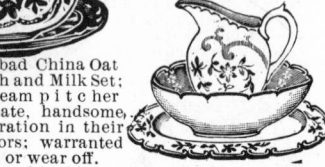

54435 Carlsbad China Oat meal or Mush and Milk Set; 3 pieces; cream pitcher bowl and plate, handsome, flower decoration in their natural colors; warranted not to wash or wear off. Price, per set of 3 pieces. $0.80

Fine Japanese Tea Services.

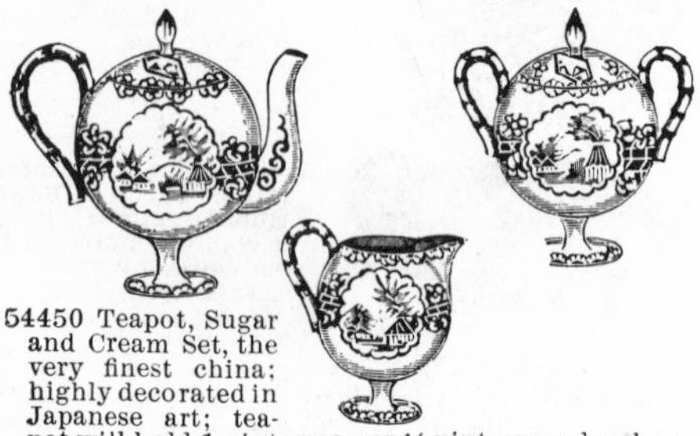

54450 Teapot, Sugar and Cream Set, the very finest china; highly decorated in Japanese art; teapot will hold 1 pint, creamer ½ pint, sugar bowl 1 pound. Price, per set.........................$3.00

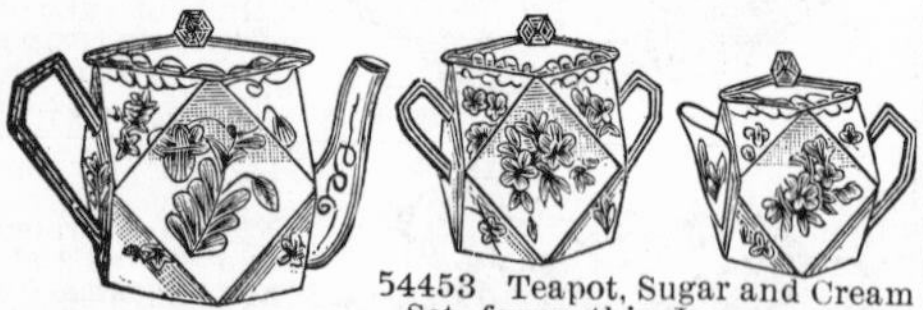

54453 Teapot, Sugar and Cream Set, fancy thin Japanese ware, highly decorated; capacity of teapot 1 pint, creame ½ pint, sugar bowl ½ pound. Per set..$2.00

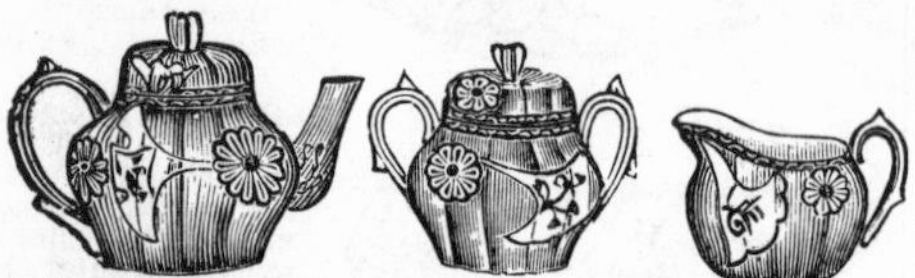

54455 Teapot, Sugar and Cream Set, highly decorated, fancy thin china; capacity of teapot 1 pint, creamer ½ pint, sugar bowl ½ pound. Price, per set $1.40

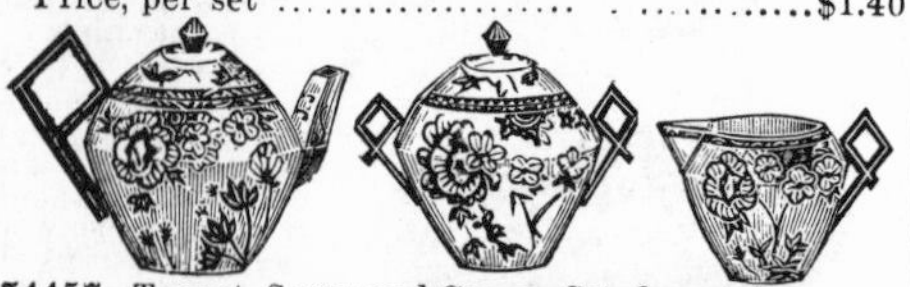

54457 Teapot, Sugar and Cream Set, fancy decorated thin Japan ware: capacity of teapot 1 pint, creamer ½ pint, sugar bowl ½ pound. Price, per set.......................................$2.00

Tea Sets—Continued.

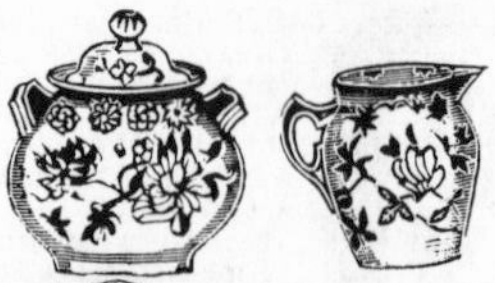

54467 Sugar Bowl and Creamer; same ware as 58465, but shape as shown in cut. Price, per set....$0.55

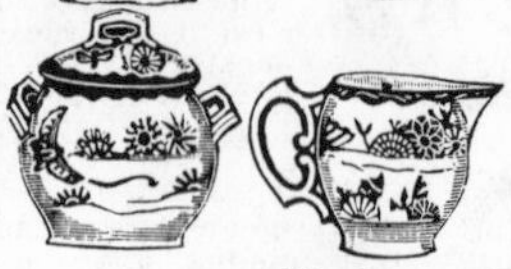

54470 Sugar Bowl and Creamer, same ware as 54467, but shape as shown in cut. Price, per set....$0.58

Tete-a-Tete.

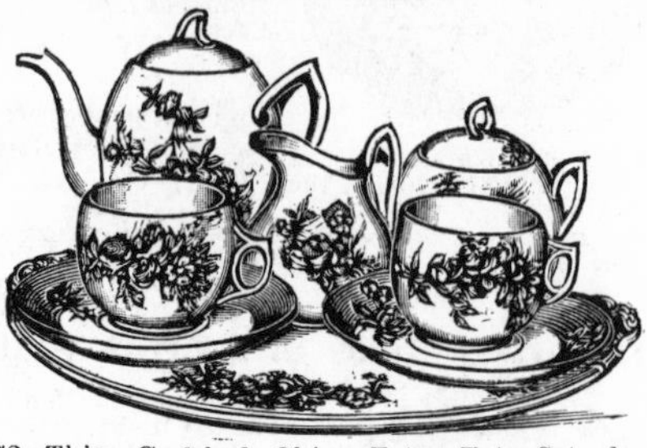

54472 Thin Carlsbad China Tete-a-Tete Set, decorated with spray of filled roses in pink color. Set consists of teapot, sugar bowl, cream pitcher and two teacups and saucers, on a fine china tray decorated to match. Per set...........$3.50

Flemish Stoneware Jugs, Etc.

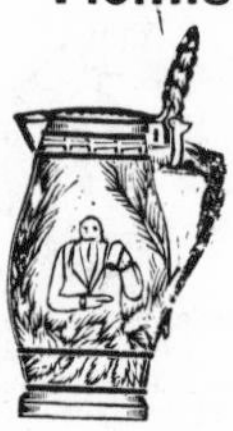

54473 Large Fancy Metal Covered Flemish Stoneware Pitcher, holds 5 pints and is artistically worked in very pleasing designs; very handy for ale, wine or in fact any liquid, as they are cool; besides, being provided with a cover, keep out dirt and insects. Price $2.00

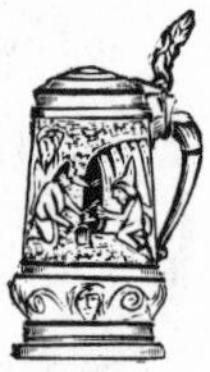

54474 Fancy Metal Covered Pitchers, tankard shape, artistically decorated, as shown in cut.

No.	1	2	3	4	5
Capacity	¾ pint.	1 pint.	1½ pint.	2 pints.	2½ pints
Price	$0.95	$1.05	$1.25	$1.40	$1.75

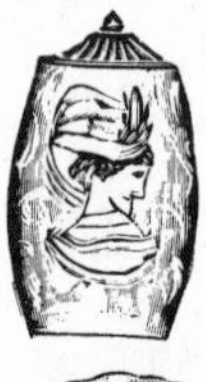

54476 Water Keg, fancy worked Flemish ttoneware. These are provided with cover, as shown in cut, and have nickel plated faucet, having rubber washer and nut, the nut to screw on from the inside of keg, making a complete and perfect fit.
2 gallon, each.......................$2.65
3 gallon, each.......................3.10
4 gallon, each.......................3.65

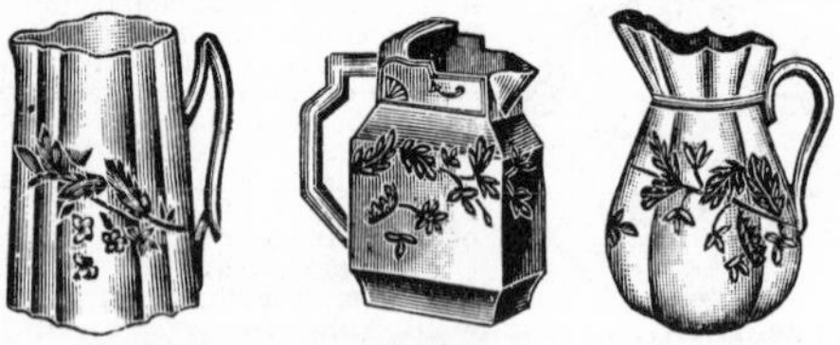

54490 54493 54497

54490 Imported China Cream Pitcher, new and pretty shape, decorated handsomely with flowers and leaves; will hold 1 pint.....................$0.28
54493 Same ware as 54490, but shape as shown in cut; will hold 1 pint...................... .25
54497 Same ware as 54490; but shape as shown in cut; will hold 1 pint .... .29

Blue Ware.

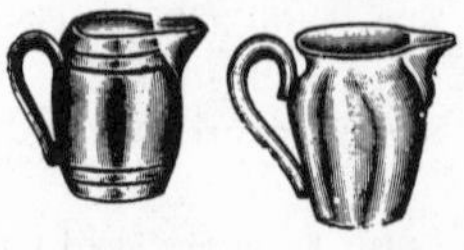

54500 54505

54500 Imported China Creamer, holds ⅓ pint, made of fine china and tinted a solid blue color, with gold handle and trimmings.
Each...............$0.25
Per dozen........ 2.70

54505 Same ware as 54500, but shape as shown in cut. Each........$0.25
Per dozen.............................. 2.70

WHAT is more attractive than a pretty face, a PRETTY DRESS and a PRETTY HAT? For the two latter qualities, look through our quotations.

Blue Ware—Continued.

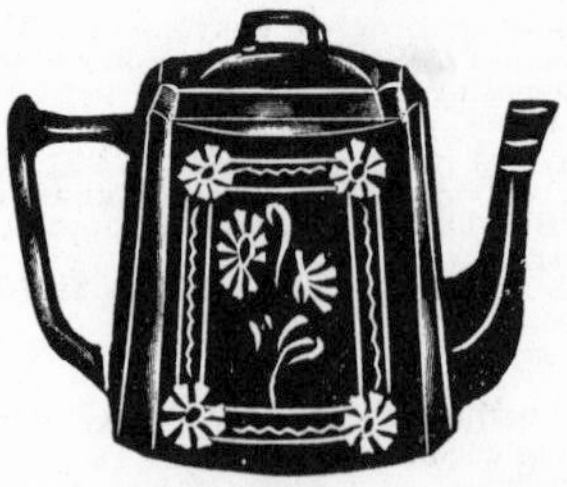

54512 Imported English Stone Porcelain Teapot, jet finish, body decorated and gold trimmed; square shape; has patent lock cover, which prevents it from dropping off when in use. Capacity, 3 pints. Price........ 1.00

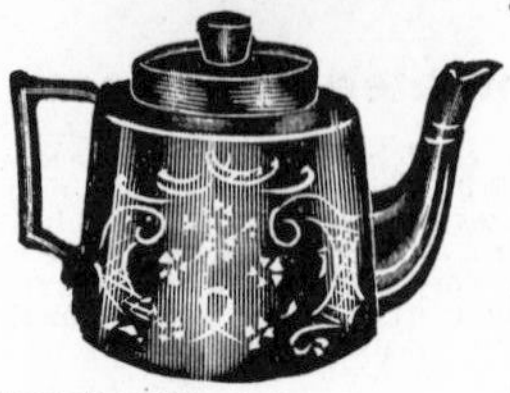

54516 Fancy Imported Teapot, English stone porcelain, jet finish, surface enameled and decorated with gold scroll work design and cluster of small pink flowers.
Capacity, 1½ pint. Price..........$0.70
Capacity, 2 pints. Price.........$0.80
Capacity, 2½ pints. Price...................... .85

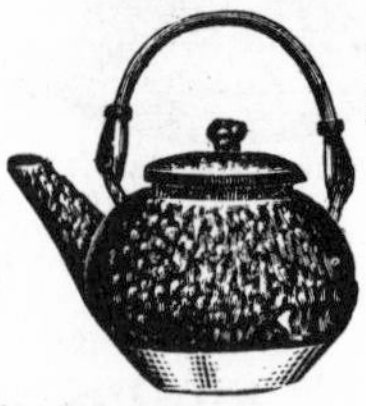

54518 Japanned Fireproof Water-drop Bamboo Handled Teapots; will draw and give tea a better flavor than any other teapot made.

No. 1, 3 pints, each.......................$0.20
No 2, 1 quart, each....................... .15
No 4, 1 pint, each....................... .10

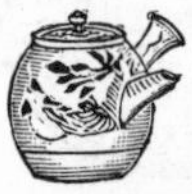

54520 Individual or Sick Room Teapot, has removable strainer, made of china and holds one cup of tea.
Each.......................$0.15

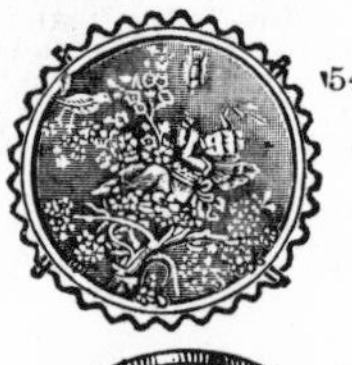

54523 Fancy Decorated Majolica Teapot Stand; 6 inches in diameter, wire back or frame, remarkably neat and strong.
Each.......................$0.13
Per dozen.................. 1.41

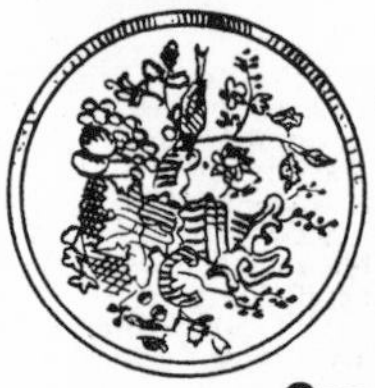

54527 Imported China Teapot Stand, delicately decorated and trimmed around the edge with a heavy gold line.
Price.......................$0.15
Price, per dozen.......... 1.70

Cracker Jars.

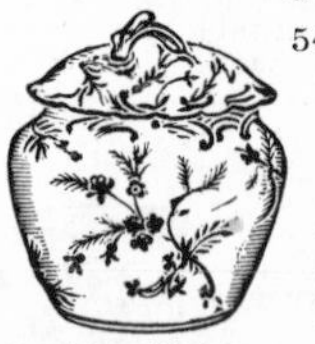

54535 This Fine Cracker Jar is made at the Royal Bon factory, Germany; the shape is exceedingly pretty, while the decoration is one of the neatest we have ever seen. It consists of clusters of small blue and red Flowers put on under the glaze, so that it is impossible to wash or wear off. It stands 6½ inches high and measures 5½ inches in diameter. Price.......................$1.00

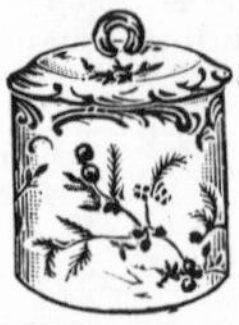

54540. This jar is made from the same material as No, 54535 and decorated in the same manner, but is of a different shape and much smaller. It stands 4½ inches high and measures 4¼ inches in diameter. Price.................$0.55

China Novelties and Blue Ware.

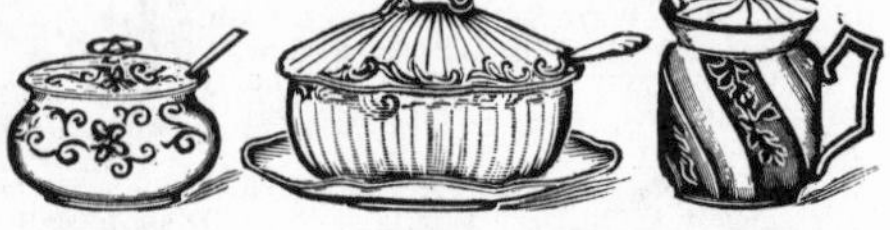

54552 54554 54556

54552 Imported China Mustard Pot, Cover and Spoon. Price.......................$0.23
54554 Imported China Mustard Pot, Cover and Spoon. This is a neat shell pattern, oblong in shape. Price .... .28
54556 Imported China Mustard Pot, decorated and gold trimmed, a very neat and dainty pattern. Price....................... .30

China Novelties—Continued.

54575 China Decorated Bon-Bon or Jewel Box; 5 inches long, 3 inches high. Each..........$0.30

54575   54580

54580 Same ware as No 54575, but shape as shown by cut, and 3 inches long by 2 inches high. Each, $0.25

54585 Imported China Hand-Decorated Candlestick, gold trimmed edges and handle. Each......$0.23 Per doz.... 2.49

54585   54590

54590 China Blue Ware Candlestick, tinted a beautiful dark blue, and elegantly gold trimmed. Each.....................$0.35

54593 China Blue Ware Ash Receiver, solid color of dark blue, gold trimmed. Each.....................$0.25

54593

54598 Japanese Match Safe, shape of suspended watch, very pretty, decorated and gold lined. Each............$0.20

Butter Dishes.

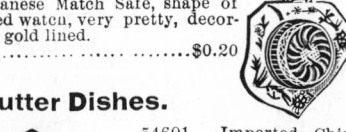

54601 Imported China Covered Butter Dish, fancy fluted shape, blossom spray decoration, in assorted colors. Price................$0.60

54603 Imported China Covered Butter Dish, with inside drainer, corrugated pattern, embossed scroll work, richly gold traced. Price................$1.00

54604 Imported China Butter Dish, new shell pattern; it consists of dish, cover and plate, the body of the ware, is pure white, profusely decorated with gold and colored flowers. It is of good size and will hold one pound of butter. Each................$0.85

54605—Child's Plate Sets, nursery rhymes; stone china, nicely decorated and lettered Something that is

54605   54610

sure to please the children; three pieces—cup, saucer and plate. Plate, 6 in; cup and saucer regular tea size. Per set.....................$0.25

54610 Child's Plates and Mug, stone china; plate, 6 inches; mug, good size; nicely decorated with alphabet and Bible pictures.   Each.   Per doz.
Plates................$0.10 $1.08
Mug...................06   .65

54620 Imperial German Bon Ware Bowls, decorated both in and outside with chrysanthemums in dark blue, put on under the glaze. We have them in the following sizes. Measurements are taken across top.   Each.   Per doz.
7-inch................$0.20 $2.16
6-inch.................15   1.62

Cuspidors.

54622 Earthenware Cuspidor, painted and decorated with leaves and flowers. Each............$0.20

Cuspidors—Continued.

54623 Earthenware Cuspidor, new shape, hand painted in natural colors. Each............$0.30

54625 Ironstone China Cuspidor, heavy and not easy to tip over, nicely decorated in floral design. Each......$0.48
54626 China Cuspidor, decorated

in very delicate frieze work. This is a cuspidor fit for the finest service. Each....$1.00

54625

54627 China Cuspidor, fluted and decorated with leaves and flowers in bright colors, and remarkably cheap. Each..............$0.70

54628 Fancy High New Shape Cuspidor, large size, stands 8 inches high and is nicely decorated. This is a very pretty article and a change from the ordinary every day style cuspidor.
Price.......................$ 1.00
Per dozen............ 11.00

54629 China Cuspidor, very light and handsome, novel shape and nicely hand-painted with floral designs. Price.....................$0.65

Chamber Sets Etc.

54632 China Croton or Washstand Set; consists of covered soap dish, brush vase and drinking mug; all the pieces are delicately decorated in colors. Per set.......................$1.00

54633 Fancy Soap Stand; the soap dish is decorated majolica, 8 inches long and 4 inches wide; the frame is made of iron wire, lacquered and bronzed, and is so formed that it will hold hair brush, tooth brush and comb; this is certainly a very useful as well as necessary article and remarkably cheap. Each........$0.20
Per dozen............. 2.16

54636 Round Decorated Soap Dish and Brush Stand with wire frame, japanned and bronzed; dish measures 5 inches across, and is large enough for a good size cake of soap. Each........$0.10
Per dozen............. 1.08

54638 English Decorated Chamber Set, ivory body, new shape, handsome panel and flower decorations, in either of the following colors: Brown, steel gray or dark green. Set consists of wash bowl and pitcher, chamber and cover, mug and soap dish, 6 pieces in all.
Price, per set.....................$1.98
Slop Jar without cover, as illustrated, to match. 1.60

Chamber Sets—Continued.

54641 English Stone China Chamber Set, nice shape and decoration of landscape scenery, in either brown, blue or pink. Set consists of the following pieces: Wash bowl and pitcher, chamber and cover, soap dish and mug.
Per set.....$2.20
Slop jar and cover to match.... 1.75

54646 The Perth Semi-Porcelain Chamber Set, manufactured by Doulton & Co., England. The shape is new, with a handsome printed decoration of cactus flowers in dark royal blue, or a light brown color; as will be noticed the composition of this set varies from the ordinary 6-piece set. It consists of the following pieces: wash bowl and pitcher, chamber and cover, soap slab and slop jar, without cover. Price, per set.........$4.50

Poppy.

54648 English Stone Pocelain Chamber Set, white body, underglazer decoration of poppy flowers and leaves in either pink, brown or slate colors. Set consists of washbowl and pitcher, chamber and cover, water pitcher, drinking mug, brush vase, soap dish with cover and drainer, 10 pieces in all. Price per set......$2.80
Slop Pail, with drop cover to match. 1.95

Royal.

54650 English Stone Porcelain Chamber Set, white body, underglaze decoration of printed flowers and leaves in either blue, brown or slate color. Set consists of washbowl and pitcher, chamber and cover, water pitcher, drinking mug, brush vase, soap dish with cover and drainer, 10 pieces in all. Price, per set.........$3.15
Slop Jar and cover to match...................2.10

Pearl.

54652 Genuine English Semi-Porcelain Ware, snow white body, handsome scroll work design, relieved with gold tracings. All the pieces match. Set consists of washbowl and pitcher, chamber and cover, slop jar and cover, water pitcher, drinking mug, brush vase, soap dish, with cover and drainer. 12 pieces in all.
Price, per set.....................$7.35

Chamber Sets—Continued.

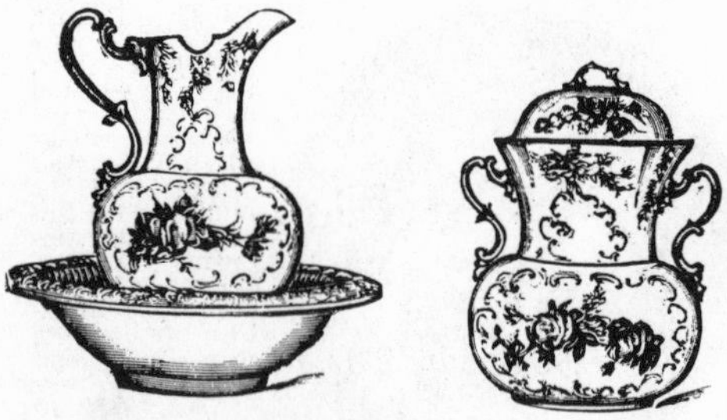

Triumph.

54654 Genuine English Semi-Porcelain Ware, handsome shape, pure white body with heavy, raised scroll work, illuminated with stippled gold and decorated with roses in blue, pink or green, all the pieces match. Set consists of washbowl and pitcher, slop jar and cover, chamber and cover, water pitcher, drinking mug, brush vase and soap dish with cover and drainer. 12 pieces in all. Per set.........$8 75

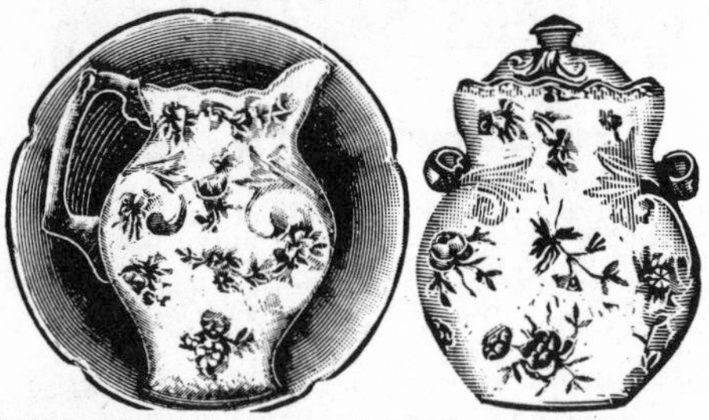

54656 Imported Chamber Set made of semi-porcelain and artistically decorated with small bunches of flowers in dark blue colors and stippled gold work. This is one of the handsomest shapes ever brought out and is entirely new. All the pieces are decorated to match; set consists of ewer and basin, chamber and cover, slop jar and cover, soap dish cover, and drainer, water pitcher, mug and brush vase; 12 pieces in all. Per set........ ....$9.50

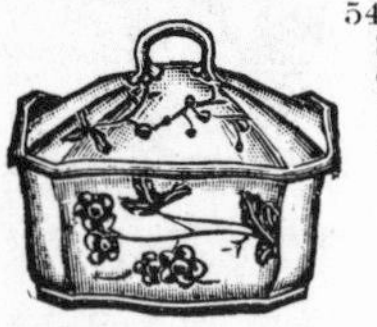

54658 Fancy China Decorated Soap Dish with cover and drainer. The decoration is a peach blossom put on by hand and neatly tinted. Price......$0.40

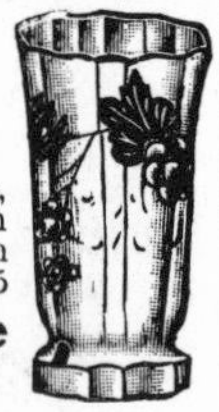

54659 Fancy China Decorated Brush Vase, decorated by hand with a peach blossom in natural colors, guaranteed not to wash or wear off. Price.... . ...$0.35

Genuine English White Stone China.

Climax Shape.

We sell nothing but the first quality of English stone china. We are bound to keep to the front and have adopted the climax shape, a new and very pretty design. Although this is more expensive than the old shape, our prices will be found as low as heretofore.

RULE FOR MEASURING.

Bowls, tureens, oval dishes, nappies, etc., are taken from one extreme edge to the other. Plates, platters, etc., are taken from outer rim on one side to inner rim on opposite side.

We have taken considerable pains to give the exact weight of stone china ware, so that hereafter but little trouble need be taken to find the weight of an order.

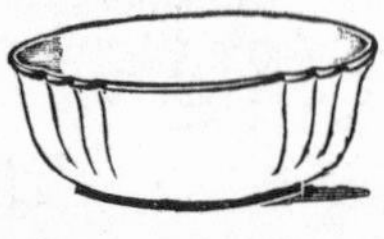

54700—

Size, inch.	Weight. oz.	Each.	Per doz.
5	12	$0.09	$1.00
6	16	.11	1.25
7	23	.14	1.51
8	29	.20	2.26
9	42	.27	3.00
10	53	.35	3.75

Nappies are convenient dishes, the small ones for bowls, etc., and larger ones for bake dishes.

Tea, Dinner and Soup Plates.

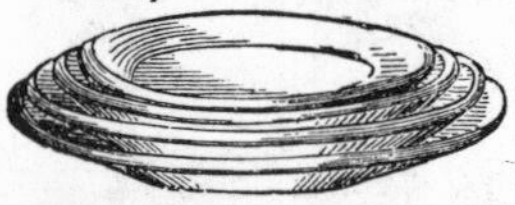

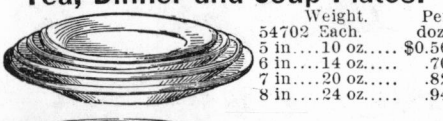

54702	Weight. Each.	Per doz.
5 in	10 oz	$0.56
6 in	14 oz	.70
7 in	20 oz	.82
8 in	24 oz	.94

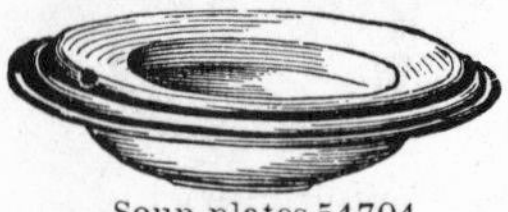

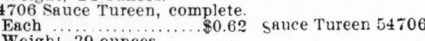

Soup plates 54704

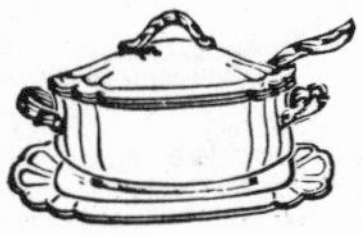

Sauce Tureen 54706

54704 7 in. Per doz.....$0.82 Weight, 14 ounces.

54706 Sauce Tureen, complete. Each ....$0.62 Weight, 39 ounces.

Chinaware—Continued.

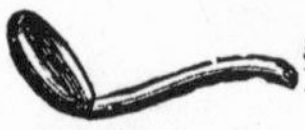

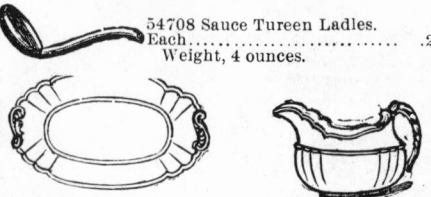

54708 Sauce Tureen Ladles. Each............................ .20 Weight, 4 ounces.

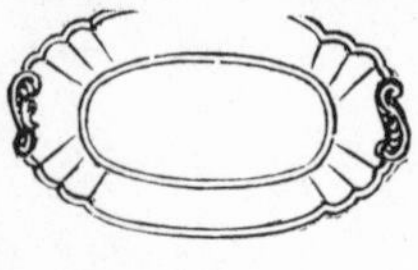

54710

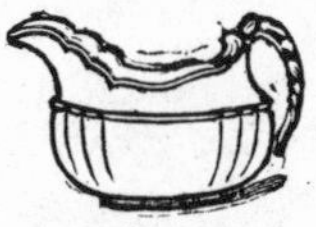

54712

54710 Pickle Dishes, assorted styles. Each.......$0.15 Weight, 16 ounces.

54712 Sauce Boat. Each.......................... .19 Weight, 14 ounces.

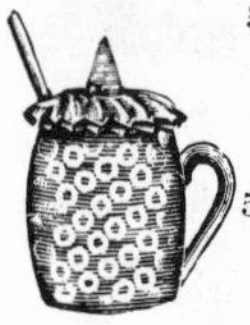

54715 China Mustard Pot and Spoon, similar to cut with delicate floral decoration. Weight, 6 ounces. Each.................$0.15 Per dozen.... .... 1.68

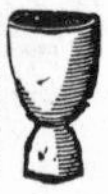

54717 Egg Cups, double. Per dozen............. .95

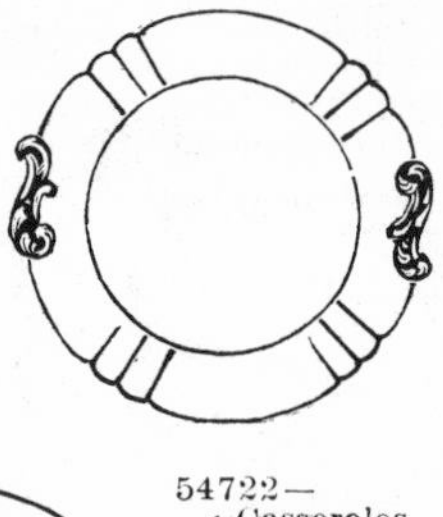

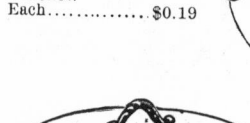

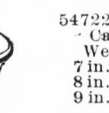

54720 Bread Plate, 8 inches. Each..............$0.19

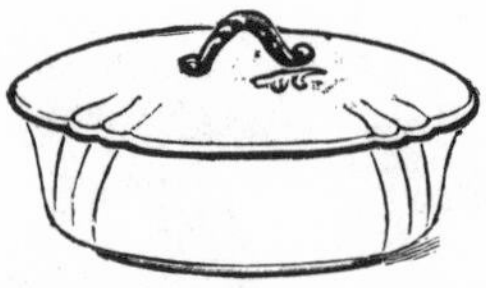

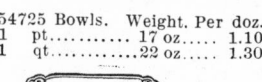

54722—Casseroles

	Weight	Each.
7 in.	49 oz	$0.55
8 in.	59 oz	60
9 in.	69 oz	.67

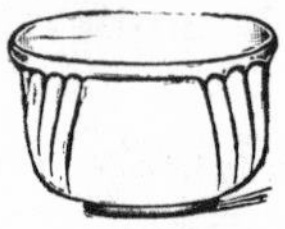

54725 Bowls.

	Weight.	Per doz.
1 pt	17 oz	1.10
1 qt	22 oz	1.30

Bowls.

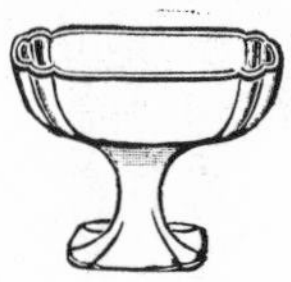

54727 Comport or Fruit and Cake Stand. Each.$0.54

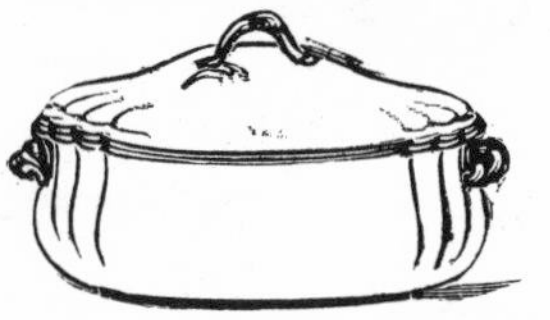

54730 Covered Dishes.

	Each.
7 inch, weight, 42 oz	$0.45
8 inch, weight, 49 oz	.52
9 inch, weight, 64 oz	58
10 inch, weight, 67 oz	.65

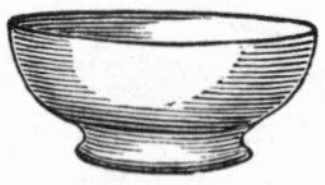

54731 Oyster Bowls, "Thick," 1 pint; weight, each, 22 oz. Per dozen............$1.10 1 quart, weight, each, 27 oz. Per dozen.... .... 1.30

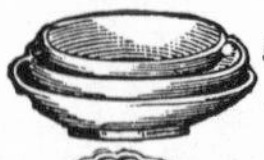

54732 Ice Cream Dishes, round sides, 4 inches, weight, each, 8 ounces. Per dozen.....................$0.35

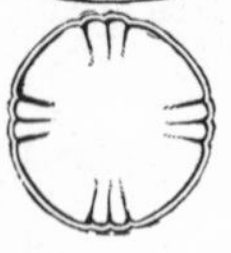

54734 Sauce Dishes, straight sides, 4 inches; weight, each, 4 ounces. Per dozen.......................$0.37

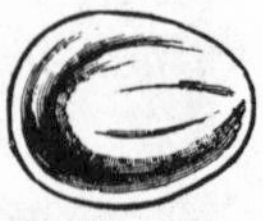

54736 Oval Nest Eggs; weight, 1 oz. each. Per dozen.....$0.30

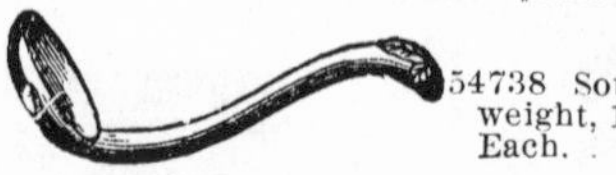

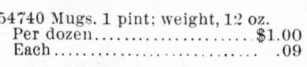

54738 Soup Ladles; weight, 18 ounces. Each. $0.39

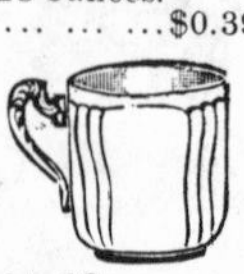

54740 Mugs. 1 pint; weight, 12 oz. Per dozen.......................$1.00 Each............................ .09

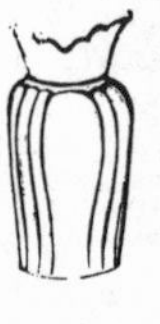

54745 Brush Vases; weight, 13 oz. Each $0.35

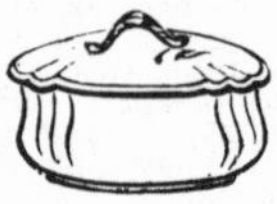

54747 Covered Soap Dishes, oval, loose drainers; weight, 25 oz. Each... ......$0.35

Chinaware—Continued.

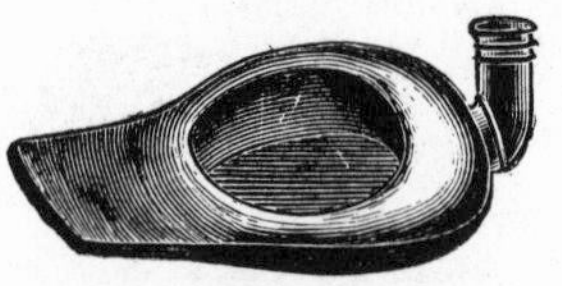

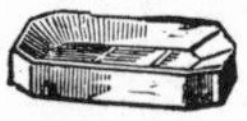

54750 Soap Slabs; weight, 9 oz. Each.......$0.07

54751 White Granite Invalids' Bed Pan. Each.. 1.00

White Stone China.

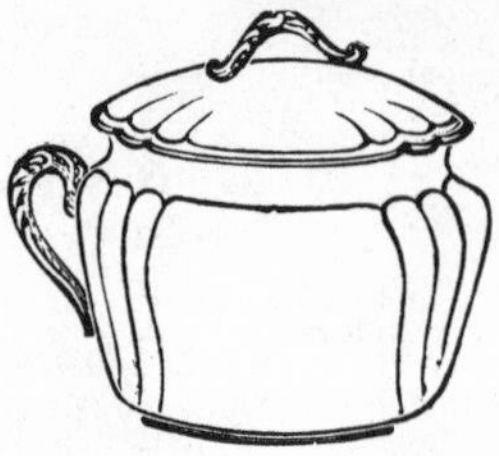

54752 Chambers, covered, medium. 5 lbs......... $0.52

54754 Chambers, uncovered, medium. 3½ lbs. $0.38

54755 Chambers, covered, large, 6 lbs. $0.65

54757 Chambers, uncovered, large, 3½ lbs. $0.45

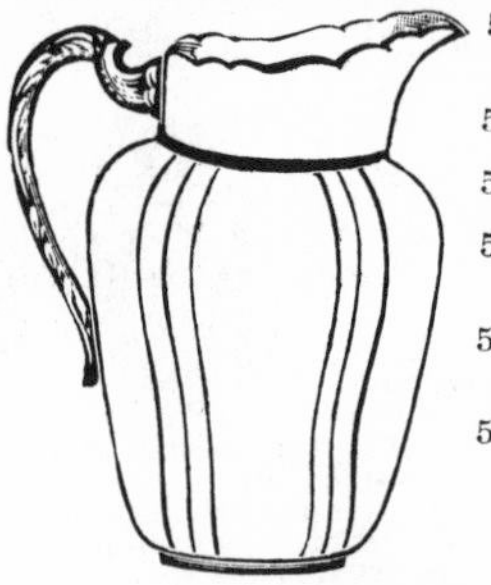

54766-71

54765 Wash Bowl and Pitcher, medium size. Each...............$0.90

54766 Chamber Pitcher, only medium $0.60

54768 Wash Bowls only medium...... .....$0.48

54769 Wash Bowl and Pitcher, large. Each...............$1.10

54771 Chamber Pitchers only, large. Each...... ....$0.65

54773 Wash Bows only, large. Each.. .... $0.50

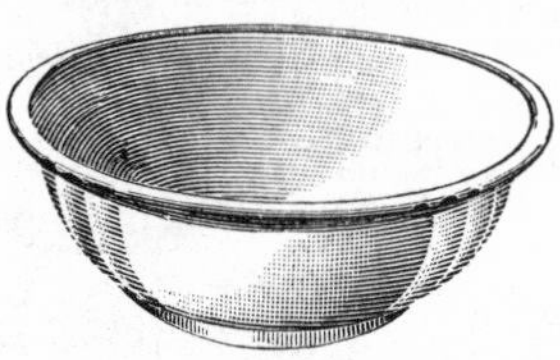

54768-73

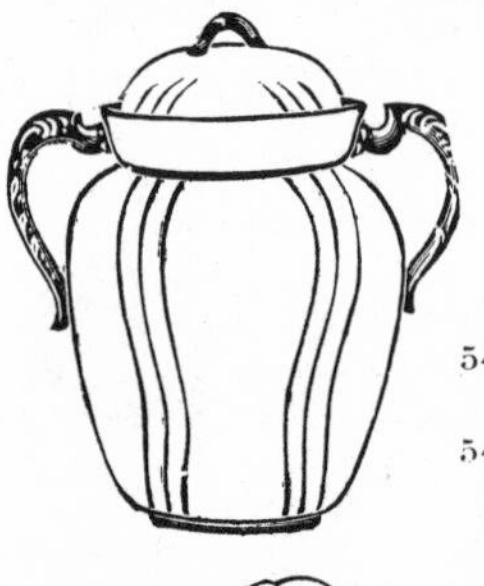

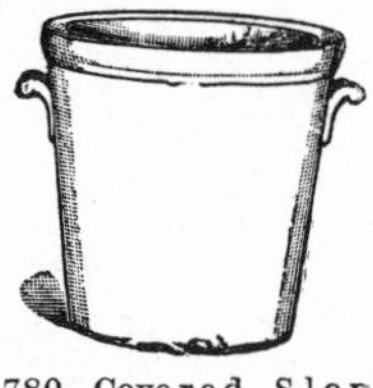

54780 Covered Slop Jar, very large. Each........... $2.25

54782 Covered Slop Pail, medium. Each.. ... .$1.50

Pitchers.

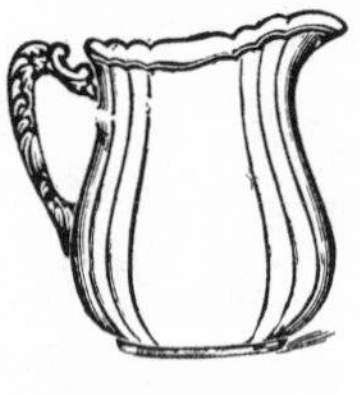

54785—

	Weight.	Each.	Per doz.
1 pt.	14 oz.	12c.	$1.25
1½ pts	16 oz.	14c.	1.55
1 qt.	26 oz.	16c.	1.95
2 qts.	36 oz.	28c.	3.10
3 qts.	48 oz.	43c.	4.65
4 qts.	64 oz.	62c.	6.75

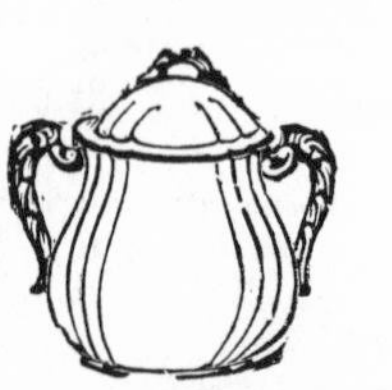

54790 Sugar Bowls 1 quart, Each..........$0.35

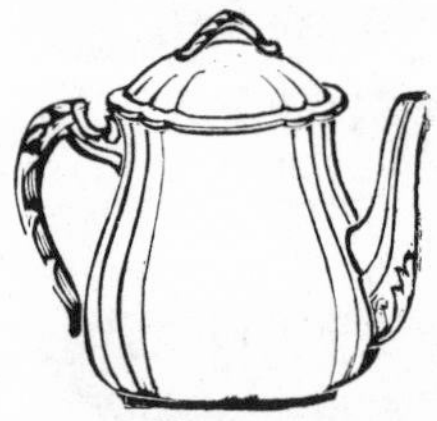

54792 Teapots, 1 qt. Each $0.40

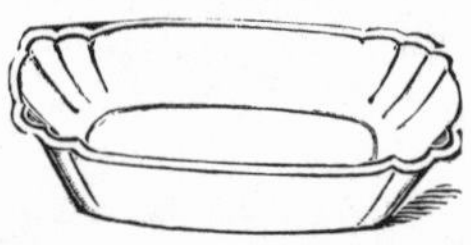

54800 Bakers.

Size	4 in.	5 in.	6 in.	7 in.	8 in.	9 in.	10 in.
Weight	9 oz.	10 oz.	11 oz.	14 oz.	18 oz.	28 oz.	32 oz.
Each	8c.	9c.	1 c.	14c.	22c.	28c.	35c.
Per doz	88c.	$1.00	1.25	1.55	2.26	3.0	3.72

Chinaware--Continued.

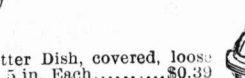
54802 Butter Plates, individual.
Per dozen........$0.28

54803 Butter Dish, covered, loose
drainer, 5 in. Each.......$0.39
Weight, each, 30 oz.

54805 Coffee Cups and Saucers,
with handles. Per set of 6 cups
and 6 saucers (wt., per set. 7½
lbs.) Per set.............$0.65
54809 Tea Cups and Saucers with
handles. Per set of 6 cups and
6 saucers (wt., per set, 6½ lbs.)
Per set $0.57
54812 Coffee Cups and Saucers
with handles. Per set of 6 cups
and 6 saucers (wt., per set. 7½
lbs.) Per set.............$0.65
54815 Without handles. Per set
(wt., per set, 7½ lbs.). $0.56
54820 Tea Cups and Saucers, with
handles. Per set of 6 cups and 6
saucers (wt., per set, 6½ lbs.) Per set....$0.57
54825 Without handles. Per set (wt., per set, 6 lbs.) .48

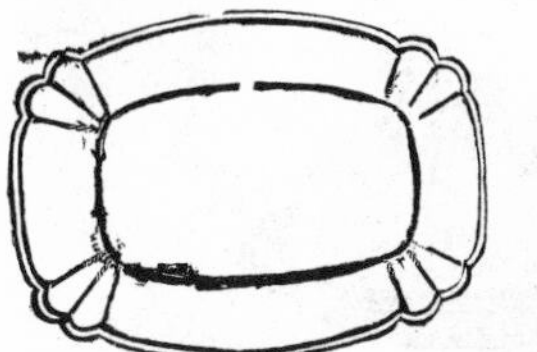

54830 Platters.

	Wt.	Each.
8 in.	1 lb.	$0.12
9 in.	1½ lb.	.15
10 in.	2 lb.	.22
11 in.	2½ lb.	.25
12 in.	2¾ lb.	.32
14 in.	4 lb.	.49
16 in.	6 lb.	.78
18 in.	7 lb.	1.00

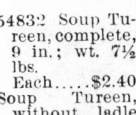

54832 Soup Tureen, complete,
9 in.; wt. 7½ lbs.
Each....$2.40
Soup Tureen, without ladle
or stand, 9 in.;
wt. 4 lbs.
Each....$1.35

Brown or Rockingham Ware.
Rockingham Pitchers.

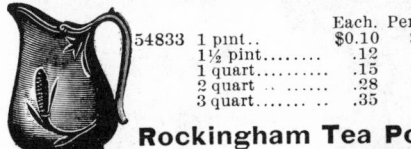

54833		Each.	Per doz.
	1 pint..	$0.10	$1.08
	1½ pint........	.12	1.30
	1 quart..........	.15	1.62
	2 quart.	.28	3.00
	3 quart........ .	.35	3.78

Rockingham Tea Pots.

54834	Each.	Per doz
1 pint.........	$0.25	$2.74
1 quart.........	.28	3.00
3 pint..........	.30	3.24
2 quart.........	.40	4.32
3 quart.........	.45	4.86

Rockingham Oval Bakers.

	Each.	Per doz.
54835 Oval Bakers, 7 inch..........	$0.08	$0.87
Oval Bakers, 8 inch..	.10	1.08
Oval Bakers, 9 inch..	.12	1.30
Oval Bakers, 10 inch.	.14	1.52
Oval Bakers, 11 inch.	.17	1.84

Rockingham Pie Plates.

		Per doz.
54836 Pie Plates,	8 inch.	$0.72
Pie Plates,	9 inch.	.85
Pie Plates,	10 inch.	.91

Yellow Ware.

Each.
54837 Yellow Chambers,
uncovered, small.......$0.12
54838 Yellow Chambers,
uncovered, medium.... .20
54839 Yellow Chambers,
uncovered, large........ .25
54840 Yellow Chambers,
covered, large............. ...$0.35
54841 Yellow Chambers, covered, medium..... .30

Yellow Nappies.

54842 Nappies, yellow, 6
inch. Each........$0.07
Per dozen... .... .76
Nappies, yellow, 7-
inch. Each........ .09
Per dozen........ .98

	Each.	Per doz.
Nappies, yellow, 8 inch........	$0.11	$1.19
Nappies, yellow, 9 inch	.12	1.32
Nappies, yellow, 10 inch........	.14	1.52
Nappies, yellow, 11 inch........	.16	1.73
Nappies, yellow, 12 inch.	.20	2.16

Yellow Bowls.

The larger sizes of yellow bowls will be found very
useful as mixing bowls.

			Each.	Per doz.
54843	Yellow Bowls,	½ pint............	$0.04	$0.44
	Yellow Bowls, 1	pint............	.05	.54
	Yellow Bowls, 1	quart.	.07	.76
	Yellow Bowls, 1½	quart.........	.10	1.00
	Yellow Bowls, 2	quart.........	.19	2.06
	Yellow Bowls, 3	quart.........	.28	3.00
	Yellow Bowls, 4	quart.........	.40	4.32
	Yellow Bowls, 6	quart.........	.45	4.86
	Yellow Bowls, 8	quart.........	.65	7.02
	Yellow Bowls, 10	quart............	1.00	10.80

Jardinieres.

54850 Fancy Jardinieres'
made of fancy clay, hand-
somely decorated and
tinted. These make very
handsome window orna-
ments when filled with
plants or ferns.
6-inch....... $0.25
7-inch....... .35
8-inch.... .45

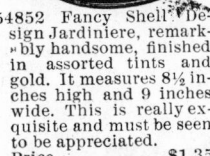
54852 Fancy Shell De-
sign Jardiniere, remark-
ably handsome, finished
in assorted tints and
gold. It measures 8½ in-
ches high and 9 inches
wide. This is really ex-
quisite and must be seen
to be appreciated.
Price.......... ....$1.35

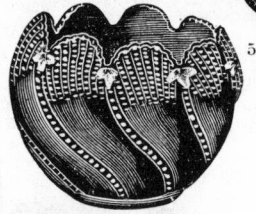
54854 Fancy Shell De-
sign Jardinieres, finished
in the same exquisite
manner as 54852; design
is well shown by cut.
Price.......... ...$1.35

Flower Pots.

54856 Fancy Flower Pots,
finished in white and red
and gold leaf. Our price is
for pots and saucers. We cannot sell them separate.
5 inch, per dozen.....$1.75
6 inch.... .... 2.75

54858 Flower Pots, soft burnt
light buff color. We do not
sell less than one dozen.
Per dozen.
Pots only, 3 inch..........$0.20
Pots only, 4 inch......... .30
Pots only, 5 inch......... .50
Pots only, 6 inch......... .60
54860 Flower Pot Saucers, soft
burnt, light buff color. We do
not sell less than one dozen.
3 inch, per dozen......$0.20
4 inch, per dozen.. ...... .20
5 inch, per dozen..$0.30   6 inch, per dozen... .30

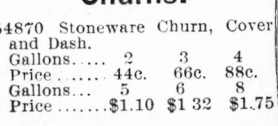
54862 Hanging Baskets, soft
burnt, light buff color,
scalloped and fluted.
Each $0.20
Per dozen......... 2.16
54864 Chain for Hanging
Basket, complete.
Each.................$0.10
Per dozen.......... 1.08
54866 Fancy Hanging Bask-
ets, finished and painted
white and red and trimmed
in gold leaf, C. R. B.
Price, each........... $0.35

Churns.

54870 Stoneware Churn, Cover
and Dash.

Gallons....	2	3	4
Price......	44c.	66c.	88c.
Gallons....	5	6	8
Price......	$1.10	$1 32	$1.75

Boston Bean Pots.

54872 Boston Bean Pots, for baking
beans; in two sizes, with covers.
½ gallon, each...........$0.25
Weight, each, 3½ lbs.
1 gallon, Each.............. .35
Weight, each, 5¼ lbs.

Fire Clay Beef Roasters and Stew
Pans.

54882 Fire Clay Beef
Roasters will cook meats
of any kind, either in
the oven or on the top of
a range. The clay from
which they are made is
thoroughly fireproof and
can be placed in the hot-
test fire without danger
of breaking.

11 inches in diameter, each.................$0.35
13 inches in diameter, each.................... .60

54884 For cooking cereals or
any kind, such as oatmeal,
cracked wheat, etc., it has
no equal; neither has it for
boiling bread and milk,
cooking meat and vege-
tables. It will neither discolor nor change the flavor
of any article cooked in it
in any manner.
Price, one gallon........ ...$0.20
Price, half gal. .... .15

54885 Stoneware Butter Jars,
light brown color.

Size.....	1lb.	2lb	4lb	8lb.	16lb.
Each ..	5c.	6c.	8c.	12c.	24c.
Per doz,	60c.	70c.	90c.	$1.40	$2.75

54886 Stoneware Water Cool-
ers, with cover and wooden
faucet, complete.

Size..3 gal.	4 gal.	6 gal.	8 gal.
Price..65c.	80c.	$1.15	$1.45

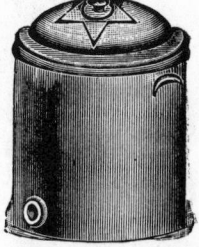
54887
54887 Stoneware Chicken
Fountains; cannot easily be
upset. Keeps the water free
from dirt, as the poultry cannot step into it.

Size........................	½ gal.	1 gal.	1½ gal.
Price, each.....	20c.	32c.	45c.

54886

Fruit Jar Rubbers.

54889 Rubber Rings, for Mason fruit jars; will
fit pint, quart and half gallon size. Per doz..... .06 
54890 Earthenware Money Bank, same
shape, size and color as an orange.
Each.........................$0.05
Per dozen.......................... .55

GLASSWARE DEPARTMENT.

Genuine Rich Cut Glass.

The demand for cut glass has induced us to offer a few items of the best value to be found. The Strawberry Diamond and Fan "Cutting" is one of the most beautiful patterns, every piece splendidly cut and highly polished in the most brilliant manner. It is as useful as silverware and is more beautiful to offer for presents, wedding gifts, etc. The illustrations are not expected to do it justice, as it is beyond comparison with the ordinary pressed glassware.

54900 Cut Glass Salad Bowl, 8 inches in diameter, genuine Strawberry diamond and fan cutting. Each.....$6.65

54901 Cut Glass Salad Bowl, 7 inches in diameter. Each.....................$5.35

54903 Cut Glass Berry or Fruit Bowl, 8 inches in diameter, genuine strawberry diamond and fan cutting Each.....$5.35

54904 Cut Glass Handled Nappie Jelly or Olive Dish, genuine strawberry diamond and fan cutting. Each.....................$2.75

54905 Cut Glass Vinegar Bottle, genuine strawberry diamond and fan cutting. Each...$1.70

54906 Cut Glass Table Tumbler, genuine strawberry diamond and fan cutting. Each...................$0.42

54907 Cut Glass, Sugar and Cream Tete-a-tete or afternoon tea size; genuine strawberry diamond and fan cutting Per set.....$5.35

55017 Genuine cut glass strawberry diamond and fancutting. Globe shape, silver plated top, salt and pepper shakers. Each, 25 cents, per dozen.............$2.70

Czarina Crystal Pattern.

An exact imitation of the celebrated strawberry diamond and fan genuine cut glass pattern, which came into prominence during the World's Fair. The shapes are very pleasing and novel. Color of glass pure crystal. We guarantee finish to be the very best obtainable. This is undoubtedly the handsomest pattern out this season and one we feel sure will please you in every respect.

55018 Table set, containing four pieces as illustrated. Per set...........$0.55

55021

55019 Czarina Half Gallon pitcher. Each....$0.40
55021 Czarina Half Pint Table Tumblers. Per dozen.........$0.68

55019

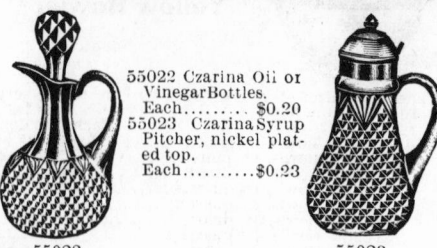
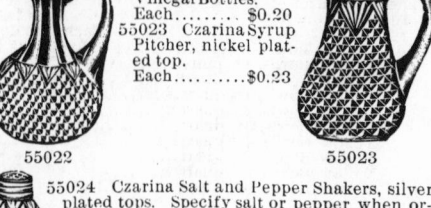

55022   **55023**

55022 Czarina Oil or Vinegar Bottles. Each.......$0.20
55023 Czarina Syrup Pitcher, nickel plated top. Each.........$0.23

55024 Czarina Salt and Pepper Shakers, silver plated tops. Specify salt or pepper when ordering. Each...........................$0.10
Per dozen..............................1.08

55026 Czarina Berry Dishes.

Inches in diameter.	Price, each.
6 inches	$0.10
7 inches	.17
8 inches	.22
9 inches	25

55027 Czarina Small Berry Nappies, used generally with large size nappies or dishes.

Inches in diameter.	Price, per doz.
4 inches	$0.40
4½ inches	.54
5 inches	.65

55030— Czarina Celery Tray. Each..$0.20

55031 Czarina Cake Salver. 9 inch, each..$0.30
10 inch, each.. .35

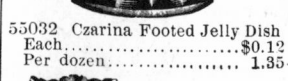

55032 Czarina Footed Jelly Dish Each...........................$0.12
Per dozen..................... 1.35

55034 Czarina Flower Vases.

	Each.	Per doz.
7 inches high	$0.15	$1.62
8 inches high	.18	1.95
10 inches high	.30	3.24

Czarina Ruby and Crystal Pattern.

The shapes in this pattern are the same as our crystal czarina. We recommend this pattern above all others to lovers of colored ware. The ruby is put on in a very pleasing manner, aside from this the prices are lower than any other pattern ever produced in ruby and crystal colors.

55035 Ruby and Crystal Czarina Table Set, same number of pieces and same shape as No. 55018. Per set.................................$1.05
55036 Ruby and Crystal Czarina Half Gallon Pitcher, for illustration see No. 55019. Each................................... 1.00
55038 Ruby and Crystal Czarina Half Pint Tumblers, see No. 55021 for illustration. Per dozen............................ 1.35
55039 Ruby and Crystal Czarina Oil or Vinegar Bottles, see No. 55022 for illustration. Each'.................................. .35
55040 Ruby and Crystal Czarina Salt and Pepper Shakers plated top,, specify salt or pepper, when ordering see No. 55024 for illustration. Each.... .... .18
Per dozen............................ 1.95
55042 Ruby and Crystal Czarina 8-inch Berry Dishes, see No. 55026 for illustration. Each.. .40
55043 Ruby and Crystal Czarina 4½-inch Berry Nappie. See No. 55027 for illustration. Per dozen........................... 1.25
55046 Ruby and Crystal Czarina Celery Tray, for illustration see No. 55030. Price ...r....... .50

St. Bernard Pattern.
Crystal Engraved.

We aim at all times to offer the latest and most pleasing patterns. As a novelty the St. Bernard pattern cannot be equaled. All the covered pieces have handles. The figure, as illustrated, is the image of a St. Bernard dog. The plain surface is decorated with a very attractive engraving, which with part of surface in figured relief, makes the effect a very pleasing one. All the pieces are extra large, and finished by the latest and best process known to manufacturers.

55048 St. Bernard Engraved Table Set Containing four pieces as illustrated. Per set.........$0.75
55050 St. Bernard engraved berry bowls.

Diameter	Price.
6 inches	$0.20
7 inches	.30
8 inches	.35

55052 St. Bernard Engraved Covered Berry Bowls.

Diameter	Price.
7 inches	$0.50
8 inches	.62

55054 St. Bernard Engraved Half Gallon Water Pitcher. Each..............$0.50

55056 St. Bernard Engraved Half Gallon Tankard. Each....$0.50

55059 St. Bernard Engraved Half Pint Tumbler. Per dozen $1.00

55060 St. Bernard Engraved Celery Holder. Each................$0.24

55063 St. Bernard Engraved 4½-inch Berry Dishes. Per dozen....$0.90

55067 St. Bernard Engraved Oil or Vinegar bottle. Each.... ......$0.22

Glassware—Continued.

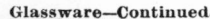

55068 St. Bernard Engraved Pickle Dish. Each.. $0.12

55069 St. Bernard Engraved Salt and Pepper Shakers, specify if salt or pepper is wanted. Each....................$0.08
Per dozen............................. .95

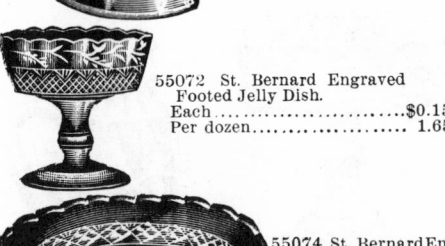

55071 St. Bernard Engraved Cake Salver, 10 inches across top. Each.......... $0.39

55072 St. Bernard Engraved Footed Jelly Dish.
Each...........................$0.15
Per dozen..................... 1.65

55074 St. Bernard Engraved Berry Nappie, 8 inches in diameter. Each...........$0.35

Alexis Pattern.

It is impossible for descriptive matter or illustrations to do this pattern justice. Nothing like it has been produced in glass heretofore and it is safe to say that nothing will ever come out to surpass it. To see the pattern is to admire it. Extra heavy, well made and not a seam to be found on any of the pieces; pronounced by everyone to be the best pattern ever manufactured in pure crystal glass.

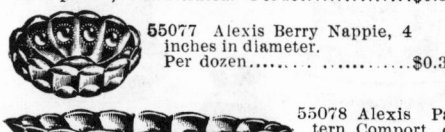

55076 Alexis Pattern Table Set, consisting of four pieces, as illustrated. Per set..............$0.54

55077 Alexis Berry Nappie, 4 inches in diameter. Per dozen........ ....$0.33

55078 Alexis Pattern Comport, or low footed Berry Dish.
Diameter. Price.
7 inches....$0.14
8 inches.... .19

55079 Alexis Pattern Berry or Fruit Bowls.
Diameter. Price.
7 inches....$0.22
8 inches.... .31

Glassware—Continued.

55080 Alexis Pattern Cake Salver, basket pattern, a new and stylish piece of glassware. Each...$0.40

55082 Alexis Pattern Half Gallon Water Pitcher, tankard shape. Each.. $0.39

55084 Alexis Pattern Half Pint Glass Tumbler. Per doz..$0.63

55085 Alexis Pattern Tall Celery Holder. Each...................$0.18

55086 Alexis Pattern Salt and Pepper Shakers, be sure and say if salt or pepper is wanted. Each....................$0.05
Per dozen........... .... .54

55087 Alexis Pattern Smooth Glass Lip and Metal Covered Syrup Pitcher.
Each.........................$0.25

55088 Alexis Pattern Oil or Vineger Botle. Each.............$0.15

55089 Alexis Pattern Pickle Dish. Each................$0.60

Excelsior Ruby and Crystal Ware.

This ware is without doubt the most attractive ever produced. The dark part as shown by cut is a deep ruby, the lower part a very sparkling crystal; there is no other article of table ware that can be compared with it; order a table or water set as a sample and we are sure you will want more.

55090 Excelsior Ruby and Crystal Table Set, consisting of covered butter dish, sugar bowl, cream pitcher and spoon holder.
Per set $1.00

55091 Excelsior Ruby and Crystal Berry Set, consisting of one 8-inch dish and six 4-inch dishes. Price...$1.10

55094 Excelsior Ruby and Crystal Berry Set, consisting of one 8-inch dish and twelve 4-inch dishes.....$1.65

55096 Excelsior Ruby and Crystal Half-gallon Pitcher, the prettiest jug made. Price....................................$1.00

55097 Excelsior Ruby and Crystal Tumblers to match pitcher. Per dozen...... ....1.50

55098 Excelsior Ruby and Crystal Celery holder. .50

Nellie Pattern Glassware.

55100 The Nellie Pattern Glass Set, neat and sparkling consists of butter dish, cream pitcher, sugar bowl and spoon holder. Per set,....$0.25
Per dozen sets..$2.80

55104 Nellie Bread Plate, 9 inches in diameter; this is a very useful article and remarkably cheap. Price...........$0.10

55106 Nellie Celery Tray, 8 inches long; can also be used as pickle dish. Price $0.15

55108 Nellie Square Fruit or Jelly Dish, 8 inches long. Price.................$0.12

55109 Nellie Footed Comport, a very convenient piece of tableware, 7 inches in diameter. Price............$).10

55110 Nellie 4-inch Footed Comport used as a berry dish. Per dozen..........$0.28

55111 Nellie Sauce Dish, 5 inches in diameter; used in conjunction with the footed comport makes a very pretty berry or ice cream set. Price.................... . . $0.27

55112 Nellie Footed Bowl, 7 inches in diameter, very useful as a cake or fruit stand. Price $0.22

55113 Nellie Half Gallon Pitcher; matches all the other pieces of Nellie ware. Price.... .... $0.23

55114 Nellie Pickle Dish, oblong in shape and measures 7 inches. Price........$0.05

55115 Imitation Strawberry and Fan Cut Glass Table Set. So close does this pattern resemble the genuine article that it is difficult to distinguish the difference at a distance of a few yards; set consists of four articles, as illustrated.
Per set...$0.55
Per dozen sets........ .... 5.95

Glassware—Continued.

55117— Imitation Cut Glass Berry Set; this is a very handsome pattern and resembles cut glass closer than any other pattern on the market; set contains one 8-inch and twelve 4-inch nappies. Price, per set.................$0.85

55118 Same as 55117, but contains one 8-inch and six 4-inch nappies. Price, per set...........$0.55

55120 Imitation Cut Glass Half Gallon Pitcher; a very handsome piece of glassware. Each.......$0.35

55122 Imitation Cut Glass footed Fruit Bowl; measures 8 inches in diameter. Price...........$0.35

Table Sets.

55124 The Boston Pattern Glass Set, a plain, neat and attractive table set; consisting of four pieces, as illustrated. Per set.................$0.30

55126 The Boston Table Set, Engraved. This is, we think, the best engraved table set in the market for the money. Price........................$0.48

55128 The Ray Table Set; exceedingly neat and attractive, very smooth and every piece perfect. Per set........................$0.50

IF CAREFULLY LOOKED THROUGH

This Catalogue will be found to contain more good things than ever before.

Glassware—Continued.

55130 Angelus Table Set, a neat attractive pattern in pure crystal glass; all the pieces well proportioned. Priced to suit the times. Per set.........................$0.49

55132 Holland Table Set; a low priced, desirable article, neat and attractiv in appearance. Per set........................$0.28

Parian Glassware "Ruby."

55133 The Parian Glass Assortment contains nothing but useful pieces of glassware, such as come constantly into use, as will be seen by the following articles They are all hand-made, of the very best quality lead-blown glass, and warranted perfect: Table set, consisting of butter dish, sugar bowl, spoon holder and cream pitcher; one large berry dish, six small sauce dishes, one half-gallon pitcher, six tumblers, one oil bottle, one syrup can, one small night lamp, three salt bottles, three pepper bottles and one toothpick holder. They are packed securely in a strong wooden box and weigh about 40 lbs. Per set........................$5.40

The Vigilant Glass Assortment.

Plain and engraved. Cuts show it engraved.

55134 This line of glassware is pronounced by experts to greatly excel all efforts in the past in the way of plain patterns, and is the acme of perfection. It is extra heavy, substantial and undoubtedly pretty; every piece is oil finished and perfect in shape. We pack them in assortments containing the following pieces: one butter dish, one sugar bowl, one spoon holder, one cream pitcher, six table tumblers, ½ gallon tankard, one 8-inch berry dish, six small sauce dishes, 1 7-inch footed bowl, one pickle dish, one celery holder, one molasses or syrup pitcher, one oil or vinegar bottle and three, each salt and pepper shakers.
Price, plain....................$3.25
Price, engraved..................4.50

Florence Assortment.

55136 Our Florence Assortment is composed of pieces of glassware most commonly used on the table. the pattern is pretty and substantial; all the pieces are finished perfectly smooth. The following is a complete list of the articles it contains: One butter dish, one sugar bowl, one cream pitcher, one spoon holder, one 9-inch berry dish, 12 small sauce dishes, one tall fruit bowl, one cake salver, six salt and six pepper bottles, one celery holder, six goblets, one half gallon pitcher and six table tumblers. It is packed by experienced packers in a good strong box, so that there is very little danger of breakage. Weight, 50 lbs. Price. **$3.60**

Hero Ruby and Engraved Assortment.

Glassware—Continued.

55137 Hero Ruby Engraved Combination Glass Assortment: the smooth part of this pattern is of a rich, ruby color, engraved in a pretty design, as shown by cuts. Engraving on ruby is very effective, as the part engraved is clear crystal, and the combination of crystal and ruby is very striking. Another thing that makes this pattern extra desirable is on account of the figured part being clear crystal, well finished glass; in fact, it must be seen to be appreciated. It is composed of the following pieces: One butter dish, one sugar bowl, one cream pitcher, one spoon holder, one large sauce or berry dish, six small sauce or berry dishes, one half gallon pitcher, six tumblers, one bon bon or candy dish, one vinegar or oil bottle, and three, each salt and pepper shakers. We pack it securely in a strong box, and it weighs ready for shipment about 35 pounds. Price..............$5.50

Water or Lemonade Sets.

55140

55140 Crystal Glass, consisting of 5 pieces, as follows: One-half-gallon pitcher, 2 tumblers, 1 bowl, and 13-inch embossed white metal tray. Per set..$0.62

55141 Engraved Water or Lemonade Set; consists of ⅛ gallon tankard shape jug, 6 engraved tumblers, and 13 inch hammered brass tray.......$1.95

55143 These handsome sets are made of the best quality lead glass and are decorated by hand with a beautiful flower and spray and warranted not to wash off. They are equal in quality and appearance to the finest imported ware that sells at three times the price we ask for these: set consists of half gallon pitcher, six tumblers and fine embossed white metal tray. Ruby, per set. $2.50. Green, $2.25.

Glassware—Continued.

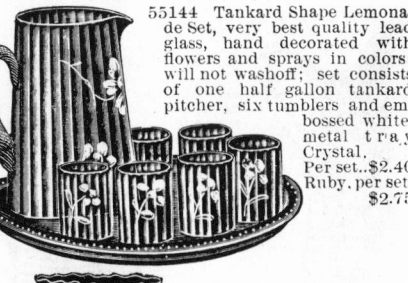

55144 Tankard Shape Lemonade Set, very best quality lead glass, hand decorated with flowers and sprays in colors; will not washoff; set consists of one half gallon tankard pitcher, six tumblers and embossed white metal tray. Crystal. Per set..$2.40 Ruby, per set, $2.75

55146 Polka Dot Thin Blown Colored Glass Water Set, globe shape pitcher with tumblers to match. Set is complete with ½-gallon pitcher, 6 tumblers and 1 13-inch embossed white metal tray. Ruby, per set...............................$1.50 Crystal opal or blue opal, per set.................. 1.00

55148

55148 A Combination of Ruby and Crystal; the crystal part has the effect of beautiful etching and makes the set appear, double the value at which we offer it: 1 ½-gallon pitcher, 6 tumblers, and 13-inch engraved pewter tray. Per set..$1.80

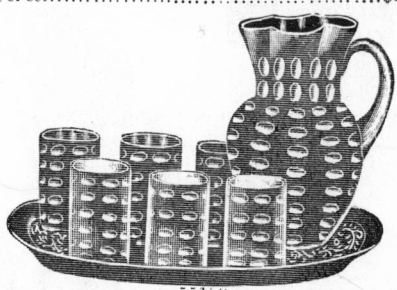
55150

55150 Water and Lemonade Set: a new pattern just out, made of fancy colored glass: the colors are very bright, and with raised scroll work design make it a handsome article for table service as well as a useful ornament. Set consists of ½-gallon pitcher, 6 tumblers, and 13-inch embossed white metal tray. Crystal opal or blue opal, per set.................$1.20 Ruby opal, per set................................ 1.50

55152

55152 Water or Lemonade Set, bottom half of each piece is pure crystal and upper part of a light ruby color. A very effective set at a medium price. All the pieces match; 6 tumblers, ½ gallon pitcher and 13-inch embossed white metal tray.

Ruby and crystal, per set	$1.75	Emerald, per set	$1.35
Violet, per set	1.35	Blue, per set	1.35

Water Pitchers.

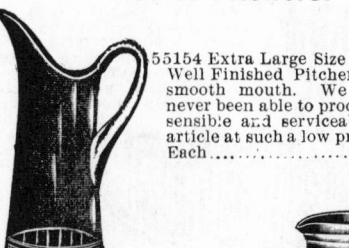

55154 Extra Large Size Heavy Well Finished Pitcher, good smooth mouth. We have never been able to procure so sensible and serviceable an article at such a low price. Each............$0.34

55156 Made of light blown glass resembling in every way the imported article. which costs more than double the money we ask for this. Entirely plain, smooth body, decorated with a neat engraving. Price............$0.37

55158 Glass Pitcher, finely engraved, very delicate and handsome pattern. The glass is of a very fine quality and heavy. Price.$0.65

55159 Hob-Nail, Half Gallon Pitcher, very strong, made of good, clear glass. Price.........$0.22

55162 Imitation Cut Glass, Half Gallon Water Pitcher, rich and sparkling, well finished and heavy. Price..........$0.39

55163 Plain Blown Glass Half-Gallon Water Pitcher, made of the very best material. and equal in every respect to an imported article. Each................$0.27

55165 Plain, Heavy Glass Water Pitcher, holds ½ gallon, heavy and well finished. We consider this the most sensible shaped pitcher on the market. Price.............$0.42

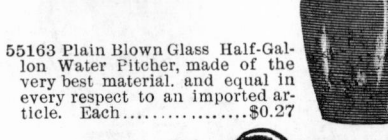

55166 Palace Water Pitcher, holds half gallon. This is one of the most sensible pitchers we have ever offered; it is almost strong enough to drive nails, and is attractive in shape. Each..$0.37

55167 Ruby and Crystal Half Gallon Pitcher. This is a very attractive as well as most useful piece of glassware. Price........................$1.10

Tumblers, Pressed and Blown.

55169

55169 Sand Blast Engraved and Etched Tumblers, pure lead blown glass, very thin, rings like a bell. The engravings are handsome and of assorted designs, six different patterns in every set. Sold by the dozen only and put up in paper box containing 12 compartments, which makes a convenient receptacle for them when not in use. Per dozen............ ....$0.78

55170   55171   55173   55174

55170 Tumblers, 8 ounces fluid measure, ornamented in bottom with a horseshoe, adding attractiveness to the article. Many tumblers of this design are supplied entirely unfinished and of poor color glass, whereas ours is an oil finished article and the color is pure crystal. Per dozen...........................$0.30

55171 Plain Table Tumbler, capacity, 7 ounces fluid measure, crystal glass of extra good quality and manufacture, imitation of cutting at bottom; the sides are nearly straight and give it a neat appearance. Per dozen................... .31

55173 Table Tumbler engraved with band as shown in cut, capacity, 7 fluid ounces. Aside from the band engraving this tumbler is in every respect like No. 55171. Per dozen.............................. .38

55174 Table Tumbler, handsomely engraved; the engraving is well executed. We offer this tumbler as the best, purest crystal glass, well finished and nattiest appearing article ever offered at the price. Per dozen...... .... .46

55176   55177   55178   55179.

55176 Perfectly Plain Table Tumblers, made of good glass and well finished; capacity, 7 fluid ounces. Per dozen.........................$0.37

55177 Glass Tumbler, capacity, 7 ounces, engraved with band as shown in cut. Per dozen........................ .... .39

55178 Engraved Water Tumbler, a very popular article, as it is the cheapest tumbler ever offered and is a pretty shape and handsome design of engraving. Per dozen...........................$0.56

55179 Table Tumbler, capacity, 10 ounces, fluid measure, made of extra heavy pure crystal glass with bottom strong enough to drive nails with, commonly called the neverbreak. Per dozen... .52

55181   55182   55183   55186

55181 Table Tumbler, capacity, 9 ounce, fluid measure; medium in weight, bottom is ground and polished. For a medium priced fancy tumbler we have nothing better to offer. Per dozen.$0.55

55182 Plain Table Tumbler, capacity, 9 ounces, fluid measure, bottom is ground and polished with sides nearly straight. Where an extra fine entirely plain table tumbler is desired at a medium price, this is the article to purchase. Per dozen...... .... .58

55183 Table Tumbler, capacity, 9 ounce, fluid measure, one of the best imitations of cut glass ever produced, and at our price should be very popular as it is well made with bottom ground and polished. Per dozen...................... .62

55186 Virginia Table tumbler, 9 ounce, fluid measure, the pattern is imitation of genuine block cutting, bottom is finished perfectly smooth. Per dozen...................... ....$0.65

Tumblers—Continued.

  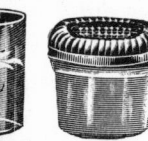

55187   55188   55190   55192

55187 Plain Blown Table Tumbler, capacity, 10 ounce, fluid measure, made of pure lead glass of egg shell thickness. This grade is growing more popular every day, and as we offer an extra good article at an extra low price we anticipate large sales. Per dozen.... ....$0.37

55188 This is in every respect like No. 55187 with the exception of a very neat engraving as shown in illustration. Per dozen........... .... .54

55190 Engraved Blown Table Tumbler, same in every respect with exception of engraving as No. 55188. Per dozen................................ .67

55192 Queen Squat Jelly Tumbler, glass cover, capacity, 10 ounces. This is the article to use in putting up jelly; it is much more desirable than with tin cover; they are made of strong, heavy glass. Per dozen................................... .64

55194 Ruby and Crystal Half Pint Tumblers; when used in conjunction with ½-gallon jug, No. 55167, makes a very handsome water set. Per dozen........ 1.85

55196   55197   55198

55196 Tin Top Jelly Tumblers, with covers which can readily be removed and put on; we mention this as many tin covers fit either too tight or too loose causing any amount of inconvenience. ¼ pint, per dozen.....................$0.29
½ pint, per dozen.................... .33

55197 Glass Tumblers, assorted colors, amber, crystal and blue, elegant goods for the money. Per dozen.............................. .47

55198 Blue Optic Half Pint Tumbler. Per dozen.................................. 1.35

Goblets. Plain and Engraved.

55199 Goblet, full size, good weight the pattern is pretty and good value at our price. Per dozen.................... ....$0.45

55200   55201   55202   55203

55200 Plain Goblet, extra large, plain bowl with stem imitation cut glass, equal value cannot be procured elsewhere. Per dozen.................$0.50

55201 A plain every day goblet, popular shape and size. Per dozen....................... .51

55202 Banded Goblet, a great favorite as it looks very rich and neat. Per dozen.................. .6

55203 Same as No. 55202, but with fancy engraving. Per dozen............................. .63

Goblets—Continued.

55205   55207   55209   55211

55205 Plain Water Goblet, heavy throughout, with extra heavy stem and foot. Per dozen...$0.52
55207 Railroad Goblet, sometimes called nut cracker, on account of its being made of extra thick glass. Per dozen.......................... .62
55209 This is another heavy goblet and is very popular; no reason why a dozen of these should not last a lifetime. Per dozen.................... .68

55211 Goblet, popular shape good weight; this goblet is used from Maine to California and is considered as staple as wheat. Doz-$0.95
55213 When you want an extra heavy, tasty goblet of medium size and good finish, order this one. Per dozen............$0.70
55215 The bowl of this goblet is extra large and the shape good; it is generally known as old reliable.

55213   55215   Per dozen.......... $0.79

Oil and Vinegar Bottles.

55217 Teutonic Vinegar Bottle, imitation of cut glass, finely finished, and at a very low figure.
Each.............$0.11
Per dozen 1.20

55219 Jeanette Vinegar Bottle, another fine imitation of cut glass, very heavy. Each.......$0.10
Per dozen.......... 1.15

55217   55219

55220   55222   55224

55220 Masonic Vinegar Bottle, new this season, handsome shape, not easily upset. Each.......$0.10
Per dozen.......... 1.16
55222 Ray Vinegar Bottle, nothing prettier made where a partly plain article is desired.
Each.........$0.09
Per dozen.......... .98

55226   55228

55224 A new pattern just out, made in fancy colored glass. The colors are very bright and with raised scroll work design make it a handsome article for the table service, as well as one that is useful; stopper is hand cut. Each. Per Doz.
Crystal opal....................$0.30 $3.24
Blue opal....................... .29 3.14
Ruby opal....................... .28 3.04
55226 Blown Glass, oil or vinegar, crystal glass cut stopper; plain glass of this description is always in good taste. Each................. .33
Per dozen....   3.57
55228 Blown Glass Ruby Oil or Vinegar Bottle, with cut stopper, a very rich looking bottle.
Each...................   .35

Pickle Jars.

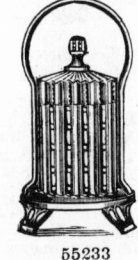

55230   55232   55233

Pickle Jars—Continued.

55230 Majestic Covered Pickle Jar, a very rich sparkling figured design resembling cut glass; nothing handsomer in the market. Each........$0.13
Per dozen..........................   1.41
55232 Pillar Pickle Jar and cover; fluted pattern of neat design. Each.................... .08
Per dozen..........................   .87
55233 The Nellie Crystal Glass Pickle Caster, with removable white metal handle; stands 10 inches high. Price....................$0.25
Per dozen..........................   2.75

Syrup Pitchers.

55235 Mascotte Syrup Pitcher; crystal glass, has patent spring cover made correct in shape to prevent dripping. Each....$0.10
Per dozen....... 1.15
55236 Syrup Pitcher crystal glass, attractive appearing, in large size.
Each.........$0.13
Per dozen....... 1.45

55235   55236

55238   55240   55241

55238 Syrup Pitchers, crystal glass, large size good shape, fitted with new patent spring cover nicely plated, nothing better for the money.
Each...........................$0.18
Per dozen..........................   1.95
55240 Syrup Pitcher, large size, nicely engraved, new patent spring cover, nicely plated.
Each..............................   .26
Per dozen..........................   2.85
55241 Blue Optic Syrup or Molasses Pitcher, has patent drip and nickel-plated top.
Price, each.........................$0.30

55243   55244   55246

55243 Scotch Decorated Syrup Pitcher, opal glass, fancy rib pattern, handsome floral decoration, good nickel plated top. Each,..........$0.34
Per dozen..........................   3.75
55244 Glass Lip Syrup Pitcher, clear crystal glass, medium weight, large size and has patent glass lip which still retains its popularity gained years ago; Brittania metal cover. Each........ .24
Per dozen..........................   2.65
55246 Syrup Pitcher in assorted colors, as follows: Opal, turquoise, canary and pink; patent dome, white metal cover. Each.................. .36
Per dozen..........................   3.89

Table Casters.

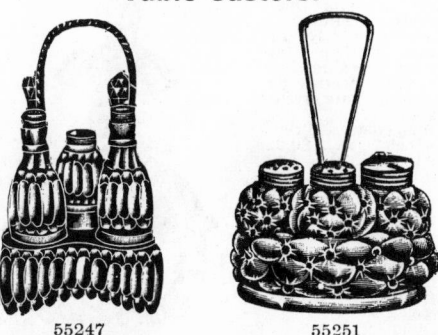

55247   55251

We Want Above all things to correct any mistakes which we may make, but we can't do it unless you tell us about them.

Casters—Continued.

55247 Huntington Five-Bottle Caster, made of strong clear glass with fancy wire handles, has 2 pepper, 2 vinegar and 1 mustard bottle; this is one of the prettiest casters ever offered at a popular price. Each.$0.65
Per dozen 7.25
55251 Three Bottle Table Caster, quilt pattern. Consists of pepper, salt and mustard bottles; the handle and tops of bottles are nickel plated. This is a very handsome article. We can furnish them in rose and turquoise blue. Price.......$0.75

55253

55253 Glass Caster, pepper, vinegar and mustard bottles, and place at top for tooth picks: a very pretty pattern. Each....................$0.45
Per dozen..........................   4.85

Pickle Dishes.

55255 Yale Pickle Dish, crystal glass, very heavy and of extra value.
Each.........$0.05
                         .54

Per dozen....................

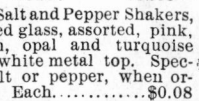

55257 I.H.C.Pickle dish a very handsome pattern very much resembling cut glass.
Each...........$0.06
Per dozen........ .66
55259 Crystal Glass Pickle Dish. 8 in. long, has handle as shown in cut. This is a remarkably pretty piece of glass ware. Each...$0.30
Same as No. 55259, but is trimmed on the edges with gold. Each...$0.60
55262 Crystal Glass Dish, oblong shape. Makes a nice low salad or canned fruit dish. This is a really pretty piece. 8 in.
Each $0.25

Mustard Pot.

55264 Glass Mustard Pot, dewdrop pattern, a very strong article.
Price..........................$0.08

Salt and Pepper Shakers.

55266   55267   55269   55271

55274   55277

55266 Salt and Pepper Shakers, colored glass, assorted, pink, lemon, opal and turquoise blue, white metal top. Specify salt or pepper, when ordering. Each...........$0.08
Per dozen.................. .87
55267 Salt and Pepper Shakers, made of crystal blown glass, extra large capacity, and well adapted for kitchen as well as table use. Specify salt or pepper when ordering. Each........... $0.06
Per dozen..........................   .65
55269 Teutonic Salt and Pepper Shakers, top is silver plated, body of crystal glass imitating to a remarkable degree a high price finely cut article. Each.......................... .10
Per dozen..........................   1.10
55271 Majestic Pattern Salt and Pepper Shakers, closely imitate cut glass, fitted with genuine silver plated top. Each......................... .12
Per dozen..........................   1.35
55274 Salt and Pepper Shakers, egg shape, handsomely tinted and decorated, the latest pattern out, finely nickel plated top. Each............ .25
Per dozen..........................   2.70
55277 Salt and Pepper Shakers, the celebrated tomato pattern, is handsomely decorated, and considered the prettiest shaker now in use.
Price.............................   .30
Per dozen..........................   3.24

55279   55281   55283

55279 Crystal Glass Salt and Pepper Shakers, beaded edge, metal top. Each...................$0.05
                                              .54
55281 Crystal Glass Salt and Pepper Shakers, very heavy, prism pattern, metal top. Each... .05
Per dozen..........................   .54
55283 Crystal Glass Salt and Pepper Shakers, large, sensible and heavy. Each................ .05
Per dozen..........................   .55

Salt Shakers—Continued.

55287   55289   55291

55287 Opal Fluted Salt and Pepper Shakers, a very handsome design. Each..................$0.08
Per dozen.................................. .90
55289 Alden Family Salt Shaker, with patent salt breaker. Each............................ .10
Per dozen..... 1.08
55291 Alden Individual Salt, with patent breaker, white metal top. Per dozen............ .97

Sugar Sifters.

55293 Sugar Sifter, large size, quilt pattern, very attractive and neat, nickel plated top. Can furnish either rose or turquoise blue. Price.............................$0.25
55295 Sugar Sifter, medium size, made of opalescent glass, with nickel plated top. Each.....$0.10
Per dozen..................... 1.10

55293   55295

Table and Individual Salts.

55297   55299   55301

55297 Crystal Glass Extra Heavy Table Salt.
Each.............................$0.06
Per dozen................................. .65
55299 Crystal Glass Medium Weight Table Salt.
Each..................................... .05
Per dozen................................. .54
55301 Crystal Glass Medium Weight Table Salt. cabinet pattern. Each....... .05
Per dozen................................. .52

55303   55304   55307

55303 Octagon Individual Glass Table Salt.
Per dozen................................. $0.16
55304 Diamond Individual Glass Table Salt.
Per dozen... .17
55307 Pavonia Individual Imitation Cut Glass Table Salt. Per dozen........................ .22

Condiment Sets.

55309   55311

55309 Majestic Condiment or Salt, Pepper and Vinegar Set, four pieces as illustrated.
Per set......................... $0.27
55311 Fan Two Bottle Caster, shaker salt and pepper bottle in a frame, very ornamental, made entirely of crystal glass. Each.................$0.17
Per dozen..... 1.90

Sugar Bowls.

55313 Crystal Glass Covered Sugar Bowl, pretty in design and very cheap.
Each.....................$0.08
Per dozen.. .... .87
55314 Empire Crystal Glass Covered Sugar Bowl, extra heavy and very large.
Each...................$0.15
Per dozen......... 1.65

55313   55314

Cream Pitchers.

55317 Crystal Glass Cream Pitcher, neat figured design, medium size.
Each....$0.06
Per doz. .65
55319 Teutonic Pattern Cream Pitcher. Your neighbors will say it is genuine cut glass; it looks so much like it. Each $0.10
Per dozen. 1.15

55317   55319

Butter Dishes.

55321   55322

55321 Boston Pattern Plain Crystal-Glass Covered Butter Dish, medium size, very cheap.
Each.........$0.10 Per dozen..........................$1.15
55322 Celtic Crystal Glass Covered Butter, attractive, both in style and price. Each.......... 1.07
Per dozen.................................. .76

Spoon Holders.

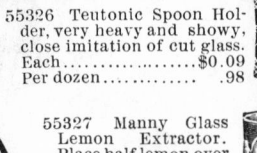

55324

55324 Crystal Glass Spoon Holder, nothing to equal it at the price. Each...$0.05
Per dozen............. .54
55326 Teutonic Spoon Holder, very heavy and showy, close imitation of cut glass.
Each....................$0.09
Per dozen............. .98

55326

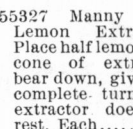 

55327 Manny Glass Lemon Extractor. Place half lemon over cone of extractor, bear down, give it a complete turn; the extractor does the rest. Each.....$0.10
Per dozen.............................$1.10
55328 Fawn Mug, made in crystal glass; something sure to please the little ones. Each........ .05
Per dozen................................. .55

55327   55328

Cake Salvers.

55331 Palace Glass Cake Salver, figured glass, extra heavy, strong and solid, 9 in. in diameter.
Each..$0.32

55333 Plain Glass Cake Salver, smooth surface, well finished, extra strong stem. Any of the following sizes in diameter.

	8 in.	9 in.	10 in.	11 in.	12 in.	14 in.
Each....	$0.23	$0.27	$0.30	$0.42	$0.55	$1.10

55334 Ruby and Crystal Footed Cake Salver, measures 9 inches in diameter. Price.....$1.35

Footed Bowls

55337 Charm Open Bowl, medium in weight, exactly correct in shape, finished like a mirror; a very effective design, in pure crystal glass.
Diameter.   Price.
8 inch..........$0.22
9 inch........... .30

55339 Charm Covered Bowl, a very useful table article used as a receptable for fruit, nuts, candy, cake etc.
Diameter.   Price.
7 inch.............$0.35
8-inch............... .40

55341 Engraved Open or Footed Berry or Fruit Bowl, measures about 7 inches across. A piece of engraved Tableware is always desirable.
Each..... ....$0.50

55343 Ruby and Crystal Footed Bowl, square shape used extensively on the table for fruit or cake. It measures 8 inches in diameter. Price.........$0.98

Berry Bowls.

55346 Engraved Covered Berry or Fruit Dish; will also answer as a honey or cheese cover.
Price....................$0.50

55349 Blue Optic Bowl, 9 inches in diameter; is used for salad, berries, or any such service.
Price, each.$0.50

55353

55351 Large Fruit or Berry Dish, made in crystal glass of such a good quality and so perfectly finished that it is difficult to distinguish from genuine strawberry, diamond and fan cut glass.

55351

Diameter.   Price.
9 inches......................................$0.17
11 inches................................... .22
55353 Small Sauce or Fruit Nappie made to match No. 55351 and when used together make an unusually handsome berry set.
Diameter.   Price per doz.
4 inches.....................................$0.38
5 inches..................................... .42

55354 Princeton Fruit or Berry Dish, 10 inches in diameter. This article was patterned after one of the most popular cut glass designs ever produced; well finished and strong.
Each...$0.50

55356 Princeton 5 inch Sauce Dish, used with No. 55354 makes a nice berry set, as they are a perfect match. Per dozen.............$0.45

55357 Square Berry or Fruit Bowl, 8 inches in diameter; can be used separate or with the small dishes, when it makes a handsome berry or ice cream set.
Price........................$0.65

55359 Square Sauce or Berry Dish, 4 inches in diameter; a very handy article, as it can be put to many uses.
Per dozen.......................$1.35

55362 Engraved Low Nappie or Fruit Bowl; used with our small nappies they make a very handsome berry set.
Each...................$0.39

55364 Engraved Sauce Nappie, 4 inches in diameter. Per dozen.........$0.85

55366 Jeannette Berry Set, 7 pieces, one large dish and six small ones; this is a very fine imitation of cut glass, large nappie measures 9 inches, small one 4½ inches diameter. Per set.........................$0.25

Nappies and Comports.

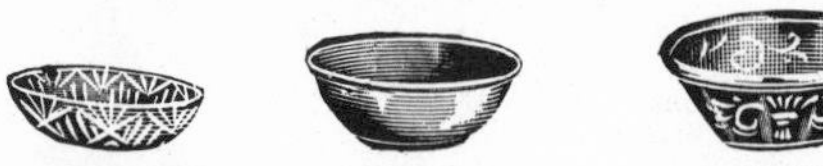

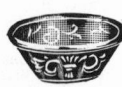

55368 55371 55373

55368 Glass Berry Sauce Dish, 4½ inches in diameter, great value.
Per dozen.......................................$0.20

55371 Glass Berry or Sauce Dish entirely plain, heavy weight, 4 inches diameter.
Per dozen.......................................19

55373 Glass Berry or Sauce Dish, neat figured design, pure crystal, medium weight.
Per dozen.......................................18

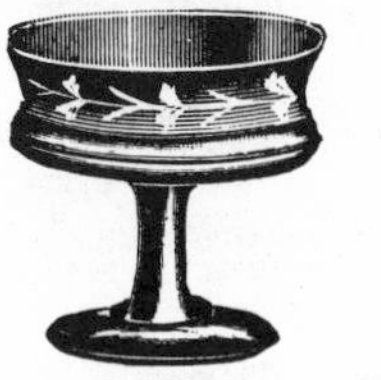
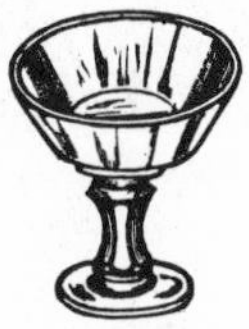

55375 55376

55375 Crystal Glass Engraved Footed Jelly Bowl, a very neat and substantial article, 5 inches in diameter. Each.......................$0.12
Per dozen.......................................1.38

55376 Crystal Glass Footed Jelly Bowl, 5 inches in diameter, substantial and neat. Each.......$0.07
Per dozen.......................................75

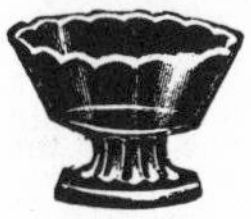
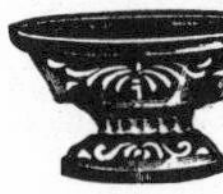

55377 55381

55377 Crystal Glass Sauce Comport, plain and heavy, polished smooth, 4 inches in diameter.
Per dozen.......................................$0.75

55381 Crystal Glass Sauce Comport, pretty pattern heavy and smooth.
Per dozen.......................................40

Celery Holders.

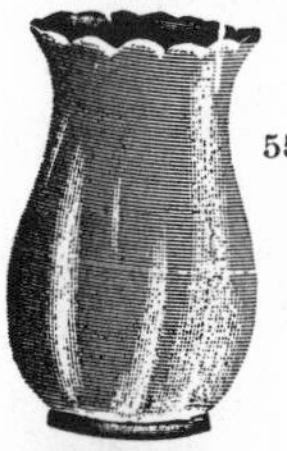

55384 Plain Glass Celery Holder, tall and heavy, medium size.
Each.......................................$0.12

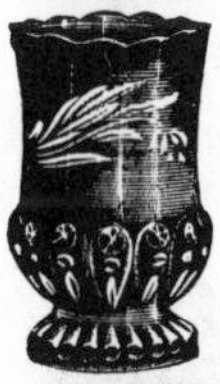

55387 Engraved Celery Holder. A very pretty piece of tableware and remarkably cheap.
Price..........$0.25

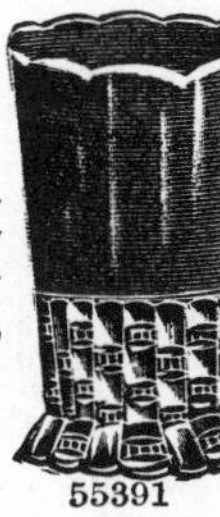

55391

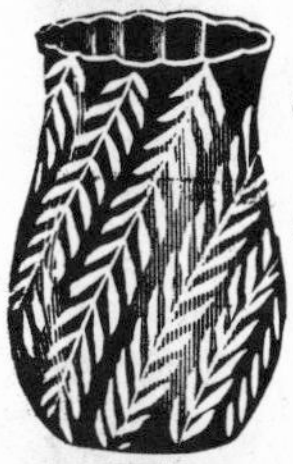

55389 Blue Optic Celery Holder, a very useful as well as ornamental piece of glassware.
Price, each.......................................$0.30

55391 Tall Glass Celery Holder, a very heavy and desirable pattern.
Each.......................................$0.17

Finger Bowls.

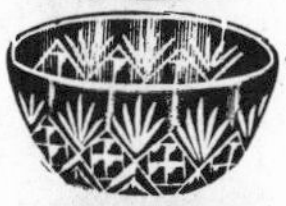

55393 Majestic Finger Bowl, a splendid imitation of a popular cut glass pattern in crystal glass.
Each.......................................$0.10
Per dozen.......................................1.08

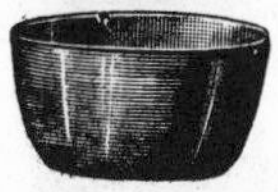

55395 Fine Thin Glass Finger Bowls, plain crystal. This is always in style and can be used with the finest servic Each.......................$0.20

55396 Same as No. 55395, with assorted engravings. Each..$0.25

55397 Same as No. 55395 either blue, green, amber or canary.
Each.......................................20

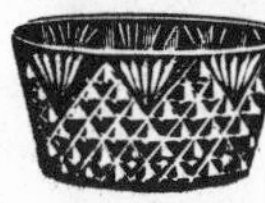

55399 Czarina Finger Bowl, fine imitation of strawberry, diamond and fan cutting; pure crystal glass, strong and well made.
Each.......................................$0.10
Per dozen.......................................1.15

35--2nd

Egg Cups.

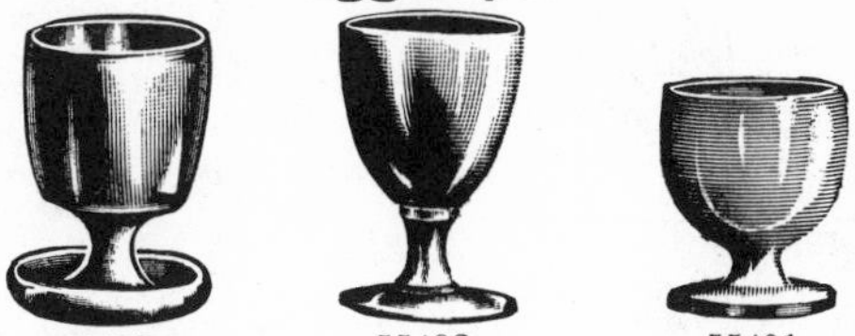

55403 55402 55401

55402 Glass Egg Cups, hold 2 or 3 eggs; a very neat and popular shape. Each.......................$0 06
Per dozen.......................................65

55403 Glass Egg Cup with saucer foot, will hold several eggs, neat design, and a very useful article. Each.......................................07
Per dozen.......................................75

55401 Southern Hotel Egg Cup, one of the never break variety. Holds 4 eggs, made of crystal glass.
Per dozen.......................................67

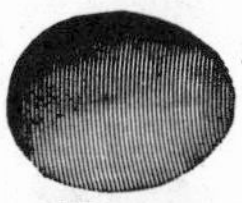

55405 Opal Nest Eggs, perfectly made, same size and appearance as a hen's egg.
Per dozen.......................................$0.30

Toothpick Holders.

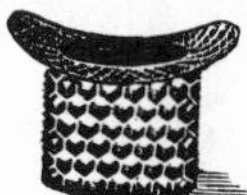

55406 Glass Hat Toothpick Holder, blue crystal or amber.
Each.......................................$0.05
Per dozen.......................................54

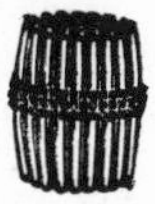

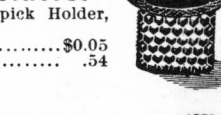

55407 Our Own Toothpick Holder; this is a very neat and substantial holder, and is not easily broken; comes in crystal.
Each.......................................$0 05
Per dozen.......................................55

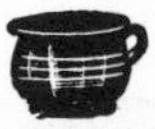

55409 Toy Chambers, yellow earthen ware; used as cigar-ash receivers.
Each.......................................$0.08
Per dozen.......................................87

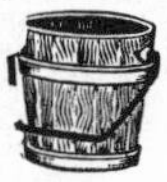

55411 Toy Bucket Toothpick Holder; assorted colors—crystal, blue and amber.
Each.......................................$0.05
Per dozen.......................................54

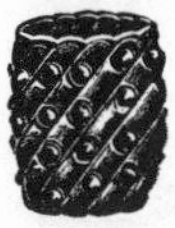

55412 Ceylon Toothpick Holder, crystal glass.
Each.......................................$0.05
Per dozen.......................................54

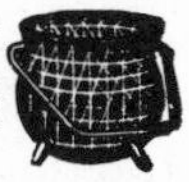

55414 Toy Toothpick Holder, gypsy kettle crystal, amber and blue.
Each.......................................$0.05
Per dozen.......................................54

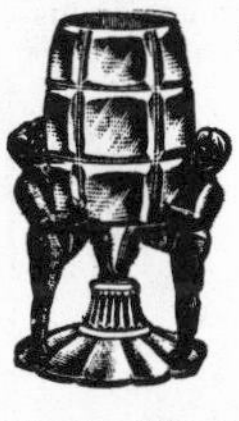

55416 Peek-a-boo Toothpick Holder, made of fine crystal glass.
Each.......................................$0.05
Per dozen.......................................54

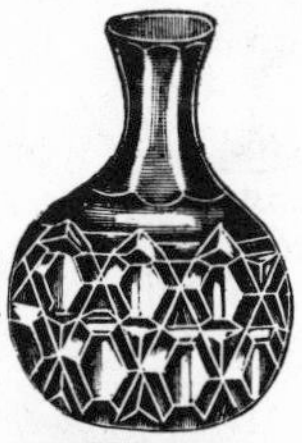

55418 Virginia Water Bottle, pure crystal glass, very heavy, a well executed imitation of the popular block cut pattern.
Each.......................................$0.30

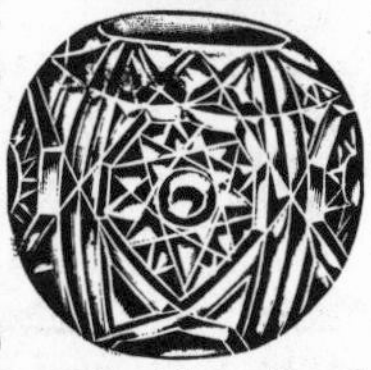

55419 Queen Rose Bowl, 6½ inch, imitation of heavy cut glass; sparkles like a diamond.
Each.......................................$0.30

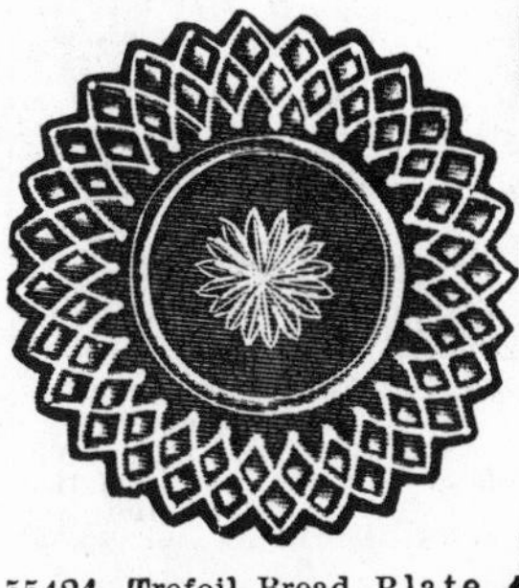

55422 Gem Bread Plate, bright, new pattern of crystal glass, full size and medium weight.
Each.......................................$0.10
Per dozen.......................................1.15

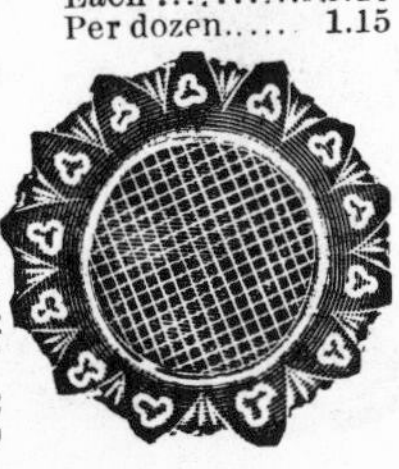

55424 Trefoil Bread Plate, pure white opal glass, has open edge through which colored ribbons may be drawn, producing an effect that makes the plate appear of much higher value.
Each.......................................$0.12
Per dozen.......................................1.30

Toothpick Holders—Continued.

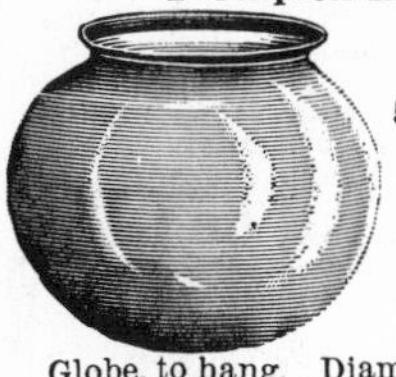

55426 Hanging Fish Globes, made of pure, lead blown glass, extra large opening at top to afford plentiful air supply for the fish. This is a necessary caution as fish need plenty of air.

Globe, to hang. Diameter.	Capacity.	Price.
8-inches	½ gallon.	$0.40
9-inches	¾ gallon.	.47
10-inches	1 gallon.	.55

55428 Globe, with foot.
1 gallon.......................................1.10
1½ gallon.......................................1.25
2 gallons.......................................1.50
3 gallons.......................................2.75

Measuring Glass.

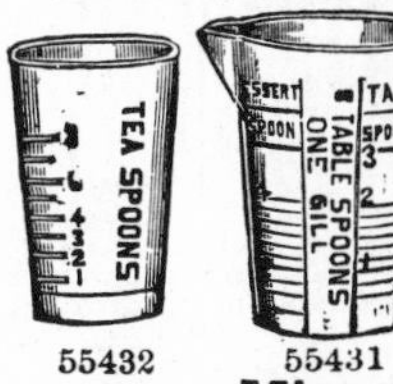

55432 55431

55431 Measuring Glass, very convenient.
Each.......................................$0.05
Per dozen.......................................54

55432 Medicine Glass, indispensable to every well regulated family.
Each.......................................$0.05
Per dozen.......................................54

Miscellaneous.

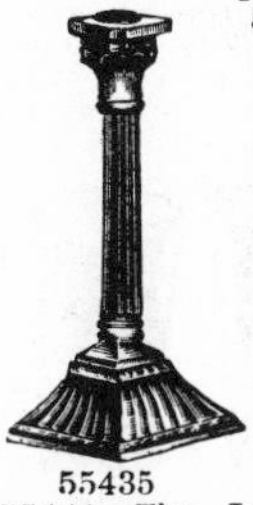

55435

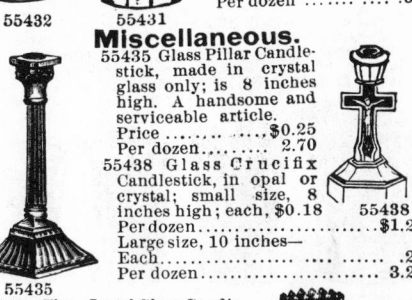

55435 Glass Pillar Candlestick, made in crystal glass only; is 8 inches high. A handsome and serviceable article.
Price.......................................$0.25
Per dozen.......................................2.70

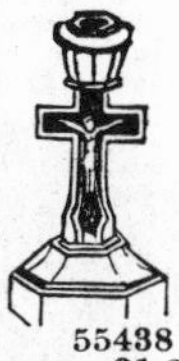

55438

55438 Glass Crucifix Candlestick, in opal or crystal; small size, 8 inches high; each, $0.18
Per dozen.......................................$1.29
Large size, 10 inches—
Each.......................................29
Per dozen.......................................3.24

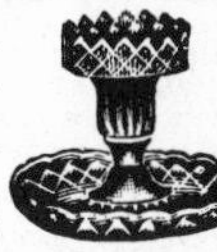

55441 The Jewel Glass Candlestick, 3½ inches high, made in crystal only; has large saucer, which prevents grease from falling over the side.
Price.......................................$0.20
Per dozen.......................................2.16

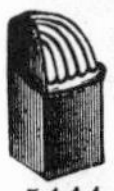

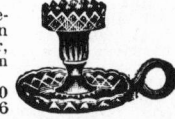

55442 Glass Bird Seed Bottles, to set in wire loop. Each.......................................$0.05
Per dozen.......................................50

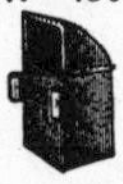

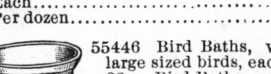

55444 Glass Bird Seed Bottles, with lugs.
Each.......................................$0.05
Per dozen.......................................50

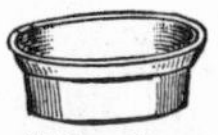

55446 Bird Baths, white or opal for large sized birds, each, 6c; per dozen, 62c. Bird Baths, small size, each 5c; per dozen, 50c. Less than ½ dozen will be charged at each price.

Mason Jars, Porcelain Lined Caps.

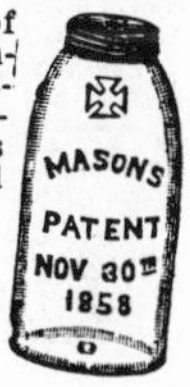

55449 Our Mason Jars are the product of the best makers. The caps are the genuine Boyd Porcelain Lined. We call attention to this, as many dealers are handling inferior jars, the caps in many cases being poorly finished, light in weight, and imperfect in fit.

THE BEST IS THE CHEAPEST.

Pints, ½ gross in case
Quarts, ⅜ gross in case.
½ Gallon, ½ gross in case
No charge for cases.
Prices quoted on application.

Globe Jars, Glass Top.

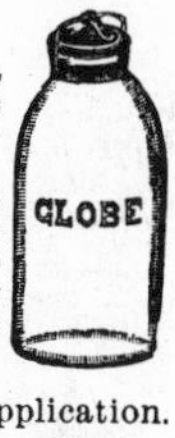

55451 Owing to frequent inquiries for a self-sealing jar without any metal to come in contact with the fruit, we decided to purchase the Globe Glass Top Jar.

Having carefully investigated the merits of this jar, we can fully recommend it to our customers as being one of the best glass top jars in the market, the construction of same being so simple that anyone can readily seal or open it.

Pints, ½ gross.
Quarts, ½ gross in case. } Prices quoted on application.
½ Gallon, gross in case.
No charge for cases.

55454 Plain Half-pint Tin Top Jelly Tumblers.
Per case of six dozen.......................................$1.95

Lemonade, Beer, Wine and Whisky Glasses.

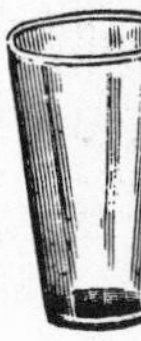

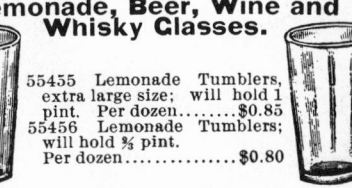

55455 Lemonade Tumblers, extra large size; will hold 1 pint. Per dozen.......$0.85

55456 Lemonade Tumblers; will hold ⅔ pint.
Per dozen.......................................$0.80

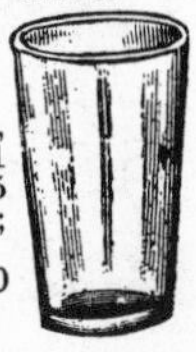

Tumblers—Continued.

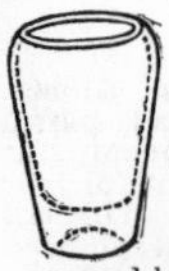

55459 Fine Pressed Glass Cupped Soda Water Tumbler. Holds 12 ounces. Has heavy bottom and will fit a plated holder such as are used with soda fountains.
Per dozen $1.00

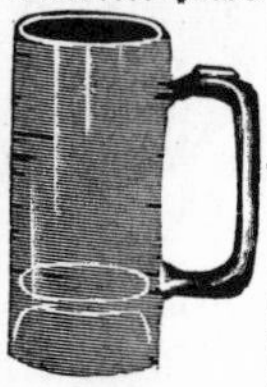

55461 Handled Beer Mugs, made of pure crystal glass, good weight and very strong, large size handle, ground bottom finished very smooth.

Capacity.	Price.
3-ounce	$0.53
5-ounce	.60
8-ounce	.78
10-ounce	.90
12-ounce	1.15
14-ounce	1.25
16-ounce	1.80

55461

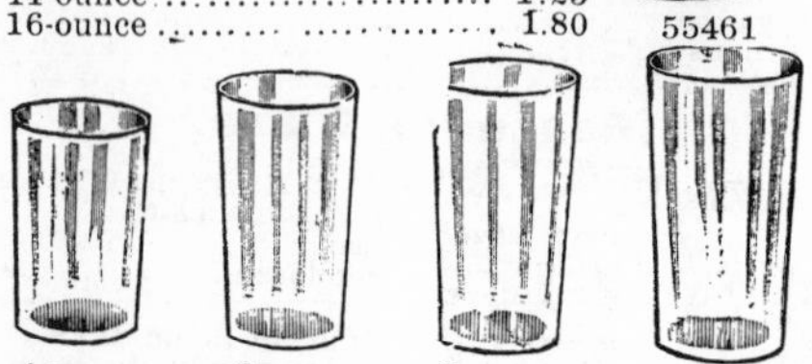

4 oz. 6 oz. 8 oz. 10 oz.

55462 Ale Tumblers, sometimes used for seltzer, cider or beer. They are nicely finished and made of good clear glass.

	4 oz.	6 oz.	8 oz.	10 oz.
Price, per dozen	$0.55	.57	.70	.85

55463 Same shape as No. 55462, but made of thin blown best quality lead glass and of the following sizes:

sizes:	5 oz.	6 oz.	7 oz.	9 oz.
Price, per dozen	$0.55	.60	.65	.85

10½ oz. 9½ oz. 7½ oz. 5¾ oz.

55466 Blown Glass Bell Shape Ale Tumblers, made of thin blown lead flint glass, bell shape now so popular.

Capacity.	Price per doz.	Capacity.	Price per doz.
4½-ounce	$0.45	9½-ounce	$0.62
5¾-ounce	.50	10½-ounce	.70
7½-ounce	.53		

55468 Crystal Glass Custard, Sherbet or Punch Glass. Pressed and fire polished.
Each $0.10
Per dozen 1.00

55471 Fine Blown Crystal Glass Sherbet or Custard Cup.
Each $0.18
Per dozen 1.95

2½ oz. 2 oz. 1½ oz. 1 oz.

55473 Glass Whisky Tumblers, with fluted bottom, as shown in cut, made of good clean pressed glass, heavy bottom. 1 oz. 1½ oz. 2 oz. 2½oz
Price, per dozen 60c. 65c 75c. 85c

2½ oz. 2 oz. 1¾ oz.

55476 Glass Whisky Tumblers, fine polished glass, heavy bottom and plain as shown by cut.

	1¾ oz.	2 oz.	2½ oz
Price, per dozen	60c.	65c.	70c.

55478 Same shape as above but made of best quality blown lead glass, very thin and tough and of the following sizes:

	2 oz.	2½ oz.	3 oz.
Price, per dozen	60c.	65c.	70c.

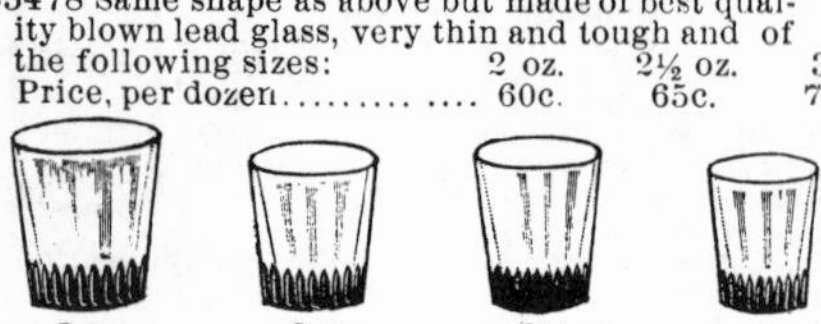

3 oz. 2 oz. 2½ oz. 1 oz

55481 Glass Whisky Tumblers, good quality, plain glass, heavy bottom, finely fluted, as shown in cut.

	1½ oz.	2 oz.	2½ oz.	3 oz
Price, per dozen	60c.	65c.	70c.	75c.

55482 Extra Heavy Sham Bottom Liquor Glasses, generally used for brandy or small whiskies; holds 1½ ounces.
Per dozen $0.55

Tumblers—Continued.

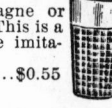

55483 Fancy Pressed Glass Champagne or Sherry Tumbler. Holds 4 ounces. This is a remarkably pretty pattern and a close imitation of cut glass.
Per dozen $0.55

55486 Fancy Pressed Glass Champagne or Sherry Tumbler. Holds 4 ounces; fluted bottom, as shown in cut.
Per dozen $0.52

55488

55488 Coctail Glass, very fine quality clear crystal glass, extra strong stem.
Per dozen $0.80

55491

55491 Coctail Glasses, standard size and very pretty shape.
Per dozen $0.82

55492 55494 55495 55497

55492 Hot Whiskey Glass, very neat shape bowl, is so light hot water will not break it.
Per dozen $0.82
55494 Hot Whiskey, thin bowl, new shape, hot water proof. Per dozen .... .81
55495 Rhine or Apple Wine Glass. Correct in size and shape. Per dozen .... .85
55497 Rhine or Apple Wine Glass. New shape and very pretty. Per dozen .... .84

55499 55505 55506

55499 Wine Glass, plain, handsome pattern, finished very smooth and bright. Per dozen $0.50
55505 Fancy Pattern Wine Glass, strong stem, a well finished and serviceable article. Per dozen $0.42
55506 Wine Glass, a neat and quiet pattern, well illustrated in cut. Per dozen $0.41

55507 55508 55509 55511

55507 Wine Glass. Entirely plain, strong and well made at a popular price. Per dozen......$0.32
55508 Wine Glass, engraved with a neat band.
Per dozen .... .39
55509 Wine Glass, with neat, figured engraving.
Per dozen .... .48
55511 Wine Glass, new and artistic shape.
Per dozen .... .49

55513 55515 55516 55517

55513 Wine Glass, very desirable, nicely figured and extra heavy. Per dozen $0.38
55515 Wine Glass, entirely plain, imitation cut stem. Per dozen .... .44

55516 Wine Glass, decorated with a handsome engraving.
Per dozen $0.60
55517 Alexis Wine Glass, the very latest shape in the market. Per dozen $0.50

Wine Sets.

55519 The Roman Wine Set made of good quality crystal glass; consists of one decanter, six wine glasses and glass tray.
Per set. $0.58

Wine Sets—Continued.

55521 The Lilly Wine Set, 1 quart decanter and six wine glasses on glass tray; a very pretty and serviceable set.
Price, complete $0.50

Decanters.

55522 55523

55522 Imported Thin Glass Decanter, handsomely engraved with Greek and star engravings as shown in cut; genuine cut stopper; cut neck and cut flutes.
1 pt. Each $1.25
1 qt. Each 1.40
55523 Pressed Glass, Wine or Liquor Decanter, genuine cut glass stopper.
1 qt. Price $1.00

Custard or Sherbet Cups.

55525

55527

55525 Glass Egg, Custard or Sherbet Glass, neat, plain, and handsomely finished. Each $0.07
Per dozen .... .75
55527 Glass Egg, Custard or Sherbet Glass, very thin and light, made to resemble fine imported ware: the flutes on bottom are made to resemble the most popular cutting ever brought out. Each..........$0.05
Per dozen .... .85

Vases.

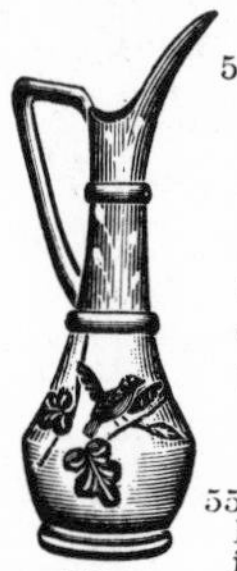

55528

55528 Imported Art Vase, imitation of the genuine Crown Derby ware, decorated in colors and gold in very pretty designs. Stands 10 inches high, makes a very rich parlor ornament.
Price, each......$0.65
Price, per pair.. 1.15

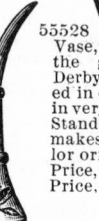

55529

55529 Imported Art Vase, imitation Royal Worcester, 7½ in. high, decorated in colors and gold. The body is finely tinted and cannot readily be detected from the genuine and expensive article. Each. $0.60
Per pair 1.10

55532

55532 Imported Flower Vase, made of Bohemian glass, tinted and decorated with floral designs: 7½ inches high; a very neat shape and remarkably cheap. Each..$0.25
Per pair............. .45

55533

55533 Flower Vase, genuine Bohemian glass, 7 in high, rich royal blue color, hand decorated with gold and colored flowers; a very pretty parlor ornament and remarkably cheap. Each $0.15
Per pair... .... .25
Per dozen pairs..... 2.70

55535

55535 Flower Vase, very pretty design, made of Bohemian glass, tinted and decorated with flowers, hand painted in natural colors, stands 8 in. high. Each........$0.30
Per pair............ .54

55537

55537 Decorated Bohemian Flower Vase, tinted and decorated with leaves and flowers; all hand work; stands 7 in. high; a very pretty receptacle for flowers or dried ferns and grasses. Each..$0.25
Per pair .... .45

55539

55539 Flower Vase, genuine Bohemian glass, imitation alabaster, 6 inches high, gold and flower decorations; an entirely new shape and very pretty.
Each................$0.15
Per pair. .. .. .25
Per dozen pair....... 2.70

55540

55540 Flower Vase, genuine Bohemian glass, same color and decoration as No. 55539, only different in shape. Each $0.15
Per pair............. .25
Per dozen pair...... 2.75

Vases—Continued.

55542 Flower Vase, made of Bohemian glass of a milky white color and beautifully decorated, 9 inches high. This makes a handsome ornament, and would be appreciated as a wedding or birthday gift. Each ....$0.25 Per pair......... .45

55543 Flower Vase, made of etched or dull finished Bohemian glass, gold lines and hand painted decorations. There is nothing nicer to give as birthday or holiday present; stands 9 in. high. Each .....$0.27 Per pair......... .50

55544 Flower Vase, etched or dull Bohemian glass, new and handsome pattern hand decorated with leaves and flowers in colors and gold; stands 9 in. high. Don't forget to order a pair when selecting your holiday gifts.

Each.............$0.25 Per pair......... .45

Genuine Imported Bisque Figures.

55547 Imported Bisque Figure, stands 7½ inches high; subjects are children in various costumes. These are not toys, but real works of art, and at the price we ask for them are remarkably cheap. Price........$0.25 Per dozen..........$2.70

Bisque Figures—Continued.

55551 Swing Bisque Figure, 3 inches high, beautifully tinted and decorrated. Each.......$0.36 Per dozen.......... 3.24

55555 Bisque Figure, representing a boy carrying a small sail boat; these make pretty mantel ornaments; they stand 7 inches high and are handsomely colored. Each.................$0.20 Per pair........ .... .38

55557 Bisque Toothpick Holders; this is a very neat article and represents a child with a willow basket strapped on her back, nicely colored and stands five inches high.$0.10

55555

Art Majolica Ware.

55559 English Majolica Vase, gold trimmed and ornamented with raised work flowers and leaves. This makes a very handsome ornament, as it is quite large, standing 14 inches high.

Price........................$1.50 Per dozen...................16.20

55557

Majolica Ware—Continued.

55561 English Majolica Double Handled Vase, raised ornamentation of flowers and leaves. This is a very handsome piece of ware and will be sure to be appreciated wherever seen. It stands 10½ inches high.

Price...................$1.25 Per dozen.............13.50

55562 English Majolica Handled Vase, stands 8 inches high; it is ornamented with raised flowers and leaves in very pleasing colors. This makes a very handsome mantel ornament.

Price................. ....$0.65 Per dozen. 7.05

55565 English Majolica Flower Vase; it is ornamented in the same manner as the larger ones; it stands 5½ inches high and is used largely for cut flowers, dried grass, etc. Price............$0.25 Per dozen 2.70

55570 English Majolica Flower Vase or Bouquet Holder, ornamented with raised work flowers and leaves, tinted in natural colors; it stands 4½ inches high and makes a very desirable, low priced article.

Price ... .$0.20 Per dozen 2.16

LAMP DEPARTMENT.

We respectfully call our customers' attention to the handsome line of hanging, table, piano and banquet lamps we are offering this season. We think they are finer than any we have yet shown. They are entirely new designs, and from the low prices we are enabled to offer them at, we predict a large sale. They are packed by experienced and careful men and the chance of breakage is very slight.

55573 Polished bronze metal, ball weight hanging lamp; length closed, 44 inches, extended 59 inches; complete with 14 inch opal cone shade, No. 2 Sun burner, taking one inch wick and ordinary No. 2 chimney.

Price $1.75

55576

55576 Polished Bronze Metal Hanging Lamp, improved spring extension; length, closed, 32 inches; extended, 80 inches, complete with 14 inch plain white dome shade, No. 2 chimney and burner.

Price $2.15

55578 Polished bronze metal, patent improved extension; length, closed, 35 inches, extended 81 inches, fancy hand decorated and-tinted 14 inch dome shade and fount to match, with climax burner, chimney and 1¼ inch wick, giving a large and steady light.

55578   Price $2.75

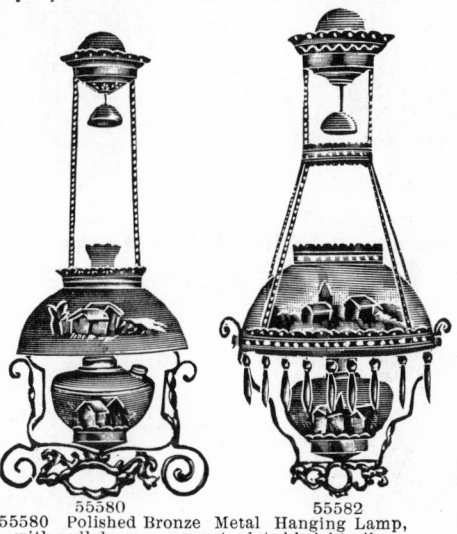

55580   55582

55580 Polished Bronze Metal Hanging Lamp, with pull-down ornament, plated bright silver, patent improved spring extension; length, closed, 37 inches, extended; 83 inches, fancy tinted and decorated 14 inch dome, shade and fount to match, fitted with large burner taking 1½ inch wick and chimney; a good light giver and sure to please. Price................... ...$3.00

55582 Polished Bronze Metal Hanging Lamp, patent spring extension; length, closed, 35 in.; extended, 81 in.; fancy hand decorated and tinted 14-inch dome shade and fount to match; cut glass crystal prisms, climax burner, chimney and 1½ inch wick, gives a brilliant light.

Price $3.65

55585 Polished Bronze Metal Hanging Lamp, patent improved spring extension; length, closed, 34 inches, extended, 80 inches, hand decorated satin finish 14-inch dome shade and fount to match; fitted with climax burner and chimney, giving large light; cut glass crystal prisms around edge of shade.

Price.... ....$3.90

55587 Polished Bronze Metal Hanging Lamp, patent improved spring extension; length, closed, 38 inches; extended,84 inches,tinted decorated satin finish 14-inch dome shade and fount to match, cut glass crystal prisms, climax burner and chimney.

Price $4.15

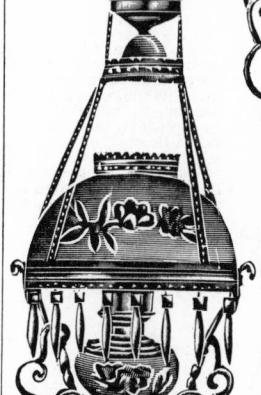

55590 Polished Bronze Metal Hanging Lamp, with cast brass silver plated ornaments, patent spring extension, length, closed,37 inches; extended, 83 inches; crystal cut glass prisms, fancy decorated 14-inch dome,shade and fount to match, trimmed with climax burner and chimney.....$4.25

55592 Polished Bronze Metal Hanging Lamp, with pull-down ornaments plated bright silver, patent improved spring extension; length, closed,39 inches; extended, 85 inches; handsome satin finished hand-decorated 14-inch dome shade and vase to match; removable oil fount fitted with 80 candle power central draft burner giving an extra large light; takes number 2 Rochester chimney and wick; crystal glass cut prisms.

Price. $6.15

Write Us Upon Any Business Topic.
=:= =:= =:= =:=

Lamps—Continued.

55593 Polished Bronze Metal Hanging Lamp, with strap work on harp and pull-down, ornaments plated bright silver, improved spring extension; length, closed, 39 inches; extended, 85 inches, satin finish fancy hand decorated 14-inch dome shade and vase to match, removable oil founts (easy to clean and fill), central draft burner giving 80 candle power light; cut glass crystal prisms. Price................$5.45

55598 Polished Bronze Metal Hanging Lamp, improved spring extension; length, closed, 39 inches; extended, 85 inches; adapted for either high or low ceilings, satin finished decorated 14-inch dome shade and vase to match, large central draft burner giving 80 candle power light; ornamented with cut glass crystal prisms. Price............$4.95

55600 Polished Bronze Metal Hanging Lamp, improved spring extension; length, closed, 38 inches; extended, 84 inches; adapted for either high or low ceilings; handsome hand-decorated and tinted; 14-inch dome shade and vase to match, on satin finish body; has removable oil fount (easy to fill or trim); fitted with central draft, 80 candle power burner, which throws a powerful light; ornamented around shade with cut glass crystal prisms. Price............$4.60

55602 Polished Bronze Metal Hanging Lamp, improved spring extension; adapted to low or high ceilings; length, closed, 38 inches; extended, 84 inches; satin finish; 14-inch dome shade and vase to match; removable oil fount (easy to fill and clean); fitted with central draft 80 candle power burner; ornamented with cut-glass crystal prisms. Price............$4.75

Lamps—Continued.

55604 Zenith

55604 Polished Bronze Metal,; length, closed, 26 inches; length, extended, 47 inches. Has Sun burner with pearl top lead glass chimney. Choice of etched crystal globe, ruby globe, or blue, pink, rose or crystal opalescent globe, all at same price. This is the cheapest and best article we have ever been able to offer in the line of a moderate size hall lamp, and is the latest production. Price............$1.80

55606 Hall Lamp, made of polished bronze metal and trimmed with pink rose globe and No. 1 Sun burner. Length, closed, 30 inches; extended, 48 inches. Price............$2.50

55606

55608 Hall Lamp, polished bronze, fitted complete with crystal etched globe and No. 1 Sun burner and chimney; length, closed, 30 inches; extended, 48 inches. Price.........$2.45

55609 Polished Bronze Metal Hall Lamp; length, closed, 29 inches; extended, 47 inches; square shape, with crystal etched glass; size of glass 6x8 inches; trimmed with No. 1 Sun burner and chimney, Price.........$2.65

55608   55609

Lamp and Chandelier Hooks.

GENEVA BRONZED.
55610 Lamp or Chandelier Hook, with plate, and 4 in. screw. Each.........$0.10
Per dozen.............1.05

Ceiling Hooks.

55612 We recommend the use of our rich gilt ceiling hook, as it compels the chandelier or lamp to remain exactly where placed on hook.
Each...................$0.22
Per dozen.... ....,2.50

Chandeliers.

55615 Polished Bronze Extension Chandelier, complete with crystal etched pan globes and embossed metal central draft burner, which gives four times the light of an ordinary burner. This is an ornamental fixture for the parlor and is used extensively in churches, halls, etc. Always gives good satisfaction.
3-light trimmed, complete $16.50
4-light trimmed, complete. 20.00

Mail Order Methods

✠ AS CONDUCTED BY US HAVE PROVEN SATISFACTORY TO MILLIONS OF PEOPLE.

Chandeliers—Continued.

55616 Chandeliers, antique brass, with patent spring extension; length, closed, 37 in extended, 55 inches; spreads 30 inches; is fitted with unique burners which enable you to light it without removing chimney or globe

We can furnish this chandelier with either etched or colored globes as desired.
Price, three-light, complete...................$11.25
Price, four-light, complete 13.25

55618 Polished Bronze Metal Chandelier, improved spring extension, adapted to either high or low ceilings; length, closed, 40 inches; extended, 58 inches; spread of arms, 30 inches; fitted with 4 inch wave top-etched globes and No. 2 Unique burners, which can be lighted without removing chimney or globe.
2-light, trimmed, complete $7.95
3 light, trimmed, complete 10.00
4-light, trimmed, complete.................12.00
55620 Same Chandelier as No. 55618, but fitted with metal oil founts, having 50-candle power burner, which gives an extra brilliant light. This fixture meets all requirements, and is suitable for dwellings, churches and halls.
2-light, trimmed, complete...................... 9.25
3-light, trimmed, complete......... ....12.00
4-light, trimmed, complete............. ....15.00

Piano Lamps.

55621 Gold Finish metal Piano Lamp; has extension rod which runs through center of table, which prevents it from being easily tipped over. Genuine Mexican onyx top, 8x8 inches, fitted with removable oil fount, and large central draft burner and handsome 20-inch silk shade, with 8-inch lace border. Height to top of chimney, 59 inches; extended, 75 inches. Price.........$12.85

Piano Lamps—Continued.

Lamp Stands—Continued.

Banquet Lamps—Continued.

55623 Gold Finish Metal Piano Lamp; an extra heavy strong table, with extension rod running through the center, genuine Mexican onyx top, 10x10 inches. The frame is heavy cast brass highly finished in rich gold, fitted with fancy 20-inch silk shade, with 8-inch chiffon border embroidered in colors; has removable oil fount with large central draft burner and chimney; height to top of chimney, 60 inches; extended, 76 inches. Price.........$19.15

55625 Gold Finish Piano Lamp, complete with 12-inch linen umbrella shade holder and chimney, 75 candle power, central draft, burner, very convenient to read by, as it can be raised or lowered to any dsired height. Price.. ......$5.75

55627 Gold Finish Piano or reading Lamp trimmed, complete with 12-inch brochatelle linen umbrella shade and 75-candle power central draft burner. Price.. .. ..$6.95

Lamp Stands.

55628 Onyx Top Fancy brass Table, onyx, measures 8x8 inches, fancy new rope pattern legs; all the metal work finished in rich gold; this is an extra strong and desirable low priced table; it stands 28 inches high. Price.....$6.25

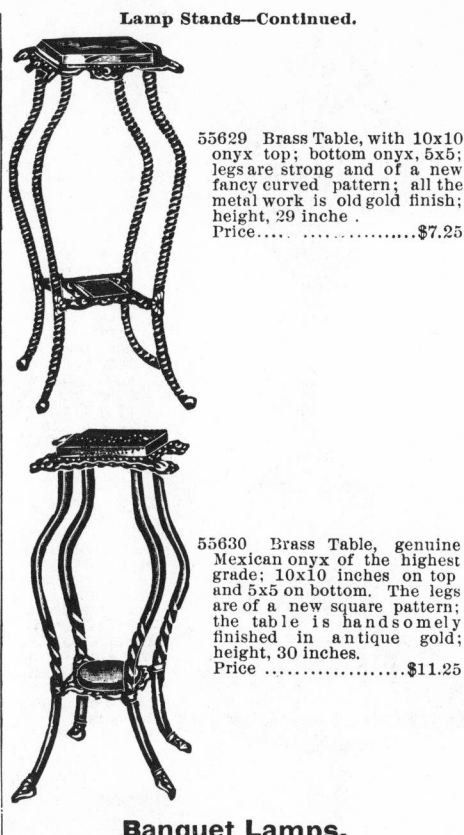

55629 Brass Table, with 10x10 onyx top; bottom onyx, 5x5; legs are strong and of a new fancy curved pattern; all the metal work is old gold finish; height, 29 inche . Price.... ....$7.25

55630 Brass Table, genuine Mexican onyx of the highest grade; 10x10 inches on top and 5x5 on bottom. The legs are of a new square pattern; the table is handsomely finished in antique gold; height, 30 inches. Price $11.25

Banquet Lamps.

The demand for Banquet Lamps increases every year, and this season we offer a very attractive line, carefully selected from the several leading factories

55635 Gold Finish Metal Banquet Lamp, cupid center piece, extra heavy cast foot; cast open work head, removable oil fount, with 80 candle power, central draft burner, 18 inchs fancy silks hade with 8 inch chiffon border embroidered in colors. An extra heavy, massive lamp and one of the handsomest designs brought out this season. Height to top of chimney, 31 inches. Price.. $10.50

55637 Gold Finish Metal Banquet Lamp; Ingomar figure, silver plated, solid cast head, removable oil fount, 80 candle power, central draft burner, trimmed with elegant 18-inch silk shade with 8-inch chiffon border embroidered in colors, a large lamp, very artistic and well made; height to top of chimney, 33 in. Price......$9.15

55639 Gold Finish metal Banquet Lamp, onyx column, cast open work head; fitted with removable oil fount, 80 candle power, central draft burner, trimmed with fancy 15-inch silk shade with 6-inch chiffon border, embroidered in colors; height to top of chimney, 30 in. Price 7.30

55640 Banquet Lamp; the column is cream de verde finish, the latest production of artistic metal work, predominent colors are: White, green and old rose variegated, which with metal side ornaments, heavy foot and cast open work, head finished in rich gold and trimmed with 18-inch fancy silk shade, with 8-inch embroidered chiffon border, combined to make it an exceedingly handsome lamp in every particul r. Has removable oil fount, fitted with 80-candle power, central draft burner; height to tip of chimney, 30 inches. Price.................................$10.50

55645 Gold Finish Metal Banquet Lamp complete with 16 inch Isabella linen shade and 80-candle power, central draft burner, takes No. 2 Rochester chimney and wick, gives immense white light; height to top of chimney, 28 inches, very neat design and good value. Price.....$3.60

55650 Gold Finish Banquet Lamp, trimmed with 10-inch crown linen shade, 80-candle power, center draft burner, taking No. 2 Rochester chimney and wick; height to top of chimney, 28 inches. Price .. .$3.45

Banquet Lamps—Continued.

55651 Banquet Lamp, made of solid wrought iron; very handsome designs; will wear forever and is always in style; trimmed with 15-inch fancy silk shade, ornamented with 6-inch chiffon edge embroidered in colors, has removable oil fount fitted with 80-candle power center draft burner; height to top of chimney, 30 in. Price.....$7.35

55652 Glass Banquet Lamp, fine tinted solid colors; the foot is antique finished; cast brass; the column bowl and globe are of glass handsomely tinted in solid colors to match, fitted with a fine duplex burner and extinguisher. This is an exceedingly pretty lamp. It comes in three colors: Blue, canary and pink; height to top of chimney, 31 inches. Pink, price.....$3.49
Canary, price..... .... 3.35
Blue, price.................... 3.10

55653 Banquet Lamp, gold finish, statue center piece, cast open work head with removable oil fount, and 80-candle power center draft burner; trimmed with handsome 15-inch silk shade, with 6-inch silk border, height to top of chimney, 29 inches. Price............................$5.75

55654 Bugle Cupid Metal Banquet Lamp, heavy cast base, embossed fount fitted with 80 candle power center draft burner, finished in rich gold, trimmed with 16-inch fancy linen shade, silk fringe; a very neat and remarkably low-priced lamp. Price $3.15

Banquet Lamps—Continued.

55655 Metal Banquet lamp, nickel plated, complete with 10-inch linen shade; silk fringe; has 80-candle power central draft burner; gives immense light, takes No. 2 Rochester chimney and wick; this is a serviceable lamp and one that will give good results; height to top of chimney, 26½ inches. Price....$2.00

55657 Banquet Lamp, hand decorated satin finish bisque column and oil fount, brass foot, trimmed with 16-inch Isabella shade and burner taking 1½ in. wick; height to top of chimney, 29 inches. Price... $2.45

55658 Fancy Hand Decorated and Tinted Parlor Vase Lamp, antique brass metal fount, trimmed with 10-inch dome shade decorated to match vase, removable oil fount fitted with 80-candle power center draft burner, which emits a very white flame. This is a very desirable lamp, not only on account of its light-giving qualities but for its rich and attractive appearance; height, 21 inches. Price..............$4.15

55659 Fancy Decorated Parlor Lamp, handsome hand decorated and tinted vase and 10 inch dome shade to match, satin finished surface, cast metal foot, antique brass finish, removable oil fount, fitted with 80 candle power center draft burner; gives as much light as four ordinary burners; height, 19½ inches. Price........ ...$2.75

55659

55660 Decorated Parlor Vase Lamp, satin finish, 10-inch, decorated dome shade to match, removable oil fount, fitted with 80-candle power center draft burner; height, 19½ inches. Price......... .....$2.25

Parlor Lamps—Continued.

55661 Parlor Vase Lamp, hand decorated and tinted bisque body; width, 10 inches; decorated dome shade to match; fitted with fine burner, taking 1½-inch wick and gives a large, clear light. Price...... .....: ..$1.50

55662

55662 Decorated Parlor Vase Lamp, tinted and decorated, satin finished, 8½-inch dome shade to match, fitted with No. 2 Sun burner and chimney; height, 17½ inches. Price........$1.15

55663 Decorated Parlor Vase Lamp, complete, with 7-inch decorated dome shade to match vase, fitted with No. 2 Sun burner and chimney; height, 17 inches.

55663   Price....... ....$0.98

55664 Decorated Stand Lamp, fancy iron foot and decorated stem; height, 20 inches. This makes a very desirable lamp for use on kitchen table or to sew by; it is trimmed with No. 2 Sun burner and fancy engraved chimney.
Price, complete $0.85

55664

55665 Decorated Stand Lamp, fancy iron foot and decorated cylinder, trimmed, complete, with fancy folding paper shade and No. 2 burner and chimney; height, 20 inches. Price. $0.95

55666   **55667**

55666 Decorated Stand Lamp, height, 22 inches; colored center, cast brass foot, antique finish, crystal oil fount, trimmed with fancy Japanese paper dome shade and No. 2 Sun burner and chimney. Price...................................$0.95

55667 Decorated Stand Lamp, metal foot, Japan finish, colored center and crystal glass fount, complete with folding paper shade, No. 2 Sun burner and chimney; height to top of chimney, 21½ inches. Price 90

Lamps—Continued.

55668   55669

55668 Decorated Stand Lamp, metal foot, Japan finish, colored center and crystal glass fount, complete, with No. 2 Sun burner, chimney and fancy Japanese paper dome shade; height to top of chimney, 21 inches. Price.... ... .$0.85

55669 Crystal Glass Stand Lamp; neat, plain pattern. We keep three sizes.
19 inches high to top of chimney, and trimmed with No. 2 burner, chimney and wick, complete. Price.................................... .35
18 inches high to top of chimney, and trimmed with No. 2 burner, chimney and wick, complete. Price.............................. .30
16 inches high to top of chimney trimmed and with No. 1 burner, chimney and wick, complete. Price.............................. .25

55670 Crystal Glass Stand Lamp has clinch collar put on under several hundred pounds pressure; no cement or plaster clinched on collars, never come off, and the process of putting them on breaks all the imperfect lamps, consequently a clinch collar lamp is superior and safer than those having collars put on with plaster paris.
19 inches high to top of chimney and trimmed with number 2 burner; chimney and wick, complete. Price.......$0.45
18 inches high to top of chimney and trimmed with number 2 burner; chimney and wick, complete. Price.......$0.37
16 inches high to top of chimney and trimmed with number 1 burner; chimney and wick, complete. Price.......$0.30

55671 Crystal Glass Night, Lamp; will hold enough oil to burn all night and is fitted with a burner, wick and chimney, complete. Price..........$0.16

55672 Footed Crystal Glass Hand Lamp, heavy foot, not easily upset, complete with No. 1 Sun burner, chimney and wick. Price .... .20

55671   55672

55673 Footed Crystal Glass Hand Lamp, with patent clinch collar, put on under several hundred pounds pressure; no cement or plaster; can never come off; extra heavy foot; complete with No. 1 Sun burner, chimney and wick. Price. ...$0.25

Fancy Metal Table Lamps.

55674 Metal Parlor Table Lamp; bright silver finish; a very handsome and substantial lamp; made of heavy cast metal, open work design; has removable oil fount fitted with 80 candle power center draft burner, 10 inch; handsome, tinted and decorated satin finished dome shade; height to top of chimney, 20½ in. Price......$6.00

Lamps—Continued.

55675 Metal Parlor Table Lamp, rich gold finish, extra heavy metal cast open work design, removable oil fount, fitted with 80 candle power center draft burner, giving a large and brilliant light, 10-inch dome shade, handsomely tinted and decorated; height to top of chimney, 19 inches. Price..............$4.50

55675

55676 Metal Parlor Table Lamp, silver finish, trimmed with 10-inch tinted and decorated dome shade; has 80 candle power center draft burner; height to top of chimney, 18 in. Price..............$3.50

55676

Montgomery Ward & Co.'s Chief Central Draft Metal Table and Hand Lamps.

We have selected this burner (after a careful comparison with all others) as being the very best; it will give more light according to the amount of oil consumed than any other lamp made. Try one and you will be more than pleased.

No. 2 Chief 80 Candle Power Central Draft Stand Lamp Complete, with opal dome shade 10-inch, shade holder and chimney; height to top of chimney, 20 inches, : takes No. 2 Rochester round wick and chimney.

Why use an inferior lamp when one guaranteed by a reputable firm can be purchased at price quoted? Order one and return at our expense if it does not bear out the following description:

1st. Gives a strong, steady white light.
2d. Easiest wicking device invented.
3d. Wick never sticks and can be raised and lowered instantly.
4th. Well made and shapely throughout.

55677 Brass finish Price..............$1.50
55678 Nickel finish. Price.......... $1.75

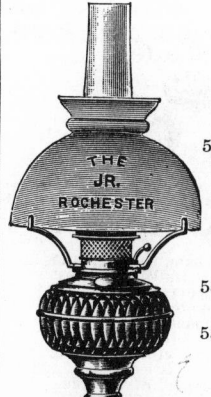

55679 The Rochester Junior is designed for a night or bedroom lamp. It stands about 9½ inches to top of burner and is fitted with 6-inch plain dome shade. It will not smoke or smell if turned low and will hold sufficient oil to burn all night. Price....$0.90
55680 Plain White Dome Shades, to fit 55679 lamp. Each.....................$0.20
55681 Chimneys to fit 55679 lamp. Each........ $0.05
Per dozen... .... .55

See Last Page for Prices of Kerosene Oil.

Student Lamps.

55682 This is the best Student or Library Lamp we know of. Gives a perfect and uniform light, is cool, absolutely safe, is adjustable in height and is in every way a perfect lamp. Price, complete, packed for shipping. *Each $3.50. Extra chimneys for students' lamp.
Per bundle of 6.....$0.20

55683 Rochester Study Lamp, detachable fount, with wick, chimney and 10-inch plain dome shade, not ribbed as shown in cut. Add 40 cents to prices below if wanted with decorated dome shade.
Brass $5.75
Nickel plated........ 6.00
Weight, 25 lbs. packed.

55684 Central Draft Bracket Lamp, made entirely of polished brass, furnished with chimney and wick (no shade). Price...........................$1.90

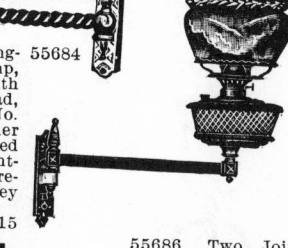

55685 Brass Swinging Bracket Lamp, 55684 square arm, with 12 in. spread, trimmed with No. 2 unique burner and 5 in. etched globe: can be lighted without removing chimney or globe. Price........$2.15

55686 Two Joint Brass Swinging Bracket Lamp, closed 12 in., extended 20, trimmed complete with fancy colored dew drop globe in blue or light ruby: has No. 2 unique burner and chimney, and can be lighted without removing either. Price.........$2.75

55687 Non-explosive Hand Lamp, bronze finish. This lamp is absolutely non-explosive; can be carried around without the slightest danger; it gives an excellent light; furnished complete with wick and chimney as shown in cut. Price $0.85

Genuine Rochester Bracket and Harp Lamp.

55688 Rochester Bracket or side lamp, metal fount, 9 inches high, holds 2 qts. of oil, gives immense light for factories, mills, engine rooms, etc. Complete bracket, reflector, 8 in. metal fount, wick and chimney. Each.$2.00

55688   55689

55689 Rochester Lamp, complete with tin shade and wire harp, 30 inches in length, to hang from shops, factories, stores etc.; fount trimmed with wick and chimney complete. Each $2.25
Per dozen...................... 24.50

55690 Rochester Lamp, same as No. 55688, with wire harp; 30 inches in length and with tin shade, to hang from ceiling; for shops, factories, stores, etc. Fount complete, with wick and chimney. Each......................$2.10
Per dozen...................... 22.75

Lamps—Continued.

55691 The Rochester Combination Oil Stove and Lamp The oil fount holds 2½ quarts and will burn twenty hours. When used as a stove it will boil water in a few minutes. The chimney is of Russia iron, having mica window and malleable iron base. The whole top easily lifts off and a glass chimney can be put on, thus changing it into a real Rochester lamp. There is real merit in this article, as it combines two of the most useful and necessary household utensils.
Price.............. ....$2.50

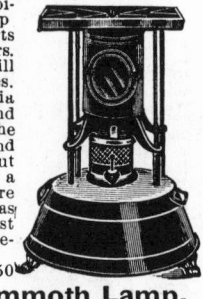

The Banner Mammoth Lamp.

400 Candle Power Light.
55692 The Mammoth Lamp gives a strong and brilliant light, and has a fount holding one gallon of oil; it is the only mammoth lamp with extra wick feeder to supply oil to the burning wick; suitable for all places where a large and steady light is required; 20 inch embossed tin shade harp, smoke bell and chimney; ready for use.
Price $3.25

55693 The Mammoth Lamp, with spring extension and 14 inch white porcelain shade; this makes a very neat appearing lamp and is especially adapted for use in churches, school houses, halls, etc.
Price.................$4.75

Extra Chimneys to fit mammoth lamp. Each.....$0.25

Steel Frame Kitchen and Night Lamps.

55694 Reflector Lamp made of steel, riveted together; will last a lifetime; the polished tin reflector is removable, and if at any time it is not required can be taken off; it is fitted as shown in cut, complete with glass fount, number 2 burner, wick and chimney. Price $0.46
Per dozen.... .... 5.52

55695 All Steel Side Lamp with polished tin reflector; it is fitted with handled glass fount which can be taken from frame when required; this will be found to be a very convenient lamp; it is fitted with number 2 burner, chimney and wick complete.
Price.................$0.40
Per dozen.......... .... 4 35

55696 All Steel Side or Reflector Lamp, very useful, as it may be hung up or placed on shelf; the frame is so constructed that it can be carried in the hand without the least danger of upsetting; fitted complete with glass fount No. 2 burner, chimney and wick. Price.............$0.35
Per dozen................... 3.80

Lamps—Continued.

55697 Swing Bracket Lamp, made of steel and riveted together, finished in black enamel and bronze stripes, fitted with glass fount, No. 2 burner, 8-inch reflector and chimney complete,
Each..........$0.65
Per dozen.... 7.00
Same as No. 55697, but without reflector. Each....$0.49
Per dozen 5.40

55698 Swing Bracket Lamp, all steel and riveted together, finished in black enamel and bronze stripes; fitted with glass fount No. 2 burner, illuminator and shade, as shown in cut; does not require any chimney,
Price..... .. $0.84
Per dozen.... 8.60

Lamp Shades.

55700   **55701**
55700 Porcelain Lamp Shade, plain white, 7 in., for standing lamps. This pattern is intended to be used on illuminator. Each, plain $0.25
Same as above, decorated .... .40
55701 Porcelain Lamp Shades, cone shapes, 10 and 14 inches. Plain and decorated, assorted decorations, not all like cut; 10 inch for parlor stand lamp; 14 inch for hanging or library lamps. Size ..10 in. 14 in.
Plain, each................................. 55c. 73c.
Decorated............................. 80c. 90c.

55702 Porcelain Lamp Shades, dome shape, 10 and 14 inch. Plain and decorated, assorted decoration; 10 inch for parlor stand lamps; 14 inch for library lamps.
Size.. 10 in. 14 in.
Plain 50c 75c..
Decorated. 75c. $1.00

Paper Shades.

55703 The Queen Folding Paper Shade, to cover the ordinary plain cone shade table lamp and give it the appearance of a nice shade lamp. There are innumerable uses to which the Queen may be put, such as covering up unused stove pipe holes, decorating the walls, covering flower pots, etc. Can be had in red, blue or green. Each, $0.15 Dozen.$1.62
55704 Holders for Queen Folding Shade; will fit any chimney. Each, $0.10 Per dozen....... 1.08

Linen and Silk Piano and Banquet Lamp Shades.

55705 Fancy Silk Shades for banquet and piano lamps, latest styles and artistically made; best China silk used; top cannot be ruffled or damaged by heat, as it is protected by a metal band. The frame on which they are made fits any four inch holder. Choice of the following colors: Red, lemon, orange, pink, nile green, old rose.
15-inch, with 6-inch lace border. Price...........$1.85
15-inch, with 6-inch embroidered chiffon border. Price 2.10
15 inch with 6-inch embroidered chiffon border in colors. Price 2.25
18-inch, with 8-inch lace border. Price........... 2.75
18-inch, with 8-inch embroidered chiffon border. Price.. 3.15
18-inch, with 8-inch embroidered chiffon in colors. Price.. 3.40
NOTE—15-inch shades are used on banquet lamps; 18 on piano lamps.

Lamp Shades—Continued.

55706 The Same material is used in the construction of this shade as 55705, the difference being in shape only.
15-inch, with 6-inch lace border, Price..... ...$1.85
15-inch, with 6-inch chiffon border. Price.......2.10
15-inch, with 6-inch chiffon border, embroidered in colors. Price 2.25
18-inch, with 8-inch lace border. Price........ 2.75
18-inch, with 8-inch embroidered chiffon border. Price.. 3.15
18-inch, with 8-inch embroidered chiffon borders in colors. Price................... 3.40
20-inch, with 8-inch lace border. Price......... 3.50
20-inch, with 8-inch embroidered chiffon border. Price.. 3.90
20-inch, with 8-inch embroidered chiffon border, in colors.................. . ... 4.25

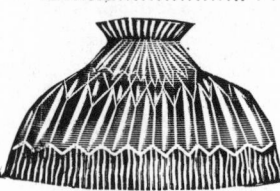

55707 Isabella Linen Shades and holder for banquet lamps; entirely new shape, made of best quality linen with 3-inch silk fringe; it comes only in one size, 16 inches in diameter, and can be had in any of the following colors: Red, lemon, orange, pink and nile green.
Price. with holder, complete.....................$0 65

55740 Linen Shades, 7-inch with 2-inch silk fringe and holder, complete.
Each....$0.25
Per doz.. 2.70
55742 Linen Shade, 9 in., with 3-inch silk fringe and holder complete. Each $0.40
Per dozen 4.32
55743 Linen Shade, 12-inch with 3-inch silk fringe. Each... .... .50
Per dozen................................... 5.40
55744 Linen Shade, 14-inch with 3-inch silk fringe. Each... .... .67
Per dozen................................... 7.42
55745 Brass Shade Holders, suitable for 10, 12, or 14 inch shades, and will fit any chimney. Each. .35

Firemen's Lanterns.

55748 This lantern is made of solid brass of extra heavy quality, and intended for firemen's use; the shield on top of globe is for the purpose of keeping water and steam from entering the globe when in burning buildings; it is fitted with number one burner, taking ⅝ inch wick, and uses the ordinary lantern globe.
Solid brass, each................$1.65
Solid brass nickel plated, each. 2.10

Stockmen's and Shippers' Lanterns.

55749 This lantern is made especially for rough use, being used very extensively on railroads by car inspectors, as they need a very strong light; it is made of the very best quality block tin, nicely japanned; it has a 4-inch silver plated reflector and five inch beveled edge, front glass; the oil pot is large, holding sufficient oil to burn all night; we recommend it wherever a strong and powerful light-giving lantern is desired.
Price..........................$1.80

The Gem Driving Lamp.

IMPROVED.

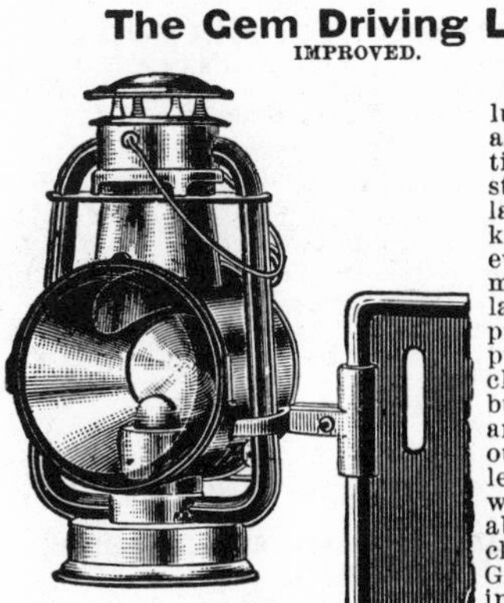

This is absolutely the best and most scientifically constructed driving lamp on the market, or that was ever made. So many driving lamps have been presented to the public as "first class" in their burning qualities and have turned out to be worthless things, that we take a justifiable pride in claiming for the Gem the following points: That it is superior in construction and finish, that it is a perfect lantern in its burning qualities, the light produced is stronger and brighter than the light produced by any lamp using a ½ inch burner, it will not smoke or blow out, nor is it possible to jar it out over rough roads; the reflector is conical, like those used on locomotive headlights, and is of solid copper, heavily silver plated, the lens is extra thick and of the best quality plate glass, with beveled edge. So confident are we of the merits of the Gem that should any purchaser find or prove after using that they are not exactly as represented by us, they may be returned and money will be cheerfully refunded. 55750. Brass..........$2.50

55752 Nickel plated........................... 3.00

55753 Japan finish to match dash and finish of buggy or coach. Each........................... 2.45

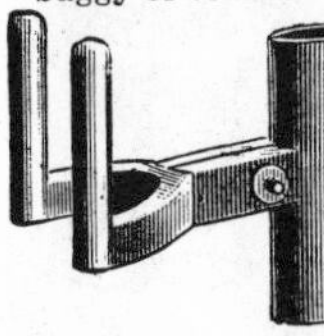

55754 Clamps for fastening Gem Lamp to dash. Each..................$0.25

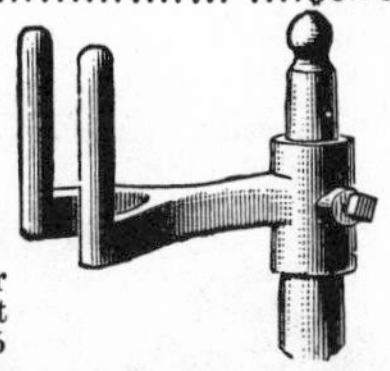

55756 Seat Rod Bracket for fitting Gem Lamp to upright rod at end of seat. Each.$0.25

Conductors' Lanterns

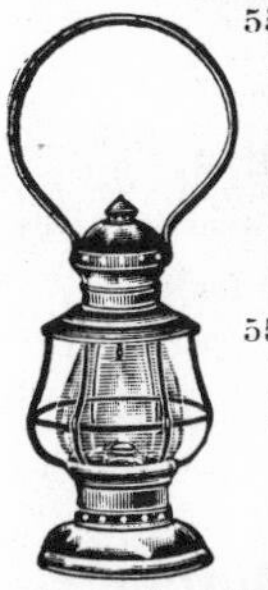

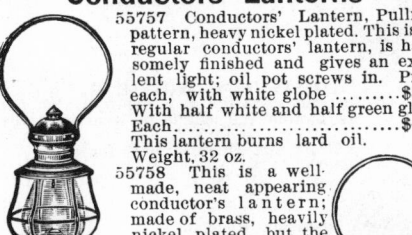

55757 Conductors' Lantern, Pullman pattern, heavy nickel plated. This is the regular conductors' lantern, is handsomely finished and gives an excellent light; oil pot screws in. Price, each, with white globe $3.35
With half white and half green globe. Each..............................$4.85
This lantern burns lard oil. Weight, 32 oz.

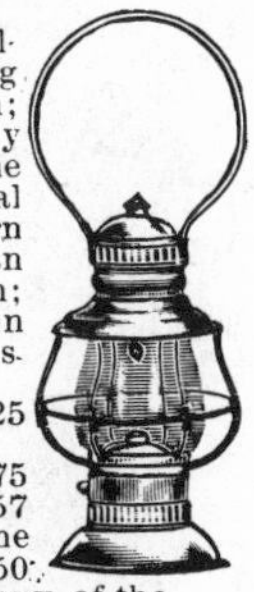

55758 This is a well-made, neat appearing conductor's lantern; made of brass, heavily nickel plated, but the material and general make-up of the lantern is much lighter than our Pullman pattern; the oil well, instead of screwing in fastens by a catch, as shown in illustration.
With white globe, price..........$2.25
With half green and white globe, price.............................. 3.75

55761 Plain Crystal Globe to fit 55757 lantern; they are hand made from the best lead glass. Each $0.50

55763 Globes to fit 55757 lanterns in any of the following colors: Half green and white, half blue and white, or half red and white; the very best quality made. Each 1.75

55765 Engraving name in Old English on globe to fit 55757 lantern. Per name.......... .55

55767 Engraving name in Old English and encircling it in fancy engraved wreath. Per name and wreath.................... .80

Extra globes and engraving for 55758 lantern furnished at same price as charged for 55757.

Raiload and Stockmen's Lanterns.

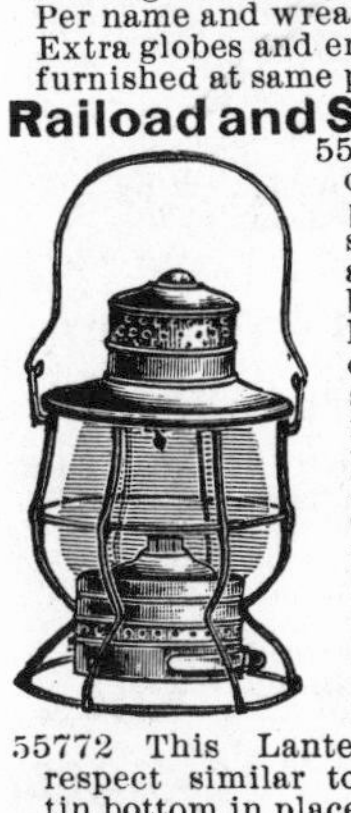

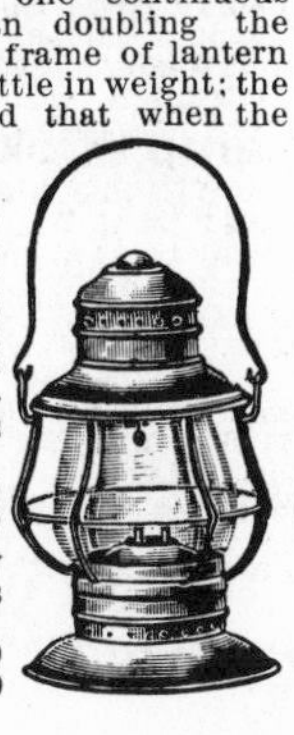

55770 This Lantern is made of double wire in one continuous piece, more than doubling the strength of the frame of lantern and adding but little in weight; the bail is so arranged that when the lantern is set down the bail stands upright in position, to be instantly grasped, or it can be thrown on the base of the lantern if required; burns lard oil.
Price $0.50
Per dozen. 4.50

55772 This Lantern is in every respect similar to 55770, but has tin bottom in place of wire.
Price.............................$0.50
Per dozen........................ 5.40

Tubular or Barn Lantern.

To Burn Kerosene.

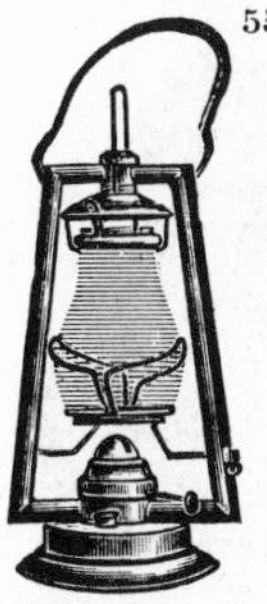

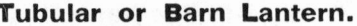

55775 Our New Clipper Lift is a thoroughly serviceable lantern in every respect, strongly made and nicely finished; the oil pot is retinned to prevent leakage; the burner being locked makes it an absolutely safe lantern; the lift movement is simple and efficient; the globe is very easily removed, making it without doubt the easiest handled lantern on the market.
Price.........$0.35
Per dozen... 3.95

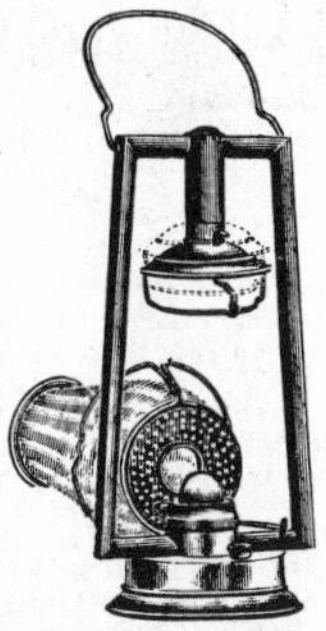

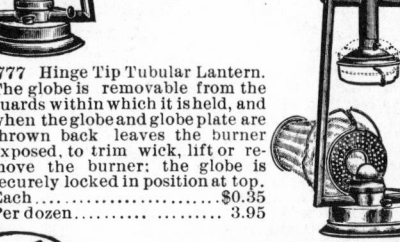

55777 Hinge Tip Tubular Lantern. The globe is removable from the guards within which it is held, and when the globe and globe plate are thrown back leaves the burner exposed, to trim wick, lift or remove the burner; the globe is securely locked in position at top.
Each $0.35
Per dozen.......................... 3.95

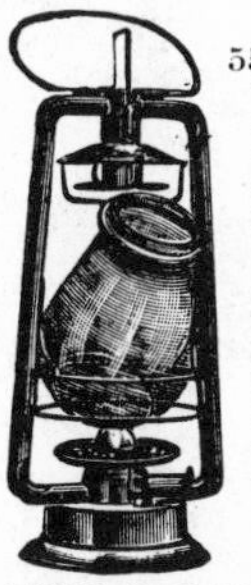

55779 Side Spring or Square Lift Lantern with new inside guard and locked glass flange and burner; the side spring securely locks the globe up when raised, and firmly holds the globe on to the glass flange when lowered. No rust can ever form to cause the lift to stick or work hard. This lantern has a patent one piece tube without elbows or joints, extra large oil pot, retinned to prevent leakage; a well-made and easy working lantern.
Each..............................$0.39
Per dozen.............................. 4.45

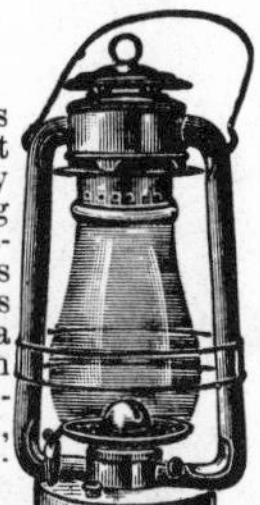

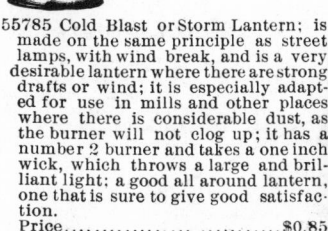

55785 Cold Blast or Storm Lantern; is made on the same principle as street lamps, with wind break, and is a very desirable lantern where there are strong drafts or wind; it is especially adapted for use in mills and other places where there is considerable dust, as the burner will not clog up; it has a number 2 burner and takes a one inch wick, which throws a large and brilliant light; a good all around lantern, one that is sure to give good satisfaction.
Price.................................$0.85
Per dozen................................ 9.25

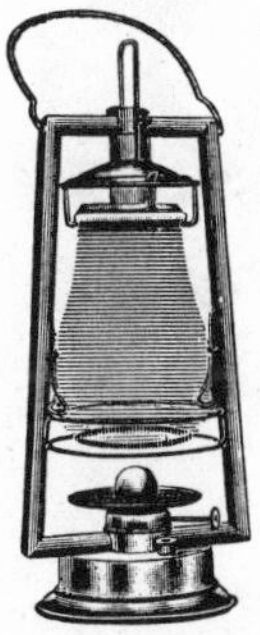

55786 Solid Brass Side Spring Safety Tubular Lantern, perfect in every detail; no rust can ever form to cause the lift to stick or work hard. The glass flange is securely locked so that the burner cannot become detached without first unlocking the glass flange; the globe is removable without taking off the guard.
Each...............................$1.00
Per dozen................................10.80

Tubular Dash Lanterns.

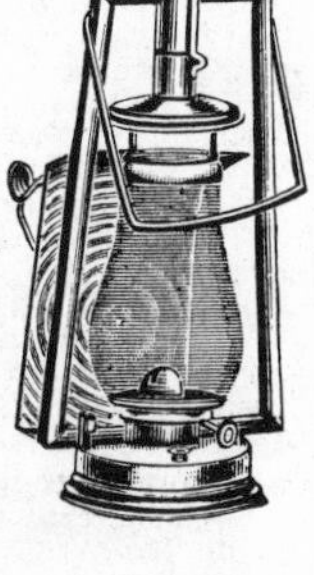

55787 Safety Tubular Dash Lantern, with patent globe lifting attachment that holds globe up while trimming or lighting by turning one side of the thumbpiece on lifting attachment; has spring fastening on back for dash boards; it can also be hung on a nail and makes a good barn lamp; burns kerosene and makes a big light.
Each.............................$0.50
Per dozen.......................... 5.60

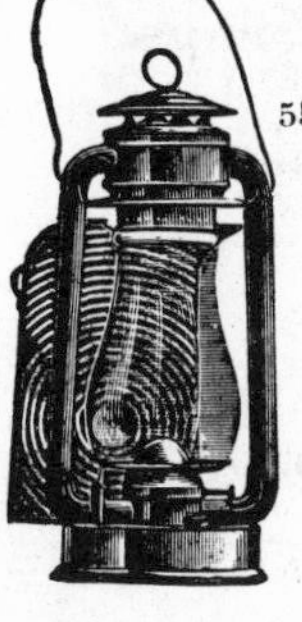

55789 Cold Blast Storm, Dash or Farm Wagon Lantern; will not blow out in the strongest wind; can be used either on front of wagon, or if hung underneath will throw a good light ahead of the team. It is fitted with a number 2 burner, taking a one-inch wick.
Price..................................$1.00
Per dozen................................10.80

Tubular Side Reflector Lamps.

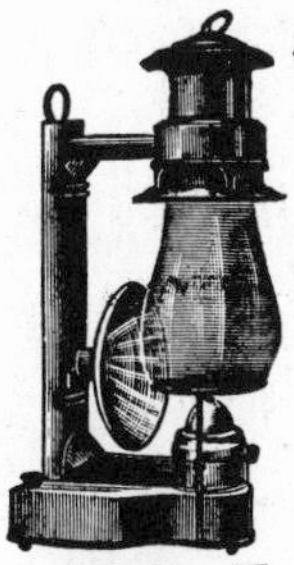

55792 Tubular Side Reflector Lamps, can be hung against the wall indoors or any convenient place out of doors, or carried in the hand; has patent wind break and will stand the wind in exposed places without smoking or blowing out; produces a very strong light. Can be filled, lighted or trimmed without removing the globe; especially adapted for use in stores, warehouses, barns, engine or boiler rooms, or any place where a strong light is required; finish in blue Japan, takes 1 inch wick. Each........................$1.00
Per dozen........................ 10.85

Globe Tubular Street Lamps.

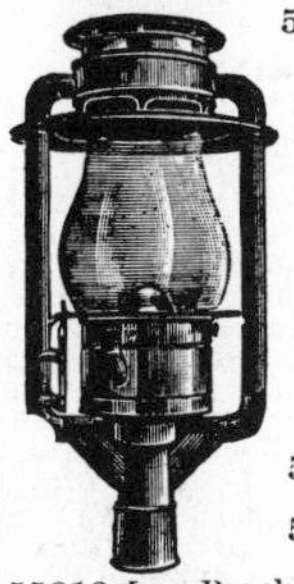

55797 Our globe street lamps have many new and modern improvements, solid elbows, automatic time extinguisher, bottom lift attachment, etc.; also our new wind break around top of lamp, making it impossible for the wind to extinguish the light. By the use of the automatic extinguisher the lamp can be set, when lighted, to burn a certain number of hours; it will then go out of its own accord. Burns 4 hours for 1 cent.
Price, each.............................$3.45

55800 Turned Wood Posts for above lamp. Each.............. 1.50

55810 Iron Cross Bars for posts. Each .... .40

55812 Iron Brackets, 24 inches long, for fastening lamp to building. Each........................ 1.00

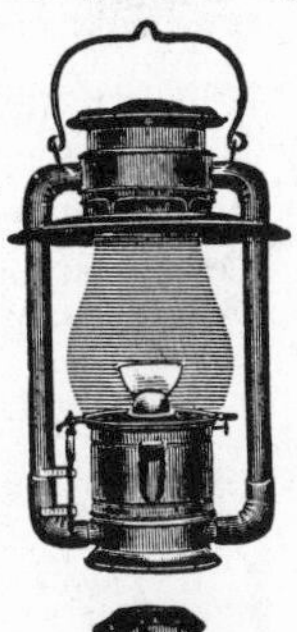

55815 Globe Tubular Hanging Lamp, built on the same principle as our globe street lamp, but is intended to hang by the bail instead of fitting on post. It will be found very convenient, as it can be moved from time to time as occasion requires. Each..... ....$2.85

New Improved Square Tubular Street Lamp.

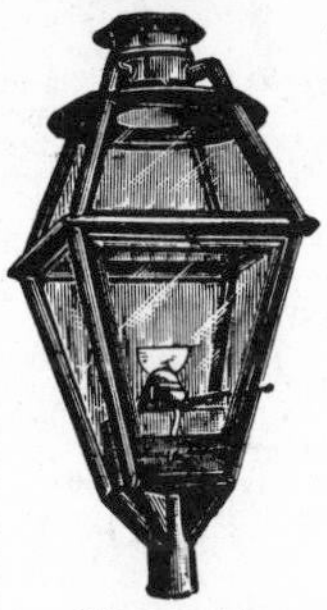

55820 This lamp is constructed on the same principle as the globe street lamp. It will not freeze up in cold weather, and will not smoke or blow out in the hardest winds. The burner is set corner wise across the lamp so that the flat side of the flame is shown from each of the four sides, thereby giving an equal light in all directions, and which also prevents the flame from striking the top lights of glass, which in other lamps is a serious defect. This lamp is beautiful in its proportions, strongly and well made and of the best material One trial will satisfy all of its superiority. Each.........$4.65

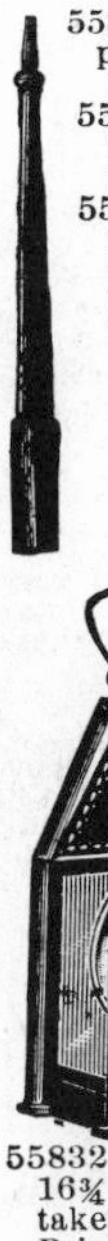

55822 Turned Wood posts for above lamps Each...........$1.50

55824 Iron Cross Bars for posts. Each $0.40

55826 Iron brackets, 24 inches long, for fastening lamp to buildings or posts. Each $1.00

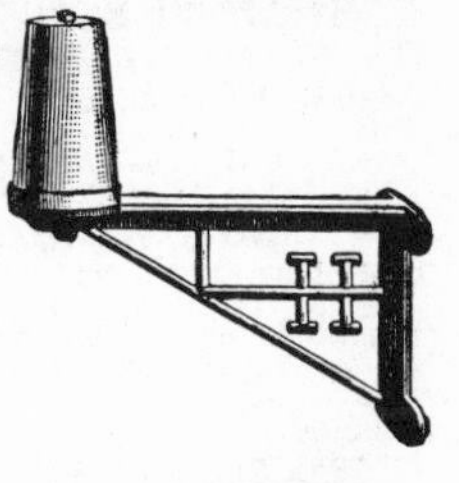

Improved Square Tubular Lamp.

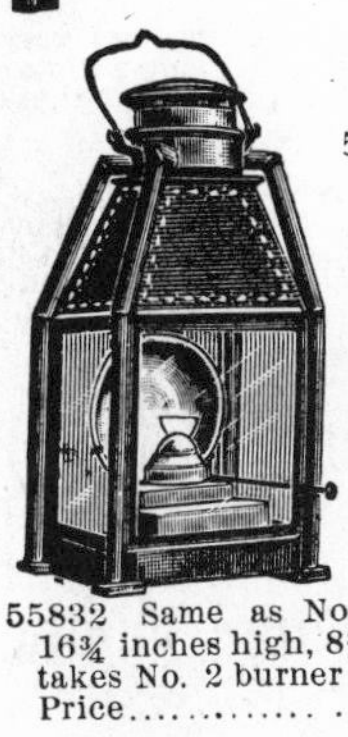

55830 This lamp gives a clear and steady light and will not smoke or blow out in strongest wind; especially adapted for use in warehouses, packing houses, sawmills, lumber yards, freight yards, or in any place where a good, strong light is required; height, 32 inches; width, 11¼ inches; depth, 10½ inches; burner takes 1½ inch wick. This makes an excellent stable lamp; weight, boxed, 22 pounds. Price.................................$3.60

55832 Same as No. 55830, but is smaller; measures 16¾ inches high, 8¾ inches wide and 7½ inches deep, takes No. 2 burner and one inch wick.
Price...................................$2.60

Ten-inch Square Headlight.

For Traction Engines.
Guaranteed to give satisfaction or money refunded.

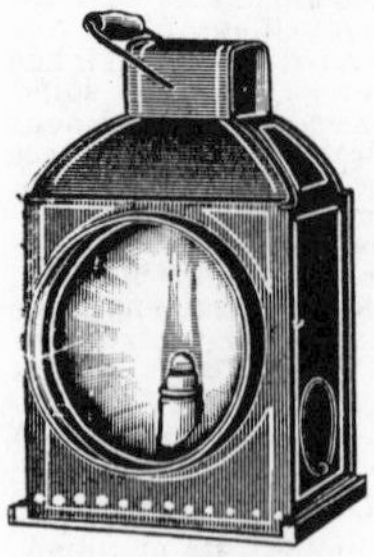

55835 This headlight is especially adapted for this purpose, as it gives a very strong light; it is built on scientific principles and will not blow or jar out. It throws a strong and bright light over 400 feet. They are packed ready for shipment complete with all the parts for fitting to engine.
Price.............................$ 9.00

Tubular "Search Light."

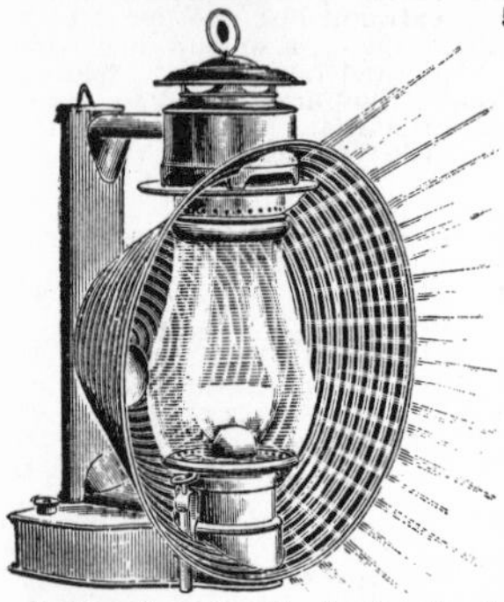

55836 This will be found just the lamp where a strong light is required over a large space, as in stables, mills, warehouses, picnic grounds, summer resorts, etc. It throws a brilliant and steady light out of doors as well as inside, without smoking or flickering, and is not affected by the wind or strong drafts. It is also an excellent lamp for kitchen or cellar use. It is a very desirable lamp to be used in the bow of a small boat, for hunting or spearing fish in the night, as the light can be thrown ahead and the rest of the boat kept in darkness; unlike the gasoline torch much used for this purpose, it does not emit any smell or smoke; the oil pot is large and holds sufficient kerosene to burn all night. It takes a regular lantern globe and is trimmed with a strong brass burner, taking a 1-inch wick. Price............$1.60
Fitted with bullseye globe..........................1.65

Chimney Cleaners.

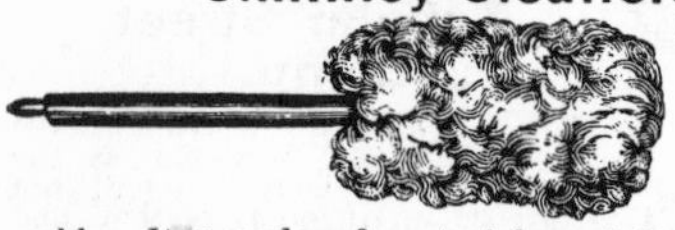

55837 The New Era Chimney Cleaner will be found useful and very desirable. It is made of material specially suited to this purpose; with it you can clean a chimney better and quicker than by any other means.
Price..$0.10
Per dozen...1.08

Lamp Chimneys.

Lamp chimneys cannot be packed safely with other goods. They must be packed in a box by themselves. *For this reason we positively will not sell less than a box of 3 dozen.* They come in cases of 3 and 6 dozen, and at the low price we sell them almost any one can afford to buy 3 dozen. If you cannot use this many, club with your neighbor. No allowance made for breakage. Be sure and give size wanted.

Straight Sun Chimneys—Not Hinged.

55840 Best Flint Straight Sun Chimneys (not hinged).

No.	0	1	2
Per Case of 3 doz.....	$1.26	$1.37	$1.90
Per Case of 6 doz.....	2.47	2.64	3.60

Sun-Hinge Chimneys.

55842 Best Flint Sun Hinge.

Chimneys.	Per case 3 doz.	Per case 6 doz.
No. 0	$1.32	$2.55
No. 1	1.44	2.76
No. 2	2.04	3.75

La Bastie Lamp Chimneys.

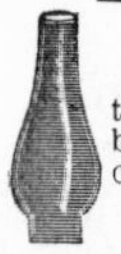

La Bastie Chimneys, patented process, very tough, can be thrown across a room without breaking. We will sell any quantity of these chimneys.

	Each.	Per doz.
55843 No. 1 Sun La Bastie Chimneys..	$0.12	$1.30
55845 No. 2 Sun La Bastie Chimneys..	15	1.62

BARB WIRE.

Send for our latest price list of Barb Wire and you will see that our prices are low. Worth your while to write us before buying elsewhere.

Dark or Police Lanterns.

Burn Sperm Oil.

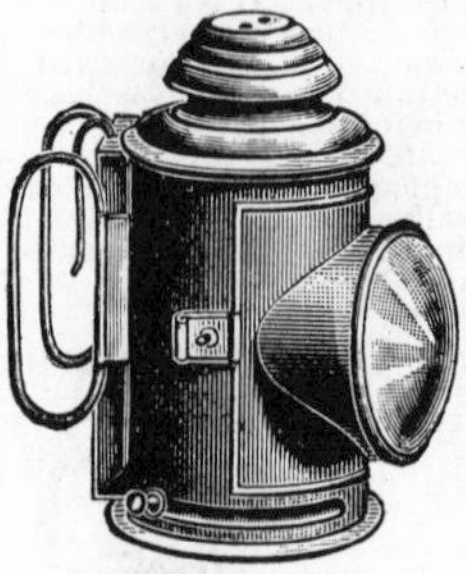

55850-52

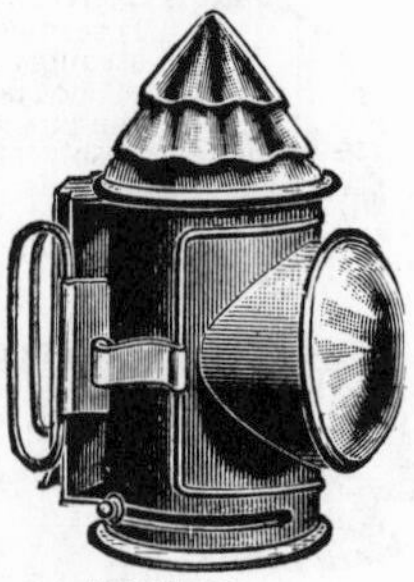

55855-60

55850 Police or Dark Lanterns, 2¾ inch bull's eye. (Weight, 22 oz.) Each............$0.45
55852 Police Lanterns, 3 inch bull's eye. (Weight, 26 oz.) Each..............................60
55855 Special Quality Dark Lanterns, made of heavy tin, nickel plated. These are considered the finest finish and strongest in the market; each lamp is furnished with the best quality fire polished lens.
With 2½ inch lens, each..............................90
With 3 inch lens, each..............................1.15
55860 Same as No. 55855, but is made of polished brass. With 2½ inch lens, each..............1.90
With 3 inch lens, each..............................2.45

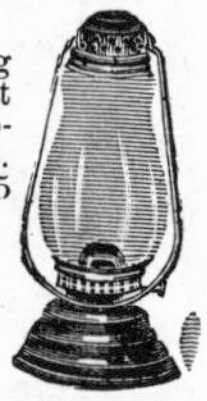

55865 The Cadet Lantern; just the thing for a lady around the house or short journeys on dark nights; burns kerosene, and stands 6¾ inches high. Brass. Price..............................$0.45

Cigar Lighters.

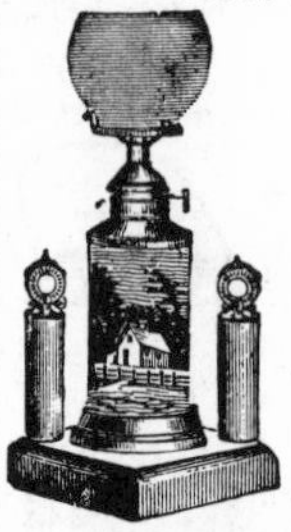

55867 Cigar Lighter, complete with colored globe, either amber, white, blue or ruby. There are two lighters, to be used with alcohol. The vase is hand decorated. Each..............................$1.10

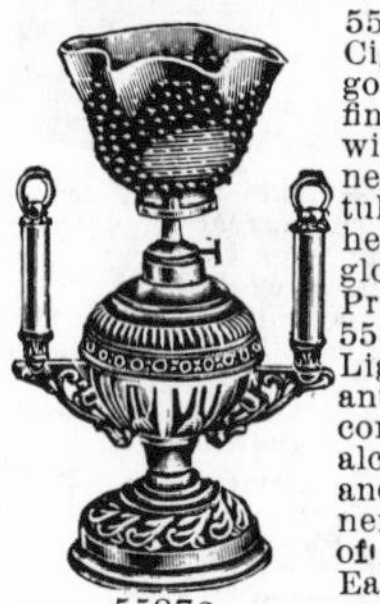

55872

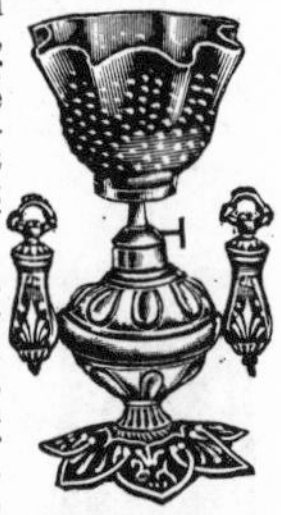

55870

55870 Metal Cigar Lighter, gold and silver finish, complete with alcohol burner and ruby dot tulip globe; height to top of globe, 10 inches Price $1.95
55872 Cigar Lighter, brass in antique finish, complete with alcohol burner and ruby dot burner; height to top of globe, 12 inches. Each..............................$2.10

Lantern Globes.

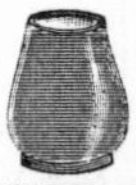

55874 Railroad Lantern Globes; height, 5⅛ inches; across the top, 2$\frac{11}{16}$ inches; across the bottom 3¼ inches.
Price..............................$0.10
Per dozen..............................1.08
55876 Ruby Railroad Lantern Globes; will fit all our railroad lanterns. Each..............................30
Per dozen..............................3.24

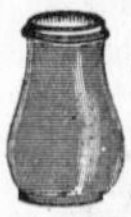

55878 Tubular Lantern Globes; height, 6½ inches; across the top, 2⅞ in.; across the bottom, 3⅛ in.
Price, each..............................$0.07
Per dozen..............................75
55880 Ruby Tubular Lantern Globes; will fit any tubular lantern.
Each..............................30
Per dozen..............................3.24

Globes for Street Lamps.

55881 Large Globes to fit 55797 and 55815 street lamps. Each..............................$0 50

Rochester Chimneys.

55882 No. 2.
Each..............................$0.09
Per doz..............................98
55885 No. 1.
Each..............................06
Per doz..............................65
55886 No. 3 fits our Mammoth Store Lamp.
Each..............................25

Rochester Wicks.

55887 No. 2. Per dozen..............................$0.25
55888 No. 1. Per dozen..............................20
55889 No. 3. Per dozen..............................75

Sun Burners (Not Hinged).

Sun Burners (not hinged), for sun chimneys.
This burner takes an ordinary straight bottom chimney and cannot be used with any other.

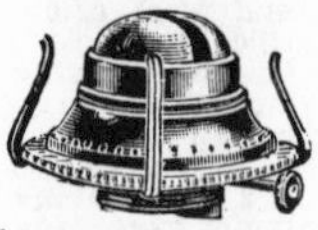

55893 No. 0, brass.
Each..............................$0.05
Per dozen..............................50
Weight, 1 oz.
55895 No. 1, brass.
Each..............................05
Per dozen..............................55
Weight, 1½ oz.
55897 No. 2 Brass.
Each..............................08
Per dozen..............................87
Weight, 1½ oz.

Tubular and Railroad Lantern Burners.

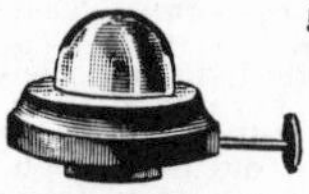

55900 Tubular Lantern Burners will fit all regular tubular lanterns.
Each..............................$0.08
Per dozen..............................89

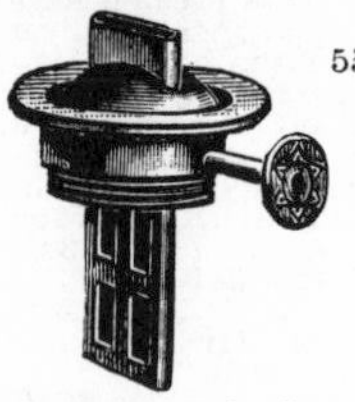

55905 Ratchet Burner for railroad lanterns, will burn kerosene or sperm oil.
Each..............................$0.10
Per dozen..............................1.08

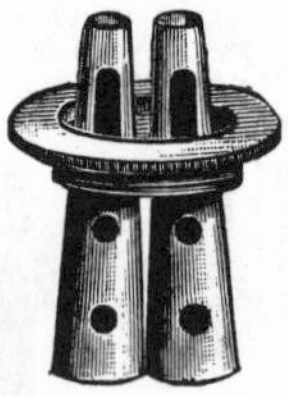

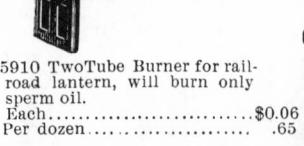

55910 TwoTube Burner for railroad lantern, will burn only sperm oil.
Each..............................$0.06
Per dozen..............................65

Climax Burner.

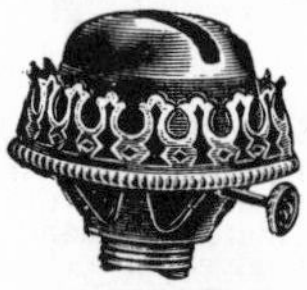

55915 Climax Burner, fits No. 2 or 3 lamp collar; takes 1½ inch wick, gives a powerful light and takes an ordinary No. 2 chimney.
Each..............................$0.15
Per dozen..............................1.65

Sun-Hinge Burners.

This burner takes a sun-hinge chimney, which has flange on the bottom and cannot be used with any other.
55920 No. 1 Brass Sun-Hinge Burners for sun-hinge chimneys.
Each..............................$0.07
Per dozen..............................75
Weight, 2 oz.
55922 No. 2, Brass Sun-Hinge Burners.
Each..............................12
Per dozen..............................1.30
Weight, 2½ oz.

The P. & A. Duplex Burner

This burner takes a special chimney and cannot be used with any other.

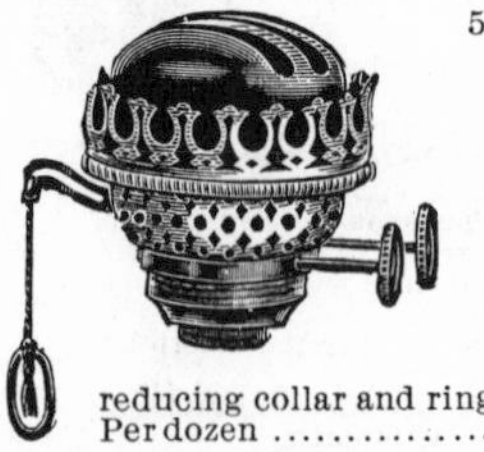

55930 This is, without doubt, the most complete, strongest and best constructed burner now in use. It takes two wicks, has a patent extinguisher to put out the light, emits a large brilliant and steady light and is suitable for fine parlor, vase or library lamps.
Price, with extinguisher, reducing collar and ring for globe..........$0.80
Per dozen..............................8.64
Return at our expense if not satisfactory.
55932 Extra chimneys for P. & A. Duplex Burner. Each $0.08 Per dozen..............................87
Weight, 12 ounces.

Prisms.

55934 Crystal Glass Prisms, for ornamenting hanging lamps. We do not have them in any other color. Each..............................$0.03
Per dozen..............................35

Lamp Wicks and Candle Wicking.

55940 Candle Wicking, per pound..............................$0.22
55941 Lamp Wicks' No. 0, ⅜ inch, per doz..............................03
55946 Lamp Wicks, No. 1, ⅝ inch, per doz..............................04
55949 Lamp Wicks, No. 2, 1 inch, per doz..............................05
55950 Lamp Wicks, No. 3, 1½ inch, per doz..............................08
55953 Lamp Wicks to fit No. 55692 and 55693 lamps, per doz..............................75
55954 Lamp Wicking No. 0, ⅜ inch, roll 32 yds..............................27
55955 Lamp Wicking No. 1, ⅝ inch, roll 32 yds..............................35
55956 Lamp Wicking No. 2, 1 inch, roll 32 yds..............................60
55957 Lamp Wicking No. 3, 1½ inch, roll 32 yds..............................80

Have your Mail Packages insured. See page 1.

BICYCLE DEPARTMENT.

Our bicycle department is one of our most prominent and we are sure that our large experience in selling cycles and appliances enable us to offer our customers the best that is to be had at the price. We publish a special bicycle catalogue and advise all interested to send for it. It is nicely illustrated and explains very fully the details of construction of our bicycles.

55975 Hawthorne Safety. Strictly high grade.

Price, complete.................................$65.00

We assert without fear of contradiction that the Hawthorne is equal to any $100 cycle in the market. Money cannot build a better wheel.

Specifications.

Bearings—All ball, adjustible and dust proof, ₇⁄₁₆-inch balls in front wheel, ¼ inch balls in crank hanger and rear wheel.

Chain—₅⁄₆-inch, Humber pattern, hardened blocks, adjustable at rear, fork ends.

Cones—Turned from bars of finest tool steel, hardened clear through and carefully tempered, then accurately ground into perfect shape by special machinery.

Cranks—Round pattern, detachable, 6½ inch throw, drop forged from carbon steel, and given a spring temper by being hardened in oil.

Crank Hanger—Drop forged from the best steel, machined down until very light, but designed so as to give great strength and rigidity; fitted with hardened tool steel cups, accurately ground and polished after being inserted in the bracket, thus insuring perfect alignment of both rows of balls—a very important feature.

Finish—Finest black enamel, hand rubbed and polished, all bright parts polished, coppered, nickel plated and buffed.

Frame—Deep diamond, built on latest and most approved lines of the best cold drawn weldless steel tubing and drop forgings throughout, with all connections thoroughly reinforced.

Gear—63 or 66½ inches.

Handle Bar—Curved upward medium drop or full drop as preferred, fitted with best cork grips.

Head—9⅞ inches between the ball races.

Hubs—Turned from special bar steel and fitted with best tool steel cups, carefully tempered and accurately ground.

Pedals—Dust proof, ball bearing, rubber or rat trap as desired; rat trap sent unless otherwise ordered.

Rims—Wood.

Saddle—Garford or Hunt, road pattern.

Spokes—Tangent, of Torrington make, double swagged, of best quality needle wire, nickel plated, 32 to front and 36 to rear wheels, tied at intersections.

Sprockets—Rear sprocket turned from solid bar of tool steel, hardened and tempered clear through; front sprocket steel, drop forged, fastened to crank axle with our patent corrugated fastening, warranted never to work loose or give trouble, and doing away with the necessity of heating the crank axle, as is the case when the sprocket is brazed to the shaft.

Tires—Morgan & Wright pneumatic, 1895 model.

Wheels—28-inches.

Weight—With all on ready to ride, 24 pounds.

Accessories—Tool bag, inflater, oil can, spanner, wrench and tire repair outfit.

Hawthorne Ladies' Safety.

Strictly high grade; the best that money can buy.

This machine is identical with the Hawthorne for men, except that it has our patent duplex drop frame for ladies' use. The cranks are 6 inch, the gear 56 inches, and the distance from seat post to crank shaft is 21 inches. The equal of this machine is not to be purchased elsewhere for less than $100.00. Price, complete...............$65.00

White Star, No. I.

55985 A first class all around Bicycle; up to date in every detail. This wheel will compare in workmanship and quality with other wheels retailing at $75.00 to $85.00. Weight, 27 pounds. Price... ....$45.00

SPECIFICATIONS.

Frame—1895 pattern, deep frame, with long head and wheel base, narrow tread, made from cold drawn seamless steel tubing and steel forgings.

Wheels—28-inch, with wood rims, fitted with 1¾-inch M. & W. pneumatic tires, steel rims furnished, if desired.

Steering Fork—Cold drawn steel tubing, with steel drop forged crown, adjustable nickeled coasters.

Handle Bar—Made of ₇⁄₈ cold drawn seamless steel tubing, drop or upturned pattern, fitted with cork handles, with German silver ferrules.

Bearings—Ball bearings to every part, made from high grade steel, carefully hardened, all dust proof.

Cranks—Round, 6½-inch throw.

Pedals—Dust proof, fitted with large moulded rubbers, rat-trap pedals furnished when so ordered.

Chain—Humber pattern, ₅⁄₁₆-inch block chain, hardened, rear adjustment.

Gear—Sprocket wheels, detachable, geared to 63 inches.

Saddle—Garford, model M. 2.

Finish—All bright parts finely nickeled, japanned with our own special enamel, which produces the best finish that can be obtained.

Tool Bag—Fitted with wrench, oil can and pump. This wheel will be furnished with an entirely detachable brake, when so ordered.

White Star, No. 2.

55990 A Light Medium Grade Ladies' Wheel. Weight, 31 pounds. Price.. $45.00

The specifications are identical with White Star No. 1, except that the frame is a double dropped tube, as shown. The cranks are 6 inch and the gear 60 inch. Others ask $75.00 or $85.00 for identical machines.

White Star, No. 3.
FOR BOYS.
Weight, 24 pounds.

Price. $38.50

55592
55992—   SPECIFICATIONS.

Frame—Improved 1895 pattern, deep frame; made of steel tubing, with important parts of steel drop forgings.

Wheels—26-inch with wood rims, with nickeled tangent spokes, fitted with 1½ inch Morgan & Wright pneumatic tires.

Steering Fork—Made of steel tubing, with steel drop forged crown. Adjustable nickeled coasters.

Handle Bar—Made of steel tubing, properly curved; cork handles with nickeled ferrules.

Bearings—Ball Bearings to every part made from high grade steel, carefully hardened; all dust proof.

Cranks—Round, detachable, 5½ inch throw.

Pedals—Dust proof; made of steel and hardened; fitted with moulded rubbers.

Chain—Humber pattern, ₅⁄₆ inch block chain true to gauge. Rear adjustment.

Gear—Sprocket wheels detachable, geared to 56-inch.

Saddle—Garford.

Finish—All bright parts finely nickeled; japanned with our own special enamel, which produces the best finish that can be obtained.

Tool Bag—Wrench, oil can and pump.

White Star, No. 4.

For Girls.

This wheel is strong enough to carry ladies of light weight and small stature.

Weight, 27½ pounds.

Price, $38.50

55594

55994 This wheel is the same as the White Star No. 3, except that it has a double drop frame, as shown. It cannot be duplicated elsewhere for less than $60.00.

White Star, No. 5.

For Boys, 7 to 15 Years Old
Weight, 21 1-2 pounds.

Price....$35.00

55996

55996   SPECIFICATIONS

Frame—Improved 1895 pattern, deep frame; made of steel tubing, with important parts of steel drop forgings

Wheels—24 inch, with wood rims, nickeled tangent spokes, fitted with 1½ inch Morgan & Wright pneumatic tires.

Steering Fork—Made of steel tubing, with steel drop forged crown, adjustable nickel coasters.

Handle Bar—Made of steel tubing, properly curved, cork handles with nickel ferrules.

Bearings—Ball bearings to every part, made from high grade steel carefully hardened, all dust proof.

Cranks—Round, detachable, 5-inch throw.

Pedals—Dust proof, made of steel and hardened, fitted with moulded rubbers.

Chain—Humber pattern, ₅⁄₁₆ block chain, true to gauge, rear adjustment.

Gear—Sprocket wheels, detachable, geared to 51 inches.

Saddle—Garford.

Finish—All bright parts finely nickeled, japanned with our own special enamel, which produces the best finish that can be obtained.

Tool Bag—Wrench, oil can and pump.

White Star, No. 6.

For Girls, 7 to 14 Years Old.
Weight, 25 1-2 pounds.

Price..$35.00

55998—
This wheel is identical with the White Star No. 5, except that it has a double dropped frame as shown, for girls use.

The Youth's Companion.

Ball Bearing Bicycle.

This bicycle is suitable for boys or girls from 5 to 12 years of age. It is not intended for grown people.

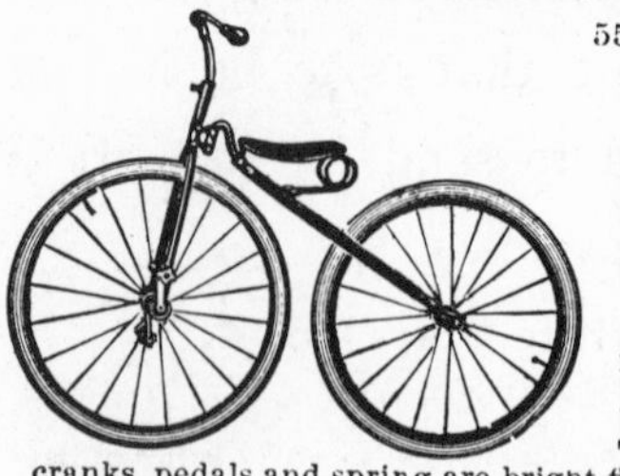

55999 This bicycle is strong and substantial, at the same time being light in weight. The frame is made of the best quality of wrought steel and malleable iron, and is finished with best quality of black enamel. The handle bar, cranks pedals and spring are bright finish, and rims painted, making a very tasty appearance. The wheels are ball bearing, with highest grade bearings. The back bone head is forged steel, and is closely fitted to the foot casting, making the bicycle very rigid. Morgan & Wright tires are used same as those on our White Star machines. Considering price and quality, this is the best bicycle yet put on the market for boys. The tires on these machines are covered by the manufacturers' guarantee the same as our regular safeties. Price, with 24-inch front wheel......$14.00
Price, with 28-inch front wheel 18.00

Stylish Bicycle Clothing.

English Bloomer Suits—Tailor made.
For Coats give breast measurement. For Pants give waist measurement.

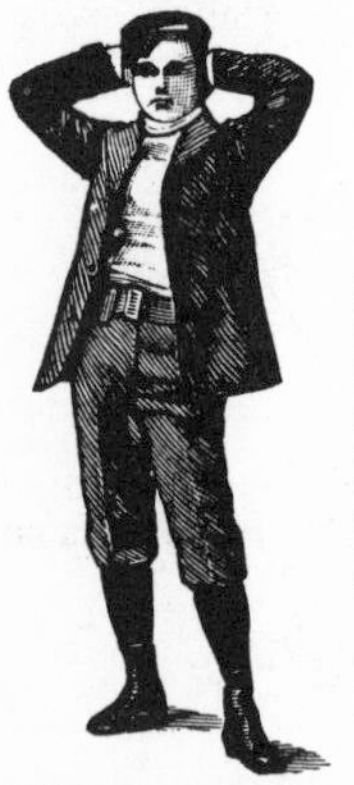

The almost universal use of the wheel as a means of pleasure has developed a great demand for strongly made, neat and tasty clothing, which has enough uniform appearance to distinguish the wearer as a rider, at the same time makes a neat business or street suit. Our goods are selected and made up with this view, and we can assure riders that nothing in the market is better made or more tasty in shape.

56001 Extra Fine Wool Cassimere, very dressy in small gray or brown checks, coat, four button sack, two lower, one cash and one pump pockets. Pants bloomer, two hip pockets with buttoned flap.
Price, per suit..$9.33
Price, coat separate.............................. 5.66
Price, pants separate.............................. 3.67
56003 Fine Woolen Mixture in gray and brown, gray and black checks and plain black, rich and handsome, coat, four button sack, with two lower, one cash and one pump pockets. Pants bloomer with two hip pockets, with buttoned flap. Price, per suit.................................$7.33
Price, coat separate.............................. 4.67
Price, pants separate.............................. 2.66
56005 Brown Check Imitation Scotch Tweed, medium weight, very handsome in coloring and designs, coat three-button sack, with four patch pockets. Pants bloomer, reinforced seat, two hip pockets.
Price, per suit...$5.33
Price, coat separate.............................. 3.16
Price, pants separate.............................. 2.17
56007 Same as No. 56005, but is gray mixed.
Price, per suit.............................. 5.33
Price, coat separate.............................. 3.16
Price, pants separate.............................. 2.17
56009 Light Brown Mixed Chevoit, neat, strong and good wearing. Coat, three-button sack, four patch pockets. Pants, bloomer style with two hip pockets, buckles and straps at knee.
Price, per suit.............................. 4.66
Price, coat separate.............................. 2.66
Price, pants separate.............................. 2.00
56011 Same as No. 56009, but is oxford or black mixed.
Price, per suit.............................. 4.66
Price, coat separate.............................. 2.66
Price, pan s separate.............................. 2.00

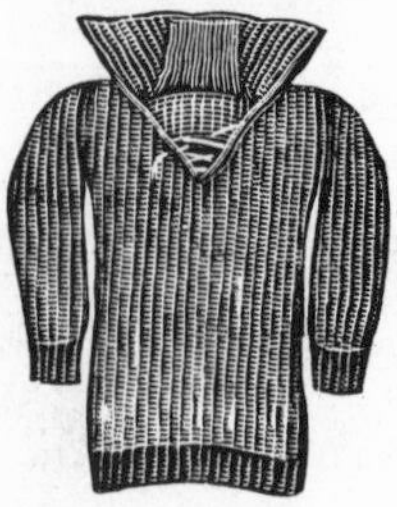

Sweaters, Wool and Worsted.

All sizes, colors and weights. Give chest measure when ordering shirts or sweaters, waist measure when ordering pants.
56012 The New Turtle Neck Sweater is the kind to get. It is full knit worsted, just what a scorcher wants. It comes in black, white and navy blue, and in sizes, from 34 to 44. Weight, about 1 pound and 14 ounces. Price..$3.49

Sweaters—Continued.

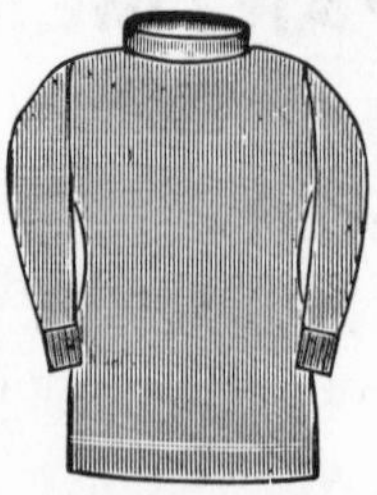

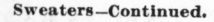

56015 Extra Fine Heavy Worsted Sweater, full fashioned, equal in value to those generally sold for $5.00. Colors: White, black and navy blue. Sizes. 34 to 44. Weight about 1 pound 12 ounces. Price......$3.15

56016 Cotton Sweater. full knit, high collar; nothing like it for hot weather. Colors: Ecru or dead grass only. Sizes, 34 to 44. Price.. .... $0.35
56018 Worsted Sweater. full knit, fast colors, black and white and navy blue. Sizes, 34 to 44. Weight, 1¼ pounds. Price.............. 2.10
56021 Wool Sweaters. full knit, high collar. Colors: Black and navy blue only. Sizes, 34 to 44. Weight, 1 pound. Price.................. 1.50

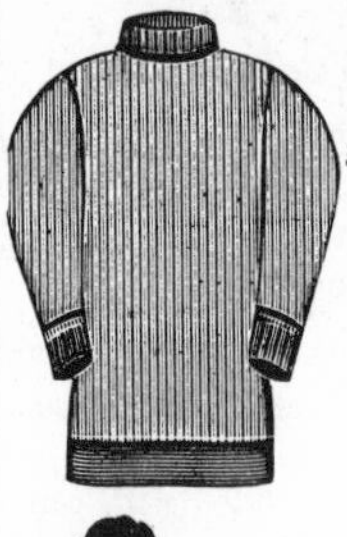

56023 Worsted Sweater, full knit, in plain body, with stripes at collar, cuffs and bottom; a very nobby article. Colors: Black, white and navy blue. Sizes, 34 to 44. Weight, 1½ ounds. Price.............................$2.79

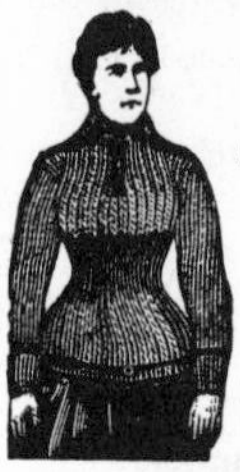

56025 Ladies' Sweaters, fine worsted, laced collar, full fashioned, striped collars and cuffs, same as in cut. Colors: Black, white, navy blue and French gray. Sizes, 30 to 40. Weight, 1 pound. Price... ....$2.80

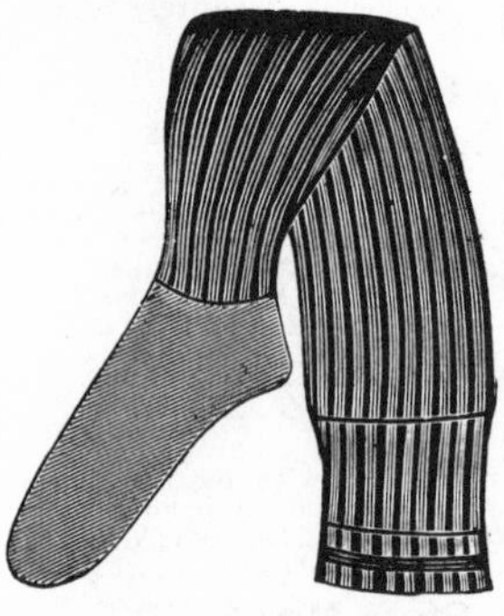

56027 Bicycle Stocking, extra stout ribbed, all wool. Shawknit; the most durable, made, black only. Per pair.....$0.95
56030 Bicycle Stocking, superfine worsted hose, extra length, derby ribbed, seamless, black, navy, blue or gray. Per pair.....$0.65
56033 Bicycle Stockings, Shawknit, cotton; absolutely fast black, ribbed, seamless. Per pair... .$0.35

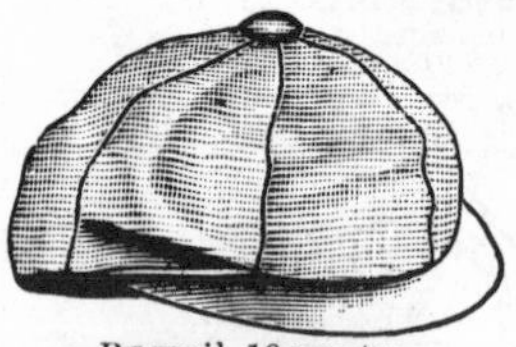

56036 Cap, hook down, made of fine flannel with sweat band, black or navy blue. Each..$0.40

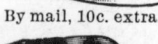

By mail, 10c. extra.

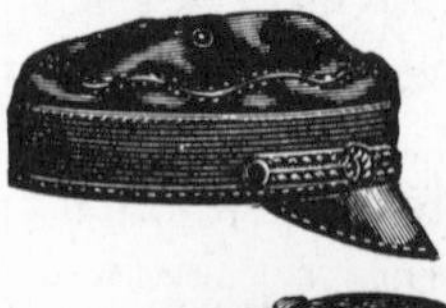

56038 Cap, Boston Club style. Color: Navy blue. Each $0.85

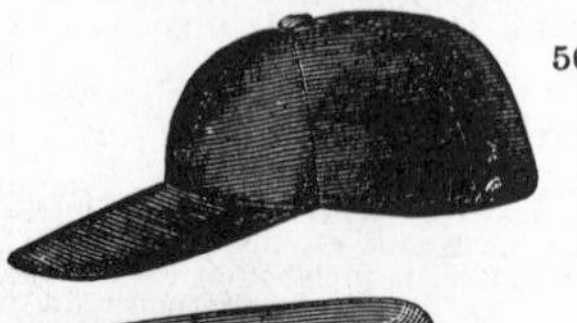

56042 Scorchers' Cap, made of flannel, either blue or black, and in all sizes; extra long beak to shade the eyes. Price.$0.50

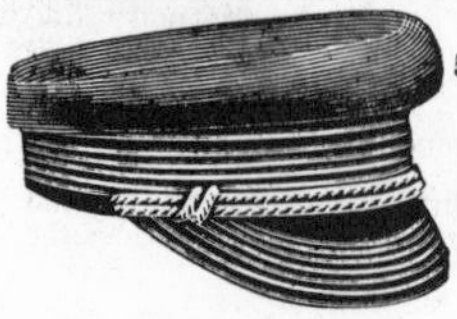

56043 Stanley or Yachting Cap, made of fine flannel, in either blue, black or mixed colors, and all sizes. Sate size and color wanted when ordering. Ptrice $0.55

Morgan & Wright Pneumatic Tires.

The Morgan & Wright tire for 1895 is as perfect in every detail as possible to make it, and it is worthy the confidence of every rider. This tire is guaranteed by the makers in the only way which really serves the rider's interests, and the terms of the guarantee given below should be carefully considered. We shall furnish all our bicycles with these tires unless otherwise ordered.

Guarantee.

We shall continue in 1895 our custom of repairing all tires of our manufacture, free of charge.
We shall replace defective parts when, in our judgment, the defect is from our fault. In no case will we replace when worn out in service or injured by accident.
Make your request direct to us, and not through the makers of your wheel.
Express charges on tires must be prepaid in every instance. If return by mail is desired, postage at the rate of one cent per ounce must come with the request for repairs. ☞ **Do not send the wheel with the tire.**
See that every package sent has your address securely fastened to package.
Any pneumatic tire ever made, or to be made, will some time need repairs, and will ultimately wear out in service. MORGAN & WRIGHT,
331 to 339 West Lake St., Chicago, Ill.

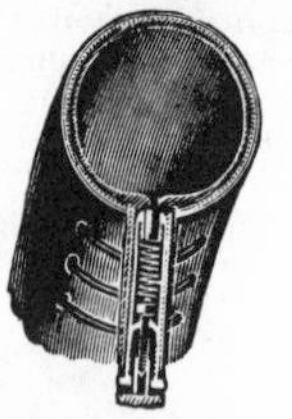

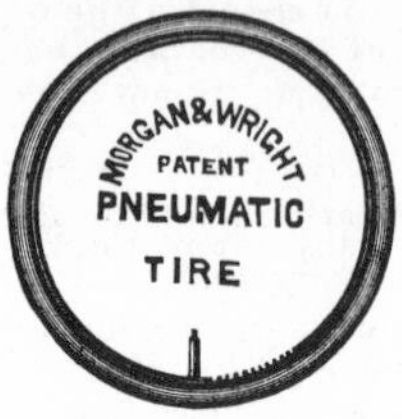

Showing construction of tire and valve.

56045 Morgan & Wright Tires, styles A, X, B, D, M, N, S 2 and O, complete with inner tubes, valves and pump, 28 or 30 inches. Per pair....$9.75
56046 Same styles as above but 24 and 26 inches. Per pair.............................. 8.75
56048 Morgan & Wright Tire, style H; weight, 6 pounds per pair and made to fit wide flat section rims. Per pair.............................. 12.50
56050 Morgan & Wright Tire, style C, sectional size 1¾ inches deep, 1⅝ inches wide, made to take the place of 1¼ inch cushion tires without remodeling rims, made for 28 or 30 inch wheels. Price, per pair........ .... 10.75
56051 Inner Tubes complete with valve stem and valve for 24, 26, 28 or 30 inch tires. Each.... 2.00
56053 Outer Casing for 24 or 26 inch Morgan & Wright tires. Each.............................. 2.75
56054 Outer Casing for 28 or 30 inch Morgan & Wright tires. Each.............................. 3.00

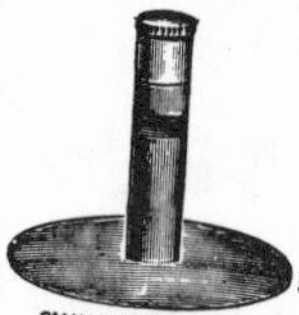

SMALLVALVE & STEM ACTUAL SIZE
56055

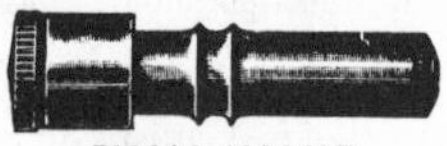

SMALL VALVE
ACTUAL SIZE
56056

56055 Valve Stems for Morgan & Wright tires. Each..............$0.10
56056 Valves for Morgan & Wright tires. Each..................$0.15

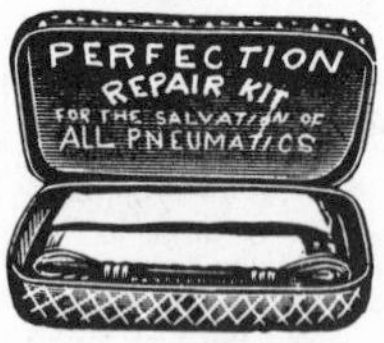

56058 Pneumatic Tire Repair Outfit contains a liberal supply of everything needed to make a quick and sure repair. Each.....................$0.25

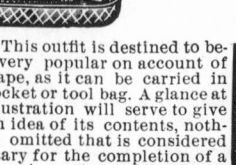

56060 This outfit is destined to become very popular on account of its shape, as it can be carried in the pocket or tool bag. A glance at the illustration will serve to give you an idea of its contents, nothing is omitted that is considered necessary for the completion of a good repair outfit. Price...$0.15

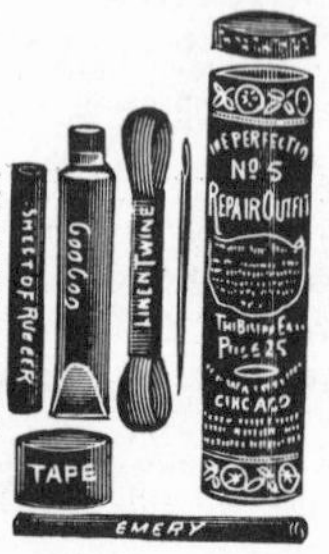

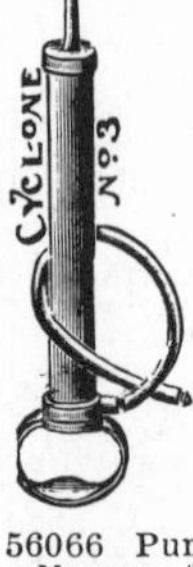

56062 This pump is intended for the dealer, re pairman and rider; it is very powerful. it has 1½x12 inch nickeled cylinder, steel plunger, cupped leather packing and steel ball valve. The new valve fastening with which this pump is furnished is the most satisfactory on the market as it fits nearly all valves. Price.................................$1.00

56066 Pumps to fit Morgan & Wright pneumatic tire. Price.........$0.30

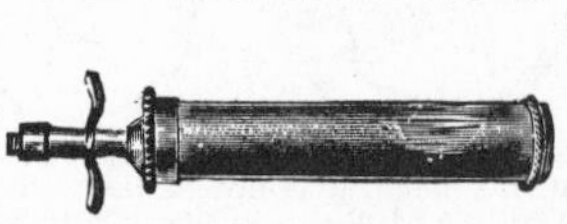

Saddles.

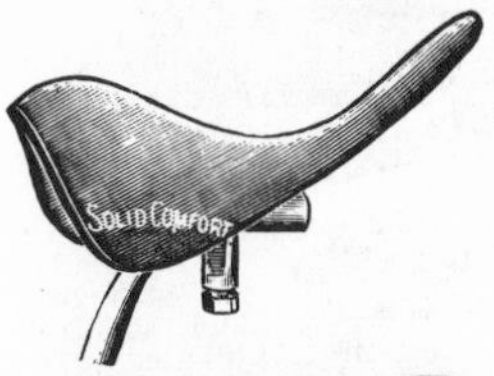

56068 Track or Racing Saddle, round steel spring frame, weight, 15½ ounces. Price.... ....$1.75

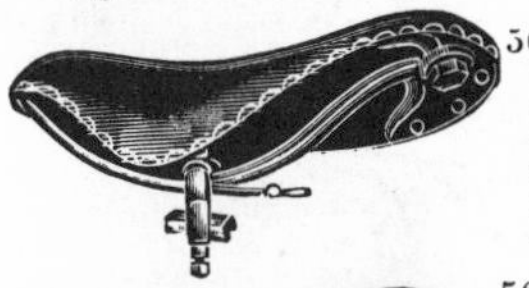

56071 This saddle we have selected from among the many good ones brought out this season; is easy, strong and cheap. Price..............$200

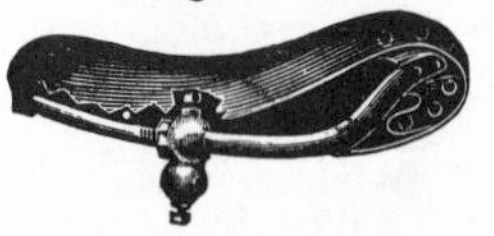

56073 This saddle is intended for the scorcher or light weight rider, although it will sustain a person of any weight who may wish to use it. Price..$1.50

Belts.

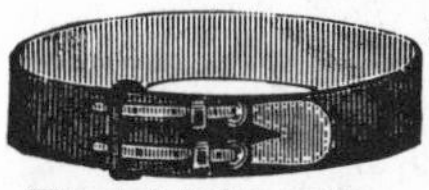

56076 Our belts are made especially for cylists, of fine worsted or cotton webbing. Made in sizes 32 to 38 inches, in all colors.

Worsted Belts, each.............................. $0.35
Per dozen.. 3.75
Cotton Belts, each.................................... .25
Per dozen.. 2.70

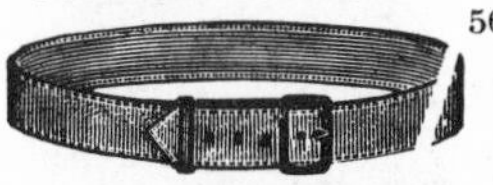

56079 Leather Bicycle Belt, 2 in wide, made of good stock and in sizes from 32 to 40; the buckle is large and leather covered. Each..........$0.40

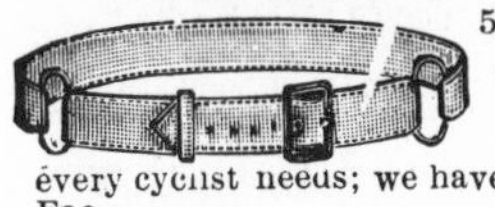

56081 Leather Bicycle Belt, 1⅞ inch wide, covered buckle and rings. This is a good strong servicable belt and what every cyclist needs; we have it in all sizes. Eac $0.50

New Departure Bicycle Bells.

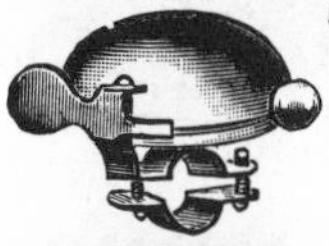

56083 This is a small sized bell, measuring 1¾ inches across and is generally used on juvenile w. eels. It fastens to the handle bar by means of screws, as shown by illustration. Price......$0.30

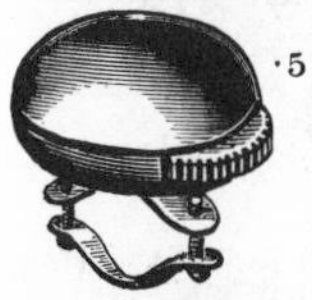

56086 This bell measures 1¾ inches in diameter and weighs 3 ounces. It will give a single, double or continuous sound. It fastens to the handle bars with screws, as shown. Price. .55

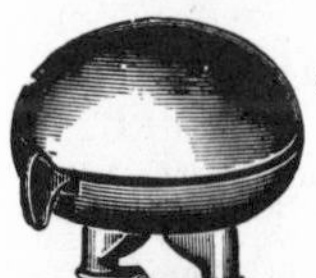

56088 This is a very popular bell. It measures 2⅛ inches in diameter and weighs 4½ ounces, It gives a double electric response and makes a loud noise. Price......... .80

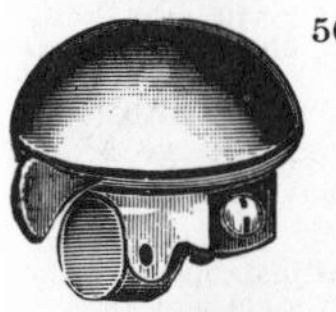

56091 This is a favorite bell and always pleases the buyer. It gives a double electric alarm for each pressure of the lever. It measures 2⅛ inches across, and locks to the handle bar with a key. Price....... .... .95

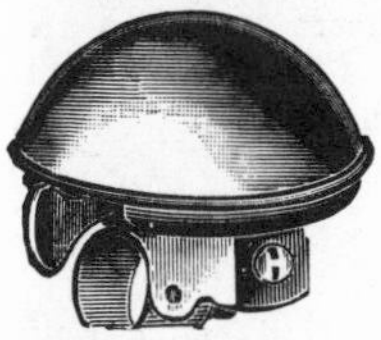

56095 This bell, if we are to judge from our past sales, is the most popular of the many now on the market. It is 2¾ inches in diameter, and weighs 7½ ounces. It fastens with a key and gives a double electric stroke. Price...... .... 1.10

THIS CATALOGUE

Offers to a greater degree than any other method

... **THE OPPORTUNITIES** ...

REQUIRED

By those people who desire the good things of this life.

Bicycle Lamps.

Our lamps all have finely polished front and heavy ruby side lights, detachable reflectors and noiseless spring backs, and all are formed with locked and folded seams and joints, no solder being used except in the oil reservoir, so that they cannot be melted apart. Use headlight or a special lantern oil, as they will not burn coal oil and give satisfaction.

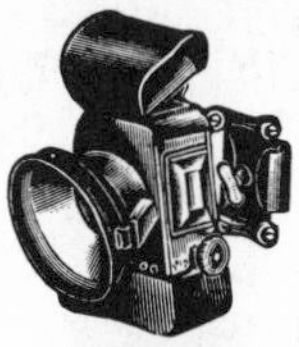

Horoscope.

56096 This is a very light lamp, having a powerful lens and finely silver plated reflector. It tapers on the inside similar to a locomotive headlight; it has a noiseless spring back; the burner is Self-locking, which holds the wick in place. It gives a strong and brilliant light and is considered the very best lamp money can buy. Price.........$2.75

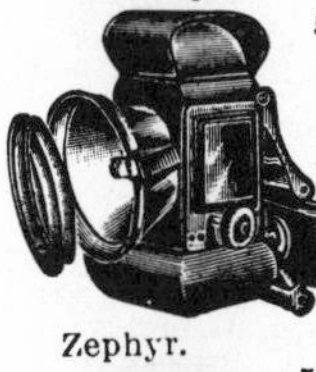

Zephyr.

56098 This lamp we consider next to the Horoscope, both in make-up and light giving qualities. Detachable reflector, finely ground lens opening in front, rubber lined noiseless bracket fastening. Price............... 2.10

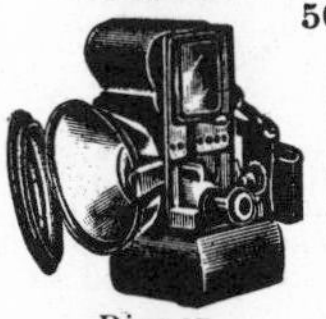

Ripper.

56100 This lamp is built on the same principle as the Zephyr, but is not so elabarately finished, neither does it possess such a fine lens. It throws a good light, however, and is extensively used. Price...................... 1,25

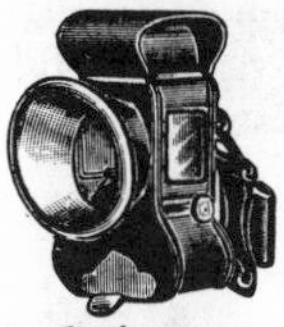

Cyclone.

56101 This lamp is regarded as one of the best made. It gives a good light, but does not have the improvements such as are put on the higher priced ones. It is fitted with a noiseless rubber lined fastening. front opens at bottom. Price........................... .89

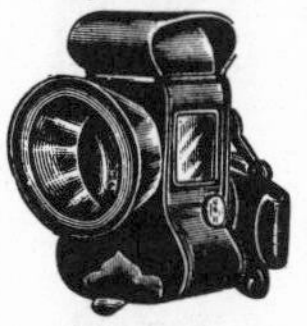

Demon.

56103 This lamp is fitted with a plate glass lens instead of a fine polished one as is the case with higher priced lamps. It will give a good light We handle it to accommodate those who do not care to invest a larger amount in a more expensive lamp. Price 55

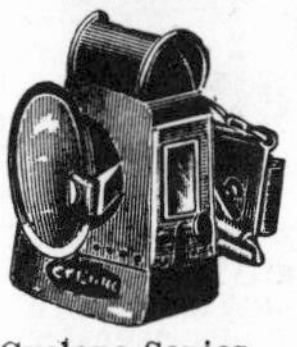

Cyclone Senior.

56104 This is absolutely the neatest and best bicycle lamp on the market. The lens, which is imported, and the very best money can buy, costs more than a great many lamps to produce. It is very light, weighing about 11 ounces, has a ¾ inch wick, but will throw more light than the majority of lamps with 1 inch wick. The fount slides and is locked in place by the sliding side light. To those in search of a superior lantern, one that will be sure to give good satisfaction, we strongly recommend the Cyclone Senior. It comes nicely jappanned with nickel trimmings. Price......... 2.50

Tool Bags.

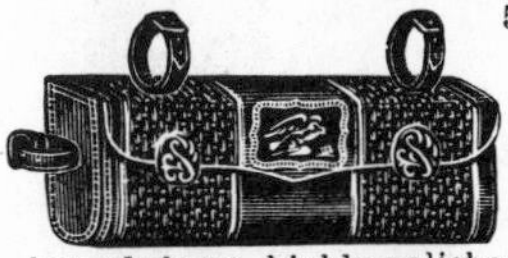

56106. This style bag will, we believe, be the most popular: it is made of russet grain leather, highly embossed, stitched ends, embossed clasps, highly polished. Price $0.45

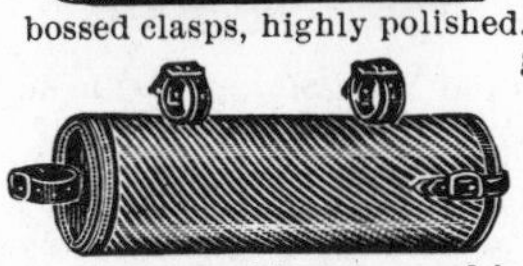

56108 This bag is make from the best quality of russet polished leather, round telescope style, fitted with straps and buckles, handsomely finished. Price .... .46

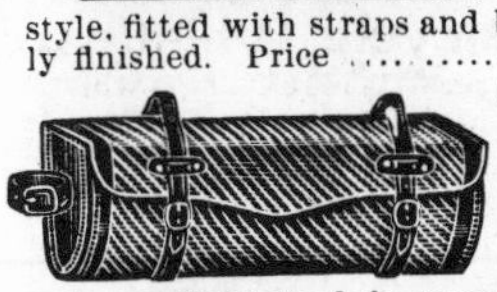

56111 We present here a tool bag designed for use on light machines. It is made from good, yet very light stock in russet color. Price...... .48

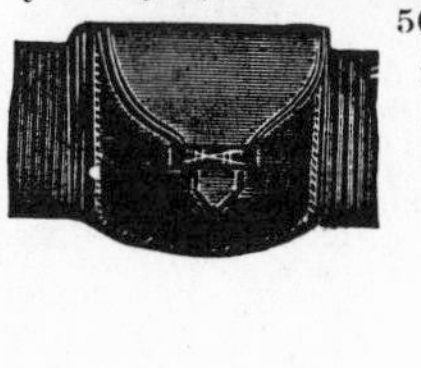

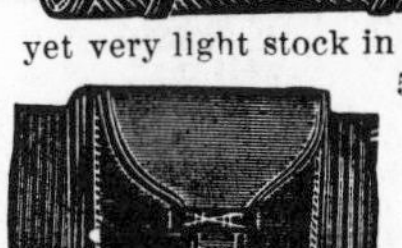

56112 Cyclists' Belt Pouch, a convenient means of carrying watch, wrench or money without fear of their being lost or damaged, made of first quality leather. Price.....................$0.75

Tool Bags—Continued.

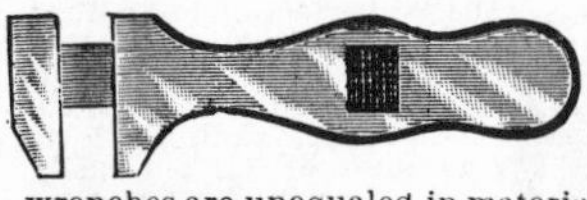

56115 Tower & Lyon Pocket Wrench, drop forged from bar steel and case hardened. These wrenches are unequaled in material, strength and efficiency and are warranted in all respects a first-class article. Nickeled, each $0.50
Per dozen 5.40

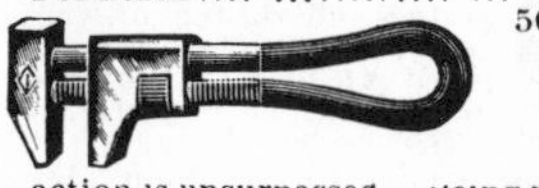

56117 The Vulcan Bicycle Wrench for strength, durability and easy action is unsurpassed. Being made entirely of iron it will stand more hard usage than the ordinary wood cushion handle monkey wrench. It measures 4½ inches long. Price................ .25

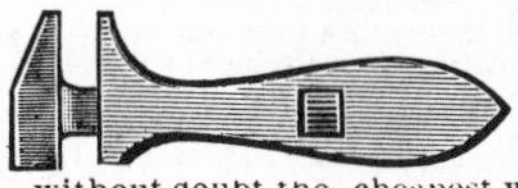

56118 This wrench is made of malleable iron case hardened and is without doubt the cheapest wrench of any account in the market. It is about four inches long and can be carried in the vest or hip pocket. Price .... .20

Bicycle Locks.

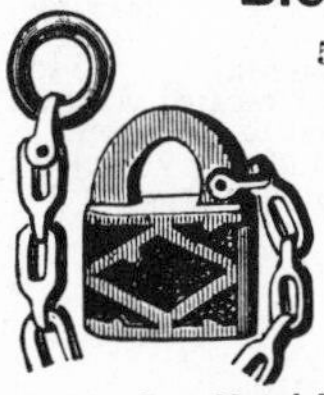

56121 Pure Aluminum Bicycle Lock; all are finished with raised parts highly polished and depressed parts luster polished. They are spring, self-locking with spring shackles and fitted with 16-inch strong and shapely chain.
Each $0.35
Per dozen 3.80

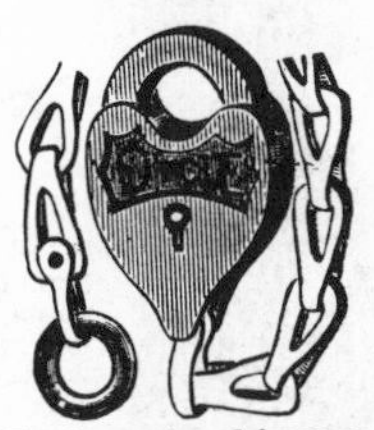

56123 Gun Metal Bicycle Lock made on same principle as railroad switch lock; all parts very stout and strong and nickel plated. The chain is 16 inches long, made of stout hard cut steel, spring self-locking, spring hinged shackles.
Each $0.45
Per dozen.. .... 4.86

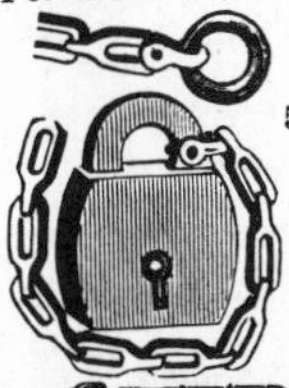

56125 Bicycle Lock, made of bronze metal, highly polished and nickel plated, spring self-locking, with automatically opening pivoted shackles, fitted with 17-inch steel chain.
Each $0.25
Per dozen......... .... 2.75

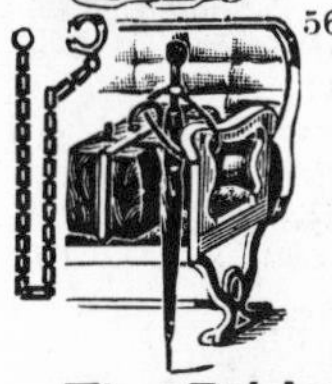

56127 This is a new idea in the way of a bicycle lock. It is made of steel and weighs about one ounce. The chain is two feet long and very strong. The key is flat and will unlock a car seat. It is used very extensively for fastening grips and umbrellas to car seats as shown by cut. Price........ ....$0.45

The Bridgeport Cyclometer.

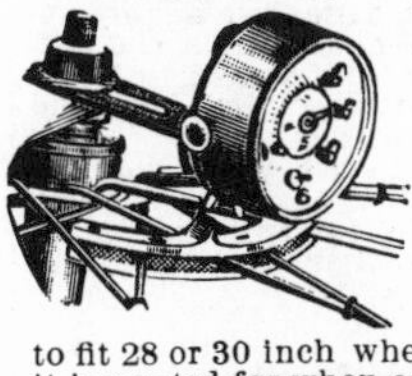

56129 The Bridgeport Cyclometer registers accurately up to 1,000 miles and repeats, or can be set back at will, adjustable to any bicycle and can be read from the saddle. We guarantee it to be absolutely reliable and equal in quality and durability to any. It weighs only 6¾ ounces and is made to fit 28 or 30 inch wheels. Be sure to say what size it is wanted for when ordering. Price $2.20

Standard Cyclometer.

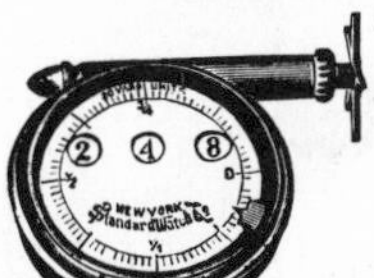

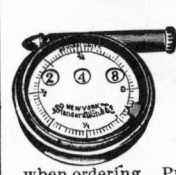

56133 The Standard Cyclometer registers 1,000 miles and repeats, adjustible to read from any position on the saddle, noiseless in action, dust and water proof; has white ivory enamel dial, same as a watch, they are made for 28 or 30-inch wheels, be sure and say which is wanted when ordering. Price........................ $1.75

Bicycle Watch.

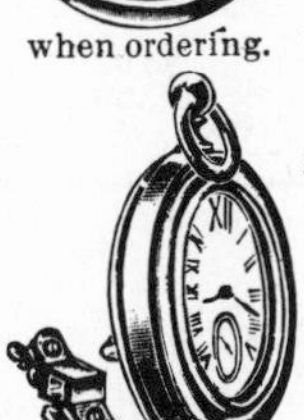

56136 Bicycle Watch, with adjustable clamp on back for fastening it to the frame or handle bar of any machine in any position. The watch is guaranteed to keep good time; it is well made and very neat in appearance, and will be found very useful as it enables the rider to tell exactly what speed he is making. Price $1.50

Oils, Lubricating and Illuminating

56138 Perfection Solid Burning oil is vastly superior in every respect to the old fashioned liquid oil; it cannot waste, spill, soil the clothes, or jar out easily. The compound is practically a solid substance until the wick is lighted, when the heat at once melts the oil around the top of wick sufficiently to allow it to feed freely. When the light is turned out, the oil becomes solid again, is sweet, clean and odorless; put up in tins containing 8 ounces. Price, per can.........................$0.15

56141 Regular illumingating oil made especially for bicycle lamps, and put up in pint cans. Per can...30

56143 Electric Cycle Oil, a very fine preparation put up especially for oiling bicycle bearings, small cans with screw top. Per can............20

56144 Electric Cycle oil, 4 ounce screw top cans. Per can ....,...... .12

Wood Rim Cement.

56146 With the advent of wood rims a quick and rapidly growing demand for a liquid cement, which can be used for fastening the tire to such rims has been created. It frequently is necessary to re-cement a tire to the rim, and every cyclist should have a supply in readiness. Put up in 4 ounce tins. Price, per tin...................$0.20

Rubber Cement.

56148 Rubber Cement for cementing cuts in or splicing rubber tires, this is the very best quality made, and will work on any kind of rubber goods equally as well as on rubber tires; can contains one pint. Price, per can .. $0.40

56151 For the convenience of those needing only a small quantity of rubber cement we have put it up in collapsible tubes as shown in illustration.

Tubes, size, 6x1-inch. Each, 12c. Per dozen..$1.35
Tubes, size, 3½x¾-inch. Each, 10c. Per dozen, . 1.05
Tubes, size, 3x½-inch. Each, 6c. Per dozen.... .65

Tire Cement.

56153 We handle nothing but the very best quality tire cement, and will guarantee it in every particular. Per pound............................$0.55

56155 Two ounce cake sufficient for one pair of tires. Per cake....................................07

Chain Graphite.

56156 We offer in this Graphite a very superior article. It is peculiarly rich and lasting and must not be confounded with the cheap compounds; it is in stick form and easily applied; it works into every link bearing preventing uneven wear and rust. Price, per stick........................$0.10

56157 Chain Graphite, in dry form put up in two ounce bottles. Per bottle...... .10

Bicycle Balls.

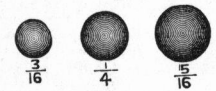

3/16   1/4   5/16

56159 Steel Balls, perfectly true and case hardened, for bicycle bearings.

Size	3/16	1/4	5/16
Each	$0.02	$0.02	$0.03
Per dozen	.20	.20	.30

56162 Tire Tape, thin as paper, strong as leather; is used to fasten a loosened tire quickly, and without heat. It is one of the essential accessories, and should be found in every cyclist's tool bag. Per package $0.10
Per dozen packages.................................. 1.05

56163 Star Enamel, easily applied with a flat brush, produces a brilliant and lasting surface like ivory, and is as washable as porcelain. One can is sufficient to enamel a bicycle. It comes in the following colors: Pure white, ivory white, blue, pink, green, yellow, red and black   Per can....$0.18   Per dozen cans 1.95

Pedals.

56163 High Grade Ball Bearing Roadster, Rat Trap Pedals, covered center, hardened cups, cones perfectly true, dust proof caps, coppered and nickel plated, Per pair..............$2.50

56167 High Grade Ball Bearing Racing Rat Trap Pedals, new pattern with properly hardened cups and perfectly true cones, coppered and nickel plated. Per pair..............$2.75

56169 High Grade Rubber Ball Bearing Pedals, covered cups and cones, ground perfectly true, dust proof cap, coppered and nickel plated, Per pair.... ....$2.35

Hose Supporters.

56171 Hose Supporter; consists of a belt to go around the waist with elastic straps, with patent fastenings to attach to the hose to hold them smoothly in their place. They are adjustable. to waist and length of limb State size of waist when ordering. Per pair, $0.35

56173 Shoulder Stocking Supporter; an article that meets the popular demand of wheelmen. These supporters do away with elastic bands which bind upon the limbs, causing numbness or swollen veins. Adjustable for any size person. Price, per pair..........................$0.45

Oilers.

PERFECT POCKET OILER

56176 Perfect Pocket Oiler. The cleanest and handsomest pocket oiler in the world. Price $0.23

56178 Bicycle Oiler, can be carried in pocket. Price $0.08 Each, nickeled . 12

56179 The .Little Beauty Oiler square. like cut, emits only a small quantity at each pressure. The needle which screws into spout keeps it always free and clear from dirt and grit.

56178
Each.................................$0.15
Per dozen................... 1.62

56179

Tire Heater.

56181 Perfection Tire Heater, a practical article for cementing rubber tires   Price $0.50

Spoke Grip.

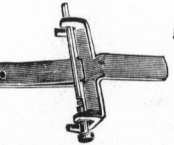

56183 The Chicago Spoke Grip. Best on earth. Price......................$0.50

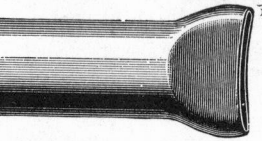

56186 The Staythere Nipple Grip for tightening the nipples on tangent spoke wheels. This is a standard article of necessity, a great labor saver and useful tool. Price..$0.25

Bicycle Whistles.

56187 This whistle is known as the Develine and will produce any kind of a sound. from a groan to a shriek, at the will of the operator; it is well made, of a convenient size and handsomely nickel plated. Price...... ....$0.20 Per dozen.. ....$2.16

56188 The Duplex Whistle; gives two clear and distinct notes; made of brass, heavily nickel plated, complete with chain and hook. Price.. . ...$0.18

Bicycle Whistles—Continued·

56191 The Gem Whistle, gives a soft, loud alarm; a favorite whistle. Price, with chain .... $0.17 Per dozen .. 2.16

56193 Single Tube Whistle, the strongest and shrillest whistle in use.   The slightest effort is all that is required to use it. Price..................................$0.20

Bicycle Horns.

56196 Bicycle Horns. No. 1, 7 in. long $0.85

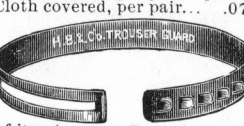

56198 The Perfect Trouser Guard, a neat and handy device for saving the pants from dirt and grease.

Enamel finish, per pair.. $0.05   Per dozen pairs.. $0.54
Cloth covered, per pair... .07   Per dozen pairs.. .76

56200 The Hulbert Trouser Guard; used in the same manner as 56198, but can be hooked as tight as desired. without any danger of its slipping. Per pair............................$0.04
Per dozen pairs......................... .45

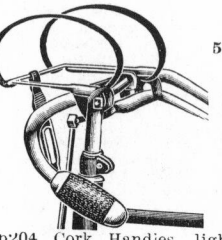

56202 The Lamson Bundle Carrier; can be attached to the bicycle in a moment, and when not attached can be used as a shawl strap; it weighs a mere trifle, and can be easily carried in the pocket when not in use. Price.................$0.85

56204 Cork Handies, light and easy to grip. nickel plated ferrule on each end. When ordering give diameter of handle. Per pair, $0.35

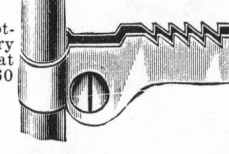

56206 Adjustable Foot-Rests or Coasters, very light, but strong and neat in design. Per pair. $0.60

56208 Toe Clips, best spring steel, tempered and heavily nickel plated; every rider using rat trap pedals ought to have a pair of these. Per pair.....................$0.30

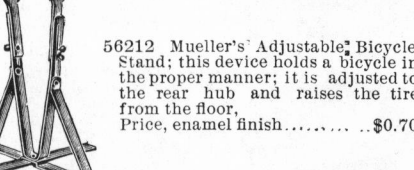

56210 The Little Beauty Child's Seat is recognized as the only safe device for giving the little children the benefit of the joy and health to be found in cycling. Each $3.25

56212 Mueller's Adjustable Bicycle Stand; this device holds a bicycle in the proper manner; it is adjusted to the rear hub and raises the tire from the floor, Price, enamel finish......... ..$0.70

56214 Griswold's Patent Folding Rubber Mud Guard. Very few manufacturers of bicycles are fitting their wheels with mud guards, as the Griswold is fast taking the place of the old style iron or steel guard. Price—
Per set..$1.50

BABY CARRIAGES.

{ We will send, upon receipt of 4 cents to pay postage, our special Baby
Carriage Catalogue, showing nearly sixty different styles.

Special Information.

Silk plushes can be furnished in the following shades with parasols to match: Cardinal, bronze gold, peacock blue, olive, pomegranate, wine, electric blue, golden brown, nile green and salmon pink.

Silk damasks in the following shades: Cardinal, peacock blue, wine, bronze gold, golden brown, electric blue, pomegranate and olive.

Imported mottled corduroys in the following shades: Golden brown, electric blue, olive, pomegranate, peacock blue. Egyptian damasks in the following shades: Cardinal, peacock blue, wine, bronze gold, golden brown, electric blue, pomegranate, olive.

We ship carriages knocked down and crated. They weigh about 50 pounds. We make no charge for crating. For rubber tire, steel wheels, add $1.50 in addition to price quoted with plain steel wheels.

If better or cheaper parasols than those quoted with carriage are desired, we can furnish them at difference in price, which may be found quoted on page 561.

We keep all parts for our carriages and will quote prices on application.

56301 Willow House Carriage, a medium size carriage for children under 3 years; strong, wood handle and axles, as shown in cut; just the thing for the country. Wheels 15 inches in diameter. Price, complete.............$1.25

56306 Baby Carriage, bleached reed body, bottom 12x24, oil cloth carpet, body lined with cretonne, upholstered seat, silesia parasol, painted gear and tinned wheels, 18x18 inches.........$3.70

56308 Baby Carriage, reed and maple body, finished; upholstered in fancy cretonne, oilcloth mat on bottom; sateen unlined carasol, 4 S springs and 20x22 brightly plated steel wheels. Price $4.65

56311 Baby Carriage, reed body, bleached, upholstered in fancy cretonne, oilcloth mat on bottom, sateen unlined parasol, four S springs and 20x22 brightly plated steel wheels........$4.80

56314 Baby Carriage, reed body, bleached, upholstered in Egyptian damask, with silk plush roll, brussels carpet on bottom, sateen parasol with lace edge, 20x22 inch steel wheels brightly plated. Price.....................................$5.70

56317 Same as 56314, but is upholstered in cretonne with silk plush roll, has oilcloth mat and sateen parasol without lace edge. Price..... 5.30

56321 Baby Carriage, reed body, shellaced, upholstered in silk plush, silk satin unlined parasol with lace edge; springs and 20x22 inch steel wheels, brightly plated, Price....   ...$6.85

56322 Same as 56321, but is upholstered in Egyptian damask with plush roll, brussels carpet, sateen unlined parasol with lace edge..6.10

56326 Baby Carriage, reed body, shellaced, upholstered in silk plush, silk satin unlined parasol with lace edge, springs and 20x22 inch steel wheels, brightly plated. Price.......   .....$7.50

56328 Same as 56326, but is upholstered in Egyptian damask with silk plush, plush roll, brussels carpet, sateen parasol with lace edge. 6.35

56331 Baby Carriage, reed body, shellaced, upholstered in silk plush rolls, silk satin parasol with lace edge, springs and 20x22 inch steel wheels, brightly plated. Price............$7.85

56333 Same as 56331, but is upholstered in Egyptian damask, in combination with silk plush, brussels carpet, sateen parasol, with lace edge, springs and 20x22 inch steel wheels, brightly plated. Price................. 6.75

56337 Baby Carriage, reed body, shellaced, upholstered in silk plush, brussels carpet, silk satin parasol, unlined, with lace edge; springs and 20x22 inch steel wheels, brightly plated, $8.50

56338 Same as 56337, but is upholstered in Egyptian damask, with silk plush roll, silk satin parasol, unlined, with lace edge; springs and 20x22 inch steel wheels, brightly plated........ 7.85

56342 Baby Carriage, reed body, shellaced upholstered in silk plush, brussels carpet, silk satin parasol, unlined, with lace edge: springs and 20x22 inch steel wheels brightly plated. $8.90

56343 Same as 56342, but is upholstered in Egyptian damask, with silk plush roll, brussels carpet mat, silk satin parasol, unlined, with lace edge: springs and 20x22 inch steel wheels, brightly plated. Price............................ 8.35

56346 Baby Carriage. reed body, shellaced, upholstered in silk plush, brussels carpet, silk satin parasol, lined with silesia, with lace edge: springs and 20x22 inch steel wheels, brightly plated. Price. $9.55

56347 Same as 56346, but is upholstered in Egyptian damask, with silk plush roll. brussels carpet, silk satin parasol, lined with silesia, with lace edge: springs and 20x22 inch steel wheels, brightly plated. Price......................$9.00

56350 Baby Carriage, reed body, shellaced, upholstered in silk plush, brussels carpet, silk satin, parasol lined with silesia, with lace edge; springs and 20x22 inch steel wheels, brightly plated. Price......................$9.85

56351 Same in every respect as 56350, but is upholstered in Egyptian damask, with silk plush roll. Price..................................... 9.30

56355 Baby Carriage, reed body, shellaced. upholstered in silk plush, brussels carpet, silk satin parasol lined with silesia, with lace edge; springs and 20x22 inch steel wheels, brightly plated. Price.... ....$9.85

56357 Same in every respect as 56355, but is upholstered in Egyptian damask, with silk plush roll. Price...................... .... 9.30

56359 Baby Carriage. reed body, shellaced, upholstered in silk plush, brussels carpet. silk satin parasol lined with silesia, with lace edge, springs and 20x22 in. steel wheels, brightly plated. Price............ ....$10.25

56361 Same in every respect as 56364, but is upholstered in Egyptian damask, with silk plush roll. Price.... .... 9.55

56366 Baby Carriage. reed body, shellaced, upholstered in silk plush, brussels carpet, silk satin parasol, lined with silesia, with lace edge, springs and 20x22-inch steel wheels, brightly plated. Price $10.35

56367 Baby Carriage, reed body, shellaced, upholstered in silk plush, brussels carpet. silk satin parasol, lined with silesia, and silk lace edge. springs and 20x22-inch steel wheels, brightly plated. Price.. ....$11.45

56368 Same as No. 56366, but is upholstered in imported silk damask. Price...................$11.75

56371 Baby Carriage, reed body, shellaced, upholstered in silk plush, brussels carpet, silk satin parasol, with silk lace edge, and lined with silesia; springs and 20x22 inch steel wheels, brightly plated. Price.... ... .$11.95

56373 Same as No. 56371, but is upholstered in imported silk damask. Price...................$12.25

56374 Baby Carriage, reed body, shellaced, upholstered in silk plush, brussels carpet, silk satin parasol, with silk lace edge, and lined with silesia: springs and 20x22 inch steel wheels, brightly plated. Price......................$12.50

56376 Same as No. 56374, but is upholstered in imported silk damask. Price................... 12.58

Baby Carriages—Continued.

56378 Baby Carriage, reed body, shellaced, upholstered in silk plush, brussels carpet; fine silk satin parasol, with silk lace edge, and lined with sateen; springs and 20x22 inch steel wheels, brightly plated. Price.............$12.95
56379 Same in every respect, as 56378, but is upholstered in imported silk damask. Price.. 13.15

56381 Baby Carriage, reed body, shellaced, upholstered in silk plush, brussels carpet, fine silk satin parasol, with silk lace edge, and lined with sateen; springs and 20x22 inch steel wheels, brightly plated. Price.............$13.60
56383 Same in every respect, as 56381, but is upholstered in imported silk damask. Price. 13.85

56386 Reed body, shellaced, upholstered in fine quality silk plush, lined outside with fine woven cane webbing, cane bottom; fine silk satin parasol, lined with sateen, with silk lace edge; front springs nickeled; steel wheels, 20x22 inches in diameter; spring cushion seat. Price $16.25
56387 Same as No. 56386, but is upholstered in imported silk damask. Price................. 16.25
36—2nd

Baby Carriages—Continued.

56390 Reed body, shellaced, upholstered in fine quality silk plush, lined outside with fine woven cane webbing, cane bottom; fine silk satin parasol, lined with satin, with silk lace edge; front springs nickeled; steel wheels 20x22 inches in diameter; spring cushion seat. Price $20.50
56391 Same as No. 56390, but is upholstered in imported silk damask. Price. 20.50

56393 Reed body, shellaced, upholstered in fine quality silk plush, lined outside with fine woven cane webbing, cane bottom, fine silk satin parasol lined with satin, with silk lace edge, front springs nickeled, steel wheels 20x 22 inches in diameter, spring cushion seat. Price............................$21.65
56394 Same as No. 56393, but is upholstered in imported silk damask. Price............. .....$21.65

56396 Canopy Top Baby Carriage, reed body shellaced, upholstered in good quality silk plush, brussel carpet on bottom, hood lined with plush to match. steel wheels 20x22 inches in diameter. Price.................................$12.75

Price List of Parts.

56398 Front C springs tinned, each............ ...$0.18
56400 Back S springs, tinned, each................. .75
56402 Back J springs, tinned, each........ .. ... .21
56404 Parasol rods with fixtures, tinned.......... .45
56406 Parasol rods with fixtures, nickeled....... .60
56408 Steel wheels, tinned, 18x20, per set of four. 1.44
56410 Steel wheels,t inned, 20x22, per set of four. 1.44
56412 Steel wheels, with rubber tires, 18-20 or 22 inches. Each................................ .72

Description and Price List of Parasols.

N. B. Prices quoted below are for parasols only. No Rod. Parasols will fit only rods same as those used on our carriages.

All satin parasols can be furnished to match upholstering in the following colors: Cardinal, bronze, gold, olive, peacock blue, pomegranate, light tan, wine, gobelin blue, golden brown and light coral.

The silesia and satin parasols can be furnished in all colors but gobelin blue, light coral and light tan.

56420 Silesia Parasol..........................$0.36
56425 Sateen Parasol.............................. .45
56429 Sateen Parasol, with lace edge..... .... .70
56430 Silk Satin Parasol, unlined, with lace edge.. 1.15
56431 Silk Satin Parasol, lined with silesia, with lace edge.............................. 1.40
56433 Silk Satin Parasol, fine quality, lined with sateen, with silk lace edge 1.60
56436 Fine Silk Satin Parasol, lined with sateen, with silk lace edge 2.00
56439 Fine Silk Satin Parasol, lined with satin, with deep silk lace edge.................. 3.75
56442 Pongee Silk, ecru color only, lined with silesia 1.60
56445 Pongee Silk, ecru color only, lined with silesia, with silk lace edge 1.80

Lace Covers.

56460 No. 1 Nottingham........................$0.25
56462 No. 2 Nottingham .... .40
56465 No. 3 Nottingham .... .60
56467 No. 4 Nottingham.......................... .80
56469 Dotted Net, full ruffle, point edge.... ... 1.75
56471 Plain Net, three ruffles. .... .85
56473 Net Point, handsomely embroidered.... 1.25
56476 Chiffon, with three ruffles and embroidered in sprays and leaves 1.75
56478 Chiffon, with three ruffles and fancy embroidery................................... 2.25
56480 High Grade Chiffon, with six flounces.... 3.35

Eiderdown and Flannel Baby Carriage Robes.

Pinked edges, fancy embroidered.

56481 Shaker flannel, pinked edge and embroidered center. Size, 28x32 inches. Price $0.38
56483 Eiderdown, pinked edge and embroidered center. Size, 28x32 inches. Price....... .50
56484 Eiderdown, pinked edge and embroidered center, in fancy designs with gold cord. Size, 28x32 inches. Price 75
56488 Fine flannel pinked edge, center embroidered with soft pink rosebuds and pale yellow leaves. Size, 28x32 inches. Price...... .75
56490 Eiderdown, pinked edge, center embroidered, with moss roses. Size, 28x32 inches. Price....................................... 1.00
56491 Eiderdown, pinked edge, embroidered flowers and the word "Baby" in center in neat letters. Size, 28x32 inches. Price 1.15
56492 Fine flannel, pinked edge, flower embroidery in center, and the word "Baby" worked in silk, also two silk ribbons sewed lengthwise. Size, 28x32 inches. Price.... .... 1.50

Children's Carriage and Parasol Protector.

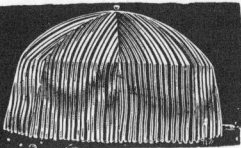

56493 The Protector is made of the best waterproof material and will protect both parasol and baby if caught out in the rain; when not in use it may be folded and carried under the seat. Price.......$1.00

Tothill's Spring Chair.

For Children and Infants.

This chair is by far the most simple, practical and durable of anything of the kind yet offered to the public. It can be readily adjusted to any position desired, and combines both chair and crib, in which the youngest infant can be placed with no possibility of falling or getting out. As can be seen at a glance, it is simple and practical; it is provided with a foot rest, which, by a slight adjustment, either increases the width of the seat or acts as a footboard to the crib. Should the child fall asleep while occupying the chair, it will not be aroused or disturbed by adjusting the chair to a bed, as it can readily be changed from an upright to a reclining position

56495 Price, with veneer seat and back........$1.50
56496 Price, with cretonne upholstered seat and back.......................... 2.00

Baby Swings or Jumpers.

Baby Swing, made of wood, smoothly finished, seat upholstered in cretonne; can be hung up anywhere, in a doorway or from a bracket or support of any kind. The swing is so arranged that it is impossible for the child to fall out; folds into a very small space and weighs about 4 pounds complete with hooks and cotton rope.

56497 Price, each..........$0.38
     Per dozen 4.15
56498 Baby Swing Springs, coil steel springs: diameter, 1⅛ in., length, 15 inches.
     Each.........................$0.40

Tothill's Improved Child's Lawn Swings.

56501 This Swing is absolutely safe for children's use; they are strong, durable and made of the best material; the chair and frame are put together with bolts. They are well painted in bright colors. Price............................$4.75

Tothill's Reclining Chair Lawn Swnigs.

56502 For ease and comfort these swings cannot be excelled; they are strong and made of the best material; the chairs are made of hardwood and are well painted in bright colors and put together with bolts. If you have children and wish to provide them with a pleasant and healthy form of exercise you cannot do better than purchase a Tothill Swing. They are so constructed that it is impossible for even the smallest child to get hurt. Prices are for swing without canopy.

	Price.
8-foot chair, seat 18 inches wide.............	$ 7.50
10-foot chair, seat 20 inches wide.............	9.00
12-foot chair, seat 22 inches wide	10.75
14-foot chair, seat 24 inches wide ·····	14.25
16-foot chair, seat 26 inches wide.............	17.00

Sun Shade or canopy to fit any swing, $2.00 extra.

OUR CLAIM⇒✦

That this Catalogue opens the markets of the world to you is no idle boast.

NOWHERE ELSE

Can you find such a variety of things at such reasonable prices.

Boys' Velocipedes.

WROUGHT IRON FRAME.

The frame is made of wrought iron with malleable iron head and neck, cow horn handle bars; suspension saddle with coil springs, metal pedals and detachable pedal pins.

We have selected this velocipede as being the best of the many now on the market. Weight, from 12 to 25 pounds.

PATENT STEEL WIRE WHEELS.

56504	16-inch drive wheel	Price $1.35
	20-inch drive wheel.	Price............. 1.75
	24-inch drive wheel.	Price............. 2.25
	26-inch drive wheel.	Price............. 2.75
	28-inch drive wheel.	Price........... ... 3.00

Rubber Tire Velocipedes with Patent Steel Wheels. Note reduced prices.

56505	16-inch drive wheel.	Price.............$3.00
	20-inch drive wheel.	Price............. 3.75
	24-inch drive wheel.	Price............. 4.15
	26-inch drive wheel.	Price............. 4.50
	28-inch drive wheel.	Price 5.00

Little Beauty Tricycle.

The cut fully illustrates the Little Beauty Tricycle for girls. The frame is made of tubing, very strong and light. The propelling is by means of levers pivoted to the center frame, and connected to the double crank shaft, which is made of steel. The seat can be adjusted in height without the use of a wrench, a handle being attached to the set screws for that purpose. Has a very elastic spring. The tricycle is highly finished; the frame is black, neatly striped; wheels, handles, levers and springs are brightly tinned. Weight, from 30 to 45 pounds.

56507	Steel Wheel Tricycle.		56508	Rubber Tire Steel Wheel Tricycle.	
Front wheel.	Rear wheel.	Price.	Front wheel.	Rear wheel.	Price.
12 in.	20 in.	$ 3.95	12 in.	20 in.	$6.70
12 in.	24 in.	5.40	12 in.	24 in.	8.25
14 in.	28 in.	6 50	14 in.	28 in.	10.00
14 in.	32 in.	7 50	14 in.	32 in.	11.75
No charge made for crating.					

BOYS' WAGONS, WHEELBARROWS, CARTS, ETC.

NEW PATENT IRON WAGON.

The handsomest and best boy's wagon made All iron.
56509 Body, 11x22 in., wheels, 8x11.
     Price............$1.40
     Weight, 15 to 25 lbs

56510 Body, 12x24 inches, wheels, 9x12 inches,
     Price.........................$1.57
56512 Body, 13x26 in.; wheels, 10x14. Price.. 1.75
56515 Body, 14x28 in.; wheels, 12x16. Price.. 2.00
56519 Body, 15x30 in.; wheels, 14x18. Price.. 2.25

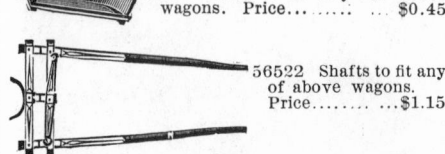

56520   Seat to fit any of above wagons. Price... ....$0.45

56522   Shafts to fit any of above wagons. Price........ ..$1.15

Have your Mail Packages Insured.
See Page 1.

Police Patrol Wagon.

56523 An exact imitation of the patrol wagon used by the police department of all large cities, strong and well made-body 21x38 inches, with front seat, also two seats running lengthways of wagon, brass rails along side, seats are upholstered, has a brass gong and whip socket in front, a step on the rear and one in the front, are strongly braced with iron, wheels are extra heavy, 15 inches in front and 22 in rear, welded tires, staggered spokes and hub caps, all parts are nicely painted the body in blue and running gear in red. Price.....................$7.50

Boy's Farm Wagon.

56524 An exact imitation of a regular farm wagon, body, 18x36 inches, with hardwood frame, the sides and ends can be taken off, leaving bed with stakes. The gearing is made like a farm wagon, having bent hounds and adjustable reach; all parts are strongly ironed and braced; wheels are 14 and 20 inches, heavy welded tires hub boxes and hub caps, has seat, handle and a pair of hardwood shafts for dog or goat. It is handsomely ornamented with landscapes and scroll work, and is without doubt the handsomest, strongest and best made boy's wagon in the market. Price..................................$6.75

56525 Wood Axle Wagon, body, 12x25 inches; front wheels turn under body; varnished and stenciled, with rim and base painted red, wheels 10 and 14 inches. Weight, 12 lbs. Price. $0.75

56527 Same as 56525 but has iron axle in place of wood. Weight, 12 lbs. Price ... ... .85

56530 Steel Wheel Express Wagon, with wooden body, 12x 25 inches; wheels, 10x 14 inches, body nicely striped and varnished, with rail on top and bottom edges painted red. Has malleable iron handle connection and fifth wheel, making a very neat, durable wagon. Weight, 15 pounds. Price........................$1.70
56532 Body 14x28 inches, otherwise same as 56530. Weight, 15 pounds. Price............. 2.00

56534 Wagon with dashboard and seat, body, 15x30 inches, handsomely painted and scrolled, wheels, 12x18, iron boxes in hub, heavy iron axles; bolsters are well-braced with heavy iron; tin malleable iron draw and circle plate; a very fine and substantial wagon Weight, 24 pounds. Price.....$2.25
Same as 56534 with steel wheels...... .... 2.95

56535 Rack Dray, made of hardwood, capable of sustaining a heavy load; it slopes in toward the center, and will carry boxes or baskets without being tied on; body measures 18x 36 inches; has iron axles and 11x12 inch strong wood spoke wheels, has malleable iron tongue fastening and fifth wheel, iron braces and bent handle, nicely striped and varnished. Weight, 16 lbs. Price..................................$1.65
56537 Toy Cart, body, 6½x11 in., 6, in. wheels; painted and striped in assorted colors. Each..........$0.14
Per dozen.... ... ... 1.45

Hook and Ladder Truck.

56539 Hook and Ladder Truck, 5 feet long, wheels, 10 and 12 inches, sweet sounding bell on steel spring, side ladders, 4 feet; middle ladder 5 feet; side ladder coupled together 7½ feet, heavy iron axles and braces. Hardwood throughout, strongly constructed and firmly bolted together. The running gear is bright red, the ladders navy blue. The splendid contrast of colors, with the artistic striping and varnishing, makes it a handsome and very fascinating toy. Weight 35 lbs. Price.....................$2.25

Doll Carriages.

56540 Doll Carriage willow body; 18 in. long, made of selected white willow; wheels, 6 inches oilcloth mat. No parasol or rod.
Each............$0.45
Per dozen 4.86
56545 Same as above, with parasol and rod.
Each..........$0.65
Per dozen.. .....7.02

56547 Doll Carriage, body 21 inches, wheels 10 inches, oil cloth mat and spring bars.
Each......$0.70
Per doz,....7.50
56548 Same as 56547 Doll Carriage, but fitted with parasol and rod.
Each.........$0.90
Per dozen.... 9.00
56550 Same as above but has folding parasol with plated rod; lined half way around and trimmed with lace, upholstered seat. Each.$1.00
Per dozen..... 10.70

56551 White Enameled Doll Cab, body, 21 inches long, carpet mat, lined body and upholstered seat, steel springs, axles and wheels, front 10 and rear 12 inches in diameter, folding parasol.
Each.........$1.50
Per dozen... 16.80

Improved Garden Wheelbarrow.

The body is made of sheet steel with edges wired with suitable wire. The frame is made of well seasoned material; no amount of knocking around can hurt it. Nicely painted and ornamented.
Each.
56554 Body, 9x12 by 5 inches high, wheel, 8 inches....................$0.75
56556 Body, 11x14 by 5½ inches high; wheel, 10 inches...........................85
56558 Body, 13x16 by 6 inches high; wheel, 13 inches...........................1.00

Improved Dump Wheelbarrow.

Solid steel body, strong hardwood shafts well bolted painted and ornamented very tastily. A good and serviceable article.
Each.
56560 Body, 12x13, wheel, 8 inches............$0.75
56562 Body, 13x16, wheel, 10 inches............85
56564 Body, 16x18, wheel, 12 inches.... ....1.00

Improved truck, made very substantial and is without doubt the strongest truck made, nicely painted and ornamented; guaranteed to carry 400 pounds; the sideboards, stakes and standard can be removed; gear and wheels painted black.
56566 Platform, 13x28, wheels, 8 and 10 inches.$3.00
56568 Platform, 14x31, wheels, 8 and 10 inches. 3.50
56570 Platform, 15x33, wheels, 10 and 12 inches. 3.75

Goat Sulky.

Goat or Dog Sulky, is made entirely of hardwood and painted vermilion, has patent steel wheels and springs; will carry safely 125 pounds; this is without doubt the finest article on the market, and is suitable for children from 3 to 15 years old. Weight, crated, 25 lbs.
56572 22 inch steel wheels.
Each....................................$3.50
56574 28-inch steel wheels.
Each...................... ... . 5 00

Goat or Dog Harness.

56575 Fine set of goat or dog harness, lines and bridle, made of good strong harness leather, are adjustable to fit any size dog or goat.
Price.................... ....$1.98

Patent Swinging Shoo-Fly Rockers.

56585 Swinging Shoo-fly, easy to operate, no danger of child falling out, nicely upholstered in cretonne and painted dapple gray.
Each......$1.80
56586 Same as above, but extra large.
Each....... $2.25

Shoo-Fly Rockers.

56587 Shoo-fly 12x40 inches; painted and dappled, has painted hardwood seat, bent rocker and hair tail.
Price...............$0.75
56588 Shoo-fly, same as 56587, but is upholstered in cretonne.
Price...............$0.90

56589 Shoo-fly, 12x44 inches, neatly painted and dappled, has box in front, to hold a child's toys, and is upholstered in cretonne; hair tail, bent rocker. Price................................. $1.10
56590 Shoo-fly, same as 56589, except that it is upholstered in satin finished damask, and is extra trimmed. Price............................. 1.35

TRUNKS.

If you cannot make a selection from among this assortment of trunks, we will mail upon request a special trunk catalogue, showing over 60 different styles. In describing our trunks we give length, the width and height is always in proportion. Trunks vary in weight according to size and quality. If you wish to know the weight of any particular trunk we shall be pleased to answer any inquiry.

Patent Square.

Imitation leather.
56600 Round top, iron bound, spring lock.

Inches.	Wgt.	Price.
24	13 lbs.	$0.50
26	15 lbs.	.70
28	17 lbs.	.90
30	18 lbs.	$1.00
32	20 lbs.	1 10
34	22 lbs.	1.20

Patent Crown Prince.

Imitation leather—men's trunk

56602 Barrel stave top, iron bound, long, hardwood slats, bumpers, hasp lock with patent bolt lock on each side, stitched leather handles with caps, rollers, iron hinges, high set up tray, covered and nicely trimmed.

28 inch....$1.60 30 inch....$1.85 32 inch....$2.05

Crystal Globe.

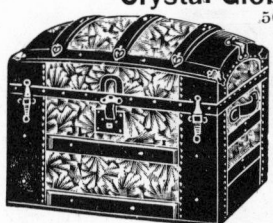

56604—
Barrel Stave Top Trunk; corner double iron bound, reverse strips on top, hasp lock, bolt locks on each side; tray with covered bonnet or hat box; a good, substantial trunk for the money.

	Each.		Each.
26 inches	....$1.65	32 inches	....$2.40
28 inches	1.95	34 inches	2.65
30 inches	2.10		

Crystal Superior.

IRON BOTTOM.

56607 Extra High and Wide Trunk; iron bottom cross bar, slats on top and on front. Flat steel key lock, buckle bolts, set-up tray with covered bonnet box

	Each.		Each.
28 inches	....$2.25	34 inches	....$2.95
30 inches	2.50	36 inches	3.20
32 inches	2.70		

Crystal Don.

56608 Extra High and Wide Trunk, wide iron bound, five cross bar slats on top, body and end slats, malleable iron corner shoes, bumpers, cross strip clamps, skeleton bands, rollers, large double hasp spring lock, patent bolts, stitched leather handles; covered tray with bonnet or hat box, parasol case and side compartment, fall in top, glove box; all linen faced.

	Each.		Each.
28 inches	....$4.85	34 inches	....$5.90
30 inches	5.15	36 inches	6.40
32 inches	5.50	38 inches	7.25

Crystal Maine.

56609 Barrel stave top, double iron bound corners, four reversed hardwood strips on top and front, valanced all around, stitched leather handles, hasp lock, bolt locks on each side, iron bottom; deep tray, with covered hat box, hardwood bottom cleats.

	Each.		Each.
26 inches	....$2.15	32 inches	....$2.95
28 inches	2.40	34 inches	3.15
30 inches	2.65		

56615 Fancy metal covered flat top with front and back rounded, hardwood reverse bent slats over entire top, body and end seats, metal corner bumpers, clamps, bottom rollers, good strong lock and patent bar bolts, heavy strap hinges; tray with bonnet box, all in top and side compartment, all separately covered.

	Each.		Each.
28 inches	....$3.00	34 inches	....$3.75
30 inches	3.25	36 inches	4.00
32 inches	3.50		

We quote a good line of

Ladies' and Men's Traveling Cases.

They are very convenient things to have.

See Index on Pink Pages.

Trunks—Continued.

56617 Barrel Stave Top Trunk, wide iron bound, five cross bar slats on top, and upright on front, end slats malleable iron corners and shoes, stitched leather handles, Excelsior lock, patent bolts; covered tray with bonnet box, parasol case and side compartment, fall in top.

	Each.		Each.
28 inches	$3.40	34 inches	$4.15
30 inches	3.65	36 inches	4.40
82 inches	3.90		

Crystal Gibson.

56620 Barrel stave, top, fancy zinc covered, double iron bound, iron bottom, five cross strips on top, two on front, also on end, good spring lock, covered body; tray with covered hat box, fall in top, extra large and well made. Iron bottom.

	Each.		Each
30 inches	$3.45	34 inches	$4.00
82 inches	3.70	36 inches	4.35

Crystal Magic.

56625 Large barrel stave top, corners double, wide iron bound, five heavy hardwood strips reversed on top and front, and two on ends, all tipped with Russia iron and braced with new style of malleable iron corners and scroll binding, stitched sliding leather handles, iron bottom, three hardwood bottom cleats, heavy malleable iron corner rollers, valance all around, heavy strap hinges, Monitor lock, heavy patent bolt locks on each side, malleable iron corner clamps on valance; hinged body tray, with separate parasol case, packing partition and bonnet box all covered, large glove box and fall in top faced with linen.

30 in	$6.25	32 in	$6.75	34 in	$7.25
36 in	7.75	38 in	8.50		

56627 Large barrel stave top, double iron bound corners, five wide hard wood strips reversed on top and front, all tipped with heavy iron, all corners and strips protected with new style malleable iron corners and clamps, extra heavy malleable iron corners on valance, brass Excelsior lock, heavy side bolts, stitched leather sliding handles, japanned iron bottom; with three hardwood bottom cleats, heavy malleable iron corner rollers; deep hinged body tray with hat box, packing partition and separate parasol case, all covered, large glove box and fall in top, faced with linen, extra dress tray.

Sizes.	30	32	34	36	38
Prices	$7.75	$8.25	$8.75	$9.25	$10.00

Trunks—Continued.

56630 High Barrel Stave Top Trunk, corners double iron bound, heavy hardwood strips reversed on top, front and ends, fancy scroll binding, heavy malleable iron corners, Excelsior lock, iron bottom and hardwood bottom cleats, hinged body; tray with hat box, covered, packing partition and parasol case, fall in top.

28 in	$4.00	30 in	$4.25
34 in	4.75	36 in	5.00

56632 New Style Trunk, flat top with round corners, double iron bound, reverse strips on front, ends and top, the latter bent to extend over round corner, from front to back valance, strap hinges, half Excelsior lock, with flat steel key, iron bottom, hardwood bottom cleats, stitched leather handles, bottom rollers, hinged body tray, with covered hat box, packing partition, fall in top, neatly faced and trimmed.

28 inches	$4.00	34 inches	$4.90
30 inches	4.30	36 inches	5.20
32 inches	4.60		

Round Top, Black Enameled Iron.

56634 Extra High and Wide Trunk, reverse slats on top and bent to shape, five upright slats on front, two lengthwise on end, full set of malleable iron trimmings throughout, bumpers, skeleton iron work on ends, corner shoes and rollers, large brass Excelsior lock, tray with bonnet box, parasol case, drop tray, glove and jewelry box in top, linen finished.

Size	30	32	34	36
Price	$6.75	$7.25	$7.75	$8.25

Black Enameled Iron Trunk.

56635 High and Wide Trunk, covered with heavy, black enameled iron, flat top, with front and back rounded, hardwood bent slats; oriental top, upright on front, end slats all protected with tinned clamps, bumpers, cross strip clamps, fancy skeleton iron work on ends, heavy brass locks; side bolts, stitched leather handles, heavy hinges, covered tray, with bonnet box and side compartment, separately covered, fall in top.

30 inches	$4.00	32 inches	$4.25
34 inches	4.50	36 inches	4.75

Crystal Square.

56637 Square Top Crystal Trunk, 4 top slats and 4 on front, hasp lock, iron corners and slat protections. A very roomy and good trunk for the money.

28 inches	$2.50
30 inches	2.75
32 inches	3.00
36 inches	3.50
34 inches	$3.25

Black Zinc, Square.

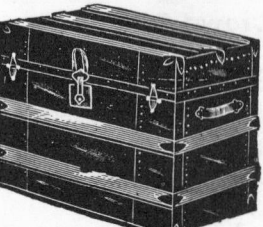

56639 Extra Large Well Made Trunk, 3 slats on top, 2 running all around, all steel corner protections, high set up tray, with covered hat box.

28 inches	$3.29
30 inches	3.55
32 inches	3.95
34 inches	4.40
36 inches	4.80

Square, Zinc Covered.

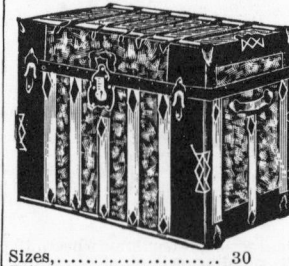

56642 Large Full Size Square Trunk five strips on top and front; three on each end, all protected with malleable iron trimmings; high set up tray with bonnet box, parasol case, etc; fall in top; this is a well made trunk and will stand any amount of hard usage.

Sizes	30	32	34	36
Price	$5.65	$6.10	$6.65	$7.15

Crystal Milan.

IRON BOTTOM.

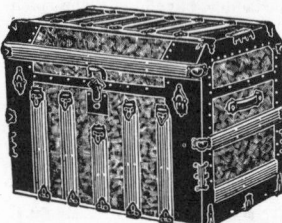

56645 Extra Large and Well Built Flat Top Trunk. Double iron bound corners, heavy hardwood strips, hasp lock, patent bolts on each side, bottom rollers, leather handles, iron bottom, hardwood bottom cleat, round body; tray with round partition; Parasol case in rear.

30 inches	$4.00	34 inches	$4.70
32 inches	4.35	36 inches	5.05

Flat Top, Beveled Corners.

Black Enameled, Iron Covered.

56650 Extra Large and High Trunk. The strips on top and front run lengthwise, and are well protected with malleable corners; high set up tray with compartments, heavy tumbler, Excelsior lock, patent bolts, stitched leather sliding handle, iron bottom; a very serviceable and remarkably cheap trunk.

Sizes	30	32	34	36
Price	$4.25	$4.50	$4.85	$5.25

Canvas Traveler.

56652 Large square box made of the best basswood, covered with extra heavy duck and painted; long hardwood slats full length of trunk, 3 on top, corners bound with selected heavy leather, leather center band and neatly scalloped, stitched leather sliding handles, heavy leather straps around trunk; slats, corners and valance protected by heavy brass clamps; heavy strap hinges, large buckle bar bolts, fine Excelsior lock, three hardwood bottom cleats, corner rollers; high set up covered hinge tray with bonnet box and partition, extra dress tray below; 36 and 38 inch have four slats on top and 38 inch has two extra dress trays. A most handsome ladies' trunk.

Size.	Price.	Size.	Price
32 inches long	$15.50	36 inches long	$17.50
34 inches long	16.50	38 inches long	19.00
		40 inches long	22.00

Square, Canvas Covered.

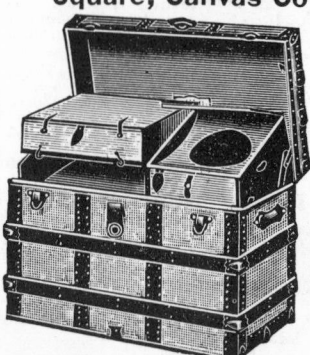

56655 Flat top, heavy duck cover, painted, double wide iron bound, two center bands, hardwood slats on top and body, end slats, all protected with heavy iron bumpers, corner shoes, etc. Excelsior lock and patent buckle bolts, heavy hinges, rollers, etc., stitched leather handles; high combination tray, hat box with removable frame, hinged shirt box on side and compartment underneath, all covered, linen finish.

Sizes	30 in.	32 in	34 in.
Price	$5.50	$5.95	$6.50

Square, Canvas Covered.

56658 Square top wide iron bound, hardwood slats full length of trunk, body and end slats, best steel bumpers and corner shoe clamps, hinges, rollers, etc., fine brass Excelsior Yale lock, two iron center bands on top and body, heavy bolts. iron body, high set up covered tray, with hat box and other compartments, linen lined.

28 inches	Price	$5.25
30 "	"	5.75
32 "	"	6.25
34 "	"	6.75
36 "	"	7.25
38 "	"	8.00

Square, Canvas Covered.

56660 Square top, wide iron bound, heavy hardwood slats full length of trunk, body and end slats, steel bumpers and clamps, rollers, etc. Excelsior lock, heavy bolt locks, iron centre band on top and body, high set up covered tray with bonnet box and other compartments, linen faced.

28 inches	Price	$4.00	34 inches	Price	$4.90
30 "	"	4.30	36 "	"	5.20
32 "	"	4.60			

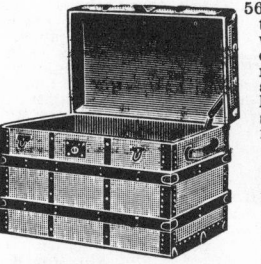

56664 This trunk is intended to meet the wants of parties who desire a large, well made trunk for storing away goods or who have no use for an inside tray such as are fitted in trunks of this character; it will hold a large quantity of goods, and stand hard usage; heavy sheet iron bound; two iron center bands around entire trunk, strong lock, side bolts and hinges, hardwood slats on top. Body, ends and bottom of trunk are protected with heavy steel clamps; a good quality of heavy canvas is used for covering and painted to protect it from rain and weather.

36 inches	Price	$3.45	40 inches	Price	$4.25
38 "	"	3.85			

56665 Large square top, canvas covered wide, iron bound, four hardwood slats on top and two on body the full length of trunk body, and end slats; heavy steel bumpers and clamps, Excelsior lock and heavy bolt locks, wide iron center band on top and body, high set up tray, with bonnet box and side compartments separately covered; linen finished, with extra dress tray. This is without doubt the best value in a square canvas trunk ever offered by us.

28 inches	Price	$4.30	34 inches	Price	$5.05
30 "	"	4.55	36 "	"	5.35
32 "	"	5.80			

56667 Leather-Bound Basswood Trunk, covered with extra heavy canvas duck, painted; large box, heavy hardwood slats full length of trunk, two extra leather center bands, slats corner and balance protected by black japanned steel clamps and shoes, strap hinges, fine brass Excelsior lock, keys all different; heavy bolt locks, high set up hinged tray, with bonnet-box and other partitions; also a portfolio in lid. It is cloth lined throughout and has an extra dress tray.

32 inches	Price	$10.50	36 inches	Price	$12.00
34 "	"	11.25	38 "	"	13.00

Trunks—Continued.

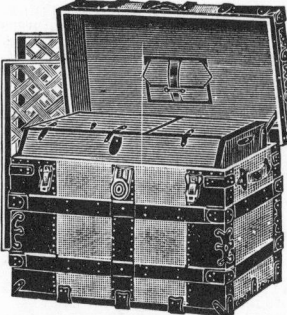

56669 Large, Square Trunk, heavy duck cover, painted, bound with heavy iron, full set of steel trimmings, bumpers, clamps, corner shoes, braces, etc., iron center bands on top and body, heavy brass Excelsior lock, side bolts, heavy leather handles, strap hinges, set-up covered tray, with bonnet box, two extra dress trays. This is a light and durable trunk.

32 inch	Price	$9.00	38 inch	Price	$11.50
34 "	"	9.75	40 "	"	12.50
36 "	"	10.50			

Men's Special Leather Bound Brass Trimmed Trunk.

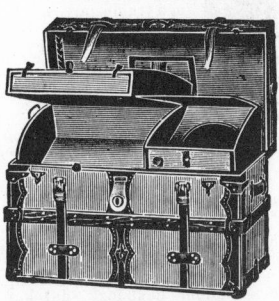

56672 A very elegant trunk, made of basswood, covered with canvas and painted; barrel stave top, hardwood slats, corners bound with heavy leather, extra leather center band, all neatly scalloped. Long heavy straps over trunk; slats, corners and valance protected by heavy brass clamps, heavy buckle bolt locks, fine Excelsior lock, high set up combination tray with elegant silk hat box, covered hinged tray divided with compartments underneath for collars, cuffs and shirts, linen, lined throughout; an elegant, gentleman's trunk.

Size, 32 in.; price..$13.50 Size, 34 in.; price..$14.50

Ladies' Special Leather Bound Brass Trimmed Trunk.

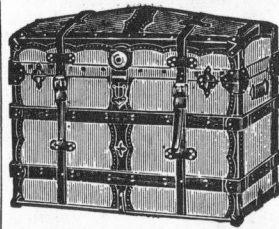

56674 Made of selected basswood, covered with heavy canvas and painted; barrel stave top, long hardwood slats, three on top, corners bound with wide heavy leather, extra leather center band neatly scalloped, long heavy leather straps over trunk, stitched leather sliding handle; slats, corners and valance protected by brass clamps, strap hinges, heavy buckle bar bolt locks, fine Excelsior locks, hardwood bottom cleats, corner rollers, high set up patent hinged tray with bonnet box, portfolio in top, cloth-lined throughout, extra dress tray; light weight ladies' trunk.

Size, 34 inch. Price............$15.75
Size, 36 inch. Price............ 17.50

Carriage Trunks.

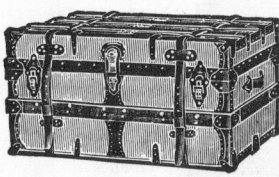

56675 Canvas Covered and Leather Bound Steel Trimmed, Carriage Trunk; very convenient for short journeys; it is higher than a steamer and lower than a full size trunk; it is full linen lined, has a tray with two partitions, partitioned in body for a lady's or gentleman's hat, but partition can be removed if desired; Excelsior lock, heavy leather bindings, scalloped edges, heavy steel clamps, heavy leather straps all the way around.

Size, 34 inches. Price............$11.50
56676 Same as No. 56675 but solid brass trimmings.
Size, 34 inches, Price.............$13.00

State Room Trunk, Canvas Edges.

56678 State Room or Steamer Trunk; corners double iron bound, long hardwood strips tipped with Russia iron, malleable iron corners and clamps, iron bottom, leather handles, heavy hasp lock, set-up tray, linen faced.

	30 in.	32 in	34 in	36 in
Length	30 in.			
Height	14 in.	14 in.	14 in.	14 in.
Width	21 in.	21 in.	21 in.	21 in.
Price, each	$4.00	$4.35	$4.75	$5.10

State Boom, Leather Corners and Covered.

56680 This trunk is made of selected basswood, covered with heavy canvas and paint; bound with extra heavy russet leather, center band scalloped, solid brass corners and clamps, valance all around. Excelsior lock, protected with patent bolts on each side; covered set up tray, adjustable partition for hat, linen lined throughout, convenient for short trips or ocean travel.

Size.	Price.	Size.	Price
30 inches long	$7.50	34 inches long	$8.50
32 inches long	8.00	36 inches long	9.00

"Major," Leather Covered.

IRON BOTTOM.

56682 Handsomely Finished Men's Trunk, cross bar, slat top and front, end slats, best plated malleable iron trimmings, bumpers, corner shoes, etc.; large plate lock, patent bolts, covered tray, with hat box and side compartment separately covered; front three pockets in cloth, faced and handsomely finished, leather covered.

Size.	Price.	Size.	Price
30 inches	$6.00	34 inches	$6.80
32 inches	6.40	36 inches	7.20

"President," Leather Covered.

IRON BOTTOM.

56684 Leather Covered Barrel Stave Top, five reverse slats on top and front, malleable iron, chain iron top, Excelsior lock and strong bolts, has top fall tray, covered body tray, with covered hat box, linen faced. This trunk is extra well made and has a row of nails from top to bottom on every corner

30 inches	$6.50
32 inches	$7.00	36 inches	8.00
34 inches	7.50	38 inches	8.75

"Sultan," Leather Covered.

56685 Leather Covered Barrel Stave Top Trunk, made over very large basswood box; has five cross slats on top and front, malleable iron chain, iron all around the trunk, extra malleable corner hinges and valance clamp, fine brass Excelsior lock and large bolts; inside full Empress finish with glove box, jewelry drawer, web tray, parasol case and other compartments; faced with Irish linen.

32 inches	$9.50
34 inches	$10.00	38 inches	11.25
36 inches	10.50	40 inches	12.00

The Monarch, Leather Covered.

56687 A New, Large Size trunk, round corners on top, five reverse hardwood strips on top and front, three on ends, all braced with fancy clamps, extra center strip and clamps on top, malleable iron scroll binding on top and body, heavy valance all around long strap hinges, heavy tumbler lock, patent bolt-locks, stitched.

Size.	Price.	Size.	Price.
30 inches	$6.00	34 inches	$7.00
32 inches	6.50	36 inches	7.50

Sole Leather Trunks.

56690 Canvas covered, sole leather bottom, heavy leather bound corners riveted, linen lined, steel springs; high set up tray with hat box, with sateen finish, large packing partition, linen lined throughout, leather bound duck cover.

30 inches	$19.00
32 "	20.00
34 "	21.00

56692 Genuine sole leather, heavy duck leather bound cover, iron frame, steel springs, hand stitched, French edge, Excelsior lock with sole leather protector, sole leather bottom; high set up combination tray with elegant silk hat box, covered tray, divided with compartments underneath for collars, cuffs, shirts, etc., all red morocco faced. The trunk is Holland linen lined throughout. The finest men's sole leather trunk in the market.

30 inches	$33.00
32 inches	$35.00
34 inches	37.00

Portmanteau.
SOLE LEATHER.

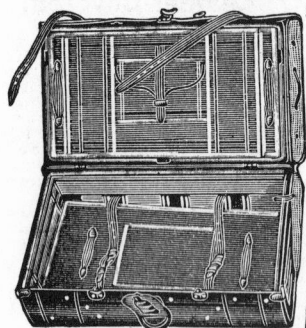

56694 Iron frame, steel springs hand stitched French edge, Excelsior lock, with sole leather lock protector, hand stitched sliding handles. The trunk opens in the center and is lined throughout with linen. The interior is especially arranged for tourists.

26 inches	$27.00
28 "	29.00
30 "	31.00
32 "	33.00

Straight Back Trunks.
SOMETHING NEW.

56696 The straight back or wall trunk, canvas covered, iron bound, steel clamps, generally known as the wall trunk, as the lid opens straight up without pulling from the wall; has a heavy brass lock, all steel clamps and heavy side bolt locks, linen faced, heavy iron centre band around body and hoop iron band on each end; a serviceable, convenient and in every respect a practical trunk for either home or traveling purposes. See cut of 56697 for closed appearance.

32 inches long, price......$7.50
34 " " " 8.00

56697 Wall Trunk, see cut of 56696 for open appearance; canvas covered, iron bound, steel clamps; this is an elegant and strongly made trunk, best Excelsior lock and heavy side bolts, steel corner clamps, and linen lined throughout; it is also provided with a linen web dress tray.

32 inches long, price......$9.00
34 " " " 9.50

OUR LINE OF
KITCHEN UTENSILS
WILL PLEASE ANY HOUSEKEEPER.

Trunks—Continued.

56699 Canvas Covered Wall Trunk, leather bound, brass trimmings; has solid brass clamps, heavy brass Excelsior lock, is full linen lined and an extra dress tray beneath a large body tray. This is a neat, compact and very desirable trunk; has a stylish appearance and is well built. See cut of 56696 for open appearance.

32 inch. long, price. $13.00   34 inch. long, price. $14.00

Crain Leather and Canvas Satchels, Telescopes, Coat Cases, Etc.
Note reduced prices.

The Gladstone style of traveling bag is the most desirable of any, as under the straps on the outside as much can be secured as the inside will hold; convenient for carrying shawls, blankets, etc. Satchels weight from 3 to 5 lbs.

56705 Gladstone Traveling Bag, soft brown leather, imitation alligator, japanned frame, large nickel plated double hasp lock; English grain leather handle, cloth lined portfolio on partition

	Each		Each
14 inches	$1.55	20 inches	$2.4)
16 inches	1.75	22 inches	2.75
18 inches	2.00	24 inches	3.00

56707 "Gladstone," soft brown grain leather, with long straps outside, cloth lined pocket on inside flap, double hasp lock, flat key, English nickel side catches, nickel plated, heavy leather handle.

	Each		Each
14 inch	$2.55	20 inch	$3.56
16 inch	2.85	22 inch	3.90
18 inch	3.23	24 inch	4.75

56710 Grained Leather Gladstone, leather covered frame, nickel lock, spring catch, patent corner protections. This bag is lined with pigskin, the outside straps are stitched, and has an English handle; is handsomely finished and very strong and durable.

	Each		Each
14 inches	$4.75	20 inches	$6.25
16 inches	5.25	22 inches	6 75
18 inches	5.75	24 inches	7.25

56712 Fitted Gladstone Bag, made of best selected leather, Spanish olive or light brown, leather covered steel frame with English corner snap catches, bottom shoes, handsome lock and trimmings, full leather lined with fine set of toilet trimmings.

Length.	Price.
16 inches	$8 67
18 inches	9.35
20 inches	10.00
22 inches	10.67

56715 Large Size Bag made from bright rubber cloth, alligator grained, heavy double flange frame, long lock, nickel trimmings, strong handle, leather straps all around, muslin lined.

	Each.		Each.
14 inches	$1.10	20 inches	$1.45
16 inches	1.25	22 inches	1.55
18 inches	1.35		

Satchels—Continued.

56719 Canvas "Gladstone" Traveling bag, made of drab canvas duck, with outside straps, nickel lock, corners bound with grained leather, cloth lined; will outwear a leather satchel.

	Each.		Each.
14 inches	$1.40	20 inches	$1.92
16 inches	1.50	22 inches	2.25
18 inches	1.67	24 inches	2.50

56720 Cabin Canvas Bag, made strong and substantial. This makes a very handy and desirable bag at a very low cost. It opens on the top and is fastened by means of three spring clasps, one on top and one on each end.

14 inches price	$0.75	20 inches, price	$1.10
16 inches, price	.85	22 inches, price	1.25
18 inches, price	1.00		

56722 The "Cabin," a new and very popular satchel, opens on top, very easy to pack, as the top of the two sides open up the full width of the satchel; is very stylish and roomy; made of the best quality grained leather, lined with leather, strong English handle, strong nickel lock and catches. This is considered the best bag on the market for the money.

12 inches Each	$4.35	16 inches Each	$5.80
14 inches Each	5.00	18 inches Each	6.25

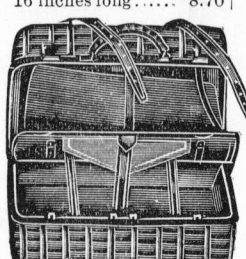

56724 Grain Leather Cabin Bag, japanned frame, strong leather English handle and brown imitation leather lining; this is a very popular style bag and is fast taking the place of the Gladstone shape.

14 inches, each	$3.35
16 inches, each	4.00
18 inches, each	4.50
20 inches, each	5.25

56725 English Oxford Alligator Bag, natural brown color, entirely new style, very high and wide. The very best selected skins are used in this bag; heavy steel frame, covered, hand stitched around entire frame, best lock and trimmings. English catches and inside stay to hold bag open; neat leather lining.

	Price.
14 inches long	$8.00
15 inches long	8.35
16 inches long	8.70
17 inches long	$8.95
18 inches long	9.25

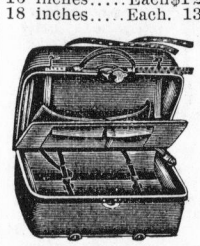

56727 Genuine Alligator Skin Gladstone Bag, made from selected stock, leather covered steel frame hand sewed to bag, heavy polished brass set in lock and snap catches, patent double jointed bottom shoe, heavy straps all around, English alligator handle, full leather lined, English style pocket on one side of flap, and shirt pocket on the other.

16 inches	Each $12.50	20 inches	Each $14.50
18 inches	Each 13.50	22 inches	Each 15.50

56729 English Sewed Frame Gladstone Traveling Bag, steel frame, padlock and chain; made from choice stock with heavy leather covered steel frame, to which bag is hand stitched: heavy nickel plated padlock with chain, nickel plated snap catches, double jointed bottom shoe, full leather lined, large portfolio on one side of flap and shirt pocket on the other, heavy English handle. The strongest and best bag made.

16 inches.	Each $11.25	20 inches.	Each $12.75
18 inches.	Each 12.00		

Satchels—Continued.

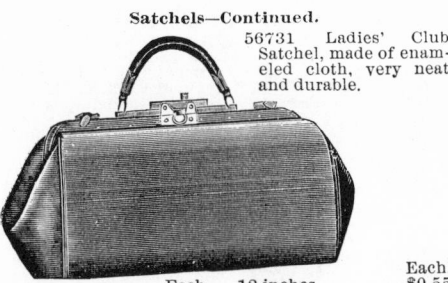

56731 Ladies' Club Satchel, made of enameled cloth, very neat and durable.

	Each.		Each.
10 inches	$0.48	12 inches	$0.55
11 inches	.50	14 inches	.60
		16 inches	.65

56732— Ladies' Satchel, "The Club." Orange colored leather, imitation alligator, japanned frame, large

nickel plated hasp lock, cloth lined.

	Each.		Each.
10 inches	$0.69	14 inches	$1.00
11 inches	.75	15 inches	1.10
12 inches	.82	16 inches	1 25
13 inches	.90		1.50

56734 Ladies' "Club" Satchel, solid grained leather, linen lined, nickel trimmings, plated hasp and lock, flat key.

	Each.
10 inches	$1.10
11 inches	1.20
12 inches	1.35
13 inches	1.50
14 inches	1.80
15 inches	1.99
16 inches	2.25

56738 Grain Leather Club, heavy leather covered frame, patent catches, English handle with rings, full leather lined, patent hinge stays, nickeled trimmings.

	Each.		Each.
10 inches	$2.28	13 inches	$3.45
11 inches	2.50	14 inches	3.45
12 inches	2.80	16 inches	4.00

56739 English Club Bag, stitched in frame, large size and made of selected stock, heavy leather covered steel frame, to which bag is hand stitched; set in English lock and English snap catches, full leather lined, heavy inside hinge stay, large pocket, heavy handle, a bag altogether suitable for steady travel. All finely mounted.

	Each.		Each.
12 inches	$4.75	16 inches	$6.25
13 inches	5.13	17 inches	6.63
14 inches	5.50	18 inches	7.00
15 inches	5.88		

56742 Genuine Alligator Club Bag, made from selected skins, covered frame, snap catches, inside hinge stay, leather lined, inside pocket, English handle, with rings and heavy lock

	Each.
13 inches	$4.50
14 inches	5.00
15 inches	5.50
16 inches	6.00
17 inches	6.50

Canvas Tele- scope Cases.

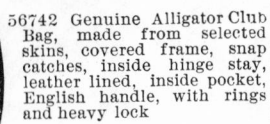

56744 Canvas Telescope Cases, plain canvas, leather corner protectors, leather straps and handle, linen lined.

LENGTH	WIDTH	HEIGHT, CLOSED	HEIGHT, OPEN	PRICE.
16 in.	8½ in.	7 in.	13 in.	$0.60
18 in.	9¾ in.	7½ in.	14 in.	.70
20 in.	11 in.	8½ in.	15 in.	.85
22 in.	12 in.	9 in.	17 in.	.95
24 in.	13½ in.	10 in.	18 in.	1.20

56746 Canvas Telescope Cases, extra heavy canvas, leather bound and extra leather corners, stitched and riveted, leather straps and handle, linen lined.

LENGTH.	WIDTH.	HEIGHT, CLOSED.	HEIGHT, OPEN.	PRICE.
16 in.	8½ in.	7 in.	13 in.	$1.35
18 in.	9¾ in.	7½ in.	14 in.	1.50
20 in.	11 in.	8½ in.	15 in.	1.65
22 in.	12 in.	9 in.	17 in.	1.80
24 in.	13½ in.	10 in.	18 in.	1.95

Canvas and Leather Dress Suit Cases.

56749 Extra strong and well made canvas telescope, designed for rough and constant wear; the edges are bound with sole leather, hand sewed; the handle is extra strong and securely fastened from the inside by a steel plate; it is impossible to wear it out or pull it loose from the top; the straps are made of heavy selected leather and sufficiently long for all purposes.

LENGTH	WIDTH	HEIGHT, OPEN	HEIGHT, CLOSED	PRICE.
16 in	11 in.	15 in.	8½ in.	$1.75
18 in.	12 in.	17 in.	9½ in.	2.00
20 in.	13 in.	19 in.	10½ in.	2.35
22 in.	14 in.	21 in.	11½ in.	2.75
24 in.	15 in.	23 in.	12½ in.	3.00

56755 Canvas Coat Case, made of heavy canvas, leather bound, riveted ends, heavy grain leather straps and handles, linen lined. This is without doubt the most convenient thing in the market; it will hold all the wearing apparel necessary for a short journey, and will not crush or wrinkle.

LENGTH	DEPTH	WIDTH CLOSED	WIDTH OPEN	PRICE
18 in.	12 in.	4½ in.	8 in.	$2.00
20 in.	12 in.	5 in.	9 in.	2.25
22 in.	13 in.	5½ in.	10 in.	2.50
24 in.	13½ in.	6 in.	11 in.	2.75

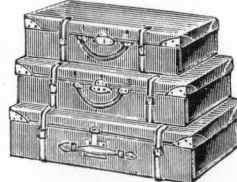

56757 Leather Coat or Dress Suit Case, heavy leather corner protections, brass lock, sliding stitched handle, linen lined, strong straps, very light and substantial

Length.	Price.
20 inches	$4.33
22 inches	4.90
24 inches	5.45

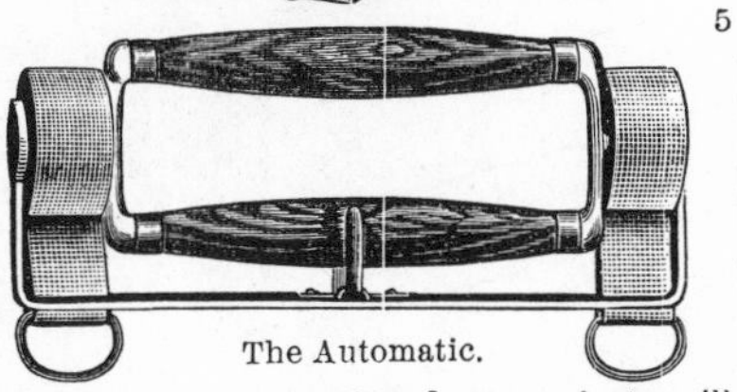

56765— Automatic Shawl Strap (see cut). Wood handles, nickel trimmings,

The Automatic.

web straps, compact and convenient, will adjust itself readily to any ordinary package; when not in use takes up less room than the old style strap. Each ....$0.17 Per dozen.........$1.84

Shawl Straps—Continued.

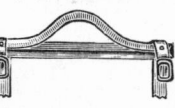

56768 Shawl Strap, covered shield, 7 inches long, leather handle, riveted to shield. Two russet straps, 30 inches long, ½ inch wide
Each $0.10
Per dozen........... 1.05

56769 Shawl Strap, covered shield, 8 in. long, with leather handle, two grain leather straps, 36 inches long, ½ inches wide, passing through loop of handle. Each. ....$0.15 Per dozen 1.65

56772 Shawl Strap, grain russet leather shield, stitched on both sides, leather covered iron handle, two grain leather straps, 36 inches long, ½ inch wide. Each......$0.20 Per dozen........ 2.20

56775 Shawl Strap, grain russet leather, covered shield, 8 inches long, grain leather handle, two grain leather straps, 48 inches long and ⅝ inch wide. Each......$0.25 Per dozen........ 2.70

56779 Shawl Strap, stiff leather covered, stitched shield, 10½ inches long, very strong, adjustable handle, stitched on both sides, two grain leather straps 48 inches long, ¾ inch wide.
Each ....$0.50 Per dozen............. 5.50

56781 Shawl Strap, leather covered shield, 12 inches long, stitched on both sides, fancy adjustable handle, two handsome hand-creased loops, attached to two fine russet grain straps 48 inches long, ⅞ inch wide, two roller buckles with billet under buckle. Price................................ .75

Tourists' Straps.

56785 Tourist's Strap 48 in. long, ⅝ in. wide, tinned loop buckle and snap made of best orange leather. Each.........$0.10
Per dozen...................... 1.15

56787 Tourist's Strap, 48 inches long, ¾ inch wide, made of best orange leather, has nickel buckle and snap. Each... $0.20 Per dozen... 2.15

56789 Tourist's Strap, same as No. 56787, but ⅞ inch wide. Each....$0.25 Per dozen...... 2.70

56792 Tourist's Strap, 48 inches long, ⅞ inch wide, made of finest stock with extra swivel and snap. Each....$0 35 Per dozen........... 3.75

Leather Trunk Tags.

56795 Trunk Tags, made of russet leather with strap to attach to trunk handles; has panel for name and address, will hold a tag or card 2¼x4 inches, with panels or openings large enough for a name and address to be written on it plainly. It cannot get lost, torn off or injured by water. Each.....$0.12 Per dozen. 1.30 If sent by mail, postage 2c.

56796 Small Name Tags for satchels, made of good strong russet leather. Each..............$0.08

Trunk Straps.

Trunk Straps, heavy russet leather.

		Each.	Per doz.
56797	7 feet long, 1¼ inches wide...	$0.45	$4.75
56798	8 feet long, 1½ inches wide...	.58	6.30
56799	9 feet long, 1½ inches wide...	.62	6.80

DAIRY SUPPLIES.

Under this heading will be found an assortment of machinery and utensils largely used in the manufacture of butter and cheese, but, realizing that the list is far from complete, we request our customers to write us for information and prices on anything in this line not found in our catalogue.

We publish a Special Catalogue of Cream Separators, both separately and in combination with various steam, horse and dog powers. This catalogue gives many reasons showing why every owner of more than five cows should have a separator. Mailed free upon request. Be sure to specify "CREAM SEPARATOR CATALOGUE."

Davis Hand and Belt Power Separator

56815 The Davis is the simplest separator on the market. Every machine is warranted to do all we claim for it. It has many improvements over the old style machines, doing away entirely with the skim milk tubes and pans or discs on the inside of the bowl, which reduces the amount of work in keeping it clean to the minimum. In place of cheap tin covers for cream and skim milk, ours are made of spun metal, well plated, thus making it impossible for them to rust. The ball bearing reduces the friction to such an extent that the machine runs very easily after getting up to full speed. Is self-oiling,

thick or thin cream can be made with change of one screw. You run no risk in purchasing a separator from us as we guarantee them to be perfect in every particular and to do all we claim for them. These machines received the award of World's Fair judges for excellence of design, ease of operation, highest standard of material and workmanship; capacity, cream and skimming qualities perfect.

CAPACITIES AND PRICES.

Capacity	Price.
150 pounds per hour for 1 to 5 cows	$ 64.68
200 pounds per hour for 3 to 15 cows	86.25
300 pounds per hour for 5 to 20 cows	107.80
400 pounds per hour for 15 to 25 cows	129.38
600 pounds per hour for 15 to 40 cows	172.50
800 pounds per hour for 25 to 50 cows	215.63

The first four sizes can be operated by hand with ease but we would advise the use of a dog power like that quoted under No. 56830; a stronger power is needed for the two larger sizes. For single pulley attachment for power for 150, 200 and 300 pound sizes add $2.00 to price of machine; for 400, 600 and 800 pound sizes add $2.50; for tight and loose pulleys with belt guard add $9.00 to price of machine.

Small Cream and Cheese Vats.

CURTIS' IMPROVED CHANNEL.

56819 These vats are made to meet the wants of a large class of dairymen who make up their own milk on the factory or creamery plan. The bottom of this vat inclines toward the center channel or groove, which gradually increases in depth throughout its entire length to the outlet, draining the contents from the vat completely. The channel or grooves, being swaged in the bottom tin, stiffen the vat bottom, thus rendering it less liable to move up and down as steam is applied, breaking the joints and causing the vat to leak. The water space underneath the tin vat will be appreciated by everyone who has had any experience in cooling or warming up vats of cream or milk. They are made in a superior manner. Perfection gates are used, and no expense is spared to make them the best vats the dairy public has seen.

Sizes and prices:
25-gallon vat, with ice box on end.............$18 00
50-gallon vat, with ice box on end.............. 21.00
We can quote prices on large vats, same as above, holding from 100 to 800 gallons.

Curtis' Improved Self-Heating Cheese Vats.

56821—This vat is designed for large and small dairies. It is built same as No. 56819 vat.

Sizes. | Prices.
25 gallon.............. ....$21.00
50 gallon............ .... 24.50
We can quote prices on self-heating cheese vats holding from 75 to 600 gallons.

Standing Press for Cheese.

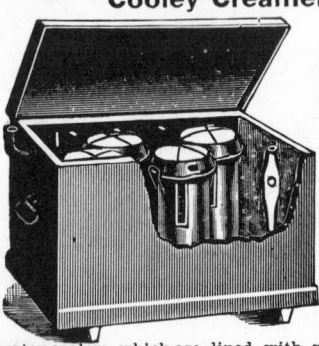

The above illustration shows the method of making a good standing press for cheese factory or private dairy. The construction is so simple that any person familiar with the use of saw and hammer can make it. It consists of a frame, which is supported on legs and the loose boards on which the hoops stand, and which is grooved to allow the whey to run off. For making a four-hoop press, as shown, it takes five sets of rods and saddles, four heavy press screws and four hoops and followers. The rods pass up one side and over the iron saddles shown on the top of the press and down on the other. Holes are bored through the top timber to allow the screws to project up through when raised to allow the removal of the hoops. The divisions between the hoops are made of two-inch plank and support the upper timber when the screws are raised. The presses can be made any length desired.
56823 Rods, Saddles and Washers, per set.......$1.50
56824 Screws, 1¾ by 20 inches long, per set..... 2.75
Prices quoted on all sizes of hoops and followers.

Cooley Creamer.

56826 The above is an illustration of the Cooley system of setting milk in submerged cans. These cans are 20 inches deep and 8½ inches in diameter; the covers are fastened down, and the air under the rims of the covers prevent the passage of any water into the cans. The cans are set in the water coolers, which are lined with metal and fitted with inlet and overflow for using flowing spring water. A thermometer is inserted in the front of each cooler, in order that the temperature can be ascertained without raising the cover. This apparatus is very simple, dispensing with costly milk rooms, as but little room is required.

If the temperature of the water in the cooler is kept at 45 to 50 degrees in spring and summer, and at 40 degrees or below in winter, the cream will rise in 12 hours, in which case only cans enough to hold a single milking are required. By this system of setting milk we have sweet cream from sweet milk, raised in the shortest possible space of time. Prices include cans with bottom faucet, and glass panel in the side of can, showing depth of cream.

SIZE, CAPACITY AND PRICES.

No. 0, for 1 can, milk of 1 cow, 18 quarts........$15.10
No. 00, for 2 cans, milk of 2 to 4 cows, 36 quarts 21.00
No. 1. for 3 cans, size, 25x32 inches, milk of 6 to 9 cows, 51 quarts.......................... 23.50
No. 2, for 4 cans, size 28x38 inches, milk of 9 to 12 cows, 68 quarts.......................... 25 20
No. 3, for 6 cans, size, 28x49 inches, milk of 12 to 18 cows, 102 quarts..................... 33 60
No. 4, for 8 cans. size, 28x61 inches, milk of 18 to 24 cows, 136 quarts.................... 42.00
No. 5, for 10 cans, size, 28x72 inches, milk of 24 to 30 cows, 170 quarts................... 50.00
No. 6, for 12 cans, size, 28x84 inches. milk of 30 to 36 cows, 204 quarts................... 58.80
In connection with the Cooley Creamer, if Boyd's Automatic Fermenting Can and Automatic Ripening Cream Vat are used, nothing can be more simple for making prime butter every day in the year. It is making butter by rule. No process in the world like it.

Skimming Bench.

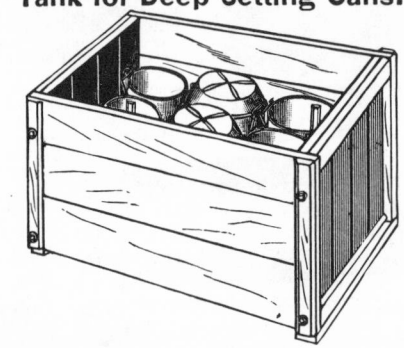

This cut shows a simple device to be used with Cooley creamer upon which to place the cans when drawing off the milk and cream, by the Cooley process of skimming. This bench should be set with one end against the creamer, so that the cans, as they are lifted out, can be readily placed upon it, thus avoiding any drip on the floor. This is an inexpensive arrangement and can easily be made by any one who can handle a saw, plane and hammer.

Tank for Deep Setting Cans.

56827 These tanks are made from two-inch lumber, the ends securely clamped and fastened with rods and have a hinged cover not shown in cut. It is fitted with an inlet and overflow. Painted both outside and inside. It is made strong and substantial and will hold Cooley or any deep setting can.
Sizes and prices.
To hold 4 cans.......... ....$5.50
To hold 6 cans...... .... 6.65
To hold 8 cans 7.50
To hold 10 cans................................ 8.45

Boyd's Automatic Cream Vat and Fermenting Can for Farm Use.

56828 This cut represents Boyd's Automatic Cream Vat for farm use, and it can truthfully be said that no other known process will produce as much and as good butter from a given amount of cream. It accomplishes for butter making what has never been done before. It enables the butter maker to work to a given rule every day in the year, and produces absolutely uniform results. It does away entirely with the necessity of coddling the cream around the stove. This vat is so constructed that when the cream is put into the vat the temperature of the cream will scarcely vary over three or four degrees in twenty-four hours. It is a perfect refrigerator vat with a cover. Quotations are for ripening vats only. Fermenting cans are quoted separately.

Price.		Price.
10 gallon vat.......$15.10	100 gallon vat.....$35.30
15 gallon vat....... 17.65	150 ga lon vat.. .. 40.35
20 gallon vat....... 20.10	200 gallon vat...... 45.30
30 gallon vat....... 22.68	250 gallon vat...... 50.40
50 gallon vat.. .... 25.20	300 gallon vat..... 55.45
75 gallon vat........ 30.25	400 gallon vat...... 63.00

Boyd's Automatic Fermenting Can.

56829 The Boyd process of fermenting is very simple, yet more scientific than appears at first sight. It consists of making a lactive ferment from sweet skimmed milk, dives ed of its butter fat, taken from a fresh cow or cows. The milk is treated to a warm water bath and brought to a certain required temperature, when it is placed in the fermenting can and the vessel closed tightly. In a given time the lactive ferment is ready for use. A small percentage of this ferment is placed in the cream at a required temperature, and the cream vat is closed in the same manner as the fermenting can. In so many hours the result is ripe cream, that is, cream of one chemical condition. The operation is uniform; so also is the result. If the rules are strictly obeyed, the operator is at all seasons master of the situation. He has perfect control over the conditions, consequently his work is all down to rule, nothing being left to chance or good luck. The Automatic Fermenting Can and Automatic Ripening Cream Vat are sold only in connection with each other, and are essential to the process.
Fermenting cans holding 1 gallon, price. $3.80
Fermenting cans holding 2 gallons, price........ 4.20
Fermenting cans holding 3 gallons, price........ 4.65
Fermenting cans holding 4 gallons, price........ 5.10
Fermenting cans holding 5 gallons, price........ 5.50
Fermenting cans holding 6 gallons, price........ 5.90
Fermenting cans holding 8 gallons, price........ 6.35

Lamb's Adjustable Animal Powers.

For Churns, Separators, Etc.

The powers are quickly and easily attached to any kind of churn, or can be used for doing a great deal of farm labor, usually done by the man or maid, or the farmer's wife. You can just as well save the wife and maid this ever tiresome task, as well as the time that is expended in churning and like work, by making your dog, goat or sheep do all this labor, as well as the labor required in many of the farm duties. The powers are built with special reference to durability, and they are finished and painted in the best manner; all shafts and bearing are lathe fitted. Special care is given in their construction, that they may be *strong, perfect* and *durable*

56830 This power is built to be operated by two dogs, sheep or goats, and will furnish sufficient power to run a "Safety" separator, corn sheller, fan mill, sawing machine, churn, pump, washing machine, etc. Balance wheel is banded for 2½ and 3 inch belt; weight, crated, 180 pounds. Price.............$23.00

First Prize Dog Power.

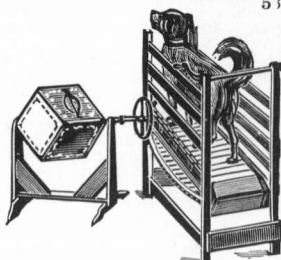

53831 This power can be operated by a dog, goat or sheep; yields 25 per cent. more power from a given weight of animal than any other, and with adjustable bridge to regulate the required power and motion, a 30 pound animal will do the churning; if you keep a dog make him "work his passage." The power can be connected to any churn sold by us. Price.......................$15.00

The illustration above shows how the double dog power can be used in operating a cream separator; when the separator is not in use and you desire to churn connect it to tumbling rod sent with machine. A corn sheller, fan mill or sawing machine, can be connected by belt from balance wheel. Separators require a high gear and for this purpose we recommend our steel pulley, 3½ by 36 inches, this we can furnish at $6.00 extra. If iron coupling rod and coupling as shown in illustration are desired to connect and run cream separator, we can furnish them at $3.00 extra.

The Peerless Creamery.

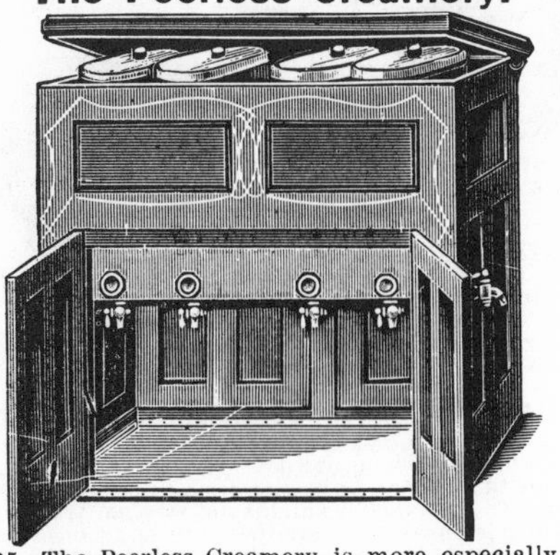

56835 The Peerless Creamery is more especially intended for water alone. The cans are oblong, 14 inches long, 5 inches wide and 14 inches deep, thus giving larger cooling surface. We have a large ice space in rear of and also between the cans; in the No. 4 we have the space between the two middle cans, 7 inches; also, in all the other sizes we have a large space between the second and third, fourth and fifth, and sixth and seventh. In these, as in the round can creamers, we use a straight faucet underneath, which is easily cleaned. The glass to observe the cream is in the nut and not in the can, so is easily repaired if accidentally broken. In the No. 3 and larger sized creameries the faucet for drawing water from the tank is placed outside of creamery, as shown in illustration Where ice is not used, we would suggest emptying tank of water about a half hour after milk has been placed in cans, and refilling tank with cold water. This will save a few hours' time in the gathering of cream. Furnished complete, with cream pail, strainer and dairy thermometer.

PRICE LIST.—Capacity of cans. 18 quarts each.

No.	No. of cans.	No. of cows.	Height, inches.	Length, inches.	Width. inches.	Weight, pounds.	Price.
2......	2	4 to 6	35	25	23	100	$17.85
3..	3	7 to 9	35	34	23	125	21.80
4......	4	10 to 12	35	41	23	160	26.40
5......	6	13 to 18	35	61	23	220	34.32
6	8	19 to 24	35	77	23	280	42.65
7......	10	25 to 30	35	80	23	320	49.40
8......	12	31 to 36	35	96	24	440	56.30

Our prices on these creameries are 40 per cent. below factory prices.

Cedar Box Factory Churn.

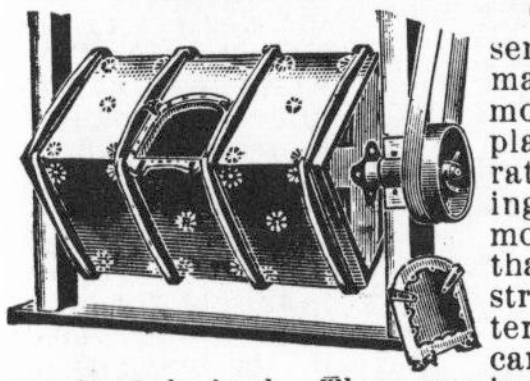

This cut represents our new churn, made of white cedar. The mouth of this churn is placed to one side, or rather at one corner, making it much easier to remove the butter and clean than the usually constructed churn of this pattern; in fact, the butter can be dumped into a tray or tub, if desired. The cover is simple and very strong, and is secured in its place by four bolts, with thumbscrews, two of which only need be loosened to remove or replace the lid, which is done very quickly. This is the most convenient and strongest cover that has yet been made.

The white cedar of which this churn has been manufactured is acknowledged by all who have had experience to be the very best material of which to make vats, tanks, churns, tubs, etc., as the wood is light, will not water-soak, and is the most lasting for such purposes.

All the woodwork is tongued and grooved together, to secure durability and tightness in all the joints. All the ironwork in the cover, and all bolt heads coming in contact with the cream, are galvanized. The flanges and shaft by which the churns are hung, are heavy and substantial.

With each churn is furnished a tight and loose pulley (18x4), with two substantial boxes for the shafting, but no frames, as that must be adapted to the place where the churn is to be used, as may be seen in the engraving; 30x4 pulleys can be furnished for $5.00 extra.

About 50 revolutions per minute is the average speed used with these churns, but that may be varied according to the judgment of the operator, and the thickness and condition of the cream.

No. 56842— SIZES AND PRICES.

Size.	Will hold, gallons.	Will churn, gallons.	Inches square outside.	Inches long outside.	Price.
No. 1	100	50	34	33	$18.15
No. 1½........	150	75	34	44	21.17
No. 2	200	100	34	55	24.20
No. 2½........	250	125	34	66	26.46
No. 3	300	150	34	76	30.24
No. 3½........	350	175	34	86	34.00
No. 4	400	200	34	96	37.80
No. 4½........	450	225	34	106	41.50
No. 5	500	250	34	116	45.36

Our prices on these churns are fully 30 per cent. below factory prices.

Sturges Steel Churn.

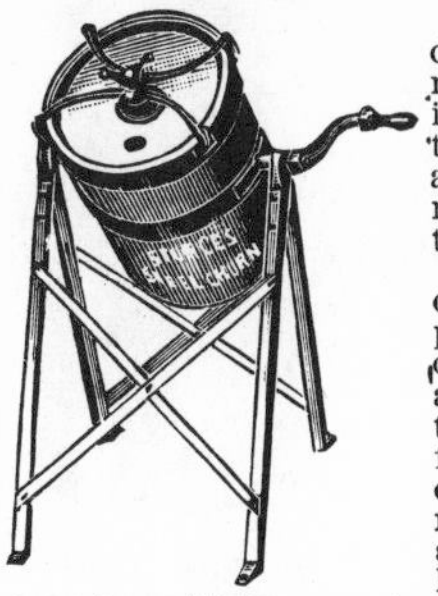

The latest and best thing out. It is exceptionally well made, being heavily coated inside with chemically pure tin, while the stand, which is also steel, is tastefully decorated in colors to brighten the home of the housewife.

An important feature, and one that cannot but be appreciated by those desirous of keeping their churn sweet and clean, is the diameter of this churn's mouth which is full size. The inside of the churn is perfectly smooth, making it as easy to clean as a crock. The cover has a half inch cork lining around the edge which prevents any possibility of a leak. A glass vent and peep hole adorns the cover for the purpose of determining when butter comes and also to let off the gases.

56845 Five Gallon Sturges Steel Churn, for one to four gallons of cream. Price.....................$5.00

56847 Nine Gallon Sturges Steel Churn, for four to seven gallons of cream. Price..................$8.00

The Star Barrel Churn.

This style of churn is old, tried and reliable, easy to operate and keep clean; it is absolutely impossible for this churn to leak as the wear can be taken up as simply as any one can turn a thumb nut. The fastenings are attached to the outside of the churn, and it will be seen from the cut that the bails and cover fastening is a compound leverage which increases the pressure ten times more than any other make of churn.

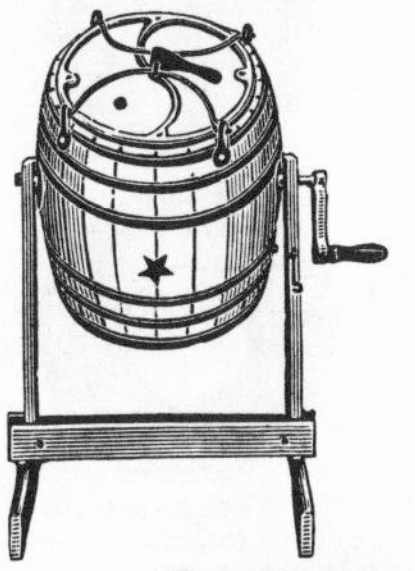

56850 Five Gallon Barrel Churn, for one or two gallons of cream. Each.$3.00

56852 Nine Gallon Barrel Churn, for 1 to 4 gallons of cream. Each......$3.25

56854 Fifteen Gallon Barrel Churn, for 2 to 7 gallons of cream. Each.$3 50

56856 Twenty Gallon Barrel Churn, for 3 to 9 gallons of cream Each.$4.00

56859 Twenty-five Gallon Barrel Churn, for 4 to 12 gallons of cream.... $4,95

56860 Thirty-five Gallon Barrel Churn for 5 to 16 gallons of cream...$6.00

Rectangular Churns.

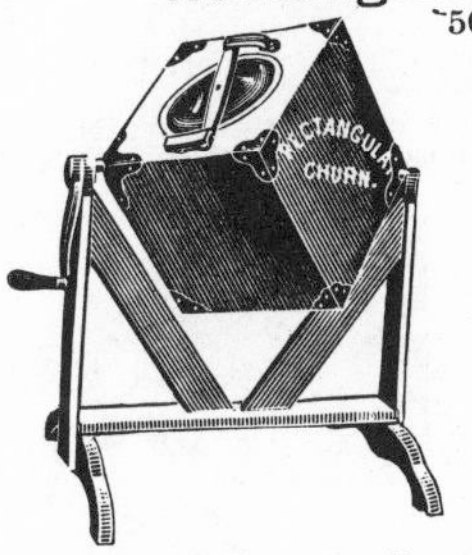

56861 The Rectangular Churn works the easiest and quickest of any churn on the market. At the Dairy Fair, held in Chicago, December 1878, it received the highest award, a cash premium and diploma in competition with the world. Wisconsin butter won five medals at the Centennial Exhibition, at Philadelphia, and four of these were awarded to butter made in the Rectangular Churn.

No. 0	holding	7 gallons.	Price	....	$3.50
No. 1	"	10 "	"	....	4.00
No. 2	"	12 "	"	....	4.35
No. 3	"	20 "	"	....	4.80
No. 3½	"	26 "	"	....	6.00
No. 4	"	40 "	"	....	12.80
No. 5	"	60 "	"	....	18.40

The Nos. 4 and 5 are adapted for use in small creameries and large dairies, and fitted with cranks at both end and so arranged that a pulley can be attached for connecting with power. Full capacity of churns are given; when in use they should be only half full.

Curtis' Improved Square Box Churn.

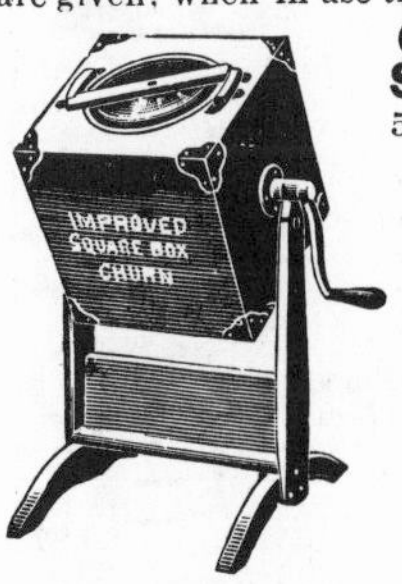

56862 Its compactness, durability and efficiency make it very desirable for a dairy of one cow or fifty. It is a great favorite and has been improved in many respects, until it is believed to be absolutely the most perfect box churn to be found anywhere. The cover is of heavy tin and securely fastened. The corners are protected with iron caps and are so constructed that when the buttermilk is drawn out and cleansed it will drain perfectly dry.

Holding	7 gal. churns	from 1 to 3 gal.	Price	..$3.50
"	10 " "	" 2 to 4 "	"	.. 4.05
"	12 " "	" 2 to 6 "	"	.. 4.35
"	20 " "	" 3 to 9 "	"	.. 4.80
"	26 " "	" 4 to 12 "	"	.. 6.00
"	40 " "	" 6 to 20 "	"	..12.80
"	60 " "	" 8 to 30 "	"	..18.40
"	80 " "	" 10 to 40 "	"	..20.80

The three largest sizes are adapted to large dairies. They have a crank on one side, a long gudgeon for pulleys on the other; strong bands and rods running around the churn make them very substantial. Light and loose pulleys are worth $6.00 extra.

Union Churn.

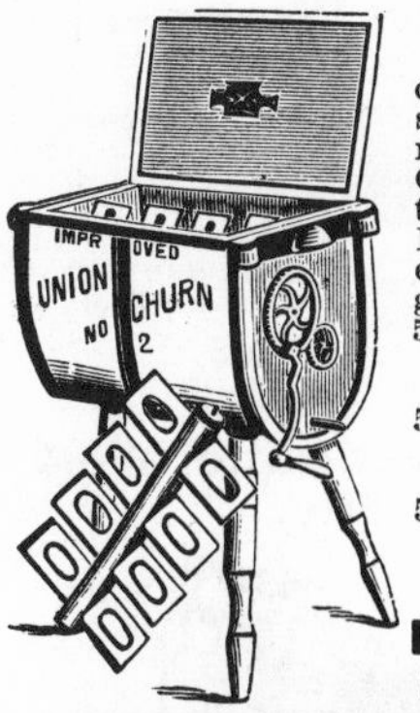

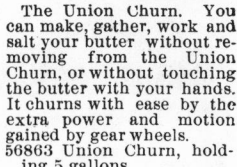

The Union Churn. You can make, gather, work and salt your butter without removing from the Union Churn, or without touching the butter with your hands. It churns with ease by the extra power and motion gained by gear wheels.

56863 Union Churn, holding 5 gallons. Each.................$4.00

56864 Union Churn, holding 7 gallons. Each....... ....$4.25

56866 Union Churn, holding 10 gallons. Each...............$4.75

Improved Cedar Cylinder Churn.

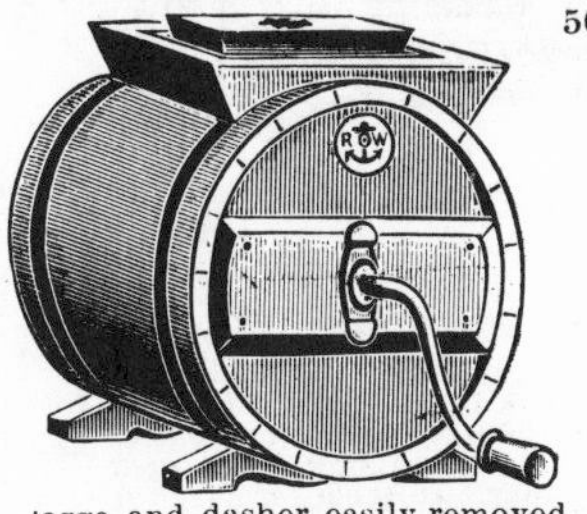

56869 This we consider by far the best small, cheap churn on the market It is made from the best Virginia cedar; it has a double dasher, and the crank is locked to the churn with a clamp and thumbscrew, which prevents leakage. Lock cannot break. The top is large and dasher easily removed. The hoops are of galvanized iron and will not rust.

No	1	2	3	4
Will hold. ...	3	4	7	10 gallons
Will churn. .	2	3	4	5 gallons
Price.........	$1.50	$1.90	$2.25	$2.50

Dash Churns.

Common Dash Churns. A long handle goes through the cover at the top, with a dasher at the bottom, which is worked up and down inside the churn.

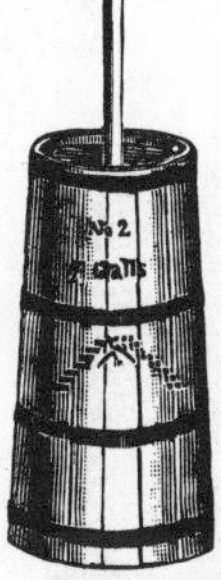

	Each.	Per doz.
56870 3-gallon dash churn...........	$0.56	$6.00
56872 4-gallon dash churn............	.70	7.56
56874 5-gallon dash churn...	.85	9.18
56875 6-gallon dash churn	.96	10.37

Dash Churns, Striped Cedar, with Brass Hoops.

	Each.	Per doz.
56878 3-gallon....	$0.95	$10.26
56880 4-gallon ...	1.00	10 80
56882 5-gallon....	1.10	11.88
56885 6-gallon....	1.20	12.26

See Index for Stoneware Dash Churns.

Reid Butter Workers.

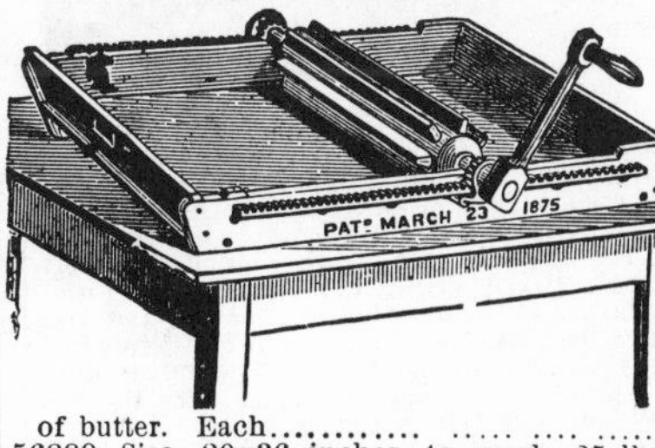

56887—Size 14 x23 inches, to work 8 lbs. of butter. Each, $3.60

56888 Size 17 x27 inches, to work 18 lbs. of butter. Each......................$4.25

56889 Size, 20x36 inches, to work 25 lbs. of butter. Each. 4.80

56890 Size, 23x36 inches, to work 50 lbs. of butter. Each...................... 5.75

Lever Butter Workers.

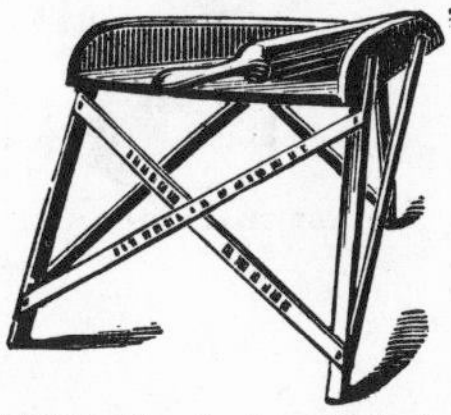

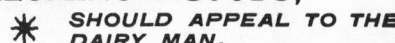

56891 The Lever Butter Worker; its simplicity, saving of time, ease of operation and very low price, commend it as an indispensable adjunct to every dairy.

No. 0 size, 20 inches wide, works 15 lbs. Each.... ....$3.50

No. 1 size, 30 inches wide, works 25 lbs. Each... .... $4.35

56892 No. 2 size, 40 inches wide, works 35 lbs. Each..... .... 5.00

ALUMINUM GOODS,

SHOULD APPEAL TO THE DAIRY MAN.

Cottage Butter Workers.

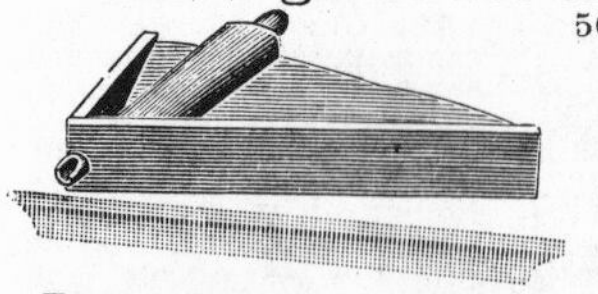

56893 A convenient low-priced worker that is placed upon a table when in use. The end is placed over the side of the table and the drip falls into a vessel upon the floor.

For 1 or 2 cows $2.50
For 2 or 3 cows 3.00
For 4 or 5 cows 3.50

Fairlamb's Improved Butter Worker Dairy Size.

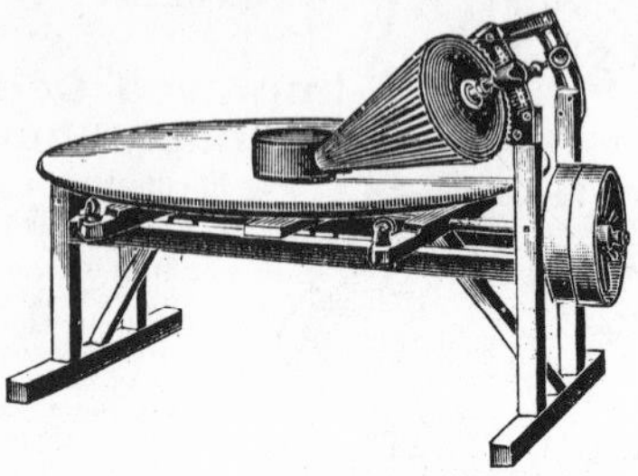

56894 The increase of the use of the small separators in the dairy has created a demand for hand or power workers of smaller capacity than those generally used; we are now prepared to fill orders for them, suitable for farm or dairy use. It is sent out complete as shown in cut and can be used with power or by hand. 3 foot table. Price.............................. $21.85

Cheese Factory Milk Cans.

56895 GENUINE STEEL.

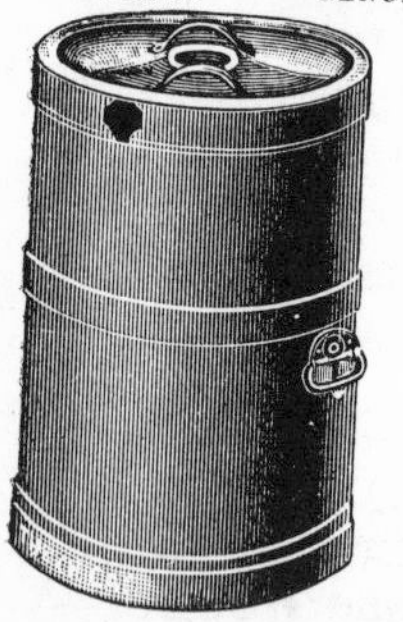

Holds	Gallons.	Price.
15	"	$3.90
20	"	4.32
30	"	4.92
40	"	5.76

Weighing Cans.

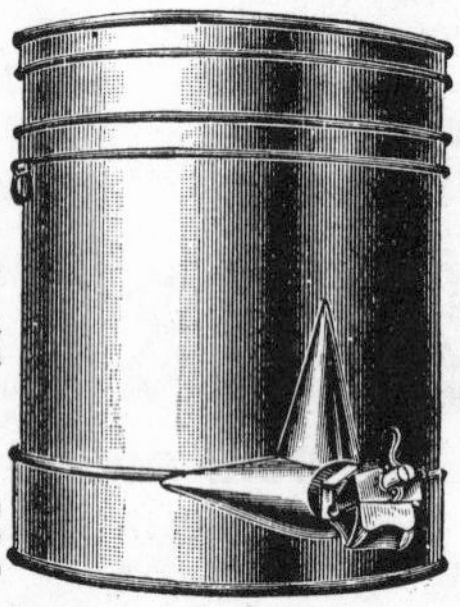

56898 Made of heavy tin with 3 inch perfection gate and sloping bottom.

Holds	Gallons	Price.
40	"	$6.00
60	"	7.20
80	"	8.40

Milk Cans.

The illustration below shows the improved breast used on all our milk cans; the most important feature is to make a breast that is proof against being "jammed in." Our heavy half oval hoop accomplishes this; the hoop is forced on the breast in the block, securely fastened and afterward retinned, which makes it absolutely safe against being knocked off. We have also adopted a new seamless neck on all our cans; this you will observe, is drawn in one piece. The advantages of the New Seamless Neck, as compared with the old style bowl and neck in two pieces are many. There are no seams to come unsoldered, no edges or joints to rust, no bowl to work loose. Adds to weight of your can, being heavier material. Strengthens the weakest part of your can. Is perfectly smooth inside and out.

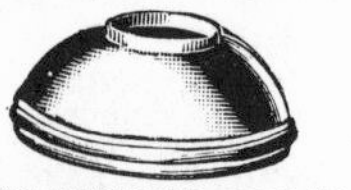

THE IMPROVED BREAST

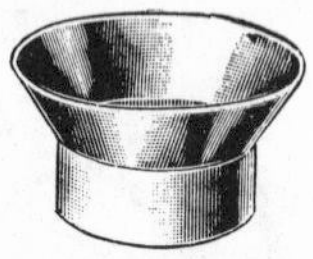

NEW SEAMLESS NECK.

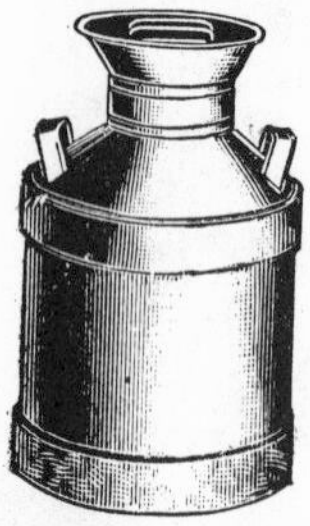

56901 Sturges' or Teet's Pattern Railroad Milk Can, with improved breast and new seamless neck.

	Wgt.	Each	Per doz.
8 gallons,	15½ lbs.	$1.98	$22.58
10 gallons,	17½ lbs.	2.10	23.95

Milk Cans—Continued.

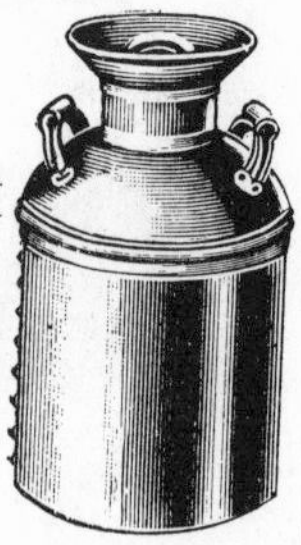

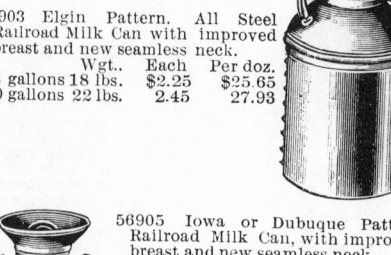

56903 Elgin Pattern. All Steel Railroad Milk Can with improved breast and new seamless neck.

	Wgt..	Each	Per doz.
8 gallons	18 lbs.	$2.25	$25.65
10 gallons	22 lbs.	2.45	27.93

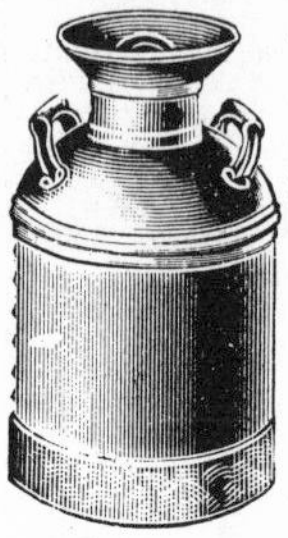

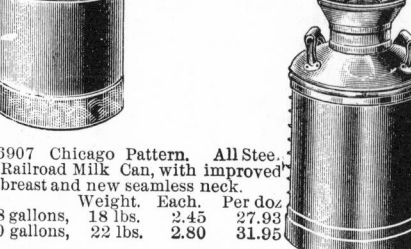

56905 Iowa or Dubuque Pattern Railroad Milk Can, with improved breast and new seamless neck.

	Weight.	Each..	Per doz.
8 gallons,	18 lbs.	$1.98	$22.75
10 gallons,	21 lbs.	2.10	23.95

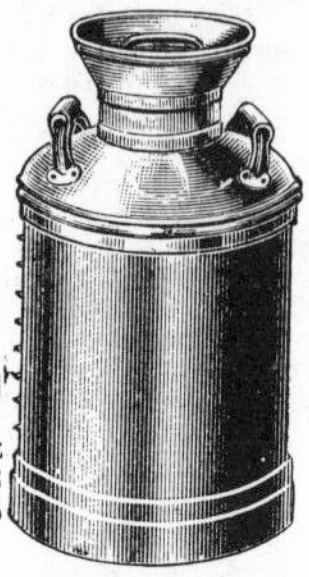

56907 Chicago Pattern. All Steel Railroad Milk Can, with improved breast and new seamless neck.

	Weight.	Each.	Per doz
8 gallons,	18 lbs.	2.45	27.93
10 gallons,	22 lbs.	2.80	31.95

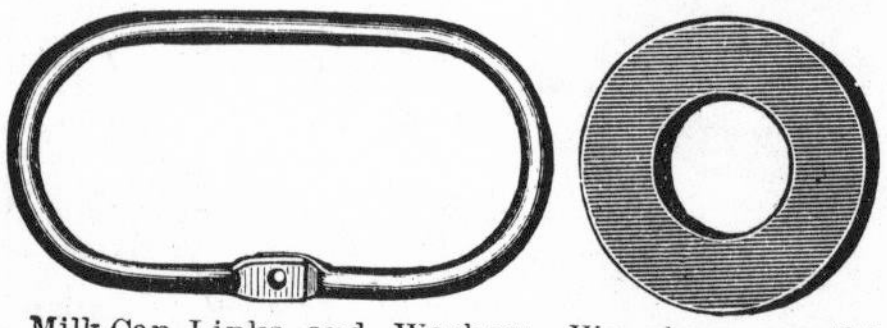

Milk Can Links and Washers. We always use this washer to strengthen can and prevent its wearing. We can fit any of our milk cans with link and washer at an additional charge of 5 cents per can.

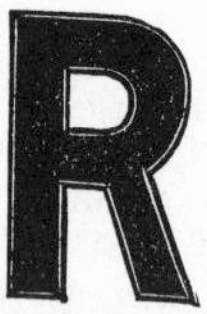

Brass or Copper Milk Can Letters; size, 1⅝ inches, soldered onto can at 1½ cents per letter; when ordering state which is desired, otherwise copper letters will be used.

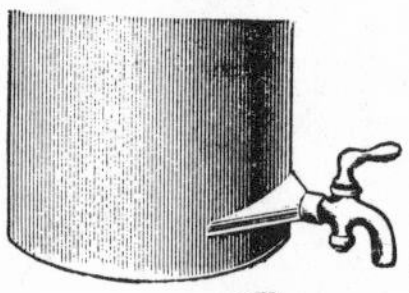

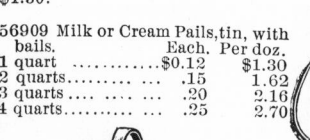

The above illustration shows ⅞ inch brass faucet fitted to milk can for delivery purposes. When desired it can be put on any of our cans at an additional cost, "including price of faucet and labor," for $1.50.

56909 Milk or Cream Pails, tin, with bails.

	Each.	Per doz.
1 quart	$0.12	$1.30
2 quarts	.15	1.62
3 quarts	.20	2.16
4 quarts	.25	2.70

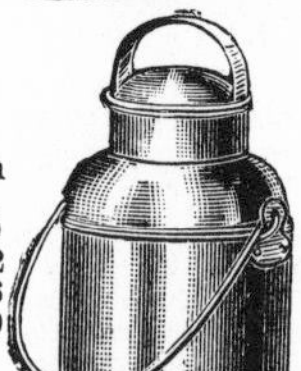

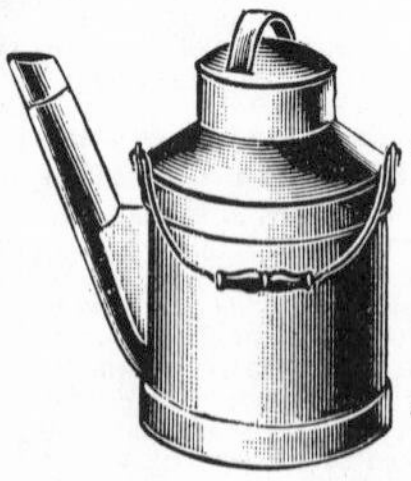

56911 Milk Peddling Cans. They are made of 4X tin with heavy brass hoop on top and bottom, spout tipped with brass; a very strong and serviceable article. Capacity two gallons. Each....................$1.56

56913 Milk Measure graduated, made of good quality tin and holds 1 quart. Each....$0.08 Per dozen $0.87

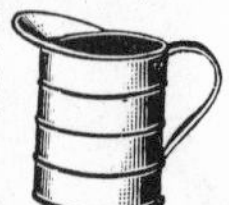

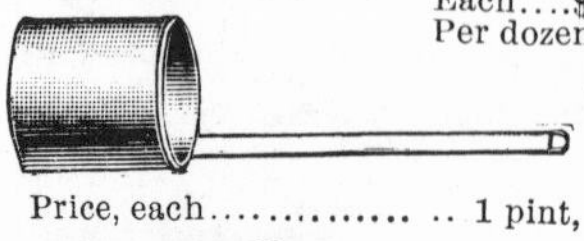

56915 Milk Dippers, made of tin, with long handle.

Price, each.............. 1 pint, 10c.; 1 quart, 15c.

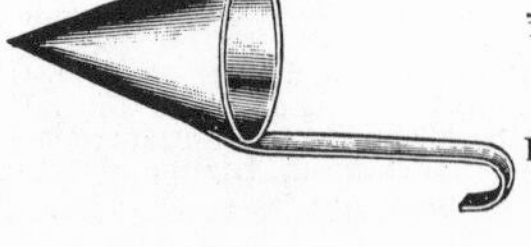

56917 Conical Milk Skimmer, well made of good stock. Each.......... $0.08 Per dozen.... .90

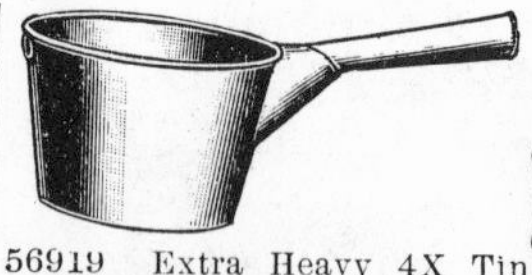

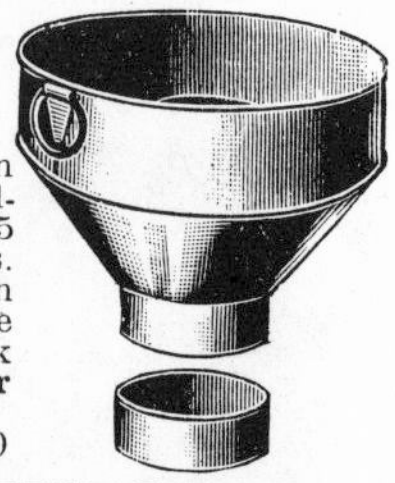

56919 Extra Heavy 4X Tin Milk Dippers, capacity, 1 gallon. Each...............$0.45

56921 Milk Can Strainers. These are made of heavy tin and have a 4-inch brass wire strainer; it will fit a milk can, Cooley or our regular cream setters. Each..................$0.80

Curtis' Improved Milk Strainer.

56922 This strainer is adapted for use in all kinds of vessels where milk is set to raise cream. It sets in a tin pan or in an 8-inch deep setting pail. The metal cone shields the strainer from getting jammed. The strainer is made from superior silvered wire cloth, while the tube which projects below has a band, where a cloth is readily put on, straining the milk twice at one operation. The bowl of the strainer is stamped from one piece of heavy plate and then retinned, making it smooth, and as near perfect as a strainer can be. Price $1.30

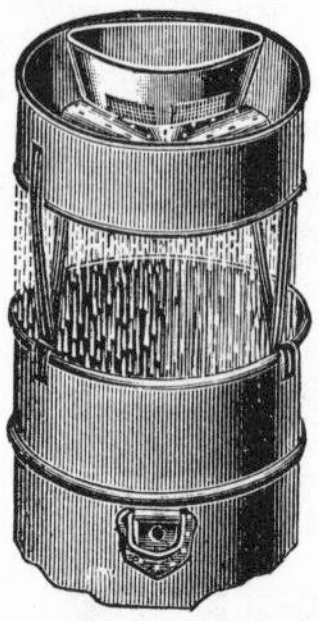

Howard Patent Milk Cooler.

56923 This valuable implement is made to fit any can. As the milk is poured into one side it is strained and runs in very fine streams into the can below. It cools the milk in the operation, and takes from it the animal odor. Each......................$2.40

Milk Cooler and Aerator.

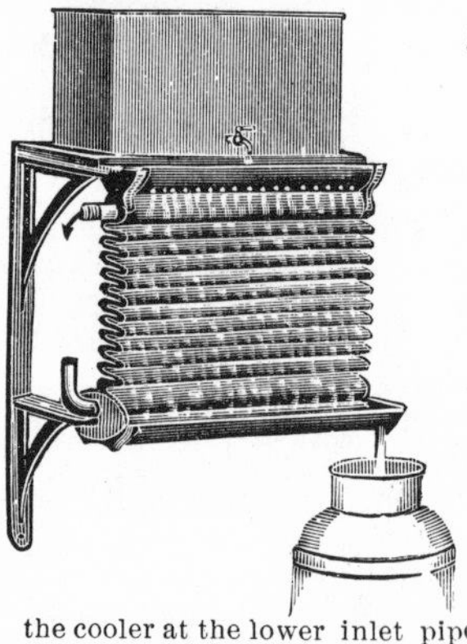

56924 Especially designed to cool and ærate new milk or cream from separator, with or without the use of ice. It cools the milk quickly, or as fast as milked, to within 2 degrees of the temperature of the water used; at the same time removes animals and garlic odors, and adds greatly to the keeping qualities of the milk. As shown in the cut, the cooler being suspended by the brackets to a wall or post, the cold water enters the cooler at the lower inlet pipe from a barrel or reservoir, flows to the opposite side, then up through the corrugations and passes out at the top. The milk in the reservoir flows out at the faucet and is distributed by the perforated trough, and flows down over the outside of the cooler in a thin film and passes into the can below. The cooler is easily cleaned, it being hinged at one end, so need not be taken down to wash. And having no sides or ends to the corrugations, there are no corners to clean. The corrugations are of sheet copper and brass, and are made in a a substantial and workmanlike manner. Satisfaction is guaranteed.

Price, with milk tank, water faucet, brackets and 6 feet ¾-inch water hose, as follows;

No. 1.. $16.25
No. 2.. 20.00
No. 3.. 24.00

Perfect Milk Pail.

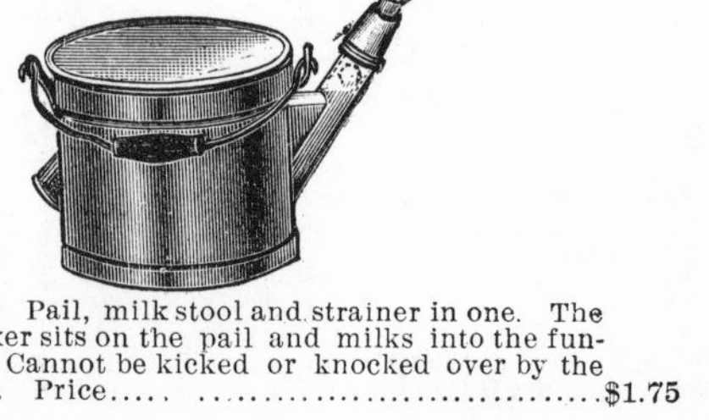

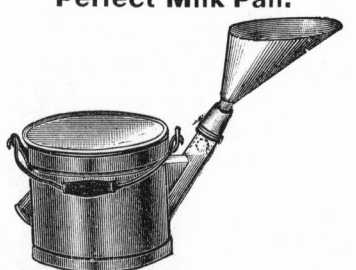

56925 Pail, milk stool and strainer in one. The milker sits on the pail and milks into the funnel. Cannot be kicked or knocked over by the cow. Price..$1.75

Curtis Babcock Farm Tester.

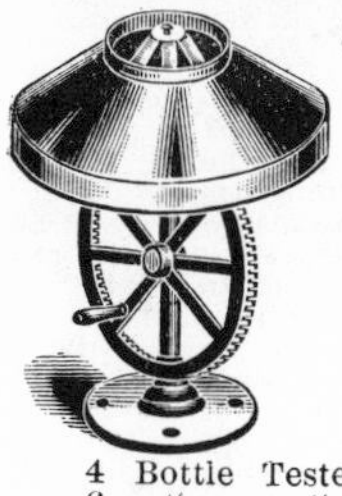

56926 Every dairyman or farmer who keeps a half dozen cows ought to provide himself with one of these milk testers, if he cares the snap of his finger to know whether he has a cow in the herd that is worth keeping. (More than one cow "eats her head off" every year she is kept.) This tester is designed expressly for farm use, and so low a price put on it that every man who owns two cows can have a four bottle machine.

4 Bottle Tester, complete. Price........$5.00
6 " " " " ......: 6.00
8 " " " " 7.00

With each machine there is a pipette acid measure, a bottle of acid and directions for operating.

Babcock Milk Test.

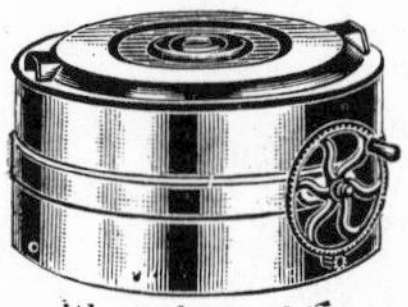

With Roe's improved swinging heads.
56927 4-Bottle Tester, complete. Price......$8.00
8-Bottle Tester, complete Price.......... 10.00
12-Bottle Tester, complete. Price......... 14.00
24-Bottle Tester, complete Price.......... 21.00

ith each machine is included testing bottles, pipette acid measure and acid for 50 to 200 tests, according to size, and full directions for operating.

Strainer Pails, Tin.

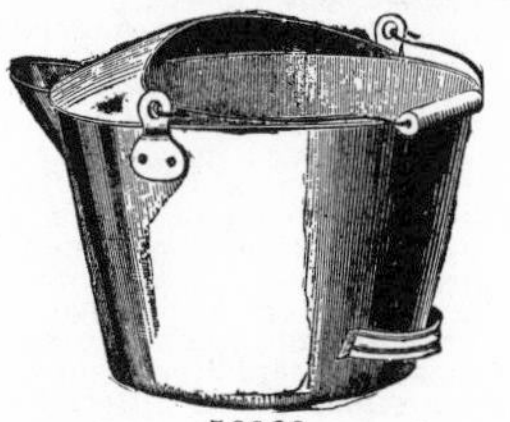

56929

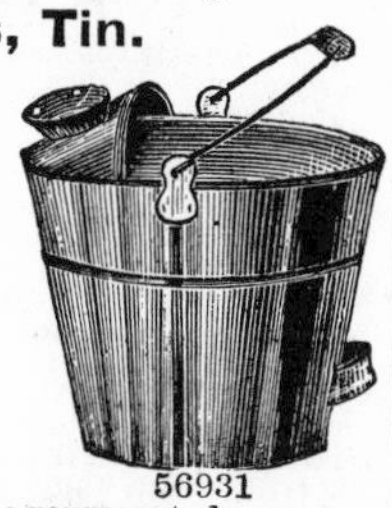

56931

They will not hold as much as represented.
56929 10 quarts ....$0.25 14 quarts $0.30
56931 Milk Pail, with strainer, extra heavy tin, stamped seamless, holds 12 quarts.
Each ....$0.90 Per dozen........... 9.72

The Dairyman's Favorite.

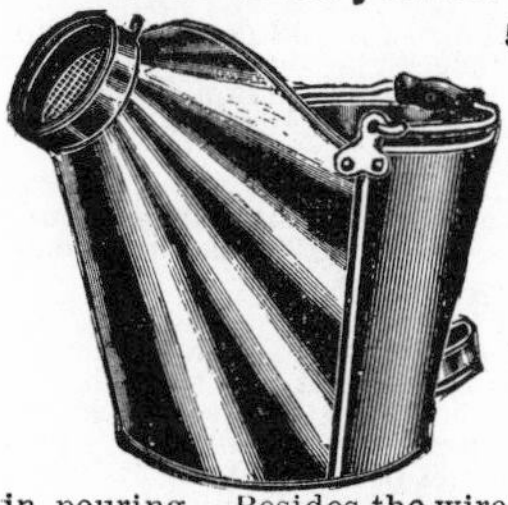

56933 The accompanying cut represents an article having all the essential points of a perfect Strainer Pail. Among its points of excellence we mention the breast and front half of the pail being formed in one piece, making but two up and down seams in the body. It will be noticed that the breast is funnel-shaped, and will not slop over in pouring. Besides the wire gauze strainer there is a brass spring clamping around the mouth to hold a cloth, thus making a double strainer without extra labor or loss of time. Another important feature is—there is no part but what can be thoroughly washed, and no rough and unsoldered seams in which dirt can accumulate and sour.

12 quarts, per dozen. ..$5.40 Each................$0.50
14 quarts, per dozen 6.05 Each.................. .56

The Chicago Milk Pail Holder.

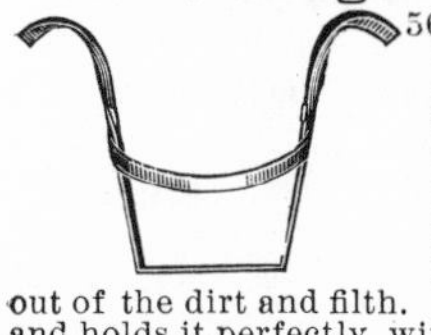

56934 Milking made easy and rest while you milk. The above cut represents a new and useful article for holding a milk pail. So simple that any person can use it without a moment's waste of time. Saves the pail from being kicked over and keeps it up out of the dirt and filth. Fits any size or style of pail and holds it perfectly without cramping the limbs, by simply hanging the holder over the knees with hoop in front, and placing the pail inside. By allowing the holder to rest against the foot the pail can be placed in any desirable position. Made of 1½ inch band iron, enameled or galvanized.

Enameled, each..........$0.25 Per dozen......$2.70
Galvanized, each.......... 0.30 Per dozen...... 3.24

Cream Setter.

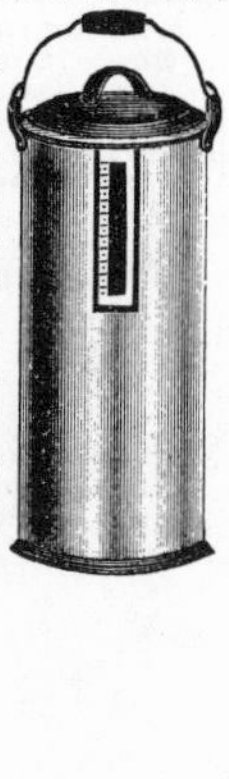

56935 This Cream Setter has tinned iron bottom, glass panel in graduate case. The glass panel in can is graduated so that if parties are buying cream two degrees will make one pound of butter. Thousands of them are in successful and satisfactory operation. They are easily cleaned and raise as much cream and as quickly as any other cream setting can in the market. The can has a bail on it so that a man can carry two of them at a time. Size, 8¼x20 inches. Weight, 4¼ lbs.

Each........$0.60 Per dozen.....$6.48
56937 Cream Setters, same as above, without gauge. Each.$0.55 Per doz.$5.95

For dairy thermometers, see Index.

Plain Cooley Can.

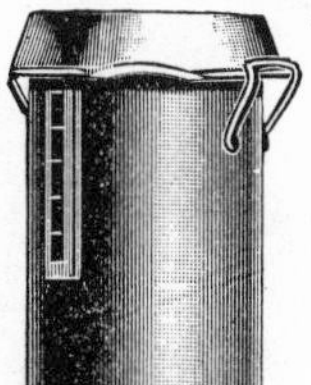

56938 The submerged system of setting milk for gathered cream is recognized everywhere as a superior way of raising cream. The milk is away from the flies and dust, and any foul odors that may be floating in the air from the barnyard or pig sty. The milk is set in cold water immediately after milking. The cream is all thrown up in twelve hours. The can holds 18 quarts. Each..$1.25

Cooley Can With Bottom Faucet.

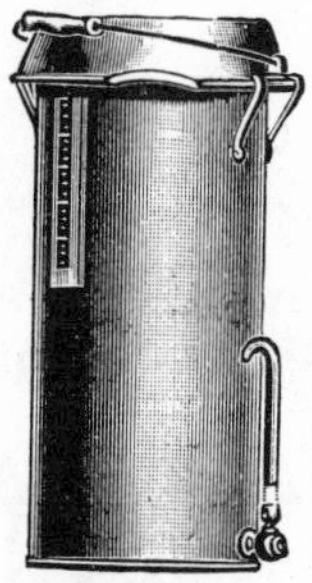

56939 For private dairies this can has no equal. The milk is drawn off through the bottom faucet, leaving the cream in the can to be poured into the cream pail. The value of sweet skim milk over sour milk for feeding purposes will more than pay for the cans every three months. All of the Cooley cans are made from the best tin obtainable. They hold 18 quarts. Each............$1.75

Family Cheesemaking Apparatus.

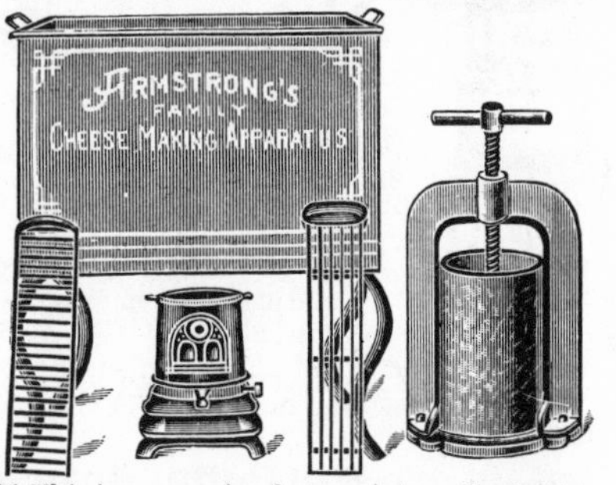

56941 This is a very simple apparatus, adapted to the wants of all farmers or dairymen who keep from two to ten cows or more. It will make from two to ten pounds of cheese each operation, according to the quantity of milk; so simple that any boy or girl of average intelligence can learn the process in a very few operations. It makes a perfect cheese each time, whether two pounds or ten pounds.

You will admit that two cows give at least six quarts at a milking, making six gallons a day. A gallon of milk will make a pound of cheese. Six gallons make six pounds—for 30 days is 180 pounds of cheese, which at 10c. per pound is $18 for one month. This is a low wholesale price. The milk is heated by a coal oil lamp, which is easily kept under control. The heating vat is so constructed that the lamp gives all the heat that is necessary. The management of the heat is the secret of success in making good cheese. The entire apparatus is so light in weight that a lady can move it from one place to another with ease. It does not take up quite as much room as an ordinary kitchen table. A lady can make cheese in the kitchen or pantry and carry on her household work at the same time. With each machine we send simple and full instructions how to make cheese successfully. Each apparatus is complete with heating vat, press, curd knives, lamp and thermometer; made of good material, strong and well finished. The apparatus is guaranteed to do the work exactly as represented. We also include sufficent rennet tablets, bandage and cheese color to make a nice little batch of cheese.

No. 1, holding 10 gals. Weight, 20 lbs. Price, $12.00
No. 2, holding 20 gals. Weight, 30 lbs. Price, 20.00
No. 3, holding 30 gals. Weight, 35 lbs. Price, 25.60

Flat Side Curd Pail.

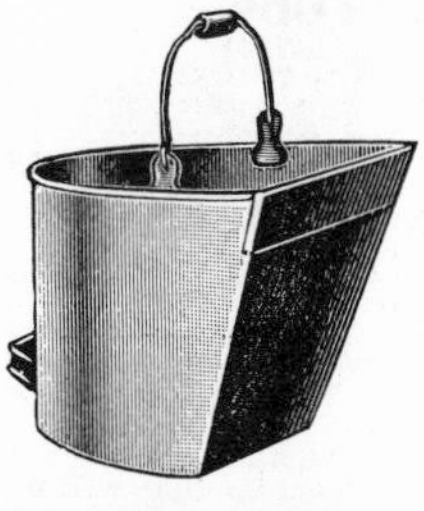

56943 This is a strongly built pail from the best 4X tin, used for lifting the curd from the vat. Price.................$0.95

Curd Scoop.

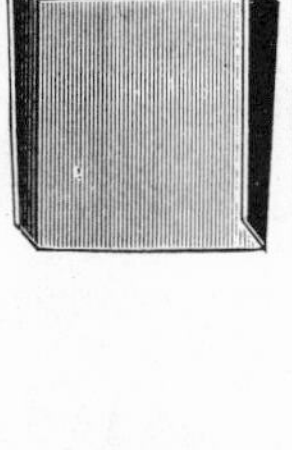

56945 These scoops are made of heavy tin and all seams and wire carefully soldered. Price....$0.50

Improved Curved Knives.

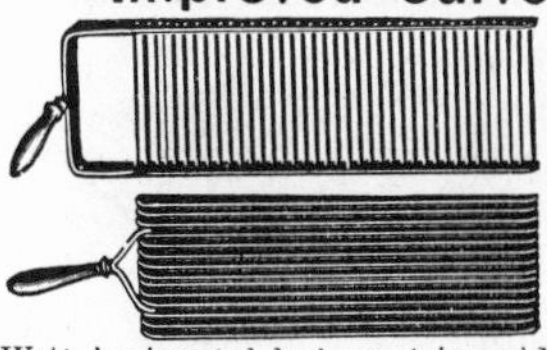

56947 These knives have no wood about them except the handles. The blades are of steel, ground to an edge, and tinned over to prevent rusting.

	Price.
With horizontal knives, 4 in. wide, 20 in. long..	$2.85
With horizontal knives, 6 in. wide, 20 in. long...	3.57
With horizontal knives, 8 in. wide, 20 in. long...	4.46
With horizontal knives, 10 in. wide, 20 in. long..	545
With horizontal knives, 12 in. wide, 20 in. long..	6.50
56949 With perpendicular knives, 4 blades, 20 in. long	1.80
With perpendicular knives, 6 blades, 20 in. long	2.15
With perpendicular knives, 8 blades, 20 in. long	2.50
With perpendicular knives, 10 blades, 20 in. long	2.70
With perpendicular knives, 12 blades, 20 in. long	3.25
With perpendicular knives, 14 blades, 20 in. long	3.60
With perpendicular knives, 15 blades, 20 in. long	3.95
With perpendicular knives, 20 blades, 20 in. long	4.50

Butter or Lard Trowel.

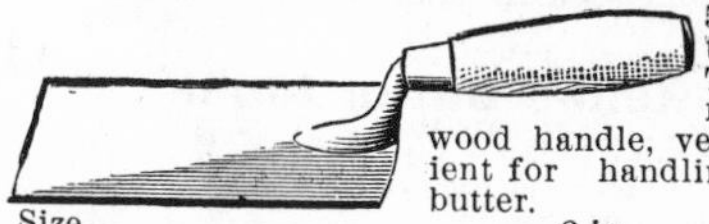

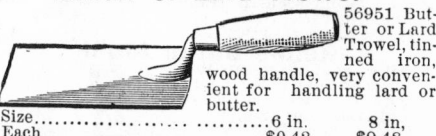

56951 Butter or Lard Trowel, tinned iron, wood handle, very convenient for handling lard or butter.

Size	6 in.	8 in.
Each	$0.42	$0.48
Per dozen	4.55	5.20

Cheese and Butter Triers.

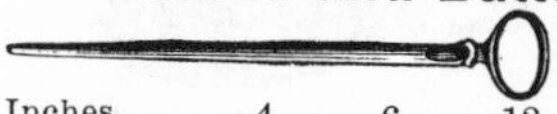

56954 Cast Steel, nickel plated.

Inches	4	6	12	18	21	24
Each	$0.22	$0.25	$0.35	$0.42	$0.50	$0.55

Fancy Square and Round Butter Molds.

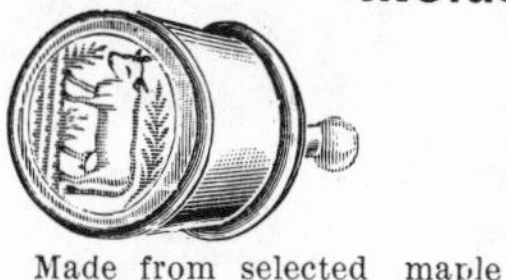

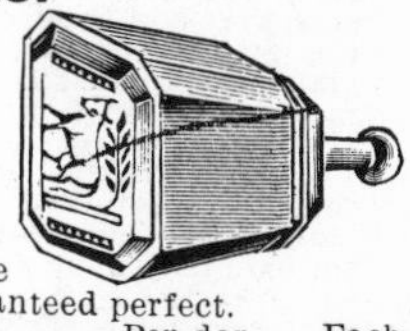

Made from selected maple wood, and every one guaranteed perfect.

	Per doz.	Each
56956 2 lb. mold, fancy carving, round.	$2.16	$0.20
56957 2 lb. mold, Jersey cow, round....	3.40	.20
56959 1 lb. mold, fancy carving, round.	1.70	.13
56961 1 lb. mold, Jersey cow, round ...	2.85	.26
56963 ½ lb. mold, fancy carving, round	1.35	.12
56965 ½ lb. mold, Jersey cow, round...	2.60	.22
56967 1 lb. mold, fancy carving, square	2.85	.26
56969 ½ lb. mold, fancy carving, square,	2.60	.23

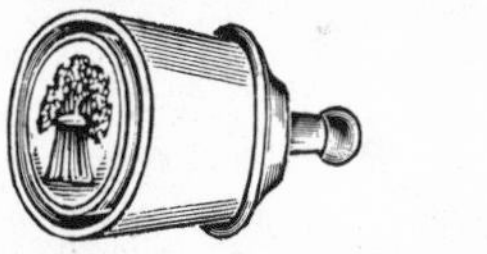

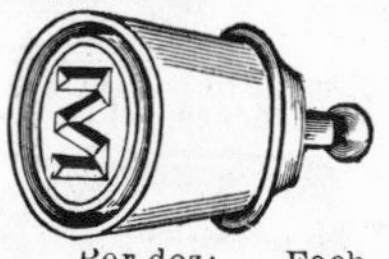

	Per doz:	Each.
56971 Individual mold, fancy carving, round........................	.75	.08
56973 Individual mold, fancy carving, with any initial letter, round..........	.85	.10
56974 Individual mold, fancy carving, square...	1.55	.14

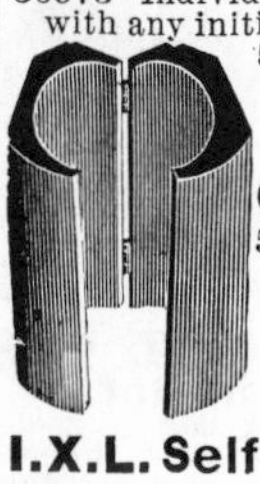

California Butter Molds.

56976 This cut represents a very popular mould, and is used very extensively in all parts of the country. Made in two pound size only

Price, each.. ....$0.25
Per dozen 2.16

I.X.L. Self-Gauging Butter Printer.

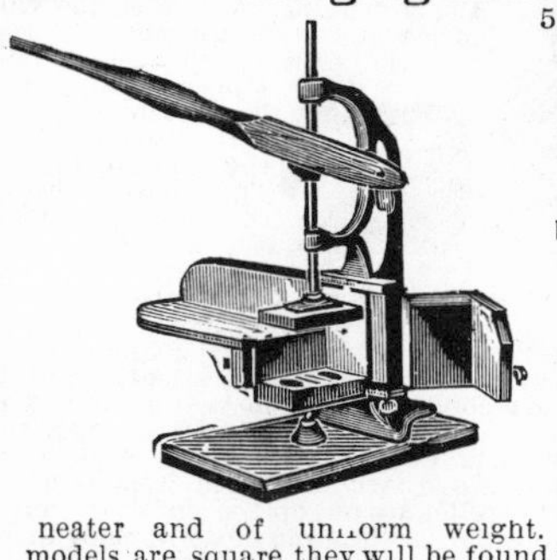

56977 This print is designed not only to print the butter, which it does very neatly and quickly, but also weighs or gauges it into pounds or half pounds, as desired, thus it does in one quarter the time it can be done by hand, making the prints neater and of uniform weight. As the models are square they will be found very convenient to pack for transportation.

Either pound or half pound printer. Price....$ 8.40
Pound and half pound printer combined. 10.95
Two pound printer. Price...................... 8.95

Either initial or monogram can be carved on at an extra charge of $1.00.

The Blanchard Butter Mold.

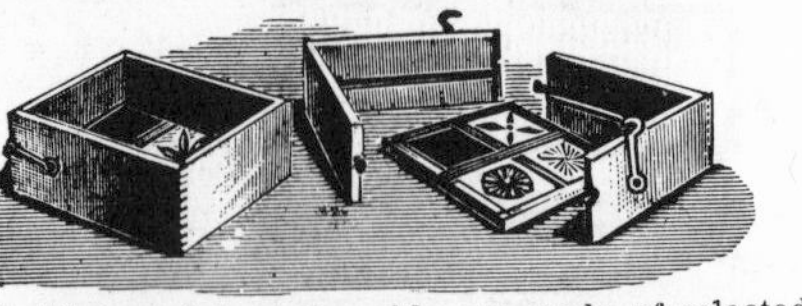

56978 These celebrated molds are made of selected white birch, and only brass hooks and screws are used throughout, so that there is no possibility of rust and consequent discoloration of the wood. The bottom is prevented from warping by strong wooden cleats, while the sides are grooved sufficiently deep to allow for swelling when in use, and are "lock-cornered" together, thus securing the utmost possible rigidity. One great advantage of these molds over most other patterns on the market, is that the prints are released by a single motion, and in perfect shape, instead of being pushed forcibly through a form by a plunger, which injures the grain.

Half-pound size, print 5 inches long, 2¼ inches wide, 1¼ inches deep. Price........................$0.85
One-pound size, print 5 inches long, 4½ inches wide, 1¼ inches deep. Price........................1.00
Two-pound size, 10 inches long, 4½ inches wide, 1¼ inches deep. Price........................1.40

Reid's Butter Mold.

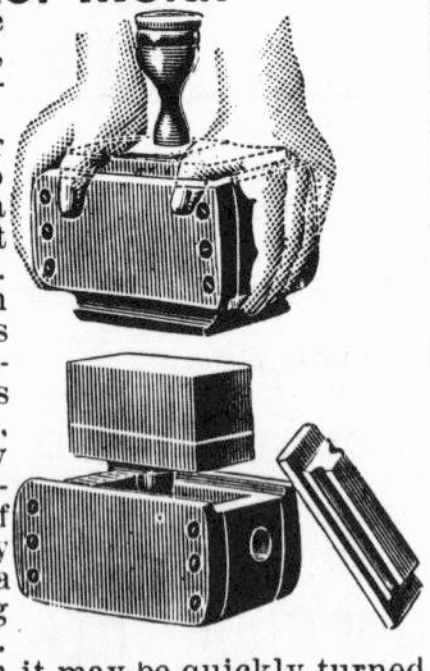

56980 Fig. 1 represents the butter as being in the mold, and the hands of the operator in the act of pressing. Fig. 2 shows the butter *molded* on the print, ready to be taken and turned on to a tray or elsewhere, when it will show the printed face. With this mold very firm butter may be printed. As shown in Fig. 1, the operator can not only put his entire weight on the print, but at the same time he may clasp the base with his fingers, thus add the power of the grip; and, further, by giving the print block a rocking motion by pressing alternately with each hand. The mold with the butter in it may be quickly turned the other side up by lifting it with a finger of each hand in the small depressions in ends of box, when the base may be removed and the butter pushed out as shown in Fig. 2.

Half-pound size, each........................$1.25
One-pound size, each........................1.35
Two-pound size, each........................2.10

Mrs. Bragg's Butter Fork.

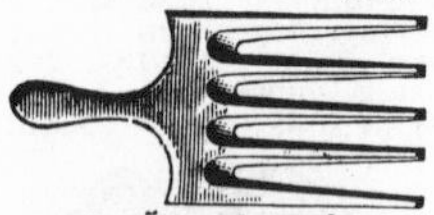

56981 A useful and convenient article to remove butter from the churn. In general use throughout the country in creamery and dairy, and considered almost indispensable; made of hard maple and well finished. Length, 12 inches; width, 5 inches. Each........................$0.15

Butter Tray.

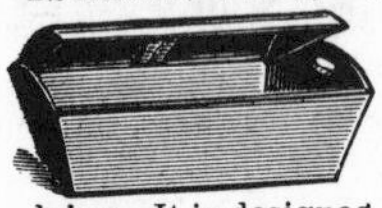

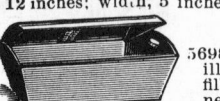

56984 The Butter Tray here illustrated is believed to fill the vacant place in nearly every creamery and dairy. It is designed to hold the butter when taken from the churn to be reworked and packed for market. The oval cover, which increases the capacity of the tray one-third, is made to fit tight, to exclude bad air and dust. They are strong and durable.

To hold 20 pounds, price........................$1.87
To hold 40 pounds, price........................2.35
To hold 60 pounds, price........................2.80
To hold 75 pounds, price........................3.00
To hold 125 pounds, price........................3.65
To hold 175 pounds, price........................4.65

Curtis' Shipping Box for Print Butter.

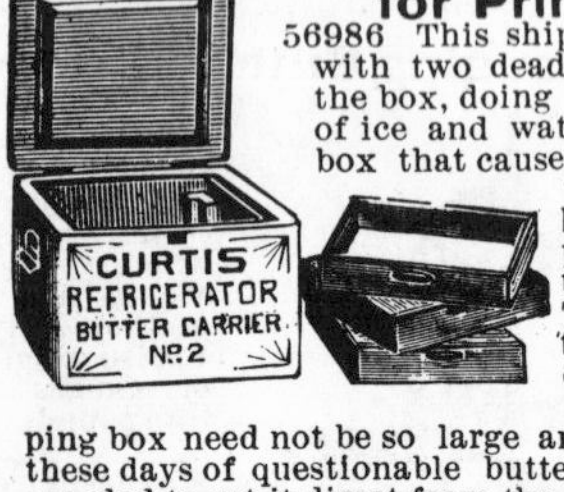

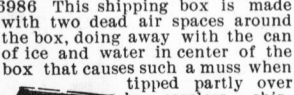

56986 This shipping box is made with two dead air spaces around the box, doing away with the can of ice and water in center of the box that causes such a muss when tipped partly over by careless shippers, often injuring the sale of butter. The butter being thoroughly protected, no ice is needed, and the shipping box need not be so large and cumbersome. In these days of questionable butter, parties who buy are glad to get it direct from the farmer or creameryman, put up in nice prints. A little attention in this matter secures a good customer the year around. The boxes are made in the most substantial manner, the trays being dove-tailed together, and all inside work being of white wood, which is free from taint or smell. Chest handles are put on the ends for convenience in handling. A shipping box will many times pay for itself in three or four shipments.

Capacity 15 pounds, price........................$3.25
Capacity 20 pounds, price........................4.20
Capacity 30 pounds, price........................5.00
Capacity 45 pounds, price........................6.00
Capacity 60 pounds, price........................6.75
Capacity 80 pounds, price........................7.65

Lee's Shipping Box for Print Butter.

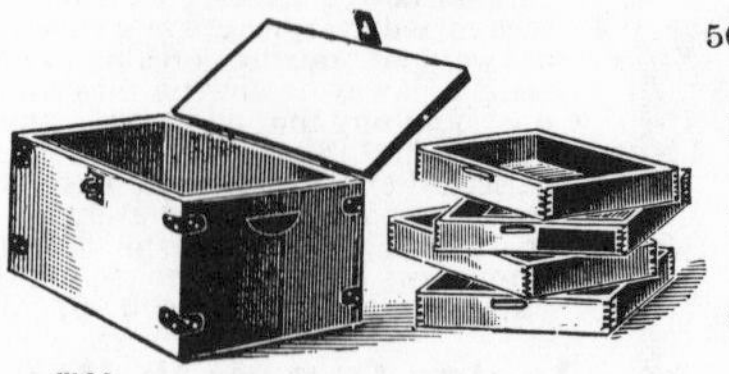

56987 We offer the above as a low priced shipping box for large shippers; it is made strong and is durable.
Price........................$1.20

Wooden Butter Spades and Ladles

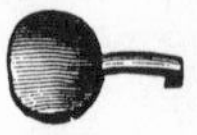
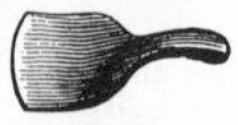
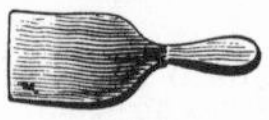

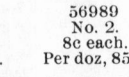

56988	56989	56991
No. 1.	No. 2.	No. 3.
8c. each.	8c each.	8c. each.
Per doz. 85c.	Per doz, 85c,	Per doz, 85c.

Maple Butter Plates.

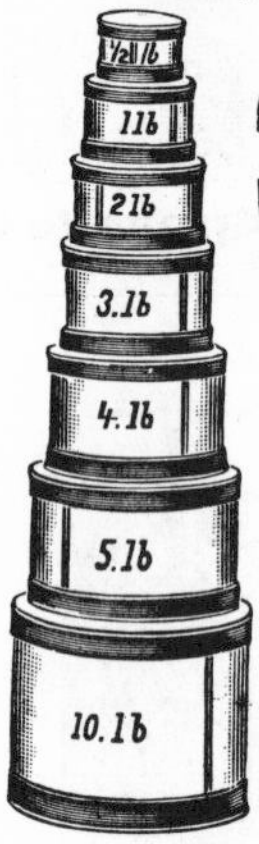

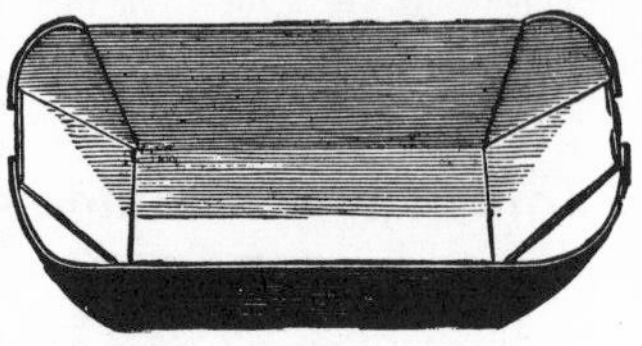

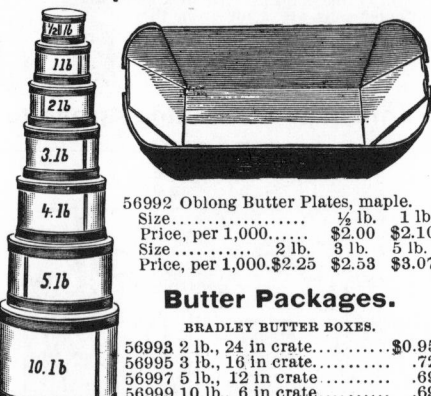

56992 Oblong Butter Plates, maple.

Size	½ lb.	1 lb.
Price, per 1,000......	$2.00	$2.10
Size...........	2 lb.	3 lb.
Price, per 1,000.	$2.25	$2.53

(Size 5 lb. — Price, per 1,000 $3.07)

Butter Packages.

BRADLEY BUTTER BOXES.

56993 2 lb., 24 in crate........................$0.95
56995 3 lb., 16 in crate........................72
56997 5 lb., 12 in crate........................69
56999 10 lb., 6 in crate........................69

Bradley's Bail Butter Boxes.

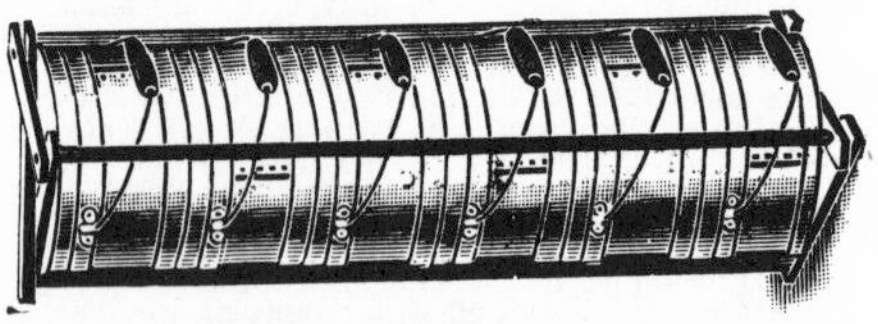

57001 8 lb. bail butter boxes .... } 50cts. per crate
57003 9 lb. bail butter boxes........................ }
57005 10 lb, bail butter boxes........................ }

Creamery Butter Tubs.

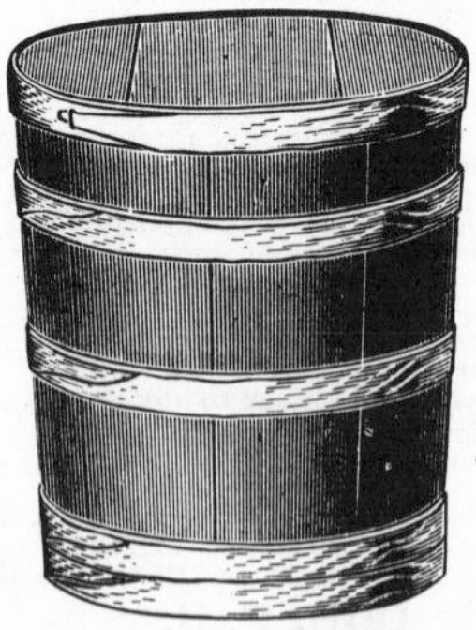

57006 Butter Tubs, spuce, 10 pounds........................$0.15
57007 Butter Tubs, spruce, 20 pounds........................18
57008 Butter Tubs, spruce, 30 pounds........................22
57009 Butter Tubs, spruce, 50 pounds........................23

Ash Butter Tubs.

57011 60 lbs., 5 hoop........................$0.24
57013 40 lbs., 4 hoop........................22
57014 25 lbs., 4 hoop........................19½
57015 10 lbs., 4 hoop........................15

Cheese Box Machine.

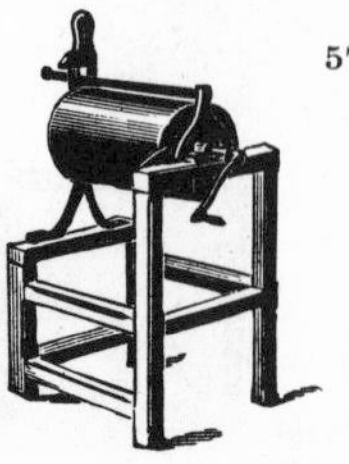

57016 For the manufacture of material into cheese boxes, machinery of some nature is required. The variety at present are as a rule too intricate and expensive. We have endeavored to present a machine that will meet the requirements of the small as well as the large maker. It has a large capacity, and is moderate in price.
Price, complete........................$14.50

Cheese Box Hoops Rims, and Headings.

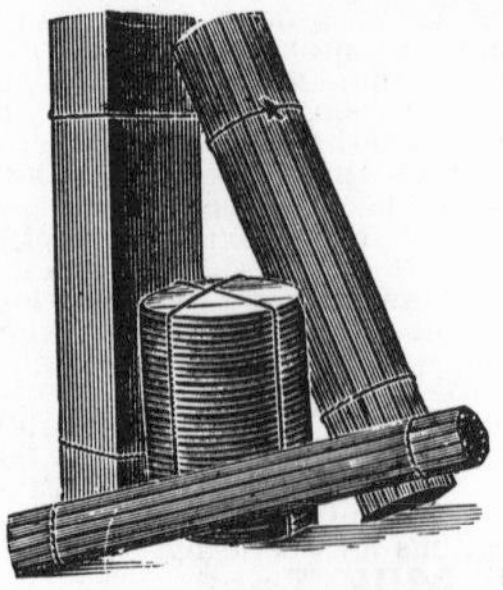

57017 Cheese makers living some distance from a cheese box factory will find it a great saving in buying the material in the "Knock down" and putting up their own boxes. The cut represents material for 50 complete boxes; average weight, 250 pounds.

	Per 1,000.	Per 100.
6 inch box any diameter. Price..	$51.00	$5.10
7 inch box any diameter. Price..	53.00	5.30
8 inch box any diameter. Price..	55.00	5.50
9 inch box any diameter. Price..	57.00	5.70
10 inch box any diameter. Price..	59.00	5.90
10¼ inch box any diameter. Price.	60.00	6.00
11 inch box any diameter. Price..	61.00	6.10
12 inch box any diameter. Price..	63.00	6.30

We cannot furnish less than 50 of any size.
57018 Swedes Iron cheese box tacks. Per pound..$0.06
57019 Cut cheese box tacks Per pound........................05
57020 Wire cheese box tacks Per pound........................06

Preservaline.

57023 This is the only article that can be used by creameries, dairies, milkmen, farmers, ice cream manufacturers, and all those requiring pure, sweet milk and cream. Preservaline is a harmless substance, which, when added to milk or cream in accordance with directions accompanying each package, will keep milk and cream for weeks in an absolutely perfect and wholesome state in any kind of weather—even through thunder storms—without requiring ice or any refrigerator; absolutely tasteless, odorless, simple and cheap to use; does not effect the flavor or qualities of the milk; for preserving composite samples of milk for test purposes, Preservaline is unsurpassed; if used in the manufacture of butter, Preservaline will hold the fine, natural flavor of the butter and prevent it from spoiling; butter put up with Preservaline will never get rancid, and can be held years or exported anywhere. We furnish two kinds of Preservaline for the use of creameries and dairies.

Preservaline for using in milk, for drinking and which is made into ice cream and also buttermilk.
1-lb. packages........................35c
5, 10 and 25-pound packages......32 cents per pound
50 and 100-pound packages......30 cents per pound

Preservaline for using in milk and cream and which is intended to be made into butter and cheese and for keeping butter and cheese.
1-lb. packages........................28c
5, 10, 25-pound packages........25 cents per pound
50 and 100-pound packages.......23 cents per pound

Ozaline.

57024 The finest disinfectant for creameries and dairies. Has no smell and gives out none. Removes every offensive smell at once. Positively marvelous in its actions. The only perfect disinfectant for creameries, dairies, stables, pig-pens, out-houses, etc. Cheap and reliable. Prevents flies in creameries. Its use in creameries and dairies is of untold advantage, as it kills all germs in the air, gives off oxygen and thus keeps the air pure, and by this means helps to keep butter, milk and cream sweet. Positively odorless and ever active. Contains no carbolic acid or chloride of lime. in use by hundreds of creameries. A small quantity of Ozaline sprinkled on dung heaps and in manure pits, and on offal in outhouses, and on anything having a bad odor, will remove all smell at once and for good. A great advantage of Ozaline is that it is a valuable fertilizer. If used alone it is equal to the highets grades of fertilizers. It will also prevent chicken lice.

In small quantities, 5 cents per pound.
In 100 pound sacks, 3 cents per pound.
In 250 pound sacks, $7.50 per sack.

Hansen's Butter Colors, Rennet, Cheese Colors, Etc.

	Per doz.	Each
57026 Hansen's Rennet Extract, 1 gallon bottles........................		$2.00
57027 Rennet Tablets, per box of 100, No. 1 Tablets........................		3.75
57028 Rennet Tablets, per box of 200 No. 2 Tablets........................		2.00
57031 Sample boxes, containing 50 No. 2 Tablets........................		.70
57033 Hansen's Household Rennet Tablets, for making junket or curd and whey 12 tablets in glass........	1.20	.15
57034 Bavarian Rennets, dry........	1.20	.12
57036 Hansen's Cheese Color, 1 gallon bottles........................		1.90
57038 Hansen's Cheese Color, 4 oz. sample bottle........................	1.90	.16

Hansen's Danish Butter Color.

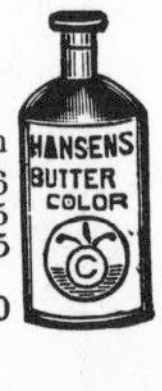

	Per doz.	Each
57040 4 oz. bottles..............	$1.80	$0.16
57041 9 oz. bottles..............	3.75	.35
57042 20 oz. bottles............	8.10	.75
57043 Gallon square jacket cans........................		2 90

Wells, Richardson's Improved Butter Color.

57044 Large, $1.00 size........ ......$0.75
57045 Medium, 50c. size............ .37
57046 Small, 25c. size............ .18

Fairlambs' Butter Color.

57047 1 Gallon Cans. per gallon....$2.15
5 Gallon Cans, per gallon......... 2.04
10 Gallon Cans, per gallon......... 1.95
Barrel lots, per gallon............ 1.85

Fairlambs' Cheese Color.

57048 1 Gallon Cans, per gallon...................$1.35
5 Gallon Cans, per gallon......................... 1.20
10 Gallon Cans, per gallon......................... 1.10
Barrel lots per gallon......................... .98

Fairlambs' Rennet Extract.

57049 1 Gallon Cans, per gallon...................$1.62
5 Gallon Cans, per gallon......................... 1.50
10 Gallon Keg, per gallon............ 1.40
Barrel lots, per gallon............ 1.30

Butter Paper.

57050 Waxed Butter Paper, grease proof, 9x12
inchss, 480 sheets $0.20
12x18 inches, 480 sheets .... .40

Parchment Dairy Paper.

Cut in the sizes as quoted and put up in packages of
1,000 sheets.

57051—	Price,	Price,
Size.	1,000 sheets.	5,000 sheets.
12x12	$1.30	$6.28
10x10........	.96	4.47
9x12........	1.05	4.99
8x11.... ...	.92	4.37
9x 9....	.87	4.13
8x 8	.70	3.33
6x 6 ...	.35	1.67

Write for our prices on large lots.

Parchment Paper Circles.

57052—	Price,		Price,
Diameter.	per 1.000.	Diameter	per 1,000.
4 inches............	$0.30	11 inches........	...$1.88
5 inches............	.40	12 inches.........	2.22
6 inches............	.53	13 inches.........	2.58
7 inches............	.72	14 inches.........	3.00
8 inches............	.97	15 inches.........	3.45
9 inches............	1.25	16 inches.........	3.95
10 inches	1.50	17 inches	4.28

½-inch sizes between can be furnished at 10 cents per
1,000 extra. Write for our prices on large lots

Cloth Circles.

We guarantee count and every one to be a perfect circle.

57053—	Price.		Price,
Diameter.	per 1,000.	Diameter	per 1,000
4 inches......	$0.59	11 inches........	3 91
4½ inches......	.70	11½ inches........	4.33
5 inches...	.91	12 inches........	4.78
5½ inches...	1.07	12½ inches........	4.95
6 inches...	1.20	13 inches........	5.36
6½ inches...	1.35	13½ inches........	5.77
7 inches...	1.65	14 inches........	6.19
7½ inches...	2.06	14½ inches........	6.47
8 inches...	2.27	15 inches........	6.60
8½ inches...	2 47	15½ inches........	7.01
9 inches...	2.77	16 inches........	7 42
9½ inches...	3.10	16½ inches........	7.84
10 inches'........	3 46	17 inches........	8.25
10½ inches...	3.71		

Write for our prices on large lots.

Butter Cloth, Best Grade.

57054—
28-inch, per piece 120 yards, 3 cents per yard.
36-inch, per piece 120 yards, 3½ cents per yard.
42-inch, per piece 120 yards, 3¾ cents per yard.
45-inch, per piece 120 yards, 4 cents per yard.

Butter Cloth (Medium Grade).

57055—
36-inch, per piece, 120 yards.....3 cents per yard
42-inch, per piece, 120 yards.....3½ cents per yard
45-inch, per piece, 120 yards.....3⅞ cents per yard

The Common Sense Milk Jar.

57056 This milk bottle is giving the best of satisfaction, as it combines economy of time, labor and expense of materials; it discards the use of glass or metal tops, wire bails or other fastenings which render the ordinary milk jar so difficult to keep clean and in good order, and reduces the cost of manufacture and breakage to the smallest degree possible, and requires no washer; the old style attached cover interferes to a considerable extent with washing the jars; this jar, having no cover, either attached or detached, is cleansed thoroughly and with dispatch, having only a slight shoulder within the neck of the jar which serves to hold the cap or cover in position when adjusted, and is all glass without separate parts; the cap or cover is made of heavy wood fibre prepared so as to resist the moisture from within and without, and when pressed into the neck of the jar to the shoulder with the thumb or finger it forms a tightly fitting cover; the operation of capping is quickly and easily accomplished, and when completed is perfectly tight and can be handled in any position and transported without danger of leakage; the disc can be removed when the milk is required for use by inserting the blade of a pen-knife or any other sharp instrument and lifting the cap out; the cap can again be used and will seal the jar reasonably tight, but their nominal cost allows the dealer to discard them after using them once; large dealers or milk depots can stamp the cap with date, etc., giving the producer a number that will enable them to keep a thorough record of milk, and trace the same to the producer when the milk proves unsatisfactory.

Quarts, per dozen....$1.50 Per gross.........$16.00
Pints, per dozen. ... 1.25 Per gross......... 14.00

Instruments For Testing Milk.

57057 These instruments are used very largely by factorymen to find out who puts the most water in his milk. They are very good detectives. Directions showing how to operate sent with each set.
Per set.................$1.90

Heavy Milk Test Glasses.

57058 These tubes are used by factorymen to test their patrons' milk; showing the relative value of each by the cream thrown up. 5 x 1¼ inches.
Per doz..$0.65

Classware for Babcock Milk Tester.

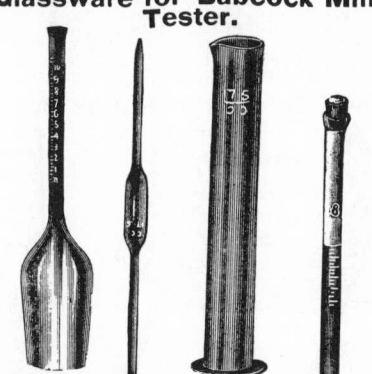

57059 Babcock bottles, each...................$0.40
57060 Milk pipette, each....................... .10
57061 Acid measure, each....................... .10
57062 Test churn tube, each....................... .10

WOODENWARE.

Wooden Measures.

	Per doz.	Each.
57063 ½ Bushel, iron bound........	$2.50	$0.23
57064 Peck............................	2.25	.20
57065 ½ Peck...........................	2.00	.18

Pails.

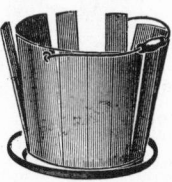 

Common pail—hoops off. Ours—hoops off.

	Per doz.	Each.
57066 2 Hoop, A1 ware....................	$1 40	$0.13
57067 3 Hoop, A1 ware....................	1.75	.16
57068 Extra Dairy, A1 ware..............	4.50	.40
57069 Large, flush bottom..............	2.75	.25
57070 Cedar, stripped, 2 brass countersunk hoops	4.10	.38
57071 Cedar, all red, 2 brass countersunk hoops.............	5.25	48

Tubs—Pine.

	Per doz.	Each.
57072 Extra Large. 27 in. diameter at top	8.80	0.80
57073 No. 1, A1 ware	7.25	.65
57075 No. 2, A1 ware......	6.25	.58
57077 No. 3, A1.........	5.25	.50

King Oak Well Buckets.

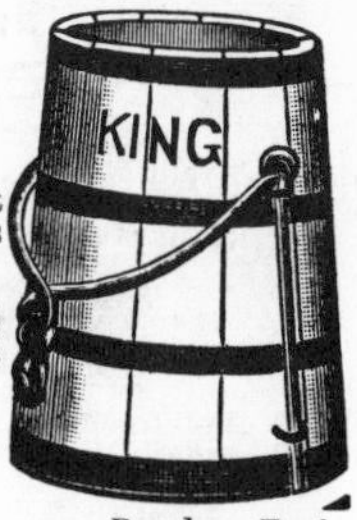

Every bucket is like the cut shows, full iron bound, and is the most durable made.

		Doz.	Each.
57081 Wrought ears.	$3.60	$0.32
57083 Swivel	4.00	.36

Sugar Buckets.

Wood Hoops.

		Per doz.	Each.
57085 10 lbs...............	$2.75	$0.28
57087 25 lbs...............	...... 3.50	.32
57091 50 lbs...............	4.00	.36

Cedar Sugar Buckets.

Brass Hoops.

Cover turned from solid piece of wood, very strong and durable.

	Doz.	Each.
57093 10 lbs...............	$4.00	$0.38
57095 15 lbs..... ...	5.00	.48
57097 20 lbs...............	6.00	.55

Metal Plug Cedar Water Can.

Entirely New, Galvanized Iron Hoops.

The Farmer's Friend. You drink from the spout; the water is kept cool and clean.

	Doz.	Each.
57098 2 gal........	$3.50	$0.35

Egg Cases and Fillers.

Cases to hold 30 dozen.
57100 No. 1, white pine, with fastener, no fillers.
Each ...$0.23
Per doz. 2.63
57102 No. 2, white pine, without fastener, no fillers.
Each...$0.14
Per doz. 1.60
NOTE.—Above cases, knocked down, at 2½ cents each, reduction boards.

57104 No. 1 Fillers, 10 sections, 8 division
boards. Per set..........................$0.09
Per dozen......................... 105
57106 No. 2 Fillers, 10 sections, 8 divisions
boards. Per set $0.7½
Per dozen .... .85
Get our quotations on large quantities.

Chopping Bowls.

Extra quality with heavy rims, prevents checking.

57115 Chopping Bowls,	13	15	17	19 inches
Each.................	$0.08	.14	.21	.26
Dozen.................	.87	1.50	2.20	2.86

57117 Hardwood Patent Oblong Chopping Trays,

	11x22		10x20		9x18	
	Per doz.	Each.	Per doz.	Each.	Per doz.	Each.
	$4.00	$0.40	$3 00	$0.28	$2.50	$0.25

Steak Mauls.

		doz.	Each.
57119 Steak Mauls.....	$0.60	$0.06

Lemon Squeezers.

57121 Hardwood Lemon Squeezers.
Each.................$0.10
Per dozen............ 1.00

Sundries.

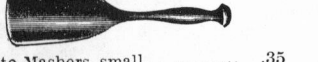

	Doz.	Each.
57123 Kraut Forks	$0.75	$0.08
57125 Combined Clothes Pounder and Kraut Stamper	2.50	.25

57127 Potato Mashers, small	.35	.03
57129 Potato Mashers, large	.44	.04

57130 Napkin Rings, plain hardwood in assorted designs, finely polished.
Per dozen...........$1.50
Each..............14

	Per doz.	Each.
57131 Wood Kitchen Spoons, 14 in. long	$0.55	$0.06

Rolling Pins.

57133 Rolling Pins, plain	$0.55	$0.05
57135 Rolling Pins, revolving	.60	.06
57137 Maple Butter Triers, 29 inches long, made same shape as steel trier, strong and durable	2.50	.25

Clothes Pins.

	Per box	Per doz.
57139 Clothes Pins, round head, 30 doz. in box		$0.32
57141 U. S. Clothes Pins, patent spring, latest patent, guaranteed to please; will last a lifetime. Note price. 12 doz. in a box	.85	$0.08

Tooth Picks.

	Case.	Box.
57143 Wood Tooth Picks, double points, 2,500 in a box, 100 boxes in case	$2.40	.04

	Pkg.	Each.
57145 Quill Tooth Picks, 40 bunches in package	$1.00	.03

STEP LADDERS.

57147 Gardner Patent Step Ladder has wrought iron connecting bands. This prevents the ladder from spreading without the useless appendage of strings or braces. These ladders are all made from selected lumber, and put together for constant service.

Weight	Length.	Each.	Weight.	Length.	Each
9 lbs.	3 foot	$0.45	27 lbs.	10 foot	$1.05
10 lbs.	4 foot	.55	37 lbs.	12 foot	1.25
11 lbs.	5 foot	.65	50 lbs.	14 foot	
14 lbs.	6 foot	.75		extra heavy	2.00
18 lbs.	7 foot	.85	65 lbs.	16 foot	
21 lbs.	8 foot	.95		extra heavy	2.35

57149 The Victor Step Ladder, designed for outdoor and where ladders are used roughly; it is made of the best seasoned Norway pine, braced with iron at the intersection of every piece. This is considered the very best ladder made.

Weight.	Size.	Each.
15 lbs.	5 foot	$1.35
18 lbs.	6 foot	1.50
22 lbs.	7 foot	2.10
26 lbs.	8 foot	2.50
35 lbs.	10 foot	3.00
40 lbs.	12 foot	3.95
60 lbs.	14 foot	4.95
75 lbs.	16 foot	5.50

Step Ladder, with Shelf Attachment.

57151 Step Ladder with shelf attachment. The shelf is so adjusted as not to interfere with the spread of the ladder; folds up readily when not in use, costs but a trifle, and is a valuable [adjunct to the ladder.

Weight.	Size.	Each.	Weight.	Size.	Each.
10 lbs.	3	$0.55	23 lbs.	8	$1.15
12 lbs.	4	.65	29 lbs.	10	1.25
13 lbs.	5	.75	34 lbs.	12	1.50
16 lbs.	6	.95	35 lbs.	14	2.15
20 lbs.	7	1.05	65 lbs.	16	2.55

Extension Ladders.

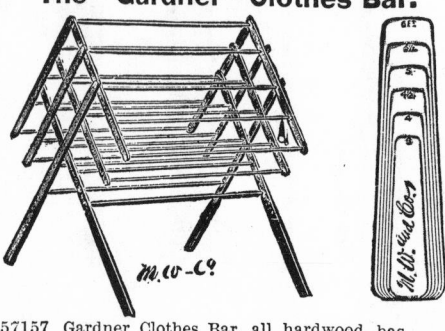

57153 Extension Ladders are made from selected Norway pine and hickory rungs. Put together with screws; gotten up in a tasty manner, of sufficient strength for safety, and not too heavy to carry. Extension ladders all lengths.
Per foot.........$0.20

Extension Step Ladder.

57155 Cut shows ladder extended; upper part can be instantly lowered, making an ordinary step ladder. When in position as a step ladder, two persons can work on it at the same time; being very strong and well braced does not require strings to keep it from spreading. It is easily adjusted to the position as a long ladder, and often of great convenience in reaching high ceilings or skylights. Can also be used as a trestle, and in the several positions can readily be appreciated by the carpenter, painter and fruit grower. It recommends itself to everyone who has use for a ladder.

Length.	Weight.	Each.
6 ft. step, extended, 11 ft.	20 lbs.	$1.75
7 ft. step, extended, 12 ft.	23 lbs.	2.00
8 f.t step, extended, 15 ft.	26 lbs.	2.25
9 ft. step, extended, 17 ft.	30 lbs.	2.50
10 ft. step, extended, 19 ft.	35 lbs.	2.75
11 ft. step, extended, 21 ft.	40 lbs.	3.00
12 ft. step, extended, 23 ft.	46 lbs.	3.25

The "Gardner" Clothes Bar.

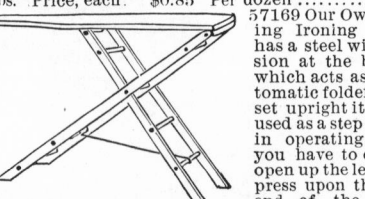

57157 Gardner Clothes Bar, all hardwood, has 60 lineal feet drying surface; something new; weight, 17 lbs. Each..$0.70 Per dozen........$7.56

57163 Ironing Boards, made of poplar wood:

Length.	Weight.	Each.	Per doz.
3 feet	3 lbs.	$0.25	$2.70
4 feet	6 lbs.	.33	3.57
4½ feet	7 lbs.	.37	4.00
5 feet	7½ lbs.	.42	4.54
5½ feet	9 lbs.	.46	4.97
6 feet	11 lbs.	.50	5.40

Cut shows board closed (opens to table height).
57164 The Excelsior Folding Skirt Board, all hardwood, adjustable to standing or sitting position, and folds up closely. Many thousands sold, meets with general favor. Weight, 15 lbs. Price, each. $0.85 Per dozen.........$9.00

57169 Our Own Folding Ironing Board, has a steel wire tension at the bottom, which acts as an automatic folder; when set upright it can be used as a step ladder; in operating it all you have to do is to open up the legs, then press upon the large end of the board. Give it a trial and you will have no other, as it certainly is the most complete table in use.
Price, each.........$1.00 Per dozen.........$10.90
Weight, 18 pounds.

57170 The Champion Bosom Board and Stretcher; the most complete in the market. After you have once used this board you will never be without one.
Price.........$0.40

Eureka Adjustable Clothes Bar.

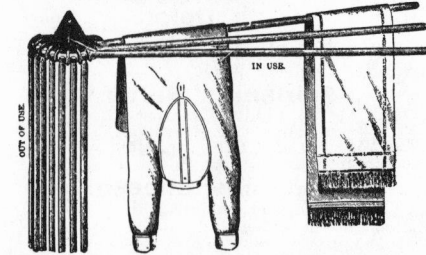

57171 Eureka Adjustable Clothes Bars, intended to fasten to the wall. When not in use takes the space of an ordinary broom. The bars are three feet in length, with gilt tips; a very convenient household article. Weight, 4 pounds.
Each.........$0.39 Per dozen.........$4.22
57173 Same as 57171 with 6 bars, 2 feet long.
Each.........$0.25 Per dozen.........$2.70

57175 The Excelsior Clothes Dryer; is made of picked ash bars ⅛ of an inch thick, folds up snug against the wall when not in use, takes up less space and has more capacity than any other bar made.
10 bars, 36 inches long.
Each.........$0.30
Per dozen.... 3.24
6 bars, 24 inches.
Each.........$0.27
Per dozen.... 2.92

Curtain Stretcher.

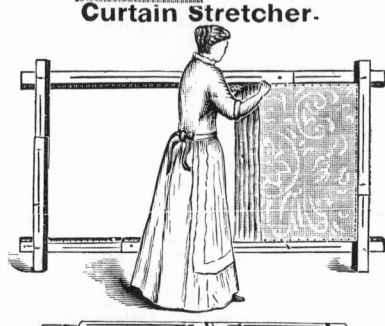

57177 Folding Curtain Stretcher, made of poplar, for stretching lace curtains, shawls, blankets, etc. Adjustable to any size. As will be observed, the frame is secured at the corners with adjustable screw clamps, and the bars are provided with plate hooks 1½ inches apart, set in coped recess below the surface, so that the bars pass each other, allowing a free extension and contraction. Each.........$1.75

Schmuck's Mop Wringer.

57178 Schmuck's Mop Wringers for simplicity, durability, dry wringing and adaptability have no equal. They are manufactured of wrought iron, the rollers made of hard maple chemically treated, and will fit any size pail. It is self-wringing, and while mopping, gloves can be used, as the hands do not come in contact with water; in fact, what has heretofore proven the dirtiest work in and about a house is now made the easiest and cleanest by the use of this mop wringer. Price is for wringer with pail.
Each.........$2.25

57181 The Globe Perfect Self-Wringing Mop. The mop is made of cotton coils, large and full size. We believe this to be the most acceptable and best wearing wringing mop ever offered for sale.
Each.........$0.25
Dozen.... 2.80
57182 Mop Stick and Brush Holder, combined.
Each.........$0.08 Per dozen.........$0.85

Hand Laundry Steam Generators.

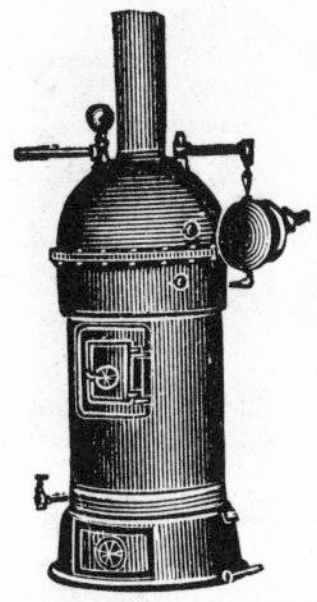

57183 These steam generators are intended for heating water, boiling clothes, making starch, etc., in hand laundries. They are tested at about forty pounds pressure. The water supply to the boiler is automatically regulated by a brass float and valve which shuts off the water when it reaches the right height and allows more to enter as needed. The float and valve are placed in an iron float-box (Z) outside of the dome, but attached to the latter by pipes (2, 4). Where the generators are to be used in cities or towns having waterworks the water supply pipe (B) is attached directly to a hydrant. Where there is no hydrant pressure a strong, tight barrel or tank is placed on a support opposite the top of the generator, and filled with water from a hole in the head, which is then plugged up. A small pipe from the dome carries steam to the top of the barrel to force the water into the generator through a pipe from the bottom of the barrel. A pipe (E) carries steam to where it is needed for use: more pipes can be used if desired. The safety valve (N) is combined with a vacuum valve to prevent matter being sucked up into the boiler through the steam pipe when there is no steam up. Full instructions for setting up and using are sent with every generator. Please state in ordering whether the water connection will be made with a hydrant or supply barrel. The fixtures include an ash box, grate, shaker, combined safety and vacuum valve, gauge cocks, blow-off valve, and 3½ feet of ¾ inch, steam hose, with 2½ feet of iron pipe to convey steam for heating. We also furnish ⅜ inch angle valve and nipple to connect with a water supply pipe for a hydrant, or 5½ feet of ½-in. rubber hose and 4⅜-inch iron nipples to make the two connections with a water supply barrel. Two horse power, diameter 22 inches, height, 56 inches, size of fire box, 16x26 inches. Weight, 900 pounds.
Price..$50.00

Troy Hand Cylinder or Washing Machines.

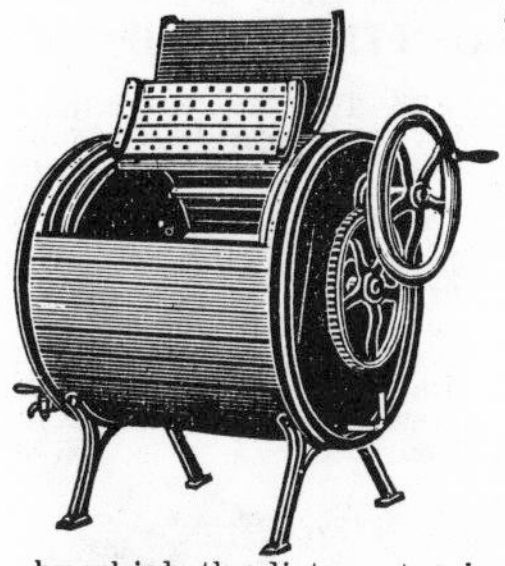

57189 This machine is intended for use in hand laundries, hotels, boarding houses, etc.; capacity is from 20 to 24 shirts, or 15 to 18 sheets. Inside measurement of cylinder, 24x44 inches. Floor space, 28x48 ins. The cylinder should make about 25 turns a minute. It can be connected to water front of stove for convenience in filling, if desired, and is provided with faucet in opposite end by which the dirty water is run off. Weight, 400 lbs.
Price..$35.00

Montgomery Ward & Co.'s Improved Western Star Washing Machine.

(Note Reduced Price)

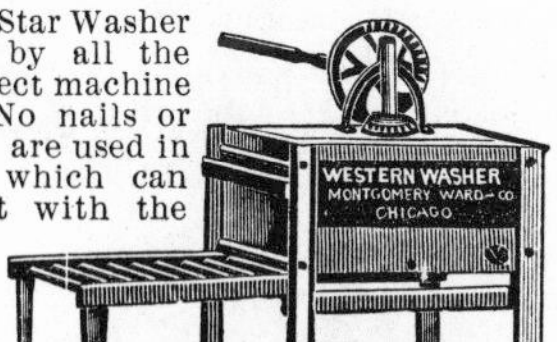

57191 The Western Star Washer is acknowledged by all the best and most perfect machine on the market. No nails or iron of any kind are used in its construction which can come in contact with the clothes, causing iron rust on the linen, as is the case with other machines; this, together with other improvements that have been made in this machine and not contained in any other, are of the greatest importance and must be seen to be appreciated. If you desire a more complete description of this machine send for descriptive circular, which will be mailed on application. Price...$2.75
Weight, 65 lbs.

Anthony Wayne Washer.

Note reduced price.

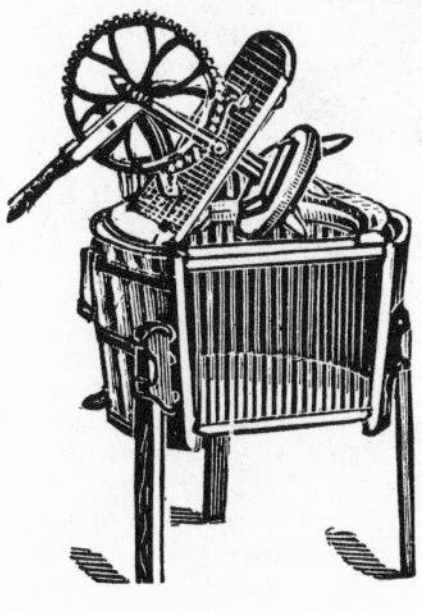

57193 The Anthony Wayne Washer, with corrugated stave and bottom. This is the best round washer made. Some prefer the round washer to the square; we have selected the Anthony Wayne as being the best on the market, and we offer it at a price which places it within reach of all.
Price.....................$2.75
Weight, 50 lbs.

New Combination Washer.

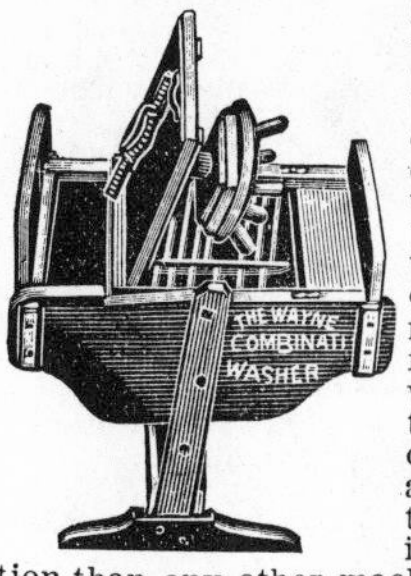

57194 We herewith present, as we believe, the best invention yet made, the Wayne Combination Washer. This machine combines the reciprocal pin-wheel motion, so well-known that we have no need of further describing it, with an oscillating movement of the whole sudbox. The main advantage that we claim for this machine is that it works fully one-third easier than any other machine that operates with a pin-wheel agitator, that it takes less water (only three pails), and that it is more simple in construction than any other machine now on the market. The machine, when open, locks itself so that a wringer can be attached on the wringer-board without tilting it; a small key inserted in the gear will prevent it from tilting when full to prevent accidents of any kind. The machine is well made out of the best of yellow poplar, finished in superior and excellent style, and we can recommend it and will warrant the same as the best family washer that we know of. Weight, 60 lbs...$4.00

Cline's Improved Steam Washer.

57195 Cline's Improved Steam Washer has several new features that the Windsor does not have. Has a corrugated cylinder; sliding cover and a faucet attached to the boiler for removing the water without lifting the boiler from the stove, which is a decided advantage. Weight, 32 lbs. Price, each..................$6.00

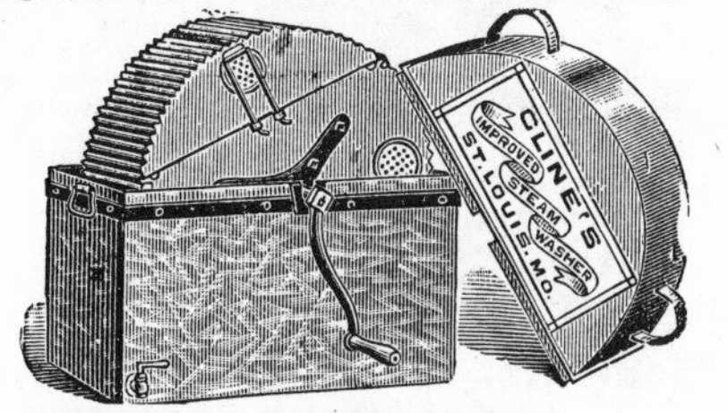

American Household.

Mangle and Wringer.

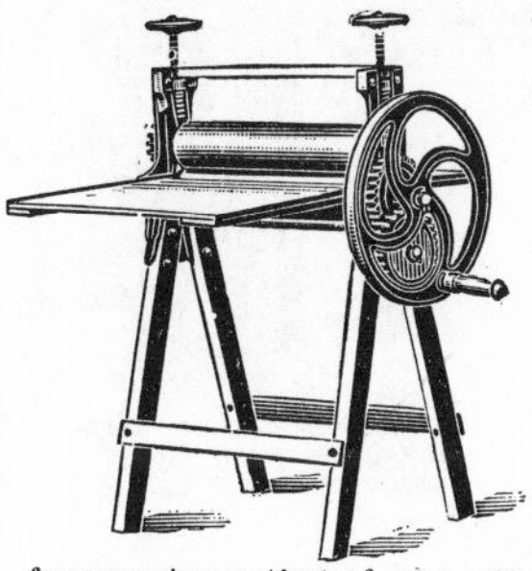

57196 In the saving of labor and the perfection of work, these machines hold the same relative position in the laundry that the sewing machine does in its place in the household economy. They are specially adapted for ironing table linens, bedding, underclothes and all plain ironing, and save a wonderful amount of labor. The driving gear is far superior to that of any other mangle ever offered, and the power required to operate it is about half that necessary to work any other. Every family should possess one of these machines, and our price is such as to place them within the reach of all. Directions for use furnished with every machine. Description: Hard wood rolls, 24 inches long 5 inches in diameter; the machine stands 4 feet high and weighs 125 pounds. Price..................................$19.00

The "Pearl" Ironer, Hotel Model.

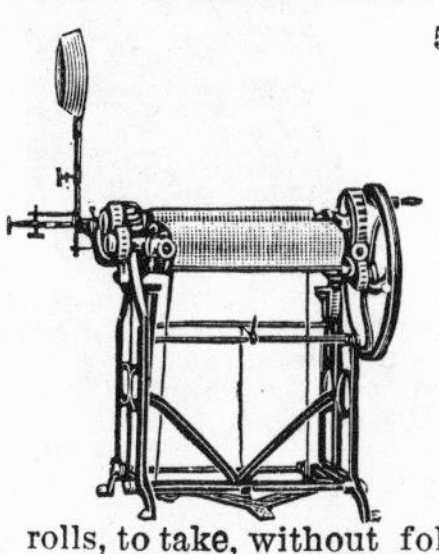

57197 The "Pearl" is designed especially to do all the flat work of hotel, institution or laundry, from a lady's handkerchief to a counter piece, or from a napkin to a lace curtain. We believe it is the greatest labor saver ever offered to these establishments. We guarantee it will do the work of a dozen girls, and do it better and with much less wear on the goods. The Pearl is made in two sizes, 45-inch and 29-inch rolls, to take, without folding, 1½ and ¾ yards respectively. It can be heated by gas, gasoline or steam at a trifling cost. Gasoline or gas burner supplied at $6.00 extra. Large size, 45-inch roll, price..$100.00
Small size 29-inch roll, price 75.00

Alliance Unbleached Sheetings.

MADE FOR AND SOLD ONLY BY

MONTGOMERY WARD & CO.

25 YARDS IN A BOLT.

See Quotations.

The Household Favorite Ironer.

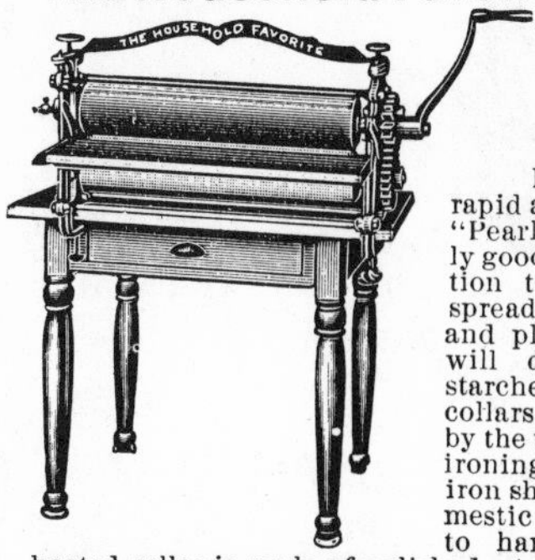

57199 The "Household Favorite" is designed especially to do family work, while it is not as rapid a machine as the "Pearl" will do equally good work. In addition to doing sheets, spreads, table cloths and plain underwear, will do straight starched work, such as collars and cuffs, and by the use of a pliable ironing board, will iron shirt bosoms, domestic finish superior to hand work. The heated roller is made of polished steel, and works in connection with a single soft covered roller, making a cushion that relieves the fabric of strain and wear. To operate this machine it is estimated that the cost of fuel will be as follows: Gas, 5 cents per day; gasoline, 3 cents per day; steam, nothing if you already have a boiler. Gasoline burner or gas burner can be attached to the machine at an additional cost of 6 dollars. The table is not furnished with the machine.
Large size, 37-inch roll. Price.................$45.00
Small size, 22-inch roll. Price................. 35.00

Jewel Shirt, Collar and Cuff Ironer

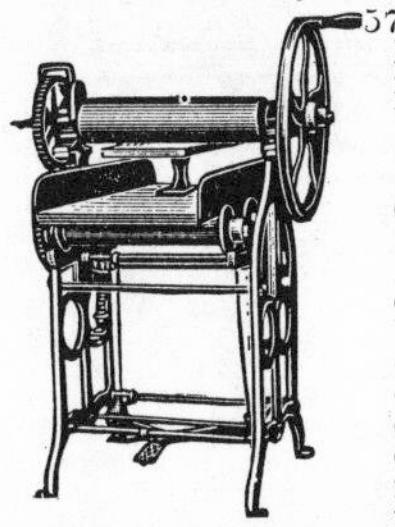

57200 This is without doubt the highest grade hand machine made; it differs in construction from other makes, in having rollers the same size (4½-inch) over and under, while others have a large drum working with a large gear. Our gear differs a little in size. By changing this gear, which can be done easily and quickly, we change the friction, and by so doing command domestic gloss or high polish. The bosom or collar board is guided by flanges on the roller, instead of the slide used in other machines. Our machine runs much easier than any other ironer made, and is much simpler and cheaper, and less liable to get out of order. One turn of the wheel passes the board full length of the bosom of the shirt or length of collar. The construction prevents any possibility of oil getting on the clothes, a point which we wish to emphasize. Floor space, 26x42 inches; weight crated, 330 pounds
Price, with gas burner, shirt, cuff and collar boards..$70.00
Price, with gasoline burner, extra.......... ... 6.00
Price, with steam connection for heating, extra.12.50
Price, with power pulleys instead of hand drive wheel, extra...... .... 12.50

The Economic Starcher.

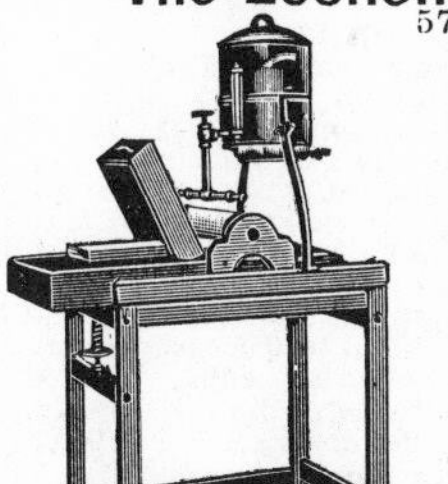

57201 This starcher is the most practical, and at the same time, the simplest of its kind made. The shirt goes direct from the wringer to the starcher, is finished on the board, and is then ready for the drying room; floor space, 36x52 inches, weight, crated ready for shipment, 75 pounds
Price, complete, with gas burner $40.00
Price, with gasoline burner, extra........................ 6.00

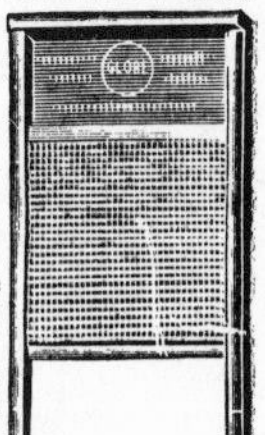

Wash Boards.

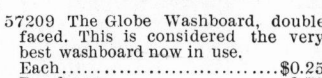

57209 The Globe Washboard, double faced. This is considered the very best washboard now in use.
Each.......................................$0.25
Per dozen......................... 2.70

57210 The Single Diamond, with protector at top. One of the best boards in the market. Each.........$0.18 Per dozen..........$1.95
57212 Wilson's single, light, strong and effective. Each.........$0.16 Per dozen.........$1.73

Folding Wash Benches.

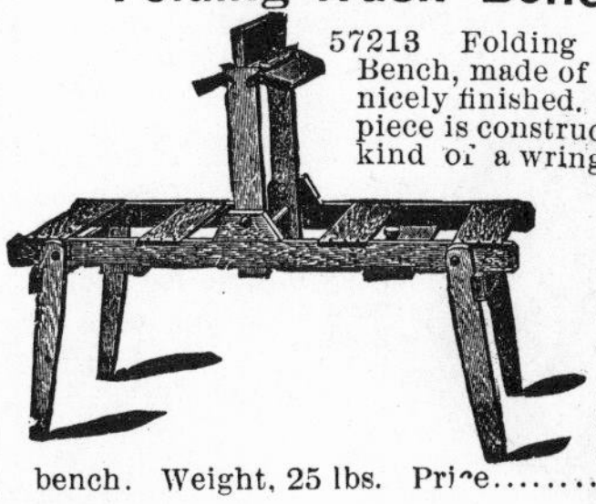

57213 Folding Double Wash Bench, made of hardwood and nicely finished. The upright piece is constructed so that any kind of a wringer can be fastened to it, and room enough each side of it for tubs. When not in use it may be folded up so it will occupy much less space than an ordinary wash bench. Weight, 25 lbs. Price.........................$1.54

Wash Benches—Continued.

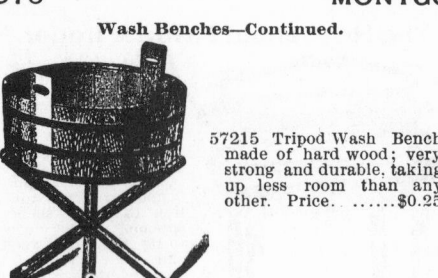

57215 Tripod Wash Bench made of hard wood; very strong and durable, taking up less room than any other. Price. $0.25

Hat and Coat Racks.

57217 The Perfection Iron Hook Hat Rack, with wood frame, to hang on the wall; the long or extension hooks can be used for hats, the shorter ones for clothing

	Each	Per doz	Weight.
Five hooks	$0.18	.95	22 oz.
Seven hooks		.22	2.16	29 oz.

57219 The Improved Hat Rack will hold any kind of a hat. The iron hooks are japanned or lacquered, and the wood frame nicely finished, two sizes only.

	Each.	Per doz.	Weight.
Six hooks	$0.20	$2.16	34 oz.
Seven hooks	.30	3.24	38 oz.

57221 Hat and Coat Racks, iron hooks, wood frame, to hang on the wall, 4 and 6 hooks.

	Each.	Per doz.	Weight.
Four hooks	$0.07	$0.76	13 oz.
Six hooks	.08	.87	18 oz.

Lap Cutting Boards.

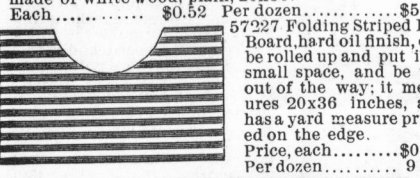

57223 Lap Cutting Board, striped, oil finished and polished, with yard measure stamped on it; size, 20x36.
Each $0.65
Per dozen.............7.05
Weight,, 4½ lbs.

57225 Lap Cutting Board, same shape as 57120, made of white wood, plain, 20x36.
Each ....$0.52 Per dozen.............$5.94

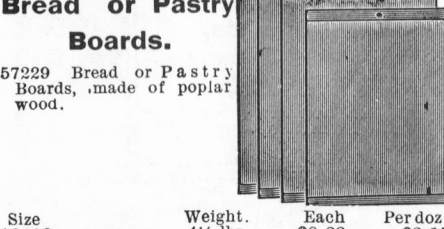

57227 Folding Striped Lap Board, hard oil finish, can be rolled up and put into small space, and be put out of the way; it measures 20x36 inches, and has a yard measure printed on the edge.
Price, each.........$0.85
Per dozen.......... 9 .20

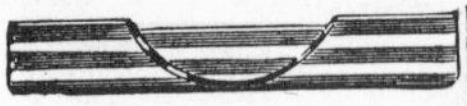

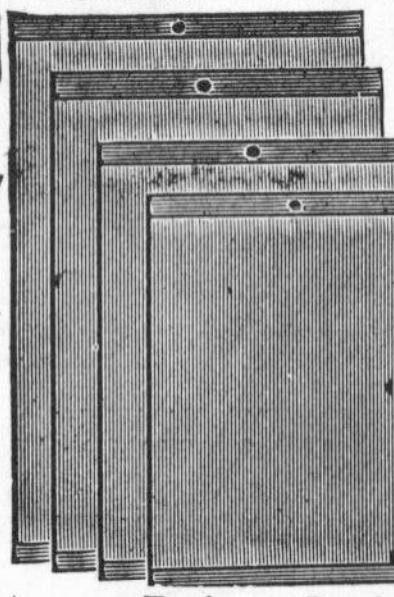

Bread or Pastry Boards.

57229 Bread or Pastry Boards, made of poplar wood.

Size	Weight.	Each	Per doz.
16x22	4½ lbs.	$0.28	$3.15
18x24	5¼ lbs.	.33	3.60
20x27	5¾ lbs.	.42	4.50
20x30	6½ lbs.	.46	4.95

57231 Fancy Hardwood and Hand Carved Bread Plate. Everybody needs one of these for slicing bread.
Each.............$0.18
Per dozen......... 1.93

Pastry Boards—Continued.

57232 Maple Pie Plates, no pic-nic complete without them, no weight and no danger of breaking.
7-inch, price, per 1,000.......................$2.60
8-inch, price, per 1,000 .... 2.70
9-inch, price, per 1,000.......................... 2.95

Slaw Cutters.

57233 Slaw Cutters, one knife.
Each........ $0.22
Per dozen ... 2.56

Adjustable Knife Krout Cutters.

57235 Kraut Cutters, 8x26inches, 3 cast steel knives, with slide box.
Each...........$1.00   Per dozen..........$10.95
57237 Kraut Cutters, 30x9 inches; 3 cast steel knives, with slide box.
Each...........$1.75   Per dozen...........$19.00

Matador Meat Slicers.

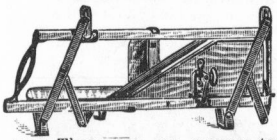

57238 This machine is intended to cut or slice boneless meats, bread, vegetables, etc., and is without doubt the best yet brought out for this purpose. There are no grooves to conceal dirt; all parts easily accessible for cleaning. Instant paralel, lateral adjustment of thickness gauge. The knife frame is carried by parallel motion levers, gauge is adjustable lengthwise to take up wear of knife. Price............ ....$4.25

Medicine, Spice Cabinets and Salt Boxes

57239 Medicine Cabinet, made of oak, antique finish, and varnished, Size, 18x11, depth, 5 inches. This is a very neat and strong cabinet and will match with the finest furniture. Price, each........ $0.85
Weight. 8 lbs.

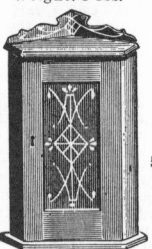

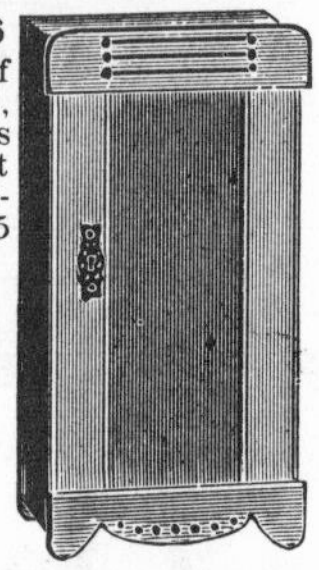

57243 Corner Medicine Cabinet, made of ash and varnished.
Price, each..................$0.75
Weight, 5 lbs.

57245 Fancy Salt and Spice Cabinet, made of ash and smooth finished, four double drawers for spices, porcelain knobs, large box at bottom for salt; size, 19x10¾ inches, 8 inches at base.
Weight, 9 lbs. Price, each.$0.85

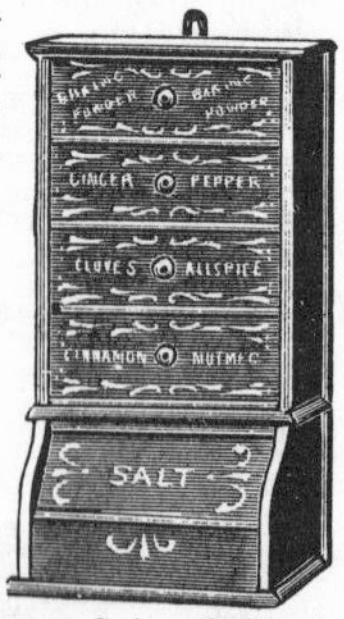

57247 Fancy Spice Cabinet, made of ash, smooth finished, four double drawers for spices; porcelain knobs. Size, 16x10¾x5¼ inches.
Price, each........ ...$0.65
Weight, 7 lbs.

57249 Spice Cabinet, neatly constructed, an ornamental cabinet for holding and preserving spices. Eight drawers marked for contents. Very handsome for any use to which a cabinet can be put. Made of ash, oil finish; size, 12x18.
Each... . ...$0.90
Per dozen............... 9.70
Weight, 6 lbs.

Cabinets—Continued.

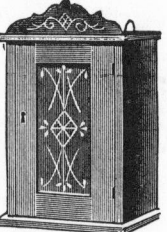

57251 Medicine or Handy Cabinet, 12x16, made of ash, nicely trimmed, for holding medicine bottles or anything that necessity or convenience may suggest. Every family should have one.
Each......................$0.75
Per dozen..... .... 8.10
Weight, 3 lbs.

Combination Spice and Salt Box.

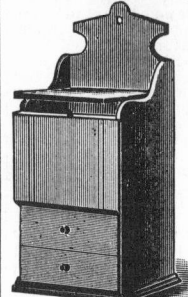

57253 Spice and Salt Box, made of oak, varnished, has two drawers, 5x5 inches, divided into four compartments each, giving room for eight different kinds of spices, and also lots of room for salt. Height, 15 inches; width, 6 inches; depth, 6 inches.
Price....................$0.45
Per dozen................ 5.00

57255 Salt Box, made of nice clear wood, is 6 inches square and will hold two small bags of salt. Each..........$0.15
Per dozen....... ...... 1.65

Coffee Spice and Drug Mills.

57257 This mill is suitable for hotels, boarding schools or large institutions; height, 13½ inches; weight, 13½ pounds; diameter of fly wheel, 9¾ inches; will grind about ½ pound of coffee per minute; is nicely painted and ornamented, and can be instantly adjusted to grind coarse or fine. Price..........$2.40

57259 This will be found a very desirable mill for large families or boarding houses; height, 13½ inches; weight, 10 pounds; diameter of fly-wheel, 9¾ inches. It is nicely painted and ornamented. Can be instantly adjusted, and will grind about ½ pound of coffee per minute. Price $1.95

57261 Columbian Coffee Mill; holds 1 pound; ornamental raised iron dome; always ready for use; this is the handsomest and best 1-pound mill in use; the crank being on the side is a great improvement over all others; the grinding qualities are superior. The highly finished hardwood box has rounded corners, with convenient handles attached.
Price.......................................$1.35

57263 Arcade Royal Mill, all iron simple locking device, requiring no screws or bolts in its construction; patent grinding regulator, detachable cup with each mill.
Each.................................$0.33
Case of six...................... 1.78

Coffee Mills—Continued.

57267 Arcade Side Mill, medium size, board back, crystalized metal hopper, japanned iron work.
Each.... ....$0.25
Per case of six............ 1.35
57269 Arcade Favorite Mill, size, 6x6x3¾; whitewood box, iron hopper. The lowest price ever named on a coffee mill of any description. Each.... .. ..$0.22
Per case of six........................ 1.32

57271 Favorite (small size), raised hopper, no cover, japanned iron, hardwood box. Never before sold for less than 60 cents to our knowledge. Usually retails at 75 cents. Best value for the money in the market.
Each...................$0.29
Per case of six.. ... 1.57
57273 Arcade Favorite, same as No. 57271, only large No. 77x4¼ inches. Each............ ...$0.35
Per case of six 1.89
57275 Arcade Favorite, retinned hopper, with patent shield to prevent coffee from snapping out, new patent regulator and pulverizing burr, hardwood box, dovetailed corners, polished and finely made; size, 7x7x4½ inches. Each...... .... $0.45
Per case of six...... .... 2.43

57277 Arcade Favorite, wood top with iron hopper and cover, similar to cut, hardwood box.
Each............ ......$0.43
Per case of six........ 2.20
57279 Arcade Favorite, with ornamental top and hinged cover. Finely finished, patent regulator and pulverizing burr.
Each............ .....$0.45
Per set of six................ .... 2.43

57281 Arcade Imperial, sunk hopper, all iron top, hinged cover-hardwood box, dovetailed and finely finished; has patent regulator and pulverizing burr, largest size made, 7x7x5¼ inches.
Each..............$0.50
Per case of six......2.70

57283 Imperial, sunk hopper, hinged cover, iron, finished with French gold bronze, white walnut box. Each.................................. .45
Per case of six.................................. 2.40
57285 Imperial, sunk hopper, hinged cover, nickel plated trimmings, white walnut box. Each .... .58
Per case of six................................ 3.14

Wood Faucets.

	DOZ.	EACH.
57287 Faucets, wood, cork-lined........	$0.40	$0.05
57289 Faucets, wood, cork-lined.......	.45	.06
57291 Faucets, wood, cork-lined.......	.55	.07

Redlich's—Cork-lined and Rubber-soaked.

	DOZ.	EACH
57293 7 inches long......................	$0.65	$0 07
57295 9½ inches long....................	1.10	.10
57297 10½ inches long...................	1.30	.12
57301 11½ inches long...................	1.50	.14
57303 12½ inches long......	2.25	.20

Wood Faucet—Metal Lock and Key.

	DOZ.	EACH
57305 8 inches long.....	$2.75	$0.25
57307 9 inches long.........	3.25	.28
57309 12 inches long.........	3.75	.33

57310 Redlich Bottle Corker. This is a very useful article, and although cheap will do as good work as the most expensive styles. Price........$0.50

The Special Catalogues

As Listed on Inside Rear Cover May Interest You.

37--2nd

Fancy Work Baskets, Mats, Etc.

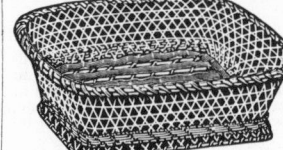

57313 Woven Split Willow Round Corner Baby Toilet Basket, 14½ inches wide, 18 inches long, well made and finished. Each..$0.75

57315 Woven Split Willow Square Shaped Baby Toilet Basket, with handles on each end; 14½ inches wide, 19 inches long, strongly made, Each . $0.75

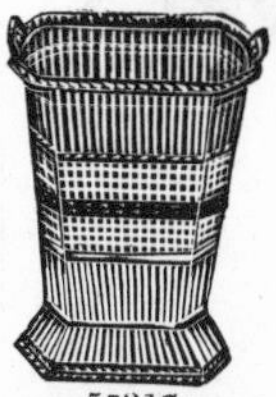

57317 Fancy Hexagon Shaped Willow and Rush Waste Paper Baskets, 12 inches high, 10½ inches wide. The rush is stained in bright colors; the willow is of fancy open work pattern, capable of being handsomely trimmed. Each...............$0.65

57317

57321

57319

57319 Fancy Square Heaped Willow and Rush Waste Paper Basket, neat design with pointed edges, it stands about 13 inches high; is about 12 inches wide. the rush is stained in bright colors. $0.65
57321 Toilet Splasher for protecting wall above washstand, etc., waterproof, made of sewed wood splints, to roll up, hand painted center; size, 16½x34
Each................. ......$0.09
Three for 25
Per dozen............ .90
57323 Table Mats, to roll up, made of woodsplints, sewed very flexible and light, flower painted in center, waterproof; set of six, two each, small, medium and large or platter size.
Per set of six $0.23
Per doz. sets 2.25
Extra by mail, per set.. .08

57325 Knife and Fork Basket, made of palm leaf and willow, handsomely and strongly woven together; a very fine basket for the money. Each.$0.35
Per dozen 3.00
57327 Heavy Straw Braid Lunch Basket, same shape as cut; 8¼ inches long, 6 in. high, dark brown color. Each $0.30
Per dozen.......... 3.24

57328 Square Plain Palm Leaf Lunch Basket, 9 inches long, 6 inches high; the strongest basket ever made.....$0.35
Per dozen..... ... 3.78

57329 Fancy Woven Rush and Cane Wall and Paper Rack, fancy square openwork of stained and varnished rushes. This is a very handsome as well as useful article. Many people trim and work them with fancy wool and ribbons; it is quite large, measuring 13x14.
Each ...,....,...$0.75

57331 Rush and Cane Music Stand, made in fancy openwork patterns; is quite large and stands about 13 inches high by 12 inches long. This is a very handy article and will be found useful where a piano or organ is used. Each...........$0.75

57332 Fine Woven Cane and Rush Music, Rack, richly ornamented and made very strong, stands 18 inches high, 13 long and 6 wide, a partition in center and fancy openwork which may be trimmed with ribbons or bows to suit taste of purchaser. Each.......$1.75

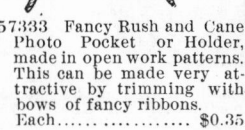

57333 Fancy Rush and Cane Photo Pocket or Holder, made in open work patterns. This can be made very attractive by trimming with bows of fancy ribbons.
Each..... .... $0.35

Carpet Beaters.

57337 Woven Cane Carpet Beater, strong and durable, will last a lifetime; three feet long. Each.$0.18

Ladies' Work Baskets.

57338 Ladies' Work Basket, made of woven straw and willow of various colors; two inside pockets, 8 pointed, and measures about 12 inches in diameter.
Each.... ...$0.55
Per dozen.... 5.94

57339 Ladies' Work Basket, fancy woven straw and stained willow, scalloped edge, two inside pockets 10½ inches square
Each.......... $0.50
Per dozen..... 5.40

57341 Ladies' Work Basket, fancy straw and willow, stained in colors, measures 12 inches in diameter and hexagon shape.
Each...... $0.45
Per dozen... 4.86

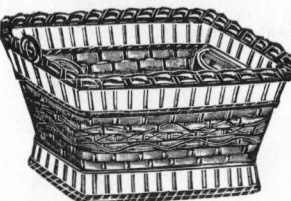

57343 Ladies' Work Basket, fancy woven straw, scalloped edge. two inside pockets, pink indestructible ribbon running around center, 11 inches long, 8 inches wide.
Each.......$0.57
Per dozen. 6.15

Oak Creek Splint Corn Baskets.

57344 This basket is stronger and can be used for more purposes around a farm than any other on the market, we carry it in a full line of sizes and shall be glad to have your order for any quantity you may desire.

Sizes, bushel........	¾	1.	1½	2.	3.	4.	6.
Price, each........	$0.40	50	62	78	1.00	1.35	1.65
Per dozen.	$4.56	5.70	7.05	8.90	11.40	15.39	18.81

Measuring Baskets.

	Per doz.	Each.
57345 Racine Corn Basket, patent stave, ½ bushel, with handle..	$1.35	$0.18
57347 Racine Corn Basket, patent stave, 1 bushel......	2.20	.22
57348 Racine Corn Basket, patent stave, 1½ bushels....	2.60	.25
57349 Racine Corn Basket, patent stave, 2 bushels........	3.25	.33
57355 Splint, 1 bushel..........	2.25	.20
57357 Splint, 1½ bushel.......	2.75	.25

Clothes Baskets.

	Per dz.	Each.
57358 Clothes, willow, small ...	$7.00	$0.65
57359 " " medium	8.00	.75
57360 " " large	9.50	.85

Market Baskets.

	Per doz.	Each.
57361 Market, willow, small....	$3.00	$0.27
57362 Market, willow, medium	3.50	.32
57363 Market, willow, large..	4.00	.38

	Per dz.	Each.
57365 Market, woven splint, wood bottom, oval, small........	$2.50	$0.25
57366 Market, woven splint, wood bottom, oval, medium	2.75	.27
57367 Market, woven splint, wood bottom, oval, large......	3.00	.28
57368 Market, common elm	.50	.05
57369 " extra elm.......	1.00	.10
57370 " elm, covered, medium....	2.00	.20
57371 " elm, covered, large	2.25	.22

Ladies' Work Stands.

57375 Ladies' Work Stand, fancy braided straw and willow, similar to cut; 30 inches high, 10 inches wide, 6 inches deep. Price, each..................$0.75

57377 Ladies' Work Stand, fancy braided straw and stained wood, 27 inches high, 12 inches wide, 6 inches deep, with handle as per cut. Price, each...................$1.00

Workstands—Continued.

57379 Ladies' Work Stand, fancy braided willow and tinsel cord with celluloid ribbon interwoven and small basket at bottom; 29 inches high, 9 inches wide, 4 inches deep. Price each.... ..$2.00

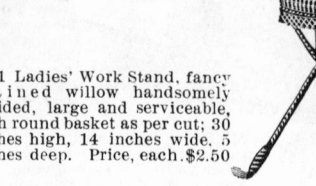

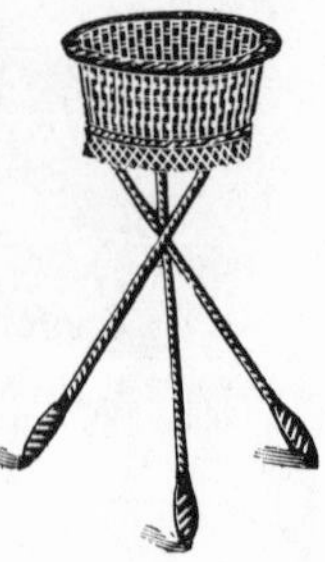

57381 Ladies' Work Stand, fancy stained willow handsomely braided, large and serviceable, with round basket as per cut; 30 inches high, 14 inches wide, 5 inches deep. Price, each.$2.50

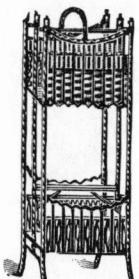

57385 Music Stand, made of stained willow, cord and braided straw artistically woven, 31 inches high, similar to cut...................2.45

FIBRE WARE.

Indurated Wood Fibre Ware.

Is without joint or seam, being in one piece from wood fibre.

Has been subjected to a hardening process that renders it impervious to liquids, hot or cold, kerosene, benzine or naphtha.

Cannot shrink, warp, swell, leak, watersoak or rust.

Is absolutely tasteless and odorless, and will not taint water, milk, or other liquids.

Has no hoops to drop off or rust off; being seamless bottom, cannot fall out.

Is light, will float, is very ornamental, and with ordinary care will last longer than any other.

Pails.

The only water pail that will hold water. No hoops or staves, all one piece. Light, ornamental, durable, will not shrink, warp, swell, watersoak, leak or rust. Absolutely tasteless and odorless.

		Crates contain	Price per dz.	Price each
57400	Buggy or 8 qt..........	1 doz.	$2.70	$0.25
57402	Ladies' or Weavers', 6 qt....	1 "	2.70	.25
57403	Star Standard Plain....	½ "	3.15	.30
57405	Deck or Masons' Heavy Wire Pail, 12 qt..........	½ "	3.60	.35
57406	Railroad or Factory, 14 qt. plain..........	½ "	4.05	.38
57408	Railroad or Factory, Stenciled, For Fire only.............½		4.05	.38
57409	Special Fire Bucket, for R.R. Cars, height, 12 in., diam., 8½ in..½	"	3.60	.35
57412	Milk or Dairy, 14 qt ....½	"	4.05	.38
57413	Stable, Flush Bottom, 14 qt.½	"	4.50	.42
57414	Stable, Flush Bottom, 16 qt.½	"	5.40	.50
57415	Stable, Flush Bottom, 20 qt.½	"	6.75	.62
57416	Covers for Star or R.R. Pails.		2.25	.25

Wash Tubs.

	Diam. in.	In. deep.	Crates contain.	Per doz.	Each
57418	23½	13½	½ doz.	$15.75	$1.38
57419	21	12	½ "	13.50	1.18
57422	19½	11	½ "	12.00	1.05
57425	18½	9½	½ "	10.50	.95
				Per nest	
57430	Nest 0 to 3 (4 tubs)		⅓ "	$4.30	
57431	Nest 1 to 3 (3 tubs)		¼ "	3.00	

Keelers.

			Price per doz.	each
57432	Diam. 20 in., 7 in. dp..	½ doz.	$8.10	$0.75
57435	Diam. 18½ in., 7 in. dp..	½ doz.	7.20	.65
57437	Diam. 17½ in., 7 in. dp..	1 doz.	6.75	.62
57439	Diam. 15½ in., 6 in. dp..	1 doz.	6.30	.58
57440	Diam. 13½ in., 5 in. dp	1 doz.	5.40	.52

Bread or Butter Bowls.

		Crates contain	Price per doz.	Price each
57450	15 inch........	1 doz.	$3.60	$0.35
57451	17 inch........	1 doz.	4.50	.45
57452	19 inch........	½ doz.	5.40	.52

Spittoons.

57453	16 in....	⅓ doz.	$7.50	$0.68
57455	13 in....	½ doz.	4.95	.46
57457	12 in....	½ doz.	4.50	.43
57459	9½ in....	½ doz.	4.05	.38

Handy Dishes.

57460	8 qt.	1 doz.	$2.95	$0.28
57462	6 qt.	1 doz.	2.65	.27
57464	4 qt.	1 doz.	2.50	.26

Milk Pans.

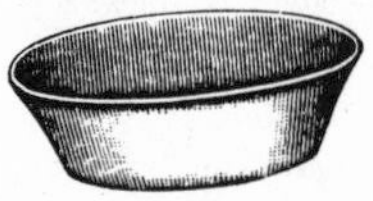

57466 Standard size, 3 dozen in crate.
Per dozen $2.25
Each.................... .22

Wash Basins.

57467 12½ inch (one size only).2 doz. in crate. Each........$0.20
Per dozen.......... ...... 2.15

Slop Jars.

57469 12 quart (one size only), ¼ dozen in crate.
Each.................$0.67
Per dozen............... 7.65

Slop Jar Mats.

57470 17 inch; crate contains 1 doz. Each......$0.33
Per dozen.................. 3.60
57471 21 inch; crate contains 1 doz. Each ... .45
Per dozen................... 4.95

Chamber Pails.

57475 12 quart, concave tops; crate contains ½ dozen.
Each.................$0.67
Per dozen.......... .... 7.65

BUGGY AND WAGON DEPARTMENT.

Prices quoted in the latest edition of this catalogue stand in correction and take preference over prices named in Catalogue B and C. which are only printed annually.

We handle a greater variety and wider range of vehicles than any other house.

We have every quality from the common to the most expensive. We class our grades as common, medium, standard, standard extra and special, the last named ranking with the very finest work sold, though our prices are much lower than dealers obtain for this high grade of work.

For full description of our different vehicles see our special catalogue, C, which we mail upon receipt of 3 cents to pay postage.

WIDTH OF TRACK.

There are two standard tracks in use, measured from center to center of tire on the ground, one narrow track, 4 ft. 8 in., and one wide, 5 ft. 2 inches. These two tracks are in use often in the same section, and it is frequently impossible to decide which is wanted, unless stated in the order. If purchasers fail to state which track is wanted, we cannot be responsible for the selection made, or for delays incident in writing for width of track, where we are in doubt as to which is required.

IN ORDERING ALWAYS GIVE WIDTH OF TRACK.

Buggies and spring wagons crated are usually shipped at *once and one-half first-class rate, actual weight.* Purchasers must pay their own freight from Chicago. We mail freight rates, which will show cost of delivery. Nothing is gained by prepaying freight. We make no charge for crating or cartage.

Top Buggy, Elliptic Springs.

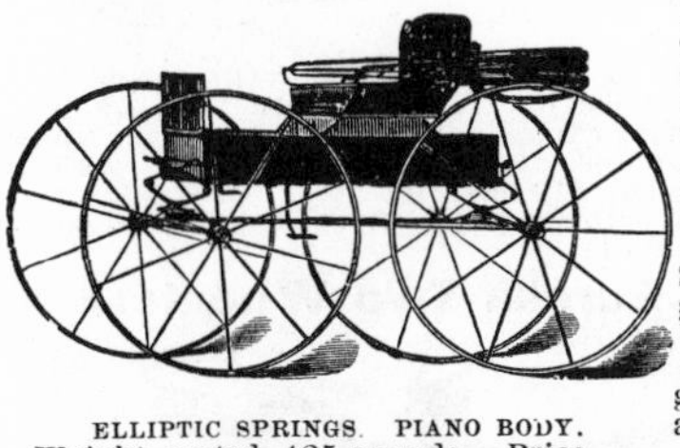

ELLIPTIC SPRINGS. PIANO BODY.

70002 Price, F.O.B. cars, crated, medium grade, $47.60 Standard grade .....$54.40 Standard Extra Grade ......$58.90 Special grade $69.50 Without top (open buggy) Standard grade Weight, crated, 425 pounds. Price...........$44.50

Indiana Piano Box, End Spring. Indiana Piano Box, Brewster Spring.

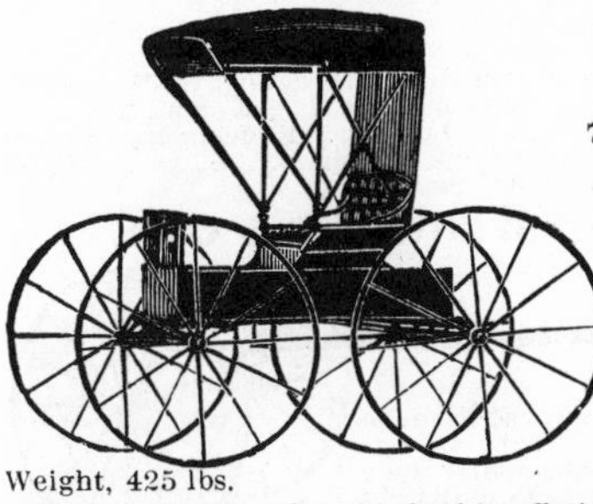

70004 Indiana Piano Box, end springs. 70005 Indiana Piano Box, Brewster springs. Price of either of these buggies, $45.75 Silver hub bands and silver dash rail $2.00 extra.

Weight, 425 lbs.

We propose to take the lead in offering the largest and best variety of buggies ever catalogued, and at prices from which any of our customers can make a satisfactory selection. These two Indiana buggies are a new addition to our list. Vehicles both alike, except style of springs; weight and price the same.

Best leather quarter top, heavy English cloth trimming.

Back of body covered with a good rubber boot.

Furnished only according to these specifications. No changes made.

AXLES—Double collar, swedged, made of steel, 15/16 inch, ⅞ inch boxing.

BODY—25x50 inches; made from the best of materials and superior workmanship.

DASH—No. 1 Patent Leather

FORGINGS, CLIPS AND BOLTS are all of Norway iron.

GEAR—Made from best second growth hickory, ironed with Norway iron; double reach.

Bodies black; gear dark green.

TOP—Best leather quarter, lined with broadcloth. Always shipped with 3 or 4 bowed top, as ordered.

TRACK—4 ft. 8 in., or 5 ft. 2 in., whichever is ordered.

TRIMMING—Cushions and back, English body cloth; upholstered with hair; Brussels carpet; boot and storm apron.

WHEELS—Sarven or Shell Band, bolted between each spoke; 3 ft. 4 in. in front, 3 ft. 8 in. in rear, ⅞ in. tread.

Brewster Springs, Corning Buggy.

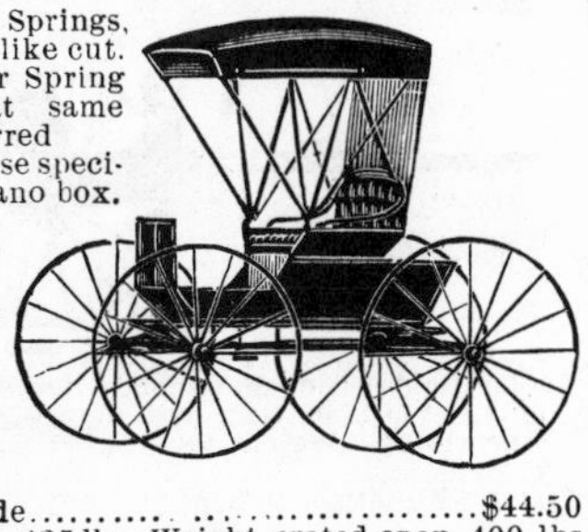

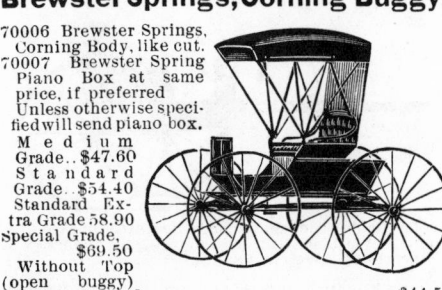

70006 Brewster Springs, Corning Body, like cut. 70007 Brewster Spring Piano Box at same price, if preferred Unless otherwise specified will send piano box.

Medium Grade..$47.60 Standard Grade..$54.40 Standard Extra Grade 58.90 Special Grade, $69.50 Without Top (open buggy) Standard Grade.......... ....$44.50 Weight, crated, 435 lbs. Weight, crated, open, 400 lbs

Top Buggy, Cross or Timken Spring.

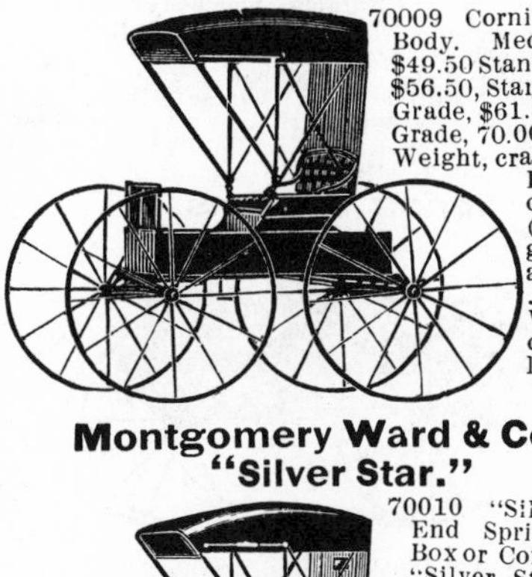

70009 Corning or Piano Body. Medium Grade $49.50 Standard Grade, $56.50, Standard Extra Grade, $61.87; Special Grade, 70.00. Weight, crated, 440 lbs. Price without top (open buggy), Standard Grade, ... $45.50 Weight, crated, 410 lbs.

Montgomery Ward & Co.'s "Silver Star."

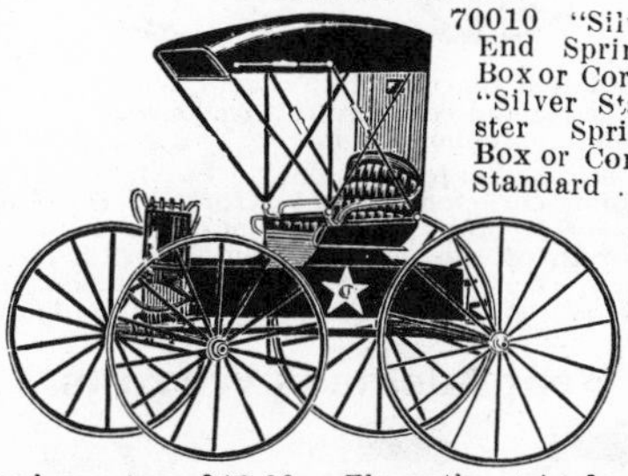

70010 "Silver Star," End Spring, Piano Box or Corning Body. "Silver Star," Brewster Spring Piano Box or Corning body. Standard ..... $53.25 Weight, Crated, 440 lbs. Standard Extra, $60. Special, $74.00. Weight, crated open, 410 lbs; Standard, no top, $48.00. Elegantly striped and highly ornamented; has silver hub bands, silver axle nuts silver dash rail, silver handles on seat, silver whip socket, silver trimmed boot on back, silver joints on brace irons to top, silver top nuts, silver fastenings to back curtains. Ornamental silver star and monogram showing initials of purchaser on both sides of body. Be sure to give initials wanted, and make them plain.

Top Buggy, Maud S Springs.

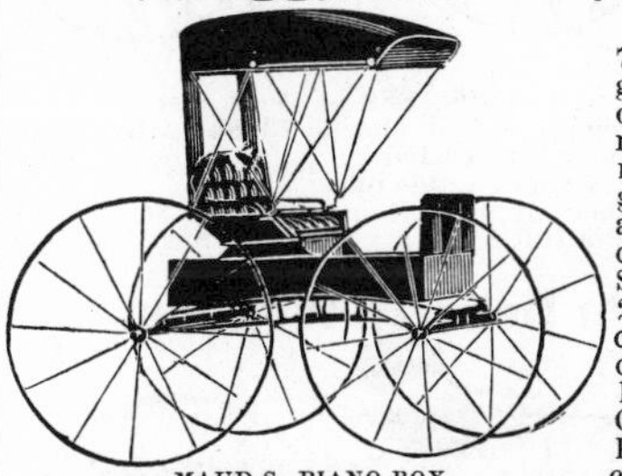

MAUD S. PIANO BOX.

70014 The great length of the springs makes them ride with great ease and evenness of motion Size of body 25x50, larger cannot be used on this gear. Piano Box or Corning body. Price. F. O. B. cars, crated.

Medium Grade...$58.00
Standard Grade, $62.00 Standard Extra Grade, 66.50
Special Grade...75.00
Weight, 415 lbs. Crated 445 lbs.
Without top (open buggy) Standard Grade... 51.00

Texas Ranger.

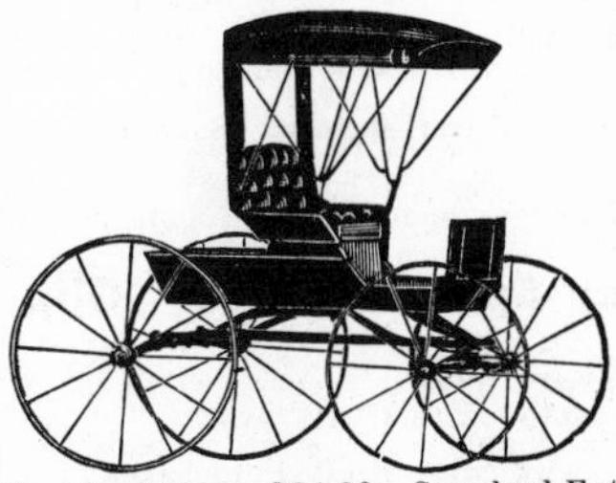

70015 Corning or Piano Box Body; extra long body and reach, hung on long Concord Springs, 1⅛ axles, 1-inch tire; made heavy and strong to withstand hard usage. Weight, crated, 520 lbs.

Standard Grade, $64.00. Standard Extra Grade, $68.50
Special Grade...83.00

Heavy Concord, Piano Box.

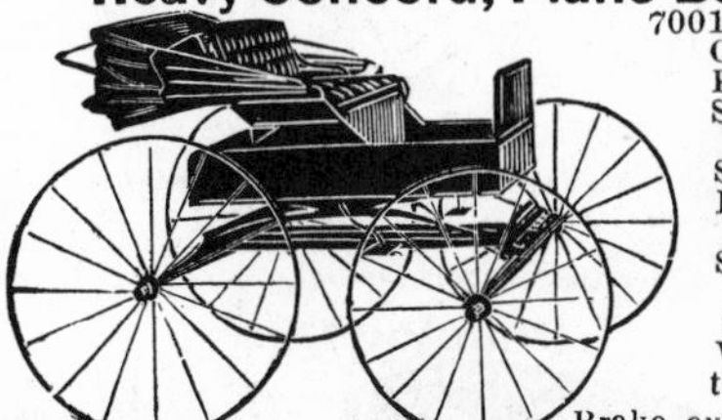

70016 Heavy Concord. Price, Standard, $65.25 Standard Extra, $69.75 Special, $84.50 Standard, Without top, $54.24 Brake, extra, $5.00

Hung on heavy Concord spring made especially for drummers' and livery use. Springs, 1½ inches, 5 plate, with equalizers, body of extra width and length and extra roomy seat. Height above ground, 34 inches; will carry 600 pounds. Body length, 54 ins; breadth, 28 ins.; depth, 8½ ins.; width of seat inside at bottom, 29 ins.; between axles. 56 in.; wheels, front, 42 ins.; rear, 46 ins.; 1 inch tire; axles, 1⅛ ins., with 1⅛ spindle; hub, 7x3 in.; actual weight, 425 lbs.; shipping weight, crated, 500 pounds.

Economy Business Wagons.

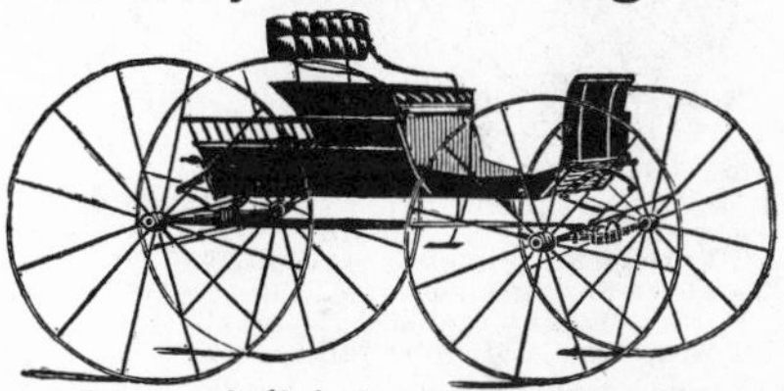

70017 Roomy spindle body on end springs. Sarven patent wheels. Medium Grade, Price, $32.50. Standard Grade, $37.50. f.o.b.. Chicago. For description of grade see Vehicle Catalogue C. State whether narrow track. 4 feet 8, or wide, 5 feet 2, is wanted. Price is with shafts. Pole, whiffletrees and yoke adds $3.00 to price. Weight, crated, 350 lbs,

Road Wagons.

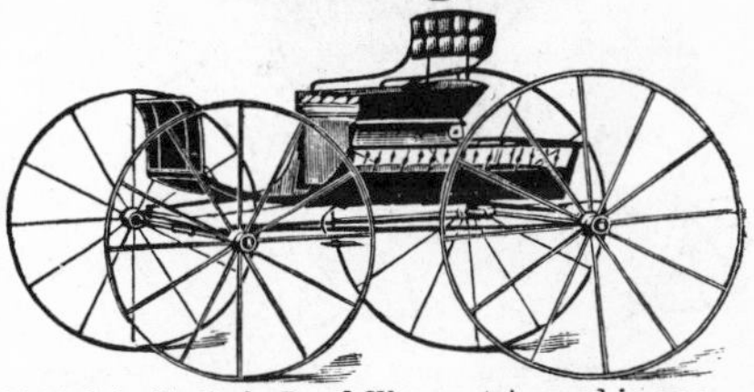

70018 Spindle Body Road Wagon, trimmed in corduroy or imitation leather. Long side springs, end springs, or Brewster springs, as preferred; 1 in. axle, 1⅛ inch spoke, felloe ⅞ inch wide; full width of tire 1 inch, weight with shafts 300 pounds. Price, medium grade $31.00
Common Grade 28.00
With rubber top, add to price.. .... 8.50
With lined leather quarter top, add to price.... 13.50
Pole in place of shafts adds $3 to price

Jump Seat Buggy.

Weight, boxed for shipment 500 lbs. (Cut shows vehicle with two seats.) Jump Seat. Three Springs.

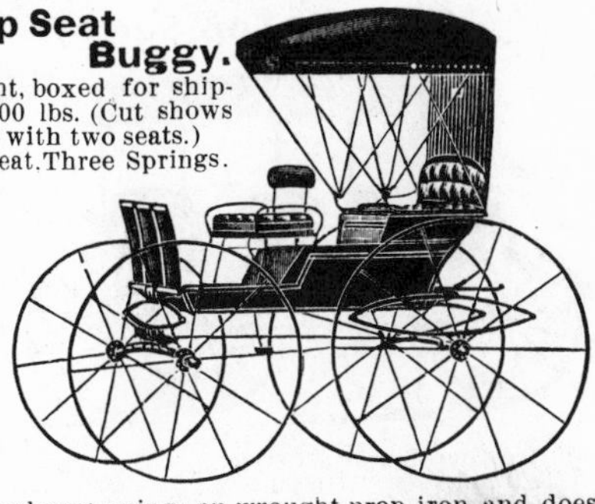

The back seat swings on wrought prop iron and does not mar the body like those moved on slides. 1⅛ axle and shafts are furnished with this buggy at following price:

	Medium.	Standard.	Standard Extra.	Special
70019 Jump Seat, three springs, Corning body.	$70.25	$76.00	$80.50	$91.50
70020 Jump Seat, side bar	70.25	76.00	80.50	91.50
Pole in place of shafts................				4.00

We devote special attention to the quotation of prices, by letter on goods not regularly quoted in our price lists; and encourage correspondence on any business topic.

Elliptic Spring Road Wagon with Top.

70021 Medium grade imitation leather or corduroy trimming, low hung, steel axles with wood beds, shafts; weight, 400 lbs. Price, with rubber top, Medium Grade $40.00
Common Grade................................. 36.00
Price, with leather quarter top 45.00

Phaetons.

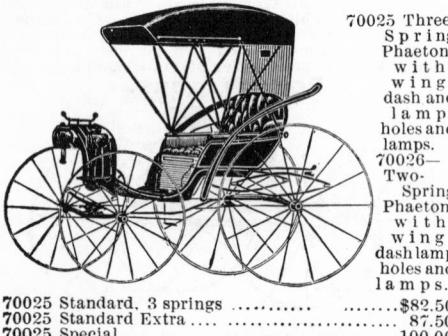

Brewster Phaeton, superior in style of body and strength of gear to any in the market. Body is hung low, making it very easy of access. Very popular with ladies, elderly persons and physicians. High, full back and very roomy.

Three-Spring Phaeton,

	Standard. Standard. Extra.	Special.
70022 Two-Spring Phaeton..$70.0 / $75.00 / $87.00
70023 Three-Spring Phaeton. 75.00 / 80.00 / 92.00
Weight, crated, 525 pounds.
Fine wing dash and silver rail, extra... ..... 4.00

Three-Spring Phaetons.

70025 Three-Spring Phaeton, with wing dash and lamp-holes and lamps. 70026—Two-Spring Phaeton, with wing dash lamp holes and lamps.

70025 Standard, 3 springs $82.50
70025 Standard Extra 87.50
70025 Special 100.00
70026 Standard, 2 springs................... 77.50
70026 Standard Extra "   " 82.50
70026 Special "   " 95.00
Weight, crated, 537 pounds.
Above prices are with shafts; pole, extra, in place of shafts... .... 4.00
State whether narrow track, 4 ft. 8; or wide, 5 ft. 2, is wanted. Delivered free on board, Chicago.

Canopy Top Surrey.

70027—Canopy Top Surrey, straight sills on end springs. 70028—Canopy Top Surrey, straight sills on Brewster springs

Price same for either style.
Medium grade, with pole.......................$78.75
Standard grade, with pole...................... 99.00
Special grade, with pole......................122.00
Weight, crated, 775 pounds.
A very nice carriage. State whether wide or narrow track is wanted. 1¼ in. axle in place of 1⅛ in., adds $3.00.   1⅝ in. wheels instead of 1 in., adds $1.50.

No charge for Cases or Cartage.

Family Carriages.

70029 Four-Passenger Extension top Carriage, substantial, light and durable. The body hangs low and is easy of access. Very roomy; light enough for one horse, furnished with lamps, leather fenders and pole, three spring gear, best construction. Full back on front seat if preferred. Standard grade. $140.00
Special grade................... .... 155.00
Shipping weight, 650 lbs.

Spring Wagons.

70033 Two-Seated Platform Half-Spring Wagon, pole, whiffletree and yoke,two full backs, leather trimming throughout.   Price, ...$49.50
The very best wagon for the money ever offered, drop end gate, round-cornered body; 1⅜ springs, 1¼ tire. This is a special vehicle, built in standard grade only The best wagon of this pattern made. Best Sarven patent wheels. Weight, crated, 625 lbs., intended to carry 1,000 lbs.; body, 88 inches long, 33 wide; body from ground, 32 inches.

Two-Seat Business Wagons.

70034 Price, with shafts, $32.00 Pole, whiffle-trees and yoke in place of shafts, adds to price, $3.00 Weight, 500 pounds, crated.
Made in the common grade only.
Drop axles and single half-end springs. Sarven patent wheels.   For full description, see our Special Buggy Catalogue.

Light Delivery Wagons.

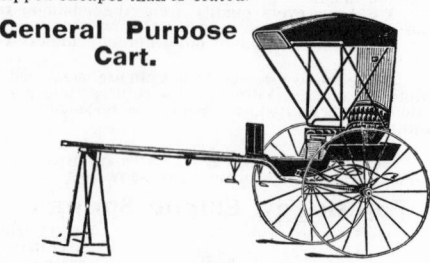

70035 Price, with shafts, $32.00. Pole, whiffle-trees and yoke in place of shafts, adds to price $3.00 Weight, 500 lbs , crated.
Drop axles and half-end springs. Sarven patent wheels.
Has side boards or wings on body; very handy for light or medium delivery up to 600 lbs. Made only in the common grade.

Studebaker Spindle Body "Clipper."

70044 Length of body, 5 feet 3 inches; width, 2 feet 4 inches; depth of box, 4½ inches. The axles are 1 inch double collar steel; wheels, Sarven patent, with steel tires; Studebaker's veneer seat, nicely trimmed. Wine, carmine or green, gearing, natural wood finish body and seat. For cut see our Buggy Catalogue. This is a standard grade job, finely finished, and should have a large sale, as price is low considering quality. Price, with shafts $32.00
Weight, crated, 300 lbs.

Insure mail packages see page 1.

Road Carts.

Road carts are usually shipped crated at one and one-half first-class freight. Wrapped, not crated, double first-class. Light carts can often be wrapped and shipped cheaper than if crated.

General Purpose Cart.

70045 "General Purpose Cart," with three bow top. Price, rubber top $39.50
Leather quarter top.... .... 40.50
Full leather top 45.00
Weight, crated, 319 lbs.
Spring heavy, to carry top. One of the most popular top carts made.

The Eureka Two Wheeler.

70048 Absolutely without horse motion.

Easier to ride in than a buggy A more useful cart would be hard to find. It has the utility of a road cart, and is as roomy as a buggy. Made and finished in best buggy style. Weight, 250 pounds; with top, 300 pounds. Price, open...$30.00
Price, with rubber top......................... .40.00
Weight, crated, 305 pounds.

The Favorite No. 3 Cart.

70050 Our Improved Favorite Road Cart. This is one of the most popular low-priced carts made;built light and neat; Sarven patent wheels, double collar steel axle braced throughout. Long oil tempered spring hung over the axle. Finish natural wood only. Weight, wrapped for shipment, 120 pounds; width of seat, from rail to rail, 30 inches. Price $9.00

The Studebaker Road Cart.

70052 The Studebaker Coil Spring Road Cart. The construction of the cart is of the well-known Studeoaker style. Substantial and well made. The frame and seat rests are of angular steel and supported at four points by elastic springs, ⅞ inch axle, painted in wine or finished in natural wood, striped and well varnished; weight, about 125 pounds; crated, 150 pounds. Price, crated, on board car.................... .... $17.00

The "Dream."

70055 Double bent shafts, body mounted on axle only. Width of seat, rail to rail, 32 inches. Easy riding. Weight, 280 lbs.
Price.. ....$29.00
70056 Miniature Dream, for pony............$29.00

Write us for freight rates to your town, we have recently enlarged our methods of giving this sort of information.

Carts—Continued.

70060 Our Improved No. 4½ Phaeton Cart.
Price............$14.50
Shipping weight, 150 lbs.

This is one of the most saleable carts we handle, long spring hung on loops under shafts, good wheels and axles, dash board, cushion and lazy back. Upholstered in imitation leather, box under seat for halter, etc. Seat, 30 inches wide. A good reliable cart.

No such cart sold anywhere at less than 30 to 40 per cent. advance on our price.

Universal Tire Setter.

WEST'S TIRE SETTER MONTGOMERY WARD & CO.

70061 This implement will set a tire on any buggy or wagon with a tire up to 4 in. wide. It is made of the best steel and galvanized iron and neatly finished. No injury whatever need be done in tightening tires by this tire setter to the finest painted wheels. Weight, 10 lbs.
Price for tire up to 3½ in. wide.................$1.75
70061½ For tire over 3½ in. wide.............. 2.00
Felloes are immersed in boiled linseed oil; kerosene is burned under tank. Oil cannot catch afire.

Our Celebrated Racine Farm Wagon.

Shipped at first-class freight, actual weight.
70062 Is made on our special order by one of the largest and best known builders in the country, and whose name alone is a guarantee of perfection in material and excellence in construction. This wagon has a national reputation, well known and in use in every state.

	No. 1.	No. 3.	No. 5.	No. 7.	No. 9
Size of skein:	2½x8	2¾x8½	3x9	3¼x10	3⅞x11

Capacity:

No. 1	No. 3	No. 5	No. 7	No. 9
1,500	2,000	2,500	3,800	4,500

Price, gears, pole and whiffletrees, and weight:

No. 1	No. 3	No. 5	No. 7	No. 9
$28.90	$30.90	$33.28	$34.78	$37.00
575 lb.	625 lb.	700 lb.	725 lb.	750 lb.

Price of wagon, top box and seat. If brake is on gear it adds to price, $5.00; on box, $2.50.

No. 1.	No. 3.	No. 5.	No. 7.	No. 9.
$39.95	$42.80	$45.59	$47.47	$49.70
790 lb.	840 lb.	915 lb.	1,025 lb.	1,085 lb.

70063 Our Reliable Clinton Farm Wagon, following prices are without brake; brake on box extra........................ ....$2.50
On gears................................ 5.00

This wagon has a good local reputation, and on account of low price is a desirable wagon to order. We have sold hundreds and they invariably give the best of satisfaction. Weight and capacity about the same as No. 70062.

	No. A.	No. B.	No. C.	No. D.	No. E.
Size of skein:	2½x8	2¾x8½	3x9	3¼x10	3½x11

Price of gears, with whiffletrees and yoke.

$24.00	$26.50	$28.00	$30.50	$32.50

Price, with box, top box and spring seat.

$35.00	$37.50	$39.00	$41.50	$43.50

AGRICULTURAL IMPLEMENT DEPARTMENT.

Montgomery Ward & Co.'s Duplex Mill With Stand.

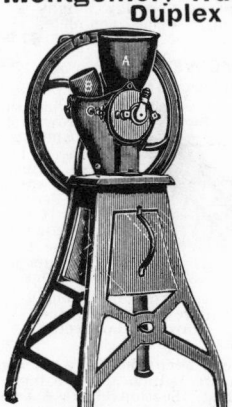

Send for our new special Agricultural Catalogue, containing 225 pages of the most desirable farm implements and machinery. One of the most complete catalogues of its kind. Postage, 4 cents.
70302 Weight, 50 lbs. without stand....$4.80
70303 Same as above on stand wt.105lbs.$7.25
Shells corn and grinds all kinds of grain.
Where a corn sheller and a family grist mill are both required it is much better to have them combined in one machine. The corn sheller is better because the shelled corn can not scatter and the balance wheel makes it more efficient. If mounted on bench or table, make opening at least 3 inches long or cobs will not discharge. We recommend our customers to buy these mills mounted on stand. All grinding and bone mills are shipped second-class freight.

Dump Cart.

Shipped 1st class.

70065.	WITH WOOD AXLE.		
Number	74.	76.	78.
Size of Skeins	2¾x8½	3x9	3¼x10
Size of Tire	1½x½	1½x-⅝	1⅝x-⅝
Capacity, pounds	1,000	1,300	1,600
Weight, pounds	445	495	565
Price	$32.50	$35.00	$37.50

Iron axle adds to price $2.50.

M. W. & Co.'s Farm Truck.

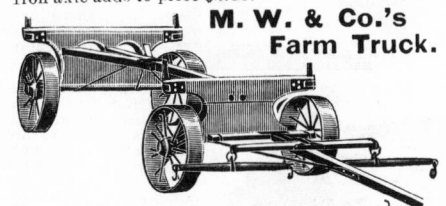

70066 Weight, 750 pounds; capacity, 3 tons.
Price, 24-inch wheels.........................$33.50
Price, 30-inch wheels......................... 35.50
Price, 36-inch wheels........ .... 37.50
The wheels have 5-inch tires; the hub bearings are chilled and are 7½ inches long; hubs have inside and outside sand bands and are fastened on axle with collar and split pin; the axles are solid two-inch stock and turned tapering to fit the hole in the hub: the bolster and bunks are 2¾ inches thick and faced on the top with heavy band iron; the stakes are round and are 2¼ inches in diameter, are removable instantly. When 36-inch wheels are used furnish bolsters of regular width; wheels do not run under bolster.

Our Scoop Board.

70079 The simplest, best, cheapest and strongest board made; used for corn, potatoes, turnips, cobs, etc.; wood bottom, steel sides, iron braces and supports. Weight, 45 lbs.
Price $2.00

Tornado Tank Pump.

For Steam Thresher Use. 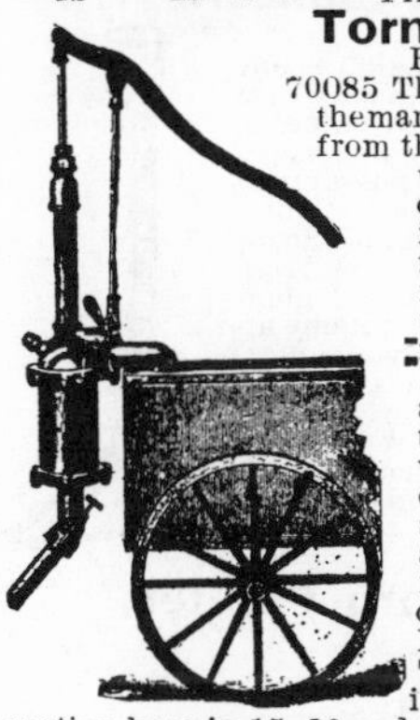
70085 This is the only tank pump in the market that has a tight discharge from the cylinder to the tank, and with a shut-off valve in this discharge to close when using the pump to wash out or fill the boiler with or transfering water from one tank to another. Also has a clevis for the 2-inch suction hose. It can also be taken entirely apart, even to the bucket in the cylinder and shut off valve and repacked with one common wrench. It is a strong, simply constructed and easy working pump for raising and forcing large quantities of water quickly. It has important advantages. Tank pump only, as shown in cut, $9.90. 2-inch suction hose in 15, 20 and 25 foot length, per foot, 45c ; 1-inch discharge hose, per foot, 12c.. Brass couplings and nozzle to screw on, for discharge hose, 50c. Strainer for 2-inch suction, hose, 65c. 1-inch discharge hose is used in case of fire.

Montgomery Ward & Co.'s Triple Bone Mill, Grain Mill and Corn Sheller Combined

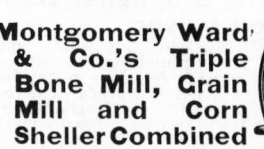

Will not grind green bones.

Triplex Mill.
70304 Shells corn, grinds all kinds of grain, and grinds dry bones and oyster shells for chickens
Mounted on stand same as 70303, wt. 112 lbs $8.95
70305 Same mill without stand, wt. 65 lbs....... 6.50
This mill has three hoppers; one B to shell corn; one A for shelled corn or any other kind of grain, and one C for dry bones or oyster shells. A family grist mill and bone grinder on legs; a corn sheller separate would cost $13.30. We here have them all in one machine on stand for $8.95 or for $7.25 without the bone grinder attachment.

Any information as to weights, shipping facilities, of freight and Express rates will be promptly furnished

Wilson's Hand Bone Mill No. 1.

70308 We have sold thousands of these mills and our customers speak only their praise.
The teeth of a bone mill are strong and coarse and will not grind grain for family use.
Allow fresh bones to dry before grinding. Will not grind green bones. Weight, 35 lbs. Our price, each..$4.00

70310 Wilson's Patent Bone Mill. No. 1, same as above, but with iron legs; weight, 65 lbs.
Price, each........$5.85
70311 No. IXL Bone Mill, weight, 30 lbs. A little lighter and easier to handle than No. 1. Grinds dry oyster shells and dry bones perfectly.
Price..............$3.60

I X L Bone Mill.

Mann's Bone Cutter.

These mills are bone planers or cutters. Will cut perfectly green bones as they come from the butcher; prepares butchers' refuse perfectly as food for poultry.
70313 Mann's No. 2 mill, weight, 140 pounds $16.50
70315 Mann's No. 6 mill, weight, 100 pounds. $16.00

No. 2 Stand.      No. 6 Post.

Our Family Grist Mill.

70316 If you own one of these mills you can have at all times fresh graham flour, fresh corn meal, fresh hominy, split peas, cracked wheat, fine table or butter salt. In fact, everything that is ground at a custom mill except fine bolted family flour.
The grinding surfaces are of a very hard material, especially made for this purpose, and are ground off perfectly true on emery wheels and will last for years. Burrs, 4½ in. diameter.
This is the same mill as is combined with our grinder and sheller No. 70302-5.
Every one guaranteed to work as represented.
Will not grind bones.
Weight, 30 lbs. Price, each.............$3.80
Burrs, per pair, Weight, 1 lb.................... 75

Oriole Farm Grist Mill No. 2½.

Shipped second-class freight.

70320 Weight, 150 lbs. Can be run with one or two horse power. For grinding corn, fine corn meal and graham flour for table use. It is made in the most durable way possible, runs easy and has an automatic feed.
This mill will grind from 5 to 8 bushels per hour. One set of burrs will grind 2,000 bushels of grain before they are worn out. They can be replaced for $1.25. Speed of this mill is about 800 revolutions per minute. Size of pulley, 8 in.; diameter of burrs, 7 in. An extra set of burrs furnished with each mill free of charge. Does not grind bones. Price.................. ....$20.00
Burrs, per set 1.25
70322 No. 3 Farm and Bone Mill combined. Similar in appearance to No. 2½ above. See large cut in Agricultural Implement Catalogue. Will grind green bones direct from butcher, dry bones, greasy bones, corn and cob and grain. Capacity on bones from 500 to 1,000 lbs. per day. Capacity on grain from 5 to 12 bushels per hour. Weight, 300 lbs Price.....$ 45.00 Burrs, per set..... 1.25

Daisy Bone Cutter.

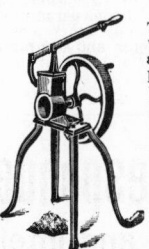

70324 Knives operate like a common wood hand-plane; except that they are notched and cut bone into small pieces. The knives can be taken out when dull, sharpened and replaced in a few minutes. A large or small bone can be cut up at once. Very little pressure on the lever is required. The cutter is always ready for work. Turns easy, cuts fine and fast. Is simple in construction; nothing to get out of order. Can be turned by hand or power, by running a belt on hand wheel. Capacity by hand, ½ lb. per minute; by power, about 60 lbs. per hour.
Weight. 140 lbs.
Price, with stand...$15.00 Without stand .. $13.00

The Little Giant Green Bone Cutter.

FOR HAND POWER ONLY.

Weight, with stand, 66 pounds. Price........$9.00
Weight, without stand, 36 pounds. Price.....7.00
Height, 45 inches. Capacity, 30 pounds per hour.
70326 This mill is adapted expressly for poultrymen and farmers, and is so low in price that anybody having use for one can easily afford to get it.

BIG GIANT.

Improved Grinding Mills.

All mills shipped second-class freight.

A mill with the greatest capacity and most even grinding of all kinds of grain ever offered to the farmer. Automatic in feeding, simple in construction, scientific in principle, looked upon by feeders as the gem of all grinders; requires from 2 to 10 horse power, according to size and speed.
70344 The No. 1 size Belt Mill, 5¾ in. burrs; capacity, 10 to 20 bushels per hour; weight, 175 pounds. Price, burrs, $1.00 per set. Mill......$20.75

70346 The No. 2 size, 5¾ inch burrs, geared for attachment to tumble rod; capacity, 10 to 20 bushels per hour; weight, 225 pounds. Price, burrs, $1.00 per set. Price of Mill.....$23.75
70348 The No. 3 size Belt Mill, 7¼ inch burrs; weight, 290 pounds, capacity, 20 to 30 bushels per hour. Price, burrs, $1.25 per set. Mill....$30.00
70352 The No. 4 size, geared for attaching to tumbling rod; 7¼ inch burrs; capacity, 20 to 30 bushels per hour; weight, 225 pounds. Price, burrs, per set, $1.25. Mill......32.75
70353 No. 5 Double Belt Mill has just double the capacity of No. 3 belt mill; two sets of 7¼ inch burrs in operation at one time, one on each end of shaft; illustration in Agricultural Catalogue; weight, 300 pounds. Burrs, $1.25 per set. Price......45.50
Nos. 2 and 4 have 12 inch pulley to connect with corn sheller.

Montgomery Ward & Co.'s

Lightning Grinding Mills.

All Grinding Mills second-class freight.
Pulley, 6¼ inches in diameter; 4 inch face.

70354 Is made of iron and steel, has few wearing parts, is not liable to get out of order, will not choke up, will empty without injury to the burrs, which is an important feature. The burrs are so arranged that if nails or any other hard substance gets in the grain they will pass through without breaking the mill. Grinds all kinds of grain; makes the best cornmeal or graham flour. Will grind from 6 to 15 bushels per hour if run from 600 to 1,200 revolutions per minute. Can be run by geared windmills or any other power. The burrs are 5½ inches in diameter and accurately fitted. Price of mill with extra set of burrs...$17.50
Extra burrs, per set of 2......75
Weight, 90 pounds.

Grinding Mills—Continued.

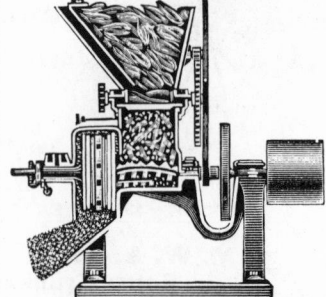

70354½ The Kelly Duplex Grinding Mill. See description in our Agricultural Catalogue B. Particularly recommended for grinding shuck corn, as well as corn in the ear and all kinds of small grain. Prices named on application.

70356 Corn and Cob Mill; will grind corn and cob, oats, barley, wheat, screenings, etc. Has removable grinding rings which can be replaced for $4.00, when first set is worn out. Weight, 410 lbs. Is intended for grinding feed only. Price......$19.00
Cast Burrs, extra, per pair......$4.00

Corn Planters.

Shipped first-class freight.

70357 Champion Hand Corn Planter; has pumpkin seed attachment. Glass slide shows just how many kernels are ready to drop in next hill. Every miss hill can be avoided; no blank hill with this planter; weight, 4½ lbs. Price......$1.50

The "Chatauqua" Corn, Bean and Seed Planter.

70358 We believe one of the best hand corn, bean and seed planters. The cuts explain its operation. It is guaranteed to do good work. Automatic. The simple act of stepping forward from this position will plant the seed without any attention on your part. Weight, 4½ lbs.
Price, each.. ...$1.25
70359 The well known Eagle corn planter, with extra revolving disks. Price .each......$1.25

Triumph Corn Planter.

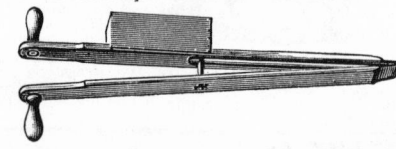

70360 Kent's Patent Triumph Hand Corn Planter; can be used on sod or plowed ground. Weight, 4½ lbs. Price, each......$0.75

The Little Giant Broadcast Hand Seed Sower.

70361 With this seeder, when properly used, you can distribute wheat 56 feet to a round, flaxseed 36 feet, clover seed 36 feet, timothy 27 feet, oats 36 feet. It will also sow rye, barley, millet, Hungarian corn, or any grain or seed that can be sown broadcast. This seeder has a light centrifugal wheel at the bottom, 11 inches in diameter, that is revolved rapidly in opposite directions by means of a bow, scattering the seed with great velocity. Weight 3 pounds. Price, each......$1.50

The Niagara Broadcast Seeder.

Shipped first-class freight.
A Positive Force Feed.

70362 The "Niagara" combines all the latest improvements in sowers. The machine is attached to an end gate that fits any wagon. Attach sprocket to left hind wheel, put on link chain and go ahead. Save grain and seed by sowing it evenly. Time is money. Early seeding is what tells. Don't spend your time with the old style seeder when four times the amount of seed can be evenly distributed with the "NIAGARA." Weight, 125 lbs. Price......$9.00

The New Five-Hoe One-Box Grain Drill.

70363 The New Five-Hoe One-Box Grain Drill. Used principally for drilling between corn rows, or putting in grain with one horse. Part of the holes can be stopped, which makes it an excellent corn, bean or pea drill; also for beets and other coarse seed. Weight, 140 lbs. Price $14.00

The Granger Seeder.

All seeders shipped first-class freight.

70364 The Granger Broadcast Hand Seeder, for sowing all kinds of grain and grass seed; sows on an average of 6 acres per hour at a common walking gait. The bag and hopper will hold about 22 quarts. Weight, 5½ pounds. Price......$3.25
70364½ The Improved Calhoun Broadcast Hand Seeder; weight, 5½ pounds (retail price, $5.00). Our price, each..$3.00

The Cyclone Hand Seeder.

70365 This is somewhat simpler and cheaper made than the Granger, but works on the same general plan. It will sow with ease to the operator 60 acres of grain or grass seed per day. Has a shake feed, and sows perfectly accurate. Weight, 4 lbs. Price $2.25

70366 Wheel barrow Clover and Grass Seeder
The box is 14 feet long and is carried so close to the ground that the wind has no effect on the seed; 20 to 30 acres can be sown per day; weighs 40 pounds and runs light. Price, complete, clover and grass seeder......$7.00

Harrows.

Shipped second-class freight.

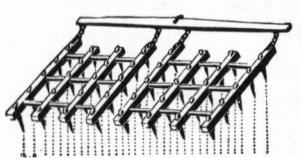

We sell a fine line of harrows, both wood and steel frames, with ridged, adjustable and spring teeth. See our Agricultural Implement Catalogue for descriptions and illustrations.
70368 Three Section Vibrating Harrow, oak beams and spools, 45 half inch square steel teeth; nine beams in three sections. Draw bar connected with chains.
We furnish extra teeth to either of the above harrows at 3½ cents each. Teeth are ½-inch steel, 9 inches long; no other size furnished. Sections have 4 bars, 20 teeth to a section.

		Feet.	Weight.	Price.
A 194, 1 section, 20 teeth, cuts.		3½	50 lbs.	$ 2.50
A 195, 2 sections, 40 teeth, cuts.		7	100 lbs.	5.00
A 196, 3 sections, 60 teeth, cuts.		10½	150 lbs.	7.50
A 197, 4 sections, 80 teeth, cuts.		14	200 lbs.	10.00

We Invite Correspondence On any business subject, and will try to answer all inquiries promptly and intelligently, as we employ a large and experienced force of correspondents for this purpose.

Our Adjustable Frame Lever Harrow.

The rails are made of channel steel, very light and very strong. The teeth can be easily taken out to change the teeth or reverse them, but cannot come out in ordinary use. This harrow has bars passing on the under side of the beams, which makes it very strong and forms a truss that makes the frame rigid.

Teeth can be set slanting at any angle or perpendicular, as desired, and can be reversed.

Three sections to any one of our harrows costs one-half more than two sections. Four sections cost twice as much as two sections. Drawbar furnished to match number of sections ordered.

	Feet.	Weight.	Price.
A 186, 1 section, 32 teeth, cuts	5	100 lbs.	$ 4.25
A 187, 2 sections, 64 teeth, cuts	10	200 lbs.	8.50
A 188, 3 sections, 96 teeth, cuts	15	300 lbs.	12.75
A 189, 4 sections, 20 teeth, cuts	20	400 lbs.	17.00

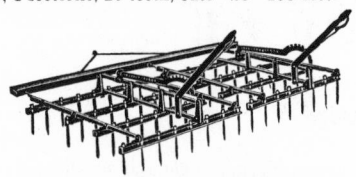

Safety Spring Flexible Frame Lever Harrow.

Shipped second-class freight.

70371 The teeth to this harrow can be set at any angle. By means of the safety springs, however, the teeth will give back to clear roots, stones and other obstructions.

This harrow can be changed so as to dispense with the spring when occasion requires, and then operates precisely like No. 70369. To do this a pin is changed from hold in front of casting to hole through the casting, thus giving the operator both styles of harrows.

	Feet.	Weight.	Price.
A 183, 1 section, 32 teeth, cuts	5	105 lbs.	$ 4.75
A 184, 2 sections, 64 teeth, cuts	10	210 lbs.	9.50
A 185, 3 sections, 96 teeth, cuts	15	315 lbs.	14.25
A 185½. 4 sect's, 128 teeth, cuts	20	425 lbs.	19.00

70372 Our Disk Harrows are made to turn to or from the center; can be spread to cultivate corn. Seeder box for sowing grain attached if desired, but must be ordered with harrow.

Shipped second-class.   Price.
No. 36, 12—16-inches disks, cut 6 feet; weight, 350 lbs............................$20.00
No. 37, 14—16-inch disks, cut 7 feet; weight, 400 lbs............. 22.00
No. 38. 16—16-inch disks, cut 8½ feet; weight, 425 lbs............. 25.00
No. 39, 12—20-inch disks, cut 6½ feet; weight, 400 lbs............. 22.00

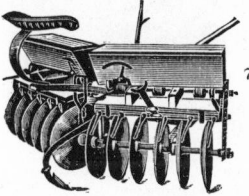

70373 Combined Disk Harrow and Broadcast Seeders.

12—16-inch disks, cuts 6½ feet.................$36.50
12—20-inch disks, cuts 6½ feet................. 38.50

70374 Spring Tooth Harrow, practically adapted to stony and stumpy ground or tough sod. The spring tooth will cultivate the ground thoroughly. Now furnished with steel frame in place of wood. Average weight, 200 lbs.
16 Tooth.............$11.50 | 20 Tooth.........$14.50
18 Tooth............. 12.50 | 24 Tooth......... 17.00
For description and price of iron frame and lever spring tooth harrows, see our Agricultural Catalogue.

Field Rollers.

Second-class freight.

70376 The Sherwin Field Roller, made of solid butt-cut white oak logs; weight is in the rolls, not in the box, to bring extra strain on the bearings: turns as easily as a wagon; each roll acts independently.
2-horse, 8½ ft., weight, 1,500. Price $20.00
$5.00 less where parties furnish their own log rollers

70378 Star Section Land Roller, iron disks for the ends, around which are bolted heavy oak staves; draft low, direct from heavy iron shaft on which roller revolves; 7½ ft. long, 30 inches in diameter; weight, 750 lbs. Each..$17.00
70380 Star flexible, three sections, land roller, constructed like 70378, but mounted like 70376. Price................ .... 22.00
Grass Seed Attachment, extra.... .... 6.00

The "Planet, Jr.," Combined Hill Dropping and Fertilizer Drill and Corn and Bean Planter.

Planters, drills and hand cultivators, first-class freight.

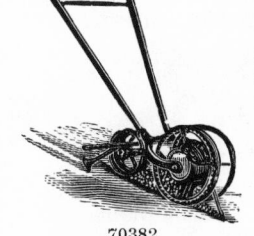

70381 This implement will drop any kind of seed neatly in hills 4, 6, 8 or 12 inches apart; distance easily regulated. The fertilizer attachment holds one peck and deposits the fertilizer either above or below the seed, as desired. Weight, 40 lbs. Price Planet Hill Dropper.....$ 8.20
With Fertilizing Attachment................... 11.20

70382 The Planet Jr., No. 2 Seed Drill. Can be regulated to plant any kind of garden seed; weight, 40 lbs.; sows seeds only, does not cultivate.
Price..... ....$5.90

70384 The Planet, Jr., Combined Drill, Wheel Hoe, Cultivator, Rake and Plow. This implement combines a complete set of easy working garden tools and no one raising a garden crop should be without one of them; weight, 46 pounds. Both sows and cultivates.
Price.....$7.70

70382

70385 The Planet Jr., Double Wheel Hoe, Cultivator, Rake and Plow combined; consists of one pair of curved point hoes, 1 pair of rakes, 1 pair of plows, 1 pair of 4-inch sweeps, 1 pair of cultivator teeth, 1 pair of detachable leaf guards; weighs 35 pounds. Cultivator only, does not sow seed.
Price........................$5.30

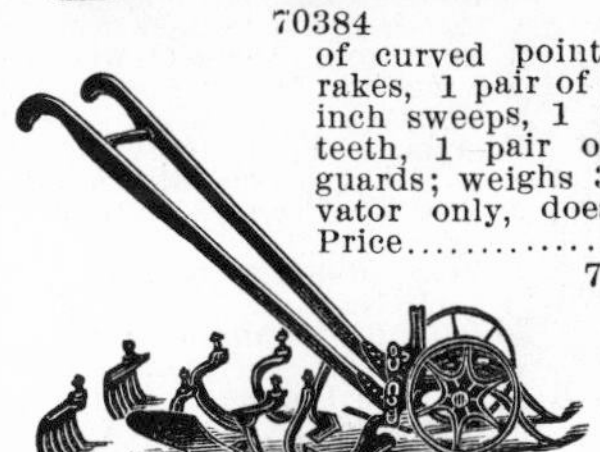

70384

70387 The Planet, Jr., Double Wheel Hoe, no attachments, but one pair of hoes. Weight 24 lbs.
Price........$3.20

70388 The Planet, Jr., Single Wheel Hoe Cultivator, Rake and Plow combined, consisting of 2 pairs of curved hoes, 1 pair of rakes, 1 pair of 4-inch unequal sided sweeps, 1 broad cultivating tooth, 1 large garden plow, 1 detachable leaf guard. Weight, 26 lbs.
Each.....$4.10

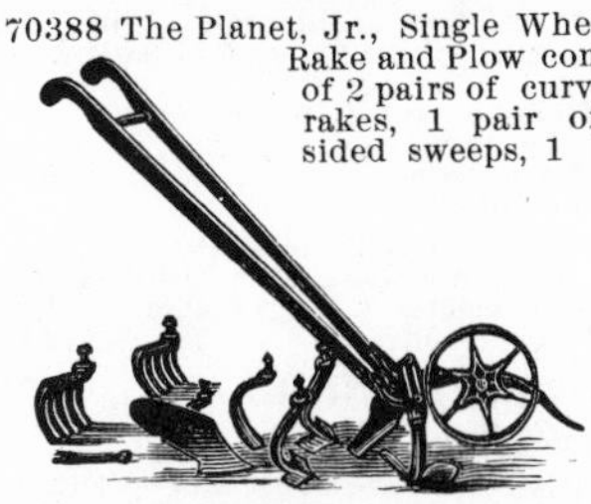

70388

The "Fire Fly" Single Wheel Hoe, Cultivator and Plow Combined.

70389 This convenient tool has rapidly convinced gardeners of its high merits. It combines lightness and strength with great adjustability, while its highly polished and tempered tools make gardening comparatively a pleasure. The tools are all made after the most perfect models and are: First, a pair of admirable hoes, which can be set to work to and from the row, and to any desired depth. Next, a set of three reversible cultivator teeth, to be used together or singly, or in conjunction with the hoes. Third, a large excellent garden plow. The whole tool is light and strong, attractive in appearance, and capable of standing hard usage for years, while the price is its final recommendation. Weight, 22 lbs. Price........................$3.50

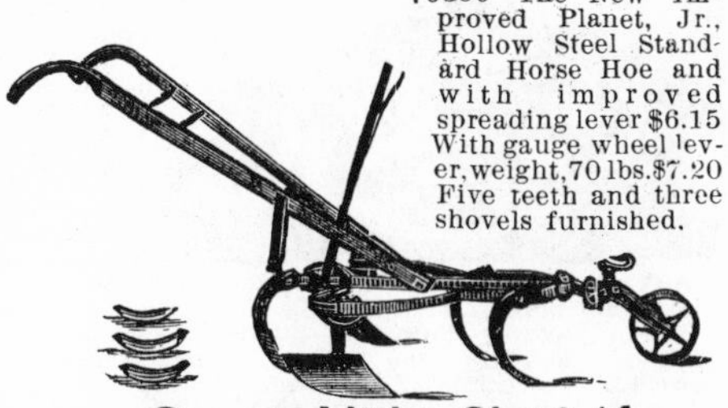

70390 The New Improved Planet, Jr., Hollow Steel Standard and Horse Hoe and with improved spreading lever $6.15 With gauge wheel lever, weight, 70 lbs. $7.20 Five teeth and three shovels furnished.

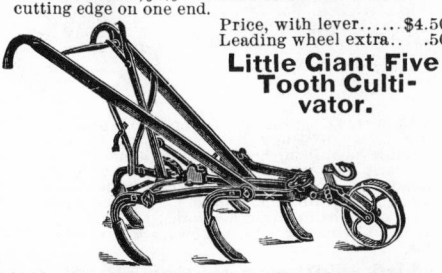

Little Giant 14-Tooth Harrow.

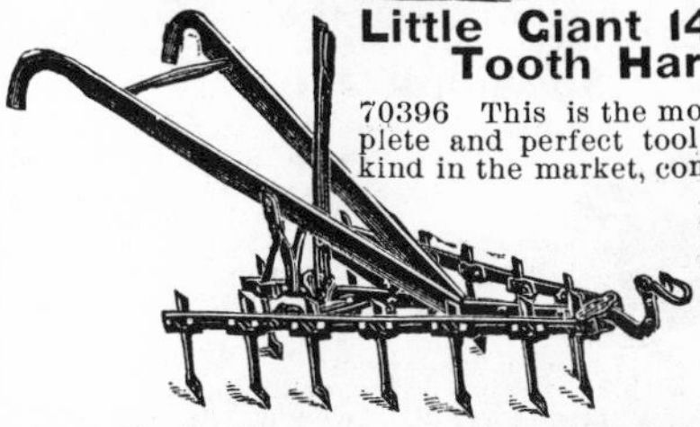

70396 This is the most complete and perfect tool of the kind in the market, combining as it does a field cultivator, garden harrow and pulverizer. The teeth are so arranged that one end is the cultivator and pulverizer, while the other end is the harrow. By a very simple device, the slant of the teeth can be changed so that the tool can be made a perfect smoothing harrow. It has fourteen ⅝x⅞ diamond teeth drawn to a cutting edge on one end.

Price, with lever......$4.50
Leading wheel extra.. .50

Little Giant Five Tooth Cultivator.

70398 This cultivator has all the latest improvements, and is the best and most perfect shaped cultivator made, provided with a lever for changing the width of its cut instantly and easily while the tool is at work. It can be expanded from 8 inches to over 2 feet. Price, complete with wheel and lever. Weight, about 70 lbs. $4.25. Without wheel, 3.75. Plain, without wheel or lever 3.00
Illustrations of above cultivators shown in our Agricultural Catalogue.

Horse Powers.

Shipped first-class freight.

When ordering machinery to be run by horse power state the number of revolutions the tumbling rod makes to one turn of the horses, and whether the rod turns against or with the team; also size of hole in coupling.

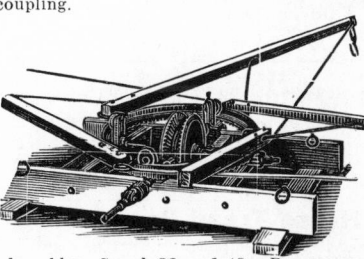

70400—The New Deal Horse-Power, complete with 4 levers and one long and one short tumbling rod with knuckles. Speed, 32 and 10. Power can be taken from fast or slow motion: weight, 1100 pounds. Price................................$35.00
70402 The New Deal 2-Horse Power, same in construction as the 4-horse power, but lighter. Has two sweeps, two lead poles, one long and one short tumbling rod, with couplings; weight, 800 pounds Speed, 33 to 10. Price................$26.00

70404 One-Horse Power, for churning, pumping water, grinding feed, shelling corn, etc., one 9 and one 5 foot length of tumbling rod, 24 revolutions to one turn of the horse; weight, 400 pounds. Price $18.00

Horse Powers—Continued.

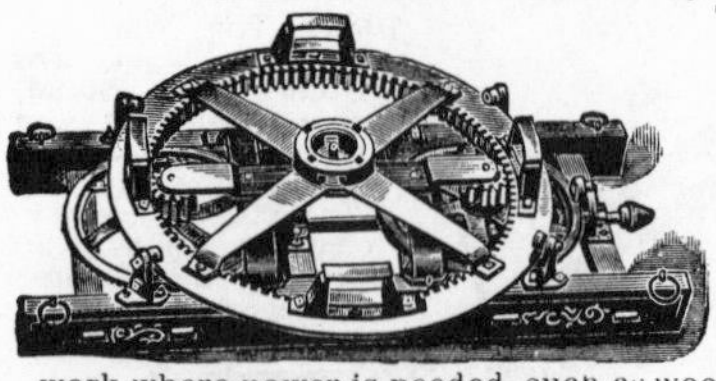

70406 The Carey Pitts Horse Power, for 2, 4 or 6 horses; is strong enough for 8 horses. This power is especially adapted for farm work where power is needed, such as wood sawing, cider making, feed cutting and grinding. Weight of power 1,500 lbs., number of revolutions, 52, and 80 to one turn of horses. Four sweeps. Two tumbling rods and 3 couplings go with each power. Main wheel, 4 feet in diameter. Price..................................$47.00

Speeding Jacks.

Shipped first-class.

70408 Bevel Jacks, used only in connection with a horse power to increase the speed. Is connected to end of tumbling rod, and transmits motion in the same direction. Furnished with 15-inch pulley, made in one size. For 2 or 4 horse-power only; weight, 100 lbs....$9.00

70409 Spur Jack; transmits motion at right angles to the tumbling rod to which it is attached. For two or four horse-power only; weight, 100 lbs.......$9.00

70410 Bevel Speeding Jack for 4 to 8 horse power; iron frame, bearings all on one casting, a strong durable jack, furnished with slip knuckle; particularly recommended for four to eight horses. Geared 2¾ to one turn of tumbling rod; any sized pulley furnished up to 24 inches; state size of hole in coupling wanted. This jack adapted to our Cary Pitts Power; weight, 185 lbs. Price..................................12.00

Link-Belt Box Water Elevator.

Shipped third-class.

70411 For irrigation, greatest possible amount of water elevated for power expended. If you intend to purchase, see description and large illustration in our Agricultural Catalogue (B).

No. Elevator	Gallons per minute.	Stm. H.P. for 10 foot lift.	Price of Elevator Complete with Wood Work but without Driving Machinery or Connections.					Weight, per foot.
			10 ft.	15 ft.	20 ft.	25 ft.	30 ft.	
B	600	2	For wood and iron work.					53lbs.
			$48.00	$55.00	$62.00	$69.00	$76.00	
			Iron work alone.					23
			$40.00	46.00	52.00	58.00	64.00	
E	1,100	3½	For wood and iron work.					75
			$79.00	84.00	99.00	110.00	119.00	
			Iron work alone.					65
			$67.00	75.00	85.00	92.00	100.00	

Horse Tread Powers.

70412 Tread Powers, complete. Illustrations appear in our Agricultural Catalogue.
One horse, weight, 1,200.....................$75.00
Two horse, weight, 2,200.......................87.00
Three horse, weight, 3,600...................115.00
Four horse, weight, 4,200....................205.00

Indiana Sawing Machine.

70413 This machine is sold at a low price, and is an efficient and easy running implement. Furnished with the very best Disston Champion Tooth Saw. Has all the advantages of any hand power cross cut saw made. The uncomfortable bent position when sawing in the usual way is overcome, and a natural upright position secured, enabling the full force and weight of the body to be thrown on the saw. Weight, 44 lbs. Price, with one 5-foot saw.......................$7.50

Circular Sawing Machine.

Shipped first-class

70414—All of our different styles are illustrated in our Agricultural Implement Catalogue by large cuts. As customers often want different sizes of saws we quote price of saw tables separately. Swing Table Saw Frame complete, with 85 lbs. balance wheel.....$17.00 Weight 275 lbs.
Swing Table Saw Frame, with 85 lbs. balance wheel.......................................$16.00
Sliding Table Saw Frame, with hood.........17.50
Pole Table Balance Wheel and Counter Shaft below table...22.00
125 lb. Balance wheel in place of 85 lbs. adds to price..1.50
Saw arbor is fitted to saw with 1⅜ inch hole. Total length of shaft 4 ft. 4in; between saw and balance wheel, 3 ft. 6 inches.
70415 Best quality of circular saws fitted to above frames. 20 inch $4.68
22 inch 5.50
24 inch 6.60
26 inch 7.75
28 inch 8.80
30 inch 9.90
Same must be filed according to our directions or warrantee does not hold.
70416 Saw mandrel alone, with pulley, balance wheel and two boxes, where parties desire to construct their own frames. Weight, 170 lbs.$10.00
Balance wheels alone, made to order, keyed and fitted, per lb......................................05

Drag Saw Machines.

Shipped second-class.

Our Drag Sawing Machine can be attached to any kind of power or motion, tumbling rod or belt. The self-feed moves carriage with logs any desired distance for sawing stave lengths, cord wood, stave bolts, heading, etc. Can be used with two or four horse power. Capacity of self-feeding machine, 30 to 40 cords of wood per day; one saw sent with each machine. Price to attach to tumbling rod or belt.
70417 Hand feed, weight, 1,050 lbs. Price......$40.00
70418 Self-feed, weight, 1,100 lbs. Price.......56.00
70419 Extra saw for Drag Saw Machine.........5.25
See description and illustrations of our Drag Saws in Agricultural Implement Catalogue.

Improved Cider Mill.

Shipped second-class.

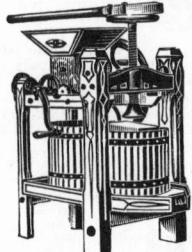

70420 These mills have hard wood frames strongly bolted together. The beams are heavy cast iron; the screws are wrought iron, capable of standing the most severe pressure applied by the lever; have long crushing roller and large crates. Made in three sizes.
Price of Senior, weight, 410 lbs..............$20.50
Price of Medium, weight, 230 lbs.............17.50
Price of Junior, weight, 165 lbs..............13.75

Lard and Wine Presses.

70421 The inside crate is 12½ inches in diameter, and 10 inches deep. The screw is 1¼ inches in diameter, and 18 inches long.
Price. iron beam.............. $7.50
Wood beam.....................6.75
Weight, 75 lbs.
70422 Cider and Cheese Press Screws Cast iron whole length; 4 foot screw, 3¾ diameter. Weight, about 50 lbs. Price, each................$14.00

Fanning Mills.

Shipped K. D., first-class.

"Minnesota Chief" Fanning Mill, shipped knocked down so as to secure a lower rate of freight; just as good a mill as there is made. Made by a well-known manufacturer; 1 wire wheat hurdle (3 sieves), wheat screen, wheat grader, corn and oat sieve and barley sieve.
Identically the same mill, No. 1, is sold by agricultural dealers for $20 00 to $25.00, which we sell for $11.90.
70424 No. 1 Farm Mill, 120 lbs., sieves 24 in. wide, 60 to 90 bushels per hour.................$11.90
70426 No. 2 Farm Mill, 125 lbs., sieves 30 in. wide, 100 to 125 bushels per hour..............15.85
70428 No. 2 Warehouse Mill, 175 lbs., sieves 40 in. wide, 200 to 300 bushels per hour..........34.00
70430 No. 3 Warehouse Mill, sieves 48 in. wide, 300 to 400 bushels per hour..........43.50
For price of grass seed attachments, see our Agricultural Catalogue.

Paint Mills.

Shipped second-class.

70432 Paint Mills for grinding colors in oil.
No. 1 Large power mill with clutch....................$36.00
No. 3 Small power mill...................11.25
No. 4 Medium hand mill..................9.00
No. 5 Small hand mill...7.50

Corn Shellers.

Shipped first-class.

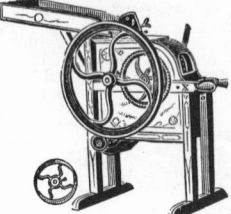

70434 The "Sheller" Valley is the best one-hole corn sheller in the market. Has the largest balance wheel put upon any sheller, being 27 inches in diameter and weighing 35 lbs.; is a right hand sheller with end delivery. One-Hole Sheller, with fan and feed table. Right hand sheller. Weight, 150 lbs. Price..................$5.40
Pulley, extra, 50c.
70436 Hocking Valley Two Hole Sheller, with fan, feed table and pulley. Weight, 225 lbs..$15.45
70438 Hocking Valley Two-Hole Sheller, complete with fan, feed table, pulley and cob carrier. Weight, 325 lbs.........................18.75

All Steel Road Scrapers.

Shipped third-class.

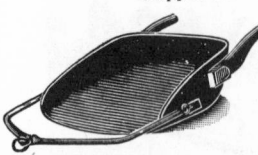

70442 No 1 carries 7 feet of earth; weight, complete, 110 lbs. Price, each..$5.40
70444 No. 2 carries 5½ feet of earth; weight, 100 lbs. Price, each..$4.90
70445 No. 3 carries 4 feet of earth; weight, about 90 lbs.............4.40
All our scrapers are furnished with runners on bottom without charge; these increase durability and ease of hauling.

SEE INDEX

For Sewing Machines

EVERY HOUSEKEEPER

SHOULD HAVE ONE.

Spray Pump--The Advance.

70446 Outfit consisting of pump (barrel not included); 6 feet of hose fitted with couplings and brass spray nozzle. Price.....$11.90 This pump can be attached to any good, sound barrel and the barrel hung on either of our barrel carts and used for spraying plants, shrubbery, vines and trees, washing buggies, watering gardens, lawns, etc. It has an agitator which commences as soon as the pump-handle is worked, preventing the settling of any mixture with which the water is charged.

Shipped first-class. 70447 Combination Barrel and Utility Cart. Weight, 100 lbs. Price, with box and irons for 1 barrel......$6.00 Irons for each additional barrel..... 1.00 Barrels have iron gudgeons bolted to each side. Cart will pick up barrel or body in a moment; change instantaneous. One cart answers for any number of barrels required

Barrel Carts, for use in the garden and for feeding purposes; can be attached to any good sound barrel; one cart required for each barrel used. Height of wheels, 3 ft. axle stubs bolted direct to barrel. Wood or iron frame. Wood wheels and frame probably strongest. Weight, 65 lbs. 70448 Barrel Cart, steel wheels. Price.....$3.25

70449 Barrel Cart, wood wheels. Price.....$3.25

Hand Carts.

70450 36-inch wheels, box 24x36, 10 inches deep. Weight, 85 lbs. Removable end boards, bent handles, iron foot rest, iron hubs, well painted and striped. A first-class job. Very useful about barn, stable or garden. Price.....$5.00

Steel Hand Cart Wheels.

Shipped First-class. 70451 We furnish a pair of light steel wheels suitable for hand cart and other purposes. Tire, 1½ inch, half oval. 38 inches high, to fit 1⅛ axle. Weight, 40 lbs. Price, per pair.....$2.25 70451½ Iron Axles for above wheels. Weight, 15 lbs. 25 cents each.

PLOWS.

We publish a special plow, cultivator and general implement catalogue of nearly 225 pages. Postage, 4 cents. This gives complete illustrations and descriptions of Plows, Cultivators, etc. Right hand plows shipped in every case unless left hand is specially ordered. Whiffletrees and neck yoke and rolling coulter furnished with sulky plows. All Walking Plows set up, shipped first class; K. D., second-class. Coulter and extra share with breaking plows. Our Chilled Plows are of the latest and most improved pattern, and sold at a price that barely pays for handling.

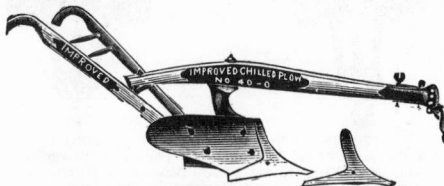

70452 M. W. & Co.'s Full Chilled Plows. In all sections where chilled plows are used, our plows will be readily recognized, and our price on plows and repairs appreciated. See the following prices;

Plows—Continued.

		Turns furrow, inches.	Depth of furrow.	Weight, pounds.	Price.
A	Right	8	4½	50	$3.60
B	Right	10	5	65	4.80
10	Right	11	5½	70	5.25
13	Right or left	11	6	80	6.00
19	Right or left	12	6½	100	6.25
20	Right or left	14	7	112	6.50
E1	Right or left	14	7	125	6.75
40	Right or left	16	9	130	6.75
	Price of jointer				1.50
	Lead wheel and standard				1.00

70453 Price of repairs for the Oliver Chilled Plows, warranted to fit any of the chilled plows we send out. Be sure and state whether plows or shares are wanted to turn furrow to the right or to the left.

	Right.	Standard.	Moldboard.	Lan'side	Shares, plain
A	"	$0.95	$0.95	$0.30	$0.20
B	"	1.13	1.32	45	.20
10	"	1.50	1.50	45	.25
13	Right or left	1.68	1.68	.50	25
19	"	1.68	1.88	.56	25
20	"	1.68	2.10	56	25
E1	"	1.88	2.25	56	25
40	"	1.88	2.25	56	.25

Jointer Points, 15c.   Moldboards, 40c.

70454 Breaking Plow, solid cast steel mold board; share unhardened, but of high natural temper, wood beam furnished with gauge wheel, rolling coulter, patent three-horse adjustable clevis, extra share.

Size, inches	12	14	16
Weight, lbs.	130	148	155
Each	$10.00	11.00	13.00

70455 Sod Breakers, steel beam, 2 shares, 2 fine cutters, gauge iron. 12 in. $5.75; 14 in. $6.00; 16 in. $6.25.

70456 Stubble Plow, wood beam, capped standard welded handle brace, wrought frog and welded bar and hardened land share; beam adjustable for 2 or 3 horses; medium landside. Warranted to scour in any soil.

Size.	Single shin.	Double shin.	Weight.
12 in.	7.00	$8.00	80 lbs.
14 in.	8.00	9.40	90 lbs.
16 in.	9.50	10.50	110 lbs.
18 in.		2.00	125 lbs.

0458 Stubble Plow, steel beam, very strong, will stand the greatest strain without bending and so curved as not to foul, or choke in weedy land; all parts carefully fitted; no chance for it to become rickety: medium landside.

Size.	Single shin.	Double shin.	Weight.
12 in	7.50	8.50	88 lbs.
13 in	8.50	9.50	100 lbs.
14 in	9.00	10.00	105 lbs.
16 in	10.00	11.00	109 lbs.
18 in		12.00	120 lbs.

70460 Brush or Timber Land Plow, also used as a road plow, works well in all kinds of land. Strong and durable, all steel.

11 inch, 83 lbs. ....$7.75 | 13 inch, 100 lbs.....$ 9.00
12 inch, 88 lbs.......8.12 |

Subsoil Plows.

70461 Indispensable for fruit culture and deep cultivation; should be used on every farm. Weight 90 lbs. Cast points.....$8.00

ERRORS.

We make them, but desire to make them right. Should one occur, don't fail to let us know about it.

Light All-Steel Plows.

70463 Designed for either stubble or light sod, doing both kinds of work in the most perfect manner; very light draft; scours in any soil. Is also adapted to the cultivation of corn, cotton, and fruit orchards. This plow does decidedly more work than its width of cut would indicate. Has a curved steel standard and cap, an extra steel share furnished with every one of these plows.

Price.
Pony, 7 inch share, 10½ moldboard, 38 lbs......$3.00
A. O., 8 inch share, 11 moldboard, 42 lbs....... 3.50
B. O., 9 inch share, 12 moldboard, 50 lbs....... 4.25
C. O., 9 inch share, 14 moldboard, 60 lbs....... 5.00
D. O., 9½ inch share, 15½ moldboard, 65 lbs.... 5.50

Sulky Plows.

For illustration of our New Three-Wheel Sulky

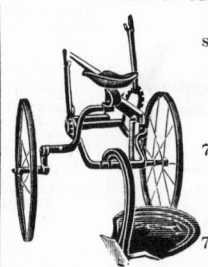

see our special Implement Catalogue for 1895. All wheel plows furnished with rolling coulters, whiffletrees, evener and yoke.
THE OLD NATIONAL TWO WHEEL SULKY.
70464 Has 40 inch steel wheels, 16 inch cutters. New spring lift, land side cut out and no friction in bottom of furrow. Prices: 14 inch 2 wheel sulky, weight, 500 lbs..$30.00
70464½ Plow Sulky, you can plow, wood or steel beam. Price.....$20.00

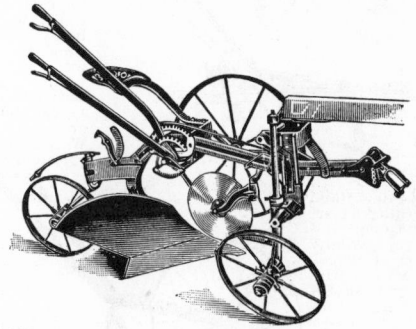

70465 The Plow Boy Three-Wheeled Sulky Plow,
12 inches. Price.....$25.50
14 inches. Price..... 26.50
16 inches. Price..... 27.50
If turf and stubble bottom is wanted it adds $1.00 to the above.
Has all the points of excellence of any three-wheeled plow; turns square corners. Complete with whiffletrees and yoke-steel share and moldboard.

70466 Steel Frame Walking Gang Plow, weight, 300 pounds, turns 27 inches. Price with steel moldboards and shares.....$19.50
With chilled cast moldboards and shares...... 16.00

70470 Shovel Plow, with hinged wings; can be adjusted to suit any width of row. Wood beam, is well made and strongly put together; Weighs, about 65 lbs. Price.....$3.50

70472 Double Shovel Plow, wood beam, weighs 35 lbs. Price.....$2.50

Contractors' Plows.

70473 This is built especially for road and contract work: it is very strong and durable, used by the principal contractors in the United States. Weight, 155 lbs.
Price.................................$10.00

Clipper Potato Digger.

70474 These diggers are put up with three rods on each side, with extra plates attached for two rods, which are sometimes used where the soil is heavy. The depth of digger is regulated by the rod from heel of shoe through end of beam. Weight, 75 lbs. Price.. ...... $7.00

Ditching Plows.

70475 Will loosen the dirt in the bottom of ditch 4ft. deep: use long evener, one horse on each side of ditch.

Dirt after being loosened is thrown out with a hand shovel. Weight, 120 lbs. Price.................$10.00

Cultivators.

All cultivators shipped as first class freight.

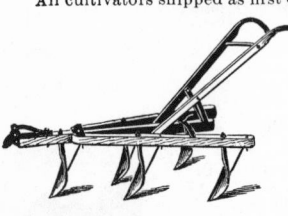

70477 Five tooth cultivator, cast steel teeth; with heavy braced standards: the teeth are reversible and the frame can be expanded or contracted. Weight, 60lbs. Price...$3.00

70479 Hand Cultivator, "Queen of the Garden" steel wheel, wrought iron shafts. With combination shovel moldboard, shovel weeder.

Weight, 28 lbs. Price............ ....$4.00
70480 Dexter Cultivator, similar to Queen, but lighter. Weight, 23 lbs. With all attachments.
Price................................$3.00

70481 Double Standard Tongueless Walking Cultivator; furnished with wood or iron beams as desired; a first class cultivator Weight, 150 pounds. Price....................................$9.50

70482— Our Dandy Steel Beam Cultivator. Has coil spring lift. Weight, 180 lbs. $12.25

Tongueless Cultivators, best pattern, steel beam.
Price..$10 00

Mowers.

Mowers shipped third-class.

70484-- The Advance Iron Mower. Weight, 500 lbs. Price, 4 feet cut, $36.00; 4 ft. 6 in. cut. Weight, 540 lbs.

Price.................................$36.00
70486 Wide Cut Mower, with bar carrying spring. This is a heavier and wider cut machine than above. Pressure of bar on ground relieved by spring. It has many advantages See cut in Agricultural Catalogue; weight, 675 lbs
Price, 4 ft. 6 in cut, $40.00; 5 ft. cut, $42.00; 6 ft. cut, $45.00

The Boss Sickle Grinder.

Shipped as second-class.

70488 The Boss Sickle Grinder, one of the most successful grinders made It costs but little more than an ordinary mounted grindstone and can be used for all grindstone purposes; size of stone, 18 in. diameter, 2¾ thick; weight, 123 lbs. Price..$3.50
70489 Perfection Emery Wheel, sickle grinder, light and handy; weight, 18 lbs. Price.................$3.00
70490 The Well-known Duttor Sickle Grinder, latest pattern. Wgt. 16 lbs $6.00

Hay Rake.

All Hay Rakes and Hay Tedders shipped first-class.

70492 The Revolving Horse Hay Rake, turned head and teeth. Weight, 70 lbs., 18 teeth.

Weight, 80 lbs. Price $4.00

70493 The Reliable Lock Lever Sulky Rake, steel wheels, poles and shafts. 20 teeth, 8 foot wide. Weight, 250 lbs. Price...$13.00
With 24 teeth, 10 feet wide; weight, 275 lbs. Price.... $14.00

70494 The Superior Self Dump Hay Rake, 9ft. Furnished with combination pole and shafts, 20 teeth, 8 feet wide, steel wheel, Price.. $18.00 10 feet wide, with 24 teeth, Price $20.00 Weight, 350 lbs.

Hay Tedder.

04??— The Perfection Hay Tedder. Price, 6 forks, $23.00 Weight, 450 lbs. Price, 8 forks, $28.00 Weight, 500 lbs.

The employees in our Gun Department are all sportsmen of national fame, who know nothing so well as they do sporting goods.

Horse Hay Pitching Apparatus.

Shipped as second-class freight.
No farmer who has ever used the Horse Hay Fork for unloading hay, either in the barn or on the stack, will ever go back to pitching by hand. Those who neglect to adopt it are wasting time and money every year. The best Double Harpoon Fork we sell for 63 cents, and good Pulleys for 15 cents each.

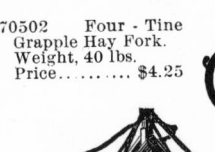

70498 Standard Double Harpoon Hay Fork, all iron and steel and very durable. The best fork in the market; standard size, regular length of tines from cross bar, 25 inches; known and used everywhere; weight, 18 pounds.
Price... ....$0.63
70500 Extra Long Tined Double Harpoon Hay Fork, for loose straw, etc.; longer than needed for hay: tines 32 inches from cross bar. Weight, 20 lbs Price, each............. $1.30

70502   Four - Tine Grapple Hay Fork. Weight, 40 lbs. Price......... $4.25

70504   Six-Tine Grapple Horse Hay Fork. Weight, 55 lbs. Price.....$5.25

70505 Fourteen Tined Combined Hay and Manure Grapple Fork, 8 tines are removable. For handling hay in connection with our stacking outfit. This fork will load or handle manure with the greatest facility. Weight, 87 lbs. Price $9.25

Harpoon Hay Forks.

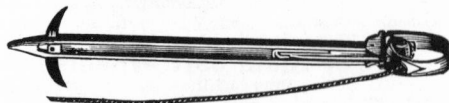

70506   The improved Single Harpoon Hay Fork. Weight, 7 lbs.   Price.....................$1.75

The Milwaukee Improved Reversible and Double Swivel Wood Track Hay Carriers.

All hay tools shipped as second class freight.
These carriers will run on 4x4 or 3x4 or 2x4 track, and will work either way from the stop without change —as it will pass the stop to right or left as well.

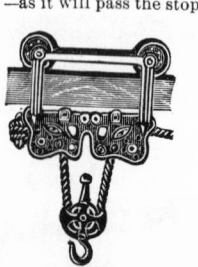

70508   70510
70508 Is reversed by threading the rope through and attaching horse to the other end of rope. Milwaukee Improved Reversible Hay Carrier. Weight, 27 lbs.......... ....$3.00
70510 Leader Double Swivel Hay Carrier, is reversed by merely swinging the pulleys around, leaving fork and horse attached. Weight, 30 lbs. Price........ .... 3.50

Leader Rod or Cable Hay Carrier.

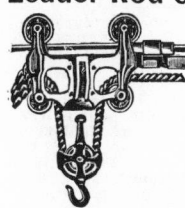

70512 Rod or Cable Track. This carrier is perfectly simple in its construction and will work either way from the stop without changing on the track; the only carrier that will do this on rod and cable, in the barn or on the stack. It is strong, well made. Weight, 20 lbs.
Each..............................$3.00
70513 Trip Pulley with either of above carriers furnished free. Ordered separate..........$0.75

Sling Pulley.

70514 To be used with our new leader double swivel wood track or cable track carrier, with our Standard wagon sling. Weight, 10 lbs.
Price, for pulley only................$2.00

Standard Wagon Sling.

70516 Used in connection with sling pulley in place of horse hay fork. Weight, 12 lbs.
Price, each..........................$2.25
Two of these slings remove a load in two parts, one sling being placed on bottom of wagon and the other in the middle of the load. Many use three slings and hoist the load in three divisions.

Hay Sling Trip Locks.

70518 Which unite the two parts of the slings in the center. Pull the trip and the sling divides in the middle. If you wish to make your own slings order these trip locks. Weight, 1 lb.
Price, each..........................$0.75

Barn and Stack Hay Pitching Outfit.

For the harvest of '93 and '94 we sold hundreds of hay pitching outfits which work equally well in the barn or in the field. Only one set need be bought for both purposes. We offer the combined outfit for a less price than either has been sold singly. Our apparatus can be put up in barn or field much quicker and works as effectually as any made. Hay can be stacked beside the barn when the barn is empty in midwinter, the apparatus can be put up part in the barn and part over stack and barn refilled. This is a most ingenious invention and has a wide range of usefulness. Illustrations shown in our special Agricultural Catalogue.

For barn, two pieces 2x6 plank, 2½ ft. long, spiked to rafters on far side, with holes for tension hooks on which to hang cable, are required.

For stack, four poles 24 to 30 ft. long, with holes 6 inches from end for tension hooks on which to string cable. Fence posts set slanting in the ground make good end stakes.

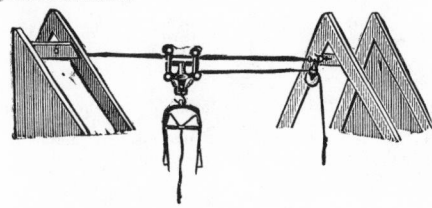

Parts required for hay pitching apparatus for barn using cable up to 50 feet in length.
70519 50 ft. cable with clamps and
eye-bolts, ready to hang..............$2.08
5 knot passing pulleys..........25c. each 1.25
120 ft ¾ manilla rope......... 2c. per ft. 2.40
75 ft. check rope.........................40
1 Double harpoon hay fork.................63
1 Cable carrier........................3.50
6 Floor hooks............................42
Hanging hooks, rafter irons, cords,
rings and eyes...........................30
                                       _____
                                       $10.98

Hay Carrier at work in the field on wire cable derrick

Parts required for *stack*, using 50 ft. of cable.
70520 50 ft. of cable, clamps and eye-
bolts, ready to hang..................$2.08
2 knot passing pulleys........25c. each .50
120 ft. ¾ manilla rope........ 2c. per ft. 2.40
75 ft. check rope.........................40
1 Double harpoon fork.....................63
1 Cable carrier........................3.50
2-50 ft. guys, loops and clamps......2.47
Complete stacking outfit furnished
entire as above........................11.98

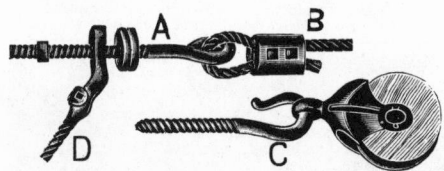

A- Is the tension eye-bolt with nut and washers at-

tached to cross plank on rafters in barn, or to the top of sheer poles when stacking. Price 20c.
B—Is the cable on which the carrier runs, used both in barn and over stack. Clamp B alone, 20c.
C— Is hook and pulley fastened to timbers near to A
D—Is one end of two 50-foot cable guys and clamps, which extend from the top of the sheer poles outward to ground. Castings and clamp D alone, 10c.
Cable is all cut to 50-foot lengths or longer; no deduction for shorter lengths.

Rafter Irons, Etc.

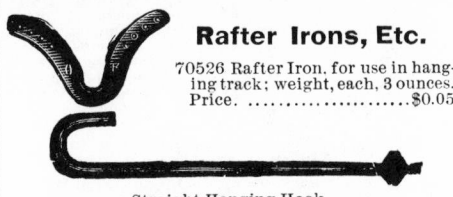

70526 Rafter Iron, for use in hanging track; weight, each, 3 ounces.
Price. $0.05

Straight Hanging Hook.
70527 Straight Hanging Hook.............$0.05
Above two parts used in barns having no ridge pole.

70528 Jointed Hanging Hook, for use in hanging track in barn with ridge poles. Each.........$0.10
Weight, each, 1½ pounds.

70530 Floor Hook, for screwing into the floor or beams for holding pulleys. Weight, 1½ pounds. Each..........$0.07

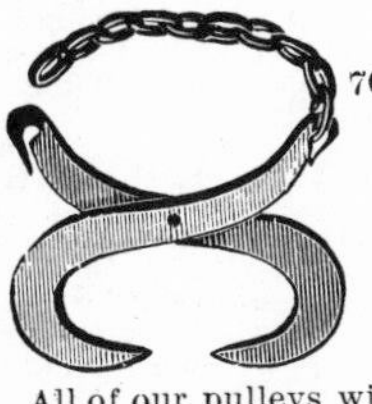

Grapple Hook.

70532 Solid Steel Grapple Hook, for hooking over rafter or beam where holes cannot be bored, for use in holding pulleys. Weight, 4½ pounds.
Each......................$0.75

Hay Fork Pulleys.

All of our pulleys will take 1-inch rope. We, however, recommend ¾ as being more pliable, more durable and better adapted to the purpose; 100 feet of ¾-inch manilla rope weighs 17 pounds.

Pulleys.

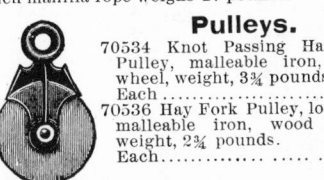

70534 Knot Passing Hay Fork Pulley, malleable iron, wood wheel, weight, 3¾ pounds.
Each........................$0.25
70536 Hay Fork Pulley, loose pin, malleable iron, wood wheel; weight, 2¾ pounds.
Each........................$0.15

70538 All Iron Pulleys, iron wheels or shives; weight, 4 pounds.
Each.......................$0.25
70540 Hay Fork Pulley, self-oiler, wood shell and wheel, wrought iron strap and steel swivel hook or eye.
Weight, 2¾ pounds.
Each.......................$0.25

Snatch Pulley Block.

70541 Snatch Pulley Block. This device shortens the travel of the horse without reducing the elevating power. Tie a knot in the rope so that when the hay is going up the horse has a direct pull, but when the carrier is unlocked and the hay begins to move along the track the rope doubles around the snatch pulley attached to the whiffletree; you will see that the horse travels only one-half of the distance the hay is carried, a great saving; also the rope can be thrown off of the snatch pulley and *fork be instantly returned to the load* without waiting for the return of the horse. Thus, when the horse pulls direct on the rope, the rope takes up just as far as the horse travels. But when the rope doubles around the pulley the rope takes up just double the distance the horse walks. Very useful where long track or cable is used, or where room to move horse is limited. Weight, 5 pounds.
Price...........................$0.60

Pulley Blocks—Continued.

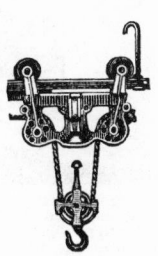

70542 Steel Track Hay Carrier and Steel Track. The best and most durable steel track in the market; carrier works either way; widest and strongest part of track directly under the wheels.
Carrier...............$3.00
Double track, per ft. 12
Hanging hooks and rafter irons, complete......11
Weight, 23 lbs.
Complete outfit for 40 foot barn, with steel track, double harpoon fork and all necessary parts.. ....$14.10
Wood track...........9.30

M. W. & Co.'s Steam or Belt Power Press.

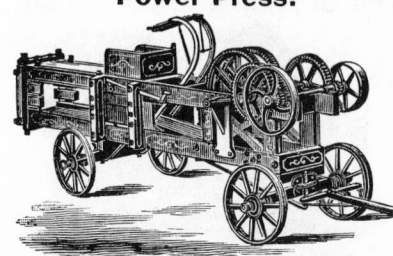

70543 This machine is a most wonderful success, far exceeding our most sanguine expectations, giving perfect satisfaction in every instance. We will fully warrant this machine to be superior in every respect to anything of its class now made. A bale every minute. Size of bale, 17x20 inches. Will put into a three-foot bale 150 to 175 pounds, or a less quantity, to suit the party baling. Weight, about 4,000 lbs.
Price, net cash, no discount................. $235.00

Montgomery Ward's & Co.'s Full Circle Double Stroke Continuous Baler.

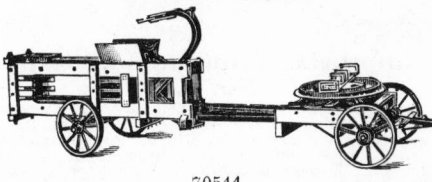

70544

The Only Full Circle Hay Press that Gives Two Complete Strokes of the Plunger Block to One Round of the Horse.

Capacity, 8 to 12 tons per day. Special circular mailed on request. Weight, about 3,500 lbs.
Price, net cash, no discount.........$225.00
Above prices on Hay Presses are f. o. b. at factory. Freight rates quoted to all points, shipped at third-class freight.

The National Hay.

70544½ Cut shows press in operation. More convenient to remove wheels than sink them in frozen ground. Jack furnished for raising and lowering press. This press sent on trial to any good and responsible party. We pay return charges if not accepted. Net cash price....................$180.00
Deposited in bank during trial. Weight, 2,500 lbs.

Bale Ties.

70545 Dimension Duck Head Hook and Adjustable Bale Ties. All sizes and lengths. Bundles of 250 ties. For price, see Agricultural Catalogue.
70545½ Annealed Wire, for Baling Ties; from 50 to 75 lbs. in bundle; we do not break bundles.
No. 10, price per 100 pounds $2.40
No. 11, price per 100 pounds 2.40
No. 12, price per 100 pounds 2.52
No. 13, price per 100 pounds 2.64
No. 14, price per 100 pounds 2.74
No. 15, price per 100 pounds 2.76
No. 16, price per 100 pounds 2.88

Success Corn Harvester.

70546 On The Success Corn Harvester, the cutting wings are pivoted to the center of the harvester and are readily and quickly thrown in under the platform witL the levers, by the operators while in motion, standing on the platform, and thus close them quickly to pass gallow hills, or obstructions, or to prevent an accident to man or horse. This is a safety and advantage possessed by no other.

No. 3 with levers, no wheel.....................$16.50
No. 4 with both levers and wheel, like cut..... 18.00

The Cummings Feed Cutter.

This cut represents Cummings Cutter, No. 3 or 4, with crusher attachment. Smaller sizes are similar in construction. See full particulars in our Agricultural Cataloguue. We have this cutter in a number of sizes, from the ordinary hand up to the heaviest power machine. We furnish elevators, also the new masticator or crusher attachment, which grinds corn fodder so it will be entirely consumed by stock.

70547 No. 1, length of cut ⅜ and ⅞ inch. Weight, 200 lbs. Capacity, 1,400 lbs. per hour; hand machine only.

Manufacturer's price.............................$25.00
Our price......... 14.75

Improved Cummings Cutter, No. 2.

70548 This cutter has four 10-inch knives, is intended for hand and power and has no equal; used in either way. Length of cut, ⅜ and ⅞ inch. Power required, two horse. Capacity, about 2,000 pounds per hour of dry feed. Speed 400 to 600 revolutions per minute. Weight, 300 pounds.

	Manufacturers' price.	Our price.
Price as hand machine..A	$30.00	$16.00
Price as power machine..B	35.00	19.00
Price with crusher attachment..C	55.00	30.00
Price of carrier, 12 feet and under..D	30.00	16.00
Over 12 feet, extra, per foot..E	1.60	1.00

Improved Cummings Cutter, No. 3.

70550 With the patent safety fly wheel. Length of knives, 12 inches. Cuts four lengths—¼, ½, ¾, and 1 inch. Size of pulley, 14 inches, diameter, 5½ inches face. Any size pulley furnished when ordered. Speed 300 to 600 revolutions. Power required, two-horse tread power. Capacity, 3,000 lbs. dry feed per hour. Weight, 500 lbs. Retail price. Our price.

	Retail price.	Our price.
Price	$70.00	$37.00
Price, with crusher	95.00	52.00
Price of 12 foot carrier (or under)	30.00	16.00
Over 12 feet, extra per foot	1.60	1.00

The Improved Cummings Cutter, No. 4.

70552 Capacity, about 5 tons per hour. Weight, 800 pounds. Length of knives, 16 inches. Number of knives, 3 or 4; size of pulley, 14 inches in diameter, 5½ inches face.

	Retail price.	Our price.
Price	$120.00	$62.00
Price with crusher	150.00	80.00
Carrier, 12 feet long or under	30.00	16.00
Over 12 feet long, extra, per foot	1.60	1.00

Carriers for all sizes are made to angle right or left or straightaway. State which is wanted.

The Clipper Cutter.

70554 We offer the Clipper as the lightest running hand cutter made. The knife is spiral, giving it a splendid cut at the least expense of power. Manufacturer's price $18.00
Our price ... 9.50
Weight, 130 pounds.

Lever Cutter.

70556 To those in want of a good cheap lever feed cutter for cutting for one horse or cow, we would recommend our Lever Cutter. It is made on the most approved pattern with an adjustable gauge to regulate the length of cut. We now furnish an improved pattern of the cutter shipped knocked down to save freights.
Mfg's price....$6.00
Our price....... 2.80

Stump Pullers.

70557 The Windlass Stump Machine; warranted the strongest windlass machine made; one or two horses can be used; 50 feet of best English plow steel cable and hook; weight, 500 lbs. Prices.
One horse power, ¾ cable, capacity, 27 tons....$42.50
70558 Benett's Stump Puller and Rock Extractor. One man can lift 20 tons.
No. 1 machine, 15 inch wheel, complete for 1 man
No. 2 machine, 18 inch wheel, complete for two men
No. 3 machine, 20 inch wheel, complete for three men
No. 4 machine, 23 inch wheel, complete for four men
Large cut of this machine in Agricultural Catalogue. Prices quoted on application.
70559 The Screw Power Stump Puller. Wrought screw, four sizes: Weight, 1,000 to 2,800 pounds. The most powerful machine made. Prices quoted, and special circular mailed on application.

The Montgomery Ward & Co.'s Wind Mill.

70560 This is a solid wood wheel with the proper dish to secure strength maintained by iron rods. To put the mill out of motion the vane is swung around parallel with the wheel, which turns edge to the wind and remains firm and motionless.
Price, complete, except tower, 10 foot mill.$24.40
Price complete, except tower, 12 foot mill.$30.00
Shipping weight of mill, 574 pounds; will furnish complete tower for 10 foot mill at 40 cents per foot.
12 foot mill at 45 cents per foot.

Montgomery Ward & Co.'s All Steel Mill.

70561 This mill is geared back one-half, so that it makes two turns to one stroke of the pump; diameter of wheel, eight feet; it is very simple in construction. Anyone can put it together; it is made of the best material and hand painted; guaranteed to stand the test of all kinds of weather and to equal in power any other make of mill of similar size.
Weight about 300 lbs.
8-foot, painted.........................$25.00
8-foot, galvanized....................... 26.25
10-foot, painted........................ 33.75
12-foot, painted.. 43.75
Gas pipe tower, 30 feet high........... 22.00
Additional height of tower, 75 cents per foot.
Metal anchor posts, set of four.................. 3.00
Wind mills shipped as first-class freight. Towers ready to set up, third-class.
70562 Our $73.00 Windmill Irrigation Pumping Outfit. For this price we furnish our 12 foot, back geared steel mill, with either of the following three sizes of pumps complete.
A Mill, pipes and pump, with a 10-inch cylinder to raise water 12 feet...........................$73.00
B Mill, pipes and pump, with an 8-inch cylinder to raise water 15 feet............................. 73.00
C Mill, pipes and pump, with a 6-inch cylinder to raise water 20 feet............................. 73.00
Parties to furnish their own tower, or metal tower by us at 22 cents per foot.

Pumping Jacks.

70563 Pumping Jack. For operating wind mill pump in times of light wind or calms; can be connected to any horse power; stroke 4 to 16 inches; balance wheel, 300 pounds comptete, Jack weight, 600 lbs. Price.................$18.00
70564 Our $10.00 Wind Mill Grinder. We furnish an elbow to connect this mill to the pump rod. Adapted to a large farm with 50 head of cattle. Weight, 75 lbs. Price.................$10.00
70566 Tallerdey Automatic Wind Mill Regulator. Weight, 50 lbs. Price.................$4.00

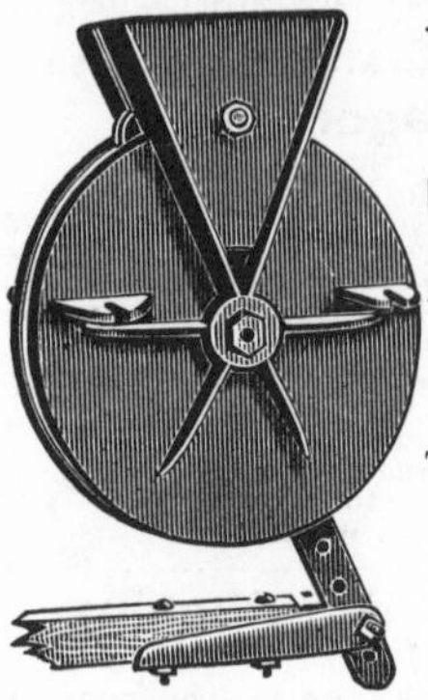

Broom Machinery.

70568 Broom Corn and Hay Press. Bales 30x24x 45 inches; weight, 300 lbs. Weight of press, 1,300 lbs. Price...$74.00
70570 Hand Broom Corn. Scraper; weight, 185 lbs. Price.................$30.00

Wagon Jacks.

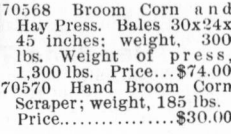

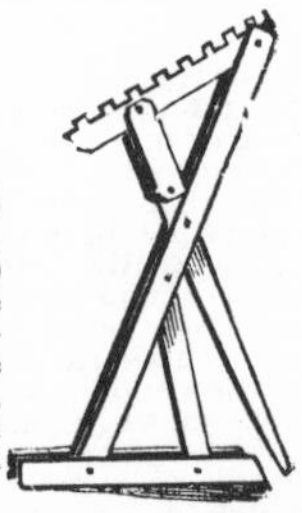

70574 The Eclipse Wagon Jack. strong and substantial. good enough for all practical purposes, weight, 7 lbs. Each............$0.70
A wagon jack is made only to raise the axle of a wagon. Elevating capacity limited to about 3 inch by one stroke of lever. To raise buildings, buy a *Jack Screw* or use our Maxon Lever Jack. Wagon jack shipped third class.

70575 The Miller Wagon Jack, can be moved and adjusted with one hand; many prefer it to all others.
No. 1 weighs 10 lbs. Price......... $1.00
No. 2 weight, 13 lbs. Price............. $1.25

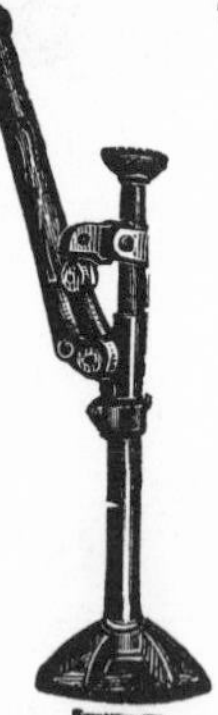

70576 The Improved Meeker Wagon Jack, strongest and lightest, most compact and neatest. All metal but the handle. It has a perfectly straight lift; will lift more and is easier to operate than any jack made. No. 1 for threshers and portable engines; weight, 40 pounds; will lift 3,500 pounds This is only a wagon jack; lifts high enough to remove wheel for greasing. Price.............$3.40
No. 2, heavy trucks; weighs 24 pounds will lift 2,000 pounds. Price....$2.90
No. 3, farm wagons; weighs 13 pounds will lift 3,000 pounds. Price....$1.20
No. 4, carriages and light wagons; 7 pounds. Price........ ....$1.00

70577 The Maxon Lever Jack. This jack differs from a wagon jack. The weight can be lifted 10 to 12 inches, capacity, 2 to 6 tons, lower claw can be inserted under a sill or stone in a 2-inch space.

No.	Tons.	Height inches.	Rise inches.	Weight pounds.	Price.
1	2	16	10	32	$ 6.50
3	6	19	12	60	10.00

No. 1 is for threshing machines, portable engines, etc.
No. 3 is for buildings, stone yards ond heavy work.

Portable Platform Scales.

Freight paid by us to all points east of the west line of Dakota, Kansas, Nebraska and Louisiana. To points farther west we apply $1 00 on the payment of freight and the purchaser pays the balance.

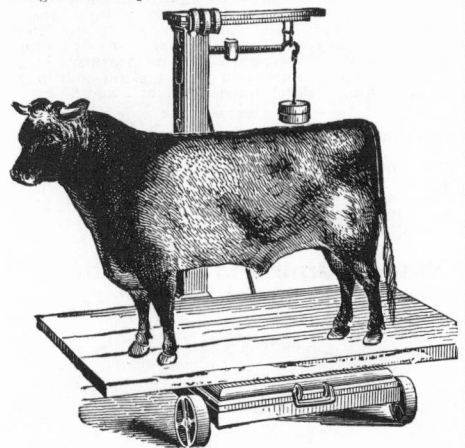

Order No. 70578   WITH WHEELS.

No.	Capacity.	P.atform.	Price
74	¼ to 600 lbs.	16x24	$13.80
75	¼ to 800 lbs.	16x25	15.00
76	¼ to 1,000 lbs.	17x25	16.25
77	¼ to 1,200 lbs.	17x26	17.50
78	¼ to 1,400 lbs.	19x28	21.25
79	¼ to 1,600 lbs.	20x29	23.75
80	¼ to 2,000 lbs.	21x29	27.50

Dairymen's Scales.

70580   WITH DOUBLE BEAM. NO WHEELS.

			Price.
No. 81	Capacity ¼ to	600 lbs.	$13.90
No. 82	Capacity ¼ to	800 lbs.	15.25
No. 83	Capacity ¼ to	1,000 lbs.	16.30

70581   DOUBLE BEAM WITH WHEELS.

No. 84	Capacity ¼ to	600 lbs.	$14.08
No. 85	Capacity ¼ to	800 lbs.	16.00
No. 86	Capacity ¼ to	1,000 lbs.	17.25

Montgomery Ward & Co.'s Hay and Stock Scale.

Montgomery Ward & Co.'s Wagon Scale.

70582   Five ton platform, 8x14.   Price.........$53.50
　　Cash with order................................... 51.90
70583   Four ton platform, 8x14.   Price......... 49.50
　　Cash wish order................................... 48.51
70584   Three ton platform, 8x14.   Price........ 46.00
　　Cash with order................................... 45.00

Shipping weight of five ton scale is 780 lbs.; four ton, 700 lbs.; three tons, 620 lbs. Are shipped as second class freight.

We ship these scales, freight paid by us, to any railroad station or steamboat landing in the United State east of the west line of Kansas and Nebraska, North and South Dakota and Louisiana. To points farther west we pre-pay $5.00 on the amount on the freight bill and the purchaser pays any balance of freight over this $5.00 paid by us on receipt of scale. No such value for this amount of money has ever before been offered the purchaser of scales. We furnish a highly finished, double brass beam and a neatly painted beam box. Our scales have double truss rods on the levers. The cheap scales sold throughout the country have single truss rods with light beams about one-half the weight of ours, which imparts a trembling and uncertain motion to the scale beam. A heavy scale is positive and accurate in its movement, and has none of the vibrating motion of a cheap scale.

We recommend our heavy-double truss rod 5-ton scale where parties do custom weighing and for town or village scales, or where farmers club together. Also for ranches, mining. and other purposes where great durability and strength are required.

Test Weight.

70590 A 50 pound test weight, sealed by an authorized sealer of weights, which can be used to test any scale. Cost on cars at Chicago.........................$2.75

Shipped as fourth class freight..

Scale Books.

Howe, U. S. Standard and Fairbanks' Scale Books (500 tickets each) post paid, 68 cents.

Howe Trucks.

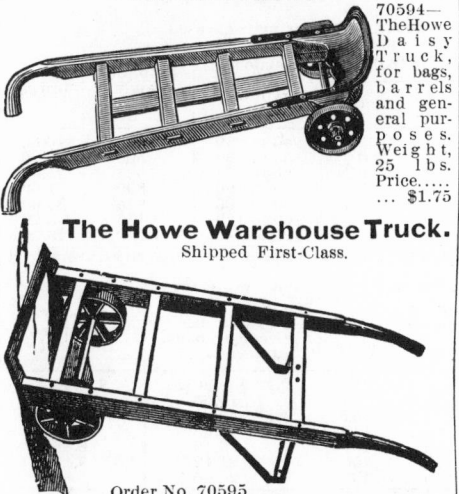

70594—The Howe Daisy Truck, for bags, barrels and general purposes. Weight, 25 lbs. Price.... $1.75

The Howe Warehouse Truck.

Shipped First-Class.

Order No. 70595
No. 1, weight, 43 lbs.   Length, 3½ ft.   Price.....$3.00
No. 2, weight 56 lbs.   Length, 4 ft.   Price....- 4.00
No. 3, weight, 77 lbs.   Length, 4¼ ft.   Price..... 5.50

The Montgomery Ward & Co.'s Road Grader.

Shipped first-class.

70596   Weight, about 1,500 lbs.   Price, without trucks...$65.00
Farm wagon gears, whiffletrees and yoke on which to mount this grader, 3¼ inch skein, weight, 725 lbs.   Price....................... .. 30.50
3½ inch skein, weight, 750 lbs................43.50
Any ordinary farm wagon gears can be used.

We warrant this grader to be strong and durable, and to stand any strain that can be brought to bear on it. Warranted a perfect and thoroughly made implement, or no sale.

This road grader with two men and four horses will do more work, and far better in t he same time, than the full road district crew of a dozen men and half dozen teams, working with a common scraper, plow, shovel, and- hoe in the usual manner. Save the money from delinquent road taxes and buy Montgomery Ward & Co.'s road grader.

Good roads render farming profitable; you can market your products at good prices when others cannot move a mile from home. Good roads enhance the value of your property, invite strangers to invest and settle in your community, and are the best evidence of an intelligent, wide awake and progressive community.

☞ We would like to correspond with the Chairman of any Town Board whose town could be interested in profitable road working machinery. Please send your address. Special circular mailed free on request.

The Great Western Feed Steamer.

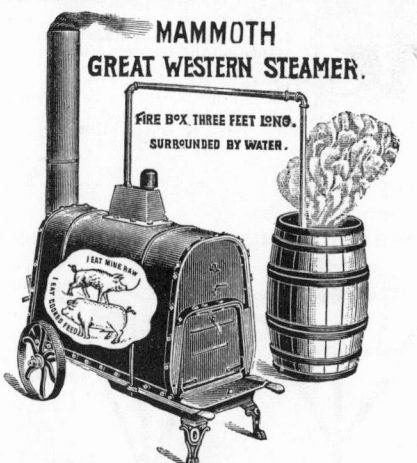

The Great Western has a large, convenient fire box, the whole length of the boiler, 40 inches, being covered with water entirely over the top and down both sides to the bottom, which gives the full benefit of all the heat from the fuel, thus making it of greater capacity than other steamers
70597   Size of boiler, 40 inches long.   Weight, 350 lbs. Price $28.50

Wood Dale Cast Iron Pig Trough.

INDESTRUCTIBLE AND EVERLASTING.

In each trough there are eight separate compartments, eight large hogs can eat at one time. Different kinds of feed can be fed at the same time, the bowls preventing their mixing. Hogs cannot upset them and waste their feed, nor is there any leaking, but great economy and satisfaction in using these troughs.

70598   Weight, 165 lbs.   Height, 24 inches.   Width, 32 inehes.   Price $4.90

70600   Kemp's Manure spreader. Most successful machine for the purpose intended.   Retail p ice, $85.00 to $135.00, as to size and capacity.   Full information to intending purchasers.

Electro Vapor Engine.

GAS OR GASOLINE FOR FUEL.

70612 No fire; no boiler; no engineer; no danger. You turn the switch, engine does the rest. Engine run by spark from small battery. The cost of running: In computing the cost of running, the following facts should be taken into consideration.
I.   No expense until started.
II.   No necessity of starting until the power is required.
III Expense while running always in exact proportion to amount of power used.
IV.   The moment engine stops all expense stops.
When running at maximum speed and power, our engine consumes about one-eighth gallon of gasoline per horse-power per hour, or, when illuminating gas is used, twenty cubic feet of gas per indicated horsepower per hour.

PRICE OF ENGINE ALONE.

No.	Size. Actual H. P.	Floor Space.	Revolutions per Minute.	Shipping Weight.	Price.
1	½	25 x 40 in.	250	600	$127.00
2	2	31 x 51 "	250	876	187.00
3	3	38½x 55½ "	250	1,201	262.00
4	4	40 x 64 "	225	1,654	337.00
5	6	57 x 82 "	200	2,203	450.00
6	8	61 x 90 "	200	3,097	525 00
7	10	76 x105 "	200	4,402	600.00

Engine and Pump combined on one base.

No.	Size. Actual H. P.	Floor Space.	Shipping Weight.	Capacity Gallons. per Hour.	Price.
1	½	25 x40 in	700	500	$131.00
2	2	31 x51 "	1,127	1,000	225.00
3	3	38½x55½ "	1,501	2,500	300.00
4	4	40 x64 "	2,054	4,500	375.00
5	6	57 x82 "	2,703	10,000	525.00

WATCH AND JEWELRY REPAIR DEPARTMENT.

We have the best of workmen in this department, and are prepared to do all kinds of repairing and altering at reasonable prices. We guarantee all work.

Montgomery Ward & Co.'s Perfection Cane Mill.

NO EXPENSIVE BREAKAGES.
Both top and bottom journals run in brass boxes. The gearing is encased.

Order No. 70622.   SIZES, WEIGHT AND PRICES.

No.	Power.	Size of rolls in inches.			Estimated capacity not guarant'd. Gallons, per hour.	Shipping weight, pounds	Prices.
		Diam. large.	Diam. small.	Length.			
0	Light One-Horse	8¼	5½	5⅝	40 to 50	400	$16.00
1	One-Horse	9½	6⅜	6	50 to 60	500	20.00
2	One-Horse	11½	6¾	6⅝	60 to 75	625	25.00
3	Two-Horse	13	7⅓	7⅜	75 to 90	800	31.00
4	Two-Horse	13	7⅓	8¾	90 to 100	850	35.00
5	Heavy Two-Horse	14	8¾	9¼	100 to 120	1,150	43.00
6	Extra Heavy Two-Horse	14	8¾	11½	120 to 140	1,250	48.00

Cane mills are shipped at third-class rates. Observe that we are furnishing these mills, on an average, at less than 4 cents per pound, actual weight.

Order No. 70625.   PRICES FOR COPPER AND GALVANIZED IRON PANS, WITH TWO SKIMMERS.

No.	Size of pan, inches.	Estimated capacity for day of 12 hours, gallons syrup.	Weight, pounds.		Price of heavy copper pans.	Price of galvanized iron pans.
			Copper.	Galvanized iron		
1	44x 66	20 to 30	97	71	$ 9.90	$ 4.40
2	44x 72	30 to 40	110	84	10.56	4.75
3	44x 90	40 to 52	135	101	13.20	5.94
4	44x108	50 to 80	150	119	15.88	7.15
5	44x126	75 to 120	165	137	18.48	8.36
6	44x144	100 to 140	195	155	21.12	9.46
7	44x180	125 to 175		191	26.40	11.88

Nos. 4 and 5 pans, for brick arch have one gate and one high ledge.
Nos. 6 and 7 pans, for brick arch, have two gates and two high ledges.

CARRIAGE HARDWARE AND SUPPLIES.

Carriage Trimmers', Wagon Makers', Blacksmiths' and Farriers' Hardware, Wood Stock and Supplies.

Special Notice.

The weights given in the following pages are ESTIMATED SHIPPING weights and are not guaranteed to be accurate. The weight of timber depends so much on its dryness and the weight of metal on its density and form that it is impossible to give weights that would be correct in all cases, even where the dimensions of articles are the same.

We make our figures as close to the average as we can to give you an idea of what transportation charges will be and of the character of the goods.

Instructions for Measuring Seat.

For tops, backs, cushions and falls as here stated.

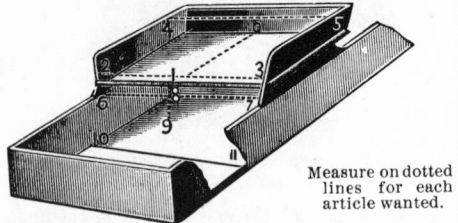

Measure on dotted lines for each article wanted.

For Buggy Tops give measure across seat at top of flare as per dotted line between figures 4 and 5 in cut. For cushions, give measure on bottom of seat as per dotted lines between figure 0....1 and 2....3. For falls to cushions give measure as per dotted lines between 6–7, 8–9, 10–11. State if seat is round or square corner.

Buggy Tops.

The three sizes quoted below are carried in stock, and are to fit seats from 34 to 39 in. wide, other sizes must be made to order, which requires about five days' time.

70699 Special Lined Rubber Buggy Tops, for one-seated buggy, made in large lots on special contract. Steel bow sockets, rubber top, lined with good cloth, rubber curtains carried in stock, ready for immediate shipment. This special top made only to fit buggies with seat out to out on top of flare 33 to 38 inches. No other sizes of this grade furnished.
Price, only...........................$8.50
70700 Leather quarter-top, lined with good broadcloth, except curtains, which are of rubber. Top for single seated buggy 33 to 38 inches.
Price, only...........................$13.75
70701 Full leather top, lined rubber side curtains, all lined with heavy broadcloth, padded top, hand-stitched front and back, 33 to 36 inches. Top for single seated buggy. Price, only...........$21.90

We have the above top made in carload lots, which enables us to maintain the remarkably low price for the quality of the tops offered. We sold over two carloads of No. 70699 alone during 1894.

Buggy Tops to Order.

Allow one week to have made.
Tops for two seated carriages weigh about 50 lbs.
Tops for single seated buggies weigh about 35 lbs.
70708 Rubber Top, made of 24 ounce rubber, lined with a good quality of broadcloth except curtains, which are made of colored rubber; back stays stiffened with buckram and made to show no raw edges, enameled front valance, silver or japanned nuts and rivets, steel bow sockets, malleable rails and joints, top nicely padded.
Top for single seated buggy.............$12.50
Top for two-seated buggy.................17.00
70714 Leather Quarter Top, lined with good broadcloth, except curtains which are of rubber. Top for single seated buggy.............18.00
Top for two seated buggy.................30.00

70716 Same top as above, except is better made, has better broadcloth lining, top handstitched welts inside and side laced pinked.
Top for single seated buggy.............22.00
Top for two seated buggy................36.00
70718 Full Leather Top, same as above, all lined with heavy broadcloth, padded top, hand stitched front and back. Top for single seated buggy........24.80
Top for two seated buggy...............38.00
We cannot furnish covers to fit old tops. They must be sent to us to be re-covered.

70720 Canopy Tops, made of solid bent wood, corners slightly rounded, covered with 8 oz. black enameled cloth, 4 iron props well braced, made only with straight standards. Give width and length of top and length of each standard.
Price, scalloped cloth fringe..$16.00 } Weight, crated.
Price, with fancy cord fringe. 19.00 } 100 lbs.
Side and back curtains, extra. 5.00

All buggy tops have to be made to order to fit the measurement sent. Other goods ordered with tops will be detained about one week until top is finished.

Above tops are made by a special carriage top maker. If ordered to fit any of our wagons, customers have to screw irons (all of which we furnish) to the seats they are ordered to fit.

In measuring for extension tops give measure from out to out on top of seat same as you see in cut from 4....5; then give measure from the back of the back seat to the front of the front on top, and state if front seat is higher than back seat at level of seat.

These tops are made in a special factory in Chicago. If wanted to fit jobs we advertise without tops, customers will have to bolt the rails and irons on to the seats of such vehicles, which can readily be done.

West's Carriage Top Dressing.

Makes an old top look as good as new.
70723 A Top Dressing of just sufficient body to render the leather waterproof and no more. A goods that will not accumulate a hard substance on the leather after repeated applications. An article that will dry in a few hours with a natural leather finish and not be sticky. A jet black waterpoof finish which will not crack, harden or injure the finest leather or rubber top.

Price, each.
½ pint cans will dress 1 buggy top............$0.40
1   "   "   "   2   "   "...........80
1 quart   "   "   4   "   "............. 1.50

Wagon, Buggy or Cart Tops.

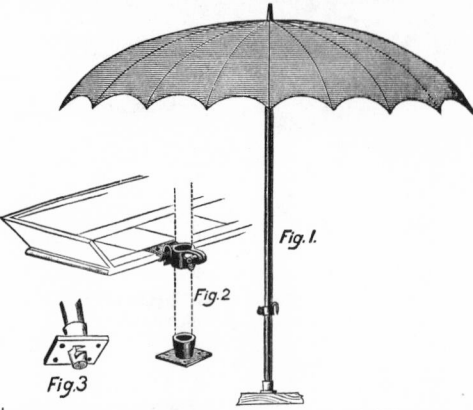

This is the latest, strongest and most durable top of this kind ever produced, and a most handsome shaped top. It does not require the services of a mechanic to attach them to the seat. You can do the work yourself in a
No. 4
very few minutes' time, and when the top is attached to the seat, you can, while sitting in the seat, lower, raise or close the top from the inside. It is not necessary to leave the seat to operate this top. You can throw this top forward or backward, or leave it standing straight up. It will stand in any position you desire to put it WHEN OPEN OR CLOSED. The top is furnished complete with irons ready to attach to the seat. The irons will fit any kind of a seat. *In ordering tops give length of seat on top.* The sizes we keep in stock are for seats measuring from 32 to 44 inches. For extra wide tops the additional cost of making will be added. Weight, about 20 lbs.

PRICES:
70724 Covered with brown duck and fringed, see cut No. 4.........................$3.75
70726 Covered with awning strip and fringed, see cut No. 4........................4.25
70728 Covered with enameled drill and fringed. see cut No. 4........................3.85
70730 Covered with rubber and fringed........4.50

Wagon Umbrella with Fixtures and Socket.

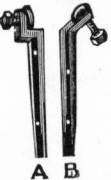

Fig. 1.
Fig. 2
Fig. 3

FOR WAGON UMBRELLAS. (Patent Applied For.)
70731 The most complete fixture yet produced. Made of the best malleable iron, light and strong, quickly applied, and holds the umbrella secure. Our umbrellas are all supplied with these fixtures without extra charge.

PRICE LIST OF UMBRELLAS WITH SOCKET AND SEAT FIXTURES COMPLETE.

36-inch, 8-rib with fixtures. Each..............$1.90
36-inch, 10-rib with fixtures. Each.............. 2.05
40-inch, 10-rib with fixtures. Each............. 2.40
In blue, drab, buff or black heavy muslin.
40-inch, 10-rib, double face duck, green inside, buff outside, with fixtures. Each............ 3.20

Best quality heavy steel ribs and fixtures. Handles 1¼ in. white ash, oiled and varnished.

Patent Leather Dashes.

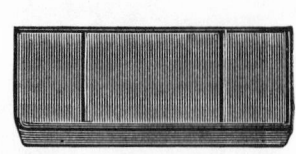

A   B

70732 For Piano Box Buggies, we send dash irons A. For Flaring End Buggies, we send angled irons B. State which is wanted.

Will fit any wagon or buggy: state size wanted. These are fine dashes, 10 stitches to the inch, dash, feet irons and bolts included in price. We send irons for square bodies, unless ordered for flaring end.

Dash Price List.

Size.	Price	Size.	Price	Size.	Price	Size.	Price
21x11	$1.19	21x13	$1.29	21x15	$1 43	21x17	$1.59
22x11	1 22	22x13	1.33	22x15	1.48	22x17	1 65
23x11	1.25	23x13	1.37	23x15	1.53	23x17	1.71
24x11	1.27	24x13	1.41	24x15	1 59	24x17	1.77
25x11	1.32	25x13	1.48	25x15	1.66	25x17	1.84
26x11	1 36	26x13	1.53	26x15	1.71	26x17	1 90
27x11	1.39	27x13	1.58	27x15	1.77	27x17	1 97
28x11	1.43	28x13	1.62	28x15	1.81	28x17	2 02
29x11	1.49	29x13	1.68	29x15	1.86	29x17	2.08
30x11	1 54	30x13	1.73	30x15	1.92	30x17	2.12
31x11	1 60	31x13	1.78	31x15	1.98	31x17	2.20
32x11	1.63	32x13	1.82	32x15	2.04	32x17	2.25
33x11	1.66	33x13	1.86	33x15	2.10	33x17	2.33
34x11	1.71	34x13	1.91	34x15	2.16	34x17	2.39
35x11	1.75	35x13	1.96	35x15	2.22	35x17	2.45
36x11	1 80	36x13	2 02	36x15	2.28	36x17	2.51
37x11	1.84	37x13	2.07	37x15	2.34	37x17	2.58
38x11	1.89	38x13	2.12	38x15	2.39	38x17	2 64
39x11	1.93	39x13	2.17	39x15	2.45	39x17	2.70
40x11	1.98	40x13	2.22	40x15	2.51	40x17	2.76
41x11	2.02	41x13	2.27	41x15	2.56	41x17	2.83
42x11	2.05	42x13	2.32	42x15	2.63	42x17	2 91

Dash Leather and Whip Sockets.

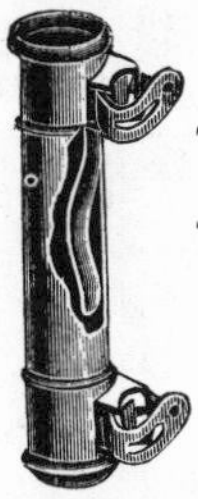

70733 Dash Leather, per square foot, 30 cents. In ordering state length and width of piece wanted.
70734 Whip Sockets—metal; can be attached to wood or leather dash; has a spring inside to hold whip securely from rattling; black japanned. 7 inches long.
Each $0.10
Per dozen 1.00

Whip Socket and Reinholder.

70734½ This useful article prevents the reins from getting in the mud or under the horses feet. Always ready for use, will be sent for leather dash unless otherwise ordered. For wood or leather dash. Japanned.
Each $0.24
Per dozen 2.60

Bow Sockets.

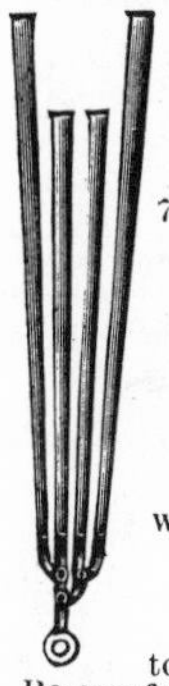

70735 Black Enameled Steel Tubular Bow Sockets.
3 Bow, buggy (one seat). Per set $1.25
4 Bow, buggy (one seat). Per set 1.50
4 Bow, extension top (two seat).
Per set 1.75
Back Tubes, with steel. Each........ .30
All other tubes for buggies. Each.... .25
Main Irons for Extension Tops. Each. .30
Always state whether right or left hand are wanted, and whether for 3 or 4 bow top.

We measure bows from center of pivot hole to the top of middle or shortest bow.
Be careful to use for the back bow the tube marked "Back Bow," as it has a steel strip welded in to prevent bending at the prop.
70738 Top Props, without nuts, 4 to a set, 2 long and 2 short.

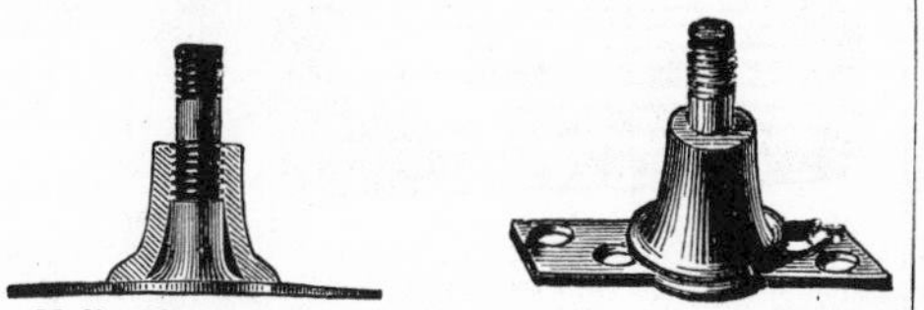

Malleable, ⅜ and $\frac{7}{16}$ shank. Each $0.04
Per set .... .15
If less than a full set is wanted, state whether long or short shanks are needed.

Cushions, Falls and Full Backs.

The following Cushions, Falls, and Curtains are made only to order.
Buggy cushions, square cornered, come 26, 28, 30 or 32 inches in length. All sizes the same price.
☞ *We will fill no order for cushions unless length of seat on bottom is given.*

	Without falls.	With falls.
70740 Buggy Cushions, rubber drill..	$1.05	$1.88
70742 Buggy Cushions, enameled duck	1.57	2.32
	Without falls	With falls.
70744 Buggy Cushions, enameled leather	2.75	3.50
70746 Buggy Cushions, Corduroy..	1.62	2.47
70748 Buggy Cushions, cloth, good quality	3.50	4.25

Plain Full Backs to match above cushions cost *extra* the same price as the cushions. This does not include lazy backs, irons or wood, for which we make an additional charge of $1.00.
(EXAMPLE.) Suppose you wish to furnish a plain seat with cushion No. 70740, $1.05. Back cushions to match, $1.05, woods and irons to back, $1.00; the amount to remit would be $3.10; or if only the *back* and seat *cushion*, $2.10.

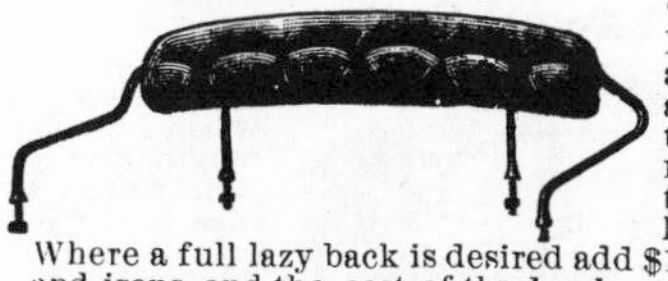

70749 Lazy Back, woods and irons, alone, $1.00; trimmed in rubber $1.50; trimmed in leather, $2.00.
Where a full lazy back is desired add $1.00 for wood and irons, and the cost of the **back cushion**, which is the same price as seat cushions without falls. Weight, about 10 lbs.

Curtains.

Side curtains for buggy tops.
70750 Side Curtains, made of 18 oz. rubber drill, colored back; weight, 18 oz. Each $1.25
70752 Side Curtains, made of rubber drill, lined with cloth; weight, 21 oz. Each...... ...... 1.87
70754 Side Curtains, made of leather, lined with cloth; weight, 36 oz. Each 4.12
Back Curtains to match side curtains, same price and weight as one side curtain. Send paper patterns of both back and side curtains, showing position of eyelet holes.

Storm Aprons.

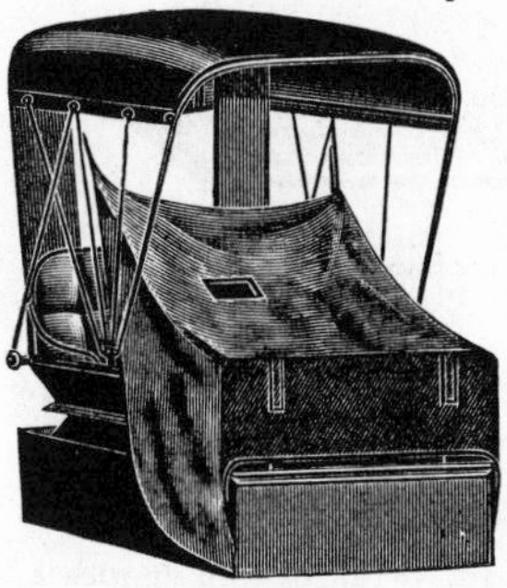

These aprons are held fimly in position on the dash by two oil tempered steel springs attached to the under side, thus forming an unbroken water-shed over front of dash. No mud, snow or rain can settle inside of carriage. Warranted to fit the dash of any wagon, carriage or buggy; 42 inches usual length.
70755 Best Rubber Drill, each ..$1.40
70756 Good Grade Rubber Drill..$0 95

Curtain Lights.

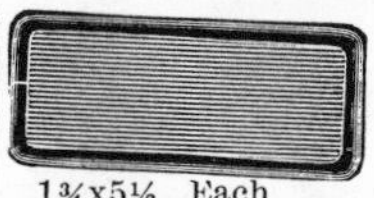

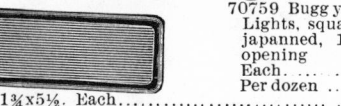

70759 Buggy Curtain Lights, square corners, japanned, 1¼x5 inch opening
Each $0.07
Per dozen .... .75
1¾x5½. Each .... .10
Per dozen 1.00

Button Holes.

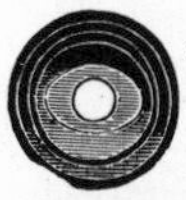

70760 Talcott's Elastic Button Holes for carriage or wagon curtains, oval hole.
Per dozen $0.30
Per gross 3.24

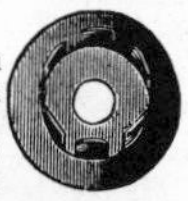

Knob Eyelets--With Leather Centers.

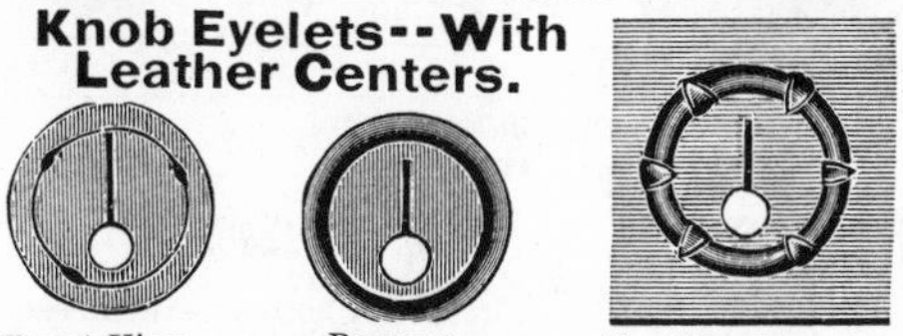

Front View. Reverse. Showing Fastener.
70760½ Knob Eyelets consist of a black japanned metal fastener, with outside prongs to pass through the curtain, and inside prongs to hold the leather eyelet, also a black japanned ring on which the outside and inside prongs are clinched. Best Goat Leather Centers. Per doz., $0.10
Per gross .... .95

Patent Buckle and Strap Loops.

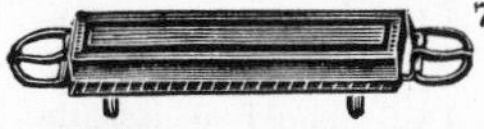

70761 Double Buckle Loop.
Each $0.05
Per dozen 0.40

Curtain Straps and Fasteners.

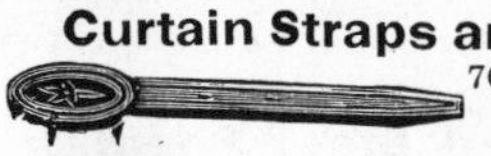

70761½ Each $0.03
Per dozen. 0.25

Carriage Knobs.

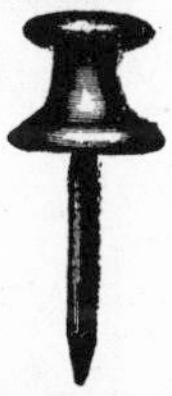

70762 To drive, per dozen..........$0.05
Per gross .... .45
70764 To screw, for double or single curtains, per dozen .... .08
Per gross. .... .80

Tufting Buttons and Lining Nails.

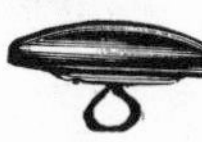

70766 Japanned Tufting Buttons, 22 line.
Per paper, of 1 gross $0.20
Per dozen papers 2.10
Weight, per dozen, 3 oz.

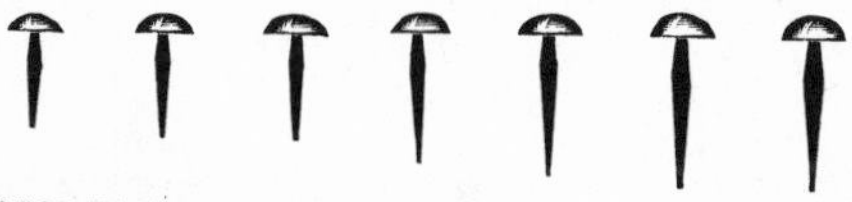

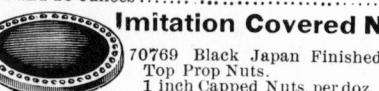

70768 Lining Nails, japanned.
Per paper, 4, 6, 8, 10, 12 ounces $0.08
14 and 16 ounces .... .10

Imitation Covered Nuts

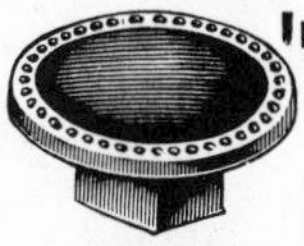

70769 Black Japan Finished Top Prop Nuts.
1 inch Capped Nuts, per doz. 15c.
1⅛ inch Capped Nuts, per doz. 16c.
1¼ inch Capped Nuts, per doz. 17c.

Pike's Patent Nut Locks.

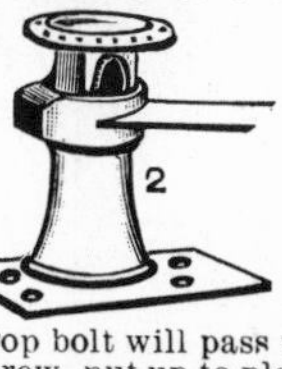

2

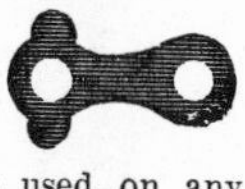

70769½ Can be used on any buggy or carriage top and absolutely insures against loosing top nuts. Bend lock over the end of prop socket so that prop bolt will pass through both holes of lock. Screw nut up to place and bend lugs on lock up on opposite sides of nut. Price, per dozen......$0 08

Rubber Drill.

70770 Rubber Drill, for covering or patching buggy tops, cushions, etc. Per yard.
18 oz, 50 in. wide $0.38
28 oz, very heavy, 50 in. wide .... .50
18 oz, green back, 50 in. wide .... .48
28 oz, green back, 50 in. wide .... .60
70771 Back finished to represent fine broad cloth, no lining necessary. Per yard .... .58
Flock Back Drill, 50 inches wide. Per yard.... .70

Enameled Cloth.

Per yd.
70771½ Black Muslin, glazed, shot or Leather grain, 45 inch wide $0.15
Imitation Rubber Muslin, smooth glazed, shot or leather grain, 45 inches wide 15
Black Drill, glazed, shot, pebble or leather grain, 45 inches wide .... .19
Black Drill, glazed, shot, pebble or leather grain, 50 inches wide .... .21
Black Drill, glazed, shot, pebble or leather grain, 54 inches wide .... .26
Tan Back Glazed Drill, 50 inches wide .... .27
Tan Back Glazed Mole Skin, 45 inches wide .64

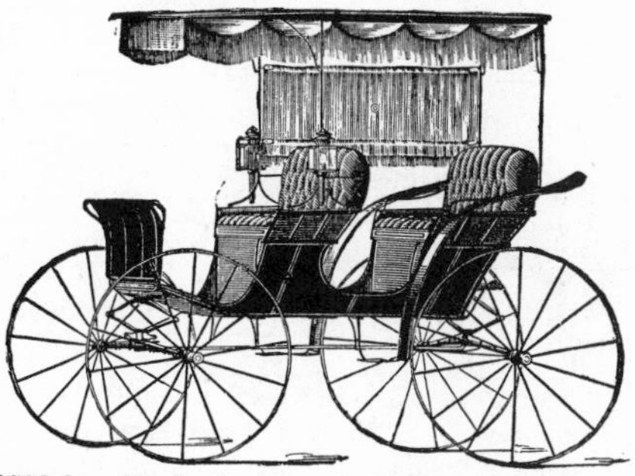

70772 Sun Shade Curtains for canopy top surreys, 60 inches long; fit any canopy top. No surrey complete without one.
Silesia, each $1.00
Cloth, each 1.50

Carriage Lamps.

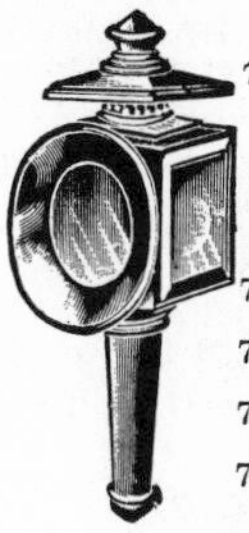

70773 Carriage Lamp, square body with round flange, round cornered head, with fancy canopy and bright cap, side glass beveled and grooved, candle burners, size of side glass, 3⅛x3½; diameter of flange, 4½ inches.
Per pair $2.60
70774 Better quality, size 3⅛x3½; flange, 4½. Price 3.00
70775 Better quality, size, 3⅛x3½; flange 4½. Price 4.00
70776 Better quality, size, 3¾x4¾; flange 5. Price 4.50
70777 Better quality, round side light; flange 5 in. Price 4.90

Carriage Fringe.

FAST COLORS—WORSTED BOULLION IN BLUE OR GREEN.

70778 Worsted Boullion 4 inches wide.
Per yard $0.22
Worsted Boullion, 5 in. wide.
Per yard $0.25
Worsted Boullion, 5½ inches wide.
Per yard $0.27

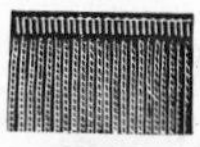

70778

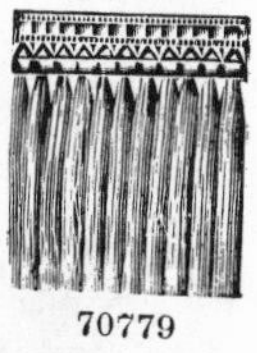

70779

FANCY HEAD GENNAPPE—BLUE OR GREEN.
70779 Fancy Head Gennappe, 5 inches wide.
Per yard $0.42

Buggy Bodies, Unpainted.

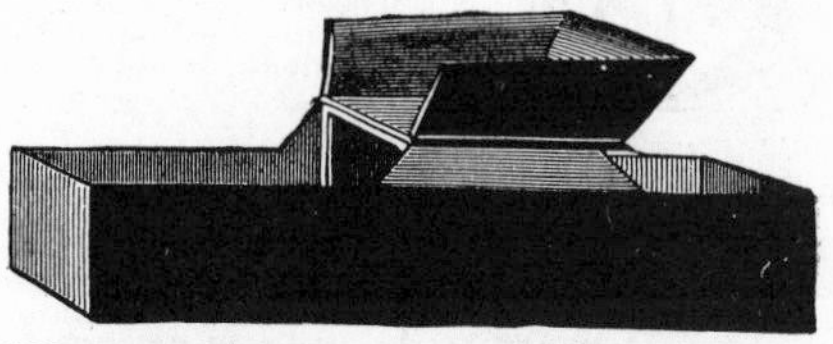

70780 Piano Buggy Body, 25 inches wide, 50 inches long, corner irons on top, panels 8 in. deep, not finished.
Weight. 50 lbs. Each $3.95
70782 Two Seated Spring Wagon Body, 28 inches wide on bottom, 5 feet 3 inches long, 8 inches deep outside. 10.00
70784 Two seat, square cornered, 2 feet 8 inches wide.—6, 6½ and 7 feet long. 2 feet 10 inches wide—6, 6½, 7, 7½ and 8 feet long, 3 feet wide, 6½, 7, 7½ and 8 feet long. 7 feet and longer kept in stock, with drop end gate, panels, 8 inches deep outside. Price 11.00
70786 Platform Spring Wagon Body, two seats ironed, patent leather dash, ready for paint, plain panel, 2 feet 10 inches or 3 feet wide, 6½, 7 or 7½ feet long $15.00
70788 Same as above, but with two rows of panels 16.65
With three rows of panels 17.50
See cuts of these bodies in our special buggy list.

Buggy Seats, Unpainted.

When ordering give size of buggy box from outside to outside.

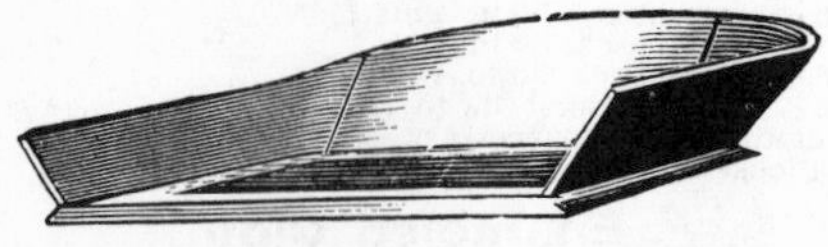

70790 Buggy Seats, not painted or ironed, but in the white, all ready for finishing, round corners, 30 to 42 inches wide on the bottom, 15 inches deep; weight, 11 pounds. Each................$1.25

Buggy Seats—Continued.

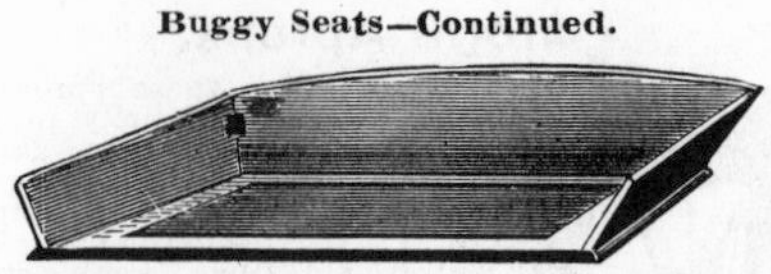

70792 Buggy Seat, not painted or ironed, but in the white, all ready for finishing, square corners, 30 to 42 inches wide on bottom, 15 inches deep; weight, 11 pounds. Each..........................$1.00

An extra singletree is a good article to have. We carry a complete line. Order a few put in with your other goods. See Page 597 for quotations.

Buggy Wheels.

Sarven patent. with all flange hub finished in the white, not painted, ironed or boxed.

Front wheels are carried in stock up to four feet high, and rear up to 4 ft. 4, We cannot furnish wheels of greater diameter than the above except at extra cost and then they must be made to order, requiring one to two weeks' time.

70793—

Light Sarven Wheels, Not Tired.

Spoke.		Hub.		Rim.		Maximum height.		Price, Per Set.				Weight. per set.
No. Flange	Size.	Diam	Length.	Tread.	Depth.	Front.	Rear.	A	B	C	D	
01	15/16	2 15/16	6½	¾ to ⅞	1 to 1¼	4 ft.	4 ft. 4	$10.10	$8.30	$6.55	$5.35	80 lbs.
0	1	3	6½	⅞	1⅛ to 1¼	4 ft,	4 ft. 4					
1	1 1/16	3 1/16	6½	⅞ to 1	1⅛ to 1¼	4 ft.	4 ft. 4					
3	1⅛	3 3/16	6½	1 to 1⅛	1¼ to 1⅜	4 ft.	4 ft. 4					
7	1 3/16	3 7/16	6½ & 7	1 to 1⅛	1¼ to 1⅜	4 ft.	4 ft. 4	11.30	9.50	7.15	6.00	100 lbs.
9	1¼	3⅝	7 & 7½	1⅛ to 1¼	1⅜ to 1½	4 ft.	4 ft. 4					
13	1⅜	3⅞	7 & 7½	1¼ to 1⅜	1⅜ to 1⅝	4 ft.	4 ft. 4	12.50	10.75	8.30	6.60	150 lbs

Prices of heavy Sarven wheels and of ordinary farm wagon wheels quoted on application

Tired and Banded Wheels (Sarven Patent).

Do not condemn your buggy simply because the wheels are worn out and rattle. It s by far cheaper to purchase a can of carriage paint, a few yards of rubber drill (70770), to recover the top and a set of new wheels at the very reasonable prices quoted below, making practically a new buggy at a small outlay.

Our wheels are the **celebrated Royer brand** tired with a round edge steel tire, firmly bolted between each spoke. Each flange and hub band cast in one piece so as to completely encase the hub with iron. No rim or sand bands being required, Take the boxes out of your old hubs, drive them into the new, paint the wheels and they are ready for use.

If your axles are worn buy a set of stubs and have welded on old axle (70950).

With a little work and small cost you can fix your buggy up yourself.

We cannot furnish painted wheels or set the boxes.

	Thickness of tire.	Size of spoke.	Length of hub	Width of rim.	Depth of rim.	Height of front wheel.	Height of rear wheel.	Price.	Weight, per set.
70797	3/16	1 1/16	6½	⅞	1⅛	3 ft. 8	4 ft.	$ 7.75	90 lbs.
70798	¼	1⅛	6½	1	1¼	3 ft. 8	4 ft.	8.00	100 lbs.
70799	5/16	1¼	7	1⅛	1⅜	3 ft. 8	4 ft.	9.50	125 lbs.
70800	⅜	1⅜	7½	1¼	1½	3 ft. 8	4 ft.	11.25	160 lbs.

The above four sizes are carried in stock ready for immediate shipment. No other size of tired wheels furnished.

Steel Truck Wheels.

70801 Steel wheels for trucks and farm wagons where low wheels and wide tires are desired.

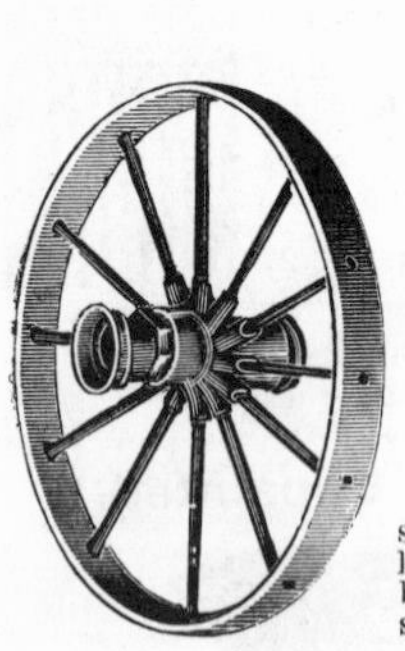

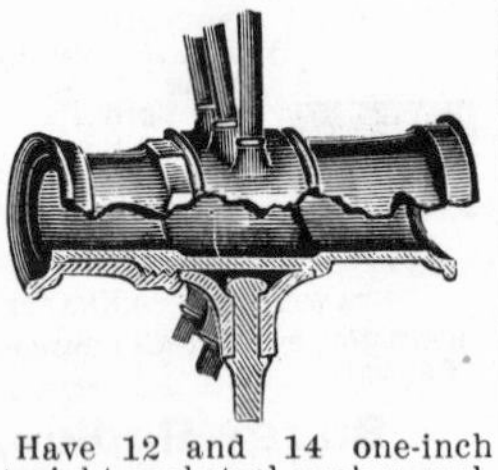

Have 12 and 14 one-inch straight oval steel spokes, malleable hubs, with removable boxes to fit all sizes of standard skeins.

30-inch wheels. Each..................$3.15 } For
34-inch wheels. Each.................. 3.60 } 9-inch
38-inch wheels. Each.................. 4.00 } skeins.

For 10-inch skeins add 5c. each 11-inch add 10c. each. 12-inch add 15c. We recommend them wherever a strong, durable wheel is required. In ordering give dimensions as indicated below.

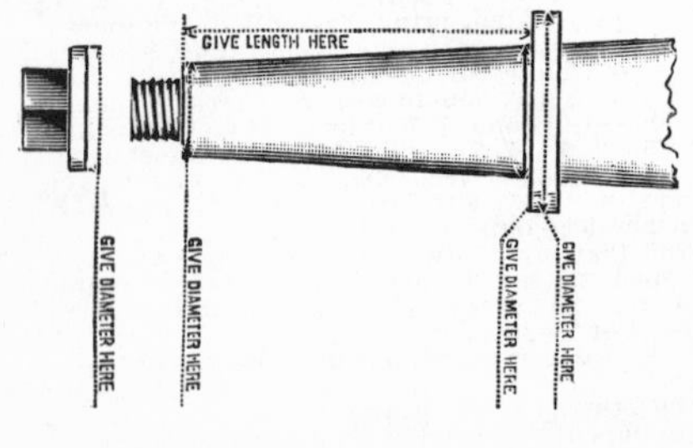

Cold Die-Rolled Steel Shafting.

70804 We are prepared to furnish it accurate to size, absolutely straight, polished surface and machine cut ends. United States Standard Gauge, April 1, 1890.

Diameter.	Weight, per ft.	per lb.
¼	.167	
5/16	.259	$0.08
⅜	.370	
7/16	.510	
½	.666	.06½
9/16	.843	
⅝	1.05	.05½
11/16	1.25	
¾	1.50	
13/16	1.757	
⅞	2.03	.04½
15/16	2.34	
1	2.64	
1 1/16	3.00	
1⅛	3 33	
1 3/16	3.74	
1¼	4.16	
1 5/16	4.61	.04¼
1⅜	5.048	
1 7/16	5.50	
1½	6.00	
1 9/16	6.52	
1⅝	7.04	
1 11/16	7.60	
1¾	8.16	
1 13/16	8.78	
1⅞	9.39	
1 15/16	10.00	
2	10.65	
2 1/16	11.15	
2⅛	12.07	
2 3/16	12.79	
2¼	13.49	
2 5/16	14.00	
2⅜	15 07	.04¼
2 7/16	15.83	
2½	16.68	
2⅝	18 32	
2¾	20.18	
2 15/16	22.96	
3	24.06	

When short lengths are ordered an extra charge of 25 cents for cutting must be allowed.

Wagon Hubs.

70810 Made of selected oak and birch, cupped patterns, measurements are made inside of hub, the cupping not being included in the lengths given. Always give sizes.

Size.		Style Mortise.	Price, per set.		Weight, per set. lbs.
Diam. In.	Length In.		Oak.	Birch.	
6	7	Part Dodged			20
6	7½	"			20
6	8	"			20
6½	7½	"	$0 85	$0.85	25
6½	8	"			25
6½	8½	"			25
7	8	Straight & "			30
7	8½	"	.97	.91	30
7	9	"			30
7½	8½	"	1.12	1.00	35
7½	9	"			35
8	9	"	1.18	1.12	40
8	10	"	1.25	1.18	40
8¼	10	"	1.31	1.25	45
8½	10	"	1.37	1.31	50
8½	11	Straight.	1.44	1.37	50
9	11	"	1.50	1.44	60
9	12	"	1.56	1.44	60
9½	11	"	1.56	1.44	75
9½	12	"	1.56	1.50	75
10	12	"	1.87	1.68	85
10½	12	"	2.18	1.81	95
11	13	"	3.25	2.25	110
12	14	"	3.68	2.87	125

These hubs are bored for thimble skeins and will be sent that way unless it is specified that they are wanted for in axles. Be sure and give dimensions in ordering.

Buggy Hubs.

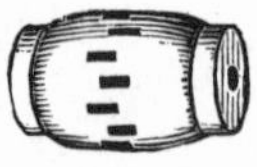

70811 Buggy and Spring Wagon Hubs, elm plain ends. 4 to a set.

	Price, per set.	Weight.
3 to 4 In. Diam	$0.60	4 to 7 lbs.
4¼ to 5 "	.66	8 to 11 lbs.
5¼ to 5¾ "	.78	12 to 14 lbs.
6 to 6¾ "	.96	15 to 18 lbs.
7 to 7¾ "	1.20	25 to 30 lbs.
8 to 8¾ "	1.63	37 to 43 lbs.
9 to 9¾ "	1.92	45 to 55 lbs.

Buggy Spokes.

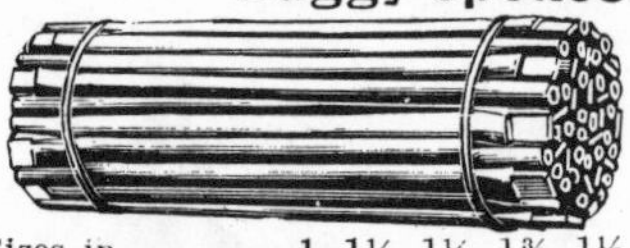

70826 Buggy spokes, hickory, 1 to 1⅜ 60 to a set, 1½ to 2 inch, 52 to set.

Sizes, in	1	1⅛	1¼	1⅜	1½	1⅝	1¾	1⅞	2
Weight, per set lbs.	25	28	32	35	40	46	48	54	60

Price, C Grade, $1.25 per set; B. select, $2.00; A, extra select, $2.50.

Wagon Spokes.

70828 Wagon Spokes, forest oak, 52 to a set.

Size. In.	Price per Set. C	B	B select	A	A select.	Weight
2 .		$1 80	$2.19	$2.69	$2.72	55 lb
2⅛ to 2½	$1.44	1.80	2.19	2.69	2.72	60-80lb
2⅝ in.	1.75	2.12	2.50	3.00	3.13	90 lb
2¾ in.	1.75	2.12	2.50	3.00	3.13	95 lb
3 in.	1.75	2.12	2.50	3.00	3.13	110 lb

Front bundles are half the price of a full set.

Hind bundles are half the price of a full set, plus 25c.

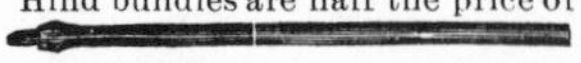

70830 Sarven Wheel Spokes; not put up in sets; will sell any quantity at prices quoted.

Size		A	B	C
¾ to 1¼,	price, each....	$0.09	$0.06	$0.05
" 1 5-16 to 1⅜,	price, each....	10	.07	.05
" 1 7-16 to 1½,	price, each....	.11	.08	.06
" 1 9-16 to 1⅝,	price, each....	.12	.09	.07
" 1¾,	price, each....	.16	.13	.11
" 1⅞,	price, each....	.17	.14	.12
" 2⅛,	price, each....	.18	.15	.13

70831 Club Spokes up to 1½ inch 1 cent each less than Sarven spokes. Do not carry over 1½ inch.

70832 Sulky Spokes, 29 inches long, 36 to set, size, ¾ to 1½ inclusive; extra select, per set, $2.00; second growth, ¾ to 1½, per set, $3.00; all white, ¾ to 1¼, per set, $3.50

Sawed Felloes.

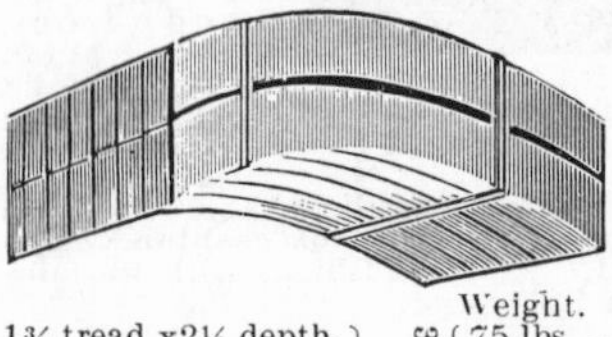

70834 Sawed Felloes, select white oak, rough; 26 to set. Nothing less than one front or one hind bundle furnished.

		Weight.	Per Set.
1¾ tread x2¼ depth,	3 ft., 8in. and 4 ft., 6 in.	75 lbs	$1.25
1¾ tread x2½ depth,		80 lbs	1.30
2 tread x2½ depth,		85 lbs	1.35
2 tread x2⅝ depth,		90 lbs	1.35
2 tread x2¾ depth,		95 lbs	1.40
2¼ tread x3 depth,		130 lbs	2.00
2½ tread x3 depth,		160 lbs	2.30
2¼ tread x3 depth,	3 ft. 2 in 4 ft. 2 in	130 lbs	2.00
2½ tread x3 depth,		160 lbs	2.30

Special diameters sawed to order. Prices on application.

Bent Felloes or Rims.

Nothing less than rims for two wheels furnished in each diameter.

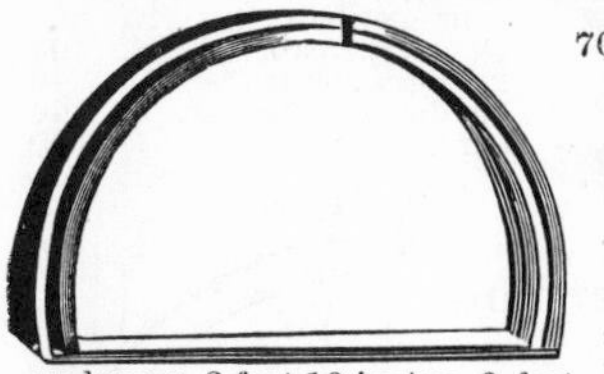

70836 All Select Hickory Rims; 1¼ inch and under are made 3 feet 8 inches and 4 feet circles; 1⅜ inch are made 3 feet 8 inches and 4 feet, 2 inches, circles. All Black Hickory Rims 1⅜ inch and under are 2 feet 10 inches, 3 feet, 3 feet 2 inches, 3 feet 4 inches, 3 feet 6 inches, 3 feet 8 inches, 3 feet 10 inches, 4 feet, or 4 feet 2 inches; 1½ and 1⅝ inch rims are 3 feet, 3 feet 2 inches, 3 feet 4 inches, 3 feet 6 inches, 3 feet 8 inches, 4 feet, or 4 feet 2 inches; 1¾ inch and over are 3 feet, 3 feet 4 inches, 3 feet 8 inches, 4 feet, or 4 feet 2 inches circles.

PRICE, PER SET (4 WHEELS).

Size.	Select Hickory.	Black Hickory.	Weight.
1 x inch square	$0.70	$0.90	25 lbs.
1⅛x inch square	.70	.90	30 lbs.
1¼x inch square	.78	1.00	35 lbs.
1⅜x inch square	.85	1.25	45 lbs.
1½x inch square	.95	1.30	50 bls.
1⅝x inch square	1.10	1.52	55 lbs.
1¾x inch square	1.30	1.75	65 lbs.
1⅞x inch square	1.70	2.12	75 lbs.
2 x inch square	1.75	2.31	80 lbs.

Bent Truck and Wagon Rims.

70837 Select White Oak.

Tread size,	Depth.	Price, per set.	Weight.
3 inch.	1¾ inch.	$2.00	120 lbs.
3	2	2.25	125 lbs.
4	1¾	2.65	155 lbs.
4	2	2.88	160 lbs.

Stock sizes; 38, 42, 44, 50 and 54 inch circles.

Buggy Singletree Woods.

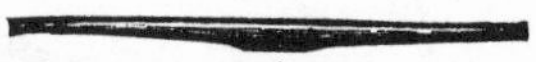

70840 Buggy Singletree Woods, forest hickory, 1½, 1⅝ 1¾, 1⅞ inch center. *Give size when ordering.* Each..............$0.12 Per dozen..........$1.30 Second Growth Hickory, Each, 18c. Per doz., $2.00.

Bent Heel Buggy or Cutter Shafts.

70841 In Rough. Price, per pair.

Size.	Weight.	XXX.	Black Hickory
1⅜x2	17 lbs.	$0.38	$0.60
1½x2¼	20 lbs.	.54	.78
1⅝x2¼	23 lbs.	.64	.90

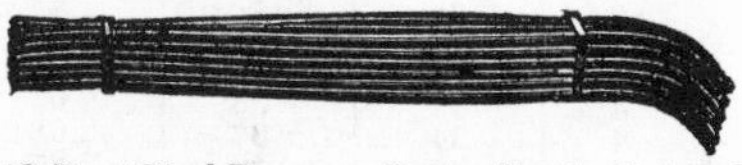

70842 Bent Heel Buggy or Cutter Shafts, finished, bars included. *Give size when ordering.*

Size.	Weight.		XXX	Blk Hick'y
1⅜x1⅞	11¼ lbs.	Per pair,	80c.	$1.05
1⅜x2	12¼ lbs.			
1½x2	12½ lbs.			
1½x2¼	14½ lbs.			
1⅝x2¼	15 lbs.			

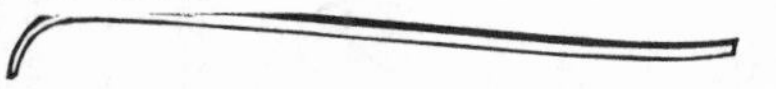

70842½ Finished Cart Shafts. 1⅝x2⅛, 9 feet 6 inches long. Per pair.....................$1.75

Buggy Poles.

70843 In the Rough.

Size.	Weight.	Select.	Black Hickory.
1¾x2¼	15 lbs.	$0.55	$0.90
2x2½	18 lbs.	.55	.90
2x2¾	21 lbs.	.75	1.05
2x3	24 lbs.	.75	1.05
2¼x3	28 lbs.		1.30
2¼x3½	35 lbs.		1.50

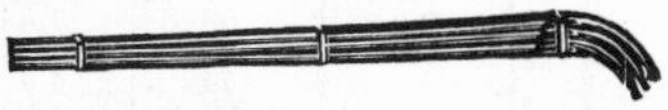

Buggy Poles, finished, including finished circles. The prices below are for one pole and circle, which are called a set.

70843½—

Size.	XXX	Black Hickory.	Weight.
1¾x2¼	$0.75	$0.95	14 lbs.
2 x2½	.80	1.05	15 lbs.
2 x2¾	.92	1.25	17 lbs.
2 x3	.95	1.28	19 lbs.

Double Bend Poles, add 5 cents to price of single bend.

Buggy Neck Yokes.

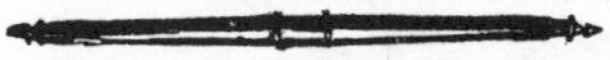

70844 Buggy Neck Yoke Woods, 40 in long, second growth of hickory. Acorn tips, 1⅝ to 2 inch center. Each, $0.25. Per dozen, $2.50. Weight, 2¼ lbs.

70846 Carriages and Express Neck Yoke Woods, Hickory, 2¼ inches in center. Each.....................$0.30 Per dozen............$3.50. Weight, 3 lbs.

38—2nd

Neck Yokes—Continued.

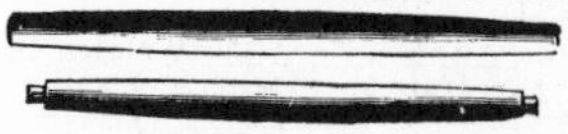

70848 Singletree Woods, round hickory, not ironed; 2½ in.; center weight, 3½ lbs, Each...$0.09 Per doz. $1.00

70850 Singletree Woods, oval hickory, not ironed, 2½ in., center weight, 3¾ lbs. Each.......... .09
Per dozen.......... 1.00

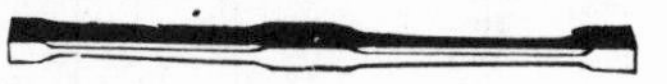

70852 Wagon Evener Woods, hickory, not ironed, 2x4 in, 4 feet long, weight, 7¾ lbs. Each $0.19
Per dozen.......... 2.05
Same, 2½x4½, weight, 10 lbs. Each.......... .27
Per dozen.......... 3.00

70853 Plow Eveners, 1¾x3½; weight, 5 lbs.
Each.......... .13
Per dozen.......... 1.40

70854 Buggy and Express Wagon Evener Woods, not ironed, but dressed and rounded. Select hickory.

Width	2¼ in.	2½ in.	3 in.
Length	4 ft.	4 ft.	4 ft.
Price, each	$0.17	$0.17	$0.17
Per dozen	1.85	1.85	1.85

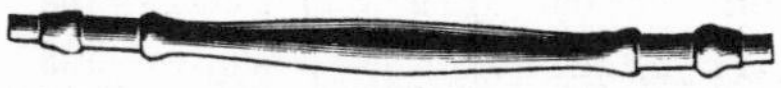

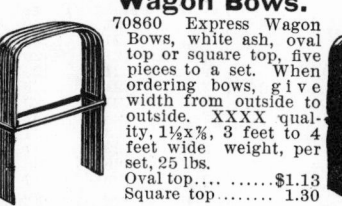

70856 Wagon Neck Yoke Wood, round hickory, 2 inch center, 38 inches long, not ironed, weight, 3 lbs. 3 oz. Each..........$0.10
Per dozen.......... 1.10

Buggy Gearing.

70857 Buggy gearing in the rough, made of carefully selected stock from the best timber sections of the country.

	Size	Length	Price, each. Black Hickory	Second growth.
Axle beds bent	1½x2 in.	4 ft. 6 in.	$0.23	$0.27
Axle beds bent	1½x2¼ in.	4 ft. 6 in.	.24	.29
Axle beds bent	1⅝x2¼ in.	4 ft. 6 in.	.25	.31
Spring bars	1½x2 in.	3 ft.	.12	.17
Spring bars	1¾x2¼ in.	3 ft.	.13	.18
Head blocks	1¾x2¼ in.	2 ft.	.08	.14
Reaches. str'ig't	1 x1 in.	6 ft.	.10	.14
Reaches, str'ig't	1⅛x1⅛ in.	6 ft. 6 in.	.12	.15
Reaches, str ig't	1¼x1¼ in.	6 ft. 6 in.	.13	.17
Reaches, str'ig't	1½x1½ in.	6 ft. 6 in.	.14	.18
Side bars	1½x2 in.	60 in. (1 s't)	.28	.34
Side bars	1¾x2¼ in.	72 in. (2 s't)	.34	.45
Side bars	2 x2½ in.	72 in. (2 s't)	.34	.45

Wagon Gearing, Rough.

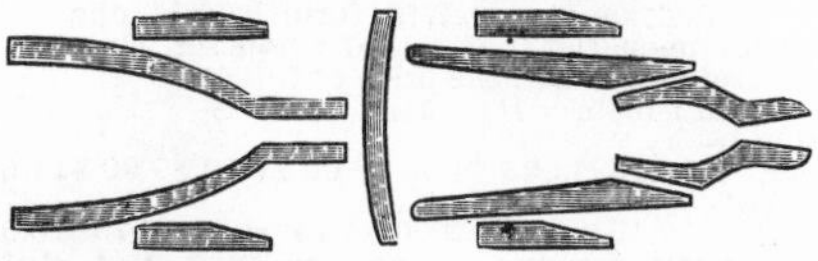

70858 Wagon Gearing, sawed select oak, consisting of
2 front hawns, per pairs..........$0.25
2 hind hawns, per pair.......... .27
2 tongue hawns, per pair.......... .25
1 sway bar, each.......... .12
4 stakes. per set.......... .10
Set complete.......... .99
(Weight, per set, 55 pounds)

70859 Lent Hawns, wide or narrow track, 2x3 in. Weight, 20 lbs. Each..........$0.51

Wagon Bows.

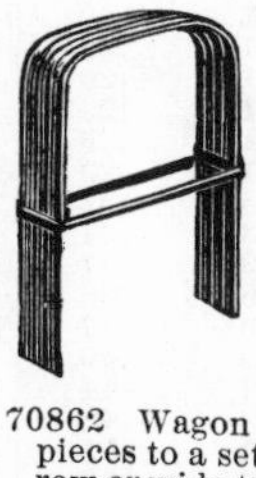

70860 Express Wagon Bows, white ash, oval top or square top, five pieces to a set. When ordering bows, give width from outside to outside. XXXX quality, 1⅛x⅝, 3 feet to 4 feet wide weight, per set, 25 lbs.
Oval top.......$1.13
Square top........ 1.30

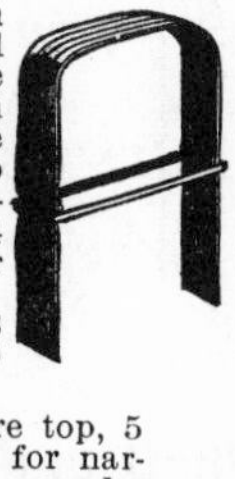

70862 Wagon Bows, round or square top, 5 pieces to a set (be sure to say whether for narrow or wide track); weight, per set, 30 pounds; Size, 1⅞x⅝ inches. Per set, round top........$0.60
Per set, square top.......... .65

Wagon Axles, Rough.

70872 Wagon Axles, Shell Bark hickory.

Size.	Weight per pair.	Per pair.
3x4 in. by 6 ft. long	48 lbs.	$0.70
4x5 in. by 6 ft. long	80 lbs.	1.40
4x6 in. by 6 ft. long	96 lbs.	1.65
5x6 in. by 6 ft. long	120 lbs.	2.25
5x7 in. by 6 ft. long	142 lbs.	2.65

Wagon Reaches.

70874 Wagon Reaches, select white oak in the rough.

Size.	Length.	W't.	Each.	Size.	Length,	W't.	Each.
2x4	8 ft.	11 lbs.	25c	2½x4½	12 ft.	47 lbs.	57c
2x4	10 ft.	13½lbs.	33c	2½x5	10 ft.	45 lbs.	50c
2x4	12 ft.	16 lbs	38c	2½x5	12 ft.	57 lbs.	60c
2½x4½	8 ft.	31 lbs.	38c	3x5	12 ft.	60 lbs.	71c
3¼x4½	10 ft.	40 lbs.	43c				

Wagon Bolster.

70876 Wagon Bolsters, select white oak in the rough.

Size	Length.	Weight.	Each.
2½x3 in.	4 ft	14 lbs.	$0.13
3x4 in.	4 ft	16 lbs.	.16
3x4 in.	4½ ft.	18 lbs.	.20
3½x4½ in.	4 ft.	21 lbs.	.18
3½x5 in.	4 ft.	23 lbs.	.21
4x5 in.	4½ ft.	27 lbs.	.26
4x6 in.	4 ft.	33 lbs.	.28
3½x4½ in.	4 ft.	21 lbs.	.26
4x5 in.	4 ft.	28 lbs	.35
4x6 in.	4½ ft	36 lbs.	.45

Wagon Tongues.

70878 Wagon Tongues, select white ash, rough, size at butt, 3x3, tip, 2x3, 12 feet long; weight, 30 lbs. Each..........$0.75

70880 4x4, 12 feet long; tip, 2x4, weight, 50 lbs. Each.......... .80

Bob Woods.

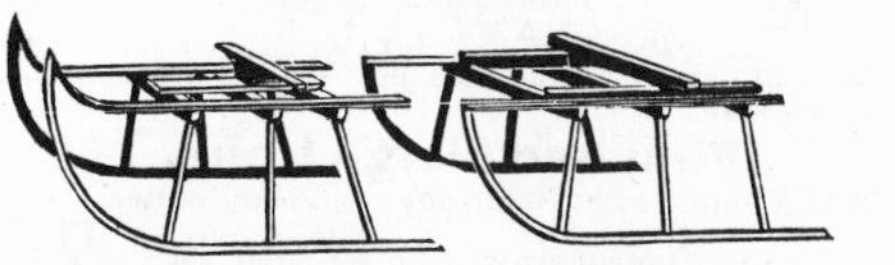

70890 Finished Grocery Bob Woods, all made with 3 knees front and 2 hind, extra well finished, not ironed or painted, but ready for finishing.
1⅛x1½ tread, per set..........$5.95
1¼x1¾ tread, per set.......... 6.85

Bob Runners, Stock Sizes.

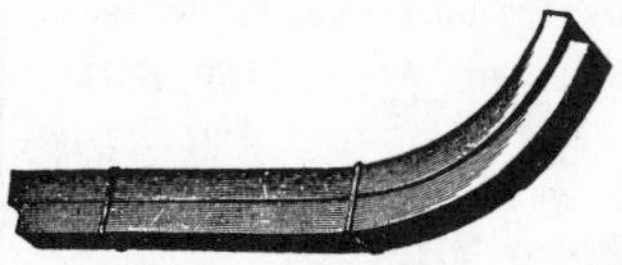

70892 Bob Sleigh Runeners, bent, entire length, 5½ feet.

	Weight.	Per set.		Weight.	Per set.
2x3.	45 lbs.	$1.44	2½x3½,	75	$1.92
2x3½,	60 lbs.	1.68	2x4,	65	2.08

Cast Iron Bob Sleigh Shoes.

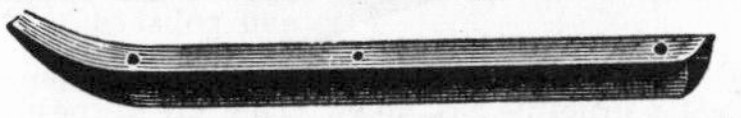

Cast Iron Bob Sleigh Shoes, interchangeable for right or left hand.

	Length.	Weight, per set of four.	Per set.
70894	36 inches.	64 pounds	$1.28
	38 inches.	66 pounds	1.32
	40 inches.	68 pounds	1.36
	42 inches.	70 pounds	1.40
	44 inches.	72 pounds	1.44
	48 inches.	76 pounds	1.52

Sleigh Shoe Bolts.

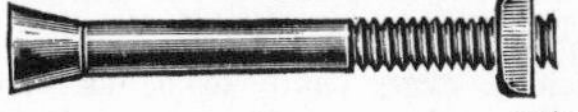

70895

Length.	Diameter.	Price, per Set of 16
4½ in.	7/16	$0.26
5 in.	7/16	.28
5½ in.	7/16	.31
6 in.	7/16	.38

Long Sleigh Runners, Solid.

70896 Bent, white oak, 10½ feet long.

	Per pair.		Per pair.
1⅜x2	$1.00	2 x3	$2.00
1⅝x2¼	1.10	2 x3½	2.10
1¾x2½	1.49	2½x4	2.40
2x2¾	1.60	2⅝x4½	2.80

Cutter Stuff.

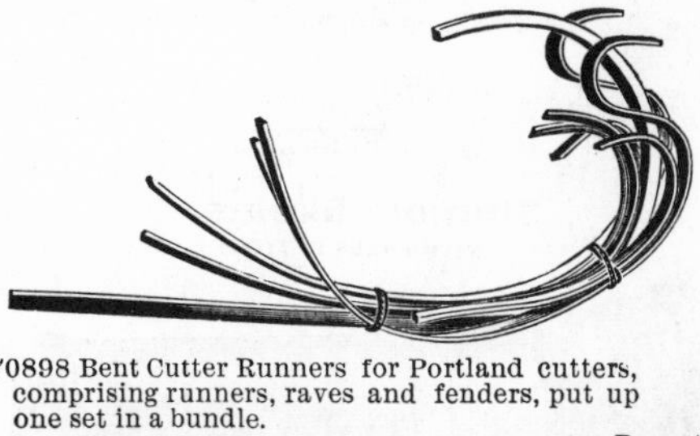

70898 Bent Cutter Runners for Portland cutters, comprising runners, raves and fenders, put up one set in a bundle.
Per set.
1¼ inch, one seat, weight, 35 lbs..........$1.00
1½ inch, two seat, weight, 40 lbs.......... 1.10

70899 Same for swell body cutters.
1¼ inch, one seat, weight, 35 lbs.......... 1.50
1½ inch, two seats, weight, 40 lbs.......... 2.20

70899½ Same for square box cutter.
1¼ inch, one seat, weight, 30 lbs.......... .85
1½ inch, two seats, weight, 35 lbs.......... .95

For cutter irons see 70916.

Bob Sleigh Gearing.

Per set.

70900 Bob Beams, 5 to a set, 3x3½; weight, 60 pounds...$0.72

70902 Bob Knees, 10 to a set, 3x3½x18; weight, 40 pounds... .40

70904 Bob Raves, 4 to a set, 1¾x6¾x54; weight, 40 pounds... .68

70906 Bob Rollers, 2 to a set, 3x3½x36; weight, 5 pounds... .23

70908 Bob Saddles, 1 to a set, 2x12x24; weight, 10 pounds...... .... .17

70910 Bob Reaches, 1 to a set, 2x4x48; weight, 7½ pounds... .10

70912 Sawed Bob Benches, white oak; wide, 3 feet 6; narrow, 3 feet 2 track; 3x9; each, 45c; 3½x9, each, 54c; 4x9, each, 63c.
Bob benches weigh 120 pounds to a set.

Cutter Shoes.

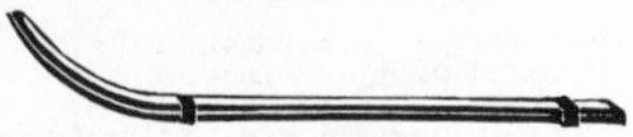

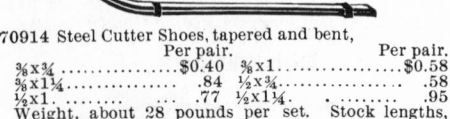

70914 Steel Cutter Shoes, tapered and bent,

Per pair.		Per pair.	
⅜x¾	$0.40	⅜x1	$0.58
⅜x1¼	.84	½x¾	.58
½x1	.77	½x1¼	.95

Weight, about 28 pounds per set. Stock lengths, 6, 6½ and 7 feet.

Finished Sleigh Irons.

70916 Complete Set Irons, for swell body cutter. Per set.................. ....$3.57

70917 Same for square box cutter. Per set..... 3.25

70918 Same for Portland cutter.................. 3.25

Iron and Steel Tires.

Iron and Steel Tire, in sets of 54 feet. Prices subject to change of market.

70920 IRON TIRE.

Size	1¼x⅜	1⅜x⅜	1½x½	1⅝x½	1¾x½	2x½
Wg'ht Per set	85 lbs.	94 lbs	137 lbs.	148 lbs.	160 lbs.	180 lbs
Price Per set	$1.48	$1.53	$2.40	$2.60	$2.80	$3.15

70922 STEEL TIRE.

Size	¾x$\frac{3}{16}$	⅞x$\frac{3}{16}$	1x¼	1¼x¼
Weight, per set	27 lbs.	30 lbs.	48 lbs.	60 lbs.
Price, per set	$0.50	$0.55	$0.84	$1.05

Plow Shares.

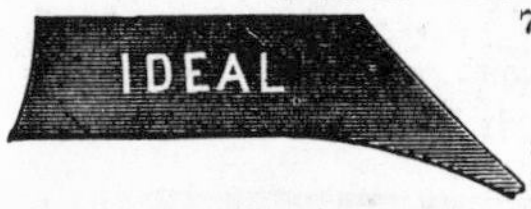

70925 What is the use of hammering out your shares when you can get shares, drawn, shaped and polished, ready to weld? They are made of the best soft center and solid crucible cast steel. They are the best shape, have an upset edge and can be easily fitted to any plow.

No. 1 Shares, double shinned, for old ground plows, made from soft center steel, 12, 14 or 16 inch cut. Each.. .... $1.32 $1.62 $1.85

No. 1 Shares, single shinned, for old ground plows, made from soft center steel, 12, 14 or 16 inch cut. Each..........................$1.11 $1.28 $1.45

No. 2 Shares, double shinned, for old ground plows, made from solid crucible cast steel, 12, 14 or 16 inch cut. Each.........90c. $1.13 $1.20

No. 2 Shares, single shinned, for old ground plows, made from solid crucible cast steel, 12, 14 or 16 inch cut. Each.............88c. $1.05 $1.18

We guarantee every share to be as represented.

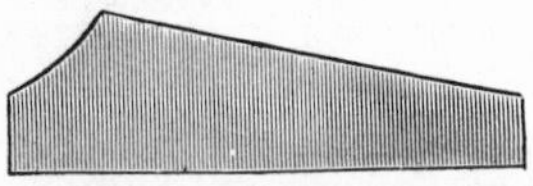

70926 No. 1 Landside Plates, ready for use for 14 or 16 inch plow, made of soft center steel.
14-inch, each.....$0.80 16-inch, each.............$0.90

70927 No. 2 Landside Plates, ready for use for 14 or 16 inch plow, made of crucible cast steel.
14 inch, each.........$0.45 16-inch each.......$0.55

Harrow Teeth.

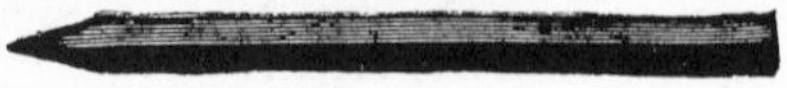

Steel Harrow Teeth, square, plain. Give length when ordering.

	Sizes.	Per dozen.
70928	½x8, 8½, 9 in.	$0.25
	$\frac{9}{16}$x8½, 9 in	.30
	⅝x8½, 9, 9½ and 10 in.	.40
	¾x10 and 11 in.	.90

Thimble Skeins.

WITH BOXES TO FIT.

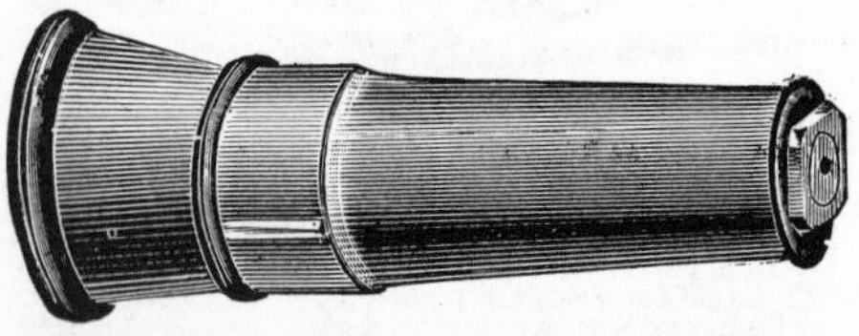

70929 Thimble Skeins, seamless, prices include nuts. Will furnish one skein only at one-quarter the price of full set or one-half a set at one-half the price of full set; when ordering one skein only, state whether right or left is wanted.

Thimble Skeins—Continued.

Size. Inches.	Weight, lb. Iron.	Price Per Set. Iron.	Price Per Set. Steel.	Weight, lb Steel.
2 x 6	24	$0.82		
2 x 6½	26	.82		
2⅛x 6½	26	.88		
2¼x 7	28	.94	$3 74	44
2¼x 7½	30	1.00	3.80	46
2⅜x 7	30	1.00		
2⅜x 7½	32	1.00		
2½x 7	32	1.13		
2½x 7½	34	1.13	3.80	48
2½x 8	36	1.19	3.87	50
2¾x 8	40	1.32	4.07	51
2¾x 8½	48	1.35	4.14	53
2¾x 9	52	1.50	4.20	60
3 x 9	56	1.50	4.34	66
3 x10	60	1.60	4.47	70
3¼x 9	65	1.75	4.96	70
3¼x10	70	1.88	5.00	76
3¼x11	74	1.94	5.06	80
3½x10	74	2.00	5.54	80
3½x10½	80	2.00	5.60	88
3½x11	84	2.08	5.67	94
3½x12	92	2.20	6.00	100
3¾x11	92	2.25	6.66	100
3¾x12	96	2.35	6.66	108
4 x12	116	2.65	8.00	112
4¼x12	122	3.75	8.67	135
4½x12	130	4.50		
4½x13	138	5.00	12.00	150

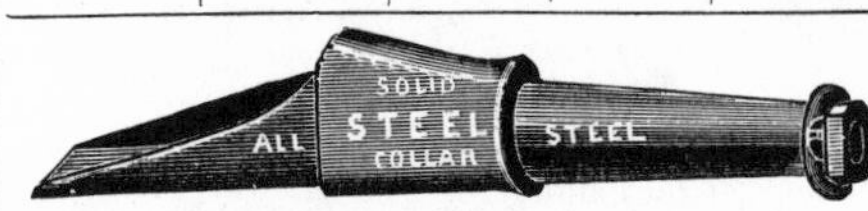

Wagon Wrenches.

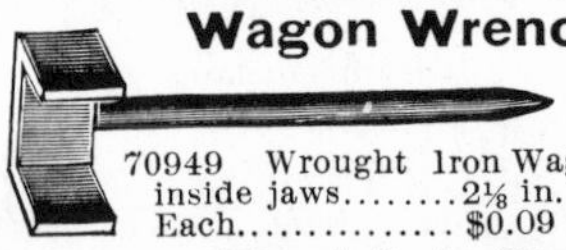

70949 Wrought Iron Wagon Wrenches, sizes inside jaws........2⅛ in. 2¼ in. 2¾ in.
Each...............$0.09 $0.11 $0.13

Steel Axle Stubs.

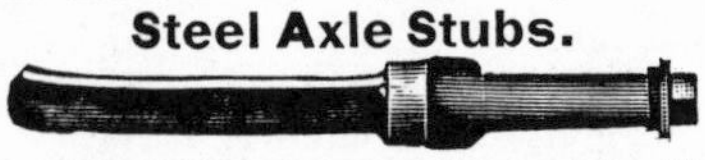

70950 A set consists of four stubs complete with boxing, that when welded together make a pair of axles. The long bed is intended to be welded together; the short bed is to weld on old axles. These axles have half patent solid collar swelled shoulder. Will furnish only one stub at one-quarter the price of whole set. One-half a set at one-half the price of full set.

Sizes..	⅞ to 1 inch.	1⅛	1¼	1⅜	1½	1⅝	1¾
Long bed— Per set,	$2.75	$3.25	$4.00	$6.00	$7.50	$9.00	$11.50
Short bed— Per set,	2.15	2.50	3.00	4.75	6.25	7.75	10.00

In ordering parts of sets be sure and state whether right or left hand is wanted.

Sand Bands.

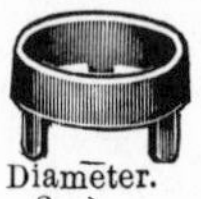

70951 Straight Patterns. To drive. For use on patent wheels.

Diameter.	Set-
2, 2⅛, 2¼, 2⅜, 2½	$0.08
3⅝, 2¾, 3	.10
3¼, 3½, 3¾, 4	.15

Rim Bands.

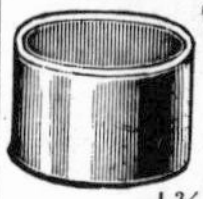

70953 Turned Malleable Carriage Rim Bands.

Diameter.	1¾-in. Deep. Per set.	2-in. Deep. Per set.
2	0.21	0.29
2⅛	.21	.29
2½	.21	.29
2⅜	.21	.29
2½	.21	.29
2⅝	.21	.29
2¾	.23	.31
2⅞	.23	.31
3	.23	.31
3⅛	.26	.36
3¼	.29	.37
3⅜	.32	.40
3½	.36	.44
3⅝	.40	.48
3¾	.45	.53
3⅞	.50	.58
4	.55	.63

Shaft and Pole Couplings.

70954 Wire Anti-Rattler, made of steel wire; prevents rattling of the shafts.
Price, per pair............$0.05
Price, per dozen pairs..... .50

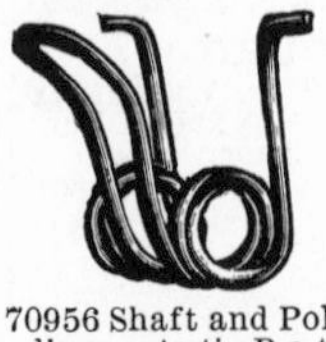

70956 Shaft and Pole Couplings. Anti-Rattlers "The Dandy," made of steel, the head strengthened by a plate riveted on to place in position set the lower part in the coupling and drive them in; they will not break; the corrugation on the side prevents them from working out. Per pair..... $0.10
Per doz pair. 1.00

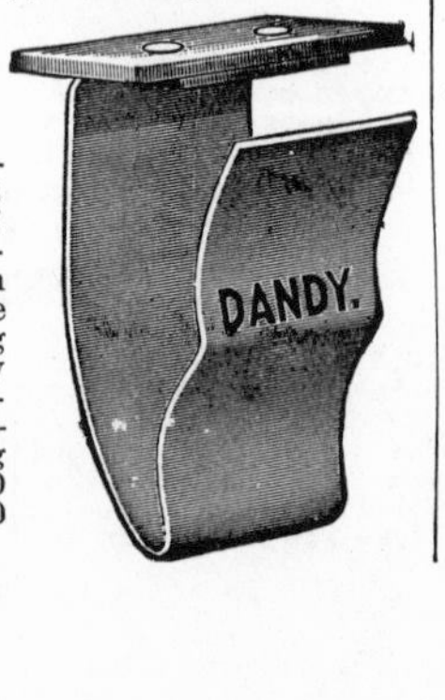

Shaft and Pole Couplings—Continued.

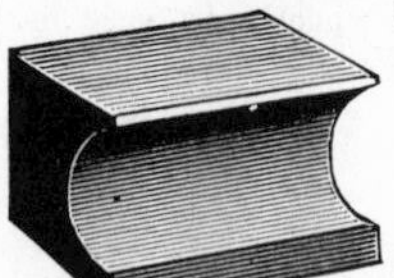

70957 Common pattern, rubber anti-rattlers
⅝ in., per pair.. ......$0.04
1 in., per pair......... .04
1⅛ in., per pair........ .05
Per dozen pairs......... .40
Per dozen pairs......... .40
Per dozen pairs .... .50

This Is What You Want.

EVERY ONE OWNING A BUGGY OUGHT TO HAVE A PAIR.

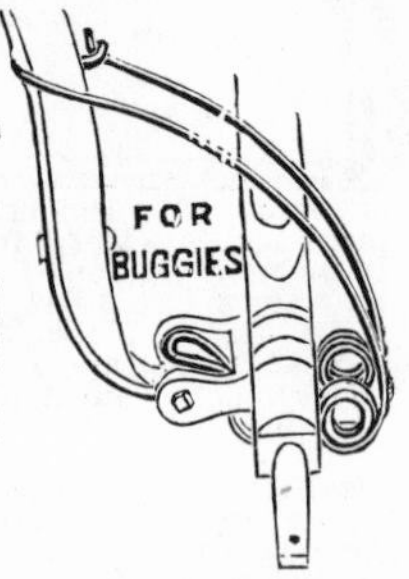

70959 The only shaft support and anti-rattler that will work on both buggies and spring wagons. No wear on harness no weight on horse's back, and no anti-rattler required.

WILL HOLD THE SHAFT AT ANY HEIGHT.

HOW TO ATTACH THE ANTI-RATTLER. SHAFT SUPPORT TO ANY BUGGY.

Drive out the old spring or rubber with a nail or punch. Put in spring from below in place of other; let the other end pass over axle; connect spring to the shaft; have spring slide between the nuts on shaft; oil shaft where holder slides.

Buggy size, per pair..............................$1.00
Spring wagon size, per pair................. .... 1.80
Surrey size, per pair.................................. ..... 1.60

Carriage Springs.

Oil Tempered; Half Bright.

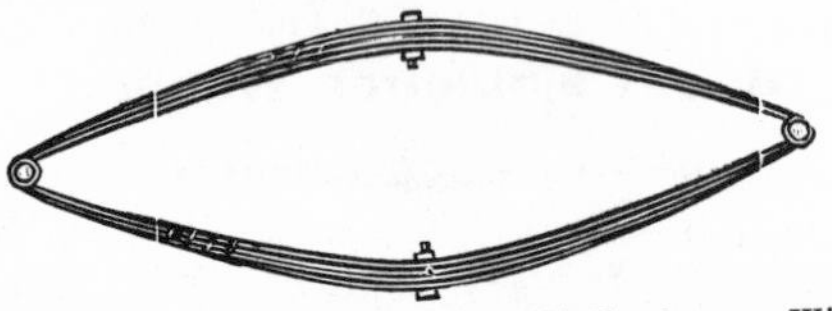

70960 Carriage Springs, regular elliptic shape. Will furnish only one spring at half the price of pair. Double sweep same price as single.

Width, Inches.	No. of Leaves.	Length, Inches.	Av. Weight Per Pair.	Price, Per Pair.
1⅛	3	32	28	$1.49
1⅛	4	32	30	1.62
1¼	3	32	32	1.75
* 1¼	3	34	33	1.82
* 1¼	3	36	35	1.95
1¼	4	32	36	2.01
* 1¼	4	34	37	2.08
* 1¼	4	36	40	2.27
* 1¼	5	36	43	2.47
1⅜	3	34	36	2.01
* 1⅜	3	36	38	2.14
* 1⅜	4	34	40	2.40
* 1⅜	4	36	45	2.53
* 1⅜	5	36	47	2.73
1½	3	34	39	2.21
* 1½	3	36	41	2.24
1½	4	34	46	2.60
* 1½	4	36	47	2.73
1½	4	38	51	2.99
1½	5	34	53	3.12
* 1½	5	36	55	3.25
1½	5	38	56	3.31
* 1½	6	36	63	3.83
1½	6	38	69	4.16
* 1¾	4	36	55	3.25
1¾	4	38	58	3.44
* 1¾	5	36	65	3.90
1¾	5	38	71	4.29
1¾	6	36	74	4.48
1¾	6	38	80	4.87
* 1¾	7	36	82	5.00
1¾	7	38	85	5.20
2	4	36	59	3.51
2	4	38	65	3.90
* 2	5	36	74	4.48
2	5	38	81	4.94
* 2	6	36	84	5.13
2	6	38	90	5.52
* 2	7	36	91	5.59
2	7	38	95	5.95
2¼	6	36	100	6.17
2¼	7	36	107	6.63
2¼	8	36	120	7.97
2½	7	36	165	10.40
2½	8	36	200	12.35

Springs marked * are stock sizes. All other sizes must be made to order, for which allow five days.

Sweet's Seat Springs.

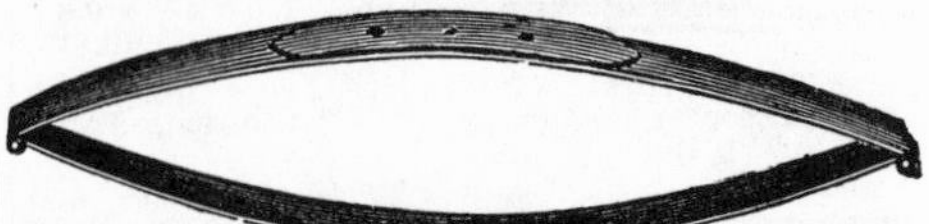

70962 Seat Spring, two leaf, 1½x26 inches.
Weight, per pair, 12 lbs.
Price, per pair...$0.65

Fig. 1.

Fig. 2.

The Brewster Patent Springs.

70963 Two each of figs. 1 and 2 constitute a set.

Per set.
1¼ by 2 and 3 leaf, stock lengths, 24 25, 26, 27 and 28 in.................................$1.90
1¼ by 3 and 4 leaf, stock lengths 25, 26, 27, 28, 28½, 29 and 30 in.......................1.90
1⅜ by 3 and 4 leaf, lengths 29 and 30 in. 2.15
1⅜ by 4 and 5 leaf, stock lengths............2.81
1½ by 3 and 4 leaf, stock lengths, 30, 31 and 32 in....2.81
1½ by 4 and 5 leaf, stocks lengths, 30 and 32 in.....3.75
1½ by 4 and 5 leaf, stock lengths, 33 and 34.....4.06
1½ by 5 and 6 leaf, stock lengths............4.10

The Brewster Springs we carry in stock are all full bright, with bushings and malleable shackles.
The length of Brewster Springs is always measured from center to center of side bars

Timken Patent Side-Bar Springs.

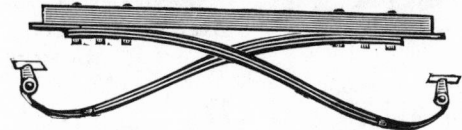

Order No. 70965.

No.	Width Front.	Plate	Width Back	Plate	Width Across Bottom	Size of Vehicle.	Price, per set.
1	1¼	3	1⅜	3	22 to 27 in.	Light top or no top buggy	$3.12
2	1⅜	3	1⅜	4	24 to 27 in.	Buggy with or without top	3.44
2¼	1⅜	3	1½	4	24 to 27 in.	Whitechapel buggy	3.75
2¾	1⅜	4	1½	4	24 to 27 in.	Livery buggy¹......................	4.06
3	1½	4	1½	5	26 to 32 in.	Two-seat sq. box wagon, with or without top ...	4.65
4	1½	4	1¾	6	26 to 32 in.	Two-seat surrey	5.00

The above prices are for bright finish, with malleable swinging and wrought permanent shackles and brass bushings, such as we carry in stock.

Special Notice.

We do not furnish single leaves for any of the preceding springs, as it is impossible to guarantee their fitting the bend of old springs they are intended to repair.

Platform Springs.

70970 Long side spring for buggy, each........$1.65
70972 One side of platform spring or one-half of duplex spring, each.....................1.75
70974 Long road cart spring to hang in stirrups, each..........1.25

In ordering the above three springs give drawings, number of leaves and measurements of all dimensions, including size of hole, and allow two weeks to have springs made.

There being so many different styles of platform springs manufactured we will positively not fill an order unless a drawing showing the exact curve and giving all the dimensions is sent. Do not try and describe the spring you want. Make a drawing, and be sure your name is marked on it, so we will know who sent it.

70976 Duplex Bolster Spring never strikes; has all the elasticity of a regular elliptic spring.

Capacity.	Size.	
1,000 lbs.	1½x4 Leaf	$6.60
1,500 lbs.	1½x5 Leaf	7.25
2,000 lbs.	1¾x4 Leaf	7.90
2,500 lbs.	1¾x5 Leaf	8.60
3,000 lbs.	2 x5 Leaf	8.90
4,000 lbs.	2 x6 Leaf	9.25
5,000 lbs.	2 x7 Leaf	9.90

Bolster Springs.

70978 For use on farm wagons.
When ordering state width between bolster stakes, and weight you wish wagon to carry.
These heavy spring steel leaves are more durable and far superior to coil springs and are taking their place wherever tested. Fits any farm wagon.

Per pair.
No. 0, 1,000 lbs. capacity, weight, 30 lbs.........$3.00
No. 1, 2,000 lbs. capacity, weight, 40 lbs. 3.50
No. 2, 4,000 lbs. capacity, weight, 50 lbs. 4.50
No. 3, 6,000 lbs. capacity, weight, 75 lbs..........5.50
Price is for two springs.

Clips and Block Plates.

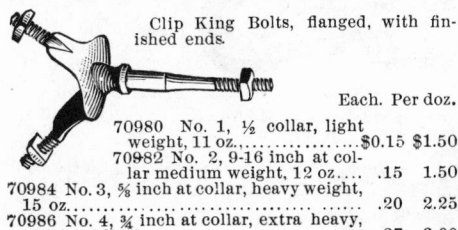

Clip King Bolts, flanged, with finished ends.

Each. Per doz.
70980 No. 1, ½ collar, light weight, 11 oz................$0.15 $1.50
70982 No. 2, 9-16 inch at collar medium weight, 12 oz.....15 1.50
70984 No. 3, ⅝ inch at collar, heavy weight, 15 oz.................20 2.25
70986 No. 4, ¾ inch at collar, extra heavy, weight, 1 lb. 4 oz. 27 3.00

Saddle Clips, half round pattern; a set consists of two clips and one top plate. The flat part of clips are 2, 2½, 2¾, 3, 3¼ and 3½ inches long for 1¼-inch springs, and run from 2¼ up to 4 inches for 1⅜-inch springs, and from 2½ to 4½ for 1½-inch springs. Give the length of flat part wanted when ordering

Per set. Per doz.
70990 For 1¼-inch spring................$0.13 $1.40
70992 For 1⅜-inch spring................14 1.50
70994 For 1½-inch spring.................15 1.60

Block Plates.

70996 Head Block Plates, single reach, finished ends, for ½ and 1⁄16 inch king bolts and 1¼ in. springs, for ⁹⁄16 and ⅝ king bolt and 1⅜ springs, for ⅝ king bolt and 1½ inch springs.
Each, any of the above sizes, $0.48 Per doz ...$5.50
70997 Same for double reach.
Each, any of above sizes.....$0.51 Per dozen.. 5.90

70998 Axle Clips, flat part 2½, 2¾, 3¼, 3¾, 4¼, 4¾ inches long, ⅜ inch wide and 1⁄16 inch shank. Clips, 2½ and 2¾; weight, 3 oz. each, 3¼ to 4¾, 5 oz. each.
Each up to 3¾ in . . $0.03 Per dozen.... $0.30
4¼ and 4¾ each.......05 Per dozen.........50
70999 Same, ⅜ shank.

		Per dozen	
Flat part 1⅜x4	......	.04	Per dozen.......	.45
Flat part 1⅜x4½	.....	.04	Per dozen.......	.45
Flat part 1⅜x5	......	.05	Per dozen.......	.55
Flat part 1⅜x5½	.....	.05	Per dozen.......	.55
Flat part 1⅜x6	......	.06	Per dozen.......	.65
Flat part 1⅜x6½	.....	.06	Per dozen.......	.65
Flat part 1⅜x7	......	.07	Per dozen.......	.75
Flat part 1⅜x7½	.....	.07	Per dozen.......	.75

71000 Axle Clip Yokes or Ties, wrought iron, punched holes, ⅞ to 1¼ inches between holes; have 1⁄16 inch holes, 1 to 2 have ⅜, 1⅛ to 2¼ have 7⁄16 inch holes. Weight, 2, 3 and 4½ ounces each. Per pair, 3c., 5c., 7c. Per dozen pairs, 25c., 50c., 75c.

71002 Stone's Shaft and Pole Shackle Jack, invaluable for fitting poles or shafts to vehicles where anti-rattlers are used.
Each......................$0.60

Shaft Couplings, Etc.

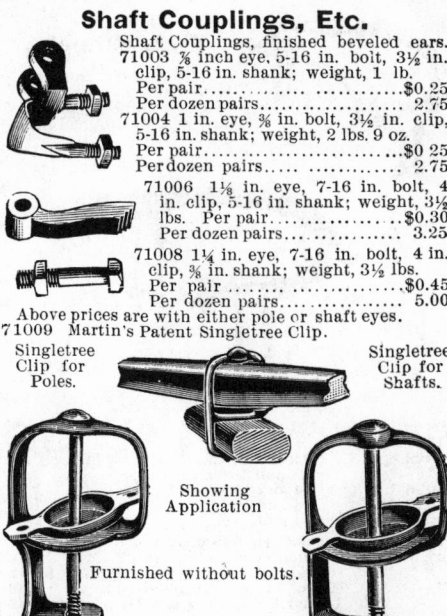

Shaft Couplings, finished beveled ears.
71003 ⅞ inch eye, 5-16 in. bolt, 3½ in. clip, 5-16 in. shank; weight, 1 lb.
Per pair............. ....$0.25
Per dozen pairs................... 2.75
71004 1 in. eye, ⅜ in. bolt, 3½ in. clip, 5-16 in. shank; weight, 2 lbs. 9 oz.
Per pair............................$0 25
Per dozen pairs....................2.75
71006 1⅛ in. eye, 7-16 in. bolt, 4 in. clip, 5-16 in. shank; weight, 3½ lbs...............$0.30
Per dozen pairs...............3.25
71008 1¼ in. eye, 7-16 in. bolt, 4 in. clip, ⅜ in. shank; weight, 3½ lbs.
Per pair $0.45
Per dozen pairs...............5.00

Above prices are with either pole or shaft eyes.
71009 Martin's Patent Singletree Clip.

Singletree Clip for Poles.   Singletree Clip for Shafts.

Showing Application

Furnished without bolts.

For 1¾ or 1⅜ in. singletree and cross bar, 1⅜ in. thick.
For 1⅝ or 1¾ in. singletree and cross bar, 1½ in. thick.
For 2¼ in. singletree and cross bar, 1⅞ in. thick.
Each................$0.07 Per dozen........$0.75

71010—Whiffletree Couplings, low pattern.

Width.	Length.	Size of hole.	Weight, oz.	Per pair.	Per doz. pair.
1½	4	⅜	4	$0.04	$0.25
1¾	4¾	⅜	8	.05	.30
2	4¾	⅜	9	.05	.30
2½	5¼	7⁄16	10	.06	.40
3	6½	7⁄16	15	.06	60

Whiffletree Bolts.

71011 Whiffletree Bolts, bent, black pattern.
⅜x3½ ⎫
⅜x4   ⎬ Each $0.04
7⁄16x3½ ⎪ Per dozen............42
7⁄16x4 ⎭

71011½ Shaft Bolts.   Each   Per doz.
1½ to 2 in. x ¼ in $0.02 $0.20
2 to 3 in. x 5⁄16 in...........03 25

Bolster Plates.

71012 Bolster Plates, wrought iron, common pattern.

Width	2¾	3	3¼	3¼
Weight	5½ lb.	5½ lb.	5½ lb.	6 lb.
Per set	20c.	25c.	30c.	32c.

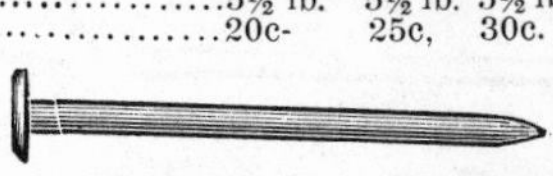

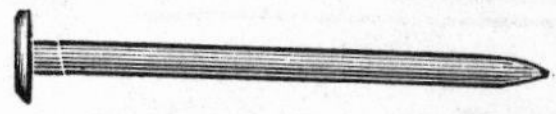

71013 Button Head Steel Wagon King Bolts,

Per doz.
⅞ inch. Each.....................$0.15 $1.50
1 "   " 20 2.00
1⅛ "   " 25 2.50
1¼ "   " 30 3.00

71014 Whiffletree Plates, 3¼ inches long, 5⁄16 round hole; weight, per set, 4 oz.
Per set $0.04
Per dozen sets.........................25

71016 Felloe Plates, Philadelphia pattern, wrought iron.

Sizes...	¾	⅞	1	1¼	1⅜	1½	1⅝	1¾	2 inches.
Per doz...	5	6	8	12	16	18	20	24	27 cents.
Weight ..	6	7	11	15	21	21	22	35	36 oz.

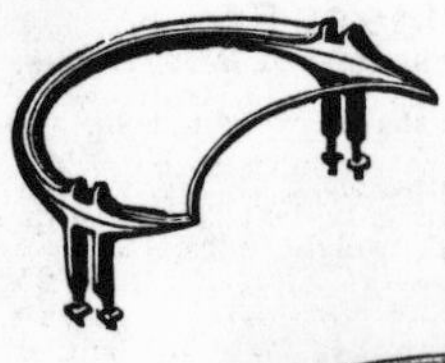

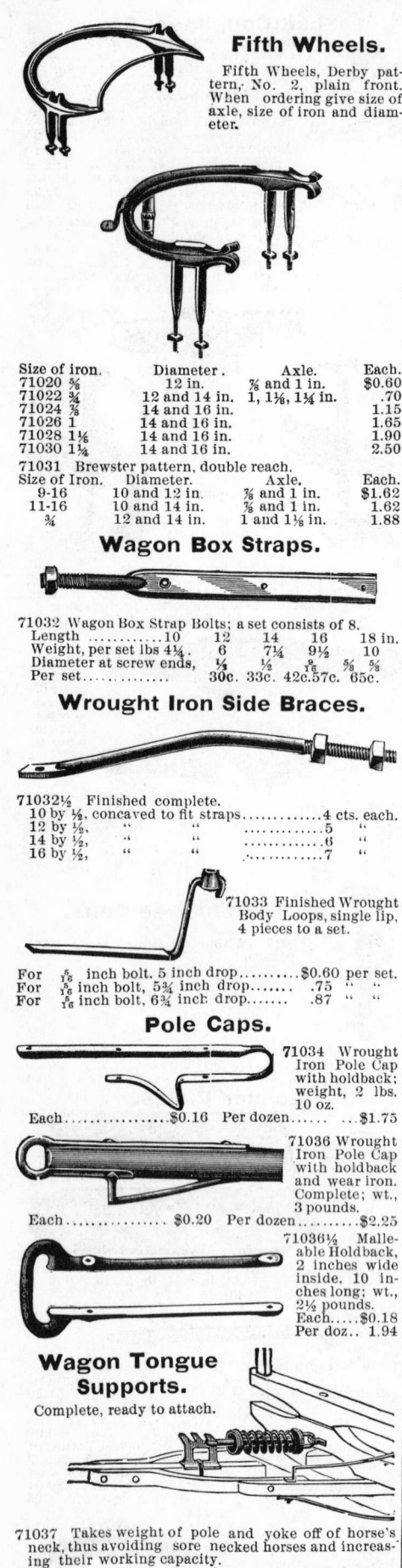

Fifth Wheels.

Fifth Wheels, Derby pattern, No. 2, plain front. When ordering give size of axle, size of iron and diameter.

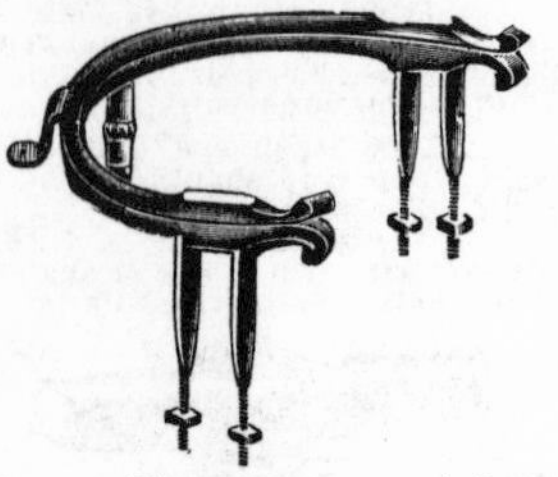

Size of iron.	Diameter.	Axle.	Each.
71020 ⅝	12 in.	⅞ and 1 in.	$0.60
71022 ¾	12 and 14 in.	1, 1⅛, 1¼ in.	.70
71024 ⅞	14 and 16 in.		1.15
71026 1	14 and 16 in.		1.65
71028 1⅛	14 and 16 in.		1.90
71030 1¼	14 and 16 in.		2.50

71031 Brewster pattern, double reach.

Size of Iron.	Diameter.	Axle.	Each.
9-16	10 and 12 in.	⅞ and 1 in.	$1.62
11-16	10 and 14 in.	⅞ and 1 in.	1.62
¾	12 and 14 in.	1 and 1⅛ in.	1.88

Wagon Box Straps.

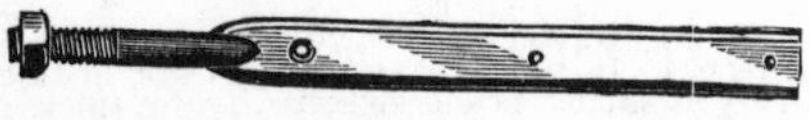

71032 Wagon Box Strap Bolts; a set consists of 8.

Length	10	12	14	16	18 in.
Weight, per set lbs	4¼	6	7¼	9½	10
Diameter at screw ends,	⅜	½	$\frac{9}{16}$	⅝	⅝
Per set	30c.	33c.	42c.	57c.	65c.

Wrought Iron Side Braces.

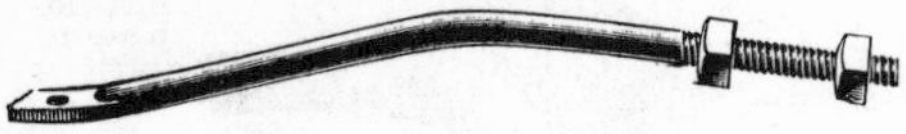

71032½ Finished complete.
10 by ⅛, concaved to fit straps ....4 cts. each.
12 by ½, " " ....5 "
14 by ½, " " ....6 "
16 by ½, " " ....7 "

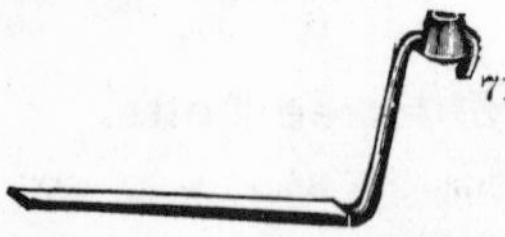

71033 Finished Wrought Body Loops, single lip, 4 pieces to a set.

For $\frac{5}{16}$ inch bolt, 5 inch drop ....$0.60 per set.
For $\frac{5}{16}$ inch bolt, 5¾ inch drop....... .75 " "
For $\frac{5}{16}$ inch bolt, 6¾ inch drop....... .87 " "

Pole Caps.

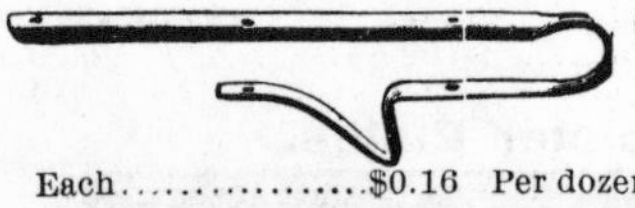

71034 Wrought Iron Pole Cap with holdback; weight, 2 lbs. 10 oz.
Each ....$0.16 Per dozen $1.75

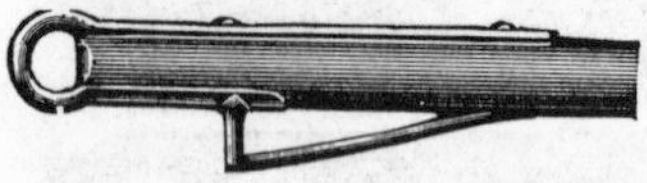

71036 Wrought Iron Pole Cap with holdback and wear iron. Complete; wt., 3 pounds.
Each .... $0.20 Per dozen $2.25

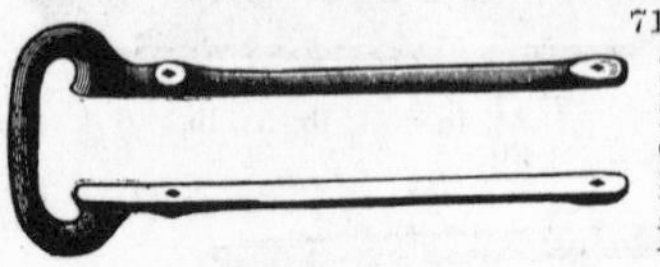

71036½ Malleable Holdback, 2 inches wide inside. 10 inches long; wt., 2½ pounds.
Each.....$0.18
Per doz.. 1.94

Wagon Tongue Supports.

Complete, ready to attach.

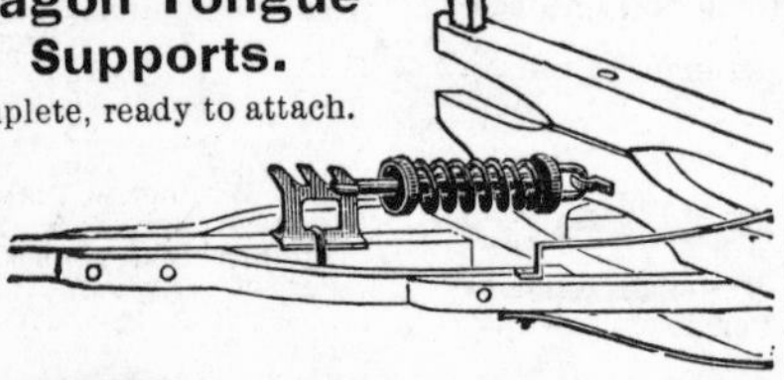

71037 Takes weight of pole and yoke off of horse's neck, thus avoiding sore necked horses and increasing their working capacity.
For light spring wagon and express wagon tongues .... $1.10 each,
For ordinary farm wagons .... 1.50 "
For heavy farm wagons........ .... 1.70 "

Pole Tips.

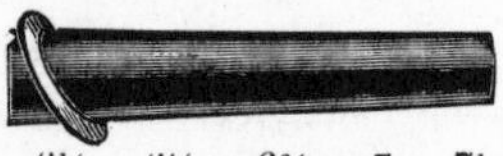

71038 Length	6¼	6½	6¾	7	7¼
Size of hole	1	1⅛	1¼	1⅜	1½
Weight, oz	14	14	17	18	23
Silver plated, each	$0.60	65	70	75	95
71039 Plain malleable. Each	.12c.	16c.	22c.	28c.	33c.

The Rider Safety Pole Tip.

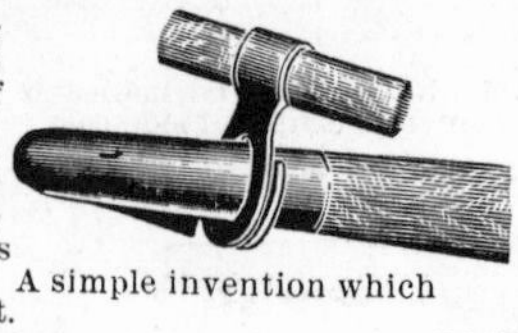

71039½ Has a spring lug which prevents neck yoke coming off pole. Simply press the lug up, to get the yoke off, there being a spring inside the cap which always keeps the lug down. A simple invention which fills a long-felt want.
Try one. 1⅛ $0.20
1¼ .... .24
1⅜ .... .28

Something New.

See No. 71150 for buggies in the white, all ironed and finished. Trim them up yourself and save money.

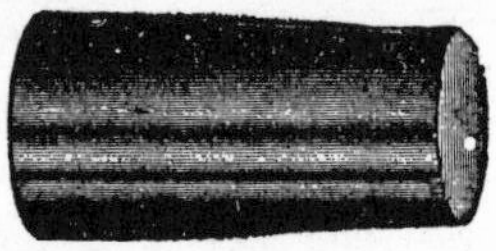

Shaft Tips.

71040 Size of hole	⅞x1¾ in.	1x2 in.
Weight	6 oz.	7 oz.
Silver plated, per pair	$0.06	$0.08
" " per doz. pair	.56	.85
71041 Wrought brass, per pair	.07	.08
" " per doz. pair	.68	.85

Size of hole, ⅞x1¾ in.
71041½ Malleable shaft tips, bright plate........$0.06
" per doz. pair .... .57

Whiffltree Hooks and Ferrules.

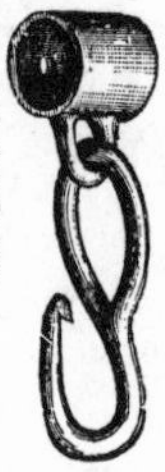

71042 Singletree Hook and Ferrule; wrought iron hook, malleable ferrule. 1¼ inch
Weight, each, 11 oz. Each $0.05
Per dozen .... .50
1½ inch. Each .... .06
Per dozen .... .60

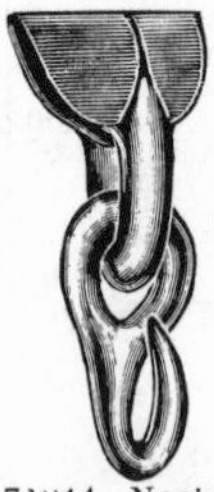

71043 Welded End Clip and Hook for 2½ in. singletree.

Size, Round part of clip.	Size of iron in hook.
$\frac{7}{16}$	⅜
⅜	$\frac{5}{16}$
Price Each.	Per Doz.
$0.05	$0.55
.04	.40

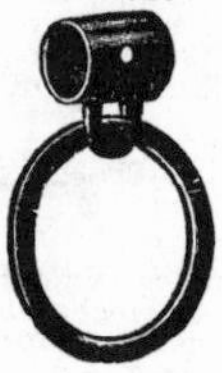

71044 Neck Yoke Ferrule and Ring; wrought iron ring, malleable ferrule. Weight each, 10 ounces.
Each $0.06
Per dozen .... .65

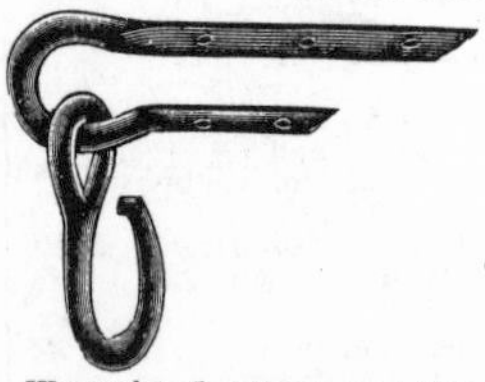

71045 Singletree Strap and hook, designed to rivet through singletree

	Each.	Per doz.
Wrought, for strap and ⅜ hook	$0.07	$0.75
" singletree strap only	.05	.55
" ⅜ hook	.03	.32

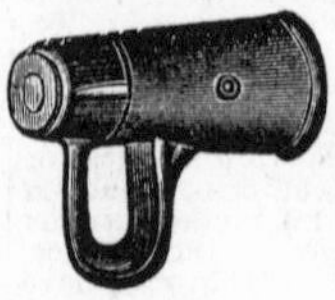

71046 Hawley's Patent Whiffletree Hooks.
Diameter, ⅞, 1, 1⅛, 1¼, 1⅜ in.
Per pair, 21c 23c 30c 33c 39c
Weight, per pair, 11, 12, 13 oz. 1 lb., 1⅛ lb.
Per dozen pairs.
$2.80, 3.00, 3.25, 3.66, 4.22.

Whiffletree Tips.

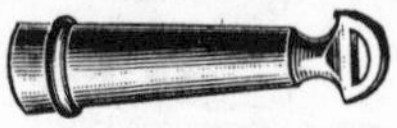

71048 Length	3¼	3½	4	4	4
Size of hole	¾	⅞	1	1⅛	1¼
Weight, per pair	8 oz.	8	13	14	21
Silver plated, per pr.	$0.45	.46	.53	.80	1.13
Silver plated, dz. pr.	4.85	4.90	5.73	8.65	12.15

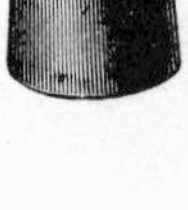

71049 Closed End—Core. Malleable.

Size inside large end	¾	⅞	1	1⅛	1¼ in.
Depth	1	1	1⅛	1$\frac{5}{16}$	1½ in.
Price, each	4c.	4c.	5c.	5c.	6c.
Price, doz	40c.	40c.	50c.	50c.	60c.

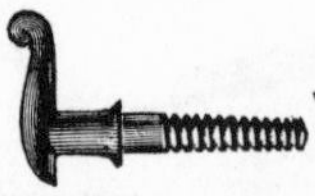

Malleable Whiffletree Tongues

71049½ With shoulder to screw.
3 inches long, $\frac{7}{16}$ in. shank. Each, 2c. Per doz., 15c
2⅞ inches long, ⅜ in. shank. Each. 3c. Per doz., 24c

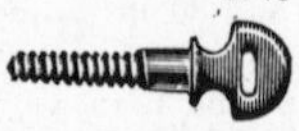

WITH SHOULDER TO SCREW.
71049¾ 2¾ inches long, $\frac{5}{16}$ in. shank. Each....$0.02
Per dozen .... .15
3¼ inches long, ⅜ in. shank. Each .... .02
Per dozen .... .20
For heavy work, 3¾ inches long, $\frac{7}{16}$ in. shank.
Each .... .03
Per dozen .... .24

Center Clips.

For 2 to 3 inch singletrees.

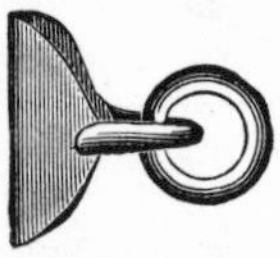

71050 Wrought Iron Center Clip with rings.

⅝x$\frac{9}{16}$	Each	$0.08	Per doz	$0.87
$\frac{9}{16}$x½	Each	.07	Per doz	.77
½x$\frac{7}{16}$	Each	.05	Per doz	.50

71051 Twisted and Welded Center Clip.

⅝ inch	Each	$0.06	Per doz	$0.68
$\frac{9}{16}$ inch.	Each	.05	Per doz	.55
½ inch.	Each	.05	Per doz	.50

Malleable Clevises.

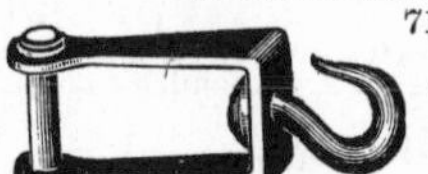

71052 Evener Clevis, with swivel hook, 2½ inches inside measurement, 9 inches extreme length. Weight, 3 lbs. 9 oz.
Each $0.15
Per doz 1.62

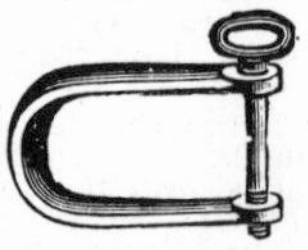

71054 Malleable Clevis, with screw pin, 2½ in. inside measure, 4½ in. in length. Weight, 1 lb. 10 oz.
Each $0.10
Per doz .... .90
71056 Malleable Plow Clevis, for 2½-inch beam, extreme length, 8¼ inch. Weight, 3¼ lbs.
Each ....$0.20 Per dozen $2.10

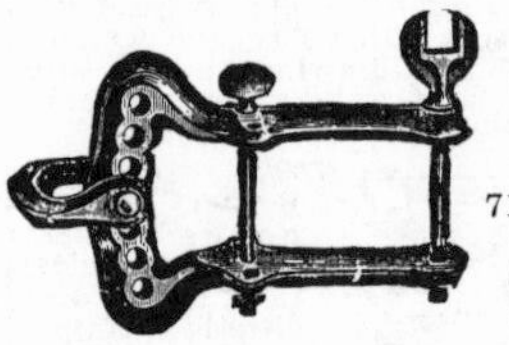

For 2¾-inch beam, extreme length, 8¾ inch. Weight, 3¼ lbs.
Each $0.22
Per doz 2.30
71058 Malleable End Clevis, inside measure, ¾ inch. Weight. 12oz.
Each $0.04
Per dozen .... .44

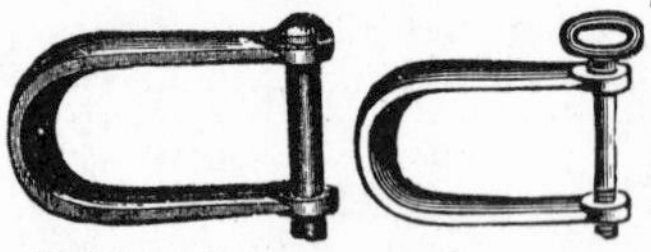

71060 Malleable Patent Self-Fastening Pin Clevis, inside measure, 2½ in.; whole length, 5½ inches.
Weight, 1 lb. 12 oz. Each $0.10
Per dozen 1.00
71062 Malleable Clevis, round pin, with eye; inside measure, 2¼ inches, whole length, 5½ in.
Weight, 1 lb. 12 oz. Each .... .10
Per dozen 1.00

Swivel Clevis.

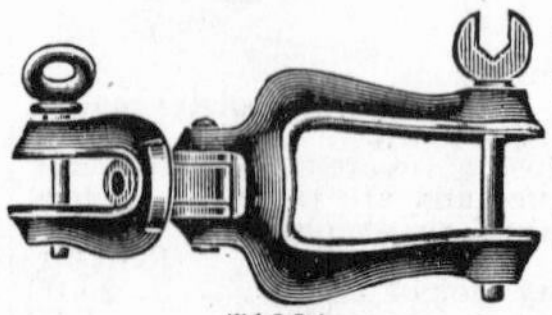

71064
Swivel Hook.

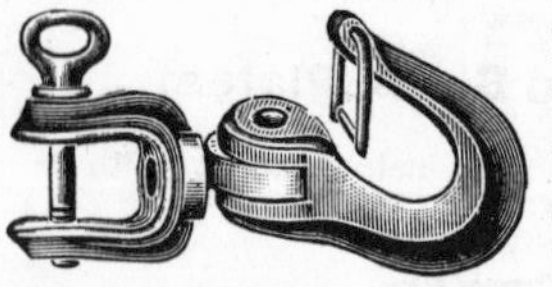

71065

These devices can be attached to any implement where hook or clevis is needed, without a link, adapting themselves to any position desired. The whiffletrees retain their proper position while you handle the plow anyway you wish. In passing stumps or trees, the doubletree will accommodate itself to any angle without disturbing the plow.

A harrow, with this device, can be raised to any angle, or turned over if necessary, without effecting the position of the doubletree.

71064 Swivel Clevis. Each $0.21
71065 Swivel Hook. Each .... .23

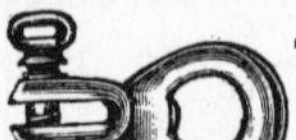

71067 New Swivel End Clevis; can be attached to any plow clevis.
Each $0.15
Per dozen 1.50

Clevises—Continued.

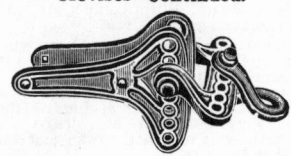

71069 Malleable Iron Plow Clevis, for 3 inch.
wood beam, 4¾ inch to center of beam holes,
weight, 5¼ pounds.
Each...$0.38

71071 Cross Link for iron heavy
plow clevis.

A.	B.	C.	
2¼	2½	3½ in. wide inside lugs.	
5	6	6½ inches long.	
6	7	8	holes.
5	7	10	cents, each.

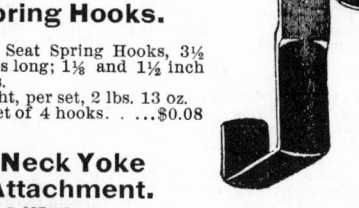

71072 Three Horse
attachment for iron
beam plow clevis,
malleable iron.

A.	B.	C.	
2	2⅜	3⅜ in. wide inside lugs	
7¾	9¼	9⅜ in. long.	
9	11	11	holes.
8	10	14	cents each.

Malleable Seat Spring Hooks.

71074 Seat Spring Hooks, 3½
inches long; 1⅛ and 1½ inch
hooks.
Weight, per set, 2 lbs. 13 oz.
Per set of 4 hooks. $0.08

Neck Yoke Attachment.

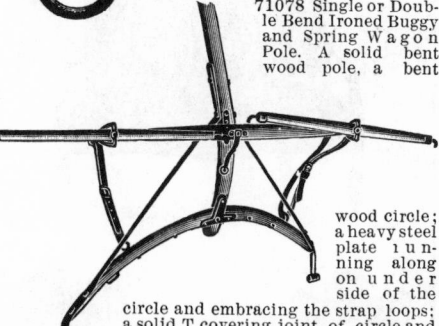

71076 Wrought Iron Neck Yoke
Attachment, with plates com-
plete. Weight, 2½ lbs.
Each.............................$0.15
Per dozen................. 1.50

71078 Single or Dou-
ble Bend Ironed Buggy
and Spring Wagon
Pole. A solid bent
wood pole, a bent
wood circle;
a heavy steel
plate run-
ning along
on under
side of the
circle and embracing the strap loops;
a solid T covering joint of circle and
pole stick. The staunchest pole made.
Buggy size, 1-inch eye, unpainted
complete...............................$3.25
Spring wagon size, 1⅛-inch eye, painted complete, with neckyoke............................ 3.50
Painted buggy size................................ 4.50
Painted spring wagon size......................... 5.75
45 inches wide at heel.

Acme Adjustable Pole.

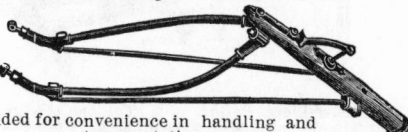

Folded for convenience in handling and
transportation.

71079 The best adjustable pole ever on the market. It can be adjusted without tools from 2 to
47 inches by merely pulling it apart or pressing
it together as required. It is interchangeable
with all sizes of eyes. The circle is made of
extra heavy tubing. The braces are of the best
quality of steel. The eyes are of the very best
forgings. It fits any wagon, carriage or sleigh
ever made. This pole is not furnished regularly
with our buggies, but is a special manufacture.
Price, with whiffletree and neck yoke...........$7.50
Weight, 30 pounds.

Stay Straps.

71080 Best Quality Leather, with Japanned
buckles. Per pair.................................$0.42

Trimmed Neck Yokes.

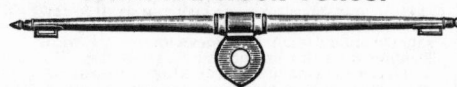

71082 Trimmed Neck Yokes, Leather Center,
acorn tips. 42 inches long; weight, 2 pounds
10 ounces. Each..................................$0.50

71083 Malleable Center Yoke, made of select
hickory, 1⅞ x42 long. Each................. $0,44
71085 Plain Leather Neck Yoke Centers,
made for 3 inch groove in sizes to
fit 1¾, 1⅞ and 2 inch yokes. Has galvanized metal collar, and can be attached by any
one with a common screw driver.
Price, each, $0.29 Per dozen.................... 3.25

Shafts.

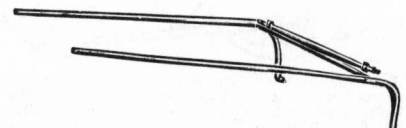

71087 All finished and ironed, in the white ready
to trim and paint.
Buggy size. Per pair.............................$1.25
Spring wagon size. Per pair...................... 1.45

Singletrees and Neck Yokes. Ironed.

71089 Single-
trees, 26 inch
plow, hickory
ironed, weight,
3¼ lbs. Each $0.17 Per dozen...............$1.84
71090 Singletrees, 30 inch plow, hickory, ironed;
weight, 3¾ pounds. Each.$0.19. Per dozen 2.00
71091 Singletrees, 36 inch wagon, hickory, ironed
with ferrules and hooks; weight, 6 pounds.
Each $0.32 Per dozen......................... 3.25
We can furnish any of the above singletrees with
twisted center clip instead of ring, at same price.

Strap End Singletrees.

71092 Have ½-inch strap, riveted on both sides
and ⅝ hook, extra strong, 2⅝x36.
Each.................. $0.35 Per dozen.......$3.60

Davis Safety Singletrees.

71093 With Davis Patent Hooks. Impossible
for the trace to become unhooked. Close connection and easily unhooked when desired.
2½x36. Each...........$ .33 Per dozen $3.45
2¼x30. Each.......... .21 Per dozen....... 2.18

71095 Neck Yokes, 38 inch; hickory, ironed complete, weight, 6¾ lbs. Each....$0.40 Per dozen$4.50

Perfection Wagon Doubletrees.

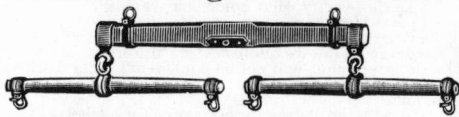

71097 Ironed, complete, with stay chain clips
and plates, on both sides of evener; woods oiled.
Evener 48 inches long. Singletrees 36 inches
long. Has adjustable clips. Suitable for wagons, threshers, engines, water tanks, etc. Quality guaranteed. Price, per set...............$1.75

ALL KINDS OF TOOLS
will be found quoted in our Hardware Department.

WE SELL ONLY GOOD TOOLS.

Pefection Plow Whiffletrees.

71098 Ironed, complete, ready for use. Evener
40 inches long. Singletree 34-inches long.
Suitable for general farm work. Adjustable
clips. Are made of best seasoned hickory,
thoroughly oiled, and the best quality malleable
clips No holes are bored in the wood to fasten
clips, thus preserving full strength of the wood.
Price, per set..................................$1.50

Ironed Evener.

71100 2x4x48 Wrought Iron Plates and malleable clevis, complete as shown in cut, oiled.
Each..$0.42
71101 Evener, Neck Yoke and Singletrees, with
clevises, complete sets ironed, and painted one
coat; weight, 30 lbs.; per set...... .... 1.50

71102 The Dandy Plow Doubletrees; 38 inches, hickory, evener and hickory singletrees with patent clips
and all irons complete. Price, only........ ....$0.90

Stay Chains.

71104 Wagon Stay Chains, black finish, wrought
iron, ⁵⁄₁₆ iron, 24 or 26 inches long. Per pair....$0.25

Wagon Box Rods.

71105 Wagon Box Rods, narrow track, 3 feet 3
inches long, with patent collar. Weight, each,
1¾ pounds. Price, each.......$0.09
Per dozen...................... .98

Wagon Bow Staples.
To Drive.
71107 Wagon Bow Staples; 1½,
1¾ and 2 inch. Weight, per doz,
15 oz. Per dozen............$0.07
Per gross..................... .80

Wagon Bow Staple.
To Rivet.

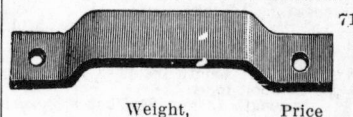

71108 Wagon
Bow Staples
(to rivet).

	Weight, doz.	Price doz.	Price gross.
1½	17 oz.	$0.07	$0 80
1¾	20 oz.	.08	.90
2	24 oz.	.09	1.00

Stake Irons.

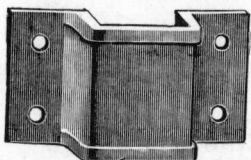

71110 2¾-inches deep.
For stake. 1½ x 3
inches. Malleable Iron,
weight, 4 pounds.
Each.............$0.16

Stake Rings.

71111 Stake, ⅞—1—1⅛-inch.
Ring, 1⅛—1¼—1½. Either
size. Per set of 8........ $0.10

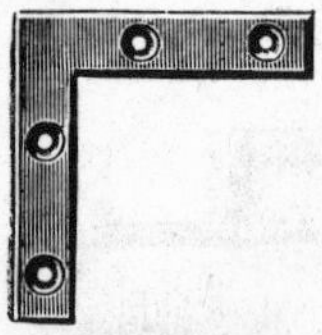

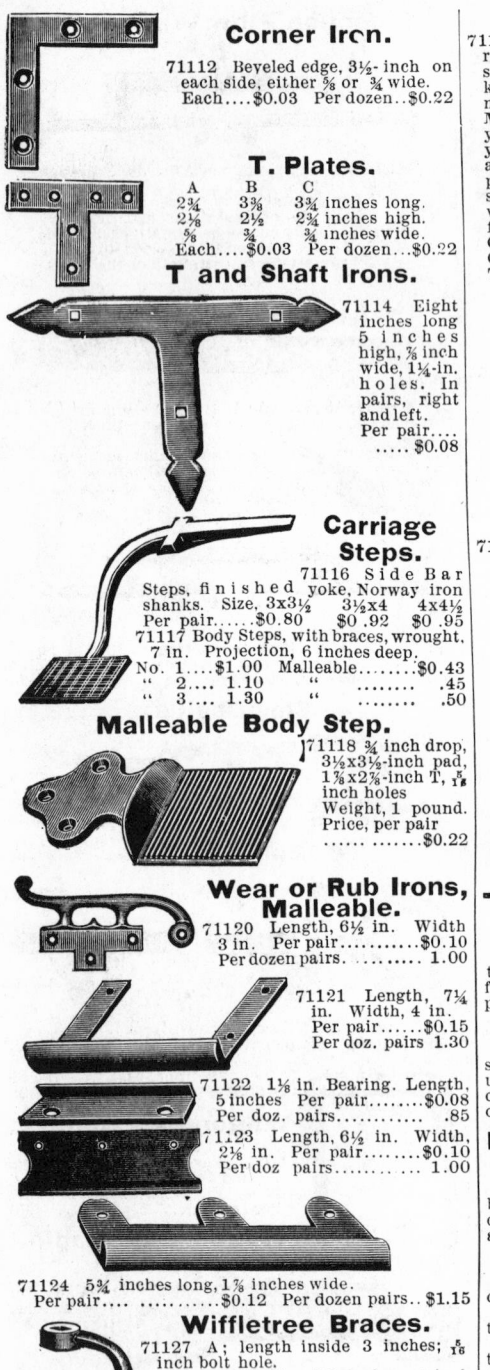

Corner Iron.

71112 Beveled edge, 3½-inch on each side, either ⅝ or ¾ wide. Each....$0.03 Per dozen..$0.22

T. Plates.

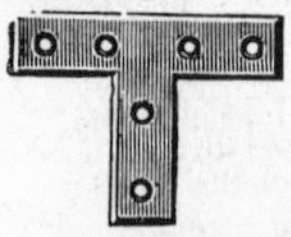

	A	B	C
	2¾	3⅜	3¾ inches long.
	2⅞	2½	2¾ inches high.
	⅝	¾	¾ inches wide.

Each....$0.03 Per dozen...$0.22

T and Shaft Irons.

71114 Eight inches long 5 inches high, ⅞ inch wide, 1¼-in. holes. In pairs, right and left. Per pair.... .....$0.08

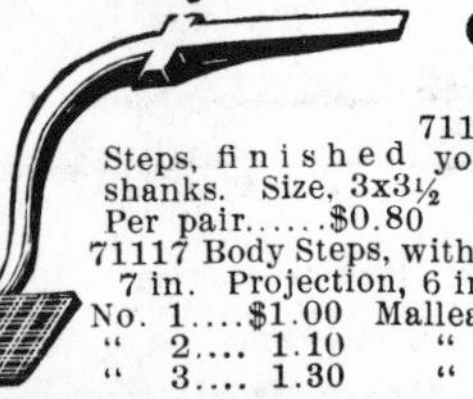

Carriage Steps.

71116 Side Bar Steps, finished yoke, Norway iron shanks. Size, 3x3½ 3½x4 4x4½

Per pair......$0.80 $0 .92 $0 .95

71117 Body Steps, with braces, wrought, 7 in. Projection, 6 inches deep.

No.			
No. 1....	$1.00	Malleable........	$0.43
" 2....	1.10	"	.45
" 3....	1.30	"	.50

Malleable Body Step.

71118 ¾ inch drop, 3½x3½-inch pad, 1⅞x2⅞-inch T, 5/16 inch holes Weight, 1 pound. Price, per pair $0.22

Wear or Rub Irons, Malleable.

71120 Length, 6½ in. Width 3 in. Per pair..........$0.10 Per dozen pairs.......... 1.00

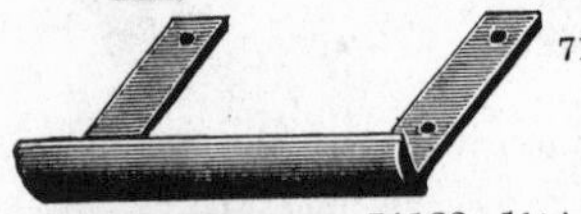

71121 Length, 7¼ in. Width, 4 in. Per pair......$0.15 Per doz. pairs 1.30

71122 1⅛ in. Bearing. Length, 5 inches Per pair........$0.08 Per doz. pairs............ .85

71123 Length, 6½ in. Width, 2⅛ in. Per pair........$0.10 Per doz pairs.......... ... 1.00

71124 5¾ inches long, 1⅞ inches wide. Per pair.... ....$0.12 Per dozen pairs.. $1.15

Wiffletree Braces.

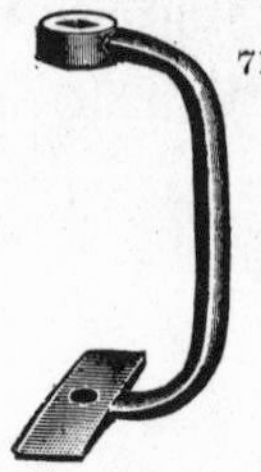

71127 A; length inside 3 inches; 5/16 inch bolt hole.
B; length inside, 3¾ inches; 5/16-inch bolt hole.
Weight, ¾ lb.
Each.............. ....$0.08

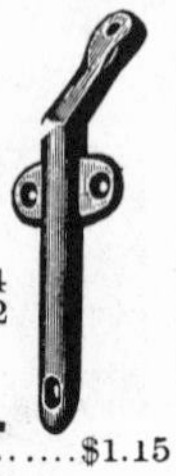

Seat Brace.

71129 Malleable iron, 4¾ inches long.
Each.......................... . ...$0.04
Per dozen............... .... .32

Blacksmiths' Aprons.

71140 Sheepskin. Each..........................$1.15

Horseshoers' Aprons.

71141 Calfskin, extra heavy, well tanned, with strap and buckle. Each.......... ....$1.50
This apron fills a long-felt want among horseshoers, it being made to withstand the severe usage to which they are subjected.

Mechanics' Aprons.

71142 Made of a good quality of bed ticking, 30 inches wide, by 36 inches in length, with pockets and shoulder and waist straps. Each..$0.20 Stamped Montgomery Ward & Co., Chicago, plainly on the front of each apron. The price without our name would be 50c each.

Carriage Covers.

71144 In our repository we keep our sample carriages protected from dust and recommend the same to our customers. It goes a long way toward keeping the paint bright and new looking. We make these covers of the well-known **Pepperill Mills Sheeting.** A buggy requires twenty square yards of material and a carriage, 30 square yards. We furnish them complete, with cords and screw eyes, so that all you have to do is to put the four screw eyes into your ceiling, and stretch the cords, through them (five minutes work). Remove dust with a feather duster before putting buggy away.
Complete outfit, for one-seated buggy............$2.00
Complete outfit, for two-seated buggy............. 3.00
These prices are net. No discount on covers.

Not Painted.

71150 Latest Style of Brewster or End Spring Buggy, completely ironed and finished, ready to paint and trim; dash included. This class of work offers exceptional opportunities to small country shops, where you have not the proper facilities for building a complete job. You can order one of these vehicles from us, trim and paint to suit your fancy, or as ordered by your customer, and then put your own nameplate on. Your customer will be satisfied for we claim this work to be equal to first class hand made jobs, and far superior to the work turned out by the majority of country shops. At the low price we offer this work, you will be able to clear a reasonable profit above all expenses. A good trimmer can easily finish one of these jobs to sell from $50 to $100 according to the quality of material used in the trimming. If you are in need of a buggy but cannot afford to pay fancy prices for one and are not over-particular as to finish, why not do this work yourself? You certainly have the time, and by so doing can obtain a first class buggy at a total cost not exceeding $40.00
DESCRIPTION: Body, 20, 23 or 25 inches wide; axles, 13/16 or 15/16: wheels banded hub or Sarven patent, with ¾ or ⅞ steel tire. Elliptic end springs as shown in cut. Brewster springs if desired.

NOTE—Unless otherwise instructed we will fill all orders with body 25 inches wide, 15/16 axles, 4 ft. 8 inch track and banded hub wheels.

☐ Be sure to state whether you want wide or narrow track, and elliptic or Brewster springs. Either style at same price. Free aboard cars at Chicago........$30.25

Shipped with body attached to the gear and crated. Wheels tied in bundles. ......

Three Spring Business Wagon.

71152 Description; Body, 33 inches wide, 78 inches long, axles, 1⅛ inch, heavy wheels. Banded hub or Sarven patent with 1 inch steel tire. Makes a fine combination business and pleasure vehicle. Just the thing for hunting trips. When necessary the rear seat can be removed and light merchandise carried behind. This vehicle cannot be purchased finished for less than $54.00
Our price aboard cars at Chicago $37.00 cash.
For canopy top woods and irons allow $7.40 additional.
The wheels are selected B grade and warranted. The woodwork is carefully fitted to the irons and finished smooth. Only the very best forgings used.

GUARANTEE.

We warrant these vehicles, with fair and reasonable usage, for one year, and if any part gives out by reason of defective material or workmanship, we will send a duplicate part free of charge.

We cannot trim or paint these jobs. For finished vehicles see our special Buggy Catalogue. A special catalogue showing cuts of over twenty other different styles of vehicles, which we can furnish in the white, will be mailed on application.

Our Dandy Doubletree, No. 71102, cannot be beaten for the price. Try one.

FURNITURE DEPARTMENT.

Send for our new special Furniture Catalogue. It contains a larger assortment than ever, of all kinds of furniture, new designs and new prices which will surprise you.

Upholstered Parlor Furniture.

All parlor furniture is made "to order." This insures clean, fresh goods, made exactly as wanted. It usually takes two to six days to complete furniture orders, depending upon the amount of work required on the goods ordered.

Explanation of Grades of Upholstering.

The prices of upholstered furniture are designated by letter. The letters represent the various grades of covering. Under each article will be found the price and quality of cover.

Grade D. Cotton tapestry and imported cretone.
Grade E. Imported cotton tapestry.
Grade F. Domestic crushed plush, wool tapestry and cotton tapestry.
Grade G. Silk and cotton brocatelle, imported wool tapestry, silk plush, figured corduroy.
Grade H. Fine mohair, crushed plush, silk faced tapestry, imported wool tapestry, fancy wide ribbed corduroy.
Grade K. Plain mohair (car) plush, heavy imported silk tapestry.
Grade L. Silk brocatelle, satin damask,.
Grade P. Imported silk damask, imported three tone brocatelle.
Grade S. Finest imported silk damask, brocatelle and brocades.

Specify exactly what colors are wanted.

Be very particular to specify style of covering wanted from the grades you order, as you will see under some grades we quote several different coverings.

Countermands will not be considered after work has commenced, as we make all upholstered furniture to order.

We make no charge for cartage or for burlaps.

Any single piece furnished out of a parlor suit at prices given, unless otherwise stated. Can furnish all the standard colors in upholstery.

Samples of upholstery sent free upon request. State what you want samples of clearly, or we shall have to guess at it.

Casters furnished with all furniture requiring same.

A parlor suit weighs about 220 pounds, as follows: sofa, 55 pounds; arm chair, 35 pounds; rocker, 40 pounds; divan, 50 pounds; two parlor chairs, 40 pounds.

NO CHARGE FOR CASES OR CARTAGE.

720 1 Five-Piece Parlor Suit. This is the greatest bargain ever offered in a parlor suit. Frame is made of solid oak, richly carved and has a good gloss finish; every piece has spring seats, is covered with a good grade of domestic crushed plush or cotton tapestry, and trimmed with silk plush; is well made and very comfortable. Samples of coverings of above suit sent upon application free of charge. We can furnish above in all standard colors. Where can you buy such a suit in the world at this price? Weight, about 170 pounds. We will sell above suit complete, or either piece separate. at the following prices;

Sofa..	$ 5.73
Arm chair..	3.12
Rocker..	4.76
Parlor chair..	2.07
Parlor chair..	2.07

Suit complete, 5 pieces.......................$17.50

Parlor Furniture—Continued.

Parlor Furniture—Continued.

Parlor Furniture—Continued.

72002 Parlor Suit. Here is a beautiful reception or parlor suit, made of solid oak, natural birch or imitation mahogany, and richly upholstered in brocacatelle, tapestry or plush; samples mailed free; frame is nicely carved and well braced. This is just the thing for a small house. Weight, about 125 pounds. Suit consists of sofa, arm chair and parlor.

Grade.	H.	K.	L.	P.	S.
Sofa	$7.00	$7.30	$7.45	$8.20	$8.75
Arm chair.	4.75	5.05	5.25	5.85	6.35
Parlor	3.18	3.35	3.50	3.95	4.25
					—A
	$14.93	$15.70	$16.20	$18.00	$19.35

72003 Suit. This is a very ornamental and pretty reception suit. Made in natural birch, imitation mahogany or solid oak; hand carved and nicely finished. Samples of covering mailed free. The stock in this suit is very select and handsome, very comfortable and well made. Weight, about 150 pounds. Suit consists of sofa, arm chair, rocker and parlor.

	F.	G.	H.	K.	L.	P.	S.
Sofa	$8.25	$8 45	$8.64	$9.02	$9.20	$10.16	$12.07
Armchair	4.91	5.00	5.08	5.27	5.40	6.03	7.00
Rocker.	5.87	5.97	6.03	6.22	6.35	7.00	7.90
Parlor...	3.50	3.56	3.62	3.75	3.81	4.00	5.00
	$22.53	22.98	23.37	24.26	24.76	27.19	31.97

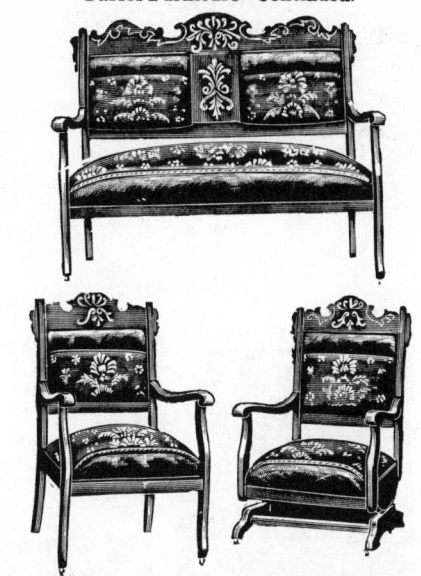

72004 Parlor Suit, made of solid oak and finished antique or imitation mahogany; covered with plush tapestry and trimmed with silk plush; has spring edge which is very comfortble. This is a beauty for the money; weight, about 220 pounds. Samples mailed free upon request.

	D.	E.	F.	G.	H.
Sofa	$6.50	$6.85	$7.40	$7.75	$8.05
Arm chair...	3.50	3.70	3.90	4.05	4.15
Rocker	4.55	4.95	5.10	5.25	5.40
Divan	4.95	5.10	5.25	5.55	5.85
Parlor	2.60	2.70	2.80	3.00	3.12
Parlor	2.60	2.70	2.80	3.00	3.12
Suit comp.					
6 pieces.	$24.70	$26.00	$27.25	$28.60	$29.69

72005 Parlor Suit. This suit is nicely upholstered in plush or tapestry and trimmed in good silk plush; richly fringed, very handsome and durable. Weight, about 200 pounds. The corner chair in this suit is very artistic and pretty. This is the cheapest suit of this style on the market. This suit has arm chair same style as rocker, in place of corner chair as cut shows it. Consists of five pieces as follows:

	Grade D.	Grade E.	Grade F.	Grade G.	Grade H.	Wilton Rug.
Sofa	$8.06	$8.32	$8.65	$9.30	$10.55	$13.00
Arm chair....	5.26	5.60	5.85	6.50	7.45	8.05
Rocker	6.17	6.50	6.90	7.45	7.80	8.65
Parlor	3.25	3 45	3.50	3.70	4.05	5 85
Parlor	3.25	3.45	3.50	3.70	4.05	5.85
Suit comp.						
5 pieces.	$25.99	$27.32	$28.40	$30.65	$33.90	$41.40

TO the best of our knowledge and belief we sell more **Baby Carriages** than any other one firm in America, outside of wholesalers. We are able, therefore, to secure the latest styles and designs, the best workmanship and the lowest prices.

We Give What We Get.

72006 Parlor Suit. made of solid oak, carved and nicely finished, well braced and very durable. Richly upholstered in plush, tapestry or brocatelle, samples mailed free, upon request. This is a beautiful and showy suit for little money. Weight, 220 pounds.

	D.	E.	F.	G.	H.	K.
Sofa	$8.32	$8.65	$8.95	$9.30	$9.55	$10.20
Arm chair...	4.68	4.75	4.95	5.15	5.35	5.65
Rocker...	5.90	6.00	6.20	6.35	6.55	6.95
Divan	5.60	5.90	6.20	6.55	6.95	7.65
Parlor	3.45	3.60	3.70	3.85	3.95	4.25
Parlor	3.45	3.60	3.70	3.85	3.95	4.25
Suit comp.						
6 pieces.	$31.40	$32.50	$33.70	$35.05	$36.30	$38.95

72007 Parlor Suit, extra large and heavy. Made of solid oak, finished antique or imitation mahogany. Frames are all hand RUBBED and richly carved. This suit is well braced and very strong. Seats have spring edges. Weight, about 225 pounds. Extra good value.

	D.	E.	F.	G.	H.	K.	L.
Sofa	$10.15	$10.45	$10.80	$11.40	$11.75	$12.70	$13.35
Arm chair	5.40	5.52	5.70	6.00	6.35	7.00	7.30
Rocker	6.65	6.80	7.00	7.30	7.60	8.25	8.55
Divan	7.00	7.30	7.60	8.05	8.40	9.45	9.85
Parlor	3.80	4.00	4.15	4.30	4.55	5.05	5.40
Parlor	3.80	4.00	4.15	4.30	4.55	5.05	5.40
Suit, 6 pcs. complete.	36.80	38.07	39.40	41.35	43.20	47.50	49.85

Parlor Furniture—Continued.

72008 Parlor Suit, well made of solid oak, richly hand carved and highly polished. Spring seats and edges; top of backs and front of seats are buttoned tufted. Is very large and comfortable. Weight 220 pounds. Good value. Extra heavy and select stock used in this suit.

	D.	E.	F.	G.	H.	K.	L.
Sofa—	$11.10	$11.50	$11.75	$12.35	$13.00	$13.95	$14.60
Arm chair—	$5.40	5.70	5.85	6.00	6.35	7.00	7.30
Rocker—	$5.70	6.65	7.20	7.30	7.60	8.25	8.55
Divan—	$7.95	8.5	8.55	9.30	9.65	10.45	11.10
Parlor—	$4.10	4.25	4.55	4.75	4.89	5.40	5.55
Parlor—	$4.10	4.25	4.55	4.75	4.89	5.40	5.55
Suit complete, 6 pieces—	$38.35	$40.60	$42.45	$44.45	$46.38	$50.45	$52.65

72009 Parlor Suit. This is one of the most *beautiful* and *ornamental* designs we have, spring seats and edges. Backs are richly tufted, frames are made of solid oak, richly hand carved and highly polished. Weight, 225 pounds. This is a bargain.

	D.	E.	F.	G.	H.	K.	L.
Sofa—	$11.40	$11.75	$12.05	$12.75	$13.35	$14.60	$15.24
Arm Chair—	$6.65	7.00	7.30	7.60	7.95	8.55	8.90
Rocker—	$7.95	8.25	8.55	8.90	9.20	9.85	10.15
Divan—	$8.85	9.20	9.50	10.00	10.55	11.55	12.05
Parlor—	$4.10	4.30	4 55	4.70	4.95	5.46	5.70
Parlor—	$4.10	4.30	4.55	4.70	4.95	5.46	5.70
Suit complete, 6 pieces—	$43.05	$44.80	$46.50	$48.60	$50.95	$55.47	$57.79

Divans.

72016 Divan, made of solid oak, richly hand carved and polished, spring seat and edges, length, 3 feet. Very pretty and ornamental. Weight, about 50 pounds.

	D.	E.	F.	G.	H.	K.	L.
Prices.	$8 85	$9.20	$9.50	$10.00	$10.55	$11.55	$12.00

72017 Divan, richly upholstered in damask, tapesty or plush and trimmed in silk tassels and heavy fringe. Length, 3 feet; very ornamental and rich. Weight, 50 pounds.

	F.	G.	H.	K.	L.
Prices	$9.30	$10.00	$10.60	$12.50	$13.40

Students' Chairs.

72020 Students' Chair, a popular pattern at a very low figure, walnut, upholstered in ramie cloth, tufted. Weight, 60 pounds..............$4.50
Grade D.............$4.70 | Grade E............$7.45
Grade F.................. 8.45
72021 Arm Chair, walnut, oak or imitation mahogany, handsomely engraved, polished, spring seat and back. Weight, 80 pounds.
Grade F.............$9.40 | Grade G............$10.10
Grade G...... 9.70 |
Wilton rug........................ 15.60

72024. Arm Chair, spring seat, back and edges, frames walnut, oak or imitation mahogany. Weight, 80 pounds.
Grade F............$13.90 | Grade K............$16.38
Grade G .. 14 45 |
72030 Rocker, made of walnut or oak, spring seat and back. Weight, 80 pounds.
Grade D $9.30
Grade E............10.35
Grade F............11.65

72031 Patent Rocker; a model; walnut, oak or imitation mahogany, spring seat and back. Weight, 80 pounds.
Grade F.................$ 9.95
Grade H................ 11.25
Wilton rug............. 16.80

Chairs—Continued.

72035   72036

72035 Patent Rocker, a model of elegance and comfort; nothing made in the way of chairs begins to approach this for luxury and positive ease; has spring edges, spring seat and spring back. Frames, oak finished, antique. Weight, 80 pounds.
Grade F.....................................$13.00
Grade G..................................... 13.60
Leather..................................... 20.70
Grade H..................................... 14.25
Grade K..................................... 15.50
72036 Patent Rocker, spring seat and back. Walnut, oak or imitation mahogany. Weight, 80 pounds.
Grade F $15.50
Grade G 15.75
Grade H.................. 16.65

Lounges.

We ship lounges with back and legs off, as otherwise the freight would be twice as much. Any one can put them together in a few minutes.

72100 Single Lounge, oak or walnut frame, spring seat. Weight, 75 pounds.
Brussels carpet....$4.70 | Grade F............$5.55
Velvet carpet...... 5.85 | Grade G............ 6.50
Moquette 5.90

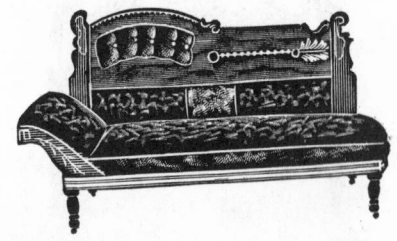

72102 Single Lounge, oak frame, The back is very high and has a very neat beading on top and center of back. Has silk plush band on front of seat and tapestry center piece in back, as shown in cut; spring seat. Weight, 75 pounds.
Brussels carpet......$8.00 | Grade G............$ 8.75
Grade F............. 8.35 | Grade H............ 10.00

72104 Single Lounge. Frame is made of solid oak and nicely finished. Carved back, ornamented with spindles and beaded molding. When upholstered in plush, corduroy or silk faced tapestry, this lounge has a silk plush border on front and silk plush piping on top of back. Spring seat. Weight, 75 lbs.
Brussels carpet.... $8.75 | Grade F............$7.80
Velvet Carpet...... 9.45 | Grade G.......... 8.75
Moquette........... 9.35 | Grade H.......... 9.75

Lounges—Continued.

72106 Couch. Made of solid oak and covered with Javenese rug, which is very pretty; is also a very durable covering. Width, 22 inches; length, 6 feet. The springs used in our couches are of the best steel; weight, about 70 lbs. Very comfortable and a bargain. Price only in Javanese Rug, $6.35; Brussels Carpet, $5.15; Velvet Carpet, $6.00; Grade F, plush.................$5.15

72107 Couch. This couch is upholstered in grade F, crushed plush, wool tapestry or cotton tapestry, and trimmed with a good grade of fringe. All spring seat and edges. Width, 22 inches; length, 6 feet. A bargain at our price. Weight, about 75 lbs. Samples sent free.
Price, in grade F.................$5.90
Price, in grade G, corduroy.................. 6.35

72108 Tufted Couch. This couch is upholstered in grade G, corduroy, silk and cotton brocatelle or wool tapestry, and trimmed with a good grade of fringe. Width, 22 inches; length, 6 feet. Sample of covering mailed free upon request. The filling of this couch consists of good moss. Weight 80 lbs. Grade D, $5.00; Grade F, $6.45; Grade G.................$7.05

72109 Couch. This couch is upholstered with a fine Wilton rug and trimmed with silk plush and a good grade of fringe. Spring seat and edges. A very comfortable couch and an exceedingly durable covering; filling consists of moss. Width, 25 inches; length, 6 feet. Well made and cheap. Weight, 80 pounds.
Price, in Wilton rug.................$10.98

We show a much larger assortment of couches in our new special Furniture Catalogue, which we mail for 8 cents.

72110 Tufted Couch. This beautiful couch is richly upholstered in grade G figured corduroy, silk and cotton brocatelle, or imported wool tapestry, and trimmed with tassels and a fine grade of fringe. Filling consists of our best moss. Width, 26 inches; length, 6 feet 2 inches. Samples of covering sent free upon request; all standard colors. Is extra large and exceedingly comfortable. Price, in grade G covering $12.80

72111 Tufted Couch. This beautiful, rich couch is upholstered in grade G corduroy, silk and cotton brocatelle, or imported wool tapestry, and trimmed with tassels and extra fine grade of fringe. The filling consists of the very best steel spring and our best moss, is very soft, and will guarantee it for comfort. Width, 27 inches; length, 6 feet 2 inches. Samples of covering mailed free; all colors. Extra good value. Weight, 90 pounds.
Price, in grade G covering.................$17.95

Lounges—Continued.

72112 Wardrobe Couch. Upholstered in all grades and trimmed with a fine grade of fringe. The filling consists of our best springs and moss. By lifting the top the inside is nicely finished, which can be used for storing clothing, or closet and wardrobe purposes. All spring seat and edges. Price includes two large pillows, which are covered with same covering as couch. Samples of covering mailed upon request. Is exceedingly comfortable and well made. Width, 30 inches; length, 6 feet 2 inches; weight, about 125 pounds.

Grade.	D.	E.	F.	G.	H.	K.	L.
Price.	$27.00	$29.00	$32.00	$34.00	$37.00	$42.00	$45.00

We can furnish above couch without pillows for $4.00 less.

Bed Lounges.

Bed lounges weigh about 125 lbs. and vary in length from 6 feet to 6 feet 6 in. All our bed lounges have a spring bed on both sides, and make as comfortable a bed as one can wish for. They are strong and well made, and are, perhaps, the most necessary convenience that a family could have. We ship lounges with backs and legs taken off, as otherwise the freight would be twice as much. Anyone can put them together in a few minutes' time.
How is this in Solid Oak for $6.25.

72115 A good bed lounge for little money. Made of solid oak, carved and has a good gloss finish. Length, 6 feet, width, when open, 39 inches. Has spring bed on both sides. Very comfortable and well made. Weight, 125 pounds. A great bargain at the following prices.
Brussels carpet, only.......................$6.25
Grade F crushed plush, only........ 7.25

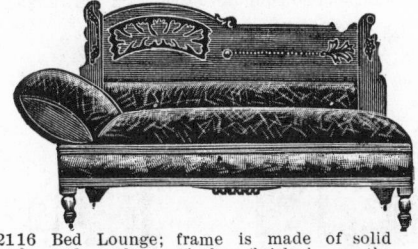

72116 Bed Lounge; frame is made of solid oak and walnut nicely finished, neatly carved and has turned legs. Length, 6 feet; width, when open, 41 inches; spring bed on both sides, a cotton top mattress and a woven wire bed. This is the best, lowest priced bed lounge made. It retails for double our price. Weight, 125 pounds.

Brussels carpet......$ 7.45	Grade F .... $ 8.70
Velvet carpet....... 10.00	Grade G 9.35
Moquette 9.25	Grade H......... 10.40

72117 Bed Lounge; this lounge is one of the best bargains in our catalogue. We have contracted for a large quantity, which enables us to sell it at such a low price. Frame is made of solid oak and polished. Has springs in bed and a cotton top mattress. Size of lounge, when closed, 24 inches wide, 6 feet long.
Size when open, 4 feet wide, 6 feet long.
Can be upholstered in all kinds of plush and carpet. Is richly trimmed in silk plush. Weight, 125 pounds. Note prices.

Brussels carpet....$10.50	Grade F............$14.62
Velvet carpet 12.30	Grade G...... ..... 15.95
Moquette.......... 12.40	Grade H............ 18.52

Bed Lounges—Continued.

72118 Bed Lounge, made of solid oak, richly carved and polished. Has springs in bed and a cotton top mattress. Length, 6 feet. Width, when open, 45 inches. Covered in carpet and plush and trimmed with silk plush, also fitted with a woven wire mattress, which makes it very comfortable. Weight, 125 pounds.

Brussels carpet....$11.55	Grade F............$11.85
Velvet carpet. 13.45	Grade G............ 12.85
Grade D............10.95	Grade H............ 13.75
Grade E............ 11.50	

72119 Bed Lounge, made of solid oak, richly hand carved and highly polished. Has a woven wire bed with springs and a cotton top mattress. Length, 6 feet, width, when open, 45 inches. Covered with carpet and plush and richly trimmed with plush. A very heavy and durable couch. Weight, 125 pounds.

Brussels carpet....$11.85	Grade F............$12.20
Velvet carpet..... 13.75	Grade G............ 13.10
Grade D........... 10.95	Grade H............ 14.05
Grade E····... .... 11.55	

72120 Bed Lounge, oak frame, highly polished and carved; has springs in bed, and a cotton top mattress; very showy and pretty Length, 70 inches; width, when open, 45 inches. This lounge has a woven wire bed in it. Weight, 125 pounds.

Brussels carpet....$11.35	Grade G..............$14 00
Velvet carpet...... 12.67	Grade H.............. 14.65
Grade F............ 13.35	

72121 Bed Lounge, solid oak frame neatly carved and highly polished. Has springs in bed and a cotton top mattress. Width, when open, 43 inches; length, 5 feet 8 inches, with a woven wire bed in it. Has a very pretty and fancy back. Weight, 125 pounds.

Brussels carpet....$13.00	Grade G $14.20
Velvet carpet...... 13.65	Grade H........... 15.30
Grade F 12.35	

Bed Lounges—Continued.

72122 Bed Lounge, made of solid oak, richly hand carved and polished. Has a woven wire bed with springs and a cotton top mattress. Length, 6 feet; width, when open, 45 inches; covered with carpet and plush. Samples mailed free of charge. Well made and cheap. Weight, 125 pounds.

Brussels carpet......$12.20	Grade F.........$12.50
Velvet carpet...... 14.05	Grade G......... 13.45
Grade D............. 11.55	Grade H......... 14.40
Grade E............. 12.20	

72123 Bed Lounge; frame is made of oak, carved and polished. Has springs in bed and a cotton top mattress; also a woven wire bed. Back is richly tufted in silk plush. Size, when open, width, 43 inches; length; 5-feet 8 inches. Weight, about 125 pounds. Very ornamental and pretty.

Brussels carpet....$14.30	Grade F...........$13.65
Velvet carpet 14.95	Grade G........... 14.95
Grade D............. 13 65	Grade H........... 16.60

72124 Bed Lounge; frame is made of oak, hand carved and highly polished. Size of lounge, when open, width, 45 inches; length, 6 feet 10 inches; spring in bed and a cotton top mattress; also has a woven wire bed; back is richly tufted in silk plush, has extra heavy oak legs; very massive and well made. Weight, 150 pounds.

Brussels carpet......$16.25	Grade F......... $15.60
Velvet carpet........ 16.90	Grade G......... 16.90
Grade D............. 15.60	Grade H......... 18.55

Foot Rests and Hassocks.

72151 Hassock. These hassocks are made only from such pieces of carpet as are too small to be used in the manufacture of other goods, which enables us to sell at such low figures. A remarkably good hassock for the price; 9 inches square, 5 inches high. Weight, 5 pounds.
Each . .$0.25 Per doz ..$2.75

72152 Hassock, made of tapestry carpet, 12½ inches square, 6 inches high. Each $0.55
Weight, 7 pounds.

72153 Ottoman, made of carpet and plush. Extra large; 10 inches high.
Tapestry carpet........$0.80
Velvet carpet.......... 1.00
Weight, 12 pounds.

72154 Foot Rest, sizes 10x12, 8 inches high. Top is covered with best mohair plush; white metal legs, all colors of plush. Weight, 15 pounds. Each....$0.75
72155 Foot Rests, made of solid oak, highly polished. Height, 8½ in.; size of seat, 10x13½ in. Well made, very pretty. Each. $0.20
Weight, 5 pounds.

Foot Rests—Continued.

72156 Foot Rest, made of tapestry carpet. Very comfortable.
Each........ ......$0.65
Per dozen........ 7.00
Weight, 5 pounds.

Blacking Cases.

72157 Blacking Case, size, 10x14 inches, height, 16 inches. Carpet top. Heavy foot rest: space for brushes. Strong, fine and cheap. Each...$0.85
Weight, 20 pounds.

72158 Combination Blacking Case and Slipper Box. This is a handsome piece of furniture as well as useful. When closed presents the appearance of an elegant ottoman. Size, 16x19 inch. Tapestry carpet, Each... ....$3.25
Velvet carpet,.. each 3.60
Weight, 25 pounds

Commodes.

72161   72160

72160 Commode, made of solid oak; has water tight joint, odorless pan. Size, 17x17 inches, nicely finished. Extra fine. Weight, about 30 pounds. Each....... ....$2.50
72161 Commode, made of solid oak, highly polished with tight joint, odorless pan; size of top, 17x17 inches; well made and cheap. Weight about 30 pounds. Price, each..........$3.50

ABSOLUTELY ODORLESS.

THOROUGHLY TESTED.

72163   72163

72163 Commode. Affords all the conveniences of the most elaborate water-closet, without deadly sewer gas. Absolutely necessary where there are no sewers. The effect on health is so great and expense so little that every family should have one. Made of solid oak, polished, with galvanized buckets, non-corrosive, and all necessary fittings. Is absolutely odorless, and can be set up in any room, having a chimney or stove-pipe, by any one. Needs no expensive plumbing. Costs nothing to keep in order. Not a luxury, but a necessity; a saver of doctor's bills. Much sickness of women and children is caused by outdoor closets. Weight, 40 pounds. Price, complete, $10.75

Furniture Polish.

72175 Cleaning Compound. It brings out the finest polish and leaving no grease on the surface will gather no dust. It is unsurpassed for cleaning and polishing all kinds of furniture, pianos, organs, carriages, bicycles, gold, silver, brass or enameled surfaces, mirrors, window glass, oil paintings and all polished surfaces of both wood and metal.

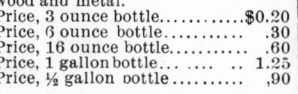

Price, 3 ounce bottle...........$0.20
Price, 6 ounce bottle.......... .30
Price, 16 ounce bottle.......... .60
Price, 1 gallon bottle...... .. 1.25
Price, ½ gallon bottle.......... .90

The Flexible Security Bed Clothes Fastener.

72180 Bed Clothes Fasteners. The most complete yet simple device for securing the clothing on the children's bed. Is neatly designed in nickel plate, easily adjusted, to regulate the amount of bed clothes necessary, or in case of sickness, should the occupant of the bed become restless, the flexible material will yield so as to conform to every movement, allowing the clothes to move, not only free, but will return to their original place. By the use of this fastener children are saved from colds and sickness. All mothers will appreciate it. Fasten to bed same as shown in above cut.
Postage on above, 4 cents.
Price, per pair............................ ....$0.35

Bedroom Furniture.

We present in the following quotations what we consider the most desirable line of low and medium priced bedroom furniture ever shown by any one house. We have selected the most desirable styles from all the large western factories, and as our furniture trade has grown to immense proportions. we are able to buy in quantity.

Remember that we come to you with our stock bought for cash direct from the makers. No middlemen are represented in the transaction.

All prices, include casters, packing for shipment, and delivery to railroad depots here.

A chamber suit weighs about 300 pounds, as follows: Bedstead, 100 pounds; dresser, 125 pounds; washstand, 75 pounds. These are average weights, some weighing less and some more.

DESCRIPTION OF FINISH.

Gloss Finish—Pores of wood filled and varnished.
Rubbed Finish—Pores of wood filled and varnished, afterward rubbed down fine with pumice stone.
Polished Finish—Pores of wood carefully filled. next shellacked, then varnished ; lastly water-rubbed and polished by hand. This gives a mirror like and lasting polish.

Bedsteads.

Slats and castors furnished with every bed.

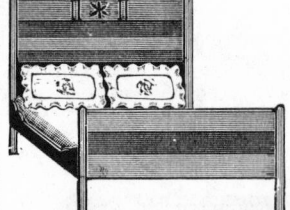

72200 Bed, made of hardwood; height, 4 feet; slat, 4 feet, 4 inches; neatly carved and finished antique. Well made and cheap; weight, 80 pounds. Price, complete $1.75

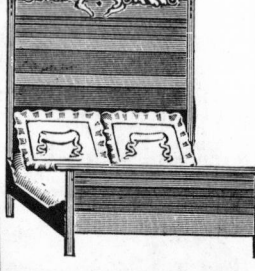

72201 Bed, made of hardwood, height 5 feet; slat, 4 feet 4 inches; carved and finished antique, good value; weight, 90 pounds. Price, complete.....$2.55

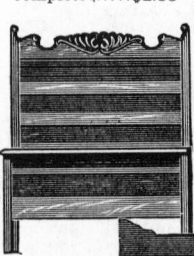

72202 Bed, made of *solid oak* and has a good gloss finish; height, 5 feet 4 inches; slat 4 feet 4 inches, carved and finished antique. Extra good value; weight, about 100 pounds. Price, complete........$3.55

Look through our CROCKERY DEPARTMENT with care. Choice bargains to be had.

Bedsteads—Continued.

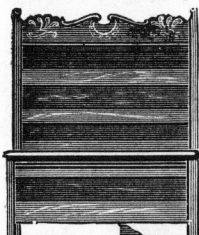

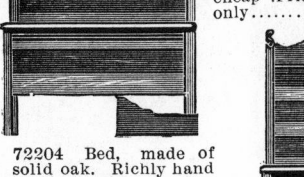

72203 Bed, made of solid oak, richly carved, and has a fine gloss finish. Height, 5ft. 10 in; slat, 4 ft. 4 in. Finished antique; weight 100 pounds; very showy and cheap. Price, complete, only.................. $4.20

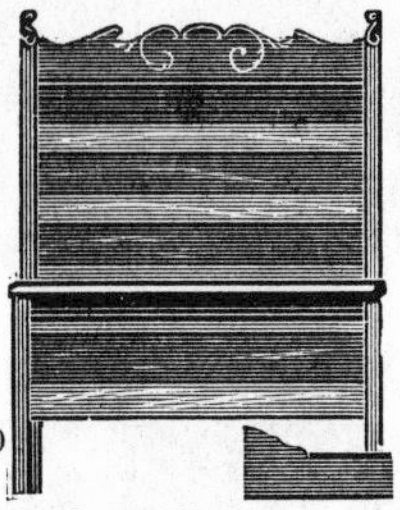

72204 Bed, made of solid oak. Richly hand carved and has a fine gloss finish. Height, 6 ft; slat 4ft 6 in; weight, about 100 pounds. Price, complete........ $4.50

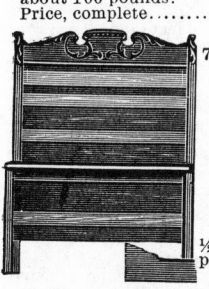

72205 Bed. This is a beauty, very large and heavy. We consider it one of the best bargains we have. Made of solid oak, richly hand carved and nicely finished. Height, 6ft. 2 in: slat, 4 ft. 6 in; weight, about 100 pounds. Price, only............. $5.25

We can furnish above beds in ½ or ¾ size, if desired, at same prices.

Iron Beds.

We want especially to call the attention of our customers to our large and carefully selected line of *iron beds*. The make is of the best and the *prices* are positively *lower than any others quoted.* Finish guaranteed. We show a larger line in our new special furniture catalogue, which we mail for 8 cents to pay postage.

Slats not included in price and not necessary. provided you select springs adapted for same, (see Index for springs). We make our springs to fit iron beds at catalogue prices. If slats are preferred, the charge is 35 cents extra.

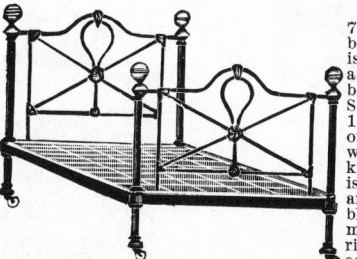

72224 Iron bed. This is a beauty and a great bargain. Size of posts 1 in. thick, ornamented with brass knobs. Finished in japan. Colors, black, blue, maroon, or richly finished in white enamel. Very fancy, well made and cheap; This bed will give perfect satisfaction. Clean, no chance for vermin. Weight, about 100 pounds. Note price.

Size, 3 x6½ feet, $4.65.
Size, 3½x6½ feet,   4.70.
Size, 4 x6½ feet,   4.75.
Size, 4½x6½ feet,   4.90.
Slats for above 35 cents extra.

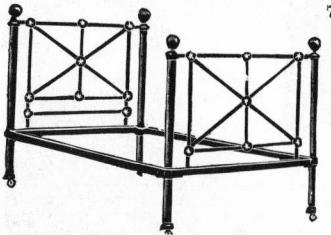

72225 Iron Bed, extra good value and a bargain. This bed is made of all iron and nicely ornamented, with brass knobs; size of posts, 1 inch. Finished in white enamel, well made and cheap, will guarantee satisfaction. Size, 4 feet 6 inches wide, 6 feet 6 inches long, weight, 100 pounds. Price only.................... $4.80
Slats for above bed 35 cents.

72225½ Iron Bed, has brass top rods and knobs, post 1 inch thick and has the extended foot rails. Finished in white enamel, well made and cheap. Weight, 100 pounds. Extra good value and a bargain. It will more than please you. Size, 4 feet 6 inches wide. Length, 6 feet 6 inches. Price only.................... $8.00

Bedsteads—Continued.

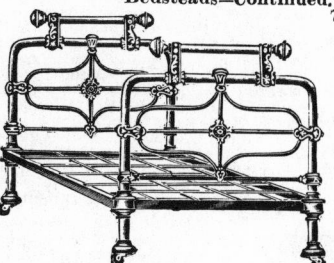

72226 Iron Bed, is extra heavy and showy, richly ornamented with brass rod and knobs, finished in japan, colors: Black, blue, maroon and enameled white, very ornamental and cheap. Weight about 100 pounds. Perfectly clean no chance for vermin. Note new prices.

Size, 3 x6½ ft.......................... $8.60
Size, 3½x6½ ft.   8.65
Size, 4 x6½ ft.   8.70
Size, 4½x6½ ft.   8.75
Slats for above 35 cents extra.

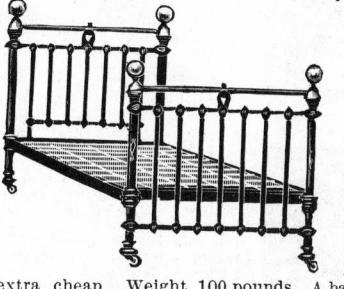

72227 Iron Bed. This is extra good value. Has brass top rods and knobs Finished in Japan; colors, black, blue, maroon and enameled white. Posts are 1 inch thick and has the extended foot rail. Very neat, durable and extra cheap. Weight, 100 pounds. A bargain.

Size, 3 x6½ ft.......................... $8.80
Size, 3¼x6½ ft.   8.85
Size, 4 x6½ ft.   8.90
Size, 4½x6½ ft.   8.95
Slats for above 35 cents extra.

72253 Iron Bed with brass top rods, knobs and brass rosettes, ornamented in gold. Finished in japan, colors: Black, blue and maroon, enameled white. A beauty. Weight, 100 pounds.

Size, 3½x6½ feet................ $12.70
Size, 4 x6½ feet................ 12.75
Size, 4½x6½ feet................ 12.80
We can furnish No. 72253 bed with canopy, if desired, for $4.00 extra.
Above prices do not include slats to iron bed. If desired, 35 cents extra.

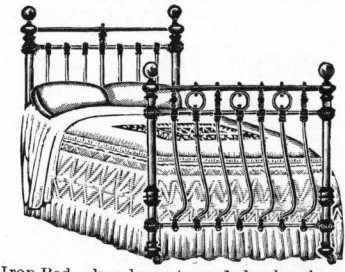

72254 Iron Bed, has brass top rods, knobs, rings and extended foot rail. Finished in all colors and enameled white. Very heavy and rich. Posts are 1 inch thick. Weight, 100 pounds.
Size, 3½x6½ feet.......................... $13.65
Size, 4 x6½ feet.......................... 13.70
Size, 4½x6½ feet.......................... 13.75
Slats for above 35 cents extra.

72255 Iron Bed, with brass top rods and knobs, and richly ornamented with 28 brass rosettes, and has the extended foot rail. Finished all colors and enameled white. Massive design. Weight, about 100 pounds.

Size, 3½x6½ feet.......................... $14.45
Size, 4 x6½ feet.......................... 14.50
Size, 4½x6½ feet.......................... 14.55
Slats for above 35 cents.

Bedsteads—Continued.

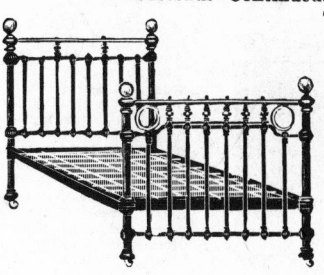

72256 Iron Bed, has brass top rods, knobs and rings. This bed is fine enough for any one, is very heavy and elegant. Richly finished in white enamel. Has the extended foot rail. Weight, about 100 pounds.

Size, 3½x6½ feet.......................... $16.10
Size, 4 x6½ feet.......................... 16.15
Size, 4½x6½ feet.......................... 16.20

Mantel Folding Beds.

We have selected from the many factories the neatest and most compact Mantle Beds made. Is just the right height to make a nice looking piece of furniture, with enough room for mattress and bedding. We use automatic inside locks, which holds the bed securely closed, and the bed stands on four legs when open, making it steady and safe. We show a larger assortment of mantel beds in our new special furniture catalogue, which we will mail on receipt of 8 cents to pay postage.

72302 Curtain Mantel Bed. Size, when open, 4 feet wide, 6 feet long. Made of oak, with woven wire mattress. Has brass rod and curtain. Finished in antique only. Weight, 125 lbs. Without curtains, only........ $7.00

72303 Mantel Folding Bed, made of hardwood and nicely finished. Size, when open, 4 feet wide, 6 feet long; has a woven wire supported spring and mattress holders attached. Well made and cheap. Weight, about 190 pounds. Price, only...... $10.40

72304 Mantel Folding Bed, made of solid oak and has a good gloss finish. Size, when closed, 4 ft. 6 inches, 5 ft. high; size, when open 4 ft. wide, 6ft. long. Has a woven wire supported spring and mattress holders attached. This is extra good value. Weight, 200 pounds. Retail price..... $16.00
Our price............... 12.15

72305 Mantel Folding Bed, made of solid oak, nicely finished and richly carved. Has a 10x10 inch French bevel miror in top; fitted with woven wire supported spring. Size, when open, 4 feet wide, 6 long; size, when closed, 4 feet 8 inches wide, 5 feet 11 inches high. Very ornamental and cheap. Weight, 200 pounds. Price, only............. $14.60

72306 Mantel Folding Bed, made of solid oak, and has a good gloss finish, French bevel mirror 12x28 inches; also fitted with a fine woven wire supported spring. Size, when closed, 4 feet 8 inches wide, 6 feet 3 inches high: size, when open, 4 feet wide and 6 feet long; finish antique. Weight, 225 pounds. Price, only............... $15.85

72307 Mantel Folding Bed, made of solid oak, nicely finished and richly carved; has a good 16x28 inch German bevel miror; fitted with a fine woven wire supported spring. Size, when closed, 4 feet 8 inch wide, 6 feet 5 inches high; size, when open, 4 feet wide and 6 feet long; nicely ornamented with brass trimmings. Weight, about. 225 pounds. Price, complete only.... $16.20

Wardrobe Folding Bed.

72308 Combination Wardrobe and Folding Bed combined. The front view shows a very handsome wardrobe, which has 6 large hooks, is 4 feet wide, 8 feet high, 14 inches deep. By turning the article around you let the bed down as any ordinary folding bed, whereby you have two very handsome pieces of furniture in one at the cost of one piece. Made of hard wood. Has 18x40 inch bevel mirror. Size when bed is open, 4 feet wide, 6 feet 3 inches long. Finished in antique only. Weight, about 400 pounds.
Each $25.00
Same, without mirror. 20.00
Price, solid oak and mirror..................27.50

72309 Combination Folding Bed, wardrobe and bookcase combined, made on same principle as 72308 bed, except is much finer, made of solid oak, highly polished and richly carved. Has a fine 18x40 inch German bevel mirror, and an extra fine woven wire spring in bed. Size of bed, when open, 4 feet wide, 6 feet 3 inches long. Has 2 drawers with locks, and a large space for books. Weight, about 450 pounds. Price, only........$34.95

72311   72310

72310 Combination Folding Bed, wardrobe, desk and bookcase combined, made on same principle as 74308, except is much finer; well made of quarter sawed oak, hand carved and polished; door contains a large 18x40 inch German bevel mirror. Desk is nicely partitioned with pigeon holes and drawer, all doors and drawers have locks. Size of bed when open is 4 feet wide, 6 feet 3 inches long. Bed contains a fine woven wire mattress; weight, about 450 pounds. Extra fine. Price in elm.............36.95
Price in quarter sawed oak.................$39.95
72311 Combination Folding Bed, bookcase and desk combined, made on same principle as 72308 bed. Well made of quarter sawed oak, richly carved and highly polished. Has a mirror 18x22 inches. Desk is nicely partitioned with pigeon holes and drawers; all shelves are adjustable; bed contains a fine woven wire mattress. Size of bed, when open, 4 feet wide, 6 feet 3 inches long; weight, about 450 pounds.
Price, complete in solid oak.....................44.90

72312 Combination Folding Bed, wardrobe and desk combined; made of solid oak, richly hand carved and hand polished. Has 20x48 inch French bevel mirror, and 3 large drawers as shown in cut; made on the same principle as No. 72308 bed, except is a much finer bed. Size of bed, when open, 4 feet 2 inches wide, 6 feet 3 inches long. Has a fine woven wire mattress; finished antique; weight, about 525 pounds.
Price, complete....$52.00

Something New.

"The Success" Combination Folding Bed. Highest award given at World's Columbian Exposition, consisting of diploma and medal. The Success bed is the easiest working and most simply constructed folding bed on the market. Pull out slide at bottom. The bed is made to turn on its base, only requiring the space it occupies against the wall to turn in. It can be turned in space less than five feet. No wear and tear on carpets and is not removed from wall to let down. Action is so free that a child can operate it. When turned round with bed outward it lets down like other folding beds. If bed is wanted to turn from left side remove guide pin to the opposite end of platform, which can be reached from back when bed is let down, so that guide will run in slot on opposite side. To take bed apart for moving remove screws from corner irons, which hold back to the front; this makes it convenient to get through narrow and crooked places. All beds are fitted with best steel coil springs.

72313 Success Combination Folding Bed, Desk and Bookcase. Made of solid oak and highly hand polished. Size of bed, when open, 4 feet wide, length, 6 feet 1 inch. Has a good 18x20 French bevel mirror. Desk is nicely partitioned, with pigeon holes and drawers. Shelves in bookcase are adjustable. Legs fold automatically and bed is also locked when open, making it perfectly safe. See above description for operating bed. Weight about 580 lbs. Bed is fitted with a fine coil spring. This is extra good value and cheap.
Price, complete, only $32.50
72314 Success Combination Folding Bed, Desk and Bookcase. Made of solid oak, richly carved and highly hand polished. Size of bed, when open, 4 feet wide; length, 6 feet 1 inch. Has a fine 20x20 inch French beveled mirror. Desk has large drop leaf and inside is nicely partitioned with pigeon holes and drawer. All shelves in bookcase are adjustable. Legs fold automatically and bed is also locked when open, making it perfectly safe. If bed is wanted to turn from back see description above 72313 bed. Weight, about 580 lbs.
Price, complete, only.................$42.05

72315 Success Combination Folding Bed, Desk and Wardrobe. Made of solid oak, carved and highly hand polished. Size of bed, when open, 4 feet wide, 6 feet 1 inch long. Has an extra large 20x36 French bevel mirror in door and one 20x26 above desk. Desk has large drop leaf and inside is nicely partitioned with pigeon holes. Wardrobe space is quite large and nicely fitted with hooks. The legs fold automatically and the bed is locked when open, which makes it perfectly safe. For method of operating this bed see description above 72313 bed. Weight, about 580 lbs
Price, complete, only................$47.50

Upright Folding Beds.

The beds are perfectly balanced and fitted with self-locking legs and automatic lock, which prevents the bed from closing accidentally or from tipping over, making it absolutely safe. The case is strongly made with box rails front and rear, and the fulcrum on which the bed turns in opening is flanged together, so that it cannot get out of order either in use or transit.

72400 Upright Folding Bed, well made and has a good gloss finish. Richly carved and has an 18x40 inch German bevel mirror; also fitted with a woven wire supported spring. Outside size, 6 feet 6 inches high; 4 feet 9 inches wide and 25 inches deep. Inside size, 4 feet 2 inches wide and 6 feet long. Has mattress clamps and automatic lock. Weight, about 400 pounds.
Price, in elm....... .$20.80
Price, in oak........ 22.10

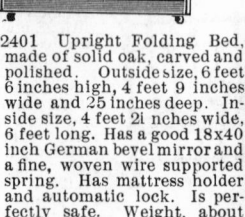

72401 Upright Folding Bed, made of solid oak, carved and polished. Outside size, 6 feet 6 inches high, 4 feet 9 inches wide and 25 inches deep. Inside size, 4 feet 2 inches wide, 6 feet long. Has a good 18x40 inch German bevel mirror and a fine, woven wire supported spring. Has mattress holder and automatic lock. Is perfectly safe. Weight, about 400 pounds. A fine bed for the money.
Price, only............$23.95

72402 Upright Folding Bed, made of quarter sawed oak, carved and polished. Inside size, 4 feet 2 inches wide and 6 feet long. Has an 18x40 inch German bevel mirror and a woven wire supported spring. Has mattress holders and automatic lock. Weight, 400 pounds. Well made and cheap.
Price............ ......$26.60

72403 Upright Folding Bed, made of quarter sawed oak, beautifully hand carved and highly polished. Inside size, 4 feet 2 inches wide and 6 feet long. Has a good 18x40 inch German bevel mirror and a fine woven wire supported springs. Also fitted with mattress holders and automatic lock. Weight, about 400 pounds. Very showy and pretty.
Price, only........$29.95
We show a much larger assortment of folding beds in our new special furniture catalogue, which we mail for 8 cents to pay postage.

Chiffoniers.

Extra *good value* in chiffoniers; very large, roomy and cheap. We show a much larger line in our new special furniture catalogue, which we mail for 8 cents to pay postage.

72500 Chiffonier, well made of hardwood, carved and polished. Has five large drawers with locks. Height, 5 feet 1 inch, width 3 feet 3 inches. Very large and roomy and exceedingly cheap; good value; weight, about 100 pounds
Price, only................$5.25

72500

72501 Chiffonier, made of hardwood, carved and highly polished. Has a good 10x17 German bevel mirror. Height, 5 feet 9 inches, width, 3 feet 3 inches. Has 5 large drawers with locks. Quite ornamental and cheap. Weight, about 125 pounds. Price, only......7.95

72501

72502 Chiffonier, well made of solid oak; richly carved and polished. Has 3 large drawers, 2 small and a large cabinet with 2 doors. A good design and price extremely low. Cabinet work guaranteed. Weight, about 100 pounds. Height, 5 feet 2 inches, width, 3 feet 3 inches. A bargain. Price, only $8.10

72502

72503 Chiffonier, made of solid oak, highly hand polished and richly hand carved. Height, 6 feet 3 inches, width, 3 feet 3 inches. Has a good large 14x24 inch German bevel mirror; 3 large drawers, 2 small and a large cabinet with 2 doors. We are sure this will please you. Weight, about 150 pounds Our price, only........$11.55

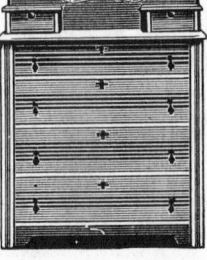

72503

Bureaus and Dressers.

72550 Bureau, antique finish, four drawers, no mirror; height, 3 ft. 7 in.; width, 3 ft. 1 in.; weight, about 75 pounds.
Price, complete.....$5.00

A good line of dressers to go with iron beds.

Dressers—Continued.

72551 Dresser, well made, of hardwood, and has a good gloss finish. Size of dresser top, 18x38 inches. Has a good 20x24 German beveled mirror and 3 large drawers. Weight, about 125 pounds. It is good value and price is extremely low. Price, only $5.70

72552 Cheval Dresser. Same as 72551, except has an upright large German bevel mirror, 17x30 inches. Price, only.......................$6.95

72553 Dresser, made of hardwood, richly carved and has a good gloss finish. Size of drawer top, 19x42 inches. Has a good 24x30 inch German bevel mirror and 3 large drawers. A good design and very cheap. Weight about 125 pounds. Has an extra large mirror, and price is only........................$7.55

72554 Cheval Dresser. Same as 72553, except has upright large mirror, 18x40. German bevel. Price.......................$9.45

72555 Dresser. Here is a bargain. Well made of solid oak, richly carved and nicely finished. Size of dresser top, 19x42 inches. Has a good, large 24x30 German bevel mirror and 3 large drawers with locks. Weight, 150 pounds. A good thing for little money. Price, only..................$8.20

72556 Cheval Dresser. Same as 72555, except has a large upright 18x40 German bevel mirror. Price, only $10.00

72557 Dresser. Very artistic design and cheap, well made of solid oak, carved and highly polished. Size of dresser top, 19x42 inches. Has a good large 24x30 German bevel mirror, and three large drawers. Weight about 150 pounds. Our price is very low for this style; good value. Price, only ..$10.00

72558 Dresser, made of solid oak, hand carved and polished. Has a beautiful large oval mirror 24x30 inches, and 3 large drawers. Dress top, 21x43 inches. Weight, 150 pounds, just the thing to go with an iron bed. Price, in ash..........$12.60 Price, in solid oak 14.70

Washstands.

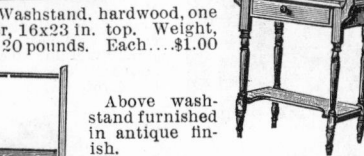

72600 Washstand, hardwood, one drawer, 16x23 in. top. Weight, about 20 pounds. Each....$1.00

Above washstand furnished in antique finish.

72601 Washstand, made of hardwood and has a good gloss finish. Size of top, 16x30. Has one large drawer, two small and a cabinet. Weight, about 50 pounds. Price, only......................$2.70

72602 Washstand. Same as 72601 except has 3 large drawers and no cabinet. Price, only........ 2.75

72604 Toilet Washstand, well made, of solid oak: size of top, 18x32 in. Has one large drawer, two small and a door. Also has a good large 18x20 in. German bevel mirror. Finished antique. Weight, about 75 pounds. Price......$6.50

72605 Toilet Washstand, made of solid oak; richly carved, and nicely finished. Has large 18x20 German bevel mirror; size of top, 18x32 inches, well made and cheap. Finished antique. Weight, about 75 pounds. Price.$7.75

72604   72605

Chamber Suits.

Send 8 cents for our new Special Furniture Catalogue. We show about 50 new beautiful designs in chamber suits. Our prices include packing, casters and delivered to freight house here.

Our New Style Palmer House Chamber Suit.

72700 Chamber Suit. This is the best suit in the world for the money, and the greatest bargain in our catalogue. Made of hardwood and finished antique. Has extra heavy carving and heavy brackets on posts. Bed is 6 ft. high, slats 4 ft. 6 in. Dresser has a good 20x24 German bevel mirror, and three large drawers. Well made and strong. Price, complete, packed for shipment, only.........$10.90

We will ship one of our 72700 suits to any railroad point within 500 miles of Chicago, with the express understanding that if not entirely satisfactory, after examination, the suit can be returned to us at our expense and purchase money will be refunded. If there is a bank at your town you need not send the money with order unless you desire to, as we will ship, when so directed, to our own address in care of the bank and draw on you for the amount of your bill. The bank will deliver bill of lading to you, which will enable you to get the goods.

We make these offers to show our faith in our own goods.

72701 Chamber Suit. This neat suit is made of solid oak, richly carved and nicely finished. Bed is 6 ft. 2 inches high, slat 4 ft. 6 in. Dresser has a good 20x24 German bevel mirror, and three large drawers. Suit consists of bed, dresser and commode. We have purchased a large quantity of this suit and are giving you the benefit of hard times prices. Weight, 300 pounds. Finished antique. Remember this suit is made of *solid oak* and the price is only......$13.85

72702 Chamber Suit, Here is value for you. Another one of our new styles at a price. This suit is well made of solid oak, richly carved and nicely finished. Height of bed 6 ft, slat, 4 ft. 6 in. Dresser has a good large 24x30 German bevel mirror. Very heavy and pretty. A good sensible suit for little money. Weight, 300 pounds. Suit consists of bed, dresser and commode. Price, complete, only...............$14.80 This is a rich suit for the money.

Chamber Suits—Continued.

72703 Look at the Design and then look at the Price. Made of solid oak, elaborately hand carved and polished, height of bed, 6 feet; slat, 4 feet 6 inches. Dresser has a large 24x30 inch German bevel mirror. The foot of bed is richly carved as well as head. Suit consists of bed, dresser and commode. Weight, 300 pounds. Dresser and commode are made with double tops and are extra heavy. You make no mistake in ordering this. Price, complete, only...$16.10

72704 Chamber Suit, made of solid oak, neatly carved and polished. Height of bed; slat, 4 feet 6 inch. Dresser has a good 24x30 German mirror. Suit consists of bed, dresser and commode. Weight, 200 pounds. Price, complete..$17.50

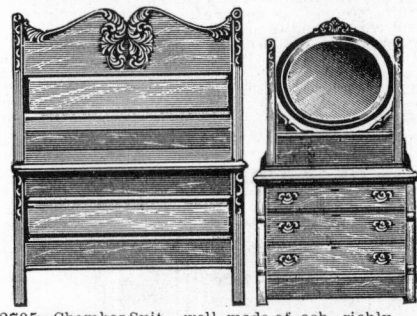

72705 Chamber Suit, well made of ash, richly hand carved, and polished, bed is 6 feet 2 inches high; slat, 4 feet 6 inch. Dresser has a fine 24x30 oval French bevel mirror. A very artistic design. Suit consists of bed, dresser and commode. Weight, 300 pounds. Price extremely low. Only..........................$17.99

72706 Chamber Suit, take particular *notice of the size of mirror and the price of this suit*. Made of solid oak, richly hand carved and polished. Height of bed, 6 feet 2 inches, slat, 4 feet 6 inches. Dresser has extra large German bevel mirror, 28x34 inches, three large drawers and double top. Suit consists of bed, dresser and commode. Weight about 300 pounds. *Well made and cheap.* Price, complete, only........$18.75

No charge for cases or cartage.

Write for freight rates to your town.

Chamber Suits—Continued.

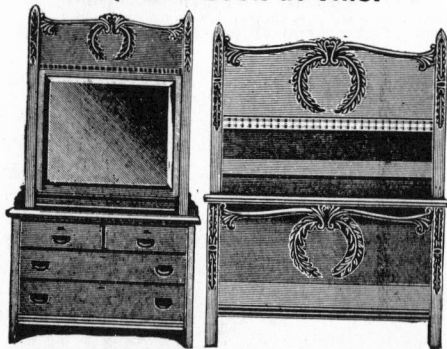

72707 Chamber Suit, made of solid oak highly polished and hand carved. Height of bed, 6 ft.; slat, 4 feet 6 inches. Dresser has a good 24x30 oval French bevel mirror, 3 large drawers and double tops. Suit consists of bed, dresser and commode. Weight, 300 pounds. Price, complete, only................$23.25

Stop and Look at This.

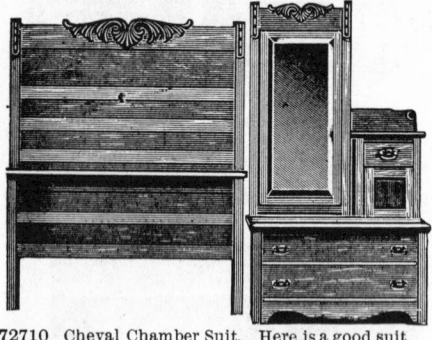

72708 Chamber Suit. Here is the greatest bargain of the times. "It's an ill wind that blows nobody good." The recent hard times are the direct means of your having this elegant suit offered to you for this low price, at which it is greater value for the money than anything ever before offered. Is made of solid oak, richly hand carved, and the finish on this suit is as fine as a piano polish. Bed is 6 feet 4 inches high; slat, 4 feet 6 inches. Dresser has a fine, large 30x36 French bevel mirror. The drawers in this dresser are extra large. Suit consists of bed, dresser and commode. Finished antique oak or birch natural finish. Birch is a new finish which resembles natural cherry. Weight, 300 pounds. Our price on this suit is only........$28.00

Cheval Chamber Suit.

72710 Cheval Chamber Suit. Here is a good suit at a bargain. Well made of hardwood, richly carved and nicely finished. Height of bed, 6 feet; slat, 4 feet 6 inches. Dresser contains a large 18x40 German bevel mirror. Well made and cheap. Suit consists of bed, dresser and commode. Weight, 300 pounds. Price, complete, only... ....$12.60

72711

Chamber Suits—Continued.

72711 Cheval Chamber Suit, made of solid oak, richly hand-carved and highly polished. We think this is one of the best of our new designs, and you will see by the *price* you are getting a bargain. Bed is 6 feet 2 inches high; slat, 4 feet 6 inches. Dresser has a good 18x40 inch German bevel mirror. This style of dresser is very convenient for ladies. The head and footboard of bed are very elaborately carved. Suit consists of bed, dresser and commode. Weight, 300 pounds. You make no mistake in ordering this. Our price on this suit, which is made of solid oak, is only........................$17.50

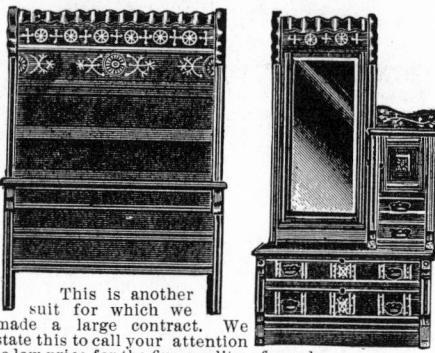

This is another suit for which we made a large contract. We state to call your attention to low price for the fine quality of goods.

72713 Solid Oak Cheval Chamber Suit. Beadstead 6 feet high; slats, 4 feet 6 inches. Dresser has 18x40 German bevel mirror. Richly carved suit consists of bed, dresser and commode. Finished antique. Weight, 300 pounds.
Retail price.....................................$30.75
Our price, only............................. 19.75

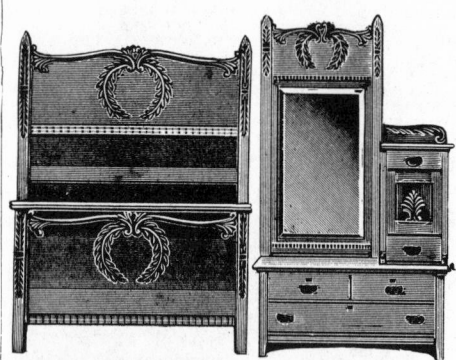

72720 Cheval Chamber Suit. Here is a bargain for you. If you buy this suit your neighbors will all envy you. It is impossible to show the value by the above cut. Made of solid oak; richly hand carved; the finish is as fine as a piano polish. Bed is 6 feet 4 inches high; slats, 4 feet 6 inches; size of dresser top, 50x24 inches; dresser has a beautiful large 24x40 inch French bevel mirror. The head and foot boards of bed have heavy carving. Suit consists of bed, dresser and commode. Weight, 300 pounds. Finished antique. This suit is also made in red birch, natural finish, which is beautiful. Birch is a new finish which resembles natural cherry. This handsome suit is a bargain at the price we offer it. Only...............................$30.80

72724 Chamber Suit, well made of solid oak, richly hand carved and highly hand polished; extra select stock in this suit. Height of bed is 6 feet 4 inches high; slat, 4 feet 6 inches; dresser has an extra large French bevel pattern plate mirror, 30x40 inches. Size of top of dresser, 22x48 inches; suit consists of bed, dresser and commode. Good value; satisfaction guaranteed. Weight, 300 pounds.
Price, only......................................$31.55

Chamber Suits—Continued.

72725 Chamber Suit, well made of quartersawed oak, hand carved and hand polished; the stock in this suit is very select and beautiful. Height of bed, 6 feet 4 inches; slat, 4 feet 6 inches. Dresser has a fine oval 30x40 French bevel mirror, and two large drawers, with locks. Suit consists of bed, dresser and commode. Weight, 300 pounds. Price, complete, only...$36.50

Sideboards.

Our sideboards are all extra good value. Made of solid oak, hand carved and hand polished. Prices include packing and casters. We show a much larger line of sideboards in our special furniture catalogue which we mail for 8 cents to pay postage.

72800 Sideboard, well made of solid oak, richly hand carved and highly polished. Size of top, 23x48 inches. Has a fine 14x28 in. French bevel mirror. One drawer lined with velvet for silverware. Extra large and good value. We will guarantee satisfaction on this board. Weight, about 200 pounds. A beauty for the money. Our price. only......$13.45

72801 Sideboard, made of solid oak, highly polished and richly hand carved. Size of top, 20x48 inches. Has a fine large mirror, 18x36 inches, one drawer lined with velvet for silverware. Very ornamental and extra good value. Weight, about 200 pounds. A bargain. Price, only..........$14.50

72802 Sideboard, well made of solid oak, richly carved and highly polished. Has an *extra large* 18x36 inch German bevel mirror. Size of top, 21x46; one drawer lined with velvet for silverware. A very neat design. Weight, about 200 pounds. Good value. Price, only..........$16.75

72803 Sideboard. This is a very artistic design, made of solid oak, elaborately hand carved and highly polished. Has a fine 18x32 inch French bevel mirror; also an 8x20 French mirror in top. One drawer lined with velvet for silverware. Very showy and pretty. Size of top, 21x46 inches. Weight, about 225 pounds. Price, only.$19.60

72804 Sideboard, well made of quarter sawed oak, hand carved and highly polished. Has a fine 16x30 inch French mirror; one drawer lined with velvet for silverware. Size of top, 25x48 inches; very large and massive; weight, about 225 pounds. Price, only..........$20.55

Sideboards—Continued.

72805 Sideboard, made of quarter sawed oak, richly carved and polished. Size of top, 25x46 inches; has a fine 18x36 inch French bevel mirror. One drawer lined with velvet for silver ware. This board has a great deal of carving, and the price is extremely low; weight, about 250 pounds. Price, only........$22.75

Kitchen Cabinets.

Very useful about a house where a "shortage" of closets or cupboards is felt.

72900 Kitchen Cabinet or Cupboard, height, 6 feet; width, 3 feet 1 inch; made of hardwood; has two upper and lower cupboards with shelves inside and two drawers in center, as shown in cut. Finished antique. Each'....$4.45 Weight, 95 lbs.

72900

72905 Cupboard made of solid oak, finished antique; has two glass doors above and two panel doors below, with two drawers in center, height, 6 feet 11 inches; width, 3 feet 4 inches. Used by many families as a crockery closet for dining room purposes. Weight, 110 pounds. Price, complete.$7.75

72905

Wardrobes.

We shall have a larger assortment of wardrobes in our new special furniture catalogue, which we mail for 8 cents to pay postage.

72908 Wardrobes, made of solid oak, strong and well made. Has 2 large doors and drawer at bottom; 76 inches high; 38 inches wide; 15 in. deep. Price ..$6.30

72908

Weight, 115 lbs. This is a bargain.

72909 Wardrobes. This is extra good value, made of solid oak, and has a good gloss finish. Height, 6 feet 3 inches; width, 3 feet 3 inches. Has 2 doors and a large drawer. Weight, 125 pounds. Price...$7.70

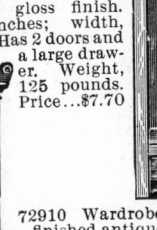

72909

72910 Wardrobe, made of ash finished antique, neatly carved. and has a good gloss finish. Height, 6 feet 10 inches; width, 3 feet 5 inches; depth 17 inches. Has 2 doors and a large drawer, well made and exceedingly deep, Weight, about 125 pounds. Price, only.............$7.00

72910

72911 Wardrobes, well made of solid oak and nicely finished Height, 6 feet, 10 inches; width, 3 feet 5 inches, depth, 17 inches. Has two doors and drawer below, very large and roomy. A very low price for an oak wardrobe. Weight, 125 pounds. Price, only $9.25

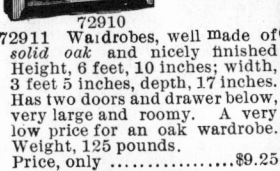

72911

Revolving Book Stands.

72955 Revolving Book Stand, made of solid oak, highly polished; top, 19 inches square, 45 inches high. Shelves, 7½x9¼; 11 inches high. Holds 75 to 90 volumes average size books; finished antique. Weight, 70 lbs. Price...................$9.25

Book Stands—Continued.

72956 Revolving Book Stand, made of solid oak and highly polished. Size of top, 19 inches square; height, 48 inches; shelves are 9, 10 and 12 inches high. Very large and exceedingly cheap. Perfect in every respect. Weight, 60 pounds. Price.$7.15

Folding Book Cases.

72960 Folding Book Rack, made of solid oak and highly polished. Height, 35 inches; width, 20 inches; depth, 8 inches. Has rod with rings for curtain. Hangs on the wall. and is very strong. Three shelves fold and close automatically. Weight, about 10 pounds. Price, without curtain......$1.50

72965 Folding Book Case, made of solid oak, carved and polished. Height, 56 inches; width, 25 inches; depth, 10 inches. Has rod with rings for curtain. Four shelves fold and close automatically. Very handy and cheap. No screws or nails needed. Weight, about 30 pounds. Price, without curtain........$2.80

Bookcases.

73000 Curtain Library Case, made of hardwood, finished antique; brass rods and rings for curtain, adjustable shelves, polished finish; height, 5 feet; width, 2 feet 8 inches. Weight, about 80 pounds. Price, complete...... ....$4.05

73001 Curtain Bookcase, made of solid oak, neatly carved and polished; height, 5 feet 2 inches' width, 2 feet 9 inches has French mirror, 6x10 in.; brass rod and rings for curtain; adjustable shelves. Weight, about 90 pounds. Price...... ....$6.00

73002 Bookcase, made of solid oak, *carved* and *polished*. Height, 5 feet; width, 2 feet 6 inches, size of glass in door 24x40 inches. All shelves are adjustable, well made and cheap. A good case for little money Weight, 95 pounds. Price, only...................$6.95

73003 Bookcase, made of quarter sawed oak, neatly carved and highly hand polished; width, 33 inches; depth, 12 inches; height, 6 feet; has one door, and shelves are adjustable; well made and cheap. We consider this a bargain. Weight, about 100 pounds. Our price, only........ .....$10.50

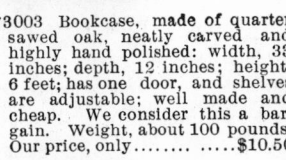

73004 Bookcase, made of quarter sawed oak, carved and highly polished. Has a 10x12 inch French bevel mirror. All shelves are adjustable. Height, 5 feet 6 inches; width, 3 feet 2 inches. Glass in the doors are extra heavy, well made and cheap. Weight, about 150 pounds. Price.......$10.75

Bookcases—Continued.

73005 Bookcase, made of quarter sawed oak, richly carved and polished. Width, 3 feet 6 inches; depth, 12 inches; height, 5 feet 5 inches: has two doors with lock and shelves are adjustable. This is a beautiful large case for the money, and exceedingly cheap Weight about 175 pounds. Price only $11.20

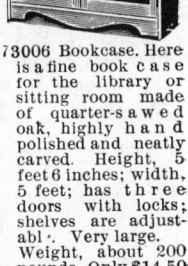

73006 Bookcase. Here is a fine book case for the library or sitting room made of quarter-sawed oak, highly hand polished and neatly carved. Height, 5 feet 6 inches; width, 5 feet; has three doors with locks; shelves are adjustable. Very large. Weight, about 200 pounds. Only $14.50

73006

73007 Bookcase, made of quarter sawed oak, richly carved and highly polished. Height, 5 feet 2 inches; width, 3 feet 3 inches. All shelves are adjustable. Extra good value and cheap. Weight, about 175 pounds. Price...................$10.80

73007

73008 Bookcase, made of quarter sawed oak, richly carved and highly hand polished. Height, 6 feet 8 inches; width, 3 feet 6 inches; depth, 13 inches. Has two doors with locks and shelves are adjustable. Has a fine French mirror 12x24 inches. Very ornamental and well made. Note low price on this bookcase. Weight, about 200 pounds. Our price, only........$16.80

73008

73009 Bookcase, made of quarter sawed oak, highly hand polished and richly hand carved. Height, 6 feet 4 inches; width, 4 feet; depth, 13½ inches. Has two large glass doors with locks; shelves are adjustable. Has a fine French bevel mirror, 10x24 inches. This is a beautiful bookcase and is extra well made. Weight, about 200 pounds. Only... $19.20

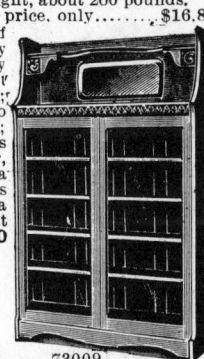

73009

73009½ Bookcase, well made of quarter sawed oak, richly carved and highly hand polished. Height, 6 feet 2 inches; width, 3 feet 8 inches. All shelves are adjustable. Has two glass doors with locks and two drawers below. French bevel mirror, 8x20 inches, in top. Very ornamental and cheap. Extra large and good value. Weight, 200 lbs.$16.90

Combination Bookcase and Writing Desks.

These designs are new, well made of oak and curly birch and the prices are *low*.

73010 Combination Bookcase and Writing Desk. Here is a bargain for you. This case is highly hand polished and made of solid oak. The shelves are all adjustable and the desk is nicely partitioned, with pigeon holes and drawers. Has a French bevel mirror, 10x14 inches. Size of case: Height, 5 feet 5 inches; width, 3 feet 1 inch. This is a good design and a beauty for the money. Look at the price. Weight, about 150 pounds. Price, only $10.50

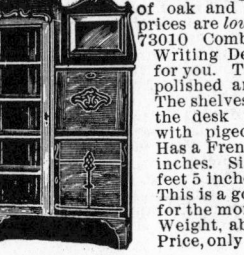

Bookcases—Continued.

73011 Combination Bookcase and Writing Desk, made of solid oak, richly carved and polished. Height, 6 feet; width 3 feet 8 inches. Interior of desk is nicely fitted with pigeon holes and drawers, shelves are adjustable. Has a good French bevel mirror, 14x16 inches; weight, about 175 pounds. This is extra good value, well made and cheap. Price. only.$14.85

73012 Combination Bookcase. richly carved and richly polished. Height, 6 feet; width 3 feet 8 inches. Has a fine French bevel mirror, 14x18 inches. All shelves are adjustable. Inside of desk is nicely partitioned with pigeon holes and drawers. Weight, 200 pounds. Finished antique. Price, complete.$16.50

73013 Combination Bookcase and Writing Desk, well made of solid oak, richly hand carved and highly hand polished. Height, 6 feet; width 3 feet 6 inches. Has a fine French bevel mirror, 14x16 inches. All shelves are adjustable. Desk is nicely partitioned with pigeon holes and drawers. Very ornamental and cheap. Weight, about 200 pounds. Price, only.$17.69

73014 Combination Bookcase and and Writing Desk, well made of solid oak, richly hand carved and highly polished. Height, 6 feet 3 inches; width, 3 feet 5 inches. Has 2 French bevel mirror,10x16 inches. All shelves are adjustable, inside of desk is nicely partitioned with pigeon holes and drawers. This case is very ornamental and a good design. Weight, 200 pounds. Price .$18.95

73015 Combination Bookcase and Writing Desk, made of quarter sawed oak, richly carved and polished. is extra large; height, 6 feet 6 inches; width, 3 feet 8 inches; has a fine French bevel mirror. 14x16 inches, shelves are adjustable; desk is nicely partitioned with pigeon holes and drawers. An extra fine case for little money. Weight, 200 pounds. Price.$20.25

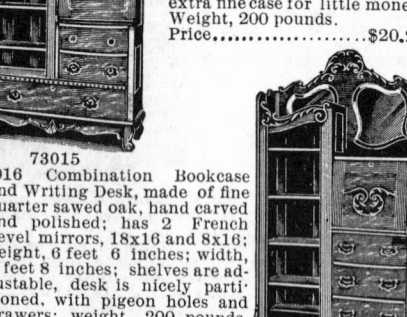
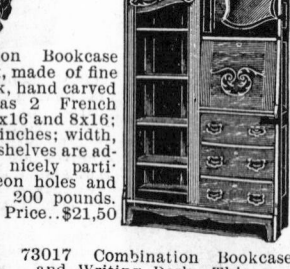

73015

73016 Combination Bookcase and Writing Desk, made of fine quarter sawed oak, hand carved and polished; has 2 French bevel mirrors, 18x16 and 8x16; height, 6 feet 6 inches; width, 3 feet 8 inches; shelves are adjustable, desk is nicely partitioned, with pigeon holes and drawers; weight, 200 pounds. This is a beauty. Price..$21,50

73017 Combination Bookcase and Writing Desk, This case is handsomely hand carved and polished like a piano; is made of solid oak and curly birch. The wood used in this case is select and beautiful; the design is artistic and fine enough for anyone; height, 5 feet 11 inches; width, 3 feet 8 inches; has a fine French bevel mirror. 15½x22 inches. The drop leaf desk is extra large and inside is nicely partitioned with pigeon holes and drawers; all shelves are adjustable. This case is high grade, very ornamental, and we are sure it will please you. Weight, about 200 pounds.
Price in quarter sawed oak.$23.50
Price, in curly birch.26.75

Bookcases—Continued.

73018 Combination Bookcase and Writing Desk. The finish on this case is as fine as a piano finish. Is made of quarter sawed oak and curly birch. The stock is extra selected and handsome. The design is artistic and rich. Height, 5 feet 10 inches; width, 3 feet 6 inches. Has a pretty French bevel mirror. 12x20 inches. The drop leaf is extra large and inside is nicely partitioned with pigeonholes and drawers. All shelves are adjustable. This case is a piece of art. If you want something fine we will guarantee this to give perfect satisfaction. Weight, 200 pounds.
Price, in quarter sawed oak.$26.75
Price, in curly birch.29.95

73019 Combination Bookcase and Writing Desk. well made, of solid oak richly hand carved and polished. Height, 6 feet 2 inches; width, 5 feet 4 inches. Has a French bevel mirror, 14x18 inches. All shelves are adjustable. Desk is nicely partitioned off with pigeon holes and drawers. This case is extra large and well made. Weight, 250 pounds. Price, complete, only.$24.75

73028 Combination Bookcase and Writing Desk, made in solid oak, neatly carved and polished; height, 6 feet 10 inches; width, 3 feet: size of glass in doors, 14 x 30 inches. Has a drop leaf desk with 3 large drawers; shelves are adjustable. Finished antique. The best and cheapest combination bookcase in the market. Weight, 175 pounds.

73028
Price, only....   **73029**
.$14.85

73029 Combination Bookcase and Writing Desk, made in walnut or solid oak, richly carved and nicely polished; height, 7 feet 2 inches; width, 2 feet 11 inches. Has a cylinder desk, nicely partitioned with pigeon holes and drawers; shelves are adjustable. Size of glass in doors, 13x30 inches. Well made and cheap. Weight, 175 pounds. Price.$20.90

73031 Combination Bookcase and Writng Desk, made in walnut or solid oak; richly carved and polished; height, 7 feet 6 inches; width, 3 feet 4 inches; size of glass in doors, 15x32 inches; has a cylinder desk nicely partitioned with pigeon holes and drawers; shelves are adjustable. Weight, 200 lbs. Price.$24.90

73031

Ladies' or Parlor Desks.

We show a much larger line of Parlor Desks in our new special furniture, which we mail for 8 cents to pay postage.

73100 Ladies' or Parlor Desks, well made of solid oak. carved and highly polished. Height, 4 feet; width, 2 feet 3 inches. Has drop leaf and one drawer. Inside is nicely partitioned with pigeon holes and drawers. Weight, about 40 pounds. A bargain. Price, only.$5.65

73101 Ladies' or Parlor Desk, Made of quartersawed oak. Richly hand carved and highly polished. Height, 4 feet; width, 2 feet 4 inches. Has large drop leaf and one drawer. Inside is nicely partitioned with pigeon holes and drawers. Weight, about 50 pounds. A good design, and extra well made. Price,only $6.95

Desks—Continued.

73105 Parlor Desk. Here is a beauty for little money. Made of quartersawed oak. Hand carved and highly polished. Height. 4 feet: with 2 feet 4 inches. Has a good French bevel mirror, 6x18 inches. The drop leaf and drawer has locks. Inside is nicely partitioned with pigeon holes and drawers. Very ornamental and cheap. Weight, about 50 pounds. Price, only. .$7.95

73106 Here is a good sensible desk for little money. Well made of quartersawed oak, hand carved and polished. Height, 4 feet, 2 inches; width, 2 feet, 6 inches. The French mirror in top is quite large, size 8x24 inches. Has 3 extra large drawers and a large drop leaf. Inside is nicely partitioned with pigeon holes and drawers. Weight, 75 pounds. A beauty for the money. Price, only.$10.65

We Lead The World on Office Desks.

We have the best made desk in the market. *Money refunded if desk is not perfectly satisfactory.* Cabinet work and finish warranted.

We show a much larger line of desks in our new special Furniture Catalogue. We can furnish pasteboard filing boxes to fit pigeon holes for 15 cents each, extra

73125 Low Curtain Office Desk. Here is a bargain for you. Well made. of solid oak, and polished. Length, 4 feet width 32 inches; height, 45 inches. Has lap joint, dust and knife proof curtain, a solid oak writing bed, painted on the back to prevent warping, 2 sliding arm rests, automatic drawer lock operated by curtain. All drawers are 10½ inches wide inside, and 2 drawers are partitioned in each pedestal. Book racks in pedestal are 17 inches, high and 11½ inches deep. Inside measure of pigeon holes, in top 3x4 inches. Price includes packing and casters. Extra good value. Weight, about 225 pounds. This desk has open back. Price, only.$15.75
We can furnished above desk with drawers on both sides if desired at same price.

73126 Low Curtain Office Desk, same as 73125, except it is 4 feet 6 inches long. Well made and and cheap. Weight, about 235 pounds. Price.$18.00

73127 Low Curtain Desk, same as 73125, except is 5 feet long. Weight, about, 245 pounds. Price, only.19.75
We have desks with drawers on both sides if desired.

73128 High Curtain Office Desk. This is the best desk in America for the money. Height, 47 inches; length, 4 feet; width, 32 inches. Extra well made of solid oak and highly polished; Has lap joint, dust and knife proof curtain. A solid oak writing bed, painted on the back to prevent warping; 2 sliding arm rests, automatic drawer lock, which is operated by curtain. All drawers are 10½ inches inside, and two drawers are partitioned in each pedestal. Book racks in pedestal are 17 inches high and 11½ inches deep. Price includes packing and casters. This desk has closed back, nicely finished. Satisfaction guaranteed or money refunded. Weight, about 245 pounds. Price, only.$17.90
We can furnish above with drawers on both sides, if desired at the same price

73129 High Curtain Office Desk, same as 73128, except is 4 feet 6 inches long. A bargain. Weight, about 255 pounds. Price, only.$19.55

73130 High Curtain Desk, same as 73128, except is 5 feet long. This desk will more than please you. The standard size, very large and roomy. Price is extremely low. Weight, about 270 pounds. A bargain, only.$20.50
We can furnish above with drawers on both sides, if desired, at same price.

Desks—Continued.

73131 Extra High Curtain Office Desk. This desk is very large and roomy and the price is extremely low; well made of oak and highly polished. Length, 4 feet; width 32 inches; height 51 inches. Has lap joint, dust and knife proof curtain; a solid oak writing bed, paint on the back to prevent warping, 2 sliding arm rests, automatic drawer lock, which is operated by curtain; all drawers are 10½ inches wide inside, and 2 drawers are partitioned in each pedestal; book racks in ped estal are 17 inches high and 11½ inches deep inside measure of pigeon holes in top, 3x4 inches. Price includes packing and casters; satisfaction guaranteed or money refunded. Weight, about 250 pounds.

Price, only.................................$20.75

We can furnish above desk with drawers on both sides, if desired at same price.

73132 Extra High Curtain Office Desk, same as 73131, except is 4 feet 6 inches long. Weight, about 265 pounds. Price, only................ 22.65

73133 Extra High Curtain Office Desk, same as 73131, except is 5 feet long; extra good value at our price and is perfect in every respect. Money refunded if not satisfactory. Weight, about 230 pounds.

Price, only..... .... 25.00

Above desk with drawers on both sides at same price if desired. We can furnish paste-board filing boxes to fit pigeon holes for 15 cents each, extra.

Typewriter Cabinets.

In these cabinets the machine is always on a level, thus saving it from the bad effect of being constantly tipped over and so getting out of order. The cabinet will accomodate any size machine, and protect it from dust. When the machine is not in use it can be dropped out of sight, thus the cabinet serves the double purpose of a typewriter cabinet and an office desk. We show a larger assortment of cabinets in our new special Furniture Catalogue, which we mail on receipt er 8 cents to pay postage.

73134 Typewriter Cabinet. This cabinet is well made of solid oak, and highly hand-polished. Height, 31 ins.. size. of top, 30x36 inches; width of drawers, 10 inches. Has one extension slide and combination lock. Weight, about 150 pounds; finished antique. Price, complete...

....$16.25

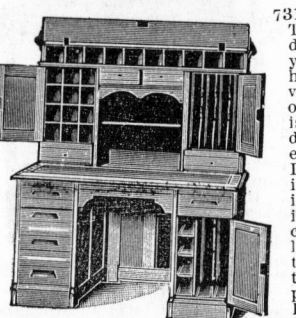

73135 Office Desk. This cut shows the desk open, which you can see is very handy and convenient. Made of oak and nicely finished. All the doors and drawers have locks. Length, 4 feet 4 in.; width, 2 ft. 7 in. Writing bed is covered with cloth or imitation leather. Has slant top. Finished antique. Weight, 200 pounds.

Price, only $21.00

73140 Flat Top Office Desk, made of oak. Length, 4 feet; width, 2 feet 6 inches. Has two extension slides. Finished in polished wood top. Back is open in place of closed. Weight, 175 lbs.

Price $9.50

73141 Flat Top Office Desk, same as 73140, except is 4 feet 6 inches long. Weight, about 180 pounds. This is well made and bargain.

Price, only......................................$10.50

73142 Flat Top Office Desk, same as 73140, except is 5 feet long. Weight. about 185 pounds. Very large and exceedingly cheap.

Price, only....................... ....$11.70

39—2nd

Desks—Continued.

73145 Men's Drop Leaf Desk. nicely partitioned with pigeon holes and drawers. Made of hardwood and finished antique. Height, 5 feet 6 inches; width, 2 feet 6 inches, A very convenient article to have in any house. Weight, 100 pounds.

Price...... ....$9.50

73150 Salesman or Student's Desk, well made of solid oak. Length, 32 inches; width, 26 inches. Has slanting wood bed and 2 drawers, with locks. Paper pocket can be hung at either end. Weight, about 100 pounds.

Price. only......$6 50

73160 Desk, made of oak, finished antique. Has all the conveniences of a large, expensive desk. Takes up no floor space; can be set on a shelf, table or can be fastened to the wall with two screws. Height, 29 inches; width, 25 inches; depth, 10 inches; size of drop leaf, 17x22 inches. Weight, 35 pounds.

Price, only......$3.50

Hat Racks

73177 Hat Back, made of solid oak, rubbed and polished, 36 in. long. 15 in. high; 10 brass plated hooks It can be folded flat for packing.

French bevel mirror. Price, each................$2.25 Weight. about 10 pounds.

73178 Hat Rack, made of solid oak, finely finished antique; size, 16x 28 inches, with 4 large hooks and a French bevel mirror, 10x14 inches. Very neat, cheap and well made. Weight, 8 pounds

Price, only $2.50

73179 Hat Rack, made of solid oak, finished antique; size, 13x36 inches, has 6 large hooks and a French bevel mirror, 6x6 in.

Weight, 6 pounds. Each, only..................$1.60

73185 Toilet or Shaving Cabinet, Well made of quarter sawed oak, carved and richly finished. Size, 17x29 inches, Door opens on side. Has a fine 12x16 French bevel mirror. Large shelf under mirror and roller for towels. Can be used for medicine cabinet. Well made and a good bargain. Weight, about 12 pounds.

Price.................. .....$2 75

73190 Umbrel'a Holder, made of oak, and nicely finished. Has removable brass pan at bottom. Height, 32 inches; width, 12 inches. Quite ornamental and very cheap. Weight, about 5 pounds.

Price, only.....................$1.00

Racks—Continued.

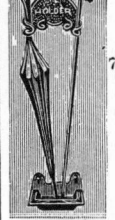

73191 Umbrella Holder. a very handy and cheap article, made of cast to fasten to wall. If the umbrella is wet the drip is all caught in a cast pan at bottom. Is very complete and takes but little room. Just the thing you want.

Price, only.........................$0.25

Hall Trees.

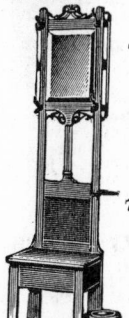

73200 Hall Tree, made of solid oak, gloss finish. Height, 6 feet 4 inches; width, 2 feet 4 inches; depth, 13 inches. Has a German mirror, 10x17 inches. Very neat and cheap; weight, 35 pounds.

Price $4.65

73201 Hall Tree, made of solid oak, and has a good gloss finish. Height, 6 feet 5 inches width, 2 feet 2 inches; depth, 14 inches. Has a fine French bevel mirror 14x18 inches; 4 large hooks and an um

73200   73201

brella holder: well made. Finished antique. Weight. 45 pounds. Price.........$6.75

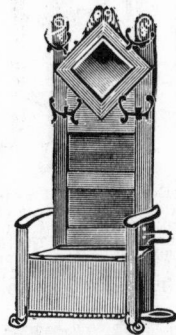

73202 Hall Tree, made of solid oak, richly hand carved and polished. Height. 6 feet 10 inches; width 2 feet 10 inches Has a good French bevel mirror 14x14 inches, umbrella holder and 4 double hat hooks. Has a box with lid for rubbers. Weight about 75 pounds.

Price, only................$9.80

73203 Hall Tree. well made of quarter sawed oak, richly hand carved and highly hand polished. Height, 6 feet 10 inches; width, 2 feet 10 inches. Has large 18x30 French bevel mirror, umbrella holder and 4 double hat racks. Has a box with lid for rubbers. Weight, about 80 pounds. Price, only......$14.90

Mirrors.

73250— Plain French Mirror. Frame is made of solid oak, and nicely finished.

73250   73251

Size	Weight		Each
Size, 9x12 in.	Weight, 4 pounds.	Eac	$0.50
Size, 10x17 in.	Weight, 5 pounds.	Each	.75
Size, 12x20 in.	Weight, 6 pounds.	Each	.95
Size, 14x24 in.	Weight, 7 pounds.	Each	1 25
Size, 17x30 in.	Weight, 10 pounds.	Each	2.45
Size, 18x36 in.	Weight, 13 pounds.	Each	2.85

73251 Pier Mirror made of molding, finely ornamented in imitation of carved wood, and finished in all silver and gold, or enameled white finished in all silver and gold. Very rich and showy. Weight, about 20 pounds.

Price, with 18x40 in. plain German mirror.......$5.50
Price, with 18x40 in. German bevel mirror....... 6.00
Price, with 18x40 in. plain French mirror......... 5.75
Price, with 18x40 in. French bevel mirror......... 6.75

Mirrors—Continued.

73252 Pier Mirror Frame, is made in oak or walnut, richly carved and polished. Weight, 18 pounds
Price, with 18x40 inches, plain German.......... $6.75
Price, with 18x40 in. German bevel. $7.50
Price, with 18x40 in. plain French $7.25
Price, with 18x40 in. French bevel $8.00

73252　　　**73253**

73253 Parlor Pier Mirror, made in solid oak, richly carved and polished. A new design, very attractive and cheap. Weight, about 40 pounds.
Price, with 20x60 inch plain French plate.... $13.50
Price, with 20x60 inch French bevel plate..... 15.55
We show a large selection of Pier Mirrors in our new Furniture Catalogue.

Parlor Stands and Library Tables.

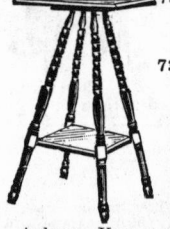

73275 Parlor Stand, made of solid oak. Size of top, 15x15 inches. Finished in antique. Weight, 10 pounds. Each..... $0.70

73300 Parlor Stand, well made of solid oak. Size of top, 16x20 in.; finished antique, well made and has two lower shelves. Very strong and price extremely low. Weight, about 15 pounds. Price. $1.20

73300

73301 Parlor Stand, well made of quarter sawed oak, and highly polished. Size of top, 20x20 inches; shelf, 15x15 inches. This is a beauty for the money. Weight, about 15 pounds. Price, only..... $2.35

73302 Parlor Stand, well made of quarter sawed oak and highly polished. Size of top, 21x21. Has lower shelf. Well braced and strong. Good value. Weight, 20 pounds. Price, only....... $2.80

73305 Parlor Stand, made of solid oak, nicely finished. Size of top, 24x24 in. Finished antique. Well made and cheap. Weight, 30 pounds. Price.... .... $1.40

72316 Sitting Room or Bed Room Stand, well made of solid oak and nicely finished. Well braced and has 1 drawer. Size of top, 22x30. Strong and cheap. Weight, 30 pounds. Price, only... $2.25

73317 Parlor or Sitting Room Stand, made of solid oak; nicely finished and quite fancy. Size of top, 22x30 inches; lower shelf, 24x16 inches. Very large and cheap. Weight, 30 pounds. Price, only...... $2.35

Parlor Stands—Continued.

73318 Parlor Stand. This is extra good value, made of quarter sawed oak, and highly hand polished. Size, of top, 26x26 inches; lower shelf, 20x20 inches. Well braced and strong. Has large top and is a good, durable table.
Weight, 30 pounds
Price, only $2.95

73325 Brass Stand, with a fine onyx top, 8x8 inches. Finished in gold lacquer. Height, 30 inches; very ornamental and cheap. Price, only $4.95

73325

73326 Brass Stand, has a fine onyx top, 8x8 inches. Size of lower onyx shelf, 6x6 inches. Height, 29½ inches; finished in gold lacquer; very pretty and nicely finished. Price $7.00

73327 Brass Stand, very showy and well made. Has a fine onyx top. 12x12 inches. Finished in gold lacquer. Height. 30 inches. Very ornamental and cheap. Good value. Weight, about 32 pounds.
Price............. $10.25

73326

73327½

73327½ Parlor Table made of solid oak and highly polished. Size, 26x26 inches. Well made and a bargain. Weight, about 30 lbs. Price, only..... $2.65

73327¾ Parlor Table, made of solid oak and highly polished. Size of top, 22x30 inches Extra heavy and well made, and very large Weight, 40 pounds. Price, only.... $2.80

73328 Parlor Stand, well made of solid oak and highly hand polished; size of top, 24x24 inches, with large lower shelf. Has heavy metal claw feet, strong and cheap. Weight, about 30 pounds. Price. only....... $2.35

73329 Fancy Parlor Stand very artistic and pretty made of solid oak and highly polished. Richly carved. Size of top, 24x24 inches. Has lower shelf, good and strong. Weight, about 30 pounds. Price, only...$2.60

73331 This is a beautiful Parlor Stand, made of quarter sawed oak, neatly carved and highly hand polished; size of top, 26 x 26 inches; with lower shelf; very stylish and pretty. This is a bargain; weight, about 25 pounds.
Price, only...... $3.75

Parlor Stands—Continued.

73332 Parlor Stand. This table will more than please you. Made of quarter sawed oak, hand carved and highly polished. Height, 30 inches. Size of top, 20x30 inches; satisfaction guaranteed, very ornamental. Weight, 30 pounds.
Price, only....... $3.85

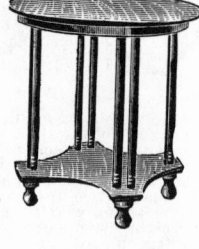

73333 Round Parlor Stand well made of quarter sawed oak, has round top, size, 30x30 inches, and lower shelf; plain and rich, highly hand polished; very select stock in this table. Weight, 30 pounds.
Price, only........... $4.40

73346 A Good Parlor or Sitting Room Table, made of solid oak, highly polished; size of top, 26x26 inches, with large lower shelf; well made and cheap weight, about 35 pounds.
Price, only..... $3.80

73346

73347 This is a beautiful parlor table, with French legs; made of select oak, highly hand polished. Size of top, 26x26 inches. Has lower shelf, connected with brass brackets. This is one of the most stylish tables we have; well made and cheap. Weight, about 35 pounds.
Price, only...... $4.40

73348 Here is an artistic table made of quarter sawed oak, and highly hand polished. Size of top, 18x36 inches. Well made and cheap. Weight, 30 pounds. Price, only.... $4.90

73348

73350 Parlor Stand, made of quarter sawed oak, highly polished. Size, of top, 20x26 inches. Has brass trimmings. The stock used in this table is select and beautiful. Weight, 30 pounds
Price, in quartered oak.... .... $4.90
Price, in solid mahogany.......... 6.30

73351

73351 A Fine Parlor Table with large turned legs. Richly hand carved and highly polished. Made of quarter sawed oak. Size of top, 26x26 inches, with lower shelf. A good, sensible table for little money. Weight, 35 pounds.
Price, only........ $4.75

73352 Here is a rich table for little money, made of quarter sawed oak or bird's eye maple. Hand carved and highly hand polished. Size of top, 26x26. This table is almost round, and is a beauty. The stock is beautiful and select. Weight, 35 pounds.
Price, only................. $4.90

Tables—Continued.

73353 Parlor or Library Table, made of quarter sawed oak, richly carved and hand polished. Size of top, 28 x28 inches. Very large and massive; well made and cheap; finished antique. Weight, 40 pounds. Our price, only $4.95

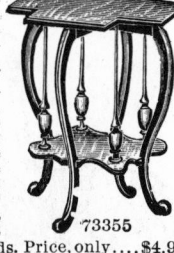

73354 Here is a beautiful little parlor table, round, made of solid mahogany, and top inlaid with birdseye maple. Size of top, 22 x22 in. This is a perfect

73354   **73355**

beauty. Weight, about 25 pounds. Price, only....$4.90
73355 How is this for an artistic design, fancy parlor table, made of birch finished imitation mahogany. Size of top, 25x25 inches, very pretty and ornamental. Weight, 30 pounds. Price, only..................... ....$6.95

Library Tables.

73356 Library or Sitting Room Table, well made of ash, and highly polished. Size of top, 25x36 inches, has large lower shelf and drawer, very heavy and well made. Extra good value. Weight, about 35 pounds.

Price, only....................................$3.85

73357 Sitting Room or Library Table, made of fine quartersawed oak, and hand polished. Size, of top, 24x36, with large lower shelf, supported with brass brackets; has large brass claw feet, well made and cheap. Weight 40 pounds.

Price, only.......................................$4.75

73358 Library Table made of quarter sawed oak, highly polished. Size, of top, 26x 38 inches, has lower shelf and drawer, good heavy stock in this table. Weight, 45 pounds. Price $4.90

73359 Library Table, made of quarter sawed oak, highly hand polished. Size of top, 26 x36, has lower shelf and one drawer, good size and style, extra value. Weight, 40 pounds. Price, only......$6.30

Tables—Continued.

73360 Library Table, made of quarter sawed oak Highly polished. Size of top, 28x44 inches. Has lower shelf and one drawer. Extra heavy stock and well made. Satisfaction guaranteed. Weight, 50 pounds. Price, only.............. .. ..$6.40

73361 Large Library Table, made of quarter sawed oak. and polished like a piano. Has extra large lower shelf and one drawer. Size, of top, 32x48 inches. This is extra heavy and a massive design. Weight, 90 pounds. Price, only.................$9.75

Folding Tables.

73410 Folding Table, hardwood top, with a yard measure neatly stamped on the same. The cheapest, light, strong, serviceable folding table made; indispensable to families where considerable sewing is done; also makes a nice card table. Weight, about 10 pounds. Price, only, $0.66

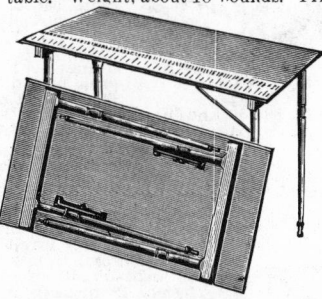

73411 Folding Table, much finer than 73410, is made of ash, finely finished antique, and mounted on casters; size, 36 inches long, 20 inches wide and 26 inches high. The folding device is constructed in such a manner as to form a complete brace from the leg to the center of the table, rendering great strength. Weight, about 15 pounds. Price $1.25

73415 Folding Table, well made of solid oak, and highly polished. Size of top, 24x37 inches; height, 29 inches. Table folds perfectly flat, which enables us to ship it K. D. It makes a fine sewing table, and is just the thing for restaurant service, church sociables, parties and club rooms. Well braced and will sustain a weight of over 500 pounds. Weight, about 20 pounds. Price, only.. ....$1.65

Dining Room Tables.
(We wish to call special attention to our prices.)

73500 Extension Table, oval drop leaves, 42x30 inch, top closed, made of solid oak and finished in antique only. Comes in 6, 8, 10 or 12 foot lengths. Weight, 10 foot table, 100 pounds. This table is well made, has rubber top and is extra good value. Price, per foot...................................$0.55

Tables—Continued.

73501 Extension Table, square, 42x30 in. top closed, made of solid oak and finished in antique only. Extra good value. Comes in 6, 8, 10 or 12 foot lengths.
Weight, 10 foot table, 100 pounds.
Price, per foot........... ....$0.55

73502 Extension Table. Here is a bargain for you. Made of solid oak and well finished. Size of top, when closed, 42x44 in. Carved and a good durable table for little money. Well braced and strong. Weight of 10 foot table, 125 pounds.
Price of 8 foot table................. ....$5.75
Price of 10 foot table........................ 7.00
Price of 12 foot table...................... 8.40

73503 Extension Table. This is extra good value. Made of solid oak and polished. Has extra heavy turned legs, well braced. Size of top, when closed, 42x44 inches.
Weight, 10 foot table, 125 lbs.
Price, 8 foot table.......................$6.20
Price, 10 foot table.. .... 7.70
Price, 12 foot table............................. 9.25

73504 Extension Table, extra heavy and a massive design. Well made of solid oak, richly hand carved and highly polished. Size of top, when closed, 42x44 inches. Has extra heavy turned legs, well braced. This table is worth double our price. Weight, 10 foot table, 125 pounds. A bargain.
Price, 8 foot table.........................$11.20
Price, 10 foot table........................... 13.50
Price, 12 foot table........................... 16.20

73505 Extension Table, well made of quarter sawed oak richly carved and highly hand polished; has extra heavy legs 4 inches thick, well braced and a massive design. Size of top, when closed, 42x42 inches. Good value. We are sure this will please you. Weight, 10 feet, 125 pounds.
Price, 8 foot table.........................$11.30
Price, 10 foot table........ .... 13.25
Price, 12 foot table........................... 15.00

Extension Tables—Continued.

73506 Extension Table. made of solid oak, and highly hand polished. Has extra heavy turned legs 6 inches thick. Extra large. Size of top when closed 48x48 inches. A good table for little money Fitted with double casters. Weight, 10 ft table, 125 pounds.
Price, 8 foot table.................$11.70
Price, 10 foot table..................13.80

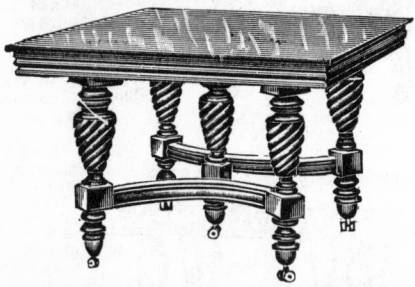

73507 Extension Table, well made of quarter sawed oak. Highly hand polished. Has extra heavy turned legs 6 inches thick. Well braced and a good sensible design. Size of top when closed, 48x48 inches. Fitted with double casters. Weight, 10 foot table, 125 pounds.
Price, 8 foot table..........................$13.25
Price, 10 foot table.........................15.65
Price, 12 foot table.........................19.10

73508 Extension table, extra well made of quarter sawed oak. Beautifully hand carved and highly hand polished. Has extra heavy turned legs 8 inches thick. Well braced and fitted with double fox casters, Size of top when closed, 48x48 inches. Weight, 10 foot table, 125 pounds.
Price, 10 foot table........................$23.60
Price, 12 foot table........................25.00

Kitchen Tables.

Each.
73515 Kitchen Table, all hardwood, turned legs. molded edge, with drawer.......................$1.30
73516 Fall-Leaf Table, square leaf at each end, folds down, made of hardwood. Size, open, 42 x52 inches.................................2.40
73517 Same as 73516, round leaf, making an oval table when all leaves are up; made of hardwood; size, open, 42x62.........................3.50

73518 Kitchen Cabinet table. The most handy household article we have. Made of elm, with maple top. Has a molding board, spice and cutlery drawer, sugar and groceries drawer. flour drawer with zinc bottom that holds 100 pounds of flour, and a cupboard for cooking utensils. Finished antique. Length, 4 ft. 4 in.; width, 2 ft. 4 in.; height, 2 ft 8 in. Well made and cheap. Price, only..........$6.95

Our Line is Very Complete and our styles are the best.

Invalid Rolling Chairs.

We are prepared to supply our customers with Invalid Chairs of all kinds at manufacturers' prices. We illustrate some of the styles most commonly used, but our limited space prevents our showing more of the extensive line which we carry. For the benefit of those who cannot find here what they think would suit their particular ailment we will mail on application a special catalogue.
73530 An Invalid's Commode or Sick Room Chair, has large arms, very strong and made of hardwood, finished light, dark or antique. No sick room should be without it. A door on the back of it will admit any ordinary commode. Weight, 20 pounds
Price...................$2.40

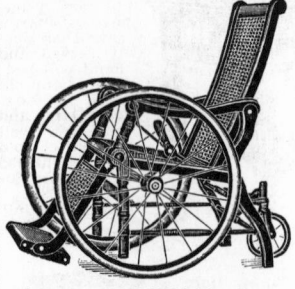

73550 A very commonly used chair for out or in door use. Iron boxed hickory wheels, oak frame, cane seat and back. Best malleable iron castings. strong enough for the heaviest adult; will pass through any door 28 in. wide; weight, 45 pounds.
Price............$16.00
Hand rims, same as on 73555, can be placed on the wheels of 73550 chair for $2.00 extra.

73551 Same pattern as 73550 for children, age 13 or 14 or under. Weight, 30 pounds. Price, $16.00

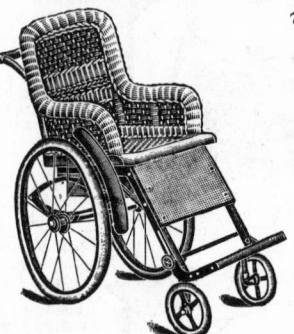

73552—
The World's Fair Rolling Chair. Here is a bargain in an invalid chair. These were used at the World's Fair. Have all been put in good shape and are almost as good as new. They have a shellaced reed body, ball bearing cushioned rubber tired bicycle wheels, on springs with a push handle. These sold at the World's Fair for $65.00, and our customers can have them until they are all sold for only.....$24.00

73553 Invalid or Reclining Chair. You can lie down or sit up in it at any angle. This is the best, most comfortable cheapest and the one used more than any other for invalids. Height of back from seat, 33 inches; width or seat inside, 19 inches. Will pass through a door 28 inches wide. Is made of antique oak, frame hickory and oak, iron boxed wheels; weight, 50 lbs.
Each..........$25.00
With outside hand rims, same as 73555, for $2.00 extra.
Springs can be had on this chair same as shown on 73555 at an additional cots of $3.00.

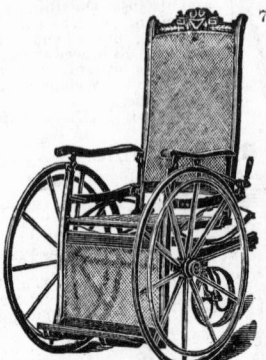

73554 Child's Invalid or Reclining Chair, same as 73553, for children of 15 years or younger. Weight, 35 pounds.
Price............$20.00
73555 Invalid's or Reclining Chair. The above chair, while being the same as 73553, is a better chair; the particular advantage is in the easy manner in which invalids can change to different positions and still be very comfortable. Otherwise it is the same in all particulars as 73553. Weight, 55 pounds.
Price, complete; as shown in cut $37.00
Price, with band rims, and without springs.... 35.00
Price, with springs and without hand rims.... 34.00
Price, without springs and without hand rims 32.00

73555 shown in cut

Invalid Chairs—Continued.

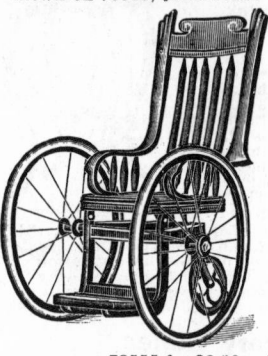

73556 A new Invalid or Reclining Chair. You can lie down or sit up at any angle. Made of solid oak, with rubber-tired bicycle wheels. A model invalid's chair; seat, 19 in. wide; will pass through a door 29 inches wide; strong and easy running. Weight, about 50 pounds. Price only.$31.00 With side hand rims, same as shown on 73555, $2.00 extra.

73557 A new style of Invalid Chair. Cane Seat, polished antique, solid oak bolted frame, has cushion tired ball bearing bicycle wheels. Back is high enough to rest anyone's head on. Very comfortable, strong and one of the best and cheapest chairs ever made for the money Large size for adult's use, will pass through a door 29 inches wide, weight, about 55 pounds. Price, only..$23.50 Hand rims can be placed on the wheels same as on 73555 for $2.00 extra.

Chairs.

Chairs are shipped to the best advantage when tied in pairs, hence it is the best not to order less than two of a kind. This, of course, does not apply to arm chairs, rockers, rattan goods, etc. We fill orders for any quantity and see that they are packed in good shape for shipping. The risk of break and damage is very slight, but such as it is, it must be assumed by the purchaser. Our responsibility ceases when we have obtained a clean receipt from the transportation company. Quarters or half dozen lots may be had at dozen rates.

Chair Cane.

73560 Chair Cane, 1,000 feet in a bunch which is enough to cane 3 ordinary chair seats.
Per bunch..............................$0.75

Kitchen and Dining Chairs—All Wood.

73600 Our Columbian Diner, very stylish, medium high back, strong and very cheap. Made of hardwood, finished antique. Weight, 10 pounds.
Each.................0.50
Per dozen................5.80
73600½ Ladies' Wood Seat Rocker to match 73600 chair. very comfortable. Finished antique. Weight, 13 pounds. Each........$0.82
This chair is extra large and heavy and a bargain at our price.

73600

73601 Bent Back Dining Chair, has 3 spindles, made of hardwood, scooped seat, double stretchers all around, plain light, dark or antique finish. Weight, about 10 pounds.
Each.......................$0.37
Per dozen...................4.30
Above chair in lots of 100 or more. Per dozen........$3.95

73601

This chair is extra strong and just the thing for public halls, school rooms, etc. Price in lots of 50 or more, $4.20 per dozen.
73602 Bent Back Dining Chair. Same size as 73601 chair; back has 4 spindles, is striped and decorated and better finished; antique, light or dark. Weight, 10 pounds.
Each.........................$0.40
Per dozen...................4.70
73603 Ladies' Rocker to match No. 73602. Light or dark finish. Weight, 12 pounds...........$0.65

73602

Chairs—Continued

73604 Pioneer Dining Wood seat, beaded double bent bow 5 spindles, extra heavy and strong. light or dark finish. Weight, 11 pounds.
Each................$0.60
Per dozen.............. 6.75

73605 Dandy High Back Diner, perforated seat and back, made in imitation walnut, antique and light finish. Weight, 11 pounds. Each............$0.80
Per dozen............. 9.00
73606 Chair, same style as 73605, only a little smaller.
Each..... .... $0.70
Per dozen............ .. 8.00

73607 A Very Strong, Medium High Back, Wood Seat, Exceed ingly Comfortable ladies rocker, finished antique, hard wood, Weight, 15 pounds.
Price, only $1.00
73608 A Dandy High Back, Large Seat, Strong and Comfortable dining chair to match 73607. Made of hardwood, finished antique. Weight, 12 pounds.
Each $0 59
Per dozen..... .... 6.80

73660 Double Black Wood Seat Kitchen Chairs, light or dark finish, most suitable for resting ironing board. Each..... $0.62
Per dozen.................. 7.00

Cane Seated Dinner and Cottage Chairs.

73700 Half Grecian Cottage or Dining Chairs, cane seat, finished in imitation walnut, and light and antique finish; weight, 9 lbs...$0.68
Per dozen... .... 8.00

73720 Very Attractive Cane Seat Dining and Chamber Chair, made of hardwood and finished imitation antique oak, carved top; weight, 12 pounds. Each only.0.85
Per dozen.................... 9.75
73721 Same as 72720 only has plain top instead of carved, and has strong brace arms. $ 0.89
Per dozen 10.00

73722 A Strong and Attractive Ladies' Rocker, made of hardwood and finished imitation antique oak to match 73721; weight, about 15 pounds. Plain top$1.20
Plain top with arms........ 1.30

73723 A Fine Medium, Dining, Sitting and Chamber Chair, has bolted brace arms, very strong aud comfortable, made of hardwood, finished antique, cane or wood seat. Cane seat, each..$0.89
Per dozen..................... 10.00
Wood seat, each .... .69
Per dozen.................. 8.00
73724 Very Comfortable Ladies' Rocker to match 73723, just the thing for nursing and sewing, rocker. Cane seat, only....$1.20
Wood seat, only 1.00

Chairs—Continued.

73725 A Very Showy Dining and Sitting Room Chair, very strong, large size, cane seat, made of elm, finished antique, a beauty. Weight, 12 pounds. Each $1.30
Per dozen...................14.50
73725½ A Fine High Back Ladies' Cane Seat Rocker to match 73725, a desirable rocker for all purposes. Weight, 15 pounds.
Each......................$1.89
73726 A Very Showy Dining and Sitting Room Chair, caneseat, made of hardwood, richly carved and nicely finished; very durable; weight, about 12 pounds; hasbracearms.
Each.....$1.20
Per doz. 13.50

73727 A Beautiful Ladies' Cane Seat Brace Arm Rocker, high back and very strong; made of hardwood and finished antique; weight, 15 pounds; a bargain. Only...........$1.80

73730 A Dandy Solid Oak, Carved Top, Dining or Sitting Room Chair, cane seat, very strong, pretty and stylish. Weight, 12 pounds.
Each...... ....$1.20
Per dozen.....................13.25
73735 Rocker to match 73730, a beautiful ladies' high back, brace arm, cane seat, oak rocker.
Price, only... ....$1.80

73739 How is this for the money? A set of hardwood, antique finish dining room chairs, cane seat; the cheapest and best made for the money. Exceedingly comfortable and very strong, most appropriate for farmers' use and made in cane.
| | Each. | Per doz. |
| Dining chair, weight, 10 pounds.....$1.10 | $12.00 |
| Arm chair, weight, 16 pounds .... 2.00 |
| One set, 5 chairs and 1 arm chair to match...... 7.00 |
73737 Rocker to match 73736 chair, finished antique; very comfortable. Weight, 15 pounds.
Price...................... 1.50
73738 A Most Magnificent Men's Large Arm Rocker, showy. bolted arms; in cane or wood seat. Made of hardwood finished antique. Strong and comfortable. Weight, about 20 pounds
Cane seat, each......$2.70
Wood, seat each 2.40

73740 A Men s Household Comfort; large arm rocker. Cane seat, strong and very comfortable; made of hardwood and finished antique. with wide, flat arms. Weight, 20 pounds.
Carved top, only........$2.10
Plain top, only......... 2.00

Chairs Continued

73742 A Very High Back, Men's Arm Rocker; very showy, well braced and bolted, beautifully finished and made of solid oak. Weight, 20 pounds.
Cane seated, only.......$3.19

Here is a Bargain for You.

73745 Cane Seat Dining Room, Sitting Room or Parlor Chair; stylish high back, richly carved and very showy; made of hardwood, finished antique; never sold for less than $1.50 each by anyone. Weight, 10 pounds.
Our price, each.............$0.98
Per dozen 11.50

73747 A Delightful Ladies' Rocker, well braced, strong and comfortable. To match 73745. Hardwood, finished antique. Good value. Weight, 14 pounds.
Price, only...............$1.70

Oak Dining Chairs.
Our Famous Mansion Pattern and the Hard Times Oak Dining Chair. A Bargain.

73750 Mansion Dining Cane Seat Chair. Good for all purposes, dining room, sitting room, and chamber; made of solid oak, heavy stock, brass arms, stylish high back, nicely finished antique; weight, 10 pounds, sold everywhere for $2.00 Each.....$ 0.98
Per dozen....................11.50

73750½ Same as 73750, only the seat is made of genuine sole leather, "cobbler seat," a very stylish and strong chair; weight, 12 pounds.
Each, $1.60 Per doz..$19.00
73754 Ladies' Rocker to match 73750 chairs, made of solid oak and nicely finished antique. Has brace arms. No better ladies' rocker sold anywhere in the country for less than $3.00. Weight, 16 pounds.
Our price, only........$1.60

73752 Rocker, same as 73751 except it has a cobbler sole leather seat; very attractive and strong; weight, 17 pounds. Price, only.................$2.20
73753 A Fine Solid Oak Cane Seat Chair; handsomely carved, and has a gloss finish; especially attractive and durable; weight, 12 pounds. Always sells for $1.85 You will be most delighted with this chair when you see it.
Our price, only. Each......$ 1.35
Per dozen................... 15.50

73754 A strong and beautiful oak rocker, has extra high back; a fine sewing or nurse rocker; weight, 16 pounds.
Price........ ....$1.90

Chairs—Continued.

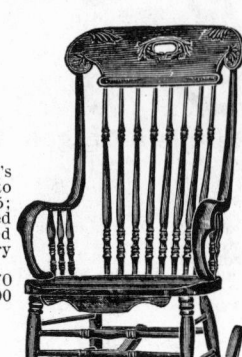

73755 Dining Chair. If you want an easy sitting chair, and at the same time a beauty, this is one; made of hardwood and finished antique, highly polished and very strong; weight, about 14 pounds.
Wood seat, each.........$ 1.40
Per dozen.............. 16.00
Cane seat, each......... 1.60
Per dozen.............. 18.00

73756 Ladies' or Men's Large Arm Rocker, to match chair No. 73755; hardwood, has bolted arm, is highly polished and very strong; is very comfortable.
Wood seat, each. .$2.70
Cane seat, each.... 3.00

73757 A Fine Saddle Wood Seat Chair, can be used for dining or sitting room, more comfortable than cane seat; is made to fit; hardwood, finished antique; weight, about 13 pounds.
Each.....................$ 1.30
Per dozen.... .... 14.50

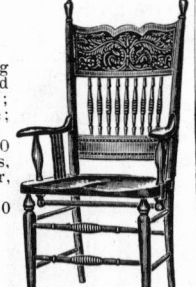

73758 An Exceedingly Strong and Comfortable Saddle Wood Seat Arm Chair to match 73757; hardwood, finished antique; weight, about 20 pounds.
Price, each..............$2.60
One set, five No. 73757 chairs, and one No. 73758 arm chair, complete dining room set.
Price $8.50

73760 The Very Best Dining Room Set, made in the country for the money, very stylish; made of solid oak, nicely finished and very durable; finished antique.
Dining chair, weight, 13 pounds. Each......... 1.50
Per dozen............. 17.00
Arm chair, weight, 18 pounds
Each................... $2.40
One set, 5 chairs and 1 arm chair to match.........$9.25

73761 A Fine Quarter Sawed Oak Dining Room Set; highly polished and well made, cane seats, plain top and very rich and artistic.
	Each.	Per doz.
Dining chair; weight, 13 pounds....	$1.80	$21.00
Arm chair; weight, 18 pounds.......	3.00	
One set 5 chairs and 1 arm chair to match, only...................... $11.00

Chairs—Continued.

73762 How is this for a fine Dining Room Set? Made of quarter sawed oak, highly polished and richly hand carved; boxed and bolted cane seat, well made and strong.
	Each.	Per doz.
Dining chair, weight, 13 pounds....	$ 2.40	27.00
Arm chair, weight, 20 pounds........	4.25	
One set, 5 chairs and 1 arm chair to match, only.... ... .15.00
Above set, with leather seats for...... 22.00

73763   73764

73763 If you want the best dining room set that can be had better get this. Perfect gems, carved selected oak or solid mahogany, all hand polished and water rubbed, leather back, with full spring leather seat. No better or finer goods made than this.
Diner, each, in oak.....................$ 7.00
Diner, each, in mahogany................. 8.50
Arm chair, each, in mahogany 12.00
Arm chair, each, in oak 10.00

73770 A Large and Comfortable Wood Rest Dining and Sitting-room Chair, very showy and strong; a bargain; made of hardwood and finished antique. Weight, 12 pounds.
Each, only.............. $0.95
Per dozen.............. 11.00
73775 Large Arm Rocker, to match 73770; very showy and strong, well made and nicely finished. Weight, 18 pounds.
Price, only................$2.20

73798 A Very Showy Cane Seat Sitting Room or Chamber Chair, hardwood, strong and comfortable; finished antique. Weight, 12 pounds.
	Each.	Per doz.
	$1.09	$12.00
Same in wood seat...........	.90	10.00

73799 Men's Large Easy Rocker, very showy, strong and comfortable; finished antique. Weight, about 20 pounds.
Price, only........$2.25

Chairs—Continued.

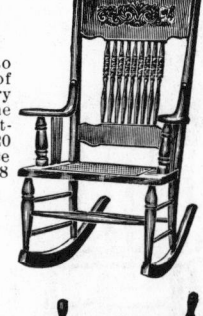

73801 A Large Arm Rocker to match 73753 chair. Made of solid oak, finely finished, very best make. Has a fine cane seat. Strong and comfortable. Weight, about 20 pounds. A bargain. Price only $2.98

73802   73802½

This is extra good value and will guarantee satisfaction,
73802 Fine Dining Room Set, made of solid oak, cane seat, backs are richly carved, very showy and pretty. Weight, about 12 pounds.
Dining chair, each, $1.60 Per dozen..... ....$18.00
Arm chair, each...... .. .. 3.00
Weight, about 25 pounds.
One set, 5 chairs and 1 arm chair to match.....10.25
73802½ Dining Room Set same as 73802 except made of elm, finished antique; 5 chairs and one arm chair for.................................... 9.00
73803 Ladies' Rocker to match 73802, with brace arm, made of oak and finished antique; never sold for less than $3.00. Weight, 15 pounds.
Our price... 2.00

73810

73810 Rocking or Nurse Rocker, cane seat and back, maple stained imitation walnut, light and antique finish; weight, 13 pounds, Each......$1.40
73811 Rocker, same as 73810 except it has brace arms; weight, 14 pounds. Each 1.70
73820 Large Cane Seat and Back Rocker, bolted arms, well made, finished in imitation walnut, antique and light finish; weight, 20 pounds.... 2.00
73821 Rocker, same as 73820, except is made in solid oak and carved top; weight, 20 pounds. 2.40

73820

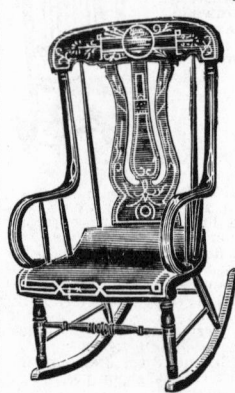

73850 Large Wood Rocker, swell seat, scroll back, strong and comfortable, neatly decorated, finished in light or dark colors. This is a much more comfortable chair than it looks; we can recommend it; weight, 19 pounds.
Each........ ......$2.00

Chairs—Continued.

73855 A Beautiful Reception and chamber Chair, very attractive and artistic. Made in antique oak, polished finish, or natural birch or birch finished mahogany; cane seat. Weight, 10 pounds. Price............$1.80
Per dozen..................$20.00
73855½ A Small Artistic Ladies' Reception Rocker to match 73855 Suitable for parlor chair. Weight, 10 pounds, cane seat.
Price, only................$2.40

73856 How is this for a bargain in a showy fancy rocker for all purposes? A very fancy reed and oak back and all oak frame, upholstered in plush or tapestry; weight, 15 pounds. Price, only....$1.80
73857 Chair to match 73856 rocker. Well made, strong and very pretty. Price only....$1.75

73858 Ladies' Parlor and Reception Chair. Very fancy and comfortable. Full size. Plush or tapestry seat; weight, 15 pounds. Price. A bargain........$2.25
73859 Ladies' Attractive rocker to match 73858. Has brace arms, strong and comfortable.
Price.....................$2.35

Ladies' Carpet Seat Rocker.

73859½ Ladies' Sugar Maple Rocker, made of 1¼ inch maple stock; selected carpets, seat webbed and fringe across front, arms screwed on; fancy turned parts; and one of the most popular rockers ever placed upon the market. Width between arms, 16 inches; height of back post, 38 inches; weight, about 16 pounds. Finished in ebony and gilt, or mahogany and gilt. Price, complete..$1.60

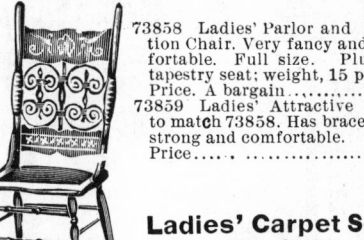

73860 A Very Large Oak and Reed Rocker, made strong, well braced, has plush or tapestry seat. Exceedingly fancy and showy for the money. Cheapest rocker of its kind on earth. Weight, 20 pounds.
Price, only.... ....$3.65

73860

73861 Large Ladies' Rocker, solid oak, carved back. Has spring seat covered with plush or tapestry. Good style and price low. Weight, 15 pounds.
Price..... ... .$2.95

73861

73862 Here is a Beautiful Large Gent's Spring Seat Rocker, made of quarter sawed oak, carved and nicely finished. A good parlor rocker. Plush or tapestry seat. Weight, 20 pounds.
Price, only............$4.75

Fine Solid Oak Polished Cobbler and Wood Seat Rockers.

No wearing out of plush or tapestry on these rockers. Our prices are extremely low on this line. We also show a much larger assortment of fancy rockers in our new special Furniture Catalogue, which we mail for 8 cents to pay postage. It will pay you to have one.

This is the Cheapest Cobbler Seat Rocker in America.

73870 Fine Parlor or Sitting Room Men's or Ladies' Arm Rocker; perfect comfort, made of quarter sawed solid oak, with cobbler embossed sole leather shoemaker's seat; no wearing out of plush or tapestry on this rocker, and just as handsome; finished antique, and highly polished; never sold for less than $4.75; weight, 18 pounds.
Our price, only. ..$2.68

73871 Here is a good bargain for you, well made of solid oak, carved and highly polished, exceedingly comfortable and has the cobbler embossed sole leather seat; very stylish and cheap. Weight, 18 pounds, ladies' size and plenty large for gentlemen.
Price, only............$2.90

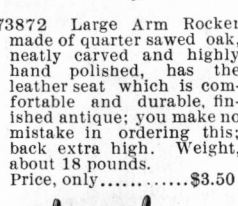

73872 Large Arm Rocker made of quarter sawed oak, neatly carved and highly hand polished, has the leather seat which is comfortable and durable, finished antique; you make no mistake in ordering this; back extra high. Weight, about 18 pounds.
Price, only..........$3.50

73872

73873 Extra High Back Arm Rocker, well made of solid oak, carved and highly hand polished. Has the cobbler seat made of sole leather; very large and good value, satisfaction guaranteed. Weight, about 18 lbs. Price, only...$3.75

73873

73874 Large Arm Rocker, made of solid oak, richly carved and highly hand polished, has the cobbler seat, made of sole leather. This rocker is extra heavy and exceedingly comfortable. Weight, 18 pounds.
Price, only............$3.90

73875 Here is just the thing for your parlor. Large Arm Rocker, made of quarter

73874

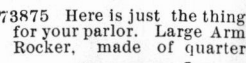

sawed oak, richly carved and has an extra fine polish finish. Seat is made of sole leather which extends over the front and gives it a rich appearance. Extra well made; will last for years. Weight, about 20 lbs. Our price, only..$4.20

73875

73876 This is an Extra Fine Quarter Sawed Oak Rocker, richly hand-carved and polished like a piano. The stock used in this rocker is select and beautiful. Height, 41 inches; width, 17 inches. Has the cobbler seat, made of sole leather; exceedingly comfortable, well made and cheap. Weight, about 20 pounds.
Our price, only.....$4.90

73876½ A Beautiful Parlor Rocker for ladies, made of curley birch or imitation mahogany, richly carved and hand polished; has the cobbler's seat made of genuine sole leather. The wood used in this rocker is something beautiful and must be seen to be appreciated. Very comfortable and well made. Weight, 17 pounds.
Retail price...... ...$6.75
Our price.............. 4.95

73877 Large Arm Rocker, for the parlor or sitting room, made of quarter sawed oak, hand carved and highly hand polished. Has sole leather seat. Height, 31 inches; width, between arms, 17 inches. This rocker is of extra heavy and fine stock and is worth double our price. Weight, about 22 pounds.
Price, only...... ...$5.60

Polished Wood Seat Rockers.

73878 Large Arm Rocker, has the saddle wood seat, which is exceedingly comfortable; made of solid oak, and highly hand polished, well made and braced. Weight, about 18 pounds.
Price, only..........$3.50

73879 Extra High Back Arm Rocker, has the saddle wood seat, which is very comfortable, made of quarter sawed oak, highly hand polished and carved; ornamental and cheap. Weight, 20 pounds.
Price, a bargain...... ...$3.85

FANCY PLUSH AND TAPESTRY SEAT ROCKERS.

All Spring Seats, Polished and Cheap.

Nothing like it for the price. How is this for value and style?

73900 Ladies' Extra High Back Rocker, made of quarter sawed oak, carved and highly hand polished, seat is covered with a fine grade of silk plush or silk tapestry, has large seat and is very comfortable. This is extra good value and a bargain. Weight, 18 pounds.
Price, only..............$2.99

73901 Here is a pretty and ornamental rocker made of solid oak, carved and highly polished, seat is covered with silk plush or tapestry and has a silk plush pad for the back; very comfortable and a bargain. Weight, about 18 pounds.
Price, only........ ......$3.50

Insure your Mail Packages. See remarks regarding mail insurance on page 1.

Rockers—Continued.

73902 Lady's Fancy Rocker made of quarter sawed oak, highly polished and nicely carved, has extra high back and large spring seat, covered with silk plush or tapestry, all colors, a beauty for the money. Weight, 18 pounds. Price, only............$3.80

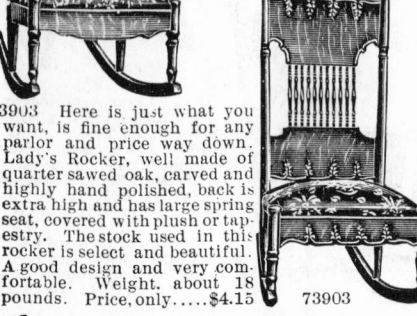

73903 Here is just what you want, is fine enough for any parlor and price way down. Lady's Rocker, well made of quarter sawed oak, carved and highly hand polished, back is extra high and has large spring seat, covered with plush or tapestry. The stock used in this rocker is select and beautiful. A good design and very comfortable. Weight, about 18 pounds. Price, only.....$4.15

73903

73904 Lady's Rocker. This is a beautiful rocker in fancy woods; made of curly birch and bird's eye maple. The stock used in this rocker is select and beautiful, which will more than please you. Richly hand carved and highly hand polished, seat is covered with extra fine imported tapestry, damask and brocatelle; satisfaction guaranteed. Weight, about 18 pounds. A bargain at our price, only.. ....$4.25

73904

73905 How is this for a bargain? A Large Arm Rocker, made of solid oak and polished, seat is covered with a good grade of silk plush and tapestry; large, comfortable and exceedingly cheap. Weight, 22 pounds. Price, only..........$3.50

93905

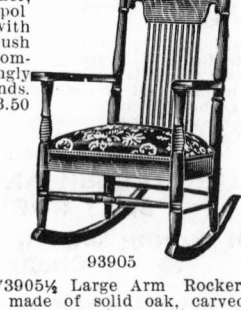

73905½ Large Arm Rocker, made of solid oak, carved and polished, extra high back and large spring seat covered with silk plush or tapestry, well made and cheap; weight, 30 pounds. Price, only..............$4.45

73905½

73906 A Beautiful Large Arm Rocker for little money, made of solid oak, carved and highly hand polished, back extra high, and has large spring seat, which is covered with silk plush or tapestry. Extra good value. Weight, 25 pounds. Price, only.$3.85

73906

73907 Large Arm Rocker, well made of solid oak, carved and highly polished, seat is covered with silk plush or tapestry; very large, comfortable and cheap. Weight, 20 pounds. Price, only $4.20

Rockers—Continued.

73909 Here is good value. A Large, Showy Arm Rocker, made of solid oak, carved and highly polished, seat is covered with good silk plush or silk tapestry; very strong and a pretty design. Weight, 20 pounds. A bargain. Only................$4.30

73909

73915 Large Arm Rocker, well made of solid oak, carved and highly polished. Seat is covered with silk plush or silk tapestry, and has a large, silk plush pad for the back. Is exceedingly comfortable and cheap. Weight, 25 pounds. Our price is only......$4.55

73915

73920 Large Arm Rocker, made of solid oak, carved and highly hand polished. Has spring seat and extra high back. Seat is covered with silk plush or silk tapestry. Very strong and well made. Weight, about 25 pounds. Price.....................$5.00

73920

73925 Here is a perfect gem. Large Arm Rocker, made of solid, quarter sawed oak, carved and polished. Back is extra high and exceedingly comfortable. Has large spring seat. Well made and a beauty for the money. Weight, 25 pounds. Price, only $5.55

73925

73927 This is the most ornamental we have for a parlor. Made of curly birch or bird's eye maple. The stock is select and beautiful. This rocker is polished like a piano. Seat is covered with our best imported silk tapestry, damask or brocatelle. Fine enough for anyone. Weight, 25 pounds. A bargain. Price, only.........$5.60

73927

73929 Extra Large Arm Rocker, made of quarter sawed oak, carved and highly hand polished. Back is extra high and seat is extra large. Upholstered in silk plush or silk tapestry. This is extra good value. Stock very select. Weight, 25 pounds. You make no mistake in ordering this. Price, $6.95

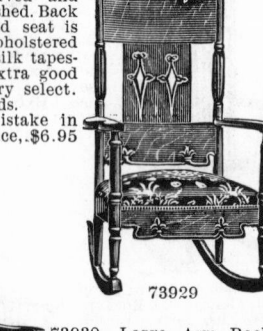

73929

73930 Large Arm Rocker, made of quarter sawed oak, richly carved and polished. Very large and has extra high back. Has cushion seat and pad for back made of silk plush or tapestry. We especially recommend this for comfort. Weight, 30 pounds. A bargain. Only... ...$8.20

THE McLEAN PATENT SWING ROCKER.
Most Comfortable Rocker Made.

73954 McLean Patent Swing Rocker, well made of solid oak and richly carved. Has spring seat covered with a fine grade of velvet carpet. Back is extra high. We recommend this for SOLID COMFORT. Weight, about 30 pounds. A bargain. Only......................$3.25

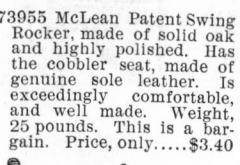

73955 McLean Patent Swing Rocker, made of solid oak and highly polished. Has the cobbler seat, made of genuine sole leather. Is exceedingly comfortable, and well made. Weight, 25 pounds. This is a bargain. Price, only.....$3.40

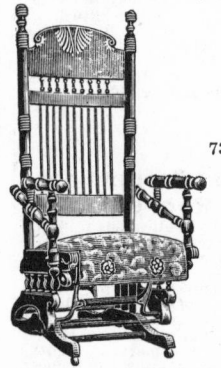

73956 McLean Patent Swing Rocker, made of solid oak and nicely finished. Has a woven wire seat with seven springs; covered with fine velvet or moquette carpet. Has extra high back and is exceedingly comfortable. Weight, 25 pounds. Price, only.....$3.80

73957 McLean Patent Swing Rocker. Well made of solid oak. Very heavy and strong. Has a good spring seat covered with fine silk plush. Back is also upholstered with silk plush. This is a very showy and comfortable rocker. Extra high back. Weight, about 30 pounds. Price, only.............$4.35

73958 McLean Patent Swing Rocker. This rocker is very pretty, made of solid oak, richly carved and nicely finished. Has a woven wire seat with springs covered with a fine grade of velvet or moquette carpet; a well made and comfortable rocker for the sitting room. Weight, about 25 pounds. Price, only.............$4.40

73960 McLean Patent Swing Rocker, made of quarter sawed oak, finished antique; richly carved and nicely finished; Seat and back are covered with a fine grade of plush, has a woven wire seat with springs; back is extra high and exceedingly comfortable; well made and cheap. Price, only....$5.10

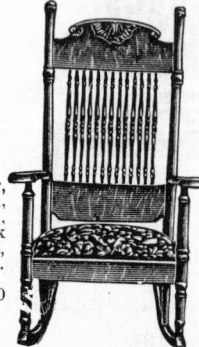

Lawn Furniture.

74175 Ladies' Veranda Rocker; back and seat is made of reed, posts are made of hardwood, is nicely varnished; well made and cheap. Weight, about 14 pounds.
Price, only.........$1.85

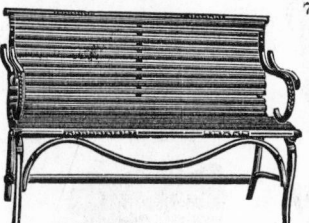

74176 Ladies' Veranda Rocker, has large flat arms, back and seat reed, posts hardwood. Extra cheap; weight, 20 pounds.
Price.........$2.00

74177 Gent's Large Arm Rocker, same style as 74176, except much larger. Exceedingly comfortable and cheap. Weight, 20 pounds.
Price.........$2.25

74178 Arm Chair to match 74177 rocker; very large and roomy. Weight, 20 pounds
Price, only....$2.25

74176-7

74200 Lawn Chair, high back, comfortable and durable; will stand outdoor use. Painted in red, green and maroon, or stained light and antique. Weight, 16 pounds.
Price.........$3.00

74205 Lawn Rocker to match No. 74200 chair. Weight, 17 pounds.
Price.........$3.60

74200

74210 Lawn Settee. Finely ornamented. Finished in light or in colors. Length, 4 feet. Weight, 28 lbs. Each.....$3.00
Length, 5 feet. Weight, 32 lbs. Each.....$3 30
Length, 6 feet. Weight, 36 lbs, Each.....$3.60

Office and Hotel Chairs.

74250 Office Chair, hardwood, finished antique, has screw for raising or lowering seat, spring which can be adjusted to weight of user. Weight, 32 pounds.
Wood seat, each.......$2.70
Cane seat, each.........3.00

74253 Office Chair. This is the best office chair ever made for the money. Polished quarter sawed oak, strong and comfortable; well braced and bolted. Has screw for raising or lowering seat, spring which can be adjusted to weight of user. Weight, 40 pounds.
Price, only.............$4.25

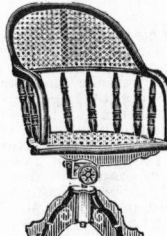

74255 Office Chair, has a half cane back and screw and spring. Most comfortable office or library chair we have. Made in light or dark or antique finish. Weight, 30 pounds.
Each.........$4.20

74260 Office Chair. Adjustable office chair. Can be raised or lowered and adjusted according to the weight and height of user. Cheapest, best and most durable and comfortable chair made for the money. Made of solid oak. Weight, 35 pounds. Polish finished. Cane seat.
Each.................$4.80
Leather seat, each.....6.25
Saddle wood seat.........4.50

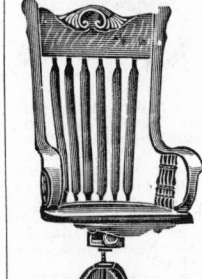

74261 A Large Strong Arm Office Chair. Very high back, well bolted. Hardwood finish antique. Has screw and spring. Extra large and cheap; weight, 40 pounds. Wood seat.
Price.................$3.90
Cane seat, price.......4.25

74262 Store Stool, well made and perfect in every respect. Suitable for a counter, stool in all stores. Japanned iron base. 21 inches high, oak wood top.
Each.................$1.10
21 inches high, nickel rim, wood center. Each.................1.50

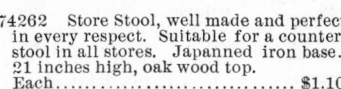

74300 Buckeye Arm Chair (see cut), rock elm, cane seat, strong and substantial. This is the well-known hotel or office chair; very comfortable for house and veranda use. Weight, 14 pounds. Each.......$1.50
74305 Buckeye Arm Chair; same as 74300, with arms; rodded wood seat. Weight, 16 pounds. Each....$1.20

Folding Camp Beds.

74350 Frame and canvas are connected in such a way that the cot can be opened and closed without any separation of its parts. It is the most desirable cot in the market for durability and strength, and must be seen to be appreciated. When folded it is but three feet in length. Weight, about 20 pounds. Price.......$1.95

Hammock Chair.

74375 Folding Hammock Garden Chair. All hardwood frame, nicely varnished; covered with fancy striped canvas; will fold to less than 2 inches in thickness. It weighs but 8 pounds. Can readily be adjusted to any position desired, and is just the thing for a garden, lawn, piazza, house or to use in place of a hammock. Weight, about 10 pounds.
Each.................$0.60
Per dozen....... 7.00

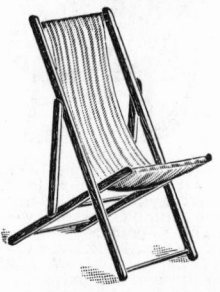

74380 Hammock Chair, same as 74375, except has arms, which make it much more comfortable. Weight, about 12 pounds. Each.........$0.75
Per dozen.................8.50

Camp Stools.

74385 Camp Stool, canvas top; height when open, 18 inches; weight, about 5 pounds. Price, each...$0.18
Per dozen... 2.00

74390 Camp Stool with back; canvas top; height of back from seat, 14½ inches. Good and strong. Weight, 10 pounds.
Price, each.........$0.25
Per dozen.................2.75

Folding Camp Chair.

74395 Has the slat seat, which is a recent invention: is much superior to the old style of seating, it being stronger, more durable and better resisting weather exposure. Slats are mortised into the seat frame and will not become loose or warp; is finished on the wood in three coats: has malleable iron folding castings. Weight, about 12 pounds. Each.........$0.75
Per dozen.... 7.50

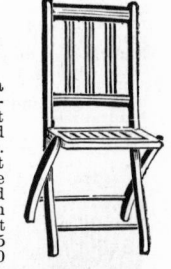

Rattan and Reed Furniture.

We are prepared to give our customers a larger selection and better goods for less money than ever before. These goods are made of the imported reed, which resembles bamboo. The outside or bark is cut off and is the cane used in making cane seats in chairs. Cutting the bark or cane off the reed leaves a porous surface, and this inside is the reed used in making these goods. On account of the reed being porous we finish these goods in different colors, as it beautifies them and makes them more durable. The new and stylish finish we call shellac, which leaves a natural color to the reed. We are prepared to fill orders at once in shellac finish, but antique, cherry and sixteenth century finishes takes about 4 days generally to finish after receipt of your order. Our goods are all new; no shopworn goods among them, and are of the very best manufacture.

For parlor and sitting room use there is nothing more comfortable, durable and beautiful than these goods.

We show a larger assortment of rattan rockers in our special Furniture Catalogue, which we mail upon receipt of 8 cents to pay postage.

74400 Lady's Reed Rocker. Here is a bargain. Look at the work on it. Is very strong and comfortable. Never sold for less than $3.50. Weight, about 11 pounds. Our price, in natural reed. $2.00
New shellac finish.........2.45

74400

74401 New Pattern of Lady's Rocker, medium size. strong and very attractive for the money. Never sold for less than $3.50. Weight, about 12 pounds.
Our price, in natural reed.........$2.25
Price in new shellac finish.........2.67

74401

74402 Lady's Reed Rocker, has hardwood frame and side arms; very showy. Weight, 11 pounds
Natural reed, only.....$2.25
New shellac finish........2.65

74402

74403 How is this for a stylish Sewing and Parlor Rocker? Very comfortable and strong enough for any ordinary adult's use. Well braced and exceedingly showy for the money, one of our best bargains. Weight, about 12 pounds.
Natural reed.............$2.45
New shellac finish.......2.89

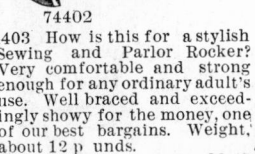

74403

Rockers—Continued.   **Rockers—Continued.**   **Rockers—Continued.**

74404 A Lady's Reed Rocker, good size, a great deal of work on it, with fine braids, well braced, making it very strong and very attractive; one of the newest styles, retails for double our price. Weight, about 11 pounds.
Natural reed, only.........$2.67
Shellac finish............. 3.10

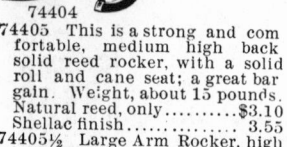

74405 This is a strong and comfortable, medium high back solid reed rocker, with a solid roll and cane seat; a great bargain. Weight, about 15 pounds.
Natural reed, only.........$3.10
Shellac finish............. 3.55
74405½ Large Arm Rocker, high back, strong and comfortable.
Natural reed.............$4.45
Shellac finish............. 5.35

74406 Lady's Reed Rocker; a very pleasing pattern and a great amount of work on it, with side arms and very showy back. Never sold for less than $4.00. Weight, 11 pounds.
Our price, natural reed..$2.90
New shellac finish....... 3.15

74407 A Large Size Lady's Reed Rocker; very showy and strong and exceedingly low in price. The handsome wide braid all around this rocker adds to its durability and makes it very attractive and comfortable. Weight, about 12 pounds.
Natural reed.............$3.10
New shellac finish....... 3.55

74407½ Here is a perfect beauty of a Lady's Reed Rocker; a great deal of hand work on it, making it attractive and showy, has a white maple base. You can't possibly make any mistake in ordering this. Weight, about 15 pounds
Natural reed, only.......$3.35
Shellac finish............. 4.00

74408 Lady's Reed Rocker. Here is another of our many new and cheap rockers. A rich design, made strong and comfortable. Its equal never sold for less than $6.00. Weight, about 12 pounds. Our price, in natural reed is only.............$4.25
New shellac finish........ 4.90

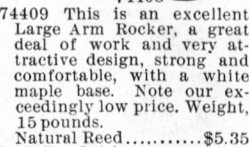

74409 This is an excellent Large Arm Rocker, a great deal of work and very attractive design, strong and comfortable, with a white maple base. Note our exceedingly low price. Weight, 15 pounds.
Natural Reed...........$5.35
Shellac finish............ 6.20
74409½ Ladies' Reed Rocker to match 74409, a gem for the money in all respects, you will make no mistake in buying this for your wife.

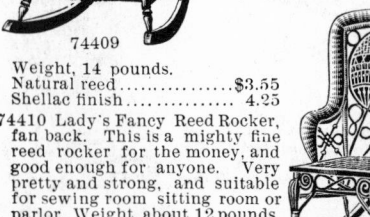

Weight, 14 pounds.
Natural reed.............$3.55
Shellac finish............. 4.25
74410 Lady's Fancy Reed Rocker, fan back. This is a mighty fine reed rocker for the money, and good enough for anyone. Very pretty and strong, and suitable for sewing room sitting room or parlor. Weight, about 12 pounds.
Natural reed, only.........$4.45
New shellac finish.... .. 5.35

74410½ Lady's Fancy Reed Rocker, a perfect little beauty. Lots of fine work and very showy. Very strong and comfortable. Weight, 11 pounds.
Price, natural reed........$4.00
New shellac finish....... 4.90
74411 Man's Large Arm Rocker, same as 74410½, except much larger. Very showy and durable. Weight, about 15 pounds.
Natural reed, only.......$5.77
New shellac finish........ 6.65

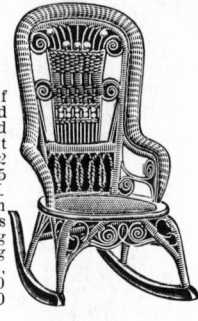

74412 Lady's Rocker, made of very fine reed, with a full solid roll. Exceedingly strong and has high back. An ornament to any home. Weight, 12 pounds. Natural reed...$4.25
New shellac finish..... 5.10
74413 Gentleman's Large Arm Rocker of the same pattern as 74412 High back; very strong and very comfortable, strong enough for any man. Weight, 16 pounds. Natural reed.$6.00
New shellac finish....... 6.90

74414 A Lady's Full Roll Comfort Rocker, solid roll all around the rocker, with a reed seat. These comfort rockers are the most complete and most durable of any rocker made. Has a good high arm and medium high back. Weight, 12 pounds. Never sold less than $6.00.
Our price, natural reel.$4.45
New shellac finish..... 5.35
74415 Gentleman's Large Arm Rocker, same style and pattern as 74414; high back and very comfortable; a household comfort. Never sold for less than $8.00. Weight, 15 pounds.
Our price, natural reed.............$5.75
New shellac finish................ 6.65

74416 A Lady's Reed Rocker. Is suitable for any purpose, well braced. Has basket reed seat, and high enough back for a head rest. A pleasing rocker and very durable. Weight, about 16 pounds.
Natural reed.............$4.45
New shellac finish....... 5.25

74417 A Large Size Ladies Rocker; very handsome, well made, all piece reed, cane seat and a great bargain for any one. Weight, about 16 lbs.
Natural reed...... ....$4.65
Shellac finish...... ..... 5.60

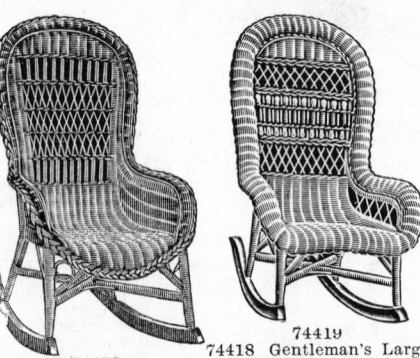

74418 Gentleman's Large Arm Rocker, high back, all reed, with what we call a full flat roll; high arm and a very comfortable and durable rocker; well made and very cheap. Weight, 15 pounds.
Natural reed, only $4.90
New shellac finish............................ 5.80
74419 Lady or Gentleman's Rocker, has extra high back, a very fine quality of reed; full solid roll, fine work, no better quality made. Never sold before for less than $8.50. Weight, 14 pounds. Our price, natural reed.............$5.35
New shellac finish 6.20

74420 Gentleman's Large Arm Rocker, full solid roll, extra high back, full reed seat. If you want strength and comfort, this is what you are after. Never sold less than $9.00. Weight, 16 lbs.
Our price, in natural reed, only.........$5.75
New shellac finish. 6.65
74421 Ladies' Full High Arm Full Reed Rocker to match 74420. Weight, 12 pounds. Natural reed.............$4.45
New shellac finish. 5 35

74422 This is a beautiful Ladies' Reed Rocker, is extra fine and perfect in every respect. Is the most showy and really the best ladies' reed rocker we show. This cut does not begin to do it justice. It pays to buy the best; very ornamental. Weight, about 14 pounds. Natural reed.$5.77
New shellac finished.... 6.65
74423 Man's Large Arm Rocker, same style as 74422, except much larger. Weight, 16 pounds. Natural reed...$7.00
New shellac finish.... . 9.00

74424 Another Handsome Pattern of the Old Reliable Comfort Ladies' Reed Rocker, has high back, solid strong roll, and exceedingly comfortable. Always have sold for $7.00 and $8.00. Weight, 20 pounds. Our price, natural reed, only............. ....$4.90
Shellac finish...... ...... 5.75

74425 Large Size Rocker to match 74424. This rocker will be a comfort to a man's declining days. Extra heavy and comfortable.
Natural reed.............. ....$5.75
Shellac finish........................... 6.65

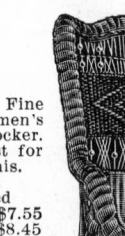

74426 A Lady's Large Size Reed Rocker, very fancy; a great deal of work on it, made very strong and one of the best bargains we have shown in these goods. Weight, 20 pounds.
Natural reed.... ....$4.90
Shellac finish.............. 5.75

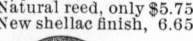

74427 An Extra Fine Pattern of Gentlemen's Very Large Arm Rocker. If you want the best for all purposes, buy this. Weight, 10 pounds. Price in natural reed $7.55
New shellac finish $8.45
74428 Lady's Reed Rocker same style and quality as 74427. Very comfortable. Weight, about 12 pounds.
Natural reed, only $5.75
New shellac finish, 6.65

74429 Gentleman's Rocker. Best quality, very fancy and durable. Extra high back. Never sold for less than $10.00. Weight, 16 pounds
Natural reed.............$7.55
New shellac finish.. 8.45
74430 Lady's Fine Reed Rocker, same pattern and quality as 74429; exceedingly comfortable; you make no mistake by ordering this rocker. Weight, 13 pounds.
Natural reed, only...$5.75
New shellac finish. . 6.65

Chairs—Continued.

74430½ A Gentleman's Big High Back Easy Arm Chair. Just the thing to take comfort in. Well made and cheap. Weight, about 18 pounds.
Natural reed.........$6.25
New shellac finish....7.10

74431 A Beautiful Reception Hall or Corner Chair. Very ornamental, comfortable and strong. A bargain, never sold before for less than $7.50. Weight, about 15 pounds. Our price, in natural reed,..... $4 45
New shellac finish........ 5.35
Finished in gold leaf...... 7.30

74432 Corner or Odd Chair, made of reed, exceedingly showy. Considering the work, style and durability it is very cheap. Weight, about 16 pounds,
Natural reed...............$5.35
New shellac finish........ 6.25
Finished in gold leaf....,. 8.25

74433 Child's Reed Rocker, strong and comfortable; hardwood frame; weight, 6 pounds. Price, natural reed $1.35
74434 High Chair with table to match 74433. Has same kind of table as shown on 74439 chair. Weight, about 12 pounds. Natural reed, only......................$1.75

74435 Child's Fancy Reed Rocker; a little beauty; very comfortable; best quality; weight, 7 pounds. Price, in natural reed, only...$2.45

74436 A Very Attractive Child's Reed Rocker. Durable and comfortable. Weight, 6 pounds. Price of natural reed, only......................$2.00
74437 Child's High Chair, to match 74436, with table same pattern as shown on 74439; strong and durable. Weight, 10 pounds. Natural reed...................$2.65

74438 A Very Pretty Child's Reed Rocker. A good pattern, strong and comfortable. Weight, about 10 pounds. Price, natural reed....$2.45

74439 Child's Reed High Chair, with table. A perfect chair. The table is the best made. New feature with bent arms, so it swings high over the head of the child. No fear of ever unfastening. The legs have a wide spread, so there is no tipping over. Weight, 10 pounds. Price, in natural reed, only $2.45
74440 Child's Reed Rocker to match 74439 an attractive pattern; very comfortable. Weight, about 10 pounds. Price, in natural reed....$1.75

Chairs—Continued.

74441 Child's High Chair, with table; reed back and solid oak frame; same table, spread of legs as on 74439 chair. This chair is a bargain. Weight, 10 pounds. Finished in antique oak
Only.... ....$1.50

74550 Baby Walker, made of willow, on casters, just the right size and thing for a baby when learning to walk. An article that everyone should have in their home. Weight, about 10 pounds.
Each.............. $1.75

74551 Baby Walker, made of hardwood, with shelf. If you want to teach your baby how to walk without trouble, at its delight, get one of these. All colors. Weight, about 15 pounds.
Each $2.40

74551

74555 Chair. Cabinet Nursery Chair. Willow, with lifting shelf and seat. Our sales on this chair are so great that it is almost impossible to supply the demand. Weight, about 5 pounds. Each.. ....$0.75
Per dozen..................... 8.00

Children's chairs.

74650 Child's High Chair, wood seat with table; light, dark or in colors. Weight, 15 pounds.
Each......................$0.85
74651 Same, with perforated veneer back. Weight, 11 pounds.
Each $0.95
Either of the above without table, 20 cents less.

74650-1

74653 A Very Handsome Child's High Chair, hardwood, cane seat, large size, with table, finished antique. Weight, 14 pounds.
Each......................$1.80

74653

74654 Child's High Chair, a beauty, finished in all colors, red, light, antique and dark; very strong, wood seat. Weight, 12 pounds. Each.............$1.20
Cane seat. Each. 1.40

74654

74655 Child's High Chair, with table, made of hardwood, finished antique. Weight, 12 pounds.
Price, cane seat..........$1.20
Price, wood seat.. .... 1.00

Chairs—Continued.

74656 A Very Showy Cane and Wood Seat High Chair, bent arm, carved back, strong and good. Weight, 12 pounds.
Wood seat....................$1.20
Cane seat.................... 1.40

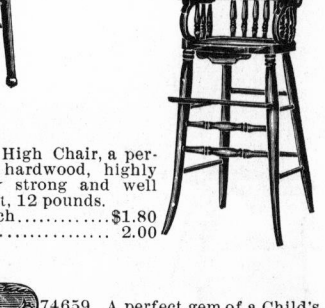

74658 Child's High Chair, a perfect beauty, hardwood, highly polished, very strong and well made. Weight, 12 pounds.
Wood seat, each............$1.80
Cane seat 2.00

74659 A perfect gem of a Child's Rocker, showy, strong, will delight the heart of any little one. Extra cheap. Hardwood, finished antique. Weight, 8 pounds.
Wood seat, each...........$1.60
Cane seat, each 1.80

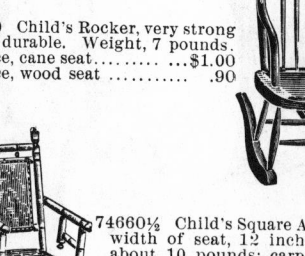

74660 Child's Rocker, very strong and durable. Weight, 7 pounds.
Price, cane seat......... ...$1.00
Price, wood seat .... .90

74660½ Child's Square Arm Rocker; width of seat, 12 inches; weight, about 10 pounds; carpet seat and back; best value for the money in the market; finished in ebony and gilt. Each, only..............$0.85

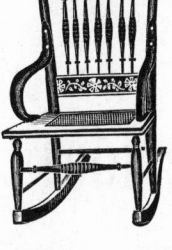

74661 A Child's beautiful Rocker; large size, strong and made of solid oak; cane seat; weight, 10 pounds. Price........$1.70

74662 A Very Attractive Youth's or Misses' Half High Chair. Made of hardwood. Finished antique. Weight, 10 Pounds. Cane seat.
Each............................$1.50

74665 Child's Nursery Chair; wood seat, light, dark or in, colors. Weight, 6 pounds
Each........................$0.65
74670 Same with shelf (or table) in front.
Weight, 8 pounds.
Each........................$0.85

Child's Rockers—Continued.

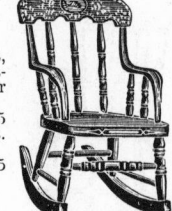

74675 Child's Rocker, wood seat, bent pillars, striped and ornamented; finished light, dark or in colors. Weight, 8 pounds.
Each........................$0.95
74680 Same as 74675; cane seat. Weight, 6 pounds.
Each......................$1.25

74675

74685 Kindergarten Chair, finished in red, light, antique and dark; made in two heights.
Height of seat from floor, 14 inches; height of seat from floor, 10 inches. Weight, 6 pounds.
Each........................$0.45
Per dozen.................. 5.00
74690 Child's Toy Chair, ornamented in colors. Weight, 3 pounds. Each..............$0.30

74685

Combination Chair and Ladder.

74695

74695 The above cut fully illustrates our combination Step Ladder and Chair. The one on the left is the form of a step ladder, and the one on the right that of a chair, which you will see at once is a neat and convenient article, and useful in many ways in every household and office.
The chair is made of dried elm, finished in natural wood with two coats of varnish. Every joint glued and nailed, making it a strong and safe ladder. when in use for that purpose. Weight, about 20 pounds. Price, each.................$1.00
Per dozen.......................11.50

Our Whole Idea

is to save you money. If we can't do it, we don't expect your trade; if we can do it we do expect your trade. You should buy in the cheapest market, the same as others do.

Best Steam Cured Feathers.

If the Feathers and Pillows we send you are not odorless free from dust and quills, and not perfectly satisfactory, they may be returned at our expense.
Our feathers are put up in sacks containing one pound and upward; no charge for sacks.
74720 Odorless Feathers. A fair grade of mixed geese feathers, free from dust and quills.
Per pound.................................$0.39
74721 Odorless Feathers. A good grade of mixed geese feathers. Per pound .... .42
74722 Odorless Feathers. Slightly mixed prime live geese feathers. Per pound.. .... .51
74723 Odorless Feathers. Extra steam dressed, prime live geese feathers. Per pound.......... .57
74724 Odorless Feathers. Selected prime live geese feathers. Per pound................ .59
74725 Very Choice Extra Selected Prime Live Geese Feathers. Per pound .... .63
74726 Odorless One-half Feathers and One-half Down; extra fine and downy, Per pound....... .73
74727 Domestic Geese Down. Per pound......... .90
74728 Domestic Geese Down; extra fine, white.
Per pound.............................. 1.25

Down Sofa Pillows.

Our Sofa Pillows are covered with Domestic Sateen or plain muslin and filled with an extra fine grade of down.

74730 Size,	16x16,	18x18,	20x20,	22x22,	24x24,	26x26
Down Pillow. Price e'ch	$0.42	$0.56	$0.84	$1.12	$1.40	$1.68

Pillows.

Only finest quality of ticking and newest patterns used on our pillows.

74731 Size		18x25,	20x26,	21x27	
Weight of each pillow.		3	3½	4	
With Hen feathers. Anchor Grade. Price		$0.45	$0.55	$0.60	
74732 Size		18x25,	20x26,	21x27.	
Weight of each pillow.		3	3½	4	
With Turkey feathers. Jewel Grade. Price		$0.55	$0 65	$0.70	
74733 Size		19x26,	21x26,	22x27.	
Weight of each pillow.		3	3½	4	
With Mixed Duck and Turkey feathers Champion Grade Price.		$0.65	$0.75	$0 90	
74734 Size	19x26,	20x27,	22x28,	24x28	26x28
Weight of each pillow.	2	2½	3	3½	4
With Mixed Geese feathers. Price.	$0.78	$0.98	$1.17	$1.37	$1.56
74735 Size	19x26,	21x27,	23x28,	25x29	27x30
Weight of each pillow.	2	2½	3	3½	4
With good Mixed Geese feathers. Price.	$0.84	$1.05	$1.26	$1.47	$1.68
74736 Size	19x26,	21x27,	23x28,	25x29,	27x30
Weight of each pillow.	2	2½	3	3½	4
With prime Live Geese feathers. Price.	$1.02	$1.28	$1.53	$1.79	$2.04
74737 Size	19x26,	21x27,	23x28,	25x29,	27x30
Weight of each pillow.	2	2½	3	3½	4
With extra steam dressed prime Live Geese feathers. Price.	$1.14	$1.42	$1.71	$1.99	$2.28
74738 Size	20x26,	22x27,	24x28,	26x29,	28x30
Weight of each pillow.	2	2½	3	3½	4
With selected prime Live Geese feathers. Price.	$1.18	$1.47	$1:77	$2.06	$2.36
74739 Size	20x26,	22x27,	24x28,	26x29,	28x30
Weight of each pillow.	2	2½	3	3½	4
With extra selected prime Live Geese feathers. Price.	$1.26	$1.58	$1.89	$2.21	$2.52
74739½ Size	20x27,	22x28,	24x29,	26x30,	28x31
Weight of each pillow.	2	2½	3	3½	4
With one-half feathers and one-half down. Extra fine. Price.	$1.46	$1.82	$2.19	$2.55	$2.92

Wire Mattresses.

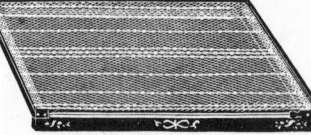

74740 The Regular Standard Corded Steel Wire Woven Mattresses, perfectly tight joint between end rail and bottom. No putty used. A good clean mattress. Weight, 40 pounds. Each....$1.15

74741 Woven Wire Mattress, supported by heavy steel spiral springs, resting upon slats, not connected with the side rails, but attached securely to strips of iron, which are firmly fastened to the end rails. It will not sag. Weight, 50 pounds.
Price, only..$1.50
Be sure to send length of slats when ordering springs.

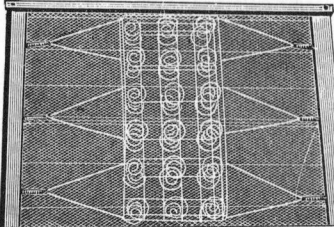

74742—Woven Wire Mattress, supported by 3 rows of heavy steel springs. The fabric is of the best mattress wire, finely woven The frame is made of kiln-dried hard maple, finely finished. This spring will give perfect satisfaction. Be sure to give size of slat. Weight, 50 pounds.
Price, only....................................$2.10

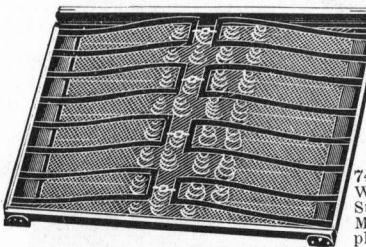

74743—Woven Wire Supported Mattress. In place of the ordinary cross slats, it has a band-iron support, each two pieces being yoked together as shown, this construction preventing any lateral motion. Each pair of supports are connected with the pair at the opposite ends of the mattress by a screw-thread swivel joint, as shown in cut. By the use of this construction a much deeper spring can be used than in the ordinary supported mattress, hence a very much greater degree of elasticity is imported to the supporting surface. The springs are fastened directly to the band iron supports at the bottom and to the fabric at the top and cannot by any possibility get out of place. We are sure this will please you as it is very durable and a comfortable bed. Weight, 50 pounds.
Price, only.......................................$2.50
Be sure to give size wanted.

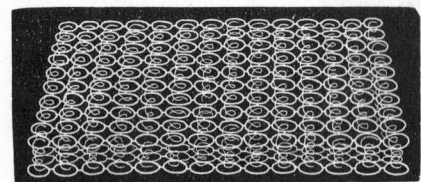

74744 This mattress is made from double cone springs standing close together, connected by broad steel clasps. The top and bottom surfaces are alike. The bed is elastic and yielding in all its parts, conforming perfectly to the form and weight of the sleeper, and is very durable. A full size has 117 springs. Leave all slats in bedstead. Weight, 40 pounds.
Each...$1.55
74745 Spring, same style as 74744, except is made of much finer wire, and has 140 springs, also folds in the center, which is much easier to handle. Weight, 40 pounds. Price, only..........................$2.50

74746 Spring Mattress; has 140 spiral springs stretching, and at the same time held firmly in place by a woven wire fabric. It has no rivets, chains, links, or other connections to become displaced or broken. No sagging in the center, no place for vermin. Durable, light, noiseless, easy to handle, elastic and springy; 40 pounds. Price, each........$4.50

Wire Mattresses—Continued.

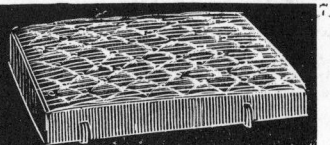

74747 Box Spring; has 72 spiral steel japanned springs covered with a thickness of 3 inches of tow, moss or hair. Best ticking used. Be sure and give length of slat when ordering. Weight, about 100 pounds.

Price, with tow top, each.....................$10.50
Price, with moss top, each.....................11.50
Price, with hair top, each.....................16.00

Send for our new special Furniture Catalogue. It contains the largest assortment of all kinds of furniture of any book issued in the world.

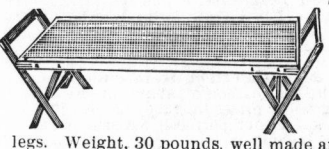

74750 Woven Wire Cot, strong and substantial in every way. Head and foot are raised by opening the legs. Weight, 30 pounds, well made and strong. A bargain.

Size, 2 feet 6 inches wide by 6 feet long $1.10
Size, 3 feet wide by 6 feet long.................1.25
This cot can be used for a regular bed as it is full size.

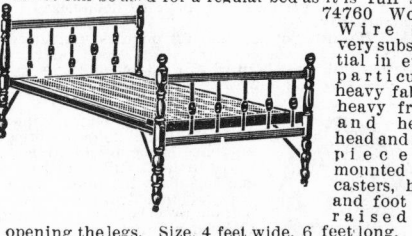

74760 Woven Wire Cot, very substantial in every particular; heavy fabric, heavy frame and heavy head and foot pieces, mounted on casters, head and foot are raised by opening the legs. Size, 4 feet wide, 6 feet long, made of maple and nicely finished. Weight, about 40 pounds. Price, only...................$2.80

Mattresses.

Our mattresses are all covered with an *extra good grade of ticking*, and the filling consists of pure and wholesome material. They average about 40 pounds in weight. Price includes them well packed in burlap and delivered to freight house here. Be sure to give size of bed when ordering mattresses.

74800 Mattresss, all excelsior, which makes a clean and comfortable bed (good ticking used). Only.$1.75
74801 Mattress, excelsior, with pure white cotton top. This mattress is covered with extra good ticking. 2.05
74802 Mattress, plain husk; a very durable and exceedingly healthy mattress. Price.......... 2.70
74803 Mattress, plain husk with pure white cotton top. Price........ 3.10
74804 Mattress, plain palm leaves. Price........ 3.50
74805 Mattress, palm leaves with pure white cotton top. Price............................ 4.00
Palm leaf is imported from Africa and has a very pleasant odor. A new material for mattresses, used exclusively in Europe, and said to make a healthful, pleasant and durable bed.
74806 Mattress, No. 2, wool, soft and comfortable$3.30
74807 Mattress, No. 1, wool, very comfortable and filled with a good grade of wool. Price....... 4.20
74808 Mattress, our best extra carded wool. 5.25
74809 Mattress, sanitary sea moss. This mattress is made of imported sea moss and possesses to a remarkable degree the tonic properties of the salt water, and is recommended for the use of delicate or nervous persons, Price, only........ 4.65
74810 Mattress, Grade XX moss. (Fair quality of moss and good ticking.) Makes a healthy and comfortable bed. Price...................... 5.75
74811 Mattress, Grade XXX moss. (Good quality of moss and and best ticking.) This is extra good value. Price...................... 6.10
74812 Mattress, Grade XXXX moss, This is our very best grade of moss and is covered with our best Amoskeag ticking. Price, only 6.80
74813 Mattress, No. 1 cotton. We guarantee this mattress to be made entirely of pure white cotton. Price...................... 6.40

Extra Value in Hair Mattresses.

It is impossible to duplicate the quality at our *prices*.
74814 Mattress, mixed hair. This mattress is made of long and short hair, and covered with the best Amoskeag ticking. You make no mistake by ordering this mattress, as it is extra good value, and will make you an exceedingly comfortable bed. A bargain. Price, only......$7.50
74815 Mattress, Grade 1, long black curled hair. 40 pounds. Price.....................11.15
74816 Mattress. Grade 2, long black curled hair. 40 pounds. Price.....................15.95
74817 Mattress, Grade 3, long black curled hair. 40 pounds. Price.....................18.50
74818 Mattress. Grade 4, long black curled hair. 40 pounds. Price 20.50

THE LATEST.
Our Patent Machine Made Sanitary Spring Mattress.

Cut Showing Inside of Mattress.

74820 Sanitary Spring Mattress. This mattress has for its central section 88 extra tempered double conical, black steel springs, with a woven wire top and bottem. This spring center is enclosed in burlaps, and the mattress filling (hair, moss, cotton, or any desired filling) is placed all around it, and tufted in the usual manner, making a beautiful spring mattress. The burlap covered spring in the center makes an air space the length and breadth of the mattress, which, from the standpoint of health, is invaluable, inasmuch as it affords a circulation of air through the entire mass of filling. Every time a weight is placed upon the mattress the springs yield, making the air space less and forcing the air out through the filling and tick, which of course are not airtight. When the weight is removed or lessened, the space immediately enlarges by the action of the springs, and air from the outside is drawn into the hollow, central space. We place in this central space a powerful antiseptic powder, which is brought into contact with the air constantly passing through the mattress, keeping it in a thoroughly healthful, antiseptic condition, clean and absolutely odorless. This being a spring mattress, it may be used without any other spring, or it can be used precisely like any other mattress, with a woven wire or other spring. The arrangment of the filling around the spring center renders packing well nigh impossible. The sanitary sea moss filling, possessing as it does the tonic properties of sea salt, is recommended for delicate and nervous persons.

Price
With cotton top excelsior filling.......$6.25
With cotton top husk filling..... 7.35
With combination hair filling 7.50
With combination cotton filling 7.55
With combination moss filling 8.85
With long, black moss filling.... 9 80
With sanitary sea moss filling 10.00
With all hair filling.
No. 1, short, soft hair (no hog hair)..............10.25
Black or gray mixed............................11.20
XX Gray ...... .14.50 CC Gray.............16.90
Pure, South American horse hair............19.50
Superior bleached, extra long drawings.. ... 22.00

Children's Beds and Cribs.

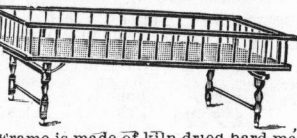

74855 Child's Crib. The legs fold under which enables us to ship it K. D. All castings are malleable iron. Frame is made of kiln-dried hard maple and supplied with a steel woven wire mattress, and patent adjustable brace for legs. Finished in natural maple and supplied with a steel woven wire mattress, and patent adjustable brace for legs. Finished in natural maple. Weight, 20 pounds.
Price, size 30x54 inches, only.............. ...$1.95
Price, size, 40x60 inches, only................. 2.60

74856 Child's Crib Has folding sides and ends which contain the bedding when folded. The legs fold under, which enables us to ship it K. D. All castings are malleable iron. Frame is made of kiln-dried hard maple, and supplied with a steel woven wire mattress and patent adjustable brace for legs. Body 12 inches deep. Finished in natural maple. Weight, 25 pounds. Size, 30x54 inches. Price..$2.80
74857 Child's Crib. Same style as 74856, only larger. Size, 40x60 inches. Weight, 30 pounds. 3.25

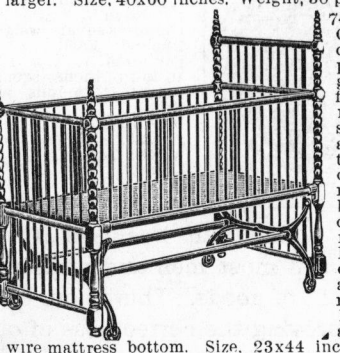

74858 Child's Cradle, made of hard maple and has a good gloss finish. Is very rigid and strong. It has a glide motion instead of the rock, making the body of the cradle remain level. Is mounted on casters and easily moved about. Fitted with a fine woven wire mattress bottom. Size, 23x44 inches, and 14 inches deep. Weight, 25 pounds. Price, only..$3.50

Children's Beds—Continued.

74858½—Cradle, bent wood ends, plain spindles, well made and substantial, finished in light or dark wood. Weight, 15 pounds. Price. $1.25

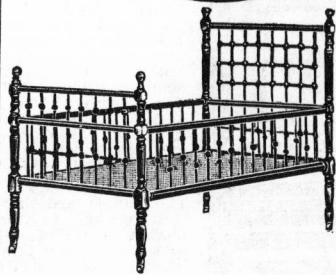

74859 Child's Bed very fancy, well made of solid oak. It is not only an ornament to a room, but is a first-class article in every respect; is also fitted with a good woven wire mattress.

Size, 30x60; 12 inches deep. Price, in oak.....$5.10
Size, 40x60; 12 inches deep. Price, in oak,.... 5.95

Open.   Closed.

74860 Child's Folding Bed Crib, well made of hard maple and has a good gloss finish; all castings are malleable iron and will not chip or mar; has rod and rings for curtain and fitted with a fine woven wire mattress. Weight, about 35 pounds.
Size, 30x60 inches. Price, only................$4.20
Size, 40x60 inches. Price, only................ 4.90

74861 This bed is made for curtain front and has all the advantages of a full sized folding bed; has a woven wire mattress. It is light, neat, tasteful and substantial. Size of bed, when open, 30x54 in. outside measure; height, 60 in.; width, 34 inches, depth, 14 inches; finished in antique only. Weight, 55 pounds. Price, complete..$6.25

74861-2

74862 Folding Bed, same as No. 74861, except in larger size—36x60 inches. Weight, 60 lbs. Price, complete...........................$6.75

Wall Pockets.

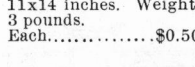

74900 Wall Pocket, made of ornamented gilt molding, neat painted flower; japanned. Size, 11x14 inches. Weight, 3 pounds.
Each...............$0.50

74901 Wall Pocket. This handsome, new pocket is fitted with a steel engraving under glass, in upright style. The outside frame is 1¾ and inside frame is 1½; molding heavily ornamented and finished in enamel and gilt; size, 16x19 inches. Weight, 5 pounds. Each..................$0.90

Wall Pockets—Continued.

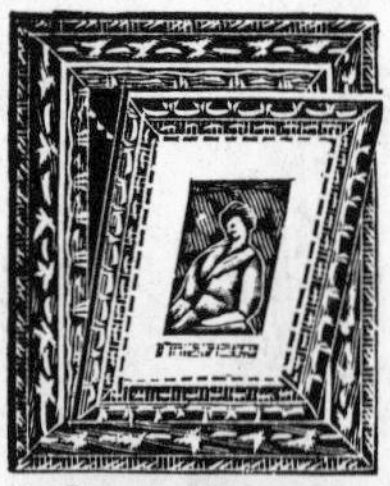

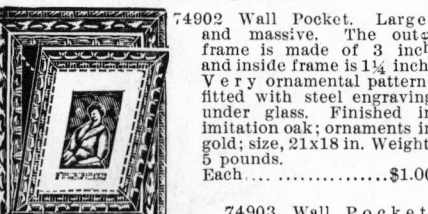

74902 Wall Pocket. Large and massive. The outside frame is made of 3 inch and inside frame is 1¼ inch. Very ornamental pattern; fitted with steel engraving under glass. Finished in imitation oak; ornaments in gold; size, 21x18 in. Weight, 5 pounds. Each....................$1.00

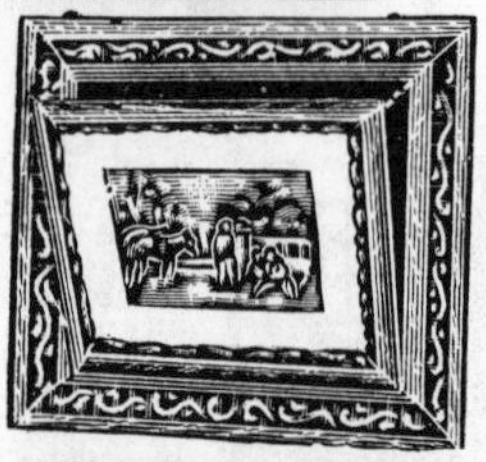

74903 Wall Pocket. The outside frame is made of 3 inch imitation oak, with heavily ornamented center. The inside frame is made of 1½ inch solid oak, with front ornament cut out and finished in silver, making a very handsome and strong pocket. Fitted with a 11x14 inch photogravure under glass. Outside measure, 19x22 inches. Weight, 5 pounds.$1.15

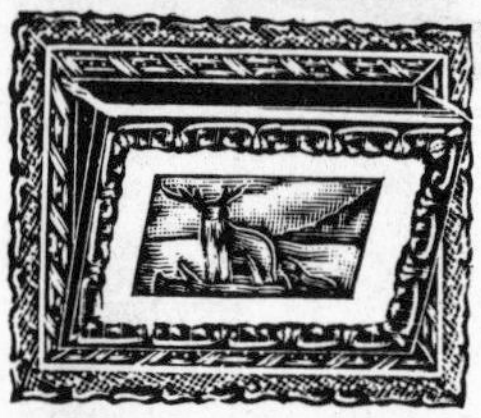

74904 Wall Pocket. The newest and prettiest pocket in the market; made of 2½ inch outside frame; finished in best white enamel and gilt, pink shaded, with 1¼ inch front molding, cut out pattern and finished in enamel and silver, and fitted with 10x14 inch steel engraving under glass; outside measure is 17x20 inches. Weight, 5 pounds. Each....................$1.25

Easels.

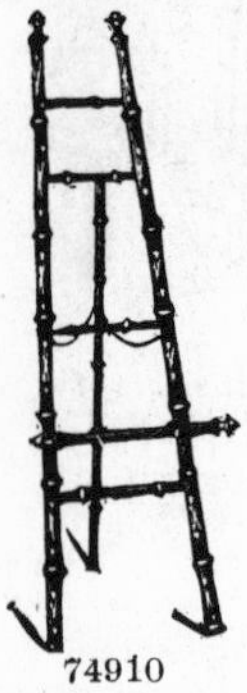

74910

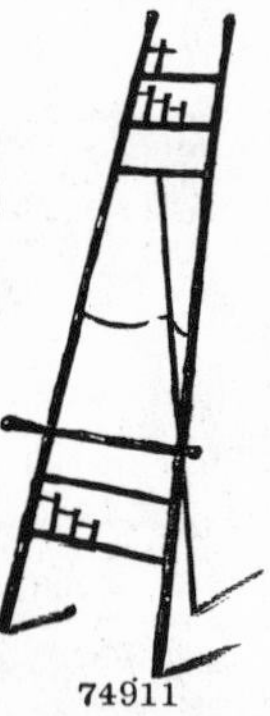

74911

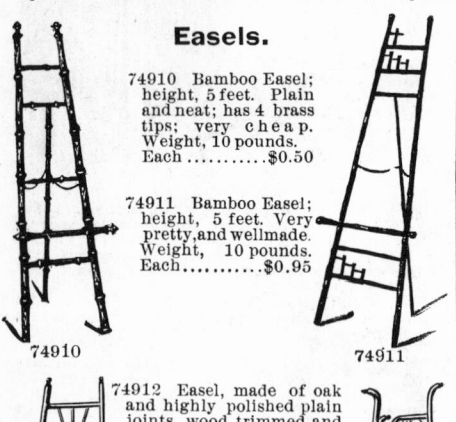

74910 Bamboo Easel; height, 5 feet. Plain and neat; has 4 brass tips; very cheap. Weight, 10 pounds. Each..........$0.50

74911 Bamboo Easel; height, 5 feet. Very pretty, and well made. Weight, 10 pounds. Each..........$0.95

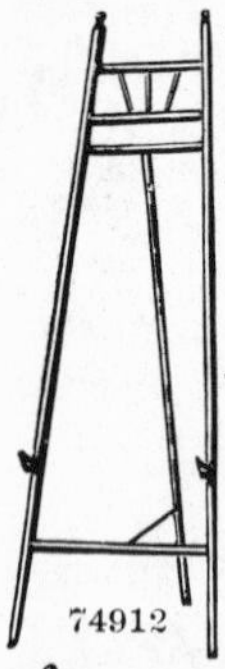

74912

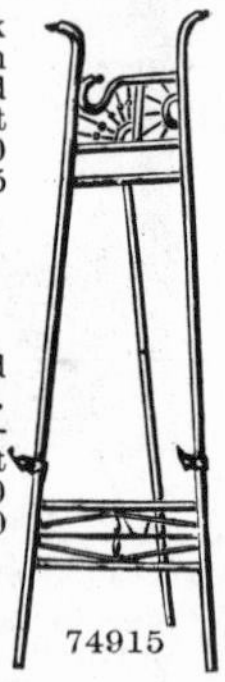

74915

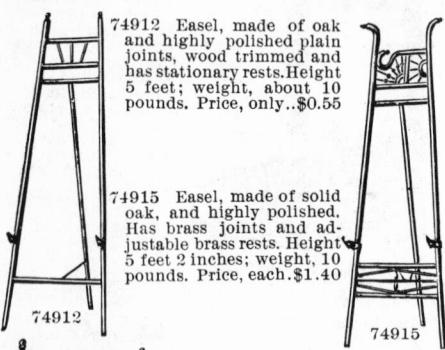

74912 Easel, made of oak and highly polished plain joints, wood trimmed and has stationary rests. Height 5 feet; weight, about 10 pounds. Price, only..$0.55

74915 Easel, made of solid oak, and highly polished. Has brass joints and adjustable brass rests. Height 5 feet 2 inches; weight, 10 pounds. Price, each.$1.40

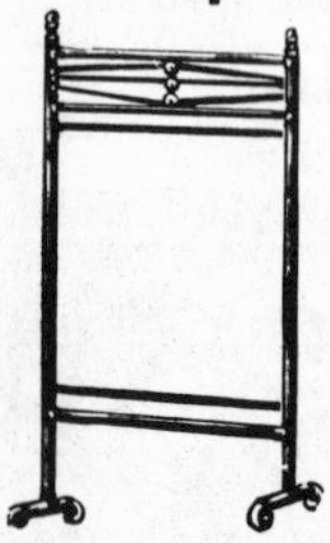

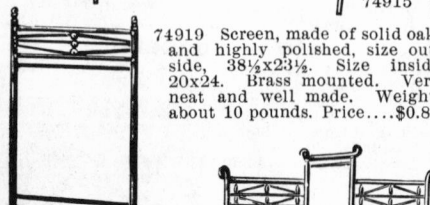

74919 Screen, made of solid oak, and highly polished, size outside, 38½x23½. Size inside 20x24. Brass mounted. Very neat and well made. Weight, about 10 pounds. Price....$0.80

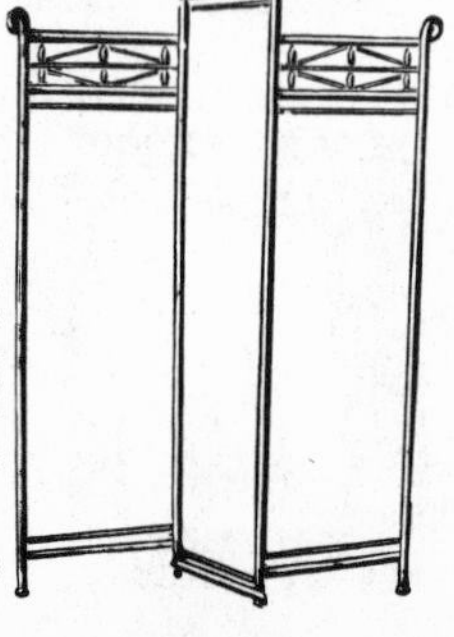

74921 Screens, made of solid oak, and highly polished, made with three separate folds, size, 64 inches high, 58 inches wide. Outside panel opening, 18x47. Inside panel opening, 18x60. Very large and cheap. Weight, about 10 pounds. Price, only..........$1.50

Towel Rack and Holders.

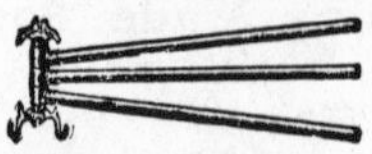

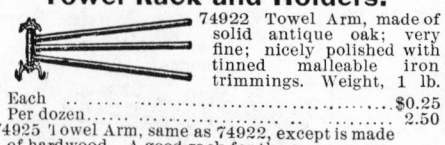

74922 Towel Arm, made of solid antique oak; very fine; nicely polished with tinned malleable iron trimmings. Weight, 1 lb.
Each $0.25
Per dozen..2.50

74925 Towel Arm, same as 74922, except is made of hardwood. A good rack for the money.
Each..$0.15
Per dozen..1.62

Towel Rollers.

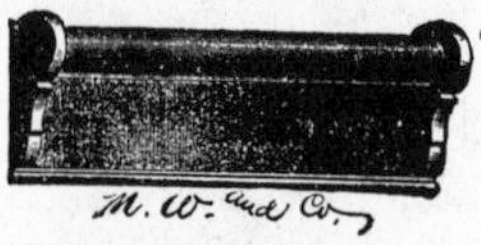

74935 Towel Rollers, made of ash, solid and fine; size, 19x5½ inches. Weight, 1½ pounds.
Each..........$0.25
Per dozen..........2.50

74940 Towel Roller, same style as 74935, except it is not varnished nor finished quite so fine; made in light only. Each..........................$0.15
Per dozen..........................1.50

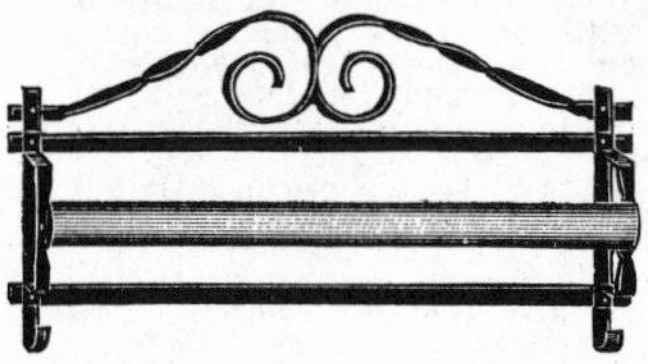

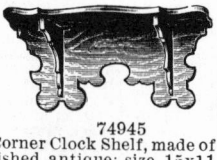

74941 Towel Roller. Frame is made of heavy steel and riveted; roller is made of good hardwood. Frame is nicely japanned. Size, 10x19 inches. Weight, 2 pounds. Each..........................$0.30

Clock Shelves.

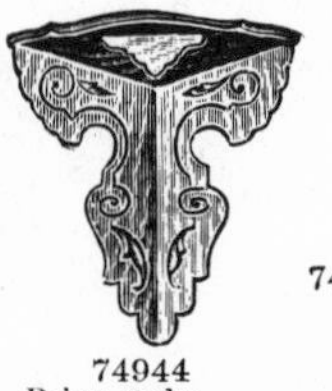

74944

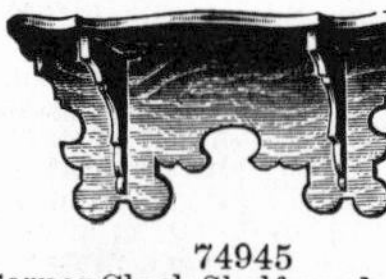

74945

74944 Corner Clock Shelf, made of ash; finished antique; size, 15x11 inches; neat and well made. Weight, 3 pounds.
Price, only.......................... $0.40

74945 Clock Shelf, made in elm, finished antique; size, 6x18 inches; well made and cheap; weight, about 3 pounds. Price..........$0.25

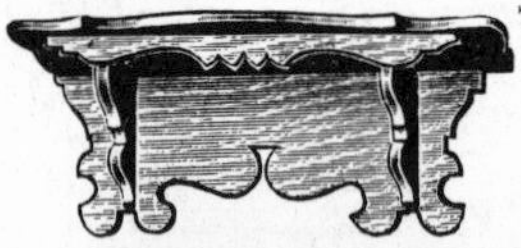

74946 Clock Shelf, made in elm; finished antique; size, 7½x24½ inches. Weight about 4 pounds.
Price..........$0.50

74947 Mantel Shelf, made of solid oak. Size, 8x28 inches. Richly carved and nicely finished antique. Well made and cheap. Weight, about 7 pounds. Price..........$0.80

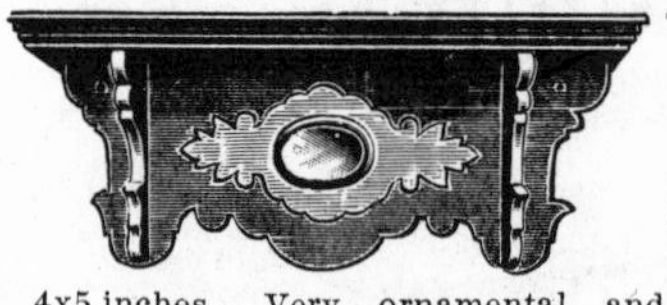

74948, Mantel Shelf, made in solid oak; finished antique. Size of shelf, 8x28 inches, with a bevel mirror 4x5 inches. Very ornamental and cheap. Weight, about 15 pounds. Price..........$1.00

Chair Bottoms.

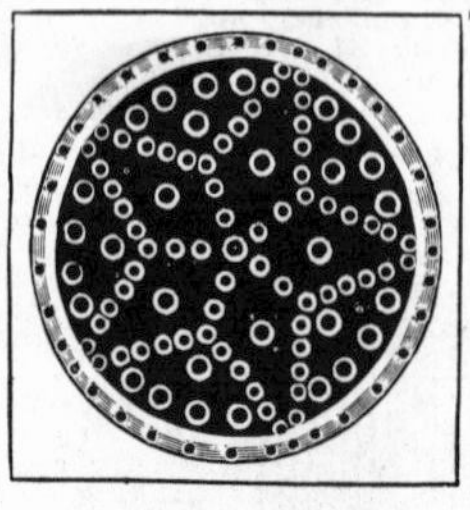

74950 Three-Ply Perforated wood chair seats.
12 inches square; weight, ½ pound. Each....$0.09
Per dozen.......... .90
15 inches square; weight, 1 pound. Each....$0.11
Per dozen.......... 1.00
16 and 17 inches square, weight, 1¼ pounds.
Each..........$0.13
Per dozen.......... 1.25
20 and 24 inches square, weight, 1¾ pounds.
Each..........$0.20
Per dozen.......... 2.00

WE would quit business if we couldn't sell most men and women a second bill of goods. This is our only way of proving the correctness of our prices and methods.

Kerosene Oil.

No charge for barrels. Barrels contain about 52 gallons.

We do not solicit Kerosene Oil trade in the State of Iowa, owing to the annoying inspection laws. The only oil we can ship into Iowa is our 175 degree fire, test, and all Kerosene Oil shipped into Iowa is entirely at the purchaser's risk.

	Per Gal. by Bbl.
G2420 M. W. & Co's White Swan Brand, 150 degrees. A fine white oil	$0.09½
G2421 Illinois Legal Test, Prime White, 150 degrees test	.09
G2422 Illinois Water White	.09
G2423 Snow White, 150 degrees	09
G2424 Indiana Legal Test, Prime White	.10½
G2425 Indiana Legal Test, Water White	.11
G2426 Michigan Legal Test, Prime White	.10½
G2427 Michigan Legal Test, Water White	.10½
G2428 Wisconsin Legal Test, Prime White	.08¾
G2429 Wisconsin Legal Test, Water White	09
G2430 Headlight Carbon Oil, 175 Legal Test	.10
G2431 **M. W. & Co.'s Perfect Kerosene Oil** is absolutely the best carbon oil at any price. No need paying fancy prices for fancy names. Fully guaranteed. If not perfectly satisfied after trying return at our expense	$0.12½
G2433 M. W. & Co.'s Perfect Oil, in cases containing two five gallon cans. Per case	1.90
G2435 Gasoline, 88 degrees, best on earth for gas machines, barrels only	.15
G2436 Stove gasoline, 74 degree, deodorized, barrels only	.09
G2437 Naphtha, or benzine, 63 degrees, barrels only	.07

We can tell you about what a barrel of kerosene oil will cost you laid down at your nearest station. Write us.

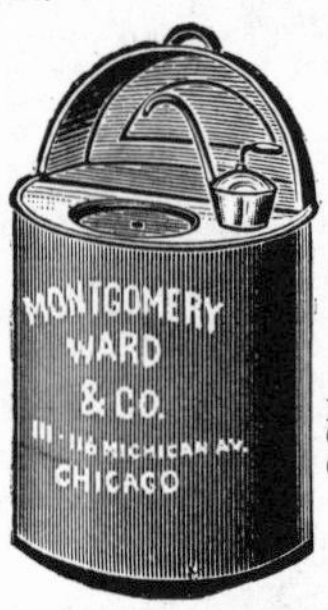

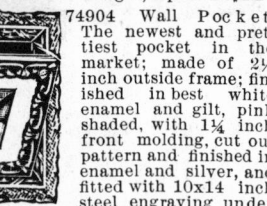

G 2524 Family Oil Tank. Capacity 60 gals.; Diam., 25½ in.; height, 40½ in. Force pump diam., 1½ in. Will hold full barrel of oil, and 10 gallons to square. Made of best galvanized iron in body and bottom, wood bottom under metal, tin hood, painted, portable, steady stream pump for pumping from barrels Weight, crated for shipment, 50 lbs.

Price, with Pump complete..........$4.50

G2525 **Extra Pumps, each** 1.50

G2526 **Gasoline Tanks,** holding 60 gallons, 4-in. screw top, ½-in. brass faucet, each.......... 4.00

Harness Oil.

Cans extra.	Per gal., bbls. & ½ bbls.	Per gal., less quantities.
G2458 **M. W. & Co.'s** Perfect Harness Oil No. 1, contains no acid; it preserves the leather and keeps it pliable. It is a better oil than usually sold at retail for $1.50 per gallon. Our price	$0.55	$0.60

M. W. & Co.'s Harness Oil

Is guaranteed equal to anything in the market for softening and preserving leather, harness, etc., etc., though it is sold at a lower price than any other make.

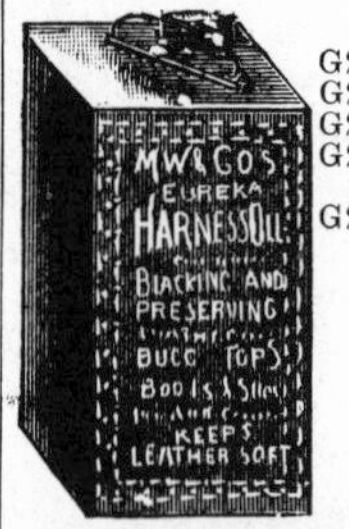

	Per can.	Per doz.
G2510 Pt. cans	$0.18	$1.95
G2511 Quart cans	.28	3.00
G2512 Gallon cans	.70	8.20
G2513 1-5 gal. can, price per 5 gals		3.10
G2514 2-5 gal. cans, price per 10 gals		6.00

Machine Oil.

(Cans extra.)	Price per bbls. & ½ bbls.	Price less quantity.
G2460 **Excelsior Machine Oils,** our price	$0.30	$0.35
G2461 Summer Black Oil, our price	.10	.15
G2462 15 degrees black oil, our price	.12	.17
G2463 Zero Black Oil, our price	.14	.19
G2465 **Castor, No. 1 White,** very best grade used for medicinal use, etc.	1.45	1.50
G2466 **Castor, No. 3,** for lubricating, etc.	1.12	1.17
G2467 **Castor, Lubricating**	54	.59
G2468 **Castor, Machine**	.30	.35
G2469 **Castor, Machine No. 1**	.28	.33
G2470 **Spirits Turpentine**	.35	.40

Price subject to market changes.

G2471 **Cup Grease.** Hard or Soft.
10 lb. pails..........$1.50
25 lb. pails.......... 3.25
50 lb. pails.......... 5.50

Price subject to market changes.

For Quotations on Lard, Neats Foot, Cylinder Engine, Linseed, Java and Baltic Oils, Turpentine, Etc., see our Monthly Grocery List, sent Free.

We have as complete a Grocery List as is made up in the United States. We revise it every month. We can save you money on everything in the Grocery line. Write us for one and examine it. Mailed free.

M. W. & Co.'s Harvester Oil.

	Per can.	Per doz.
G2490 For threshing machines, wind mills, harvesters, mowers and heavy farm machinery of all kinds. Is highly recommended by those who have used it. Quart cans, 1 dozen in case	$0.21	$2.50
G2491 Gallon cans,6in case	.55	6.20
G2492 Five gallon cans, price, per case of ten gallons		4.35
G2493 5 gal.can, in 1 case, price, for 5 gal.		2.30
G2494½ bbl., 28 gallons, no charge for packages, 33 cents per gallon. Bbls., 52 gallons; price, per gallon		.29

M. W. Co.'s Absolutely Pure Prepared Paint.

Our contract for the year 1895 is the largest we ever made. We fully guarantee our prepared paint to give better satisfaction as to durability and appearance than any paint mixed by hand. Write us for our *1895 Color Card and Hints on Selecting Colors*, showing 16 combinations selected with careful regard to harmony which can be relied upon as being in good taste. *Remember* the Montgomery Ward & Co.'s Barn Floor and Carriage Paint is equally as good as the house paint. The manufacturers guarantee every gallon of full *weight and measure*, to give perfect satisfaction if properly used, and any failure to do so will be made good. If it pleases you, as we are sure it will, kindly tell your neighbors about it, what it costs, and how they can get it.

☞One gallon of this paint will cover (two coats) over 300 square feet of surface.

NO.	COLOR.	NO.	COLOR.
100	Outside White.	124	Austrian Drab.
101	Inside white.	125	Light Lavender.
102	Black.	126	Gold Brown.
103	Straw.	127	Quaker Drab, Dark.
104	Quaker Drab, Medium,	128	Cream.
105	Light Blue.	129	Fawn.
106	Olive.	130	Dark Yellow Stone.
107	Apple Green.	131	Terra Cotta, Dark.
108	Dark Olive.	132	Green Stone.
109	Willow Green.	133	Yellow Drab.
110	Light Yellow.	134	Light Flesh.
111	Red Brown.	135	Seal Brown.
112	Buff.	136	Light Drab.
113	Terra Cotta, Light	137	White Tint.
114	Dark Red.	138	Cold Drab.
115	Golden Yellow.	139	Medium Blue,
116	Sage.	140	Ecru Yellow.
117	Drab, Dark.	141	Medium Brown.
118	Tuscan Red,	142	Light Stone.
119	Warm Brown.	143	Ecru.
120	Leather Brown.	144	Emerald Green.
121	Warm Drab.	145	French Gray.
122	Medium Stone.	146	Deep Blue.
123	Pure Gray.	147	English Vermilion.

Prices for all Colors Except Nos. 118, 144, 146 and 147.

G2550 1 Quart cans, each $0.35
G2551 2 Quart cans, each .... .60
G2552 1 Gallon cans, each 1.15
G2553 5 Gallon kits, per gal 1.10
G2554 10 Gallon kits, per gal 1.10
G2555 25 gallon bbls., per gal 1.05
G2556 50 gallon bbls., per gal 1.00

	1 Qt.	2 Qt	1 Gal.
G2558 No. 118, Tuscan Red	$0.45	$0.85	$1.60
G2559 No. 144, Emerald Green,	.50	.95	1.80
G2560 No. 146 Deep Blue	.40	.70	1.35
G2561 No. 147 Eng. Vermilion	.65	1.20	2.25

M. W. & Co.'s Paste Paints for 1895.

G2562—

Quality guaranteed equal to any in the world. A new departure in our paint and oil department for 1895. Paste paints are made in all colors same as M. W. & Co.'s Pure Prepared paint except the following four: Emerald Green, Vermilion, Deep Blue and Tuscan Red. Parties who wish to do their own mixing will find our paste paints to be the very best quality, being made from the very best pigments ground in pure linseed oil, and are ready for immediate use with the addition of oils for thinning. Packed in 12½ and 25 lb. pails. Directions: With every 25 lb. pail of paste paint add 2½ gallons of Boiled Linseed Oil for the first coat (priming coat). For every additional coat add only 2 gallons of Boiled Linseed Oil. Price for all colors, 12½ lb. pails, $1.00; 25 lb. pails, $1.75.

Color card sent free on application.

M. W. & Co.'s Liquid Floor Paints.

Floor paints improved for 1895. New colors. Made from the very best pigments by the latest and most improved machinery. Absolutely the best floor paint made; guaranteed to please or can be returned at our expense. Paint will dry over night with hard cement finish.

Colors.
No. 148 Red Brown
No. 149 Lgt. Brown
No. 150 Dark Drab
No. 151 Slate
No. 152 Dark Brown
No. 153 Yellow

G2570 1 Gals $1.15
G2571 ½ Gals .... .60
G2572 Quart cans .... .35

Discount on larger packages same as liquid house paints.

M. W. & Co.'s Roof, Fence and Barn Paints.

These are composed of the most durable mineral paints, finely ground and thinned with linseed oil. They are recommended for their durability. Color card upon application. The colors are: No. 154 yellow, 155, Princess Mineral, 156 dark brown, 157 red, 158 blue slate, 159 red slate.

	Per gal
G2575 1 gal. cans	$0.75
G2576 5 gal. kits	.70
G2577 10 gal. kits	.70
G2578 25 gal. barrels	.60
G2579 50 gal. barrels	.55

M. W. & Co.'s Buggy Paints.

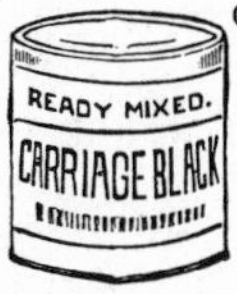

Ground in best Coach Varnish, ready for use. Prepared expressly for painting buggies, coaches, carriages, garden chairs, settees, benches, etc. One coat will make a beautiful and durable finish. No varnishing required. An assortment at dozen prices.

Colors—Dark Green, Wine, Brewster Green, Yellow, Black and Blue.

	Each.	Per doz.
G2585 Quart cans	$0.60	$6.00
G2586 Pint cans	.35	3.25
G2587 Half pint cans	.20	2.25
Also best vermilion and white.		
G2588 Quart cans	.75	8.50
G2589 Pint cans	.40	4.50
G2590 Half pint cans	.25	2.85

Enamel Paint.

In 12 beautiful and delicate shades, also white, adapted for general decorative purposes, especially desirable for picture frames, chairs, tables, flower pots, wicker work and bric-a-brac. Dries hard in 48 hours, with a very high luster. Send for color card and specify enamel.

	Each.	Per doz.
G2591 ½ pound bottles	$0.20	$2.00
G2592 1 pound cans	.40	
G2593 1 quart cans	.75	
G2594 1 gallon cans	2 50	

Liquid Wood Filler.

Dries quickly, fills pores absolutely, makes a hard, smooth finish. Superior to any in the market in color, working qualities and durability.

	Per gal.
G2600 By the bbl	$1.15
G2601 " " ½ bbl	1.20
G2602 " " 10 gal. can	1.25
G2603 " " 5 gal. can	1.30
G2604 " " 1 gal. can .... Each,	1.40
G2605 " " quart can .... "	.40

No charge for packages.

Varnish Stains.

Perfect imitations of natural woods, cherry, rosewood, mahogany, walnut, ebony, light oak, dark oak, specially intended for refinishing wood work in the interior of homes. Can be applied over any surface.

	Per gal.	Per can.
G2635 Gallons	$1.45	
G2636 Half gallons		$0.80
G2637 Quarts		.45
G2638 Pints		.30
G2639 Half Pints		.20

Pure Colors Ground in Oil.

Ready for use with addition of oils, etc., for thinning.

	1 lb. cans.	5 lb. cans.
G2640 Drop Black	$0.16	$0.75
G2645 Ivory Black	.16	.75
G2646 Coach Black	.16	.75
G2647 Prussian Blue	.36	1.65
G2648 Ultramarine Blue	.20	.95
G2649 Italian Sienna, Raw or Burnt	.14	.65
G2650 Turkey Umber, Raw or Burnt	.12	.55
G2651 Van Dyke Brown	.14	.65
G2652 Chrome Green	.16	.75
G2653 Scarlet Vermilion	.26	1.20
G2654 Tuscan Red	.20	.95
G2655 Venetian Red	.08	.35
G2656 Indian Red	.15	.70
G2657 Chrome Yellow	.20	.90
G2658 Yellow Ocher	.10	.45
G2630 Graining Colors (Antique, Mahogany, Cherry, Walnut)	.15	.70
G2661 Red Lead	.13	.60

Dry Colors.

We handle only best qualities.

	By bbl. pr lb.	Per lb.
G2700 Rochelle Ochre, 400 lbs. to bbl	$0.01¼	$0.02
G2701 Golden Washed Ochre, 400 lbs.	.01	.02
G2702 Italian Buff (light) 500 lbs.	.01	.02
G2703 Cookson English Venetian Red, 336 pounds to barrel	.01⅜	0.2½
G2704 Imperial English Venetian Red, 336 pounds to barrel	.01⅜	.02½
G2705 Snow White Wood Filler, 550 lbs. to bbl	.01½	.02¼
G2706 Silver White Wood Filler, 550 lbs. to bbl	01½	.02½
G2707 White Mineral Primer, 550 lbs. to bbl	.01½	.02½
G2708 Lampblack (Germantown) 35 lbs	.10	.11
G2709 Burnt Umber, 350 lbs.	.05	.06
G2710 Raw Umber, 350 lbs.	.05	.06
G2711 Burnt Sienna, 350 lbs.	.08	.09
G2712 Red Lead	.09	.10
G2713 Raw Sienna, 350 lbs.	.08	.09
G2714 Chrome Green		.10
G2714½ Chrome Yellow		.15

Iron Paints.

G2715 Dark Red Iron Paint, 350 lbs. to bbl	$0.01¼	$0.02
G2716 Rossie Red (genuine), 350 lbs.	.01¼	.02

VARNISHES, COLORS IN OILS, STAINS, ETC., ETC.

WOOD STAINS.

No charge for package.

	Pt cans ea.	Pint cans, per doz.	Qt. cans, ea.	Qt. cans, per doz	½ gal. can, each	½ gal. can, per doz.	1 gal. cans, each.	1 gal. cans, per doz.	5 gal. cans, each.	10 gal. cans, each.	½ bbls. 25 gal., per gal.	Bbls. 50 gal., per gal.
G2619 Oil stains, new line. In all colors as follows: Walnut, Mahogany, Cherry, Rosewood, Light oak and Dark oak.	$0.25	2.50	.44	4.80	.78	8.50	1.44	16.00	6.25	11.50	1.10	1.00

Chicago Varnish Co.'s Varnishes, Etc.

We have obtained the agency for this celebrated brand of goods, which are guaranteed equal in quality to any like goods made, and have placed them on the market at prices that will at once command your attention. Put up in all sizes, from pts. to 50 gallon barrels. No charge for packages.

	Pints, each.	Pints, doz.	Quarts, each.	Quarts, doz.	½ gal., each	½ gal., doz.	1 gal., each	5 gal., each	10 gal., each	½ barrel, 25 gallons, Per gal.	Barrels, 50 gallons, Per gal.
G2620 Outside Body Varnish	$0.55	$6.00	$1.00	$11.00	$1.60	$18.00	$3.00	$12.50	$25.00	$2.40	$2.35
G2621 Inside Coach Rubbing Varnish	.35	3.75	.65	6.25	1.00	11.00	1.80	8.00	16.00	1.55	1.50
G2622 Benzine Dryer	.18	2.00	.25	2.50	.35	3.60	.60	2.25	4.50	.40	.35
G2623 No. 1 Coach Varnish	.25	2.50	.45	4.25	.85	8.50	1.60	6.25	12.50	1.05	1.00
G2624 No. 1 Furniture Varnish	.22	2.25	.40	3.50	.60	6.00	1.00	4.50	9.00	.80	.75
G2625 Light Hard Oil Finish	.25	2.35	.45	4.00	.80	8.25	1.50	6.00	12.00	1.15	1.10
G2626 Extra Light Coach Varnish	.30	3.00	.55	5.50	.90	9.25	1.60	7.00	14.00	1.35	1.30
G2627 Coach Body Varnish	.50	5.00	.85	8.50	1.50	15.00	2.75	13.00	25.50	2.45	2.40
G2628 Rubbing Body Varnish	.40	3.50	.75	7.00	1.30	12.50	2.55	11.50	23.00	2.20	2.15
G2629 Supremis Floor Varnish	.35	3.25	.65	6.25	1.20	11.50	2.30	10.50	21.00	2.00	1.95
G2630 Pure T'rp'ntine Demar Varnish	.30	3.20	.55	5.50	.90	9.50	1.60	7.50	15.00	1.45	1.40
G2631 No. 1 Black Asphaltum	.20	2.20	.30	2.50	.50	4.75	.80	3.50	7.00	.65	.60
G2632 Turpentine Japan Dryer	.25	2.35	.35	3.00	.60	6.00	.90	4.50	8.25	.75	.70
G2633 Enamel Leather Top Dressing, ½ pts. 25c. each, $2.50 per doz	.40	4.00	.75	7.75	1.35	13.00	2.59	10.00	20.00	2.20	2.10
G2634 Shellac. Varnish, Orange. Grain Alcohol	.50		.85				3.15				
G2634½ Shellac Varnish, Orange, Wood Alcohol	.40		.75				2.50				

For prices of paint and varnish brushes, see Index.

White Lead.

	Per lb.
G2720 M. W & Co.'s Strictly Pure St. Louis White Lead in oil, 12½, 25, 50 and 100 lb. kegs, guaranteed	$0.05¾
G2721 M. W. & Co.'s special brand. Warranted to give as good satisfaction as strictly pure. 12½, 25, 50 and 100 lb. kegs	.05½
G2722 American White Lead, 1 to 5 lb. cans	.08

Zinc and Putty.

G2725 Pure Red Seal French Zinc, in Oil, 12½ and 25 lb. cans	$0.11½
G2726 Strictly pure French Zinc, in Oil, 1 to 5 lb. cans	.15
G2727 Zinc, in Oil, American Snow White; 12½ and 25 lb. pails	.08
G2728 Putty, in bladders, 10 to 15 lbs., each	.03

For Complete Quotations on Varnishes, Paints and Oils, see our Grocery List. Sent free upon application.

Montgomery Ward & Co.'s Kalsomine Colors.

1st. It is the only strictly Sanitary Kalsomine in the world and contains the best Hygienic disinfectant known to science.

2nd. It is prepared dry, and made ready for use by simply adding hot water. Full directions on every package, and can be applied by an inexperienced person.

3rd. It can be applied to old, hard finished walls and make them as good as new. It can be used on iron, wood, brick, stone or plaster walls, wooden partitions, &c.

4th. Our White, of which no sample is shown. is a purer white than ordinary kalsomine, and will remain so much longer.

Will always make a perfect finish, one package covering about 400 square feet.

16 Kalsomine Tints and White.

G2729—

White, per pkg	$0.30
Tints, per pkg	.35
25 packages in case, white	7.00
25 packages in case, tints	7.50
100 lb. drum, white	6.00
100 lb. drum, tints	6.50

4 Fresco Colors, for Bordering, Striping, Etc.

No. 22, per ½ lb	$0.20
No. 21, per ½ lb	.40
No. 25, per ½ lb	.35
No. 23, per ½ lb	.30

Write us for Kalsomine Color Card.

Buy where you can buy best.

Monarch Iron Paint.

For Metal Roofs.

Can not be excelled for general durability and preservative qualities. It is made especially for covering all kinds of metal work, dries rapidly with a hard glossy, black finish and is absolutely water and acid proof. One gallon will cover about 300 square feet.

G2750—	Per gal.
2-Gallon cans	$0.80
5-Gallon cans	.68
10-Gallon cans	.60
25-Gallon barrels	.47
50-Gallon barrels	.35

Can furnish only in black.

Lime, Cement, Tar, Etc.

		Per bbl.
G2770	Lime	$1.10
G2771	Cement, natural	1.25
G2772	Portland Cement, imported	3.40
G2773	Plaster Paris	2.00
		Per bushel.
G2774	Hair, washed	$0.30
G2775	Pine Tar, Carolina, bbls. only, per bbl. about 30 gallons	2.50
G2776	Coal Tar, per bbl	7.50

Elastic Cement.

G2776½ You can apply elastic cement yourself with a putty knife or paddle, no tinner or roofer required. When once applied it will stay. The weather does not affect it and it lasts for years. It is perfectly elastic and will not shrink or become hard and crack with age. Contains no inflammable ingredients, will not freeze, melt or run, and consequently has no equal for flashing around chimneys, porches, etc., also repairing gutters, eavetroughs, etc., or repairing leaks on shingle, iron, tin, slate, glass, paper, tile or gravel roofs; stopping leaks in boats, around steam exhaust or water pipes; in fact, can be applied to any thing or place desired to be made air or water tight. Price, 2 pound cans | $0.30

Price, 5 pound cans | .60

Axle Grease.

M. W. & Co.'s Perfection Axle Grease.

We have secured control of the total product of the best equipped axle grease factory in the United States, and can now offer you a grease that will outwear by 5 to 15 days any grease in the market. No matter how this price may seem to you, we have faith enough in the goods to place *our name on every package*, and if not satisfactory, you may return the goods at *our expense*.

		Per case.	Each.
G2800	Trial box. 1 doz. 1 lb. boxes	$0.55	$0.05
G2801	2 doz. in case 1 lb. boxes	1.00	.05
G2802	3 doz. in case 1 lb. boxes	1.45	.05
G2803	½ doz. in crate 10 lb. bkts	2.20	.40
G2804	1 doz. in crate 10 lb. bkts	4.10	.40
G2805	½ doz. in crate 25 lb. bkts	5.00	.90
G2806	1 doz. in crate 25 lb. bkts	9.00	.90
G2807	Kegs, about 60 lbs	2.10	
G2809	100 lb. kegs	3.25	

For General Household Purposes.

M. W. & Co.'s *Old Fashioned Dirt Killer*. An extra quality German mottled soap, and better than any we have seen.

60 1-pound bars in a box for $2.10 per box.

For the Laundry Mrs. Hannah Cobb's Improved Soap.

We guarantee it as good as any soap in the market and for the money it can not be surpassed.

100 12 oz. Bars, wrapped in box, $3.35 per box.
30 12 oz. Bars. wrapped in box, $1.15 per box. Trial or family size.

For the Toilet and Bath.

M. W. & Co.'s Co Co White Floating Soap. As pure a soap as made, for washing the hands, face fine, woolens, laces or anything you are particular about.

100 6-oz cakes in box (neatly wrapped) $3.50 per box.
50 6-oz cakes in box (neatly wrapped) $1.85 per box.

NOTICE: Until September 1,1895 we will furnish with all express on freight orders *one cake M. W. & Co.'s Co Co* soap FREE on request. We cannot send it by mail.

Prices of Window Glass

ARE GIVEN IN OUR

GROCERY LIST.

Published Monthly.   Free Upon Request.

We have no compunctions in asking you to try the Mail Order system. The convenience of purchasing whatever you may happen to want all at one store, the advantage of selecting from assortments that comprise every desirable range in quality, styles and sizes, and the fact that the prices at which you can buy these goods are lower than you can secure them for elsewhere, backed by our offer to refund purchase price for everything returned to us as not satisfactory, should appeal to your own sound, hard sense, if you are looking out for your own interest, and most everybody is.

BINDER TWINE —CONSULT US THIS YEAR SURE.

Prices will be found in Grocery List.

PARIS GREEN.

THIS WILL BE THE BIGGEST POTATO YEAR ON RECORD, YOU WILL NEED PARIS GREEN.

The Effect of a Large Contract is that we can make a very low price.   See Grocery List.

Montgomery Ward & Co.,

111, 112, 113, 114. 115, 116 Michigan Avenue,   CHICAGO.